CHILTON'S TRUCK and VAN REPAIR MANUAL

CHILTON BOOK COMPANY
Chilton Way, Radnor, Pa. 19089

Manufactured in USA

ISBN 0-8019-6910-7
Library of Congress Catalog Card No. 78-52225

1 2 3 4 5 6 7 8 9 0 9 8 7 6 5 4 3 2 1 0

CONTENTS

DOMESTIC TRUCK SERVICE

DOMESTIC TRUCK GENERAL REPAIR SECTIONS

IMPORT TRUCK SERVICE

DOMESTIC TRUCK SECTION

INDEX

ENGINE IDENTIFICATION CODE

10-20-30 Series (Light Duty Trucks)

NOTE: On 1973-78 vehicles, a combination Vehicle Identification Number and rating plate used on all models is located on the left door lock pillar of C, K, and G models. On forward control models it is attached to the dash and toe panel. On 1979-80 vehicles the Vehicle Identification Number is stamped on a plate which is attached to the left top of the instrument panel on C, K, and G models, and is visible through the windshield. On P-10, 20, 30 models the plate is attached to the front of the dash and toe panel to the left of the steering column.

The third symbol of the Vehicle Identification Number is the engine code. Refer to the chart for the corresponding engine cubic inch displacement.

YEAR	250 Cu. In. L-6/1 bbl.	292 Cu. In. L-6/1 bbl.	305 Cu. In. V-8/2 bbl.	307 Cu. In. V-8/2 bbl.	350 Cu. In. V-8/2 bbl.	350 Cu. In. V-8/4 bbl.	400 Cu. In. V-8/4 bbl.	454 Cu. In. V-8/4 bbl.	454 Cu. In. V-8/4 bbl.	350 Cu. In V-8/Diesel
1973	Q	T	—	X	—	Y	—	Z①	—	—
1974	Q	T	—	—	V	Y	—	Z①	—	—
1975	Q	T	—	—	V	Y	M	Z①	L②	—
1976	D	T	Q	—	V	L	U	S①	Y②	—
1977	D	T	U	—	—	L	R	S③	Y④	—
1978	D	T	U	—	—	L	R	S	—	Z
1979-80	D	T	U	—	M	L	R	S	—	Z

40 through 90 Series (Medium and Heavy Duty Trucks)

NOTE: A combination Vehicle Identification and Rating plate is used on all 1973-78 50-90 series trucks. It is attached to the left-hand door pillar on most models. Bus models have their plates attached to the air intake plenum panel. In 1979 and 1980, the Vehicle Identification Number plate for all 40-70 series truck is located on the top of the instrument panel and is visible from the driver's side looking through the windshield. A combination Vehicle Identification and Rating plate, used on all 80-90 series trucks, is attached to the left-hand door pillar on most models. Bus models have their plates attached to the air intake plenum panel.

For 1973-78 medium and heavy duty trucks, the third symbol of the Vehicle Identification Number is the engine code. For 1979-80 medium and heavy duty trucks, the fifth symbol of the Vehicle Identification Number is the engine code. Refer to the chart for the corresponding, applicable engine.

ENGINE	1973-78	1979-80
6 Cyl. Gasoline	S	T
V-8 Gasoline	E	—
350 Cu. In. Gasoline	—	A
366 Cu. In. Gasoline	—	B
427 Cu. In. Gasoline	—	E
454 Cu. In. Gasoline	—	S
3406 Caterpillar Inline 6 Cyl. Diesel	R	R
3208 Caterpillar V-8 Diesel	Y	Y
Cummins KT-450 Inline 6 Cyl. Diesel	L	L
Cummins Turbocharged 6 Cyl. Diesel	C	C
Cummins V-8 Diesel	B	—
Detroit Diesel 4-53 Series	D	D
Detroit Diesel Inline 6 Cyl.	I	—
Detroit Diesel 6-71 Series	—	I
Detroit Diesel V6-53 Series	V	V
Detroit Diesel V6-92 Series	J	J
Detroit Diesel V-8	H	—
Detroit Diesel 8V-71 Series	—	H
Detroit Diesel V8-92	K	K
Detroit Diesel V12	P	—
Glider Kit—Less Engine	—	X

① 6000 lbs. and under GVWR
② Over 6000 lbs. GVWR
③ Conventional models only
④ Motor Home Chassis only

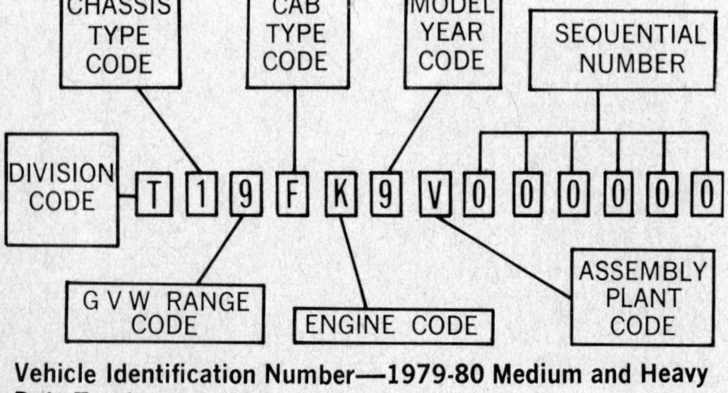

Vehicle Identification Number—1979-80 Medium and Heavy Duty Trucks (typical)

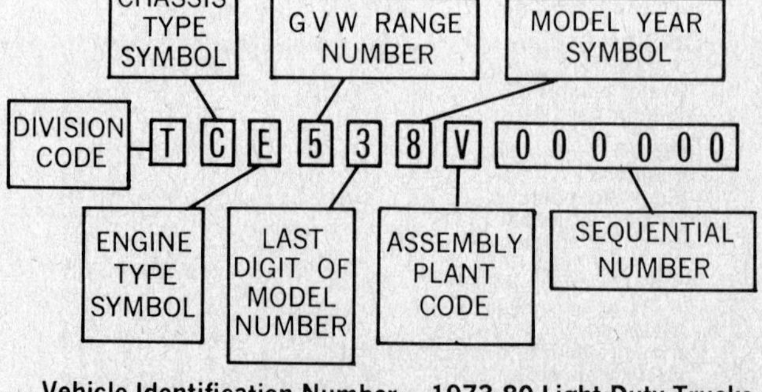

Vehicle Identification Number—1973-80 Light Duty Trucks and 1973-78 Medium and Heavy Duty Trucks (typical)

TUNE-UP SPECIFICATIONS

Note: Refer to the emission control label before making any final adjustments, as the label may reflect changes in engine tune-up specifications which occurred after the initial tune-up information was released for publication.

Up to and including the model year 1978, Federal light duty emission requirements affected only vehicles up to 6,000 lbs. GVW. Beginning with the model year 1979, Federal light duty emission requirements have been extended to include vehicles up to 8,500 lbs. GVW.

CU. IN. DISPLACEMENT (cu. in.)	YEAR	SPARK PLUG GAP (in.)	DISTRIBUTOR POINT DWELL (deg.)	DISTRIBUTOR POINT GAP (in.)	IGNITION TIMING (DEGREES)	CRANKCASE COMP. PRESSURE	VALVE CLEARANCE Int. Exh.	NO LOAD GOV. RPM (rpm)	PUMP FUEL PRESS (psi)	IDLE SPEED* (rpm) STD.	IDLE SPEED* (rpm) AUTO.
SIX CYLINDER											
250	1973	0.035	31-34	0.019	6B①	130	Hyd.		3.5-4.5	700	600②
	1974	0.035	31-34	0.019	8B③	130	Hyd.		3.5-4.5	850④	600
	1975 (Fed./Calif.)	0.060	Elec.	Elec.	10B	130	Hyd.		3.5-4.5	900N	550D
	1976 (Fed.)	0.035	Elec.	Elec.	⑤	130	Hyd.		3.5-4.5	900N	550D
	1976 Calif.)	0.035	Elec.	Elec.	⑥	130	Hyd.		3.5-4.5	1000N	600D
	1977 (Fed.)	0.035	Elec.	Elec.	⑦	130	Hyd.		4.5-6.0	750N	⑧
	1977 (Calif.)	0.035	Elec.	Elec.	⑨	130	Hyd.		4.5-6.0	850N	600D
	1978 (Fed.)	0.035	Elec.	Elec.	⑩	130	Hyd.		4.5-6.0	⑪	⑪
	1978 (High Alt.)	0.035	Elec.	Elec.	⑫	130	Hyd.		4.5-6.0	750N	600D
	1978 (Calif.)	0.035	Elec.	Elec.	⑬	130	Hyd.		4.5-6.0	750N	600D
	1979-80 (Fed.)	0.035	Elec.	Elec.	10B	130	Hyd.		4.5-6.0	750N	600D
	1979-80 (Calif.)	0.035	Elec.	Elec.	⑭	130	Hyd.		4.5-6.0	750N	600D
292	1973	0.035	31-34	0.019	4B⑮	130	Hyd.		3.5-4.5	700⑯	700⑯
	1974	0.035	31-34	0.019	8B	130	Hyd.		3.5-4.5	700	700
	1975 (Fed.)	⑰	Elec.	Elec.	8B	130	Hyd.	3800-4000	⑱	600N	——
	1976 Fed./Calif.)	0.035	Elec.	Elec.	8B	130	Hyd.	3800-4000	⑱	600N	——
	1977-78 (Fed./Calif.)	0.035	Elec.	Elec.	8B	130	Hyd.	4000	4-5	600N	600N
	1979-80 (Fed./Calif.)	0.035	Elec.	Elec.	8B	130	Hyd.		4-5	700N	700N
305C (V6)	1973	0.040	31-34	0.019	7-½B	125	0.012-0.018	3600	5.0-7.0	550	550
	1974	0.035	31-34	0.019	7-½B	125	0.012-0.018	3600	5.0-7.0	600	600
379 (V6)	1973	0.035	31-34	0.019	8B	125	0.012-0.018	4000	5.0-7.0	550	550
	1974	0.035	31-34	0.019	6B	125	0.012-0.018	4000	5.0-7.0	575	575
432 (V6)	1973	0.035	31-34	0.019	8B	125					
	1974	0.035	31-34	0.019	6B	125	0.012-0.018	3200	5.0-7.0	525	525
EIGHT CYLINDER											
305	1977 (Fed.)	0.045	Elec.	Elec.	8B	⑲	Hyd.		7.5-9.0	600N	500D
	1978 (Fed.)	0.045	Elec.	Elec.	⑳	⑲	Hyd.		7.5-9.0	600N	500D
	1979-80 (Fed.)	0.045	Elec.	Elec.	6B	⑲	Hyd.		7.5-9.0	700N	600D
307	1973	0.035	29-31	0.019	4B㉑	150	Hyd.		5.0-6.5	900㉒	600
350	1973	0.035	29-31	0.019	㉓	150	Hyd.		5.0-6.5	900㉔	600㉔
	1974	0.035	29-31	0.019	㉕	150	Hyd.		5.0-6.5	900㉖	600㉖
	1975 (2 bbl) (Fed.)	0.060	Elec.	Elec.	6B	150	Hyd.		7-8.5	——	600D
	1975 (4 bbl) (Fed./Calif.)	0.060	Elec.	Elec.	6B	150	Hyd.		7-8.5	800N	600
	1975 (Fed.)*	0.060	Elec.	Elec.	8B	150	Hyd.		7-8.5	600N	600N
	1975 (Calif.)*	0.060	Elec.	Elec.	2B	150	Hyd.		7-8.5	700N	700N
	1975-76**	0.035	31-34	0.019	4B	150	Hyd.	㉗	7-9	600N	600N
	1976 (2 bbl) (Fed.)	0.045	Elec.	Elec.	㉘	150	Hyd.		7-8.5	800N	600D
	1976 (4 bbl) (Fed.)	0.045	Elec.	Elec.	8B	150	Hyd.		7-8.5	800N	600D
	1976 (4 bbl) (Calif.)	0.045	Elec.	Elec.	6B	150	Hyd.		7-8.5	800N	600D
	1976 (Fed.)*	0.060	Elec.	Elec.	8B	150	Hyd.		7-8.5	600N	600N
	1976 (Calif.)*	0.060	Elec.	Elec.	2B	150	Hyd.		7-8.5	600N	600N
	1977 (Fed.)	0.045	Elec.	Elec.	8B	150	Hyd.		7-8.5	700N	500D
	1977 (High Alt.)	0.045	Elec.	Elec.	6B	150	Hyd.		7-8.5	——	600D

TUNE UP SPECIFICATIONS (Cont'd)

CU. IN. DISPLACE-MENT (cu. in.)	YEAR	SPARK PLUG GAP (in.)	DISTRIBUTOR POINT DWELL (deg.)	DISTRIBUTOR POINT GAP (in.)	IGNITION TIMING (DEGREES)	CRANKCASE COMP. PRESSURE	VALVE CLEARANCE Int. Exh.	NO LOAD GOV. RPM (rpm)	PUMP FUEL PRESS (psi)	IDLE SPEED* (rpm) STD.	IDLE SPEED* (rpm) AUTO.
	1977 (Calif.)	0.045	Elec.	Elec.	6B	150	Hyd.		7-8.5	700N	500D
	1977 (Fed.*)	0.045	Elec.	Elec.	8B	150	Hyd.		7-8.5	700N	700N
	1977 (Calif.)	0.060	Elec.	Elec.	2B	150	Hyd.		7-8.5	700N	700N
	1977**	0.035	Elec.	Elec.	4B	150	Hyd.	4100	7-9	600N	600N
	1978 (Fed.)	0.045	Elec.	Elec.	8B	150	Hyd.		7-8.5	600N	500D
	1978 (High Alt.)	0.045	Elec.	Elec.	8B	150	Hyd.		7-8.5	—	500D
	1978 (Calif.)	0.045	Elec.	Elec.	8B	150	Hyd.		7-8.5	700N	500D
	1978 (Fed.)*	0.045	Elec.	Elec.	8B	150	Hyd.		7-8.5	700N	700N
	1978 (Calif.)*	0.045	Elec.	Elec.	2B	150	Hyd.		7-8.5	700N	700N
	1978-80 (Fed.)**	0.045	Elec.	Elec.	4B	150	Hyd.	4000	7.5-9	600N	600N
	1978-80 (Calif.)**	0.035	Elec.	Elec.	4B	150	Hyd.	4000	7.5-9	600N	600N
	1979-80 (Fed./ Calif.)	0.045	Elec.	Elec.	㉙	150	Hyd.		7.5-9	700N	500D
366	1973	0.035	28-32	0.019	8B	150	Hyd.		5.0-6.5	550㉚	550㉚
	1974	0.035	28-32	0.019	8B	150	Hyd.		5.0-6.5	600	600
	1975 (Fed.)	0.035	28-32	0.019	8B	150	Hyd.	㉛	7-9	700	700
	1975-76 (Calif.)	0.060	Elec.	Elec.	8B	150	Hyd.	4100	7-9	700	700
	1977** (Fed./ Calif.)	㉜	Elec.	Elec.	8B	150	Hyd.	4100	7-9	700N	700N
	1978-80** (Fed./ Calif.)	㉜	Elec.	Elec.	8B	150	Hyd.	4075	8¼	700N	700N
400	1975-78 (Fed.)*	㉝	Elec.	Elec.	4B	150	Hyd.		7-8.5	700	700
	1975-78 (Calif.)*	㉝	Elec.	Elec.	2B	150	Hyd.		7-8.5	700	700
	1979-80 (Fed./ Calif.)	0.045	Elec.	Elec.	4B	150	Hyd.		7-8.5	700N	500D
427	1973	0.035	28-32	0.019	8B	150	Hyd.		7.0-8.5	550㉚	550㉚
	1974	0.035	28-32	0.019	8B	150	Hyd.		7.0-8.5	600	600
	1975-76 (Fed.)**	0.035	28-32	0.019	8B	150	Hyd.	㉞	7-9	700	700
	1975-76 (Calif.)**	0.060	Elec.	Elec.	8B	150	Hyd.	4100	7-9	700	700
	1977 (Fed.)**	0.035	Elec.	Elec.	8B	150	Hyd.	㉟	7-9	700N	700N
	1977 (Calif.)**	0.060	Elec.	Elec.	8B	150	Hyd.	㉟	7-9	700N	700N
	1978 (Fed.)**	0.045	Elec.	Elec.	8B	150	Hyd.	4075	8¼	700N	700N
	1978 (Calif.)**	0.060	Elec.	Elec.	8B	150	Hyd.	4075	8¼	700N	700N
	1979-80 (Fed./ Calif.)**	0.045	Elec.	Elec.	8B	150	Hyd.	4075	8¼	700N	700N
454	1973 (Fed.)	0.035	28-32	0.019	10B	150	Hyd.		7.0-8.5	900②	600②
	1973 (Calif.)	0.035	28-32	0.019	㊱	150	Hyd.		7.0-8.5	900②	600②
	1974	0.035	29-31	0.019	10B㊲	150	Hyd.		7.0-8.5	800②	600②
	1975 (Fed.)	0.060	Elec.	Elec.	㊳	150	Hyd.		7-8.5	—	650D
	1975 (Fed./ Calif.)**	0.060	Elec.	Elec.	8B	150	Hyd.		7-8.5	700	700
	1976 (Fed.)	0.045	Elec.	Elec.	㊴	150	Hyd.		7-8.5	—	600D
	1976-78 (Fed./ Calif.)*	0.045	Elec.	Elec.	8B	150	Hyd.		7-8.5	700N	700N
	1977 (Fed.)	0.045	Elec.	Elec.	4B	150	Hyd.		7-8.5	—	600D
	1978 (Fed.)	0.045	Elec.	Elec.	8B	150	Hyd.		7-8.5	—	550D
	1978 (Calif.)	0.045	Elec.	Elec.	8B	150	Hyd.		7-8.5	—	㊵
	1979-80 (Fed./ Calif.)	0.045	Elec.	Elec.	㊶	150	Hyd.		7-8.5	㊷	㊷
	1979-80 (Fed./ Calif.)**	0.045	Elec.	Elec.	8B	150	Hyd.	4075	7-8.5	700N	700N

TUNE UP SPECIFICATIONS (Cont'd)

— Not Applicable
Elec.—Electronic Ignition
Hyd.—Hydraulic valve lifters (one turn down from zero lash)
N—Neutral
D—Drive
B—BTDC

① 4B All C,K-20 except Suburban; all C,P-30 series and all G-30 except Sportvan
② 700 RPM all C,K-20 except Suburban; all C,P-30 series and all G-30 except Sportvan
③ 6B all C,K-20 series except Suburban; all C,P-30 series and all G-30 except Sportvan
④ 600 RPM all C,K-20 except Suburban; all C,P-30 series and all G-30 except Sportvan
⑤ C-10 w/4 Spd. or Auto trans.—10B (light duty emission)
C,G-10 w/3 Spd. trans.—6B (light duty emission)
C,K-10 (all trans.) w/heavy duty emission systems—6B
⑥ C,G-10 w/manual trans.—6B
C,G-10 w/auto. trans.—10B
⑦ C-10 (code TBA) and G-10 (code TBF) w/man. trans.—8B (light duty emission)
C-10 (code TBB) and G-10 (code TBH) w/auto. Trans.—12B (light duty emission)
⑧ 550D w/o A/C, 600D with A/C
⑨ C-10 (code TBI) and G-10 (code TBJ) w/man. trans.—6B
C-10 (code TBD) and G-10 (code TBK) w/auto. trans.—10B
⑩ C-10 (code TAC) and G-10 (code TAF) w/man. trans.—8B
C-10 (code TAB) and G-10 (code TAH) w/auto. trans.—8B
⑪ man. trans.—750N
auto. trans.—550D (No A/C), 600D (A/C)
⑫ man. trans.—8B
auto. trans.—12B
⑬ man. trans.—8B
auto. trans.—10B
⑭ man. trans.—6B
auto. trans.—8B
⑮ California—8B
⑯ California—600 RPM
⑰ light duty trucks—0.060 in.
medium and heavy duty trucks—0.035 in.
⑱ light duty trucks—3.5-4.5 psi
medium and heavy duty trucks—4-5 psi
⑲ The lowest acceptable compression pressure reading must be within at least 70% of the highest pressure reading for any given cylinder. Example: If 7 out of 8 cylinders indicate pressures of 150 psi/cyl., then a pressure of 105 psi is acceptable in the eighth cylinder. A pressure lower than 105 psi would indicate that repairs are necessary.
⑳ 4B (light duty emission systems)
6B (heavy duty emission systems)
㉑ 8B all 10 series, C,K-20, Suburban, G-20,30 Sportvans w/auto. trans. TDC all others
㉒ 600 RPM all C,K-20 except Suburban, and all C,P-30 series and all G-30 except Sportvan
㉓ C-20 Suburban—2B
All 10 series, K-20 Suburban, G-20, and G-30 Sportvan:
w/manual transmission 8B
w/automatic transmission 12B
All others 4B
㉔ All C,K-20 except Suburban; all C,P-30 series, all G-20,30 except Sportvan—700 RPM
㉕ Federal except C,K-10,20 Suburban and G-20, 30 Sportvan—8B
Federal C,K-10,20 Suburban and G-20,30 Sportvan:
w/automatic transmission 12B
w/automatic transmission (except Suburban) 8B
Suburban (w/manual transmission) 6B
California:
w/automatic transmission 8B
Suburban (w/manual transmission) 6B
w/manual transmission 4B
㉖ All C,K-20 except Suburban, all C,P-30 series and all G-20,30 except Sportvan 600 RPM
㉗ Auto. trans. 540—4000 RPM
Auto. trans. 475—3600 RPM
㉘ Auto. trans.—6B
Man. trans.—2B
㉙ 8B (all vehicles except Fed. G-30 and C,K,P-20,30 with carburetor 17059213, 17059215, and distributor 1103375—4B)
㉚ California—700 RPM
㉛ GMC carb. 792870, Holley carb. R7264A—3750 RPM
GMC carb. 717721, Holley carb. R6928A—4000 RPM
㉜ 0.045 (Fed.)
0.060 (Calif.)
㉝ 0.060—1975-76
0.045—1977-78
㉞ GMC carb. 795092, Holley carb. R7266A—3600 RPM
GMC carb. 717722, Holled carb. R6929A—4000 RPM
㉟ 4150 RPM—manual trans.
3500 RPM—RT613 trans.
㊱ All 10 series, C,K-20 Suburban, G-20,30 Sportvan 10B
All C,K-20 except Suburban, all C,P-30 series and all G-30 except Sportvan:
w/manual transmission 5B
w/automatic transmission 8B
㊲ All C,K-20 except Suburban, all C,P-30 series and all G-30 except Sportvan 8B
㊳ w/Catalytic Converter—16B
w/o Catalytic Converter—10B
㊴ w/Catalytic Converter—12B
w/o Catalytic Converter—8B
㊵ C-20 (code TRM)—700N
C-10,20 (code TSS) and C-20 (code TRF)—550D
㊶ C-30 w/man. trans.—4B
C-20 (code ZWZ) and C,P-30 w/auto. trans.—4B
C-20 w/man. trans. and C-10,20 w/auto. trans.—8B
㊷ All except C-10,20 w/auto. trans.—700N
C-10,20 w/auto. trans.—550D

*Vehicles equipped with heavy duty emission systems
**Medium and heavy duty trucks only

FIRING ORDER

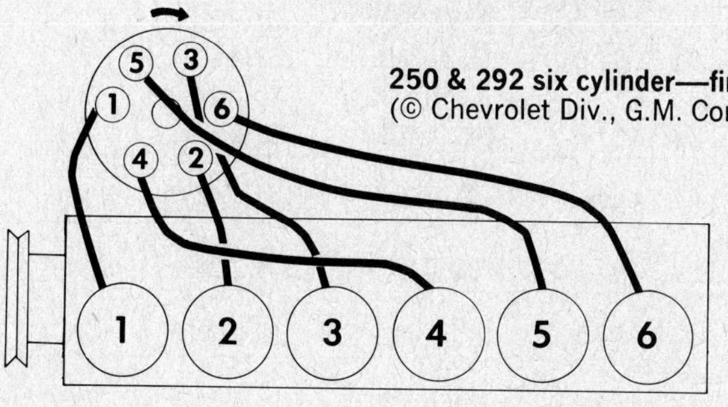

250 & 292 six cylinder—firing order 1-5-3-6-2-4
(© Chevrolet Div., G.M. Corp.)

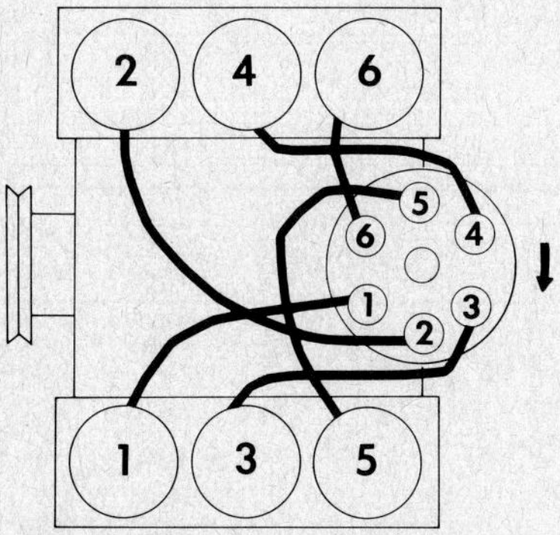

305, 379, & 432 V6 engines—firing order 1-6-5-4-3-2
(© Chevrolet Div., G.M. Corp.)

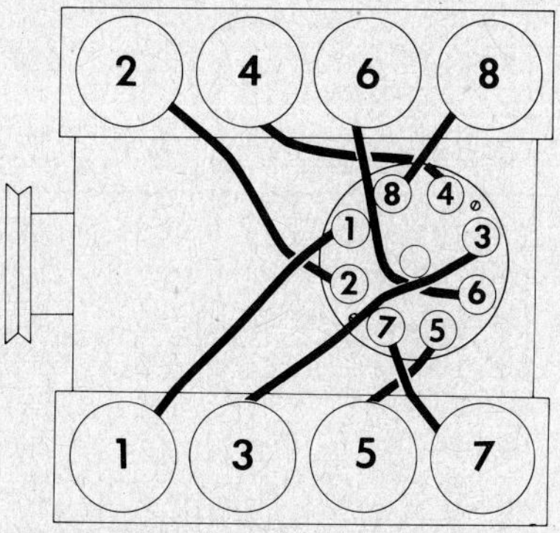

305, 350, 366, 400, 454 engines—firing order 1-8-4-3-6-5-7-2
(© Chevrolet Div., G.M. Corp.)

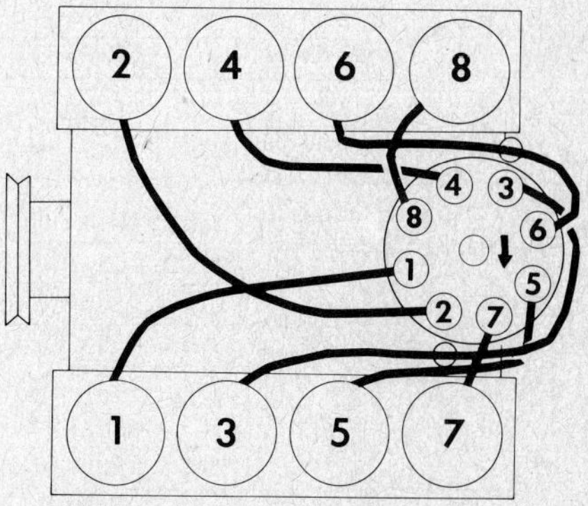

307, 350, 366, 427, 454 engines—firing order 1-8-4-3-6-5-7-2
(© Chevrolet Div., G.M. Corp.)

GENERAL ENGINE SPECIFICATIONS

CU. IN. DISPLACEMENT	YEAR	BORE X STROKE	FIRING ORDER	HORSEPOWER @ R.P.M.	TORQUE @ R.P.M.	COMPRESSION RATIO	CARBURETOR	VALVE LIFTER TYPE	NORMAL OIL PRESSURE
				SIX CYLINDER					
250	1973-74	3.875 x 3.53	1-5-3-6-2-4	100 @ 3600	175 @ 2000	8.25	1V	Hyd.	40-60
	1975	3.875 x 3.53	1-5-3-6-2-4	105 @ 3800	185 @ 1200	8.25:1	1V	Hyd.	40-60
	1976 (L.D.)	3.875 x 3.53	1-5-3-6-2-4	105 @ 3800	185 @ 1200	8.25:1	1V	Hyd.	40-60
	1976 (H.D.)	3.875 x 3.53	1-5-3-6-2-4	100 @ 3600	175 @ 1800	8.25:1	1V	Hyd.	40-60
	1977-78 (L.D.)	3.87 x 3.53	1-5-3-6-2-4	110 @ 3800	195 @ 1600	8.3:1	1V	Hyd.	40-60
	1977-78 (H.D.)	3.87 x 3.53	1-5-3-6-2-4	100 @ 3600	175 @ 1800	8.0:1	1V	Hyd.	40-60
	1979-80	3.87 x 3.53	1-5-3-6-2-4	①	②	8.3:1	2V	Hyd.	40-60
292	1973-74	3.875 x 4.125	1-5-3-6-2-4	120 @ 3600	225 @ 2000	8.0	1V	Hyd.	40-60
	1975	3.87 x 4.12	1-5-3-6-2-4	120 @ 3600	215 @ 2000	8.0:1	1V	Hyd.	40-60
	1976-78	3.87 x 4.12	1-5-3-6-2-4	120 @ 3600	215 @ 2000	8.0:1	1V	Hyd.	40-60
	1979-80	3.87 x 4.12	1-5-3-6-2-4	115 @ 3400	215 @ 1600	8.0:1	1V	Hyd.	40-60
305C (V6)	1973-74	4.250 x 3.58	1-6-5-4-3-2	148 @ 4000	238 @ 1600	7.5	2V	Mech.	57
379 (V6)	1973-74	3.56 x 3.86	1-6-5-4-3-2	170 @ 3600	280 @ 1600	7.5	2V	Mech.	57
432 (V6)	1973-74	4.875 x 3.86	1-6-5-4-3-2	190 @ 3200	331 @ 1600	7.5	2V	Mech.	60
				EIGHT CYLINDER					
305	1977-78	3.74 x 3.48	1-8-4-3-6-5-7-2	145 @ 3800	245 @ 2400	8.5:1	2V	Hyd.	40
	1979-80	3.74 x 3.48	1-8-4-3-6-5-7-2	③	④	8.4:1	2V	Hyd.	45
307	1973	3.875 x 3.25	1-8-4-3-6-5-7-2	115 @ 3600	205 @ 2000	8.5	2V	Hyd.	30
	1973	3.875 x 3.25	1-8-4-3-6-5-7-2	130 @ 4000	220 @ 2200	8.5	2V	Hyd.	30
350	1973	4.00 x 3.48	1-8-4-3-6-5-7-2	145 @ 4000	255 @ 2400	8.5	2V	Hyd.	40
		4.00 x 3.48	1-8-4-3-6-5-7-2	155 @ 4000	255 @ 2400	8.5	4V	Hyd.	40
		4.00 x 3.48	1-8-4-3-6-5-7-2	175 @ 4000	260 @ 2800	8.5	4V	Hyd.	40
	1974	4.00 x 3.48	1-8-4-3-6-5-7-2	145 @ 3600	250 @ 2200	8.5	2V	Hyd.	40
		4.00 x 3.48	1-8-4-3-6-5-7-2	160 @ 3800	255 @ 2400	8.5	4V	Hyd.	40
	1975 (2 bbl)	4.00 x 3.48	1-8-4-3-6-5-7-2	145 @ 3600	250 @ 2200	8.5:1	2V	Hyd.	40-60
	1975 (4 bbl)	4.00 x 3.48	1-8-4-3-6-5-7-2	160 @ 3800	250 @ 2400	8.5:1	4V	Hyd.	40-60
	1976	4.00 x 3.48	1-8-4-3-6-5-7-2	160 @ 4000	265 @ 2400	8.0:1	2V	Hyd.	40-60
	1977-78 (L.D.)	4.00 x 3.48	1-8-4-3-6-5-7-2	165 @ 3800	260 @ 2400	8.5:1	4V	Hyd.	40
	1977-78 (H.D.)	4.00 x 3.48	1-8-4-3-6-5-7-2	165 @ 3800	255 @ 2800	8.5:1	4V	Hyd.	40
	1979-80 (Fed.)	4.00 x 3.48	1-8-4-3-6-5-7-2	165 @ 3600	270 @ 2000	8.2:1	4V	Hyd.	45
	1979-80 (Calif.)	4.00 x 3.48	1-8-4-3-6-5-7-2	155 @ 3600	260 @ 2000	8.2:1	4V	Hyd.	45
366	1973-74	3.937 x 3.76	1-8-4-3-6-5-7-2	200 @ 4000	310 @ 2800	8.0	4V	Hyd.	40-55
	1975	3.937 x 3.76	1-8-4-3-6-5-7-2	200 @ 4000	305 @ 2800	8.0:1	4V	Hyd.	40-55
	1976-78 (single exh.)	3.937 x 3.76	1-8-4-3-6-5-7-2	195 @ 4000	290 @ 2800	8.0:1	4V	Hyd.	40-55
	1976-78 (dual exh.)	3.937 x 3.76	1-8-4-3-6-5-7-2	200 @ 4000	305 @ 2800	8.0:1	4V	Hyd.	40-55
	1979-80 (single exh.)	3.937 x 3.76	1-8-4-3-6-5-7-2	180 @ 4000	290 @ 2400	7.6:1	4V	Hyd.	40-55
	1979-80 (dual exh.)	3.937 x 3.76	1-8-4-3-6-5-7-2	190 @ 4000	305 @ 2400	7.6:1	4V	Hyd.	40-55
400	1975	4.125 x 3.75	1-8-4-3-6-5-7-2	175 @ 3600	290 @ 2800	8.5:1	4V	Hyd.	40-60
	1976-78	4.125 x 3.75	1-8-4-3-6-5-7-2	175 @ 3600	290 @ 2800	8.5:1	4V	Hyd.	40-60
	1979-80 (Fed.)	4.125 x 3.75	1-8-4-3-6-5-7-2	⑤	⑥	8.5:1	4V	Hyd.	40
	1979-80 (Calif.)	4.125 x 3.75	1-8-4-3-6-5-7-2	170 @ 3600	305 @ 1600	8.5:1	4V	Hyd.	40
427	1973-74	4.25 x 3.76	1-8-4-3-6-5-7-2	230 @ 4000	360 @ 2800	8.0	4V	Hyd.	40-55
	1975	4.25 x 3.76	1-8-4-3-6-5-7-2	220 @ 4000	360 @ 2400	8.0:1	4V	Hyd.	40-55
	1976-78	4.25 x 3.76	1-8-4-3-6-5-7-2	220 @ 4000	360 @ 2400	8.0:1	4V	Hyd.	40-55
	1979-80	4.25 x 3.76	1-8-4-3-6-5-7-2	220 @ 4000	360 @ 2400	7.5:1	4V	Hyd.	40-55
454	1973	4.251 x 4.00	1-8-4-3-6-5-7-2	240 @ 4000	355 @ 2800	8.25	4V	Hyd.	40
		4.251 x 4.00	1-8-4-3-6-5-7-2	245 @ 4000	375 @ 2800	8.25	4V	Hyd.	40
		4.251 x 4.00	1-8-4-3-6-5-7-2	250 @ 4000	365 @ 2800	8.25	4V	Hyd.	40
	1974	4.251 x 4.00	1-8-4-3-6-5-7-2	230 @ 4000	350 @ 2800	8.25	4V	Hyd.	40
		4.251 x 4.00	1-8-4-3-6-5-7-2	245 @ 4000	365 @ 2800	8.25	4V	Hyd.	40

GENERAL ENGINE SPECIFICATIONS, continued

CU. IN. DISPLACEMENT	YEAR	BORE X STROKE	FIRING ORDER	HORSEPOWER @ R.P.M.	TORQUE @ R.P.M.	COMPRESSION RATIO	CARBURETOR	VALVE LIFTER TYPE	NORMAL OIL PRESSURE
	1975 (L.D.)	4.251 x 4.00	1-8-4-3-6-5-7-2	215 @ 4000	350 @ 2400	8.15:1	4V	Hyd.	40
	1975 (H.D.)	4.251 x 4.00	1-8-4-3-6-5-7-2	245 @ 4000	355 @ 3000	8.15:1	4V	Hyd.	40
	1976-78 (L.D.)	4.251 x 4.00	1-8-4-3-6-5-7-2	245 @ 3800	365 @ 2800	8.15:1 ⑦	4V	Hyd.	40
	1976-78 (H.D., Fed.)	4.251 x 4.00	1-8-4-3-6-5-7-2	240 @ 3800	370 @ 2800	8.15:1	4V	Hyd.	40
	1976-78 (H.D., Calif.)	4.251 x 4.00	1-8-4-3-6-5-7-2	250 @ 3800	385 @ 2800	8.15:1	4V	Hyd.	40
	1979-80	4.25 x 4.00	1-8-4-3-6-5-7-2	245 @ 4000	380 @ 2500	7.6:1	4V	Hyd.	40-55

Fed.—Federal (all states except California)
Calif.—California only
L.D.—Light duty emissions (under 6,000 lb GVW)
H.D.—Heavy duty emissions (over 6,000 lb GVW)
① 130 @ 3800 light and medium duty emissions (all states except California)
125 @ 4000 light duty emissions 10 series only (California)
130 @ 4000 light and medium duty emissions, all except 10 series (California)
② 210 @ 2400 light and medium duty emission (all states except California)
205 @ 2000 light duty emission, 10 series only (California)
205 @ 2000 light and medium duty emissions, all except 10 series (California)
③ 160 @ 4000 all except California (4 bbl)
155 @ 4000 California only (4 bbl)
140 @ 4000 all 10-30 series (2 bbl)
④ 235 @ 2400 all except California (4 bbl)
225 @ 2400 California only (4 bbl)
240 @ 2000 all 10-30 series (2 bbl)
⑤ 185 @ 3600 light and medium duty (up to 8500 lbs. GVWR)
180 @ 3600 heavy duty (8501 lbs. GVWR and above)
⑥ 300 @ 2400 light and medium duty (up to 8500 lbs. GVWR)
310 @ 2400 heavy duty (8501 lbs. GVWR and above)
⑦ 8.25:1 on C-10 w/H.D. chassis and C-10,20 Suburban

CRANKSHAFT BEARING JOURNAL SPECIFICATIONS

CU. IN. DISPLACEMENT	YEAR	MAIN BEARING JOURNALS: JOURNAL DIAMETER	OIL CLEARANCE	SHAFT END PLAY	THRUST ON NO.	CONNECTING ROD BEARING JOURNALS: JOURNAL DIAMETER	OIL CLEARANCE	END PLAY
SIX CYLINDER								
250	1973-78	2.2983-2.2993	.0003-.0029	.002-006	Rear	1.999-2.000	.0007-.0027	.006-.017
	1979-80	2.2979-2.2994	①	.002-.006	Rear	1.999-2.000	.0010-.0030	.006-.017
292	1973-78	2.2983-2.2993	.0008-.0034	.002-.006	5	2.099-2.100	.0007-.0027	.006-.017
	1979-80	2.2979-2.2994	①	.002-.006	5	2.099-2.100	.0010-.0030	.006-.017
305C (V6)	1973-74	3.1247-3.1237②	.0013-.0039	.003-.008	—	2.8112-2.8122	.001-.003	.006-.011
379 (V6)	1973-74	3.1247-3.1237②	.0023-.0039③	.003-.008	—	2.8112-2.8122	.0015-.0035	.006-.011
432 (V6)	1973-74	3.1247-3.1237②	.0023-.0039③	.003-.008	—	2.8112-2.8122	.0015-.0035	.006-.011
EIGHT CYLINDER								
305	1977	④	⑤	.002-.006	5	2.199-2.200	.0013-.0035	.008-.014
	1978-80	④	⑤	.002-.006	5	2.0988-2.0998	.0013-.0035	.008-.014
307	1973	2.4484-2.4493⑥	⑤	.002-.006	5	2.199-2.200	.0013-.0035	.008-.014
350	1973-76	2.4484-2.4493⑥	⑤	.002-.006	5	2.199-2.200	.0013-.0035	.008-.014
	1977	④	⑤	.002-.006	5	2.199-2.200	.0013-.0035	.008-.014
	1978-80	④	⑤	.002-.006	5	2.0988-2.0998	.0013-.0035	.008-.014
366	1973-80	2.7481-2.7490⑦	.0013-.0025⑧	.006-.010	5	2.1985-2.1995	.0014-.0030	.019-.025
400	1975-76	2.4484-2.4493⑥	⑤	.002-.006	5	2.199-2.200	.0013-.0035	.008-.014
	1977	⑨	⑤	.002-.006	5	2.199-2.200	.0013-.0035	.008-.014
	1978-80	⑨	⑤	.002-.006	5	2.0988-2.0998	.0013-.0035	.008-.014
427	1973-80	2.7481-2.7490⑦	.0013-.0025⑧	.006-.010	5	2.199-2.1998	.0014-.0030	.019-.025
454	1973-80	2.7485-2.7494⑩	.0013-.0025⑪	.006-.010	5	2.1985-2.1995	.0009-.0025	.013-.023

① Nos. 1-6 .0010-.0024
No. 7 .0016-.0035
② Rear 3.1229-3.1239
③ No. 4 .0031-.0047
④ No. 1 2.4484-2.4493
Nos. 2,3,4 2.4481-2.4490
No. 5 2.4479-2.4488
⑤ No. 1 .0008-.0020 (.002 maximum)
Nos. 2,3,4 .0011-.0023 (.0025 maximum)
No. 5 .0017-.0032 (.0035 maximum)
⑥ Rear 2.4479-2.4488
⑦ Rear 2.7473-2.7483
⑧ Rear .0029-.0045
⑨ Nos. 1,2,3,4 2.6484-2.6493
No. 5 2.6479-2.6488
⑩ Nos. 2,3,4 2.7481-2.7490
No. 5 2.7478-2.7488
⑪ No. 5 .0024-.0040

RING SIDE CLEARANCE (IN.)

ENGINE (cu. in.)	YEAR	TOP COMPRESSION	BOTTOM COMPRESSION	OIL CONTROL
250	1973-80	.0012-.0027	.0012-.0032	.0000-.0050
292	1973-80	.0020-.0040	.0020-.0040	.0005-.0055
305 (V6)	1973-74	.0030-.0050	①	.0010-.0040
379 (V6)	1973-74	.0030-.0045	②	.0025-.0040
432 (V6)	1973-74	.0030-.0045	②	.0025-.0040
305 (V8)	1977-80	.0012-.0032	.0012-.0032	.002-.007
307	1973	.0012-.0027	.0012-.0032	.0000-.0050
350	1973-80	.0012-.0032	.0012-.0032	.002-.007
366	1973-80	.0018-.0032	.0018-.0032	.0020-.0035
400	1975-80	.0012-.0032	.0012-.0032	.002-.007
427	1973-80	.0018-.0038	.0018-.0038	.002-.0035
454	1973-80	.0017-.0032	.0017-.0032	.005-.0065

①—2nd compression—.0030-.0045
3rd compression—.0025-.0040

②—2nd compression—.0025-.0040
3rd compression—.0025-.0040

RING GAP SPECIFICATIONS (IN.)

ENGINE	YEAR	TOP COMPRESSION	BOTTOM COMPRESSION	OIL CONTROL
250	1973-80	.010-.020	.010-.020	.015-.055
292	1973-80	.010-.020	.010-.020	.015-.055
305 (V6)	1973-74	.017-.027	①	No Gap
379 (V6)	1973-74	.022-.032	②	No Gap
432 (V6)	1973-74	.024-.034	③	No Gap
305 (V8)	1977-80	.010-.020	.010-.025	.015-.055
307	1973	.010-.020	.010-.020	.015-.055
350	1973-80	.010-.020	.013-.025	.015-.055
366	1973-80	.010-.020	.010-.020	.010-.023
400	1975-76	.010-.020	.010-.020	.010-.035
	1977-80	.010-.020	.010-.025	.015-.055
427	1973-80	.010-.020	.010-.020	.010-.023
454	1973-76	.010-.020	.010-.020	.010-.030
	1977-80	.010-.020	.010-.020	.015-.055

①—2nd compression—.015-.025
3rd compression—.015-.025

②—2nd compression—.022-.032
3rd compression—.015-.025

③—2nd compression—.024-.034
3rd compression—.015-.025

VALVE SPECIFICATIONS

CU. DISPLACE-MENT	YEAR	LASH (HOT) (INCHES) INT.	EXH.	ANGLE (DEGREES) FACE	SEAT	STEM DIA. (INCHES) INT.	EXH.	STEM CLEARANCE INTAKE	EXHAUST	CAM LOBE LIFT (INCHES)	VALVE SPRING TENSION (LBS @ INCHES) OPEN	CLOSED	FREE LENGTH (INCHES)
							SIX CYLINDER						
250	1973-76	①	①	45	46	.342	.3413	.0010-.0027	.0015-.0032	.2217	185 @ 1.27	60 @ 1.66	1.90
	1977	①	①	45	46	.342	.3413	.0010-.0027	.0015-.0032	.2217	185 @ 1.27	60 @ 1.66	2.08
	1978-80	①	①	45	46	.342	.3413	.0010-.0027	.0015-.0032	.2217	170 @ 1.26	60 @ 1.66	1.88
292	1973-76	①	①	45	46	.342	.3413	.0010-.0027	.0015-.0032	.2315	180 @ 1.30	90 @ 1.69	1.90
	1977	①	①	45	46	.342	.3413	.0010-.0027	.0015-.0032	.2315	180 @ 1.30	90 @ 1.69	2.08
	1978-80	①	①	45	46	.342	.3413	.0010-.0027	.0015-.0032	.2315	175 @ 1.26	82 @ 1.66	1.90
305C (V6)	1973-74	.012	.018	—	30	.341	.340	.0015-.003	.002-.0035	.454②	203 @ 1.50	80 @ 1.92	2.27
379 (V6)	1973-74	.012	.018	—	30	.373	.438	.0015-.003	.0019-.0036	.454②	203 @ 1.50	80 @ 1.92	2.27
432 (V6)	1973-74	.012	.018	—	30	.373	.438	.0015-.003	.0019-.0036	.454②	203 @ 1.50	80 @ 1.92	2.27

VALVE SPECIFICATIONS

CU. DISPLACEMENT	YEAR	LASH (HOT) (INCHES) INT.	EXH.	ANGLE (DEGREES) FACE	SEAT	STEM DIA. (INCHES) INT.	EXH.	STEM CLEARANCE INTAKE	EXHAUST	CAM LOBE LIFT (INCHES)	VALVE SPRING TENSION (LBS @ INCHES) OPEN	CLOSED	FREE LENGTH (INCHES)
EIGHT CYLINDER													
305 (V8)	1977	①	①	45	46	.341	.341	.0010-.0027	.0010-.0027	③	④	⑤	2.03
	1978-80	①	①	45	46	.341	.341	.0010-.0027	.0010-.0027	⑥	④	⑤	2.03
307	1973	①	①	45	46	.341	.341	.001-.003	.001-.003	③	189 @ 1.20	80 @ 1.61	1.91
350	1973-76	①	①	45	46	.341	.341	.0010-.0027	.0010-.0027	⑦	⑧	⑤	⑨
	1977-80	①	①	45	46	.341	.341	.0010-.0027	.0010-.0027	⑦	④	⑤	2.03
366	1973-80	①	①	45	46	.3718	.372	.0010-.0027	.0012-.0029	.234	220 @ 1.40	90 @ 1.80	2.05
400	1975-80	①	①	45	46	.371	.371	.0010-.0027	.0012-.0029	⑦	④	⑤	2.03
427	1973-80	①	①	45	46	.372	.372	.0010-.0027	.0019-.0022	⑩	220 @ 1.40	90 @ 1.80	2.05
454	1973-80	①	①	45	46	.372	.371	.0010-.0027	.0012-.0029	.234	300 @ 1.38	80 @ 1.88	2.12

① One complete turn down from zero lash
② Exhaust .464
③ Intake .2485
Exhaust .2733
④ Intake 200 @ 1.25
Exhaust 200 @ 1.16
⑤ Intake 80 @ 1.70
Exhaust 80 @ 1.61
⑥ Intake .2484
Exhaust .2667
⑦ Intake .260
Exhaust .273
⑧ Intake 200 @ 1.25
Exhaust 190 @ 1.20
⑨ Intake 2.03
Exhaust 1.91
⑩ Intake .2343
Exhaust .2530

TORQUE SPECIFICATIONS

CU. IN. DISPLACEMENT	YEAR	CYLINDER HEAD BOLTS (FT. LBS.)	ROD BEARING BOLTS (FT. LBS.)	MAIN BEARING BOLTS (FT. LBS.)	CRANKSHAFT BALANCER BOLT (FT. LBS.)	FLYWHEEL TO CRANKSHAFT BOLTS (FT. LBS.)	MANIFOLDS (FT. LBS.) INTAKE	EXHAUST
SIX CYLINDER								
250	1973-78	95	35-45	65	Pressed on	60	①	①
	1979-80	95	35	65	Pressed on	60	②	②
292	1973-78	95	40	65	Pressed on	55-65	①	①
	1979-80	95	40	65	60	110	②	②
305C (V6)	1973-74	60-65	55-65	170-180③	180-200	100-110	30-35	15-20
379 (V6)	1973-74	90-100	55-65	170-180③	240-260	100-110	30-35	15-20
432 (V6)	1973-74	90-100	55-65	170-180③	240-260	100-110	30-35	15-20
EIGHT CYLINDER								
305 (V8)	1977-80	65	45	80④	60	60	30	20
307	1973	65	45	70	Pressed on	60	30	20⑤
350	1973-76	65	45	70	60	60	30	20⑤
	1977-80	65	45	80④	60	60	30	20⑤
366	1973-80	75-85	⑥	100-110	80-90	60-70	25-35	25-30
427	1973-80	75-85	⑥	100-110	80-90	60-70	25-35	25-30
454	1973-80	80	50	110	85	65	30	20

① Outer 20 ft. 1 lb., others 30 ft. lbs.
② Exhaust 30 ft. lbs.
Exhaust to intake 45 ft. lbs.
Manifold to cylinder head 40 ft. lbs.
③ Rear 90-100 ft. lbs.
④ Intermediate outer bolts 70 ft. lbs.
⑤ Inside bolts 30 ft. lbs.
⑥ 7/16" 67-73 ft. lbs.
⅜" 45-55 ft. lbs.

WHEEL ALIGNMENT SPECIFICATIONS

IMPORTANT: A. It is recommended that the alignment adjustments be made with the vehicle "loaded", as caster, camber, and toe-in specifications represent the true dimensions for a vehicle carrying its design load. A simulated load condition during adjustments can improve tire wear and increase the life of the tires.

B. All caster specifications are given based on a frame angle of zero. If the frame of the vehicle isn't perfectly level, compensation must be made (for the frame angle) as the position of the frame directly affects the caster angle. A distinction must be made between the caster reading as it appears on the alignment measuring equipment and the "actual" caster reading, which is the true caster angle of the vehicle, obtained after compensating for the effect of the frame angle on the caster angle. In order to determine the "actual" caster reading prior to adjustment, you must first measure the angle between the frame and an imaginary horizontal line. The following rules apply to the usual combinations of frame angle and caster reading:

1. Subtract a DOWN IN REAR frame angle from a positive caster reading.
2. Add an UP IN REAR frame angle to a positive caster reading.
3. Add a DOWN IN REAR frame angle from a negative caster reading.
4. Subtract an UP IN REAR frame angle from a negative caster reading.

After the necessary alignment adjustments have been made, it will, again, be necessary to determine the "actual" caster reading. Remember, the reading on the alignment equipment must be mathematically corrected (actual) in order to determine the "actual" caster reading, as the direct reading from the alignment equipment does not reflect any compensation for the frame angle. Therefore, it will be necessary to repeat the "actual" caster reading procedure (according to the above mentioned rules) after adjustments have been made.

C. Measure the distance between the bump stop bracket and the frame (Dimension "A"—see illustration). Refer to the CASTER SPECIFICATION chart for the correct caster setting as it corresponds to Dimension "A". (Light duty trucks only)

D. Ordinarily, a shim pack will leave at least two threads of the bolt exposed beyond the nut. If, in order to properly align the front wheels, it is necessary to build the shim pack beyond the two thread minimum, then check for damaged control arms and related parts. The difference, in thickness, between the front shim pack and the rear shim pack must not exceed 0.30 inch. The front shim pack must be at least 0.24 inch. (Light duty trucks only)

10-20-30 SERIES (LIGHT DUTY)

MODEL	YEAR	CASTER (deg.)	CAMBER (deg.)	TOE-IN (inches)	TURNING ANGLE	KINGPIN INCLINATION
C-10, 20, 30	1973-78	①	+¼°	3⁄16"	⑥	⑦
	1979-80	①	+0.2°	3⁄16"	⑥	⑦
G-10, 20, 30	1973-78	①	+¼°	3⁄16"	⑥	⑦
	1979-80	①	+0.2°	3⁄16"	⑥	⑦
P-10, 20, 30	1973-74	①	+¼°	3⁄16"	⑥	⑦
	1975-78	①	⑧	3⁄16"	⑥	⑦
	1979-80	①	+0.2°	3⁄16"	⑥	⑦
K-10, 20	1973-74	①	+1½°⑨	3⁄16"⑩	⑥	⑦
	1975-76	①	+1½°⑨	0	⑥	⑦
K-10, 20, 30	1977-78	①	+1½°⑨	0	⑥	⑦
K-10, 20	1979-80	①	+1°⑨	0	⑥	⑦
K-30	1979-80	①	+½°⑨	0	⑥	⑦

CAMBER SPECIFICATIONS (MODELS P-10, 20, 30 ONLY)

Dimension "A" in Inches	2½"	2¾"	3"	3¼"	3½"	3¾"	4"	4¼"	4½"	4¾"	5"	5¼"	5½"
1975-78 P-10	0°	0°	+¼°	+¼°	+¼°	+¼°	+¼°	0°	0°	0°	−¼°	−½°	−¾°
1975-78 P-20, 30	0°	0°	+¼°	+¼°	+¼°	+¼°	+¼°	+¼°	0°	0°	−¼°	−½°	−¾°

CASTER SPECIFICATIONS
(See important note above)

Dimension "A" in Inches	1½"	1¾"	2"	2¼"	2½"	2¾"	3"	3¼"	3½"	3¾"	4"	4¼"	4½"	4¾"	5"
1973-78 C-10	—	—	—	—	—	—	+2°	+1½°	+1¼°	+1°	+¾°	+½°	+¼°	0°	−½°
1973 C-20, 30	—	—	—	—	+2°	+1½°	+1¼°	+1°	+1¾°	+½°	+¼°	0°	−¼°	−½°	−¾°
1974-78 C-20, 30	—	—	—	—	+1½°	+1¼°	+1°	+¾°	+½°	+¼°	0°	−¼°	−½°	−¾°	−1°
1979-80 C-10	—	—	—	—	+2.4°	+2.1°	+1.8°	+1.5°	+1.2°	+1.0°	+0.7°	+0.5°	+0.2°	+0.1°	−0.3°
1979-80 C-20, 30	—	—	—	—	+1.5°	+1.2°	+0.9°	+0.6°	+0.3°	+0.1°	0°	−0.1°	−0.7°	−1.0°	−1.2°
1973-77 G-10, 20, 30	—	—	—	—	+2¼°	+2°	+1½°	+1¼°	+1°	+¾°	+½°	+¼°	0°	−¼°	−½°
1978 G-10, 20	—	—	—	—	+3¼°	+3°	+2¾°	+2½°	+2½°	+2¼°	+2°	+2°	+1¾°	+1½°	+1½°
1978 G-30	—	—	—	—	+2¼°	+2°	+1½°	+1¼°	+1°	+¾°	+½°	+¼°	0°	−¼°	−½°
1979-80 G-10, 20	+2.9°	+2.7°	+2.3°	+2.2°	+2.0°	+1.8°	+1.6°	+1.4°	+1.3°	+1.1°	+0.9°	+0.7°	—	—	—
1979-80 G-30	+3.4°	+3.0°	+2.7°	+2.4°	+2.1°	+1.8°	+1.5°	+1.3°	+1.0°	+0.7°	+0.4°	+0.2°	—	—	—
1973 P-10	—	—	—	—	—	—	+2°	+1½°	+1¼°	+1°	+¾°	+½°	+¼°	0°	−½°
1973 P-20, 30	—	—	—	—	+2°	+1½°	+1¼°	+1°	+¾°	+½°	+¼°	0°	−¼°	−½°	−¾°
1974 P-10, 20	—	—	—	—	—	—	—	+1½°	+1¼°	+1°	+¾°	+½°	+¼°	0°	−¼°
1974 P-30	—	—	—	—	+2¼°	+2°	+1½°	+1¼°	+1°	+¾°	+½°	+¼°	0°	−¼°	−½°
1975-78 P-10, 20, 30	—	—	—	—	+2½°	+2¼°	+2°	+1¾°	+1½°	+1°	+¾°	+½°	+¼°	0°	−¼°
1979-80 P-10	—	—	—	—	+2.3°	+2.0°	+1.7°	+1.5°	+1.2°	+0.9°	+0.6°	+0.4°	+0.1°	−0.1°	−0.3°
1979-80 P-20, 30	—	—	+2.9°	+2.6°	+2.3°	+2.0°	+1.7°	+1.4°	+1.2°	+0.9°	+0.6°	+0.4°	+0.2°	+0.1°	—
1973-76 K-10, 20	+4° No provision for adjustment														
1977-80 K-10, 20, 30	+8° No provision for adjustment														

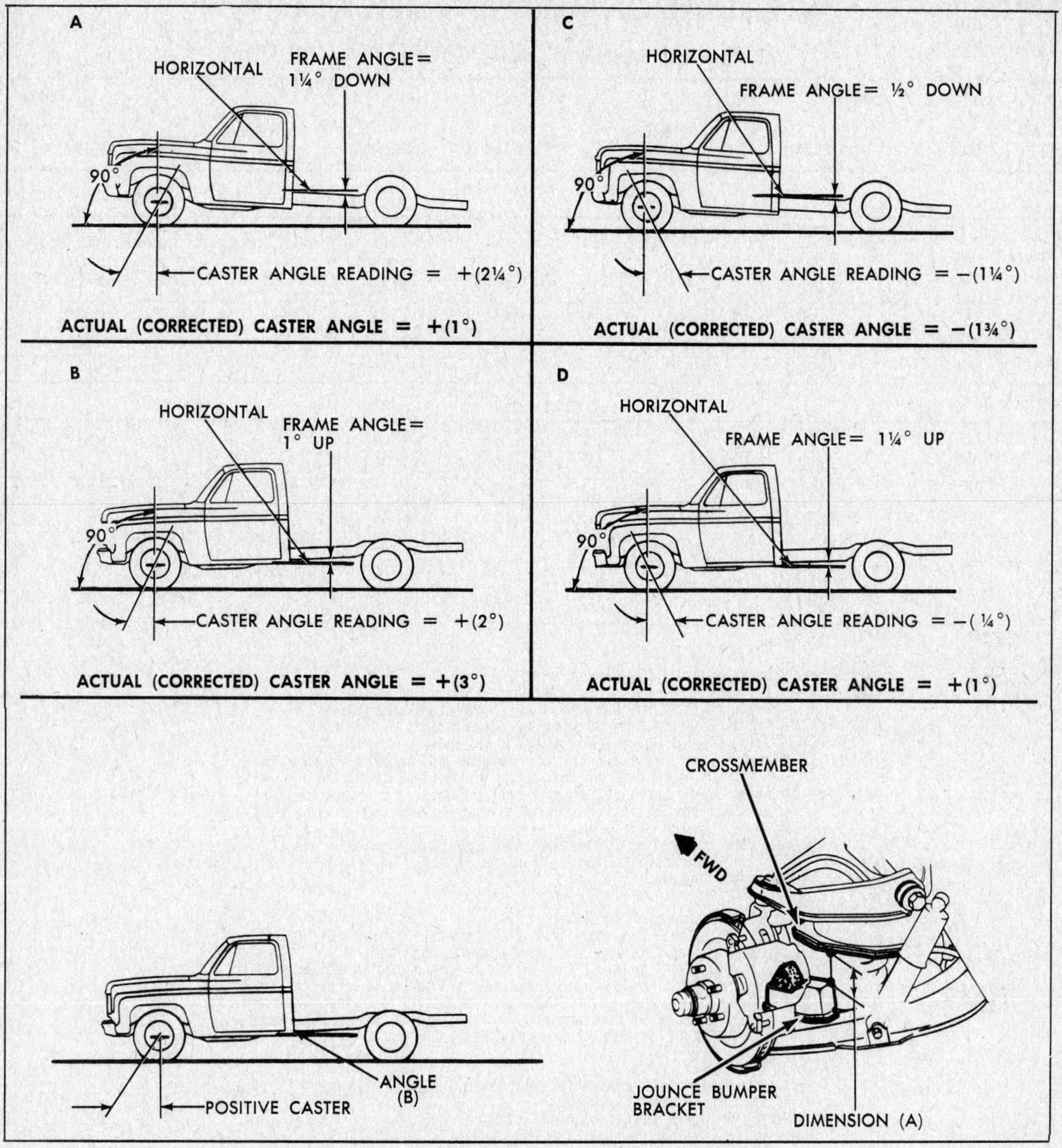

WHEEL ALIGNMENT SPECIFICATIONS

40-65 Series (Medium Duty)

MODEL	YEAR	AXLE (19)	CAMBER (3) L.H.	CAMBER (3) R.H.	CASTER (3)	TOE-(16)IN (13)	TURNING ANGLES (12) INSIDE	TURNING ANGLES (12) OUTSIDE	KING PIN INCLINATION LEFT	KING PIN INCLINATION RIGHT
C-50	1973	F-050	+1°	+1°	+2½°	⅛"-3/16"	20°	17¾°	7¼°	7¼°
	1974	F-050	+1°	+1°	+2½°	1/16"-⅛" (11)	20°	17¾°	7¼°	7¼°
S/C-60	1973	F-050, 055, 070	+1°	+1°	+2½°	3/32"-3/16"	20°	17¾°	7¼°	7¼°
	1974	F-050, 055, 070	+1°	+1°	+2½°	1/16"-⅛"	20°	17¾°	7¼°	7¼°
C/M-65	1973-74	F-070	+1°	+1°	+2½°	3/32"-3/16" (14)	20°	17¾°	7¼°	7¼°
C/M-65	1973-74	F-090, 120	+¼°	–¼°	+2½°	⅛"-7/32" (15)	20°	17¾°	5¾°	6¼°
T-60	1973-74	F-070	+1½°	+1½°	+1¼°	⅛"-¼" (14)	39°	27¾°	7°	7°
T-60	1973-74	F-090	+¼°	–¼°	+1¼°	⅛"-¼"	39°	27¾°	5¾°	6¼°
T-65	1973-74	F-170	+1½°	+1½°	+1¼°	⅛"-¼" (14)	39°	27¾°	7°	7°
T-65	1973-74	F-090	+¼°	–¼°	+1¼°	⅛"-¼"	39°	27¾°	5¾°	6¼°
T-65	1973-74	F-120	+¼°	–¼°	+1¼°	⅛"-¼"	39°	27¾°	5¾°	6¼°
P-40, 45	1974	F-050, 055	+1°	+1°	+2½°	1/16"-⅛"	20°	17¾°	7¼°	7¼°

WHEEL ALIGNMENT SPECIFICATIONS

P-40,45 and Medium Duty Conventional (C/M)

MODEL	YEAR	AXLE⑲	CAMBER③ L.H.	CAMBER③ R.H.	CASTER③	TOE-⑯IN⑬	TURNING ANGLES⑫ INSIDE	TURNING ANGLES⑫ OUTSIDE	KING PIN INCLINATION LEFT	KING PIN INCLINATION RIGHT
LBS. RATE⑲ (Axle)										
5000	1975-80	F-050	+1½°	+1½°	+2½°	⅛"-¼"	⑫	⑫	7°10′	7°10′
5500	1975-78	F-055	+1½°	+1½°	+2½°	⅛"-¼"	⑫	⑫	7°10′	7°10′
7000	1975-80	F-070	+1½°	+1½°	+2½°	⅛"-¼"	⑫	⑫	7°10′	7°10′
9000	1975-80	F-090	+¼°	−¼°	+2½°	⅛"-¼"	⑫	⑫	5¾°	6¼°
9000	1975-80	F-120⑰	+¼°	+¼°	+2½°	⅛"-¼"	⑫	⑫	5¾°	6¼°⑱
12000	1975	F-120	+¼°	+¼°	+2½°	⅛"-¼"	⑫	⑫	5¾°	6¼°⑱
Steel Tilt (T)										
7000	1975-80	F-070	+1½°	+1½°	+4°	⅛"-¼"	⑫	⑫	7°10′	7°10′
9000	1975-76	F-090	+¼°	−¼°	+4°	⅛"-¼"	⑫	⑫	5¾°	6¼°
	1977-80	F-090	+½°	−¼°	+4°	⅛"-¼"	⑫	⑫	5¾°	6¼°
9000	1975-76	F-120⑰	+¼°	+¼°	+4°	⅛"-¼"	⑫	⑫	5¾°	6¼°
	1977-80	F-120⑰	+½°	+¼°	+4°	⅛"-¼"	⑫	⑫	5¾°	6¼°
12000	1975-76	F-120	+¼°	+¼°	+4°	⅛"-¼"	⑫	⑫	5¾°	6¼°
	1977-80	F-120	+½°	+¼°	+4°	⅛"-¼"	⑫	⑫	5¾°	6¼°

① Refer to the Caster Specifications chart.
② Caster and camber must not vary more than ½° from side to side.
③ A reading of ±½° from specified setting is acceptable (see chart).
④ Always set toe-in after caster and camber adjustments.
⑤ A setting of ±1⁄16" from specified setting is acceptable.
⑥ Also known as toe-out-on-turns. No dimensions are available, however, the turning angle of the inner wheel is always greater than the turning angle of the outer wheel. The turning angles are not adjustable. If a scuffing condition is evident, check the steering arms for damage. If a steering arm is damaged in any way, it must be replaced.
⑦ Also known as steering axis inclination. This angle is not adjustable.
⑧ See Camber Specifications chart for "P-10, 20, 30 only".
⑨ No provision for adjustment.
⑩ K-10 with full time four wheel drive, toe-in is "0".
⑪ Axle toe-in measured at 20" diameter.
⑫ Adjustment of stop screw must provide ⅝" minimum clearance of tire with any chassis components, regardless of maximum turning angles.
⑬ Toe-in measurements must be made at the horizontal axis of the wheel. If, for any reason, the vehicle has been jacked up, it will be necessary to neutralize the front suspension. Roll the vehicle forward 12 to 15 feet. By doing so, all tolerances in the front suspension will be taken up, and the suspension will then be in normal operating position (neutralized).
⑭ 1974 toe-in 1⁄16" - ⅛"
⑮ 1974 toe in ⅛" - ¼"
⑯ Vehicles equipped with steel belted radial tires will have zero toe-in.
⑰ 12,000 lbs. axle rated at 9,000 lbs.
⑱ 1979-80, right side king-pin-inclination is 5¾°
⑲ Refer to illustrations for correct axle identification

DISTRIBUTOR

Detailed information on direction of distributor rotation, cylinder numbering, firing order, point gap, cam dwell, spark plugs, and idle speed will be found in the Specifications tables.

Engine diagnosis is found in the General Repair Section.

H.E.I. System—1975-80

1975-80 light duty Chevrolet truck engines use a High Energy Ignition system. Two types are used. V8 and 1978 and later six-cylinder distributors combine all ignition components in one unit. The coil is in the distributor cap and connects directly to the rotor. The 6 cylinder distributor through 1977 has an externally mounted coil. Both units operate in basically the same manner. The module and pick-up coil replace the conventional breaker points. The module automatically controls the dwell, stretching it with increased engine speed. The system also features a longer spark duration due to the greater amount of energy stored in the primary coil.

The centrifugal and vacuum advance mechanisms are basically the same type of unit as on a conventional ignition distributor.

NOTE: The 292 engine uses both centrifugal and vacuum advance mechanisms, while the 350, 366, and 427 engines use only a centrifugal advance mechanism (medium duty trucks).

The electronic module is serviced by complete replacement.

WARNING: Do not remove the spark plug wires with the engine running. Severe shock could result.

Distributor Removal and Installation

Inline Engines

1. Remove distributor cap, primary wire and vacuum line.
2. Scribe a mark on the distributor body, locating the position of the rotor. Scribe another mark on the distributor body and engine block, showing the position of the body in the block.
3. Remove the distributor hold-down screw and lift the distributor up and out of the engine.

NOTE: As the distributor is removed from engine, the rotor will turn counterclockwise slightly. When reinstalling be sure to allow for this.

4. If the crankshaft was rotated, turn the engine until the piston of No. 1 cylinder is at the top of its compression stroke.
5. Position the distributor in the block so that the vacuum control unit is in its normal postion.
6. Position the rotor to point toward the front of the engine (with distributor held out of the block, but in installed position). Turn rotor counterclockwise about one-eighth turn and push distributor down to engage camshaft drive. It may be necessary to move the rotor one way or the other to mesh the drive and driven gears properly.
7. While holding the distributor down in place, kick the starter a few times to make sure the oil pump shaft is engaged. Install hold-down clamp and bolt and snug up the bolt.
8. Once again, rotate the crankshaft until No. 1 cylinder is on the compression stroke and the harmonic balancer mark is on 0°.
9. Turn distributor body slightly until points open. Tighten distributor clamp bolt.
10. Place distributor cap in position and see that the rotor lines up with the terminal for the No. 1 spark plug.
11. Install cap, distributor primary wire, and double check plug wires in the cap towers.
12. Start engine and set timing according to the Tune-up chart.
13. Reconnect vacuum hose to vacuum control assembly.

CAUTION: When using an auxiliary starter switch for bumping the engine into position for timing or compression test, the primary distributor lead must be disconnected from the negative post of the ignition coil and the ignition switch must be on. Failure to do this may cause damage to the grounding circuit in the ignition switch. This will also prevent the sudden starting of engine and possible serious injury.

V8 Engines

If it becomes necessary to remove the distributor, carefully mark the

INTERIM 1978 AND LATER

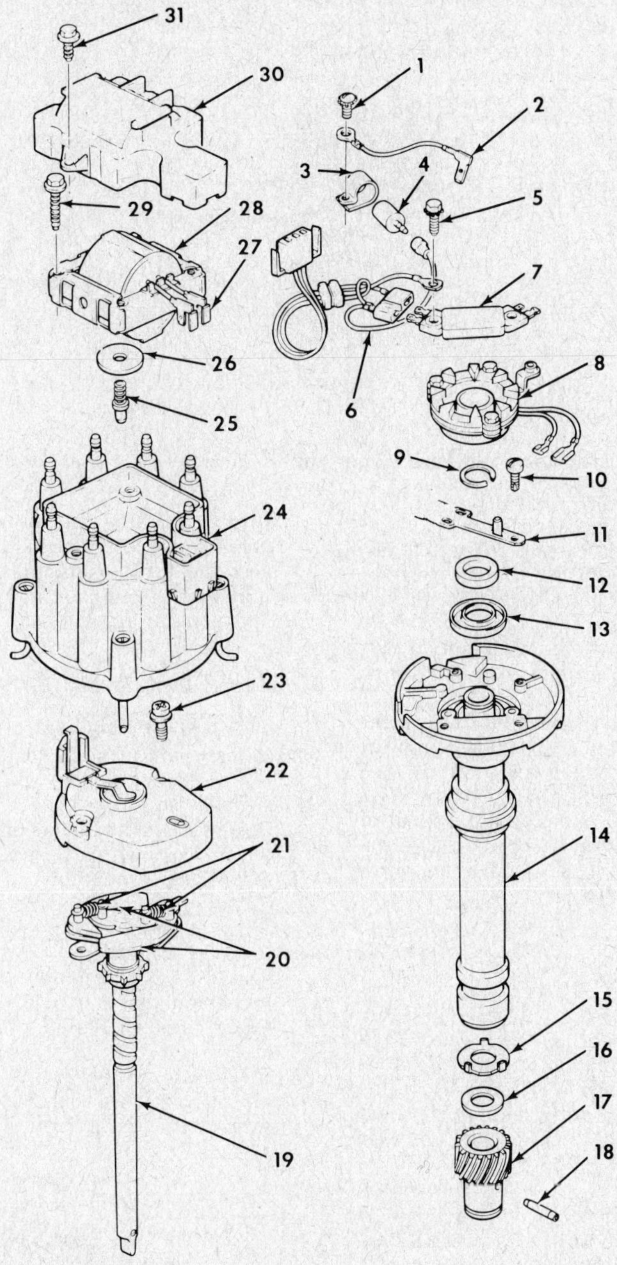

HEI distributor w/o vacuum advance—V8 engine (typical)
(© Chevrolet Div., G.M. Corp.)

1 Screw
2 Wiring Lead
3 Capacitor Clamp
4 Capacitor
5 Screw
6 Wiring Harness Module Leads
7 Module
8 Pick-Up Coil Magnet Assembly
9 Thin "C" Washer
10 Screw
11 Plastic Retainer
12 Felt Washer
13 Felt Retainer
14 Housing
15 Thrust Washer
16 Shim
17 Driven Gear
18 Roll Pin
19 Shaft
20 "Centrifugal Advance" Weights
21 Springs
22 Rotor
23 Screw
24 Cap
25 Spring & Button Assembly
26 Seal
27 Coil Terminals
28 Coil
29 Screw
30 Cover
31 Screw

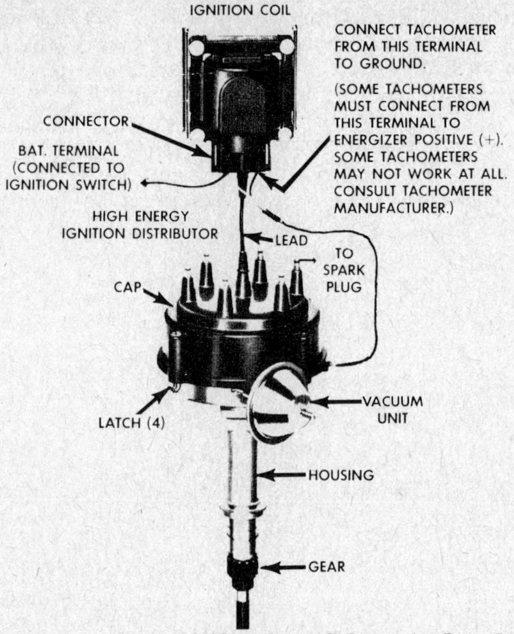

HEI Distributor—inline and V6 engines (© Chevrolet Div., G.M. Corp.)

position of the rotor so that, if the engine is not turned after the distributor is taken out, the rotor can be returned to the position from which it was removed without difficulty.

1. To remove the distributor, take off the carburetor air cleaner, disconnect the coil primary wire and the vacuum line, remove the distributor cap, take out the single hold-down bolt located under the distributor body. With a pencil, mark the position of the body relative to the block, and then work the distributor up out of the block.

NOTE: If necessary, remove secondary leads from cap after first marking cap tower for No. 1 lead.

2. Remove No. 1 spark plug and, with finger on plug hole, crank the engine until compression is felt in No. 1 cylinder. Continue cranking until pointer lines up with the timing mark on the crankshaft pulley.
3. Position distributor in opening of the block in normal installed attitude; have rotor pointing to front of engine.
4. Turn the rotor counterclockwise about one-eighth of a turn (from straight front toward the left cylinder bank). Push the distributor down to engage the camshaft and while holding, turn the engine with the starter so that distributor shaft engages the oil pump shaft.
5. Return engine to compression stroke of No. 1 piston with timing mark on pulley aligned with the pointer. Adjust the distributor so that the points are opening. Install the cap being sure the rotor points to the contact for No. 1 spark plug. Connect the timing light and check that spark occurs as timing mark and pointer are aligned.

Contact Point Replacement

Inline Engines

1. Release distributor cap hold-down screws, remove cap.
2. Remove rotor.
3. Pull primary and condenser lead wires from contact point quick disconnect terminal.
4. Remove condenser hold-down screw and replace condenser.
5. Remove contact set attaching screw, lift contact point set from breaker plate.
6. Clean breaker plate of oil and dirt.
7. Place new contact point assembly in position on breaker plate, install attaching screw.

CAUTION: Carefully wipe protective film from point set prior to installation.

NOTE: Pilot on contact set must engage matching hole in breaker plate.

8. Connect primary and condenser lead wires to quick disconnect terminal on contact point set.
9. Check and adjust points for proper alignment and breaker arm spring tension. Use an aligning tool to bend *stationary contact support* if points need alignment.
10. Set point gap.
11. Reinstall rotor and distributor cap.
12. Start engine and check dwell.

V8 Engines

1. The contact point set is replaced as one complete assembly and only dwell angle requires adjustment after replacement. Breaker lever spring tension and point alignment are factory set.
2. Remove the distributor cap by placing a screw driver in the slot head of the latch, press down and turn 1/4 turn in either direction. Remove two attaching screws, which hold rotor to weight base, and remove rotor.

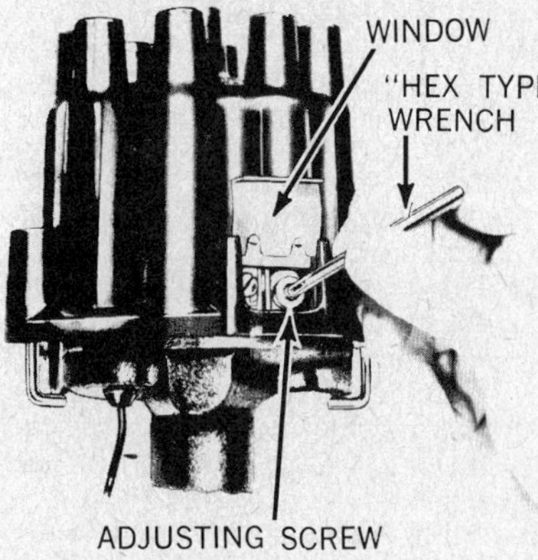

Ignition point adjustment—V8 engines (© Chevrolet Div., G.M. Corp.)

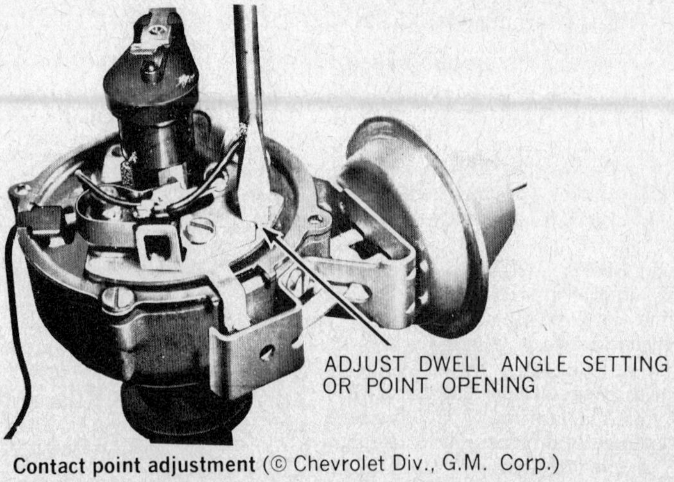

Contact point adjustment (© Chevrolet Div., G.M. Corp.)

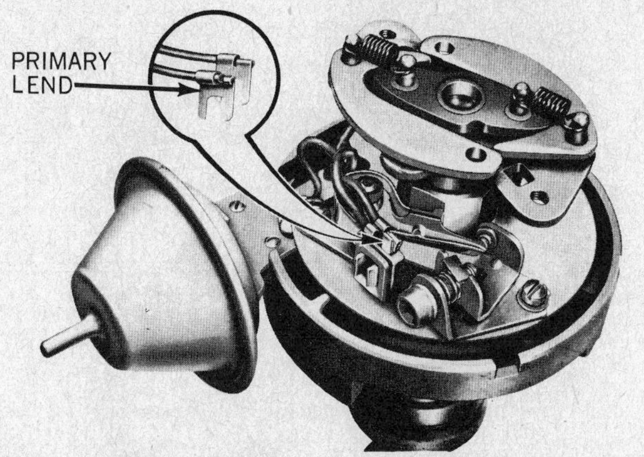

Primary circuit and condenser—electrical leads (correctly installed) (© Chevrolet Div., G.M. Corp.)

3. (On '73-'74 models, remove the two screws which hold R.F.I. shield in place, and remove shield.) Remove the two attaching screws which hold the base of the contact set assembly in place.
4. Remove the primary and condenser leads from their nylon insulated connection in contact set.
5. Reverse Steps 2, 3 and 4 to install new contact set.

CAUTION: **Improper installation of the primary and condenser leads will cause lead interference between the cap, weight base and breaker advance plate.**

6. Start engine and check the dwell.

With the engine running at idle and operating temperatures normal ized, the dwell is adjusted by raising the window provided in the cap and inserting a "Hex" type wrench into the adjusting screw head.

Turn the adjusting screw until the specified dwell angle is obtained.

Dwell Angle—H.E.I. System (1975 and later)

The dwell angle is fixed and is not adjustable. No attempt should be made to adjust the unit.

Timing Light Connections—H.E.I. System

Timing light connections should be made in parallel using an adapter at the distributor No. 1 terminal.

Tachometer Connections—H.E.I. System

There is a "tach" terminal on the distributor cap or on the remote-mounted coil. Connect the tachometer to this terminal and ground. Follow the tachometer manufacturer's instructions.

CAUTION: **Grounding the tach terminal could damage the H.E.I. ignition module.**

Ignition Timing

On conventional ignition engines, remove the spark plug wire from No. 1 plug and attach a timing light between the wire and the plug. On H.E.I. systems, connect the timing light in parallel at the No. 1 tower on the distributor cap. Disconnect the distributor spark advance hose and plug the vacuum opening. Start the engine and run it at idle speed. Aim the timing light at the degree scale just over the harmonic balancer. The markings on the scale are in 2° increments with the greatest number of markings on the *before* side of the 0. Adjust the timing by loosening the securing clamp and rotating the distributor until the desired ignition advance is achieved, then tighten the clamp. To advance the timing, rotate the distributor opposite to the normal direction of rotor rotation. Retard the timing by rotating the distributor in the normal direction of rotor rotation.

NOTE: On conventional ignition engines, if engine miss or rough idle occurs, connect the dwell meter and accelerate the engine to 1700 rpm. If the dwell reading varies more than 3°, check the distributor for worn distributor shaft, worn bushings or a loose distributor breaker plate.

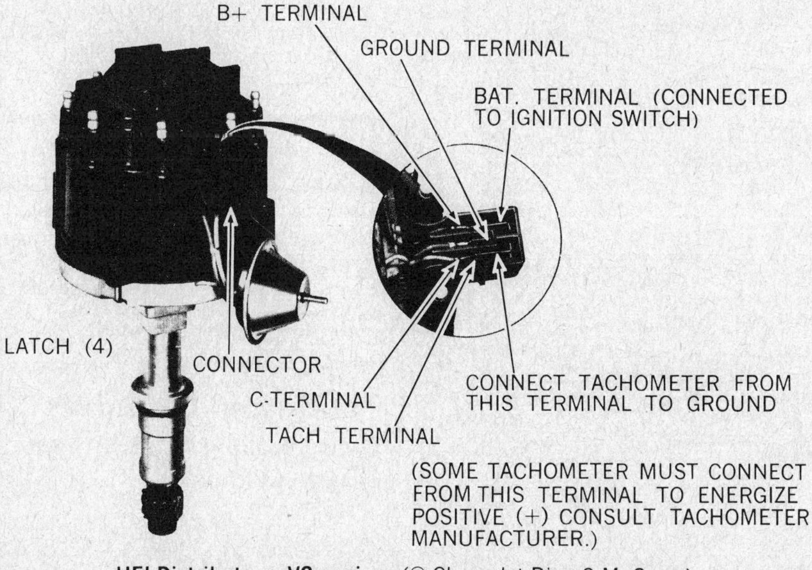

HEI Distributor—V8 engines (© Chevrolet Div., G.M. Corp.)

ALTERNATOR

Delcotron, the alternator by Delco-Remy is used on Chevrolet trucks. These units are furnished in two types with companion voltage regulators, which will be a two-unit external regulator or transistorized internal regulator.

Repair and test details on the alternator and its regulators are covered in the General Repair Section.

Alternator Removal and Installation

1. Disconnect the battery ground strap at battery to prevent damaging diodes or wiring harness (also prevents accidentally reversing polarity).
2. Disconnect wiring leads at Delcotron.
3. Remove the alternator brace bolt, (if power steering equipped, loosen pump brace and mount nuts) then detach drive belt(s).
4. Support the generator and remove alternator mount bolt (6.2" Delcotron uses 2 mounting bolts) or bolts and remove from vehicle.
5. Reverse the removal procedure to install, then adjust drive belt(s).
6. If no belt tension tool is available, force alternator away from the engine until fan belt has 5/16 in. deflection when forced downward from normal position with light pressure applied between the alternator and the fan.

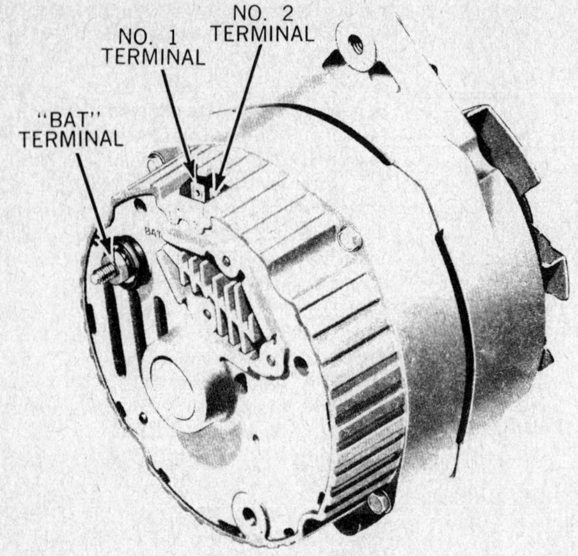

Alternator wiring terminals (© Chevrolet Div., G.M. Corp.)

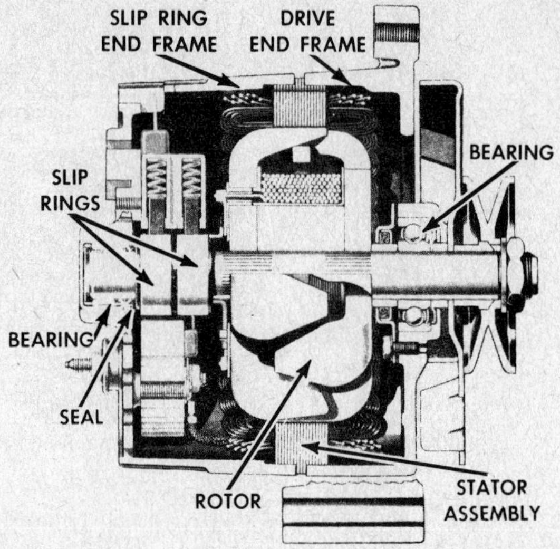

Cross section of alternator (© Chevrolet Div., G.M. Corp.)

CAUTION: Since the Delcotron and regulator are designed for use on a single polarity system, the following precautions must be observed:

1. The polarity of the battery, generator, and regulator must be matched and considered before making any electrical connections in the system.
2. When connecting a booster battery, be sure to connect the negative battery terminals with one another, and the positive battery terminals with one another.
3. When connecting a charger to the battery, connect the charger positive lead to the battery positive terminal. Connect the charger negative lead to the battry negative terminal.
4. Never operate the Delcotron on uncontrolled open circuit. Be sure that all connections in the circuit are clean and tight.
5. Do not short across or ground any of the terminals on the Delcotron regulator.
6. Do not attempt to polarize the Delcotron.
7. Do not use test lamps of more than 12 volts for checking diode continuity.
8. Avoid long soldering times when replacing diodes or transistors. Prolonged heat is damaging to these units.
9. Disconnect the battery ground terminal when servicing any AC system. This will prevent the possibility of accidentally reversing polarity.

STARTER

Starter Motor Removal and Installation

The following procedure is a general guide for all vehicles and will vary slightly depending on the truck series and model. (On Forward Control Vans, vehicle must be raised and supported.)

1. Disconnect battery ground cable at the battery.
2. Disconnect engine wiring harness and battery leads at solenoid terminals.
3. Remove starter mounting bolts and retaining nuts and disengage starter assembly from the flywheel housing. Light duty gasoline powered engines use conventional nose housing or pad mounting. Intermediate and heavy duty use conventional flange. On these, scribe mark on flange and flywheel housing as nose housing can be mounted in several positions.
4. Position starter motor assembly to the flywheel housing and install the mounting bolts and retaining nuts. Torque the mounting bolts 25 - 35 ft. lbs.
5. Connect all wiring leads at the solenoid terminals.
6. Connect the battery ground cable and check operation of the unit.

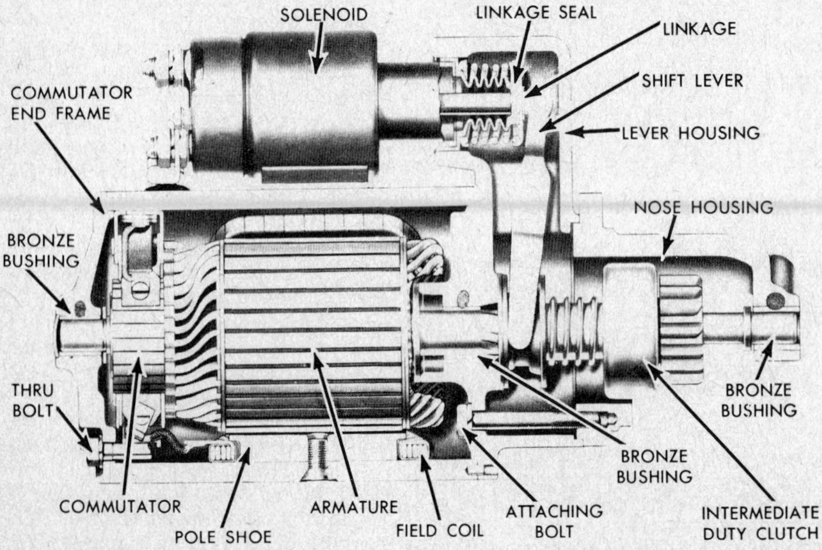

Starter motor—overrunning clutch type (© Chevrolet Div., G.M. Corp.)

BRAKES

Specific information will be found in General Brake Section on adjustments, bleeding, master cylinder and wheel cylinder overhaul procedures and trouble shooting.

Refer to Power Brake Section for details concerning power brakes.

Master Cylinders

Twin (Brake & Clutch) Type Master Cylinder

Removal

1. Disconnect clutch and brake pedal return springs.

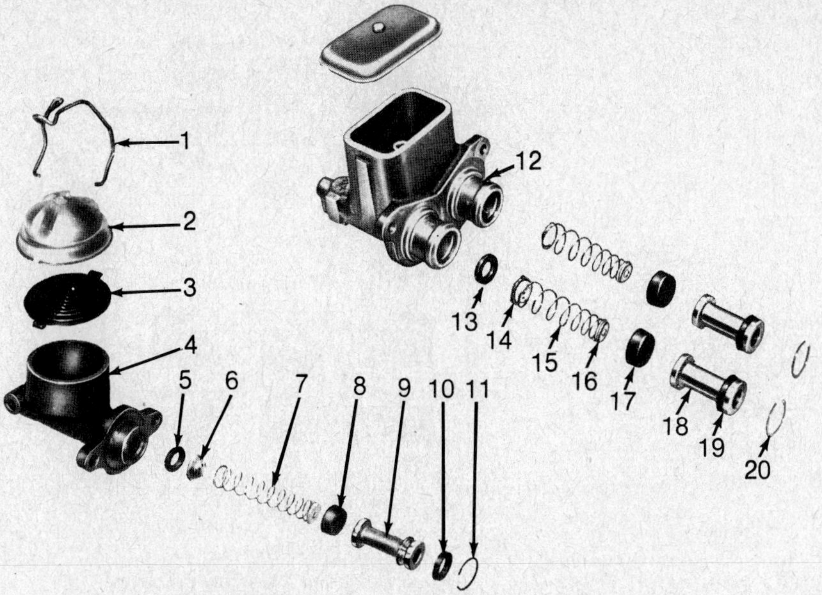

Single & Clutch assist master cylinders (© Chevrolet Div., G.M. Corp.)

1 Bail wire
2 Reservoir cover
3 Seal
4 Body
5 Valve seat
6 Valve assembly
7 Spring
8 Primary cup
9 Piston
10 Secondary cup
11 Lock ring
12 Housing
13 Seal
14 Check valve
15 Return spring
16 Retainer
17 Primary cup
18 Piston
19 Piston seal
20 Snap ring

2. Detach push rod boots from cylinders.
3. Remove clutch and brake hydraulic lines.
4. Remove three bolts holding cylinder to dash and slide cylinder off push rod.

NOTE: Wipe hydraulic fittings clean and place dry cloth under lines to absorb any fluid spillage. Cover fittings and lines to prevent any foreign matter from entering system.

Installation

1. Place new gaskets and push rod boots over cylinder tubes.
2. Hold cylinder next to dash and insert push rods, making sure they are centered.
3. Bolt assembly loosely to dash. This freedom of assembly will allow hydraulic lines to be started in cylinder without stripping fittings.
4. Tighten assembly and hydraulic lines securely.
5. Replace pedal return springs.
6. Fill reservoir and bleed both clutch and brake cylinders.
7. Check pedal free play and operation.

Standard Conventional Single Master Cylinder

Removal

1. Clean area at fitting and place dry cloth under line to absorb leakage.
2. Disconnect hydraulic line at cylinder and cover ends with clean cloth to prevent any foreign matter from entering system.
3. Disconnect push rod from pedal.
4. Remove the two nuts and washers holding cylinder to firewall. Remove Cylinder.

Installation

1. Position cylinder at dash, align push rod through boot and secure loosely. This freedom of assembly will allow hydraulic line and push rod to be installed with minimum of effort.
2. Tighten nuts and line. Check free play.
3. Fill cylinder and bleed. Bleeding can be accomplished by slowly pressing down on brake pedal and at same time tightening the hydraulic line fitting. Any air still trapped in line at fitting can be expelled by pressing hard on brake pedal to a point of just below free play. By having a slight pressure on pedal, the piston is held forward enough to clear ports in reservoir and check valve is held off its seat, so air can be released.
4. Final check of fluid and brake operation.

Standard Dual Master Cylinder

Removal

1. Clean area at fittings and place dry cloth under lines to absorb leakage.
2. Disconnect both lines at cylinder and cover to prevent foreign matter from entering system.
3. Disconnect any stop light or brake warning light wires.
4. Unbolt cylinder and remove, allowing push rod to fall loose.

Installation

1. Install new boot on push rod.
2. Position cylinder making certain push rod and boot are in proper position and fasten loosely to firewall. This freedom of assembly will allow both hydraulic lines to be started easily.
3. Tighten mounting nuts and lines. Check free play.
4. Connect any stop light or brake warning light wires.
5. Fill reservoir and bleed. Test brakes before moving truck.

Wheel Cylinders

Four types of cylinders are used identified by type of brake system

Duo servo—One double-end cylinder mounted at toe ends of shoes.

Twinplex—Two double-end cylinders mounted between shoes at toe and heel.

Wagner F (FA)—Two single end cylinders (single piston, single direc-

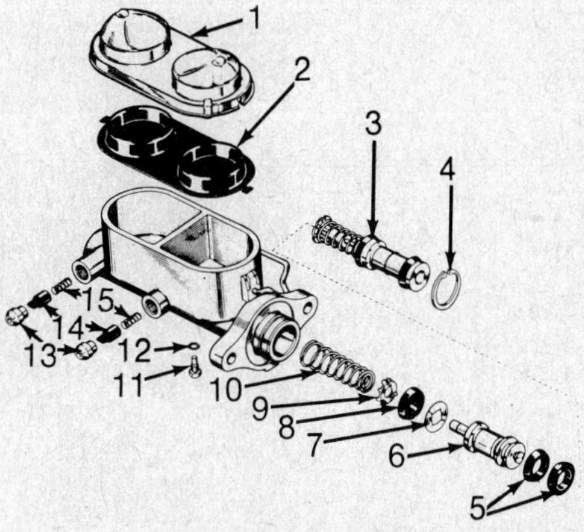

1 Cover
2 Diaphragm
3 Rear piston assembly
4 Snap ring
5 Secondary cups
6 Front piston
7 Cup protector
8 Primary cup
9 Cup retainer
10 Front piston return spring
11 Piston top screw
12 "O" ring
13 Tube seat inserts
14 Check valves
15 Check valve springs

Dual master cylinder (© Chevrolet Div., G.M. Corp.)

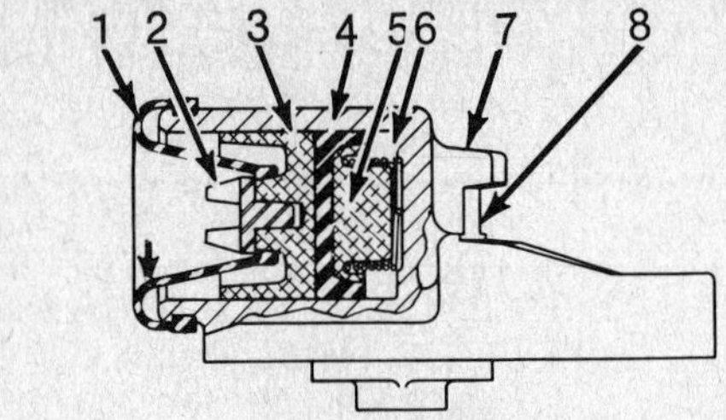

TYPE "F"

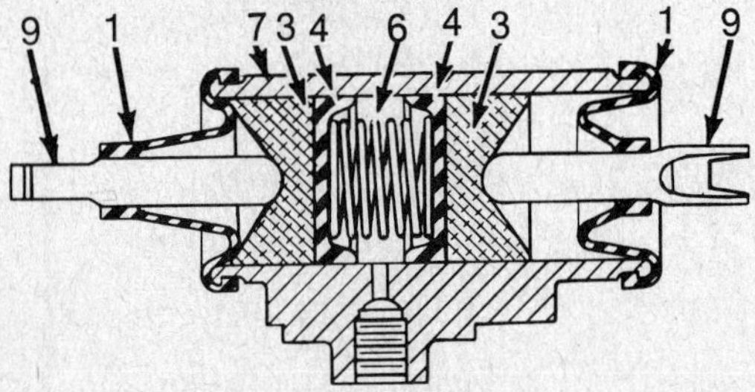

TYPE "FR-3"

Wheel cylinder used with "F", "FA", "FR3", & "FR3A" brakes (© Chevrolet Div., G.M. Corp.)

1 Boot
2 Brake shoe guide
3 Piston
4 Piston cup
5 Cup filler
6 Piston spring
7 Cylinder
8 Brake shoe anchor slot
9 Push rod

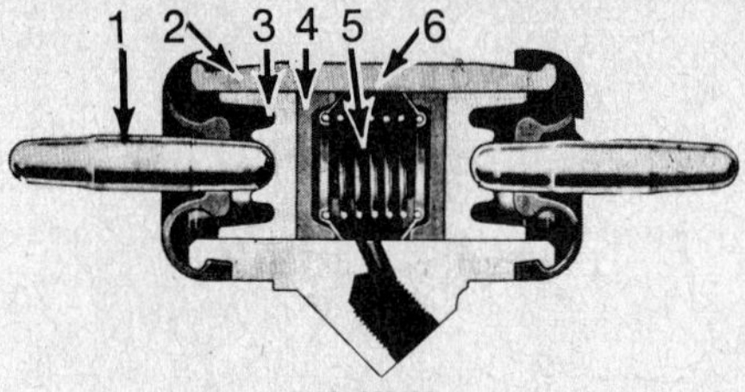

DUO-SERVO

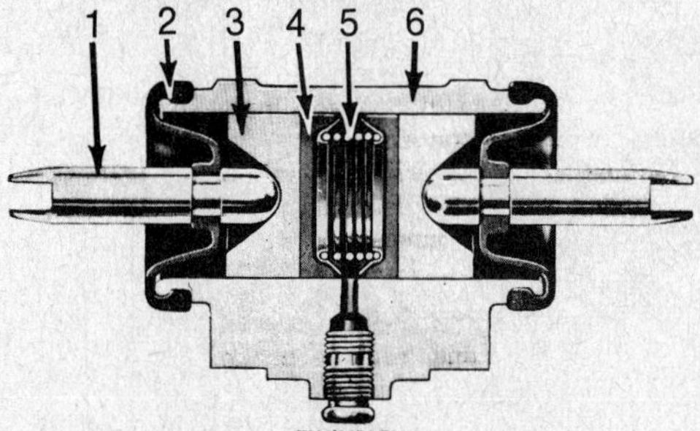

TWINPLEX

Duo servo and Twin Plex cylinders (© Chevrolet Div., G.M. Corp.)

1 Push rod
2 Boot
3 Piston
4 Piston cup
5 Spring
6 Housing

tion) mounted so as to be an anchor for one and powering other.

Wagner FR3 (FR3A)—Two double-end cylinders mounted between shoes.

Wheel Cylinder

Removal

1. Jack up axle and support. Remove wheel and drum.

NOTE: To remove drum it may be necessary to back off brake adjustment, also if rear drum, release hand brake cable if so equipped.

CAUTION: To gain access to adjusting starwheel, a knockout lanced area is located in web of drum. After knocking out metal be sure to clean all metal particles from brake compartment. A new cover plug must be installed.

2. Release shoe return springs and spread shoes to clear wheel cylinder links. Make sure any lubricant or brake fluid does not get on facings by covering same.
3. At front—Disconnect metal line from flexible hose and remove hose if accessible or remove hose later after cylinder is removed. At rear—Disconnect metal line from cylinder.
4. Remove shield over cylinder and connecting line between cylinders, if so equipped.
5. Remove cap screws and washers holding cylinder to backing plate. Remove cylinder being careful of any fluid spillage.

Installation

1. Clean mounting surface and reverse above procedures.
2. Bleed and readjust brakes. Check pedal before moving vehicle.

NOTE: Twinplex—Upper and lower cylinders are not interchangeable due to position of connector tube openings. Upper cylinder has threaded bleeder valve opening drilled at outer edge of bore.

Wagner F & FA—Two wheel cylinder (upper and lower) are identical, however cylinders on right and left brakes have opposite castings.

Wagner FR3 & FR3A—Upper and lower cylinders on both right and left brakes are interchangeable.

Bleeding Hydraulic Brakes

Pressure Bleeding

Light Duty Trucks

NOTE: The manufacturer specifically advises that the pressure bleeding equipment be of the diaphragm type, i.e., there must be a rubber diaphragm between the air supply and the brake fluid to prevent contaminants, such as air, moisture, oil, etc., from entering the hydraulic system. Furthermore, the equipment used must be capable of exerting 20 to 30 psi hydraulic pressure on the brake system.

1. Be certain that the brake fluid in the bleeder equipment is at the operating level.
2. Remove all dirt from the top of the master cylinder, and remove the cylinder cover and rubber diaphragm.
3. Attach a brake bleeder adapter or an equivalent tool for the frame mounted boosters to the master cylinder.
4. Connect a hose from the bleeder equipment to the bleeder adapter, and open the release valve on the bleeder equipment.

NOTE: The combination valve (front brake metering valve) must be held in the open position

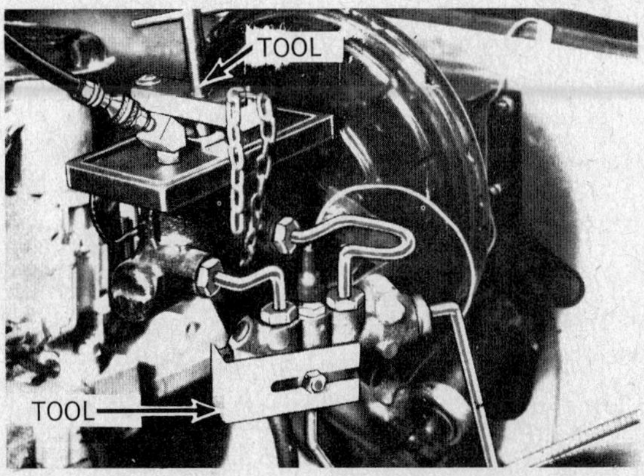

Brake Bleeder Adapter Installed (© Chevrolet Div., G.M. Corp.)

while bleeding. Install tool or an equivalent device with the open slot under the mounting bolt and pushing in on the pin in the end of the valve.

5. Bleed the brakes in the following order: right rear, left rear, right front, and left front.
6. Fill a transparent container with a sufficient amount of brake fluid to ensure that the submerged end of the bleeder hose will remain below the surface of the fluid.
7. Place a brake bleeder wrench over the first bleeder valve, and install one end of the bleeder hose over the valve.
8. Place the loose end of the bleeder hose in the container of brake fluid. Make sure that the hose end remains submerged in the brake fluid.
9. Open the bleeder valve by turning the bleeder wrench 3/4 turn counterclockwise, and allow fluid to flow until no air is seen in the fluid.
10. Close the bleeder valve tightly, and proceed in the same manner with the remaining bleeder valves until there is no longer any air in the brake system.
11. Disconnect the brake bleeder equipment from the adapter at the master cylinder, and remove the adapter from the master cylinder.
12. Fill the master cylinder reservoir(s) to within 1/4" of the top rim, and install the master cylinder diaphragm and cover.

Medium Duty Trucks—1973

CAUTION: Stop engine and relieve vacuum or exhaust pressure from system before following procedures.

1. Make certain fluid in pressure tank is above the petcock outlet and that tank is chraged with 40 to 50 psi of air.
2. Clean dirt from around master cylinder filler cap. Connect pressure tank hose to filler cap or cover opening. Bleed air from hose before tightening connection. Open valves at both ends.
3. Bleed slave cylinder and control valve first. (when used). Slip end of bleeder hose over bleeder valve No. 1 and place other end in glass jar containing enough hydraulic fluid to cover end of hose. Open bleeder valve with wrench and observe flow of fluid. On 40-50 series vehicles, start engine and make at least two power brake applications with bleeder valve open to force air out of slave cylinder. Close bleeder valve as soon as bubbles stop and fluid flows in solid stream. Stop engine and relieve vacuum from system.
4. Bleed valve No. 2 (on power cylinder control valve), then bleed wheel cylinders in sequence. Repeat bleeding operations at power cylinder. On 40-50 series vehicles, repeat power brake applications with engine running as in Step (3).
5. If, after bleeding the pedal "feel" is not satisfactory, inspect

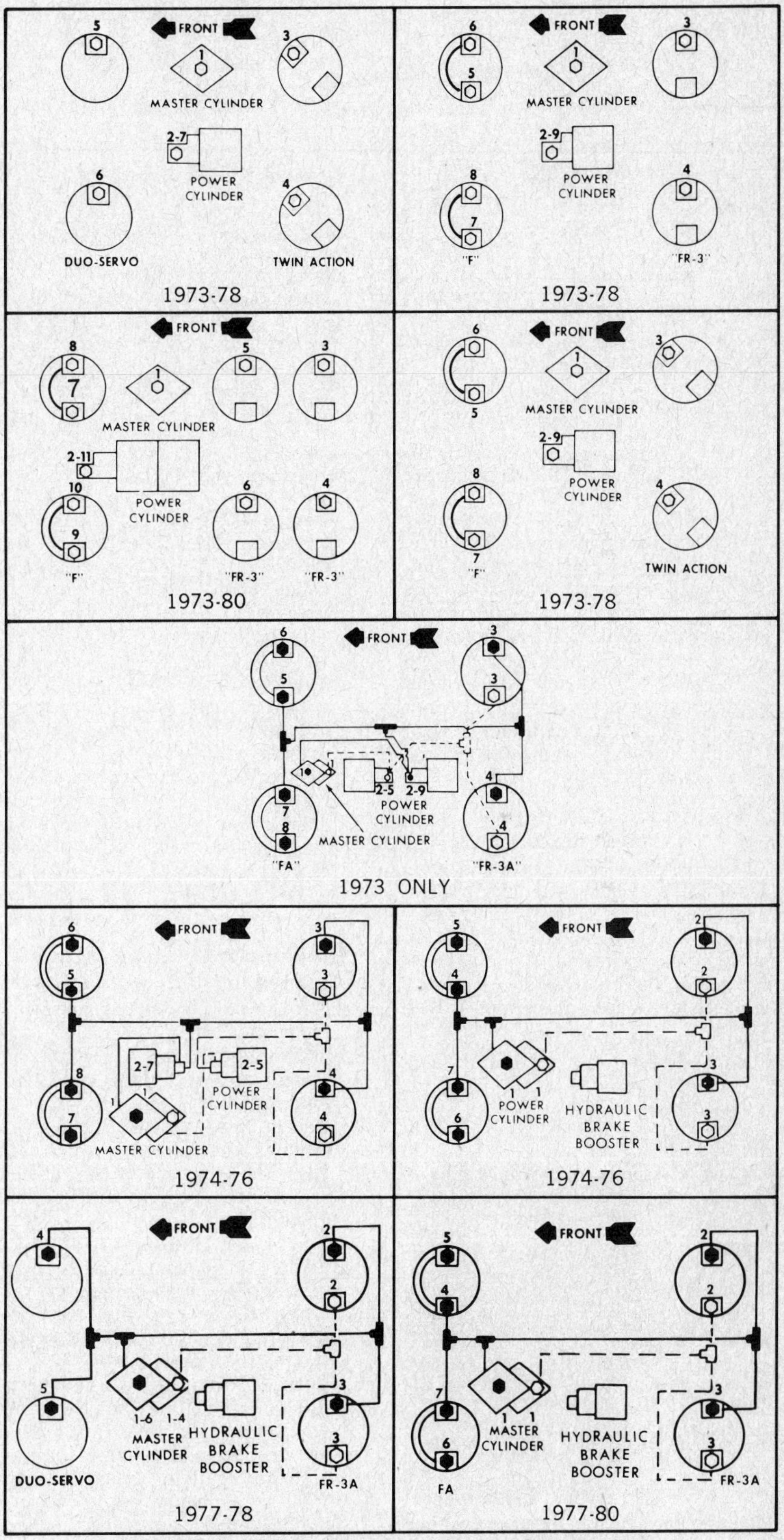

Hydraulic Brake Bleeding Sequence—Medium Duty Trucks (common brake systems 1973-80) (© Chevrolet Div., G.M. Corp.)

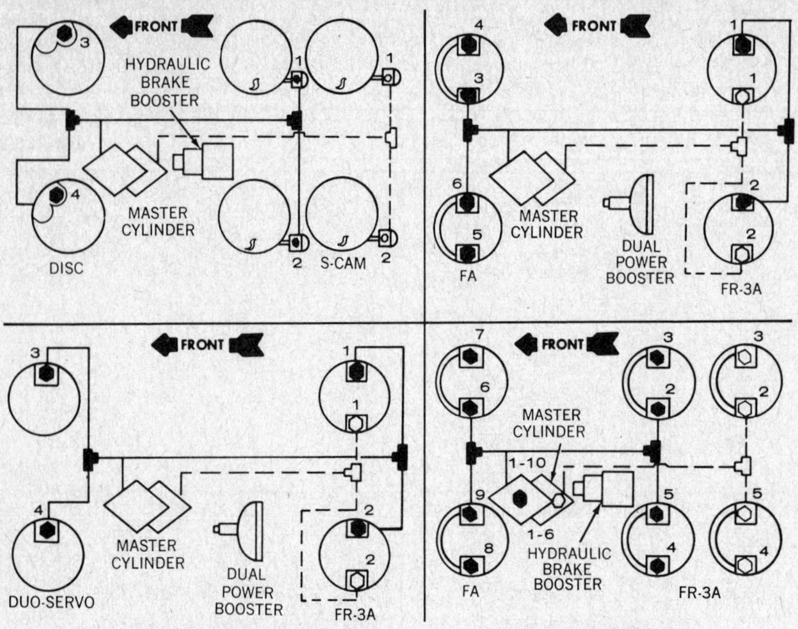

Hydraulic Brake Bleeding Sequence—Medium Duty Trucks (typical of 1979-89 vehicles) (© Chevrolet Div., G.M. Corp.)

residual check valve in the master cylinder and the check valve in the power cylinder piston. Improper operation of either or both of these valves will result in same pedal "feel" as air in the system, since malfunction permits recirculation of fluid through compensating line and back to master cylinder reservoir. Refer to applicable procedures for repair.

Medium Duty Trucks (w/Disc Brakes)

The pressure bleeding procedure for medium duty trucks with disc brakes is essentially the same as the procedure for light duty trucks with the following exceptions:

1. Install special tool or an equivalent tool on the metering valve, which is located at the frame crossmember. This step is necessary to hold the metering valve open, because when a bleeder valve is opened, the pressure drops allowing the metering valve to close, which stops the flow of fluid to the front brakes.
2. Install a brake bleeder adapter or an equivalent tool on the master cylinder.
3. Begin bleeding the system at the valve nearest the master cylinder, then proceed to the next nearest, and so on until all of the valves have been bled. If the master cylinder has bleeder valves, bleed these valves first.

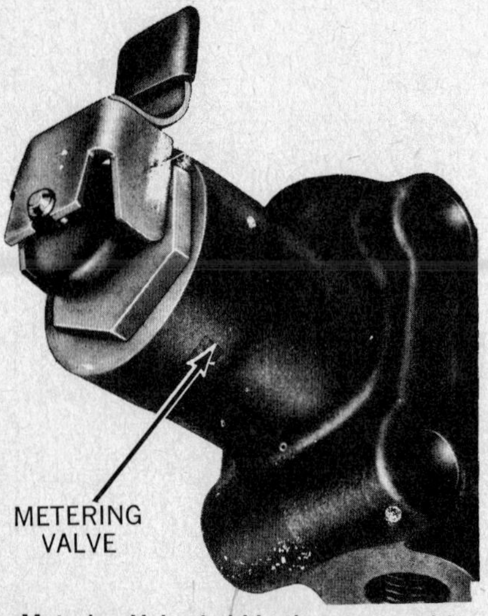

Metering Valve held in the open position —Medium Duty Trucks (w/disc brakes) (© Chevrolet Div., G.M. Corp.)

Bleeding Hydro-Boost System Medium Duty Trucks

1. Fill the power steering pump to the proper level.
2. Start the engine for approximately two seconds. Check the fluid and add if necessary.
3. Repeat step 2 until the fluid level remains constant.
4. Raise the front end of the vehicle so that the tires are clear of the ground.
5. Start the engine and run approximately 1500 rpm. Depress and release the brake pedal several times then turn the steering wheel right and left, lightly contacting the wheel stops.
6. Turn off the engine and check the fluid level in the reservoir and add fluid if necessary.
7. Lower the vehicle, start the engine and run at approximately 1500 rpm. Depress and release the brake pedal several times and turn the steering wheel to full right and left.
8. Turn the engine off and check the fluid level in the reservoir. Add fluid if necessary.

NOTE: If the fluid is extremely foamy, or there is an erratic pedal feel allow vehicle to stand a few moments with the engine off and repeat the above procedure.

Manual Bleeding

Manual bleeding follows the same procedures as pressure bleeding, except that brake fluid is forced through lines by pumping the brake pedal instead of by air pressure. Fluid in master cylinder must be replenished after bleeding at each valve. Brake pedal should be pumped up and down slowly, and should be on downstroke as valve is closed. Metering valve must be held in the open position.

Split System ("S" Models)

The system consists of a dash mounted master cylinder and two power cylinders mounted on the frame. The main system consists of the front wheel brakes and one cylinder on each rear wheel brake. The secondary system consists of one cylinder on each secondary wheel brake. Each system must be bled separately.

Disc Brakes

Disc Brakes are used on the light trucks, light vans, and on four wheel drive units.

Specific information will be found in the Disc Brake Sections on replacement and overhaul.

Power Brakes

Power Hydraulic

Specific information will be found in Power Brake Section on adjustments, bleeding, overhaul and trouble shooting.

Various vacuum-hydraulic or air-hydraulic brake systems are used, although sizes and shapes differ the basic function is the same.

Dual vacuum booster
(© Chevrolet Div., G.M. Corp.)

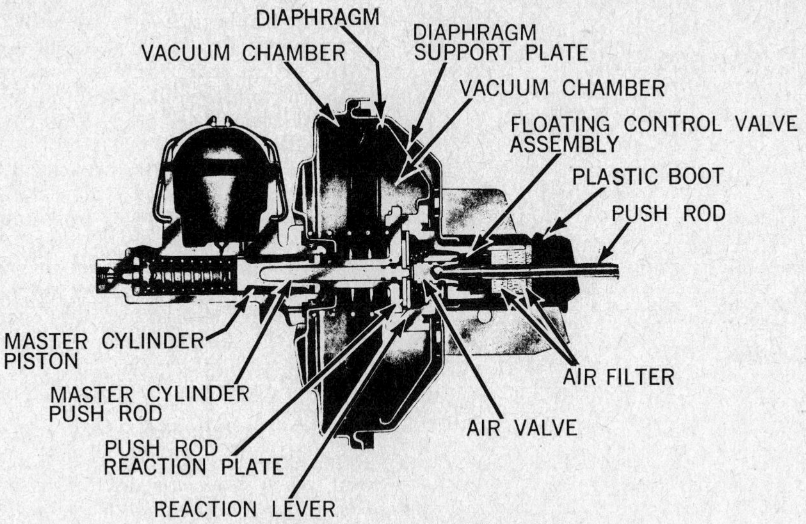

Moraine power unit (© Chevrolet Div., G.M. Corp.)

Dual Power Brake System

(Medium Duty Conventional Cab)

The Dual Power Brake System (DPB) is a system which utilizes two power boosting units in series to provide the power assist necessary to stop the vehicle. This is accomplished by combining a vacuum operated booster with a hydraulically operated booster in tandem arrangement with a standard dual master cylinder. Assist power generated by the vacuum booster is transmitted forward to the hydraulic booster, where the apply power is, again, assisted or augmented by the hydraulic booster. Doubly assisted power available at the hydraulic booster is transmitted to the master cylinder, thereby developing hydraulic pressure up to a maximum of approximately 600 psi.

NOTE: The entire dual power assembly may be removed as one unit (master cylinder, hydraulic booster, and vacuum booster), individual units, or combinations of units.

Hydraulic Booster

Removal and Installation

1. Prevent the vehicle from moving by blocking the wheels.
2. Disconnect the battery ground.
3. Disconnect the electrical connection at the flow switch.
   NOTE: It is advised that a container of suitable size be placed under the master cylinder and booster assembly prior to disconnecting any fluid lines.
4. Remove, if necessary, the brake line clamps, clips, and supports to allow movement of the master cylinder.
5. Remove the master cylinder mounting bolts, and position the master cylinder out of the way.
   NOTE: Support the master cylinder in an upright position in order to relieve strain on the brake lines and prevent spillage of hydraulic fluid.
6. Disconnect the fluid lines at the booster inlet and flow switch.
7. Remove the nuts which secure the hydraulic booster to the vacuum booster, and remove the hydraulic booster.
8. Install in the reverse order of removal.
9. Torque the hydraulic booster to vacuum booster retaining nuts to 23 ft. lbs.
10. Torque the master cylinder mounting bolts to 23 ft. lbs.
11. Bleed the system.
12. Connect the battery ground.

Vacuum Booster

Removal and Installation

1. Prevent the vehicle from moving by blocking the wheels.
2. Disconnect the battery gruond.
3. Remove, if necessary, the brake line clamps, clips, and support to allow movement of the master cylinder.
4. Remove the three nuts which retain the hydraulic booster to the vacuum booster.
5. Position the master cylinder and hydraulic booster out of the way.
   NOTE: Support the master cylinder and hydraulic booster in an upright position in order to relieve strain on the hydraulic lines and prevent spillage of hydraulic fluid.
6. Disconnect the vacuum hose from the check valve.

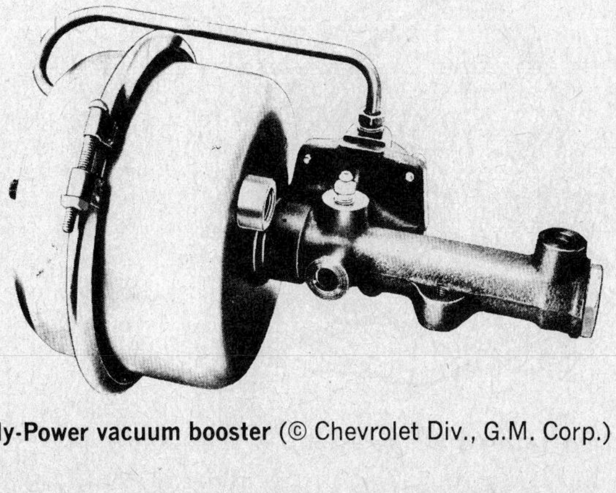
Hy-Power vacuum booster (© Chevrolet Div., G.M. Corp.)

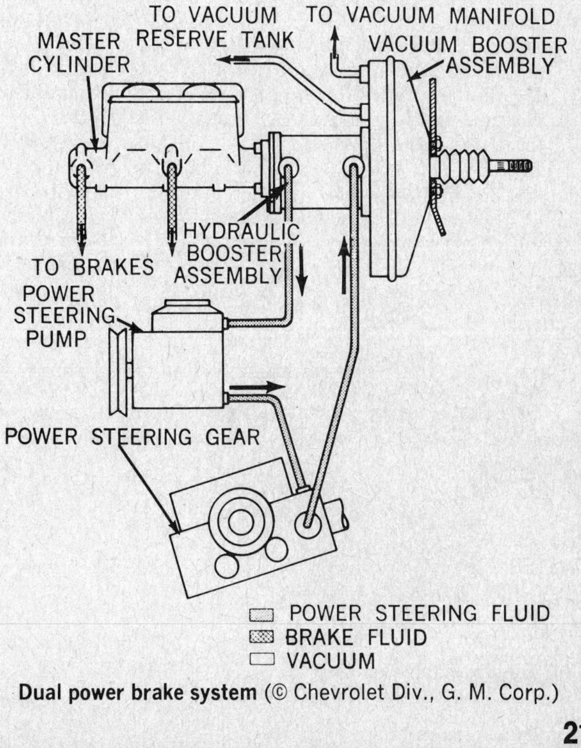

Dual power brake system (© Chevrolet Div., G. M. Corp.)

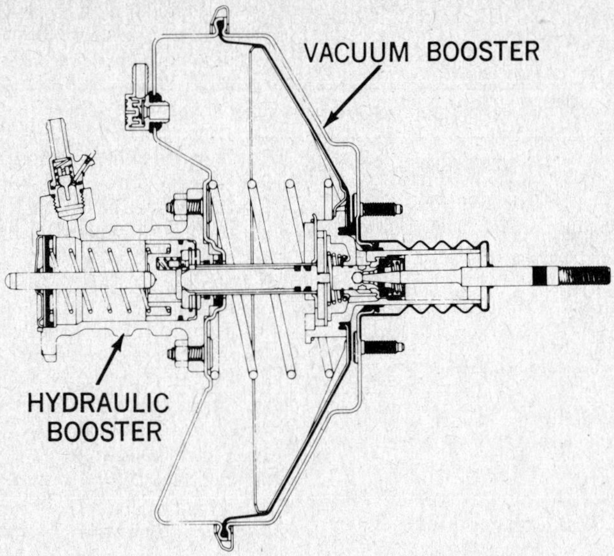

Dual power booster (© Chevrolet Div., G.M. Corp.)

7. Disconnect the vacuum hose at the elbow.
8. Position the vacuum hose out of the way in order to prevent contamination.
9. Disconnect the push rod (apply rod) at the brake pedal.
10. Working from inside the cab, remove the four muonting studs which secure the vacuum booster to the cab. Pull the booster away from the cowl, and remove it from the vehicle.
11. Install in the reverse order of removal.
    NOTE: It will be necessary to gauge the hydraulic booster piston push rod. For information concerning the gauging procedure, refer to the BRAKE portion of the General Repair Section.
12. Torque the vacuum booster mounting stud nuts to 18 ft. lbs.
13. Torque the hydraulic booster to vacuum booster mounting nuts to 23 ft. lbs.

Master-Vac

The Master-Vac, a self contained hydraulic and vacuum unit is used on light duty trucks. This hydrovac is of the diaphragm type. The multi-vac-unit was designed for use with the low input-high output system, while the newer hydrovac is used in equal displacement system. In equal displacement hydraulic system the fluid displaced by the master cylinder is equal to the fluid displaced by the power cylinder. Vacuum powered cylinders on 40-50-60 series, with hydraulic brakes, are either single or tandem diaphragms. The tandem diaphragm unit is used with single master cylinder. Single diaphragm units, two used, are on dual cylinder units. One for each system.

Single Diaphragm Hydrovac

The Single Diaphragm Hydrovac is a self contained vacuum hydraulic power brake unit designed for use on a vehicle with a vacuum source such as the intake manifold vacuum of a conventional gasoline engine. The Hydrovac is comprised of three basic elements:

1. A vacuum power chamber which consists of a power diaphragm and a push rod that connects the power diaphragm to the hydraulic piston.
2. A hydraulic cylinder (slave cylinder) which contains a hydraulic piston with a drilled passage to permit the filling of the hydraulic cylinder and return of the fluid to the master cylinder upon release of the brakes.
3. A vacuum control valve built integrally with the hydraulic cylinder which controls the power output of the vacuum power chamber in accordance with the hydraulic pressure developed with the vehicle master cylinder.

Power-Vacuum

Removal

NOTE: Wipe hydraulic fittings clean, place dry cloth under lines to absorb any fluid leakage, cover lines to keep system clean.

1. Disconnect push rod clevis at pedal, if clearance hole in dash is not large enough, remove clevis. (mark position)
2. Remove vacuum hose from unit. (check valve)
3. Disconnect hydraulic lines, if necessary.
4. Remove any stop light wires.
5. Remove 4 nuts and washers holding unit to firewall, remove unit (and bracket)

Installation

1. Mount unit in place and install loosely. Secure push rod to pedal and check free-play.
2. Tighten mounting nuts and hydraulic lines.
3. Install vacuum line.
4. Connect any stop light wire.
5. Bleed brakes, (bench-bleed unit before installing, units with 2 bleeder valves. Bleed valve nearest to shell first).

CAUTION: **Pressure bleeding must be done with engine off (no vacuum). In manual bleeding, use engine (start engine, allow vacuum to build up).**

6. Check brakes and stoplight before moving vehicle.
7. Units requiring lubrication, remove ⅛ inch pipe plug in front end of shell (engine off).

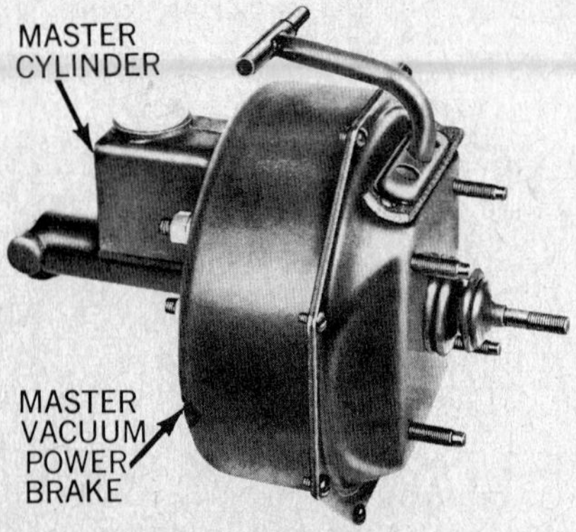

Bendix master vac unit
(© Chevrolet Div., G.M. Corp.)

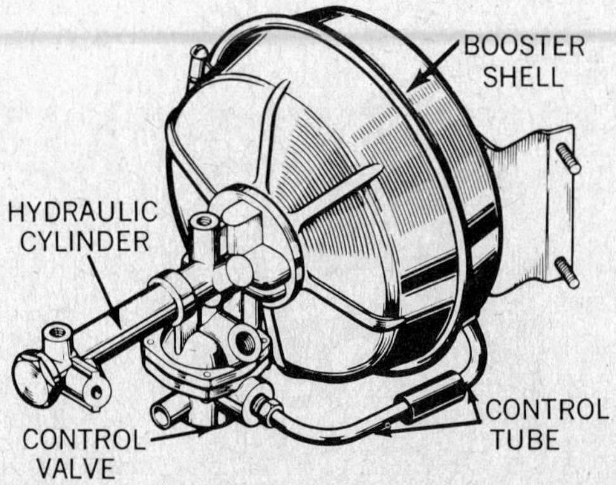

Single Diaphragm Hydrovac (© Chevrolet Div., G.M. Corp.)

Fill with vacuum cylinder oil until oil runs out filler hole.

Hydro-Boost

Specific information will be found in the Power Brake portion of the General Repair Section on adjustments, overhauling and troubleshooting.

The Hydro-boost system was designed to eliminate the need for the remote frame mounted boosters. It utilizes power steering fluid in place of engine vacuum to provide a power assist that operates a dual master cylinder brake system. A spring accumulator is used in conjunction with the hydraulic brake booster. The accumulator is a sealed hydraulic cylinder with a port at each end. On 1974 models the accumulator and booster are mounted separately. In 1975 all "C" model vehicles equipped with the hydro-boost incorporate an accumulator which is integral with the booster. All 1976 and later hydro-boost vehicles will incorporate an accumulator which is integral with the booster.

CAUTION: **The accumulator used on 1974-77 vehicles contains a spring compressed under high pressure. Any attempt to disassemble or cut into the accumulator could cause severe personal injury. The accumulator used on 1978 and later hydro-boost vehicles contains compressed gas. DO NOT apply heat to the accumulator. NEVER attempt to repair an inoperative accumulator; always replace the accumulator with a new unit.**

In order to dispose of an inoperative accumulator, drill a 1/16" diameter hole through the end of the accumulator can opposite the "O" ring. (compressed gas type only)

Hydraulic Brake Booster Removal and Installation

Motor Home Chassis

1. Make sure all pressure is discharged from the accumulator by depressing and releasing the brake pedal several times.
2. Raise the vehicle on a hoist.
3. Clean all the dirt from the booster at the hydraulic line connections and master cylinder.
4. Remove the nuts and lockwashers that secure the master cylinder to the booster and support bracket. Support the master cylinder leaving the hydraulic lines attached to the master cylinder.
5. Disconnect and plug the hydraulic lines from the booster ports.
6. Remove the cotter pin, nut, bolt and washers that secure the operating lever to the vertical brake rod.
7. Remove the six nuts, lockwashers and bolts that secure the booster linkage bracket to the front and rear support brackets, then slide the booster off the rear support studs and remove the booster from the vehicle.
8. Remove the cotter pin, nut, washer and bolt that secures the operating lever to the pedal rod.
9. Remove the brake pedal rod lever nut and bolt and then remove the lever, sleeve and bushings.
10. To install reverse the removal procedures. Bleed the booster-power steering hydraulic system and check the brake pedal and stoplamp switch adjustment.

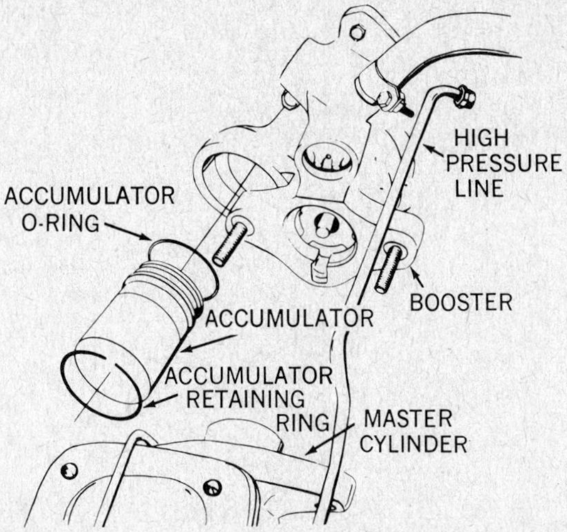

Accumulator installation—compressed gas type (© Chevrolet Div., G.M. Corp.)

Conventional Cab & Suburban

1. Make sure all pressure is discharged from the accumulator by depressing and releasing the brake pedal several times.
2. Remove the nuts and lockwashers that secure the master cylinder to the booster and support bracket. Support the master cylinder leaving the hydraulic lines attached to the master cylinder.
3. Remove the booster pedal push rod cotter pin, and washer and disconnect the push rod from the brake pedal.
4. Remove the booster support bracket.
5. Remove the booster bracket to dash panel or support bracket nuts and remove the booster assembly.
6. To install reverse the removal procedure. Bleed the booster-power steering hydraulic system and check brake pedal and stoplamp switch adjustment.

Forward Control Chassis—(Vans)

1. Make sure all pressure is dis-

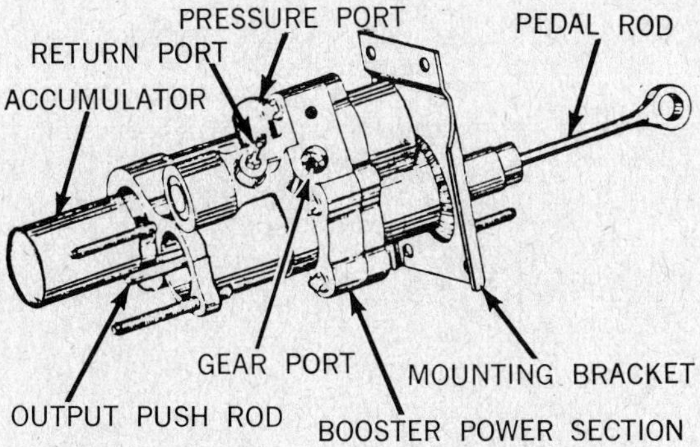

Hydro-Boost—Cab Over & Suburban—typical (© Chevrolet Div., G.M. Corp.)

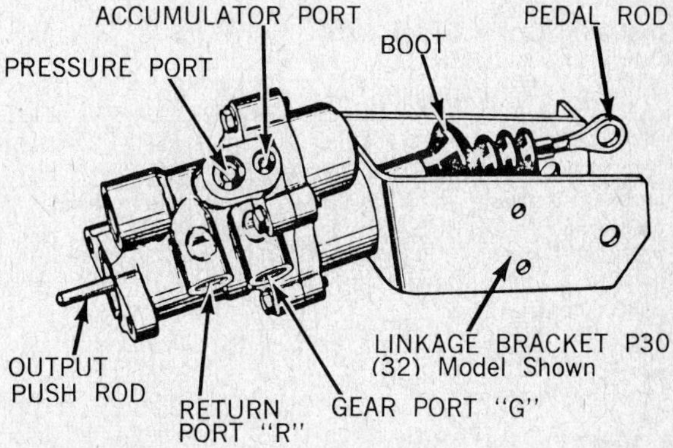

Hydro-Boost—typical (© Chevrolet Div., G.M. Corp.)

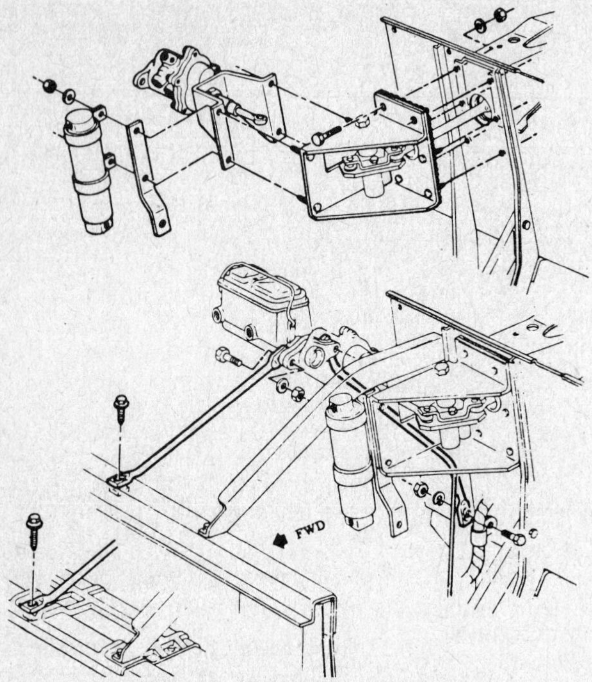

Booster installation—P models
(© Chevrolet Div., G.M. Corp.)

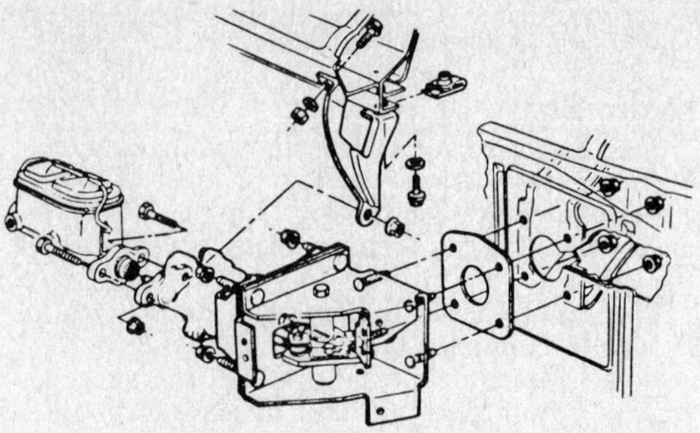

Booster installation—Vans
(© Chevrolet Div., G.M. Corp.)

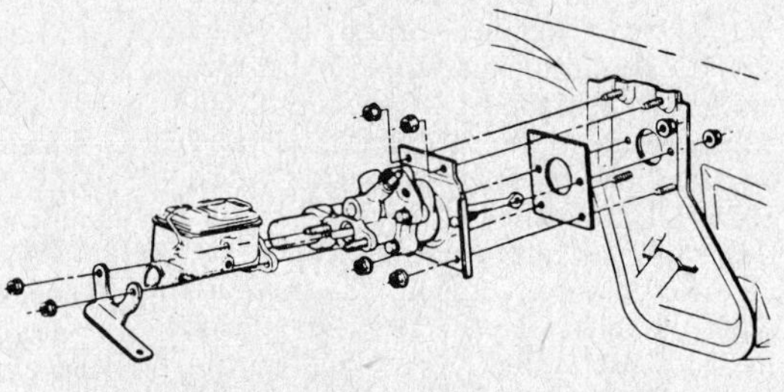

Booster installation—Cab & Suburban
(© Chevrolet Div., G.M. Corp.)

charged from the accumulator by depressing and releasing the brake pedal several times.

2. Clean all the dirt from the booster at the hydraulic line connections and master cylinder.
3. Remove the nuts and lockwashers that secure the master cylinder to the booster and the support bracket. Support the master cylinder leaving the hydraulic lines attached to the master cylinder.
4. Remove the booster pedal push rod cotter pin and washer and disconnect the push rod from the booster bracket pivot lever.
5. Remove the booster supper braces.
6. Remove the booster bracket nuts and remove the booster.
7. To install reverse the removal procedure. Bleed the booster-power steering hydraulic system and check the brake pedal and stop lamp switch adjustment.

Brake Pedal Adjustment

Motor Home Chassis

1. With brake pedal pull back spring installed, brake pedal hard into bumper, brake master cylinder assembly and brake pedal rod lever at full return, install the preassembled brake pedal rod assembly (rod end at boot) and adjust to 31.75″.
2. Turn the brake pedal rod end and adjust the free pedal travel to .06″ to .36″.
3. Fasten the boot to the floor pan assembly and compress the boot to 2.54″ installed height.

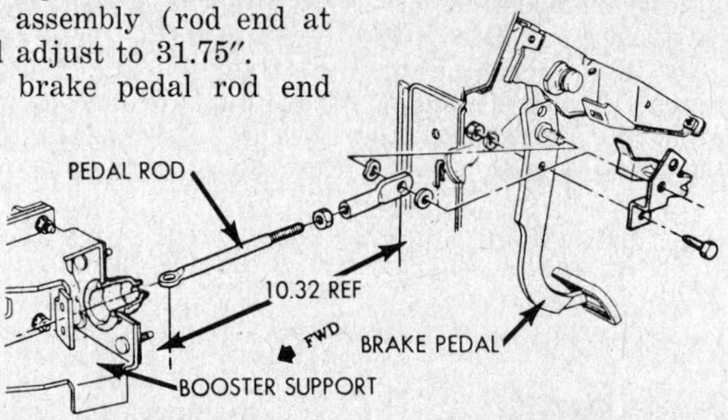

Brake pedal adjustment—G models (© Chevrolet Div., G.M. Corp.)

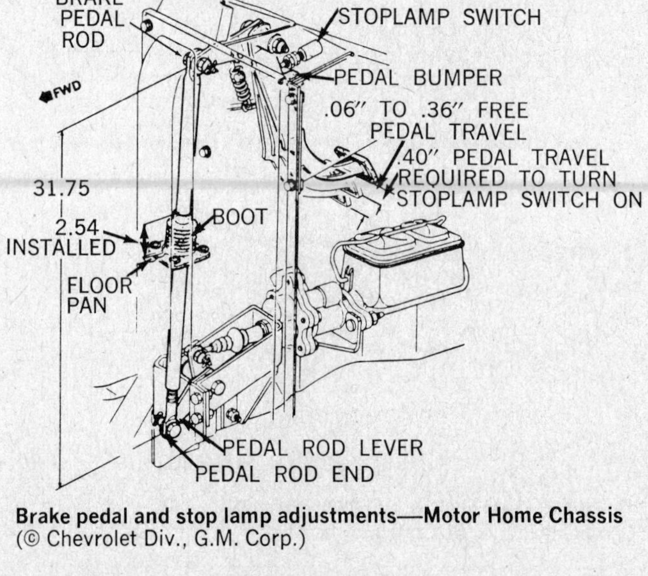

Brake pedal and stop lamp adjustments—Motor Home Chassis
(© Chevrolet Div., G.M. Corp.)

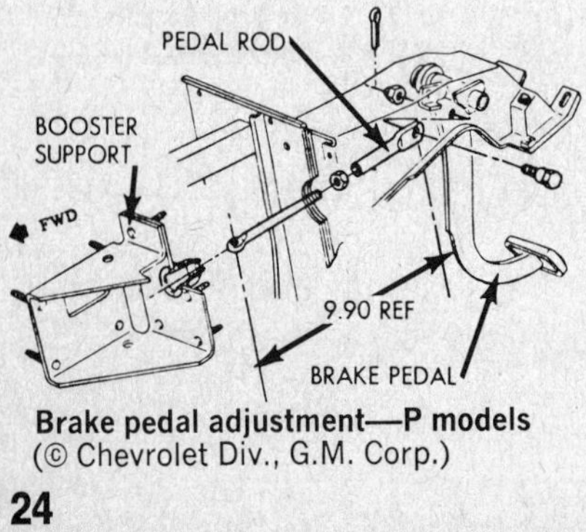

Brake pedal adjustment—P models
(© Chevrolet Div., G.M. Corp.)

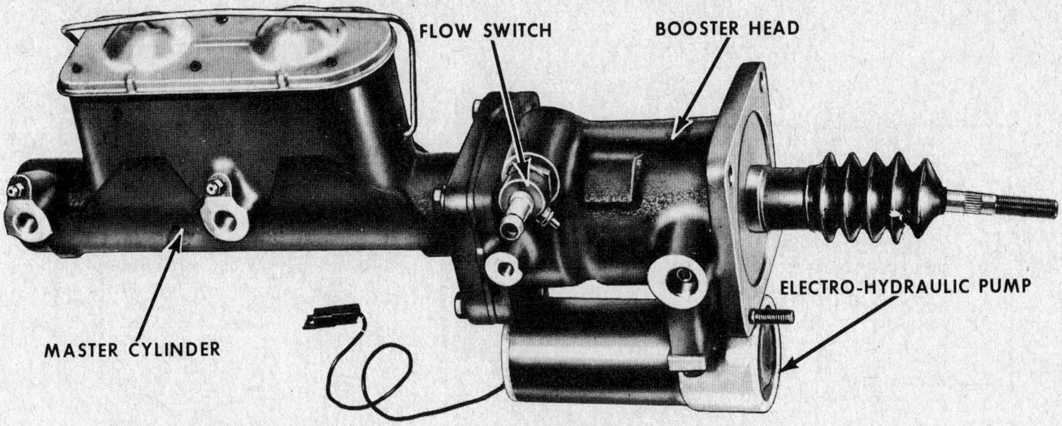

Electro-Hydraulic brake booster and master cylinder (© Chevrolet Div., G.M. Corp.)

Forward Control Chassis (P and G Models)

1. Adjust the length of the pedal rod to 10.32" on G models.
2. Adjust the length of the pedal rod to 9.90" on P models.

NOTE: The brake pedal push rod is not adjustable on conventional cab models.

Electro-Hydraulic

The booster unit is hydraulically operated with an electrical pump attached as a back-up unit in the event of primary pump failure. The booster system features a dual braking system, increased pressure output, excellent pedal feel, separate hydraulic pump, and an electrically powered back-up system.

The hydraulic booster is powered by a standard power steering vane type pump.

Electro-Hydraulic Pump Removal

NOTE: The pump may be removed from the booster assembly while in the vehicle.

1. Block vehicle wheels.
2. Disconnect battery ground.
3. Disconnect E.H. pump lead.
4. Position a container to catch fluid and remove bracket-to-booster 9/16 in. hex-head bolt.
5. Remove two 9/16 in. hex-head mounting bolts. Remove pump and two O-rings.

Installation

1. To install reverse the removal procedure. Use new O-rings and torque the two 3/8-16 x 1 1/8 in mounting bolts to 16-30 ft. lbs.

Booster Assembly Removal
Conventional Cab

1. Block vehicle wheels.
2. Disconnect battery ground cable.
3. Disconnect electrical leads to E.H. pump and flow switch.

NOTE: Booster head may be removed from vehicle without removing master cylinder and disconnecting brake lines. Remove two nuts retaining brake line clips to line support. Remove bolt and clips in booster head. Remove four 9/16 in. hex head master cylinder to booster head mounting bolts and move master cylinder forward from booster. Secure in an upright position. Complete booster assembly removal procedure following:

4. Disconnect hydraulic lines from booster. Use a container to catch fluid. DO NOT reuse fluid.
5. Remove cotter key from push rod pin. Remove nut and bolt from pedal push rod eye. Thread push rod and nut from booster push rod.
6. Remove line and hose supports from booster head.

NOTE: Use care when proceeding to next two steps. This is a heavy unit, approximately 50 pounds including master cylinder, and should be handled as such. After removing from vehicle, use care in handling so that flow switch or E.H. pump is not damaged and bail or cover on master cylinder is not damaged.

7. Remove two 3/8-24 thread hex-head nuts and washers from inside cab at dash panel.
8. Remove upper two mounting bolts and washers from booster head at dash. Remove booster assembly.
9. Remove four 9/16 in. hex-head bolts which attach brake master cylinder to booster head. Remove master cylinder, gasket, and brake line support.

Installation

1. To install reverse the removal procedure. Torque the four 3/8-16 x 1 3/8 in. hex-head bolts attaching the master cylinder to the booster head to 16-30 ft lbs. The two hex-nuts on the 3/8-24 in. studs are torqued to 25-30 ft lbs. The two mounting bolts are torqued to 25-30 ft lbs.

Tilt Cab

1. Block vehicle wheels.
2. Disconnect battery ground cable.
3. Disconnect electrical lead to E.H. pump.
4. Disconnect hydraulic lines from booster and master cylinder. Use a suitable container to catch fluid. Do not reuse fluid.
5. Loosen nuts on each end of push rod extension. Turn extension until free of booster push rod. Bellcrank ball joint may have to be removed to facilitate turning extension.
6. Remove two 9/16 in. hex-head bolts and nuts retaining support to cab sill.
7. Remove two 9/16 in. hex-head bolts and nuts retaining bracket to sill.
8. Remove booster assembly. Move push rod end forward and down while revolving unit to clear E.H. pump, support, and bracket.
9. Remove four 9/16 in. hex-head bolts which attach brake master cylinder to booster head and remove master cylinder and gasket.

Flow Switch Removal

1. Position container to catch fluid from disconnected hose at flow switch.
2. Loosen outer hose clamp at switch and remove hydraulic line from hose. Drain fluid into previously placed container. DO NOT reuse fluid.
3. Loosen inner hose clamp at switch and remove hose.
4. Disconnect electrical lead to switch.
5. Remove switch using a one-inch thin blade wrench.

Installation

1. Use a new O-ring seal and torque to 20-30 ft lbs.

Stop Lamp Switch Adjustment

1. Release the brake pedal to its normal position.

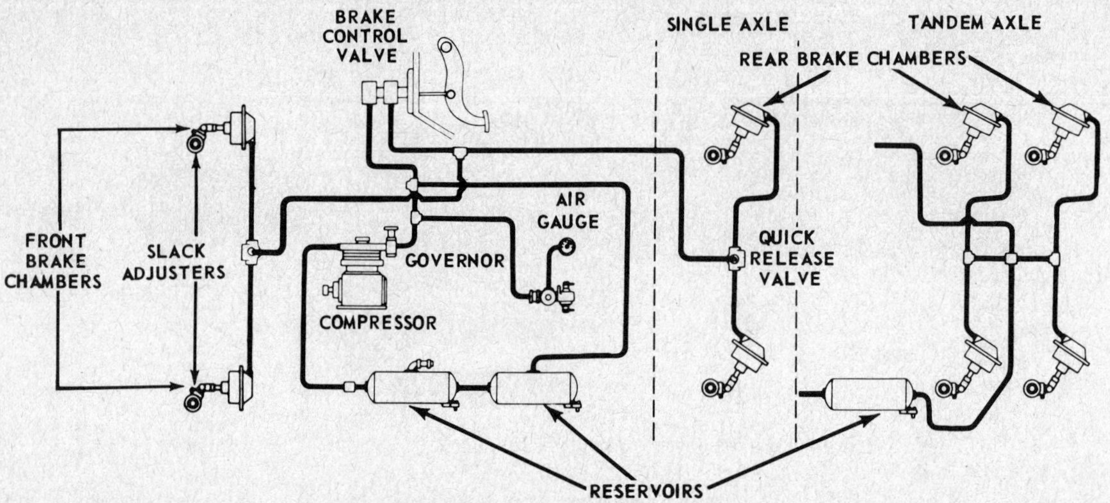

Full air brake system (© Chevrolet Div., G.M. Corp.)

2. Loosen the switch locknut and rotate the switch in its bracket. Electrical contact should be made when pedal travel is ³⁄₈"-⁵⁄₈".

Air Brakes

Specific information will be found in Air Brake Section on adjustments, overhauling and troubleshooting.

Full air brakes completely replace ALL hydraulic parts with more durable components, capable of producing and using greater braking energy.

Brakes are applied by pushing on the pedal, which controls the application valve. Varying amounts of pressurized air will fill the brake chambers depending on brake pedal travel. Cam type shoe actuators (wedge type on stopmaster) are connected to push rods attached to diaphragms in the brake chamber. When air pressure is passed to brake chambers, the diaphragm then converts air pressure energy to mechanical force, the pressured diaphragms move the cam type actuators (wedge type on stopmaster) spreading the brake shoes and thereby applying brakes.

When the brake pedal (application valve) is released, a rapid discharge of air pressure from brake chambers is necessary to speed brake shoe release. A front and rear quick release valve aids in this function.

Many safety devices are used. A low air pressure warning buzzer sounds when pressure falls below a safe level. An air pressure gauge on dash shows the air pressure in system. Normal air pressure, for brake application, is at least 70 lbs. "Wet" and "dry" reserve tanks (also called primary and secondary) serve to remove moisture from air and also to provide a reserve of braking power. Drain cocks in tanks are provided to drain condensation. A pressure relief valve on the "wet" tank will release pressures over 150 lbs. A check valve located ahead of "wet" tank will retain air pressure in event of compressor failure or leaks.

Components

Compressor

Belt driven on gas engines and usually gear driven on diesel.

The air compressor serves only to supply and maintain sufficient pressure for brakes and air operated accessories. When pressure in system reaches top of normal range, an unloading valve opens and nullifies compressor action.

The average compressor is a single stage reciprocating piston type, usually one cylinder. Larger units are two cylinders. Compressors are lubricated by the engine system.

NOTE: Water cooled compressors, in event of freezing weather, must be drained as well as engine block.

Governor

Controls load and unload mechanism to automatically maintain maximum and minimum air pressures in reservoirs. Pressure ranges or settings are adjustable. The governor, by regulating the load and unloading mechanism, establishes an intermittent compressor pumping cycle.

Brake Control (Application) Valve (Foot Operated)

Provides quick and sensitive control of air pressure (FORCE) from reservoir to brake chambers. The amount of force applied to brakes is proportional to the amount of pedal depression.

Reservoir(s)

"Wet and Dry" tanks serve to remove moisture and provide a sufficient reserve of air under pressure for several brake applications (safety factor). Drain cocks are provided to drain condensed moisture. A dash mounted gauge will show amount of reservoir pressure.

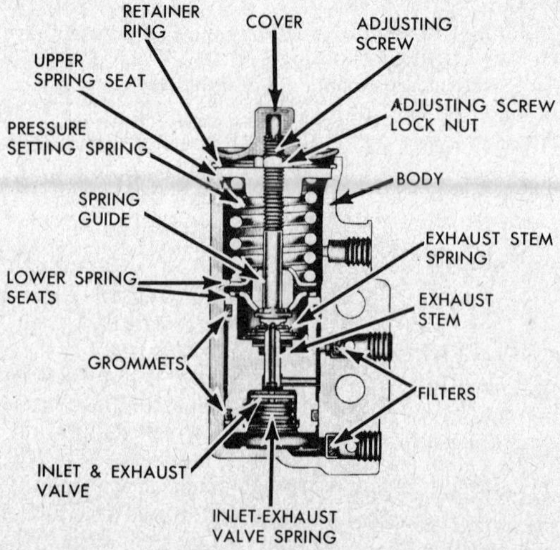

Governor assembly (© Chevrolet Div., G.M. Corp.)

Safety Valve

Usually mounted on reservoir, allows air to escape when air pressure exceeds a predetermined setting (adjustable).

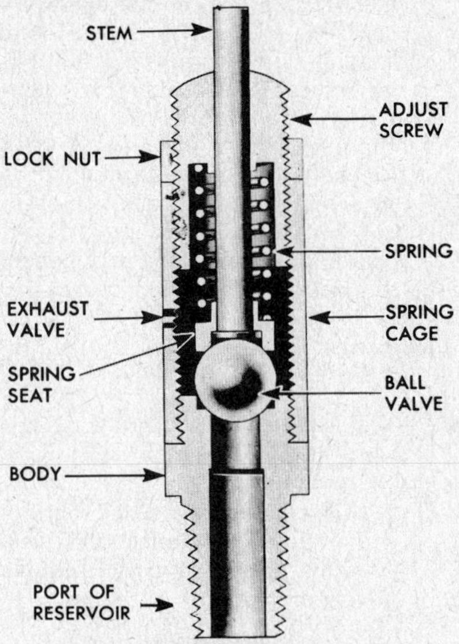

Safety valve
(© Chevrolet Div., G.M. Corp.)

Check Valve

Between "Wet" tank and compressor to retain air pressure in the event of compression (compressor or lines) failure.

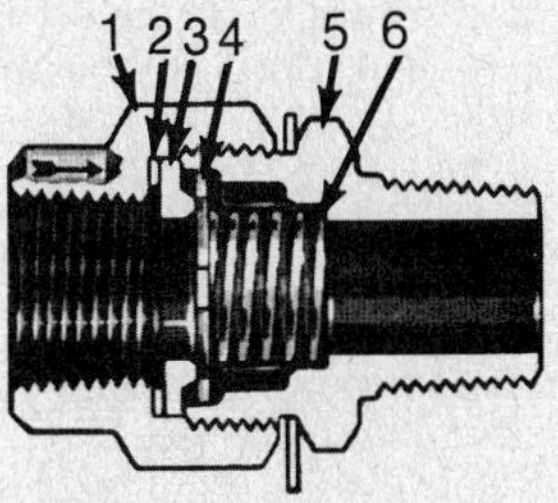

Air tank check valve
(© Chevrolet Div., G.M. Corp.)

1 Valve body
2 Washer
3 Valve seat
4 Valve disc
5 Screws cap
6 Valve spring

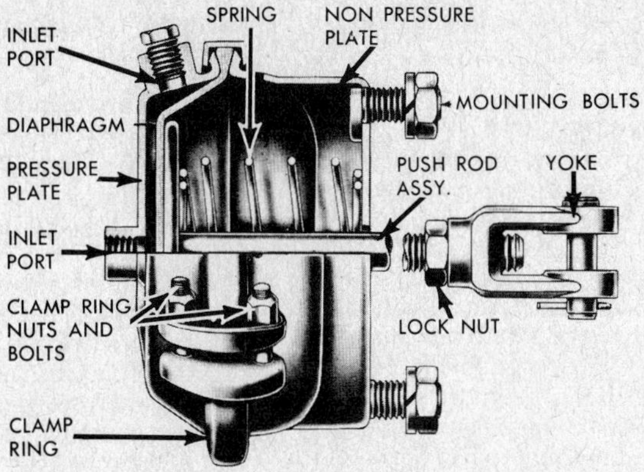

Air brake chamber (© Chevrolet Div., G.M. Corp.)

Low Pressure Signal

A safety device (buzzer) sounds when air pressure is absent or low.

Air Gauge

Located on instrument panel, shows air pressure in system, works in conjunction with low pressure switch to warn of low pressure.

Pressure Protection Valve

Mounted in the delivery port of application valve. Its function is to close all air lines to auxiliary systems in event of loss of air pressure.

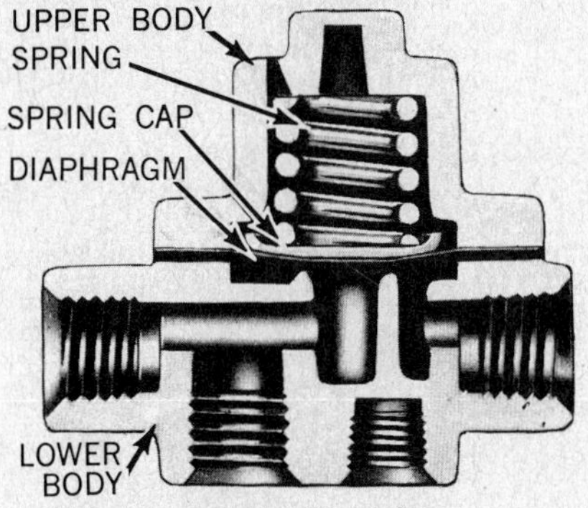

Pressure protection valve
(© Chevrolet Div., G.M. Corp.)

Relay Valve

A relay station to speed the application and release of brakes because of long air lines and volume of air necessary. A relay valve is usually at rear wheels. It is connected to application valve and meters air directly to rear brake chambers from an auxiliary reservoir.

Quick Release Valve

When brake pedal is released, a rapid discharge of air is necessary to speed the return of brake shoes. Two valves are used, one with front brake chambers and one with rear chambers.

Moisture Ejector Valve

Mounted on bracket on cab step support close to wet air tank. Valve operates when brakes are applied and released to evacuate moisture from system.

Brake Chambers

Converts energy of compressed air into mechanical force required for brake application.

Cam Type

Air, admitted by control valve, enters brake chamber and pressurizes diaphragm with attached push rod. Push rod rotates lever arm of slack adjuster exerting a turning force on camshaft with an "S" design on end. This "S" cam operates between rollers on free ends of brake shoes and

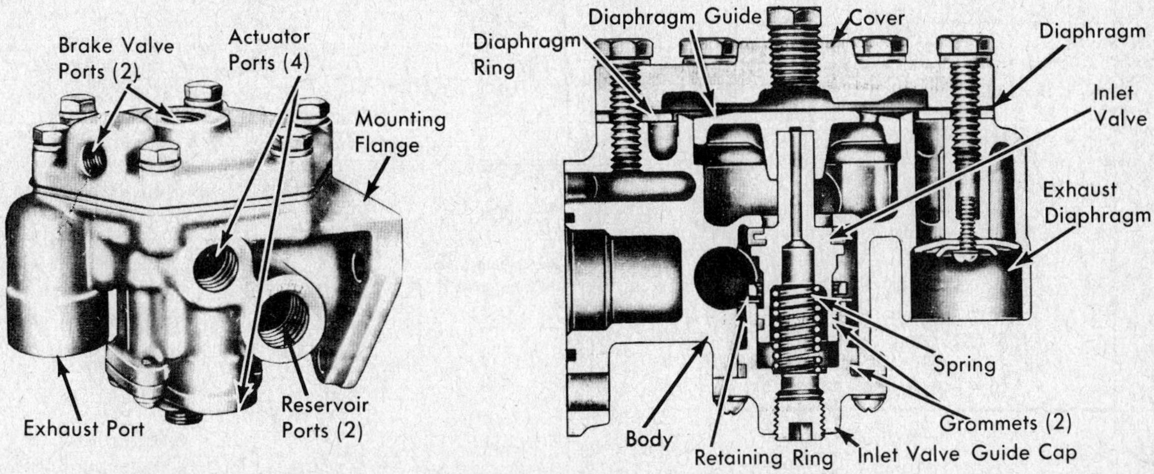

Relay valve components (© Chevrolet Div., G.M. Corp.)

serves to expand shoes. Adjustment is manual at slack adjusters.

Wedge Type

Features two brake chambers per wheel. Wedge type actuators, operating between roller assemblies, force *each* shoe evenly against drum. Stopmaster brakes have automatic adjusters and do not need slack adjusters. *Fail-Safe* and *Super Fail-Safe* can be operated by either air or spring pressure, with additional features such as spring applied parking brake and is a safety factor in event of air brake failure.

NOTE: These units have a manual release bolt, in center of chamber cap, to permit safe handling for service. See note and caution under R&R.

Slack Adjusters

Used with cam type brakes to provide convenient means of adjustment for brake lining wear. With brakes APPLIED the angle formed by slack adjuster lever and brake chamber push rod should be approximately 90 degrees, and all adjusters to be about the same angle. Excessive travel of push rod shortens the life of chamber diaphragms and also results in slow braking response. Some slack adjusters have a locking sleeve, which engages head of worm shaft adjusting bolt, that must be pushed in to clear bolt head in order to make brake adjustments. Re-engage sleeve when finished.

Belt Driven Compressor

Removal

1. Block or hold vehicle by means other than air brakes.
2. Drain air from system, usually at reservoirs.
3. If water cooled, drain cooling system.
4. Disconnect ALL lines. (air, water and oil).
5. Loosen belt adjusting stud and remove drive belt.
6. Remove mounting bolts, remove compressor.

Installation

1. Run engine briefly to clear and check oil supply lines. Clean oil return lines and passages. Check coolant supply and lines (if used).
2. Clean mounting surface and replace gasket, be sure oil holes in gasket are aligned.
3. Install compressor with mounting cap screws loose, compressor will be movable to allow fittings on lines to be started.
4. Make sure air cleaner is cleaned and properly installed.
5. Align compressor, check drive belt.
6. Tighten mounting bolts and adjust belt tension.
7. Tighten all lines, fill cooling system if drained.
8. Run engine and check compressor for noises, leaks and output. Soapy water will help pin-point any air leaks. Check build-up time and governor.

Gear Driven Compressor

Removal

1. Block or hold vehicle by means other than air brakes.
2. Drain air from system.
3. Drain engine block.
4. Disconnect ALL lines (air, water, oil).
5. Remove four nuts and washers from mounting studs, pull compressor back off studs and remove.

Installation

1. Run engine briefly to clear and check oil supply lines. Check oil return lines and passages. Check coolant supply and lines. Inspect drive gears and coupling.

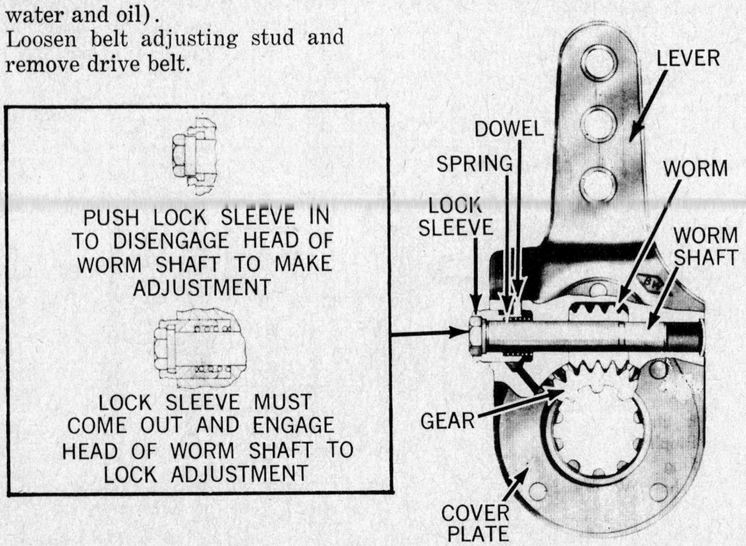

Slack adjusters (© Chevrolet Div., G.M. Corp.)

2. Make sure mating surfaces of compressor and housing are clean. Place new gasket on studs.
3. Install drive coupling on hub and position compressor on mounting studs. Guide compressor into mesh with driven disc, making sure coupling teeth engage disc. Install nuts and washers and torque to 65 foot pounds.
4. Connect water, air and oil lines securely, fill cooling system.
5. Run engine and check compressor for noise, leaks and output. Check build-up time and governor action.

Governor

Removal

1. Block or hold vehicle by means other than air brakes.
2. Drain air system.
3. Remove dirt and grease from air line fittings, disconnect air lines.
4. Remove mounting bolts, remove governor.

Installation

1. Make sure both air lines, to governor, are clean and open.
2. Place governor in position with exhaust port towards ground, tighten bolts finger-tight allowing unit to move. Start fittings.
3. After fittings are started, tighten governor mounting bolts then securely tighten fittings.
4. Test governor and check for leaks.

Application Control Valve

Removal

1. Block or hold vehicle by means other than air brakes.
2. Exhaust air system.
3. Remove all lines and wires.
4. Remove pedal clevis pin and pedal.
5. Remove mounting bolts, remove valve.

Installation

1. Mount valve in position, fasten loosely.
2. Start all fittings, connect stop lite wires. *NOTE. Keep any sealant compound off first two threads of fittings.*
3. Tighten mounting bolts, then securely tighten all lines.
4. Replace pedal.
5. Run engine and charge air system.
6. Check all fittings with pedal depressed with soapy water solution.
7. Check (and adjust) pedal free play.
8. Check valve action.

Reservoir

Removal

1. Block or hold vehicle by means other than air brakes.

2. Exhaust air system, open drain cocks.
3. Disconnect all air lines, remove drain cock and valves.
4. Remove mounting bracket bolts and nuts, remove tank.

CAUTION: Where inside of reservoir is sludged and steam is used to clean, do not plug up reservoir or use excessive steam pressure.

NOTE—In cold weather, more attention should be given to draining of moisture.

Installation

1. Install reservoir in place loosely.
2. Start all fittings, valves and drain cock.
3. Tighten all mounting bolts and nuts to make sure reservoir does not vibrate in service. (Vibration causes premature line failures).
4. Securely tighten all lines, drain cock and valves.
5. Run engine, charge air system.
6. Check for leaks.

Valves, Signals, and Gauges

Removal

1. Block or hold vehicle by means other than air brakes.
2. Exhaust air system, make certain ignition is off.
3. Clean work area, remove any wires, air lines and brackets. Remove unit.

Installation

1. Position replacement unit in system, making certain of any markings showing air flow direction, and secure.
2. Connect any wires and air lines.
3. Run engine and charge air system.
4. Test for leaks and operation of unit.

Cam Type Chamber (Uses Slack Adjusters, one per wheel)

Removal

1. Disconnect air hose from chamber.
2. Remove clevis pin from yoke.
3. Remove nuts and washers from mounting studs.
4. Remove chamber.

Installation

1. Place chamber on mounting bracket and secure with stud nuts and lock washers.
2. Connect air hose.
3. Install slack adjuster yoke clevis pin, after adjusting for minimum travel. (Angle made by push rod and slack adjuster lever should *not* be less than 90°, brakes applied). Lock yoke with locking nut. Push rod travel should be as short as possible without brakes dragging.
4. Check for leaks, and possible brake shoe adjustment.

Wedge Type Chamber (Two per Wheel)

Removal

1. Block or hold vehicle by means other than air brakes.
2. Disconnect air hose from chamber.
3. Remove lock washer tangs from notches in spanner nut and spider housing.
4. Loosen spanner nut and unscrew air chamber from housing.

Installation

1. Screw air chamber in spider housing until it "bottoms", then back off (no more than one turn) until chamber air port aligns with air hose. The plastic guide will assure proper position of wedge. Lock brake chamber in position with spanner nut and lock washer.
2. Start engine, charge air system check for leaks. Pump brake pedal to allow automatic adjusters to adjust brakes.

NOTE: When brakes are equipped with "fail-safe" brake chambers, cage power spring before starting any disassembly or removal of wheels or drums to avoid possible injury. When a vehicle is disabled, due to low or lost air pressure, cage power spring before attempting to move the vehicle. Cage the power spring by rotating the release bolt approximately 18 to 21 turns clockwise. Caging and uncaging can be made easier by applying air pressure, 65 lbs needed (if possible). This takes spring load off release bolt.

CAUTION: Before removing or caging brake chamber, block wheels since parking brake will not be applied.

Slack Adjuster

Removal

1. Remove clevis pin at lever.
2. Remove lock ring and washer on splined camshaft (some front slack adjusters are held on by a retaining screw).
3. Slide adjuster off splined shaft.

Installation

1. Make sure spacer washers are in place (if used).
2. Slide slack adjuster on splined camshaft, lock in place with snap ring and washer. If held on by retaining screw, allow .010" end play. Stake edge of screw to lock.
3. Connect yoke clevis pin. Angle made by push rod and slack adjuster lever should NOT be less than 90° brakes applied. Push rod travel should be as short as possible without brakes dragging.
4. Lubricate adjuster.

Hy-Park System

The Hy-Park brake system is comprised basically of a hydraulic service brake system in conjunction with a hydraulically released, spring applied parking brake.

Hydraulic brake fluid from the master cylinder is used to actuate the rear S-cam service brakes. A hydraulic pump (power steering pump on medium duty trucks) delivers power steering fluid, under pressure, to compress the power spring in the Hy-Park actuator (chamber). Application and release of the parking brake is controlled by a hand valve, which is located in the cab. The rear brake is a conventional S-cam brake such as the type found on vehicles equipped with air brakes. This unit is not covered in the General Repair section of this manual.

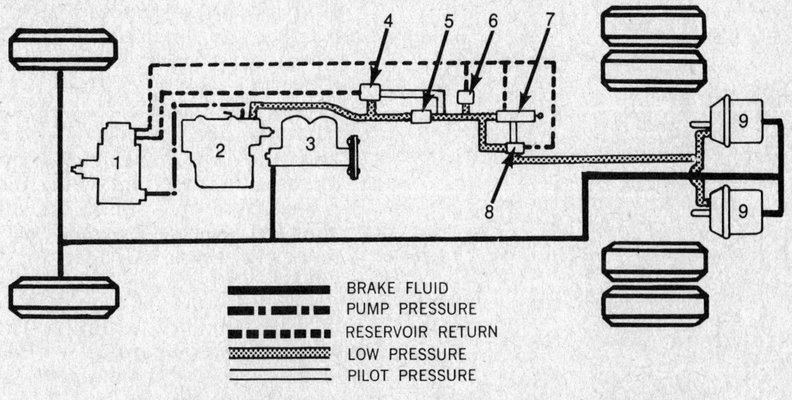

Hy-Park Brake System—typical (© Chevrolet Div., G.M. Corp.)

1 Hydraulic Pump
2 Steering Gear
3 Master Cylinder
4 Diverter Valve
5 Check Valve
6 Relief Valve
7 Hand Control Valve
8 Relay Valve
9 Hy-Park Actuators (Chambers)

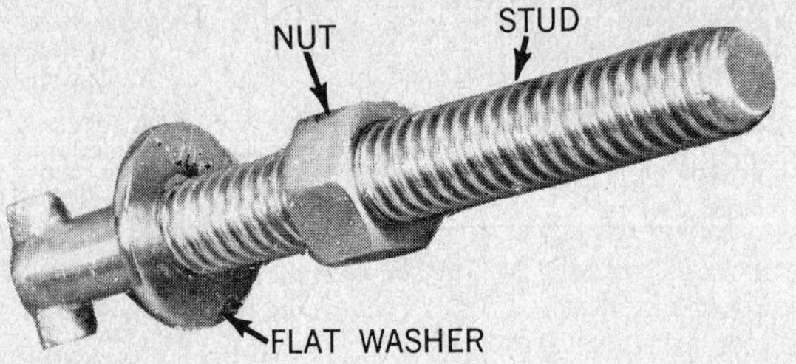

Release stud, nut, and washer (© Chevrolet Div., G.M. Corp.)

Caging Hy-Park Actuator Power Spring

IMPORTANT: Failure to properly cage the spring before removal or dissassembly could result in serious personal injury, as the load on the compressed power spring is approximately 2,000 pounds.

NOTE: Two special release studs, nuts, and washers will be needed to cage one power spring (illustration).

Caging With Engine Operating

1. Prevent the vehicle from moving by blocking the wheels or by whatever means is safe and convenient.
2. Start the engine.
3. Release the parking brakes by using the cab control valve.
4. Install a washer on a release stud, and thread a nut on the stud for a few turns.
5. Remove the dust caps from the slots in the rear of the actuator, and insert a release stud, nut, and washer assembly until there is metal to metal contact. DO NOT force.
6. Turn the release stud 1/4 turn clockwise, and pull outward to engage the stud in the recess in the diaphragm support assembly.
7. While pulling outward on the release stud with a slight force, try rotating the stud in either direction. If the stud has been properly installed, it will not turn. Continue holding the stud firmly in this position.
8. Thread the nut on the stud until the nut and washer contact the rear housing. Hand tighten to ensure that there is a firm contact.
9. Repeat steps 4 through 8 for the other release stud assembly.

   NOTE: If the system has been operating properly, i.e., if the power spring has been hydraulically compressed, then the release studs are now in position to properly contain (cage) the power spring, and the engine may be shut off. With the engine not running and the parking brake applied, the power spring will begin to expand, but it will be prevented from expanding as the release studs now hold the spring in the caged position.
10. Continue tightening the release stud nuts until the diaphragm support assembly bottoms out against the rear housing.

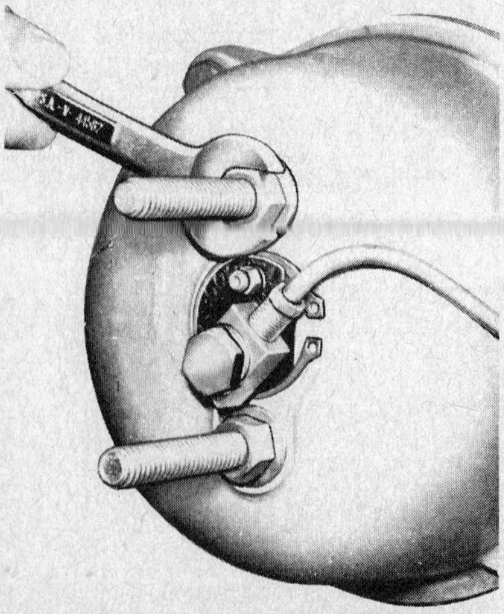

Release studs—installed
(© Chevrolet Div., G.M. Corp.)

Caging With Engine Not Operating

NOTE: In the event of a parking brake hydraulic system malfunction, manually release the parking brakes, and cage the power spring by following the steps of the previous procedure noting the following exceptions.

1. Only start the nut onto the threads of the release stud. This is done because almost the full length of the studs will be required to reach the diaphragm support assembly.
2. Tighten the release nuts in an alternate and gradual manner until the power spring is compressed. Continue tightening the release stud nuts until the diaphragm support assembly bottoms out against the rear housing.

CAUTION: Failure to tighten the release stud nuts alternately could cause the sleeve and diaphragm supprot assembly to tilt and bind in the housing.

NOTE: Bottoming out will occur when the extension of the end of the stud beyond the housing is approximately 2 7/8".

Hy-Park Actuator

Removal and Installation

CAUTION: The Hy-Park actuator houses two types of hydraulic fluid: (1) brake fluid, and (2) power steering fluid. These two very different types of hydraulic fluid are not compatible, and should not be allowed to come into contact with one another, nor should they be allowed to come into contact with components of the system for which they are not intended. If, at any time during removal or installation, either fluid contacts a rubber sealing component of the wrong system, i.e., should power steering fluid contaminate the apply piston double lip seal, or, if brake fluid should contaminate the actuator diaphragm or boot, then the affected seal(s) should be dscarded, as the fluid will attack the seal and cause it to deteriorate. If care is not exercised to isolate these two fluids, then inevitable deterioration will result, causing leakage at the seals and eventual system malfunction.

1. Prevent the vehicle from moving by blocking the wheels.
2. Disconnect the battery ground.
3. Disconnect the brake fluid line from the piston housing, located at the rear of the actuator.
4. Disconnect the power steering fluid line from the front of the housing.

   NOTE: After disconnecting the fluid lines, cover the openings immediately to contain the fluid and prevent contamination.
5. Disconnect the push rod clevis pin from the slack adjuster.
6. Remove the nuts and lock washers from the mounting studs.
7. Remove the actuator from the mounting bracket.
8. Drain all remaining fluid
9. Install in the reverse order of removal.

   NOTE: During installation, position the actuator so that the brake bleeder valve is above the brake line.

Relay Valve

Removal and Installation

1. Disconnect the battery ground.

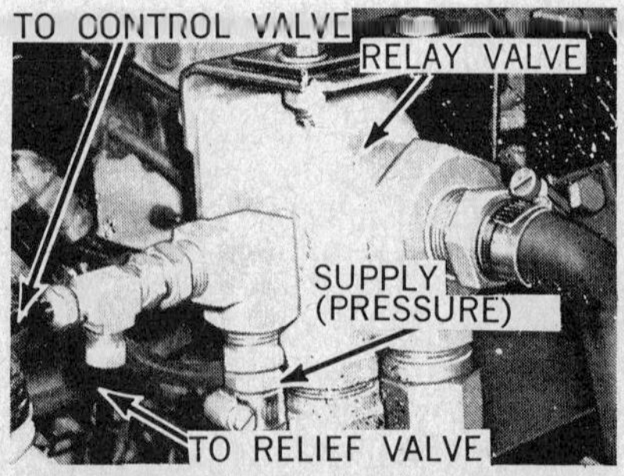

Relay valve—installed (Aluminum conventional cab)
(© Chevrolet Div., G.M. Corp.)

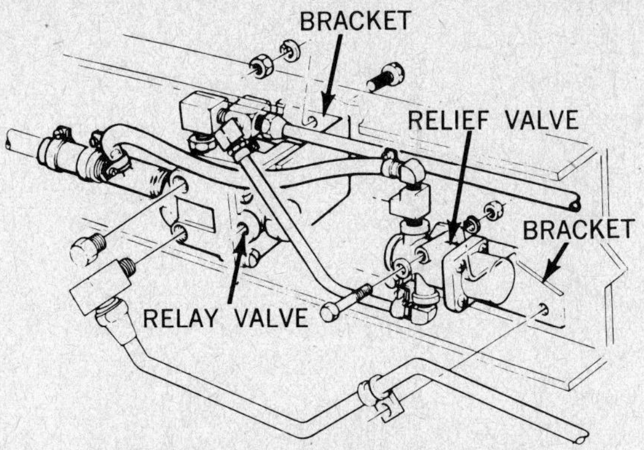

Pressure relief and relay valves—installed (medium duty conventional cab)
(© Chevrolet Div., G.M. Corp.)

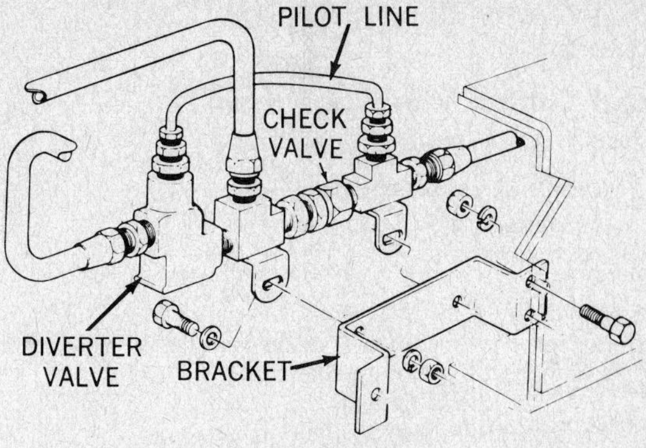

Installation of check and diverter valves (medium duty conventional cab)
(© Chevrolet Div., G.M. Corp.)

2. Pull the control valve knob outward, and set the parking brakes.
3. Disconnect the return line.
4. Disconnect the remaining lines.
   NOTE: Cap all open lines.
5. Remove the two, valve-to-frame, attaching bolts and nuts on conventional cab models. Remove the two, valve-to-support, attaching bolts and nuts on aluminum conventional cab models.
6. Disconnect the actuator delivery lines from the base of the valve, and remove the valve.
7. Remove the bracket from the valve.
8. Install in the reverse order of removal.

Pressure Relief Valve

Removal and Installation

1. Disconnect the battery ground.
2. Disconnect the hydrualic lines at the valve, and plug the lines.
3. Remove the bracket-to-frame attaching bolts and nuts.
4. Remove the valve-to-bracket attaching bolts and nuts.
5. Install in the reverse order of removal.
6. Torque the valve mounting bolt nuts to 75 in. lbs.

Check Valve

Removal and Installation

1. Disconnect the battery ground.
2. Disconnect the lines from the "T" fitting on the end of the valve.
3. Remove the fittings from the "T" as necessary.
4. Remove the check valve by unscrewing it in a counterclockwise direction.
5. Remove the "T" from the check valve.
6. Install in the reverse order of removal.

Diverter Valve

Removal and Installation

1. Disconnect the battery ground.
2. Disconnect the return line.
3. Disconnect the pilot line.
   NOTE: Cap all open lines.
4. For conventional cab models, remove the check valve, and then thread the diverter valve from the pressure line. For aluminum conventional cab models, turn the valve down 90 degrees, turn the valve outwards 180 degrees, and thread the diverter valve from the bushing and elbow.
   NOTE: In order to allow movement of the line to provide cleranace for valve movement, it may be necessary to remove the clip on the hydraulic pressure line to the booster.
5. Install in the reverse order of removal.

Reservoir

Removal and Installation

1. Disconnect the battery ground.
2. Disconnect one line at the bottom of the reservoir, and allow the reservoir to drain.
3. Disconnect the remaining lines. Plug all open lines.
4. Remove the reservoir attaching bolts and nuts, and remove the reservoir.
5. Install in the reverse order of removal. Torque the mounting bolts to 27 ft. lbs.
6. Using new power steering fluid, fill the reservoir to the sight

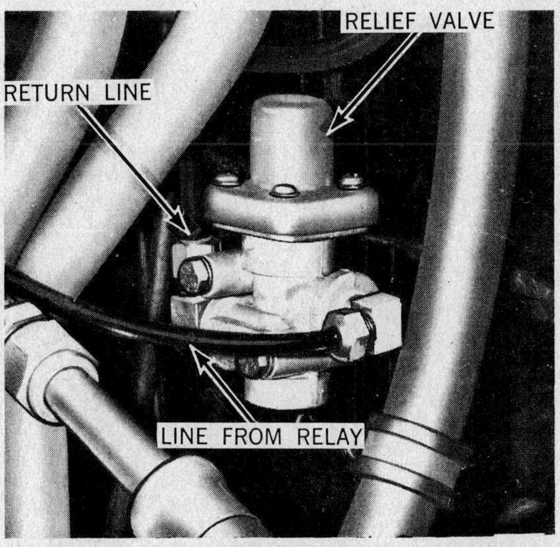

Pressure relief valve–installed (aluminum conventional cab)
(© Chevrolet Div., G.M. Corp.)

Removal of diverter valve (© Chevrolet Div., G.M. Corp.)

glass with the park brake released.

Hand Control Valve and Knob (Aluminum Conventional Cab)

Removal and Installation

1. Disconnect the battery ground.
2. Disconnect the lines from the valve.
   NOTE: Cap all open lines.
3. Loosen the control cable set screw, and disconnect the control cable from the end of the valve.
4. Remove the nut from behind the bracket, and remove the valve.
5. Drill the roll pin out from the knob, and remove the knob.
6. Remove the valve mounting plate.
7. Remove the hexagonal nut from the plate, and pull the cable assembly through the plate.
8. Install in the reverse order of removal. Be certain that there are no kinks or sharp bends in the cable when installing.

Hand Control Valve and Knob (Medium Duty Conventional Cab)

Removal and Installation

1. Disconnect the battery ground.
2. Drive the roll pin out from the control valve knob, and remove the knob.
3. Remove the mounting plate attaching screws.
4. Remove the nut securing the valve to the plate.
5. Disconnect the lines at the valve. Cap all open lines.
6. Install in the reverse order of removal.

Hydraulic Pump (Gear Driven Type)

Removal

1. Disconnect the battery ground.
2. Remove the engine access cover from inside the cab.
3. Disconnect the exhaust pipe from the exhaust manifold and the rear coupling.
4. Move the pipe forward and away from the pump.
5. Disconnect the lines at the pump. Cap all open lines.
6. Remove the six pump-to-engine attaching bolts, and discard the mounting gasket.
7. Remove the coupling from the pump drive hub.
   NOTE: The coupling may remain on the engine drive hub.
8. Remove the $^3/_4$ inch hexagonal nut from the pump shaft, and remove the pump drive hub.
9. Remove the three, adapter-to-pump, attaching bolts, and remove the adapter from the pump. Discard the seal ring.

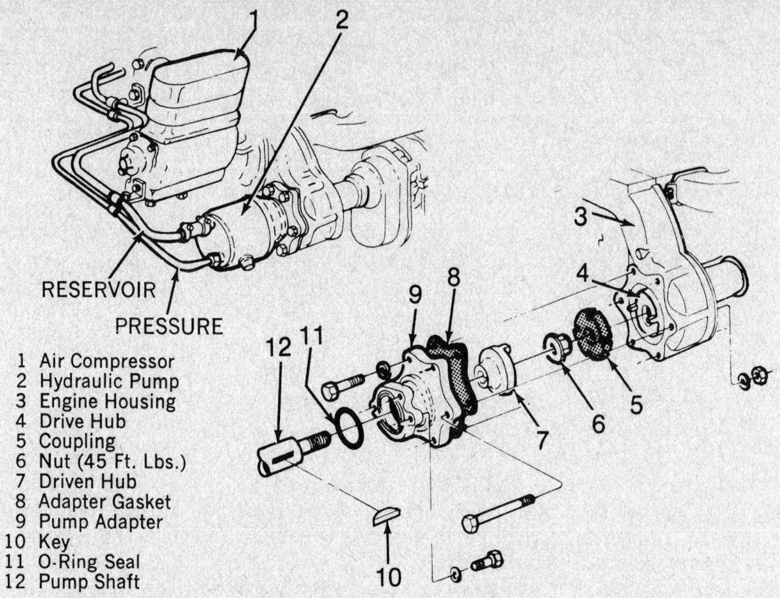

Installation of hydraulic pump (© Chevrolet Div., G.M. Corp.)

Installation

1. Position a new seal ring in the adapter housing groove.
2. Position the adapter in its correct position on the pump, and install the three attaching bolts and washers. Torque the bolts to 27 ft. lbs.
3. Position the pump drive hub over the pump shaft and woodruff key.
4. Thread the hexagonal nut onto the pump shaft, and torque to 45 ft. lbs.
5. Install the coupling on the pump drive hub, and position a new gasket on the adapter flange.
6. Position the pump assembly onto the engine, and install the six attaching bolts and washers. Make sure that the slots in the coupling are aligned with the tabs on the engine drive hub. Torque the nuts and bolts to 27 ft. lbs.
7. Connect all fluid lines to the pump.
8. Install the exhaust pipe.
9. Connect the battery ground.
10. Install the engine access cover.

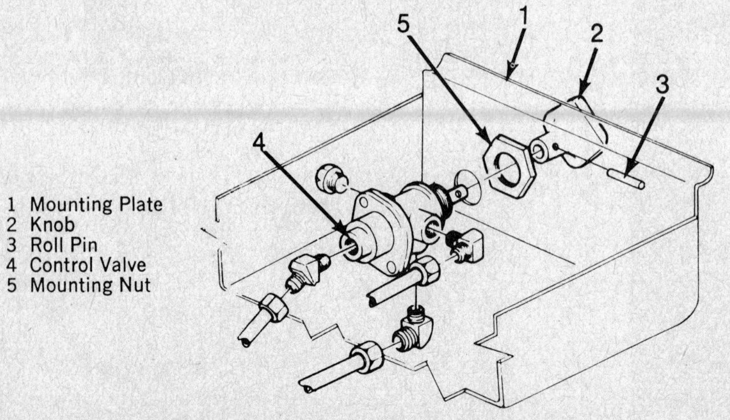

Installation of control valve (medium duty conventional cab)
(© Chevrolet Div., G.M. Corp.)

Parking Brake Adjustment

NOTE: Except in case of an emergency, set parking brake only after vehicle is brought to a complete stop. Parking brakes are not designed to take the place of service brakes.

Drive Shaft—Band Type

This type, using external band and drum mounted on rear of transmission, provides a hand controlled brake independent of service brakes. Band, with lining, is centered on transmission bracket (anchor) and both sides are arranged to contract equally. Brake is actuated by lever and rod, or cable, to a cam and "J" bolt.

1. Block wheels and release hand brake.
2. Remove locking wire from anchor bolt (19) and adjust to obtain .010″ clearance between lining and drum—rewire anchor.

Contracting band (external) parking brake
(© Chevrolet Div., G.M. Corp.)

1 Brake band	11 Adjusting nut
2 Cams	12 Lock nut
3 Links	13 Lock washer
4 Clevis pins	14 Brake lining
5 Cam shoe	15 Release spring
6 Lock nut	16 Brake drum
7 Adjusting nut	17 Adjusting bolt
8 Locating bolt	18 Anchor bar
9 Tension spring	19 Anchor screw
10 Washer	20 Lock wire

Internal expanding type brake
(© Chevrolet Div., G.M. Corp.)

1 Return springs	7 Brake shoe
2 Anchor pin link	8 Plate bolt
3 Camshaft	9 Adjusting screw spring
4 Control lever	10 Adjusting screw
5 Link	11 Support plate
6 Relay lever	

3. Loosen lock nut (6) on locating bolt and tighten adjusting nut (7) until there is a clearance of .020" between lining and drum. Measure clearance about 3 inches from end of lining. Tighten lock nut.
4. Loosen lock nut (12) on adjusting "J" bolt (17) and tighten adjusting nut (11) to obtain a clearance of .020" approximately 3 inches from end of lining. Tighten lock nut.
5. Check hand brake operation by applying lever. If more than ½ the number of notches on sector are needed to lock the propeller shaft, make final adjustment on lever rod, at clevis end. Remove blocks.

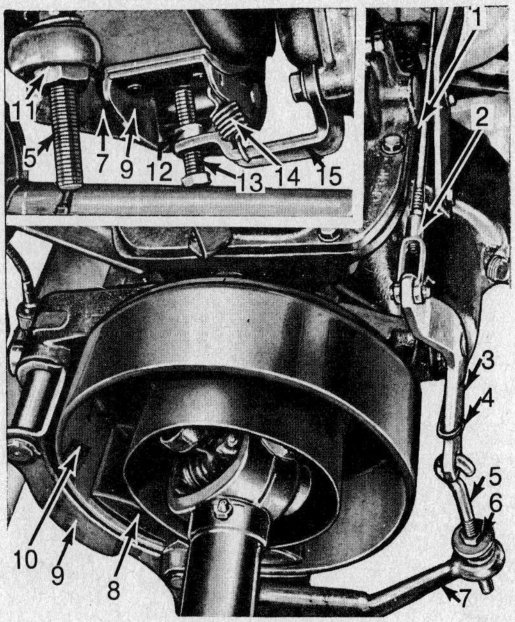

Two Shoe (Duo Grip) parking brake (© Chevrolet Div., G.M. Corp.)

1 Brake cable	6 Lock nut	11 Adjusting nut
2 Adjusting clevis	7 Operating lever	12 Lock nut
3 Connecting lever	8 Inner shoe	13 Adjusting bolt
4 Return spring	9 Outer shoe	14 Return spring
5 Link	10 Brake drum	15 Adjuster bracket

Propeller Shaft—Shoe Type

Hand brake drum is mounted on rear of transmission with internal and external shoes (duo-grip) or with two internal expanding shoes. Shoes are forced against drum by lever and cam actuated by cable. Propeller shaft brakes lock the driveline for parking.

Duo-Grip

1. Block wheels and release hand brake.
2. Loosen lock nut (12) and tighten adjusting bolt (13) to obtain .010" clearance between outer shoe lining and drum at this point. Hold bolt and lock nut securely.
3. Loosen lock nut (6) and tighten adjusting nut (11) to obtain .010" between inner shoe lining and drum, at center of shoe. Hold nut (11) and tighten nut (6).

NOTE: Some vehicles, such as tilt cab, use a compound hand brake lever with flexible cable that features a cable adjustment. This allows the operator to adjust the "over-center" position of lever required to lock parking brake.

Two Shoe Internal Expanding

1. Block wheels and release hand brake, it may be necessary to remove clevis pin to assure full release of shoes.

Internal expanding type adjustment
(© Chevrolet Div., G.M. Corp.)

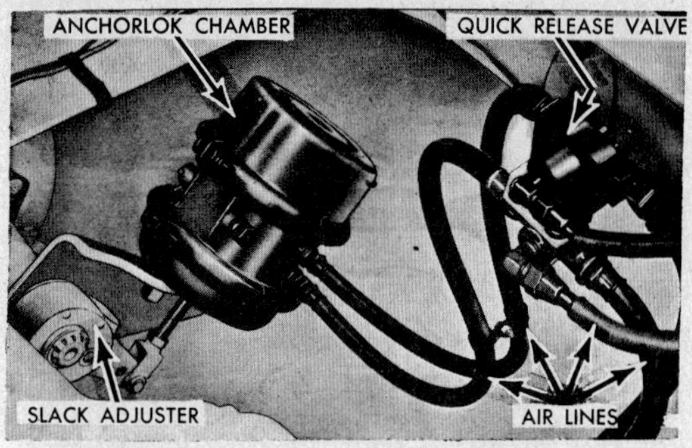

Anchor Lock brake chamber—installed
(© Chevrolet Div., G.M. Corp.)

2. Align slot in drum with star wheel adjuster. Knock out lanced area in drum, if necessary to gain access to star wheel. Be sure to remove all metal from brake compartment.
3. Engage star wheel with brake spoon and rotate star wheel to obtain a .010″ clearance between lining and drum. Moving handle end of spoon down expands shoes. Check with .010″ feeler gauge rotating drum. Shoes can be expanded so as to lock drum then backed off 5 notches similar to a wheel adjustment. Check drum, jack up one rear wheel, for free rotation.
4. Replace clevis, install drum hole cover, remove jack and blocks.

Rear Wheel—Cable Type

Hand lever or foot pedal operated, cable actuated, rear wheel service brakes are used for parking brakes.

1. Block front wheels and apply hand brake two notches from released position.
2. Jack up both rear wheels.
3. All cables and linkage connected, pull back spring in place, loosen cable adjusting lock nut and tighten adjusting nut until a slight drag is felt when rotating rear wheels. Tighten lock nut.
4. Fully release parking brake and check both rear wheels. No drag should be present.
5. Remove jack and blocks.

NOTE: Adjustment of cable should only be made when service brakes are in full adjustment. Cables should be lubricated when rear drums are off.

Rear Wheel—Air Brake

NOTE: For stopmaster fail-safe and super fail-safe information see brake chamber section. (automatic adjusters)

Anchorlok

Anchorlok chamber is mounted "piggy back" on service chamber. It contains a diaphragm under air pressure (60 pounds or more) to contain a powerful spring in compression in normal opration. When air pressure drops below 60 pounds, the coiled spring starts to move out. If air pressure continues to drop, the spring will keep expanding to apply brakes until at approximately 30 pounds the spring will have applied the brakes sufficiently to bring the vehicle to a safe, even stop.

Spring compressor assembly—installed
(© Chevrolet Div., G.M. Corp.)

To permit moving vehicle, when air pressure is not available to compress spring, a caging tool consisting of a stud and nut will be found stored on service chamber housing. Remove rubber plug in center of anchorlok and insert stud $\frac{1}{4}$ turn. Turning nut on stud will cage spring.

CAUTION: Cage spring before removing or servicing anchorlock.

TRU-STOP (Disc Type)

This type brake is used only on models equipped with an auxilliary transmission. It uses a ventilated brake disc which is mounted between the propeller shaft flange and the auxiliary transmission shaft companion flange. The brake shoes are mounted in the opposed positions with the brake disc between. When the brake is applied the shoes are forced against the disc.

1. Disconnect the brake cable or rod clevis from the brake lever.
2. Tighten the adjusting nut until the spring exerts enough pressure to bring the lever against the front lever arm.

1 Brake support bracket
2 Parallel adjusting screws
3 Front lever arm pin
4 Pin retaining screw
5 Brake cable clevis
6 Brake lever
7 Brake shoe pin retainer
8 Brake shoe pin
9 Front brake shoe
10 Rear brake shoe
11 Front lever arm
12 Brake disc
13 Tension spring
14 Spring
15 Rear lever arm
16 Adjusting nut
17 Tie rod

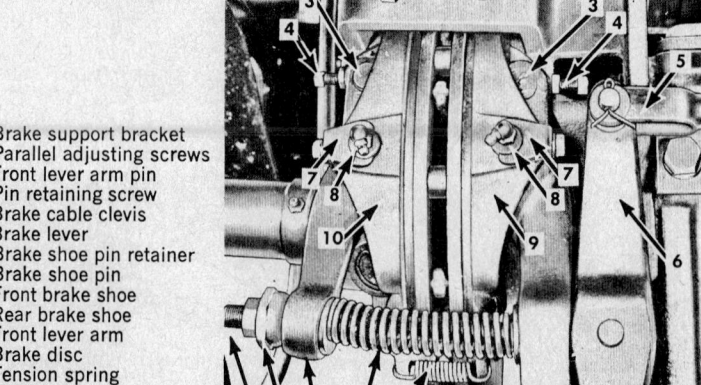

Tru-stop parking brake (© Chevrolet Div., G.M. Corp.)

3. Insert a 1/32″ shim between the rear shoe lining and brake disc.
4. Tighten the adjusting nut until the front shoe lining is firmly against the disc yet still allowing removal of the shim.
5. Make sure that the tensions spring is in place. Make sure that both linings are parallel with the disc by adjusting the parallel adjusting screws. This provides 1/64″ clearance between the front and rear shoelinings and brake disc at all points.
6. Check to see that brake lever in the cab is in the full released position. Adjust the clevis on the brake cable as necessary to permit installation of the clevis pin through the clevis and brake lever without changing position of the lever. Install the clevis pin and cotter pin.
7. Make sure the lock nuts on the brake cable and adjusting screws are firmly tightened.

FUEL SYSTEM

This section contains brief information on removal, installation and minor external adjustments. For more detailed information see carburetor general section.

Carburetor

Various carburetors are designed to meet requirements of engine, transmission and vehicle; therefore carburetors may look alike but are not always interchangeable. All carburetors have conventional float, idle, low speed, power or high speed and accelerating circuits with either manual or automatic chokes.

NOTE: Some symptoms indicate carburetor trouble but in reality are ignition. Before any extensive repairs on carburetor, check first—heat riser, intake manifold and ignition.

Removal

1. Remove air cleaner.
2. Disconnect fuel, vacuum, spark control and governor lines.
3. Disconnect choke and hand throttle controls.
4. Disconnect throttle and automatic transmission linkage at carburetor. Remove pull back spring.
5. Remove mounting nuts and washers.
6. Lift carburetor off manifold and drain. Discard gasket.

Installation

1. Clean carburetor mounting surface.
2. Install new gasket on manifold. Be sure vacuum port and gasket slots are aligned.
3. Place carburetor on manifold, reconnect finger-tight all lines before (evenly) tightening carburetor mounting nuts.
4. Tighten all lines.
5. Reconnect choke and hand throttle controls, replace throttle and automatic transmission linkage, reconnect all vacuum and electrical lines. Connect pull back spring. Check choke and throttle operation.
6. Install air cleaner, check element.
7. Start engine and warm to operating temperature. During warm-up time, torque intake manifold.
8. Adjust idle mixture and idle speed screws, be sure choke is fully open.

CAUTION: **Do not force idle mixture screw against seat, this will damage needle. On transmission controlled spark engines (TCS), fast idle adjustment must be set with electrical leads disconnected at solenoid and transmission in neutral.**

NOTE: If possible (safely), fill carburetor bowl before installing. This will save time and battery drain as well as reducing possible backfiring. Dirt is greatest troublemaker for carburetors. Check all filters. Use starter briefly to clear fuel lines (before reconnecting) of any metal flakes that are always present when fuel lines (metal) are disturbed.

NOTE: For Idle Speed and Mixture adjustments (see Tune-Up decal) in the engine compartment. For all other adjustments refer to the appropriate carburetor in the General Repair Section.

Fuel Pump

Two types of pumps are used, mechanical and electric. Mechanical pump is diaphragm type, consisting of a single fuel chamber or a combination fuel and vacuum chambers. In-line engines the pump is actuated by an eccentric lobe on camshaft, V6 eccentric is attached to front of camshaft, V8 engines use a push rod between eccentric lobe on camshaft and pump rocker arm. The single pump is non-serviceable while the combination pump is rebuildable. Electrical pumps are used with step fuel tanks or as stand-by emergency units.

NOTE: In order to minimize the possibility of vapor lock, some fuel pumps are equipped with a special metering outlet for a vapor return system. Any vapor which forms is returned to the fuel tank along with hot fuel through a separate line.

Removal

(Diaphragm Type)

1. Disconnect fuel lines at pump, also vacuum lines on combination unit. Be ready to cap gas feed line should it be necessary (trucks without shut-off valve).
2. Remove two cap screws and washers holding pump to block. Remove pump and mounting gasket. Be careful of push rod on V8's.

Installation

1. Crank engine to position camshaft lobe on lowest point.
2. Check feed line for restrictions.
3. On V8s—place heavy grease on one end of push rod and slide into position.
4. Hold fuel pump, with new gasket, in position and start two cap screws finger tight. CAUTION: **Be sure rocker arm contacts eccentric in correct position.**
5. Start fuel line fittings, using flexibility of pump to insure against crossing threads, also start vacuum lines if dual pump.
6. Tighten mounting bolts and lines. Start engine and check for leaks. (open shut-off valve if closed)

CAUTION: **When engine is cranked at starter with jumper cable, remove distributor lead from negative post on coil and ignition switch must be on. Failure to do this can result in damage to the ground circuit of ignition switch.**

(Electric)

1. Disconnect battery ground cable.
2. Disconnect wiring harness from pump connector.
3. Remove fuel line from pump.

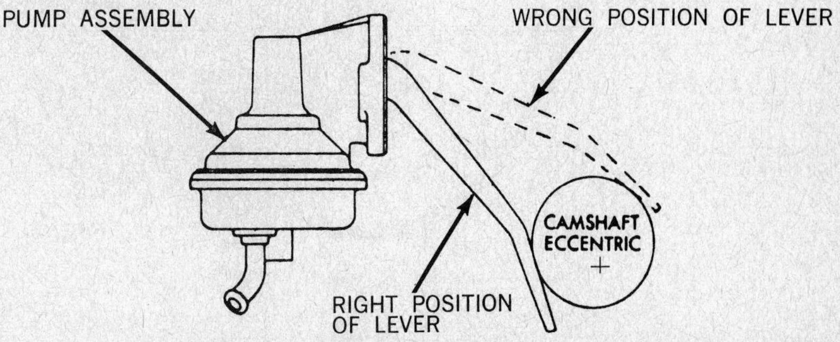

Fuel pump installation (© Chevrolet Div., G.M. Corp.)

4. Remove bolts and washers holding pump to tank, rotate pump 90 degrees counterclockwise and remove from tank.

Installation

1. Carefully position pump into tank opening. Reconnect fuel outlet line to fitting.
2. Install attaching bolts and torque to 4-6 ft.-lbs.
3. Reconnect pump wiring harness and battery ground cable.
4. Check operation of pumps by using pump selector switch.

Fuel Tank

Following procedure is intended only as a guide. It will vary according to truck model and tank type.

Removal and Installation

1. On trucks with dual tanks check shut-off valve position.
2. Be sure ignition switch is off or battery ground is disconnected.

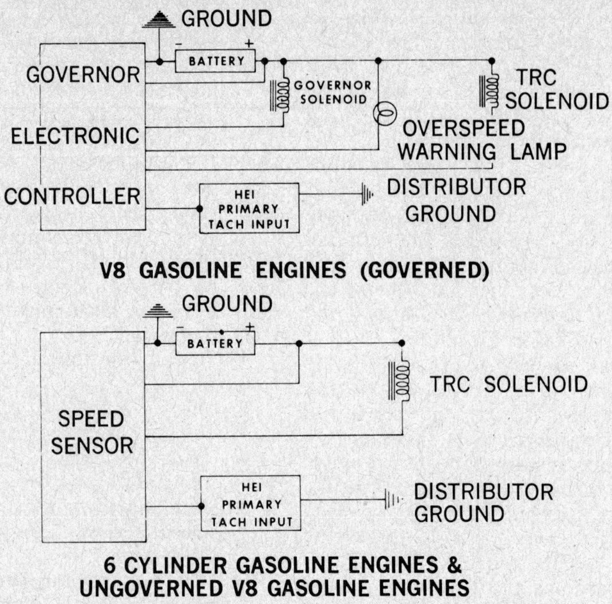

Governor electronic controller—wiring schematic—1979 (typical) (© Chevrolet Div., G.M. Corp.)

3. Remove seat back rest if cab mounted.
4. Drain tank. If tank does not have a drain plug, disconnect gas line and use opening to drain tank. If not accessible, siphon fuel. Do not siphon by mouth. Use equipment for that purpose, or make a siphon hose as shown below and use air pressure if available.
5. Remove filler neck, cap and vent hose.
6. Disconnect tank gage wire and any ground lead.
7. Remove tank support straps or mounting bolts. Remove tank.
8. Clean all lines, check filters. (Blow clean only after disconnecting other end of line).
9. To install, reverse removal procedures.

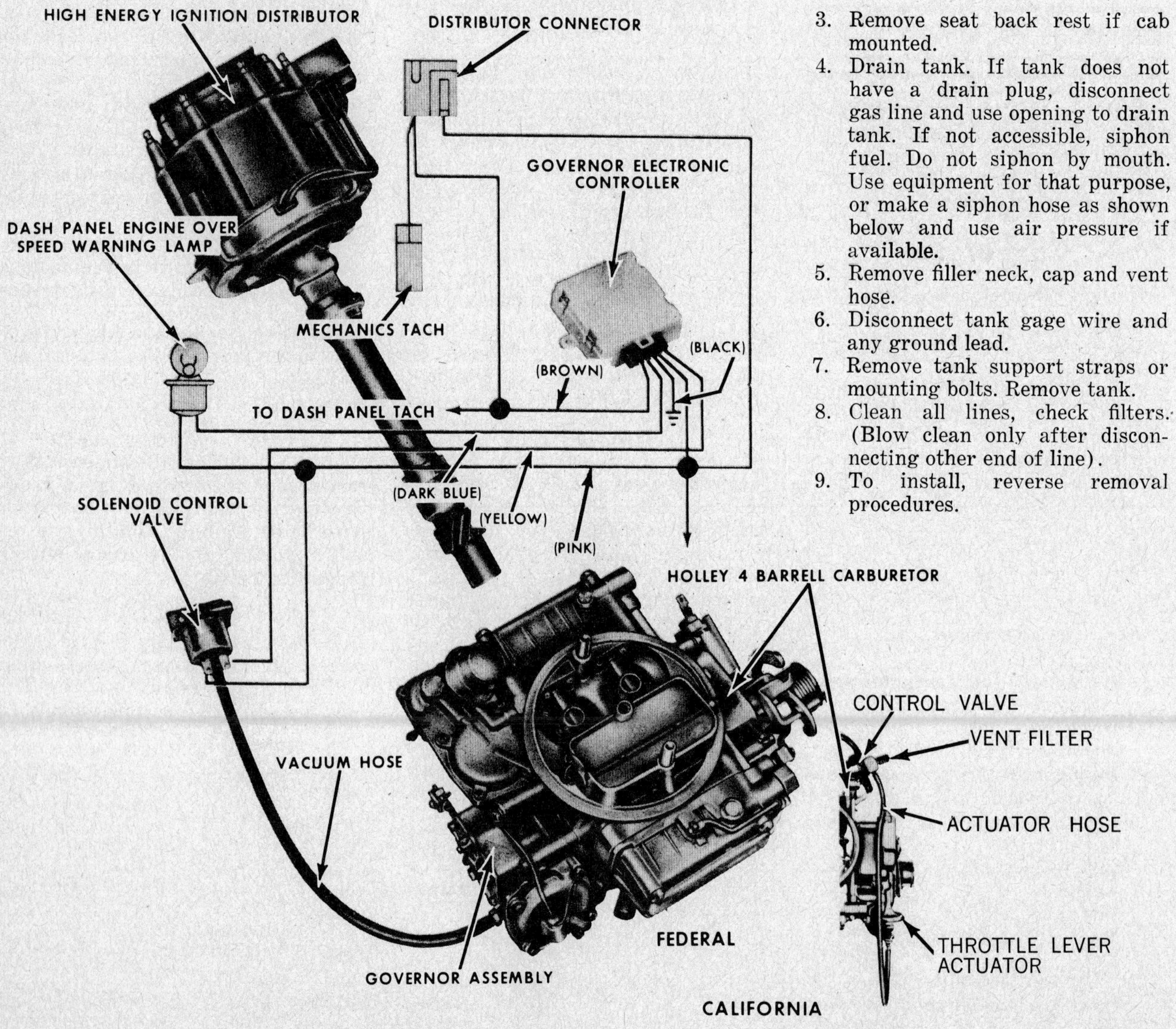

Governor Electric Controller—1977 (typical) (© Chevrolet Div., G.M. Corp.)

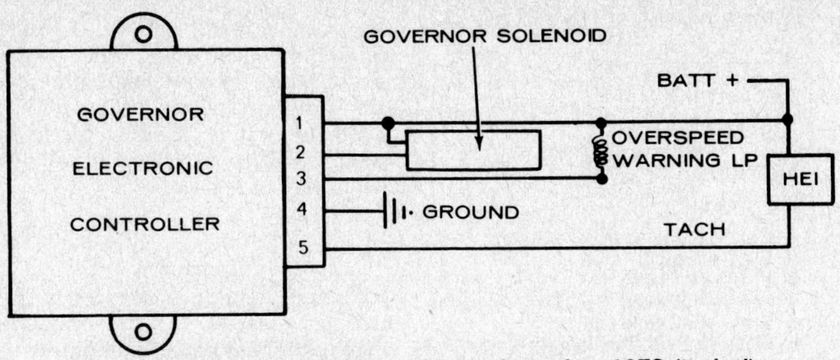

Governor electronic controller—wiring schematic—1978 (typical)
(© Chevrolet Div., G.M. Corp.)

CAUTION: Do not use drop cord in area. A bulb breakage could have disastrous effects. Use only safety cans for fuel storage. Do not overtighten lines, as this could distort or twist and lead to leaks.

Governors

Electronic Governor

Beginning with the 1977 model year, the governor system is integrated with the HEI system in order to electronically regulate governor operation. The governor system is comprised of three basic components: governor, electronic controller, and solenoid control valve. The governor regulates current to the solenoid control valve, and the solenoid control valve is responsible for creating governor vacuum. The electronic controller is not adjustable.

NOTE: Governor RPM is preset at the factory, and is not adjustable. Any deviation from normal operation will require testing of the system.

In order to achieve electric current regulation at the solenoid control valve, the controller monitors the HEI tachometer signal and compares it to an internal reference; the internal reference is proportional to the desired governor setting. If the tachometer signal exceeds the controller reference, then current is allowed to flow to the solenoid control valve, thereby closing the valve. When this happens, governor vacuum reduces the engine rpm to the preset govenor speed.

Solenoid Control Valve Test

1. Disconnect the battery ground.
2. Disconnect the wiring harness from the solenoid control valve at the governor.
3. Measure the resistance across the solenoid terminals with an ohmmeter.

   NOTE: For all 1977 vehicles, the resistance should be 25-35 ohms. Beginning with the 1978 model year, the required resistance, measured in ohms, for the two barrel carburetor will be differene from the required resistance for the four barrel carburetor. Resistance for the two barrel carburetor should be 25-35 ohms. and resistance for the four barrel carburetor should be 47-53 ohms.
4. Replace the solenoid control valve if the measured resistance is not within these limits.

   NOTE: If the measured resistance is below these limits, the controller may be damaged. Perform the electronic controller test.
5. To test for an internal short circuit, connect one lead of the ohmmeter to either terminal of the valve and the other to the metal case of the valve. The resistance should be 800 ohms or higher. If the resistance is lower than 800 ohms, then a short circuit condition probably exists within the valve. If the measured resistance falls within the required limits, then proceed to check for proper governor operation.

Electronic Controller Test

1. Disconnect the battery ground.
2. Disconnect the wiring harness from the electronic controller.
3. Attach one lead of an ohmmeter to the ground terminal in the wiring harness connector and the other lead to the chassis ground. The measured resistance should be less than 3 ohms.

   NOTE: If there is an open circuit between the connector and the chassis ground, look for a problem in the ground wire connectors and terminals.
4. Connect the battery ground.
5. Turn the ignition switch to the ON position, but DO NOT start the engine.
6. Using a voltmeter, measure the voltage between the ground terminal in the harness connector and the terminals connecting the HEI tachometer, the solenoid control valve, and ignition (battery +). The reading at all four terminals should be equivalent to battery voltage. If the reading at any of these terminals is less than battery voltage, then check the appropriate circuit for damage, corrosion, or poor insulation. Repair damaged or defective circuitry.

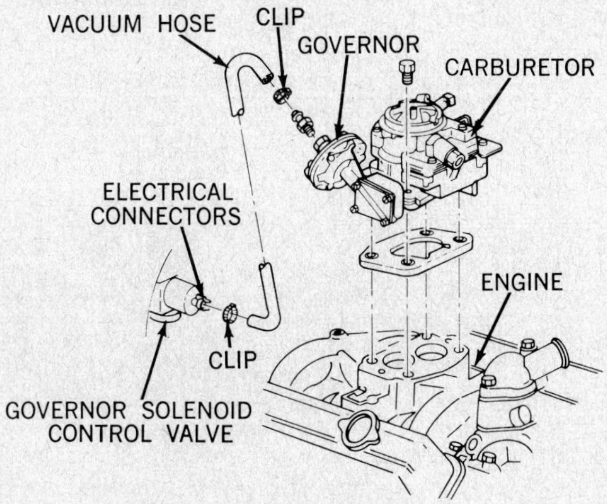

Governor solenoid control valve
(© Chevrolet Div., G.M. Corp.)

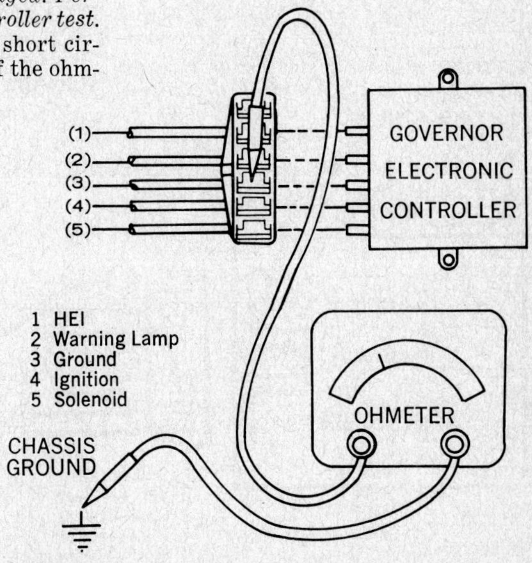

Governor electronic controller terminal connector identification—1978 (© Chevrolet Div., G.M. Corp.)

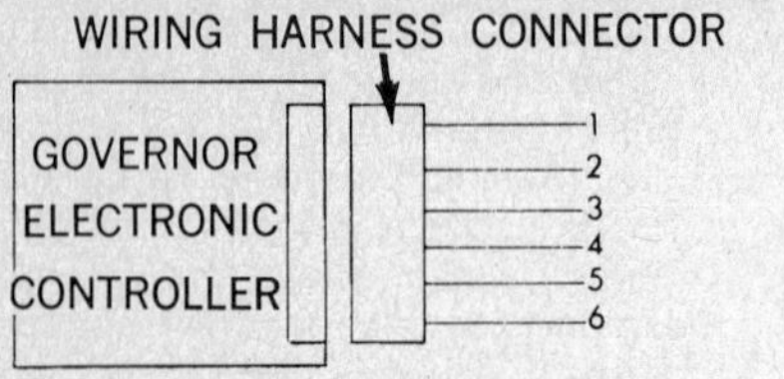

1 Brn —Signal Input (Tach)
2 Blk —Ground
3 Blue—Engine Overspeed Warning Lamp
4 Yel —Governor Solenoid
5 Grn —TRC Solenoid
6 Pink—12 Volt Positive (+) Input

V8 ENGINES (GOVERNED)

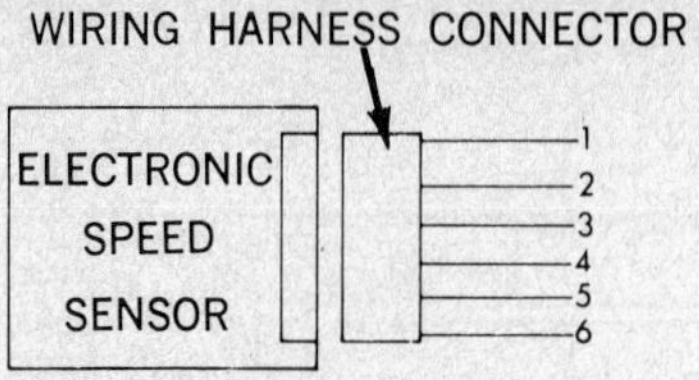

1 Brn —Signal Input (Tach)
2 Blk —Ground
3 Blue—Not Used
4 Yel —Not Used
5 Grn —TRC Solenoid
6 Pink—12 Volt Positive (+) Input

V8 & 6 CYLINDER ENGINES (UNGOVERNED)

Controller ground circuit resistance test and terminal connector identification—1977 (© Chevrolet Div., G.M. Corp.)

NOTE: Allow for a very slight voltage drop between the battery voltage and the reading at the voltmeter, as this may only be the result of minor resistance in the chasis ground circuit.

7. If, after checking the wiring harness, solenoid control valve, tubing, electrical fuse and governor, the governor still does not govern properly, then replace the electronic controller.

Overspeed Warning System

This system was designed to alert the driver of excessive engine speeds such as would be caused by down-hill operation when the wheels may begin to drive the engine.

A red warning lamp, located in the instrument panel will light when activated by a signal from the governor electronic controller.

When the ignition key is returned from the START position, the ignition switch ground circuit is broken and the light will go out. The warning lamp will remain unlighted until the engine rpm reaches the predetermined governed speed.

NOTE: Some ungoverned V-8 and 6 cylinder engines are equipped with a similar sensing device which is designed to warn the operator of excessive engine speeds.

Velocity Type

Governor is mounted between carburetor and intake manifold and automatically governs the maximum speed of engine which in turn limits maximum speed of vehicle.

Operation

Governor is operated by vacuum intake manifold opposing a calibrated (adjusting) spring, which in turn is connected to a throttle shaft and valve. Velocity of gas mixture from carburetor tends to close valve but this action is opposed by governor spring tension. The calibration of velocity versus spring tension is very sensitive.

Adjustment

Adjustment of spring pull is accomplished by number of spring coils operating (active). Turn adjusting cap counter-clockwise for higher speeds. If too sensitive use special hollow wrench to turn adjusting screw nut. Caps are usually wire locked and sealed.

Vacuum Spinner Type

Governor consists of two components connected by tubing. One is in distributor housing and other on carburetor throttle body. This type permits full horsepower usage without excessive engine speeds. An overspeed warning device is usually incorporated in system.

Operation

To limit engine speed while permitting greater throttle openings when additional power is required.

Vacuum is applied to diaphragm in carburetor chamber on throttle housing by internal passages. This vacuum is controlled by distributor air valve thru inter-connecting tube. Distributor centrifugal air valve, by spring pressure, remains open until desired governor speed is reached. Then adjustable centrifugal weight will close air valve in opposition to spring, thereby allowing vacuum to be applied to diaphragm which in turn acts to close throttle valve in opposition to carburetor governor tension.

Increased engine load results in lower distributor speed which allows air valve to open, permitting vacuum to drop, which will in turn allow governor spring to open throttle wider, increasing engine power to meet load increase.

Adjustment

Since governor speed is a function of both distributor and carburetor the best method of setting speed is to adjust spinner on vehicle. The spinner mechanism can be adjusted by holding slotted end of ballast weight with screw driver and turning adjusting nut on other end.

Increase speed by turning nut clockwise, decrease — counter-clockwise.

NOTE: Efficiency of governor depends on keeping all passageways clean and tight, also distributor air filter clean.

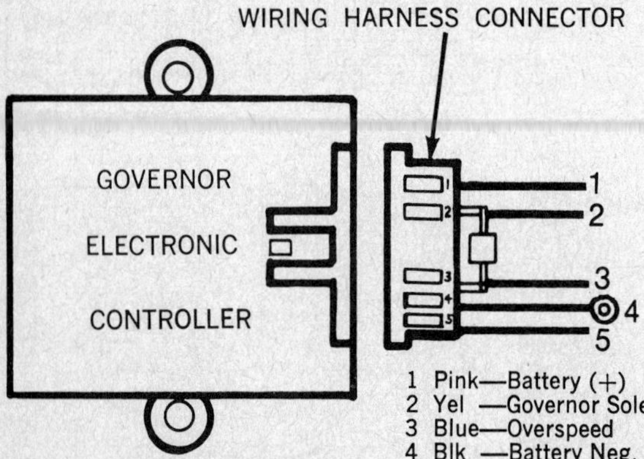

1 Pink—Battery (+)
2 Yel —Governor Solenoid
3 Blue—Overspeed
4 Blk —Battery Neg. (−)
5 Brn —Tachometer

Terminal connector wiring identification—1979 and later (© Chevrolet Div., G.M. Corp.)

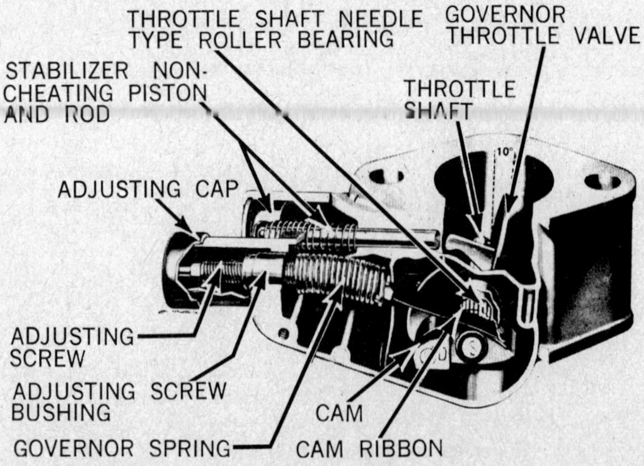

Cross section of governor (© Chevrolet Div., G.M. Corp.)

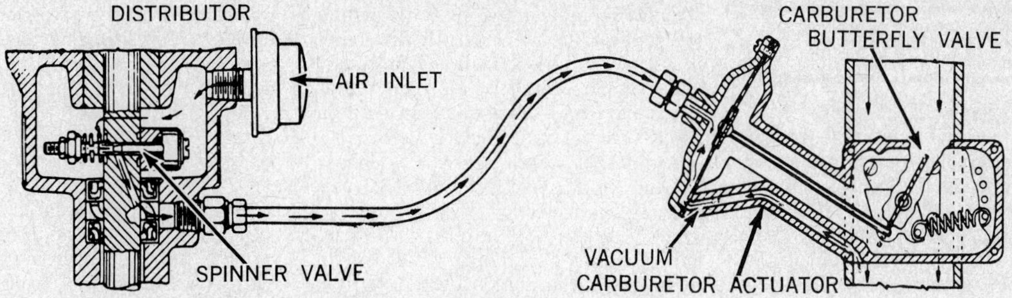

Spinner type governor installation (© Chevrolet Div., G.M. Corp.)

COOLING SYSTEM

All models have pressurized cooling system, thermostatically controlled bypass, sealed by radiator cap. System is designed to operate with coolant's boiling point raised which increases efficiency of radiator. Pressure cap contains both pressure and vacuum relief valves, spring loaded. Pressure valve allows excess pressure out overflow and vacuum valve relieves when system cools off. Thermostat is pellet or poppet construction designed to open and close at predetermined temperatures, and incorporates a by-pass. Two types of cores are used, down-flow and cross-flow, according to vehicle needs and design.

Water Pump

Pump is belt driven, centrifugal vane impeller type. Bearings are permanently lubricated and sealed against water and dirt. Pump requires no care other than keeping air vent, on top of housing, and drain hole in bottom, open.

Removal

1. Drain system.
2. Remove lower radiator and heater hoses.
3. Loosen alternator and remove fan belt (and idler belt if so equipped).
4. Remove fan blade bolts, remove blades and pulley. **CAUTION—Thermostatic fans are to be kept in "on the car" position to avoid loss of silicone fluid.**
5. Remove pump attaching bolts (or nuts) and pull pump cautiously out of block recess, avoid any contact that might damage impeller.

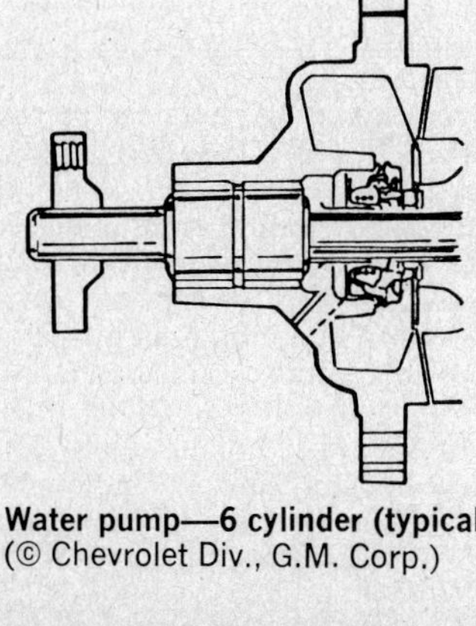

Water pump—6 cylinder (typical) (© Chevrolet Div., G.M. Corp.)

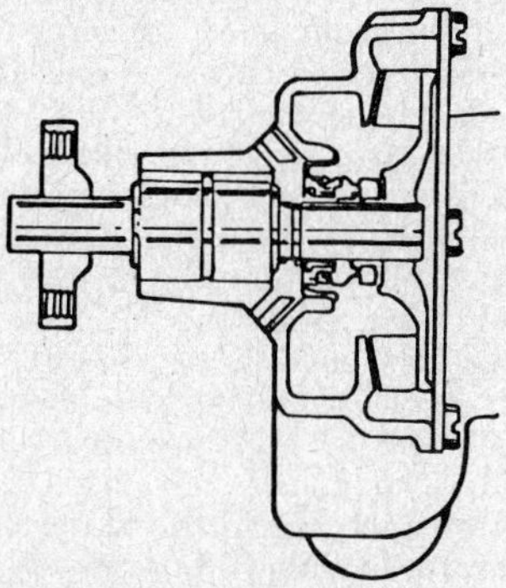

Water pump—V8 typical) (© Chevrolet Div., G.M. Corp.)

Installation

1. Clean gasket surface on block and install new pump-to-block gasket, sealed on *both* sides.
2. Guide pump into position and secure evenly.
3. Connect all hoses, use a good sealer.
4. Replace fan blades and pulley.
5. Install fan belt and adjust.
6. Fill cooling system and check for leaks, check heater operation.

NOTE: A 5/16 x 1" SAE cap screw (with head removed) will make a guide stud to help align fan blades, pulley and hub.

Heater Core

NOTE: Due to the many vehicle models the following are general removal and installation procedures for the heater core with or without air conditioning. Care should be exercised when removing the air distribution duct assembly, to avoid breakage of the housing due to hidden screws. Replace any sealer that is broken or removed during the disassembly.

Removal and Installation

With Air Conditioning

1. Disconnect the negative battery cable and drain the cooling system. Plug the heater core outlets to avoid leakage.
2. Remove the glove box and door assembly.
3. Remove the center duct to selector duct and instrument panel screws. Remove the center lower and upper ducts.
4. Disconnect the Bowden cable at the temperature door.
5. Remove the nuts from the three selector duct studs, projecting into the engine compartment.
6. Remove the selector duct to dash panel screw, (inside the vehicle).
7. Pull the duct assembly rearward to clear the dash panel by the heater core tubes.
8. Lower the unit to gain access to the electrical and vacuum harnesses and disconnect them.
9. Remove the duct assembly from the vehicle. Remove the core straps and remove the heater core.
10. To install, reverse the procedure. Refill the cooling system, start the engine, and check the heater system for proper operation.

Without Air Conditioning

1. Disconnect the negative battery cable, drain the coolant and plug the core tubes.
2. Remove the nuts from the distribution duct studs projecting into the engine compartment.
3. Remove the glove box and door assemblies and disconnect the temperature and air-defrost cable.
4. Remove the floor outlet, the defroster duct to air distribution duct screws and the distribution duct to dash panel screws.
5. Pull the assembly to the rear and remove the wiring harness.
6. Remove the heater distribution unit from the vehicle and remove the core retaining screws.
7. Remove the heater core from the distribution unit.
8. To install, reverse the procedure. Refill the cooling system, start the engine, and check the heater system for proper operation.

ENGINE

Emission Control

Emission control systems are designed to control the emissions of Hydrocarbons (HC), Carbon Monoxide (CO), and Oxides of Nitrogen (NO_X), at the levels specified by the federal and state governments. Emission control systems vary in their usage, in relation to the engine, transmission, and series application.

The units are covered in the Emission Control Section of the General Repair Section.

Evaporative Emission System

This system was designed to reduce fuel vapor emissions that are normally vented into the atmosphere from the gas tank and the carburetor fuel bowl, through the use of a carbon canister and liquid-vapor separator.

Transmission Controlled Spark System (TCS)

This system controls emissions by eliminating distributor vacuum advance in neutral, reverse, and low forward gears. By limiting vacuum advance in these gear ranges, a more efficient combustion level is reached, therefore a lower level of pollution.

Vacuum advance is controlled *directly* by a vacuum advance solenoid which is a two position vacuum switch with a provision for venting the advance unit to atmospheric pressure when the vacuum advance solenoid is de-energized. By allowing atmospheric pressure at the vacuum advance unit, the vacuum advance is prevented from becoming locked in the advanced position.

Vacuum advance is controlled *indirectly* by a series of switches which are operated thermostatically, mechanically, or electrically. These are: cold overide switch (coolant temperature switch), transmission switch, and 20 second time relay switch.

At temperatures below 93 degrees F., the cold override switch closes, thereby completing the circuit to ground. When this happens, the vacuum advance solenoid, which is in series with the cold override switch, is activated and the plunger shifts to the vacuum ON position, permitting vacuum advance. At temperatures above 93 degrees F., the cold override switch opens, the circuit through the vacuum advance solenoid is interrupted, the plunger shifts to the OFF position, and manifold vacuum to the advance unit is denied.

When the ignition switch is first turned ON, a circuit, through the vacuum advance solenoid and to ground, is completed through the time relay switch, a bi-metallic ON/OFF switch. This circuit, which is an extension of the cold override circuit, is independent from the thermostatically operated overide, and allows current to activate the vacuum advance solenoid even when the coolant temperature is above 93 degrees F. The circuit is closed during engine start-up for a period of approximately 20 seconds. The purpose of this additional circuit is to facilitate start-up at temperatures above 93 degrees F., as the thermostatic override switch is then eliminated from the system. If the engine does not start during the 20 seconds time limit, the circuit through the vacuum advance solenoid and to ground will be interrupted and the engine may not start. This is because the time relay bi-metallic switch has been allowed to overheat, thereby opening the circuit to ground. If this happens, a waiting period will be necessary to allow time for the relay to cool before the engine can be started.

NOTE: The time relay circuit will stay OPEN as long as the ignition switch remains in the ON position.

A fourth device, the transmission switch, which is situated on the outside of the transmission, permits current to flow through the vacuum advance solenoid and to ground only when the transmission is operating in high gear. When the transmission is operated in high gear, the switch closes, completing the circuit through the vacuum advance solenoid and to ground. When this happens, the plunger shifts to the vacuum ON position, permitting distributor vacuum advance. When the transmission is shifted to neutral, or is operating in any of the low gear ranges or reverse, the mechanically operated transmission switch is moved to the open position, preventing current from activating the vacuum advance solenoid.

NOTE: In order to compensate for the retarded spark condition, carburetor throttle opening is wider at idle. However, wide throttle blade settings can contribute to engine dieseling. To overcome the attendant dieseling condition, idle stop solenoids have been installed on vehicles equipped with the TCS system. The electrically activated idle stop solenoid supports the throttle at idle and allows the throttle to relax beyond the normal idle position when the ignition switch is turned OFF.

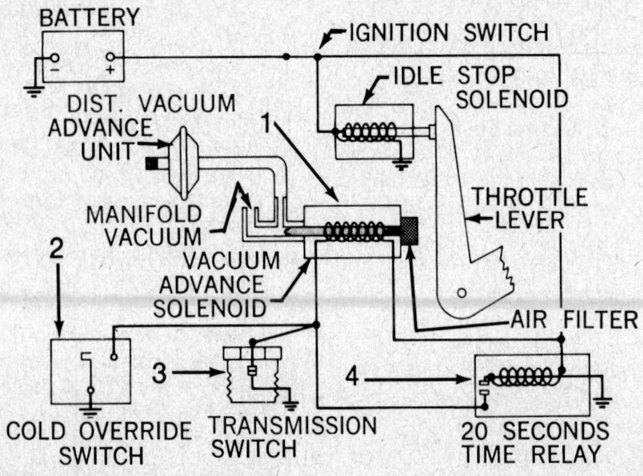

Transmission controlled spark system—high gear operation—typical
(© Chevrolet Div., G.M. Corp.)

1 Vacuum circuit open to advance unit when solenoid electrical circuit is closed. Vacuum circuit closed to advance unit when solenoid electrical circuit is open. Vacuum circuit closed to advance unit when ignition switch is OFF.
2 Circuit open at coolant temperatures above 93 degees F. Circuit closed at coolant temperatures below 93 degrees F.
3 Circuit closed in high gear operation. Circuit open in low gear ranges, reverse, and neutral.
4 Circuit closed when ignition switch is OFF. Circuit open when ignition switch is ON, but remains closed for first 20 seconds.

Throttle Return Control System (TRC)

Ordinarily, engine deceleration is controlled by the operator of the vehicle, as he regulates the throttle blade position through a system of accelerator linkage components. This system, though thoroughly operational, is not entirely efficient. In conventional carburetion systems, there is usually some mechanical force which opposes accelerator application, i.e., there is some device which returns the throttle blade to the idle position whenever the accelerator is released. This is, in a great many cases, accomplished with the aid of a return spring.

Even though the accelerator return spring is an effective decelerator, it, nevertheless, contributes to pollution because of its rapid rate of deceleration. If the throttle blade is rapidly returned to idle, a very low pressure develops in the intake manifold area. When this happens, an unnecessarily high proportion of liquid fuel is drawn into the combustion area, and then exhausted before complete burning can occur. Also, when wheel rotation, transmitted through the dif-

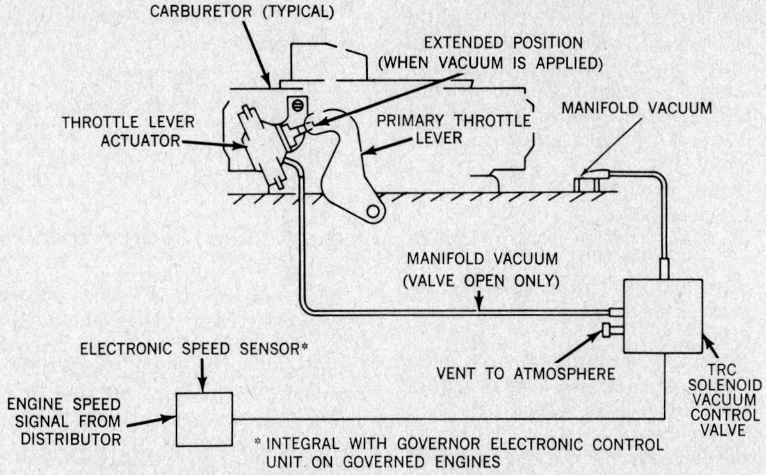

Throttle return control system (© Chevrolet Div., G.M. Corp.)

ferential and transmission, drives the engine (coasting), very high manifold vacuum levels are attained, and, again, an unnecessarily high volume of liquid fuel is introduced into the combustion area.

In order to overcome the problem of rapid deceleration and non-volatile fuel consumption during coasting, the TCR system has been installed on some V-8 and 6 cylinder engines. The system consists of three major components; they are the throttle lever actuator, solenoid vacuum control valve, and the electronic speed sensor.

The throttle lever actuator, located at the carburetor, is vacuum operated, and controls the position of the primary throttle plates a preset amount in excess of curb idle when engine vacuum is applied to it.

The electronic speed sensor monitors engine speed at the distributor, and will supply a continuous electrical signal to the solenoid vacuum control valve whenever speed is in excess of the preset value.

The solenoid vacuum control valve is an ON/OFF vacuum valve which is held open above a preset engine speed by a signal from the electronic speed sensor. When this happens, vacuum at the throttle lever actuator causes the actuator to open the throttle blade, only slightly, admitting more air to ensure more complete burning of the air/fuel mixture.

NOTE: TRC activation value is 1825 rpm ± 65 rpm. Deactivation value is at least 10 rpm below activation, or not less than 1700 rpm.

TRC System Test

Throttle Lever Actuator Operates Outside Normal RPM Range:

1. Connect a tachometer to the distributor "TACH" terminal.
2. Start the engine, and shift the transmission into neutral.
3. Advance the throttle until the engine speed is 1890 rpm. The throttle lever actuator should be extended at this speed.
4. Decrease the engine speed to 1700 rpm. The throttle lever actuator should be retracted at this speed.
5. If the throttle lever actuator operates outside of the 1890-1700 rpm range, then the electronic speed sensor is out of calibration and should be replaced.

Throttle Lever Does Not Operate At Any Speed:

1. Start the engine, and shift the transmission into neutral.
2. Connect the negative lead of a voltmeter to the engine ground, and insert the positive lead into the connector cavities of either the solenoid control valve or the electronic speed sensor. In either case the voltage should measure 12-14 volts.
3. If the voltage measured at the speed sensor is approximately equivalent to battery voltage (12-14 volts), but the voltage measured at the solenoid control valve is 0, then a problem exists somewhere in the engine wiring harness. Repair is necessary.
4. If the voltage measured at either device is 0 (no voltage), then check the engine harness connections at the distributor and/or the bulkhead connector. Repair as necessary.
5. If battery voltage is present at both the solenoid control valve and the speed sensor, then connect one end of a jumper wire to the solenoid control valve-to-speed sensor connecting wire terminal at the solenoid vacuum control valve and the other end of the jumper wire to ground. With the engine running, the throttle lever actuator should extend.
6. If the throttle lever actuator does not extend, then disconnect the actuator vacuum hose at the solenoid vacuum control valve side port. Check for any blockage or obstruction in the port. Clean as necessary.
7. If there is no vacuum obstr tion in the vacuum line (vacuum passage is clear), then replace the solenoid vacuum control valve.

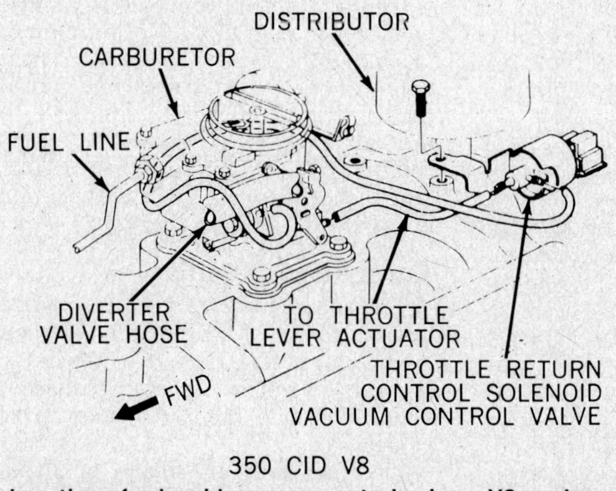

Location of solenoid vacuum control valve—V8 engines (© Chevrolet Div., G.M. Corp.)

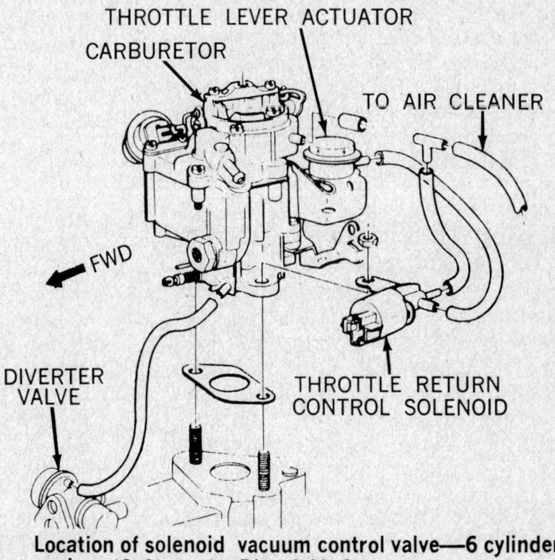

Location of solenoid vacuum control valve—6 cylinder engine (© Chevrolet Div., G.M. Corp.)

If the actuator extends after performing step no. 5, then connect one end of a jumper wire to the solenoid control valve-to-speed sensor connecting wire terminal at the speed sensor and the other end of the jumper wire to ground. If the throttle lever actuator does not extend, then repair the wire which connects the speed sensor to the solenoid vacuum control valve. If the actuator does extend, then connect one lead of the voltmeter to the speed sensor ground wire at the speed sensor and the other lead to ground. The voltmeter should indicate 0 volts (no voltage drop). If any voltage is indicated on the voltmeter, then there is resistance in the speed sensor-to-ground circuit, or, possibly, an open circuit. Repair as necessary.

Throttle Lever Actuator Extended At All Speeds

1. Disconnect the wire connector from the solenoid vacuum control valve.
2. If the actuator remains in the extended position, then check the solenoid side vacuum port for blockage. Clean as necessary.
3. Reattach the wire connector and the vacuum hose to the solenoid control valve, and recheck system operation.
4. If the actuator remains in the extended position, again, disconnect the wire connector from the solenoid vacuum control valve. If the actuator does not retract, then replace the solenoid vacuum control valve.
5. If the actuator retracts with the solenoid control valve wire connector disconnected, then reattach the connector, and disconnect the speed sensor wire connector. If the actuator retracts from the extended position, then replace the speed sensor. If the actuator does not retract, then a short circuit condition (to ground) probably exists in the solenoid-to-speed sensor wire located within the wiring harness. Repair as necessary.

Testing Throttle Lever Actuator

NOTE: The throttle lever actuator can be vacuum leak tested in the conventional manner by using an ordinary vacuum hand pump/gauge tool.

1. Disconnect the valve-to-actuator vacuum hose at the solenoid vacuum control valve.
2. Connect the disconnected end of the vacuum hose to a vacuum hand pump/gauge tool or any external vacuum source equipped with a vacuum gauge.
3. Manually, check the throttle linkage, lever, and shaft for binding or sticking. Repair as necessary.
4. Start the engine with the transmission in neutral, and operate until normal operating temperature is reached. Note the idle rpm.
5. Apply vacuum (20 inches Hg.) to the actuator.
6. Manually, open the throttle slightly, and allow the throttle to close against the extended actuator plunger. Again note the engine rpm.
7. Open the actuator vacuum hose to atmospheric pressure (vacuum cancelled), and reapply vacuum (20 inches Hg.). DO NOT assist the actuator. Note the increase in engine rpm.
8. If the rpm noted in step no. 7 is not within 150 rpm of that noted in step no. 6, then the actuator plunger may be binding due to foreign material, corrosion, etc. Also, the actuator diaphragm tension may have weakened. Correct any binding condition. Replace the actuator if proved to be weak.
9. Again, open the actuator vacuum hose to atmospheric pressure (vacuum cancelled). The engine speed should return to within 50 rpm of the idle speed noted in step no. 4. If not, the plunger may be binding. If the binding condition cannot be rapaired, then replace the actuator.
10. If the engine rpm noted in step no. 6 is not within the specified TRC speed range, then adjust the throttle lever actuator (see chart).

TRC Idle Speed Ajdustment

NOTE: Check the throttle linkage, lever, and shaft to be certain that they are free from binding or sticking.

1. Disconnect the valve-to-actuator vacuum hose at the solenoid vacuum control valve.
2. Connect the disconnected end of the vacuum hose to a vacuum hand pump/gauge tool or any external vacuum source equipped with a vacuum gauge.
3. Apply vacuum (20 inches Hg.) to the actuator.
4. Manually, open the throttle slightly, and allow the throttle to close against the extended actuator plunger. Note the engine rpm.
5. Adjust by turning the actuator plunger screw on 350 CID and 292 CID engines, or by loosening the jam nut on the mounting bracket for the 366, 427, and 454 CID engines and turning the actuator body in the appropriate direction. Repeat steps no. 3 and 4 until the specified speed range is obtained.

TRC SPEED

Engine	Throttle Setting—RPM
292 CID 6 cyl.	1475-1525
350 CID V-8	1375-1425
366, 427, 454 CID V-8	1375-1425

Exhaust Gas Recirculation System

This system helps reduce nitrogen oxides emitted by the engine exhaust. This is accomplished by releasing small amounts of exhaust gas into the cylinders by means of the E.G.R. valve. This lowers the peak combustion temperatures, reducing the amounts of oxides produced.

Air Injection Reactor

The A.I.R. system injects compressed air into the exhaust system, close enough to the exhaust valves to continue the burning of the normally unburned segment of the exhaust gases. To do this it employs an air injection pump and a system of hoses, valves, tubes, etc., necessary to carry the compressed air from the pump to the exhaust manifolds. Carburetors and distributors for A.I.R. engines have specific modifications to adapt them to the air injection system; these components should not be interchanged with those intended for use on engines that do not have the system.

A diverter valve is used to prevent backfiring. The valve senses sudden increases in manifold vacuum and ceases the injection of air during fuel-rich periods. During coasting, this valve diverts the entire air flow through the muffler and during high engines speeds, expels it through a relief valve. Check valves in the system prevent exhaust gases from entering the pump.

Early Fuel Evaporation System

1975 and later models are equipped with this system to reduce engine warm-up time, improve driveability, and reduce emissions. On start-up, a vacuum motor acts to close a heat valve in the exhaust manifold which causes exhaust gases to enter the intake manifold heat riser passages. Incoming fuel mixture is then heated and more complete fuel exaporation is provided during warm-up.

Catalytic Converters

The converters are used to oxidize hydrocarbons (HC) and carbon monoxide (CO). They are necessary because of even stricter emission standards for the 1975 and later models.

The catalysts are made of noble metals (platinum and palladium) which are bonded to either a monolithic (one-piece) element or to individual pellets. The catalyst causes the HC and CO to break down without taking part in the reaction; hence, a catalyst life of 50,000 miles is expected.

Some engines equipped with the converters require an air injection pump to supply air for the reaction; others will not.

For more detailed information refer to the General Section.

Engine Removal and Installation

NOTE: Due to the varied engine-transmission combinations used in the Chevrolet truck line, the procedures for removal and installation of the engines are given as a general outline. It may be necessary to alter the procedures somewhat to compensate.

Conventional Cab, Pickups, Panel and 4 Wheel Drive

Removal

1. Disconnect and remove battery.
2. Drain cooling system.
3. Drain engine oil.
4. Remove air cleaner and ducts.
5. Remove hood and radiator (also shroud if equipped) on larger models (1½ ton and up) it will be necessary to remove front end sheet metal. *NOTE: Scribe alignment marks on hood hinges.*
6. Disconnect wires at:
   Starter solenoid.
   Delcotron.
   Temperature switch.
   Oil Pressure switch.
   Transmission controlled spark solenoid.
   Coil.
   Neutral safety switch.
7. Disconnect:
   Accelerator linkage.
   Choke cable at carburetor (if so equipped).
   Fuel line to fuel pump. (capline).
   Heater hoses.
   Transmission dipstick and tube, plug hole (if so equipped).
   Oil pressure line to gauge. (if so equipped).
   Oil fill tube (and dipstick).
   Vacuum or air lines.
   Parking brake cable (if used).
   Power steering lines (if so equipped).
   Engine ground straps.
   Exhaust pipe (support if necessary).
8. Loosen fan belt, remove fan blades and pulley.
9. Remove clutch cross-shaft or disconnect clutch slave cylinder (if so equipped).
10. Remove road draft tube (if so equipped).
11. Remove rocker arm cover (s) and attach engine lifting tool. Take engine weight off mounting bolts.
12. Remove propeller shaft and plug end of transmission housing on light trucks. On 1½ ton and up, support transmission and disconnect from engine.
13. On light duty trucks, disconnect speedometer cable at transmission, shift linkage and any clutch linkage as required.
14. Disconnect transmission cooler lines (if so equipped).
15. On light trucks equipped with automatic or 4 speed transmission, remove rear engine mount bolts and rear crossmember.
16. Remove front engine mount bolts. **CAUTION: Make final check that all necessary disconnects have been made.**
17. On light trucks, raise engine and transmission and pull forward until removed. Larger trucks remove rear mounting bolts, raise engine and pull forward until disconnected from transmission continue to raise engine until removed from vehicle. Be careful not to damage clutch disc.

Installation

Install in reverse order of removal, fill cooling system and crankcase (check transmission). Start engine and check for leaks and operation. Adjust carburetor and road test.

Van (Panel and Sport)

Removal

Because of its location, the engine is removed from below and both engine and transmission removed as a unit.

1. Disconnect battery ground cable.
2. Drain cooling system.
3. Remove engine cover.
4. Disconnect:
   Air cleaner, extensions and heat tubes.
   Accelerator linkage.
   Choke cable at carburetor (if used).
   Transmission controlled spark solenoid (if used)
   Primary wire at coil.
   Oil fill tube (and dipstick).
   Starter solenoid.
   Temperature sender at unit.
   Delcotron.
   Oil pressure line or sender switch.
   Transmission dipstick and tube, plug hole (if so equipped).
   Evaporative Control System lines at air cleaner and carburetor.
5. Remove upper radiator hose and heater hoses.
6. Loosen fan belt, remove blades, pulley and shroud (if used).
7. Remove distributor cap and spark plug wiring harness. *NOTE: Disconnect any wiring harness retaining clips.*
8. Raise vehicle on hoist, drain crankcase and disconnect:
   Engine splash shields (if used).
   Engine ground straps.
   Lower radiator hose.
   Neutral safety switch, at transmission (if equipped).
   Fuel line to fuel pump. (capline).
   Transmission controlled spark switch, at transmission (if used).
   Transmission cooler lines (if used).
   Speedometer cable at transmission (and plug).
   Power steering hoses (if equipped).
   Parking brake cable (if used).
   Steering idler and pitman arms.
   Positive battery cable at starter.
9. Disconnect exhaust pipe, support if necessary or block out of way.
10. Remove propeller shaft at transmission and plug extension housing to prevent oil leakage.
11. On manual transmissions, disconnect shift levers and clutch linkage; on automatics, shift linkage.

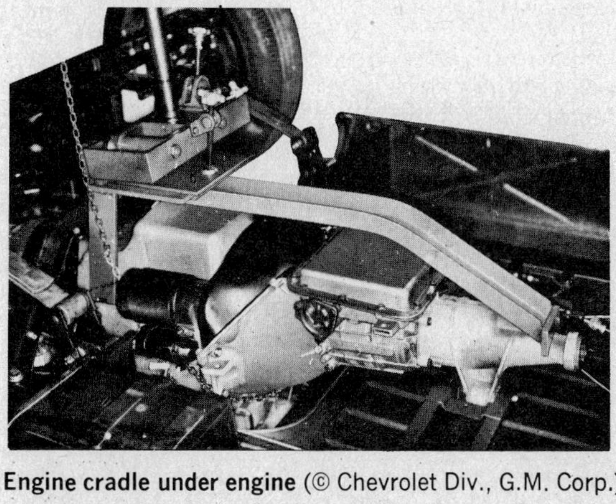

Engine cradle under engine (© Chevrolet Div., G.M. Corp.)

12. Place jack, with engine cradle attached, under engine and take weight off mounting bolts. **CAUTION: Place cradle under engine as far as possible, (to the fifth oil pan cap screw from flywheel at least) and secure with chain over flywheel housing.**
13. Remove engine front mounting bolts (and brackets for additional room).
14. Remove bolts at rear mount to crossmember.
15. Remove transmission support crossmember bolts and remove crossmember. **CAUTION: Make final check that all necessary disconnects have been made.**
16. Lower engine and transmission assembly slowly, pulling to rear to clear front crossmember, and move unit out from under vehicle.

NOTE: On 1974 and later Chevy-Van and Sportvan, provisions have been made so that the grille, filler panels and tie bars can be removed easier than on previous models. This allows removal of the engine from the front of the vehicle instead of from underneath, which makes engine R & R quicker and easier.

Installation

Install in reverse order of removal, fill cooling system and crankcase (check transmission). Start engine and check for leaks and operation. Adjust carburetor and road test.

Step Vans

Removal

1. Disconnect battery and remove.
2. Drain cooling system, drain engine oil.
3. Remove engine box, drivers seat, floor panels at stepwells, floor panel around steering column and pedals, and inspection plate on firewall above engine box.
4. Remove air cleaner (and any ducts).
5. Remove radiator and shroud.
6. Loosen fan belt and remove fan blades.
7. Remove engine splash pans (if used).
8. Disconnect neutral safety wire at converter (if used).
9. Remove upper and lower radiator hoses.
10. Disconnect wires at:
    Starter solenoid.
    Delcotron.
    Transmission controlled spark solenoid (if used).
    Temperature switch.
    Oil pressure switch.
    Coil.
11. Disconnect:
    Accelerator Linkage.
    Choke cable at carburetor (if so equipped).
    Fuel line to pump.
    Heater hoses.
    Oil pressure gauge line (if so equipped).
    Parking brake cable (if used).
    Vacuum or airlines.
    Power steering lines (if so equipped).
    Engine ground straps.
    Exhaust pipe (support if necessary).
12. Remove clutch cross-shaft or disconnect clutch slave cylinder (if so equipped).
13. Remove oil fill tube and dipstick also transmission dipstick and tube, plug holes (if used)
14. Remove rocker arm cover (s) and attach engine lift tool.
15. Push arm of engine lift crane in right side door opening. Attach to lifting device or sling and take engine weight off mounts. **CAUTION: Make final check that all necessary disconnects have been made.**
16. Support transmission and remove shift controls (cover opening), speedometer cable (plug hole), transmission spark control switch wire and oil cooler lines (if used).
17. Remove propeller shaft at transmission. Plug extension housing to prevent leakage.
18. Remove 2 top transmission to clutch housing cap screws and insert 2 guide pins. NOTE: Take 2 bolts, the same diameter and threads as just removed, but at least 4" long and cut heads of bolts off. Using a hack saw, slot ends just cut for screwdriver and use for guides.
19. Remove 2 lower transmission to clutch housing cap screws and slide transmission back until clear of clutch disc. When transmission is free from engine, lower and remove from under vehicle.
20. Remove engine mounting bolts, front and rear.
21. Raise engine slightly and push forward to clear crossmember, then lift up and remove engine through door opening.

Installation

A careful check of clutch components should be made. Install in reverse order of removal, fill cooling system and crankcase (check transmission). Start engine and check for leaks and operation. Adjust carburetor and road test.

Tilt Cab

Removal

1. Tilt cab to expose engine area and secure.
2. Block wheels and exhaust air (if so equipped).
3. Disconnect battery ground cable.
4. Drain cooling system.
5. Drain crankcase.
6. Remove air cleaner and any ducts.
7. Remove radiator and heater hoses.
8. Remove radiator support and shroud assembly.
9. Disconnect hoses and remove surge tank.
10. Disconnect choke cable at carburetor.
11. Disconnect hand throttle at carburetor.
12. Disconnect shift linkage at control island.
13. Remove control island bolts and swing island out of way.
14. Remove both right and left island supports.
15. Disconnect cab safety lock and remote cab support.
16. Disconnect emergency brake cable.
17. Remove any engine splash shields.
18. Disconnect wires at:
    Starter solenoid.
    Delcotron.
    Temperature sender.
    Oil pressure sender.
    Coil.
    Governor speed warning.
    Transmission controlled spark solenoid at carburetor.
19. Remove:
    Accelerator linkage.
    Fuel line to pump.
    Lines or wires to dash guages.
    Vacuum or air lines at engine.
    Power steering lines at pump (if equipped).
    Engine ground straps.
    Exhaust pipe or crossover pipe (support if necessary).
20. Remove fan blades, pulley and support bracket assembly.
21. Remove clutch cross-shaft or disconnect clutch slave cylinder.
22. Remove rocker arm covers and install lift tool or sling.
23. Hoist engine and take engine weight off motor mounts.

NOTE: According to work to be performed select either of the following.

Removal of Engine and Transmission as a Unit

24. Disconnect speedometer (and plug).
25. Disconnect shift linkage at transmission (cover opening).
26. Disconnect any clutch linkage not yet removed.
27. Disconnect and drop propeller shaft at transmission, also any power take-off or auxiliary transmission couplings (cover or plug all openings).
28. Disconnect oil cooler lines or transmission spark control switch (if so equipped).

29. On Roadrangers remove air lines and parking brake drum (if used).
30. Remove all engine mounting bolts and raise slightly to support transmission weight. **CAUTION: Make final check that all necessary disconnects have been made.**
31. Remove any transmission to support bolts.
32. Raise engine and transmission assembly out of chassis as a unit.

Removal of Engine Only

24. Support transmission, remove flywheel under-pan, and disconnect from engine. *NOTE: If possible, install transmission guide pins in top (transmission to clutch housing) holes to allow engine to slide forward to clear clutch disc splines. This will prevent bending clutch hub.*
25. Remove all engine mounting bolts. **CAUTION: Make final check that all necessary disconnects have been made.**
26. Raise slightly and pull forward until clear of transmission.
27. Continue to raise engine until high enough to clear chassis.

Installation

Install in reverse order of removal, fill cooling system and crankcase (check transmission). Start engine and check for leaks and operation. Make any minor adjustments and road test.

Engine Manifolds

NOTE: The use of a good chemical solvent on exhaust manifold bolts and nuts will facilitate the operation.

CAUTION: Pay particular attention to heat risers, their failure increases warm-up time and failure to open can cause lean mixtures at higher speeds.

Inline Engines (Combination Manifold)

Removal

1. Remove air cleaner (and any ducts).
2. Disconnect throttle controls, rods, linkage and return spring.
3. Disconnect fuel and vacuum lines at carburetor, also choke cable or control (if used).
4. Disconnect crankcase ventilation valve, vacuum brake or transmission spark control hoses (if used).
5. Remove carburetor.
6. Remove oil filter support bracket and swing filter to one side (if so equipped).
7. Disconnect exhaust pipe at flange and support if necessary (discard gasket or packing).
8. Remove manifold attaching bolts and clamps, remove manifold assembly (be careful of locating rings). Discard gaskets.

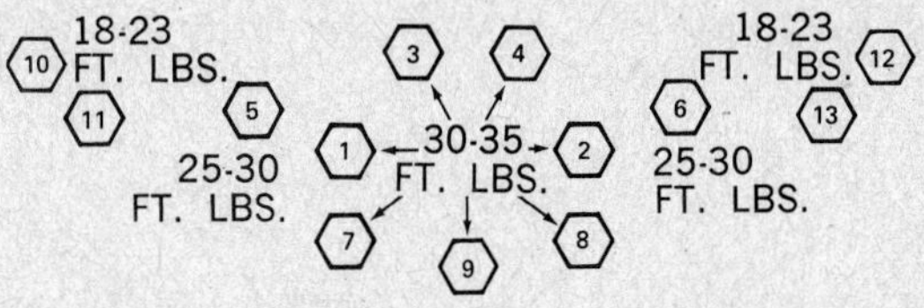

Exhaust manifold to cylinder head tightening sequence—6 cylinder
(© Chevrolet Div., G.M. Corp.)

Installation

Reverse removal procedures after cleaning all gasket surfaces, checking for cracks, check heat riser and alignment. Lay straight edge on manifold to head surface to check. If intake and exhaust are not in line, loosen center bolts where they are joined and do not tighten until assembly is bolted to head, then retighten). Install finger-tight, check that pilot or locating rings and gaskets are in place, then torque to specifications in proper sequence.

Warm engine, adjust idle and check for leaks.

V8 Engines—Intake Manifold

Removal

1. Drain radiator, remove top hose at thermostat housing also any bypass or heater hoses.
2. Remove battery ground cable.
3. Remove carburetor air cleaner and any ducts.
4. Remove oil fill tube and cap.
5. Disconnect gas line, all vacuum hoses, throttle linkage and return spring, choke cable and crankcase ventilation valve.
6. Disconnect wires to temperature sender, coil and transmission spark controlled solenoid (if so equipped).
7. Remove carburetor.
8. Remove distributor cap and mark position of rotor. Remove distributor.
9. Exhaust air and remove air compressor, disconnect oil drain line at manifold (if so equipped and interferes).
10. Remove manifold attaching bolts, remove manifold.

NOTE: If manifold is not to be replaced, some components can be left on such as carburetor, oil fill tube, thermostat housing and temperature sender.

Installation

Clean gasket and seal surfaces on manifold, block and heads. Install new gaskets and seals, coated with a good sealer particularly at water passages. Position manifold, use guide pins to prevent gaskets moving, and check mating angle at heads. (Angle could be incorrect due to excessive cylinder head resurfacing)

Install bolts finger tight, then torque to specifications in proper sequence. Reverse the removal procedures fill radiator, warm engine, adjust timing and carburetor idle if necessary and check for leaks.

V8 Engines—Exhaust Manifold

Removal

1. Use a good liquid penetrant freely on attaching bolts and nuts.
2. Remove the carburetor heater if so equipped.
3. Remove exhaust pipe (support if necessary).
4. Open french locks and remove manifold attaching bolts.

   NOTE: A 9/16", thin wall, 6 point socket sharpened at leading edges, placed over head of bolt then tapped with hammer will speed the opening of french locks.
5. Remove Delcotron (on left side), remove manifold.

NOTE: On 366 and 427 engs. spark plugs must also be removed before removing manifold.

Installation

Clean mating surfaces, install new

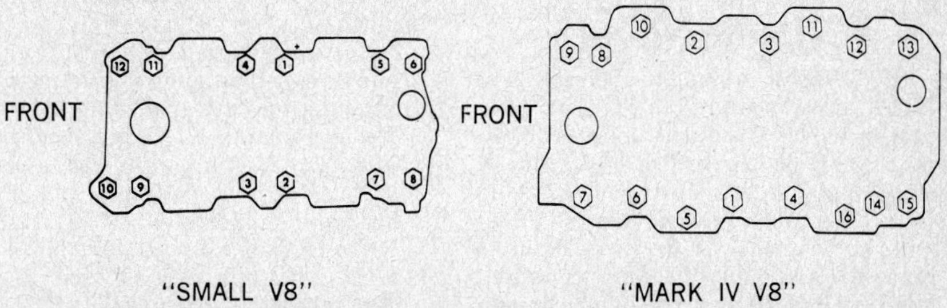

Intake manifold—bolt torquing sequence (© Chevrolet Div., G.M. Corp.)

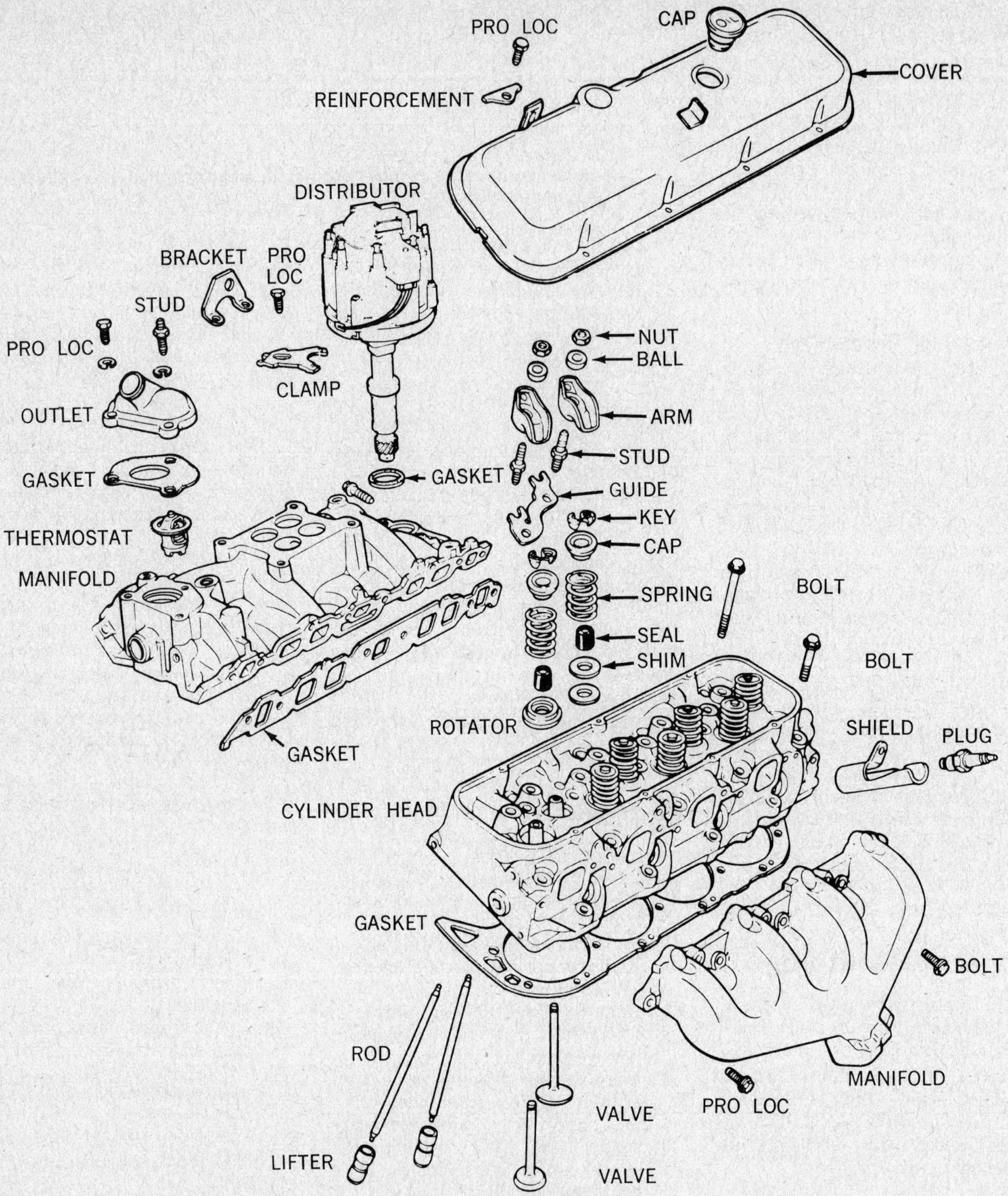

Upper engine components—454 CID V8 (© Chevrolet Div., G.M. Corp.)

gaskets where used, check heat riser and check for cracks. Reverse removal procedures. Start engine and check for leaks.

Cylinder Head

WARNING: **All engines except 305 series have sodium-cooled type exhaust valves. Sodium-cooled valves must not be discarded with other scrap metal. If a sodium-cooled valve is accidentally broken, the sodium will react violently with water, resulting in fire and explosion. Serious burns will result if sodium or sodium oxide comes in contact with the skin.**

Inline Engines

Removal

1. Drain cooling system and remove battery ground strap at head.
2. Remove air cleaner and any ducts.
3. Remove choke cable, accelerator rod and return spring, fuel and vacuum lines at carburetor.
4. Remove manifold to head bolts and clamps, pull manifold and carburetor assembly clear of head and support.
5. Remove fuel and vacuum lines from retaining clip at thermostat housing.
6. Disconnect temperature sender wire, remove wiring harness from rocker cover clip. Remove coil wires and coil.
7. Remove top radiator hose, at thermostat housing.
8. Remove spark plug wires and distributor cap.
9. Remove rocker arm cover.

CAUTION: Never pry rocker arm cover loose—bump cover rearward in a gasket shearing manner.

10. Engines with rocker arm shafts, back off adjusting nuts, rotate rocker arm to clear push rod and remove push rods. Engines using pedestal rocker arms, remove rocker arm ball nuts, arms and push rods.

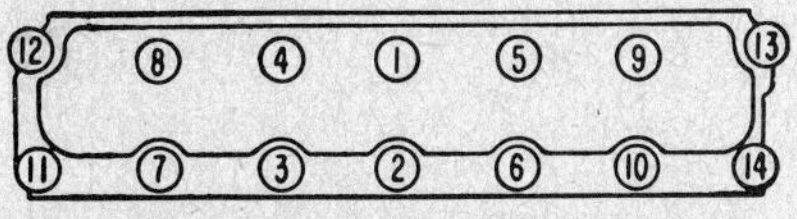

Torquing sequence—inline 6 cylinder engines (© Chevrolet Div., G.M. Corp.)

11. Remove push rod cover.
12. Remove cylinder head bolts, cylinder head and discard gasket.

NOTE: Place rocker arm mechanism and cylinder head bolts in a rack so they can be re-installed in same locations. (mated)

Check cylinder head for warpage with a straight edge. Inspect for cracks and burnt valves.

Installation

Reverse removal procedures and adjust valves after cleaning gasket surfaces. Engines using a steel (shim) gasket, coat both sides with a good sealer, bead side up. Do not reuse gaskets. Cylinder head bolt threads in block and threads on bolts must be clean. Coat threads on bolts with sealer before installing. Tighten each cylinder head bolt a little at a time, in correct sequence, until specified torque is reached. Engines using composition (steel asbestos) gaskets must have heads retorqued after warm-up. (retightening heads effects valve lash) Refer to specifications at beginning of this section for nut tightening sequence.

V8 Engines

Removal

1. Remove intake manifold (with carburetor) and exhaust manifold—see manifolds R & R. *NOTE: If only one head is to be removed, remove inlet manifold bolts on that side only and leave inlet manifold assembly in place.*
2. Loosen belt and remove power steering pump (if so equipped).
3. Remove rocker arm covers. **CAUTION: Never pry rocker arm cover loose—bump cover rearward in a gasket shearing manner.**
4. Loosen rocker arm adjusting nut, turn rocker arm to clear push rods and remove push rods. Exhaust push rods are longer than intake push rods in some engines so to be sure—place in sequence so that they can be installed in same location (mated).
5. Remove cylinder head bolts, cylinder head and discard gasket.
6. Check cylinder head for warpage with a straight edge. Inspect for cracks and burnt valves.

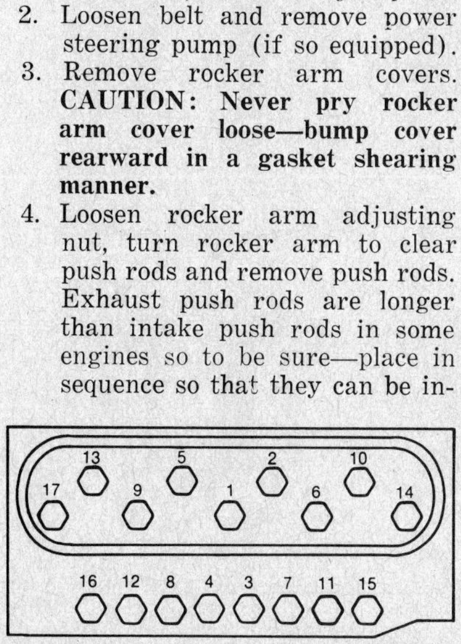

Torquing sequence—307, 350, & 305 V8 engines (© Chevrolet Div., G.M. Corp.)

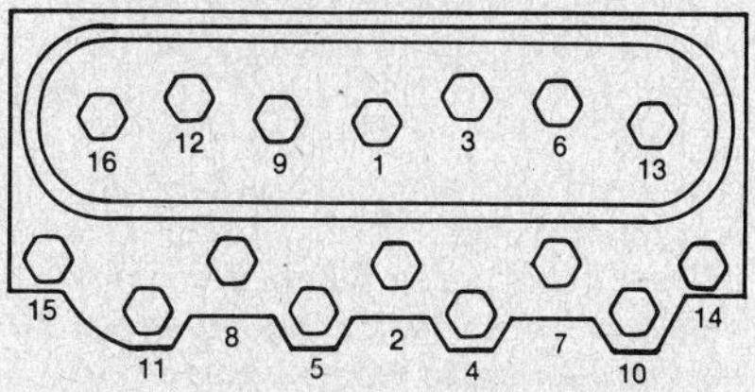

Torquing sequence— 366, 400, 427 & 454 V8 engines (© Chevrolet Div., G.M. Corp.)

Installation

Reverse removal procedures and adjust valves, after cleaning gasket surfaces. If heads are to be resurfaced check alignment at intake manifold. Cylinder head bolt threads in block and threads on bolts must be clean, coat threads with sealer. Tighten each cylinder head bolt a little at a time, in correct sequence, until specified torque is reached. Engines using steel (shim) gasket, coat both sides with a good sealer, bead side up. Engines using composition (steel asbestos) gaskets must be retorqued after warm-up (retightening heads effects valve lash).

Refer to specifications at beginning of this section for nut tightening sequence.

Valve System

Adjustments—Hydraulic lifters

Engine Running

1. Run engine to normalize (stabilize oil temperature), remove rocker cover (s) bump off—do not pry off). Leave old gasket on head to aid against oil overflow or use oil deflector clips.
2. Reduce engine idle as low as possible, tighten cylinder head bolts (and rocker supports if used). Check camshaft lobe lift.
3. Back off rocker arm adjusting nut until rocker arm starts to clatter, then turn nut down slowly until clatter stops. This is zero lash position.
4. Turn adjusting nut down ¼ turn and pause 10 seconds until engine runs smoothly. Repeat operation 3 more times until 1 full turn down from zero lash position is reached. *NOTE: This 1 turn pre-load adjustment must be done slowly and in stages to allow hydraulic lifter to adjust itself to prevent possibility of internal interference or bent push rods.*

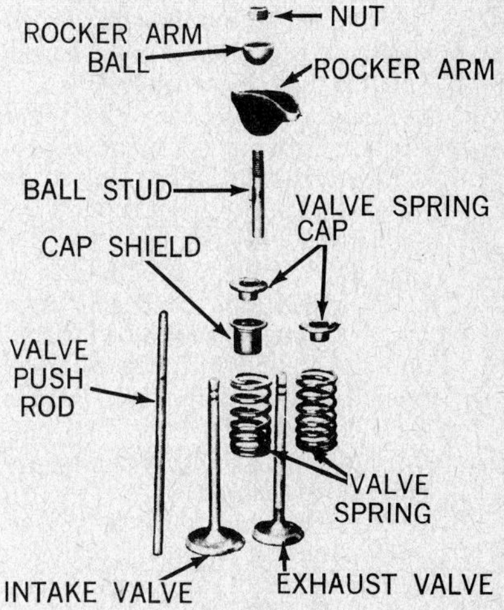

Valve system—V8 engines (© Chevrolet Div., G.M. Corp.)

5. Repeat for each valve, the use of a vacuum gauge is recommended.
6. Install new rocker cover gaskets and torque rocker covers. Reset engine idle.

Engine Not Running

1. Remove rocker cover (s) (bump off—do not pry off).

Valve adjustment (© Chevrolet Div., G.M. Corp.)

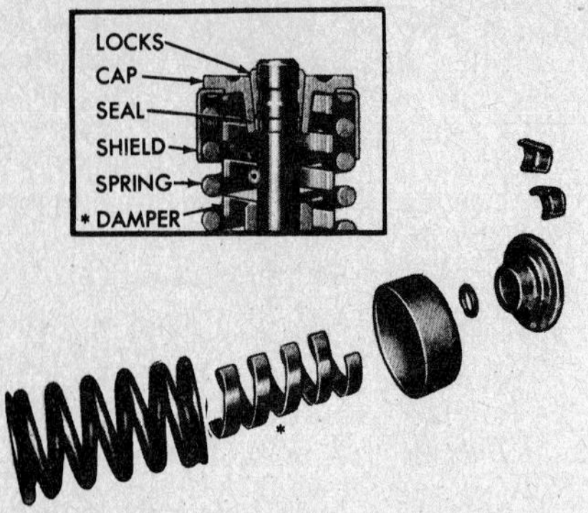

Valve spring installation—inline & small V8 engines (© Chevrolet Div.,G.M. Corp.)

2. Tighten cylinder head bolts (and rocker arm supports if used).
3. Disconnect primary wire at negative terminal of coil.
4. Mark distributor housing with chalk at each spark plug tower (double mark no. 1 cylinder).
5. Remove distributor cap and crank engine until rotor points to No. 1 chalk mark. (No. 1 cylinder is approximately at TDC and both valves can be adjusted). Valve adjustment is made by backing off rocker arm nut until push rod can be rotated and then slowly tightened until push rod does not turn. This is zero lash position. Turn adjusting nut down 1 full turn to complete adjustment.
6. Adjust the remaining valves, one cylinder at a time (following firing order) in same manner.
7. Install distributor cap.
8. Install new rocker cover gasket (s) and torque rocker cover (s).

Noisy Lifters

Locate a noisy lifter by using a mechanic's stethoscope or hose, can also be detected by placing finger on valve spring retainer (a distinct shock will be felt each time valve returns to seat). Forcing push rod down will cause lifter check valve to unload and remain open. A noisy or defective push rod is usually indicated by a free-spinning push rod.

Rocker Arms

Rocker arms are trough shaped, pressed steel levers that transfer lifter motion to valves. Rocker arms are supported on individual pedestals and have an oval hole in center to fit over stud and pivot on ball seats. Oil is fed to rocker arms by means of hollow push rods. Whenever arms or ball seats are being installed, coat all bearing surfaces with engine oil.

Rocker arm studs are pressed in cylinder head and are available in oversize for replacement.

CAUTION: Do not try to press oversized stud in head without reaming stud hole first.

Pressed in studs can be replaced by a stud threaded on both ends. Head is to be threaded in stud hole to accept threaded stud.

Checking Engine Valve Timing

6 cyl. (Inline Engine)

1. Remove the valve rocker arm cover and the push rod front cover.
2. Loosen the nut and the no. 2 intake valve rocker arm, swing the rocker arm away from the push rod and remove the push rod and valve lifter.
3. Temporarily install a flat face mechanical lifter in place of the hydraulic lifter.
4. Turn the crankshaft until the no. 2 exhaust valve opens and the notch on the pulley dampner is aligned with the "O" mark on the timing pointer.
5. Position a deal indicator to measure lifter movement and set the indicator at zero. Turn the crankshaft to 360 degrees and read the indicator. On engines that are correctly timed the indicator will read as follows:
   250 engines . . . . 0.014″
   292 engines . . . . 0.016″

If the reading is not as above, reset the indcator at zero and turn the crankshaft 360 degrees, then read the indicator again. If the read is now correct, the engine is timed properly. The following chart shows indicator readings result from improperly indexed gears.

6. If after checking an out-of-time condition exist, remove the engine front cover and check for proper indexing of time marks on gears.

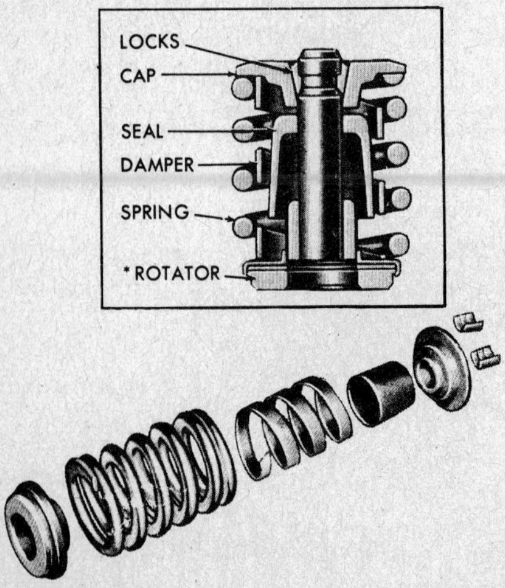

Exhaust valve spring installation–Mark IV V8 engines (© Chevrolet Div., G.M. Corp.)

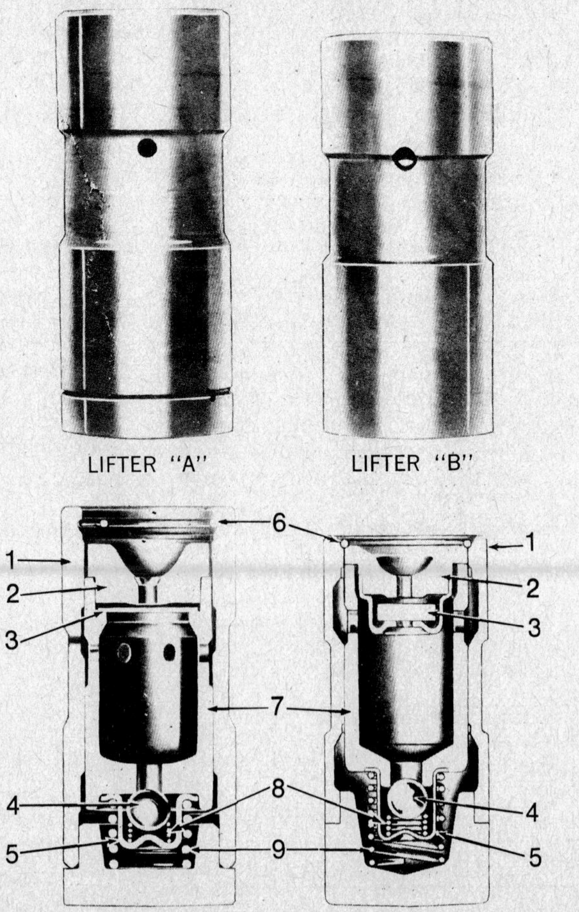

1 Lifter body
2 Push rod seat
3 Metering valve (Lifter A)
Inertia valve (Lifter B)
4 Check ball
5 Check ball retainer
6 Push rod seat retainer
7 Plunger
8 Check ball spring
9 Plunger spring

Hydraulic valve lifters (© Chevrolet Div., G.M. Corp.)

Engine (Cu. In.)	Camshaft Part No. & Valve Lift	Gears Properly Indexed	One Tooth Adv.	One Tooth Ret.
250	3864896-.388	.014″ ± .004″	.0351″	.0055″
292	384800-.405	.016″ ±.004″	.0379″	.0068″

V6 Engine

1. Remove the left-hand rocker cover.
2. Facing the front of the engine turn the engine clockwise to the top dead center No. 1 mark at the crankshaft pulley on the compression stroke. Both the intake and the exhaust valve on the No. 1 cylinder will then be closed.
3. On all V-6 engines adjust the clearance to exactly 0.099 inches at the No. 1 exhaust valve (front valve).
4. Turn the engine clockwise until the No. 1 exhaust valve opens and begins to close, then with fingers, try turning the push rod of the No. 1 exhaust valve as the engine is cranked slowly. When the push rod rotates with finger pressure, the 5-degree (before top dead center mark) on the pulley should be at the pointer. This will be about one revolution from the starting point. If the pushrod can be rotated at any point between the 10-degree mark and the top dead center No. 1 mark, the valve timing is correct. After making the timing check be sure to adjust the exhaust valve clearance to 0.018″.

NOTE: If the timing chain has been installed improperly, there will be a 15 degrees out-of-time condition for each mismatched tooth on the sprocket.

V8 Engine

1. Remove the rocker arm covers.
2. Turn the crankshaft so that the timing mark is at the "O" mark on the pointer and the No. 1 cylinder is ready to fire.
3. Move the crankshaft, and the exhaust valve in the No. 6 cylinder will just close and the intake valve will just begin to open.
4. If the exhaust valve or the intake valve is open when the pointer is at the "O" timing mark the camshaft is out of time
5. When the No. 6 cylinder is ready to fire and the pointer is at the "O" timing mark the No. 1 cylinder exhaust valve will have just closed and the intake valve will begin to open.

Timing Gears and Chain

Crankshaft Pulley or Damper

Removal

1. Drain radiator; remove hoses.
2. Remove radiator—See Radiator R & R

NOTE: On V-8 engines if additional operations such as camshaft removal are not being performed, radiator removal will not be necessary.

3. Loosen fan belt and remove any accessory drive.
4. Use puller to remove pulley or damper.

NOTE: On some early models, pulley is bolted to Hub. Remove pulley first then, using pulley holes, remove hub. More recent models have the hub bonded to inertia weight. Care must be exercised when using a puller.

Installation

1. Clean area, inspect oil seal in cover. (Now would be good time to install new seal even if just for preventative maintenance).
2. Coat timing case cover oil seal with light oil, inspect hub for seal (grooved) wear.
3. Position damper (or hub) on crankshaft, aligning keyway, and tap lightly into position.
4. Pull damper (or hub) into position with damper retaining bolt and washer. (Make sure damper retaining bolt has good thread engagement before applying force). Torque to specifications.
5. Reverse balance of removal steps.

Timing Cover Oil Seal Replacement

1. Remove torsional damper—see damper R & R.
2. Pry old seal out, be careful not to mar crankshaft or bend cover.
3. Install new seal (lip of seal toward block), tap lightly into position. Coat seal with oil.
4. Reverse removal procedures.

Timing Gear Replacement

Inline Engines

NOTE: When necessary to install a new camshaft gear the camshaft should be removed. However gear can be removed from camshaft without removing camshaft from engine. Cam gear can be split and hub section pulled off but extreme care must be taken not to allow any impact, either removing or installing gear, on the shaft. Camshaft must be totally blocked so as not to allow any movement to disturb oil sealing welsh plug at camshaft rear bearing.

Removal

1. Drain and remove radiator.
2. Remove front end sheet metal or grille.
3. Remove damper or pulley.
4. Remove oil pan (See Oil Pan R & R).
5. Remove timing case cover (2 bolts inside oil pan at front main bearing cap).
6. Remove rocker arm cover(s) and remove lifters.
7. Remove fuel pump and distributor (mark position of rotor).

Removing torsion damper (© Chevrolet Div., G.M. Corp.)

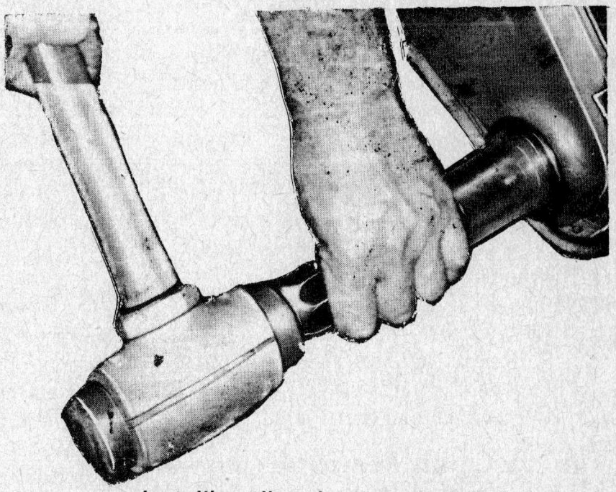

Installing oil seal—cover installed (© Chevrolet Div., G.M. Corp.)

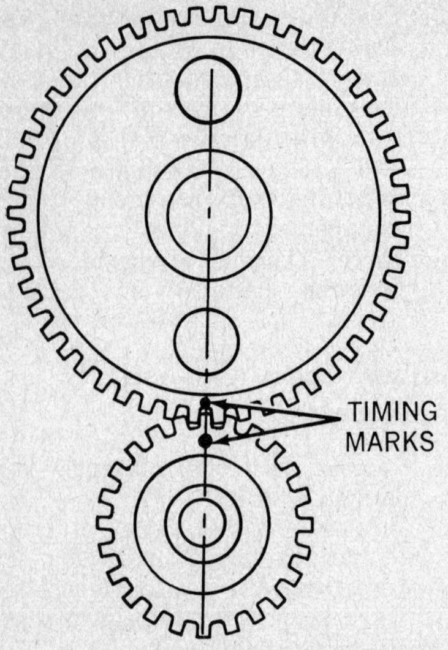

Timing mark alignment—inline engines
(© Chevrolet Div., G.M. Corp.)

8. Align timing gear marks (check rotor mark) then remove 2 thrust plate screws by reaching through 2 holes in camgear.
9. Remove camshaft and rear assembly by pulling and turning shaft carefully so lobes will not mar bearings and will clear lifters.
10. Use press to remove cam gear using caution not to damage thrust plate by woodruff key.
11. Clean all gasket surfaces and inspect.
12. Check camshaft alignment and lobes for wear. Check camshaft bearings in block, check crank gear and oil spray nozzle.

Installation

1. Support camshaft at back end of front bearing in a press, place thrust plate over end of shaft, install woodruff key in key way, align camgear with key and press gear on shaft until clearance at thrust plate (and front end of front bearing) is .001-.003″.
2. Install camshaft and gear assembly in block, turning shaft carefully so lobes clear lifters and bearings, until it almost bottoms. *NOTE: Coat lobes and bearing surfaces with engine oil.*
3. Turn camshaft and mesh timing marks, tighten thrust plate.
4. Check cam gear for runout (should not exceed .005″).
5. Check backlash at gears. (.004-.006″).
6. Reverse remaining removal procedures.
7. Fill radiator, and oil and start engine. Adjust valves, check timing and inspect for leaks.

Timing Chain Removal

V8 Engines

1. Drain and remove radiator.
2. Remove torsional damper.
3. Remove oil pan (see oil pan R & R).
4. Remove water pump or pulley if necessary.
5. Remove timing case cover.
6. Align timing marks.
7. Remove (3) camshaft sprocket bolts.
8. Remove sprocket and chain. *NOTE: Sprocket is a light press fit on-camshaft, especially at dowel pin. If sprocket is tight, tap lightly with plastic hammer on lower edge of sprocket.*
9. Clean all gasket and seal areas and inspect.
10. Check teeth on both sprockets for wear.

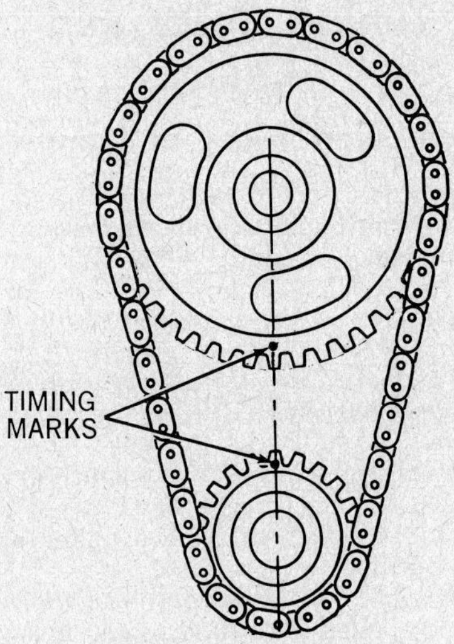

Valve timing—V8 engines
(© Chevrolet Div., G.M. Corp.)

Installation

1. Suspend chain on camshaft sprocket with timing mark in approximate position.
2. Place chain over crankshaft sprocket and position camshaft sprocket on dowel. Recheck timing marks.
3. Draw camshaft sprocket in place using the three mounting bolts. Torque to specifications. **CAUTION: do not drive sprocket on camshaft as welsh plug at rear of camshaft can be dislodged.**
4. Lubricate chain with engine oil, make sure oil slinger is in place.
5. Reverse removal procedures.
6. Fill radiator, add engine oil and start engine. Check for leaks.

Check for Worn Chain

1. Check fan belt tension, adjust if too loose.
2. Remove distributor cap, loosen spark plugs.
3. Move fan blades until rotor moves. Mark distributor housing and balancer at pointer.
4. Move fan in opposite direction until rotor moves, remark both units.
5. Marks in excess of 4° apart, 2 graduations (usually) on balancer, indicate excess wear.

Pistons and Connecting Rods

Pistons

Pistons are of various designs, flat, cup, hump and dome. Heads are usually notched to indicate front or pistons are marked on pin boss.

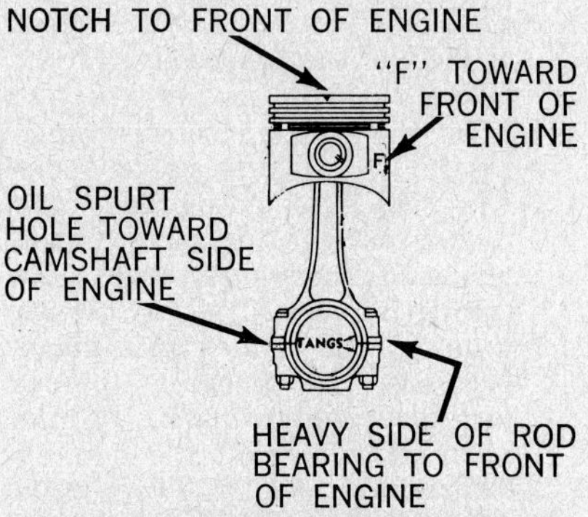

Correct relationship of piston and rod on 250 engine (© Chevrolet Div., G.M. Corp.)

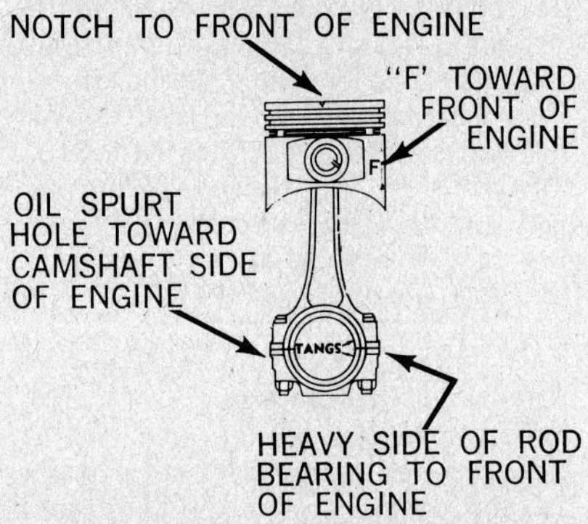

Correct relationship of piston and rod—292 engines (© Chevrolet Div.,G.M.Corp.)

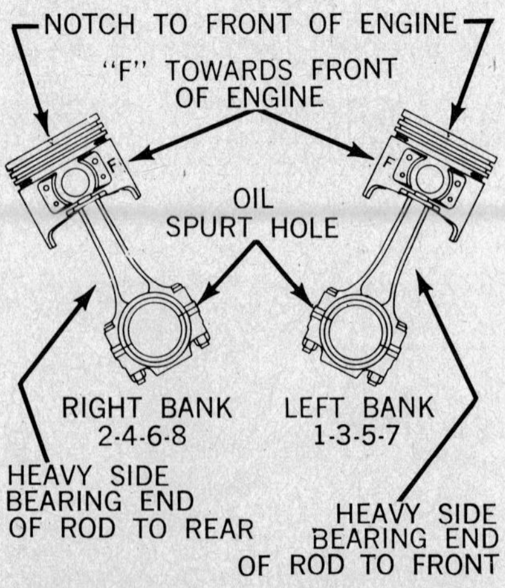

Correct relationship of piston and rod on the 307, 305, and 350 engines
(© Chevrolet Div., G.M. Corp.)

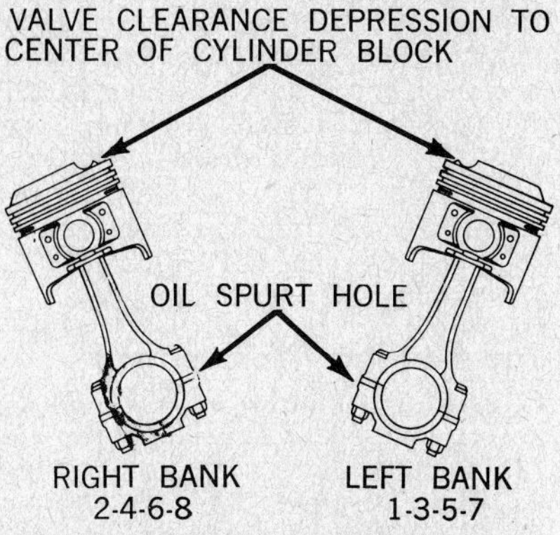

Correct relationship of piston and rod on 366, 400, 427, and 454 engines
(© Chevrolet Div., G.M. Corp.)

Connecting Rods

Rod forging and cap have mating numbers and must be on same side when installed or cap is on "backwards." Rod number on in-line en-

Installing piston and rod assembly
(© Chevrolet Div., G.M. Corp.)

gines go to camshaft side. Numbers on "V" engines go to outside of block. The oil spurt (cylinder wall oiling) hole goes toward camshaft. On in-line engines the spurt hole and number are both on camshaft side. On "V" engines the spurt hole is in center, toward camshaft, and numbers to outside.

Removal

1. Drain cooling system and remove cylinder head(s). See cylinder head removal.
2. Drain crankcase oil and remove oil pan. See Oil Pan Removal.
3. Remove any ridge and/or deposits from upper end of cylinder bores with a ridge reamer. *NOTE: Move piston to bottom of its travel and place a cloth on top of piston to collect cuttings. After ridge and/or deposits are removed turn crankshaft until piston is at top of its stroke and carefully remove cloth with its cuttings.*
4. Check connecting rods and pistons for cylinder number identification and if necessary, mark them.
5. Remove conecting rod nuts and caps. Push rods away from crankshaft and install caps and nuts loosely to their respective rods.
6. Push piston and rod assemblies away from crankshaft and out of cylinders. See Engine Rebuilding—General Section.

Installation

1. Lightly coat pistons, rings and cylinder walls with light engine oil, making sure everything is clean and free of dirt and foreign material.
2. With bearing caps removed, and ring compressor tool installed, install each piston in its respective bore.
3. Install bearing caps and check bearing clearance. See Engine Rebuilding—General Section.
4. Install oil pan gaskets, seals and oil pan. See Oil Pan Installation.
5. Install cylinder head gasket(s) and head(s). See Cylinder Head Installation.
6. Refill crankcase and cooling system and check for leaks.

Measuring connecting rod side clearance V8 engines (© Chevrolet Div.,G.M. Corp.)

Piston Rings

Piston rings are available in standard size as well as .020″, .030″, and .040″ oversizes.

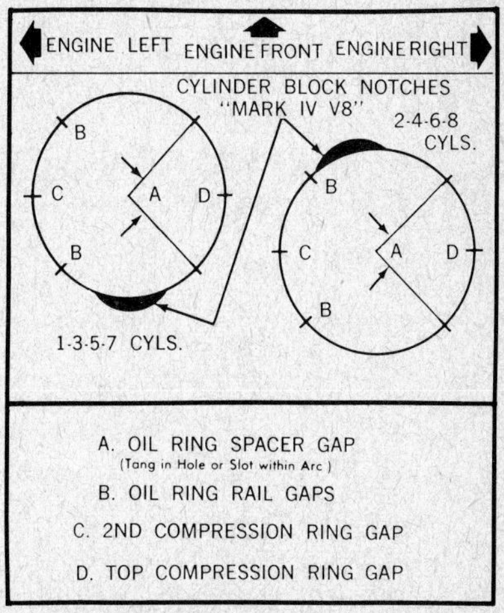

Ring gap location—V8—typical
(© Chevrolet Div., G.M. Corp.)

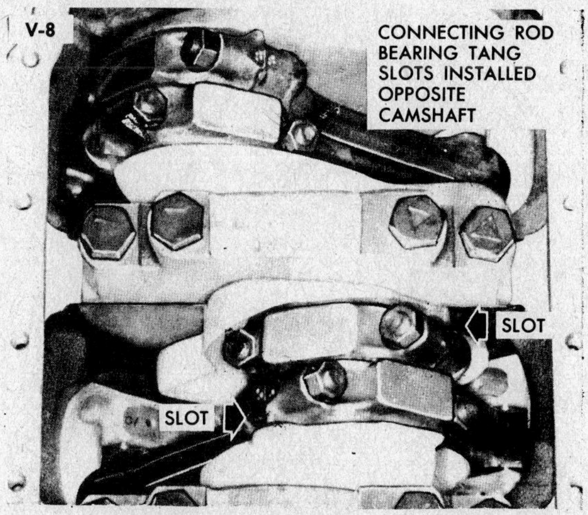

Connecting rods installed—V8 engines
(© Chevrolet Div., G.M. Corp.)

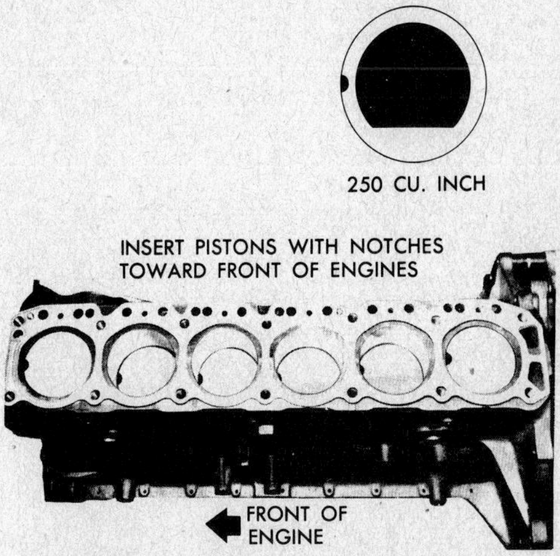

Pistons installed—inline engines
(© Chevrolet Div., G.M. Corp.)

Removal

1. With pistons removed from cylinders, remove piston rings by expanding them and sliding them off piston.
2. Clean piston ring grooves by removing all particles of carbon. Check for burrs or nicks that might cause rings to hang up.

Installation

See Engine Rebuilding—General Section.

Main and Rod Bearings

Main bearings and connecting rod bearings are replaceable inserts, precision fit and held in place by locking tangs. Excessive bearing clearances reduce oil pressure. Never replace the lower half of any bearing without replacing the upper half. Do not file any bearing cap. Make sure, on main bearings, the upper half oil hole is aligned. Be certain oil passages in the crankshaft are open. Mark rod caps and upper forgings, also main caps and block, in numerical order to aid in reassembly. Rod bearings are available in standard size as well as .001″, .002″, .010″ and .020″ undersizes. Main bearings are furnished in standard size and .001″, .002″, .009″, .010″, .020″ and .030″ undersizes.

Rod Bearing Replacement

1. Drain crankcase oil and remove oil pan. See Oil Pan Removal.
2. Remove connecting rod bearing cap.
3. Wipe bearing shell and crankpin clean of oil.
4. Inspect bearings for evidence of wear or damage. (Bearings showing the above should not be installed).
5. Measure crankpin for out-of-round or taper with a micrometer. If within specifications measure bearing clearance with plastigage or its equivalent. See Engine Rebuilding—General Section.
6. Install bearing in connecting rod and cap.

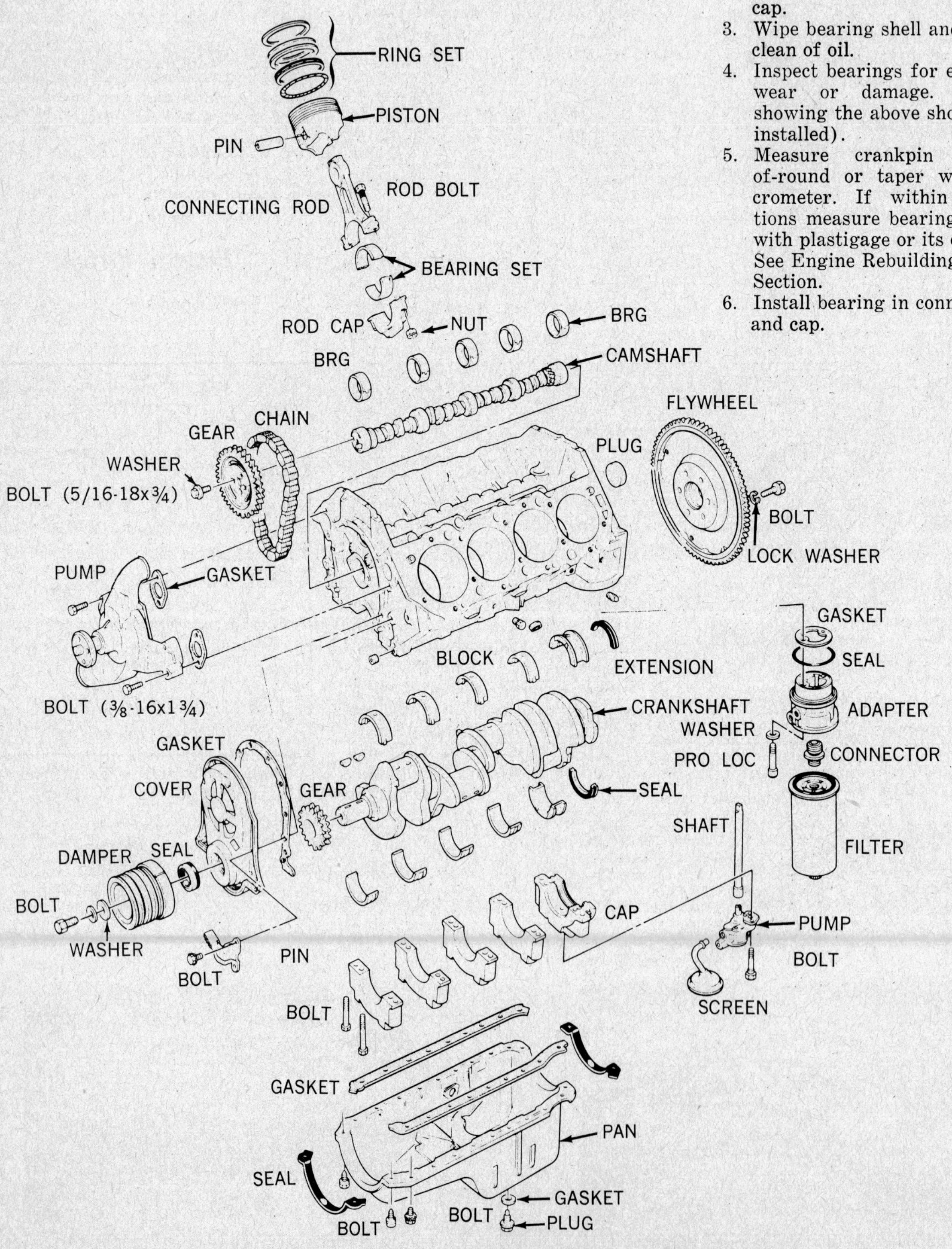

Short engine assembly—454 CID V8 (© Chevrolet Div., G.M. Corp.)

Removing upper half of rear main bearing (© Chevrolet Div., G.M. Corp.)

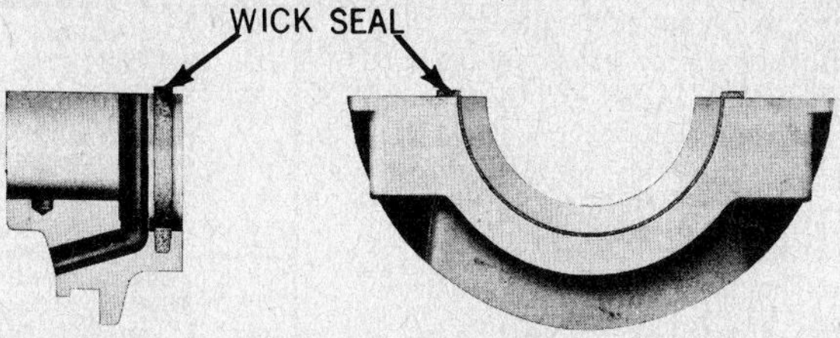

Rear main oil seal installation (© Chevrolet Div., G.M. Corp.)

7. Coat bearing surface with oil, install rod cap and torque nuts to specifications.
8. Rotate crankshaft after bearing adjustment to be sure bearings are not too tight. Check side clearance.
9. Install oil pan gaskets, seals and oil pan. See Oil Pan Installation.

Main Bearing Replacement

NOTE: Main bearings may be replaced with or without removing crankshaft.

(Engine in Vehicle)

1. Drain crankcase oil and remove oil pan. See Oil Pan Removal.
2. Remove oil pump.
3. Loosen or remove spark plugs for easier crankshaft rotation.
4. Starting with rear main bearing, remove bearing cap and wipe oil from journal and cap.
5. Inspect bearings for evidence of wear or damage.
6. Measure bearing clearance with plastigage or its equivalent. The crankshaft should be supported at damper and flywheel to remove clearance from upper bearing. Total clearance can then be measured between lower bearing and journal. See Engine Rebuilding—General Section.
7. Remove bearing shell from cap.
8. On in-line engine crankshaft, rear main bearing has no oil hole. Replace rear main bearing upper half as follows:
   a. Use a small drift punch and hammer to start upper bearing half rotating out of block.
   b. Use a pair of pliers (with taped jaws) to hold bearing thrust surface to oil slinger and rotate crankshaft to remove bearing.
   c. Oil new selected size upper bearing and insert plate (unnotched) and between crankshaft and indented or notched side of block.
   d. Use pliers as in removing to rotate bearing into place. The last ¼ movement may be done by holding just the slinger with pliers or tap in place with a drift punch.
9. All other crankshaft journals (in-line and "V" models) have oil holes. Replace main bearing upper half as follows:
   a. Install a main bearing removing and installing tool in oil hole in crankshaft journal. *NOTE: If such a tool is not available, a cotter pin (with head flattened) may be used.*
   b. Rotate crankshaft clockwise as viewed from front of engine. This will roll upper bearing out of block.
   c. Oil new selected size upper bearing and insert plain (unnotched) end between crankshaft and indented or notched side of block. Rotate bearing into place and remove tool from oil hole in crankshaft journal.
10. Oil new lower bearing and install in bearing cap.
11. Install main bearing cap according to markings. Torque bearing cap bolts to specifications.
12. Install oil pump and oil pan. Refill crankcase. Install and tighten spark plugs.

Rear Main Bearing Oil Seal Replacement (Engine in Vehicle)

1. Raise vehicle and drain oil.
2. Remove oil pan and oil pump. See oil pan and oil pump removal.
3. Remove rear main cap and discard seal.
4. Loosen all mains (except no. 1) and block crankshaft down for maximum clearance at rear main.
5. Use wooden dowel, so as not to mar journal, tap lightly until

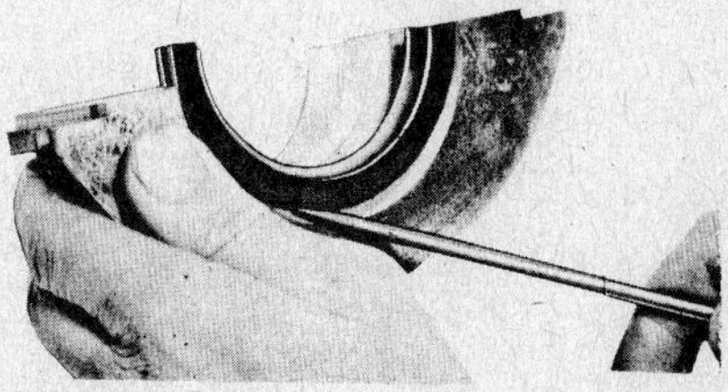

Removing lower half of rear oil seal (© Chevrolet Div., G.M. Corp.)

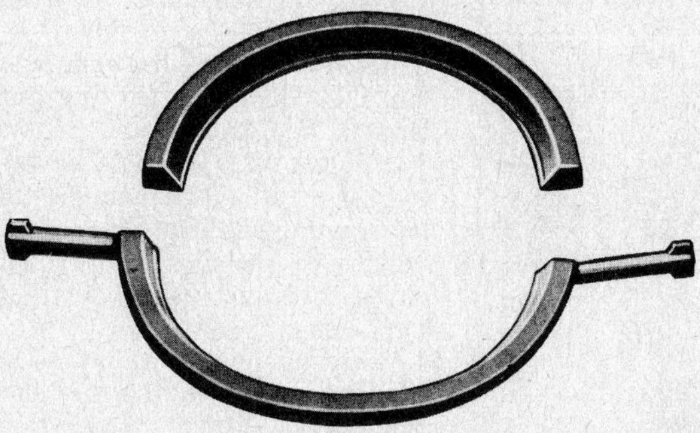

Rear main oil seal—6 cylinder engines (© Chevrolet Div., G.M. Corp.)

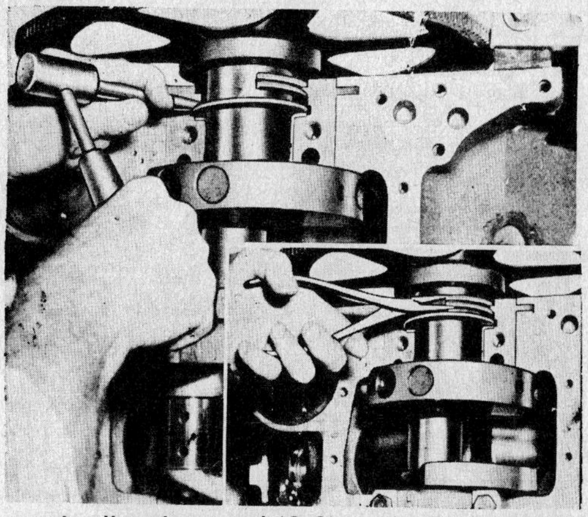

Rear main oil seal removal (© Chevrolet Div., G.M. Corp.)

seal can be gripped and removed. Rotating shaft may help.

6. Wick type seal: Use "Chinese Finger" type of tool, or insert a piece of soft wire through seal approximately 1/4 from end, then wrap end with wire. Insert wire through seal opening in crankcase and around crankshaft. Start upper half of seal in place, lubricated with light sealer. Pull seal into place (rotating shaft may help) until centered. Cut each end of seal so that 1/4" protrudes. Install new lower half of oil seal in cap and roll or pack into position. Cut ends flush with cap parting face. Replace cap. Molded type seal: Insert new upper half, lubricated with light sealer, into channel and apply firm pressure with hammer handle until seal is centered. (Lip of seal facing toward front of engine.) Install lower half of oil seal in cap (lip toward front), lubricate lip with oil and install cap.
7. Torque all mains, check for drag.
8. Replace oil pump, oil pan and add oil.
9. Start engine and check for leaks.

Oil Pan

Removal and Installation

Vans

1. Support on stands.
2. Disconnect battery ground cable, loosen fan belt and remove radiator shroud top belt.
3. Remove radiator fan and pulley.
4. Raise vehicle, clean road dirt from oil pan.
5. Drain oil, replace drain plug gasket.

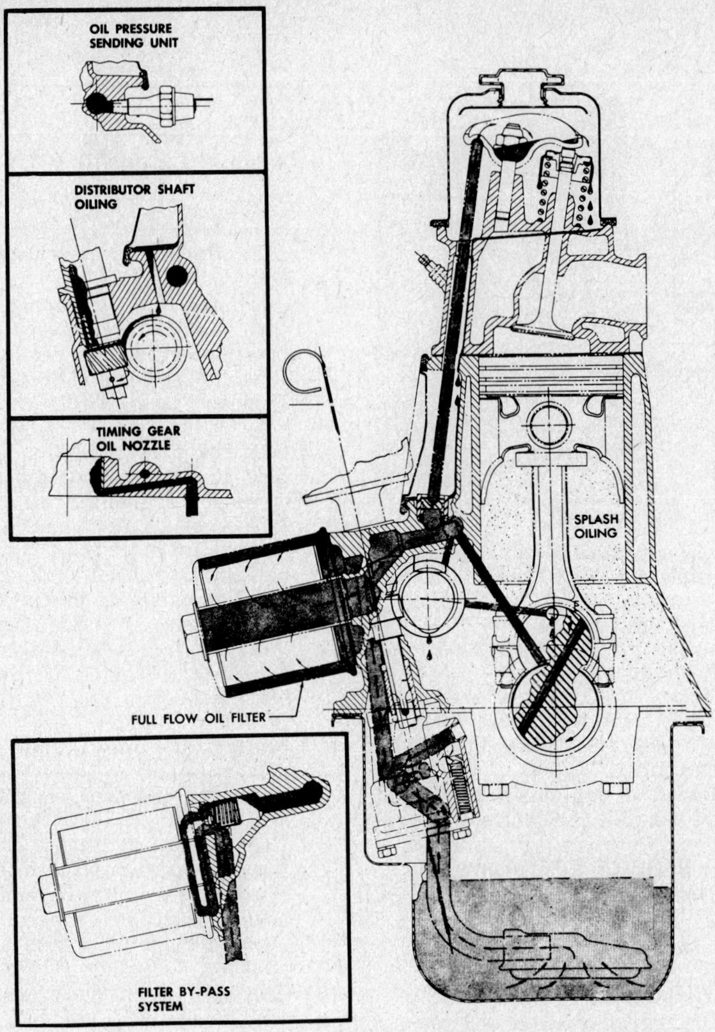

Engine lubrication—inline 6 cylinder engines (© Chevrolet Div., G.M. Corp.)

6. Remove engine splash shields if equipped.
7. Remove starter, leave electrical connections intact, swing out of way.
8. Automatic transmisson models —remove oil cooler lines and converter pan.
9. Remove front motor mount bolts.
10. Remove accessory drive pulley (if used).
11. Engines with radiator shroud—drain radiator, remove lower radiator hose, remove lower shroud bolts and lower shroud out of way.
12. Using a jack, raise and support front of engine.
13. Remove crossmember to frame bolts, remove crossmember.
14. Remove oil pan bolts, remove oil pan. **CAUTION: If any prolonged operations are planned (with pan off), it would be safer to re-install crossmember and lower engine on mounts.**
15. Reverse removal steps to install after cleaning gasket and seal surfaces.
16. Lower vehicle, fill crankcase and radiator, start engine and check for leaks. *NOTE: Use gasket sealer as a retainer to hold side gaskets in place on block. Bolts in front cover should be installed*

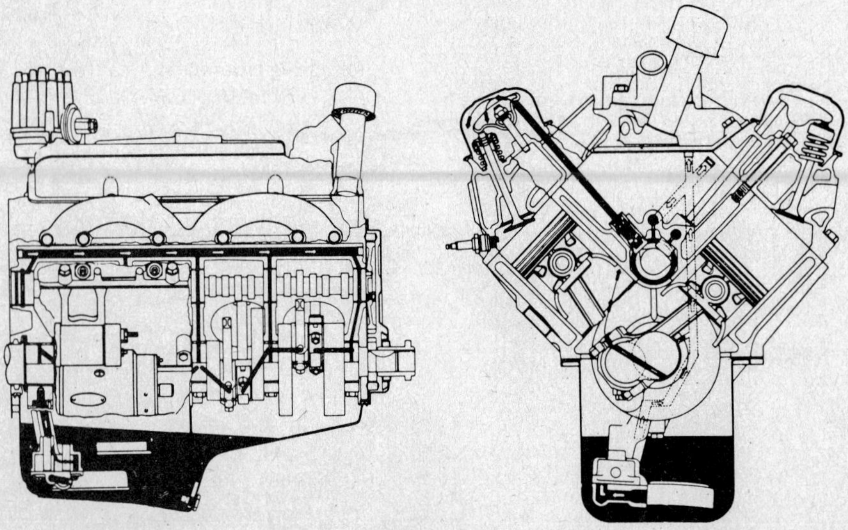

Engine lubrication—305, 307, and 350 engines (© Chevrolet Div., G.M. Corp.)

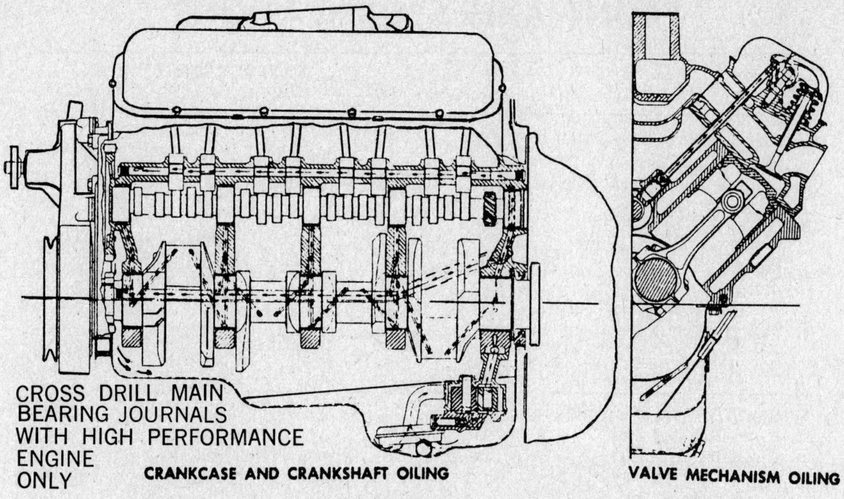

Engine lubrication—454 V8 engine (© Chevrolet Div., G.M. Corp.)

last. They are installed at an angle and holes line up after rest of pan bolts are tightened.

(Except Vans)

1. Raise front of vehicle and support on stands.
2. Remove road dirt from pan and drain plug.
3. Drain oil, replace drain plug gasket.
4. Remove converter pan on automatic transmission.
5. Remove battery ground cable, remove starter (leave electrical connections intact and swing aside).
6. V8—Remove dipstick and tube, remove exhaust crossover pipe.
7. C10-30—Remove front motor mount bolts, using a block of wood under oil pan, raise engine with a jack high enough to insert blocks at motor mounts.
8. Remove oil pan and discard gaskets and seals.
9. Reverse removal steps to install after cleaning all gasket and seal surfaces.
10. Lower vehicle, fill crankcase to level, start engine and check for leaks.

NOTE: Use gasket sealer as a retainer to hold side gaskets in place on block.

Oil Filter

Oil filters are related to oil change periods, which in turn are related to quality of oil used, type of service and operating conditions. Severe conditions such as frequent and prolonged idle periods may warrant more changes. Heavy sludge in pan or filter indicates oil change intervals should be shortened. Filter replacements should be made at time of oil change. It is recommended that filter be replaced with initial oil change and every second oil change thereafter.

Filters on in-line engines are located at right front of engine, "V" engines at left rear.

Replacement

Element Type

1. Remove drain plug (some models) in shell and drain, replace drain plug (if used).
2. Remove center stud, withdraw shell and empty (if no drain plug).
3. Lift out element and clean inside of shell thoroughly.
4. Clean base and replace shell gasket, check bypass valve.
5. Install new element (with element gasket) in shell.
6. Install shell on base, drain plug away from engine, and tighten retaining bolt to engine and check for leaks, check oil level.

Disposable (Spin-on) type

1. Turn filter from mounting base and discard.
2. Clean base and inspect gasket area.
3. Apply oil film to gasket and turn filter on stud until gasket seats then tighten ½ turn more.
4. Run engine, check for leaks, check oil level.

NOTE: On some vans the right hand engine splash shield will have to be removed.

Oil Pump

The pumps used are distributor driven gear type. Oil pump consists of two spur gears and a relief valve in a two piece housing. On in-line engines, pump is mounted on cylinder block while on "V" engines pump is mounted on rear main cap inside oil pan. Pump gears and body are not serviced separately, replace pump as a unit. A baffle, incorporated on the pickup screen, eliminates oil pressure loss due to surging.

Removal and Installation

1. Remove oil pan—see oil pan removal.
2. In-line engines—Remove oil suction pipe at housing.

   CAUTION: Do not disturb screen on pick up pipe.
3. Remove two flange mounting bolts, remove pump.
4. Reverse removal steps to install, using new pan gasket, watch slot alignment with distributor tang.

   NOTE: Pump should slide easily into place, if not, remove and relocate slot.
5. Refill with oil, start engine and check for leaks.

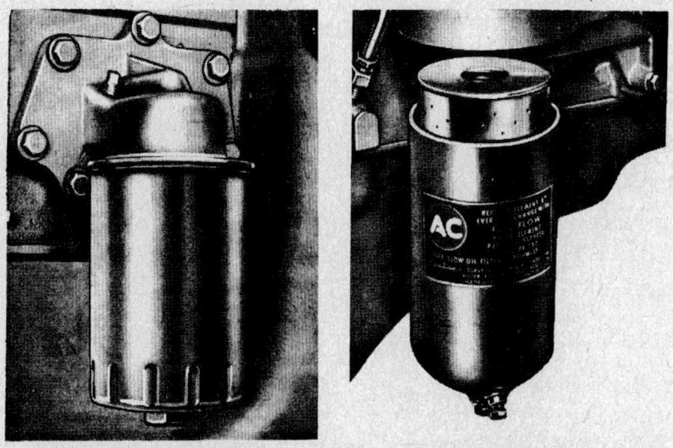

THROW-AWAY TYPE　　REPLACEABLE ELEMENT TYPE

Engine oil filters (© Chevrolet Div., G.M. Corp.)

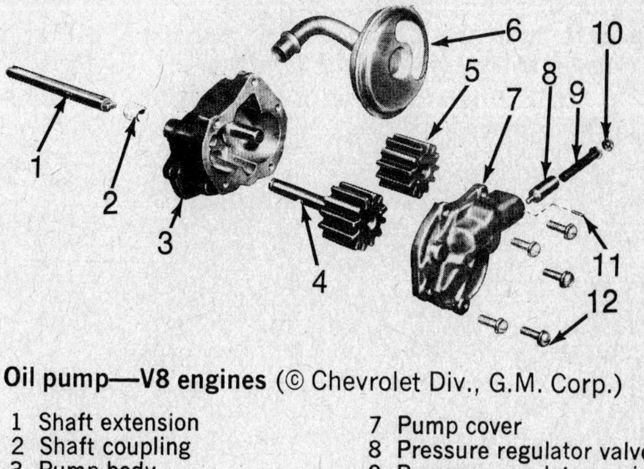

Oil pump—V8 engines (© Chevrolet Div., G.M. Corp.)

1 Shaft extension
2 Shaft coupling
3 Pump body
4 Drive gear and shaft
5 Idler gear
6 Pickup screen and pipe
7 Pump cover
8 Pressure regulator valve
9 Pressure regulator spring
10 Washer
11 Retaining pin
12 Screws

FRONT AXLE AND SUSPENSION

Procedures covering front end alignment are not covered in this manual.

Figures covering the caster, camber, toe-in, kingpin inclination, and turning radius can be found in the Wheel Alignment table of this section.

FRONT AXLE SPECIFICATIONS

	FRONT AXLE MODELS F-050/F-055	F-070	F-090	F-120
Steering Knuckle To Axle Center Clearance:				
Factory Tolerance (inches)	.001-.010	.001-.010	.004-.012	.005-.015
Service Tolerance (inches)	.015-.030	.015-.030	.015-.030	.015-.035
Spacing Washers Available				
No. 1	—	—	.114-.116	.0478
No. 2	—	—	.121-.123	—
No. 3	—	—	.128-.130	—
Spacing Shims Available				
No. 1	.005	.005	.005	.005
No. 2	—	—	.010	.010

⑲ Refer to illustrations in FRONT SUSPENSION section for correct axle identification.

I-Beam Front Axle

This type of front axle is a one-piece steel forging in which dowel pins are installed to locate spring seats. Both ends of the axle are machined to accept the steering knuckle and kingpin assemblies, and the kingpin inclination is a built-in angle.

Spring

Removal and Installation

1. Wire brush all road dirt from threaded areas on U bolts, shock absorbers and stabilizer links, apply a good penetrant on threads.
2. Disconnect shock and stabilizer link at lower bracket.
3. Loosen both spring U bolts.
4. Using jack under I-beam, raise front of vehicle and support at frame side rail with stand. Finish removing U bolts and rebound bumper. Lower jack until spring clears I-beam or tire rests on ground. Remove any caster wedges (shims) and set aside for installation.

   NOTE: Thick end of shim goes to rear of vehicle for increased caster.
5. Remove front spring eye bolt.
6. Remove rear shackle (and hanger cam if equipped).
7. Remove spring, inspect hangers and spring seat (center bolt index).
8. Reverse removal procedures to install after placing spring on axle with center bolt head indexed in seat and caster shims in place. Torque all nuts and lubricate.

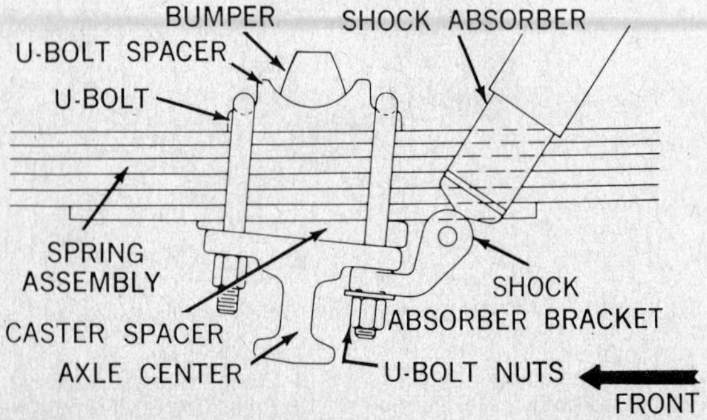

Spring center mount—leaf type—steel tilt model (typical of most models) (© Chevrolet Div., G.M. Corp.)

Steering Knuckle and Kingpin Assembly

F-050, F-055, and F-070 Axles

CAUTION: **Steering knuckle bushings are of a split type and are constructed of thermoplastic polyester. Bushings can be cleaned in most conventional solvents, except ketone or chlorinated types.**

Removal

1. Support the frame of the vehicle in a raised position, high enough so that the tires clear the floor.
2. Remove the wheels, hubs, and bearings.
3. Remove brake components as necessary.
4. Disconnect the tie-rod from the steering arm.
5. Remove the two lower steering arm-to-axle flange bolts, and swing the steering arm out of the way.
6. Remove the two upper bolts from the axle flange, and remove the brake backing plate.
7. Remove the kingpin draw key nut and washer.
8. Thread the draw key nut onto the draw key far enough to protect the threads from damage.
9. Drive the draw key loose by striking the nut with a brass hammer.
10. Finish driving the draw key out with a brass drift.
11. Remove the kingpin bearing cap scews.
12. Remove the kingpin bearing caps and gaskets.
13. Using a brass hammer, drive the kingpin out of the axle.
14. Remove the steering knuckle, thrust bearing, shims, and the O-ring.

NOTE: Steering knuckle bushinas can be hand pressed into the knuckle bore until flush with the top.

Installation

1. Position the steering knuckle on the axle, and insert the thrust bearing.
2. Install a new O-ring seal at the bottom of the upper bushing.

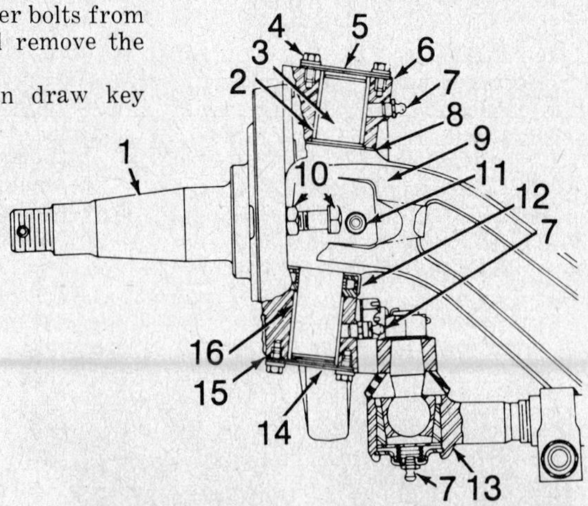

F-070 Axle 1973-80 (© Chevrolet Div., G.M. Corp.)

1 Steering Knuckle Spindle
2 Kingpin Bushing (Upper)
3 Kingpin
4 Cap Screw
5 Kingpin Bearing Cap (Upper)
6 Gasket
7 Lube Fitting
8 Shim
9 Axle Center
10 Stop Bolt and Lock Nut
11 Draw Key
12 Thrust Bearing
13 Tie Rod End Assembly
14 Kingpin Bearing Cap (Lower)
15 Gasket
16 Kingpin Bushing (Lower)

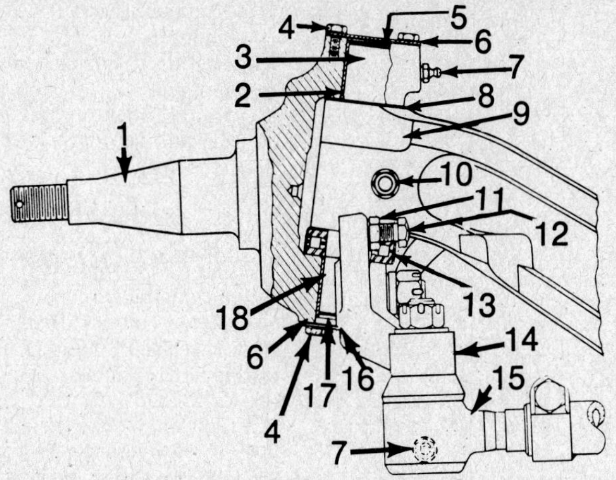

F-050 and F-055 Axle 1973-80 (© Chevrolet Div., G.M. Corp.)

1 Steering Knuckle Spindle
2 Upper Bushing
3 Kingpin
4 Cap Screw
5 Upper Kingpin Bearing Cup
6 Kingpin Bearing Cup Gasket
7 Lubrication Fitting
8 Shim
9 Axle Center
10 Draw Key
11 Stop Screw Nut
12 Stop Screw
13 Thrust Bearing
14 Lower Steering Arm
15 Tie Rod End Assembly
16 Lower Kingpin Bearing Cap
17 Spacer—Steering Knuckle Bushing
18 Lower Bushing

3. Align the steering knuckle yoke, axle end, and the thrust bearing to accept the kingpin; start the kingpin through the top of the assembly.
4. With the axle center firmly secured, jack up the steering knuckle until there is zero clearance between the steering knuckle lower yoke, thrust bearing, and the axle center.
5. Check the clearance between the top of the axle center and the knuckle upper yoke. Select shims which will provide the correct thrust clearance as indicated in the Front Axle Specification Chart.
6. From the top, insert the kingpin through the steering knuckle yoke, shim, thrust bearing, and axle center end. Press the kingpin down until the machined slot in the kingpin aligns with the draw key hole.
7. Insert the draw key into the axle center, and install the washer and nut.

CAUTION: If, after tightening the draw key nut, the kingpin is not secured, then replace the draw key.

NOTE: On models using steering knuckle bushing spacer, install spacer at lower end of the kingpin.

8. Using new gaskets, install upper and lower kingpin bearing caps and cap screws.
9. Lubricate the kingpin with chassis lubricant.
10. Secure the brake backing plate to the axle flange with the top two axle flange bolts.
11. Swing the steering arm into position, and secure it to the axle flange with two lower flange bolts.
12. Install brake components.
13. Install hubs and bearings.
14. Install wheels.
15. Lower the vehicle, and check front end alignment. Make necessary adjustments.

Steering Knuckle and Kingpin Assembly

F-090 Axle (F-120 Axle—Similar)

NOTE: The steering knuckle is supported on a solid kingpin which is tapered at the center. The kingpin bushing is constructed of steel, and the knuckle bushings are constructed of steel backed bronze.

Removal

1. Support the frame of the vehicle in a raised position, high enough so that the tires clear the floor.
2. Remove the wheels, hubs, and bearings.
3. Remove brake components as necessary.
4. Disconnect steering linkage components as necessary.
5. Remove the axle flange-to-steering knuckle bolts, and remove the brake backing plate.
6. Remove the dust cap and gasket.
7. Remove the lower expansion plug retainer and plug.

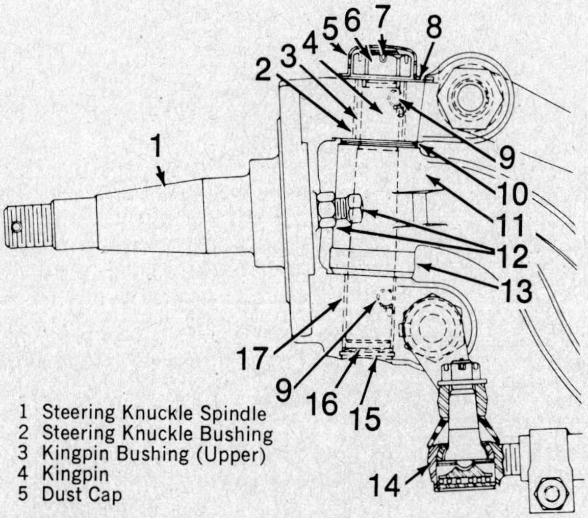

1 Steering Knuckle Spindle
2 Steering Knuckle Bushing
3 Kingpin Bushing (Upper)
4 Kingpin
5 Dust Cap

F-090 Axle 1973-80 (© Chevrolet Div., G.M. Corp.)

6 Kingpin Nut
7 Cotter Pin
8 Gasket
9 Lube Fitting
10 Washers or Shims
11 Axle Center
12 Stop Bolt and Lock Nut
13 Thrust Bearing
14 Tie Rod Assembly
15 Plug Retainer
16 Expansion Plug
17 Kingpin Bushing (Lower)

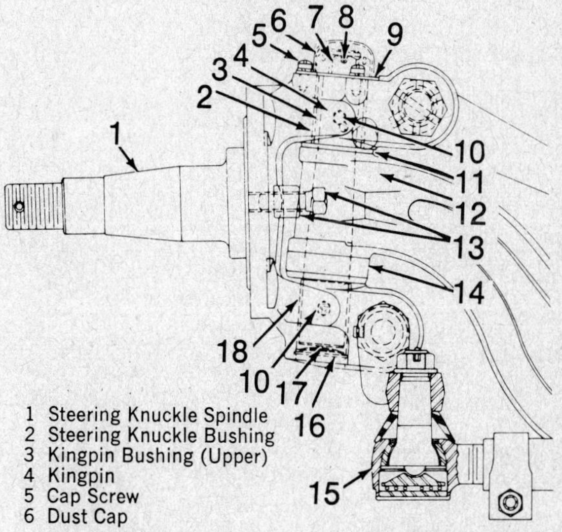

1 Steering Knuckle Spindle
2 Steering Knuckle Bushing
3 Kingpin Bushing (Upper)
4 Kingpin
5 Cap Screw
6 Dust Cap

F-120 Axle 1973-74 (© Chevrolet Div., G.M. Corp.)

7 Kingpin Nut
8 Cotter Pin
9 Gasket
10 Lube Fitting
11 Spacers or Shims
12 Axle Center
13 Stop Bolt and Lock Nut
14 Thrust Bearing
15 Tie Rod End Assembly
16 Plug Retainer
17 Expansion Plug
18 Kingpin Bushing (Lower)

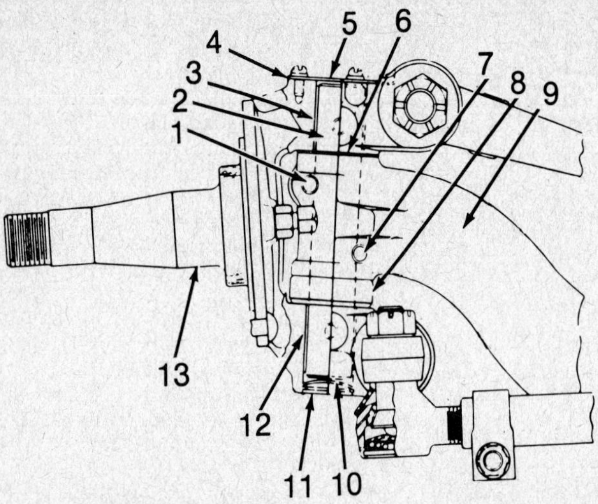

F-120 Axle 1975-80 (© Chevrolet Div., G.M. Corp.)

1 Upper Draw Key (Short)
2 Kingpin
3 Upper Bushing
4 Cap Gasket
5 Kingpin Cap
6 Spacing Shim
7 Lower Draw Key
8 Thrust Bearing
9 Axle Center
10 Expansion Plug
11 Lock Ring
12 Lower Bushing
13 Steering knuckle

NOTE: If the plug does not remove freely after the retainer has been removed, it will come out along with the kingpin when the kingpin is driven out.

8. Remove the cotter pin, kingpin nut, and the steel washer.
9. Drive the kingpin down and out of the axle with a brass drift.
10. Remove the steering knuckle, thrust bearing, and spacers from the axle.

NOTE: Bushing replacement can be accomplished with the use of an arbor press.

Installation

1. With the steering knuckle positioned on the axle center end, insert the thrust bearing assembly between the lower face of the axle center and the steering knuckle lower yoke.

   NOTE: Be sure that the retainer is on top of the bearing with the lip of the retainer facing down.
2. Align the knuckle yoke and axle center to accept the kingpin.
3. With the axle center firmly secured, jack up the steering knuckle until there is zero clearance between the steering knuckle lower yoke, thrust bearing, and the axle center.
4. Check the clearance between the top face of the axle center end and the face of the upper steering knuckle yoke. Select shims which will provide the correct thrust clearance as indicated in the Front Axle Specification Chart.

   NOTE: Kingpin, kingpin bore, and component parts must be thoroughly cleaned and dry.
5. Insert the kingpin up through the bottom yoke of the steering knuckle, and drive it into place with a soft hammer.
6. Position the kingpin bushing over the kingpin, and press into place. Bushing must be flush with the knuckle.
7. Install the kingpin nut and cotter pin.
8. Install a new inverted expansion plug in the lower hole.
9. Install the plug retainer. Retainer must be seated securely in groove.
10. Install the kingpin dust cap and gasket.
11. Connect steering linkage components.
12. Install backing plate to axle flange.
13. Install brake components.
14. Install the hubs, bearings, and wheels.

Independent Front Suspension

This suspension consists of upper and lower control arms, pivoting on steel threaded bushings on upper and lower control arm inner shafts which are attached to the crossmember. Control arms are connected to the steering knuckle by ball joints. A coil spring is seated between the upper and lower control arms, thus the lower control arm is the load carrying member.

Coil Spring

Removal and Installation

1. Raise vehicle and place (high) stands under frame allowing control arm to hang free.
2. Disconnect shock absorber (and stabilizer if used) at lower end.
3. Using a floor jack, under center of lower control arm inner shaft, raise and remove tension from shaft. **CAUTION: Install a safety chain through spring.**
4. Remove both clamps or "U" bolts securing inner shaft to crossmember.
5. Release jack very cautiously, slowly lowering arm with spring until spring is free. Remove safety chain, remove spring.
6. Inspect front end especially at

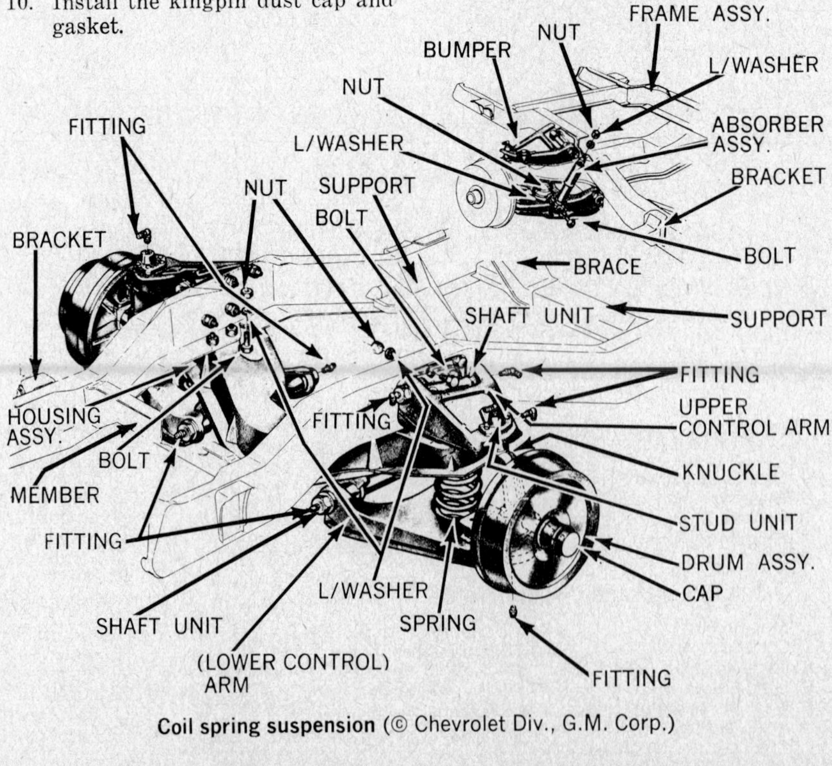

Coil spring suspension (© Chevrolet Div., G.M. Corp.)

ball joints and both upper and lower control arm inner shaft bushings.

7. Reverse removal steps to install, use a long tapered drift to align holes of inner control arm shaft and crossmember while slowly jacking arm into place.

Upper Control Arm (All Vehicles)

Removal

1. Hoist the vehicle, and remove the front wheels.
2. Position an adjustable jackstand under the outboard side of the lower control arm, and adjust the height of the jackstand so that the uppermost extremity of the jackstand comes in contact with the metal undersurface of the lower control arm.
3. Remove the cotter pin from the upper control arm ball joint stud and nut.
4. Loosen the stud nut approximately one full turn.
5. If the ball joint stud does not unseat from the steering knuckle, it may be necessary to press the control arm and ball joint stud away from the knuckle, using a tool designed for that purpose.
6. Remove the nut from the ball stud, and swing the upper control arm up and away from the steering knuckle.

   NOTE: It may be necessary to remove the brake caliper assembly from the steering knuckle in order to facilitate upper control arm removal and installation.
7. Remove the nuts securing the control arm pivot shaft to the frame, and remove the control arm.
8. Tape the alignment shims together, and tag them in order to properly relocate them during installation.

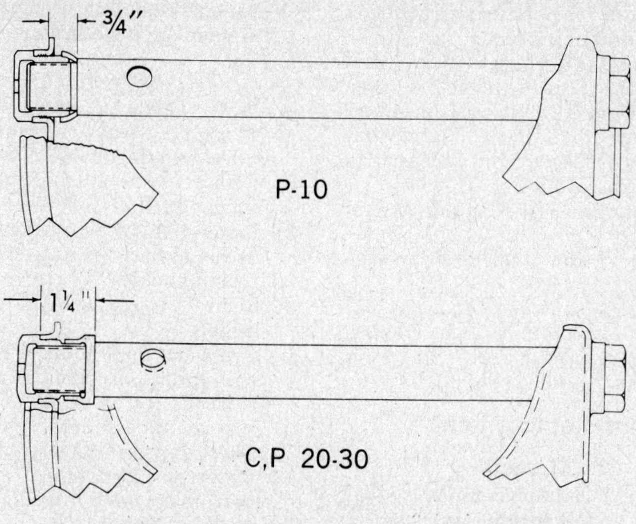

Correctly positioned lower control arm steel bushings
(© Chevrolet Div., G.M. Corp.)

Installation

NOTE: Special pivot shaft aligning washers must be positioned with the concave and convex sides together.

1. Situate the upper control arm against its normal mounting position, and install the pivot shaft nuts. DO NOT tighten the nuts.
2. Install the alignment shims in their respective positions as noted during removal.

   NOTE: Tighten the nut on the thinner shim pack first. This will improve shaft to frame clamping force and torque retention.
4. Insert the ball joint stud into the bore and the steering knuckle, and install the nut and cotter pin.
5. Install the brake caliper assembly.
6. Remove the adjustable jackstand from under the lower control arm.
7. Install the wheel and tire assembly.
8. The vehicle may now be positioned to check front end alignment.

NOTE: Ordinarily, a shim pack will leave at least two threads of the bolt exposed beyond the nut. If, in order to properly align the front wheels, it is necessary to build the shim pack beyond the two thread minimum, then check for damaged control arms and related parts. The difference, in thickness, between the front shim pack and the rear shim pack must not exceed 0.03 inches. The front shim pack must be at least 0.24 inches.

Lower Control Arm

Removal

1. Raise the vehicle on a hoist, and remove the front coil spring (see Coil Spring/Removal and Installation).
2. Support the disconnected. inboard end of the lower control arm after the spring is removed.
3. Remove the cotter pin from the lower ball joint stud, and loosen the stud nut approximately one full turn.
4. Press the control arm and ball joint stud away from the steering knuckle, using a tool designed for that purpose.

   NOTE: It may be necessary to remove the brake caliper assembly from the steering knuckle in order to facilitate lower control arm removal and installation.
5. Remove the lower control arm.

Installation

1. Insert the lower ball joint stud

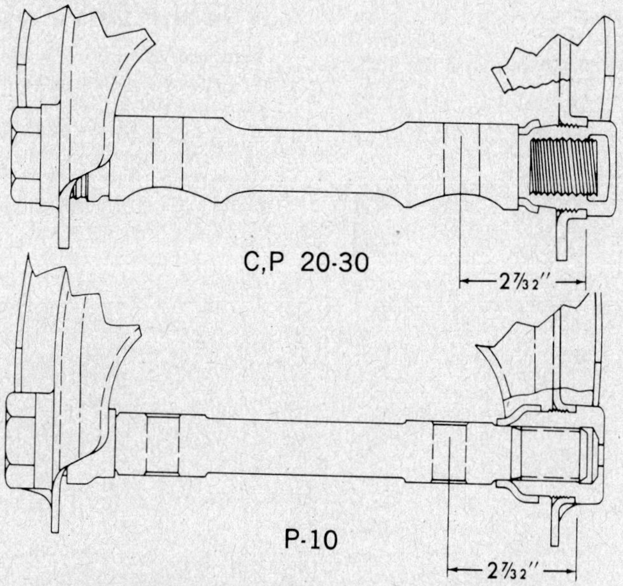

Correctly positioned upper control arm steel bushings
(© Chevrolet Div., G.M. Corp.)

through the steering knuckle, and tighten the nut.
2. Install the coil spring and reattach the inboard end of the lower control arm to the cross member.
3. Be sure that the ball joint stud nut is properly tightened, and install the cotter pin.
4. Install the brake caliper assembly.
5. Remove the vehicle from the hoist.

NOTE: It is always advisable that the front end alignment be checked after any component of the front suspension has been replaced.

Ball Joint Replacement

Upper

1. Place jack under lower control arm, at coil spring, and raise vehicle until tire clears floor.
2. Remove tire, wheel and drum assembly.
3. Remove upper ball stud nut and break the stud taper from the steering knuckle by rapping sides of knuckle flats at stud. Separate stud from knuckle.
4. Remove rivets and bolt in new ball joint. Rivets can be chiseled off, ground off or drilled out.
   CAUTION: Use special hardened bolts only when installing joint (furnished with joint).

AXIAL MOVEMENT

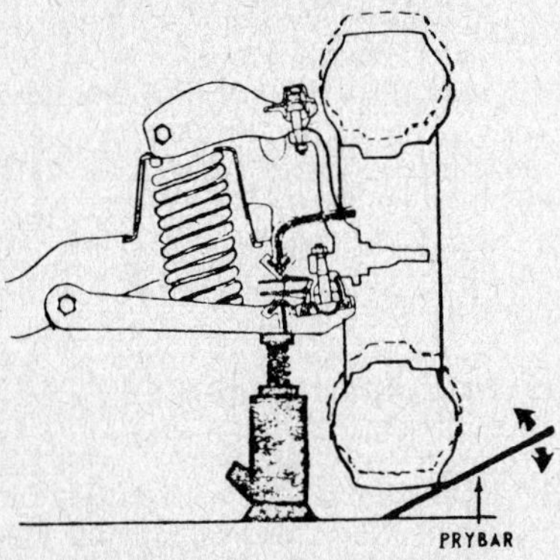

Checking ball joint—unloaded
(© Chevrolet Div., G.M. Corp.)

TIRE SIDEWALL MOVEMENT

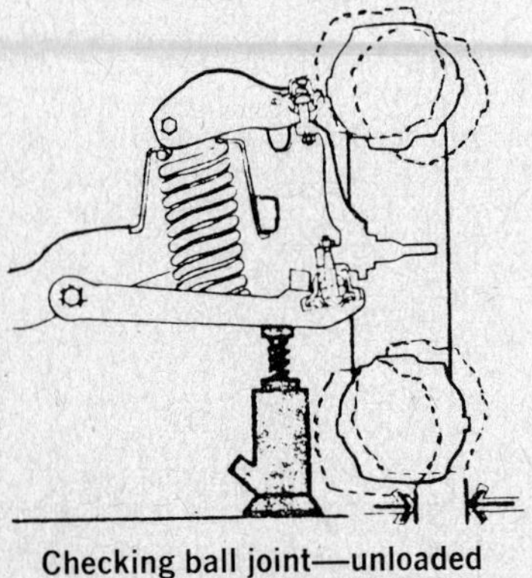

Checking ball joint—unloaded
(© Chevrolet Div., G.M. Corp.)

5. Reverse remaining removal steps to complete installation.

Lower

1. Jack vehicle at lower control arm spring seat and remove tire, wheel and drum assembly.
2. Remove coil spring, see coil spring R&R.
3. Remove ball stud nut at knuckle, use stud jack or rap stud loose from knuckle.
4. Remove lower control arm assembly.
5. Press out ball joint. Press new ball joint into arm. Make sure ball joint assembly is fully seated and square with arm. Check inner shaft bushings.
6. Reverse remaining removal steps to complete installation.

Wheel Bearing Adjustment

1. Check the bearing for a tight or loose fit by gripping the wheel at the top and bottom and moving the wheel in and out on the spindle. The end play should be .001 to .005 inch.
2. If adjustment is needed, remove the cotter pin and tighten the spindle nut to 12 ft. lbs. to fully seat the bearings.
3. Loosen the nut until either hole in the spindle lines up with the slot in the nut.
4. Install the cotter pin and bend the ends against the nut. The end play should be between .001 and .005 inch.
5. Install the dust cover and wheel cover, if equipped.

Shock Absorbers

Shock absorbers are used to dampen the rebound of the two types of springs used: coil and leaf.

Leaf Type

The top of the shock absorbers are mounted to the frame and the bottom is usually mounted to the U bolt bracket at the axle area or to a bracket welded to the axle housing.

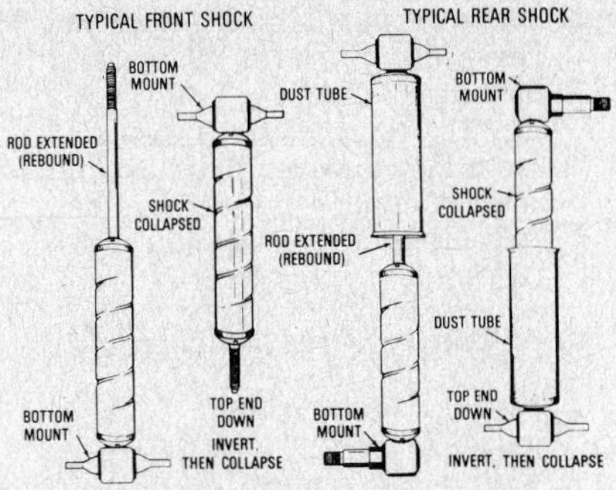

Purging air from shock absorbers
(© Chevrolet Div., G.M. Corp.)

Coil Spring

Front

The shock absorbers are usually attached to the lower control arm at the bottom and to the frame rail at the top. On some models, the shock absorbers may be mounted through the coil spring.

Rear

The top of the shock absorber is mounted to the body or to a crossmember with the bottom mounted to a stud or bracket welded or mounted on the axle housing.

Removal and Replacement

Removal and replacement is accomplished by the removing of the attaching retainers at the top and bottom of the shock absorber, and withdrawing the shock. Replacement is the reverse of removal. Air should be purged from the shock absorber by extending it in the upright position and then inverting and collapsing the shock.

Front Drive Axle

The front axle is a hypoid type gear unit equipped with either ball joint or kingpin steering knuckles, and is powered through a transfer case which may be one of two types. A full-time four wheel drive unit (model 203 transfer case) is used

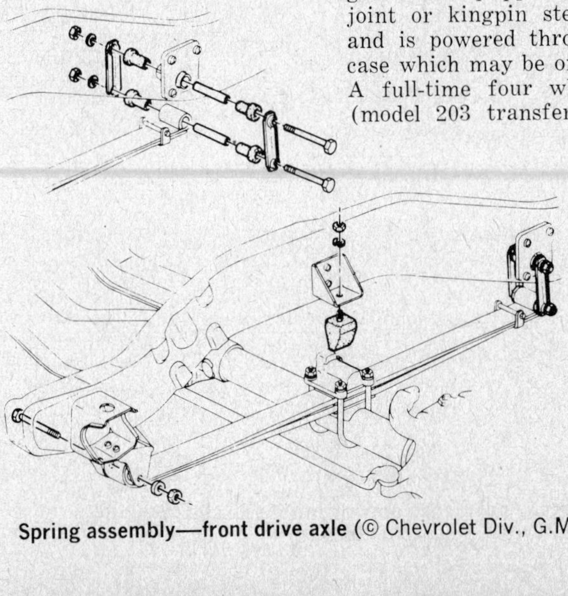

Spring assembly—front drive axle (© Chevrolet Div., G.M. Corp.)

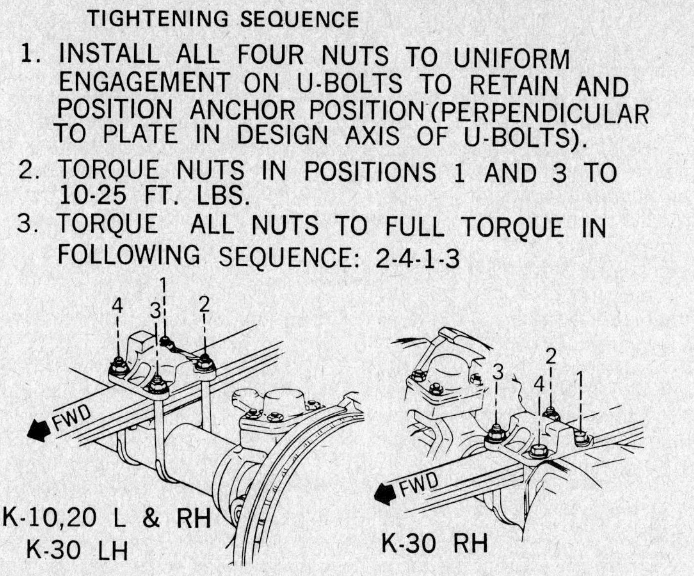

U-bolt tightening sequence—front drive axle (© Chevrolet Div., G.M. Corp.)

mainly with V-8 engines and automatic transmission. The other type is a conventional part-time four wheel drive system.

A yoke and a trunnion universal joint, as part of the drive axle, allows a continous power flow to each wheel, regardless of the turning angle.

Free-wheeling hubs are available on the front wheels except those vehicles equipped with the full time four wheel drive transfer case.

For repairs to the hypoid gear unit, refer to the General Repair Section.

Spring

Removal

1. Raise the vehicle on a hoist.
2. Position an adjustable jack under the front axle.
3. Situate the axle so that all tension is removed from the spring.
4. Remove shackle retaining bolt (upper).
5. Remove the front eye bolt from the spring.
6. Remove the U-bolt nuts, and remove the spring, lower plate and spring pads.
7. Remove the spring-to-shackle bolt, and remove the bushings and shackle.

Installation

1. Install the shackle bushings in the spring, and attach the shackle. DO NOT tighten bolt.
2. Place the upper cushion on the spring.
3. Position the front of the spring in its mounted position at the frame, and stall the bolt. DO NOT tighten bolt.
4. Position the shackle bushings in the frame, and attach the rear shackle. DO NOT tighten bolt.
5. Install the lower spring pad.
6. Install the spring retainer plate. Tighten bolts.
7. Tighten front and rear spring eye and shackle bolts.
8. Remove the vehicle from the hoist.

Locked Hub (Full-Time)

K-10, 20, 30

Removal

1. Remove the hub cap and the snap ring.
2. Remove the drive gear.

   NOTE: Remove the pressure spring on K-10, 20 models.
3. Remove the wheel bearing outer lock nut, lock ring, and the wheel bearing inner adjusting nut.
4. Remove the hub and disc assembly.
5. Remove the outer wheel bearing and the spring retainer plate.
6. Drive the inner bearing cone and oil seal from the hub with the use of a brass drift. Discard the oil seal.
7. Using a brass drift, remove the inner and outer bearing cups.

Installation

1. Install the outer wheel bearing cup into the wheel hub.
2. Install the inner wheel bearing cup into the wheel hub.
3. Pack the wheel bearing cone with a suitable wheel bearing grease (high melting point type).
4. Install the cone into the cup.
5. Install a new grease seal into the inboard end of the hub.
6. Lubricate the wheel bearings; install the hub and disc and the bearings on the spindle.
7. While rotating the hub and disc, torque the inner adjusting nut to 50 ft. lbs.
8. Back off the inner adjusting nut.
9. While rotating the hub and disc, torque the inner adjusting nut to 35 ft. lbs.
10. Again, back off the inner adjusting nut a maximum of 3/8 turn.

K-10, 20 models: Assemble the adjusting nut lock by aligning the nearest hole in lock with the

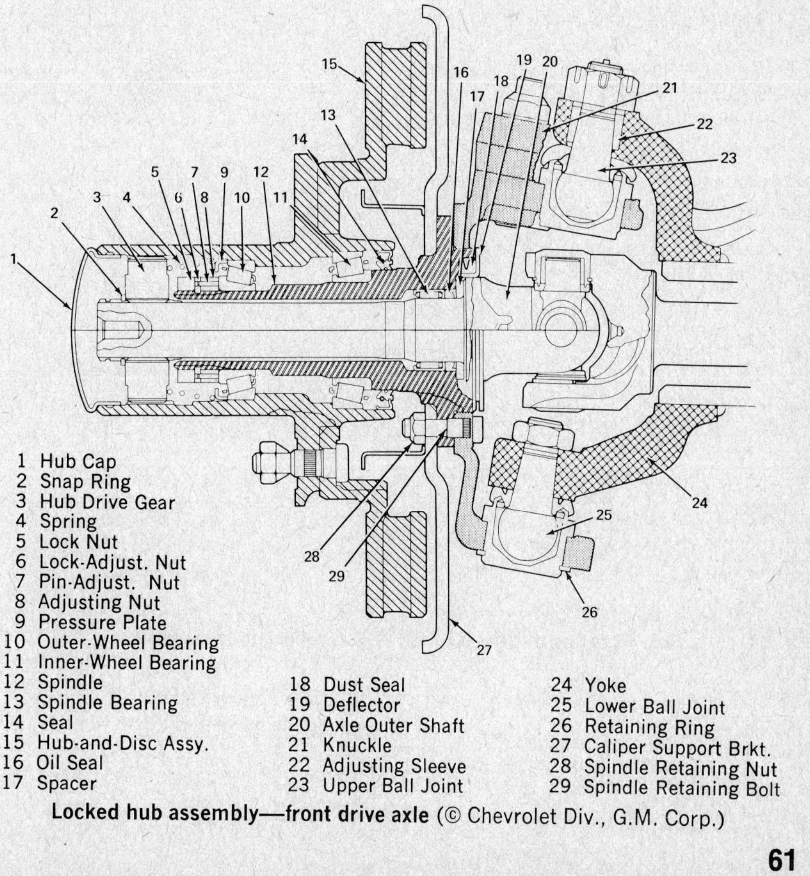

Locked hub assembly—front drive axle (© Chevrolet Div., G.M. Corp.)

adjusting nut pin. Install the outer lock nut torque to 80 ft. lbs.

K-30 models: Assemble the lockwasher and outer locknut. Torque the outer locknut to 65 ft. lbs. Bend one tab of the lockwasher over the inner nut a minimum of 30 degrees. Bend one tab of the lockwasher over the outer nut a minimum of 60 degrees.

NOTE: End play for all models is .001-.010 inch.

11. Install the pressure spring, drive gear, snap ring and hub cap.

Free-Wheeling Hub (Part-Time)

The engagement and disengagement of free-wheeling hubs is a manual operation which must be performed at each front wheel. The transfer case control lever must be in 2-wheel drive position when locking or unlocking hubs. Both hubs must be in the fully locked or fully unlocked position. They must not be in the free-wheeling position when low all-wheeldrive is used as the additional torque output in this position can subject the rear axle to severe strain, and rear axle failure may result.

K-10 All

K-20 (Current Models)

Removal

1. Turn the actuator to the LOCK position.
2. Raise the vehicle on a hoist.
3. Remove the six retaining plate bolts.
4. Remove the retaining plate, actuator knob, and O-ring.
5. Remove the internal snap ring, outer clutch retaining ring, and actuating cam body.
6. Remove the axle shaft snap ring.

   NOTE: It may be necessary to first relieve pressure from the axle shaft snap ring.
7. Remove the wheel bearing outer lock nut and lock ring.
8. Remove the wheel bearing inner adjusting nut.
9. Remove the hub and disc assembly, outer wheel bearing, and the spring retainer plate.
10. Drive the inner bearing cone and oil seal from the hub with a brass drift. Discard the oil seal.
11. Using a brass drift, remove the inner and outer bearing cups.

Installation

NOTE: All parts should be lubricated with an ample amount of high speed grease prior to installation.

1. Install the outer wheel bearing cup into the wheel hub.
2. Install the inner wheel bearing cup into the wheel hub.
3. Pack the wheel bearing cone with a suitable wheel bearing grease (high melting point type).
4. Install the cone into the cup.
5. Lubricate the wheel bearings; install the hub and disc and the bearings on the spindle.
6. While rotating the hub and disc, torque the inner adjusting nut to 50 ft. lbs.
7. Back off the inner adjusting nut.
8. While rotating the hub and disc, torque the inner adjusting nut to 35 ft. lbs.
9. Again, back off the inner adjusting nut a maximum of 3/8 turn.
10. Assemble the adjusting nut lock by aligning the nearest hole in lock with the adjusting nut pin.
11. Install outer lock nut and torque to 50 ft. lbs.

    NOTE: Hub end play should be .001-.010 inch.
12. Install the spring retainer plate over the spindle nuts with the flange side facing the bearing, and seat the retainer against the bearing outer cup.
13. Install the pressure spring.

    NOTE: The large diameter of the spring seats against the retaining plate. When the spring is seated, it extends past the spindle nuts by approximately 7/8".
14. Install the inner clutch ring and bushing into the axle shaft sleeve and clutch ring; install unit as an assembly onto the axle shaft.
15. While pressing in on the assembly, install the axle shaft snap ring.

    NOTE: To facilitate snap ring installation, thread a 7/16 x 20 bolt in the end of the axle shaft, and pull outward on the axle shaft.
16. Install the actuating cam body. Cam faces outward.
17. Install the outer clutch retaining ring and the internal snap ring.
18. Install the O-ring on the retaining plate.
19. Install the actuating knob and retaining plate.

    NOTE: Actuating knob should be installed in the LOCK position. The grooves in the knob must fit into the actuator cam body.
20. Install the six cover bolts and seals. Torque bolts to 30 ft. lbs.
21. Turn the actuating knob to the FREE position, and check free-wheeling operation.
22. Remove vehicle from hoist.

K-20 (Early Models)

Removal

1. Raise the vehicle on a hoist. Turn the hub key knob to "Free" position.
2. Remove the allen head bolts, and remove the hub cap assembly and gasket from the wheel hub. Remove the exterior sleeve extension housing and gasket.
3. Turn the hub key knob to the locked position. Drive out the key knob retainer roll pin.
4. Remove the outer clutch gear assembly.
5. Remove the lock ring. Remove the slotted adjustment sleeve.

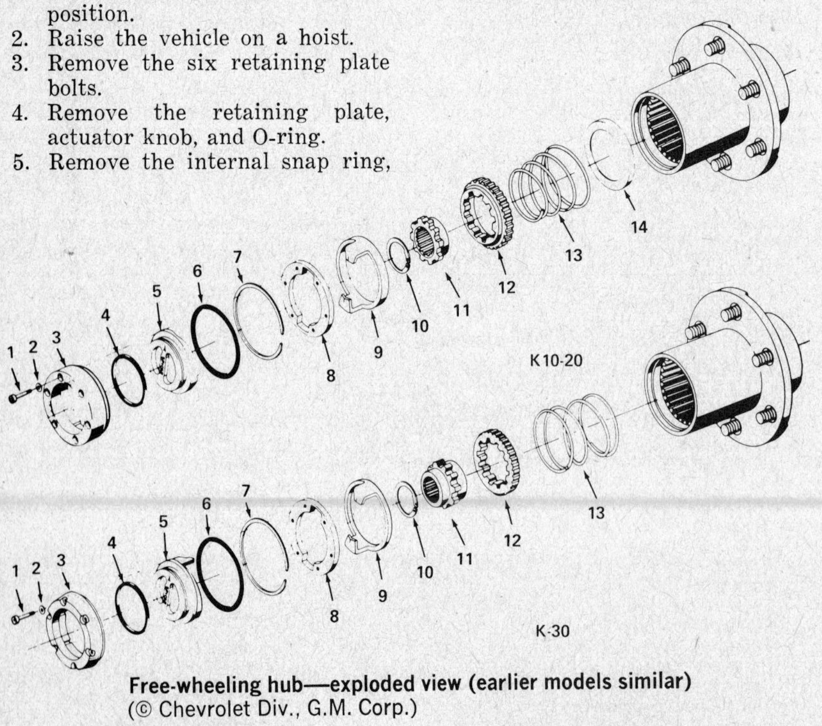

Free-wheeling hub—exploded view (earlier models similar)
(© Chevrolet Div., G.M. Corp.)

1 Retaining Plate Bolts
2 Washer
3 Hub Ring Retaining Knob
4 Actuator Knob O-Ring
5 Actuator Knob
6 O-Ring
7 Internal Snap Ring
8 Outer Clutch Retaining Ring
9 Actuating Cam Body
10 Axle Shaft Snap Ring
11 Axle Shaft Sleeve And Ring
12 Inner Clutch Ring
13 Pressure Spring
14 Spring Retainer Plate

6. Remove the spring, and then remove the lock ring securing the plastic key knob to the hub retainer cap.
7. Remove the O-ring from the plastic hub key knob.
8. Remove the snap ring from the end of the axle shaft. Pull the internal clutch gear and its collar.

Installation

1. Apply a high speed grease to both faces of the bushing, the splines, the teeth of the inner and outer clutch gears, and to the actuating cam.
2. Install the internal clutch collar and gear. Install the lock ring at the end of the axle shaft.
3. Lubricate the O-ring and install it in the groove of the plastic hub key knob. Insert the knob into the retainer cap.
4. Install the lock ring into the hub retainer cap. Push outward on the plastic knob to ensure that the lock ring is fully engaged, and correct its position as necessary.
5. Install the slotted adjustment sleeve with the two tabs outward.
6. Install the key knob retaining roll pin with the knob in the locked position. Install the spring.
7. Place the outer clutch gear assembly on top of the spring, compress the spring, and install the lock ring at the sleeve end. Turn the key knob to the "Free" position.
8. Install a 3/8" bolt 5 inches long into one of the hub housing bolt holes.
9. Install the new exterior sleeve extension housing gasket and the housing and retainer cap assembly and gasket. Install the allen head bolts, and tighten securely.
10. Turn the hub key knob to the locked position and check for proper engagement. Install the wheel and tire.

Axle Assembly

Removal

1. Disconnect the drive shaft from the front axle. Raise the vehicle far enough to take the weight off the front springs and place jack stands under the truck.
2. Disconnect the connecting rod at the steering arms.
3. Disconnect the brake hoses at the frame fittings, and cover all open ends.
4. Disconnect the shock absorbers at the axle brackets.
5. Disconnect the axle vent tube clip at the differential housing.
6. Unfasten the U-bolts, raise the truck further, as necessary, and roll the axle out from underneath.

Installation

1. With truck on axle stands, roll the axle under the truck. Lower the truck until axle and truck are in proper relative positions. Again support the vehicle with axle stands.
2. Attach the shock absorbers to the axle brackets. Connect the brake hoses to the frame fittings and fill and bleed the brake system.
3. Attach the steering connecting rod at the steering arms.
4. Connect the drive axle to the front differential.

Axle Shaft Assembly

Removal

1. Remove the free-wheeling hubs as outlined, if so equipped.
2. Remove the wheel bearing outer lock nut, lock ring, and inner adjusting nut.
3. Remove the hub assembly from the spindle.
4. Remove the spindle retaining bolts and tap the end of the spindle with a soft faced hammer, to separate the spindle from the knuckle.
5. Remove the axle shaft and joint assembly by pulling outward on the shaft.
6. Repairs to the wheel hub assembly and to the axle universal joint can be accomplished at this time.

Installation

1. Install a new grease seal onto the slinger of the axle shaft, with the lip of the seal facing toward the spindle.
2. Install the axle shaft into the housing and engage the splines with the pinion side gears of the differential.
3. Place the bronze thrust washer on the axle shaft with the chamfered edge towards the slinger and install the spindle onto the knuckle.
4. Torque the spindle nuts to 45 ft. lbs. and assemble the hub to the spindle. Torque the inner adjustment nut to 50 ft. lbs. while rotating the hub. Back off the inner nut an additional 3/8 of a turn maximum.
5. Assemble the lock washer and the outer lock nut to the spindle. Torque the outer lock nut to 50 ft. lbs. minimum. The hub should have .001 to .010 inch end play.
6. If the vehicle is equipped with free-wheeling hubs, refer to the installation procedure for correct installation and if not equipped, install the hub cap assembly.

Steering Knuckle (With Ball Joints)

K-10, 20

Removal

1. With the spindle and axle removed, as previously outlined, disconnect the tie rod end from the steering arm.
2. If necessary for working clearance, remove the steering arm from the knuckle.

   NOTE: If the steering arm is removed, discard the three self-locking nuts and replace them with new self locking nuts upon assembly.
3. Remove the upper and lower ball joint retaining nuts.

   NOTE: The upper ball joint stud and nut have a cotter pin retainer, while the lower ball point stud and nut have none.
4. With a wedge type tool, separate the lower ball joint stud from the knuckle. Repeat this operation for the upper ball joint stud.
5. Remove the snap ring retainer from the lower ball joint. With the aid of a "C" clamp tool, press the lower ball joint from the knuckle.

   NOTE: The lower ball joint must be removed before any service can be performed on the upper ball joint.
6. With the aid of the "C" clamp tool, press the upper ball joint from the knuckle. Replacement of the knuckle can be accomplished at this point in the disassembly.

Installation

1. Press the lower ball joint into the knuckle with the aid of the "C" type tool and install the snap ring retainer on the lower ball joint.
2. Install the upper ball joint into the knuckle with the aid of the "C" clamp tool.
3. Position the ball joint studs in their respective openings on the yoke and install the new nuts finger tight.

   NOTE: The castellated nut is placed on the upper ball joint stud.
4. Torque the lower ball joint stud nut to 70 ft. lbs. while exerting upward pressure on the knuckle.
5. Torque the upper ball joint stud adjusting sleeve to 50 ft. lbs. using a spanner type socket.
6. Torque the upper ball joint stud nut to 100 ft. lbs. Apply additional torque if necessary to align the cotter pin hole in the nut and stud.
7. Reassemble the steering arm, if removed, tie rod ends, spindle,

1 Retaining Plate
2 O-Ring
3 Actuator Knob
4 Retaining Plate Bolt
5 Axle Shaft Snap Ring
6 Actuating Cam Body
7 Internal Snap Ring
8 Outer Clutch Retaining Ring
9 Axle Shaft Sleeve And Clutch Ring
10 Inner Clutch Ring
11 Spring
12 Lock Nut
13 Lock-Adjust. Nut
14 Pin-Adjust. Nut
15 Adjusting Nut
16 Pressure Plate
17 Outer-Wheel Bearing
18 Inner-Wheel Bearing
19 Spindle
20 Spindle Bearing
21 Seal
22 Hub-And-Disc Assy.
23 Oil Seal
24 Spacer
25 Dust Seal
26 Deflector
27 Axle Outer Shaft
28 Knuckle
29 Adjusting Sleeve
30 Upper Ball Joint
31 Yoke
32 Lower Ball Joint
33 Retaining Ring
34 Caliper Support Brkt.
35 Spindle Retaining Nut
36 Spindle Retaining Bolt

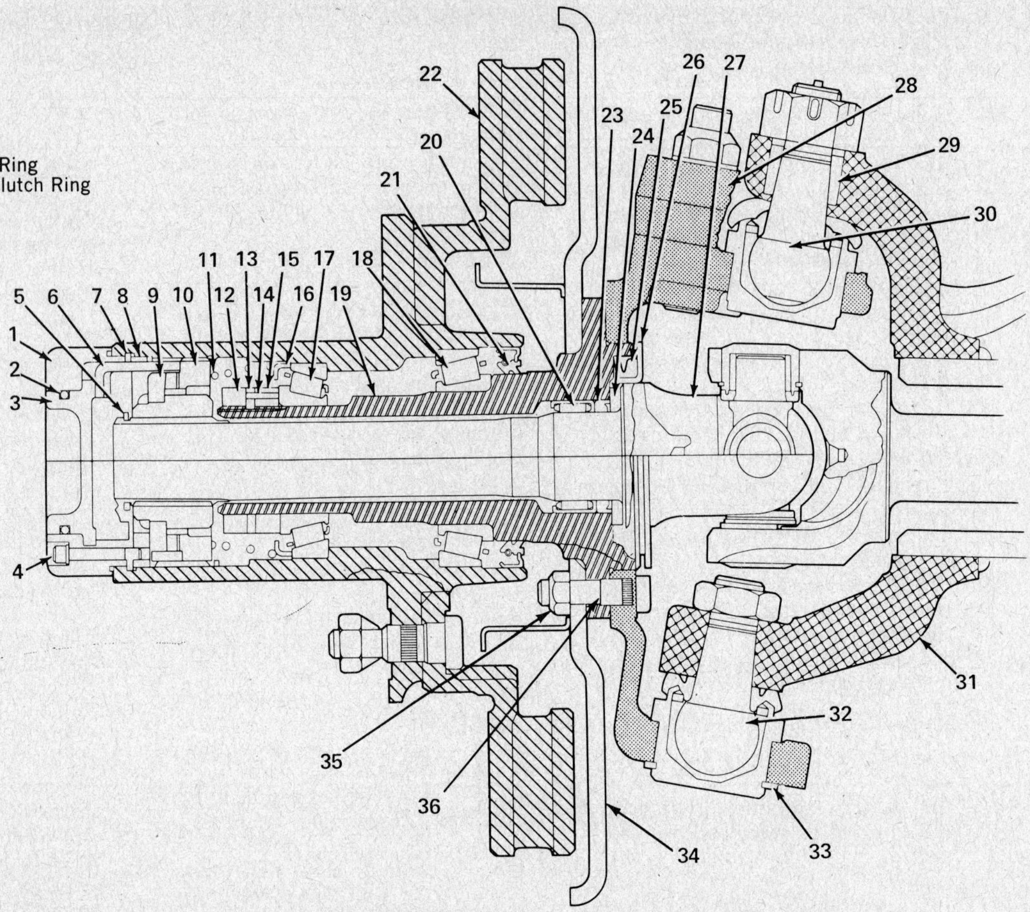

Steering knuckle/ball joint assy. (with free-wheeling hub) (© Chevrolet Div., G.M. Corp.)

axle and hub as outlined previously.

8. Torque the steering arm nuts to 90 ft. lbs. and the tie rod nut to 45 ft. lbs. and install the cotter pin.

Steering Knuckle (With King Pins)

K-30

Removal

1. Remove the hub and spindle.
   NOTE: It may be necessary to tap lightly on the spindle with a rawhide hammer in order to free it from the knuckle.
2. Remove the four cap nuts from the upper king pin.
   NOTE: Spring pressure will force the cap up.
3. Remove the cap, spring and gasket. Discard the gasket.
4. Remove the four cap screws from the lower king pin bearing.
5. Remove the cap and the lower king pin.
6. Remove the upper king pin bushing.
7. Remove the knuckle from the yoke.
8. Remove the king pin felt seal.
9. Remove the upper king pin from the yoke with a very large

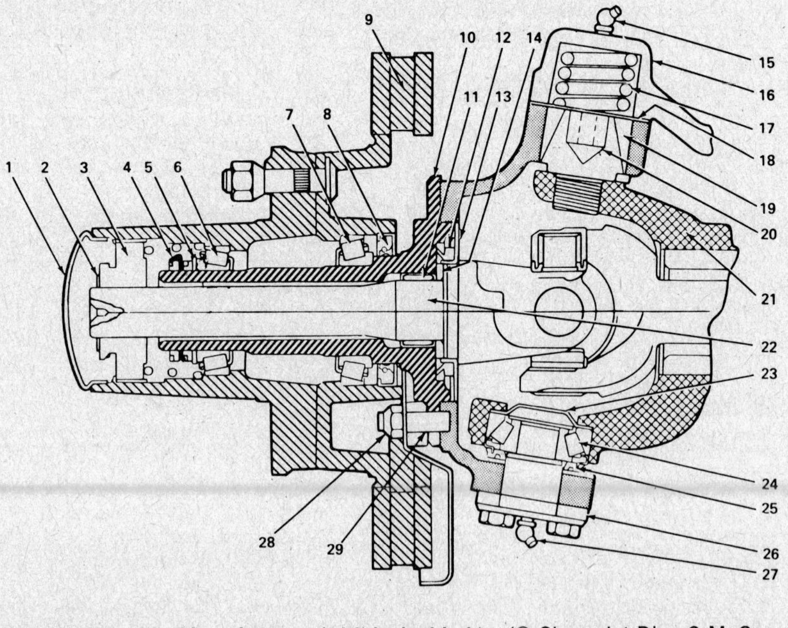

Steering knuckle/king pin assy. (with locked hub) (© Chevrolet Div., G.M. Corp.)

1 Hub Cap
2 Snap Ring
3 Hub Drive Gear
4 Adjusting Nut Assembly
5 Washer
6 Outer Wheel Bearing
7 Inner Wheel Bearing
8 Seal
9 Hub-And-Disc Assembly
10 Spindle
11 Spindle Bearing
12 Seal
13 Deflector
14 Spacer
15 Lube Fitting
16 Upper Bearing
17 Pressure Spring
18 Gasket
19 Kingpin Bushing
20 Kingpin
21 Yoke
22 Outer Axle Shaft
23 Grease Retainer
24 Lower Bearing
25 Seal
26 Bearing Cup
27 Lube Fitting
28 Spindle Attaching Nut
29 Spindle Attaching Bolt

breaker bar and any suitable adapter designed to fit the king pin.

NOTE: Considerable force will be required to remove the king pin from the yoke as the king pin is originally torqued to 500-600 ft. lbs.

10. Remove the lower king pin bearing cup, cone, grease retainer, and seal. Discard the seal. Discard the grease retainer if damaged.

Installation

1. Install the lower king pin bearing cup and a new grease retainer.
2. Fill the grease retainer with grease.
3. Lubricate the bearing cone with grease. Install the bearing cone.
4. Install a new oil seal for the lower king pin bearing.

Installing oil seal—front drive yoke w/king pins
(© Chevrolet Div., G.M. Corp.)

NOTE: The oil seal will protrude slightly from the surface of the yoke flange when fully installed.

5. Install the upper king pin, and torque to 500-600 ft. lbs.
6. Assemble the felt seal to the king pin.

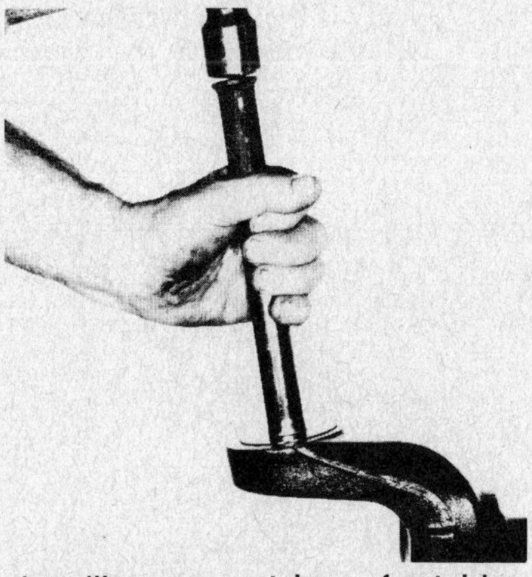

Installing grease retainer—front drive yoke w/king pins
(© Chevrolet Div., G.M. Corp.)

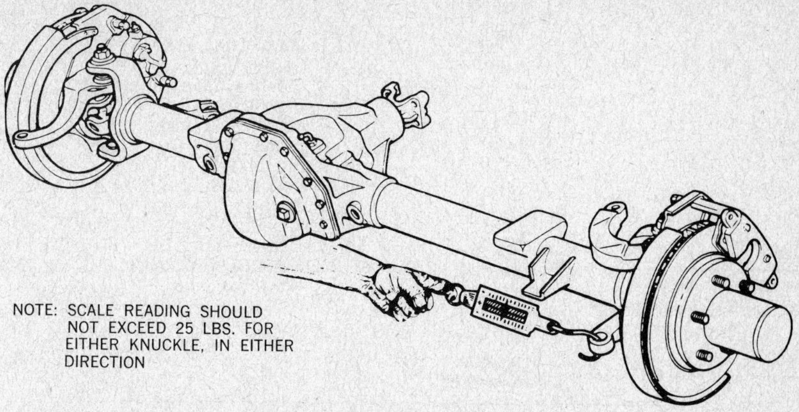
NOTE: SCALE READING SHOULD NOT EXCEED 25 LBS. FOR EITHER KNUCKLE, IN EITHER DIRECTION

Checking front drive axle ball joint adjustment (© Chevrolet Div., G.M. Corp.)

7. Position the steering knuckle over the king pin, and install the tapered bushing over the king pin.
8. Install the lower king pin and the lower bearing cap. Torque the cap screws to 70-90 ft. lbs.
9. Position the compression spring over the upper king pin bushing.
10. Install the upper bearing cap with a new gasket. Torque the nuts to 70-90 ft. lbs.

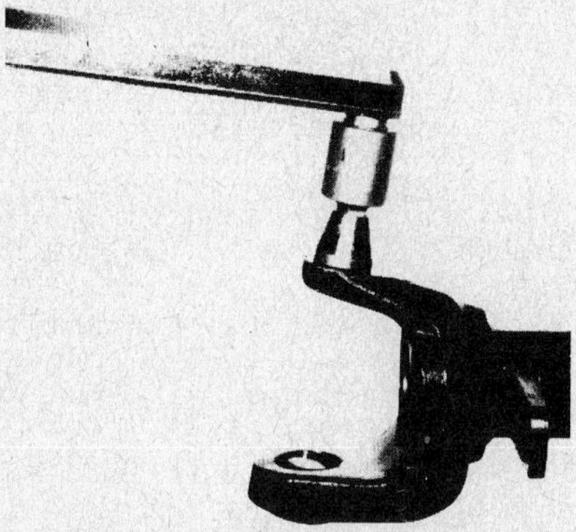

Installing upper king pin—front drive axle (© Chevrolet Div., G.M. Corp.)

Ball Joint Adjustment

K-10, 20

1. Raise the vehicle on a hoist.
2. Disconnect the connecting rod and the tile rod to allow the steering knuckle to move freely.
3. Attach a spring scale to the tie rod mounting hole of the steering arm.
4. Move the knuckle to the straight-ahead position.
5. Determine the right angle pull required to keep the knuckle turning after initial movement from standing still. The pull should not exceed 25 lbs. for each knuckle assembly.
6. If the effort required to maintain turning movement is in excess of 25 lbs., then remove the upper ball stud nut, and loosen the ball stud adjusting sleeve as required. Tighten the ball stud nut and recheck the turning effort.

Wheel Bearing Adjustment

Refer to the Installation procedures under Locked Hub (Full-Time) or Free-Wheeling Hub (Part-Time) for the corresponding wheel bearing adjustment instructions.

STEERING GEAR

Manual Steering Gear

Instructions covering the overhaul of the light duty steering gear will be found in the General Repair Section.

Power Steering Gears

Troubleshooting and repair instructions covering power steering gears are given in the General Repair Section.

Standard Steering Gear

Medium and Heavy Trucks

Removal

1. Disconnect steering linkage from pitman arm.
2. Scribe alignment marks on worm shaft and clamp yoke for reassembly.
3. Remove bolts attaching clamp yoke or coupling to steering gear worm shaft.

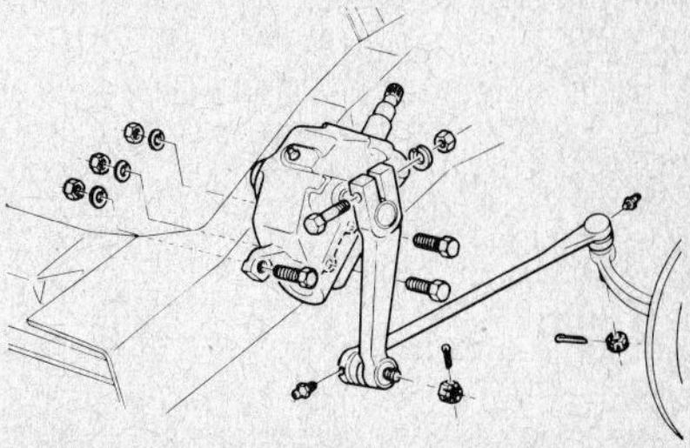

Manually operated steering gear P models
(© Chevrolet Div., G.M. Corp.)

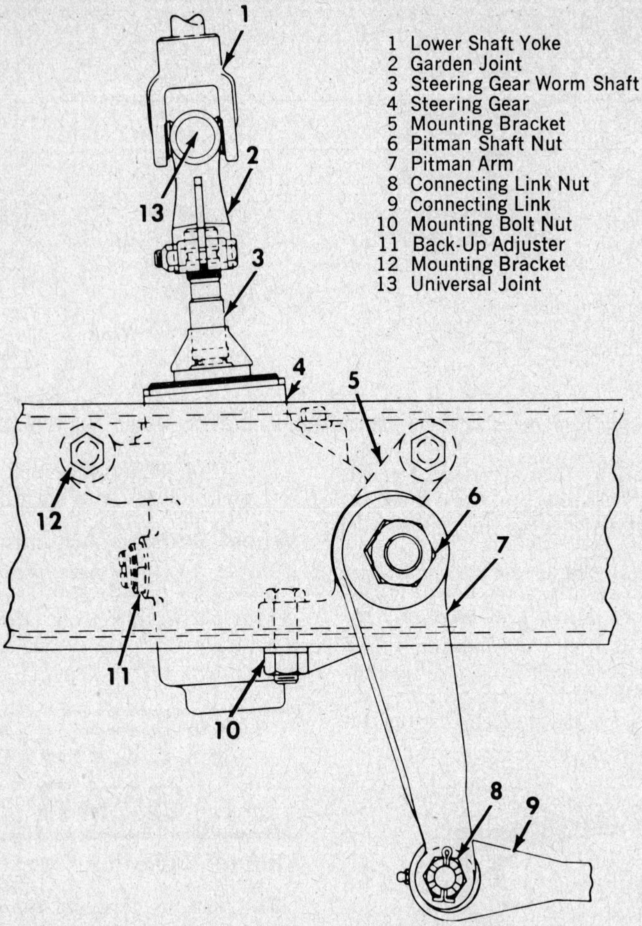

Manually operated steering gear installed—steel tilt (© Chevrolet Div., G.M. Corp.)

4. Remove pitman arm nut and washer, then use a puller to remove arm.
5. Remove attaching bolts, nuts and washers, then remove steering gear.

Installation

1. Turn steering wheel to straight-ahead position and center steering gear.
2. Position the steering gear, matching the alignment marks.
3. Install attaching bolts, washers and nuts.
4. Connect clamp yoke or coupling to steering gear worm shaft with attaching parts and torque to specifications.
5. Align pitman arm and shaft; press arm onto shaft and torque to specifications.

Light Duty Trucks

Removal

1. Drive the vehicle a short distance and move the wheels to the straight ahead position.
2. On P models, remove the lower universal joint pinch bolt. On C and K models, remove the bolts from the flexible coupling to steering shaft flange. Mark the relationship between the universal yoke and wormshaft.
3. Mark the relationship between the pitman arm and the pitman shaft, and remove the pitman shaft nut or pitman arm pinch bolt.
4. Remove the pitman arm from the shaft with a special puller.
5. Remove the bolts between steering gear and frame. Remove the steering gear.
6. On C and K models, remove the flexible coupling pinch bolt and remove the coupling from the wormshaft.

Installation

1. On C and K models:
   a. Install the flexible coupling onto the steering gear wormshaft. The flats in the coupling and on the shaft must line up. Then, push the coupling onto the shaft until the wormshaft bottoms on the coupling reinforcement. Install the pinch bolt. *Note that the coupling bolt must pass through the shaft undercut.*
   b. Position the steering gear, guiding the coupling bolt into the steering shaft flange.
   c. Install the steering gear to frame bolts. Torque to 65 ft. lbs.
   d. In cases where plastic spacers are used on the flexible coupling alignment pins, make sure they are bottomed on the pins, torque the flange bolt nuts, and then remove the spacers.
   e. If plastic spacers are not used, center the pins in the steering shaft flange slots, and install and torque the flange bolt nuts.
2. On P models:
   a. Position the steering gear, guiding wormshaft into the U-joint assembly. Line up the marks made at removal. In cases where a new steering gear is being installed, line up the mark on the worm-

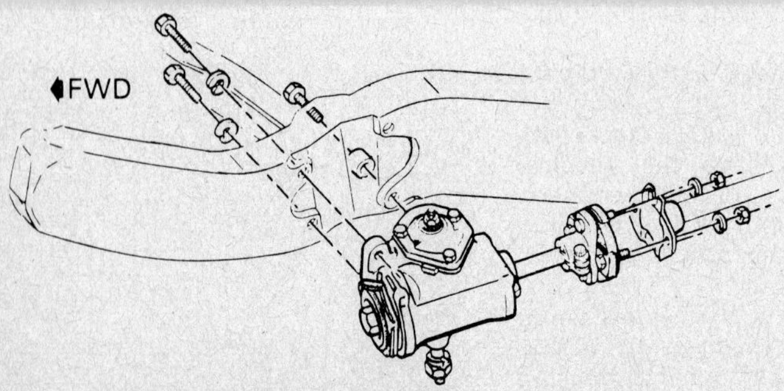

Manually operated steering gear—C, K models
(© Chevrolet Div., G.M. Corp.)

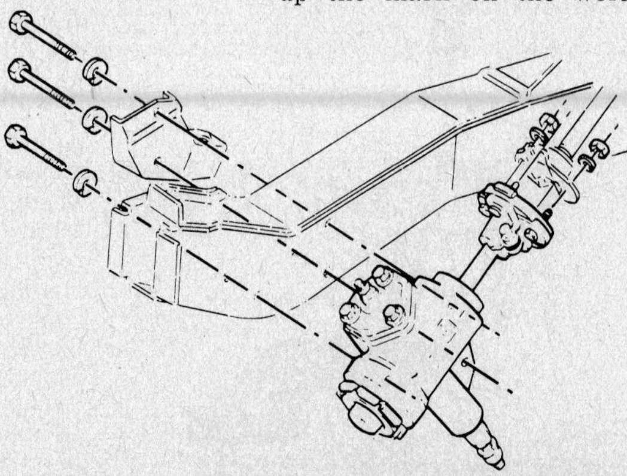

Manually operated steering gear—G, P models
(© Chevrolet Div., G.M Corp.)

shaft with the slit in the yoke of the U-joint.

b. Install the steering gear to frame bolts, and torque to 65 ft.-lbs.

c. Install and torque the universal joint pinch bolt. Make sure the bolt passes through the shaft undercut.

3. Install the pitman arm onto the shaft, lining up marks made at removal. Install the shaft nut or pinch bolt and torque to 140 ft. lbs.

Adjustments (On Vehicle)

1. Check tire pressure and inspect steering linkage.
2. Check gear housing for lubricant, tighten cover side plate.
3. Check steering gear housing to frame rail bolts.
4. Set wheels in straight ahead position.
5. Disconnect drag link from pitman arm, remove pitman arm on Vans.
6. Loosen sector (cross) shaft lock nut and back off lash adjuster 1/4 turn. This lessens steering worm bearing load by reducing tooth mesh contact.
7. Check load on steering gear by measuring pull on steering wheel with scale. Pull is measured at rim of wheel with scale tangent to rim of wheel (1/2 to 3 lb. pull according to size of truck).
8. If pull is not within limits, adjust worm bearings. Loosen worm bearing lock nut and turn adjusting nut in until there is no perceptible end play. Tighten lock nut. Using an inch-pound torque wrench and socket on steering wheel nut (remove horn wire and button), measure torque (3 inch pounds to 14 inch pounds according to size of truck). A rough feeling when rotating steering wheel indicates defective worm bearings. Some early heavy duty steering gears use shims under steering gear housing top cover, and also use a back-up adjuster. Removal of shims decreases worm bearing end play. Back-up adjuster setting is made last. After adjusting worm bearings and lash, then tighten back-up adjuster until adjuster bottoms against ball nut return guide clamp, then back-off adjuster 1/8 to 1/4 turn and secure with lock nut.
9. After proper adjustment of worm bearings is obtained, center steering wheel by turning wheel gently from one stop to the other, counting the number of turns. Turn wheel back exactly half way to center position (high point). Mark steering wheel rim at top or bottom center with tape. Turn lash (slotted) adjuster clockwise to take out all lash in gear teeth and tighten lock nut. Check steering free play. *NOTE: If maximum adjustment is exceeded, turn lash adjuster screw back (counter-clockwise) and then come in (clockwise) slowy on adjustment.* **CAUTION: Do not bounce steering wheel hard against stops with drag link removed, worm ball guide damage can result.**
10. Connect drag link or replace pitman arm, road test and check steering.

Power Steering Gear

Medium and Heavy Trucks

Integral Type 553-DU—Removal

1. Mark steering gear worm shaft and clamp yoke or coupling for reassembly.
2. Remove connecting rod from pitman arm.
3. Remove attaching pinch bolt, nuts and washers from pitman arm; press pitman arm from shaft.
4. Drain as much fluid as possible from steering gear.
5. Disconnect all tubes from the control valve ports. Plug all tubes and cover all ports to prevent any dirt from entering the system.
6. Remove attaching bolts, nuts and washers from the steering gear and control valve assembly. Remove steering gear.

Installation

1. Center steering wheel and steering gear.
2. Install steering gear by reversing the removal procedure. Make certain to match all alignment marks and to torque all nuts to specifications.
3. Bleed the system and fill reservoir to the proper level.

Integral Type 710-D Removal

1. Center steering gear by positioning tires straight ahead and remove Pitman arm clamp bolt.
2. Install Pitman arm puller and remove Pitman arm.

   NOTE: It may be necessary to spread the Pitman arm clamp bosses slightly to remove arm. Install a dial indicator as shown. Insert a wedge shaped tool and spread clamp bosses .004 in.
3. Remove pot joint to stub shaft clamp bolt (conventional cab) or carden joint to stub shaft clamp bolt (school bus model). Remove steering column plastic cap and metal cover at dash. Remove column clamp cap screws. Pull steering shaft up until shaft coupling clears stub shaft.

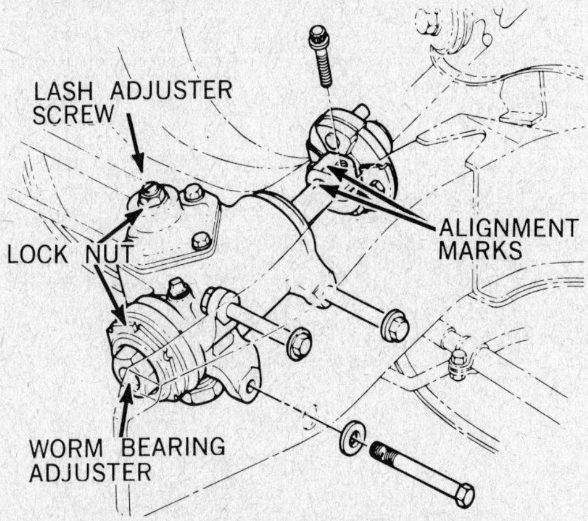

Steering gear adjustments—typical
(© Chevrolet Div., G.M. Corp.)

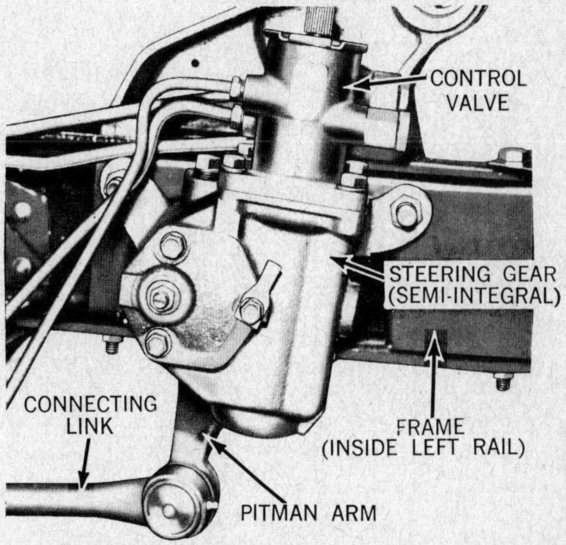

Semi-integral power steering gear—steel tilt cap
(© Chevrolet Div., G.M. Corp.)

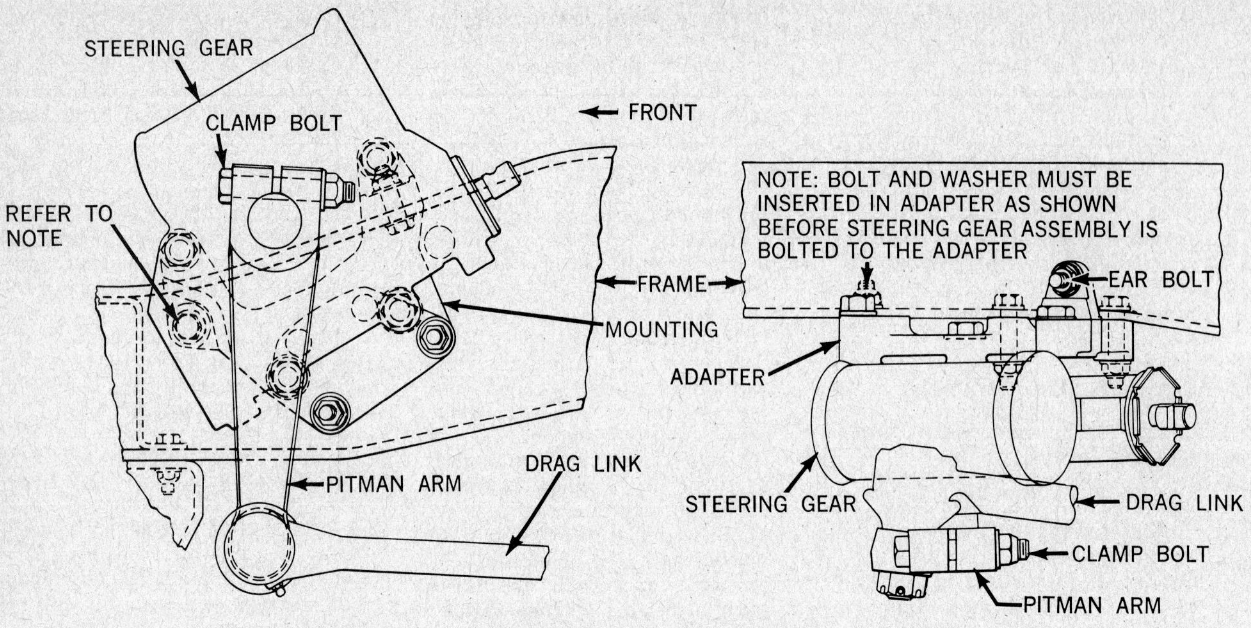

Integral power steering gear (© Chevrolet Div., G.M. Corp.)

4. Remove steering gear mounting bolts. It will be necessary to use two persons to remove ear bolt as shown.
5. Disconnect lines from steering gear and plug lines. Turn gear in a vertical position (stub shaft up) and work gear down between frame and inner fender panel and remove gear.
6. Remove adapter to gear bolts.

Installation

1. Install adapter to gear with washers under bolt heads and torque bolts to specifications.

   NOTE: One adapter plate to frame bolt and washer (lower forward bolt as shown) must be installed before adapter is bolted to the gear.
2. Holding gear in the vertical position (stub shaft up) push gear up between inner fender panel and frame and position ear on adapter plate over frame and push the bolt previously installed into frame and install washer and nut only finger tight. With gear loose, reach between gear and frame and remove line plugs and install line fittings to gear.
3. Install steering gear to frame mounting bolts with washers and torque to specifications.
4. With one person inside cab centering steering wheel and one at steering gear with steering gear centered, install pot joint or carden joint over stub shaft. Push steering shaft down until coupling lines up with the cross groove in stub shaft. Install clamp bolt and adjust pot joint to 3.08 in. Tighten steering column clamp cap screws, replace metal cover panel and column plastic cap.
5. Install Pitman arm to Pitman shaft, install clamp bolt and torque to 180 ft. lb.
6. Bleed the system and fill reservoir to the proper level.

Light Duty Trucks

Removal

1. Disconnect the hoses at the gear and secure the open ends in a raised position.
2. Cap the open ends of the hoses and plug the openings of the steering unit.
3. Remove the flexible coupling to flange bolts on G, C, and K models, or the U-joint pinch bolt on P models. Mark the relationship between the universal yoke and stub shaft.
4. Mark the relationship between the pitman arm and shaft. Remove the shaft nut or pinch blot from the pitman arm.
5. Remove the arm from the shaft with a special puller.
6. Remove the steering gear mounting bolts, and remove the gear. On G, C, and K models, also remove the pinch bolt from the flexible coupling, and remove the coupling.

Installation

1. Where applicable, install the flexible coupling, aligning the flats in coupling and on shaft. Make sure the stub shaft bottoms on

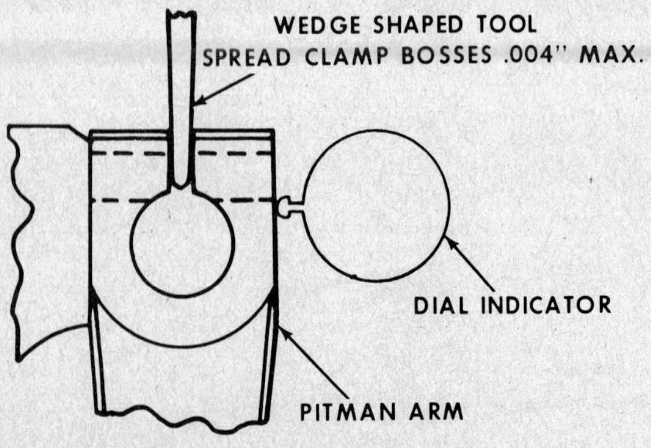

Pitman arm removal—dial indicator and wedge shape tool installed (© Chevrolet Div., G.M. Corp.)

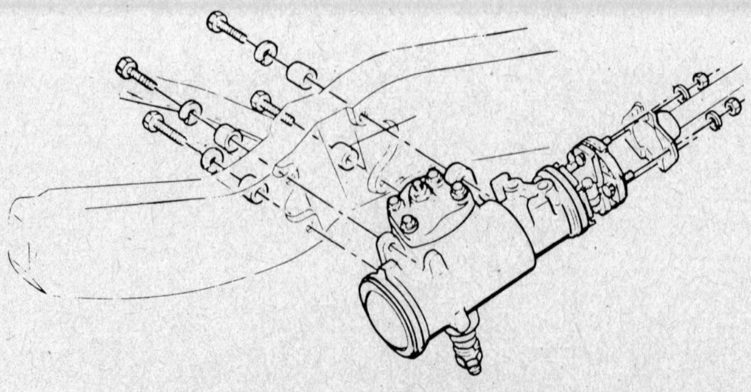

Power steering gear—light duty trucks—typical (© Chevrolet Div., G.M. Corp.)

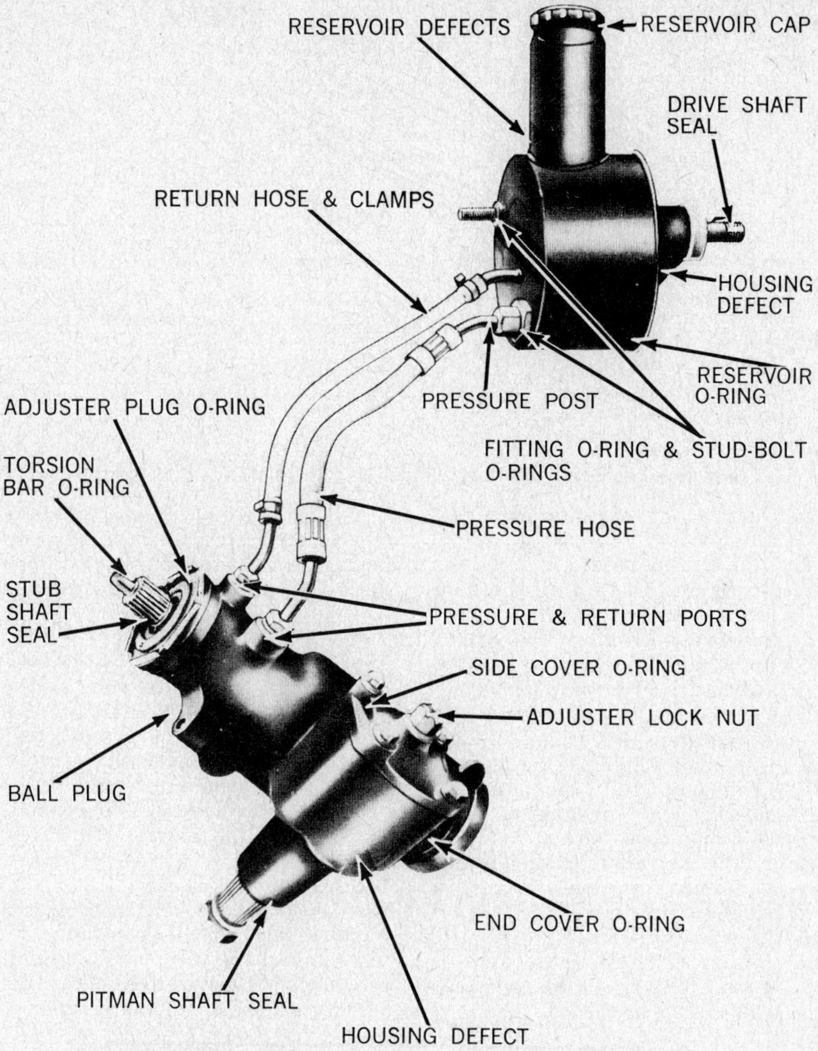

Potential leakage areas—light duty power steering system
(© Chevrolet Div., G.M. Corp.)

the coupling reinforcement. Install the pinch bolt and torque to 18 in lbs. Make sure the bolt passes through the shaft undercut.

2. Position the steering gear, guiding the coupling bolt into the shaft flange.
3. Install the mounting bolts and torque to 65 ft-lbs. (110 ft-lbs on G series).
4. If plastic spacers are used in the flexible coupling, make sure they are bottomed on the pins, tighten the flange bolt nuts to 18 in-lbs. (20 ft-lbs. on P series), and then remove the spacers. Where plastic spacers are not used, center the pins in the steering shaft flange slots and install the bolt nuts and torque as above.
5. On P Models:
   a. Position the steering gear, guiding the stub shaft into the U-joint assembly and lining up marks made at removal or, with a new unit, lining up the mark on the stub shaft with the mark on the universal yoke.
   b. Install the gear to frame bolts and torque to 65 ft-lbs.
   c. Install the U-joint pinch bolt and torque to 20 ft-lbs. Make sure the bolt passes through the shaft undercut.
6. Install the pitman arm, lining up the marks made at removal. Install the shaft nut or pinch bolt and torque to 180 ft-lbs. on C series, 90 ft-lbs. on K series, and 180 ft-lbs. on G and P series.
7. Remove the plugs and caps from the fluid fittings and reinstall both hoses.

Adjustments

Light Duty Trucks

Power steering gear is adjusted in the same manner as manual steering gear however, sector lash adjustment is the only power steering gear adjustment that can be made on the vehicle. In order to make this adjustment, it is necessary to check the combined valve drag and worm bearing preload.

1. Check power steering fluid level, check belt tension and hose for leaks or kinks.
2. Remove drag link from pitman arm.
3. Disconnect horn wire, remove horn button assembly.
4. Center steering wheel—turn through its full travel then locate wheel at center of its travel.
5. Loosen sector lash adjusting screw locknut and back off (slotted) adjusting screw to the limit of its travel.
6. Check combined valve drag and worm bearing preload with inch-pound torque wrench and socket on steering shaft nut, by rotating wheel approximately 20° in each direction. Note highest reading.
7. Tighten sector lash adjusting screw until torque at steering wheel meets specifications (4 to 18 inch pounds according to truck size). Secure lock nut. *NOTE: If maximum adjustment is exceeded, turn lash adjuster screw back (counter-clockwise) and then come in (clockwise) slowly on adjustment.* **CAUTION: Do not bounce steering wheel hard against stops with drag link removed, worm ball guide damage can result.**
8. Replace drag link, horn button assembly and connect horn wire.
9. Road test and check steering.

Adjustments—Type-533-DU

The only adjustment that can be made on the vehicle is the over-center adjustment.

1. Disconnect pitman arm from shaft, marking the alignment positions.
2. Loosen pitman shaft adjusting screw nut and turn screw out to its limit of travel.
3. Disconnect battery ground cable.
4. Remove horn button.
5. Center steering wheel.
6. Check combined ball and thrust bearing preload by using an in. lbs. torque wrench. Note the highest reading.
7. Tighten pitman shaft adjusting screw and torque steering shaft nut to specifications.
8. Install horn button and connect battery ground cable.
9. Connect pitman arm to shaft, making certain to match alignment marks.

NOTE: There are no on-vehicle adjustments of the type 710-D steering gears.

Power Cylinders

Power cylinders are used to assist in lowering the steering effort for the vehicle operator. Two types are used, side mounted and axle mounted.

The side mounted unit is attached to the frameside rail at one end and to the pitman arm at the other end. The axle mounted cylinder is attached to the front axle at one end and to the steering tie rod at the other.

A control valve mounted on the steering gear housing, directs oil pressure from the belt driven oil pump to either the right or left sides of the piston within the power cylinder, depending upon the turn being made. If a hydraulic failure occurs with this type unit, the steering reverts to manual with no hydraulic assist.

Overhaul of the light duty power cylinder is detailed in the Power Steering Section of the General Repair Section.

Removal and Installation

Removal and installation of the power cylinder is accomplished by the removal of the power cylinder hydraulic lines, and the attaching bolts at each end of the cylinder. A container should be placed under the lines to catch the fluid that will drain from the lines.

To install the cylinder, reverse the procedure, fill the power steering reservoir, and bleed the system of air.

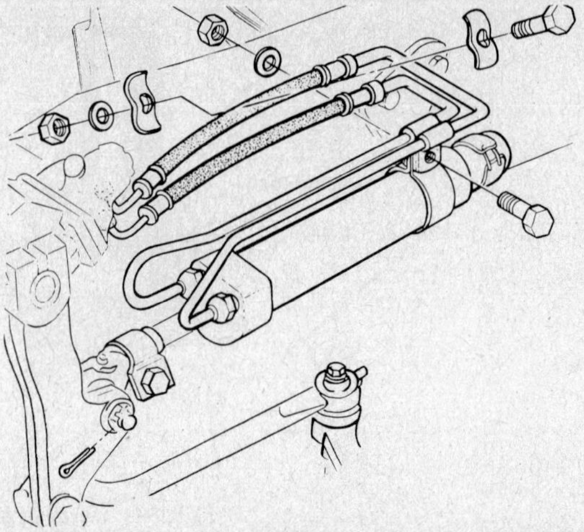

Side mounted power steering cylinder (© Chevrolet Div., G.M. Corp.)

Bleeding Hydraulic System

Light Duty Trucks

1. Fill the reservoir to the proper level, and allow the fluid to stand for at least two minutes; any air bubbles trapped in the fluid will rise and separate from the fluid.
2. Operate the engine for a few seconds.
3. Add fluid as needed.
4. Repeat the above until the fluid level remains constant.
5. Support the front of the vehicle in the raised position, so that the wheels are off of the ground.
6. Increase the engine speed to approximately 1500 rpm.
7. Operate the steering mechanism from right to left, contacting the steering stops only lightly.
8. Add fluid as needed.
9. Lower the vehicle to the ground, and turn the wheels from full right to full left.
10. Add fluid as needed.
11. Repeat all of the above steps as many times as necessary. Keep adding fluid as needed.

NOTE: If, after repeated attempts to bleed the system, air is still present in the fluid (fluid is foamy), then check the hydraulic system for leaks.

Semi-Integral System—Medium and Heavy Duty Trucks

1. Fill the fluid reservoir to the proper level: FLUID LEVEL mark on integral pumps; half full on remote mounted reservoir.
2. Allow the fluid to stand undisturbed for at least two minutes.
3. Operate the engine for a few seconds.
4. Add fluid as needed.
5. Repeat the above steps until the fluid level remains constant.
6. Support the front of the vehicle in the raised position, so that the wheels are off of the ground.

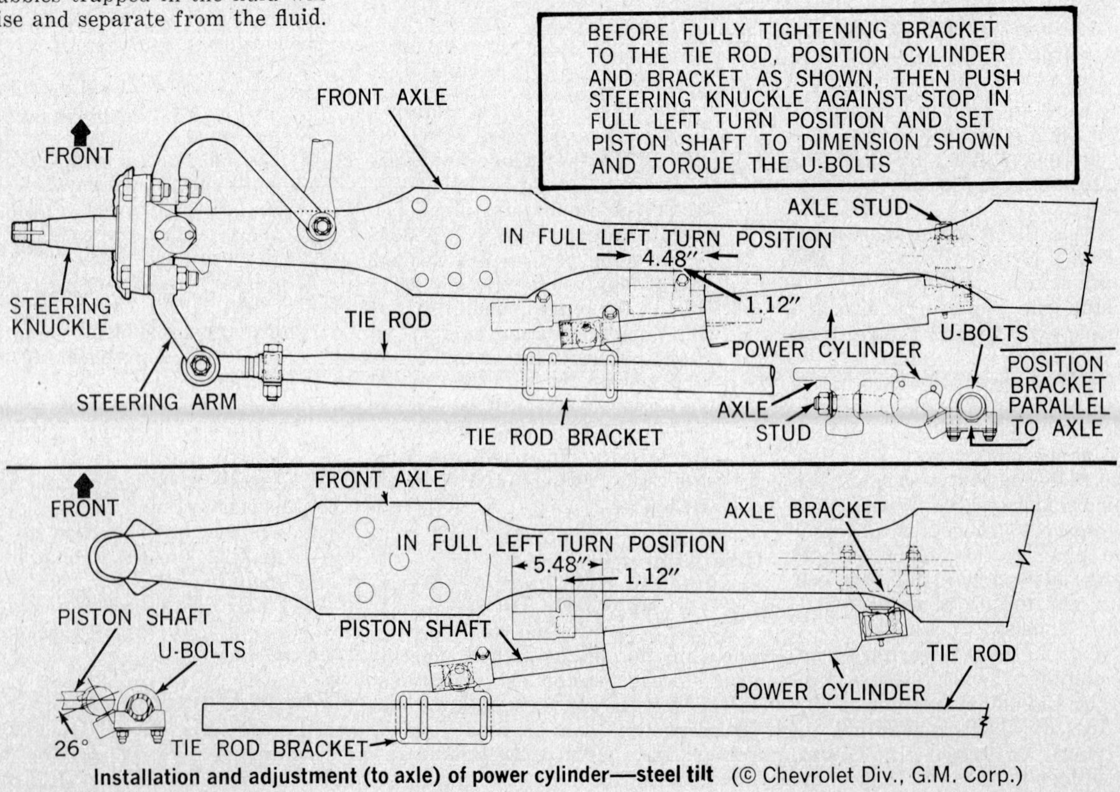

Installation and adjustment (to axle) of power cylinder—steel tilt (© Chevrolet Div., G.M. Corp.)

7. Operate the steering mechanism from stop to stop. Continue this operation until fluid is noticeably clear and free of air bubbles.
8. Add fluid as needed.
9. Increase the engine speed to approximately 1500 rpm, and, again, operate the steering mechanism from stop to stop. Continue until the fluid is clear.
10. Lower the vehicle to the ground.

NOTE: If, after repeated attempts to bleed the system, air is still present in the fluid (fluid is foamy), then check the hydraulic system for leaks.

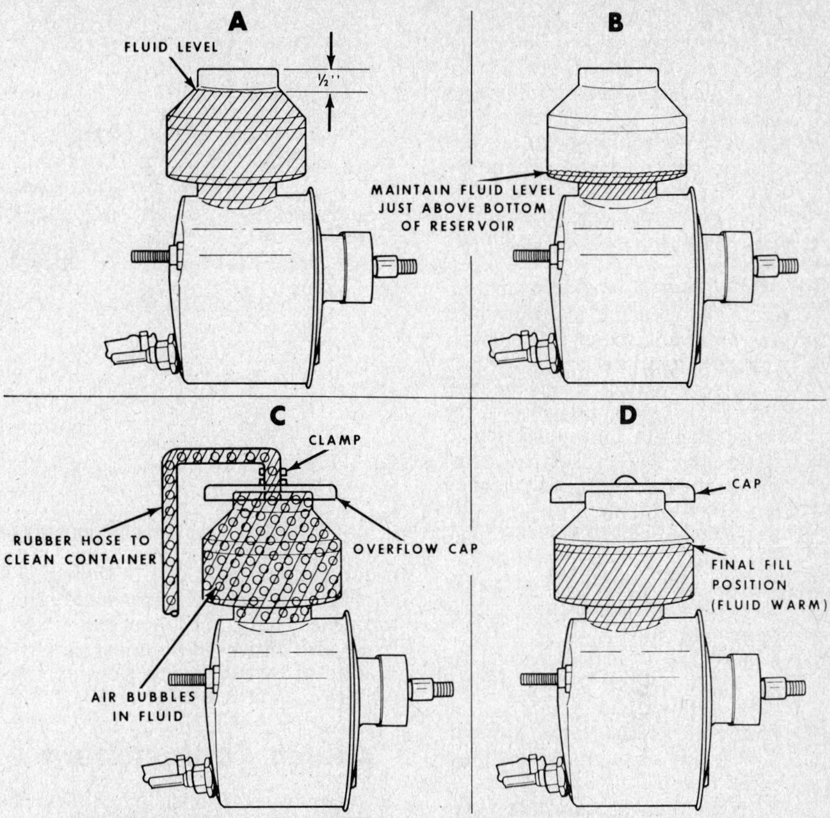

Integral reservoir fluid level (follow in alphabetical order when bleeding hydraulic system) (© Chevrolet Div., G.M. Corp.)

Integral System—Medium Duty Trucks

1. Remove the drag link at the pitman arm.
2. Fill the reservoir to within one-half inch of the top with power steering fluid, and leave the cap off. On vehicles equipped with a remote reservoir, squeeze the hose starting at the pump and work up to the reservoir to remove trapped air.

NOTE: An improvised overflow cap can be installed during the bleednig procedure before the engine is stopped. Overflow can be directed to a clean container. To fabricate an overflow cap:

A. Drill a 3/16" hole through the center of the top of the reservoir cap.

B. Solder a piece of 3/16" O.D. pipe onto the cap at the drilled area.

C. Attach a length of 3/16" I.D. hose to the pipe, which is long enough to reach the external container. Secure the hose in place with a clamp.

3. Pour power steering fluid into the reservoir the moment the engine starts.

NOTE: It may be necessary to have someone ready to assist in this operation.

4. Operate the engine for approximately 3 seconds and then shut it off.
5. Allow the fluid to stand undisturbed for at least one minute.
6. Add fluid as necessary.
7. Repeat the above two more times.

NOTE: DO NOT install the standard reservoir cap during the bleeding procedure, as air may be trapped in the system. If this were to happen, the trapped air would force power steering fluid out of the breather hole in the cap.

8. Start the engine again. Make sure that the fluid level is up to the bottom of the reservoir.

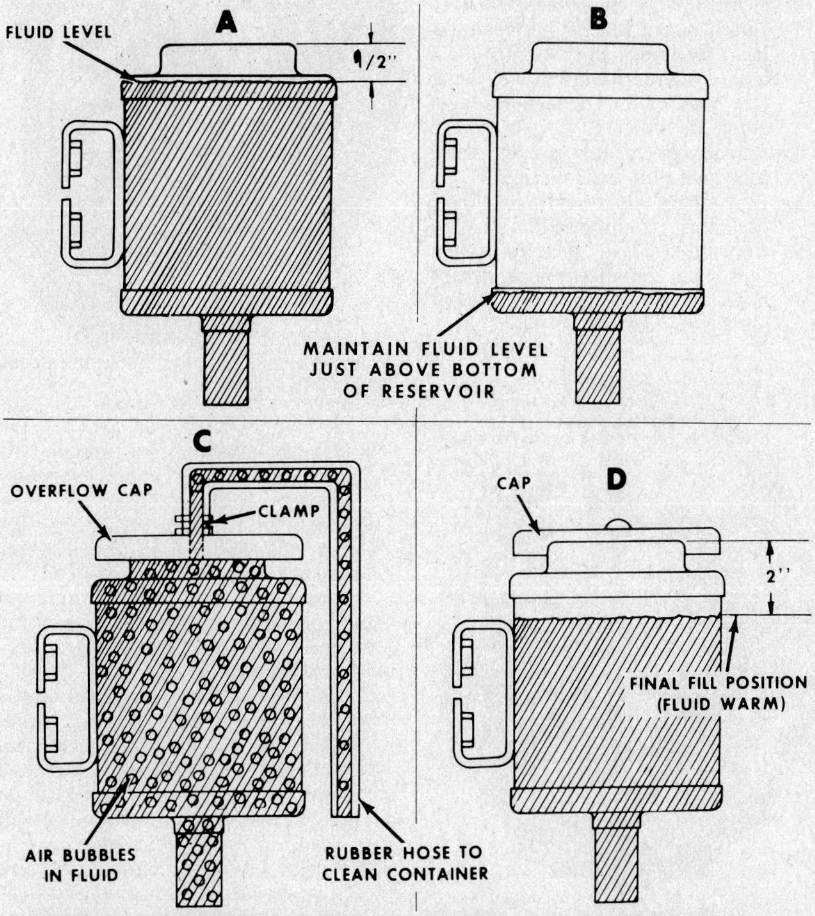

Remote reservoir fluid level (follow in alphabetical order when bleeding hydraulic system) (© Chevrolet Div., G.M. Corp.)

NOTE: The fluid level should be maintained at the bottom of the reservoir to prevent pump aeration during the bleeding procedure.

9. On vehicles equipped with a hydraulic brake booster, pump the brake pedal a minimum of 3 times with the engine running. This will purge air from the booster.
10. Allow the engine to idle, and operate the steering mechanism in one direction, either full right or full left, against the stop. Turn the steering away from the stop only slightly, and return it to the stop. Repeat this operation 5 times. DO NOT force the steering against the stop, as this may damage the pump.
11. Repeat step no. 10 for the opposite side.
12. Maintain the fluid level at a point just above the bottom of the reservoir.
13. Center the steering wheel, and allow the engine to idle. Install the overflow cap.
14. Shut the engine off. Air will bubble out through the overflow cap.
15. Remove the cap, and start the engine.
16. Add fluid as needed to maintain the fluid level just above the bottom of the reservoir.
17. Repeat steps nos. 3 through 16 as many times as necessary, until there is no more than a one inch rise in the fluid level with the engine shut off.
18. Start the engine, and center the steering wheel.
19. Connect the drag link to the pitman arm.
20. Idle the engine at approximately 1500 rpm, and operate the steering mechanism from stop to stop.
21. Shut the engine off, and fill the reservoir to the proper level.

CLUTCH

Clutches used on inline engines are single (driven) disc with either of two types of pressure (drive) plates, diaphragm or coil spring. "V" engines use a single disc with coil spring pressure plate. Heavy duty clutches use two discs. The two plate clutch consists of three basic assemblies, the cover with rear pressure plate assembly, front pressure plate and two discs. The front pressure plate, located between the two driven discs, has two friction surfaces and is coupled to rear pressure plate through steel drive straps bolted at each of its four driving bosses. Diaphragm spring covers operate with light pedal pressure while coil spring levers combine operating ease and high torque capacity. The operating controls are either mechanical or hydraulic. Discs have torsion spring centers.

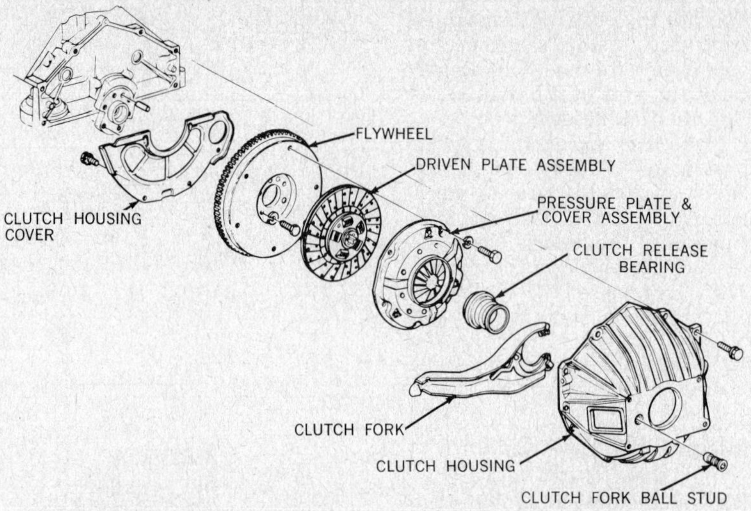

Clutch system components (© Chevrolet Div., G.M. Corp.)

Clutch Replacement

1. Remove transmission.
2. Block clutch fingers down on coil spring covers for additional clearance. On heavy duty clutches use blocks between release bearing and spring plate hub. On Lipe-Rollaway use bolts and washer in three holes provided
3. Disconnect pedal linkage and fork arm pull back springs.
4. Disconnect slave cylinder from fork arm (if equipped).
5. Remove release bearing from fork arm or disconnect grease hose and remove bearing assembly from yoke.

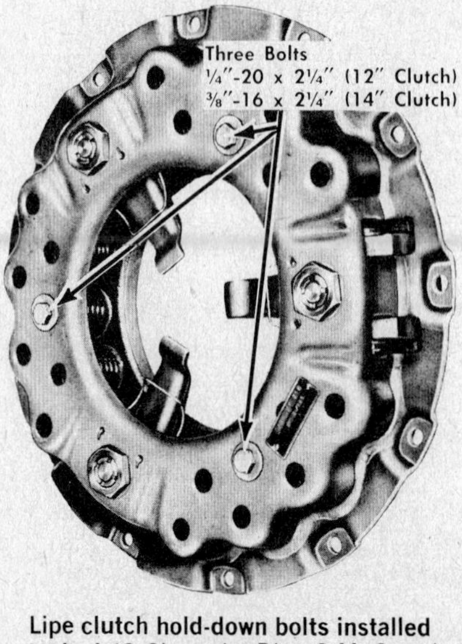

Lipe clutch hold-down bolts installed typical (© Chevrolet Div., G.M. Corp.)

6. Remove fork arm from ball stud or remove yoke and shaft.
7. Fork arm ball stud can be removed if necessary.
8. Punch mark cover and flywheel for alignment if cover assembly is to be re-used.

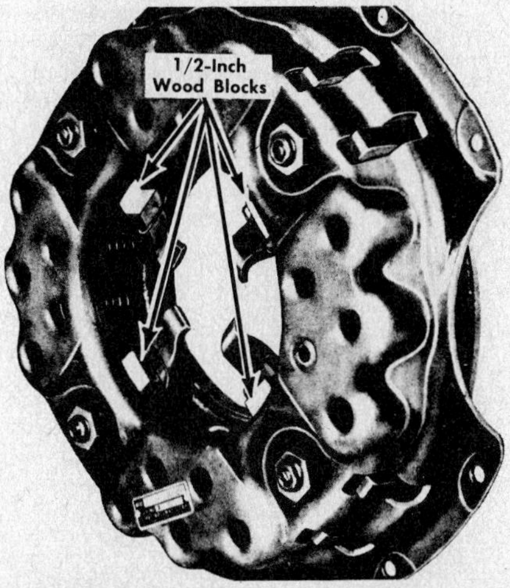

Wooden blocks installed between release levers and cover
(© Chevrolet Div., G.M. Corp.)

9. Loosen cover bolts a turn or two at a time to prevent cover distortion. Support cover and disc with pilot tool (or sling) to prevent damage to clutch when last cover bolt is removed. A good practice on heavy units is to remove one cover bolt and install a support stud. Rotate flywheel and locate stud at top, loosen all other bolts evenly until pressure is released from disc(s). Disc(s) can be removed and marked for positions. Remove remaining cover bolts and slide cover assembly off stud. Stud will also aid in installation.
10. Clean flywheel and pressure plates, check for scores and heat cracks. Excessive bluing indicates abnormally high operating

temperatures. Torque flywheel bolts.

11. Check pilot bearing or bushing (lubricate sparingly), check splines on clutch shaft, check release bearing (do not wash bearing).
12. Reverse removal steps to install. Use pilot tool or dummy shaft to align disc(s). Be certain of disc's position in relation to flywheel. Tighten cover bolts evenly. Do not try to pull clutch into place with impact wrench. This procedure can crack or break pilot shoulders on bolts. Lubricate with a light coat of grease, fork arm ball seat and inside of release bearing. Make sure spring retainer (if used) for release fork ball stud is in correct position. Install retainer with high side up, away from bottom of ball socket and with open end of retainer horizontal. After clutch and transmission are installed and clutch pedal free travel adjusted, check disc(s) for release. This can be done by putting transmission in gear and pulling down slowly on clutch pedal while applying torque to transmission propeller shaft flange. If release can be felt, then complete installation.

Adjustment

Free Pedal Travel

This adjustment is for the amount of pedal travel (measured at pedal) before clutch release bearing contacts the levers, or fingers of a coil spring cover or the diaphragm spring of a diaphragm clutch cover. This is called free-play. With normal clutch wear the amount of free-play is reduced and in time this will cause the release bearing to be in constant contact with the cover. This in turn will cause clutch disc slippage resulting in premature failure of disc and release bearing. It is necessary to maintain sufficient free pedal travel for clutch efficiency and long life.

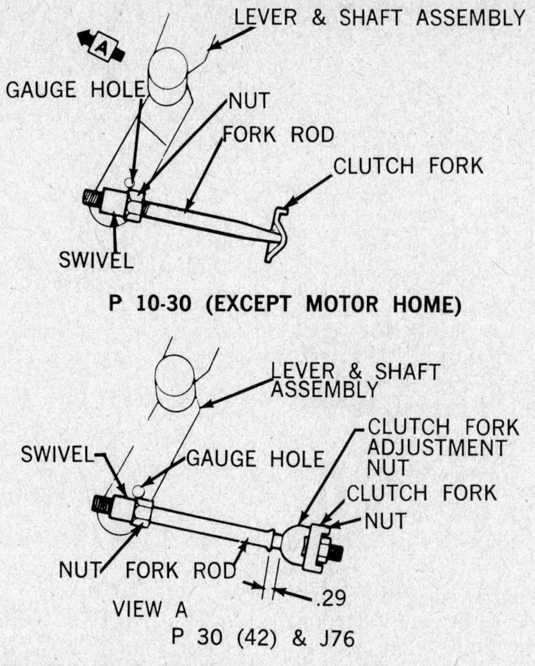

Free pedal travel—P models (© Chevrolet Div., G.M. Corp.)

C, K, and P Models (Except P-30 W/J76)

1. Disconnect the clutch fork return spring.
2. Rotate the clutch lever assembly until the clutch pedal stops against the rubber bumper on the brake pedal bracket.
3. Position the clutch fork so that the release bearing lightly contacts the pressure plate levers.
4. Loosen the apply rod lock nut, and adjust the rod length so that the swivel slips easily into the gauge hole (upper hole) on the clutch lever.
5. Continue lengthening the push rod until all lash is removed from the clutch linkage.
6. Remove the swivel from the gauge hole, and insert it into the lower hole on the clutch lever.
7. Install the washers and cotter pin. Tighten the lock nut.
8. Install the clutch fork return spring. Check clutch pedal free travel.

NOTE: Pedal travel for C and K models should be $1\frac{3}{8}$-$1\frac{5}{8}$ inches; pedal travel for P models should be $1\frac{1}{4}$-$1\frac{1}{2}$ inches.

P-30 W/J76

1. Disconnect the clutch fork return spring.
2. Loosen the lock nut at the apply rod swivel.
3. Move the clutch fork rearward to remove all clearance between the release bearing and the pressure plate levers.
4. Rotate the clutch lever assembly until the clutch pedal stops against the bumper on the brake pedal bracket.
5. Adjust the apply rod until the distance between the shoulder on the apply rod and the adjustment nut is approximately $\frac{1}{4}$-$\frac{5}{16}$ (.29) inch.
6. Tighten the lock nut, and install the return spring.
7. Check clutch pedal free travel.

NOTE: Free travel should be $1\frac{3}{8}$-$1\frac{5}{8}$ inches.

G Models

1. Check linkage for excessive wear.
2. Disconnect fork arm return spring.

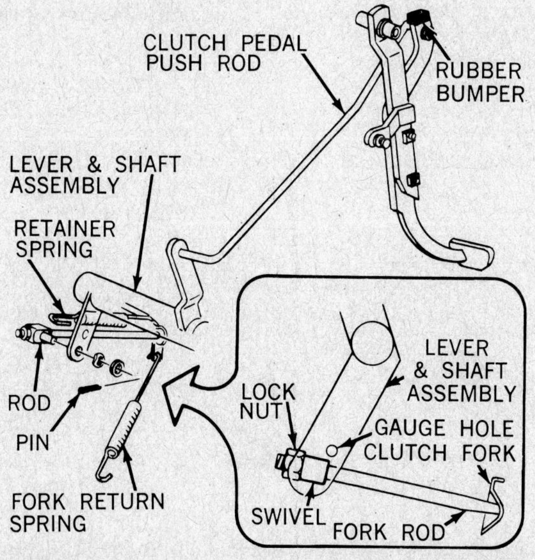

Free pedal travel—C, K models (© Chevrolet Div., G.M. Corp.)

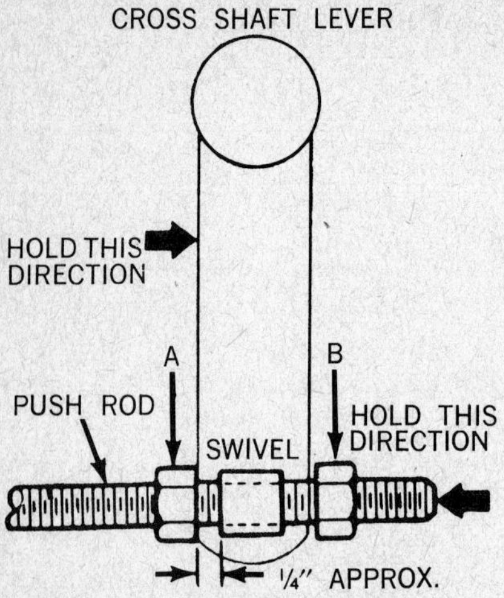

Free travel adjustment—G models
(© Chevrolet Div., G.M. Corp.)

3. Back off locknut "A" at least 1/2" from swivel.
4. Hold fork push rod against fork to keep release bearing touching fingers (or diaphragm). Push rod will slide through swivel at cross shaft.
5. Adjust nut "B" to obtain approximately 3/16" to 1/4" clearance between nut "B" and swivel.
6. Release push rod, connect pull back spring at fork and tighten nut "A" to lock swivel against nut "B".
7. Check clutch pedal free travel. Free travel should be 1 1/4-1 1/2 inches.

Medium Duty Trucks W/427 CID Engine (Others Similar)

1. Loosen the lock nuts.
2. Apply a force of approximately five pounds to the push rod in the direction of arrow (D) to take up all clearances in the linkage.

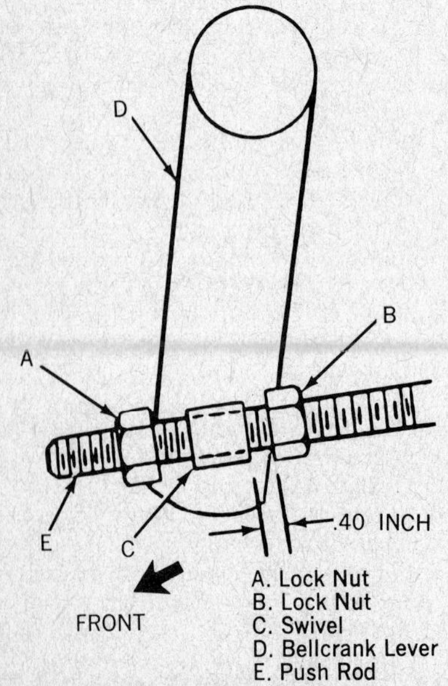

Clutch linkage adjustment except models equipped with 427 CID engine
(© Chevrolet Div., G.M. Corp.)

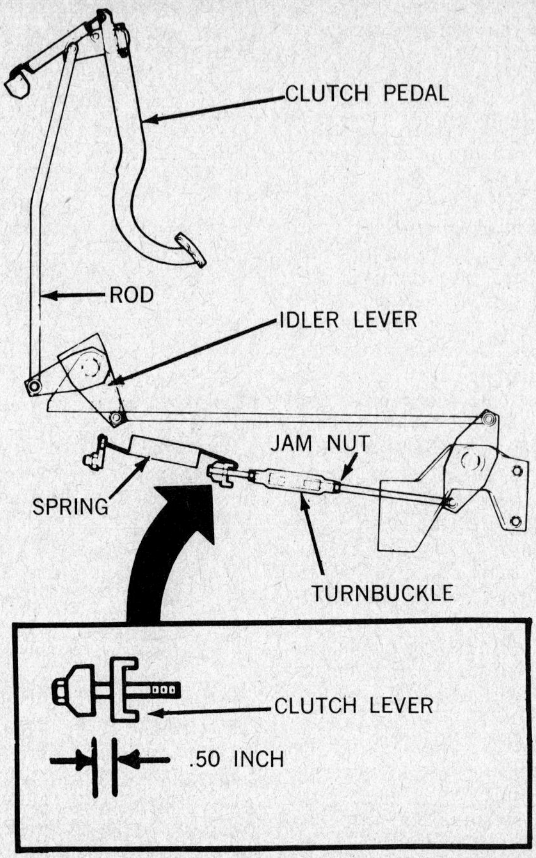

Clutch linkage adjustment—medium duty steel cab w/427 V8, 454 V8, and 4-53T (© Chevrolet Div., G.M. Corp.)

3. Apply a force of approximately five pounds to the clutch lever in the direction of arrow (F) to eliminate the clearance between the release bearing and the internal release levers.
4. Turn the lock nut (B) to obtain a clearance of 0.40 inch between the nut and swivel. Free travel should be approximately 3/4-1 inch.

   NOTE: The clearance for vehicles equipped with either an RT 613 or an RT 610 transmission is 0.45 inch. Free travel should be 1 7/8 inches.
5. While holding the nut (B), release the clutch lever, and tighten the other nut (A).
6. Check clutch operation.

Slave Cylinder Push Rod

1. Disconnect the slave cylinder return spring.
2. Push the slave cylinder push rod into the slave cylinder, until it bottoms.
3. Move the clutch fork in the direction away from the slave cylinder. This will bring the release bearing into contact with the clutch release levers.
4. Check the clearance between the wedge and the adjusting nut.

   NOTE: Clearance should be as follows:

   4-53 Diesel Engine 0.40 inch
   V-8 Gasoline Engine 0.40 inch
5. Loosen the jam nut and the adjusting nut.
6. Turn the adjusting nut to obtain

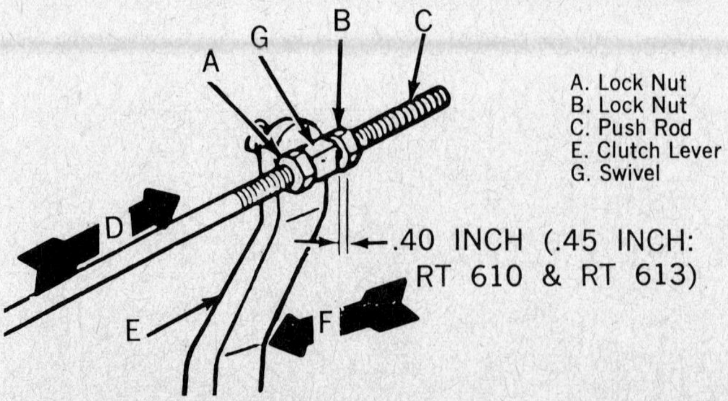

Clutch linkage adjustment—models equipped with 427 CID gasoline engine
(© Chevrolet Div., G.M. Corp.)

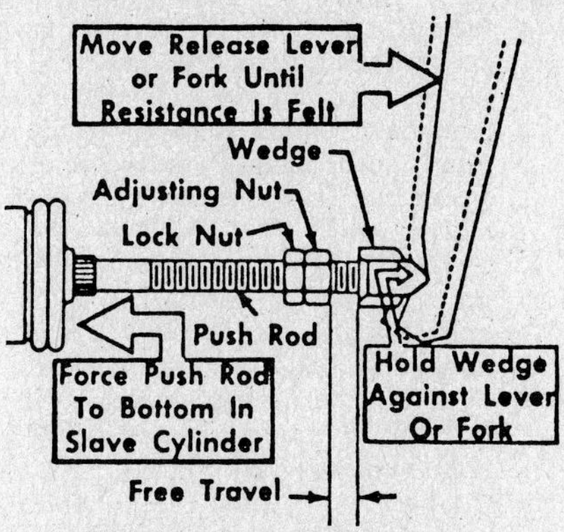

Clutch slave cylinder adjustment
(© Chevrolet Div., G.M. Corp.)

the proper clearance, and then tighten the jam nut against the adjusting nut.

7. Connect the return spring, and check clutch operation.

Cover Assemblies

While no wear adjustment is needed (except Spicer), original settings at time of manufacture must be retained for good clutch operation. If a diaphragm clutch cover fails to release properly, after first checking pedal travel and pedal lash and linkage for looseness, replace diaphragm retracting springs. This can be done in the vehicle. If trouble still persists the diaphragm is probably overstressed.

TRANSFER CASE

Information on repair and overhaul of light duty transfer cases can be found in the General Repair Section.

Removal

1. Raise and support vehicle on hoist. Drain transfer case.
2. Disconnect speedometer cable, back-up lamp and TCS switch.
3. Remove skid plate and crossmember supports as necessary.
4. Disconnect rear prop shaft from transfer case and tie up away from work area.
5. Disconnect front prop shaft from transfer case and tie up shaft away from work area.
6. Disconnect shift lever rod from shift rail link. On full time 4 wheel drive models, disconnect shift levers at transfer case.
7. Remove transfer case to frame mounting bracket bolts.
8. Support transfer case and remove bolts attaching transfer case to transmission adapter.
9. Move transfer case to rear until input shaft clears adapter and lower assembly from vehicle.

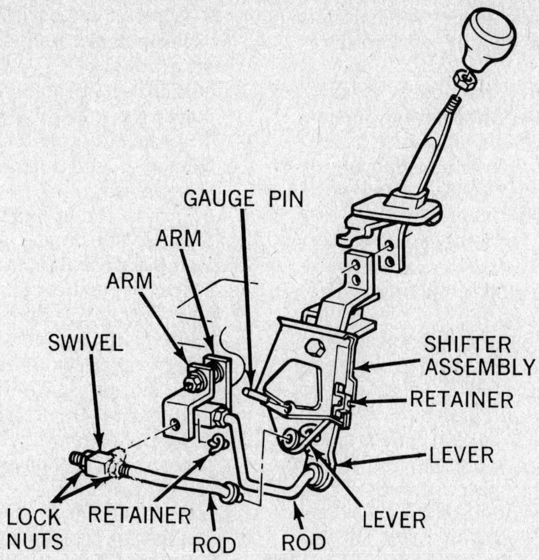

Transfer case linkage—model 203 (© Chevrolet Div., G.M. Corp.)

Installation

1. Support transfer case in suitable stand and position case to transmission adapter. Install bolts attaching case to adapter and torque to 45 ft. lbs.
2. Remove stand as required and install bolts attaching transfer case to frame rail. Bend lock tabs after assembly.
3. Install connecting rod to shift rail link or connect shift levers to transfer case, as applicable.
4. Connect front prop shaft to transfer case front output shaft.
5. Connect rear prop shaft to transfer case rear output shaft.
6. Install crossmember support and skid plate, If removed.
7. Connect speedometer cable, back-up lamp and TCS switch.
8. Fill transfer case to proper level with lubricant.
9. Lower and remove vehicle from hoist.

CAUTION: **Check and tighten all bolts to specified torques.**

NOTE: Before connecting prop shafts to companion flanges be sure locknuts are torqued to specifications.

Linkage Adjustment

Model 203

1. Align the gauge holes in the shift levers with the gauge hole in the shifter assembly, and insert the alignment pin (gauge pin). This will place the levers in the NEUTRAL position.
2. Position the transfer case arms in the vertical position (straight up and down).
3. Loosen the swivel lock nuts on the outer shift rod, and rotate the swivel on the rod until the distance between the end of the rod and the swivel is exactly the same as the distance between the hole in the transfer case arm and the hole in the corresponding shift lever.
4. Install the shift rod. The shift rod swivel must fit easily into the hole in the transfer case arm. DO NOT force it into the hole. If it is necessary to force the swivel into the hole, then the swivel is not properly adjusted.
5. Lock the swivel in place with a retainer.
6. Repeat steps nos. 1 through 5 for the inner rod.
7. Remove the gauge pin, and check the operation of the transfer case and shifter.

MANUAL TRANSMISSION

Troubleshooting and repair of light duty manual transmissions are covered in the General Repair Section.

3 and 4 Speed Light Duty Transmission

3 Speed Except Van and Blazer with 4 Wheel Drive

Removal

1. Raise vehicle and support on jack stands.
2. Drain transmission.
3. Disconnect speedometer cable, TCS switch and back-up lamp wire at transmission.
4. Disconnect shift control levers from transmission.
5. Disconnect parking brake lever and controls (if used).
6. Remove drive shaft after marking position of shaft to flange.

7. Position jack under transmission to support weight of transmission.
8. Remove crossmember. Visually inspect to see if other equipment, brackets or lines, must be removed to permit removal of transmission. *NOTE: Mark position of crossmember when removing to prevent incorrect installation.*
9. Remove flywheel housing underpan.
10. Remove the top two transmission to housing bolts and insert two guide pins. *NOTE: The use of guide pins will not only support the transmission but will prevent damage to the clutch disc. Guide pins can be made by taking two bolts, the same as those just removed only longer, and cutting off the heads. (Slot for screwdriver)*
11. Remove two remaining bolts and slide transmission straight back from engine. Use care to keep the transmission drive gear straight in line with clutch disc hub. *NOTE: Be sure to support release bearing when removing transmission to avoid having bearing fall into flywheel housing.*
12. When transmission is free from engine, move from under vehicle.

Installation

1. Place transmission on guide pins, slide forward starting main drive gear into clutch disc's splines. *NOTE: Place transmission in gear and rotate transmission flange or output yoke to aid entry of main drive gear into disc's splines. Make sure clutch release bearing is in position.*
2. Install two lower transmission mounting bolts, and flywheel lower pan (if equipped).
3. Remove guide pins and install upper mounting bolts.
4. Install propeller shaft, watch align marks.
5. Connect parking brake, back-up lamp and T.S.C. switch (if used).
6. Connect shift levers, see section on adjustment if needed.
7. Connect speedometer cable, refill transmission.
8. Lower vehicle and road test.

Vans

Removal

1. Place heavy cardboard between radiator core and fan blades as a precautionary measure.
2. Raise and support vehicle on stands or hoist, drain transmission.
3. Disconnect speedometer cable at transmission.
4. Disconnect parking brake, back-up lamp and T.S.C. switch (if used).
5. Disconnect propeller shaft and power take off (if equipped).
6. 3 Speed (Column Shift)
   a. Remove shift controls from transmission.

   4 Speed (Floor Shift)
   a. Remove floor mat.
   b. Remove floor pan.
   c. Place transmission in neutral and remove gearshift lever by sliding open side of tool over lever, engage lugs of tool in the open slot of retainer, press down on tool and turn to left to disengage the lugs on retainer. Cover transmission opening. Be careful of pivot pin.
   d. Remove reverse lever cable and bracket at transmission.

   4 Speed (Column Shift)
   a. Remove shift controls from levers.
   b. Remove reverse lever cable and bracket at transmission.
7. Remove clutch shaft frame bolts and accelerator linkage at manifold bellcrank.
8. Place jack under bell housing and raise enough to relieve weight at transmission rear support.
9. Remove transmission rear support crossmember or on early models, remove support bolt and lower engine carefully to allow transmission rear mount to clear support bracket.
10. Position jack under transmission and adjust to carry weight of transmission (if 4 speed).
11. Remove 2 top transmission to bell housing bolts and install 2 guide pins to prevent damaging clutch disc.
12. Remove two lower transmission mounting bolts.
13. Visually inspect to determine if other equipment or lines need to be removed.
14. Slide transmission back on guide pins, four speed units aided by jack (support release bearing), until transmission clears engine. Remove transmission from under vehicle.

CAUTION: If other work is to be performed support engine more securely after transmission is removed.

Installation

1. Clean bell housing and transmission mating surfaces, lightly lubricate main drive gear bearing retainer and clutch pilot bushing or bearing. Make sure release bearing is in position.
2. Move transmission into position on guide pins, shift transmission into any gear.
3. Slide transmission forward rotating transmission flange or yoke to aid entry of main drive gear into clutch disc splines.
4. Install two lower transmission mounting bolts. Remove guide pins and install two upper mounting bolts. Remove transmission jack.
5. Carefully raise engine and transmission to normal position and install transmission rear mounting bolt or crossmember. Remove jack from under bell housing. Remove cardboard from radiator.
6. Connect speedometer cable, parking brake, back-up light and T.S.C. switch (if equipped).
7. Connect propeller shaft and power take off (if equipped).
8. Connect clutch shaft and accelerator linkage.
9. Reinstall shift controls on transmission or gearshift lever on four speed. Install reverse cable and bracket. See section on shift linkage adjustment if needed.
10. Replace floor mat and floor pans on four speed units.
11. Refill transmission, lower vehicle and road test.

4 Wheel Drive (Including Blazer)

Removal and Installation

1. Floor shift models.
   a. Remove shift lever boots and retainers on both transfer case and transmission.
   b. Remove floor mat or carpet, seat and accelerator pedal.
   c. Center console models: remove center outlet from heater distributor duct and remove console.
   d. Remove transmission floor cover, shift transfer case lever into neutral and rotate floor cover approximately 90° while lifting to clear transfer case lever.
   e. Slide open side of tool over transmission gearshift lever, engage lugs of tool in open slot of retainer, press down and turn counter-clockwise to remove lever. Do same for transfer case lever. Be careful of any pivot pins. Cover transmission openings.
2. Raise vehicle and support on stands or hoist vehicle.
3. Drain transmission and transfer case.
4. Disconnect back-up light and T.S.C. switches (if equipped).
5. Disconnect parking brake.
6. Disconnect speedometer cable (at transfer case on some models).
7. Disconnect front and rear auxiliary drive shafts at transfer case and tie up out of work area.
8. Remove bolts attaching transfer

case to adapter (remove side access cover to reach two bolts).
9. Support rear of engine with jack.
10. Support transfer case on cradle or dolly. Remove two transmission adapter mounting bolts.
11. Remove transfer case mounting bolts, remove transfer case (all except Blazer).
12. Column Shift Models:
   a. Disconnect shift control rods from levers at transmission.
   b. On 4 speed, remove reverse cable and bracket at transmission.
13. Remove two upper transmission mounting bolts and install two guide pins (longer bolts with heads cut off and slotted). Use of guide pins will prevent damage to clutch disc.
14. Remove flywheel under pan and remove two lower transmission mounting bolts.
15. On V-8 engines, remove exhaust crossover pipe.
16. On Blazer, remove transmission frame crossmember bolts. Remove crossmember (rotating to clear frame rails).
17. Visually inspect to determine if other equipment or lines need to be removed.
18. Slide transmission and adapter (transmission with transfer case on Blazer) back on guide pins, aided by transmission dolly, until main drive gear clears clutch (watch clutch release bearing), remove from under vehicle.
19. Lubricate pilot bushing or bearing, make sure clutch release bearing is in position, use guide pins to align transmission and rotate main drive gear to enter clutch disc splines without forcing. Reverse removal procedures to install.

4 and 5 Speed, Heavy Duty Transmissions

The procedures required to remove and install the transmissions covered in this section are dependent upon types of cabs, engines and chassis used, also what equipment is available in repair shop. Other operations may be necessary if vehicle has special equipment, therefore, procedures contained herein will serve only as a guide. It is important to note that vehicles covered in this section will have either an "apron" or "S.A.E. 2" type of flywheel housing. The apron type is identified by sheet metal pan, also note it is a one piece housing. The "S.A.E. 2" type completely surrounds the flywheel. A separate clutch housing is used in addition to the flywheel housing. Transmission replacement procedures are different for each type of flywheel housing used.

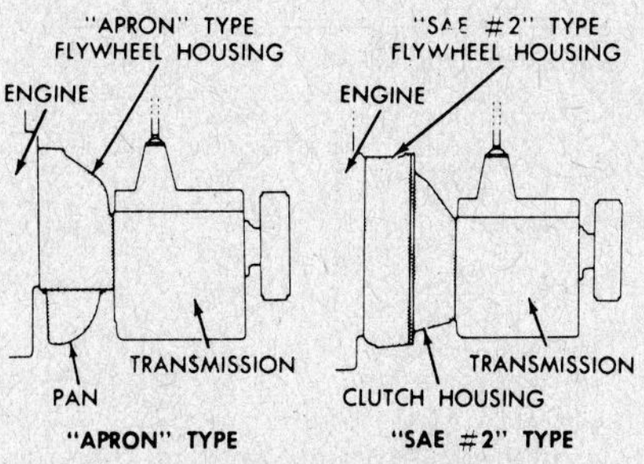

Flywheel housing identification
(© Chevrolet Div., G.M. Corp.)

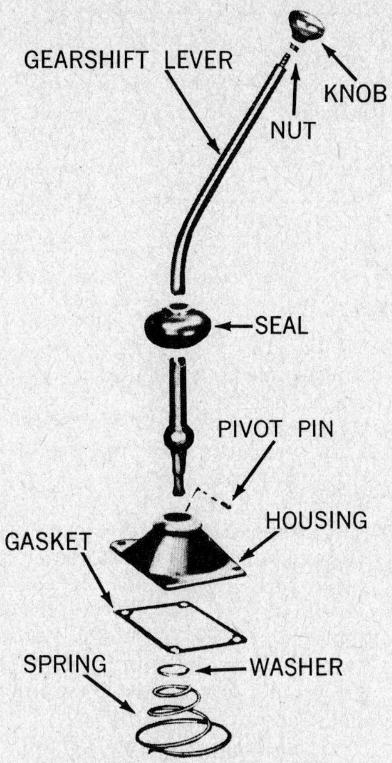

Gearshift lever and housing
(© Chevrolet Div., G.M. Corp.)

Removal

1. Drain transmission.
2. On transmission equipped with remote controls.
   a. Disconnect control rods from shift levers at transmission.
3. On transmissions with a conventional floor gearshift lever.
   a. Remove steering jacket grommet from floor and slide grommet up mast jacket out of way (if used).
   b. Remove floor mat and accelerator pedal.
   c. Disconnect and remove parking brake lever.
   d. Remove transmission floor pan (s), place gearshift lever in neutral.
   e. Remove gearshift lever (and control tower on some models).

NOTE: On models with New Process Transmissions remove lever by sliding open side of tool over lever. Engage lugs of tool in open slot of retainer, press down on tool and turn to left to disengage lugs on retainer. Lift lever out of cover, be careful of pivot pin. Cover opening in transmission.

On Spicer models, press down on shift lever cup and drive locking pin out of lever. Lift off cup, spring, cap and seal. Remove snap ring from groove on lever housing and tap out slotted pin. Lift lever out of housing and cover opening.

On Clark models remove shift lever housing cover to transmission bolts. Lift lever and control tower from transmission. Cover transmission opening.

On Air Control Shift models, bleed air tanks, remove range shift lines at air valve on transmission. Remove gearshift lever and control tower assembly from transmission. Cover transmission opening and tape or plug air valves.

4. Disconnect and drop propeller shaft at transmission.
5. If unit is equipped with power take-off, disconnect drive shaft and controls.
6. Remove reverse shift control cable and bracket on 4 speed units.
7. Disconnect any clutch control linkage on transmission.
8. Disconnect speedometer cable at transmission.
9. Remove engine ground strap, back up lamp switch and "T.S.C." switch (if used).
10. Place transmission jack into position and adjust to carry weight of transmission. Use locking chain to secure transmission to jack. *NOTE: On vehicles which have rear engine mountings attached to the clutch housing (except "apron" type flywheel housing models), position a jack under flywheel housing and adjust to carry the weight of the engine. Remove rear engine mounts.*
11. Remove bolts attaching transmission to rear crossmember support brackets (if used).
12. Remove clutch housing-to-flywheel housing bolts. (except on "apron" type flywheel housing models) *NOTE: On models with "apron" type flywheel housing, remove flywheel housing under pan (also access panel on Spicer) and transmission to flywheel housing bolts. The use of guidepins in two top holes of "apron" type flywheel housing or in two top side holes on "S.A.E." type will maintain alignment during both removal and installation of transmission.*
13. Visually inspect to determine if other equipment or lines must be removed.

14. Move transmission straight back, using guide pins to keep transmission main drive gear in alignment with clutch disc, until free from engine. Be sure to support clutch release bearing during removal of transmission. Lower transmission and move from under the vehicle.

Installation

1. Clean transmission mating surfaces and apply a light film of grease to main drive gear bearing retainer and clutch pivot bearing.
2. Place transmission on jack and move into position.
3. On "apron" type, place clutch release bearing and support assembly inside flywheel housing. Be sure clutch fork engages bearing. On "S.A.E. 2" type, make sure clutch release bearing is in position.
4. Using guide pins to align transmission main drive gear with clutch disc, move transmission forward rotating main drive gear so gear can enter clutch disc splines without forcing.
5. Reverse removal procedures to install.

NOTE: On transmissions having remote controls make the following control island shift mechanism adjustments if necessary.

1. Place transmission selector and shift levers in neutral.
2. Adjust selector and shift rods to provide 90° angle at the lower end of the gearshift lever to the control island panel. Adjustment is made by rotating the adjustable clevis at either the control island or transmission end of the selector and shift rods. Tighten lock nuts.
3. Check adjustments by moving gearshift lever through shift pattern.

NOTE: On 4 speed transmissions with reverse idler eccentric. To adjust the position of the reverse idler gear, the transmission must be fully assembled except for power take-off cover. Then proceed as follows:

1. Loosen the eccentric nut and rotate the eccentric, using a screwdriver in the slot with end of electric, until slot with dot on end is to the rear. This places the reverse idler in its extreme rear position and will provide for maximum engagement when the transmission is shifted into reverse.
2. Shift transmission into second. Check for interference between reverse idler and first and reverse gear. If interference exists, rotate eccentric in a counter-clockwise direction to obtain approximately 1/32" clearance This clearance can be checked through the power take-off opening.
3. Shift transmission into reverse and check clearance between reverse idler gear and transmission case. If necessary, rotate the eccentric an additional amount, in counter-clockwise direction, to obtain running clearance at this point.
4. Tighten eccentric nut and lock.
5. Install power take-off cover and new gasket.

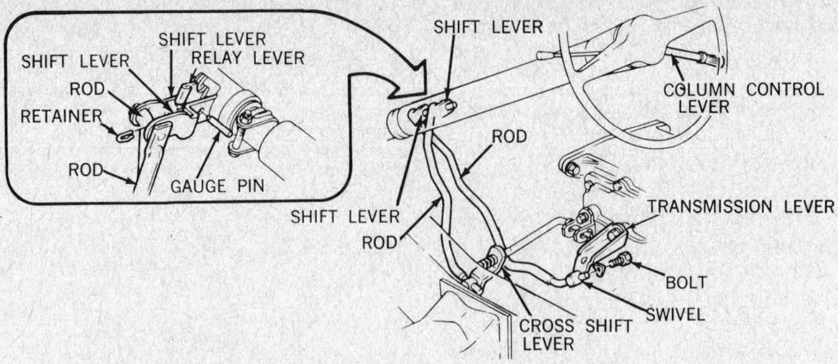

Column shift linkage—C, K models (© Chevrolet Div., G.M. Corp.)

Shift Linkage Adjustment

3 Speed Column Shift

1. Raise vehicle and support on stands.
2. Disconnect control rods at transmission levers.
3. Place transmission shift levers in neutral (neutral detents in cover must be fully engaged).
4. Place gearshift lever in neutral, on early models remove housing cover at base of mast jacket and make sure shifter gates and inner levers are aligned. If alignment is off, loosen first and reverse control rod swivel clamp at housing outer lever and adjust swivel until shifter gates are aligned.
5. Adjust swivels on control rods until swivels (or rods) enter transmission shift lever holes. Make sure levers remain in neutral position. Lock control rods.
6. Lower vehicle and move gearshift lever through all gear positions to check (keep clutch pedal depressed to aid shifting).

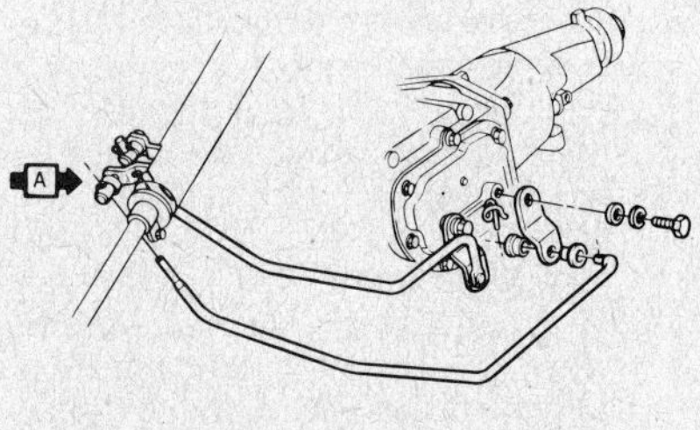

Column shift linkage—P models
(© Chevrolet Div., G.M. Corp.)

4 Speed Column Shift

1. Place gearshift lever in neutral. Raise vehicle on hoist.
2. Disconnect first and second shift rod from cross shaft lever. Disconnect third and fourth shift rod from transmission lever. Disconnect reverse cable from reverse lever by removing "C"

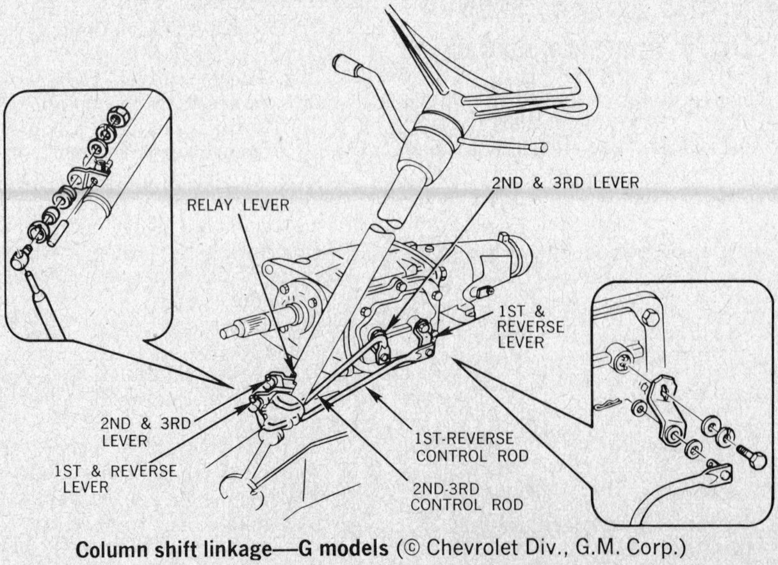

Column shift linkage—G models (© Chevrolet Div., G.M. Corp.)

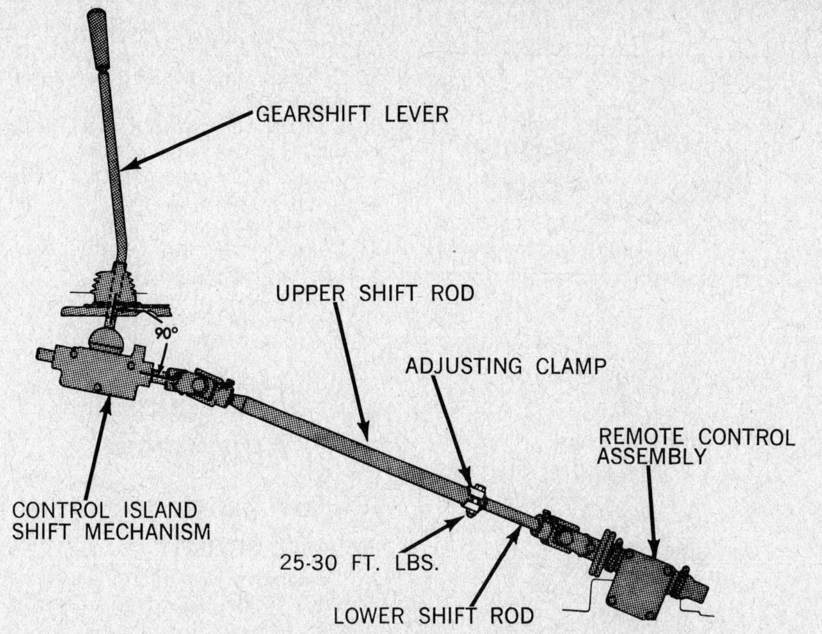

Gearshift linkage w/one piece shift rod tilt cab models (© Chevrolet Div., G.M. Corp.)

clip. Manually shift all transmission controls into neutral, including reverse lever.

3. Remove engine splash shield. Install a fabricated pin (see illustration for details) through upper control shaft bracket into cutouts in shift levers and into hole provided at base of control shaft as shown.
4. Adjust swivel on end of first and second rod to freely enter cross shaft lever hole. Reconnect rod to lever.
5. Adjust swivel on end of third and fourth rod to freely enter transmission lever. Reconnect rod to lever.
6. Adjust swivel on end of reverse cable to freely enter reverse lever hole. If more adjustment is needed at swivel, adjust cable assembly by using cable to bracket attaching nuts. Install washer and "C" clip. Tighten swivel lock nut.
7. Remove fabricated pin, replace splash shield, lower vehicle and move gearshift lever through all gear positions to check. Depressing clutch pedal will aid in shifting.

Van Column Shift

1. Raise vehicle and support on stands.
2. Remove control rods at transmission levers.
3. Move both transmission levers until transmission is in neutral. Neutral detents must be fully engaged.
4. Move gearshift lever into neutral position, align shifter relay levers on mast jacket, install pin in holes of levers to hold levers in alignment and in neutral position.
5. Adjust swivel on end of low and reverse control rod until swivel enters transmission lever freely,

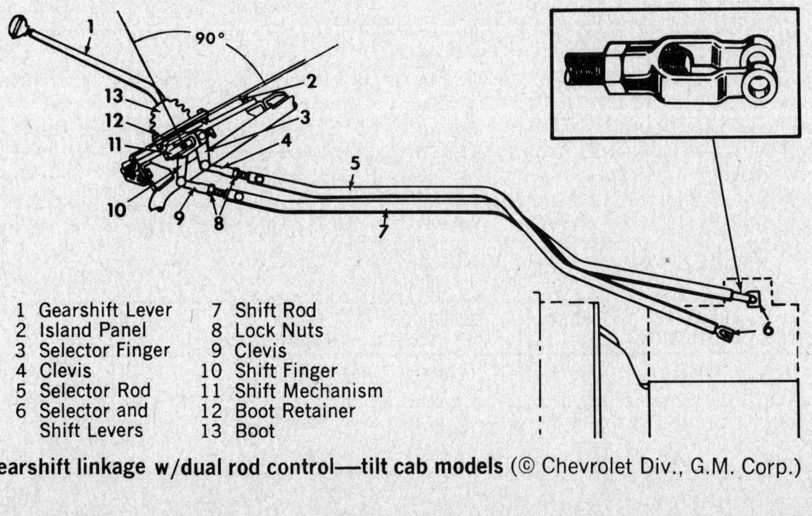

Gearshift linkage w/dual rod control—tilt cab models (© Chevrolet Div., G.M. Corp.)

lock with retaining ring, tighten swivel locknut.

6. Similarly, install second and third control rod, be sure levers remain in neutral.
7. Lower vehicle and move gearshift lever through all gear positions to check. Keep clutch pedal depressed to aid in shifting.

Tilt Cab (w/Dual Rod Control)

1. Position the transmission selector and shift levers in NEUTRAL.

   NOTE: The position of the selector and shift levers (in NEUTRAL) is critical, and must be maintained throughout the adjustment procedure.

2. Disconnect the clevis of either control rod (both if necessary) at the transmission, and rotate the clevis(es) to the length required to bring the lower end of the gearshift lever into a 90 degree relationship with the control island panel.
3. Connect the control rods to the transmission.
4. Check adjustment by shifting through the gear ranges.

Tilt Cab (w/One-Piece Shift Rod)

1. Shift the transmission into NEUTRAL, and tilt the cab forward.
2. Remove the lock wire and set screw from the U-joint at the shift rod.
3. Secure the gearshift lever to maintain a 90 degree angle between the lower end of the lever and the control island shift mechanism. Adjust the position of both U-joints to retain the 90 degree angle.
4. Install the set screw and the lock wire.

Tilt Cab (w/Two-Piece Shift Rod)

NOTE: This operation is similar to the one for tilt cabs equipped with a one-piece shift rod. The only difference is the point of adjustment. On vehicles equipped with the two-piece shift rod, the adjustment is made by loosening the adjusting clamp to achieve the 90 degree gearshift lever angle, and then tightening the clamp to retain the angle.

Auxiliary Transmissions

The spicer auxiliary transmission is supported at the front by a support bracket attached to the frame side rails and at the rear by a support beam attached to frame brackets. The gears are shifted by a lever in the cab, which is interconnected to

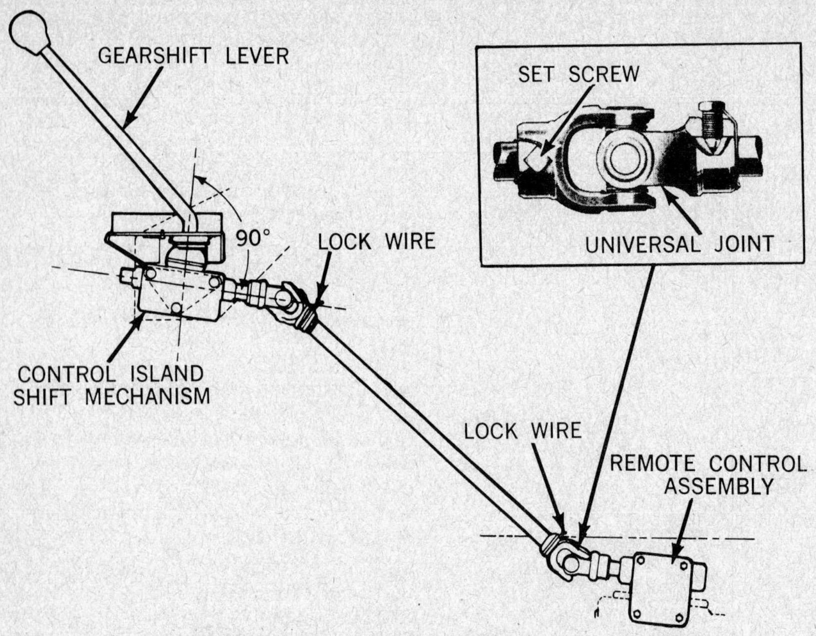

Gearshift linkage—w/two piece shift rod—tilt cab models
(© Chevrolet Div., G.M. Corp.)

the auxiliary transmission with control rods. The hand brake and speedometer drive gear are located at the rear of the transmission.

Removal

1. Drain the lubricant.
2. Disconnect and support the propeller shafts from the input and output ends of the transmission.
3. Disconnect the shift control rods from the front of the transmission.
4. Disconnect the speedometer cable from the adapter at the rear of the transmission.
5. Disconnect the parking brake linkage if applicable.
6. Remove all connections to the auxiliary transmission power take-off.
7. Place a suitable dolly or jack under the transmission and adjust its position so it can safely carry the weight.
8. Disconnect the front and rear mountings and lower the transmission away from the chassis.

Installation

1. Make sure the tapered surface of the front mount face the front of the vehicle as shown in the illustration.
2. Move the transmission into position under the vehicle and adjust the front and rear height. (See alignment Data Chart)
3. Torque the attaching parts to the proper specifications (See
4. Reconnect the propeller shafts to the input and output ends of the transmission.

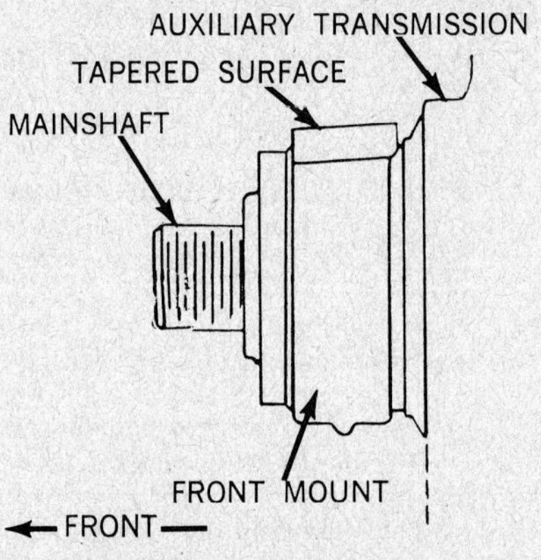

Front mount installed
(© Chevrolet Div., G.M. Corp.)

NOTE: It is important that all angles of the driveline be checked with a bevel protractor. Also the auxiliary transmission must be the same as the engine and main transmission. Adjustments may be made by raising or lowering the front or rear of the auxiliary transmission or by adding plates, washers spacers etc. (See Drive shaft alignment in U-joints-Drive Line Section.

5. Connect the power take-off if applicable.
6. Connect the parking brake linkage.
7. Connect the speedometer cable to the adapter at the rear of the transmission.
8. Connect the shift control rods and adjust if necessary.
9. Refill the transmission with the recommended lubricant.

Shift Linkage Adjustment

Auxiliary Transmission

SP6041 & SP7041

1. Disconnect the control rods from the shift control tower under the cab.
2. Place the auxiliary transmission gearshift lever and shift rods in the "Neutral" position.
3. Adjust the length of each control rod by rotating its adjustable clevis to provide a free clevis pin fit.
4. Reconnect the control rods to the control tower and shift the transmission through its entire shift pattern.
5. Replace any worn or damaged cotter pins, tighten the locknuts firmly and lubricate the control linkage.

Auxiliary Transmission AT1202

1. Remove the clevis pin, and disconnect the control rod from the shift lever.

   NOTE: Make sure that the shift lever mounting bracket bolts are tight.
2. Place the transmission shift rail in the NEUTRAL position.
3. While holding the lower end of the shift lever in a 90 degree angle relationship with the cab floor, adjust the clevis position on the threaded end of the shift rod to provide for free clevis pin entry.
4. Install the clevis pin and cotter pin.
5. Check the transmission shifting operation.

   NOTE: Check for free pin rotation in each gear. If the pin does not turn freely, then a bind-

MODELS	ENGINE	MAIN TRANSMISSION	AUXILIARY TRANSMISSION	FRONT MOUNTING	DIMENSION "A" INCHES	REAR MOUNTING	DIMENSION "A" INCHES
ME65	366 V-8	NP542 CL285V	SP6041	View A	2-1/2	View B	3-1/4 (3-3/16 W/209"WB)
ME65	427 V-8	CL325V SP5652B NP7590	SP7041	View B	3-7/16 (2-7/8 W/209"WB)	View B	4

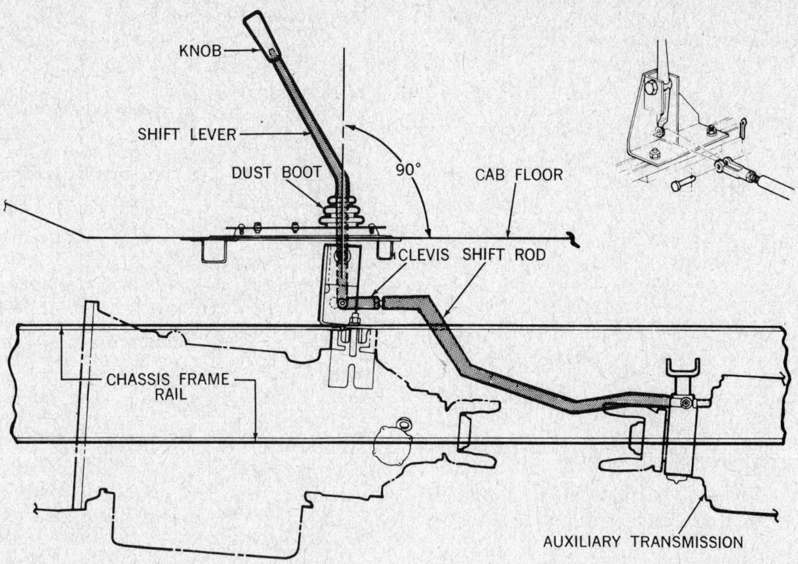

Gearshift linkage—auxiliary transmission AT-1202 (© Chevrolet Div., G.M. Corp.)

ing condition exists. Readjust the clevis if necessary.

6. Tighten the jam nut against the clevis, and spread the cotter pin ends to retain the pin.

AUTOMATIC TRANSMISSION

See specific chapter in General Repair Section for overhaul procedures for each make.

Transmission

Removal and Installation

CAUTION: **The temperature of the transmission fluid, after the vehicle has been in operation, can exceed 350 degrees F.**

Turbo Hydra-Matic 350 (Except 4 Wheel Drive)

Removal

1. With vehicle on hoist drain by removing pan or drain plug (if so equipped). *NOTE: Fluid can be drained after transmission is removed if so desired.*
2. Remove the vacuum modulator line and speedometer cable from the transmission and secure out of way.
3. Remove detent cable and manual control lever from the transmission.
4. Disconnect the drive shaft and remove.
5. Place suitable jack or other support under transmission and secure transmission to it.
6. At transmission extension disconnect rear engine mount and then remove support crossmember.
7. Remove converter underpan. Place marks on the flywheel and converter to insure proper installation and then remove the flywheel-to-converter bolts.
8. Support engine at oil pan rail with jack capable of supporting the weight of the engine when transmission is removed.
9. Lower rear of the transmission slightly so that upper, housing-to-engine, transmission bolts can be reached with a long extension and universal socket. Remove upper bolts. *NOTE: Have an assistant watch upper engine parts to make sure everything clears when rear of transmission is being lowered.*
10. Remove remaining transmission-to-housing bolts.
11. Remove transmission by moving it slightly to the rear and downward. Remove from under vehicle.

CAUTION: **Watch converter when removing transmission to be sure that it moves with transmission. If it does not move pry it free from flywheel before proceeding any further.**

NOTE: On those vehicles so equipped, disconnection of the catalytic converter may be necessary to provide adequate clearance for transmission removal.

NOTE: Keep transmission front upward when removing transmission to prevent converter from falling out. Install converter holding tool after removal from engine.

For overhaul procedures—see General Repair Section.

Installation

1. Mount transmission on transmission lifting equipment installed on jack or other lifting device.
2. Remove converter holding tool. **CAUTION: Do not permit converter to move forward after removal of holding tool.**
3. Raise transmission into place at rear of engine and install transmission case to engine upper mounting bolts, then install remainder of the mounting bolts.
4. Remove support from beneath engine, then raise rear of transmission to final position.
5. If scribed during removal, align scribe marks on flywheel and converter cover. Install converter to flywheel attaching nuts and bolts.
6. Install converter underpan.
7. Reinstall transmission support crossmember to transmission and frame.
8. Remove transmission lift equipment.
9. Connect propeller shaft to transmission.
10. Connect manual control lever rod and detent cable to transmission.
11. Connect vacuum modulator line. and speedometer drive cable to transmission.
12. Lower vehicle.
13. Refill transmission.
14. Check transmission for proper operation and for leakage. Check and, if necessary, adjust linkage.
15. Remove vehicle from hoist.

Turbo Hydra-Matic 350 (4 Wheel Drive)

Removal

1. With vehicle on hoist drain by removing pan or drain plug (if so equipped). *NOTE: Fluid can be drained after transmission removal if so desired.*
2. Remove shift lever and rod from transfer case.
3. Remove speedometer cable and vacuum modulator line from transmission and secure out of way.
4. Disconnect detent cable and manual control lever rod from transmission.
5. Remove front and rear drive shafts from transfer case.
6. Place jack or other support under transfer case and remove transmission - to - adapter case bolts.
7. Place jack or other support under transmission and secure transmission to it.
8. Remove transfer case-to-frame bracket bolts and remove transfer case.
9. On V8 engines remove exhaust crossover pipe.

10. Disconnect and remove rear transmission crossmember.
11. Remove converter underpan. Place marks on the flywheel and converter to insure proper installation and then remove the flywheel-to-converter bolts.
12. Support engine at oil pan rail with jack capable of supporting engine weight when transmission is removed.
13. Lower rear of transmission slightly so that upper housing-to-engine transmission bolts can be removed with a long extension and universal socket. Remove upper bolts. *NOTE: Have an assistant watch upper engine parts to make sure everything clears when transmission is lowered.*
14. Remove the remaining transmission-to-housing bolts.
15. Remove the transmission by moving it slightly to the rear and downward. Remove from under vehicle.

CAUTION: Watch converter when removing transmission to make sure converter moves with transmission. If it does not, pry it loose from flywheel before proceeding any further.

NOTE: Keep transmission front upwards when removing from engine to prevent converter holding tool after removal from engine. See General Repair Section for overhaul procedures.

Installation

1. Mount transmission on transmission lifting equipment installed on jack or other lifting device.
2. Remove converter holding tool. **CAUTION: Do not permit converter to move forward after removal of holding tool.**
3. Raise transmission into place at rear of engine and install transmission case to engine upper mounting bolts, then install remainder of the mounting bolts.
4. Remove support from beneath engine, then raise rear of transmission to final position.
5. If scribed during removal, align scribe marks on flywheel and converter cover. Install converter to flywheel attaching bolts.
6. Install flywheel cover.
7. Place transfer case and adapter assembly at rear of transmission on suitable lift equipment and install transfer case to frame bracket attaching bolts.
8. Reinstall transmission to transfer case adapter attaching bolts and remove lift equipment.
10. Connect front and rear axle propeller shafts to transfer case.
11. Install exhaust system cross pipe.

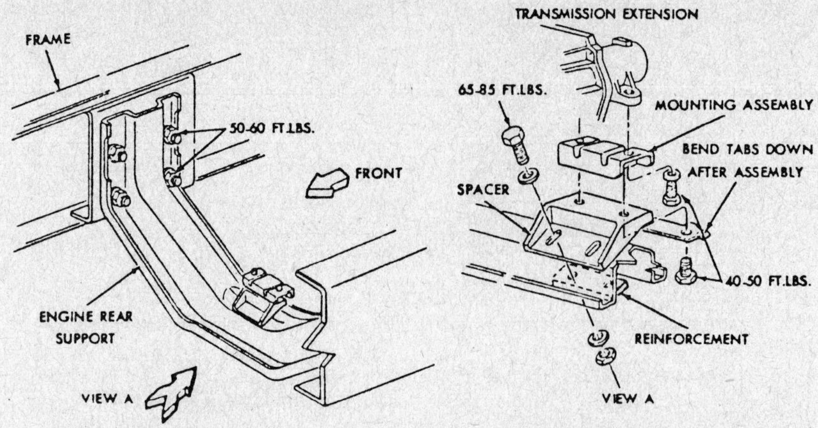

Engine rear mounting—AT-475 tranmission (© Chevrolet Div., G.M. Corp.)

12. Connect manual control lever rod and detent cable to transmission.
13. Connect vacuum modulator line and speedometer drive cable to transmission.
14. Assemble rod on transfer case shift lever before installing rod to transfer case shift linkage.
15. Lower vehicle.
16. Refill transmission.
17. Check transmission for proper operation and for leakage. Check, and if necessary, adjust linkage.
18. Remove from hoist.

Turbo Hydra-Matic 400/475

Removal and Installation

Before raising the truck, disconnect the battery and release the parking brake.

1. Raise truck on hoist.
2. Remove propeller shaft.
3. Disconnect speedometer cable, electrical lead to case connector, vacuum line at modulator, and oil cooler pipes.

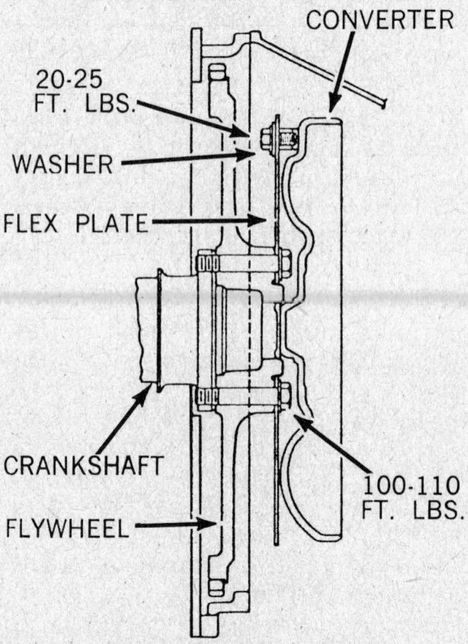

Flex plate installed—AT-475 transmission w/V6 engines (© Chevrolet Div., G.M. Corp.)

4. Disconnect shift control linkage.
5. Support transmission with transmission jack.
6. Disconnect rear mount from frame crossmember.
7. Remove two bolts at each end of frame crossmember and remove crossmember.
8. Remove converter under pan.
9. Remove converter to flywheel bolts.
10. Loosen exhaust pipe to manifold bolts approximately ¼ inch, and lower transmission until jack is barely supporting it.
11. Remove transmission to engine mounting bolts and remove oil filler tube at transmission.
12. Raise transmission to its normal position, support engine with jack and slide transmission rearward from engine and lower it away from vehicle.

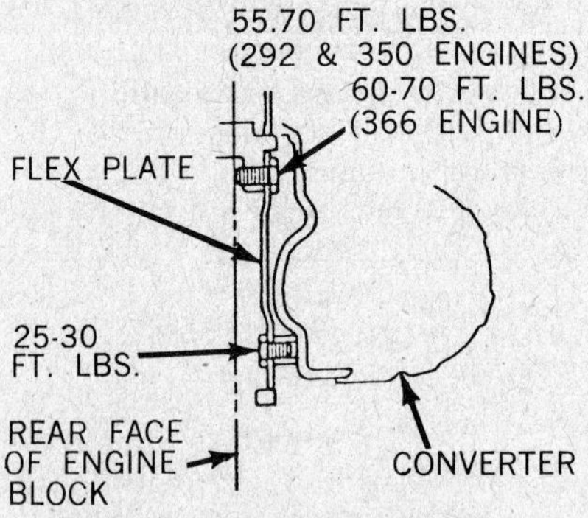

Flex plate installed—AT-475 transmission (all except V6 engines) (© Chevrolet Div., G.M. Corp.)

CAUTION: Use converter holding tool when lowering transmission or keep rear of transmission lower than front so as not to lose converter.

The installation of the transmission is the reverse of the removal with the following additional steps.

Before installing the flex plate to converter bolts, make certain that the weld nuts on the converter are flush with the flex plate and the converter rotates freely by hand in this position. Then, hand start all three bolts and tighten finger tight before torquing to specification. This will insure proper converter alignment.

NOTE: After installation of transmission check linkage for proper adjustment and check for leaks.

Draining and Refilling Automatic Transmission

Turbo Hydra-Matic 350, 375/400/475

CAUTION: The temperature of the transmission fluid, after the vehicle has been in operation, can exceed 350 degrees F.

1. Raise the vehicle and support safely.
2. Place a fluid receptacle under the transmission pan. Remove the pan attaching bolts from the front and side of the pan.
3. Loosen the rear pan attaching bolts approximately four turns and pry the pan loose to allow the fluid to drain.
4. Remove the remaining pan screws and remove the pan and gasket. Discard the gasket.
5. Remove the strainer to valve body screws and remove the strainer (filter) and gasket and discard.

NOTE: On the 400/475 transmissions, remove the filter retaining bolt, filter, and intake pipe O ring. When installing, replace the filter and the intake pipe O ring. Tighten the retaining bolt to 10 ft. lbs.

6. Install the new strainer and gasket and install the strainer to valve body screws and tighten.
7. Install a new gasket on the oil pan and install the oil pan. Tighten the pan bolts to 12 ft. lbs. torque. Connect and tighten the filler tube.
8. Lower the vehicle and install 2.5 quarts of transmission fluid into the transmission and start the engine.
9. Move the selector lever through the detents for each range. Add fluid to bring the level to 1/4 inch below the ADD mark on the dipstick.

Turbo Hydra-Matic 350, 400, 475

Shift Linkage Adjustment

Cabs, Suburbans, 4-wheel drive 1974 and Later—Forward Control exc. Vans

1. Place gearshift lever in Drive (D), as determined by transmission detent. Obtain Drive position by rotating transmission lever counterclockwise to low

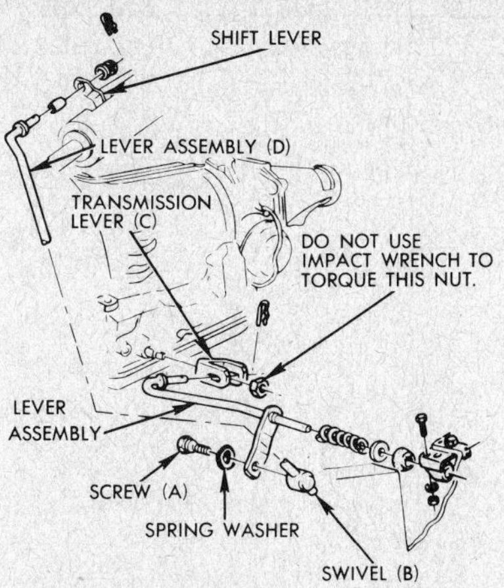

Turbo-Hydramatic control rod linkage—C & K models
(© Chevrolet Div., G.M. Corp.)

detent, then clockwise two detent positions to Drive.

2. Loosen adjustment swivel at mast jacket lever and rotate transmission lever so that it contacts the Drive stop in the steering column.
3. Tighten swivel and recheck adjustment.
4. Readjust indicator pointer, if necessary, to agree with transmission detent positions.
5. Readjust Neutral safety switch if necessary.

1973—Forward Control 1973-74—Vans

1. Set transmission lever in Drive position. Obtain Drive position by rotating transmission lever counter-clockwise to Low detent, then clockwise two detent positions to Drive.
2. Attach control rod to lever and shaft assembly with retainers.
3. Assemble ring, washers, grommet, swivel, retainer and nut loosely on shaft.
4. Insert control rod in swivel and retainer, attach opposite end to tube and lever assembly.
5. Set tube lever assembly in Drive position and tighten nut.

NOTE: When above procedure is done, the following conditions must be met by manual operation of the gearshift lever. From Reverse to Drive position travel, the transmission detent feel must be noted and related to indicated position on dial. When in Drive and Reverse position, pull lever toward steering wheel and then release. It must drop back into position with no restriction.

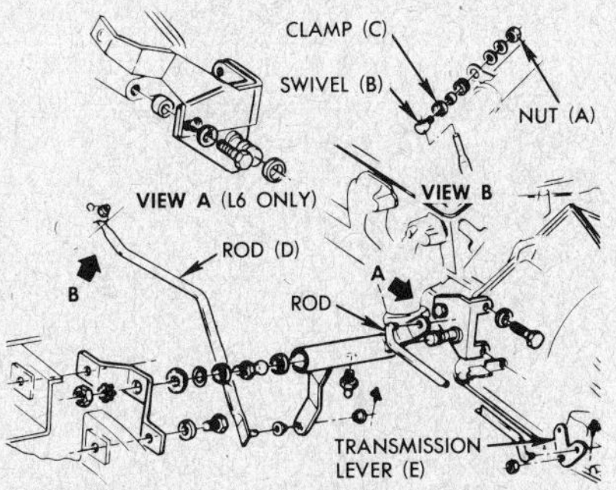

Turbo-Hydramatic control rod linkage—early G models
(© Chevrolet Div., G.M. Corp.)

1975 and Later Vans

1. The shift tube and lever assembly must be free in the mast jacket.
2. Set transmission lever (C) in "neutral" position by one of the following optional methods.

NOTE: Obtain "neutral" position by moving transmission lever (C) counter-clockwise to "LI" detent, then clockwise three detent positions to "neutral" or obtain "neutral" position by moving transmission lever (C) clockwise to the "park" detent then counter-clockwise two detents to "neutral".

3. Set the column shift lever in "neutral" position. This is obtained by rotating shift lever until it locks into mechanical stop in the column assembly.

NOTE: Do not use indicator pointer as a reference to position the shift lever.

4. Attach rod (A) to shaft assembly (B) as shown.
5. Slide swivel (D) and clamp (E) onto rod (A) align the column shift lever and loosely attach as shown.
6. Hold column lever against "neutral" stop "park" position side.
7. Tighten nut (F) to 18 foot pounds.
8. Readjust indicator needle if necessary to agree with the transmission detent positions.
9. Readjust neutral start switch if necessary to provide the correct relationship to the transmission detent positions.

CAUTION: Any inaccuracies in the above adjustments may result in premature failure of the transmission due to operation without controls in full detent position. Such operation

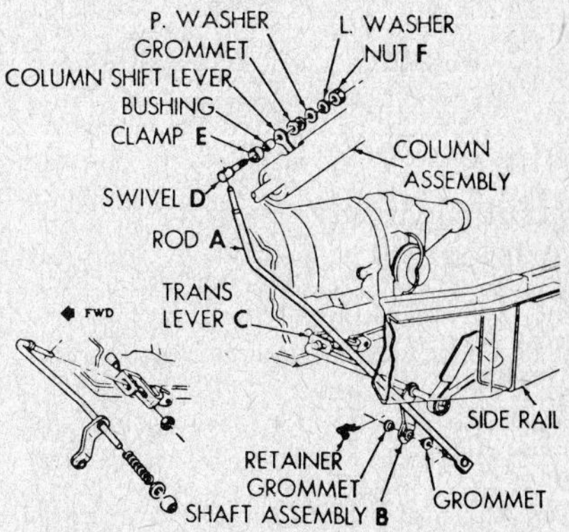

Turbo-Hydramatic control rod linkage G models—1975 and later
(© Chevrolet Div., G.M. Corp.)

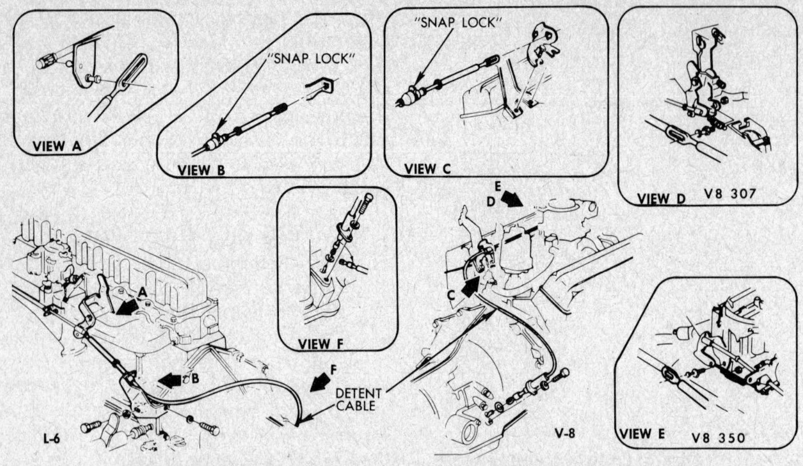

Detent cable adjustment—G models—other models similar
(© Chevrolet Div., G.M. Corp.)

results in reduced oil pressure and partial engagement of clutches.

Kickdown or Detent Switch Adjustment

Turbo Hyrda-Matic 350

1. Disengage the snap lock on the detent cable.
2. Place the carburetor in the wide open position.
3. Holding the carburetor in the wide open position, push the snap lock on the detent cable downward until the top is flush with the cable.

Turbo Hydra-Matic 400/475

A detent solenoid, activated by an electrical switch on carburetor, controls downshifts.

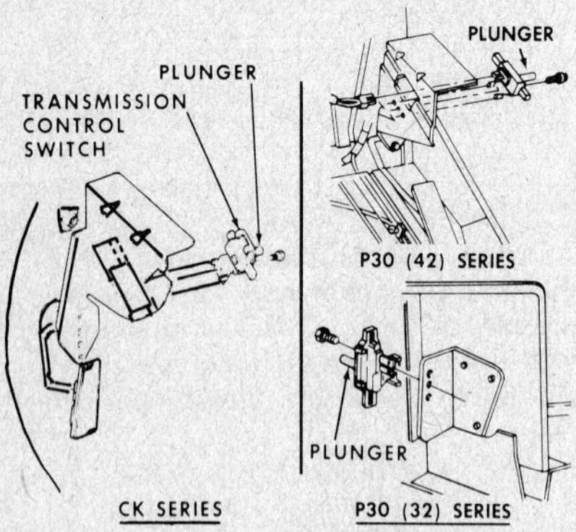

Detent switch adjustment
(© Chevrolet Div., G.M. Corp.)

Neutral Safety Switch Adjustment

Column Mounted

1. Place gearshift lever in Neutral (N).
2. Loosen retainer screws holding switch, install 3/32″ drill (or pin) through hole in lower switch arm and bracket. Adjust position of switch until engine turns over (with ignition switch in start).

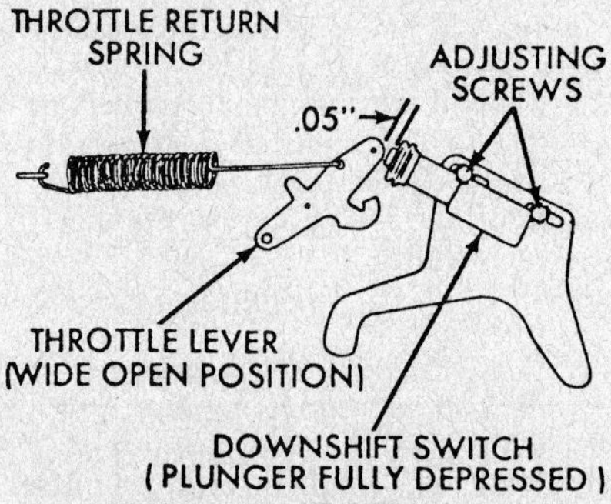

Downshift linkage AT-475 transmission
(© Chevrolet Div., G.M. Corp.)

Transmission Mounted

1. Place gearshift lever in Neutral (N), loosen transmission lever extension bolt.
2. Pin switch lever in Neutral position with 3/32″ drill or pin.
3. Install rod into switch lever, adjust swivel on rod to allow free entry of rod into lever.
4. Secure rod with retainer, tighten transmission lever extension bolt.
5. Check adjustment by testing for cranking in both Neutral and Park.

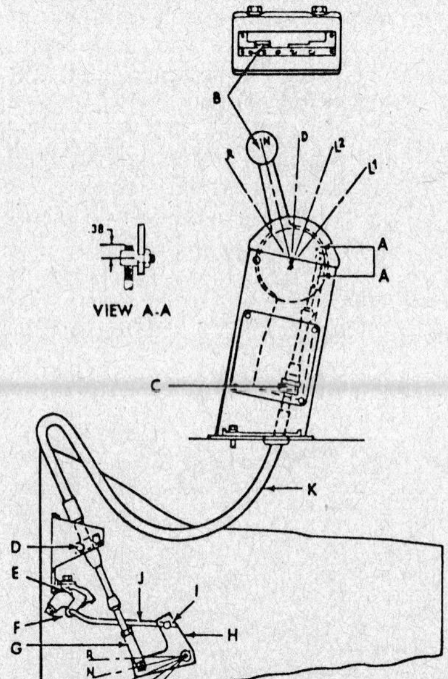

Shift linkage—AT-475 transmission
(© Chevrolet Div., G.M. Corp.)

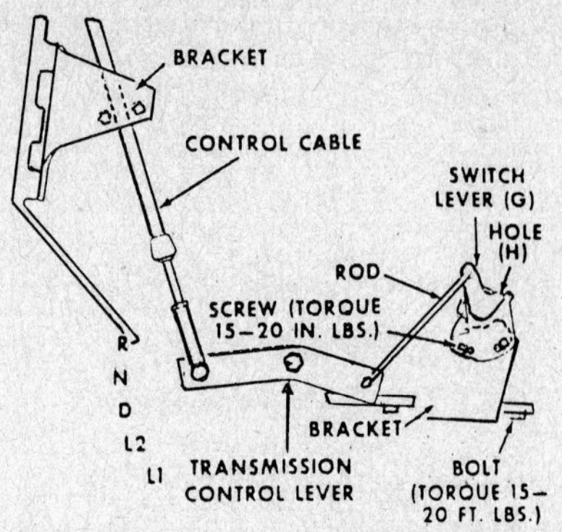

Neutral safety and back-up lamp switch 1975-76 AT-475 transmission
(© Chevrolet Div., G.M. Corp.)

Allison Transmission

Removal and Installation

AT540 Removal

NOTE: It may be necessary to remove the air tanks, fuel tanks, special equipment, etc., on some vehicles to provide clearance before the transmission is removed.

1. Block vehicle so that it cannot move. Disconnect ground strap from battery negative (—) post. Remove the spark plugs so the engine can be turned over manually.
2. Remove the level gauge (dipstick). Drain transmission by

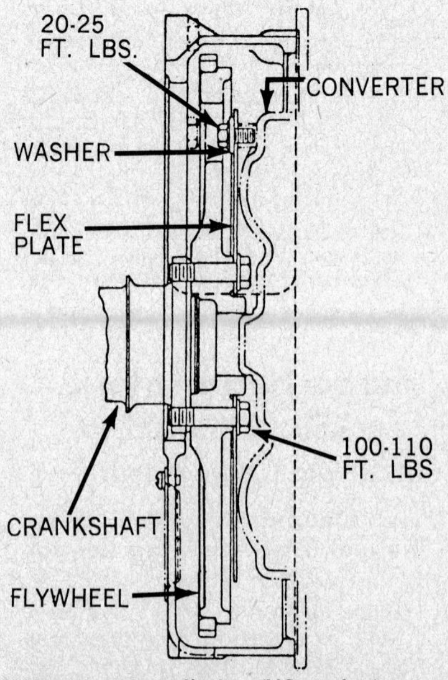

Flex plate installation (V6 engine)—AT-540 (© Chevrolet Div., G.M. Corp.)

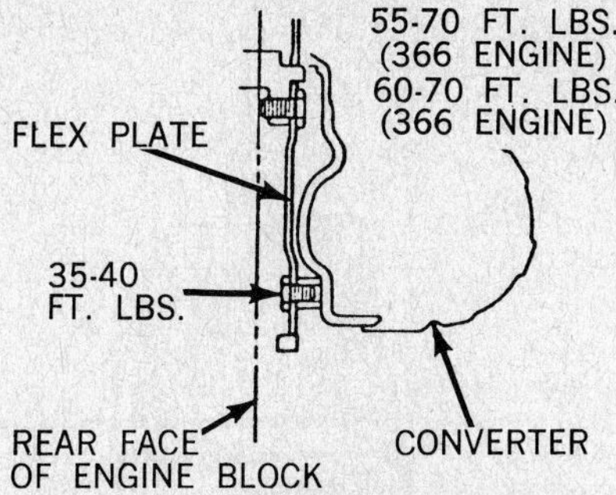

Flex plate installation (V8 engine)
AT-540 (© Chevrolet Div., G.M. Corp.)

disconnecting filler tube at right side of transmission pan. Remove bracket holding filler tube to transmission and remove filler tube from vehicle. Replace dipstick in tube and cover the pan opening to prevent entry of foreign material.

3. Disconnect cooler lines from fittings on right side of transmission case. Plug line ends and case openings with lint-free material.
4. Disconnect the range selector cable from shift lever at left-side of transmission.
5. Disconnect vacuum modulator line from modulator. Also, on conventional cab models, disconnect wiring from neutral safety and back-up lamp switches.
6. Disconnect the speedometer shaft fitting from adapter at rear of transmission.
7. Disconnect the propeller shaft from transmission.
8. Disconnect the mechanical parking brake linkage at the right side of the transmission (if used).
9. Through the opening in the flywheel housing, use a pry-bar, as necessary to manually turn the flywheel. As the flywheel is rotated, remove the six bolts retaining flywheel flex plate assembly to converter cover.
10. Support the transmission with a 500-pound (minimum) transmission floor jack. The jack must be positioned so transmission oil pan will not support the weight of transmission. Fasten a safety chain over top of transmission and to both sides of jack.
11. Place a support under rear of engine and remove transmission case - to - crossmember support bolts. Raise the engine to remove weight from the engine rear mounts.
12. Remove the transmission case-to-flywheel housing bolts and washers.
13. Carefully inspect transmission and surrounding area to be sure no lines, hoses, or wires will interfere with transmission removal.

NOTE: When removing transmission, keep rear of transmission lower than the front so as not to lose converter.

14. Move transmission assembly from the engine, lower the assembly carefully and move it out from the vehicle.

Installation

1. Raise vehicle sufficiently to allow installation of transmission. With transmission assembly mounted on transmission jack move transmission into position aligning converter with flywheel. Check for and clean away any foreign material in flywheel pilot hole, flywheel flex-plate assembly, and front face of transmission case. Rotate flywheel as necessary so that the six bolt holes in flex-plate are aligned with bolt holes in converter cover. Carefully move transmission assembly toward engine so flex-plate-to-converter cover bolts can be loosely installed and so that pilot on transmission converter enters pilot hole in center of flywheel.
2. Install bolts and washers that attach transmission case to flywheel housing. Tighten bolts to 25-30 foot-pounds torque.
3. Tighten the six flex-plate-to-converter cover bolts to 35-40 foot-pounds torque.
4. Carefully lower engine and transmission assembly onto engine rear mounts. Tighten engine rear mounting bolts to 60-70 foot-pounds torque. Then bend lock tabs down over head of each bolt. Remove lifting equipment from beneath vehicle.
5. Remove plugs from oil cooler lines and transmission case fittings. Be sure fittings are clean and lint-free, then connect oil cooler lines to transmission.
6. Install oil filler tube and bracket on right side of transmission. Install oil level gauge (dipstick).
7. Connect the speedometer shaft fitting to adapter at rear of transmission.
8. Connect propeller shaft to transmission.
9. Connect parking brake linkage (if used) at side of transmission.
10. Connect the range selector cable to shift lever at left side of transmission.
11. Connect the vacuum modulator line to modulator. Also, on conventional cab models, connect wiring to neutral safety and back-up lamp switches.

NOTE: Make sure the ignition switch is in the off position before proceeding to the next step.

12. Install spark plugs and connect battery ground strap, previously disconnected.
13. Connect any other lines, hoses, or wires which were disconnected to aid in transmission removal.
14. Adjust the shift linkage. (see "Shift Linkage Adjustment")
15. Refill the transmission with the proper lubricant.

MT640, MT650, MT654

Removal

NOTE: It may be necessary to remove the air tanks, fuel tanks, special equipment, etc., on some vehicles to provide clearance before the transmission is removed.

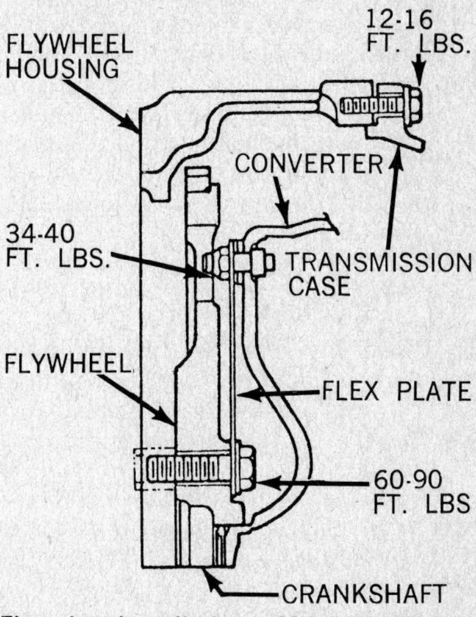

Flex plate installation—MT-640, MT-650
(© Chevrolet Div., G.M. Corp.)

1. Block vehicle so that it cannot move. Disconnect ground strap from battery negative (—) post. Remove the spark plugs so the engine can be turned over manually.
2. Remove the level gauge (dipstick). Drain transmission by disconnecting filler tube at right side of transmission pan. Remove bracket holding filler tube to transmission and remove filler tube from vehicle. Replace dipstick in tube and cover the pan opening to prevent entry of foreign materials.
3. Disconnect cooler lines from fittings on right side of transmission case. Plug line ends and case openings with lint-free material.
4. Disconnect shift cable from shift lever at left side of transmission.
5. Disconnect vacuum modulator line from modulator. Also, disconnect wiring from back-up lamp switch (right side of transmission) and neutral safety switch (left side of transmission).
6. Disconnect the speedometer shaft fitting from adapter at rear of transmission.

7. Disconnect the propeller shaft from transmission.
8. Disconnect the mechanical parking brake linkage at the right side of the transmission (if used).
9. Through access opening in the flywheel housing, use a pry bar, as necessary to manually turn the flywheel. As the flywheel is rotated, remove the six nuts retaining flex-plate assembly to converter cover.
10. Support the transmission with a 750-pound (minimum rating) transmission floor jack. The jack must be positioned so transmission oil pan will not support the weight of transmission. Fasten a safety chain over top of transmission and to both sides of jack.
11. Place a support under rear of engine and remove transmission case-to-crossmember support bolts. Raise the engine to remove weight from the engine rear mounts.
12. Remove the transmission case-to-flywheel housing bolts and washers.
13. Carefully inspect transmission and surrounding area to be sure no lines, hoses, or wires will interfere with transmission removal.

NOTE: When removing transmission keep rear of transmission lower than the front so as not to lose converter.

14. Move transmission assembly from the engine, lower the assembly carefully and move it out from the vehicle.

Installation

1. Raise vehicle sufficiently to allow installation of transmission. With transmission assembly mounted on transmission jack move transmission into position aligning converter with flywheel. Check for and clean away any foreign material in flywheel pilot hole, flex-plate assembly, and front face of transmission case. Rotate flywheel as necessary so that the six studs in converter cover are aligned with holes in flex plate. Carefully move transmission assembly toward engine so flex-plate-to-converter cover nuts can be loosely installed and so that pilot on transmission converter enters pilot hole in center of flywheel.
2. Install bolts and washers that attach transmission case-to-flywheel housing. Tighten bolts to 12-16 foot-pounds torque.
3. Tighten the six flex-plate-to-converter cover nuts to 34-40 foot-pounds torque.
4. Carefully lower engine and transmission assembly onto engine rear mounts. Tighten engine rear mounting nuts to 190-210 foot-pounds torque. Remove lifting equipment from beneath vehicle.
5. Remove plugs from oil cooler lines and transmission case fittings. Be sure fittings are clean and lint-free, then connect oil cooler lines-to-transmission.
6. Install oil filler tube and bracket on right side of transmission. Install oil level gauge (dipstick).
7. Connect the speedometer shaft fitting to adapter at rear of transmission.
8. Connect propeller shaft to transmission.
9. Connect parking brake linkage (if used) at side of transmission.
10. Connect shift cable to shift lever at left side of transmission.
11. Connect the vacuum modulator line to modulator. Also, connect wiring to neutral safety switch (left side of transmission) and back-up lamp switch (right side of transmission).

NOTE: Make sure the ignition switch is in the off position before proceeding to the next step.

12. Install spark plugs and connect battery ground strap, previously disconnected.
13. Connect any other lines, hoses, or wires which were disconnected to aid in transmission removal.
14. Adjust the shift linkage. (see "Shift Linkage Adjustment")
15. Refill the transmission with the proper lubricant.

Shift Linkage Adjustment

AT540, MT640, MT650 Transmissions

Gas and Diesel Engines

1. Disconnect clevis from transmission shift lever by removing cotter pin and clevis pin.

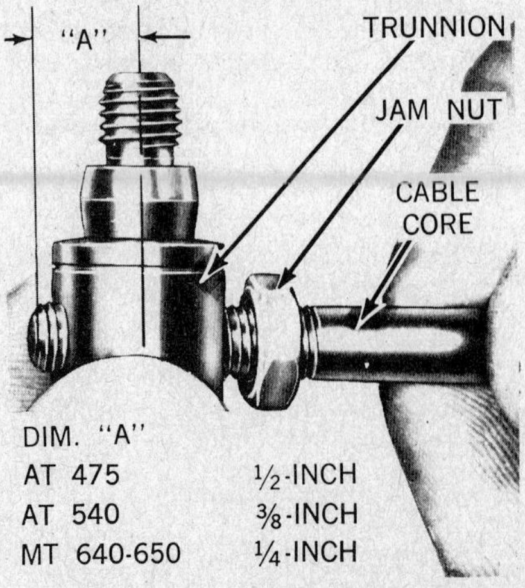

Trunnion adjustment Allison transmission (© Chevrolet Div., G.M. Corp.)

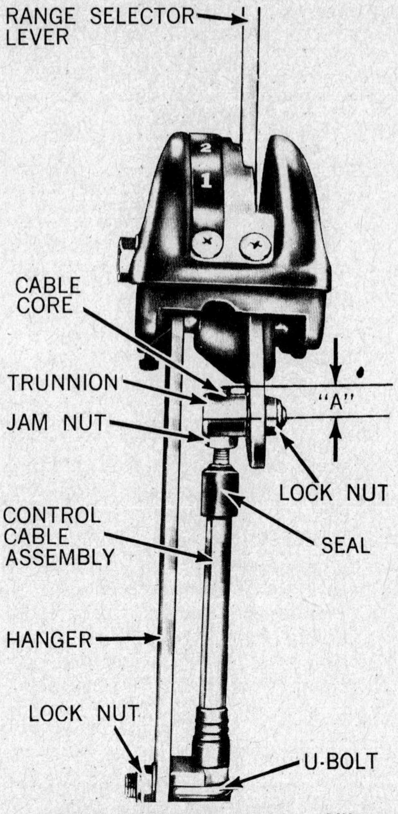

Trunnion and Cable Assembly—Allison transmission
(© Chevrolet Div., G.M. Corp.)

2. Disconnect control cable from anchor point at bracket on transmission and remove cable retainer clips from underside of cab.
3. Remove four cross recess screws retaining range selector cover to tower or bracket, depending on truck model. Lift range selector assembly out to inspect cable attachment at range selector lever and hanger.
4. Check cable at trunnion for dimension "A" as shown. This dimension is necessary to allow for proper cable length at clevis. If adjustment is necessary, remove cable from range selector lever and hanger assembly as follows:
   a. Remove ½-inch locknut from trunnion.
   b. Disconnect cable from anchor

Clevis adjustment—Allison transmission
(© Chevrolet Div., G.M. Corp.)

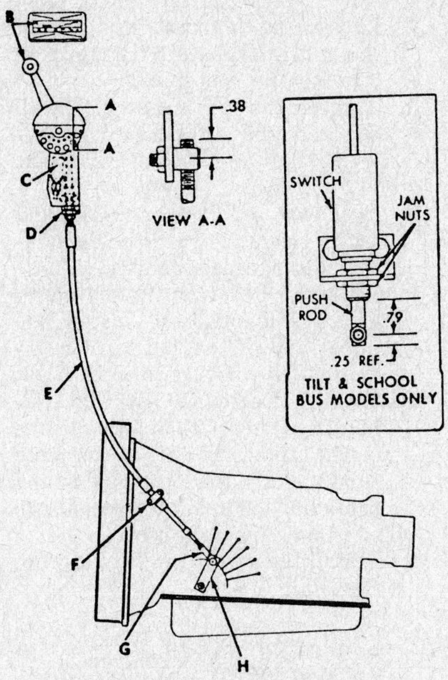

Shift linkage—AT-540 transmission
(© Chevrolet Div., G.M. Corp.)

point on hanger by removing two locknuts and U-bolt.

NOTE: Locknuts can be removed and reinstalled up to six times before their replacement becomes necessary.

c. Mark location of trunnion. Remove trunnion with attached cable core from lever.

CAUTION: **The trunnion has been placed in the proper hole at the factory. Any change in the location could cause vehicle operation to be dangerous.**

5. With control cable removed, loosen jam nut at trunnion.

NOTE: Do not use pliers on cable core when loosening jam nut or when adjusting trunnion. Cable core finish may be damaged resulting in cable core seal damage.

6. Turn trunnion clockwise, or counterclockwise to attain dimension "A". Tighten jam nut against trunnion.
7. Install trunnion in its original hole and tighten locknut securely.
8. Anchor cable to hanger with U-bolt, washers and locknuts. Tighten locknuts 3-5 foot-pounds torque.
9. Install shift control cover in tower or bracket depending on truck model. Install four cross recess screws. Tighten screws 3-5 foot-pounds torque. Install cable clips to underside of cab.
10. Anchor cable to bracket at transmission. Tighten two cross recess screws securely.
11. Locate transmission shift lever in "R" (Reverse) position.

NOTE: "R" position if full counterclockwise (except on AT 475 "full clockwise") movement of lever.

12. Locate range selector lever against stop in "R" (Reverse) position.
13. Loosen jam nut at clevis. Turn clevis clockwise or counterclockwise on threaded cable core until holes in clevis align with hole in shift lever. Install clevis pin, note that pin should enter freely, if it does not, adjust clevis slightly by $1/2$ turn in each direction until pin does enter freely.
14. Turn clevis one full turn clockwise to allow for cable backlash.
15. Connect clevis to shift lever with clevis pin and a new cotter pin, but do not spread cotter pin at this time.
16. Move the range selector lever through all drive ranges. The transmission detents should fully engage just before the range selector lever hits the stops incorporated in the shift control cover.

Model MT 654

NOTE: If the shift linkage can not be adjusted satisfactorily, it may be necessary to replace the shift linkage cable.

1. Move the range selector against the stop in the REVERSE postion.
2. Remove the cotter pin from the shift lever clevis, and disconnect the clevis.
3. Place the shift lever in the REVERSE position.
4. Loosen the jam nut, and turn the clevis until the holes in the clevis align with the hole in the shift lever. The clevis pin should install easily.
5. Turn the clevis one full turn clockwise to allow for cable backlash.
6. Connect the clevis pin to the shift lever. Install the clevis pin and the cotter pin.
7. Check shifter operation.

NOTE: The transmission detents should fully engage just before the range selector lever contacts the stops in the shift control cover.

Throttle Valve Linkage Adjustment

Early Models

1. Apply parking brake and block vehicle's driving wheels.
2. Disconnect upper TV cable end from accelerator cross shaft.
3. Push upper cable end toward transmission modulator until seated against the stop.
4. Assemble slotted clevis end to cable with locknut.
5. With accelerator linkage in "IDLE" position, upper end of the slotted clevis must be against the clevis pin on the cross shaft lever.
6. Shorten cable at slotted clevis by turning clevis three complete turns clockwise to locate lower end of the cable in actuator $1/8$-inch from idle stop.
7. Tighten locknut securely.
8. Assemble slotted clevis to cross shaft lever with clevis pin and a new cotter pin.
9. Attach TV return spring to bracket.

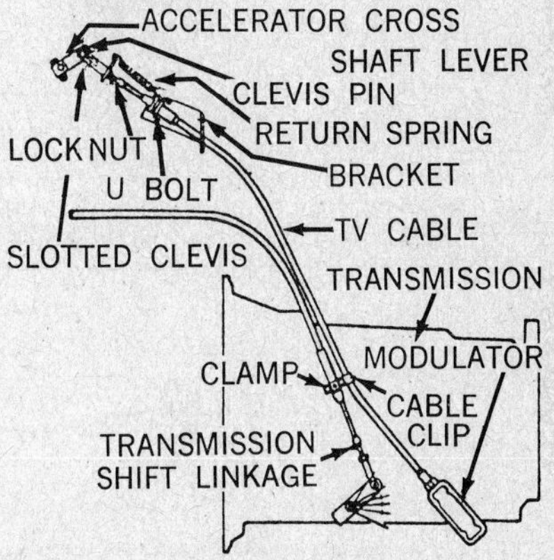

Throttle valve linkage (diesel engine)—Allison transmission
(© Chevrolet Div., G.M. Corp.)

Medium Duty Trucks w/Diesel Engine

NOTE: Make sure that the throttle

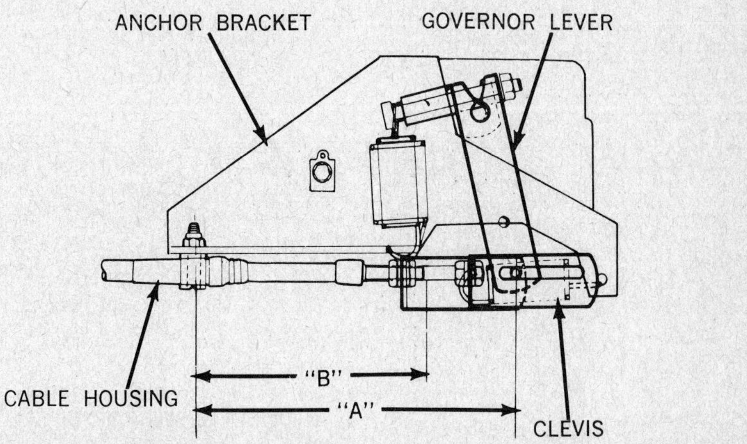

Throttle valve linkage adjustment medium duty trucks (© Chevrolet Div., G.M. Corp.)

valve cable housing is secured to the control anchor bracket.

1. Disconnect the throttle valve cable clevis from the governor lever.
2. Measure distance "A" ($6\frac{5}{8}$ inches) with the governor lever in the idle position. Adjust if necessary, and torque the clamp bolt to 9 ft. lbs.
3. Disconnect the clevis and lever return springs.
4. Move the governor lever to the full throttle position, and hold. Check for free pin entry.

   NOTE: The hole in the lever must align at the forward end of the slot with free pin entry. Adjust the position of the clevis accordingly, and tighten the jam nut against the clevis.

6. Connect the clevis and governor lever return springs. Check lever operation.

Conventional Cab Models w/Diesel Engine

NOTE: Make sure that the cable assembly is properly secured at the support bracket.

1. Disconnect the cable return spring and clevis from the bellcrank.
2. Measure distance "A": $33\frac{5}{32}$ inches—aluminum conventional cabs, and $29\frac{5}{8}$ inches—steel conventional cabs.

   NOTE: If distance "A" is correct and valve operation is normal, adjustment is not necessary.

3. Disconnect the rod end from the accelerator cross shaft lever.
4. Loosen the jam nut, and adjust the rod to the desired length by turning the rod end.
5. Tighten the jam nut, and install the rod end on the accelerator lever. Torque the attaching nut to 11 ft. lbs.
6. Push the modulator cable end (with clevis) toward the modulator, and against the stop.
7. With the bellcrank in the accelerator idle position, install the upper end of the slot (in clevis) against the clevis pin in the bellcrank. Decrease the overall length of the cable by turning the clevis adjusting nuts 3 complete turns; locate the lower end of the cable in the modulator a distance of $\frac{1}{8}$ inch from the stop.
8. Install the cotter pin through the clevis pin.

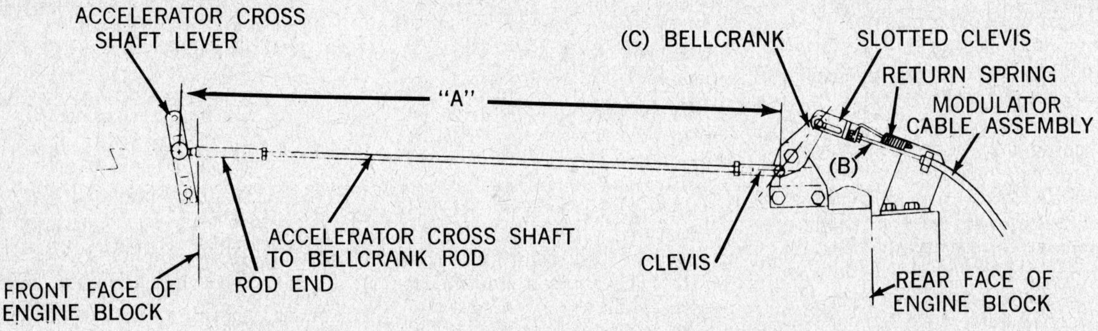

ALUMINUM CONVENTIONAL CAB MODELS W/DIESEL ENGINE

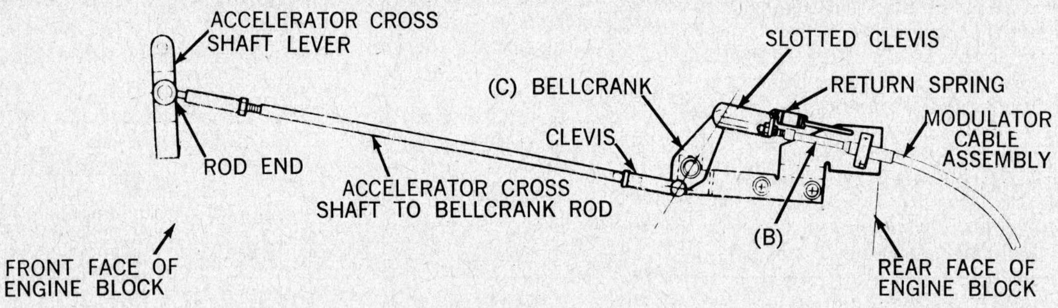

CONVENTIONAL CAB MODELS W/DIESEL ENGINE

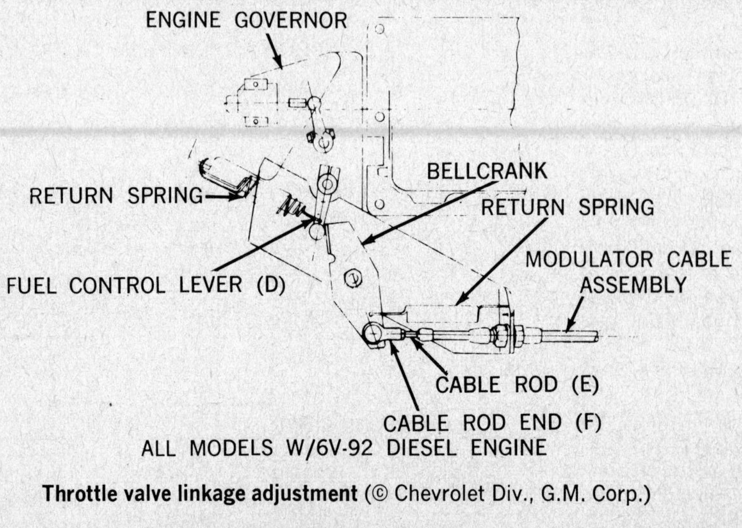

ALL MODELS W/6V-92 DIESEL ENGINE

Throttle valve linkage adjustment (© Chevrolet Div., G.M. Corp.)

9. Tighten the jam nut against the clevis, and install the return spring.
10. Check the operation of the linkage assembly.

All Models w/6V-92 Engine

NOTE: Make sure that the cable assembly is properly secured at the support bracket. Be sure that the bellcrank bolt is tight.

1. Rotate the fuel control lever to the full throttle position.
2. Pull cable "E" until it is bottomed out.
3. Adjust the cable rod end to permit free pin entry in the bellcrank.
4. Check linkage for proper return to the idle position.
5. Check cable travel "E": $1\frac{3}{16}$ inch minimum, and $1\frac{9}{16}$ inch—maximum.

Neutral Safety and Backup Lamp Switch Adjustment

Allison—(AT450) Transmission Tilt & Schoolbus Models

NOTE: "Shift Linkage Adjustment" should be performed as described previously, prior to adjustment of the neutral safety and backup lamp switch.

1. Block driving wheels, apply parking brake, and perform the following to prevent the vehicle from accidentally starting.

NOTE: Pull the secondary wire out of center socket in the distributor cap and ground wire to prevent possible damage to coil.

2. Move selector lever (B) to "N" (Neutral) position. Then, loosen jam nuts and adjust length of push rod to dimension shown.
3. With switch push rod properly adjusted, tighten jam nuts securely.
4. Check each range position of shift linkage to make sure the starter does not operate with the selector lever in any position other than "N." Have assistant check for proper operation of back-up lights with selector lever in "R." If necessary readjust switch.
5. Reconnect secondary wire to distributor cap.

NOTE: The neutral safety and back-up lamp switches are non-adjustable on the Allison-MT-640, MT-650 trans. and all diesel engines with automatic transmissions.

Fluid and Filter Changes

AT and MT Models

1. Have the transmission at normal operating temperature (160 to 220 degrees F), and the transmission in neutral.
2. Remove the fill tube from the pan or the drain plug from the right side of the transmission pan. Allow the fluid to drain into a large container.

NOTE: Do not allow the fluid to spill and splash. Burns can result.

3. Remove the pan bolts, loosen and remove the pan and gasket. Discard the gasket.
4. Remove the one screw that retains the filter, remove the filter and discard.

NOTE: Later models will have a suction tube that separates from the filter. Retain the tube for use with the new filter, the tubes will have a sealring. Replace with a new sealring upon installation.

5. To clean or replace the governor feed screen, the valve body must be removed on the AT Models, and the screen taken from the governor feed bore. Refer to the valve body removal and installation procedures outlined in the General Repair Section. The MT Models have discontinued the use of the primary governor screen, and if one is found in the governor feed tube area of the valve body, discard it.
6. The MT Models have the main governor screen located in the rear cover. Early models will have a screen to be cleaned and reinstalled while the later models will have a replaceable cartridge type filter.

NOTE: The screen or filter is inserted into the rear cover open end first.

7. Retain the screen or filter with the plug or cap.
8. Install the new filter, suction tube and seal ring in the sump area and secure with the retaining bolt. Torque to 10 to 15 ft. lbs. for the MT models and 10 to 13 ft. lbs. for the AT models.
9. Install the pan with a new gasket. Torque the pan bolts to 10 to 15 ft. lbs. for the MT models and 10 to 13 ft. lbs. for the AT models.
10. Install the filler tube or drain plug into the transmission or pan.
11. Install 10 quarts of transmission fluid into the AT models, and 15 quarts into the MT models. Start the engine, check for leaks, move the selector through the gear positions, and recheck the fluid level of the transmission and refill to the full mark on the dipstick.

DRIVESHAFT

Tubular type drive shafts and needle bearing type universal joints are used on all model trucks. An internally splined sleeve which compensates for variation in distance between rear axle and transmission is located at the forward end of single or rear shafts.

The number of shafts used is dependent upon the wheel base of the vehicle. On vehicles which use two or more shafts, each shaft (except the rear) is supported near its splined end in a rubber cushioned ball bearing which is mounted in a bracket attached to a frame cross member. The ball bearing is a permanently sealed and lubricated type.

An extended-life universal joint, which does not require periodic inspection and lubrication, has been incorporated in several applications on the 10 and 20 series vehicles.

This extended-life universal joint is identified by the absence of the lubrication fitting, which is present on all trunnions not equipped with the extended-life feature.

A lubrication fitting is also pro-

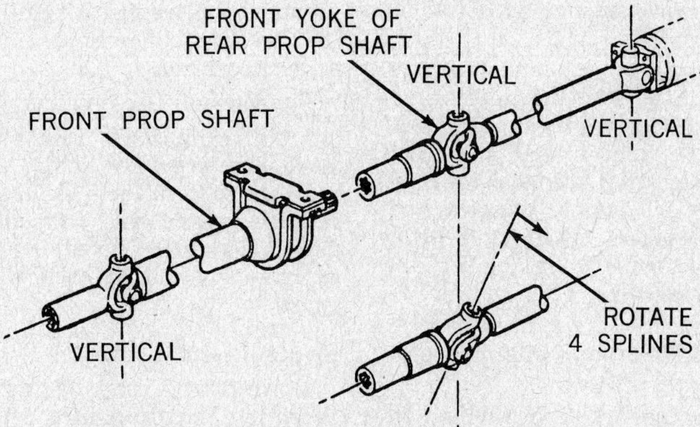

Aligning universal joints (© Chevrolet Div., G.M. Corp.)

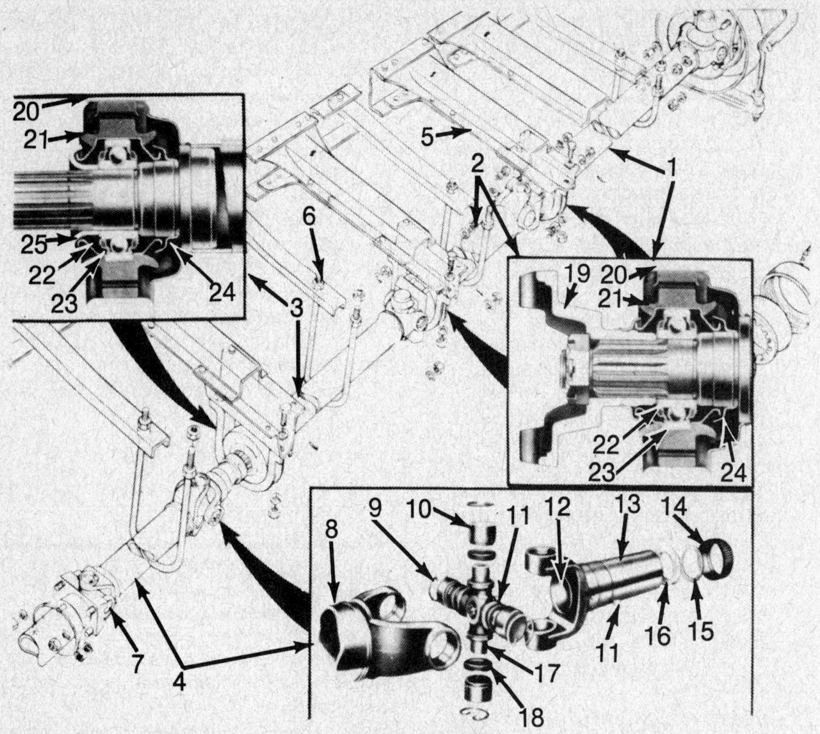

Propeller shafts, universal joints and bearing supports (© Chevrolet Div., G.M. Corp.)

1 Front propeller shaft and bearing support assy.
2 Front intermediate propeller shaft and bearing support assy.
3 Rear intermediate shaft and bearing support assy.
4 Rear propeller shaft and sleeve assy.
5 Frame crossmember
6 Guard
7 "U" clamp
8 Rear propeller shaft
9 Lock ring
10 Bearing assembly
11 Lubrication fitting
12 Plug
13 Sleeve
14 Retainer
15 Washer
16 Cork packing
17 Trunnion
18 Seal ring
19 Flange and deflector assy.
20 Bracket
21 Cushion
22 Slinger
23 Grease retainer
24 Inner deflector
25 Dust shield

vided on each sliding sleeve to lubricate the splines. A plug is staked into the yoke end of sleeve to retain lubricant and a small hole is drilled in the end of this plug to relieve trapped air. The opposite end of the sleeve is sealed by means of a cork packing in a retainer which screws on the end of the sleeve.

Shaft Removal

Single or Rear

Remove rear trunnion "U" clamps, lower the rear of shaft and pull back to disengage the sleeve at front of shaft. Remove shaft from under vehicle.

Front

Remove four front flange nuts at transmission and, if equipped with intermediate shaft, remove the rear trunnion "U" clamps. Remove nuts and lock washers attaching bearing support to frame crossmember and pull shaft assembly from vehicle.

Intermediate or Rear Intermediate Shaft

Remove the front trunnion "U" clamps and the bearing support mounting bolt nuts and lock washers. Lower the front of the shaft and pull forward to disengage splines at rear of shaft. Remove shaft and bearing support assembly from under vehicle.

Front Intermediate Shaft

Remove the front and rear trunnion "U" clamps and the bearing support mounting bolt nuts and lock washers. Lower shaft and bearing support assembly from vehicle.

Inspection

Wash ends of propeller shaft in cleaning solvent, inspect for damage and excessive wear on splines, trunnions and bearings. Examine sleeve seal, washer and retainer for damage or deterioration.

CAUTION: When trunnion bearing "U" clamps are removed to remove the propeller shaft, tape the bearings to keep them clean and from becoming damaged. Propeller shaft guards may be removed, if necessary, by removing nut at each end of the guard.

Shaft Installation

Drive shafts may be installed by reversing the procedure used in removal when the following notes are observed.

NOTE 1: Before installing a rear shaft and sleeve assembly, slide seal retainer, steel washer and cork seal on spline of mating shaft. Assemble these parts to sleeve by turning retainer onto sleeve after rear propeller shaft is installed.

NOTE 2: Over torquing "U" clamp nuts will result in bearing cap distortion which will reduce roller bearing life.

NOTE 3: To prevent excessive driveline vibration on some models, the rear propeller shaft must be installed so that centerline of sleeve yoke is positioned from vertical to 7 splines clockwise from vertical. The centerline of either yoke at the transmission end is perpendicular to the ground.

NOTE 4: The shaft to pinion flange fastener is an important attaching part in that it could affect the performance of vital components and systems and/or could result in major repair expense. It must be replaced with one of the same part number or with an equivalent part if replacement becomes necessary. Do not use a replacement part of lesser quality or substitute design. Torque values must be used as specified during reassembly to assure proper retention of this part.

Universal Joints

Snap Ring Type

Disassembly

1. Remove trunnion bearings from propeller shaft yoke as follows:
   a. Remove lock rings from yoke and lubrication fitting from trunnion.
   b. Support yoke in a bench vise.
   c. Using soft drift and hammer, drive on one trunnion bearing to drive opposite bearing from yoke.
   NOTE: The bearing cap cannot be driven completely out.
   d. Grasp cap in vise and work out.
   e. Support other side of yoke and drive other bearing cap from yoke and remove as in step d.
   f. Remove trunnion from propeller shaft yoke.
2. If equipped with sliding sleeve, remove trunnion bearings from sleeve yoke in the same manner as above. Remove seal retainer from end of sleeve and pull seal and washer from retainer.

Assembly

1. Assemble trunnion bearings to propeller shaft as follows:
   a. On extended life universal joints when performing service operations that require disassembly of the universal joint, repack bearings with grease as outlined in NOTE

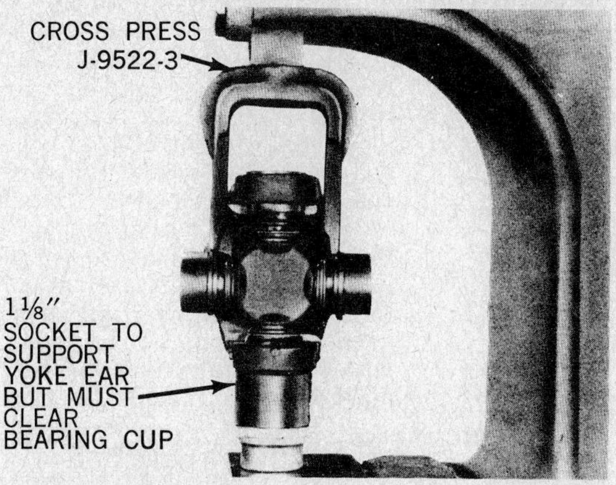

Pressing out bearing cup—plastic retaining ring type (© Chevrolet Div., G.M. Corp.)

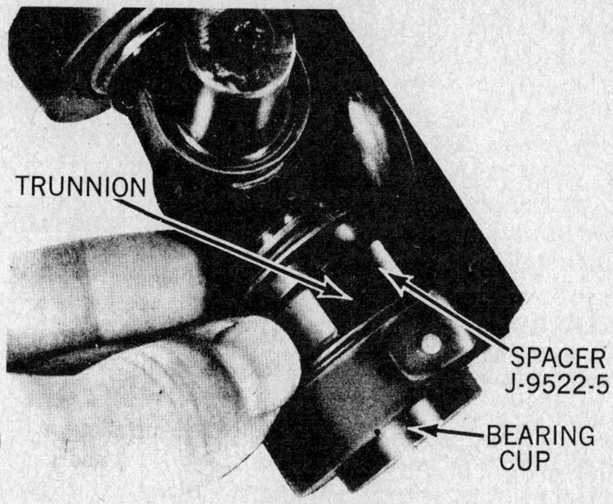

Using spacer to remove bearing cup—plastic retaining ring type (© Chevrolet Div., G.M. Corp.)

below and replace trunnion assembly dust seals.

b. On all other universal joints lubricate trunnion bearing rollers and install new seal rings.

c. Insert trunnion in propeller shaft yoke and press bearings into yoke and over trunnion hubs far enough to install lock rings.

d. Hold trunnion in one hand and tap propeller shaft yoke lightly to seat bearings against lock rings.

2. On rear propeller shafts, install sleeve yoke over trunnion hubs and install bearings in the same manner as above.

NOTE: In addition to packing the bearings, make sure the lubricant reservoir at the end of each trunnion is completely filled with lubricant. In filling these reservoirs, pack lubricant into the hole so as to fill from the bottom. This will prevent air pockets and ensure an adequate supply of lubricant

To replace trunnion dust seal, remove the old dust seal and place new seal on trunnion—cavity of seal toward end of trunnion—Press seal onto trunnion exercising caution during installation to prevent seal distortion and to assure proper seating of seal on trunnion.

Plastic Retaining Ring Type

Disassembly

1. Support the drive shaft in a horizontal position in line with the base plate of a press. Place the universal joint so that the lower ear of the shaft yoke is supported on a 1⅛″ socket. Place the cross press, J-9522-3 or equivalent, on the open horizontal bearing cups, and press the lower bearing cup out of the yoke ear as shown in the illustration. This will shear the plastic retaining the lower bearing cup.
2. If the bearing cup is not completely removed, lift the cross and insert Spacer J-9522-5 or equivalent, between the seal and bearing cup being removed, as shown in figure 2.

   Complete the removal of the bearing cup, by pressing it out of the yoke.
3. Rotate the drive shaft, shear the opposite plastic retainer, and press the opposite bearing cup out of the yoke as before, using Spacer J-9522.
4. Disengage the cross from the yoke and remove.

NOTE: Production universal joints cannot be reassembled. There are no bearing retainer grooves in production bearing cups. Discard all universal joint parts removed.

5. Remove the remains of the sheared plastic bearing retainer from the ears of the yoke. This will aid in reassembly of the service joint bearing cups. It usually is easier to remove plastic if a small pin or punch is first driven through the injection
6. If the front universal joint is being serviced, remove the pair of bearing cups from the slip yoke in the same manner.

Reassembly

1. A universal joint service kit is used when reassembling this joint. This kit includes one pregreased cross assembly, four service bearing cup assemblies with seals, needle rollers, washers, grease and four bearing retainers.
2. Make sure that the seals are in place on the service bearing cups to hold the needle rollers in place for handling.

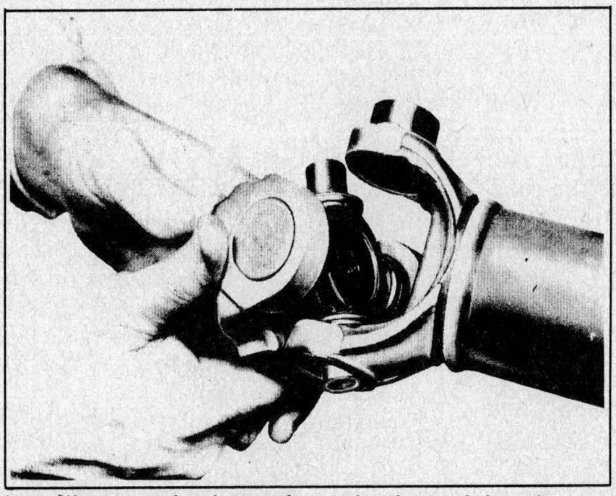

Installing trunnion into yoke—plastic retaining ring type (© Chevrolet Div., G.M. Corp.)

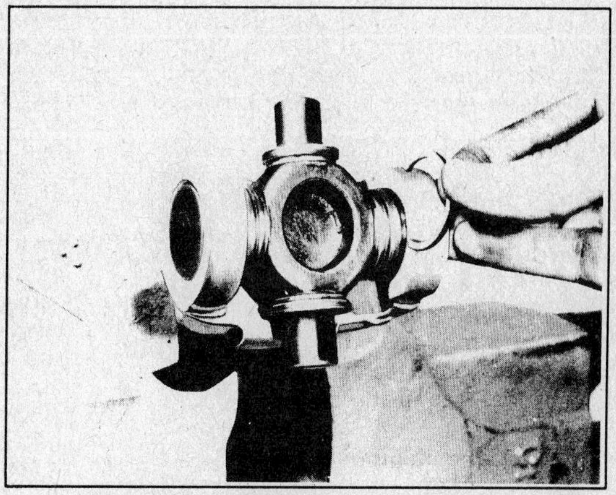

Installing snap ring to retain trunnion (© Chevrolet Div., G.M. Corp.)

3. Remove all of the remains of the sheared plastic bearing retainers from the grooves in the yokes. The sheared plastic may prevent the bearing cups from being pressed into place, and this prevents the bearing retainers from being properly sealed.
4. Install one bearing cup part way into one side of the yoke, and turn this yoke ear to the bottom.
5. Insert cross into yoke so that the trunnion seats freely into bearing cup as shown in illustration.
6. Install opposite bearing cup part way. Make sure that both trunnions are started straight and true into both bearing cups.
7. Press against opposite bearing cups, working the cross all of the time to check for free movement of the trunnions in the bearings. If there isn't, stop pressing and recheck needle rollers to determine if one or more of them has been tipped under the end of the trunnion.
8. As soon as one bearing retainer groove clears the inside of the yoke, stop pressing and snap the bearing retainer into place as shown in the illustration.
9. Continue to press until the opposite bearing retainer can be snapped into place. If difficulty is encountered, strike the yoke firmly with a hammer to aid in seating bearing retainers. This springs the yoke ears slightly.
10. Assemble the other half of the universal joint in the same manner.
11. Check the freedom of rotation of both sets of trunnions of the cross. If too tight, again rap the yoke ears as described above. This will loosen the bearings and help seat the bearing retainers.

Constant Velocity Joint

Disassembly

1. Remove front propeller shaft from vehicle.
2. Remove rear trunnion snap rings from center yoke. Remove grease fitting.
3. Place propeller shaft in vise and drive one rear trunnion bearing

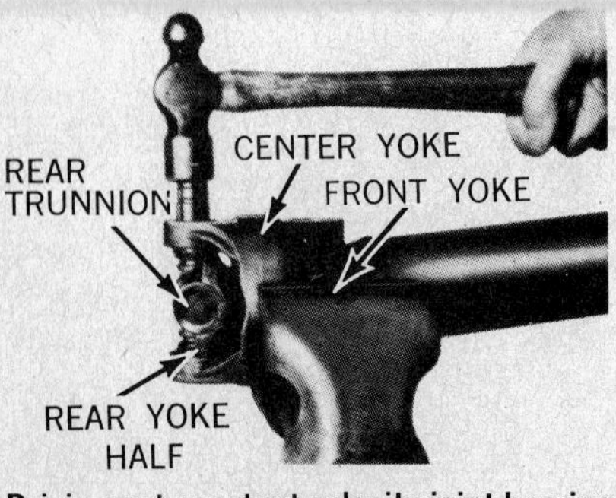

Driving out constant velocity joint bearing cups (© Chevrolet Div., G.M. Corp.)

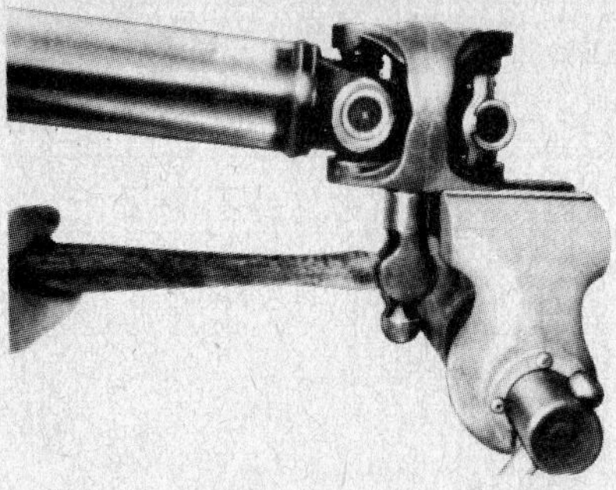
Driving yoke away from bearing cup (© Chevrolet Div., G.M. Corp.)

cap from center yoke until it protrudes approximately 3/8".

NOTE: Keep rear portion of propeller shaft up to avoid interference of rear yoke half with center yoke.

4. Once the bearing cap protrudes 3/8", release vise. Grasp protruding portion of cap in vise and drive on center yoke until cap is removed. Remove cap seal by prying off with a thin screwdriver.
5. Repeat steps 3 and 4 for remaining bearing caps.
6. Once the center yoke caps have been removed remove rear yoke half bearing caps. Remove rear trunnion.
7. Gently pull rear yoke half from propeller shaft. Remove all loose needle bearings. Remove spring seal.
8. Remove front trunnion from center and front yoke in same manner as described in Steps 2, 3 & 4.

NOTE: Before front trunnion can be removed all four (4) bearing caps must be removed.

Assembly

1. Clean and inspect all needle bearings, caps, seals, fittings, trunnions and yokes. Assemble all needle bearings in caps (27 per cap); assemble needle bearings in front yoke (28 total). Retain bearings with a heavy grease. Assemble seals to bearing caps.
2. Place front trunnion in drive shaft. Place center yoke on front trunnion. Install one bearing cap and seal assembly in front yoke. Drive in to a depth that the snap ring can be installed. Install snap ring. Install remaining cap and seal in front yoke. Install snap ring.
3. Install front trunnion bearing caps in center yoke in same manner.
4. With front trunnion completely installed, install seal on propeller shaft (large face first). Gently slip rear yoke half on propeller shaft using care not to upset rollers. Insert rear trunnion in center yoke. Install rear yoke half bearing caps on rear trunnion. Install one rear trunnion bearing cap in center yoke and press into yoke until snap ring can be installed. Install remaining cap and snap ring.
5. Before assembly is reinstalled in vehicle, grease universal at all three (3) fittings (2 conventional type and one, in rear yoke half), that requires a needle nose grease gun adapter.

Bearing Support

Removal

1. Remove dust shield, or, if equipped with flange, remove cotter pin and nut and pull flange and deflector assembly from shaft.
2. Pull support bracket from rubber cushion and pull cushion from bearing.
3. Pull bearing assembly from shaft. Remove grease retainers and slingers (if used) from bearing.
4. Remove inner deflector from shaft if replacement is necessary.

NOTE: The ball bearing is a permanently sealed and lubricated type.

Installation

1. Install inner deflector on propeller shaft, if removed, and prick punch deflector at two opposite points to make sure it is tight on shaft.
2. Pack retainers with grease. Insert a slinger (if used) inside one retainer and press this retainer over bearing outer race.
3. Start bearing and slinger assembly straight on shaft journal. Support propeller shaft and, using suitable length of pipe over splined end of shaft, press bearing and inner slinger against shoulder on shaft.
4. Install second slinger on shaft and press second retainer over bearing outer race.
5. Install dust shield over shaft, small diameter first and press into position against outer slinger or, if equipped with flange, install flange and deflector assembly as follows:
   a. Install deflector on flange, if removed, and prick punch at two opposite points to make sure it is tight on flange.
   b. Align centerline of flange yoke with centerline of propeller shaft yoke and start flange straight on splines of shaft with end of flange against slinger.
   c. Install retaining nut and tighten to 160-180 ft. lbs. torque. Install cotter pin.

6. Force rubber cushion onto bearing and coat outside diameter of cushion with brake fluid.
7. Force bracket onto cushion.

Drive Shaft Alignment

Correct drive line angles are necessary to prevent excessive torsional vibrations, especially tandem rear axle models. On some vehicles adjustable auxiliary transmission mountings are provided for adjusting the angle of the various drive line components. On vehicles not having adjustable auxiliary transmission mountings and adjustable torque rods at rear axles, proper adjustment of the angle of the drive line components must be accomplished by the use of spacers or shims at the frame crossmember or hangers. All angles must be checked with a maximum amount of exactness. The use of a bubble level is not sufficient, a bevel protractor must be used. The vehicle should be checked on a reasonably flat surface.

Clean machined surface at rear of (main) tranmission to check engine (and transmission) angle. This is the key angle and auxiliary transmission (if equipped) and rear axle pinion must be set to this angle. Make sure all drive line components from (main) transmission to rear axle are properly centered. Clean dirt and paint off machined surface of propeller shaft yoke, make sure surface is free of nicks or burrs. Set bevel protractor to zero, place protractor on yoke surface at right angle to propeller shaft and rotate shaft until bubble is centered in glass. Reposition protractor on yoke, in-line with propeller shaft, and note shaft angle.

Shaft angle must be held within a maximum of 1° less than engine. Check rear axles on machined surfaces on differential carrier housing, at right angle to pinion shaft. Make sure protractor is held straight up to

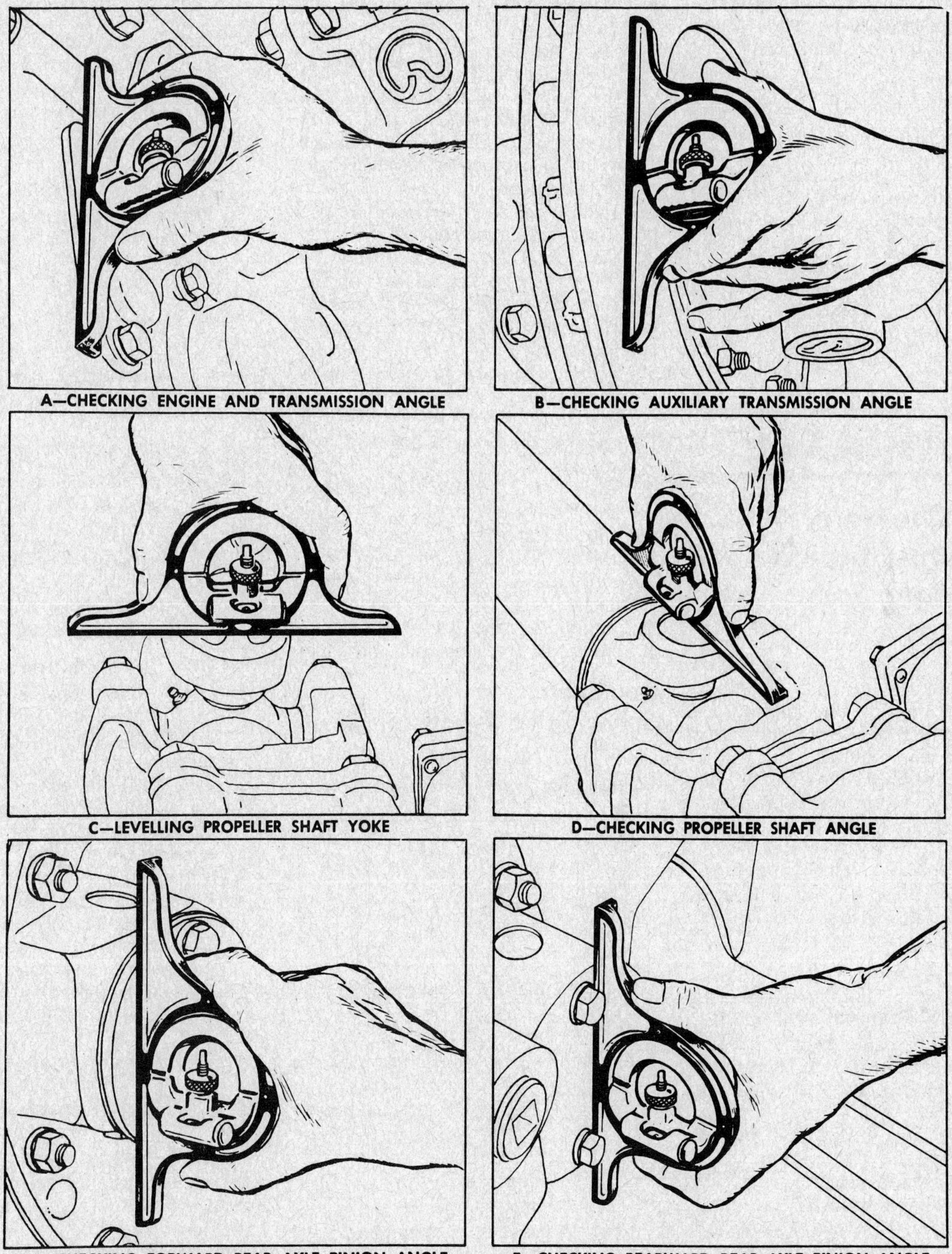

A—CHECKING ENGINE AND TRANSMISSION ANGLE

B—CHECKING AUXILIARY TRANSMISSION ANGLE

C—LEVELLING PROPELLER SHAFT YOKE

D—CHECKING PROPELLER SHAFT ANGLE

E—CHECKING FORWARD REAR AXLE PINION ANGLE

F—CHECKING REARWARD REAR AXLE PINION ANGLE

Method of checking drive line angles—typical (© Chevrolet Div., G.M. Corp.)

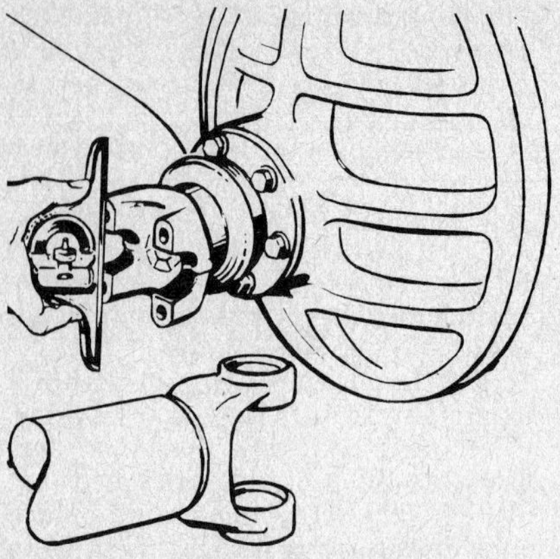

Method of checking pinion angle (single speed rear)—typical
(© Chevrolet Div., G.M. Corp.)

get correct angle. On rear axles that do not have a machined surface it will be necessary to remove propeller shaft. Rotate the pinion yoke into a vertical position, clean the four machined ends of yoke of dirt, paint, nicks and burrs. Place the protractor across ends of yoke, on either side, and in as close as possible to a vertical position. Rear axle angle should be same as engine.

REAR AXLE

Chevrolet Semi-Floating Single Speed

Two types of rear axles are used. The removable carrier type with Hotchkiss drive and the Salisbury type type with an integral carrier.

The following applies to both rear axles except where noted.

The drive pinion is mounted on two preloaded taper roller bearings. The ring gear is bolted to the differential case which is mounted on preloaded taper roller bearings. There are two side gears and two differential pinion gears.

Axle Shaft

Removal

1. Remove the brake drum.
2. Drain lubricant from the differential and remove the housing cover.
3. Remove the differential pinion shaft lock screw, pinion shaft and axle shaft spacer.
4. Push the axle shaft in and remove the "C" washer from the inner end of the axle shaft.
5. Remove the axle shaft from the housing.

Installation

NOTE: If a new axle shaft is to be installed.

1. Position the axle shaft gasket to the axle shaft flange.
2. Apply heavy shellac or paint to both sides of the gasket and axle shaft oil deflector.
3. Install the axle shaft oil deflector over the gasket aligning the oil pocket with the notch in the flange.
4. Insert six special axle shaft bolts and force the heads down to the deflector.
5. Peen the end of the shoulder on the bolts into the countersink around the bolt holes in the flange.
6. Slide the axle shaft into place.
   CAUTION: Exercise care that the splines on the end of the shaft do not cut the axle shaft oil seal and that they engage with the splines of the differential side gears.
7. Install the "C" washer on the inner end of the shaft.
8. Pry the shafts apart so that the "C" washers are seated in the counterbore in the differential side gears and install the pinion gears.
9. Select the proper axle shaft spacer to give free fit to .014" maximum clearance between the end of the axle shaft and the spacer.
10. Install the spacer and pinion shaft, locking in place with the special screw.
11. Install the axle housing cover and gasket and refill the differential.
12. Install the drum and wheel.
13. Road test for leaks and noise.

Axle Shaft (Spline Drive Type)

Removal

Procedure for removal of axle

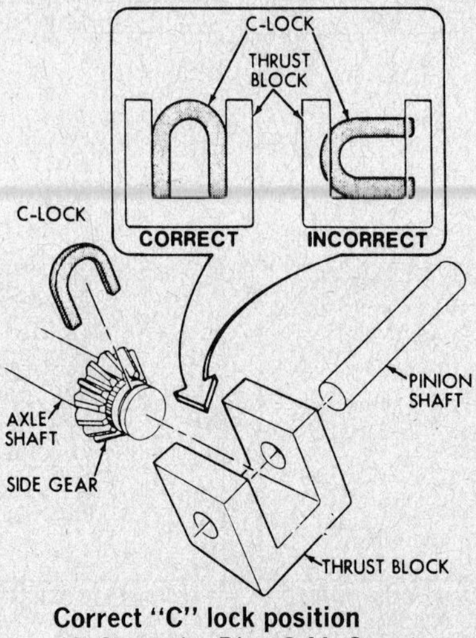

Correct "C" lock position
(© Chevrolet Div., G.M. Corp.)

shafts is same with assembly removed or installed in the vehicle.

1. Remove cap screws and hub cap from hub.
2. Install slide hammer adapter into tapped hole in axle flange.
3. Install slide hammer into adapter and remove axle shaft.

Installation

1. Dip small end of splined shaft in axle lubricant, and insert shaft into hub.
2. Turn shaft as necessary to index shaft splines with differential side gear splines. As shaft is pushed inward, rotate hub to align axle shaft flange splines to hub. Push shaft into place.
3. Install new gasket on hub cap and install hub cap to hub with cap screws. Torque cap screws 15 to 20 foot-pounds.

Axle Shaft Bearing or Oil Seal

Removal

1. Remove the wheel, drum and axle shaft (see axle shaft removal).

Bearing and oil seal removal
(© Chevrolet Div., G.M. Corp.)

2. Using a slide hammer, remove the bearing, bearing retainer and oil seal.
3. Inspect the bore and dress out the old stake points.

Installation

1. Using the proper driver, place the oil seal, bearing and inside bearing retainer on the driver in that order.
2. Place a light coat of sealer on the outside of the seal to insure proper sealing of the seal in the housing bore.
3. Start the bearing into the axle housing and tap the tool with a hammer to seat the parts.
4. Remove the driver and stake the oil seal in place with a punch.
5. Assemble the axle shafts (see Axle Shaft Installation).

Chevrolet Full Floating

Single Speed

The rear axle is a full floating type with hypoid ring gear and pinion. The full floating construction enables removal of the axle shafts without removing the truck load or jacking up the rear axle. The drive pinion is straddle mounted being supported at the rear end on a roller bearing and at the front end on a double row bearing.

The ring gear is bolted to the differential case and some models are provided with a ring gear thrust pad to prevent distortion when starting under heavy loads.

Some models have a two pinion differential while others have a four pinion differential.

Two-speed

The Chevrolet two-speed axle is available in the 15,000 and 17,000 lb. capacity. In low gear, torque is transmitted to the differential case through the planetary pinions. The straddle mounted drive pinion and the ring gears operate to produce the high range reduction, the planet and sun gears being locked to revolve with the ring gear.

Early models have a two way vacuum system for axle shifts. Later models use an electric shift system.

Maintenance and adjustments for the two speed axle are performed the same as those outlined for the Chevrolet single-speed axles.

Differential Carrier

Removal

1. Drain the lubricant from the differential.
2. Remove the axle shafts. (See Axle Shaft Removal)
3. Disconnect the rear universal

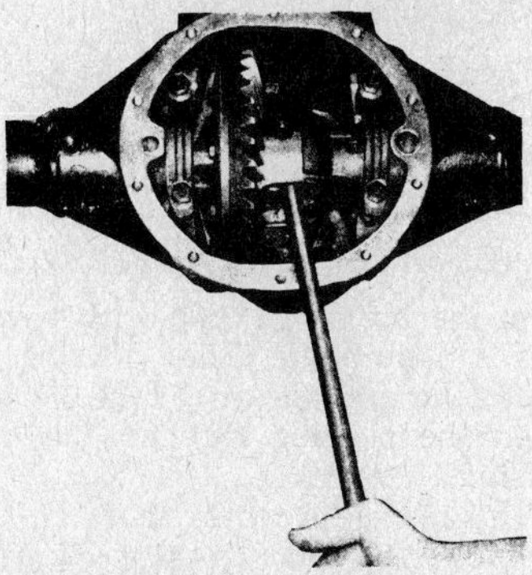

Differential case removal
(© Chevrolet Div., G.M. Corp.)

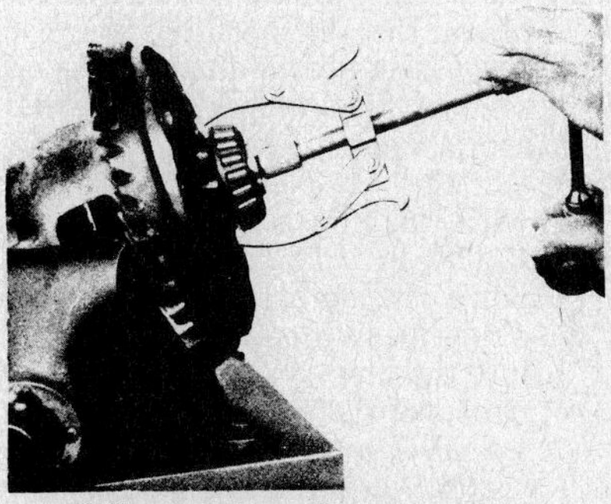

Differential bearing removal
(© Chevrolet Div., G.M. Corp.)

Installing differential shim
(© Chevrolet Div., G.M. Corp.)

joint and swing the propeller shaft to one side.
4. On two speed axles, remove the electric or vacuum lines.
5. Remove the bolts and lockwashers which retain the carrier assembly to the axle housing. Support the differential housing with a floor jack and roll it from under the truck. For overhaul—see General Section.

Installation

1. Clean the axle housing and differential housing gasket surfaces and place a new gasket over the axle housing.
2. Assembly the carrier to the axle housing, install the lockwashers and bolts and tighten securely.
3. Assemble the rear universal joint.
4. On two speed axles, connect the electric or vacuum lines.
5. Install the axle shafts. (See Axle Shaft Installation)

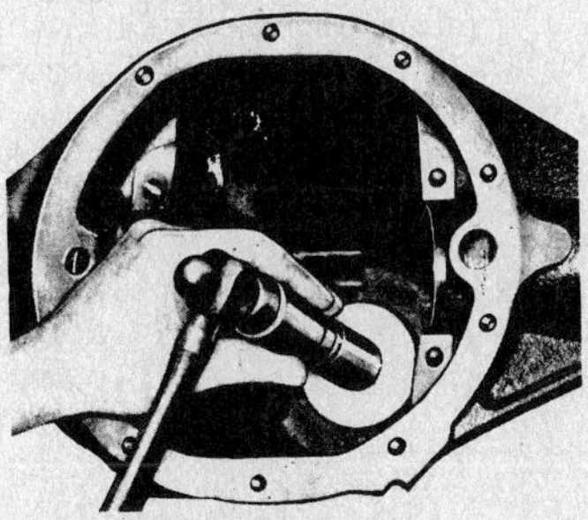

Installing bearing cap
(© Chevrolet Div., G.M. Corp.)

Drive Pinion Oil Seal

Replacement

1. Disconnect the propeller shaft and remove the pinion flange and deflector.
2. Remove the bolts retaining the oil seal retainer to the carrier, and withdraw the retainer from the pinion.
3. Pry the old seal from the bore.
4. Clean all foreign matter from the retainer.
5. Pack the cavity of the new seal with a high melting point bearing lubricant, position the seal on an installer.
6. Press the seal into the retainer until it bottoms against the shoulder.
7. Position the seal retainer over the pinion. Install and tighten the retaining bolts.
8. Reinstall the pinion flange and propeller shaft.

Axle Shaft Removal

5200 and 7200 lb. Axle

1. Remove the bolts and lockwashers that attach the axle shaft flange to the wheel hub.
2. Install two ½" - 13 bolts in the threaded holes provided in the axle shaft flange. By turning these bolts alternately the axle shaft may be started and then removed from the housing.

Installation

1. Clean both the axle flange and the wheel hub.
2. Place a new gasket over the axle shaft and position the axle shaft in the housing so that the shaft splines enter the differential side gear.
3. Install the bolts and torque to 85-95 ft. lbs.

11,000-13,500 and 1500 lb. Axle

1. Remove the hub cap and install a slide hammer and adapter in the tapped hole on the shaft flange
2. Remove the axle shaft.

Installation

1. Clean the old gasket from the hub and hub cap. Clean the axle shaft flange and mating surfaces in the wheel hub.
2. Install the axle shaft so that the shaft splines index into the hub splines.
3. Tap the shaft into position. Install a new hub cap gasket, position the hub cap to the hub and install the attaching bolts. Torque the bolts to 11-18 ft. lbs.

17,000 lb. Axle

1. Remove the axle shaft flange—to—hub nuts.
2. Strike the flange with a lead hammer to loosen the flange and dowels.
3. Remove the tapered dowels from the studs and pull the axle shaft from the housing.

Installation

1. Clean the old gasket from the wheel hub and axle shaft flange and install a new gasket over the hub studs.
2. Install the axle shaft so that the splines are aligned with the differential side gear and the flange holes index over the hub studs.

3. Install the tapered dowel over each hub stud. Install and tighten the stud nuts to 80-100 ft. lbs

Spline Drive Type

Procedure for removal of axle shafts is same with assembly removed or installed in the vehicle.

1. Remove cap screws and hub cap from hub.
2. Install slide hammer adapter into tapped hole in axle flange.
3. Install slide hammer into adapter and remove axle shaft.

Installation

1. Dip small end of splined shaft in axle lubricant, and insert shaft into hub.
2. Turn shaft as necessary to index shaft splines with differential side gear splines. As shaft is pushed inward, rotate hub to align axle shaft flange splines to hub. Push shaft into place.
3. Install new gasket on hub cap and install hub cap to hub with cap screws. Torque cap screws 15 to 20 foot-pounds.

Hub and Drum

Removal

1. Remove the wheel assembly and axle shaft. (See Axle Shaft Removal)
2. Disengage the tang of the nut lock from the slot or flat of the adjusting nut and remove the nut lock. Using an appropriate tool, remove the adjusting nut.
   NOTE: On 5200 through 15,000 lb. axles, remove the thrust washer from the housing tube.
3. Pull the hub and drum assembly straight off the axle housing.
   NOTE: On 11,000 through 17,000 lb. axles avoid dropping the outer bearing inner race and roller assembly.

Bearing and Bearing Cup

Replacement

Replace the inner cup (all axles) and outer bearing cup for 17,000 lb. axle as follows:

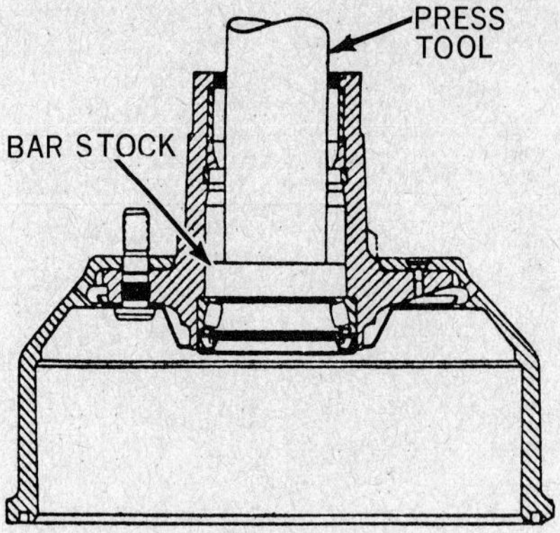

Removing hub inner bearing cup
(© Chevrolet Div., G.M. Corp.)

1. Place an appropriate press-out tool behind the bearing cup, index the tool in provided notches, and press out the cup.
   NOTE: The hub outer bearing (all axles except 17,000 lb. axle) cannot be replaced with the inner bearings in position; therefore, replace the outer bearings (if required) before proceeding.
2. Position the cup in the hub, with the thick edge of the cup toward the shoulder of the hub. Using an applicable cup installer, press the cup into the hub until it seats on the hub shoulder.

Replace the outer bearing assembly (all axles except 17,000 lb.) as follows:

NOTE: The inner bearing assembly must be removed before attempting to replace the outer bearing.

1. Using a punch, tap the bearing outer race away from the bearing retaining ring. Then remove the retaining ring from the hub.
2. On 5,200 and 7,200 lb. axles, remove the outer bearing by using a brass drift. On 11,000, 13,500 and 15,000 lb. axles, remove the bearings by driving on the axle spacer, using the splined flange cut from an old axle.
3. On 11,000, 13,500 and 15,000 lb. axles place the axle shaft spacer in the hub first. Place the inner race and roller assembly in the hub, larger O.D. towards the outer end of the hub. Position the bearing cup in the hub, then end of the cup toward the outer end of the hub. Press the cup into the hub, install the retainer ring, then press the cup into positive contact with the retainer ring.

NOTE: The bearing cup to retainer ring seating is essential to assure accurate wheel bearing adjustment.

Removing lock nut—typical (© Chevrolet Div., G.M. Corp.)

Wheel Hub Oil Seal

Replacement

Pry out the old seal from the hub bore. Pack the cavity between the new seal lips with wheel bearing grease. Position the seal in the hub bore and press the seal into the bore until it is properly seated.

With the exception of the 15,000 lb. axle with 15x4 inch brakes, the seal should be installed flush with the end of the hub. On the 15,000 lb. axle with 15x4 inch brakes the seal should be installed so that it makes contact with the bearing race.

Tightening wheel hub bearing nut
(© Chevrolet Div., G.M. Corp.)

Hub and Drum

Installation

On the 15,000 lb. axle with 4 inch brakes, install the inner bearing oil seal in the inner bearing race and position the bearing race on the axle housing.

1. Using a smooth cup grease, pack the bearings and apply a light coat of grease to the inside of the bearing hub and the outside of the axle housing tube.
2. Install the hub and drum assembly on the axle housing, exercise care so as not to damage the oil seal or dislocate other internal componants.
3. On the 11,000, 13,500, 15,000 with 15x4 inch brake, and the 17,000 lb. (single speed) axles, place the outer bearing on the axle housing and press firmly into the hub.
4. On 5,200 through 15,000 lb. with 4 inch brake axles, install the thrust washer so that the tang is in the keyway on the axle housing.

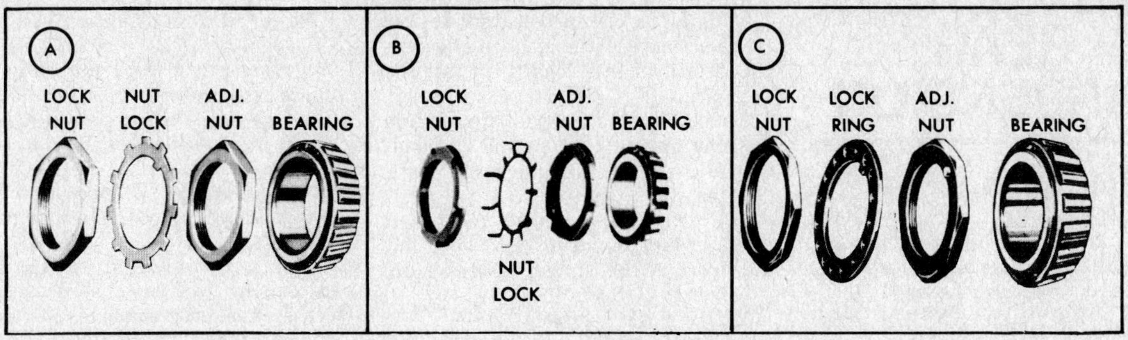

Typical lock types used on rear axle wheel bearing nuts—full floating axle systems (© Chevrolet Div., G.M. Corp.)

5. Install the adjusting nut and adjust the bearings.

Bearing Adjustment

Before checking the bearing adjustment, make sure the brakes are fully released and do not drag. Check bearing play by grasping the tire at the top and pulling back and forth, or by using a pry bar under the tire. If the bearings are properly adjusted, movement of the brake drum in relation to the brake flange plate will be barely noticeable and the wheel will turn freely. If movement is excessive, adjust the bearings as follows:

1. Remove the axle shaft and raise the vehicle until the wheel is free to rotate. (See Axle Shaft Removal)
2. Disengage the nut lock from the lock nut and remove them from the axle housing tube.
3. Using an appropriate tool, tighten the adjusting nut to specifications, at the same time rotating the hub.
   5,200 and 7,200 lb. axles—55 ft. lbs.
   11,000 and 13,500 lb. axles—90 ft. lbs.
   15,000 lb. axle
   4 inch brakes—90 ft. lbs.
   5 inch brakes—50 ft. lbs.
   17,000 lb. axle—65 ft. lbs.
   Then back the nut off $\frac{1}{8}$ to $\frac{1}{4}$ turn to align the nearest slot with the short tang on the nut lock.
3. Install the nut lock.
4. Install the lock nut and tighten to specifications.
   5,200 and 7,200 lb. axles—175 ft. lbs.
   11,000 and 15,000 lb. axles with 15x4 inch brake—250 ft. lbs.
   13,500 lb. axle—135 ft. lbs.
   15,000 lb. axle with 15x5 inch brake—135 ft. lbs.
   17,000 lb. axle—135 ft. lbs.
5. Bend the tang of the nut lock over the flat or slot of the lock nut.
   Final bearing check should show 0.001″ to 0.007″ end play.
6. Lower the vehicle and install the axle shaft. (See Axle Shaft Installation)

Eaton Full Floating

Single Speed

This axle is equipped with a straddle mounted drive pinion. Pinion bearings are of the opposed tapered roller bearing type.

A straight roller type pilot bearing is pressed onto the inner end of the drive pinion and seats in the bore of the differential case.

The differential carrier assembly may be removed, while the axle is still installed in the truck, after the axle shafts have been removed.

The differential is a conventional four pinion type. On early models the ring gear is riveted to the differential case. On later models the ring gear is bolted to the differential case.

Some models have a thrust pad mounted on the end of an adjusting screw which is threaded into an opening in the differential carrier. This thrust pad limits the deflection of the drive gear under severe loads.

Axle shaft, oil seal, wheel bearings, pinion seal and differential removal and installation are performed the same as those outlined for Chevrolet axles. Refer to Rear Axle (Chevrolet).

For overhaul—see General Section.

Two Speed

The differential and planetary assembly is installed in a two-piece support case. The ring gear is installed between the halves of the support case and retained in place by the same bolts which fasten the support case halves together.

The planetary assembly is composed of a high speed clutch plate, and four planetary pinions.

An electric power shifting arrangement is used to assist in making ratio changes. For schematic of Electric Shift see Chevrolet Two Speed Axle.

Axle shaft, oil seal, wheel bearings, pinion seal and differential removal and installation are performed the same as those outlined for Chevrolet Axles. Refer to Rear Axle (Chevrolet).

For overhaul—see General Section.

Tandem Axle

The Hendrickson type tandem axle suspension uses equalizing beams to tie the front to the rear axle and to permit independent vertical movement of each axle. The torque rods are used to maintain proper drive line alignment and to stabilize the driving and braking forces. Bolts are used on some models to hold the spring to the top saddle pad, while U-bolts are used on other models.

NOTE: When major overhaul is required, the complete tandem axle should be removed as a unit. The torque rods, springs, equalizing beam and other parts may be removed separately as required.

CAUTION: Block the vehicle securely before removal of the assembly to avoid rolling or pivoting at the equalizer beams when the torque rods are disconnected. The use of a helper is suggested, along with proper lifting tools so that personal injury does not occur.

Removal and Installation

1. Block all wheels and disconnect all applicable brake lines or hoses, differential lock lines, or electrical wiring from the rear axles.
2. Remove the rebound bolts from the rear spring brackets.
3. Remove all nuts and washers from the front spring brackets.
4. If equipped with ball stud torque rods, remove the stud nuts and tap each ball stud loose with a soft hammer. Remove the ball studs from the axle brackets.
5. If equipped with straddle mount torque rods, remove the mounting bolts from the rear axle bracket.
6. Support the rear axle differential with a floor jack, and disconnect the drive shaft from the forward rear axle.
7. Using a hoist, raise the rear of the frame high enough to clear the tandem axle assembly. Roll the assembly out from under the frame.
8. Installation is the reverse of reremoval.

REAR SUSPENSION

Coil Spring Type

Control Arm

Removal

1. Remove the load from the spring by jacking at the frame.
2. Disconnect the parking brake cable from the control arm.
3. Remove the spring clamp bolt from the underside of the control arm.
4. Remove the "U" bolt nuts and separate the shock absorber bracket from the control arm. Separate the control arm from the "U" bolts and lower the rear of the arm.
5. Remove the pivot bolt and remove the arm from the vehicle.

Installation

1. Position the bushed end of control arm and insert the pivot bolt. Place the nut on the bolt finger tight.
2. Position the clamp inside the spring, raise the control arm, then pass the bolt, with the flat washer installed, up through the control arm and clamp. Install the lock washer and nut. Torque from 40 to 50 ft. lbs.
3. Place the arm adjacent to the axle. Pass the "U" bolt over the axle and through the holes in the arm.
4. Place the shock absorber bracket on the "U" bolt, install the nuts and torque from 200 to 225 ft. lbs.
5. Lower the vehicle to put full weight of the unloaded vehicle on the front and rear suspension, torque the control arm pivot bolt from 125 to 165 ft. lbs.

Coil Spring

Removal

1. Raise the vehicle and adjust the axle to frame height so that the spring is not under tension.
2. Remove the shock absorber bolt from the mounting bracket at the control arm.
3. Remove the upper and lower clamps from the spring.
4. Lower the control arm sufficiently to permit removal of the spring.

Installation

1. Place the spring lower clamp inside the spring. Position the clamp so that the end of the spring coil is within the notch. Locate the spring and clamp over the bolt hole in the control arm.
2. Pass the clamp bolt and washer up through the hole in the control arm and loosely install the nut.
3. Position the upper clamp inside the spring and install the bolt and washer. Torque to 45-55 ft. lbs.
4. Connect the shock absorber. Torque the nut to 110-150 ft. lbs.
5. Torque the spring lower clamp bolt to 40-50 ft. lbs.
6. Lower the vehicle.

Leaf Spring Type

Spring Removal and Installation

Light Duty Trucks with Spring Hanger and Shackle Pin Lubricating Fittings

1. Jack the vehicle at the frame to relieve tension on the spring.
2. Remove the lubrication fitting from the spring eye and rear shackle pin.
3. Remove the lock bolts and nuts or pins from the shackle pin and spring eye pin.
4. Using appropriate tools, remove the spring eye pin and shackle pin.
5. Remove the "U" bolt nuts, withdraw the "U" bolts and remove the spring from the vehicle.

Installation

1. Position the spring assembly on the axle housing. Install the spacer assembly between the axle housing and spring, if so equipped, then install the "U" bolts.
2. Install the "U" bolt retaining nuts, torque the nuts alternately and evenly to properly seat the spring.
3. Jack as required to align the spring eyes; install the spring eye and shackle pins, lock bolts and nuts or lock pins and lubricating fittings. Lubricate the spring bushings and lower the vehicle.

Light Duty Trucks with Rubber Spring Hanger and Shackle Bushings

1. Jack the vehicle at the frame to relieve tension on the spring.
2. Remove the "U" bolt retaining nuts and withdraw the "U" bolts.
3. Loosen the shackle bolts and remove the lower bolt.
4. Remove the nut and bolt securing the spring to the front hanger.
5. Remove the spring from the vehicle.

Installation

1. Position the spring assembly, and spacers if so equipped, on the axle housing. *NOTE: On springs with metal encased pressed in type bushings the shackle assembly must be attached to the rear spring eye before installing the shackle to the rear hanger.*
2. Position the "U" bolts and loosely install the "U" bolt retaining nuts.
3. Jack as required to align the spring eyes with the front hanger and rear shackle, install the eye bolts.
4. Lower the vehicle.
5. Tighten the "U" bolt retaining nuts alternately and evenly to properly seat the spring, and tighten the front hanger and rear shackle bolts.

Medium Duty Trucks

1. Raise vehicle frame to take weight off the spring. Make sure vehicle is supported safely.
2. Remove rear wheels to provide access to spring assembly.
3. Safely support axle on floor jack.
4. Install a C-clamp on radius leaf, to relieve load on radius leaf eye bolt on 45 Series vehicles.
5. On 45 Series at the front and rear hanger, remove rebound pin retainer bolt, then remove retainer. Install suitable puller into tapped hole at end of rebound pin, then remove pin.
6. Remove spring U-bolt nuts, shock absorber bracket (when used) U-bolt anchor plate and U-bolts and U-bolt spacer, then lower axle slightly.
7. Remove spring eye on radius bolt nut and washer, then remove spring eye bolt from spring eye or radius leaf.

NOTE: When tapered shim is used, the position of shim thin and thick edge should be noted so that shim can be installed properly at assembly.

Installation

1. Set spring assembly and tapered shim or spacer (if used) at axle pad.

NOTE: Tapered shim must be installed on axle in same position that was noted at removal.

2. Install U-bolt spacer over center bolt.
3. Seat U-bolts in spacer grooves, then secure spring to axle by installing anchor plates, shock absorber bracket (when used) and nuts on U-bolts.
4. Lower frame until ends of spring enter the hanger and touch the cam surface of hanger. Compress radius leaf with C-clamp until radius leaf eye and hanger holes are aligned and torque to specifications.
5. Remove C-clamp from radius leaf.

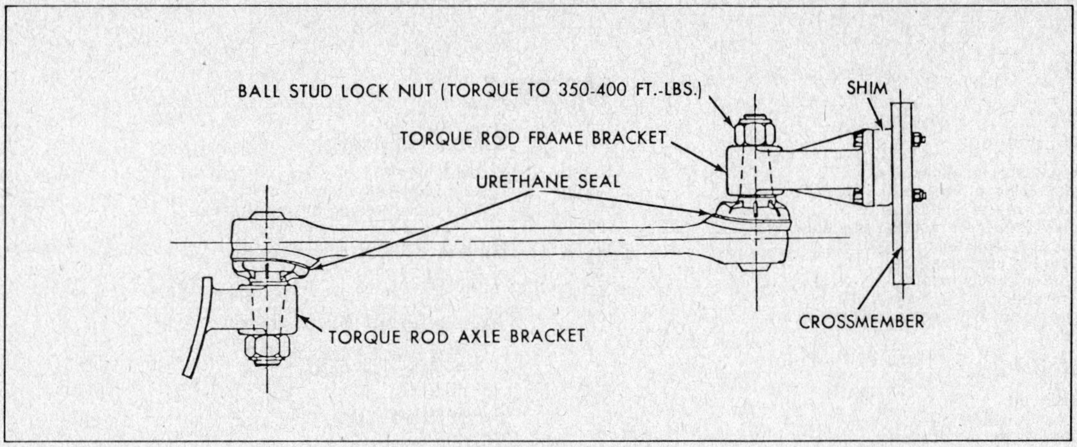

Torque rod installation (© GM Chevrolet Div.)

6. Install rebound pin at front and rear hangers. Install rebound pin retainer and secure with retainer bolt.
7. Install wheels.
8. Remove blocking and lower frame to place weight on springs. Check U-bolt nuts for proper torque.

Single or Tandem Axles Springs—Heavy Duty

1. Raise the rear of the vehicle, place floor jacks under the axle(s) and remove the dual wheels from the hubs to facilitate the removal of the spring eye pin and to expose the other nuts and bolts.
2. Remove the saddle cap stud nuts and/or spring U-bolts.
3. Remove the rebound pin locks or retainers, and then remove the rebound pins.
4. Remove the eye bolts or radius lead pin clamp bolts, then remove the lubrication fitting from the inner end of the pin, if equipped.
5. Remove the pins from the springs and lower the axle(s) or raise the frame until the spring will clear the brackets.
6. Remove the spring from the vehicle.
7. The installation is in the reverse of the removal procedure.
8. Torque the U-bolts or saddle cap stud nuts to specifications after the vehicle is lowered to the floor.

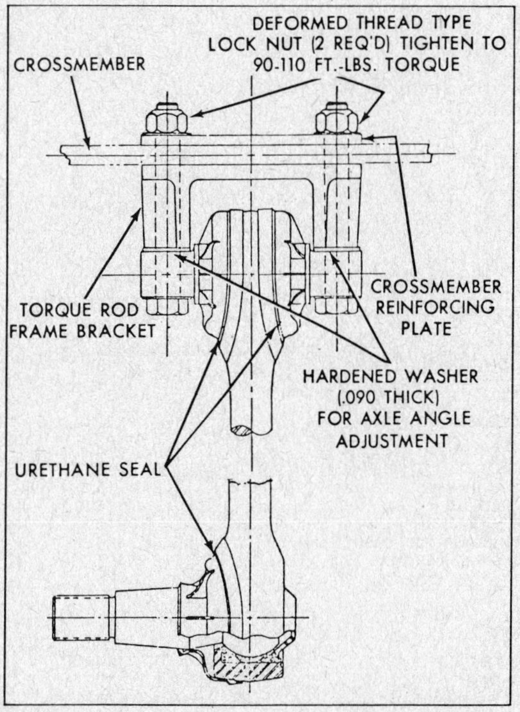

Straddle type torque rod (© GM Chevrolet Div.)

REAR SUSPENSION TORQUE SPECIFICATIONS

PART	FT. LBS TORQUE
Spring U-Bolt Nuts (All "C/S" Series)	190-210
(All "T" Series)	190-210
Shock Absorber Nuts (when used) Upper Nut	85-90
Lower Nut	25-30
Rear Spring Radius Leaf Bolt Nut	175-225
(All T Series)	290-320
(All "C/S" Series with ⅝" x 18 Bolt)	60-80
(All "C/S" Series with 1" x 14 Bolt)	150-200
Rebound Pin Retainer Bolt (All Except "T" Series)	10-14
("T" Series)	
60	5-10
65	20-25
Rear Axle Bumper Bolt Nuts (All Except "T" Series)	6-8
("T" Series)	10-12

Dodge/Plymouth—Trucks, Vans, Ramcharger and Trail Duster

INDEX

TUNE-UP SPECIFICATIONS

CU. IN. DISPLACE-MENT	YEAR	SPARK PLUG GAP	DISTRIBUTOR POINT DWELL	DISTRIBUTOR POINT GAP	IGNITION TIMING DEG. BTC (± 2°)	CRANKING COMP. PRES.	VALVE CLEARANCE INTAKE	VALVE CLEARANCE EXHAUST	GOV. RPM NO LOAD	FUEL PUMP PRESS	IDLE SPEED STD.	IDLE SPEED AUTO.
SIX CYLINDER												
225 Lt.Duty	1973	.035	Electronic		TDC	100	.012H	.024H	3600	3½-5	700 (800)	700N (800)
225 Heavy Duty	1973	.035	Electronic		TDC (2½A)	100	.012H	.024H	3600	3½-5	700 (800)	700N (800)
225 Lt. Duty	1974	.035	Electronic		TDC	100	.012H	.024H	3600	3½-5	800	750N
225 Heavy Duty	1974	.035	Electronic		2½A	100	.012H	.024H	3600	3½-5	800	750N
225 Lt. Duty	1975	.035①	Electronic		TDC	100	.012H	.024H	3600	3½-5	800	750N
225 Heavy Duty	1975	.035①	Electronic		TDC	100	.012H	.024H	3600	3½-5	700	700N
225	1976	.035①	Electronic		③	100	.012H	.024H	3600	3½-5	③	③
225 LD-1V	1977-80	.035	Electronic		2	100	.012H	.020H	3600	3½-5	750	750
225 HD-2V	1977-80	.035	Electronic		TDC	100	.012H	.020H	3600	3½-5	700	700
EIGHT CYLINDER												
318-1 Lt. Duty	1973	.035	Electronic		2½B②	100	—	—	3900	5-7	750	700(750)N
318-1 Heavy Duty	1973	.035	Electronic		5B (TDC)	100	—	—	3900	5-7	750	700(750)N
318-3 Heavy Duty	1973	.035	Electronic		2½B	100	—	—	3700	5-7	700	700N
318-1 Lt. Duty	1974	.035	Electronic		TDC	100	—	—	3900	5-7	750	750N
318-1 Heavy Duty	1974	.035	Electronic		2½A	100	—	—	3700	5-7	750	750N
318-3 Heavy Duty	1974	.035	Electronic		TDC	100	—	—	3900	5-7	700	700N
318-1 Lt. Duty	1975	.035	Electronic		2B (TDC)	100	—	—	3900	5-7	750	750N
318-1 Heavy Duty	1975	.035	Electronic		2A (TDC)	100	—	—	3800	5-7	750 (700)	750N (700)
318-3 Heavy Duty	1975	.035	Electronic		TDC (2B)	100	—	—	3800	5-7	700	700N
318	1976	.035	Electronic		③	100	—	—	3800	5-7	③	③
318-3	1976	.035	Electronic		③	100	—	—	3800	5-7	③	③
318 LD	1977-80	.035	Electronic		2	100	—	—	3800	5-7	750	750
318-1 HD	1977-80	.035	Electronic		2ATDC	100	—	—	3800	5-7	750	750
318-3 HD	1977-80	.035	Electronic		TDC	100	—	—	3800	5-7	700	700
360 Lt. Duty	1973	.035	Electronic		TDC	100	—	—	3900	5-7	750	700N(750)N
360 Heavy Duty	1973	.035	Electronic		TDC	100	—	—	3900	5-7	750	700N(750)N
360 Lt. Duty	1974	.035	Electronic		2½B	100	—	—	3900	5-7	750	750N
360 Heavy Duty	1974	.035	Electronic		TDC	100	—	—	3900	5-7	750	750N
360 Lt. Duty	1975	.035	Electronic		TDC (4B)	100	—	—	3800	5-7	750 (700)	750N (700)
360 Heavy Duty	1975	.035	Electronic		TDC	100	—	—	3800	5-7	750 (700)	750N (700)
360	1976	.035	Electronic		③	100	—	—	3800	5-7	③	③
360-3	1976	.035	Electronic		③	100	—	—	3800	5-7	③	③
360 LD	1977-80	.035	Electronic		6	100	—	—	3800	5-7	700	700
360-1 HD	1977-80	.035	Electronic		TDC	100	—	—	3800	5-7	750	750
360-3 HD	1977-80	.035	Electronic		TDC	100	—	—	3800	5-7	750	750
361-3, 4	1973	.035	Electronic		5B	100	—	—	3600	3½-5	600 (700)	700N
361-3, 4	1974-75	.035	Electronic		2½B	100	—	—	3600	6-7½	700	700N
361-3	1976	.035	Electronic		③	100	—	—	3600	6-7½	③	③
361-4 HD	1977-78	.035	Electronic		2.5	100	—	—	—	5-7	700	700
400 Lt. Duty	1973	.035	Electronic		10B	100	—	—	—	3½-5	700	700N
400 Heavy Duty	1973	.035	Electronic		2½B	100	—	—	—	3½-5	700	700N
400 Lt. Duty	1974	.035	Electronic		7½B	100	—	—	—	5-7	750	750N
400 Heavy Duty	1974	.035	Electronic		2½B	100	—	—	—	5-7	750	750N
400	1976	.035	Electronic		③	100	—	—	—	5-7	③	③
400-1 HD	1977-80	.035	Electronic		2④	100	—	—	—	5-7	700	700
400-1 HD	1977-80	.035	Electronic		8⑤	100	—	—	—	5-7	700	700
413-1	1973	.035	Electronic		5B	100	—	—	3600	3½-5	600 (700)	600N (700)N
413-2	1973	.035	Electronic		5B (2½B)	100	—	—	3600	3½-5	600 (700)	500N (700)N

TUNE-UP SPECIFICATIONS

CU. IN. DISPLACE-MENT	YEAR	SPARK PLUG GAP	DISTRIBUTOR POINT DWELL	DISTRIBUTOR POINT GAP	IGNITION TIMING DEG. BTC (± 2°)	CRANKING COMP. PRES.	VALVE CLEARANCE INTAKE	VALVE CLEARANCE EXHAUST	GOV. RPM NO LOAD	FUEL PUMP PRESS	IDLE SPEED STD.	IDLE SPEED AUTO.
413-3	1973	.035	Electronic		5B	100	—	—	3600	3½-5	600 (700)	600N (700)N
413-2	1974	.035	Electronic		2½B	100	—	—	3600	6-7½	700	700N
413-3 Heavy Duty	1975	.035	Electronic		5B	100	—	—	3600	6-7½	700	700N
413-3 Bus	1975	.035	Electronic		TDC	100	—	—	3600	6-7½	700	700N
413-3	1976	.035	Electronic		③	100	—	—	3600	5-7	③	③
413-3 HD	1977-78	.035	Electronic		5	100	—	—	—	5-7	700	700
440 Lt. Duty	1974	.035	Electronic		10B (5B)	100	—	—	—	5-7	700	700N
440 Heavy Duty	1974	.035	Electronic		7½B	100	—	—	—	5-7	700	700N
440	1975	.035	Electronic		8B	100	—	—	3800	5-7	700	700N
440	1976	.035	Electronic		③	100	—	—	—	5-7	③	③
440-3	1976	.035	Electronic		③	100	—	—	3800	5-7	③	③
440-1 HD	1977-80	.035	Electronic		8	100	—	—	—	8	700	700
478	1973	.035	28-32	.016	10B	140	—	—	3400	4-4¾	500	500N

① Uses taper seat plug without tube or gasket, torque to 10 ft. lbs.
② TDC with automatic.
③ See underhood specifications sticker.
④ 2 bbl Carb
⑤ 4 bbl Carb
LD—Light duty cycle
HD—Heavy duty cycle
Lt. Duty—Under 6,000 lbs. GVW.
Heavy Duty—Over 6,000 lbs. GVW.
Figures in parentheses are for California only.

Note: The underhood specifications sticker often reflects tune up specifications changes made in production. Sticker figures must be used if they disagree with those in this Chart.

FIRING ORDER

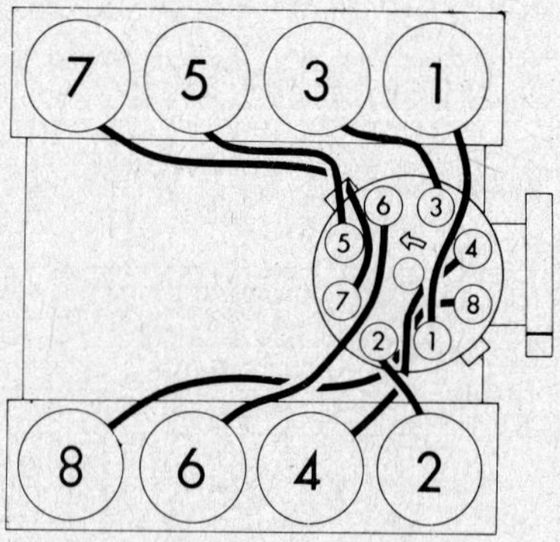

383, 400, 440, V8 engines

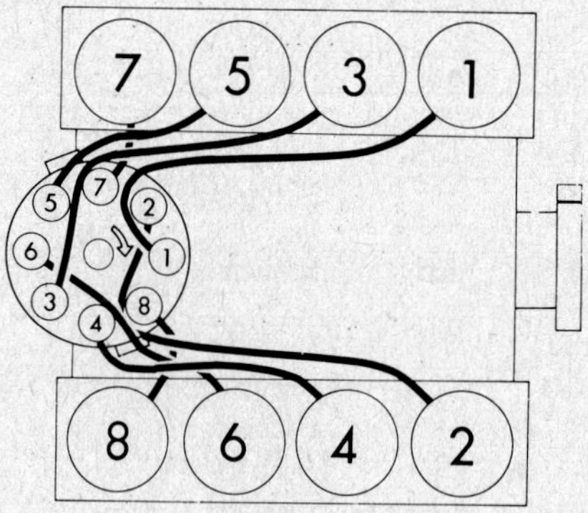

318, 340, 360, V8 engines

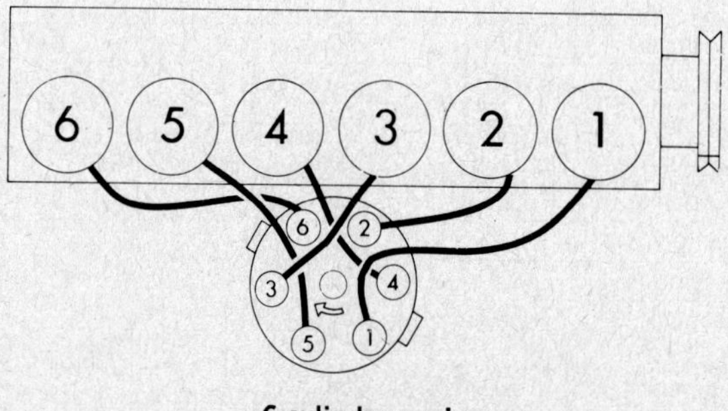

6-cylinder engine

GENERAL ENGINE SPECIFICATIONS

CU. IN. DISPLACEMENT	YEAR	BORE & STROKE	FIRING ORDER	ESTIMATED H.P. @ RPM	ESTIMATED TORQUE @ RPM	COMPRESSION RATIO	CARBURETOR	VALVE LIFTER TYPE	NORMAL OIL PRESSURE
SIX CYLINDER									
225	1973-74	3.40 x 4.125	1-5-3-6-2-4	100 @ 3900	180 @ 1600	8.4	1V	Mech.	55
225	1975-76	3.40 x 4.125	1-5-3-6-2-4	90 @ 3600	170 @ 1600	8.4	1V	Mech.	55
225	1977-80	3.40 x 4.125	1-5-3-6-2-4	100 @ 3600	170 @ 1600	8.4 x 1	1V	Std.	30-80
225	1977-80	3.40 x 4.125	1-5-3-6-2-4	110 @ 3600	180 @ 2000	8.4 x 1	2V	Std.	30-80
EIGHT CYLINDER									
318	1973-74	3.91 x 3.312	1-8-4-3-6-5-7-2	150 @ 3600	260 @ 2000	7.8/8.6	2V	Hyd.	30-80
318	1975	3.91 x 3.312	1-8-4-3-6-5-7-2	150 @ 4000	255 @ 1600	7.8/8.6	2V	Hyd.	30-80
318	1976	3.91 x 3.312	1-8-4-3-6-5-7-2	150 @ 4000	255 @ 1600	8.4	2V	Hyd.	30-80
318-3	1976	3.91 x 3.312	1-8-4-3-6-5-7-2	150 @ 4000	255 @ 1600	7.8	2V	Hyd.	30-80
318	1977-80	3.91 x 3.31	1-8-4-3-6-5-7-2	145 @ 4000	245 @ 1600	8.5 x 1	2V	Hyd.	30-80
318-3	1977-80	3.91 x 3.31	1-8-4-3-6-5-7-2	150 @ 4200	250 @ 1600	8.5 x 1	2V	Hyd.	30-80
360	1973-75	4.00 x 3.58	1-8-4-3-6-5-7-2	170 @ 4000	285 @ 2400	8.4	2V	Hyd.	30-80
360	1976	4.00 x 3.58	1-8-4-3-6-5-7-2	170 @ 4000	285 @ 2400	8.7	2V	Hyd.	30-80
360-3	1976	4.00 x 3.58	1-8-4-3-6-5-7-2	170 @ 4000	285 @ 2400	7.9	2V	Hyd.	30-80
360	1977-80	4.00 x 3.58	1-8-4-3-6-5-7-2	155 @ 3600	275 @ 2000	8.4 x 1	2V	Hyd.	30-80
360-3	1977-80	4.00 x 3.58	1-8-4-3-6-5-7-2	165 @ 3600	285 @ 2000	8.4 x 1	4V	Hyd.	30-80
361-2	1973-75	4.125 x 3.375	1-8-4-3-6-4-7-2	186 @ 4000	300 @ 2400	7.5	2V	Hyd.	70
361-3	1973-75	4.125 x 3.375	1-8-4-3-6-5-7-2	194 @ 3600	310 @ 2400	7.5	2V	Hyd.	70
361-4	1973-75	4.125 x 3.375	1-8-4-3-6-5-7-2	204 @ 3600	335 @ 2400	7.5	2V	Hyd.	70
361	1973-75	4.125 x 3.375	1-8-4-3-6-5-7-2	155 @ 3600	295 @ 2000	7.5	2V	Hyd.	70
361-4	1977-78	4.125 x 3.375	1-8-4-3-6-5-7-2	150 @ 3600	290 @ 2000	7.5 x 1	2V	Hyd.	30-80
400	1973-74	4.34 x 3.38	1-8-4-3-6-5-7-2	180 @ 3600	315 @ 2400	8.2	2V, 4V	Hyd.	30-80
400	1976	4.34 x 3.38	1-8-4-3-6-5-7-2	180 @ 3600	315 @ 2400	8.2	2V	Hyd.	30-80
400	1977-80	4.34 x 3.38	1-8-4-3-6-5-7-2	195 @ 3600	305 @ 3200	8.2 x 1	4V	Hyd.	50-75
413	1973-78	4.188 x 3.75	1-8-4-3-6-5-7-2	180 @ 3200	334 @ 2000	7.5	2V	Hyd.	70
440	1973-76	4.32 x 3.75	1-8-4-3-6-5-7-2	235 @ 4000	340 @ 2400	8.2	4V	Hyd.	30-80
440-3	1976	4.32 x 3.75	1-8-4-3-6-5-7-2	235 @ 4000	340 @ 2400	7.5	4V	Hyd.	30-80
440	1977-80	4.32 x 3.75	1-8-4-3-6-5-7-2	195 @ 3600	320 @ 2000	8.2 x 1	4V	Hyd.	30-80
478	1973	4.50 x 3.7 5	1-8-7-3-6-5-4-2	206 @ 3400	403 @ 1800	8.2	2V	Hyd.	50-70

VALVE SPECIFICATIONS

CU. IN. DISPLACEMENT	YEAR	LASH (HOT) INCHES		ANGLE DEGREE		STEM DIA. INCHES		STEM CLEARANCE		VALVE LIFT INCHES	VALVE SPRING LBS. @ INCHES		FREE LENGTH INCHES
		INT.	EXH.	FACE	SEAT	INT.	EXH.	INTAKE	EXHAUST		OPEN	CLOSED	
SIX CYLINDER													
225	1973-80	.012	.024	①	45	.372	.371	.001-.003	.002-.004	⑦	144 @ 1 5/16	53 @ 1 11/16	1.92
225	1975-76	.012	.024	①	45	.372	.371	.001-.003	.002-.004	⑧	144 @ 1 5/16	53 @ 1 11/16	1.92
EIGHT CYLINDER													
318-1	1973-74	no adj.	no adj.	①	45	.372	.371	.001-.003	.002-.004	⑨	177 @ 1 5/16	83 @ 1 11/16	2.00
318-3	1973-74	no adj.	no adj.	45	45	.372	.371	.001-.003	.002-.004	⑨	177 @ 1 5/16⑩	83 @ 1 11/16⑪	2.00⑫
318-1	1975-76	no adj.	no adj.	45	45	.372	.371	.001-.003	.002-.004	⑨	185 @ 1 1/4⑬	93 @ 1 21/32	2.00
318-3	1975-80	no adj.	no adj.	45	45	.372	.371	.001-.003	.002-.004	⑨	177 @ 1 5/16㉑	83 @ 1 11/16㉒	2.00⑫
360	1973-80	no adj.	no adj.	①	45	.372	.371	.001-.003	.002-.004	⑭	177 @ 1 5/16㉓	83 @ 1 11/16㉔	2.00
361	1973-78	no adj.	no adj.	45	45	.372	.433	.001-.003	.003-.005	.360	180 @ 1 15/32⑮	80 @ 1 55/64⑯	2.31⑰
400	1973-80	no ad.	no adj.	45	45	.372	.372	.002-.003	.002-.003	.430	200 @ 1 7/16	125 @ 1 55/64	2.63
413	1973-78	no adj.	no adj.	45	45	.372	.433	.001-.003	.003-.005	.360	180 @ 1 15/32⑮	80 @ 1 55/64⑯	2.31⑰
440	1973-74	no adj.	no adj.	45	45	.372	.372	.002-.003	.002-.003	.464	105 @ 1 55/64	105 @ 1 55/64⑯	2.31⑰
440	1975-80	no adj.	no adj.	45	45	.372	.372	.002-.003	.002-.003	.425②	200 @ 1 7/16⑲	125 @ 1 7/8⑲	2.58
478	1973	0 + 1 turn		15③	14④	.434	.434	.0015-.004	.0025-.005	—	83 @ 1 17/32	⑤	2.28

① Intake 45, Exhaust 43
② Intake .424, Exhaust .434
③ Intake, Exhaust 45
④ Intake, Exhaust 44
⑤ Inner, Outer 116.5
⑥ Inner, Outer 2.562
⑦ Intake .406, Exhaust .414
⑧ Intake .394, Exhaust .390
⑨ Intake .372, Exhaust .400
⑩ 185 @ 1 5/64
⑪ Exhaust 85 @ 1 31/64
⑫ Intake, Exhaust 1.81
⑬ Exhaust 192 @ 1 9/32
⑭ Intake .410, Exhaust .400
⑮ Intake, Exhaust 175 @ 1 21/64
⑯ Intake, Exhaust 85 @ 1 3/4
⑰ Intake, Exhaust 2.13
⑱ Intake, Exhaust 246 @ 1 23/64
⑲ Intake, Exhaust 208 @ 1 5/16
⑳ Not used
㉑ 1977-80 184 @ 1 15/16
㉒ 1977-80 88 @ 1 11/16
㉓ 1947-80 200 @ 1 11/16
㉔ 1977-80 118 @ 1 21/32

CRANKSHAFT BEARING JOURNAL SPECIFICATIONS

CU. IN. DISPLACE-MENT	YEAR	MAIN BEARING JOURNALS		SHAFT END PLAY	THRUST ON NO.	CONNECTING ROD BEARING JOURNALS		
		JOURNAL DIAMETER	OIL CLEARANCE			JOURNAL DIAMETER	OIL CLEARANCE	END PLAY
SIX CYLINDER								
225	1973-80	2.7495-2.7505	.0005-.0020①	.002-.009	3	2.1865-2.1875	.0005-.0020①	.006-.025
EIGHT CYLINDER								
318	1973-80	2.4495-2.5005	.0005-.0020	.002-.009	3	2.124-2.125	.0005-.0020	.006-.014
360	1973-80	2.8095-2.8105	.0005-.0020	.002-.009	3	2.124-2.125	.0005-.0020	.006-.014
361	1973-78	2.6245-2.6255	.0015-.0025	.002-.009	3	2.374-2.375	.001-.002	.009-.017
400	1978-80	2.6245-2.6255	.0005-.0020	.002-.009	3	2.374-2.375	.0005-.0025	.009-.017
413	1973-78	2.7495-2.7505	.002-.0022	.002-.009	3	2.374-2.375	.0005-.0020	.009-.017
440	1973-80	2.7495-2.7505	.002-.0022	.002-.009	3	2.374-2.375	.0005-.0020	.009-.017
478	1973	3.123-3.124	.0014-.0044	.004-.009	3	2.623-2.624	.0017-.0042	.010-.018

① 1979-80 (.002-.0022)

RING GAP (IN.)

YEAR	ENGINE NO. CYL. DISPLACEMENT	TOP COMPRESSION	BOTTOM COMPRESSION	OIL CONTROL
1973-80	6-225	.010-.020	.010-.020	.015-.055
1973-80	8-318	.010-.020	.010-.020	.015-.055
1973-80	8-360	.010-.020	.010-.020	.015-.055
1973-78	8-361	.013-.025	.013-.025	.015-.055
1973-80	8-400	.013-.023	.013-.023	.015-.062
1973-78	8-413	.013-.025	.013-.025	.015-.055
1973-74	8-440	.013-.052	.013-.052	.015-.062
1975-80	8-440	.013-.023	.013-.023	.015-.055

RING SIDE CLEARANCE (IN.)

YEAR	ENGINE NO. CYL. DISPLACEMENT	TOP COMPRESSION	BOTTOM COMPRESSION	OIL CONTROL
1973-80	6-225	.0015-.0030	.0015-.0030	.0002-.0050
1973-80	8-318	.0015-.0030	.0015-.0030	.0002-.0050
1973-80	8-360	.0015-.0030	.0015-.0030	.0002-.0050
1973-78	8-361	.0025-.0040	.0025-.0040	.0010-.0030
1973-80	8-400	.0015-.0030	.0015-.0030	.0002-.0050
1973-74	8-413	.0025-.0040	.0025-.0040	.0010-.0030
1975-78	8-413	.0010-.0025	.0010-.0025	.0010-.0030
1973-74	8-440	.0015-.0040	.0015-.0040	.0000-.0050
1975-80	8-440	.0015-.0030	.0015-.0030	.0000-.0050

GASOLINE ENGINES

ENGINE	YEARS AVAILABLE	ENGINE MAKE
6-225	1973-80	Own
V8-318	1973-80	Own
V8-361	1973-78	Own
V8-361	1973-78	Own
V8-400	1973-80	Own
V8-413	1973-78	Own
V8-440	1973-80	Own
V8-478	1973	IH

DIESEL ENGINES

ENGINE	ENGINE MAKE
6-243	Mitsubishi
6-71N	Detroit
8V-71N	Detroit
8V-71NE	Detroit
NH230	Cummins
NHC250	Cummins
NTC280	Cummins
NTC335	Cummins
V8-210	Cummins
V903	Cummins

TORQUE SPECIFICATIONS

CU. IN. DISPLACE-MENT	YEAR	CYLINDER HEAD BOLTS (FT. LBS.)	ROD BEARING BOLTS (FT. LBS.)	MAIN BEARING BOLTS (FT. LBS.)	CRANKSHAFT BALANCER BOLT (FT. LBS.)	FLYWHEEL TO CRANKSHAFT BOLTS (FT. LBS.)	MANIFOLD (FT. LBS.) INTAKE	MANIFOLD (FT. LBS.) EXHAUST
SIX CYLINDER								
225	1971-78	70	45	85	Press	55	10	10
EIGHT CYLINDER								
318	1973-80	95	45	85	100	55	35	20
360	1973-80	95	45	85	100	55	35	20
361	1973-78	70	45	85	135	55	45	30
400	1973-80	70	45	85	135	55	40	30
413	1973-78	70	45	85	135	55	45	30
440	1973-80	70	45	85	135	55	45	30
478	1973	90-100	60-70	100-110	—	90-100	—	30

WHEEL ALIGNMENT SPECIFICATIONS

YEAR	MODEL	CASTER (Deg.)*	CAMBER (Deg.)	TOE-IN (in.)	KING PIN INCLINATION (Deg.)
1973-80	**D100**	0 to +½	0 to +½	1/16-1/8	—
1973-78	**AW, PW, W100**	3	1½	0-1/8	7½
1973-80	**B, PB, CB, MB100 200, 300**	½⑤	+¼	1/16-1/8	—
1973-80	**D200**	0 to +½	0 to +½	1/16-1/8	—
1973-80	**W200**⑥	3	1½	0-1/8	7½
1973-80	**D300**	0 to +½	0 to +½	1/16-1/8	—
1973	**W300**	1½	3½	0-1/8	8
1974-80	**W300**⑥	3	½	0-1/8	8½
1973	**P400**	1④	2	0-1/8	7
1973-78	**D500, S500**②	½ to 2	2	0-1/8	7
1973-78	**D600**②	½ to 2	2	0-1/8	7
1973-78	**S600**	0 to +1	1	0-1/8	5½
1973-78	**W600**	2½	¾	0-1/8	8
1973-78	**D700**②	½ to 2	2	0-1/8	7
1973-78	**D700**③	0 to +1	1	0-1/8	5½
1975-78	**S700**	0 to +1	1	0-1/8	5½
1973-78	**800 All**	0-1④	1	0-1/8	5½
1973-76	**850 All**	1③	1	0-1/8	5½
1973-76	**900 All**	0 to +1④	1	0-1/8	5½
1973-76	1000 All	0 to +1④	1	0-1/8	5½

* No load
① Not used
③ 5000 lb. axle
② 7000 lb. axle
④ With power steering 4-5 degrees
⑤ 2¼ with power steering
⑥ Use W300 figures for W200 with Spicer 60 or 70F front axle

NOTE: Ramcharger and Trailduster service procedures are the same as those for conventional trucks, except where specific and separate procedures are given.

DISTRIBUTOR

Distributor—All Types

Removal

1. Disconnect primary lead wire at coil. On electronic ignition, disconnect the distributor lead wire at the connector.
2. Disconnect vacuum hose at distributor.
3. On the Holley distributor, disconnect tachometer drive and governor inlet and outlet lines.
4. Unfasten distributor cap retaining clips and remove distributor cap.
5. Scribe a line on the distributor housing and engine block to indicate positioning of the rotor and housing.

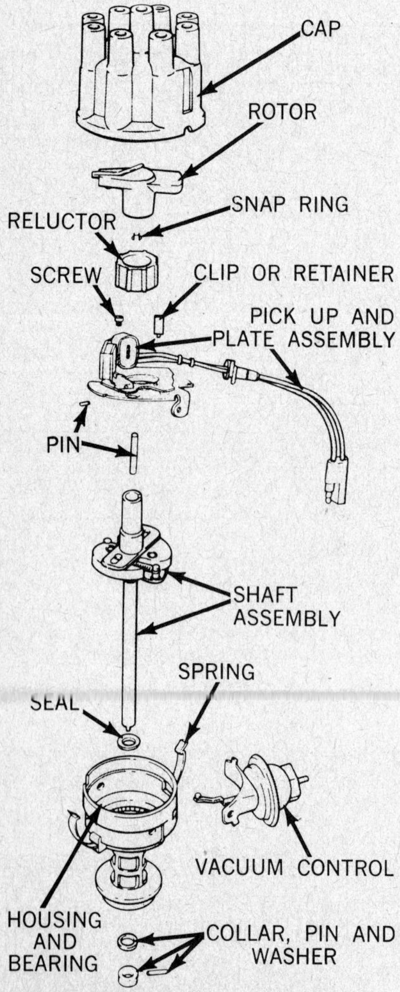

V8 electronic ignition distributor
(© Chrysler Corp.)

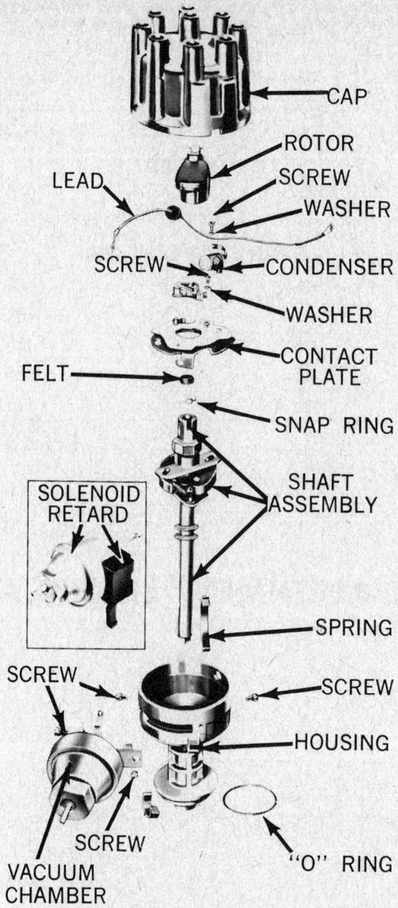

Typical dual point distributor—V8
(© Chrysler Corp.)

6. Remove distributor hold-down clamp or arm screw.
7. Carefully lift out distributor assembly.

NOTE: Do not disturb engine position.

Installation

1. If the crankshaft has not been rotated, insert distributor into block with the rotor and body aligned to the previously scribed marks. Make sure O-ring seal is in groove of shank. *NOTE: Distributors on 6 cylinder engines have the drive gear mounted on the bottom of the distributor shaft and a slight rotation will occur when installing. Allow for this rotation when aligning rotor with scribed line on housing.*
2. If engine has been cranked while distributor was removed, it will be necessary to correctly time the distributor with the camshaft. This is done by rotating the crankshaft until No. 1 piston is at top dead center of compression stroke. With rotor in No. 1 cylinder firing position with respect to the distributor cap, insert distributor into engine.
3. Connect primary lead or electronic ignition lead wire.
4. Install distributor cap and check that all high tension leads are securely in position.
5. On the Holley distributor, connect governor lines and tachometer drive cable.
6. Set ignition timing.
7. Tighten distributor arm or clamp screw.
8. Connect vacuum advance line.

Breaker Points and Condenser Replacement, Dwell Angle Adjustment

1. Remove the distributor cap and rotor and inspect them for burned or corroded conditions.
2. Loosen the terminal screw nut and remove the primary and condenser lead wires. Remove the stationary contact lockscrew and remove the point set. Be very careful not to drop any of these screws inside the distributor. If the hold-down screw is lost, it must be replaced with one that is no longer than the original to avoid interference with the distributor advance mechanism workings. Remove the point set.
3. If the points are to be reused, clean them with a few strokes of a fine file.
4. Remove the condenser retaining screw and the condenser.
5. Rub a matchhead size dab of high melting point grease on the cam lobes, and install the new condenser.
6. Replace the point set and leave the screw slightly loose. Replace the two wire terminals, making sure that the wires don't interfere with anything.
7. Check that the contacts meet squarely. If they don't, bend the tab supporting the fixed contact.
8. Turn the engine until a high point on the cam which opens the points contacts the rubbing block on the point arm.
9. There is a rectangular slot near the contacts. Insert a suitable tool and lever the points open or closed until they appear to be at about the gap specified in the "Tune-Up Specifications" chart.
10. Insert the correct size feeler gauge and adjust the gap until you can push the gauge in and out between the contacts with a slight drag, but without disturbing the point arm. Check by trying the gauges 0.001-0.002 larger and smaller than the setting size. The larger one should disturb the point arm, while the smaller one should not drag at all. Tighten the point set hold-down screw. Recheck the gap, as

it often changes when the screw is tightened.

11. Put one drop of SAE 10 oil on the felt wick in the top of the distributor shaft. Push the rotor firmly into place. It will only go on one way.
12. Replace the distributor cap.
13. Check the dwell. Dwell can be checked with the engine running or cranking. Decrease dwell by increasing the point gap; increase dwell by decreasing the gap. Dwell angle is simply the number of degrees of distributor shaft rotation during which the points stay closed. Theoretically, if the point gap is correct, the dwell should also be correct or nearly so. Adjustment with a dwell meter produces more exact, consistent results than a feeler gauge since it is a dynamic adjustment.
14. To adjust dwell, trial and error point adjustments are required. On a Holley governor distributor, dwell can be adjusted externally with a 1/8 in. Allen wrench.
15. Since changing the gap and dwell affects the ignition point setting, the timing should be checked and adjusted as necessary after each point replacement or adjustment.

Electronic Ignition System Distributor

No internal distributor maintenance is required with this system; it does not use contact points or a condenser. This system is easily identified by a double wire lead from the distributor and a control unit in the engine compartment.

NOTE: The dwell reading that is obtained with a dwell meter is of no significance in servicing the ignition system and since dwell is non-adjustable, no changes should be attempted.

Electronic Ignition Distributor Air Gap Adjustment

This adjustment is not required at regular intervals. It is not a normal tune-up service.

1. Release the spring clips and remove the distributor cap. Pull off the rotor.
2. Align one reluctor tooth with the pick-up coil tooth by turning the engine. The reluctor is the six or eight-toothed ring around the distributor shaft.
3. Insert an 0.008 in. *nonmagnetic* (brass) feeler gauge between the reluctor tooth and the pick-up coil tooth.
4. Loosen the hold-down screw and adjust the gap using the screwdriver slot in the mounting plate. Contact should be made between the reluctor tooth, the feeler gauge, and the pick-up coil tooth.
5. Tighten the hold-down screw.
6. Remove the feeler gauge. No force should be required.
7. Check the gap with a 0.010 in. *nonmagnetic* feeler gauge. It should not fit; don't force it into the gap.
8. Turn the distributor shaft and apply vacuum to the vacuum advance unit. If it is adjusted properly and nothing is bent, the pick-up coil tooth will not hit the reluctor teeth.

IGNITION TIMING

On all engines the timing plate is located on the timing case (front) cover and the timing mark is on the crankshaft pulley damper. On all models the ignition is timed to the No. 1 cylinder spark plug. Always remove and plug the vacuum advance line when setting ignition timing.

ALTERNATOR

Reference

For voltage regulator circuit tests and for alternator off-the-vehicle service, see The Electrical Section.

Alternator

Removal

1. Disconnect battery ground cable at the negative terminal.
2. Disconnect alternator output "BAT" and field "FLD" leads and disconnect ground wire.
3. Remove mounting bolts and remove alternator.

Installation

1. Install alternator and adjust drive belt.
2. Connect output "BAT" and field "FLD" leads and connect ground wire.
3. Connect battery ground cable.
4. Start engine, and observe alternator operation.
5. Test current output and adjust regulator voltage setting, if necessary. See Electrical Section.

NOTE: Late models use a non-adjustable sealed electronic regulator.

Voltage Regulator

Electronic Voltage Regulator

Removal and Installation

1. Release the spring clips and pull off the regulator wiring plug.
2. Unbolt and remove the regulator.

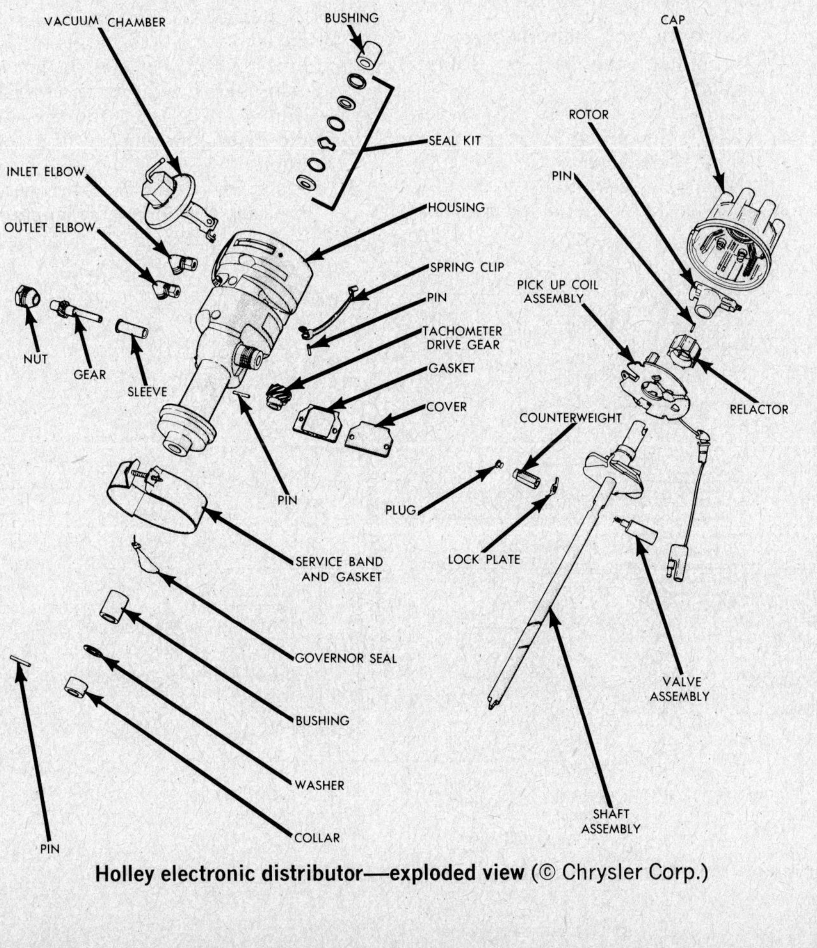

Holley electronic distributor—exploded view (© Chrysler Corp.)

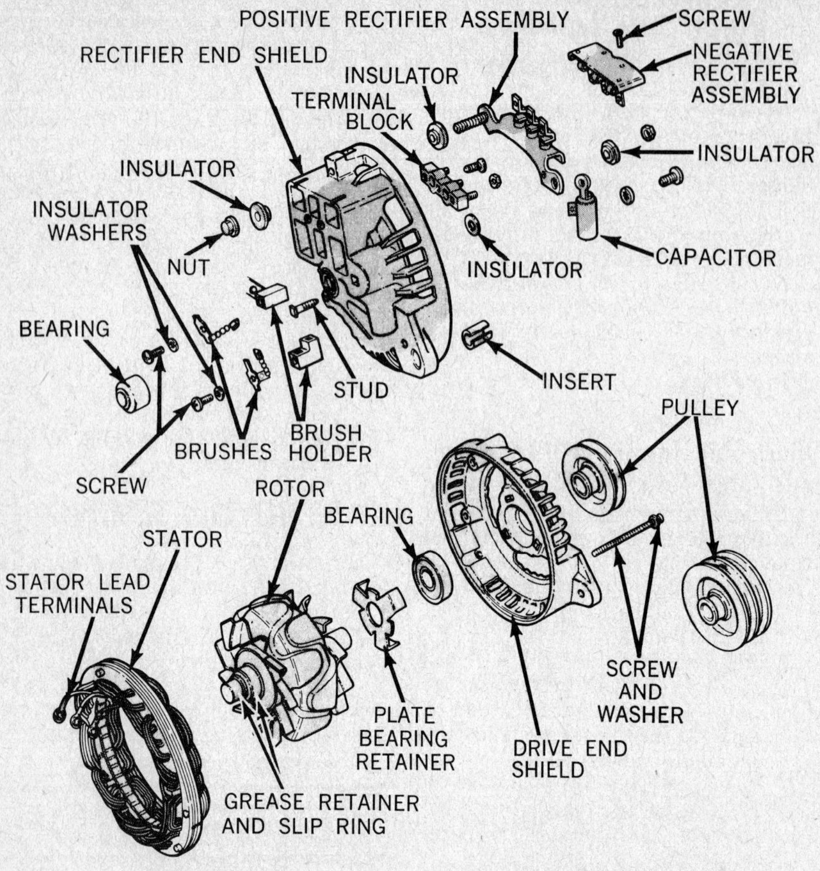

Exploded view of alternator (© Chrysler Corp.)

3. Installation is the reverse of removal. Be sure that the spring clips engage the wiring plug.

STARTER

Reference

For starter motor overhaul procedures see the Electrical Section.

Gasoline Engine

Removal and Installation

1. Disconnect the battery ground cable.
2. Remove the cable at the starter.
3. If the solenoid is mounted on the starter, disconnect the wires at the solenoid terminals.
4. Remove the starter to flywheel housing mounting bolts. Remove automatic transmission oil cooler tube bracket off the stud if necessary. Remove the starter and removable seal if so equipped.
5. Before installing the starter, make sure the starter and flywheel housing mounting surfaces are free of dirt and oil. These surfaces must be clean.
6. Install the starter to flywheel housing removable seal if so equipped.
7. Position the starter to the flywheel housing and, if necessary, install the automatic transmission oil cooler bracket. Install mounting bolts. Tighten securely.

NOTE: When tightening the mounting bolt and nut on the starter hold the starter away from the engine for correct alignment.

8. If the solenoid is mounted on the starter, connect the wires to the solenoid terminals.
9. Connect the cable to the starter terminal.
10. Connect the battery ground cable and test operation of the starter for proper engine cranking.

Diesel Engine

Removal and Installation

1. Disconnect the negative battery cable at the battery. Raise the vehicle on a hoist.
2. Disconnect the battery and solenoid wiring at the starter. Remove the bolt, nut and washer securing the starter to the engine.
3. Remove the starter and the solenoid from the engine as an assembly.
4. Before installing the starter, be sure that the mounting surfaces

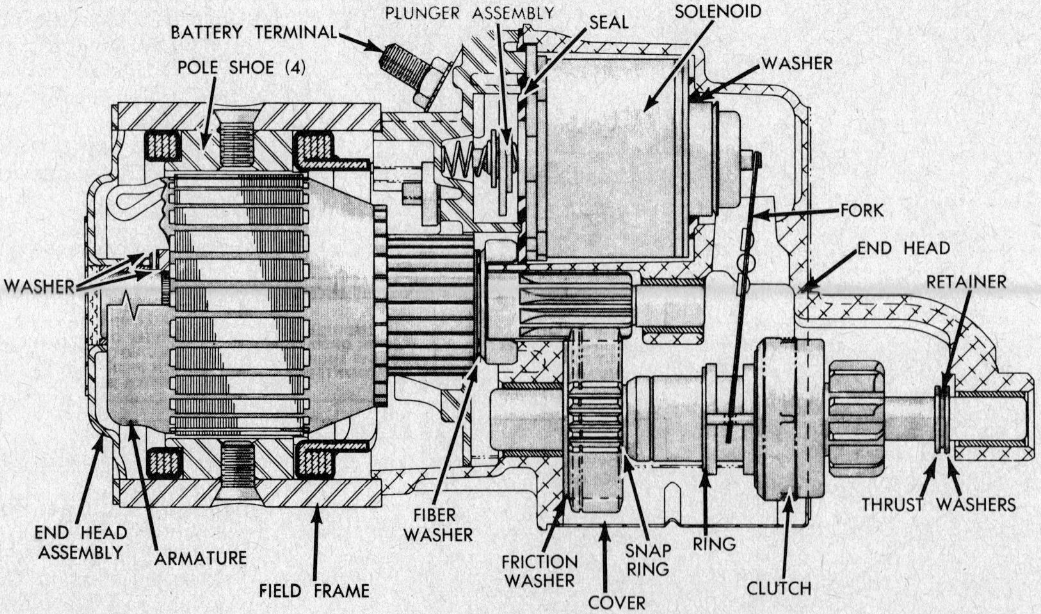

Starter motor (reduction gear type) (© Chrysler Corp.)

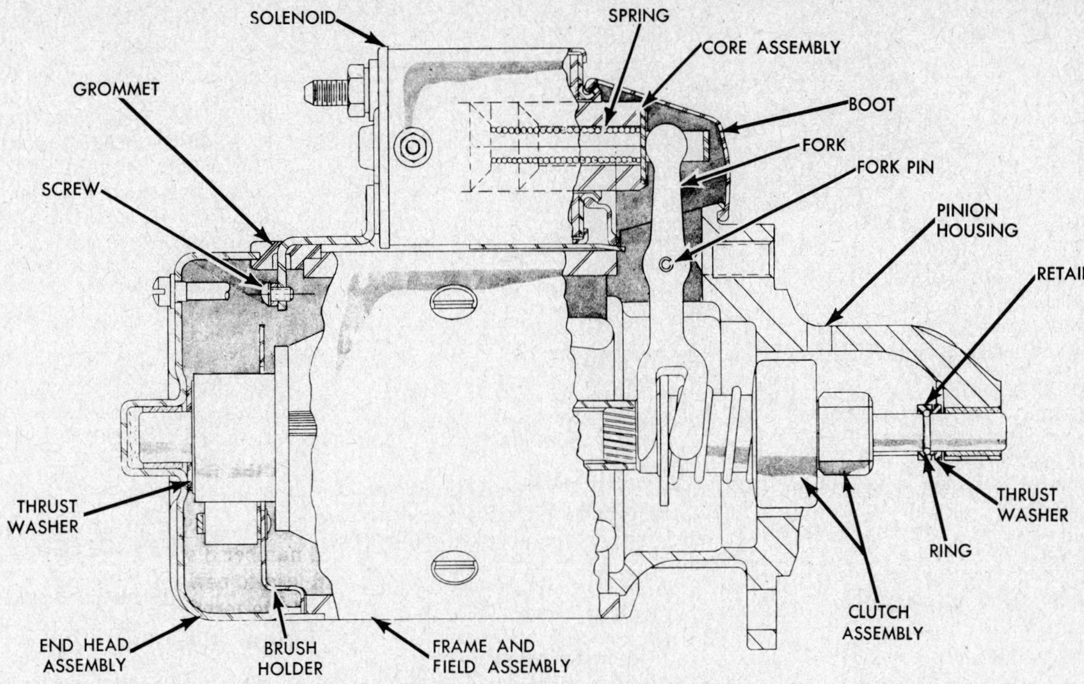

Starter motor (direct drive type) (© Chrysler Corp.)

on the drive-end housing and the flywheel housing are free of dirt and oil to ensure a good electrical contact.

5. To install the starter, reverse the removal procedures.

   NOTE: When tightening attaching bolt and nut, hold the starter away from the flywheel housing to ensure proper alignment.

6. Connect the battery ground cable and test the operation of the starter for proper engine cranking.

BRAKES

Reference

For master, wheel, slave cylinder, and disc brake caliper overhaul, brake shoe and pad replacement and service procedures, bleeding of the hydraulic system, dual master cylinder, vacuum-hydraulic booster system and the Bendix hydro-boost booster system refer to the Brake Section in the General Repair Section.

Master Cylinder

Removal and Installation

1. Disconnect the primary and secondary brake lines from the master cylinder. Install plugs in the outlets of the master cylinder.
2. On vehicles equipped with manual brakes, disconnect the stop lamp switch mounting bracket from under the instrument panel. Grasp the brake pedal and pull backward to disengage the push rod from the master cylinder piston. This will destroy the push rod retention grommet.
3. Remove the nuts that attach the master cylinder to the cowl panel or the brake booster unit.
4. Remove the master cylinder from the vehicle.

   NOTE: On vehicles equipped with manual brakes be sure to remove all traces of the old grommet from the push rod groove and piston socket.

5. To install, bleed the master cylinder before installing it on the vehicle.
6. On vehicles equipped with manual brakes, install a new push rod grommet onto the push rod. Position and install the master cylinder to the cowl panel. Connect the front and rear brake lines. From under the instrument panel, moisten the push rod grommet with a drop of water, align the push rod with the master cylinder piston and using the brake pedal, apply pressure to fully seat the push rod into the piston.
7. On all other vehicles, position the master cylinder to the power

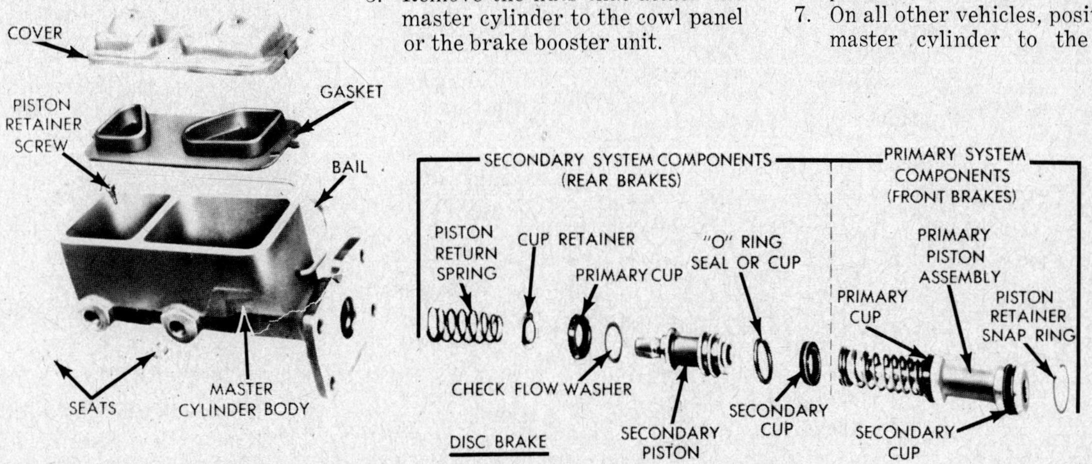

Typical tandem master cylinder—exploded view (© Chrysler Corp.)

Bleeding dual master cylinder (© Chrysler Corp.)

brake unit and install. Connect the front and rear brake lines.
8. Bleed the brake system, being sure that the proper fluid level in the master cylinder is maintained.

Wheel Cylinder

Removal

1. Remove the wheel, drum, and brake shoes.
2. Disconnect the brake hose from the brake tube at the frame bracket for front wheels, and disconnect the brake tube from the wheel cylinder for the rear wheels.
3. Remove the wheel cylinder attaching bolts and slide the cylinder from the brake support plate.
4. Overhaul or replace the cylinder as required.

Installation

1. Position the wheel cylinder on the brake support plate and install the cylinder attaching bolts.
2. On the front wheel cylinders, tighten the brake hose to the cylinder before attaching the brake tube to the hose at the frame location. Tighten the attaching bolts.
3. With the rear wheel cylinder loose on the brake support plate, connect the brake tube to the cylinder and then, tighten the attaching bolts and the brake tube to the wheel cylinder.
4. Install the brake shoes, drum, and wheel.
5. Bleed the hydraulic system.

Disc Brakes

Disc brake removal, installation, and overhaul procedures will be found in the General Repair Section under Disc Brakes.

Power Brakes

Vacuum-Hydraulic Booster

Frame Mounted

Removal and Installation

1. Depress brake pedal several times to remove all vacuum from the system.
2. Disconnect all lines, hoses and wires from the unit.
3. Remove the brake booster mounting brackets, then remove booster.
4. Position the assembly on the mounting brackets, and install the attaching bolts.
5. Connect all lines, hoses and wires to the unit. *NOTE: On Tandem Booster units, remove the lubricating plugs from the end and center the plates. Add vacuum cylinder oil to the level of the filler holes, then install the lubricating plugs.*
6. Bleed the hydraulic system.

Cowl Mounted Conventional Truck

Removal and Installation

1. Remove the master cylinder.
2. Disconnect the vacuum hose from the power brake booster.
3. From under the instrument panel, remove the nut and attaching bolt from the power brake input push rod and brake pedal blade.
4. Remove the four nuts and washers holding the booster in place. Remove the unit from the vehicle.
5. To install, reverse the removal procedures.
6. Check the stop light operation and bleed the hydraulic system if necessary.

Cowl Mounted Vans

Removal and Installation

1. Remove the master cylinder. Disconnect the vacuum hose from the check valve.

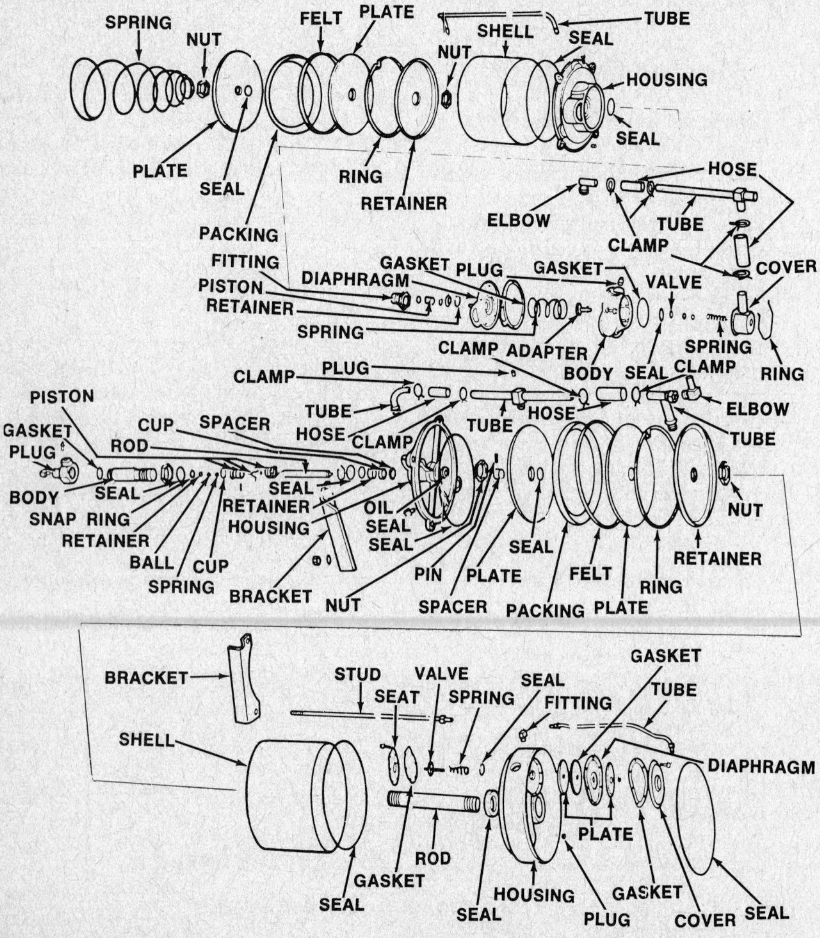

Tandem power brake unit—exploded view (© Chrysler Corp.)

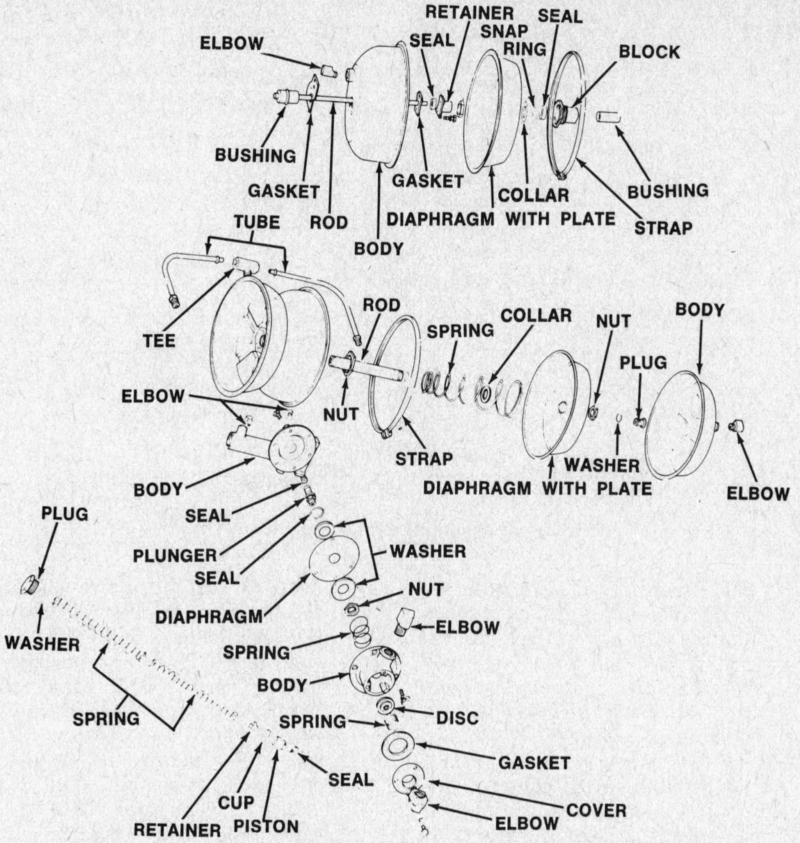

Double diaphragm power brake unit—exploded view (© Chrysler Corp.)

2. Remove the master cylinder to booster mounting nuts.
3. Remove the booster-to-hub and bellcrank pivot bolt.
4. Remove the mounting nuts from the mounting plate and remove the unit from the vehicle.
5. To install, position the booster on the mounting plate and install the coned washers and nuts. Install the pivot bolt.
6. Position and install the master cylinder.
7. Connect the vacuum hose to the check valve and check for proper operation.
8. Bleed the hydraulic system if necessary.

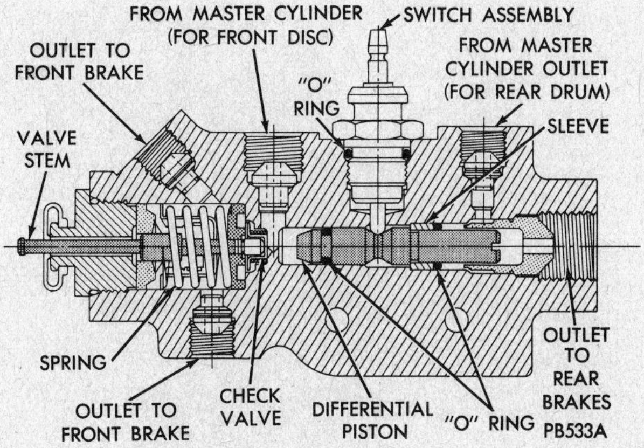

Dual brake system safety switch (© Chrysler Corp.)

Hydro-Boost Booster

Removal and Installation

1. Pump the brake pedal several times to be sure that all pressure is discharged from the accumulator prior to disconnecting the hoses from the booster.
2. Remove the nuts holding the master cylinder to the booster and lay the master cylinder aside. Be sure to avoid kinking or bending the hydraulic brake lines.
3. Disconnect and plug the tubes from the booster ports. Disconnect the brake return spring.
4. Remove the bolt from the push rod to the brake pedal. Remove the mounting nuts and the booster assembly from the vehicle.
5. To install, position the booster on the vehicle and tighten the push rod.
6. Remove the plugs from the hydraulic lines and connect them to their respective ports. Connect the brake pedal return spring.
7. Position and install the master cylinder.
8. Bleed the hydro-boost system.

Bleeding Hydraulic Brakes

Hydro-Boost Hydraulic System

1. Fill the hydraulic pump reservoir to the proper level. Allow the fluid to remain undisturbed for two minutes.

   NOTE: Leave the reservoir cap off during the bleeding operation.
2. Start the engine and run for ten seconds. Check the fluid level and add fluid, if nceessary. Repeat this procedure until the fluid level remains constant in the reservoir.
3. Raise the front end of the vehicle so that the tires clear the ground.
4. Start the engine and run at approximately 1500 RPM. Apply and release the brake pedal several times, while turning the wheels right and left lightly contacting the wheel stops.
5. Turn off the engine and check the fluid level in the reservoir. Add fluid, if necessary.
6. Lower the vehicle. Start the engine and run at approximately 1500 RPM. Apply and release the brake pedal several times, while turning the wheels right and left lightly contacting the wheel stops.
7. Turn the engine off and check the fluid level in the reservoir, add if necessary.

   NOTE: If fluid is extremely foamy, allow the vehicle to stand for an hour with the engine off.

If fluid level is low repeat the process again.

8. Replace the cover on the reservoir.

Stop Light Switch Adjustment

The stop light switch is located behind the brake pedal and adjustment is possible by moving the switch and the bracket assembly in either direction.

Air Brakes

Compressor

The air compressor used on Dodge trucks is a two cylinder single stage reciprocating type using automatic inlet valves. The compressor for the single system is rated at 7¼ cubic feet per minute at 1250 rpm and the compressor for the dual system is rated at 12 cubic feet per minute at 1250 rpm.

The compressor is belt driven and operates continuously when the engine is running with compressed air delivery controlled by the governor. The compressor is lubricated and cooled through the engine systems. Proper cooling is important in maintaining the air discharge temperatures below the maximum of 400°F.

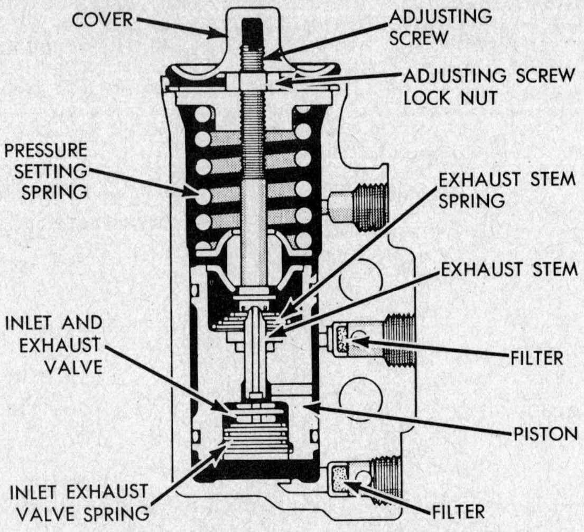

Governor assembly (© Chrysler Corp.)

Maintenance

- *Every 100 hours or 5,000 miles:* Remove the compressor air strainer and wash all parts. The strainer element should be cleaned or replaced. Saturate the element in clean engine oil and squeeze dry before replacing the strainer in the compressor. Check and adjust the belt tension, and inspect the compressor mounting bolts for tightness.
- *Every 350 hours or 10,000 miles:* On self-lubricated compressors, drain the compressor crankcase and flush and refill with clean engine oil.
- *Every 1,000 hours or 35,000 miles:* Remove the compressor discharge valve cap and nuts and check for excessive carbon deposits. Check the discharge line for carbon. If excessive carbon is found in the cylinder head, or in the above checks, the cylinder head or discharge line should be replaced. If the compressor is a self-lubricating model, service the crankcase breather by washing in a suitable solvent.
- *Every 3,000 hours or 100,000 miles:* Disassemble the compressor, clean and inspect all parts thoroughly replacing any component that is worn or damaged.

Governor

The governor is mounted at the rear of the compressor to automatically control the pressure in the air brake system. Pressure in the system

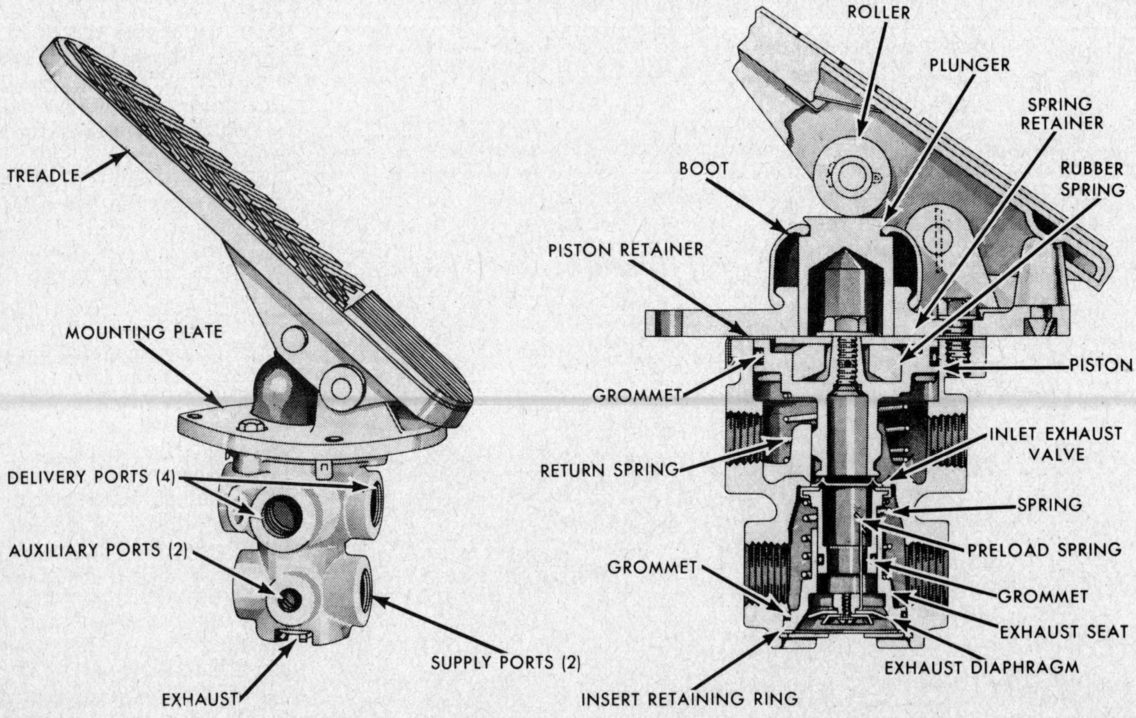

Single system air brake control valve—typical (© Chrysler Corp.)

reservoirs is maintained between the desired pressures of 80-95 psi for the single system and 95-120 psi for the dual system.

1. With the engine running, observe the registered pressure at which the governor cuts, stopping any further pressure build up in the system. The governor should cut out between 85-125 psi (depending on system desired pressure).
2. Make several brake applications and observe the gauge pressure at which the governor cuts-in. Air compression should begin between 80-125 psi.
3. Adjust the governor only if cut-out and cut-in pressures have been checked with an accurate air pressure gauge to confirm the original dash gauge readings.

Air Brake System Valves

Removal and Installation

NOTE: Removal and installation of the different valves (application, relay, quick release, and so on) in the air brake system is very straight forward. The following procedure is a general outline to be followed for all valves.

1. Block and hold the vehicle's wheels.
2. *Exhaust the air pressure from the brake system.*
3. Disconnect the air lines at the valve.
4. Remove the mounting bolts and the valve.
5. Inspect the valve ports (in use) to be sure that they are not plugged.
6. Inspect the air lines and replace any that are damaged or worn.
7. Install the valve in the reverse order of removal. *Make sure that any unused valve ports are properly sealed.*
8. Pressurize the system and check for leaks and proper operation. Road test the vehicle.

Slack Adjusters (Cam Type Brakes)

Adjustment

1. Raise the wheels.
2. Turn the adjusting screw of the slack adjuster in the direction that will rotate the camshaft in the apply direction. *NOTE: The apply direction rotation may be clockwise or counterclockwise depending on the particular installation on the rear wheels. The front brakes will be clockwise. On rear wheels if the adjustment has a locking sleeve, it will be necessary to depress, the sleeve against the spring tension with a wrench while turning the adjusting screw.*
3. Adjust the slack adjuster adjustment screw until the brake shoes are firmly against the brake drum.
4. Back off the adjusting screw just until the wheels will turn freely.
5. Bring the air pressure up to the operating limits and apply full pedal. With the brakes fully applied, check the angle of the push rod to a line through the center of the camshaft and the center of the push rod yoke pin. The angle should be 90° or slightly more, never less than 90°. *NOTE: If the push rod angle is less than 90°, proceed to step #6. If the angle is 90° or more, lower the vehicle and check the operation of the brakes.*
6. Release the brakes and back off the slack adjuster adjustment screw.
7. Loosen the clevis locknut and remove the clevis pin.
8. Adjust the slack adjuster push rod length.
9. Re-adjust the slack adjuster as detailed in steps #3 and #4.
10. Install the clevis pin and the locknut. Tighten the clevis pin locknut.
11. Lower the vehicle and check the operation of the brakes.

Removal and Installation

1. Remove the clevis pin which attaches the slack adjuster to the brake chamber. *NOTE: On vehicles with a rear wheel spring brake, the spring brake must be released to remove the clevis pin.*
2. Remove the lock ring attaching the slack adjuster to the camshaft.
3. Mark the position of the slack adjuster on the camshaft, then slide the slack adjuster off the camshaft.
4. Place the slack adjuster on the camshaft, aligning the locating marks. If there is excessive end play, install an additional spacer at the cam end of the camshaft. Install the lock ring.
5. Connect the brake chamber push rod to the slack adjuster by installing the clevis pin in the upper hole, and install the cotter pin.
6. Lubricate the slack adjuster, and adjust the brakes.

Cam Type Brake Chamber

Removal and Installation

1. Clean the outside of the brake chamber, removing all dirt and grease.
2. *Exhaust the air from the system* and disconnect the air line at the brake chamber.
3. Disconnect the push rod clevis pin from the slack adjuster.
4. Remove the mounting bolts and the brake chamber.
5. Check and if necessary, cut the push rod of the new chamber to the same length as the original. If a new chamber is being installed, transfer the brake line fittings to the replacement chamber.
6. Inspect the air line to the brake chamber, replace if worn or damaged.
7. Position the chamber assembly on the mounting bracket. Install the mounting bolts, clevis pin,

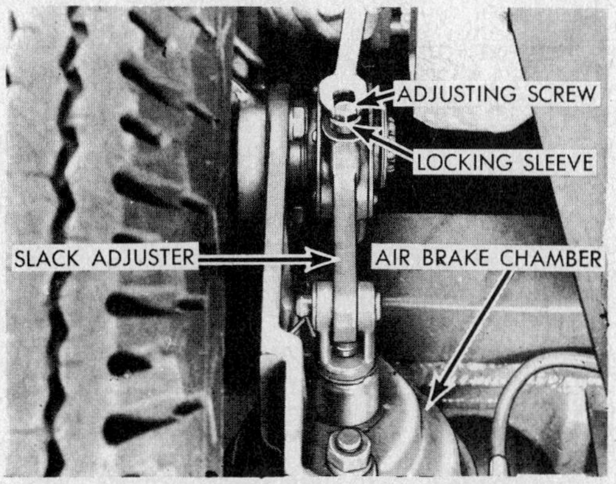

Slack adjuster adjustment (© Chrysler Corp.)

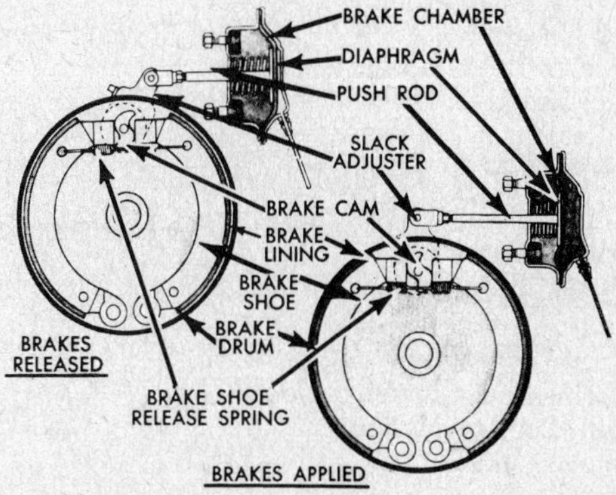

Cam type brake chamber installation (front)—typical (© Chrysler Corp.)

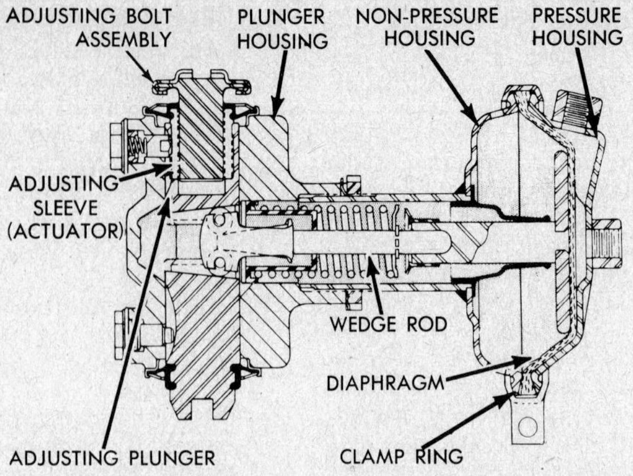

Wedge type brake chamber—typical (© Chrysler Corp.)

and cotter pin. Connect the air line to the chamber.

8. Pressurize the system and check for leaks.
9. Adjust the brakes and check their operation. Road test the vehicle.

Wedge Type Brake Chamber

Removal and Installation

1. *Exhaust the air pressure from the brake system.*
2. Disconnect the air lines.
3. Loosen the spanner nut with a drift and a light hammer.
4. Unscrew the brake chamber from the wedge housing.
   Check the position of the wedge in the plunger housing to make sure that the wedge assembly is properly seated. Be certain that the automatic adjusting identification ring on the chamber tube is replaced.
5. Screw the brake chamber into the plunger housing until it bottoms (spanner nut loose).
6. Align the connection ports with the brake lines, if necessary, unscrew the service chamber not more than one full turn.
7. Connect the brake lines.
8. Make and hold a full pressure brake application. Drive the spanner nut with a drift and hammer until it is tight against the plunger housing. Release the brake pressure.
9. Check for leaks and proper operation. Road test the vehicle.

Parking Brake

External Contracting Driveshaft Type

Removal

1. Disconnect the brake cable.
2. Remove adjusting bolt nut.
3. Remove guide bolt adjusting lock nuts.
4. Remove anchor adjusting screw.
5. Pull band assembly away from transmission and off propeller shaft.

Installation

1. Position brake band and lining assembly over propeller shaft and on brake drum.
2. Install brake band anchor adjusting screw and adjusting guide bolt nut and lock nuts.
3. Connect brake cable.

Internal Expanding Driveshaft, Type One

NOTE: This procedure is for the type brake which has an internal adjuster similar to the type used on wheel brakes. There is an adjusting screw cover plate on the bottom of the backing plate.

Removal

1. Disconnect propeller shaft at transmission.
2. Remove companion flange nut, lockwasher and flatwasher.
3. Install a suitable tool on the companion flange and remove flange and brake drum while using a holding tool to prevent rotation.
4. Disengage ball end of cable from operating lever.
5. Separate shoes at bottom, allowing brake shoe adjusting nut screws, and sleeve to drop out and release shoes.
6. Pry brake shoe return spring up and over to the right and brake shoe in.
7. Then, work spring out of assembly.
8. Pry out brake shoe retaining washer and remove outer guide.
9. Slide each shoe out from under guide spring (as shoes are removed, the operating lever strut will drop out of place).
10. Separate the operating lever from the right hand brake shoe by removing nut, lockwasher and bolt.

Installation

1. Assemble operating lever to right hand brake shoe.
2. Slide the right and left parking brake shoes under guide.
3. Spread shoes and insert operating lever.
4. Work return spring under guide spring and upward to engage retaining pin on left hand shoe.
5. Force the other end of return spring upward and over retaining pin on right hand shoe.
6. Install adjusting nut, screw and sleeve.
7. Place outer anchor guide over anchor and secure shoes with retaining washer.
8. Turn shoe adjusting nut until shoes are in a released position and install brake drum.
9. Adjust brake shoe and control cable.

CAUTION: If parking brake is adjusted incorrectly, the automatic shifting of the Load-Flite Transmission will be affected.

Internal Expanding Driveshaft, Type Two

NOTE: This procedure is for the type brake that has an external linkage clevis adjustment.

Removal

1. Disconnect the adjuster clevis at the operating lever.
2. Remove the universal joint trunnion bolts and support the driveshaft.

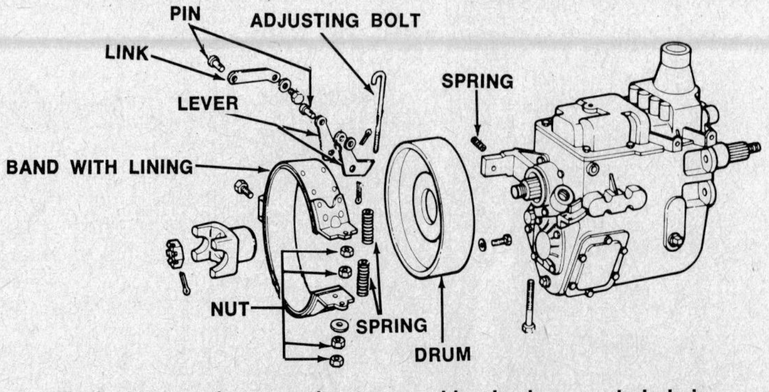

Typical external contracting type parking brake—exploded view
(© Chrysler Corp.)

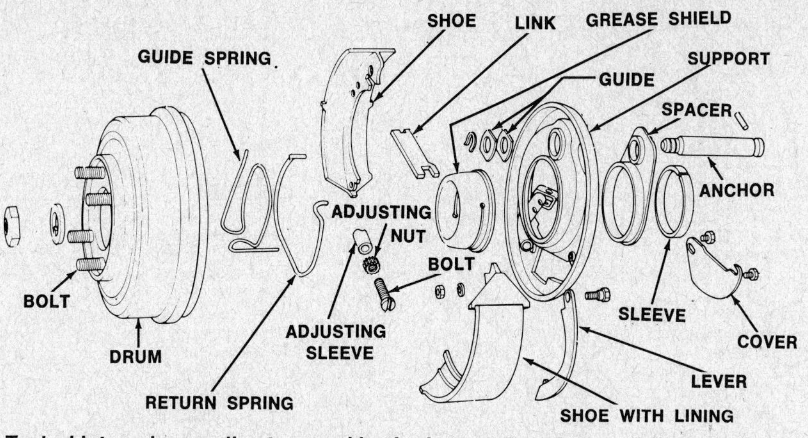

Typical internal expanding type parking brake—exploded view (© Chrysler Corp.)

3. Remove the mainshaft locknut and washer. Remove the yoke and drum.
4. Unbolt the drum from the yoke.
5. Unbolt the brake assembly from the transmission mounting flange. Separate the shoe assembly from the actuating cam and lever.

Installation

1. Place the brake assembly, with the cam lugs between the ends of the shoes, on the mounting flange.
2. Align the brake on the flange, install the mounting bolts and lockwashers, torquing to 75 ft. lbs.
3. Bolt the drum to the yoke, torquing to 75 ft. lbs.
4. Install the drum to the mainshaft. Torque the nut to 120 ft. lbs.
5. You can check drum runout with a dial indicator. If it exceeds .015 in., loosen the drum to yoke bolts 1/4 turn and tap the high side with a soft hammer. Tighten the bolts and recheck the runout. If runout persists, but doesn't exceed .018 in., make 6-8 moderate brake applications from 20 mph and recheck runout. If runout still exceeds .015 in., a new drum is required.

Air Spring Type

Reference

The air spring type parking brake is air actuated and is operated in conjunction with the rear wheel service brake air chamber. The spring is held in the retracted (or off) position by air pressure from a protected third air reservoir. As the air pressure is released from the cylinder housing, the spring is released thereby actuating the service brake push rod and applying the brakes.

Air—Removal & Installation

1. Back off slack adjuster adjusting screw.
2. Disconnect brake chamber push rod by removing clevis pin.
3. Disconnect air lines.
4. Remove nuts and washers from mounting bolts, remove brake chamber and spring brake assembly.
5. To install reverse the above procedure, and adjust brakes.

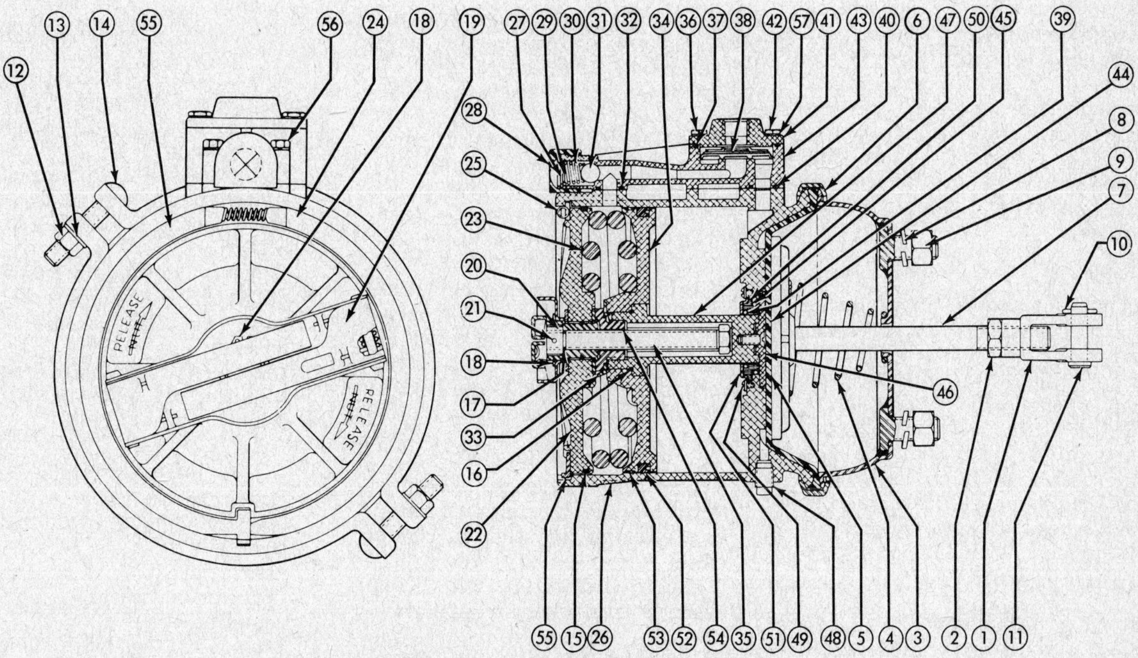

Spring type parking brake (© Chrysler Corp.)

1. Yoke
2. Jam Nut
3. Non Press Housing
4. Spring
5. Diaphragm
6. Clamp Band
7. Push Rod
8. Lockwasher
9. Nut
10. Cotter Pin
11. Clevis Pin
12. Nut
13. Washer
14. Carriage Bolt
15. O-Ring
16. O-Ring
17. O-Ring
18. Snap Ring
19. Handle
20. Nut
21. Pin
22. Cover Plate-Sub Assembly
23. Spring
24. Retaining Ring
25. Spring
26. Cylinder
27. Snap Ring
28. Boot
29. Washer
30. Spring
31. Ball
32. O-Ring
33. Tooth Washer
34. Piston
35. Release Bolt
36. Screw
37. O-Ring
38. Diaphragm
39. Screw
40. O-Ring
41. Cap
42. Screw
43. Body
44. O-Ring
45. O-Ring
46. Plunger
47. Piston Shaft
48. Pipe Plug
49. Screw
50. Bushing
51. Cap
52. O-Ring
53. Ring
54. Piston Nut
55. Retaining Ring
56. Screw
57. Lock Washer

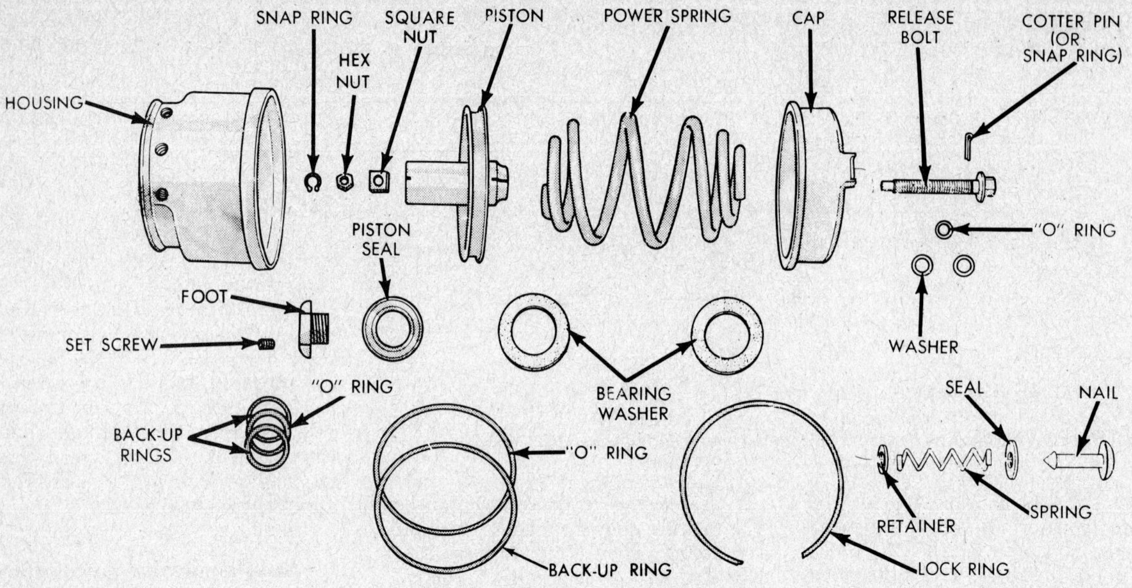

Fail safe unit (© Chrysler Corp.)

Quick Release Valve—Removal & Installation

1. Relieve air pressure. Disconnect air line.
2. Remove four capscrews and remove cap.
3. Remove remaining two capscrews holding release valve to body.
4. Remove boot from small end of body, clean all parts with solvent and blow dry with compressed air. All "O" rings and rubber parts must be replaced.
5. To install, reverse the above procedure. Tighten all six capscrews to 15 ft. lb. Connect air line pressurize system and check for leaks.

Fail-Safe

This unit is mounted "Piggy Back" on the air chamber non-pressure housing of the stopmaster brake. The power spring is held in a compressed position as long as the air pressure is 65 PSI or more. Anytime the air pressure drops below 65 PSI the power spring pushes the piston against the diaphragm plate, forcing the wedge head between the rollers, which spreads the plungers apart and applies the brake.

Removal

1. Cage power spring. Relieve air pressure and remove air lines from unit.
2. Mark non-pressure housing, pressure housing and cap with punch or chisel to aid in alignment at reassembly. Loosen or remove clamp ring and remove unit from non-pressure housing.

Installation

1. Align cap and housing with marks made during removal.
2. Position unit on non-pressure housing and install clamp ring and bolt.
3. Connect air lines and apply air pressure. Uncage power spring and check operation of system.

Shortstop Spring Brake

This spring type parking brake assembly is used in conjunction with the wedge type air brakes.

Removal

1. Bleed air from system. Disconnect air lines (mark lines for proper assembly).
2. Remove breather cap. Using a 9/16" deep socket, unscrew release bolt completely.
3. Mark clamp ring, spring brake housing and service brake housing to aid in proper alignment at assembly. Remove bolt from clamp ring. Spring brake is now free for further work.

Installation

1. Align service brake housing, spring brake housing and clamp ring. Install and tighten clamp bolt.
2. Connect and tighten air lines using marks made during removal.
3. Charge system with air, screw release bolt down.
4. Check for air leaks, clean and replace breather cap.

Rear Wheel Cable Type

In this system, the rear wheel brakes also act as parking brakes. They are operated mechanically by a lever and strut connected to a steel cable. This cable is connected to the rear wheel brake cables via an equalizer.

Removal

1. Raise the vehicle, release the brakes, and remove the rear wheels.
2. Remove the brake drum from the rear axle.
3. Remove the brake shoe return spring and brake shoe retaining springs.
4. Remove the brake shoe strut and spring from the support plate.
5. Disconnect the cable from the operating arm.
6. Compress the retainers on the end of the cable housing and remove the cables from the support plate.
7. Remove the retaining bolt and nut from the cable bracket. Remove the clips at the frame bracket.
8. Disconnect the cable from the equalizer bar, and remove the assembly.

Installation

1. Lubricate the cable with short fiber grease at the point of contact.
2. Insert the cable and housing into the frame bracket and install the retaining clips.
3. Engage the end with the equalizer bar.
4. Insert the rear end of the cable and housing into the brake support plate. Make sure the housing retainers lock firmly in place.
5. Insert the end of the cable into the brake shoe operating lever and install the brake shoes.
6. Install the retaining springs, return springs, brake drum, and wheel.

7. Connect the brake cable bracket.
8. Adjust the brakes and cable.

Parking Brake Adjustment

Internal Expanding Driveshaft Type One

Disconnect front end of propeller shaft to permit turning brake drum by hand.

1. Remove adjusting screw cover plate, loosen brake cable clamping bolt and back off the cable adjusting nut.
2. Turn adjusting nut to decrease shoe-to-drum clearances, until a slight drag is felt on drum.
3. Back off adjusting nut at least one full notch, using spanner wrench. **CAUTION: Make sure the two raised shoulders on adjusting nut are seated in the grooves on the adjusting sleeve.**
4. The cable length adjusting nut should be positioned against cable housing so there is at least .005 inch but no more than .010 inch clearance, between the operating lever and brake shoe cable. To lock adjustment, tighten cable housing clamp securely.
5. Tighten cable adjusting nut against the housing.
6. Check parking brake lever for travel.
7. Install adjusting screw cover plate and connect propeller shaft.
8. With rear wheels off the floor, start engine, apply brakes a few times, check for binding and proper adjustment.

Internal Expanding Driveshaft Type Two

1. Release the brake handle.
2. Adjustment is made by removing the pin and adjusting the length of the clevis. The brake should be free of drag when rotated. Shoe to drum clearance should be .020 in. on the 10 in. brake used on D800 and S600 models.

External Contracting Driveshaft Type

1. Remove the lockwire from the anchor adjusting screw on the left side.
2. Using a feeler gauge between drum and lining tighten or loosen adjusting screw to give .015 to .020 inch clearance. Install lock wire. **CAUTION: The lockwire which retains anchor screw must not be drawn up tight. It will cause uneven wear and poor brake application.**
3. Adjust the small diameter guide bolt on the right side to adjust the clearance of the lower part of the band.
4. Adjust the large adjusting bolt (the one with the springs) on the right side to adjust the clearance of the upper part of the band. Adjust until the drum is free with the brake released.
5. Adjust the cable as necessarv.

Rear Wheel Cable Type

1. Inspect all components and correct any deficiencies such as rust, kinks, or bent parts.
2. Raise the vehicle on a lift and release the brake.
3. Loosen the adjustment until both cables have slack.
4. Tighten the cable adjuster until a slight drag is felt while rotating the wheel. Loosen the adjuster until there is no drag, then back off two turns.
5. Apply the brake several times, then recheck the adjustment.

FUEL SYSTEM

Reference

Carburetor specifications, exploded views, and basic adjustments are found in the General Repair Section under Carburetor Repairs.

Carburetor

Removal and Installation

The following is a general removal procedure for all carburetors.

1. Disconnect the battery ground cable.
2. Remove the air cleaner.
3. Remove the fuel tank pressure-vacuum filler cap. The tank could be under a small amount of pressure.
4. Disconnect and plug the fuel lines. Use two wrenches to avoid twisting the fuel line. A container is also useful to catch any fuel which spills from the lines.
5. Disconnect the throttle and choke linkage.
6. Disconnect any vacuum lines.
7. Remove the mounting bolts.
8. Carefully remove the carburetor from the engine and carry it in a level position to a clean work place.
9. Installation is the reverse of removal. Adjust the curb idle speed.

Fuel Pump

Removal and Installation

1. Disconnect the fuel lines from the inlet and output sides of the fuel pump.
2. Plug these lines to prevent gasoline from leaking out.
3. Unbolt the retaining bolts from the fuel pump and remove the fuel pump from the engine.
4. Remove the old gasket from the engine and/or fuel pump.
5. Clean all mounting surfaces.
6. Using a new gasket, install the fuel pump. Installation is the reverse of removal.

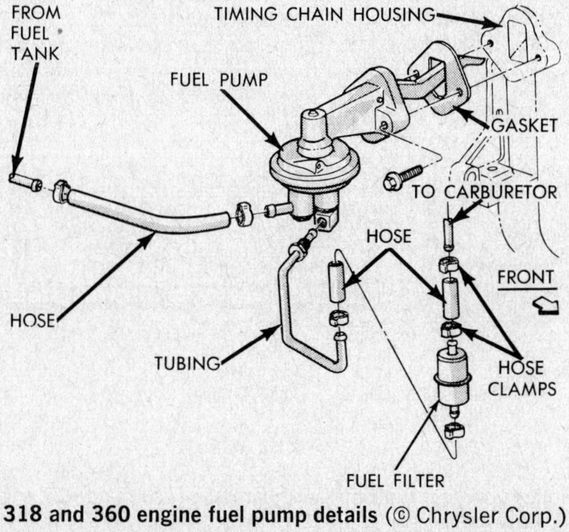

318 and 360 engine fuel pump details (© Chrysler Corp.)

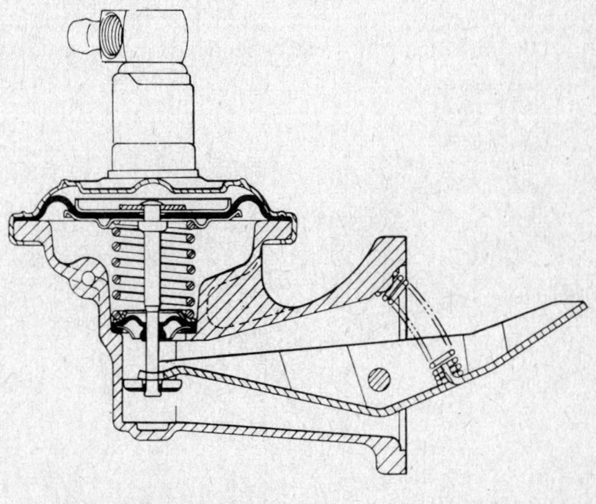

Fuel pump 6-Cylinder (© Chrysler Corp.)

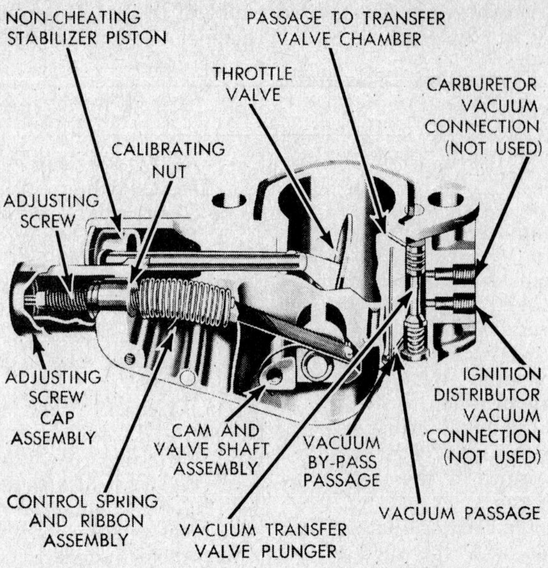

Sandwich type velocity governor (© Chrysler Corp.)

Governors

Sandwich Velocity Type Governor

Speed Adjustment

NOTE: See specifications at the beginning of this section for engine no load governed rpm.

1. Remove seal.
2. Turn speed screw adjusting cap, one-half turn at a time, counterclockwise to increase speed and clockwise to decrease speed. Each ½ turn equals approximately 150 rpm. More than two complete counterclockwise turns from factory setting is not recommended.

Surge Adjustment

1. Remove adjusting screw cap assembly and locate special hollow wrench in calibrating nut.
2. Locate hex wrench through hollow wrench into adjusting screw.
3. Block throttle linkage to produce surge at governed speed.
4. Turn calibrating nut clockwise ¼ turn at a time while holding adjusting screw with hex wrench until surge is minimized.
5. Reinstall adjusting screw cap assembly and reset governor speed if necessary.
6. Install a new seal.

Slow Action Adjustment

If governor does not cut in quickly at maximum speed or does not open promptly at governed speed when load is applied, governor is said to be slow acting. This is corrected by the same procedure as that described for surge adjustments above, except that the calibrating nut is turned counterclockwise.

Holley Governors

Adjustment

1. Connect tachometer to engine. run it up to governed speed.
2. After the engine has warmed up, run it up to governed speed.
3. Stop the engine for adjustment.
4. Remove the cover band and seal from the distributor body. Turn the engine until the governor counterweight adjusting screw is accessible.
5. Remove the plug from the counterweight with a ⅛ in. Allen wrench.
6. Insert a slotted adjusting tool into the counterweight hole and engage the adjusting tangs. Turn clockwise to decrease speed and counterclockwise to increase. ¼ turn changes governed speed about 100 rpm.
7. Remove the adjusting tool and replace the plug and cover band before starting the engine.
8. Install new band seal.

Idle Speed and Mixture Adjustment

NOTE: Adjust with the air cleaner installed.

1. Run the engine at fast idle to stabilize engine temperature.
2. Make sure that the choke plate is fully released.
3. Attach a tachometer to the engine. With electronic ignition, connect the meter to the negative primary coil terminal and to a ground.
   NOTE: Not all tachometers or dwell/tachometers will work with electronic ignition; some may be damaged. Check the manufacturer's instructions carefully.
4. Connect an exhaust analyzer to the engine and insert the probe as far into the tailpipe as possible. On vehicles with dual exhaust, insert the probe into the left tailpipe as this is the side without the heat riser valve.
5. Check ignition timing and adjust it as required.
6. If the truck has air conditioning, turn the air conditioner off. On six-cylinder engines, turn the headlights on high beam.
7. Place the manual transmission in neutral; put the automatic in Park. Make sure the hot idle compensator valve (if any) on the carburetor is fully seated in the closed position.
8. Turn the engine idle speed adjustment screw in or out to adjust idle speed to specification. If

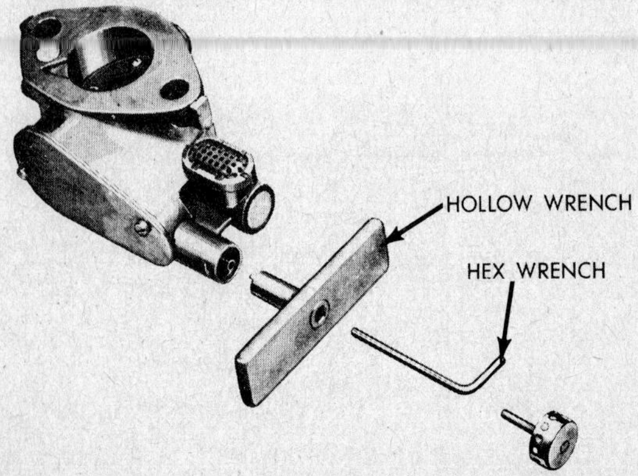

Sandwich governor surge adjustment (© Chrysler Corp.)

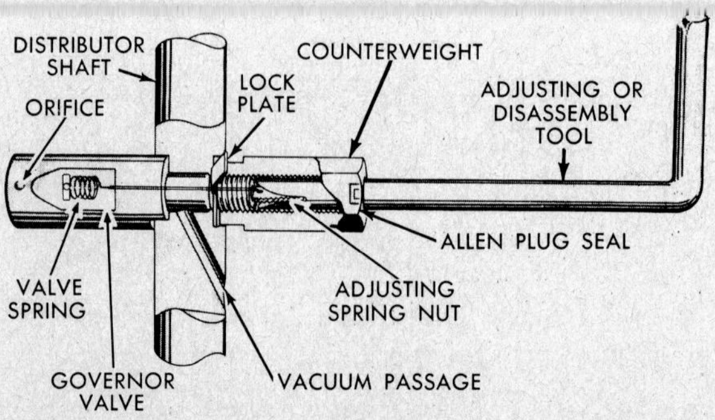

Holley governor distributor adjustment—361 and 413 engine (© Chrysler Corp.)

the carburetor has an electric solenoid, turn the solenoid adjusting screw in or out to obtain the specified rpm. Then, adjust the curb idle speed screw until it just touches the stop on the carburetor body. Now, back the curb idle speed adjusting screw out one full turn.

9. Turn each idle mixture adjustment screw 1/16 turn richer (counterclockwise). Wait 30 seconds and observe the reading on the exhaust gas analyzer. Continue this procedure until the meter indicates a definite increase in the richness of the mixture.

   NOTE: This step is very important. A carburetor that is set too lean will cause the exhaust gas analyzer to give a false reading indicating a rich mixture. Because of this, the carburetor must be known to have a rich mixture to verify the reading on the exhaust gas analyzer.

10. After verifying the reading obtained on the meter, adjust the mixture screws to get an air/fuel ratio of 14.2:1. Turn the mixture screws clockwise (leaner) to raise the meter reading or counterclockwise (richer) to lower the meter reading.

NOTE: On 1975 and later models, adjust to get the air/fuel ratio and percentage of CO indicated on the engine compartment sticker.

Idle Speed Solenoid Adjustment

This solenoid is energized whenever the ignition circuit is on. Its function is to allow the throttle plates to close farther when the ignition is switched off, thereby preventing engine over-running.

1. Bring the engine to operating temperature and attach a tachometer.
2. With the engine running, adjust the solenod screw to the proper rpm.
3. Adjust the slow curb idle screw until the screw end just contacts the stop on the carburetor body. Back the screw off one full turn.
4. Test the above procedure by disconnecting the solenoid wire at the connector. Be sure not to let the lead short to the engine. The solenoid should de-energize and idle speed should drop down below normal. Now reconnect the wire. After you reconnect the solenoid, move the throttle linkage by hand since the solenoid isn't strong enough to move it.

Propane Adjustment

1. Place the transmission in neutral position and set the parking brake. Turn all lights and accessories off. Connect a tachometer and a timing light to the engine. Start the engine and allow it to warm up on the second stop of the fast idle cam. Do this until normal operation temperature is reached, then return the engine to idle.
2. Disconnect and plug the EGR vacuum hose and the distributor vacuum hose. Check the engine timing and adjust if necessary, Disconnect the heated air door vacuum hose at the carburetor nipple and in it's place, install the propane supply hose. On 440 Cu. In. engines without the heated air system, insert the propane supply hose 12 in. into the air cleaner snorkel. Make sure that the propane bottle is in an upright and safe position. Remove the PCV valve from the cylinder head cover and disconnect the purge hose to the vapor canister at the carburetor end. Leave both open to underhood air.
3. Open the propane main flow valve. With the air cleaner in place, slowly open the propane metering valve until the maximum engine RPM is reached. When too much propane is added, the engine RPM will decrease. "Fine Tune" the metering valve to obtain the highest engine RPM.
4. With the propane still flowing, adjust the idle speed screw to attain the propane RPM specified on the emissions label. If there has been a change in the maximum RPM, readjust the idle speed screw to the specified propane RPM.
5. Turn off the propane main valve and allow the engine speed to stabilize. With the air cleaner in place, slowly adjust the idle air mixture screws to achieve the smoothest idle at the specified idle set RPM. Pause between adjustments to allow the engine speed to stabilize. If it appears necessary to remove the limiter caps to reach the idle set RPM, first check for engine malfunctions and vacuum leaks. If idle limiter caps are removed, service caps must be installed with the tang against the maximum rich stop.
6. Turn the propane main valve *on.* If the maximum speed is more than 25 RPM different than the specified propane RPM, repeat steps 3 through 6.
7. Turn both the propane main valve and the *metering valve off.* Remove the tachometer. Remove the propane supply hose and reinstall the heated air door vacuum hose (except models without heated air). Unplug and reinstall the vacuum hose to the EGR valve and to the distributor.
8. Replace the PCV valve. Reconnect the canister purge hose to it's proper place. A variation in the engine RPM may occur, *but do not readjust.*

Fuel Tank

Vans and Pick-Ups

Removal

1. Disconnect the battery ground cable.
2. Remove the fuel tank filler cap.
3. Raise the vehicle on a lift. Pump all fuel from the tank into an approved holding tank, and raise the vehicle.
4. Disconnect the fuel line and wire lead to the gauge unit. Remove the ground strap.
5. Remove the vent hose shield and the hose clamps from the hoses running to the vapor vent tube.
6. Remove the filler tube hose clamps and disconnect the hose from the tank.
7. Place a transmission jack under the center of the tank and apply sufficient pressure to support the tank.
8. Disconnect the two J-bolts and remove the retaining straps at the rear of the tank. Lower the tank from the vehicle. Feed the two vent tube hoses and filler tube vent hose through the grommets in the frame as the tank is being lowered. Remove the tank gauge unit.

Installation

1. Inspect the fuel filter, and if it is clogged or damaged, replace it.
2. Insert a new gasket in the recess of the fuel gauge opening and slide the gauge into the tank. Align the positioning tangs on the gauge with those on the tank. Install the lock ring, and tighten securely.
3. Position the tank on a transmission jack and hoist it into place, feeding the vent hoses through the grommets on the way up.
4. Connect the J-bolts and retaining straps, and tighten to 40 inch-lbs. Remove the jack.
5. Connect the filler tube and all vent hoses.
6. Connect the fuel supply line, ground strap, and gauge unit wire lead.
7. Refill the tank and inspect it for leaks. Connect the battery ground cable.

Conventional

Removal

1. Disconnect the battery ground cable. Remove the fuel tank filler cap.

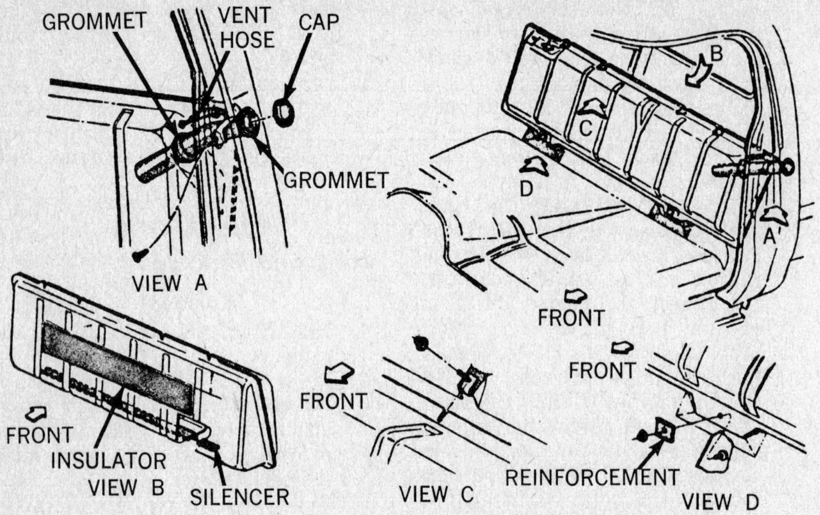

Conventional truck in-cab fuel tank (© Chrysler Corp.)

2. Pump all fuel out of the tank and the auxiliary tank (if so equipped) into a safe holding tank.
3. Remove all seat mounting nuts from under the cab, and remove the seat from the cab.
4. Disconnect the gauge wire, vent lines, and fuel line and remove the grommet from the outer end of the filler tube. If the vehicle is equipped with an auxiliary fuel tank, disconnect the two large hose clamps on the lower filler tube inside the cab and slide the hose down far enough to allow the top filler tube to be disconnected with the tank. Disconnect the auxiliary fuel tank vent hose from the filler tube.
5. Remove the screw from the filler tube mounting bracket located on the face of the cab pillar.
6. Loosen the four nuts from the mounting studs along the top of the tank and remove two bolts from the bottom of the tank.
7. Tip the bottom of the tank forward and remove the tank from the vehicle, working through the passenger side door opening.
8. Remove the tank gauge unit with a special spanner wrench. Slide the gauge unit assembly from the tank and discard the gasket.

Installation

1. Insert a new gasket and the gauge assembly into the fuel gauge opening recess. Align the gauge positioning tangs with the tangs in the tank. Install the lock ring and secure it.
2. Put the tank into position in the cab and tighten the bolts and nuts securely.
3. Connect the gauge wire, vent tubes, and fuel line. If there is an auxiliary fuel tank, connect the lower hoses and tighten the hose clamps.
4. Install the filler tube grommet over the end tube and install the retaining screw into the filler tube mounting bracket.
5. Mount the seat in the vehicle and securely install the nuts on the seat mounting studs under the vehicle.
6. Refill the fuel tank, and inspect for leaks. If no leaks are present, install the battery and ground cable and gauge wire.

Conventional Chassis Mounted

Removal

1. Disconnect the battery ground. Remove the fuel tank filler cap.
2. Pump all fuel from the tank into an approved holding tank.
3. Put the vehicle on a lift and disconnect the vent hoses and filler hose. Remove the vent hoses from the hose routing bracket.
4. Remove the nut from the outboard end of the center retaining strap, pull off the end of the strap, and allow it to hang free.
5. Place a transmission jack under the tank and apply sufficient pressure to support it.
6. Remove the two remaining outboard retaining strap nuts and lower the tank slightly to permit disconnecting the gauge wire and fuel line. Remove these, and then lower the tank further and remove it from the vehicle.

Installation

1. Place the tank on top of the transmission jack and raise it high enough to connect the fuel line and gauge wire.
2. Connect the fuel line and gauge wire. Raise the tank into position and connect the two retaining straps.
3. Remove the jack and connect the center strap. Tighten all three straps firmly, but cautiously, to avoid overstraining straps.
4. Route the vent hoses through the hose holding bracket and connect them to the adapters at the back of the cab.
5. Connect the filler hose to the adaptor at the back of the cab.
6. Refill the tank and inspect for leaks, verifying safety before reconnecting battery ground.

Ramcharger and Trail Duster

Removal

1. If there is a tank skid plate, remove it.
2. Disconnect the battery ground cable.
3. Remove the tank filler cap.
4. Pump or siphon the contents of the tank into a safe container.

CAUTION: **Siphoning should not be started by mouth. Only fuel-safe pumps should be used.**

5. Raise the vehicle on a hoist and disconnect the fuel line and tank sending unit wire. Remove the ground strap or wire.
6. Remove the hose clamps from the vent dome hose.
7. Remove the filler tube hose clamps. Detach the hoses from the tank.
8. Support the tank with a padded transmission jack.
9. Disconnect the two J-bolts and remove the straps at the rear of the tank.
10. Remove the tank gauge sending unit.

Installation

1. Use a new tank gauge sending unit gasket. Check the filter on the end of the fuel suction tube.
2. Use a new or undamaged tank to frame insulator. Raise the tank into position.
3. Connect the J-bolts and retaining straps. Tighten the bolts until about .97 in. of threads protrude.
4. Connect the filler tube and all hoses. Tighten the clamps.
5. Connect the fuel line, ground strap or wire, and tank sending unit wire. Make sure that all fuel line heat shields are in place.
6. Reconnect the battery ground cable and replace the skid plate.

COOLING SYSTEM

Water Pump

Removal and Installation

1. Drain the cooling system and remove the fan belt and fan shroud. Remove the radiator if necessary.
2. Unscrew fan blade bolts and remove fan blade, spacers and bolts as an assembly.

CAUTION: Silicone drive fans must be kept in their normal attitude. If the shaft points down, silicone fluid will contaminate the fan drive bearing.

3. Position the six-cylinder lower clamp in the center of the by-pass hose. Disconnect or remove heater and radiator hoses.
4. Remove water pump retaining bolts and remove water pump assembly.

   NOTE: On air conditioned equipped vehicles with V-8 engines, the compressor clutch assembly and the front mounting brackets may have to be removed to allow for the removal of the water pump assembly.
5. Install a new by-pass hose if necessary, with clamps positioned in the center of the hose.
6. Use a new gasket and install water pump. Install and tighten pump retaining bolts to 30 foot pounds. Position by-pass hose clamps. Install the heater and radiator hoses.
7. Install fan blade, spacer and bolt assembly. Start all bolts, then tighten to 15-18 foot pounds.
8. Install fan belt and adjust belt tension. Fill cooling system. Start the engine and check for leaks.

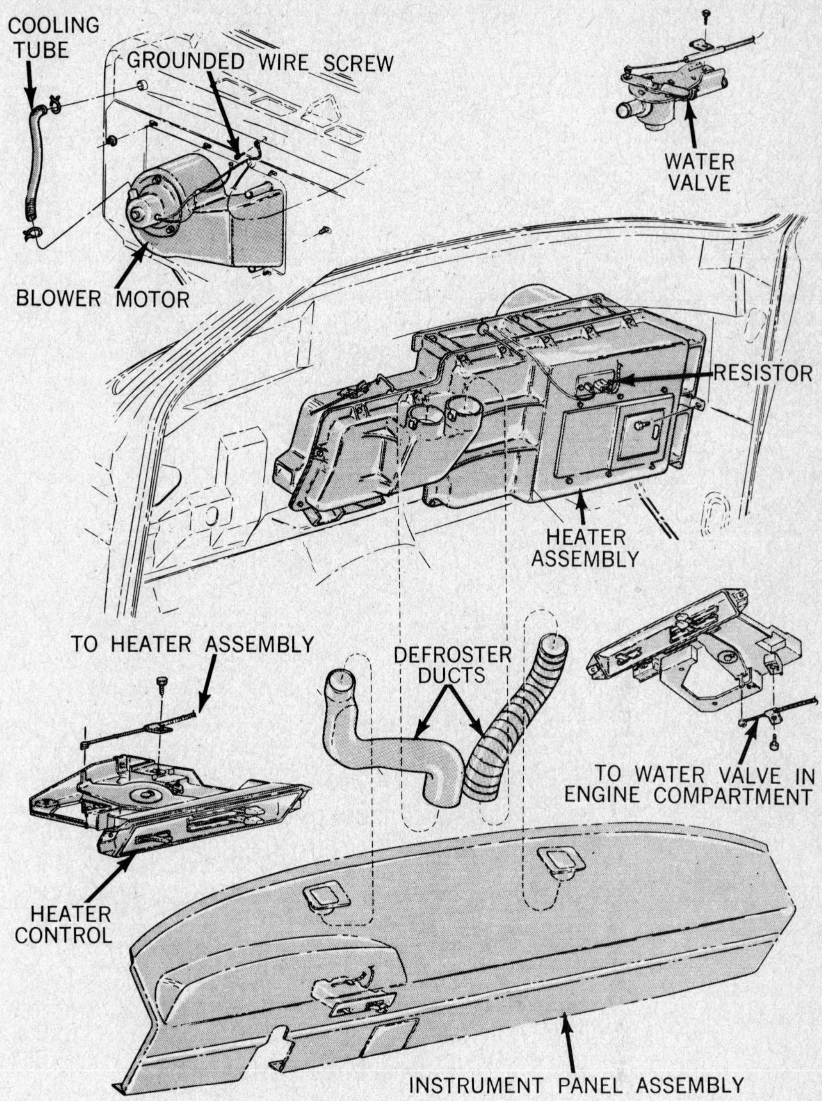

Typical heater assembly (© Chrysler Corp.)

Heater Core

Conventional Trucks without Air Conditioning

Removal and Installation

1. Disconnect the battery ground cable.
2. Drain the radiator.
3. Disconnect the heater hose from the heater.
4. Disconnect the wiring from the resistor.
5. Remove the defroster ducts.
6. Disconnect the ground wire and the cooling tube from the engine side of the blower motor.
7. Remove the bracket from the righthand side of the instrument panel and pull the panel toward the rear of the truck.
8. Remove the seven retaining nuts from the engine side of the firewall. Remove one nut from inside the truck at the right-hand kick panel.
9. Roll the heater out from its mounting.
10. Separate the front and rear housings. Two of the retaining screws are located inside the unit at the right-hand end.
11. Remove the screws at each end of the core, holding the core to the housing. Remove the screws from the front side of the housing, between the inlet and outlet tubes.
12. Installation is the reverse of removal.

Conventional Trucks with Factory Air Conditioning

Removal and Installation

1. Disconnect the battery ground cable.
2. Drain the coolant and disconnect the heater hoses at the firewall.
3. Remove the glove box and ashtray.
4. Remove the right and left ducts.
5. Remove the four screws and the distribution duct. Remove the two screws and the center air outlet and duct.
6. Disconnect the wiring harness from the resistor. Detach the vacuum lines from the housing.
7. Remove the 22 screws from the housing. Remove the two plugs in order to remove the two inside screws. Hold the defroster door to the heat position and separate the housing.
8. Remove the screw between the heater core tubes from the engine compartment firewall and the two screws from each end of the core. Slide the core out.
9. On installation, position the core and install the retaining screws.
10. Assemble the housing, holding the defroster door to the heat position and making sure that the shaft lines up in the hole.
11. Install the vacuum lines, wiring, ducts, glovebox, and ashtray.
12. Connect the heater hoses and the battery cable. Fill the cooling system.
13. Let the engine warm up with the heater on, then check the coolant level.

Vans and Pick-Ups Without Air Conditioning

Removal and Installation

1. Disconnect the battery ground cable.
2. Drain the radiator.

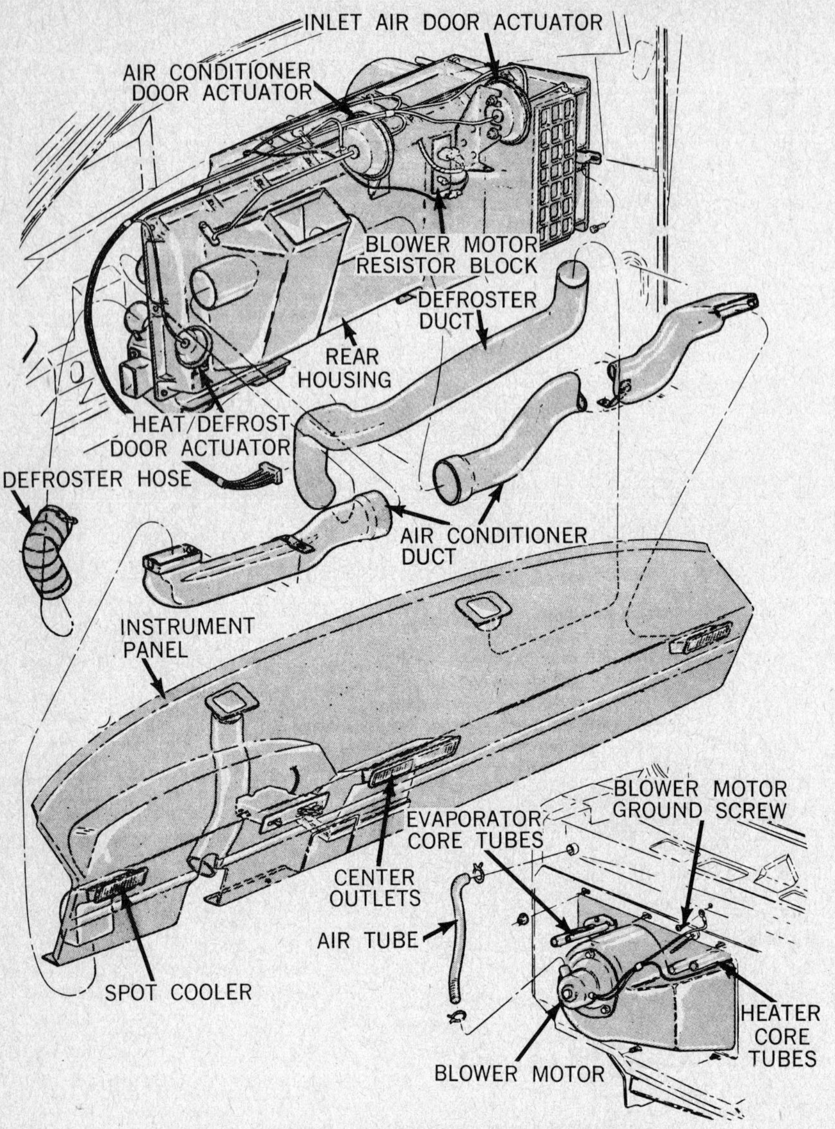

Typical heater and evaporator assembly (© Chrysler Corp.)

3. Cover the alternator with a waterproof cover.
4. Disconnect the blower motor resistor and ground wires from the heater.
5. Disconnect and plug the heater core hoses.
6. Disconnect the control cables.
7. Remove the retaining screws from the water valve. Do not disconnect the hoses from the water valve; place the water valve with hoses attached to one side.
8. Remove the blower motor cooler tube.
9. Remove the nuts holding the housing to the mounting studs and tip the complete unit out through the hood opening.

To remove the heater core:

10. Remove the 3 retaining nuts and lift the blower assembly out of the housing.
11. Remove the 4 cover retaining nuts and lift the cover off the housing.
12. Remove the 4 core retaining screws and lift the core out of the housing.
13. Installation is the reverse of removal. Fill the cooling system.
14. Let the engine warm up with the heater on, then check the coolant level.

Vans and Pick-Ups with Factory Air Conditioning

Removal and Installation

The air conditioning system must be discharged to remove the heater core. Do not attempt if you are not familiar with air conditioning servce.

1. Disconnect the battery ground cable and drain the coolant.
2. Remove the grille, condenser, and radiator.
3. Place a waterproof cover over the alternator.
4. Disconnect the heater hoses at the water valve and remove the valve and bracket. Disconnect and cap the refrigerant lines.
5. Remove the glovebox, spot cooler bezel, and appearance shield.
6. Working through the glovebox opening, remove the evaporator housing to firewall screws and nuts.
7. Remove the wiper motor. Detach all evaporator housing vacuum and electrical connections. Detach the blower motor cooling hose and the drain hoses.
8. Remove the two 2¼ in. bolts from the crossbar and the four screws from the sealplate on the front of the housing. Separate the evaporator and blower motor housings, remove the evaporator housing.
9. Remove the receiver drier and cap all the openings. Carefully pry the heater core out, leaving the air seal at the front intact.
10. On installation, connect the hoses to the core. Position the evaporator housing on top of the blower housing. Install the mounting screws and nuts.
11. Position the crossbar under the lip on the blower housing opening and install the two 2¼ in. bolts. Install the four seal plate screws at the front of the housing.
12. Replace the wiper motor and connect the vacuum and electrical lines. Connect the blower motor cooler hose and the drain hoses.
13. Connect the heater hoses to the water valve.
14. Install the receiver drier and connect the refrigerant lines.
15. Install the radiator, condenser, and grille.
16. Replace the glovebox, spot cooler bezel, and appearance shield.
17. Install the battery ground cable and fill the cooling system. Let the engine warm up with the *heater on*, then check the coolant. Charge the air conditioner.

ENGINE

Reference

Engine overhaul procedures can be found in the "Engine Rebuilding" section of this manual.

Emission Controls

Description

Two basic approaches to emission control have been used on Dodge engines. The first is engine design modifications, which apply to some extent to all engines. The second is a group of specific emission control systems, the application of which varies

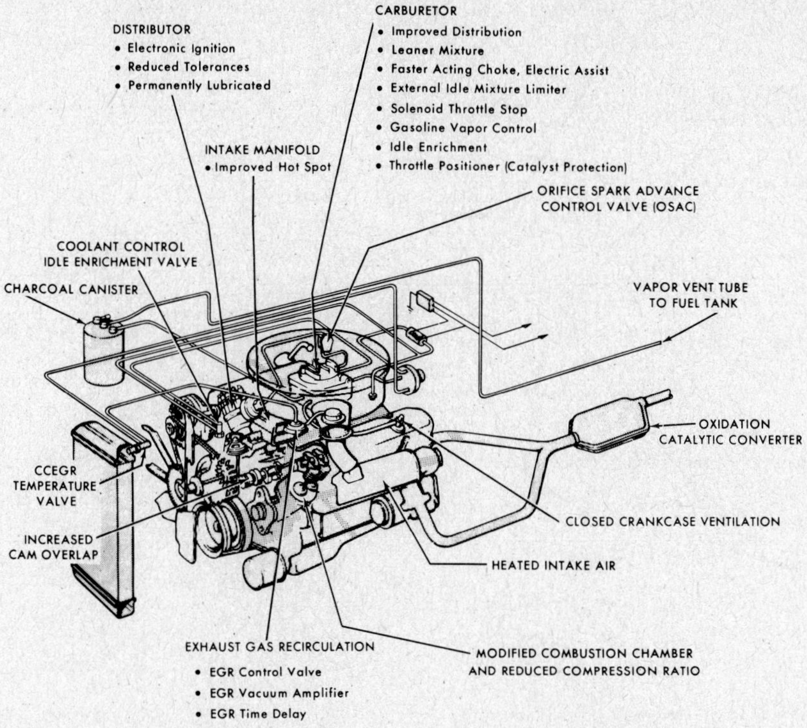

Typical vehicle emission controls (© Chrysler Corp.)

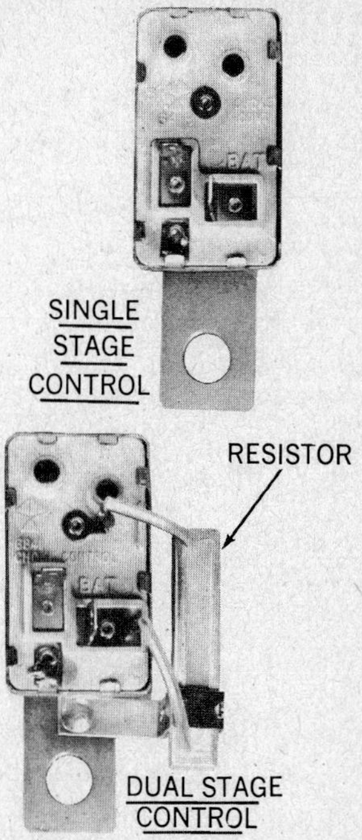

Two types of electric choke controls (© Chrysler Corp.)

with model and power train. Those models rated under a specific GVW are subject to stricter light-duty emission regulations, and therefore use more of these systems.

The design modifications and emission control systems are listed here; tests and adjustments for the systems will be found in the General Repair Section on Emission Controls.

Engine Design Modifications

Engine design modifications have been made from model year to model year, to aid in the reduction of harmful emissions.

The intake manifold has been modified to aid in the rapid vaporization of the fuel, and modification of the combustion chamber design allows better combustion of the fuel.

Compression ratios were reduced on most engines, to allow the use of a lower octane fuel, and the cam shaft design was changed to allow greater valve overlap to reduce engine emissions.

Carburetors have continually been modified to aid in fuel distribution and the Electronic Ignition System is used to reduce the need for continual adjustment of the ignition system and also provides for better and more precise spark.

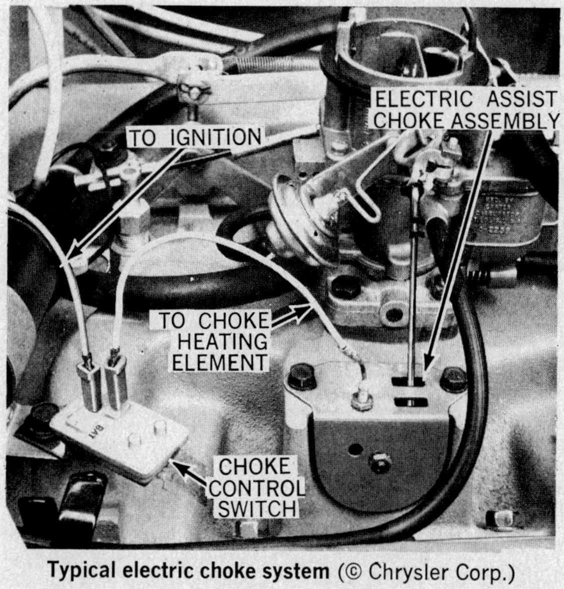

Typical electric choke system (© Chrysler Corp.)

Electric Assist Choke System

Two types of electric choke controls are used to shorten the choke duration during both winter and summer operation.

The single stage choke control operates a slower choke opening at temperatures of 58° or below, and a rapid choke opening at temperatures of 68° and higher.

The dual stage choke control provides partial power to the choke coil at temperatures of 58° and below, and full power to the choke coil at temperatures of 68° and above, and will stop the current to the choke coil at temperatures of approximately 130° and higher.

Engines started in the winter will experience three levels of current to the choke coil from the dual choke control. **LOW** during the engine warmup, **HIGH** after the engine warm-up, and **NONE** after the engine reaches normal operating temperatures. Engines started in summer weather will not have the **LOW** system in operation, nor will an engine that is restarted when hot, have a **HIGH**.

NOTE: All temperature readings are in Fahrenheit.

Single Stage Control Switch Test

1. Remove the "BAT" connector from the control unit.
2. Connect a test lamp to the small

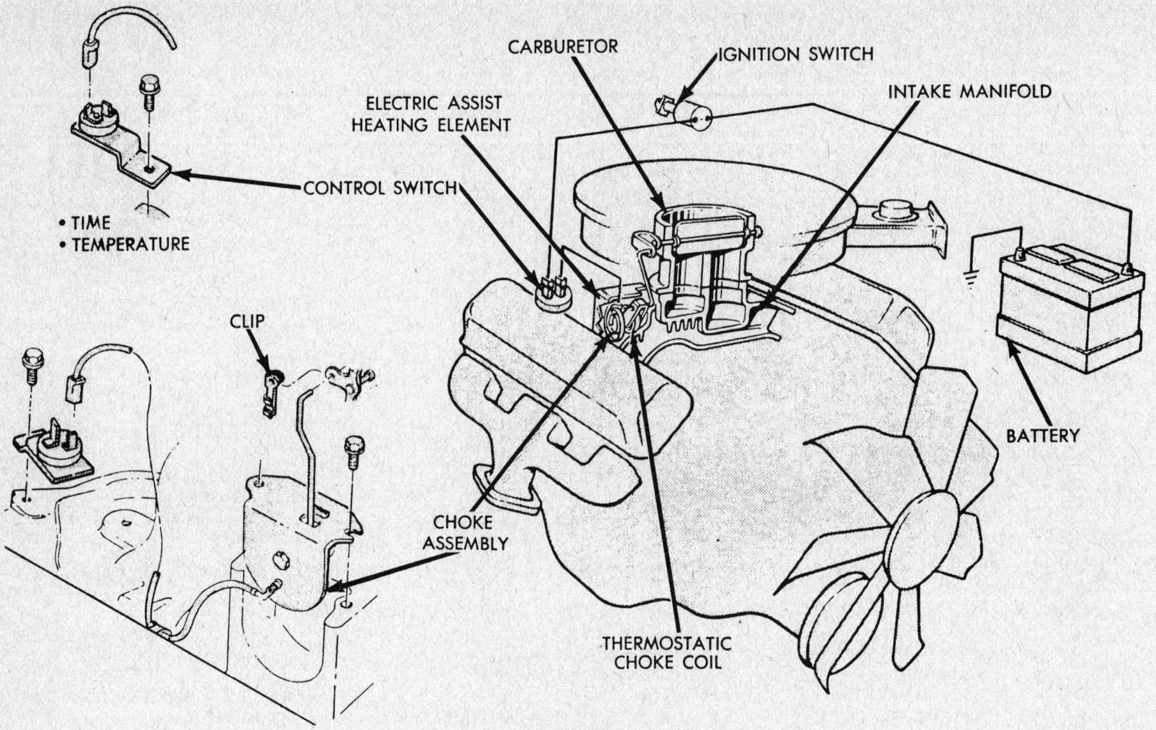

Electric assist choke system (© Chrysler Corp.)

terminal of the control to ground.

3. Start the engine and warm it up to normal operating temperature.
4. Reconnect the "BAT" terminal wire to its post on the control and observe the test lamp.
5. The test lamp should light. It may remain on for a few seconds or for a longer duration, but must not remain on for over five minutes. If so, replace the control switch.

Dual Stage Control Switch Test

1. The test procedure is the same for the dual stage control switch as for the single stage switch, except the brightness or intensity of the test lamp should match that of battery current during the test. If the intensity is less, or the light remains on for over five minutes, the control switch is defective and should be replaced.

Choke Heating Element Test

1. Disconnect the electric heating element wire at the control switch.
2. Connect an ohmmeter lead to the crimped junction of the element wire at the choke end, avoiding connection with the heater casing. Ground the other lead of the ohmmeter.
3. Resistance of twelve ohms is acceptable. Replace the unit if resistance is outside this range.
4. Make sure choke linkage moves freely when hot and when cold.

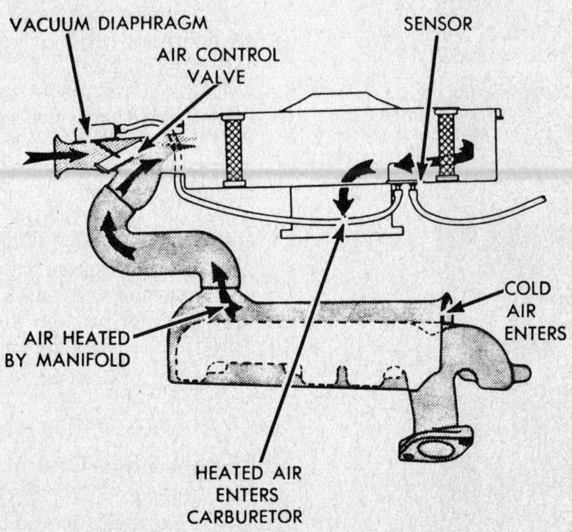

Heated air inlet system (© Chrysler Corp.)

Heated Air Intake System

The carburetor air preheater is a device which is part of the air cleaner and which keeps the air entering the carburetor at about 100° F when underhood temperatures are less than 100° F. By using this device, the carburetor can be calibrated much leaner to improve engine warm-up characteristics.

The heated air intake system is basically a two circuit airflow system. When underhood temperatures are less than 100° F, the air will flow into the stove, through a flexible connector, into the adaptor on the bottom of the snorkel, and then into the carburetor. When the underhood temperature is above 100° F, the airflow will be through the snorkel.

Modulation of the induction air is performed through the use of intake manifold vacuum, a temperature sensor, and a vacuum diaphragm which operates the heat control door in the snorkel.

Orific Spark Advance Control (OSAC)

The OSAC system is used to control NO_x. The system controls the amount of vacuum supplied to the vacuum advance mechanism of the distributor.

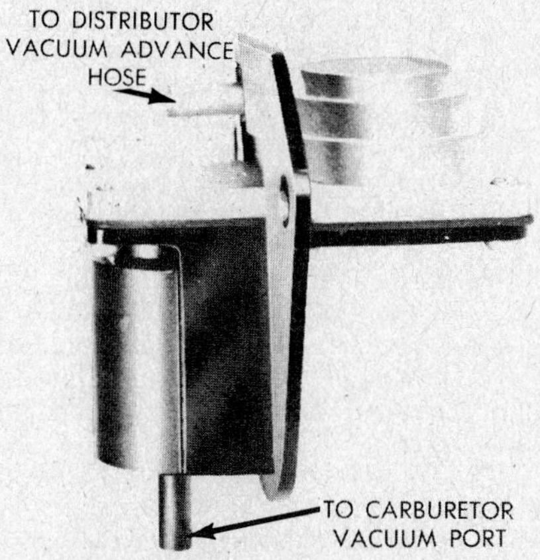

OSAC valve (© Chrysler Corp.)

Exhaust Gas Recirculation (EGR)

EGR is used in conjunction with the vacuum spark advance control to limit peak flame temperatures and thus retard the formation of NO_x. Two alternate systems are used.

Ported Vacuum Control System

This system uses a slot type port in the carburetor throttle body which is exposed to an increasing percentage of manifold vacuum by the opening movement of the throttle plate. The throttle bore port is directly connected to the EGR valve through an external nipple. The flow rate of exhaust gases is determined by manifold vacuum, throttle position, and exhaust gas backpressure. Wide open throttle recycling of exhaust gases is prevented by calibrating the valve opening point above manifold vacuum available at wide open throttle, since port vacuum cannot exceed manifold vacuum.

Venturi Vacuum Control System

This system uses a vacuum tap at the throat of the carburetor venturi to provide a control signal. Because the signal is so low however, a vacuum amplifier is used to increase the strength of the signal. The amplifier uses stored manifold vacuum to provide the source for amplification. Elimination of EGR at wide open throttle is accomplished by a "dump" diaphragm which compares venturi and manifold vacuum to determine when wide open throttle is achieved. At wide open throttle, the internal reservoir is "dumped", limiting the output of the EGR valve to manifold vacuum. As with the ported vacuum control system, the valve opening point is set above the manifold vacuum available at wide open throttle, permitting the valve to be closed at wide open throttle.

Coolant Control Exhaust Gas Recirculation Valve

Trucks with EGR are equipped with a CCEGR valve located in the top of the radiator tank. When coolant in the top radiator tank reaches 65° F, the valve opens to apply vacuum to the EGR valve to recirculate exhaust gases.

EGR Delay System

Some trucks are equipped with an EGR delay system, which is an electrical timer on the dash to control an engine mounted solenoid. The timer prevents exhaust gas recirculation for about 35 seconds after the ignition is turned on.

Air Injection System

This system adds a controlled amount of air through special passages in the cylinder head, to exhaust gases in the exhaust ports, causing oxidation of the gases and thereby reducing carbon monoxide and hydrocarbon emissions to the required levels.

The air injection system consists of a belt-driven air pump, rubber hose, a check valve to protect the hoses and pump from hot gases, injection tubes, and a combination diverter/pressure relief valve assembly.

Evaporative Control System

The function of the evaporative control system is to prevent the emission of raw gasoline vapors from the fuel tank and carburetor into the atmosphere. When fuel evaporates in the tank or float bowl, the vapors pass through lines and into the charcoal canister where they are temporarily stored until they can be drawn into the intake manifold and burned.

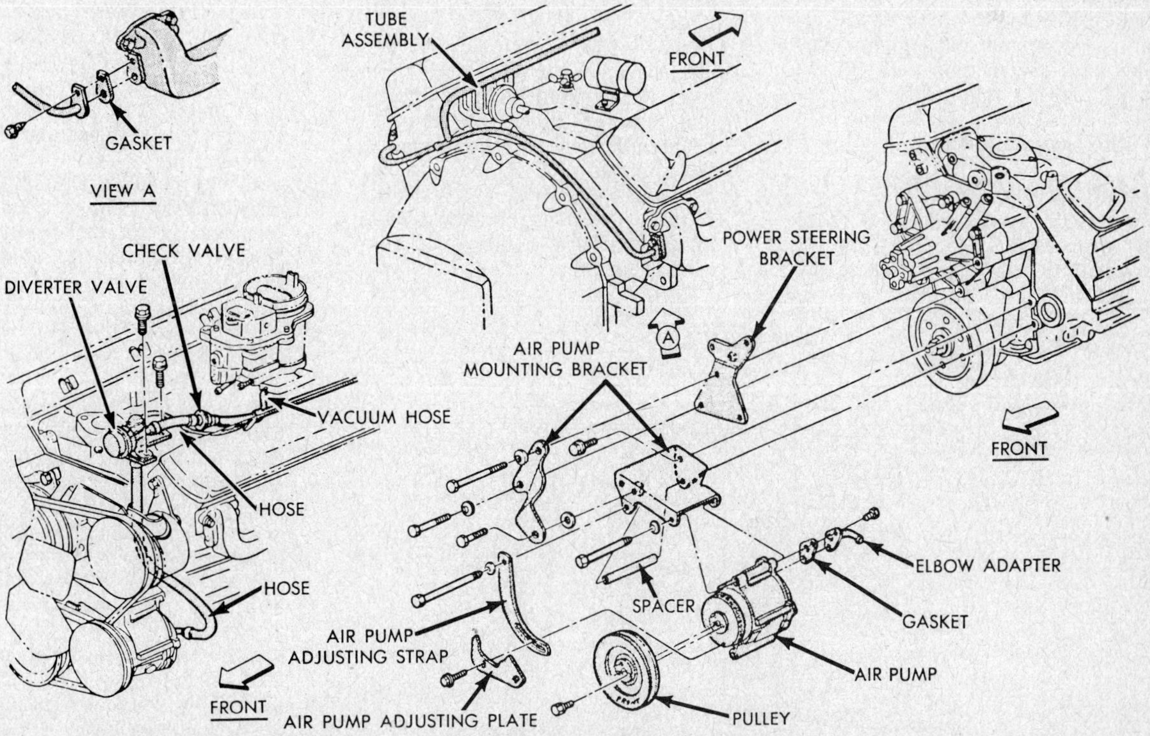

Air injection system—360 engine shown (© Chrysler Corp.)

A vacuum port located in the base of the carburetor governs vapor flow from the canister to the engine.

Closed Crankcase Ventilation System

The closed PCV system operates as follows:

In place of a vented oil filler cap, an air intake line is installed between the carburetor air filter and a crankcase opening in the valve cover.

A sealed oil filler cap and dipstick are used.

A separate PCV air filter is used. The filter is located where the intake air line connects to the valve cover.

Under normal engine operation, air enters through the intake line from the air filter. Under heavy acceleration, any excess vapors back up through the air intake line and are forced to mix with incoming air into the carburetor and are burned in the combustion chamber. Back-up fumes cannot escape into the atmosphere, creating a closed system.

The PCV valve is used to control the rate at which crankcase vapors are returned to the intake manifold. The action of the valve plunger is controlled by intake manifold vacuum and the spring. During deceleration and idle, when manifold vacuum is high, it overcomes the tension of the valve spring and the plunger bottoms in the manifold end of the valve housing. Because of the valve construction, it reduces, but does not stop, the passage of vapors to the intake manifold. When the engine is lightly accelerated or operated at constant speed, spring tension matches intake manifold vacuum pull and the plunger takes a mid-position in the valve body, allowing more vapors to flow into the manifold.

Catalytic Converter

Most 1975 and later models rated under a specific GVW, are equipped with catalytic converters. These devices are used to oxidize excess carbon monoxide (CO) and hydrocarbons (HC) in the exhaust system before they can escape out the tailpipe and into the atmosphere. The converter is installed in front of the mufflers, underneath the truck, and protected by a heat shield.

The expected catalyst life is 50,000 miles, provided that the engine is kept in tune and unleaded fuel is used.

To keep the catalyst from being overheated by an overly rich mixture during deceleration, a catalyst protection system (CPS) is sometimes used. The system consists of a throttle positioner solenoid (not to be confused with the idle stop solenoid), a control box, and an engine rpm sensor.

Any time that the engine speed is more than 2,000 rpm, the solenoid is energized and keeps the throttle butterfly from fully closing, thus preventing the deceleration mixture from becoming too rich.

Engine Removal and Installation

Vans and Pick-Ups

NOTE: Engine removal is a complicated operation. A floor jack is a necessity and you will probably have to fabricate several stands and attaching apparatus. On vehicles equipped with air conditioning, before removing the engine, have an air conditioning expert evacuate the system.

1. Disconnect the battery and drain the coolant from the radiator and engine block. Drain the engine oil. On V8s, remove the oil filter.
2. Remove the engine cover, air cleaner, and starter.
3. Remove the front bumper, grille, and support brace. Disconnect both radiator hoses and remove the radiator and support brace as a unit.
4. Remove the power steering and air pumps with the hoses attached and lay them aside.
5. Disconnect the throttle linkage, heater and vacuum hoses and all electrical connections to the ignition, alternator, and all other electrical connections.
6. Remove the alternator, fan, pulley, and drive belts.
7. Remove the heater blower motor.
8. Remove and plug the inlet line to the fuel pump.
9. Remove the oil dipstick tube. On V8s, remove the intake manifold and left exhaust manifold. If equipped with air conditioning, remove the right side valve cover.
10. To provide clearance for engine removal, the oil pan and transmission must be removed.
11. Raise the engine slightly in preparation for transmission removal. Support it with an engine lifting fixture. This tool can be fabricated from galvanized pipe fittings obtained locally. Use only galvanized parts with an inside diameter of $1\frac{1}{2}$ in. or larger. Be sure they are firmly threaded together to assure maximum strength.
12. Raise the vehicle and support it on jackstands. Remove the starter and distributor.
13. Remove the driveshaft and engine rear support. Remove the rear support by removing the rear mount through-bolt and the U-shaped bracket from the crossmember. Remove the insulator from the bottom face of the transmission housing.
14. If equipped with an automatic transmission, remove the transmission intact with the filler tube and the torque converter separated from the drive plate.
15. Raise the rear of the engine approximately 2 in. and remove the clutch or drive plate and the flywheel.

15a. On V8s, position the cut-out in the crankshaft flange at 3 o'clock. Remove the oil pan screws and lower the oil pan far enough to reach inside and turn the oil pump pick-up tube slightly to the right to clear the pan. Remove the oil pan.

16. Lower the vehicle.
17. Using a boom hoist attached to the engine with the shortest hook-up possible, take up all tension and support the engine. The boom hoist is the ideal tool to use. If one is not available, it may be possible to support the engine on a stationary hoist and roll the vehicle out from under the engine.
18. Remove the engine front mounts and insulators.
19. Carefully remove the engine from the vehicle.
20. Installation is the reverse of re-

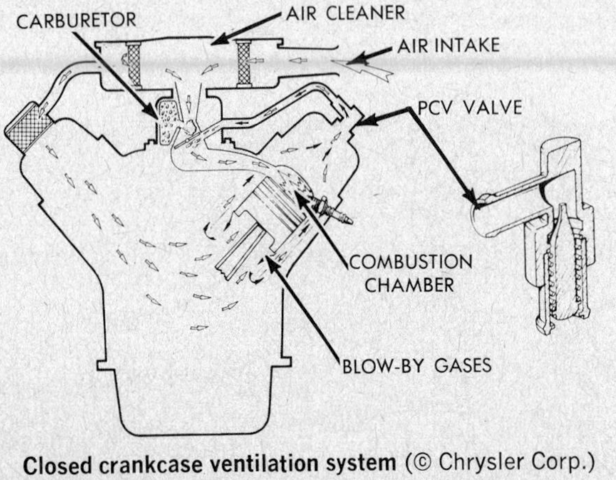

Closed crankcase ventilation system (© Chrysler Corp.)

moval. Check all fluid levels and perform all tune-up adjustments if the engine was rebuilt.

NOTE: If the engine was rebuilt or new camshaft or lifters installed, add 1 quart of Engine oil Supplement to aid break-in. This should be left in the engine for at least 500 miles.

Conventional Trucks

1. Drain the coolant.
2. Remove the battery.
3. Mark the outline of the hinges on the hood and remove it.
4. Discharge the air conditioning system safely. If you are not sure of the procedure, do not do it yourself. Disconnect and cap the compressor lines.
5. Disconnect the wiring at the alternator, coil, temperature and oil pressure sending units, starter relay, and engine ground strap.
6. Remove the air cleaner and carburetor. Install an engine lifting fixture.
7. Remove the distributor cap, rotor, and spark plug wires.
8. Disconnect and cap the fuel line.
9. Remove the fan and radiator.
10. Detach the exhaust pipe, driveshaft, linkage, and oil cooler lines.
11. Support the rear of the engine and remove the engine rear crossmember and transmission. On the 361 and 413 engines, remove the transmission only.
12. Unbolt the engine mounts and lift the engine out. On D500 and larger models, the grille and support assembly should be removed first.

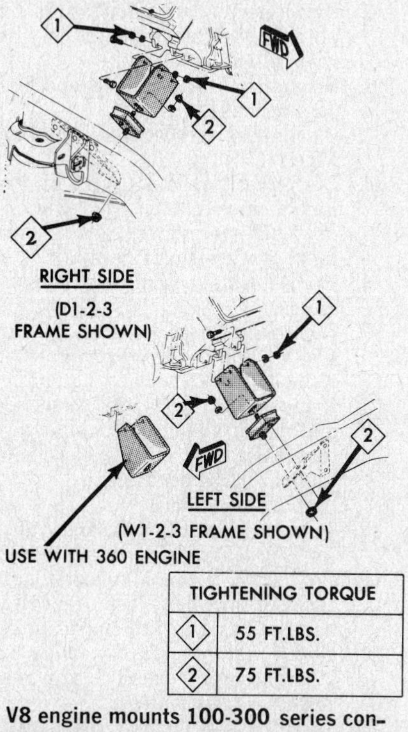

V8 engine mounts 100-300 series conventional trucks (© Chrysler Corp.)

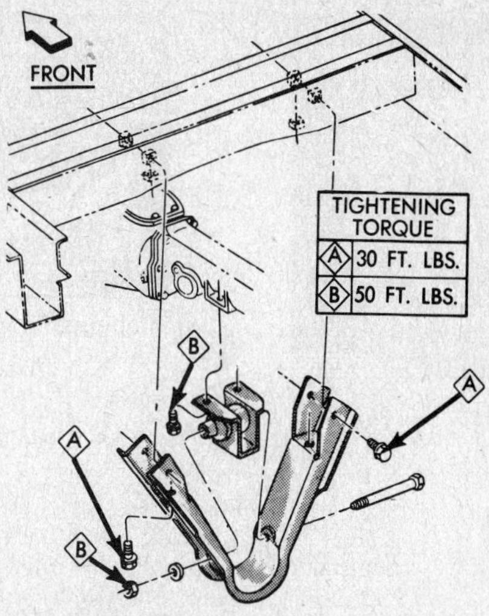

Rear engine mount—vans and wagons (© Chrysler Corp.)

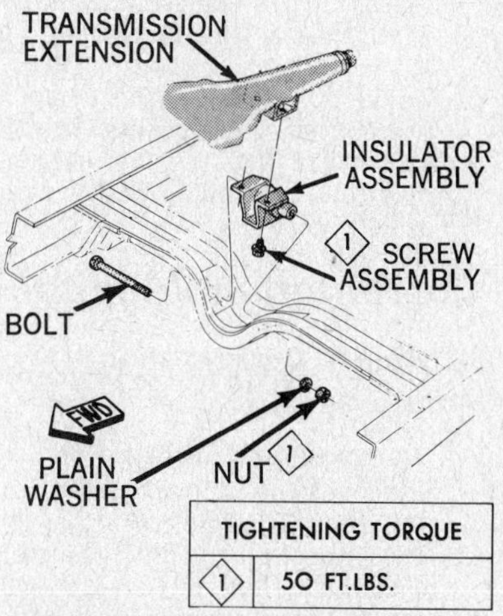

Rear engine mount—100-300 series (© Chrysler Corp.)

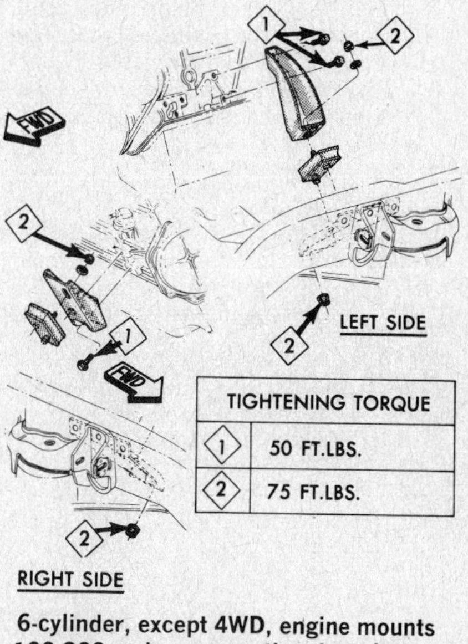

6-cylinder, except 4WD, engine mounts 100-300 series, conventional trucks (© Chrysler Corp.)

Ramcharger and Trail Duster

1. Drain the coolant from the radiator and cylinder block.
2. Disconnect the battery ground cable. Remove the battery on V8 models.
3. Scribe the outline of the hood hinges and remove the hood.
4. If equipped with air conditioning, remove the compressor with lines attached and lay it aside.

CAUTION: Do not disconnect any refrigerant lines. Bodily injury could result.

5. Disconnect the electrical connections at the alternator, ignition coil, temperature and oil pressure sending units, starter-to-solenoid, and engine/body ground.
6. Remove the air cleaner and carburetor. Install an engine lifting fixture.
7. Remove the distributor cap and rotor.
8. Disconnect and plug the fuel pump line.
9. Disconnect the radiator and heater hoses. Disconnect and plug the oil cooler lines.
10. Remove the fan, spacer, fluid drive, and radiator. Do not store the fan drive unit with the shaft pointing downward. Fluid will leak out.
11. Raise the truck and support the rear of the engine.
12. Disconnect the exhaust pipes at the manifolds.
13. Remove the starter on V8 models.
14. Remove the automatic transmission dust cover and attach a C-clamp to the front bottom of the torque converter housing to prevent it from failling out. Remove the drive plate bolts from the torque converter. On manual transmission models, remove the rear crossmember, transmission, transfer case and adapter. You can leave the transfer case in place on six-cylinder models.
15. Support the transmission and remove the transmission attaching bolts.
16. Lower the truck and attach a hoist to the engine.
17. Remove the front motor mount bolt stud nuts and washers.
18. Carefully remove the engine.
19. Installation is the reverse of removal. Fill the engine with coolant and fresh oil. Adjust the transmission linkage, carburetor, and ignition timing.

Intake Manifold

V-8 Intake Manifold

Removal and Installation

1. Drain cooling system and disconnect battery.

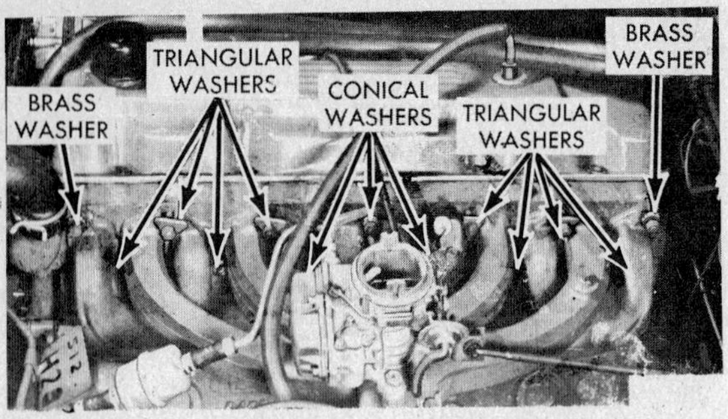

Intake and exhaust manifold installation, 6-cylinder (© Chrysler Corp.)

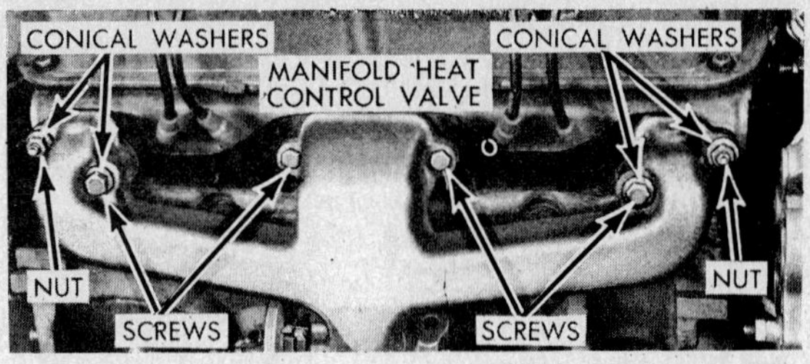

Installing 318 and 360 exhaust manifold (© Chrysler Corp.)

2. Remove alternator, carburetor air cleaner, and fuel line.
3. Disconnect accelerator linkage.
4. Remove vacuum control between carburetor and distributor.
5. Remove the distributor cap and wires.
6. Disconnect coil wires, temperature sending unit wire, heater hoses and bypass hose.
7. Remove intake manifold, ignition coil and carburetor as an assembly.
8. Installation is the reverse of the above procedure. Tighten the intake manifold to head bolts in the sequence illustrated, from center alternating out.
9. Tighten the exhaust manifold mounting nuts to the required torque which is listed in the specifications chart of this section.

Exhaust Manifold

V-8 Exhaust Manifold

Removal and Installation

1. Disconnect the exhaust manifold at the flange where it mates to the exhaust pipe.
2. If the vehicle is equipped with air injection and/or a carburetor-heated air stove, remove them.
3. Remove the exhaust manifold by removing the securing bolts and washers. To reach these bolts, it may be necessary to jack the engine slightly off its front mounts. When the exhaust manifold is removed, sometimes the securing studs will screw out with the nuts. If this occurs, the studs must be replaced with the aid of sealing compound on the coarse thread ends. If this is not done, water leaks may develop at the studs.
4. To install, reverse the removal procedures. On the center branch of the 318 and the 360 exhaust manifold, no conical washers are used.

Combination Manifold

6-Cylinder Combination Manifold

Removal and Installation

1. Remove the air cleaner, lines and tubes to the carburetor.
2. Disconnect all the linkages to the carburetor and remove the carburetor from the manifold.
3. Disconnect the exhaust pipe from the manifold, remove the manifold attaching washers and retaining nuts, and remove the manifold from the cylinder head.
4. Separate the exhaust manifold from the intake manifold, if necessary, and install a new gasket between the two upon reassembly.

NOTE: Do not tighten the three securing bolts until the manifold assembly has been installed on the cylinder head.

5. Position the manifold on the cylinder head using a new gasket, and install the conical and triangular washers, the retaining nuts, and torque the retaining nuts and the three securing bolts to the specified torque.
6. Attach the exhaust pipe to the exhaust manifold flange.
7. Install the carburetor and attach all the lines, tubes, and linkages. Install the air cleaner assembly.

Cylinder Head

6-Cylinder Engine

Removal and Installation

1. Drain cooling system.
2. Remove air cleaner and fuel line.
3. Remove vacuum line at carburetor and distributor.
4. Disconnect accelerator linkage.
5. Disconnect spark plug wires by pulling boot straight out in line with plugs.
6. Disconnect heater hose and bypass hose clamp.
7. Disconnect temperature sending wire.
8. Disconnect exhaust pipe at exhaust manifold flange. Disconnect diverter valve vacuum line on engines with air pump.
9. Remove intake and exhaust manifolds.
10. Remove closed vent system (PCV) and rocker cover.
11. Remove rocker shaft assembly.
12. Remove pushrods in sequence and mark them in such a way that they may be put back into their original positions.
13. Remove head bolts.
14. Remove spark plugs and tubes on 1973-74 models.
15. To install, clean all gasket surfaces of cylinder block and cylinder head and install spark plugs.
16. Check all surfaces with a straightedge if there is any reason to suspect leakage.
17. Install gasket, using sealer, and cylinder head.

V8 intake manifold tightening sequence (© Chrysler Corp.)

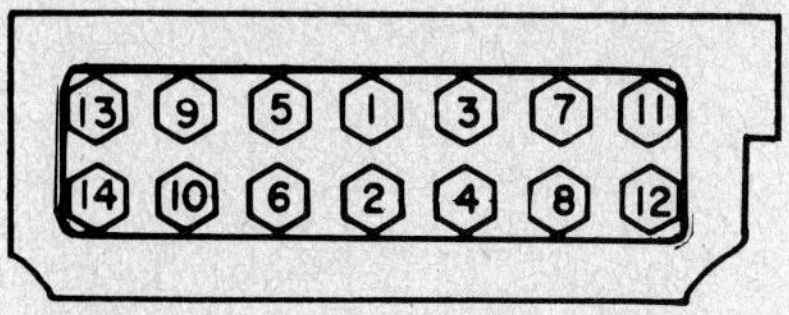

6-cylinder head bolt tightening sequences (© Chrysler Corp.)

18. Install cylinder head attaching bolts. Tighten all bolts in the sequence illustrated to 50 ft. lbs. torque, then repeat tightening sequence torquing to 70 ft. lbs.
19. Install rocker arms and shaft assembly with the flat (1973 models) or the oil hole on the end of the shaft on top and to the front. The special bolt goes to the rear. Install rocker shaft retainers between rocker arms so they seat on rocker shaft and not on extended bushing of rocker arm. Be sure to install long retainer in center position only. Tighten bolts to 25 ft. lbs. Tighten the special bolt to 200 in. lbs.
20. Loosen the 3 bolts holding intake manifold to exhaust manifold. This is necessary for proper alignment.
21. Install the manifolds as detailed under manifold removal and installation.
22. Connect heater hose and by-pass hose clamp.
23. Connect heat indicator sending unit wire, the accelerator linkage and spark plug wires.
24. Install the vacuum control tube from carburetor to distributor. Install the air tube assembly with a new gasket to the head, tightening it to 100 inch-pounds. Install the diverter valve vacuum line.
25. Connect exhaust pipe to exhaust manifold flange.
26. Install fuel line and carburetor air cleaner.
27. Fill cooling system, start and warm up engine, and adjust valve tappet clearance.
28. Install valve cover using new gasket, tightening retaining nuts to 3-4 ft. lbs.
29. Install crankcase ventilation system.

V8 Engines

Removal and Installation

1. Drain cooling system and disconnect battery. On vehicles with 361 or 413 cu. in. engines, remove battery.
2. Remove alternator, air cleaner and fuel line.
3. Disconnect accelerator linkage.
4. Remove vacuum control hose between carburetor and distributor.
5. Remove cooling and heater hoses from head and, if so equipped, remove air compressor.
6. Remove distributor cap and high tension leads as an assembly.
7. Remove heat indicator sending unit wire.
8. Remove crankcase ventilation system and valve covers.
9. Remove spark plugs and, on 361, 413 cu. in. engines, remove distributor and governor.
10. Remove intake manifold, carburetor and, if attached to manifold, ignition coil as an assembly.
11. Remove tappet chamber cover.
12. On 361, 413 cu. in. engines, remove the bolts that secure water pump housing to each cylinder head.
13. Remove exhaust manifolds. On the 361, 413 cu. in. engines, tag the center bolts for reinstallation in same hole.
14. Remove rocker arms and shaft assemblies.
15. Remove pushrods and *identify to insure installation in original location.*
16. Remove cylinder head bolts and cylinder heads.
17. Before installing cylinder heads, clean all gasket surfaces of block and heads.
18. Inspect all surfaces with a straightedge if there is any indication of leakage.
19. Coat new head gaskets with sealant and install on block.
20. Install cylinder head and head bolts. Tighten bolts in the sequence illustrated, first to 50 ft. lbs. torque, then in sequence again to the specified torque (see Specifications at the beginning of this section). **CAUTION: Do not retighten cylinder head bolts after engine has been operated if embossed steel head gaskets are used.**

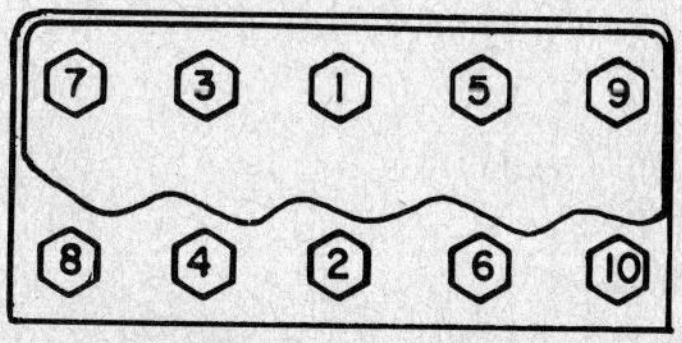

Cylinder head tightening sequence, 360 and smaller V8 (© Chrysler Corp.)

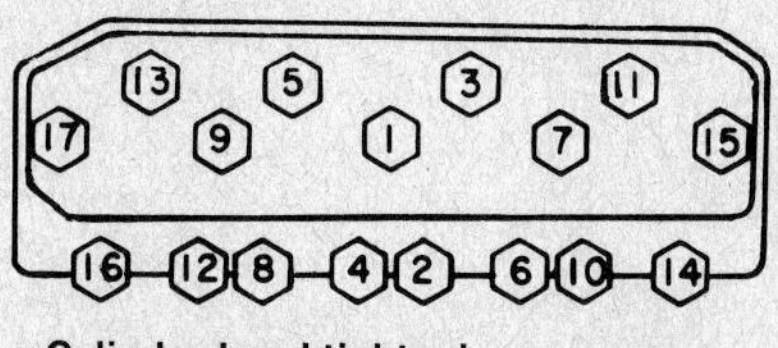

Cylinder head tightening sequence, 361 and larger V8 (© Chrysler Corp.)

21. Inspect pushrods for wear or bending and install in original positions. Use an aligning rod.
22. Install rocker shaft assembly, making sure long stamped steel retainers are in the No. 2 and No. 4 positions. Tighten rocker shaft mounting bolts to 25 ft. lbs. (17 ft. lbs on 318 and 360 cu. in. engine) torque. On the 318 and 360 cu. in. engines, make sure the "NOTCH" end of the rocker assemblies are pointing toward the centerline of the engine and toward the front on the left bank and toward the rear on the right bank.
23. Install tappet chamber cover. On the 361, 413 cu. in. engines, make sure the 1/8" gasket bleed hole at the crossover is on the right side of the engine. Tighten bolts to 7-8 ft. lbs. torque.
24. Install exhaust manifolds. Use new gaskets. On the 361, 413 cu. in. engines, be sure center bolt is inserted in its original position. Tighten bolts to the specified torque.
25. Set correct gap on spark plugs (see Tune-Up Specifications at the beginning of this section) and install, tightening to 30 ft. lbs. torque.
26. Install intake manifold and carburetor assembly, tightening bolts from center outward, first to 25 ft. lbs. torque, then again to correct torque (see Torque Specifications at the beginning of this section). On the 318 cu. in. engine, coat the gaskets with sealant and install with bead down. On 360 cu. in. engines, do not use any sealer on side composition gaskets.
27. If they were removed, install distributor and governor.
28. Install distributor cap and high tension leads.
29. Connect vacuum control hose between distributor and carburetor, throttle linkage, heat indicator sending unit wire, heater and coolant hoses, fuel line and, if so equipped, manual choke cable.
30. On the 361, 413 cu. in. engines, install bolts which secure water pump housing to each cylinder head.
31. Install rocker cover, using new gasket. Tighten bolts to 3-4 ft. lbs. torque.
32. Install crankcase ventilation system and air cleaner.
33. Install alternator and drive belts. Install air compressor if so equipped.
34. Fill cooling system and install or connect battery.

Valve Rocker Arm Shaft Assembly

6-Cylinder Engine

Removal and Installation

1. Remove the closed ventilation system.
2. Remove the evaporative control system.
3. Remove the valve cover with its gasket.
4. Take out the rocker arm and shaft assembly securing bolts and remove the rocker arm and shaft.
5. Reverse the above for installation. The flat (1973 models) or the oil hole on the end of the shaft must be on the top and point toward the front of the engine to provide proper lubrication to the rocker arms. The special bolt goes to the rear. Torque the rocker arm bolts to 25 ft. lbs. and adjust the valves.

V-8 Engines

Removal and Installation

1. Disconnect the spark plug wires.
2. Disconnect the closed ventilation and evaporative control system.
3. Remove the valve covers with their gaskets.
4. Remove the rocker shaft bolts and retainers, and lift off the rocker arm assembly.
5. Reverse the above procedure to install. The notch on the end of both rocker shafts on the 318 and 360 should point to the engine centerline and toward the front of the engine on the left cylinder head, or toward the rear on the right cylinder head. On the 361, 383, 400, 413, and 440, the rocker arm lubrication holes must point down and toward the valves. Torque the rocker shaft bolts to 17 ft. lbs. on the 318 and 316, and 25 ft. lbs. on the others.

Valve Arrangement

Front to rear
6 Cylinder
E I E I E I I E I E I E
V-8 Right
E I I E E I I E
Left
E I I E E I I E

Valve Adjustment

This adjustment is required only on the six-cylinder engine. It should be done at every tune-up. It should also be done whenever there is excessive noise from the valve mechanism.

No valve lash adjustment is necessary or possible on any other Chrysler-built engine. Hydraulic valve lifters automatically maintain zero clearance. After engine reassembly these lifters adjust themselves as soon as engine oil pressure builds up.

NOTE: Do not set the valve lash closer than specified in an attempt to quiet the valve mechanism. This will result in burned valves.

The manufacturer recommends that the valves be adjusted with the engine running, but the following procedure can also be used.

1. The engine must be at normal operating temperature. Mark the crankshaft pulley into three equal 120° segments, starting at the TDC mark.
2. Remove the valve (rocker) cover and the distributor cap.
3. Set the engine at TDC on the No. 1 cylinder by aligning the mark on the crankshaft pulley with the 0° mark on the timing cover pointer. The distributor rotor should point at the position of the No. 1 spark plug wire in the distributor cap. Both rocker arms on the No. 1 cylinder should be free to move slightly. If all this isn't the case, you have No. 6 cylinder at TDC and will have to turn the engine 360° in the normal direction of rotation.
4. The lash is measured between the rocker arm and the end of the valve.
5. To check the lash, insert the correct size feeler gauge between the rocker arm and the valve. Press down lightly on the other end of the rocker arm. If the gauge cannot be inserted, loosen the self-locking adjustment nut on top of the rocker arm. Tighten the nut until the gauge can just be inserted and withdrawn without buckling.
6. After both valves for the No. 1 cylinder are adjusted, turn the engine so that the pulley turns 120° in the normal direction of rotation (clockwise). The distributor rotor will turn 60°, since it turns at half engine speed.
7. Check that the rocker arms are free and adjust the valves for the next cylinder in the firing order, 5. The firing order is 1-5-3-6-2-4.
8. Turn the engine 120° to adjust each of the remaining cylinders in the firing order. When you are done the engine will have made two complete revolutions (720°) and the rotor one complete revolution (360°).
9. Replace the rocker cover with a new gasket. Replace the distributor cap. Start the engine and check for leaks.

Valve Stem Oil Seal Replacement

If valve stem oil seals are found to be the cause of excessive oil consumption, they may be replaced without removing the cylinder heads.

1. Remove the air cleaner.
2. Remove the rocker arm covers and spark plugs.
3. Detach the coil wire from the distributor.
4. Turn the engine so that No. 1 cylinder is at Top Dead Center on the compression stroke. Both valves for No. 1 cylinder should be fully closed and the crankshaft damper timing mark at

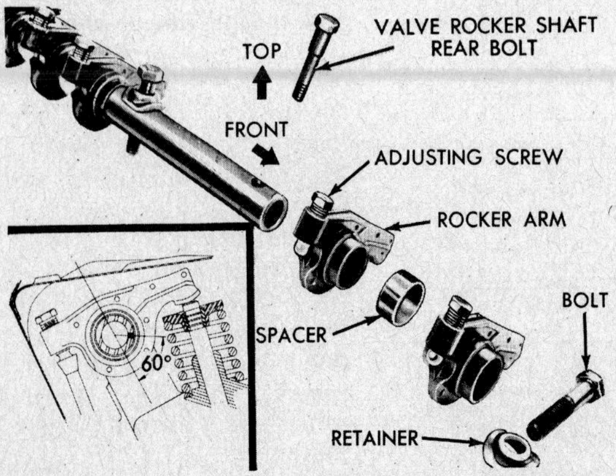

6-cylinder rocker arm shaft (© Chrysler Corp.)

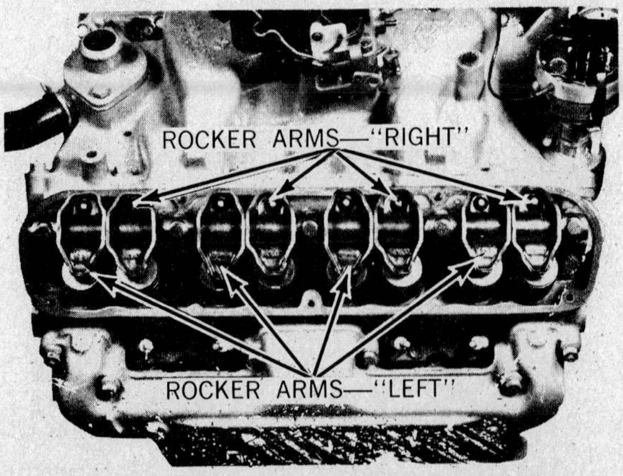

Proper rocker arm location on shaft (© Chrysler Corp.)

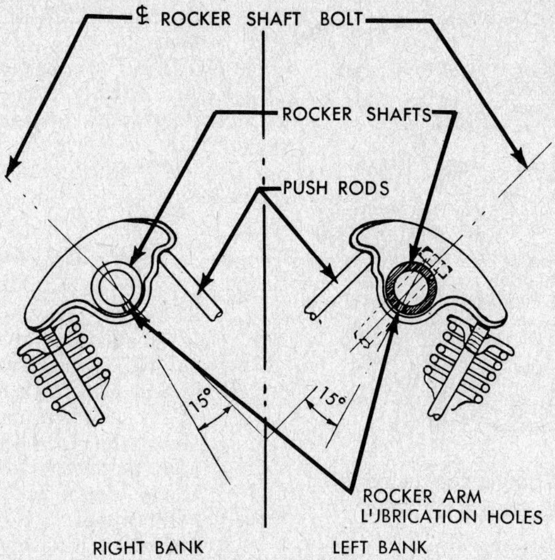

On 361 and larger V8's the rocker arm lubrication holes should be aligned as shown (© Chrysler Corp.)

TDC. The distributor rotor will point at the No. 1 spark plug wire location in the cap.

5. Remove the rocker shaft and install a dummy shaft.
6. Apply 90-100 psi air pressure to No. 1 cylinder, using a spark plug hole air hose adaptor.
7. Use a valve spring compressor to compress each No. 1 cylinder valve spring and remove the retainer locks and the spring. Remove the old seals.
8. Install a cup shield on the exhaust valve stem. Position it down against the valve guide.
9. Push the intake valve stem seal firmly and squarely over the valve guide.
10. Compress the valve spring only enough to install the lock.
11. Repeat the operation on each successive cylinder in the firing order, making sure that the crankshaft is exactly on TDC for each cylinder. See the Firing Order and Distributor Rotation illustrations in the Specifications Section of this Chapter for cylinder numbering.
12. Replace the rocker arms, covers, spark plugs, and coil wire.

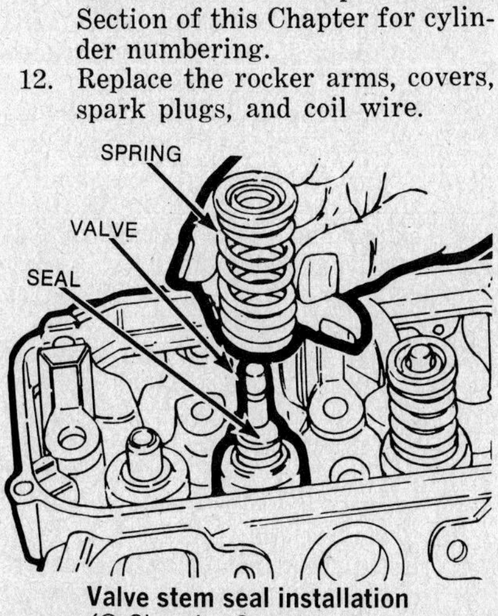

Valve stem seal installation
(© Chrysler Corp.)

Timing Cover and Chain

NOTE: On 1973-74 models it is normal to find particles of rubber collected between the seal retainer and the crankshaft oil slinger after the seal has been in service. Check the slack in the chain after installation.

6-Cylinder Engines

Removal and Installation

1. Drain the cooling system and disconnect the battery.
2. Remove the radiator and fan.
3. With a puller, remove the vibration damper.
4. Loosen the oil pan bolts to allow clearance, and remove the timing case cover and gasket.
5. Slide the crankshaft oil slinger off the front of the crankshaft.
6. Remove the camshaft sprocket bolt.
7. Remove the timing chain with the camshaft sprocket.
8. On installation: Turn the crankshaft to line up the timing mark on the crankshaft sprocket with the centerline of the camshaft (without the chain).

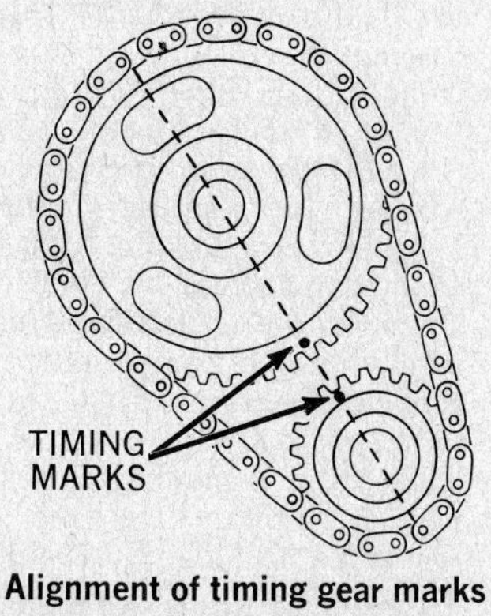

Alignment of timing gear marks 6 cylinder (© Chrysler Corp.)

9. Install the camshaft sprocket and chain. Align the timing marks.
10. Torque the camshaft sprocket bolt to 35 ft. lbs.
11. Replace the oil slinger.
12. Reinstall the timing case cover with a new gasket and torque the bolts to 17 ft. lbs. Retighten the engine oil pan to 17 ft. lbs.
13. Press the vibration damper back on.
14. Replace the radiator and hoses.
15. Refill the cooling system.

V8 Engines

Removal and Installation

1. Disconnect the battery and drain the cooling system. Remove the radiator.
2. Remove the vibration damper pulley. Unbolt and remove the vibration damper with a puller. On 318 and 360 engines, remove the fuel lines and fuel pump, then loosen the oil pan bolts and remove the front bolt on each side. On 361 and 413 engines, you will have to remove the front engine mount to get out the two front pan bolts.
3. Remove the timing gear cover and the crankshaft oil slinger.
4. On 318 and 360 engines, remove the camshaft sprocket lockbolt, securing cup washer, and fuel pump eccentric. Remove the timing chain with both sprockets. On 383, 361, 400, 413, and 440 engines, remove the camshaft sprocket lockbolt and remove the timing chain with the camshaft and crankshaft sprockets.

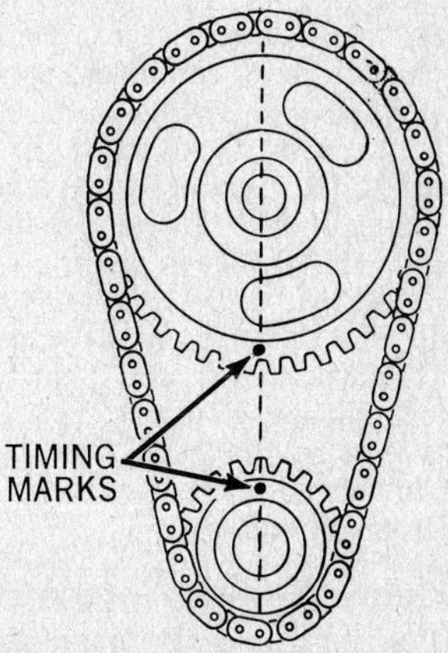

Alignment of timing gear marks V8
(© Chrysler Corp.)

5. To begin the installation procedure, place the camshaft and crankshaft sprockets on a flat surface with the timing indicators on an imaginary centerline through both sprocket bores. Place the timing chain around both sprockets. Be sure that the timing marks are in alignment.

CAUTION: When installing the timing chain, have an assistant support the camshaft with a suitable tool to prevent it from contacting the plug in the rear of the engine block. Remove the distributor and the oil pump/distributor drive gear. Position the suitable tool against the rear side of the cam gear and be careful not to damage the cam lobes.

6. Turn the crankshaft and camshaft to align them with the keyway location in the crankshaft sprocket and the keyway or dowel hole in the camshaft sprocket.

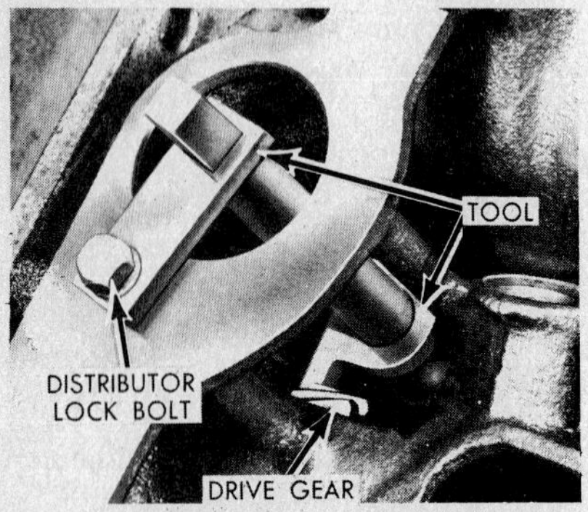

The V8 camshaft should be held forward while installing the chain and sprockets

7. Lift the sprockets and timing chain while keeping the sprockets tight against the chain in the correct position. Slide both sprockets evenly onto their respective shafts.
8. Use a straightedge to measure the alignment of the sprocket timing marks. They must be perfectly aligned.
9. On 318 and 360 engines, install the fuel pump eccentric, cup washer, and camshaft sprocket lockbolt and torque to 35 ft. lbs. If camshaft end play exceeds 0.010 in., install a new thrust plate. It should be 0.002-0.006 in. with the new plate.

On 383, 361, 400, 413, and 440 V8s, install the washer and camshaft sprocket lockbolt(s) and then torque the lockbolt to 35-40 ft. lbs. Check to make sure that the rear face of the camshaft sprocket is flush with the camshaft end.

Checking Timing Chain Slack

1. Position a scale next to the timing chain to detect any movement in the chain.
2. Place a torque wrench and socket on the camshaft sprocket attaching bolt. Apply either 30 ft. lbs. (if the cylinder heads are installed on the engine) or 15 ft. lbs. (cylinder heads removed) of force to the bolt and rotate the bolt in the direction of crankshaft rotation in order to remove all slack from the chain.

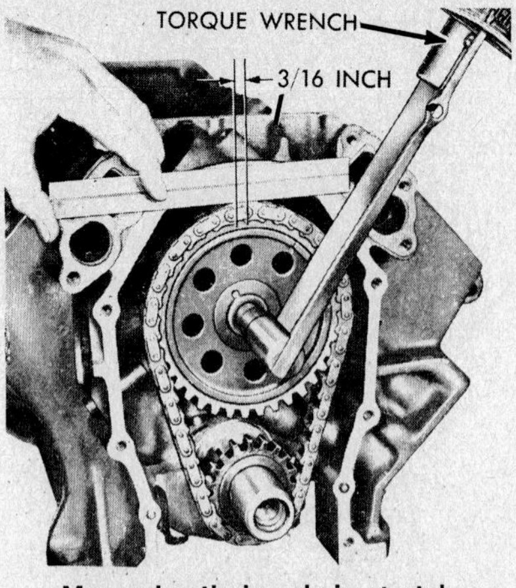

Measuring timing chain stretch
(© Chrysler Corp.)

3. While applying torque to the camshaft sprocket bolt, the crankshaft should not be allowed to rotate. It may be necessary to block the crankshaft to prevent rotation.
4. Position the scale over the edge of a timing chain link and apply an equal amount of torque in the opposite direction. If the movement of the chain exceeds 3/16 in. for all 361 and 413 engines, or 1/8 in. for 1973 and later models, replace the chain.

Timing Gear Cover Seal Replacement

NOTE: A seal remover and installer tool is required to prevent seal damage.

1. Using a seal puller, separate the seal from the retainer.
2. Pull the seal from the case.
3. To install the seal place it face down in the case with the seal lips downward.
4. Seat the seal tightly against the cover face. There should be a maximum clearance of .0014 in. between the seal and the cover. Be careful not to over-compress the seal.

Valve Timing Operation

6-Cylinder

1. Rotate the crankshaft until No. 6 exhaust valve is closing and No. 6 intake valve is opening.
2. Install a dial indicator so that the indicator pointer contacts the valve spring retainer on the No. 1 intake valve parallel to the axis of the valve stem.
3. Turn the No. 1 intake adjusting screw *in* one complete turn to remove the lash. Adjust the dial indicator to zero.
4. Rotate the crankshaft clockwise normal running direction) until the valve has lifted .029 inch.
5. The timing of the crankshaft pulley should now read from 12 degrees BTDC to DC. Readjust lash.

NOTE: If the reading is not within specified limits, inspect the sprocket index marks, inspect the timing chain for wear, and nspect the accuracy of the "DC" mark on the timing indicator.

318, 360, 400 and 440 Cu. In. Engine

1. Turn the crankshaft until the No. 6 exhaust valve is closing and the No. 6 intake valve is opening.
2. Insert a 1/4 inch spacer between the rocker arm pad and the stem tip of the No. 1 intake valve. Allow the spring load to bleed the tappet down giving, in effect, a solid tappet.
3. Install a dial indicator so that the plunger contacts the valve spring retainer as nearly perpendicular as possible. Zero the indicator.
4. Rotate the crankshaft clockwise (normal running direction) until the valve has lifted .010 inch for 318 cu. in. engines, .020 inch for 1973-77 360 cu. in. engines .034 inch for 1978-80 360 cu. in. engines, and .025 inch with 260-268 degrees camshaft for 400 and 440 cu. in. engines.

   NOTE: Do not turn the crankshaft any further clockwise as the valve spring might bottom and result in serious damage.
5. The timing of the crankshaft pulley should now read from 10 degrees BTDC to 2 degrees ATDC. Remove the spacer.

NOTE: If the reading is not within the specified limits, check the sprocket index marks, inspect the timing chain for wear, and check the accuracy of the "DC" mark on the timing indicator.

361 and 413 Cu. In. Engine

1. Check the accuracy of the TDC mark on the indicator plate by bringing the No. 1 piston to TDC by means of an indicator placed in the spark plug opening.
2. Rotate the crankshaft clockwise (normal running direction) until No. 1 intake is fully open. Install a dial indicator on the No. 1 exhaust valve so that the indicator pointer contacts the spring retainer as near to the 90 degree angle as possible.
3. Insert a 1/4 inch spacer between the rocker arm and the stem of the No. 1 exhaust valve. Allow the spring load to bleed the tappet down giving, in effect, a solid tappet.
4. Reset the dial indicator to zero. Rotate the crankshaft counterclockwise (opposite to normal running direction) until the ex-

haust valve has lifted the amount shown below.

361-4. 413-3 ....048 inch

5. The timing marks should now read from 12 degrees before TDC to TDC. If the reading is over the specified limits, check the timing gear marks and the timing chain wear.
6. After the timing has been checked, turn the crankshaft clockwise (normal running direction) until the tappet is back down to the closed valve position. Remove the spacer from between the rocker arm and the valve stem.

Camshaft

6-Cylinder Engines

Removal and Installation

1. Remove the cylinder head, timing gear cover, camshaft sprocket, and timing chain.
2. Remove the valve tappets, keeping them in order to ensure installation in their original locations.
3. Remove the crankshaft sprocket.
4. Remove the distributor and oil pump.
5. Remove the fuel pump.
6. Install a long bolt into the front of the camshaft to facilitate its removal.
7. Remove the camshaft, being careful not to damage the cam bearings with the cam lobes.
8. Prior to installation, lubricate the camshaft lobes and bearing journals. It is recommended that 1 pt. of Crankcase Conditioner be added to the initial crankcase oil fill.
9. Install the camshaft in the engine block. From this point, reverse the removal procedure.

V8 Engines

Removal and Installation

1. Remove the intake manifold, cylinder head covers, rocker arm assemblies, push rods, and valve tappets, keeping them in order to insure the installation in their original locations.
2. Remove the timing gear cover, the camshaft and crankshaft sprockets, and the timing chain.
3. Remove the distributor and lift out the oil pump and distributor driveshaft. On 361, 400, 413, and 440 cu. in. engines, remove the fuel pump to allow the push rod to drop away from the cam eccentric.
4. Remove the camshaft thrust plate (on 318 and 360).
5. Install a long bolt into the front of the camshaft and remove the camshaft, being careful not to damage the cam bearings with the cam lobes.
6. Prior to installation, lubricate the camshaft lobes and bearing journals. It is recommended that 1 pt. of Crankcase Conditioner be added to the initial crankcase oil fill. Insert the camshaft into the engine block within 2 in. of its final position in the block.
7. Have an assistant support the camshaft with a suitable tool to prevent the camshaft from contacting the plug in the rear of the engine block. Position the suitable tool against the rear side of the cam gear and be careful not to damage the cam lobes.
8. Replace the camshaft thrust plate. If camshaft end play exceeds 0.010 in., install a new thrust plate. It should be 0.002-0.006 in. with the new plate.

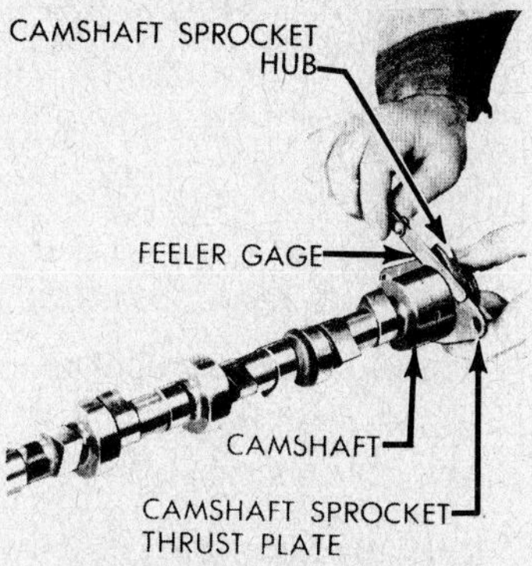

Measuring camshaft end play (© Chrysler Corp.)

9. Install the timing chain and sprockets, timing gear cover, and pulley.
10. Install the tappets, pushrods, rocker arms, and cylinder head covers. Install fuel pump, if removed.
11. Install the distributor and oil pump driveshaft. Install the distributor.
12. After starting the engine, adjust the ignition timing.

Pistons and Connecting Rods

The notch on the top of each piston must face the front of the engine.

To position the connecting rod correctly, the oil squirt hole should point to the right-side on all six-cylinder engines. On all V8 engines, the larger chamfer of the lower connecting rod bore must face to the rear on the right bank and to the front on the left bank.

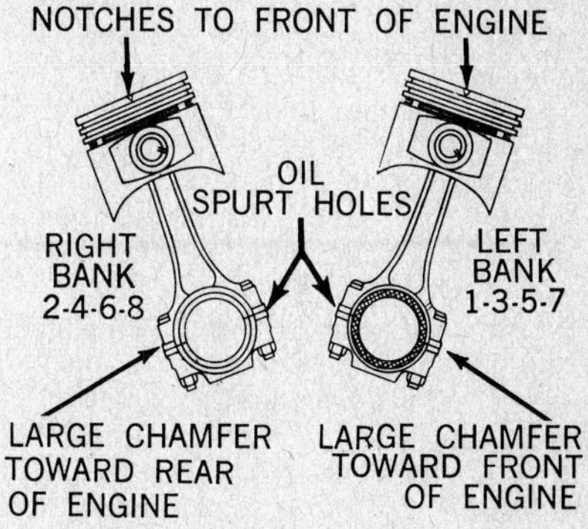

Relation of piston to rod V8 engines (© Chrysler Corp.)

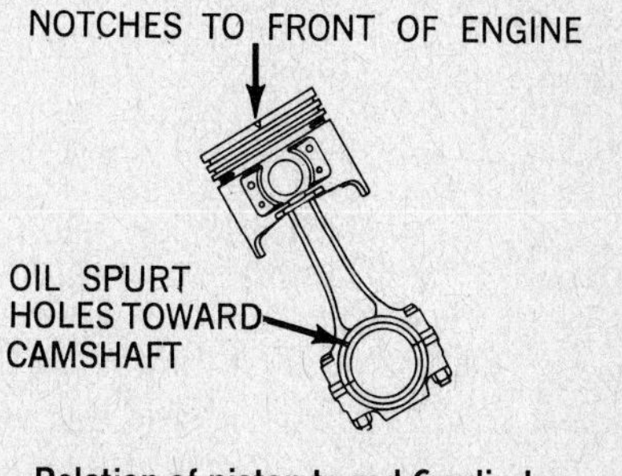

Relation of piston to rod 6 cylinder engines (© Chrysler Corp.)

Main Bearings

Reference

Detailed procedures for fitting main and rod bearings can be found in the Engine Rebuilding Section.

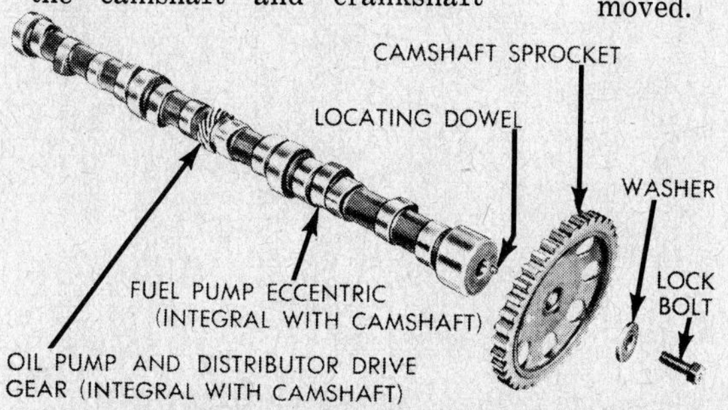

Camshaft 6 cylinder engines (© Chrysler Corp.)

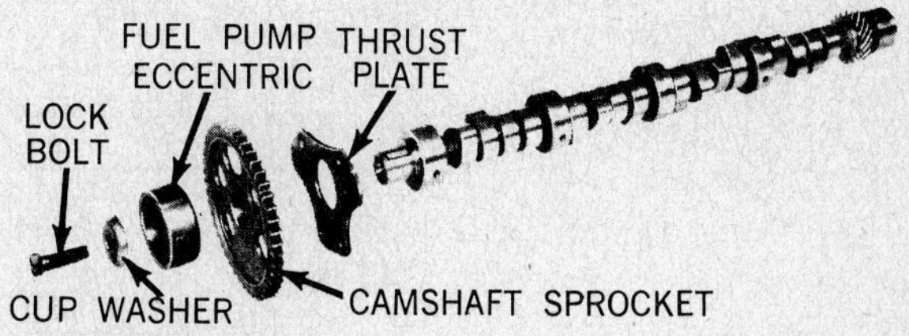

Typical V8 camshaft and sprocket assembly (318/360 shown) (© Chrysler Corp.)

6 Cylinder Engine

The maximum allowable bearing clearance is .001". No. 1, No. 2 and No. 4 lower inserts are interchangeable. No. 2 and No. 4 upper inserts are interchangeable. No. 1 upper insert has a chamfer on the tab side for timing chain oiling and is identified by the red mark on the edge of the insert. No. 3 upper and lower inserts are flanged. Bearing caps are not interchangeable and are numbered for correct installation. Maximum end play is .0085". Replace No. 3 (thrust) bearing if end play exceeds that amount.

V8 Engine

A Maltese Cross stamped on the engine (except on the 318 and 360) numbering pad indicates that the engine is equipped with a crankshaft which has one or more connecting rods and/or main bearing journal finished .001" undersize. The position of the undersize journal(s) is stamped on a machine surface of the No. 3 counterweight. The letter "R" or "M" signifies whether the undersize journal is a rod or main, and the number following the letter indicates which one it is. A Maltese Cross with an "X" indicates that all those journals are .010" undersize. On the 318 and 360 engines, .001 in. undersize journals are indicated by marks on the No. 8 crankshaft counterweight. If the "R" or "M" is followed by "X", all those journals are .010 in. undersize.

Upper and lower bearing inserts are not interchangeable on any of the V8 engines due to oil hole and V-groove in the uppers. On the 318 and 360 cu. in. engine lower bearing halves No. 1, No. 2 and No. 4 are interchangeable; No. 1, No. 2 and No. 4 upper bearing halves are interchangeable. No. 3 bearing is the thrust bearing and No. 5 is the wider rear main bearing. On 361, 383, 400, 413, and 440 cu. in. engines the No. 1,

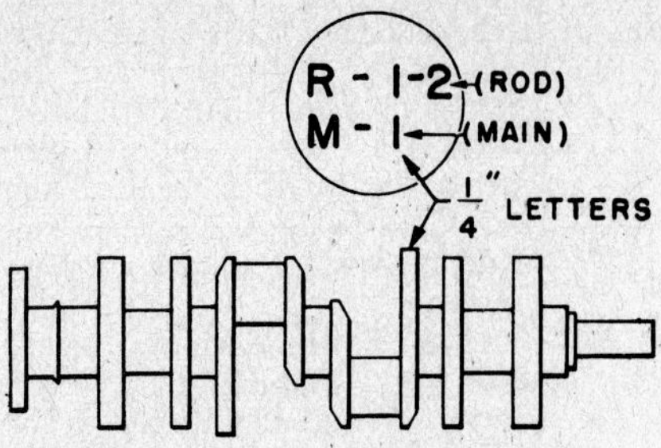

Location of undersize markings on counterweight; 318 and 360 engines are marked on the No. 8 counterweight (© Chrysler Corp.)

No. 2, No. 4 and No. 5 lower bearing halves are interchangeable; No. 2, No. 4 and No. 5 upper bearing halves are interchangeable. No. 1 upper insert has a chamfer on the tab side for timing chain oiling and is identified by the red marking on the edge. No. 3 bearing is a thrust bearing and should be replaced if end play exceeds .007".

Remove main bearing caps one at a time and check clearance. Check number of cap for proper location.

On the 361, 383, 400, 413, and 440 cu. in. engines, the rear main bearing lower seal is held in place by a seal retainer. On the 318 and 360 cu. in. engine, the rear main bearing lower seal is held in place by the rear main bearing cap. Note that the oil pump is mounted on this cap and that there is a hollow dowel which must be in place when the cap is installed.

Crankshaft Main Bearing

Removal and Installation

All Models

1. Drain the engine oil and remove the oil pan.
2. Mark the bearing caps before removing them.
3. Remove the bearing caps one at a time. Remove the upper half of the bearing by inserting a suitable tool into the oil hole of the crankshaft.
4. Slowly rotate the crankshaft clockwise forcing out the upper half of the bearing shell.

   NOTE: Only one main bearing should be selectively fitted while all other main bearing caps are properly torqued. When installing a new upper bearing shell, slightly chamfer the sharp edges from the plain side.
5. To install, start the bearing in place, and insert a suitable tool into the oil hole of the crankshaft. Slowly rotate the crankshaft counter-clockwise sliding the bearing into position. Remove the tool.
6. Continue the installation in the reverse order of the removal.
7. Fill the engine with the proper grade engine oil. Start the engine and check for leaks.

Oil Pan

Conventional Trucks

Removal and Installation

1. Remove the dipstick.
2. Raise the vehicle safely and drain the oil. On I-beam axle models, let the axle hang down on the springs.
3. Remove the optional frame reinforcement.
4. Remove the left bellhousing brace.
5. Unbolt the pan and lower it.
6. On installation, make sure that the six cylinder oil pickup screen contacts the bottom of the pan and that it is 1⅛ in. from the inside edge of the block.
7. Install the pan with new gaskets and seals.

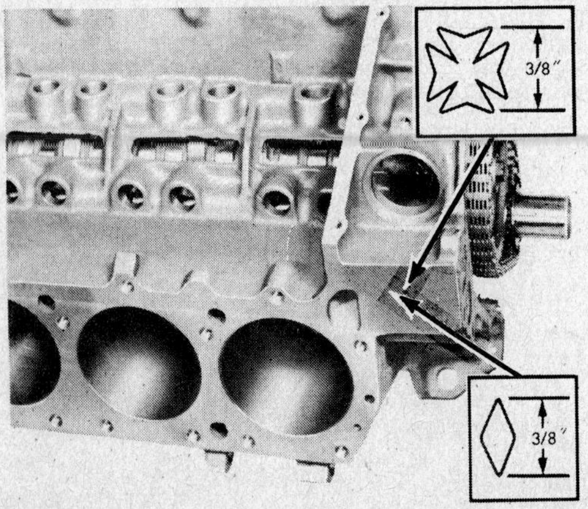

The engine number pad shows marks which indicate undersize crankshaft journals—except 318 and 360 engines (© Chrysler Corp.)

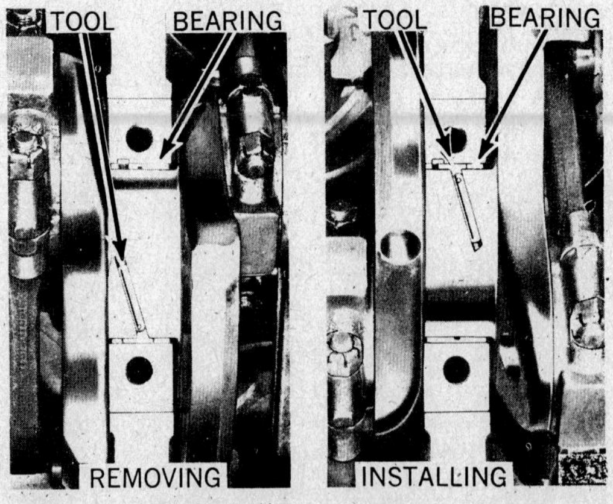

Removing and installing upper main bearings (© Chrysler Corp.)

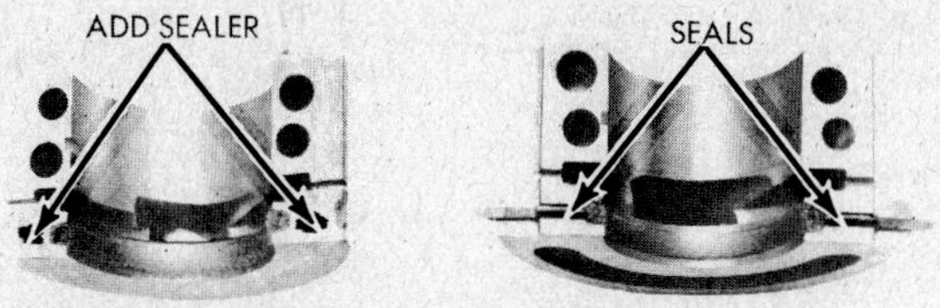

Typical rear main bearing caps (© Chrysler Corp.)

Six Cylinder Vans and Pick-Ups

1. Disconnect the battery and remove the dipstick.
2. Remove the engine cover and remove the starter and air cleaner.
3. Raise the van on a hoist and drain the crankcase oil.
4. Install an engine support as described under "Engine Removal."
5. Disconnect and tie out of the way: driveshaft, transmission linkage, and exhaust pipe at the manifold.
6. Remove the clutch torque shaft (if equipped) and the oil cooler lines (if equipped).
7. Disconnect the speedometer cable and electrical connections to the transmission.
8. Remove the support bracket, inspection plate, and drive plate-to-converter attaching screws if equipped.
9. Remove the bolts which attach the transmission to the clutch housing. Carefully work the transmission and converter rearward off the engine dowels and disengage the converter hub from the end of the crankshaft if so equipped. Remove the transmission.
10. Support the rear of the engine and raise it two inches.
11. Remove the oil pan attaching bolts. Positioning the crankshaft so that the counterweights will clear the pan, rotate the pan to the steering gear side and remove it. You may have to turn the pump pickup tube for clearance.
12. Installation is the reverse of removal. Make sure that the pickup screen contacts the bottom of the pan. Fill the engine with oil and check for leaks.
11. Remove the oil pan attaching screws and position the crankshaft so that the pan will clear the counterweights. Remove the pan.
12. Installation is the reverse of removal. Check all fluid levels and be sure that there are no leaks.

318 and 360 V8 Vans and Pick-Ups

Removal and Installation

1. Disconnect the battery ground cable. Remove the dipstick and tube, engine cover, and air cleaner.
2. Disconnect the throttle linkage at the rear of the engine and the clutch or automatic transmission linkage.
3. Raise the engine slightly and support it with the device described under "Engine Removal".
4. Raise the vehicle and drain the oil. Remove the starter.
5. Remove the driveshaft and engine rear support.
6. Remove the transmission from the van. Remove the automatic transmission with the filler tube installed and the torque converter separated from the drive plate.
7. Remove the clutch assembly and flywheel (or driveplate) from the crankshaft.
8. Raise the engine about 2 in.
9. Rotate the crankshaft so that the counterweights will clear the oil pan. Maximum clearance is with the notch in the crankshaft flange at the 3 o'clock position. Remove the oil pan. It will be necessary to reach inside the oil pan and turn the oil pick-up tube and strainer slightly to the right to clear the pan.
10. Installation is the reverse of removal. Be sure to check all fluid levels and be sure that there are no leaks.

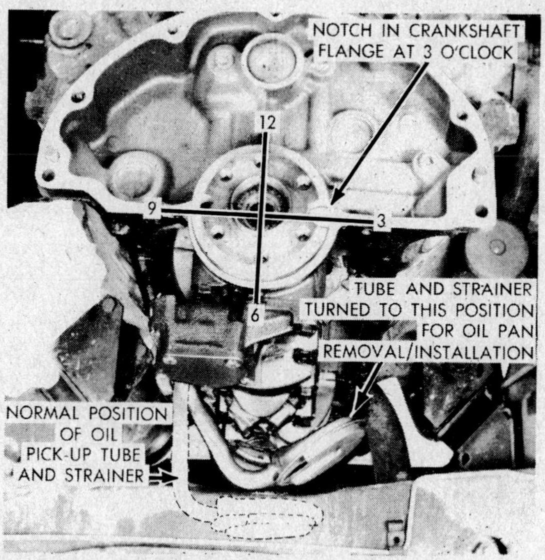

The crankshaft and oil pick up tube positioned for oil pan removal and installation (© Chrysler Corp.)

Two-wheel Drive Ramcharger and Trail Duster

Removal and Installation

1. Disconnect the battery cable and remove the dipstick.
2. Raise and support the truck.
3. Drain the oil.
4. Remove the torque converter or clutch housing brace.
5. If necessary, remove the exhaust pipe.
6. Remove the oil pan bolts and remove the pan.
7. Installation is the reverse of removal.

Four-Wheel Drive Ramcharger and Trail Duster

Removal and Installation

1. Raise vehicle on a hoist.
2. Remove the two front engine mounting bolts.
3. Remove the left-side support, connecting the converter housing and cylinder block.
4. Raise the engine approximately 2 in.
5. Drain oil.
6. Remove the oil pan bolts, lower pan down and to the rear. (Do not turn oil pickup out of position)

Oil Pump

6-Cylinder Engines

Removal and Installation

The rotor type oil pump is externally mounted on the rear right-hand (camshaft) side of the engine and is gear driven (helical) from the camshaft. The oil filter screws into the pump body.

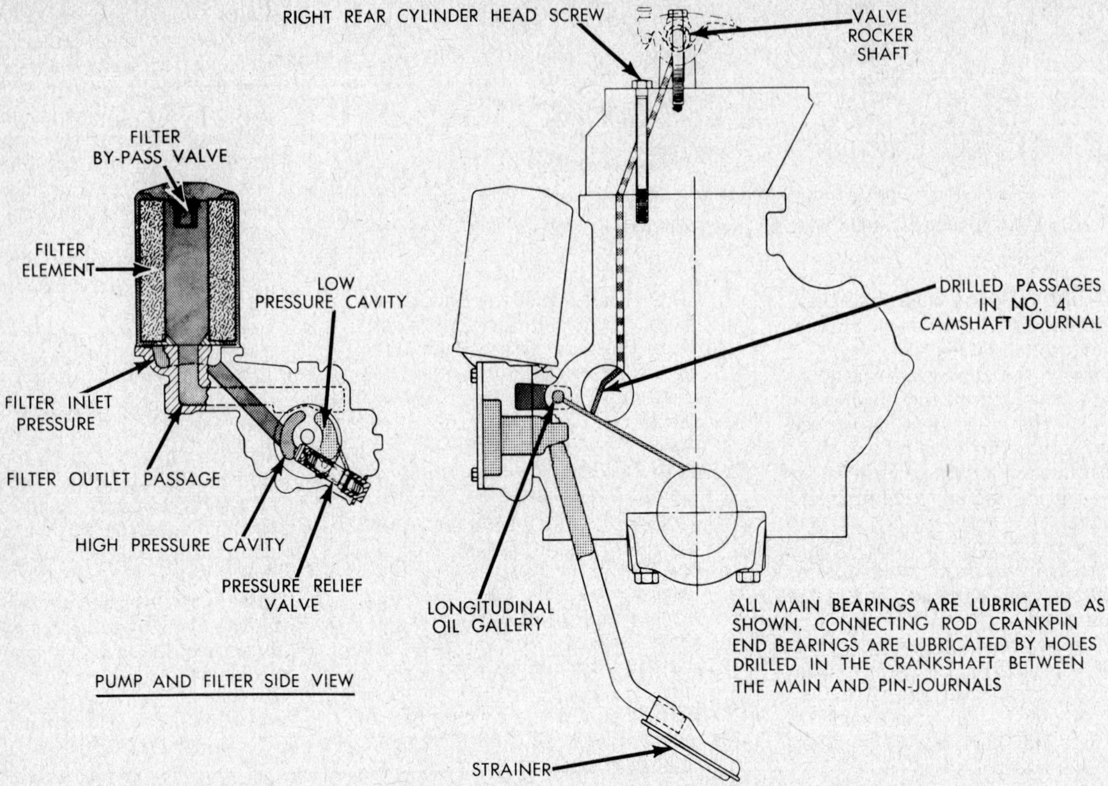

6 cylinder engine oiling system (© Chrysler Corp.)

1. Remove oil pump mounting bolts and remove pump and filter assembly from engine.
2. Disassemble the oil pump (drive gear must be pressed off) and inspect the following clearances: maximum cover wear is .0015″; outer rotor to body maximum clearance is .014″; maximum clearance between rotors is .010″. Inspect the pressure relief valve for scoring and free operation. Relief valve spring should have a free length of 2¼ in.
3. Install new oil seal rings between cover and body, tightening cover attaching bolts to 95 in. lbs.
4. Install oil pump to engine block using a new gasket and tightening mounting bolts to 200 in. lbs.

6 cylinder oil pump pick up screen on conventional trucks must be positioned 1⅛ inch from the inside edge of the block (© Chrysler Corp.)

318 and 360 Cu. In. Engines

Removal and Installation

NOTE: It is necessary to remove the oil pan, and to remove the oil pump from the rear main bearing cap to service the oil pump.

1. Drain the engine oil and remove the oil pan.
2. Remove the oil pump mounting bolts and remove the oil pump from the rear main bearing cap.
3. To remove the relief valve, drill a ⅛ inch hole into the relief valve retainer cap and insert a self-threading sheet metal screw

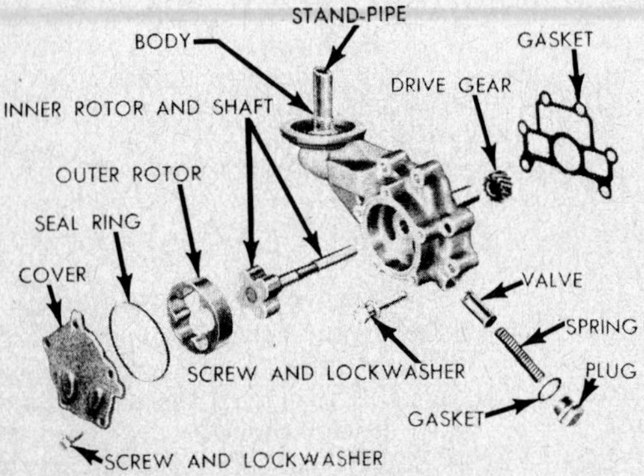

6 cylinder oil pump (© Chrysler Corp.)

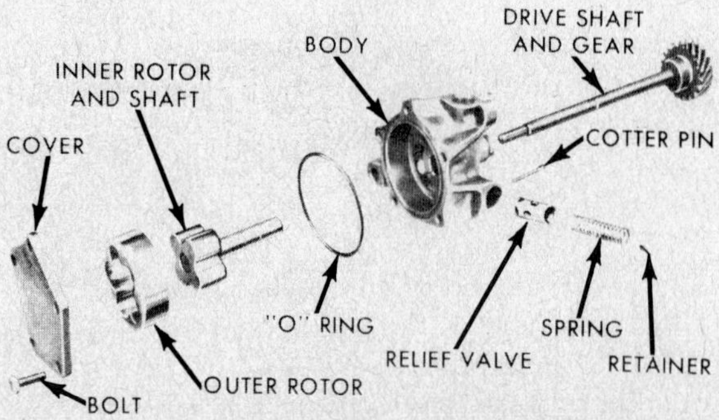

318 and 360 V8 oil pump (© Chrysler Corp.)

into the cap. Clamp the screw into a vise and while supporting the oil pump, remove the cap by tapping the pump body using a soft hammer. Discard the retainer cap and remove the spring and the relief valve.

4. Remove the oil pump cover and lockwashers, and lift off the cover. Discard the oil ring seal. Remove the pump rotor and shaft, and lift out the outer rotor.

   NOTE: Wash all parts in solvent and inspect for damage or wear. The mating surfaces of the oil pump cover should be smooth. Replace the pump assembly if this is not the case.

5. Lay a straight edge across the pump cover surface and if a .0015 inch feeler gauge can be inserted between the cover and the straight edge, the pump assembly should be replaced. Measure the thickness and the diameter of the outer rotor. If the outer rotor thickness measures .825 inch or less, (.943 inch or less on 360 cu. in. engines 1977-80) or if the diameter is 2.469 inches or less, replace the outer rotor. If the inner rotor measures .825 inch or less, (.943 inch or less on 360 cu. in. engines 1977-80) then the inner rotor and shaft assembly must be replaced.
6. Slide the outer rotor into the pump body, do this by pressing it to one side with your fingers and measure the clearance between the rotor and the pump body. If the measurement is .014 inch or more, replace the oil pump assembly. Install the inner rotor and shaft into the pump body. If the clearance between the inner and outer rotors is .010 inch or more, replace the shaft and both rotors.

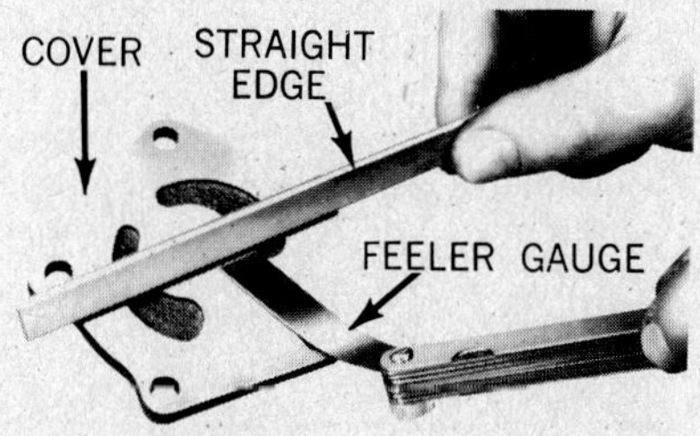

Measuring oil pump cover wear—typical (© Chrysler Corp.)

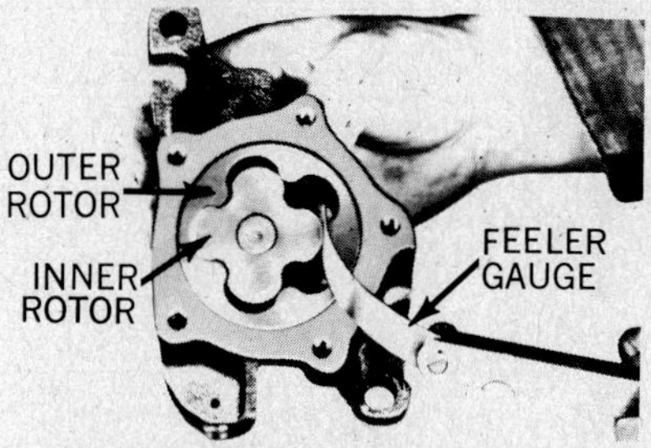

Measuring the clearance between the rotors—typical (© Chrysler Corp.)

7. Place a straight edge across the face of the pump, between the bolt holes. If a feeler gauge of .004 inch or more can be inserted between the rotors and the straight edge, replace the pump assembly.
8. Inspect the oil pressure relief valve plunger for scoring and free operation in it's bore. Small marks may be removed with 400-grit wet or dry sandpaper.
9. The relief valve spring has a free length of 2 1/32 to 2 3/64 inch and should test between 16.2 and 17.2 lbs. when compressed to 1 11/32 inch. Replace the spring if it fails to meet this specification.
10. To install, assemble the oil pump, using new parts as required. Tighten the cover bolts to 95 in. lbs.
11. Prime the oil pump before installation by filling the rotor cavity with engine oil. Install the oil pump on the engine and tighten attaching bolts to 30 ft. lbs.
12. Continue the installation in the reverse order of the removal.
13. Fill the engine with the proper grade motor oil. Start the engine and check for leaks.

361, 400, 413, 440 Cu. In Engines

Removal and Installation

The rotor type oil pump is externally mounted and gear driven from the camshaft. The oil filter screws into the pump body.

1. Drain engine oil.
2. Remove oil pump and filter assembly.
3. Disassemble and inspect pump components for wear. If 0.0015″ feeler gauge can be inserted between cover and straight edge, replace cover. Install outer rotor in pump body and holding against one side of body measure clearance between rotor and body. If clearance is greater than 0.014″, replace oil pump body. Install inner rotor into pump body and place straight edge across pump body between bolt holes. If feeler gauge greater than 0.004″ can be inserted between rotors and body, replace oil pump body. Measure clearance between tips of inner and outer rotor where they are opposed. If clearance exceeds 0.010″, replace inner and outer rotors. Use new oil seal rings between filter base and body. Tighten bolts to 10 ft. lbs. Use a new "O" ring seal on pilot of oil pump before attaching pump to engine block.
4. Install oil pump on engine using new gasket and tightening bolts to 30 ft. lbs. The distributor drive gear slot should parallel the crankshaft with no. 1 cylinder on TDC.
5. Install oil filter and fill crankcase with oil.

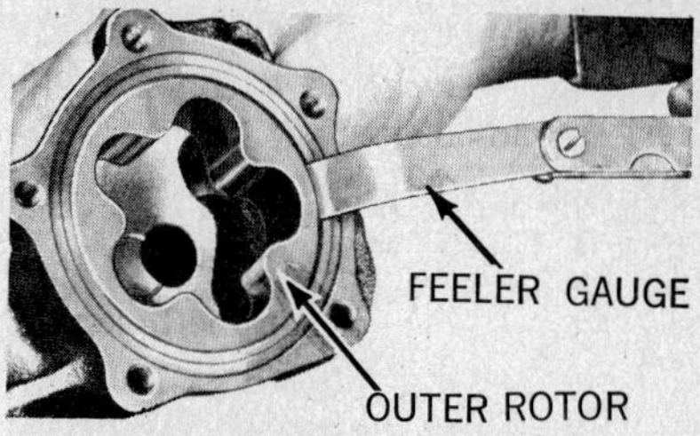

Measuring the outer rotor clearance typical (© Chrysler Corp.)

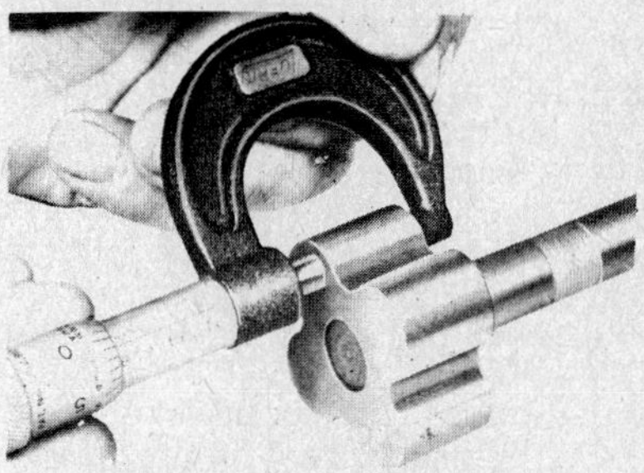
Measuring the inner rotor clearance typical (© Chrysler Corp.)

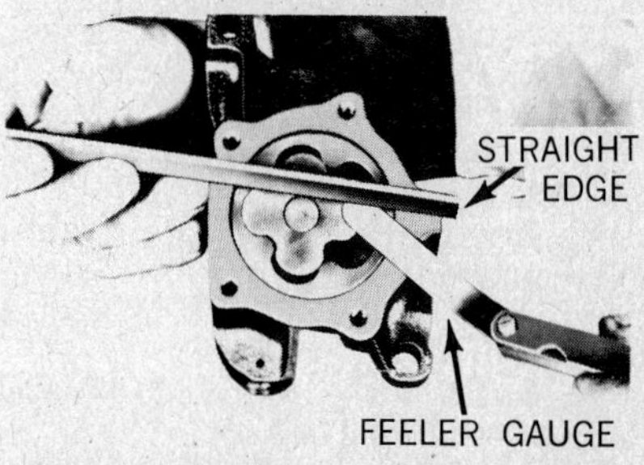

Measuring the clearance over the rotors typical (© Chrysler Corp.)

Rear Main Bearing Oil Seal

Replacement

Service replacement seals are of the split rubber type composition. This type of seal makes it possible to replace the upper rear seal without removing the crankshaft. The seal must be used as an upper and lower set and cannot be used with the rope type seal.

NOTE: Rope type seals are included in overhaul gasket sets, for use when the crankshaft has been removed, on all engines, except the 360 V-8, which uses only the composition seal.

The following procedure is for removing the rope type rear main seal and replacing it with the rubber type seal.

1. Remove the oil pan, and both the rear seal retainer and the rear main bearing cap, if separate.
2. Remove the lower rope seal from the cap or retainer by prying the seal out of the groove.
3. With the use of suitable tools, either pull or push the seal from its seat, while rotating the crankshaft, being careful not to damage the surface of the journal. If necessary, loosen all the main bearing caps slightly, to lower the crankshaft, which will aid in the removal and replacement of the seal.
4. Clean and lubricate the crankshaft journal. Hold the seal tight against the crankshaft with the painted stripe to the rear, and install the seal into the block groove.
5. Rotate the crankshaft while pushing the seal into the groove. Be careful that the sharp edges of the block groove. *Do not cut or nick the rear of the seal.*
6. Install the lower half of the seal into the lower seal retainer or the main bearing cap, if separate, with the paint stripe facing to the rear.
7. Install the lower seal retainer and/or the rear main bearing cap. Torque all main bearing caps to specifications.
8. Install the oil pan, add oil and check for oil leaks.

FRONT AXLE AND SUSPENSION

I-Beam Axle King Pin and Bushing Removal and Installation

1. Raise the front of the vehicle and safely support it on stands. Remove the wheels and drums.
2. Remove the brake support plate attaching bolts, and remove the support plate from the steering knuckle. Secure the plate to the frame so that it does not hang by the brake hose. If equipped with air brakes, disconnect the push rod and remove the air chamber.
3. Remove the steering arm from the steering knuckle.
4. Remove the pivot pin locking screw or pin from the knuckle. Some models may have two locking screws.
5. Remove the upper pivot pin oil seal plug from the knuckle and drive the pivot pin down, forcing the lower oil seal plug from its seat. *NOTE: On some models, a lock ring is used to hold the oil seal plug in place. Others have caps with hold-down screws.*
6. Remove the knuckle from the axle and if equipped with bronze bushings, press the old ones out and press the new ones in and line ream them to fit the new pin. If equipped with Delrin or Zytel type bushings, bronze bushings must be used as service replacements. Upon installation of the bushings, align the grease hole in the bushing to that of the grease fitting hole in the knuckle.
7. Install the knuckle on the axle. position the thrust bearing, and install the pivot pin through the knuckle and axle, securing it with the locking pins or screws.
8. Install the oil seal plugs and secure them by staking in four locations.
9. Complete the assembly by reversing steps one to three. Lubricate to assure grease channels are open.

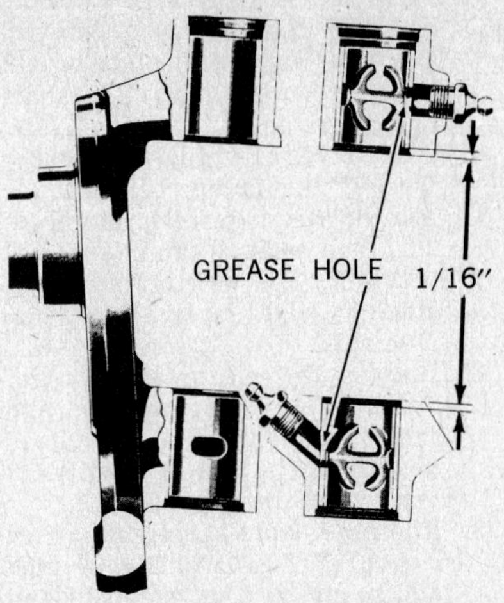

King pin bushing installation D100, 200 (© Chrysler Corp.)

Front Leaf Spring Removal and Installation

This procedure applies to all models with front leaf springs.

1. Raise truck until weight is removed from springs.
2. Install stands under side frame members as a safety precaution.
3. Disconnect the sway bar at the spring plate. Remove nuts, lockwashers and U-bolts securing spring to axle.
4. Remove spring shackle bolts, shackles and spring front eye bolt.
5. Remove spring.
6. To install, line up spring fixed eye with bolt hole in bracket and install spring bolt and nut.
7. Install shackle bolts, shackles and nuts. Tighten shackle bolt nuts and fixed eye bolt until slack is taken up.
8. Position spring on axle so spring center bolt enters locating hole in axle pad.
9. Install U-bolts, new lockwashers and nuts, tightening securely.
10. Remove stands from under frame, lower truck so weight is resting on wheels. Tighten

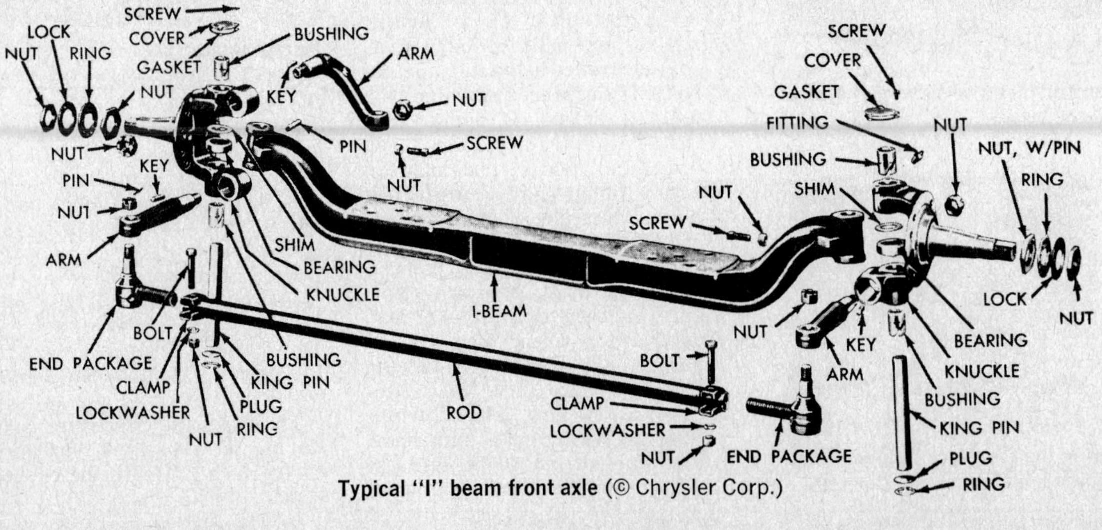

Typical "I" beam front axle (© Chrysler Corp.)

U-bolt nuts, spring eye bolt nuts and shackle bolt nuts.

11. Lubricate spring bolts and shackle bolts with chassis lubricant. *Do not lubricate rubber*

Wheel Bearing Adjustment

D100, D200, and D300

1. While rotating the wheel, tighten the adjusting nut to 360-480 inch pounds.
2. With the wheel at rest, back off the adjusting nut to completely release the bearing preload.
3. Finger tighten the adjusting nut, and install the lock nut and the cotter key.

NOTE: End play of .0001-.003 inch is acceptable. If this measurement is obtained, then the wheel bearing adjustment is satisfactory.

500, 550, 7000, and 9000 Lbs. Front Axles

1. While rotating the hub and drum, tighten the adjusting nut to 50 ft. lbs.
2. Back off the adjusting nut approximately 1/4 turn, and install the lock ring. Be sure to align the dowel with the hole in the lock ring.

   NOTE: After backingfi off the adjusting nut, be certain that the nut is only finger tight.
3. Install the lock washer and nut. Torque the lock nut to 100-150 ft. lbs.

All Others

1. Tighten the adjusting nut to 50 ft. lbs.
2. Back off the adjusting nut approximately 1/4 turn.
   NOTE: After backing off the adjusting nut, be certain that the nut is only finger tight.
3. Install the cotter key to lock in place.
4. Bend the lock washer down over one of the flats of the lock nut.

Front Drive Axle

Front Drive Axle Assembly Removal and Installation

1. Raise the truck and install stands under the frame rails, behind the front springs.
2. Disconnect front driveshaft at drive pinion yoke.
3. Disconnect steering linkage at drag link.
4. Disconnect front shock absorbers and brake line at frame. Disconnect the sway bar link assembly from the spring clip plate.
5. Remove nuts from the spring hold down bolts and remove axle assembly from under vehicle.
6. To install, place axle assembly under vehicle and line up spring center bolts with locating hole in axle housing pad.
7. Install spring clips or spring U-bolts, new lock washer and nuts.
8. Connect the shock absorbers, and the brake line at the frame.
9. Connect the steering linkage to the drag link, and the driveshaft to the pinion yoke. Check lubricants and bleed the brakes.
10. Lower the vehicle and test the operation.

Front Drive Axle Shaft Removal and Installation

Enclosed U-Joint, Pivot Pin Type

1. After removing wheel assembly and locking hubs, remove grease cap from drive flange.
2. Remove drive flange bolts and snap ring. Then, using a suitable puller, remove drive flange.
3. Remove locknut, lockwasher and adjusting nut.
4. Remove wheel hub and brake drum assembly, being careful not to damage oil seal.
5. Remove brake assembly and wire to frame, leaving hydraulic line connected.
6. Tap end of spindle with a soft hammer and remove spindle.
7. Inspect spindle and bushing for wear. Bushing is pressed on and requires no reaming for proper fit.
8. Remove axle shaft assembly. Inspect universal joint. Disassemble and replace any worn components.
9. Install axle assembly, being careful not to damage inner oil seal.
10. Lubricate flanged bushing and install spindle and brake support assembly.
11. Remove, clean, inspect and repack inner and outer wheel bearings.
12. Install inner wheel bearing, position hub, drum and wheel assembly on spindle, then install outer bearing, washer and adjusting nut.
13. Adjust bearing by tightening adjusting nut to 50 ft. lbs. torque, then back off 1/4 to 1/3 turn. Tighten locknut and bend tab of lock-washer.
14. Install drive flange, retaining nuts, snap ring and grease cup.

Exposed U-Joint, Ball Joint Type

This procedure is for disc-braked vehicles, but may be adapted to those with drum brakes.

1. Remove the locking hubs. Remove the cotter key and loosen the axle shaft nut.
2. Block the brake pedal up. Remove the wheel.
3. Remove and hang the caliper out of the way. Remove the inner pad.
4. Working through the hole in the disc hub, remove the socket head capscrews.
5. Remove the axle shaft nut and use a hub puller to remove the disc and hub.
6. Remove the O-ring from the steering knuckle. Remove the disc brake adapter from the knuckle. Punch out the inner oil seal from the rear of the knuckle.
7. Slide the axle shaft from the housing.
8. On replacement, first slide the shaft into place, then drive a new seal into the steering knuckle.
9. Install the disc brake adapter and torque the mounting bolts to 85 ft. lbs.
10. Install a new O-ring on the steering knuckle.
11. Slide the disc and hub, retainer and bearing assembly over the shaft and start it into the housing. Install the axle shaft nut.
12. Install the capscrews holding the retainer to the steering knuckle flange. Tighten them to 30 ft. lbs. in a criss-cross pattern.
13. Torque the axle shaft nut to 100 ft. lbs. and tighten further until the cotter key can be installed.
14. Locate the inner pad on the adapter with the shoe flanges in the adapter ways. Slide the caliper into position, being careful

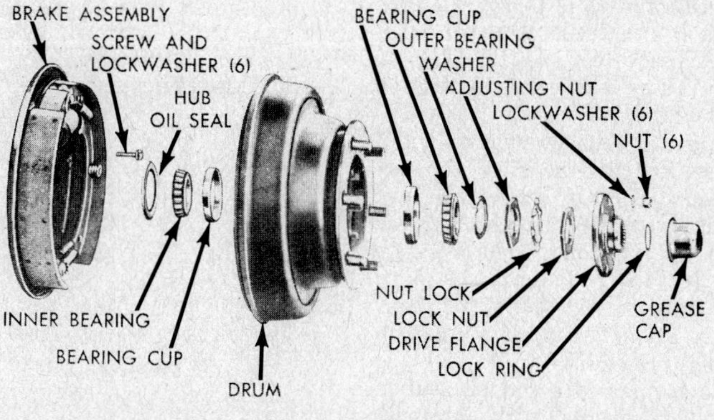

Typical brake hub and drum assembly (© Chrysler Corp.)

not to pull the dust boot from its grooves.

15. Install the anti-rattle springs, making sure that the inner one is on top of the retainer spring plate. Tighten the retaining clips to 200 in. lbs.
16. Install the wheel and lower the vehicle.

Front Drive Axle Steering Knuckle Service

Enclosed U-Joint, Pivot Pin Type

1. Remove, wheel, hub, brake drum assembly, brake support assembly, spindle and axle shaft.
2. Disconnect tie rod ends from steering knuckles and drag link from steering knuckle arm.
3. Remove steering knuckle felt and oil seal retainers.
4. Remove lower bearing cap and shims.
5. Remove upper bearing cap or knuckle arm and shims.
6. Remove knuckle housing, felt and oil seal.
7. Remove upper and lower bearing cones, then clean and inspect bearings.
8. Check bearing cups for wear and remove with drift if required.
9. To assemble, place felt and oil seal over end of axle housing.
10. Install steering knuckle arm or upper bearing cap and shim pack and tighten retaining bolts or nuts. If a new shim pack is used, use *only* one which is .060″ thick.
11. Lubricate and install cone (press in) on upper bearing pivot, making sure serration or key and slot are properly located, if so equipped.
12. Seat bearing cups in yokes of axle housing. Slide knuckle assembly over yoke and enter bronze cone in its cup.
13. Lubricate and insert lower bearing cone, tilting knuckle to provide access. Install lower bearing cap and shim pack. If a new pack is required, use *only* .025″ thick pack for 44-3F axle or .055″ thick pack for 44-3HF or 70F axle.
14. Using a torque wrench on a top outer knuckle bearing cap retaining bolt or nut, measure bearing preload as knuckle is turning. It must read 5-15 ft. lbs. for 44-3F axle and 15-35 ft. lbs. for the 44-3HDF or 70-F axles. Remove or add shims to adjust preload.
15. Attach oiled felt and oil seal to knuckle housing with retainers and screws.

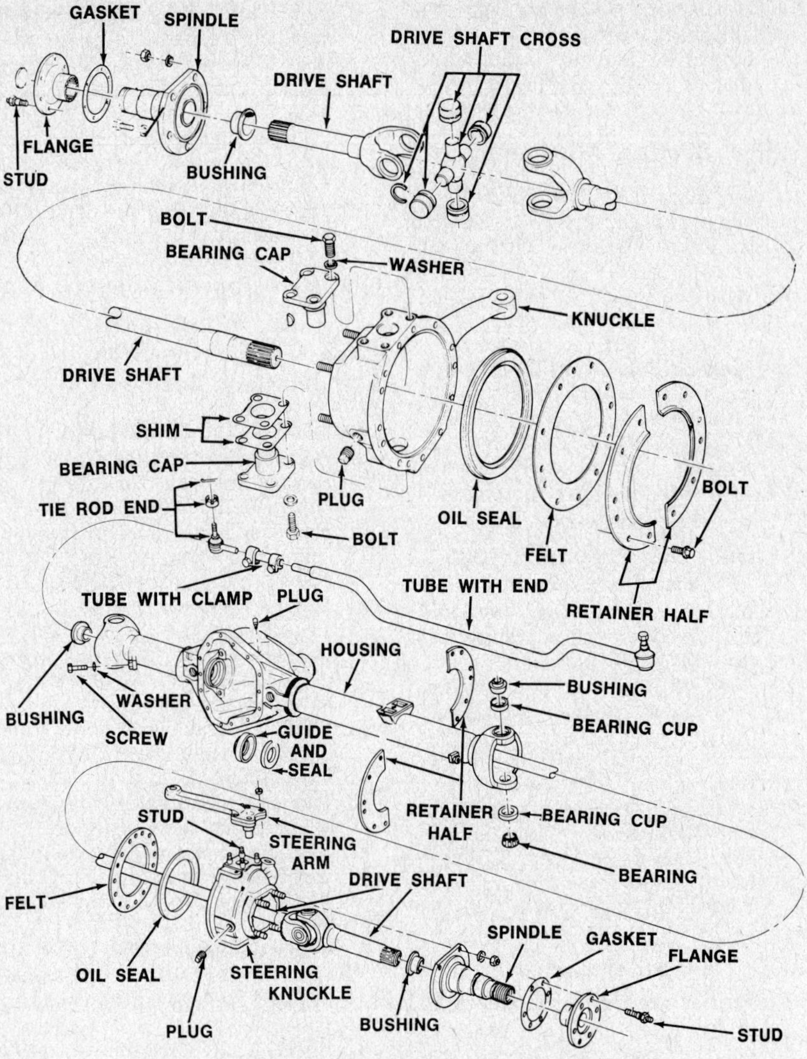

Axle housing (W500)—exploded view (© Chrysler Corp.)

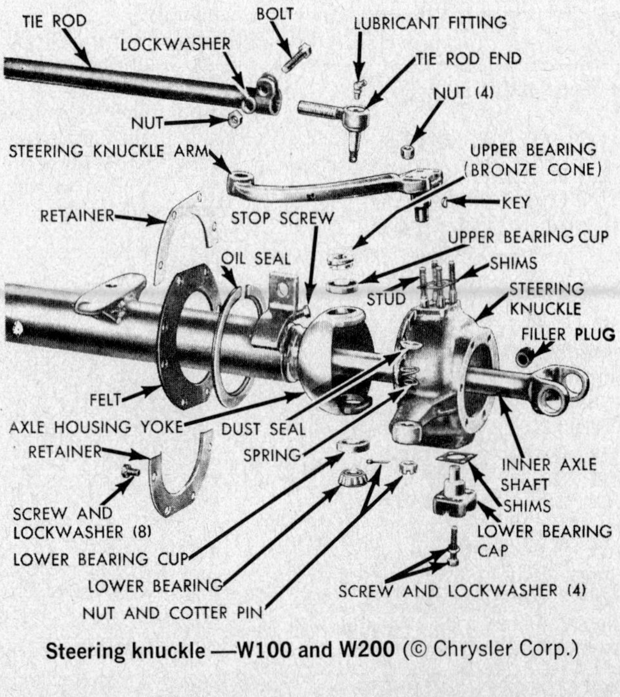

Steering knuckle —W100 and W200 (© Chrysler Corp.)

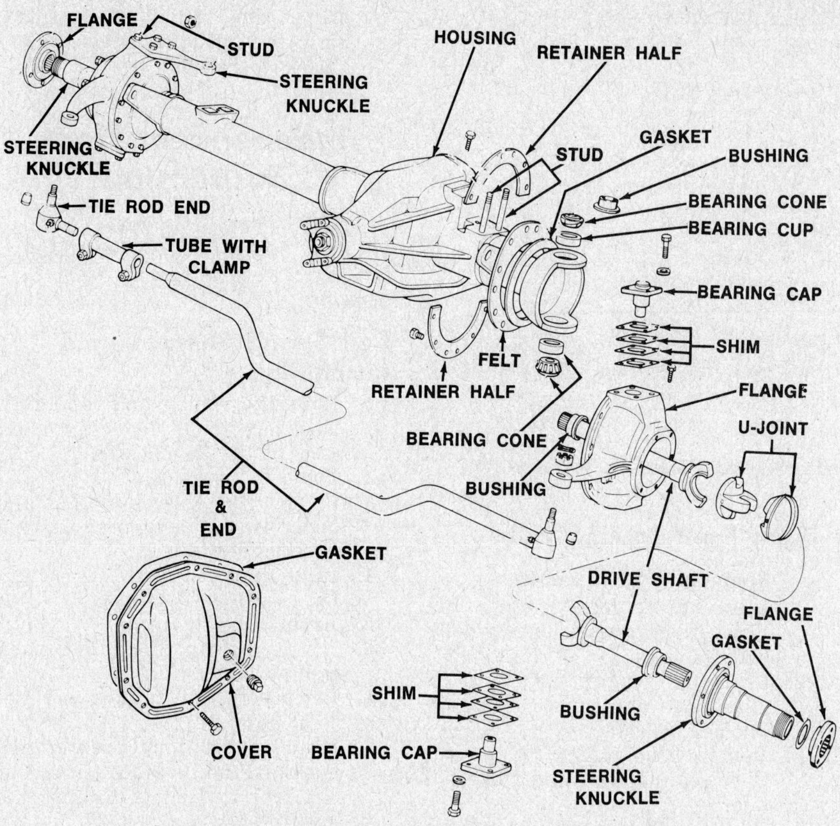

70F axle and steering knuckle—exploded view (© Chrysler Corp.)

16. Install axle shaft, spindle and brake support assembly, tightening spindle to steering knuckle flange bolts.
17. Install hub, brake drum and wheel assembly.
18. Fill steering knuckle housing with SAE 140 oil to level of filler plug opening.
19. Check and adjust toe-in and turning radius.

Exposed U-Joint, Ball Joint Type

The ball joints should be replaced if there is any looseness or end-play. The steering knckle and ball joint must be removed to replace the ball joint.

Removal

1. Refer to the "Front Drive Axle Removal and Replacement," on Exposed U-Joint, Ball Joint type, for the detailed removal of the rotor, hub and bearings, 1 through 6.
2. Remove and discard the O-ring from the steering knuckle.
3. Remove the capscrews from the brake splash shield and remove the splash shield. Remove the brake disc adaptor from the steering knuckle.
4. Disconnect the tie-rod from the steering knuckle. On the left side, disconnect the drag link from the steering knuckle arm.
5. Using a punch and hammer, remove the inner oil seal from the rear of the steering knuckle.
6. Carefully, slide the outer and inner axle shaft complete with U-joint from the axle housing.
7. On the left-side, remove the steering knuckle arm by tapping it to loosen the tapered dowels.
8. Remove the cotter pin from the upper ball joint nut. Remove the upper and lower ball joint nuts and discard the lower nut.
9. Separate the steering knuckle from the axle housing yoke with a brass drift and hammer. Remove and discard the sleeve from the upper ball joint yoke on the axle housing.
10. Position the steering knuckle upside down in a vise with soft jaws and remove the snap-ring from the lower ball joint.
11. Press the lower and upper ball joints from the steering knuckle individually.

Installation

1. Position the steering knuckle right side up in a vise with soft jaws. Press the lower ball joint into position and install the snap-ring.
2. Press the upper ball joint into position. Install new boots on both ball joints.
3. Screw a new sleeve into the upper ball joint yoke on the axle housing, leaving about two threads showing at the top.
4. Install the steering knuckle on the axle housing yoke and install a new lower ball joint nut, tightening it to 80 ft. lbs.
5. Tighten the sleeve in the upper ball joint yoke to 40 ft. lbs. Install the upper ball joint nut and tighten it to 100 ft. lbs. Align the cotter key hole in the stud with the slot in the castellated nut and install the cotter pin. Do not loosen the nut to align the holes.
6. On the left-side, position the steering knuckle arm over the studs on the steering knuckle. Install the tapered dowels and nuts. Tighten the nuts to 90 ft. lbs. Install the drag link on the steering arm. Install the nut and tighten it to 60 ft. lbs. Install the cotter pin.
7. Install the tie-rod end on the steering knuckle. Tighten the nut to 45 ft. lbs. and install the cotter pin.
8. Install the axle shaft. Install the brake splash shield and tighten the screws to 13 ft. lbs. Install the brake disc adaptor and tighten the bolts to 85 ft. lbs.
9. Install a new O-ring in the steering knuckle.
10. Clean any rust from the axle shaft splines.
11. Carefully, slide the hub, rotor and retainer, and bearing onto the axle shaft and start it into the housing. Install the axle shaft nut.
12. Align the retainer with the steering knuckle flange. Install the retainer screws and tighten them in a criss-cross pattern to 30 ft. lbs.
13. Tighten the axle shaft nut to 100 ft. lbs. Tighten the nut until the next slot in the nut aligns with the hole in the axle shaft. Install the cotter pin.
14. Install the inboard brake shoe on the adaptor with the shoe flanges in the adaptor ways. Install the caliper in the adaptor and over the disc. Align the caliper on the machined ways of the adaptor. Be careful not to pull the dust boot from its grooves as the piston and boot slide over the inboard shoe.
15. Install the anti-rattle springs and retaining clips. Torque to 16-17 ft. lbs. The inboard shoe anti-rattle spring must always be installed on top of the retainer spring plate.
16. Install the wheel, tire, and locking hub and lower the truck. Lubricate all fittings.

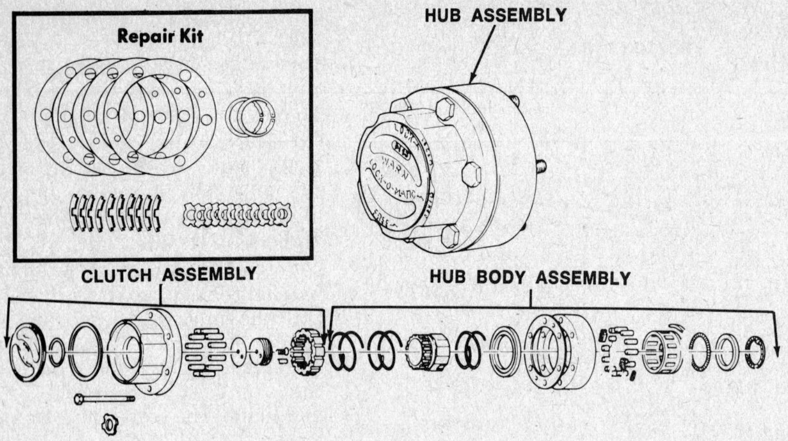

Warn locking hub—exploded view (© Chrysler Corp.)

Warn Front Locking Hubs

Removal and Disassembly

1. Straighten the lock tabs and remove the six hub mounting bolts.
2. Tap the hub gently with a mallet to remove.
3. Separate the clutch assembly from the body assembly.
4. Remove the snap ring from the rear of the body assembly, using snap-ring pliers. Slip the axle shaft hub out of the body from the front.
5. Remove the Allen screw from the inner side of the clutch, and remove the bronze dial assembly from the front side of the clutch housing assembly.
6. Remove the clutch assembly from the rear of the housing, complete with the twelve roller pins.

Assembly and Installation

1. Coat the moving parts with a water-proof grease.
2. Slide the axle shaft hub into the body from the front, and replace the snap-ring.
3. Replace the bronze dial assembly and the inner clutch. Tighten the Allen screw and stake the edge of the screw with a center punch to prevent loosening.
4. With the dial in the FREE position, rotate the outer clutch body into the inner assembly until it bottoms in the housing. Back it up to the nearest hole and install the roller pins.
5. Position the hub and clutch assembly together with a new gasket in between.
6. Position the hub assembly over the end of the axle and replace the six hub mounting bolts and lock tabs.
7. Torque the bolts to 35 foot-pounds and bend the lock tabs to anchor the bolts.
8. Verify the operation by road testing.

Dana Front Locking Hubs

Removal and Disassembly

1. Place hub in lock position. Remove Allen head mounting bolts and washers.
2. Carefully remove retainer, O-ring seal and knob. Separate knob from retainer.
3. Remove large internal snap-ring. Slide retainer ring and cam from hub.
4. While pressing against sleeve and ring assembly, remove axle shaft snap-ring. Relieve pressure and remove sleeve and ring, ring and bushing, spring and plate.
5. Inspect all parts for wear, nicks and burrs. Replace all parts which appear questionable.

Assembly and Installation

1. Slide plate and spring (large coils first) into wheel hub housing.
2. Assemble ring and bushing, sleeve and bushing. Slide complete assembly into housing.
3. Compress spring and install axle shaft snap-ring.
4. Position cam and retainer in housing and install large internal snap-ring.
5. Place small O-ring seal on knob, lubricate with waterproof grease and install in retainer at lock position.
6. Place large O-ring seal on retainer. Align retainer and retainer ring and install washers and Allen head mounting screws.
7. Check operation.

Independent Front Suspension

NOTE: These procedures apply to all vans, pick-ups, and conventional trucks with independent front suspension.

Coil Spring Removal and Installation

1. Raise the vehicle and support it with jackstands under the front ends of the frame rails.
2. Remove the wheel.
3. Remove the shock absorber and upper shock absorber bushing bushing and sleeve.
4. If equipped, remove the sway bar.
5. Remove the strut.
6. Install a spring compressor and tighten finger-tight.
7. Remove the cotter pins and ball joint nuts.
8. Install a ball joint breaker tool and turn the threaded portion of the tool to lock it against the lower stud.
9. Spread the tool to place the lower stud under pressure, then strike the steering knuckle sharply with a hammer to free the stud. Do not attempt to force the stud out of the steering knuckle with the tool.
10. Remove the tool. Slowly release the spring compressor until all tension is relieved from the spring.
11. Remove the spring compressor and spring.
12. Installation is the reverse of removal. Compress the spring until the ball joint can be properly positioned in the steering knuckle.

Shock Absorber Removal and Installation

1. Raise and support the vehicle with jackstands positioned at the extreme front ends of the frame rails.
2. Remove the wheel.

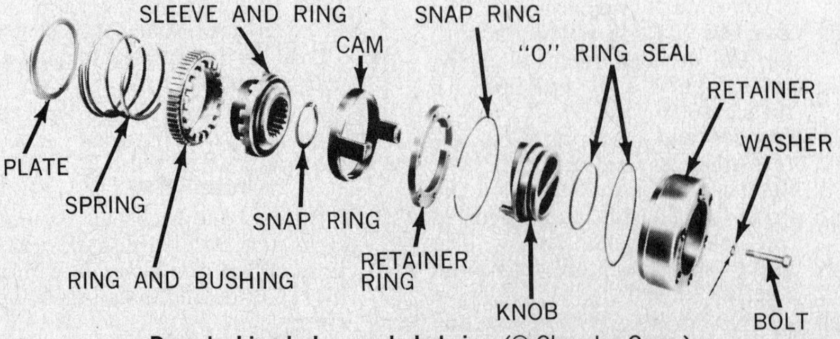

Dana locking hub—exploded view (© Chrysler Corp.)

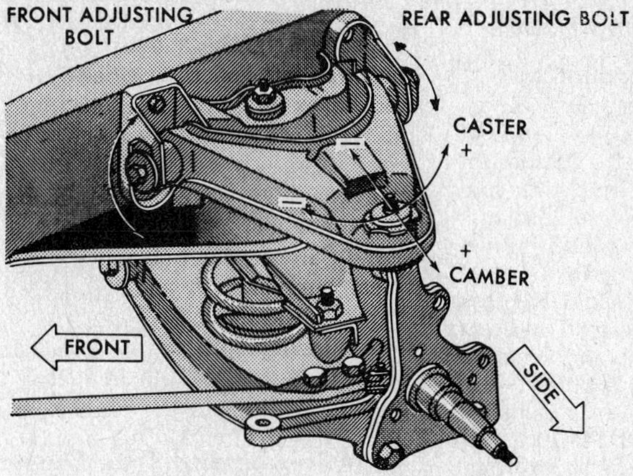

Independent front suspension alignment points (© Chrysler Corp.)

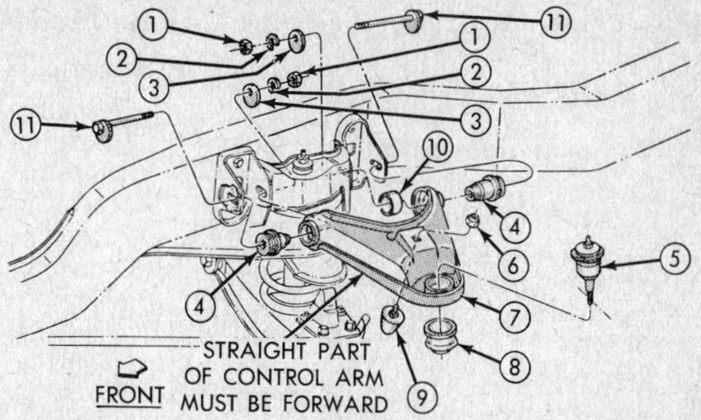

Upper control arm details (© Chrysler Corp.)

1 Nut
2 Lockwasher
3 Cam
4 Bushing Assembly
5 Ball Joint
6 Lock Nut
7 Upper Control Arm
8 Upper Ball Joint
9 Bumper Assembly
10 Sleeve
11 Cam and Bolt Assembly

3. Remove the upper nut and retainer.
4. Remove the two lower mounting bolts.
5. Remove the shock absorber.
6. Installation is the reverse of removal.

Upper Control Arm Removal and Installation

NOTE: Any time the control arm is removed, it is necessary to align the front end.

1. Raise and support the vehicle with jackstands under the frame rails.
2. Remove the wheel.
3. Remove the shock absorber and shock absorber upper bushing and sleeve.
4. Install a spring compressor and tighten it finger-tight.
5. Remove the cotter pins and ball joint nuts.
6. Install a ball joint breaker and turn the threaded portion of the tool, locking it securely against the upper stud. Spread the tool enough to place the upper ball joint under pressure and strike the steering knuckle sharply to loosen the stud. Do not attempt to remove the stud from the steering knuckle with the tool.
7. Remove the tool.
8. Remove the eccentric pivot bolts, after making their relative positions in the control arm.
9. Remove the upper control arm.
10. Installation is the reverse of removal. Tighten the ball joint nuts to 135 ft. lbs. Tighten the eccentric pivot bolts to 70 ft. lbs.
11. Adjust the caster and camber.

Lower Control Arm Removal and Installation

1. Follow the procedure outlined under "Coil Spring Removal and Installation."
2. Remove the mounting bolt from the crossmember.
3. Remove the lower control arm from the vehicle.
4. Installation is the reverse of removal. After the vehicle has been lowered to the ground, tighten the mounting bolt to 210 ft. lbs.

1 Nut
2 Retainer
3 Bushing
4 Bolt
5 Nut
6 Coil Spring
7 Shock Absorber
8 Washer
9 Bushing Assembly
10 Capscrew
11 Lower Control Arm

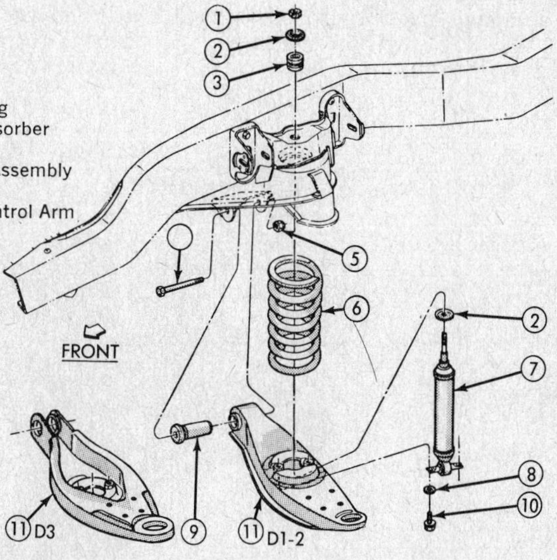

Lower control arm details (© Chrysler Corp.)

Lower Ball Joint Removal and Installation

1. Remove the lower control arm.
2. Remove the ball joint seal.
3. Using an arbor press and a sleeve, press the ball joint from the control arm.
4. Installation is the reverse of removal. Be sure that the ball joint is fully seated. Install a new ball joint seal.
5. Install the lower control arm. Be sure to install the ball joint cotter pins.

Upper Ball Joint Removal and Installation

1. Install a jack under the outer end of the lower control arm and raise the vehicle.
2. Remove the wheel.
3. Remove the ball joint nuts. Using a ball joint breaker, loosen the upper ball joint.
4. Unscrew the ball joint from the control arm.
5. Screw a new ball joint into the control arm and tighten 125 ft. lbs.
6. Install the new ball joint seal, using a 2 in. socket. Be sure that the seal is seated on the ball joint housing.
7. Insert the ball joint into the steering knuckle and install the ball joint nuts. Tighten the nuts to 135 ft. lbs. and install the cotter pins.
8. Install the wheel and lower the truck to the ground.

STEERING GEAR

Reference

Refer to the Steering chapter in the General Repair Section for the overhaul of the manual and power steering gears and the power steering pump.

Manual Steering Gear

Ross Models With Long Shaft

Removal and Installation

1. Disconnect battery negative cable at battery, horn wire at connector and any gear shift linkage or directional signal controls that are attached to steering column jacket.
2. Remove horn button.
3. Remove steering wheel and column clamp to instrument panel.
4. Disconnect drag link from steering arm. *Mark relation of arm to cross shaft before removal.*
5. Using a puller, remove steering arm from cross shaft.
6. If so equipped, remove transmission shift linkage.
7. Remove gear housing mounting bolts and lower jacket mounting bolts and remove gear and tube assembly from vehicle.
8. To install, insert gear and tube assembly from below frame.
9. Install mounting bolts.
10. Install clamp bolts and secure tube to instrument panel.
11. Tighten gear housing to frame bolts.
12. Loosen instrument panel to tube clamp bolts. Column tube will not change position if steering gear is in alignment. If column tube shifted position when clamp was loosened, relocate column tube bracket before tightening clamp.
13. Install spring, retainer, steering wheel, horn button spring, retainer and wheel nut, tightening nut to 24 ft. lbs. torque.
14. Attach directional signal switch.
15. Install spring, contact plate, horn wire spring and horn button.
16. Connect and adjust shift linkage if so equipped.
17. Install steering arm and drag link, tighten steering arm nut to 85 ft. lbs. torque.

Ross Models With Short Shaft

Removal and Installation

1. Remove bolt from column coupling clamp at upper end of steering worm shaft. Disconnect turn signal and horn wire connectors and move column upward to clear worm shaft splines.
2. *Mark relation of arm to gear shaft before removal.* Remove steering arm nut and washer from gear shaft and remove steering arm with a puller.
3. Remove steering gear housing mounting bolts. On 6D-400 models, remove two bolts at trunnion cap.
4. Remove steering gear from vehicle.
5. To install, center gear and install on the frame, aligning housing with frame. Tighten 7/16" and ½" mounting bolts to 70 ft. lbs. torque and 9/16" bolts to 100 ft. lbs. torque.
6. Install universal joint clamp to worm shaft and tighten to 30 ft. lbs. torque. On pot type joint, center the steering column shaft in the joint to insure adequate travel.
7. Set front wheels straight ahead.
8. Install steering arm (use marks made during removal to position arm in original location). Tighten bolt clamp to 170 ft. lbs. and cross shaft nut to 250 ft. lbs.

Saginaw Models

Removal and Installation

1. Unbolt the coupling clamp at the bottom of the column.
2. Remove the steering gear arm nut.
3. Use a puller to remove the steering gear arm.
4. Unbolt the steering gear from the frame and remove it. You may have to remove the grille for access on some larger models, with the Saginaw 553 steering box.
5. Align the gear in the straight-ahead position.
6. Bolt the steering gear to the frame.
7. Make sure the front wheels are straight ahead and install the steering arm but not the nut.
8. If both wheels and steering gear are in the straight-ahead position, install the steering arm nut.
9. Install the coupling clamp.

NOTE: On models with the Saginaw 553 steering box, you will have to slide the column up to install the coupling.

Ramcharger and Trail Duster

Removal and Installation

1. Remove the two bolts from the wormshaft coupling.
2. Remove the steering arm from the steering gear using a suitable tool.
3. Remove the steering gear-to-frame bolts and remove the unit from the vehicle.
4. To install, position the steering gear to the frame and install the mounting bolts.
5. Install the steering arm and place the front wheels in the straight ahead position.
6. Place the steering wheel in the straight ahead position.
7. Install the wormshaft-to-column coupling bolts.

Vans and Pick-Ups 1973-74

Removal and Installation

1. Remove the drag link from the steering arm.
2. Raise the hood and disconnect the battery. Disconnect the wires from the windshield washer motor and lift the reservoir up and out of the way.
3. Remove the steering column.
4. Remove the retaining bolts and the retaining nut which hold the gear onto the frame.
5. Remove the two bolts from the bottom of the splash shield going

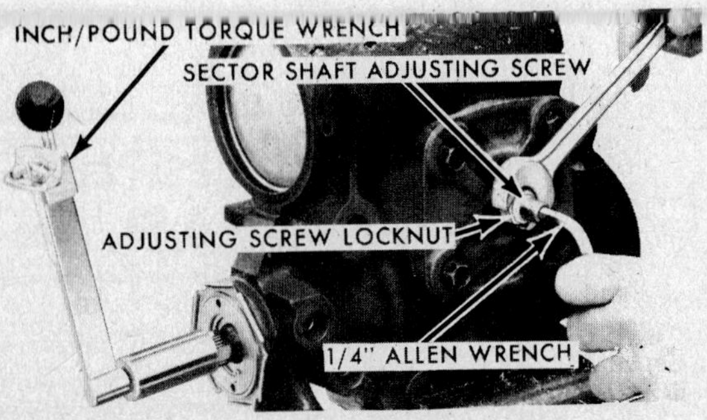

Sector shaft adjustment model 710 steering gear (© Chrysler Corp.)

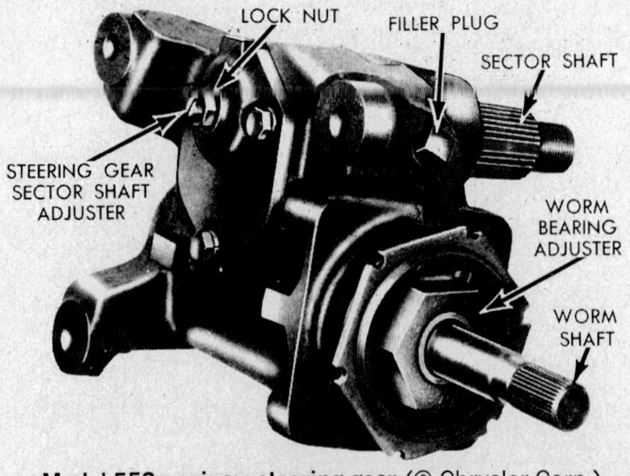

Model 553 saginaw steering gear (© Chrysler Corp.)

in under the left wheel house. Force the bottom of the shield out about ½ inch.
6. Lift the gear up off the mounting stud and out through the hood opening.
7. To replace the gear, position it to the frame in reverse of the above step, and install the mounting bolts, nut, and lockwasher. Tighten the bolts and nut to 100 ft-lbs.
8. Center the worm shaft and steering wheel.
9. Install the drag link to the steering arm.
10. Install the two splash shield bolts.
11. Install and adjust the steering column.
12. Connect the windshield washer motor wiring and battery. Mount the washer reservoir in its retaining bracket.

Vans and Pick-Ups 1975 and Later

Removal and Installation

1. Disconnect the battery.
2. Raise the vehicle on a hoist and disconnect "rubber and fabric" coupling (leaving the lower half of the coupling on the wormshaft.
3. Disconnect the shift linkage at the steering column.
4. Remove the steering arm retaining nut and washer. With a suitable tool remove the steering arm from the sector shaft.
5. Remove the three gear mounting bolts. Lower the vehicle from the hoist and remove the toe plate and column support bolts.
6. Disconnect the wiring and remove the column assembly.
7. Raise the vehicle on the hoist and remove the steering gear through the opening on the inboard side of the frame. (It may be helpful to remove the three bolts from the left idle arm bracket and move the bracket out of the way to provide additional clearance.)

   NOTE: If the lower half of the steering coupling was removed from the gear, reinstall it on the wormshaft and secure it with a roll pin before installing the gear into the vehicle.
8. From underneath the vehicle, place the steering gear in position and install the three mounting bolts.
9. Reinstall the idler arm bracket, if it was removed.
10. Install the steering arm on the sector shaft. Install the washer and retaining nut.
11. Install the steering column assembly. Connect the steering column wiring. Install the shift linkage at the steering column.
12. Connect the steering shaft coupling at the wormshaft.
13. Connect the battery.

Worm Bearing Preload Adjustment

Ross Models

1. Remove the horn button and spring.

   NOTE: Mark the relation of the steering arm to the steering gear sector shaft before removal.
2. Remove the steering arm from the steering gear cross shaft. Inspect the steering column for alignment (long wormshaft type). Correct as required.
3. Loosen the sector shaft adjusting screw locknut and back out the adjusting screw (approx. two turns). Turn the steering wheel two complete turns from the straight-ahead position.
4. Using a torque wrench and socket on the steering wheel nut, rotate the steering wheel through "lash" area (toward straight-ahead position). The torque required to keep the wheel moving indicates the worm bearing preload. This torque should be 7 to 14 inch-pounds.
5. If the preload is not within these limits, adjust by removing or adding shims beneath the lower worm bearing cover. Shims are available in .0025, .0055 and .010 inch thickness.
6. Tighten the worm cover screws to 20 foot-pounds. Recheck the preload, if necessary repeat the test using a different set of shims.

Saginaw Model 525

1. Disconnect and remove the steering gear arm from the sector shaft using a suitable tool.
2. Remove the horn pad.
3. Loosen the sector shaft adjusting screw lock nut, and back out the adjusting screw one half to two turns).
4. Turn the steering wheel to the right stop then back it off one half turn and place a torque wrench on the steering shaft nut.
5. Rotate the steering shaft from the right stop toward the straight ahead position, while testing the rotating torque with the torque wrench. The torque required to keep the wheel moving should be between 4 to 6 inch pounds.
6. If this reading is not within the specified limits, adjustment can be made as follows, with the gear in or out of the vehicle: Loosen the adjuster locknut. Turn the adjuster plug clockwise to increase preload or counterclockwise to decrease preload. While holding the adjuster plug from turning, tighten the locknut securely, then reset the worm bearing preload.

Saginaw Model 553

1. Remove the steering arm from the steering gear sector shaft.
2. Loosen the sector shaft adjuster screw locknut, and back out the adjuster screw (approx. two turns).
3. Turn the steering wheel two complete turns from the straight-ahead position.

   NOTE: Do not turn the steering wheel hard against the stops in the gear when the steering gear arm is disconnected as internal damage could result.
4. Using a torque wrench and a ¾ inch socket (12 point), rotate the steering worm shaft at least one turn (toward straight-ahead position). The torque required to keep the worm shaft moving should be between 13 and 18 inch-pounds. If the reading is not within these limits, adjustment is necessary.
5. To adjust the preload, loosen the adjuster lock nut and turn the adjuster clockwise to increase preload, or counterclockwise to decrease preload. Retighten the locknut to 70-100 foot-pounds and recheck the preload. The preload must be within the specified limits after the locknut has been tightened.

Vans and Pick-Ups

1. Disconnect the steering gear arm from the sector shaft with a suitable tool.
2. Remove the horn pad.
3. Loosen the sector shaft adjusting screw lock nut (approx. two turns).
4. Turn the steering wheel two complete turns from the straight-ahead position, and place a torque wrench on the steering shaft nut.
5. Rotate the steering shaft at least one turn toward the straight-ahead position, while testing the rotating torque with a torque wrench.
6. If the reading is not within the limits specified below, the following adjustments can be made with the gear in or out of the vehicle. Loosen the adjuster locknut. Use an adjuster wrench and turn the adjuster clockwise to increase preload, or counterclockwise to decrease preload. While stopping the adjuster from turning, tighten the lock nut securely, then reset the worm bearing preload.

1973-74 Worm Bearing
  Preload . . 1½-4½ inch pounds

1975 and Later Worm Shaft Thrust Bearing Preload ....16-24 inch ounces

Cross or Sector Gear Mesh Adjustment

This adjustment is made only after worm bearing preload is adjusted. Steering arm is still removed from cross (sector) shaft.

1. Center steering wheel (wormshaft) by counting turns from full right to full left and counting back exactly half way.
2. Loosen locknut on cross (sector) shaft adjusting screw and turn adjusting screw in until all lash is gone.
3. Check torque required to move steering wheel (torque wrench on steering wheel nut) through high-spot (center) position. See below.)
4. Readjust if necessary and retighten locknut.
5. Reinstall steering arm on cross (sector) shaft and tighten clamp bolt to 85 ft. lbs. torque.

Cross or Sector Gear Mesh (in lbs.)

Cross or Sector Gear Mesh (in.

Ross ....20-27 Total
Ross 6D-400 ....20-27 Total
Saginaw 525 ....14 Total
Saginaw 553 ....25-29 Total
Vans and Pick-Ups .....8¼-11¼ Total

Power Steering Gear

Integral Type

Conventional Trucks
Removal and Installation

1. Center the steering gear.
2. Pull off the steering gear arm with a suitable tool.
3. Disconnect the pressure and return hoses.
4. Disconnect the steering shaft coupling.
5. Unbolt the gear from the frame and remove it.
6. Install the mounting bolts finger tight on installation.
7. Connect the coupling. Align the gear to the frame to prevent binding; tighten the bolts.
8. Connect the pressure and return hoses.
9. Center the steering gear, make sure the wheels are straight ahead, replace the steering arm and nut.
10. Idle the engine and turn the steering wheel gently from stop to stop to bleed the system of air.

Vans and Pick-Ups 1973-74

Removal and Installation

1. Disconnect the battery and remove the windshield washer reservoir.
2. Remove the steering column.
3. Remove the optional steering arm shield.
4. Use a puller to remove the drag link from the steering arm.
5. Detach the hoses and raise their ends to prevent spillage.
6. Remove the two gear to frame bolts and the nut from the stud.
7. Remove the two bolts from the bottom of the splash shield (left side) and pull it out to lift the gear off the stud.
8. Turn the steering arm and lift the steering gear out through the hood opening.
9. On installation, move the parking brake cable away from the mounting stud. Position the gear. Install the mounting bolts and nut.
10. Install the drag link to the steering arm.
11. Replace the splash shield bolts.
12. Connect the hoses and check the reservoir fluid level.
13. Replace the steering column.
14. Replace the windshield washer reservoir and connect the battery.
15. Idle the engine and turn the steering wheel gently from stop to stop to bleed the system of air.

Vans and Pick-Ups 1975 and Later

Removal and Installation

1. Raise the hood and remove the battery.
2. Disconnect the wires from the windshield washer pump. Remove the windshield washer reservoir mounting screws and position the reservoir out of the way.
3. Disconnect the power steering hoses at the steering gear. Cap the fittings at the steering gear and tie the hoses above the fluid level in the pump reservoir to prevent oil leakage.
4. Raise the vehicle on a hoist and disconnect the "rubber and fabric" coupling at the steering gear (leaving the lower half of the coupling on the wormshaft).
5. Disconnect the shift linkage at the steering column.
6. Remove the steering arm shield if so equipped. Remove the nut and washer, then with a suitable tool, remove the steering arm from the sector shaft.
7. Remove the mounting bolt on the left side of the gear.
8. Lower the vehicle and remove one of the two remaining steering gear mounting bolts.
9. Remove the toe plate and column support bolts.
10. Disconnect the steering column wiring and remove the assembly.
11. Raise the vehicle on the hoist. Remove the three bolts from the left idler arm bracket and swing the bracket out of the way.
12. Remove the remaining bolt and the steering gear from underneath of the vehicle, through the opening on the inboard side of the frame.

    NOTE: Before installing the steering gear into the vehicle, install the coupling half on the wormshaft and secure it with the roll pin.
13. From the underside of the vehicle, place the steering gear into position on the mounting bracket and install the three mounting bolts.
14. Continue the installation in the reverse order of the removal.
15. Lower the vehicle, start the engine and turn the steering wheel several times from stop to stop to bleed the system of air.
16. Stop the engine and check the fluid level, correct if necessary. Inspect for leaks.

Linkage Assist Type

Removal and Installation

1. Disconnect pressure and return hoses at valve assembly.
2. Cap hoses and connections at valve assembly. Fasten hoses so that ends are above fluid level in reservoir and tag them for reinstallation identification.
3. Disconnect ball ends at steering arm and steering knuckle arm and remove control valve and drag link assembly.
4. To install, connect control valve sliding sleeve end at steering arm and install nut and cotter pin.
5. Connect drag link end to steering knuckle arm and install nut and cotter pin.
6. Connect pressure and return hydraulic lines at valve assembly, tightening securely.
7. Refill pump reservoir.
8. Bleed system by turning steering wheel back and forth several times while the engine is idling.
9. Recheck fluid level and refill if necessary.

Power Cylinder

Removal and Installation

1. Disconnect hydraulic lines at power cylinder and cap ends and connections at cylinder.
2. Remove cotter pin and nut at ball studs (and tie rod clamp U-bolts on lightweight trucks). Remove cylinder.
3. To install, insert ball stud into place on axle bracket and install nut and cotter pin, tighten nut securely.
4. Rotate steering wheel to extreme right turn position.
5. Install tie rod clamp loosely (on medium weight trucks loosen tie

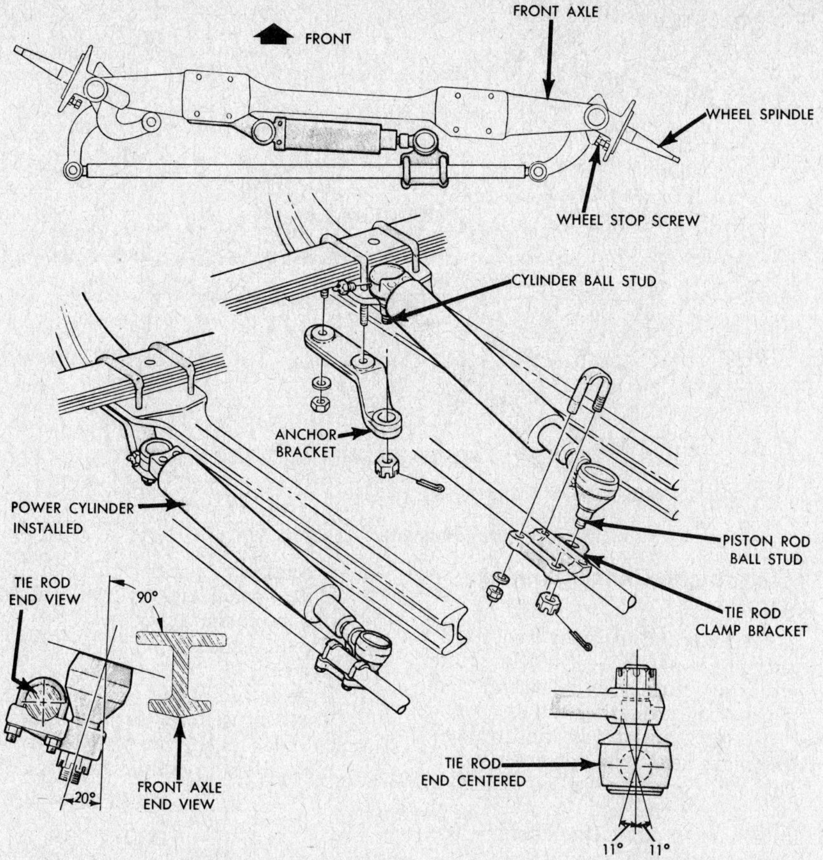

Power cylinder adjustment (© Chrysler Corp.)

rod clamp and install ball stud and nut).

6. Position cylinder piston rod in fully retracted position and tighten U-bolt clamps on tie rod. On medium weight trucks the ball stud will have to be connected to tie rod clamp bracket before tightening clamp bolts. Clamp should be mounted on tie rod at a 20° angle to the vertical. Nuts on U-bolts are torqued to 40 ft. lbs.
7. Connect hydraulic lines to power cylinder in their original positions.
8. Bleed system by turning the steering wheel back and forth several times with the engine idling.

Power Steering Pump

Removal and Installation

1. Loosen pump lower mounting and locking bolts and remove the belt.
2. Place a container under pump and disconnect both pump hoses.
3. Remove mounting and locking bolts and remove pump and brackets.
4. To install, position pump on engine and install retaining and locking bolts.
5. Install drive belt and adjust. Tighten pump brackets to 30 ft. lbs. torque.
6. Connect pressure and return hoses, routing them in the same position they were in before removal.
7. Fill pump reservoir.
8. Start engine and turn steering wheel all the way left and right to bleed the system. Stop engine and recheck fluid level, refilling if necessary.

Adjustment

The power steering gear used in conventional trucks should not be adjusted while in the chassis or filled with hydraulic fluid. The unit in vans and wagons may be adjusted in the vehicle.

Worm Thrust Bearing Adjustment

1. Remove the adjuster plug locknut.
2. Bottom the adjuster plug to 20 pounds torque to seat the thrust bearings.
3. Mark the steering housing in line with one of the tool hole locations on the adjuster plug. Measure counterclockwise 3/16 to ¼ inch and remark the housing.
4. Loosen the adjuster until the tool hole is in line with the second mark on the steering housing and install the lock nut and tighten while maintaining the alignment of the adjuster tool hole with the mark on the housing.

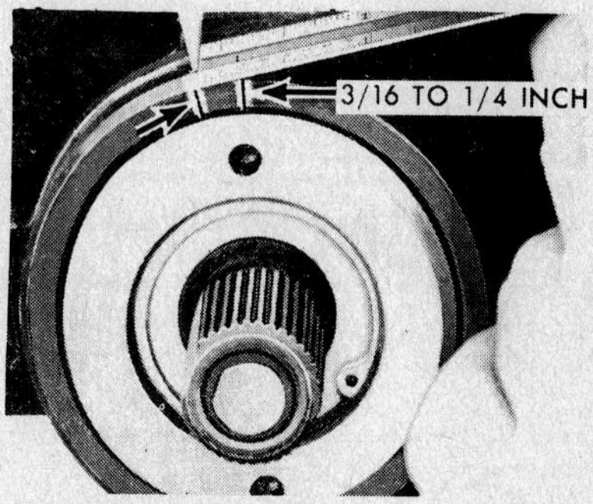

Mark housing in relationship with tool hole in the adjuster plug (© Chrysler Corp.)

5. With the aid of a torque wrench, turn the stub shaft to the right stop and back off ¼ of a turn. While turning the stub shaft evenly counterclockwise, observe the torque reading. The reading should be from 4 to 10 inch pounds.
6. Continue the adjustments as necessary to obtain the specified torque readings.

Cross Shaft Over-Center Adjustment

1. With the gear on center, loosen the adjusting nut and tighten the sector adjusting screw.
2. Tighten the lock nut and check the overcenter torque while rotating the stub shaft through an arc of 180 degrees, with a torque wrench.
3. Adjust the sector shaft accordingly until the correct torque is obtained.
   New gears—4 to 8 inch pounds, but not over 18 inch pounds combined torque.
   Used gears—4 to 5 inch pounds, but not over 14 inch pounds combined torque.

NOTE: Combined torque includes the thrust bearing adjustment reading, over-center and internal friction.

Sector Adjustment, Vans and Pick-Ups

1. Disconnect the center link from the steering gear arm.
2. Start the engine and allow to run at normal idle speed.
3. Rotate the steering wheel from lock to lock. Carefully count the number of turns required, then rotate the wheel back, exactly to the midpoint of its travel.
4. Loosen the adjusting screw until backlash in the steering gear arm becomes apparent.

NOTE: Backlash is felt by holding the end of the steering gear arm lightly between your thumb and forefinger.

5. Tighten the adjusting screw just enough so that the backlash disappears. Continue to tighten the screw for another 3/8 to 1/2 turn from this point. Tighten the locknut to 28 ft. lbs.
6. Attach the center link to the steering gear arm.

CLUTCH

Removal and Installation

All Models

1. Support the engine on a suitable jack, if necessary.
2. Remove crossmember, if necessary.
3. Remove transmission. . Remove transfer case, if equipped.
4. Remove clutch housing pan if so equipped.
5. Remove clutch fork, clutch bearing and sleeve assembly if not removed with transmission.
6. Mark clutch cover and flywheel, with a suitable tool to assure correct reassembly.
7. Remove clutch cover retaining bolts, loosening them evenly so clutch cover will not be distorted.
8. Pull pressure plate assembly clear of flywheel and, while supporting pressure plate, slide clutch disc from between flywheel and pressure plate.
9. To install, thoroughly clean all working surfaces of the flywheel and the pressure plate.
10. Grease radius at back of bushing.
11. Rotate clutch cover and pressure plate assembly for maximum clearance between flywheel and frame crossmember if crossmember was not removed during clutch removal.
12. Tilt top edge of clutch cover and pressure plate assembly back and move it up into the clutch housing. Support clutch cover and pressure plate assembly and slide clutch disc into position.
13. Position clutch disc and plate against flywheel and insert spare transmission main drive gear shaft or clutch installing tool through clutch disc hub and into main drive pilot bearing.
14. Rotate clutch cover until the punch marks on cover and flywheel line up.
15. Bolt cover loosely to flywheel. Tighten cover bolts a few turns at a time, in progression, until tight. Then tighten bolts to 20 ft. lbs. torque.
16. Install transmission
17. Install frame crossmembers and insulator, tighten all bolts.

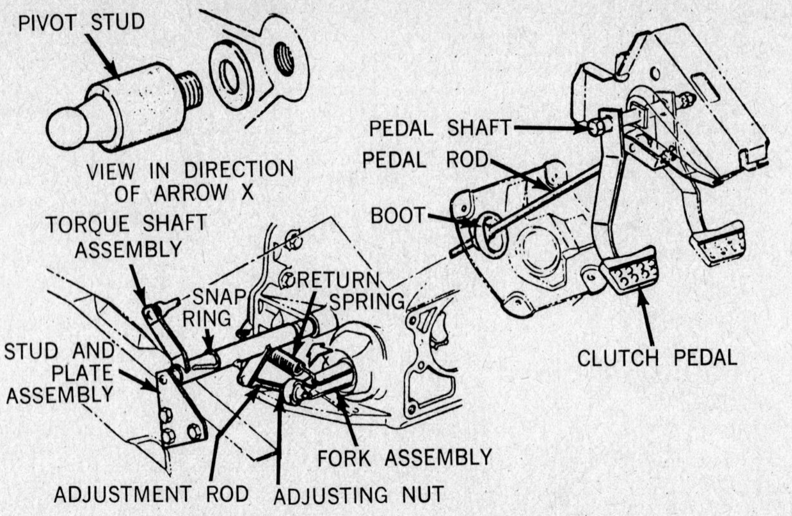

Typical clutch linkage (© Chrysler Corp.)

Mechanical Clutch Linkage Adjustment

The only adjustment required is pedal free-play. Adjust the clutch actuating fork rod by turning the self-locking adjusting nut to provide 1/8 in. (3/32 in. on vans and wagons) free movement at the end of the fork. This will provide the recommended 1 1/2 in. (1 in. on Vans, Wagons, Ramcharger, and Trailduster) free-play at the pedal.

Bleeding Hydraulic Clutch System

1. Clean away dirt from around master cylinder reservoir filler cap, remove cap and fill reservoir. Make sure to check reservoir frequently during bleeding process and fill when necessary.
2. Clean bleeder valve on slave cylinder and attach bleeder hose to valve.
3. Place other end of hose in jar half full of brake fluid.
4. Bleed intermittently as clutch pedal is being depressed by opening and closing bleeder valve. Continue bleeding until no air bubbles come from bleeder hose.

Clutch Master Cylinder Removal and Installation

1. Remove pedal return spring.
2. Disconnect push rod end at clutch pedal and hydraulic fluid line at master cylinder.
3. Unbolt master cylinder from firewall.
4. Installation is the reverse of the above procedure. Adjust master cylinder push rod to .010" free play. Bleed hydraulic system.

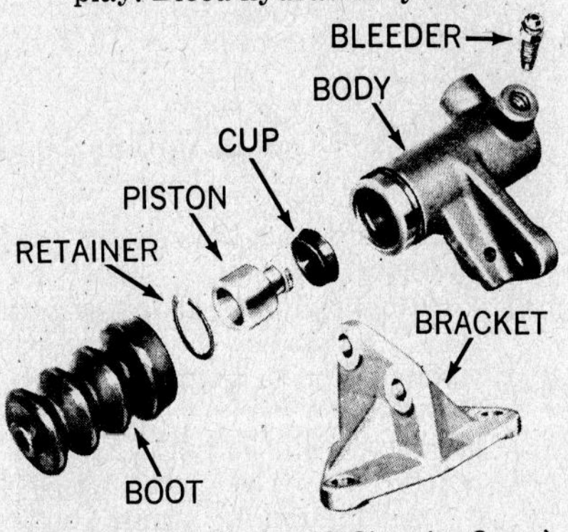

Clutch slave cylinder (© Chrysler Corp.)

Clutch Slave Cylinder Removal and Installation

Slave cylinder is located on the right side of the clutch housing. Disconnect hydraulic line, then remove

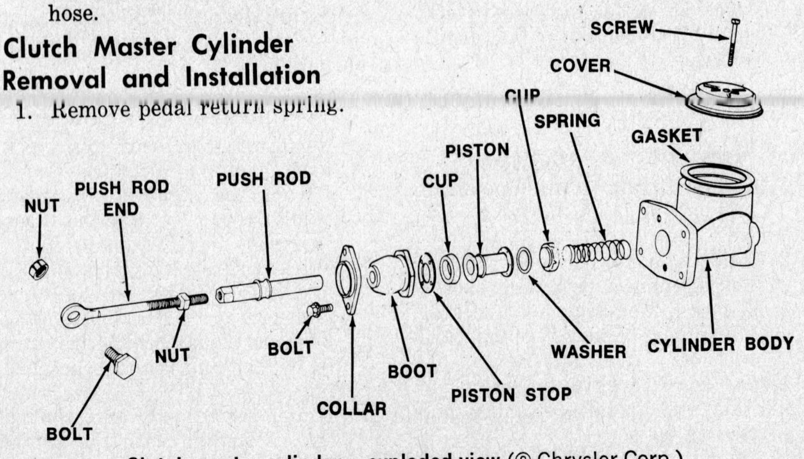

Clutch master cylinder—exploded view (© Chrysler Corp.)

cylinder mounting bolts. After installation, be sure to bleed hydraulic system and adjust as described above.

TRANSFER CASE

See General Section for Transfer Case overhaul procedures.

Transfer Case

W100, 200, 300 (1973-74)

Removal and Installation

1. Drain lubricant.
2. Disconnect speedometer cable.
3. Disconnect input and output shafts, securing driveshafts to frame.
4. Remove shift rod from shift rail link.
5. Using a suitable jack, support transfer case while removing frame crossmember.
6. Remove mounting bolts and lower transfer case from truck.
7. Installation is the reverse of the above procedure. Tighten mounting bolts to 35 ft. lbs. and driveshaft yoke bolts to 300-400 ft. lbs. torque.

W100, 200, 300 (1975 and Later) Ramcharger and Trail Duster

Removal and Installation

1. Raise and support the truck.
2. Remove the skid plate, if any.
3. Drain the transfer case by removing the bottom bolt from the front output rear cover.
4. Disconnect the speedometer cable.
5. Disconnect the front and rear output shafts. Suspend these from a convenient location; do not allow them to hang free.
6. Disconnect the shift rods at the transfer case.
7. Support the transfer case.
8. Remove the adaptor-to-transfer case mounting bolts and move the transfer case rearward to disengage the front input splines.
9. Lower and remove the transfer case.
10. Installation is the reverse of removal. Adjust the linkage.

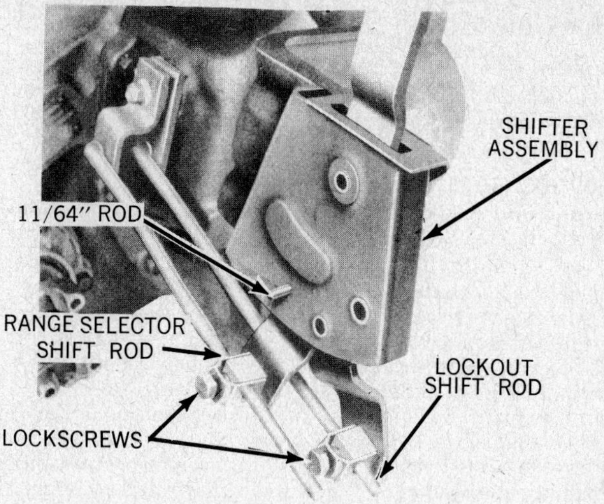

shift linkage adjustment

W500, 600

Removal and Installation

1. Drain lubricant.
2. Disconnect speedometer and parking brake cables.
3. Disconnect input and output shafts. *Do not allow shafts to hang.*
4. Remove clevis pins, disconnecting de-clutch and shift control rods from transfer case rails. Secure rods out of the way.
5. Using a jack, support transfer case while removing support bracket bolts.
6. Carefully lower transfer case from truck.
7. To install, raise transfer case with a jack and align threaded mounting bolt holes in transfer case with holes in support brackets. Install bolts and tighten securely.
8. Connect the speedometer cable. Connect and adjust the parking brake cable.
9. Install and adjust transfer case shift and de-shift rods.
10. Connect driveshafts.

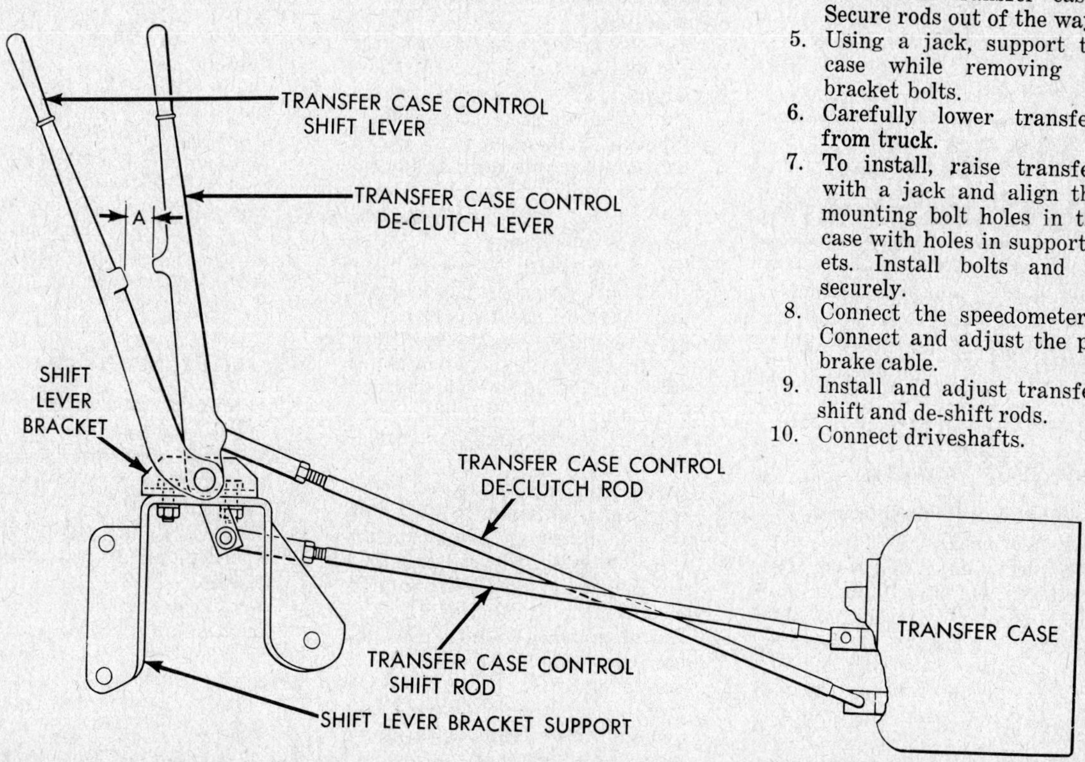

New process T-233 transfer case shift linkage adjustment, measurement A should be ¼ inch (© Chrysler Corp.)

Linkage Adjustment

W100, 200, 300 (1973-74)

There is no external linkage adjustment necessary or possible on this unit.

W100, 200, 300 (1975 and Later) Ramcharger and Trail Duster

1. Loosen the lockscrews in both swivel rod clamps at the shifter assembly. The rods must be free to slide in the swivels.
2. Place the selector lever in the cab in neutral and insert alignment rod through the alignment holes in the shifter housing.
3. Place the range shift lever (outboard lever) on the transfer case in the neutral position.
4. Place the lockout shift lever on the transfer case (the inboard lever) in the unlocked position.
5. Retighten the rod swivel screws.
6. Remove the alignment rod from the shifter housing.

W500, 600

1. Make sure that the front axle drive is engaged (the de-clutch rail on the case must be fully in). Make sure that the transfer case is in low range (the shift rail on the case must be fully out).
2. Disconnect the de-clutch and shift rods at the case by removing the clevis pins.
3. Adjust the de-clutch rod length so that the lever clears the rear end of the cab floor slot by ½ in. Replace the clevis pin.
4. Adjust the shift rod length until the distance between the lever contact surfaces is ¼ in. Replace the clevis pin.

MANUAL TRANSMISSION

Reference

For light duty Manual Transmission overhaul procedures see "Manual Transmission" in the General Service Section.

Manual Transmission

3-Speed 2WD Models

Removal and Installation

1. Drain lubricant.
2. Disconnect and match-mark the driveshaft. On the sliding spline type, disconnect driveshaft at the rear universal joint, then carefully pull the shaft yoke out of the transmission extension housing. Do not nick or scratch splines.
3. Disconnect gearshift control rods and speedometer cable.
4. Remove backup light switch if so equipped.
5. Support engine.
6. Remove crossmember and rubber insulator on 1975 and later models with A-390 transmission. On all other models. unbolt the insulator or mount from the crossmember. Support the transmission with a jack.
7. Remove transmission to clutch housing bolts.
8. Slide transmission rearward until pinion shaft clears clutch completely, then lower transmission from vehicle.
9. Installation is the reverse order of the above procedure. Before inserting transmission drive shaft into clutch, make sure clutch housing bore, disc and face are aligned. Tighten clutch housing to transmission bolts to 50 ft. lbs. torque.
10. Fill with lubricant.
11. Adjust shift linkage.
12. Road test.

4-Speed 2WD Models

Removal and Installation

1. Shift transmission into any gear.
2. Disconnect universal joint and loosen yoke retaining nut.
3. Disconnect parking brake (if so equipped) and speedometer cables at transmission.
4. Remove lever retainer by pressing down, rotating retainer counter-clockwise slightly, then releasing.
5. Remove lever and its springs and washers.
6. Support the rear of the engine and remove the crossmember. Remove transmission to clutch bell housing retaining bolts and pull transmission rearward until drive pinion clears clutch, then remove transmission.
7. To install, place ½ teaspoon of short fibre grease in pinion shaft pilot bushing, taking care not to get any grease on flywheel face.
8. Align clutch disc and backing plate with a spare drive pinion shaft or clutch aligning tool, then carefully install transmission.
9. Install transmission to bell housing bolts, tightening to 50 ft. lbs. torque. Replace the crossmember.
10. Install gear shift lever, shift into any gear and tighten yoke nut to 95-105 ft. lbs. torque.
11. Install universal joint, speedometer cable and brake cable.
12. Adjust clutch.
13. Install transmission drain plug and fill transmission with lubricant.
14. Road test.

3 and 4-Speed-4WD Models

Removal and Installation

1. Raise and support the truck.
2. Remove the skid plate, if any.
3. Disconnect the speedometer cable.
4. Disconnect and match-mark the front and rear driveshafts. Suspend each shaft from a convenient place; do not allow them to hang free.
5. Disconnect the shift rods at the transfer case. On 4-speed transmissions, remove the shift lever retainer by pressing down and turning it counterclockwise. Remove the shift lever springs and washers.
6. Remove the rear driveshaft. Matchmark the driveshaft and rear U-joints before removing the driveshaft.
7. Support the transfer case.
8. Remove the extension-to-transfer case mounting bolts.
9. Move the transfer case rearward to disengage the front input shaft spline.
10. Lower and remove the transfer case.
11. Disconnect the back-up light switch.
12. Support the engine.
13. Support the transmission.
14. Remove the transmission crossmember.
15. Remove the transmission-to-clutch housing bolts.
16. Slide the transmission rearward until the mainshaft clears the clutch disc.
17. Lower and remove the transmission.
18. Installation is the reverse of removal. The transmission pilot bushing in the end of the crankshaft requires high-temperature grease. Multipurpose grease should be used. Do not lubricate the end of the mainshaft, clutch splines, or clutch release levers. Adjust the gearshift linkage on 3-speed transmissions.

5-Speed Transmission

Removal and Installation

1. Drain lubricant.
2. Remove gearshift lever, floor mat and floor cover over transmission.
3. Disconnect parking brake cable, speedometer cable and driveshaft.
4. Loosen flange nut and drop center bearing if so equipped.
5. Position a transmission jack under transmission and remove clutch housing-to-transmission bolts.
6. Slide transmission rearward until pinion shaft clears clutch

(about 6"), then lower jack slightly. Move transmission to the left just enough for the main drive pinion to clear clutch housing, then lower transmission.
7. Installation is the reverse order of the above procedure. Align clutch backing plate and disc with a spare drive pinion shaft or clutch aligning tool before inserting transmission drive pinion and be sure splines on shaft align with clutch hub splines before inserting. Tighten bell housing-to-transmission bolts to 100 ft. lbs. torque and driveshaft flange nut to 125 ft. lbs. torque.
8. Fill with lubricant and adjust clutch.
9. Road test.

Heavy Duty Transmission —Five Speed, Six Speed and Up

Removal and Installation

1. a. *Conventional Gearshift Lever:* Remove the floor mat and transmission pan cover and place the gearshift lever in the neutral position. Remove the gearshift lever and control tower assembly from the transmission.
   b. *Range or Splitter Power Shift:* Bleed the air tanks and disconnect the air lines at the air valve on the transmission. Remove the gear shift lever and control tower assembly from the transmission. On Tilt cab models, disconnect the shift control linkage from the remote control assembly at the transmission or remove the cover assembly.
2. Place a clean lint free cloth over the opening in the transmission to keep dirt out.
3. Disconnect the wire from the back-up light switch mounted on the transmission (if equipped).
4. Drain the transmission lubricant.
5. Disconnect the speedometer cable at the transmission adapter.
6. Disconnect the clutch control linkage.
7. Disconnect the parking brake lever and controls (if equipped).
8. Disconnect the propeller shaft from the transmission.
9. Remove any exhaust system brackets mounted on the transmission.
10. If necessary, support the saddle tanks and remove the tank cross struts.
11. Remove the engine ground strap and the battery cable support clip if attached to the transmission or clutch housing.
12. Remove the power take off unit and controls if equipped.
13. On vehicles equipped with range or splitter air power shift, disconnect the air lines from the intake at the air filter, the air input, and shift control. Cover the air filter opening to keep dirt out.
14. Position a transmission jack or dolly under the transmission and adjust to carry the weight of the transmission.
15. Remove the parts that attach the transmission to the rear mount, if used.
16. Visually inspect to determine if other equipment, lines or brackets must be removed to permit removal of the transmission.
17. On vehicles which have a rear engine mounting attached to the clutch housing, it will be necessary to support the engine with a suitable jack positioned under the flywheel housing. Remove the engine rear mounting as necessary to free the transmission.
18. Remove the clutch housing-to-flywheel housing bolts or the transmission-to-flywheel housing bolts if equipped with an apron type flywheel housing.
19. Move the transmission assembly straight back from the engine until the main drive gear shaft is clear. Be careful to keep the transmission main shaft in alignment with the clutch disc.
20. Lower the transmission and remove from the vehicle. If additional clearance is needed, raise the rear wheels of the vehicle.
21. Inspect the clutch components and replace any worn or damaged parts.
22. Apply a light film of multi-purpose grease to the main drive gear retainer and the splined portion of the main shaft to assure smooth assembly. *NOTE: Do not apply an excessive amount of grease to the mainshaft components as under operating conditions the grease would be thrown onto the clutch facings causing clutch failure.*
23. Shift the transmission into direct drive.
24. Mount the transmission on a jack and move into position under the vehicle. *NOTE: With the apron type flywheel housing, position the clutch release bearing and support assembly inside the flywheel housing. Be sure that the clutch fork properly engages the clutch release bearing.*
25. Align the transmission mainshaft with the clutch disc hub by rotating the companion flange. Move the transmission forward, guiding the mainshaft into the clutch disc splines.

NOTE: Avoid springing the clutch when the transmission is being installed on the engine. Do not force the transmission into the clutch disc splines. Do not let the transmission drop or hang unsupported in the splined hub or clutch release bearing.

26. Install the clutch housing-to-engine flywheel housing mounting bolts and lock washers, tighten to specification.
27. Install the engine mountings if they were removed and tighten.
28. Install the remaining parts and components in the reverse of removal.

Linkage Adjustment

Conventional Trucks

1. Remove both shift rod swivels from transmission shift levers. Make sure transmission shift levers are in neutral (middle detent) position.
2. Move shift lever to line up locating slots in bottom of steering column shift housing and bearing housing. Install suitable tool in slot, if any.
3. Place a suitable tool between crossover blade and second-third lever at steering column so that both lever pins are engaged by crossover blade.
4. Set first-reverse lever on transmission to reverse position (rotate clockwise).
5. Adjust first-reverse rod swivel by loosening clamp bolt and sliding swivel along rod so it will enter first-reverse lever at transmission. Install washers and clip. Tighten swivel bolt.
6. Remove gearshift housing locating tool and shift column lever into neutral position.
7. Adjust second-third rod swivel by loosening clamp bolt and slidenter second-third lever at transmission. Install washers and clip. Tighten swivel bolt.
8. Remove tool from crossover blade at steering column, and shift through all gears to check adjustment and crossover smoothness.

Vans and Pick-Ups

A-230, A-250

1. Adjust the length of the 2-3 shift rod so the position of the shift lever on the steering column will be correct.
2. Assemble the 1st-reverse and 2-3 shift rods, and place each in its normal position, secured with a clip. Loosen both swivel clamp bolts.
3. Move the 2-3 shift lever into 3rd position (this means moving the forward lever forward). Move the steering column lever until it is about five degrees above the horizontal. Tighten the shift rod swivel clamp bolt.

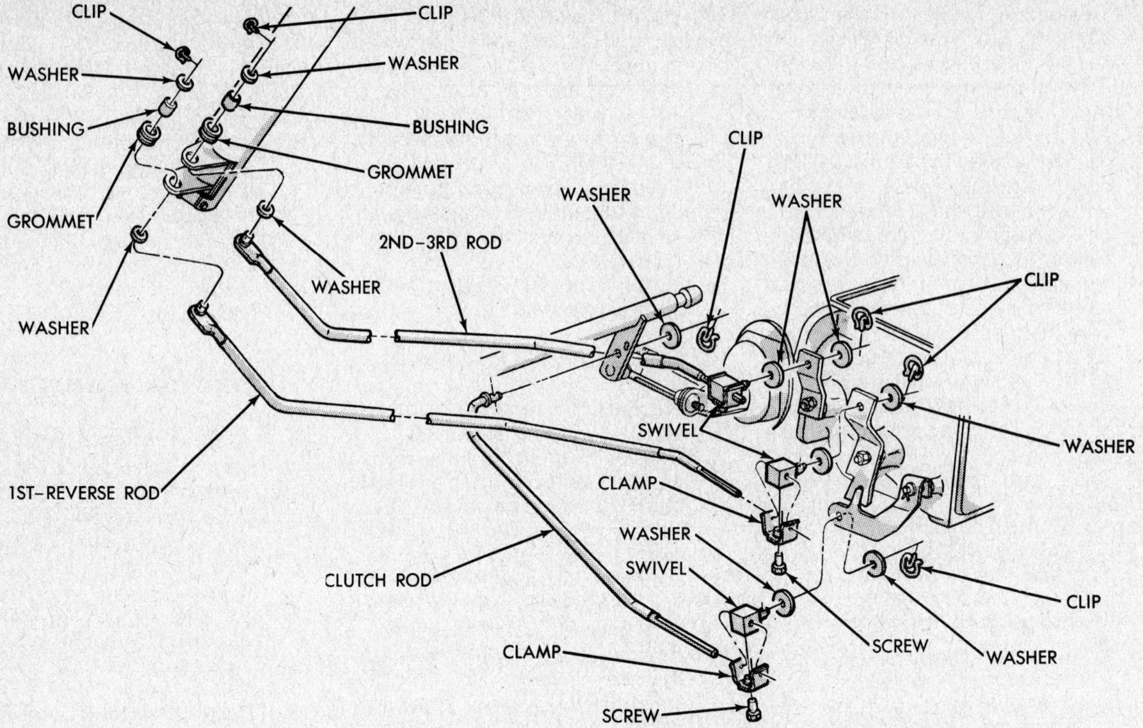

A-250 transmission linkage with clutch interlock—van with 6 cylinder engine (© Chrysler Corp.)

4. Shift the transmission to neutral. Place a suitable tool between the crossover blade and the 2-3 lever at the steering column so that both lever pins are engaged by the crossover blade.
5. Set the 1st-reverse lever in neutral. Tighten the swivel clamp bolt.
6. Remove the tool from the cross over blade, and check all shifts for smoothness.

Ramcharger and Trail Duster

A-230

1. Remove both shift rod swivels from the transmission shift levers. Make sure that the transmission shift levers are in the neutral position (middle detent).
2. Move the shift lever to line up the locating slots in the bottom of the steering column shift housing and bearing housing.
3. Place a suitable tool between the crossover blade and the 2nd and 3rd lever at the steering column, so that both lever pins are engaged by the crossover blade.
4. Set the 1st-reverse lever on the transmission to the reverse position (rotate clockwise).
5. Adjust the 1st-reverse rod swivel by loosening the clamp bolt and sliding the swivel along the rod so it will enter the 1st-reverse lever at the transmission. Install the washers and the clip. Tighten the swivel bolt.
6. Remove the gearshift housing locating tool, and shift the transmission into the neutral position.
7. Adjust the 2nd-3rd rod swivel by loosening the clamp bolt and sliding the swivel along the rod so it will enter the 2nd-3rd lever at the transmission. Install the washers and the clip. Tighten the swivel bolt.
8. Remove the tool from the crossover blade at the steering column and shift the transmission through all the gears to check the adjustment and the crossover smoothness.

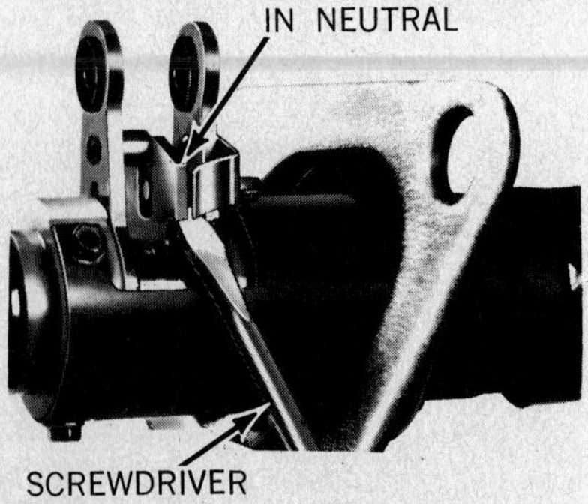

Holding the three speed column shift linkage in the neutral position
(© Chrysler Corp.)

All Models

A-390

1. Loosen both shift rod swivels. Make sure that the transmission shift levers are in the neutral position (middle detent).
2. Move the shift lever to line up the locating slots in the bottom of the steering column shift housing and bearing housing. Install a suitable tool in the slot.
3. Place a suitable tool between the crossover blade and the 2nd-3rd lever at the steering column so that both lever pins are engaged by the crossover blade.
4. Tighten both rod swivel bolts. Remove the gearshift housing locating tool.
5. Remove the tool from the crossover blade at the steering column and shift the transmission through all gears to check adjustment and crossover smoothness.
6. Check for proper operation of the steering column lock in reverse. With the proper linkage adjustment, the ignition should lock in reverse only, with hands off the gearshift lever.

Clutch Interlock

Adjustment

A-250 3-Speed

This adjustment is required only on the A-250 3-speed transmission. This is a top cover unit used only as base equipment on light duty six cylinder models. It has synchromesh only on second and third gears.

1. Disconnect the clutch rod swivel from the interlock pawl. Adjust the clutch pedal free play.
2. Shift the transmission to neutral. Loosen swivel clamp bolt

and slide the swivel onto the rod untl the pawl is positioned fully within the slot in the first-reverse lever. Install the washers and clip.

3. Hold the interlock pawl forward and tighten the swivel clamp bolt. The clutch pedal must be in fully returned position during the adjustment. *NOTE: Do not pull the clutch rod rearward to engage the swivel in the pawl.*
4. Shift the transmission into first and reverse and release the clutch pedal while in either gear to check for normal clutch action. Then, shift halfway between neutral and either gear and release clutch. The interlock should hold it to within one or two inches of the floor.

AUTOMATIC TRANSMISSION

Reference

For complete light duty overhaul procedures see "Automatic Transmission" section of the General Repair Section.

Loadflite and New Process

Removal

1. Remove the transmission and converter as an assembly; otherwise the converter drive plate pump bushing, and oil seal will be damaged. The drive plate will not support a load. Therefore, none of the weight of transmission should be allowed to rest on the plate during removal. Remove the transfer case, as necessary.
2. Attach a remote control starter switch to the starter solenoid so the engine can be rotated from under the vehicle.
3. Disconnect high tension cable from the ignition coil.
4. Remove cover plate from in front of converter assembly to provide access to the converter drain plug and mounting bolts.

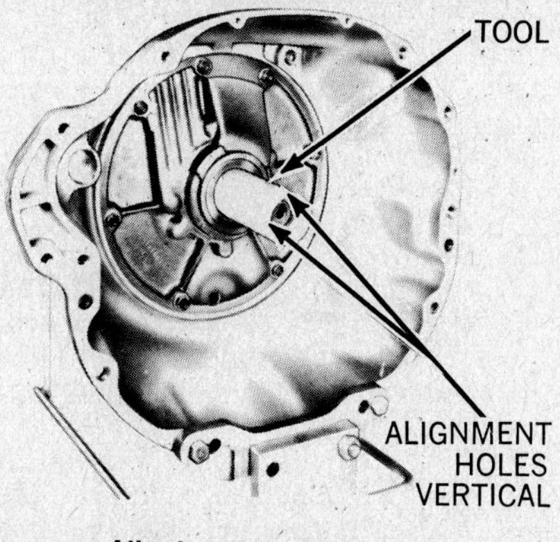

Aligning the pump rotors (© Chrysler Corp.)

5. Rotate engine to bring drain plug to "6 o'clock" position. Drain the converter and transmission.
6. Mark converter and drive plate to aid in reassembly.
7. Rotate the engine with the remote control switch to locate two converter to drive plate bolts at "5 and 7 o'clock" positions. Remove the two bolts, rotate engine again and remove the other two bolts. **CAUTION: Do not rotate converter on drive plate by prying with a screwdriver or similar tool as drive plate might become distorted. Also the starter should never be engaged if drive plate is not attached to converter with at least one bolt or if transmission case to engine block bolts have been loosened.**
8. Disconnect battery ground cable. Remove engine to transmission struts, if necessary. You may have to drop the exhaust system on some models.
9. Remove the starter.

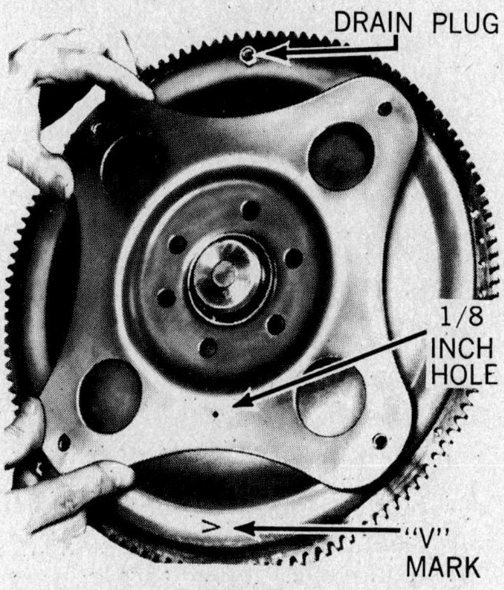

Converter and drive plate markings typical (© Chrysler Corp.)

10. Remove wire from the neutral starting switch.
11. Remove gearshift cable or rod from the transmission and the lever.
12. Disconnect the throttle rod from left side of transmission.
13. Disconnect the oil cooler lines at transmission and remove the oil filler tube. Disconnect the speedometer cable.
14. Disconnect the driveshaft.
15. Install engine support fixture to hold up the rear of the engine.
16. Raise transmission slightly with jack to relieve load and remove support bracket or crossmember. Remove all bell housing bolts and carefully work transmission and converter rearward off engine dowels and disengage converter hub from end of crankshaft. **CAUTION: Attach a small "C" clamp to edge of bell housing to hold converter in place during transmission removal; otherwise the front pump bushing might be damaged.**

Installation

NOTE: Install transmission and converter as an assembly. The drive plate will not support a load. Do not allow weight of transmission to rest on the plate during installation.

1. Rotate pump rotors until the rotor lugs are vertical.
2. Carefully slide converter assembly over input shaft and reaction shaft. Make sure converter impeller shaft slots are also vertical and fully engage front pump inner rotor lugs.
3. Use a "C" clamp on edge of converter housing to hold converter in place during transmission installation.
4. Converter drive plate should be free of distortion and drive plate to crankshaft bolts tightened to 55 ft. lbs. torque.
5. Using a jack, position transmission and converter assembly in alignment with engine.
6. Rotate converter so mark on converter (made during removal) will align with mark on drive plate. The offset holes in plate are located next to the 1/8" hole in inner circle of the plate. A stamped "V" mark identifies the offset hole in converter front cover. Carefully work transmission assembly forward over engine block dowels with converter hub entering the crankshaft opening.
7. Install converter housing to engine bolts and tighten to 28 ft. lbs.
8. Install the two lower drive plate to converter bolts and tighten to 270 in. lbs. torque.
9. Install engine to transmission struts, if required. Install starting motor and connect battery ground cable.
10. Rotate engine and install two remaining drive plate to converter bolts.
11. Install crossmember and tighten attaching bolts to 90 ft. lbs. torque. Lower transmission so that extension housing is aligned and rests on the rear mount. Install bolts and tighten to 40 ft. lbs. torque.
12. Remove transmission jack and engine support fixture, then install tie-bars under the transmission.
13. Replace the driveshaft.
14. Connect oil cooler lines, install oil filler tube and connect the speedometer cable.
15. Connect gearshift cable or rod and torqueshaft assembly to the

transmission case and to the lever.
16. Connect throttle rod to the lever at left side of transmission bell housing.
17. Connect wire to back-up and neutral starting switch.
18. Install cover plate in front of the converter assembly.
19. Refill transmission with fluid.
20. Adjust throttle and shift linkage.

Allison

Removal and Installation

NOTE: The following general procedures apply to all vehicles. It may be necessary to remove the air tanks, fuel tanks, special equipment, etc. on some vehicles to provide clearance for removal.

1. Block and hold the vehicle wheels.
2. Disconnect the battery ground cable and remove the spark plugs so that the engine can be turned over manually.
3. Remove the dipstick. Drain the transmission by disconnecting the oil filler tube at the right side of the transmission oil pan. Remove the bracket holding the oil filler tube to the transmission and remove the filler tube. Cover the oil pan opening to prevent entry of foreign material.
4. Disconnect the oil cooler lines from the fittings on the right side of the transmission case. Plug the ends of the lines and the fittings in the transmission case.
5. Disconnect the range selector cable from the shift lever.
6. Disconnect the vacuum modulator line from the modulator.
7. Disconnect the speedometer shaft fitting from the adapter.
8. Disconnect the propeller shaft from the transmission.
9. Disconnect the mechanical parking brake linkage (if equipped).
10. Remove the bolts holding the flywheel flex plate to the converter by working through the opening in the flywheel housing and turning the flywheel manually.
11. Support the transmission with a 500 lb. (minimum) transmission floor jack. The jack should be positioned so that the transmission oil pan will not support the weight of the transmission. Fasten a safety chain over the transmission.
12. Place a support under the rear of the engine and remove the transmission case-to-crossmember support bolts. Raise the engine to remove the weight from the rear engine mounts.
13. Remove the transmission case-to-flywheel housing bolts and washers.
14. Carefully inspect the transmission and surrounding area to be sure that there are no lines, hoses, or wires which will interfere with the transmission removal.

CAUTION: During removal of the transmission keep the rear of the transmission lower than the front to prevent the loss of the converter.

NOTE: Position the jack or hoist sling relative to the transmission center of gravity. The torque converter is free to move forward when the transmission is disconnected from the engine. Be sure that the converter is not allowed to separate from the transmission while the assembly is being removed. Install a retainer strap to hold the converter in place as soon as the transmission is clear of its mountings.

15. Move the transmission assembly straight away from the engine and lower the assembly carefully. Remove the transmission from the vehicle.
16. Install the transmission in the reverse order of removal.

Shift Linkage Adjustment

LoadFlite

1. Place the gearshift lever in the Park position.
2. Move the shift control lever on the transmission all the way to the rear (in the Park detent).
3. Set the adjustable rod to the proper length and install it with no load in either direction. Tighten the swivel bolt.

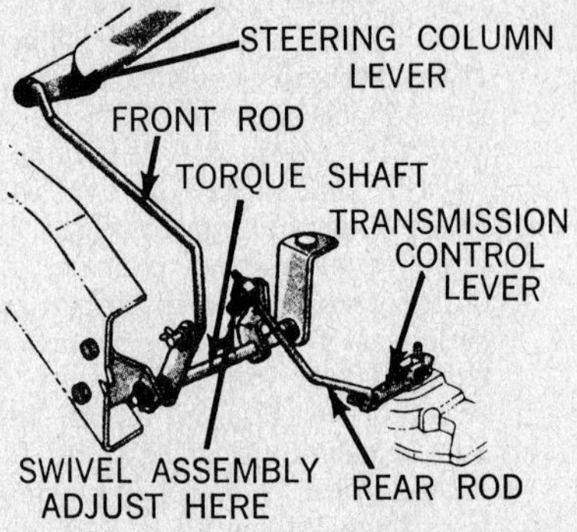

Typical loadflite transmission shift linkage (© Chrysler Corp.)

4. The shift linkage must be free of binding and be positive in all positions. Make sure that the engine can start only when the gearshift lever is in the Park or Neutral position. Be sure that the gearshift lever will not jump into an unwanted gear.

New Process A-345

1. Detach the clevis from the transmission lever by removing the pin.
2. Place the shift lever in Neutral.
3. Place the transmission lever in Neutral, the second detent from the rear.
4. Adjust and install the clevis.
5. Make sure that the engine can only be started in Neutral.

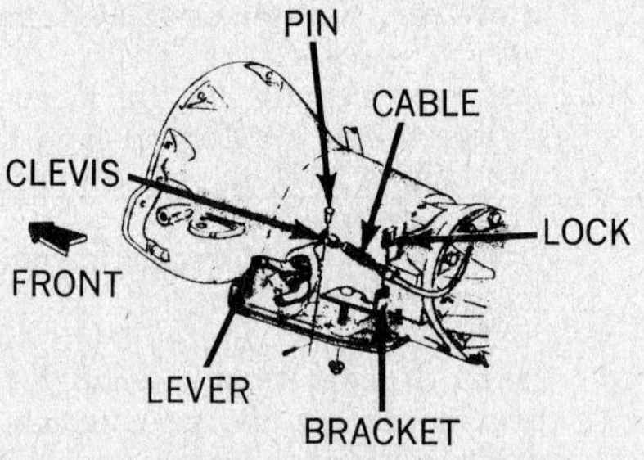

A-345 4 speed automatic transmission shift linkage (© Chrysler Corp.)

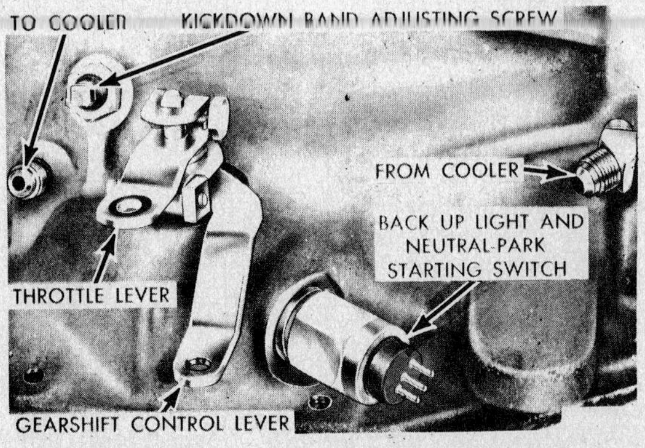

Loadflite external adjustments (© Chrysler Corp.)

Allison

1. Place the selector lever in the R (reverse) position.
2. Remove the cotter pin from the connection at the transmission selector lever. Move the connector out of the way, then shift the lever all the way forward (toward the front of the vehicle).
3. With both the selector lever in the cab and the lever on the transmission in the reverse ("R") position, the pin in the cable connector should be

aligned with the hole in the transmission lever.

4. If alignment is not correct, loosen the jam nut at the connector and turn the connector in or out until alignment is obtained and the connector pin can be installed easily.
5. Secure the connector pin with a cotter pin and tighten the jam nut securely at the connector.
6. Test the selector operation in all positions.

Band Adjustments

LoadFlite

Kickdown Band

The kickdown band adjusting screw is located on the left-hand side of the transmission case near the throttle lever shaft.

1. Loosen the locknut and back it off about five turns. Be sure that the adjusting screw is free in the case.
2. Torque the adjusting screw to 72 in. lbs.
3. Back off the adjusting screw 2 turns. On 1973 and later six-cylinder engines, and 1974 and later conventional truck V8s back off 2½ turns. On 1974 and later 440 V8, V8 van and wagon, and A-345 four-speed back off 2 turns. Then, keep the screw from turning and torque the locknut to 35 ft. lbs.

Low and Reverse Band

The pan must be removed from the transmission to gain access to the low and reverse band adjusting screw.

1. Remove the skidplate, if any. Drain the transmission and remove the pan.
2. Loosen the band adjusting screw locknut and back it off about five turns. Be sure that the adjusting screw turns freely in the lever.
3. Torque the adjusting screw to 72 in. lbs.
4. Back off the adjusting screw 2 turns. Keep the screw from turning and torque the locknut to 30 ft. lbs.

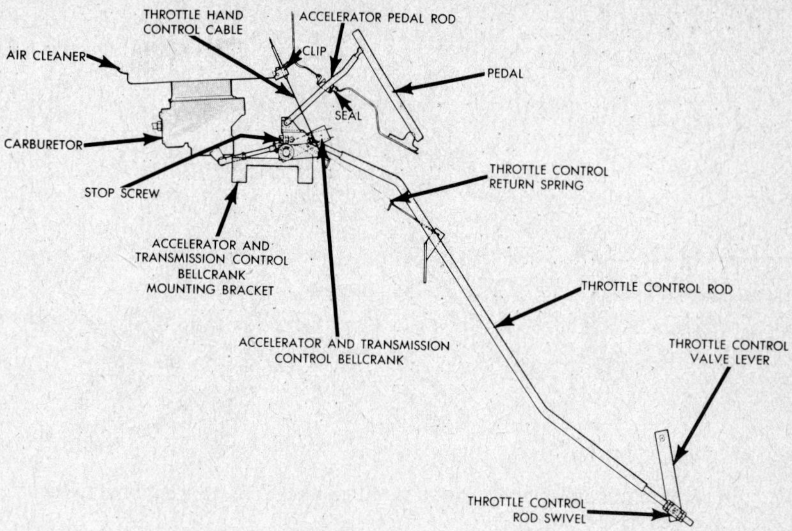

Throttle linkage assembly—typical (© Chrysler Corp.)

5. Using a new gasket, install the pan and torque the pan bolts to 150 in. lbs. Refill the transmission.

Throttle Adjustment

LoadFlite

1973 and Later Conventional Trucks, Six-Cylinder

1. Block the choke valve fully open and release the fast idle cam.
2. Hold the transmission lever forward firmly against its stop while adjusting the linkage. If there is a solenoid idle stop, the plunger must be fully entended.
3. Loosen the slotted link lock bolt and pull forward on the slotted adjuster link until it contacts the carburetor lever pin and all slack is removed.
4. Tighten the lock bolt.
5. Check the adjustment by moving the slotted adjuster link all the way back and releasing it slowly. It should return to the full forward position.

1973 and Later Conventional Trucks, V8

1. Set the idle speed to specifications.

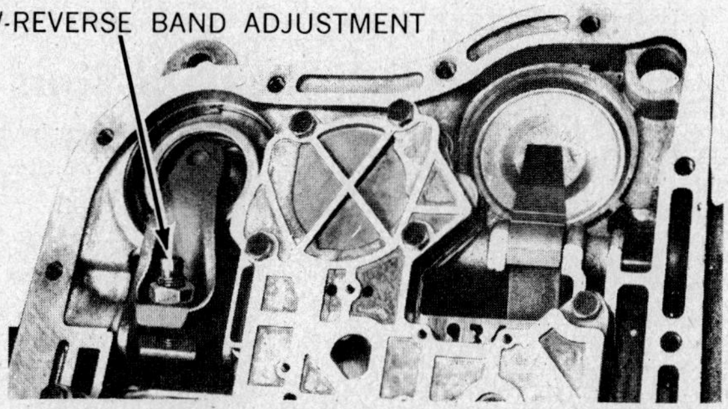

Loadflite low-reverse band adjustment—A-345 similar (© Chrysler Corp.)

2. Disconnect the choke at the carburetor or block the choke open in the wide open position.
3. Open the throttle slightly to release the fast idle cam and return the carburetor to curb idle.
4. It is important that the transmission lever remain firmly against the stop during the next two steps. Have an assistant hold the transmission throttle lever forward against the stop while the adjustment is made. On engines with solenoid idle stops, the solenoid plunger must be fully extended.
5. With a 3/16 in. diameter rod placed in the holes in the upper bellcrank and lever, adjust the length of the intermediate transmission rod by means of the threaded adjustment at the upper end. The ball socket must align with the ball end with a slight downward pressure on the rod.
6. Assemble the ball socket to the ball end and remove the 3/16 in. rod from the upper bellcrank and lever.
7. Disconnect the return spring, clip, and washer and adjust the length of the carburetor rod by pushing rearward on the rod and turning the threaded adjustment. The rear end of the slot should contact the carburetor lever pin with no backlash when the slotted adjuster link is in its normal operating position.
8. Assemble the slotted adjustment to the carburetor lever pin and install the washer and retainer clip. Install the transmission linkage return spring.
9. Check the freedom of operation by moving the slotted link at the carburetor to the full rearward position and allow it to return

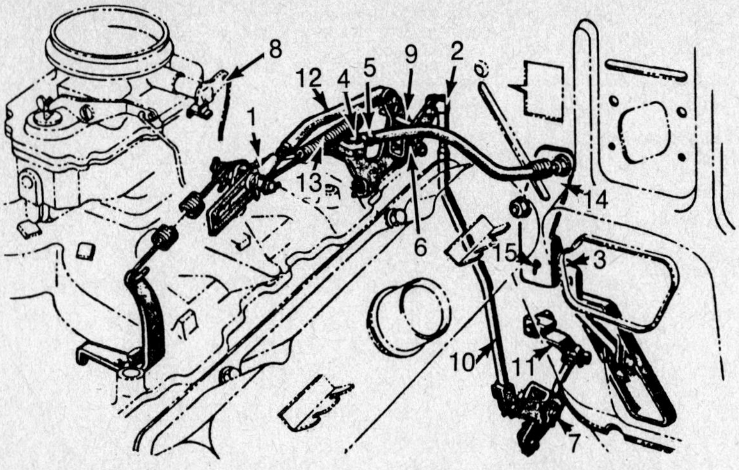

Loadflite transmission kickdown throttle linkage, V8 conventional truck
(© Chrysler Corp.)

1 Adjuster
2 Ball socket
3 Accelerator pivot
4 Clamp bolt
5 Ferrule
6 Upper bellcrank
7 Pivot pin
8 Choke
9 3/16 in. adjusting rod
10 Intermediate transmission rod
11 Transmission throttle lever
12 Carburetor rod
13 Transmission linkage return spring
14 Throttle base
15 Retaining pin

slowly. Be sure that it returns to the full rearward position.

10. Connect the choke rod or unblock the choke plate.

Vans and Pick-Ups

1. Warm the engine to operating temperature.
2. Block the choke plate fully open.
3. Remove the throttle return spring from the carburetor.
4. Remove the clip, washer and slotted throttle rod from the carburetor pin.
5. Rotate the threaded end of the rod so that the rear edge of the slot in the rod contacts the carburetor pin when the transmission throttle lever is held forward against its stop.
6. Install the washer and clip to retain the throttle rod to the carburetor.
7. Install the throttle rod return spring.
8. Check the transmission linkage for freedom of operation and unblock the choke plate.

New Process A-345

1. Block the choke valve fully open and release the fast idle cam.
2. Hold the transmission lever forward against its stop while adjusting the linkage.
3. Remove the spring from the stabilizer and retainer (not the throttle return spring) and loosen the bolt attaching the upper end of the slotted rod to the retainer.
4. Push gently backward on the rod to remove all slack.
5. Tighten the bolt at the retainer and replace the spring.
6. Check that the linkage works freely.

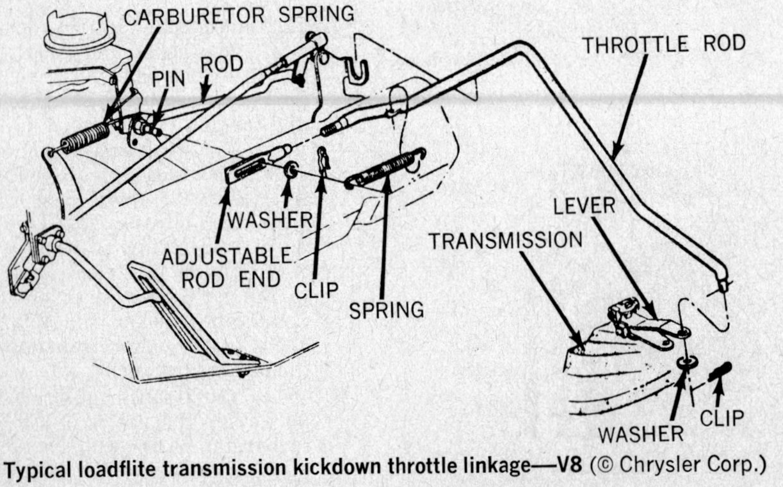

Typical loadflite transmission kickdown throttle linkage—V8 (© Chrysler Corp.)

Allison

1. Remove the throttle control return spring and governor arm spring (if equipped).

   CAUTION: **Do not stretch or distort the governor spring in any way as it will throw off the governor calibration.**
2. At the transmission, remove the throttle control shift rod swivel cotter pin and withdraw the swivel from the TV lever on the transmission.
3. Remove the carburetor air cleaner.
4. Place the carburetor linkage in the idle position.
5. Adjust the throttle control rod so that the accelerator control bell crank stop is against the bracket.
6. Tighten the nuts on the throttle control rod.
7. Move the carburetor throttle lever to the wide open position.
8. The wide open throttle stop bolt must be adjusted so that the bolt head contacts the bell crank when the throttle is in the wide open position.
9. With the throttle control shaft pushed upward until the travel of the rod is halted by the wide open throttle stop, rotate the transmission throttle control lever forward until the TV lever is firm against the internal stop in the transmission. In this position the swivel pin should freely enter the lower hole in the transmission throttle valve (TV) control lever. Finger tighten the front and rear adjusting nuts against the swivel.
10. Loosen the swivel 3 turns to back off the valve. Connect the linkage and tighten the nuts.
11. On all models the through detent pedal stop, located on the throttle control bell crank, must be adjusted so that the pedal forces cannot be applied to the TV linkage. To do this, adjust the stop so that it contacts the bracket bolted to the engine at the same time the TV lever contacts the stop in the transmission. Turn the bolt 1/16" further to eliminate any force being applied through the linkage from the stop in the transmission.

Neutral Start Switch Adjustment

LoadFlite

The neutral safety switch is mounted in the transmission case. When the gearshift lever is placed in either the Park or Neutral position, a cam, which is attached to the transmission throttle lever inside the transmission, contacts the neutral safety

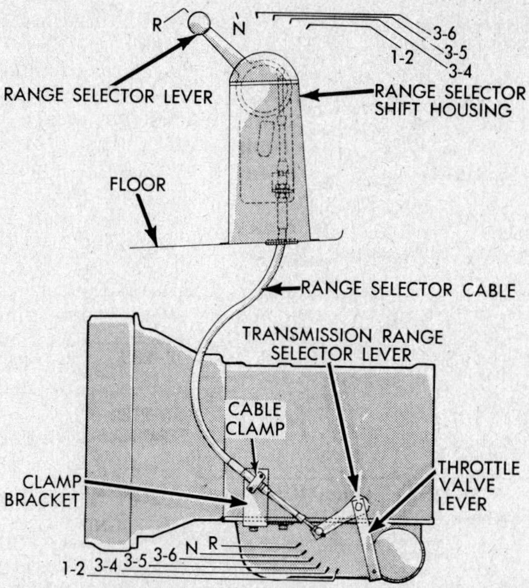

Selector lever adjustment—typical (© Chrysler Corp.)

switch and provides a ground to complete the starter solenoid circuit.

The back-up light switch is incorporated into the neutral safety switch. The center terminal is for the neutral safety switch and the two outer terminals are for the back-up lamps.

There is no adjustment for the switch. If a malfunction occurs, the switch must be removed and replaced.

To remove the switch, disconnect the electrical leads and unscrew the switch. Use a drain pan to catch the transmission fluid. Using a new seal, install the new switch and torque it to 24 ft. lbs. Refill the transmission.

Allison

1. Check the starter circuit at all range selector lever positions by positioning the lever and turning the starter switch to the "Start" position.
2. The engine should start only with the selector lever in the neutral ("N") position. If it is necessary to make an adjustment, first loosen the neutral safety switch bracket screws and rotate the switch clockwise so the starter circuit is closed when the selector lever is placed in the neutral position. Be sure that the switch mounting screws are tightened securely.
3. If the engine fails to start with the selector lever in neutral, check the switch lead wires and switch with a test light.

Pan Removal and Installation, Filter Change

1. Operate the transmission until it is thoroughly warmed up.
2. Remove the skidplate, if any. Unbolt the pan. Be ready with a large container to drain the fluid.

NOTE: If the fluid removed smells burnt, serious transmission troubles, probably due to overheating should be suspected.

3. Remove the access plate in front of the torque converter. Rotate the engine clockwise to bring the converter drain to the bottom. Position the container under the converter, remove the drain plug, and allow the fluid to drain. Drain the compounder housing on the A-345.

Replace the converter drain plug and torque it to 110 in. lbs. for a 7/16 in. head plug and 90 in. lbs. for a 5/16 in. plug. Install the access plate.

4. Unscrew and discard the filter.
5. Install a new filter. The proper torque is 35 in. lbs.
6. Clean out the pan, being extremely careful not to leave any lint from rags inside.
7. Replace the pan with a new gasket. Tighten the bolts to 150 in. lbs. in a crisscross pattern.
8. Pour six quarts (eight on the A-345) of the proper type automatic transmission fluid through the dipstick tube.
9. Start the engine in Neutral and let it idle for two minutes or more.
10. Hold your foot on the Brake and shift through D,2,1, and R and back to N.
11. Add enough fluid to bring the level to the ADD ONE PINT mark.
12. Operate the truck until the transmission is thoroughly warmed up, then check the level. It should be between FULL and ADD ONE PINT. Add fluid as necessary.

NOTE: The manufacturer recommends automatic transmission sealer be added to reduce fluid leakage resulting from hardening or shrinking of the seals in high-mileage vehicles.

DRIVESHAFT

Single Section Type

Removal and Installation

This driveshaft has a universal joint at either end and no external supports.

1. Raise and support the truck with the rear higher.
2. Matchmark the shaft and pinion flange to assure proper balance at installation.
3. Remove both rear U-joint roller and bushing clamps from the rear axle pinion flange. Do not

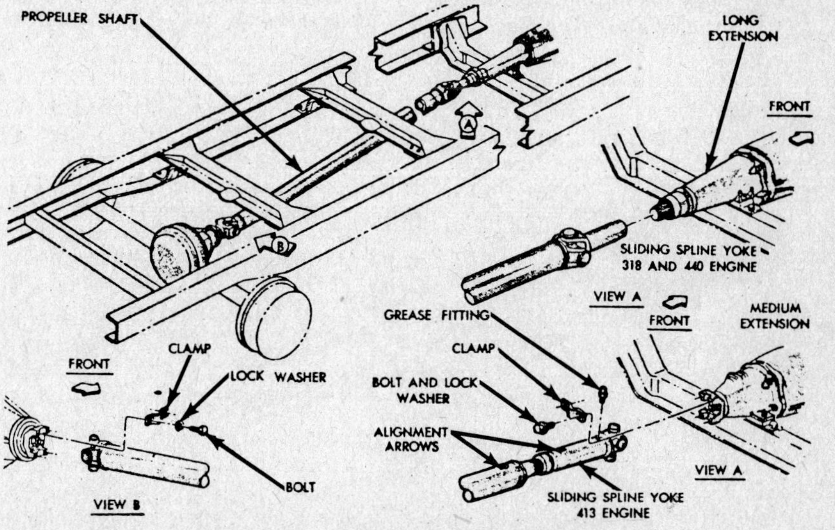

Single section driveshaft (© Chrysler Corp.)

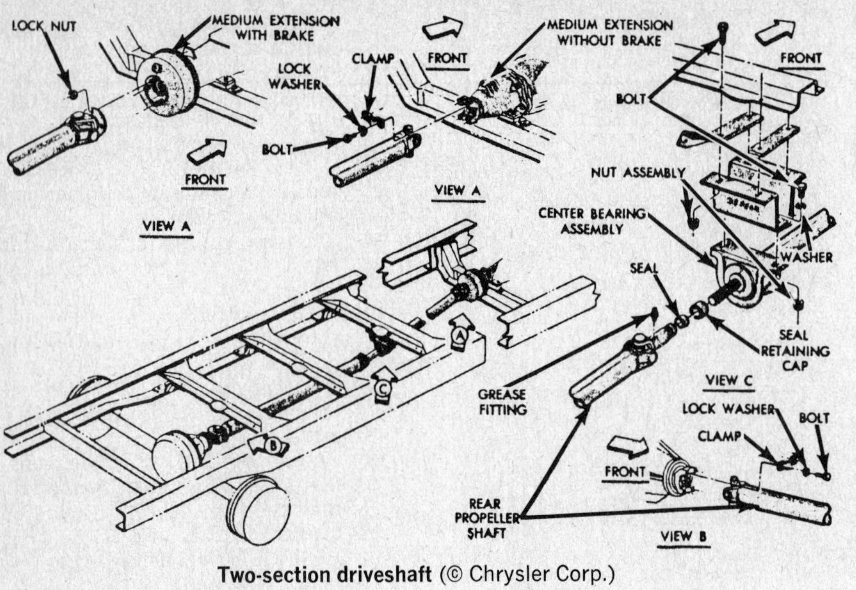

Two-section driveshaft (© Chrysler Corp.)

disturb the retaining strap which holds the bushing assemblies on the U-joint cross.

NOTE: Do not allow the driveshaft to hang during removal. Suspend it from the frame with a piece of wire. Before removing the driveshaft, raise the rear end of the truck to prevent loss of transmission fluid.

4. Slide the driveshaft, with the front sliding yoke, off the transmission output shaft.
5. Installation is the reverse of removal. Align the matchmarks made during removal.

Two-Section Type

Removal and Installation

This driveshaft has a universal joint at either end, with a third universal joint and a support bearing at the center.

1. Matchmark the shaft and the rear axle pinion hub yoke. Matchmark the center bearing spline and slip yoke.

NOTE: Do not allow the driveshaft to hang down during removal. Suspend it from the frame. Raise the rear of the truck to prevent loss of transmission fluid.

2. Remove both rear U-joint roller and bushing assembly clamps from the rear axle pinion yoke. Do not disturb the retaining strap used to hold the bushing assemblies on the U-joint cross.
3. Slide the rear half of the shaft off the front shaft splines at the center bearing. Remove the rear half.
4. At the transmission end of the front half, remove the bushing retaining bolts and clamps, after matchmarking. If there is a driveshaft brake, there will be flange nuts.
5. Unbolt the center bearing mounting nuts and bolts and remove the front half of the shaft.
6. On installation, align the matchmarks at the transmission and start all the bolts and nuts at the front U-joint and the center support bearing.
7. Tighten 1/4 in. clamp bolts to 170 in. lbs, and 5/16 in. bolts to 300 in. lbs. Tighten driveshaft brake flange nuts to 35 ft. lbs. Leave the center bearing bolts just snug.
8. Align the rear shaft matchmarks and slide the yoke onto the front shaft splines.
9. Align the rear U-joint matchmarks and install the bushing clamps and bolts. Tighten the bolts to the torque given in Step 7. Grease the joints and splines.
10. Jack up the rear wheels and let the engine drive the shaft. The center support bearing will align itself.
11. Tighten the center bearing bolts to 50 ft. lbs.

Four-Wheel Drive Front Driveshaft

Removal and Installation

This applies to Ramcharger and Trail Duster, W100, 200, and 300.

1. Remove the four flange retaining bolts and lockwashers from the constant velocity U-joint at the transfer case. Mark the parts to reinstall them in the same position. To prevent the constant velocity joint from turning while removing the nuts, use a press bar.
2. Remove the nuts and lockwashers from the U-bolts at the differential flange and remove the U-bolts.
3. Support the driveshaft and separate the U-joint at the front the driveshaft joint backward to clear the flange. The driveshaft should never be allowed to hang by either universal joint.
4. Remove the driveshaft.
5. Installation is the reverse of removal.

Universal Joint Replacement

The Lock Ring and the Snap Ring Type

The lock-ring type and the snap-ring type universal joints are basi-

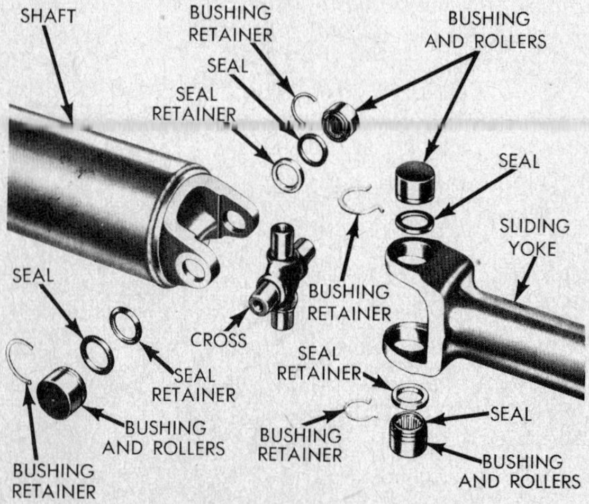

Lock ring type universal joint (© Chrysler Corp.)

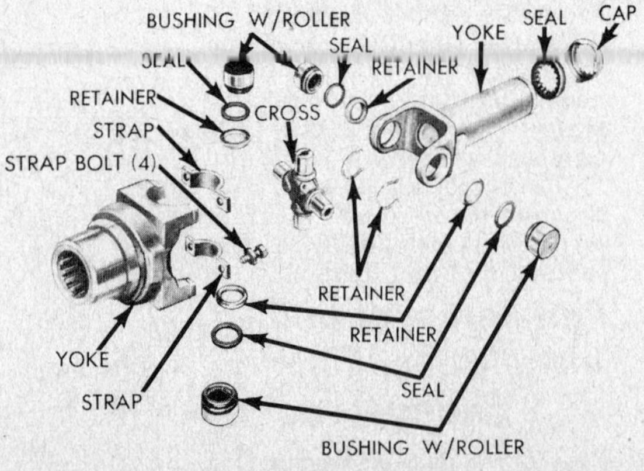

Strap clamp type universal joint (© Chrysler Corp.)

cally the same, except for the locations of the retainers. The lock-ring retainers hold the bearing cups in the yoke by being installed in a machined groove on the bearing cup, which is located on the inner side of the yoke when the joint is assembled.

The snap-ring type retainer holds the bearing cup in the yoke by being installed in a machined groove in the upper area of the bearing bore of the yoke.

The disassembly and assembly are as follows:

1. Hammer the bushings (roller cups) slightly inward to relieve pressure on the retainers. Remove the retainers.
2. Place the yoke in a vise with a socket bigger than the bushing on one side and one smaller than the bushing on the other side.
3. Apply pressure, forcing one bushing out into the larger socket.
4. Reverse the vise and socket arrangement to remove the other bushing and the cross.
5. On installation, press the new bushings in just far enough to install the retainers.

Strap Clamp Type (Rear Axle Yoke)

Unbolt strap bolts and remove straps, bushings, seals and washer retainers. Install new components as required. When assembling, grease bearings. Install with grease fitting parallel to other fittings in drive train. Tighten strap bolts to 20 ft. lbs. torque.

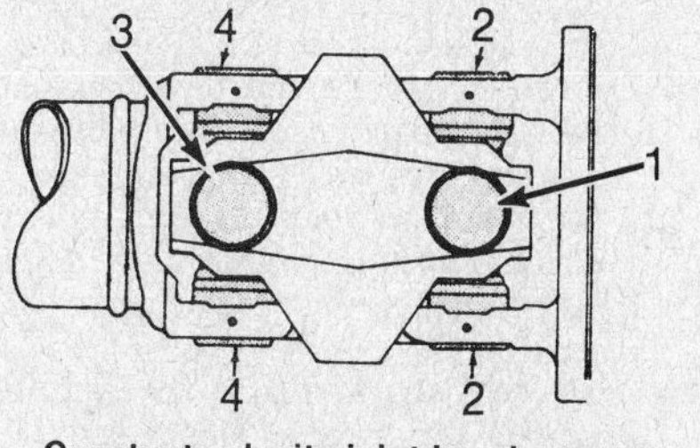

Constant velocity joint bearing cup removal sequence (© Chrysler Corp.)

Constant Velocity U-Joint

This is the double universal joint used in the front driveshaft on four-wheel drive models. These are disassembled in the same way as the snap-ring type U-Joint. Original equipment U-joints are held together by plastic retainers which shear when pressed out. The bearing cups in the center part of the joint should be pressed out before those in the yoke. Original equipment constant velocity joints cannot be reassembled. Replacement part kits have bearing cups with grooves for retaining rings.

Slip Joints

When reassembling slip joints make sure that arrows stamped on each side are matched. This will assure proper universal joint alignment.

REAR AXLE

Reference

See the General Repair Section for overhaul procedures for rear axles.

Axle Assembly

Removal and Installation

1. Raise vehicle and support at front of rear springs.
2. Block brake pedal in the up position.
3. Remove rear wheels.
4. Disconnect hydraulic brake hose at "T" fitting or at each wheel.
5. Disconnect parking brake cable.

   NOTE: to insure proper drive line balance when reassembling, make scribe marks on the driveshaft universal joint and differential pinion flange before removal.
6. Disconnect driveshaft at rear universal joint bearing clamps and secure with wire to prevent damage to front universal joint.
7. Disconnect shock absorbers and remove rear spring nuts and U-bolts.
8. Remove assembly from vehicle.
9. To install, position rear axle assembly spring pads over the spring center bolts.
10. Install U-bolts and tighten nuts securely.
11. Connect shock absorbers.
12. Connect parking brake cable.
13. Connect hydraulic brake lines. Install brake drums and adjust. Bleed hydraulic brake system.
14. Connect driveshaft universal joint in its original position, matching scribe marks made during removal. Tighten universal joint clamp bolts.

Differential Service

For service and overhaul procedures on light duty differentials see "Drive Axles" in the General Repair Section.

Axle Shaft

Removal and Installation

8⅜ and 9¼ in. Axles

NOTE: There is no provision for axle shaft end-play adjustment on this axle.

1. Raise the vehicle and remove the rear wheels.
2. Clean all dirt from the housing cover and remove the housing cover to drain the lubricant.

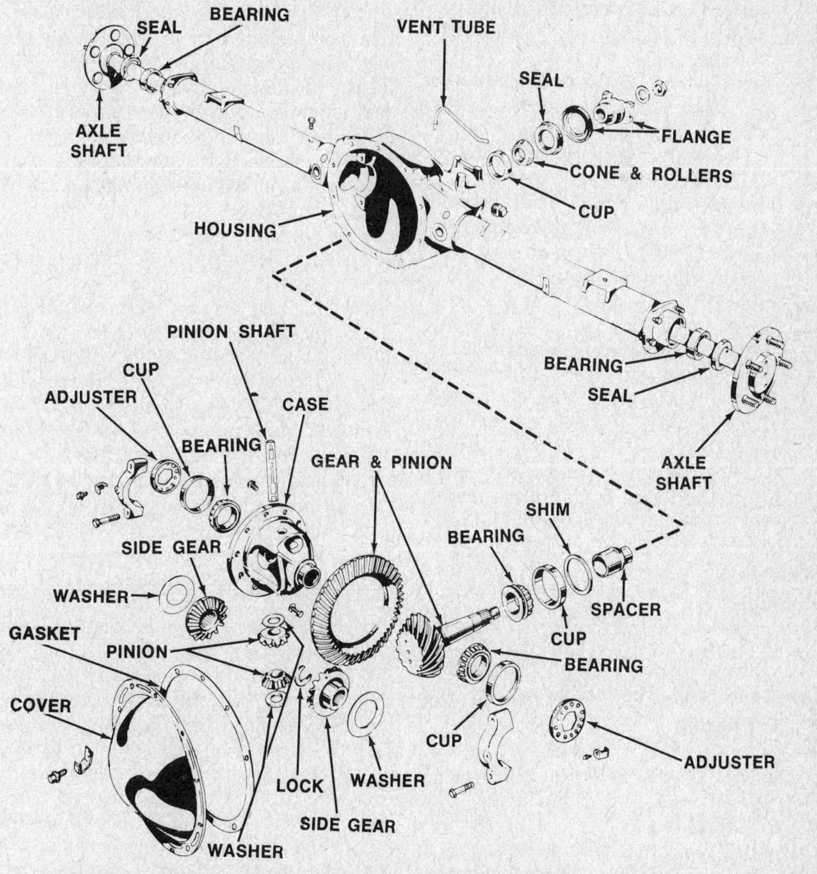

8⅜ inch rear axle, the 9¼ inch is similar (© Chrysler Corp.)

3. Remove the brake drum.
4. Rotate the differential case until the differential pinion shaft lockscrew can be removed. Remove the lockscrew and pinion shaft.
5. Push the axle shafts toward the center of the vehicle and remove the C-locks from the grooves on the axle shafts.
6. Pull the axle shafts from the housing, being careful not to damage the bearing which remains in the housing.
7. Inspect the axle shaft and bearings and replace any doubtful parts. Whenever the axle shaft is replaced, the bearings should also be replaced.
8. Remove the axle shaft seal from the bore in the housing.
9. Remove the axle shaft bearing from the housing.
10. Check the bearing shoulder in the axle housing for imperfections, and should be corrected.
11. Clean the axle shaft bearing cavity.
12. Install the axle shaft bearing in the cavity. Be sure that the bearing is seated firmly against the shoulder.
13. Install the axle shaft bearing seal. It should be seated beyond the end of the flange face.
14. Insert the axle shaft, making sure that the splines do not damage the seal. Be sure that the splines are properly engaged with the differential side gear splines.
15. Install the C-locks in the grooves on the axle shafts. Pull the shafts outward so that the C-locks seat in the counterbore of the differential side gears.
16. Install the differential pinion shaft through the case and pinions. Install the lockscrew and secure it in position.
17. Install the cover and a new gasket.

NOTE: Replacement gaskets may not be available for differential covers. In this case, the use of a gel type nonsticking sealant is recommended.

Be sure that the rear axle ratio identification tag is replaced under one of the cover bolts. Refill the axle with the specified lubricant to ½ in. below the filler plug hole. Do not overfill.

18. Install the brake drum and wheel.
19. Lower the vehicle to the ground and test the operation of the brakes.

8¾ in. Axle

NOTE: Whenever this axle assembly is serviced, both the brake support plate gaskets and the inner axle shaft oil seal must be renewed.

1. Raise the rear of the vehicle and remove the rear wheels.

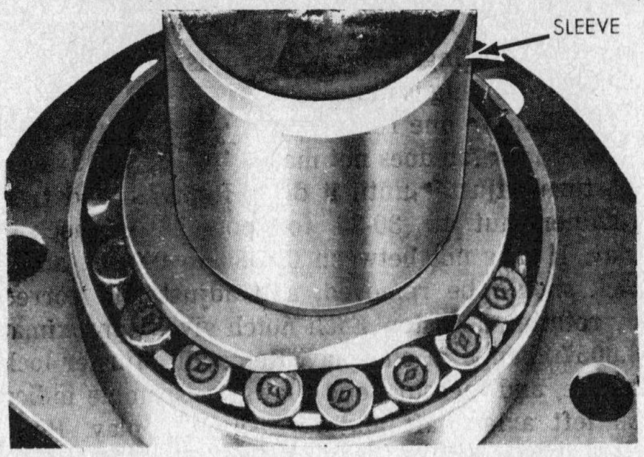

Grind the flange off the inner cone to remove the ¾ in. axle bearing rollers (© Chrysler Corp.)

2. Detach the clips which secure the brake drum to the axle shaft studs and remove the brake drum.
3. Through the access hole in the axle shaft flange, remove the axle shaft retaining nuts. The right-side axle shaft has a threaded adjuster in the retainer plate and a lock under one of its studs which should be removed at this time.
4. Remove the parking brake strut.
5. Attach a puller to the axle shaft flange and remove the axle shaft.
6. Remove the brake assembly from the axle housing.
7. Remove the axle shaft oil seal from the axle housing.

CAUTION: It is advisable to position some sort of a protective sleeve over the axle shaft seal surface next to the bearing collar to protect the seal surface. Never use a torch or other heat source as an aid in removing any axle shaft components; this will result in serious damage to the axle assembly.

8. Wipe the axle housing seal bore clean. Install a new axle shaft oil seal.

NOTE: All 8¾ in. rear axle shaft bearings are packed with a special lubricant at the factory. If the roller bearing must be repacked, the factory lubricant must be washed out. The service lubricant is not compatible with the factory lubricant.

9. Place the axle shaft retainer retaining collar in a vise. With a chisel, cut deeply into the retaining collar at 90° intervals. Remove the retainer.
10. Remove the bearing roller retainer flange by cutting off the lower edge with a chisel.
11. Grind or file a section off the flange of the inner bearing cone and remove the bearing rollers.
12. Pull the bearing roller retainer down as much as possible and cut it off with side cutters.
13. Remove the roller bearing cup with its protective sleeves.
14. To prevent damage to the seal journal when the bearing cone is removed, protect the journal with a single wrap of 0.002 in. thick shim stock held in place by a rubber band.
15. Using a puller, remove the bearing cone. Remove the seal in the bearing retainer plate and replace it.
16. To assemble the axle, first install the retainer plate and seal assembly on the axle shaft.
17. Grease the wheel bearings and install them.
18. Install a new axle shaft bearing cup, cone, and collar on the shaft. Check the axle shaft seal journal for imperfections and if necessary, polish with No. 600 crocus cloth.
19. Thoroughly clean the axle housing flange face and brake support. Install a new rubber/asbestos gasket onto the axle housing studs. Next, install the brake support plate assembly on the left side of the axle housing.
20. Lightly grease the outside edge of the bearing cup. Install the bearing cup in the bearing bore.
21. Replace the foam gasket on the studs of the left-side axle housing and very carefully slide the axle shaft assembly through the oil seal and engage the splines of the differential side gear.
22. Using a non-metallic hammer, lightly tap the axle shaft bearing in the recess end of the axle housing. Install the retainer plate over the axle housing studs and, starting with the bottom securing nut, torque the nuts to 30-35 ft. lbs.
23. Repeat steps 19-22 for the right-side axle housing.
24. At the right side of the axle housing, back off the threaded adjuster until the inner face of the adjuster is flush with the inner face of the retainer plate. Very carefully slide the axle shaft assembly through the oil seal and engage the splines of the differential side gear. Then repeat step 22.

25. Mount a dial indicator on the left brake support. Turn the adjuster clockwise until both wheel bearings are seated and there is zero end-play in the axle shafts. Back off the adjuster about four notches to establish proper end-play (0.008-0.018).
26. Lightly tap the end of the left axle shaft with a non-metallic hammer. This will seat the right wheel bearing cup against the adjuster. Turn the axle shaft several times so that a true end-play reading is obtained.
27. Remove one retainer plate nut and install the adjuster lock. If the lock tab does not mate with the notch in the adjuster, turn the adjuster slightly until it does. Refit the nut and torque it to 30-35 ft. lbs.
28. Recheck the axle shaft end-play. If it is not within specifications, repeat the adjustment. When the adjustment is complete, remove the dial indicator.
29. Install the parking brake strut. Replace the brake drum and retaining clips.
30. Install the rear wheels and lower the vehicle.

RA115, Spicer 60 and 70, F147, F140D, Eaton 2-Speed Axles

1. Remove axle shaft flange nuts and washers.
2. Rap axle shafts sharply in center of flange with hammer to free dowels.
3. Remove tapered dowels and axle shafts.
4. Clean gasket contact area with suitable solvent and install a new flange gasket.
5. Install axle shaft into axle housing.
6. On axles having an outer wheel bearing seal, install new gaskets on each side of seal mounting flange.
7. Install tapered dowels, lock washers and nuts. Torque the nuts to 30-35 ft. lbs. on the RA115, 40-70 ft. lbs. on Spicer axles with 7/16 in. thread size, and 65-105 on Spicer with ½ in.

Wheel Bearing Adjustment

Semi-Floating Axles

NOTE: Both of the rear wheels must be off the ground to measure and set the axle shaft end play.

1. Remove the tire, wheel and drum assembly. Remove the adjuster lock from the right shaft.
2. Using the dial indicator mounted on the left brake support, turn the adjuster clockwise until both wheel bearings are seated and there is zero end play in the axle shafts. Back off the adjuster counterclockwise approximately four notches to establish an axle shaft end play of .005-.0015 inch.
3. Tap the end of the left axle shaft lightly with a non metalic mallet to seat the right wheel bearing cup against the adjuster. Rotate the axle shaft several revolutions so that a true end play reading is indicated. Install the adjuster lock. If the tab on the lock does not mate with the notch in the adjuster, turn the adjuster slightly until it does. Install and tighten the nut.
4. Recheck the axle shaft end play. If it is not within the tolerance of .005-.0015 inch, repeat the procedure.
5. Remove the dial indicator, install the drum, wheel and tire assembly and lower the vehicle.

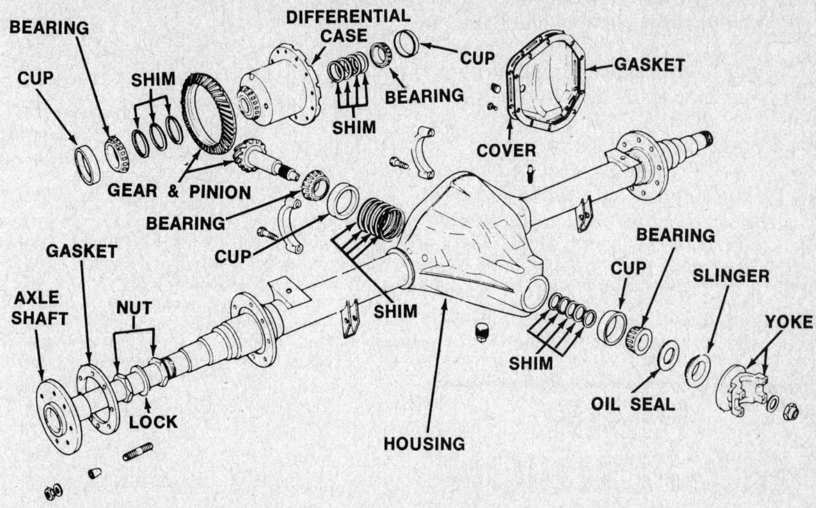

Spicer (Dana) 60, 60HD rear axle—exploded vew (© Chrysler Corp.)

Full-Floating Axles

1. Raise the wheel to be adjusted and remove the axls shaft, gasket or seal.
2. Straighten the tang on the lock ring, if so equipped and using a suitable wrench, remove the outer lock nut and lock ring.
3. While revolving the wheel and tire tighten the inner nut until

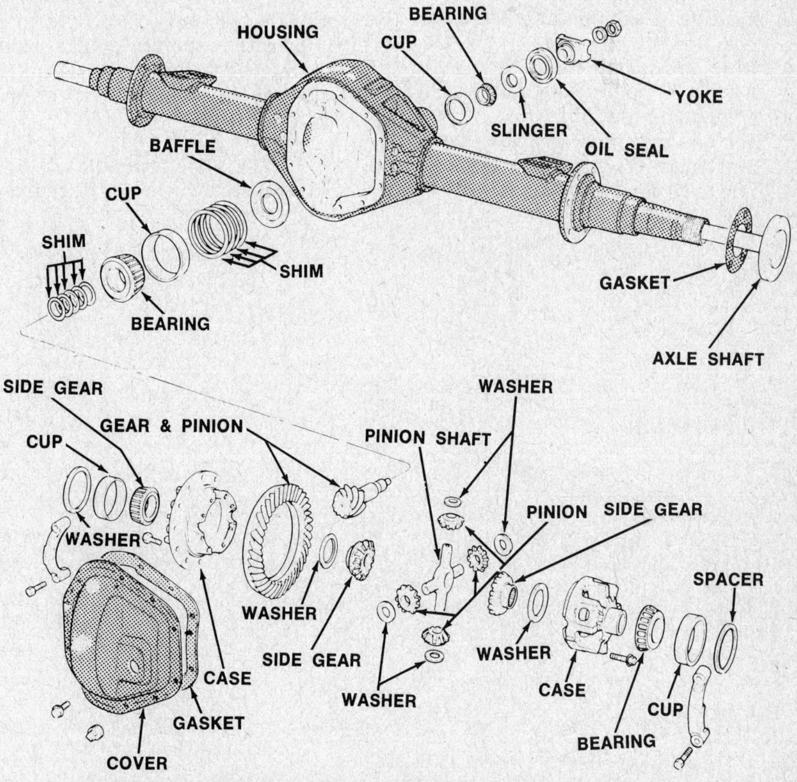

Spicer (Dand) 70 rear axle—exploded view (© Chrysler Corp.)

a slight bind is evident. Back off the nut 1/6 of a turn so that the wheel will rotate freely without excessive end play.

4. Install the lock ring and the outer nut.

   NOTE: Be careful in tightening the outer nut not to force the inner nut forward on the threads affecting the adjustment.

5. Bend the tang on the lock ring if so equipped. Install a new gasket or seal. Install the axle shaft. Lower the vehicle.

REAR SUSPENSION

Rear Spring Removal and Installation

Conventional Trucks, 100-300

1. Raise rear of truck until weight is removed from springs, wheels just touching the floor.

NOTE: Truck must be lifted by jack or hoist under frame side rail at crossmember behind the axle being careful not to bend flange of side rail.

2. Place stands under side frame members as a safety precaution.
3. Remove nuts, lockwashers and U-bolts securing spring to axle.
4. Remove spring shackle bolts, shackle and spring front bolt, then remove spring.
5. To install, position spring on axle so spring center bolt enters locating hole in axle housing pad.
6. Line up spring front eye with bolt hole in bracket and install spring bolt and nut.
7. Install the rear shackle, bolts and nuts. Tighten shackle bolt nut until slack is taken up.

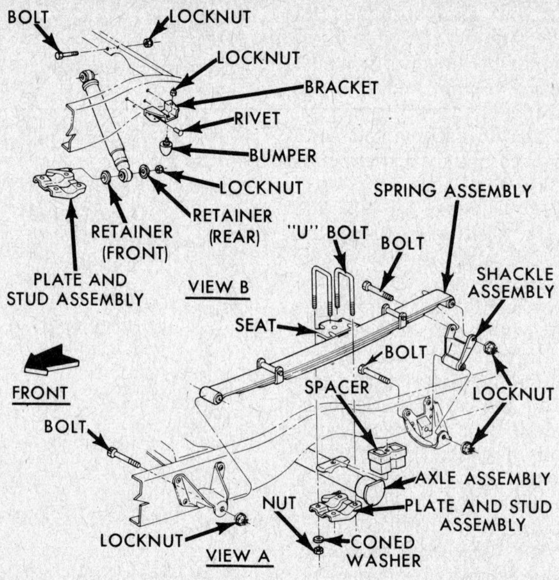

Rear suspension Ramcharger and Trail Duster (© Chrysler Corp.)

8. On headless type spring bolts install the bolts with lock bolt groove lined up with lock bolt hole in bracket. Install lock bolt and tighten lock bolt nut. Install lubrication fittings.
9. Install U-bolts, new lockwashers and nuts, tightening until nuts push lockwashers against axle. Align auxiliary spring parallel with main spring.
10. Remove stands from under vehicle, lower truck so weight is resting on wheels. Tighten U-bolt nuts, spring eye nuts and shackle bolt nuts.
11. Lubricate spring bolts and shackle bolts with chassis lubricant when equipped with lubrication fittings.

Vans and Pick-Ups

1. Raise the vehicle until springs are accessible. Place jackstands under the bumper brackets.
2. Remove U-bolt nuts, U-bolts, and plate.
3. Remove the front pivot bolt nut. Remove the bolt.
4. Remove the rear shackle bolt nuts. Remove the shackle plate.
5. Remove the outer shackle and bolt assembly from the hanger. Remove the spring. On vehicles equipped with one piece shackles, remove the nut, remove the shackle to spring bolt, and remove the spring.
6. To install, position the spring and shackle assembly in the rear hanger.
7. Install the shackle plates and nuts, tightening the nuts to 40 ft-lbs. On vehicles with the one piece shackle, first position the

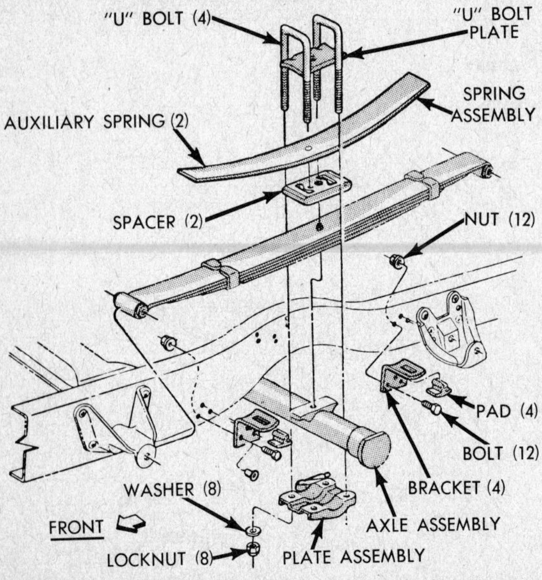

Rear suspension, D100, 200 shown (© Chrysler Corp.)

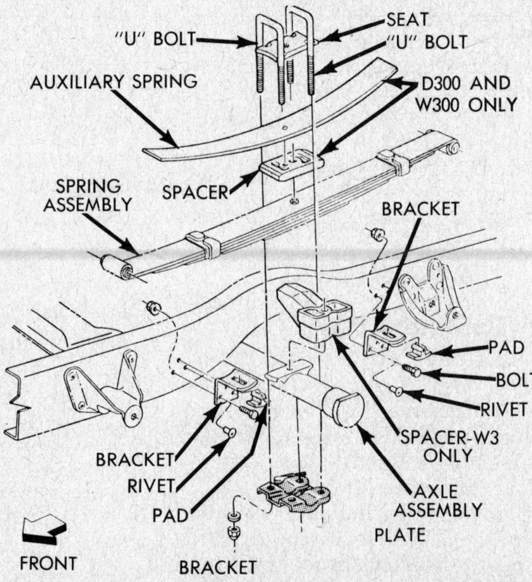

Rear suspension, W200, W300, and D300 shown (© Chrysler Corp.)

spring to the shackle, and then install the bolt and nut.

8. Position the spring in the front pivot hanger and install the bolt and nut.
9. Position the spring properly on the axle and install the U-bolt plate.
10. Install the U-bolts and nuts. Make sure the shackled end of the spring is above the shackle bracket pivot.
11. Lower the vehicle to the floor, and tighten all nuts.

Installing New Leaf

1. Clamp spring in a vise, remove center bolt and bend clamp type clips back from spring leaves.
2. Insert long drift in center bolt hole and release vise slowly.
3. Remove assembly from vise and replace broken leaf.
4. Place spring assembly in vise, slowly tightening vise while holding spring leaves in alignment with drift.
5. Remove drift and install new center bolt.
6. Install nut, tightening to 15 ft. lbs. torque.
7. Remove spring from vise.

Medium Duty Models, 400-800

1. Raise truck frame until weight is off rear springs with wheels still touching the ground.
2. Remove nuts from spring clips and remove spring clip plate. Remove spring clips.
3. If truck is so equipped, remove the auxiliary spring and spacer.
4. Install a "C" clamp on radius leaf to relieve load on spring eye bolt. Remove front eye bolt retaining nut.
5. Remove spring eye bolt and slowly release tension on radius leaf.
6. Remove rebound pin retaining lock from front bracket. Remove spring rebound pin. Repeat for rear rebound pin.
7. Remove rear spring.
8. If necessary, replace radius leaf eye rubber bushing.
9. To install, position spring in front bracket and install rebound pin. Install retaining lock.
10. Position spring in rear bracket, and install rebound pin. Install retaining lock.
11. Align spring eye and install spring eye bolt and nut. It may be necessary to draw the radius leaf eye into position with a "C" clamp.
12. Install auxiliary spring assembly if so equipped.
13. Install spring U-bolt plate and U-bolt seat. Install spring clips and nuts and washers, tightening nuts until they are snug.
14. Lower truck to the floor and tighten spring U-bolts.

REAR SPRINGS

Truck Model Designation		D100	D200	D300
Rear Spring (Type)		Progressive	Progressive	Progressive
Width (Inches)		2.5	2.5	2.5
Length Std. (inches)		52	52	52
Aux. (inches)		35.68	35.68	35.68
Type of Bushings		Rubber	Rubber	Rubber
Capacity (lbs.) 6-8 Cyl.	Standard	1350/1520	1950/2175	2500/2820
	Extra	1650/1820	2500/2725	3250/3650
	Extra		2500/2750	
No. of Leaves	Standard	4	5	6
	Extra	5	6	7
Aux. .262 in. thick		1	1	N/A
Capacity (lbs.)		365	365	365
Camper Aux. .423 in. thick			1	1
Capacity (lbs.)			585	585

Truck Model Designation	W100	W200	W300
Standard Equipment			
Rear Spring Type	Progressive	Progressive	Single Stage
Length (inches)	52	52	52
Width (inches)	2.5	2.5	2.5
No. of Leaves	5	5	7
Type of Bushings	Rubber	Rubber	Rubber
Capacity (lbs.) 6-8 Cyl.	1350/1570	1750/1970	3250/3650
Extra Equipment			
Length (inches)	52	52	
Width (inches)	2.5	2.5	
No. of Leaves	5	6	1 Aux.
Type of Bushings	Rubber	Rubber	Rubber
Capacity (lbs.) 6-8 Cyl.	1750/1970	2200/2425	585 Aux.

Ford—Trucks, Vans and Jimmy

INDEX

TUNE-UP SPECIFICATIONS
1973-78

CU. IN. DISPLACE-MENT	YEAR	SPARK PLUG GAP	DISTRIBUTOR POINT DWELL	DISTRIBUTOR POINT GAP	IGNITION TIMING DEGREES	CRANKING COMP. PRESSURE	VALVE CLEARANCE INLET	VALVE CLEARANCE EXHAUST	GOV. R.P.M. NO LOAD	FUEL PUMP PRESS.	IDLE SPEED STD.	IDLE SPEED AUTO.
SIX CYLINDER												
200	1973-75	.034	37	.027	6B	175	Zero		—	4-6	500	650
240	1973	.034	33-39	.027	①	⑫	Zero		4000	4-6	①	①
	1974	①	①	①	①	⑫	Zero		①	4-6	①	①
300	1973	.034	33-39	.027	①	⑫	Zero		—	4-6	①	①
	1974-78	①	①	①	①	⑫	Zero		—	4-6	⑨	⑨
EIGHT CYLINDER												
302	1973	.034	24-30	.017	①	150	Zero		—	5	①	①
	1974-78	①	①	①	①	⑫	Zero		—	5	①	①
330	1973	.030	24-30②	.017③	①	140	Zero		3900	4½-6½	①	①
	1974-78	①	①	①	①	⑫	Zero		3900	4½-6½	①	①
351W	1976-78	①	⑪	⑪	①	⑫	Zero		—	4½-6½	①	①
351M	1977-78	①	⑪	⑪	①	⑫	Zero		—	4½-6½	①	①
360/359	1973	.034	24-30	.017	①	⑫	Zero		—	4½-6½	①	①
	1974-78	①	①	①	①	⑫	Zero		—	4½-6½	①	①
361	1974-78	①	①		①	⑫	Zero		3800	4½-6½	①	①
390	1973	.034	24-30	.017	①	⑫	Zero		3800	4½-6½	①	①
	1974-76	①	①	①	①	⑫	Zero		3800	4½-6½	①	①
391/389	1973	.030	26-31②	.017③	①	140	Zero		3800	4½-6½	550①	500①
	1974-78	①	①	①	①	⑫	Zero		3800	4½-6½	①	①
400	1977-78	①	⑪	⑪	①	⑫	Zero		—	4½-6½	①	①
401	1973-74	.030	26-31②	.017③	8①	150	.020	.020	3600	④	525①	500D①
	1975-78	①	①	①	①	⑫	.020	.020	①	⑧	①	①
460	1974-78	①	①	①	①	⑫	Zero		—	4½-6½	①	①
475	1977-78	①	①	①	①	⑫	.020	.020	①	⑧	①	①
477	1973-74	.030	26-31②	.017③	8①	150	.020	.020	3400	④	525①	500D①
	1975-78	①	①	①	①	⑫	.020	.020	①	⑧	①	①
534	1973-74	.030	22-24	.020	8①	150	.020	.020	3200	④	550①	500①
	1975-78	①	①	①	①	⑫	.020	.020	①	⑧	①	①

1979-80

For 1979 and later Tune-Up Specifications consult the Vehicle Emissions Control Label, which is located on the engine of the vehicle. This decal will contain a calibration number which when used in conjunction with the chart below will yield the required tune-up information.

NOTE: If the information given in this chart disagrees with the information on the decal, use the information on the decal.

CALIBRATION	SPARK PLUG GAP	IGNITION TIMING	FAST IDLE RPM HIGH CAM	FAST IDLE RPM KICK DOWN	CURB IDLE RPM A/C⑤ OFF/ON	CURB IDLE RPM NON-A/C	TSP OFF RPM A/C	TSP OFF RPM NON-A/C
9-51G-RO	.042-.046	6°BTDC	—	1600	700	700	500	500
9-51J-RO	.042-.046	6°BTDC	—	1600	700	700	500	500
9-51K-RO	.042-.046	6°BTDC	—	1600	700	700	500	500
9-51L-RO	.042-.046	6°BTDC	—	1600	700	700	500	500
9-51M-RO	.042-.046	6°BTDC	—	1600	700	700	500	500
9-51S-RO	.042-.046	6°BTDC	—	1600	700	700	500	500
9-51T-RO	.042-.046	6°BTDC	—	1600	700	700	500	500
9-52G-RO	.042-.046	10°BTDC	—	1600	550	550	500	500
9-52J-RO	.042-.046	10°BTDC	—	1600	550	550	500	500
9-52L-RO	.042-.046	10°BTDC	—	1600	550	550	500	500
9-52M-RO	.042-.046	10°BTDC	—	1600	550	550	500	500
9-53G-RO	.042-.046	6°BTDC	2000	—	700	700	—	—
9-53H-RO	.042-.046	4°BTDC	2000	—	700	700	—	—
9-54G-RO	.042-.046	8°BTDC	2000	—	600	600	550	550
9-54H-RO	.042-.046	6°BTDC	2000	—	600	600	550	550
9-54J-RO	.042-.046	6°BTDC	2000	—	600	600	550	550
9-54R-RO	.042-.046	6°BTDC	2000	—	600	600	550	550
9-54S-RO	.042-.046	8°BTDC	2000	—	650	650	550	550

TUNE-UP SPECIFICATIONS

CALIBRATION	SPARK PLUG GAP	IGNITION TIMING	FAST IDLE RPM HIGH CAM	FAST IDLE RPM KICK DOWN	CURB IDLE RPM A/C⑤ OFF/ON	CURB IDLE RPM NON-A/C	TSP OFF RPM A/C	TSP OFF RPM NON-A/C
9-54T-RO	.042-.046	6°BTDC	2000	—	600	600	550	550
9-54U-RO	.042-.046	6°BTDC	2000	—	650	650	550	550
9-59H-RO	.042-.046	10°BTDC	2000	—	650	650	—	—
9-59J-RO	.042-.046	10°BTDC	2000	—	650	650	—	—
9-59K-RO	.042-.046	10°BTDC	2000	—	650	650	—	—
9-59S-RO	.042-.046	8°BTDC	2000	—	650	650	—	—
9-59T-RO	.042-.046	10°BTDC	2000	—	650	650	—	—
9-60G-RO	.042-.046	6°BTDC	2000	—	550	550	—	—
9-60H-RO	.042-.046	6°BTDC	2000	—	550	550	—	—
9-60J-RO	.042-.046	6°BTDC	2000	—	550	550	—	—
9-60L-RO	.042-.046	6°BTDC	2000	—	550	550	—	—
9-60M-RO	.042-.046	6°BTDC	2000	—	550	550	—	—
9-60S-RO	.042-.046	10°BTDC	2100	—	550	550	—	—
9-61G-RO	.042-.046	10°BTDC	2000	—	650	650	—	—
9-61H-RO	.042-.046	10°BTDC	2000	—	650	650	—	—
9-62J-RO	.042-.046	6°BTDC	1900	—	550	550	—	—
9-62M-RO	.042-.046	6°BTDC	1900	—	550	550	—	—
9-63H-RO	.042-.046	4°BTDC	—	1500	800	800	500	500
9-64G-RO	.042-.046	10°BTDC	2200	—	600	600	500	500
9-64H-RO	.042-.046	12°BTDC	2200	—	600	600	500	500
9-64S-RO	.042-.046	8°BTDC	2200	—	600	600	500	500
9-66G-RO	.042-.046	14°BTDC	—	1600	650⑥	650	800⑦	800
7-76J-R11	.042-.046	6°BTDC	—	1700	650	650	525⑤	525
7-93J-RO	.042-.046	10°BTDC	2500	—	600	600	—	—
7-95J-RO	.042-.046	10°BTDC	2500	—	600	600	—	—
9-71J-RO	.042-.046	6°BTDC	1750	—	600	600	—	—
9-72J-RO	.042-.046	12°BTDC	2000	—	600	600	500	500
9-73-RO	.042-.046	3°BTDC	1750	—	600	600	—	—
9-74J-RO	.042-.046	3°BTDC	2000	—	600	600	500	500
9-77J-RO	.042-.046	12°BTDC	—	1600	700	700	500	500
9-77M-90	.042-.046	12°BTDC	2550	—	—	700	—	500
9-78J-RO	.042-.046	12°BTDC	—	1600	550	550	500	500
9-83G-RO	.042-.046	6°BTDC	2200	—	—	600	—	—
9-83H-RO	.042-.046	2°BTDC	2500	—	—	600	—	—
9-87G-RO	.042-.046	8°BTDC	2700	—	—	600	—	—
9-97J-RO	.042-.046	8°BTDC	—	1600	650	—	—	—
9-97J-R11	.042-.046	8°BTDC	—	1600	650	—	—	—

① Set to specifications shown on engine decal.
② Transistor Ignition 22-24.
③ Transistor Ignition .020.
④ Electric.
⑤ Only for A/C-TSP equipped, A/C compressor electromagnetic clutch de-energized.
⑥ Energize A/C electromagnetic clutch.
⑦ De-energize A/C electromagnetic clutch.
⑧ .021 w/Dual Diaphragm Distributor.
⑨ 26-31 on F-250 and 1972 Models.
⑩ TSP-Dash Pot Throttle Positioner
⑪ Electronic ignition.
⑫ Take the highest reading and compare it to the lowest reading. The lower reading must be within 75% of the highest.

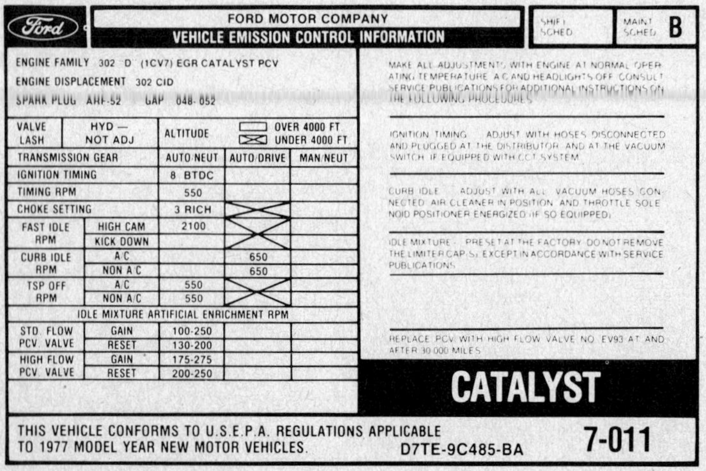
FORD MOTOR COMPANY
VEHICLE EMISSION CONTROL INFORMATION

SHIFT SCHED | MAINT SCHED B

ENGINE FAMILY 302 D (1CV7) EGR CATALYST PCV
ENGINE DISPLACEMENT 302 CID
SPARK PLUG AHF-52 GAP .048-.052

VALVE LASH	HYD — NOT ADJ	ALTITUDE	OVER 4000 FT / ☒ UNDER 4000 FT	
TRANSMISSION GEAR		AUTO/NEUT	AUTO/DRIVE	MAN/NEUT
IGNITION TIMING		8 BTDC		
TIMING RPM		550		
CHOKE SETTING		3 RICH		
FAST IDLE RPM	HIGH CAM	2100		
	KICK DOWN			
CURB IDLE RPM	A/C		650	
	NON A/C		650	
TSP OFF RPM	A/C	550		
	NON A/C	550		
IDLE MIXTURE ARTIFICIAL ENRICHMENT RPM				
STD. FLOW PCV. VALVE	GAIN	100-250		
	RESET	130-200		
HIGH FLOW PCV. VALVE	GAIN	175-275		
	RESET	200-250		

MAKE ALL ADJUSTMENTS WITH ENGINE AT NORMAL OPERATING TEMPERATURE A/C AND HEADLIGHTS OFF. CONSULT SERVICE PUBLICATIONS FOR ADDITIONAL INSTRUCTIONS ON THE FOLLOWING PROCEDURES.

IGNITION TIMING — ADJUST WITH HOSES DISCONNECTED AND PLUGGED AT THE DISTRIBUTOR AND AT THE VACUUM SWITCH IF EQUIPPED WITH CCT SYSTEM.

CURB IDLE — ADJUST WITH ALL VACUUM HOSES CONNECTED, AIR CLEANER IN POSITION, AND THROTTLE SOLENOID POSITIONER ENERGIZED (IF SO EQUIPPED).

IDLE MIXTURE — PRESET AT THE FACTORY. DO NOT REMOVE THE LIMITER CAP(S) EXCEPT IN ACCORDANCE WITH SERVICE PUBLICATIONS.

REPLACE PCV WITH HIGH FLOW VALVE NO. EV93 AT AND AFTER 30,000 MILES.

CATALYST

THIS VEHICLE CONFORMS TO U.S.E.P.A. REGULATIONS APPLICABLE TO 1977 MODEL YEAR NEW MOTOR VEHICLES.
D7TE-9C485-BA
7-011

Typical emission certificate (tune-up specification) decal (© Ford Motor Co.)

FIRING ORDER

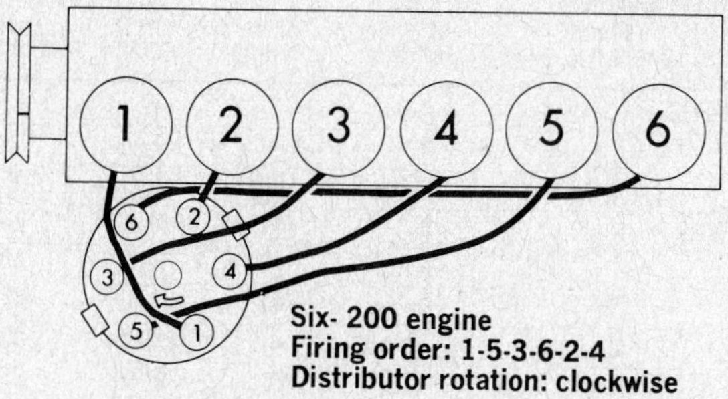

Six- 200 engine
Firing order: 1-5-3-6-2-4
Distributor rotation: clockwise

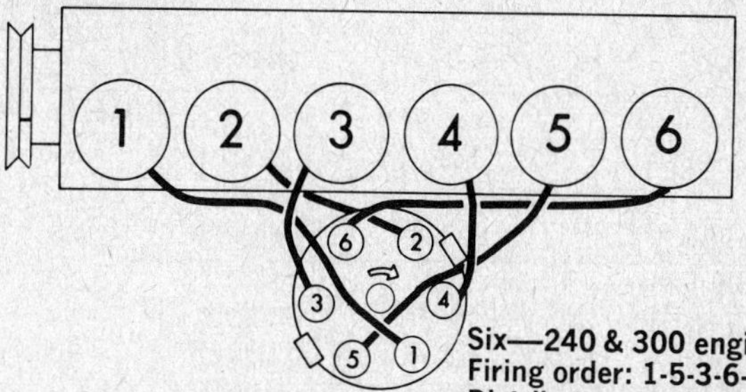

Six—240 & 300 engines
Firing order: 1-5-3-6-2-4
Distributor rotation: clockwise

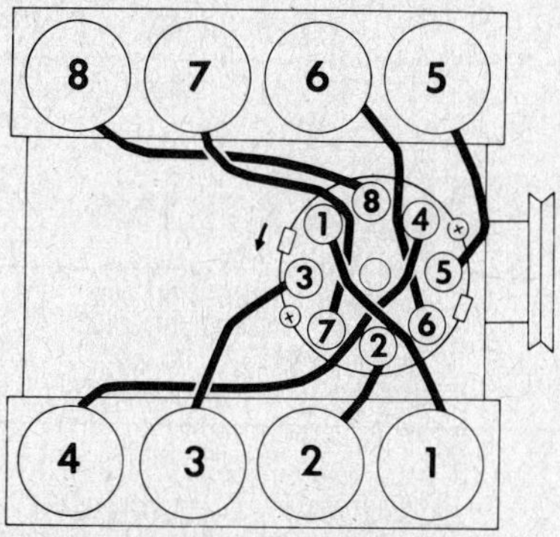

V8—351, 351W & 400 engines
Firing order: 1-3-7-6-5-4-8
Distributor rotation counterclockwise

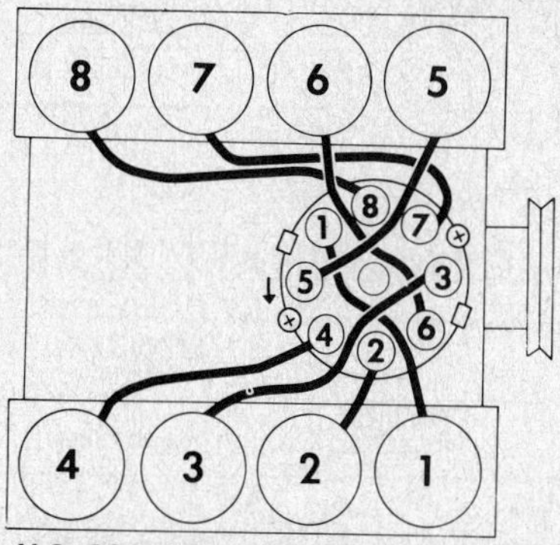

V-8- 302, 330, 359, 360, 361, 370, 389, 390, 401, 429, 460, 475, 477, & 534 engines
Firing order: 1-5-4-2-6-3-7-8
Distributor rotation: counterclockwise

GENERAL ENGINE SPECIFICATIONS

CU. IN. DISPLACE-MENT	YEAR	BORE AND STROKE	FIRING ORDER	DEVELOPED HORSE POWER @ R.P.M.	DEVELOPED TORQUE @ R.P.M.	COM-PRESSION RATIO	CARBU-RETOR	VALVE LIFTER TYPE	NORMAL OIL PRESSURE
				SIX CYLINDER					
200	1973-75	3.683 x 3.26	153624	84 @ 3600	151 @ 1800	8.3	2V	Hyd.	35.55
240	1973-74	4.00 x 3.18	153624	119 @ 3800	190 @ 2200	8.5	1V	Hyd.	40-60
300	1973	4.00 x 3.98	153624	128 @ 3600	234 @ 1600	7.9	1V	Hyd.	40-60
	1973	4.00 x 3.98	153624	132 @ 3600	241 @ 1800	7.9	1V	Hyd.	40-60
	1973-80	4.00 x 3.98	153624	N.A.	N.A.	N.A.	1V	Hyd.	40-60
				EIGHT CYLINDER					
302	1973	4.00 x 3.00	15426378	157 @ 4000	249 @ 2600	8.2	2V	Hyd.	40-60
	1974-80	4.00 x 3.00	15426378	N.A.	N.A.	N.A.	2V	Hyd.	40-60
330	1973	3.875 x 3.50	15426378	154 @ 3600	276 @ 2000	7.4	2V	Hyd.	35-60
	1973	3.875 x 3.50	15426378	155 @ 3600	262 @ 2600	7.4	2V	Hyd.	35-60
	1974-78	3.815 x 3.50	15426378	N.A.	N.A.	N.A.	2V	Hyd.	35-60
351W	1975-80	4.00 x 3.50	13726548	N.A.	N.A.	N.A.	2V	Hyd.	40-65
351M	1977-80	4.00 x 3.50	13726548	N.A.	N.A.	N.A.	2V	Hyd.	50-75
360	1973	4.05 x 3.50	15426378	189 @ 4600	287 @ 2400	8.0	2V	Hyd.	35-60
	1974-76	4.05 x 3.50	15426378	N.A.	N.A.	N.A.	2V	Hyd.	35-60
361	1973	4.05 x 3.50	15426378	169 @ 3600	290 @ 2400	7.2	2V	Hyd.	35-75
	1974-78	4.05 x 3.50	15426378	N.A.	N.A.	N.A.	2V	Hyd.	35-75
370	1979-80	4.050 x 3.590	15426378	N.A.	N.A.	N.A.	2V	Hyd.	40-65
	1979-80	4.050 x 3.590	15426378	N.A.	N.A.	N.A.	4V	Hyd.	40-65
390	1973	4.05 x 3.78	15426378	195 @ 4400	319 @ 2400	8.2	2V	Hyd.	35-75
	1974-76	4.05 x 3.78	15426378	N.A.	N.A.	N.A.	2V	Hyd.	35-75
391/389	1973	4.05 x 3.79	15426378	192 @ 3600	333 @ 2400	7.2	4V	Hyd.	35-75
	1974-78	4.05 x 3.79	15426378	N.A.	N.A.	N.A.	4V	Hyd.	35-75

GENERAL ENGINE SPECIFICATIONS

CU. IN. DISPLACE-MENT	YEAR	BORE AND STROKE	FIRING ORDER	DEVELOPED HORSE POWER @ R.P.M.	DEVELOPED TORQUE @ R.P.M.	COM-PRESSION RATIO	CARBU-RETOR	VALVE LIFTER TYPE	NORMAL OIL PRESSURE
				EIGHT CYLINDER					
400	1977-80	4.00 x 4.00	13726548	N.A.	N.A.	N.A.	2V	Hyd.	50-75
401	1973	4.125 x 3.75	15486372	185 @ 3400	293 @ 3000	7.3	4V	Mech.	35-60
	1974-76	4.125 x 3.75	15486372	N.A.	N.A.	N.A.	4V	Mech.	35-60
429	1979-89	4.360 x 3.590	15426278	N.A.	N.A.	N.A.	4V	Hyd.	40-65
460	1974-80	4.36 x 3.85	15426378	N.A.	N.A.	N.A.	4V	Hyd.	40-65
475	1977-80	4.50 x 3.75	15486372	N.A.	N.A.	N.A.	4V	Mech.	35-60
477	1973	4.50 x 3.75	15486372	209 @ 3200	353 @ 2800	7.20	4V	Mech.	35-60
	1974-80	4.50 x 3.75	15486372	N.A.	N.A.	N.A.	4V	Mech.	35-60
534	1973-80	4.50 x 4.20	15486372	222 @ 3000	400 @ 1800	7.3	4V	Mech.	35-65

CRANKSHAFT BEARING JOURNAL SPECIFICATIONS

CU. IN. DISPLACE-MENT	YEAR	MAIN BEARING JOURNALS				CONNECTING ROD BEARING JOURNALS		
		JOURNAL DIAMETER	OIL CLEARANCE	SHAFT END PLAY	THRUST ON NO.	JOURNAL DIAMETER	OIL CLEARANCE	END PLAY
				SIX CYLINDER				
200	1973	2.2482-2.2490	.0005-.0026	.004-.008	5	2.1232-2.1240	.0002-.0024	.0035-.0105
240	1973-74	2.3982-2.3990	.0005-.0022	.004-.008	5	2.1228-2.1236	.0008-.0024	.006-.013
300	1973-80	2.3982-2.3990	.0009-.0028	.004-.008	5	2.1228-2.1236	.0009-.0027	.006-.013
				EIGHT CYLINDER				
302	1973-80	2.2482-2.2490	.0005-.0015	.004-.008	3	2.1228-2.1236	.0010-.0015	.010-.020
330 MD	1973-78	2.7484-2.7492	.0011-.0031	.004-.008	3	2.4380-2.4388	.0006-.0023	.010-.020
HD	1973-78	2.7479-2.7487	[1]	.004-.010	3	2.4377-2.4385	.0009-.0027	.010-.020
351W	1976-80	2.9994-3.002	[3]	.004-.008	3	2.3103-2.311	.0008-.0026	.010-.020
351M	1977-80	2.9994-3.0002	.0008-.0025	.004-.008	3	2.3103-2.3111	.0008-.0025	.010-.020
360/359	1973-76	2.7484-2.7492	.0005-.0024	.004-.010	3	2.4380-2.4388	.0008-.0026	.010-.020
370	1979-80	2.9994-3.0002	.0008-.0026	.004-.008	3	2.4992-2.5000	.0008-.0028	.010-.020
361	1973-78	2.7479-2.7487	[1]	.004-.010	3	2.4377-2.4385	.0010-.0029	.010-.020
390	1973-78	2.7484-2.7492	.0005-.0024	.004-.010	3	2.4380-2.4385	.0008-.0026	.010-.020
391/389	1973-78	2.7479-2.7487	.0012-.0033	.004-.008	3	2.4377-2.4385	.0012-.0033	.006-.016
400	1977-80	2.9994-3.0002	.0008-.0025	.004-.008	3	2.3103-2.3111	.0008-.0025	.010-.020
401	1973-76	3.1246-3.1254	.0018-.0025	.004-.008	3	2.7092-2.7100	.0017-.0036	.006-.014
429	1979-80	2.9994-3.0002	.0008-.0026	.004-.008	3	2.4992-2.5000	.0008-.0028	.010-.020
460	1973-79	2.9994-3.002	.0008-.0026 [4]	.004-.008	3	2.4992-2.500	.008-.0015	.010-.020
475	1977-80	3.1246-3.1254	.0018-.0039	.004-.008	3	2.7092-2.7100	.0017-.0036	.006-.014
477	1973-80	3.1246-3.1254	.0018-.0039	.004-.008	3	2.7092-2.7100	.0017-.0036	.006-.014
534	1973-80	3.1246-3.1254	.0018-.0039	.004-.008	3	2.7092-2.7100	.0017-.0036	.006-.014

MD—Medium Duty.
HD—Heavy Duty.

1—No. 1, 3 .0012-.0036, No. 2, 4, 5 .0010-.0033.
2—No. 1. .0007-.0031, others .0005-.0028.
3—No. 1—.0005-.0015; All others .0008-.0015.
4—No. 1 only—All others, .0008-.0015.

VALVE SPECIFICATIONS

CU. IN. DISPLACE-MENT	YEAR	LASH (HOT) INCHES INT.	LASH (HOT) INCHES EXH.	ANGLE DEGREE FACE	ANGLE DEGREE SEAT	STEM DIA. INCHES INT.	STEM DIA. INCHES EXH.	STEM CLEARANCE INTAKE	STEM CLEARANCE EXHAUST	VALVE LIFT INCHES	VALVE SPRING LBS. @ INCHES OPEN	VALVE SPRING LBS. @ INCHES CLOSED	SPRING FREE LENGTH INCH
						SIX CYLINDER							
200	1973-75	Zero		44	45	.3103	.3101	.0008-.0025	.0010-.0027	.245	150 @ 1.22	55 @ 1.59	1.79
240	1973-74	Zero		44	45	.3420	.3420	.0010-.0027	.0010-.0027	.249	197 @ 1.30	80 @ 1.70	1.99
300	1973	Zero		44	45	.3420	.3420	.0010-.0027	.0010-.0027	.249	192 @ 118	80 @ 1.58②	1.99①
	1974-80	Zero		44	45	.3420	.3420	.0010-.0027	.0010-.0027	.249	192 @ 118	80 @ 1.58②	1.99①

VALVE SPECIFICATIONS

CU. IN. DISPLACE-MENT	YEAR	LASH (HOT) INCHES INT.	LASH (HOT) INCHES EXH.	ANGLE DEGREE FACE	ANGLE DEGREE SEAT	STEM DIA. INCHES INT.	STEM DIA. INCHES EXH.	STEM CLEARANCE INTAKE	STEM CLEARANCE EXHAUST	VALVE LIFT INCHES	VALVE SPRING LBS. @ INCHES OPEN	VALVE SPRING LBS. @ INCHES CLOSED	LENGTH INCH FREE
EIGHT CYLINDER													
302	1973-76	Zero		44	45	.3420	.3415	.0010-.0027	.0015-.0032	.2303③	200 @ 1.31	80 @ 1.69	1.94④
	1977-78	Zero		44	45	.3420	.3415	.0010-.0027	.0015-.0032	.2375⑤	200 @ 1.31	80 @ 1.58⑥	1.94①
	1979-80	Zero		44	45	.3420	.3415	.0010-.0027	.0015-.0032	.2375⑤	200 @ 1.36	78 @ 1.18⑥	2.04④
330 MD	1973-75	Zero		44	45	.3715	.3705	.0010-.0027	.0020-.0040	.2446⑨	189 @ 1.42	99@ 1.82	2.20
	1976-77	Zero		44	45	.3715	.3705	.0010-.0027	.0020-.0037	.2446⑨	220 @ 1.38	90 @ 1.82	2.12
330 HD	1973-76	Zero		44	45	.3715	.4343	.0010-.0027	.0020-.0040	.2446⑨	185 @ 1.24	80 @ 1.67	2.00
	1977	Zero		44	45	.3715	.4343	.0010-.0027	.0020-.0040	.2446⑨	200 @ 1.38	90 @ 1.82	2.12⑩
330	1978	Zero		44	45	.3715	.4343	.0010-.0027	.0020-.0040	.2446⑨	200 @ 1.38	80 @ 1.67	2.12⑩
351 W	1975-76	Zero		44	45	.3420	.34.15	.0010-.0027	.0015-.0032	.2303③	200 @ 1.34	75 @ 1.79	2.06⑪
	1977-78	Zero		44	45	.3420	.34.15	.0010-.0027	.0015-.0032	.2600	200 @ 1.34	75 @ 1.79	2.06⑪
	1979-80	Zero		44	45	.3420	.34.15	.0010-.0027	.0015-.0032	.2600	200 @ 1.36	78 @ 1.78	2.04④
351 M	1977-80	Zero		44	45	.3420	.34.15	.0010-.0027	.0015-.0032	.2350⑭	226 @ 1.39	80 @ 1.82⑬	2.06
359	1974-75	Zero		44	45	.3715	.4343	.0010-.0027	.0020-.0040	.2448	220 @ 1.38	90 @ 1.82⑮	2.12
360	1973-76	Zero		44	45	.3715	.3715	.0010-.0024	.0020-.0034	.2470	221 @ 1.30	80 @ 1.67	2.12
361	1973-78	Zero		44	45	.3715	.4343	.0010-.0027	.0020-.0040	.2448	220 @ 1.38	90 @ 1.82⑮	2.12⑩
370	1979-80	Zero		44	45	.3715	.3705	.0010-.0027	.0020-.0037	.2530⑯	225 @ 1.26	80 @ 1.72⑰	1.97⑫
389	1976	Zero		44	45	.3715	.4343	.0010-.0024	.0020-.0040	.2448	180 @ 1.24	80 @ 1.67	2.00
	1977	Zero		44	45	.3715	.4343	.0010-.0024	.0020-.0040	.2448	220 @ 1.38	90 @ 1.82	2.12
390	1973-76	Zero		44	45	.3715	.3715	.0010-.0024	.0020-.0034	.2480	200 @ 1.37	90 @ 1.67	2.12
391	1973-78	Zero		44	45	.3715	.4343	.0010-.0024	.0020-.0040	.2448	220 @ 1.38	90 @ 1.82⑱	2.12⑩
400	1977-80	Zero		44	45	.3420	.3415	.0010-.0027	.0015-.0032	.2480	225 @ 1.39	80 @ 1.82⑲	2.06
401	1973-76	.020	.020	44	45	.4354	.4340	.0010-.0026	.0024-.0040	.2780	185 @ 1.28	77 @ 1.70	2.07
429	1979-80	Zero		44	45	.3715	.3708	.0010-.0027	.0016-.0035	.2530⑩	225 @ 1.26	80 @ 1.72⑰	1.97
460	1974-80	Zero		44	45	.3420	.3420	.0010-.0027	.0010-.0027	.2530	252 @ 1.33	80 @ 1.81	2.07㉑
475	1973-80	.020	.020	44	45	.4354	.4340	.0010-.0026	.0024-.0040	.2780	185 @ 1.28	77 @ 1.70	2.02
477	1973-80	.020	.020	44	45	.4354	.4340	.0010-.0026	.0024-.0040	.2780	185 @ 1.28	77 @ 1.70	2.02
534	1973-80	.020	.020	44	45	.4354	.4340	.0010-.0026	.0024-.0040	.2780	185 @ 1.28	77 @ 1.70	2.02

MD—Medium Duty
HD—Heavy Duty
W—Winsdor
M—Modified (Formerly C)
① Exhaust 1.87 in.
② Intake Open—1.95 @ .30, Closed—80 @ 1.70
③ Exhaust .2375 in.
④ Exhaust 1.85 in.
⑤ Exhaust .2474 in.
⑥ Exhaust Open—200 @ 1.20, Closed—80 @ 1.60
⑦ Not Used
⑧ Not Used
⑨ Exhaust .2328 in.
⑩ Exhaust 2.0 in.
⑪ Exhaust 1975—2.12 in., 1977—1.87 in.
⑫ Exhaust 2.03 in. w/2 bbl. carb.
⑬ 1979-80 Exhaust Closed—83 @ 1.68
⑭ 1979-80 Exhaust 1.93 in.
⑮ Exhaust Open—190 @ 1.24, Closed—80 @ 1.67
⑯ Exhaust .265 in.
⑰ Exhaust Open—225 @ 1.32, Close—80 @ 1.78
⑱ Exhaust Open—185 @ 1.24, Closed—80 @ 1.70
⑲ 1978 Exhaust Open—225 @ 1.25, 1979-80 Exhaust Closed—84 @ 1.68
⑳ Exhaust .278 in.
㉑ 1974-76 Intake and Exhaust 2.03 in.

RING SIDE CLEARANCE SPECIFICATIONS

ENGINE (CU IN.)	YEAR	TOP COMPRESSION (IN.)	BOTTOM COMPRESSION (IN.)	OIL CONTROL (IN.)
200-6	1973-75	.0019-.0036	.0025-.0045	Snug
240-6	1973-74	.0019-.0036	.0025-.0045	Snug
300-6	1973-80	.0019-.0036	.0025-.0045	Snug
302-V8	1973-80	.002-.004	.002-.004	Snug
351W-V8	1975-80	.002-.004	.002-.004	Snug
351M-V8	1977-80	.0019-.0036	.002-.004	Snug
330-V8	1973-78	.0024-.0046	.003-.005	Snug①
360-V8	1973-76	.002-.004	.002-.004	Snug
370-V8	1979-80	.0019-.0039	.002-.004	Snug③
361-V8 359-V8	1973-78	.002-.005	.002-.005	.003-.0046
390-V8	1973-78	.002-.004	.002-.004	Snug

ENGINE (CU IN.)	YEAR	TOP COMPRESSION (IN.)	BOTTOM COMPRESSION (IN.)	OIL CONTROL (IN.)
391-V8②	1973-78	.003-.005	.003-.005	.003-.0046
400-V8	1977	.0019-.0036	.002-.004	Snug
429-V8	1979-80	.0019-.0036	.002-.004	.002-.0035
401-V8 477-V8 534-V8	1973-76	.0029-.0046	.0029-.0046	.0014-.0031
475-V8 477-V8 534-V8	1977-80	.0029-.0046	.0025-.0045	.0014-.0031
460-V8	1976-79	.002-.004	.002-.004	Snug

① 330 Heavy Duty—.0036-.0039
② Intermediate compression same as others
③ 1979-80 4 bbl. Carb—.0015-.003

Ford—Trucks, Vans and Bronco

RING GAP SPECIFICATIONS

ENGINE (CU IN.)	YEAR	TOP COMPRESSION (IN.)	BOTTOM COMPRESSION (IN.)	OIL CONTROL (IN.)
200-6	1973-75	.010-.020	.010-.020	.015-.055
240-6	1973-74	.010-.020	.010-.020	.015-.055
300-6	1973-80	.010-.020	.010-.020	.015-.055
302-V8	1973-80	.010-.020	.010-.020	.015-.055
351W-V8	1975-80	.010-.020	.010-.020	.015-.055
351M-V8	1977-80	.010-.020	.010-.020	.010-.035⑤
330-V8①	1973-78	.010-.015	.010-.015	.015-.055
360-V8①	1973-76	.015-.023	.010-.015	.015-.055
370-V8	1979-80	.010-.022	.010-.023	Steel Rails
359-V8 361-V8	1973-78	.015-.023	.010-.020	.015-.025
390-V8①	1973-78	.015-.023	.010-.020	.015-.055
391-V8	1973-78	.015-.023	.010-.020	.015-.025
400-V8	1977-80	.010-.020	.010-.020	.010-.035⑤
429-V8	1979-80	.013-.025	.010-.020	.013-.028
460-V8	1975-79	.010-.020	.010-.020	.015-.055③④
401-V8 477-V8 534-V8	1973	.018-.028	.018-.028②	.013-.028
401-V8 477-V8 534-V8	1974-76	.018-.028	.015-.025②	.013-.028
475-V8 477-V8 534-V8	1977-80	.018-.028	.015-.025	.013-.028

① If equipped with intermediate ring, gap is .015-.023 in.
② Intermediate ring same as bottom compression
③ 1979—.10-.035
④ 1977-78—.010-.030
⑤ 1978—.010-.055

TORQUE SPECIFICATIONS

CU. IN. DISPLACE-MENT	YEAR	CYLINDER HEAD BOLTS (FT. LBS.)	ROD BEARING BOLTS (FT. LBS.)	MAIN BEARING BOLTS (FT. LBS.)	CRANKSHAFT BALANCER BOLT (FT. LBS.)	FLYWHEEL TO CRANKSHAFT BOLTS (FT. LBS.)	MANIFOLD (FT. LBS.) INTAKE	MANIFOLD (FT. LBS.) EXHAUST
SIX CYLINDER								
200	1973-75	70-75	19-24	60-70	85-100	75-85	—	13-18
240	1973-74	70-75	40-45	60-70	130-150	75-85	23-28	23-28
300	1973-80	70-85②	40-45	60-70	130-150	75-85	22-32	28-33
EIGHT CYLINDER								
302	1973-80	65-72③	19-24	60-70⑦	70-90	75-85	23-25	18-24
330 MD.	1973-78	70-90⑫	40-45	95-105	70-90⑬	75-85	40-45	18-24
HD.	1973-78	70-90⑫	40-45	95-105	150-175⑬	75-85	40-45	18-24
351 W	1975-80	65-70⑧	19-24⑨	60-70⑪	70-90	75-85	23-25	18-24
351 M	1977-80	95-105④	40-45	35-45⑪	70-90	75-85	⑤	18-24
360	1973-76	80-90	40-45	95-105	70-90①	75-85	32-35	12-18
370	1979-80	70-140⑭	45-50	95-105	150-175	75-85	22-32	28-33
361/359	1973-78	70-90⑫	40-45	95-105	150-175	75-85	40-45	18-24
390	1973-76	70-90⑫	40-45	95-105	70-90①	75-85	40-45	12-18
391/389	1973-78	70-90⑫	40-45	95-105	150-175	75-85	40-45	18-24
400	1977-80	95-105④	40-45	35-45⑪	70-90	75-85	⑤	18-24
401	1973-76	170-180⑥	60-65	150-165	130-175	100-110	23-28	23-28
429	1979-80	70-140⑭	45-50	95-105	150-175	75-85	22-32	28-33
460	1974-80	130-140	40-45	95-105	70-90	75-85	25-30	28-33
477/475	1973-80	170-180⑥	60-65	130-150	130-175	100-110	25-32	22-32
534	1973-80	170-180⑥	60-65	150-165	130-175	100-110	25-32	22-32

MD—Medium Duty.
HD—Heavy Duty.
① 1975-76—130-150.
② Torque in steps; first to 55 ft. lbs., then to 65, final 70-85.
③ Torque in steps; first to 55-65 ft. lbs., then to 65-72.
④ Torque in steps; first to 75, then 95, final 105 ft. lbs.
⑤ ⅜ in-22-32 ft. lbs.; 5/16"-17-25 ft. lbs.
⑥ Torque in steps; first to 140 ft. lbs., then to 160 ft. lbs., final 170-180 ft. lbs.
⑦ 1978 (95-105)
⑧ 1976 torque in steps; first to 50, then to 60, finals to 65-70
1977-80 torque in steps first to 85, then to 05, final to 105-112
⑨ 1977-80 (40-45)
⑩ Not Used
⑪ 1978-80 (95-105)
⑫ 1973-80 torque in steps first to 70, then to 80, final to 90
⑬ 1974-79 ⅝" (130-150)
¾" (150-175)
⑭ 1979-80 torque in steps; first to 70-80; then to 100-110; final to 130-140

WHEEL ALIGNMENT SPECIFICATIONS — EXCEPT BRONCO

YEAR	MODEL	CASTER (deg) MAXIMUM	CASTER (deg) MINIMUM	CASTER (deg) OPTIMUM	CAMBER (deg) MAXIMUM	CAMBER (deg) MINIMUM	CAMBER (deg) OPTIMUM	TOE-IN (in.)
1973	E-100, 200	8½P	3½P	—	3½P	½P	—	⅛
	E-300	7½P	3½P	—	3½P	½P	—	⅛

WHEEL ALIGNMENT SPECIFICATIONS — EXCEPT BRONCO

YEAR	MODEL	CASTER (deg) MAXIMUM	CASTER (deg) MINIMUM	CASTER (deg) OPTIMUM	CAMBER (deg) MAXIMUM	CAMBER (deg) MINIMUM	CAMBER (deg) OPTIMUM	TOE-IN (in.)
	F-150, 250, 350	8½P	3½P	—	3½P	½P	—	⅛
	F-100 (4WD)	4¼P	2¾P	3½P	2P	1P	½P	5/32
	F-250 (4WD)	4½P	3½P	2½P	2P	1P	½P	5/32
	P-350 P-3500	5¼P	3¾P	4½P	⅞P	⅜P	⅝P	⅛
	P-400, 4000 P-500, 5000	4¼P	2¾P	3½P	1P	0	½P	⅛
1974	E-100, 150, 200, 250	8½P	2½P	—	3½P	½P	—	⅛
	E-300, 350	7½P	2½P	—	3½P	½P	—	⅛
	F-150, 250	8½P	½P	—	2½P	½N	—	⅛
	F-350	8½P	½P	—	3P	0	—	⅛
	F-100 (4WD) F-150 (4WD)	4¼P	2¾P	3½P	2P	1P	1½P	5/32
	F-250 (4WD)	4½P	3½P	4P	2P	1P	1½P	5/32
	P-350 P-3500	5¼P	3¾P	4½P	⅞P	⅜P	⅜P	⅛
	P-400, 500 P-4000, 5000	4¼P	2¾P	3½P	1P	0	½P	⅛
1975	E-100, 150, 250	8½P	½P	—	2½P	½N	—	⅛
	E-350	7½P	2½P	—	3½P	½P	—	⅛
	F-100, 250	8½P	½P	—	2½P	½N	—	⅛
	F-350	8½P	½P	—	3P	0	—	3/32
	F-100 (4WD)	4¼P	2¾P	3½	2P	1P	1½P	5/32
	F-250 (4WD)	4½P	3½P	4P	2P	1P	1½P	5/32
	P-350, 3500	5¼P	3¾P	4½	⅞P	⅜P	⅝P	⅛
	P-400, 500, 4000, 5000	4¼P	2¾P	3½	1P	0	½P	⅛
1976	E-100, 150, 260	8½P	½P	—	3½P	½P	—	⅛
	E-350	7½P	2½P	—	3½P	½P	—	⅛
	F-100, 250	8½P	½P	—	2½P	½N	—	⅛
	F-350	8½P	½P	—	3P	0	—	⅛
	F-100, 150 (4WD)	4¼P	2¾P	4½P	2P	1P	1½P	5/32
	F-250 (4WD)	4½P	3½P	4P	2P	1P	1½P	5/32
	P-350	5¼P	3¾P	4½P	⅞P	⅜P	⅝P	⅛
	P-400, 500	4¼P	2¾P	3½P	1P	0	½P	⅛
1977	E-100, 150	5¾P	2P	—	1¾P	¾N	—	⅛
	E-250, 350	8¼P	4P	—	2¼P	½N	—	⅛
	F-100, 150, 250 (6200-6900 GVW)	9P	4P	—	3P	1N	—	⅛
	F-250 (7800-8000 GVW) F-250 Super Cab	8½P	3¼P	—	3¼P	0	—	⅛
	F-250 (8100 GVW S.C.) F-350	9P	3¼P	—	3¾P	0	—	⅛
	F-150 (4WD)	4¼P	2¾P	3½P	2P	1P	1½P	5/32
	F-250 (4WD)	5P	3P	4P	1½P	½P	1P	5/32
	P-500	4¼P	2¾P	3½P	1P	0	½P	⅛
1978	F-250 (4WD) F-150 (4WD) P-600	5P 4¼P 4¼P	2⅛P 2¾P 2¾P	4P 3½ + 8P 3½P	½P 2P 1P	½P 1P 0	½P 1½P ½P	5/32 3/32 ⅛
1979-80	F-150 (4WD) F-150 (4WD) S/C① F-250 (4WD) F-350 (4WD)	9½P 5½P 5½P 5½P	6½ 2½P 2½P 2½P	3½ + 8P 4P 4P 4P	3P 3P 3P 3P	1P 0 0 0	1½P ½P ½P ½P	3/32 3/32 3/32 3/32

Note: Maximum variation between wheels—½°

P—Positive

N—Negative

① S/C—Super Cab

WHEEL ALIGNMENT SPECIFICATIONS — EXCEPT BRONCO

1978-80

The front wheel specifications and the method of checking caster, camber and toe alignments are determined with the vehicle at its normal operating height and altitude, provided the front ride height within the range shown in the charts below. The only exceptions to this method of front wheel alignment are models F-150-250 (4x4) and P-600.

1978

RIDE AT LEAST	HEIGHT NOT MORE THAN	F-100/150/250* 6200-6900 GVW② REGULAR CAB				F-250 7800-8000 GVW REGULAR CAB*② 6350-7800 GVW SUPER CAB			
		CAMBER		CASTER		CAMBER		CASTER	
		MIN.①	MAX.	MIN.①	MAX.	MIN.①	MAX.	MIN.①	MAX.
2.75	3.00	−1°	+½°	8¼°	9⅝°	−½°	+1°	7⅝°	8⅞°
3.00	3.25	−½°	+1°	7¾°	9°	−¼°	+1½°	6⅞°	8⅜°
3.25	3.50	−¼°	+1½°	7°	8⅜°	0°	+1¾°	5⅜°	7¾°
3.50	3.75	0°	+1¾°	6¼°	7⅜°	+½°	+2¼°	5¾°	7°
3.75	4.00	+½°	+2¼°	5¾°	7°	+¾°	+2½°	5°	6½°
4.00	4.25	+¾°	+2½°	5°	6½°	+1¼°	+3°	4½°	5⅞°
4.25	4.50	+1¼°	+3°	4½°	5⅞°	+1¾°	+3¼°	3⅞°	5⅛°
4.50	4.75	+1⅝°	+3¼°	3¾°	5°	+2°	+3½°	3⅛°	4½°
4.75	5.00	+2°	+3¾°	3⅛°	4½°	+2⅜°	+4⅛°	2½°	4°
5.00	5.25	+2⅜°	+4⅛°	2½°	4°	+2¾°	+4½°	2°	3¼°
5.25	5.50	—	—	—	—	—	—	—	—
5.50	5.75	—	—	—	—	—	—	—	—

F-350 (ALL)*② F-250 8100 GVW SUPER CAB F-250 SUPER CAB W/RPO SUSPENSION				E-100/150*④				E-250/350*③			
CAMBER		CASTER		CAMBER		CASTER		CAMBER		CASTER	
MIN.①	MAX.	MIN.①	MAX.	MIN.①	MAX.	MIN.①	MAX.	MIN.①	MAX.	MIN.①	MAX.
−⅜°	−¼°	9¾°	10⅞°	—	—	—	—	—	—	—	—
−1°	+⅝°	9°	10¼°	—	—	—	—	—	—	—	—
−½°	+1°	8¼°	9⅝°	—	—	—	—	—	—	—	—
−¼°	+1½°	7⅝°	8⅝°	—	—	—	—	—	—	—	—
0°	+1¾°	6⅞°	8⅜°	—	—	—	—	—	—	—	—
+½°	+2¼°	6⅜°	7¼°	−¾°	+½°	+3¾°	+6½°	−1°	+¾°	+6¼°	+9°
+¾°	+2½°	5¾°	7°	−½°	+¾°	+3¼°	+5¾°	−½°	+1¼°	+5¾°	+8¼°
+1¼°	+3°	5⅛°	6½°	0°	+1¼°	+2½°	+5¼°	0°	+1¾°	+5¼°	+7¾°
+1¾°	+3¼°	4½°	5⅞°	+½°	+1¾°	+2°	+4½°	+½°	+2¼°	+4½°	+7¼°
+2°	+3¼°	3⅞°	5⅛°	+1¼°	+2½°	+1¼°	+4°	+1°	+2¾°	+4°	+6½°
—	—	—	—	+1¾°	+3¼°	+¾°	+3¼°	+1½°	+3¼°	+3¼°	+6°
—	—	—	—	+1½°	+3¾°	0°	+2¾°	—	—	—	—

* Toe-in should be checked using a trammel bar with frictionless plates
① All vehicles with normal operating altitudes
② Toe-in range for these vehicles is 1/32″ out to 7/32″ in (3/32″ nominal)
③ Toe range for these vehicles is 3/32″ out to 5/32″ in (1/32″ nominal)
④ Toe range for these vehicles is 0 to ¼″ in

NOTE: MEASURE FROM BOTTOM FLANGE OF SPRING SEAT LOWER SURFACE, (AT INSIDE AREA OF JOUNCE BUMPER BRACKET), TO TOP OF FRONT AXLE BEAM.

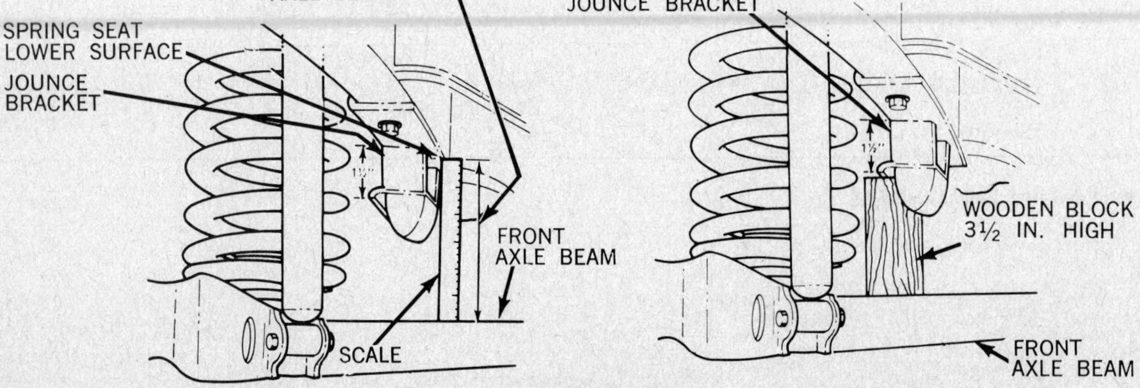

Ride height measurement procedure—E-100-E-350 Vehicles (© Ford Motor Co.)

1979-80

RIDE AT LEAST	HEIGHT NOT MORE THAN	F-100 (ALL) F-150 (ALL) ①② F-250 (6200-6800 GVW				F250 R/C 7700-7900 GVW F-250 S/C 6300-7800 GVW ①②			
		CAMBER		CASTER		CAMBER		CASTER	
		MIN.	MAX.	MIN.	MAX.	MIN.	MAX.	MIN.	MAX.
2.75	3.00	−2°	−¼°	8⅜°	9⅝°	−1⅞°	−¼°	7¾°	9°
3.00	3.25	−1½°	+⅛°	7¾°	9°	−1½°	+⅛°	7°	8⅜°
3.25	3.50	−1⅛°	+½°	7°	8⅜°	−1⅛°	+½°	6⅜°	7¾°
3.50	3.75	−¾°	+1°	6¼°	7⅝°	−¾°	+⅞°	5⅞°	7⅛°
3.75	4.00	−⅜°	+1¼°	5⅞°	7⅛°	−⅜°	+1¼°	5⅛°	6½°
4.00	4.25	0°	+1⅝°	5⅛°	6½°	0°	+1⅝°	4½°	5⅞°
4.25	4.50	+⅜°	+2°	4½°	5⅞°	⅜°	+2°	3⅞°	5¼°
4.50	4.75	+¾°	+2⅜°	3¾°	5¼°	⅞°	2½°	3¼°	4⅝°
4.75	5.00	1¼°	+2¾°	3¼°	4⅝°	1¼°	2¾°	2⅝°	4°
5.00	5.25	1⅞°	+3⅞°	2½°	4°	1⅝°	3⅛°	2°	3⅜°
5.25	5.50	—	—	—	—	—	—	—	—

F-350 (ALL) F-250 S/C 3100 GVW①② F-250 S/C RPO SUSPENSION				E-100/150①③				E-250/350①③			
CAMBER		CASTER		CAMBER		CASTER		CAMBER		CASTER	
MIN.	MAX.	MIN.	MAX.	MIN.	MAX.	MIN.	MAX.	MIN.	MAX.	MIN.	MAX.
−2⅛°	−⅝°	9⅝°	11°	—	—	—	—	—	—	—	—
−1¾°	−¼°	8⅞°	10⅜°	—	—	—	—	—	—	—	—
−1⅜°	+⅛°	8⅜°	9¾°	−1¾°	−¼°	6¼°	8°	−1¾°	−¼°	9°	10½°
−1⅛°	+½°	7¾°	9°	−1½°	−¼°	5¾°	7¼°	−1½°	+¼°	8½°	9¾°
−¾°	+¾°	7°	8⅜°	−1°	+¾°	5°	6¾°	−1°	+¾°	7⅞°	9°
−¼°	+1¼°	6⅜°	7¾°	−½°	+1¼°	4½°	5¾°	−½°	+1¼°	7⅛°	8½°
0°	+1⅝°	5¾°	7⅛°	0°	+1¾°	4°	5¼°	0°	+1¾°	6½°	7¾°
+⅜°	+2°	5⅛°	6½°	+½°	+2¼°	3¼°	4½°	+½°	+2¼°	5¾°	7°
+¾°	+2⅛°	4½°	5⅞°	+1°	+2¾°	2½°	4°	+1°	+2¾°	5¼°	6½°
+1¼°	+2¾°	3⅞°	5¼°	+1½°	+3¼°	2°	3¼°	+1½°	+3¼°	4⅝°	6°
—	—	—	—	+2°	+3¾°	1½°	2¾°	+2°	+3¾°	4°	5½°

① All vehicles with normal operating altitude
② Toe setting is 3/32″ in
③ Toe setting is 1/32″ in

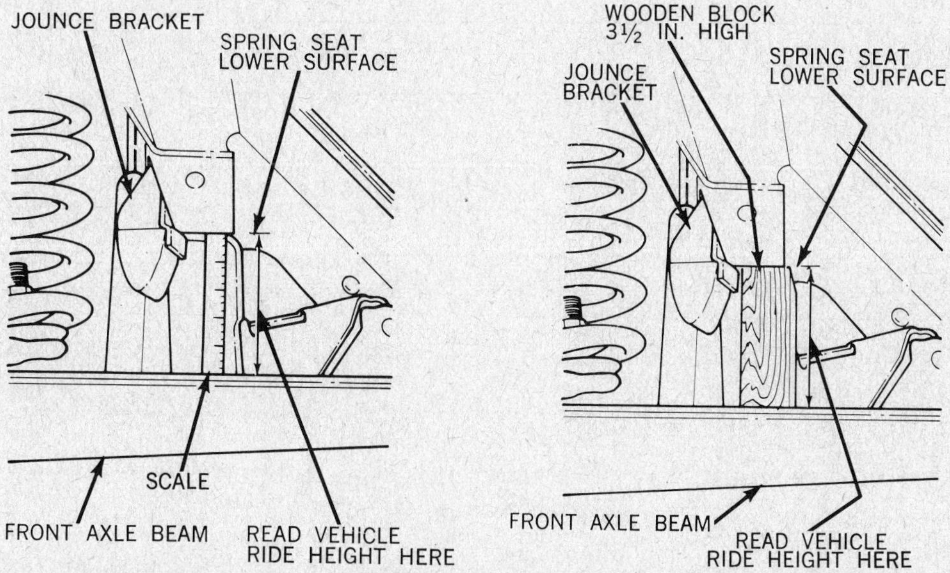

Ride height measurement procedure—F-100-F-350 Vehicles (© Ford Motor Co.)

CASTER SPECIFICATIONS — MEDIUM AND HEAVY DUTY TRUCKS

VEHICLE	AXLE CAPACITY (lbs)	YEAR	CASTER (deg) ① Minimum	CASTER (deg) ① Maximum
F-B 700, 750	All	1973-76	3P	4P
L-N 500, 750	All	1973-76	4P	5P
C-CT Series	6000, 7000, 9000, 12000 Conventional, 15000	1973-76	2½P	3½P
	12000 Center-Point	1973-76	0	1P
L-LT-LN-LNT	6000, 7000	1973-76	3¼P	4¼P
800-900, 9000	9000,	1973-76	3½P	4½P
	16000, 18000, 20000	1973-76	3P	4P
	12000 Conventional 12000 Steer-Ease	1973-76	1 15/16P	3 1/16P
W-WT 9000	12000 Conventional 15000 Conventional	1973 1973-76	3P	4P
	12000 Center-Point	1973	0	1P
	12000 Conventional	1974-76	2½P	3½P
F-600 (4WD)	7500	1973-76	2½P	3½P

① Vehicle unladen
P—Positive
N—Negative

Note: Caster Specifications are for a level frame front to rear. If the frame is lower at the rear, subtract the frame angle from the angle on the checking equipment. If the frame is lower at the front, add the frame angle to the angle on the checking equipment.

CASTER SPECIFICATIONS —MEDIUM AND HEAVY DUTY TRUCKS

VEHICLE	YEAR	AXLE CAPACITY (lbs)	CASTER (deg.)
F-600, LN-600 Hydraulic Brakes	1977-80	5000 5500	3½° ± ½° F-B Series 4½° ± ½° LN Series
B-600, F-C-B-LN-600-700, LT-LNT-800, LT-800, F-C-LN-6000, F-B-C-7000, L-800-900, LN-800 Hydraulic Brakes	1977-80	6000 7000	3½° ± ½° F-B Series (Medium) 4½° ± ½° LN (Medium) 3¾° ± ½° L-LN (Heavy) 3° ± ½ °C Series
F-600-700, B-LN-600-700, LN-F-B-700, F-B-LN-7000, F-800 Air Brakes	1977-80	7000 Medium	3° ± ½° F-B 3°30′ ± ½° L
F-C-L-LN-700-7000, LT-800, C-L-LT-LTS-800-900, CT-LN-LNT-800 Hydraulic Brakes	1977-80	9000	4° ± ½° All Except C Series 3° ± ½° C Series
L-LT-LN-LNT-800, L-LN-LNT-8000, LNT-9000, L-LN-LNT-900, F-LT-LNT-800, C-600-700, C-7000 Air Brakes	1977-80	7000 Heavy	2°51′ ± ½° C (9.5 Frame) 4°30′ ± ½° C (9.76 Frame) 5° ± ½° L (Except Drop Frame) 3°30′ ± ½° LN-LNT w/Drop Frame
F-LN-700-7000, F-800 Air Brakes	1977-80	9000 Medium	3° ± ½° F-B 3°30′ ± ½° LN
L-LT-LTS-LN-LNT-800-900—8000-9000, LT-LNT-800, C-700-800-9-00—7000-8000, CT-800-900-8000 Air Brakes	1977-80	9000 Heavy	5° ± ½° All L Except Drop Frame 3°30′ ± ½° LN-LNT w/Drop Frame 2°51′ ± ½° C w/9.5 Frame 4°30′ ± ½°C w/9.76 Frame
L-LT-LTS-LN-LNT-C-CT-800-900, L-LT-LTS-LN-LNT-8000-9000, LNT-LT-800, C-8000, CT-8000, W-WT-9000 Air Brakes	1977-80	12000	3° ± ½° C w/9.5 Frame L-W w/2° Wedge 3°30′ ± ½° L w/Drop Frame 4°30′ ± ½° C w/9.76 Frame
C-900, CT-800-900, CT-8000, LT-800-900, LTS-LN-LNT-8000-9000, LNT-LT-800, C-8000, CT-8000 Air Brakes	1977-80	16000 18000 20000	3° ± ½° w/1600 Axle 3½° ± ½° All w/16-18-20000 lb. Axles Except C

CAMBER SPECIFICATIONS — MEDIUM AND HEAVY DUTY TRUCKS

VEHICLE	AXLE CAPACITY (lbs)	YEAR	CAMBER (deg)① Minimum	CAMBER (deg)① Maximum
All	5000, 5500, 6000, 7000	1973-76	¼P	1P
All Except L-LT-LTS-LN-LNT 800-9000	9000, 12000 Conventional	1973-76	D(L), ½N(R)	¾P(L), ¼P(R)
	12000 Center-Point	1973-76	⅛P(L), ⅜N(R)	⅞P(L), ⅜(PR)
	15000	1973-76	¼P	1P
L-LT-LTS-LN-LNT 800-9000	9000, 12000 Conventional, 12000 Steer-Ease, 16000, 18000, 20000	1973-76	¼P	1P
F-600 (4WD)	7500	1973-76	½P	1½P
F-600, LN-600 Hydraulic Brakes	5000 5500	1977-80	¼P	1P
B-600, F-C-B-LN-600-700, LT-LNT-800, LT-800, F-C-LN-6000, F-B-C-7000, L-800-900, LN-800 Hydraulic Brakes	6000 7000	1977-80	¼P	1P
F-600-700, B-LN-600-700, LN-F-B-700, F-B-LN-7000, F-800 Air Brakes	7000 Medium	1977-80	¼P	1P
F-C-L-LN-700-7000, LT-800, C-L-LT-LTS-800-900, CT-LN-LNT-800 Hydraulic Brakes	9000	1977-80	0 ¼N ¼P	¾P② ½P③ 1P④
L-LT-LN-LNT-800, L-LN-LNT-8000, LNT-9000, L-LN-LNT-900, F-LT-LNT-800, C-600-700, C-7000 Air Brakes	7000 Heavy	1977-80	¼P	1P
F-LN-700-7000, F-800 Air Brakes	9000 Medium	1977-80	¼P	1P
L-LT-LTS-LN-LNT-800-900—8000-9000, LT-LNT-800, C-700-800-900—7000-8000, CT-800-900—8000 Air Brakes	9000 Heavy	1977-80	¼P	1P
L-LT-LTS-LN-LNT-C-CT-800-900, L-LT-LTS-LN-LNT-8000-9000, LNT-LT-800, C-8000, CT-8000, W-WT-9000 Air Brakes	12000	1977-80	¼P	1P
C-900, CT-800-900, CT-8000, LT-800-900, LTS-LN-LNT-8000-9000, LNT-LT-800, C-8000, CT-8000 Air Brakes	16000 18000 20000	1977-80	¼P	1P

① Vehicle Empty
P—Positive
N—Negative
L—Left
R—Right

② LH C Series
③ BW C Series
④ All except C Series

TOE-IN SPECIFICATIONS — MEDIUM AND HEAVY DUTY TRUCKS

VEHICLE	AXLE CAPACITY (lbs)	YEAR	TOE-IN (in.)① Minimum	TOE-IN (in.)① Maximum
All Exc. w-wt w/Center Point	5000, 5500, 6000, 7000, 12000 Center-Point	1973-80	3/16	5/16
All Exc. L-w-wt Series conventional or Steer-Ease	9000, 12000 Conventional, 12000 Steer-Ease, 15000, 16000, 18000, 20000	1973-80	5/16	7/16
W-WT 9000 w/Center-Point	1200 Center-Point②	1973-80	3/16	11/16
F-600 (4WD)	7500	1973-80	1/16	3/16
L-w-wt Series w/12000 Conv. or 12000 Steer-Ease	12000 Conventional 12000 Steer-Ease	1973-80	3/16	5/16

① Vehicle Unladen
② No part of the tie-rod clamp can be in the area between 10 o'clock and 2 o'clock.

BRONCO WHEEL ALIGNMENT

YEAR	CASTER① (Deg.)	CAMBER① (Deg.)	TOE-IN (In.)	KIN PIN INCLINATION (Deg.)
1973-75	3½	1½	5/32	8½
1976	4½	1½	5/32	8½
1977-78	3½	1½	5/32	8½
1978-80	+ 3½ Min. + 8 Max.	1½	3/32	8½

① The Caster and Camber angles are designed into the front axle and can not be adjusted.

ENGINE IDENTIFICATION SPECIFICATIONS

The Engine Identification Code letter is the fourth character in the vehicle identification number for Ford vehicles. See the charts below for code letter information.

GASOLINE ENGINE CODES

Engines	Model Year & Engine Code 1973	1974	1975	1976	1977	1978	1979-80
200—6 Cylinder 1V	T	T	T	—	—	—	—
240—6 Cylinder 1V	A	A	—	—	—	—	—
300—6 Cylinder 1V	B	B	B	B	B	B	B
HD Light Truck	—	—	—	—	—	—	K
Heavy Truck	—	—	—	—	—	G	G
302—V8 2V	G	G	G	G	G	G	G
330—V8 2V	C	C	C	C	C	C	—
Heavy Truck	D	D	D	D	D	D	—
351—V8 2V	—	—	H	H	H	H	—
359—V8 2V	—	K	K	—	—	—	—
360—V8 2V	Y	Y	Y	Y	—	—	—
361—V8 2V	E	E	E	P	P	P	—
4V	—	—	—	E	E	E	—
370—V8 2V Medium Truck	—	—	—	—	—	—	C
Heavy Truck	—	—	—	—	—	—	A
4V Medium Truck	—	—	—	—	—	—	M
Heavy Truck	—	—	—	—	—	—	B
389—V8 4V	—	—	—	F	F	—	—
390—V8 2V	H	H	H	H	—	—	—
V8 4V	—	M	M	—	—	—	—
391—V8 4V	F	F	F	F	F	F	—
400—V8 2V	—	—	—	—	S	S	S
401—V8 2V	H	H	H	H	—	—	—
429—V8 4V	—	—	—	—	—	—	C
460—V8 4V Econoline	—	—	A	A	A	A	A
4V Light Truck	J	J	J	J	J	J	J
475—V8 4V	J	J	J	J	J	J	J
477—V8 4V	K	K	K	K	K	K	K
534—V8 4V	L	L	L	L	L	L	L

DIESEL ENGINE CODES

CATERPILLAR

Engines	Model Year & Engine Code 1973	1974	1975	1976	1977	1978	1979-80
522 V8 150HP	U	U	U	U	—	—	—
522 V8 175HP	V	V	V	V	—	—	—
573 V8 200HP	4	4	4	4	—	—	—
636 V8 225HP	C	C	C	C	C	C	C
636 3208 175HP	—	—	—	—	B	B	B
636 3208 200HP	—	—	—	—	Q	Q	Q
636 3208 210HP	—	—	—	—	D	D	D
893 3400 280HP 1900RPM	—	—	—	—	J	J	J
893 3400 280HP 2100RPM	—	—	—	—	H	H	H
893 3400 325HP	—		—	--	M	M	M

DIESEL ENGINE CODES

DETROIT

Engines	Model Year & Engine Code 1973	1974	1975	1976	1977	1978	1979-80
159 3V-53N 94HP	K	K	K	K	—	—	—
318 6V-53N 195HP	8	8	—	—	—	—	—
318 6V-53T 230HP	—	—	—	—	—	—	1
318 6V-53TT 210HP	—	—	—	—	—	1	—
318 6V-53TT 225HP	—	—	—	—	—	0	—
426 6-71N 228HP	—	—	—	—	—	2	2
552 8V-71N 263HP	—	—	—	—	7	7	—
552 8V-71N 280HP	—	—	—	—	6	6	—
552 8V-71N 304HP	—	—	—	—	T	T	T
552 8V-71T 308HP	—	—	—	—	N	N	—
552 8V-71T 335HP	—	—	—	—	E	E	—
552 8V-71T 350HP	—	—	—	—	Y	Y	Y
552 8V-71TT 305HP	—	—	—	—	4	4	4

CUMMINS

Engines	Model Year & Engine Code 1973	1974	1975	1976	1977	1978	1979-80
555 V8 210HP	—	A	—	A	—	—	—
555 V8 225HP	—	H	H	H	—	—	—
855 NH230 230HP 1900RPM	—	—	—	—	R	—	—
855 NTC230 230HP 1900RPM	—	—	—	—	—	X	X
855 NTC230 230HP 2100RPM	—	—	—	—	—	9	9
855 NTC250 250HP 1900RPM	—	—	—	—	2	5	—
855 NTC250 250HP 2100RPM	—	—	—	—	F	F	F
855 NTC270PT 270HP	—	—	—	—	K	K	—
855 NTC290 255HP 1900RPM	—	—	—	—	9	—	—
855 NTC290 255HP 2100RPM	—	—	—	—	3	—	—
855 NTC290 290HP 1900RPM	—	—	—	—	U	U	U
855 NTC350 290HP 2100RPM	—	—	—	—	V	V	V
855 NTC350 300HP 1900RPM	—	—	—	—	X	—	—
855 NTC350 300HP 2100RPM	—	—	—	—	W	—	—
855 NTC350 320HP 1900RPM	—	—	—	—	G	3	—
855 NTC350 335HP 1900RPM	—	—	—	—	I	—	—
855 NTC350 335HP 2100RPM	—	—	—	—	0	—	—
855 NTC350 350HP 1900RPM	—	—	—	—	P	P	P
855 NTC350 350HP 2100RPM	—	—	—	—	L	L	L
903 V903 295HP	—	—	—	—	—	G	—

General Information

All 1973-74 engines are equipped with Motorcraft dual advance distributors. Starting in 1975, all light trucks began using the Motorcraft electronic ignition system. The medium and heavy duty trucks with gas engines continued to have standard point type ignition systems.

Starting in 1979, all trucks are equipped with the Dura Spark II, solid state breakerless system, with the exception of Super Duty vehicles. The system incorporated in these vehicles is the solid state breakerless system with standard distributor cap and wires.

Rotation is clockwise on the six cylinder engines and counterclockwise on the V8 engines.

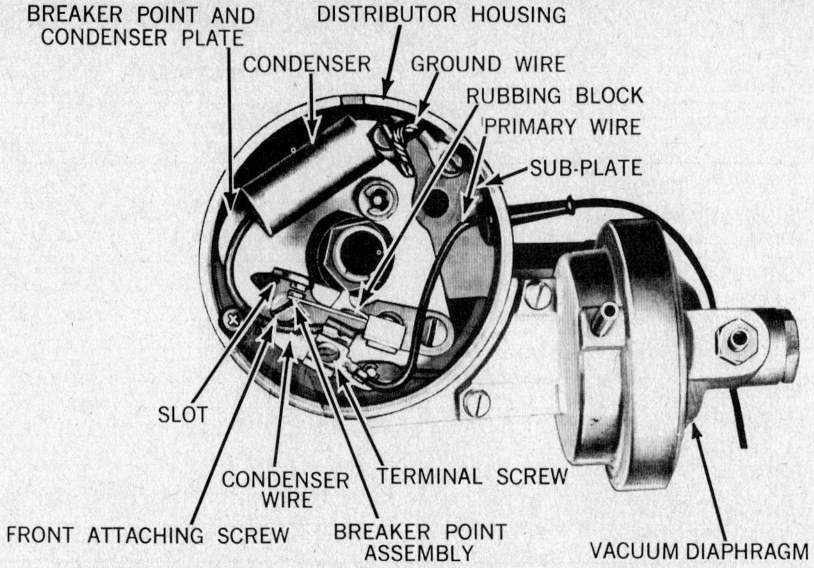

Autolite dual diaphragm distributor—6 cylinder (© Ford Motor Co.)

DISTRIBUTOR

Distributor Removal & Installation

All Types

1. a. On a conventional ignition system, disconnect the primary wire at the coil.
   b. On a transistor ignition system, disconnect the primary wire from quick disconnect terminal.
   c. On a electronic ignition, disconnect the primary wire from the wiring harness.
2. Disconnect the vacuum line(s) at the distributor.
3. Remove the distributor cap.
4. Scribe a mark on the distributor body, indicating the position of the rotor. Scribe another mark on the body and engine block, indicating the position of the body in the block. These marks will insure that the distributor will be correctly timed when it is reinstalled.
5. Remove hold down bolt and clamp or retaining bolt and lockwasher and lift the distributor out of the block. *NOTE: Do not rotate the crankshaft while the distributor is removed, or it will be necessary to time the engine.*
6. To install, position the distributor in the block with the rotor aligned to the mark previously scribed on the distributor and the marks on the distributor and block aligned.
7. If the crankshaft has been rotated while the distributor was removed, the distributor must be timed with respect to the crankshaft.

   a. For Conventional and Transistor ignitions: Rotate the engine until the No. 1 piston is at TDC of the compression stroke. Position the distributor in the block with the rotor in the No. 1 firing position. Rotate the distributor until the points just about open. *NOTE: Make sure the oil pump intermediate shaft properly engages the distributor shaft. It may be necessary to crank the engine with the starter after the distributor gear is engaged in order*

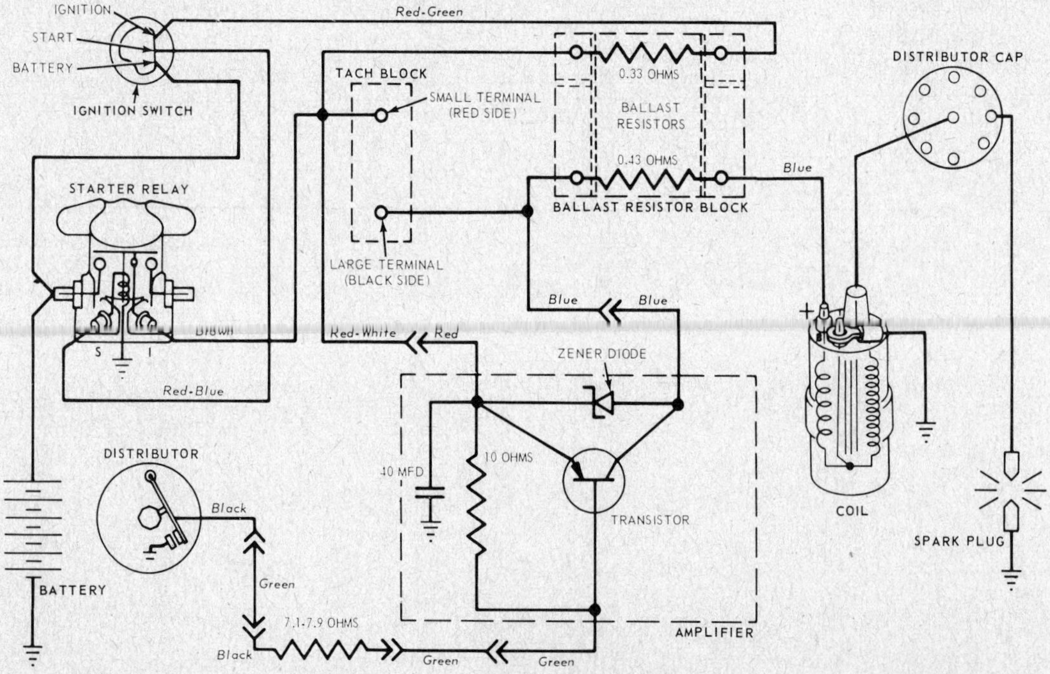

Transistor ignition system (© Ford Motor Co.)

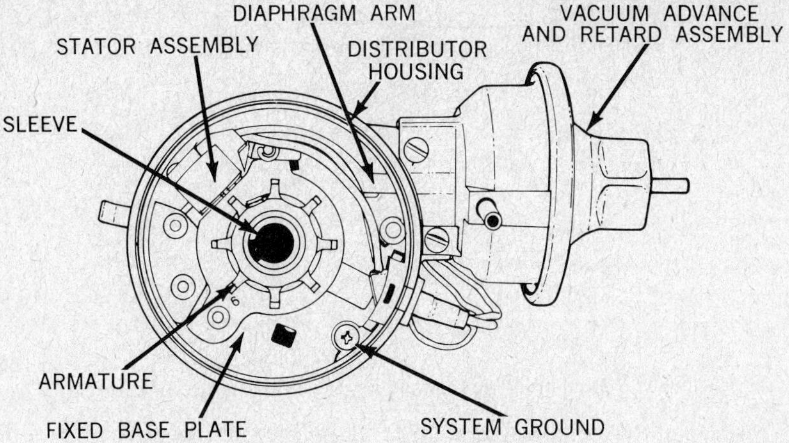

Electronic ignition distributor (© Ford Motor Co.)

to engage the oil pump intermediate shaft.

b. For Electronic ignition systems: Rotate the engine until the No. 1 piston is at TDC on the compression stroke. Align the correct initial timing mark with the pointer on the crankshaft damper. Position the distributor in the block with one of the armature segments aligned with the pickup on the stator and the rotor in the No. 1 firing position. The terminal housing is marked with an embossed "No.1" at the No. 1 terminal. *NOTE: Make sure the oil pump intermediate shaft properly engages the distributor shaft.* It may be necessary to crank the engine with the starter after the distributor drive is partially engaged in order to engage the oil pump intermediate shaft. If the previous step was necessary, return the crankshaft to the initial timing alignment.

8. Install retaining clamp and bolt or retaining bolt and lockwasher, but do not tighten. On electronic ignition distributors, rotate the distributor to advance the timing to the position where the armature tooth is properly aligned.
9. Connect primary wire and install distributor cap.
10. Check and reset ignition timing as described below.
11. Tighten hold down clamp bolt or retaining bolt.
12. Connect vacuum hose(s).

Breaker Point Replacement

1. Remove the distributor cap and rotor.
2. Disconnect the primary and condenser wires from breaker point assembly.
3. Remove the breaker point assembly and condenser retainer screws and lift the breaker point assembly and condenser out of the vehicle.
4. To install, place breaker point assembly and condenser in position and install retaining screws. Be sure to place the ground wire under the breaker point assembly screw farthest from the breaker point contacts on V8 engine distributor or under the condenser retaining screw on 6-cylinder engine distributor.
5. Align and adjust the breaker points.
6. Connect primary and condenser wires to the breaker point assembly.
7. Install rotor and distributor cap.
8. Set ignition timing to specifications.

Transistor Ignition System

The tachometer block is used to connect a tachometer or other test equipment into the circuit.

CAUTION: Do not connect test equipment into the circuit in any other manner, or reading will be inaccurate and damage may occur to the resistor, or change its operating characteristics.

Connect the tachometer red lead to the tachometer block small terminal and black lead to the large terminal when making tests.

Ignition timing and breaker point gap are set in the conventional manner as described above.

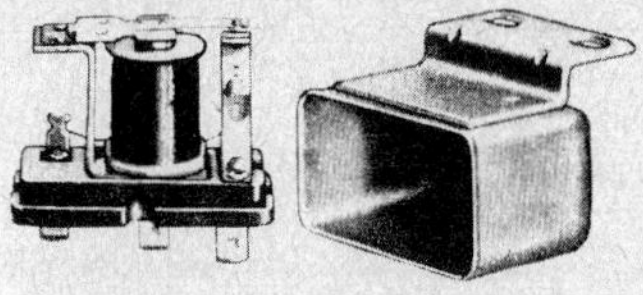

Field relay transistor ignition (© Ford Motor Co.)

Breakerless Distributor (Solid State)

Starting in 1975 all light truck engines are equipped with the breakerless type electronic ignition system. The convenitonal contact breaker points and condenser in the distributor are replaced by a permanent magnet low-voltage generator. The generator consists of an armature with four or six gear-like teeth mounted on the top of the distributor shaft, and a permanent magnet inside a small coil. The coil is riveted in place to provide a preset air gap with the armature. The distributor base, cap, rotor and vacuum and centrifugal spark advance are about the same as the conventional system.

The distributor is wired to a solid state module in the engine compartment. Inside the module is an electronic circuit board which consists of inner connecting resistors, capacitors, transistors and diodes. The module senses a signal from the magnetic generator to perform the switching function of conventional points and it senses and controls dwell.

Unless a malfunction occurs, or the distributor is moved or replaced, the initial ignition timing remains constant. Because the low voltage coil in the distributor is riveted in position, the air gap adjustment with the rear tooth armature is not possible.

Tachometer-to-Coil Connection—Electronic Ignition

The new solid state ignition coil connector allows a tachometer test

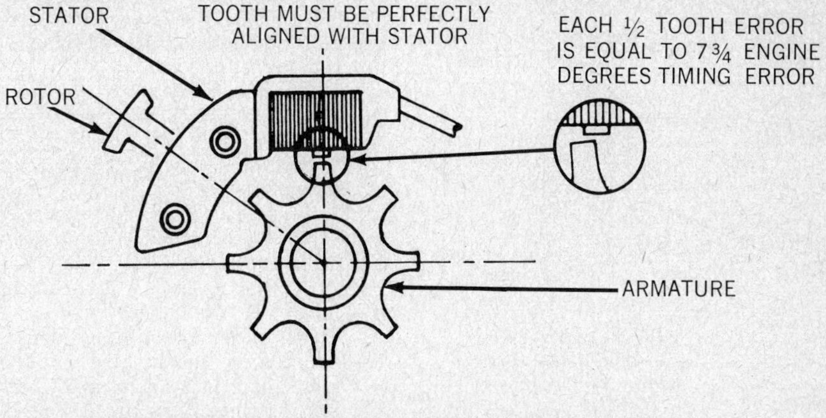

Electronic ignition static timing position (© Ford Motor Co.)

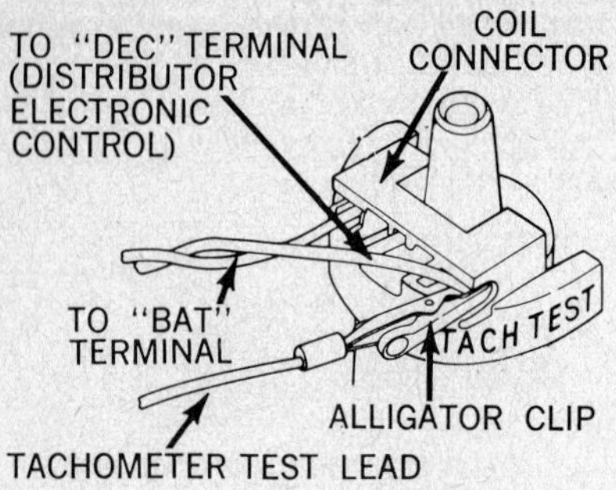

Tachometer to coil connection—Electronic ignition (© Ford Motor Co.)

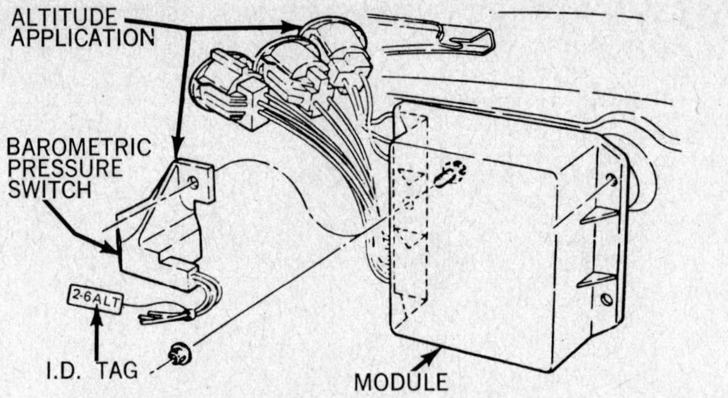

Dual mode timing module (© Ford Motor Co.)

lead with an alligator-type clip to be connected to the DEC (Distributor Electronic Control) terminal without removing the connector.

When engine rpm must be checked, install the tachometer alligator clip into the "TACH TEST" cavity as shown. If the coil connector must be removed, grasp the wires and pull horizontally until it disconnects from the terminals.

Module Test

If the electronic module is suspected of being defective, proceed as follows:

1. Without removing the existing module from the vehicle, unplug the connectors from the electronic module. Connect a known good module. The substitute module does not have to be fastened to the vehicle to operate properly.
2. Attempt to start the engine. If the engine starts and accelerates properly, proceed to step three. If the engine will still not start, the fault is in the wiring or other vehicle systems. Inspect and repair as necessary.
3. Reconnect the original module. Again attempt to start and run the engine. If the engine once again will not start, remove the original module and replace with a new one. If, however, the engine will now start and run on the original module, the module is not defective.
4. With the engine operating, check all connections in the primary wiring of the ignition system for such faults as poor wire crimp to terminal or improper engagement. The faulty connection will be observed when the engine misfires or stops. Correct as necessary.

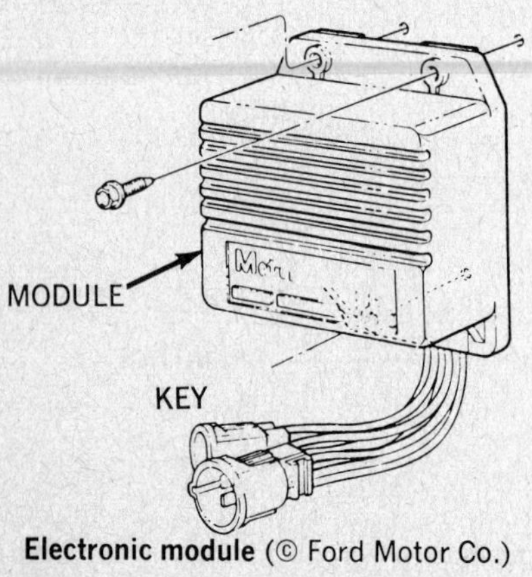

Electronic module (© Ford Motor Co.)

Dual Mode Timing Ignition Module

On some applications, a special Dura-Spark II ignition module is used with altitude compensation. This special module plus the barometric pressure switch allows the base engine timing to be modified to suit altitude conditions. All other elements and performance characteristics of this module are identical in both modes of operation to the basic Dura-Spark II system. All Dura-Spark II Modules equipped with altitude feature have three connectors instead of the normal two. A barometric switch provides an automatic retard signal to the module at different altitudes, giving appropriate advanced timing at higher altitude and retard mode for spark knock control at lower altitudes.

Setting Ignition Timing

Before checking and adjusting the ignition timing, on conventional systems inspect the breaker points for alignment and adjust if necessary. Rotate the distributor until breaker rubbing block rests on the peak of a cam lobe and check the breaker point gap, adjusting if necessary. See Specifications at the beginning of this section for correct gap setting.

NOTE: The higher coil charging currents from the Dura Spark II ignition system can cause false triggering of timing lights with capacitive coupled pickups. The false triggering will result in apparent multiple sparks or an erratic timing indication. Timing lights with inductive pickup should be used for correct readings.

1. Clean and mark timing marks. All timing marks are on the crankshaft belt drive pulley, except on the 240 cu. in. engine in Econoline models and 240 and 300 cu. in. engines in P series models, where the marks are on the flywheel or flexplate (automatic transmission).
2. Disconnect vacuum line(s) and plug the disconnected line(s).
3. Connect a timing strobe light to the No. 1 spark plug lead and install a tachometer.
4. Start engine and set idle speed.
5. Loosen hold down clamp bolt or retainer bolt and rotate distributor housing until timing is correctly set.
6. Check the operation of the centrifugal advance by accelerating the engine to 2000 rpm. If the timing does not advance 9-14 degrees, the mechanical advance mechanism is faulty and must be removed for service.
7. Unplug vacuum line(s) and connect to distributor diaphragm. Momentarily accelerate engine to 2000 rpm and note timing advance. If it is not considerably more than the mechanical advance alone, the disphragm must be replaced.
8. Remove timing light and tachometer. Reset idle to correct speed.

Monolithic Timing

A number of engines were equipped with the Monolithic Timing receptacle during the 1974 model year, and made standard on all 1975 and later engines; while still retaining the Conventional Timing method. The "Monolithic" system employs a timing receptacle designed to accept an electronic probe that is connected to a digital read-out meter. The recep-

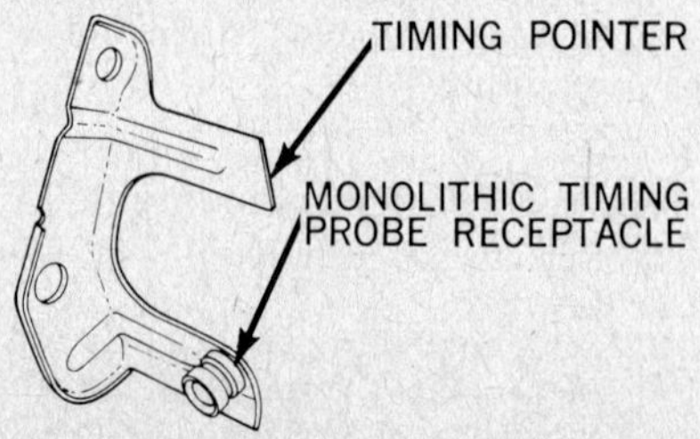

Monolithic timing pointer and receptacle (© Ford Motor Co.)

tacle is located in the front of the engine, so the probe is next to the balancer pulley. To time the engine with the Monolithic Timing Equipment, follow the procedure below.

1. Install monolithic timing equipment to engine as per manufacture's instructions.
2. Disconnect all vacuum lines at the distributor and plug. Loosen distributor hold down bolt.
3. Start engine—warm up and reduce idle speed to 600 RPM.
4. Adjust initial timing to specification noted on engine decal, by rotating the distributor against rotor rotation to advance timing or with rotor rotation to retard timing. Tighten hold down bolt, and recheck engine timing.
5. Check centrifugal advance by accelerating engine (in neutral) to 2500 RPM. If ignition timing advance is noted during acceleration the centrifugal advance mechanism is functional. Refer to the engine decal for this specification. If out of specification remove distributor and make required repairs.
6. To check vacuum advance—unplug and reinstall carburetor source vacuum line (removed in step 2) to outer diaphragm (on dual diaphragm distributors). Accelerate engine to 2500 RPM. Total advance should be greater now than in prior step (centrifugal only) if advance mechanism is functional. Remove distributor and make required repairs if no additional advance is observed and vacuum is noted at the line to the diaphragm.
7. To check vacuum retard operation (dual diaphragm) connect the intake manifold line (removed in step 2) to the inner diaphragm side of the distributor. With the engine at normal idle, a 6 or 12 degree retard should be noted, depending on shuttle, if the retard mechanism is working properly. If the retard function is not evident, remove distributor and make required repairs.
8. Reconnect all distributor lines properly and check curb idle, reset if necessary.
9. Remove engine tachometer and monolithic timing equipment.

ALTERNATOR

Reference

Procedures for diagnosis and repair of the charging system can be found in the "Electrical Section" in the General Repair portion of this manual.

Alternator Removal and Installation

1. Disconnect battery ground cable.
2. Loosen the alternator mounting bolts and remove the adjustment arm to alternator attaching bolt.
3. Remove the electrical connectors from the alternator. The stator and field connectors are of the push-on type and should be pulled straight off to prevent damage to the terminal studs.
4. Disengage the alternator belt.
5. Remove the alternator mounting bolt and alternator.
6. To install, first install the wiring harness, then position the alternator on engine, installing spacer (if used) and mounting bolt. Tighten bolt only finger tight.
7. Install the adjustment arm to alternator attaching bolt.
8. Adjust belt tension as described below.
9. Tighten adjusting arm bolts and mounting bolt to 22-32 ft. lbs. torque.

Alternator Belt Adjustment

1. Loosen the alternator mounting bolt to a snug position and loosen the adjusting arm bolt.
2. *Apply pressure on the alternator front housing only* and tighten the adjusting arm to alternator bolt.
3. Check for correct tension. Belt tension is correctly adjusted when belt can be deflected by hand ½-¾". Readjust if necessary.
4. Tighten all mounting bolts to 22-32 ft. lbs. torque.

Regulator Removal and Installation

NOTE: If vehicle is equipped with an electric choke, be sure to disconnect electric choke wire from starter terminal of the alternator when working on the charging system. Check electric choke wire for a ground condition. Removing the connector from an un-grounded regulator with the ignition switch on will destroy the regulator.

1. Remove battery ground cable.
2. Remove the regulator mounting screws.
3. Disconnect the regulator from the wiring harness.
4. To install, connect wiring harness.
5. Mount the regulator to the regulator mounting plate. The radio supression condenser (electro-mechanical regulator) mounts under one of the mounting screws. The ground lead mounts under the other mounting screw.
6. Connect battery ground cable and test the charging system for proper voltage regulation. See the "Electrical Diagnosis" in the General Repair Section for testing procedures.

Regulator Adjustments

Motorcraft

The Motorcraft electro-mechanical regulator used on 38, 42, 44, 55 and 61 Ampere alternators is not adjustable and must be replaced if charging system tests indicate that it is defective.

Transistorized Regulator—1973

1. Remove regulator mounting screws and regulator.

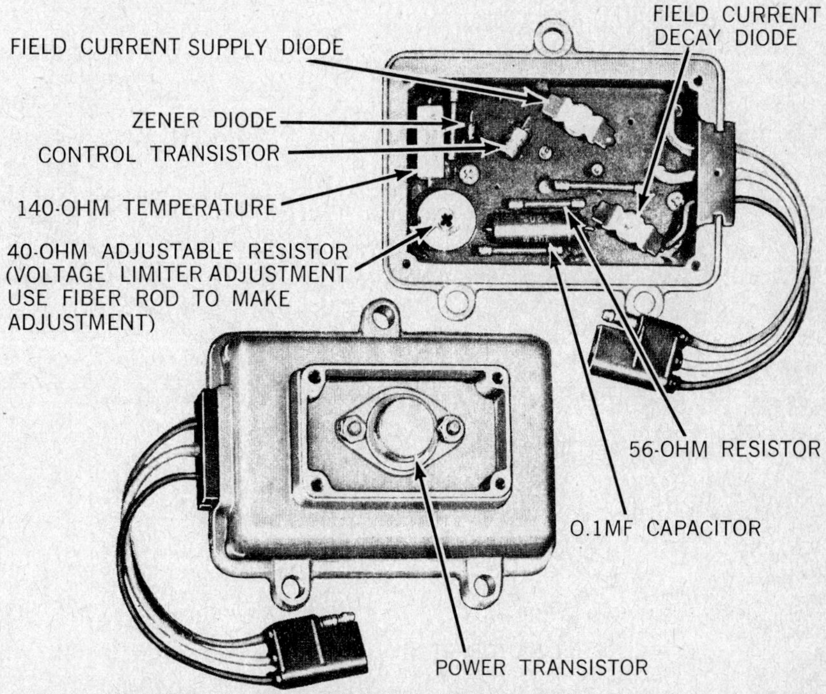

1973 Transistorized alternator regulator (© Ford Motor Co.)

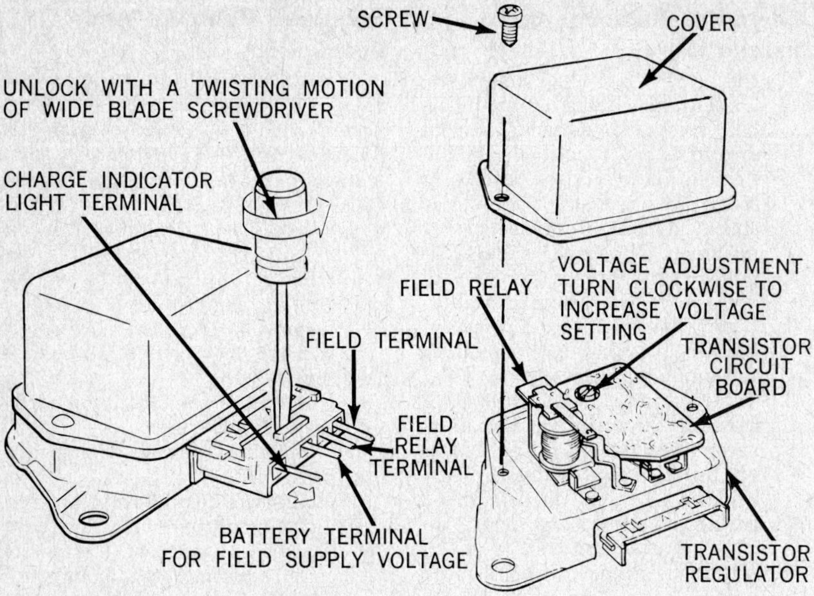

1974-80 Transistorized alternator regulator (© Ford Motor Co.)

2. Remove bottom cover from regulator.
3. With regulator at nomal operating temperature, use a fiber rod as a screwdriver to turn 40-ohm adjustable resistor.
4. Install bottom cover and mount regulator.

Transistorized Regulator—1974-78

NOTE: The only adjustment that can be made on this regulator is the voltage limiter adjustment.

1. With the regulator at normal operating temperature, remove the cover screws and cover.
2. Using a fiber rod as a screwdriver, turn the voltage adjusting screw clockwise to increase voltage setting or counterclockwise to decrease the setting.
3. Reinstall the cover.

Electronic Voltage Regulator—1979-80

The new electronic voltage regulator is completely solid state, consisting of transistors, diodes, and resistors. This new regulator will be released under two separate part numbers with two color codes. The units will look alike, but will not be interchangeable with the new regulator wiring harness due to different connector plugs. One of these units will be used on vehicles equipped with an ammeter and the other used for alternator warning-indicator-lamp equipped cars. These regulators are calibrated and preset by the manufacturer. No adjustment is required or possible on these units.

NOTE: Some Medium and Heavy trucks may incorporate an integral voltage regulator, when a high ampere output alternator is used in the charging system.

Fuse Link

The fuse link is a short thin length of insulated wire integral with the engine compartment wiring harness. If there is a heavy reverse current flow (such as caused by an improperly connected booster battery or when a short occurs in the wiring harness), the fuse link burns out and thus protects the alternator from damage. Production fuse links are black and replacement are green or black. All have the words FUSE LINK printed on the insulation. Burn-out of a fuse link may be evidenced by disfigured or bubbled insulation or by bare wire ends protruding from the insulation.

To test continuity of the fuse link (Bronco and F-Series LD) check that the battery is OK, then check with a voltmeter for voltage at the BAT terminal of the alternator. No voltage indicates that the fuse link is probably burned out. On P-Series trucks, disconnect the battery ground cable and, using an ohmmeter or a self-powered test light, check for continuity. A good fuse link will light the test bulb or show zero resistance on the ohmmeter. If fuse link is burned out, replace as described below.

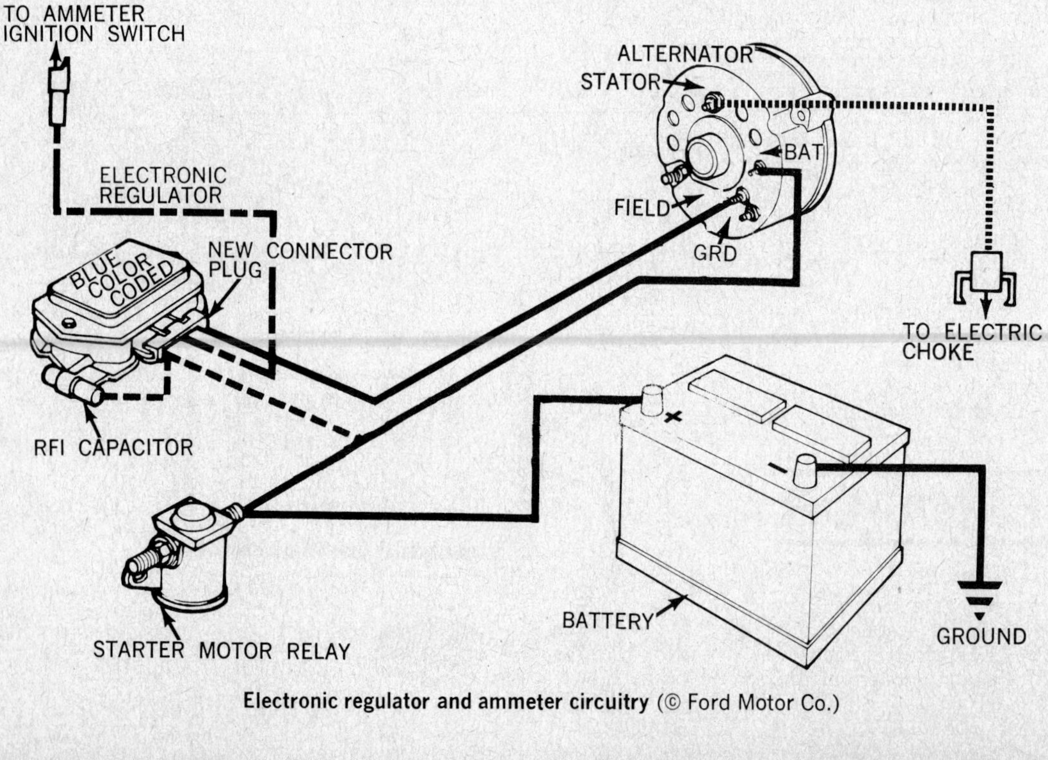

Electronic regulator and ammeter circuitry (© Ford Motor Co.)

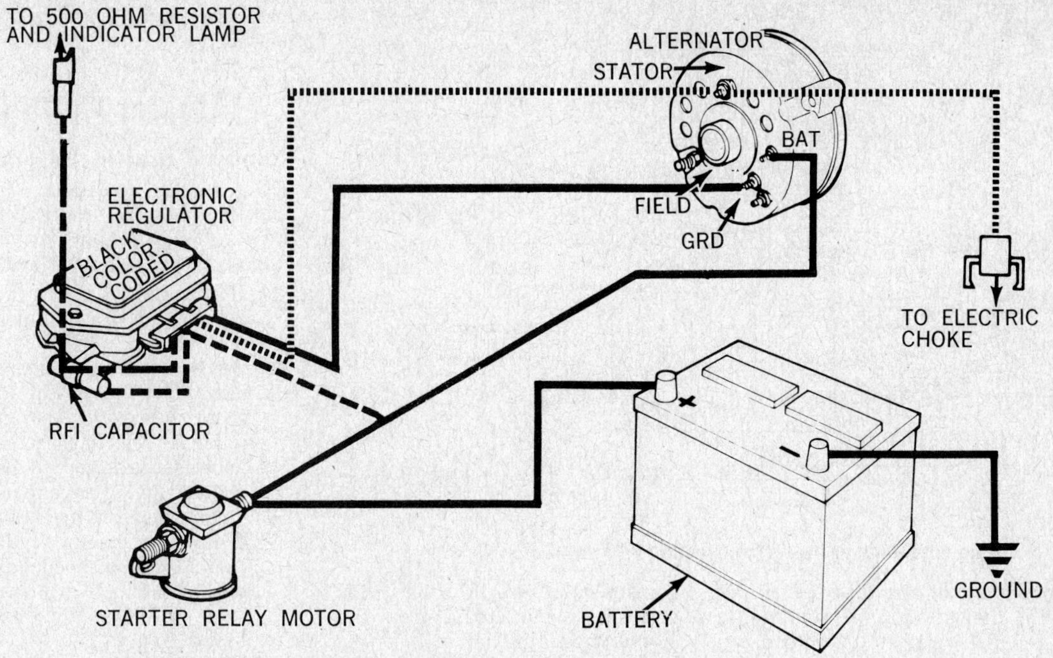

Electronic regulator and warning lamp indicator circuitry (© Ford Motor Co.)

Fuse Link Replacement

1. If the 5/16″ eyelet terminal is not required, cut it off as close to the terminal as possible.
2. Disconnect battery ground cable.
3. Disconnect the fuse link terminal at the starter relay (alternator on P-Series).
4. Remove the complete fuse link at the splice, when applicable, remove the old terminal from the battery stud of the starter relay.
5. Cut out original splice(s), then splice and solder the new fuse link with the existing wires from the original splice(s). See illustration. Wrap splice completely with tape. If there were two wires connected to the fuse link eyelet, cut link from eyelet and position the second wire with the eyelet back on the starter relay terminal.
6. Install all other wires removed during service.
7. Connect battery ground cable.

STARTER

Reference

For complete diagnostic and overhaul procedures on light duty truck starter motors, see the "Starters" group in the General Repair section.

Autolite & Motorcraft Positive Engagement Starter

Removal and Installation

1. Disconnect starter cable at the starter terminal.
2. Remove the starter mounting bolts.
3. Remove the starter assembly.
4. To install, insert the starter into the pilot hole in the flywheel housing, making sure that the starter housing pilot completely enters the pilot hole all the way around, and that the starter housing face is square and tight to the engine rear cover plate. Install mounting bolts.
5. Snug all bolts, torquing them to 23–28 ft. lbs.
6. Connect starter cable.

Motorcraft Solenoid Actuated Starter

Removal and Installation

1. Disconnect the battery ground cable and raise the vehicle.
2. Disconnect the cable and wires at the solenoid terminals.
3. Turn the front wheels all the way to the right and remove the bolts attaching the idler arm to the frame.
4. Remove the starter mounting bolts and the starter.
5. Position the starter on the mounting plate and start the bolts.
6. With the starter held firmly against the mounting surface and fully in the pilot hole, run the mounting bolts in until they are snug.
7. Tighten the mounting bolts to 15-20 ft-lbs.
8. Connect the cable and wires to the solenoid terminals. The battery cable should be tightened to 45-95 in-lbs.
9. Install the idler arm bracket on the frame and tighten the bolts to 28-35 ft-lbs.
10. Lower the vehicle and connect the battery ground cable.

Delco Remy Starter

Removal and Installation

1. Disconnect the battery cables.

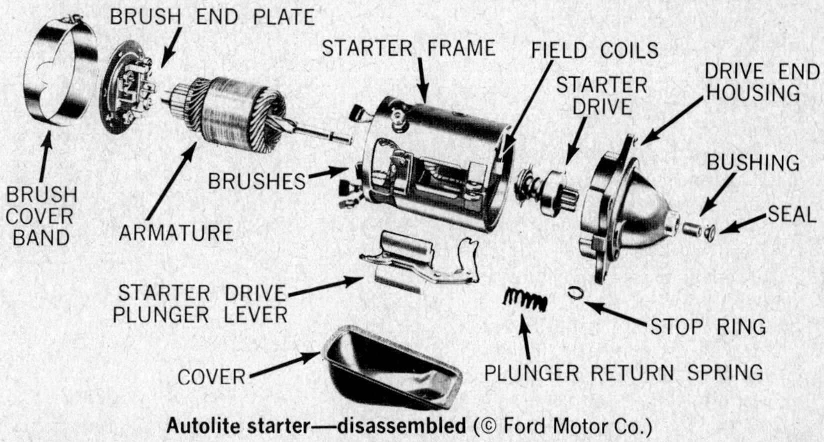

Autolite starter—disassembled (© Ford Motor Co.)

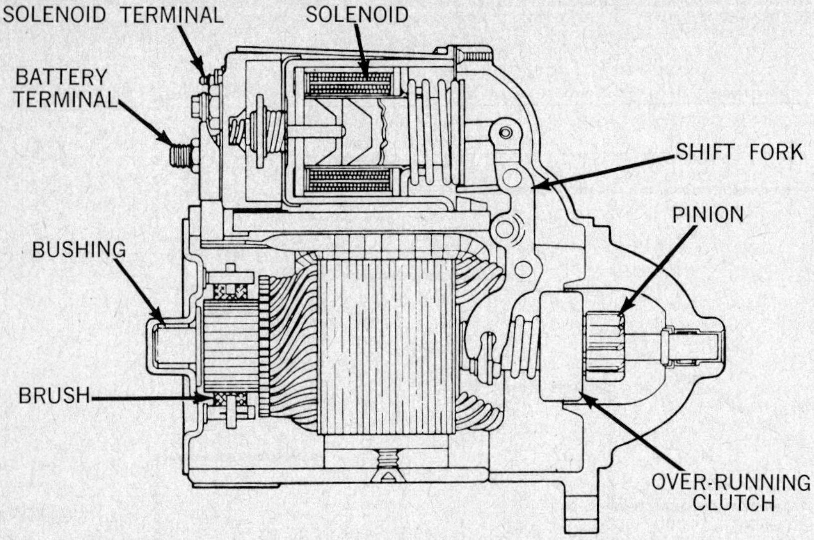

Solenoid actuated starter—cross section (© Ford Motor Co.)

2. Remove one bolt and lockwasher securing the battery cable retainer to the right rear cylinder head cover.
3. Remove the starter upper mounting bolt.
4. Remove the clamps securing the resonator inlet pipes to the exhaust manifolds, and position the inlet pipes out of the way.
5. Remove the starter shield retaining bolts.
6. Disconnect starter and solenoid wires. Tag the wires to insure proper reinstallation.
7. Remove the two remaining starter mounting bolts and lockwashers.
8. Remove starter.
9. To install, position the starter on engine and install three mounting bolts and lockwashers. Tighten to 23–28 ft. lbs. torque.
10. Connect solenoid wire to starter terminal.
11. Install starter shield on engine block with two retaining bolts.
12. Connect the remaining starter wires to the terminals.
13. Connect the resonator inlet pipes to the exhaust manifolds, and secure with clamps.
14. Connect the battery cables and close battery box.
15. Check operation of starter.

Prestolite Starter

Removal and Installation

1. Disconnect the starter cable at the starter terminals.
2. Remove the heat shield from the manifold.
3. Remove the starter mounting bolts.
4. Tilt the starter slightly so the starter drive clears the flywheel housing and remove the starter
5. Installation is the reverse of removal. On trucks with automatic transmission the dipstick tube bracket is mounted under the starter mounting bolt.

BRAKES

Reference

Complete overhaul and service information for hydraulic brake components can be found in the "Hydraulic Brake", "Power Brake" and "Disc Brake" sections of the Unit Repair portion of this manual.

No service or overhaul operation for air brake systems are included in the General Repair section of this book.

Master Cylinder

Removal and Installation

On models equipped with power boosters, depress brake pedal while engine is not running to expell vacuum or air from booster system.

1. If stoplight switch is mounted on the master cylinder, disconnect wires.
2. On dash-mounted master cylinders, disconnect the dust boot from the rear of the master cylinder at the dash panel. If the boot is connected to the master cylinder only, leave it in place.
3. Disconnect the hydraulic line(s) from the master cylinder and pump the brake pedal all the way several times to evacuate all fluid from the master cylinder into a suitable container.
4. Disconnect the pushrod from the brake pedal. On dash-mounted master cylinders the pushrod is connected to the brake pedal lever with a bolt, and there may be a stoplight switch mounted by that bolt. Remove the bolt and stoplight switch. If the master cylinder is under the floorboard, remove clevis pin from pushrod yoke. Mark or tag bushings and spacers for correct position.
5. On trucks equipped with conventional brakes, remove the master cylinder mounting bolts and master cylinder. If the truck is

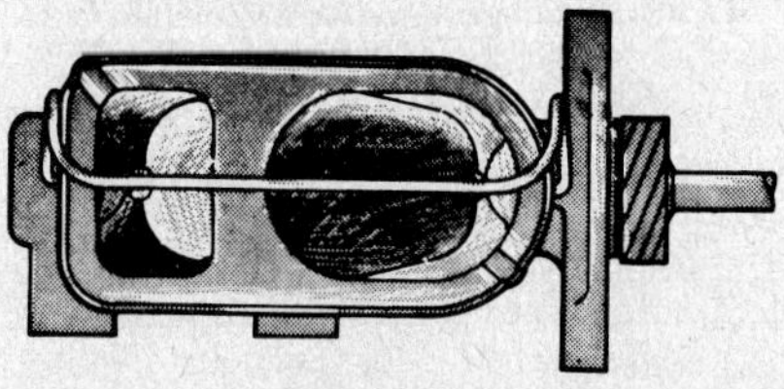

BENDIX

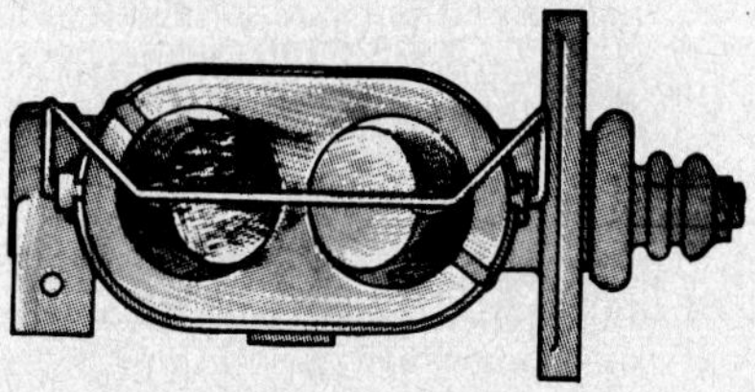

GPD

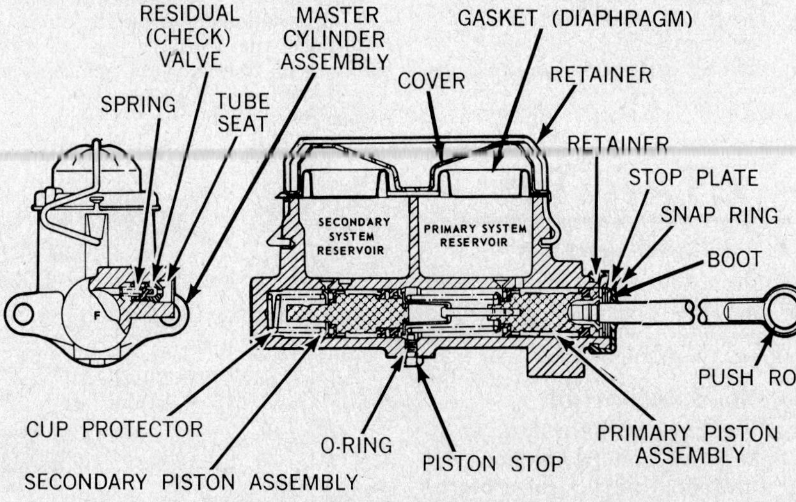

Typical dual master cylinder (© Ford Motor Co.)

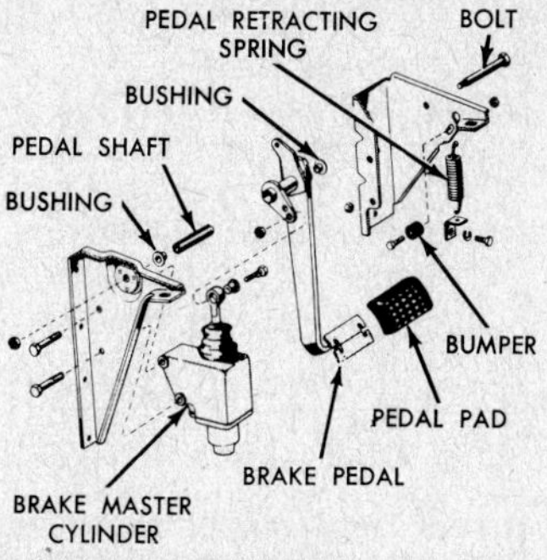

Brake cylinder installation—C-Series (© Ford Motor Co.)

equipped with a dash-mounted booster, remove the retaining nuts and washers and pull master cylinder off mounting studs.

6. Bleed the master cylinder before installing it on the vehicle as follows:
   a. Support the master cylinder body in a soft-jawed vise, and fill both reservoirs with extra heavy duty brake fluid.
   b. Loosely install plugs in the front and rear outlet ports. Depress the primary piston several times until air bubbles no longer appear in the brake fluid.
   c. Tighten the plugs and try to depress the piston. Depressing the piston should be harder after all the air in the brake reservoir is expelled.
   d. Remove the plugs. Install the cover and diaphragm assembly, making sure the cover retainer is tightened securely.
7. Position master cylinder so that mounting bolts or retainer nuts may be installed. Tighten mounting bolts or nuts securely.
8. Connect hydraulic line(s) loosely to master cylinder fitting(s).
9. If rubber dust boot attaches to both cylinder and dash, make sure it is properly installed at this time.
10. Connect pushrod to brake pedal lever. If there is a bushing in the hole at the end of the pushrod, lubricate bushing. Install stoplight switch at this time if it was removed when disconnecting pushrod from brake pedal lever. Make sure all bushings and spacers are properly installed.
11. Connect stoplight switch wires.
12. Bleed hydraulic system, and tighten hydraulic line(s) to master cylinder fitting(s).

Wheel Cylinder

Removal and Installation

1. Remove the wheel, drum, and brake shoes.
2. Remove the cylinder-to-shoe connecting links.
3. Disconnect the brake line from the wheel cylinder.
4. Remove the wheel cylinder retaining bolts and remove the cylinder from the brake backing plate. On two-cylinder brake assemblies remove the wheel cylinder cover with the brake cylinder.
5. Position the brake cylinder on the backing plate and install the retaining bolts and lockwashers.
6. Install a new gasket on the brake line (if equipped) and connect the line to the wheel cylinder.
7. Install the brake shoes and the connecting links between the shoes and cylinder. Install the brake drum and wheel.
8. Adjust the brakes and bleed the system. Check pedal operation before moving the vehicle.

Disc Brakes

Floating Caliper

Caliper Removal and Installation

1. Raise and secure the vehicle.
2. Remove the wheel and tire assembly.
3. Disconnect the brake hose from the caliper.
4. Remove the pins and nuts holding the caliper to the anchor plate, remove the caliper.
5. Coat the mounting pins with a light film of chassis lube. Place the caliper assembly on the anchor plate and install the retaining pins and nuts. Tighten the nuts to 17-23 ft-lbs. torque.
6. Place a new copper washer on the brake hose fitting and install the brake hose.
7. Install the wheel and tire assembly.
8. Bleed the brake system and lower the vehicle.

Mounting Pin Bushing Removal and Installation

1. Insert a suitable tool under the outer lip of the bushing steel shell and pry the bushing out of the support boss.
2. Using a caliper mounting pin fitted with a ½ in. washer, press the new bushing into the support boss.

Sliding Caliper

Removal and Installation

1. Siphon or dip part of the brake fluid out of the large section of the master cylinder to avoid overflow when the caliper piston is pressed into the cylinder bore.
2. Raise the vehicle and remove the tire and wheel assembly.
3. Position a 8 in. C-clamp on the caliper and tighten the clamp to bottom the piston in the caliper cylinder bore.
4. Remove the key retaining screw.

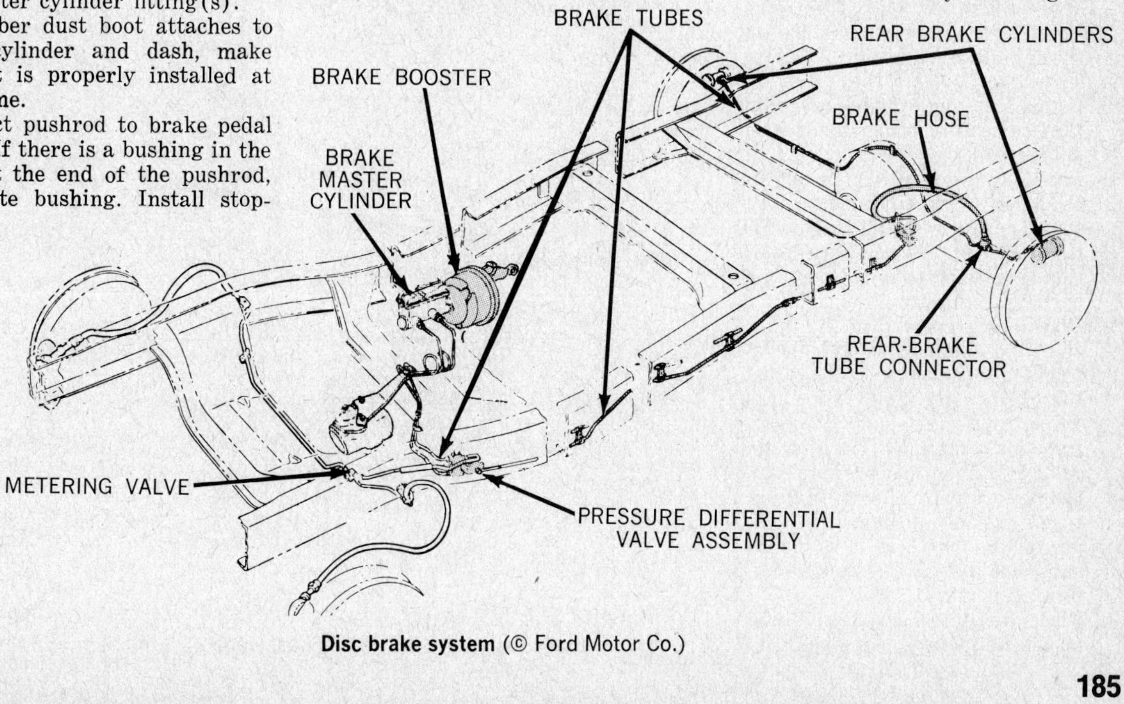

Disc brake system (© Ford Motor Co.)

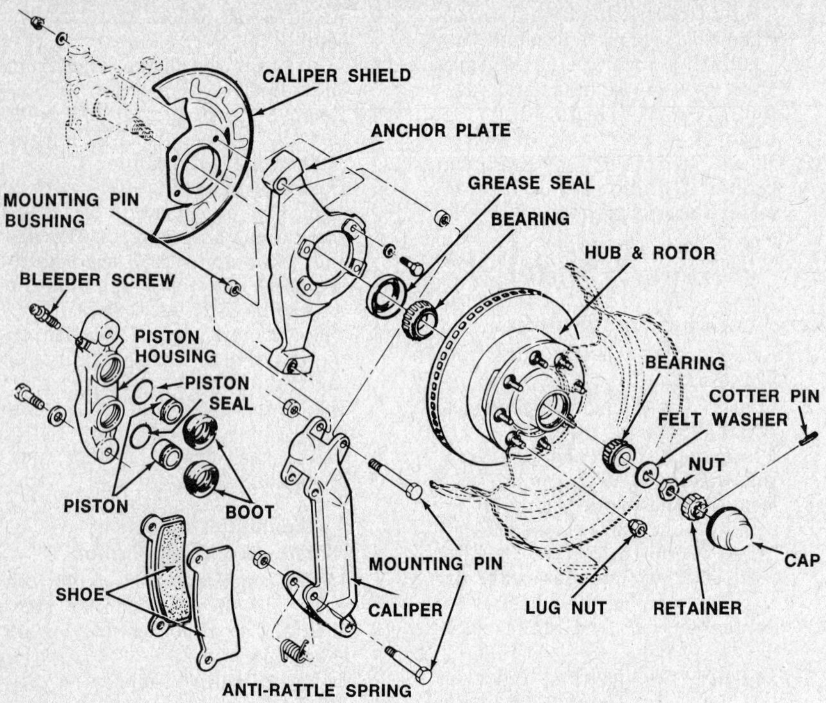

Exploded view of floating caliper assembly (© Ford Motor Co.)

5. Drive the caliper support key and spring out with a brass rod and light hammer.
6. Disconnect the brake hose from the inlet port. Cap the hose and inlet port to prevent fluid leakage.
7. Remove the caliper from the spindle assembly by pushing it downward against the spindle and rotating the upper end upward out of the spindle assembly.
8. Remove the outer shoe and lining from the caliper. Remove the inner shoe and lining from the spindle assembly. Remove the shoe antirattle clip from the lower shoe abutment surface on the spindle assembly.
9. Thoroughly clean the areas of the caliper and spindle assembly that come in contact during the sliding action of the caliper.
10. Position a new anti-rattle clip in the lower shoe abutment in the spindle assembly. Make sure that the tabs on the clip are positioned properly and the loop-type spring is away from the rotor.
11. Place the lower end of the inner shoe and lining in the spindle assembly shoe abutment against the anti-rattle clip. Slide the Upper end of the shoe into position. Make certain that the clip is still in the proper position.
12. Check to be sure that the caliper piston is fully bottomed in caliper piston pore. If it is necessary, use a 8-in. C-clamp to bottom the piston.
13. Place the outer shoe and lining on the caliper and using your fingers, press the shoe tabs into place. If the shoe cannot be pressed into place by hand, use a C-clamp to press the shoe into position. Be careful not to damage the lining.
14. Place the caliper on the spindle assembly by pivoting the caliper around the spindle upper mounting surface. Be careful not to tear or cut the boot as it slips over the inner shoe.
15. Using a brake adjusting tool, hold the upper machined surface of the caliper against the surface of the spindle assembly. Install a new caliper support spring and a new caliper support key. Drive the key and spring assembly into position with a soft faced mallet. Install the key retaining screw.
16. Install new copper washers on the brake hose fittings. Connect the brake hose to the caliper inlet port.
17. Bleed the brake system, install the wheel and tire assembly, and lower the vehicle.

Rail Slider Two Piston Sliding Caliper

Removal and Installation

1. Raise and secure the vehicle. Remove the wheel and tire assembly.
2. Disconnect the brake hose from the caliper and plug the hose and ilnet port.
3. Remove the key retaining screw.
4. Using a brass rod and light hammer drive out the key and spring.
5. Remove the caliper from its support assembly by rotating the key and spring end out and away from the rotor. Slide the opposite end of the caliper clear of the slide in the support end of the rotor.

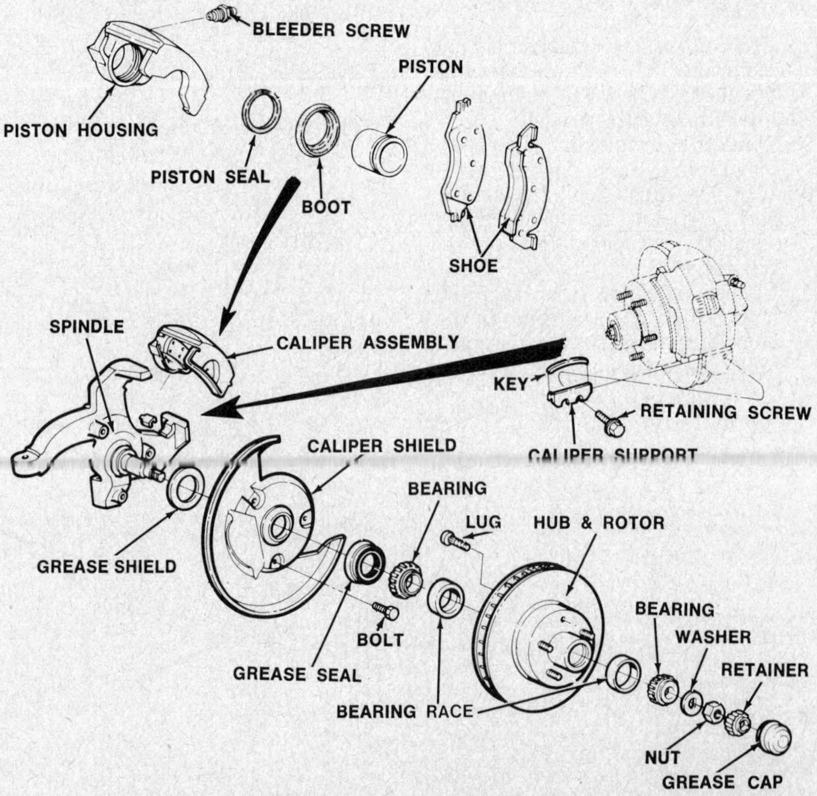

Exploded view of sliding caliper assembly (© Ford Motor Co.)

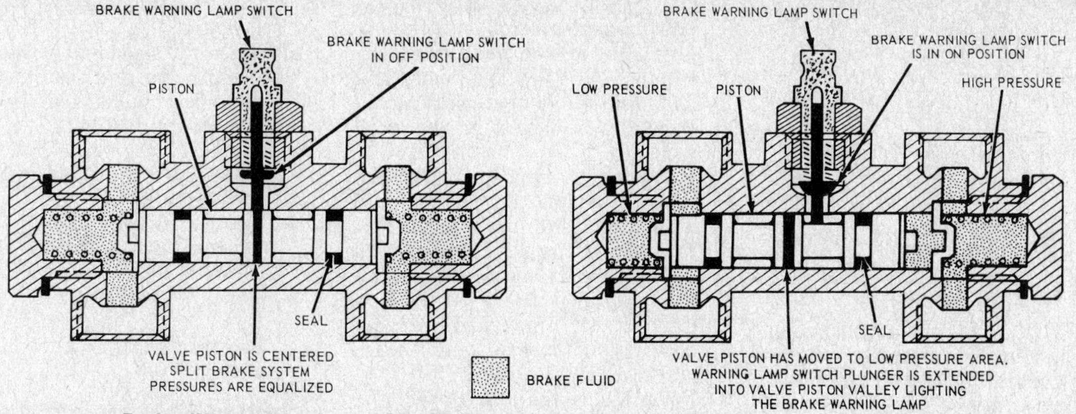

Brake differential valve—500-900 Series w/split hydraulic brakes (© Ford Motor Co.)

6. Clean the areas of the caliper and support that come in to contact during the sliding action of the caliper.
7. Clean any brake fluid, grease or grit off the rotor breaking surface.
8. Place the caliper rail into the slide on the support and rotate the caliper into the rotor.
9. Position the key and spring between the caliper and support assembly and start in by hand. Note that the spring is between the key and caliper and that the spring tangs overlap the ends of the key. Use a break adjusting tool to hold up the caliper against the support assembly.
10. Using a hammer, drive the key and spring into position aligning the correct notch with the existing hole in the support.
11. Secure the key to the support with the key retaining screw. Tighten the screw to 20 ft-lbs.
12. Place new copper washer on the brake hose fitting and connect to the caliper inlet port.
13. Bleed the system, lower the vehicle, and refill the master cylinder if necessary.

Heavy Duty Two Piston Sliding Caliper

Removal and Installation

1. Raise the vehicle and remove the wheel and tire assembly.
2. Remove the four screws holding the caliper mounting plate and remove the plate.
3. Lift the caliper off the hub and rotor assembly.
4. Disconnect the brake hose and cap the hose and caliper inlet port.
5. Remove the inner shoe and lining from the anchor plate.
6. Remove the spring, pin and cup from the caliper and remove the outer brake shoe.
7. Install new inner shoe into the anchor plate. Take care that the shoes do not fall out prior to installing the caliper.
8. Using a block of wood over the pistons and a large C-clamp, push the pistons to the bottom of the cylinder bore.
9. Place the outer shoe in the caliper assembly and install the retaining pin, spring and cup.
10. Install the caliper assembly over the rotor assembly and position in the anchor plate grooves.
11. Install the caliper hold down plate and tighten the attaching screws to 40 ft-lbs.
12. Install new copper washer on the brake hose fitting and connect the brake hose to the caliper inlet port.
13. Install the wheel and tire assembly and bleed the system.
14. Lower the vehicle and top off the master cylinder.

Differential Valve

Removal and Installation

1. Raise the vehicle on a hoist.
2. Disconnect the brake warning light from the pressure differential valve assembly switch.

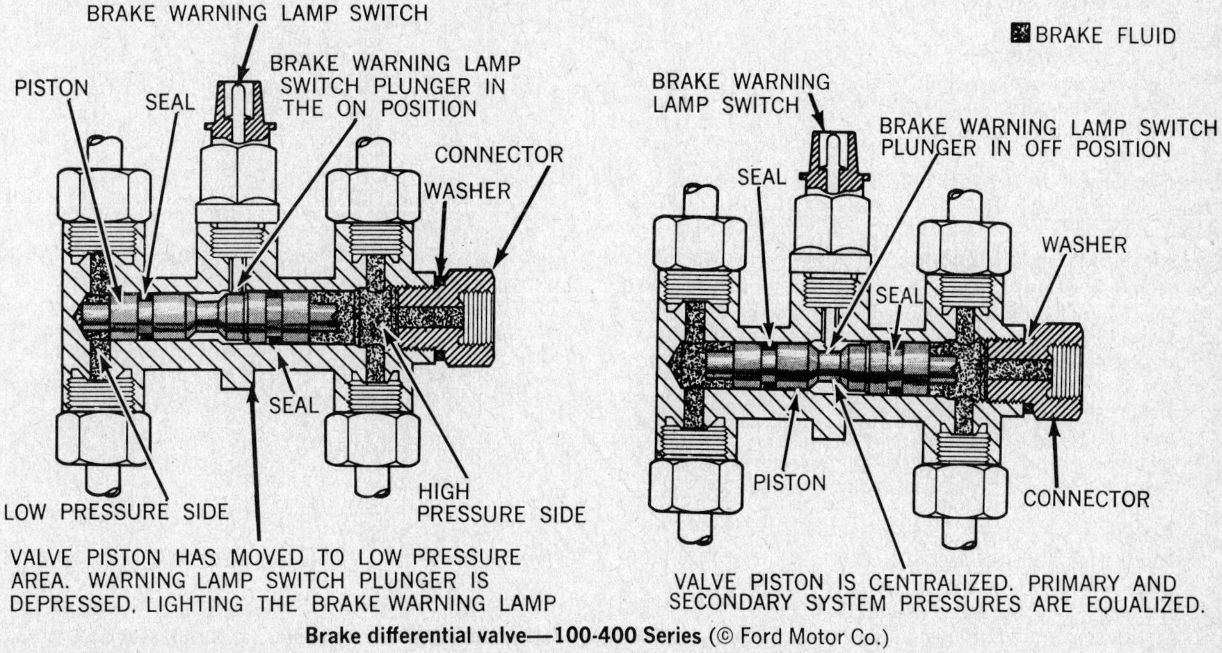

Brake differential valve—100-400 Series (© Ford Motor Co.)

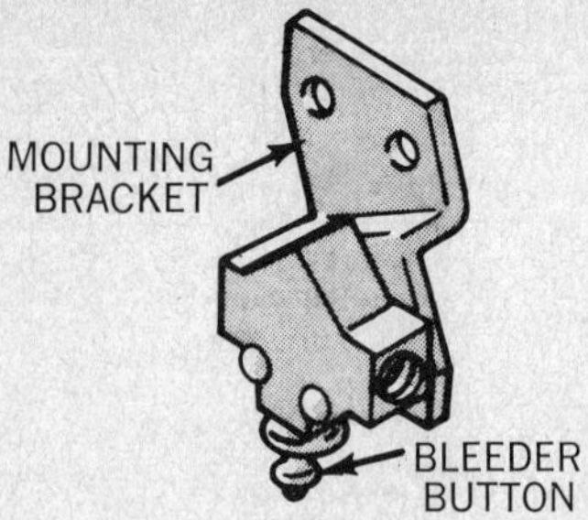

Brake metering valve (© Ford Motor Co.)

CAUTION: To prevent damage to the brake warning switch wire connector, expand the plastic lugs to allow removal of the shell-wire connector from the switch body.

3. Disconnect the brake hydraulic lines from the differential valve assembly.
4. Remove the screw retaining the pressure differential valve assembly to the frame side rail and remove the valve assembly.
5. Differential valve and switch are separate units and are serviced separately. Remove warning light switch from valve to replace either unit.
6. To install, mount the pressure differential valve assembly on the frame side rail and tighten the attaching bolt.
7. Connect the brake hydraulic lines to the differential valve and tighten the tube nuts securely.
8. Connect the shell-wire connector to the brake warning light switch. Make sure plastic lugs on the connector hold the connector securely to the switch.
9. Bleed the brakes and centralize the pressure differential valve as described above.

Power Boosters

Reference

No power booster overhaul procedures are included in the General Repair section of this book.

Bendix Dash-Mounted Vacuum Booster

Removal and Installation

1. Remove retaining nuts and master cylinder from booster.
2. Loosen hose clamp and remove manifold vacuum hose from booster.
3. From inside the cab, remove the attaching bolt, nut and plastic bushings and disconnect the booster pushrod from the brake pedal.
4. Remove nuts that retain the booster mounting bracket to the dash panel.
5. Remove the booster assembly from engine compartment.
6. To install, mount the booster and bracket assembly to the engine side of the dash panel by sliding the bracket mounting bolts and valve operating rod in through the holes in the dash panel.
7. From inside the cab, install the booster mounting bracket to dash panel retaining nuts.
8. Position the master cylinder to the booster assembly and install the retaining nuts.
9. Connect the manifold vacuum hose to the booster and secure with clamp.
10. From inside the cab connect the booster valve operating rod to the brake pedal with the attaching bolt, nut and plastic bushings.
11. Start engine and check operation of the brake system.

Midland-Ross Dash-Mounted Vacuum Booster

Removal and Installation

Removal and installation procedure for the Midland-Ross booster is the same as that described for the Bendix booster.

Bendix Frame Mounted Vacuum Booster

Removal and Installation

1. Depress the brake pedal several times to remove all vacuum from the system.
2. Loosen the booster air inlet tube clamp and remove the tube.
3. Disconnect the hydraulic lines and vacuum lines from the booster.
4. Remove the booster mounting bolts and booster from the bracket.
5. Place the booster on the mounting bracket and secure with the mounting bolts. Use new lockwashers on the bolts.
6. Connect the hydraulic lines. Make sure that the connections are tight.
7. Connect the air inlet tube to the booster. Be sure that the hose clamp is tight.
8. Bleed the brake system.
9. Connect the vacuum line to the booster and tighten the clamp securely.

Midland-Ross Frame Mounted Vacuum Booster

Removal and Installation

Removal and installation procedure for the Midland-Ross booster is the same as that described for the Bendix vacuum booster.

Brake Pedal Adjustment

1973-80 Dash Mounted Booster

1. Remove the master cylinder.
2. Fabricate the gage illustrated and place it against the master cylinder mounting surface on the booster body.
3. Adjust the push rod screw until the end of the screw just touches the inner edge of the slot in the gauge.
4. Install the master cylinder.

Bleeding System

Conventional Hydraulic Brake System

NOTE: On trucks with frame mounted boosters, engine must be off

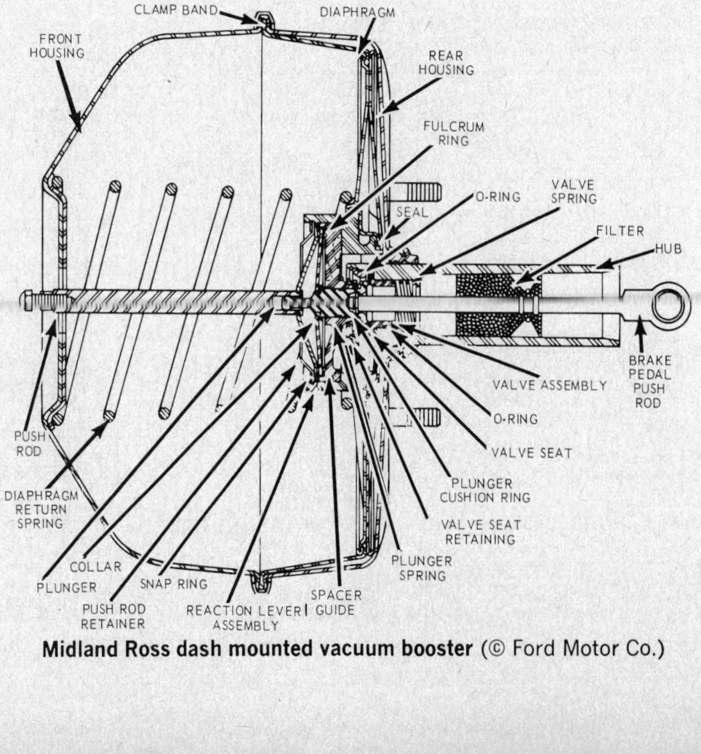

Midland Ross dash mounted vacuum booster (© Ford Motor Co.)

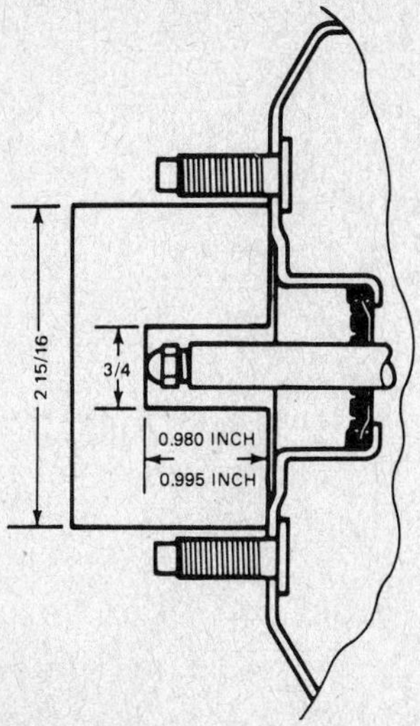

Pushrod (brake pedal) adjustment—Bendix dash mounted brake booster, Midland Ross similar (© Ford Motor Co.)

and all vacuum depleted from the system prior to bleeding.

1. Fill master cylinder reservoir with fluid. Check level of fluid frequently during bleeding procedure.
2. If hydraulic system is equipped with a vacuum booster, bleed the booster before bleeding the rest of the system.
3. If vehicle is equipped with dual slave cylinders, bleed the upper one first. If there are two bleeder screws, bleed the one nearest the power chamber first.
4. Bleed the wheel cylinder with the longest hydraulic line first.
5. Attach bleeder tube to bleeder screw and place other end of tube in a container partially filled with fluid.
6. Loosen bleeder screw, then slowly depress the brake pedal by hand, allowing it to return slowly to the fully-released position. Repeat until all bubbles cease to flow from bleeder tube.
7. Close bleeder screw and remove tube.
8. Repeat this procedure at each wheel until system is completely free of air bubbles.

Dual Hydraulic Brake Systems

The primary and secondary hydraulic brake system are individual systems and are bled separately. Bleed the longest line first on the individual system being serviced. Be sure to keep reservoir filled during bleeding operation.

After bleeding it is necessary to centralize the pressure differential valve. On 500-900 series trucks, remove the brake warning light switch from the pressure differential valve to prevent damage to the switch assembly.

NOTE: On trucks with frame mounted boosters, engine must be off and all vacuum depleted from the system prior to bleeding.

1. Bleed master cylinder at the outlet port side of the system being serviced. If there are no bleed screws, loosen the hydraulic line nut. Do not use the secondary piston stop screw located on the bottom of the master cylinder—the stop screw or piston could easily be damaged.
2. Operate pedal slowly until fluid is free of air bubbles, then tighten bleed screw.
3. Follow Steps 1 through 8 of Conventional Bleeding procedure.
4. Centralize the pressure differential valve. Turn the ignition switch to ACC or ON position. Loosen the pressure differential valve inlet tube nut on the system opposite the system which was bled last. This will result in unequal pressure in the other direction and allow the valve to center. Slowly depress brake pedal until light goes out. Tighten inlet tube nut. On 500-900 series trucks, disconnect wires from warning light switch on the differential valve, remove switch. Springs inside valve will center valve. Replace switch and wire.
5. Check fluid level in reservoir and fill to within 1/4″ of top.

Disc Brake Hydraulic System

The hydraulic system may be bled in the conventional manner, with the following additional steps.

1. First bleed master cylinder, then rear brake cylinders (longest line first).
2. On front disc brakes, the bleeder button on the metering valve must be depressed to allow the brake fluid to reach the caliper assemblies. When the bleeding operation is complete, fill the reservoir to within 1/4″ of top.
3. Centralize the pressure differential valve as described in "Bleeding Dual Hydraulic Brake Systems".

Stop Light Switch Adjustment

F-100—F-350, Bronco 1978-80

Stop light switch should be checked on vehicles with dragging or locking brakes. An improperly positioned stop light switch may restrict the brake pedal from returning to its non-applied position and prevent the brake fluid from returning to the master cylinder reservoir which can cause dragging or locked brakes.

Check switch for proper seating by pulling the brake pedal with no more than 25 lbs. force, which will seat the switch properly and may relieve these conditions.

When installing a new stop light switch be sure to insert the switch into the retainer on the brake pedal by pushing the switch rearward until it bottoms in the brake switch bracket. Then manually pull the brake pedal rearward against stop to set switch in proper position.

Air Brakes

Adjustments

Governor

Before adjusting the pressure settings of the governor, determine the

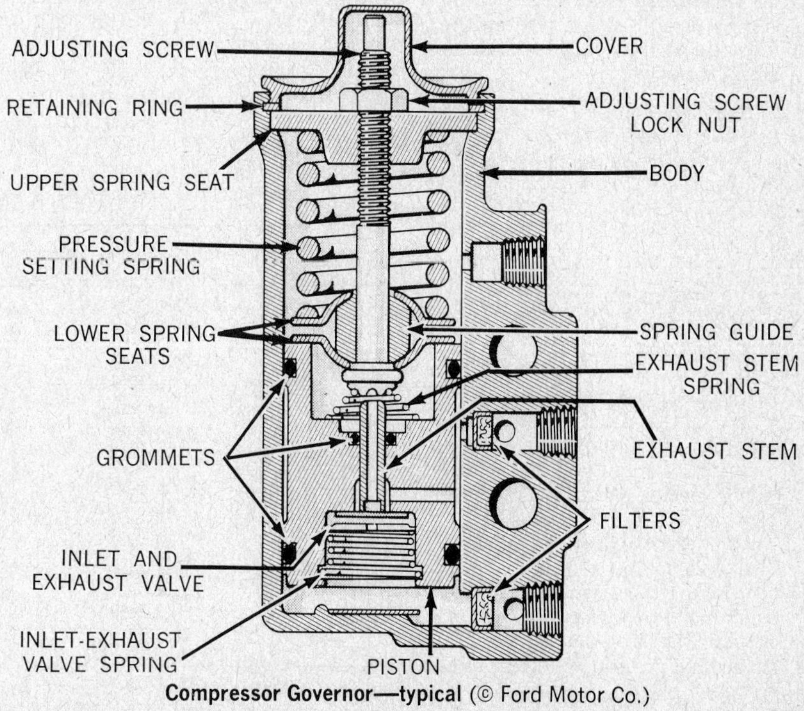

Compressor Governor—typical (© Ford Motor Co.)

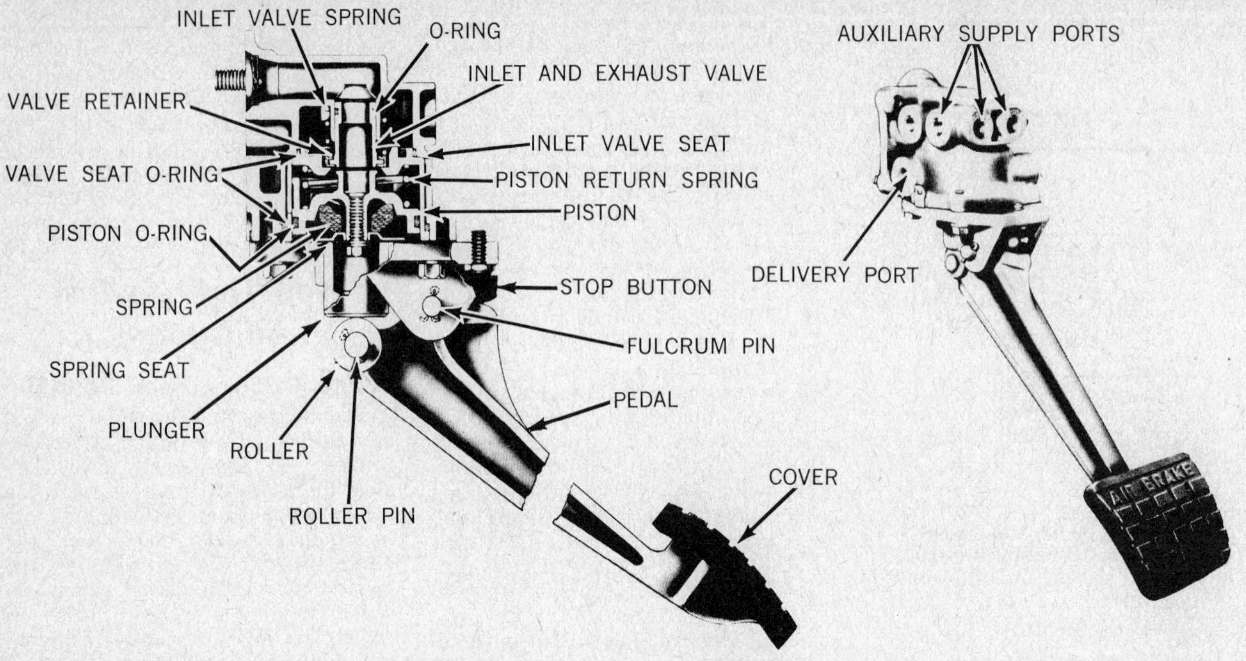

Foot control valve—typical (© Ford Motor Co.)

accuracy of the dash gauge by checking the readings against an accurate test gauge. The cut-in cut-out setting is made at the adjusting screw.

1. With the engine running, build up pressure in the system and observe the pressure registered by the dash gauge.
2. If the pressure build-up continues beyond 125 psi before the governor cuts-out, remove the cover from the top of the governor and loosen the locknut. Turn the adjusting screw clockwise to lower the cutout pressure, and counter clockwise to increase the cut-out pressure. After adjusting the cut-out pressure, tighten the adjusting screw locknut and install the cover.

NOTE: The air pressure range between the cut-out pressure (maximum) and the cut-in pressure (minimum) is fixed at about 20-25 psi and cannot be adjusted.

Foot Control Valve

To determine if the brakes are applying properly, proceed as follows:

1. Install a pressure gauge anywhere in the circuit between the control valve and brake chamber, or install the gauge in one of the extra service ports (upper row of ports).
2. Fully depress the brake pedal. The test gauge reading should approximate reservoir pressure as indicated by the dash gauge.
3. Adjust the stop button on the suspended pedal to eliminate free travel.

Slack Adjuster-Cam Operated Brakes

Apply the brakes and measure the travel of the brake chamber push rod. If the vehicle is equipped with Maxi brake unit, the minimum air pressure should be 90 psi while measuring the travel.

The travel should be kept to the minimum possible without causing the brakes to drag. The maximum travel should not exceed the following dimensions:

NOTE: Adjustment of the yoke on the brake chamber push rod should not be changed. When new, the yoke is adjusted so that the slack adjuster brake chamber push rod angle is slightly greater than 90° when the brakes are properly adjusted and the brakes are applied. Brake lining wear will not change this angle as long as the slack adjusters are kept adjusted to compensate for lining wear.

Front: This procedure applies only to trucks equipped with the S-cam operated brakes. Push rod travel which reaches or exceeds the maximum listed above indicates the need of adjustment. Turn the adjusting screw clockwise until the push for travels ¾ in. in, going from released to fully applied position. When making the adjustment, turn the screw in quarter turns.

Rear: This procedure applies to vehicles equipped with either standard or Maxi brake S-cam slack adjusters. Push rod travel which reaches or exceeds the maximum listed above indicates the need of adjustment. Depress the lock sleeve and turn the hex head of the wormshaft clockwise until the push rod travels one inch in, going from released to fully applied position. Be sure that the lock sleeve comes back out of the wormshaft so that the adjustment is locked.

Slack Adjuster Data

Brake Chamber Type	Year	Maximum Stroke at Which Brake Should Be Adjusted①	Maximum Stroke After Adjustment①
#9	1973-74 1975-80	1⅜ in. 1½ in.	1 in. 1⅛ + ⅛ in. at 100 PSI
#12	1973-74 1975-80	1⅜ in. 1½ in.	1 in. 1⅛ + ⅛ in. at 100 PSI.
#16	1973-74 1975-80	1⅜ in. 1½ in.	1 in. 1⅛ + ⅛ in. at 100 PSI.
#20	1973-74 1975-80	1¾ in. 1¾ in.	1¼ in. 1½ + ⅛ in. at 100 PSI.
#24	1973-74 1975-80	1¾ in. 1¾ in.	1¼ in. 1½ + ⅛ in. at 100 PSI.
#30	1973-74 1975-76 1977-80	2 in. 1⅞ in. 2 in.	1¼ in. 1⅝ + ⅛ in. at 100 PSI. 1⅝ + ⅛ in. at 100 PSI.
#36	1977-80	2¼ in.	1⅝ + ⅛ in. at 100 PSI.

① Push rod stroke is measured from chamber or chamber mounting bracket to push rod clevis.

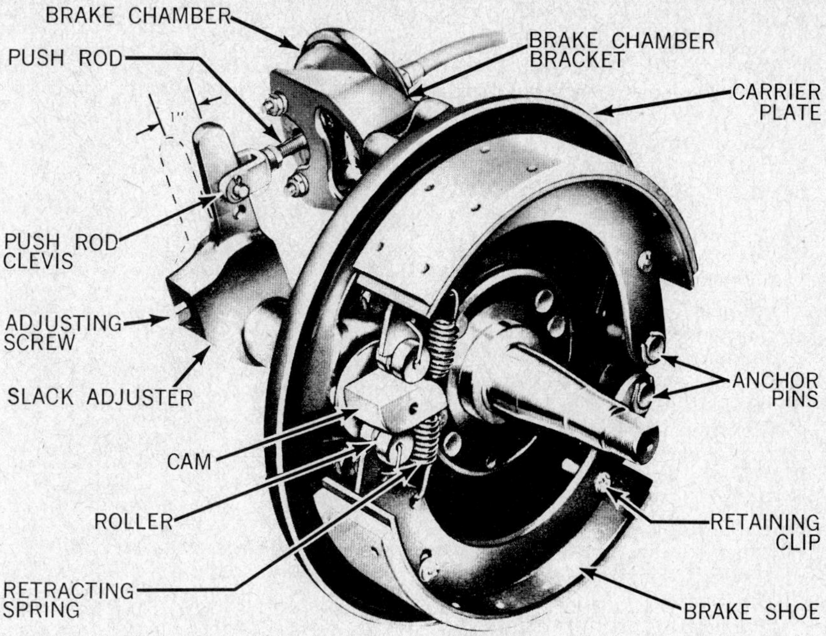

Cam type brake assembly (front) showing slack adjuster adjustment
(© Ford Motor Co.)

NOTE: When adjusting either the front or rear slack adjuster, raise the wheels and make sure that there is no brake drag.

Stop Light Switch (Air Brake)

If the stop lamp does not operate, connect a jumper wire across the switch terminals. If the lamp lights with the jumper wire connected, remove the wire and replace the switch. If the lamp still does not light, repair or replace the switch lead wires.

Air Compressor

Removal and Installation

NOTE: The following operations are for Ford gasoline engine vehicles only. No R&R procedures on Diesel engine models are included in the General Information Repair section of this book.

Depending on the particular truck model and engine, compressors are mounted in various locations. The procedures for removal and installation differ between vertically mounted units and side mounted units.

The following procedures apply generally to liquid cooled compressors, but air cooled installations are similar.

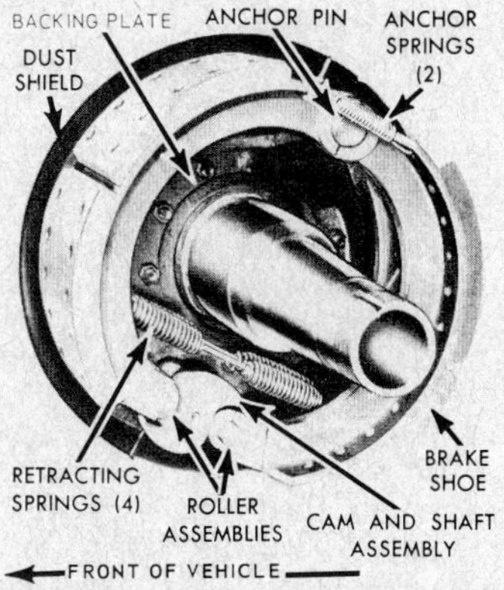

Cam type brake assembly (rear)
(© Ford Motor Co.)

Vertically Mounted Compressor— Removal and Installation

1. Open the reservoir drain cocks to exhaust air pressure from the system.
2. Drain the cooling system.
3. Disconnect the compressor air outlet line, the water inlet and outlet lines, the oil feed and return lines at the compressor.
4. Since the reservoir hose is difficult to remove at the governor, disconnect the hose at the fitting on the opposite end. If the hose is to be replaced, disconnect it from the compressor after compressor removal.
5. Remove the compressor-to-base plate bolts, then slide the compressor inward on the base plate. Disengage the drive belt and remove the compressor.
6. Transfer the pulley, Woodruff key and attaching nut to the new compressor.
7. Transfer the air outlet elbow and gasket, water outlet fittings, and oil inlet and outlet fittings to the new sealer. Apply sealer to all parts.
8. Transfer the governor and gasket to the new compressor and apply sealer. If the reservoir pressure hose is being replaced, connect it to the governor.
9. Transfer the air inlet filter and gasket to the new compressor and apply sealer.
10. Position the compressor on the base plate and engage the drive belt to the pulley.
11. Install the attaching bolts and slide the compressor away from the fan pulley until a ½ inch belt deflection is obtained. Tighten the bolts.
12. Connect the compressor air outlet line, water inlet line, and water outlet line to the compressor.
13. Connect the oil feed and return lines to the compressor.
14. Connect the hose from the governor to the fitting on the reservoir pressure line.
15. Fill the cooling system, close the reservoir drain cocks, start the engine and check for oil, air, or coolant leaks.

Side Mounted Compressor— Removal and Installation

1. Drain the cooling system, and open the reservoir drain cocks to exhaust the air pressure from the system.
2. Loosen the idler pivot bolt and adjusting bolt, remove the compressor drive belt.
3. Disconnect all oil, air, and coolant lines from the compressor and the reservoir pressure line from the governor.
4. Remove the bracket bolt at the cylinder head and the bracket bolt and washer at the manifold. Remove the bracket between the exhaust manifold and the cylinder head.
5. On vehicles with power steering, remove the attaching bolt, nut and lockwasher from the clip at the frame side rail. Remove the power steering hose retainer bolt, nut, and lockwasher at the frame crossmember and place the hoses out of the way.
6. Remove the front compresor-to-base attaching bolts. *There is very little clearance between the compressor base plate and the engine mount.*
7. Remove the remaining bolts.
8. Remove the air compressor from underneath the vehicle in a rearward direction. Discard the base gasket.
9. Remove the compressor pulley cotter pin and Woodruff key, and remove the pulley from the shaft with a suitable puller.
10. On C-series models, install the compressor pulley on the new compressor. On all other models with a side-mounted compressor, install the pulley after the compressor is installed.
11. Transfer all air, water, and oil fittings to the replacement compressor. Coat the threads with sealer.
12. Transfer the air inlet strainer

and gasket to the replacement compressor and apply sealer.
13. Transfer the governor and gasket to the new compressor and apply sealer.
14. Clean the compressor base and cylinder block base plate.
15. Apply sealer to both sides of the compressor base gasket.
16. Install pilot studs in the two rear bolt holes of the base plate mounting surface on the cylinder block. Position the base gasket on the base plate over the studs. From underneath the vehicle, install the compressor on the pilot studs and install the three attaching bolts. Remove the pilot studs and install the remaining bolts.
17. On vehicles with power steering, position the power steering hose on the frame rail and secure with the attaching bolt, washer, and nut.
18. Connect the water outlet line to the compressor.
19. Position the steering tube clips on the frame side rail and secure with the attaching nut, bolt, and lockwasher.
20. Connect the water inlet line to the compressor.
21. On all vehicles except C-series, loosen the power steering belt adjustment bolts and loosen the belt to provide clearance for installing the compressor pulley. Install the pulley on the shaft and secure with the nut and cotter pin.
22. Position the power steering belt on the pulleys and adjust the belt tension.
23. Position the air compressor drive belt on the pulleys and adjust the belt tension.
24. Connect the air outlet line to the compressor.
25. Connect the reservoir pressure line at the governor.
26. Fill the cooling system, close the air reservoir drain cocks, and build up pressure in the system. Check for air, oil, and coolant leaks.

Governor

Removal and Installation

1. Exhaust the air from the system.
2. On vertically-mounted compressors, disconnect the governor hose from the fitting in the reservoir pressure line. On side-mounted compressors, disconnect the pressure line at the governor.
3. Remove the attaching bolts and the governor.
4. On vertically-mounted compressors, transfer the hose to the replacement governor.
5. Install the governor, gasket, and the attaching bolts. Apply sealer to the threads.
6. On vertically-mounted compressors, connect the hose to the fitting on the reservoir pressure line. On side-mounted compressors, connect the pressure line to the governor.
7. Test the governor as detailed under "Adjustments".

Pressure Indicator Valve

Removal and Installation

1. Exhaust the air from the system.
2. Disconnect the wire at the buzzer switch.
3. Disconnect the air lines to the wiper control as required.
4. Unscrew the pressure indicator fitting and remove the assembly.
5. Install the pressure indicator valve assembly.
6. Connect the buzzer switch wire. Turn on the ignition switch to test that the buzzer and light are functioning properly before building up pressure in the system.

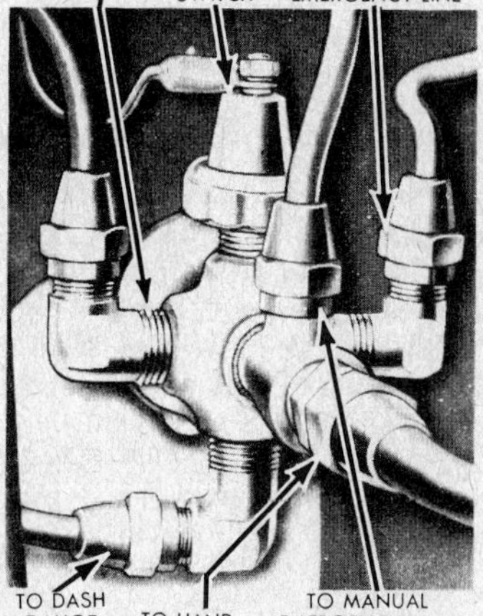

Pressure indicator valve
(© Ford Motor Co.)

Foot Control Valve

Removal and Installation

1. Open the reservoir drain cocks to exhaust the air from the system.
2. Disconnect all but one line from the valve ports. Loosen, *but do not disconnect,* the remaining line. This will prevent the valve from falling when the attaching bolts are removed.
3. Remove the cotter pin and pivot pin that connect the brake tredle to the control valve mounting plate.
4. Remove the control valve attaching bolts.
5. Disconnect the remaining air line from the control valve, and remove the control valve.
6. If the valve is being replaced, transfer all brass fittings and the stop light switch to the new valve. Apply sealer to the threads before installation.

Brake treadle and mounting plate—typical integral type (© Ford Motor Co.)

7. Remove the actuating button and rubber seal from the control valve mounting plate to allow installation of the new valve.
8. Position the new valve on the lower dash panel and mounting plate and install the attaching bolts.
9. Install the actuating button in the mounting plate bore, and install the rubber seal to the button and mounting seal.
10. Install the brake treadle on the control valve mounting plate with the pivot pin and cotter pin.
11. Connect the brake service lines to the upper ports of the valve.
12. Start the engine to build up pressure in the system. Check for leaks.

Quick Release Valve

Removal and Installation

1. Exhaust the air from the system.
2. Disconnect the air lines at the valve.
3. Remove the valve mounting bolts and the valve.
4. Install the valve and tighten the bolts and nuts.
5. Check the exhaust port to be sure that it is not plugged.
6. Connect the air lines.

Relay Valve

Removal and Installation

1. Block the wheels.
2. Exhaust the air from the system.
3. Disconnect the air lines from the relay valve.
4. Remove the valve mounting bolts and remove the valve.
5. Remove the insert (inlet and exhaust valve assembly), by removing the four exhaust cover cap screws and cover. Pull the insert out.

6. Clean and inspect the relay valve air lines. Replace any lines which are damaged or connecting hoses which are deteriorating or show signs of chafing.
7. Mount the relay valve and secure with the attaching bolts.
8. Connect the air lines to the valve.
9. Build up pressure in the system. Test the valve for correct operation and air leaks.

Brake Shoes

Reference

No information on the trouble-shooting and repair of anti-skid systems is included in this book.

Anti-Skid System

Reference

Information on the trouble-shooting and repair of "Anti-Skid System" units will be found in the "Anti-Skid section of the General Repair portion of this manual.

Brake Service Air Chamber

Wedge Type Brakes—Removal and Installation

1. Exhaust all air from the system.
2. Disconnect the air inlet line from the brake chamber.
3. Using a drift and a light weight hammer, loosen the spanner nut.
4. Unscrew the brake chamber from the wedge housing.
5. Check the position of the wedge in the plunger housing to be sure that the wedge assembly is properly seated.
6. Replace the automatic adjusting identification ring on the brake chamber tube. Thread the spanner nut into the power unit tube.
7. Screw the service chamber into the plunger housing until it bottoms (spanner nut loose).
8. Align the connection ports with the brake lines, if necessary, unscrewing the brake chamber not more than one full turn.
9. Connect the air lines.
10. Make and hold a full pressure brake application. Drive the spanner nut with a drift and hammer until it is tight against the plunger housing. Release the brake pressure.
11. Check for leaks at all connections.

Cam Type Brakes—Removal and Installation

1. Exhaust all air from the system.
2. Disconnect the air line at the brake chamber.
3. Disconnect the push rod clevis pin from the slack adjuster.
4. Remove the attaching nuts, and remove the brake chamber assembly.
5. Check and if necessary, cut the push rod of the new chamber to the same length as on the removed brake chamber.
6. If the chamber is being replaced, transfer the brake line fitting to the new brake chamber.
7. Position the brake chamber assembly on the mounting bracket and install the attaching nuts.
8. Install the clevis and cotter pin.
9. Connect the air line to the brake chamber.
10. Build up pressure in the system and inspect for leaks.
11. Adjust the brakes.

Slack Adjuster-Cam Type Brakes

Removal and Installation

1. Remove the clevis pin (on vehicles with a rear wheel spring brake, the spring brake must be released to remove the clevis pin) attaching the slack adjuster to the brake chamber push rod.
2. Remove the lock ring attaching the slack adjuster to the camshaft.
3. Mark the position of the slack adjuster on the camshaft, then slide the slack adjuster off the shaft.
4. Place the slack adjuster on the camshaft, aligning the locating marks. If there is excessive camshaft and play, install an additional spacer at the cam end of the camshaft. Install the lock ring.
5. Connect the brake chamber push rod to the slack adjuster by installing the clevis pin in the upper hole, and installing the cotter pin. The distance from the clevis to the mounting face of the chamber should be 2.60 in.
6. Lubricate the slack adjuster. Build up pressure in the system, check operation of brake assembly and for air leaks. Adjust the brakes.

Air-Hydraulic Intensifier

Master Cylinder Removal and Installation

1. Clean the dirt from around the discharge fitting and the inlet fitting of the master cylinder.
2. Disconnect the inlet (hydraulic reservoir) line from the master cylinder inlet port and plug both the line and port.
3. Disconnect the discharge line and plug the descharge port of the master cylinder. The open brake line should be plugged to prevent contaminats from entering the line or fluid loss.
4. Unscrew the four ⅜ in. screws holding the master cylinder onto the rotochamber. Remove the master cylinder.
5. Bolt the new master cylinder onto the rotochamber. Tighten the cap screws.
6. Remove the plug from the brake line and connect the line to the discharge port on the master cylinder.
7. Remove the plug from the reservoir line and connect it to the master cylinder inlet port.
8. Clean the dirt from around the hydraulic reservoir lid. Unfasten the bail wire from the reservoir lid and remove the lid. Add brake fluid until it is level with the tops of the four vertical ribs in the reservoir.
9. Connect a bleeder bottle to the bleed screw on the master cylinder and allow the unit to gravity bleed. Close the bleed screw when the fluid is flowing freely with no air bubbles.
10. If pressure bleeding is performed on the system, the warning switch on the rotochamber may be tripped and cause the brake light on the instrument panel to come on. After pressure bleeding is complete, manually reset the switch by pushing in the plunger located in the middle of the switch.
11. Fill the fluid reservoir, install the lid, and fasten the bail wire in place.
12. Check the installation for leaks as follows:
    a. Make sure that system pressure is at least 90 psi.
    b. Make a full brake application, hold for 5-10 seconds, then release.
    c. Check for fluid leaks around the discharge line, and bleeder screw on the master cylinder.

Intensifier Unit

Removal and Installation

1. Disconnect and cap hydraulic lines. Plug the port in the master cylinder.
2. Discharge the secondary system reservoir and exhaust chamber.
3. Remove the air line and cap to prevent the entry of dirt.
4. Remove the bracket mounting bolts and remove the assembly from the vehicle.
5. Mount the intensifier unit in the vehicle with the bracket attaching bolts and tighten securely.
6. Attach air lines and hydraulic lines, tighten securely.
7. Apply air pressure and hold. Leak test air line connections and intensifier with soap suds.
8. Pressure bleed front brakes at caliper bleed screws.

9. Fill the master cylinder reservoir to ½-¼ inch below the top of the unit with specified brake fluid.

Parking Brakes

NOTE: No detailed description of Maxi-Brake or MGM Stopgard parking brakes is included in this book.

Adjustment

Orscheln Lever

The Orscheln parking brake is the over center locking type. It is adjusted (in the fully released position) by turning the lever knob. When properly adjusted, it pulls over center with a distinct click. No other adjustment is normally required.

Cable Actuated Rear Wheel Type

Adjust service brakes before attempting to adjust the parking brake cables. Place parking brake lever in fully released position, then check for slack in the parking brake two rear cables. Cables are properly adjusted when the rear brake shoes are fully applied when parking brake is applied, and the brake shoes fully release when the parking brake lever is released.

To tighten cables, loosen locknut and tighten adjusting nut on equalizer. Tighten locknut when proper adjustment is obtained.

External Band Type

1. On cable controlled parking brakes, move the parking brake lever to the fully released position. On a vehicle with a rod type linkage, set the lever at the first notch.
2. Check the position of the cam to make sure that the flat portion is resting on the brake band bracket. If the cam is not flat with the bracket, remove the clevis pin from the upper part of the cam and adjust the clevis rod to allow the flat portion of the cam to rest on the brake band bracket. Install the clevis pin and cotter pin.
3. Remove the lock wire from the anchor adjusting screw, and turn the adjusting screw clockwise until a clearance of 0.100″ is obtained between the brake lining and the brake drum at the anchor bracket. Install the lock wire in the anchor adjusting screw.
4. Adjust the clearance on the upper and lower halves of the band in a similar manner. See illustration for location of adjusting screws. Adjust for a 0.010" clearance between band and drum.

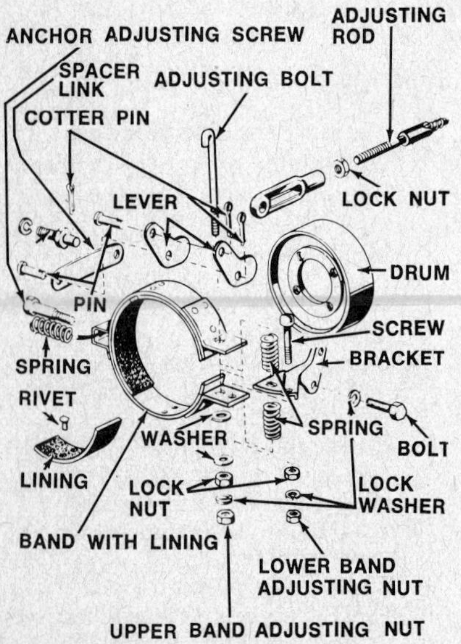

Exploded view of external band type parking brake (© Ford Motor Co.)

Internal Shoe Type 9″ Drum

1. Release parking brake lever.
2. Remove cotter pin from the parking brake linkage adjusting clevis pin and remove the clevis pin.
3. Lengthen or shorten adjusting link by turning the clevis. There should be a 0.010″ clearance between the drum and the band all the way around when the clevis pin is installed.
4. Install a new cotter pin in the clevis pin and check brake operation.

12″ Drum

There is no internal adjustment on this brake. Adjust the linkage as follows:

1. Remove clevis pin, loosen the nuts on the adjusting rod and turn clevis until a ¼″—⅜″ free play is obtained at the brake lever with pin installed.
2. Tighten locknuts on adjusting rod and reinstall clevis pin.

Internal Shoe Type Parking Brake Drum and Shoe

Removal and Installation

1. Remove the drive shaft. Disconnect the parking brake actuating lever from the linkage.
2. Remove the transmission spline flange and drum. Remove the bolts holding the carrier plate to the transmission housing. Slide the plate with the brake shoes and retaining springs off the transmission.
3. Remove the actuating lever, shoe retaining springs, and shoes.
4. Install the brake shoe lower retaining of the shoes.

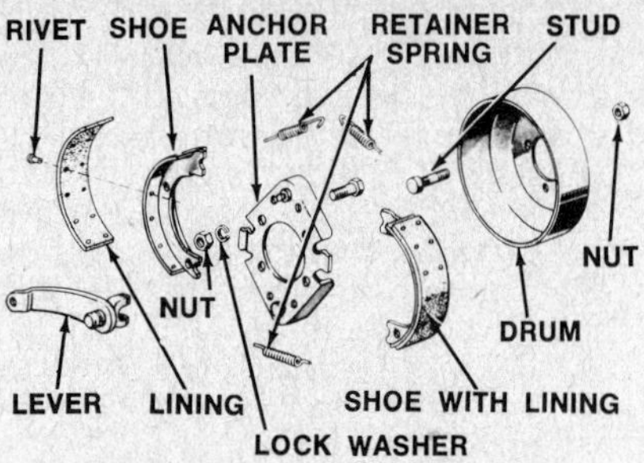

Exploded view of internal shoe type parking brake (© Ford Motor Co.)

5. Position the shoes and lower retaining spring on the back of the carrier plate and install the shoe upper retaining springs and the actuating lever. Place the assembly on the transmission with the lever properly positioned at the ball socket and shoe ends.
6. Install the brake mounting bolts and lockwashers.
7. Install the transmission drum, spline flange, nut, and cotter pin.

   NOTE: If the drum mounting bolts are pressed into the companion flange the drum can be mounted during the following step.
8. Install the drive shaft and brake drum.
9. Connect the actuating lever to the parking brake linkage. Check the brake operation and adjust if necessary.

Transmission Mounted External Band Shoe

Removal and Installation

1. Put the transmission in low gear and disconnect the driveshaft flange from the transmission.
2. Apply the parking brake and remove the nut attaching the transmission output shaft flange. Release the parking brake.
3. Disconnect the adjusting rod from the cam by removing the cotter and clevis pins.
4. Remove the cotter and clevis pins and remove the cam link from the cam.
5. Remove the lockwire and anchor adjusting screw.
6. Remove the brake band adjusting nuts and bolts.
7. Lift the brake band and lining from the drum.
8. The lining should be replaced if the lining is less than 1/32 in. off the top of the rivet.
9. Installation is the reverse of removal. Adjust the parking brake.

FUEL SYSTEM

Reference

Information of application and

major adjustments can be found in the "Carburetor" sections of this manual.

Idle Mixture Adjustments

Idle Fuel Settings—Engine Off—1973

1. Set idle mixture screw(s) and limiter cap(s) to full counterclockwise position.
2. Back off idle speed adjusting screw until throttle plate(s) seat in throttle bore(s).
3. Be sure dashpot or solenoid (if so equipped) plunger is not interfering with the throttle lever. It may be necessary to loosen the dashpot to allow the throttle plate to seat in the throttle bore.
4. Turn the idle speed adjusting screw inward until it just makes contact with stop on throttle shaft and lever assembly, then turn screw inward $1\frac{1}{2}$ turns to establish a preliminary idle speed adjustment.

Idle Fuel Settings—Engine Running—1973

1. Set parking brake, start engine and position idle screw on the intermediate step of the fast idle cam to obtain an engine speed of 1500 rpm. Let the engine run for at least 20 minutes so that engine and underhood temperatures are stabilized.
2. Check ignition timing and advance as described above in this section. These settings must be accurate.
3. On manual transmission model, idle setting is made with transmission in *neutral*. On automatic transmission models, set selector lever in DRIVE position and parking brake on, except as noted when using an exhaust gas analyzer.
4. Be sure choke plate is in full open position.
5. On carburetors equipped with a hot idle compensator or where the idle compensator is in the crankcase ventilation hose, be sure the compensator is seated to allow for proper idle adjustment.
6. Turn headlights on so that alternator is under load.
7. Turn air conditioner OFF for final idle speed adjustment.
8. Adjust curb idle rpm to specifications (see Specifications at the beginning of this section or in the Carburetor section of the General Repair Section). Use a tachometer and leave the air cleaner on. On Carter model YF 1-v with solenoid throttle modulator, turn solenoid plunger screw to obtain correct curb idle. Disconnect solenoid lead wire at bullet connector near the loom (*not* at solenoid), then adjust the throttle stop screw for 500 rpm. Reconnect solenoid lead wire and open throttle by hand: the throttle plunger should follow the throttle lever and remain in the fully extended position as long as the ignition is on and the solenoid energized. If it is impossible to adjust idle speed with the air cleaner on, remove it to adjust, then reinstall it and check speed, repeating the process until correct idle speed is obtained.
9. Turn idle mixture adjusting screw(s) inward to obtain the smoothest possible idle within range of limiter(s). On 2- and 4-barrel carburetors, turn idle mixture limiters and equal amount. Check for smoothness only with the air cleaner installed.

Additional Idle Speed and Mixture Procedures—1973

If a satisfactory idle is not obtained with the above normal procedures, make the following checks, making corrections if necessary:

1. Vacuum leaks, ignition wiring continuity, spark plugs, breaker point dwell angle, breaker point gap and initial ignition timing.
2. If a satisfactory idle condition is still not obtained with the checks and corrections of Step 1 above, check: fuel level, crankcase ventilation system, valve clearance and engine compression.
3. If the above procedures fail to produce a satisfactory idle condition, it may be due to a lean idle mixture. Check air-fuel mixture with an exhaust analyzer and adjust as described below.

Use of Exhaust Gas Analyzer—1973

1. Connect analyzer in accordance with manufacturer's instructions. All exhaust gas analyzers must be checked for calibration.
2. Observe reading with *air cleaner installed*. Refer to specifications below for correct air-fuel ratio.
3. Turn idle mixture adjusting screw(s) to obtain specified air-fuel ratio. On 2- and 4-barrel carburetors, turn the idle limiters equal amounts. Be sure to check idle speed frequently, correcting if necessary. Allow at least 10 seconds after each mixture adjustment for the analyzer to properly respond and stabilize.
4. If the air-fuel ratio is not to specifications, as shown by analyzer reading, it may be corrected by altering the controlled limits of the idle mixture system. See following paragraph for limiter cap replacement procedure.

Replacing Idle Limiter Caps—1973

1. Cut plastic cap with a knife or side-cutter pliers, then carefully pry limiter apart. On some carburetors it may be necessary to remove the carburetor to remove the limiters. On Holley 4-barrel carburetors, pry limiters out of metering block with a screwdriver.
2. After limiters are removed, set the carburetor to the correct fuel-ratio, using exhaust gas analyzer.
3. When air-fuel ratio is within specified value, install limiter caps. Install cap so that it is the maximum counterclockwise position with the tab of the limiter against the stop on the carburetor. Be careful not to turn the screw, installing cap with a straight, forward push.
4. Recheck air-fuel ratio with the analizer.

Idle Fuel Setting-Exhaust Gas Analyzer—1974-76

NOTE: The following operations are for vehicles without catalytic converters or with related partial catalyst equipped vehicles.

1. Operate the analyzer as recomended by the manufacturer's instructions.
2. Operate the engine for a minimum of 20 minutes at fast idle to normalize engine temperature.
3. Check and make sure that the engine timing and idle speed are as specified on the engine decal. All vacuum hoses must be connected.
4. If the vehicle is equipped with a dual spark delay valve, the DSDV must be disconnected and plugged.
5. Disconnect the evaporative emission purge line to the air cleaner.

   NOTE: The air cleaner must be in position when the readings are taken for valid results.
6. Disconnect the thermactor system air hose from the by-pass valve to the check valve at the check valve connection.
7. Place the transmission in neutral or park with the parking brake on. Start the engine and accelerate to 1500 rpm. Place your hand over the by-pass valve connection, air flow should be felt and heard.
8. With your hand held over the by-pass valve connection for 5 to 8 seconds, pinch off the vacuum hose at the by-pass valve to duplicate the air by-pass cycle. Release the pinched vacuum hose. Air flow should be felt and heard

to diminish or stop for a short period of time then resume as before. The length of time required to resume normal flow cannot be specified since the time interval is dependant on the engine vacuum and length of time the vacuum line is pinched off. Air will be discharged through the exhaust ports in the side of the valve silencer cover. If this complete cycle does not occur, the valve must be replaced.

9. Insert the probe of the prepared "CO" analyzer into the tail pipe of a non-catalyst vehicle according to the manufacture's instructions.
10. With the brake pedal depressed, or the wheels blocked, increase the engine speed slightly and allow the throttle to return to the normal closed position. If the vehicle is equipped with an automatic transmission, place the selector in the drive position.
11. Observe the readings on the analyzer after allowing at least 10 seconds for the instrument to stabilize.

    NOTE: All readings must be completed in 60 seconds to preclude incorrect readings caused by engine overheating.

12. If the reading in step 11 is not within specifications, recheck the instrument calibrations according to the manufacture's instructions and adjust if required. Repeat steps 10 and 11, after stabilization of the engine temperature.
13. If the readings are still not within specifications, proceed as follows:
    a. Remove the air cleaner.
    b. Adjust the idle mixture screws to provide the correct "CO" reading. If necessary, remove the limiter caps.
    c. If necessary, correct the idle speed immediately to specifications. The thermactor system must be connected each time the curb idle speed is adjusted.
    d. Install the air cleaner and tighten the nut.
    e. If necessary, re-stabilize the engine temperature by operating the vehicle at fast idle speed.
14. Repeat steps 10 thru 13 until the correct "CO" reading and idle speed has been obtained.
15. Install blue service limiter caps if caps were removed. The limiter caps should be installed so that they are against the stops and it is not possible to turn them counter clockwise.
16. Re-check the "CO" reading to be sure the reading has not changed during installation of the limiter caps.
17. Remove all test equipment and connect the evaporative emission hose and the thermactor air hose.

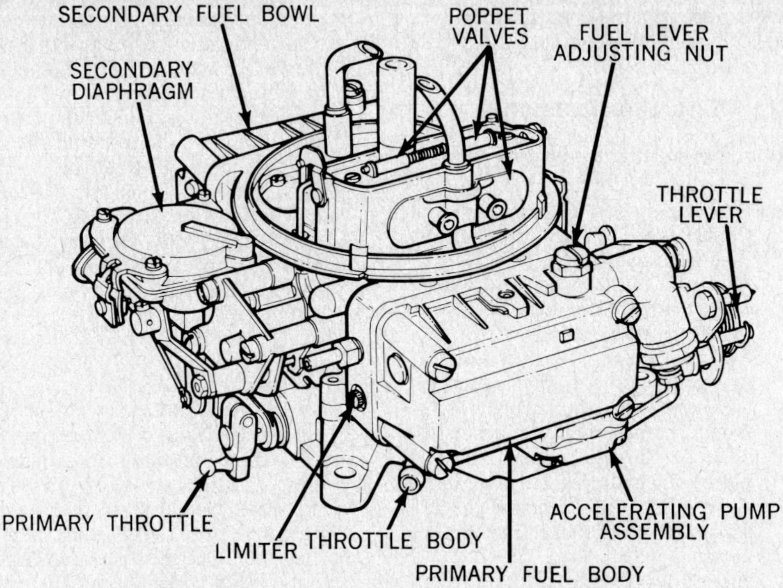

Holley 4 BBL—adjustment locations (© Ford Motor Co.)

Idle Mixture Setting-Propane Enrichment Method—1975 and Later

NOTE: Remove the air cleaner when necessary to perform adjustments.

1. Bring the engine to normal operation temperature and connect a tachometer.

   NOTE: If vehicle is equipped with the Dura Spark II *ignition system, be sure to use a tachometer rated for this type of ignition system.*

2. Disconnect the evaporative emission purge hose from the air cleaner. Disconnect the PCV closure hose from the air cleaner and plug the hose.
3. Adjust the curb idle speed to specifications on engine decal.

   NOTE: With the transmission in neutral, run the engine at 2500 rpm for 15 seconds before each speed check. The idle speed must be adjusted with the air cleaner in place.

4. If vehicle is equipped with Thermactor System, revise the dump valve vacuum hoses as follows:
   a. For dump valves with two vacuum fittings, disconnect and plug the hose(s).
   b. For dump valves with one fitting, remove the hose at the dump valve and plug it. Connect a slave hose from the dump valve vacuum fitting to an intake manifold vacuum fitting.
5. Place the special gas tool into the air cleaner evaporative purge nipple. *With the engine idling, slowly open the propane valve until the engine speed reaches a maximum and then begins to drop. Note the maximum speed increase. If the speed will not drop, check the bottle gas supply. If necessary, repeat the operation with a new bottle gas supply.
   a. If the speed increase is within specifications, but not "O" rpm, proceed to step 6. If the speed increase is "O" and minimun specification is "O", proceed to step 5d.
   b. If the speed increase is higher than specification enrich the mixture without propane by turning the mixture limiter screws counterclockwise in equal amounts until the rpm increases as necessary. Example: If the increase was 80 rpm and the desired reset is 50 rpm, the mixture screws should be richened to attain a 30 rpm increase. Repeat steps 3 and 5.
   c. If the speed increase is lower than specifications proceed as follows; lean the mixture without propane by turning the mixture screws clockwise in equal amounts until the rpm decreases as necessary. Example: If the increase was "O" rpm and the desired reset increase is 20 rpm, the mixture screws should be leaned to attain a 20 rpm decrease. Reepat steps 3 and 5.
   d. If the speed increase is "O" rpm and the minimum speed gain specification is "O", perform the following speed drop test; Turn the mixture

limiters counterclockwise to the maximum rich position. (If the limiters have been removed, do not enrich; assume the mixture screws are already set at the maximum rich position.) Lean the idle fuel mixture by turning the screws clockwise equally as specified. Note the drop in engine rpm.

e. If the speed drop is equal to or greater than the specified minimum speed drop, return the mixture limiters to the maximum rich position or the mixture screws to the "assumed" maximum rich position. If the engine speed before mixture adjustment was 650 rpm and the speed drop specification is 100 rpm minimum, proceed to step 6 if the engine speed drops to at least 550 rpm or stalls.

f. If the speed drop is less than the specified minimum speed drop, leave the mixture limiters or screws in the adjusted position and repeat steps 3 and 5.

6. If the idle limiters were removed, install new blue service limiters at the maximum rich stop. Check the speed increase after installation of the limiters to be certain that the settings were not disturbed. If the setting is within specification, proceed to step 7, if not correct as required.
7. Remove the gas tool from the nipple and connect all system components that were removed.
8. Set the curb idle speed to specification if step 3 required an idle speed adjustment.
9. Turn off the engine and disconnect the tachometer.

* Every time propane is administered, place the transmission in the range specified on the engine decal.

† Remove the limiter caps with appropriate tool if required.

Idle Fuel Setting-Optimum Idle Method—1977 and Later

NOTE: This alternate method is to be used only when propane enrichment equipment is not available. Remove the air cleaner when necessary to perform adjustments.

1. Bring the engine to normal operation temperature and connect a tachometer.

   NOTE: If vehicle is equipped with the Dura Spark II *ignition system, be sure to use a tachometer rated for this type of ignition system.*
2. Disconnect the evaporative emission purge hose from the air cleaner.
3. If vehicle is equipped with Thermactor System, revise the dump valve vacuum hoses as follows:
   a. For dump valves with two vacuum fittings, disconnect and plug the hose(s).
   b. For dump valves with one fitting, remove the hose at the dump valve and plug it. Connect a slave hose from the dump valve vacuum fitting to an intake manifold vacuum fitting.
4. Remove the idle mixture limiter.
5. With the transmission in neutral, run the engine at 2500 rpm for 15 seconds.
6. Block the wheels or apply the brake. With the transmission in drive for automatic and neutral for manual, adjust the idle to curb idle RPM plus the optimum idle speed range RPM (if the specified optimum idle speed range is "O" rpm, simply adjust to the curb idle rpm).
7. With the transmission in drive for automatic and neutral for manual, adjust the idle mixture screws to the maximum idle rpm, leaving the screws in the leanest position that will maintain this "maximum idle rpm."
8. Repeat steps 5, 6, and 7 until further adjustment of the idle mixture screws does not increase the idle rpm.
9. If the specified optimum idle speed rpm is "O" proceed to step 11. Otherwise proceed to the next step.
10. With the transmission in drive for automatic and neutral for manual, turn the mixture screws equally in the lean direction until the curb idle rpm is obtained.
11. Install new blue service limiter caps at the maximum rich stops. Check the idle speed to insure that the limiter cap installation did not disturb the setting. Correct if necessary.
12. Turn off the engine, disconnect the tachometer, reinstall the system components, and make sure that the air cleaner attaching nut is tight.

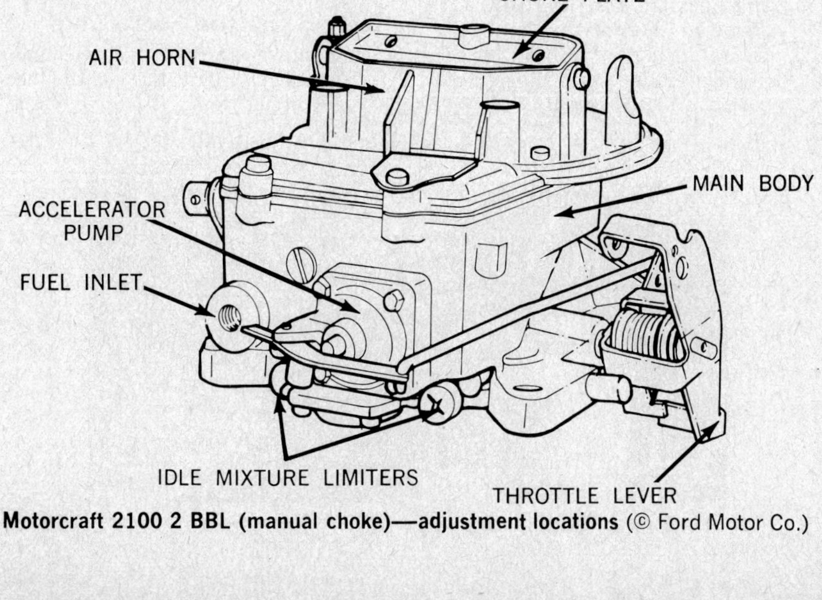

Motorcraft 2100 2 BBL (manual choke)—adjustment locations (© Ford Motor Co.)

Carburetor

Removal and Installation

1. Remove the air cleaner.
2. Remove the throttle cable or rod from the throttle lever. Disconnect the distributor vacuum line, EGR vacuum line, if so equipped, the inline fuel filter and the choke heat tube at the carburetor.
3. Disconnect the choke clean air tube from the air horn. Disconnect the choke actuating cable, if so equipped. Disconnect the electric choke wire at the connector, if so equipped. Disconnect the governor throttle control lines and governor wire connector at the carburetor, if so equipped.
4. Remove the carburetor retaining nuts then remove the carburetor. Remove the carburetor mounting gasket, spacer (if so equipped), and the lower gasket from the intake manifold.
5. Before installing the carburetor, lean the gasket mounting surfaces of the spacer and carburetor. Place the spacer between two new gaskets and position the spacer and gaskets on the intake manifold. Position the carburetor on the spacer and gasket and secure it with the retaining nuts. To prevent leakage, distortion or damage to the carburetor body flange, snug the nuts, then alternately tighten each nut in a criss-cross pattern.
6. Connect the inline fuel filter, throttle cable, choke heat tube, distributor vacuum line, EGR vacuum line, choke cable, electric choke wire and governor throttle control lines and wire.

NOTE: On some carburetors, be sure the end of the choke cable is bent downward to prevent interference with the bottom of the air cleaner. Failure to do this will restrict the opening of the choke plate.

7. Connect the choke clean air line to the air horn.
8. Adjust the engine idle speed, the idle fuel mixture and anti-stall dashpot (if so equipped). Install the air cleaner.

Idle Speed Adjustment

1. Start the engine and run it until it reaches operating temperature.
2. If it hasn't already been done, check and adjust the ignition timing. After you have set the timing, turn off the engine.
3. Attach a tachometer to the engine.
4. Turn the headlights on to high beam.
5. On trucks with manual transmissions, engage the parking brake and place the transmission in Neutral; vehicles equipped with automatic transmission, engage the parking brake, and place the gear selector in Drive. Block the wheels.
6. Make sure that the choke plate is in the fully open position.
7. Adjust the engine curb idle rpm to the proper specifications. The tachometer reading must be taken with the carburetor air cleaner in place. If it is impossible to make the adjustment with the air cleaner in position, remove it and make the adjustment. Then replace the air cleaner and check the tachometer for the proper rpm reading.

On carburetors equipped with a solenoid throttle positioner, loosen the jam nut on the solenoid at the bracket and rotate the solenoid in or out to obtain the specified curb idle rpm. Disconnect the solenoid lead wire at the connector, set the automatic transmission in Neutral, then adjust the carburetor throttle stop screw to obtain 500 rpm. Connect the solenoid lead wire and open the throttle slightly by hand. The solenoid plunger will follow the throttle lever and remain in the fully extended position as long as the ignition is on and the solenoid energized.

Fuel Pump

All engines except the 330, 359, 361, 389, 391, 401, 475, 477 and 534 cu. in. are equipped with mechanical fuel pumps which are driven by an eccentric on the camshaft. On 6-cylinder engines it is located on the lower, left center of the block. On V-8 engines mechanical pumps are mounted on the left side of the cylinder front cover. Some fuel pumps have an integral filter. Other models have an inline filter assembly. Filters are replaced (see owner's manual for specified replacement interval) by unscrewing the filter housing and replacing the old filter.

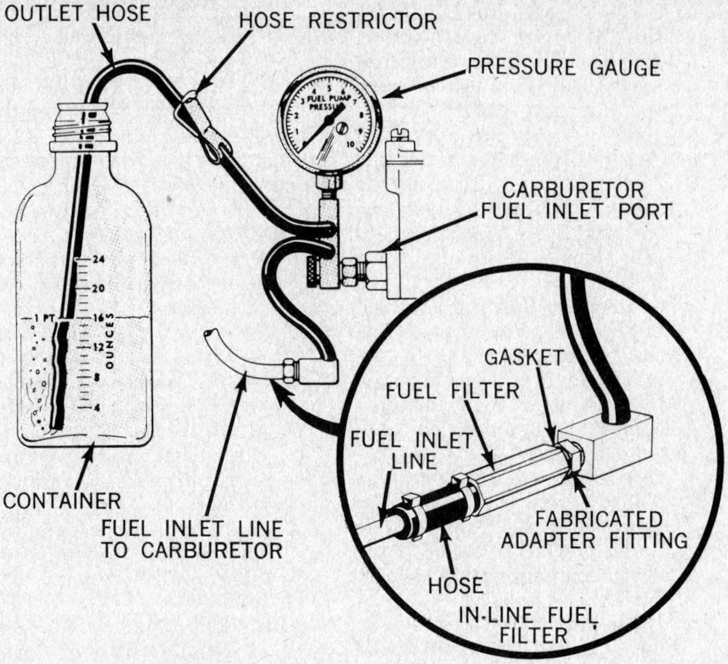

Testing mechanical fuel pump (© Ford Motor Co.)

Testing Mechanical Fuel Pump

Install a new filter element before making the following tests. Tests are made with the fuel pump installed on the engine, with the engine warmed up to normal operating temperature, and with the engine idling at proper idle speed.

1. Remove air cleaner assembly and disconnect fuel inlet line at the carburetor. *Avoid fuel spillage due to risk of fire.*
2. Connect pressure gauge and fitting, flexible hose and restrictor clamp as illustrated.
3. Operate engine at idle speed. Momentarily open restrictor clamp to bleed system of air.
4. Close restrictor and note reading after pressure has stabilized. See Tune-Up Specifications at the beginning of this section for correct fuel pump pressure. If pressure is below specified value, fuel pump must be replaced or rebuilt.
5. If fuel pump is producing correct pressure, leave engine idling and proceed with volume test.
6. Open restrictor clamp and note time required to expell one pint into the container. It should take no more than 30 seconds.
7. If it takes more than 30 seconds, check for restriction in the fuel line from the tank by connecting pump to an external fuel source. If the volume test still takes more than 30 seconds per pint, then the fuel pump must be replaced.

Testing Electric Fuel Pump

1. Remove air filter and disconnect the fuel inlet line at the carburetor.

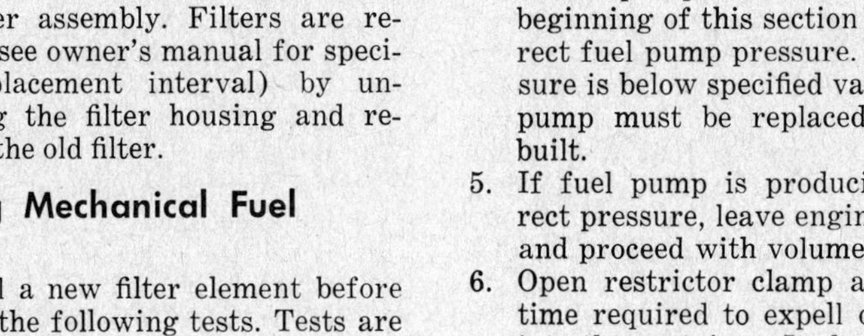

Testing electric fuel pump (© Ford Motor Co.)

2. Using ¼″ pipe fittings (smaller diameter will restrict the flow), connect the pressure gauge, gate valve and flexible hose as illustrated. Use a suitable container to collect expelled fuel.
3. Operate fuel pump with primer switch. *Be sure the battery is fully charged.* Adjust gate valve for a reading of 2 psi, then note time required to expell 1 quart of fuel.
4. If the time required to expell one quart exceeds that specified in the table below, repeat the same test at the outlet at the tank to establish whether or not there is restriction in the fuel line.

Engine	*Time (Sec.)*
330	40
359/361	37
389/391	34
401/475	36
477	33
534	30

5. If the fuel pump does not fill the quart container fast enough, the pump must be replaced as a unit.
6. Remove test equipment, connect fuel line and install air cleaner.

Mechanical Fuel Pump

Removal and Installation

1. Disconnect inlet and outlet lines from pump.
2. Remove pump mounting bolts and remove pump and gasket. Discard gasket.
3. To install, clean away all gasket material from mounting pad and pump flange. Apply sealant to new gasket and threads of bolts.
4. Position pump and gasket on the mounting pad, being sure the rocker arm is riding on the cam eccentric. Turn engine over until eccentric is on low side of stroke.
5. Install mounting bolts and tighten securely.
6. Connect fuel lines.
7. Operate engine and check for leaks.

Electric Fuel Pump

Removal and Installation

1. Disconnect the battery.
2. Disconnect the fuel outlet line at the pump cover.

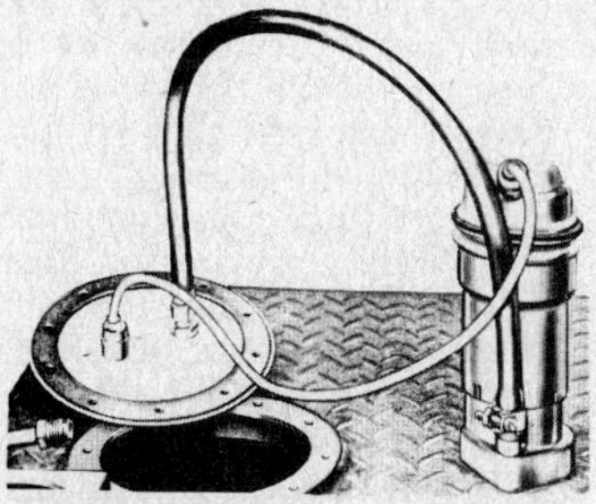

Electric fuel pump installation
(© Ford Motor Co.)

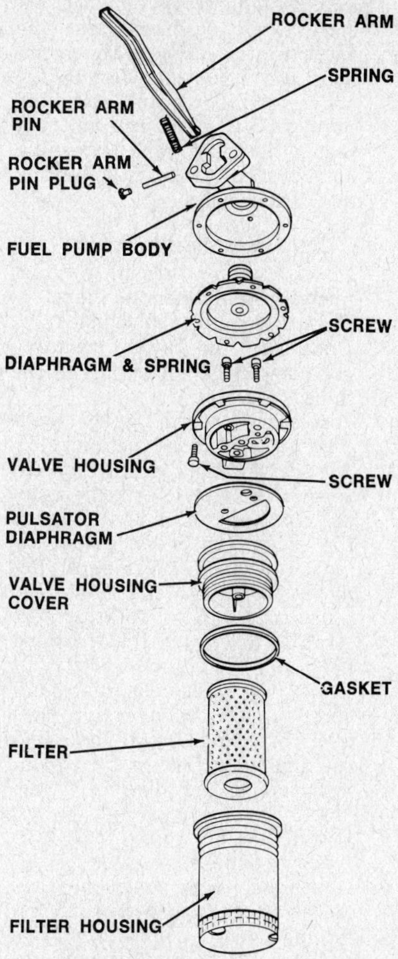

Typical mechanical fuel pump
(© Ford Motor Co.)

3. Remove wire harness housing cover from the fuel pump cover and disconnect the wires.
4. Remove fuel pump cover and reach down into the tank and disconnect the toggle clamp which secures the pump in the retaining bracket and remove the fuel pump.
5. Disconnect the fuel outlet tube and the wire assembly at the cover and at the pump.
6. To install, remove the old gasket from the cover and install a new gasket.
7. Connect the fuel outlet tube and the wire assembly to the pump cover and to the pump.
8. Install fuel pump in the bracket in the tank and fasten the toggle clamp.
9. Position the pump cover assembly on the tank and install the attaching bolts and wire clamps.
10. Connect the fuel line to the fitting on the cover.
11. Position the wiring harness in its housing on the cover and install the wire harness housing cover.
12. Connect the battery and operate the pump and truck engine to check for leaks.

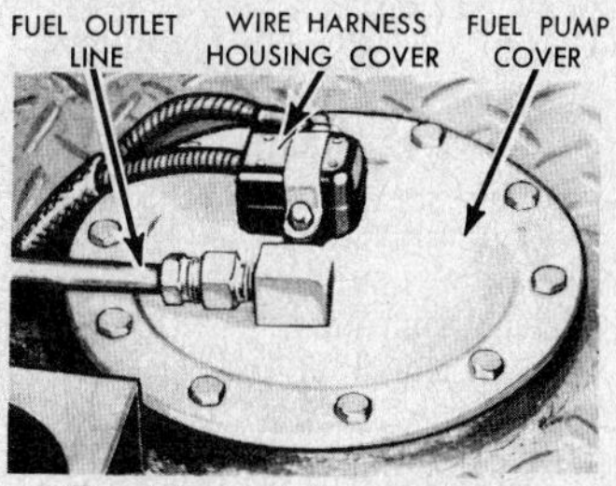

Electric fuel pump wiring
(© Ford Motor Co.)

Fuel Tank

Removal and Installation

1973-77 Bronco

The following procedure can be used to remove either the main or auxiliary fuel tanks.

1. Insert a siphon through the filler neck and drain the fuel into a suitable container.
2. Raise the rear of the vehicle. If you are removing the auxiliary tank, raise the left side of the vehicle.
3. To avoid any chance of sparking at or near the tank(s), disconnect the ground cable from the vehicle battery. Disconnect the fuel gauge sending unit wire at the fuel tank.
5. Loosen the clamp on the fuel filler pipe hose at the filler pipe and disconnect the hose from the pipe.
5. Loosen the hose clamps, slide the clamps forward and disconnect the fuel line at the fuel gauge sending unit.
6. If the fuel gauge sending unit is to be removed, turn the unit retaining ring, and gasket, and remove the unit from the tank.
7. Remove the strap attaching nut at each tank mounting strap, swing the strap down, and lower the tank enough to gain access to the tank vent hose.
8. Disconnect the fuel tank vent hose at the top of the tank. Disconnect the fuel tank-to-separator tank lines at the fuel tank.
9. Lower the fuel tank and remove it from under the vehicle.
10. To install the fuel tank: Position the forward edge of the tank to the frame crossmember, and connect the vent hose to the top of the tank. Connect the fuel tank-to-separator tank lines at the fuel tank.
11. Position the tank and mounting straps, and install the attaching nuts and flat washers.
12. If the fuel gauge sending unit was removed, make sure that all of the old gasket material has been removed from the unit mounting surface on the fuel

tank. Using a new gasket, position the fuel gauge sending unit to the fuel tank and secure it with the retaining ring.

13. Connect the fuel line at the fuel gauge sending unit and tighten the hose clamps securely. Install the drain plug. if so equipped.
14. Connect the fuel gauge sending unit wire to the sending unit.
15. Connect the filler pipe-to-tank hose at the filler pipe and install the hose clamp.
16. Connect the vehicle battery ground cable.
17. Fill the tank and check all connections for leaks.
18. Lower the vehicle.

Econoline-Frame and Body Mounted Tanks

1. Drain the tank with a siphon inserted through the fuel filter pipe.
2. Raise and secure the vehicle.
3. Disconnect the battery negative cable to avoid sparking at the tank. Disconnect the fuel gauge sending unit wire at the tank.
4. Loosen the clamps on the filler and vent hoses. Disconnect the hoses at the tank.
5. Disconnect the fuel line hose from the fuel gauge sending unit.
6. a. On body mounted tanks: Support the tank in position. Remove the nuts the mounting straps to the J-bolts. *NOTE: the J-bolts are attached to body brackets located at the rear of the tank.* Disengage the straps from the J-bolts and the front body brackets. Lower the tank enough to gain access to the vapor valve.
   b. On frame mounted tanks: Support the tank in position. Remove the nuts and bolts that attach the tank supports to the frame. Disengage the straps from the front frame support and the rear crossmember. Lower the tank enough to gain access to the vapor valve.
7. Disconnect the vapor hose from the vapor control valve.
8. Lower the fuel tank and remove it from the vehicle.
9. If the fuel gauge sending unit is to be removed from the tank, turn the unit retaining ring counterclockwise and remove the sending unit, retaining ring, and gasket.
10. If the vapor control valve is to be removed, pull it out of the grommet located in the top of the tank, and remove the grommet.
11. Install the tank in the reverse order of removal. Use a new sealing gasket at the sending unit if the unit was removed. Install a new grommet for the vapor control valve if the grommet was removed. Torque the body mounted J-bolt attaching nuts to 6-8½ ft lbs. and the frame mounted tank attaching bolts to 25-34 ft lbs. Fill the tank and check for leaks.

Econoline-Midship Tank

1. Insert a siphon through the fuel filler pipe and drain the fuel.
2. Raise and secure the vehicle.
3. Disconnect the battery negative cable to avoid sparking at the tank.
4. Disconnect the fuel gauge sending unit wire at the fuel tank.
5. Support the tank in position and remove the restrictor brace from the front of the tank. Disengage the mounting strap ends attached to the frame side rail. Remove the other end from the tank support by rotating the strap to disengage the L-shaped hook end.
6. Lower the tank enough to gain access to the vapor valve, fuel filler hose, fuel vent hose, and fuel line hose. Loosen the attaching clamps and disconnect the hoses.
7. Lower the tank and remove it from the vehicle.
8. If the fuel gauge sending unit is to be removed, turn the unit retaining ring counterclockwise and remove the sending unit, retaining ring and gasket.
9. If the vapor control valve is to be removed, turn the unit retaining ring counterclockwise and remove the vapor valve, retaining ring and gasket.
10. Install the tank in the reverse order of removal. Use a new gasket at the sending unit or vapor valve if they were removed. Torque the stud end nuts to 26-31 ft lbs. and the restrictor brace bolts to 12-18 ft lbs. Fill the tank and check for leaks.

F-100, 150, 250, 350 In-Cab Fuel Tank

1. Siphon the fuel from the tank into a suitable container through the filler neck.
2. Move the seat to the full forward position and tilt the seat forward.
3. Disconnect the fuel gauge sending unit wire and fuel line from the tank. Disconnect the vapor vent chamber and vapor lines of the fuel evaporative emission control system.
4. Loosen the filler neck hose clamp at the tank end of the hose, and pull the filler neck away from the tank.
5. Remove the fuel tank retaining nuts and bolts and lift the tank out of the cab. If the tank is being replaced, remove the fuel gauge sending unit and install it in the new tank.
6. Install the fuel tank in the reverse order of removal.

F100, 150, 250, 350 In-Frame Fuel Tank

1. Drain the fuel from the tank into a suitable container by either removing the drain plug, if so equipped, or siphoning through the filler cap opening.
2. Disconnect the fuel gauge sending unit wire and fuel outlet line.
3. Disconnect the air relief tube from the filler neck and fuel tank.
4. Loosen the filler neck hose clamp at the fuel tank and pull the filler neck away from the tank.
5. Remove the retaining strap mounting nuts and bolts and lower the tank to the floor.
6. If a new tank is being installed, change over the fuel gauge sending unit to the new tank.
7. Install the fuel tank in the reverse order of removal.

F100, 150, 250, 350 Behind-the-Axle Fuel Tank

1. Raise the rear of the truck.
2. Disconnect the negative battery cable.
3. Disconnect the fuel gauge sending unit wire at the fuel tank.
4. Remove the fuel drain plug or siphon the fuel from the tank into a suitable container.
5. Loosen the fuel line hose clamps, slide the clamps forward and disconnect the fuel line at the fuel gauge sending unit.
6. If the sending unit is to be removed, turn the unit retaining ring counterclockwise and remove the sending unit, retaining ring and gasket. Discard the gasket.
7. Loosen the clamps on the fuel filler pipe and vent hose as necessary and disconnect the filler pipe hose and vent hose from the tank.
8. If the tank is the metal type, support the tank and remove the bolts attaching the tank supports to the frame. Carefully lower the tank and disconnect the vent tube from the vapor emission control valve in the top of the tank. Finish removing the filler pipe and filler pipe vent hose if not possible previously. Remove the tank from under the vehicle.
9. If the tank is the plastic type, support the tank and remove the bolts attaching the combination skid plate and tank support to the frame. Carefully lower the tank and disconnect the vent

tube from the vapor emission control valve in the top of the tank. Finish removing the filler pipe and filler pipe vent hose if it was not possible previously. Remove the skid plate and tank from under the vehicle. Remove the skid plate from the tank.
10. Install the tank in the reverse

F series and 1973-77 Bronco auxiliary fuel tank

NOTE: The Bronco auxiliary fuel tank is made of a high density plastic, and is not repairable. If this tank leaks, it must be replaced.

1. Insert a siphon through the filler neck and drain the fuel.
2. Disconnect the negative battery cable to avoid sparking when the tank is removed. Remove the skid plate if equipped.
3. Disconnect the fuel gauge sending unit wire from the unit.
4. Remove the clamps and disconnect the hoses connected to the tank. On vehicles equipped with a fuel evaporative emission control system, disconnect the vapor line from the control valve.
5. Remove the nuts and bolts from the retaining straps and lower the tank to the floor. Replace any worn or damaged parts.
6. Install the tank in the reverse order of removal. *NOTE: On the Bronco, tightening the nuts for the J-bolts until there is 1¼ of thread exposed below the nut. This procedure applies to vehicles with and without a skid plate.* Fill the tank and check for leaks.

Medium & Heavy Duty Trucks Outside Frame Fuel Tanks

1. Drain the fuel by either removing the drain plug (if equipped), or by siphoning through the filler cap opening.
2. Disconnect the negative battery cable to avoid sparking during removal.
3. Disconnect the fuel gauge sending unit wire and fuel lines.
4. Disconnect the electric fuel pump wires if so equipped.
5. Disconnect the fuel return lines if so equipped.
6. In vehicles equipped with dual fuel tanks, disconnect the line connecting the tanks.
7. If the vehicle is equipped with a filler neck and connecting hose, loosen the hose clamp at the tank and disconnect the hose.
8. Support the tank in position and remove the tank retaining strap bolts and straps. Remove the fuel tank. Replace any worn or damaged parts.
9. If the fuel tank is to be replaced, remove the fuel gauge sending unit, shut off valve (if so equipped), and electric fuel pump (if equipped).
10. Install the tank in the reverse order of removal. Install new gaskets for fuel sending unit, shut off valve, and electric fuel pump. Make sure that the tank is properly aligned and that the insulators are properly centered under the straps and brackets. Fill the tank and check for leaks.

Medium & Heavy Duty Trucks Saddle Tanks

1. Drain both sides of the tank.
2. Disconnect the wires from the fuel gauge sending units, and the electric fuel pump (if equipped). Disconnect the fuel lines.
3. Remove the nuts and bolts retaining the air line and hose bracket to the forward edge of the tank.
4. Remove the bolt, nut, flat washer and spring from each fuel tank mounting bracket.
5. Hook a lifting chain to the four corners of the fuel tank, near the mounting brackets and remove the tank with a hoist.
6. If a replacement is being installed, transfer all equipment to the new tank. Install new gaskets on transferred parts.
7. Install the tank in the reverse order of removal. Replace any damaged insulators. Fill the tank and check for leaks.

Air Cleaners—Oil Bath Type

On vehicles that are equipped with oil bath air cleaners, air from the air intake duct assembly enters the air cleaner, passing down over the oil reservoir. The air is then deflected up through the filter element, and then down the center of the air cleaner to the carburetor. Large, heavy dust particles fall into the oil, while the remaining dust particles are trapped in the oil-wetted air filter element. Oil bath carburetor air cleaner oil should be changed every 15,000 miles, and more often if vehicle is operated under severe dust conditions.

Governors

Adjusting Velocity Governors

1. Connect a tachometer to the engine, warm up the engine then read engine rpm at wide-open throttle. If governed speed is not within the range stamped on the governor plate, adjustment is required.
2. Remove the governor seal.
3. To increase rpm, turn the cap counterclockwise; to decrease the rpm turn it clockwise.
4. If the truck is to be operated at a consistent altitude, cut the seal wire and remove the adjusting cap. *Do not rotate the cap during removal.* Use a mirror and light to observe the position of the slots in the adjusting bushing. *Do not disturb the center post or adjusting bushing*—if the tool does not engage the slots easily, remove the tool and realign it. For an increase in the average altitude of operation rotate the inserted tool the amount specified in the table below in the counterclockwise direction.

Aver. Operating Altitude—Feet	*Amount of Tool Rotation*
2000	1/3 turn (120°)
3000	1/2 turn (180°)
4000	2/3 turn (240°)
5000	5/6 turn (300°)
6000	1 turn (360°)

60° or 1/6 turn rotation is equivalent to one flat of the tool hex head.

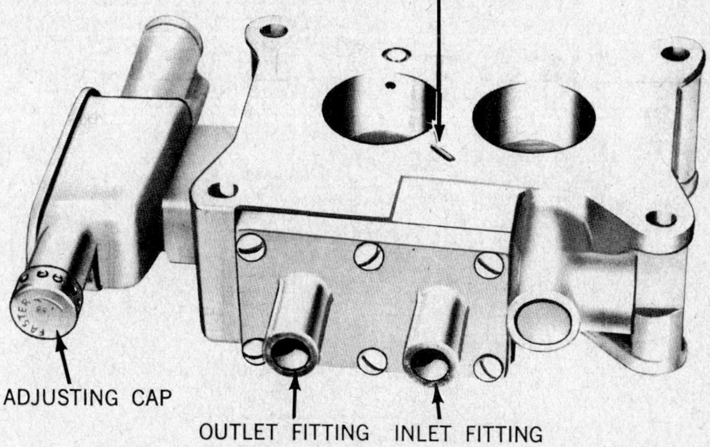

Coolant heated velocity governor (© Ford Motor Co.)

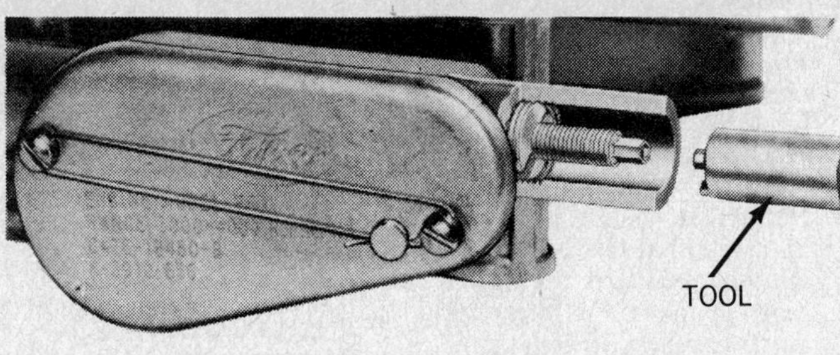

Altitude compensation adjustment—Velocity type governor (© Ford Motor Co.)

5. Remove tool and install cap, but *do not turn the adjusting cap.*
6. Install a tachometer and check and adjust the no-load setting. It should be 3900 for no-load at altitude and 3600 for load at altitude. Load and no-load speed should be slightly above these speeds if the governor is being adjusted above anticipated operating altitude and slightly below if it is being adjusted below anticipated operating altitude.
7. If load rpm is below 3600 rpm at operating altitude, repeat Step 4 turning the tool counterclockwise. If load governed speed is above 3600 rpm, repeat Step 4 turning the tool clockwise.
8. Seal adjusting cap to the governor body using service governor seal wire.
9. If the engine is to be operated at varying altitudes, adjust the governor for 3800 rpm no-load for sea-level. Using the adjusting cap only, adjust the no-load speed for 4100 rpm at the anticipated altitude by turning the adjustment cap ¼-turn (clockwise) for each 1000′ difference between the adjusting and anticipated altitudes. If the maximum operating altitude of the truck is lower than the altitude at which the adjustment is being made, adjust the no-load speed to 4100 rpm with the adjusting cap.

Adjusting Vacuum Governor

1. Warm up the engine until normal operating temperature is reached, then connect a tachometer.
2. Momentarily operate engine at wide-open throttle (governed speed) and note rpm reading.
3. If governed speed is not at the correct value (see Tune-Up Specifications at the beginning of this section), turn off the ignition switch and remove adjusting hole cover from the controlling unit (distributor).
4. Crank engine by hand until adjusting nut is aligned with access hole.
5. Turn adjusting nut clockwise to increase speed and counterclockwise to decrease speed. One full turn equals about 150 rpm.
6. Repeat above procedure until proper governed speed is obtained.
7. Install adjusting access hole cover and tighten securely.
8. Install new locking wire and lead seal.

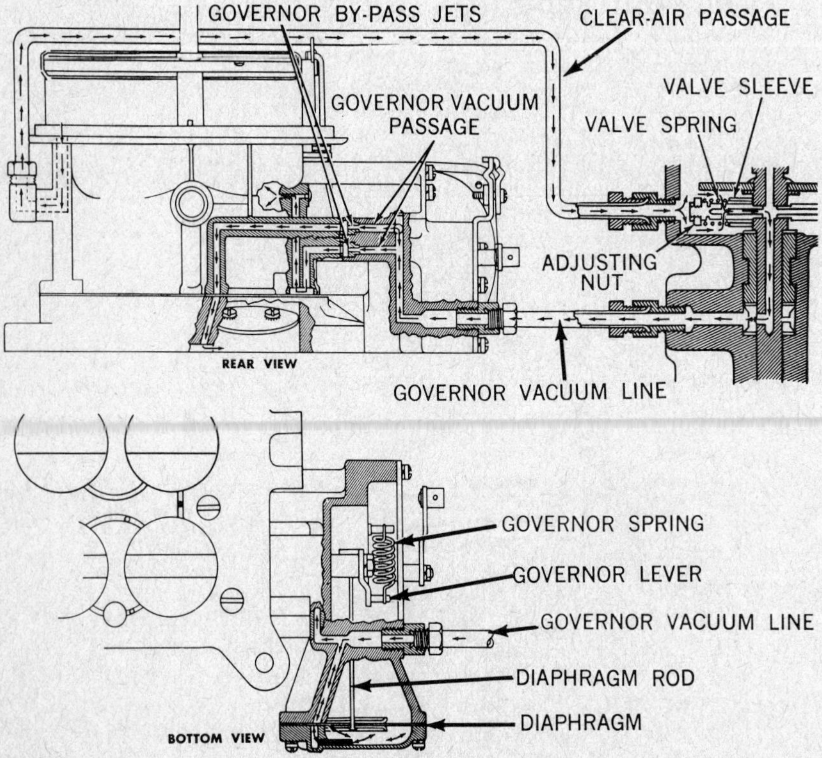

Vacuum governor system (© Ford Motor Co.)

Adjusting Mechanical Governor

1. Disconnect the throttle control rod at the carburetor.

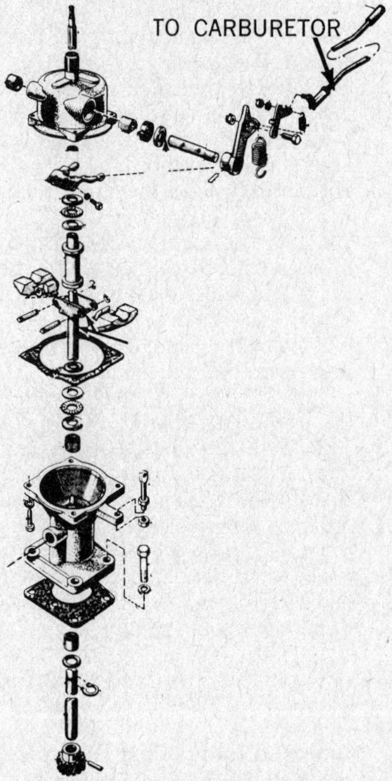

Mechanical governor (© Ford Motor Co.)

2. Loosen the top nut on the primary spring adjusting eye bolt.
3. Tighten the bottom nut finger tight, then turn it in two additional turns to pre-load the spring. Tighten the top nut.
4. Move the throttle to the wide-open position and connect the governor throttle control rod to the carburetor control arm.
5. Adjust the governor throttle control rod so that the governor throttle control auxiliary lever is full forward, then back off (shorten) the rod one full turn.
6. Check the throttle linkage to be sure that the throttle is wide-open when pedal is depressed to the floor. Be sure the rod or cable is attached to the proper hole in the throttle lever.
7. Check operation of choke plate for proper adjustment. On C- AND W-Series trucks the choke plate does not completely close when the dash knob is fully out.

8. To adjust speed, operate the engine (parking brake on) until normal operating temperature is reached. With throttle wide-open, adjust main spring (higher tension increases rpm and lower tension decreases rpm). Sensitivity of the governor can be sharpened by installing the governor spring in the hole closest to the lower arm pivot. Adjust governed speed after changing spring position.

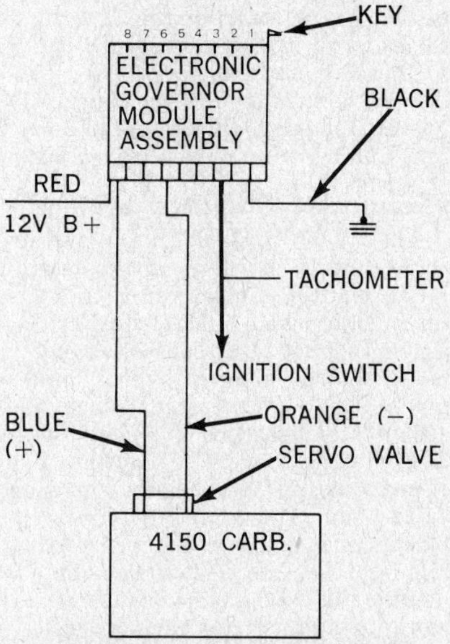

Electronic governor system wiring (typical) (© Ford Motor Co.)

Electronic Governor Control

The function of the electronic governor control system is to limit engine speed to a predetermined maximum and still allow full power output upon demand close to governed speed. The governor mechanism on the carburetor utilizes engine vacuum to provide the actuating force to modulate throttles, and precise control of the system is achieved by regulating governor and secondary diaphragm vacuum levels with a solenoid valve actuated by an electronic control unit.

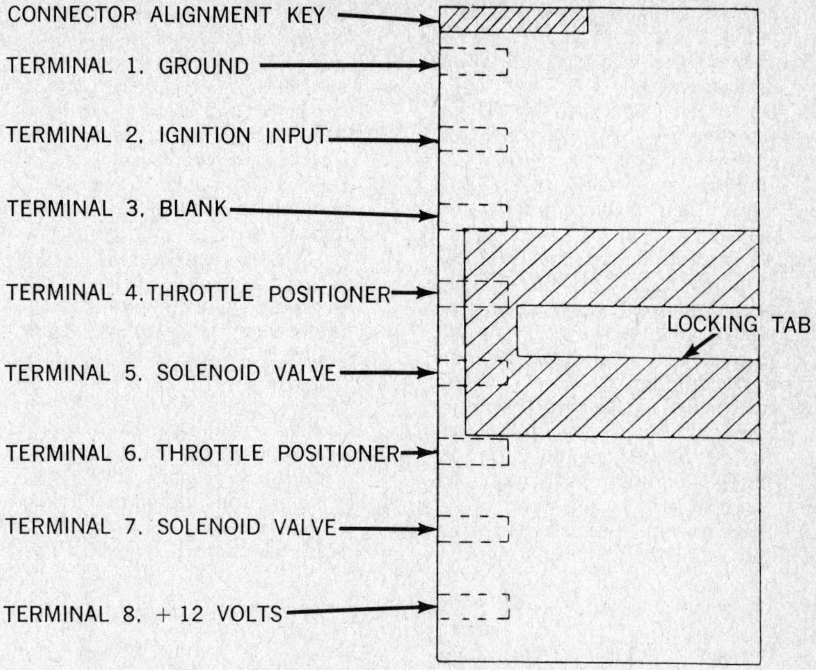

Electronic governor module edge connector (© Ford Motor Co.)

The electronic control governor system is composed of an electronic governor module (EGM) and a carburetor control subsystem.

The following checks should be made initially in response to any complaint about governor operation:

NOTE: It is important that the electronic governor module receives 12 volts across pins 1 and 8 of the edge connector. Pin 2 of the edge connector is an ignition input from the negative primary side of the ignition cell. Pins 5 and 7 of the edge connector are a square wave output to the carburetor mounted vacuum solenoid.

1. Check throttle linkage and carburetor primary throttle plates to confirm proper idle position (closed throttles) and proper wide open position.
2. Check carburetor hose from governor solenoid assembly to secondary diaphragm housing for proper attachment and leaks.
3. Check governor solenoid and cover assembly attachment to governor housing (4 screws) for secure assembly.
4. Check secondary operating lever and shaft assembly to ensure that it's properly connected and operating freely.
5. Check electrical connections for breaks or loose wires at harness-to-EGM junction and also at harnesss-to-carburetor "pigtail" junction.

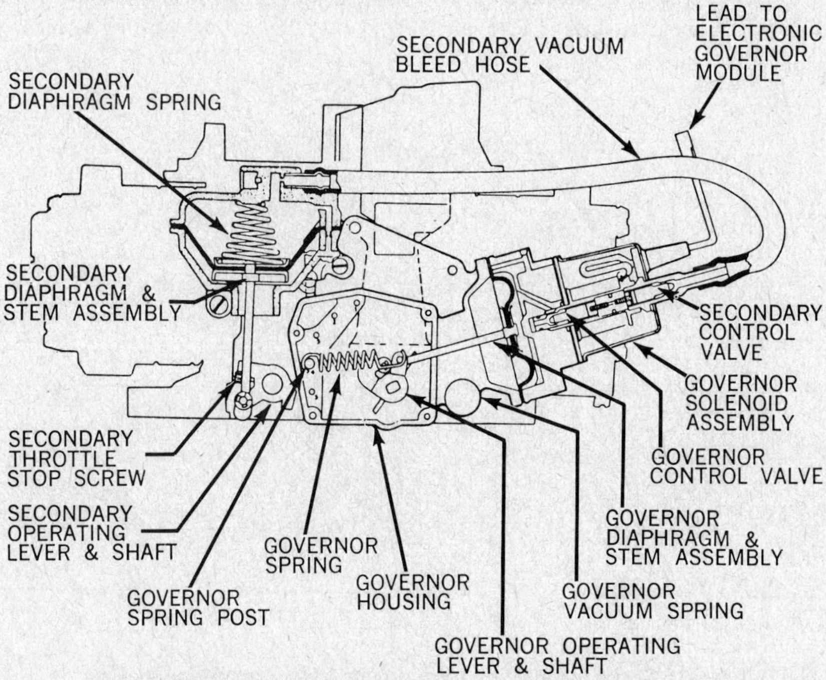

Typical electronic governor system (© Ford Motor Co.)

COOLING SYSTEM

Water Pump

Removal and Installation

6-Cylinder Engines

1. Drain cooling system.
2. Disconnect radiator lower hose

and heater hose at the water pump.
3. Remove fan belt, fan and water pump pulley.
4. On trucks equipped with air compressors, remove the air compressor belt.
5. Remove water pump retaining bolts, then remove pump and gasket.
6. To install, clean gasket surfaces of pump body and engine block.
7. If a new water pump is being installed, remove the fittings from the old pump and install them on the new pump.
8. Coat new gasket with water-resistant sealer on both sides and install gasket and pump on engine. Tighten mounting bolts securely.
9. Install water pump pulley, fan and fan belt, adjusting fan belt tension.
10. If so equipped, install air compressor belt.
11. Connect radiator and heater hoses.
12. Fill cooling system and operate engine to bleed air. Check for leaks and recheck coolant level.

V8 Engines except 401, 475, 477, and 534

Removal and Installation

1. Drain the cooling system and disconnect the battery. On the Econoline models remove the air cleaner and the intake duct assembly, including the P.C.V. hose.
2. Loosen and remove the drive belt(s). Disconnect the radiator hose(s), heater hose and water by-pass hose at the water pump.
3. Remove the bolts securing the fan shroud to the radiator, if so equipped.
4. On engines with water-pump mounted fans, remove the fan, spacer and pulley. Let the fan blade rest down in the shroud. On high-fan engines, remove the fan and bracket assembly. On low-fan engines, remove the bolts securing the fan assembly to the crankshaft damper. Remove the fan assembly.
5. On various engines it may be necessary to remove the air brake compressor, if so equipped. Remove the air brake compressor attaching bolts and position the compressor on the frame rail. Remove the air compressor mounting bracket. Loosen air pump and alternator brackets as required.
6. On vehicles with power steering, loosen the power steering pump and position it to one side, leaving the hoses attached.
7. On various engines it may be necessary to remove the air conditioning compressor, if so equipped. Loosen air conditioning compressor top bracket attaching bolts and remove bracket. Remove air conditioner idler arm and bracket assembly.
8. Remove the water pump attaching bolts and remove the water pump.
9. To install, clean all old gasket material from the cylinder front cover and the water pump.
10. Using a new gasket, and sealer, install the water pump.

    NOTE: Vehicles with 351M-V8 and 400-V8 engines, coat the threads of the attaching screws with oil resistant sealer before installing the water pump.
11. Complete the installation in the reverse order of removal. Fill and bleed the cooling system. Check for leaks.

401, 475, 477, and 534 Engines

1. Drain the cooling system. Disconnect the lower radiator hose, heater hose, and water by-pass hose at the water pump. Remove the fan belt(s).
2. Remove the fan and pulley and lower them into the bottom of the radiator shroud. Remove the bolts attaching the water pump to the water pump housing and remove the pump with the old gaskets.

    NOTE: On C-Series vehicles, remove the water pump attaching bolts and remove the water pump, pulley, and gaskets as an assembly.
3. To install, clean all old gasket material from the water pump housing and the water pump.
4. Position new gaskets coated on both sides with sealer, on the water pump housing, and install the water pump.
5. Complete the installation in the reverse order of removal. Fill and bleed the cooling system. Check for leaks.

Radiator Automatic Shutter

The automatic shutter controls engine temperature by regulating air flow through the radiator. It provides faster engine warm-up and less variation in operating temperature.

There are three methods of operating the shutters, a thermostatically operated system, an air operated system, and a vacuum operated system.

Thermostat Operated System

The thermostat operated system consists of a shutter control assembly, a shutter control rod or a shutter control cable and a shutter assembly. The shutter control assembly has a power element which works much like a thermostat. When the coolant temperature is below operating temperature, the shutters are closed because of the spring tension at the end of the control rod or cable. As the coolant reaches operating temperature, the power element expands and opens the shutters by working against the spring tension.

Air Operated System

The air operated shutter system consists of the shutter assembly, an air cylinder which operates the shutter, and a thermostatically controlled air valve called a shutterstat. With no air pressure on the system, springs in the shutter assembly will hold the shutter blades in the open

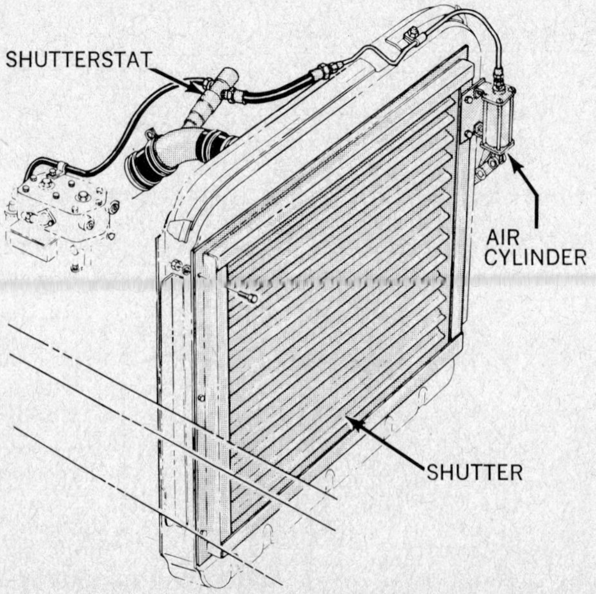

Typical C-Series radiator shutter assembly, air-operated type shown (© Ford Motor Co.)

position. With normal air pressure and the engine below operating temperature, the shutter blades close. As the engine coolant heats to the operating temperature setting of the shutterstat, an air valve in the shutterstat closes, cutting off air to the air cylinder. The air in the air cylinder is then exhausted through the shutterstat and the shutter assembly springs open the shutter blades. Always release the air from the brake system before removing a shutter air line.

Vacuum Operated System

The vacuum operated shutter system consists of the shutter assembly, a vacuum power cylinder which operates the shutter, and thermostatically controlled vacuum valve called a shutterstat. Operation of this system is the same as for air with the exception that vacuum power is the operating medium.

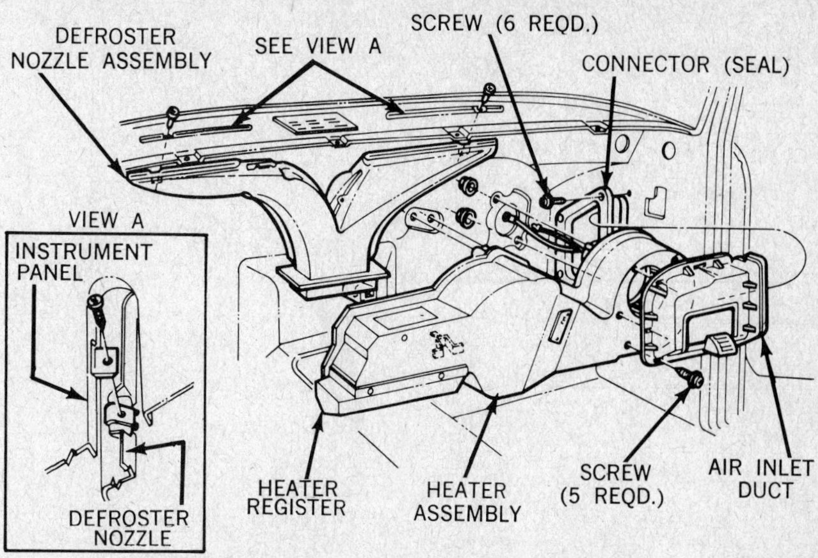

F-100-350 heater installation (© Ford Motor Co.)

Heater Core

Heater Core Without Air Conditioning—Removal & Installation

F-500-880 1973-80

1. Drain the cooling system and disconnect both heater hoses at the heater.
2. Remove the three nuts and washers that hold the heater assembly to the dash panel.
3. Remove the glove box.
4. Remove the screws that hold the air inlet duct to the cowl, pull the heater assembly from the dash panel, and disconnect both defroster nozzles from the heater.
5. Disconnect the wire lead to the blower motor and resistor.
6. Disconnect the wire and control cables from the heater, and remove the assembly to a bench.
7. Remove the core cover stop bracket. Remove the retaining clip and the heater core from the case.
8. Transfer the pad to the new core (no glue) and position the core in the heater case. Install the clip and heater core cover.
9. Position the heater assembly on the dash and cowl, and start one heater to dash retaining nut.
10. Connect the blower motor and resistor wire lead. Install the duct to side cowl retaining screws.
11. Connect the control cables and the defroster nozzles to the heater assembly.
12. Install the remaining heater to dash nuts at the engine side of the dash panel and tighten all the nuts.
13. Position the pads on the core tubes, connect the heater hoses, and fill the cooling system.

1973-79 F-100, 150, 250, 350

1. Disconnect the temperature and air door Bowden cables from the heater housing. *This must be done to prevent damage to the cables.*
2. Disconnect the wires from the blower resistor and the blower motor.
3. Remove the screws attaching the air inlet (vent) duct to the heater housing.
4. Disconnect the blower motor wires.
5. Drain the radiator and remove the heater hoses from the heater core.
6. Remove the heater stud retaining nuts and remove the heater assembly.
7. Remove the gasket between the heater hose ends and the dash panel at the core tubes.
8. Remove the heater core cover and gasket.
9. Pull the heater core and lower support out of the heater assembly.
10. Place the foam gaskets on the heater core and install the core in the heater assembly.
11. Install the core seal and cover plate.
12. Position the heater assembly in the vehicle and install the stud retaining nuts.
13. Connect the heater hoses to the heater core and fill the radiator.
14. Connect the blower motor wires.
15. Place the defroster nozzle on the heater assembly so that the defroster and heater openings are in the up position and there is no air leak around the seal.
16. Install the air inlet (vent) duct on the heater assembly. Push the duct firmly against the seal on the side cowl and tighten the attaching screws.
17. Connect the wires to the blower motor resistor and blower motor.
18. Connect the temperature and air door cables to the heater, and adjust the cables.
19. Install the gasket between the heater hose ends and the dash panel at the core ends.
20. Check the heater operation.

1973-77 Bronco

1. Drain the cooling system.
2. Disconnect the heater hoses at the heater assembly.
3. Remove the nuts and star washers holding the heater assembly to the dash panel.
4. Disconnect the right and left defroster hoses at the plenum.
5. Disconnect the fresh air inlet at the cowl. Rest the heater assembly on the floor.
6. Disconnect the heat/defrost door cable at the door crank arm.
7. Disconnect the outside air door cable at the crank arm.
8. Disconnect the electrical wires at the connector.
9. Remove the heater assembly from the vehicle.
10. Remove the screws holding the rear cover. Remove the clip retaining the cover. Remove the clip holding the heater core in the case, and remove the core.
11. Transfer the seals from the old heater core to the replacement core.
12. Position the heater core in the case. Install the retaining clip. Position the cover and install the screws.
13. Position the heater assembly on the floor of the vehicle. Connect the electrical wire connector.
14. Connect and adjust the heat/defrost door cable and the outside air door control cable.

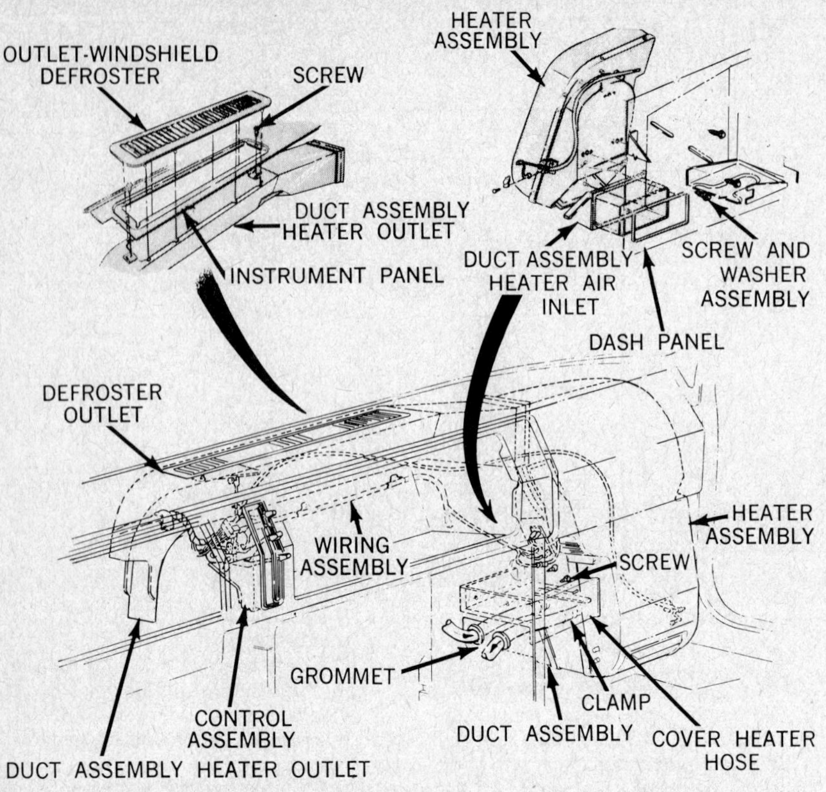

1973-74 Econoline heater installation (© Ford Motor Co.)

15. Position the heater assembly on the dash panel and install the nuts and washers.
16. Place the heater core pads over the door and connect the hoses.
17. Connect the defroster hoses and the fresh air intake.
18. Fill the cooling system. Check the heater operation.

Econoline 1973-74

1. Remove the battery.
2. Drain the cooling system.
3. Disconnect the heater hoses at the heater.
4. Disconnect the heater resistor and motor leads.
5. From under the hood, remove the heater to dash mounting bolts. Move the heater out of position to gain access to the control cable and disconnect the cable.
6. Separate the two halves of the heater case.
7. Remove the heater core.
8. Transfer the core pads to the replacement heater core and position the core in the case.
9. Position both halves of the heater case together and install the screws and clip.
10. Place the heater controls in the OFF position. Place the heater on the wheel housing as near as possible to the installed position. Pull the air door closed (toward the rear of the vehicle) and connect the control cable.
11. Position the heater on the dash, and install the mounting bolts. Use an assistant and make certain that the housing openings line up with the defroster and fresh air openings.
12. Connect the resistor and blower motor leads.
13. Connect the heater hoses, and fill the cooling system.
14. Install the battery. Check the operation of the heater.

Econoline 1975-80

1. Drain the cooling system and remove the battery.
2. Disconnect the resistor wire and the blower motor wire at the harness.
3. Remove the ground wire screw from the dash panel.
4. Disconnect the heater hoses from the core tubes. Remove the plastic strap retaining the heater hoses to the heater assembly.
5. Remove the five heater mounting screws inside of the vehicle.
6. Remove the heater assembly.
7. Cut the seal at the top and bottom edge of the heater core retainer, and remove the retainer.
8. Slide the core and seal assembly out of the heater case.
9. Insert the replacement heater core and seal assembly into the heater case, and install the attaching screws.
10. Install the heater assembly with the mounting screw from inside the vehicle.
11. Connect the heater hoses to the heater core and install the plastic strap.
12. Install the ground wire to the dash panel.
13. Connect the resistor and blower motor leads.
14. Install the battery.
15. Fill the cooling system and check the heater operation.

C-Series

1. Drain the cooling system.
2. Disconnect the defroster hoses at the plenum chamber.
3. Disconnect the blower motor wires at the connectors. Remove the glove compartment liner to

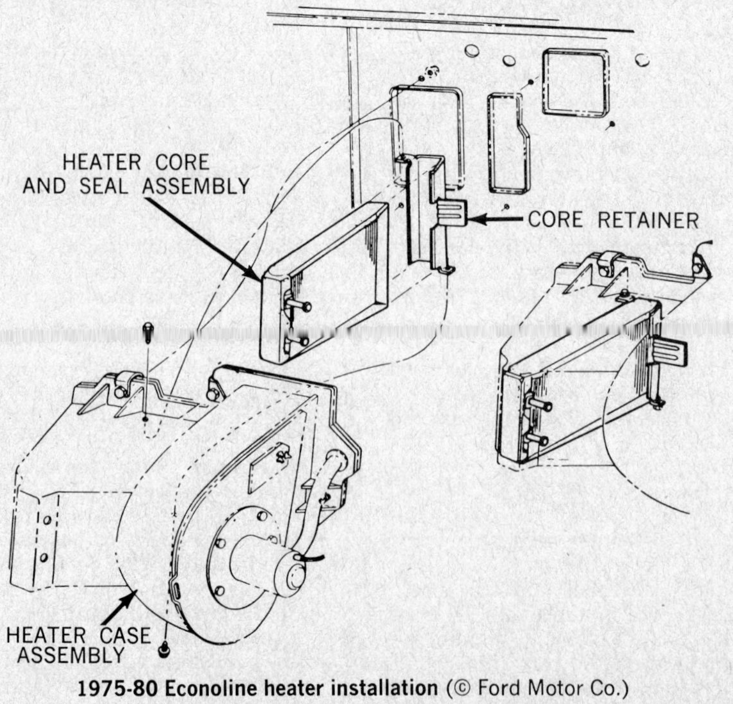

1975-80 Econoline heater installation (© Ford Motor Co.)

gain access to the heater wire connectors.
4. Disconnect the heater hoses at the heater.
5. Remove the heater lower mounting bolts, nuts and lockwashers.
6. Remove the upper mounting screws and move the heater assembly away from the dash. Disconnect the Bowden cable from the air inlet door and remove the heater assembly from the vehicle.
7. Remove the heater assembly top cover.
8. Remove the heater core mounting screws and remove the core from the housing.
9. Install the heater core assembly in the reverse order of removal.

L-Series

1. Drain the cooling system and disconnect the heater hoses at the heater core.
2. Disconnect the control cable at the top of the heater assembly.
3. Disconnect the motor wire leads, and remove the heater front cover.
4. Pull the heater core out of the heater assembly. Transfer the core pads to the replacement core and push the replacement core into the heater assembly.
5. Route the motor leads through the front of the cover assembly, position the cover on the heater assembly, and install the retaining screws.
6. Connect the blower motor leads.
7. Connect the control cable at the top of the heater assembly and adjust the cable.
8. Connect the heater hoses and fill the cooling system.
9. Check the heater operation.

W-Series

1. Drain the cooling system and unlock and tilt the cab.
2. Disconnect both heater hoses at the core and the control valve tubes.
3. Lower the cab.
4. Remove the top cover from the heater assembly, and the register from the side of the heater assembly.
5. Remove the cable retaining clip and disconnect the cable at the fresh air door.
6. Remove the cable from the fresh air door.
7. Remove the seal from the top of the blower housings.
8. Remove the clip holding the defroster door cable to the heater housing, and disconnect the cable at the defroster door.
9. Remove the blower motor hold-down strap secured by tow nuts. One nut also holds the blower motor ground wire.
10. Disconnect the wires at the heater switch.
11. Remove the screws holding the blower housing to the heater housing and the center plate.
12. Lift out the blower housings, motor and cages as an assembly.
13. Remove the defroster door pivot plate.
14. Remove the heater core top retaining plate. Note the defroster cable routed between the plate and the heater core.
15. Remove the screws holding the heater core to the left side of the heater assembly.
16. Remove the clip from the switch and control valve cable and disconnect the cable at the valve.
17. Remove the screws securing the valve and bracket to the heater housing.
18. Lift the heater core, valve and bracket out of the heater housing as a unit.
19. Transfer the valve, bracket and hose to the replacement heater core. (Disconnect the valve hose at the core tube.)
20. Install the heater core assembly in the reverse order of removal.

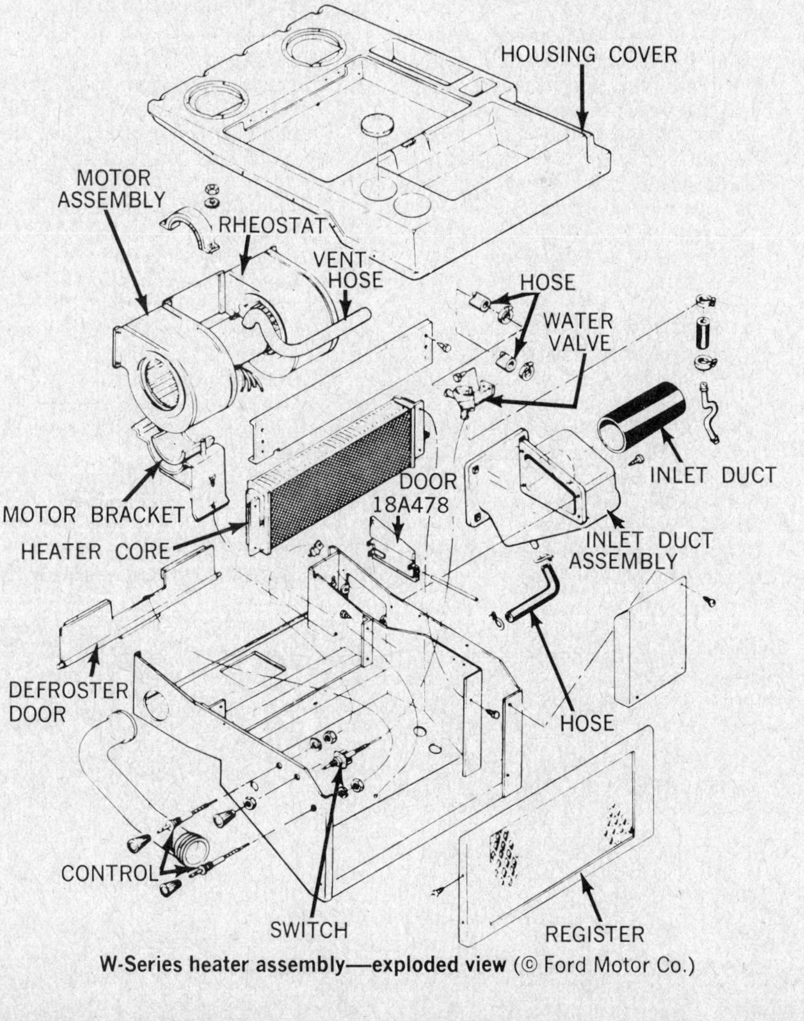

W-Series heater assembly—exploded view (© Ford Motor Co.)

Heater Core With Air Conditioning—Removal and Installation

1973-74 F-100-350 and Bronco

1. Disconnect the battery cable, remove the carburetor air cleaner, and drain the coolant system.
2. Remove the heater hoses from the heater core.
3. Remove the A/C hose support from the cowl.
4. Remove the insulation tape from the expansion valve. Remove the cover plate and seal from the evaporator housing at the expansion valve.
5. Remove the glove box liner and the right A/C duct. Pull the duct from the register and release the clip at the plenum for duct removal.
6. Disconnect the vacuum hose from the fresh air door vacuum motor.
7. Remove the evaporator rear housing dash panel and fresh air inlet boot. Install one upper nut to hold the evaporator front housing to the dash after the housing is removed.
8. Remove the icing switch and the icing switch mounting plate. Push the wire grommet out of the mounting plate.
9. Remove the plenum from the evaporator front housing and lower the plenum.

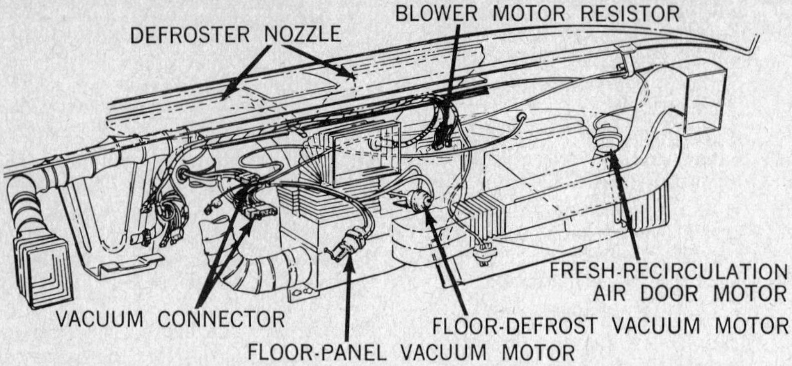

1975-80 F-100-350 and Bronco heater-A/C installation (© Ford Motor Co.)

10. Remove the screws attaching the evaporator core to the housing. Pull the core away from the housing and position up and rearward from the housing. *NOTE: This can be done by tying twine to one of the core end tubes, routing the twine through the glove box opening, and connecting it to the steering wheel.*
11. Remove the heater core from the evaporator housing.
12. Install the heater core in the reverse order of removal. Be sure to test the operation of the heater-air conditioning system when assembly is completed.

1975-79 F-100, 150, 250, 350 and 1978-79 Bronco

1. Disconnect the battery cable, remove the carburetor air cleaner, and partially drain the cooling system.
2. Remove the heater hoses from the heater core.
3. From under the hood, remove the A/C support bracket from the cowl.
4. Remove the insulation tape from the expansion valve. Then remove the cover plate and seal from the evaporator housing at the expansion valve.
5. Remove the glove box liner and remove the A/C duct by pulling from the instrument panel register and releasing the clip at the plenum.
6. Disconnect the right hand cowl fresh air inlet vacuum hose from the fresh air inlet vacuum door vacuum motor.
7. Remove the evaporator rear housing from under the instrument panel. Remove the fresh air inlet tube from the evaporator rear housing and install one upper nut to retain the evaporator housing-to-dash after the rear housing is removed.
8. Disconnect the wires from the icing switch and pull the capillary tube out of the evaporator core. Remove the icing switch mounting plate and remove the plenum.
9. Remove the screws retaining the plenum-to-dash (above transmis sion tunnel) and the screws to evaporator case. Remove the plenum.
10. Install a piece of protective tape on the "A" pillar inner cowl panel, at the lower right corner of the instrument panel.
11. Remove the lower right instrument panel-to-"A" pillar bolt an lower the center instrument panel brace, bolt and nut.
12. Position the instrument panel rearward and install the "A" pillar bolt to hold the panel in the rearward position.
13. Remove the evaporator retaining screws.
14. Position the evaporator away from the case and secure it rearward and upward. Remove the evaporator sealing grommet.
15. Remove the heater core.
16. Install the heater core and evaporator housing components in the reverse order of removal. Be sure to test the operation of the heating and A/C systems after the installation is completed.

Econoline 1975-80

1. Disconnect the electrical leads from the resistor on the front face of the A/C blower.
2. Disconnect the vacuum line from the fresh air/recirculated air door vacuum motor.
3. Remove the A/C blower cover.
4. Remove the push nut and washer from the fresh air/recirculated air door shaft.
5. Remove the control cable from the bracket and slide over the bracket. Remove the cable wire loop from the blend door shaft.
6. Remove the A/C blower motor housing.
7. Remove the blend door housing.
8. Partially drain the cooling system.
9. Remove the heater hoses from the heater core.
10. Remove the heater core retaining brackets.
11. Remove the heater core and seal assembly.
12. Install the heater core and related parts in the reverse order of removal. Check the operation of the heating and A/C system after installation is completed.

L-Series

1. Drain the cooling system.
2. Discharge the A/C system.
3. Disconnect the battery ground cable. **CAUTION: Before any refrigerant lines or hoses are disconnected, be sure that the air conditioning system is fully discharged.**
4. Disconnect the refrigerant low pressure line at the dash panel and remove the fitting retaining nut and lockwasher.
5. Remove the bolts holding the A/C-heater assembly to the dash panel.
6. Disconnect the drain tube at the bottom of the assembly housing.
7. Disconnect the heater hoses at the bottom of the assembly housing.
8. Disconnect the refrigerant high pressure hose at the side of the assembly housing.
9. Lower the assembly to the vehicle floor and disconnect the control cables from the A/C-heater assembly.
10. Disconnect the wires from the blower switch and remove the A/C-heater assembly from the vehicle.
11. Remove the wire harness from the A/C-heater assembly.
12. Remove the blower resistor from the A/C housing.
13. Remove the screws retaining the

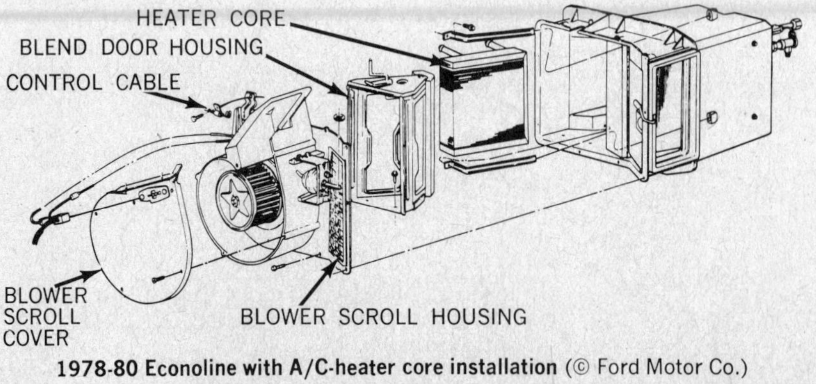

1978-80 Econoline with A/C-heater core installation (© Ford Motor Co.)

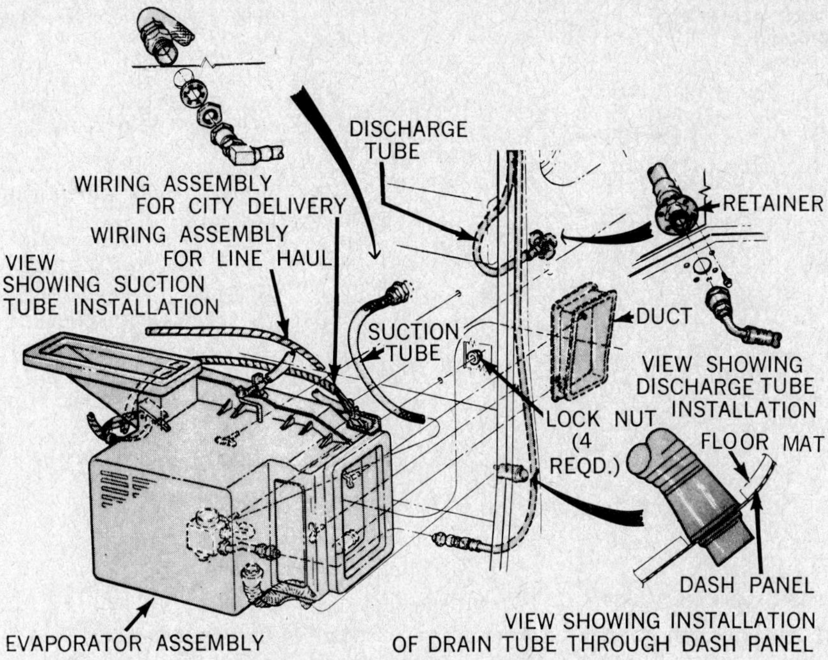

L-Series heater-A/C installation (© Ford Motor Co.)

evaporator core air deflector to the air inlet end of the housing.

14. Remove the housing cover retaining screws and remove the cover.
15. Remove the evaporator core retaining screws and remove the evaporator core and hoses.
16. Remove the blower and adapter plate attaching screws, and remove the blower and adapter plate.
17. Remove the screws attaching the A/C door lever retainers to the door and remove the door from the bellcrank.
18. Remove the screws attaching the evaporator core air deflector to the housing and remove the assembly from the housing.
19. Remove the heater baffle from the housing.
20. Remove the heater core retainer attaching screws and remove the heater core.
21. Remove the insulators from the heater core.
22. Install the assembly in the reverse order of removal. Be sure to leak test, evacuate, and charge the A/C system when the installation is completed. Test the system operation.

ENGINE

Description

All Ford truck engines are of the conventional overhead valve design, either of six-cylinder in-line or V-8 configuration.

The 240 cu. in. (1973-74) and 300 cu. in. (1973-80) 6-cylinder engines are the large block units found in most medium and some heavy duty trucks. The 300 HD Six has a lower compression ratio to meet the higher torque requirements of heavier vehicles. These are the most common Ford power units.

The 330 cu. in. engine became the most popular V-8 option in medium and heavy duty trucks. The difference between the medium and heavy duty models is that the HD has a longer crankshaft in front.

The 302 cu. in. was the V-8 for both Econoline and Bronco models. The 351W was added in 1975, the 460 was added in 1973, and the 351M and 400 were added in 1977.

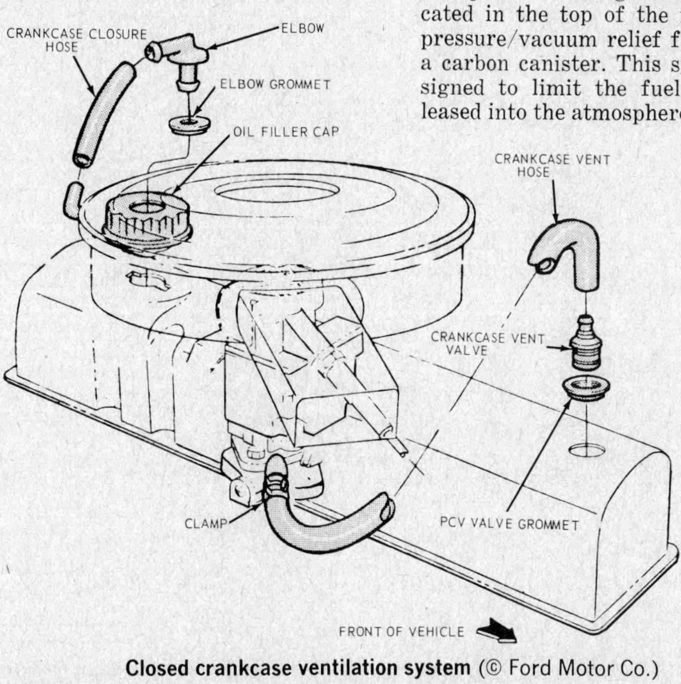

Closed crankcase ventilation system (© Ford Motor Co.)

New for 1979 is the 370 cu. in. V-8 and the 429 cu. in. V-8 engines. The 370 cu. in. engine is available with either a 2 bbl. or a 4 bbl. carburetor. The 429 cu. in. engine is only available with a 4 bbl. carburetor.

The large block Super Duty 401, 475, 477 and 534 cu. in. V-8 engines are used mainly in heavy trucks and will not be considered here.

Reference

Tune-up and general specifications for Ford truck engines may be found at the beginning of this section. Engine overhaul procedures can be found in the "ENGINE REBUILDING" section in the General Repair portion of this manual.

Emission Control

Crankcase Emission Controls

The crankcase emission control equipment consists of a positive crankcase ventilation (PCV) valve, a crankcase air filter that is vented to the air cleaner, and the hoses that connect the equipment.

When the engine is running, a small amount of the gases formed in the combustion chamber leak by the piston rings and enter the crankcase. The PCV system pulls these gases back into the intake manifold allowing fresh air to flow into the crankcase through the filter and filler cap. For service to the PCV system, refer to the "Emission Control" chapter in the General Repair section of this manual.

Evaporative Emission Control

The Evaporative Emission Control system consists of a sealed fuel tank, a vapor controlling orifice valve located in the top of the fuel tank, a pressure/vacuum relief fuel cap, and a carbon canister. This system is designed to limit the fuel vapors released into the atmosphere.

The open orifice valve is used to control the flow of fuel vapor and to minimize the amount of liquid gasoline entering the fuel vapor delivery line. The delivery line conducts the vapor forward to the carbon canister where the vapor is stored. During normal driving, the engine compartment mounted canister is purged of the fuel vapor by means of a hose connected to the air cleaner assembly. The vapors are drawn into the engine's induction system. The fuel cap is sealed and contains a vacuum and pressure relief valve. The vacuum valve relieves tank vacuum caused by consumption or cooling and the pressure relief valve prevents excessive fuel tank pressurization due to any system component failure or operation extremes.

Air Injector System—"Thermactor"

The air injection exhaust emission control system "Thermactor" consists of a air supply pump, external air manifold or cylinder head/exhaust manifold with internal air passages, air by-pass valve, check valve, and the hoses necessary to connect the components.

The air injection system reduces the carbon monoxide and hydrocarbon content of the exhaust gases by injecting fresh air into the hot exhaust gas stream as it leaves the combustion chamber. A pump supplies the air under pressure to the exhaust port near the exhaust valve by either an external air manifold or through an internal drilled passages in the cylinder head or exhaust manifold. The oxygen in the fresh air plus the heat of the exhaust gases cause further burning which converts the exhaust gases into carbon dioxide and water.

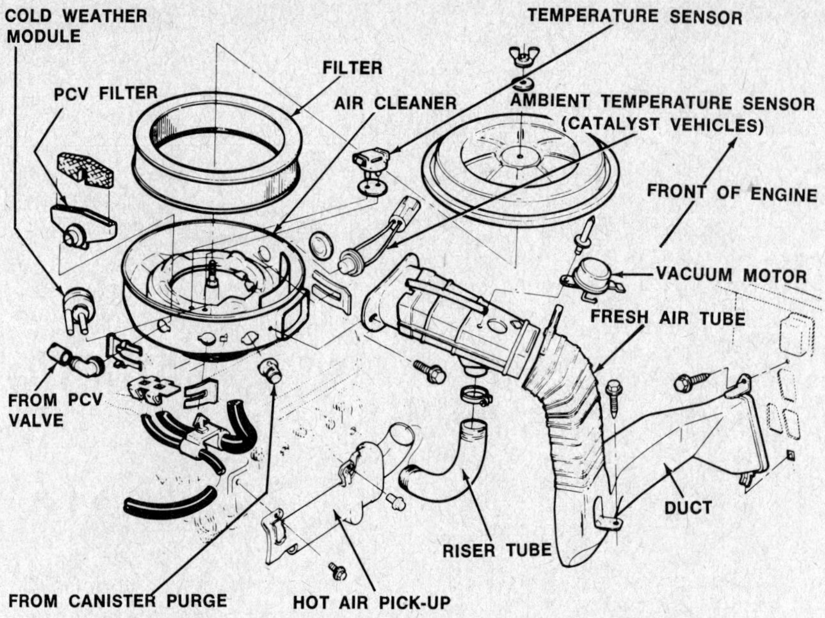

Typical thermostatically controlled air cleaner (TAC) (© Ford Motor Co.)

For service on the air injection system, refer to the "Emission Control" chapter in the General Repair section of this manual.

Catalytic Converter

The catalytic converter is a muffler type device installed in the vehicles exhaust system which contains a chemical catalyst. When the hot exhaust gas passes over and through the catalyst, it heats up to a high temperature and the chemical reaction which occurs breaks down the exhaust into harmless elements. For service on the catalytic converter, refer to the "Emission Control" chapter in the General Repair Section of this manual.

Thermostatically Controlled Air Cleaner System (TAC)

This system consists of a heat shroud which is integral with the right-side exhaust manifold, a hot air hose and a special air cleaner assembly equipped with a thermal sensor and vacuum motor and air valve assembly.

The purpose of TAC is to get hot air into the carburetor as soon as possible because the engine will emit less pollutants on a lean mixture.

Dual Diaphragm Distributor

The dual diaphragm distributor has two diaphragms which operate independently. The outer (primary) diaphragm makes use of carburetor vacuum to advance the ignition timing. The inner (secondary) diaphragm uses intake manifold vacuum to provide additional retardation of ignition timing during closed-throttle decleration and idle, resulting in the reduction of hydrocarbon emissions.

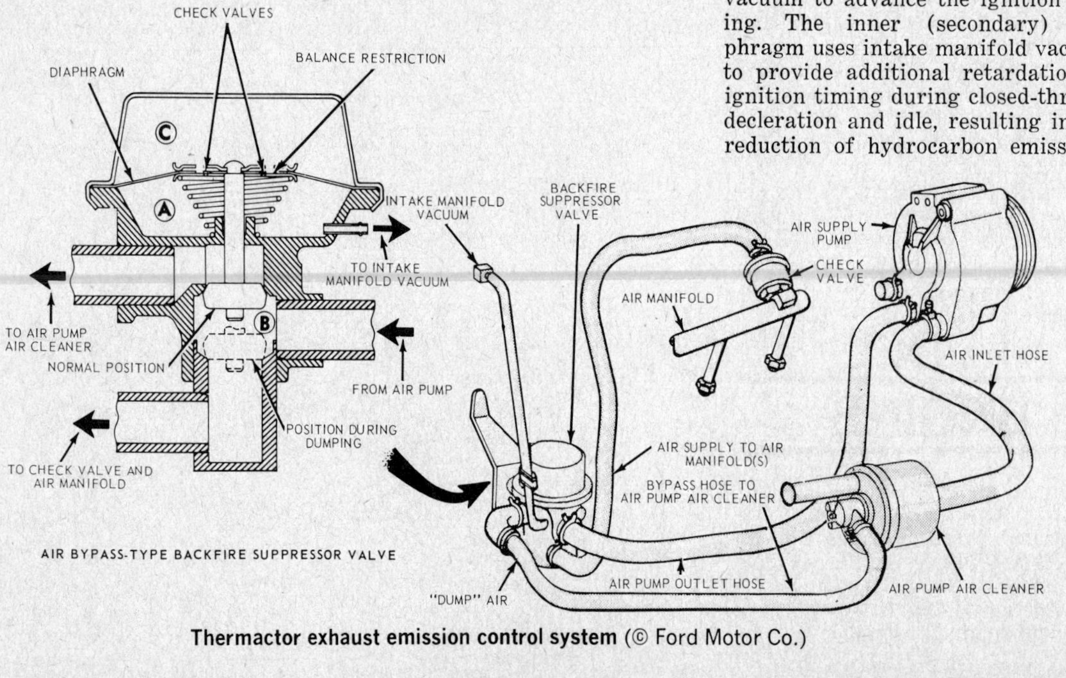

Thermactor exhaust emission control system (© Ford Motor Co.)

Ported Vacuum Switch Valve (PVS)

The PVS valve is a temperature sensing valve usually found on the distributor vacuum advance line, and is installed in the coolant outlet elbow. During prolonged periods of idle, or any other situation which causes engine operating temperatures to be higher than normal, the valve, which under normal conditions simply connects the vacuum advance diaphragm to its vacuum source within the carburetor, closes the normal source vacuum port and engages an alternate source vacuum port. This alternate source is from the intake manifold which, under idle conditions, maintains a high vacuum. This increase in vacuum supply to the distributor diaphragm advances the timing, increasing the idle speed. The increase in idle speed causes a directly proportional increase in the operation of the cooling system. When the engine has cooled sufficiently, the vacuum supply is returned to its normal source, the carburetor.

These switches are used in several places in the emission systems. They can have anywhere from two to four ports and can be used to turn vacuum on and off, or to switch between two vacuum sources for a third delivery point.

Deceleration Valve

Some engines were equipped with a distributor vacuum advance control valve (deceleration valve) which is used with dual diaphragm distributors to further aid in controlling ignition timing. The deceleration valve is in the vacuum line which runs from the outer (advance) diaphragm to the carburetor, the normal vacuum supply for the distributor. During deceleration, the intake manifold vacuum rises causing the deceleration valve to close off the carburetor vacuum source and connect the intake manifold vacuum source to the distributor advance diaphragm. The increase in vacuum provides maximum ignition timing advance, thus providing more complete fuel combustion and decreasing exhaust system backfire.

Exhaust Gas Recirculation System (EGR)

In this system, a vacuum-operated EGR flow valve is attached to the carburetor spacer (except on the 302 V8). A passage in the carburetor spacer mates with a hole in the mounting face of the EGR valve or the intake manifold. The EGR valve on the 302 V8 is located on the rear of the intake manifold. On all engines except the 302 V8, the system allows exhaust gases to flow from the exhaust crossover, through the control valve and through the spacer into the intake manifold below the carburetor. For those engines where exhaust gases cannot be picked up from the exhaust crossover (6 cylinder) as described above, the gases are picked up from the choke stove located on the exhaust manifold or directly from the exhaust manifold. The exhaust gases are routed to the carburetor spacer through steel tubing.

The vacuum signal which operates the EGR valve originates at the EGR vacuum port in the carburetor. This signal is controlled by at least one, and sometimes, two series of valves.

A water temperature sensing valve (the EGR PVS) which is closed until the water temperature reaches either 60° F or 125° F, depending on application, is always used.

Another system working in conjunction with the EGR system is the EGR/CSC system. This system regulates both the distributor spark advance and operation of the EGR valve according to the temperature of the engine coolant. The system consists of: a 95° EGR valve, a spark delay valve, and a vacuum check valve.

When the engine coolant is below 82° F, the EGR PVS valve admits carburetor EGR port vacuum directly to the distributor advance diaphragm through a one-way check valve. At the same time, the EGR PVS valve shuts off carburetor EGR vacuum to the EGR valve and transmission diaphragm.

When the engine coolant temperature is above 95° F, the EGR PVS valve is actuated and directs carburetor EGR vacuum to the EGR valve and transmission instead of the distributor.

The spark delay valve (SDV) delays carburetor spark advance vacuum to the distributor advance diaphragm by restricting the vacuum through the SDV valve for a predetermined time. During normal acceleration, little or no vacuum is admitted to the distributor advance diaphragm until acceleration is completed, because of the time delay of the SDV valve, and the re-routing of the EGR port vacuum, if the engine coolant temperature is 95° F or higher. The check valve blocks vacuum from the SDV valve to the EGR PVS valve so that carburetor spark vacuum will not be dissipated when the EGR PVS valve is actuated above 95° F. increases and the increase in coolant circulation and fan speed cools the engine.

Cold Temperature Activated Vacuum System

The cold temperature activated vacuum (CTAV) system was used beginning in 1974 on 460 V8 engines in F-100 trucks built for sale in California.

The CTAV system more accurately marches spark advance to the engine requirements under cold ambient temperature conditions. The system can select from two vacuum sources

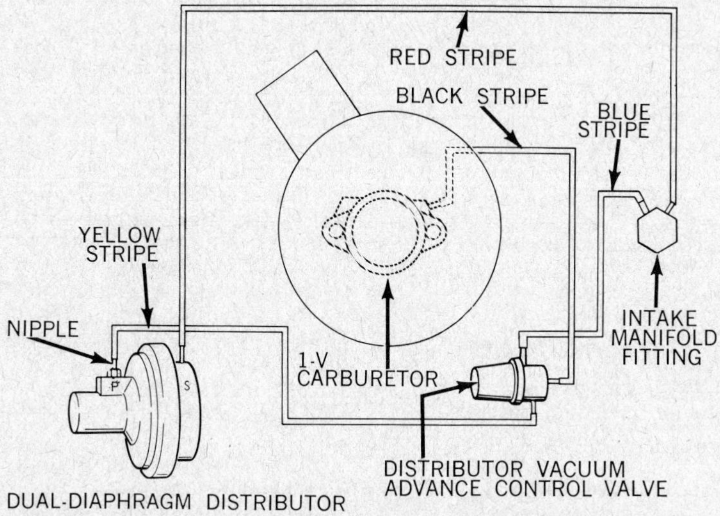

Ignition vacuum system with Imco emission (© Ford Motor Co.)

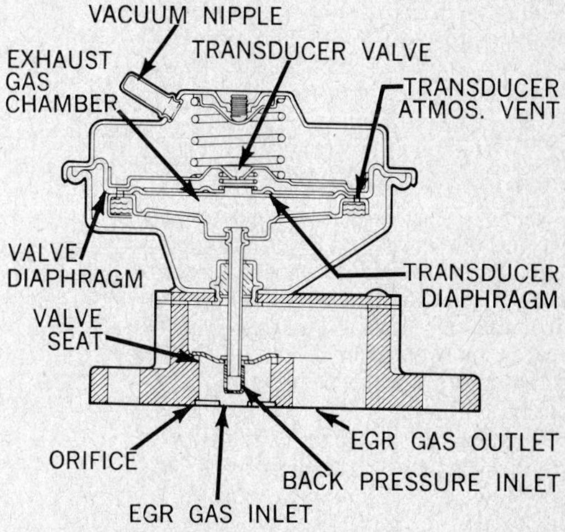

Integral transducer back pressure EGR (exhaust gas recirculation) valve
(© Ford Motor Co.)

for spark advance depending on the ambient temperature: below 45° F—carburetor spark port vacuum, above 65° F—EGR vacuum. In between these two temperature ranges the system will select either source of vacuum, depending on the cycle it is in.

The CTAV system consists of an ambient temperature switch, a three-way vacuum switch, inline vacuum bleed, and a latching relay.

The vacuum from both the spark port of the carburetor and the EGR port is supplied to the three-way solenoid valve. The ambient temperature switch provides the signal that determines which of the sources will be selected. The latching relay provides for only one cycle each time the ignition switch is turned on.

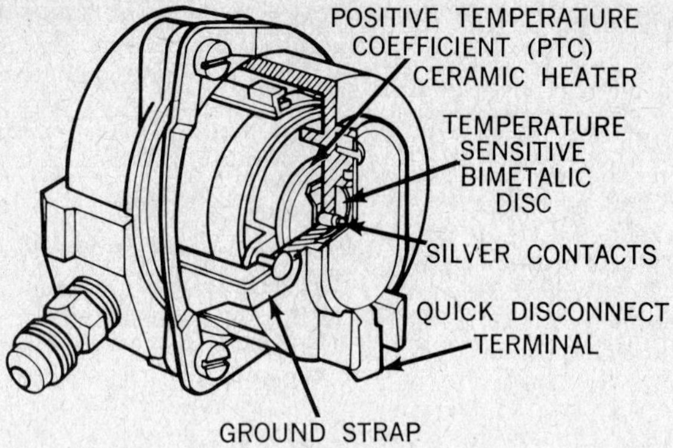

Electric assisted choke (© Ford Motor Co.)

Vacuum and Spring Controlled Heat Control Valve

The heat control valve, commonly known as the heat riser, is mounted between the exhaust pipe and the exhaust manifold. The purpose of the device is to provide a quick warm-up of the carburetor and the rest of the induction system.

Fuel will condense on the cold surfaces of the induction system, which causes air/fuel ratios to fluctuate. These variations can cause uneven acceleration and increased emissions. The exhaust control valve, which is thermostatically-controlled, is closed when the engine is cold and routes hot exhaust gases through a passage under the carburetor and over to the opposite exhaust manifold which has no heat control valve and thus no restriction to block the flow of exhaust gases. This quickly warms the air/fuel mixture delivery passages and provides improved mixture control and driveability. As the engine warms up, the valve opens and reduces the flow of exhaust gases through the warm-up passage.

The valve is either operated by a bimetal temperature sensitive spring or vacuum motor operated by intake manifold vacuum routed through a PVS switch.

Electrically-Assisted Choke

Some pick-ups use an electrically heated choke thermostatic spring housing as an aid to fast choke release and better emission characteristics during engine warm-up. The heater operates from a lead off the alternator only when the engine is actually running.

The heater element only operates when ambient temperatures are above 60° F (when long periods of choke operation are not necessary for engine driveability). When temperatures are blow 60° F, the choke thermostatic spring is heated in the normal manner: via a tube running from an exhaust manifold heat stove.

Vacuum Delay Valves

Retard Delay Valves (RDV) and Spark Delay Valves (SDV)

Delay valves are found in many places on 1974 and later engines. The delay valves work to slow the air flow in the vacuum lines, thus providing closer control on vacuum operated equipment. The SDV is normally used to delay the opening function of a vacuum device and the RDV is used to delay the closing of a vacuum device. The delay valves have an interval sinterted orifice; the check valve and filter pack must be installed in the correct direction in each system.

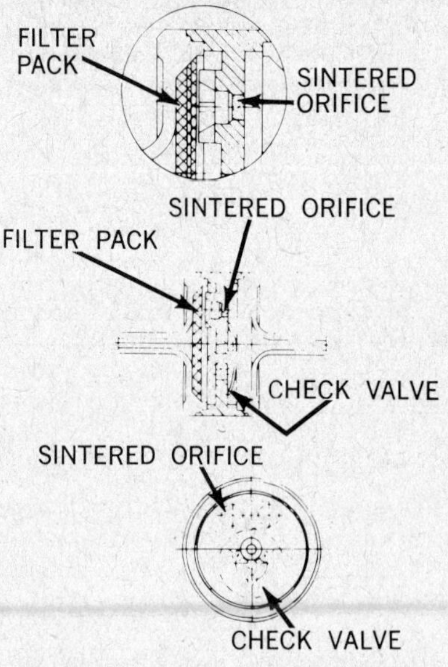

Typical spark delay valve (SDV)
(© Ford Motor Co.)

Engine Removal and Installation

NOTE: For the 1978 and later Bronco, use F-150 4 x 4 procedures.

Bronco 170 cu. in. 6-Cylinder

1. Drain cooling system and remove air cleaner.
2. Disconnect battery ground cable from the battery.
3. Disconnect upper and lower hoses at the engine, remove the four radiator mounting bolts, then remove radiator.
4. Disconnect the heater hose at the water pump and at the rear of the carburetor spacer.
5. Disconnect battery ground cable and alternator ground wire from the cylinder block.
6. Remove fan belt and alternator.
7. Disconnect the starter cable at starter, then remove the starter.
8. Remove U-clamp holding exhaust head pipe to the block, remove manifold stud retaining nuts, and remove pipe from the exhaust manifold.
9. Disconnect wiring at the coil and oil and temperature sending units.
10. Disconnect throttle and choke cables from the carburetor.
11. Remove windshield wiper vacuum home from fuel pump.
12. Remove the crimped clamp, then the flex line from fuel pump.
13. Remove the retaining screws from the equalizer shaft bracket at the block and clutch housing, and remove the bracket.
14. Remove nut and washer from each of the engine mounts.
15. Loosen clutch housing to block bolts just enough so that they may be hand removed later.
16. Remove clutch housing cover retaining bolts.
17. Lower vehicle to the floor.
18. Position a jack under the transmission, and remove the clutch housing to block bolts.
19. Carefully remove engine.
20. To install, lower engine assembly carefully aligning the transmission shaft with the clutch disc splines.
21. Remove hoisting equipment and transmission jack
22. Raise vehicle on a hoist.
23. Install lower clutch housing to block bolts securely
24. Install clutch housing cover to clutch housing retaining bolts.

25. Install engine mount washers and retaining nuts, tightening securely.
26. Lubricate the clutch equalizer shaft and bracket and position the bracket and install the retaining bolts.
27. Lower vehicle.
28. Connect flex line (use a new clamp) and vacuum line to fuel pump.
29. Connect and adjust choke and throttle cables.
30. Connect the wiring at the coil and at the oil and temperature sending units.
31. If they were removed, install the water pump pulley, spacer and fan.
32. Place a new gasket on the exhaust inlet pipe, connect the pipe to the exhaust manifold, install the remaining nuts and tighten securely.
33. Install the U-bolt clamp to retain the inlet pipe to the block.
34. Install the starter and starter cable.
35. Install alternator and belt. Adjust belt.
36. Connect battery and alternator ground cables to block.
37. Connect heater hose at the rear of carburetor spacer and at the water pump.
38. Install radiator and, using a water-resistant sealer, connect upper and lower hoses to engine.
39. Connect battery ground cable and install air cleaner.
40. Fill cooling system and bleed all air.
41. Fill crankcases with lubricant.
42. Operate engine and check for fuel, lubricant and coolant leaks.

240, 300 Cu. In. 6-Cylinder

All Trucks Except 1973-80 Econoline

The engine and transmission are disattached in the following engine removal procedure.

1. Drain cooling system and crankcase.
2. Remove hood or tilt the cab.
3. Remove air cleaner. On C-series, remove the oil filler tube.
4. Disconnect the battery positive cable.
5. Disconnect the heater hose from the water pump and coolant outlet housing.
6. Disconnect flexible fuel line from the fuel pump.
7. Remove the radiator.
8. Remove the cooling fan, water pump pulley and fan drive belt.
9. Disconnect the accelerator cable and the choke cable at the carburetor. Remove the cable retracting spring.
10. On a vehicle with power brakes, disconnect the vacuum line at the intake manifold.
11. On a vehicle with automatic transmission, disconnect the transmission kickdown rod at the bellcrank assembly.
12. Disconnect exhaust manifold from the muffler inlet pipe.
13. Disconnect the body ground strap and the battery ground cable at the engine.
14. Disconnect the engine wiring harness at the ignition coil, water temperature and oil pressure sending units.
15. Remove alternator mounting bolts and position the alternator out of the way, leaving wires attached.
16. On a vehicle with power steering, remove the power steering pump from the mounting brackets and position it right side up and to one side, leaving the line attached.
17. If equipped with an air compressor, bleed the air system and disconnect the two air lines at the compressor.
18. Raise vehicle and remove starter and, if so equipped, remove the automatic transmission fluid filler tube.
19. Remove engine rear plate upper right bolt.
20. On a vehicle with manual transmission, remove all the flywheel housing lower attaching bolts. Disconnect the clutch retracting spring.
21. On vehicles with an automatic transmission, remove the converter housing access cover assembly. Remove the flywheel to converter nut and secure the converter assembly in the housing. Remove the transmission oil cooler lines from the retaining clip at the engine. Remove the converter housing to engine lower attaching bolts.
22. On F-100, 350, remove the insulator to intermediate support bracket nut from each engine front support. On other vehicles, remove the engine from support insulator bolt.
23. Lower the vehicle and position a transmission jack under the transmission. Remove the remaining flywheel or converter housing to engine bolts.
24. Attach engine lifting hook and raise the engine slightly and carefully pull it from the transmission. Lift engine out of the chassis.
25. To install, place a new gasket on the muffler inlet pipe.
26. Lower engine carefully into chassis. Make sure the studs on the exhaust manifold are aligned with the holes in the muffler inlet pipe and the dowels in the block engage the holes in the flywheel or converter housing.
27. On a vehicle with an automatic transmission, start the converter pilot into the crankshaft. Remove the retainer securing the converter in the housing.
28. On a vehicle with standard transmission, start the transmission input shaft into the clutch disc. It may be necessary to adjust the position of the transmission with relation to the engine if the transmission input shaft will not enter the clutch disc. If the engine hangs up after the shaft enters, turn the crankshaft slowly (with transmission in gear) until the shaft splines mesh with the clutch disc splines.
29. Install the converter or flywheel housing upper attaching bolts. Remove the transmission jack.
30. Lower the engine until it rests on the engine support(s) and remove the lifting hook.
31. On the F-100, 350, install engine left and right support insulator to intermediate support bracket retaining nuts, tightening securely. Install the front engine mount bolt and nut on other vehicles.
32. Install the transmission oil cooler lines bracket, if so equipped.
33. Install remaining converter or flywheel housing attaching bolts.
34. Connect clutch return spring.
35. Install starter and connect cable.
36. If so equipped, install transmission fluid filler tube bracket.
37. On a vehicle with automatic transmission, install transmission oil cooler lines in the bracket at the engine block.
38. Install exhaust pipe to exhaust manifold, tightening bolts securely.
39. Connect engine ground strap and battery ground cable.
40. On a vehicle with automatic transmission, connect the kickdown rod to the bellcrank assembly on the intake manifold.
41. Connect the accelerator linkage to the carburetor and install the retrackting spring. Connect the choke cable to the carburetor and hand throttle if so equipped.
42. On a vehicle with power brakes, connect the brake vacuum line to the intake manifold.
43. On a C-series vehicle, install the oil filler tube.
44. Connect coil primary wire, oil pressure and water temperature sending units, flexible fuel line, heater hoses and battery positive cable.
45. Install alternator on mounting bracket. On a vehicle with power

steering, install the power steering pump on the mounting brackets.
46. Install water pump pulley, spacer, cooling fan and drive belt, tightening bolts securely.
47. Install radiator.
48. Connect air compressor lines.
49. If so equipped, connect oil cooler lines.
50. Install and adjust hood.
51. Fill and bleed cooling system, checking for leaks.
52. Adjust the carburetor idle speed and mixture.
53. Adjust clutch pedal free travel or automatic transmission control linkage and check transmission fluid level.
54. Install air cleaner.

Econoline—1973-74

1. Disconnect the battery and drain the cooling system. Remove the engine cover and the right hand seat. Remove the grille and bumper.
2. Remove the hood lock support bracket, right and left headlight doors, and grille.
3. Disconnect all hoses and lines to the radiator, and remove the battery deflector. Remove the radiator.
4. Disconnect
   A. The heater hoses, at the engine.
   B. Temperature, oil, and ignition wires.
   C. Starter solenoid, neutral safety switch, and back-up light wiring.
5. Remove the engine oil dipstick and oil filler tube. Remove hoses connecting the rocker cover and air filter. Remove the air cleaner and brackets.
6. Disconnect the choke and accelerator cables at the carburetor. Disconnect the auxiliary heater hose at the front heater. Disconnect the hoses at the right front of the engine, and position them out of the way.
7. Disconnect the fuel pump discharge line at the pump. Disconnect the alternator, and remove it from the brackets.
8. Disconnect the ground wires at the block, and the muffler inlet pipe at the manifold. Disconnect the modulator line at the intake manifold.
9. Put the vehicle on a hoist. Drain the crankcase and remove the oil filter.
10. Disconnect the starter wiring, and remove the starter.
11. Position an engine support bar to the chassis and engine, and adjust it.
12. On manual transmission vehicles:
    A. Disconnect the driveshaft, and remove it. Install a plug in the transmission extension housing.
    B. Disconnect the speedometer cable and housing, and secure the assembly out of the way.
    C. Remove the nut and bolt holding the rear support to the crossmember. Raise the transmission, remove the mounting bolts, and remove the crossmember.
    D. Remove the clutch equalizer arm bolts from the engine. Disconnect the retracting spring, and move the assembly away.
    E. Remove the bolts connecting transmission and clutch, and remove the transmission.
13. On automatic transmission vehicles:
    A. Remove the bolts connecting the adapter plate and inspection cover to the torque converter.
    B. Unbolt and remove the transmission dipstick tube. Drain the transmission.
    C. Remove the nuts attaching the converter to the flex plate. Disconnect the oil cooler and modulator lines at the transmission.
    D. Disconnect the driveshaft at the companion flange.
    E. Disconnect the speedometer cable and housing from the transmission. Disconnect the shift rod at the lever on the transmission. Jack the transmission up slightly.
    F. Remove the nuts and bolts attaching the rear engine mount bracket to the crossmember. Remove the side support bolts, and remove the crossmember.
    G. Secure the transmission to the jack with a safety chain, remove the remaining bolts attaching the transmission to the cylinder block, and remove the transmission from the vehicle.
14. Remove the nuts which attach the engine front support insulator, remove the bellcrank bolt from the block, and position it out of the way.
15. Lower the vehicle, and remove the fan spacer, and water pump pulley. Lift the engine from the vehicle with a lifting hook. Remove the clutch housing on vehicles with manual transmission.
16. Install the clutch housing on manual transmission vehicles. Hoist the engine into the vehicle, and allow it to rest on the front supports and support tool.
17. Raise the vehicle on a hoist.
18. On manual transmission equipped
    A. Raise the transmission and position it behind the clutch housing. Install the mounting bolts.
    B. Raise the transmission slightly further, position the crossmember to the chassis and rear support, and install the attaching bolts. Torque crossmember to body bolts to 20-30 ft-lbs.
    C. Remove the jack and engine support tool. Connect the shift linkage and the speedometer cable housing.
    D. Install and connect the drive shaft.
19. Install the engine front support insulator bolts, and torque to 45-55 ft-lbs.
20. Install the transmission bellcrank.
21. On automatic transmission equipped vehicles:
    A. Position the transmission against the block and install the mounting bolts. Torque to 23-33 ft-lbs.
    B. Position the crossmember to the rear mount bracket and frame side members. Install the attaching nuts and bolts, and torque to 20-30 ft-lbs.
    C. Remove the transmission safety chain, and remove the jack. Remove the engine support bar.
    D. Install the converter to the flex plate. Connect the vacuum and oil cooler lines to the transmission.
    E. Install the dipstick and tube into the transmission oil pan. Install the tube and vacuum line bracket attaching bolt to the block.
    F. Connect the driveshaft to the transmission companion flange. Connect the speedometer cable and housing to the transmission. Connect the shift rods to the transmission levers.
    G. Install the adapter plate and inspection cover.
22. Install the starter. Connect the muffler inlet pipe at the manifold.
23. Install the clutch equalizer arm bracket (on manual transmission models). Install the attaching bolts, and connect the retractor spring.
24. Lower the vehicle to the floor, install the remaining automatic transmission mounting bolts.
25. Install the starter ground wire and remaining starter attaching bolt. Connect the starter cable at the starter.
26. Install the water pump pulley, spacer, and fan assembly.
27. Install the alternator onto its mounting brackets, and install and tension the V-belt.
28. Connect the alternator wiring,

and back-up light and neutral safety switch leads.
29. Connect the alternator and battery ground wires to the block.
30. Connect the transmission modulator line to the manifold.
31. Connect the fuel line from the tank to the fuel pump.
32. Connect the choke and accelerator cables to the carburetor. Install the dipstick tube, and bolt it to the cylinder head.
33. Connect remaining neutral safety switch and back-up light wires. Position the wiring harness, and connect the coil, oil, and temperature leads.
34. Connect the auxiliary heater hoses. Connect the oil filler tube to the rocker arm cover and install the retaining clamp. Install the filler tube bracket to the dash panel.
35. Install the radiator and battery deflector. Connect the radiator hoses and oil cooler lines.
36. Install the grille, head light and hood lock bracket.
37. Fill the crankcase and cooling system. Fill the automatic transmission.
38. Connect the positive battery cable, and operate the engine to check for leaks. Adjust idle speed and mixture, and automatic transmission linkage.
39 Install the air cleaner and brackets, engine front cover, and right front seat, grille and bumper.

Econoline—1975-80

1. Remove the engine cover, drain the coolant, remove the air cleaner and disconnect the battery.
2. Remove the front bumper. Remove the grille and lower the gravel deflector as an assembly.
3. Disconnect top radiator hose at the engine. Remove the alternator splash shield. Remove the lower radiator hose at the radiator.
4. If equipped, disconnect the automatic transmission oil lines at the radiator.
5. Remove the radiator and the radiator shroud, if so equipped.
6. Disconnect the heater hoses at the engine. Disconnect the alternator and move it aside.
7. Remove the power steering pump belt, then remove the power steering pump and support bracket from the engine, and set aside.
8. Disconnect and plug the fuel line at the fuel pump. Disconnect the distributor and sender unit wires from the engine.
9. Disconnect the brake booster hose at the engine. Disconnect the accelerator cable and remove the bracket from the engine.
10. Disconnect the automatic transmission kickdown at the bell crank.
11. Remove the exhaust manifold heat deflector. Remove the inlet pipe to manifold nuts.
12. Disconnect both ends of the transmission vacuum line from the intake manifold and junction. Remove the upper transmission to engine bolts.
13. Remove the automatic transmission, dipstick tube support bolt at the intake manifold.
14. Raise the vehicle on a hoist and drain the engine oil. Disconnect the starter wires and remove the starter. Remove the flywheel inspection cover.
15. Remove the converter nuts. Remove the front engine support nuts. Remove the oil filter.
16. Complete the removal of the engine to transmission bolts.
17. Lower the vehicle on the hoist. Install the lift chain and remove the engine from the engine compartment.
18. To install, position the engine and lower it into place. Start the engine mounting bolts. Remove the lifting chain and connect the exhaust inlet to the manifold.
19. Connect the transmission dipstick tube to the intake manifold. Install the manifold heat shield.
20. Connect the automatic transmission kick down rod, then install the upper transmission to engine bolts.
21. Connect the transmission vacuum line at the junction. Install the accelerator cable and bracket assembly.
22. Connect the distributor and sender unit wires to the engine. Connect the brake booster hose. Unplug and connect the fuel line to the fuel pump.
23. Connect the transmission vacuum line to the manifold. Reinstall the alternator wires. Connect the heater hoses to the engine. Install the power steering pump and support bracket.
24. Install the power steering belt and adjust it to its proper tension. Install the radiator and shroud assembly. Position the grille and lower gravel deflector assembly.
25. Connect the upper radiator hose, then install the grille and gravel deflector assembly. Install the bumper, then raise the vehicle on the hoist.
26. Install the converter nuts, then install the flywheel inspection cover. Connect the starter wires and install the starter assembly. Install the oil filter.
27. Install the front support nuts, and the lower engine to transmission bolts. Connect the lower radiator hose. Connect the transmission cooler lines to the radiator. Install the alternator splash shield.
28. Lower the vehicle on the hoist. Fill the cooling system, connect the battery and fill the crankcase with the proper grade oil. Start the engine and check for leaks. Install the engine cover.

302, 351M, 351W, & 400 V8
F-100-F-350, Bronco

The engine removal and installation procedures are for the removal of the engine only, without the transmission attached.

1. Drain the cooling system and the crankcase. Disconnect the battery and alternator ground cables from the cylinder block.
2. Remove the air cleaner and intake duct assembly, including the PCV hose and carbon canister hose.
3. Disconnect the radiator hoses at the radiator. If equipped, disconnect automatic transmission cooler lines.
4. If so equipped, discharge the air conditioning system and remove the air conditioner condenser. Disconnect the air conditioning lines at the compressor.
5. Unbolt the fan shroud and position it over the fan. Remove the radiator. Remove the fan shroud, fan spacer, belts and pulley. Remove the alternator bolts and allow the alternator to swing down and out of the way.
6. Disconnect the oil pressure sending unit wire from the sending unit. Disconnect and plug the fuel tank line. Disconnect evaporative emission hoses at carburetor bowl vent and vacuum harness.
7. Disconnect the accelerator cable from the carburetor. Disconnect the transmission kick down rod and remove the retracting spring, if so equipped.
8. Disconnect the heater hoses from the intake manifold and the water pump. Disconnect the water temperature sending unit wire from the sending unit.
9. Remove the flywheel housing-to-engine upper bolts.
10. Disconnect the primary wire from the ignition coil. Remove the wire harness from the left rocker arm cover and position the wires out of the way. Disconnect the ground strap from the cylinder block.
11. Raise the front of the vehicle. Disconnect the starter cable from the starter and remove the starter.
12. Disconnect the muffler inlet pipes from the exhaust manifolds. Disconnect the engine support in-

sulators from the brackets on the frame underbody.
13. On vehicles with automatic transmission, remove the converter inspection plate. Remove the torque converter-to-flywheel attaching bolts.
14. Remove the remaining flywheel housing-to-engine bolts.
15. If so equipped, disconnect air conditioning compressor magnetic clutch load wire.
16. Lower the vehicle and support the transmission.

NOTE: A left and a right lifting bracket are used to remove the engine, the left bracket is placed on the left cylinder head and the right bracket is placed on the right cylinder head. A sling is attached to each bracket to lift out the engine.

17. Raise the engine slightly and carefully pull it from the transmission. Carefully lift the engine out of engine compartment so that the rear cover plate is not bent or any other components damaged.
18. To install, lower the engine carefully into the engine compartment. Make sure the dowels in the block are through the rear cover plate, then engage the holes in the flywheel housing.
19. On a vehicle with manual transmission, start the transmission main drive shaft into the clutch disc. It may be necessary to adjust the position of the transmission in relation to the engine if the input shaft will not enter the clutch disc.

NOTE: If the engine hangs up after the shaft enters, turn the crankshaft slowly (transmission in gear) until the shaft splines mesh with the clutch disc splines.

20. Install the flywheel housing upper bolts.
21. Install the engine support insulator-to-bracket washers and attaching nuts. Disconnect the engine lifting sling and remove.
22. Raise the front of the vehicle. Connect both exhaust manifolds to muffler inlet pipes. Position and install the starter and the starter cable.
23. Install the remaining flywheel housing-to-engine bolts.
24. If equipped with automatic transmission, install the converter-to-flywheel attaching bolts. Install the converter inspecting plate.
25. Remove the support from the transmission, and lower the vehicle.
26. If equipped, connect the air conditioning compressor magnetic clutch lead. Connect the wiring harness to the left valve rocker arm cover and connect the coil wire.
27. Connect the water temperature sending unit wire.
28. Connect the bellcrank to the intake manifold. Connect the transmission shift rod and install the retracting spring. Connect the accelerator rod.
29. Remove the plug from the fuel tank line and connect the fuel line and the oil pressure sending unit wire. Reconnect the evaporative emission hoses at the carburetor bowl vent and vacuum harness.
30. Install the pulley, belt, spacer and fan. Position the fan shroud over the fan.
31. Position the alternator and install the alternator bolts. Connect the alternator and battery ground cables. Connect the air conditioning lines to the air conditioning compressor, if so equipped.
32. Install the radiator. Connect the radiator hoses. Connect the transmission oil cooler lines, if so equipped. Install the fan shroud.
33. If so equipped, install air conditioning condenser to the radiator. Connect the heater hoses at the water pump.
34. Fill and bleed the cooling system. Fill the crankcase with the proper grade and quanity of oil.
35. Operate the engine at fast idle and check all gaskets and hose connections for leaks.
36. Install the air cleaner and air intake duct assembly including the PCV hose and carbon canister hose.
37. Evacuate and charge the air conditioning system, if so equipped.

Econoline—1973-74

In this procedure the engine is removed without the transmission attached.

1. Remove engine cover.
2. Remove right front seat.
3. Drain cooling system.
4. Remove air cleaner and intake duct assembly (later models), including crankcase ventilation hose.
5. Disconnect battery and alternator ground cables at block.
6. Remove oil filler tube at dash panel and disconnect at the rocker arm cover.
7. Disconnect radiator upper and lower hoses at the radiator and automatic transmission cooler lines (if so equipped).
8. Remove radiator.
9. Disconnect heater hoses at the engine.
10. Remove fan, spacer, pulley and drive belt.
11. Disconnect accelerator linkage at accelerator shaft assembly on the left cylinder head.
12. Disconnect automatic transmission kickdown rod at the carburetor and vacuum line at the intake manifold, if so equipped.
13. Disconnect wiring harness from left rocker arm cover.
14. Remove upper nut attaching right exhaust manifolds to exhaust pipe.
15. Raise vehicle on hoist.
16. Drain crankcase and remove filter.
17. Disconnect fuel pump inlet line at the pump.
18. Disconnect oil dipstick tube bracket from exhaust manifold and oil pan.
19. On vehicles with standard transmission, remove bolts attaching the equalizer arm bracket to cylinder block and clutch housing (this includes clutch linkage disconnection and retracting spring).
20. Disconnect starter cable at starter and remove starter.
21. On a vehicle with standard transmission, disconnect driveshaft at the rear axle and remove driveshaft. Install plug in transmission end.
22. On a vehicle with automatic transmission, disconnect driveshaft at companion flange.
23. Disconnect speedometer cable and transmission linkage at transmission.
24. Position a transmission jack under transmission. Raise transmission and remove bolts attaching crossmember to chassis. Lower transmission slightly and remove bolt which attaches rear engine support to frame crossmember. Remove crossmember.
25. On a vehicle with standard transmission, remove bolts attaching transmission to clutch housing. Remove transmission.
26. On a vehicle with automatic transmission, remove the lower front cover from converter housing. Remove transmission dipstick tube and drain transmission. Install plastic bag in transmission oil pan. Remove nuts attaching transmission converter to flywheel. Disconnect oil cooler lines and vacuum lines at transmission. Remove remaining bolts fastening transmission to engine. Remove transmission.
27. Position engine support bar (tool T65E-6000-J) to engine and chassis, or improvise a suitable support.
28. Disconnect exhaust pipes at exhaust manifold.
29. Remove front engine mount attaching nuts and washers.
30. Remove bellcrank bolt from side of engine block and position bellcrank aside.
31. Lower vehicle.
32. Remove bolts which fasten alter-

nator and adjusting arm to the block and water pump. Set alternator aside.
33. Remove carburetor air horn stud. Disconnect fuel line at fuel pump.
34. Install engine lifting apparatus and remove engine through side door.
35. On vehicle with standard transmission, remove bolts which fasten adapter plate to clutch housing. Remove clutch housing from block.
36. To install, connect fuel line to fuel pump.
37. On models with manual transmission, position clutch housing to block and install mounting bolts. Install adapter plate to clutch housing.
38. Position alternator and adjusting arm to cylinder block and water pump. Install and tighten attaching bolts.
39. Lift engine and position to chassis and supporting tool.
40. Raise vehicle on hoist.
41. Install front engine support retaining nuts and washers, tightening securely.
42. On vehicle with automatic transmission, position bellcrank assembly to engine block and install attaching bolt, tightening securely. Position transmission to engine and install attaching bolts, tightening securely.
43. On vehicle with standard transmission, position transmission to clutch housing and install attaching bolt, tightening securely.
44. Remove engine support bar.
45. Position rear engine support crossmember to chassis and install retaining bolts. Position transmission with rear engine support attached to crossmember. Install bolt and nut. Tighten all bolts and nuts securely.
46. On vehicle with automatic transmission, install and tighten converter-to-flywheel attaching nuts. Connect oil cooler and vacuum lines at transmission. Install transmission dipstick tube in pan. Install dipstick tube and vacuum line retaining bracket bolt to engine block.
47. Connect transmission shift linkages and speedometer cable.
48. On vehicle with automatic transmission, connect driveshaft to transmission companion flange.
49. On vehicle with standard transmission, remove plug from transmission and install driveshaft yoke into transmission. Connect rear end of driveshaft at rear axle.
50. Install starter and connect cable to starter.
51. Install the exhaust pipe to exhaust manifold, installing all bolts except upper nut on right exhaust manifold.
52. On a standard transmission, install the bolts connecting equalizer arm bracket to block and clutch housing (including clutch linkage connection and retracting spring).
53. Install oil filter, then oil dipstick tube bracket to oil pan and exhaust manifold.
54. Connect fuel line at fuel pump.
55. Lower the vehicle.
56. Install upper nut attaching right exhaust manifold to exhaust pipe.
57. Connect engine wire harness at left rocker arm cover.
58. Connect battery and alternator ground cables at block.
59. If applicable, connect automatic transmission vacuum line at intake manifold and transmission kickdown rod at carburetor.
60. Connect accelerator linkage at accelerator shaft assembly on left cylinder head.
61. Install drive belt, pulley, spacer and fan.
62. Connect heater hoses at engine, then install radiator and connect hoses.
63. Install oil filler tube by connecting to left rocker arm cover and dash panel.
64. Install air cleaner and intake duct assembly, including the crankcase ventilation hose.
65. Fill and bleed cooling system.
66. Fill crankcase and automatic transmission (if so equipped).
67. Install right front seat and engine cover.
68. Operate engine at fast idle and check for leaks.

Econoline—1975-80

1. Remove the engine cover. Disconnect the battery and drain the cooling system. Remove grille assembly and gravel deflector.
2. Remove the upper grille support bracket, hood lock support and air conditioning condenser upper mounting brackets.
3. If so equipped, discharge the air conditioning system, and remove the air conditioning condenser. Disconnect the air conditioning lines at the air conditioner compressor, and remove the accelerator cable bracket. Disconnect the engine heater hoses.
4. Disconnect the radiator hoses at the radiator. If equipped with automatic transmission, disconnect the oil cooler lines at the radiator.
5. Remove the fan shroud and fan assembly. Remove the radiator. Pivot the alternator inward. Disconnect the alterator lead wires at the alternator.
6. Remove the air cleaner assembly, the duct and valve assembly and the exhaust manifold shroud. Remove the flex tube from the exhaust manifold stove.
7. Disconnect the throttle at the carburetor and remove the accelerator cable bracket from the engine. Disconnect the transmission shift rod if so equipped.
8. Disconnect the fuel line, choke lines, and then remove the carburetor and the carburetor spacer (includes disconnecting vacuum lines). Where applicable, disconnect evaporative emission hoses from the front of the carburetor pad and/or the top of the PCV valve. Disconnect hose from evaporative canister to vacuum harness at the harness.
9. Raise the vehicle on the hoist, drain the engine oil and remove the oil filter.
10. Disconnect the muffler inlet pipe at the exhaust manifolds. Remove the bolts retaining the transmission filler tube bracket to the right cylinder head.
11. Remove the engine mount attaching bolts and nuts. Remove the starter and disconnect the starter cable.
12. On vehicles equipped with manual transmission, remove the housing-to-engine bolts. On vehicles with automatic transmission, remove the torque converter inspection cover bolts.
13. Remove the nuts attaching the converter to the flex plate. Remove the bolts retaining the adapter plate to the converter housing.
14. Remove four converter housing-to-cylinder block lower bolts. Remove the bolt retaining the ground cable to the cylinder block. Lower the vehicle and support the transmission.
15. If so equipped remove the power steering front bracket bolts and remove the belt.
16. Disconnect only one vacuum line at the rear of the intake manifold. Disconnect the engine wire loom and position it out of the way.
17. Remove the speed control servo and the accelerator cable bracket from the intake manifold, and position them out of the way.
18. If so equipped disconnect the air conditioning compressor magnetic clutch load wire. Remove two converter housing-to-cylinder block upper bolts.
19. Position a floor jack under the transmission for support. Position a floor crane to the vehicle and connect it to the lifting bracket device.

NOTE: A left and a right lifting bracket are used to remove the engine, the left bracket is placed on the left cylinder head and the right bracket is placed on the right cylinder head. A sling is attached to each bracket to lift out the engine.

Remove the engine from the vehicle.

20. To install, on vehicles with automatic transmission, connect a a floor crane to the engine and position it into the vehicle aligning the transmission converter to the flywheel (or flex plate) and lower the engine dowels to the transmission. Lower the engine to the chassis brackets, and align.
21. On vehicles equipped with manual transmission, start the transmission main clutch drive shaft into the clutch disc.

    NOTE: It may be necessary to adjust the position of the transmission in relation to the engine if the input shaft will not enter the clutch disc. If the engine hangs up after the shaft enters, turn the crankshaft slowly (transmission in gear) until the shaft splines mesh with the clutch disc splines.

    Align the housing on the engine and insert the housing-to-engine bolts. Tighten to specification.
22. If equipped with automatic transmission, install two converter-to-cylinder block lower bolts. Remove the lifting bracket from the intake manifold.
23. Remove floor jack from under the transmission.
24. Connect the flex tube to the exhaust manifold stove. Install the accelerator cable mounting bracket and the speed control servo to the intake manifold.
25. Position the engine wire harness in retainers and connect at respective locations. Connect vacuum lines at the rear of the intake manifold.
26. Connect heater hoses. If so equipped re-install the power steering front face bracket and the power steering pump.
27. Install the fan assembly and spacer, and position the fan shroud over the fan assembly.
28. Raise the vehicle on a hoist. Install ground cable to cylinder block. Install four lower converter housing-to-cylinder block lower bolts. Install nuts retaining the flex plate. Install the converter inspection cover.
29. Install the starter and connect the starter motor cable. Install the engine mount attaching bolts. Install transmission filler tube bracket. Connect the muffler inlet pipe at the exhaust manifolds. Install a new oil filter.
30. Lower the vehicle on the hoist. Install the carburetor and gasket, connect the fuel line, choke line, vacuum lines and the choke lead wires. Reconnect evaporative canister hose to carburetor bowl vent vacuum harness and intake manifold or PCV valve.
31. Connect the throttle and transmission linkage. Connect the alternator lead wires. If so equipped, connect air conditioning lines to the air conditioner compressor and install the accelerator cable bracket to the dash. Attach compressor magnetic clutch lead.
32. Install the radiator. Complete installation of the fan shroud. Connect the oil cooler lines to the radiator, if so equipped. Connect the radiator hoses to the radiator.
33. Install the air conditioner condenser to radiator support, if so equipped. Install the grille upper support bracket, hood lock support and air conditioner condenser upper mounting brackets.
34. Install the grille assembly. Fill the engine with the proper grade oil. Fill the cooling system. Connect the battery, start the engine and check for leaks. Adjust idle speed and mixture.
35. Evacuate and charge the air conditioner, if so equipped. Install the air cleaner assembly. Install the engine cover.

460 V8

1. Remove the hood.
2. Drain the cooling system, the radiator, and the cylinder block.
3. Disconnect the negative battery cable and remove the air cleaner assembly.
4. Disconnect the upper and lower radiator hoses and the transmission oil cooler lines from the radiator.
5. Remove the fan shroud from the radiator and remove the fan from the water pump. Remove the fan and shroud from the engine compartment.
6. Remove the upper support and remove the radiator.
7. If the truck is equipped with air conditioning, remove the compressor from the engine and position it out of the way. If the compressor must be removed completely, loosen the air conditioning service valves (disconnect) carefully to discharge the air conditioning system. Remove the compressor.
8. Remove the power steering pump from the engine, if so equipped, and position it to one side. Do not disconnect the fluid lines.
9. Disconnect the fuel pump inlet line from the pump and plug the line.
10. Remove the alternator drive belts and disconnect the alternator from the engine, positioning it aside.
11. Disconnect the ground cable from the right front corner of the engine.
12. Disconnect the heater hoses.
13. Remove the transmission fluid filler tube attaching bolt from the right side valve cover and position the tube out of the way.
14. Disconnect all vacuum lines at the rear of the intake manifold.
15. Disconnect the speed control cable at the carburetor, if so equipped. Disconnect the accelerator rod and the transmission kick-down rod and secure them out of the way.
16. Disconnect the engine wiring harness at the connector on the fire wall.
17. Raise the vehicle and disconnect the exhaust pipes at the exhaust manifolds.
18. Disconnect the starter cable and remove the starter. Bring the starter forward and rotate the solenoid outward to remove the assembly.
19. Remove the access cover from the converter housing and remove the fly-wheel-to-converter attaching nuts. Remove the lower converter housing-to-engine attaching bolts.
20. Remove the engine mount through bolts attaching the rubber insulators to the frame brackets.
21. Lower the vehicle and place a jack under the transmission to support it.
22. Remove the converter housing-to-engine block attaching bolts (left-side).
23. Disconnect the coil wire and remove the coil and bracket assembly from the intake manifold.
24. Attach the engine lifting device and carefully lift the engine from the engine compartment.
25. Install the engine in the reverse order of removal.

330, 350, 360, 361, 389, 390, 391 Cu. In. V-8

All Models

1. On D, F and FT series trucks, remove engine hood assembly from vehicle; on C and CT vehicles, release cab lock and tilt the cab forward. On N and NT series vehicles, position a suitable support in front of the truck to accept the hood and fender assembly when it is fully forward, then raise the hood and fender assembly.
2. Disconnect the ground cable from the battery. On N and NT series trucks, disconnect and remove the battery.

3. Drain cooling system and crankcase.
4. On N and NT series trucks, disconnect the check cable assemblies and let the hood swing forward out of the way, resting on the support. Remove radiator to cowl support rod, disconnect water hoses and unbolt and remove radiator.
   On C and CT series trucks, remove the heater hoses from the radiator, transmission oil cooler lines (automatic transmission), disconnect upper and lower radiator hoses, disconnect and remove vent line between radiator and supply tank and hose between water outlet housing and supply tank, remove fan (leaving it lay in the shroud), then remove the radiator, shroud and fan as an assembly. Remove radiator supply tank from cab rear support.
   On B, F and FT series trucks, disconnect the upper and lower hoses from the engine and water pump, remove the fan, disconnect the transmission oil cooler hoses (if applicable), then unbolt and remove radiator.
5. On a vehicle with power steering, disconnect the power steering pressure line from the pump reservoir and return line from the pump housing. Drain oil, then loosen and remove the power steering drive belt.
6. On N and NT series trucks, remove fan.
7. On N, NT, C and CT series truck, disconnect heater hoses at engine.
8. Remove air cleaner and, if applicable, vent hose from carburetor.
9. Disconnect choke and throttle cables and accelerator linkage.
10. Disconnect tachometer cable (and bracket, if so attached) and position out of the way.
11. Remove ignition coil.
12. On a vehicle with an air compressor, relieve pressure from the system and disconnect main line from the compressor and treadle valve. Remove drive belt if it is still in place.
13. Disconnect fuel line (from tank) at the fuel pump and cap line.
14. Disconnect wires from the alternator and remove wiring harness from engine (or disconnect from junction block).
15. Disconnect cable from starter and remove starter. Remove flywheel lower housing attaching bolts first on L and LT truck. Disconnect engine-to-body ground strap.
16. Unbolt exhaust pipes from right and left exhaust manifolds.
17. Disconnect vacuum lines from intake manifold.
18. Remove clutch return spring and hydraulic clutch slave cylinder attaching bolts on C and CT trucks.
19. Remove driveshaft center bearing retainer (except on C and CT series) and position a jack under transmission.
20. Remove flywheel housing cover.
21. On B, F and FT series trucks, remove lower clutch housing attaching bolts. Secure lifting apparatus. Remove front engine mount nuts. Remove remaining clutch housing bolts. Raise engine high enough to remove the bolts that attach the engine front mount bracket to the upper insulator. Carefully lift engine away from the transmission and chassis. On C and CT vehicles, remove flywheel housing to engine attaching bolts. Remove nuts and bolts from front engine mount and upper insulator. Attach lifting apparatus and remove engine from chassis. On N and NT trucks, remove flywheel upper housing to engine attaching bolts. Remove the bolt(s) attaching the front engine mounting plate to the front engine mount. Attach lifting apparatus. Raise engine sufficiently to remove the front support bracket-to-upper insulator bolt and nuts. Remove engine.
22. To install, carefully lower engine into chassis, aligning clutch disc splines with transmission shaft and aligning front engine mount bracket with upper insulator.
23. Install flywheel housing to engine attaching bolts, tightening securely.
24. Install flywheel housing cover.
25. Lower engine and remove jack from under transmission, being careful to keep front engine mounting aligned.
26. Install and tighten front engine mount bolts and nuts. On N and NT trucks, install front engine mount to mounting plate.
27. Remove lifting apparatus.
28. Install driveshaft center bearing support to frame crossmember.
29. On vehicle with power steering, install power steering unit if it was removed.
30. Install starter motor and starter cable, attaching engine-to-frame ground cable if applicable.
31. Install left and right exhaust pipes to exhaust manifolds, using new gaskets.
32. Connect alternator wires and engine wiring harness wires. Secure engine wiring harness to bracket on engine.
33. On C and CT trucks, install hydraulic clutch slave cylinder to the flywheel housing and attach the clutch return spring.
34. Secure coil and bracket to cylinder head and connect all leads.
35. Connect vacuum line(s) to intake manifold.
36. Connect fuel line to fuel pump.
37. On C and CT trucks install radiator supply tank to cab rear support.
38. Connect accelerator linkage, choke and throttle cables and tachometer cable. Adjust linkage and cables if necessary.
39. Connect heater hoses.
40. On vehicles equipped with air system, install and connect all components.
41. Connect engine-to-body ground strap.
42. On N and NT series trucks, install fan. On B, F, FT, C and CT trucks, place fan in radiator, shroud, then install radiator, shroud and fan (loose) in vehicle. Secure all attaching bolts, insulators and radiator supports. Make sure belts are ready to be installed. Install fan and belts.
43. Connect radiator upper and lower hoses. On C and CT series trucks, connect hoses to radiator supply tank.
44. On vehicle with automatic transmission, connect transmission oil cooler lines to radiator lower tank.
45. On vehicle with power steering, install and tighten the drive belt and connect power steering pressure line to the pump reservoir and return line to the pump housing.
46. On C and CT series trucks, attach the heater hoses, throttle cable, choke cable and tachometer cable to the radiator.
47. Install air cleaner.
48. Install (if removed) and connect battery cables.
49. Fill crankcase and cooling system.
50. On B, F and FT series trucks, install the hood.
51. On N and NT series trucks, raise hood and connect check cables.
52. Adjust clutch as required.
53. Operate engine and check for lubricant and coolant leaks.

370, 429 Cu. In. V-8

NOTE: The Removal and Installation procedures for the Super Duty engine are similar to the procedures below.

B, F, and LT-Series

1. Drain the cooling system and the engine crankcase. Disconnect the ground cable from the battery. Remove the hood from the vehicle.
2. Disconnect the radiator hoses.

Remove the fan. Remove the air cleaner and vent hose from the carburetor.

3. If the vehicle is equipped with automatic transmission, disconnect the oil cooler lines. Remove the radiator.
4. Disconnect the wires from the alternator. Drain the air system and disconnect the air line at the compressor. Disconnect the starter motor cable and remove the starter.
5. Disconnect the muffler inlet pipes from the exhaust manifolds. Disconnect the body-to-engine ground strap from the engine.
   Disconnect the accelerator linkage at the dash. Disconnect the choke cable (manual choke) and the throttle cable from the carburetor. Disconnect the heater hose from the engine. Disconnect the treadle valve air line.
6. Disconnect and plug the fuel line. Disconnect the wiring harness from the engine. Remove the ignition coil and it's mounting bracket.
7. Disconnect the drive shaft center bearing retainer from the cross member to permit raising or lowering of the transmission. Position a jack under the transmission to support it.
8. Remove the cover from the lower end of the clutch housing. Remove the bolts from the lower half of the clutch housing. Remove the nuts that secure the engine support to the upper insulator. Remove the retaining clutch housing attaching bolts.

   NOTE: A left and a right lifting bracket are used to remove the engine, the left bracket is placed on the left cylinder head and the right bracket is placed on the right cylinder head. A sling is attached to each bracket to lift out the engine.
9. Secure the lifting sling to the lifting brackets and raise the engine high enough to remove the bolts that attach the engine front support bracket to the upper insulator. Carefully lift the engine away from the transmission and out of the vehicle.
10. To install, lower the engine into the vehicle. Align the clutch hub splines with those on the transmission input shaft. Position the engine in place against the clutch housing and install the attaching bolts. Remove the jack from under the transmission.
11. Lower the engine and align the engine front and rear supports with the upper insulator, and secure. Remove the engine lifting sling and brackets.
12. Secure the drive shaft center bearing support to the frame crossmember. Install the cover on the lower end of the clutch housing. Position a new gasket on each exhaust manifold flange. Secure the muffler inlet pipes to the exhaust manifolds.
13. Install the starter motor and the starter cable. Reconnect the alternator wires to their proper place on the alternator. Secure the coil and it's bracket to the left cylinder head. Unplug and connect the fuel line.
14. Connect the accelerator linkage to the dash panel. Connect the treadle valve air line. Connect the choke cable (manual choke) and the throttle cable to the carburetor and adjust both.
15. Connect the engine wiring harness to the respective connectors. Connect the engine-to-body ground strap to the rear of the engine. Connect the heater hoses. Connect the main air line to the compressor.
16. Position the fan in the radiator shroud. Install the radiator. Position the fan on the water pump pulley (or high mount), and secure it in place with the attaching bolts. Connect the radiator hoses. Fill and bleed the cooling system.
17. Fill the engine with the proper grade of oil. Connect the battery cables. Adjust the clutch as required. Start the engine and check for leaks. Install the air cleaner and vent hose. Install the hood.

C- and CT-Series

1. Release the cab lock and tilt the cab forward. Drain the cooling system and the crankcase. Disconnect the battery ground cable.
2. Remove the clamps holding the throttle, choke, and tachometer cables. Remove the clamps securing the heater hoses to the radiator.
3. Remove the air cleaner. Disconnect the accelerator rod, throttle cable and choke cable (manual choke) from the carburetor and position it out of the way. If vehicle is equipped with an air compressor remove the belt.
4. Remove the fan from the crankshaft damper and lay it inside the fan shroud. If equipped with automatic transmission, disconnect the transmission oil cooler lines at the radiator.
5. Disconnect the radiator hoses. Disconnect and remove the vent line between the radiator and the supply tank and the hose between the water outlet housing and the supply tank.
6. Remove the radiator attaching bolts and insulators from the top brackets and the nuts and insulators from the bottom support rods. Remove the radiator, shroud and fan as an assembly.
7. Disconnect the heater hoses at the water pump and intake manifold and position them out of the way. Remove the ignition coil. Remove the radiator supply tank from the cab rear support.
8. Disconnect and plug the fuel line. Disconnect the windshield wiper and vacuum brake hoses from the intake manifold. If vehicle is equipped with an air compressor, release the air pressure and disconnect the main air line from the compressor.
9. Disconnect the wires from the alternator and the engine wires at the junction block. Remove the clutch return spring. Remove the hydraulic clutch slave cylinder attaching bolts.
10. Remove both muffler inlet pipes from the exhaust manifolds. Disconnect the starter motor cable from the starter and remove the starter. (Ground strap is held by one starter bolt).
11. If equipped with power steering, remove the power steering pump and reservoir and position it out of the way.
12. Position a jack under the transmission. Remove the flywheel housing inspection cover. Remove the flywheel housing-to-engine attaching bolts. Remove the engine front and rear support bolts.
13. Attach the lifting brackets and sling and remove the engine from the vehicle.

    NOTE: A left and a right lifting bracket are used to remove the engine, the left bracket is placed on the left cylinder head and the right bracket is placed on the right cylinder head. A sling is attached to each bracket to lift out the engine.
14. To install, position the engine in the vehicle using a floor crane. Engage the clutch hub splines with the transmission input shaft and slide the engine back against the transmission.
15. Install the flywheel housing-to-engine bolts. Install the flywheel housing inspection cover. Remove the jack from under the transmission.
16. Lower the engine and align the front support bracket with the upper insulator, and install the bolts and nuts. Remove the engine lifting sling and brackets.
17. If so equipped, install the power steering unit. Install the starter and the ground strap. Attach the starter cable to the starter. Install the muffler inlet pipes to the exhaust manifolds, using new gaskets.

18. Install the hydraulic clutch slave cylinder to the flywheel housing, and attach the clutch return spring. Connect the alternator wires to their respective terminals. Connect the engine wiring harness to the junction block. On vehicles equipped with an air compressor, connect the main air line.
19. Connect the brake hose to the intake manifold vacuum connections. Unplug and connect the fuel line. Install the radiator supply tank to the cab rear support. Install the ignition coil to the left cylinder head. Connect the heater hoses to their respective locations.
20. Install the radiator, shroud, and fan (loose inside shroud) in the chassis. Secure the radiator with insulators and nuts to the bottom support rods and insulators and bolts to the top brackets.
21. Connect the radiator-to-supply tank vent tube. Connect the radiator hoses to their respective locations. Install and connect the water outlet housing-to-supply tank hose.
22. If equipped with automatic transmission, connect the oil cooler lines to the radiator. Install the fan on the crankshaft damper. Install and adjust the air compressor belt, if so equipped.
23. Connect the accelerator rod, throttle cable, and choke cables (manual choke) to the carburetor. Install the air cleaner.
24. Connect the ground cable to the battery. Fill the engine with the proper type oil. Fill the cooling system. Operate the engine at fast idle and check for leaks. Lower the cab and lock it into position.

LN- and LNT-Series

NOTE: Position a suitable support in front of the truck to hold the hood and fender assembly when it is fully forward.

1. Raise the hood and fender assembly. Disconnect and remove the battery.
2. Disconnect the check cable assemblies and allow the hood to swing forward, resting on the previously positioned support. Remove the radiator-to-cowl support rod.
3. If vehicle is equipped with power steering, disconnect the power steering pressure line from the pump reservoir and return line from the pump housing. Drain the power steering fluid.
4. Disconnect the upper radiator hose from the thermostat housing and the lower hose from the water pump. Remove the radiator attaching bolts and insulators from the top radiator support brackets and the nuts and insulators from the bottom support rods. Remove the radiator. Remove the bolts attaching the fan blade to the water pump hub (or high-mount fan hub).
5. If equipped with an air compressor, release the air pressure from the system. Disconnect the main air line from the air compressor. Disconnect the main air line from the treadle value.
6. Remove the air cleaner. Disconnect the heater hoses from the engine. Disconnect and plug the flexible fuel line.
7. Disconnect the choke control cable (manual choke) and the throttle control cable at the carburetor. Disconnect the accelerator linkage.
8. Remove the ignition coil. Disconnect the vacuum line from the intake manifold. Disconnect the wiring harness. Disconnect the wires from the alternator.
9. Remove the flywheel housing cover, and the lower flywheel housing bolts.
10. Disconnect the starter cable from the starter. Remove the starter, dust cover and the engine ground strap.
11. Remove both muffler inlet pipe attaching nuts from the manifold and disengage the inlet pipes.
12. Remove the drive shaft center bearing retainer, to permit raising and lowering of the drive shaft and transmission. Position a jack under the transmission. Remove the flywheel housing-to-engine upper bolts. Remove the bolt(s) attaching the engine front mounting plate to the engine front mount.
13. Attach engine lifting equipment.

    NOTE: A left and a right lifting bracket are used to remove the engine, the left bracket is placed on the left cylinder head and the right bracket is placed on the right cylinder head. A sling is attached to each bracket to lift out the engine.

14. Raise the engine just enough to remove the front support bracket-to-upper insulator bolts and nuts. Remove the engine from the vehicle.
15. To install, position the engine to align the front support bracket with the upper insulator. Install the bolts and nuts. Install the flywheel housing-to-engine bolts. Lower the engine and remove the transmission jack. Remove the engine lifting brackets.
16. Install the bolt(s) attaching the engine mounting plate to the engine front mount. Install the dirve shaft center bearing retainer. Install the flywheel housing cover bolts.
17. Place new gaskets on the end of the muffler inlet pipes and install both exhaust manifolds.
18. Install the starter, engine ground strap and dust cover. Connect the starter cable to the starter. Connect the wires to the alternator and the wiring harness to the engine. Connect the vacuum line to the intake manifold.
19. Position the tachometer cable on the engine, attaching the two clamps, and connect the tachometer cable to the distributor. Install the ignition coil.
20. Connect the choke cable (manual choke) and the throttle cable to the carburetor. Connect the accelerator linkage. Unplug and connect the fuel line. Connect the heater hoses to the engine. Install the air cleaner.
21. If equipped with air brakes, connect the main air line to the compressor and the air line to the treadle valve.
22. Install the fan blade on the hub. Install the radiator. Connect the radiator hoses to their respective locations.
23. If equipped with power steering, install and tighten the drive belt. Connect the power steering pressure line to the pump housing and the return line to the pump reservoir.
24. Install the radiator support rod to the cowl and radiator. Fill the engine with the proper oil. Fill the cooling system.
25. Raise the hood and check cables. Install and connect the battery. Start the engine and check for oil and water leaks.

Manifolds

Exhaust Manifold—

Removal and Installation

302 and 351W V8

1. Remove air cleaner, intake duct and crankcase ventilation hose as an assembly.
2. Remove air cleaner inlet duct attaching bolts (Bronco and F-100) and oil dipstick tube bracket on right exhaust manifold.
3. Disconnect exhaust pipes from manifolds.
4. Remove heat shield, if equipped.
5. Remove bolts, washers and manifolds.
6. To install, clean mating surfaces of cylinder head and manifolds. Clean out exhaust pipe flange of manifolds and exhaust pipe.
7. Apply graphite grease to mating surfaces of manifolds.
8. Install manifolds, heat shield,

tab washers, and bolts, tightening from the center out to 12-16 ft. lbs. torque. Bend tabs to lock bolts.
9. Install exhaust pipe to flange on manifold, using a new gasket.
10. Install air cleaner inlet duct (Bronco and F-100) and oil dipstick tube bracket on the right exhaust manifold.
11. Install air cleaner and intake duct, including crankcase ventilation hose.

351M and 400 Cu. In. V8

1. If the right manifold is being removed, remove the air cleaner, intake duct and heat stove. If the left manifold is being removed, remove the oil filter.
2. On vehicles equipped with column selector and automatic transmission, disconnect the selector lever cross shaft for clearance.
3. Disconnect the muffler inlet pipe or the catalytic converter at the exhaust manifold. Remove the spark plug heat shields.
4. Remove the exhaust manifold attaching bolts and remove the manifold.
5. Clean the mating surfaces of the exhaust manifold and cylinder head. Clean the mounting flange of the exhaust manifold and muffler inlet pipe or catalytic converter.
6. Apply a graphite grease to the mating surfaces of the exhaust manifold.
7. Position the exhaust manifold on the head and install the attaching bolts. Working from the center to the ends, tighten the bolts to specification.
8. Install the spark plug heat shields.
9. Install the spacer between the inlet pipe and the exhaust manifold.
10. Connect the muffler inlet pipe or the catalytic converter at the exhaust manifold. Tighten the nuts to specification.
11. If the left exhaust manifold is being installed, install the oil filter.
12. On vehicles with automatic transmissions and column selector, connect the selector cross shaft at the chassis and cylinder block.
13. If a right manifold is being installed, install the air cleaner heat stove.
14. Install the air cleaner and intake duct.
15. Start the engine and check for exhaust leaks.

330, 359, 360, 361, 370, 389, 390, 391, 429 and 460 Cu. In. V-8 —All Models

1. Remove air cleaner and disconnect exhaust pipes from manifolds.
2. On all engines except the 460, disconnect the power steering pump bracket from the cylinder block and move it out of the way. Position the pump so that the oil will not drain out. Remove dipstick and tube assembly.
3. Remove attaching bolts, washers of cylinder head, manifold, manifold pipe flange and exhaust pipe.
4. To install, clean mating surfaces.
5. Apply graphite grease to mating surface of manifold, then install manifold, tab washers and bolts. Tighten bolts from the center out to specifications. Bend tabs to lock bolts.
6. Install dipstick and tube assembly.
7 Install power steering pump bracket and adjust belt tension.
8. Connect exhaust pipes to manifolds, using new gaskets.
9. Install air cleaner.

Intake Manifold Removal and Installation

302 and 351 W Cu. In. V-8

1. Drain cooling system.
2. Remove air cleaner and intake duct assembly, including crankcase ventilation hose.
3. Disconnect accelerator rod, choke cable and automatic transmission kickdown rod (if applicable) at the carburetor. Remove the accelerator retracting spring, where so equipped. Disconnect the electric choke and carburetor solenoid wires, if so equipped.

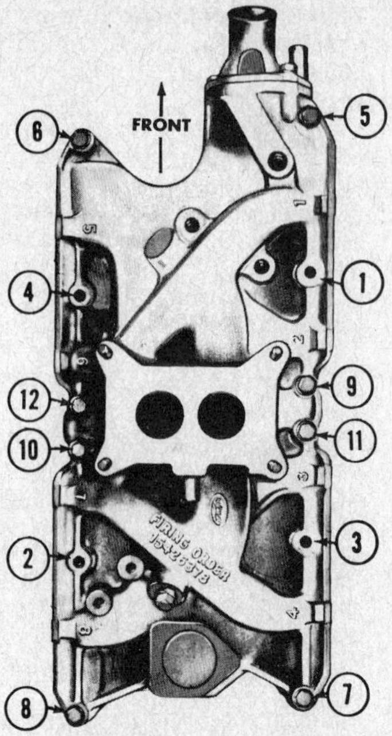

Intake manifold torque sequence—302 V8 (© Ford Motor Co.)

4. Disconnect high tension lead and wires from the coil.
5. Remove spark plug wire from plugs and harness brackets, then remove distributor cap and spark plug wire assembly.
6. Disconnect fuel inlet line at carburetor.
7. Disconnect distributor vacuum hoses and remove distributor.
8. Remove heater hose, radiator hose and water temperature sending unit wire from manifold.
9. Remove water pump bypass hose from coolant outlet housing.

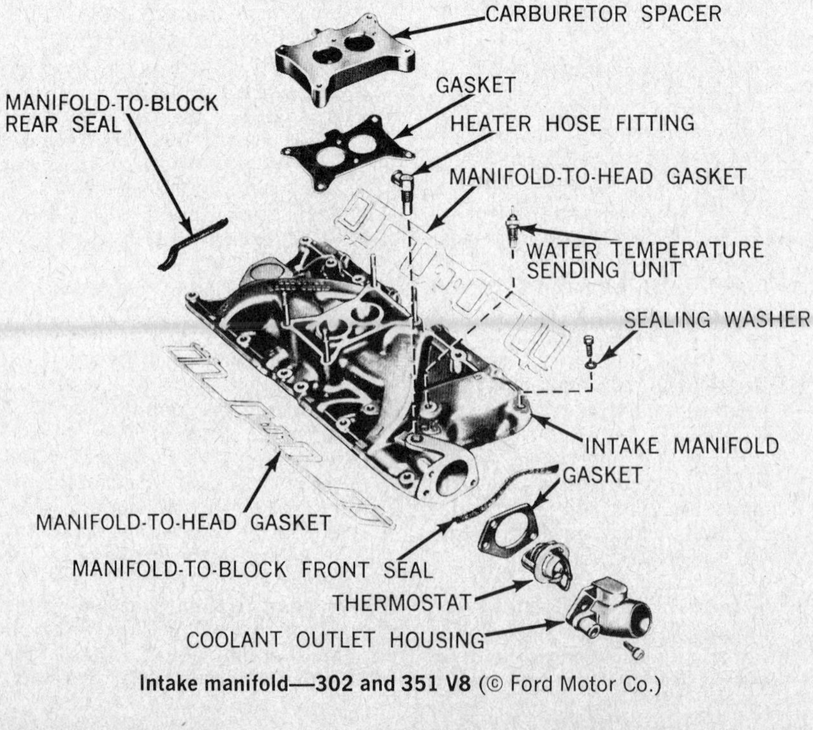

Intake manifold—302 and 351 V8 (© Ford Motor Co.)

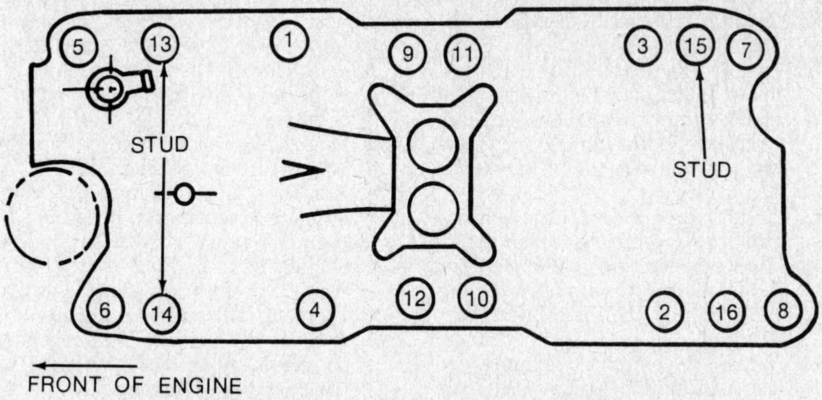

Intake manifold torque sequence—351 V8 (© Ford Motor Co.)

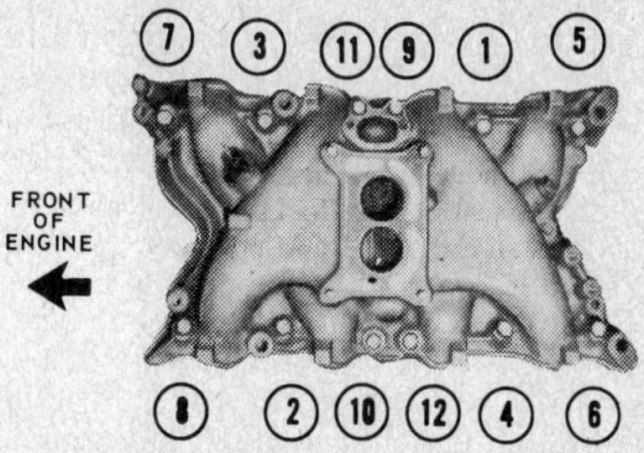

Intake manifold torque sequence—351M & 400 V8 engines
(© Ford Motor Co.)

10. Disconnect crankcase ventilation hose from valve rocker cover.
11. Remove intake manifold and carburetor as an assembly, prying manifold from cylinder head if necessary. Throw away gaskets and bolt sealing washers.
12. When disassembling, identify all vacuum hoses before disconnecting them. Remove coolant outlet housing and gasket. Remove ignition coil and engine identification tag, temperature sending unit, carburetor, spacer, gasket, vacuum fitting, accelerator retracting spring bracket and choke cable bracket.
13. To install, first assemble manifold/carburetor unit by installing all components removed in Step 12 above, making sure vacuum lines are positioned correctly.
14. Clean all mating surfaces, using a suitable solvent to remove all oil. Apply block surfaces with adhesive sealer.
15. Position new gaskets and front and rear seals, using a nonhardening sealer at four gasket-seal junctions. Interlock gaskets with seal tabs and be sure all holes are aligned.
16. Carefully position manifold, making sure that gaskets and seals do not shift. Install bolts and new bolt seal washers, tightening in the sequence illustrated. *Retighten after engine has been operated until warmed up.*
17. Install water bypass hose to coolant outlet housing, radiator upper hose and heater hose.
18. Install distributor. Install distributor cap and spark plug wires, positioning wires in harness brackets on valve rocker covers.
19. Connect crankcase ventilation hose, high tension lead and coil wires, accelerator rod and retracting spring, choke cable and automatic transmission kickdown rod (if applicable). Connect electric choke and carburetor solenoid wires, if so equipped.
20. Fill and bleed cooling system.
21. Adjust ignition timing.
22. Connect vacuum hoses at distributor.
23. Operate engine until warmed up, checking for leaks.
24. Retorque manifold bolts.
25. Adjust transmission throttle linkage, if so equipped.
26. Install air cleaner and intake duct assembly including closed crankcase ventilation hose.

351M and 400 Cu. In. V8—All Models

1. Remove the air cleaner and intake duct. On vehicles with air conditioning, isolate and remove the compressor.
2. Disconnect the high tension lead and wires from the coil. Disconnect the engine harness and move it out of the way.
3. Disconnect the spark plug wires from the plugs. Remove the distributor cap and spark plug wire assembly.
4. Remove the air pump by pass valve and hose from the check valve.
5. Remove the carburetor fuel inlet line.
6. Remove the heater hoses from the retainers and position the hoses out of the way.
7. Remove the ignition coil, vacuum solenoid valve and bracket.
8. Disconnect the crankcase emission hose at the left rocker arm cover.
9. Disconnect the vacuum lines from the intake manifold.
10. Disconnect the distributor vacuum hose from the distributor. Remove the distributor as detailed in the "Distributor" section of this chapter. Block the distributor hole with a rag to prevent foreign material from entering the crankcase.
11. Disconnect the accelerator linkage and the transmission downshift linkage and position out of the way.
12. Remove the carburetor.
13. Remove the manifold attaching bolts, and remove the manifold. Remove and discard the manifold gasket and seals.
14. If the manifold assembly is to be disassembled, disconnect the vacuum hoses.
15. Clean the mating surfaces of the intake manifold, cylinder head and engine block.
16. Apply a 1/8 in. bead of silicone rubber sealer at the edge of the seal mounting surface on the cylinder block and cylinder head. Apply the sealer at all four seal ends. **CAUTION: Do not apply the sealer to the waffle section of the end seals as the sealer will rupture the seal material.**
17. Position new seals on the cylinder block and press the seal locating extensions into the holes in the mating surface.
18. Apply a 1/6 in. bead of silicone rubber sealer to the outer end of each manifold seal, (above previous sealer application), along the full length of the seal end.

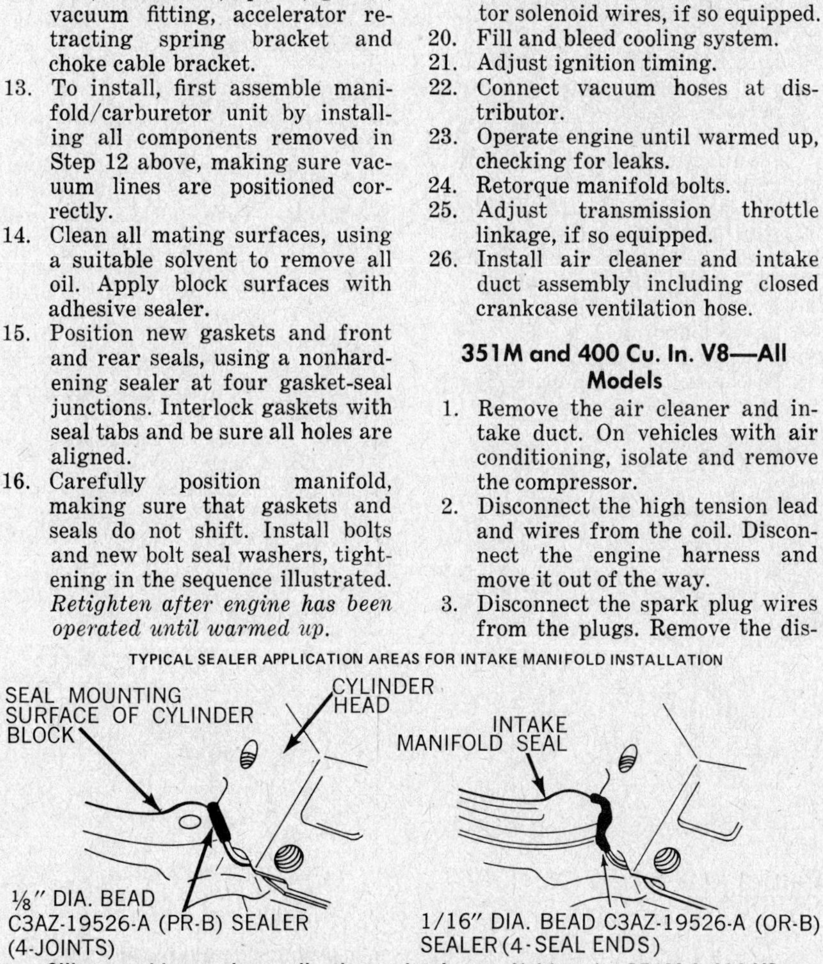

Silicone rubber sealer application on intake manifold seal—351M & 400 V8 engines (© Ford Motor Co.)

CAUTION: Do not apply the sealer to the waffle section of the end seals as the sealer will rupture the seal material. The sealer sets up in 15 minutes so it is very important that the assembly be completed quickly.

19. Position the intake manifold gasket on the block and cylinder heads with the alignment notches under the dowels on the cylinder head. Be sure that the holes in the gasket are aligned with the holes in cylinder head.
20. Carefully lower the intake manifold into position on the cylinder block and heads.
21. Check and make sure that the holes in the manifold gaskets and the manifold are in alignment. Install the intake manifold attaching bolts. Tighten the intake bolts in three steps in sequence and to proper torque specifications.
22. Install the carburetor and gasket.
23. Install the distributor as detailed in the "Distributor" section of this chapter.
24. Install the accelerator linkage and the transmission downshift rod.
25. Install the vacuum solenoid valve and the ignition coil.
26. Connect the vacuum lines at the manifold. Install the air pump bypass air supply hose.
27. Position the wiring harness under the hold down clips on the left rocker arm cover and connect the wires to the ignition coil, water temperature sending unit and throttle solenoid.
28. Connect the PCV line at the left rocker arm cover.
29. Install the heater hoses in their retainers.
30. Connect the fuel inlet pipe to the carburetor.
31. Install the distributor cap and spark plug wires. Position the spark plug wires in the harness brackets on the rocker arm covers and connect the wires to the spark plugs.
32. Install the air conditioning compressor, if vehicle is so equipped.
33. Start the engine and check for leaks. Adjust the ignition timing and connect the distributor vacuum line.
34. When the engine temperature has stabilized, adjust the idle mixture and speed.
35. *Retorque the intake manifold in sequence and to specifications.*
36. Install the air cleaner and recheck the idle speed.

330, 359, 360, 361, 389, 390, and 391 Cu. In. V8—All Models

1. Drain cooling system.
2. Remove air cleaner and crankcase vent hose(s).
3. Disconnect accelerator linkage at the carburetor.
4. If so equipped, remove the accelerator cross shaft bracket from the intake manifold.
5. Disconnect fuel line and distributor vacuum line at the carburetor.
6. Disconnect all leads at the coil and oil pressure and water temperature sending units.
7. Remove wiring harness from the retaining clips on the left valve rocker cover.
8. Disconnect spark plug wires, remove wires from harness brackets, remove distributor cap and spark plug wire assembly.
9. Disconnect and remove distributor vacuum line.
10. Remove distributor.
11. Disconnect radiator upper hose(s) at the water outlet housing, heater hoses and, on C series vehicle, the coolant supply tank hose at the water outlet housing.
12. Disconnect water pump bypass hose(s) at the water pump.
13. Remove valve rocker covers and crankcase ventilation hoses.
14. Remove valve rocker shaft assembly as described in the section, "Rocker Arm Shaft Assembly Removal and Installation."
15. Remove and identify pushrods so that they can be put back in their original positions.
16. Remove manifold attaching bolts.
17. Install eyebolts (5/16-18 thread) in the left front and right rear rocker arm cover screw holes and attach lifting sling.
18. Carefully lift out intake manifold, then remove seals and gaskets.
19. Remove water pump bypass hoses (s), water outlet housing, carburetor, gaskets spacer and water temperature sending unit.
20. Before installing, assemble components removed in Step 19. Use a new gasket and sealing compound when installing water outlet (thermostat) housing. Use electrical-conductive sealer when installing water temperature sending unit.
21. Thoroughly clean all manifold, cylinder head and block mating surfaces (use solvent to remove all traces of oil). Coat block seal surfaces with quick-setting seal adhesive and coat mating surfaces of cylinder heads and block with non-hardening Oil-resistant sealer. Position new seals on block and cylinder heads, *making sure they are properly aligned.* Position manifold gasket slots over the end tabs on the seals and coat these junctions with non-hardening sealer.
22. Install eyebolts in intake manifold and attach lifting sling, then carefully lower manifold

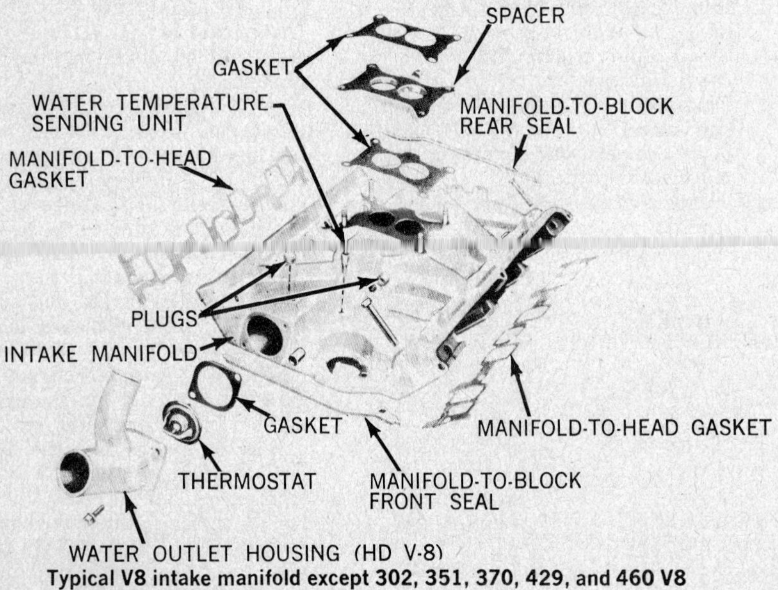

Typical V8 intake manifold except 302, 351, 370, 429, and 460 V8
(© Ford Motor Co.)

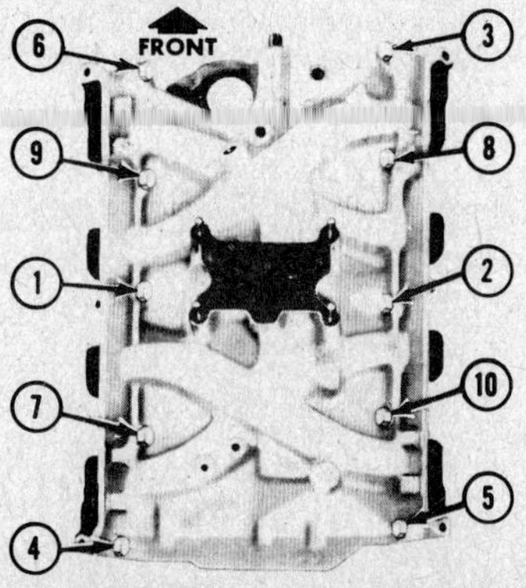

Intake manifold torque sequence—V8 except 302, 351, 370, 429 and 460
(© Ford Motor Co.)

onto engine. Position manifold by inserting distributor and check that seals and gaskets are still properly aligned and that all holes line up.

23. Install manifold attaching bolts, coating under side of bolt heads with non-hardening sealer. Tighten bolts to 32-35 ft. lbs. torque in the sequence illustrated. Retorque bolts after engine has been run and warmed up. Remove distributor, lifting sling and eyebolts.
24. Connect water pump bypass hose (s) to water pump, radiator upper hose, heater hoses, water temperature sending unit and, on C series trucks, coolant supply tank hose.
25. Apply lubriplate to both ends of pushrods and install them in their original positions. Install valve rocker shaft as described in "Rocker Arm Shaft Assembly Removal and Installation."
26. Install the distributor as described in "Distributor Removal and Installation."
27. Install rocker covers, using new gasket and sealer, tightening to 10-12 ft. lbs., waiting two minutes then torquing again.
28. Connect crankcase ventilation hoses.
29. Install carburetor fuel inlet line, spark plug wires, wiring harness, distributor vacuum line and distributor cap.
30. Connect oil pressure sending unit wire and coil wire and lead.
31. Install accelerator cross shaft bracket (if applicable) and accelerator rod.
32. Fill and bleed cooling system.
33. Install air cleaner and vent hose.
34. Start engine, then check ignition timing idle speed and idle fuel mixture, then let engine warm up.
35. Retorque intake manifold bolts to specifications.

370, 429 and 460 V-8

1. Drain the cooling system and remove the air cleaner assembly.
2. Disconnect the upper radiator hose at the engine.
3. Disconnect the heater hoses at the intake manifold and the water pump. Position them out of the way. Loosen the water pump by-pass hose clamp at the intake manifold.
4. Disconnect the PCV valve and hose at the right valve cover. Disconnect all of the vacuum lines at the rear of the intake manifold and tag them for proper reinstallation.
5. Disconnect the wires at the spark plugs, and remove the wires from the brackets on the valve covers. Disconnect the high-tension wire from the coil and remove the distributor cap and wires as an assembly.
6. Disconnect all of the distributor vacuum lines at the carburetor and vacuum control valve and tag them for proper installation. Remove the distributor and vacuum lines as an assembly.
7. Disconnect the accelerator linkage at the carburetor. Remove the speed control linkage bracket, if so equipped, from the manifold and carburetor.
8. Remove the bolts holding the accelerator linkage bellcrank and position the linkage and return springs out of the way.
9. Disconnect the fuel line at the carburetor.
10. Disconnect the wiring harness at the coil battery terminal, engine temperature sending unit, oil pressure sending unit, and other connections as necessary. Disconnect the wiring harness from the clips at the left valve cover and position the harness out of the way.
11. Remove the coil and bracket assembly.
12. Remove the intake manifold attaching bolts and lift the manifold and carburetor from the engine as an assembly. It may be necessary to pry the manifold away from the cylinder heads. Do not damage the gasket sealing surfaces.
13. Install the intake manifold in the reverse order of removal. Clean all gasket material from the mating surfaces of the manifold and cylinder heads and block. Glue the intake manifold end seals in place before installing the manifold. Use sealer at each end of the intake manifold-to-cylinder head gaskets for the full width of the gasket. When the manifold is placed on top of the engine run your fingers around the end seal areas to make sure that the end seals have not shifted. If they have, remove the manifold and reposition the seals. Tighten the intake manifold bolts in two stages in the proper sequence; first to 15 ft lbs, and then to 25-30 ft lbs. After the engine has been started and has reached normal operating temperature, retorque the intake manifold bolts.

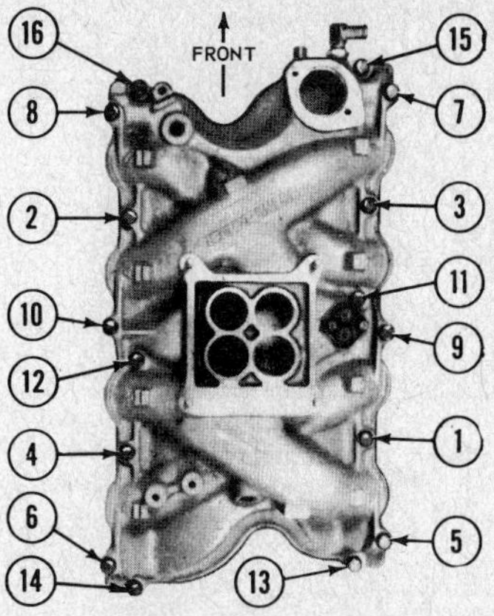

Intake manifold torque sequence—370, 429 & 460 V8 (© Ford Motor Co.)

Intake/Exhaust Manifold Removal and Installation

200 Cu. In. 6-Cylinder

1. Remove air cleaner and, if so equipped (later models), hot air duct.
2. Disconnect exhaust pipe from manifold.
3. Remove retaining bolts and manifold.
4. To install, clean mating surfaces of head and manifold and scrape gasket material from manifold exhaust pipe flange and pipe.
5. Apply graphite grease to the mating surface of the exhaust manifold.
6. Install manifold, retaining bolts and tab washers, tightening bolts from the center out to 13-18 ft. lbs. Bend tabs to lock bolts.
7. Install exhaust pipe on manifold, using new gasket.
8. Install air cleaner and hot air duct.
9. Start engine and check for exhaust leaks.

240 and 300 Cu. In. 6-Cylinder

1. Remove air cleaner and hot air ducts.

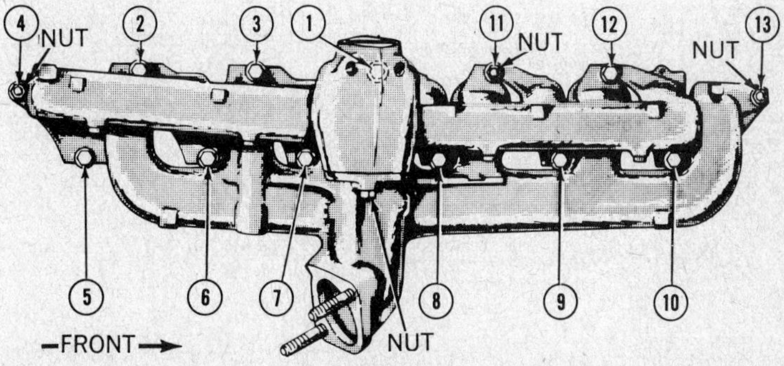

Manifold tightening sequence—240 & 300 engines (© Ford Motor Co.)

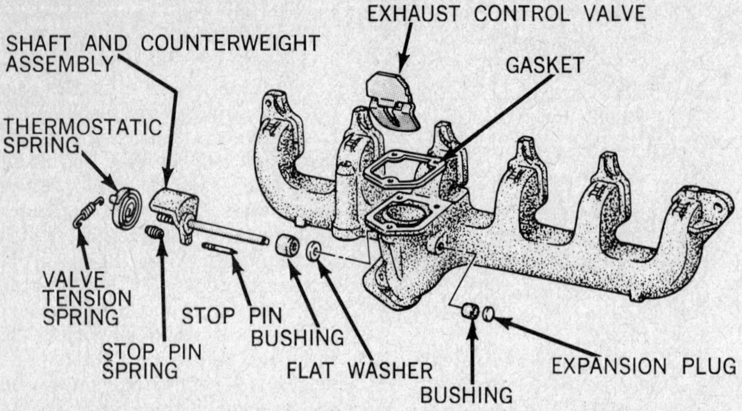

Exhaust control valve assembly—240 & 300 engines (© Ford Motor Co.)

2. Disconnect choke cable and accelerator rod or cable at the carburetor. Remove accelerator retracting spring.
3. On LN series vehicles, disconnect the battery and remove the alternator.
4. On vehicle with an automatic transmission, remove the kickdown rod retracting spring and remove the accelerator rod bellcrank assembly.
5. On C series vehicle, remove the engine oil dipstick and tube.
6. Disconnect fuel inlet line and distributor vacuum line from the carburetor, exhaust pipe from the manifold and, if so equipped, power brake vacuum line.
7. Remove manifold attaching bolts and lift manifolds from engine.
8. To separate manifolds, remove the nuts joining the intake and exhaust manifolds. Discard all gaskets.
9. If the exhaust control valve requires replacement, see "Exhaust Control Valve Removal and Installation" below.
10. To install, clean the mating surfaces of cylinder head and manifolds.
11. If a new manifold is to be used, remove the tube fittings on the old manifold and install them on the new one.
12. Before joining exhaust and intake manifolds, coat the mating surfaces lightly with graphite grease. Use a new gasket and tighten the nuts finger tight.
13. Coat the mating surfaces with graphite grease and install the manifold assembly on the cylinder head. Use a new intake manifold gasket. Tighten the bolts and nuts to 23-28 ft. lbs. torque in the sequence illustrated.
14. Tighten the intake to exhaust manifold stud nuts to 28-33 ft. lbs. torque.
15. Connect exhaust pipe to manifold, tightening nuts to 25-30 ft. lbs. torque.
16. Connect crankcase vent hose to intake manifold inlet tube, fuel inlet line and distributor vacuum line to carburetor, accelerator rod or cable and choke cable to carburetor. Install the accelerator retracting spring.
17. On LN series trucks, install the alternator and belts and connect the battery.
18. On C series trucks, install the dipstick and tube.
19. On a vehicle with an automatic transmission, install the bellcrank assembly and kickdown rod retracting spring. Adjust the transmission control linkage.
20. Install the air cleaner and hot air duct.
21. Adjust idle speed and idle fuel mixture.

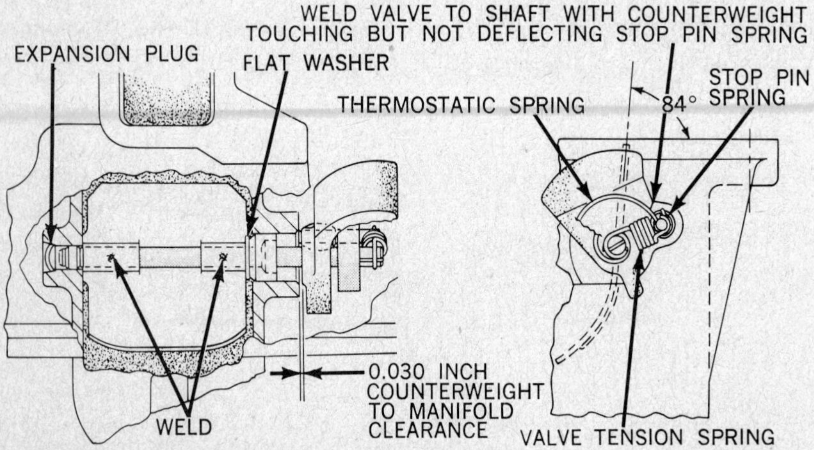

Exhaust valve plate position & counterweight clearance (© Ford Motor Co.)

Exhaust Control Valve Removal and Installation

240 and 300 Cu. In. 6-Cylinder

1. Separate intake and exhaust manifolds.
2. Remove valve tension spring, thermostatic spring and stop pin.
3. The valve shaft must be cut with a torch on each side of the valve plate. Remove valve plate and expansion plug.
4. Remove bushings and install new ones. There are two sizes of replacement bushings (OD) so make sure the right ones are used. Ream the ID of bushings to 0.51-0.253″. The shorter bushing (front) is installed 0.010-0.015″ below inside surface of the manifold and the longer bushing (rear) protrudes into the manifold cavity 0.020″ (note that beveled end points inward).
5. Slide new shaft into the bushings, flat washer and valve plate. Note that the flat washer is between the valve plate and the long (rearward) bushing. Install a new stop pin spring on the stop pin.
6. Rotate the counterweight and shaft assembly clockwise until the counterweight contacts the stop pin spring, then place a 0.030″ feeler gauge between the counterweight and the manifold to maintain the specified clearance. Hold the valve plate at a 84 degree angle to the top surface of the manifold as illustrated and tack-weld the plate to the shaft, *using stainless steel welding rod.*
7. Check for free movement of the valve and install expansion plug in the bushing bore.
8. Install the thermostatic spring, positioned so that it will be necessary to wind the spring ½ turn clockwise to hook it over the stop pin.
9. Install a new valve tension spring on the exhaust control valve shaft and the stop pin.

Cylinder Head

Cylinder Head Removal and Installation

200 Cu. In. 6-Cylinder

1. Drain cooling system, remove the air cleaner and oil filler tube, and disconnect the battery cable at cylinder head.

2. Disconnect exhaust pipe from manifold.
3. Disconnect accelerator rod retracting spring, choke control cable and accelerator rod at the carburetor, transmission kickdown rod (automatic transmission), accelerator linkage at bellcrank, fuel inlet line at fuel filter hose, distributor vacuum line at the carburetor and other vacuum lines as necessary for accessibility (identify them for proper reinstallation).
4. Remove upper radiator hose at the coolant outlet housing.
5. Disconnect the distributor vacuum line at the distributor and carburetor fuel inlet line at the fuel pump.
6. Disconnect spark plug wires at the plugs and temperature sending unit wire at the unit.
7. Remove PCV valve and hose from valve rocker cover and disconnect the other end of the hose from the intake manifold.
8. Remove the valve rocker arm cover, then remove the rocker arm shaft support bolts by loosening them two turns at a time in sequence.
9. Lift off rocker arm shaft.
10. Remove cylinder head bolts and cylinder head. *Do not pry.*
11. Before installing, clean gasket surfaces of cylinder head and engine block, install guide studs at each end of block, apply cylinder head gasket sealer evenly to both sides of the head gasket, and run the gasket down the guide studs into position on the engine block.
12. Put a new gasket on the flange of the exhaust pipe, then carefully lower the head down the guide studs onto the block, guiding the exhaust manifold studs into the exhaust pipe.
13. Coat the threads of the cylinder head right side end bolts (Nos. 12 and 13 in the illustration) and install them finger tight to hold the head and gasket in position. Install the rest of the head bolts finger tight, then tighten in steps to 55 ft. lbs, 65 ft. lbs. and 70-75 ft. lbs., following the sequence illustrated for each step.

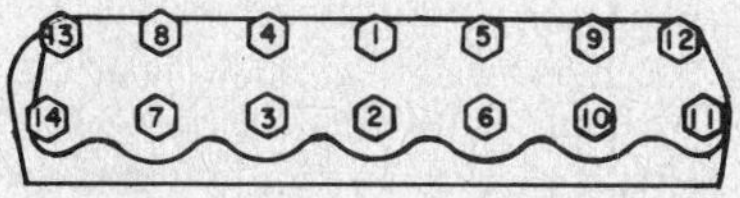

Cylinder head torque sequence—200 cu. in. 6-cylinder (© Ford Motor Co.)

14. Apply Lubriplate to both ends of their original locations.
15. Apply Lubriplate to the rocker arm follower pads and to the valve stem tips, then position rocker arm shaft assembly on the head.
16. Install the rocker arm shaft support bolts and tighten them in sequence two turns at a time until they are torqued to 30-35 ft. lbs.
17. Check and adjust the preliminary (cold) lash as described in "Valve Clearance Adjustment."
18. Install lockwashers and nuts to exhaust manifold to exhaust pipe studs and tighten to 25-35 ft. lbs. torque.
19. Connect radiator upper hose at the coolant outlet housing.
20. Install vacuum lines(s) and fuel line.
21. Connect accelerator linkage at the bellcrank assembly, transmission kickdown rod, accelerator rod retracing spring, battery cable at the cylinder head, choke control cable and accelerator rod at carburetor, temperature sending unit wire and spark plug leads. Adjust choke cable.
22. Temporarily install rocker cover and PC valve, then operate engine until it is warmed up. Adjust final (hot) valve lash as described in "Valve Clearance Adjustment."
23. Clean rocker cover and head gasket surfaces and install cover using a new seal coated on both sides with oil-resistant sealer. Tighten cover retaining bolts to 3-5 ft. lbs. torque, wait two minutes, then retorque to the same value.
24. Connect one end of the crankcase vent hose to the carburetor spacer and the valve end to the rocker cover.
25. Install oil filler tube and air cleaner.
26. Start engine and check for coolant and oil leaks.

240 and 300 Cu. In. 6-Cylinder

1. Drain cooling system and remove air cleaner and crankcase ventilation valve.
2. Disconnect the following: the vent hose at the intake manifold inlet tube, carburetor fuel inlet line, distributor vacuum line, choke cable, accelerator cable and heater hose at the coolant outlet elbow. Remove accelerator cable retracting spring.
3. On a vehicle with automatic transmission, disconnect the kickdown rod at the carburetor.
4. Disconnect upper radiator hose and exhaust pipe.
5. Remove the coil and the valve rocker cover and disconnect spark plug wires.
6. Loosen the rocker arm stud nuts so that the rocker arms can be twisted aside, then remove the pushrods, identifying each so that it may be installed in its original position.
7. Remove head bolts and remove the cylinder head. *Do not pry between head and block.*
8. Before installing, clean mating surfaces of block, cylinder head and exhaust pipe.
9. Position new gasket over the dowel pins on the cylinder block, then carefully lower head into place on the block. Remove lifting apparatus.
10. Oil the threads and install head bolts. Tighten the bolts in three steps, following the sequence illustrated in each step: first to 50-55 ft. lbs., then to 60-65 ft. lbs, and finally to 70-75 ft. lbs.

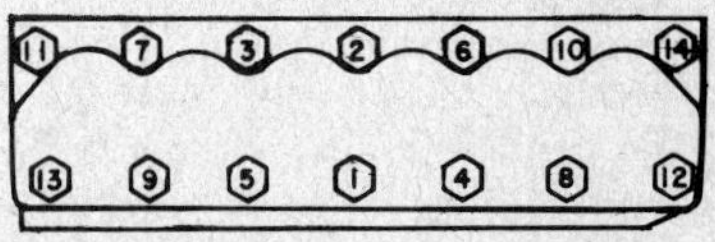

Cylinder head bolt tightening sequence—6 cylinder—240 & 300 engines
(© Ford Motor Co.)

11. Connect exhaust pipe to manifold flange, using a new gasket and tighten the nuts to 25-30 ft. lbs.
12. Apply Lubriplate to both ends of the pushrods and install them in their original positions.
13. Apply Lubriplate to both the rocker arm fulcrum seat and the fulcrum seat socket of each rocker arm and install the rocker arms, tightening the stud nuts just enough to hold the pushrods. Adjust the valve lash as described in "Valve Clearance Adjustment."
14. Install the rocker cover, using oil-resistant sealer and a new gasket. Tighten the retaining bolts to 4-7 ft. lbs.
15. Connect the spark plug wires to the plugs, crankcase vent hose to the intake manifold, PCV valve in the valve rocker cover, fuel inlet line, distributor vacuum hose, accelerator cable and choke cable. Install accelerator cable retracting spring.
16. On a vehicle with automatic transmission, connect the kickdown rod to the carburetor.
17. Connect radiator upper hose to the coolant outlet housing and the heater hose to the coolant outlet housing, leaving the clamp loose.
18. Fill the cooling system and bleed. Then tighten the heater hose clamp.
19. Operate the engine until it is warmed up, checking for leaks.
20. Adjust engine idle speed and idle fuel mixture.

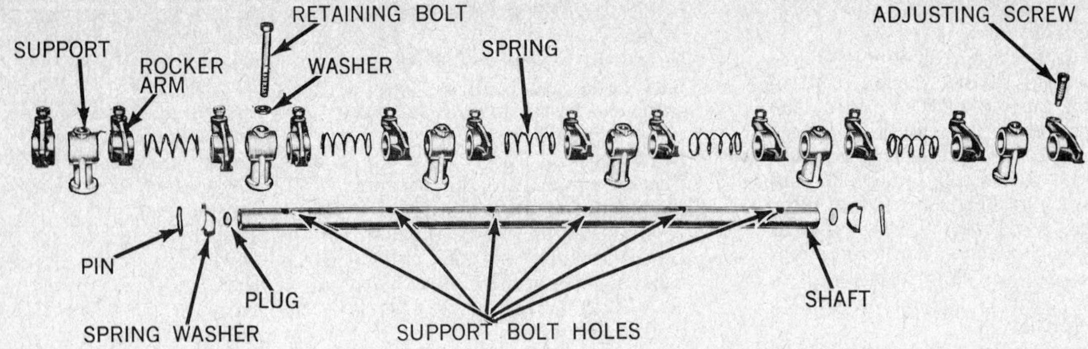

Rocker arm shaft assembly—6 cylinder—typical (© Ford Motor Co.)

302 and 351W Cu. In. V-8

1. Remove the intake manifold and carburetor as an assembly as described in "Intake Manifold Removal and Installation."
2. Remove rocker arm cover.
3. To remove right cylinder head, loosen alternator adjusting arm bolt and remove the alternator mounting bracket bolt and spacer. Swing alternator down out of the way. On Bronco and Econoline trucks, remove the coil and air cleaner inlet duct from the right head. To remove left cylinder head, remove accelerator shaft fastening bolts at the front of the head. On some later models, it may be necessary to remove the air conditioning compressor bracket.
4. Disconnect exhaust pipe from the manifold.
5. Loosen rocker arm stud nuts and twist rocker arms so that the pushrods may be removed. Identify the pushrods when removing so that they may be reinstalled in their original locations.
6. Remove exhaust valve stem caps, on 320 engines. On 1979 and later E-100 - E-350 models, remove the thermactor air supply manifold, pump valve, and hose as an assembly. On 1979 and later F-100 - F-150 models, disconnect the thermactor supply hoses at the check valves and plug the check valves.
7. Install cylinder head holding fixtures, remove head bolts and lift off head.
8. To install, clean all gasket surfaces of block, head and rocker cover. Position new head gasket over the dowels onto the block (do *not* use sealer on this composition gasket). Install head and remove holding fixture.
9. Install head bolts and tighten in three steps: first to 50 ft. lbs, then to 60 ft. lbs, and finally to 65-72 ft. lbs. Tighten in the sequence illustrated for each step.
10. Clean pushrods, blowing out oil passage, and check them for straightness. Lubricate pushrod ends, valve stem tips and rocker arm cups, fulcrum sets and followers. Install pushrods in their original positions, install exhaust stem caps and install rocker arms. Adjust the valve clearance as described in "Valve Clearance Adjustment."
11. Connect the exhaust pipe to the manifold, using new gasket and tightening nuts to 25-35 ft. lbs. torque.
12. On right cylinder head, position the alternator and install the attaching bolt and spacer, ignition coil (Bronco and Econoline) and air cleaner inlet duct. Adjust drive belt tension. On left cylinder head, install accelerator shaft assembly, and air conditioning compressor bracket.
13. Install rocker cover using new gasket and tightening cover bolts to 3-5 ft. lbs.
14. Install intake manifold and carburetor assembly as described in "Intake Manifold Removal and Installation."
15. Install the thermactor air supply assembly where necessary.

330, 359, 360, 361, 389, 390 and 391 Cu. In. V-8

Removal and installation of cylinder heads on the larger V-8's is essentially the same procedure as that described above for the 302 and 351W cu. in. engines. The intake manifold and carburetor assembly and rocker arm shaft assembly are removed first (see "Intake Manifold Removal and Installation"). When installing new head gasket, note the word "front" on the gasket and install accordingly. The head bolts are tightened in three steps, first to 70 ft. lbs., then to 80 ft. lbs., and finally to 85-90 ft. lbs. Tighten in the sequence illustrated for each step.

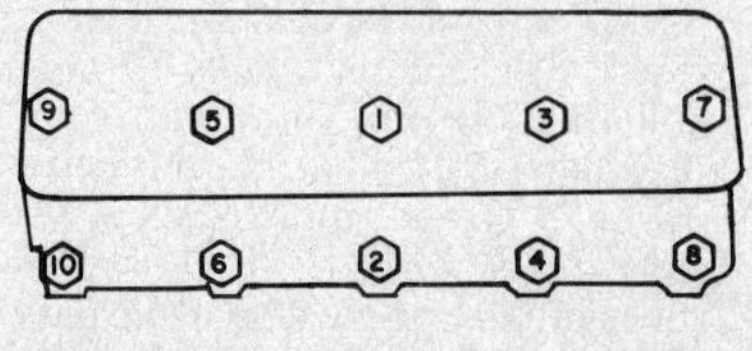

Cylinder head bolt tightening sequence —all V8 engines (© Ford Motor Co.)

351M and 400 Cu. In. V8

1. Remove the intake manifold and carburetor as an assembly. This procedure is described earlier in "Intake Manifold Removal and Installation."
2. Remove the rocker arm cover.
3. If the left cylinder head is being removed; isolate and remove the air conditioning compressor (if so equipped), disconnect the power steering pump bracket, and remove the drive belt from the pump pulley. Position the power steering pump out of the way and in a position that will prevent the fluid from draining out.
4. If the right cylinder head is being removed; remove the alternator mounting bracket through bolt and the air cleaner duct from the cylinder head assembly. Disconnect the ground strap from the rear of the cylinder head.
5. Disconnect the muffler inlet pipe or catalytic converter from the exhaust manifold.
6. Remove the rocker arm bolts, oil deflectors, fulcrum seats, rocker arms, and push rods in sequence so that they may be installed in there original positions.
7. Remove the cylinder head attaching bolts and lift the head off the cylinder block. Remove and discard the head gasket.
8. Clean the cylinder head, intake manifold, rocker arm cover and cylinder head mounting surface. If the cylinder head was removed to replace the head gasket, check the flatness of the head and cylinder block.
9. Position a new head gasket over

the cylinder dowels on the block. Place the cylinder head on the block and install the attaching bolts.

10. The cylinder head bolts are tightened in three progressive steps. Tighten all the bolts in sequence to 75 ft-lbs., then to 95 ft-lbs. and finally to 105 ft-lbs. It will not be necessary to retorque the bolts after extended operation.
11. Clean the push rods and blow out the oil passages. Check the ends of the push rods for nicks, grooves, roughness or excessive wear. Visually check the push rods for straightness or check runout with a dial indicator. If the runout exceeds the maximum limit, replace the push rod. *Do not attempt to straighten a push rod.*
12. Lubricate and install the push rods in their original positions.
13. Lubricate and install the rocker arms, fulcrum seats, oil deflectors, and rocker arm bolts.
14. Connect the muffler inlet pipe or catalytic convertor to the exhaust manifold. Tighten the nuts to specification.
15. Install the alternator mounting bracket through bolt and air cleaner inlet duct on the right cylinder head. Connect the ground strap at the rear of the right cylinder head.
16. Install the power steering pump bracket and air conditioning compressor (if equipped) on the left cylinder head.
17. Adjust the drive belts to specification.
18. Apply sealer to the rocker arm cover gasket to hold the gasket in place. Position the gasket on the cover aligning the holes in cover and gasket. Install the rocker arm cover.
19. Install the intake manifold assembly as described earlier in this section, "Intake Manifold Removal and Installation."

370, 429, 460 V-8

1. Remove the intake manifold and carburetor as an assembly.
2. Disconnect the exhaust pipe from the exhaust manifold. Some applications may require the removal of the exhaust manifold at the cylinder heads.
3. Loosen the air conditioning compressor drive belt, if so equipped.
4. Loosen the alternator attaching bolts and remove the bolt attaching the alternator bracket to the right cylinder head.
5. Disconnect the air conditioning compressor from the engine and move it aside, out of the way. Do not discharge the air conditioning system, if possible.
6. Remove the bolts securing the power steering reservoir bracket to the left cylinder head. Position the reservoir and bracket out of the way. Remove air brake and thermactor brackets as necessary.
7. Remove the valve rocker arm covers. Remove the rocker arm bolts, rocker arms, oil deflectors, fulcrums and pushrods in sequence so that they can be reinstalled in their original positions.
8. Remove the cylinder head bolts and lift the head and exhaust manifold off the engine. If necessary, pry at the forward corners of the cylinder head against the casting bosses provided on the cylinder block. Do not damage the gasket mating surfaces of the cylinder head and block by prying against them.
9. Remove all gasket material from the cylinder head and block. Clean all gasket material from the mating surfaces of the intake manifold. If the exhaust manifold was removed, clean the mating surfaces of the cylinder head exhaust port areas and install the exhaust manifold.
10. Position the two long cylinder head bolts in the two rear lower bolt holes of the left cylinder head. Place a long cylinder head bolt in the rear lower bolt hole of the right cylinder head. Use rubber bands to keep the bolts in position until the cylinder heads are installed on the cylinder block.
11. Position new cylinder head gaskets on the cylinder block dowels. Do not apply sealer to the gaskets, heads, or block.
12. Place the cylinder heads on the block, guiding the exhaust pipe connections. Install the remaining cylinder head bolts. The longer bolts go in the lower row of holes.
13. Tighten all the cylinder head attaching bolts in the proper sequence in three stages: 75 ft lbs, 105 ft lbs, and finally, to 135 ft lbs. When this procedure is used, it is not necessary to retorque the heads after extended use.
14. Connect the exhaust pipes to the exhaust manifolds.
15. Install the intake manifold and carburetor assembly. Tighten the intake manifold attaching bolts in the proper sequence to 25-30 ft lbs.
16. Install the air conditioning compressor to the engine.
17. Install the power steering reservoir to the engine.
18. Apply oil-resistant sealer to one side of the new valve cover gaskets and lay the cemented side in place in the valve covers. Install the covers.
19. Install the alternator to the right cylinder head and adjust the alternator drive belt tension.
20. Adjust the air conditioning compressor drive belt tension.
21. Fill the radiator with coolant.
22. Start the engine and check for leaks.

Valve Rocker Arm Shaft Assembly

Removal and Installation

330, 359, 360, 361, 389, 390 and 391 Cu. In. Engine

1. Remove air cleaner, disconnect spark plug leads and remove leads from bracket on the valve rocker cover.
2. Remove crankcase ventilation hose from rocker cover, then remove rocker cover. On left rocker

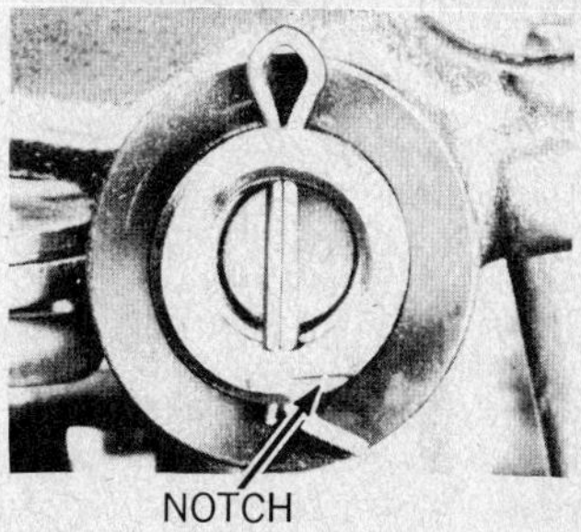

Rocker arm shaft identification notch (© Ford Motor Co.)

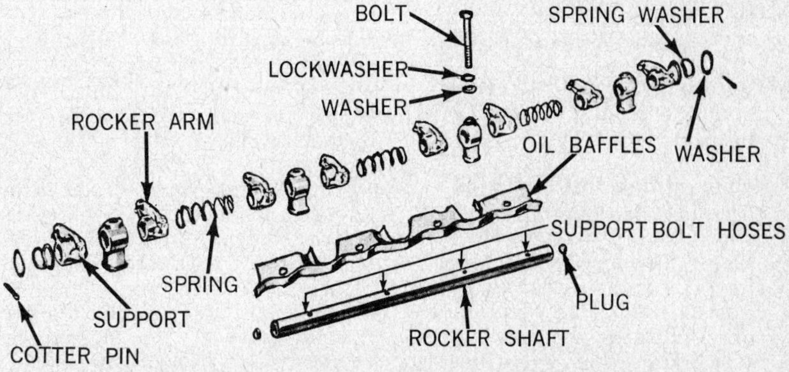

Valve rocker arm shaft assembly V8—typical (© Ford Motor Co.)

cover the wiring harness must be removed.

3. On right side, start at No. 4 cylinder (rearmost) and loosen the support bolts in sequence, two turns at a time. Remove the shaft assembly and baffle plate after all the bolts have been loosened. The same procedure is followed on the left bank, except that the bolt-loosening sequence starts with the No. 5 cylinder (foremost).

    CAUTION: The above bolt-loosening procedure must be followed to avoid damage to the rocker arm shaft.

4. To install, apply Lubriplate to the pad end of the rocker arms, to the tip of the valve stems and to both ends of the pushrods.
5. Rotate engine to 45 degrees *past* No. 1 cylinder TDC.
6. With the pushrods in place, position rocker arm shaft assembly and baffle plate on the cylinder head such that *oil holes are on the bottom and identification notch is down and toward the front on the right bank and toward the rear on the left bank.* Tighten support bolts finger tight.
7. On the right bank, start at No. 4 cylinder and tighten the support bolts two turns at a time in sequence (4-3-2-1) until the supports are fully in contact with the cylinder head. Then tighten the support bolts to 40-45 ft. lbs. torque. The same procedure is followed on the left valve rocker arm shaft support bolts, starting with the No. 5 cylinder. This procedure allows imes for the hydraulic lifter leakdown and thus prevents damage to pushrods, valves and rocker arms.
8. Check valve clearances and adjust if necessary.
9. Install rocker cover, using new gaskets and sealer.
10. Tighten cover retaining bolts to 10-12 ft. lbs, wait two minutes, then tighten to the same torque again.
11. Install crankcase ventilation regulator valve and hose(s), connect spark plug wires and crankcase vent hose, and install air cleaner.

Valve Rocker Arm

6-Cylinder

Removal and Installation

1. Disconnect the inlet air hose at the oil fill cap. Remove the air cleaner. Disconnect the accelerator cable at the carburetor, and remove the cable retracting spring. Remove the accelerator cable bracket from the cylinder head.

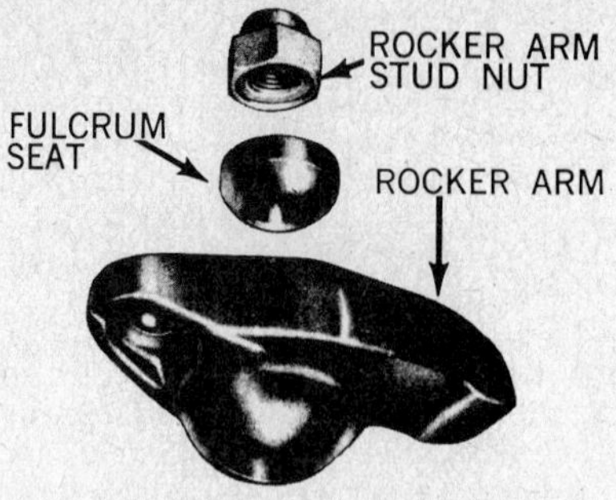

Stud/nut type rocker arm
(© Ford Motor Co.)

2. Remove the PCV valve from the rocker arm cover. Remove the valve rocker arm cover. Remove the valve rocker arm stud nut, fulcrum seat and rocker arm.

    NOTE: Inspect the rocker arm cover bolts for worn or damaged seals under the bolt heads and replace as necessary.

3. To install, apply Lubriplate (or Equivalent) to the top of the valve stem, at the push rod guide in the cylinder head, to the rocker arm fulcrum seat and the fulcrum seat socket in the rocker arm.
4. Install the valve rocker arm, fulcrum seat and stud nut. Adjust the valve clearance as outlined in "Preliminary Valve Adjustment, 6-Cylinder" in this section.
5. Using a new gasket, install the cover on the cylinder head. Partially tighten the cover bolts in sequence, starting with the middle bolts. Then tighten to specification in the same order.
6. Install the PCV valve. Install the accelerator cable bracket on the cylinder head and connect the cable to the carburetor. Connect the inlet air hose to the oil fill cap. Install the air cleaner.
7. Start the engine and check for oil leaks.

8-Cylinder

Removal and Installation

1. Remove the air cleaner and the intake duct assembly, including the crankcase ventilation hoses.
2. Disconnect all appropriate hoses, wires and equipment necessary to remove the rocker arm valve cover(s).
3. Disconnect the spark plug wires, and remove them from the bracket on the valve rocker arm cover.
4. Remove the valve rocker arm cover. Remove the valve rocker arm stud nut (or bolt), oil deflector (if equipped), fulcrum seat and rocker arm.
5. To install, apply Lubriplate (or equivalent) to the top of the valve stems, rocker arm and fulcrum seats.

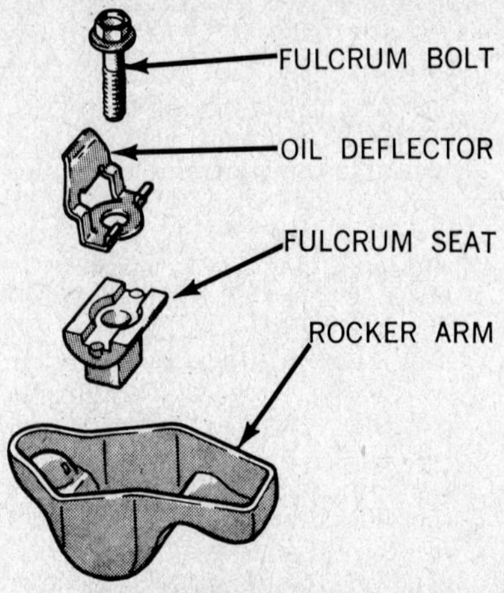

Bolt and fulcrum rocker arm
(© Ford Motor Co.)

6. Install the valve rocker arm and attaching parts. Adjust the valve clearance as outlined in this section.
7. Continue the installation in the reverse order of the removal.
8. Start the engine and check for leaks.

Valve Train

Valve Arrangement

200-Six: E-I-E-I-E-E-I-E-I-I-E

240, 300 Six: E-I-E-I-E-I-E-I-E-I-E-I

302, 351W, 351M, 370, 400, 429, 460-V8:
RT I-E-I-E-I-E-I-E
LT E-I-E-I-E-I-E-I

330, 359, 360, 361, 389, 390, 391-V8:
RT E-I-E-I-E-I-E-I
LT E-I-E-I-E-I-E-I

401, 475, 477, 534-V8:
RT E-I-E-I-I-E-I-E
LT E-I-E-I-I-E-I-E

Valve Adjustment

Valve Clearance (Lash) Adjustment

All engines used in full-size Ford products are equipped with hydraulic valve lifters except the 401, 475, 477, 534 cu. in. versions. Valve systems with hydraulic valve lifters operate with zero clearance in the valve train, and because of this the rocker arms are non-adjustable. The only means by which valve system clearances can be altered is by installing .060 in. over-or undersize pushrods; but, because of the hydraulic lifter's natural ability to compensate for slack in the valve train, all components of the valve system should be checked for wear if there is excessive play in the system.

Preliminary Valve Adjustment

A .060 inch shorter push rod or a

.060 inch longer push rod are available for service to provide a means for compensating for dimensional changes in the valve mechanism.

Valve stem to valve rocker arm clearance should be within specifications with the hydraulic tappet completely collapsed. Repeated valve reconditioning operations (valve and/or valve seat refacing) will decrease the clearance to the point that if it is not compensated for, the lifter will cease to function and the valve will be held open.

To determine whether a shorter or a longer push rod is necessary, make the following check.

6-Cylinder

1. Crank the engine until the TDC mark on the crankshaft damper is aligned with timing pointer on the cylinder front cover.
2. Scribe a mark on the damper at this point.
3. Scribe two more marks on the damper, each equally spaced from the first mark (see illustration).
4. With the engine on TDC of the compression stroke (mark A aligned with the pointer), back off the rocker arm adjusting nut until there is end-play in the pushrod. Tighten the adjusting nut until all clearance is removed, then tighten the adjusting nut one additional turn. To determine when all clearance is removed from the rocker arm, turn the pushrod with the fingers. When the pushrod can no longer be turned, all clearance has been removed.
5. Repeat this procedure for each valve, turning the crankshaft 1/3 turn to the next mark each time and following the engine firing order of 1-5-3-6-2-4.

STEP 1—SET NO. 1 PISTON ON T.D.C. AT END OF COMPRESSION STROKE ADJUST NO. 1 INTAKE AND EXHAUST

STEP 4—ADJUST NO. 6 INTAKE AND EXHAUST

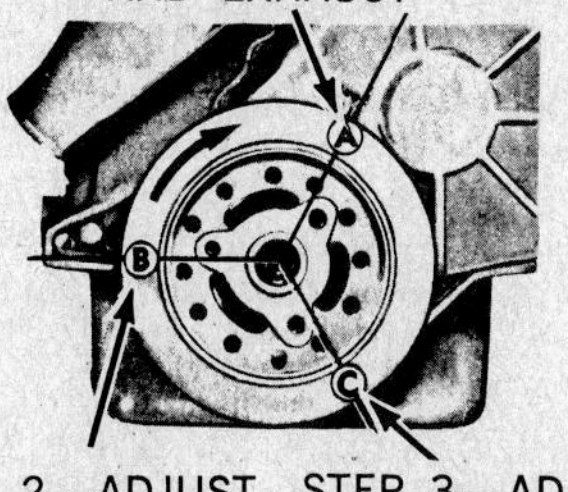

STEP 2—ADJUST NO. 5 INTAKE AND EXHAUST

STEP 3—ADJUST NO. 3 INTAKE AND EXHAUST

STEP 5—ADJUST NO. 2 INTAKE AND EXHAUST

STEP 6—ADJUST NO. 4 INTAKE AND EXHAUST

6-cylinder preliminary valve adjustment (© Ford Motor Co.)

8-Cylinder Engines

All Except 330, 359, 360, 361, 370, 389, 390, 391 and 429 Cu. In. Engines

1. Install an auxiliary starter switch. Crank the engine with the ignition switch OFF until No. 1 piston is on TDC after the compression stroke.
2. With the crankshaft in the positions designated in steps 5, 6 and 7, position a hydraulic tappet compressor tool on the rocker arm.
3. Slowly apply pressure to bleed down the hydraulic tappet until the plunger is completely bottomed. Hold the tappet in this position and check the available clearance between the rocker arm and the valve stem tip with a feeler gauge.

Checking valve clearance—hydraulic lifters (© Ford Motor Co.)

4. If the clearance is less than specification, install a shorter push rod. If clearance is greater than specification, install a longer push rod.
5. With the No. 1 piston on TDC at the end of the compression stroke, Position 1 in the illustration, check the following valves:

302, 460 cu. in.

No. 1 intake No. 1 exhaust
No. 7 intake No. 5 exhaust
No. 8 intake No. 4 exhaust

351 and 400 cu. in.

No. 1 intake No. 1 exhaust
No. 4 intake No. 3 exhaust
No. 8 intake No. 6 exhaust

6. After these valves have been checked rotate the crankshaft to Position 2 in the illustration and check the following valves:

302, 460 cu. in.

No. 5 intake No. 2 exhaust
No. 4 intake No. 6 exhaust

351, 400 cu. in.

No. 3 intake No. 2 exhaust

WITH NO. 1 AT TDC AT THE END OF THE COMPRESSION STROKE MAKE A CHALK MARK AT POINTS 2 AND 3 APPROXIMATELY 90 DEGREES APART.

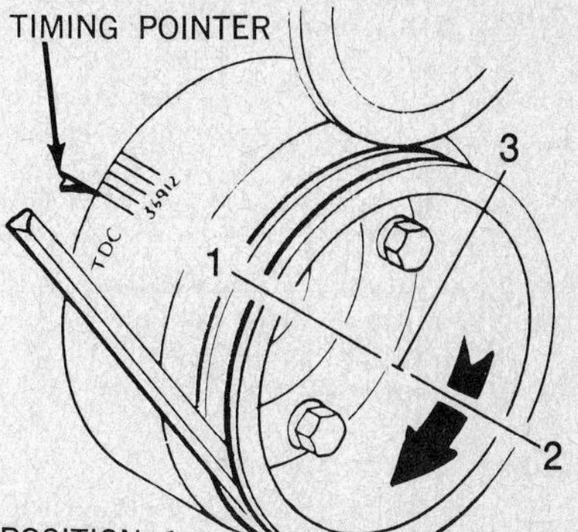

POSITION 1—
NO. 1 AT TDC AT THE END OF THE COMPRESSION STROKE

POSITION 2—
ROTATE THE CRANKSHAFT 180 DEGREES (ONE HALF REVOLUTION) CLOCKWISE FROM POSITION 1

POSITION 3—
ROTATE THE CRANKSHAFT 270 DEGREES (THREE QUARTER REVOLUTION CLOCKWISE FROM POSITION 2

Position of crankshaft for adjusting valve clearance (© Ford Motor Co.)

No. 7 intake No. 6 exhaust

7. After these valves have been checked rotate the crankshaft to Position 3 in the illustration and check the following valves:

302, 460 cu. in.

No. 2 intake No. 7 exhaust
No. 3 intake No. 3 exhaust
No. 6 intake No. 8 exhaust

351, 400 cu. in.

No. 2 intake No. 4 exhaust
No. 5 intake No. 5 exhaust
No. 6 intake No. 8 exhaust

330, 359, 360, 361, 370, 389, 390, 391 and 429 Cu. In. Engines

1. Install an auxiliary starter switch. Crank the engine with the ignition switch OFF until No. 1 piston is on TDC after the compression stroke.
2. With the crankshaft in the positions designated in steps 5, and 6, position a tappet compressor tool on the rocker arm.
3. Slowly apply pressure to bleed down the hydraulic tappet until the plunger is completly bottomed. Hold the tappet in this position and check the available clearance between the rocker arm and the valve stem tip with a feeler gauge.
4. If the clearance is less than specification, install a shorter push rod. If clearance is greater than specification, install a longer push rod.

5. Rotate the crankshaft until No. 1 piston is on TDC at the end of the compression stoke and check the following valves:
   No. 1 intake No. 1 exhaust
   No. 3 intake No. 4 exhaust
   No. 7 intake No. 5 exhaust
   No. 8 intake No. 8 exhaust
6. After these valves have been checked rotate the crankshaft 360 degrees and check the following valves:
   No. 2 intake No. 2 exhaust
   No. 4 intake No. 3 exhaust
   No. 5 intake No. 6 exhaust
   No. 6 intake No. 7 exhaust

Valve Overhaul

See the General Repair Section for complete valve overhaul procedures. All valves are removed by compressing the spring with a valve spring compressing tool, then removing the keepers from the end of the valve stem. Most models utilized an O-ring or cup type oil seal as illustrated. Valve spring, stem and seal specifications may be found in the Valve Specifications Table at the beginning of this section.

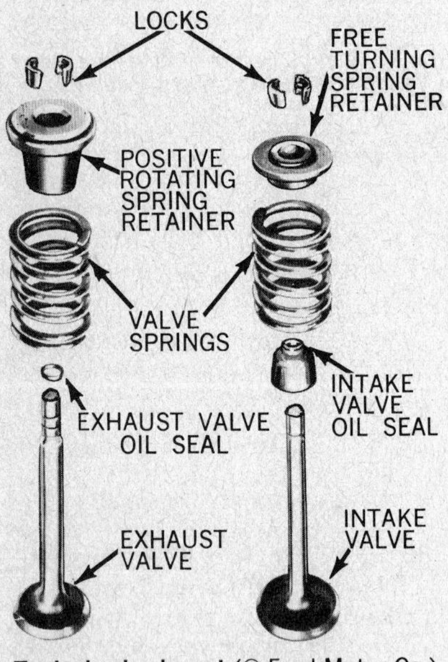

Typical valve layout (© Ford Motor Co.)

Timing Gears and Chain

Timing (Front) Cover and Seal Removal and Installation

200 Cu. In. 6-Cylinder

1. Drain cooling system, disconnect the radiator upper hose at the coolant outlet elbow and remove the two radiator upper attaching bolts.
2. Raise vehicle and drain crankcase.
3. Remove splash shield (if applicable) and radiator as described above.

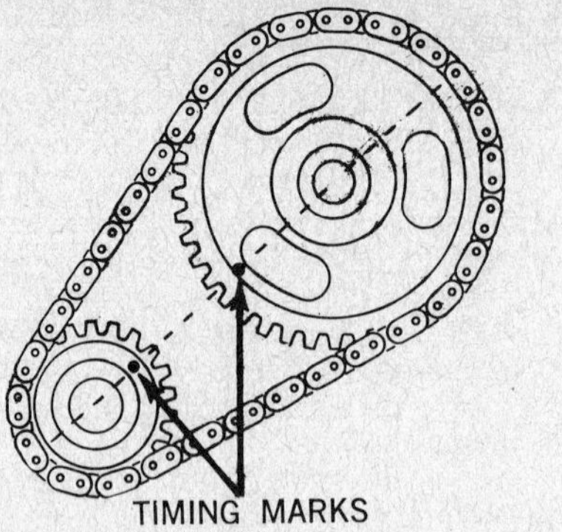

Timing mark alignment—200 cu. in. 6-cylinder (© Ford Motor Co.)

4. Remove drive belts, fan, pulley and crankshaft damper (use a suitable puller).
5. Remove front cover attaching bolts. Before removing the cover, cut the oil pan gasket. Remove cover.
6. Check timing chain deflection and camshaft endplay as described below. Endplay should be within 0.001-0.007″ and chain deflection should not exceed 0.500″.
7. Rotate crankshaft until sprocket timing marks are aligned, then remove camshaft sprocket attaching bolt and washer. Slide off sprockets and chain.
8. Drive out the old seal with a pin punch and clean out seal recess.
9. Coat new seal with grease and install using a suitable installing tool.
10. Clean and oil chain and sprockets, then install as an assembly with timing marks aligned as illustrated. Install camshaft sprocket retaining bolt and washer, tightening to 34-45 ft lbs.
11. Cut and install a piece of new gasket to go between front cover and oil pan, using sealer on all surfaces.
12. Install front cover and new seal, coating all surfaces with sealer. It may be necessary to force the cover downward to compress the new piece of oil pan gasket. Coat threads of cover attaching screws with oil-resistance sealer and install them finger-tight. While holding the front cover in alignment (using an aligning tool if available), tighten oil pan to cover attaching to 7-9 ft. lbs. Tighten the rest of the mounting bolts to the same torque.
13. Apply Lubriplate to the hub of the crankshaft and install damper, tightening attaching bolt to 85-100 ft. lbs.
14. Install fan, pulley, drive belt (adjust), radiator, radiator lower hose and splash shield.
15. Lower the vehicle and connect upper hose.

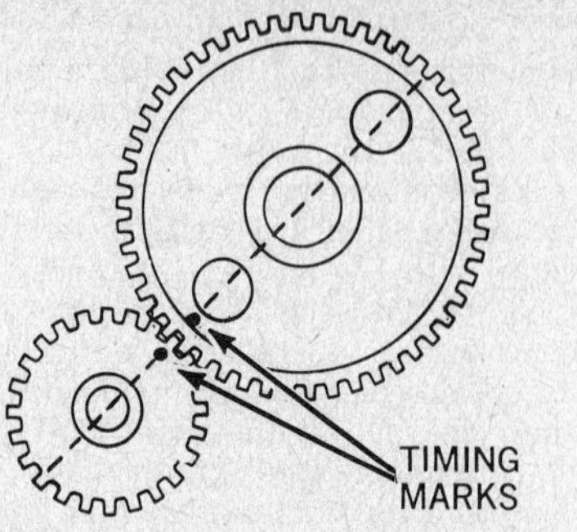

Timing mark alignment—6 cylinder 240 & 300 engines (© Ford Motor Co.)

16. Fill and bleed cooling system.
17. Fill crankcase.
18. Operate engine and check for leaks.

240 and 300 Cu. In. 6-Cylinder

1. Drain the cooling system.
2. Remove the radiator and shroud.
3. Remove the alternator adjusting arm bolt, loosen the drive belt and swing the alternator arm aside. Remove the fan, drive belts and pulleys.
4. Remove the screw and washer from the end of the crankshaft, remove the crankshaft damper.
5. Remove the front oil pan and front cover attaching screws.

NOTE: Be careful not to get foreign material in the crankcase during service work, or the crankcase oil will have to be changed.

6. Remove the cylinder front cover and discard the gasket. It is a good idea to replace the crankshaft oil seal when the cylinder front cover is removed.
7. Drive out the crankshaft oil seal with a pin punch. Clean the seal bore in the cover.
8. Coat a new crankshaft oil seal with grease and install the seal in the cover. Drive the seal in until it is fully seated in the seal bore.
9. Cut the old front oil pan seal flush at the cylinder block/pan junction and remove the old seal material.
10. Clean all gasket surfaces.
11. Cut and fit a new pan seal flush to the cylinder block pan junction. Use the old seal as a pattern.
12. Coat the gasket surfaces of the block and cover with a oil resistant sealer. Position a new front cover gasket on the cylinder block.
13. Align the pan seal locating tabs with the pan holes. Pull the seal tabs through until the seal is completely seated. Apply a silicone sealer to the block/pan junction.
14. Position the front cover assembly over the end of the crankshaft and against the cylinder

block. Start the cover and pan attaching screws. Slide the cover alignment tool over the crank stub and into the seal bore of the cover. Install the alternator adjusting arm, tighten all attaching screws to specification.

NOTE: Tighten the oil pan screws first (compressing the pan seal) to obtain the proper alignment of the cover.

15. Lubricate the crank stub, damper hub I.D. and the seal rubbing surface with Lubriplate. Align the damper keyway with the key on the crankshaft and install the damper.
16. Install the washer and capscrew into the damper and tighten to specification.
17. Install the pulleys, drive belts, and fan. Adjust all drive belts to correct tension.
18. Install the radiator and shroud. Connect all cooling system hoses.
19. Fill and bleed the cooling system. If no foreign material has entered the crankcase during service work, it is not necessary to change the engine oil.
20. Operate the engine at fast idle and check for coolant and oil leaks.

302 and 351W Cu. In. V8—All Trucks Except Econoline

1. Drain the cooling system.
2. Remove the fan shroud to radiator attaching bolts. Position the shroud over the fan.
3. Disconnect the radiator lower hose, heater hose and by-pass hose at the water pump. Remove the drive belts, fan, fan spacer, and pulley.
4. Remove the fan shroud.
5. Loosen the alternator pivot bolt and bolt attaching the alternator adjusting arm to the water pump.
6. Remove the crankshaft pulley from the crankshaft vibration damper. Remove the damper attaching bolt and washer. Install a puller on the vibration damper and remove the damper.
7. Disconnect the fuel pump outlet line from the fuel pump. Remove the fuel pump to one side with the flexible fuel line still attached.
8. Remove the oil dipstick and the bolt attaching the dipstick to the exhaust manifold.
9. Remove the oil pan to cylinder front cover attaching bolts. Use a knife with a thin blade to cut the oil pan gasket flush with the cylinder block face prior to separating the cover from the cylinder block. Remove the cylinder front cover and water pump as an assembly.
10. Discard the cylinder front cover gasket. Remove the crankshaft front oil slinger.

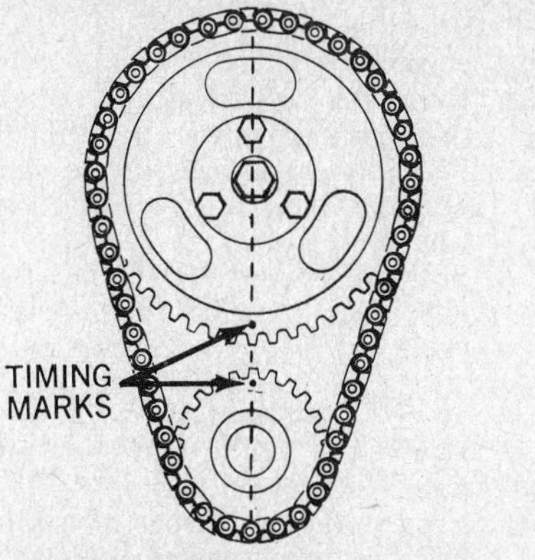

V8 engine timing mark alignment
(© Ford Motor Co.)

11. Check the tining chain deflection. The method for checking timing chain deflection is outlined at the end of this section. If the deflection exceeds specification, replace the chain and sprockets as follows:
    a. Crank the engine until the timing marks on the sprockets are correctly aligned.
    b. Remove the camshaft sprocket capscrew, washers, and fuel pump eccentric. Slide both sprockets and the timing chain forward and remove the chain and sprockets as an assembly.
    c. Position the sprockets and timing chain on the camshaft. Be sure that the timing marks are properly aligned.
    d. Install the fuel pump, eccentric, washers, and camshaft sprocket capscrew. Tighten the capscrew to specification.
12. Install the crankshaft front oil slinger.
13. Clean the cylinder front cover, oil pan and block gasket surfaces. Clean the oil pan gasket surface where the oil pan and front cover fasten.
14. Install a new crankshaft front oil seal.
15. Lubricate the timing chain and fuel pump eccentric with a heavy engine oil.
16. Coat the gasket surface of the oil pan with sealer, then cut and position the required sections of a new gasket on the oil pan and apply sealer at the corners. Install the pan seal as required. Coat the gasket surfaces of the block and cover with sealer, and position a new gasket on the block.
17. Position the cylinder front cover on the cylinder block. Use care when installing the cover to avoid seal damage or possible gasket dislocation.
18. Install the cylinder front cover to seal alignment tool.
19. It may be necessary to force the cover downward to slightly compress the pan gasket. This operation can be facilitated by using a suitable tool at the front cover attaching hole locations.
20. Coat the threads of the attaching bolts with a oil-resistant sealer and install the bolts. While pushing in on the alignment tool, tighten the oil pan to cover attaching bolts to specification. Tighten the cover to block attaching bolts to specification. Remove the alignment tool.
21. Apply Lubriplate or equivalent to the oil seal rubbing surface of the vibration damper inner hub to prevent damage to the seal. Apply a white lead and oil mixture to the front of the crankshaft for damper installation.
22. Line up the crankshaft vibration damper keyway with the key on the crankshaft. Install the vibration damper on the crankshaft. Install the capscrew and washer and tighten to specification. Install the crankshaft pulley.
23. Lubricate the fuel pump lever with heavy engine oil and install the pump using a new gasket. Connect the fuel pump outlet pipe.
24. Install the alternator pivot bolt and bolt attaching the alternator adjusting arm to the water pump.
25. Position the fan shroud over the water pump. Install the pulley, spacer and fan. Install and adjust the drive belts and adjust to specified tension. Connect the radiator, heater, and by-pass hoses. Position the fan shroud on the radiator and install the attaching bolts.
26. Fill and bleed the cooling system.
27. Run the engine at fast idle and check for coolant and oil leaks. Check the coolant level. Check and adjust the ignition timing.
28. Install the air cleaner and intake duct assembly including the crankcase ventilation hose.

302 and 351W Cu. In. V8-Econoline

1. Drain the radiator.
2. Remove the air conditioning idler pulley, bracket and drive belt if equipped.
3. Remove the upper radiator hose. Remove the fan and shroud as an assembly. Raise the vehicle on a hoist.
4. Loosen the thermactor and alternator drive belts.
5. Disconnect the lower radiator hose at the water pump. Disconnect the fuel line at the fuel pump and remove the pump. Lower the vehicle.
6. Remove the by-pass hose. Remove the power steering pump

drive belt if equipped. Remove the water pump pulley and disconnect the heater hose at the water pump.

7. Remove the air condition compressor upper bracket and the power steering pump mount.
8. Remove the crankshaft pulley. Remove the oil pan to front cover bolts. Remove the front cover.
9. Check timing chain deflection, as outlined at the end of this section. If the deflection exceeds specification, replace the chain and sprockets as follows:
   a. Crank the engine until the timing marks on the sprockets are correctly aligned.
   b. Remove the camshaft sprocket capscrew, washers, and fuel pump eccentric. Slide both sprockets and the timing chain forward and remove the chain and sprockets as an assembly.
   c. Position the sprockets and timing chain on the camshaft. Be sure that the timing marks are properly aligned.
   d. Install the fuel pump, eccentric, washers, and camshaft sprocket capscrew. Tighten the capscrew to specification.
10. Clean the front cover, fuel pump, and damper. Lubricate the crankshaft front seal. Clean the gasket surface at the pan and trim the gasket. Clean the front cover gasket surface at the block.
11. Replace the oil seal in the front cover. Position the gasket on the front cylinder cover. Apply a silicone sealer to the oil pan and cylinder block junction. Cut the pan gasket and postion on pan and front cover.
12. Install the front cover, fuel pump, and crankshaft pulley.
13. Install the power steering pump and water pump by-pass hose. Connect the heater hose at the water pump.
14. Install the air conditioning compressor upper bracket, water pump pulley and power steering drive belt.
15. Install the alternator belt, thermactor belt, and fan/shroud assembly.
16. Adjust the power steering pump drive belt tension to specification.
17. Install the air conditioning drive belt idler pulley and bracket. Install the air conditioning drive belt and tighten to specification.
18. Install the upper radiator hose.
19. Raise the vehicle on a hoist. Install the fuel pump with a new gasket and connect the fuel line.
20. Install the lower radiator hose. Adjust the alternator and air injection pump drive belts to specified tension.
21. Drain the crankcase and replace the oil filter. Lower the vehicle.
22. Fill the crankcase and cooling system. Check and adjust ignition timing.
23. Start the engine and run at a fast idle, check for oil and coolant leaks.

351M and 400 Cu. In. V8

1. Drain the cooling system and disconnect the battery.
2. Remove the fan shroud attaching bolts and move the shroud to the rear.
3. Remove the fan and spacer from the water pump shaft.
4. Remove the air conditioner compressor drive belt lower idler pulley and the compressor mount to water pump bracket.
5. Loosen the alternator and power steering pump and remove the drive belts.
6. Remove the water pump pulley.
7. Remove the alternator and power steering pump brackets from the water pump and position them out of the way.
8. Disconnect the lower radiator and heater hose from the water pump.
9. Remove the crankshaft pulley from the crankshaft vibration damper. Remove the vibration damper attaching screw. Install a puller and remove the damper.
10. Remove the timing pointer.
11. Remove the bolts attaching the front cylinder cover to the cylinder block. Remove the front cover and water pump assembly.
12. Disconnect the fuel pump outlet line from the pump. Remove the fuel pump attaching bolts and lay the pump to one side with the flexible line still attached.
13. Discard the cylinder front cover gasket and oil pan seal.
14. Check the timing chain deflection, as outlined at the end of this section.
15. If the timing chain deflection exceeds specification, proceed as follows:
    a. Crank the engine until the timing marks on the sprockets are aligned.
    b. Remove the camshaft sprocket capscrew, washer, and two piece fuel pump eccentric. Slide both sprockets and the timing chain forward, and remove them as an assembly.
    c. Postion the sprockets and timing chain on the camshaft and crankshaft. Be certain that the timing marks on the sprockets are correctly aligned.
    d. Install the two piece fuel pump eccentric, washers, and camshaft sprocket capscrew. Tighten the camshaft capscrew to specification. *Make sure that the outer fuel pump eccentric sleeve rotates freely.*
16. Coat a new fuel pump gasket with oil resistant sealer and position the fuel pump and gasket on the cylinder block with the fuel pump arm resting on the eccentric outer sleeve. Install the pump attaching bolt and nut and tighten to specification. Connect the fuel pump outlet line.
17. Remove the front crankshaft seal from the front cover. Clean the cylinder front cover and the engine block gasket surfaces.
18. Coat the gasket surfaces of the block and cover with sealer, and position a new gasket on the cylinder block alignment dowels.
19. Position the cylinder front cover and water pump assembly on the cylinder block alignment dowels.

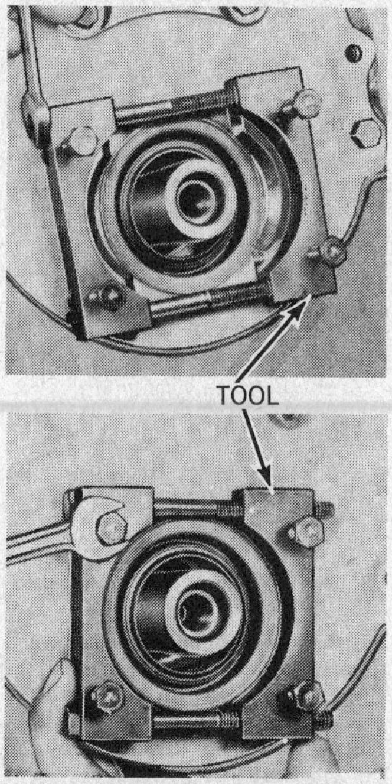

Removing the crankshaft front seal—351M & 400 engines (© Ford Motor Co.)

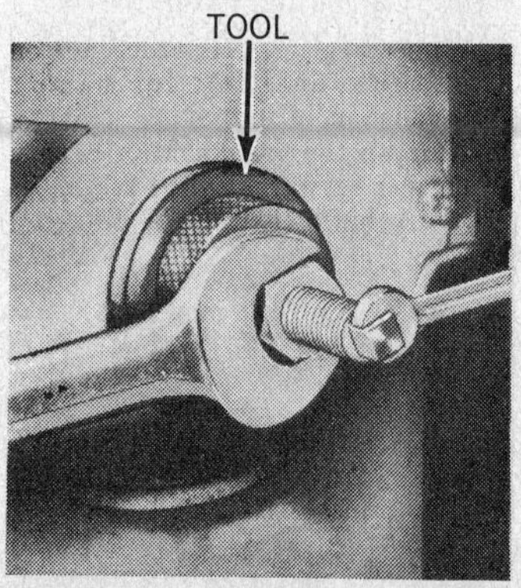

Installing the crankshaft front seal—351M & 400 V8 engines (© Ford Motor Co.)

20. Coat the threads of the attaching bolts with an oil resistant sealer and install the timing pointer and attaching bolts. Tighten the bolts to specifications.
21. Install the front cover oil seal into the cylinder front cover.
22. Apply lubriplate or its equivalent to the oil seal rubbing surface of the vibration damper inner hub to prevent damage to the seal. Apply a white lead and oil mixture to the front of the crankshaft for damper installation.
23. Line up the crankshaft vibration damper keyway with the key on the crankshaft. Install the vibration damper on the crankshaft by pressing on with appropriate tool. Install the capscrew and washer, tighten to specification. Install the crankshaft pulley.

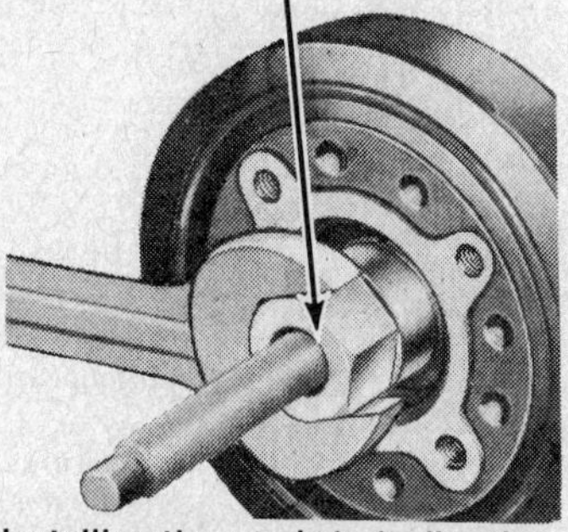

Installing the crankshaft vibration damper—351M & 400 V8 engines (© Ford Motor Co.)

24. Connect the heater hose and the lower radiator hose to the water pump.
25. Install the air conditioner compressor to water pump bracket and lower idler pulley.
26. Position the alternator bracket and power steering pump bracket on the water pump and install the bolts.
27. Position the water pump pulley on the water pump shaft and install the drive belts.
28. Place the fan shroud over the pulley, and install the fan and spacer.
29. Position the fan shroud over the radiator and install the attaching bolts.
30. Adjust the drive belts to specification.
31. Raise the vehicle and remove the oil pan and install new gaskets and seals as described in "Oil Pan Removal and Installation" in this section.
32. Lower the vehicle. Fill the crankcase. Fill and bleed the cooling system. Connect the battery cable.
33. Operate the engine until normal operating temperature has been reached and check for oil or coolant leaks.

330, 359, 360, 361, 370, 389, 390, 391, and 429 Cu. In. V8

1. Drain the cooling system and the crankcase. Remove the air cleaner. Disconnect the battery ground cable and the distributor vacuum line.
2. Disconnect the upper radiator hose at the thermostat housing and the lower radiator hose at the water pump.
3. Disconnect the transmission oil cooler lines if equipped.
4. Remove the radiator and support as an assembly. If the vehicle is equipped with an automatic radiator shutter, leave it attached to the radiator assembly.
5. Disconnect the heater hose at the water pump. Remove the water pump by-pass hose. On a high fan installation, remove the cooling fan and drive belt.
6. Remove the power steering pump and position it to one side, leaving the hoses attached.
7. If equipped with an air compressor, disconnect the air lines and remove the compressor.
8. Remove the alternator adjusting arm bolt at the alternator. Remove the drive belts. Disconnect the wiring and remove the alternator from the support bracket.
9. Remove the water pump and cooling fan drive belts. Remove the water pump and fan as an assembly. On C-series vehicles, remove the cooling fan from the crankshaft damper.
10. Remove the cap screw and washer from the end of the crankshaft. Install a puller on the crankshaft damper and remove the damper.

    NOTE: L-800, C, F, B and LN Models. Equipped with 370 and 429 CID engines, remove crankshaft pulley bolts.
11. Disconnect the carburetor fuel inlet line at the fuel pump.
12. Remove the fuel pump attaching bolts and lay the fuel pump to one side with the flexible fuel line still attached.
13. Remove the bolts attaching the cylinder front cover to the cylinder block and oil pan. Using a knife with a thin blade, cut the oil pan gasket flush with the cylinder block to oil pan junction prior to separating the cover from the block.

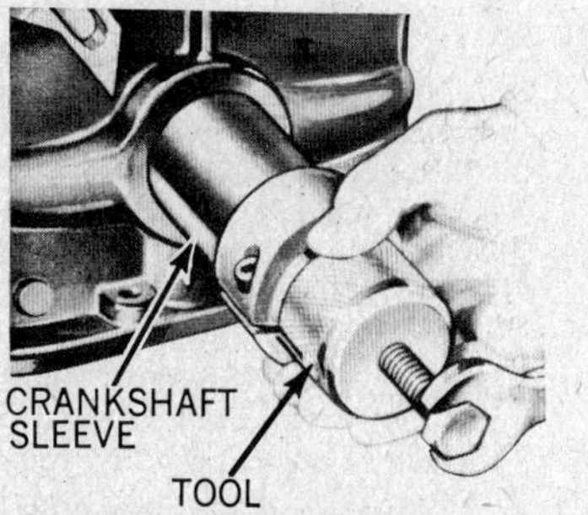

Removing crankshaft sleeve—330 engine (© Ford Motor Co.)

14. Remove the cylinder front cover, alternator support bracket and adjusting arm, and the engine front support bracket.
15. Discard the cylinder front cover gasket. Remove the oil slinger.
16. Check the timing chain deflection and camshaft end play, as outlined at the end of this section.
17. If the timing chain deflection exceeds specification, proceed as follows:
    a. Crank the engine until the timing marks on the sprockets are correctly aligned.
    b. Remove the camshaft sprocket capscrew and the fuel pump eccentric.
    c. Slide both sprockets and the timing chain forward and remove the sprockets and timing chain as an assembly.
    d. Clean the sprockets and chain replace any worn or damaged parts. Clean the crankshaft damper.
    e. Position the sprockets and timing chain of the camshaft and crankshaft. Be sure that the timing marks are in alignment.
    f. Install the fuel pump eccentric and the camshaft sprocket cap screw. Tighten the capscrew to specification.

    If a new thrust plate was installed on the camshaft to bring end play within specifications, check the camshaft end play.
18. Install the crankshaft front oil slinger.
19. Clean all oil pan and cylinder block to front cover gasket surfaces.
20. Coat the gasket surface on the oil pan with sealer. Cut and position the required section of a new gasket on the oil pan. Apply silicone sealer at the corners.
21. Coat the gasket surface of the cylinder block and front cover with sealer and position a new gasket on the cylinder block.
22. Position the cylinder front cover on the cylinder block. Be careful during installation of the cover to avoid dislocation or damage to the gasket.
23. Install the cylinder front cover-to-seal alignment tool in its proper position. It may be necessary to force the cover downward to slightly compress the pan gasket. This operation can be faciliated by using a suitable tool at the cover attaching bolt hole locations in the cylinder block. Position the engine front support bracket and alternator

mounting bracket and adjusting arm bracket on the cylinder front cover. Install the attaching bolts.
24. When pushing on the alignment tool, align the oil pan surfaces on the cylinder front cover and cylinder block. Tighten the attaching bolts to specification. Remove the alignment tool.
25. Clean the oil seal rubbing surface on the crankshaft sleeve with solvent and polish with crocus cloth. Examine for grooves, nicks, and burrs which could damage the seal. Lubricate the seal rubbing surface with grease and install the crankshaft sleeve.
26. Lubricate the damper hub and line the damper keyway with the key on the crankshaft. Install the damper on the crankshaft.
27. Install the damper capscrew and washer and tighten the capscrew to specification.
28. Install the power steering pump pulley on the damper and tighten the attaching bolts to specification.
29. Clean the water pump gasket surfaces. Coat the new gaskets with a water resistant sealer and position the gaskets on the cylinder front cover or water pump. Install the water pump and fan assembly. Tighten the attaching bolts to specification. On C-series vehicles, install the cooling fan on the crankshaft damper.
30. Install the alternator and the alternator drive belt. Adjust the alternator and water pump drive belts to the correct tension.
31. Install the power steering pump and drive belt, adjust the drive belt to the correct tension.
32. Install the air comrpessor and connect the air lines. Install the air compressor drive belt and adjust tension to specification.
33. On a high-fan installation, install the fan and drive belt and adjust the tension to specification.
34. Install the fuel pump using a new gasket.
35. Connect the carburetor fuel inlet line to the fuel pump.
36. Connect the heater hose to the water pump and install the by-pass hose.
37. Install the radiator, radiator support, and shutter assembly (if equipped) as an assembly. Connect the upper and lower radiator hoses.
38. Connect the transmission oil cooler lines and the battery ground cable.
39. If any coolant has entered the oil pan when separating the cylinder front cover from the block, it will be necessary to flush the crankcase.
40. Fill and bleed the cooling system.
41. Fill the crankcase with the correct grade and qualtity of oil.
42. Install the air cleaner and operate the engine at a fast idle to check for coolant or oil leak. Adjust the ignition timing and connect the vacuum line to the distributor.

460 V-8

1. Drain the cooling system and crankcase.
2. Remove the radiator shroud and fan.
3. Disconnect the upper and lower radiator hoses, and the automatic transmission oil cooler lines from the radiator.
4. Remove the radiator upper support and remove the radiator.
5. Loosen the alternator attaching bolts and air conditioning compressor idler pulley and remove the drive belts with the water pump pulley. Remove the bolts attaching the compressor support to the water pump and remove the bracket (support), if so equipped.
6. Remove the crankshaft pulley from the vibration damper. Remove the bolt and washer attaching the crankshaft damper and remove the damper with a puller. Remove the woodruff key from the crankshaft.
7. Loosen the by-pass hose at the water pump, and disconnect the heater return tube at the water pump.
8. Disconnect and plug the fuel inlet and outlet lines at the fuel pump, and remove the fuel pump.
9. Remove the bolts attaching the front cover to the cylinder block. Cut the oil pan seal flush with the cylinder block face with a thin knife blade prior to separating the cover from the cylinder block. Remove the cover and water pump as an assembly. Discard the front cover gasket and oil pan seal.
10. Transfer the water pump if a new cover is going to be installed. Clean all of the gasket sealing surfaces on both the front cover and the cylinder block.
11. Check the timing chain deflection, as outlined at the end of this section. If timing chain deflection exceeds specification, proceed as follows:
    a. Crank the engine until the timing marks on the sprockets are aligned.
    b. Remove the camshaft sprocket capscrew, washer, and two piece fuel pump eccentric. Slide both sprockets and the timing chain forward, and remove them as an assembly.
    c. Position the sprockets and timing chain on the camshaft and crankshaft. Be certain that the timing marks on the sprockets are correctly aligned.
    d. Install the two piece fuel pump eccentric, washers, and camshaft sprocket capscrew. Tighten the camshaft capscrew to specification.
12. Coat the gasket surface of the oil pan with sealer. Cut and position the required sections of a new seal on the oil pan. Apply sealer to the corners.
13. Coat the gasket surfaces of the cylinder block and cover with sealer and position the new gasket on the block.
14. Position the front cover on the cylinder block. Use care not to damage the seal and gasket or mislocate them.
15. Coat the front cover attaching screws with sealer and install them.

    NOTE: It may be necessary to force the front cover downward to compress the oil pan seal in order to install the front cover attaching bolts. Use a drift to engage the cover screw holes through the cover and pry downward.
16. Assemble and install the remaining components in the reverse order of removal. Tighten the front cover bolts to 15-20 ft lbs, the water pump attaching screws to 12-15 ft lbs, the crankshaft damper to 70-90 ft lbs, the crankshaft pulley to 35-50 ft lbs, fuel pump to 19-27 ft lbs, the oil pan bolts to 9-11 ft lbs for the 5/16″ screws and to 7-9 ft lbs for the ¼″ screws, and the alternator pivot bolt to 45-57 ft lbs.

Checking Timing Chain Deflection

To measure timing chain deflection, rotate crankshaft clockwise to take up slack on the left side of chain. Choose a reference point and measure distance from this point and the chain. Rotate crankshaft in the opposite direction to take up slack on the right side of the chain. Force the left (slack) side of the chain out and measure the distance to the reference point chosen earlier. The difference between the two measurements is the deflection.

Timing chain should be replaced if deflection measurement exceeds specified limit. On 330, 361, and 391 cu. in. engines, the deflection measurement should not exceed 11/16 in., on all other engines the deflection measurement should not exceed ½ in.

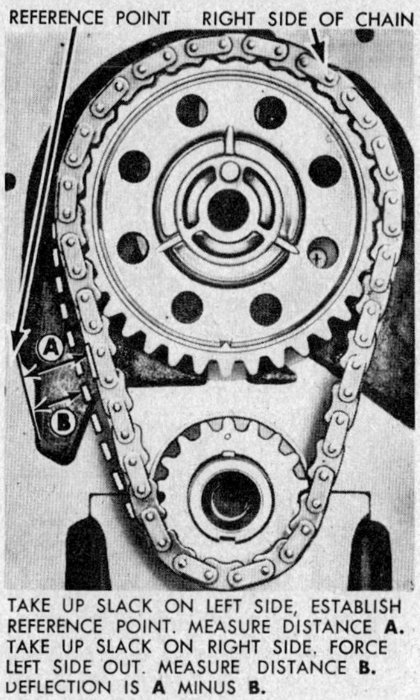

REFERENCE POINT
RIGHT SIDE OF CHAIN
A
B
TAKE UP SLACK ON LEFT SIDE, ESTABLISH REFERENCE POINT. MEASURE DISTANCE A. TAKE UP SLACK ON RIGHT SIDE, FORCE LEFT SIDE OUT. MEASURE DISTANCE B. DEFLECTION IS A MINUS B.

Checking timing chain deflection (© Ford Motor Co.)

Camshaft Endplay Measurement

The fiber camshaft gears used on some engines is easily damaged if pried upon while the valve train load is on the camshaft. Loosen rocker arm nuts or rocker arm shaft support bolts before checking camshaft endplay.

Push camshaft toward rear of engine, install and zero a dial indicator, then pry between camshaft gear and block to pull the camshaft forward. If endplay is excessive, check for correct installation of spacer. If spacer is installed correctly, then replace thrust plate.

Checking camshaft gear runout (© Ford Motor Co.)

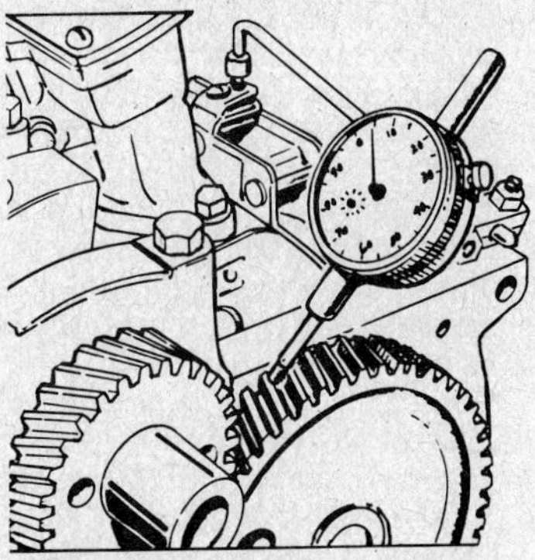

Checking timing gear backlash (© Ford Motor Co.)

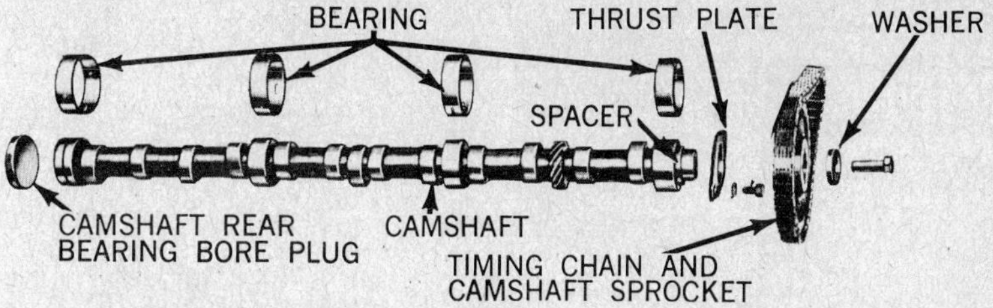

Camshaft 200 cu. in. 6-cylinder (© Ford Motor Co.)

Measuring Timing Gear Backlash

Use a dial indicator installed on block to measure timing gear backlash. Hold gear firmly against the block while making measurement. If excessive backlash exists, replace both gears.

Camshaft

Camshaft Removal and Installation

200 Cu. In. 6-Cylinder

1. Remove in order front cover, timing chain, cylinder head, distributor and fuel pump. Detailed removal and installation procedures for these components may be found in this section under each component heading.
2. Remove tappets with a magnet.
3. Remove dipstick, headlights, parking lights and the grill and hoodlock assembly.
4. Remove camshaft thrust plate and carefully slide camshaft from block.
5. Blow out rocker arm oil supply passages in the block with compressed air. Oil camshaft journals and apply Lubriplate to lobes. If a new camshaft is being used, transfer the spacer and dowel from old camshaft. Carefully slide camshaft into place.
6. Install thrust plate, tightening bolts to 12-15 ft. lbs.
7. Install timing sprockets, chain and all related front cover components as described in front cover removal and installation procedures above. Be sure to install a new front cover oil seal.
8. Install in reverse order all components removed, following instructions for each component group described topically in this section.
9. Start engine, adjust ignition timing, set idle speed and check for leaks.

240 and 300 Cu. In. 6-Cylinder

1. Remove the front cover following procedure described in "Front Cover Removal and Installation".
2. Remove the oil pan and oil pump as detailed in "Oil Pan Removal and Installation."
3. Remove air cleaner and crankcase vent tube at the rocker cover.
4. Disconnect accelerator cable, choke cable and hand throttle cable (if so equipped). Remove accelerator cable retracting spring.
5. If applicable, remove air compressor and power steering belts.
6. Disconnect oil filler hose from rocker cover.
7. Remove distributor cap and wiring as an assembly, then disconnect vacuum line and primary wire and remove distributor.
8. Remove fuel pump.
9. Remove valve rocker cover, loosen rocker arm stud nuts and move rocker arms to one side. Remove pushrods, identifying each so that they may be installed in their original locations.
10. Remove pushrod cover and valve lifters, identifying the position of each.
11. Turn crankshaft to align timing marks, remove camshaft thrust plate bolts and carefully pull camshaft and gear from block. Metal camshaft gear (300 HD) is bolted onto camshaft and fiber

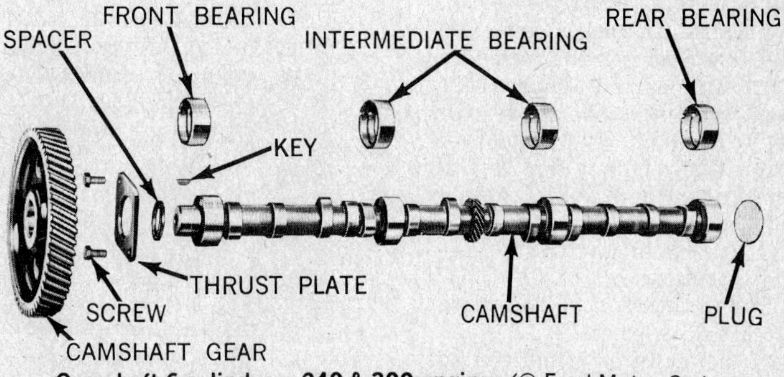

Camshaft 6 cylinder—240 & 300 engines (© Ford Motor Co.)

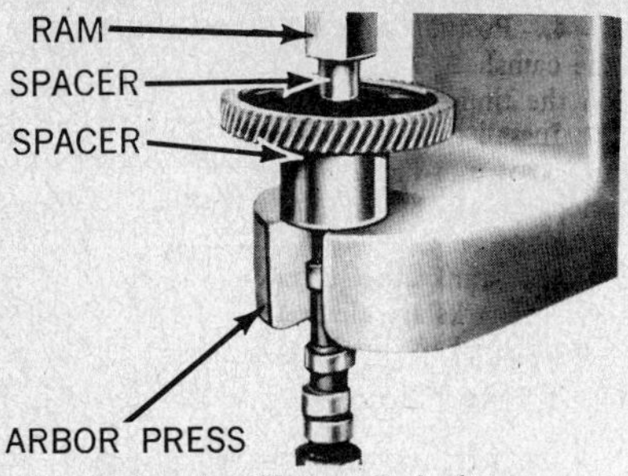

Removing fiber camshaft gear
(© Ford Motor Co.)

gear (240 and 300 LD) is pressed on and must be removed with an arbor press.

12. To install camshaft, oil journals and apply Lubriplate to lobes, then carefully install camshaft, spacer, thrustplate and gear as an assembly, making sure timing marks are aligned, then tightening thrustplate bolts to 19-20 ft. lbs. Do not rotate crankshaft until distributor is installed.
13. Install front cover, referring to "Front Cover Removal and Installation" for correct procedure.
14. Install valve lifters, then the pushrods in their original locations. Apply heavy engine oil to the lifters and Lubriplate to the pushrods.

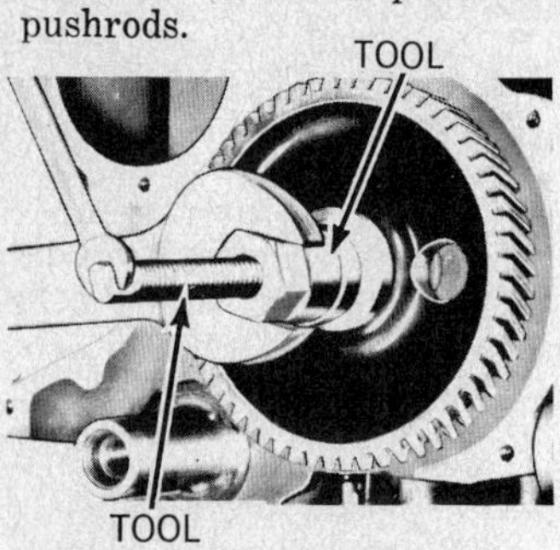

Installing camshaft gear
(© Ford Motor Co.)

15. Install in order the following components, referring to appropriate sections by topic for detailed instructions if necessary and using new gaskets with sealer: pushrod cover, valve rocker cover (adjust valve lash first), distributor (rotor in No. 1. cylinder firing position), fuel pump, distributor cap and wiring assembly, crankcase ventilation valve (in rocker cover), oil filler hose, accelerator cable and retracting spring, choke cable, hand throttle cable, front cylinder cover, oil pump, oil pan, water pump pulley, fan, belt, air compressor and power steering belts, radiator, hood latch, grill and air cleaner.
16. Fill crankcase.
17. Fill and bleed cooling system, checking for leaks.
18. Set the ignition timing, then connect distributor vacuum line.

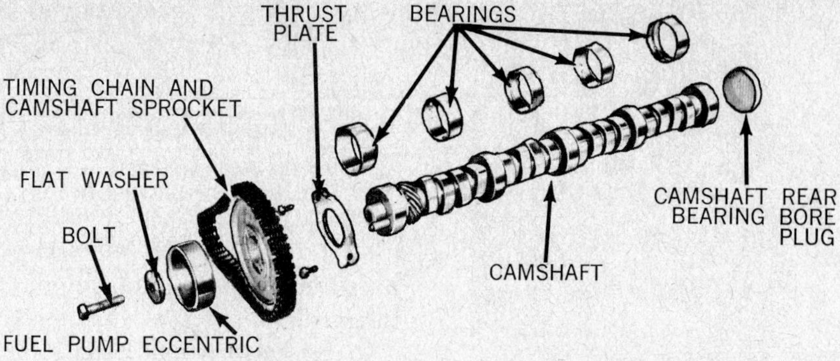

Typical camshaft—V8 engines (© Ford Motor Co.)

19. Adjust carburetor idle speed and idle fuel mixture.

V-8 Engines

1. Remove the intake manifold and valley pan, if so equipped. On Econolines, remove the grill.
2. Remove the rocker covers, and either remove the rocker arm shafts or loosen the rockers on their pivots and remove the pushrods. The pushrods must be reinstalled in their original positions.
3. Remove the valve lifters in sequence with a magnet. They must be replaced in their original positions.
4. Remove the timing gear cover and timing chain and sprockets, as detailed in "Timing Cover and Seal Removal and Installation."
5. In addition to the radiator and air conditioning condenser, if so equipped, it may be necessary to remove the front grille assembly and the hood lock assembly to gain the necessary clearance to slide the camshaft out the front of the engine.
6. Remove the camshaft thrust plate attaching screws and carefully slide the camshaft out of its bearing bores. Use extra caution not to scratch the bearing journals with the camshaft lobes.
7. Install the camshaft in the reverse order of removal. Coat the camshaft with engine oil liberally before installing it. Slide the camshaft into the engine very carefully so as not to scratch the bearing bores with the camshaft lobes. Install the camshaft thrust plate and tighten the attaching screws to 9-12 ft lbs. Measure the camshaft end-play. If the end-play is more than 0.009 in., replace the thrust plate. Assemble the remaining components in the reverse order of removal.

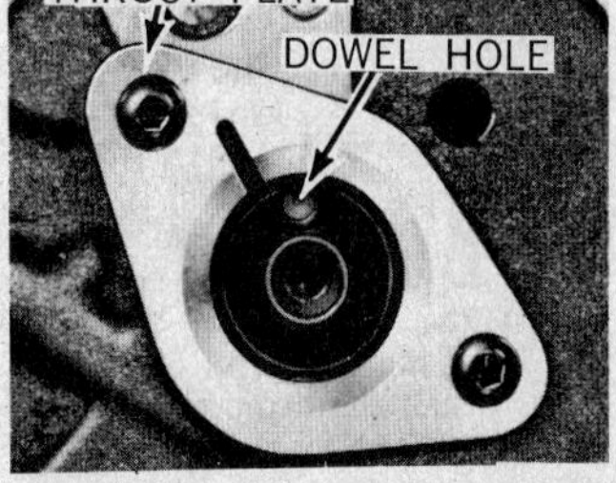

Camshaft thrustplate & spacer—330 engine (© Ford Motor Co.)

Camshaft Bearings and Valve Lifters

Reference

For detailed procedures for camshaft bearing replacement and hydraulic lifter service see the General Repair Section.

Pistons and Connecting Rods

Reference

Instructions for fitting of rings and rod bearings, ridge reaming and cylinder honing may be found in the General Repair Section.

Piston and Rod Removal and Installation

All Models

1. Drain cooling system and crankcase.
2. Remove the cylinder head.
3. Remove oil pan, oil pump pick-up tube and screen assembly and oil pump.
4. Turning crankshaft so that piston is at the bottom of its stroke, then ridge ream the top of the cylinder. *Never cut into the ring travel area in excess of 1/32" when removing ridges.*
5. Mark each rod bearing cap before removal so that it can be installed in its original location, then remove cap. Caps and rods are numbered on some models.
6. Push connecting rod and piston assembly out the top of the cylinder.
7. Make sure piston is assembled in correct relation to the connecting rod, that is, that the notch on the top of the piston and the oil hole in the rod are positioned as illustrated. Align ring gaps as illustrated and oil the piston

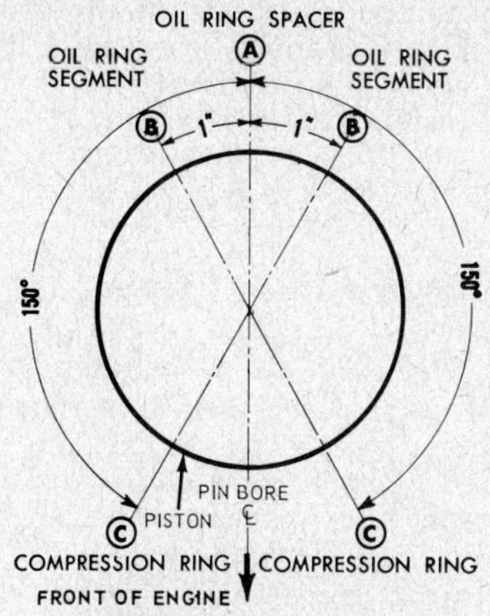

Piston ring gap spacing (© Ford Motor Co.)

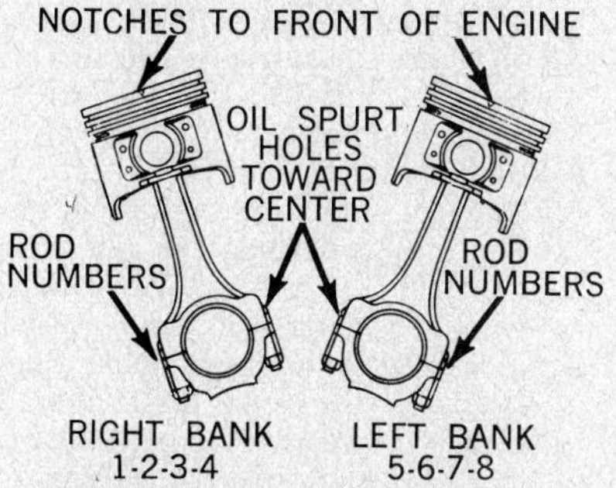

Piston-to-rod relationship—302 and 351M V8 (© Ford Motor Co.)

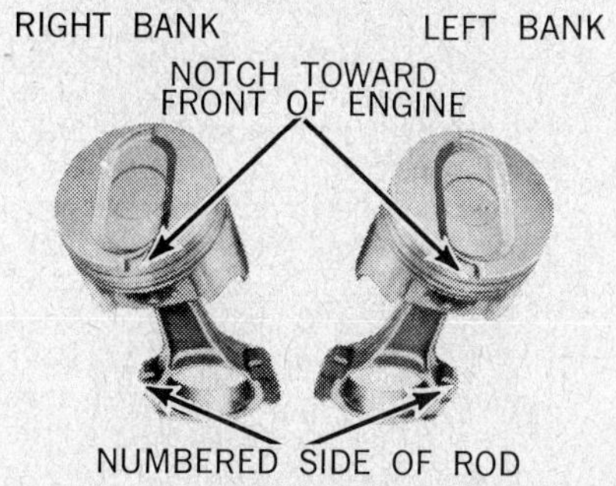

Piston and rod relationship—370, 429, and 460 V8 engine (© Ford Motor Co.)

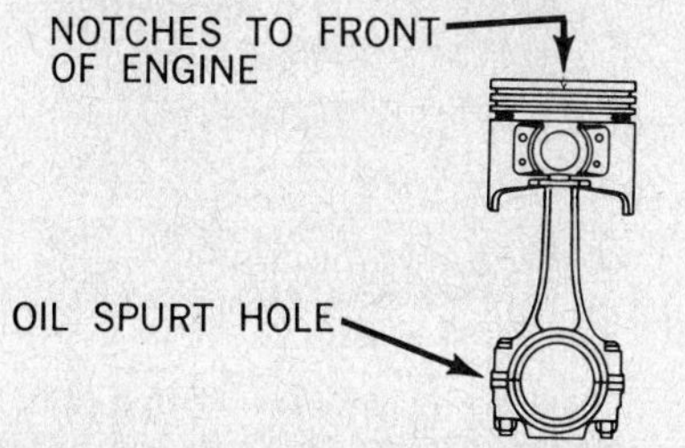

Piston-to-rod relationship—200 cu. in. 6-cylinder (© Ford Motor Co.)

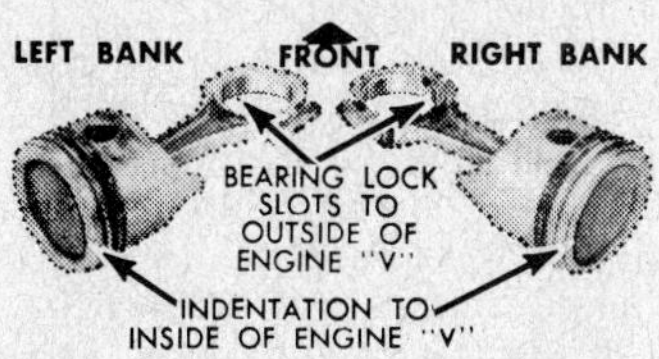

Piston and rod relationship—330, 359, 360, 361, 389, 390, and 391 V8 engines (© Ford Motor Co.)

rings, pistons and cylinder walls.

8. Install a ring compressor and push the piston and rod assembly into the cylinder (if reinstalling an old piston, make sure it is in the same cylinder). On all but the 330, 359, 360, 361, 389, 390 and 391 cu. in. V-8 engines the piston is installed with the notch on the crown toward the front of the engine. On the 330, 359, 360, 361, 389, 390 and 391 cu. in. engines the notch faces in (toward "V").
9. Fit rod bearings, apply oil to journals and bearings, then install bearings and cap, tightening cap bolts to specified torque (see Specifications at the beginning of this section).
10. Check rod bearing side clearance.
11. Thoroughly clean oil pump assembly, then prime it by filling and rotating shaft until pump is full. Install pump assembly.
12. Install oil pan, cylinder head and intake manifold (V-8 engines).
13. Fill and bleed cooling system.
14. Fill crankcase.
15. Set ignition timing and operate engine to check for leaks.
16. Make final (hot) valve lash adjustment.

Main Bearings

Main Bearing Removal and Installation

Remove oil pan and oil pump assembly (see Engine Lubrication System below). Replace one bearing at a time. Remove cap and insert special Ford tool #6331 (-E) or similar bearing removing tool into the crankshaft journal oil hole. Slowly rotate crankshaft in its running direction to force upper bearing insert out of its seat. Fit new bearings (0.001" and 0.002" undersize available) for specified main bearing clearance, then oil journal and bearings and install cap, tightening cap bolts to specified torque (see Specifications).

To seat thrust bearing fit bearing inserts, then install bearings and cap, tightening cap bolts finger-tight. While prying crankshaft forward and bearing cap rearward (see illustration), tighten the cap bolts to specified torque.

If the rear main bearing is replaced, install a new rear oil seal as described below. For more information see the General Repair Section for main bearing fitting procedure.

Rear Oil Seal Removal and Installation

All Engines Except 240 and 300 Cu. In. 6-Cylinder

On all models, remove the oil pan

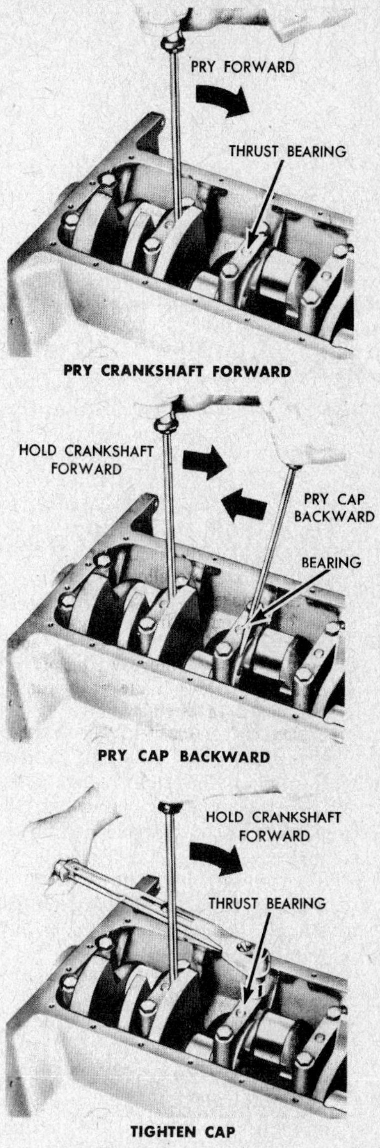

Aligning thrust bearing (© Ford Motor Co.)

as described below. In some cases it may be necessary to remove the oil pump pick-up and screen or the whole pump assembly.

Use only the split-lip type crankshaft rear oil seal as a replacement.

1. Loosen all main bearing caps, lowering the crankshaft slightly, but not more than 1/32".
2. Remove the rear main bearing cap.
3. Remove the seal halves from cap and block. Use a seal removing tool on the block half or install a small metal screw in one end so that the seal may be pulled out. **CAUTION: Do not damage or scratch the crankshaft seal surfaces.**
4. If so equipped (not used on split-lip type), remove the oil seal retaining pin from the bearing cap.
5. Thoroughly clean seal grooves in

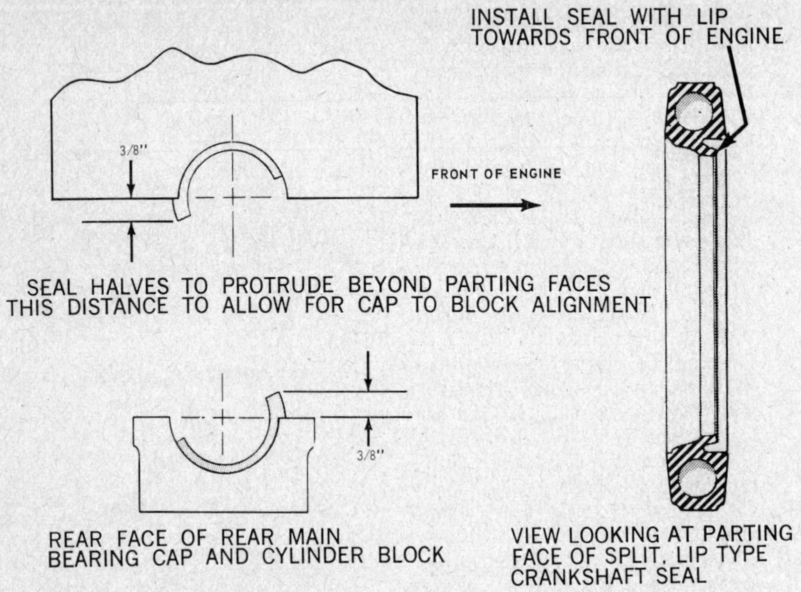

Crankshaft rear oil seal installation (© Ford Motor Co.)

block and cap with brush and solvent.

6. Dip seal halves in engine oil.
7. Carefully install upper half of seal with the lip facing toward the *front* of the engine until 3/8″ is left protruding below parting surface. Be careful not to scrape seal.
8. Tighten all but the rear main bearing caps to specified torque.
9. Install lower seal half in the rear main bearing cap with the lip facing toward the *front* of the engine. Apply a light coat of oil-resistant sealer to the rear of the top mating surface of the cap. Do not apply sealer to the area forward of the side seal groove.
10. Install rear main bearing cap and tighten bolts to specified torque.
11. Install side seals on the 330, 360, 361, 390 and 391 cu. in. V-8. Dip side seals in oil (do not use sealer as these seals expand when in contact with oil and sealer would retard or stop the expansion). Install seals in grooves, lightly tapping them if necessary. Do not cut off projecting ends. After allowing sufficient time for the seals to expand, squirt oil over the seal end and blow compressed air against the seals from inside the block to check for leakage.
12. Install oil pump and oil pan.
13. Fill crankcase and operate engine to check for leaks.

240 and 300 Cu. In. 6-Cylinder

NOTE: If the oil seal is being replaced in conjunction with a rear main bearing replacement, the engine must be removed from the vehicle according to Ford Motor Co.

1. Remove the starter.
2. Remove the transmission (see Transmission Removal and Installation). On standard transmission, remove pressure plate and cover assembly and the clutch disc.
3. Remove flywheel and engine rear cover plate.
4. Punch two holes with an awl on each side of the crankshaft just above the bearing cap to cylinder block splint line.
5. Install two sheet metal screws, then pry on both at once to remove seal. Be careful not to damage or scratch oil seal surface. Clean out seal recess in cap and block.
6. Lightly oil crankshaft and seal, then install seal with tool as illustrated. Carefully drive the seal straight in.
7. Install engine rear cover plate and flywheel. Coat the flywheel attaching bolt threads with oil-resistant sealer and torque to 75-85 ft. lbs.
8. On standard transmission, install the clutch disc and pressure plate assembly (see Clutch Removal and Installation).
9. Install transmission.

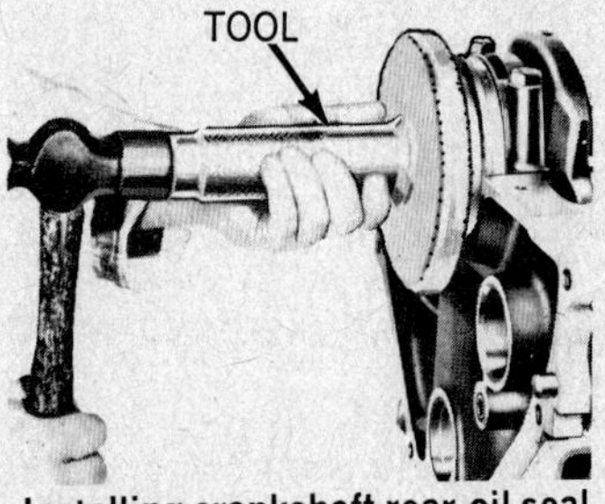

Installing crankshaft rear oil seal (© Ford Motor Co.)

Oil Pan

Removal and Installation

200 Cu. In. 6-Cylinder

On some earlier models there is no frame crossmember under the oil pan. Therefore, some of the steps of the following procedure will not be applicable in certain cases.

1. Drain crankcase and cooling system and remove dipstick.
2. Remove fan and water pump pulley.
3. Disconnect the radiator upper and lower hoses, flex fuel line at the fuel pump and starter cable at the starter.
4. Remove the starter.
5. Remove nuts from both front engine support insulators and raise the front of the engine with a transmission jack and wood block. Remove crossmember from beneath the pan and install blocks between front support insulators and side rails. Lower and remove jack.
6. Remove the oil pan attaching bolts and pan.
7. Clean all gasket surfaces and remove seals from their grooves in the front cover and rear main bearing cap.
8. Position oil pan gasket, then pan front seal on front cover, making sure that the tabs on the seal are over the oil pan gasket. Position oil pan rear seal on the rear main bearing cap, making sure the tabs on the seal are over the oil pan gasket.

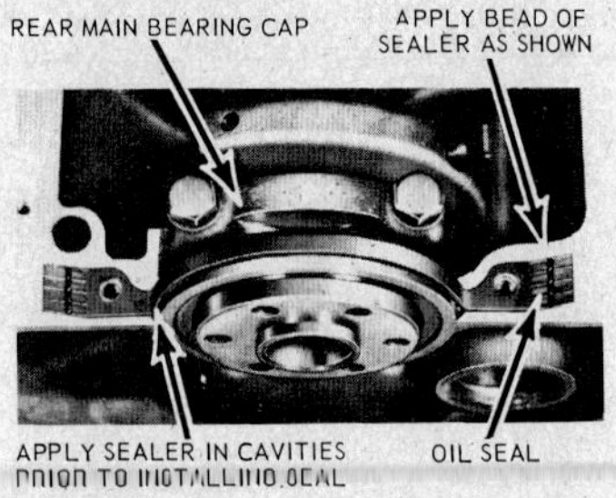

Installing oil pan seal—240 & 300 engines (© Ford Motor Co.)

9. Install oil pan, tightening bolts to 7-9 ft. lbs.
10. Raise the engine with a transmission jack and remove the blocks. Install crossmember and lower the engine. Install washers and nuts on the insulator studs and tighten to 30-40 ft. lbs.
11. Install starter and connect starter cable.
12. Connect radiator hoses and fuel pump flex line.

13. Install water pump pulley, fan and drive belt. Adjust belt.
14. Install dipstick.
15. Fill and bleed cooling system.
16. Fill crankcase.
17. Operate the engine and check for leaks.

F-100, 250, 350 and 1980 Bronco

240 and 300 Cu. In. 6-Cylinder

1. Drain the crankcase.
2. On the F-100-250, also drain the cooling system.
3. Remove radiator from F-100-250 vehicles.
4. Raise vehicle on a hoist. On F-100-250 trucks disconnect and remove the starter.
5. On F-100-250, remove engine front support insulator to support bracket nuts and washers. Use a transmission jack to raise the front of the engine, then install blocks (1″ thick) between the front support insulators and support brackets. Lower engine onto blocks and remove jack.
6. Remove the attaching bolts and oil pan. It may be necessary to remove the oil pump inlet tube and screen assembly in order to free the pan.
7. Remove the rear main bearing cap and front cover seals. Clean out the seal grooves and all gasket surfaces.
8. Apply oil-resistant sealer in the spaces between the rear main bearing cap and the block as illustrated. Install new rear cap seal, then apply a bead of sealer to the tapered ends of the seal.
9. Install new oil pan side gaskets with sealer and position the front cover seal.
10. Clean oil pump pick-up assembly and place it in the pan.
11. Position pan under the engine and install pick-up assembly.
12. Install pan and attaching bolts, tightening to 10-12 ft. lbs.
13. Raise engine enough with a jack and remove wood blocks. Lower engine and install washers and nuts on the support insulator studs, tightening to 40-60 ft. lbs. on LD trucks and 110-150 ft. lbs. on MD and HD trucks.
14. Install starter and starter cable on F-100-250 trucks.
15. Lower vehicle and install radiator if it was removed.
16. Fill crankcase and cooling system and start engine to check for leaks.

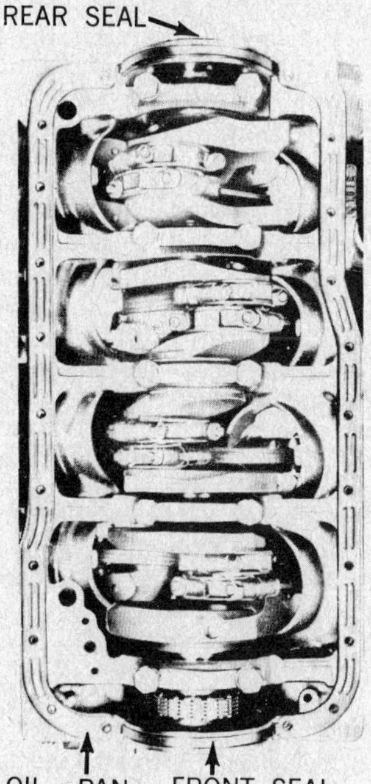

Oil pan gasket and seals—typical V8
(© Ford Motor Co.)

E-100-E-350

1976-78

1. Remove the engine cover. Remove the air cleaner and carburetor.
2. Remove retaining bolts and position the radiator shroud on the fan.
3. Remove exhaust inlet pipe to manifold nuts.
4. Raise the vehicle on a hoist and remove the fuel line from the frame retainer.
5. Remove the alternator splash shield, front engine support nuts, and the starter.
6. Hoist the engine and place blocks under the engine support. Remove the oil pan dipstick tube. Remove the oil pan.
7. Clean the oil pan, tube and screen assembly and the gasket surfaces of the block and oil pan.
8. If removed, install the oil pump screen and tube assembly. Cement a new oil pan gasket on the oil pan. Position a new oil pan to cylinder front cover seal on the oil pan. Position the rear seal to the rear bearing cap and apply sealer. Install the oil pan.
9. Install the dipstick tube and lower the engine. Install the support nuts, starter and position the fuel line in the retainer.
10. Install the alternator splash shield and remove the hoist. Install the carburetor. Connect the exhaust and install the radiator.
11. Fill the cooling system. Replace the oil filter and fill the crankcase with the proper grade oil. Start the engine and check for leaks. Adjust the carburetor curb idle speed. Install the air cleaner.

1979 and Later

1. Remove the engine cover. Remove the air cleaner and the carburetor.
2. If equipped with air conditioning, discharge the system and remove the compressor.
3. If the vehicle is an E-350, disconnect the thermactor check valve inlet hose and remove the check valve. Remove the EGR valve.
4. Remove the radiator hoses. Unbolt the fan shroud and position the on the fan. If equipped with automatic transmission, disconnect the cooler lines and remove the oil filler tube.
5. Remove exhaust inlet pipe to manifold nuts. Raise the vehicle on a hoist and disconnet and plug fuel pump inlet line. Remove the starter. Remove alternator splash shield and front engine support nuts.
6. Remove the power steering return line clip which is located in front of the No. 1 crossmember.
7. Raise the engine and place 3 in. blocks under the engine mounts. Remove the oil pan dipstick tube.
8. Remove the oil pan bolts and remove the oil pan. Remove the pickup tube and screen from the oil pump.
9. Clean the oil pan, tube and screen assembly and the gasket surfaces of the block and oil pan.
10. Install the oil pump and screen assembly, if removed. Cement a new oil pan gasket on the oil pan. Position a new oil pan to cylinder front cover seal on the oil pan. Position the rear seal to the rear bearing cap and apply sealer. Install the oil pan.
11. Install the dipstick tube and lower the engine. Install the support nuts, starter, and connect the fuel line.
12. Install the lower radiator hose. Connect the transmission cooler lines and the transmission fill tube, if equipped.
13. Install the power steering return line clip and position the line.
14. Install the alternator splash shield and lower the host. Install the EGR valve and the carburetor. Connect the exhaust.
15. On E-350 models, install the thermactor check valve and connect the inlet hose.
16. Install the fan shroud and the upper radiator hose. Fill the cooling system.
17. Install the air conditioning compressor and charge the system.
18. Replace the oil filter and fill the crankcase. Start the engine and check for leaks. Adjust the carburetor curb idle speed. Install the air cleaner.

302, 351W V8 Engines

1973-77 Bronco V8

1. Remove the air cleaner and duct assembly. Remove the oil dipstick tube. Drain the engine oil.

2. Remove the oil pan bolts and remove the oil pan.
3. To install, clean the oil pan and the cylinder block of all old gasket material. *Position a new oil pan gasket and end seals to the cylinder block.*
4. Clean and install the oil pump pick-up tube and screen assembly, if removed.
5. Install the oil pan to the cylinder block. Install the oil dipstick tube, air cleaner and duct assembly.
6. Fill the crankcase with the proper oil. Start the engine and check for leaks.

F series and 1978-80 Bronco

1. Remove the oil dipstick. Remove the bolts attaching the fan shroud to the radiator and position the shroud over the fan.
2. Remove the nuts and lockwashers attaching the engine support insulators to the chassis bracket.
3. Disconnect the oil cooler line at the left side of the radiator, if equipped with automatic transmission.
4. Raise the engine and place wood blocks under the engine supports. Drain the crankcase.
5. Remove the oil pan bolts and lower the oil pan onto the crossmember.
6. Remove the oil pump pick-up tube and screen. Lower this assembly into the oil pan. Remove the oil pan.
7. To install, clean the oil pan, inlet tube and gasket surfaces. *Position a new oil pan gasket and seals to the cylinder block.*
8. Install the oil pick-up tube and screen to the oil pump, and install the lower attaching bolt and gasket loosely. Place the oil pan on the crossmember. Install the upper pick-up tube bolt. Tighten both pick-up tube bolts.
9. Install the oil pan. Remove the wood blocks and lower the engine.
10. Install the insulator-to-chassis bracket nuts and washers.
11. Connect the automatic transmission cooler line, if equipped. Install the fan shroud attaching bolts.
12. Fill the crankcase with oil. Install the oil dipstick. Start the engine and check for leaks.

Econoline 1973-75

1. Raise vehicle on a hoist. Remove the bolts holding the oil dipstick tube and position it aside. Drain the crankcase and remove the oil filter.
2. Disconnect steering rod end at idler arm.
3. Remove nuts and washers attaching front engine support crossmember.

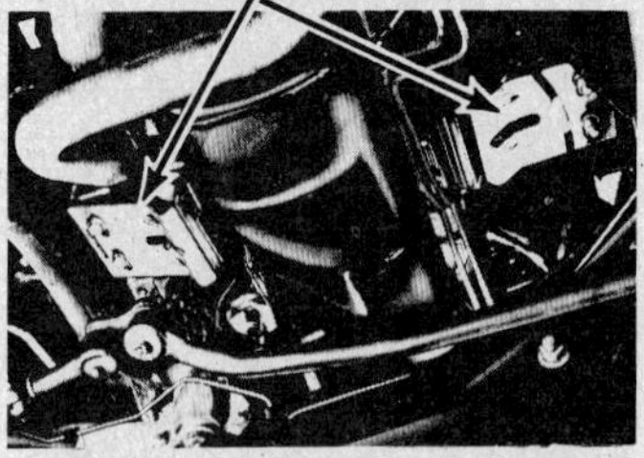

Engine support tools—Econoline
(© Ford Motor Co.)

4. Position a support jack under the damper and raise the engine as required. Remove nuts attaching engine support crossmember to side rails and frame. Remove engine support crossmember.
5. Position engine support tools (T68E-6038-A or equivalent) to side rails and front engine supports. Install washers and nuts fastening support tools to side rails. Lower the support jack.
6. Remove the oil pan bolts. Remove
7. To install, clean oil pan, inlet tube and gasket surfaces. *Position a new oil pan gasket and end seal to the cylinder block.* Install the oil pump inlet tube. Install the oil pan.
8. Complete the installation in the reverse order of removal.
9. Install a new oil filter and fill the crankcase with the proper grade oil. Start the vehicle and check for leaks.

Econoline 1976 and Later

1. Disconnect the battery and remove engine cover. Remove the air cleaner. Drain the cooling system.
2. If equipped with power steering remove the pump and position it out of the way. If so equipped, remove the air conditioning compressor retainer and position the compressor out of the way.
2. Disconnect the radiator hoses. Remove the fan shroud bolts and oil filler tube. Remove the oil dipstick bolt. Raise the vehicle on a hoist.
4. Remove the alternator splash shield. If equipped, disconnect the automatic transmission cooler lines at the radiator.
5. Disconnect and plug the fuel line at the fuel pump. Remove the engine mount nuts. Drain the engine oil. Remove the dispstick tube. Disconnect the muffler inlet pipe from the exhaust manifolds.
6. If equipped, remove the automatic transmission dipstick and tube. Disconnect the manual linkage at the transmission. Remove the center driveshaft support and remove the driveshaft from the transmission.
7. Place a transmission jack under the oil pan and insert a wooden block between the pan and jack.

CAUTION: The engine and transmission assembly will pivot around the rear engine mount. The engine assembly must be raised four inches (measured from the front motor mounts). The engine must remain centered in the engine compartment to obtain this much lift.

8. Raise the engine and transmission assembly. Insert wooden blocks to support the engine in its uppermost position.
9. Remove the oil pan bolts and lower the oil pan. Unbolt the oil pump and the oil pick-up tube and lay them in the oil pan. Remove the oil pan from the vehicle.

NOTE: The oil pump must be removed along with the removal of the oil pan. When installing the oil pump refer to the procedure for "Oil Pump removal and installation."

10. To install, clean the oil pan, oil pick-up tube, oil pump and gasket surfaces. *Position new gasket and seals to the engine block.*
11. Position the oil pan with the oil pump to vehicle and install the oil pump. Install the oil pan.
12. Continue the installation in the reverse order of removal.
13. Install a new oil filter and fill the crankcase with the proper grade oil. Fill the cooling system. Start the engine and check for oil and water.

351M, 400 V8 Engines

1. Remove the oil dipstick. Remove the fan shroud bolts and position the shroud over the fan.
2. Raise the vehicle. Drain the crankcase. Disconnect the starter cable and remove the starter.
3. Place a jack and a wood block under the oil pan and support the engine. Remove the engine front support through blots.
4. Raise the engine and place wood blocks between the engine supports and the chassis brackets. Remove the jack.
5. If equipped with an automatic transmission, position the oil cooler lines out of the way.
6. Remove the oil pan attaching bolts and remove the oil pan.
7. To install, clean the gasket surfaces of the block, oil pan, oil pick-up tube, and screen. Coat the block surface and the oil pan gasket with sealer. *Position the oil pan gasket to the cylinder block.*
8. Position the oil pan front seal on the cylinder front cover plate. Position the oil pan rear seal on the rear main bearing cap. Be sure that the tabs on both the front and rear seals are over the oil pan gasket.

9. Position and install the oil pan. Continue the installation in the reverse order of removal.
10. Fill the crankcase. Start the engine and check for oil leaks.

330, 359, 360, 361, 370, 389, 390, 391, and 429 V8 Engines

1. Drain the crankcase and remove the oil dipstick and the dipstick tube.
2. Remove the oil pan bolts and lower the oil pan to the axle. Position the crankshaft so that the counterweight will clear the oil pan.
3. Remove the oil pump and the inlet tube bolts. Place the oil pump, inlet tube screen and intermediate drive shaft into the oil pan. Remove the oil pan and the oil pump.

   NOTE: The oil pump must be removed along with the oil pan. When installing the oil pump refer to the procedure for "Oil Pump removal and installation."
4. To install, clean the oil pan and block gasket surfaces. Position a new gasket on the oil pan.
5. Remove the inlet tube screen from the oil pump. Clean the oil pump and inlet tube screen. Position a new oil pump inlet tube gasket on the oil pump and install the inlet tube.
6. Place the oil pump in the oil pan and position the oil pan on the crossmember. Position a new oil pump gasket on the cylinder block and install the oil pump. Position and install the oil pan. Install the dipstick tube and the dipstick.
7. Replace the engine oil filter element. Fill the crankcase. Start the engine and check for oil leaks.

460 V8 Engine

All Except Econoline

1. Disconnect the battery ground cable. Disconnect the radiator shroud and position it over the fan.
2. Raise the vehicle on a hoist and drain the crankcase. Remove the oil filter.
3. Remove the through bolt from each engine support. Place a floor jack under the front edge of the oil pan, with a block of wood between the jack and the oil pan. Raise the engine just high enough to insert 1¼" blocks of wood between the insulators and the brackets. Remove the floor jack.
4. Remove the oil pan bolts and remove the oil pan. It may be necessary to rotate the crankshaft to provide clearance between the pan and the crankshaft counterweights.
5. To install, clean the gasket surfaces of the block and the oil pan. Coat both surfaces with sealer. *Position the oil pan gasket on the cylinder block.* Position the oil pan front seal on the cylinder front cover. Position the oil pan rear seal on the rear main bearing cap. Be sure that the tabs on both the front and rear seals are over the oil pan gasket.
6. Position and install the oil pan. Continue the installation in the reverse order of removal.
7. Replace the oil filter and fill the crankcase. Start the engine and check for oil leaks.

Econoline

1. Remove the engine cover, disconnect the battery and drain the cooling system.
2. Remove the air cleaner assembly. Disconnect the throttle and transmission linkage at the carburetor. Disconnect the power brake vacuum lines.
3. Disconnect the fuel line, choke lines and remove the carburetor air cleaner adaptor from the carburetor.
4. Disconnect the radiator hoses. If equipped, disconnect the oil cooler lines. Remove the fan assembly and remove the radiator. If equipped, remove the power steering pump and position it aside.
5. Remove the front engine mount attaching bolts. Remove the engine oil dipstick tube from the exhaust manifold. Remove the oil filler tube and bracket.
6. If so equipped, rotate the air conditioning lines (at the rear of the compressor) down to clear the dash (or remove them).
7. Raise the vehicle on a hoist, drain the crankcase and remove the oil filter.
8. Remove the muffler inlet pipe assembly. Disconnect the manual and kickdown linkage from the transmission. Remove the driveshaft and coupling shaft assembly. Remove the transmission tube assembly.
9. Remove the dipstick and tube from the oil pan. Place a transmission jack under the engine oil pan. Insert a wood block between the jack surface and the oil pan. Jack the engine upward, pivoting on the rear mount until the transmission contacts the floor. Block the engine in position.

   NOTE: The engine must remain centralized to obtain the maximum height. The engine must be raised four inches at the mounts to remove the oil pan.
10. Remove the oil pan bolts and lower the oil pan. Remove the oil pump and pick-up tube attachments and drop them into the oil pan. Remove the oil pan rear-

    NOTE: The oil pump must be remove when removing the oil pan. When installing refer to the procedure for "Oil Pump removal and installation."
11. To install, clean the oil pan gasket surface at the cylinder block, the oil pan assembly, the oil pump pick-up tube, and the screen.
12. *Position the oil pan gaskets and end seals to the cylinder block using sealer.* Position the oil pan with the oil pump and pick-up tube assembly to the chassis and install the oil pump assembly. Position and install the oil pan. Continue the installation in the reverse order of the removal.
13. Fill the cooling system, replace the oil filter, fill the crankcase and connect the battery. Start the engine and check for oil and water leaks.

Oil Pump

Removal and Installation

1. Remove the oil pan, refer to the procedures on "Oil Pan removal and installation."
2. Remove the oil pump mounting bolts and remove the oil pump from the cylinder block.
3. To install, prime the pump by filling the inlet port with engine oil. Rotate the pump shaft to distribute oil within the pump body. Install the distributor intermediate shaft in the oil pump rotor shaft.
4. Insert the intermediate shaft into the distributor shaft hex bore. Make certain that the intermediate shaft is properly seated. Do not force the pump into position if it will not seat readily. The intermediate shaft hex may be misward from the vehicle.
aligned with the distributor shaft. To align, rotate te inter-

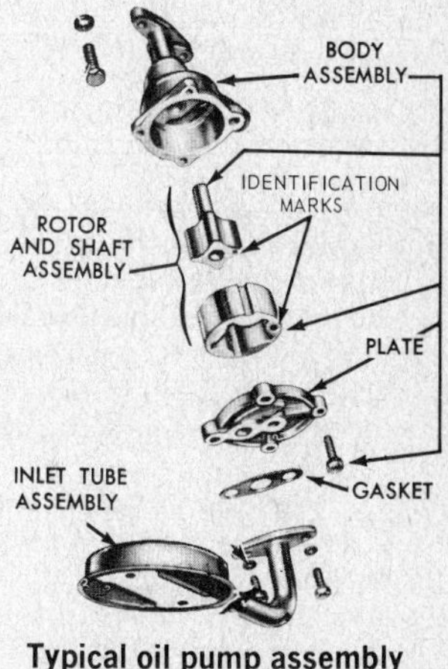

Typical oil pump assembly
(© Ford Motor Co.)

OIL PUMP CLEARANCES

Year	Engine Cu. In.	Relief Valve Spring Pressure Lbs. @ Specified Length	Driveshaft to Housing Clearance	Retail Valve to Housing Clearance	Rotor Assembly End Clearance	Outer Race to Housing Clearance
1973-75	200	9.0-10.1 @ 1.078	.0015-.0030	.0015-.0030	.001-.0040	.001-.013
1973-80	240/300	2.06-22.6 @ 2.49	.0015-.0030	.0015-.0030	.001-.0040	.001-.013
1973-80	302	10.6-12.2 @ 1.704	.0015-.0030	.0015-.0030	.001-.0040	.001-.013
1975-80	351W	18.2-20.2 @ 2.49	.0015-.0030	.0015-.0030	.001-.0040	.001-.013
1973-77	330 MD	8.7-9.5 @ 1.560	.0015-.0030	.0015-.0030	.001-.0040	.001-.013
1973-78	330 HD	11.1-11.8 @ 1.560	.0015-.0030	.0015-.0030	.001-.0040	.001-.013
1973-78	359/361	11.1-11.8 @ 1.560	.0015-.0030	.0015-.0030	.001-.0040	.001-.013
1973-77	360	8.7-9.5 @ 1.560	.0015-.0030	.0015-.0030	.001-.0040	.001-.013
1973-78	389/391	11.1-11.8 @ 1.560	.0015-.0030	.0015-.0030	.001-.0040	.001-.013
1973-77	390	8.7-9.5 @ 1.560	.0015-.0030	.0015-.0030	.001-.0040	.001-.013
1977-80	351M	20.6-22.6 @ 2.49	.0015-.0030	.0015-.0030	.001-.0040	.001-.013
1979-80	370	20.6-22.6 @ 2.49	.0015-.0030	.0015-.0030	.001-.0040	.001-.013
1977-80	400	20.6-22.6 @ 2.49	.0015-.0030	.0015-.0030	.001-.0040	.001-.013
1979-80	429	20.6-22.6 @ 2.49	.0015-.0030	.0015-.0030	.001-.0040	.001-.013
1974-79	460	20.6-22.6 @ 2.49	.0015-.0030	.0015-.0030	.001-.0040	.001-.013
1973-80	401/477/475/534	10.7-11.9 @ 1.07	.0015-.0030	.0015-.0030	.001-.0040	.006-.011

mediate shaft until it can be seat.

5. Secure the oil pump to the cylinder block and tighten the bolts. Install the oil pan and other related parts.

Oil Pump Clearances—Checking

Thoroughly clean all parts in solvent and dry with compressed air. Check the inside of the pump housing for obvious wear or scoring. Check mating surfaces of pump cover and rotors, replacing the cover if it is scored or grooved.

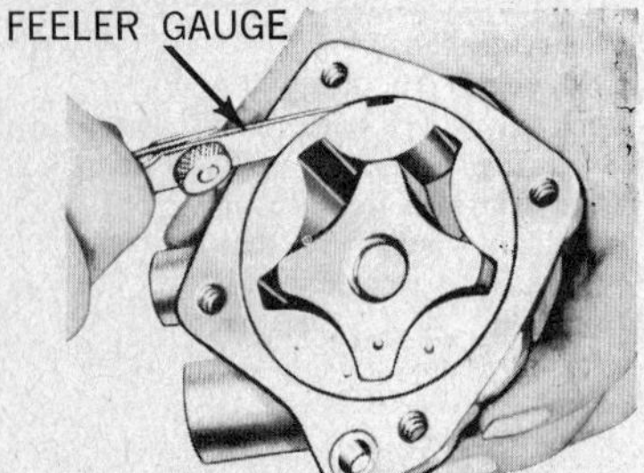

Checking outer race-to-housing clearance (© Ford Motor Co.)

Measure outer race to housing clearance and clearance (rotor endplay) between a straightedge and the rotor. The outer race, shaft and rotor are replaceable only as an assembly.

Measure the driveshaft to housing clearance by comparing shaft OD to housing bearing ID.

Inspect relief valve spring for collapsed or worn condition. Check the spring tension. Replace the spring if weak or worn.

Check relief valve piston and bore for scores and free operation.

FRONT AXLE AND SUSPENSION

Solid I-Beam

Front Spring Removal and Installation

P-500 Series Trucks

1. Raise the vehicle frame until the weight is off the springs with the wheels still resting on the floor.
2. Remove spring U-bolts, nuts, an plate.
3. Remove the nut from the spring-to-frame bracket bolt and drive the bolt out of the spring bracket with a drift.
4. Remove the nut from the lower shackle bolt and drive the bolt out of the spring and shackle bars.
5. Remove the grease fittings from the shackle bolts.
6. Remove the spring, noting the position of any caster wedges.
7. Install new bushings in the spring and shackle bracket if required.
8. Install the caster wedges, if so equipped. Position the caster wedges with the thick edge in the same direction as they were before removal. Install the spring on the spring eye.
9. Position the spring eye between the shackle bars and install the lower shackle bolt and nut. *Do not tighten at this point.*

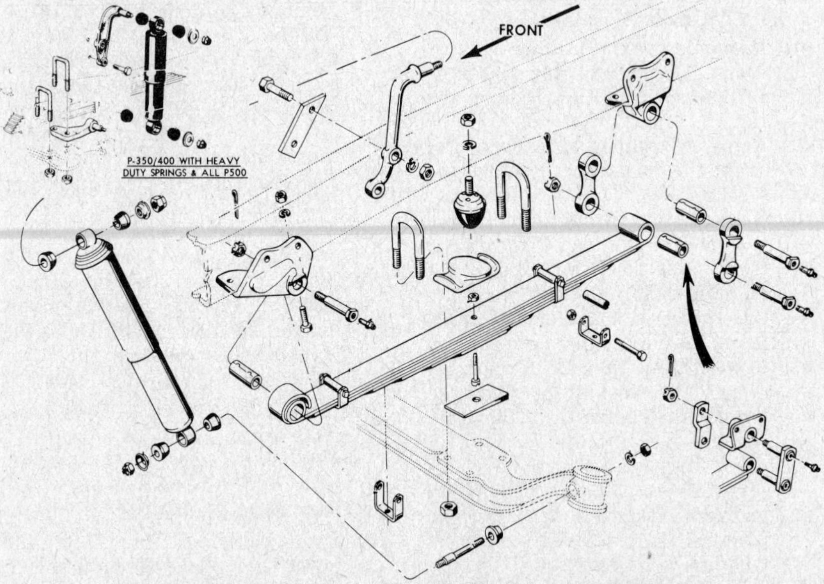

Front spring installation—P 350-500 (© Ford Motor Co.)

10. Position the spring eye in the bracket and install the bolt through the bracket and spring, with the bolt head toward the outside of the vehicle. *Install but do not tighten the nuts.*
11. Install the grease fittings in the shackle bolts.
12. Place the U-bolts and nuts in position over the spring plate and through the holes in the axle. *Make sure that the spring tie bolt is centered in the recess on the axle.*
13. Install the U-bolt nuts and lower the vehicle to the floor.
14. Tighten the lower shackle nut, spring bracket nut, and U-bolt nuts. *The nuts must be tightened in the order given.*

LN-500 to 750 Series Trucks

1. Raise the vehicle frame until the weight is off the front springs, with the wheels still touching the floor.
2. Remove the shock absorber.
3. Remove the cotter pin from the support bracket and remove the stud from the front bracket.
4. On trucks equipped with hydraulic brakes, remove the cotter pin and drive out the spring pin.
5. On trucks equipped with air brakes, remove the cotter pin and nut from the rear bracket shackle bolt and drive out the bolt.
6. Remove the nuts from the two spring clips (U-bolts) holding the spring on the axle.
7. Position the spring on the spring seat and align the spring eye with the spring bracket.
8. Prior to installation, coat the bushings with lubricant. Drive the stud through the bracket and the eye of the spring.

   NOTE: The lubrication opening in the stud should face inward.
9. Install the attaching nut. Tighten the nut to 31-42 ft-lbs. then back it off one castellation. Install a new cotter pin.
10. Install the lubrication fitting.
11. Raise the opposite end of the spring leaf into the spring rear bracket.
12. On vehicles with hydraulic brakes, install the spring pin in the bracket and secure the pin with a new cotter pin.
13. On vehicles with air brakes, install the spring retaining bolt, washer, nut, and new cotter pin.
14. Place the spring clips (U-bolts) in position over the spring clip plate and through the holes in the axle. *Make sure that the spring tie bolt is centered in the recess of the axle.*
15. Install the nuts on the spring clips. Lower the vehicle to the floor and tighten the spring clip nuts. Lubricate the front pin.

F-500 thru 750

1. Raise truck until weight is off front springs, but with wheels still touching ground.
2. Support front axle.
3. Remove attaching nuts and U-bolts.
4. Remove rear hanger cotter pin, nut, washers and bolt.
5. Remove securing cotter pin, then remove spring front hanger pin.
6. Remove spring.

Installation is a reversal of the removal procedure, in addition to noting the following:

1. Make certain that front U-bolt enters shock absorber lower bracket.
2. Raise or lower axle to align spring eye with bolt hole in rear hanger. Install bolt and one washer on each side of bracket; then, with the weight of the truck on the springs, tighten rear hanger bolt nut and install cotter pin.

   NOTE: Do not back-off nut to align castellation with cotter pin hole. If necessary, tighten nut.

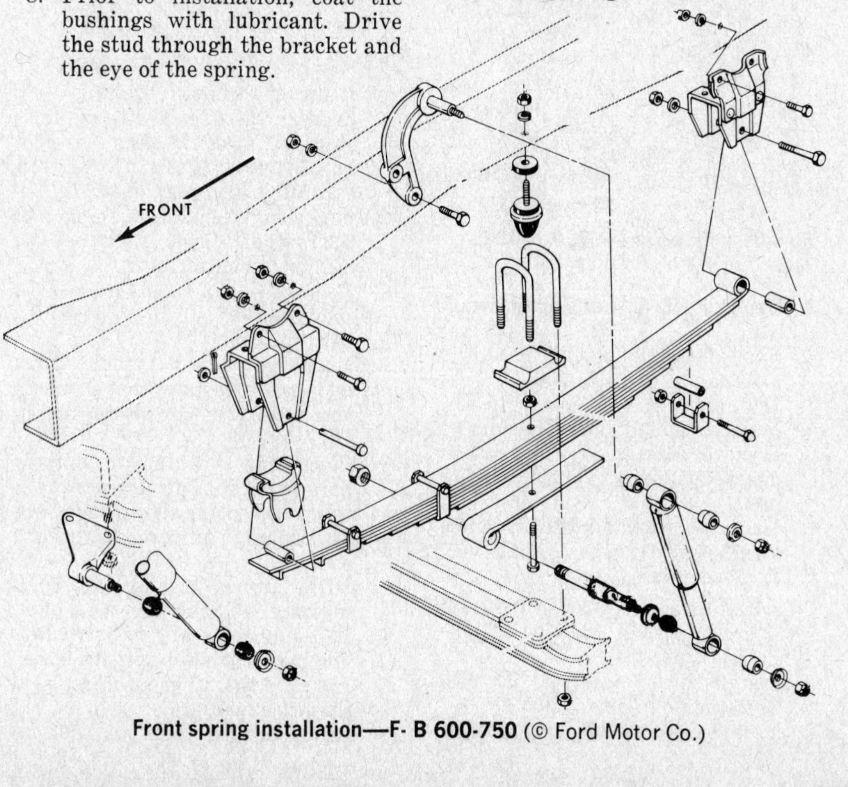

Front spring installation—F- B 600-750 (© Ford Motor Co.)

L-LT-LN-LNT-800-900, 8000-9000, C-CT And W Series

1. Raise the vehicle until the weight is off the front springs, with the wheels still touching the floor. Remove the shock absorber, if equipped.
2. On all vehicles except the C-series, remove the bolt securing the spring pin in the front bracket.
3. Remove the retaining pin from the bracket. On C-series trucks, remove the cotter pin and nut from the spring stud and drive the stud out of the front hanger bracket and spring eye.
4. On all vehicles except C-series, remove the four through bolts and then the two shackle pins securing the shackle assembly. Remove the shackle from the spring and rear bracket. On C-series trucks, remove the two shackle retaining nuts and slide the shackle assembly out of the shackle bar, hanger and the spring eye.
5. Remove the two U-bolts that attach the spring to the axle.
6. Lift the spring off of the axle, noting the position of any caster wedges or spacers.
7. Position the spring on the spring seat and align the spring front eye with the spring bracket.
8. On all vehicles except C-series, remove the lubricating fitting from the retaining pin. Position the pin with the notches aligned with the attaching bolt holes in the front bracket, and the lubricator opening facing outward. Drive the pin through the bracket and spring, then install the attaching bolt, lockwashers, and nuts. Install the lubricator fittings in the pin. On C-series vehicles, remove the lube fittings from the retaining stud and drive the stud through the front hanger bracket and spring eye. Install the lube fitting on the outer end of the stud and the nut and cotter pin on the inner end.
9. On C-series vehicles, raise or lower the rear end of the spring as required to insert the shackle into the spring eye and rear bracket. Position the shackle bar

to the inner side of the rear bracket, and drive the shackle assembly pins through the hanger bracket, spring eye and shackle bar. Install the two shackle retaining nuts and cotter pins.

10. On all vehicles except C-series, align the shackle assembly upper holes with the rear bracket holes and the shackle lower holes with the spring eye. Drive one shackle pin through the upper hole and bracket and the other pin through the lower hole and spring eye.

    NOTE: Be sure that the notches in the shackle pins are aligned with the attaching (pinch) bolt holes in the shackle and that the lube openings face outward.

11. Install the pinch bolts and nuts, tighten.
12. On vehicles equipped with a spacer, place it on the axle.
13. On vehicles equipped with caster wedge, place it on the axle in the same position as removed.
14. Position the U-bolts over the spacer and through the holes in the axle.

    NOTE: Make sure that the spring tie bolt is centered in the recess of the axle, spacer or caster wedge.

15. Install the shock absorber lower bracket to the underside of the axle, except C-series vehicles, with the spring clip (U-bolt) ends entering the holes in the bracket. Install the flat washers and lock nuts on the spring clip.
16. Lower the vehicle to the floor and tighten the clip nuts. Lubricate the shackle bolts.

Spindle

Removal and Installation

P Series, C

1. Raise truck until wheels clear floor. Place a support under axle.
2. Remove wheel, drum, bearing and hub assembly.

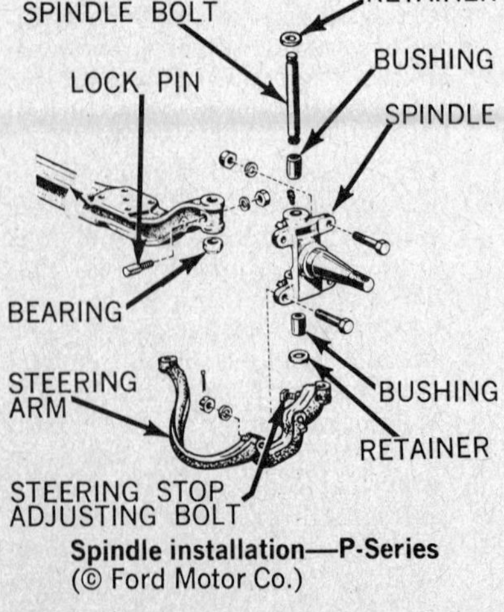

Spindle installation—P-Series (© Ford Motor Co.)

NOTE: It may be necessary to back-off brakes adjustment in order to remove drum.

3. Remove brake backing (carrier) plate, then remove spindle arm bolt and nut. Tie plate and arm to frame with wire.
4. Remove attaching nut, lockwasher and spindle bolt locking pin.
5. Remove top spindle bolt seal, then drive bolt out from top of axle. Remove the spindle from the axle.

Installation is a reversal of the removal procedure, in addition to noting the following:

1. Coat all spindle parts with oil.
2. Pack bearing with chassis lubricant.
3. Install bearing with open end of seal facing downward.
4. Install a new top spindle bolt seal.
5. Make certain that notch in spindle bolt is aligned with locking pin hole in axle.
6. Install new bottom spindle bolt seal.
7. After lowering truck, check and adjust toe-in.

C, F, N Series (5000, 5500, 6000, 7000 Lb. Axles)

1. Raise truck and support front axle.

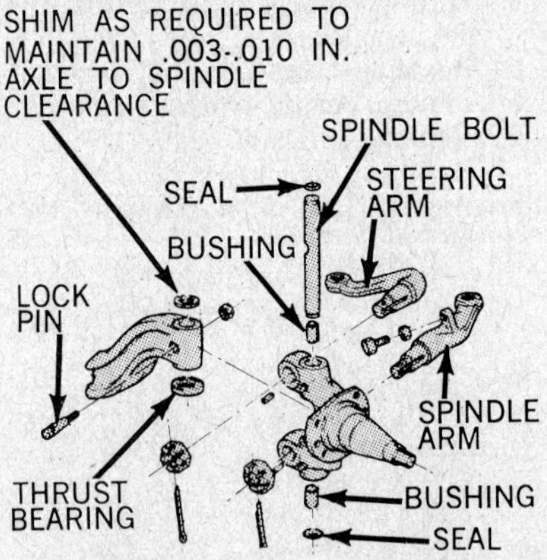

Spindle installation—6000-7000 lb. axles (© Ford Motor Co.)

2. Remove wheel, hub, drum bearing.
3. Remove brake backing plate. Tie plate to frame with wire.
4. Disconnect spindle arm.
5. Remove top spindle bolt seal.
6. Remove attaching nut, then drive out spindle bolt locking pin.
7. Using a suitable drift, drive out spindle bolt from top of axle.
8. Remove spindle assembly.

Installation is a reversal of the removal procedure, in addition to noting the following:

1. Install thrust bearing with seal (retainer) lip downward.
2. Late model trucks, excluding F

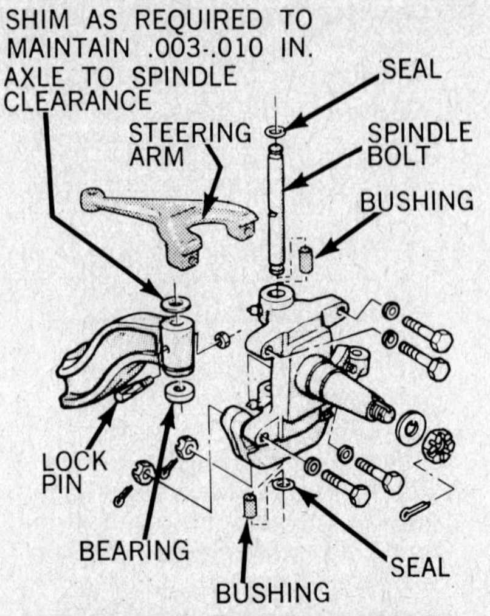

Spindle installation—5000-5500 lb. axles (© Ford Motor Co.)

Series, are equipped with shims between top of axle and spindle. A clearance of .003-010" between axle and spindle must be maintained on all models.

3. Excluding F Series, install spindle bolt with letter "T" upward.
4. Install new top and bottom spindle bolt seals.
5. On 5000 and 5500 lb. axles. excluding F Series, make certain that hardened flat washers, of the same type removed, are placed between backing plate and attaching bolt heads.
6. On 6000 lb. and larger axles, install spindle arm before backing plate.
7. Lubricate spindle bushings.
8. Adjust front wheel bearings and toe-in.

Spindle Bushing Replacement

1. Remove bronze bushings by driving them out with a drift slightly smaller than spindle bore. If a drift is not available, carefully drive a small center punch between the bushing and the spindle bore. Collapse the bushing, then remove.
2. Remove Delrin bushings, using a small center punch as described in Step 1.
3. Thoroughly clean spindle bores and make certain that lubrication holes are not obstructed in any way.
4. Place new bushing in spindle bore with lubricating holes properly aligned. Position open end of bushing oil groove toward axle.
5. Drive bronze bushing into spindle bore, using a drift as a pilot.
6. It is not necessary to drive Delrin bushings into spindle bores.
7. Install remaining bushing(s) in the same manner.
8. Ream bronze bushings .001 to

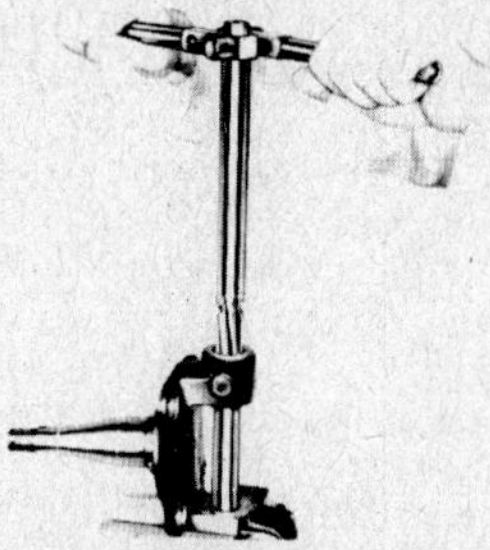

Reaming bronze bushing
(© Ford Motor Co.)

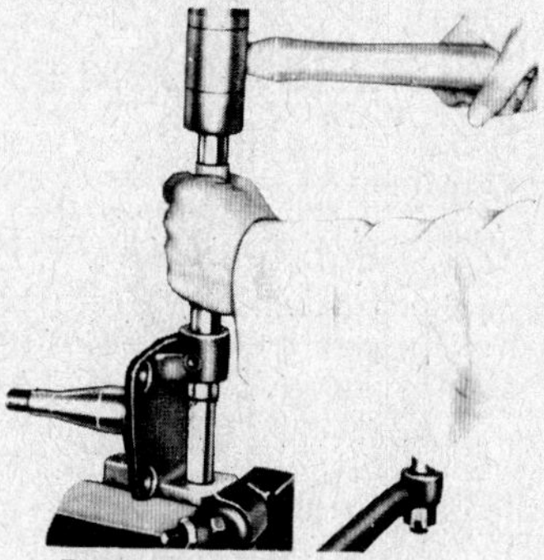

Removing bronze bushing
(© Ford Motor Co.)

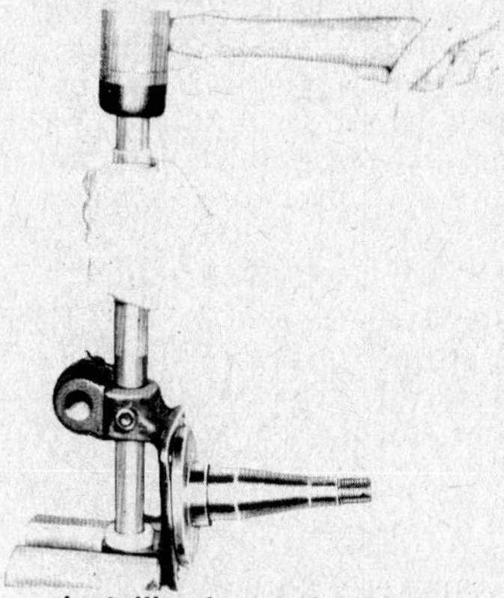

Installing bronze bushing
(© Ford Motor Co.)

.003″ larger than spindle bolt diameter.
9. DO NOT ream Delrin bushings.
10. After reaming bronze bushings, clean out spindle bore to remove metal shavings.
11. Apply a light coat of oil to all bushings before spindle assembly and installation.

Twin I-Beam

NOTE: F-100 and F-250 models with standard brakes utilize Delrin spindle bolt bushings.

NOTE: F-250, F-350 and E-300 models with BX or disc brakes are equipped with an integral arm and spindle.

Front Coil Spring

Removal and Installation Econoline 1973-75

1. Remove floor mat retainer from lower end of door opening.

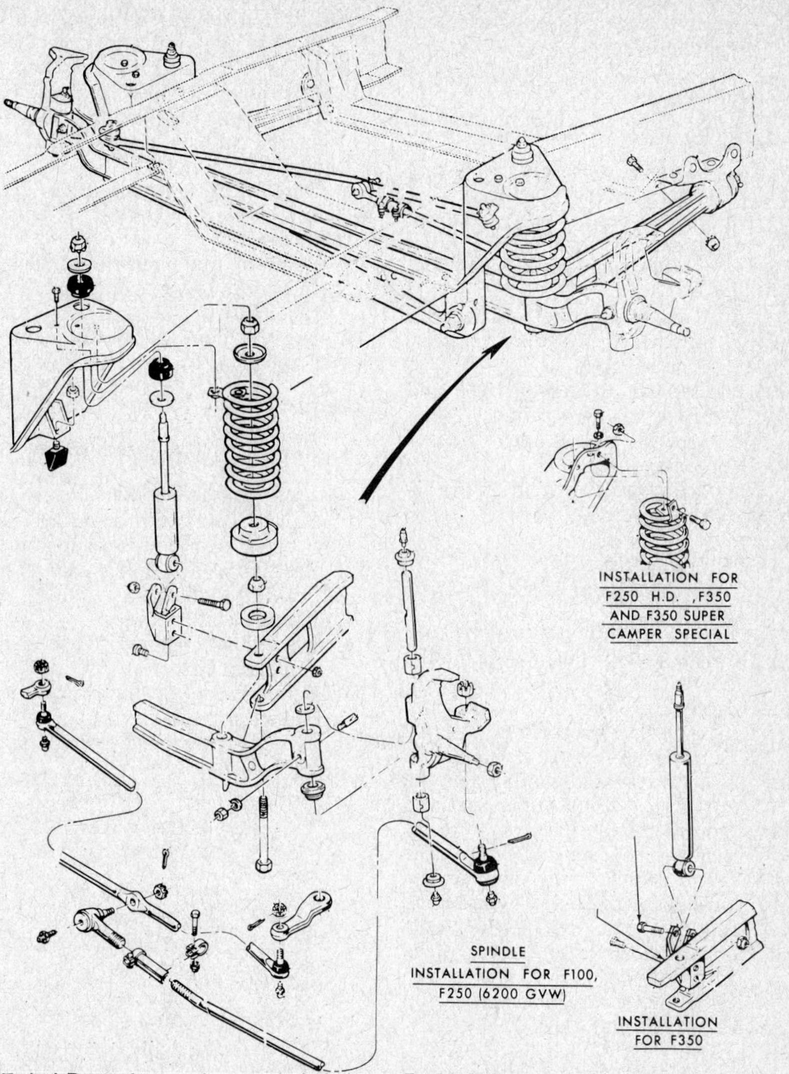

Twin I-Beam front axle—exploded view—F-100-350 shown (© Ford Motor Co.)

2. Fold mat to one side, then remove attaching screws and shock absorber cover plate.
3. Remove spring upper retainer attaching screws, insulator and clamp.
4. Support frame side rails with a jack stand.
5. Position a floor jack under axle, then remove lower retainer attaching bolt, retainer and spring support.
6. Slowly lower axle to release tension, then remove spring.
7. Installation procedure is given in steps 8-14.
8. Position spring on axle with pigtails toward rear end of truck.
9. Position spring lower support and retainer. Install attaching bolt loosely.
10. Place upper insulator on spring.
11. Raise jack to apply light spring pressure.
12. Install upper retainer and clamp.

NOTE: Make certain that all upper retainer parts are correctly seated.

13. Remove jack stand.
14. Install shock absorber cover plate and floor mat retainer.

Econoline 1976 and Later

1. Raise and support the front of the van. Support the front axle.
2. Disconnect the shock absorber from the lower bracket.
3. Remove the 2 upper spring attaching bolts from the upper spring seat. Remove the retainer.
4. Remove the nut from the lower spring retainer and remove the retainer.
5. Install a spring compressor.
6. Lower the axle carefully, and remove the spring.
7. Installation is the reverse of removal.

F-100, 150, 250, 350 1973-74

Removal and Installation

1. Raise front end of truck and support frame with floor stands.
2. Position a jack under axle.
3. Disconnect shock absorber from lower bracket.

4. Remove attaching bolt, nut and rebound bracket.
5. On F-100 and F-250, perform the following:
   a. Remove attaching bolts and retainer.
   b. Remove attaching nut and lower spring retainer.
   c. Lower axle and remove spring.
6. On F-350, perform the following:
   a. Remove bolts attaching upper spring clip to seat. Remove clip.
   b. Remove attaching nut and lower spring retainer.
   c. Lower axle and remove spring.

Installation is a reversal of the removal procedure.

F100, 150, 250 & 350 1975 and Later

Removal and Installation

1. Raise the vehicle and support the axle with a jack.
2. Disconnect the shock absorber from the lower bracket.
3. Remove the two spring upper retainer attaching bolts from the top of the spring upper seat and remove the retainer.
4. Remove the nut attaching the spring lower retainer to the lower seat and axle, remove the retainer.
5. Lower the axle and remove the spring.
6. Place the spring in position and raise the front axle.
7. Position the spring lower retainer over the stud and lower seat. Install the attaching nut.
8. Position the upper retainer over the spring coil and against the spring upper seat. Install the two attaching bolts.
9. Tighten the upper retainer bolts and lower retainer attaching nut.
10. Connect the shock absorber to the lower bracket and install the rebound bracket.
11. Remove the jack and safety stands.

Radius Arm

Removal and Installation

All Models

1. Raise front end of truck and support frame with floor stands.
2. Position a jack under axle or appropriate wheel.
3. Remove coil spring.
4. Disconnect steering rod from spindle arm.
5. Remove coil spring lower seat and shim.
6. Remove radius arm front attaching bolt and nut.
7. Remove cotter pin, nut and washer from radius arm rear attachment.
8. Remove bushing (insulator) from rear end of arm.
9. Remove radius arm.
10. Remove inner bushing (insulator).

Installation is reversal of the removal procedure.

Refer to Wheel Alignment Specifications for toe-in, caster, camber and kingpin (spindle bolt) inclination values.

Front Drive Axle

Description

1973-77 Bronco

The Dana Model 44-1F drive axle is used on Bronco trucks. The axle has an open yoke welded to the outer ends of the axle housing. Cardan-type universal joints transmit power to the front driving wheels.

1973-79 F-100, 150 and 1978-79 Bronco

The Dana Model 44-7F drive axle is used on F-100, F-150 four wheel drive trucks. The axle has an open spindle assembly, utilizing Cardan-type universal joints to transmit power to the front drive wheels.

1973-79 F-250

Dana Models 44-6BF and 44-7BF-HD are used on early F-250 four wheel drive trucks. The axle has a spherical, closed spindle and enclosed universal joint.

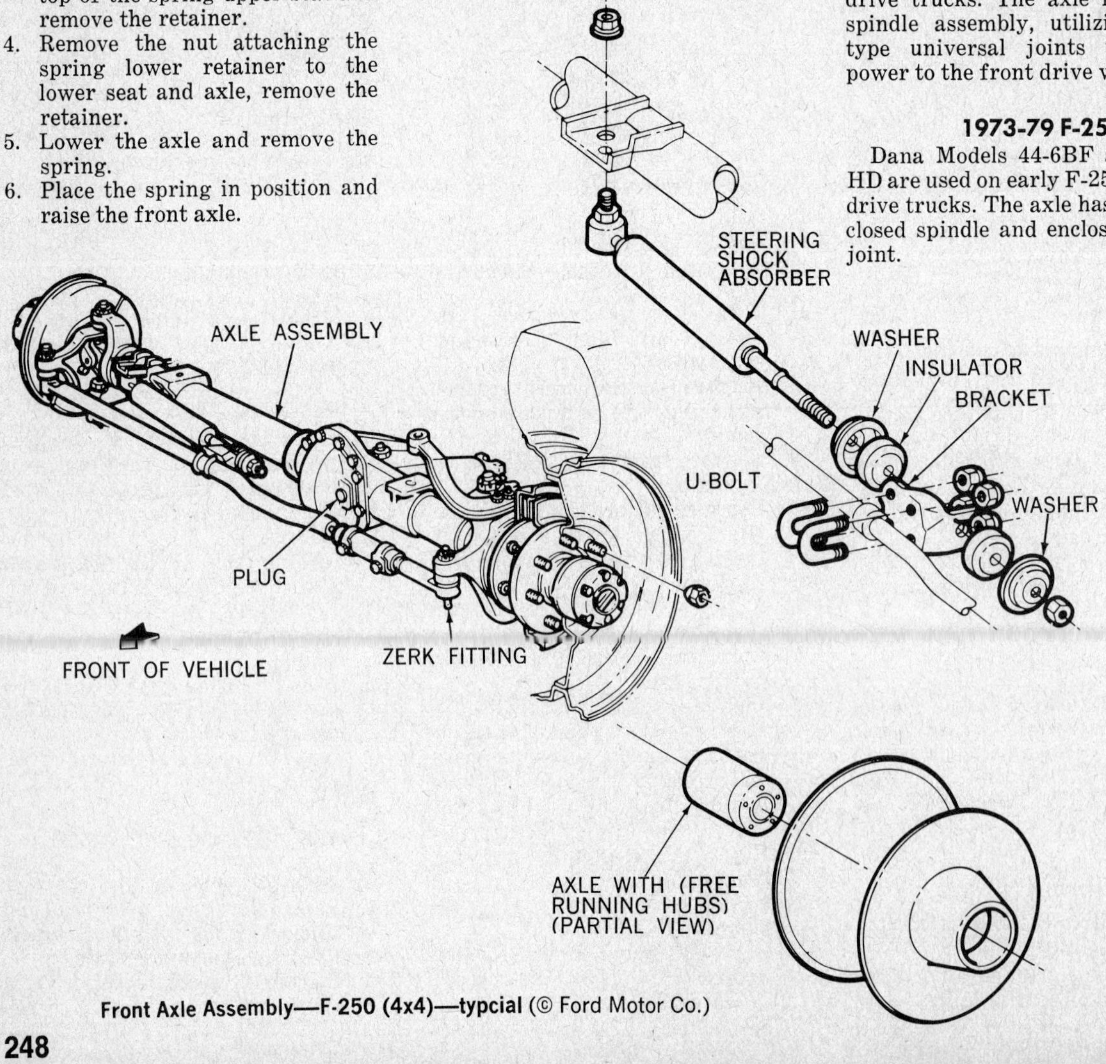

Front Axle Assembly—F-250 (4x4)—typcial (© Ford Motor Co.)

Late model trucks use the Dana model 44-6CF or model 44-6CF-HD. These axles are identical to the other 44 series except for a few minor differences.

F-600

The Rockwell-Standard Single-Reduction Final Drive Axle is used on F-600 trucks. The axle has a heavy duty spiral bevel or hypoid pinion and gear. The differential and gear assembly is carried in tapered roller bearings.

Refer to the General Repair Section for complete overhaul procedures on the front wheel drive axles.

With the exception of specialized components required for front drive application, the Dana and Rockwell-Standard models are identical to their rear axle counterparts (i.e. Dana 44-7F—Dana Model 44, Rockwell - Standard Single - Reduction—same, etc.). Spicer and Dana front drive axles are identical. The Dana Model 44IF, used on Bronco models, is similar to the other Dana axles except in size.

Axle Shaft and Steering Knuckle

1973-79 F-100, 150 and 1973-77 Bronco

1. Raise vehicle on a hoist.
2. Remove front hub grease cap. Remove driving hub retaining snap-ring, then slide splined driving hub from between axle shaft and wheel hub.
3. Remove driving hub spring. *NOTE: If equipped with free-wheeling hubs, see hub removal.*
4. Remove lock nut, washer, and wheel bearing adjusting nut from spindle. Remove wheel, hub and drum as an assembly. The wheel outer bearing will be forced off the spindle at the same time. Remove wheel inner bearing cone.
5. Remove capscrews that attach brake backing plate and spindle to steering knuckle. Remove brake backing plate and secure it to one side. Carefully remove the spindle.
6. Pull shaft assembly from axle housing, working universal joint through bore in steering knuckle.
7. To remove steering knuckle (housing), disconnect the steering connecting rod end from the steering knuckle and remove the bearing caps. Remove the steering knuckle.
8. Remove the three retaining nuts and remove the steering arm. Remove the cotter key from the upper ball socket.
9. Remove the nut from the upper ball socket. Remove the nut from the lower ball socket.

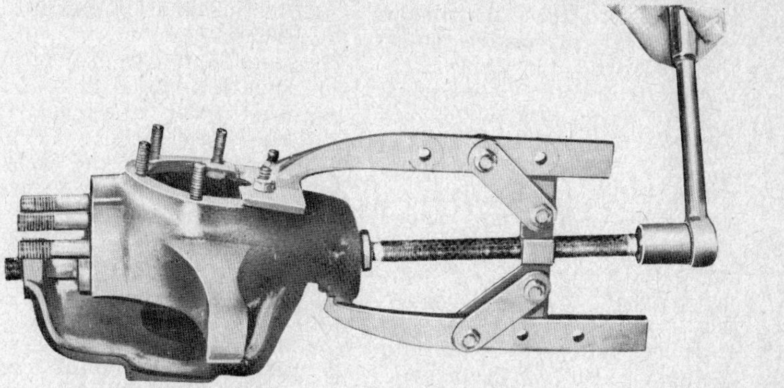

Knuckle removal (© Ford Motor Co.)

NOTE: Discard the nut from the bottom socket.

10. Remove the knuckle from the yoke. If the top socket remains in the yoke it can be dislodged with a rawhide hammer.
11. Remove the bottom socket, the adjusting sleeve and the top socket from the knuckle. On F-100, F-150 remove the snap-ring before removing the socket.
12. Installation is given in steps 13 thru 30.
13. Place knuckle in vise and assemble bottom socket. Place new socket into knuckle making sure it is not cocked; place the driver over the socket; place forcing screw into driver as shown. Apply torque to screw and force socket into knuckle.
14. Make sure socket shoulder is seated against knuckle. Use a .0015″ feeler gauge between socket and knuckle. Feeler gauge is not to enter at minimum area of contact.
15. Assemble top socket into knuckle. Assemble holding plate onto backing plate screw. Tighten nuts snug. Place new socket into knuckle. Be sure socket is straight and not in a cocked position. Place driver over socket.

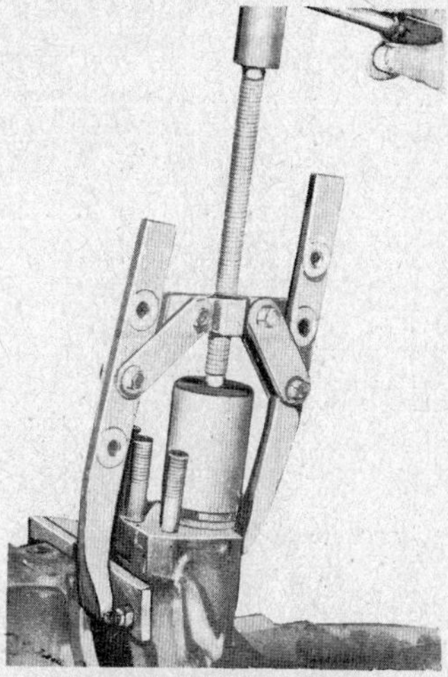

Top socket assembly (© Ford Motor Co.)

16. Make sure socket shoulder is seated against knuckle. Use a .0015″ feeler gauge between socket and knuckle. Feeler gauge is not to enter at minimum area of contact.
17. Assemble new adjusting sleeve into top of yoke. Leave approximately two threads exposed. This will protect the threads in the yoke.
18. Assemble knuckle with sockets to yoke. Assemble new nut to bottom socket. Tighten nut finger loose. This will serve as a holding device.
19. Place spanner wrench and step plate over adjusting sleeve. Position puller, and turn forcing screw. This will pull the knuckle assembly into the yoke. With torque still applied, tighten the bottom nut on the socket. Torque nut to 70-90 ft. lbs. *NOTE: If the bottom stud should turn with the nut, add more torque to the puller forcing screw.*
20. Torque adjusting sleeve to 50 ft. lbs. Remove spanner wrench.
21. Assemble top socket nut. Torque to 100 ft. lbs. Line up cotter key hole of stud with the castellation or slot of the nut. Tighten nut when it is being lined up with the hole of the stud. Do not loosen nut. Assemble cotter key.
22. Assemble steering arm, three stud adapters, and three nuts. Torque nuts to 80-100 ft. lbs.
23. Assemble the tie rod to the knuckle arm. Torque the nut to specifications and install the cotter key.
24. Assemble the protective inner slinger on to the axle shaft. The outer wheel bearing spindle nut will serve as a guide to assemble the slinger. Place the nut in a vise and the slinger on the end of the shaft. Tap on the shaft with a rawhide hammer until the slinger is seated.
25. Assemble the protective outer slinger on to the shaft. One of the wheel spindles will serve as a guide. Place the spindle in a vise. Do not clamp on the bear-

ing diameters. Place the slinger on the shaft. Tap on the end of the shaft with a rawhide hammer until the slinger is seated.

NOTE: Take care not to damage the seal diameter of the slinger.

26. Assemble the axle shaft joint assembly into the housing.
27. Place the spindle in a vise and install the needle roller bearings, using driver and rawhide hammer.
28. Assemble the grease seal into the spindle, flush with the spindle face.
29. After assembly of the needle bearing and oil seal, pack wheel bearing grease around the needle bearing and lip of the seal.
30. Assemble the axle shaft joint assembly, bronze spacer and spindle to the knuckle.

NOTE: The chamfer of the spacer should be inboard against the shaft.

F-250 1973-75

1. Raise the vehicle and support it with jackstands placed under the frame side rails.
2. Remove the front wheel free-running hub. Remove the hub and brake drum.
3. Place a drain pan under the steering knuckle assembly.
4. Remove the capscrews which hold the brake backing plate and spindle to the steering knuckle. Remove the backing plate and spindle. Support the brake backing plate with a piece of wire so that the tension is removed from the brake fluid hose.
5. Slide the axle shaft out through the opening in the steering knuckle.
6. Disconnect the steering drag link from the steering knuckle.
7. Disconnect the spindle tie-rod at both ends.
8. Remove the unitized seal from the steering arm of the steering knuckle, if so equipped.
9. Remove the upper and lower kingpin bearing caps and shims. Keep the shims in the same order side-to-side in which they are removed for proper installation.
10. Remove the steering knuckle from the axle housing and remove the bearings.
11. If the bearing cups (races) are to be removed from the housing, tap them out with a hammer and drift.
12. Place a new steering knuckle seal over the axle housing tube, if the seal is being replaced. The seal is attached to the rear of the steering knuckle with the split facing up to prevent leakage. Do not attach the seal until the steering knuckle turning torque is checked.
13. Install and assemble the steering knuckle and axle shaft in the reverse order of removal. Install the shims under the kingpin bearing caps in the same order in which they were removed and tighten the cap attaching bolts to 30-40 ft lbs on the Dana Model 44-6CF and 80-90 ft lbs on the Dana Model 44-6CF-HD.
14. Place a torque wrench on the inside/forward bearing cap retaining bolt and check the torque required to turn the steering knuckle. The torque required should be 5-10 ft lbs on the 44-6CF and 10-15 ft lbs on the 44-6CF-HD. Adjust the number and thickness of the shims under the bearing cap to obtain the correct turning breakaway torque.

NOTE: Check the steering turning torque with the seal not yet attached to the back of the knuckle, the axle shaft removed, and the steering linkage unattached.

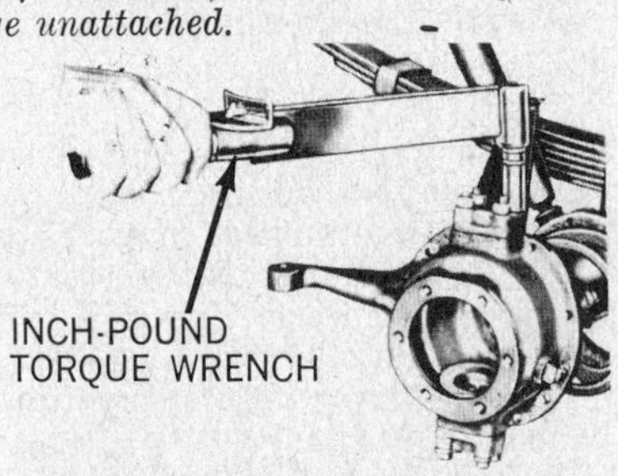

Checking steering knuckle bearing preload (© Ford Motor Co.)

F-250 1976 and Later

Removal and Installation

1. Raise and support the front of the truck.

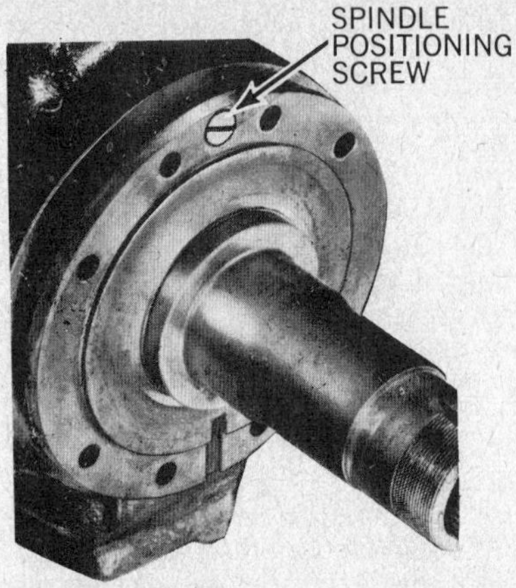

Spindle in position (© Ford Motor Co.)

2. Remove the wheel.
3. Remove the caliper from the rotor and suspend it from the frame.
4. Remove the dust cap, cotter pin, nut, washer and outer bearing and remove the rotor from the spindle.

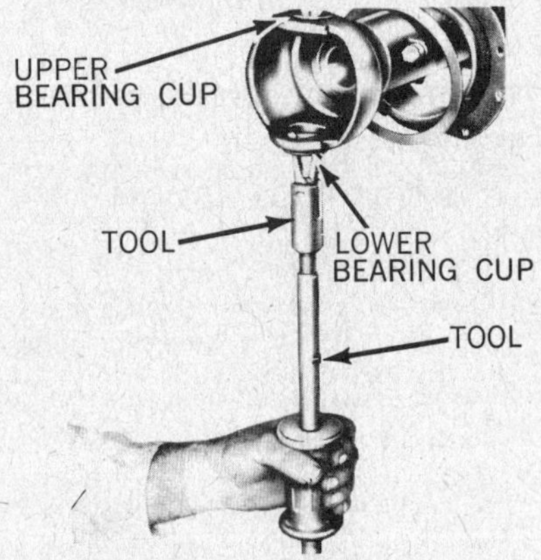

Removing king pin bearing cup (© Ford Motor Co.)

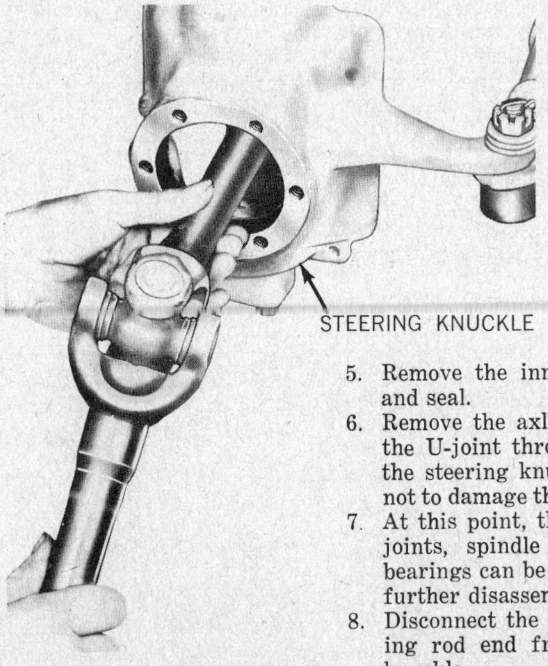

Removing axle shaft (© Ford Motor Co.)

5. Remove the inner bearing cone and seal.
6. Remove the axle shaft, working the U-joint through the bore of the steering knuckle. Be careful not to damage the seal.
7. At this point, the axle shaft, U-joints, spindle bore seals and bearings can be replaced without further disassembly.
8. Disconnect the steering connecting rod end from the steering knuckle.

Removing or installing steering knuckle (© Ford Motor Co.)

9. Remove the cotter key from the upper ball socket. Loosen the nuts from the upper and lower ball sockets and discard the nuts.
10. Remove the knuckle from the yoke. If the top socket sticks in the yoke, it can be removed with a plastic mallet.
11. Remove and discard the bottom socket.
12. Remove and discard the adjusting sleeve.
13. Remove the top socket from the knuckle.
14. Place a new knuckle in a vise and install a new bottom socket. The socket shoulder should be seated against the knuckle so that a .0015 in. feeler blade cannot be inserted between the socket and the knuckle.
15. Install the top socket as in Step 14.
16. Install a new adjusting sleeve, leaving about 2 threads exposed.
17. Assemble the knuckle to the yoke and tighten the nut finger-tight.
18. Pull the knuckle assembly into the yoke and tighten the bottom nut on the socket to 70-90 ft lbs.
19. Tighten the adjusting sleeve to 40 ft lbs.
20. Assemble the top socket nut. Tighten it to 100 ft lbs and align the keyway with the castellations on the nut. Tighten the nut to align the holes. Install a new cotter pin.
21. Test the steering knuckle turning effort with a spring scale hooked at the tie rod hole. If it is more than 26 lbs, the ball joints should be replaced.
22. Connect the steering rod to the steering knuckle and tighten the nut.
23. Further installation is the reverse of removal. Adjust the wheel bearings.

F-600

Removal and Installation

1. Raise and support the vehicle.
2. Remove the plug from the bottom of the axle housing and drain the lubricant. Replace the plug.
3. Disconnect the drive shaft at the pinion shaft.
4. Remove one front wheel from the hub and drum assembly.
5. Remove the outer hub cap retaining screws and remove the cap.
6. Remove the retaining lock ring.
7. Remove the retaining screws and remove the splined drive plate.
8. Bend the tab of the lock washer from the lock nut and remove the lock nut.
9. Remove the lockwasher and discard it. Remove the adjusting nut.
10. Remove the drum and hub assembly from the axle spindle.
11. Remove the brake backing plate retaining screws and carefully lift out the backing plate and wire it up out of the way.
12. Remove the spindle positioning screw and remove the spindle.
13. Remove the axle shaft from the housing.
14. Remove the four upper bearing cap retaining screws.
15. Remove the bearing cap and steering arm and set them aside. Do not drop or lose the shims.
16. Remove the bearing from the socket and set it aside.
17. Remove the four lower bearing cap retaining screws.
18. Remove the cap and bearing from the socket and set them aside. Do not drop or lose the shims.
19. Remove the steering knuckle from the yoke.
20. Position the knuckle on the yoke.

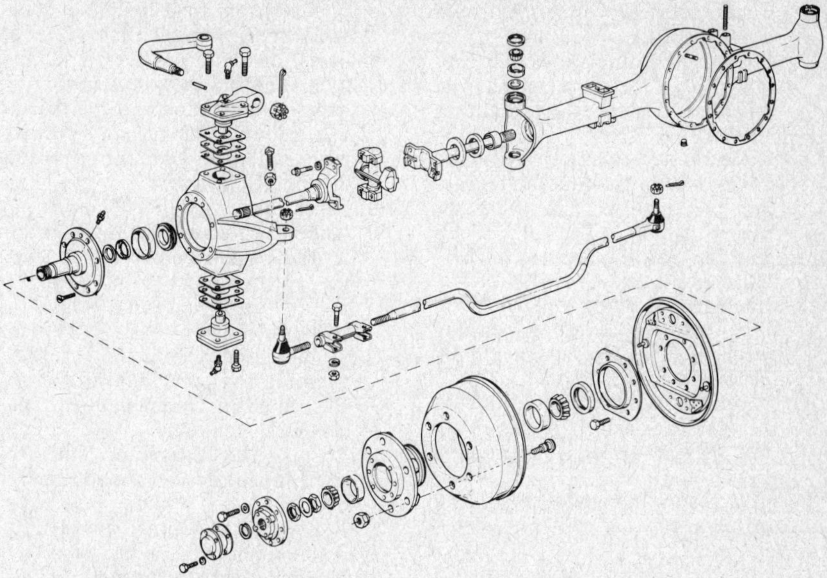

F-600 front driving axle housing—exploded view (© Ford Motor Co.)

Axle shaft removal—F-600 (© Ford Motor Co.)

21. Clean, lubricate and install the upper bearing.
22. Position the shims, bearing cap, and the steering arm on the knuckle. Install the retaining screws.
23. Clean, lubricate and position the lower bearing, shims and bearing cap. Install the retaining screws.
24. Tighten the capscrews to 185-235 ft-lbs. torque.
25. Check the steering knuckle bearing preload with a torque wrench. The preload should be between 11-15 ft-lbs.
26. Adjust the shim thickness at the bearing caps as required to bring the bearing preload to specification.
27. The remaining installation procedures are the reverse of removal.

Front Drive Axle

Removal and Installation

1973-77 Bronco

1. Raise the vehicle on a hoist or jack and install safety stands under the radius arm brackets.
2. Follow the procedure given in Axle Shaft and Steering Knuckle Removal and remove the front wheels, tires, brake drums or brake calipers, brake backing plates, spindles and axle shaft.
3. Remove the hydraulic brake line brackets from each end of the axle without breaking the hydraulic connection. Disengage the hydraulic lines from the axle clips. Tie the lines to the frame to keep them out of the working area.
4. Disconnect the steering tie rod at the knuckle connecting rod ends and tie it out of the working area. Disconnect the axle stablizer bar.
5. Disconnect the front drive shaft at the pinion companion flange and universal joint. Secure the drive shaft out of the working area.
6. Lower the vehicle onto the safety stands and place a jack under the axle to support it while disconnecting it from the radius arms.
7. Each radius arm and cap is numbered from 1 through 100 for proper assembly, since they are manufactured as matched pairs. Remove the bolts attaching the radius arms to the radius arm caps. Remove the rubber insulators and roll the axle form under the vehicle.
8. Installation is given in steps 9 thru 15.
9. Position the front drive axle under the vehicle, using a floor jack, and install the radius arms, insulators and caps to the axle. The numbers enscribed on cap and arm should be matched. Torque the attaching bolts to specifications, tightening them diagonally in pairs.
10. Raise the vehicle to working height and install the drive shaft to the pinion companion flange at the universal joint. Torque the universal joint U-bolt nuts to specifications.
11. Connect the axle stabilizer bar. Connect the steering tie rod to the steering knuckle by the steering connecting rod ends. Torque the attaching nuts to specifications, then install cotter pins.
12. Follow the procedure detailed in Axle Shaft and Steering Knuckle Installation and install the axle shafts, spindles and brake backing plates.
13. Position the hydraulic brake lines and brackets, then install the retaining clips.
14. Install the front brake drums, wheels and tires. Adjust the front wheel bearings. Install the dust cap or locking hub cap and the wheel cover on each front wheel.
15. Lower the truck and fill the axle housing with the specified lubricant.

F-100, 150 and 1978-79 Bronco

Removal and Installation

1. Raise the vehicle on a hoist or jack and install safety stands under the radius arm brackets.
2. Follow the procedure detailed in Axle Shaft and Steering Knuckle Removal and remove the front wheels, tires, brake drums, brake carrier plates, spindles and axle shafts.
3. Remove the hydraulic brake line brackets from each end of the axle without breaking the hydraulic connection. Disengage the hydraulic lines from the axle clips. Tie the lines to the frame.
4. Disconnect the steering tie rod at the spindle connecting rod ends. Disconnect the axle stabilizer bar.
5. Disconnect the front drive shaft at the pinion companion flange and universal joint. Secure the drive shaft out of the working area.
6. Lower the vehicle onto the safety stands and place a jack under the axle to support it while disconnecting it from the radius arms.
7. Each radius arm and cap is marked, since they are manufactured as matched pairs (parts are numbered 1 through 100). Remove the bolts attaching the radius to the radius arm caps. Remove the rubber insulators and roll the axle from under the truck.
8. Installation is given in steps 9 thru 15.
9. Position the front drive axle under the vehicle, using a floor jack, and install the radius arms, insulators and caps to the axle. Numbers on radius arm and cap should be matched. Torque the attaching bolts to specifications, tightening them diagonally in pairs.
10. Raise the vehicle to working height and install the drive shaft to the pinion companion flange at the universal joint. Torque the universal joint U-bolt nuts to specifications.
11. Connect the axle stablizer bar. Connect the steering tie rod to the spindle arms by means of the steering connecting rod ends. Torque the attaching nuts to specifications, then install the cotter pins.
12. Follow the procedure detailed in Axle Shaft and Spindle Arm Installation and install the axle shafts, spindles and brake backing plates.
13. Position the hydraulic brake lines and brackets, then install the retaining clips.
14. Install the front brake drums, wheels and tires. Adjust the front wheel bearings. Install the dust cap or locking hub cap and the wheel cover on each front wheel. NOTE: If a dust cap is used, install it with a coat of non-hardening sealer on the sealing surface.
15. Lower the truck and fill the axle housing with the specified lubricant.

F-250

Removal and Installation

1. Raise the vehicle on a hoist so that no weight is supported by the front axle.
2. Remove the hubs, rotors, brake carrier plates, axle shafts and steering knuckle as given in Axle Shaft and Steering Arm.
3. Disconnect both front axle shock absorbers at their lower ends.
4. Disconnect the front axle drive shaft at the pinion flange.
5. Support the front axle on a transmission jack, then remove the spring clip (U-bolt) nuts and the spring seats.
6. Lower the axle assembly and roll it from under the truck.
7. Installation is given in steps 8 thru 11.
8. Position axle under truck and

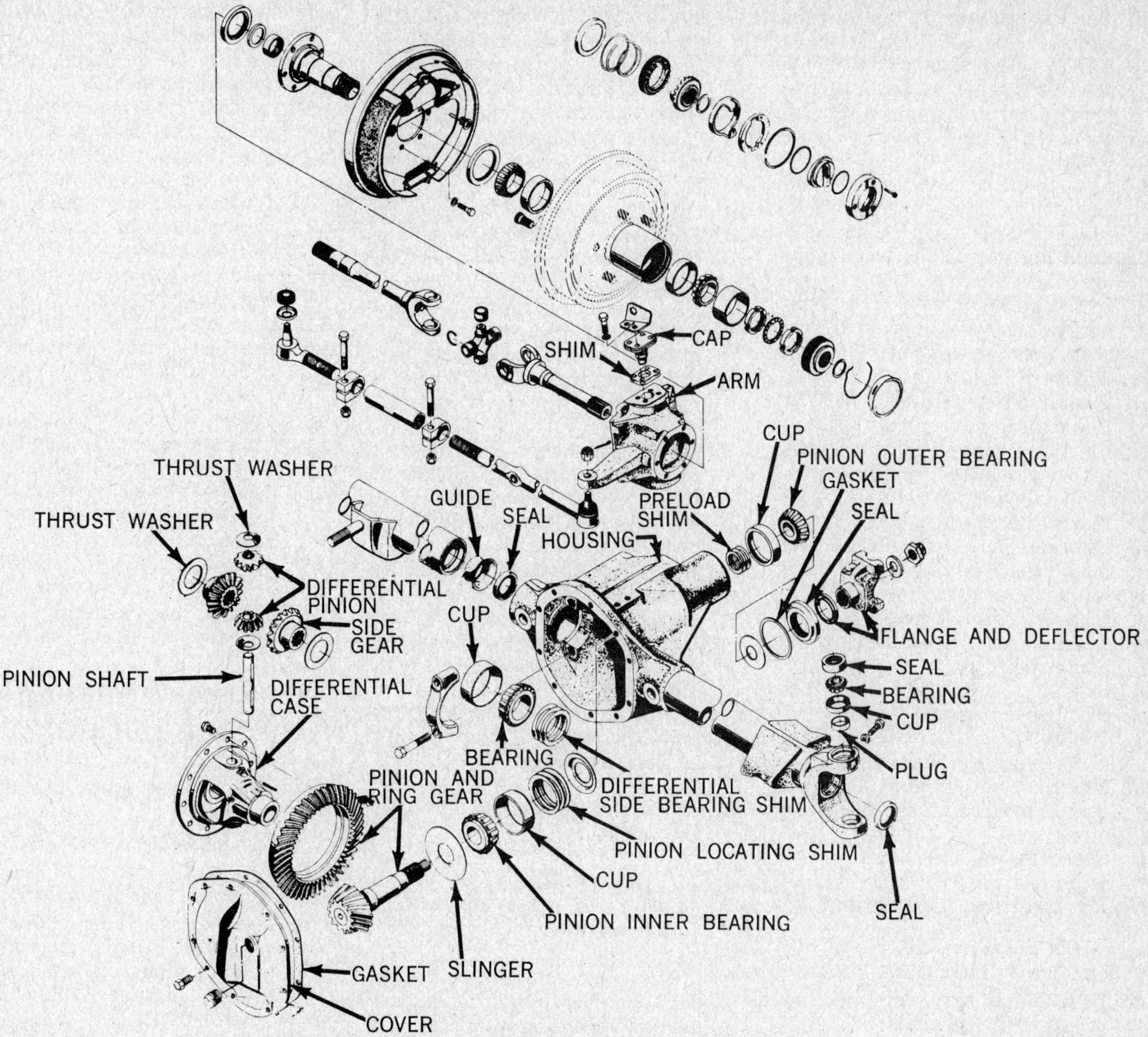

Front drive axle—F-100 and F-150 (© Ford Motor Co.)

raise it so that the spring clips and spring seats can be installed.

9. Connect the front axle shock absorbers.
10. Connect the front axle drive shaft.
11. Complete the assembly as given in Axle Shaft and Steering Knuckle Installation.

F-600

Removal and Installation

1. Raise the vehicle and support with safety stands.
2. Remove the plug from the bottom of the axle housing and drain the lubricant.
3. Disconnect the driveshaft at the pinion shaft.
4. Remove one front wheel from the brake drum and hub assembly.
5. Remove the outer hub cap retaining screws and cap.
6. Remove the retaining lock ring.
7. Remove the retaining screws and the splined drive plate.
8. Bend the tab of the lockwasher from the locknut, then remove the locknut.
9. Remove lockwasher and discard. Remove the adjusting nut.
10. Remove the drum and hub assembly from the spindle.
11. Remove the brake backing plate retaining screws and carefully lift out the backing plate and wire it out of the way.
12. Remove the spindle positioning screw and spindle.
13. Remove the axle shaft from the housing.
14. Repeat steps 4 thru 13 to remove the opposite axle shaft.
15. Remove the carrier to housing stud nuts and washers. Loosen two top nuts and leave on studs to prevent carrier from falling.
16. Break carrier loose from axle housing with rawhide mallet.

    NOTE: A roller jack should be positioned and fastened to the carrier at this point.

17. Remove the top nuts and washers, then work the carrier free. A small pinch bar may be used to straighten the carrier in the housing bore. However, the end must be rounded to prevent identing the carrier flange. A roller jack may be used to facilitate removal of the carrier.
18. Installation is given in steps 21 thru 39.
19. Remove all traces of old gasket material from the carrier and housing surfaces, then position a new gasket over the housing mounting studs.
20. Using a roller jack, ease the carrier into position in the housing bore.
21. Position two washers and run two nuts part way on to the studs to hold the carrier; then align it properly with the housing.
22. Install the housing stud nuts and torque them to specifications.
23. Install one axle shaft in the housing.
24. Install the spindle and secure it with the positioning screw.
25. Position the brake backing plate, install the retaining screws and torque to specifications.
26. Carefully position the drum, and hub assembly on the axle spin-

dle, and tighten the adjusting nut.
27. Adjust wheel bearing. Position a new lockwasher against the adjusting nut and apply a film of oil to the outer face of the lockwasher.
28. Run the lock nut against the lockwasher, then torque it to specifications.
29. Bend one tab of the lockwasher over the adjusting nut.
30. Bend other tab of the lockwasher (in the opposite direction) over the lock nut.
31. Apply Silastic Sealer to the front and rear mounting faces of the splined drive plate. Position the drive plate and install the plate retaining screws, then torque to specifications.
32. Install the retaining lock ring.
33. Position the outer hub cap and install the retaining screws, then torque to specifications.
34. Install the front wheel.
35. Connect the drive shaft at the pinion shaft.
36. Repeat steps 23 through 34 for the other axle shaft assembly.
37. Make sure that the housing drain plug has been installed.
38. Fill the axle housing with the correct grade and quantity of lubricant.
39. Lower the vehicle.

Wheel Bearing Adjustment

F-100, F-150, F-250, F-350, Econoline P-350-500—(2WD)

1. Remove the hub cap and hub grease cap.
2. Clean the end of the spindle and remove the cotter pin and nut-lock.
3. While rotating the wheel, torque the adjusting nut to 17-25 ft lbs. (40-55 ft lbs.—P-350-500), to seat the bearings.
4. Install the nut-lock so that the cotter pin hole in the spindle is aligned with the hole in the nut-lock.
5. Back the adjusting nut off, 2 slots and install the cotter pin. Be sure that the wheel rotates freely with no noticeable endplay.
6. Install the grease cap and hub cap.

4-Wheel Drive Except F600

1. Raise the vehicle and support with safety stands.
2. Back off the brake adjusting screw, if necessary. Remove the wheel cover.
3. Remove the front hub grease cap. Remove the driving hub retaining snap-ring and slide the splined driving hub from between the axle shaft and the wheel hub. Remove the driving hub spacer. *NOTE: If equipped with free-wheeling hubs, see Free-Wheeling Hub Removal.*
4. Remove lock nut and lock ring from the spindle.
5. Tighten the bearing adjusting nut to 50 ft. lbs., while rotating the wheel back and forth to seat the bearings.
6. Continue rotating the wheel and then, loosen and re-torque the adjusting nut to 30-40 ft. lbs.
7. Back the adjusting nut off approximately ¼ turn (90 degrees). Assemble the lock ring by turning the nut to the nearest notch where the dowel pin will enter.
8. Install the outer lock nut and torque to 50 ft. lbs. (80-100 ft. lbs—1973-78). Final endplay of the wheel on the spindle should be 0.001 to 0.010.
9. Install the driving hub, spacer, snap-ring and hub grease cap. Apply a thin coat of non-hardening sealer to the seating edge of the grease cap before installation.
   NOTE: If equipped with free-wheeling hubs, installation refer to Free-Wheeling Hub.
10. Adjust the brake.
11. Remove safety stands and lower the vehicle.

F-600

1. Remove the outer hub cap retaining screws, then remove the cap.
2. Remove the retaining lock ring.
3. Remove the retaining screws and the splined drive plate.
4. Bend the tab of the lockwasher away from the locknut, then remove the locknut.
5. Remove the lockwasher and discard.
6. While rotating the wheel back and forth to correctly seat the bearings, torque the adjusting nut to 50 ft. lbs.
7. Back-off the adjusting nut from ¼ to 1/3 turn.
8. Position a new lockwasher against the adjusting nut and apply a film of oil to the outer face of the lockwasher.
9. Run the lock nut up against the lockwasher, then torque it to 100-150 ft. lbs.
10. Bend one tab of the lockwasher over the adjusting nut.
11. Bend other tap (in the opposite direction) over the lock nut.
    NOTE: Use a blunt tool when bending the tabs.
12. Apply Silastic Sealer to the front and rear mounting faces of the spined drive plate.
13. Position the drive plate, install the retaining screws and torque to specifications.
14. Install the retaining lock ring.
15. Position the outer hub cap and install the retaining screws. Torque to specifications.

Free-Wheeling Lock-out Hubs

Free Wheeling Hub

1973-79 except H.D.

Removal and Installation

1. Remove the three screws (six screws on Bronco) attaching the lock-out actuating knob and retaining plate assembly to the wheel hub. Remove the actuating knob and retaining plate assembly and large O-ring.
2. Remove the large internal snap-ring, the outer clutch retaining ring and the actuating cam body.
3. While pressing inward against

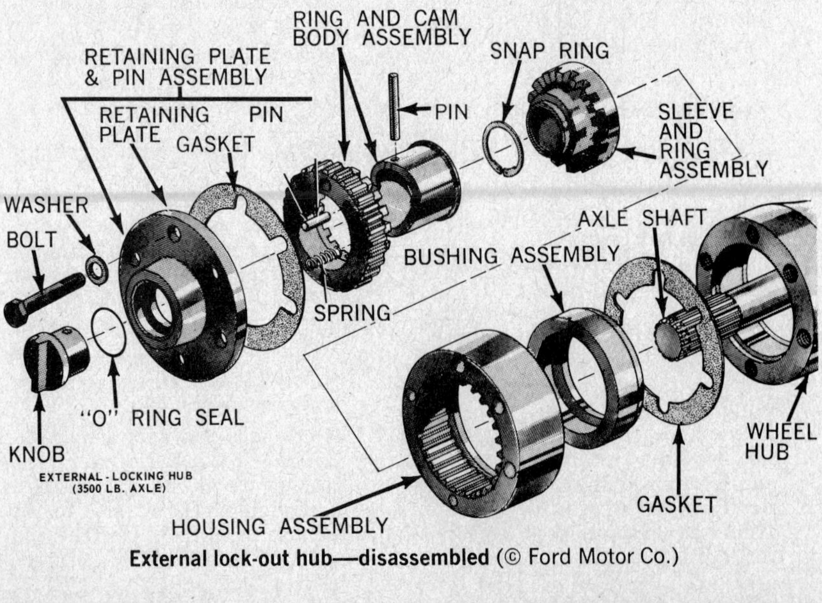

External lock-out hub—disassembled (© Ford Motor Co.)

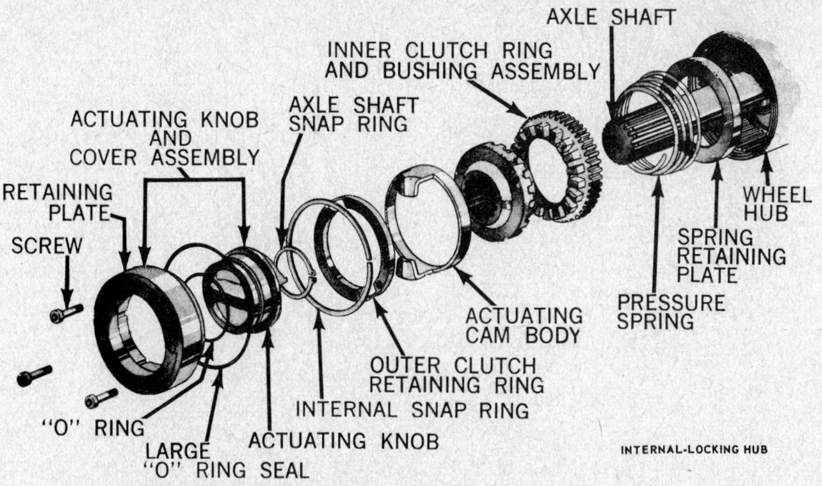

Internal lock-out hub—disassembled (© Ford Motor Co.)

the axle shaft sleeve and ring assembly, remove the snap-ring that secures the axle sleeve and ring assembly to the axle shaft.
4. Remove the axle shaft sleeve and ring assembly and the inner clutch and bushing assembly.
5. Remove the pressure spring (or spacer) and spring retainer plate.
6. Installation is given in steps 7 thru 13.
7. Insert the spring retainer plate into the wheel hub with the flange side facing inward. Be sure spring retainer plate bottoms against the outer wheel hub bearing cap.
8. Position the pressure spring (or spacer), with the large end seating against the spring retainer plate, inside the wheel hub.
9. Assemble the inner clutch ring and bushing assembly to the axle shaft sleeve and ring assembly, sliding both assemblies as a unit on to the axle shaft splines. Using a new axle shaft snap-ring, lock the axle shaft sleeve and ring assembly to the shaft.
10. Place the actuating cam body in position against the axle shaft sleeve and ring assembly, inside the wheel hub.
11. Install the outer clutch retaining ring and the internal snap-ring into position in the wheel hub. Make certain the snap-ring is well seated in the groove on the inside diameter of the hub.
12. Coat the large O-ring seal with O-ring lubricant. Install the large O-ring seal onto the actuating knob and retaining plate and place the knob and retaining plate assembly into position in the wheel hub.
13. Install the three (six on Bronco) knob and retaining plate assembly attaching screws and copper washers. Tighten screws securely.

F-250 Heavy-Duty

Removal and Installation

1. Remove the free-running hub screws and washers.
2. Loosen the gear hub housing and slide it away from the hub and drum assembly.
3. Remove and discard the inner metal gasket, remove the gear hub housing, and remove and discard the outer gasket. Wipe the exposed parts clean with a clean rag.
4. Remove the snap-ring while holding pressure on the clutch gear.
5. The actuator knob should be in the lock position while performing this operation. Ease the clutch gear and pressure spring out of the assembly.
6. Turn the actuator knob to the free position. Drive the cam lock pin out of the assembly with a drift.
7. Remove the actuating cam from the knob.
8. Remove the knob retainer snap-ring and remove the knob from the knob retainer.
9. Using a capscrew, pull out slightly on the axle shaft and remove the snap-ring which retains the bushing and inner clutch gear assembly.
10. Remove the inner clutch gear and the bushing behind it. Replace these two components as a set if excessive wear or damage is evident.
11. Inspect the splines of the axle shaft for nicks or burrs. Clean the threaded holes in the wheel hub.
12. Apply Moly XL Hi-Speed grease to the back face and thrust face of the bushing and the splines of the inner clutch gear.
13. Assemble the inner clutch gear into the bushing.
14. Install the bushing and inner clutch gear onto the axle shaft mating the splines of the axle and the gear.
15. Install a new snap-ring to retain the bushing and gear. It may be necessary to pull out the axle with a capscrew to gain clearance for the snap-ring to be installed. Make sure that the snap-ring is fully seated.
16. Apply a small amount of O-ring lubricant on the actuator knob and assemble the O-ring to the actuator knob.
17. Install the actuating knob into the knob retainer with the arrow pointing to the free position.
18. Install the knob retainer snap-ring.
19. Install the actuating cam onto the knob, aligning the ears of the cam with the slots of the retainer. Position the parts on a small block of wood.
20. Assemble the cam lock pin through the groove of the cam and the holes in the actuating knob. Be sure that the ends of the pin are flush with the outside diameter of the cam.
21. Turn the actuator knob to the lock position and apply a small amount of Moly XL Hi-Speed grease to both grooves of the cam.
22. Install the pressure spring and outer clutch gear. Compress the pressure spring by forcing the clutch gear down, then install the snap-ring. Be sure that the snap-ring is fully seated in the groove.
23. Turn the actuator knob to the free position. Assemble the six dished washers to the six retaining screws.
24. Install two screws with washers into the knob retainer to properly align the parts. Apply a small amount of Moly XL Hi-Speed grease to the outer spline and teeth of the outer clutch gear. Remove any excess lubricant from the gasket surface of the retainer.
25. Install a new outer retainer gasket. Assemble the gear hub housing by aligning the splines of the housing with those on the outer clutch gear. Then install a new inner metal gasket on the hub housing.
26. Position the free-running hub assembly to the axle and tighten the two installed retaining screws. Turn the actuator knob to the lock position.
27. Install the remaining four retainer screws with washers and tighten all screws in sequence to 30-36 ft lbs.

NOTE: The hubs may be hard to engage and disengate at first, but should loosen up after some use. Make sure that both the hubs are either engaged or disengaged before driving the truck.

Reference

Front wheel and steering alignment procedures may be found in the General Repair Section.

STEERING GEAR

Manual Steering Gear

Reference

Manual steering overhaul procedures for light trucks are found in the General Repair section of this book.

Steering Gear

Removal and Installation

Econoline 1973-74

1. Raise the vehicle on a hoist.
2. Remove the flex coupling lower attaching bolt.
3. Disconnect the pitman arm from the drag link.
4. Remove the three attaching bolts and remove the gear.
5. Remove the pitman arm attaching nut and remove the pitman arm.
6. To install, center the input shaft (approximately three turns from either stop).
7. Install pitman arm pointing downward, tightening attaching nut securely.
8. Fill the steering gear to the proper level with lubricant.
9. Position the steering gear in the truck, aligning the input shaft splines to engage the flexible coupling. Install and tighten the three steering gear mounting bolts.
10. Connect drag link to pitman arm. Install attaching bolt and tighten securely. Install cotter pin.

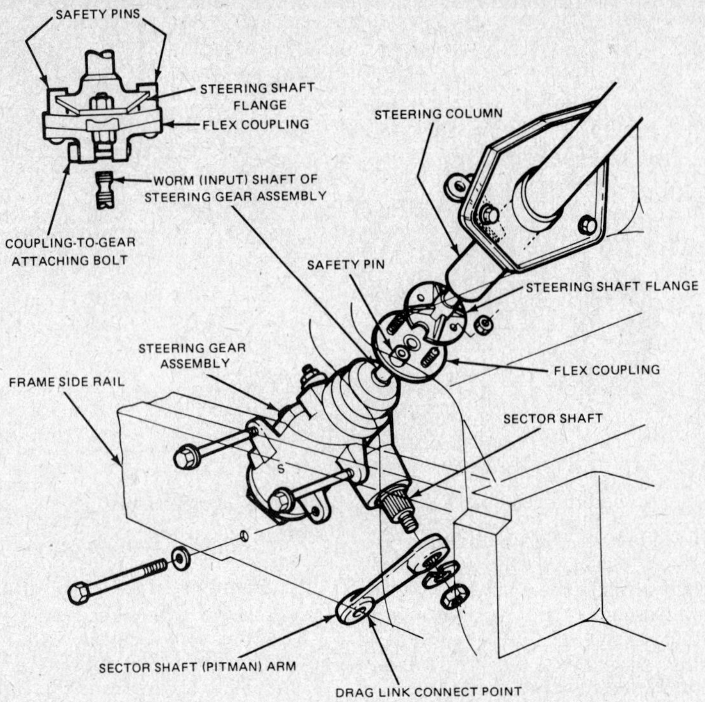

1975-80 Econoline manual steering gear installation (© Ford Motor Co.)

11. Install flexible coupling attaching bolt and tighten securely.
12. Lower vehicle.

Econoline 1975 and Later

1. Raise the vehicle.
2. Disconnect the flex coupling from the steering shaft flange by removing the two attaching nuts.
3. Disconnect the drag link from the sector shaft arm.
4. Support the steering gear and remove the bolts and washers that attach the steering gear assembly to the frame side rail. Lower the steering gear from the vehicle.
5. Remove the coupling to gear attaching bolt from the lower half of the flex coupling and remove the coupling from the steering gear assembly.
6. Remove the pitman arm-to-sector shaft attaching nut and washer. Remove the pitman arm from the sector shaft.
7. Install the flex coupling on the worm shaft of the gear assembly. Install a new coupling-to-gear attaching bolt and tighten.
8. Center the input shaft. The center position is approximately three turns from either stop.
9. Assemble the pitman arm on the sector shaft pointing downward. Install the attaching nuts and washers. Tighten the nuts.
10. Position the steering gear assem-

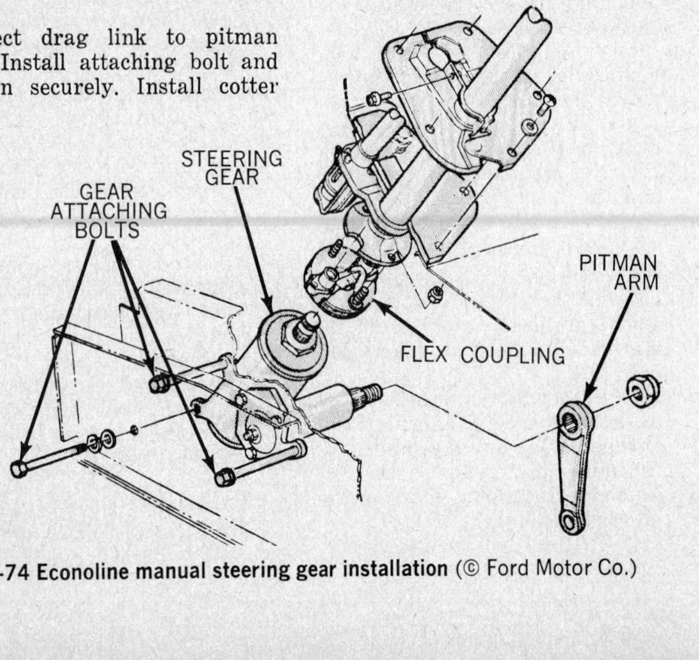

1973-74 Econoline manual steering gear installation (© Ford Motor Co.)

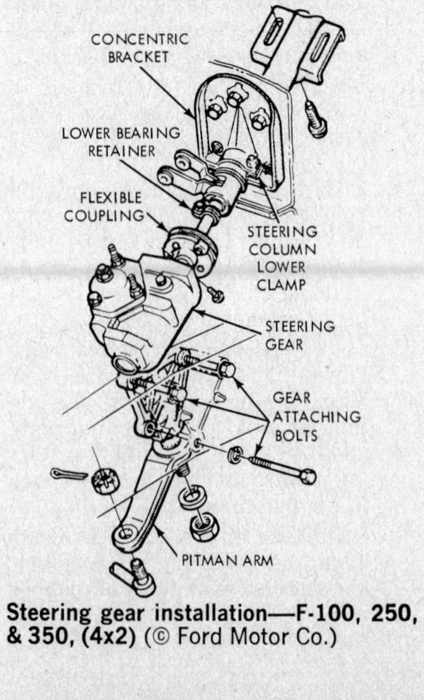

Steering gear installation—F-100, 250, & 350, (4x2) (© Ford Motor Co.)

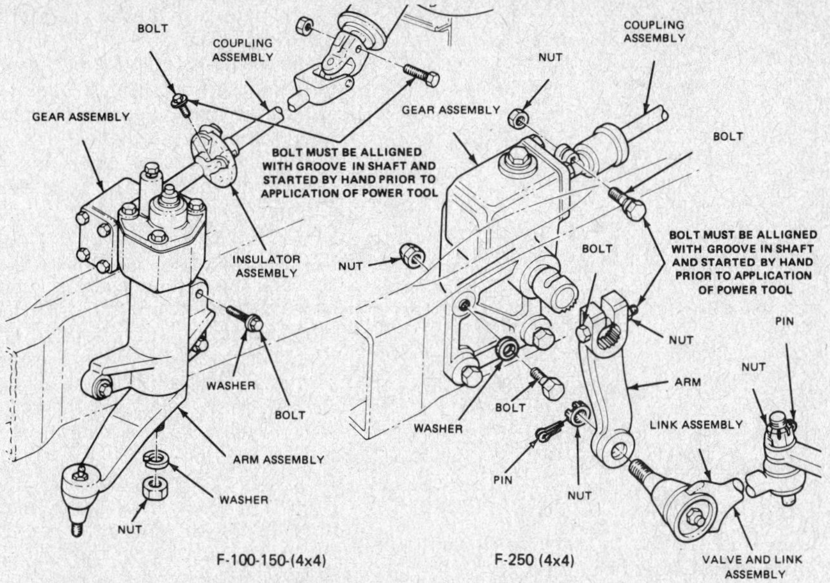

F-100, F-150, & F-250 manual steering gear installation (© Ford Motor Co.)

bly so that the stud bolts on the flex coupling enter the bolt holes in the steering shaft flange, and the holes in the mounting bosses of the gear match the bolt holes in the frame side rail.

11. While supporting the gear in the proper position, install the gear-to-frame side rail attaching bolts and washers, tighten.
12. Connect the drag link to the pitman arm. Install the drag link ball stud nut and tighten the nut. Install the cotter pin.
13. Secure the flex coupling to the steering shaft flange with the two attaching nuts and tighten.

F-100, 150, 250, 350 (4x2)

1. Remove flex joint attaching bolt and remove the brake line bracket.
2. Raise the front of the vehicle, and install safety stands.
3. Disconnect the pitman arm from the sector shaft.
4. Remove the steering gear attaching bolts and the gear.
5. Before installing gear, align the wheels and the sector shaft to the straight-forward position.
6. Install steering gear, tightening attaching bolts securely.
7. Install the brake line bracket to the gear cover studs.
8. Connect the pitman arm to the sector shaft.
9. Install and tighten flex coupling bolt.
10. Remove the steering gear filler plug and housing lower cover bolt. Turn the steering wheel to the left to move the ball nut away from the filler hole. Fill the steering gear with lubricant (until lubricant comes out of the housing cover lower bolt hole). Install filler plug and cover bolt.

1973-79 Bronco and F-100 thru 350 4x4

1. Raise the vehicle on a hoist.
2. Remove the pitman arm.
3. Remove the three gear to frame attaching bolts, then lower the vehicle.
4. Remove the flex coupling clamp bolt at the steering gear input shaft and loosen the other clamp bolt (steering column). Remove the coupling from the steering gear input shaft. Discard clamp, bolt and nut.
5. Remove the steering gear from the vehicle.
6. When installing, first mount the steering gear to the frame, but do not tighten attaching bolts.

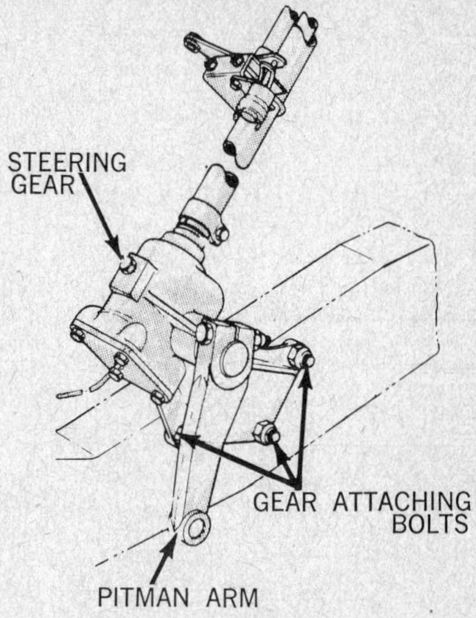

P-Series manual steering gear installation (© Ford Motor Co.)

7. Install steering shaft flex coupling to the gear input shaft using a new clamp and bolt. Tighten bolt securely.
8. Install the flex coupling to the steering column shaft with a new clamp and bolt. Tighten bolt securely.
9. Raise the vehicle and tighten the steering gear attaching bolts securely.
10. Install the pitman arm on the steering gear sector shaft, tightening attaching nut securely.
11. Lower the vehicle and fill the steering gear with lubricant.

P Series

1. Remove the steering wheel.
2. Remove the steering column bracket bolts from the instrument panel.

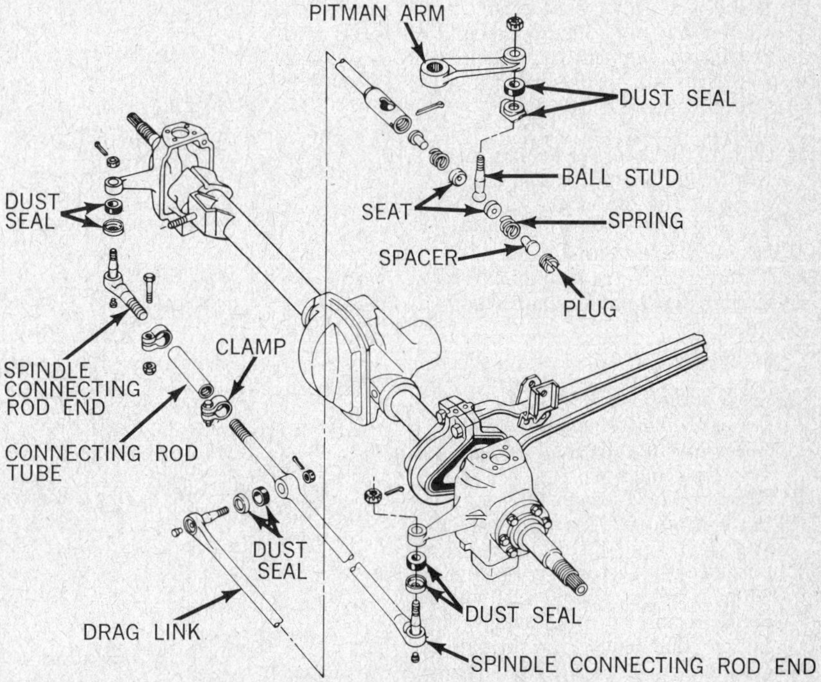

Steering linkage—F-100 & (4x4) Bronco (© Ford Motor Co.)

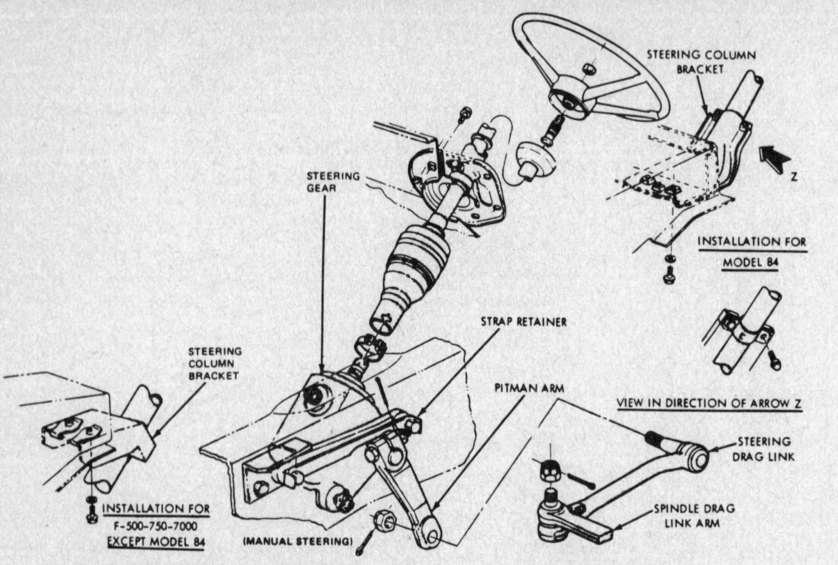

F- B 500-750 manual steering gear installation (© Ford Motor Co.)

3. Raise the front of the vehicle 10 inches and support with safety stands.
4. Remove the sector shaft arm from the sector shaft and remove the steering gear attaching bolts. It may be necessary to spread the sector shaft opening in the arm.
5. Loosen the steering column lower clamp and disconnect the horn wire.
6. Move the steering gear to the left and remove it from beneath the vehicle.
7. Place the steering gear in the steering column tube and partially tighten the lower clamp.
8. Install the steering gear attaching bolts finger tight and connect the horn wire.
9. Install the sector shaft arm and tighten the nut. Spread the split portion of the arm if necessary.
10. Loosely install the steering column tube bracket bolts.
11. Install the steering wheel.
12. Adjust the steering column tube to provide a 1/16 inch clearance between the top of the tube and the steering wheel hub. Tighten the instrument panel bolts.
13. Tighten the lower clamp bolt and tighten the steering gear attaching bolts.
14. Lower the vehicle.

F-B Series—500 and Up

1. Loosen the steering column lower clamp and slide the clamp down the column.
2. Remove the pitman arm retaining bolt and nut from the sector shaft.
3. Loosen the steering column 9000 lb axles, remove the nuts, bolts, cotter pin, and strap retainer that hold the steering gear housing on the frame side member.
4. Remove the steering gear from under the vehicle.
5. Install the steering gear assembly from underneath the vehicle and tighten the mounting bolts, nuts, and strap retainer finger tight.
6. Connect the steering column lower clamp and tighten.
7. Tighten the nuts that attach the upper steering gear housing to the frame.
8. Install the bottom nut and cotter pin and tighten to 50-70 ft-lbs.
9. Install the pitman arm on the sector shaft and tighten.

L-N, L-LT-LNT-W-WT Series

1. Place the steering wheel and the front wheels in the straight ahead position.
2. Remove the bolt, nut and cotter pin holding the pitman arm to the sector shaft. Remove the pitman arm from the shaft.
3. Mark the steering gear input shaft and the U-joint yoke for alignment.
4. Remove the cotter pin, bolt and nut holding the U-joint to the steering gear input shaft, and slide the joint up and off the input shaft.
5. Remove the bolts, nuts, cotter pin, and strap retainers holding the steering gear or steering gear bracket to the frame side rail.
6. Remove the steering gear.
7. Place the gear (or gear and bracket) on the side rail. Install the bolts, nuts and strap retainers and tighten. Advance the nut to the next castellation if necessary and install the cotter pins.
8. Align the marks on the input shaft and U-joint yoke and place the steering shaft U-joint on the steering shaft U-joint on the steering gear input shaft and install a new nut and bolt.

   NOTE: Be sure the bolt engages in the slot on the steering gear input shaft. Tighten the nuts. Advance to the next castellation if necessary and install the cotter pin.
9. Place the pitman arm on the steering shaft and install the bolt and nut. On W and L series vehicles, align the slash marks on the pitman arm with the ser-

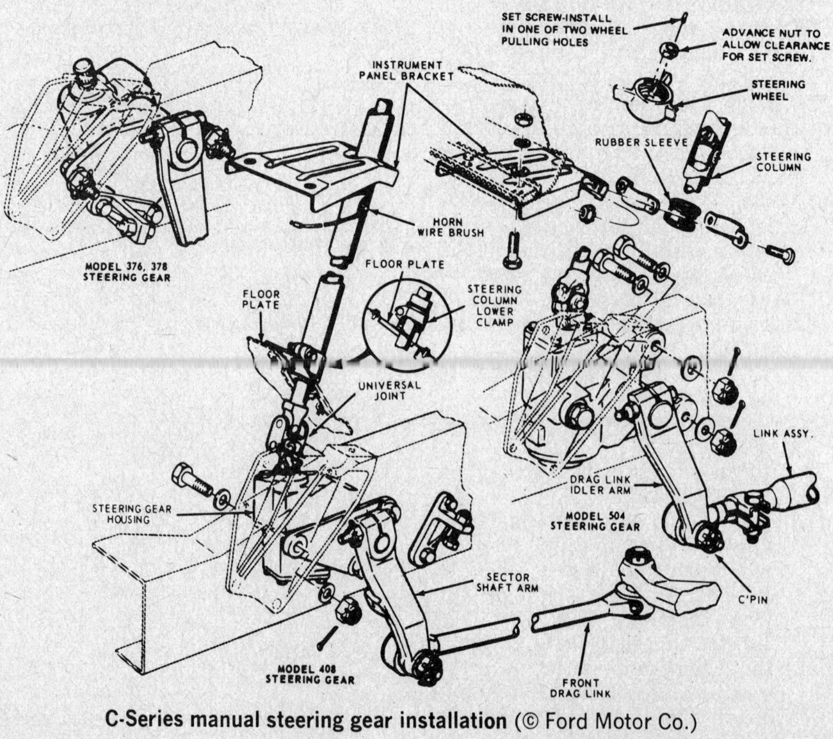

C-Series manual steering gear installation (© Ford Motor Co.)

rations on the sector shaft. Tighten the bolts. Advance the nut to the castellation if necessary and install the cotter pin.

C-Series

1. Tilt the cab up and remove the horn wire brush from the steering column just below the instrument panel bracket.
2. Remove the bolt that attaches the U-joint to the steering gear.
3. Turn the wheels all the way to the right. Remove the sector arm attaching nut and bolt. Pry the sector arm off the sector shaft. Spread the sector shaft opening in the arm if necessary.
4. Remove the steering gear housing attaching bolts and remove the gear.
5. Place the steering gear housing on the frame side rail and install the attaching bolts. Tighten the nuts and install the cotter pins.
6. Center the steering gear input shaft. Turn the steering wheel to position the lower spoke in a vertical position.
7. With a helper, push the steering shaft down until the U-joint is in position on the steering gear input shaft. Install and tighten the U-joint attaching bolt and nut.
8. Install the sector shaft arm on the sector shaft. Make sure it is in line with the lock bolt slot in the sector shaft. Install and tighten the bolt and nut. Spread the sector shaft opening in the arm if necessary.
9. Connect the hornwire. Road test the vehicle in check for proper steering operation.

Worm Bearing Preload Adjustment

F-100, 150, 250, 350 (4x2)

Always check and adjust worm and roller mesh after check checking and adjusting worm bearing preload (see below for worm and roller mesh adjustment).

1. Remove the pitman arm from sector shaft and the horn button and spring from the steering wheel. Disconnect the horn wire at the relay.
2. Turn steering wheel to end of travel.
3. Use a torque wrench on the steering wheel nut and measure the lowest torque required to move the wheel at a constant speed. This torque is the worm bearing preload.
4. If the preload is not 4-5" lbs. (manual) or 3-4" lbs. (power assist), adjust the preload as follows: loosen the steering shaft bearing adjuster locknut and turn adjuster to set the preload.
5. Tighten bearing adjuster locknut, install the pitman arm and horn components.

F-100 (4x4)

Follow Steps 1 through 3 of the procedure for F-100, 250, 350 (4x2) above. If adjustment is necessary, remove or add shims between the worm shaft bearing retainer cover and the steering gear housing. If erratic readings are experienced, disconnect the steering shaft joint at the steering gear and check torque required to rotate the steering shaft. If that torque is measurable, add it to the preload specification.

1973-77 Bronco

Remove the gear from the vehicle, loosen locknut and back off the mesh and roller adjusting nut. Check the torque required to rotate the input shaft 1½ turns either side of center. If bearing preload is not 5-10" lbs., add or remove shims between the worm shaft bearing retainer cover and the steering gear housing until proper preload is obtained.

F and C-Series

Remove the steering gear and use a 12-point socket and torque wrench on the lower steering serrated shaft to measure preload at a constant speed rotation. If bearing preload is not within 9-11" lbs. (C-series) or 5-9" lbs. (F-series), add or remove gasket shims between the worm shaft bearing retainer and the gear housing. Adjust the worm and roller mesh preload. Install steering gear in vehicle.

Worm and Roller Mesh Adjustment

Always check and adjust worm bearing preload before making the mesh adjustment (see above).

1. Remove the steering gear from the vehicle.
2. Measure the torque required to move the gear through middle (straight-ahead) position with a torque wrench on the input shaft. The highest reading is used. If it is not 24-29" lbs. (C-series), 14-22" lbs. (F-500-750) or 12-21" in. lbs. (F-100 4x4 and Bronco), loosen locknut and turn adjusting screw until correct mesh load is obtained. Tighten locknut.
3. Recheck mesh load, install steering gear in vehicle and fill gear with lubricant.

Steering Worm and Sector Adjustment

Econoline 1973-74

1. Remove the steering gear from the vehicle.
2. Loosen locknut on the sector shaft adjusting screw and turn adjusting screw out (counterclockwise) approximately three turns.
3. Using a torque wrench on the input shaft, rotate shaft about 1½ turns either side of center. If the preload is not 4-5" lbs. (manual) or 3-4" lbs. (power assist), loosen input shaft bearing adjuster locknut and tighten or loosen bearing adjuster to obtain the correct bearing preload. Tighten locknut and recheck preload.
4. Center the input shaft (turn against stops gently as it is easy to damage the ball return guides).
5. Turn sector shaft adjusting screw clockwise until an over-center meshload of 9-10" lbs. (manual) or 8-9" lbs. (power assist) is obtained (measured at input shaft). Tighten the locknut.
6. Check the total gear lash by holding the sector shaft solid in the center position and pulling with the torque wrench 15 in. lbs. in each direction. If the travel of the wrench exceeds 1¼", then the whole gear must be replaced.
7. Recheck total over-center preload, then install steering gear in vehicle.

Econoline 1975 and Later

1. Remove the steering gear.
2. Tighten the worm bearing adjuster plug until all end-play is removed. Loosen it ¼ turn.
3. Using a socket on an in. lb torque wrench, turn the worm shaft full right and back ½ turn.
4. Tighten the adjuster plug until 5-8 in. lbs is reached. Tighten the locknut to 85 ft. lbs.
5. Turn the worm shaft from stop to stop, counting the number of turns. Turn the shaft back exactly half the number of turns to the center position.
6. Turn the sector shaft adjuster screw clockwise to remove all lash between the ball nut and sector teeth. Tighten the locknut.
7. Using a socket and in. lb torque wrench, note the highest reading required to rotate the gear through the center position, which should be 16 in. lbs.
8. If necessary, adjust the sector shaft adjuster screw to obtain the proper torque and recheck it.

Power Steering Gear

Reference

Power steering gear overhaul procedures for light duty trucks are found in the General Repair section of this book.

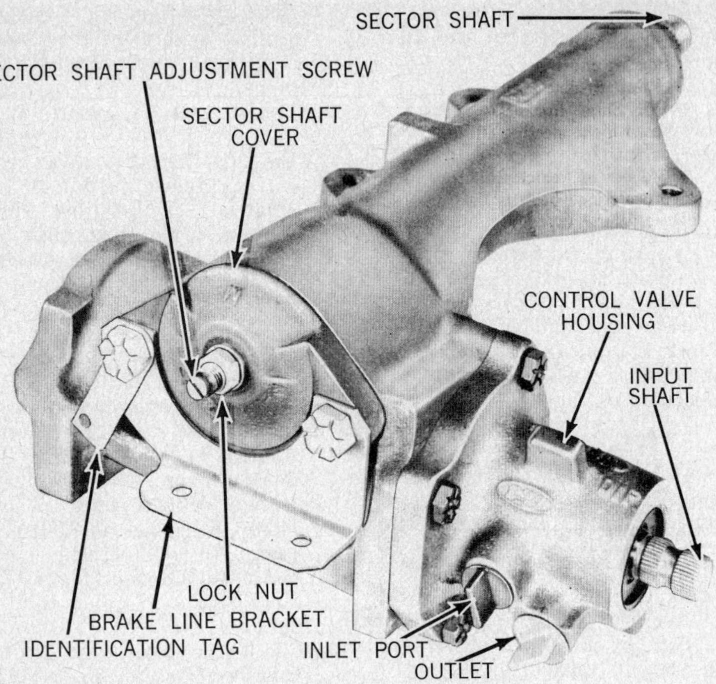

Ford integral power steering gear (© Ford Motor Co.)

Ford Integral Power Steering Gear

F series and 1978-80 Bronco

Over Center Preload Adjustment

1. Disconnect pitman arm from the sector shaft.
2. Disconnect the fluid return line at the reservoir and cap the reservoir return line.
3. Place the end of the return line in a clean container and cycle the steering wheel in both directions to discharge the fluid from the gear.
4. Turn the steering wheel to 45-degrees from the left stop and measure the torque (at the steering wheel nut) required to turn 1/8-turn from there.
5. Determine the torque required to turn the steering gear through center position. Loosen adjusting screw locknut and turn adjusting screw to obtain a torque reading 11-18 in. lbs. greater than the torque 45-degrees from the stop.
6. Hold adjusting screw while tightening locknut.
7. Install the pitman arm and steering wheel hub cover.
8. Connect the fluid return line and fill reservoir with fluid.

Removal and Installation

1. Disconnect pressure and return lines from the steering gear, *being sure to tag them for identification.* Plug lines and ports.
2. Remove brake lines attached to bracket on the steering gear.
3. Remove the two bolts that secure the flex coupling to the steering gear and to the column steering shaft assembly.
4. Raise the vehicle.
5. Remove the pitman arm from the sector shaft, using a puller if necessary.
6. If vehicle has a standard transmission, remove the clutch release lever retracting spring.
7. Remove the steering gear attaching bolts and steering gear, working the steering gear free of the flex coupling.
8. To install, slide the flex coupling into place on the bottom of the steering shaft.
9. Set the steering wheel so that the spokes are horizontal and center the steering gear input shaft.
10. Slide the steering gear input shaft into the flex coupling. Install the three steering gear attaching bolts and tighten them securely.
11. With wheels in the straight ahead position, install the pitman arm on the sector shaft.
12. Install the flex coupling and tighten the bolts securely.
13. Connect fluid pressure and return lines to steering gear. Reinstall brake lines on bracket on steering gear.
14. Remove the coil wire, fill the power steering pump reservoir and, while engaging the starter, cycle the steering wheel to distribute the fluid. Add fluid if reservoir is not full.
15. Connect the coil wire, start the engine and check for leaks while cycling the steering wheel.

Integral Power Steering Gear (Saginaw)

Mesh Load Adjustment

1. On Econolines, remove the drag link from the Pitman arm and remove the horn pad. On Broncos, disconnect the Pitman arm from the sector shaft and remove the horn pad.
2. Disconnect the fluid return line and cap the reservoir return line. Put the end of the return line in a clear container and cycle the wheel several times to discharge fluid from the gear.
3. Using an in. lb torque wrench on the steering wheel nut, check the torque required to rotate the wheel through a 180° arc on each side of center. The new gear over center torque should be 4-8 in. lbs greater than the end readings but the total should not exceed 18 in. lbs. Used gears should be 4-5 in. lbs greater than the end reading, but should not exceed 14 in. lbs.
4. To adjust, make sure the Pitman shaft over center adjusting screw is backed all the way out. Turn it in 1/2 turn.
5. Rotate the shaft from one stop to the other. Count the number of turns and locate the center position. Check the combined preload on the ball and thrust bearing by rotating the shaft through the center of travel. Note the highest reading.
6. Tighten the adjusting screw until the torque wrench reads 3-6 in. lbs, higher than the reading in Step 5. The total should not exceed 14 in. lbs.
7. Hold the adjusting screw and tighten the locknut to 35 ft lbs.

Removal and Installation

1973-77 Bronco

1. Disconnect the pressure and return lines and plug the lines and ports.
2. Raise the truck and disconnect the Pitman arm.
3. Remove the Pitman arm.
4. Unbolt the gear from the frame rails and lower the truck.
5. Remove the pinch-bolt from the flange and insulator.
6. Unbolt the horn and hold it outward.
7. Remove the attaching bolts and remove the gear from the truck, with the shaft and joint assemblies as a unit.
8. Remove the pinch-bolt from the shaft and joint.
9. Remove the shaft and joint from the gear.
10. Installation is the reverse of removal.
11. Remove the coil wire, fill the

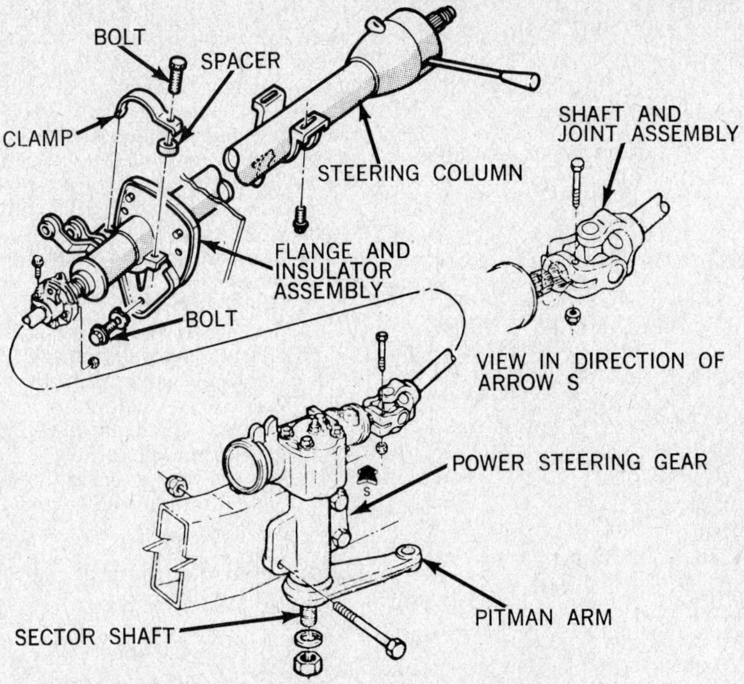

Bronco power steering gear installation (© Ford Motor Co.)

power steering pump reservoir and, while engaging the starter, cycle the steering wheel to distribute the fluid. Add fluid if reservoir is not full.

12. Connect the coil wire, start the engine and check for leaks while cycling the steering wheel.

Econoline

1. Disconnect the pressure and return lines and plug the ports.
2. Raise the van and remove the drag link from the Pitman arm.
3. Unbolt the flex coupling from the steering shaft.
4. Support the gear and remove the attaching bolts.
5. Remove the pinch bolt from the flex coupling and remove the coupling from the gear.
6. Remove the Pitman arm from the sector shaft.
7. Installation is the reverse of removal.
8. Remove the coil wire, fill the power steering pump reservoir and, while engaging the starter, cycle the steering wheel to distribute the fluid. Add fluid if reservoir is not full.
9. Connect the coil wire, start the engine and check for leaks while cycling the steering wheel.

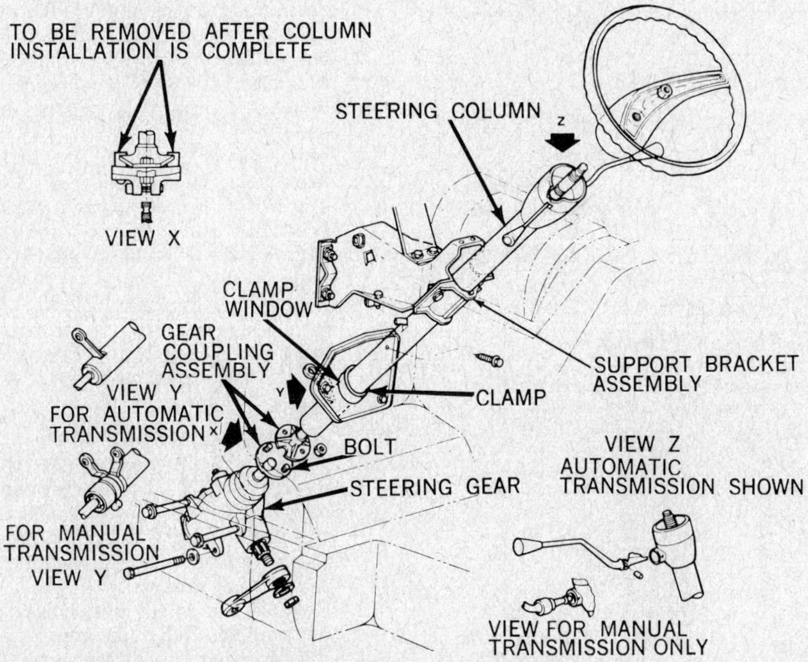

Econoline power steering gear installation (© Ford Motor Co.)

Ross HF-54 and HF-64 Integral Power Steering Gears

F, B, L-500 through 9000 Series

Unloader Valve Adjustment

This adjustment is made for *right turn only* on the HF-54 gear and for *both turns* on the HF-64 gear.

Before making this adjustment, establish the straight-forward center of the steering system by driving the truck forward with hands off the wheel until the steering finds its own center. Stop the truck and mark the steering column to steering wheel with chalk or masking tape.

1. With wheels straight ahead engine warm and idling, turn the steering wheel 1¾ turns to the right (HF-54), 1½ turns (2 port HF-64) or 1¼ turns (4 port HF-64). Hold this position.
2. Loosen locknut and turn the unloader valve pressure adjusting screw until an audible hiss is heard. Tighten locknut.
3. While vehicle is moving, let the steering wheel center (straight-forward), then stop the truck and turn the wheel the prescribed number of turns (Step 2 above) and listen for audible hiss. Repeat Step 2 if necessary.

   NOTE: The pitman arm on the HF-64 must not contact the stop cast on the gear housing prior to contacting the unloader valve. The distance between the pitman arm and the stop should be 1/16" to ⅛" when the hiss is heard.
4. To adjust the unloader valve for left turn (HF-64 ONLY), repeat Steps 1 through 3 above turning the steering wheel to the left.

Sector Shaft Adjustment

1. Disconnect the drag link from the pitman arm and center the steering wheel. Check for lash between the sector shaft and the rack piston by moving the pitman arm. If there is noticeable lash, remove the gear from the vehicle.
2. Loosen the sector shaft adjustment screw locknut on the side cover.
3. Rotate the input shaft through its full travel at least five times, then adjust the sector shaft adjusting screw for a 15–20 in. lb. (20-25 in. lbs. 1974-76) torque as shaft is rotated 90 degrees each side of center.
4. Back off adjusting screw one turn and note torque required to move the input shaft 90 degrees each side of center. Move the adjusting screw in to provide for

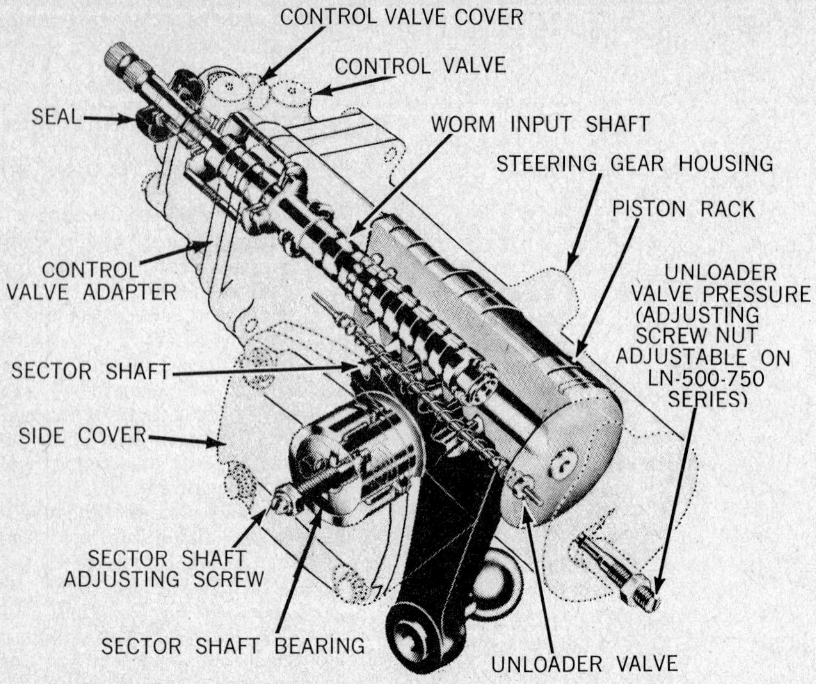

Ross model HF-54 integral steering gear (© Ford Motor Co.)

an increase of 2-4 in. lbs. at a point within 45 degrees each side of center after locknut is first tightened snugly. Torque locknut to 20–25 ft. lbs.

5. Input torque of assembled gear (no fluid) should not exceed 15 in. lbs. over the full travel of output shaft.
6. Install steering gear in the vehicle.
7. Connect the drag link to the pitman arm.
8. Connect the pump lines and fill the system with fluid.

Removal and Installation

1. Position a drain pan under the steering gear and disconnect the pressure line from the gear, the return line from the gear and the turning hoses if so equipped. Mark all lines for identification.
2. Remove the pitman arm from the sector shaft.
3. Disconnect the universal joint from the input shaft of the gear, sliding it up and off the shaft.
4. Remove the steering gear attaching bolts and remove the gear.

On Ford B-6000-7000 and F-800 with manual transmission: The front engine mount must be loosened. Remove the exhaust pipes shields and loosen the exhaust pipes. Remove the clutch spring bracket, from under the left side pipe. Unbolt the transmission mount and jack the transmission. Remove the mounting pads. Unbolt the clutch bracket from the steering gear. Unbolt the gear from the frame. Remove the floor board covering the gearshift and brake levers. Move the engine and transmission to the right and remove the gear.

5. To install, first position gear in vehicle and install and tighten attaching bolts.
6. Connect universal joint to the steering gear input shaft.
7. Install pitman arm on the sector shaft.
8. Connect all hydraulic lines in their original locations.
9. Fill power steering hydraulic system, start engine and check for leaks.

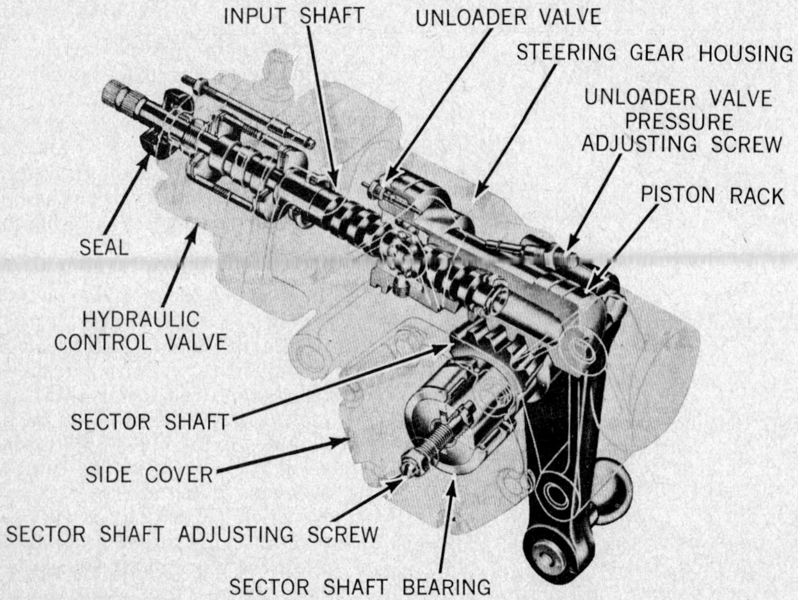

Ross model HF-64 integral steering gear (© Ford Motor Co.)

Ross HFB-52 Integral Power Steering Gear

C-Series

Sector Shaft Adjustment

NOTE: If access to the steering gear is possible, the sector shaft adjustment can be made with the steering gear installed in the vehicle. If access is not possible the steering gear will have to be removed from the vehicle. If the steering gear is to be adjusted while installed on the vehicle, disconnect the input coupling and pitman arm. Leave plumbing connected and start the engine and allow the vehicle to idle while performing the adjustment.

1. Loosen the locknut on the side cover adjusting screw. Adjust the screw to provide 23-28 in. lbs torque at the worm shaft as the steering gear is moved 90 degrees on each side of center.
2. Back the adjusting screw out one turn and note the torque required to move through 90 degrees on each side of center.
3. Move the adjusting screw in to provide a rise in torque of 2 to 4 in. lbs at a point within 45 degrees on each side of center. Tighten the locknut to 40-45 ft. lbs.
4. After tightening the locknut, the torque to rotate the worm shaft must not exceed 26 in. lbs at any point of the steering gear travel.

Removal and Installation

1. Place a drain pan under the steering gear. Disconnect the power steering pressure line at the gear and the return line at the gear. If equipped, disconnect the turning hoses.
2. Remove the cotter pin, bolt and nut (or castellated nut and cotter pin) holding the pitman arm to the sector shaft, and remove the

pitman arm from the sector shaft.

3. Remove the U-joint yoke and input shaft bolt and nut (or castellated nut and cotter pin). Mark for re-installation.
4. Remove the bolts and nuts holding the steering gear or the steering gear bracket to the frame side rail. Remove the unit from the vehicle.
5. To install, place the gear (or gear and bracket) on the side rail. Install the bolts, nuts and lock straps (if equipped). Advance the nuts to the next castellation, if necessary, and install the cotter pins.
6. Continue the installation in the reverse order of the removal.
7. Fill the power steering pump reservoir with fluid. Start the engine, turn the steering wheel from left to right, and check for fluid leaks.

Ross HPS-70 Semi-Integral Power Steering Gear

W Series

Mesh Load Adjustment

To provide close adjustment in the straight ahead position, the groove of the cam is cut shallower and narrower in the mid-position range of stud travel.

NOTE: Always adjust the mesh load with the wheels in the straight ahlead position. Backlash will occur if the wheels are turned to either side.

1. Disconnect the drag link and the power steering cylinder from the pitman arm and the universal joint from the gear input shaft.
2. Loosen the adjusting screw lock nut. Turn the adjusting screw clockwise until a 15 in. lb. torque is required to turn the steering gear through mid-position.
3. Turn the adjusting screw counterclockwise 1/8 turn.
4. Holding the adjusting screw in place, tighten the locknut to 15-20 ft-lbs. to lock the adjustment.
5. Turn the gear from left to right with the engine off then check the adjustment. The torque at the input shaft should be 2-8 in-lb. for the full travel.
6. Connect the drag link and power steering cylinder to the pitman arm, and the universal joint to the steering gear input shaft.

Removal & Installation

1. Remove the grill from the front of the cab.
2. Unlatch the cab and raise it to the full tilt position.
3. Mark the power steering hose location, and disconnect the hoses from the steering gear control valve fittings.
4. Remove the cotter pin and nut attaching the hydraulic cylinder to the pitman arm. Remove the cylinder stud from the pitman arm. Place the cylinder to one side.
5. Remove the cotter pin and nut attaching the drag link to the pitman arm. Remove the drag link stud from the pitman arm and place the drag link out of the way.
6. Remove the steering shaft universal joint nut, bolt, and flat washer. Separate the joint from the steering gear input shaft.
7. Remove the bolts that attach the gear and bracket to the frame bracket. Remove the nuts, flat washers, and cotter pins and remove the gear and bracket from the vehicle.
8. Secure the gear and bracket in a vise and remove the pitman arm from the output shaft.
9. Remove the bolts and nuts attaching the gear to the bracket. Separate the gear from the bracket.
10. Place the gear on the bracket. Install and tighten the bolts and nuts.
11. Install the pitman arm on the output shaft with the notches on the output shaft and pitman arm aligned. Tighten the clamp bolt and install the cotter pin.
12. Place the steering gear and bracket on the frame bracket and install the bolts, washers, and nuts. Tighten the nuts and install the cotter pins.
13. Connect the drag link to the pitman arm. Tighten the nut on the pitman arm and install the cotter pin.
14. Connect the hydraulic cylinder to the pitman arm and tighten the nut. Install the cotter pin.
15. With the front wheels and steering gear in the straight ahead position, place the steering shaft universal joint on the steering gear input shaft. Install a new bolt, nut, and hardened washer, tighten the nut to 31-32 ft-lbs. *Be sure that the bolt passes through the slot on the steering gear input shaft.*
16. Connect the hoses to the control valve.
17. Fill the fluid reservoir. Lower the cab. Start the engine and turn the steering wheel from left to right three or four times to bleed the air from the system.
18. Install the grill on the front of the cab.

Linkage Assist

Removal and Installation

NOTE: See "Power Steering" in the General Repair Section for control valve overhaul and service procedures.

1. Disconnect pressure and return hoses at valve assembly.
2. Cap hoses and connections at valve assembly. Fasten hoses so that ends are above fluid level in reservoir and tag them for reinstallation identification.
3. Disconnect ball ends at steering arm and steering knuckle arm and remove control valve and drag link assembly.
4. To install, connect control valve sliding sleeve end at steering arm and install nut and cotter pin.
5. Connect drag link end to steering knuckle arm and install nut and cotter pin.
6. Connect pressure and return hydraulic lines at valve assembly, tightening securely.
7. Refill pump reservoir.
8. Bleed system by turning steering wheel back and forth several times while the engine is idling.
9. Recheck fluid level and refill if necessary.

Power Cylinder

Removal and Installation

1. Disconnect hydraulic lines at power cylinder and cap ends and connections at cylinder.
2. Remove cotter pin and nut at ball studs (and tie rod clamp U-bolts on leightweight trucks). Remove cylinder.
3. To install, insert ball stud into place on axle bracket and install nut and cotter pin, tighten nut securely.
4. Rotate steering wheel to extreme right turn position.
5. Install tie rod clamp loosely (on medium weight trucks loosen tie rod clamp and install ball stud and nut).
6. Position cylinder piston rod in fully retracted position and tighten U-bolt clamps on tie rod. On medium weight trucks the ball stud will have to be connected to tie rod clamp bracket before tightening clamp bolts. Clamp should be mounted on tie rod at a 20° angle to the vertical. Nuts on U-bolts are torqued to 40 ft. lbs.
7. Connect hydraulic lines to power cylinder in their original position.
8. Bleed system by turning the steering wheel back and forth several times with the engine idling.

Power Steering Pump

Removal and Installation

NOTE: See "Power Steering" in General Repair Section for power steering pump overhaul procedures.

1. Loosen pump lower mounting and locking bolts and remove the belt.

2. Place a container under pump and disconnect both pump hoses.
3. Remove mounting and locking bolts and remove pump and brackets.
4. To install, position pump on engine and install retaining and locking bolts.
5. Install drive belt and adjust. Tighten pump brackets.
6. Connect pressure and return hoses, routing them in the same position they were in before removal.
7. Fill pump reservoir.
8. Start engine and turn steering wheel all the way left and right to bleed the system. Stop engine and recheck fluid level, refilling if necessary.

CLUTCH

9.37", 10", 11", 11.5", 12" and 13" Single Disc

Removal & Installation

1. Disconnect the release lever retracting spring and pushrod at the lever.
2. If so equipped, remove the slave cylinder attaching bolts.
3. Remove the transmission.
4. If there is no dust cover on the flywheel housing remove the starter. Remove the release lever and bearing and remove the housing.
5. If the flywheel housing has a dust cover, remove it with the housing. Remove the release lever and bearing from the clutch housing. Mark the presure plate and cover assembly and the flywheel, so that the parts can be reinstalled in the same position.
6. Loosen the pressure plate attaching bolts evenly until the springs are loose then remove the bolts, pressure plate assembly and clutch disc. Do not remove the pilot bushing unless it is to be replaced.
7. To install, position the disc on the flywheel and install a pilot tool or spare transmission spline shaft.
8. Install the pressure plate assembly over the aligning tool and align the marks made during removal. Install the retaining bolts, tightening securely.
9. Remove pilot tool and apply a light coat of lithium-base grease to the hub splines of the clutch disc.
10. Apply lithium-base grease to the sides of the driving lugs.
11. Position throwout bearing and bearing hub on the release lever and install release lever on the trunnion in the flywheel housing.
12. Apply a light film of lithium-base grease to the release lever fingers and to the lever trunnion or fulcrum. Fill the angular groove of the release bearing hub with grease.
13. If removed, install the flywheel housing, tightening bolts securely.
14. Install the starter motor if it was removed.
15. Apply a light film of lithium-base grease to the transmission front bearing retainer and install the transmission assembly on the clutch housing, tightening attaching bolts securely.
16. Install the slave cylinder, if applicable.
17. Adjust the clutch linkage and install the clutch housing dust cover.

14" Single Plate Clutch

Removal & Installation

1. Disconnect the clutch pedal assist spring, removing the left-hand exhaust pipe from the manifold if necessary.
2. Disconnect the release lever retracting spring and remove the slave cylinder attaching bolts, if applicable.
3. Remove the transmission.
4. Insert two ¾" wood blocks between the throwout bearing housing and the rear surface of the pressure plate assembly.
5. Remove the clutch to flywheel bolts and remove the flywheel ring and pressure plate assembly. Remove the clutch disc.
6. To install, position the clutch disc and pressure plate assembly on the flywheel and start the bolts. NOTE: the long hub of the clutch disc faces the rear.
7. Insert a spare transmission splined shaft or a disc aligning tool through the disc and into the pilot bushing. Tighten pressure plate bolts evenly and securely.
8. Remove the wood blocks and aligning tool or shaft.
9. Install the transmission.
10. Install the clutch slave cylinder.
11. Connect the release lever retracting spring and exhaust pipe.
12. Connect the clutch pedal assist spring.
13. Check internal clutch adjustment, linkage adjustment and correct if necessary.

13" Double Disc Clutch

Removal & Installation

1. Disconnect the clutch pedal reacting spring.
2. Remove the muffler inlet pipe if necessary.
3. Remove the bolts that attach the slave cylinder to the clutch housing.
4. Disconnect the slave cylinder push rod at the release lever. Disconnect the release lever retaining spring.
5. Remove the transmission as detailed in "Manual Transmission Removal and Installation."
6. Remove the dust cover from the clutch housing.
7. Remove the clutch release bearing and hub from the release lever.
8. Mark the center drive plate, pressure plate, cover assembly, and flywheel so that the parts may be installed in the same relative position.
9. Loosen the pressure plate and cover attaching bolts evenly until the pressure plate springs are expanded. Remove the bolts.
10. Remove the pressure plate and cover, the discs, and the intermediate pressure plate through the opening in the bottom of the clutch housing.
11. *Remove the pilot bearing only if replacement is necessary.*
12. Install the pilot bearing if it was removed.

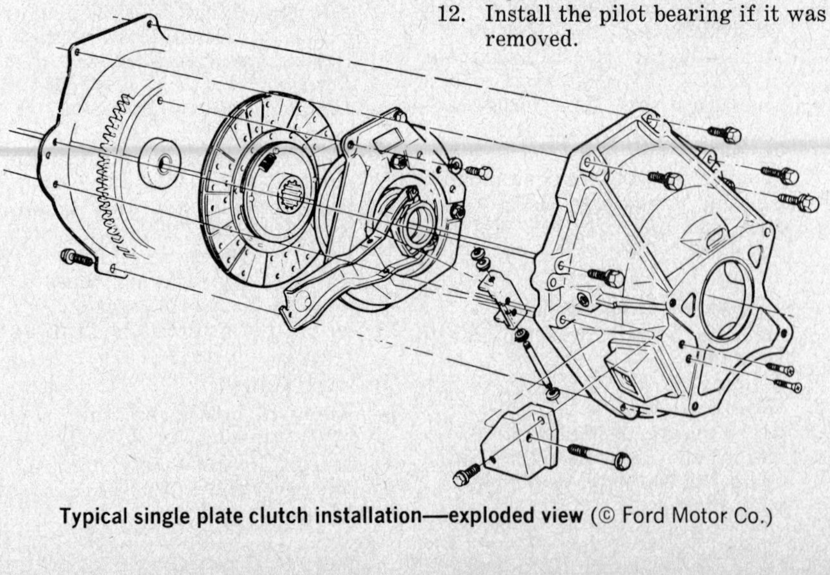

Typical single plate clutch installation—exploded view (© Ford Motor Co.)

13. Position the discs and second pressure plate on the flywheel so that the pilot tool can enter the clutch pilot bushing. *When installing the original pressure plate and cover assembly, align the assembly and flywheel according to the match marks made during the removal operations. The long end of the clutch disc hub must face the rear of the transmission.* The front (flywheel) side of the center drive plate is stamped "flywheel side" on one of the lugs.
14. Position the clutch discs, center drive plate, pressure plate and cover assembly on the flywheel and install the retaining bolts that fasten the assembly to the flywheel. Tighten the bolts to specification. Remove the clutch pilot tool.
15. Position the clutch release bearing and hub on the release lever.
16. Install the transmission assembly on the clutch housing and tighten the bolts to specification.
17. Install the slave cylinder and tighten the bolts.
18. Adjust the slave cylinder push rod. Connect the release lever reacting spring and (if removed) install the muffler left inlet pipe. Connect the clutch pedal reacting spring.
19. Lubricate the release bearing through the grease fitting with ½ oz of the specified lubricant.
20. Install the clutch housing dust cover.

14" and 15½" Double Disc Clutches

Removal & Installation

1. Disconnect the clutch pedal assist spring. If necessary, remove the left muffler inlet pipe.
2. Disconnect the release lever reacting spring. Remove the bolts that attach the slave cylinder. Remove the slave cylinder.
3. Remove the transmission as detailed in "Manual Transmission Removal and Installation."

NOTE: Pull the transmission straight out until it is clear of the clutch assembly. An unsupported, partially removed or installed transmission can spring or damage the clutch plates.

4. Insert two ¾ in. wood blocks between the release bearing housing and the rear surface of the pressure plate assembly.
5. Remove the clutch-to-flywheel bolts and remove the flywheel ring and pressure plate assembly.
6. Remove the rear disc, intermediate plate, and the front disc from the engine. If necessary, remove the clutch drive pin retaining set screw and remove the four intermediate pressure plate drive pins.
7. Install the pressure plate drive pins in the flywheel if they were removed. Make sure they are a press fit. Oversize pins are available for service. Install the intermediate pressure plate and check the clearance between the pin heads and slots in the pressure plate. A clearance of .006-.010 in. is required, measured on the same side of all pins. Replace the pins or plate if necessary. Remove the intermedidate plate, and using an adjustable square to maintain pin head alignment, install the pin set screws.
8. Place the front driven disc (shorter hub than rear disc) in the flywheel with the hub facing the rear. Set the intermediate pressure plate in the flywheel, aligning the slots with the pins. The side marked FRONT should face the engine. Position the read driven plate in the flywheel with the long end of the splined hub toward the rear. Insert the clutch disc aligning tool through the two discs and into the pilot bushing. Place the main (rear) pressure plate and flywheel ring assembly in position and start the bolts. Tighten the pressure plate bolts evenly and tighten them to specification.
9. Remove the wood blocks from the release bearing housing and pressure plate. Remove the spline aligning tool.
10. Install the transmission.
11. If the vehicle is equipped with a slave cylinder, install the slave cylinder on the clutch housing. Connect the release lever reacting spring and the left-hand muffler inlet pipe if it was removed.
12. Connect the clutch pedal assist spring. Check the internal clutch adjustment, and make necessary correction.

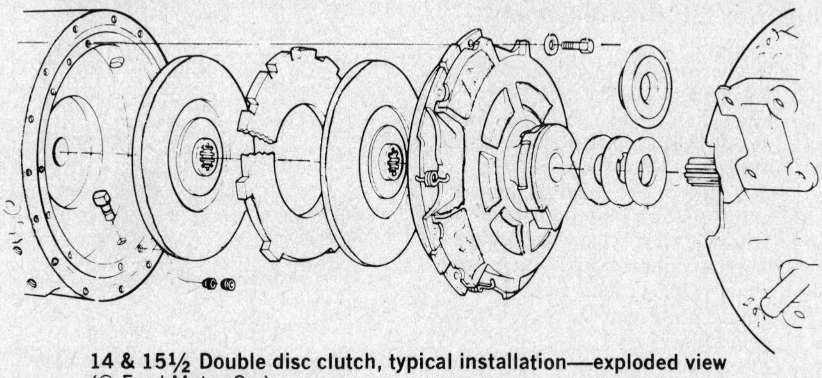

14 & 15½ Double disc clutch, typical installation—exploded view
(© Ford Motor Co.)

Adjustment

Mechanical Clutch Linkage Adjustment

The clutch pedal free travel is the distance between the clutch pedal in the fully released position and the pedal position at which the clutch release fingers contact the clutch release bearing (this can be felt).

The clutch pedal total travel is the distance between the floor pan and the top of the pedal when the clutch is in the fully released position.

Only the clutch pedal free travel is adjusted. If the pedal free travel is not within 11/16" to 1⅛", adjust the clutch release rod until correct free travel is obtained.

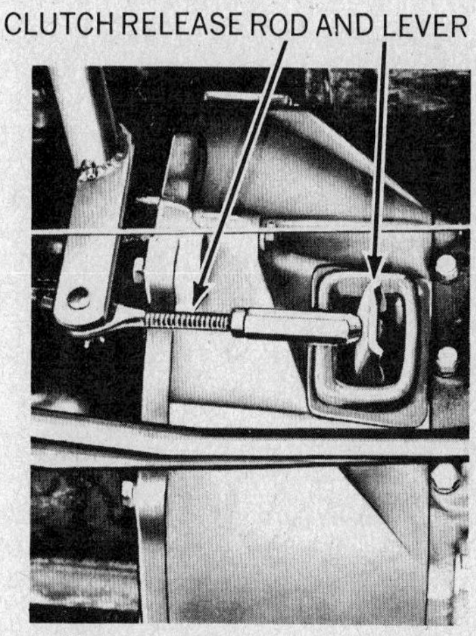

Clutch adjustment—Econoline
(© Ford Motor Co.)

Econoline

First the clutch pedal total travel is adjusted. It should be between 7½" and 7¾". Adjustment is made by loosening the locknut on the pedal stop eccentric bolt and turning the eccentric bolt until correct total travel is obtained. Tighten locknut.

Check the clutch pedal free travel. It should be 1⅛" to 1⅜". Adjustment is made at the clutch release rod turnbuckle.

1973-77 Bronco

If the clutch pedal total travel is not within 6 11/16" or 6¾" to 7", move the clutch pedal bumper and bracket up or down to obtain required free travel.

Check and adjust pedal free travel. It should be ¾″ to 1½″. Adjustment is made at the clutch release rod turnbuckle.

F- and N-Series

Total pedal travel is adjusted at the pedal bumper stop. Pedal free travel is made at the clutch release rod.

F-Series

1. Measure the clutch pedal free-play by depressing the pedal slowly until the free-play between the release bearing assembly and the pressure plate is removed. Note this measurement. The difference between this measurement and when the pedal is not depressed is the free-play measurement.
2. If the free-play measurement is less than ¾″, the clutch linkage must be adjusted.
3. Loosen the two jam nuts on the release rod under the truck and back off both nuts several turns.
4. Loosen or tighten the first jam nut (nearest the release lever) against the bullet (rod extension) until a free-play measurement of ¾-1½″ is obtained. A free-play measurement closer to 1½″ is more desirable.
5. When the correct free-play measurement is obtained, hold the first jam nut in position and securely tighten the other nut against the first.
6. Recheck the free-play adjustment.

NOTE: Total pedal travel is fixed and is not adjustable.

Hydraulic Actuated Clutch Adjustment

Before adjusting hydraulic clutch, check the level of fluid in the master cylinder reservoir, filling to within ½″ of the top if necessary. Bleed the hydraulic system as descibed below.

Bleeding Hydraulic Clutch

1. Attach a funnel to the bleeder screw of the slave cylinder by means of a transparent bleeder hose. The funnel must be higher than the master cylinder.
2. Pour fluid into the funnel as the system is filling, *being careful not to pour bubbles in the fluid.* Bleeder screw must be open.
3. Close the bleeder screw when master cylinder reservoir is full.
4. Check the slave cylinder pushrod total travel which should be 1⅛″.
5. The clutch master cylinder relief port must be open in order to bleed the system. Clutch master cylinder pushrod lash of ¼″ is required on the P-500 and 5000 series vehicles to permit the conventional type master cylinder piston to return to the piston stop ring and open the relief port. The clutch master cylinder cannot be adjusted on the P-350, 400, 3500 and 4000 series vehicles. In the case of tilt-cab (C-series) master cylinder, the O-ring seal on the end of the pushrod must not seat against the piston. Uncovering of the piston port is accomplished by adjustment of the pushrod to a piston lash of ¼″. Forcing the clutch pedal to compress the pedal bumper more than normal by jamming a suitable tool between the pedal pad and the floor insures a complete uncovering of the relief port.

Hydraulic Clutch Adjustment

There are two adjustments for obtaining clutch pedal free travel. The initial pedal free travel should be ¼″ for all models. On F, N, NT, and T Series vehicles the pedal height is first adjusted to 8-1/16″ to 8-3/16″ at the pedal stop. Turn eccentric bolt on pedal to obtain an initial pedal free travel of 3/16″ to ⅜″. Remove retracting spring, push slave cylinder pushrod as far forward as possible and release lever back until it contacts the release fingers. Adjust the nut on the pushrod for a clearance of ¼″ between pushrod adjusting nut and release lever. A total pedal travel of at least 2″ should result.

On P and C Series trucks, the initial pedal free travel is that distance of pedal travel before the master cylinder pushrod contacts the piston. On C Series vehicles this adjustment is made with the eccentric bolt and on P Series it is made by rotating the master cylinder pushrod. Obtain an initial pedal free travel of ¼″. With the retracting spring removed, the slave cylinder pushrod held completely forward and the release lever held in contact with the release fingers, turn adjusting nut on the slave cylinder pushrod to obtain a final pedal free travel of approximately 2″.

Internal Clutch Adjustment

1. Remove inspection cover from the bottom of the clutch housing.
2. Disconnect the retracting spring and hold the release lever against the throwout bearing. Measure the distance between the throwout bearing and the clutch spring hub (synchromatic transmission) or clutch brake (non-synchromatic transmission). On vehicles with the 14″ single plate clutch, this distance should be 11/32″ to 13/32″. On all Spicer clutches, also adjust the adjusting ring to obtain a ⅛″ clearance between release yoke fingers and the throwout bearing.

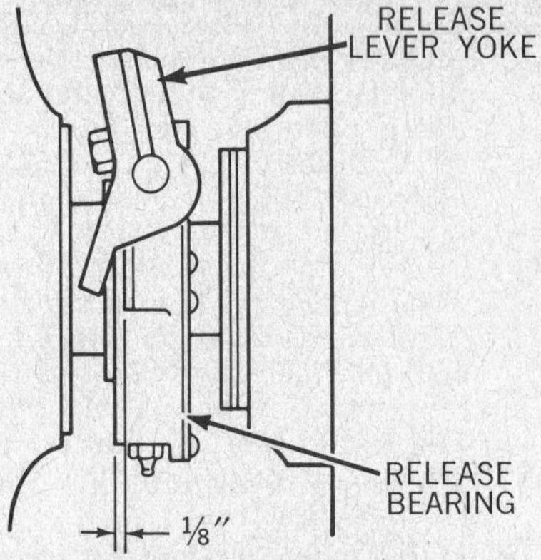

Spicer clutch adjustment
(© Ford Motor Co.)

3. If adjustment is necessary, rotate the clutch assembly to get at the adjusting lockring and bolt. Remove the bolt and lockring.

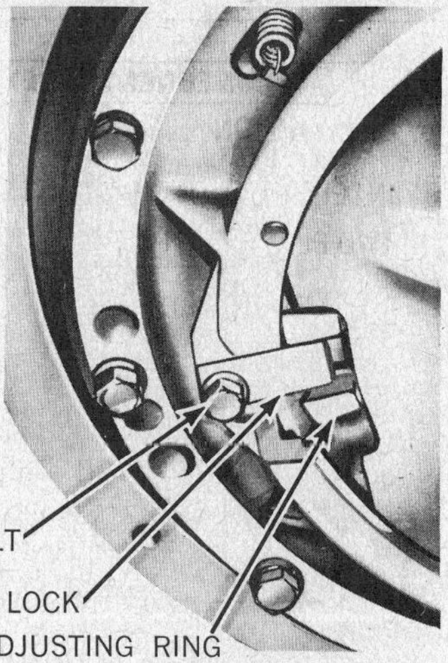

Internal clutch adjustment
(© Ford Motor Co.)

4. With clutch pedal held or blocked in the released position, rotate the adjusting ring (use a pry bar) clockwise to move the throwout bearing toward the flywheel or counterclockwise to move the throwout bearing away

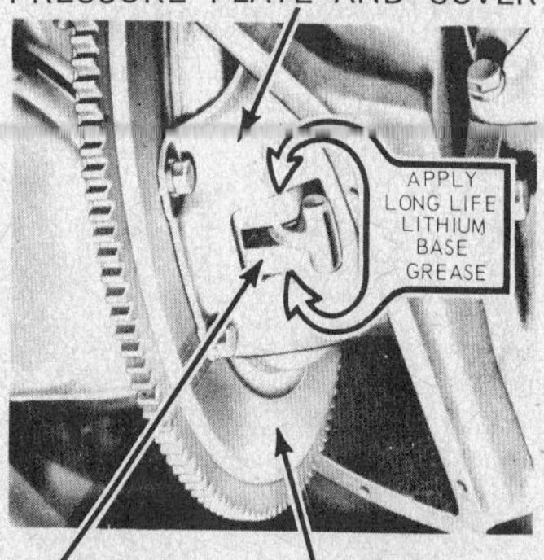

Pressure plate lubrication point
(© Ford Motor Co.)

from the flywheel. Rotating the adjusting ring one lug position moves the throwout bearing about 1/32″.

5. Let clutch pedal return to engage the clutch, then recheck clearance.
6. Install lock and bolt.
7. Adjust clutch linkage.
8. Connect the retracting spring and replace the clutch housing cover.

TRANSFER CASE

Reference

Transfer case overhaul procedures for light duty trucks are found in the General Repair section of this book.

Transfer Case

Dana 20

1. Shift the transfer case into neutral and remove the fan shroud. Raise vehicle, support transfer case shield, then remove shield.
2. Drain the transmission and transfer case lubricant then disconnect driveshafts from transfer case.
3. Disconnect speedometer cable and shift rods.
4. A tool must be placed in the transmission shift levers to keep the input shaft roller bearings from falling out.
5. Remove the frame crossmember from side frame and transfer case, first raising transmission and removing adapter insulators.
6. Disconnect the shift rod from the transfer case shift lever bracket.
7. Remove the shift lever bracket to transfer case adapter bolt and let the assembly hang.
8. Position a transmission jack under the transfer case, remove the transfer case to transmission attaching bolts, then pull the transfer case back until it clears the transmission output shaft.
9. To install, place the transfer case in position and install the attaching bolts, tightening securely.
10. Install the shift lever to transfer case adapter. Connect the shift rod to the shift lever bracket.
11. Raise the transmission and transfer case high enough to provide clearance for installing the crossmember. Position the upper insulators on the crossmember, install the crossmember, then lower the transmission and install the bolts, tightening securely.
12. Remove fabricated tool from shift levers and install the shift rods.
13. Connect the speedometer cable.
14. Install the forward and rear driveshafts.
15. Fill the transmission and transfer case with lubricant.
16. Install transfer case shield.

Dana 21

1. Raise the vehicle on a hoist and disconnect the front and rear driveshafts.
2. Disconnect the shift rod from transfer case shift lever.
3. Remove transmission extension housing to transfer case attaching bolts and remove the transfer case.
4. To install, position transfer case and new gasket to extension housing and install attaching bolts.
5. Connect shift rod to shift lever.
6. Connect the front and rear driveshafts.
7. Lower vehicle and check for proper operation.

Dana 24

1. Raise the vehicle on a hoist and drain transfer case lubricant.
2. Disconnect front and rear driveshafts, speedometer cable and shift rods.
3. Position a transmission jack under the transfer case and remove mounting bolts. Remove transfer case.
4. To install, raise transfer case on the jack and install nuts on mounting studs.
5. Connect shift rod, speedometer cable and driveshafts.
6. Fill transfer case to filler plug with lubricant.

New Process Model 205

1. Drain the Transfer case and remove the rear drive shaft.
2. On F-250 models remove the front drive shaft from the transfer case. On F-100 models remove the front drive shaft and remove the transmission adapter to transfer case bolts.
3. Disconnect the shift rod and speedometer cable. Disconnect the reaction bar.
4. Support the transfer case with a jack and remove the transfer case mounting bolts.
5. Remove the transfer case from the vehicle.
6. To install reverse the removal procedures. Fill transfer case to the filler plug with the proper lubricant.

Rockwell (223-C9, 223-C11 & 223-C1)

1. Drain transfer case and disconnect speedometer cable.
2. Disconnect front and rear driveshafts and secure with wire or rope *so that they do not hang*.
3. Disconnect parking brake at the bellcrank and secure rod out of the way.
4. Disconnect de-clutch and shift rods.
5. Support the transfer case with a transmission jack and remove the support bracket bolts. Remove transfer case.
6. Install with the use of a transmission jack. Install and tighten mounting bolts.
7. Connect and adjust parking brake rod at the bellcrank.
8. Connect de-clutch and shift rods.
9. Connect front and rear driveshafts.
10. Connect speedometer.
11. Fill transfer case with lubricant.

New Process Model 203

1. Drain the transfer case by removing the power take-off lower bolts and the front output rear cover lower bolts.
2. Disconnect the front axle driveshaft from the flange at the transfer case.
3. Disconnect the shift rods from the transfer case.
4. Disconnect the speedometer cable and lockout light switch wire from the transfer case rear output shaft housing.
5. On F-250 pick-ups (1975-77), disconnect the front input and output shafts from the transfer case flanges. On all others, remove the transfer case-to-transmission adapter attaching bolts. Disconnect the rear axle driveshaft at the transfer case flange.
6. Position a transmission jack under the transfer case and secure it with a chain.
7. Remove the transfer case mounting bolts and remove the unit from the vehicle. On F-250 models (1975-77), remove the stabilizer bar-to-transfer case attaching bolt before lowering the case.
8. Install the transfer case in the reverse order of removal. Fill the transfer case to the filler plug with the proper lubricant.

Transfer Case Shift Linkage Adjustment

New Process Model 205—F-250

Manual Transmission

Adjust the length of the shift rod between the transfer case and the shift lever with the lever in 4WD-Low so that the distance between the rear face of the transmission and the shift lever-to-rod clevis pin is 3.94 to 3.82″.

Automatic Transmission

Adjust the length of the shift rod between the transfer case and the shift lever with the lever in 4WD-Low so that the distance between the upper surface of the automatic transmission extension housing and the upper horizontal edge of the shift lever is 0.640 to 0.600″.

New Process 203 Full-Time 4WD

F-100, F-150 (1975-77)

1. Place the shift lever in the Low position.
2. Remove the adjusting stud nuts from the shift rods under the truck.
3. Disconnect the front driveshaft at the transfer case.
4. Remove the transfer case shifter.
5. Unsnap the top snap of the splash boot, peel the boot back and install a new adjustment pin in the rear of the shifter bracket. The pin is 1.5″ long, ¼″ in diameter and must be of breakable material. The pin cannot be reached once the shifter is installed.
6. Reinstall the shifter. tightening the rear bolt to 12-17 ft lbs and the front bolt to 70-90 ft lbs.
7. Move the lower lever on the transfer case completely forward and the upper lever completely rearward.
8. Install new adjusting stud nuts and tighten them to 20-25 ft lbs.
9. Connect the front driveshaft.

F-250 (1975-77)

1. Move the transfer case shifter to the low position.
2. Loosen the adjusting stud nuts.
3. Unsnap the top splash boot snap and peel the boot back. Install a new adjustment pin in the rear of the shifter bracket. The pin is the same size as previously mentioned for the F-100. If the pin is made of steel, it must be removed after tightening the adjusting studs.
4. Move the lower lever on the transfer case completely forward and the upper lever completely rearward.
5. Install new adjusting nuts and tighten them to 15-20 ft lbs.

1978-79 F series and Bronco

1. Place the shifter lever in neutral Remove the two adjusting nut studs.
2. Install 0.25 inch diameter alignment pin (1.25 in. long) through the shifter assembly.
3. Align as follows:
   a. Bottom lever, (lock lever)—rotate clockwise to the forward position.
   b. Top lever, (range lever)—place in the mid-pisition or the neutral position.
4. Re-position the two shift rods and tighten new adjusting stud nuts to 15-20 ft. lbs.
5. Remove the alignment pin from the shifter assembly.

Rockwell (C223-C9, 223-C11 & 223-C1)

1. Before adjusting transfer case shift linkage, set the engaged and disengaged rod to 41.52 in. (dimension A) and the high-neutral-low rod to 40.18 in. (dimension A).

RODS ARE TO BE SET TO THESE DIMENSIONS PRIOR TO INSTALLATION	A
ENGAGED & DISENGAGED ROD	41.52
HIGH NEUTRAL—LOW ROD	40.18

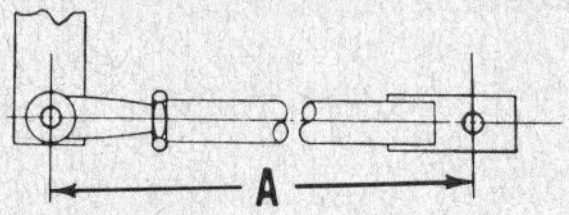

Rockwell transfer case rod adjustments (© Ford Motor Co.)

2. Run the jamnut on each clevis to full thread. Install clevises in transfer case so they bottom in shift rails.
3. Back off clevises (not over 90 degrees) so clevis pins are horizontal to the ground. Tighten the jamnuts.
4. When adjusting the control and shift lever rods the levers should be ¾ in. from the seat cushion frame with the seat in full forward position. The shift rails in the transfer case should be located in detent disengage and low position.

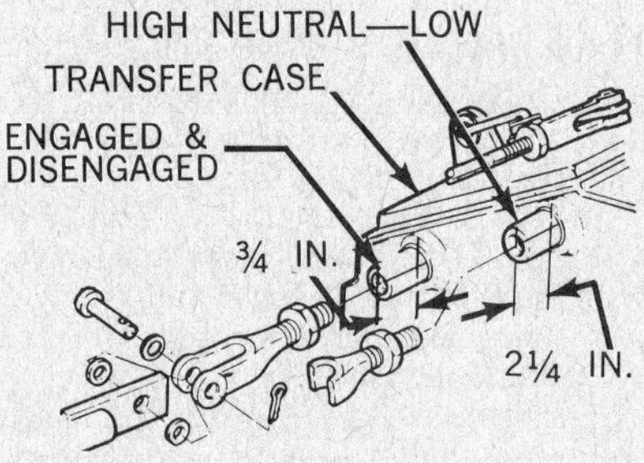

Transfer case control lever rod and shift lever rod (© Ford Motor Co.)

MANUAL TRANSMISSION

Reference

Manual transmission overhaul procedures for light duty trucks are found in the General Repair section of this book.

Transmission

Ford 3.03 3-Speed

1973-77 Bronco
Removal and Installation

1. Shift the transfer case into Neutral.
2. Remove the bolts attaching the fan shroud to the radiator support, if so equipped.
3. Raise the vehicle on a hoist.
4. Support the transfer case shield with a jack and remove the bolts that attach the shield to the frame side rails. Remove the shield.
5. Drain the transmission and transfer case lubricant. To drain the transmission lubricant, remove the lower extension housing-to-transmission bolt.
6. Disconnect the front and rear driveshafts at the transfer case.
7. Disconnect the speedometer cable at the transfer case.
8. Disconnect the T.R.S. switch, if so equipped.
9. Disconnect the shift rods from the transmission shift levers. Place the First-Reverse gear shift lever into the First gear position and insert the fabricated tool. The tool consists of a length of rod. the same diameter as the holes in the shift levers, which is bent in such a way to fit in the holes in the two shift levers and hold them in the position stated above. More important, this tool will prevent the input shaft roller bearings from dropping into the transmission and output shaft. THIS TOOL IS A MUST
10. Support the engine with a jack.
11. Remove the two cotter pins, bolts, washers, plate and insulators that secure the crossmember to the transfer case adapter.
12. Remove the crossmember-to-frame side support attaching bolts.
13. Position a transmission jack under the transfer case and remove the upper insulators from the crossmember. Remove the crossmember.
14. Roll back the boot enclosing the transfer case shift linkage. Remove the threaded cap holding the shift lever assembly to the shift bracket. Remove the shift lever assembly.
15. Remove the two lower bolts attaching the transmission to the flywheel housing.
16. Reposition the transmission jack under the transmission and secure it with a chain.
17. Remove the two upper bolts securing the transmission to the flywheel housing. Move the transmission and transfer case rearward and downward out of the vehicle.

18. Move the assembly to a bench and remove the transfer case-to-transmission attaching bolts.
19. Slide the transmission assembly off the transfer case.
20. To install, position the transfer case to the transmission. Apply an oil-resistant sealer to the bolt threads and install the attaching bolts. Tighten to 42-50 ft lbs.
21. Position the transmission and transfer case on a transmission jack and secure them with a chain.
22. Raise the transmission and transfer case assembly into position and install the transmission case to the flywheel housing.
23. Install the two upper and two lower transmission attaching bolts and torque them to 37-42 ft lbs.
24. Position the transfer case shift lever and install the threaded cap to the shift bracket. Reposition the rubber boot.
25. Raise the transmission and transfer case high enough to provide clearance for installing the crossmember. Position the upper insulators to the crossmember and install the crossmember-to-frame side support attaching bolts.
26. Align the bolt holes in the transfer case adapter with those in the crossmember, then lower the transmission and remove the jack.
27. Install the crossmember-to-transfer case adapter bolts, nuts, insulators, plates and washers. Tighten the nuts and secure them with cotter pins.
28. Remove the engine jack.
29. Remove the fabricated tool and connect each shift rod to its respective lever on the transmission. Adjust the linkage.
30. Connect the speedometer cable.
31. Connect the T.R.S. switch. if so equipped.
32. Install the front and rear driveshaftshafts to the transfer case.
33. Fill the transmission and transfer case to the bottom of the filler hole with the recommended lubricant.
34. Position the transfer case shield to the frame side rails and install the attaching bolts.
35. Lower the vehicle.
36. Install the fan shroud, if so equipped.
37. Check the operation of the transfer case and the transmission shift linkage.

Econoline

Removal and Installation

1. Raise the vehicle on a hoist and drain the lubricant from the transmission by removing the drain plug if the vehicle is so equipped. For models without drain plugs, remove the lower extension housing-to-transmission bolt.
2. Disconnect the drive shaft from the flange at the transmission. Secure the front end of the drive shaft out of the way with lock wire.
3. Disconnect the speedometer cable from the extension housing and disconnect the gear shift rods from the transmission shift levers. Remove the wire to the TCS switch if so equipped.
4. Position a transmission jack under the transmission. Secure the transmission to the jack.
5. Raise the transmission slightly and remove the four bolts retaining the transmission support crossmember to the frame side rails. Remove the bolt retaining the transmission extension housing to the crossmember.
6. Remove the four transmission-to-flywheel housing bolts.
7. Position engine support bar (Tool T65E-6000-J) to the frame.
8. Lower the transmission.
9. To install, make certain that the machined surfaces of the transmission case and the flywheel housing are free of dirt, paint and burrs.
10. Install a guide pin in each lower mounting bolt hole.
11. Start the input shaft through the release bearing. Align the splines on the input shaft with the splines in the clutch disc. Move the transmission forward on the guide pins until the input shaft pilot enters the bearing or bushing in the crankshaft. If the transmission front bearing retainer binds up on the clutch release bearing hub, work the release bearing lever until the hub slides onto the transmission front bearing retainer. Install the two transmission-to-flywheel housing upper mounting bolts and lock washers. Remove the two guide pins and install the lower mounting bolts and lock washers.
12. Raise the jack slightly and remove the engine support bar.
13. Position the support crossmember on the frame side rails and install the retaining bolts. Install the extension housing-to-crossmember retaining bolt.
14. Connect the gear shift rods and the speedometer cable.
15. Install the drive shaft and torque the attaching bolts to specification.
16. Fill the transmission to the bottom of the filler hole with the recommended lubricant.
17. Adjust the clutch pedal free travel and shift linkage as required.

F-100, 250 and 1978-80 Bronco

Removal and Installation

1. Raise the vehicle and position safety stands. Support the engine with a jack and wood block placed under the oil pan.
2. Drain the transmission lubricant by removing the drain plug if the vehicle is so equipped. For models without drain plugs, remove the lower extension housing-to-transmission bolt.
3. Position a transmission jack under the transmission.
4. Disconnect the gear shift linkage at the transmission.
5. If the vehicle has a four-wheel drive, remove the transfer case shift lever bracket from the transmission.
6. Disconnect the speedometer cable.
7. Disconnect the drive shaft from the transmission.
8. Remove the transmission-to-clutch housing attaching bolts.
9. Move transmission to the rear until the input shaft clears the clutch housing and lower the transmission. *Do not depress the clutch pedal while the transmission is removed.*
10. Before installing the transmission, apply a light film of lubricant to the clutch disc splines, release bearing inner hub surfaces, release lever fulcrum and fork and the transmission front bearing retainer. Exercise care to avoid contaminating the clutch disc with excessive grease.
11. Place the transmission on a transmission jack. Raise the transmission until the input shaft splines are in line with the clutch disc splines. The clutch release bearing and hub must be properly positioned in the release lever fork.
12. Install a guide stud in each lower clutch housing-to-transmission case mounting bolt and align the splines on the input shaft with the splines on the clutch disc.
13. Slide the transmission forward on the guide studs until it contacts the clutch housing.
14. Install the two transmission to flywheel housing upper mounting bolts and nuts. Remove the two guide studs and install the lower mounting bolts.
15. Connect the speedometer cable and the driven gear.
16. Install the drive shaft.
17. Connect each shift rod to its respective lever on the transmission.
18. If the vehicle is equipped with

four-wheel drive, install the four-wheel drive shaft bracket.
19. Fill the transmission to the proper level with an approved lubricant.
20. Adjust the clutch pedal free travel and shift linkage as required.

Warner T-87G

Removal and Installation

1. Raise and support the truck.
2. Drain the lubricant.
3. Support the transmission with a jack.
4. Disconnect the gearshift linkage at the transmission.
5. If the vehicle is a 4WD, remove the transfer case shift lever bracket from the transmission.
6. Disconnect the brake cable clevis at the cam and remove the cable clamp.
7. Disconnect the speedometer cable.
8. Remove the driveshaft and wire it aside.
9. Remove the transmission attaching bolts and remove the transmission.
10. Installation is the reverse of removal.
11. Fill the transmission with the proper lubricant. Lower the vehicle.

Warner T-18, T-19 4-Speed

Removal and Installation

1. Disconnect the back-up light switch located at the rear of the gearshift housing cover.
2. Remove the rubber boot, floor mat, and the body floor pan cover, and remove the transmission shift lever. Remove the weather pad and pad retainer.
3. Raise the truck and position safety stands. Position a transmission jack under the transmission, and disconnect the speedometer cable.
4. If the truck is equipped with band-type parking brake, disconnect the brake cable clevis at the cam. Remove the brake cable conduit clamp.
5. Remove the front U-joint flange attaching bolts. Remove the bolts that attach the coupling shaft center support to the crossmember and wire the coupling shaft and drive shaft to one side. On F-100-350 Series trucks, remove the transmission rear support.
6. Remove the transmission attaching bolts.
7. Move the transmission to the rear until the input shaft clears the clutch housing, and lower the transmission.

Before installing the transmission, apply a light film of lubricant to the clutch disc splines, release bearing inner hub surfaces, release lever fulcrum and fork, and the transmission front bearing retainer. Care must be exercised to avoid excessive grease from contaminating the clutch disc.

8. Place the transmission on a transmission jack, and raise the transmission until the input shaft splines are aligned with the clutch disc splines. The clutch release bearing and hub must be properly positioned in the release lever fork.
9. Install guide studs in the clutch housing and slide the transmission forward on the guide studs until it is in position on the clutch housing. Install the attaching bolts and nuts. Remove the guide studs and install the two lower attaching bolts.
5. Connect the speedometer cable and driven gear and parking brake clevis. Install the brake cable conduit clamp, and shift linkage.
6. Install the bolts attaching the coupling shaft center support to the crossmember.
7. Install the bolts attaching the front U-joint flange to the transmission output shaft flange. On F-100-350 Series trucks, install the transmission rear support.
8. Connect the back-up light switch.
9. Install the shift lever and lubricate the spherical ball seat with lubricant.
10. Install the weather pad and pad retainer. Install the floor pan cover, floor mat and boot.

F-150-F-250 (4x4)—With T-18 Transmission

1. Open the door and cover seat. Remove the shift knobs. Remove the transmission shift lever boot assembly.
2. Remove the screws holding the floor mat. Remove the screws holding the access cover to the floor pan. Place the shift lever in reverse and remove the cover.
3. Remove the insulator and the dust cover. Remove the transfer case shift lever. Remove the bolts holding the shift cover and the gasket.
4. Cover the shift cover opening to protect the transmission from dirt during the removal procedure.
5. Raise the vehicle on a hoist. Drain the transmission.
6. Disconnect the front and the rear driveshaft from the transfer case and wire them out of the way. Remove the cotter pin that holds the shift link in place and remove the shift link.
7. Remove the speedometer cable from the transfer case. Position a transmission jack under the transfer case. Remove the bolts holding the transfer case to the transmission and remove the transfer case from the vehicle.
8. Remove the bolts that hold the rear support bracket to the transmission.
9. Position a transmission jack under the transmission and remove the rear support bracket and brace. Remove the bolts that hold the transmission to the bell housing and remove the transmission.
10. To install, place the transmission on a transmission jack and install it in the vehicle. Install two guide pins in the bell housing top holes, to guide the transmission in place.
11. Install the two lower bolts, remove the guide pins and install the upper two bolts.
12. Continue the installation in the reverse order of the removal. Fill the transfer case and the transmission with lubricant. Lower the vehicle.

Four-Speed Overdrive Transmission

Removal and Installation

1. Raise the vehicle on a hoist. Mark the driveshaft so that it may be installed in the same position. Disconnect the driveshaft from the U-joint flange. Slide the driveshaft off the transmission output shaft and install the extension housing seal installation tool into the extension housing to prevent the transmission lubricant from leaking out.
2. Disconnect the speedometer cable at the extension housing. Remove the retaining clips, flat washers, and spring washers that secure the shift rods to the shift levers. Remove the bolts connecting the shift control to the transmission extension housing. Remove the nut connecting the shift control to the transmission case.

   NOTE: A '6' and '8' is stamped on the transmission extension housing by the shift control plate bolt holes. The '6' and '8' refer to either a 6 or 8 cylinder engine application. The shift control plate bolts must be placed in the right holes for proper plate positioning dependent upon the engine used in the vehicle.
3. Remove the rear transmission support connecting bolts attaching the support on the crossmember to the transmission extension housing. Support the engine with a transmission jack and remove the extension housing-to-engine rear support attaching bolts.
4. Raise the rear of the engine high

enough to relieve the weight from the crossmember. Remove the bolts retaining the crossmember to the frame side supports and remove the crossmember.
5. Support the transmission on a jack and remove the transmission-to-flywheel housing bolts. Move the transmission and the jack rearward until the transmission input shaft clears the flywheel housing. Lower the engine enough to obtain clearance for transmission removal and remove the unit.

NOTE: Do not depress the clutch pedal while the transmission is removed.
6. To install, make sure that the mounting surfaces of the transmission and the flywheel housing are free of dirt, paint, and burrs. Install two guide pins in the flywheel housing lower mounting bolt holes. Move the transmission forward on the guide pins until the input shaft splines enter the clutch hub splines and the case is positioned against the flywheel housing.
7. Install the two upper transmission mounting bolts, remove the guide pins and install the lower mounting bolts.
8. Continue the installation in the reverse order of the removal.
9. Fill the transmission to the proper level with lubricant. Lower the vehicle. Check the shift and crossover motion for full shift engagement and smooth crossover operation.

New Process 435 4-Speed

Removal and Installation

1. On C-, P-600, F-, LN- or B-Series truck, remove the rubber boot and floor mat.
2. On C-, P-600, F-, LN- or B-Series truck, remove the floor pan transmission cover plate. Remove the weather pad and pad retainer. It may be necessary first to remove the seat assembly.
3. Disconnect the back-up light switch located in the rear of the gearshift housing cover.
4. Raise the truck and position safety stands. Position a transmission jack under the transmission, and disconnect the speedometer cable.
5. Disconnect the parking brake lever from its linkage, and remove the gearshift housing. On a C-Series truck, disconnect parking brake cable and bracket at the transmission.
6. Disconnect the drive shaft. Remove the bolts that attach the coupling shaft center support to the cross-member and wire the coupling shaft and drive shaft to one side. In F-100-350 Series Trucks (1973-78), remove the transmission rear support. On Bronco, F-150- F-250 (4x4) remove the transfer case.
7. Remove the two transmission upper mounting nuts at the clutch housing.
8. Remove the transmission attaching bolts at the clutch housing, and remove the transmission.
9. Before installing the transmission, apply a light film of lubricant to the clutch disc splines, release bearing inner hub surfaces, release lever fulcrum and fork, and the transmission front bearing retainer. Care must be exercised to avoid excessive grease from contaminating the clutch disc.
10. Place the transmission on a transmission jack, and raise the transmission until the input shaft splines are aligned with the clutch disc splines. The clutch release bearing and hub must be properly positioned in the release lever fork.
11. Install guide studs in the clutch housing and slide the transmission forward on the guide studs until it is in position on the clutch housing. Install the attaching bolts and nuts. Remove the guide studs and install the two lower attaching bolts.
12. Install the bolts attaching the coupling shaft center support to the crossmember.
13. Connect the drive shaft and the speedometer cable. Install transmission rear support, if removed. Install transfer case, if removed.
14. Connect the parking brake to the transmission.
15. Connect the back-up light switch.
16. On an C-, P-600, F-, LN- or B-Series truck, install the weather pad, the pad retainer and the transmission cover plate. Install the seat assembly if it was removed.
17. On an C-, P-600, F-, LN- or B-Series truck, install the weather pad, the pad retainer, the floor mat and rubber boot.

New Process 542 5-Speed

Removal and Installation

1. Remove the floor mat and the floor plate. Loosen the two nuts that secure the top of the transmission to the clutch housing studs. If the vehicle is not raised on a hoist, it may be necessary to remove the parking brake lever before the transmission can be removed.
2. Remove the shift lever and drain the transmission.
3. Disconnect the drive shaft or coupling shaft at the parking brake drum. If the vehicle is equipped with a coupling shaft support, disconnect the support bracket and remove the coupling shaft.
4. Disconnect the parking brake adjusting rod and the speedometer cable.
5. Remove the dust cover from the bottom of the clutch housing. Position a transmission jack under the transmission. Remove the top nuts, and the bottom bolts and lockwashers that hold the transmission to the clutch housing.
6. Remove the transmission rearward until the input shaft splines clear the clutch housing. Be careful that the clutch release bearing and hub do not drop out of the release lever fork. Lower the transmission to the floor.
7. Place the transmission on the transmission jack and raise the transmission until the input shaft splines are aligned with the clutch disc splines. The clutch release bearing and hub must be properly positioned in the release lever fork. Slide the transmission forward until it is in position on the clutch housing.
8. Install the lock washers and the top nuts and the bottom bolts and tighten to specification.
9. Install the dust cover on the bottom of the clutch housing. Connect the speedometer cable.
10. Connect the parking brake adjusting rod.
11. Install the coupling shaft in the support bracket and connect the support bracket to the support plate. Connect the coupling shaft or drive shaft at the transmission. Install the shift lever.
12. Lower the vehicle to the floor and install the floor plate and the floor mat. Fill the transmission to the correct level with the correct lubricant.
13. Check the clutch pedal free travel and adjust if necessary.

Clark, Fuller, and Spicer 5 Speed Transmissions

Removal and Installation

1. Remove the floor mat and floor plate. On spicer transmissions, remove the 1st-reverse lockout plunger retainer, spring and plunger. Remove the gear shift lever housing and disconnect the parking brake lever (if so equipped). Cover the case opening to prevent foreign material from entering the case.
2. On C-series vehicles, shift the transmission into neutral, release the lock and tilt the cab forward. Remove the rear cross-

shaft housing bolts. Tie the housing so that it does not fall. If necessary, raise the rear of the vehicle and install saefty stands to provide room for the removal of the transmission. Block the wheels on W-series vehicles, remove the cross shaft housing bolts and tie the housing out of the way.

3. Drain the transmission. Disconnect the drive shaft or coupling shaft at the parking brake drum. If the vehicle is equipped with a coupling shaft support, disconnect the support bracket and remove the coupling shaft.
4. Disconnect the parking brake rod (if so equipped) and the speedometer cable. Remove the speedometer driven gear. Check the speedometer driven gear bushing in the mainshaft rear bearing cap on Spicer transmissions.
5. Disconnect the clutch linkage at the release arm. If the truck is equipped with a slave cylinder, disconnect the slave cylinder return spring, remove the slave mounting bolts, and set the slave cylinder out of the way.
6. Remove the dust cover from the bottom of the clutch housing.
7. a. *For Clark and Spicer transmissions;* position a transmission jack under the transmission. Remove the top nuts and the bottom bolts and lockwashers that attach the transmission to the clutch housing.

   b. *For Fuller transmissions;* position a jack under the transmission and raise it slightly to relieve the pressure at the side rail mounting brackets. Remove the side rail bracket stud nuts, insulators and reinforcements. Remove the side rail brackets and the bolts that attach the clutch housing to the engine.
   On W-series vehicles, remove the bolts and lockwashers that attach the transmission support to the frame side rail brackets. Mark the washers so that they can be re-installed in there original position. Remove the lock wire and the transmission support-to-transmission case bracket bolts, washers, and insulators. Remove the support and attach a chain hoist to the transmission. Remove the bolts that attach the clutch housing to the engine.
8. Move the transmission to the rear until it is clear and lower (or hoist on W-series vehicles) out of the chassis.
9. Install the transmission in the reverse order of removal.

NOTE: On Clark and Fuller transmissions when installing the gear shift lever housing, always lower it straight down onto the gear shift housing.

Fuller and Spicer Transmissions—6 Speed and Up

Removal and Installation

1. Bleed the air reservoir and disconnect the air line at the rear of the transmission. Drain the transmission lubricant.
2. Disconnect the drive shaft at the transmission companion flange.
3. Disconnect the speedometer cable at the transmission.
4. Clean the area around the cross shaft housing. Remove the housing and tie it out of the way. Cover the opening in the gear shft housing to prevent foreign material from entering.
5. Remove the shift control cable. Remove the retaining clamps for the speedometer and fuel line.
6. Disconnect the nylon cables at the air valve and shift cylinder. Tie the air cables next to the chassis frame to prevent damage to the cables when the transmission is removed.
7. Disconnect the clutch linkage at the clutch release arm. Remove all but two of the clutch attaching bolts at the engine. Remove the clutch housing dust cover.
8. Place a jack under the transmission and raise slightly to relieve the pressure at the side rail mounting brackets. Remove the bolts attaching the transmission support to the frame side rail brackets. After removing the lockwire, remove the transmission support-to-transmission case bolts, washers, insulators, and spacers. Remove the support.
9. Remove the remaining clutch housing attaching bolts. Pull the transmission rearward to clear the input shaft.
10. Raise the rear of the vehicle and support with safety stands. Remove the transmission from the vehicle.
11. Install the transmission in the reverse order of removal.

NOTE: If the pilot bearing was removed, the new bearing must be pressed approximately 1/16 of inch beyond the flush position.

When installing the air lines to the cab control valve, relative to the piston air valve, keep the air lines with the protective cover at least four inches from the exhaust manifold. Heat will melt the protective cover and the air lines. Sharp bends in the air lines will restrict the required air pressure of 50-55 psi.

Gearshift Linkage Adjustment

Ford 3.03 3-Speed

E and F Series & Bronco

1. Place the shifter in the Neutral position and insert a gauge pin (3/16″ diameter) through the steering column shift levers and the locating hole in the spacer.
2. If the shift rods at the transmission are equipped with threaded sleeves, adjust the sleeves so that they enter the shift levers on the transmission easily with the shift levers in the Neutral position. Now lengthen the rods seven turns of the sleeves and insert them into the shift levers.
3. If the shift rods, are slotted, loosen the attaching nut, make sure that the transmission shift levers are in the Neutral position, then retighten the attaching nuts.
4. Remove the gauge pin and check the operation of the shift linkage.

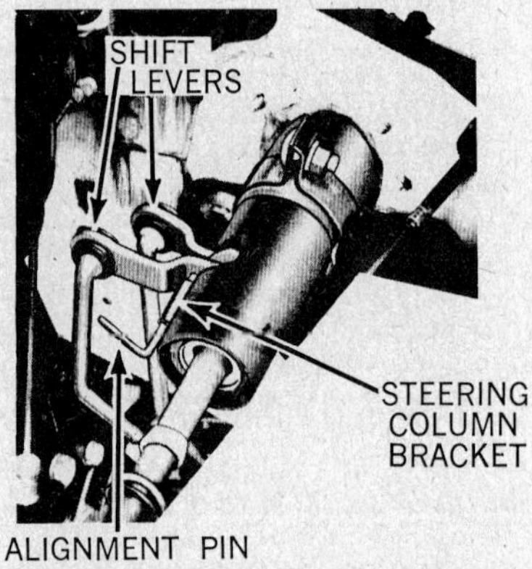

Gearshift linkage adjustment—Bronco (© Ford Motor Co.)

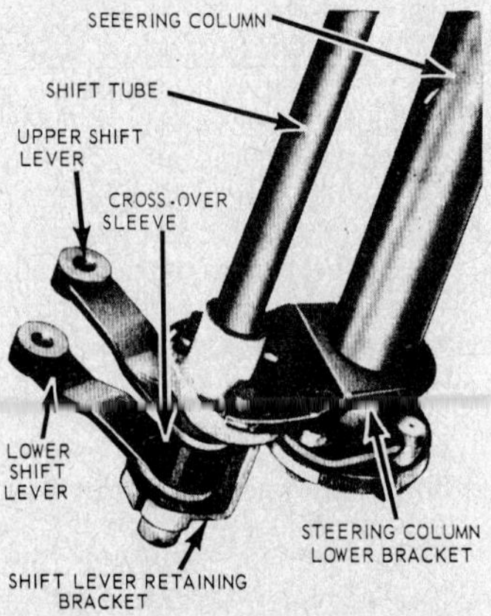

Gearshift linkage adjustment—Econoline (© Ford Motor Co.)

Four-Speed Overdrive

F Series & E-100-E-350

1. Disconnect the shift rods from the shifter assembly.
2. Insert a .25 in. diameter pin

through the alignment hole in the shifter assembly.

NOTE: Make sure that the levers are in the neutral position.

3. Align the transmission levers as follows:
   a. Forward lever (3rd-4th lever) in the mid-position (neutral).
   b. Rearward lever (1st-2nd lever) in the mid-position (neutral).
   c. Middle lever (reverse lever) rotate counterclockwise to the neutral position.
4. Rotate the output shaft to assure that the transmission is in neutral.
5. Attach the slotted end of the shift rods over the slots of the studs in the shifter assembly and tighten the locknuts.
6. Remove the alignment pin and check for proper operation.

Auxiliary Transmission

Spicer Auxiliary Transmission

Removal and Installation

1. Position the vehicle so that the auxiliary transmission can be easily reached. Drain the lubricant.
2. Remove the cotter pins and the clevis pins from the auxiliary transmission shift rods as follows:
   a. Move each shift rod into the forward position.
   b. Remove the pins and push each shaft to the neutral position.
3. Disconnect the U-joint at the front of the auxiliary transmission. Disconnect the U-joint at the rear of the auxiliary transmission and position the drive shaft out of the way.
4. Disconnect the speedometer cable from the transmission. If the speedometer cable cannot be readily disconnected, remove the parking brake drum and linkage, then disconnect the speedometer cable.
5. Remove the parking brake adjusting rod clevis pin and disconnect the parking brake lever to cam connector.
6. Position a transmission jack under the transmission and fasten the transmission to the jack with a safety chain.
7. Remove the transmission mounting stud (or bolt), insulator nut, cotter pins and nuts.

   NOTE: When studs are used, do not disturb the stud-to-mounting bracket nuts.
8. Lower and remove the auxiliary transmission from the vehicle.
9. To install, position the insulators and reinforcements, if used, on the transmission mounting brackets and raise the transmission into place. Install the remaining insulators, retaining nuts and washers.
10. Adjust the auxiliary transmission so that it is parallelled to the main transmission within plus or minus ½ degree. The coupling shaft between the two transmissions must be parallel to the transmissions from zero degree to one degree up at the auxiliary transmission end.

    NOTE: The front two adjusting bolts and the rear two adjusting bolts must have final adjusting dimensions within ⅛ in. of each other respectively.
11. Install the speedometer cable. If the parking brake drum has been removed, install the drum and the linkage. Attach the parking brake connector to the adjusting rod with a clevis pin.
12. Position the drive shaft and connect the rear U-joint. Connect the gear shift connecting rods to the transmission shift rods with clevis pins and new cotter pins. Connect the U-joint at the front of the auxiliary transmission.
13. Fill the transmission with the proper lubricant. Adjust the parking brake and shift linkage if required.

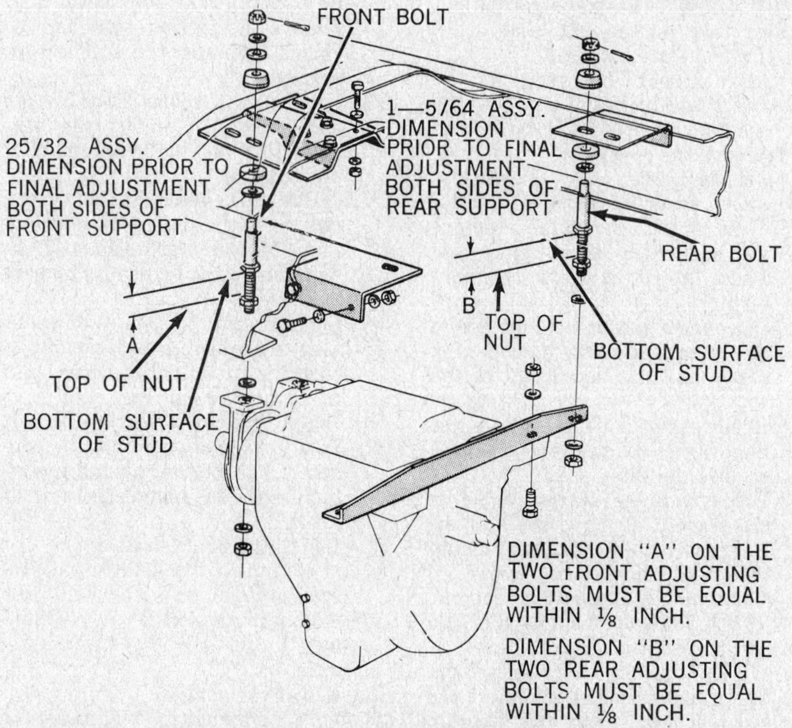

Transmission mounting details (© Ford Motor Co.)

AUTOMATIC TRANSMISSION

Reference

Automatic transmission overhaul procedures for light duty trucks are found in the General Repair section of this book.

Automatic Transmission

C4 Automatic Transmision

Removal and Installation

F-100, 150, 250

1. Raise the vehicle and disconnect the transmission fluid filler tube from the pan. Drain the transmission fluid.
2. At the front lower edge of the converter housing, remove the cover attaching bolts and remove the dust cover. Remove the splash shield at the control levers.
3. Remove the drive shaft or coupling shaft. Remove the converter drain plug. Allow the converter to drain and install the drain plug.
4. Disconnect the oil cooler lines from the transmission.
5. Disconnect the manual and downshift linkage rods from the transmission control levers.
6. Remove the speedometer gear from the extension housing.
7. Remove the four converter to flywheel attaching nuts. Disconnect the starter cable. Remove the three starter to converter housing attaching bolts. Remove the starter.
8. Disconnect the vacuum line from

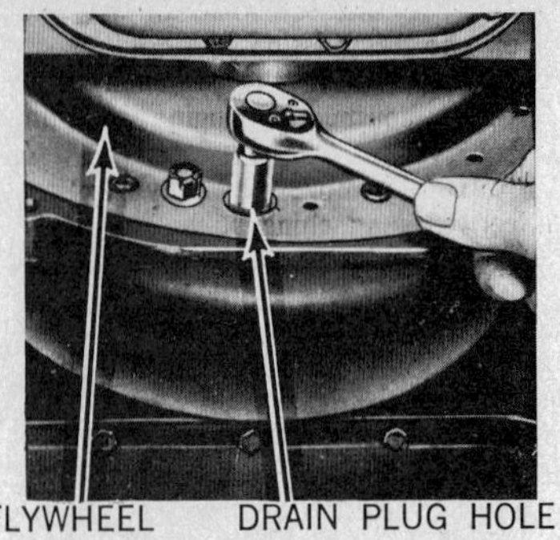

Converter drain plug location
(© Ford Motor Co.)

the diaphragm unit and the vacuum line retaining clip.
9. Position the transmission jack to support the transmission. Install the safety chain to hold the transmission on the jack.
10. Remove the two engine rear support crossmember-to-frame attaching bolts.
11. Remove the two engine rear support-to-extension housing attaching bolts.
12. Raise the transmission and remove the rear support. Remove the six converter housing-to-engine attaching bolts.
13. Move the transmission away from the engine. Lower the transmission and remove it from under the vehicle.
14. To install, secure the transmission on a transmission jack. Align the transmission with the engine and move it into place, using care not to damage the flywheel and the converter pilot.

    NOTE: The converter must rest squarely against the flywheel. This indicates that the converter pilot is not binding in the crankshaft.
15. Install the six converter housing-to-engine attaching bolts. Install the converter-to-flywheel ataching nuts.
16. Install the rear support. Install the rear support-to-extension housing attaching bolts.
17. Position the starter into the converter housing and install the three attaching bolts. Install the starter cable.
18. Remove the transmission jack.
19. Connect the transmission filler tube to the transmission pan. Connect the oil coolers lines to the transmission.
20. Install the speedometer driven gear in the extension housing.
21. Connect the transmission linkage rods to the transmission control levers.

    NOTE: When making transmission control attachments, new retaining rings and grommets should be used.
22. Install the drive shaft or coupling shaft.
23. Install the vacuum line in the retaining clip. Connect the vacuum line to the diahragm unit.
24. At the front lower area of the converter housing, install the lower cover and the control lever dust shield. Install the attaching bolts.
25. Secure the fluid filler tube to the pan.
26. Lower the vehicle.
27. Fill the transmission to the proper level.
28. Raise the vehicle and check for transmission fluid leakage. Lower the vehicle and adjust the throttle and manual linkage.

Econoline
Removal and Installation

1. Working from inside the vehicle, remove the engine compartment cover.
2. Disconnect the neutral start switch wires at the plug connector.
3. If the vehicle is equipped with a V8 engine, remove the flex hose from the air cleaner heat tube.
4. Remove the upper converter housing-to-engine attaching bolts (three bolts on 6-cylinder engines; four bolts on 8-cylinder engines).
5. On V8 engines, remove the upper muffler inlet pipe-to-exhaust manifold flange nut (right side of engine).
6. Raise the vehicle on a hoist.
7. On V8 engines, remove the three remaining muffler inlet pipe-to-exhaust manifold flange nuts and allow the exhaust pipe to hang.
8. Disconnect the transmission filler tube at the pan and drain the transmission fluid.
9. At the front lower edge of the converter housing, remove the dust cover attaching bolts and remove the cover.
10. Remove the converter-to-flywheel attaching nuts. As the flywheel is being rotated, remove the converter drain plug and drain the fluid from the converter.
11. Disconnect the drive shaft from the transmission companion flange and position it out of the way.
12. Remove the bolt retaining the fluid filler tube to the engine and remove the tube.
13. Disconnect the starter cable at the starter. Remove the starter-to-converter housing attaching bolts and remove the starter.
14. Position the engine support bar (Tool T65E-6000-J) to the side rail and engine oil pan flanges.
15. Disconnect the cooler lines from the transmission. Disconnect the vacuum line from the vacuum diaphragm unit.
16. Remove the speedometer driven gear from the extension housing.
17. Disconnect the manual and downshift linkage rods from the transmission control levers.
18. Install the converter drain plug. If the converter is not going to be cleaned, torque the drain plug to specification.
19. Position a transmission jack to support the transmission. Install the safety chain to hold the transmission on the jack.
20. Remove the bolt and nut securing the rear mount to the crossmember. Remove the four bolts retaining the crossmember to the side rails. Then, with the transmission jack, raise the transmission and remove the crossmember.
21. Remove the remaining converter housing-to-engine attaching bolts. Lower the transmission and remove it from under the vehicle.
22. Position the transmission on the jack and secure the transmission and converter to the jack with the safety chain.
23. Raise the transmission and guide the transmission and converter into position. The converter-to-flywheel retaining studs must line up with the holes in the flywheel. The converter hub must enter the end of the crankshaft.
24. Install the converter engine attaching bolts. Install the converter-to-flywheel attaching nuts.
25. Install the crossmember. Install the rear mount-to-crossmember attaching bolt and nut.
26. Remove the safety chain and remove the jack from under the vehicle. Remove the engine support bar.
27. Connect the cooler lines to the transmission. Connect the vacuum line to the vacuum diaphragm unit.
28. Install the speedometer driven gear into the extension housing.
29. Connect the transmission linkage rods to the transmission control levers.
30. Connect the transmission filler tube to the transmission pan. Secure the tube to the engine with the attaching bolt.
31. Install the converter dust cover.
32. Position the starter into the converter housing and install the attaching bolts. Install the starter cable.
33. Install the drive shaft.
34. If equipped with a V8 engine, install the muffler inlet pipe on the exhaust manifolds and install and torque the three retaining nuts.
35. Lower the vehicle.
36. On V8 engines, install and torque the upper muffler inlet pipe-to-

exhaust manifold flange nut.
37. Install the upper converter housing-to-engine attaching bolts.
38. On V8 engines, install the flex hose to the air cleaner heat tube.
39. Connect the neutral start switch wires at the plug connector.
40. Fill the transmission to the proper level with the specified fluid.
41. Raise the vehicle and check for transmission fluid leakage. Lower the vehicle and adjust the throttle and manual linkage.
42. Install the engine compartment cover.

1973-77 Bronco

Removal and Installation

1. Working from the engine compartment, remove the screws retaining the fan shroud to the radiator.
2. Raise the vehicle on a hoist. Remove the transfer case shield, if equipped. Drain the transfer case.
3. Remove the fluid filler tube from the transmission oil pan and drain the transmission fluid.
4. Remove the converter drain plug access cover.
5. Remove the converter-to-flywheel nuts. Place a wrench on the crankshaft pulley bolt to turn the converter to gain access to the nuts.
6. With the wrench on the crankshaft pulley bolt, turn the converter to gain access to the drain plug. Drain the fluid and replace the drain plug.
7. Disconnect the rear drive shaft at the transfer case and move it out of the way. Disconnect and remove the front drive shaft.
8. Disconnect the complete exhaust system. Remove the speedometer gear from the transfer case. Disconnect the oil cooler lines from the transmission.
9. Disconnect the manual and downshift linkage rods from the transmission control levers.
10. Disconnect the neutral safety switch wires from the retaining clamps and connectors.
11. Disconnect the starter cable. Remove the starter-to-converter housing bolts. Remove the starter.
12. Remove the vacuum hoses from the transmission vacuum unit. Disconnect the vacuum lines from the retaining clip.
13. Remove the bolts, washers, plates and insulators that secure the crossmember to the transfer case adapter.
14. Remove the crossmember-to-frame side support bolts. Position a transmission jack to support the transmission and the transfer case.
15. Raise the transmission and the transfer case assembly and remove the bolts securing the left side support bracket to the frame. Remove the side support bracket, crossmember and upper crossmember insulators from the vehicle.
16. Raise the transmission and the transfer case slightly and disconnect the shift rod from the transfer shift lever bracket.
17. Remove the shift lever bracket-to-transfer case adapter bolts and allow the assembly to hang by the shift lever.
18. Secure the transmission and the transfer case assembly to a transmission jack and remove the converter housing-to-engine bolts.
19. Move the transmission and the transfer case assembly away from the engine. Lower the assembly and remove it from the vehicle.
20. To install, position the converter to the transmission making sure the converter drive flats are fully engaged in the pump gear.
21. With the converter properly installed, position the transmission and the transfer case assembly on a transmission jack and secure the assembly in place.
22. Rotate the converter until the studs and the drain plug are in alignment with their holes in the flywheel.
23. With the transmission and the transfer case mounted on a transmission jack, move the assembly forward into position, using care not to damage the flywheel and the converter pilot.

    NOTE: The converter must rest squarely against the flywheel. This indicates that the converter pilot is not binding in the engine crankshaft.
24. Continue the installation in the reverse order of the removal. When the transmission linkage rods are connected to the transmission control levers, always install new retaining rings and grommets.
25. Fill the transfer case with lubricant. Fill the transmission to the proper level with the specified fluid. Adjust the manual and downshift linkage as required.

C-6 Automatic Transmission

Removal and Installation

F-100-F-350, Bronco

1. Drive the vehicle on a hoist, but do not raise at this time.
2. Remove the two upper converter housing-to-engine bolts.
3. Remove the bolt securing the fluid filler tube to the engine cylinder head.
4. Raise the vehicle and drain the fluid from the transmission and converter.
5. Disconnect the coupling shaft or driveshaft from the transmission companion flange and position it out of the way.
6. Disconnect the speedometer cable from the bearing retainer.
7. Disconnect the throttle and manual linkage rods from the levers at the transmission.
8. Disconnect the oil cooler lines from the transmission.
9. Remove the vacuum hose from the vacuum unit. Remove the vacuum line retaining clip.
10. Disconnect the cable from the terminal on the starter motor. Remove the three attaching bolts and remove the starter motor.
11. Remove the four flywheel attaching nuts. Place a wrench on the crankshaft pulley attaching bolt to turn the converter to gain access to the nuts.
12. On F-150- F-250 (4x4) and Bronco remove the transfer case, if equipped.
13. Remove the two engine rear support crossmember-to-frame attaching bolts.
14. Remove the two engine rear support-to-extension housing attaching bolts.
15. Remove the eight bolts securing the No. 2 crossmember to the frame side rails.
16. Raise the transmission with a transmission jack and remove both crossmembers.
17. Secure the transmission to the jack with the safety chain.
18. Remove the remaining converter housing-to-engine attaching bolts.
19. Move the transmission away from the engine. Lower the transmission and remove it from under the vehicle.
20. To install, tighten the converter drain plug. Position the converter on the transmission making sure the converter drive flats are fully engaged in the pump gear.
21. With the converter properly installed, place the transmission on the jack. Secure the unit to the jack with a chain.
22. Rotate the converter so that studs and drain plug are in alignment with those in the flywheel.
23. Move the transmission toward the cylinder block until they are in contact.

    NOTE: The converter must rest squarely against the flywheel. This indicates that the converter pilot is not binding in the engine crankshaft.
24. Install the converter housing-to-engine bolts.
25. Remove the transmission jack

safety chain from around the transmission.

26. Position the No. 2 crossmember to the frame side rails. Install the attaching bolts.
27. If equipped, install the transfer case.
28. Position the engine rear support crossmember to the frame side rails. Install the rear support to extension housing mounting bolts.
29. Lower the transmission and remove the jack.
30. Secure the engine rear support crossmember to the frame side rails with the attaching bolts.
31. Connect the vacuum line to the vacuum diaphragm making sure that the metal tube is secured in the retaining clip.
32. Connect the oil cooler lines to the transmission.
33. Connect the throttle and manual linkage rods to their respective levers on the transmission.
34. Connect the speedometer cable to the bearing retainer.
35. Secure the starter motor in place with the attaching bolts. Connect the cable to the terminal on the starter.
36. Install a new O-ring on the lower end of the transmission filler tube and insert the tube in the case.
37. Secure the converter-to-flywheel attaching nuts. Use a wrench on the crankshaft pulley attaching nut to rotate the flywheel. Do not use a wrench on the converter attaching nuts to rotate it.
38. Install the converter housing dust shield and secure it with the attaching bolts.
39. Connect the coupling shaft drive shaft.
40. Adjust the shift linkage.
41. Lower the vehicle. Then install the two upper converter housing-to-engine bolts.
42. Position the transmission fluid filler tube to the cylinder head and secure with the attaching bolt.
43. Fill the transmission to the correct level with the specified lubricant. Start the engine and shift the transmission thru all ranges, then re-check the fluid level.

Econoline

Removal and Installation

The removal and installation procedure for Econoline's equipped with the C-6 automatic transmission is the same as Econoline's equipped with the C-4 automatic transmission.

Refer to the C-4 automatic transmission section for the removal and installation procedures.

F-600 and C-600

Removal and Installation

1. Remove the six floor covering molding retaining screws from the left side of the vehicle and remove the molding.
2. Remove the three body bolt cover retaining screws and remove the cover. Remove the body bolt and nut.
3. Remove the two rear body bolt covers and loosen the body bolts.
4. Raise the left side of the body with a jack and place a 1⅝ in. piece of wood between the frame and the body mounting surfaces. Lower the jack.
5. Connect a remote control starter button to the solenoid.
6. Remove the rear support-to-crossmember bolts.
7. With a transmission jack positioned at the rear of the engine, raise the engine and transmission high enough to remove the rear supports.
8. Drain the automatic transmission fluid.
9. Remove the converter drain plug access cover bolts from the lower end of the converter housing.
10. Remove the converter-to-flywheel nuts. Crank the engine to turn the converter to gain access to the nuts.
11. Crank the engine to gain access to the converter drain plug. Drain the fluid and replace the drain plug.
12. Disconnect the starter cable from the starter. Remove the starter retaining bolts. Remove the starter.
13. Disconnect the drive shaft at the transmission and move it aside.
14. Disconnect the speedometer cable. Disconnect the parking brake linkage. Disconnect the shift cable from the manual lever at the transmission.
15. Remove the bolts that secure the shift cable bracket to the converter housing and move the cable and bracket aside.
16. Disconnect the downshift rod from the transmission downshift lever.
17. Disconnect the vacuum hose from the vacuum diaphragm at the rear of the transmission. Remove the vacuum line from the retaining clip at the transmission.
18. Disconnect the oil cooler lines at the transmission case. Remove the transmission filler tube and dipstick.
19. Position a transmission Jack under the transmission and secure the transmission to the jack with a safety chain.
20. Remove the converter housing-to-engine bolts.
21. Move the transmission assembly away from the engine. Tilt the assembly forward, and with the jack guide it over the crossmember. Lower the jack and remove the assembly from the vehicle.
22. To install, tighten the converter drain plug. Position the converter to the transmission making sure the converter drive flats are fully engaged in the pump gear.
23. With the converter properly installed, place the transmission on the jack. Secure the transmission to the jack with a safety chain.
24. Rotate the converter until the studs and the drain plug are in alignment with their holes in the flywheel.
25. Raise the transmission and position it over the crossmember to the engine.

    NOTE: Be careful not to damage the flywheel and converter pilot. The converter must rest squarely against the flywheel. This indicates that the converter pilot is not binding in the engine crankshaft.

28. Continue the installation in the reverse order of the removal. When replacing the transmission filler tube be sure to use a new O-ring.
27. Fill the transmission to the correct level with the proper fluid. Adjust the transmission control linkage, as required. Check the transmission, converter and oil cooler lines for leaks.

FMX Automatic Transmission

Removal and Installation

1. Drive the vehicle onto a hoist, but do not raise it at this time.
2. After removing the converter access hole covers, remove the two upper bolts and lockwashers which attach the converter housing to the engine.
3. Raise the vehicle, and remove the cover from the lower front side of the converter housing.
4. Remove the converter drain plug. Drain the converter and reinstall the plug. If desired, the converter may be drained after the unit has been removed from the vehicle.
5. Disconnect the fluid filler tube from the transmission pan.
6. When the fluid has stopped draining from the transmission, remove the flywheel to converter bolts. Wedge the converter to hold it in place when the transmission is removed.
7. Disconnect the starter cable from the starter, and disconnect the transmission to body ground cable from the transmission. Remove the starter.
8. On a transmission that has an oil cooler in the radiator, disconnect the fluid lines. On models

equipped with a sidemounted cooler, disconnect the radiator-to-cooler coolant lines at the cooler. Plug the lines to prevent coolant loss from the radiator.

9. Disconnect the manual and throttle linkages from the transmission.
10. Remove the vacuum hose from the vacuum unit. Remove the vacuum line retaining clip.
11. Disconnect the speedometer cable from the extension housing, and remove the drive shaft and/or coupling shaft.
12. Remove both engine rear support bolts.
13. With the transmission jack, raise the engine and transmission high enough to remove the engine rear supports.
14. Lower the engine against a floor stand or engine support bar so that the converter housing is clear of the cross member when all weight is off the transmission jack.
15. Remove the remaining converter housing to engine attaching bolts.
16. Remove the flywheel to converter attaching bolts. Then move the assembly toward the rear and lower it, leaving the flywheel attached to the crankshaft. If additional clearance is needed, tilt the rear of the assembly upright slightly and to the rear (enough to allow removal of the six flywheel to crankshaft bolts). Move the assembly to the rear, and remove it.
17. If the converter has been removed from its housing, position the converter in the housing, and install a wedge to prevent the converter from slipping out of the housing.
18. Rotate the converter until the studs are in the vertical position. Position the flywheel on the crankshaft flange and install the six attaching bolts.
19. Raise the transmission and converter with the jack to align it with the engine. Remove the wedge from the converter housing. Carefully move the transmission toward the engine and at the same time engage the converter studs with the holes in the flywheel.
20. Install the converter engine lower bolts.
21. Raise the engine and transmission with the transmission jack, and remove the engine support stand or support bar.
22. Place the engine rear supports in position on the cross member.
23. Lower the engine and transmission against the supports, and at the same time install the support bolts.
24. Rotate the flywheel, and tighten the attaching bolts.
25. Install the four converter-to-flywheel attaching nuts. Install the converter drain plug and the access plate.
26. Connect the oil cooler inlet and outlet lines to the transmission or side-mounted cooler.
27. Install the vacuum line and retaining clip. Install the vacuum hose on the vacuum unit.
28. Coat the universal joint knuckle with transmission fluid, and install the drive shaft and/or coupling shaft.
29. Connect the speedometer cable to the transmission.
30. Connect the manual linkage rod to the transmission manual lever.
31. Connect the throttle linkage to the transmission throttle lever.
32. Install the linkage splash shield.
33. Install the starter motor. Connect the transmission to frame ground cable to the transmission.
34. Connect the fluid filler tube to the pan.
35. Lower the hoist. Then install the upper two converter housing-to-engine bolts.
36. Install the access hole covers, and position the floor mat.
37. Fill the transmission with fluid.
38. Check the transmission converter assembly, and oil cooler lines for fluid leaks. Then adjust the transmission control linkage.

Allison AT-540 Automatic Transmission

Removal and Installation

1. Remove the right and left door sill scuff plates. Move the floor mat out of the way. Remove the bolts securing the transmission access cover to the floor pan and remove the cover.
2. On a one-piece drive shaft, disconnect the shaft from the yoke at the parking brake drum. On vehicles with a two-piece drive shaft, disconnect the coupling shaft from the yoke at the parking brake drum. Remove the center support bearing bracket. Move the forward end of the drive shaft out of the way.

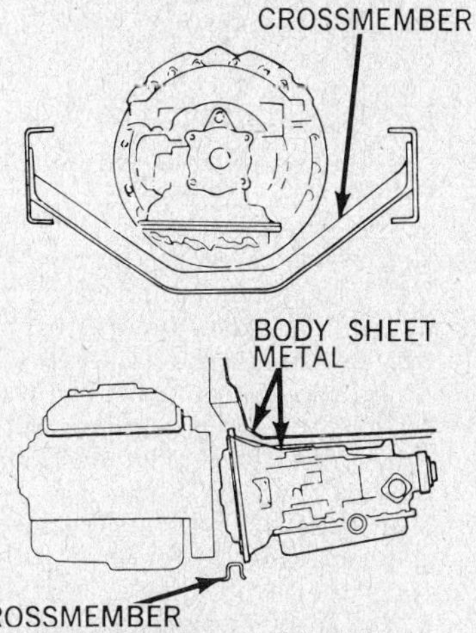

Removal or installation of Allison AT-540 transmission (© Ford Motor Co.)

3. Disconnect the parking brake linkage and remove the parking brake drum from the output shaft flange.
4. Remove the parking brake handle and brackets from the transmission case.
5. Place a drain pan under the transmission and drain the fluid.
6. Disconnect the speedometer cable from the rear of the transmission.
7. Disconnect the oil cooler lines at the transmission.
8. Disconnect the vacuum line from the vacuum modulator.
9. Remove the vacuum modulator retainer bolt and remove the retainer. Remove the vacuum modulator valve actuating rod from the case.
10. Disconnect the shift cable from the manual selector lever at the transmission.
11. Remove the two bolts holding the shift cable bracket to the transmission and position the cable and bracket out of the way.
12. Remove the inspection cover from the bottom front side of the flywheel housing.
13. Remove the six converter to flywheel attaching bolts. It may be necessary to turn the engine over manually.
14. Remove the four upper and two lower converter housing to flywheel attaching bolts.
15. Remove the bolts and nuts securing the two rear engine supports to the cross member. Remove the lower insulators and flat washers.
16. Loosen the front engine support bolts.
17. Position a transmission jack under the transmission and secure the transmission to the jack with a chain.
18. Place a jack under the engine. Raise both jacks to relieve the pressure on the cross member.
19. Remove the two upper engine rear support insulators from the crossmember.
20. Remove the bolts securing the engine rear support brackets to the transmission and remove the brackets.
21. With both jacks supporting the engine and transmission, remove the remaining converter housing to flywheel attaching bolts.
22. Pull the transmission rearward until the converter housing touches the body sheet metal.

Then, tilt the rear of the transmission upward until the bottom of the converter housing clears the crossmember. Lower the transmission assembly and remove it from the underside of the vehicle. If necessary, raise the rear of the vehicle to permit the transmission to clear the chassis.

NOTE: Prior to installing the transmission, it is mandatory that the flexplate be checked for runout. The maximum T.I.R. should be .020 in. In addition, the flywheel housing transmission mounting face alignment inspection should be made on the engine flywheel housing transmission surface. The face and bore runout should not exceed .008 in T.I.R.

23. Position the torque converter on the transmission, engaging the turbine shaft with the stator and the hub with the oil pump drive gear.
24. Place the transmission on a jack and secure with a chain.
25. Raise the converter and transmission of the jack and move the transmission assembly into position over the cross member. Align the holes in the converter with the holes in the flywheel.
26. Install six converter housing-to-flywheel attaching bolts, three on each side. Tighten the bolts to specification.
27. Lower the engine jack and remove it from the vehicle.
28. Position the engine rear support brackets on the side of the transmission and secure with the attaching bolts.
29. Position the two upper engine rear support insulators on the crossmember. Position the lower insulators and flat washers on the cross member and install the rear support-to-cross member bolts and nuts. Tighten the bolts to specification.
30. Lower the transmission jack and remove it from the vehicle.
31. Install the four upper and two lower conver housing-to-flywheel attaching bolts.
32. Tighten the front engine support bolts to specification.
33. Install the six converter to flywheel attaching bolts. Tighten the bolts to specification.
34. Install the inspection cover on the bottom front side of the flywheel housing.
35. Position the shift cable bracket on the transmission and install the attaching bolts.
36. Connect the shift cable to the manual lever on the transmission.
37. Install the vacuum modulator actuating rod and vacuum modulator into the case. Install the vacuum modulator retainer and secure with the attaching bolt.
38. Connect the vacuum line to the vacuum modulator.
39. Connect the oil cooler lines to the transmission.
40. Connect the speedometer cable.
41. Install the fluid filler tube on the oil pan.
42. Position the parking brake handle and bracket on the transmission and secure with the attaching bolts.
43. Install the parking brake drum and connect the parking brake linkage.
44. Install the drive shaft, center support bearing bracket and the coupling shaft. Connect the coupling shaft to the parking brake drum and tighten all bolts.
45. Position the transmission access cover on the floor pan and secure with the attaching screws.
46. Add enough automatic transmission fluid to the transmission to bring the fluid level to the full mark on the transmission.
47. Check the transmission, converter assembly and oil cooler for leaks.

Allison MT-Series Automatic Transmission

Removal and Installation

NOTE: Nothing fastens the torque converter to the transmission. A retaining strap must be used for handling. The torque converter and the transmission must be removed from and installed in the vehicle as the unit. The transmission cannot be removed from or installed on the converter in the vehicle.

1. Remove the filler tube from the oil pan and drain the oil from the transmission.
2. Install a protective plug in the drain hole.
3. On vehicles with a one piece drive line, disconnect the shaft from the pinion shaft flange and from the yoke at the parking brake drum. *Do not remove the bolt that attaches the flange to the transmission output shaft.* On vehicles with two piece drive shafts, disconnect the coupling shaft from the yoke at the parking brake drum, and then remove the center support bearing bracket. Move the forward end of the drive shaft out of the way.
4. Disconnect the speedometer cable from the rear of the transmission.
5. Disconnect the throttle control rod and the selector lever cable from the levers on the left side of the transmission housing. Remove the cable clamp bracket from the transmission.
6. Disconnect the parking brake linkage.
7. Disconnect the oil cooler lines from the fittings on the retarder valve body, then remove the forward fitting. Plug the lines and valve body openings. If desired, the lines and valve body can be drained, but they should be plugged before removing the transmission assembly from the vehicle.
8. Remove the dust shield from the bottom front side of the flywheel housing.
9. Remove the nuts and flat washers that hold the converter pump cover to the engine flywheel. The nuts and washers can be reached through an opening in the lower right side of the flywheel housing. The flywheel must be turned to remove all the nuts and washers.

CAUTION: The ignition system should be disconnected during the operation to prevent accidental starting of the engine.

10. Cut the lock wires and remove the two bolts and nuts that hold the converter housing to the frame crossmember.
11. Cut the lock wire and remove the two bolts, washers, and insulators from the top of the transmission rear support and cross member.
12. Place an engine support under the rear of the engine, then raise the engine to take the weight off the cross member.
13. Support the transmission with a 1000-lb. transmission jack. The jack should be placed so that the oil pan does not support the entire weight of the transmission. Fasten a safety chain over the top of the transmission and to both sides of the jack.
14. Remove the two bolts from each end of the transmission rear support crossmember, and remove the crossmember.
15. Remove the bolts and lockwashers that attach the converter housing the flywheel housing.
16. Move the transmission assembly away from the engine until the converter clears the crossmember. If necessary raise the floor pan slightly to permit the converter housing to clear the crossmember.

NOTE: If the engine, flywheel housing has been replaced, check the housing alignment and flywheel shim adjustment before installing the torque converter and transmission.

The flywheel housing transmission mounting face alignment inspection should be made on the engine flywheel housing transmission surface. The bace bore runout should not exceed .008 in T.I.R.

17. Raise the transmission assembly on the jack, then move the unit into position over the crossmember that supports the converter. Align the studs in the converter with the holes in the flywheel. Install the two guide studs in the flywheel housing, then push the unit forward so that the converter studs enter the holes in the flywheel.
18. Install the bolts, except the fluid filler tube support bracket bolt, and lockwashers that attach the converter housing to the flywheel housing. Torque the bolts to 23-28 ft-lbs.
19. Install six new self locking nuts and flat washers to attach the converter to the engine flywheel. Torque the nuts to 34-40 ft-lbs.
20. Install the dust shield on the bottom front side of the flywheel housing.
21. Install the transmission rear support crossmember on top of the frame brackets, then install the bolts on the cross member and tighten to 40-45 ft-lbs. torque.
22. Lower the jack, and remove it from under the vehicle. Remove the engine support.
23. Install the nuts and bolts that hold the converter housing to the frame crossmember and tighten the bolts to 70-91 ft-lbs. torque. Install the lock wire.
24. Install the bolts, washers, and insulators at the transmission rear 60 ft-lbs. torque and install the support. Tighten the bolts to 40-lock wire.
25. Install the oil cooler lines.
26. Install the selector lever cable bracket on the left side of the transmission and tighten the attaching screws to 8-10 ft-lbs. torque.
27. Connect the selector lever cable to the lever on the left side of the housing.
28. Connect the selector lever cable to the lever on the left side of the housing.
28. Connect the fluid filler tube to the oil pan, then install the tube support bracket bolt.
29. Push the breather hose across the top of the transmission and connect the hose to the fitting above the left PTO plate. Tighten the hose clamp.
30. Connect the parking brake linkage.
31. If the exhaust system was removed or disconnected during transmission removal, install and connect the parts.
32. Install the drive shaft, center bearing support bracket, and the coupling shaft. Connect the coupling shaft to the parking brake drum. Tighten all nuts and bolts.
33. Connect the speedometer cable to the rear of the transmission.
34. Adjust the selector lever linkage.
35. Check all fluid line connections for tightness, and lower the vehicle to the floor.
36. Add enough automatic transmission fluid to the converter and transmission to bring the fluid level up to the full mark on the dipstick.

Shift Linkage Adjustment

Shift Linkage Adjustment

Bronco, Econoline, F-100-F-350 and F-100-F-250 (4x4) 1973 and Later

1. With the engine stopped, place the transmission selector lever at the steering column in the D position and hold aganst the "D" stop by applying an eight pound weight to the selector lever knob.
2. Loosen the shift rod adjusting nut at the transmission lever.
3. Shift the manual lever at the transmission to the D position, two detents from the rear. On an F-100 with 4WD, move the bellcrank lever.
4. With the selector lever and transmission manual lever in the D position, tighten the adjusting nut to 12-18 ft lbs. Do not allow the rod or shift lever to move while tightening the nut.
5. Check the operation of the shift linkage, after you have removed the eight pound weight from the selector lever knob.

NOTE: It is not permissible to adjust the linkage in any position other than the "D" position.

P-Series

1973-78

1. With the engine stopped, disconnect the upper end of the manual shift rod from the shift lever.
2. Position the selector lever with the pointer against the steering column stop in the N position.
3. Shift the manual lever on the transmission to the N position, by moving the lever all the way rearward then forward three detents.
4. Rotate the trunnion on the manual shift rod until the pin can be easily inserted in the lever. Turn the trunnion two full turns counterclockwise to lengthen the rod.
5. Connect the trunnion to the shift lever. Operate the shift lever in all positions. Re-adjust the manual shift rod, if required, one turn at a time.

F-600

1. With the engine stopped, position the transmission selector lever in the D position.
2. Disconnect the shift cable clevis at the transmission manual level.

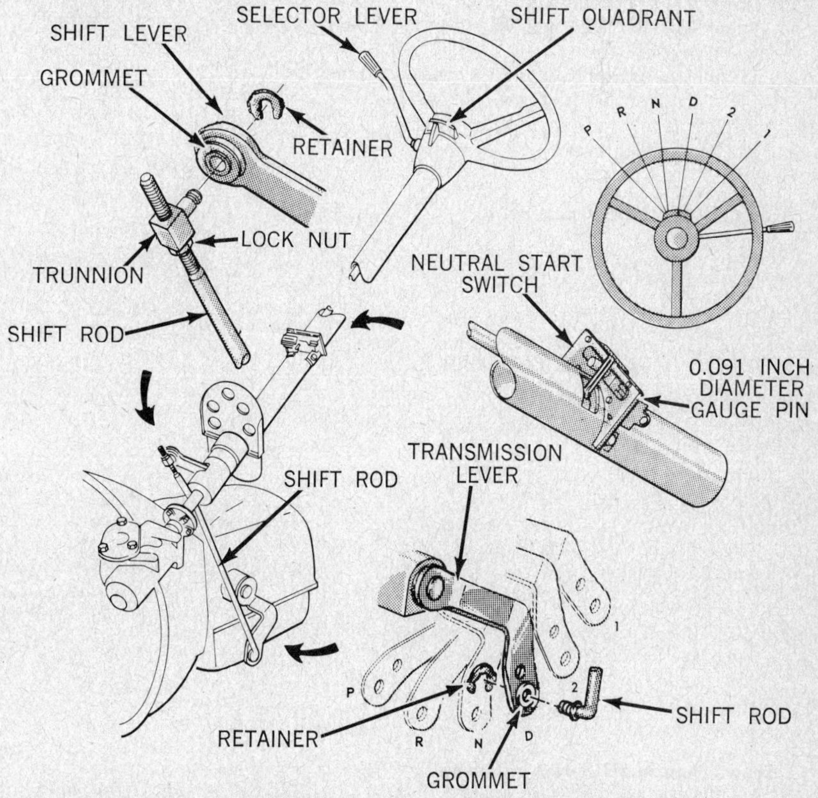

Manual linkage adjustment F-100-250-350 (© Ford Motor Co.)

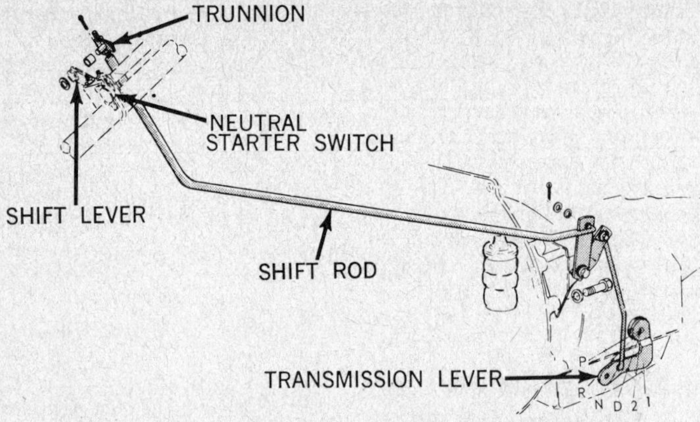

Manual linkage adjustment—P-Series (© Ford Motor Co.)

Move the transmission manual lever to the D position.

3. With the transmission manual lever in the D position, adjust clevis until it freely enters into the hole of the manual lever.
4. Connect the clevis to the manual lever and secure it with the flat washers, spring washer and cotter pin.
5. Operate the shift lever in all positions. It may be necessary to re-adjust the clevis slightly to obtain the detent position in all drive ranges.

Allison Automatic Transmission

1. With the engine off, position the selector in the "R" position.
2. Disconnect the shift level cable sleeve at the transmission manual shift lever.
3. Shift the transmission manual lever to "R" (all the way forward and upward).
4. With the manual lever in the "R" position, adjust the sleeve until it freely enters into the hole in the manual lever.
5. Connect the sleeve to the manual lever with the flat washers, spring washers, and cotter pin.
6. Operate the shift lever in all positions to make certain that the manual lever at the transmission is in full detent at all gear ranges. It may be necessary to re-adjust the sleeve slightly to obtain the detent position in all drive ranges.

Band Adjustments

C-4 Automatic Transmission

Intermediate Band Adjustment

1. Clean adjusting screw, apply penetrating lubricant and remove and discard locknut.
2. Install a new locknut (loosely) and torque adjusting screw to 10 ft. lbs., then *back off 1 3/4 turns.*
3. Hold adjusting screw and tighten locknut.

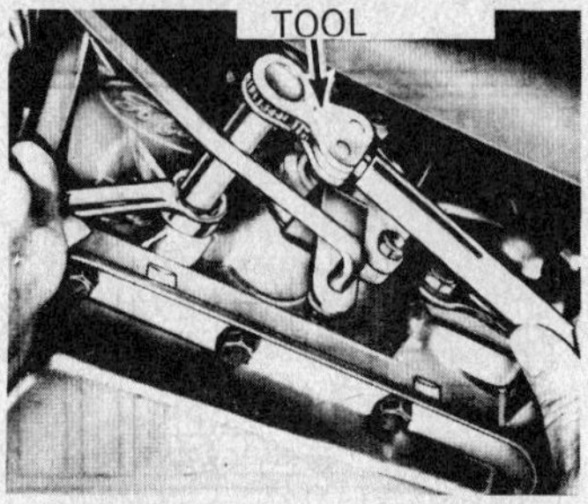

Adjusting intermediate band
(© Ford Motor Co.)

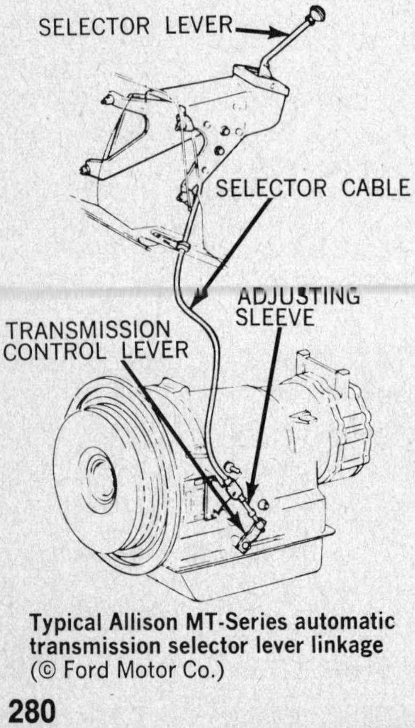

Typical Allison MT-Series automatic transmission selector lever linkage
(© Ford Motor Co.)

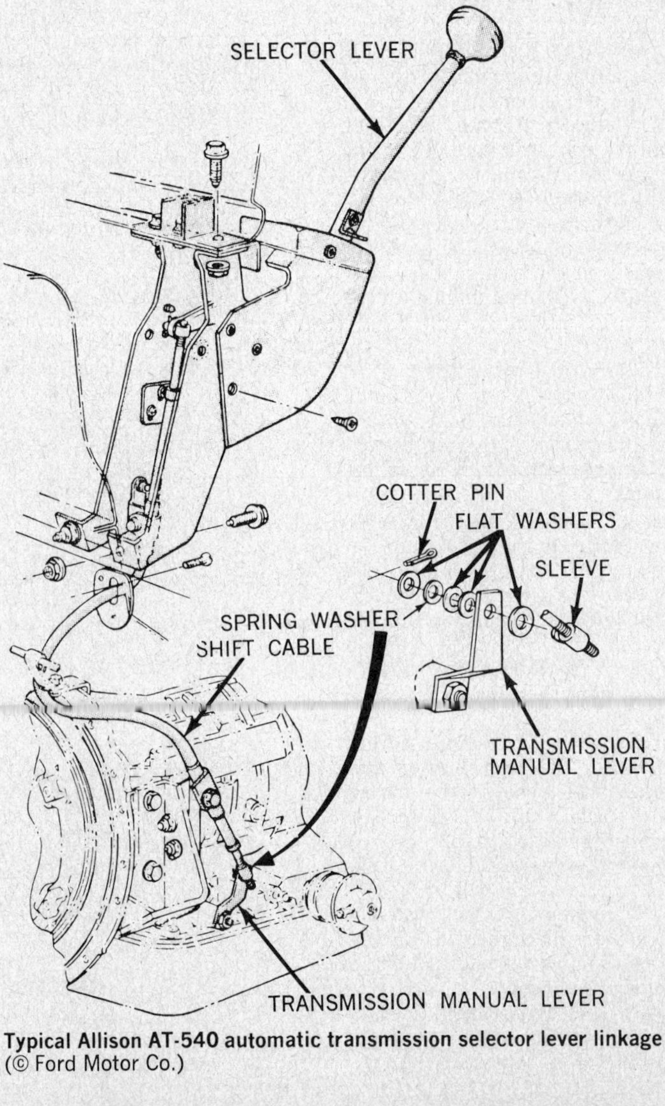

Typical Allison AT-540 automatic transmission selector lever linkage
(© Ford Motor Co.)

Low-Reverse Band Adjustment

The adjusting procedure is exactly the same as that described for the intermediate band above except the *adjusting screw is backed off 3 full turns.*

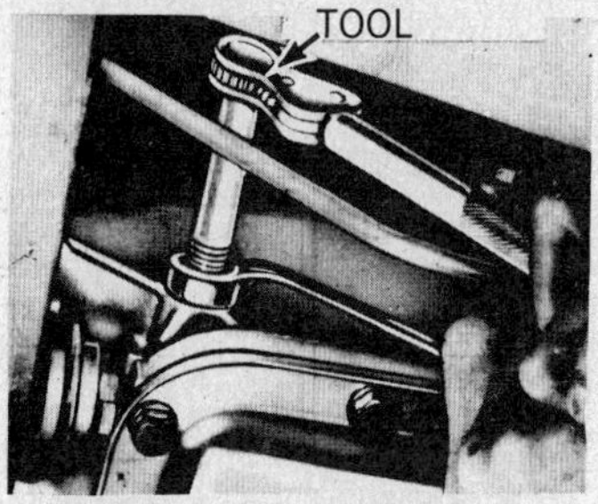

Adjusting low-reverse band
(© Ford Motor Co.)

C-6 Automatic Transmission

Intermediate Band Adjustment

F-100, 150, 250, 350

The adjusting procedure is exactly the same as that described for the C4 intermediate band adjustment above except that the adjusting screw is *backed off 1 1/2 turns.*

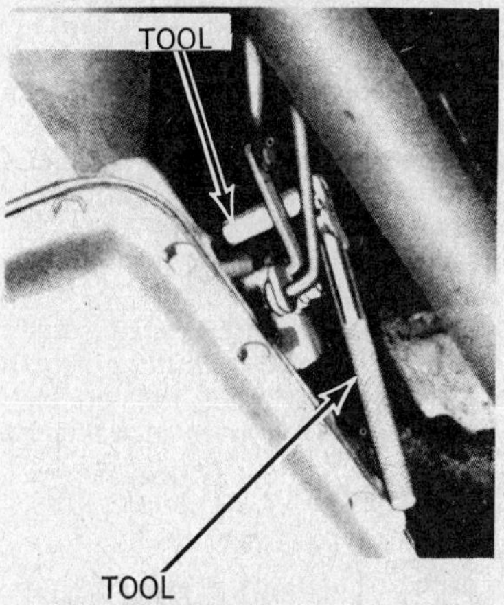

C6 intermediate band adjustment
(© Ford Motor Co.)

FMX Automatic Transmission

Front Band Adjustment

1. Remove the transmission oil pan.
2. Loosen the front servo adjusting screw locknut.
3. Pull back on the actuating rod, and insert a ¼″ spacer between the adjusting screw and the servo piston stem.
4. Tighten the adjusting screw to 10″ lbs.
5. Remove the spacer and tighten the adjusting screw an additional ¾ turn.
6. Hold the adjusting screw stationary and tighten the locknut. Tighten the locknut to 20-25 ft lbs.
7. Install the oil pan and a new gasket in the reverse order of removal.

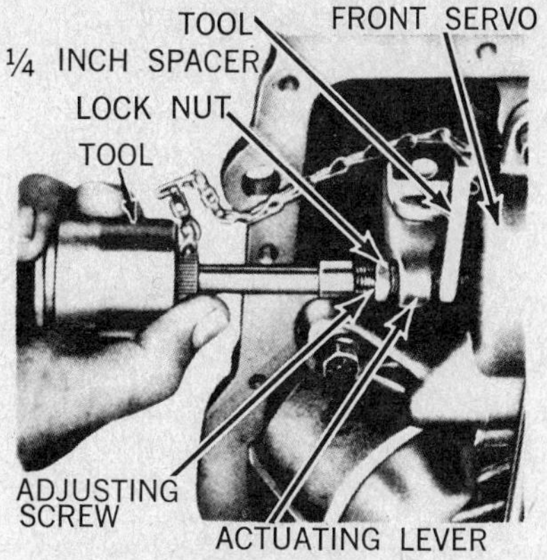

FMX front band adjustment
(© Ford Motor Co.)

Rear Band Adjustment

1. Remove all dirt away from the adjusting screw threads then oil the threads.
2. Loosen the rear band adjusting screw locknut.
3. Tighten the adjusting screw to 10 ft lbs.
4. Back off the adjusting screw *exactly 1 1/2 turns.*
5. Hold the adjusting screw stationary and tighten the adjusting screw locknut to 35-40 ft lbs.
6. Reinstall the oil pan and a new gasket.

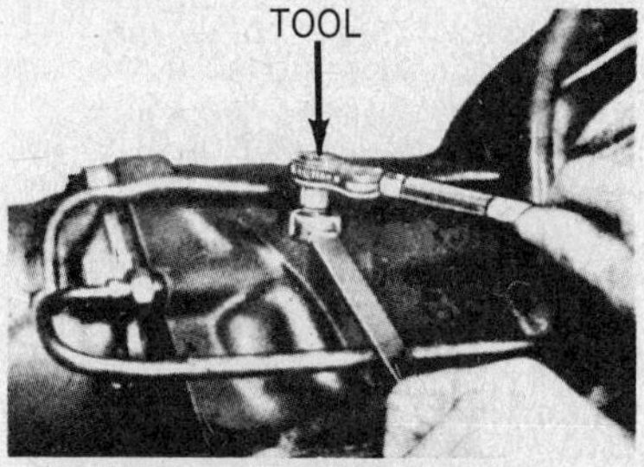

FMX rear band adjustment
(© Ford Motor Co.)

Neutral Safety Switch Adjustment

F-100-350

1. Loosen the two neutral start switch attaching screws.
2. Hold the selector lever against the neutral stop.
3. Move the sliding block on the neutral switch to the neutral position. Working from the rear side of the switch, insert a .091 inch diameter gauge pin (#43 drill) in the gauge pin hole.
4. Slide the switch, as required, to permit the switch actuating lever to contact the switch sliding block.
5. Tighten the two switch attaching screws and remove the gauge pin.
6. Check the operation of the switch. The engine should start only with the selector lever in the "N" (neutral) or "P" (park) positions.

E-100-350 and Bronco (1973-80) F-150-350 (1979-80)

1. With the manual linkage properly adjusted, loosen the two switch attaching bolts.
2. Place the transmission selector lever in neutral. Rotate the switch and insert .091 in. (#43 drill) gauge pin into the gauge pin holes. The gauge pin has to be inserted a full 31/64 in. into the three holes in the switch.
3. Tighten the two neutral start switch attaching bolts and remove the gauge pin from the switch.
4. Check the operation of the switch. The engine should start only with the selector lever in the "N" (neutral) or "P" (park) position.

P-500

1. Place the selector lever in neutral.
2. Loosen the two neutral start switch attaching bolts.
3. Move the neutral start switch until the switch lever is in the neutral detent position. Tighten the attaching screws.
4. Check the operation of the switch in each selector lever position. The engine should start only with the selector lever in the "N" (neutral) or "P" (park) positions.

F-500-600

1. Check the starter at all selector

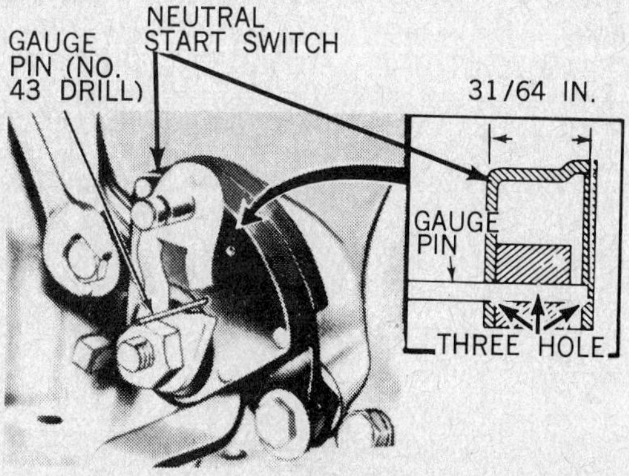

Neutral safety switch adjustment (© Ford Motor Co.)

lever positions. The circuit must be open at all positions except "N" (neutral).
2. To adjust, loosen the neutral switch to bracket attaching screws.
3. Position the switch so that the starter circuit is closed when the selector lever is in the "N" (neutral) position.

Allison Automatic Transmissions

1. Check the starter circuit at all selector positions. The circuit must be open in all positions except the N (neutral) position.
2. Loosen the switch-to-bracket attaching screws.
3. Position the switch so that the starter circuit is closed when the selector lever is at N.

NOTE: Refer to the Automatic Transmission Section of this manual for the throttle or modulator adjustment, the transmission oil pan removal and installation and maintenance services.

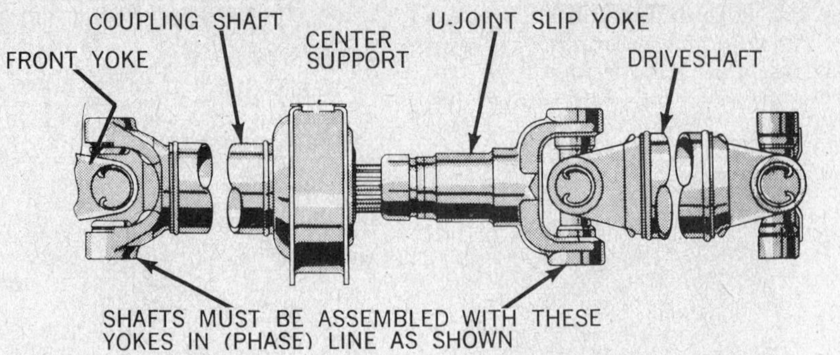

Drive shaft components—132″ wheelbase (© Ford Motor Co.)

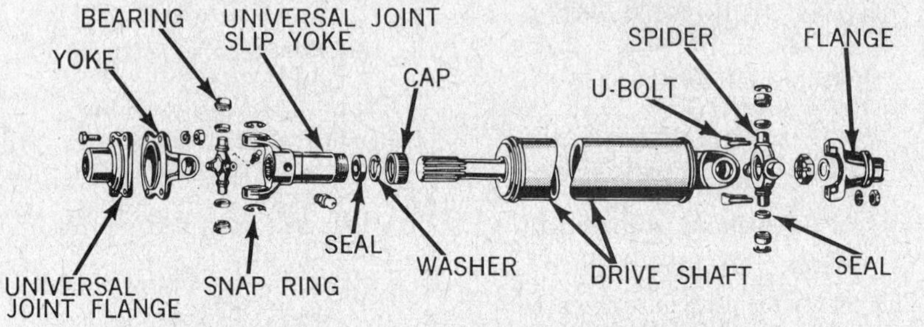

Drive shaft components—115″ wheelbase (© Ford Motor Co.)

DRIVESHAFT

All Except One Piece Drive Shaft Models

Removal and Installation

NOTE: Mark the relationship of the rear drive shaft yoke and axle pinion flange before disassembly, to maintain driveline balance.

Driveshaft

Single Snap Ring U-Joint Type

1. Disconnect the driveshaft from the rear axle flange.
2. If vehicle has a coupling shaft, slide the driveshaft off the coupling splines.
3. Working from the center support nearest to the rear of the vehicle, remove the two attaching bolts and support the bearing.
4. On a vehicle with more than one coupling shaft, disconnect the rear shaft from the front one.
5. Remove the remaining center support attaching bolts and support the bearing.
6. Remove the transmission coupling shaft flange attaching nuts and remove the shaft and center bearing(s) as an assembly.
7. Thoroughly clean all driveshaft components before installing.
8. To install, connect the front flange or joint to the transmission flange.
9. Secure the center bearing to the frame bracket, tightening the bracket attaching bolts securely.
10. If vehicle has more than one cou-

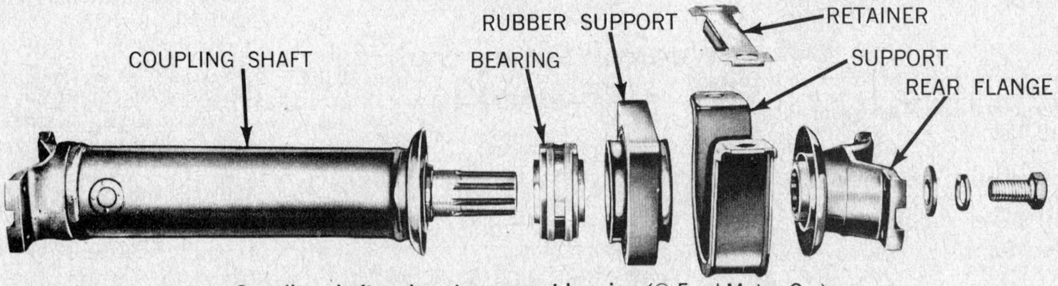

Coupling shaft and center support bearing (© Ford Motor Co.)

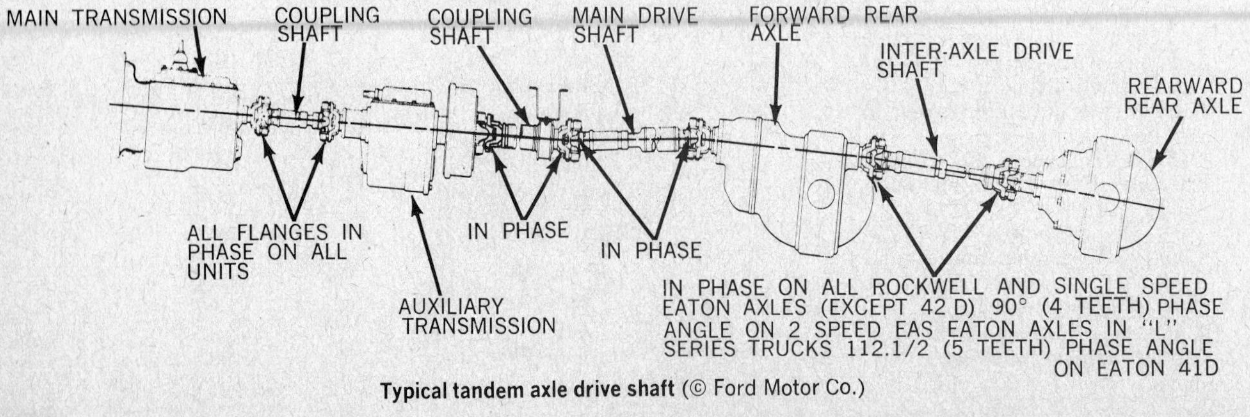

Typical tandem axle drive shaft (© Ford Motor Co.)

pling shaft, connect the rear shaft to the forward one, then install the remaining center support.

11. Connect the rear universal to the rear axle flange, tightening nuts or bolts securely.
12. Be sure all driveshaft and coupling shaft yokes are in phase.

One Piece Drive Shaft Models

Removal and Installation

1. If the yellow alignment marks are not visible, mark the relationship of the rear drive shaft yoke and the drive pinion flange of the axle in line with the drive shaft so that they may be re-installed in the same position.
2. Disconnect the rear U-joint from the companion flange. Wrap tape around the loose bearing caps to prevent them from falling off the spider. Pull the drive shaft toward the rear of the vehicle until the slip yoke clears the transmission extension housing and the seal. Install the appropriate tool in the housing to prevent the lubricant or fluid from leaking.
3. To install, reverse the removal procedure, taking note that if either the rubber seal on the output shaft or the seal in the end of the transmission extension housing is damaged it must be replaced. Also if the lugs on the axle pinion flange are shaved or distorted so that the bearings silde, replace the flange.
4. Install the U-bolts and torque the nuts to 8-15 foot lbs.

NOTE: If a vibration should exist, the drive shaft should be disconnected from the axle, rotated 180 degrees and re-installed.

Double Cardan U-Joint Type

Removal and Installation

1. To remove the front or rear drive shaft, disconnect the double cardan joint from the flange at the transfer case.
2. Disconnect the single U-joint from the flange at the axle. Remove the drive shaft.
3. To install, position the single U-joint end of the drive shaft to the axle, before the cardan end. Install and tighten all U-bolts, nuts, bolts and lockwashers.

Single Bearing Cap, Bolt/ Bolted End Cap U-Joint Type

Removal and Installation

1. Disconnect the drive shaft from the flange at the rear axle.
2. If working on a vehicle equipped with a coupling shaft, slide the drive shaft off the coupling shaft splines. On some Mechanics, Rockwell, and heavy duty Spicer assemblies, remove the attaching bolts.
3. Working from the center support nearest to the rear of the vehicle, remove the two attaching bolts and support bearing. Different types of support brackets are used. Some have elongated mounting holes. This permits close adjustment.
4. If working on a vehicle equipped with more than one coupling shaft, disconnect the rear shaft from the front one.
5. Remove the remaining center support attaching bolts and support the bearing.
6. Remove the nuts that attach the coupling shaft flange to the transmission, and remove the shaft and center bearing assembly.
7. Thoroughly clean all drive shaft components before installation.
8. Connect the front flange or joint of the drive shaft or coupling shaft to the flange on the transmission.
9. Secure the center bearing to the frame bracket with the center support and attaching bolts. Note that L-series vehicles are adjustable with two-piece center support brackets. Tighten all bolts.
10. If working on a vehicle with more than one coupling shaft, connect the rear shaft to the forward one, then install the remaining center support. Make sure all splines are properly lubricated.
11. Connect the U-joint to the rear axle flange and tighten the nuts or bolts.
12. Make sure that all drive shaft and coupling shaft yokes are properly in phase.

U-Joints

Single Snap Ring Type U-Joint & Double Cardan Type U-Joint

Disassembly and Assembly

1. Mark the position of the spiders, the center yoke, and the centering socket as related to the stud yoke which is welded to the front of the driveshaft tube. The spiders must be assembled with the bosses in their original positions to provide proper clearance.
2. Remove the snap-rings that secure the bearings in the front of the center yoke.
3. Position the driveshaft in a vise so that the bearing caps that are pressed into the center yoke can be pressed or driven out with a drift and hammer. Do this for all of the spiders.
4. Clean all the serviceable parts in cleaning solvent. If you are using a repair kit, install all of the parts supplied with the kit.

   NOTE: If the driveshaft is damaged in any way, replace the complete driveshaft to insure a balanced assembly.
5. Assemble the U-joints in the reverse order of disassembly.

Bearing Cap and Bolt Type U-Joint

Disassembly and Assembly

1. Remove the cap screws attaching the bearing caps to the U-joint flange and yoke. Remove the bearing caps and bearings from the spider.
2. Remove the grease seals and retainers from the spider.
3. Clean the assembly thoroughly and check for damage or wear.
4. Pack the recess in the spider with the proper grade of grease.
5. Install the grease seals on the spider.
6. Position the needle bearings in the bearing cap, then position the caps on the spider. Place the spider in the yokes, and then install the bearing caps.
7. Lubricate the U-joints with the proper grade of grease.

Bolted End Cap Type U-Joint

Disassembly and Assembly

1. Bend the tangs on the lock plates away from the capscrews.
2. Remove the capscrews and lock plates holding the bearing caps to the U-joint flange. Remove the bearing caps and bearings from the flange and spider.

   If the bearing caps are integral, tap the bearing cap lightly clockwise and, using a screw driver, pry under first one end of the bearing cap and then the other until the bearing comes out of the yoke. Turn the joint over, and remove the opposite bearing in the same way.

   If the bearing cap and bearing are separate, the bearing cap will come off with a light tap. Remove the bearings by first tapping with a round soft drift on the exposed face of one bearing until the opposite bearing comes out. Turn the joint over and tap the exposed end of the journal cross pin until the opposite bearing is free.
3. Remove the spider. All burrs on the bearing cap or yoke must be removed before replacing the spider in the yoke.
4. Clean all parts thoroughly and inspect for damage or wear.
5. Before assembling, fill the jour-

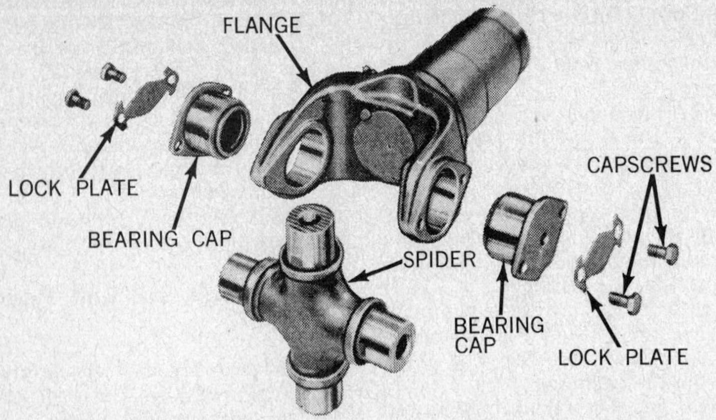

Bolted end cap type U-joint—exploded view (© Ford Motor Co.)

nal passages with a long life lubricant of the proper grade.

6. Position the needle bearings in the bearing caps.
7. Position the spider in the flange and install the bearing caps through the yoke and onto the spider. Press or tap the bearing caps into place with a soft drift.
8. Position the lock plates on the bearing caps and secure with the capscrews. Bend the tabs of the lock up against the capscrews.
9. Lubricate the U-joint with a long life grease of the proper grade.

REAR AXLE

Reference

Rear axle overhaul procedures for light duty trucks are found in the General Repair section of this book.

Integral Carrier Axle (Dana)

E250, E350, F100, F250, F350, P Series

Removal and Installation

1. Loosen the wheel stud nuts and the axle shaft retaining bolts.
2. Disconnect the rear shock absorbers from the spring seat caps. Then raise the rear end of the vehicle frame until the weight is off the rear springs. Place safety stands under the frame in this position.
3. Disconnect the flexible hydraulic line at the frame and disconnect the axle vent hose at the axle connection.
4. Disconnect the parking brake cable (if so equipped) at the equalizer, and remove the cables from the cable support brackets.
5. Disconnect the drive shaft from the rear U-joint flange.
6. Remove the nuts from the spring clips (U-bolts), and remove the spring seat caps.
7. Roll the axle from under the vehicle, and drain the lubricant. Remove the wheels. Mount the axle in a work stand.
8. Replace the hub inner grease seal. Install the axle shafts through the housing ends so that they will spline to the differential side gears. Install the shaft retaining bolts and lock washers.
9. After installing rear wheels, roll the axle assembly under the vehicle.
10. Install the spring clips (U-bolts) and spring seat caps. Torque the nuts to 165-185 ft-lbs.
11. Connect the rear shock absorbers.
12. Lower the vehicle to the floor. Connect the drive shaft to the rear universal joint flange.
13. Connect and adjust the parking brake cables (if so equipped).
14. Connect the hydrualic brake hose and bleed the brakes. Also con-

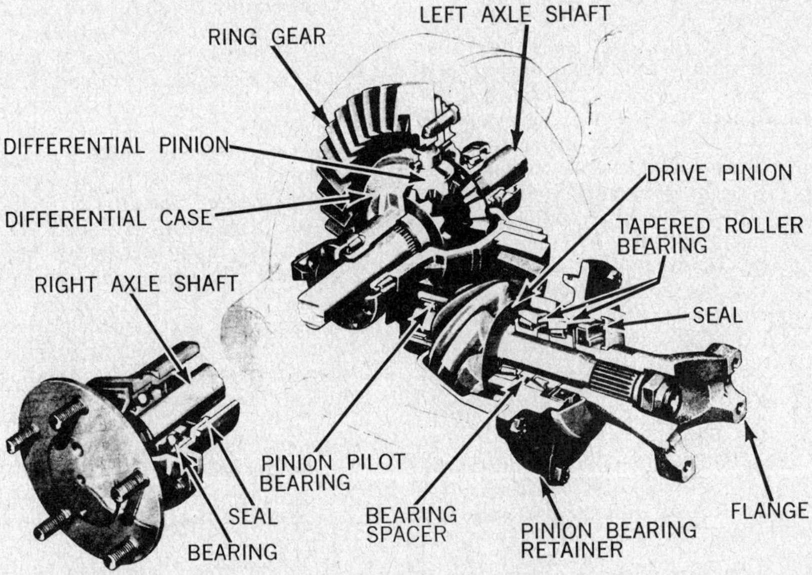

Ford banjo (removable carrier) type differential (© Ford Motor Co.)

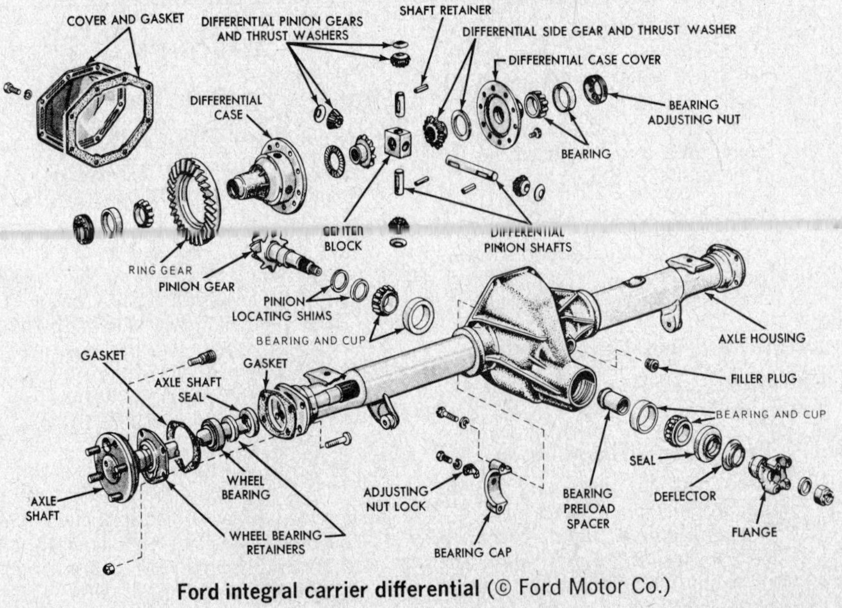

Ford integral carrier differential (© Ford Motor Co.)

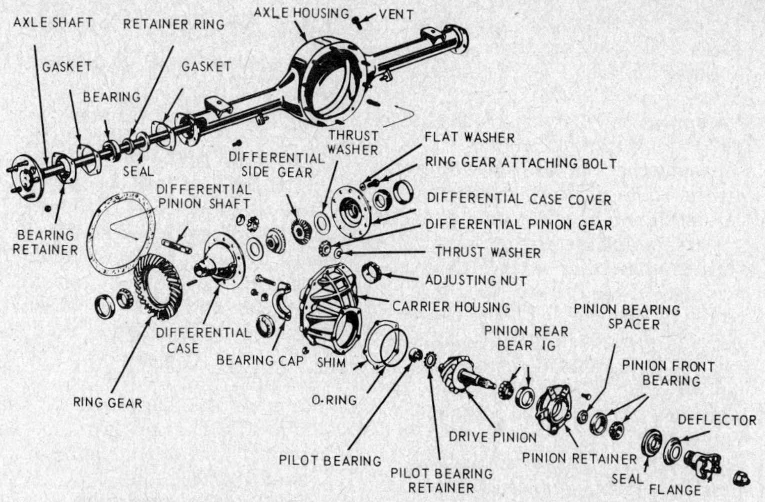

Ford banjo type differential—exploded view (© Ford Motor Co.)

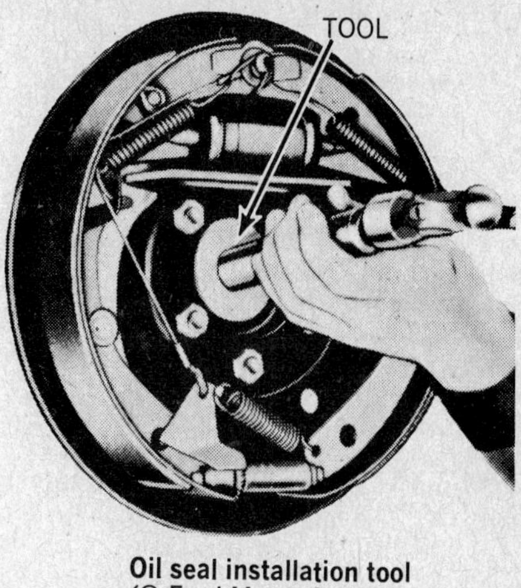

Oil seal installation tool
(© Ford Motor Co.)

nect the axle vent hose to the axle fitting.
15. Fill the axle with the proper grade and amount of lubricant.

Ford Removable Carrier Axle

Bronco, E100, F200, F100, and F150

Carrier Assembly

Removal and Installation

1. Raise the vehicle on a hoist and remove the two rear wheel and tire assemblies.
2. Remove the two brake drums (3 Tinnerman nuts at each drum) from the axle shaft flange studs. If difficulty is experienced in removing the drums, back off the brake shoes.
3. Working through the hole provided in each axle shaft flange, remove the nuts that secure the rear wheel bearing retainer plate. Pull each axle shaft assembly out of the axle housing using axle shaft remover, Tool 4235-C. Care must be exercised to prevent damage to oil seal, if so equipped. Any roughing or cutting of the seal element during removal or installation can result in early seal failure. Install a nut on one of the brake carrier plate attaching bolts to hold the plate to the axle housing after the shaft has been removed. Whenever a rear axle shaft is replaced, the wheel bearing oil seals must be replaced. Remove the seals with tool 1175-AB.
4. Make scribe marks on the drive shaft end yoke and the axle U-joint flange to insure proper position at assembly. Disconnect the drive shaft at the rear axle U-joint, remove the drive shaft from the transmission extension housing. Install oil seal replacer tool T57P-7657-A in the housing to prevent transmission leakage.
5. Place a drain pan under the carrier and housing, remove the carrier attaching nuts, and drain the axle. Remove the carrier assembly from the axle housing.
6. Synthetic wheel bearing seals must not be cleaned, soaked or washed in cleaning solvent. Clean the axle housing and shafts using kerosene and swabs. To avoid contamination of the grease in the sealed ball bearings, do not allow any quantity of solvent directly on the wheel bearings. Clean the mating surfaces of the axle housing and carrier.
7. Position the differential carrier on the studs in the axle housing using a new gasket between carrier and housing. Install the carrier-to-housing attaching nuts.
8. Remove the oil seal replacer tool from the transmission extension housing. Position the drive shaft so that the front U-joint slip yoke splines to the transmission output shaft.
9. Connect the drive shaft to the axle U-joint flange, aligning the scribe marks made on the drive shaft end yoke and the axle U-joint flange during the removal procedure. Install the U-bolts and nuts and torque to specifications.
10. Wipe a small amount of an oil-resistant sealer on the outer edge of each seal before it is installed. Do not put any of the sealer on the sealing lip. Install the oil seals in the ends of the rear axle housing with tool shown in illustration.
11. Install the two axle shaft assemblies in the axle housing. Care must be exercised to prevent damage to the oil seals. The shorter shaft goes into the left side of the housing. When installing an axle shaft, place a new gasket between the housing flange and the brake backing plate, and carefully slide the axle shaft into the housing so that the rough forging of the shaft will not damage the oil seal. Start the axle splines into the differential side gear, and push the shaft in until the bearing bottoms in the housing.
12. Install the bearing retainer plates on the attaching bolts on the axle housing flanges. Install and tighten the nuts on the bolts.
13. Install the two rear brake drums and the drum attaching nuts.
14. Install the rear wheel and tire assemblies.
15. If the rear brake shoes were backed off, adjust the brakes.
16. Fill the rear axle with lubricant.

Axle Housing

Removal and Installation

1. Remove the carrier assembly from the axle housing as outlined in the foregoing procedure.
2. Position safety stands under the rear frame members, and support the axle housing with either a floor jack or hoist.
3. Disengage the brake line from the clips that retain the line to the axle housing.
4. Disconnect the vent tube from the rear axle housing.
5. Remove the brake backing plate assemblies from the axle housing, and support them with wire. Do not disconnect the brake line.
6. Disconnect each rear shock absorber from the mounting bracket stud on the axle housing.
7. Lower the rear axle slightly to reduce some of the spring tension. At each rear spring, remove the spring clip (U-bolt) nuts, spring clips, and spring seat caps.

8. Remove the rear axle housing from under the vehicle. If the axle housing is new, install a new vent. The hose attaching portion must face toward the front of the vehicle.
9. Install new rear wheel bearing oil seals in the ends of the rear axle housing. If leather-type wheel bearing service seals are to be installed, soak the new rear wheel bearing oil seals in SAE 10 oil for ½ hour before installation.
10. Position the rear axle housing under the rear springs. Install the spring clips (U-bolts), spring seat caps, and nuts. *Torque the spring clip nuts evenly.*
11. If a new axle housing is being installed, remove the bolts that attach the carrier plate and bearing retainer from the old housing flanges. Position the bolts in the new housing flanges to hold the brake backing plates in position. Install the backing plates with new gaskets between the housing flange and the brake backing plate.
12. Connect the vent tube to the axle housing.
13. Position the brake line to the axle housing, and secure with the retaining clips.
14. Raise the rear axle housing and springs enough to allow connecting the rear shock absorbers to the mounting bracket studs on the axle housing.
15. Install the carrier assembly and the two axle shaft assemblies in the axle housing as outlined in this section.

Single-Speed, Single-Reduction Axles

Differential Carrier

Removal and Installation

1. Drain the axle lubricant.
2. Remove the axle shaft and the stud nuts and lockwasher.

   If tapered dowels are installed in the axle shaft flange, hold a short drift firmly in the center of icant.
2. Remove the axle shaft and the stud nuts and lockwasher.

   If tapered dowels are installed in the axle shaft flange, hold a short drift firmly in the center of the flange, and then strike it sharply to loosen the dowels. Remove the dowels and then remove the axle shaft.

   Tapered dowels are not used at the axle shaft flange on most of the larger vehicles, on these flanges, two threads are provided. Use one or both puller threads to remove the axle shafts.
3. Disconnect the drive shaft at the rear U-joint pinion flange.
4. Support the carrier assembly with a roller jack, then remove the carrier-to-housing stud nuts or bolts, and lock washers.
5. Tighten the puller screws, when provided in the carrier, until the carrier is losened from the housing, and then back off the puller screws. Remove and discard the gasket.
6. Place the carrier on a transmission stand.
7. Position a new gasket on the axle housing. *A dry gasket will prevent creeping between the carrier and housing under heavy loads.*
8. Place the differential carrier assembly on a roller jack, and roll the carrier into position. Start the carrier into the housing with four capscrews (or stud nuts) equally spaced.
9. Tighten the capscrews (or nuts) alternately to draw the carrier square into the housing. Install the remaining carrier-to-housing lockwashers and capscrews (or nut), then tighten.
10. Install new gaskets on the wheel hugs, then install the axle shafts. Install the dowels, lockwashers, and stud nuts.
11. Connect the drive shaft at the rear U-joint flange.
12. Fill the axle with the proper grade of lubricant.

Rear Axle Housing

Removal and Installation

1. Disconnect the drive shaft and remove the axle shafts and differential carrier as detailed above.
2. Disconnect the rear shock absorbers from the spring seal caps or shock absorber brackets. Raise the rear of the vehicle frame until the weight is off the rear springs. Place safety stands under the frame.
3. Disconnect the flexible hydraulic brake hose or air lines at the frame or frame cross member.
4. Remove the nuts from the spring clips (U-bolts), and remove the spring seat caps and shock absorber brackets.
5. Roll the axle housing and rear wheels from underneath the vehicle.
6. Remove the wheels from the axle housing.
7. Install the axle housing in the reverse order of removal.

Two Speed, Double Reduction Axles

Differential Carrier

Removal and Installation

1. Shift the axle into the low range.
2. Drain and discard the lubricant.
3. Remove the axle shafts, stud nuts and lock washers. Strike the center of each axle flange with a hammer and drift to loosen the tapered dowels, when used. Remove the axle shafts from the housing.
4. Remove the electric shift unit from the carrier housing. Disconnect the drive shaft at the rear U-joint flange.
5. Support the carrier on a roller jack. Remove the carrier-to-housing bolts and lockwashers or stud nuts.
6. Remove the carrier from the axle housing. Remove and discard the carrier-to-housing gasket.
7. Install guide studs in the axle housing. Place a new gasket over the guide studs.
8. Install the carrier in the axle housing. As the carrier-to-housing bolts are installed, remove the guide studs. Tighten the nuts and or bolts.
9. Install the axle shafts through the housing ends so that they will spline to the differential side gears. Install the tapered dowels, when used, lockwashers, and axle shaft flange stud nuts.
10. Install the electric shift unit. Connect the drive shaft at the rear U-joint flange.
11. Fill the axle with the proper grade lubricant up to the bottom of the filler hole in the rear cover, then add one pint of axle lubricant at the lubricant channel filler plug.
12. Road test the vehicle.

Rear Axle Housing

Removal and Installation

1. Disconnect the drive shaft and remove the axle shafts and differential carrier as detailed above.
2. Disconnect the rear shock absorbers from the spring seal caps of shock absorber brackets. Raise the rear of the vehicle frame until the weight is off the rear springs. Place safety stands under the frame.
3. Disconnect the flexible hydraulic brake hose or air lines at the frame or frame crossmember.
4. Remove the nuts from the spring clips (U-bolts), and remove the spring seat caps and shock absorber brackets.
5. Roll the axle housing and rear

wheels from underneath the vehicle.
6. Remove the wheels from the axle housing.
7. Install the axle housing in the reverse order of removal.

Eaton Tandem Axles

Power Divider and Carrier

Removal and Installation

1. Block the wheels.
2. Drain the power divider and axle housing.
3. Remove the vacuum or air shift components as equipped. Remove the lockout cylinder and mounting bracket from the power divider.
4. Disconnect the drive shaft at the input shaft.
5. Remove the air brake line from the right-hand forward axle brake chamber and the connector on the axle housing.
6. Remove both axle shafts.
7. Position a roller jack, with cradle, beneath the power divider and carrier. Fasten the assembly to the cradle.
8. Remove the axle carrier to housing stud nuts.
9. Disconnect the inter-axle drive shaft at the power divider output shaft flange.
10. Hold the output shaft flange, and remove the flange nut. Pull the flange out.
11. Carefully remove the power divider and carrier from the housing. As the power divider and carrier are moved out of the housing, the output shaft and roller bearing inner race must slide out of the straight rollers in the axle housing cover.
12. Remove the power divider and carrier from under the vehicle.
13. Clean the inside of the axle housing.
14. Remove the power divider output shaft flange seal from the axle housing rear cover. Remove the flange spacer and the roller bearing from the cover.
15. Mount the power divider and carrier in a roller jack.
16. Place a new gasket on the axle housing. Install the gasket dry to prevent leakage due to creeping caused by sealing compound.
17. Start the carrier housing on the axle housing studs and pull it into position with the stud nuts. Tighten the nuts.
18. Install the roller bearing outer race and cage in the housing cover. Place the spacer next to the bearing.
19. Install a new seal in the housing cover for the output shaft flange.
20. Start the flange on the output shaft. Hold the flange and pull it into position with the flange nut and flat washer. Tighten the nut and install a new cotter pin.
21. Connect the inner-axle drive shaft. Connect the drive shaft at the input shaft flange.
22. Install and connect the power divider lockout unit. Install the air line to the brake chamber.
23. Place new gaskets on the wheel hub studs and install the axle shafts. Tighten the stud nuts.
24. Fill the power divider and axle housing with the proper grade lubricant.

Rear Axle Carrier Removal and Installation

For removal and installation of the rear axle carrier, follow the procedure outlined in the Single-Speed, Single-Reduction Axle or Two-Speed, Double Reduction Axle.

Rockwell Tandem Axles

Inter-Axle Differential and Forward Carrier Removal and Installation

1. Disconnect the forward drive shaft at the inter-axle differential input shaft flange.
2. Disconnect the rear drive shaft at the through shaft flange.
3. Remove the plug from the bottom of the axle housing and drain the lubricant. Drain the lubricant from the inter-axle differential cover by removing the bottom plug.
4. Remove the axle shaft, stud nuts and lockwashers.

   If tapered dowels are installed in the axle shaft flange, hold a short drift firmly in the center of the axle shaft flange, and then strike it sharply to loosen the dowels and remove the axle shaft.

   Tapered dowels are not used at the axle shaft flange on most of the larger trucks. On these flanges, two puller threads are provided. Use one or both puller threads to remove the axle shafts.
5. Remove the attaching screws and lockwashers, and remove the shift housing assembly.
6. Remove the shift lever attaching nut, and lift out the button, shift lever, cap, and spring.
7. Remove the through-shaft, cage and flange assembly. To free the through-shaft cage from the housing bore, it may be necessary to tap the yoke with a soft mallet. While the through-shaft assembly is being drawn out from the rear of the housing, work the sliding clutch splines by hand at the shift lever opening. When the through-shaft clears the opening, lift out the clutch.
8. Remove all the carrier-to-housing nuts except the two nuts, which should be loosened but left on the studs to prevent the carrier from falling. Break the carrier loose with a rawhide mallet.
9. Place a roller jack under the carrier, and remove the two top nuts. Work the carrier free. A small pinch bar may be used to straighten the carrier in the housing bore, but the end of the bar should be rounded to prevent indenting the carrier flange.
10. Clean the inside of the axle housing and install a new gasket over the housing studs.
11. Mount the inter-axle differential and carrier assembly on a roller jack and move the assembly into position. Start the carrier into the housing with nuts and flat washers, equally spaced on the housing. Tighten the nuts enough to draw the carrier into the housing.
12. Remove the nuts and flat washers, install the lockwashers and stud nuts. Tighten the nuts.
13. Insert the through-shaft and cage, with a new gasket, into the cage bore in the rear of the axle. Move the through-shaft in until the forward end of the shaft is even with the shift lever opening.
14. Slide the splined clutch collar over the forward end of the shaft, through the shift opening, and ease the shaft through and into the forward side gear of the inter-axle differential. At the same time, pass the splined clutch collar through and onto the through-shaft clutch splines.
15. Install the through-shaft cage retaining screws and lockwashers, tighten the screws.
16. Install the shift lever spring, cup, and lever over the shift lever bolt. Properly locate the lever inner yoke in the clutch groove at this time.
17. Install the shift lever button and nut. Tighten the nut and install a new cotter pin.
18. Position the shift shaft housing with a new gasket, on the carrier. Be sure that the shift lever outer yoke is properly located in the shift shaft collar groove.
19. Install the shift housing capscrews and tighten.
20. Install the axle shafts and the retaining nuts and lockwashers.
21. Remove the fill plugs on the axle housing and inter-axle differential cover and fill the assembly with the proper grade of lubricant. Install the plugs.
22. Connect the rear drive shaft at the through shaft flange.
23. Connect the forward drive shaft at the inter-axle differential input shaft flange.

Rear Axle Carrier

Removal and Installation

For removal and installation of the rear axle carrier, follow the procedures outlined in *Single-Speed, Single-Reduction Axle Removal and Installation.*

Axle Shaft

Ford Removable Carrier

Removal and Installation

1. Raise and support the vehicle and remove the wheel/tire assembly from the brake drum.
2. Remove the nuts which secure the brake drum to the axle flange, then remove the drum from the flange.
3. Working through the hole provided in each axle shaft flange, remove the nuts which secure the wheel bearing retainer plate.
4. Using an axle puller, pull the axle shaft assembly out of the axle housing.

   NOTE: The brake backing plate must not be dislodged. Install one nut to hold the plate in place after the axle shaft is removed.
5. To install, remove the one nut which holds the brake backing plate and carefully slide the axle shaft into the housing, so that the rough forgings on the shaft will not damage the oil seal.
6. Start the axle splines into the side gear and push the shaft in until the bearing bottoms in the housing.
7. Install the bearing retainer plate and the nuts which secure it.
8. Install the brake drum and the drum attaching nuts.
9. Install the wheel/tire assembly and lower the vehicle.

Dana Integral Carrier

Removal and Installation

1. Remove the lockbolts and lockwashers which hold the axle flange to the hub and drum assembly.

   NOTE: It is not necessary to raise the vehicle to remove the axle shafts.
2. Carefully slide the axle shaft out of the axle housing.
3. Clean the mating surfaces of the axle flange and the hub and drum assembly.
4. Position a new gasket on the axle flange and carefully slide the axle shaft into the axle housing. When the splined end of the axle shaft reaches the side gear, gently rotate the shaft until it is inserted into the side gear.
5. Position the gasket between the axle flange and the hub and drum and install the lockbolts and lockwashers.

Axle Shaft Bearing

Removal and Installation (Axle Out)

NOTE: Whenever an axle shaft is removed, the oil seal should be replaced. Remove the axle oil seal with a suitable axle seal removing tool. Inspect the machine surfaces of the axle shaft and the axle housing for rough spots or other irregularities which could affect the bearing action of the oil seal.

1. Drill a ¼″ to a ½″ hole in the outside diameter of the inner retainer to a depth of appoximately ¾″ the thickness of the retainer ring.

   NOTE: Do not drill all the way through the retainer ring as the drill could damage the axle shaft.
2. After drilling the retainer ring, use a chisel positioned across the drilled hole and strike sharply to split the retainer ring. Discard the retainer, as it is not reusable.
3. Press the bearing off the axle shaft with a suitable tool.
4. To install, coat the wheel bearing bores with axle lubricant. Place the bearing retainer plate on the axle shaft, if removed.
5. Press the new wheel bearing on the axle shaft with a suitable tool. Press the bearing inner retainer ring on the axle shaft under the retainer seats firmly against the bearing.

NOTE: Do not attempt to press both the bearing and the inner retainer ring on the axle shaft at the same time.

Pinion Seal

Light Duty Vehicles

Removal and Installation

NOTE: The drive pinion oil seal can be replaced without removing the differential carrier assembly from the housing.

1. Raise the vehicle and install safety stands. Remove both rear wheels and brake drums.
2. Match mark the drive shaft end yoke and the axle U-joint flange to insure poper positioning at re-installation. Disconnect the drive shaft from the axle U-joint flange. Do not drop the loose U-joint bearing cups. Mark the cups so that they will be in their original position in relation to the flange when they are reassembled.
3. Remove the drive shaft from the transmission extension housing. Install an oil seal replacer tool in the housing to prevent the transmission fluid form leaking out.
4. Position an in.-lb. torque wrench on the pinion nut. Record the torque required to maintain rotation of the pinion shaft through several revolutions.
5. Scribe the pinion shaft and the U-joint flange inner surface for assembly re-alignment. Hold the flange with the pinion yoke holding tool and remove the integral pinion nut and washer.
6. Clean the front drive pinion bearing retainer around the oil seal. Place a drain pan under the seal, or raise the front of the vehicle higher than the rear.
7. Using the pinion yoke holding tool remove the U-joint flange.
8. Using an oil seal removal tool, remove the drive pinion oil seal. Clean the oil seal seat.
9. To install, position the new seal in the retainer, using the applicable tool.
10. Check the splines on the drive pinion shaft to be sure that they are free of burrs. If they are not remove them by using a fine crocus cloth, working in a rotational motion. Apply a small amount of lubricant to the U-joint flange and the pinion shaft.

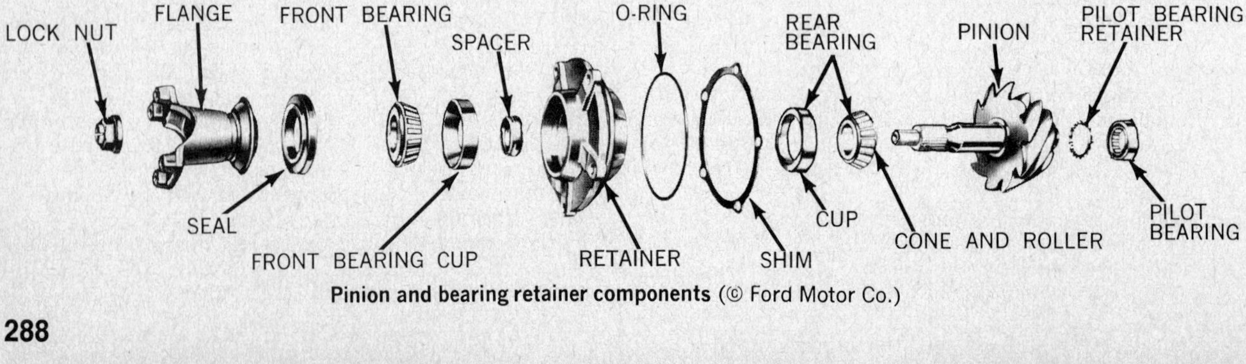

Pinion and bearing retainer components (© Ford Motor Co.)

11. Install the U-joint flange. Install a new integral nut and washer on the pinion shaft (hold the shaft with the pinion yoke holding tool while tightening the nut).
12. Tighten the pinion shaft nut, rotating the pinion occasionally to insure proper bearing seatting, and to take frequent peload readings. If the recorded preload is less than specification, (8-14 in.-lb. for the old bearing, 17-27 in.-lb. for the new bearing) tighten to specification. If the preload is higher than specification, tighten to the original reading.

    NOTE: Under no circumstances should the pinion nut be backed off to lessen the preload. If this is done, a new collapsible spacer must be installed.
13. Remove the oil seal replacer tool from the transmission extension housing and install the front end of the drive shaft on the transmission output shaft.
14. Connect the rear end of the drive shaft to the axle U-joint flange, aligning the scribe marks made on the drive shaft end yoke and the axle U-joint flange.
15. Check the lubricant level.

    NOTE: Make sure that the axle is in the running position. Add whatever amount of the proper lubricant is necessary to reach the lower edge of the filler plug hole.
16. Install the brake drum and attaching nuts. Install the wheels and tires. Lower the vehicle.

Medium and Heavy Duty Vehicles

Removal and Installation

NOTE: The drive pinion oil seal can be replaced without removing the differential carrier assembly from the rear axle or the rear axle from the vehicle.

1. Disconnect the drive shaft from the rear U-joint pinion flange.
2. With a pinion yoke holding tool installed on the U-joint flange, remove the cotter pin, nut and washer from the drive pinion shaft. Remove the flange.
3. Remove the bolts that attach the oil seal retainer and the pinion bearing retainer to the carrier. Remove the oil seal retainer and gasket.
4. Using an oil seal removal tool, remove the oil seal from the retainer.
5. To install, coat the outside edge of the new oil seal with an oil-resistant sealer and press it into the oil seal retainer, using the proper oil seal replacer tool. Apply a light coat of lubriplate to the contact areas of the seal and the drive pinion shaft.
6. Position the oil seal retainer and a new gasket against the pinion bearing retainer. Install and tighten the bolts that attach the oil seal retainer and the pinion bearing reainer to the differential carrier assembly.
7. Install and tighten the U-joint flange, nut, washer and cotter pin. Connect the drive shaft to the rear U-joint flange.
8. Check the lubricant level and fill as necessary.

REAR SUSPENSION

Rear Spring (Single Axle) E-100, 150, 200

Removal and Installation

1. Raise the rear end of the vehicle and support the chassis with safety stands. Support the rear axle with a floor jack or hoist.
2. Disconnect the lower end of the shock absorber from the bracket on the axle housing.
3. Remove the two U-bolts and plate.
4. Lower the axle and remove the upper and lower rear shackle bolts.
5. Pull the rear shackle assembly and rubber bushings from the bracket and spring.
6. Remove the nut and mounting bolt that secures the front end of the spring. Remove the spring assembly from the front shackle bracket.
7. Install new rubber bushings in the rear shackle bracket and in the rear eye of the replacement spring.
8. Position the spring assembly and connect the front eye of the spring to the front shackle bracket by installing the front mounting bolt and nut. Do not tighten the nut.
9. Mount the rear end of the spring by inserting the upper bolt of the rear shackle assembly through the eye of the spring and lower bolt through the rear spring hanger.
10. Position the spring center bolt to the pilot hole in the axle and install the plate. Install the U-bolts through the plate. Do not tighten the attaching nuts at this time.
11. Raise the axle with a floor jack or hoist until the vehicle is free of the stands and connect the lower end of the shock absorber to the bracket on the axle housing.
12. Tighten the spring front mount-

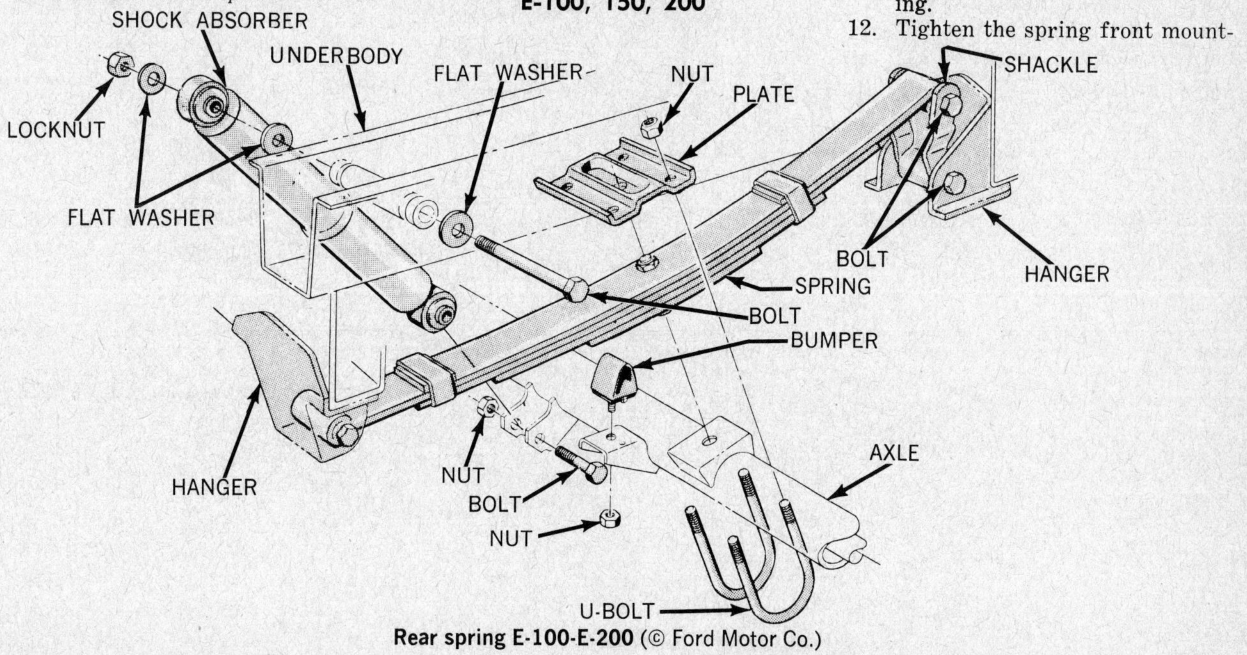

Rear spring E-100-E-200 (© Ford Motor Co.)

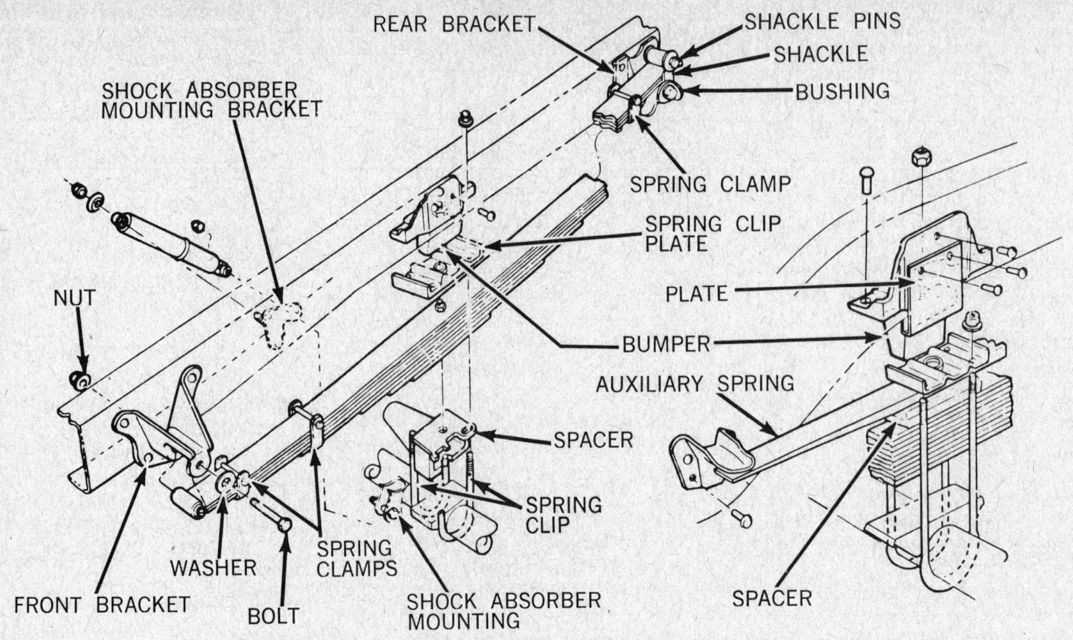

Rear suspension—F-250 4-wheel drive (© Ford Motor Co.)

ing bolt and nut, the rear shackle nuts and the U-bolt nuts.
13. Remove the safety stands and lower the vehicle.

E-250, 300, 350

Removal and Installation

1. Raise the rear end of the vehicle and support the chassis with safety stands. Support the rear axle with a floor jack or hoist.
2. Disconnect the lower end of the shock absorber from the bracket on the axle housing.
3. Remove the two spring clips (U-bolts) and the spring clip cap.
4. Lower the axle and remove the guiding it so that the center bolt spring front bolt from the hanger.
5. Remove the two attaching bolts from the rear of the spring. Remove the spring and the shackle.
6. Assemble the upper end of the shackle to the spring with the attaching bolt.
7. Connect the front of the spring to the front bracket with the attaching bolt.
8. Assemble the spring and shackle to the rear bracket with the attaching bolt.
9. Place the spring clip plate over the head of the center bolt.
10. Raise the axle with a jack and enters the pilot hole in the pad on the axle housing.
11. Install the spring clips, cap and attaching nuts. Tighten the nuts snugly.
12. Connect the lower end of the shock absorber to the lower bracket.
13. Tighten the spring front mounting bolt and nut, the rear shackle nuts and spring clip nuts.
14. Remove the safety stands and lower the vehicle.

1973-75 F and P series

Removal and Installation

1. Raise the vehicle frame until the

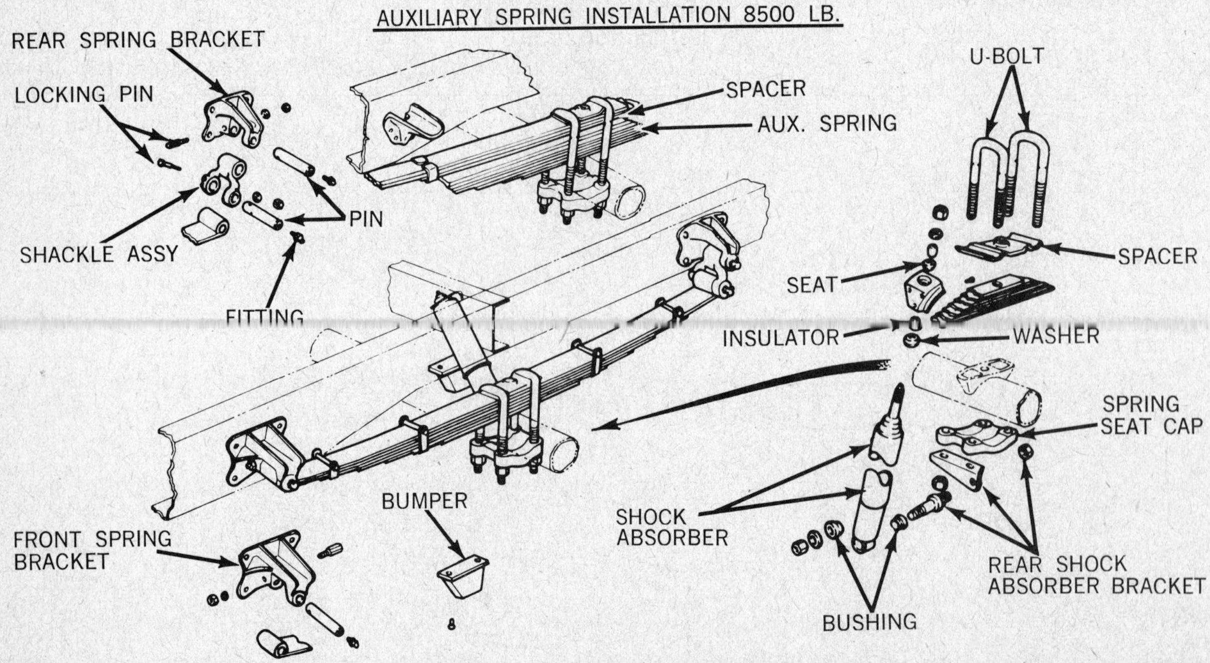

Rear suspension—P-400 (© Ford Motor Co.)

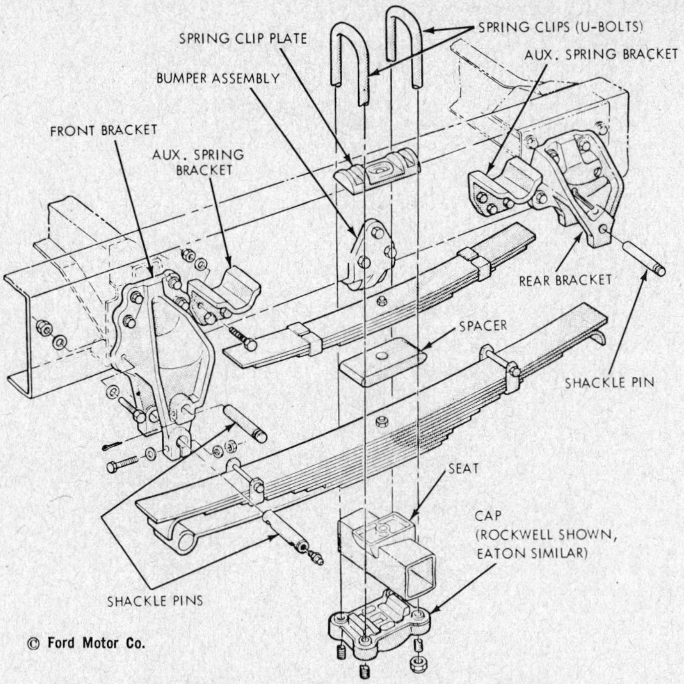

Rear Spring installation (© Ford Motor Co.)

weight is off the rear springs with the wheels still touching the floor.

2. Remove the nuts from the spring clips (U-bolts) and drive the clips out of the spring seat cap and remove the spring clip plate. If the truck is so equipped, remove the auxiliary spring and spacer.
3. Remove the shackle pin locking bolts from each end of the spring (bolt and nut on F-250 4 x 4 front eye).
4. Working from the inner side of the frame, insert a drift in the hole provided in the frame for removing the shackle pin. Drive the shackle pin out of each spring bracket (bolt on F-250 4 x 4 front eye).
5. Remove the spring and shackle from the vehicle. On F-100-250 4 x 4 models, remove the spring to axle spacer.
6. Drive out the remaining shackle pin from the rear spring eye and remove the shackle from the spring.
7. Position the shackle to the rear spring eye.
8. Install the shackle pin through the shackle and spring eye with the lubricator fitting on the shackle pin facing outward.
9. Line up the shackle pin lock bolt groove with the lock bolt hole in the shackle. Install the lock bolt, lock washer, and nut.
10. Position the spring on the axle, making sure that the spring tie bolt is in the hole provided in the axle spring seat or spacer. On F-100-250 4 x 4 models, first install the spacer between the spring seat and the spring, making sure the spacer dowel is positioned in the pilot hole of the axle spring seat.
11. Install a shackle pin through the shackle and rear bracket, with the lubricating fitting on the shackle pin facing outward. Line up the pin groove with the lock bolt hole in the bracket, and install the lock bolt, lock washer, and nut as before.
12. Repeat this operation to install a shackle pin at the front bracket and spring eye (bolt on F-250 4 x 4).
13. If so equipped, install the auxiliary spring and spacer. Place the spring clip plate on top of the spring at the tie bolt, and put the spring clips over the spring assembly and axle.
14. Position the spring seat cap, and install the nuts on the spring clips.
15. Lower the vehicle to the floor and tighten the spring clip nuts. Lubricate the fittings on the shackle pins.

1976-80 F-100, 150, 250 and 1978-80 Bronco

Removal and Installation

1. Raise the vehicle frame, until the weight is off the rear spring, with the tires still touching the floor.
2. Remove the nuts from the spring U-bolts and drive the U-bolts from the U-bolt plate. If so equipped, remove the auxiliary spring and the spacer.
3. Remove the spring-to-bracket nut and bolt at the front of the spring.
4. Remove the shackle upper and lower nuts and bolts at the rear of the spring. Remove the spring and shackle assembly from the rear shackle bracket.
5. If the bushings in the spring or shackle are worn or damaged, replace them.
6. To install, position the spring in the shackle, and install the upper shackle-to-spring bolt and nut with the bolt head facing outboard.
7. Position the front end of the spring in the bracket and install. Position the shackle in the rear bracket and install.

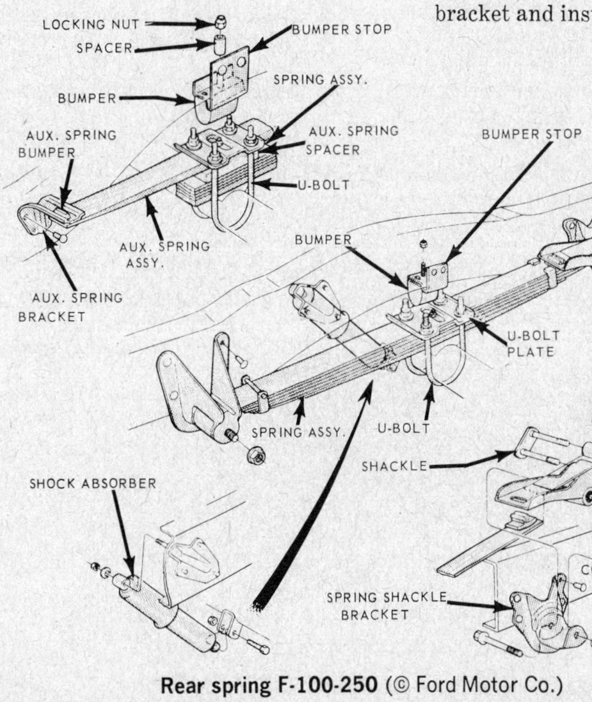

Rear spring F-100-250 (© Ford Motor Co.)

8. Position the spring on top of the axle with the spring tie bolt centered in the hole provided in the seat. If equipped, install the auxiliary spring and spacer.
9. Install the spring U-bolt plate and nuts. Lower the vehicle. Tighten the sping U-bolt nuts. Tighten the front spring bolt and nut and the rear shackle bolts and nuts.

1973-77 Bronco

Removal and Installation

1. Raise the vehicle by the axles and install safety stands under the frame.
2. Disconnect the shock absorber from the axle.
3. Remove the U-bolt attaching nuts and remove the two U-bolts and the spring clip plate.
4. Lower the axle to relieve spring tension and remove the nut from the spring front attaching bolt
5. Remove the spring front attaching bolt from the spring and hanger with a drift.
6. Remove the nut from the shackle to hanger attaching bolt and drive the bolt from the shackle and hanger with a drift and remove the spring from the vehicle.
7. Remove the nut from the spring rear attaching bolt. Drive the bolt out of the spring and shackle with a drift.
8. Position the shackle (closed section facing toward front of vehicle) to the spring rear eye and install the bolt and nut.
9. Position the spring front eye and bushing to the spring front hanger, and install the attaching bolt and nut.
10. Position the spring rear eye and bushing to the shackle, and install the attaching bolt and nut.
11. Raise the axle to the spring and install the U-bolts (when an axle cap is not used, the U-bolt shank should contact the leaf edges) and spring clip plate. Align the spring leaves.
12. Tighten the U-bolt nuts and the spring front and rear attaching bolt nuts. The U-bolts should contact the spring assembly edges or axle seat.
13. Connect the shock absorber to the axle and tighten the nut.
14. Remove the safety stands and lower the vehicle.

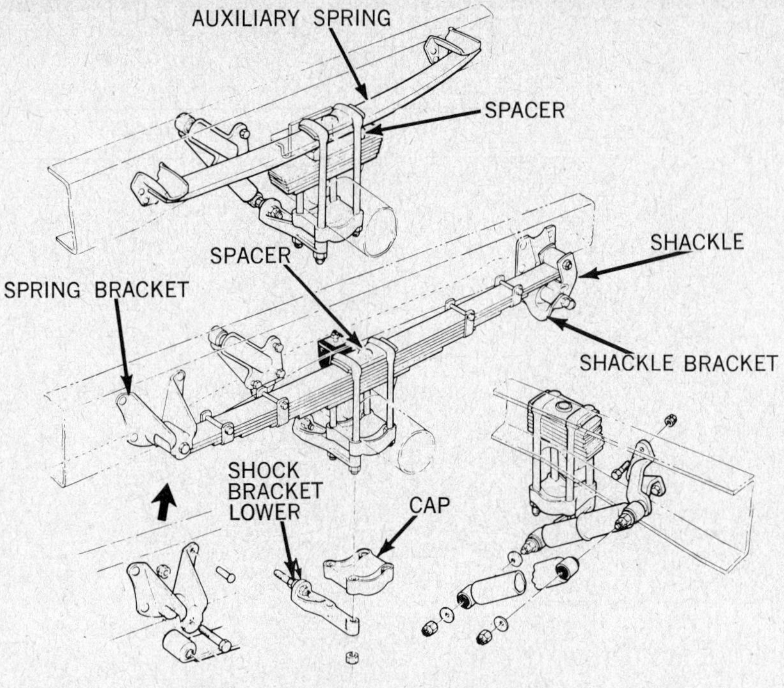

Rear spring F-350 (© Ford Motor Co.)

1973-80 F-350

Removal and Installation

1. Raise the vehicle frame until the weight is off the rear springs with the wheels still touching the floor.
2. Remove the nuts from the spring U-bolts.
3. Drive the U-bolts out of the shock absorber lower bracket and the spring cap and remove the U-bolts.
4. Remove the spacer from the top of the spring.
5. If equipped with auxiliary springs, remove the auxiliary spring and spacer.
6. Remove the shackle to bracket bolt and nut from the rear of the spring.
7. Remove the spring-to-hanger bolt and nut from the front of the spring and remove the spring.
8. Remove the shackle-to-spring bolt and nut and remove the shackle from the spring.
9. Position the shackle to the spring and install the attaching bolt and nut. The bolt must be installed so the nut is away from the frame.
10. Position the spring to the spring front hanger and install the attaching bolt and nut.
11. Position the shackle to the bracket and install the attaching bolt and nut.
12. Align the spring toe bolt with the pilot hole in the axle spring seat and, if so equipped, install the auxiliary spring and spacer.
13. Position the spacer on top of the spring and install the U-bolts over the spacer, spring and axle.
14. Position the spring cap and shock lower bracket to the axle and U-bolts. Install the U-bolt attaching nuts.
15. Lower the vehicle and tighten the front spring bracket bolt and nut and the rear shackle bolts and nuts.

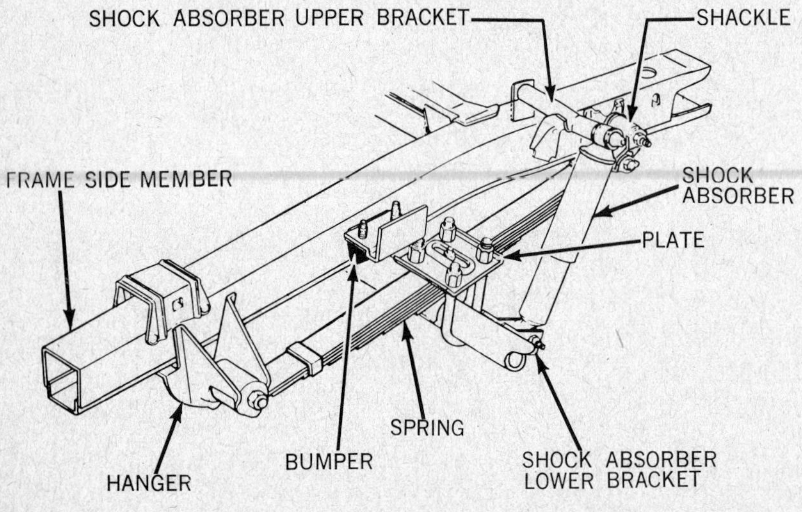

Rear suspension—Bronco (© Ford Motor Co.)

C-Series

Removal and Installation

1. Raise the vehicle frame until the weight is off the rear springs with the wheels still touching the floor.
2. Remove the nuts from the spring clips (U-bolts) and drive the clips out of the spring seat cap. If so equipped, remove the auxiliary spring and spacer.
3. Remove the shackle pin locking bolts from each spring bracket.
4. A hole is provided in the frame opposite each spring bracket for removing the shackle pin. Insert a drift from the inside of the frame through these holes and drive the shackle pin out of each bracket.
5. Remove the spring and shackle assembly from the truck. Separate the spring from the shackle by removing the locking bolt and driving out the shackle lower pin from the shackle and spring eye.
6. Remove the lubricating fittings from the shackle pins.
7. Align the upper bore of the shackle with the holes in the rear bracket. Drive the shackle upper pin through the shackle and bracket with the pin lubricator hole facing outward.
8. Line up the shackle pin groove with the locking bolt hole in the bracket and install the locking bolt, washer and nut.
9. Install the spring seat and the wedge (if so equipped) between the axle and the spring. Position the spring on the axle, being sure that the spring tie bolt is in the hole provided in the axle or spring seats. If so equipped, install the auxiliary spring and spacer.
10. Drive the shackle lower pin through the shackle and spring rear eye. Install the locking bolt, washer and nut as before. Repeat the operation to install the shackle pin through the spring front bracket and eye.
11. Place the spring clip plate on top of the spring at the tie bolt, and put the spring clips over the spring assembly and the axle.
12. Install the spring seat cap on the spring clips and install the spring clip nuts on the clips.
13. Lower the vehicle to the floor and tighten the spring clip nuts.

L-LN-B-W Series

Removal and Installation

1. Lift the vehicle until the weight is off of the rear spring but the wheels still touch the ground.
2. Remove the nuts from the U-bolts and drive the bolts out of the spring seat caps.
3. Remove the auxiliary spring and spacer.
4. Support the spring and remove the front shackle pins. The lower pin is held in place by a lock bolt and the upper is held by a cotter pin.
5. Remove the cotter pin in the rear shackle pin and remove the pin. Remove the spring from the vehicle.
6. To install place the spring in the rear shackle bracket and install the shackle pin and cotter pin.
7. With a jack or C-clamp press the front eye of the spring up into the bracket until the eye is lined up with the hole in the bracket. Install the shackle pins in the spring and secure them in place with the lock bolt or the cotter pin.
8. Install the spring seat and the wedge (if so equipped) between the axle and spring and install the U-bolts over the axle and install the nuts on the bolts after installing the spring seat cap.
9. Lower the vehicle and tighten the nuts on the U-bolts securely.

Rear Spring (Hendrickson Tandems)

Removal and Installation

1. Raise the rear of the vehicle and position the blocks under the frame behind the rear axle.
2. Remove the wheels, hub, and drum from the forward rear axle.
3. Remove the support beam bar saddle caps from the lower side of the support beam.
4. Position a jack under the front end of the support beam.
5. Remove the shackle pin lock pin from the spring front bracket and remove the shackle pin.
6. Lower the support beam and spring. Remove the spring from the support beam.
7. a. *RU and RUE suspension*: Remove the U-bolt nuts and remove the saddle and U-bolts from the spring.

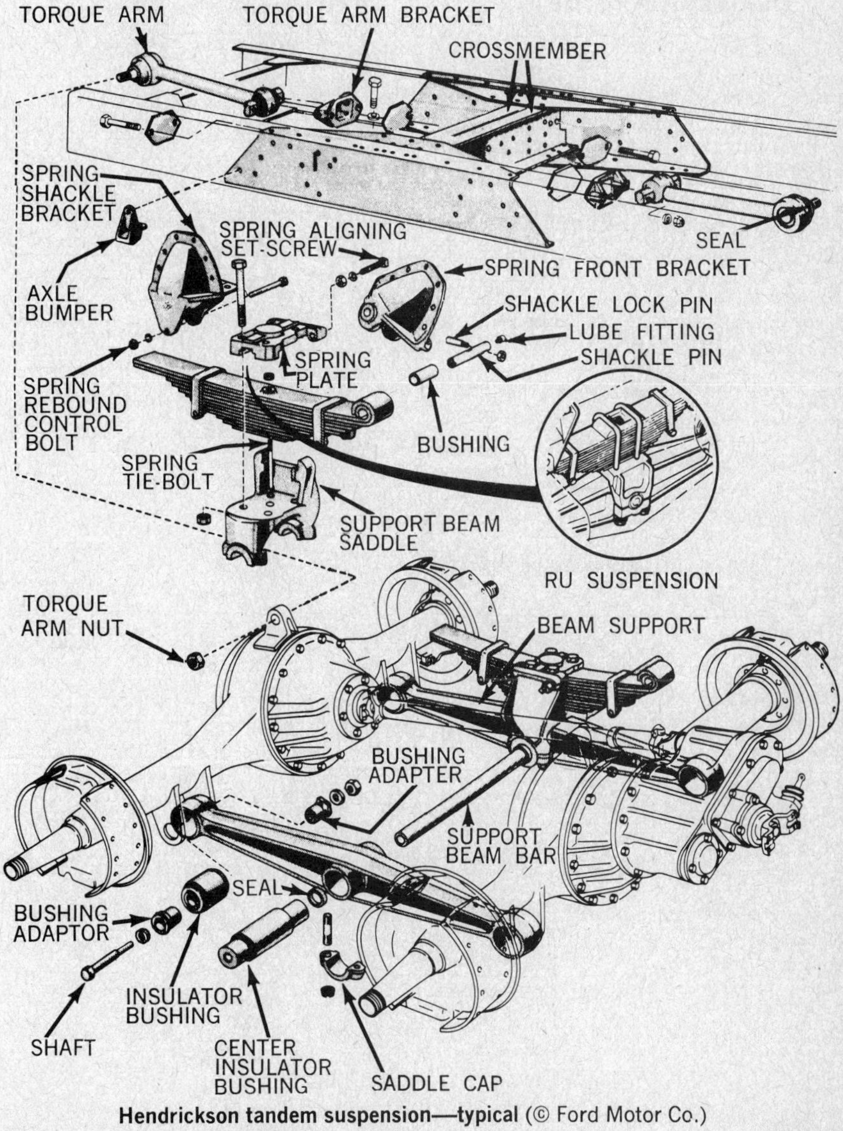

Hendrickson tandem suspension—typical (© Ford Motor Co.)

b. *RT suspension*: Remove the spring plate-to-support beam saddle attaching bolts and nuts. Remove the saddle and spring plate from the spring.

8. a. *RU and RUE suspension*: Position the saddle on the spring and install the U-bolts and nuts. Tap the U-bolts with a hammer while tightening the nuts.

   b. *RT suspension*: Position the spring plate and saddle on the spring. Snug up, but do not tighten, the saddle nuts. Tighten the spring plate set screw and lock down, then tighten the saddle nuts.
9. Position the spring and saddle on the support beam and spring rear bracket.
10. Raise the support beam and spring, and position the spring on the front spring bracket.
11. Align the spring with the front bracket and install the shackle pin.
12. Install the shackle pin lock pin and tighten the lock pin nut.
13. Install the hub, drum, and wheel on the forward rear axle.
14. Remove the jack from the support beam and the blocks from the rear of the frame. Lower the saddle on the support beam bar center insulator bushing and install the saddle caps.
15. Install the saddle caps and tighten.

NOTE: The weight of the vehicle must be on the suspension when the saddle cap attaching nuts are tightened.

Shock Absorber

Econoline and 1973-77 Bronco

Removal and Installation

1. Raise the vehicle on a hoist.
2. Remove the shock absorber lower attaching nut and bolt, and swing the lower end free of the mounting bracket on the axle housing.
3. Remove the attaching nut from the upper mounting stud, and remove the shock absorber.
4. To install, position the shock absorber with the rubber bushings and steel washers to the upper mounting bolt.
5. Swing the lower end of the shock absorber into the mounting bracket on the axle housing. Install the attaching washers, mounting bolt, and self-locking nut.
6. Install the self-locking nut on the upper mounting bolt.
7. Lower the vehicle from the hoist.

All Others

Removal and Installation

1. Remove the self-locking nut, steel washer, and rubber bushings at the upper and lower ends of the shock absorber.
2. Remove the unit from the vehicle.
3. To install, position the shock absorber on the mounting brackets with the large diameter at the top.
4. Install the rubber bushing, steel washer, and self-locking nut.

REAR SUSPENSION TORQUE LIMITS — F-SERIES, E-SERIES, BRONCO

Description	Model	Ft-Lb
Rear Shock Upper Mounting	F-100-F-250, F-150 (4x4), F-250 (4x4), E-100-350, F-350 SC, F-350, Bronco	15-25
Rear Shock Lower Mounting	F-Series, E-Series, Bronco	40-60
Rear Spring to Axle U-Bolt	F-150-F-250 (4x4),	(9/16-12 Nut)
	E-100-E-150	85-115
	F-350	110-160
	E-250-E-350	150-200
	Bronco	45-60
Rear Spring to Front Hanger	F-100, F-150 (4x2)	(9/16-12 Nut) 75-105
	F-150 (4x4), F-250, F-350	150-200
	E-100-E-350	(5/8-11 Nut) 110-160
Rear Spring to Rear Hanger	F-100-F-350 SC, Bronco, E-100-E-350, F-150-F-250 4x4	75-105

REAR SUSPENSION TORQUE LIMITS — 500-9000 SERIES

Torque limits are determined by these bolt and nut diameters	
Dia. Inches	Torque Limit
1/4	85-115 in-lb
5/16	12-17 ft-lb
3/8	31-42 ft-lb
7/16	50-70 ft-lb
1/2	75-105 ft-lb
9/16	110-150 ft-lb
5/8	150-205 ft-lb
3/4	220-300 ft-lb
7/8	360-480 ft-lb
1.0	540-730 ft-lb

TANDEM SUSPENSION TORQUE LIMITS (FT-LBS)

Hendrickson					
Description	RU-RUE-RT	RS	Description	RU-RUE-RT	RS
Beam & Adaptor to Axle	220-300	220-300	Torque Arm to Axle Taper Pin	220-300	220-300
Spring Brackets to Frame*	220-300	—	Cap to Saddle RU & RUE	110-150	110-150
Shackle Pin Lock Nut	75-100	—	Cap to Saddle RT & RS	220-300	220-330
Axle Bumper to Frame*	220-300	220-300	Hanger Assembly to Frame	—	150-205
Torque Arm to Bracket to Crossmember	150-205	150-205	Hanger Assembly to Saddle Assembly	—	220-300
Spring U-Bolt Nuts RU-RUE Only	237-302	—	Bushing Retainer Clamp Nuts	—	100-125
Spring Plate Set Screw RT Only	100-150	—	Beam End Tube Nut	—	360-480
			Saddle Nut RT Only	275-300	—

* For CT Models equipped with ⅝" bolts use 150-250 ft-lbs.

SPECIAL TOOLS

Tool Number	Description
OTCY-865	Beam Adapter Remover
T57L-4614-A	Saddle Bushing Remover
OTC-1002-L	Axle Bracket Arm Stud Remover

INDEX

ENGINE IDENTIFICATION CODE

1500-3500 Series (Light Duty Trucks)

NOTE: On 1973-78 vehicles, a combination Vehicle Identification Number and rating plate used on all models is located on the left door lock pillar of C, K, and G models. On forward control models it is attached to the dash and toe panel. On 1979-80 vehicles the Vehicle Identification Number is stamped on a plate which is attached to the left top of the instrument panel on C, K, and G models, and is visible through the windshield. On P-1500-3500 models the plate is attached to the front of the dash and toe panel to the left of the steering column.

The third symbol of the Vehicle Identification Number is the engine code. Refer to the chart for the corresponding engine cubic inch displacement.

YEAR	250 Cu. In. L-6/1 bbl.	292 Cu. In. L-6/1 bbl.	305 Cu. In. V-8/2 bbl.	307 Cu. In. V-8/2 bbl.	350 Cu. In. V-8/2 bbl.	350 Cu. In. V-8/4 bbl.	400 Cu. In. V-8/4 bbl.	454 Cu. In. V-8/4 bbl.	454 Cu. In. V-8/4 bbl.	350 Cu. In V-8/Diesel
1973	Q	T	—	X	—	Y	—	Z①	—	—
1974	Q	T	—	—	V	Y	—	Z①	—	—
1975	Q	T	—	—	V	Y	M	Z①	L②	—
1976	D	T	Q	—	V	L	U	S①	Y②	—
1977	D	T	U	—	—	L	R	S③	Y④	—
1978	D	T	U	—	—	L	R	S	—	Z
1979-80	D	T	U	—	M	L	R	S	—	Z

4000 through 9000 Series (Medium and Heavy Duty Trucks)

NOTE: A combination Vehicle Identification and Rating plate is used on all 1973-78 5000-9000 series trucks. It is attached to the left-hand door pillar on most models. Bus models have their plate attached to the air intake plenum panel. In 1979 and 1980, the Vehicle Identification Number plate for all 4000-7000 series trucks is located on the top of the instrument panel and is visible from the driver's side looking through the windshield. A combination Vehicle Identification and Rating plate, used on all 8000-9000 seres trucks, is attached to the left-hand door pillar on most models. Bus models have their plates attached to the air intake plenum panel.

For 1973-78 medium and heavy duty trucks, the third symbol of the Vehicle Identification Number is the engine code. For 1979-80 medium and heavy duty trucks, the fifth symbol of the Vehicle Identification Number is the engine code. Refer to the chart for the corresponding, applicable engine.

ENGINE	1973-78	1979-80
6 Cyl. Gasoline	S	T
V-8 Gasoline	E	—
350 Cu. In. Gasoline	—	A
366 Cu. In. Gasoline	—	B
427 Cu. In. Gasoline	—	E
454 Cu. In. Gasoline	—	S
3406 Caterpillar Inline 6 Cyl. Diesel	R	R
3208 Caterpillar V-8 Diesel	Y	Y
Cummins KT-450 Inline 6 Cyl. Diesel	L	L
Cummins Turbocharged 6 Cyl. Diesel	C	C
Cummins V-8 Diesel	B	—
Detroit Diesel 4-53 Series	D	D
Detroit Diesel Inline 6 Cyl.	I	—
Detroit Diesel 6-71 Series	—	I
Detroit Diesel V6-53 Series	V	V
Detroit Diesel V6-92 Series	J	J
Detroit Diesel V-8	H	—
Detroit Diesel 8V-71 Series	—	H
Detroit Diesel V8-92	K	K
Detroit Diesel V12	P	—
Glider Kit—Less Engine	—	X

① 6000 lbs. and under GVWR
② Over 6000 lbs. GVWR
③ Conventional models only
④ Motor Home Chassis only

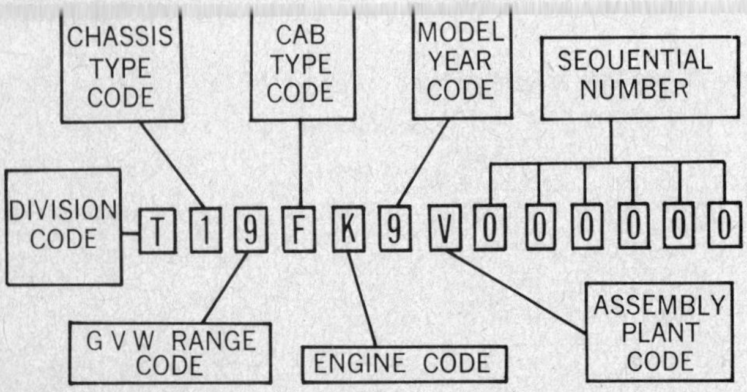

Vehicle Identification Number—1973-80 Light Duty Trucks and 1973-78 Medium and Heavy Duty Trucks (typical)

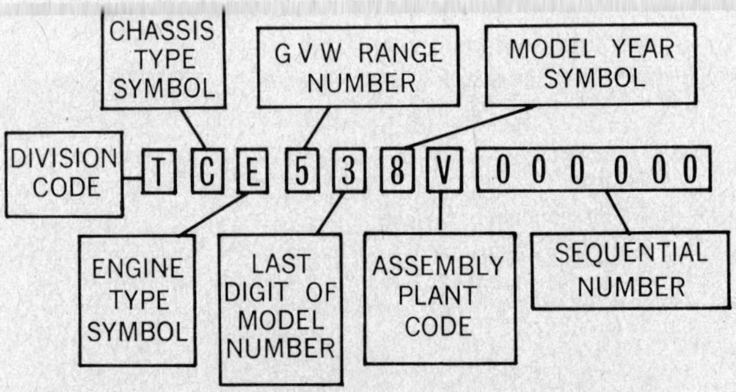

Vehicle Identification Number—1979-80 Medium and Heavy Duty Trucks (typical)

TUNE-UP SPECIFICATIONS

Note: Refer to the emission control label before making any final adjustments, as the label may reflect changes in engine tune-up specifications which occurred after the initial tune-up information was released for publication.

Up to and including the model year 1978, Federal light duty emission requirements affected only vehicles up to 6,000 lbs. GVW. Beginning with the model year 1979, Federal light duty emission requirements have been extended to include vehicles up to 8,500 lbs. GVW.

CU. IN. DISPLACE-MENT (cu. in.)	YEAR	SPARK PLUG GAP (in.)	DISTRIBUTOR POINT DWELL (deg.)	DISTRIBUTOR POINT GAP (in.)	IGNITION TIMING (DEGREES)	CRANKCASE COMP. PRESSURE	VALVE CLEARANCE Int. Exh.	NO LOAD GOV. RPM (rpm)	PUMP FUEL PRESS (psi)	IDLE SPEED* (rpm) STD.	IDLE SPEED* (rpm) AUTO.
					SIX CYLINDER						
250	1973	0.035	31-34	0.019	6B①	130	Hyd.		3.5-4.5	700	600②
	1974	0.035	31-34	0.019	8B③	130	Hyd.		3.5-4.5	850④	600
	1975 (Fed./Calif.)	0.060	Elec.	Elec.	10B	130	Hyd.		3.5-4.5	900N	550D
	1976 (Fed.)	0.035	Elec.	Elec.	⑤	130	Hyd.		3.5-4.5	900N	550D
	1976 Calif.)	0.035	Elec.	Elec.	⑥	130	Hyd.		3.5-4.5	1000N	600D
	1977 (Fed.)	0.035	Elec.	Elec.	⑦	130	Hyd.		4.5-6.0	750N	⑧
	1977 (Calif.)	0.035	Elec.	Elec.	⑨	130	Hyd.		4.5-6.0	850N	600D
	1978 (Fed.)	0.035	Elec.	Elec.	⑩	130	Hyd.		4.5-6.0	⑪	⑪
	1978 (High Alt.)	0.035	Elec.	Elec.	⑫	130	Hyd.		4.5-6.0	750N	600D
	1978 (Calif.)	0.035	Elec.	Elec.	⑬	130	Hyd.		4.5-6.0	750N	600D
	1979-80 (Fed.)	0.035	Elec.	Elec.	10B	130	Hyd.		4.5-6.0	750N	600D
	1979-80 (Calif.)	0.035	Elec.	Elec.	⑭	130	Hyd.		4.5-6.0	750N	600D
292	1973	0.035	31-34	0.019	4B⑮	130	Hyd.		3.5-4.5	700⑯	700⑯
	1974	0.035	31-34	0.019	8B	130	Hyd.		3.5-4.5	700	700
	1975 (Fed.)	⑰	Elec.	Elec.	8B	130	Hyd.	3800-4000	⑱	600N	—
	1976 Fed./Calif.)	0.035	Elec.	Elec.	8B	130	Hyd.	3800-4000	⑱	600N	—
	1977-78 (Fed./Calif.)	0.035	Elec.	Elec.	8B	130	Hyd.	4000	4-5	600N	600N
	1979-80 (Fed./Calif.)	0.035	Elec.	Elec.	8B	130	Hyd.		4-5	700N	700N
305C (V6)	1973	0.040	31-34	0.019	7-½B	125	0.012-0.018	3600	5.0-7.0	550	550
	1974	0.035	31-34	0.019	7-½B	125	0.012-0.018	3600	5.0-7.0	600	600
379 (V6)	1973	0.035	31-34	0.019	8B	125	0.012-0.018	4000	5.0-7.0	550	550
	1974	0.035	31-34	0.019	6B	125	0.012-0.018	4000	5.0-7.0	575	575
432 (V6)	1973	0.035	31-34	0.019	8B	125					
	1974	0.035	31-34	0.019	6B	125	0.012-0.018	3200	5.0-7.0	525	525
					EIGHT CYLINDER						
305	1977 (Fed.)	0.045	Elec.	Elec.	8B	⑲	Hyd.		7.5-9.0	600N	500D
	1978 (Fed.)	0.045	Elec.	Elec.	⑳	⑲	Hyd.		7.5-9.0	600N	500D
	1979-80 (Fed.)	0.045	Elec.	Elec.	6B	⑲	Hyd.		7.5-9.0	700N	600D
307	1973	0.035	29-31	0.019	4B㉑	150	Hyd.		5.0-6.5	900㉒	600
350	1973	0.035	29-31	0.019	㉓	150	Hyd.		5.0-6.5	900㉔	600㉔
	1974	0.035	29-31	0.019	㉕	150	Hyd.		5.0-6.5	900㉖	600㉖
	1975 (2 bbl) (Fed.)	0.060	Elec.	Elec.	6B	150	Hyd.		7-8.5	—	600D
	1975 (4 bbl) (Fed./Calif.)	0.060	Elec.	Elec.	6B	150	Hyd.		7-8.5	800N	600
	1975 (Fed.)*	0.060	Elec.	Elec.	8B	150	Hyd.		7-8.5	600N	600N
	1975 (Calif.)*	0.060	Elec.	Elec.	2B	150	Hyd.		7-8.5	700N	700N
	1975-76**	0.035	31-34	0.019	4B	150	Hyd.	㉗	7-9	600N	600N
	1976 (2 bbl) (Fed.)	0.045	Elec.	Elec.	㉘	150	Hyd.		7-8.5	800N	600D
	1976 (4 bbl) (Fed.)	0.045	Elec.	Elec.	8B	150	Hyd.		7-8.5	800N	600D
	1976 (4 bbl) (Calif.)	0.045	Elec.	Elec.	6B	150	Hyd.		7-8.5	800N	600D
	1976 (Fed.)*	0.060	Elec.	Elec.	8B	150	Hyd.		7-8.5	600N	600N
	1976 (Calif.)*	0.060	Elec.	Elec.	2B	150	Hyd.		7-8.5	600N	600N
	1977 (Fed.)	0.045	Elec.	Elec.	8B	150	Hyd.		7-8.5	700N	500D
	1977 (High Alt.)	0.045	Elec.	Elec.	6B	150	Hyd.		7-8.5	—	600D

TUNE UP SPECIFICATIONS (Cont'd)

CU. IN. DISPLACEMENT (cu. in.)	YEAR	SPARK PLUG GAP (in.)	DISTRIBUTOR POINT DWELL (deg.)	DISTRIBUTOR POINT GAP (in.)	IGNITION TIMING (DEGREES)	CRANKCASE COMP. PRESSURE	VALVE CLEARANCE Int. Exh.	NO LOAD GOV. RPM (rpm)	PUMP FUEL PRESS (psi)	IDLE SPEED* (rpm) STD.	IDLE SPEED* (rpm) AUTO.
	1977 (Calif.)	0.045	Elec.	Elec.	6B	150	Hyd.		7-8.5	700N	500D
	1977 (Fed.*)	0.045	Elec.	Elec.	8B	150	Hyd.		7-8.5	700N	700N
	1977 (Calif.)	0.060	Elec.	Elec.	2B	150	Hyd.		7-8.5	700N	700N
	1977**	0.035	Elec.	Elec.	4B	150	Hyd.	4100	7-9	600N	600N
	1978 (Fed.)	0.045	Elec.	Elec.	8B	150	Hyd.		7-8.5	600N	500D
	1978 (High Alt.)	0.045	Elec.	Elec.	8B	150	Hyd.		7-8.5	—	500D
	1978 (Calif.)	0.045	Elec.	Elec.	8B	150	Hyd.		7-8.5	700N	500D
	1978 (Fed.)*	0.045	Elec.	Elec.	8B	150	Hyd.		7-8.5	700N	700N
	1978 (Calif.)*	0.045	Elec.	Elec.	2B	150	Hyd.		7-8.5	700N	700N
	1978-80 (Fed.)**	0.045	Elec.	Elec.	4B	150	Hyd.	4000	7.5-9	600N	600N
	1978-80 (Calif.)**	0.035	Elec.	Elec.	4B	150	Hyd.	4000	7.5-9	600N	600N
	1979-80 (Fed./ Calif.)	0.045	Elec.	Elec.	㉙	150	Hyd.		7.5-9	700N	500D
366	1973	0.035	28-32	0.019	8B	150	Hyd.		5.0-6.5	550㉚	550㉚
	1974	0.035	28-32	0.019	8B	150	Hyd.		5.0-6.5	600	600
	1975 (Fed.)	0.035	28-32	0.019	8B	150	Hyd.	㉛	7-9	700	700
	1975-76 (Calif.)	0.060	Elec.	Elec.	8B	150	Hyd.	4100	7-9	700	700
	1977** (Fed./ Calif.)	㉜	Elec.	Elec.	8B	150	Hyd.	4100	7-9	700N	700N
	1978-80** (Fed./ Calif.)	㉜	Elec.	Elec.	8B	150	Hyd.	4075	8¼	700N	700N
400	1975-78 (Fed.)*	㉝	Elec.	Elec.	4B	150	Hyd.		7-8.5	700	700
	1975-78 (Calif.)*	㉝	Elec.	Elec.	2B	150	Hyd.		7-8.5	700	700
	1979-80 (Fed./ Calif.)	0.045	Elec.	Elec.	4B	150	Hyd.		7-8.5	700N	500D
427	1973	0.035	28-32	0.019	8B	150	Hyd.		7.0-8.5	550㉚	550㉚
	1974	0.035	28-32	0.019	8B	150	Hyd.		7.0-8.5	600	600
	1975-76 (Fed.)**	0.035	28-32	0.019	8B	150	Hyd.	㉞	7-9	700	700
	1975-76 (Calif.)**	0.060	Elec.	Elec.	8B	150	Hyd.	4100	7-9	700	700
	1977 (Fed.)**	0.035	Elec.	Elec.	8B	150	Hyd.	㉟	7-9	700N	700N
	1977 (Calif.)**	0.060	Elec.	Elec.	8B	150	Hyd.	㉟	7-9	700N	700N
	1978 (Fed.)**	0.045	Elec.	Elec.	8B	150	Hyd.	4075	8¼	700N	700N
	1978 (Calif.)**	0.060	Elec.	Elec.	8B	150	Hyd.	4075	8¼	700N	700N
	1979-80 (Fed./ Calif.)**	0.045	Elec.	Elec.	8B	150	Hyd.	4075	8¼	700N	700N
454	1973 (Fed.)	0.035	28-32	0.019	10B	150	Hyd.		7.0-8.5	900②	600②
	1973 (Calif.)	0.035	28-32	0.019	㊱	150	Hyd.		7.0-8.5	900②	600②
	1974	0.035	29-31	0.019	10B㊲	150	Hyd.		7.0-8.5	800②	600②
	1975 (Fed.)	0.060	Elec.	Elec.	㊳	150	Hyd.		7-8.5	—	650D
	1975 (Fed./ Calif.)**	0.060	Elec.	Elec.	8B	150	Hyd.		7-8.5	700	700
	1976 (Fed.)	0.045	Elec.	Elec.	㊴	150	Hyd.		7-8.5	—	600D
	1976-78 (Fed./ Calif.)*	0.045	Elec.	Elec.	8B	150	Hyd.		7-8.5	700N	700N
	1977 (Fed.)	0.045	Elec.	Elec.	4B	150	Hyd.		7-8.5	—	600D
	1978 (Fed.)	0.045	Elec.	Elec.	8B	150	Hyd.		7-8.5	—	550D
	1978 (Calif.)	0.045	Elec.	Elec.	8B	150	Hyd.		7-8.5	—	㊵
	1979-80 (Fed./ Calif.)	0.045	Elec.	Elec.	㊶	150	Hyd.		7-8.5	㊷	㊷
	1979-80 (Fed./ Calif.)**	0.045	Elec.	Elec.	8B	150	Hyd.	4075	7-8.5	700N	700N

TUNE UP SPECIFICATIONS (Cont'd)

——Not Applicable
Elec.—Electronic Ignition
Hyd.—Hydraulic valve lifters (one turn down from zero lash)
N—Neutral
D—Drive
B—BTDC

(1) 4B all C,K-2500 except Suburban; all C,P-3500 series and all G-3500 except Rally STX
(2) 700 RPM all C,K-2500 except Suburban; all C,P-3500 series and all G-3500 except Rally STX
(3) 6B all C,K-2500 series except Suburban; all C,P-3500 series and all G-3500 except Rally STX
(4) 600 RPM all C,K-2500 except Suburban; all C,P-3500 series and all G-3500 except Rally STX
(5) C-1500 w/4 spd. or auto. trans.—10B (light duty emission)
C,G-1500 w/3 spd. trans.—6B (light duty emission)
C,K-1500 (all trans.) w/heavy duty emission systems—6B
(6) C,G-1500 w/manual trans.—6B
C,G-1500 w/auto. trans.—10B
(7) C-1500 (code TBA) and G-1500 (code TBF) w/man. trans.—8B (light duty emission)
C-1500 (code TBB) and G-1500 (code TBH) w/auto. trans.—12B (light duty emission)
(8) 550D w/o A/C, 600D with A/C
(9) C-1500 (code TBI) and G-1500 (code TBJ) w/man. trans.—6B
C-1500 (code TBD) and G-1500 (code TBK) w/auto. trans.—10B
(10) C-1500 (code TAC) and G-1500 (code TAF) w/man. trans.—8B
C-1500 (code TAB) and G-1500 (code TAH) w/auto. trans.—8B
(11) man. trans.—750N
auto. trans.—550D (no A/C), 600D (A/C)
(12) man. trans.—8B
auto. trans.—12B
(13) man. trans.—8B
auto. trans.—10B
(14) man. trans.—6B
auto. trans.—8B
(15) California—8B
(16) California—600 RPM
(17) light duty trucks—0.060 in.
medium and heavy duty trucks—0.035 in.
(18) light duty trucks—3.5-4.5 psi
medium and heavy duty trucks—4-5 psi
(19) The lowest acceptable compression pressure reading must be within at least 70% of the highest pressure reading for any given cylinder. Example: If 7 out of 8 cylinders indicate pressures of 150 psi/cyl., then a pressure of 105 psi is acceptable in the eighth cylinder. A pressure lower than 105 psi would indicate that repairs are necessary.
(20) 4B (light duty emission systems)
6B (heavy duty emission systems)
(21) 8B all 1500 series, C,K-2500, Suburban, G-2500,3500 Rally STX w/auto. trans. TDC all others
(22) 600 RPM all C,K-2500 except Suburban, and all C,P-3500 series and all G-3500 except Rally STX
(23) C-2500 Suburban—2B
All 1500 series, K-2500 Suburban, G-2500, and 3500 Rally STX
w/manual transmission—8B
w/automatic transmission—12B
All others 4B
(24) All C,K-2500 except Suburban; all C,P-3500 series, all G-2500,3500 except Rally STX—700 RPM
(25) Federal except C,K-1500,2500, Suburban and G-2500,3500 Rally STX—8B
Federal C,K-1500,2500 Suburban and G-2500,3500 Rally STX:
w/automatic transmission 12B
w/automatic transmission (except Suburban) 8B
Suburban (w/manual transmission) 6B
California: w/automatic transmission 8B
Suburban (w/manual transmission) 6B
w/manual transmission 4B
(26) All C,K-2500 except Suburban, all C,P-3500 series and all G-2500, 3500 except Rally STX—600 RPM
(27) Auto. trans. 540—4000 RPM
Auto. trans. 475—3600 RPM
(28) Auto. trans.—6B
Man. trans.—2B
(29) 8B (all vehicles except Fed. G-3500 and C,K,P-2500,3500 with carburetor 17059213, 17059215, and distributor 1103375—4B)
(30) California—700 RPM
(31) GMC carb. 792870, Holley carb. R7264A—3750 RPM
GMC carb. 717721, Holley carb. R6928A—4000 RPM
(32) 0.045 (Fed.)
0.060 (Calif.)
(33) 0.060—1975-76
0.045—1977-78
(34) GMC carb. 795092, Holley carb. R7266A—3600 RPM
GMC carb. 717722, Holley carb. R6929A—4000 RPM
(35) 4150 RPM—manual trans.
3500 RPM—RT613 trans.
(36) All 1500 series, C,K-2500 Suburban, G-2500,3500 Rally STX 10B
All C,K-2500 except Suburban, all C,P-3500 series and all G-3500 except Rally STX:
w/manual transmission 5B
w/automatic transmission 8B
(37) All C, K-2500 except Suburban, all C, P-3500 series and all G-3500 except Rally STX 8B
(38) w/Catalytic Converter—16B
w/o Catalytic Converter—10B
(39) w/Catalytic Converter—12B
w/o Catalytic Converter—8B
(40) C-2500 (code TRM)—700N
C-1500, 2500 (code TSS) and C-2500 (code TRF)—550D
(41) C-3500 w/man. trans.—4B
C-2500 (code ZWZ) and C,P-3500 w/auto. trans.—4B
C-2500 w/man. trans. and C-1500, 2500 w/auto. trans.—8B
(42) All except C-1500, 2500 w/auto. trans.—700N
C-1500, 2500 w/auto. trans.—555D
* Vehicles equipped with heavy duty emission systems.
** Medium and heavy duty trucks only.

FIRING ORDER

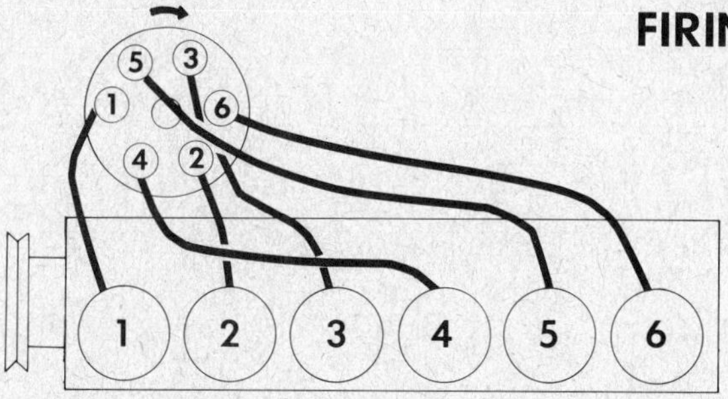

250 and 292 six cylinder firing order 1-5-3-6-2-4

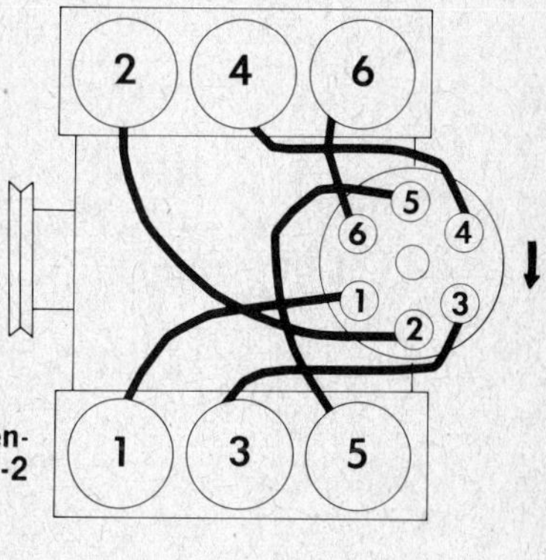

305C, 379 and 432 V6 engines firing order 1-6-5-4-3-2

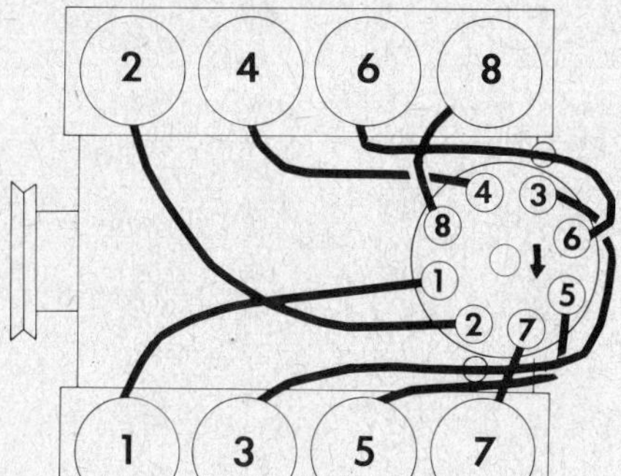

307, 350, 366, 402, 427 and 454 engines firing order 1-8-4-3-6-5-7-2

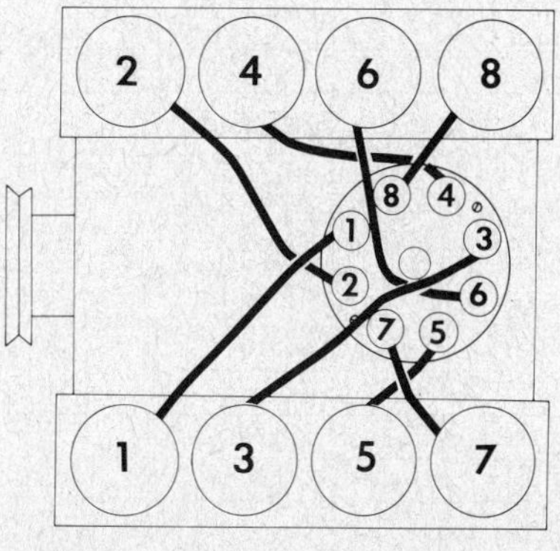

305, 350, 366, 400 ,and 454 engines firing order 1-8-4-3-6-5-7-2

GENERAL ENGINE SPECIFICATIONS

CU. IN. DISPLACEMENT	YEAR	BORE X STROKE	FIRING ORDER	HORSEPOWER @ R.P.M.	TORQUE @ R.P.M.	COMPRESSION RATIO	CARBURETOR	VALVE LIFTER TYPE	NORMAL OIL PRESSURE
SIX CYLINDER									
250	1973-74	3.875 x 3.53	1-5-3-6-2-4	100 @ 3600	175 @ 2000	8.25	1V	Hyd.	40-60
	1975	3.875 x 3.53	1-5-3-6-2-4	105 @ 3800	185 @ 1200	8.25:1	1V	Hyd.	40-60
	1976 (L.D.)	3.875 x 3.53	1-5-3-6-2-4	105 @ 3800	185 @ 1200	8.25:1	1V	Hyd.	40-60
	1976 (H.D.)	3.875 x 3.53	1-5-3-6-2-4	100 @ 3600	175 @ 1800	8.25:1	1V	Hyd.	40-60
	1977-78 (L.D.)	3.87 x 3.53	1-5-3-6-2-4	110 @ 3800	195 @ 1600	8.3:1	1V	Hyd.	40-60
	1977-78 (H.D.)	3.87 x 3.53	1-5-3-6-2-4	100 @ 3600	175 @ 1800	8.0:1	1V	Hyd.	40-60
	1979-80	3.87 x 3.53	1-5-3-6-2-4	①	②	8.3:1	2V	Hyd.	40-60
292	1973-74	3.875 x 4.125	1-5-3-6-2-4	120 @ 3600	225 @ 2000	8.0	1V	Hyd.	40-60
	1975	3.87 x 4.12	1-5-3-6-2-4	120 @ 3600	215 @ 2000	8.0:1	1V	Hyd.	40-60
	1976-78	3.87 x 4.12	1-5-3-6-2-4	120 @ 3600	215 @ 2000	8.0:1	1V	Hyd.	40-60
	1979-80	3.87 x 4.12	1-5-3-6-2-4	115 @ 3400	215 @ 1600	8.0:1	1V	Hyd.	40-60
305C (V6)	1973-74	4.250 x 3.58	1-6-5-4-3-2	148 @ 4000	238 @ 1600	7.5	2V	Mech.	57
379 (V6)	1973-74	3.56 x 3.86	1-6-5-4-3-2	170 @ 3600	280 @ 1600	7.5	2V	Mech.	57
432 (V6)	1973-74	4.875 x 3.86	1-6-5-4-3-2	190 @ 3200	331 @ 1600	7.5	2V	Mech.	60
EIGHT CYLINDER									
305	1977-78	3.74 x 3.48	1-8-4-3-6-5-7-2	145 @ 3800	245 @ 2400	8.5:1	2V	Hyd.	40
	1979-80	3.74 x 3.48	1-8-4-3-6-5-7-2	③	④	8.4:1	2V	Hyd.	45
307	1973	3.875 x 3.25	1-8-4-3-6-5-7-2	115 @ 3600	205 @ 2000	8.5	2V	Hyd.	30
	1973	3.875 x 3.25	1-8-4-3-6-5-7-2	130 @ 4000	220 @ 2200	8.5	2V	Hyd.	30
350	1973	4.00 x 3.48	1-8-4-3-6-5-7-2	145 @ 4000	255 @ 2400	8.5	2V	Hyd.	40
		4.00 x 3.48	1-8-4-3-6-5-7-2	155 @ 4000	255 @ 2400	8.5	4V	Hyd.	40
		4.00 x 3.48	1-8-4-3-6-5-7-2	175 @ 4000	260 @ 2800	8.5	4V	Hyd.	40
	1974	4.00 x 3.48	1-8-4-3-6-5-7-2	145 @ 3600	250 @ 2200	8.5	2V	Hyd.	40
		4.00 x 3.48	1-8-4-3-6-5-7-2	160 @ 3800	255 @ 2400	8.5	4V	Hyd.	40
	1975 (2 bbl)	4.00 x 3.48	1-8-4-3-6-5-7-2	145 @ 3600	250 @ 2200	8.5:1	2V	Hyd.	40-60
	1975 (4 bbl)	4.00 x 3.48	1-8-4-3-6-5-7-2	160 @ 3800	250 @ 2400	8.5:1	4V	Hyd.	40-60
	1976	4.00 x 3.48	1-8-4-3-6-5-7-2	160 @ 4000	265 @ 2400	8.0:1	2V	Hyd.	40-60
	1977-78 (L.D.)	4.00 x 3.48	1-8-4-3-6-5-7-2	165 @ 3800	260 @ 2400	8.5:1	4V	Hyd.	40
	1977-78 (H.D.)	4.00 x 3.48	1-8-4-3-6-5-7-2	165 @ 3800	255 @ 2800	8.5:1	4V	Hyd.	40
	1979-80 (Fed.)	4.00 x 3.48	1-8-4-3-6-5-7-2	165 @ 3600	270 @ 2000	8.2:1	4V	Hyd.	45
	1979-80 (Calif.)	4.00 x 3.48	1-8-4-3-6-5-7-2	155 @ 3600	260 @ 2000	8.2:1	4V	Hyd.	45
366	1973-74	3.937 x 3.76	1-8-4-3-6-5-7-2	200 @ 4000	310 @ 2800	8.0	4V	Hyd.	40-55
	1975	3.937 x 3.76	1-8-4-3-6-5-7-2	200 @ 4000	305 @ 2800	8.0:1	4V	Hyd.	40-55
	1976-78 (single exh.)	3.937 x 3.76	1-8-4-3-6-5-7-2	195 @ 4000	290 @ 2800	8.0:1	4V	Hyd.	40-55
	1976-78 (dual exh.)	3.937 x 3.76	1-8-4-3-6-5-7-2	200 @ 4000	305 @ 2800	8.0:1	4V	Hyd.	40-55
	1979-80 (single exh.)	3.937 x 3.76	1-8-4-3-6-5-7-2	180 @ 4000	290 @ 2400	7.6:1	4V	Hyd.	40-55
	1979-80 (dual exh.)	3.937 x 3.76	1-8-4-3-6-5-7-2	190 @ 4000	305 @ 2400	7.6:1	4V	Hyd.	40-55
400	1975	4.125 x 3.75	1-8-4-3-6-5-7-2	175 @ 3600	290 @ 2800	8.5:1	4V	Hyd.	40-60
	1976-78	4.125 x 3.75	1-8-4-3-6-5-7-2	175 @ 3600	290 @ 2800	8.5:1	4V	Hyd.	40-60
	1979-80 (Fed.)	4.125 x 3.75	1-8-4-3-6-5-7-2	⑤	⑥	8.5:1	4V	Hyd.	40
	1979-80 (Calif.)	4.125 x 3.75	1-8-4-3-6-5-7-2	170 @ 3600	305 @ 1600	8.5:1	4V	Hyd.	40
427	1973-74	4.25 x 3.76	1-8-4-3-6-5-7-2	230 @ 4000	360 @ 2800	8.0	4V	Hyd.	40-55
	1975	4.25 x 3.76	1-8-4-3-6-5-7-2	220 @ 4000	360 @ 2400	8.0:1	4V	Hyd.	40-55
	1976-78	4.25 x 3.76	1-8-4-3-6-5-7-2	220 @ 4000	360 @ 2400	8.0:1	4V	Hyd.	40-55
	1979-80	4.25 x 3.76	1-8-4-3-6-5-7-2	220 @ 4000	360 @ 2400	7.5:1	4V	Hyd.	40-55
454	1973	4.251 x 4.00	1-8-4-3-6-5-7-2	240 @ 4000	355 @ 2800	8.25	4V	Hyd.	40
		4.251 x 4.00	1-8-4-3-6-5-7-2	245 @ 4000	375 @ 2800	8.25	4V	Hyd.	40
		4.251 x 4.00	1-8-4-3-6-5-7-2	250 @ 4000	365 @ 2800	8.25	4V	Hyd.	40
	1974	4.251 x 4.00	1-8-4-3-6-5-7-2	230 @ 4000	350 @ 2800	8.25	4V	Hyd.	40
		4.251 x 4.00	1-8-4-3-6-5-7-2	245 @ 4000	365 @ 2800	8.25	4V	Hyd.	40

GENERAL ENGINE SPECIFICATIONS, continued

CU. IN. DISPLACE-MENT	YEAR	BORE X STROKE	FIRING ORDER	HORSEPOWER @ R.P.M.	TORQUE @ R.P.M.	COM-PRESSION RATIO	CARBU-RETOR	VALVE LIFTER TYPE	NORMAL OIL PRESSURE
	1975 (L.D.)	4.251 x 4.00	1-8-4-3-6-5-7-2	215 @ 4000	350 @ 2400	8.15:1	4V	Hyd.	40
	1975 (H.D.)	4.251 x 4.00	1-8-4-3-6-5-7-2	245 @ 4000	355 @ 3000	8.15:1	4V	Hyd.	40
	1976-78 (L.D.)	4.251 x 4.00	1-8-4-3-6-5-7-2	245 @ 3800	365 @ 2800	8.15:1⑦	4V	Hyd.	40
	1976-78 (H.D., Fed.)	4.251 x 4.00	1-8-4-3-6-5-7-2	240 @ 3800	370 @ 2800	8.15:1	4V	Hyd.	40
	1976-78 (H.D., Calif.)	4.251 x 4.00	1-8-4-3-6-5-7-2	250 @ 3800	385 @ 2800	8.15:1	4V	Hyd.	40
	1979-80	4.25 x 4.00	1-8-4-3-6-5-7-2	245 @ 4000	380 @ 2500	7.6:1	4V	Hyd.	40-55

Fed.—Federal (all states except California)
Calif.—California only
L.D.—Light duty emissions (under 6,000 lb GVW)
H.D.—Heavy duty emissions (over 6,000 lb GVW)

① 130 @ 3800 light and medium duty emissions (all states except California)
125 @ 4000 light duty emissions, 1500 series only (California)
130 @ 4000 light and medium duty emissions, all except 1500 series (California)

② 210 @ 2400 light and medium duty emission (all states except California)
205 @ 2000 light duty emission, 1500 series only (California)
205 @ 2000 light and medium duty emissions, all except 1500 series (California)

③ 160 @ 4000 all except California (4 bbl)
155 @ 4000 California only (4 bbl)
140 @ 4000 all 1500-3500 series (2 bbl)

④ 235 @ 2400 all except California (4 bbl)
225 @ 2400 California only (4 bbl)
240 @ 2000 all 1500-3500 series (2 bbl)

⑤ 185 @ 3600 light and medium duty (up to 8500 lbs. GVWR)
180 @ 3600 heavy duty (8501 lbs. GVWR and above)

⑥ 200 @ 2400 light and medium duty (up to 8500 lbs. GVWR)
310 @ 2400 heavy duty (8501 lbs. GVWR and above)

⑦ 8.25:1 on C-1500 w/H.D. chassis and C-1500,2500 Suburban

CRANKSHAFT BEARING JOURNAL SPECIFICATIONS

CU. IN. DISPLACE-MENT	YEAR	MAIN BEARING JOURNALS: JOURNAL DIAMETER	OIL CLEARANCE	SHAFT END PLAY	THRUST ON NO.	CONNECTING ROD BEARING JOURNALS: JOURNAL DIAMETER	OIL CLEARANCE	END PLAY
SIX CYLINDER								
250	1973-78	2.2983-2.2993	.0003-.0029	.002-006	Rear	1.999-2.000	.0007-.0027	.006-.017
	1979-80	2.2979-2.2994	①	.002-.006	Rear	1.999-2.000	.0010-.0030	.006-.017
292	1973-78	2.2983-2.2993	.0008-.0034	.002-.006	5	2.099-2.100	.0007-.0027	.006-.017
	1979-80	2.2979-2.2994	①	.002-.006	5	2.099-2.100	.0010-.0030	.006-.017
305C (V6)	1973-74	3.1247-3.1237②	.0013-.0039	.003-.008	—	2.8112-2.8122	.001-.003	.006-.011
379 (V6)	1973-74	3.1247-3.1237②	.0023-.0039③	.003-.008	—	2.8112-2.8122	.0015-.0035	.006-.011
432 (V6)	1973-74	3.1247-3.1237②	.0023-.0039③	.003-.008	—	2.8112-2.8122	.0015-.0035	.006-.011
EIGHT CYLINDER								
305	1977	④	⑤	.002-.006	5	2.199-2.200	.0013-.0035	.008-.014
	1978-80	④	⑤	.002-.006	5	2.0988-2.0998	.0013-.0035	.008-.014
307	1973	2.4484-2.4493⑥	⑤	.002-.006	5	2.199-2.200	.0013-.0035	.008-.014
350	1973-76	2.4484-2.4493⑥	⑤	.002-.006	5	2.199-2.200	.0013-.0035	.008-.014
	1977	④	⑤	.002-.006	5	2.199-2.200	.0013-.0035	.008-.014
	1978-80	④	⑤	.002-.006	5	2.0988-2.0998	.0013-.0035	.008-.014
366	1973-80	2.7481-2.7490⑦	.0013-.0025⑧	.006-.010	5	2.1985-2.1995	.0014-.0030	.019-.025
400	1975-76	2.4484-2.4493⑥	⑤	.002-.006	5	2.199-2.200	.0013-.0035	.008-.014
	1977	⑨	⑤	.002-.006	5	2.199-2.200	.0013-.0035	.008-.014
	1978-80	⑨	⑤	.002-.006	5	2.0988-2.0998	.0013-.0035	.008-.014
427	1973-80	2.7481-2.7490⑦	.0013-.0025⑧	.006-.010	5	2.199-2.1998	.0014-.0030	.019-.025
454	1973-80	2.7485-2.7494⑩	.0013-.0025⑪	.006-.010	5	2.1985-2.1995	.0009-.0025	.013-.023

① Nos. 1-6 .0010-.0024
No. 7 .0016-.0035

② Rear 3.1229-3.1239

③ No. 4 .0031-.0047

④ No. 1 2.4484-2.4493
Nos. 2,3,4 2.4481-2.4490
No. 5 2.4479-2.4488

⑤ No. 1 .0008-.0020 (.002 maximum)
Nos. 2,3,4 .0011-.0023 (.0025 maximum)
No. 5. 0017-.0032 (.0035 maximum)

⑥ Rear 2.4479-2.4488

⑦ Rear 2.7473-2.7483

⑧ Rear .0029-.0045

⑨ Nos. 1,2,3,4 2.6484-2.6493
No. 5 2.6479-2.6488

⑩ Nos. 2,3,4 2.7481-2.7490
No. 5 2.7478-2.7488

⑪ No. 5 .0024-.0040

RING SIDE CLEARANCE (IN.)

ENGINE (cu. in.)	YEAR	TOP COMPRESSION	BOTTOM COMPRESSION	OIL CONTROL
250	1973-80	.0012-.0027	.0012-.0032	.0000-.0050
292	1973-80	.0020-.0040	.0020-.0040	.0005-.0055
305 (V6)	1973-74	.0030-.0050	①	.0010-.0040
379 (V6)	1973-74	.0030-.0045	②	.0025-.0040
432 (V6)	1973-74	.0030-.0045	②	.0025-.0040
305 (V8)	1977-80	.0012-.0032	.0012-.0032	.002-.007
307	1973	.0012-.0027	.0012-.0032	.0000-.0050
350	1973-80	.0012-.0032	.0012-.0032	.002-.007
366	1973-80	.0018-.0032	.0018-.0032	.0020-.0035
400	1975-80	.0012-.0032	.0012-.0032	.002-.007
427	1973-80	.0018-.0038	.0018-.0038	.002-.0035
454	1973-80	.0017-.0032	.0017-.0032	.005-.0065

①—2nd compression—.0030-.0045
3rd compression—.0025-.0040

②—2nd compression—.0025-.0040
3rd compression—.0025-.0040

RING GAP SPECIFICATIONS (IN.)

ENGINE	YEAR	TOP COMPRESSION	BOTTOM COMPRESSION	OIL CONTROL
250	1973-80	.010-.020	.010-.020	.015-.055
292	1973-80	.010-.020	.010-.020	.015-.055
305 (V6)	1973-74	.017-.027	①	No Gap
379 (V6)	1973-74	.022-.032	②	No Gap
432 (V6)	1973-74	.024-.034	③	No Gap
305 (V8)	1977-80	.010-.020	.010-.025	.015-.055
307	1973	.010-.020	.010-.020	.015-.055
350	1973-80	.010-.020	.013-.025	.015-.055
366	1973-80	.010-.020	.010-.020	.010-.023
400	1975-76	.010-.020	.010-.020	.010-.035
	1977-80	.010-.020	.010-.025	.015-.055
427	1973-80	.010-.020	.010-.020	.010-.023
454	1973-76	.010-.020	.010-.020	.010-.030
	1977-80	.010-.020	.010-.020	.015-.055

①—2nd compression—.015-.025
3rd compression—.015-.025
②—2nd compression—.022-.032
3rd compression—.015-.025

③—2nd compression—.024-.034
3rd compression—.015-.025

VALVE SPECIFICATIONS

CU. DISPLACE-MENT	YEAR	LASH (HOT) (INCHES) INT.	LASH (HOT) (INCHES) EXH.	ANGLE (DEGREES) FACE	ANGLE (DEGREES) SEAT	STEM DIA. (INCHES) INT.	STEM DIA. (INCHES) EXH.	STEM CLEARANCE INTAKE	STEM CLEARANCE EXHAUST	CAM LOBE LIFT (INCHES)	VALVE SPRING TENSION (LBS @ INCHES) OPEN	VALVE SPRING TENSION (LBS @ INCHES) CLOSED	FREE LENGTH (INCHES)
						SIX CYLINDER							
250	1973-76	①	①	45	46	.342	.3413	.0010-.0027	.0015-.0032	.2217	185 @ 1.27	60 @ 1.66	1.90
	1977	①	①	45	46	.342	.3413	.0010-.0027	.0015-.0032	.2217	185 @ 1.27	60 @ 1.66	2.08
	1978-80	①	①	45	46	.342	.3413	.0010-.0027	.0015-.0032	.2217	170 @ 1.26	60 @ 1.66	1.88
292	1973-76	①	①	45	46	.342	.3413	.0010-.0027	.0015-.0032	.2315	180 @ 1.30	90 @ 1.69	1.90
	1977	①	①	45	46	.342	.3413	.0010-.0027	.0015-.0032	.2315	180 @ 1.30	90 @ 1.69	2.08
	1978-80	①	①	45	46	.342	.3413	.0010-.0027	.0015-.0032	.2315	175 @ 1.26	82 @ 1.66	1.90
305C (V6)	1973-74	.012	.018	—	30	.341	.340	.0015-.003	.002-.0035	.454②	203 @ 1.50	80 @ 1.92	2.27
379 (V6)	1973-74	.012	.018	—	30	.373	.438	.0015-.003	.0019-.0036	.454②	203 @ 1.50	80 @ 1.92	2.27
432 (V6)	1973-74	.012	.018	—	30	.373	.438	.0015-.003	.0019-.0036	.454②	203 @ 1.50	80 @ 1.92	2.27

VALVE SPECIFICATIONS

CU. DISPLACE-MENT	YEAR	LASH (HOT) (INCHES) INT.	EXH.	ANGLE (DEGREES) FACE	SEAT	STEM DIA. (INCHES) INT.	EXH.	STEM CLEARANCE INTAKE	EXHAUST	CAM LOBE LIFT (INCHES)	VALVE SPRING TENSION (LBS @ INCHES) OPEN	CLOSED	FREE LENGTH (INCHES)
						EIGHT CYLINDER							
305 (V8)	1977	①	①	45	46	.341	.341	.0010-.0027	.0010-.0027	③	④	⑤	2.03
	1978-80	①	①	45	46	.341	.341	.0010-.0027	.0010-.0027	⑥	④	⑤	2.03
307	1973	①	①	45	46	.341	.341	.001-.003	.001-.003	③	189 @ 1.20	80 @ 1.61	1.91
350	1973-76	①	①	45	46	.341	.341	.0010-.0027	.0010-.0027	⑦	⑧	⑤	⑨
	1977-80	①	①	45	46	.341	.341	.0010-.0027	.0010-.0027	⑦	④	⑤	2.03
366	1973-80	①	①	45	46	.3718	.372	.0010-.0027	.0012-.0029	.234	220 @ 1.40	90 @ 1.80	2.05
400	1975-80	①	①	45	46	.371	.371	.0010-.0027	.0012-.0029	⑦	④	⑤	2.03
427	1973-80	①	①	45	46	.372	.372	.0010-.0027	.0019-.0022	⑩	220 @ 1.40	90 @ 1.80	2.05
454	1973-80	①	①	45	46	.372	.371	.0010-.0027	.0012-.0029	.234	300 @ 1.38	80 @ 1.88	2.12

① One complete turn down from zero lash
② Exhaust .464
③ Intake .2485
Exhaust .2733
④ Intake 200 @ 1.25
Exhaust 200 @ 1.16
⑤ Intake 80 @ 1.70
Exhaust 80 @ 1.61
⑥ Intake .2484
Exhaust .2667
⑦ Intake .260
Exhaust .273
⑧ Intake 200 @ 1.25
Exhaust 190 @ 1.20
⑨ Intake 2.03
Exhaust 1.91
⑩ Intake .2343
Exhaust .2530

TORQUE SPECIFICATIONS

CU. IN. DISPLACE-MENT	YEAR	CYLINDER HEAD BOLTS (FT. LBS.)	ROD BEARING BOLTS (FT. LBS.)	MAIN BEARING BOLTS (FT. LBS.)	CRANKSHAFT BALANCER BOLT (FT. LBS.)	FLYWHEEL TO CRANKSHAFT BOLTS (FT. LBS.)	MANIFOLDS (FT. LBS.) INTAKE	EXHAUST
				SIX CYLINDER				
250	1973-78	95	35-45	65	Pressed on	60	①	①
	1979-80	95	35	65	Pressed on	60	②	②
292	1973-78	95	40	65	Pressed on	55-65	①	①
	1979-80	95	40	65	60	110	②	②
305C (V6)	1973-74	60-65	55-65	170-180③	180-200	100-110	30-35	15-20
379 (V6)	1973-74	90-100	55-65	170-180③	240-260	100-110	30-35	15-20
432 (V6)	1973-74	90-100	55-65	170-180③	240-260	100-110	30-35	15-20
				EIGHT CYLINDER				
305 (V8)	1977-80	65	45	80④	60	60	30	20
307	1973	65	45	70	Pressed on	60	30	20⑤
350	1973-76	65	45	70	60	60	30	20⑤
	1977-80	65	45	80④	60	60	30	20⑤
366	1973-80	75-85	⑥	100-110	80-90	60-70	25-35	25-30
427	1973-80	75-85	⑥	100-110	80-90	60-70	25-35	25-30
454	1973-80	80	50	110	85	65	30	20

① Outer 20 ft. 1 lb., others 30 ft. lbs.
② Exhaust 30 ft. lbs.
Exhaust to intake 45 ft. lbs.
Manifold to cylinder head 40 ft. lbs.
③ Rear 90-100 ft. lbs.
④ Intermediate outer bolts 70 ft. lbs.
⑤ Inside bolts 30 ft. lbs.
⑥ 7/16" 67-73 ft. lbs.
⅜" 45-55 ft. lbs.

WHEEL ALIGNMENT SPECIFICATIONS

IMPORTANT: A. It is recommended that the alignment adjustments be made with the vehicle "loaded", as caster, camber, and toe-in specifications represent the true dimensions for a vehicle carrying its design load. A simulated load condition during adjustments can improve tire wear and increase the life of the tires.

B. All caster specifications are given based on a frame angle of zero. If the frame of the vehicle isn't perfectly level, compensation must be made (for the frame angle) as the position of the frame directly affects the caster angle. A distinction must be made between the caster reading as it appears on the alignment measuring equipment and the "actual" caster reading, which is the true caster angle of the vehicle, obtained after compensating for the effect of the frame angle on the caster angle. In order to determine the "actual" caster reading prior to adjustment, you must first measure the angle between the frame and an imaginary horizontal line. The following rules apply to the usual combinations of frame angle and caster reading.

1. Subtract a DOWN IN REAR frame angle from a positive caster reading.
2. Add an UP IN REAR frame angle to a positive caster reading.
3. Add a DOWN IN REAR frame angle to a negative caster reading.
4. Subtract an UP IN REAR frame angle from a negative caster reading.

After the necessary alignment adjustments have been made, it will, again, be necessary to determine the "actual" caster reading. Remember, the reading on the alignment equipment must be mathematically corrected (actual) in order to determine the "actual" caster reading, as the direct reading from the alignment equipment does not reflect any compensation for the frame angle. Therefore, it will be necessary to repeat the "actual" caster reading procedure (according to the above mentioned rules) after adjustments have been made.

C. Measure the distance between the bump stop bracket and the frame (Dimension "A"—see illustration). Refer to the CASTER SPECIFICATION chart for the correct caster setting as it corresponds to Dimension "A".

D. Ordinarily, a shim pack will leave at least two threads of the bolt exposed beyond the nut. If, in order to properly align the front wheels, it is necessary to build the shim pack beyond the two thread minimum, then check for damaged control arms and related parts. The difference, in thickness, between the front shim pack and the rear shim pack must not exceed 0.30 inches. The front shim pack must be at least 0.24 inches.

1500-3500 Series (Light Duty)

MODEL	YEAR	CASTER (deg.)	CAMBER ②③ (deg.)	TOE-IN ④⑤ (inches)	TURNING ANGLE	KING PIN INCLINATION
C-1500-3500	1973-78	①	+¼°	3/16"	⑥	⑦
	1979-80	①	+0.2°	3/16"	⑥	⑦
G-1500-3500	1973-78	①	+¼°	3/16"	⑥	⑦
	1979-80	①	+0.2°	3/16"	⑥	⑦
P-1500-3500	1973-74	①	+¼°	3/16"	⑥	⑦
	1975-78	①	⑧	3/16"	⑥	⑦
	1979-80	①	+0.2°	3/16"	⑥	⑦
K-1500-2500	1973-74	①	+1½°⑨	3/16"⑩	⑥	⑦
	1975-76	①	+1½°⑨	0	⑥	⑦
K-1500-3500	1977-78	①	+1½°⑨	0	⑥	⑦
K-1500-2500	1979-80	①	+1°⑨	0	⑥	⑦
K-3500	1979-80	①	+½°⑨	0	⑥	⑦

CAMBER SPECIFICATIONS (MODELS P-1500-3500 ONLY)

Dimension "A" in inches		2½"	2¾"	3"	3¼"	3½"	3¾"	4"	4¼"	4½"	4¾"	5"	5¼"	5½"
1975-78	P-1500	0°	0°	+¼°	+¼°	+¼°	+¼°	+¼°	0°	0°	0°	−¼°	−½°	−¾°
1975-78	P-2500,3500	0°	0°	+¼°	+¼°	+¼°	+¼°	+¼°	+¼°	0°	0°	−¼°	−½°	−¾°

CASTER SPECIFICATIONS
(See IMPORTANT note above)

Dimension "A" in inches		1½"	1¾"	2"	2¼"	2½"	2¾"	3"	3¼"	3½"	3¾"	4"	4¼"	4½"	4¾"	5"
1973-78	C-1500	—	—	—	—	—	—	+2°	+1½°	+1¼°	+1°	+¾°	+½°	+¼°	0°	−½°
1973	C-2500,3500	—	—	—	—	+2°	+1½°	+1¼°	+1°	+1¾°	+½°	+¼°	0°	−¼°	−½°	−¾°
1974-78	C-2500,3500	—	—	—	—	+1½°	+1¼°	+1°	+¾°	+½°	+¼°	0°	−¼°	−½°	−¾°	−1°
1979-80	C-1500	—	—	—	—	+2.4°	+2.1°	+1.8°	+1.5°	+1.2°	+1.0°	+0.7°	+0.5°	+0.2°	+0.1°	−0.3°
1979-80	C-2500,3500	—	—	—	—	+1.5°	+1.2°	+0.9°	+0.6°	+0.3°	+0.1°	0°	−0.1°	−0.7°	−1.0°	−1.2°
1973-77	G-1500,2500,3500	—	—	—	—	+2¼°	+2°	+1½°	+1¼°	+1°	+¾°	+½°	+¼°	0°	−¼°	−½°
1978	G-1500,2500	—	—	—	—	+3¼°	+3°	+2¾°	+2½°	+2½°	+2¼°	+2°	+2°	+1¾°	+1½°	+1½°
1978	G-3500	—	—	—	—	+2¼°	+2°	+1½°	+1¼°	+1°	+¾°	+½°	+¼°	0°	−¼°	−½°
1979-80	G-1500,2500	+2.9°	+2.7°	+2.3°	+2.2°	+2.0°	+1.8°	+1.6°	+1.4°	+1.3°	+1.1°	+0.9°	+0.7°	—	—	—
1979-80	G-3500	+3.4°	+3.0°	+2.7°	+2.4°	+2.1°	+1.8°	+1.5°	+1.3°	+1.0°	+0.7°	+0.4°	+0.2°	—	—	—
1973	P-1500	—	—	—	—	—	—	+2°	+1½°	+1¼°	+1°	+¾°	+½°	+¼°	0°	−½°
1973	P-2500,3500	—	—	—	—	+2°	+1½°	+1¼°	+1°	+¾°	+½°	+¼°	0°	−¼°	−½°	−¾°
1974	P-1500,2500	—	—	—	—	—	—	—	+1½°	+1¼°	+1°	+¾°	+½°	+¼°	0°	−¼°
1974	P-3500	—	—	—	—	+2¼°	+2°	+1½°	+1¼°	+1°	+¾°	+½°	+¼°	0°	−¼°	−½°
1975-78	P-1500,2500,3500	—	—	—	—	+2½°	+2¼°	+2°	+1¾°	+1½°	+1°	+¾°	+½°	+¼°	0°	−¼°
1979-80	P-1500	—	—	—	—	+2.3°	+2.0°	+1.7°	+1.5°	+1.2°	+0.9°	+0.6°	+0.4°	+0.1°	−0.1°	−0.3°
1979-80	P-2500,3500	—	—	+2.9°	+2.6°	+2.3°	+2.0°	+1.7°	+1.4°	+1.2°	+0.9°	+0.6°	+0.4°	+0.2°	+0.1°	—
1973-76	K-1500,2500	+4° No provision for adjustment														
1977-80	K-1500,2500,3500	+8° No provision for adjustment														

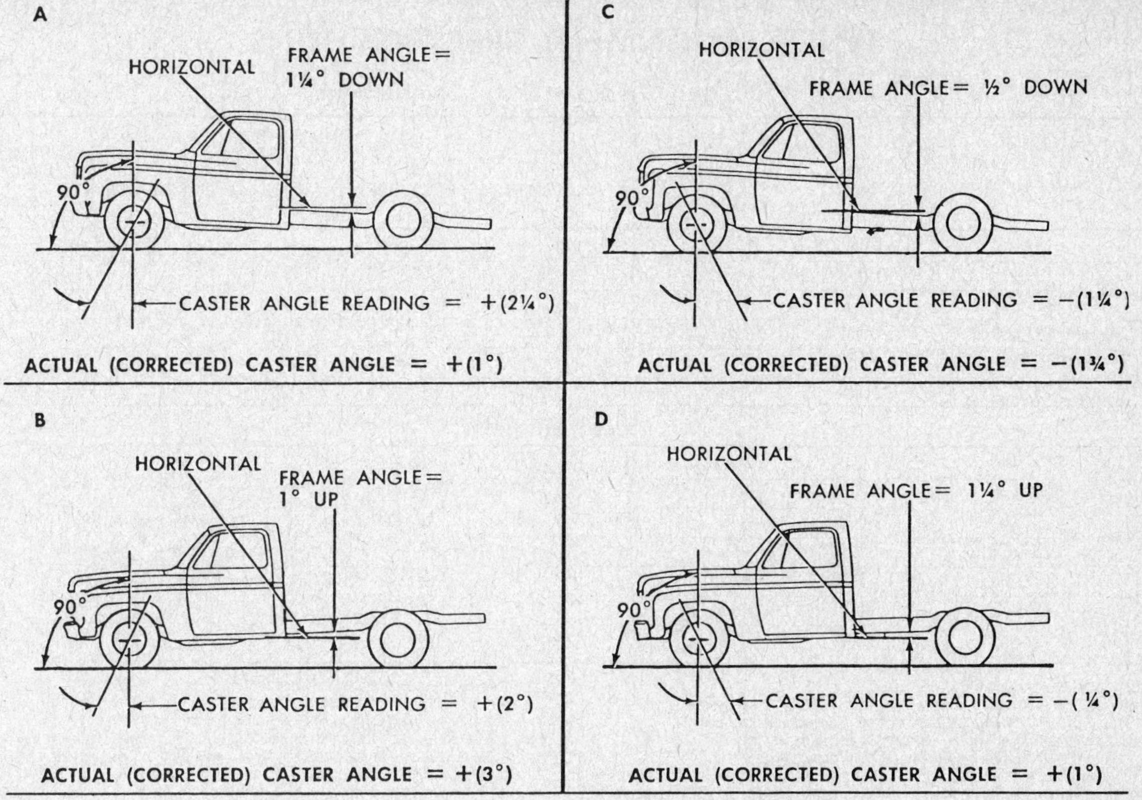

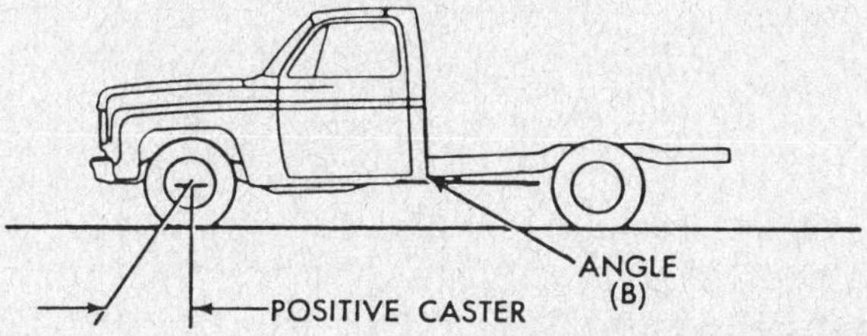

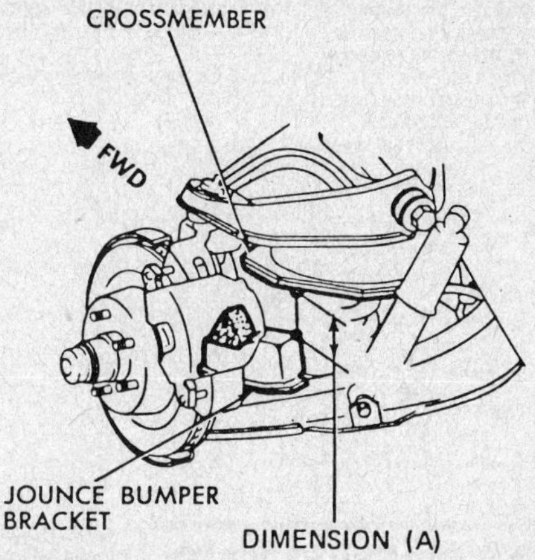

Determining Caster—Typical—1974-76—Series 1500 thru 3500

WHEEL ALIGNMENT SPECIFICATIONS

4000-6500 Series (Medium Duty)

MODEL	YEAR	AXLE(19)	CAMBER(3) L.H.	CAMBER(3) R.H.	CASTER(3)	TOE-(16)IN(13)	TURNING(12) ANGLES INSIDE	TURNING(12) ANGLES OUTSIDE	KING PIN INCLINATION LEFT	KING PIN INCLINATION RIGHT
C-5000	1973	F-050	+1°	+1°	+2½°	⅛"-3/16"	20°	17¾°	7¼°	7¼°
	1974	F-050	+1°	+1°	+2½°	1/16"-⅛"(11)	20°	17¾°	7¼°	7¼°
S/C-6500	1973	F-050, 055, 070	+1°	+1°	+2½°	3/32"-3/16"	20°	17¾°	7¼°	7¼°
	1974	F-050, 055, 070	+1°	+1°	+2½°	1/16"-⅛"	20°	17¾°	7¼°	7¼°
C/M-6500	1973-74	F-070	+1°	+1°	+2½°	3/32"-3/16"(11)	20°	17¾°	7¼°	7¼°
C/M-6500	1973-74	F-090, 120	+¼°	−¼°	+2½°	⅛"-7/32"(15)	20°	17¾°	5¾°	6¼°
T-6000	1973-74	F-070	+1½°	+1½°	+1¼°	⅛"-¼"(14)	39°	27¾°	7°	7°
T-6000	1973-74	F-090	+¼°	−¼°	+1¼°	⅛"-¼"	39°	27¾°	5¾°	6¼°
T-6500	1973-74	F-070	+1½°	+1½°	+1¼°	⅛"-¼"(11)	39°	27¾°	7°	7°
T-6500	1973-74	F-090	+¼°	−¼°	+1¼°	⅛"-¼"	39°	27¾°	5¾°	6¼°
T-6500	1973-74	F-120	+¼°	−¼°	+1¼°	⅛"-¼"	39°	27¾°	5¾°	6¼°
P-4000, 4500	1974	F-050, 055	+1°	+1°	+2½°	1/16"-⅛"	20°	17¾°	7¼°	7¼°

WHEEL ALIGNMENT SPECIFICATIONS

P-4000, 4500 and Medium Duty Conventional (C/M)

MODEL	YEAR	AXLE⑲	CAMBER③ L.H.	CAMBER③ R.H.	CASTER③	TOE-⑯IN⑬	TURNING⑫ ANGLES INSIDE	TURNING⑫ ANGLES OUTSIDE	KING PIN INCLINATION LEFT	KING PIN INCLINATION RIGHT
5000	1975-80	F-050	+1½°	+1½°	+2½°	⅛"-¼"	⑫	⑫	7°10′	7°10′
5500	1975-78	F-055	+1½°	+1½°	+2½°	⅛"-¼"	⑫	⑫	7°10′	7°10′
7000	1975-80	F-070	+1½°	+1½°	+2½°	⅛"-¼"	⑫	⑫	7°10′	7°10′
9000	1975-80	F-090	+¼°	−¼°	+2½°	⅛"-¼"	⑫	⑫	5¾°	6¼°
9000	1975-80	F-120⑰	+¼°	+¼°	+2½°	⅛"-¼"	⑫	⑫	5¾°	6¼°⑱
12000	1975	F-120	+¼°	+¼°	+2½°	⅛"-¼"	⑫	⑫	5¾°	6¼°⑱
				Steel Tilt (T)						
7000	1975-80	F-070	+1½°	+1½°	+4°	⅛"-¼"	⑫	⑫	7°10′	7°10′
9000	1975-76	F-090	+¼°	−¼°	+4°	⅛"-¼"	⑫	⑫	5¾°	6¼°
	1977-80	F-090	+½°	−¼°	+4°	⅛"-¼"	⑫	⑫	5¾°	6¼°
9000	1975-76	F-120⑰	+¼°	+¼°	+4°	⅛"-¼"	⑫	⑫	5¾°	6¼°
	1977-80	F-120⑰	+½°	+¼°	+4°	⅛"-¼"	⑫	⑫	5¾°	6¼°
12000	1975-76	F-120	+¼°	+¼°	+4°	⅛"-¼"	⑫	⑫	5¾°	6¼°
	1977-80	F-120	+½°	+¼°	+4°	⅛"-¼"	⑫	⑫	5¾°	6¼°

① Refer to the Caster Specifications chart.
② Caster and camber must not vary more than ½° from side to side.
③ A reading of ±½° from specified setting is acceptable (see chart).
④ Always set toe-in after caster and camber adjustments.
⑤ A setting of ± 1/16" from specified setting is acceptable.
⑥ Also known as toe-out-on-turns,. No dimensions are available, however, the turning angle of the inner wheel is always greater than the turning angle of the outer wheel. The turning angles are not adjustable. If a scuffing condition is evident, check the steering arms for damage. If a steering arm is damaged in any way, it must be replaced.
⑦ Also known as steering axis inclination. This angle is not adjustable.
⑧ See Camber Specifications chart for "P-1500-3500 only".
⑨ No provision for adjustment.
⑩ K-1500 with full time four wheel drive, toe-in is "0".
⑪ Axle toe-in measured at 20" diameter.
⑫ Adjustment of stop screw must provide ⅝" minimum clearance of tire with any chassis components, regardless of maximum turning angles.
⑬ Toe-in measurements must be made at the horizontal axis of the wheel. If, for any reason, the vehicle has been jacked up, it will be necessary to neutralize the front suspension. Roll the vehicle forward 12 to 15 feet. By doing so, all tolerances in the front suspension will be taken up, and the suspension will then be in normal operating position (neutralized).
⑭ 1974 toe-in 1/16" - ⅛"
⑮ 1974 toe-in ⅛" - ¼"
⑯ Vehicles equipped with steel belted radial tires will have zero toe-in.
⑰ 12,000 lbs. axle rated at 9,000 lbs.
⑱ 1979-80, right side king-pin-inclination is 5¾°
⑲ Refer to illustrations for correct axle identification.

DISTRIBUTOR

Standard Ignition

The distributor used on inline engines is driven from the engine camshaft by spiral cut gears and is located on the right side of the engine. A gasket is used between the distributor flange and cylinder block. The distributor is held in place by a hold-down clamp and cap screw. The lower end of the distributor shaft is tongued and fits a slot in the upper end of the oil pump shaft to drive the oil pump.

The distributor used on V6 and V8 engines is mounted on top center of cylinder block at the rear end, and is driven from the camshaft by spiral cut gears. A gasket is used between distributor flange and engine block. The distributor is held in place by a hold-down clamp and cap screw. The lower end of the distributor shaft has a hexagonal opening that fits the end of the oil pump shaft to drive the oil pump. Model number is stamped on distributor housing.

Distributor

Removal

1. Locate number one cylinder spark plug wire and mark the position of the wire tower on the distributor cap and body.
2. Remove the distributor cap, primary wire from the coil terminal, and the vacuum advance line from the advance unit.
3. With the use of the starter, rotate the engine until the crankshaft pulley timing marks are aligned with the pointer or timing mark tab, located on the timing cover housing.
4. The rotor segment should point toward the mark previously made on the distributor housing. If the rotor segment points 180° degrees away from the mark, rotate the engine one complete revolution and re-align the timing marks.
5. Note the position of the vacuum advance unit in relation to the engine. Remove the hold-down bracket and bolt, and lift the distributor upward until the spiral gear disengages from the camshaft gear. Remove the distributor from the engine.
6. The rotor will move a few degrees as the gears disengage. Mark the second position of the rotor segment on the distributor housing to aid in reassembly.

NOTE: Keep the distributor in the upright position so that oil from the distributor shaft will not run out onto the breaker plate and points, or the electronic units within the distributor.

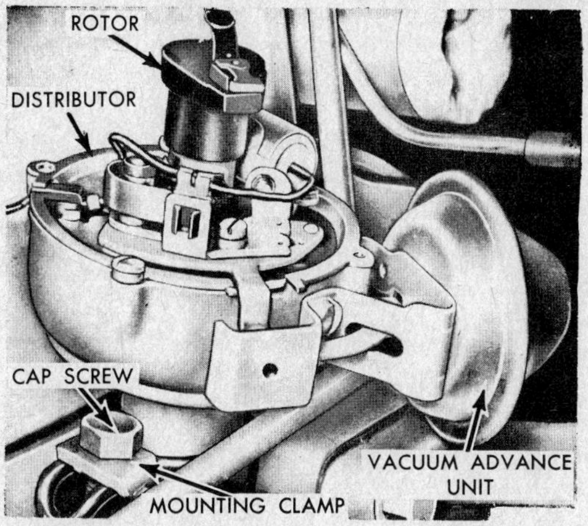

Distributor with cover removed—inline 6 cylinder engine (typical) (© G.M.C)

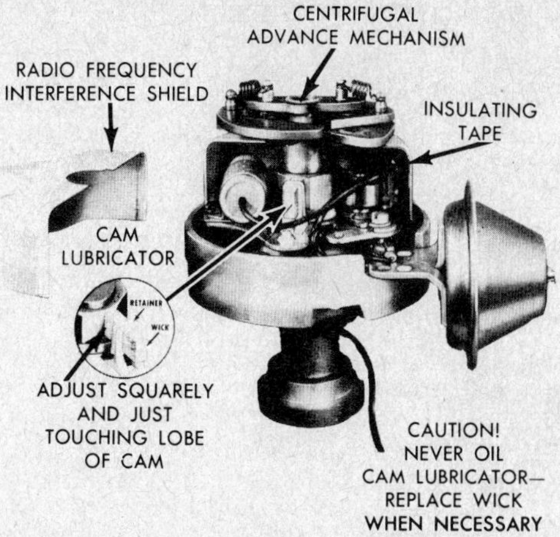

Distributor view—V8 engine (typical) (© G.M.C.)

Installation

1. Lubricate the distributor drive gear with engine oil and install a new distributor flange gasket.
2. Turn the rotor segment to point toward the mark made on the housing after the gears were disengaged. Insert the distributor into the engine while observing the previous position of the vacuum advance unit, relative to the engine.
3. As the gears engage, the rotor will rotate a few degrees and the rotor segment will align with the mark on the housing, that represents the number one cylinder spark plug wire.
4. Press down on the distributor to seat it fully against the block. If necessary, engage the starter several times to make certain the oil pump shaft is engaged.
5. Rotate the distributor body until the points begin to open with the rotor segment pointing to the number one cylinder position. Install the hold-down bracket and bolt and snug them in place.
6. Replace the primary wire to the coil terminal, the vacuum line to the advance unit, and the distributor cap to the distributor body. Start the engine, adjust the dwell and the ignition timing.

Locating Number One Firing Position

If the engine has been cranked with the distributor out, locating number one firing position can be accomplished by one of the two methods outlined below:

a. Remove number one spark plug and place a finger over the hole and crank the engine until compression can be felt. Continue cranking until the timing mark on the crankshaft pulley aligns with the pointer or the timing tab.

b. Remove the rocker arm cover over number one cylinder and crank the engine until the number one intake valve begins to close. Continue to crank the engine until the timing marks align between the crankshaft pulley and the pointer or tab.

Relocate the oil pump shaft to a position to accept the distributor gear, and install the distributor as outlined in the removal and installation section.

Contact Point Replacement

Cleaning

Dirty breaker points should be cleaned with a few strokes of a fine-cut contact file. File should be kept free of grease, dirt and should not be used on other metals. Never use emery cloth to clean breaker points. Do not attempt to file point surface smooth, just remove scale or dirt.

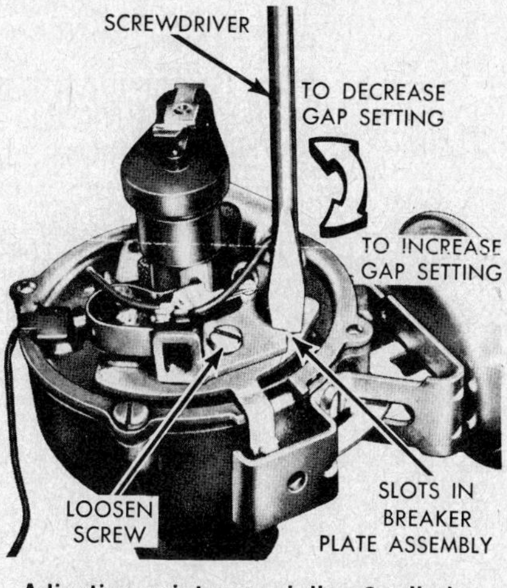

Adjusting point gap—inline 6 cylinder and V6 engines (typical) (© G.M.C.)

NOTE: Highly pitted or burnt points are often caused by improper condenser capacity.

Inline, V6 Engines—Removal

1. Remove distributor cap and place it away from work area.
2. Lift off rotor.
3. Pull primary and condenser lead wires from quick-disconnect terminal.
4. Remove attaching screws and lift breaker point set from plate.
5. Remove oil, dirt and smudge from breaker plate.

Installation

1. Carefully remove protective covering from points and place set on breaker plate. Install attaching screws.
2. Connect primary and condenser leads to terminals. Assemble clips "back to back". Do not push on spring.
3. Apply a slight amount of petroleum jelly to breaker cam and a few drops of S.A.E. #20 oil to top of shaft.
4. Check points for alignment and breaker arm spring for proper tension.
5. Set point gap to specifications.
6. Install rotor and distributor cap.

V8 Engines—Removal

1. Remove distributor cap and place it away from work area.
2. Remove two screws attaching rotor to weight assembly, then pull primary and condenser lead wires from quick-disconnect terminal.
3. Remove two screws breaker plate, point set to distributor housing, and lift out set.
4. Remove cam lubricating wick, if so equipped, with long nose pliers. Clean old lubricant from cam surface.

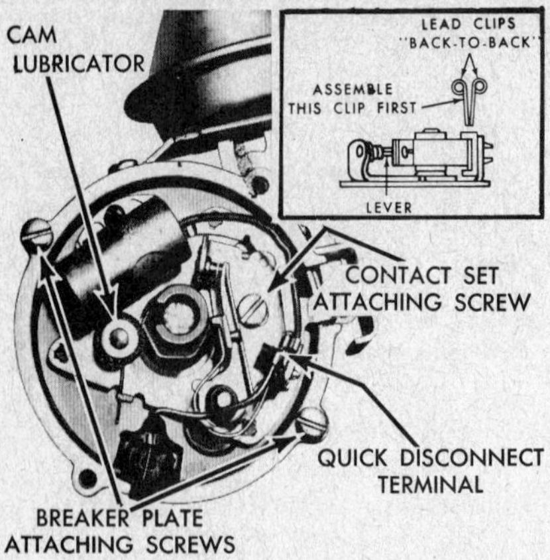

Breaker plate components (© G.M.C.)

Installation

NOTE: Breaker point set is replaced as a complete assembly; point alignment and spring tension are pre-adjusted.

1. If equipped with cam lubricator, adjust wick to touch cam lobe only.
2. Install new contact set assembly on the plate and attach with two screws.
3. Connect primary and condenser leads to terminals. Assemble clips "back to back".
4. Install rotor on weight assembly with two screws and washers.
5. Install distributor cap and lock into position with screw latches.

Ignition Timing

NOTE: To use a timing light, disconnect vacuum advance line to carburetor and tape open end. Carburetor trouble can affect ignition timing adjustments. Without a power timing unit, an accurate method of setting timing with engine stopped is by using a jumper light.

1. Remove distributor cap and rotor, set breaker gap to specifications.

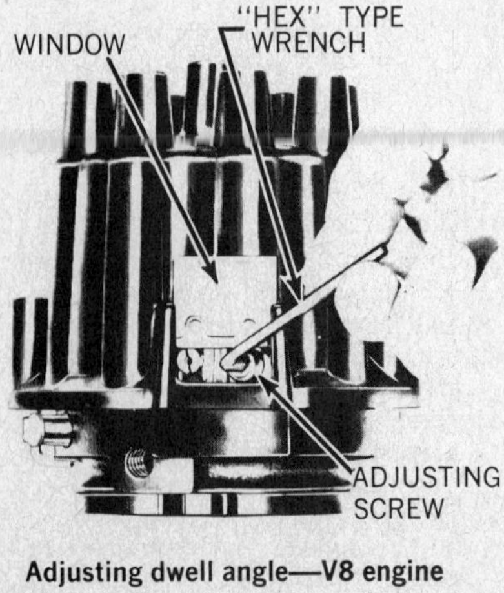

Adjusting dwell angle—V8 engine
(© G.M.C.)

INTERIM 1978 AND LATER

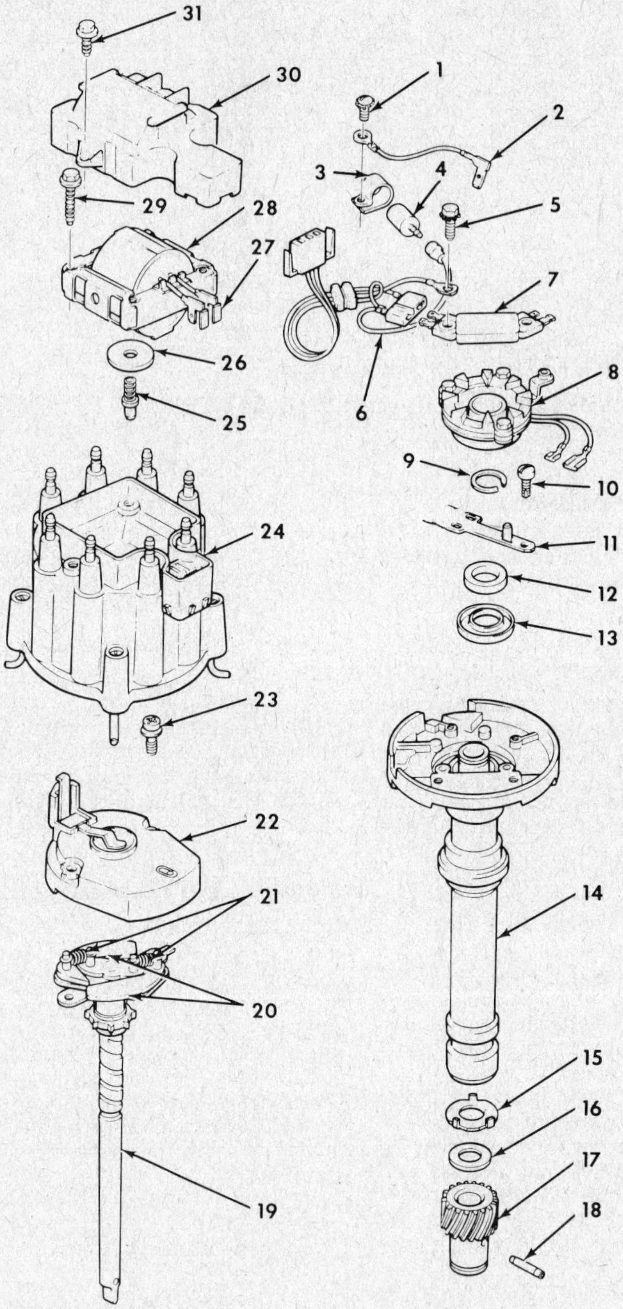

HEI distributor w/o vacuum advance—V8 engine (typical)
(© Chevrolet Div., G.M. Corp.)

1 Screw
2 Wiring Lead
3 Capacitor Clamp
4 Capacitor
5 Screw
6 Wiring Harness Module Leads
7 Module
8 Pick-Up Coil Magnet Assembly
9 Thin "C" Washer
10 Screw
11 Plastic Retainer
12 Felt Washer
13 Felt Retainer
14 Housing
15 Thrust Washer
16 Shim
17 Driven Gear
18 Roll Pin
19 Shaft
20 "Centrifugal Advance" Weights
21 Springs
22 Rotor
23 Screw
24 Cap
25 Spring & Button Assembly
26 Seal
27 Coil Terminals
28 Coil
29 Screw
30 Cover
31 Screw

2. Rotate engine until No. 1 cylinder is at firing position (timing mark on crankshaft pulley aligned with timing tab).
3. Connect jumper light between distributor ignition terminal and ground.
4. Turn on ignition.
5. Loosen distributor and move in normal rotation until light goes out (points closed), then slowly turn distributor back until light just comes on. Tighten distributor.

Reference

Refer to Troubleshooting section for ignition problem analysis.

High Energy Ignition

Beginning with 1975 and 1976 models, most GMC truck engines use a High Energy Ignition system. Two types are used. V8 distributors and 1978 and later sixes combine all ignition components in one unit. The coil is in the distributor cap and connects directly to the rotor. The 6 cylinder distributor through 1977 has an externally mounted coil. Both units operate in basically the same manner, except that the module and pick-up coil replace the conventional breaker points. The module automatically controls the dwell, stretching it with increased engine speed. The system also features a longer spark duration due to the greater amount of energy stored in the primary coil.

The centrifugal and vacuum advance mechanisms are basically the same type of unit as on a conventional ignition distributor.

NOTE: The 292 engine uses both centrifugal and vacuum advance mechanisms, while the 350, 366, and 427 engines use only a centrifugal advance mechanism (medium duty trucks).

The electronic module is serviced by complete replacement.

WARNING: *Do not remove the spark plug wires with the engine running. Severe shock could result.*

Distributor—All Models

Removal

1. Disconnect wiring harness connectors at side of distributor cap.
2. Remove distributor cap and position out of way.
3. Disconnect vacuum advance hose from vacuum advance mechanism.
4. Scribe a mark on the engine in line with rotor. Note approximate position of distributor housing in relation to engine.
5. Remove distributor hold-down nut and clamp.
6. Lift distributor from engine.

Installation

1. Install distributor using same procedure as for standard distributor.
2. Install distributor hold-down clamp and snugly install nut.
3. Move distributor housing to approximate position relative to engine noted during removal.
4. Position distributor cap to housing with tab in base of cap aligned with notch in housing and secure with four latches.
5. Connect wiring harness connector to terminals on side of distributor cap. Connector will fit only one way.
6. Adjust ignition timing.

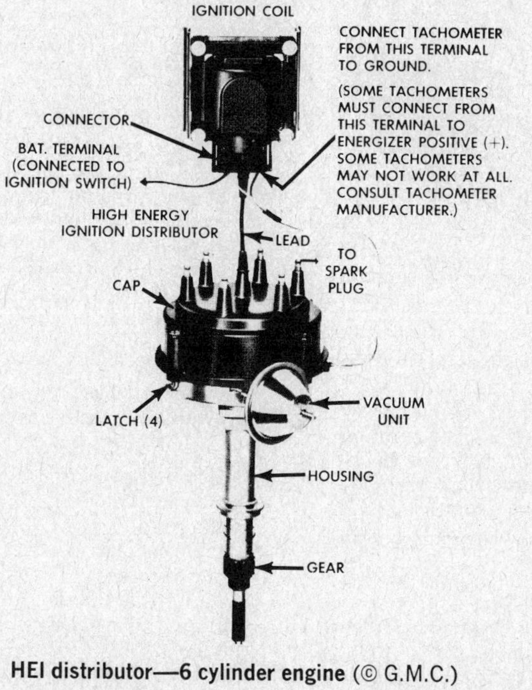

HEI distributor—6 cylinder engine (© G.M.C.)

Dwell Angle

The dwell angle is fixed and is not adjustable. No attempt should be made to adjust the unit.

Tachometer Connections

There is a "tach" terminal on the distributor cap on V8s and 1978 and later sixes. On sixes through 1977, it is on the coil. Connect the tachometer to this terminal and ground. Follow the tachometer manufacturer's instructions.

CAUTION: **Grounding the tach terminal could damage the H.E.I. ignition module.**

Ignition Timing

On H.E.I. systems, connect the timing light in parallel at the No. 1 tower on the distributor cap. Disconnect the distributor spark advance hose and plug the vacuum opening. Start the engine and run it at idle speed. Aim the timing light at the degree scale just over the harmonic balancer. The markings on the scale are in 2° increments with the greatest number of markings on the *before* side ofthe 0. Adjust the timing by loosening the securing clamp and rotating the distributor until the desired ignition advance is achieved, then tighten the clamp. To advance the timing, rotate the distributor opposite to the normal direction of rotor rotation. Retard the timing by rotating the distributor in the normal direction of rotor rotation.

ALTERNATOR

Information on trouble-shooting and overhaul of the charging system can be found in the General Repair section.

Alternator

Removal

1. Disconnect negative (-) cable from battery.

CAUTION: **Alternator will be damaged if terminals or wiring is accidentally shorted or grounded with negative (—) cable connected to battery.**

2. Depress lock and pull connector out of socket on generator. Remove rubber boot from "BAT" terminal and remove terminal nut. Disconnect wire from "GRD" terminal and remove clip.

NOTE: On 130 amp alternators, remove nuts and washers from harness leads at alternator

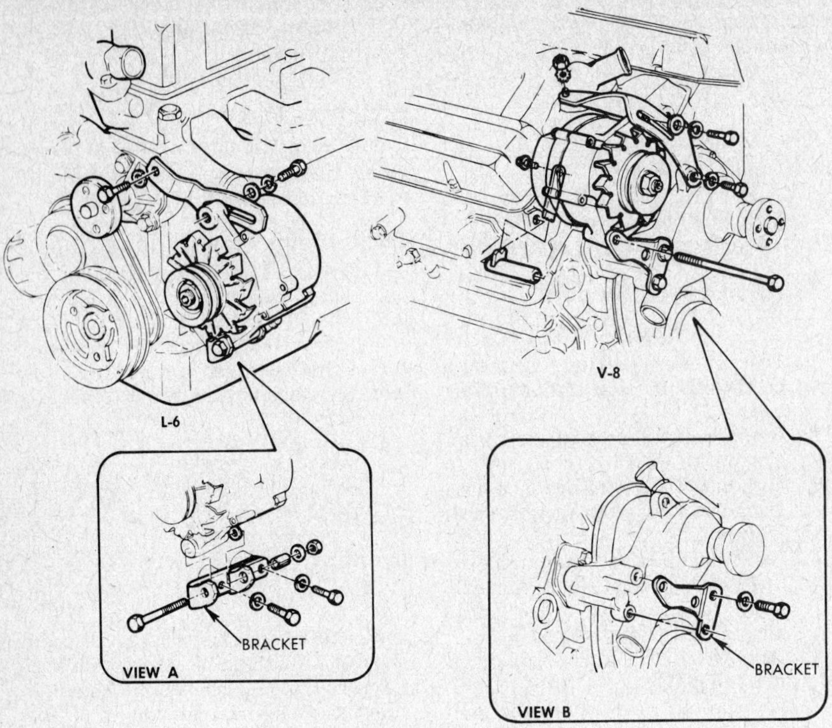

Delcotron installation (© G.M.C.)

terminals. Remove harness clip from alternator, then pull leads from terminals.

3. Loosen alternator mounting bolts and adjusting arm pivot bolt, then remove drive belt(s).
4. Remove alternator mounting bolts and adjusting arm pivot bolt. Lift alternator assembly from engine.

Installation

CAUTION: **Make certain negative (—) cable is disconnected from battery.**

1. Attach alternator to mounting bracket and install adjusting arm. Tighten lock nuts.
2. Install drive belt(s) and adjust to specifications. Torque lock nuts and mounting bolts to specifications.
3. Push connector into socket, making certain that it locks; place clip on "GRD" terminal and connect ground wire.

   NOTE: On 130 amp alternator, connect leads to respective terminals, install attaching nuts and washers.
4. Install harness clip.
5. Attach red wire to "BAT" terminal on generator and fit rubber boot.

STARTER

Information on trouble-shooting and overhaul of the starter motor can be found in the General Repair Section.

The starter motor used on all models is the over-running clutch type,

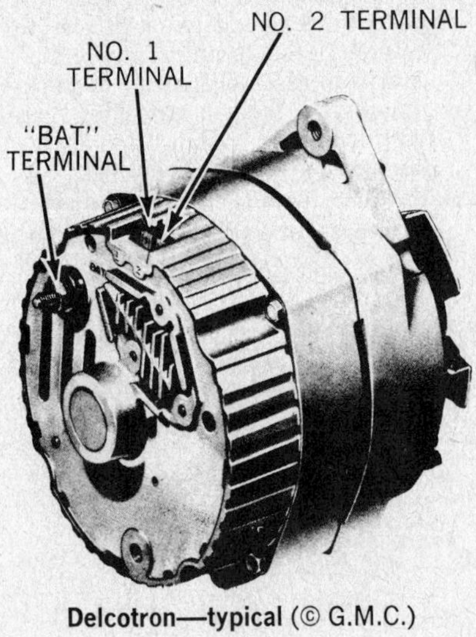

Delcotron—typical (© G.M.C.)

having an enclosed shift lever and solenoid plunger mechanism, within the extended drive end housing. A compression type lever return spring is used to operate the over-running clutch. Oil impregnated bronze bushings and oil saturated wicks provide the lubrication to the armature shaft at the commutator end and the nose housing.

Removal

1. Remove ground strap from negative (-) post on battery.
2. Disconnect wires from terminals on starter solenoid. Reinstall nuts as each wire is disconnected.
3. Loosen front bracket mounts where applicable. Remove bolts, nuts and washers attaching starter to flywheel housing.
4. Remove starter and spacer (when used).

Installation

1. Install spacer (when used) and position starter against flywheel housing.
2. Install bolts, nuts and washers and torque to specifications.
3. Connect wires to proper terminals on starter solenoid and tighten attaching nuts.
4. Connect ground strap to negative (-) post on battery.

Refer to General Section for starter motor overhaul.

BRAKES

Master Cylinder

Specific information will be found in the General Brake Section on adjustment, bleeding, master cylinder and wheel cylinder overhaul procedures and troubleshooting.

Refer to the Power Brake Section for details concerning power brakes.

Three types of master cylinders are used on GMC trucks covered by this manual.

The removal and installation of the master cylinders are covered in this chapter, while the disassembly and assembly are covered in the hydraulic brake section.

Single Reservoir Firewall Mounted Type

Removal

1. Clean the area at the fitting and place a dry cloth under the line to absorb any fluid leakage.
2. Disconnect the hydraulic line at the cylinder and cover the end to prevent any foreign material from entering the system.
3. Disconnect the pushrod from the pedal.
4. Remove the two nuts and washers holding the cylinder to the firewall and remove the cylinder.

Installation

1. Position the master cylinder at the dash and align the pushrod to the pedal.
2. Attach the nuts and washers, but do not tighten.
3. Install the fluid lines, and tighten the attaching nuts and the lines.
4. Check and adjust the pedal push-

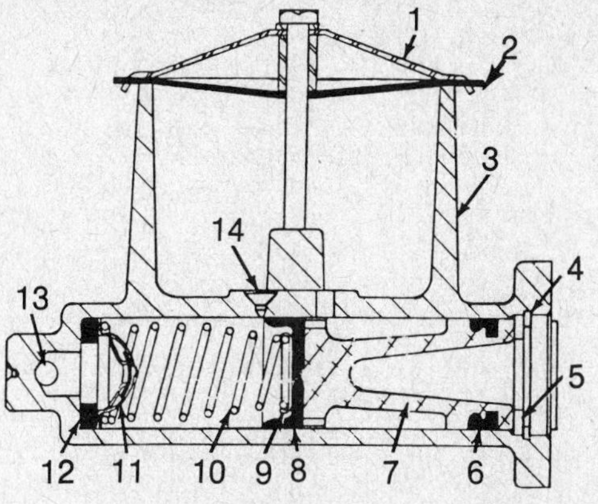

1 Cover assembly
2 Cover gasket
3 Reservoir body
4 Snap ring
5 Stop plate
6 Secondary cup
7 Piston assembly
8 Primary cup
9 Spring retainer
10 Return spring
11 Check valve
12 Check valve seat
13 Outlet port
14 By-pass port

Single reservoir master cylinder (© G.M.C.)

rod for 1/8 in. clearance between the rod and the piston of the master cylinder.
5. Fill the cylinder with brake fluid and bleed the system.

Dual Cylinder Type

Removal

NOTE: Wipe the hydraulic fittings clean and place a dry cloth under the lines to absorb any fluid leakage. Cover the lines and fittings to prevent any foreign matter from entering the system.

1. Disconnect the brake and clutch pedal return springs.
2. Remove the push rod boots from the cylinders.
3. Remove the brake and clutch hydraulic lines.
4. Remove the three bolts holding the cylinder to the firewall and slide the cylinder from the pushrods.

Installation

1. Place new pushrod rubber boots over the cylinder tubes.
2. Hold the cylinder next to the firewall and insert the pushrods, making sure the rods are centered in the pistons.
3. Bolt the assembly loosely to the dash. The movement of the assembly will allow easier attachment of the lines to the fittings with out being stripped.
4. Tighten the assembly and the hydraulic lines securely.
5. Reinstall the clutch and brake pedal return springs.
6. Check and adjust the pedal pushrods for the proper clearance and free play.
7. Fill the reservoirs and bleed both systems.

Dual Reservoir Type

Removal

1. Clean the area at the fittings and place a dry cloth under the lines to absorb any fluid leakage.
2. Disconnect both lines at the cylinder and cover them to prevent foreign matter from entering the system.
3. Unbolt the cylinder and remove, while allowing the pushrod to hang loose.

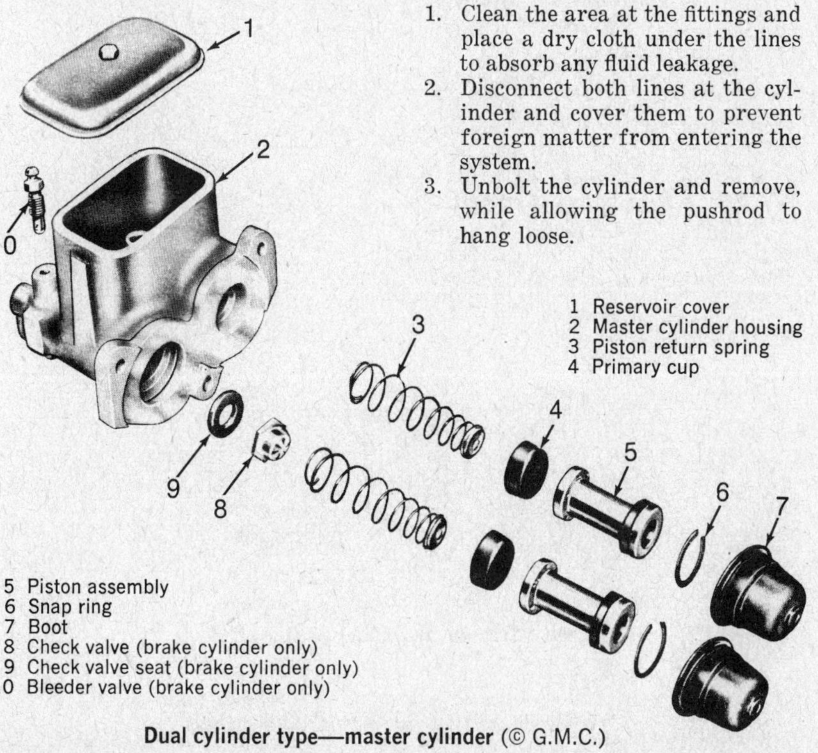

1 Reservoir cover
2 Master cylinder housing
3 Piston return spring
4 Primary cup
5 Piston assembly
6 Snap ring
7 Boot
8 Check valve (brake cylinder only)
9 Check valve seat (brake cylinder only)
10 Bleeder valve (brake cylinder only)

Dual cylinder type—master cylinder (© G.M.C.)

Installation

1. Install a new boot on the pushrod and install the boot on the cylinder.
2. Fasten the cylinder loosely to the attaching point. This freedom of the assembly will allow both hydraulic lines to be started easily.
3. Tighten the mounting bolts and the lines securely. Check for the proper pedal rod free play.
4. Fill the reservoir and bleed the system.

NOTE: To identify the reservoir for the conventional front and rear brakes, it is advisable to check the brake line routing from the master cylinder. On master cylinders with a large and small reservoir, the large reservoir is used for the disc brake system.

Wheel Cylinders

Four types of cylinders are used, identified by type of brake system used.

Duo servo—One double-end cylinder mounted at toe ends of shoes.

Twinplex—Two double-end cylinders mounted between shoes at toe and heel.

Wagner F (FA)—Two single end cylinders (single piston, single direction) mounted so as to be an anchor for one and powering other.

Wagner FR3 (FR3A)—Two double-end cylinders mounted between shoes.

Wheel Cylinder

Removal

1. Jack up axle and support. Remove wheel and drum.

   NOTE: To remove drum it may be necessary to back off brake adjustment, also if rear drum, release hand brake cable if so equipped.

   CAUTION: To gain access to adjusting starwheel, a knockout lanced area is located in web of drum. After knocking out metal be sure to clean all metal particles from brake compartment. A new cover plug must be installed.
2. Release shoe return springs and spread shoes to clear wheel cylinder links. Make sure any lubricant or brake fluid does not get on facings by covering same.
3. At front—Disconnect metal line from flexible hose and remove hose if accessible or remove hose later after cylinder is removed. At rear—Disconnect metal line from cylinder.
4. Remove shield over cylinder and connecting line between cylinders, if so equipped.
5. Remove cap screws and washers

holding cylinder to backing plate. Remove cylinder being careful of any fluid spillage.

Installation

1. Clean mounting surface and reverse above procedures.
2. Bleed and readjust brakes. Check pedal before moving vehicle.

NOTE: Twinplex — Upper and lower cylinders are not interchangeable due to position of connector tube openings. Upper cylinder has threaded bleeder valve opening drilled at outer edge of bore.

Wagner F & FA—*Two wheel cylinders (upper and lower) are identical, however cylinders on right and left brakes have opposite castings.*

Wagner FR3 & FR3A—*Upper and lower cylinders on both right and left brakes are interchangeable.*

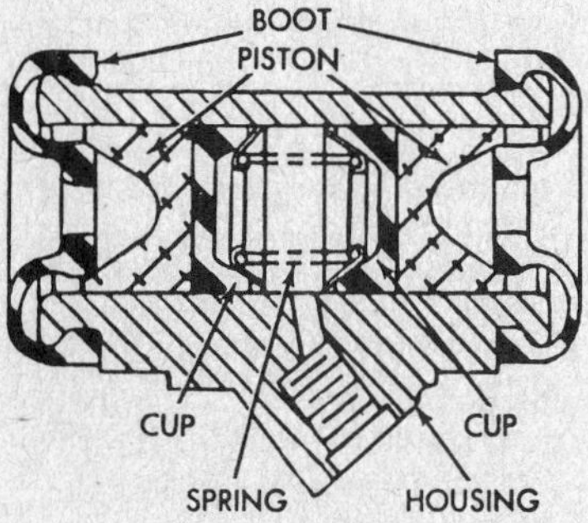

Duo-servo wheel cylinder (© G.M.C.)

Disc Brakes

Information on repair and overhaul of the disc brake components can be found in the General Repair Section.

Removal

1. Check the master cylinder fluid level and if full, siphon approximately ⅔ of the fluid from trhe reservoir and discard.
2. Raise the front of the vehicle and remove the front wheels.
3. Using a "C" clamp type tool, push the pistons back into the caliper bores.
4. Remove the two mounting bolts which attach the caliper to the support.
5. Lift the caliper assembly off the rotor and hub assembly.
6. Remove the inboard shoe, dislodge and remove the outboard shoe.
7. Position the caliper on the front suspension arm so that the brake hose does not support the weight of the caliper.
8. Remove the shoe support spring from the piston.
9. Remove the two sleeves from the inboard ears of the caliper.
10. Remove the four rubber bushings from the grooves of the caliper ears.

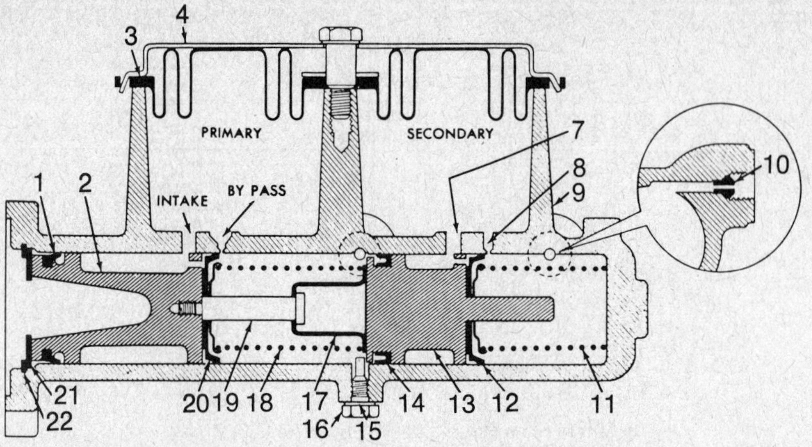

Typical split system master cylinder (© G.M.C.)

1 Primary piston seal cup
2 Primary piston
3 Cover seal
4 Reservoir cover
5 Gasket
6 Cover bolt
7 Intake port
8 By-pass port
9 Reservoir housing
10 Tube seat
11 Secondary piston return spring
12 Secondary piston pressure cup
13 Floating secondary piston
14 Secondary piston seal cup
15 Gasket
16 Stop bolt
17 Primary return spring retainer
18 Primary return spring
19 Primary piston stop pin
20 Primary piston pressure cup
21 Stop plate
22 Retainer ring

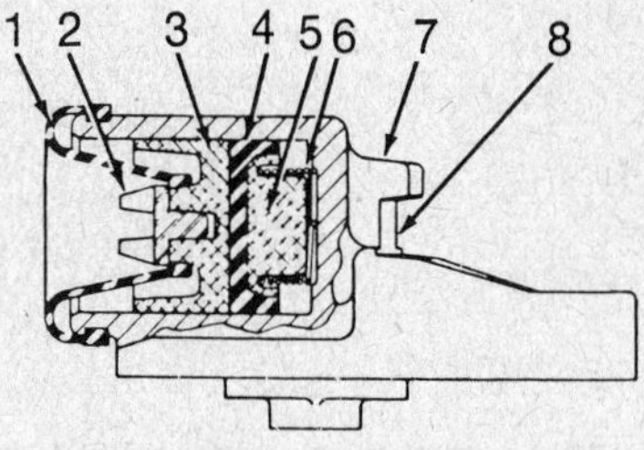

Type F and FA—front wheel cylinder

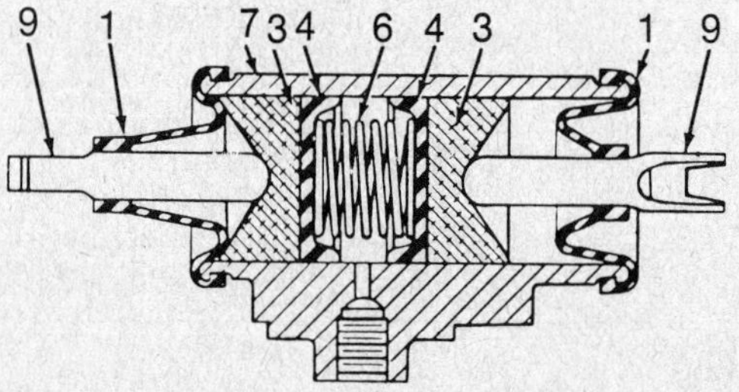

Type FR-3 and FR-3A—rear wheel cylinder (© G.M.C.)

1 Boot
2 Brake shoe guide
3 Piston
4 Piston cup
5 Cup filler
6 Piston spring
7 Cylinder
8 Brake shoe anchor slot
9 Push rod

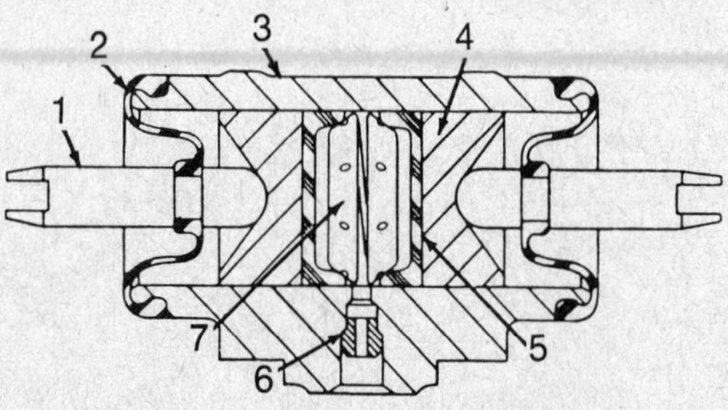

Twin action wheel cylinder (© G.M.C.)

1 Connecting rod
2 Seal
3 Wheel cylinder body
4 Piston
5 Cup
6 Connector insert
7 Spring assembly

Installation

1. Lubricate the new sleeves, rubber bushings, the bushing grooves and the ends of the mounting bolts.
2. Install the new rubber bushings in the caliper ears.
3. Install the new sleeves in the inboard ears of the caliper. Position the sleeve so that the end towards the shoe and lining assembly is flush with the machine surface of the ear.
4. Install the shoe support spring and the inboard shoe in the center of the piston cavity. Press down to lay flat on the caliper.
5. Position the outboard shoe in the caliper with the ears at the top of the shoe over the caliper ears and the tab at the bottom of the shoe engaged in the caliper cutout.
6. Making sure there is no clearance between the tab at the bottom of the outboard shoe and the caliper abutment, position the caliper over the rotor and hub assembly, lining up the hole in the caliper ears with the holes in the mounting brackets.
7. Insert the mounting bracket bolts through the sleeves in the inboard caliper ears and through the mounting bracket, making sure that the bolts pass under the retaining ears on the inboard shoe.
8. Push the mounting bolts through to engage the holes in the outboard shoes and the outboard caliper ears, and thread the bolts into the mounting bracket. Torque the mounting bolts to 35 ft. lbs.
9. Pump the brake pedal to fill the piston cavity and to force the shoes and lining against the rotors.
10. Bend both upper ears of the outboard shoes until no radial clearance exists between the shoe and the caliper housing.
11. Install the front wheels and lower the vehicle.
12. Add brake fluid to the master cylinder reservoir and pump brake pedal several times to assure a firm pedal. Recheck the master cylinder fluid level.

Bleeding Hydraulic Brakes

Pressure Bleeding

Light Duty Trucks

NOTE: The manufacturer specifically advises that the pressure bleeding equipment be of the diaphragm type, i.e., there must be a rubber diaphragm between the air supply and the brake fluid to prevent contaminants, such as air, moisture, oil, etc., from entering the hydraulic system. Furthermore, the equipment used must be capable of exerting 20 to 30 psi hydraulic pressure on the brake system.

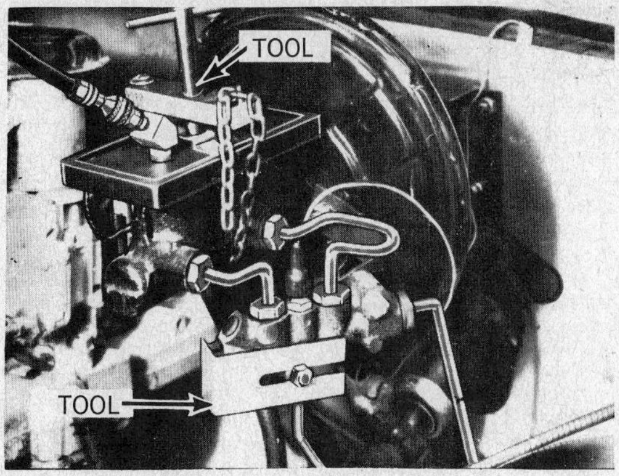

Brake Bleeder Adapter Installed (© Chevrolet Div., G.M. Corp.)

1. Be certain that the brake fluid in the bleeder equipment is at the operating level.
2. Remove all dirt from the top of the master cylinder, and remove the cylinder cover and rubber diaphragm.
3. Attach a brake bleeder adapter J-23518 or an equivalent tool (J-23339 for frame mounted boosters) to the master cylinder.
4. Connect a hose from the bleeder equipment to the bleeder adapter, and open the release valve on the bleeder equipment.

   NOTE: The combination valve (front brake metering valve) must be held in the open position while bleeding. Install tool J-23709 or an equivalent device with the open slot under the mounting bolt and pushing in on the pin in the end of the valve.
5. Bleed the brakes in the following order: right rear, left rear, right front, and left front.
6. Fill a transparent container with a sufficient amount of brake fluid to ensure that the submerged end of the bleeder hose will remain below the surface of the fluid.
7. Place a brake bleeder wrench over the first bleeder valve, and install one end of the bleeder hose over the valve.
8. Place the loose end of the bleeder hose in the container of brake fluid. Make sure that the hose end remains submerged in the brake fluid.
9. Open the bleeder valve by turning the bleeder wrench ³⁄₄ turn

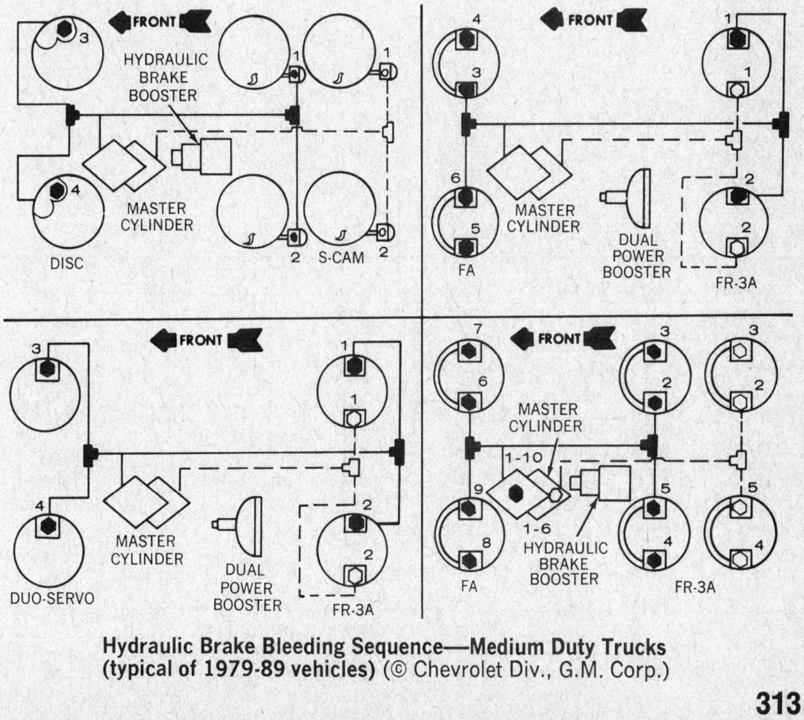

Hydraulic Brake Bleeding Sequence—Medium Duty Trucks (typical of 1979-89 vehicles) (© Chevrolet Div., G.M. Corp.)

counterclockwise, and allow fluid to flow until no air is seen in the fluid.

10. Close the bleeder valve tightly, and proceed in the same manner with the remaining bleeder valves until there is no longer any air in the brake system.

11. Disconnect the brake bleeder equipment from the adapter at the master cylinder, and remove the adapter from the master cylinder.

12. Fill the master cylinder reservoir(s) to within 1/4″ of the top rim, and install the master cylinder diaphragm and cover.

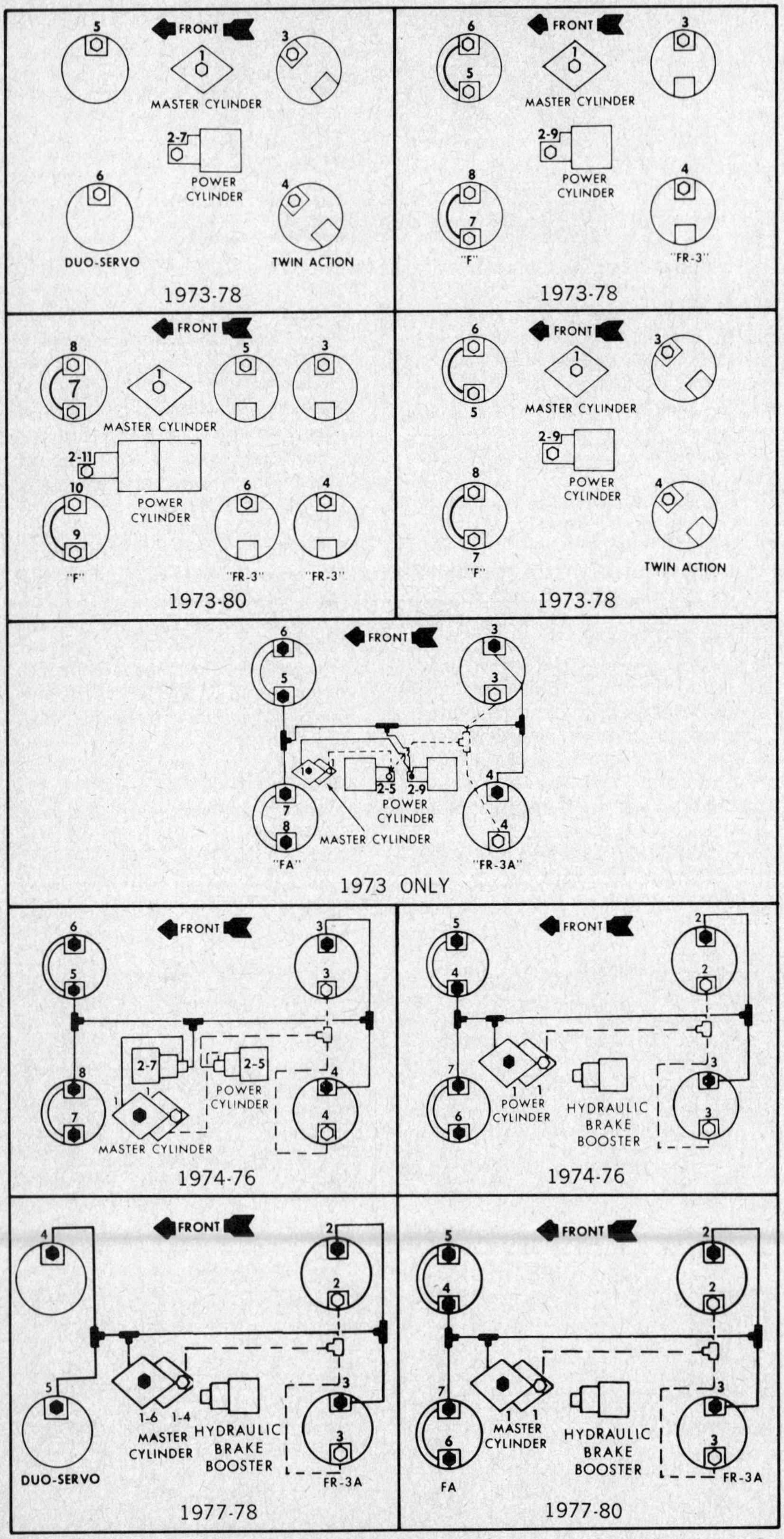

Hydraulic Brake Bleeding Sequence—Medium Duty Trucks (common brake systems 1973-80) (© Chevrolet Div., G.M. Corp.)

Medium Duty Trucks—1973

CAUTION: Stop engine and relieve vacuum or exhaust pressure from system before following procedures.

1. Make certain fluid in pressure tank is above the petcock outlet and that tank is charged with 40 to 50 psi of air.
2. Clean dirt from around master cylinder filler cap. Connect pressure tank hose to filler cap or cover opening. Bleed air from hose before tightening connection. Open valves at both ends.
3. Bleed slave cylinder and control valve first. (when used). Slip end of bleeder hose over bleeder valve No. 1 and place other end in glass jar containing enough hydraulic fluid to cover end of hose. Open bleeder valve with wrench and observe flow of fluid. On Models 4000 and 5000, start engine and make at least two power brake applications with bleeder valve open to force air out of slave cylinder. Close bleeder valve as soon as bubbles stop and fluid flows in solid stream. Stop engine and relieve vacuum from system.
4. Bleed valve No. 2 (on power cylinder control valve), then bleed wheel cylinders in sequence. Repeat bleeding operations at power cylinder. On Models 4000 and 5000, repeat power brake applications with engine running as in Step (3).
5. If, after bleeding, the pedal "feel" is not satisfactory, inspect residual check valve in the master cylinder and the check valve in the power cylinder piston. Improper operation of either or both of these valves will result in same pedal "feel" as air in the system, since malfunction permits recirculation of fluid through compensating line and back to master cylinder reservoir. Refer to applicable procedures for repair.

Medium Duty Trucks (w/Disc Brakes)

The pressure bleeding procedure for medium duty trucks with disc brakes is essentially the same as the procedure for light duty trucks with the following exceptions:

1. Install special tool J23774-01 or an equivalent tool on the metering valve, which is located at the frame crossmember. This step is

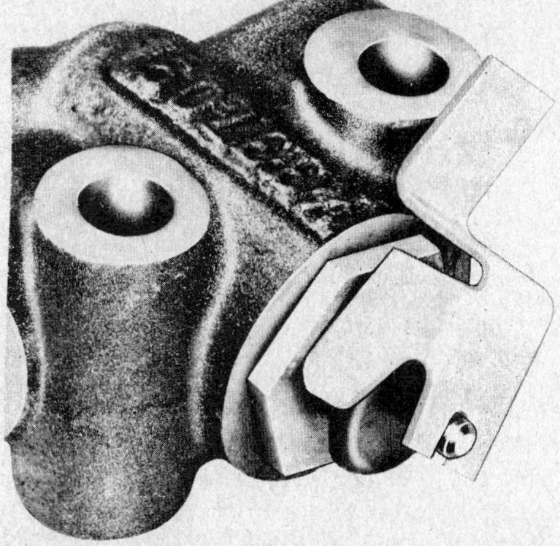

Metering Valve held in the open position—Medium Duty Trucks (w/disc brakes) (© Chevrolet Div., G.M. Corp.)

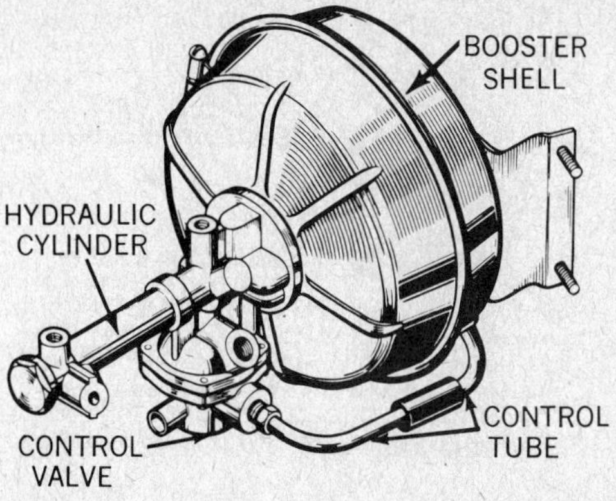

Single Diaphragm Hydrovac (© Chevrolet Div., G.M. Corp.)

necessary to hold the metering valve open, because when a bleeder valve is opened, the pressure drops allowing the metering valve to close, which stops the flow of fluid to the front brakes.

2. Install a brake bleeder adapter J-24863 or an equivalent tool on the master cylinder.
3. Begin bleeding the system at the valve nearest the master cylinder, then proceed to the next nearest, and so on until all of the valves have been bled. If the master cylinder has bleeder valves, bleed these valves first.

Manual Bleeding

Manual bleeding follows the same procedures as pressure bleeding, except that brake fluid is forced through lines by pumping the brake pedal instead of by air pressure. Fluid in master cylinder must be replenished after bleeding at each valve. Brake pedal should be pumped up and down slowly, and should be on downstroke as valve is closed.

Split System ("S" Models)

The system consists of a dash mounted master cylinder and two power cylinders mounted on the frame. The main system consists of the front wheel brakes and one cylinder on each rear wheel brake. The secondary system consists of one cylinder on each secondary wheel brake. Each system must be bled separately.

Vacuum Power Brakes

Single Diaphragm Hydrovac

The Single Diaphragm Hydrovac is a self contained vacuum hydraulic power brake unit designed for use on a vehicle with a vacuum source such as the intake manifold vacuum of a conventional gasoline engine. The Hydrovac is comprised of three basic elements:

1. A vacuum power chamber which consists of a power diaphragm and a push rod that connects the power diaphragm to the hydraulic piston.
2. A hydraulic cylinder (slave cylinder) which contains a hydraulic piston with a drilled passage to permit the filling of the hydraulic cylinder and return of the fluid to the master cylinder upon release of the brakes.
3. A vacuum control valve built integrally with the hydraulic cylinder which controls the power output of the vacuum power chamber in accordance with the hydraulic pressure developed within the vehicle master cylinder.

Power Cylinder

Removal

1. For easier accessibility, it is recommended that cab step be removed on conventional models and that cab be tilted forward on tilt cab models.
2. Clean away road dirt and grease to prevent contamination of vacuum or hydraulic systems.
3. Have a container available to catch hydraulic brake fluid which will flow from system. *Do*

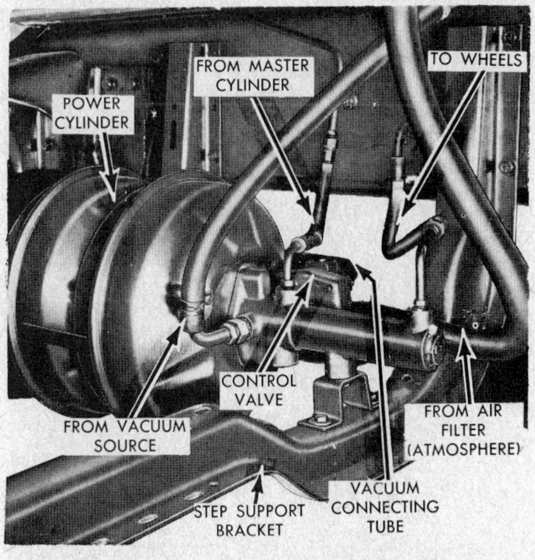

Power cylinder—conventional cab (© G.M.C.)

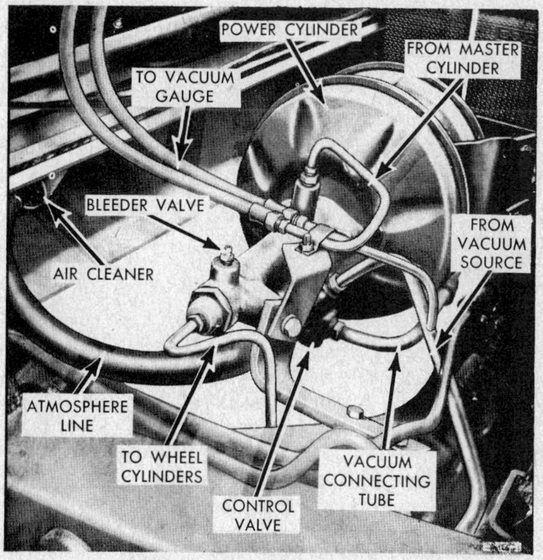

Power cylinder—tilt cab (© G.M.C.)

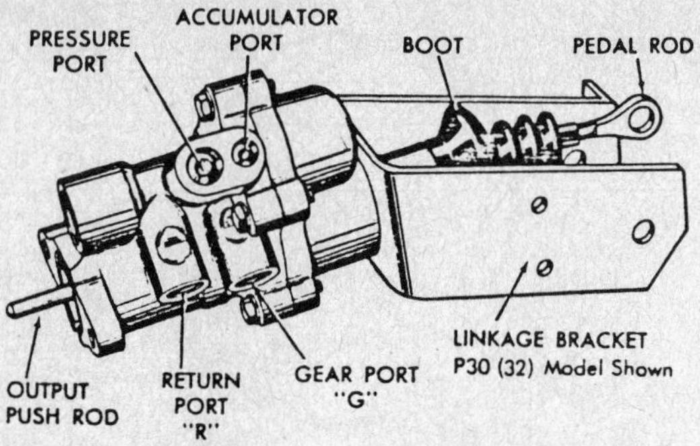

Hydro-boost—1974 (© G.M.C.)

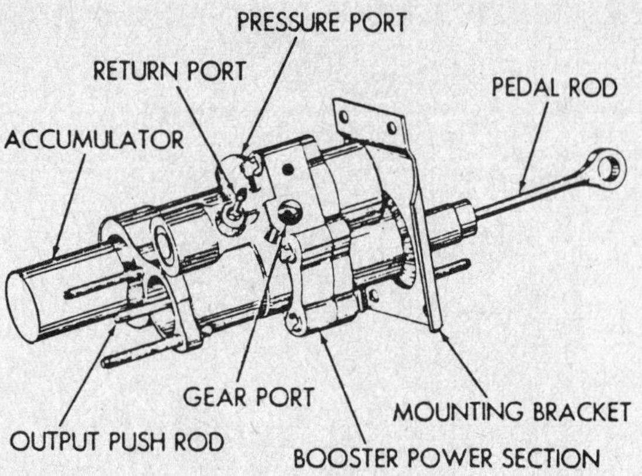

Hydro-boost—Cabs, Suburban—1975 (© G.M.C.)

not re-use this fluid.

4. Disconnect all hydraulic, vacuum and atmospheric lines and hoses from power cylinder. Plug vacuum line.
5. On light duty models, disconnect the push rod from the brake pedal. Remove bolts and nuts fastening cylinder to frame and support brackets.
6. Remove power cylinder.

Installation

1. Place power cylinder in position and fasten with nuts and bolts to frame and support brackets. Connect the push rod to the brake pedal.
2. Connect all hydraulic, vacuum, and atmospheric lines and hoses to power cylinder.
3. Bleed master cylinder and vacuum power cylinder as directed under "Bleeding Brakes." If ONLY the power cylinder has been removed, it should not be necessary to bleed the wheel cylinders IF the master cylinder and power cylinders are bled first AND lines to wheel cylinder have not been disturbed.

Hydro-Boost Power Brakes

Specific information will be found in the Power Brake portion of the General Repair Section on adjustments, overhauling and troubleshooting.

The Hydro-boost system was designed to eliminate the need for the remote frame mounted boosters. It utilizes power steering fluid in place of engine vacuum to provide a power assist that operates a dual master cylinder brake system. A spring accumulator is used in conjunction with the hydraulic brake booster. The accumulator is a sealed hydraulic cylinder with a port at each end. On 1974 models the accumulator and booster are mounted separately. In 1975 all "C" model vehicles equipped with the hydro-boost incorporate an accumulator which is integral with the booster. All 1976 and later hydro-boost vehicles will incorporate an accumulator which is integral with the booster.

CAUTION: **The accumulator used on 1974-77 vehicles contains a spring compressed under high pressure. Any attempt to disassemble or cut into the accumulator could cause severe personal injury. The accumulator used on 1978 and later hydro-boost vehicles contains compressed gas. DO NOT apply heat to the accumulater. NEVER attempt to repair an inoperative accumulator; always replace the accumulator with a new unit.**

In order to dispose of an inoperative accumulator, drill a 1/16″ diameter hole through the end of the accumulator can opposite the "O" ring. (compresssed gas type only)

Hydraulic Brake Booster Removal and Installation

Motor Home Chassis

1. Make sure all pressure is discharged from the accumulator by depressing and releasing the brake pedal several times.
2. Raise the vehicle on a hoist.
3. Clean all the dirt from the booster at the hydraulic line connections and master cylinder.
4. Remove the nuts and lockwashers that secure the master cylinder to the booster and support bracket. Support the master cylinder leaving the hydraulic lines attached to the master cylinder.
5. Disconnect and plug the hydraulic lines from the booster ports.
6. Remove the cotter pin, nut, bolt and washers that secure the operating lever to the vertical brake rod.
7. Remove the six nuts, lockwashers and bolts that secure the booster linkage bracket to the front and rear support brackets, then slide the booster off the rear support studs and remove the booster from the vehicle.
8. Remove the cotter pin, nut, washer and bolt that secures the operating lever to the pedal rod.
9. Remove the brake pedal rod lever nut and bolt and then remove the lever, sleeve and bushings.
10. To install reverse the removal procedures. Bleed the booster-power steering hydraulic system and check the brake pedal and stoplamp switch adjustment.

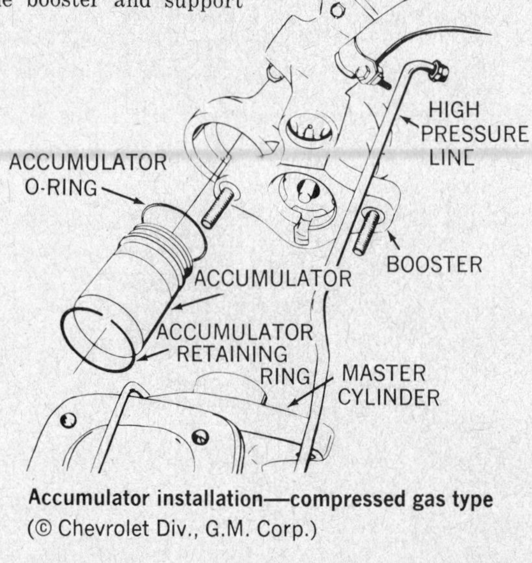

Accumulator installation—compressed gas type
(© Chevrolet Div., G.M. Corp.)

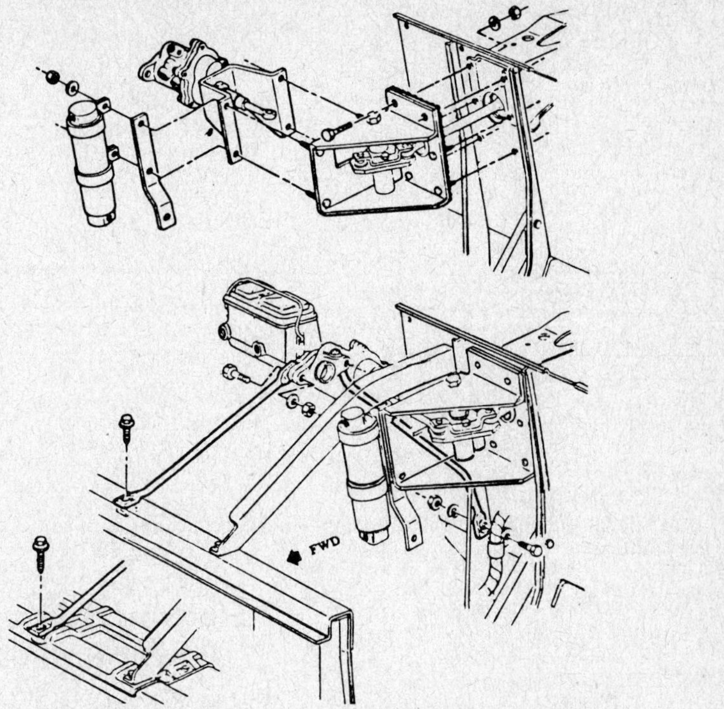

Booster installation—forward control chassis—except light duty vans (© G.M.C.)

Conventional Cab & Suburban

1. Make sure all pressure is discharged from the accumulator by depressing and releasing the brake pedal several times.
2. Remove the nuts and lockwashers that secure the master cylinder to the booster and support bracket. Support the master cylinder leaving the hydraulic lines attached to the master cylinder.
3. Remove the booster pedal push rod cotter pin and washer, and disconnect the push rod from the brake pedal.
4. Remove the booster support bracket.
5. Remove the booster bracket to dash panel or support bracket nuts and remove the booster assembly.
6. To install reverse the removal procedure. Bleed the booster-power steering hydraulic system and check brake pedal and stoplamp switch adjustment.

Forward Control Chassis (Vans)

1. Make sure all pressure is discharged from the accumulator by depressing and releasing the brake pedal several times.
2. Clean all the dirt from the booster at the hydraulic line connections and master cylinder.
3. Remove the nuts and lockwashers that secure the master cylinder to the booster and the support bracket. Support the master cylinder leaving the hydraulic lines attached to the master cylinder.
4. Remove the booster pedal push rod cotter pin and washer and disconnect the push rod from the booster bracket pivot lever.
5. Remove the booster upper braces.
6. Remove the booster bracket nuts and remove the booster.
7. To install reverse the removal procedure. Bleed the booster-power steering hydraulic system and check the brake pedal and stop lamp switch adjustment.

Bleeding Hydro-Boost System

1. Fill the power steering pump to the proper level.
2. Start the engine for approximately two seconds. Check the fluid and add if necessary.
3. Repeat step 2 until the fluid level remains constant.
4. Raise the front end of the vehicle so that the tires are clear of the ground.
5. Start the engine and run approximately 1500 rpm. Depress and release the brake pedal several times then turn the steering wheel right and left, lightly contacting the wheel stops.
6. Turn off the engine and check the fluid level in the reservoir and add fluid if necessary.
7. Lower the vehicle, start the engine and run at approximately 1500 rpm. Depress and release the brake pedal several times and turn the steering wheel to full right and left.
8. Turn the engine off and check the fluid level in the reservoir. Add fluid if necessary.

NOTE: If the fluid is extremely foamy, or there is an erratic pedal feel allow vehicle to stand a few moments with the engine off and repeat the above procedure.

Brake Pedal Adjustment

Motor Home Chassis

1. With brake pedal pull back spring installed, brake pedal hard into bumper, brake master cylinder assembly and brake pedal rod lever at full return, install the preassembled brake pedal rod assembly (rod end at boot) and adjust to 31.75 in.
2. Turn the brake pedal rod end and adjust the free pedal travel to .06 in. to .36 in.
3. Fasten the boot to the floor pan assembly and compress the boot to 2.54 in. installed height.

Forward Control Chassis (P and G Models)

1. Adjust the length of the pedal

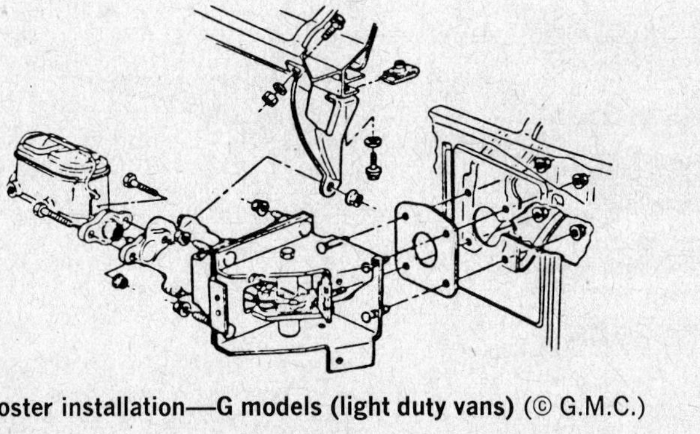

Booster installation—G models (light duty vans) (© G.M.C.)

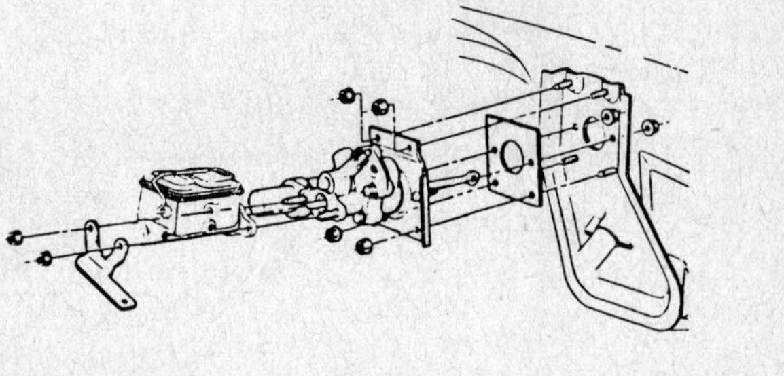

Booster installation—conventional cab and Suburban (© G.M.C.)

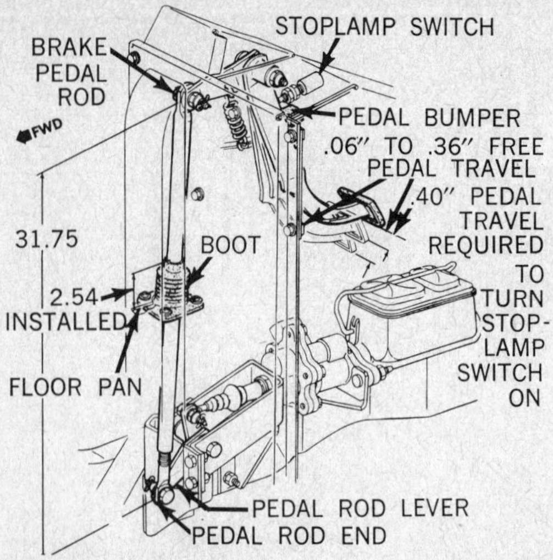

Brake pedal and stop lamp adjustments—motor home chassis (© G.M.C.)

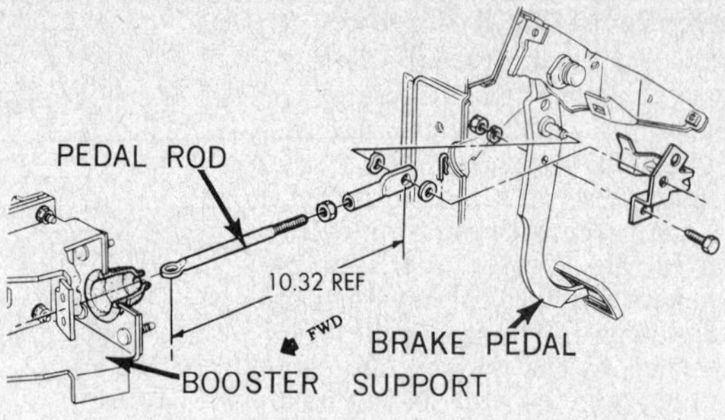

Brake pedal adjustment—vans (© G.M.C.)

rod to 10.32" on G models.

2. Adjust the length of the pedal rod to 9.90" on P models.

NOTE: The brake pedal push rod is not adjustable on conventional cab models.

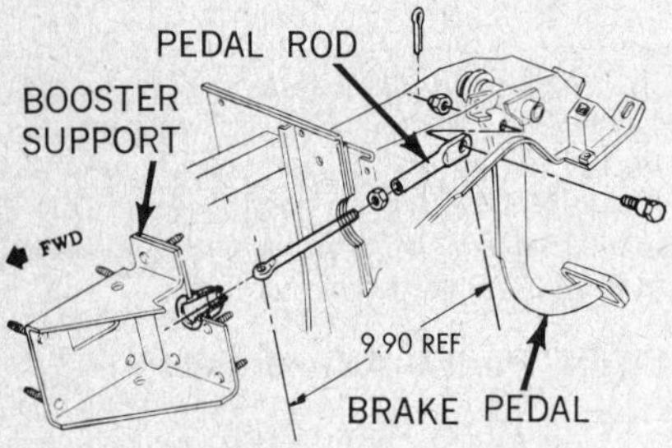

Brake pedal adjustment—forward control chassis (© G.M.C.)

Stoplamp Switch Adjustment

1. Release the brake pedal to its normal position.
2. Loosen the switch locknut and rotate the switch in its bracket. Electrical contact should be made when pedal travel is 3/8 in-5/8 in.

Electro-Hydraulic Power Brakes

The booster unit is hydraulically operated with an electrical pump attached as a back-up unit in the event of primary pump failure. The booster system features a dual braking system, increased pressure output, excellent pedal feel, separate hydraulic pump, and an electrically powered back-up system.

The hydraulic booster is powered by a standard power steering vane type pump.

Electro-Hydraulic Pump

Removal

NOTE: The pump may be removed from the booster assembly while in the vehicle.

1. Block vehicle wheels.
2. Disconnect battery ground.
3. Disconnect E.H. pump lead.
4. Position a container to catch fluid and remove bracket-to-booster 9/16 in. hex-head bolt.
5. Remove two 9/16 in. hex-head mounting bolts. Remove pump and two O-rings.

Installation

1. To install reverse the removal procedure. Use new O-rings and torque the two 3/8-16 x 1 1/8 in mounting bolts to 16-30 ft. lbs.

Booster Assembly

Conventional Cab—Removal

1. Block vehicle wheels.
2. Disconnect battery ground cable.
3. Disconnect electrical leads to E.H. pump and flow switch.

   NOTE: Booster head may be removed from vehicle without removing master cylinder and disconnecting brake lines. Remove two nuts retaining brake line clips to line support. Remove bolt and clips in booster head. Remove four 9/16 in. hex head master cylinder to booster head mounting bolts and move master cylinder forward from booster. Secure in an upright position. Complete booster assembly removal procedure following:

4. Disconnect hydraulic lines from booster. Use a suitable container to catch fluid. DO NOT reuse fluid.
5. Remove cotter key from push rod pin. Remove nut and bolt from pedal push rod eye. Thread push rod and nut from booster push rod.
6. Remove line and hose supports from booster head.

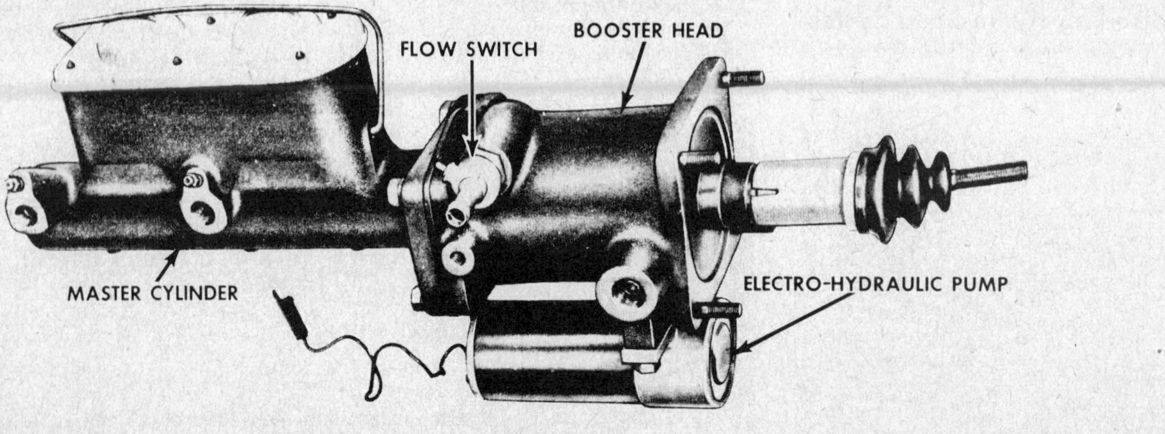

Electro-hydraulic brake booster and master cylinder (© G.M.C.)

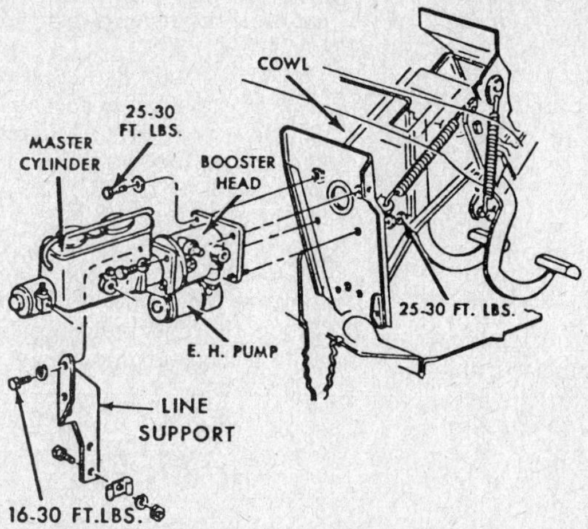

Booster assembly mounting—conventional cab (© G.M.C.)

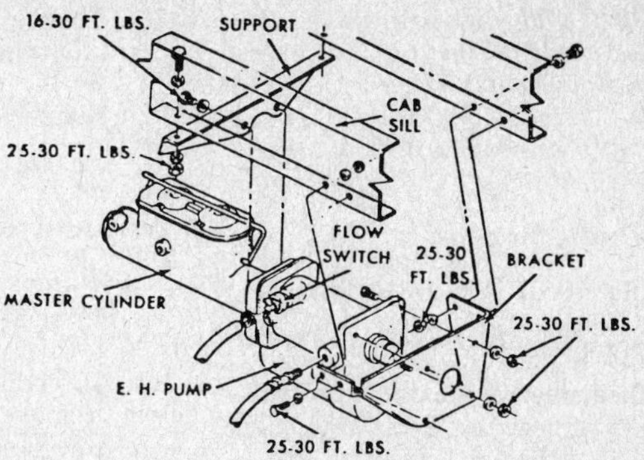

Booster assembly mounting—tilt cab (© G.M.C.)

NOTE: Use care when proceeding to next two steps. This is a heavy unit, approximately 50 pounds including master cylinder, and should be handled as such. After removing from vehicle, use care in handling so that flow switch or E.H. pump is not damaged and bail or cover on master cylinder is not damaged.

7. Remove two 3/8-24 thread hex-head nuts and washers from inside cab at dash panel.
8. Remove upper two mounting bolts and washers from booster head at dash. Remove booster assembly.
9. Remove four 9/16 in. hex-head bolts which attach brake master cylinder to booster head (Fig. 8). Remove master cylinder, gasket, and brake line support.

Installation

1. To install reverse the removal procedure. Torque the four 3/8-16 x 1 3/8 in. hex-head bolts attaching the master cylinder to the booster head to 16-30 ft lbs. The two hex-nuts on the 3/8-24 in. studs are torqued to 25-30 ft lbs. The two mounting bolts are torqued to 25-30 ft lbs.

Tilt Cab—Removal and Installation

1. Block vehicle wheels.
2. Disconnect battery ground cable.
3. Disconnect electrical lead to E.H. pump.
4. Disconnect hydraulic lines from booster and master cylinder. Use a suitable container to catch fluid. Do not reuse fluid.
5. Loosen nuts on each end of push rod extension. Turn extension until free of booster push rod. Bellcrank ball joint may have to be removed to facilitate turning extension.
6. Remove two 9/16 in. hex-head bolts and nuts retaining support to cab sill.
7. Remove two 9/16 in. hex-head bolts and nuts retaining bracket to sill.
8. Remove booster assembly. Move push rod end forward and down while revolving unit to clear E.H. pump, support, and bracket.
9. Remove four 9/16 in. hex-head bolts which attach brake master cylinder to booster head and remove master cylinder and gasket.

Flow Switch

Removal

1. Position container to catch fluid from disconnected hose at flow switch.
2. Loosen outer hose clamp at switch and remove hydraulic line from hose. Drain fluid into previously placed container. DO NOT reuse fluid.
3. Loosen inner hose clamp at switch and remove hose.
4. Disconnect electrical lead to switch.
5. Remove switch using a one-inch thin blade wrench.

Installation

1. Use a new O-ring seal and torque to 20-30 ft lbs.

Brake Hydraulic Pump

V8 Engine—Removal

1. Disconnect E.H. pump electrical lead.
2. Disconnect hydraulic lines at pump. Cap or otherwise restrict flow of fluid from lines.
3. Remove hose to reservoir (if used).
4. Remove pulley.
5. Remove adjusting nut and washers at rear of pump at bracket slot.
6. Remove adjusting bolt and washers from front of pump at bracket slot.
7. Remove front mounting bolt and washers and remove pump.

Installation

1. To install reverse the removal procedure. Use a belt tension gauge and adjust the belt to 90-100 lbs (new belt).

Six Cylinder Engine—Removal

1. Disconnect E.H. pump electrical lead.
2. Disconnect hydraulic lines at pump. Cap or otherwise restrict flow of fluid from lines.
3. Remove pulley.
4. Remove adjusting bolt and washer from slot at front bracket.
5. Remove nut and washer from support at rear of pump.
6. Remove mounting bolt at front bracket and remove pump.

Installation

1. To install reverse the removal procedure. Use a belt tension gauge and adjust the belt to 90-100 lbs (new belt).

Dual Power Brake System

(Medium Duty Conventional Cab)

The Dual Power Brake System (DPB) is a system which utilizes two power boosting units in series to provide the power assist necessary to stop the vehicle. This is accomplished by combining a vacuum operated booster with a hydraulically operated booster in tandem arrangement with a standard dual master cylinder. Assist power generated by the vacuum booster is transmitted forward to the hydraulic booster, where the apply power is, again, assisted or augmented by the hydraulic booster. Doubly assisted power available at the hydraulic booster is transmitted to the master cylinder, thereby developing hydraulic pressure up to a maximum of approximately 600 psi.

NOTE: The entire dual power booster assembly may be removed as one unit (master cylinder, hydraulic booster, and vacuum booster), individual units, or combination of units.

Hydraulic Booster

Removal and Installation

1. Prevent the vehicle from moving by blocking the wheels.
2. Disconnect the battery ground.
3. Disconnect the electrical connection at the flow switch.
   NOTE: It is advised that a container of suitable size be placed under the master cylinder and booster assembly prior to disconnecting any fluid lines.
4. Remove, if necessary, the brake line clamps, clips, and supports to allow movement of the master cylinder.
5. Remove the master cylinder mounting bolts, and position the master cylinder out of the way:
   NOTE: Support the master cylinder in an upright position in order to relieve strain on the brake lines and prevent spillage of hydraulic fluid.
6. Disconnect the fluid lines at the booster inlet and the flow switch.
7. Remove the nuts which secure the hydraulic booster to the vacuum booster, and remove the hydraulic booster.
8. Install in the reverse order of removal.
9. Torque the hydraulic booster to vacuum booster retaining nuts to 23 ft. lbs.
10. Torque the master cylinder mounting bolts to 23 ft. lbs.
11. Bleed the system.
12. Connect the battery ground.

Vacuum Booster

Removal and Installation

1. Prevent the vehicle from moving by blocking the wheels.
2. Disconnect the battery ground.
3. Remove, if necessary, the brake line clamps, clips, and supports to allow movement of the master cylinder.
4. Remove the three nuts which retain the hydraulic booster to the vacuum booster.
5. Position the master cylinder and hydraulic booster out of the way.
   NOTE: Support the master cylinder and hydraulic booster in an upright position in order to relieve strain on the hydraulic lines and prevent spillage of hydraulic fluid.
6. Disconnect the vacuum hose from the check valve.
7. Disconnect the vacuum hose at the elbow.
8. Position the vacuum hose out of the way in order to prevent contamination.
9. Disconnect the push rod (apply rod) at the brake pedal.
10. Working from inside the cab, remove the four mounting studs which secure the vacuum booster to the cab. Pull the booster away from the cowl, and remove it from the vehicle.
11. Install in the reverse order of removal.
    NOTE: It will be necessary to gauge the hydraulic booster, piston push rod. For information concerning the gauging procedure, refer to the BRAKE portion of the General Repair Section.
12. Torque the vacuum booster mounting stud nuts to 18 ft. lbs.
13. Torque the hydraulic booster to vacuum booster mounting nuts to 23 ft. lbs.

Air Brakes

Information on repair and overhaul of air brake components is not included in the General Repair Section.

Application Valve

Conventional—Removal

1. Relieve air pressure from system.
2. Disconnect all air lines from valve. On "L" models, disconnect hose from exhaust tube.
3. Remove valve as follows:
   a. All except SPA5000: Remove three attaching bolts and valve assembly.
   b. SPA5000: Remove bolts attaching valve and treadle mounting plate to toeboard and then remove the complete assembly from the truck. Remove three bolts attaching valve to mounting plate and remove valve.

Installation

a. Except SPA5000 models: Position valve assembly on mounting bracket with pushrod inserted into piston cup.

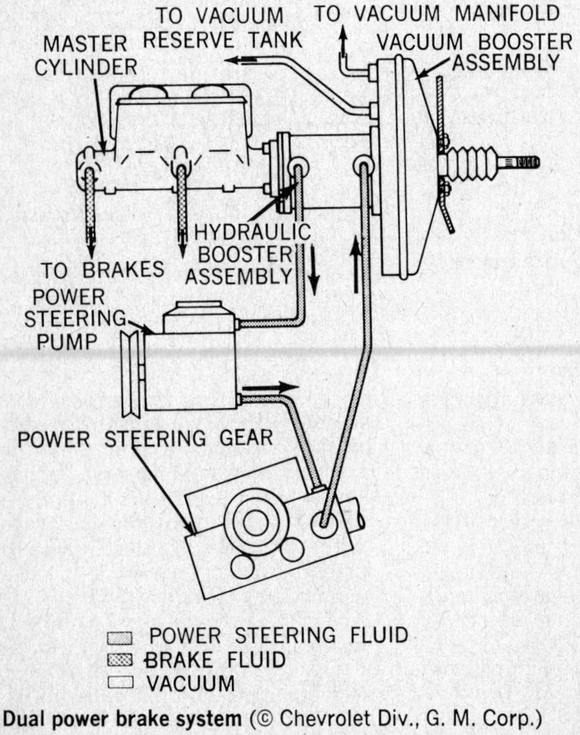

Dual power brake system (© Chevrolet Div., G. M. Corp.)

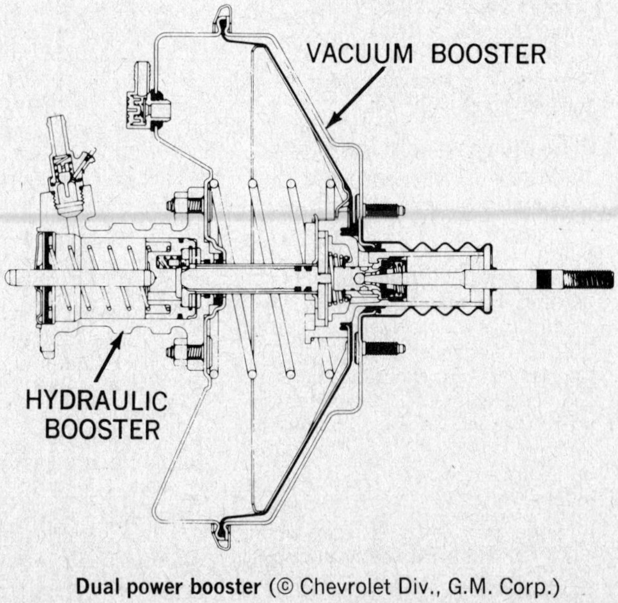

Dual power booster (© Chevrolet Div., G.M. Corp.)

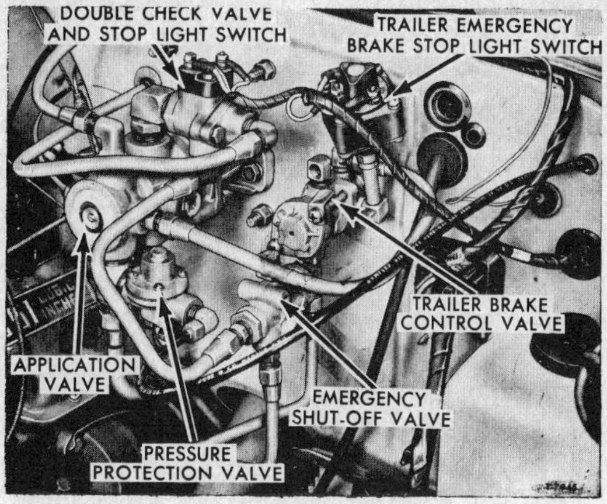

Brake treadle installation—SPA5000 (© G.M.C.)

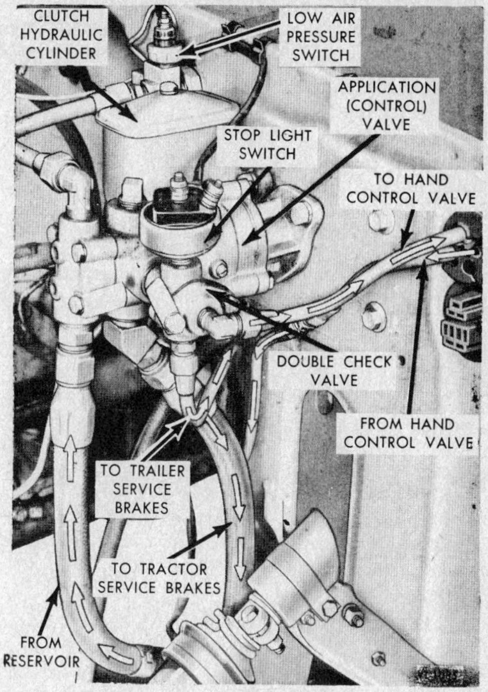

Application valve—models 1000-4500—typical (© G.M.C.)

On dash mounted units, the exhaust opening (with filter screen) must be down; on "L" models, exhaust tube must be toward right side of cab. Attach valve to mounting bracket with three bolts. Check pushrod or stop screw adjustment and correct if necessary.

b. SPA5000: Models: Connect valve assembly to mounting plate, with pushrod inserted into plate. Attach with three bolts and lock washers. Check for free travel between end of pushrod and piston cup. If necessary, remove treadle pin, then remove treadle stop bumper and add shims under bumper as necessary to remove clearance. Install treadle pin and secure with cotter pin. Install the complete assembly on toeboard and attach with three bolts, lock washers, and nuts.

Connect air lines to valve. When installing connector fittings in valve, use sealing compound on threads. *Keep sealing compound off first two threads of fittings.* Sealing compound inside the valve could foul valve seats and block compensating port. On "L" models, connect hose to exhaust tube. Build up air pressure in system and test application valve operation.

Tilt Cab 5000-6500 Models—Removal

1. Block the vehicle wheels, drain air pressure from the brake system, and disconnect the air lines from the application valve.
2. Disconnect the exhaust hose from the exhaust port of the valve.
3. Remove the bolts which attach the valve to the support bracket, and remove the valve.

Installation

1. Position the valve on the support bracket and install the attaching bolts.
2. Connect the exhaust hose to the exhaust port of the valve.
3. Connect the air lines to the valve.
4. Operate the engine until operating air pressure is built up, check for leaks, and test brakes for proper operation.

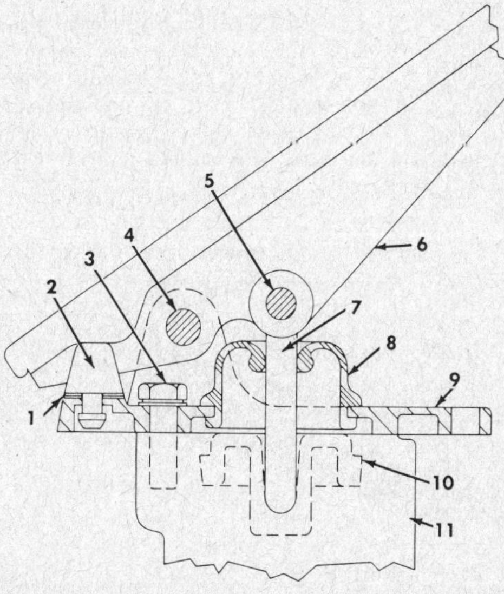

1 Shims
2 Treadle stop bumper
3 Mounting plate to application valve bolt
4 Treadle pin
5 Push rod pin
6 Treadle
7 Push rod
8 Push rod boot
9 Mounting plate
10 Application valve piston cup
11 Application valve

Application valve—models 6500—typical (© G.M.C.)

Compressor

Removal

1. Block or hold vehicle by means other than air brakes.
2. Drain air from system, usually at reservoirs.
3. If water cooled, drain cooling system.
4. Disconnect ALL lines (air, water and oil).
5. Loosen belt adjusting stud and remove drive belt.
6. Remove mounting bolts, remove compressor.

Installation

1. Run engine briefly to clear and check oil supply lines. Clean oil return lines and passages. Check coolant supply and lines (if used).
2. Clean mounting surface and replace gasket, be sure oil holes in gasket are aligned.
3. Install compressor with mount-

ing cap screws loose, compressor will be movable to allow fittings on lines to be started.
4. Make sure air cleaner is cleaned and properly installed.
5. Align compressor, check drive belt.
6. Tighten mounting bolts and adjust.

Cam Type Brake Chamber

Removal

1. Disconnect air hose from chamber.
2. Remove clevis pin from yoke.
3. Remove nuts and washers from mounting studs.
4. Remove chamber.

Installation

1. Place chamber on mounting bracket and secure with stud nuts and lock washers.
2. Connect air hose.
3. Install slack adjuster yoke clevis pin, after adjusting for minimum travel. (Angle made by push rod and slack adjuster lever should not be less than 90°, brakes applied). Lock yoke with locking nut. Push rod travel should be as short as possible without brakes dragging.
4. Check for leaks, and possible brake shoe adjustment.

Wedge Type Brake Chamber

Removal

1. Block or hold vehicle by means other than air brakes.
2. Disconnect air hose from chamber.
3. Remove lock washer tangs from notches in spanner nut and spider housing.
4. Loosen spanner nut and unscrew air chamber from housing.

Installation

1. Screw air chamber in spider housing until it "bottoms," then back off (no more than one turn) until chamber air port aligns with air hose. The plastic guide will assure proper position of wedge. Lock brake chamber in position with spanner nut and lock washer.
2. Start engine, charge air system, check for leaks. Pump brake pedal to allow automatic adjusters to adjust brakes.

NOTE: When brakes are equipped with "fail-safe" brake chambers, cage power spring before starting any disassembly or removal of wheels or drums to avoid possible injury. When a vehicle is disabled, due to low or lost air pressure, cage power spring before attempting to move the vehicle. Cage the power spring by rotating the release bolt approximately 18 to 21 turns clockwise. Caging and uncaging can be made easier by applying air pressure, 65 lbs needed (if possible). This takes spring load off release bolt.

CAUTION: Before removing or caging brake chamber, block wheels since parking brake will not be applied.

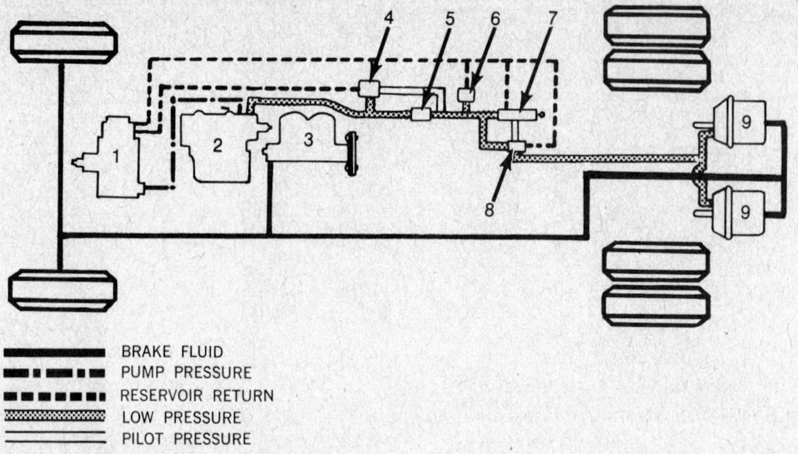

Hy-Park Brake System—typical (© Chevrolet Div., G.M. Corp.)

1 Hydraulic Pump
2 Steering Gear
3 Master Cylinder
4 Diverter Valve
5 Check Valve
6 Relief Valve
7 Hand Control Valve
8 Relay Valve
9 Hy-Park Actuators (Chambers)

Slack Adjusters

Removal

1. Remove clevis pin at lever.
2. Remove lock ring and washer on splined camshaft (some front slack adjusters are held on by a retaining screw).
3. Slide adjuster off splined shaft.

Installation

1. Make sure spacer washers are in place (if used).
2. Slide slack adjuster on splined camshaft, lock in place with snap ring and washer. If held on by retaining screw, allow .010 in. end play. Stake edge of screw to lock.
3. Connect yoke clevis pin. Angle made by push rod and slack adjuster lever should NOT be less than 90° brakes applied. Push rod travel should be as short as possible without brakes dragging.
4. Lubricate adjuster.

Hy-Park System

The Hy-Park brake system is comprised basically of a hydraulic service brake system in conjunction with a hydraulically released, spring applied parking brake.

Hydraulic brake fluid from the master cylinder is used to actuate the rear S-cam service brakes. A hydraulic pump (power steering pump on medium duty trucks) delivers power steering fluid, under pressure, to compress the power spring in the Hy-Park actuator (chamber). Applications and release of the parking brake is controlled by a hand valve, which is located in the cab. The rear brake is a conventional S-cam brake such as the type found on vehicles equipped with air brakes.

Caging Hy-Park Actuator Power Spring

IMPORTANT: Failure to properly cage the spring before removal or dissassembly could result in serious personal injury, as the load on the compressed power spring is approximately 2,000 pounds.

NOTE: Two special release studs, nuts, and washers will be needed to cage one power spring (illustration).

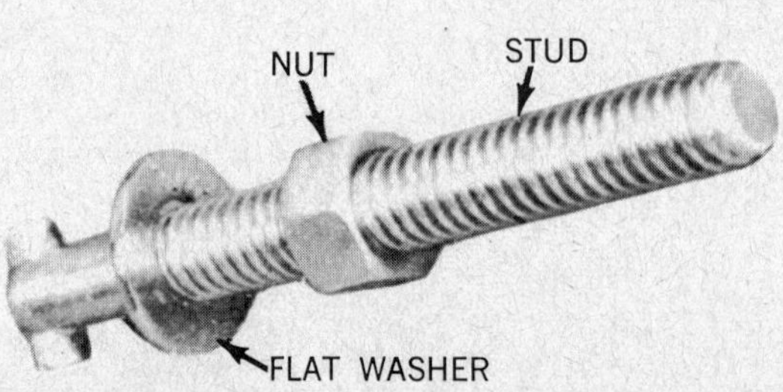

Release stud, nut, and washer (© Chevrolet Div., G.M. Corp.)

Caging With Engine Operating

1. Prevent the vehicle from moving by blocking the wheels or by whatever means is safe and convenient.
2. Start the engine.
3. Release the parking brakes by using the cab control valve.
4. Install a washer on a release stud, and thread a nut on the stud for a few turns.
5. Remove the dust caps from the slots in the rear of the actuator, and insert a release stud, nut, and washer assembly until there is metal to metal contact. DO NOT force.
6. Turn the release stud $1/4$ turn clockwise, and pull outward to engage the stud in the recess in the diaphragm support assembly.
7. While pulling outward on the release stud with a slight force, try rotating the stud in either direction. If the stud has been properly installed, it will not turn. Continue holding the stud firmly in this position.
8. Thread the nut on the stud until the nut and washer contact the rear housing. Hand tighten to ensure that there is a firm contact.
9. Repeat steps 4 through 8 for the other release stud assembly.

   NOTE: If the system has been operating properly, i.e., if the power spring has been hydraulically compressed, then the release studs are now in position to properly contain (cage) the power spring, and the engine may be shut off. With the engine not running and the parking brake applied, the power spring will begin to expand, but it will be prevented from expanding as the release studs now hold the spring in the caged position.
10. Continue tightening the release stud nuts until the diaphragm support assembly bottoms out against the rear housing.

Caging With Engine Not Operating

NOTE: In the event of a parking brake hydraulic system malfunction, manually release the parking brakes, and cage the power spring by following the steps of the previous procedure noting the following exceptions.

1. Only start the nut onto the threads of the release stud. This is done because almost the full length of the studs will be required to reach the diaphragrm support assembly.
2. Tighten the release nuts in an alternate and gradual manner until the power spring is compressed. Continue tightening the release stud nuts until the diaphragm support assembly bottoms out against the rear housing.

CAUTION: **Failure to tighten the release stud nuts alternately could cause the sleeve and diaphragm support assembly to tilt and bind in the housing.**

NOTE: Bottoming out will occur when the extension of the end of the stud beyond the housing is approximately $2\frac{7}{8}''$.

Hy-Park Actuator

Removal and Installation

CAUTION: **The Hy-Park actuator houses two types of hydraulic fluid: (1) brake fluid, and (2) power steering fluid. These two very different types of hydraulic fluid are not compatible, and should not be allowed to come into contact with one another, nor should they be allowed to come into contact with components of the system for which they are not intended. If, at any time during removal or installation, either fluid contacts a rubber sealing component of the wrong system, i.e., should power steering fluid contaminate the apply piston double lip seal, or, if brake fluid should contaminate the actuator diaphragm or boot, then the affected seal(s) should be discarded, as the fluid will attack the seal and cause it to deteriorate. If care is not exercised to isolate these two fluids, then inevitable deterioration will result, causing leakage at the seals and eventual system malfunction.**

1. Prevent the vehicle from moving by blocking the wheels.
2. Disconnect the battery ground.
3. Disconnect the brake fluid line from the piston housing, located at the rear of the actuator.
4. Disconnect the power steering fluid line from the front of the housing.

   NOTE: After disconnecting the fluid lines, cover the openings immediately to contain the fluid and prevent contamination.
5. Disconnect the push rod clevis pin from the slack adjuster.
6. Remove the nuts and lock washers from the mounting studs.
7. Remove the actuator from the mounting bracket.
8. Drain all remaining fluid.
9. Install in the reverse order of removal.

   NOTE: During installation, position the actuator so that the brake bleeder valve is above the brake line.

Relay Valve

Removal and Installation

1. Disconnect the battery ground.
2. Pull the control valve knob outward, and set the parking brakes.
3. Disconnect the return line.
4. Disconnect the remaining lines.

   NOTE: Cap all open lines.
5. Remove the two, valve-to-frame, attaching bolts and nuts on conventional cab models. Remove the two, valve-to-support, attaching bolts and nuts on alum-

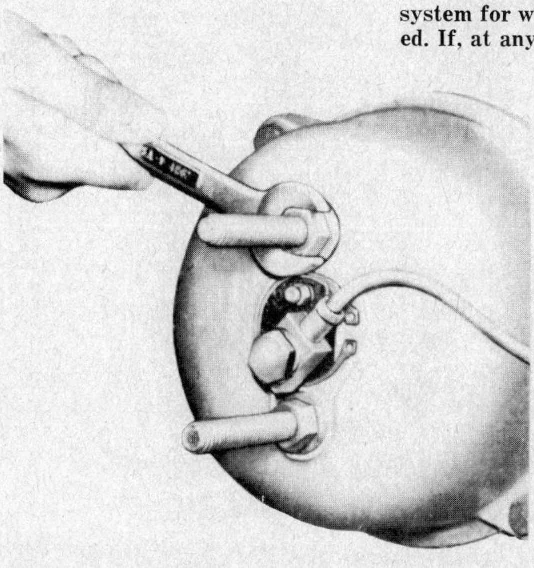

Release studs—installed (© Chevrolet Div., G.M. Corp.)

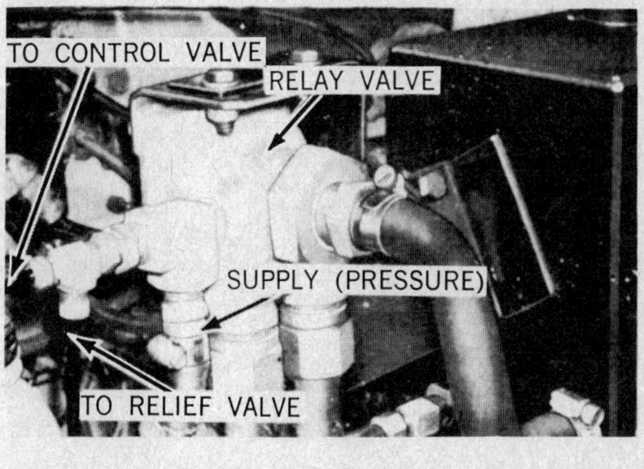

Relay valve—installed (Aluminum conventional cab)
(© Chevrolet Div., G.M. Corp.)

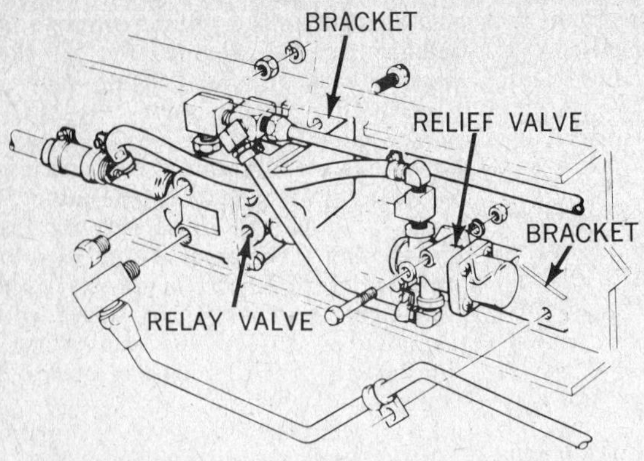

Pressure relief and relay valves—installed (medium duty conventional cab) (© Chevrolet Div., G.M. Corp.)

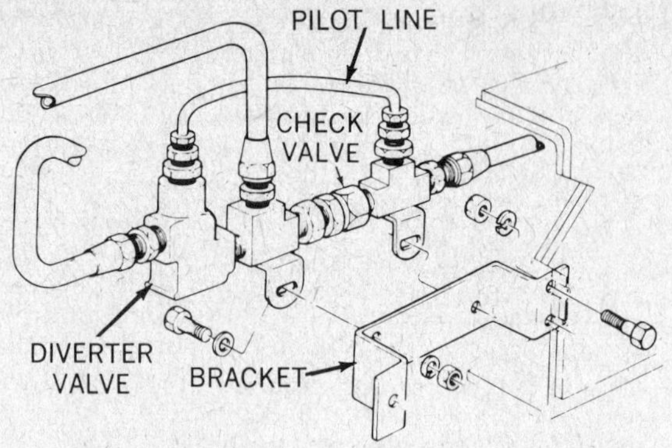

Installation of check and diverter valves (medium duty conventional cab) (© Chevrolet Div., G.M. Corp.)

inum conventional cab models.

6. Disconnect the actuator delivery lines from the base of the valve, and remove the valve.
7. Remove the bracket from the valve.
8. Install in the reverse order of removal.

Pressure Relief Valve

Removal and Installation

1. Disconnect the battery ground.
2. Disconnect the hydraulic lines at the valve, and plug the lines.
3. Remove the bracket-to-frame attaching bolts and nuts.
4. Remove the valve-to-bracket attaching bolts and nuts.
5. Install in the reverse order of removal.
6. Torque the valve mounting bolt nuts to 75 in. lbs.

Check Valve

Removal and Installation

1. Disconnect the battery ground.
2. Disconnect the lines from the "T" fitting on the end of the valve.
3. Remove the fittings from the "T" as necessary.
4. Remove the check valve by unscrewing it in a counterclockwise direction.
5. Remove the "T" from the check valve.
6. Install in the reverse order of removal.

Diverter Valve

Removal and Installation

1. Disconnect the battery ground.
2. Disconnect the return line.
3. Disconnect the pilot line.

   NOTE: Cap all open lines.

4. For conventional cab models, remove the check valve, and then thread the diverter valve from the pressure line. For aluminum conventional cab models, turn the valve down 90 degrees, turn the valve outwards 180 degrees, and thread the diverter valve from the bushing and elbow.

   NOTE: In order to allow movement of the line to provide clearance for valve movement, it may be necessary to remove the clip on the hydraulic pressure line to the booster.

5. Install in the reverse order of removal.

Reservoir

Removal and Installation

1. Disconnect the battery ground.
2. Disconnect one line at the bottom of the reservoir, and allow the reservoir to drain.
3. Disconnect the remaining lines. Plug all open lines.
4. Remove the reservoir attaching bolts and nuts, and remove the reservoir.
5. Install in the reverse order of removal. Torque the mounting bolts to 27 ft. lbs.
6. Using new power steering fluid, fill the reservoir to the sight glass with the park brake released.

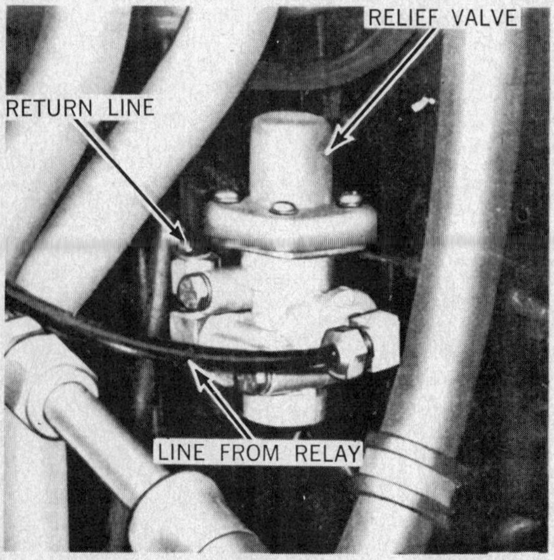

Pressure relief valve—installed (aluminum conventional cab) (© Chevrolet Div., G.M. Corp.)

Removal of diverter valve (© Chevrolet Div., G.M. Corp.)

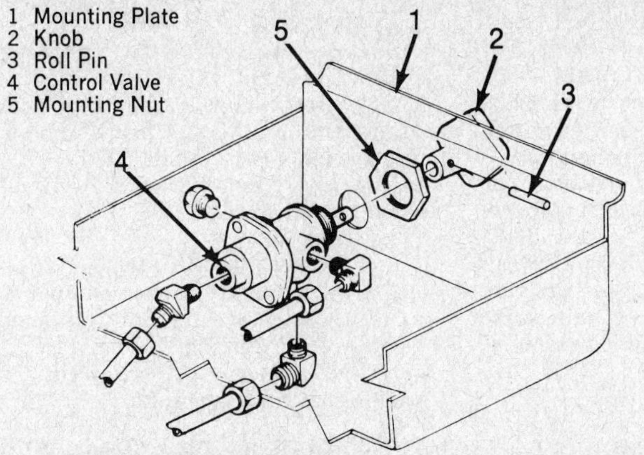

Installation of control valve (medium duty conventional cab) (© Chevrolet Div., G.M. Corp.)

Hand Control Valve and Knob (Aluminum Conventional Cab)

Removal and Installation

1. Disconnect the battery ground.
2. Disconnect the lines from the valve.
   NOTE: Cap all open lines.
3. Loosen the control cable set screw, and disconnect the control cable from the end of the valve.
4. Remove the nut from behind the bracket, and remove the valve.
5. Drive the roll pin out from the knob, and remove the knob.
6. Remove the valve mounting plate.
7. Remove the hexagonal nut from the plate, and pull the cable assembly through the plate.
8. Install in the reverse order of removal. Be certain that there are no kinks or sharp bends in the cable when installing.

Hand Control Valve and Knob (Medium Duty Conventional Cab)

Removal and Installation

1. Disconnect the battery ground.
2. Drive the roll pin out from the control valve knob, and remove the knob.
3. Remove the mounting plate attaching screws.
4. Remove the nut securing the valve to the plate.
5. Disconnect the lines at the valve. Cap all open lines.
6. Install in the reverse order of removal.

Hydraulic Pump (Gear Driven Type)

Removal

1. Disconnect the battery ground.
2. Remove the engine access cover from inside the cab.
3. Disconnect the exhaust pipe from the exhaust manifold and the rear coupling.

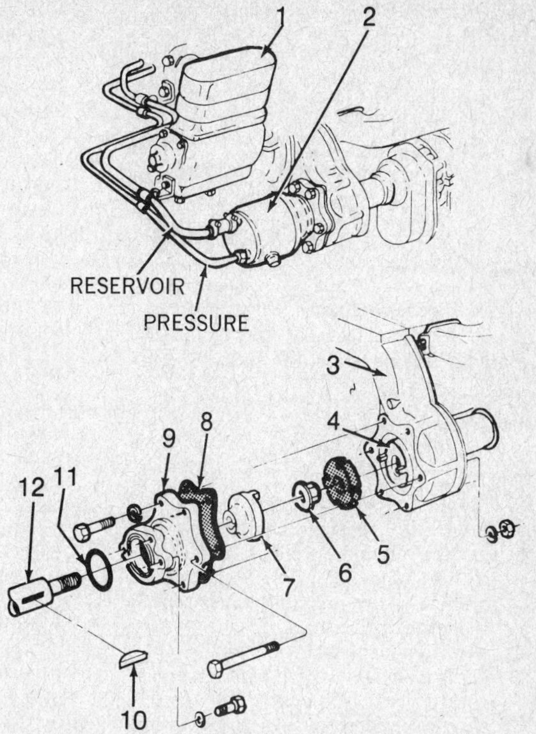

Installation of hydraulic pump (© Chevrolet Div., G.M. Corp.)

1 Air Compressor
2 Hydraulic Pump
3 Engine Housing
4 Drive Hub
5 Coupling
6 Nut (45 Ft. Lbs.)
7 Driven Hub
8 Adapter Gasket
9 Pump Adapter
10 Key
11 O-Ring Seal
12 Pump Shaft

4. Move the pipe forward and away from the pump.
5. Disconnect the lines at the pump. Cap all open lines.
6. Remove the six pump-to-engine attaching bolts, and discard the mounting gasket.
7. Remove the coupling from the pump drive hub.
   NOTE: The coupling may remain on the engine drive hub.
8. Remove the 3/4 inch hexagonal nut from the pump shaft, and remove the pump drive hub.
9. Remove the three, adapter-to-pump, attaching bolts, and remove the adapter from the pump. Discard the seal ring.

Installation

1. Position a new seal ring in the adapter housing groove.
2. Position the adapter in its correct position on the pump, and install the three attaching bolts and washers. Torque the bolts to 27 ft. lbs.
3. Position the pump drive hub over the pump shaft and woodruff key.
4. Thread the hexagonal nut onto the pump shaft, and torque to 45 ft. lbs.
5. Install the coupling on the pump drive hub, and position a new gasket on the adapter flange.
6. Position the pump assembly onto the engine, and install the six attaching bolts and washers. Make sure that the slots in the coupling are aligned with the tabs on the engine drive hub. Torque the nuts and bolts to 27 ft. lbs.
7. Connect all fluid lines to the pump.
8. Install the exhaust pipe.
9. Connect the battery ground.
10. Install the engine access cover.

Parking Brakes

Adjustment

NOTE: Parking brake adjustment can be accomplished only when service brakes are in adjustment.

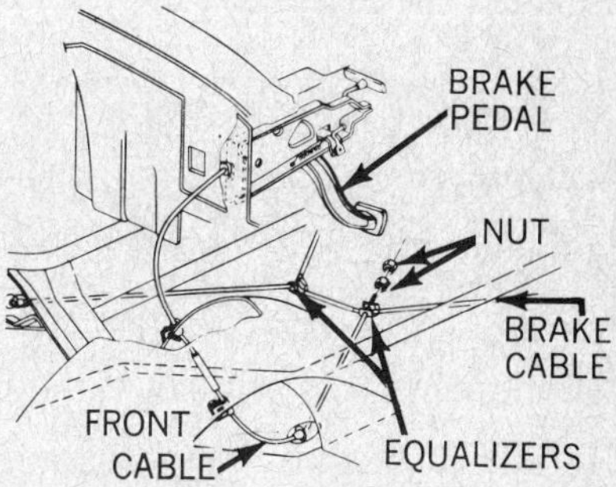

Parking brake system—C,K models (© G.M.C.)

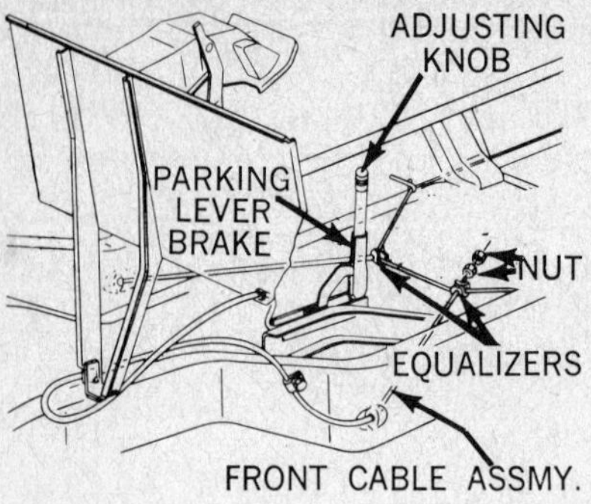

Parking brake system—P 2500-3500 models (© G.M.C.)

Foot Pedal Type

1. Jack up rear wheels.
2. Apply parking brake 1 notch from fully released position.
3. Loosen equalizer check nut and tighten the adjusting nut until moderate drag is felt when rear wheels are rotated.
4. Tighten check nut securely.
5. Fully release parking brake and rotate rear wheels. No drag should be present.

Orscheln Lever Type

1. Turn adjusting knob on parking brake lever counter-clockwise to stop.
2. Apply parking brake.
3. Jack up rear wheels.
4. Loosen lock nut at intermediate cable equalizer and adjust front nut to give light drag at rear wheels.
5. Re-adjust parking brake lever knob to give definite snap-over-center feel.
6. Fully release parking brake and rotate rear wheels. No drag should be present.

Driveshaft Type (Drum On)

1. Jack up at least one rear wheel. Block wheels and release hand brake.
2. Remove cotter pin and clevis pin connecting pull rod to relay lever.

   NOTE: It may be necessary to knock out lanced area in brake drum with punch and hammer to gain entry to adjusting screw through brake drum.
3. Rotate brake drum to bring an access hole into line with adjusting screw at bottom of shoes.
4. Expand shoes by rotating adjusting screw with screw driver. Move outer end of screw driver away from drive shaft. Continue adjustment until shoes are tight against drum and drum cannot be rotated by hand. Back off adjustment ten notches and check drum for free rotation.
5. Place parking brake lever in fully released position. Take up slack in brake linkage by pulling back on cable just enough to overcome spring tension. Adjust clevis of pull rod or front cable to line up with hole in relay levers.
6. Insert clevis pin and cotter pin, tighten clevis locknut.
7. Install new hole cover in drum to prevent dirt contamination.
8. Lower rear wheels. Remove jack and wheel blocks.

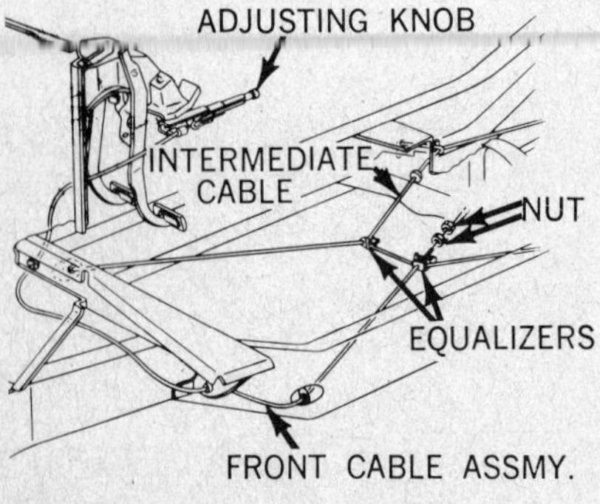

Parking brake system—P 1500 models (© G.M.C.)

Driveshaft Type (Drum Off)

1. With parking brake drum off, check diameter of drum clearance surface.
2. Turn tool to the opposite side and fit over brake shoes by turning star wheel until gauge just slides over linings.
3. Rotate gauge around brake shoe lining surface to insure proper clearance.
4. Install driveshift flange at mainshaft.
5. Lower rear wheels. Remove jack and wheel blocks.

Stopmaster "Fail-Safe" Type

Stopmaster "Fail-Safe" parking brakes are used as standard equipment on some models and as optional equipment on others. When Stopmaster service brakes with "Fail-Safe" feature are used, no other parking brake system is required.

Anchorlok Type

The "Anchorlok" brake chamber is used as optional equipment on some models. This chamber incorporates a spring applied, air pressure released parking/emergency brake.

Tru-Stop (Disc) Type

This type brake is used only on "W" models when equipped with 3-speed or 4-speed auxiliary transmission. The ventilated brake disc is mounted between propeller shaft flange and auxiliary transmission shaft companion flange. Brake shoes are mounted in opposed positions with brake disc between, as shown in illustration. When brake is applied, the shoes are forced against disc. Brake should be adjusted before a full application requires parking brake lever to be pulled to travel limit.

1. Disconnect brake cable clevis (5) from brake lever (6).
2. Tighten adjusting nut (16) until spring (14) exerts enough pressure to bring lever (6) against front lever arm (11).
3. Insert a 1/32″ shim between rear shoe lining and brake disc.
4. Tighten adjusting nut (16) until front shoe lining is firmly against disc, yet allowing removal of shim.
5. Make certain tension spring (13) is in place. Turn adjusting

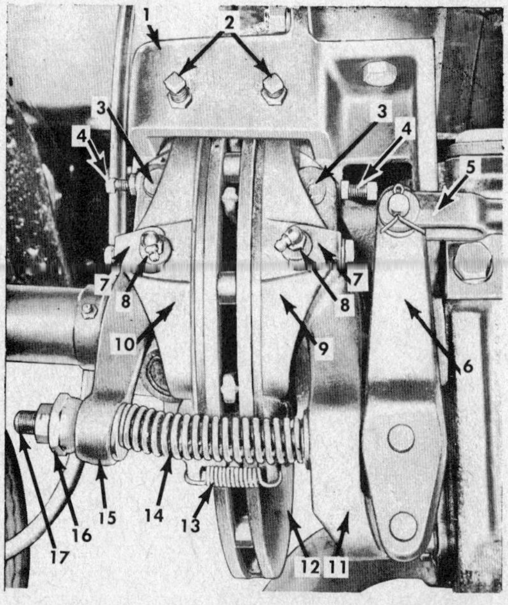

1 Brake support bracket
2 Parallel adjusting screws
3 Front lever arm pin
4 Pin retaining screw
5 Brake cable clevis
6 Brake lever
7 Brake shoe pin retainer
8 Brake shoe pin
9 Front brake shoe
10 Rear brake shoe
11 Front lever arm
12 Brake disc
13 Tension spring
14 Spring
15 Rear lever arm
16 Adjusting nut
17 Tie rod

Tru-stop parking brake (© G.M.C.)

Typical idle speed and mixture screw locations (© G.M.C.)

screws (2) so that both linings are parallel with disc. This provides 16¼″ clearance between front and rear shoe linings and brake disc at all points.

6. Make certain parking brake lever is in fully released position. Adjust clevis (5) on brake cable to permit installation of clevis pin through clevis and brake lever (6) without changing position of lever. Install clevis pin and cotter pin.
7. Make certain lock nuts on brake cable and adjusting screws are firmly tightened.

FUEL SYSTEM

This section contains information on removal, installation and minor external adjustments. For more detailed specifications, see the carburetor general section. Data on the correct engine idle speed and fuel pump pressures will be found in the specification charts at the beginning of this section.

Carburetors

Various carburetors are designed to meet requirements of engine, transmission and vehicle; therefore carburetors may look alike but are not always interchangeable. All carburetors have conventional float, idle, low speed, power or high speed and accelerating circuits with either manual or automatic chokes.

NOTE: Some symptoms indicate carburetor trouble but in reality are ignition related. Before any extensive repairs on carburetor, check first—heat riser, intake manifold and ignition.

Removal

1. Remove air cleaner.
2. Disconnect fuel, vacuum, spark control and governor lines.
3. Disconnect choke and hand throttle controls.
4. Disconnect throttle and automatic transmission linkage at carburetor. Remove pull back spring.
5. Remove mounting nuts and washers.
6. Lift carburetor off manifold and drain. Discard gasket.

Installation

1. Clean carburetor mounting surface.
2. Install new gasket on manifold. Be sure vacuum port and gasket slots are aligned.
3. Place carburetor on manifold, reconnect finger-tight all lines before (evenly) tightening carburetor mounting nuts.
4. Tighten all lines.
5. Reconnect choke and hand throttle controls, replace throttle and automatic transmission linkage reconnect all vacuum and electrical lines. Connect pull back spring. Check choke and throttle operation.
6. Install air cleaner, check element.
7. Start engine and warm to oper-

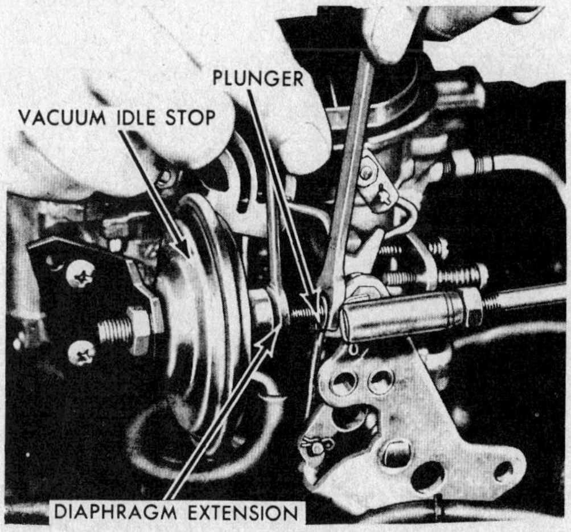

Adjusting vacuum-idle-stop (© G.M.C.)

Adjusting idle stop solenoid (© G.M.C.)

ating temperature. During warm-up time, torque intake manifold.

8. Adjust idle mixture and idle speed screws, be sure choke is fully open.

CAUTION: Do not force idle mixture screw against seat, this will damage needle. On transmission controlled spark engines (TCS), fast idle adjustment must be set with electrical leads disconnected at solenoid and transmission in neutral.

NOTE: If possible (safely), fill carburetor bowl before installing. This will save time and battery drain as well as reducing possible backfiring.

CAUTION: Dirt is greatest troublemaker for carburetors, check all filters. Use starter briefly to clear fuel lines (before reconnecting) of any metal flakes that are always present when fuel lines (metal) are disturbed.

NOTE: For Idle Speed and Mixture adjustments see the underhood tune-up specifications sticker. For all other adjustments, refer to the appropriate carburetor in the General Repair Section.

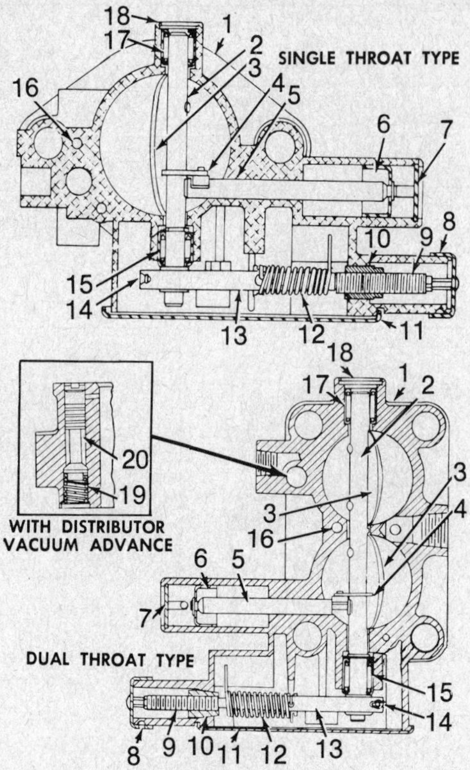

Velocity type governor (© G.M.C.)

1 Governor body
2 Valve shaft
3 Throttle valve
4 Throttle valve arm
5 Stabilizer piston rod
6 Stabilizer piston
7 Stabilizer piston plug
8 Adjusting screw cap
9 Adjusting screw
10 Adjusting screw bushing
11 Governor cover
12 Operating spring
13 Cam ribbon
14 Cam ribbon clip
15 Roller bearing
16 Vacuum by-pass passage
17 Roller bearing
18 Shaft plug
19 Transfer valve spring
20 Transfer valve

Fuel Pump

Two types of pumps are used, mechanical and electric. Mechanical pump is diaphragm type, consisting of a single fuel chamber or a combination fuel and vacuum chambers. In-line engines the pump is actuated by an eccentric lobe on camshaft, V6 eccentric is attached to front of camshaft, V8 engines use a push rod between eccentric lobe on camshaft and pump rocket arm. The single pump is non-serviceable while the combination pump is rebuildable. Electrical pumps are used with step fuel tanks or as stand-by emergency units.

NOTE: In order to minimize the possibility of vapor lock, some fuel pumps are equipped with a special metering outlet for a vapor return system. Any vapor which forms is returned to the fuel tank along with hot fuel through a separate line.

Mechanical Fuel Pump

Removal

1. Disconnect all inlet and outlet pipes from fuel pump.
2. Remove fuel pump mounting bolts.
3. Remove fuel pump and gasket.
   NOTE: On V8 engines, remove fuel pump adapter and gasket if pushrod is to be removed.
4. Transfer fittings if new pump is to be installed.

Installation

1. On V8 engines, install fuel pump pushrod and adapter.
2. Install fuel pump, using new

Governor mounting (© G.M.C.)

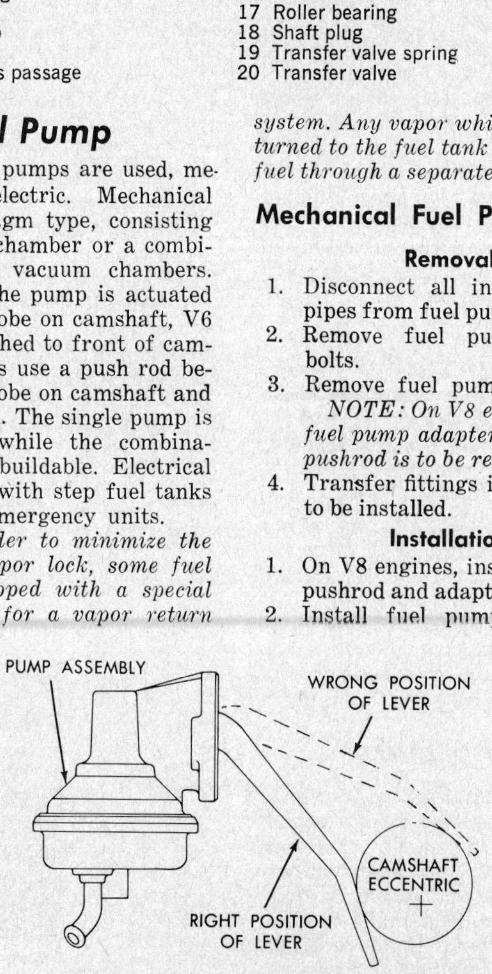

Mechanical fuel pump—V6 engine (© G.M.C.)

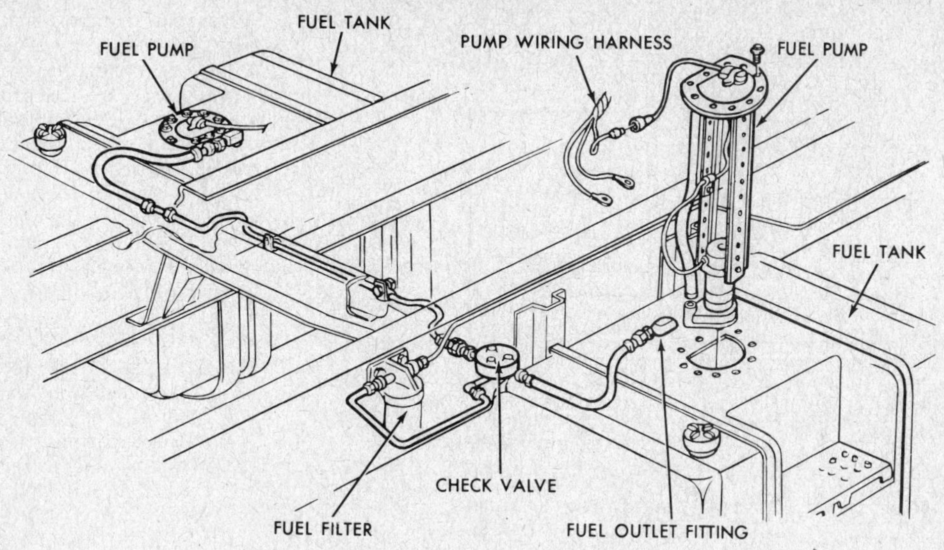

Installing electric fuel pump (© G.M.C.)

gasket and sealer on mounting bolt threads.
3. Connect fuel lines to pump.
4. Start engine and check for leaks.

NOTE: On V8 engines use mechanical fingers or heavy grease to hold push rod up while installing pump.

Electric Fuel Pump

Removal

1. Disconnect battery ground cable.
2. Disconnect pump wiring harness from connector.
3. Disconnect fuel outlet fitting from hose.
4. Remove cap screws and washers.
5. Rotate pump 90° counterclockwise and lift out.

Installation

1. Insert pump outlet line into tank and connect to fitting.
2. Carefully install fuel pump and cap screws with washers. Tighten to specifications.
3. Connect pump harness to connector.
4. Connect battery ground cable.

Governor

NOTE: On earlier models (prior to the 1977 model year), governor adjustments are pre-set at the factory. However, minor adjustments, to satisfy local conditions, may be accomplished by turning the adjusting cap counterclockwise for higher speed,

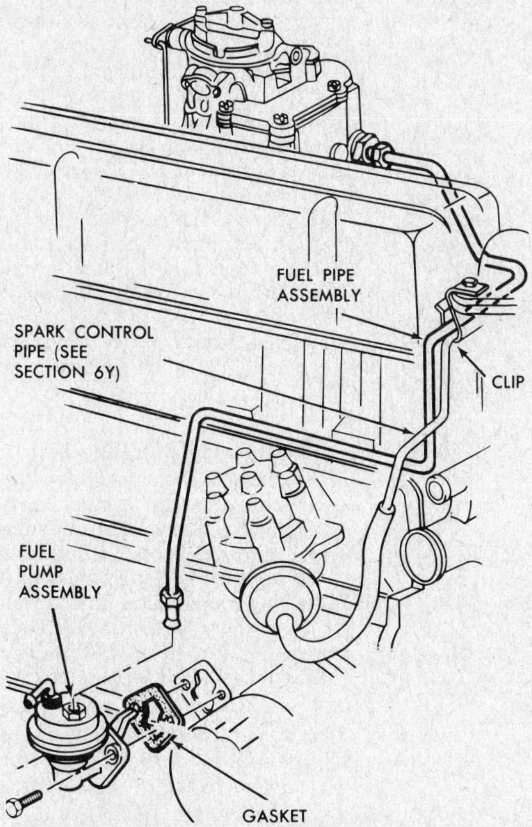

Fuel pump—inline 6 cylinder engine (© G.M.C.)

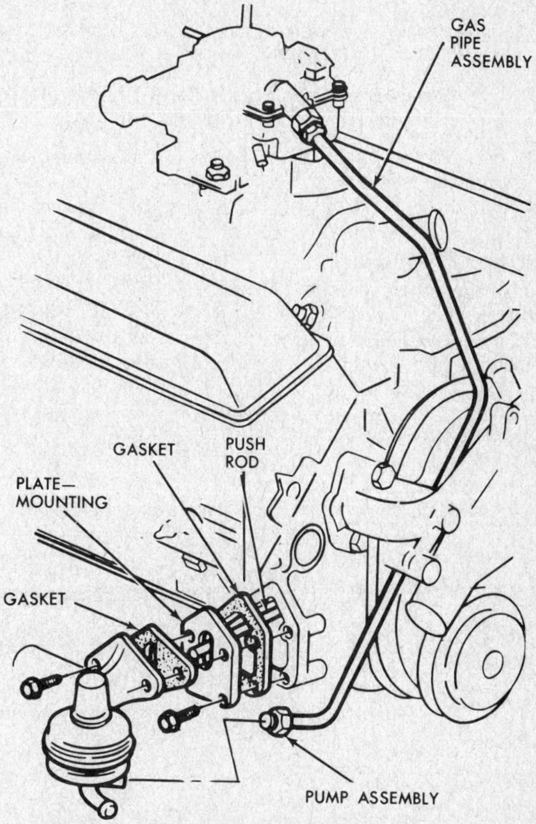

Fuel pump installation—V6 engine (© G.M.C.)

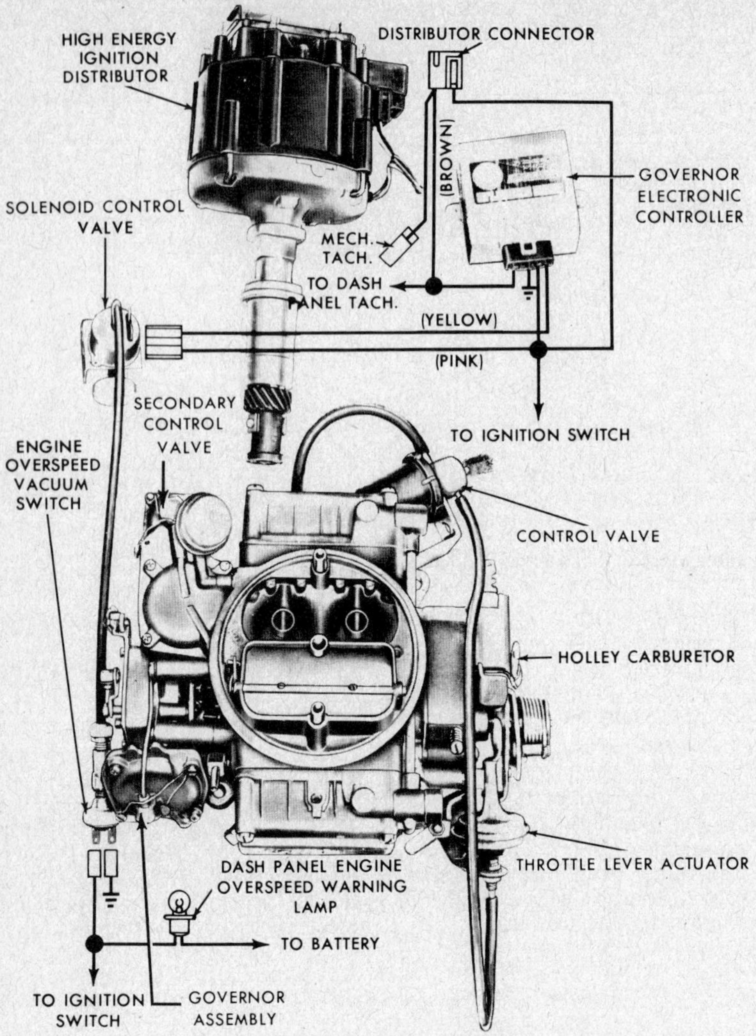

Governor electronic controller—1977 (typical) (© G.M.C.)

and clockwise for lower speed. One turn on the adjusting cap will vary speed 300-400 rpm or 4-5 mph.

Electronic Governor

Beginning with the 1977 model year, the governor system is integrated with the HEI system in order to electronically regulate governor operation. The governor system is comprised of three basic components: governor, electronic controller, and solenoid control valve. The governor regulates current to the solenoid control valve, and the solenoid control valve is responsible for creating governor vacuum. The electronic controller is not adjustable.

NOTE: Governor RPM is preset at the factory, and is not adjustable. Any deviation from normal operation will require testing of the system.

In order to achieve electric current regulation at the solenoid control valve, the controller monitors the HEI tachometer signal and compares it to an internal reference; the internal reference is proportional to the desired governor setting. If the tachometer signal exceeds the controller reference, then current is allowed to flow to the solenoid control valve, thereby closing the valve. When this happens, governor vacuum reduces the engine rpm to the preset governor speed.

Solenoid Control Valve Test

1. Disconnect the battery ground.
2. Disconnect the wiring harness from the solenoid control valve at the governor.
3. Measure the resistance across the solenoid terminals with an ohmeter.

   NOTE: For all 1977 vehicles. the resistance should be 25-35 ohms. Beginning with the 1978 model year, the required resistance, measured in ohms, for the two barrel carburetor will be different from the required resistance for the four barrel carburetor. Resistance for the two barrel carburetor should be 25-35 ohms, and resistance for the four barrel carburetor should be 47-53 ohms.
4. Replace the solenoid control valve if the measured resistance is not within these limits.

   NOTE: If the measured resistance is below these limits, the controller may be damaged. Perform the electronic controller test.
5. To test for an internal short circuit, connect one lead of the ohmmeter to either terminal or the valve and the other to the metal case of the valve. The resistance should be 800 ohms or higher. If the resistance is lower than 800 ohms, then a short circuit condition probably exists within the valve. If the measured resistance falls within the required limits, then proceed to check for proper governor operation.

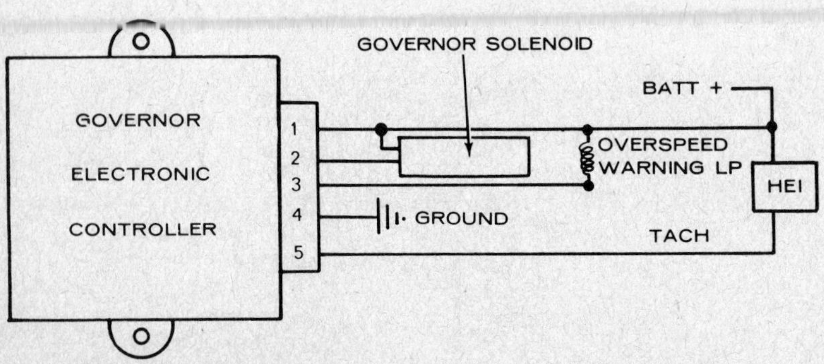

Governor electronic controller—wiring schematic—1978 (typical) (© Chevrolet Div., G.M. Corp.)

Electronic Controller Test

1. Disconnect the battery ground.
2. Disconnect the wiring harness from the electronic controller.
3. Attach one lead of an ohmmeter to the ground terminal in the wiring harness connector and the other lead to the chassis ground. The measured resistance should be less than 3 ohms.

   NOTE: If there is an open circuit between the connector and the chassis ground, look for a problem in the ground wire connectors and terminals.
4. Connect the battery ground.
5. Turn the ignition switch to the

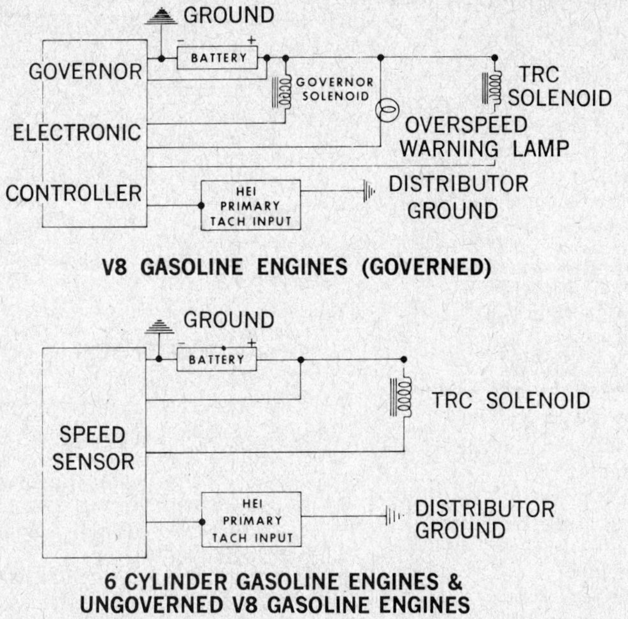

Governor electronic controller—wiring schematic—1979 (typical) (© Chevrolet Div., G.M. Corp.)

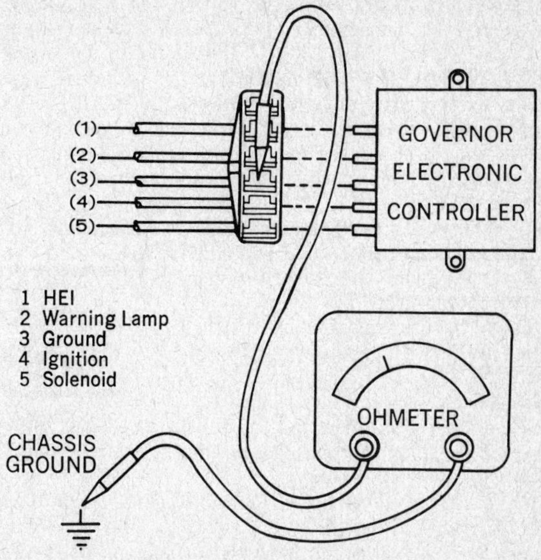

Controller ground circuit resistance test and terminal connector identification–1977 (© Chevrolet Div., G.M. Corp)

ON position, but DO NOT start the engine.

6. Using a voltmeter, measure the voltage between the ground terminal in the harness connector and the terminals connecting the HEI tachometer, the solenoid control valve, and ignition (battery +). The reading at all four terminals should be equivalent to battery voltage. If the reading at any of these terminals is less than battery voltage, then check the appropriate circuit for damage, corrosion, or poor insulation. Repair damaged or defective circuitry.

   NOTE: Allow for a very slight voltage drop between the battery voltage and the reading at the voltmeter, as this may only be the result of minor resistance in the chassis ground circuit.

7. If, after checking the wiring harness, solenoid control valve, tubing, electrical fuse and governor, the governor still does not

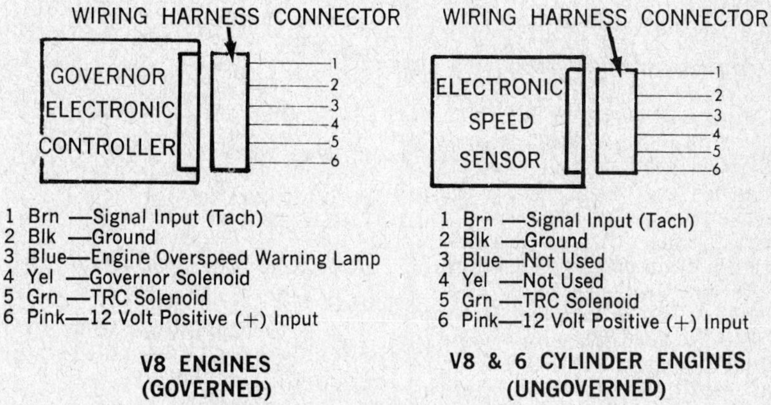

Terminal connector wiring identification—1979 and later (© Chevrolet Div., G.M. Corp.)

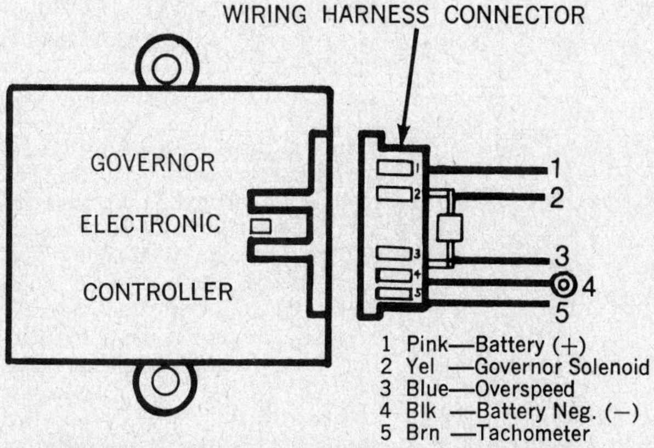

Governor electronic controller terminal connector identification—1978 (© Chevrolet Div., G.M. Corp.)

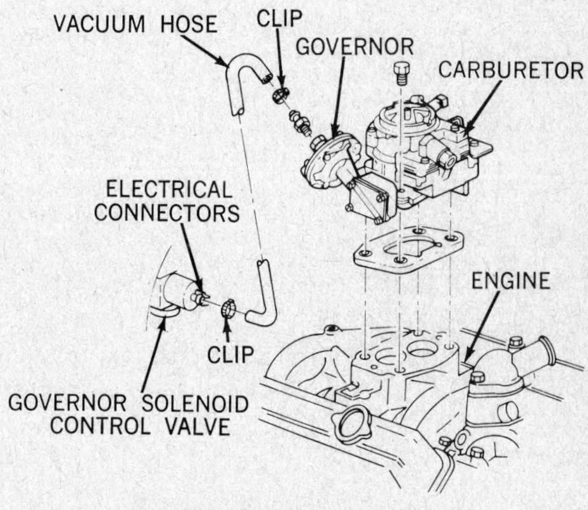

Governor solenoid control valve (© Chevrolet Div., G.M. Corp.)

govern properly, then replace the electronic controller.

Overspeed Warning System

This system was designed to alert the driver of excessive engine speeds such as would be caused by down-hill operation when the wheels may begin to drive the engine.

A red warning lamp, located in the instrument will light when activated by a signal from the governor electronic controller.

When the ignition key is returned from the START position, the ignition switch ground circuit is broken and the light will go out. The warning lamp will remain unlighted until the engine rpm reaches the predetermined governed speed.

NOTE: Some ungoverned V8 and 6 cylinder engines are equipped with a similar speed sensing device which is designed to warn the operator of excessive engine speeds.

Fuel Tank

NOTE: The following procedure is intended only as a guide. It will vary according to truck model and tank type.

Removal and Installation

1. On trucks with dual tanks check shut-off valve position.
2. Be sure ignition switch is off or battery ground is disconnected.
3. Remove seat back rest if cab mounted.
4. Drain tank. If tank does not have a drain plug, disconnect gas line and use opening to drain tank. If not accessible, siphon fuel. Do not siphon by mouth, use equipment for that purpose or make a siphon hose as shown below and use air pressure if available.
5. Remove filler neck, cap and vent hose.
6. Disconnect tank gage wire and any ground lead.
7. Remove tank support straps or mounting bolts. Remove tank.
8. Clean all lines, check filters. (Blow clean only after disconnecting other end of line).
9. To install, reverse removal procedures.

CAUTION: Do not use drop cord in area. A bulb breakage could have disastrous effects. Use only safety cans for fuel storage. Do not overtighten lines, as this could distort or twist and lead to leaks.

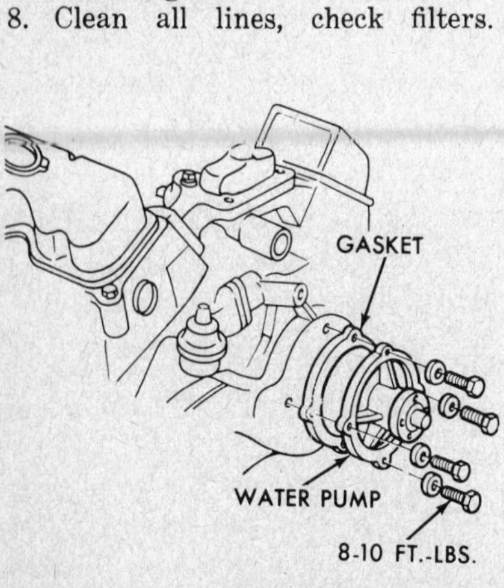

Water pump—V6 engine (© G.M.C.)

COOLING SYSTEM

Water Pump

Removal

1. Drain cooling system.
2. Remove fan spacers (when used) and pulley(s) from water pump drive hub.
3. Remove all hoses connected to water pump.
4. Remove mounting bolts and washers.
5. Remove pump and gasket.

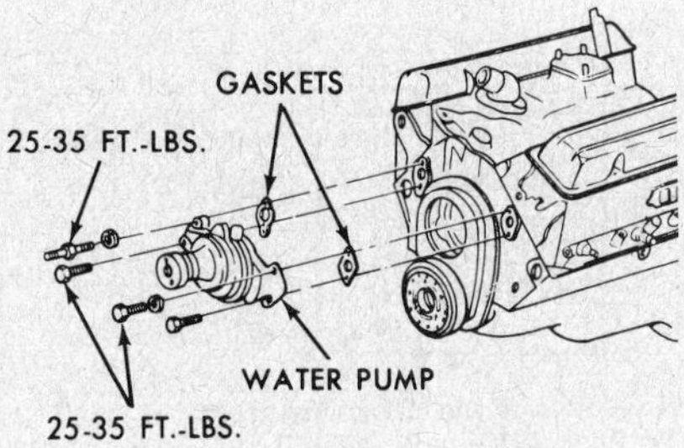

Water pump—V8 engine (© G.M.C.)

Installation

Reverse removal procedure, installing new water pump gasket.

Overhaul

Overhaul procedures vary considerably. The following basic guide may be used.

1. Support fan hub in an arbor press and press shaft out of hub.
2. Drive seal out of pump body.
3. Clean and inspect water pump components. Check all surfaces for wear and bearings for excessive play.

   NOTE: Do not clean bearing and shaft assembly in solvent as it will dissolve lubicant.
4. Replace water pump seal and necessary parts.
5. Reassemble and install water pump.

Heater Core Removal and Installation

NOTE: The following procedures are a general guide for the removal and installation of the heater core from the GMC truck line and will vary slightly depending on the truck series, model, and year.

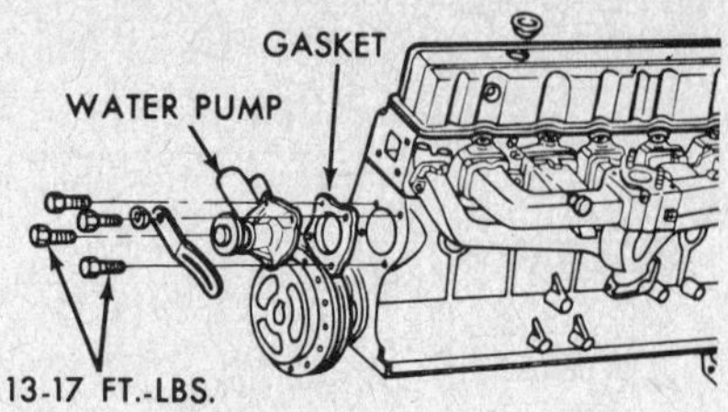

Water pump—inline 6 cylinder engine (© G.M.C.)

Series 1500 to 6500 w/o Air Conditioning

1. Disconnect the battery ground cable and drain the cooling system.
2. Disconnect the heater hoses at the core tubes and plug the outlets to prevent coolant leakage when removing the core.
3. Remove the nuts from the air distribution duct bolts extending into the engine compartment.
4. Remove the glove box and door assembly.
5. Disconnect the temperature door cable and the air-defrost cable.
6. Remove the defroster to heater distribution air duct screw and the floor outlet duct.
7. Remove the screws holding the air distribution housing to the dash. Pull the unit rearward and disconnect the wiring harness attached to the unit.

   NOTE: On van models, tilt the case rearward at the top while lifting the unit so that the bottom mounted core tubes will clear the dash opening.
8. To reinstall the unit, reverse the disassembly procedure, making sure that the case sealer is in place before installing the heater core.

Series 1500 to 6500 w/Air Conditioning

1. Disconnect the negative battery cable and drain the cooling system.
2. Remove the heater hoses from the core tubes and plug the tubes to avoid coolant spillage during the removal of the core.
3. Remove the glove box and door assembly.
4. Remove the center lower and center upper ducts by the removal of their retaining screws.
5. Disconnect the bowden cable at the temperature blend door.
6. Remove the three selector duct stud nuts projecting through the firewall and the housing retaining screw located inside the cab.
7. Pull the selector duct assembly rearward until the tubes of the core clear the dash panel opening and remove the vacuum and electrical connections.

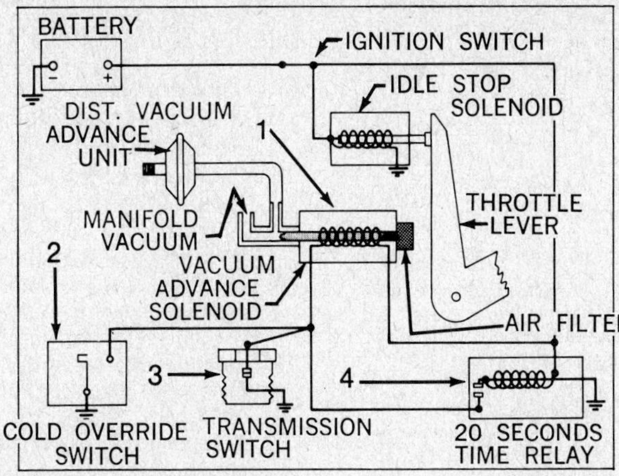

Transmission controlled spark system—high gear operation—typical
(© Chevrolet Div., G.M. Corp.)

1 Vacuum circuit open to advance unit when solenoid electrical circuit is closed. Vacuum circuit closed to advance unit when solenoid electrical circuit is open. Vacuum circuit closed to advance unit when ignition switch is OFF.
2 Circuit open at coolant temperatures above 93 degees F. Circuit closed at coolant temperatures below 93 degrees F.
3 Circuit closed in high gear operation. Circuit open in low gear ranges, reverse, and neutral.
4 Circuit closed when ignition switch is OFF. Circuit open when ignition switch is ON, but remains closed for first 20 seconds.

8. Remove the selector duct from the vehicle and by removing the core mounting strap screws, the heater core can be removed.
9. To reinstall the unit, reverse the disassembly procedure, making sure that the case sealer is in place before installing the heater core.

ENGINE

Emission Control Systems

Emission control systems are designed to control the emissions of Hydrocarbons (HC), Carbon Monoxide (CO), and Oxides of Nitrogen (NOx), at the levels specified by the Federal and State Governments. Emission control systems vary in their usage, in relationship to the engine, transmission and series application. The units are covered in the Emission Control Section of the General Repair Section.

Evaporative Emission System

This system was designed to reduce fuel vapor emissions that are normally vented into the atmosphere from the gas tank and the carburetor fuel bowl, through the use of a carbon canister and liquid-vapor separator.

Transmission Controlled Spark System (TCS)

This system controls emissions by eliminating distributor vacuum advance in neutral, reverse, and low forward gears. By limiting vacuum advance in these gear ranges, a more efficient combustion level is reached, therefore a lower level of pollution.

Vacuum advance is controlled *directly* by a vacuum advance solenoid which is a two position vacuum switch with a provision for venting the advance unit to atmospheric pressure when the vacuum advance solenoid is de-energized. By allowing atmospheric pressure at the vacuum advance unit, the vacuum advance is prevented from becoming locked in the advanced position.

Vacuum advance is controlled *indirectly* by a series of switches which are operated thermostatically, mechanically, or electrically. These are: cold override switch (coolant temperature switch), transmission switch, and 20 second time replay switch.

At temperatures below 93 degrees F., the cold override switch closes, thereby completing the circuit to ground. When this happens, the vacuum advance solenoid, which is in series with the cold override switch, is activated and the plunger shifts to the vacuum ON position, permitting vacuum advance. At temperatures above 93 degrees F., the cold override switch opens, the circuit through the vacuum advance solenoid is interrupted, the plunger shifts to the OFF position, and manifold vacuum to the advance unit is denied.

When the ignition switch is first turned ON, a circuit, through the vacuum advance solenoid and to ground, is completed through the time relay switch, a bi-metallic ON/OFF switch. This circuit, which is an extension of the cold override circuit, is independent from the thermostatically operated override, and allows current to activate the vacuum advance solenoid even when the coolant temperature is above 93 degrees F. The circuit is closed during engine start-up for a period of approximately 20 seconds. The purpose of this additional circuit is to facilitate start-up at temperatures above 93 degrees F., as the thermostatic override switch is then eliminated from the system. If the engine does not start during the 20 seconds time limit, the circuit through the vacuum advance solenoid and to ground will be interrupted and the engine may not start. This is because the time relay bi-metallic switch has been allowed to overheat, thereby opening the circuit to ground. If this happens, a waiting period will be necessary to allow time for the relay to cool before the engine can be started.

NOTE: The time relay circuit will stay OPEN as long as the ignition switch remains in the ON position.

A fourth device, the transmission switch, which is situated on the outside of the transmission, permits current to flow through the vacuum advance solenoid and to ground only when the transmission is operating in high gear. When the transmission is operated in high gear, the switch closes, completing the circuit through the vacuum advance solenoid and to ground. When this happens, the plunger shifts to the vacuum ON position, permitting distributor vacuum advance. When the transmission is shifted to neutral, or is operating in any of the low gear ranges or reverse, the mechanically operated transmission switch is moved to the open position, preventing current from activating the vacuum advance solenoid.

NOTE: In order to compensate for the retarded spark condition, carburetor throttle opening is wider at idle. However, wide throttle blade settings can contribute to engine dieseling. To overcome the attendant dieseling condition, idle stop solenoids have been installed on vehicles equipped with the TCS system. The electrically activated idle stop solenoid supports the throttle at idle and allows the throttle to relax beyond the normal idle position when the ignition switch is turned OFF.

Throttle Return Control System (TRC)

Ordnarily, engine deceleration is controlled by the operator of the vehicle, as he regulates the throttle blade position through a system of accelerator linkage components. This system, though thoroughly operational, is not entirely efficient. In con-

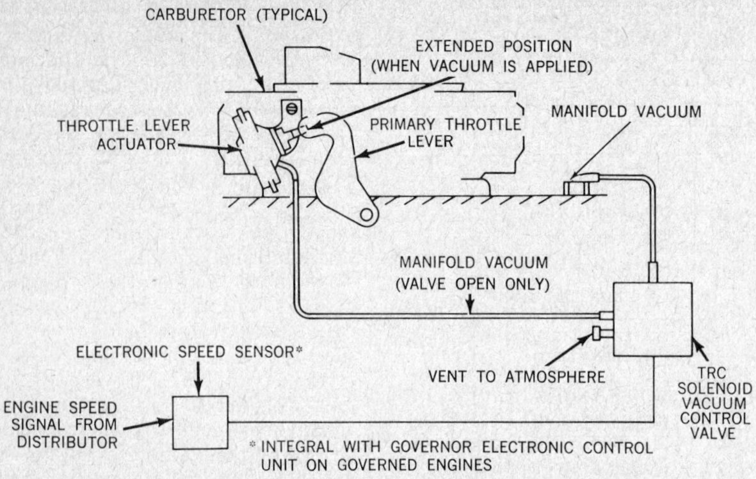

Throttle return control system (© Chevrolet Div., G.M. Corp.)

ventional carburetion systems, there is usually some mechanical force which opposes accelerator application, i.e., there is some device which returns the throttle blade to the idle position whenever the accelerator is released. This is, in a great many cases, accomplished with the aid of a return spring.

Even though the accelerator return spring is an effective decelerator, it, nevertheless, contributes to pollution because of its rapid rate of deceleration. If the throttle blade is rapidly returned to idle, a very low pressure develops in the intake manifold area. When this happens, an unnecessarily high proportion of liquid fuel is drawn into the combustion area, and then exhausted before complete burning can occur. Also, when wheel rotation, transmitted through the differential and transmission, drives the engine (coasting), very high manifold vacuum levels are attained, and, again, an unnecessarily high volume of liquid fuel is introduced into the combustion area.

In order to overcome the problem of rapid deceleration and non-volatile fuel consumption during coasting, the TRC system has been installed on some V-8 and 6 cylinder engines. The system consists of three major components; they are the throttle lever actuator, solenoid vacuum control valve, and the electronic speed sensor.

The throttle lever actuator, located at the carburetor, is vacuum operated, and controls the position of the primary throttle plates a preset amount in excess of curb idle when engine vacuum is applied to it.

The electronic speed sensor monitors engine speed at the distributor, and will supply a continuous electrical signal to the solenoid vacuum control valve whenever engine speed is in excess of the preset value.

The solenoid vacuum control valve is an ON/OFF vacuum valve which is held open above a preset engine speed by a signal from the electronic speed sensor. When this happens, vacuum at the throttle lever actuator causes the actuator to open the throttle blade, only slightly, admitting more air to ensure more complete burning of the air/fuel mixture.

NOTE: TRC activation value is 1825 rpm ± 65 rpm. Deactivation value is at least 10 rpm below activation, or not less than 1700 rpm.

TRC System Test

Throttle Lever Actuator Operates Outside Normal RPM Range:

1. Connect a tachometer to the distributor "TACH" terminal.
2. Start the engine, and shift the transmission into neutral.
3. Advance the throttle until the engine speed is 1890 rpm. The throttle lever actuator should be extended at this speed.
4. Decrease the engine speed to 1700 rpm. The throttle lever actuator should be retracted at this speed.
5. If the throttle lever actuator operates outside of the 1890-1700 rpm range, then the electronic speed sensor is out of calibration and should be replaced.

Throttle Lever Does Not Operate At Any Speed:

1. Start the engine, and shift the transmission into neutral.
2. Connect the negative lead of a voltmeter to the engine ground, and insert the positive lead into the connector cavities of either the solenoid control valve or the electronic speed sensor. In either case the voltage should measure 12-14 volts.
3. If the voltage measured at the speed sensor is approximately equivalent to battery voltage (12-14 volts), but the voltage measured at the solenoid control valve is 0, then a problem exists somewhere in the engine wiring harness. Repair as necessary.
4. If the voltage measured at either device is 0 (no voltage), then check the engine harness connections at the distributor and/or the bulkhead connector. Repair as necessary.

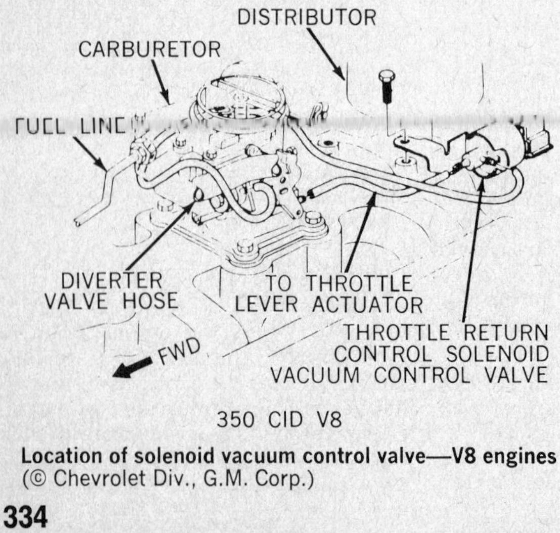

Location of solenoid vacuum control valve—V8 engines (© Chevrolet Div., G.M. Corp.)

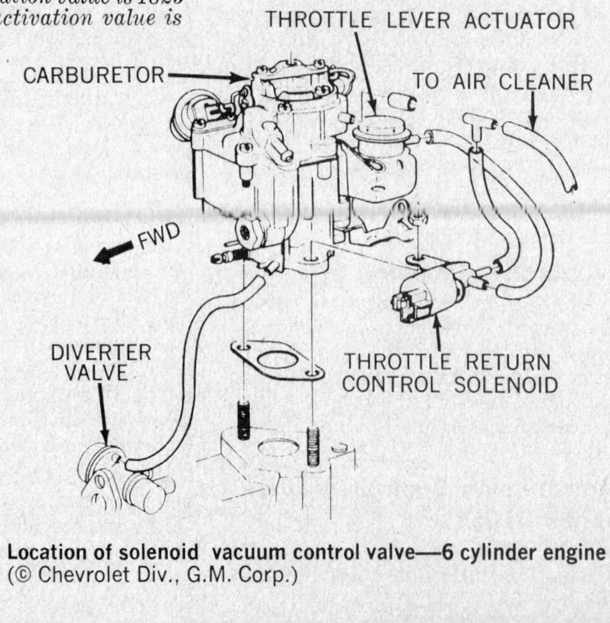

Location of solenoid vacuum control valve—6 cylinder engine (© Chevrolet Div., G.M. Corp.)

5. If battery voltage is present at both the solenoid control valve and the speed sensor, then connect one end of a jumper wire to the solenoid control valve-to-speed sensor connecting wire terminal at the solenoid vacuum control valve and the other end of the jumper wire to ground. With the engine running, the throttle lever actuator should extend.
6. If the throttle lever actuator does not extend, then disconnect the actuator vacuum hose at the solenoid vacuum control valve side port. Check for any blockage or obstruction in the port. Clean as necessary.
7. If there is no vacuum obstruction in the vacuum line (vacuum passage is clear), then replace the solenoid vacuum control valve.
8. If the actuator extends after performing step no. 5, then connect one end of a jumper wire to the solenoid control valve-to-speed sensor connecting wire terminal at the speed sensor and the other end of the jumper wire to ground. If the throttle lever actuator does not extend, then repair the wire which connects the speed sensor to the solenoid vacuum control valve. If the actuator does extend, then connect one lead of the voltmeter to the speed sensor ground wire at the speed sensor and the other lead to ground. The voltmeter should indicate 0 volts (no voltage drop). If any voltage is indicated on the voltmeter, then there is resistance in the speed sensor-to-ground circuit, or, possibly, an open circuit. Repair as necessary.

Throttle Lever Actuator Extended At All Speeds

1. Disconnect the wire connector from the solenoid vacuum control valve.
2. If the actuator remains in the extended position, then check the solenoid side vacuum port for blockage. Clean as necessary.
3. Reattach the wire connector and the vacuum hose to the solenoid control valve, and recheck system operation.
4. If the actuator remains in the extended position, again, disconnect the wire connector from the solenoid vacuum control valve. If the actuator does not retract, then replace the solenoid vacuum control valve.
5. If the actuator retracts with the solenoid control valve wire connector disconnected, then reattach the connector, and disconnect the speed sensor wire connector. If the actuator retracts from the extended position, then replace the speed sensor. If the actuator does not retract, then a short circuit condition (to ground) probably exists in the solenoid-to-speed sensor wire located within the wiring harness. Repair as necessary.

Testing Throttle Lever Actuator

NOTE: The throttle lever actuator can be vacuum leak tested in the conventional manner by using an ordinary vacuum hand pump/gauge tool.

1. Disconnect the valve-to-actuator vacuum hose at the solenoid vacuum control valve.
2. Connect the disconnected end of the vacuum hose to a vacuum hand pump/gauge tool or any external vacuum source equipped with a vacuum gauge.
3. Manually, check the throttle linkage, lever, and shaft for binding or sticking. Repair as necessary.
4. Start the engine with the transmission in neutral, and operate until normal operating temperature is reached. Note the idle rpm.
5. Apply vacuum (20 inches Hg.) to the actuator.
6. Manually, open the throttle slightly, and allow the throttle to close aganst the extended actuator plunger. Again note the engine rpm.
7. Open the actuator vacuum hose to atmospheric pressure (vacuum cancelled), and reapply vacuum (20 inches Hg.). DO NOT assist the actuator. Note the increase in engine rpm.
8. If the rpm noted in step no. 7 is not within 150 rpm of that noted in step no. 6, then the actuator plunger may be binding due to foreign material, corrosion, etc. Also, the actuator diaphragm tension may have weakened. Correct any binding condition. Replace the actuator if proved to be weak.
9. Again, open the actuator vacuum hose to atmospheric pressure (vacuum cancelled). The engine speed should return to within 50 rpm of the idle speed noted in step no. 4. If not, the plunger may be binding. If the binding condition cannot be repaired, then replace the actuator.
10. If the engine rpm noted in step no. 6 is not within the specified TRC speed range, then adjust the throttle lever actuator (see chart).

TRC Idle Speed Adjustment

NOTE: Check the throttle linkage, lever, and shaft to be certain that they are free from binding or sticking.

1. Disconnect the valve-to-actuator vacuum hose at the solenoid vacuum control valve.
2. Connect the disconnected end of the vacuum hose to a vacuum hand pump/gauge tool or any external vacuum source equipped with a vacuum gauge.
3. Apply vacuum (20 inches Hg.) to the actuator.
4. Manually, open the throttle slightly, and allow the throttle to close against the extended actuator plunger. Note the engine rpm.
5. Adjust by turning the actuator plunger screw on 350 CID and 292 CID engines, or by loosening the jam not on the mounting bracket for the 366, 427, and 454 CID engines and turning the actuator body in the appropriate direction. Repeat steps nos. 3 and 4 until the specified speed range is obtained.

TRC SPEED

Engine	Throttle setting-RPM
292 CID 6 Cyl.	1475-1525
350 CID V-8	1375-1425
366, 427, 454 CID V8	1375-1425

Exhaust Gas Recirculation System

This system helps reduce oxides of nitrogen emitted by the engine exhaust. This is accomplished by releasing small amounts of exhaust gas into the cylinders by means of the E.G.R. valve. This lowers the peak combustion temperatures, reducing the amounts of oxides produced.

Air Injection Reactor

The A.I.R. system injects compressed air into the exhaust system, close enough to the exhaust valves to continue the burning of the normally unburned segment of the exhaust gases. To do this it employs an air injection pump and a system of hoses, valves, tubes, etc., necessary to carry the compressed air from the pump to the exhaust manifolds. Carburetors and distributors for A.I.R. engines have specific modifications to adapt them to the air injection system; these components should not be interchanged with those intended for use on engines that do not have the system.

A diverter valve is used to prevent backfiring. The valve senses sudden increases in manifold vacuum and ceases the injection of air during fuel-rich periods. During coasting, this valve diverts the entire air flow through the muffler and during high engines speeds, expels it through a relief valve. Check valves in the system prevent exhaust gases from entering the pump.

Early Fuel Evaporation System

1975 models are equipped with this system to reduce engine warm-up time, improve driveability, and reduce emissions. On start-up, a vacuum motor acts to close a heat valve in the exhaust manifold which causes exhaust gases to enter the intake manifold heat riser passages. Incoming fuel mixture is then heated and more complete fuel evaporation is provided during warm-up.

Catalytic Converters

The converters are used to oxidize hydrocarbons (HC) and carbon monoxide (CO). The catalysts are made of noble metals (platinum and palladium) which are bonded to either a monolithic (one-piece) element or to individual pellets. The catalyst causes the HC and CO to break down without taking part in the reaction; hence, a catalyst life of 50,000 miles is expected.

Some engines equipped with the converters require an air injection pump to supply air for the reaction; others will not.

Engine Assembly

Inline Engines In Conventional Models

Removal

1. Drain radiator.
2. Disconnect battery.
3. Remove hood and attaching parts.
4. Remove grille and radiator support braces.
5. Remove radiator and heater hoses.
6. Remove radiator and grille assembly.
7. Disconnect fuel line at fuel pump.
8. Remove air cleaner and cover carburetor to protect it from dirt.
9. Disconnect choke control and accelerator linkage.
10. Disconnect exhaust pipe from manifold.
11. Disconnect wiring harness and battery cable.
12. Remove hand brake lever and gearshift lever from transmission.
13. Disconnect driveshaft from transmission flange.
14. Attach lifting equipment, remove mounting bolts and rear crossmember.
15. Lift out engine and transmission assembly.

Installation

1. Attach lifting equipment and lower assembly into chassis. Install support crossmember and engine mountings.
2. Connect driveshaft.
3. Install handbrake and gearshift levers.
4. Connect exhaust pipe to manifold.
5. Connect wiring harness and carburetor control linkage.
6. Install hood and attaching parts.
7. Install air cleaner, connect fuel line.
8. Fill cooling system.
9. Fill crankcase with oil to the proper level.
10. Install battery.
11. Start engine and check for leaks.

Inline Engines in Tilt Cab Models

Removal

1. Drain cooling system.
2. Disconnect battery cables.
3. Tilt cab forward; remove radiator and shroud.
4. Disconnect shift linkage at control island.
5. Disconnect throttle and choke controls at carburetor.
6. Disconnect parking brake cable and housing.
7. Remove control island mounting bolts; swing control island forward.
8. Disconnect hoses and remove surge tank.
9. Remove right and left island supports.
10. Disconnect cab safety lock, remove cab rear support.
11. Disconnect electrical wiring from engine units.
12. Disconnect all fuel, heater, oil lines from engine.
13. Disconnect exhaust pipe from manifold.
14. Remove engine fan and pulley.
15. Remove rocker arm cover and attach lifting brackets at cylinder head bolts.
16. Attach hoist and take up slack.
17. Remove engine mounting bolts and bolts attaching transmission to engine. Support transmission.
18. Move engine forward until it is disengaged from transmission.
19. Lift engine from the chassis.

Installation

Install engine by reversing the removal procedure. Be certain to maintain cleanliness and to avoid damaging the engine parts. After engine is installed, check operation of all control linkages, fill cooling system and check for leaks. Fill crankcase with oil to the proper level.

V6 Engines in Conventional Models

Removal

1. Drain radiator.
2. Disconnect battery.
3. Remove hood and attaching parts.
4. Remove grille and radiator braces.
5. Remove radiator and heater hoses.
6. Disconnect oil cooler lines (when used).
7. Remove grille, radiator, and front bumper.
8. Disconnect fuel line.
9. Disconnect air lines (when used).
10. Disconnect engine ground strap.
11. Disconnect exhaust pipes from manifolds.
12. Disconnect accelerator and choke controls from the carburetor.
13. Disconnect tachometer drive and oil gauge pressure line (when used).
14. Attach lifting equipment and take up slack.
15. Remove clutch housing to flywheel housing bolts.
16. Move engine forward to disengage transmission.
17. Lift engine from the chassis.

Installation

Install engine by reversing the removal procedure. Be certain to maintain cleanliness and to avoid damaging the engine parts. After engine is installed, check operation of all control linkages, fill cooling system and check for leaks. Fill crankcase with oil to the proper level.

V6 Engines in Tilt Cab Models

Removal

1. Drain radiator.
2. Disconnect battery.
3. Disconnect oil cooler lines (when used).
4. Disconnect electrical wiring and cables from the engine units.
5. Disconnect engine ground strap.
6. Disconnect accelerator and choke controls at the carburetor.
7. Disconnect transmission control rods, surge tank hoses, air cleaners and hoses.
8. Remove control island and rear cab support.
9. Disconnect exhaust pipes from manifolds.
10. Disconnect clutch control cylinder, parking brake control and speedometer drive from the rear of the transmission.
11. Disconnect cooling system and heater hoses.
12. Disconnect air lines from compressor (when used).
13. Disconnect driveshaft from transmission.
14. Attach lifting equipment and take up slack.
15. Remove bolts from front and rear mountings.
16. Lift assembly from the chassis.

Installation

Install engine by reversing the removal procedure. Be certain to maintain cleanliness and to avoid damaging the engine parts. After engine is installed, check operation of all control linkages, fill cooling system and check for leaks. Fill crankcase with oil to the proper lever.

V8 Engines in Conventional Models

Removal

1. Disconnect battery cables and remove battery.
2. Drain cooling system.
3. Disconnect air intake hose (when used).
4. Disconnect all wiring to engine units as necessary.
5. Disconnect radiator and heater hoses.
6. Disconnect fuel line.
7. Remove front end sheet metal, including hood.
8. Remove engine fan and drive belts.
9. Remove power steering pump.
10. Remove air compressor and disconnect air lines (when used).
11. Remove air cleaner and disconnect accelerator and choke cables at the carburetor.
12. Disconnect exhaust pipes from manifolds.
13. Disconnect clutch and transmission controls as necessary.
14. Remove valve covers and attach lifting brackets at cylinder head bolts.
15. Attach lifting equipment and take up slack.
16. Remove bolts from front and rear mountings.
17. Remove bolts attaching transmission to engine.
18. Move engine forward to disengage transmission.
19. Lift engine from the chassis.

NOTE: Engines coupled to an automatic transmission must be removed as a unit. Disconnect all transmission controls accordingly. Transmission may be removed from engine assembly after power plant removal.

Installation

Install the engine by reversing the removal procedure. Be certain to maintain cleanliness and to avoid damaging the engine parts. After engine is installed, check operation of all control linkages, fill cooling system and check for leaks. Fill crankcase with oil to the proper level.

NOTE: Engines coupled to an automatic transmission must be installed as a unit.

V8 Engines in Tilt Cab Models

Removal

1. Remove radiator, support and shroud.
2. Disconnect shift linkage at control island, accelerator and choke cables at carburetor.
3. Disconnect parking brake control.
4. Disconnect surge tank hoses.
5. Remove surge tank and control island rear support.
6. Remove cab safety lock control and cab rear support.
7. Disconnect all wiring to engine units.
8. Disconnect fuel line.
9. Disconnect heater hoses and vacuum/air lines (when used).
10. Disconnect engine ground straps.
11. Disconnect exhaust pipes from manifolds.
12. Disconnect clutch control.
13. Remove engine fan and pulley.
14. Remove valve covers and install lifting brackets at cylinder bolts.
15. Attach lifting equipment and take up slack.
16. Remove bolts attaching transmission to engine.
17. Remove bolts from front and rear mountings.
18. Move engine forward to disengage transmission.
19. Lift engine from the chassis.

Installation

Install the engine by reversing the removal procedure. Be certain to maintain cleanliness and to avoid damaging engine parts. After engine is installed, check operation of all control linkages, fill cooling system and check for leaks. Fill crankcase with oil to the proper level.

Manifolds

Inline Engine

Removal

1. Remove air cleaner.
2. Disconnect both throttle rods at bellcrank, remove throttle return spring.

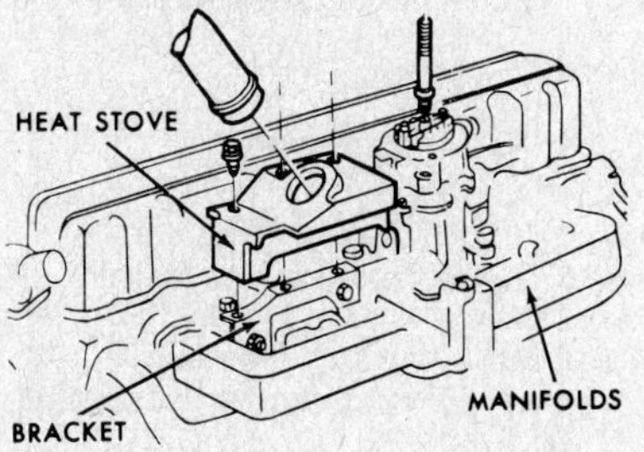

Manifold heat stove—inline 6 cylinder engine (© G.M.C.)

3. Disconnect fuel and vacuum lines, choke cable at carburetor.
4. Disconnect crankcase ventilation hose.
5. Disconnect exhaust pipe at manifold flange. Discard packing.
6. Remove heat stove (when used).
7. Remove attaching bolts and clamps and manifold.

Installation

1. Clean all surfaces.
2. Place new gasket over manifold end studs on head.
3. Position manifold and install bolts and clamps while holding manifold in place.
4. Torque bolts to specifications.
5. Connect exhaust pipe to manifold using new packing.
6. Connect crankcase ventilation hose.
7. Connect fuel and vacuum lines.
8. Connect choke cable, throttle rods, and install throttle return spring.
9. Install air cleaner.

V6 and V8 Engines

Intake Manifold Removal

1. Drain radiator and remove air cleaner.
2. Disconnect battery cables, radiator and heater hoses, water pump by-pass, accelerator linkage, choke control, and fuel line at carburetor. If necessary, remove crankcase ventilation lines and spark advance connections.
3. Where necessary, remove the distributor cap, mark the rotor position with chalk, and remove the distributor.
4. Remove, as necessary, the oil filler bracket, air cleaner bracket, air compressor and bracket, coil, accelerator return spring, and bracket, and accelerator bellcrank.
5. Remove the attaching bolts, and remove the manifold.

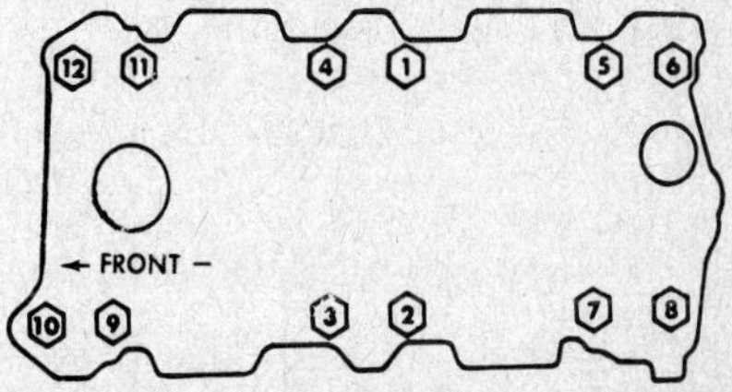

Intake manifold bolt tightening sequence —350 V8 engine (© G.M.C.)

Intake Manifold Installation

1. Clean all surfaces.
2. Install manifold seals on block and gaskets on cylinder heads.

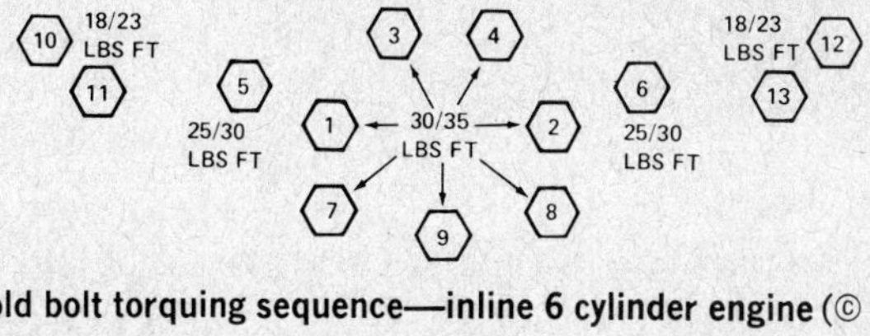

Manifold bolt torquing sequence—inline 6 cylinder engine (© G.M.C.)

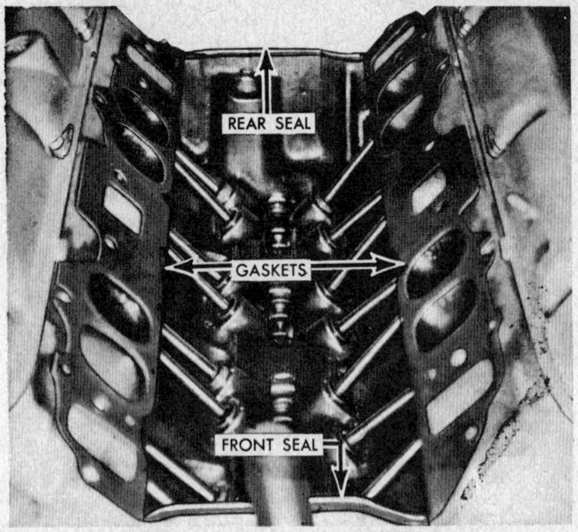

Intake manifold gaskets and seals—V8 engine (© G.M.C.)

3. Install manifold and torque bolts to specifications.
4. To finish installation, reverse removal procedure. Fill cooling system and check for leaks.

V6 and V8 Engines

Exhaust Manifold Removal

1. Remove carburetor bracket as required. Remove generator and bracket from manifold, as required.

NOTE: On large V8 engines, remove sparkplugs.

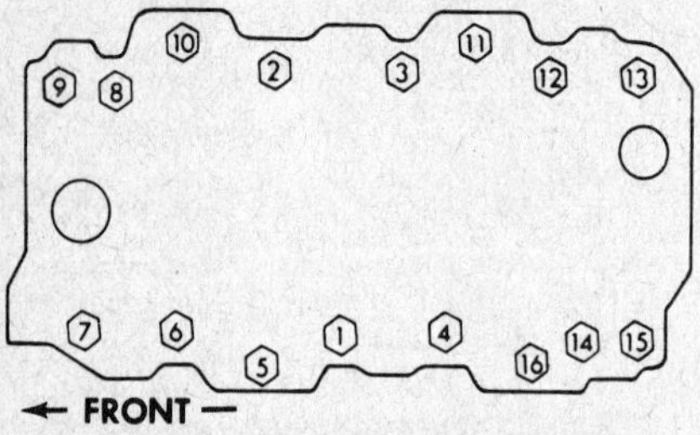

Intake manifold bolt tightening sequence —366, 427 engines (© G.M.C.)

2. Disconnect exhaust pipe from manifold.
3. On 1975-78 models remove the carburetor heat choke tube assembly.
4. Bend back bolt lock tabs and remove manifold bolts.
5. Remove exhaust manifolds.

Exhaust Manifold Installation

1. Clean all surfaces.
2. Install bolts with locks and torque in proper sequence to specifications.
3. Connect exhaust pipe to manifold with new packing.
4. On 1975-78 models install the carburetor heat choke tube with a new gasket.
5. Install generator and bracket and carburetor bracket as re-

NOTE: Install spark plugs on large engines.

Cylinder Head

WARNING: All engines except 305 series have sodium-cooled type exhaust valves. Sodium-cooled valves must not be discarded with other scrap metal. If a sodium-cooled valve is accidentally broken, the sodium will react violently with water, resulting in fire and explosion. Serious burns will result if sodium or sodium oxide comes in contact with the skin.

Inline Engines

Removal

1. Remove manifold assembly.
2. Remove valve mechanism.
3. Drain cooling system (block).
4. Remove fuel and vacuum lines from retaining clip and disconnect wires at temperature sending units.
5. Disconnect radiator hose at water outlet and ground strap at cylinder head.
6. Remove coil.
7. Remove cylinder head bolts, cylinder head and gasket.

Installation

1. Clean all surfaces and make certain there are no nicks or deep scratches. Cylinder head bolt threads must also be cleaned.
2. Place gasket over dowel pins with the bead up.
3. Place cylinder head over dowel pins carefully.
4. Apply sealer to head bolts and tighten down finger tight.
5. Tighten cylinder head bolts a little at a time in proper sequence and to torque specifications.
6. Install valve mechanism.
7. Connect wires to temperature sending units, connect fuel vacuum lines to retaining clip.

NOTE: Make certain to follow proper cylinder head tightening sequence.

V6 Engines

Removal

1. Drain cooling system.
2. Remove exhaust manifold.
3. Remove valve covers and valve mechanism.
4. Disconnect spark plug wires from plugs.
5. Remove water outlet and intake manifolds.
6. Remove cylinder head bolts, cylinder head and gasket.

NOTE: If lifters are removed, always install them in the same bores they were removed from.

Installation

1. Clean all surfaces and make certain there are no nicks or deep scratches. Cylinder head bolt threads must also be cleaned.
2. Place gasket over dowel pins, the word "top" facing up.
3. Place cylinder head over dowel pins carefully.
4. Apply sealer to head bolts and tighten down finger tight.
5. Tighten cylinder head bolts a little at a time in proper sequence and to torque specifications.

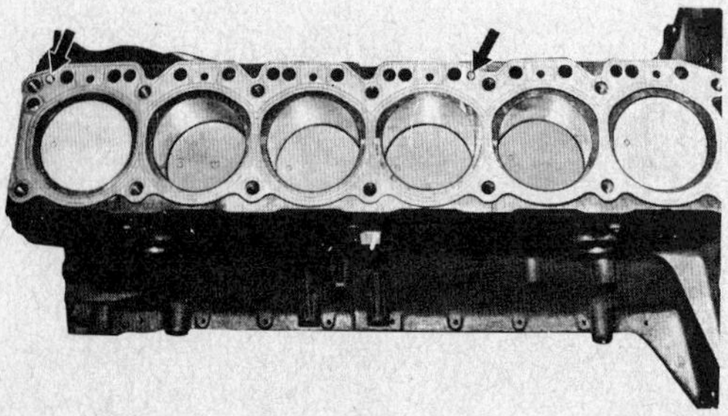

Cylinder head gasket installed—inline 6 cylinder engine (© G.M.C.)

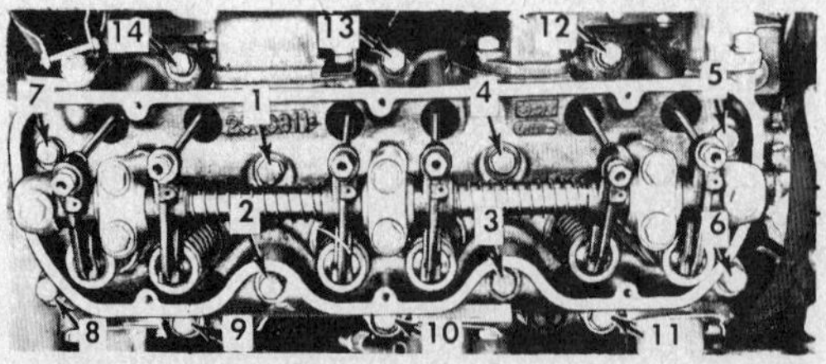

Cylinder head bolt tightening sequence—V6 engines (© G.M.C.)

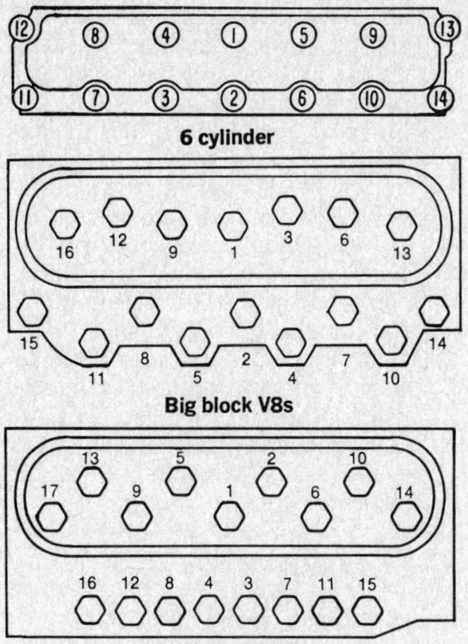

Cylinder head torque sequence
(© G.M.C.)

6. Install exhaust manifolds, using new gaskets.
7. Install intake manifold and water outlet manifold, using new gaskets.
8. Lubricate and install valve mechanism. Install valve cover with new valve cover gasket after valve adjustment.

V8 Engines

Removal

1. Drain cooling system (block).
2. Remove intake manifold.
3. Remove exhaust manifolds.
4. Remove valve mechansim.
5. Remove cylinder head bolts, cylinder head and gasket.

Installation

1. Clean all surfaces and make certain there are no nicks or deep scratches. Cylinder head bolt threads must also be cleaned.
2. Coat both sides of gasket with a thin coat of sealer.

   NOTE: Use no sealer on a composition steel-asbestos gasket.
3. Place gasket over dowel pins with bead facing up.
4. Place cylinder head over dowel pins carefully.
5. Apply sealer to head bolts and tighten down finger tight.
6. Tighten cylinder head bolts a little at a time in proper sequence and to torque specifications.
7. Install exhaust manifolds.
8. Install intake manifold.
9. Install valve mechanism and adjust.

Reference

Refer to the specifications area for proper head bolt tightening sequences and torques for all Inline, V6 and V8 engines.

Valve Train

Valve Arrangement

Front
E I I E E I I E E I I E
6 cylinder

Front
E I I E I E
E I E I I E
V6 engine

Front
E I I E E I I E
E I I E E I I E
Small block V8s

Front
I E I E I E I E
E I E I E I E I
Big block V8s

Adjustments

Inline and V8 Engines

1. Remove rocker arm cover.
2. With engine running at idle speed, install oil deflector clips to prevent oil splatter.
3. Back off rocker arm stud nut at one rocker arm until it begins to clatter, then tighten it slowly until the clatter just stops. This is zero lash position.
4. Turn nut down ¼ turn and pause for 10 seconds. Repeat this procedure until nut has been turned down for one complete revolution. This allows the hydraulic lifter to adjust itself while the valve completely closes each time.
5. Repeat the above procedure on all rocker arm assemblies.
6. Remove the oil deflector clips and install rocker arm cover using new gasket.

V6 Engines

1. Run engine until it reaches normal operating temperature.
2. Remove rocker arm covers.
3. Using a feeler gauge and a box end wrench, adjust exhaust and intake valve clearance to specifications.
4. Repeat the above procedure for all rocker arms, and check to make certain that all valve rocker arms are receiving sufficient lubrication.

Valve Rocker Arm

Inline and V8 Engines—Removal

1. Remove rocker arm cover.
2. Remove rocker arm nuts, rocker arm balls, rocker arms and push rods.

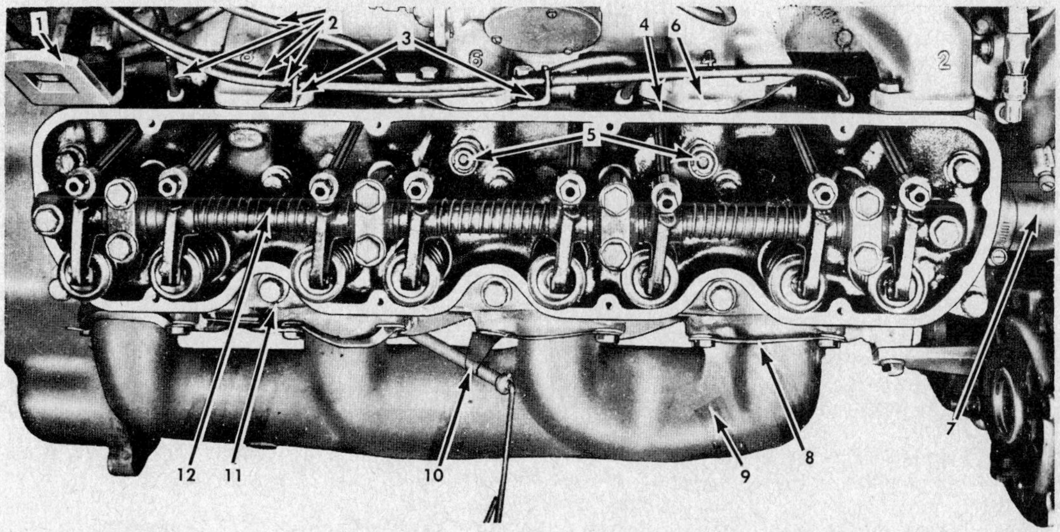

Exhaust manifold installed—V8 engine (© G.M.C.)

1 Engine lifting bracket
2 Spark plug wires
3 Plug wire supports
4 Intake manifold gasket
5 Crankcase ventilation valves
6 Intake manifold
7 Water outlet hose
8 Exhaust manifold bolt locks
9 Exhaust manifold
10 Dip stick tube clip
11 Exhaust manifold gasket
12 Rocker arms, shaft, and brackets

NOTE: Place assemblies in a specific order so that they may be installed in their previous positions.

Installation

1. Install push rods, making certain they seat in the lifter socket.
2. Install rocker arms, rocker arm balls and rocker arm nuts. Tighten all rocker arm nuts until all lash is eliminated.
3. Adjust valves.

Refer to Engine Rebuilding Section for more details.

Refer to valve specifications for valve spring, stem and seat angle specifications.

NOTE: Whenever installing new rocker arms or rocker arm balls, coat bearing surfaces with Molykote or its equivalent.

Valve Rocker Arms and Shaft

V6 Engines—Removal

1. Remove rocker arm covers.
2. Loosen rocker arm shaft bracket bolts until spring pressure is fully relieved from rocker arms.
3. Lift off rocker arm shaft and brackets as an assembly.
4. Remove push rods and place them in a specific order so that they may be installed in their original positions.

Installation

1. Install push rods in their proper positions.
2. Install rocker arm shaft and bracket assembly.
3. Set clearance between rocker arm shaft end brackets and adjacent rocker arms to specifications. Set initial valve clearance to 0.014″-intake, 0.022″-exhaust.
4. Lubricate rocker arms with engine oil, temporarily install rocker arm covers.
5. Run engine until operating temperature is reached, then stop engine.
6. Adjust valves.

Checking Engine Valve Timing

Inline Engine

1. Remove the valve rocker arm cover and the push rod front cover.
2. Loosen the nut and the No. 2 intake valve rocker arm, swing the rocker arm away from the push rod and remove the push rod and valve lifter.
3. Temporarily install a flat face mechanical lifter in place of the hydraulic lifter.
4. Turn the crankshaft until the no. 2 exhaust valve opens and the notch on the pulley dampener is aligned with the "O" mark on the timing pointer.
5. Position a deal indicator to measure lifter movement and set the indicator at zero. Turn the crankshaft to 360 degrees and read the indicator. On engines that are correctly timed the indicator will read as follows:
   250 engines ....0.014 in.
   292 engines ....0.016 in.
   If the reading is not as above, reset the indicator at zero and turn the crankshaft 360 degrees, then read the indicator again. If the reading is now correct, the engine is timed properly. The following chart shows indicator readings with gears properly indexed for each engine and indicator readings resulting from improperly indexed gears.
6. If after checking an out-of-time condition exists, remove the engine front cover and check for proper indexing of timing marks on gears.

Engine (Cu. In.)	Camshaft Part No. & Valve Lift	Gears Properly Indexed	One Tooth Adv.	One Tooth Ret.
250	3864896-.388	.014″±.004″	.0351″	.0055″
292	3848000-.405	.016″±.004″	.0379″	.0068″

V6 Engine

1. Remove the left-hand rocker cover.
2. Facing the front of the engine turn the engine clockwise to the top dead center No. 1 mark at the crankshaft pulley on the compression stroke. Both the intake and the exhaust valve on the No. 1 cylinder will then be closed.
3. On all V6 engines adjust the clearance to exactly 0.099 in. at the No. 1 exhaust valve (front valve).
4. Turn the engine clockwise until the No. 1 exhaust valve opens and begins to close. then with fingers, try turning the push rod of the No. 1 exhaust valve as the engine is cranked slowly. When the push rod rotates with finger pressure, the 5-degree (before top dead center mark) on the pulley should be at the pointer. This will be about one revolution from the starting point. If the push rod can be rotated at any point between the 10-degree mark and the top dead center No. 1 mark, the valve timing is correct. After making the timing check be sure to adjust the exhaust valve clearance to 0.018 in.

NOTE: If the timing chain has been installed improperly, there will be a 15 degree out-of-time condition for each mismatched tooth on the sprocket.

V8 Engine

1. Remove the rocker arm covers.
2. Turn the crankshaft so that the timing mark is at the "0" mark on the pointer and the No. 1 cylinder is ready to fire.
3. Move the crankshaft, and the exhaust valve in the No. 6 cylinder will just close and the intake valve will just begin to open.
4. If the exhaust valve or the intake valve is open when the pointer is at the "0" timing mark the camshaft is out of time.
5. When the No. 6 cylinder is ready to fire and the pointer is at the "0" timing mark the No. 1 cylinder exhaust valve will have just closed and the intake valve will begin to open.

Timing Gears

Timing Case Cover

Removal and Installation

1. Remove the damper and/or pulley. If necessary, remove the radiator.
2. Remove the bolts from the front cover to block and remove the two bolts from the oil pan to the front cover, if needed.
3. Carefully remove the front cover, discard the old gasket and oil seal.
4. To reassemble, clean the gasket surface and install a new gasket. Replace the oil seal in the cover.
5. Install the cover to the block and install the bolts.
6. Reinstall the damper and/or pulley, and install the radiator, if removed.

Timing Chain

V6 and V8 Engines

Removal

1. Drain and remove radiator.
2. Remove torsional damper.
3. Remove oil pan (see oil pan R & R).
4. Remove water pump or pulley if necessary.
5. Remove timing case cover.
6. Align timing marks.
7. Remove (3) camshaft sprocket bolts.
8. Remove sprocket and chain.
   NOTE: Sprocket is a light press fit on-camshaft, especially at dowel pin. If sprocket is tight, tap lightly with plastic hammer on lower edge of sprocket.
9. Clean all gasket and seal areas and inspect.
10. Check teeth on both sprockets for wear.

Installation

1. Suspend chain on camshaft sprocket with timing mark in approximate position.
2. Place chain over crankshaft sprocket and position camshaft

Timing chain alignment marks—V8 engine (© G.M.C.)

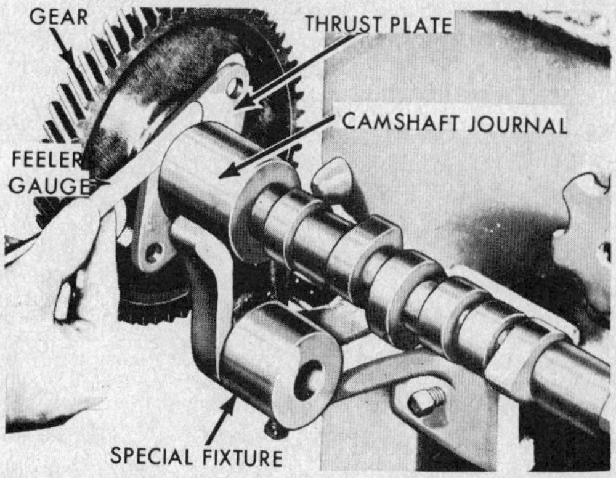

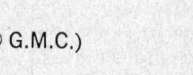

Measuring camshaft thrust plate clearance—inline 6 cylinder engine (© G.M.C.)

sprocket on dowel. Recheck timing marks.

3. Draw camshaft sprocket in place using the three mounting bolts. Torque to specifications. CAUTION: **do not drive sprocket on camshaft as plug at rear of camshaft can be dislodged.**
4. Lubricate chain with engine oil, make sure oil slinger is in place.
5. Reverse removal procedures.
6. Fill radiator, add engine oil and start engine. Check for leaks.

Check for Worn Chain

1. Check fan belt tension, adjust if too loose.
2. Remove distributor cap, loosen spark plugs.
3. Move fan blades until rotor moves. Mark distributor housing and balancer at pointer.
4. Move fan in opposite direction until rotor moves, remark both units.
5. Marks in excess of 4° apart, 2 graduations (usually) on balancer, indicate excess wear.

Inline Engines

Crankshaft Gear Removal

1. Attach gear puller to crankshaft gear (puller screw holes are provided on gear).
2. Turn puller screw and remove gear.
3. Check condition of timing gear key; replace if necessary.

Installation

1. Install key in crankshaft and coat gear seat with oil.
2. Align key way in gear to key on crankshaft with timing mark toward front of crankshaft.
3. Drive gear into place.

Camshaft Gear Removal

1. Gear is press fit on camshaft. Place in arbor press and apply pressure to front end of camshaft.
2. Press camshaft out of gear and remove key and spacer.

Installation

1. Install spacer and key, apply transmission oil on gear seat.
2. Support camshaft at journal, then position gear with timing mark forward and keyway aligned with key in camshaft.
3. Press gear on to camshaft until gear hub stops at spacer.
4. Measure clearance at thrust plate with a feeler gauge. A clearance of 0.001-0.005″ is necessary for proper lubrication.

Crankshaft Pulley or Damper

Removal

1. Drain radiator; remove hoses.
2. Remove radiator.
3. Loosen fan belt and remove any accessory drive.
4. Use puller to remove pulley or damper.

NOTE: On some early models, pulley is bolted to hub. Remove pulley first then, using pulley holes, remove hub. More recent models have the hub bonded to inertia weight. Care must be exercised when using a puller.

Timing Cover Oil Seal

Replacement

1. Remove torsional damper—See Damper R & R.
2. Pry old seal out, be careful not to mar crankshaft or bend cover.
3. Install new seal (lip of seal toward block), tap lightly into position. Coat seal with oil.
4. Reverse removal procedures.

Camshaft

Removal and Installation

Inline, V6, and V8 engines

1. Drain and remove the radiator assembly.
2. Remove the front end sheetmetal and/or grille.
3. Remove the damper and/or pulley.
4. Remove the timing case cover,. Remove the two bolts at the front of the oil pan.

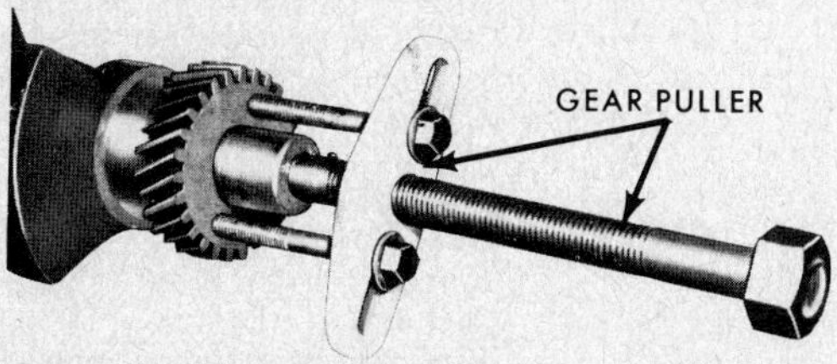

Crankshaft gear removal—inline 6 cylinder engine (© G.M.C.)

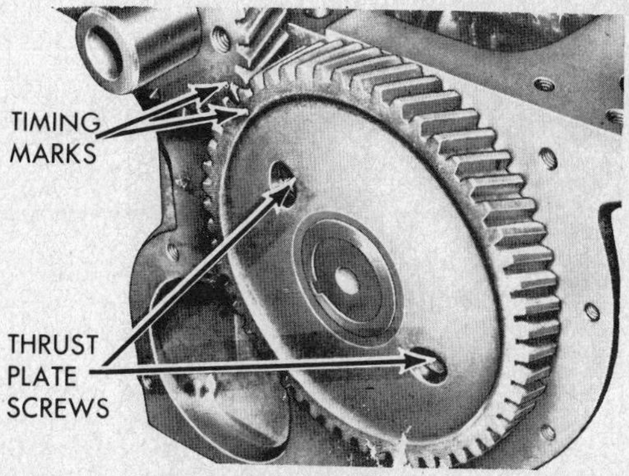

Timing gear marks and thrust plate screws—inline 6 cylinder engine (© G.M.C.)

5. Remove the rocker arm covers, the rocker arms, and push rods.
6. On 6 cylinder inline models, remove the push rod covers and remove the lifters. On the V6 and V8 engines, remove the intake manifold, and remove the lifters.
   NOTE: The lifters may be kept in their respective bores with the use of spring clothes pins, snapped around the lifter housing.
7. Align the timing gear marks on the camshaft and crankshaft gears for easier assembly when replacing the camshaft.
8. Remove two thrust plate screws by reaching through the two access holes in the camshaft gear.
9. Remove the camshaft and gear assembly by pulling and turning the shaft so the lobes will not strike and mar the camshaft bearings.
10. Use a press to remove the cam gear from the camshaft, using caution not to damage the thrust plate with the Woodruff key.
11. Clean all gasket surfaces and install the gear on the camshaft and the camshaft assembly into the engine in the reverse order of the disassembly.

Piston and Connecting Rod

Removal

1. Ream out top of bore if a piston ring travel ridge is present.
2. Position crankshaft so that a pair of connecting rods can be moved without interference.
3. Remove nuts from connecting rod cap bolts, remove rod cap and lower bearing half.
4. Mark all parts for reassembly.
5. With the aid of a length of wood or a hammer handle, push upward on the connecting rod to remove the piston from the cylinder bore.

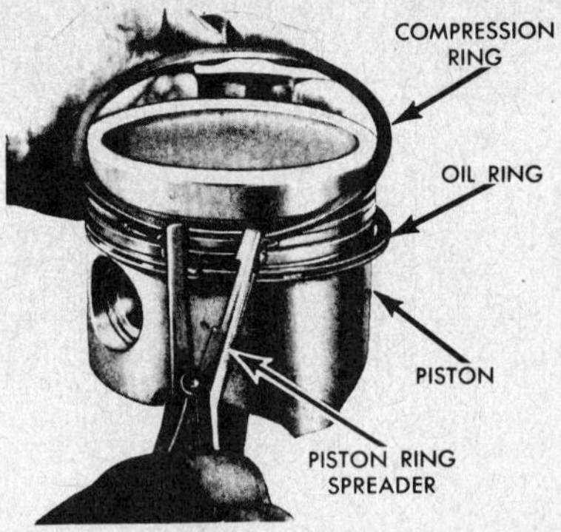

Installing piston rings with spreader tool (© G.M.C.)

Installation

1. Clean and coat piston pin, rings, and cylinder bore with engine oil.
2. Stagger piston ring gaps.
3. Place connecting rod bearing halves in rod and cap.
4. Use a ring compressor to install piston and connecting rod assembly in cylinder bore.
5. Install cap and lower bearing half. Lubricate nut threads and torque to specifications.
6. Check bearing clearances.

Refer to General Engine Rebuilding Section for further details on piston and connecting rod assembly and disassembly.

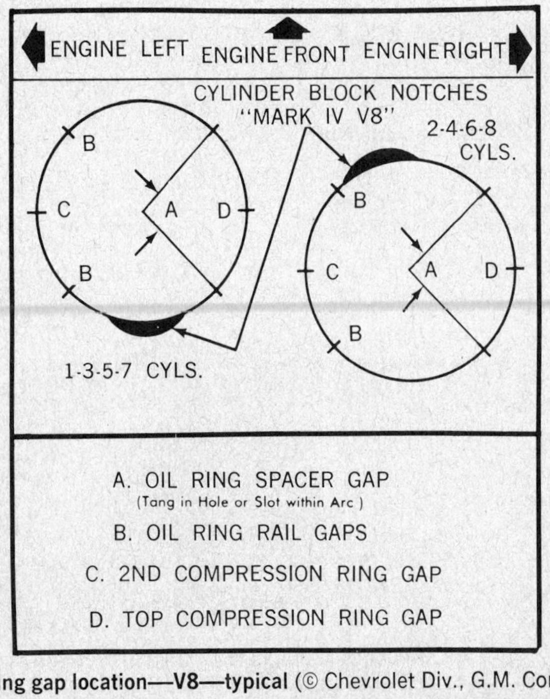

Ring gap location—V8—typical (© Chevrolet Div., G.M. Corp.)

Piston Rings

Piston rings are removed and installed with the use of a spreader tool. Use care not to break the rings.

Crankshaft Bearings

Main and Rod Bearings

Main bearings and connecting rod bearings are replaceable inserts, precision fit and held in place by locking tangs. Excessive bearing clearances reduce oil pressure. Never replace the lower half of any bearing without replacing the upper half. Do not file any bearing cap. Make sure, on main bearings, the upper half oil hole is aligned. Be certain oil passages in the crankshaft are open. Mark rod caps and upper forgings, also main caps and block, in numerical order to aid in reassembly. Rod bearings are available in standard size as well as .001″, .002″, .010″ and .020″ undersizes. Main bearings are furnished in standard size and .001″, .002″, .009″, .010″, .020″ and .030″ undersizes.

Rod Bearing Replacement

1. Drain crankcase oil and remove oil pan. See Oil Pan Removal.
2. Remove connecting rod bearing cap.
3. Wipe bearing shell and crankpin clean of oil.
4. Inspect bearings for evidence of wear or damage. (Bearings showing the above should not be installed).
5. Measure crankpin for out-of-round or taper with a micrometer. If within specifications measure bearing clearance with plastigage or its equivalent. See Engine Rebuilding—General Section.
6. Install bearing in connecting rod and cap.
7. Coat bearing surface with oil, install rod cap and torque nuts to specifications.
8. Rotate crankshaft after bearing adjustment to be sure bearings are not too tight. Check side clearance.
9. Install oil pan gaskets, seals and oil pan. See Oil Pan Installation.

Main Bearing Replacement

NOTE: Main bearings may be replaced with or without removing crankshaft.

(Engine in Vehicle)

1. Drain crankcase oil and remove oil pan. See Oil Pan Removal.
2. Remove oil pump.
3. Loosen or remove spark plugs for easier crankshaft rotation.
4. Starting with rear main bearing,

remove bearing cap and wipe oil from journal and cap.
5. Inspect bearings for evidence of wear or damage.
6. Measure bearing clearance with plastigage or its equivalent. The crankshaft should be supported at damper and flywheel to remove clearance from upper bearing. Total clearance can then be measured between lower bearing and journal. See Engine Rebuilding—General Section.
7. Remove bearing shell from cap.
8. On inline engine crankshaft, rear main bearing has no oil hole. Replace rear main bearing upper half as follows:
   a. Use a small drift punch and hammer to start upper bearing half rotating out of block.
   b. Use a pair of pliers (with taped jaws) to hold bearing thrust surface to oil slinger and rotate crankshaft to remove bearing.
   c. Oil new selected size upper bearing and insert plate (unnotched) between crankshaft and indented or notched side of block.
   d. Use pliers as in removing to rotate bearing into place. The last ¼ movement may be done by holding just the slinger with pliers or tapping into place with a drift punch.
9. All other crankshaft journals (inline and "V" models) have oil holes. Replace main bearing upper half as follows:
   a. Install a main bearing removing and installing tool in oil hole in crankshaft journal.
   NOTE: If such a tool is not available, a cotter pin (with head flattened) may be used.
   b. Rotate crankshaft clockwise as viewed from front of engine. This will roll upper bearing out of block.
   c. Oil new selected size upper bearing and insert plain (unnotched) end between crankshaft and indented or notched side of block. Rotate bearing into place and remove tool from oil hole in crankshaft journal.
10. Oil new lower bearing and install in bearing cap.
11. Install main bearing cap according to markings. Torque bearing cap bolts to specifications.
12. Install oil pump and oil pan. Refill crankcase. Install and tighten spark plugs.

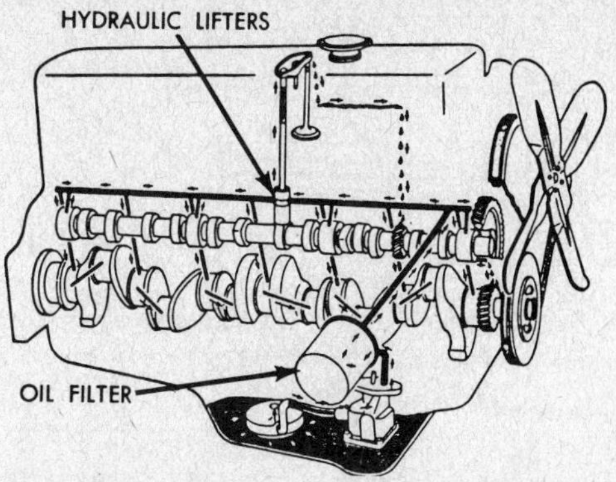

Lubrication oil circuits—inline 6 cylinder engine (© G.M.C.)

Oil Pan R & R

Series 1500-3500

6 Cyl.—Removal

1. Disconnect battery ground cable.
2. Raise vehicle on a hoist and disconnect starter at engine block—leave electrical connections intact and position starter out of way.
3. Remove bolts securing engine mounts to crossmember brackets—then, using a suitable jack with a flat piece of wood to protect oil pan, raise engine sufficiently to insert 2 in. x 4 in. wood block between engine mounts and crossmember brackets.
4. Drain engine oil and remove flywheel (converter) cover.
5. Remove engine mount spacer on C Series vehicles.
6. Remove oil pan bolts and withdraw oil pan from engine.

Installation

1. Discard old gaskets and seals, thoroughly clean all gasket sealing surfaces.
2. Install new rear seal in rear main bearing cap.
3. Install new front seal on crankcase front cover.
4. Install new side gaskets on cylinder block.
   NOTE: DO NOT USE SEALER.
5. Position oil pan to block, making sure that seals and gaskets remain in place, install and torque

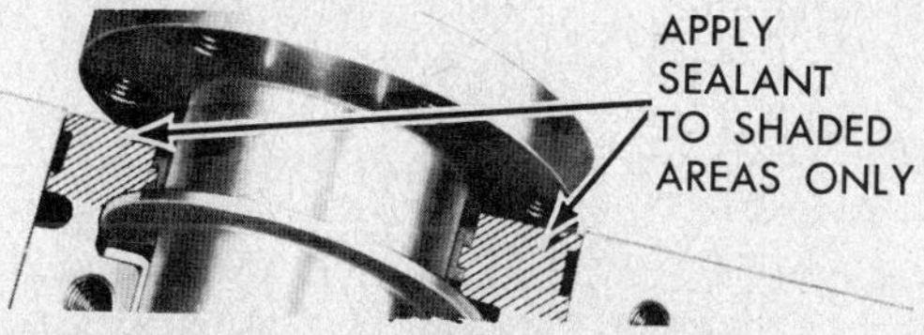

Applying sealer to rear bearing cap area (© G.M.C.)

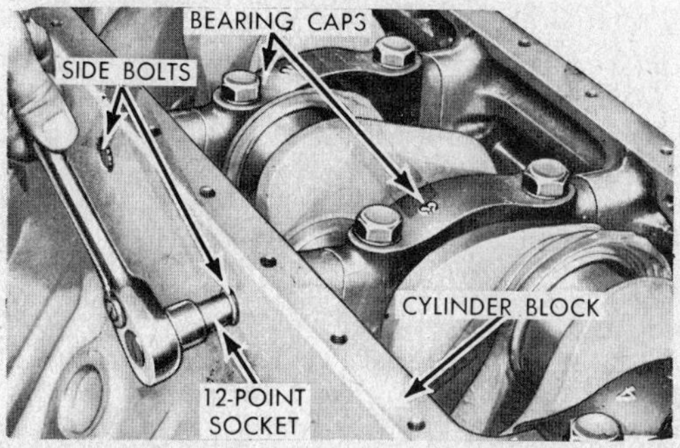

Installing bearing cap side bolts—V8 engine (© G.M.C.)

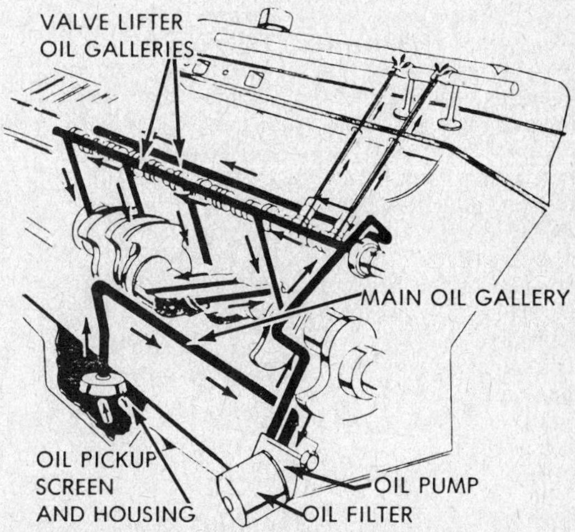

Typical lubrication oil circuits—V6 engines (© G.M.C.)

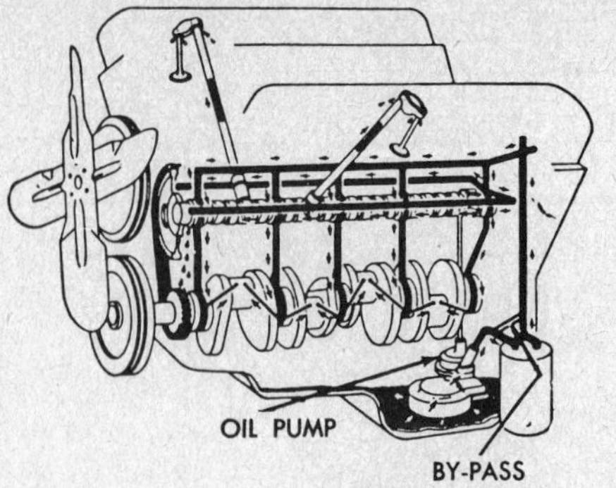

Lubrication oil circuits—small V8 engines—typical (© G.M.C.)

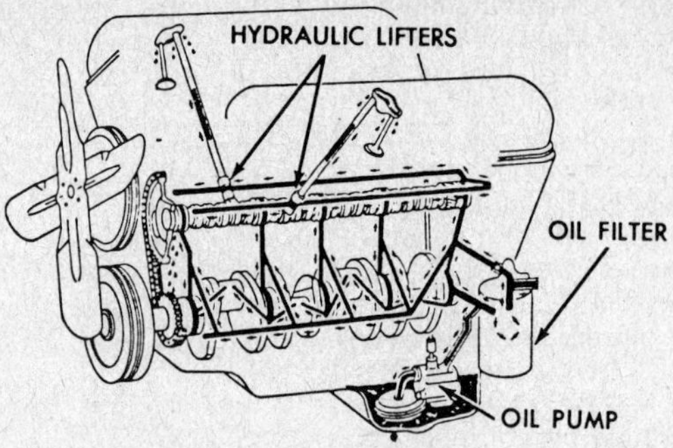

Lubrication oil circuits—Mark IV V8 engines—typical (© G.M.C.)

pan screws to specifications.

6. Raise engine as outlined above and remove blocks used to support engine.
7. Lower engine, install and torque mount-to-crossmember bracket bolts.
8. Install starter and flywheel (converter) cover.
9. Install engine mount spacer on C Series vehicles.
10. Fill engine with specified quantity of oil, then start engine and check for leaks.

V8—Removal

1. Drain engine oil.
2. Remove oil dip stick and tube.
3. On vehicles so equipped remove exhaust crossover pipe.
4. On vehicles equipped with automatic transmission remove converter housing under pan.
5. Remove starter brace and inboard bolt, swing starter aside.
6. Remove oil pan and discard gaskets and seals.

Installation

1. Thoroughly clean all gasket and seal surfaces on oil pan, cylinder block, crankcase front cover and rear main bearing cap.
2. Install new oil pan side gaskets on cylinder block using gasket sealer as a retainer. Install new oil pan rear seal in rear main bearing cap groove, with ends butting side gaskets. Install new oil pan front seal in groove in crankcase front cover with ends butting side gaskets.
3. Install oil pan and torque bolts to specifications.
4. Install starter brace and attaching bolts. Torque bolts to specifications.
5. Install converter housing under pan (if removed).
6. Install exhaust crossover pipe (if removed).
7. Install oil dip stick tube and dip stick.
8. Fill with oil, start engine and check for leaks.

Series 4500-6500

Removal

1. Clean all dirt and accumulated material from oil pan attaching bolts and drain plug.
2. Drain oil out of crankcase.
3. Remove oil pan bolts, then remove oil pan. Scrape off any portions of gaskets which adhere to oil pan flange or bolting flange on engine block and front cover. Gasket at front cover is neoprene type. Remove seal at crankshaft rear bearing cap.

Installation

1. Install seal at rear bearing cap.
2. Install front seal on timing gear cover, pressing tips into holes in cover.
3. Use grease or cement to hold side gaskets in place on cylinder block. Side gasket tabs must index with front seal on timing gear cover.
4. Install oil pan.

Oil Cooler Service

Should foreign matter be suspected of contaminating oil system, back flush oil cooler and lines, using cleaning solvent and compressed air. Do not exceed 100 psi.

Rear Main Bearing Oil Seal

Replacement (Engine in Vehicle)

1. Raise vehicle and drain oil.
2. Remove oil pan and oil pump. See oil pan and oil pump removal.
3. Remove rear main cap and discard seal.
4. Loosen all mains (except no. 1) and block crankshaft down for maximum clearance at rear main.
5. Use wooden dowel, so as not to mar journal, tap lightly until seal can be gripped and removed. Rotating shaft may help.
6. Wick type seal: Use "Chinese Finger" type of tool, or insert a piece of soft wire through seal approximately ¼ from end, then wrap end with wire. Insert wire through seal opening in crankcase and around crankshaft. Start upper half of seal in place, lubricated with light sealer. Pull seal into place (rotating shaft may help) until centered. Cut each end of seal so that ¼" protrudes. Install new lower half of oil seal in cap and roll or pack

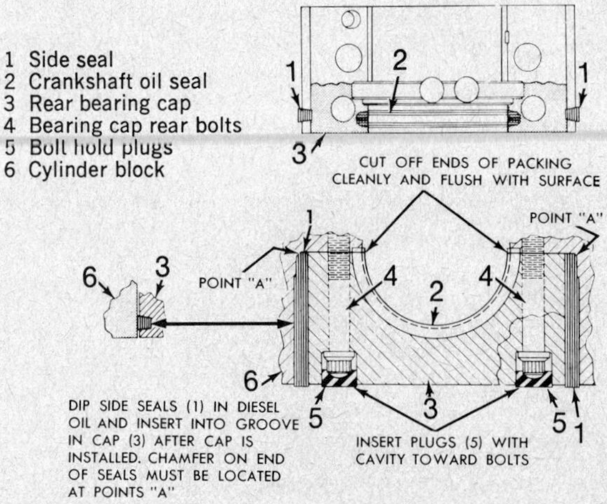

Cross section of rear seals (© G.M.C.)

into position. Cut ends flush with cap parting face. Replace cap. Molded type seal: Insert new upper half, lubricated with light sealer, into channel and apply firm pressure with hammer handle until seal is centered. (Lip of seal facing toward front of engine.) Install lower half of oil seal in cap (lip toward front), lubricate lip with oil and install cap.
7. Torque all mains, check for drag.
8. Replace oil pump, oil pan and add oil.
9. Start engine and check for leaks.

Oil Pump R & R

Inline Engines

Removal

1. Remove oil pan.
2. Remove oil suction pipe bolt and two bolts attaching the pump flange to engine.
3. Remove oil pump and screen.

Installation

1. Install oil pump, aligning drive shaft with distributor tang. Install suction pipe support bolt.
2. Install oil pan.

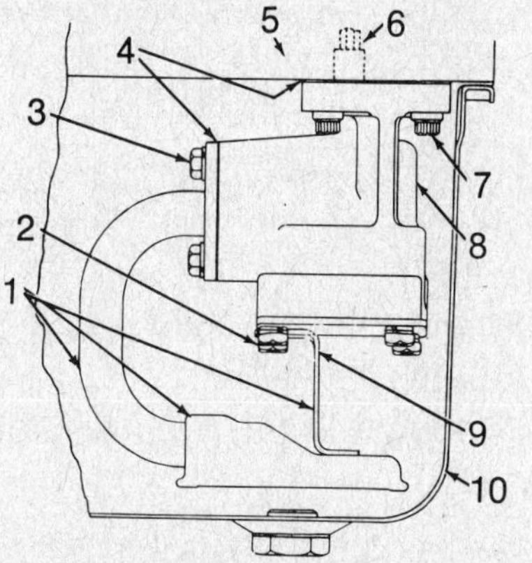

Engine oil pump installation (© G.M.C.)

1 Suction tube and screen assy.
2 Bracket bolt (20-25 ft. lbs.)
3 Flange bolts and lock washers
4 Gaskets
5 Cylinder block
6 Pump drive shaft
7 Pump to block bolts (30-35 ft. lbs.)
8 Oil pump 9 Bracket 10 Oil pan

V6 Engines

Removal

1. Remove oil pan.
2. Remove two mounting bolts and oil pump.

Installation

1. Place new gasket on pump flange and install pump, turning shaft as necessary to engage gears.
2. Install mounting bolts and torque to specifications.
3. Install oil pan.

V8 Engines

Removal

1. Remove oil pan.
2. Remove pump to rear main bearing cap bolt.
3. Remove pump and extension shaft.

Installation

1. Install pump and extension shaft, aligning slot with tang on lower end of distributor drive shaft.
2. Install attaching bolt and torque to specifications.
3. Install oil pan.

NOTE: To prime the oil pump, fill the gear cavity with petroleum jelly or with engine oil.

FRONT AXLE AND SUSPENSION

General instructions covering the front suspension and how to repair and adjust it are given in the General Repair Section.

Specifications covering the caster, camber, toe-in, king pin inclination, and turning radius can be found in the Wheel Alignment table of this section.

I-Beam Front Axle

This type of front axle is a one-piece steel forging in which dowel pins are installed to locate spring seats. Both ends of the axle are machined to accept the steering knuckle and kingpin assemblies, and kingpin inclination is a built-in angle.

Spring

Removal and Installation

1. Wire brush all road dirt from threaded areas on U bolts, shock absorbers and stabilizer links, apply a good penetrant on threads.
2. Disconnect shock and stabilizer link at lower bracket.
3. Loosen both spring U bolts.
4. Using jack under I-beam, raise front of vehicle and support at frame side rail with stand. Finish removing U bolts and rebound bumper. Lower jack until spring clears I-beam or tire rests on ground. Remove any caster wedges (shims) and set aside for installation.

NOTE: Thick end of shim goes to rear of vehicle for increased caster.

5. Remove front spring eye bolt.
6. Remove rear shackle (and hanger cam if equipped).
7. Remove spring, insert hangers and spring seat (center bolt index).
8. Reverse removal procedures to install after placing spring on axle with center bolt head indexed in seat and caster shims in place. Torque all nuts and lubricate.

Steering Knuckle and Kingpin Assembly

F-050, F-055, and F-070 Axles

CAUTION: Steering knuckle bushings are of a split type and are constructed of thermoplastic polyester. Bushings can be cleaned in most conventional solvents, except ketone or chlorinated types.

Removal

1. Support the frame of the vehicle in a raised position, high enough so that the tires clear the floor.
2. Remove the wheels, hubs, and bearings.
3. Remove brake components as necessary.
4. Disconnect the tie-rod from the steering arm.
5. Remove the two lower steering arm-to-axle flange bolts, and swing the steering arm out of the way.
6. Remove the two upper bolts from the axle flange, and remove the brake backing plate.
7. Remove the kingpin draw key nut and washer.
8. Thread the draw key nut onto the draw key far enough to protect the threads from damage.

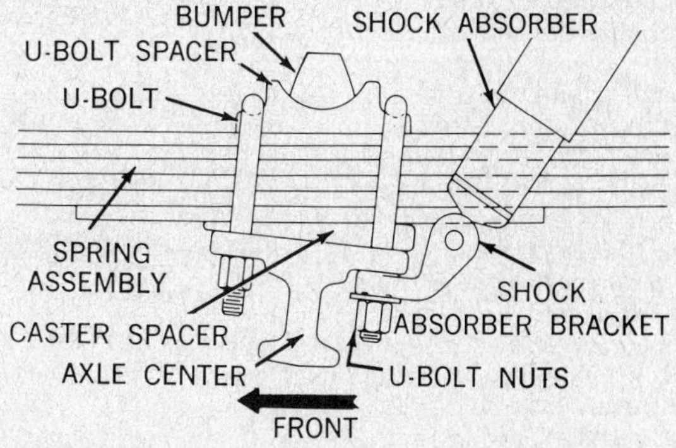

Spring center mount—leaf type—steel tilt model (typical of most models) (© Chevrolet Div., G.M. Corp.)

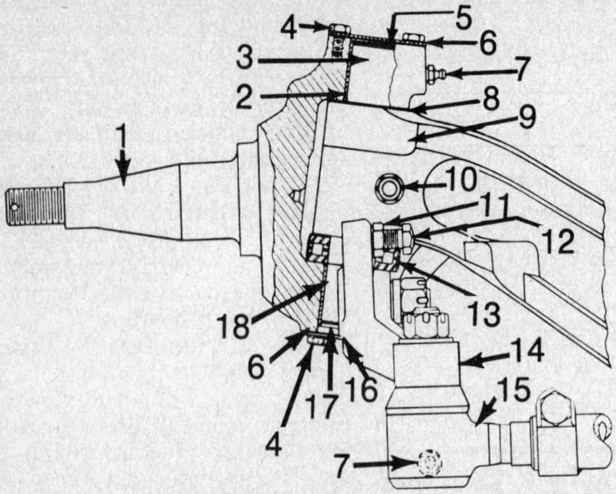

F-050 and F-055 Axle 1973-80 (© Chevrolet Div., G.M. Corp.)

1 Steering Knuckle Spindle
2 Upper Bushing
3 Kingpin
4 Cap Screw
5 Upper Kingpin Bearing Cup
6 Kingpin Bearing Cup Gasket
7 Lubrication Fitting
8 Shim
9 Axle Center
10 Draw Key
11 Stop Screw Nut
12 Stop Screw
13 Thrust Bearing
14 Lower Steering Arm
15 Tie Rod End Assembly
16 Lower Kingpin Bearing Cap
17 Spacer—Steering Knuckle Bushing
18 Lower Bushing

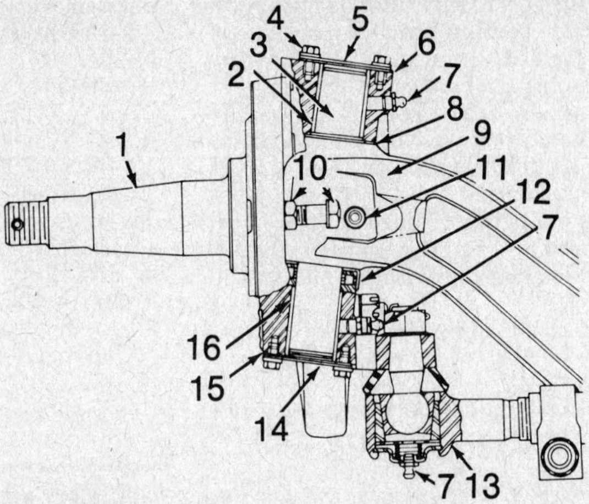

F-070 Axle 1973-80 (© Chevrolet Div., G.M. Corp.)

1 Steering Knuckle Spindle
2 Kingpin Bushing (Upper)
3 Kingpin
4 Cap Screw
5 Kingpin Bearing Cap (Upper)
6 Gasket
7 Lube Fitting
8 Shim
9 Axle Center
10 Stop Bolt and Lock Nut
11 Draw Key
12 Thrust Bearing
13 Tie Rod End Assembly
14 Kingpin Bearing Cap (Lower)
15 Gasket
16 Kingpin Bushing (Lower)

9. Drive the draw key loose by striking the nut with a brass hammer.
10. Finish driving the draw key out with a brass drift.
11. Remove the kingpin bearing cap screws.
12. Remove the kingpin bearing caps and gaskets.
13. Using a brass hammer, drive the kingpin out of the axle.
14. Remove the steering knuckle, thrust bearing, shims, and the O-ring.

NOTE: Steering knuckle bushings can be hand pressed into the knuckle bore until flush with the top.

Installation

1. Position the steering knuckle on the axle, and insert the thrust bearing.
2. Install a new O-ring seal at the bottom of the upper bushing.
3. Align the steering knuckle yoke, axle end, and the thrust bearing to accept the kingpin; start the kingpin through the top of the assembly.
4. With the axle center firmly secured, jack up the steering knuckle until there is zero clearance between the steering knuckle lower yoke, thrust bearing, and the axle center.
5. Check the clearance between the top of the axle center and the knuckle upper yoke. Select shims which will provide the correct thrust clearance as indicated in the Front Axle Specification chart.
6. From the top, insert the kingpin through the steering knuckle yoke, shim, thrust bearing, and axle center end. Press the kingpin down until the machined slot in the kingpin aligns with the draw key hole.
7. Insert the draw key into the axle center, and install the washer and nut.

CAUTION: If, after tightening the draw key nut, the kingpin is not secured, then replace the draw key.

NOTE: On models using steering knuckle bushing spacer, install spacer at lower end of the kingpin.

8. Using new gaskets, install upper and lower kingpin bearing caps and cap screws.
9. Lubricate the kingpin with chassis lubricant.
10. Secure the brake backing plate to the axle flange with the top two axle flange bolts.
11. Swing the steering arm into position, and secure it to the axle flange with two lower flange bolts.
12. Install brake components.
13. Install hubs and bearings.
14. Install wheels.
15. Lower the vehicle, and check front end alignment. Make necessary adjustments.

Steering Knuckle and Kingpin Assembly

F-090 Axle (F-120 Axle—Similar)

NOTE: The steering knuckle is supported on a solid kingpin which is tapered at the center. The kingpin bushing is constructed of steel, and the knuckle bushings are constructed of steel backed bronze.

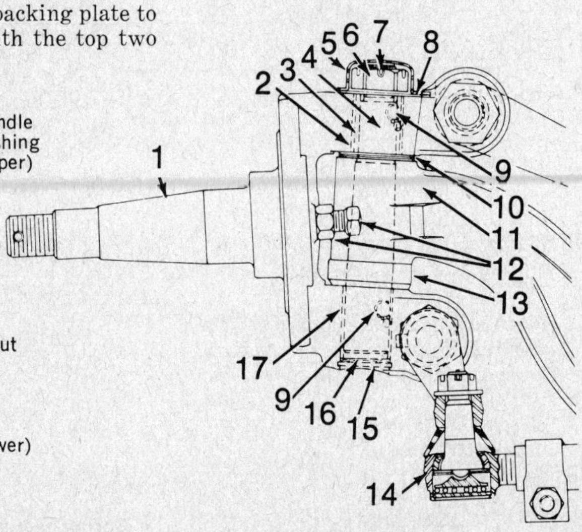

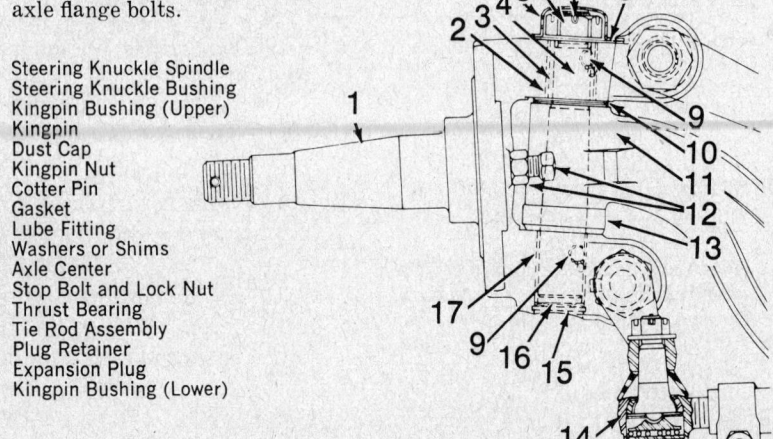

F-090 Axle 1973-80 (© Chevrolet Div., G.M. Corp.)

1 Steering Knuckle Spindle
2 Steering Knuckle Bushing
3 Kingpin Bushing (Upper)
4 Kingpin
5 Dust Cap
6 Kingpin Nut
7 Cotter Pin
8 Gasket
9 Lube Fitting
10 Washers or Shims
11 Axle Center
12 Stop Bolt and Lock Nut
13 Thrust Bearing
14 Tie Rod Assembly
15 Plug Retainer
16 Expansion Plug
17 Kingpin Bushing (Lower)

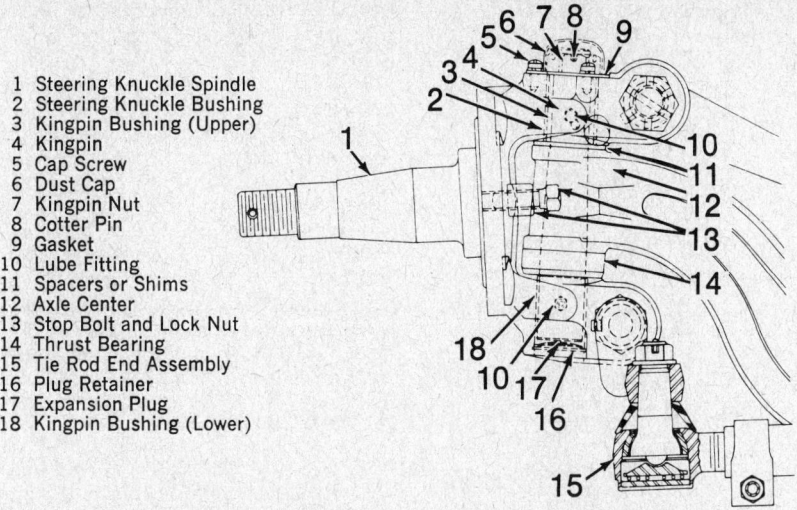

1 Steering Knuckle Spindle
2 Steering Knuckle Bushing
3 Kingpin Bushing (Upper)
4 Kingpin
5 Cap Screw
6 Dust Cap
7 Kingpin Nut
8 Cotter Pin
9 Gasket
10 Lube Fitting
11 Spacers or Shims
12 Axle Center
13 Stop Bolt and Lock Nut
14 Thrust Bearing
15 Tie Rod End Assembly
16 Plug Retainer
17 Expansion Plug
18 Kingpin Bushing (Lower)

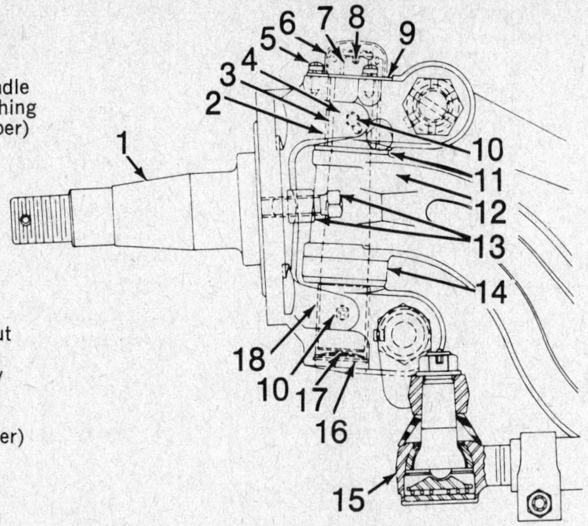

F-120 Axle 1973-74 (© Chevrolet Div., G.M. Corp.)

Removal

1. Support the frame of the vehicle in a raised position, high enough so that the tires clear the floor.
2. Remove the wheels, hubs, and bearings.
3. Remove brake components as necessary.
4. Disconnect steering linkage components as necessary.
5. Remove the axle flange-to-steering knuckle bolts, and remove the brake backing plate.
6. Remove the dust cap and gasket.
7. Remove the lower expansion plug retainer and plug.

   NOTE: If the plug does not remove freely after the retainer has been removed, it will come out along with the kingpin when the kingpin is driven out.
8. Remove the cotter pin, kingpin nut, and the steel washer.
9. Drive the kingpin down and out of the axle with a brass drift.
10. Remove the steering knuckle, thrust bearing, and spacers from the axle.

    NOTE: Bushing replacement can be accomplished with the use of an arbor press.

Installation

1. With the steering knuckle positioned on the axle center end, insert the thrust bearing assembly between the lower face of the axle center and the steering knuckle lower yoke.

   NOTE: Be sure that the retainer is on top of the bearing with the lip of the retainer facing down.
2. Align the knuckle yoke and axle center to accept the kingpin.
3. With the axle center firmly secured, jack up the steering knuckle until there is zero clearance between the steering knuckle lower yoke, thrust bearing, and the axle center.
4. Check the clearance between the top face of the axle center end and the face of the upper steering knuckle yoke. Select shims which will provide the correct thrust clearance as indicated in the Front Axle Specification chart.

   NOTE: Kingpin, kingpin bore, and component parts must be thoroughly cleaned and dry.
5. Insert the kingpin up through the bottom yoke of the steering knuckle, and drive it into place with a soft hammer.
6. Position the kingpin bushing over the kingpin, and press into place. Bushing must be flush with the knuckle.
7. Install the kingpin nut and cotter pin.
8. Install a new inverted expansion plug in the lower hole.
9. Install the plug retainer. Retainer must be seated securely in groove.
10. Install the kingpin dust cap and gasket.
11. Connect steering linkage components.
12. Install backing plate to axle flange.
13. Install brake components.
14. Install the hubs, bearings, and wheels.

1 Upper Draw Key (Short)
2 Kingpin
3 Upper Bushing
4 Cap Gasket
5 Kingpin Cap
6 Spacing Shim
7 Lower Draw Key
8 Thrust Bearing
9 Axle Center
10 Expansion Plug
11 Lock Ring
12 Lower Bushing
13 Steering knuckle

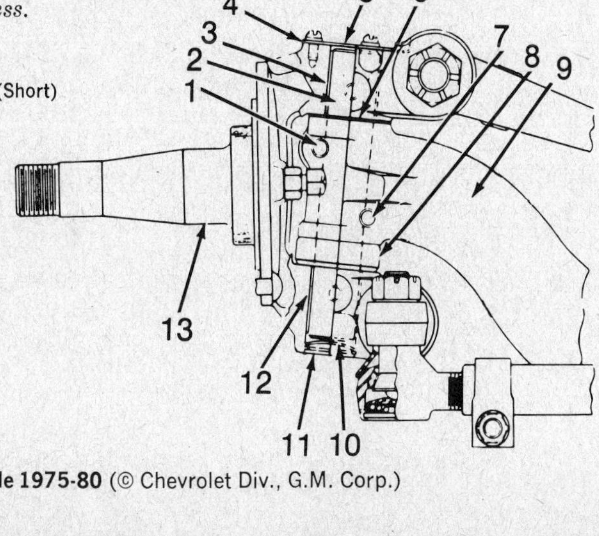

F-120 Axle 1975-80 (© Chevrolet Div., G.M. Corp.)

Independent Front Suspension

This suspension consists of upper and lower control arms, pivoting on steel threaded bushings on upper and lower control arm inner shafts which are attached to the crossmember. Control arms are connected to the steering knuckle by ball joints. A coil spring is seated between the upper and lower control arms, thus the lower control arm is the load carrying member.

Coil Spring

Removal and Installation

1. Raise vehicle and place (high) stands under frame allowing control arm to hang free.
2. Disconnect shock absorber (and stabilizer if used) at lower end.
3. Using a floor jack, under center of lower control arm inner shaft, raise and remove tension from shaft.

   CAUTION: Install a safety chain through spring and lower control arm.
4. Remove both clamps or "U" bolts securing inner shaft to crossmember.
5. Release jack very cautiously, slowly lowering arm with spring until spring is free. Remove safety chain, remove spring.
6. Inspect front end especially at ball joints and both upper and lower control arm inner shaft bushings.
7. Reverse removal step to install; use a long tapered drift to align holes of inner control arm shaft and crossmember while slowly jacking arm into place.

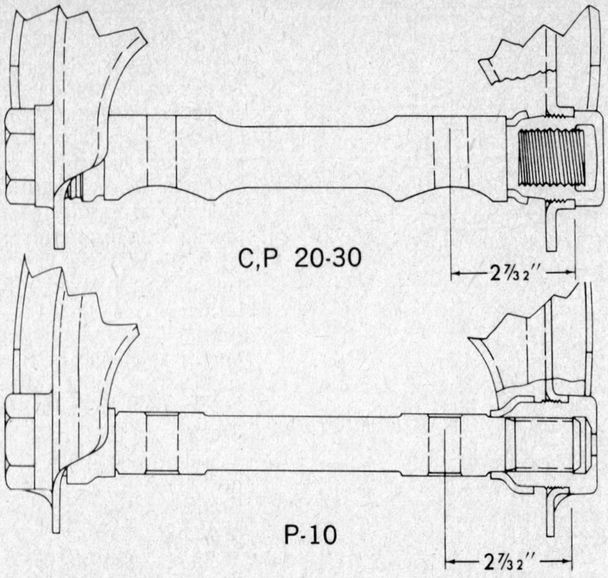

Correctly positioned upper control arm steel bushings
(© Chevrolet Div., G.M. Corp.)

Upper Control Arm (All Vehicles)

Removal

1. Hoist the vehicle, and remove the front wheels.
2. Position an adjustable jackstand under the outboard side of the lower control arm, and adjust the height of the jackstand so that the uppermost extremity of the jackstand comes in contact with the metal undersurface of the lower control arm.
3. Remove the cotter pin from the upper control arm ball joint stud and nut.
4. Loosen the stud nut approximately one full turn.
5. If the ball joint stud does not unseat from the steering knuckle, it may be necessary to press the control arm and ball joint stud away from the knuckle, using a tool designed for that purpose.
6. Remove the nut from the ball joint stud, and swing the upper control arm up and away from the steering knuckle.

   NOTE: It may be necessary to remove the brake caliper assembly from the steering knuckle in order to facilitate upper control arm removal and installation.
7. Remove the nuts securing the control arm pivot shaft to the frame, and remove the control arm.
8. Tape the alignment shims together, and tag them in order to properly relocate them during installation.

Installation

NOTE: Special pivot shaft aligning washers must be positioned with the concave and convex sides together.

1. Situate the upper control arm against its normal mounting position, and install the pivot shaft nuts. DO NOT tighten the nuts.
2. Install the alignment shims in their respective positions as noted during removal.
3. Tighten the pivot shaft nuts.

   NOTE: Tighten the nut on the thinner shim pack first. This will improve shaft to frame clamping force and torque retention.
4. Insert the ball joint stud into the bore in the steering knuckle, and install the nut and cotter pin.
5. Install the brake caliper assembly.
6. Remove the adjustable jackstand from under the lower control arm.
7. Install the wheel and tire assembly.
8. The vehicle may now be positioned to check front end alignment.

   NOTE: Ordinarily, a shim pack will leave at least two threads of the bolt exposed beyond the nut. If, in order to properly align the front wheels, it is necessary to build the shim pack beyond the two thread minimum, then check for damaged control arms and related parts. The difference, in thickness, between the front shim pack and the rear shim pack must not exceed 0.30 inches. The front shim pack must be at least 0.24 inches.

Lower Control Arm

Removal

1. Raise the vehicle on a hoist, and remove the front coil spring (see Coil Spring/Removal and Installation).
2. Support the disconnected, inboard end of the lower control arm after the spring is removed.
3. Remove the cotter pin from the lower ball joint stud, and loosen the stud nut approximately one full turn.
4. Press the control arm and ball joint stud away from the steering knuckle, using a tool designed for that purpose.

   NOTE: It may be necessary to remove the brake caliper assembly from the steering knuckle in order to facilitate lower control arm removal and installation.
5. Remove the lower control arm.

Installation

1. Insert the lower ball joint stud through the steering knuckle. and tighten the nut.
2. Install the coil spring, and reattach the inboard end of the lower control arm to the cross member.
3. Be sure that the ball joint stud

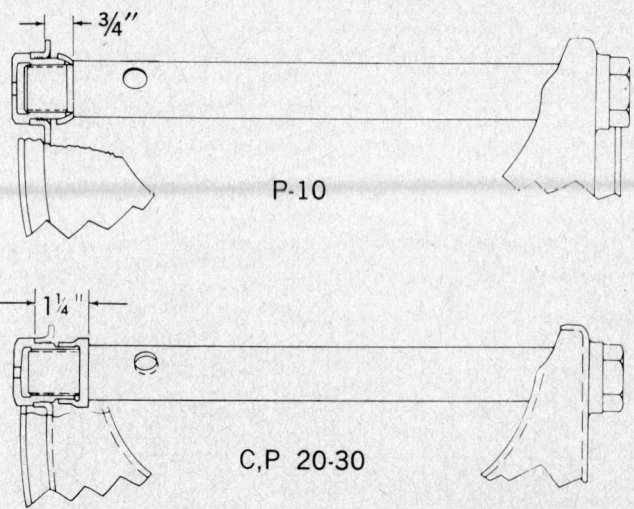

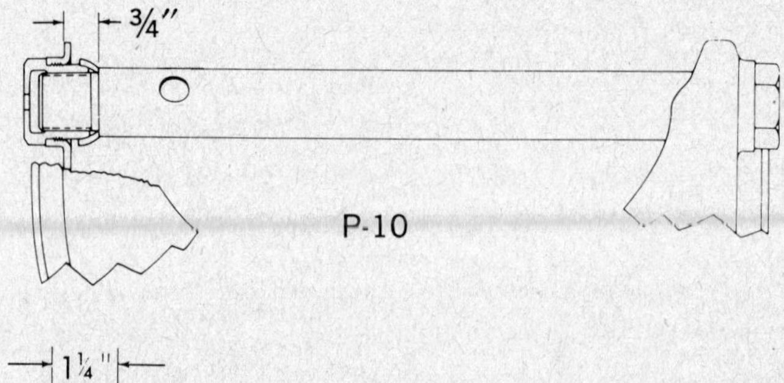

Correctly positioned lower control arm steel bushings
(© Chevrolet Div., G.M. Corp.)

nut is properly tightened, and install the cotter pin.

4. Install the brake caliper assembly.

NOTE: It is always advisable that the front end alignment be checked after any component of the front suspension has been replaced.

Adjustments

Refer to the wheel alignment specifications for necessary information.

Ball Joint Inspection

Lower Ball Joint

1. Support the control arms at the wheel hub and at the drum.
2. Measure the distance between the tip of the ball stud and the tip of the grease fitting below the ball joint.
3. Remove the support under the control arm, and measure the distance between the tip of the ball stud and the tip of the grease fitting, as in 2.
4. Subtract the smaller measurement from the larger. If the difference exceeds .094″ (or 3/32″), the ball joint must be replaced.

Upper Ball Joint

1. Check the stud for perceptible lateral shake.
2. Attempt to twist the stud in its socket with the fingers. If either test produces positive results, replace the ball joint.

Upper Ball Joint

Removal

1. Put the vehicle on a hoist. Support the lower control arm, using a floor jack, if necessary.
2. Remove the cotter pin from the upper ball stud. Loosen the stud nut just two turns.
3. Remove the brake caliper assembly and wire it to the frame for clearance.
4. Install a special tool between the ball studs, as shown.
5. Extend the bolt from the special tool to loosen the ball stud in the steering knuckle. When the stud is loose, remove the tool and stud nut.

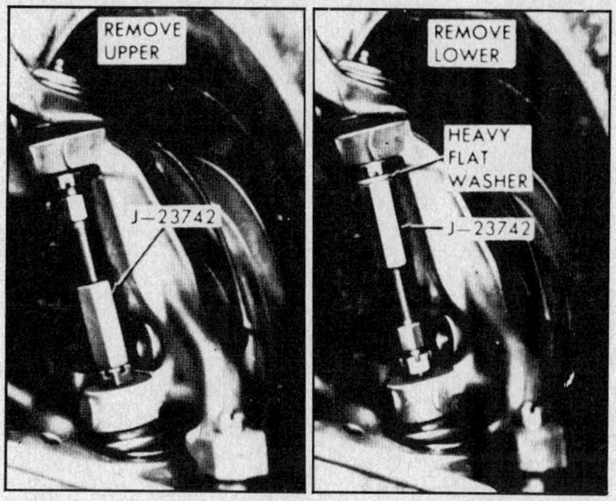

Special tool used to remove upper and lower ball joint studs (© G.M.C.)

6. Center punch the rivet heads. Drill out the rivets.
7. Remove the assembly.

Installation

1. Install a new service ball joint with fasteners supplied, torquing nuts to 45 ft lbs.
2. Install the ball stud in the steering knuckle, and install the stud nut, torquing the nuts, as specified below:
   10 Series—40-60 ft lbs
   20, 30 Series—80-100 ft lbs, plus additional torque required to cotter pin—not to exceed 130 ft lbs
3. Install a new cotter pin.
4. Install the lube fitting, and lubricate the joint.
5. Install the brake caliper assembly and tire and wheel.

Lower Ball Joint

Removal

1. Put the vehicle on a hoist. Support the lower control arm using a floor stand, if necessary.
2. Remove the tire and wheel.
3. Remove the lower stud cotter pin and loosen the stud nut just two turns.
4. Remove the brake caliper assembly and wire it to the frame for clearance.
5. Install a special tool between the ball studs, as shown.
6. Extend the bolt from the special tool to loosen the ball stud in the steering knuckle. When the stud is loosened, remove the tool and ball stud nut.
7. Pull the brake disc and knuckle assembly off the ball stud and support the upper arm with a block of wood.
8. If working on a 20 or 30 Series vehicle, cut a piece of 3″ water pipe to a length of 2⅝″. Install the special tools and, on 20 and 30 Series vehicles the pipe, as shown in the illustration.
9. Press the ball joint out of the control arm with the hex head screw. Remove the ball joint.

Installation

1. Start the new joint into the control. Then, install the special installation tools shown. Make sure bleed vent in rubber boot is inward.
2. Turn the hex head screw just far enough to seat the new joint in the control arm.
3. Lower the upper arm and start the lower ball stud into the steering knuckle.
4. Install the brake caliper assembly.
5. Install the ball stud nut and torque to 80-100 ft lbs. Then continue to torque the nut until the cotter pin hole is in alignment.

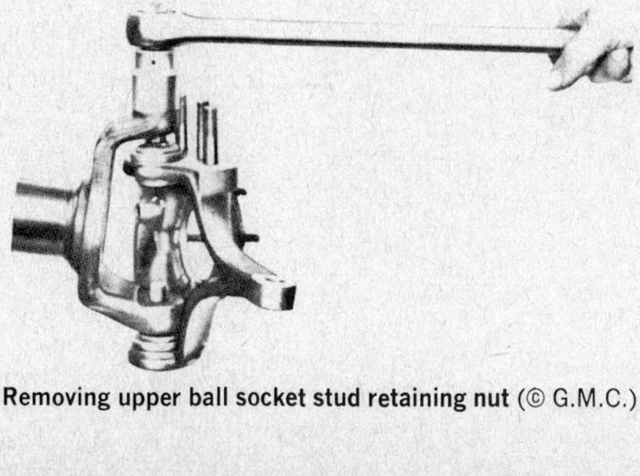

Removing upper ball socket stud retaining nut (© G.M.C.)

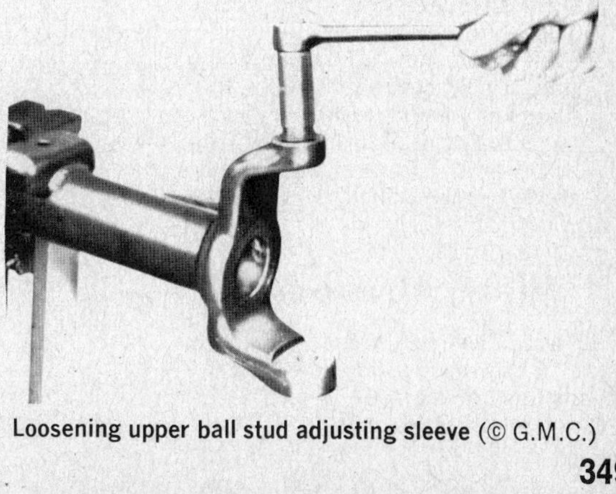

Loosening upper ball stud adjusting sleeve (© G.M.C.)

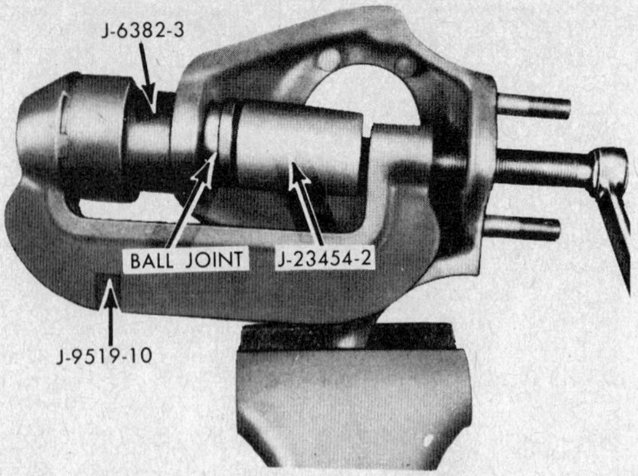

"C" clamp tool used to install lower ball joint in knuckle (© G.M.C.)

The maximum torque must not exceed 130 ft lbs.

6. Install a lube fitting and lubricate the new joint. Install the tire and wheel.

Wheel Bearing Adjustment

1500-3500 Series

1. Remove the hub cap or wheel disc from the wheel.
2. Remove the dust cap from the hub.
3. Remove the cotter pin from the spindle and spindle nut.
4. Tighten the spindle nut to 12 ft lbs. while turning the wheel assembly forward by hand to fully seat the bearings.
5. Back off the nut to the "just loose" position.
6. Hand tighten the spindle nut then loosen the spindle nut until either hole in the spindle lines up with a slot in the nut and install a new cotter pin.
7. Measure the looseness in the hub assembly. If properly adjusted the end play will be from .001-.005 in.
8. Install the dust cap, hub cap and lower the vehicle.

4500-6500 Series

1. Raise the vehicle and safely support the axle.
2. Remove the hub cap and gasket.
3. Remove the cotter pin from the adjusting nut.
4. Tighten the adjusting nut to 50 ft. lbs. while rotating the wheel in both directions.
5. Back off the nut 1/3 turn and install a new cotter pin. This adjustment should result in bearing end play of .001-.007 in.
6. Install the dust cap and wheel and lower the vehicle.

Shock Absorbers

Shock absorbers are used to dampen the rebound of the two types of springs used on the vehicles, the coil and leaf springs.

Leaf Type

The top of the shock absorbers are mounted to the frame and the bottom is usually mounted to the U bolt bracket at the axle area or to a bracket welded to the axle housing.

Coil Spring

Front

The shock absorbers are usually attached to the lower control arm at the bottom and to the frame rail at the top. On some models, the shock absorbers may be mounted through the coil spring.

Rear

The top of the shock absorber is mounted to the body or to a crossmember with the bottom mounted to a stud or bracket welded or mounted on the axle housing.

Removal and Installation

The removal and replacement is accomplished by the removal of the attaching retainers located at the top and bottom of the shock absorber, and withdrawing the shock. Replacement is the reverse of removal. Air should be purged from the shock absorber by extending with the shock absorber in the upright position, and then inverting and collapsing the shock absorber.

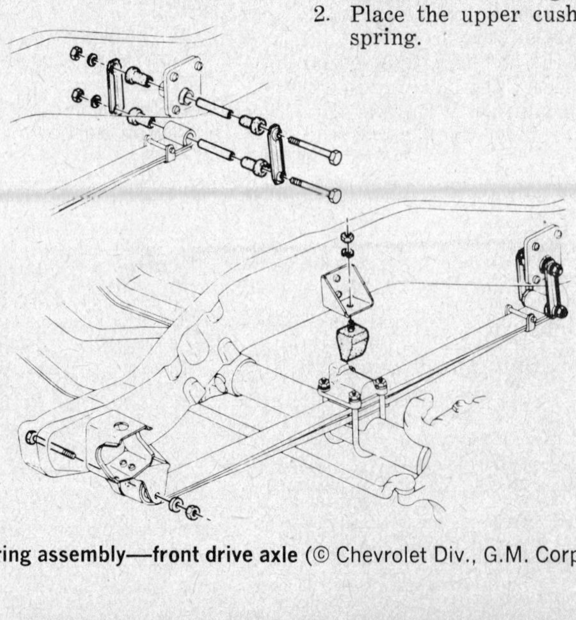

Spring assembly—front drive axle (© Chevrolet Div., G.M. Corp.)

Front Drive Axle

The front axle is a hypoid type gear unit equipped with ball joint steering knuckles, and is powered through a transfer case which may be one of two types. A full-time four wheel drive unit (New Process 203 transfer case) is used mainly with V8 engines and automatic transmission. The other type is a conventional part-time four wheel drive system.

A yoke and a trunnion universal joint as part of the drive axle, allows a continous power flow to each wheel, regardless of the turning angle.

Free-wheeling hubs are available on the front wheels except those vehicles equipped with the full time 4 wheel drive transfer case.

For repairs to the hypoid gear unit, refer to the General Repair Section.

Spring

Removal

1. Raise the vehicle on a hoist.
2. Position an adjustable jack under the front axle.
3. Situate the axle so that all tension is removed from the spring.
4. Remove shackle retaining bolt (upper).
5. Remove the front eye bolt from the spring.
6. Remove the U-bolt nuts, and remove the spring, lower plate and spring pads.
7. Remove the spring-to-shackle bolt, and remove the bushings and shackle.

Installation

1. Install the shackle bushings in the spring, and attach the shackle. DO NOT tighten bolt.
2. Place the upper cushion on the spring.

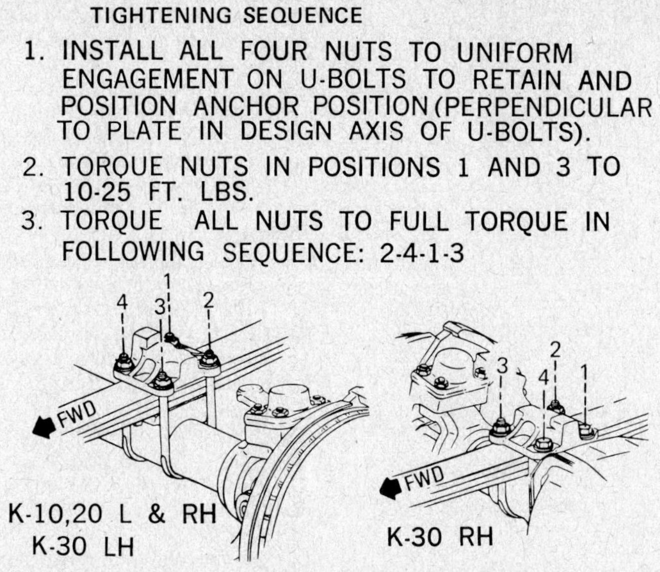
TIGHTENING SEQUENCE
1. INSTALL ALL FOUR NUTS TO UNIFORM ENGAGEMENT ON U-BOLTS TO RETAIN AND POSITION ANCHOR POSITION (PERPENDICULAR TO PLATE IN DESIGN AXIS OF U-BOLTS).
2. TORQUE NUTS IN POSITIONS 1 AND 3 TO 10-25 FT. LBS.
3. TORQUE ALL NUTS TO FULL TORQUE IN FOLLOWING SEQUENCE: 2-4-1-3
4
3
1
2
FWD
K-10,20 L & RH
K-30 LH
FWD
K-30 RH

U-bolt tightening sequence—front drive axle (© Chevrolet Div., G.M. Corp.)

3. Position the front of the spring in its mounted position at the frame, and install the bolt. DO NOT tighten bolt.
4. Position the shackle bushings in the frame, and attach the rear shackle. DO NOT tighten bolt.
5. Install the lower spring pad.
6. Install the spring retainer plate. Tighten bolts.
7. Tighten front and rear spring eye and shackle bolts.
8. Remove the vehicle from the hoist.

Locked Hub (Full-Time) K-1500-3500

Removal

1. Remove the hub cap and the snap ring.
2. Remove the drive gear.
   NOTE: Remove the pressure spring on K-1500, 2500 models.
3. Remove the wheel bearing outer lock nut, lock ring, and the wheel bearing inner adjusting nut.
4. Remove the hub and disc assembly.
5. Remove the outer wheel bearing and the spring retainer plate.
6. Drive the inner bearing cone and oil seal from the hub with the use of a brass drift. Discard the oil seal.
7. Using a brass drift, remove the inner and outer bearing cups.

Installation

1. Install the outer wheel bearing cup into the wheel tub.
2. Install the inner wheel bearing cup into the wheel hub.
3. Pack the wheel bearing cone with a suitable wheel bearing grease (high melting point type).
4. Install the cone into the cup.
5. Install a new grease seal into the inboard end of the hub.
6. Lubricate the wheel bearings; install the hub and disc and the bearings on the spindle.
7. While rotating the hub and disc, torque the inner adjusting nut to 50 ft. lbs.
8. Back off the inner adjusting nut.
9. While rotating the hub and disc, torque the inner adjusting nut to 35 ft. lbs.
10. Again, back off the inner adjusting nut a maximum of 3/8 turn.
    K-1500, 2500 models: Assemble the adjusting nut lock by aligning the nearest hole in lock with the adjusting nut pin. Install the outer lock nut and torque to 80 ft. lbs.
    K-3500 models: Assemble the lockwasher and outer locknut. Torque the outer locknut to 65 ft. lbs. Bend one tab of the lockwasher over the inner nut a minimum of 30 degrees. Bend one tab of the lockwasher over the outer nut a minimum of 60 degrees.
    NOTE: End play for all models is .001-.010 inch.
11. Install the pressure spring, drive gear, snap ring and hub cap.

Free-Wheeling Hub (Part-Time)

The engagement and disengagement of free-wheeling hubs is a manual operation which must be performed at each front wheel. The transfer case control lever must be in 2-wheel drive position when locking or unlocking hubs. Both hubs must be in the fully locked or fully unlocked position. They must not be in the free-wheeling position when low all-wheel-drive is used as the additional torque output in this position can subject the rear axle to severe strain, and rear axle failure may result.

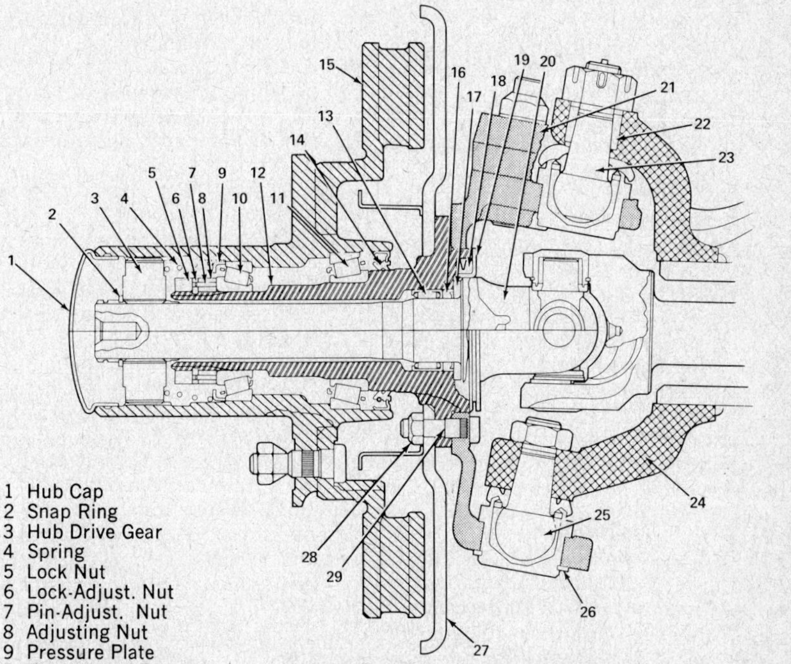

1 Hub Cap
2 Snap Ring
3 Hub Drive Gear
4 Spring
5 Lock Nut
6 Lock-Adjust. Nut
7 Pin-Adjust. Nut
8 Adjusting Nut
9 Pressure Plate
10 Outer-Wheel Bearing
11 Inner-Wheel Bearing
12 Spindle
13 Spindle Bearing
14 Seal
15 Hub-and-Disc Assy.
16 Oil Seal
17 Spacer
18 Dust Seal
19 Deflector
20 Axle Outer Shaft
21 Knuckle
22 Adjusting Sleeve
23 Upper Ball Joint
24 Yoke
25 Lower Ball Joint
26 Retaining Ring
27 Caliper Support Brkt.
28 Spindle Retaining Nut
29 Spindle Retaining Bolt

Locked hub assembly—front drive axle
(© Chevrolet Div., G.M. Corp.)

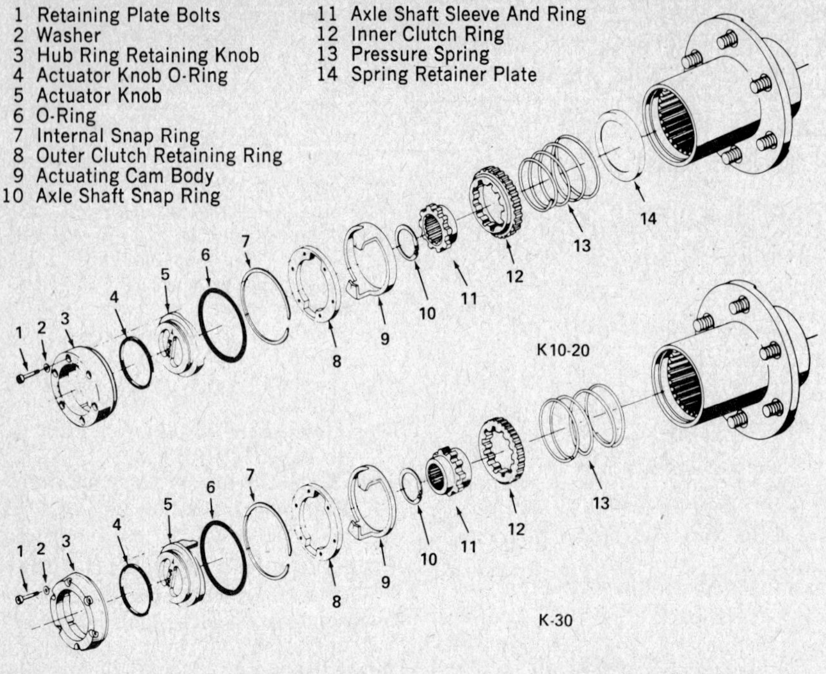

Free-wheeling hub—exploded view (earlier models similar)
(© Chevrolet Div., G.M. Corp.)

K-1500, K2500 All (Current Models)

Removal

1. Turn the actuator to the LOCK position.
2. Raise the vehicle on a hoist.
3. Remove the six retaining plate bolts.
4. Remove the retaining plate, actuator knob, and O-ring.
5. Remove the internal snap ring, outer clutch retaining ring, and actuating cam body.
6. Remove the axle shaft snap ring.

   NOTE: It may be necessary to first relieve pressure from the axle shaft snap ring.
7. Remove the wheel bearing outer lock nut and lock ring.
8. Remove the wheel bearing inner adjusting nut.
9. Remove the hub and disc assembly, outer wheel bearing, and the spring retainer plate.
10. Drive the inner bearing cone and oil seal from the hub with a brass drift. Discard the oil seal.
11. Using a brass drift, remove the inner and outer bearing cups.

Installation

NOTE: All parts should be lubricated with an ample amount of high speed grease prior to installation.

1. Install the outer wheel bearing cup into the wheel hub.
2. Install the inner wheel bearing cup into the wheel hub.
3. Pack the wheel bearing cone with a suitable wheel bearing grease (high melting point type).
4. Install the cone into the cup.
5. Lubricate the wheel bearings; install the hub and disc and the bearings on the spindle.
6. While rotating the hub and disc, torque the inner adjusting nut to 50 ft. lbs.
7. Back off the inner adjusting nut.
8. While rotating the hub and disc, torque the inner adjusting nut to 35 ft. lbs.
9. Again, back off the inner adjusting nut a maximum of 3/8 turn.
10. Assemble the adjusting nut lock by aligning the nearest hole in lock with the adjusting nut pin.
11. Install outer lock nut and torque to 50 ft. lbs.

    NOTE: Hub end play should be .001-.010 inch.
12. Install the spring retainer plate over the spindle nuts with the flange side facing the bearing, and seat the retainer against the bearing outer cup.
13. Install the pressure spring.

    NOTE: The large diameter of the spring seats against the retaining plate. When the spring is seated, it extends past the spindle nuts by approximately 7/8".
14. Install the inner clutch ring and bushing into the axle shaft sleeve and clutch ring; install unit as an assembly onto the axle shaft.
15. While pressing in on the assembly, install the axle shaft snap ring.

    NOTE: To facilitate snap ring installation, thread a 7/16 x 20 bolt in the end of the axle shaft, and pull outward on the axle shaft.
16. Install the actuating cam body. Cam faces outward.
17. Install the outer clutch retaining ring and the internal snap ring.
18. Install the O-ring on the retaining plate.
19. Install the actuating knob and retaining plate.

    NOTE: Actuating knob should be installed in the LOCK position. The grooves in the knob must fit into the actuator cam body.
20. Install the six cover bolts and seals. Torque bolts to 30 ft. lbs.
21. Turn the actuating knob to the FREE position, and check free-wheeling operation.
22. Remove vehicle from hoist.

K-2500 Early Models

Removal

1. Raise the vehicle on a hoist. Turn the hub key knob to "Free" position.
2. Remove the allen head bolts, and remove the hub cap assembly and gasket from the wheel hub. Remove the exterior sleeve extension housing and gasket.
3. Turn the hub key knob to the locked position. Drive out the key knob retainer roll pin.
4. Remove the outer clutch gear assembly.
5. Remove the lock ring. Remove the slotted adjustment sleeve.
6. Remove the spring, and then remove the lock ring securing the plastic key knob to the hub retainer cap.
7. Remove the O-ring from the plastic hub key knob.
8. Remove the snap ring from the end of the axle shaft. Pull the internal clutch gear and its collar.

Installation

1. Apply a high speed grease to both faces of the bushing, the splines, the teeth of the inner and outer clutch gears, and to the actuating cam.
2. Install the internal clutch collar and gear. Install the lock ring at the end of the axle shaft.
3. Lubricate the O-ring and install it in the groove of the plastic hub key knob. Insert the knob into the retainer cap.
4. Install the lock ring into the hub retainer cap. Push outward on the plastic knob to ensure that the lock ring is fully engaged, and correct its position as necessary.
5. Install the slotted adjustment sleeve with the two tabs outward.
6. Install the key knob retaining roll pin with the knob in the locked position. Install the spring.
7. Place the outer clutch gear assembly on top of the spring, compress the spring, and install the lock ring at the sleeve end. Turn the key knob to the "Free" position.

8. Install a 3/8" bolt 5 inches long into one of the hub housing bolt holes.
9. Install the new exterior sleeve extension housing gasket and the housing and retainer cap assembly and gasket. Install the allen head bolts, and tighten securely.
10. Turn the hub key knob to the locked position and check for proper engagement. Install the wheel and tire.

Axle Assembly

Removal

1. Disconnect the drive shaft from the front axle. Raise the vehicle far enough to take the weight off the front springs and place jack stands under the truck.
2. Disconnect the connecting rod at the steering arms.
3. Disconnect the brake hoses at the frame fittings, and cover all open ends.
4. Disconnect the shock absorbers at the axle brackets.
5. Disconnect the axle vent tube clip at the differential housing.
6. Unfasten the U-bolts, raise the truck further, as necessary, and roll the axle out from underneath.

Installation

1. With truck on axle stands, roll the axle under the truck. Lower the truck until axle and truck are in proper relative positions. Again support the vehicle with axle stands.
2. Attach the shock absorbers to the axle brackets. Connect the brake hoses to the frame fittings and fill and bleed the brake system.
3. Attach the steering connecting rod at the steering arms.
4. Connect the drive axle to the front differential.

Axle Shaft Assembly

Removal

1. Remove the free-wheeling hubs as outlined, if so equipped.
2. Remove the wheel bearing outer lock nut, lock ring, and inner adjusting nut.
3. Remove the hub assembly from the spindle.
4. Remove the spindle retaining bolts and tap the end of the spindle with a soft faced hammer, to separate the spindle from the knuckle.
5. Remove the axle shaft and joint assembly by pulling outward on the shaft.
6. Repairs to the wheel hub assembly and to the axle universal joint can be accomplished at this time.

Installation

1. Install a new grease seal onto the slinger of the axle shaft, with the lip of the seal facing toward the spindle.
2. Install the axle shaft into the housing and engage the splines with the pinion side gears of the differential.
3. Place the bronze thrust washer on the axle shaft with the chamfered edge towards the slinger and install the spindle onto the knuckle.
4. Torque the spindle nuts to 45 ft. lbs. and assemble the hub to the spindle. Torque the inner adjusting nut to 50 ft. lbs. while rotating the hub. Back off the inner nut and retorque to 35 ft. lbs. while still rotating the hub. To complete, back off the inner nut an additional 3/8 of a turn maximum.
5. Assemble the lock washer and the outer lock nut to the spindle. Torque the outer lock nut to 50 ft. lbs. minimum. The hub should have .001 to .010 inch end play.

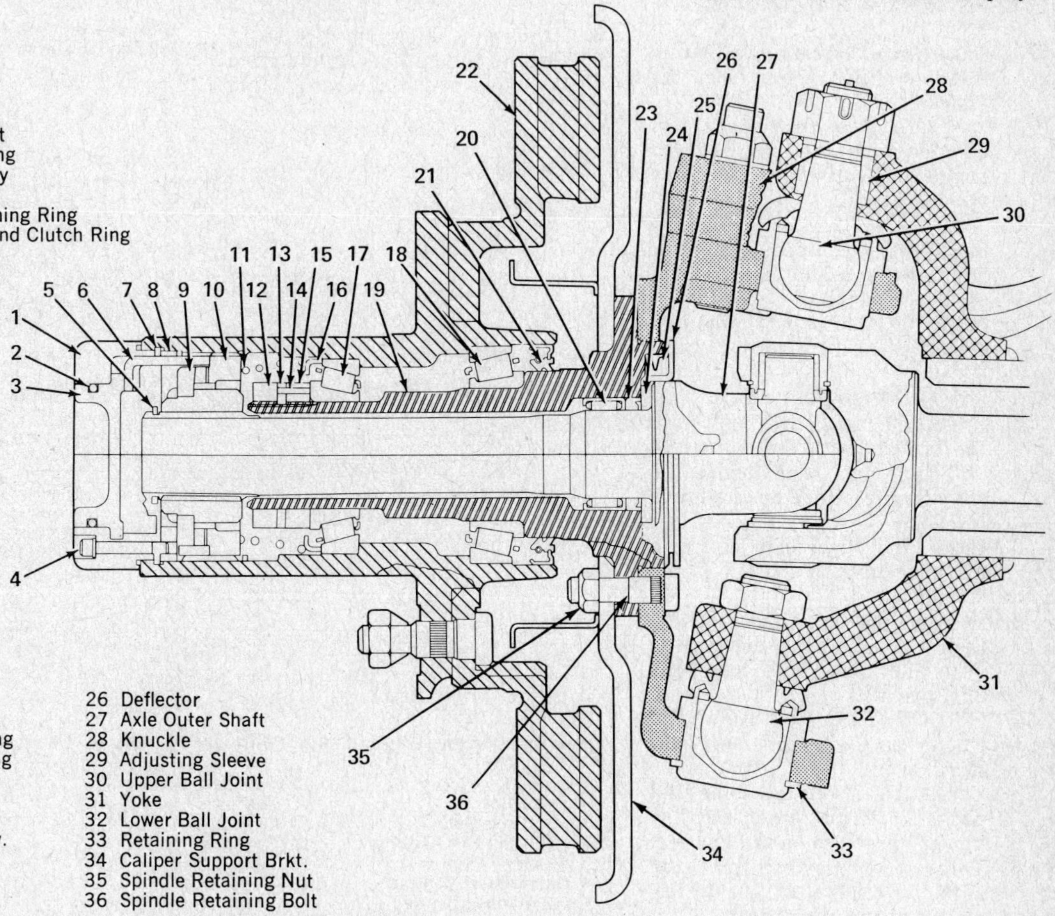

1 Retaining Plate
2 O-Ring
3 Actuator Knob
4 Retaining Plate Bolt
5 Axle Shaft Snap Ring
6 Actuating Cam Body
7 Internal Snap Ring
8 Outer Clutch Retaining Ring
9 Axle Shaft Sleeve And Clutch Ring
10 Inner Clutch Ring
11 Spring
12 Lock Nut
13 Lock-Adjust. Nut
14 Pin-Adjust. Nut
15 Adjusting Nut
16 Pressure Plate
17 Outer-Wheel Bearing
18 Inner-Wheel Bearing
19 Spindle
20 Spindle Bearing
21 Seal
22 Hub-And-Disc Assy.
23 Oil Seal
24 Spacer
25 Dust Seal
26 Deflector
27 Axle Outer Shaft
28 Knuckle
29 Adjusting Sleeve
30 Upper Ball Joint
31 Yoke
32 Lower Ball Joint
33 Retaining Ring
34 Caliper Support Brkt.
35 Spindle Retaining Nut
36 Spindle Retaining Bolt

Steering knuckle/ball joint assy. (with free-wheeling hub)
(© Chevrolet Div., G.M. Corp.)

6. If the vehicle is equipped with free-wheeling hubs, refer to the installation procedure for correct installation and if not equipped, install the hub cap assembly.

Steering Knuckle (With Ball Joints) K-1500, 2500

Removal

1. With the spindle and axle removed, as previously outlined, disconnect the tie rod end from the steering arm.
2. If necessary for working clearance, remove the steering arm from the knuckle.

   NOTE: If the steering arm is removed, discard the three self-locking nuts and replace them with new self-locking nuts upon assembly.
3. Remove the upper and lower ball joint retaining nuts.

   NOTE: The upper ball joint stud and nut have a cotter pin retainer, while the lower ball joint stud and nut have none.
4. With a wedge type tool, separate the lower ball joint stud from the knuckle. Repeat this operation for the upper ball joint stud.
5. Remove the snap ring retainer from the lower ball joint. With the aid of a "C" clamp tool, press the lower ball joint from the knuckle.

   NOTE: The lower ball joint must be removed before any service can be performed on the upper ball joint.
6. With the aid of the "C" clamp tool, press the upper ball joint from the knuckle. Replacement of the knuckle can be accomplished at this point in the disassembly.

Installation

1. Press the lower ball joint into the knuckle with the aid of the "C" type tool and install the snap ring retainer on the lower ball joint.
2. Install the upper ball joint into the knuckle with the aid of the "C" clamp tool.
3. Position the ball joint studs in their respective openings on the yoke and install the new nuts finger tight.

   NOTE: The castellated nut is placed on the upper ball joint stud.
4. Torque the lower ball joint stud nut to 70 ft. lbs. while exerting upward pressure on the knuckle.
5. Torque the upper ball joint stud adjusting sleeve to 50 ft. lbs. using a spanner type socket.
6. Torque the upper ball joint stud nut to 100 ft. lbs. Apply additional torque if necessary to align the cotter pin hole in the nut and stud.
7. Reassemble the steering arm, if removed, tie rod ends, spindle, axle and hub as outlined previously.
8. Torque the steering arm nuts to 90 ft. lbs. and the tie rod nut to 45 ft. lbs. and install the cotter pin.

Steering Knuckle (With King Pins) K-3500

Removal

1. Remove the hub and spindle.

   NOTE: It may be necessary to tap lightly on the spindle with a rawhide hammer in order to free it from the knuckle.
2. Remove the four cap nuts from the upper king pin.

   NOTE: Spring pressure will force the cap up.
3. Remove the cap, spring and gasket. Discard the gasket.
4. Remove the four cap screws from the lower king pin bearing.
5. Remove the cap and the lower king pin.
6. Remove the upper king pin bushing.
7. Remove the knuckle from the yoke.
8. Remove he king pin felt seal.
9. Remove the upper king pin from the yoke with a very large breaker bar and any suitable adapter designed to fit the king pin.

   NOTE: Considerable force will be required to remove the king pin from the yoke as the king pin is orginally torqued to 500-600 ft. lbs.
10. Remove the lower king pin bearing cup, cone, grease retainer, and seal. Discard the seal. Discard the grease retainer if damaged.

Installation

1. Install the lower king pin bearing cup and a new grease retainer.

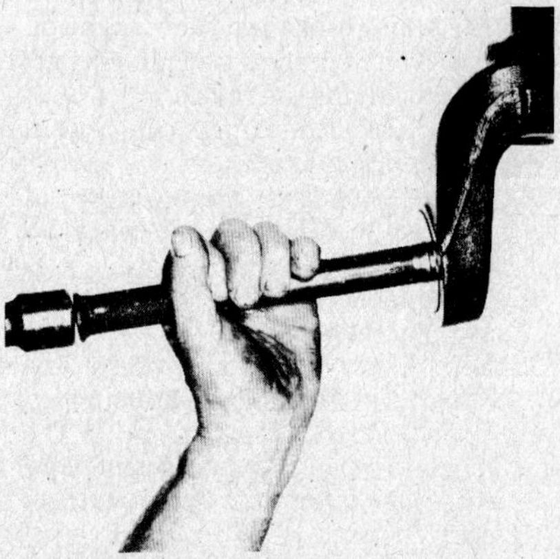

Installing grease retainer—front drive yoke w/king pins
(© Chevrolet Div., G.M. Corp.)

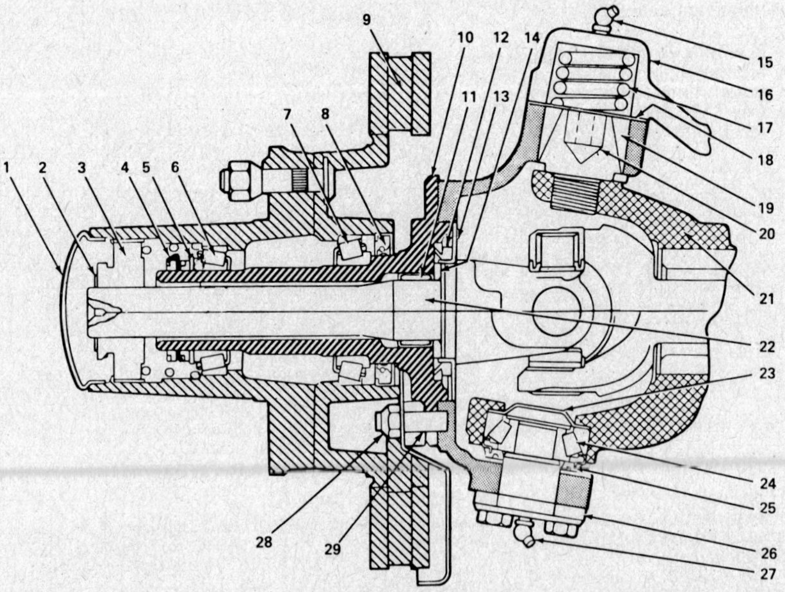

Steering knuckle/king pin assy. (with locked hub) (© Chevrolet Div., G.M. Corp.)

1 Hub Cap
2 Snap Ring
3 Hub Drive Gear
4 Adjusting Nut Assembly
5 Washer
6 Outer Wheel Bearing
7 Inner Wheel Bearing
8 Seal
9 Hub-And-Disc Assembly
10 Spindle
11 Spindle Bearing
12 Seal
13 Deflector
14 Spacer
15 Lube Fitting
16 Upper Bearing
17 Pressure Spring
18 Gasket
19 Kingpin Bushing
20 Kingpin
21 Yoke
22 Outer Axle Shaft
23 Grease Retainer
24 Lower Bearing
25 Seal
26 Bearing Cup
27 Lube Fitting
28 Spindle Attaching Nut
29 Spindle Attaching Bolt

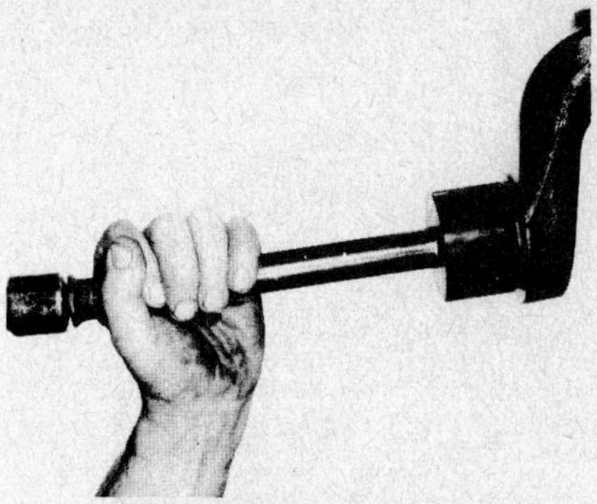

Installing oil seal—front drive yoke w/king pins (© Chevrolet Div., G.M. Corp.)

2. Fill the grease retainer with grease.
3. Lubricate the bearing cone with grease. Install the bearing cone.
4. Install a new oil seal for the lower king pin bearing.
   NOTE: The oil seal will protrude slightly from the surface of the yoke flange when fully installed.
5. Install the upper king pin, and torque to 500-600 ft. lbs.
6. Assemble the felt seal to the king pin.
7. Position the steering knuckle over the king pin, and install the tapered bushing over the king pin.

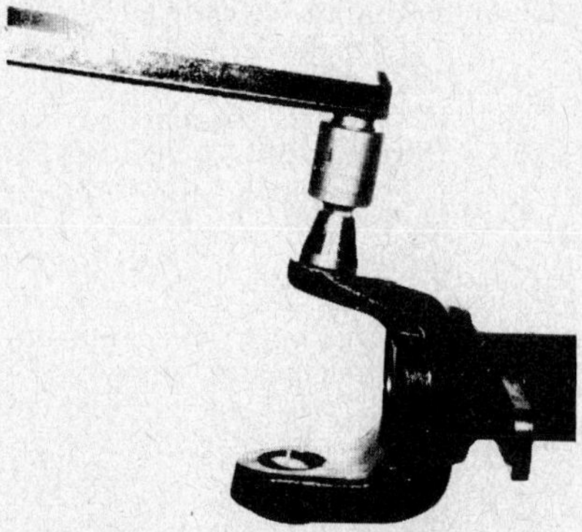

Installing upper king pin—front drive axle (© Chevrolet Div., G.M. Corp.)

8. Install the lower king pin and the lower bearing cap. Torque the cap screws to 70-90 ft. lbs.
9. Position the compression spring over the upper king pin bushing.
10. Install the upper bearing cap with a new gasket. Torque the nuts to 70-90 ft. lbs.

Ball Joint Adjustment K-1500, 2500

1. Raise the vehicle on a hoist.
2. Disconnect the connecting rod and the tie rod to allow the steering knuckle to move freely.
3. Attach a spring scale to the tie rod mounting hole of the steering arm.

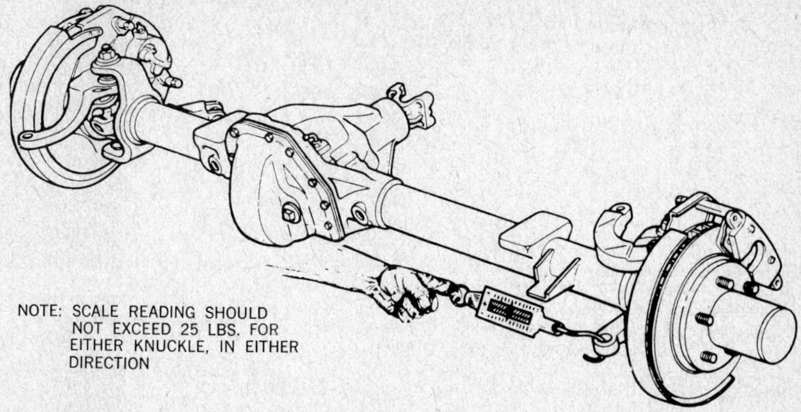

Checking front drive axle ball joint adjustment (© Chevrolet Div., G.M. Corp.)

4. Move the knuckle to the straight-ahead position.
5. Determine the rght angle pull required to keep the knuckle turning after initial movement from standing still. The pull should not exceed 25 lbs. for each knuckle assembly.
6. If the effort required to maintain turning movement is in excess of 25 lbs., then remove the upper ball stud nut, and loosen the ball stud adjusting sleeve as required. Tighten the ball stud nut and recheck the turning effort.

Wheel Bearing Adjustment

Refer to the Installation procedures under Locked Hub (Full-Time) or Free-Wheeling Hub (Part-Time) for the corresponding wheel bearing adjustment instructions.

STEERING GEAR

Instructions covering the overhaul of light duty steering gear will be found in the General Repair Section.

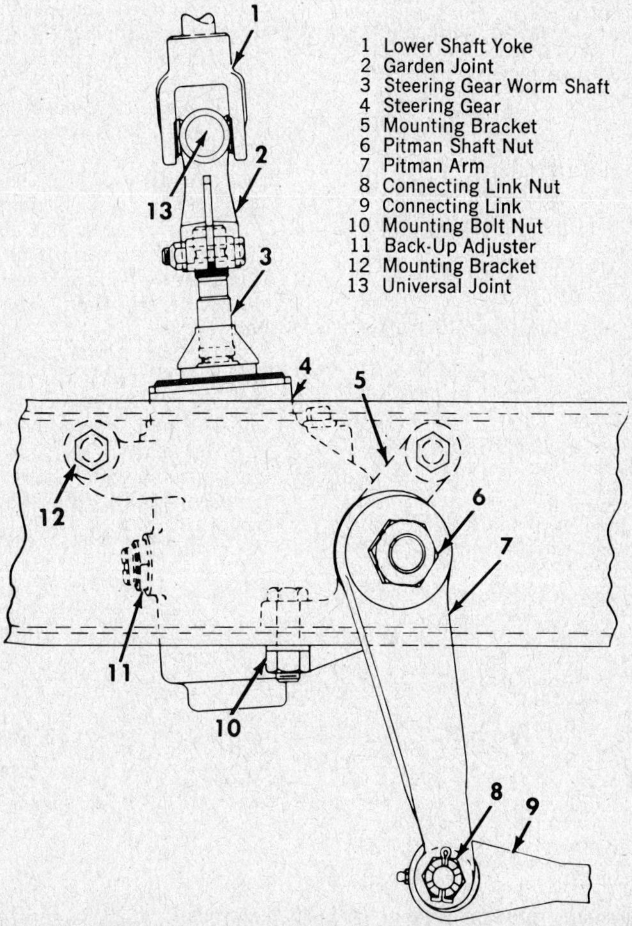

Manually operated steering gear installed—steel tilt (© Chevrolet Div., G.M. Corp.)

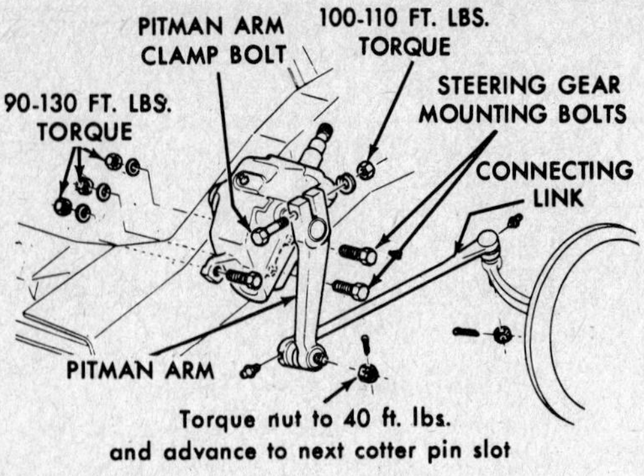

Steering gear and shaft—with flexible coupling (© G.M.C.)

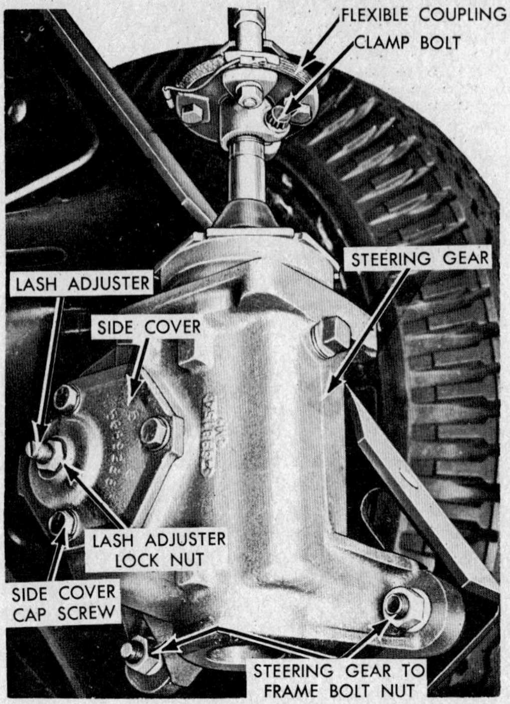

Steering gear and linkage—conventional models—typical (© G.M.C)

Standard Steering Gear

Medium and Heavy Trucks

Removal

1. Disconnect steering linkage from pitman arm.
2. Scribe alignment marks on worm shaft and clamp yoke for reassembly.
3. Remove bolts attaching clamp yoke or coupling to steering gear worm shaft.
4. Remove pitman arm nut and washer, then use a puller to remove arm.
5. Remove attaching bolts, nuts and washers, then remove steering gear.

Installation

1. Turn steering wheel to straight-ahead position and center steering gear.
2. Position the steering gear, matching the alignment marks.
3. Install attaching bolts, washers and nuts.
4. Connect clamp yoke or coupling to steering gear worm shaft with attaching parts and torque to specifications.
5. Align pitman arm and shaft; press arm onto shaft and torque to specifications.

Light Duty Trucks

Removal

1. Drive the vehicle a short distance and move the wheels to the straight ahead position.
2. On P models, remove the lower universal joint pinch bolt. On C and K models, remove the bolts from the flexible coupling to steering shaft flange. Mark the relationship between the universal yoke and the wormshaft.
3. Mark the relationship between the pitman arm and the pitman shaft, and remove the pitman shaft nut or pitman arm pinch bolt.
4. Remove the pitman arm from the shaft with a special puller.
5. Remove the bolts between steering gear and frame. Remove the steering gear.
6. On C and K models, remove the flexible coupling pinch bolt and remove the coupling from the wormshaft.

Installation

1. On C and K models:
   a. Install the flexible coupling onto the steering gear wormshaft. The flats in the coupling and on the shaft must line up. Then, push the coupling onto the shaft until the wormshaft bottoms on the coupling reinforcement. Install the pinch bolt. *Note that the coupling bolt must pass through the shaft undercut.*
   b. Position the steering gear, guiding the coupling bolt into the steering shaft flange.
   c. Install the steering gear to frame bolts. Torque to 65 ft-lbs.
   d. In cases where plastic spacers are used on the flexible coupling alignment pins, make sure they are bottomed on the pins, torque the flange

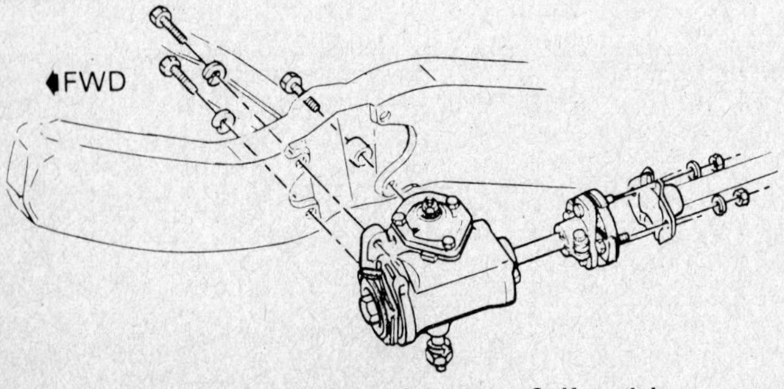

Manually operated steering gear—C, K models
(© Chevrolet Div., G.M. Corp.)

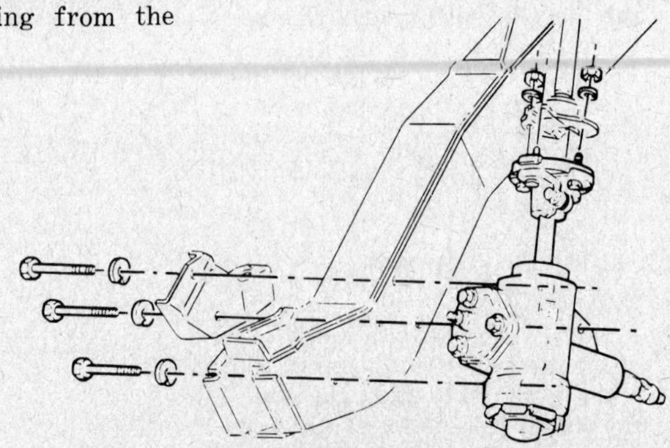
Manually operated steering gear—G, P models
(© Chevrolet Div., G.M Corp.)

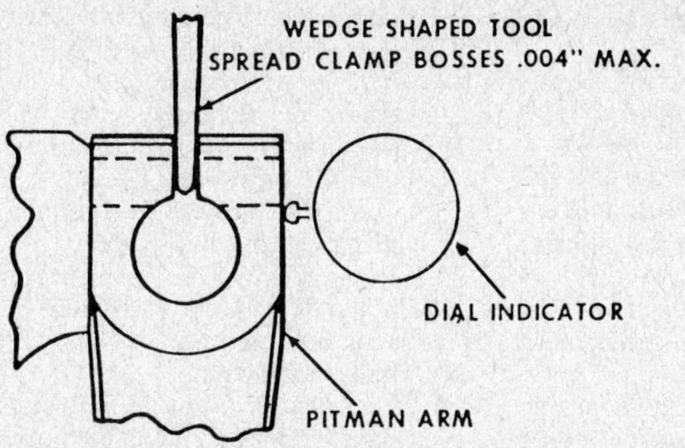

Pitman arm removal—dial indicator and wedge shaped tool installed (© G.M.C.)

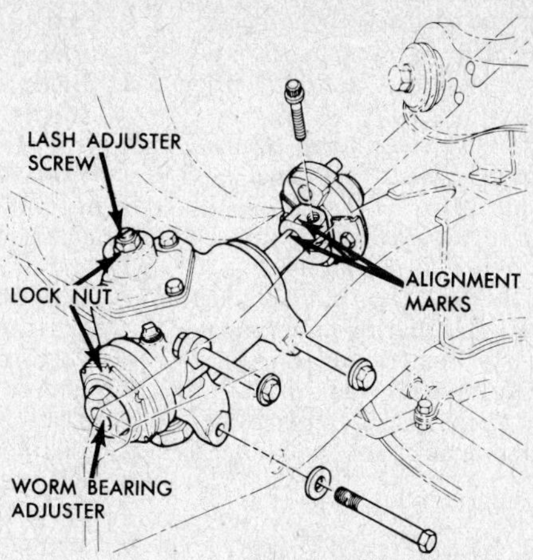

Steering gear adjustment points—typical (© G.M.C.)

bolt nuts, and then remove the spacers.

e. If plastic spacers are not used, center the pins in the steering shaft flange slots, and install and torque the flange bolt nuts.

2. On P models:
   a. Position the steering gear, guiding wormshaft into the U-joint assembly. Line up the marks made at removal. In cases where a new steering gear is being installed, line up the mark on the wormshaft with the slit in the yoke of the U-joint.
   b. Install the steering gear to frame bolts, and torque to 65 ft-lbs.
   c. Install and torque the universal joint pinch bolt. Make sure the bolt passes through the shaft undercut.
3. Install the pitman arm onto the shaft, lining up marks made at removal. Install the shaft nut or pinch bolt and torque to 140 ft-lbs.

Adjustments

1. Check tire pressure and inspect steering linkage.
2. Check gear housing for lubricant, tighten cover side plate.
3. Check steering gear housing to frame rail bolts.
4. Set wheels in straight ahead position.
5. Disconnect drag link from pitman arm, remove pitman arm on Vans.
6. Loosen sector (cross) shaft lock nut and back off lash adjuster ¼ turn. This lessens steering worm bearing load by reducing tooth mesh contact.
7. Check load on steering gear by measuring pull on steering wheel with scale. Pull is measured at rim of wheel with scale tangent to rim of wheel (½ to 3 lb. pull according to size of truck).
8. If pull is not within limits, adjust worm bearings. Loosen worm bearing lock nut and turn adjusting nut in until there is no perceptible end play. Tighten lock nut. Using an inch-pound torque wrench and socket on steering wheel nut (remove horn wire and button), measure torque (3 inch pounds to 14 inch pounds according to size of truck). A rough feeling when rotating steering wheel indicates defective worm bearings. Some early heavy duty steering gears use shims under steering gear housing top cover, and also use a back-up adjuster. Removal of shims decreases worm bearing end play. Back-up adjuster setting is made last. After adjusting worm bearings and lash, then tighten back-up adjuster until adjuster bottoms against ball nut return guide clamp, then back-off adjuster ⅛ to ¼ turn and secure with lock nut.
9. After proper adjustment of worm bearings is obtained, center steering wheel by turning wheel gently from one stop to the other, counting the number of turns. Turn wheel back exactly half way to center position (high point). Mark steering wheel rim at top or bottom center with tape. Turn lash (slot-

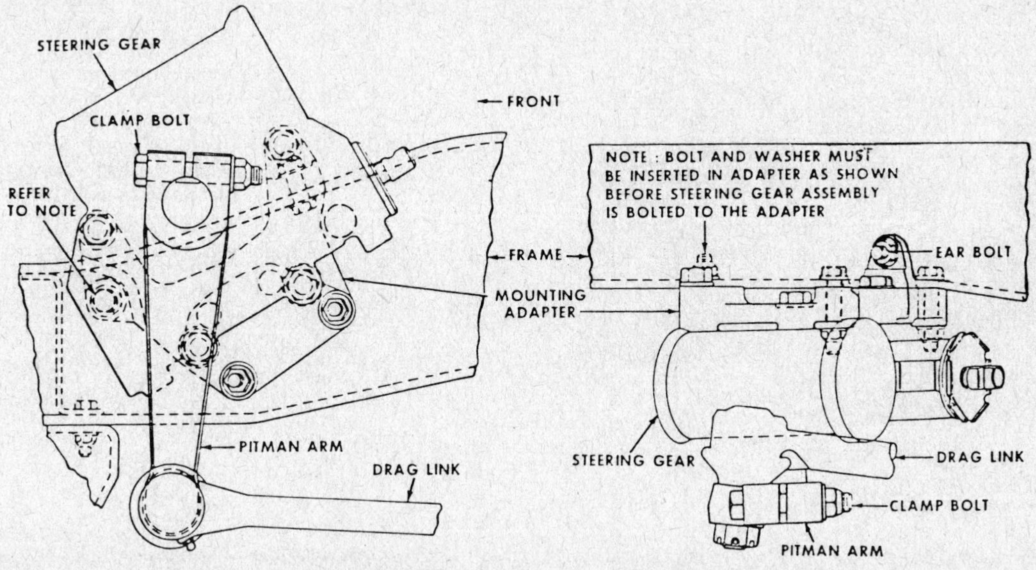

Integral power steering gear (© G.M.C.)

ted) adjuster clockwise to take out all lash in gear teeth and tighten lock nut. Check steering free play.

NOTE: If maximum adjustment is exceeded, turn lash adjuster screw back (counter-clockwise) and then come in (clockwise) slowly on adjustment.

CAUTION: Do not bounce steering wheel hard against stops with drag link removed, worm ball guide damage can result.

10. Connect drag link or replace pitman arm, road test and check steering.

Power Steering Gear

Medium and Heavy Trucks

Integral Type 553-DU—Removal

1. Mark steering gear worm shaft and clamp yoke or coupling for reassembly.
2. Remove connecting rod from pitman arm.
3. Remove attaching pinch bolt, nuts and washers from pitman arm; press pitman arm from shaft.
4. Drain as much fluid as possible from steering gear.
5. Disconnect all tubes from the control valve ports. Plug all tubes and cover all ports to prevent any dirt from entering the system.
6. Remove attaching bolts, nuts and washers from the steering gear and control valve assembly. Remove steering gear.

Installation

1. Center steering wheel and steering gear.
2. Install steering gear by reversing the removal procedure. Make certain to match all alignment marks and to torque all nuts to specifications.
3. Bleed the system and fill reservoir to the proper level.

Adjustments—Type-553-DU

The only adjustment that can be made on the vehicle is the over-center adjustment.

1. Disconnect pitman arm from shaft, marking the alignment positions.
2. Loosen pitman shaft adjusting screw nut and turn screw out to its limit of travel.
3. Disconnect battery ground cable.
4. Remove horn button.
5. Center steering wheel.
6. Check combined ball and thrust bearing preload by using an in. lbs. torque wrench. Note the highest reading.
7. Tighten pitman shaft adjusting screw and torque steering shaft nut to specifications.
8. Install horn button and connect battery ground cable.
9. Connect pitman arm to shaft, making certain to match alignment marks.

NOTE: There are no on-vehicle adjustments of the type 710-D steering gears.

Refer to the General Repair Section for overhaul procedures.

Integral Type 710-D Removal

1. Center steering gear by positioning tires straight ahead and remove Pitman arm clamp bolt.
2. Install Pitman arm puller and remove Pitman arm.

   NOTE: It may be necessary to spread the Pitman arm clamp bosses slightly to remove arm. Install a dial indicator as shown. Insert a wedge shaped tool and spread clamp bosses .004 in.

3. Remove pot joint to stub shaft clamp bolt (conventional cab) or carden joint to stub shaft clamp bolt (school bus model). Remove steering column plastic cap and metal cover at dash. Remove column clamp cap screws. Pull steering shaft up until shaft coupling clears stub shaft.
4. Remove steering gear mounting bolts. It will be necessary to use two technicians to remove gear bolt as shown.
5. Disconnect lines from steering gear and plug lines. Turn gear in a vertical position (stub shaft up) and work gear down between frame and inner fender panel and remove gear.
6. Remove adapter to gear bolts.

Installation

1. Install adapter to gear with washers under bolt heads and torque bolts to specifications.

   NOTE: One adapter plate to frame bolt and washer (lower forward bolt as shown) must be installed before adapter is bolted to the gear.

2. Holding gear in the vertical position (stub shaft up) push gear up between inner fender panel and frame and position ear on adapter plate over frame and push the bolt previously installed into frame and install washer and nut only finger tight. With gear loose, reach between gear and frame and remove line plugs and install line fittings to gear.
3. Install steering gear to frame mounting bolts with washers and torque to specifications.
4. With one technician inside cab centering steering wheel and one at steering gear with steering gear centered, install pot joint or carden joint over stub shaft. Push steering shaft down until coupling lines up with the cross groove in stub shaft. Install clamp bolt and adjust pot joint to 3.08 in. Tighten steering column clamp cap screws, replace metal cover panel and column plastic cap.
5. Install Pitman arm to Pitman shaft, install clamp bolt and torque to specifications.

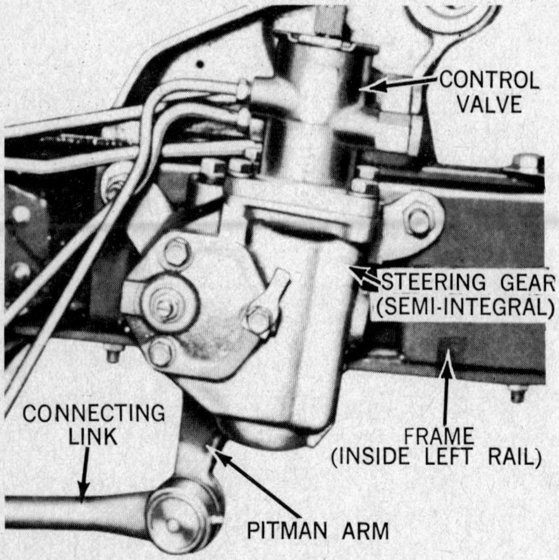

Semi-integral power steering gear—steel tilt cap
(© Chevrolet Div., G.M. Corp.)

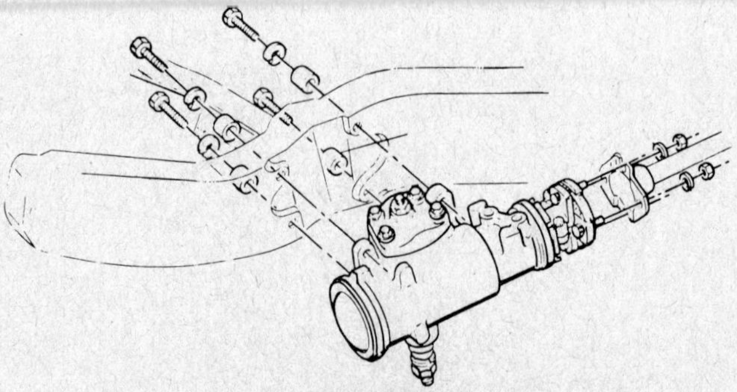

Power steering gear—light duty trucks—typical
(© Chevrolet Div., G.M. Corp.)

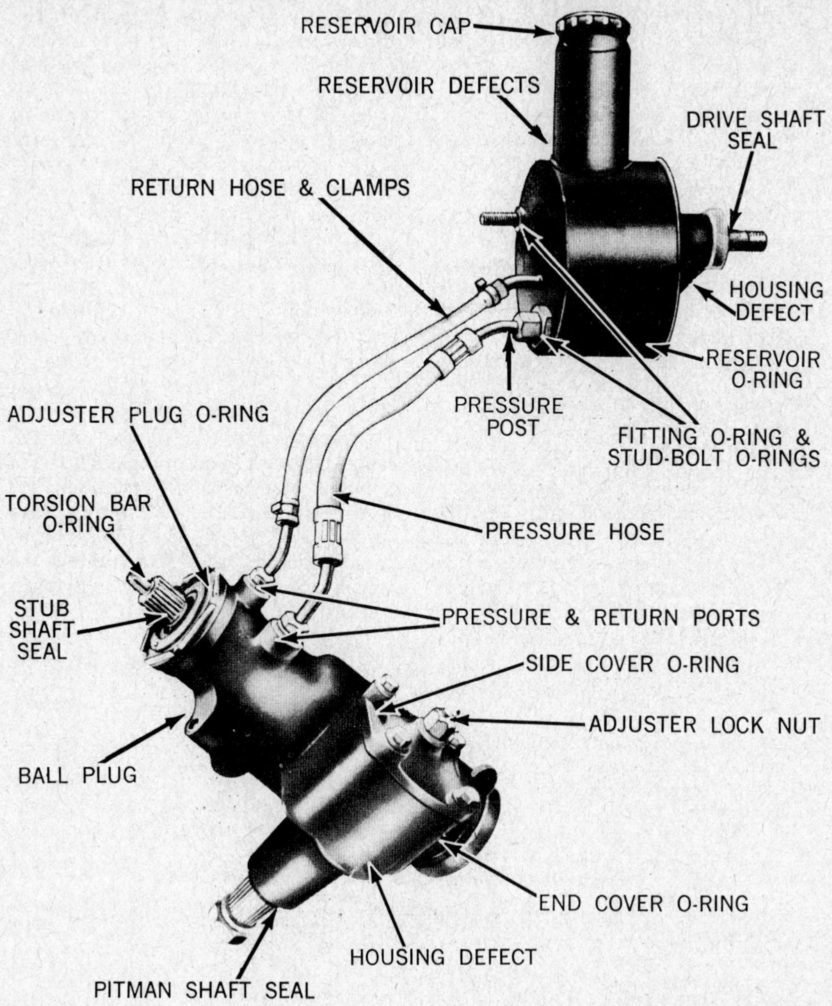

Potential leakage areas—light duty power steering system (© Chevrolet Div., G.M.C.)

6. Bleed the system and fill reservoir to the proper level.

Light Duty Trucks

Removal

1. Disconnect the hoses at the gear and secure the open ends in a raised position.
2. Cap the open ends of the hoses and plug the openings of the steering unit.
3. Remove the flexible coupling to flange bolts on G, C, and K models, or the U-joint pinch bolt on P models. Mark the relationship between the universal yoke and stub shaft.
4. Mark the relationship between the pitman arm and shaft. Remove the shaft nut or pinch bolt from the pitman arm.
5. Remove the arm from the shaft with a special puller.
6. Remove the steering gear mounting bolts, and remove the gear. On G, C, and K models, also remove the pinch bolt from the flexible coupling, and remove the coupling.

Installation

1. Where applicable, install the flexible coupling, aligning the flats in coupling and on shaft. Make sure the stub shaft bottoms on the coupling reinforcement. Install the pinch bolt and torque to 18 in lbs. Make sure the bolt passes through the shaft undercut.

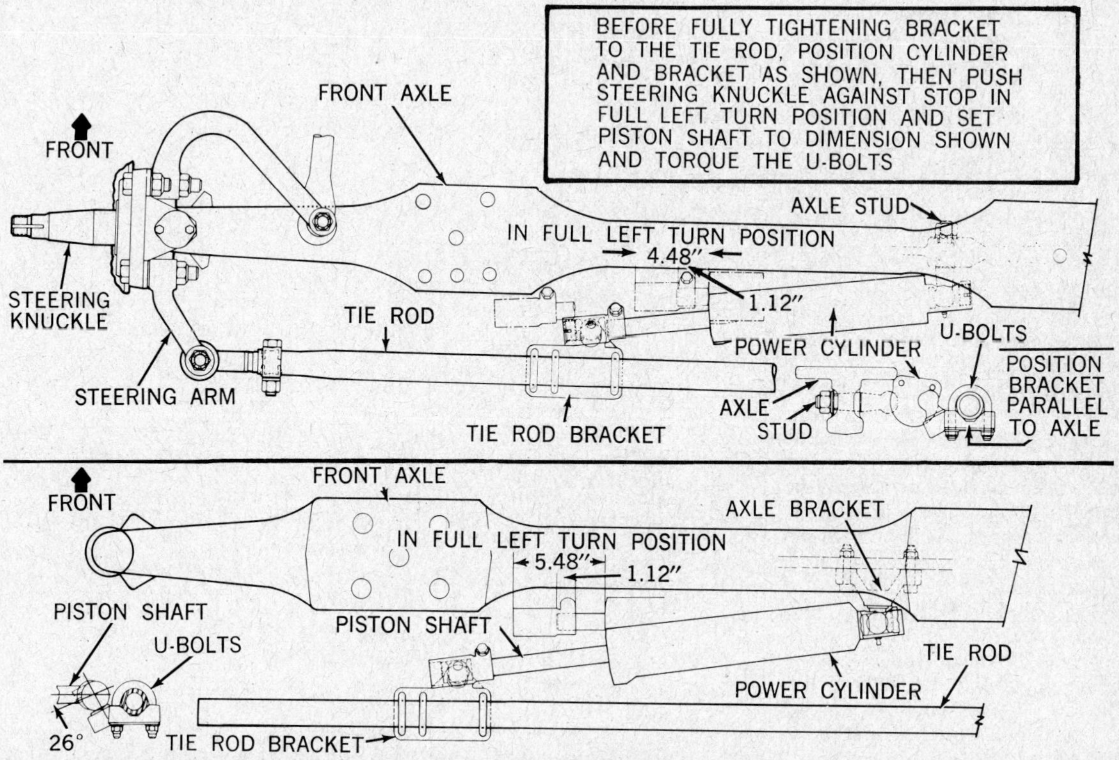

Installation and adjustment (to axle) of power cylinder—steel tilt (© Chevrolet Div., G.M. Corp.)

2. Position the steering gear, guiding the coupling bolt into the shaft flange.
3. Install the mounting bolts and torque to 65 ft-lbs. (110 ft-lbs on G series).
4. If plastic spacers are used in the flexible coupling, make sure they are bottomed on the pins, tighten the flange bolt nuts to 18 in-lbs (20 ft-lbs on P series), and then remove the spacers. Where plastic spacers are not used, center the pins in the steering shaft flange slots and install the bolt nuts and torque as above.
5. On P Models:
   a. Position the steering gear. guiding the stub shaft into the U-joint assembly and lining up marks made at removal or, with a new unit, lining up the mark on the stub shaft with the mark on the universal yoke.
   b. Install the gear to frame bolts and torque to 65 ft-lbs.
   c. Install the U-joint pinch bolt and torque to 20 ft-lbs. Make sure the bolt passes through the shaft undercut.
6. Install the pitman arm, lining up the marks made at removal. Install the shaft nut or pinch bolt and torque to 180 ft-lbs on C series, 90 ft-lbs on K series, and 180 ft-lbs on G and P series.
7. Remove the plugs and caps from the fluid fittings and reinstall both hoses.

Adjustments

Light Duty Trucks

Power steering gear is adjusted in the same manner as manual steering gear however, sector lash adjustment is the only power steering gear adjustment that can be made on the vehicle. In order to make this adjustment, it is necessary to check the combined valve drag and worm bearing preload.

1. Check power steering fluid level, check belt tension and hose for leaks or kinks.
2. Remove drag link from pitman arm.
3. Disconnect horn wire, remove horn button assembly.
4. Center steering wheel—turn through its full travel then locate wheel at center of its travel.
5. Loosen sector lash adjusting screw locknut and back off (slotted) adjusting screw to the limit of its travel.
6. Check combined valve drag and worm bearing preload with inch-pound torque wrench and socket on steering shaft nut, by rotating wheel approximately 20° in each direction. Note highest reading.
7. Tighten sector lash adjusting screw until torque at steering wheel meets specifications (4 to 18 inch pounds according to truck size.) Secure lock nut.

   NOTE: If maximum adjustment is exceeded, turn lash adjuster screw back (counterclockwise) and then come in (clockwise) slowly on adjustment.

   CAUTION: Do not bounce steering wheel hard against stops with drag link removed, worm ball guide damage can result.
8. Replace drag link, horn button assembly and connect horn wire.
9. Road test and check steering.

Power Cylinders

Power cylinders are used to assist in lowering the steering effort for the vehicle operator. Two types are used; side mounted and axle mounted.

The side mounted unit is attached to the frame side rail at one end and to the pitman arm at the other end. The axle mounted cylinder is attached to the front axle at one end and to the steering tie rod at the other.

A control valve mounted on the steering gear housing, directs oil pressure from the belt driven oil pump to either the right or left sides of the piston within the power cylinder, depending upon the turn being made. If a hydraulic failure occurs with this type unit, the steering reverts to manual with no hydraulic assist.

Overhaul of the power cylinder is detailed in the Power Steering Section of the General Repair Section.

Removal and Installation

Removal and installation of the power cylinder is accomplished by the removal of the power cylinder hydraulic lines, and the attaching bolts at each end of the cylinder. A container should be placed under the lines to catch the fluid that will drain from the lines.

To install the cylinder, reverse the procedure, fill the power steering reservoir, and bleed the system of air.

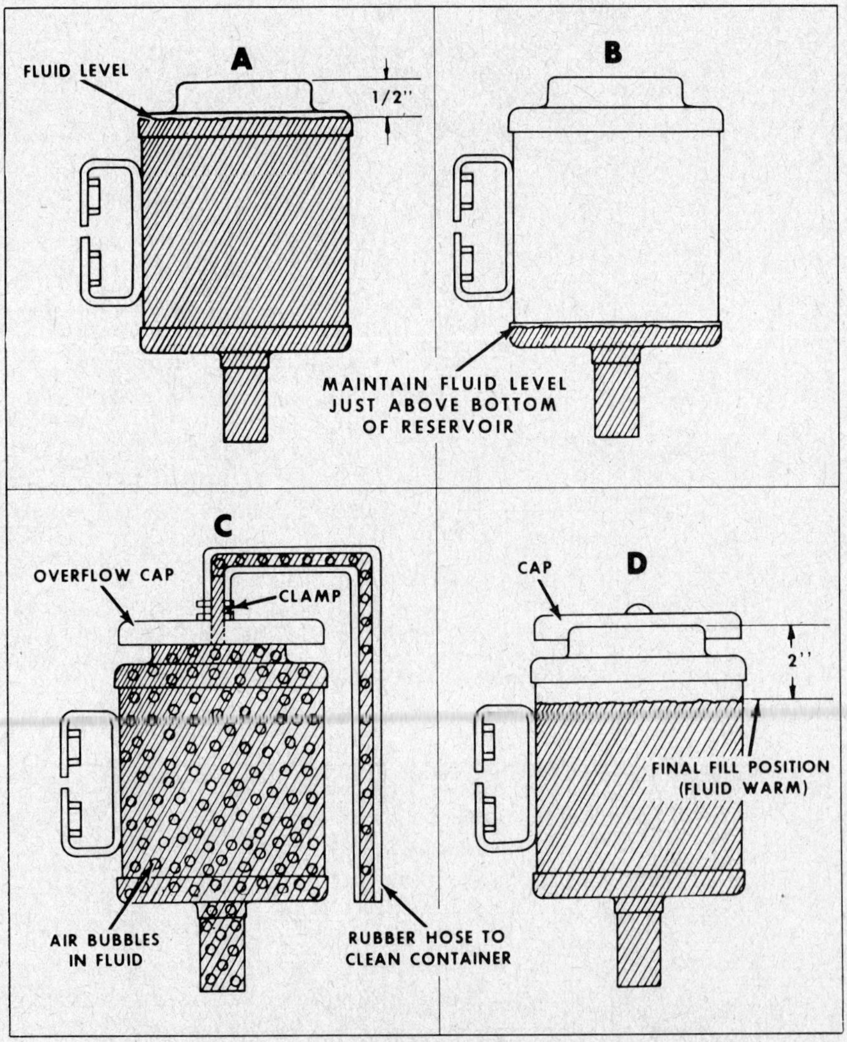

Remote reservoir fluid level (follow in alphabetical order when bleeding hydraulic system) (© Chevrolet Div., G.M. Corp.)

Bleeding Hydraulic System

Light Duty Trucks

1. Fill the reservoir to the proper level, and allow the fluid to stand for at least two minutes; any air bubbles trapped in the fluid will rise and separate from the fluid.
2. Operate the engine for a few seconds.
3. Add fluid as needed.
4. Repeat the above until the fluid level remains constant.
5. Support the front of the vehicle in the raised position, so that the wheels are off of the ground.
6. Increase the engine speed to approximately 1500 rpm.
7. Operate the steering mechanism from right to left, contacting the steering stops only lightly.
8. Add fluid as needed.
9. Lower the vehicle to the ground, and turn the wheels from full right to full left.
10. Add fluid as needed.
11. Repeat all of the above steps as many times as necessary. Keep adding fluid as needed.

NOTE: If, after repeated attempts to bleed the system, air is still present in the fluid (fluid is foamy), then check the hydraulic system for leaks.

Semi-Integral System—Medium and Heavy Duty Trucks

1. Fill the fluid reservoir to the proper level: FLUID LEVEL mark on integral pumps; half full on remote mounted reservoir.
2. Allow the fluid to stand undisturbed for at least two minutes.
3. Operate the engine for a few seconds.
4. Add fluid as needed.
5. Repeat the above steps until the fluid level remains constant.
6. Support the front of the vehicle in the raised position, so that the wheels are off of the ground
7. Operate the steering mechanism from stop to stop. Continue this operation until fluid is noticeably clear and free of air bubbles.
8. Add fluid as needed.
9. Increase the engine speed to approximately 1500 rpm, and, again, operate the steering mechanism from stop to stop. Continue until the fluid is clear.
10. Lower the vehicle to the ground.

NOTE: If, after repeated attempts to bleed the system, air is still present in the fluid (fluid is foamy), then check the hydraulic system for leaks.

Integral System—Medium Duty Trucks

1. Remove the drag link at the pitman arm.
2. Fill the reservoir to within one-half inch of the top with power steering fluid, and leave the cap off. On vehicles equipped with a remote reservoir, squeeze the hose starting at the pump and work up to the reservoir to remove trapped air.

   NOTE: An improvised overflow cap can be installed during the bleeding procedure before the engine is stopped. Overflow can be directed to a clean container. To fabricate an overflow cap:

   A. Drill a 3/16" hole through the center of the top of the reservoir cap.

   B. Solder a piece of 3/16" O.D. pipe onto the cap at the drilled area.

   C. Attach a length of 3/16" I.D. hose to the pipe, which is long enough to reach the external container. Secure the hose in place with a clamp.
3. Pour power steering fluid into the reservoir the moment the engine starts.

   NOTE: It may be necessary to have someone ready to assist in this operation.
4. Operate the engine for approximately 3 seconds, and then shut it off.
5. Allow the fluid to stand undisturbed for at least one minute.
6. Add fluid as necessary.
7. Repeat the above two more times.

   NOTE: DO NOT install the standard reservoir cap during the bleeding procedure, as air may be trapped in the system. If this were to happen, the trapped air would force power steering fluid out of the breather hole in the cap.
8. Start the engine again. Make sure that the fluid level is up to the bottom of the reservoir.

   NOTE: The fluid level should be maintained at the bottom of the reservoir to prevent pump aeration during the bleeding procedure.
9. On vehicles equipped with a hydraulic brake booster, pump the brake pedal a minimum of 3 times with the engine running. This will purge air from the booster.
10. Allow the engine to idle, and op-

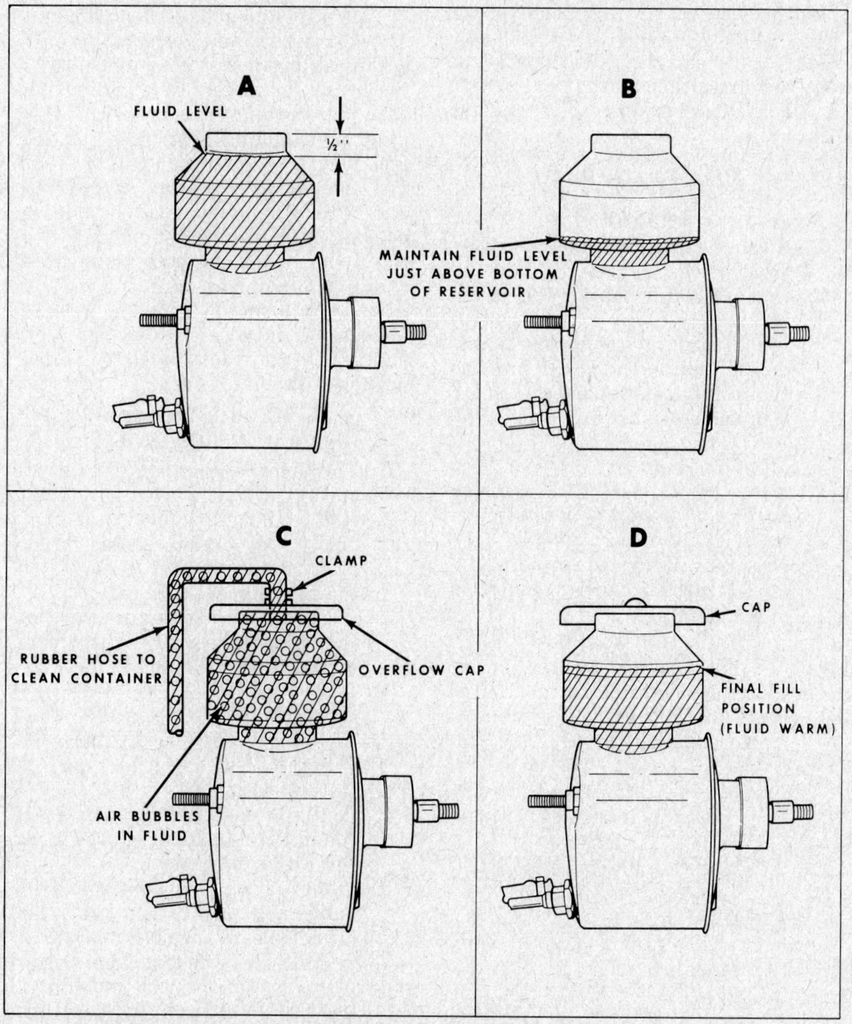

Integral reservoir fluid level (follow in alphabetical order when bleeding hydraulic system) (© Chervolet Div., G.M. Corp.)

erate the steering mechanism in one direction, either full right or full left, against the stop. Turn the steering away from the stop only slightly, and return it to the stop. Repeat this operation 5 times. DO NOT force the steering against the stop, as this may damage the pump.

11. Repeat step no. 10 for the opposite side.
12. Maintain the fluid level at a point just above the bottom of the reservoir.
13. Center the steering wheel, and allow the engine to idle. Install the overflow cap.
14. Shut the engine off. Air will bubble out through the overflow cap.
15. Remove the cap, and start the engine.
16. Add fluid as needed to maintain the fluid level fust above the bottom of the reservoir.
17. Repeat steps nos. 3 through 16 as many times as necessary, until there is no more than a one-inch rise in the fluid level with the engine shut off.
18. Start the engine, and center the steering wheel.
19. Connect the drag link to the pitman arm.
20. Idle the engine at approximately 1500 rpm, and operate the steering mechanism from stop to stop.
21. Shut the engine off, and fill the reservoir to the proper level.

CLUTCH

Clutches used on inline engines are single (driven) disc with either of two types of pressure (drive) plates, diaphragm or coil spring. "V" engines use a single disc with coil spring pressure plate. Heavy duty clutches use two discs. The two plate

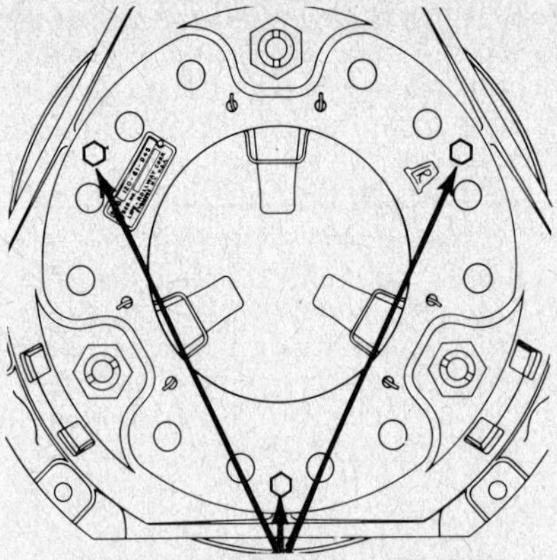

Hold down bolts installed (Lipe-Rollway) (© G.M.C.)

clutch consists of three basic assemblies, the cover with rear pressure plate assembly, front pressure plate and two discs. The front pressure plate, located between the two driven discs, has two friction surfaces and is coupled to the rear pressure plate through steel drive straps bolted at each of its four driving bosses. Diaphragm spring covers operate with light pedal pressure while coil spring levers combine operating ease and high torque capacity. The operating controls are either mechanical or hydraulic. Discs have torsion spring centers.

Clutch R & R

Removal

1. Remove transmission assembly from truck.
2. Remove clutch release fork from ball stud.
3. Install aligning tool or old transmission main drive gear into the clutch hub to support the clutch components during removal.

   NOTE: To facilitate the removal of Long or Borg and Beck clutch cover assemblies, install hardwood wedges between release levers and cover.
4. On Lipe- Rollway clutches, install three flat washers and hold down bolts.

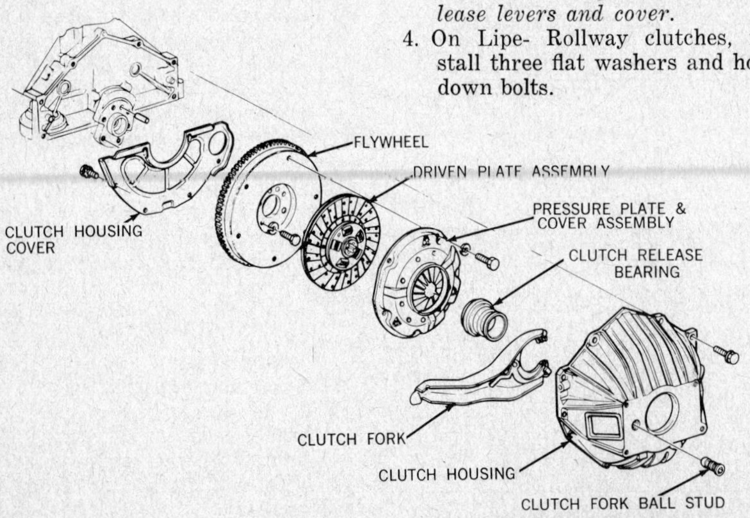

Clutch system components (© Chevrolet Div., G.M. Corp.)

5. Make alignment marks on the clutch cover and engine flywheel for reassembly.
6. Loosen the cover bolts one turn at a time and then remove the clutch assembly.

Installation

1. Install clutch assembly.
2. Install clutch cover assembly using the alignment tool or old transmission main drive gear. Make certain alignment marks match.
3. Install cover to flywheel bolts and torque slowly one turn at a time to specifications.
4. Remove aligning tool and wood wedges or hold-down bolts.
5. Connect clutch release mechanism. Lubricate clutch release bearing sparingly and apply a small amount of high temperature grease to recess in release fork. Tighten ball stud to specifications.
6. Install transmission assembly.

Refer to General Repair Section for clutch overhaul procedures.

Free Pedal Travel

This adjustment is for the amount of pedal travel (measured at pedal) before clutch release bearing contacts the levers, or fingers of a coil spring cover or the diaphragm spring of a diaphragm clutch cover. This is called free-play. With normal clutch wear the amount of free-play is reduced and in time this will cause the release bearing to be in constant contact with the cover. This in turn will cause clutch disc slippage resulting in premature failure of disc and release bearing. It is necessary to maintain sufficient free pedal travel for clutch efficiency and long life.

C, K, and P Models (Except P-3500 w/J76)

1. Disconnect the clutch fork return spring.
2. Rotate the clutch lever assembly. until the clutch pedal stops against the rubber bumper on the brake pedal bracket.
3. Position the clutch fork so that the release bearing lightly contacts the pressure plate levers.
4. Loosen the apply rod lock nut, and adjust the rod length so that the swivel slips easily into the gauge hole (upper hole) on the clutch lever.
5. Continue lengthening the push rod until all lash is removed from the clutch linkage.
6. Remove the swivel from the gauge hole, and insert it into the lower hole on the clutch lever.
7. Install the washers and cotter pin. Tighten the lock nut.
8. Install the clutch fork return spring. Check clutch pedal free travel.

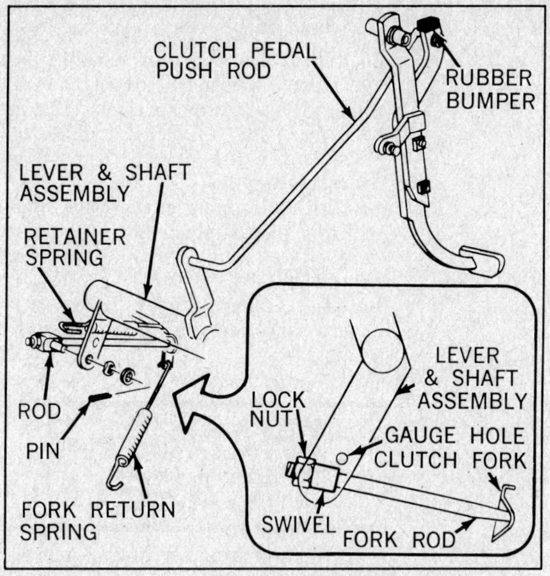

Free pedal travel—C, K models (© Chevrolet Div., G.M. Corp.)

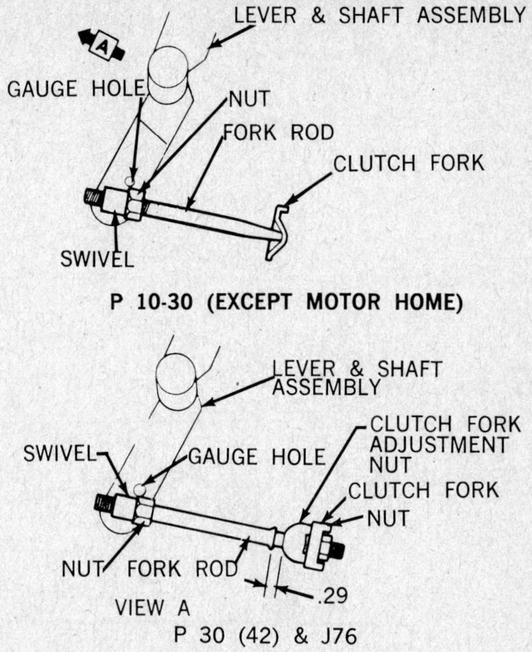

Free pedal travel—P models (© Chevrolet Div., G.M. Corp.)

NOTES: Pedal travel for C and K models should be $1\frac{3}{8}$-$1\frac{5}{8}$ inches; pedal travel for P models should be $1\frac{1}{4}$-$1\frac{1}{2}$ inches

P-3500 W/J76

1. Disconnect the clutch fork return spring.
2. Loosen the locknut at the apply rod swivel.
3. Move the clutch fork rearward to remove all clearance between the release bearing and the pressure plate levers.
4. Rotate the clutch level assembly until the clutch pedal stops against the bumper on the brake pedal bracket.
5. Adjust the apply rod until the distance between the shoulder on the apply rod and the adjustment nut is approximately $\frac{1}{4}$-5/16 (.29) inch.
6. Tighten the lock nut, and install the return spring.
7. Check clutch pedal free travel.

NOTE: Free travel should be $1\frac{3}{8}$-$1\frac{5}{8}$ inches.

G Models

1. Check linkage for excessive wear.
2. Disconnect fork arm return spring.
3. Back off locknut "A" at least ½" from swivel.
4. Hold fork push rod against fork to keep release bearing touching fingers (or diaphragm). Push rod will slide through swivel at cross shaft.
5. Adjust nut "B" to obtain approximately 3/16" to ¼" clearance between nut "B" and swivel.
6. Release push rod, connect pull back spring at fork and tighten nut "A" to lock swivel against nut "B".
7. Check clutch pedal free travel. Free travel should be $1\frac{1}{4}$-$1\frac{1}{2}$ inches.

Medium Duty Trucks W/427 CID Engine (Others Similar)

1. Loosen the lock nuts.
2. Apply a force of approximately five pounds to the push rod in the direction of arrow (D) to take up all clearances in the linkage.
3. Apply a force of approximately five pounds to the push rod in the the direction of arrow (F) to eliminate the clearance between the release bearing and the internal release levers.
4. Turn the lock nut (B) to obtain a clearance of 0.40 inch between the nut and swivel. Free travel should be approximately ¾-1 inch.

   NOTE: The clearance for vehicles equipped with either an RT 613 or an RT 610 transmission is 0.45 inch. Free travel should be $1\frac{7}{8}$ inches.
5. While holding the nut (B), release the clutch lever, and tighten the other nut (A).
6. Check clutch operation.

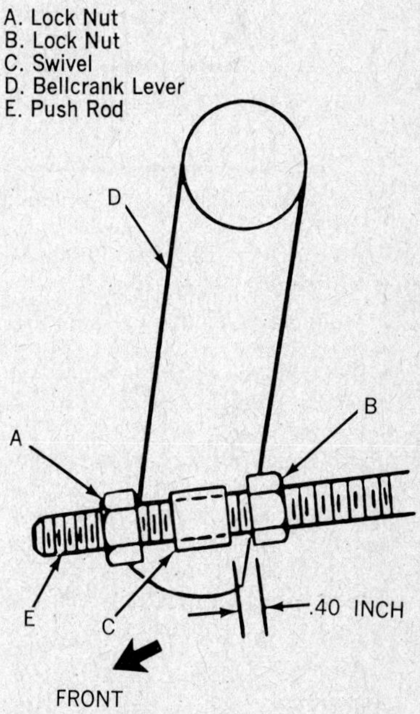

Clutch linkage adjustment—except models equipped with 427 CID engine (© Chevrolet Div., G.M. Corp.)

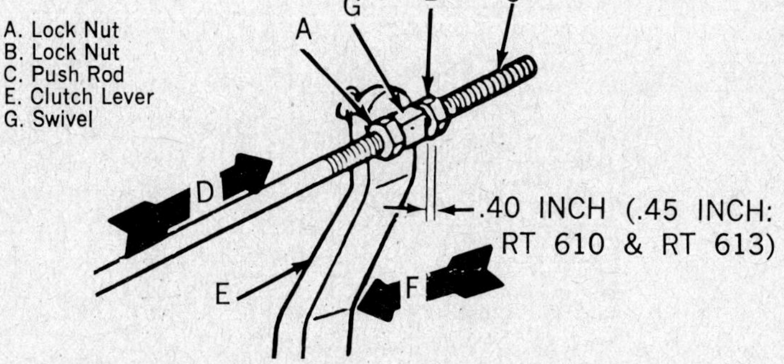

Clutch linkage adjustment—models equipped with 427 CID gasoline engine (© Chevrolet Div., G.M. Corp.)

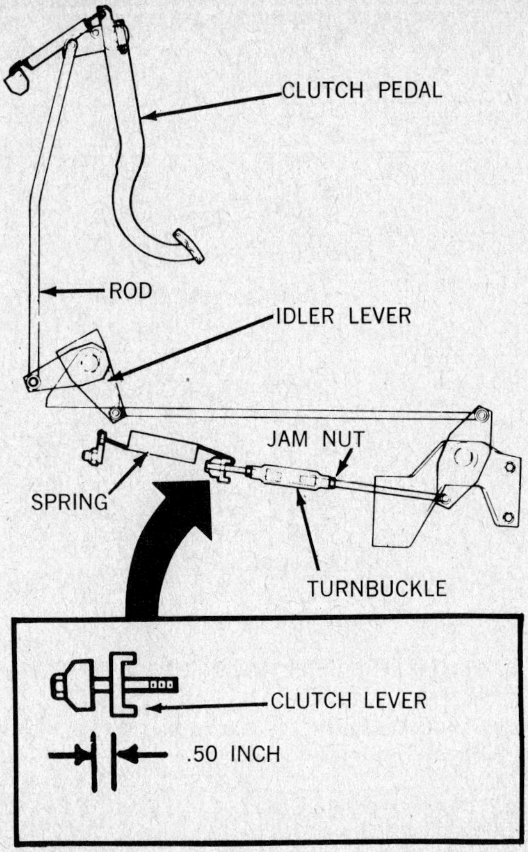

Clutch linkage adjustment—medium duty steel cab w/427 V8, 454 V8, and 4-53T (© Chevrolet Div., G.M. Corp.)

Slave Cylinder Push Rod

1. Disconnect the slave cylinder return spring.
2. Push the slave cylinder push rod into the slave cylinder, until it bottoms.
3. Move the clutch fork in the direction away from the slave cylinder. This will bring the release bearing into contact with the clutch release levers.
4. Check the clearance between the wedge and the adjusting nut.

NOTE: Clearance should be as follows:

4.53 Diesel Engine 0.40 inch
V-8 Gasoline Engine 0.40 inch

5. Loosen the jam nut and the adjusting nut.
6. Turn the adjusting nut to obtain the proper clearance, and then tighten the jam nut against the adjusting nut.
7. Connect the return spring, and check clutch operation.

Cover Assemblies

While no wear adjustment is needed (except Spicer), original settings at time of manufacture must be retained for good clutch operation. If a diaphragm clutch cover fails to release properly, after first checking pedal travel and pedal lash and linkage for looseness, replace diaphragm retracting springs. This can be done in the vehicle. If trouble still persists the diaphragm is probably overstressed.

With coil spring covers, the finger or lever adjusting screw nut is locked (staked) at time of manufacture and should not be disturbed unless rebuilding. Some Spicer heavy duty covers are internally adjusted for wear.

TRANSFER CASE

Information on repair and overhaul of light duty transfer cases can be found in the General Repair Section.

Removal

1. Raise and support vehicle on hoist. Drain transfer case.
2. Disconnect speedometer cable, back-up lamp and TCS switch.
3. Remove skid plate and crossmember supports as necessary.
4. Disconnect rear prop shaft from transfer case and tie up away from work area.
5. Disconnect front prop shaft from transfer case and tie up shaft away from work area .
6. Disconnect shift lever rod from shift rail link. On full time 4 wheel drive models, disconnect shift levers at transfer case.
7. Remove transfer case to frame mounting bracket bolts.
8. Support transfer case and remove bolts attaching transfer case to transmission adapter.
9. Move transfer case to rear until input shaft clears adapter and lower assembly from vehicle.

Installation

1. Support transfer case in suitable stand and position case to transmission adapter. Install bolts attaching case to adapter and torque to 45 ft. lbs.
2. Remove stand as required and install bolts attaching transfer case to frame rail. Bend lock tabs after assembly.
3. Install connecting rod to shift rail link or connect shift levers to transfer case, as applicable.
4. Connect front prop shaft to transfer case front output shaft.
5. Connect rear prop shaft to transfer case rear output shaft.
6. Install crossmember support and skid plate, if removed.
7. Connect speedometer cable, backup lamp and TCS switch.
8. Fill transfer case to proper level with lubricant.

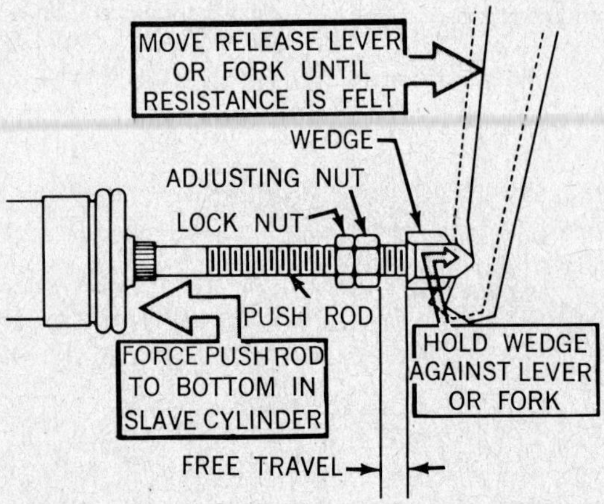

Slave cylinder push rod adjustment (© G.M.C.)

9. Lower and remove vehicle from hoist.

CAUTION: Check and tighten all bolts to specified torques.

NOTE: Before connecting prop shafts to companion flanges be sure locknuts are torqued to specifications.

Linkage Adjustment

Model 203

1. Align the gauge holes in the shift levers with the gauge hole in the shifter assembly, and insert the alignment pin (gauge pin). This will place the levers in the NEUTRAL position.
2. Position the transfer case arms in the vertical position (straight up and down).
3. Loosen the swivel lock nuts on the outer shift rod, and rotate the swivel on the rod until the distance between the end of the rod and the swivel is exactly the same as the distance between the hole in the transfer case arm and the hole in the corresponding shift lever.
4. Install the shift rod. The shift rod swivel must fit easily into the hole in the transfer case arm. DO NOT force it into the hole. If it is necessary to force the swivel into the hole, then the swivel is not properly adjusted.
5. Lock the swivel in place with a retainer.
6. Repeat steps nos. 1 through 5 for the inner rod.
7. Remove the gauge pin, and check the operation of the transfer case and shifter.

MANUAL TRANSMISSION

Reference

Information on the overhaul of light duty standard transmissions will be found in the General Repair Section.

NOTE: The following procedures for removing and installing the transmission are intended as a guide only. Procedures will vary according to optional equipment and individual

Transmission R & R

Except "K" Models

Removal

1. Remove floor mat and transmission floor pan cover, then place transmission in neutral and remove gearshift lever and control tower.

   NOTE: On trucks equipped with SM465 or New Process transmission, remove gearshift only.
2. Place a clean cloth over the transmission opening to prevent the entrance of dirt.
3. Disconnect back-up light switch at transmission and, where applicable, TCS connection.
4. Drain transmission lubricant.
5. Disconnect speedometer cable at transmission and remove parking brake controls.
6. Disconnect driveshaft from transmission.
7. Remove power take-off unit (when used) and cover opening.
8. Position a jack or dolly under the transmission and make certain that all attaching lines and brackets are disconnected.
9. Support rear of engine when mounts are located on the clutch housing.
10. Remove transmission to flywheel housing bolts.
11. Move transmission straight back from the engine, keeping mainshaft in alignment.

    CAUTION: Do not let the weight of the transmission hang on the clutch disc hub.
12. When transmission is free of the engine, lower jack or dolly and remove transmission.

Installation

1. Apply a light coating of high temperature grease to main drive gear bearing retainer and splined portion of driveshaft.

   CAUTION: Do not apply an excessive amount of grease as it will be thrown onto the clutch facings.
2. To complete transmission installation, place transmission in fourth gear, reverse the removal procedures and torque mounting bolts to specifications. Fill transmission with lubricant to the proper level.

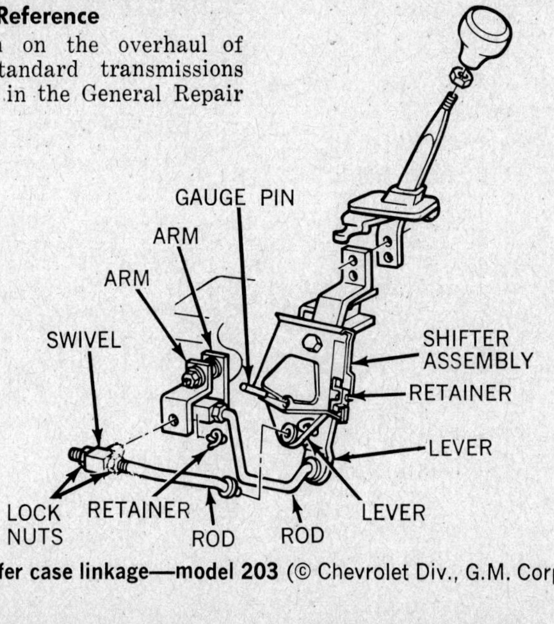

Transfer case linkage—model 203 (© Chevrolet Div., G.M. Corp.)

"K" Models (3 Speed)

Removal

1. Drain transfer case and transmission.
2. Disconnect speedometer cable and TCS connections at transmission.
3. Disconnect driveshaft at U-joint.
4. Remove attaching shift assembly bolt, then push assembly to one side.
5. Supporting transfer case in cradle, remove attaching bolts and case.
6. Disconnect shift control rods from transmission.
7. Support engine rear and remove adapter mount bolts.
8. Remove top 2 transmission to flywheel housing mount bolts and install guide pins.
9. Remove remaining mount bolts and slide transmission straight back on guide pins until it is disengaged from engine.
10. Remove transmission and adapter as an assembly.

Installation

To install transmission, reverse the removal procedures and fill with lubricant to the proper level.

"K" Models (4 Speed)

Removal

1. Remove transfer case shift lever retainer.
2. Remove floor mat, shift lever, console and heater duct (when used).
3. Remove transmission floor cover and disconnect shift lever link assembly.
4. Remove all attaching wiring and clamps.
5. Support engine. Drain transmission and transfer case.
6. Disconnect front and rear driveshafts at transfer case.
7. Remove transmission and trans-

fer case to frame bolts and place jack or dolly under transmission assembly.
8. Remove frame crossmember.
9. Remove flywheel housing cover and exhaust crossover pipe (when used).
10. Remove transmission to flywheel housing bolts. Using guide pins, slide assembly back until it disengages the engine.
11. Remove transmission assembly.

Installation

To install the transmission, reverse the removal procedure and torque mounting bolts to specifications. Fill transmission with lubricant to the proper level.

5 Speed and Larger Transmissions

Removal

1. Remove the floor mat and transmission floor pan cover. Remove the gear shift lever and control tower assembly, with the transmission in the neutral position. Cover the opening in the transmission to keep foreign material from entering.

   NOTE: On vehicles equipped with the New Process or SM465 Transmission, remove the gearshift lever only.
2. Disconnect the electrical wiring from the back-up lamp switch and remove the speedometer cable from the transmission adapter.
3. Drain the transmission assembly.
4. Disconnect the clutch linkage and the parking brake lever and controls, if used, from the rear of the transmission.
5. Match-mark the drive shaft, yoke, and/or the universal joint and remove the drive shaft from the rear of the transmission.
6. Remove the power take-off unit and controls, if equipped.
7. Position a jack or dolly under the transmission and support the weight.

   NOTE: On vehicles having the rear engine mountings attached to the clutch housing, support the weight of the engine with a suitable dolly or jack and remove the mountings.
8. Remove the bolts holding the transmission to the engine as follows:
   a. Apron type flywheel housing (has sheet metal pan covering the entire lower portion of the clutch housing). Remove the bolts retaining the transmission to the flywheel housing.
   b. S.A.E. #2 type flywheel housing (has a separate clutch housing used in addition to the flywheel housing). Remove the clutch housing to flywheel housing mounting bolts.
9. Pull the transmission assembly straight away from the engine to clear the clutch hub with the input shaft and lower the transmission and remove from under the vehicle.

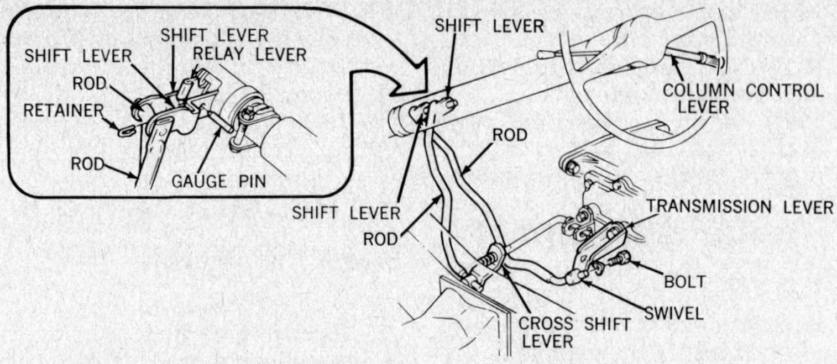

Column shift linkage—C, K models (© Chevrolet Div., G.M. Corp.)

Installation

1. Shift the transmission into high gear.
2. Place the transmission on a dolly or a jack and move into position under the vehicle.
3. Raise the transmission and align the assembly with the engine, and move the unit forward. Align the transmission main drive gear shaft with the clutch hub by rotating the transmission output shaft or yoke.
4. Move the transmission forward until the flywheel housing seats on the engine or the clutch housing.
5. On the Apron type flywheel housing, install and torque the bolts to 55 to 65 ft. lbs.
6. On the S.A.E. type flywheel housing, install and torque the bolts to 25 to 30 ft. lbs.
7. Reinstall the rear mountings, if removed, and remove the engine support. Tighten the rear engine mounting bolts.
8. Reinstall the power take-off and controls, if equipped.
9. Connect the drive shaft and align the match-marks.
10. Connect the brake control cable or rod to the parking brake unit, if equipped.
11. Connect the speedometer cable, clutch control linkage, and any other equipment that may have been removed.
12. Shift the transmission into neutral and install the gear shift lever and control tower assembly.
13. Connect the back-up light switch wires at the transmission.
14. Fill the transmission with lubricant and adjust the clutch linkage as needed.
15. Install the transmission floor pan and the floor mat.

Shift Linkage Adjustment

Column Shift

1. Disconnect central rods and align both second/third and first/reverse shifter tube levers in neutral position.

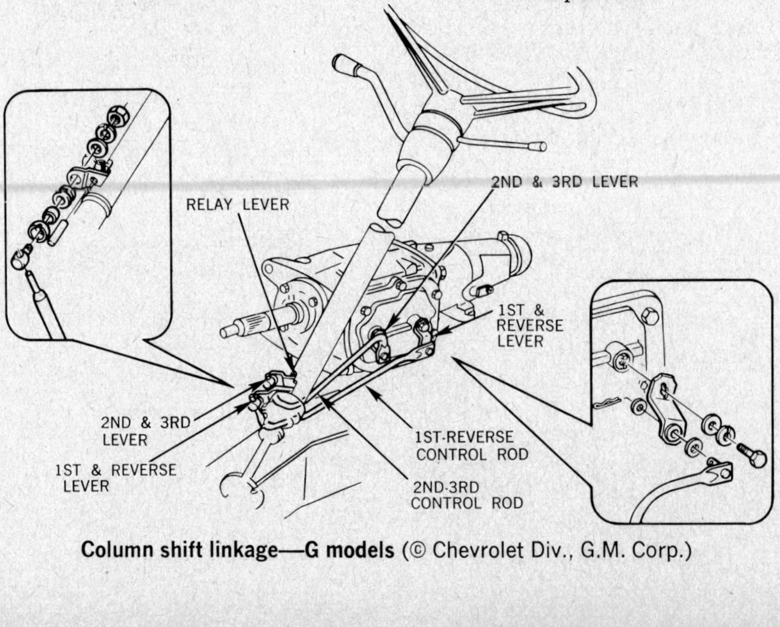

Column shift linkage—G models (© Chevrolet Div., G.M. Corp.)

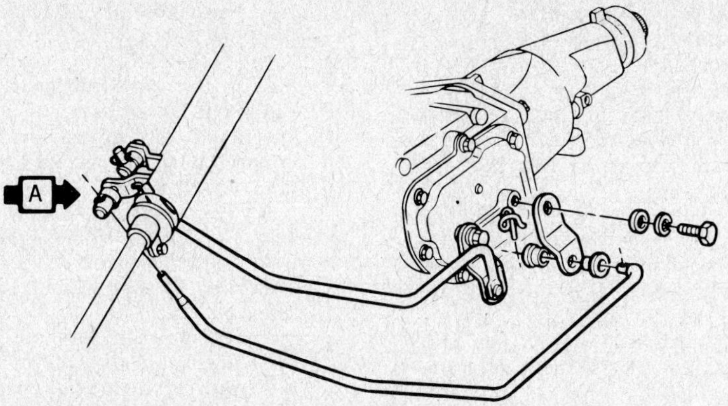

Column shift linkage—P models (© Chevrolet Div., G.M. Corp.)

2. Install gauge in holes provided to maintain alignment.
3. Position relay levers so that gearshift is in neutral position.
4. Connect control rods to tube levers and then remove gauge.
5. Move gearshift through pattern to check adjustment.

Van Column Shift

1. Raise vehicle and support on stands.
2. Remove control rods and transmission levers.
3. Move both transmission levers until transmission is in neutral. Neutral detents must be fully engaged.
4. Move gearshift lever into neutral position, align shifter relay levers on mast jacket, install pin in holes of levers to hold levers in alignment and in neutral position.
5. Adjust swivel on end of low and reverse control rod until swivel enters transmission lever freely, lock with retaining ring, tighten swivel locknut.
6. Similarly, install second and third control rod, be sure levers remain in neutral.
7. Lower vehicle and move gearshift lever through all gear positions to check. Keep clutch pedal depressed to aid in shifting.

Tilt Cab (w/Dual Rod Control

1. Position the transmission selector and shift levers in NEUTRAL.

   NOTE: The position of the selector and the shift levers (in NEUTRAL) is critical, and must be maintained throughout the adjustment procedure.
2. Disconnect the clevis of either control rod (both if necessary) at the transmission, and rotate the clevis(es) to the length required to bring the lower end of the gearshift lever into a 90 degree relationship with the control island panel.
3. Connect the control rods to the transmission.
4. Check adjustment by shifting through the gear ranges.

Tilt Cab (w/One-Piece Shift Rod)

1. Shift the transmission into NEUTRAL, and tilt the cab forward.
2. Remove the lock wire and set screw from the U-joint at the shift rod.
3. Secure the gearshift lever to maintain a 90 degree angle between the lower end of the lever and the control island shift mechanism. Adjust the position of both U-joints to retain the 90 degree angle.
4. Install the set screw and the lock wire.

Tilt Cab (w/Two-Piece Shift Rod)

NOTE: This operation is similar to the one for tilt cabs equipped with a one-piece shift rod. The only difference is the point of adustment. On vehicles equipped with the two-piece shift rod, the adjustment is made by loosening the adjusting clamp to achieve the 90 degree gearshift lever angle, and then tightening the clamp to retain the angle.

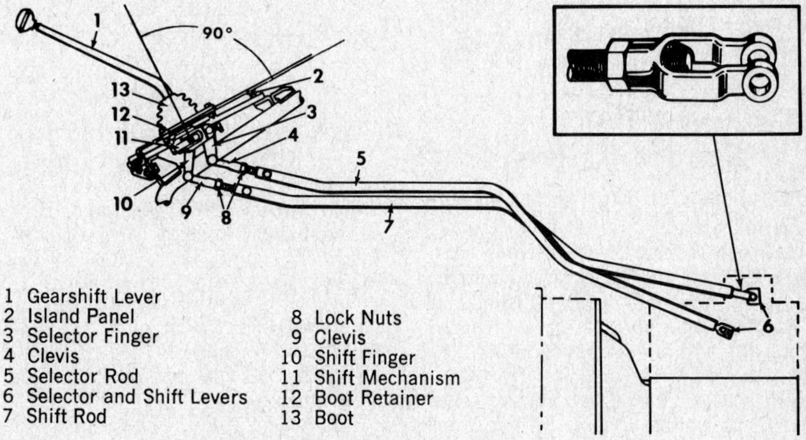

1 Gearshift Lever
2 Island Panel
3 Selector Finger
4 Clevis
5 Selector Rod
6 Selector and Shift Levers
7 Shift Rod
8 Lock Nuts
9 Clevis
10 Shift Finger
11 Shift Mechanism
12 Boot Retainer
13 Boot

Gearshift linkage—w/dual rod control—tilt cab models (© Chevrolet Div., G.M. Corp.)

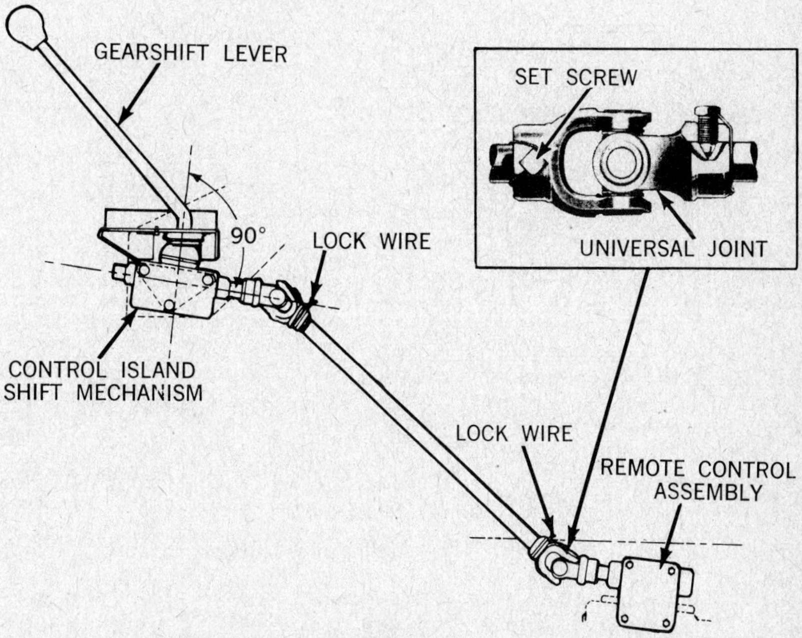

Gearshift linkage—w/one piece shift rod—tilt cab models (© Chevrolet Div., G.M. Corp.)

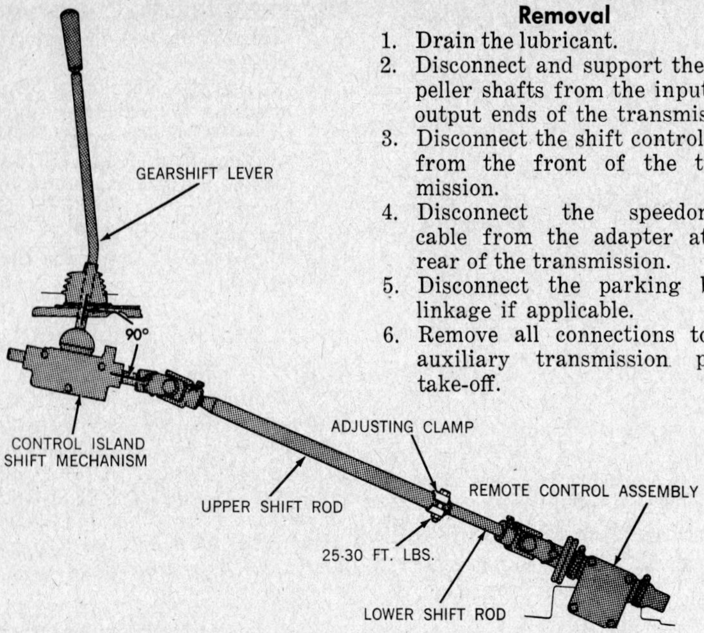

Gearshift linkage—w/two piece shift rod—tilt cab models
(© Chevrolet Div., G.M. Corp.)

Auxiliary Transmissions

The spicer auxiliary transmission is supported at the front by a support bracket attached to the frame side rails and at the rear by a support beam attached to frame brackets. The gears are shifted by a lever in the cab, which is interconnected to the auxiliary transmission with control rods. The hand brake and speedometer drive gear are located at the rear of the transmission.

Removal

1. Drain the lubricant.
2. Disconnect and support the propeller shafts from the input and output ends of the transmission.
3. Disconnect the shift control rods from the front of the transmission.
4. Disconnect the speedometer cable from the adapter at the rear of the transmission.
5. Disconnect the parking brake linkage if applicable.
6. Remove all connections to the auxiliary transmission power take-off.
7. Place a suitable dolly or jack under the transmission and adjust its position so it can safely carry the weight.
8. Disconnect the front and rear mountings and lower the transmission away from the chassis.

Installation

1. Make sure the tapered surface of the front mount face the front of the vehicle as shown in the illustration.
2. Move the transmission into position under the vehicle and adjust the front and rear height. (See alignment Data Chart.)
3. Torque the attaching parts to the proper specifications. (See alignment Data Chart.)
4. Reconnect the propeller shafts to the input and output ends of the transmission.

   NOTE: It is important that all angles of the driveline be checked with a bevel protractor. Also the auxiliary transmission must be the same as the engine and main transmission. Adjustments may be made by raising or lowering the front or rear of the auxiliary transmission or by adding plates, washers spacers etc. (see Drive shaft alignment in U-joints-Drive Line Section.)
5. Connect the power take-off if applicable.
6. Connect the parking brake linkage.

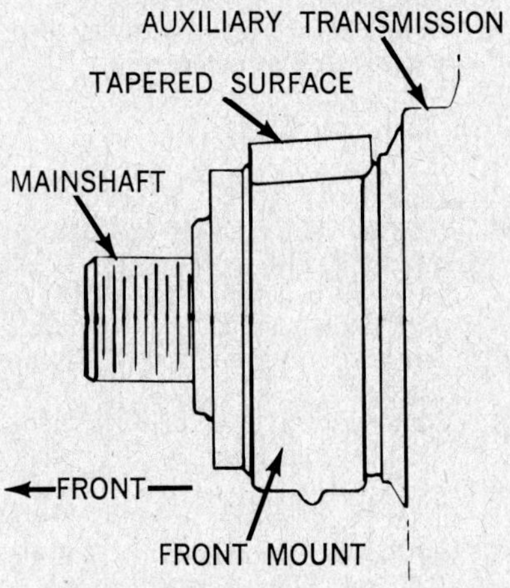

Front mount installed (© G.M.C.)

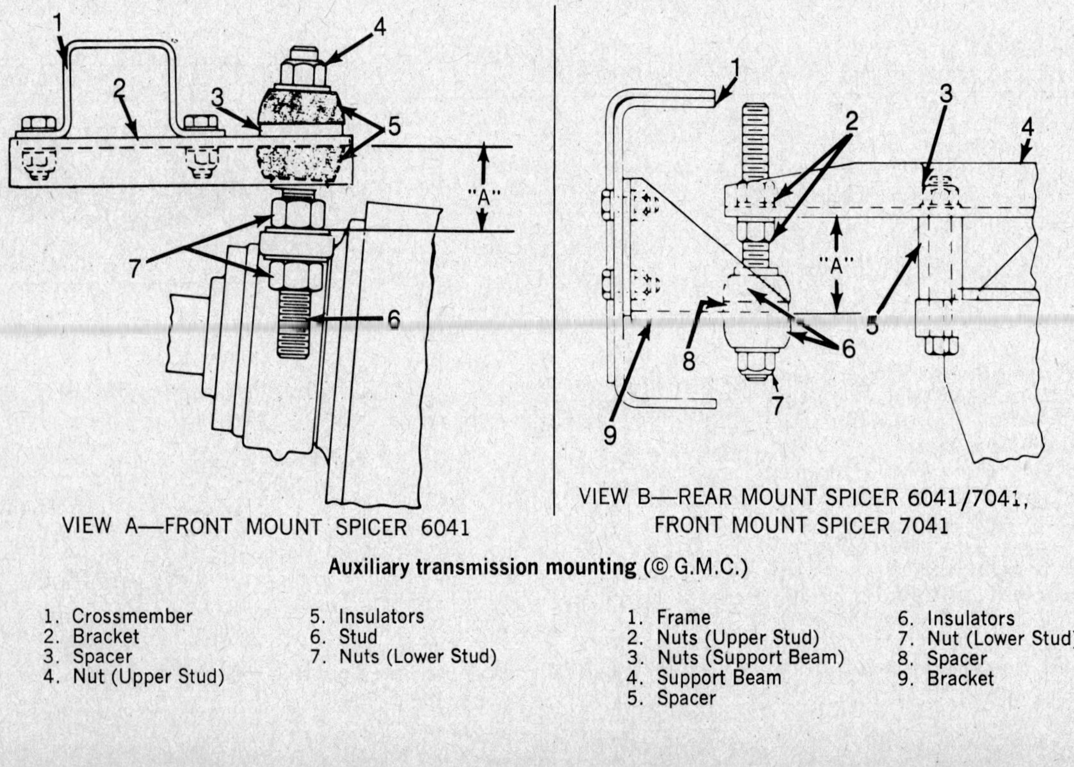

Auxiliary transmission mounting (© G.M.C.)

1. Crossmember
2. Bracket
3. Spacer
4. Nut (Upper Stud)
5. Insulators
6. Stud
7. Nuts (Lower Stud)

1. Frame
2. Nuts (Upper Stud)
3. Nuts (Support Beam)
4. Support Beam
5. Spacer
6. Insulators
7. Nut (Lower Stud)
8. Spacer
9. Bracket

7. Connect the speedometer cable to the adapter at the rear of the transmission.
8. Connect the shift control rods and adjust if necessary.
9. Refill the transmission with the recommended lubricant.

Shift Linkage Adjustment

Auxiliary Transmission SP6041 & SP7041

1. Disconnect the control rods from the shift control tower under the cab.
2. Place the auxiliary transmission gearshift lever and shift rods in the "Neutral" position.
3. Adjust the length of each control rod by rotating its adjustable clevis to provide a free clevis pin fit.
4. Reconnect the control rods to the control tower and shift the transmission through its entire shift pattern.
5. Replace any worn or damaged cotter pins, tighten the locknuts firmly and lubricate the control linkage.

Auxiliary Transmission AT1202

1. Remove the clevis pin, and disconnect the control rod from the shift lever.

   NOTE: Make sure that the shift lever mounting bracket bolts are tight.
2. Place the transmission shift rail in the NEUTRAL position.
3. While holding the lower end of the shift lever in a 90 degree angle relationship with the cab floor, adjust the clevis position on the threaded end of the shift rod to provide for free clevis pin entry.
4. Install the clevis pin and cotter pin.
5. Check the transmission shifting operation.

   NOTE: Check for free pin rotation in each gear. If the pin does not turn freely, then a binding condition exists. Readjust the clevis if necessary.
6. Tighten the jam nut against the clevis, and spread the cotter pin ends to retain the pin.

AUTOMATIC TRANSMISSION

Overhaul procedures, as they apply to both Allison and Turbo Hydra-Matic transmissions, are covered in the General Repair Section.

NOTE: The automatic transmissions covered in this section are Allison and Turbo Hydra-Matic. Removal and installation procedures are covered separately for each. It may be necessary to remove air tanks, fuel tanks, and optional equipment in order to gain access to the transmission.

Transmission R & R

CAUTION: The temperature of the transmission fluid, after the vehicle has been in operation, can exceed 350 degrees F.

Turbo Hydra-Matic 350 (Except 4 Wheel Drive)

Removal

1. With vehicle on hoist drain by removing pan or drain plug (if so equipped).

   NOTE: Fluid can be drained after transmission is removed if so desired.
2. Remove the vacuum modulator line and speedometer cable from the transmission and secure out of way.
3. Remove detent cable and manual control lever from the transmission.
4. Disconnect the drive shaft and remove.
5. Place suitable jack or other support under transmission and secure transmission to it.
6. At transmission extension disconnect rear engine mount and then remove support crossmember.
7. Remove converter underpan. Place marks on the flywheel and converter to insure proper installation and then remove the flywheel-to-converter bolts.
8. Support engine at oil pan rail with jack capable of supporting the weight of the engine when transmission is removed.
9. Lower rear of the transmission slightly so that upper, housing-to-engine, transmission bolts can be reached with a long extension and universal socket. Remove upper bolts.

   NOTE: Have an assistant watch upper engine parts to make sure everything clears when rear of transmission is being lowered.
10. Remove remaining transmission-to-housing bolts.
11. Remove transmission by moving it slightly to the rear and downward. Remove from under vehicle.

CAUTION: Watch converter when removing transmission to be sure that it moves with transmission. If it does not move, pry it free from flywheel before proceeding any further.

NOTE: On those vehicles so equipped, disconnection of the catalytic converter may be necessary to provide adequate clearance for transmission removal.

NOTE: Keep transmission front upward when removing transmission to prevent converter from falling out. Install converter holding tool after removal from engine.

For overhaul procedures—see General Repair Section.

Installation

1. Mount transmission on transmission lifting equipment installed on jack or other lifting device.
2. Remove converter holding tool.

   CAUTION: Do not permit converter to move forward after removal of holding tool.
3. Raise transmission into place at rear of engine and install transmission case to engine upper mounting bolts, then install remainder of the mounting bolts.
4. Remove support from beneath

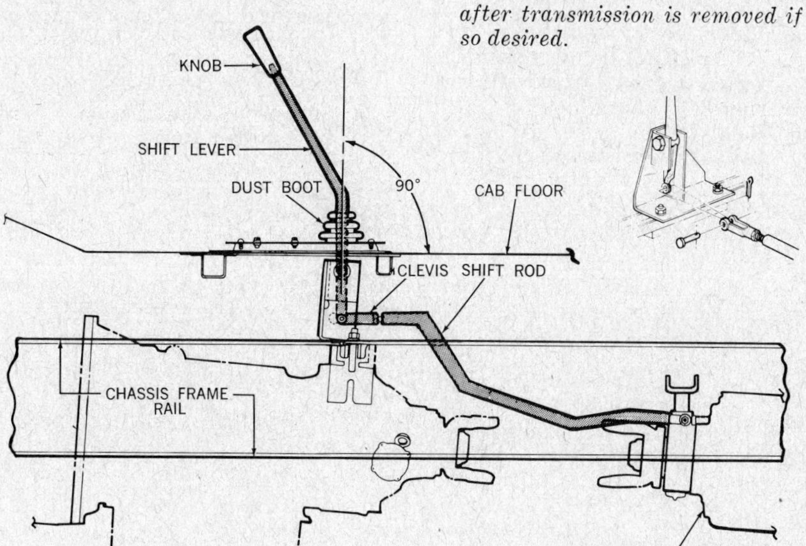

Gearshift linkage—auxiliary transmission AT-1202
(© Chevrolet Div., G.M. Corp.)

engine, then raise rear of transmission to final position.

5. If scribed during removal, align scribe marks on flywheel and converter cover. Install converter to flywheel attaching nuts and bolts.
6. Install converter underpan.
7. Reinstall transmission support crossmember to transmission and frame.
8. Remove transmission lift equipment.
9. Connect drive shaft to transmission.
10. Connect shift control lever rod and detent cable to transmission.
11. Connect vacuum modulator line, and speedometer drive cable to transmission.
12. Lower vehicle.
13. Refill transmission.
14. Check transmission for proper operation and for leakage. Check and, if necessary, adjust linkage.
15. Remove vehicle from hoist.

Turbo Hydra-Matic 350—(4 Wheel Drive) Removal

1. With vehicle on hoist drain by removing pan or drain plug (if so equipped).

   NOTE: Fluid can be drained after transmission removal if so desired.
2. Remove shift lever and rod from transfer case.
3. Remove speedometer cable and vacuum modulator line from transmission and secure out of way.
4. Disconnect detent cable and manual control lever rod from transmission.
5. Remove front and rear drive shafts from transfer case.
6. Place jack or other support under transfer case and remove transmission - to - adapter case bolts.
7. Place jack or other support under transmission and secure transmission to it.
8. Remove transfer case-to-frame bracket bolts and remove transfer case.
9. On V8 engines remove exhaust crossover pipe.
10. Disconnect and remove rear transmission crossmember.
11. Remove converter underpan. Place marks on the flywheel and converter to insure proper installation and then remove the flywheel-to-converter bolts.
12. Support engine at oil pan rail with jack capable of supporting engine weight when transmission is removed.
13. Lower rear of transmission slightly so that upper housing-to-engine transmission bolts can be removed with a long extension and universal socket. Remove upper bolts.

    NOTE: Have an assistant watch upper engine parts to make sure everything clears when transmission is lowered.
14. Remove the remaining transmission-to-housing bolts.
15. Remove the transmission by moving it slightly to the rear and downward. Remove from under vehicle.

CAUTION: Watch converter when removing transmission to make sure converter moves with transmission. If it does not, pry it loose from flywheel before proceeding any further.

NOTE: Keep transmission front upwards when removing from engine to prevent converter holding tool after removal from engine. See General Repair Section for overhaul procedures.

Installation

1. Mount transmission on transmission lifting equipment installed on jack or other lifting device.
2. Remove converter holding tool.

   CAUTION: Do not permit converter to move forward after removal of holding tool.
3. Raise transmission into place at rear of engine and install transmission case to engine upper mounting bolts, then install remainder of the mounting bolts.
4. Remove support from beneath engine, then raise rear of transmission to final position.
5. If scribed during removal, align scribe marks on flywheel and converter cover. Install converter to flywheel attaching bolts.
6. Install flywheel cover.
7. Place transfer case and adapter assembly at rear of transmission on suitable lift equipment and install transfer case to frame bracket attaching bolts.
8. Reinstall transmission to transfer case adapter attaching bolts and remove lift equipment.
9. Connect front and rear drive shafts to transfer case.
10. Install exhaust system cross pipe.
11. Connect manual control lever rod and detent cable to transmission.
12. Connect vacuum modulator line and speedometer drive cable to transmission.
13. Assemble rod on transfer case shift lever before installing rod to transfer case shift linkage.
14. Lower vehicle.
15. Refill transmission.
16. Check transmission for proper operation and for leakage.
17. Check, and if ncessary, adjust linkage.

    Remove from hoist.

Turbo Hydra-Matic 400/475 Removal & Installation

Before raising the truck, disconnect the battery and release the parking brake.

1. Raise truck on hoist.
2. Remove drive shaft.
3. Disconnect speedometer cable, electrical lead to case connector, vacuum line at modulator, and cooler pipes.
4. Disconnect shift control linkage.
5. Support transmission with transmission jack.

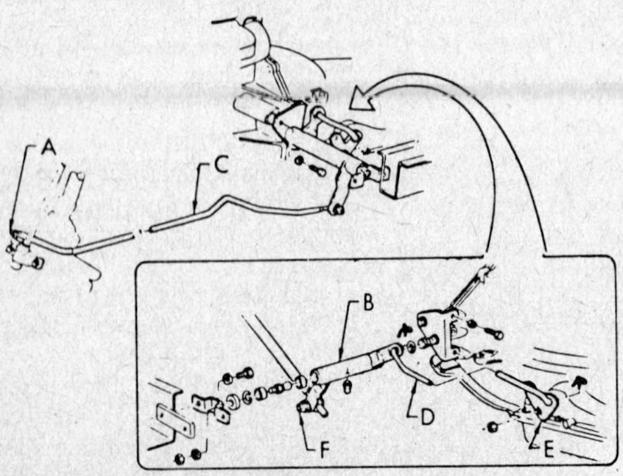

Linkage adjustment—forward control (1973), and G models (1973-74)—Turbo Hydra-Matic (© G.M.C.)

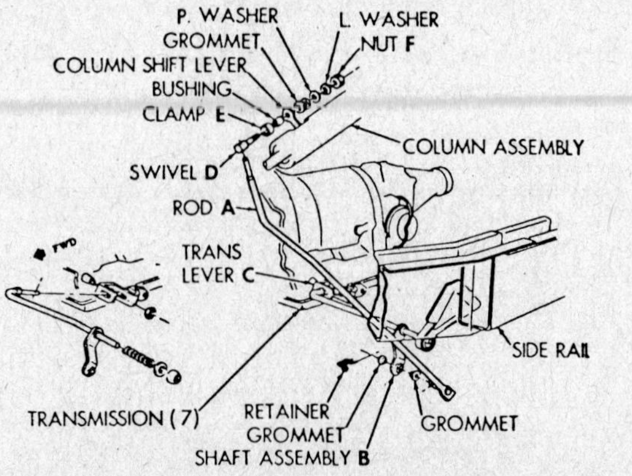

Linkage adjustment—G models (1975 and later)—Turbo Hydra-Matic (© G.M.C.)

6. Disconnect rear mount from frame crossmember.
7. Remove two bolts at each end of frame crossmember and remove crossmember.
8. Remove converter under pan.
9. Remove converter to flywheel bolts.
10. Loosen exhaust pipe to manifold bolts approximately 1/4 inch, and lower transmission until jack is barely supporting it.
11. Remove transmission to engine mounting bolts and remove filler tube at transmission.
12. Raise transmission to its normal position, support engine with jack and slide transmission rearward from engine and lower it away from vehicle.

CAUTION: Use converter holding tool when lowering transmission or keep rear of transmission lower than front so as not to lose converter.

The installation of the transmission is the reverse of the removal with the following additional steps.

Before installing the flex plate to converter bolts, make certain that the weld nuts on the converter are flush with the flex plate and the converter rotates freely by hand in this position. Then, hand start all three bolts and tighten finger tight before torquing to specification. This will insure proper converter alignment.

NOTE: After installation of transmission check linkage for proper adjustment and check for leaks.

Turbo Hydra-Matic 350, 400, 475

Linkage Adjustment— Light Duty Trucks

1973 and Later Cabs, Suburbans, 4-wheel drive

1974 and Later Forward Control exc. Vans

1. Place gearshift lever in Drive (D), as determined by transmission detent. Obtain Drive position by rotating transmission lever counterclockwise to detent, then clockwise two detent positions to Drive.
2. Loosen adjustment swivel at mast jacket lever and rotate transmission lever so that it contacts the Drive stop in the steering column.
3. Tighten swivel and recheck adjustment.
4. Readjust indicator pointer, if necessary, to agree with transmission detent positions.
5. Readjust Neutral safety switch if necessary.

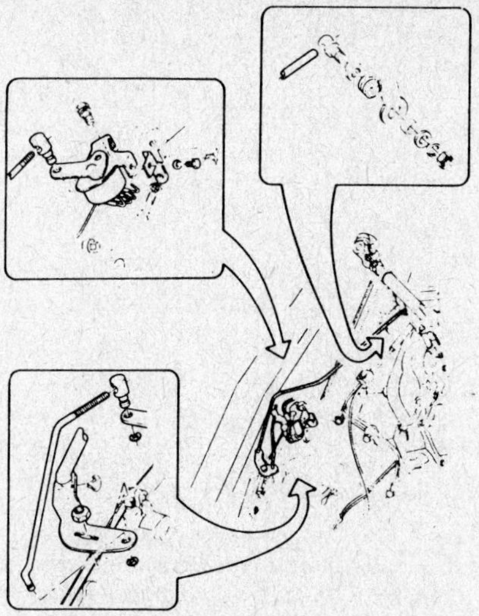

Selector linkage—P models (Turbo Hydra-Matic) (© G.M.C.)

1973—Forward Control 1973-74—Vans

1. Set transmission lever in Drive position. Obtain Drive position by rotating transmission lever counter-clockwise to Low detent, then clockwise two detent positions to Drive.
2. Attach control rod to lever and shaft assembly with retainers.
3. Assemble ring, washers, grommet, swivel, retainer and nut loosely on shaft.
4. Insert control rod in swivel and retainer, attach opposite end to tube and lever assembly.
5. Set tube lever assembly in Drive position and tighten nut.

NOTE: When above procedure is adhered to, the following conditions must be met by manual operation of the gearshift lever. From Reverse to Drive position travel, the transmission detent feel must be noted and related to indicated position on dial. When in Drive and Reverse position, pull lever toward steering wheel and then release. It must drop back into position with no restriction.

1975 and Later Vans

1. The shift tube and lever assembly must be free in the mast jacket.
2. Set transmission lever in "neutral" position by one of the following optional methods.

NOTE: Obtain "neutral" position by moving transmission lever counter-clockwise to "LI" detent, then clockwise three detent posi-

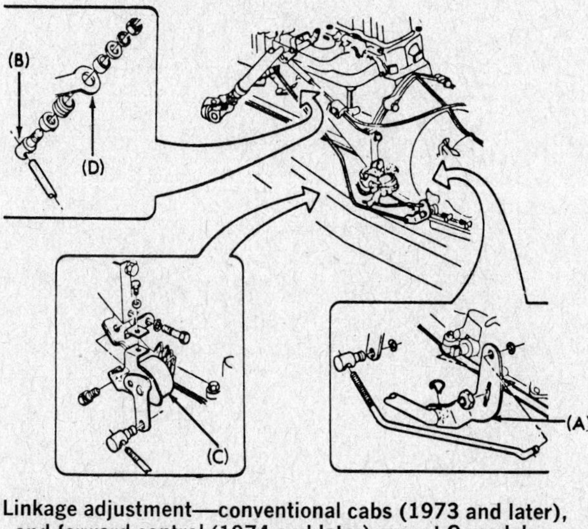

Linkage adjustment—conventional cabs (1973 and later), and forward control (1974 and later) except G models—Turbo Hydra-Matic (© G.M.C.)

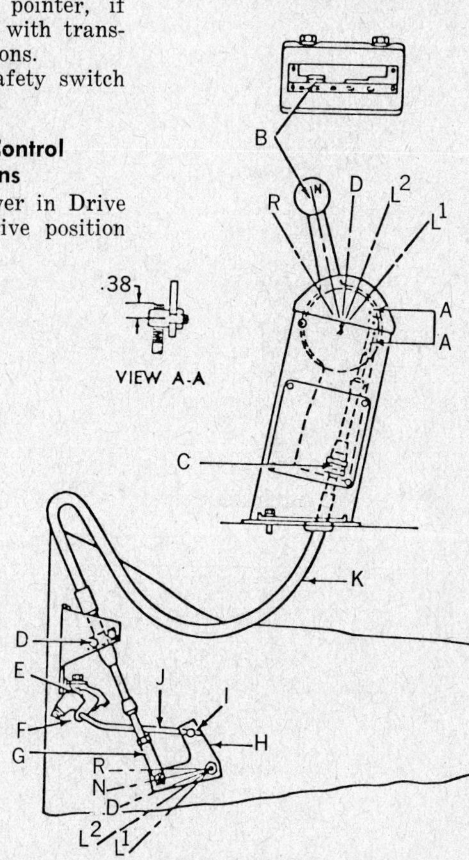

Shift linkage—AT-475 (© G.M.C.)

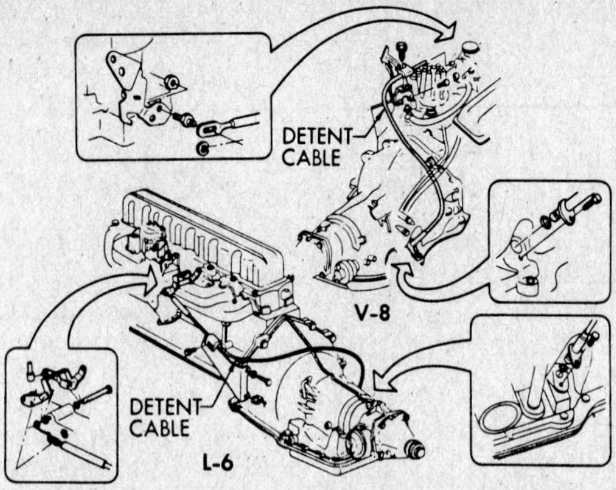

Detent cable adjustment (Turbo Hydra-Matic) (© G.M.C.)

tion to "neutral" or obtain "neutral" position by moving transmission lever clockwise to the "park" detent then counter-clockwise two detents to "neutral."

3. Set the column shift lever in "neutral" position. This is obtained by rotating shift lever until it locks into mechanical stop in the column assembly.

   NOTE: Do not use indicator pointer on a reference to position the shift lever.
4. Attach rod to shaft assembly.
5. Slide swivel and clamp onto rod, align the column shift lever and loosely attach.
6. Hold column lever against neutral stop "Park" position side.
7. Tighten nut.
8. Readjust indicator needle if necessary to agree with the transmission detent positions.
9. Readjust neutral start switch if necessary to provide the correct relationship to the transmission detent positions.

CAUTION: **Any inaccuracies in the above adjustments may result in premature failure of the transmission due to operation without controls in full detent position. Such operation results in reduced oil pressure and partial engagement of clutches.**

Downshift Switch Adjustment

Turbo Hydra-Matic 350

1. Remove air cleaner.
2. Loosen detent cable screw.
3. With choke off and accelerator linkage properly adjusted, position carburetor lever in wide open throttle position.
4. Pull detent cable rearward until wide open throttle stop in transmission is felt.

   NOTE: Cable must be pulled through detent position to reach wide open throttle stop in transmission.
5. Tighten detent cable screw and check linkage for proper operation.

Turbo Hydra-Matic 400/475

A detent solenoid, activated by an electrical switch on the carburetor linkage, controls downshift for passing speeds.

Neutral Safety Switch Adjustment

Mast Jacket Mounted

1. Place gearshift lever in Neutral (N).
2. Loosen retainer screws holding switch, install 3/32″ drill (or pin) through hole in lower switch arm and bracket. Adjust position of switch until engine turns over (with ignition switch in start).

Transmission Mounted

1. Place gearshift lever in Neutral (N), loosen transmission lever extension bolt.

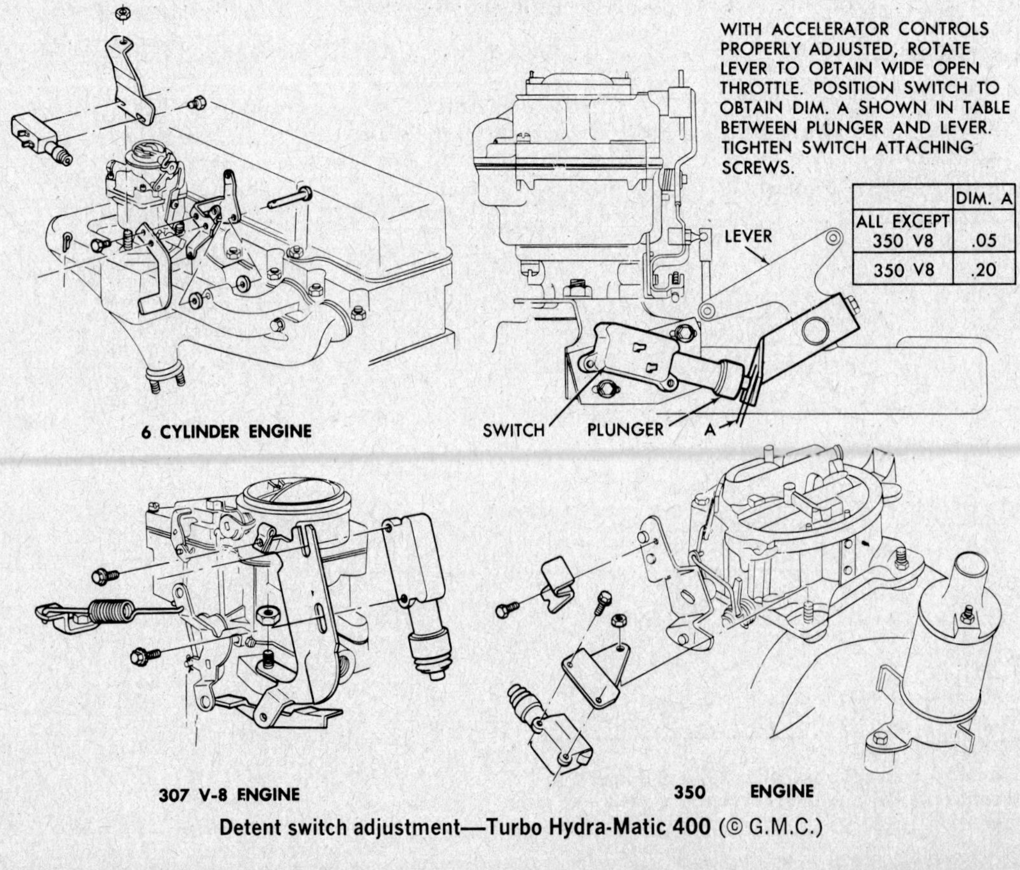

Detent switch adjustment—Turbo Hydra-Matic 400 (© G.M.C.)

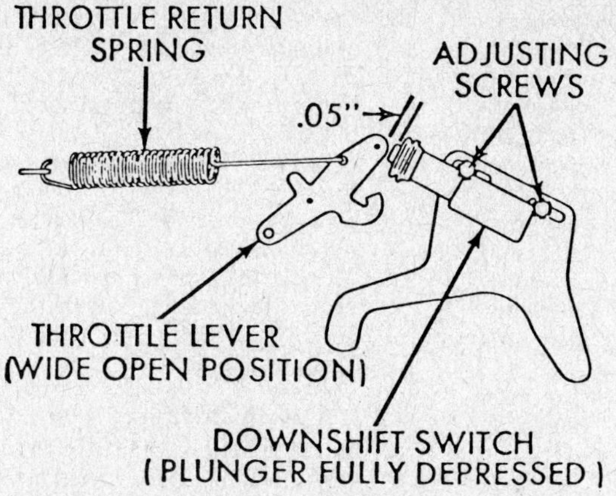

Downshift linkage—AT 475 transmission (© G.M.C.)

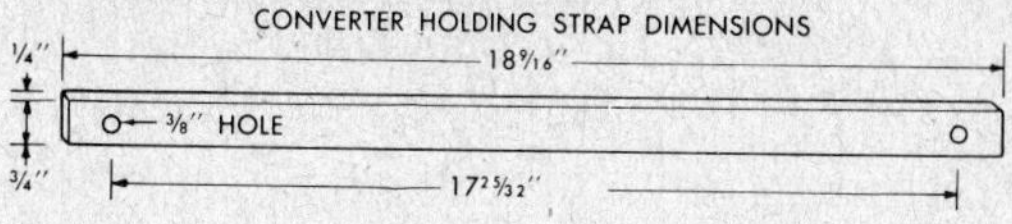

Converter holding strap (© G.M.C.)

2. Pin switch lever in Neutral position with 3/32" drill or pin.
3. Install rod into switch lever, adjust swivel on rod to allow free entry of rod into lever.
4. Secure rod with retainer, tighten transmission lever extension bolt.
5. Check adjustment by testing for cranking in both Neutral and Park.

Draining and Refilling

Turbo Hydra-Matic 350, 375/400/475

CAUTION: **The temperature of the transmission fluid, after the vehicle has been in operation, can exceed 350 degrees F.**

1. Raise the vehicle and support safely.
2. Place a fluid receptacle under the transmission pan. Remove the pan attaching bolts from the front and side.
3. Loosen the rear pan attaching bolts approximately four turns and pry the pan loose to allow it to drain.
4. Remove the remaining pan screws and remove the pan and gasket. Discard the gasket.
5. Remove the strainer to valve body screws and remove the strainer (filter) and gasket and discard.
6. Install the new strainer and gasket and install the strainer to valve body screws and tighten.

NOTE: The 400/475 transmissions use a filter retainer bolt, oil filter assembly, O-ring seal and an intake pipe. The filter and O-ring seal must be replaced when the fluid is changed.

7. Install a new gasket on the pan and install the pan. Tighten the pan bolts to 12 ft. lbs. torque. Connect and tighten the filler tube.
8. Lower the vehicle and install 2.5 quarts of transmission fluid into the transmission and start the engine.
9. Move the selector lever through the detents for each range. Add fluid to bring the level to 1/4 inch below the ADD mark on the dipstick.

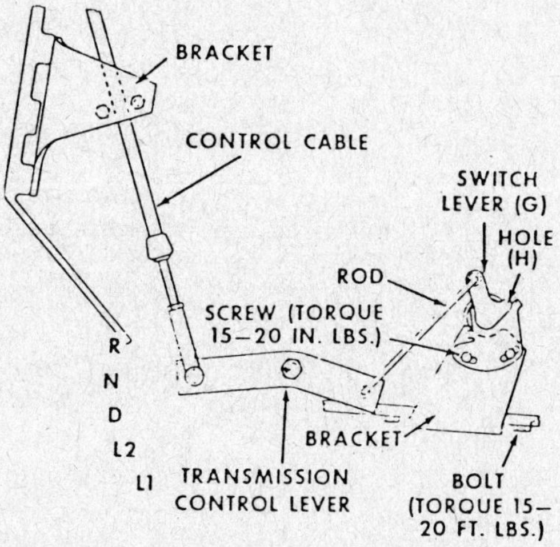

Neutral safety and back-up lamp switch—AT 475 transmission (1975-76) (© G.M.C.)

Allison—AT540, MT640, MT650 Automatic Transmission

Transmission R & R

AT540 Removal

NOTE: It may be necessary to remove the air tanks, fuel tanks, special equipment, etc., on some vehicles to provide clearance before the transmission is removed.

1. Block vehicle so that it cannot move. Disconnect ground strap from battery negative (—) post. Remove the spark plugs so the engine can be turned over manually.
2. Remove the level gauge (dipstick). Drain transmission by disconnecting filler tube at right side of transmission pan. Remove bracket holding filler tube to transmission and remove filler tube from vehicle. Replace dipstick in tube and cover the pan opening to prevent entry of foreign material.
3. Disconnect cooler lines from fittings on right side of transmission case. Plug line ends and case openings with lint-free material.
4. Disconnect the range selector cable from shift lever at left-side of transmission.
5. Disconnect vacuum modulator line from modulator. Also, on conventional cab models, disconnect wiring from neutral safety and back-up lamp switches.
6. Disconnect the speedometer

shaft fitting from adapter at rear of transmission.

7. Disconnect the drive shaft from transmission.
8. Disconnect the mechanical parking brake linkage at the right side of the transmission (if used).
9. Through the opening in the flywheel housing, use a pry-bar, as necessary to manually turn the flywheel. As the flywheel is rotated, remove the six bolts retaining flywheel flex plate assembly to converter cover.
10. Support the transmission with a 500-pound (minimum) transmission floor jack. The jack must be positioned so transmission pan will not support the weight of transmission. Fasten a safety chain over top of transmission and to both sides of jack.
11. Place a support under rear of engine and remove transmission case-to-crossmember support bolts. Raise the engine to remove weight from the engine rear mounts.
12. Remove the transmission case-to-flywheel housing bolts and washers.
13. Carefully inspect transmission and surrounding area to be sure no lines, hoses, or wires will interfere with transmission removal.

    NOTE: When removing transmission, keep rear of transmission lower than the front so as not to lose converter.
14. Move transmission assembly from the engine, lower the assembly carefully and move it out from the vehicle.

Installation

1. Raise vehicle sufficiently to allow installation of transmission. With transmission assembly mounted on transmission jack

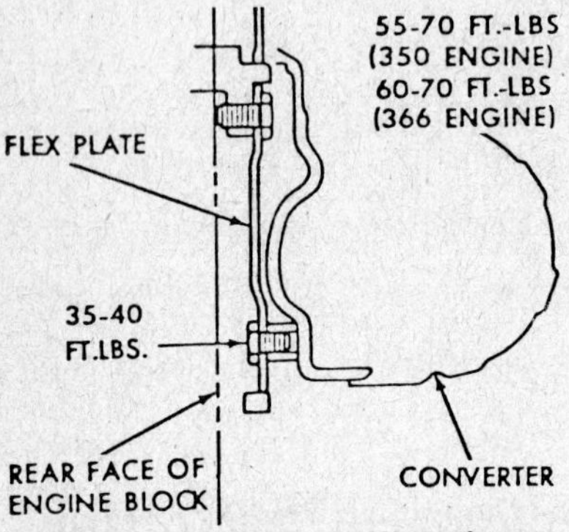

Flex plate installation—V8 engine—AT-540 (© G.M.C.)

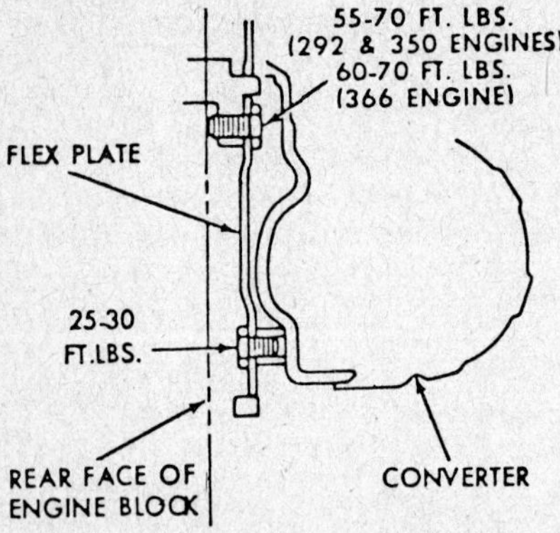

Flex plate installed—inline and V8 engines—AT 475 (© G.M.C.)

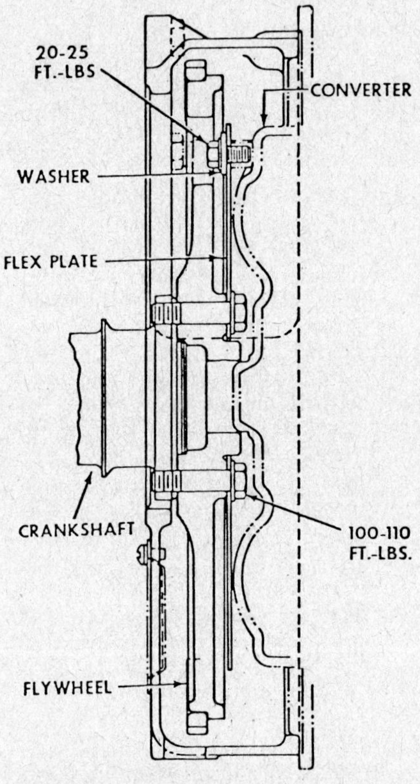

Flex plate installation—V6 engine—AT-540 (© G.M.C.)

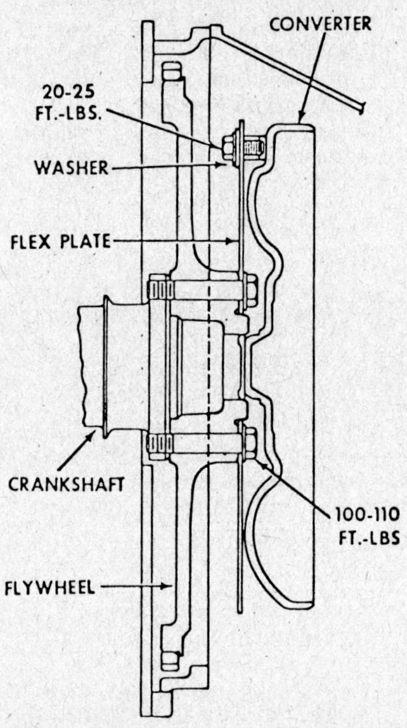

Flex plate installation—V6 engine—AT 475 (© G.M.C.)

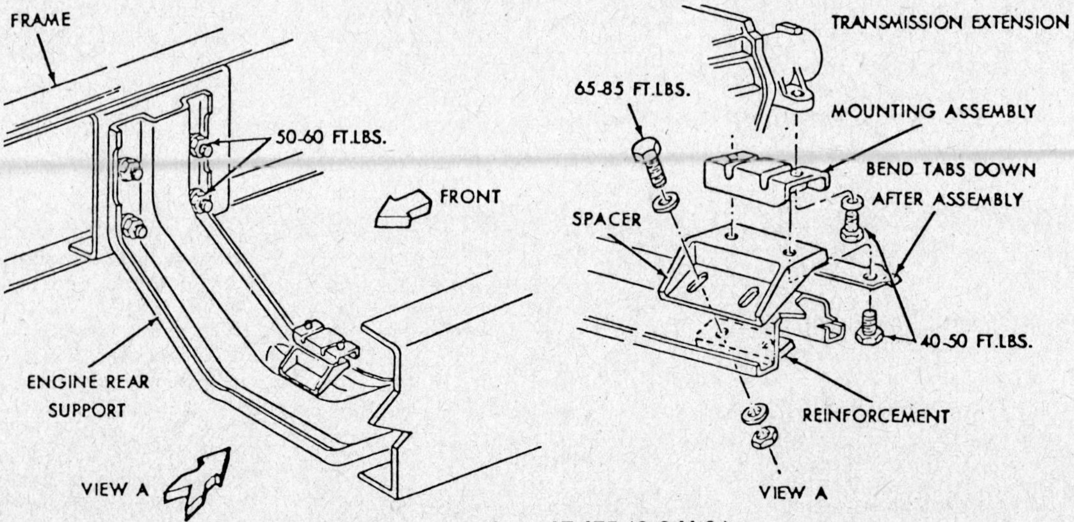

Engine rear mounting—AT 475 (© G.M.C.)

move transmission into position aligning converter with flywheel. Check for and clean away any foreign material in flywheel pilot hole, flywheel flex-plate assembly, and front face of transmission case. Rotate flywheel as necessary so that the six bolt holes in flex-plate are aligned with bolt holes in converter cover. Carefully move transmission assembly toward engine so flex-plate-to-converter cover bolts can be loosely installed and so that pilot on transmission converter enters pilot hole in center of flywheel.

2. Install bolts and washers that attach transmission case to flywheel housing. Tighten bolts to 25-30 foot-pounds torque.
3. Tighten the six flex-plate-to-converter cover bolts to 35-40 foot-pounds torque
4. Carefully lower engine and transmission assembly onto engine rear mounts. Tighten engine rear mounting bolts to 60-70 foot-pounds torque. Then bend lock tabs down over head of each bolt. Remove lifting equipment from beneath vehicle.
5. Remove plugs from cooler lines and transmission case fittings. Be sure fittings are clean and lint-free, then connect cooler lines to transmission.
6. Install filler tube and bracket on right side of transmission. Install level gauge (dipstick).
7. Connect the speedometer shaft fitting to adapter at rear of transmission.
8. Connect drive shaft to transmission.
9. Connect parking brake linkage (if used) at side of transmission.
10. Connect the range selector cable to shift lever at left side of transmission.
11. Connect the vacuum modulator line to modulator. Also, on conventional cab models, connect wiring to neutral safety and back-up lamp switches.

    NOTE: Make sure the ignition switch is in the off position before proceeding to the next step.

12. Install spark plugs and connect battery ground strap, previously disconnected.
13. Connect any other lines, hoses, or wires which were disconnected to aid in transmission removal.
14. Adjust the shift linkage. (see "Shift Linkage Adjustment")
15. Refill the transmission with the proper lubricant.

MT640, MT650, MT654—Removal

NOTE: It may be necessary to remove the air tanks, fuel tanks, special equipment, etc., on some vehicles to provide clearance before the transmission is removed.

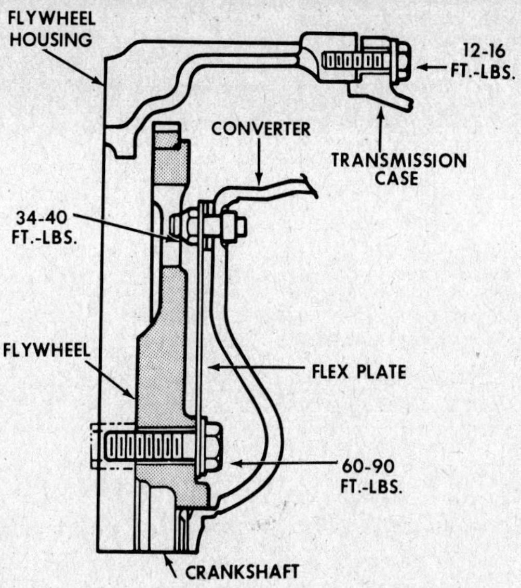

Flex plate installation—MT-640, MT-650 (© G.M.C.)

1. Block vehicle so that it cannot move. Disconnect ground strap from battery negative (—) post. Remove the spark plugs so the engine can be turned over manually.
2. Remove the level gauge (dipstick). Drain transmission by disconnecting filler tube at right side of transmission pan. Remove bracket holding filler tube to transmission and remove filler tube from vehicle. Replace dipstick in tube and cover the pan opening to prevent entry of foreign materials.
3. Disconnect cooler lines from fittings on right side of transmission case. Plug line ends and case openings with lint-free material.
4. Disconnect shift cable from shift lever at left side of transmission.
5. Disconnect vacuum modulator line from modulator. Also, disconnect wiring from back-up lamp switch (right side of transmission) and neutral safety switch (left side of transmission).
6. Disconnect the speedometer shaft fitting from adapter at
7. Disconnect the drive shaft from transmission.
8. Disconnect the mechanical parking brake linkage at the right side of the transmission (if used).
9. Through access openings in the flywheel housing, use a pry bar, as necessary to manually turn the flywheel. As the flywheel is rotated, remove the six nuts retaining flex-plate assembly to converter cover.
10. Support the transmission with a 750-pound (minimum rating) transmission floor jack. The jack must be positioned so transmission pan will not support the weight of transmission. Fasten a safety chain over top of transmission and to both sides of jack.
11. Place a support under rear of engine and remove transmission case-to-crossmember support bolts. Raise the engine to remove weight from the engine rear mounts.
12. Remove the transmission case-to-flywheel housing bolts and washers.
13. Carefully inspect transmission and surrounding area to be sure no lines, hoses, or wires will interfere with transmission removal.

    NOTE: When removing transmission keep rear of transmission lower than the front so as not to lose converter.

14. Move transmission assembly from the engine, lower the assembly carefully and move it out from the vehicle.

Installation

1. Raise vehicle sufficiently to allow installation of transmission. With transmission assembly mounted on transmission jack move transmission into position aligning converter with flywheel. Check for and clean away any foreign material in flywheel pilot hole, flex-plate assembly, and front face of transmission case. Rotate flywheel as necessary so that the six studs in converter cover are aligned with holes in flex plate. Carefully move transmission assembly toward engine so flex-plate-to-converter cover nuts can be loosely installed and so that pilot on transmission converter enters pilot hole in center of flywheel.
2. Install bolts and washers that at-

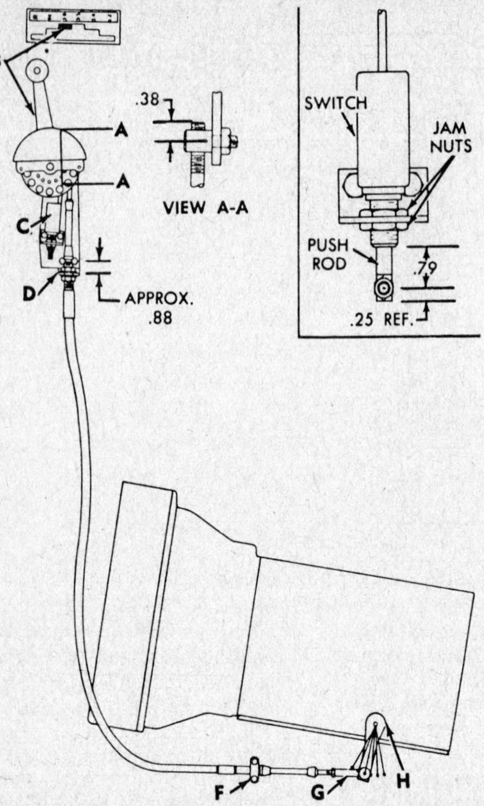

Linkage adjustment—AT-41, MT-40 (© G.M.C.)

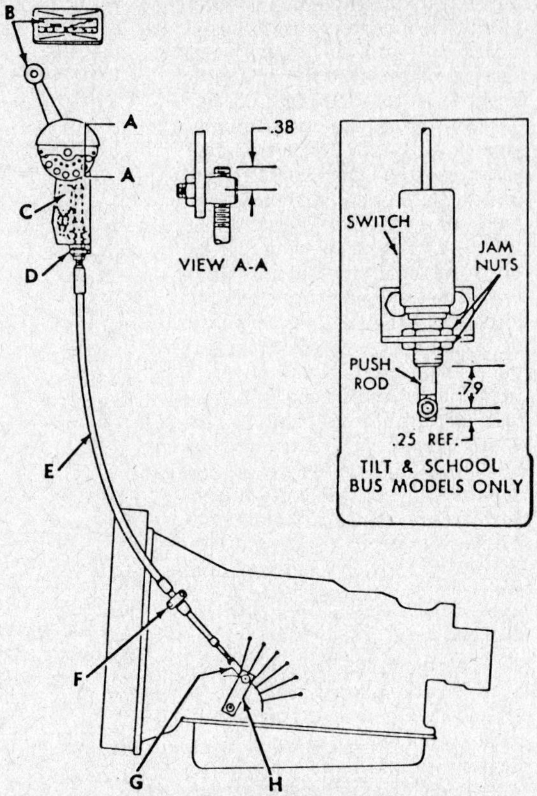

Shift linkage—AT-540 (© G.M.C.)

tach transmission case-to-flywheel housing. Tighten bolts to 12-16 foot-pounds torque.

3. Tighten the six flex-plate-to-converter cover nuts to 34-40 foot-pounds torque.
4. Carefully lower engine and transmission assembly onto engine rear mounts. Tighten engine rear mounting nuts to 190-210 foot-pounds torque. Remove lifting equipment from beneath vehicle.
5. Remove plugs from cooler lines and transmission case fittings. Be sure fittings are clean and lint-free, then connect cooler lines-to-transmission.
6. Install filler tube and bracket on right side of transmission. Install level gauge (dipstick).
7. Connect the speedometer shaft fitting to adapter at rear of transmission.
8. Connect drive shaft to transmission.
9. Connect parking brake linkage (if used) at side of transmission.
10. Connect shift cable to shift lever at left side of transmission.
11. Connect the vacuum modulator line to modulator. Also, connect wiring to neutral safety switch (left side of transmission) and back-up lamp switch (right side of transmission).

    NOTE: Make sure the ignition switch is in the off position before proceeding to the next step.

12. Install spark plugs and connect battery ground strap, previously disconnected.
13. Connect any other lines, hoses, or wires which were disconnected to aid in transmission removal.
14. Adjust the shift linkage. (see "Shift Linkage Adjustment")
15. Refill the transmission.

Shift Linkage Adjustment

With engine off and vehicle wheels blocked, shift the selector lever through each drive range while feeling for full engagement in the transmission. The transmission shift control linkage should fully engage all transmission detent positions in the transmission just before the range selector lever hits the stops incorporated in the range selector cover. Note the position of the selector lever after each shift. The transmission detent "R" (Reverse) should not engage until the selector lever is completely out of the neutral notch. If the selector lever is not properly located or operating, adjust the linkage.

Gas and Diesel Engines

1. Disconnect clevis from transmission shift lever by removing cotter pin and clevis pin.
2. Disconnect control cable from anchor point at bracket on transmission and remove cable retainer clips from underside of cab.
3. Remove four cross recess screws retaining range selector cover to tower or bracket, depending on truck model. Lift range selector assembly out to inspect cable attachment at range selector lever and hanger.
4. Check cable at trunnion for dimension "A". This dimension is necessary to allow for proper cable length at clevis. If adjustment is necessary, remove cable from range selector lever and hanger assembly as follows:
   a. Remove ½ inch locknut from trunnion.
   b. Disconnect cable from anchor point on hangers by removing two locknuts and U-bolt.

   NOTE: Locknuts can be removed and reinstalled up to six times before their replacement becomes necessary.

   c. Mark location of trunnion. Remove trunnion with attached cable core from lever.

CAUTION: The trunnion has been placed in the proper hole at the factory. Any change in the location could cause vehicle operation to be dangerous.

5. With control cable removed, loosen jam nut at trunnion.

   NOTE: Do not use pliers on cable core when loosening jam nut or when adjusting trunnion. Cable core finish may be damaged resulting in cable core seal damage.

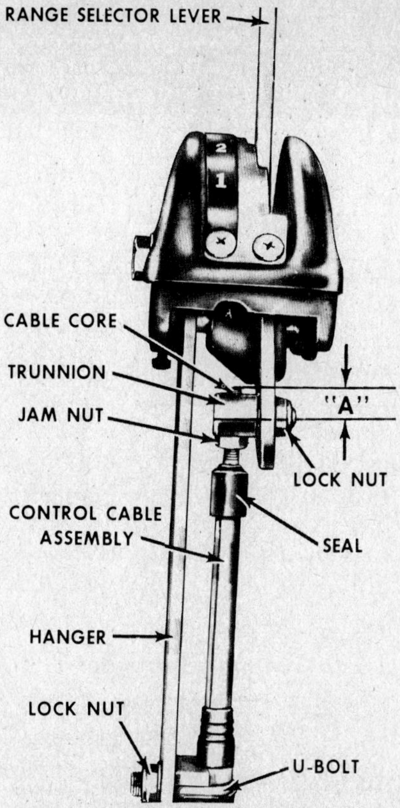

Trunnion and cable core assembly—Allison transmission (© G.M.C.)

6. Turn trunnion clockwise, or counterclockwise to attain dimension "A". Tighten jam nut against trunnion.
7. Install trunnion in its original hole and tighten locknut securely.
8. Anchor cable to hanger with U-bolt, washers and locknuts.
9. Install shift control cover in tower or bracket depending on truck model. Install four cross recess screws. Install cable clips to underside of cab.
10. Anchor cable to bracket at transmission. Tighten two cross recess screws securely.
11. Locate transmission shift lever in "R" (Reverse) position.
    NOTE: "R" position is full counterclockwise movement of lever.

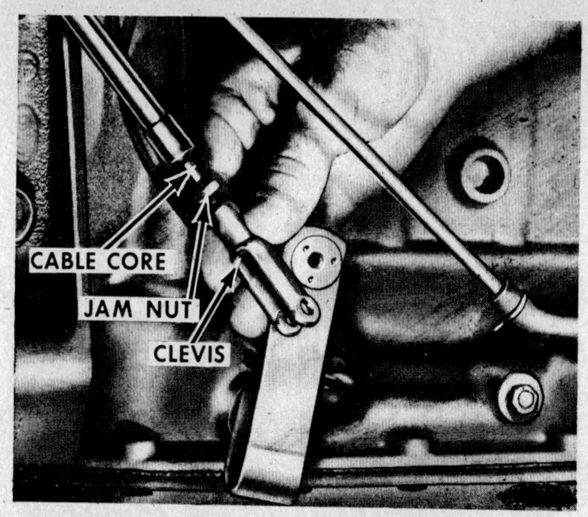

Clevis adjustment—Allison transmission (© G.M.C.)

12. Locate range selector lever against stop in "R" (Reverse) position.
13. Loosen jam nut at clevis. Turn clevis clockwise or counterclockwise on threaded cable core until holes in clevis align with hole in shift lever. Install clevis pin, note that pin should enter freely, if it does not, adjust clevis slightly by ½ turn in each direction until pin does enter freely.
14. Turn clevis one full turn clockwise to allow for cable backlash.
15. Connect clevis to shift lever with clevis pin and a new cotter pin, but do not spread cotter pin at this time.
16. Move the range selector lever through all drive ranges. The transmission detents should fully engage just before the range selector lever hits the stops incorporated in the shift control cover.

Model MT 654

NOTE: If the shift linkage can not be adjusted satisfactorily, it may be necessary to replace the shift linkage cable.

1. Move the range selector against the stop in the REVERSE position.
2. Remove the cotter pin from the shift lever clevis, and disconnect the clevis.
3. Place the shift lever in the REVERSE position.
4. Loosen the jam nut, and turn the clevis until the holes in the clevis align with the hole in the shift lever. The clevis pin should install easily.
5. Turn the clevis one full turn clockwise to allow for backlash.
6. Connect the clevis pin to the shift lever. Install the clevis pin and the cotter pin.
7. Check shifter operation.

NOTE: The transmission detents should fully engage just before the range selector lever contacts the stops in the shift control cover.

Throttle Valve Linkage Adjustment

Early Models

1. Apply parking brake and block vehicles's driving wheels.
2. Disconnect upper TV cable end from accelerator cross shaft.
3. Push upper cable end toward transmission modulator until seated against the stop.
4. Assemble slotted clevis end to cable with locknut.
5. With accelerator linkage in "IDLE" position, upper end of the slotted clevis must be against the clevis pin on the cross shaft lever.
6. Shorten cable at slotted clevis by turning clevis three complete turns clockwise to locate lower end of the cable in actuator ⅛-inch from idle stop.

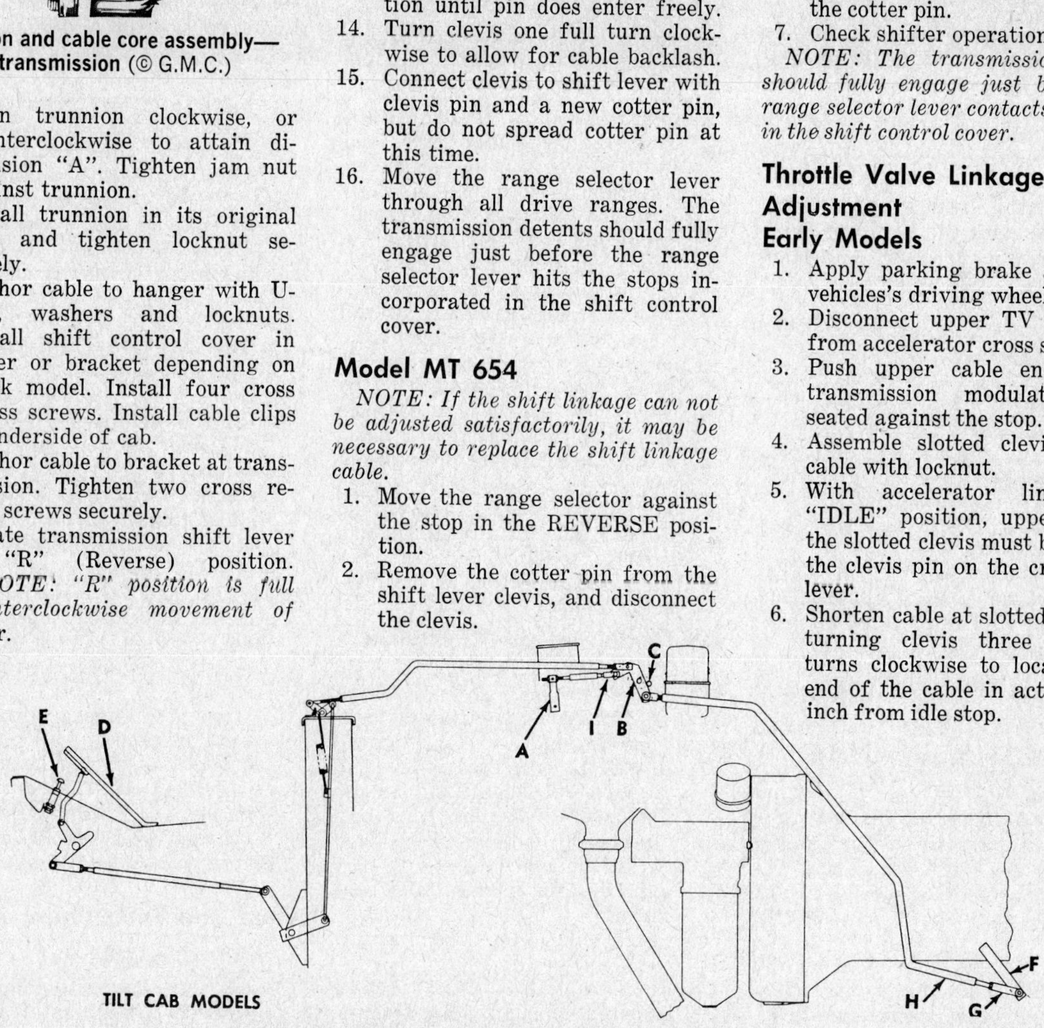

Throttle valve linkage adjustment—AT-41, MT-40 (© G.M.C.)

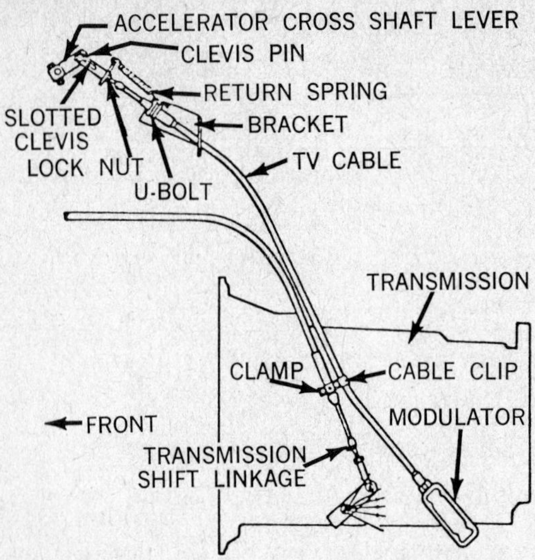

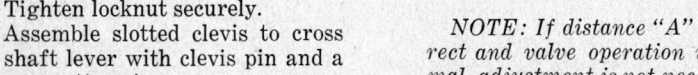

Throttle valve linkage (diesel engine)—Allison transmission
(© G.M.C.)

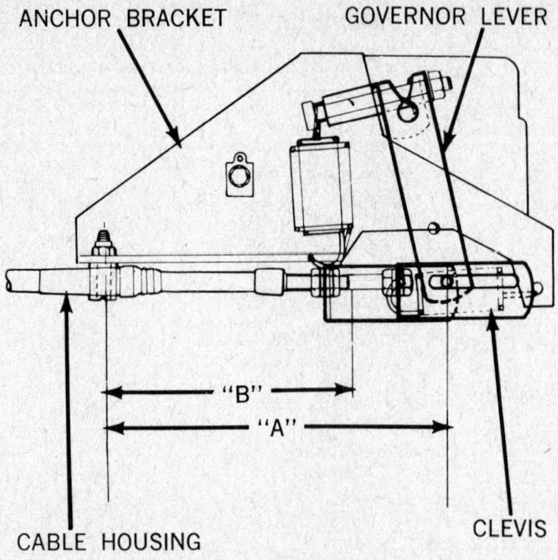

Throttle valve linkage adjustment—medium duty trucks
(© Chevrolet Div., G.M. Corp.)

7. Tighten locknut securely.
8. Assemble slotted clevis to cross shaft lever with clevis pin and a new cotter pin.
9. Attach TV return spring to bracket.

Medium Duty Truck w/Diesel Engine

NOTE: Make sure that the throttle valve cable housing is secured to the control anchor bracket.

1. Disconnect the throttle valve cable clevis from the governor lever.
2. Measure distance "A" (6⅝ inches) with the governor lever in the idle position. Adjust if necessary, and torque the clamp bolt to 9 ft. lbs.
3. Disconnect the clevis and lever return springs.
4. Move the clevis toward the transmission to achieve distance "B" (4¾ inches).
5. Move the governor lever to the full throttle position, and hold. Check for free pin entry.

   NOTE: The hole in the lever must align at the forward end of the slot with free pin entry. Adjust the position of the clevis accordingly, and tighten the jam nut against the clevis.
6. Connect the clevis and governor lever return springs. Check lever operation.

Conventional Cab Models w/Diesel Engine

NOTE: Make sure that the cable assembly is properly secured at the support bracket.

1. Disconnect the cable return spring and clevis from the bellcrank.
2. Measure distance "A": 33 5/32 inches — aluminum conventional cabs, and 29⅝ inches—steel conventional cabs.

NOTE: If distance "A" is correct and valve operation is normal, adjustment is not necessary.

3. Disconnect the rod end from the accelerator cross shaft lever.
4. Loosen the jam nut, and adjust the rod to the desired length by turning the rod end.
5. Tighten the jam nut, and install the rod end on the accelerator lever. Torque the attaching nut to 11 ft. lbs.
6. Push the modulator cable end (with clevis) toward the modulator, and against the stop.
7. With the bellcrank in the accelerator idle position, install the upper end of the slot (in clevis) against the clevis pin in the bellcrank. Decrease the overall length of the cable by turning the clevis adjusting nuts 3 complete turns; locate the lower end of the cable in the modulator a distance of ⅛ inch from the stop.
8. Install the cotter pin through the clevis pin.
9. Tighten the jam nut against the clevis, and install the return spring.
10. Check the operation of the linkage assembly.

All Models w/6V-92 Engine

NOTE: Make sure that the cable assembly is properly secured at the support bracket. Be sure that the bellcrank bolt is tight.

1. Rotate the fuel control lever to the full throttle position.
2. Pull cable "E" until it is bottomed out.
3. Adjust the cable rod end to permit free pin entry in the bellcrank.
4. Check linkage for proper return to the idle position.
5. Check cable travel "E": 1 3/16 inch minimum, and 1 9/16 inch—maximum.

Neutral Safety and Backup Lamp Switch Adjustment

Allison (AT 540) Transmission Tilt & Schoolbus Models

NOTE: "Shift Linkage Adjustment" should be performed as described previously, prior to adjustment of the neutral safety and backup lamp switch.

1. Block driving wheels, apply parking brake, and perform the following to prevent the vehicle from accidentally starting.

   NOTE: Pull the secondary wire out of center socket in the distributor cap and ground wire to prevent possible damage to coil.
2. Move selector lever to "N" (Neutral) position. Then, loosen jam nuts and adjust length of push rod.
3. With switch push rod properly adjusted, tighten jam nuts securely.
4. Check each range position of shift linkage to make sure the starter does not operate with the selector lever in any position other than "N." Have assistant check for proper operation of back-up lights with selector lever in "R". If necessary, readjust switch.
5. Reconnect secondary wire to distributor cap.

NOTE: The neutral safety and back-up lamp switches are non-adjustable on the Allison-MT-640, MT-650 transmission and all diesel engines with automatic transmissions.

Fluid and Filter Changes

AT and MT Models

1. Have the transmission at normal operating temperature (160 to 220 degrees F), and the trans-

mission in neutral.
2. Remove the fill tube from the pan or the drain plug from the right side of the transmission pan. Allow the fluid to drain into a large container.
NOTE: Do not allow fluid to spill and splash. Burns can result.
3. Remove the pan bolts, loosen and remove the pan and gasket. Discard the gasket.
4. Remove the one screw that retains the filter, remove the filter and discard.
NOTE: Later models will have a suction tube that separates from the filter. Retain the tube for use with the new filter. The tubes will have a sealring. Replace with a new sealring upon installation.
5. To clean or replace the governor feed screen, the valve body must be removed on the AT models, and the screen taken from the governor feed bore. Refer to the valve body removal and installation procedures outlined in the General Repair Section. The MT Models have discontinued the use of the primary governor screen, and if one is found in the governor feed tube area of the valve body, discard it.
6. The MT Models have the main governor screen located in the rear cover. Early models will have a screen to be cleaned and reinstalled while the later models will have a replaceable cartridge type filter.
NOTE: The screen or filter is inserted into the rear cover open end first.
7. Retain the screen or filter with the plug or cap.
8. Install the new filter, suction tube and sealring in the sump area and secure with the retaining bolt. Torque to 10 to 15 ft. lbs. for the MT models and 10 to 13 ft. lbs for the AT models.
9. Install the pan with a new gasket. Torque the pan bolts to 10 to 15 ft. lbs. for the MT models and 10 to 13 ft. lbs. for the AT models.
10. Install the filler tube or drain plug into the transmission or pan.
11. Install 10 quarts of transmission fluid into the AT models, and 15 quarts into the MT Models. Start

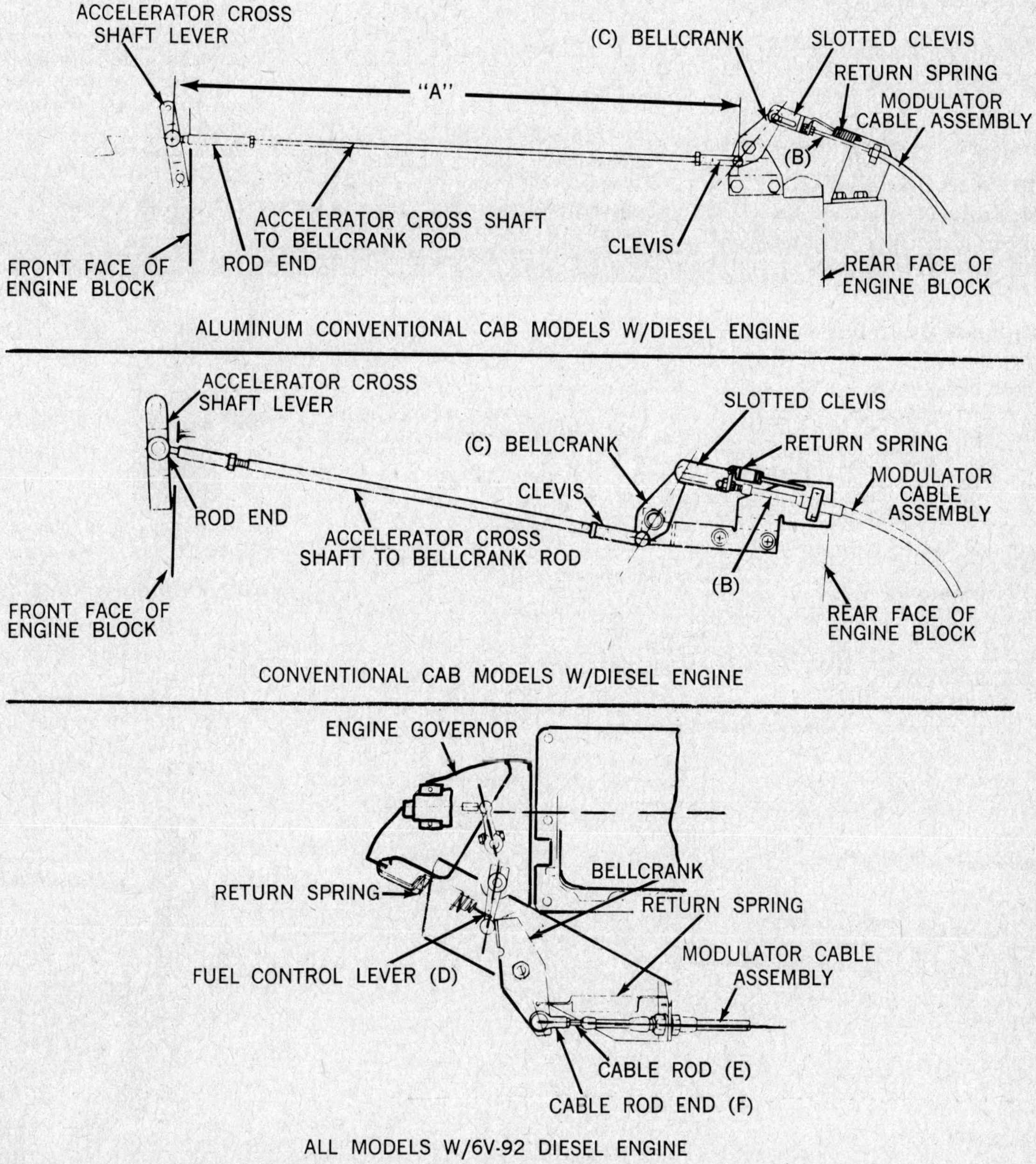

Throttle valve linkage adjustment (© Chevrolet Div., G.M. Corp.)

the engine, check for leaks, move the selector through the gear positions, and recheck the fluid level of the transmission and refill to the full mark on the dipstick.

DRIVESHAFT

Drive Shaft R & R

Removal

1. Raise vehicle.
2. Mark shaft and companion flange alignment.
3. Disconnect rear universal joint by removing attaching U-bolt or strap.
4. Remove bearing support bolts as necessary.
5. Slide driveshaft forward to disengage trunnion, then back to disengage transmission.

One Piece Driveshaft—Installation

1. Slide shaft into transmission and connect rear U-joint.
2. Torque bolts to specifications.

Two Piece Driveshaft—Installation

1. Insert front shaft into transmission and bolt support to crossmember.

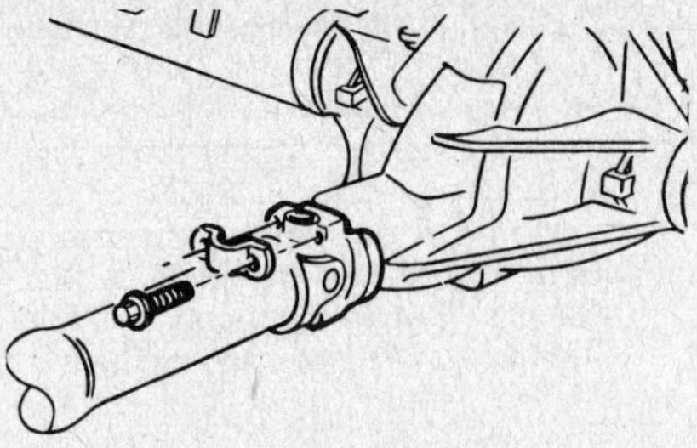

Driveshaft strap attachment (© G.M.C.)

2. Install grease cap and gasket on rear splines.
3. Align all U-joint trunnions in the same vertical position, then install rear shaft.
4. Connect rear U-joint to axle.
5. Torque all bolts to specifications and tighten grease cap.

Universal Joint Overhaul

Snap Ring Type

1500-3500 Models

1. Remove bearing lock rings.
2. Support yoke in an arbor press and apply pressure on trunnion until bearing cup is almost out.
   NOTE: Bearing cup cannot be fully pressed out.
3. Grasp cup with vise and work out of yoke.
4. Repeat procedure on the opposite side.
5. Clean and inspect all parts; replace as necessary. Pack bearings and make certain to fill lubricant reservoirs at end of each trunnion. Place dust seals on trunnions and press into position.
6. Position trunnion into yoke and partially install one bearing cup.
7. Partially install opposite cup and then press them both into place.
8. Install lock rings.

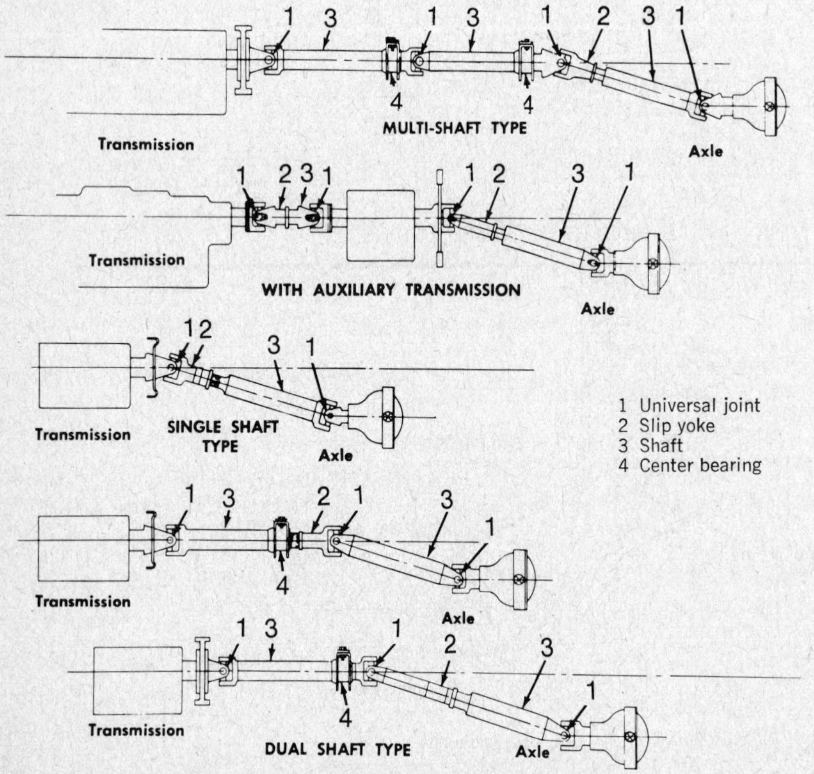

Driveshaft combinations—typical (© G.M.C.)

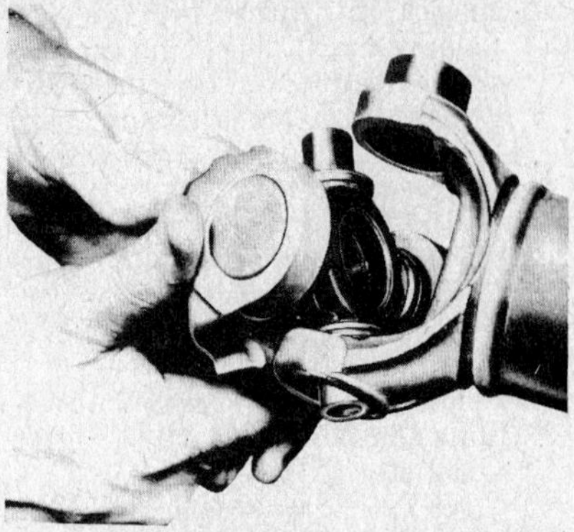

Installing trunnion into yoke—plastic retaining ring type (© Chevrolet Div., G.M. Corp.)

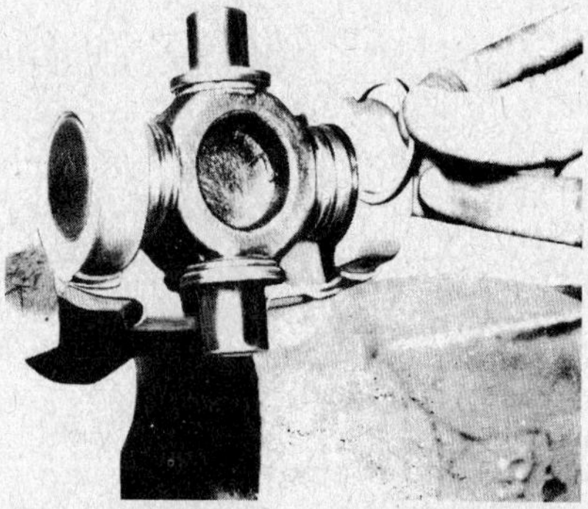

Installing snap ring to retain trunnion (© Chevrolet Div., G.M. Corp.)

Plastic Retaining Ring Type

Disassembly

1. Support the drive shaft in a horizontal position in line with the base plate of a press. Place the universal joint so that the lower ear of the shaft yoke is supported on a $1\frac{1}{8}$ in. socket. Place the cross press, J-9522-3 or

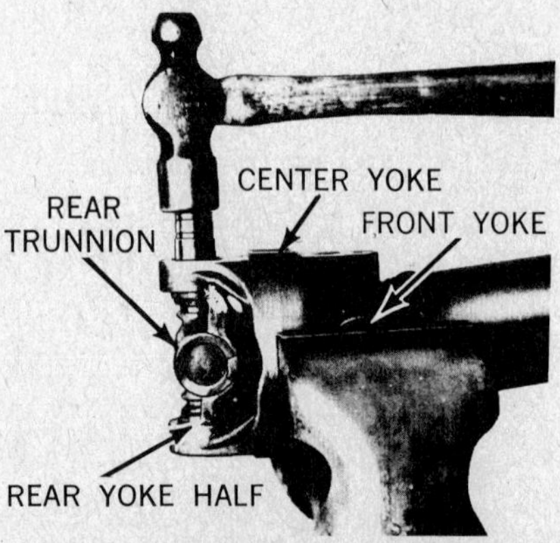

Driving out bearing caps (© G.M.C.)

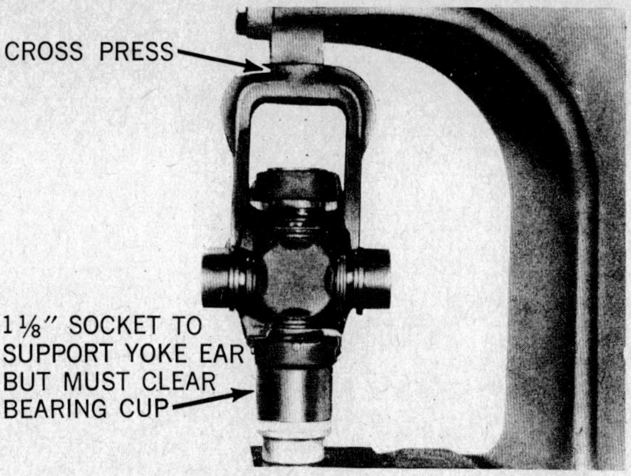

Pressing out bearing cup—plastic retaining ring type
(© Chevrolet Div., G.M. Corp.)

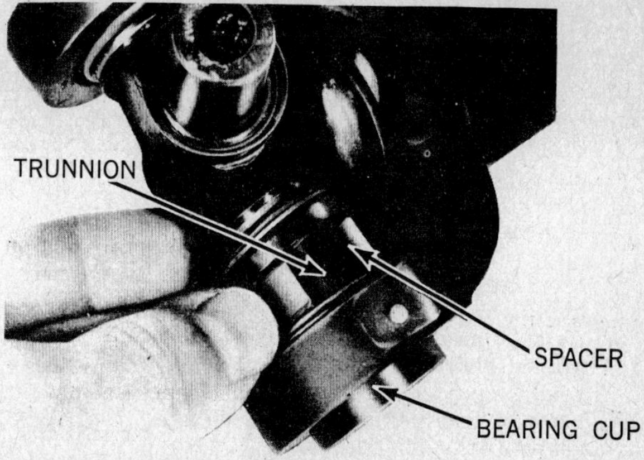

Using spacer to remove bearing cup—plastic retaining ring type
(© Chevrolet Div., G.M. Corp.)

equivalent, on the open horizontal bearing cups, and press the lower bearing cup out of the yoke ear as shown in the illustration. This will shear the plastic retaining the lower bearing cup.
2. If the bearing cup is not completely removed, lift the cross and insert Spacer J-9522-5 or equivalent, between the seal and bearing cup being removed.
   Complete the removal of the bearing cup, by pressing it out of the yoke.
3. Rotate the drive shaft, shear the opposite plastic retainer, and press the opposite bearing cup out of the yoke as before, using Spacer J-9522.
4. Disengage the cross from the yoke and remove.

NOTE: Production universal joints cannot be reassembled. There are no bearing retainer grooves in production bearing cups. Discard all universal joint parts removed.

5. Remove the remains of the sheared plastic bearing retainer from the ears of the yoke. This will aid in reassembly of the service joint bearing cups. It usually is easier to remove plastic if a small pin or punch is first driven through the injection holes.
6. If the front universal joint is being serviced, remove the pair of bearing cups from the slip yoke in the same manner.

Reassembly

1. A universal joint service kit is used when reassembling this joint. This kit includes one pregreased cross assembly, four service bearing cup assemblies with seals, needle rollers, washers, grease and four bearing retainers.
2. Make sure that the seals are in place on the service bearing cups to hold the needle rollers in place for handling.
3. Remove all of the remains of the sheared plastic bearing retainers from the grooves in the yokes. The sheared plastic may prevent the bearing cups from being pressed into place, and this prevents the bearing retainers from being properly sealed.
4. Install one bearing cup part way into one side of the yoke, and turn this yoke ear to the bottom.
5. Insert cross into yoke so that the trunnion seats freely into bearing cup as shown in illustration.
6. Install opposite bearing cup part

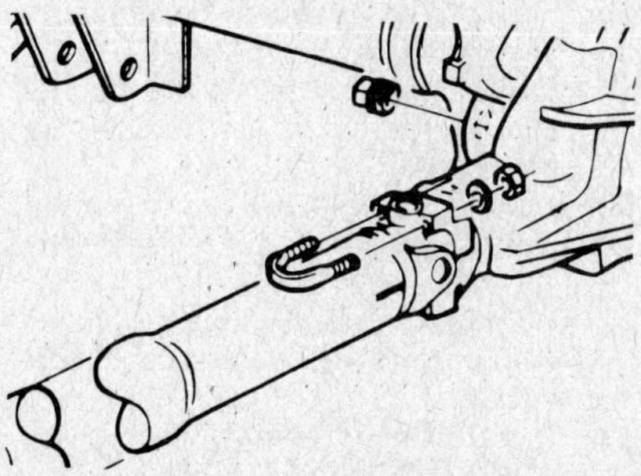

Driveshaft U-bolt attachment (© G.M.C.)

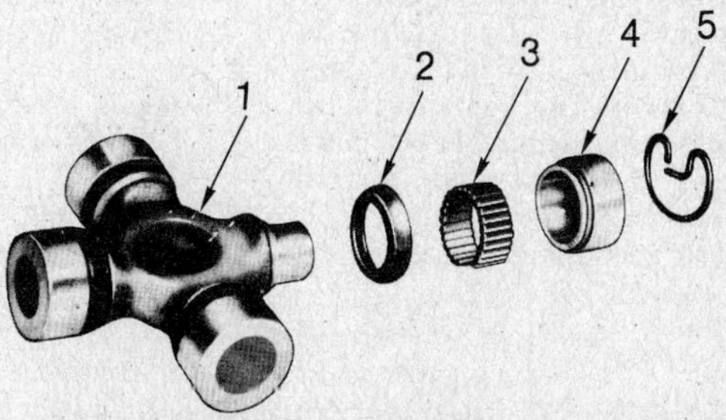

Universal joint—snap ring type (© G.M.C.)

Bearing cap removal (© G.M.C.)

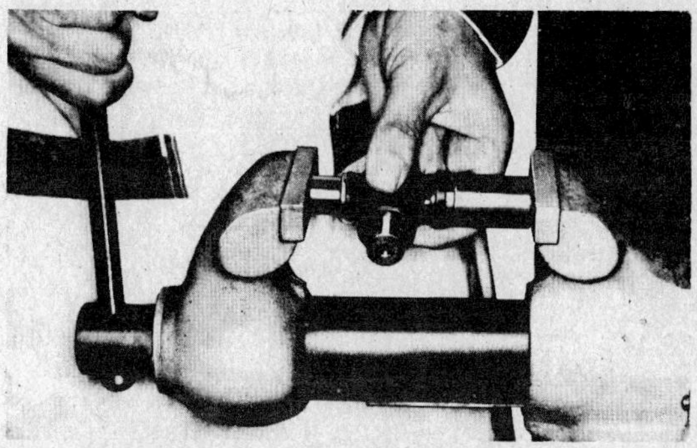

Assembling U-joint—snap ring type (© G.M.C.)

way. Make sure that both trunnions are started straight and true into both bearing cups.
7. Press against opposite bearing cups, working the cross all of the time to check for free movement of the trunnions in the bearings. If there isn't, stop pressing and recheck needle rollers to determine if one or more of them has been tipped under the end of the trunnion.
8. As soon as one bearing retainer groove clears the inside of the yoke, stop pressing and snap the bearing retainer into place as shown in the illustration.
9. Continue to press until the opposite bearing retainer can be snapped into place. If difficulty is encountered, strike the yoke firmly with a hammer to aid in seating bearing retainers. This springs the yoke ears slightly.
10. Assemble the other half of the universal joint in the same manner.
11. Check the freedom of rotation of both sets of trunnions of the cross. If too tight, again rap the yoke ears as described above. This will loosen the bearings and help seat the bearing retainers.

4500-7500 Models

1. Remove bearing retaining snap rings or U-bolts.
2. Strike one side of yoke with hammer to remove bearing. Repeat on opposite side.
3. Tilt journal and remove yoke.
4. Remove remaining bearings in the same manner as step (2).
5. Clean all parts with cleaning fluid. Make certain lubricating passages in journal cross are clear, and all old lubricant has been removed. Check for wear and any missing bearing rollers. If any excessive wear is noted, discard bearings and journal; replace with new parts. Lubricate as recommended in specifications.
6. Install lubrication fitting in journal.
7. Install journal in yoke, then install bearings using a mallet to tap them in place.
8. Install bearing retaining snap rings or U-bolts and torque nuts (when used) to specifications.

Axle shaft removal—10½″ ring gear axle (© G.M.C.)

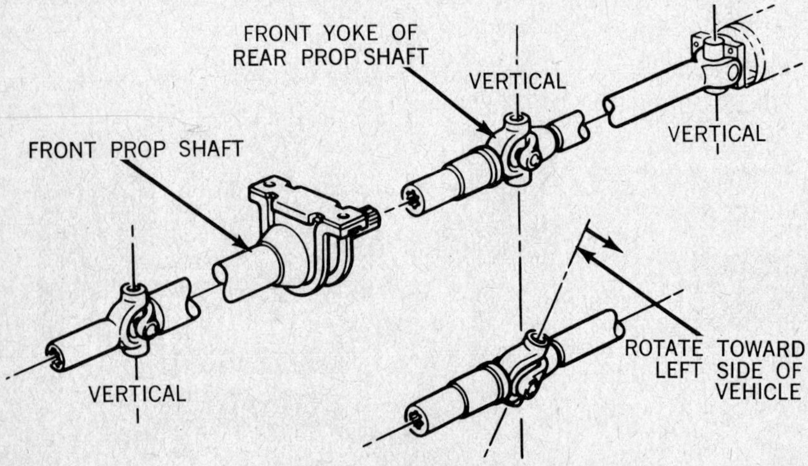

Aligning U-joints (© G.M.C.)

AXLE

Axle Shaft

Semi-Floating—8⅞ Axle

Removal

1. Remove the brake drum.
2. Drain lubricant from the differential and remove the housing cover.
3. Remove the differential pinion shaft lock screw, pinion shaft and axle shaft spacer.
4. Push the axle shaft in and remove the "C" washer from the inner end of the axle shaft.
5. Remove the axle shaft from the housing.

Installation

NOTE: If a new axle shaft is to be installed.

1. Position the axle shaft gasket to the axle shaft flange.
2. Apply heavy shellac or paint to both sides of the gasket and axle shaft oil deflector.
3. Install the axle shaft oil deflector over the gasket aligning the oil pocket with the notch in the flange.
4. Insert six special axle shaft bolts and force the heads down to the deflector.
5. Peen the end of the shoulder on the bolts into the countersink around the bolt holes in the flange.
6. Slide the axle shaft into place.
   CAUTION: Exercise care that the splines on the end of the shaft do not cut the axle shaft oil seal and that they engage with the splines of the differential side gears.
7. Install the "C" washer on the inner end of the shaft.
8. Pry the shafts apart so that the "C" washers are seated in the counterbore in the differential side gears and install the pinion gears.
9. Select the proper axle shaft spacer to give free fit to .014″ maximum clearance between the end of the axle shaft and the spacer.
10. Install the spacer and pinion shaft, locking in place with the special screw.
11. Install the axle housing cover and gasket and refill the differential.
12. Install the drum and wheel.

Full Floating—10½″ Axle

Removal

1. Remove the bolts and lock washers from the axle shaft flange to hub.
2. Tap on the axle shaft flange with a soft-faced hammer to loosen the flange from the hub.
3. Grip the axle flange and pull the axle from the axle tube.

Installation

1. Clean the hub surface and the axle flange.
2. Install a new gasket over the axle shaft and install the axle shaft into the axle tube.
3. Engage the axle splines with the

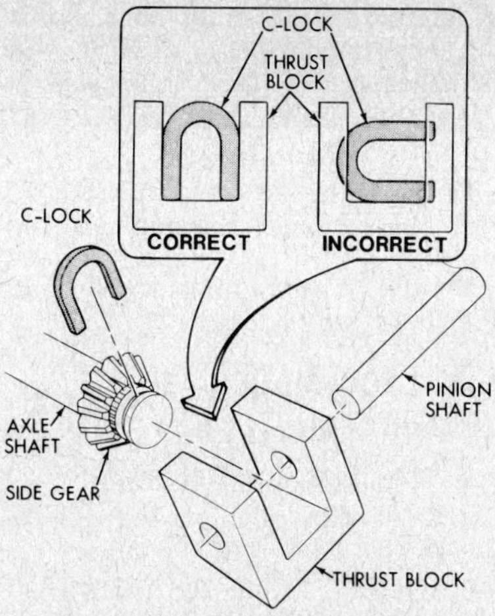

Correct "C" lock position (© G.M.C.)

splines of the differential side gear, align the bolt holes in the axle flange with the bolt holes in the wheel hub and push the axle flange to mate with the hub surface.
4. Install the bolts and lock washers. Torque the bolts to 90 ft. lbs.

Full Floating—12¼" Axle

Removal

1. Remove the bolts from the hub cap and install a side hammer assembly into the tapped hole in the axle shaft flange.
2. Remove the axle shaft with the aid of the slide hammer.

Installation

1. Clean the old gasket material from the hub and hub cap surfaces.
2. Install the axle shaft into the axle tube and align the axle splines of the differential side gear, and align the splines of the axle flange with the splines of the wheel hub.
3. Tap the axle shaft into position on the hub.
4. Install the hub cap and bolts. Torque the bolts to 15 ft. lbs.

Semi-Floating Axle Shaft Bearing or Oil Seal

Removal

1 Remove the wheel, drum and axle shaft (see axle shaft removal).
2. Using a slide hammer, remove the bearing, bearing retainer and oil seal.
3. Inspect the bore and dress out the old stake points.

Installation

1. Using the proper driver, place the oil seal, bearing and inside bearing retainer on the driver in that order.
2. Place a light coat of sealer on the outside of the seal to insure proper sealing of the seal in the housing bore.
3. Start the bearing into the axle housing and tap the tool with a hammer to seat the parts.
4. Remove the driver and stake the oil seal in place with a punch.
5. Assemble the axle shafts (see Axle Shaft Installation).

Pinion Flange, Oil Deflector and/or Oil Seal

Replacement

1. Raise the vehicle and support the frame on stand jacks, allow the axle to drop for clearance and expand the brake shoes on one wheel to lock the wheel.
2. Check the free wheel for freedom of rotation.
3. Separate the rear universal, tape the trunnion bearings to the joint and lower the rear of the propeller shaft
4. Using a one inch torque wrench, and proper socket on the pinion flange nut, rotate the pinion through several complete revolutions and record the torque required to keep the pinion turning. If the old flange is to be installed, mark the pinion and flange for reassembly in the same relative position.
5. Hold the pinion flange, remove the pinion flange nut and special washer. Discard the nut and use a new one upon reassembly.
6. Remove the pinion flange Pry the old oil seal out of the case.
7. Inspect the pinion flange for smooth oil seal surface or worn drive splines. Replace if necessary.
8. Install a new flange oil deflector if the deflector is damaged.
9. Soak the new seal in light engine oil before installation. Wipe the outside of the seal and coat the outside with sealer.
10. Install the new seal using the proper driver.
11. Install the pinion flange, aligning the marks on the pinion and flange if the old flange is being used. If the flange does not go on the shaft easily, pull the flange on the shaft using a special tool. Remove the special tool and install the special washer and new nut.
12. Tighten the nut to remove end play and continue alternately tightening and checking preload with an inch pound torque wrench until it is the same as recorded in step 4.
13. Readjust the brake on the locked wheel.
14. Connect the propeller shaft, lower the vehicle and road test for leaks and noise.

Rear Axle Assembly

3500 and 5500 lbs Capacity Axle (Models 1500-3500)

Removal

1. Raise truck and support rear axle to relieve load from springs, tie-rod, and shock absorbers.
2. Disconnect tie-rod at axle (when used).
3. Disconnect driveshaft.
   NOTE: Secure bearing caps to trunnion with tape.
4. Disconnect shock absorbers.
5. Disconnect vent hose.
6. Disconnect brake hose on axle housing. Remove brake drum and disconnect parking brake cable.
7. Make certain coil springs (when used) are compressed, then remove U-bolts, spacers and clamp plates.
8. Withdraw axle assembly.

Installation

To install axle assembly, reverse the removal procedure, bleed brake system, adjust parking brake and torque all bolts to specifications.

11,000 lb. Capacity Axle (Models 1500-3500)

Removal

1. Raise truck, support frame side rails and remove rear wheels.
2. Disconnect driveshaft.
   NOTE: Secure bearing caps to trunion with tape.
3. Disconnect brake hose and shock absorbers.
4. Remove drum and disconnect parking brake.
5. Support axle, remove spring U-bolts and then withdraw assembly.

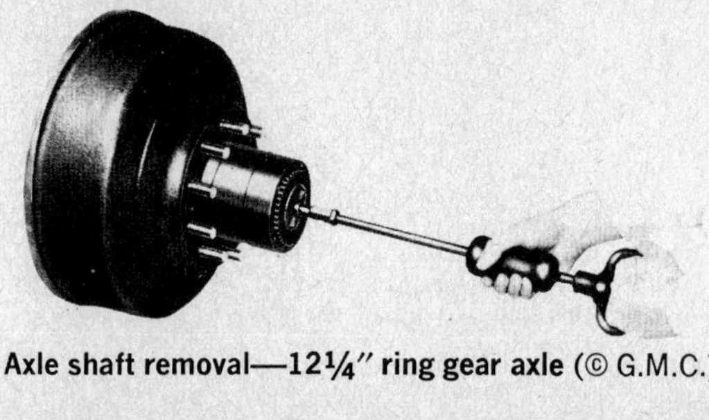
Axle shaft removal—12¼" ring gear axle (© G.M.C.)

Installation

To install axle assembly, reverse the removal procedure, bleed brake system, adjust parking brake and torque all bolts to specifications.

11,000 lb. Capacity Axle (Models 4500-7500)

Removal

1. Raise rear of truck and support frame rails.
2. Disconnect brake lines and electrical wiring.
3. Disconnect driveshaft and torque or radius rods (when used).
4. Remove spring U-bolts and withdraw axle assembly.

Installation

To install axle assembly, mount wheels and tires, roll axle under truck and reverse the removal procedure. Bleed brake system, fill axle with lubricant to proper level and torque all bolts to specifications.

Refer to General Repair Section for complete light duty overhaul procedures and out of truck adjustments.

Tandem Axle Suspension

Description

The Hendrickson type tandem axle suspension uses equalizing beams to tie the front rear axle to the rear axle and to permit independent vertical movement of each axle as required by the road surface. The torque rods are used to maintain proper drive line alignment and to stablize the driving and braking forces. Bolts are used on some models to hold the spring to the top saddle pad, while U-bolts are used on other models.

NOTE: When major overhaul is required, the complete tandem axle should be removed as a unit. The torque rods, springs, equalizing beams and other parts may be removed separately as required.

CAUTION: **Block the vehicle securely before removal of the assembly to avoid rolling or pivoting at the equalizer beams when the torque rods are disconnected. The use of a helper is suggested, along with proper lifting tools so that personal injury does not occur.**

Tandem Axle Removal and Installation

1. Block all wheels and disconnect all applicable brake lines or hoses, differential lock lines, or electrical wiring from the rear axles.
2. Remove the rebound bolts from the rear spring brackets.
3. Remove all nuts, washers from the front spring brackets.
4. If equipped with ball stud torque rods, remove the stud nuts and tap each ball stud loose with a soft hammer. Remove the ball studs from the axle brackets.
5. If equipped with straddle mount torque rods, remove the mounting bolts from the rear axle bracket.
6. Support the rear axle differential with a floor jack, and disconnect the propeller shaft from the forward rear axle.
7. Using a suitable hoist, raise the rear of the frame high enough to clear the tandem axle assembly. Roll the assembly out from under the frame.
8. The installation is in the reverse of the removal procedure.

Locking Differentials

Refer to General Repair Section for complete overhaul procedures.

REAR SUSPENSION

Leaf Spring

1500-3500 Models

Removal

1. Raise truck.
2. Loosen, but do not remove, spring to shackle retaining nut.
3. Remove shackle to spring hanger attaching bolt.
4. Remove attaching spring to front hanger bolt.
5. Remove U-bolts and then remove spring.

Installation

To install leaf spring assembly, reverse the removal procedure and torque nuts and bolts to specifications.

NOTE: Torque nuts and bolts after lowering the truck.

4500-7500 Models—Single or Tandem Axle Springs

Removal and Installation

1. Raise the rear of the vehicle, place floor jacks under the axle(s) and remove the dual wheels from the hubs to facilitate the removal of the spring eye pin and to expose the other nuts and bolts.
2. Remove the saddle cap stud nuts and/or spring U-bolts.
3. Remove the rebound pin locks or retainers, and then remove the rebound pins.
4. Remove the eye bolts or radius lead pin clamp bolts, then remove the lubrication fitting from the inner end of the pin, if equipped.
5. Remove the pins from the springs and lower the axle(s) or raise the frame until the spring will clear the brackets.
6. Remove the spring from the vehicle.
7. Installation is the reverse of removal.
8. Torque the U-bolts or saddle cap stud nuts to specifications after the vehicle is lowered to the floor.

Coil Spring

1500-3500 Models

Removal

1. Raise truck on hoist and support rear axle.
2. Disconnect shock absorber at control arm bracket.
3. Remove upper and lower spring clamps.

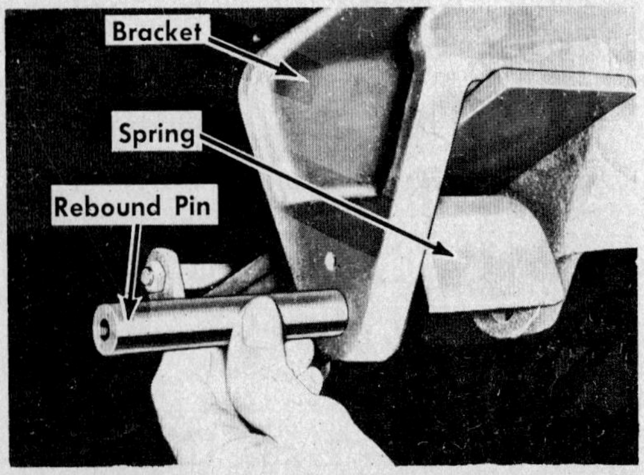

Installing rebound pin—typical (© G.M.C.)

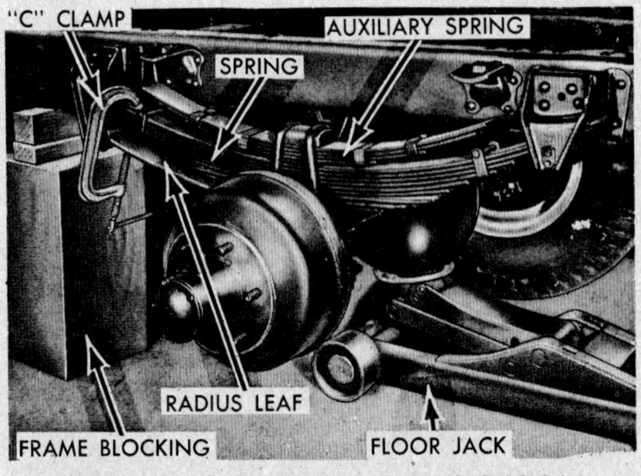

Using C-clamp at radius leaf (© G.M.C.)

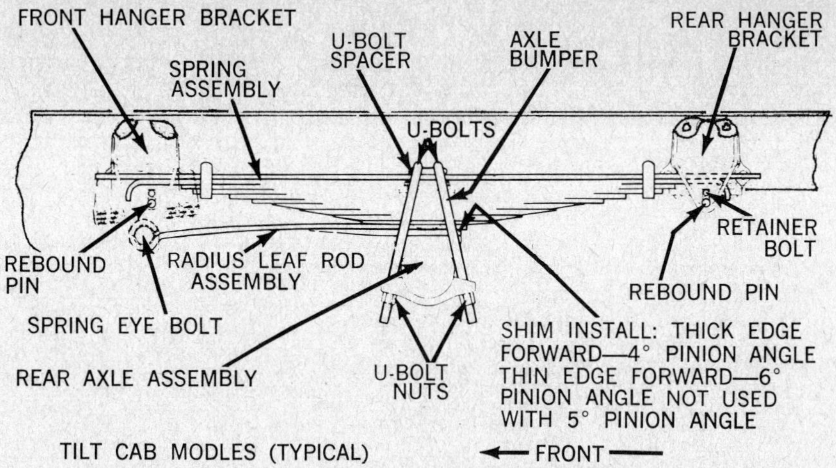

Rear leaf spring suspension (© G.M.C.)

4. Lower control arm enough to remove spring.

Installation

1. Position clamp in spring.
2. Install spring and clamp loosely; torque upper clamp nut to specifications.
3. Connect shock absorber and torque to specifications.
4. Torque lower clamp nut to specifications.
5. Remove axle support and lower truck.

Auxiliary Springs

Some models are equipped with auxiliary springs. They are mounted to brackets on the frame and are usually held to the main spring by long U-bolts. The purpose of these springs is to provide additional stability under unusual operating conditions.

Shock Absorbers

Shock absorbers used are non-adjustable and non-repairable. Maintenance operations are limited to periodic tightening and replacement of rubber mounting grommets. If a shock absorber is worn, the complete unit must be replaced.

Tie Rod

CP1500-C2500 Models

Removal

1. Raise truck.
2. Remove attaching nuts and bolts, then remove rod.

Installation

1. Position rod ends in mounting brackets, insert pivot bolts and install nuts finger tight.
2. Lower truck and torque pivot nuts to specifications.

Control Arm

CP1500-C2500 Models

Removal

1. Raise truck and relieve load on springs by supporting axle.
2. Place jack under control arm.
3. Remove spring clamp bolt from underside of arm.
4. Remove U-bolt nuts; disconnect shock absorber bracket, and lower end of control arm.
5. Disconnect parking brake lever, then remove pivot bolt and control arm.

Installation

To install control arm, reverse the removal procedure. Torque spring clamp and shock absorber BEFORE lowering truck, torque pivot bolts AFTER.

Stabilizer Shaft

P3500 Model

Removal

1. Raise truck and support axle to relieve load on U-bolts.
2. Remove the forward U-bolt retaining nuts, and remove shaft anchors.
3. Remove shaft retaining brackets and then remove shaft.

Installation

To install stabilizer shaft, reverse the removal procedure. Alternately torque all nuts and bolts to specifications.

NOTE: Make certain that both ends of shaft protrude equally from the anchors.

REAR AXLE TORQUE SPECIFICATIONS

ITEM	TORQUE (FT. LB.)
DRIVE PINION YOKE NUT	
Eaton	
1⅛″-18	320-450
1¼″-12	400-600
1½″-18	500-700
Rockwell	
1″-20	300-400
1¼″-18	700-900
1½″-18	800-1100
Corporation	
1⅛″-18	160-280
DIFFERENTIAL CARRIER TO HOUSING	
Eaton	
½″-13 Cap Screw	75-85
⅝″-11 Cap Screw	160-175
⅝″-18 Stud Nut	220-240
Rockwell	
½″-20 Stud Nut	92-118
⅝″-18 Stud Nut	185-235
Corporation	
7/16″-20 Cap Screw	75-90
9/16″-18	130-170

ITEM	TORQUE (FT. LB.)
OIL SEAL RETAINER & PINION CAGE	
Eaton	
9/16″-12	115-125
Rockwell	
7/16″-14	60-70
½″-13	80-105
9/16″-12	115-150
Corporation	
½″-13 (H135)	160-170
½″-13 (H150)	80-105
½″-13 (T150)	80-105
⅝″-11 (H110)	160-170
SHIFT CHAMBER	
Stud Nut—⅜″-24	30-35
Bolt—7/16″-14	40-50
AXLE SHAFT FLANGE	
Stud Nut—½″	50-60
Stud Nut—⅝″	90-110
Cap Screw—5/16″-24	11-18

International Harvester Pick-Up, Scout, Traveler

INDEX

TUNE-UP SPECIFICATIONS

CYL — CID	YEAR	SPARK PLUG GAP	DISTRIBUTOR POINT DWELL	DISTRIBUTOR POINT GAP	IGNITION TIMING DEGREES	CRANKING COMPRESSION PRESSURE	VALVE CLEARANCE IN	VALVE CLEARANCE EXH	GOVERNOR NO LOAD RPM	FUEL PRESS.	IDLE SPEED STD	IDLE SPEED AUTO
4-196	1975-80	.035	24-34	①	0⑥	143	0	0	4000⑦	5	575	600
6-232	1973-74	.035	32	.016⑧	TDC	130	0	0	4000⑦	5	725	650
6-258	1973-74	.035	32	.016⑧	TDC	130	0	0	4000⑦	5	675	675
8-304	1973	.030	30	.019	TDC	145	0	0	3900⑦	5	700	700N
8-304	1974-80	.030	30	.017①	TDC	145	0	0	3900⑦	5	700	650N
8-345	1973-75	.030	30	.019①	TDC②	143	0	0	3800	5	600⑪	600N
8-345	1976-80	.035	30	①	5B⑩	143	0	0	3800	5	650⑩	650⑩
8-392	1973-75	.030⑫	30	.019①	TDC⑬	140	0	0	3600	5	700	600D
8-400	1973-74	.035	30	.016	5B	140	0	0	3400	5	700	—
8-401	1973-74	.027	30	.017	7B	140	0	0	3400	5	700	—
8-404 (399)	1975-80	.030	24-34	①	9B	140	0	0	3600	5	525	575
6-406	1973-74	.030	32	.019	5B	120	.025H	.025H	2450	5	475	—
8-446	1975-80	.030	24-34	①	5B	145	0	0	3600	5	525	—
6-450	1973-74	.030	32	.019	5B	120	.025H	.025H	2800	5	525	—
8-478	1973-74	.027	32	.017	10B	135	0	0	3400	5	550	550
6-501	1973-74	.030	32	.019	5B	120	.025H	.025H	2800	5	525	—
8-537	1975-80	.030	24-34	①	7B	140	0	0	3400	5	550	—
8-549	1973-78	.027	32	.017	7B④	140	0	0	3200	5	475	—
8-605	1975-80	.030	24-34	①	7B	140	0	0	3400	5	500	550

① .008 on breakerless ignition
② LPG—10B
1975 Low compression—5B
③ with thermoquad—5B
④ FTV models—9B
⑥ With automatic transmission—5BTDC
⑦ Maximum recommended RPM
⑧ 1973—.019 inch
⑨ Idle speed shutdown—525-575N
⑩ 1976-78—Equipped with distributor numbers—
461270-C91
461271-C91
461272—C91
Idle speed (AT and ST) 650-700
Timing—TDC
⑪ 1973—700 RPM
1974—800 RPM⑨
1975—650 RPM
⑫ 1975—.035 inch
⑬ Equipped with carter carburetor and distributor number 519861—5 BTDC

FIRING ORDER AND ROTATION

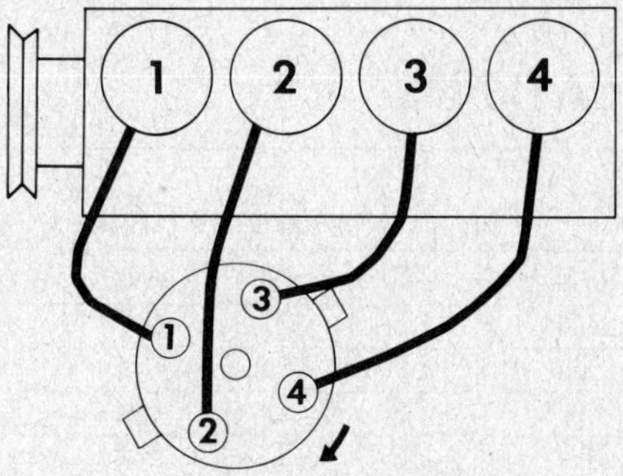

4 cylinder 4-196
1-3-4-2

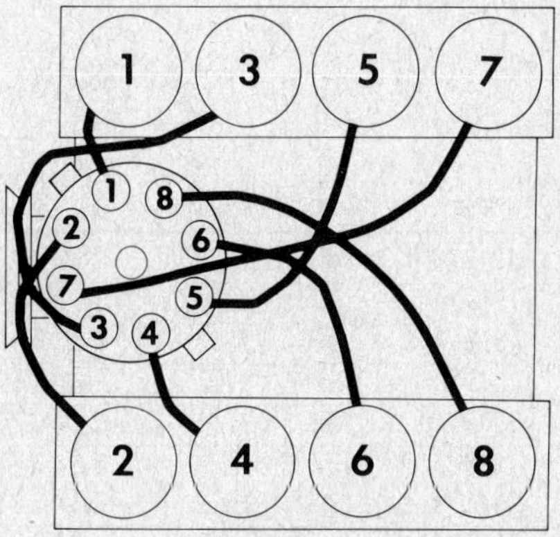

MV 404, 446
1-2-7-3-4-5-6-8

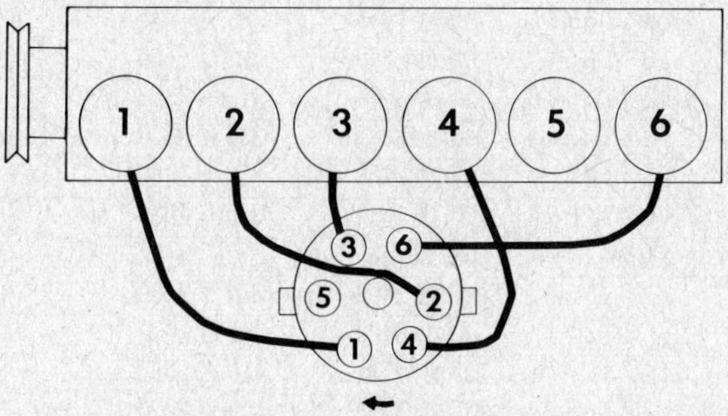

6 cylinder RD 406, 450, 501
1-5-3-6-2-4

FIRING ORDER AND ROTATION

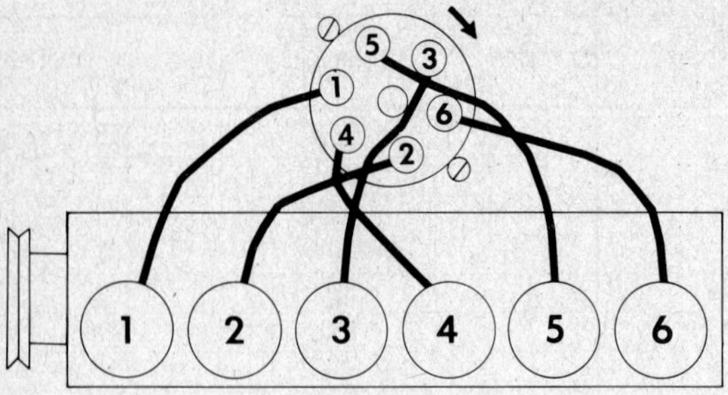

6 cylinder P-6, 232, 258
1-5-3-6-2-4

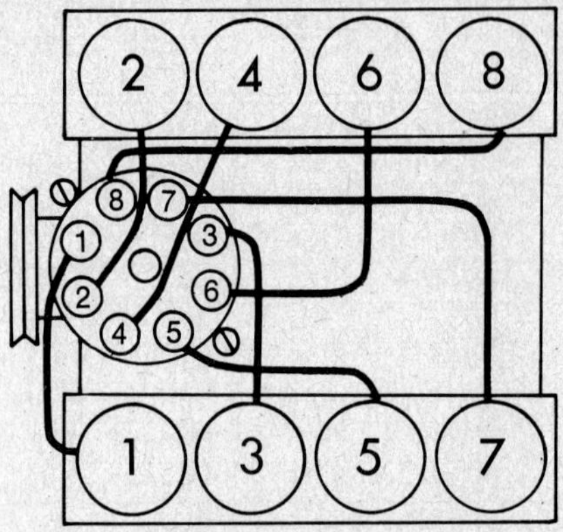

8 cylinder VS 401, 478, 549
1-8-7-3-6-5-4-2

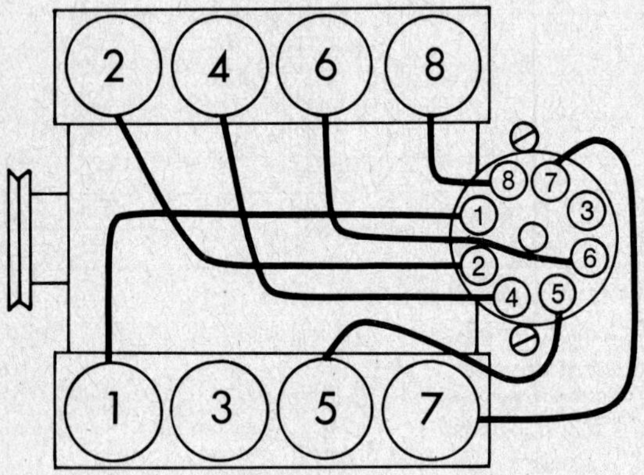

8 cylinder V 537, 605
1-8-7-3-6-5-4-2

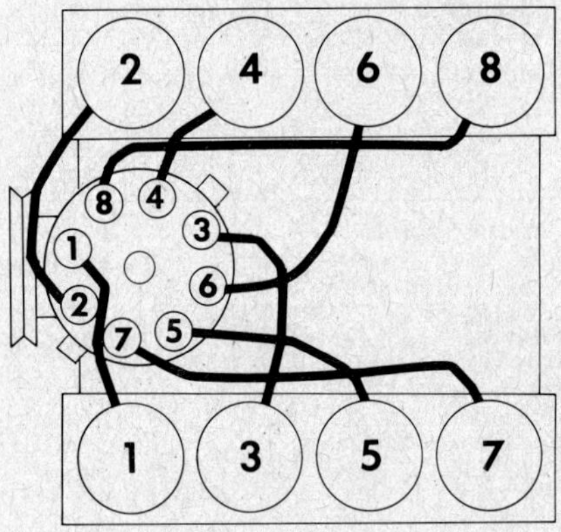

8 cylinder V 304, 345, 392
1-8-4-3-6-5-7-2

GENERAL ENGINE SPECIFICATIONS

CYL — CID	YEAR	BORE x STROKE	FIRING ORDER	SAE HORSEPOWER @ RPM	SAE TORQUE @ RPM	COMP. RATIO	CARBU-RETOR	VALVE LIFTER	OIL PRESSURE
4-196	1975-80	4.125 x 3.656	1-3-4-2	111 @ 4400	180 @ 2000	8.1	1V	Hyd.	50
6-232	1973-74	3.75 x 3.50	1-5-3-6-2-4	145 @ 4300	215 @ 1600	8.5	1V	Hyd.	32
6-258	1973-74	3.75 x 3.895	1-5-3-6-2-4	115 @ 3800	199 @ 2000	8.0	1V	Hyd.	32
8-304	1973-80	3.875 x 3.218	1-8-4-3-6-5-7-2	147 @ 3900	240 @ 2400	8.2	2V	Hyd.	45
8-304	1973-74	3.875 x 3.218	1-8-4-3-6-5-7-2	153 @ 3900	246 @ 2400	8.2	4V	Hyd.	45
8-345	1973-80	3.875 x 3.656	1-8-4-3-6-5-7-2	157 @ 3800	266 @ 2400	8.1	2V	Hyd.	45
8-345	1973-75	3.875 x 3.656	1-8-4-3-6-5-7-2	163 @ 3800	273 @ 2400	8.1	4V	Hyd.	45
8-392	1973-74	4.125 x 3.656	1-8-4-3-6-5-7-2	191 @ 3600	299 @ 2800	8.0	2V	Hyd.	45
8-392	1973-75	4.125 x 3.656	1-8-4-3-6-5-7-2	194 @ 3600	308 @ 2800	8.0	4V	Hyd.	45
8-400	1973-74	4.166 x 3.680	1-8-4-3-6-5-7-2	211 @ 4000	326 @ 2800	8.25	2V	Hyd.	50
8-401	1973-74	4.125 x 3.750	1-8-7-3-6-5-4-2	186 @ 3400	322 @ 2400	7.69	2V	Hyd.	55
8-404 (399)	1975-80	4.125 x 3.740	1-2-7-3-4-5-6-8	188 @ 3600	311 @ 2300	8.1	2V	Hyd.	55
8-404 (399)	1975-80	4.125 x 3.740	1-2-7-3-4-5-6-8	210 @ 3600	336 @ 2800	8.1	4V	Hyd.	55
6-406	1973-74	4.375 x 4.50	1-5-3-6-2-4	160 @ 2750	336 @ 1400	7.13	2V	Mech.	50
8-446	1975-80	4.125 x 4.180	1-2-7-3-4 5-6-8	235 @ 3600	385 @ 2600	8.1	4V	Hyd.	55
6-450	1973-74	4.375 x 5.0	1-5-3-6-2-4	168 @ 2600	372 @ 1400	7.1	2V	Mech.	50
8-478	1973-74	4.50 x 3.750	1-8-7-3-6-5-4-2	209 @ 3400	384 @ 2200	7.6	2V	Hyd.	55
6-501	1973-74	4.50 x 5.250	1-5-3-6-2-4	181 @ 2600	406 @ 1400	6.8	4V	Mech.	40
8-537	1975-80	4.625 x 3.750	1-8-7-3-6-5-4-2	208 @ 3200	415 @ 2000	7.5	2V	Hyd.	55
8-537	1975-80	4.625 x 3.750	1-8-7-3-6-5-4-2	236 @ 3200	429 @ 2200	7.5	4V	Hyd.	55
8-549	1973-78	4.50 x 4.312	1-8-7-3-6-5-4-2	227 @ 3200	446 @ 2000	7.6	4V	Hyd.	55
8-605	1975-80	4.625 x 4.50	1-8-7-3-6-5-4-2	227 @ 3200	446 @ 2000	7.5	4V	Hyd.	55

CRANKSHAFT SPECIFICATIONS

CYL — CID	MAIN BEARING JOURNALS: Journal Diameter	Oil Clearance	Shaft End Play	Thrust on No.	CONNECTING ROD JOURNALS: Journal Diameter	Oil Clearance	Rod Side Clearance
4-196	2.7484-2.7494	.001-.004	.003-.008	3	2.373-2.374	.0011-.0036	.004-.011
6-232	2.4981-2.500	.001-.002	.0015-.007	3	2.0934-2.0955	.001-.002	.008-.010
6-258	2.498-2.500	.001-.002	.0015-.007	3	2.0934-2.0955	.001-.002	.008-.010
8-304	2.7484-2.794	.001-.004	.003-.008	3	2.373-2.374	.0011-.0036	.008-.016
8-345	2.7484-2.794	.001-.004	.003-.008	3	2.373-2.374	.0011-.0036	.008-.016
8-392	2.7484-2.794	.001-.004	.003-.008	3	2.373-2.374	.0011-.0033	.008-.018
8-400	2.7474-2.7489	.001-.002	.003-.008	3	2.2485-.2.2464	.001-.002	.006-.018
8-401	2.124-3.125	.0008-.0038	.006-.011	3	2.623-2.624	.0017-.0042	.010-.018
8-404 (399)	3.1228-3.1236	.0010-.0036	.0025-.0085	3	2.4980-2.4990	.0011-.0036	.008-.020
6-406	3.2495-3.2505	.0013-.0043	.006-.015	7	2.751-2.752	.0012-.0037	.007-.013
8-446	3.1228-3.1236	.0010-.0036	.0025-.0085	3	2.4980-2.4990	.0011-.0036	.008-.020
6-450	3.2495-3.2505	.0013-.0043	.006-.015	7	2.751-2.752	.0012-.0037	.007-.013
8-478	3.124-3.125	.0008-.0038	.006-.011	3	2.623-2.624	.0017-.0042	.010-.018
6-501	3.2495-32505	.0013-.0043	.006-.015	7	2.751-2.752	.0012-.0037	.007-.013
8-549	3.124-3.125	.0015-.0035	.006-.012	3	2.623-2.624	.011-.036	.008-.018
8-537	3.1235-3.1245	.0008-.0038	.006-.011	3	2.623-2.624	.0017-.0042	.010-.018
8-605	3.1235-2.1245	.0015-.0035	.006-.012	3	2.623-2.624	.011-.036	.008-.018

VALVE SPECIFICATIONS

CYL — CID	ANGLE Face	ANGLE Seat	STEM DIA. In	STEM DIA. Ex	STEM-TO-GUIDE CLEARANCE In	STEM-TO-GUIDE CLEARANCE Ex	VALVE LIFT IN.	VALVE SPRING TENSION LBS @ INCHES	SPRING FREE LENGTH
4-196	⑥	⑥	.372	.415	.001-.0035	.0015-.004	①	188 @ 1.428	2.065
6-232	⑩	⑪	.371	.371	.001-.003	.001-.003	.254	190 @ 1.437	2.265
6-258	⑩	⑪	.371	.371	.001-.003	.001-.003	.254	190 @ 1.437	2.265
8-304	45	45	.372	.371	.001-.0035	.0015-.004	①	180-195 @ 1.429	2.065
8-345	45	45	.372	.371	.001-.0035	.0015-.004	①	180-195 @ 1.429	2.065
8-392	⑥	⑥	.372	.414	.001-.0035	.0015-.004	①	180-195 @ 1.429	2.065
8-400	⑥	⑥	.372	.372	.001-.003	.001-.003	.286	210-226 @ 1.365⑧	2.200⑨
8-401	⑤	⑤	.435	.434	.0015-.0035	.0025-.0045	.426	113-121 @ 1.663⑩	2.562⑦
8-404 (399)	45	45	.372	.372	.0012-.0028	.0017-.0024	.435	188 @ 1.429	2.065
6-406	②	②	.435	.434	.0015-.004	.002-.0045	.449	133-141 @ 1.703③	2.562④
8-446	45	45	.372	.372	.0012-.0028	.0017-.0024	.435	188 @ 1.429	2.065
6-450	②	②	.435	.434	.0015-.004	.002-.0045	.449	133-141 @ 1.703③	2.562④
8-478	⑤	⑤	.435	.434	.0015-.0035	.0025-.0045	.426	113-121 @ 1.663⑩	2.562⑦
6-501	②	②	.435	.434	.0015-.004	.002-.0045	.449	133-141 @ 1.703③	2.562④
8-537	②	②	.435	.434	.0016-.0034	.002-.0037	.465	200 @ 1.397	2.075
8-549	⑤	⑤	.435	.434	.0015-.0035	.0015-.0045	.426	113-121 @ 1.663⑩	2.562⑦
8-605	②	②	.435	.434	.0016-.0034	.002-.0037	.465	200 @ 1.397	2.075

① Intake .440; Exh. 395
② Intake 15; Exh. 45
③ Inner 83-88 @ 1.50
④ Inner 2.343
⑤ Intake 15; Exh. 45
⑥ Intake 30; Exh. 45
⑦ Inner 2.281
⑧ Exhaust 210-226 @ 1.183
⑨ Exhaust 2.00
⑩ Inner 79-87 @ 1.538
⑪ Face—Intake 30°
Exhaust 44°
⑫ Seat—Intake 29°
Exhaust 45°

PISTON RING SPECIFICATIONS

Cyl — CID	RING GAP Compression	RING GAP Oil Control	RING CLEARANCE Compression	RING CLEARANCE Oil Control
4-196	.013-.023	.013-.028	.0015-.003	.002-.0035
6-232	.010-.020	.015-.055①	.0015-.0035	.000-.005
6-258	.010-.020	.015-.055①	.0015-.0035	.000-.005
8-304	.010-.020	.015-.055①	.0015-.003	.000-.0084
8-345	.010-.020	.015-.055①	.0015-.003	.000-.0084

PISTON RING SPECIFICATIONS

Cyl — CID	RING GAP Compression	RING GAP Oil Control	RING CLEARANCE Compression	RING CLEARANCE Oil Control
8-392	.013-.023	.013-.028	.0015-.003	.002-.0035
8-400	.010-.020	.0015-.030①	.0015-.003	.002-.0035
8-401	.013-.025	.013-.028	.0035-.005	.001-.003
8-404	.013-.023	.013-.023	.002-.004	.002-.004
6-406	.025-.035	.013-.028	.0035-.005	.002-.0035
8-446	.013-.023	.013-.023	.002-.004	.002-.004
6-450	.025-.035	.013-.028	.0035-.005	.002-.0035
8-478	.013-.025	.013-.028	.0035-.005	.001-.003
6-501	.013-.023	.013-.028	.0035-.005	.002-.0035
8-537	.012-.022②	.012-.022	.002-.004	.002-.004
8-549	.013-.025	.013-.028	.0035-.005	.001-.003
8-605	.012-.022②	.012-.022	.002-.004	.002-.004

① Spring spacer or steel rails—no gap at joint
② 2nd compression—.014-.024

Bolt Torque Specifications (Unlisted)

Many bolts are used that have no torque specification listed. Refer to the following charts for the classification of the bolts and the allowable torque for each bolt class.

Note that torque specifications given in the chart are based on the use of clean and dry threads. Reduce the torque by 10 percent when threads are lubricated with oil and by 20 percent if new plated bolts are used.

S.A.E. CLASSIFICATION

SAE GRADE NUMBER	1 or 2	5	6 or 7	8
Capscrew Head Markings Manufacturer's marks may vary. Three-line markings on heads, for example, indicate SAE Grade 5. 	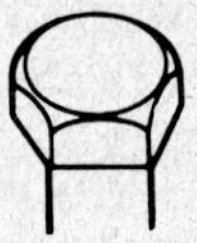			
Usage	Used Frequently	Used Frequently	Used at Times	Used at Times
Quality of Material	Indeterminate	Minimum Commercial	Medium Commercial	Best Commercial
Capscrew Body Size (Inches)—(Thread)	Torque Ft-Lb	Torque Ft-Lb	Torque Ft-Lb	Torque Ft-Lb
1/4-20	5	8	10	12
-28	6	10		14
5/16-18	11	17	19	24
-24	13	19		27
3/8-16	18	31	34	44
-24	20	35		49
7/16-14	28	49	55	70
-20	30	55		78
1/2-13	39	75	85	105
-20	41	85		120
9/16-12	51	110	120	155
-18	55	120		170
5/8-11	83	150	167	210
-18	95	170		240
3/4-10	105	270	280	375
-16	115	295		420
7/8-9	160	395	440	605
-14	175	435		675
1-8	235	590	660	910
-14	250	660		990

TORQUE SPECIFICATIONS

CYL — CID	HEAD BOLTS	ROD CAP BOLTS	MAIN CAP BOLTS	CRANKSHAFT BALANCER BOLT	FLYWHEEL BOLTS	MANIFOLDS IN.	MANIFOLDS EX.
4-196	90-100	40-45	75-80	100-110	45-55	40-45	40-45
6-232, 258	80-85	25-30	75-85	70-80	100-110	20-25	20-25
8-304	90-100	45-55	75-85	100-110	45-55	40-55	40-45
8-345, 392	90-100	45-55	75-85	100-110	45-55	40-55	40-45
8-400	110	35-40	95-105	50-60	100-110	40-45	20-30
8-401	90-100	60-70	100-110	Press-Fit	90-100	25-30	25-30
8-404 (399)	100-110	38-44	90-100	80-100	—	—	15-20
6-406	100-110	65-75	100-110	Press-Fit	150-160	25-30	25-30
8-446	100-110	38-44	90-100	80-100	—	—	15-20
6-450	100-110	65-75	100-110	Press-Fit	150-160	25-30	25-30
8-478	90-100	60-70	100-110	Press-Fit	90-100	25-30	25-30
6-501	100-110	65-75	100-110	Press-Fit	150-160	25-30	25-30
8-549	90-100	60-70	100-110	Press-Fit	90-100	25-30	25-30
8-537, 8-605	80-90	65-70	125-135	260-290	110-120	30-38	30-38

FRONT END ALIGNMENT SPECIFICATIONS

AXLE	CASTER LEVEL FRAME	CAMBER	TOE-IN	KING PIN INCLINATION
FA-1	2° ± 1° (Not Metro) 2° ± ½° (Metro)	1½° ± ½°	1/16 ± 1/16	4°
FA-3	0°	1°	3/16	8½°
FA-10	3° ± ½°	1½° ± ½°	1/16 ± 1/16	4°
FA-13	0°	1°	3/16	8½°
FA-12	2° ± 1° (Not Motor Home) 4° ± ½° (Motor Home)	½° ± ½°	1/16 ± 1/16	4°
FA-28	1° ± 1° (Not Motor Home or Metro) 4° ± ½° (Motor Home) 3° ± ½° (Metro)	½° ± ½°	1/16 ± 1/16	4°
FA-44	0°	1°	3/16	8½°
FA-48	2° ± 1° (Not Motor Home) 4° ± ½° (Motor Home)	½° ± ½°	1/16 ± 1/16	4°
FA-54	1	0°	1/16	8°
FA-57	0 ± 2	2°	0-⅜	0°
FA-59	0 ± 2	2°	0-⅜	0°
FA-68	2° ± 1°	½° ± ½°	1/16 ± 1/16	4°
FA-69	3° ± ½° (Cargostar Manual Strg.) 4½° ± ½° (Cargostar Power Strg.)	½° ± ½° ½° ± ½°	⅛ ± 1/16 ⅛ ± 1/16	4° 4°
FA-71	2° ± ½°	½° ± ½°	1/16 ± 1/16	LT 4¼° RT 4½°
FA-72	2° ± ½°	½° ± ½°		4°
FA-73	2° ± ½°	½° ± ½°	1/16 ± 1/16	LT 4¼° RT 4½°
FA-74	3° ± ½° (Manual Strg.) 4½° ± ½° (Power Strg.)	½° ± ½°	⅛ ± 1/16	LT 4¼° RT 4½°
FA-78	0 ± 2	2°	0-⅜	0°
FA-91	2° ± 1° (Not CO-190) 2° ± ½° (CO-190)	½° ± ½°	1/16 ± 1/16	4°
FA-98	2° ± (Not Fleetstar A) 2° ± ½° (Fleetstar A 4x2) 4° ± ½° (Fleetstar A 4x4)	½° ± ½°	1/16 ± 1/16	4°
FA-99	3° ± ½° (Cargostar Manual Strg.) 4½° ± ½° (Cargostar Power Strg.)	½° ± ½°	⅛ ± 1/16	4°
FA-101	2° ± ½° (Not Fleetstar 6x4) 4° ± ½° (Fleetstar 6x4)	½° ± ½° ½° ± ½°	1/16 ± 1/16 1/16 ± 1/16	LT 4¼° RT 4½° LT 4¼° RT 4½°
FA-103	3° ± ½° (Manual Strg.) 4½° ± ½° (Power Strg.)	½° ± ½°	⅛ ± 1/16	LT 4¼° RT 4½°

FRONT END ALIGNMENT SPECIFICATIONS

AXLE	CASTER LEVEL FRAME	CAMBER	TOE-IN	KING PIN INCLINATION
FA-109	Lt. ¼ + ½ Rt. 0 + ½	1°	1/16	4½ R.H. 4¼ L.H.
FA-112	3½	0°	1/16	1°
FA-136	4	0°	1/16	5½°
FA-139	Lt. ¼ ± ½ Rt. 0 ± ½	1°	1/16	4½ R.H. 4¼ L.H.
FA-182	4	0°	1/16	5½°
FA-228	4	0°	1/16	5½°
FA-309	Lt. ¼ ± ½ Rt. 0 ± ½	1°	1/16	4½ R.H. 4¼ L.H.
FA-329	3	Lt. ¼ + ½ Rt. 0 + ½	1/16	4½ R.H. 4¼ L.H.
FA-339	3	Lt. ¼ + ½ Rt. 0 + ½	1/16	4½ R.H. 4¼ L.H.

ENGINE APPLICATION BY YEAR—GASOLINE

CID	YEARS	CID	YEARS
4-196	1975-78	**8-400**	1973-74
6-232	1973-74	**8-401**	1973-74
6-258	1973-74	**8-404**	1975-80
6-406	1973-74	**8-446**	1975-80
6-450	1973-74	**8-478**	1973-74
6-501	1973-74	**8-537**	1975-80
8-304	1973-80	**8-549**	1973-78
8-345	1973-80	**8-605**	1975-80
8-392	1973-75		

ENGINE APPLICATIONS

SERIES	AXLES	ENGINES—HP RATING
SCOUT SERIES (with or without top)		
Scout II	4x2	G 86-158
Scout II	4x4	G 86-158
MULTI-STOP SERIES		
MS-1210	4x2	G 158-163
MS-1510	4x2	G 158-163
PICKUP MODELS		
150 Bonus Load, Regular	4x2	G 140-163
200 Bonus Load, Regular	4x2	G 140-163
150 Bonus Load, Regular	4x4	G 140-163
200 Bonus Load, Regular	4x4	G 140-163
TRAVELER		
150	4x2	G 187-196
200	4x2	G 187-196
150	4x4	G 187-196
200	4x4	G 187-196
LIGHT-DUTY SERIES		
150	4x2	G 140-196
200	4x2	G 140-196
500	4x2	G 140-196
150	4x4	G 140-196
200	4x4	G 140-196

SERIES	AXLES	ENGINES—HP RATING
FLEETSTAR A SERIES—S2200-2600		
2010A	4x2	G 209-227
2050A	4x2	D 170-216
2070A	4x2	D 228-290
F-2010A	6x4	G 209-227
F-2050A	6x4	D 170-216
F-2070A	6x4	D 228-290
S-2200	4x2	D 426-228
S-2500	6x4	G 537-208
S-2500	6x4	D 426-228
S-2600	6x4	G 537-208
S-2600	6x4	D 426-228
TRANSTAR SERIES		
4270	4x2	D 260-350
4370	4x2	D 290-350
F-4270	6x4	D 260-430
F-4370	6x4	D 290-450
PAYSTAR SERIES		
5050	4x4	D 190-210
5070	4x4	D 228-304
F-5050	6x4	D 190-210
F-5070	6x4	D 228-400
F-5050	6x6	D 190-210
F-5070	6x6	D 228-400

ENGINE APPLICATIONS

SERIES	AXLES	ENGINES—HP RATING
LOADSTAR SERIES—S1600-2100		
1600	4x2	G 157
1700	4x2	G 190
1750	4x2	D 150-175
1800	4x2	G 205-235
1850	4x2	D 170-210
1600	4x4	G 147
1700	4x4	G 157
F-1800	6x4	G 205-235
F-1850	6x4	D 170-210
S-1600	4x2	G 345-158
S-1700	4x2	G 345-158
S-1700	4x2	D 170-150
S-1800	4x2	G 345-158
S-1800	4x4	G 345-158
S-1800	4x4	D 190-170
S-1900	6x4	G 404-188
S-1900	6x6	G 404-188
S-1900	6x4	D 190-170
S-1900	6x6	D 190-170
S-2100	6x4	G 537-208
S-2100	6x4	D DT466-180

SERIES	AXLES	ENGINES—HP RATING
CARGOSTAR SERIES		
CO-1610B	4x2	G 157
CO-1710B	4x2	G 205
CO-1810B	4x2	G 205-235
CO-1850B	4x2	D 170-190
CO-1910B	4x2	G 209-227
CO-1950B	4x2	D 170-210
COF-1810B	6x4	G 205-235
COF-1910B	6x4	G 209-227
COF-1950B	6x4	D 170-210
CO TRANSTAR II SERIES		
CO-4070B	4x2	D 290-350
COF-4070B	6x4	D 290-450

G = Gasoline
D = Diesel

DISTRIBUTOR

Distributor Removal

1. Remove distributor cap.
2. Mark position of rotor by scribing a mark on the distributor body.
3. Mark position of distributor body on the engine block or mounting bracket.
4. If so equipped, remove vacuum advance line, governor lines, and tachometer cable.
5. Loosen clamp screw or hold-down bolt and remove distributor from engine.
6. To install, reverse the above procedure, making sure to align marks which position rotor and distributor body.
7. If the engine has been disturbed (crankshaft position unknown), rotate engine until engine is in No. 1 firing position (No. 8 on V-304, 345, and 392 engines). Compression stroke may be felt by placing finger tightly over spark plug hole as engine is rotating. Holding distributor shaft so that rotor is in No. 1 (or No. 8 on V-304, 345, 392) firing position, insert distributor, rotating slightly until it drops into keyed position.
8. Adjust ignition timing before tightening clamp screw or hold-down bolt.

Adjusting point gap slots
(© International Harvester Co.)

Breaker Points Replacement

1. Unsnap and remove distributor cap.
2. Remove rotor and dust cover if so equipped.
3. Loosen nut retaining primary and condenser leads and remove leads.
4. Remove breaker assembly mounting screws.
5. Remove breaker assembly, carefully freeing conductor spring. Do not lose eccentric screw which may fall out.
6. To install, follow the above procedure in reverse order, being sure to include eccentric screw.
7. Lightly lubricate cam with distributor cam grease.
8. Set breaker gap and ignition timing.

Breaker Point Setting

Internal Adjustment Type

1. Remove distributor cap.
2. Loosen distributor housing clamp screw or hold-down bolt.
3. Rotate distributor until cam positions breaker points at maximum gap.
4. Inspect alignment of breaker points and, if necessary, gently bend the stationary contact support (never bend arm) with needle-nose pliers.
5. Loosen lock screws which mount breaker assembly and adjust gap using a small screwdriver in slots of contact bracket and upper plate. On models without slots and with eccentric adjusting screw instead, rotate adjusting screw until proper gap is obtained.
6. Replace cap and set ignition timing.

External Adjustment Type

1. With engine idling, raise window in distributor cap and insert proper "hex" wrench into adjustment screw.
2. Turn wrench clockwise until en-

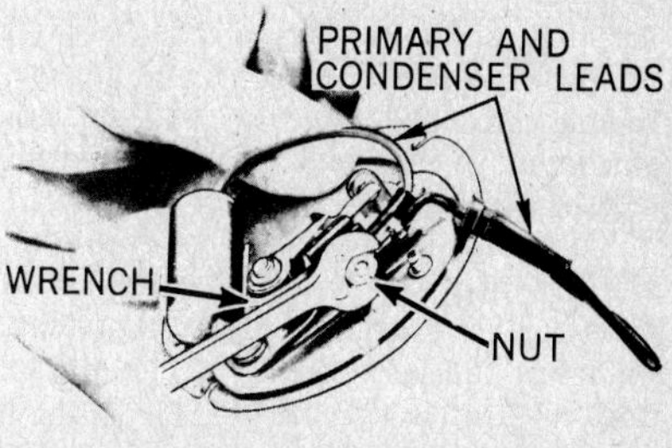

Removing primary condenser
(© International Harvester Co.)

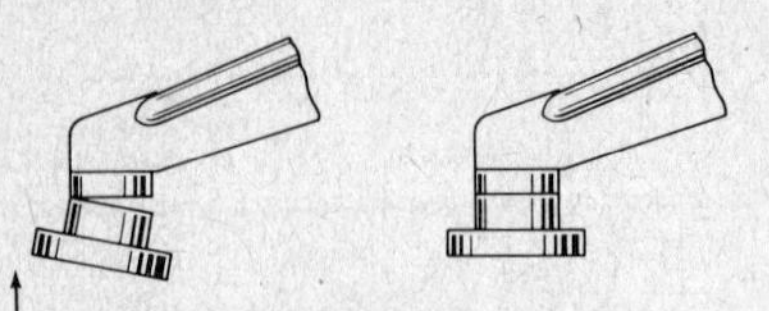

Adjusting point gap eccentric screw (© International Harvester Co.)

gine begins to miss, then back off ½ turn, or until dwell meter reads specified dwell angle. *NOTE: To remove distributor cap, press down in slot of latch head with a screwdriver and twist.*

Electronic Ignition System

The I.H. electronic ignition system contains three major components, a breakerless distributor, a standard ignition coil, and an electronic ignition control unit. The conventional cam, ignition points, and condensor are replaced by the sensor and trigger wheel, which signals the control box when to open and close the primary circuit to induce the high voltage in the ignition coil secondary circuit. This high voltage is directed in the conventional manner, to the rotor, distributor cap, spark plug cables, and to the spark plugs.

Dwell angle is determined by the angle between the adjacent teeth of the trigger wheel and by the air gap between the ends of the trigger wheel teeth and the center line of the sensor. Since no wearing surfaces exist on the trigger wheel and the sensor, dwell remains constant and no adjustment is required, after the initial sensor air gap is made.

To obtain the proper dwell reading, the air gap should be adjusted with the use of a brass feeler gauge, placed between the center line of the sensor and a aligned tooth of the trigger wheel. Attach a *modified* dwell meter to the distributor circuitry in a conventional manner, and operate the engine at curb idle. If the dwell is within specifications, the trigger wheel to sensor gap is satisfactory. If the dwell is out of specifications, stop the engine and move the sensor toward the trigger wheel to decrease dwell, and move the sensor away from the trigger wheel to increase dwell.

NOTE: Dwell is affected approximately ½ degree per each .001 inch of sensor movement.

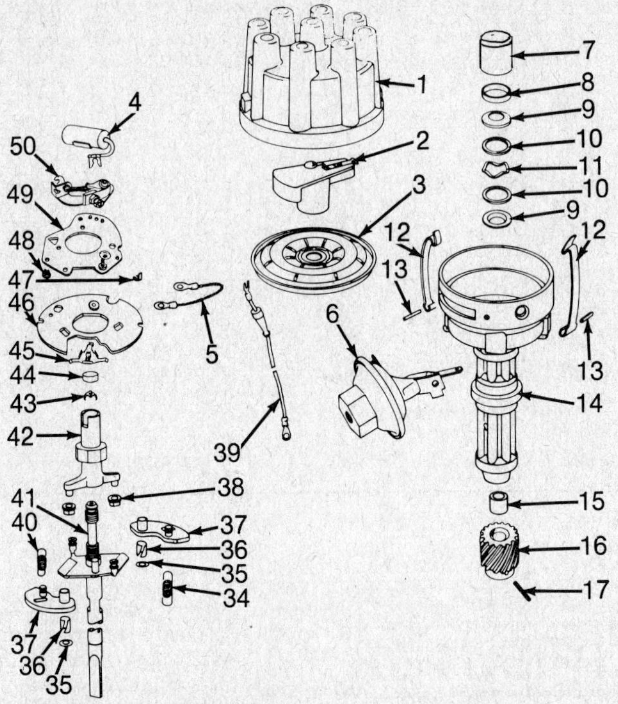

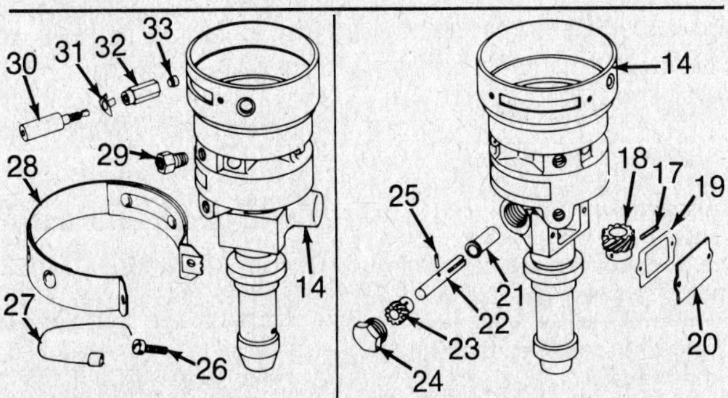

Exploded view model 1510 distributors (© International Harvester Co.)

1 Cap, assembly
2 Rotor, assembly
3 Cover, dust, assembly
4 Condenser, assembly
5 Cable, ground, assembly
6 Chamber, diaphragm, assembly
7 Bushing, drive shaft, upper
8 Retainer, seal
9 Seal, Drive shaft
10 Washer, drive shaft
11 Spacer, drive shaft
12 Clamp, cap
13 Pin, roll
14 Housing
15 Bushing, drive shaft, lower
16 Gear, drive shaft
17 Pin, roll
18 Gear, tachometer drive
19 Gasket, cover plate
20 Plate, cover
21 Bushing, tachometer drive shaft
22 Shaft, driven, tachometer
23 Gear, driven, tachometer
24 Plug, tachometer driven shaft
25 Pin, roll
26 Screw, governor clamp
27 Wire, seal
28 Clamp, governor
29 Fitting
30 Housing, with valve, governor
31 Plate, lock weight
32 Weight, governor valve counter
33 Plug, governor valve
34 Spring, weight (primary)
35 Washer
36 Bushing
37 Plate, weight, assembly
38 Block, slider
39 Cable, primary
40 Spring, weight (secondary)
41 Shaft, drive, assembly
42 Cam, breaker
43 Retainer, cam
44 Wick, shaft oil
45 Spring, retainer
46 Plate, lower breaker
47 Retainer, diaphragm rod
48 Button
49 Plate, upper breaker
50 Point set

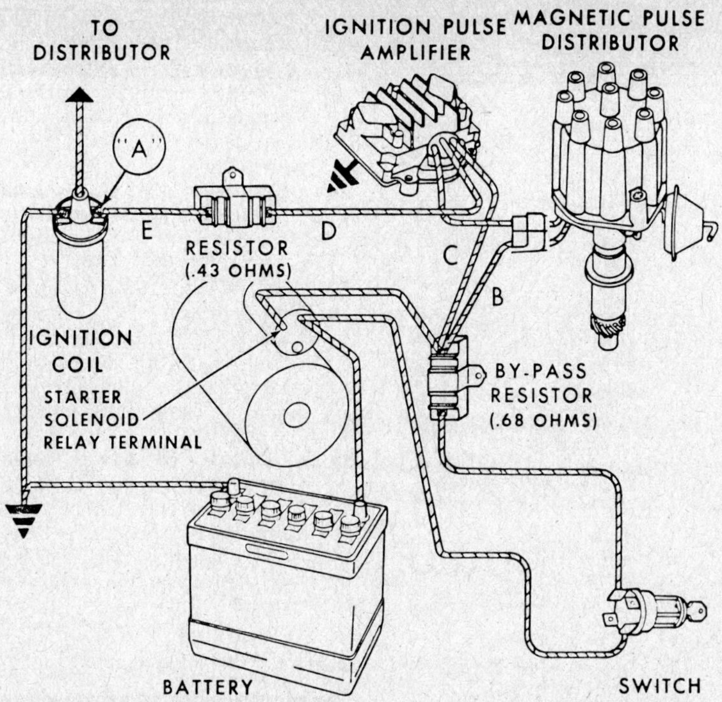

Typical transistor ignition wiring (© International Harvester Co.)

In the event of engine misfire or surging, other possible sources of trouble should be checked first, such as carburetion and fuel supply. Then check for breaks in the wiring and for corroded or loose connections.

The timing may be set in the conventional way: rotate the distributor housing while the timing marks are viewed with a timing strobe light.

If the engine will not run at all, remove a lead from one of the spark plugs and hold ½" from the engine block while cranking engine. If there is no spark, check wiring and connections.

CAUTION: Never disconnect the high voltage lead between the coil and distributor and never disconnect more than three spark plugs at a time unless the ignition switch is off.

To make compression checks, disconnect the harness plug at the control box or disconnect the lead at the negative terminal of the coil.

Ignition Timing

See tune-up specification table at the beginning of this section for timing settings. Timing light is connected to the No. 1 spark plug lead (No. 8 on V-304, 345, 392).

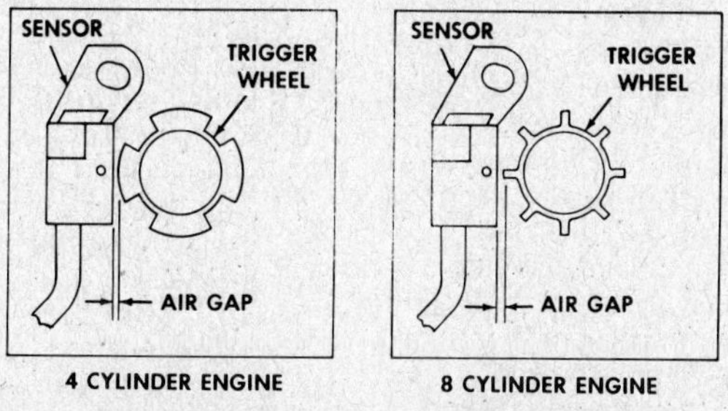

Air gap location trigger wheel to sensor (© International Harvester Co.)

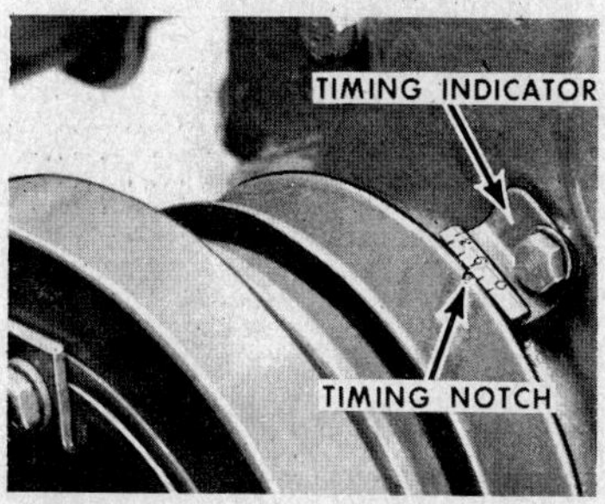

Ignition timing marks RD engine (© International Harvester Co.)

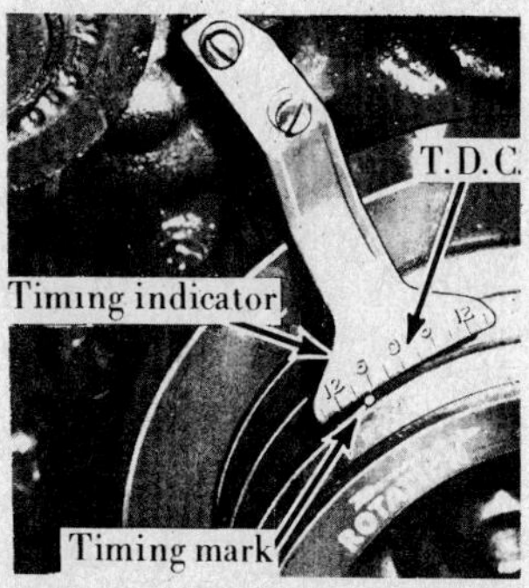

Ignition timing marks OHV4 and V8 engines (© International Harvester Co.)

ALTERNATOR

Precautions—Alternators

Rectifiers and regulators in alternator systems are easily damaged by incorrect polarity. Observe the following precautions when wiring and testing circuits:

1. Always be certain of battery polarity.
2. Always connect booster battery negative to negative and positive to positive.
3. Never ground alternator output terminal.
4. When adjusting voltage regulator, be careful not to short adjusting tool.
5. Before making any tests, turn off ignition switch and disconnect battery ground.
6. Never use a fast charge with the battery connected unless charging unit is equipped with a special alternator protector.
7. Never try to polarize the alternator regulator, this will cause severe damage to the regulator and alternator.

Alternator Removal

1. Disconnect the negative battery cable.
2. Remove the wire terminals from the rear of the alternator.
3. Loosen the adjusting strap and pivot bolts. Push inward on the alternator to loosen the belt and slip it off the pulley.
4. Remove the adjusting strap and pivot bolts, and remove the alternator from the engine.
5. Installation is in the reverse of the removal. Adjust the belt to have no more than ½ inch deflection on the longest span of the belt.

Voltage Regulators

Two types of voltage regulators are used to control the output of the alternators. One type is the internal unit, mounted with-in the alternator, and the second is an external type, normally mounted on the inner fender panel or the firewall.

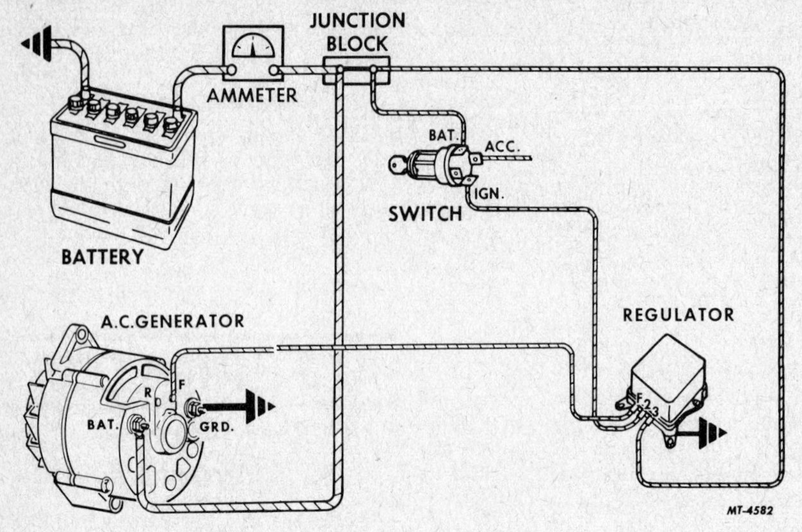

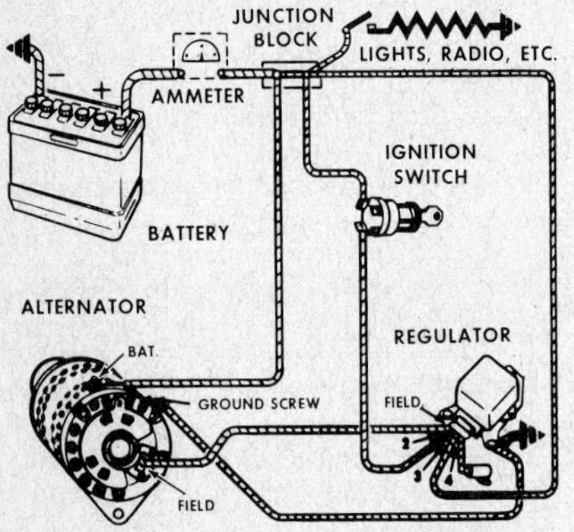

Circuit with Vibrating Contact Type Regulator

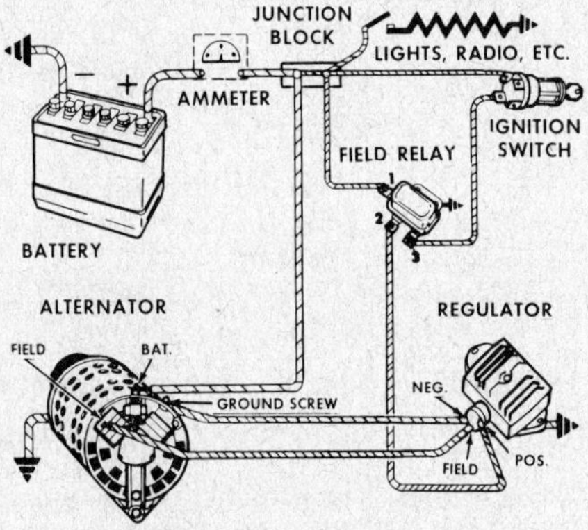

Circuit with Transistor Type Regulator

Typical circuits used for alternator charging system (© International Harvester Co.)

6. With the use of a special tool (IH*SE-2072-2) inserted through the governor adjusting hole, engage the adjusting screw tang. *NOTE: The adjusting screw is of a special design and cannot be adjusted with a screwdriver or any device, other than the special adjusting tool.*
7. Turning the adjusting screw clockwise to decrease governed speed, or counterclockwise to increase governed speed. *NOTE: ¼ turn of the adjusting screw will affect the governed speed approximately 100 RPM.*
8. When specified governed speed has been attained, reinstall the plug in the adjusting hole and tighten securely.
9. Reinstall governor clamp and gasket on the distributor housing and install a new seal wire.

Carburetor Adjustment

LPG (propane-butane) RD-501, V-304, 345, 401, & 549 Engines

Setting the idle fuel adjustment automatically gives the correct mixture for part and full throttle operation.

CAUTION: **Liquefied petroleum gas is extremely flammable. Observe all safety precautions regardless of the nature of work being performed. No work is to be done on fuel tanks except by qualified concerns who normally service such containers.**

1. Set throttle for fast idle by turning throttle stop screw in from closed position 3 or 4 turns.
2. Start engine and adjust idle adjusting screw in drag link (either end) until engine runs smoothly. Turning screw in (clockwise) enriches mixture.
3. Adjust throttle stop screw for idle of 600 rpm.
4. Readjust idle adjusting screw in drag link for maximum engine speed. If engine speed starts to go above 900 rpm, set back speed with throttle stop screw to 600 rpm and continue adjusting drag link screw for maximum engine speed.
5. Adjust idle to 400 rpm and replace cotter pin in drag link adjusting screw to lock adjustment.

Voltage Regulator Removal

External Type

1. Disconnect clamp lead at the negative terminal of battery.
2. Disconnect the wiring harness connector at regulator terminals.
3. Remove mounting screws and regulator unit from vehicle.
4. To install, reverse the above procedure.
5. Reconnect cable clamp to battery terminal, checking polarity first.

Internal Type

1. Remove the alternator as outlined.
2. Mark and separate the front housing from the rear housing.
3. Remove the diode trio screws and nuts, and remove the trio assembly.
4. Remove the two remaining screws in the regulator, and remove the brush holder and the regulator from the rear housing.
5. Installation is the reverse order of the removal, assuring that the insulated sleeves are installed on the proper screws, during installation.

STARTER

For servicing and overhauling starter motors, see Electrical Diagnosis Section of General Section.

Starter Motor—Removal

1. Disconnect cable clamp from negative terminal of battery.
2. Disconnect cable and wire leads from terminals of solenoid assembly, identifying leads with tags. If the solenoid is not mounted directly on the starter motor, disconnect the cable from the solenoid to the motor at the motor terminal.
3. Remove starter motor mounting bolts or stud nuts.
4. Pull starter assembly forward to clear housing and remove starter.
5. To install, reverse the above procedure, installing new tang lockwashers where removed.

BRAKES

Hydraulic Brakes

Late model trucks are equipped with a dual hydraulic brake system in which there are separate hydraulic systems for the front and rear brakes. In this dual system a warning light switch operates a warning light on the dashboard when there is a pressure failure in either the front or rear system. A power system may be employed to reduce the effort applied to the brake pedal. See General

Repair Section for hydraulic brake service and overhaul.

Master Cylinder R & R

1. Disconnect hydraulic lines from master cylinder.
2. Disconnect master cylinder pushrod at brake pedal and remove nuts securing cylinder to dash panel.
3. If master cylinder is mounted on power unit, remove nuts securing master cylinder to power unit and remove cylinder from vehicle.
4. Installation is the reverse of the above procedure.
5. Bleed system.

Tandem master cylinder disconnect points (© International Harvester Co.)

Resetting the Warning Light Switch

Once a difference of 85-150 psi pressure between the front and rear systems has activated the warning light switch, it will not go off by itself and must be manually reset.

1. Clean switch and disconnect wire from terminal.
2. Unscrew and completely remove switch from body. This will allow the pistons to center and hold the switch in "off" position.
3. Screw switch back into body and reconnect wire to terminal.
4. *NOTE: If fluid is in the switch cavity, press brake pedal to see if pistol O-ring seals are leaking. If there is leakage, the O-rings must be replaced.*
5. Warning light switch should be checked periodically for proper function and the presence of foreign matter and dirt.

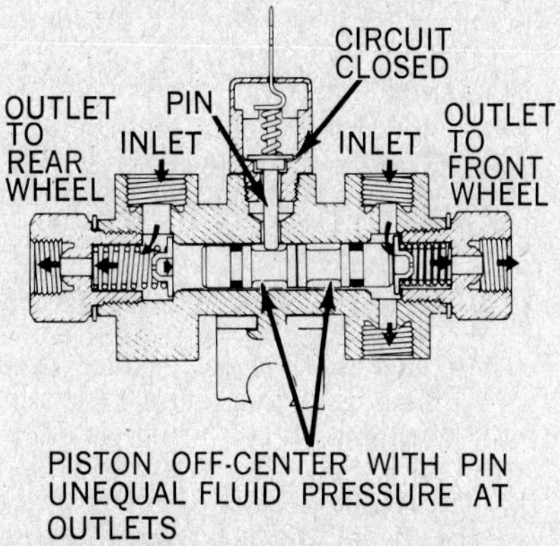

Warning light switch circuit closed (© International Harvester Co.)

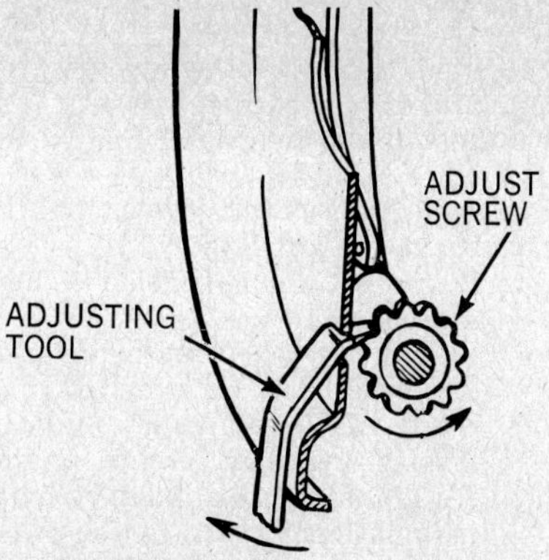

Adjusting brakes (© International Harvester Co.)

Adjusting Brake Shoes

1. Remove rubber dust cover from access hole.
2. Using an adjusting tool or screwdriver, turn star screw until shoes drag on the drum.
3. Rotate star screw back from drag position until drag is completely eliminated.
4. On brakes equipped with automatic adjusters it will be necessary to hold the adjusting lever away from the star wheel with a screwdriver while the adjustment is made.

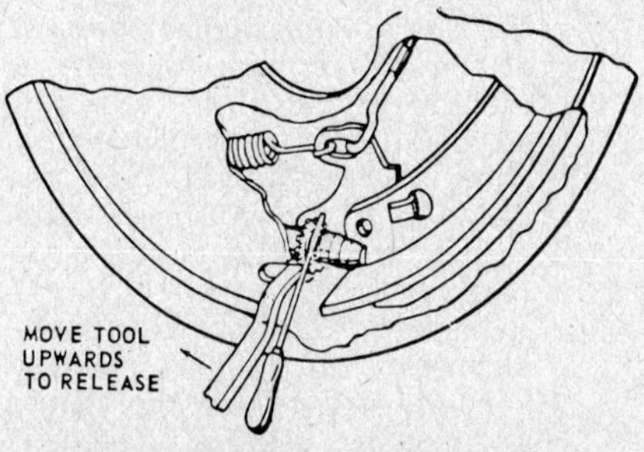

Backing off adjusting screw self adjusting brakes (© International Harvester Co.)

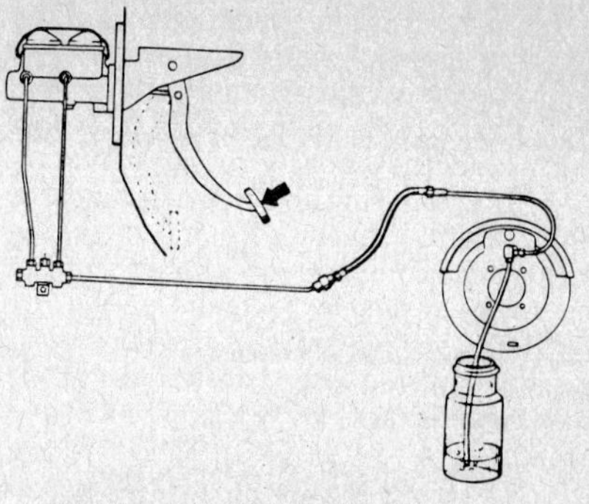

Bleeding brake system (© International Harvester Co.)

Bleeding Hydraulic Brakes

1. Before bleeding the brake system, disconnect electrical wire from warning light switch and remove any foreign material or dirt accumulation around warning light switch. Then remove the switch from body. The switch must be removed to prevent shearing of the end of the pin due to unequal pressures created between front and rear systems while bleeding.
2. Fill master cylinder reservoir (s) with clean brake fluid.
3. Attach bleeder hose to bleeder valve on wheel cylinder and place free end of bleeder hose in a jar partially filled with fluid. On some models it may be necessary to take the wheel off to get at the bleeder valve.
4. While the brake pedal is being pressed steadily, open the bleeder valve until the fluid coming from the hose is clean and free of air bubbles, then close bleeder valve and release brake pedal.

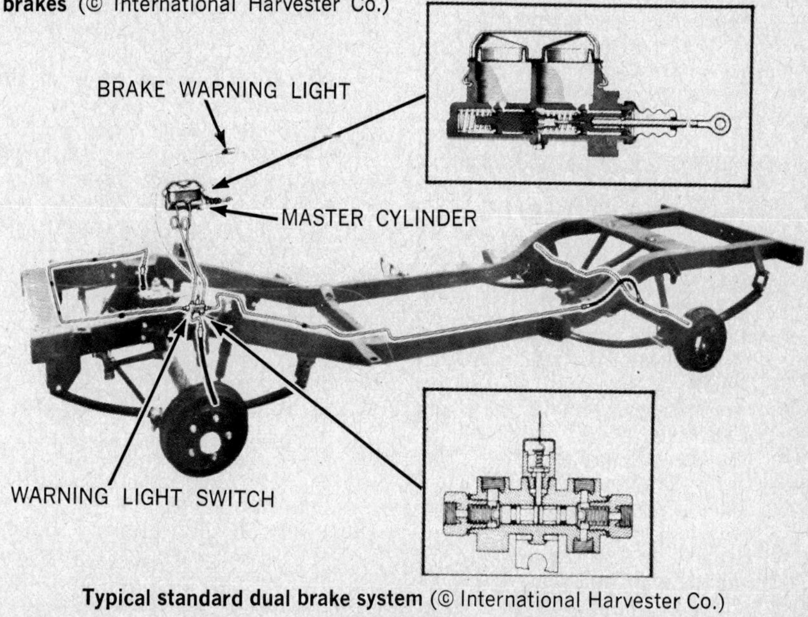

Typical standard dual brake system (© International Harvester Co.)

5. If the brake pedal goes to the floorboard before the bleeding becomes clean, more fluid will have to be added to the reservoir and the above process repeated.
6. Repeat the above procedure for each wheel cylinder, making sure to check the level of fluid in the reservoir frequently. *NOTE: On models equipped with power boosters, the booster must be bled first.*

Wheel Cylinder (Front Wheel)

Removal

1. Raise the front of the vehicle and support it safely.
2. Remove the front wheel assembly, including the drum, to expose the brake shoes.
3. Remove the brake shoes from the brake support plate.
4. Loosen or remove the hydraulic brake line. Remove the wheel cylinder from the brake support plate.

NOTE: The brake hose can be loosened at the cylinder and removed when the cylinder is loose from the support plate, or can be removed from the pipe and fitting at the frame rail, and withdrawn with the wheel cylinder from the brake support plate, to be separated later.

Installation

1. Connect the brake hose to the wheel cylinder and install the wheel cylinder to the brake support plate.
2. Install the brake lining and secure.
3. Install the drum and wheel assembly.
4. Adjust the wheel bearings and brakes.
5. Bleed the hydraulic system. Refill the master cylinder.

NOTE: The warning switch should be disconnected and removed from its seat in the switch until after the bleeding operation is completed.

Wheel Cylinder (Rear Wheel)

Removal

1. Raise the rear of the vehicle and support it safely.
2. Remove the axle shaft (if full floating), and the rear wheel assembly.
3. If necessary, remove the drum separately.
4. Remove the brake lining from the brake support plate.
5. Remove the hydraulic line from the wheel cylinder.
6. Remove the wheel cylinder attaching bolts and remove the cylinder.

Installation

1. Install the wheel cylinder on the brake support plate.
2. Install the hydraulic line to the wheel cylinder.
3. Install the brake shoes on the brake support plate.
4. Install the drum, if removed separately.
5. Install the wheel assembly and the axle shaft (if removed).
6. Bleed the system and refill the master cylinder. Refer to the *NOTE* under the front cylinder installation concerning the warning switch removal during bleeding.

Disc Brakes

The disc brakes are the sliding caliper, single piston type, and are used on the front wheels in combination with drum type brakes on the rear.

Removal

1. Raise the front of the vehicle and support it safely.
2. Remove the front wheels from the hub.
3. Remove approximately a third of the fluid from the large reservoir of the master cylinder, to avoid leakage of fluid when the pistons are forced back into the calipers.
4. Position a large "C" clamp over the caliper and engage the rear of the caliper with the shoe of the clamp, and place the screw on the outboard disc pad. Tightening the screw will cause the piston to be forced deeper in the bore, by the movement of the caliper.
5. Remove the key retaining screw and drive the support key and support spring from the caliper and support, using a brass drift and a light hammer.
6. Remove the caliper from the support bracket and support the assembly on a wire.
   CAUTION: Do not support the assembly by the brake hose.
   NOTE: It is not necessary to remove the brake hose from the caliper when only replacing the disc pads, and therefore it would not be necessary to bleed the caliper when reinstalled.
7. Remove the disc pads from the calipers.

Installation

1. Position the new disc pads into the calipers, using a new anti-rattle spring clip, and position it on the inboard pad.
2. Place the caliper assembly over the rotor and engage the anchor bracket.
3. Position the caliper support spring and support key between the bottom edge of the caliper and the anchor bracket.
4. With the use of a brass drift and hammer, drive the key and spring assembly into position and install the key retaining screw.
5. Refill the master cylinder as needed, apply the brakes several times to seat the pads, and recheck the master cylinder fluid level.
6. Install the wheels and lower the vehicle.

Brake Pedal Adjustment

There are no provisions available for the adjustment of the brake pedal height. However, it should be checked to determine if sufficient height exists. Corrections can only be made by replacement of parts, alignment, or straightening of the affected parts. To determine if sufficient pedal height exists, open a wheel cylinder bleed valve to simulate a failed system, and depress the brake pedal. The pedal should not contact the floor board during this test.

NOTE: Close the bleeder valve before releasing the brake pedal. The brake warning light switch will have to be reset after the test is completed.

Stoplight Switch Adjustment

No stoplight switch adjustments are provided. If the stop lamps are inoperative, a defective switch, defective bulbs, loose or broken connections, or an improper positioned switch would be indicated. A mechanical type switch is located on the brake pedal, at the pushrod bolt location, while the hydraulic type switch is located on or near the master cylinder, and operated by hydraulic pressure.

The air brake system on the straight truck models, utilizes two air operated switches. One switch is used on the primary brake system, and the second switch is used on the secondary brake system, to provide stop lamps in case of a failure in one of the systems. The tractor type models use a single switch, but it is mounted on a double check valve, and is operated by air being passed through from both the primary and secondary brake systems.

Vacuum Power Brakes

The vacuum power cylinder used with the single and dual hydraulic brake systems assists braking differently than a power booster in that its activation results directly from the foot pedal and not from the master cylinder. There are single and tandem dual types. Both types are

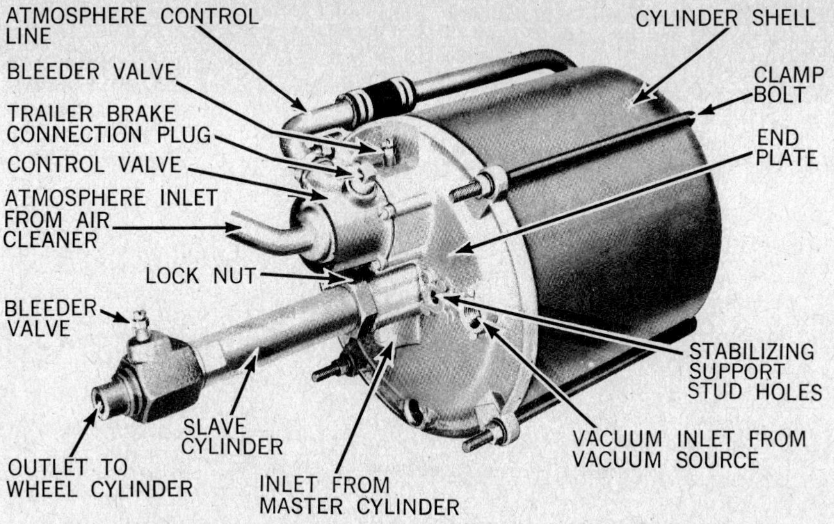

Typical single cylinder booster (© International Harvester Co.)

mounted on the engine side of the firewall.

Vacuum Power Brake Cylinder R & R

1. Disconnect vacuum hose from check valve.
2. Disconnect hydraulic lines from master cylinder.
3. Disconnect pedal link from pedal from inside the cab.
4. Remove bolts which mount the bracket to the firewall.
5. To install reverse the above procedure.

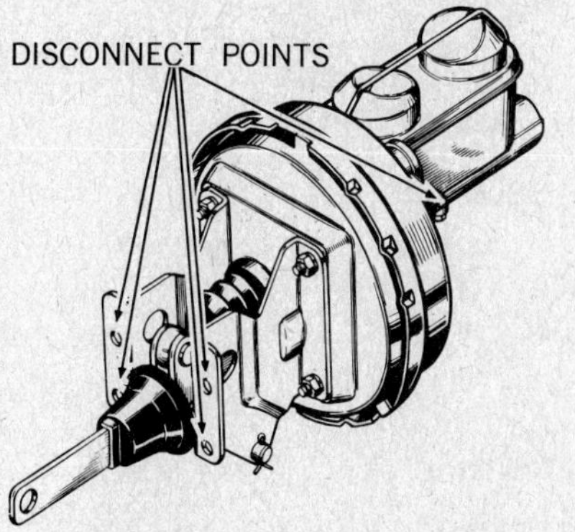

Power cylinder disconnect points
(© International Harvester Co.)

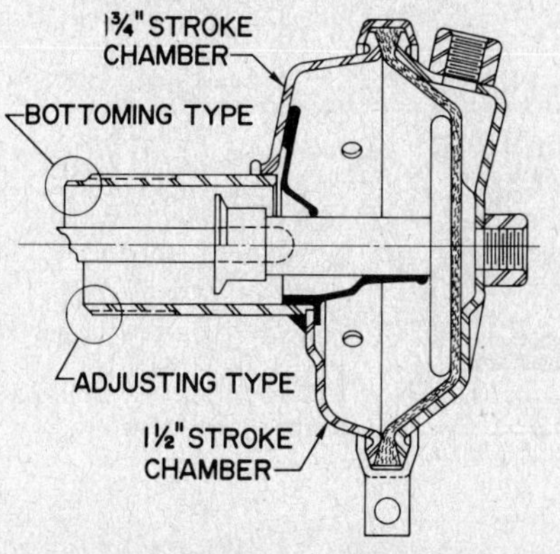

Power brake air chamber
(© International Harvester Co.)

6. Bleed master cylinder output ports while connecting tube nuts which secure lines to ports.
7. Bleed hydraulic brake system.

Vacuum Brake Boosters

Vacuum boosters add pressure to the hydraulic brake system. The activation and amount of pressure is controlled by a hydraulic line from the master cylinder.

Booster R & R

1. On units lacking integral air filter, remove air inlet hose (from engine air cleaner).
2. Disconnect vacuum inlet tube (coming from engine manifold).
3. Disconnect hydraulic line from master cylinder and hydraulic line going to wheel cylinders.
4. Remove mounting bolts and lift out vacuum unit.
5. To install, reverse the above procedure.
6. Bleed complete hydraulic system, starting with cylinder on vacuum unit as described below.

Bleeding Vacuum Booster Systems

1. The booster must be bled before proceeding to wheel cylinders.
2. All vacuum boosters have a bleed valve on the control valve as indicated in the figures by the number "1". This valve must always be bled first.
3. On boosters having an additional bleeder valve on the hydraulic cylinder indicated by the number "2", bleed this cylinder after control valve.
4. Bleed wheel cylinders as described in preceding section.

Trailer Brake Hand Control Adjustment

The advance control valve is used in conjunction with the Hydrovac and trailer brake system to vary the initial braking of the trailer.

1. Place advance plate in full released position (rotate counterclockwise).
2. While coasting on smooth road at 20 mph, apply valve by rotating clockwise until a slight drag is felt from the trailer brakes.
3. Rotate advance plate to where it just touches the valve operating handle. This releases the brakes on the trailer but sets the advance effect.
4. Leaving advance valve controls as set above, gently apply trac-

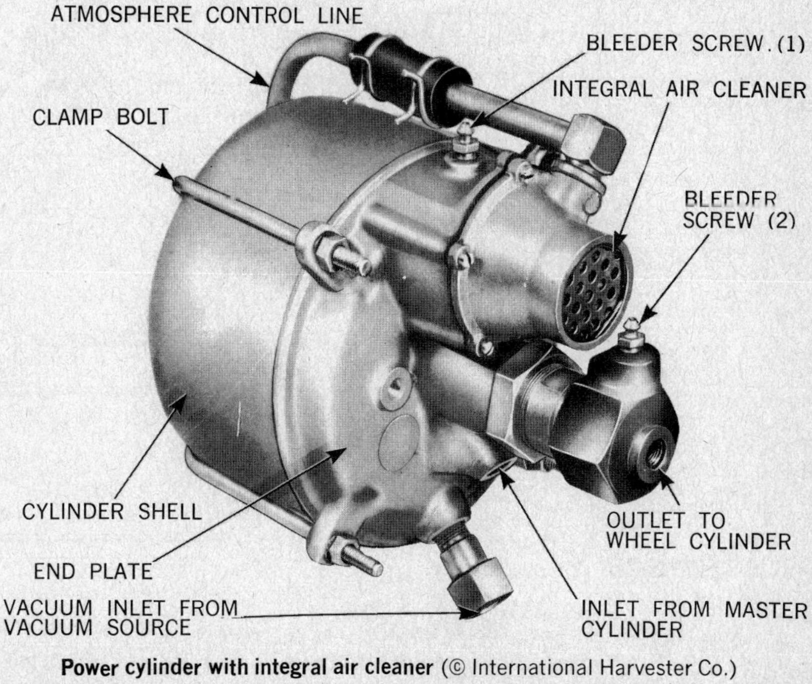

Power cylinder with integral air cleaner (© International Harvester Co.)

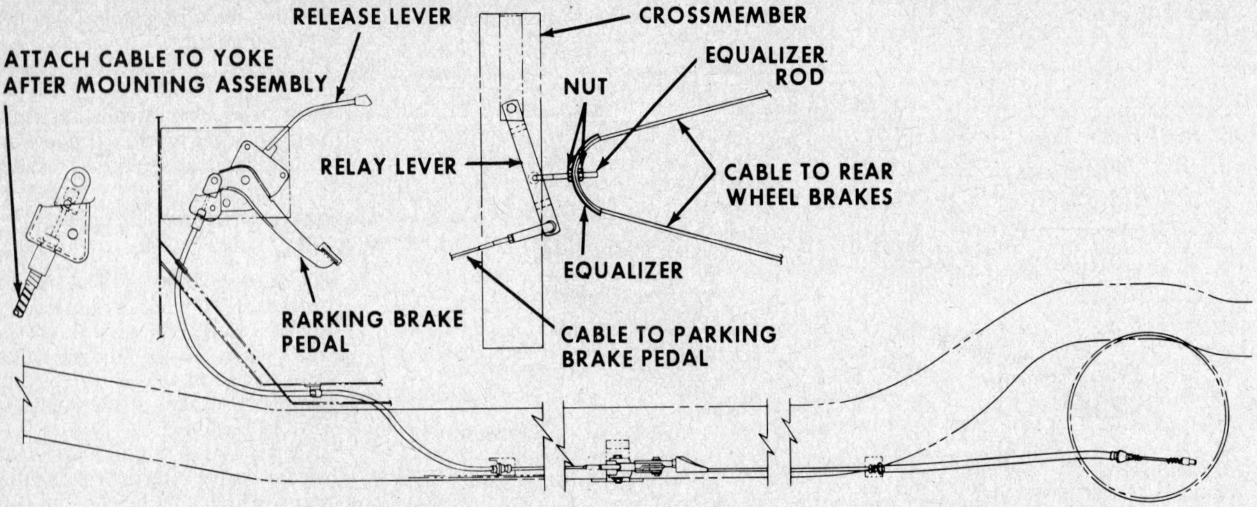

Parking brake cable adjustment (© International Harvester Co.)

tor brakes to check the "advance" of the trailer brakes.

Parking Brake Adjustment

Rear Brake Type

1. Loosen locknut on the equalizer rod and turn front nut forward several turns.
2. Turn the locknut (rear) forward just enough to remove any slack but not so much that the brake shoes lift of their anchors.
3. Tighten both nuts against the equalizer.

Drive Shaft Band Type

1. Leaving parking brake lever in the extreme release position, check that the cam lever is resting squarely on upper brake band bracket. This is adjusted by removing the clevis pin and readjusting yoke.
2. Adjust screw nut (1) until a clearance of .020-.030″ is reached.
3. Adjusting nuts (4) on bolt (5), obtain .020-.030″ clearance on lower half of lining and drum.
4. Adjust nuts (2) on bolt (3) for a clearance of .020-.030″ clearance on top half of lining.
5. Lock all adjustment with lock nuts.

Enclosed Drum Type—Driveshaft

1. Block the vehicle wheels.
2. Disconnect the clevis pin from the bellcrank and clevis at the brake assembly.
3. Move the hand brake control lever approximately 1/4 to 3/8 inch in the apply direction to compensate for the allowable freeplay.
4. Move the bellcrank lever in the apply direction until contact is

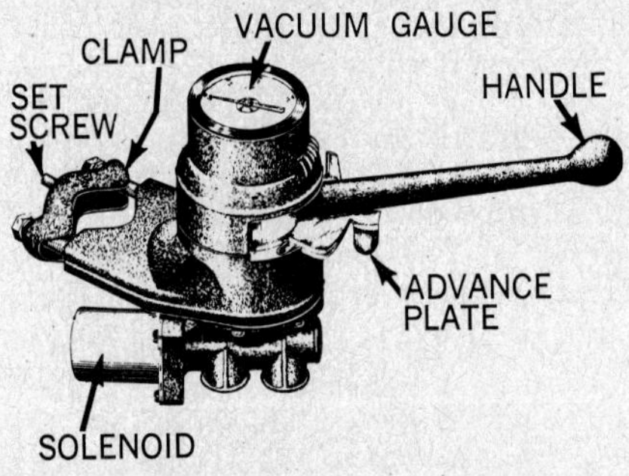

Advance control valve assembly (© International Harvester Co.)

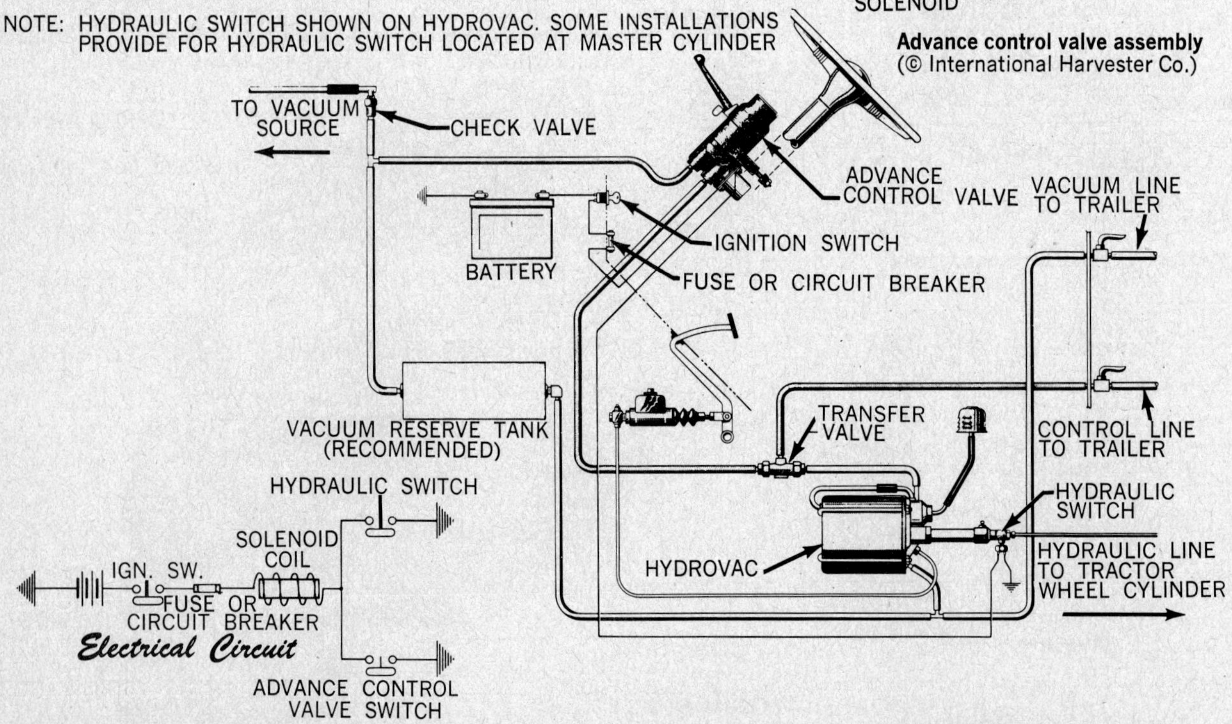

Typical advance trailer brake control valve installation (© International Harvester Co.)

made with the brake cam, without any brake shoe movement.

5. Adjust the clevis until the hole in the clevis aligns with the mating hole in the positioned bellcrank lever.
6. Assemble the clevis and bellcrank lever. Tighten the clevis locknut.
7. Recheck the freeplay and lever adjustment.

NOTE: If the vehicle is equipped with the Orschelm type parking brake lever, (over-center type), rotate the adjusting knob on the end of the lever, while in the released position, to attain a force of 90 lbs. to apply the parking brake. When properly adjusted, a distinct click will be heard when pulled over center.

Spring Actuated—Tandem Type—Air

This unit is a spring actuated type parking brake consisting of a tandem-type cylinder, connected to the brake shoes, through the air brake slack adjuster and brake camshaft. The cylinder assembly is divided into two sections. One section is the regular air brake chamber, and the second is the spring actuated chamber, containing a powerful spring, compressed by air pressure and applied by the operator with the use of a control valve. The brake adjustment is controlled by the adjustment of the slack adjuster for the regular brakes.

Air Brake System

Air brake systems are composed of a compressor, a reservoir, brake actuating chambers and a network of lines and valves which control operation. The piston-type air compressor is belt driven directly from the engine and is dependent upon the engine for its lubrication. Pressure in the system is regulated by a governor which starts loading the compressor when the system pressure drops below 95 psi and unloads the compressor when the system pressure reaches 110 psi.

Air Compressor

Removal

1. Drain all air from the reservoirs and lines.
2. Providing the compressor is water cooled, drain the engine and compressor cooling system.
3. Disconnect all air, water, and oil lines from the compressor.
4. *a. Gasoline engine models*
   Remove the compressor mounting bolts and remove the belt or belts from the pulleys. Remove the compressor.
   b. Diesel engine models
   Attach a lifting sling to the compressor and remove the mounting bolts. Slide the compressor rearward to disengage the drive gear of the compressor and lift the unit away from the engine.
5. Remove the crankshaft nut and remove the pulley or the gear from the crankshaft of the compressor, with puller.

Installation

1. Install the compressor crankshaft pulley or gear on the crankshaft and tighten the attaching nut.
2. *a. Gasoline engine models*
   Position the compressor on the engine bracket and install the mounting bolts, but do not tighten. Install the belts on the pulleys and adjust. Tighten the mounting bolts.
   b. Diesel engine models
   Mount the compressor in a sling and lift it to the rear of its mounting position. Slide the compressor forward and engage the drive gear with the idler timing gear. Install the mounting bolts and tighten.
3. Attach the air, water, and oil lines to the compressor.
4. Operate the compressor and inspect for oil, water or air leaks.

Compressor Governor Valve

Removal and Installation

The compressor governor valve can be either the remote-mounted or compressor-mounted type. The air system must be drained before any attempt is made to remove either type valve. If the governor valve is the compressor-mounted type, the reservoir line must be disconnected, and then the attaching bolts removed. If the governor valve is the remote-mount type, the unloader line and the reservoir line must be disconnected from the valve, and then the attaching bolts removed. Installation is the reverse of removal. Test the air system before the vehicle is placed in service.

Reservoir

Removal

1. Drain the air from the reservoir and lines.

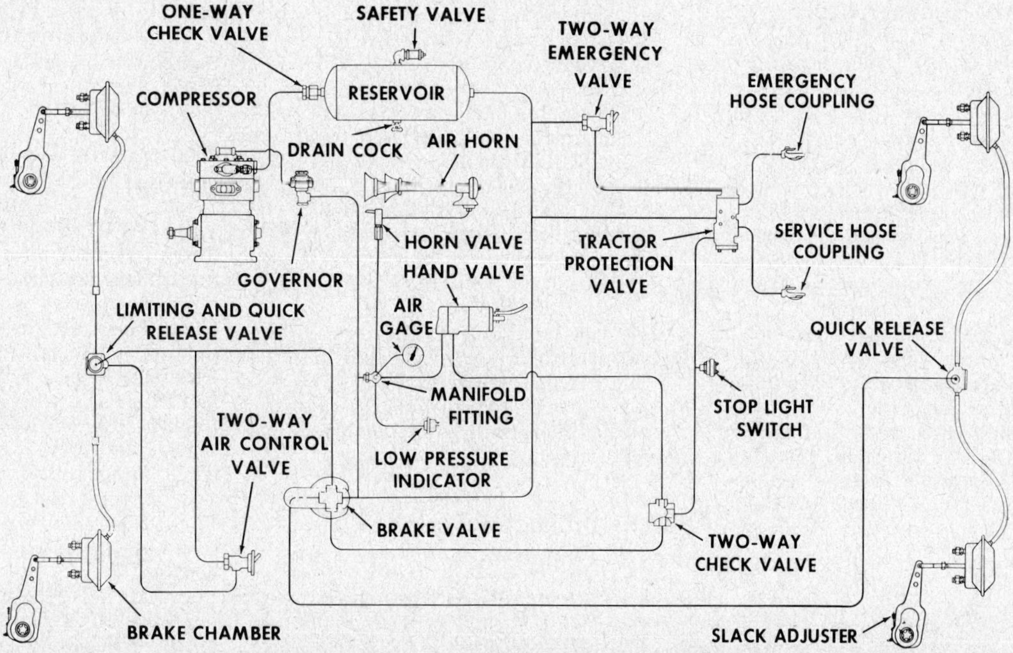

Typical air brake system (© International Harvester Co.)

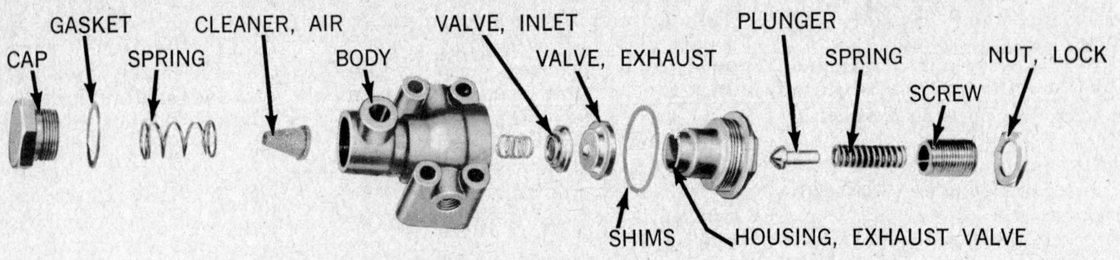

Air compressor governor—early models (© International Harvester Co.)

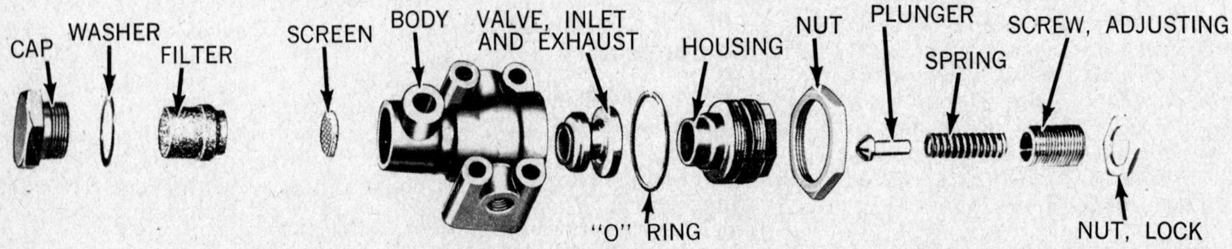

Air compressor governor late models (© International Harvester Co.)

2. Remove the air lines to the reservoir.
3. Loosen and remove the attaching straps holding the reservoir to the frame or crossmember.
4. Remove the reservoir assembly.

Installation

1. Install the reservoir and secure it with the attaching straps.
2. Attach the air lines to the reservoir.
3. Close the drain cock and build up air pressure to test air holding ability.

NOTE: The combined volume of all reservoirs and supply reservoirs must be twelve times the combined volume of all service brake chambers at maximum travel, and should never be altered.

Control and Check Valves

Removal and Installation

NOTE: Before any valve, line, or fitting is loosened or removed, all air must be drained from the system. Personal injury can result if these precautions are not adhered to.

The safety valve, pressure gauge or gauges, low pressure indicator, stop light switch, automatic reservoir drain valve, check valves, inversion valve, and quick release valves are located in the lines and may be bolted to the frame or crossmember. To remove or install the above mentioned valves, is simply a matter of disconnecting and connecting the lines from the valve, and removing or installing any attaching bolts, and repairing or replacing the affected valve. The lines must be maintained in their proper order so as not to interchange the primary and secondary air systems.

Brake Valve

Removal

1. Drain the air from the primary and secondary air systems.

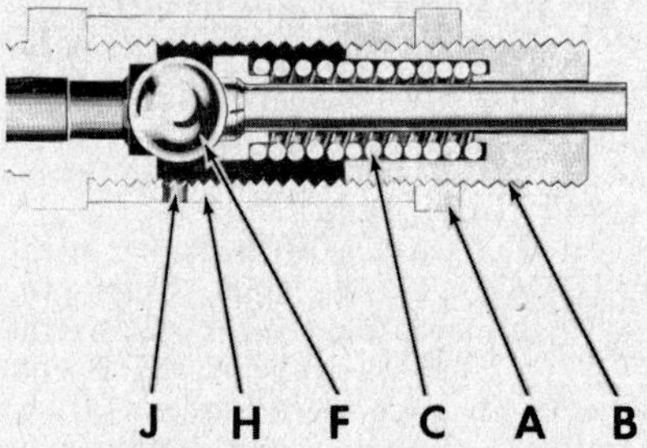

Safety valve
(© International Harvester Co.)

2. Dsisconnect all supply and delivery lines at the brake valve. Mark each line to assist in reassembly.
3. Remove the fittings from the valve and mark for reassembly.
4. Remove the valve from the vehicle.
   a. *Suspended pedal valves.* Remove the attaching nuts on the engine fire wall side and remove valve.
   b. *Treadle type valve* Remove three capscrews on the outer bolt circle of the mounting plate and lift the valve upward. The valve can be removed from the mounting plate by the removal of capscrews from the inner bolt circle.

Installation

1. The installation of the brake valve is the reverse of removal. Connect all fittings and lines in their proper order, and test the brake operation before vehicle movement.

Spring Brake Two-way Control Valve

Push and Pull—Dash Mounted

Removal

1. Drain the air from the system.
2. Loosen locknut and remove the knob and nut.
3. Disconnect the air lines at the valve.
4. Loosen and remove the valve mounting nut, and name plate.
5. Remove the valve from the rear of the instrument panel.

Installation

1. The installation is in the reverse order of the removal. Test the system before vchicle operation.

Flip Switch—Dash Mounted

Removal

1. Drain air from the system.
2. Remove the air lines from the valve.
3. Remove the machine screw securing the valve to the instrument panel and remove the valve.

Installation

1. Installation is the reverse of removal. Test the system before vehicle operation.

Air Compressor Governor Adjustment

Early Models

1. Check governor filter and supply line for any restriction.
2. Loosen adjusting screw locknut and exhaust valve housing.
3. Remove exhaust valve housing with adjusting screw locknut, and shims as a complete unit.
4. Replace exhaust valve housing, adjusting screw, locknut and three shims into governor body and tighten.
5. Turn adjusting screw until it sticks out 3/8″ from exhaust valve housing.
6. Start truck engine and build up pressure in air brake system until it reaches 115 psi then shut off engine. If governor cuts out

before 115 psi then turn adjusting screw out one complete turn and repeat this step.

7. With pressure holding at 115 psi slowly turn adjusting screw out until governor cuts out (dull pop).
8. Start truck engine and slowly bleed pressure until governor cuts in. Cut-in should be between 93-98 psi.
9. If cut-in is below 93 psi, remove exhaust valve housing unit and add shims (one shim equals 4 psi) to adjust cut-in and install as in step 4.
10. If cut-in is above 98 psi, remove exhaust valve housing unit and remove shims to lower cut-in pressure.
11. Check cut-in and cut-out pressure after each adjustment and repeat appropriate steps if necessary.
12. When adjustments are completed, tighten locknut.

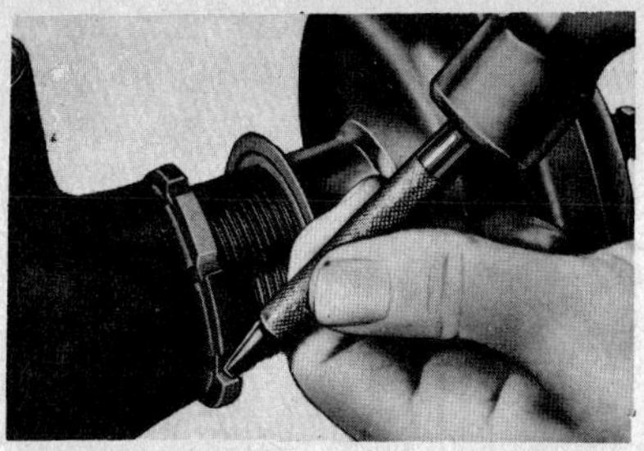

Loosening collect nut air brake power unit (© International Harvester Co.)

Air Compressor Governor Adjustment

Late Models

1. Check governor filter and supply line for any restriction.
2. Loosen adjusting screw locknut and exhaust valve housing locknut.
3. Unscrew adjusting screw four turns.
4. Screw in exhaust valve housing

Adjusting brakes
(© International Harvester Co.)

until it bottoms (do not tighten—seats are easily ruined).

5. Back off exhaust valve housing ¾ turn.
6. While holding exhaust valve housing, turn in adjusting screw three turns after it has made contact with the spring. A slight resistance should be felt when contact is made. If this contact cannot be felt, turn adjusting screw until it sticks out ⅜″ from exhaust valve housing.
7. Start engine and build up air pressure to 115 psi and shut off engine. If governor cuts out before 115 psi, turn adjusting screw out one turn and repeat this step.
8. With pressure holding at 115 psi, turn in adjusting screw until governor cuts out (dull pop).
9. Start truck engine and bleed pressure down until governor cuts in. Cut-in pressure should be 93-98 psi.
10. If cut-in pressure is below 93 psi, hold adjusting screw and turn out exhaust valve housing (1/6 turn equals 5 psi).
11. If cut-in pressure is above 98 psi, hold adjusting screw and turn in exhaust valve housing.
12. Repeat steps until proper cut-in pressure is reached.
13. Check cut-out pressure and adjust if necessary.
14. Tighten adjusting screw locknut and exhaust valve housing locknut.

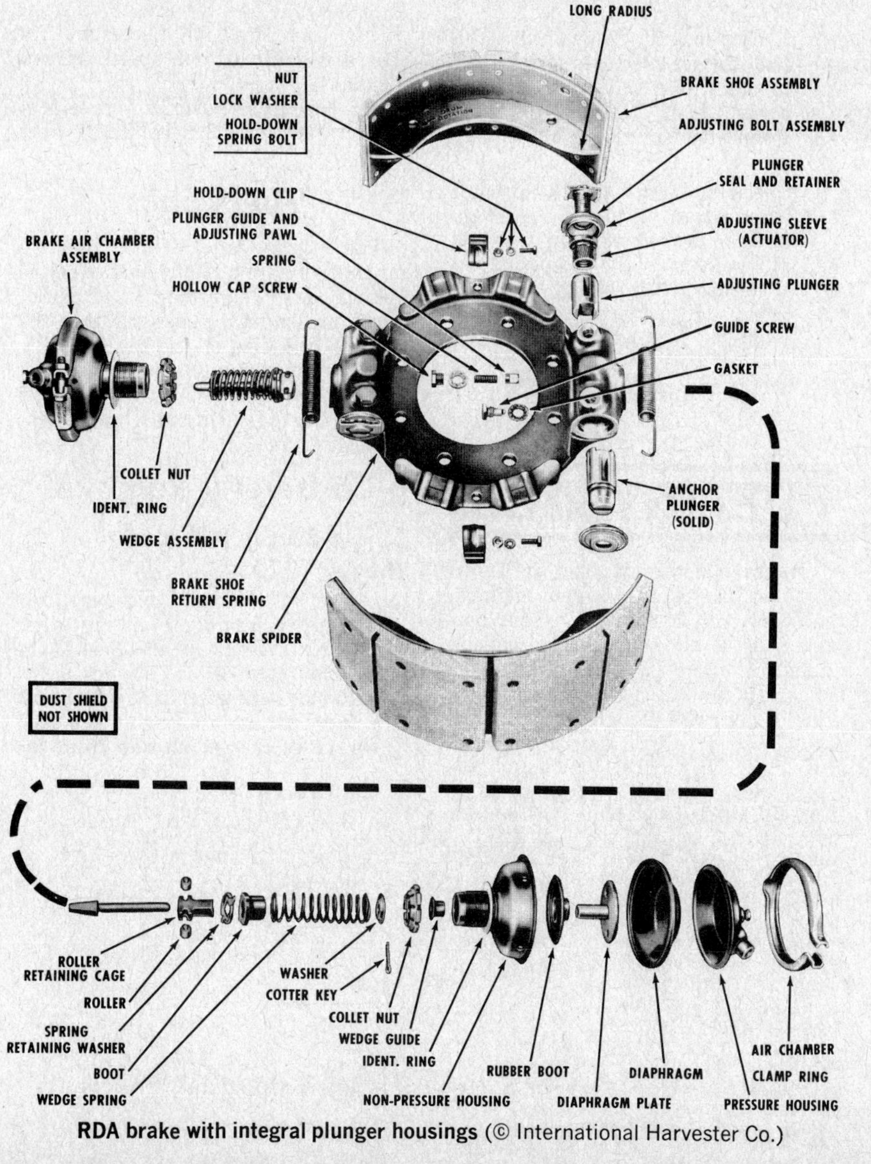

RDA brake with integral plunger housings (© International Harvester Co.)

Air Reservoir Safety Valve Adjustment

1. Connect an accurate air pressure gauge to the emergency line at the rear of the truck and open emergency line valve. With truck engine running, turn air supply valve to the air supply position to bypass governor. Let pressure rise in reservoir until 150 psi is reached then quickly shut off air supply valve.
2. If the safety valve did not blow off at 150 psi or blew off before that pressure, loosen locknut (A) and turn adjusting screw (B) either in for higher pres-

sure setting or out for lower pressure setting.

3. When adjustment is complete, tighten locknut and reduce pressure in system to normal 100 psi by applying and releasing brakes.

Plunger Actuated Brake Adjustment

1. Jack or hoist wheels free of ground.
2. Remove dust cover from adjusting slot—two places on each brake.
3. Turn the star wheel until heavy drag on drum is developed.
4. Back off bolt barely past light drag.
5. Replace dust covers in adjusting slots.
6. Repeat for other brakes.
7. If brakes are equipped with automatic adjusters, check drum to lining clearance. If it is more than .060″, adjust brakes manually until they can be serviced. See Unit Repair section for servicing air brakes.

Air Power Unit Adjustment

1. Determine whether the power unit is the adjustable or bottoming type. Bottoming units have an identification tag fastened to the clamp ring bolt of the air chamber. Adjustable units have no identification markings. Loosen collet nut.
2. Bottoming units automatically provide optimum useful chamber stroke and need only be screwed in until they bottom.
3. Adjustable units are adjusted manually by screwing the unit in until the wedge is just starting to lift the plungers off the abutment seats at the first movement of the diaphragm.
4. After screwing in air chamber unit to proper depth, tighten collet nut to lock position.

Air Brake Slack Adjusters Adjustment

Cam actuated air brakes should be adjusted for lining wear every 2000 miles. Adjustment is made by turning a worm screw on a gear which positions stack adjuster angle.

1. With wheel free to rotate, disconnect pushrod from the slack adjuster to determine whether or not it is in fully released position.
2. Reinsert clevis pin through bottomed pushrod and slack adjuster arm, adjusting worm gear if necessary.
3. Holding the locking sleeve in, adjust worm screw until shoes drag against drum, then back off enough to eliminate drag.
4. Angle that slack adjuster makes when brake is fully applied should not "go over" 90° point.

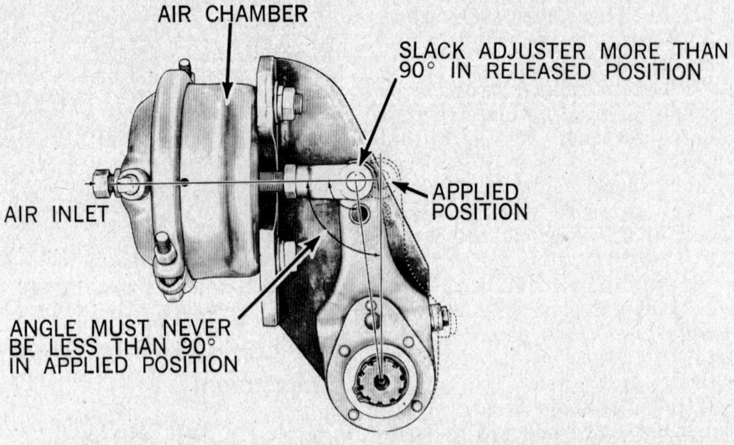

Foundation air brake slack adjuster (© International Harvester Co.)

5. If the slack adjuster goes over the 90° point the maximum force will not be exerted and the pushrod must be adjusted as follows:
6. Carefully disconnect slack adjuster from pushrod—it may snap into the air chamber with considerable force.
7. Loosen locknut on pushrod clevis and thread clevis onto pushrod towards air chamber several turns.
8. Connect pushrod and clevis with pin.
9. Check pushrod-to-slack adjuster angle again as the brake is applied to make sure that it is not still going over the 90° point.
10. Readjust if necessary.
11. When adjustment is correct tighten locknut on pushrod clevis and install cotter pin which secures clevis pin.

FUEL SYSTEM

The carburetors used on the International Harvester truck engine models, vary from one barrel to four barrels. Due to emission control regulations, different internal components and adjustments are necessary for each carburetor model, regardless of the similarity of the carburetor exteriors. When replacing or overhauling a carburetor, it is most important the model number is referred to. This number can be found either on a metal tag, fastened to a bowl cover screw, or embossed on the carburetor casting.

The Emission Control Information Label should be referred to, for the correct specifications necessary for the idle mixture and speed adjustments.

For carburetor overhaul specifications, refer to the General Repair Section.

Fuel Tanks

The location and size of the fuel tanks vary as the requirements of the vehicle vary. The removal and installation procedure will depend upon the location and size of the tanks.

When left and right tanks are used a fuel selector switch is used and is located on the floor panel or the instrument panel.

Carburetor Removal

Single-Barrel Holley Model 1920

1. Remove the air cleaner, fuel lines, vacuum lines and any other hoses and linkage attached to the carburetor.
2. Remove the attaching bolts from the base of the carburetor and remove the carburetor from the

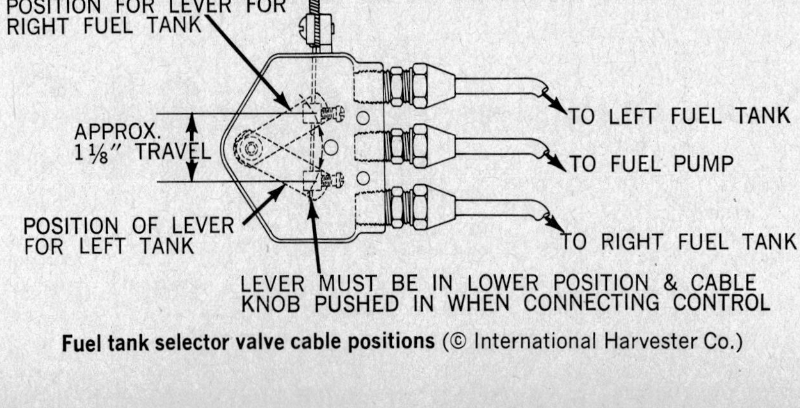

Fuel tank selector valve cable positions (© International Harvester Co.)

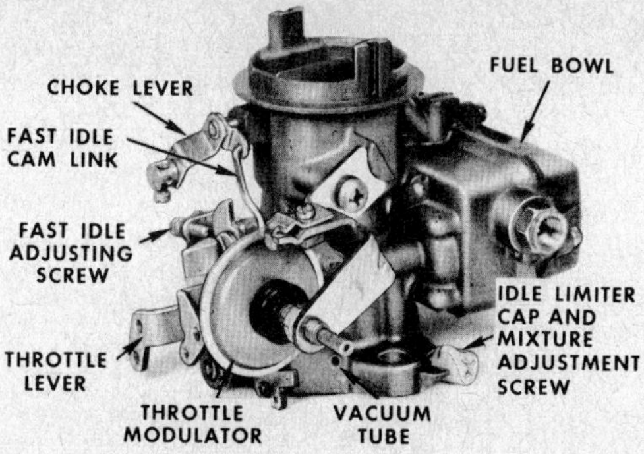

Model 1920 carburetor (© International Harvester Co.)

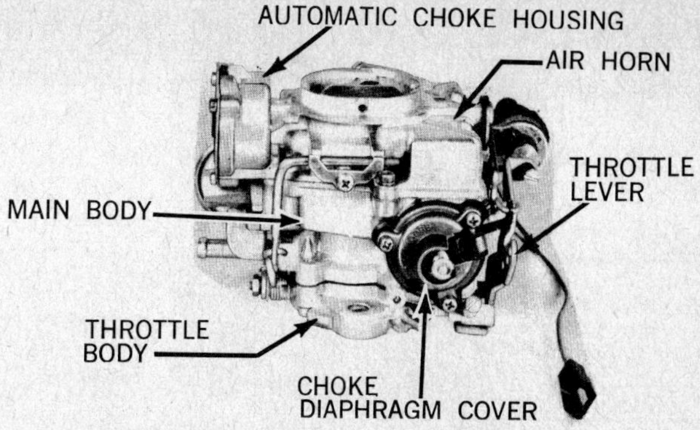

Model 1940 Holley carburetor (© International Harvester Co.)

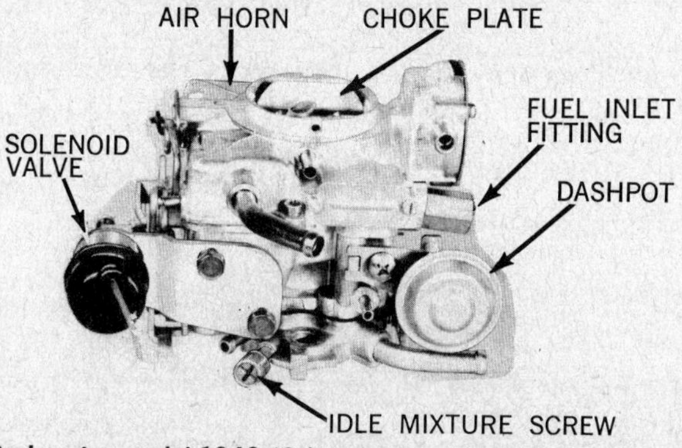

Carburetor model 1940 (© International Harvester Co.)

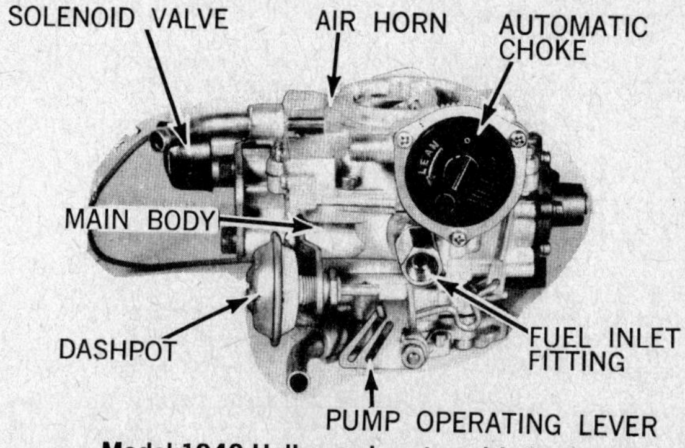

Model 1940 Holley carburetor with dashpot (© International Harvester Co.)

manifold. Remove and discard the old gasket under the base of the carburetor.

3. To install reverse the removal procedure making sure to install a new gasket under the carburetor base.

Single-Barrel Holley Model 1940

1. Remove the air cleaner, fuel lines, vacuum lines and any other lines or linkage attached to the carburetor.
2. Remove the attaching bolts from the base of the carburetor and remove the carburetor from the manifold. Remove and discard the old gasket from under the carburetor.
3. To install reverse the removal procedure making sure to install a new gasket under the carburetor base.

Two-Barrel Holley Models 2100 and Model 2210-C

1. Remove air cleaner, throttle linkage and choke cable.
2. Disconnect fuel line and distributor and governor vacuum lines.
3. Remove bolts from mounting studs and lift off carburetor.
4. To install, clean manifold mating surface and install a new flange gasket.
5. Install carburetor but do not tighten down stud nuts.
6. Connect fuel line and vacuum lines.
7. Tighten nuts on mounting studs in an alternating fashion so that flange gasket compresses evenly for a good seal.
8. Connect throttle linkage and choke cable, making sure that choke plates are fully open when the choke knob is pushed in.
9. Check throttle for complete travel.
10. Install air cleaner.
11. Adjust carburetor as described.

Two-Barrel Holley Model 852-FFG and 885-FFG

1. Remove the air cleaner, fuel lines, vacuum lines, linkage for the choke and throttle, and any

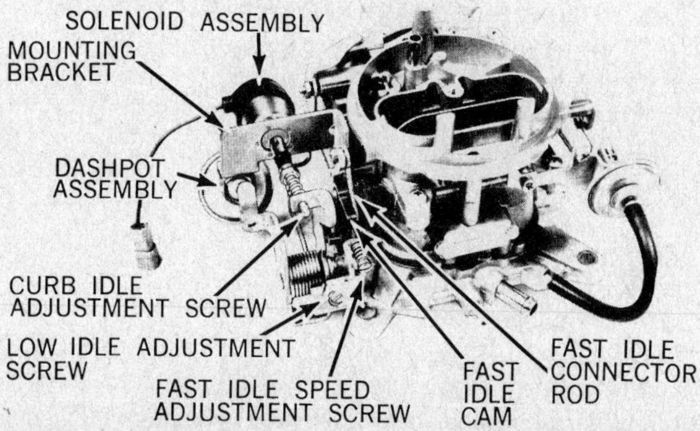

Carburetor model 2210C (© International Harvester Co.)

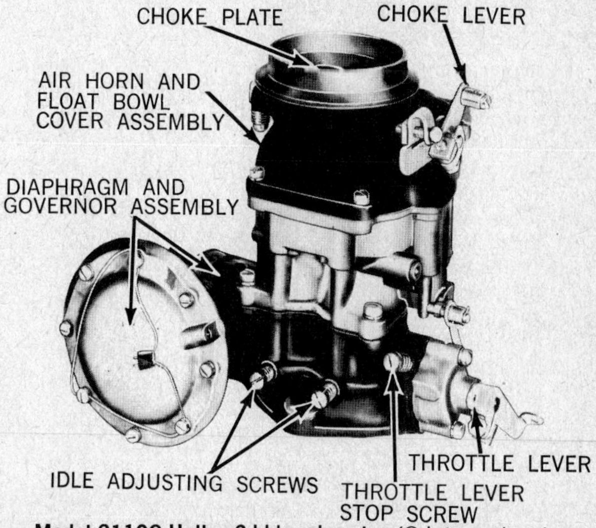

Model 2110G Holley 2 bbl carburetor (© International Harvester Co.)

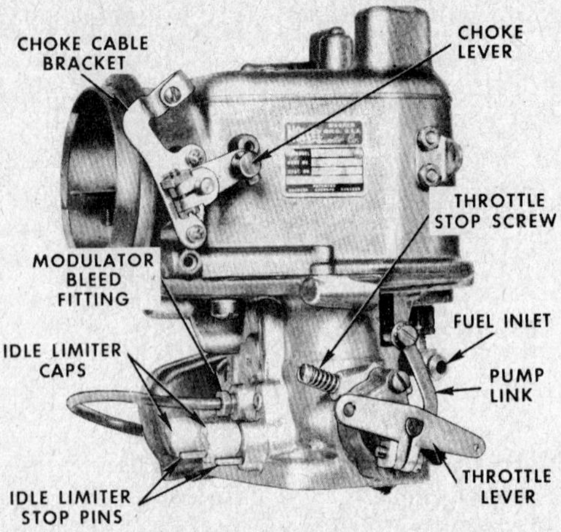

Carburetor model 885-FFG (© International Harvester Co.)

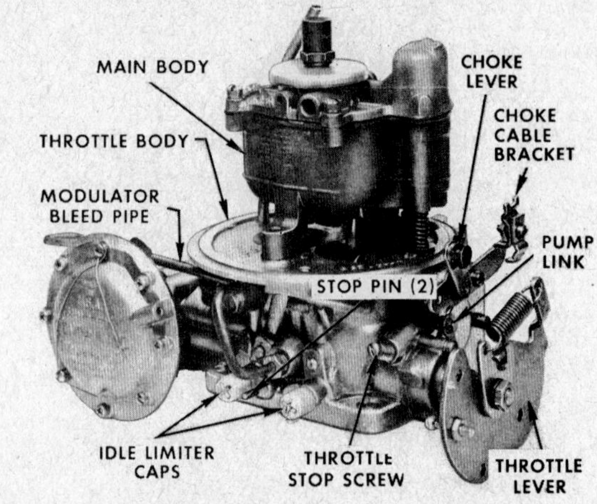

Carburetor model 2140G (© International Harvester Co.)

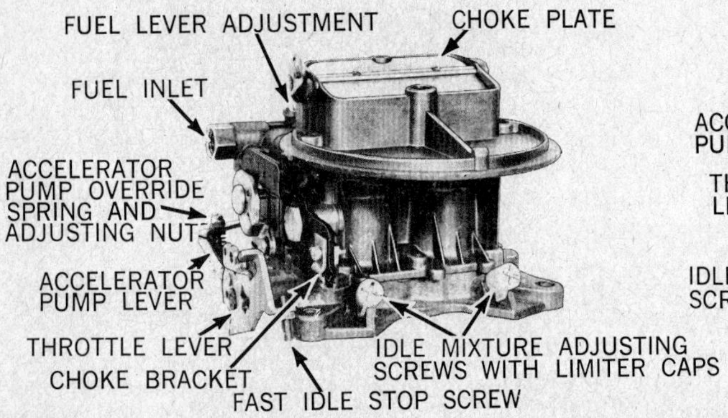

Carburetor model 2300 (© International Harvester Co.)

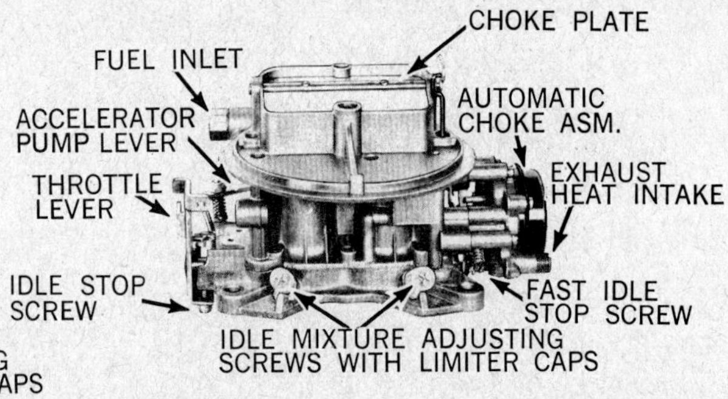

Carburetor model 2300G (© International Harvester Co.)

other lines, linkages, and hoses attached to the carburetor.
2. Remove the nuts or bolts holding the carburetor to the manifold.
3. Remove the carburetor and the base gasket. Clean any gasket particles from the base and manifold surface.
4. To install the carburetor, reverse the removal procedure.
5. Adjust the idle speed and mixture as outlined.

Two-Barrel Holley Models 2300 and 2300G

1. Remove air filter and disconnect fuel line, distributor and governor vacuum lines and throttle and choke linkages.
2. Remove mounting stud nuts and lift off carburetor.
3. Remove flange gasket and discard.
4. To install, clean manifold mating surface and install a new flange gasket.
5. Operate choke and throttle levers to be sure they are functioning properly.
6. Install carburetor and mounting stud nuts, but do not tighten nuts.
7. Connect fuel line, vacuum lines and throttle and choke linkage.
8. Tighten down mounting stud nuts in an alternating criss-cross pattern to make sure that flange gasket is compressed evenly.
9. Check to see that choke plate is fully open and dashboard knob is in when connecting choke.
10. Make all adjustments described in text.
11. Install air cleaner.

Four-Barrel Holley Model 2140G and 2140SG

1. Remove the air cleaner, throttle linkage, vacuum lines, fuel lines, choke control cable, and other hoses and linkages attached to the carburetor.
2. Remove the attaching bolts or nuts from the base of the carburetor, and remove the carburetor from the manifold.
3. Discard the base gasket and clean the base and manifold surfaces of gasket particles.
4. To reinstall the carburetor, reverse the removal procedure, using a new base gasket.

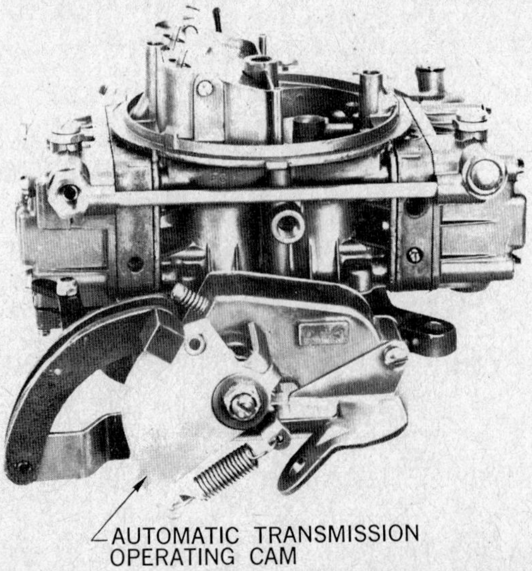

Model 4150G carburetor with automatic transmission operating cam (© International Harvester Co.)

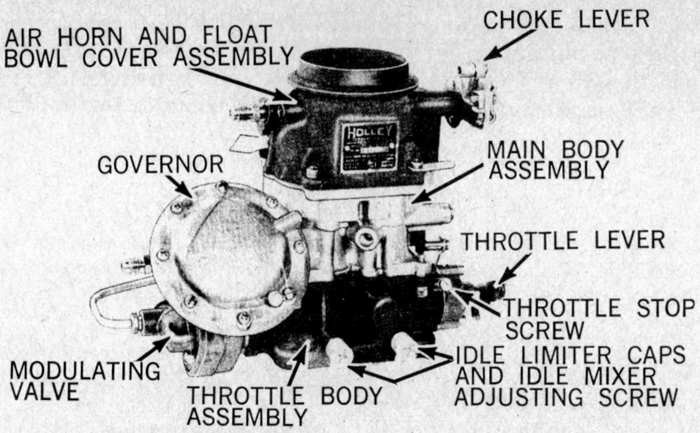

Carburetor model 852-FFG (© International Harvester Co.)

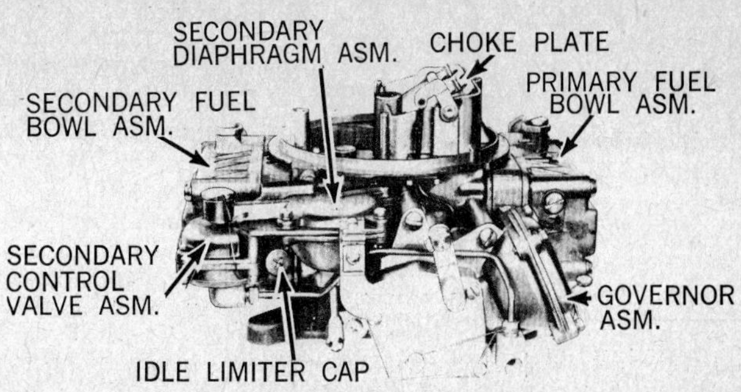

Carburetor model 4150G (© International Harvester Co.)

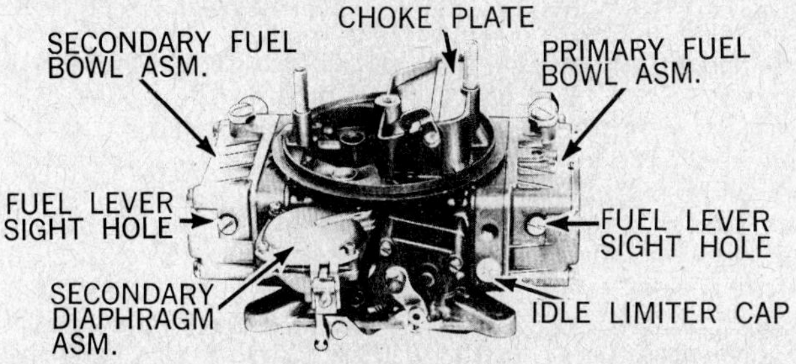

Carburetor model 4150 (© International Harvester Co.)

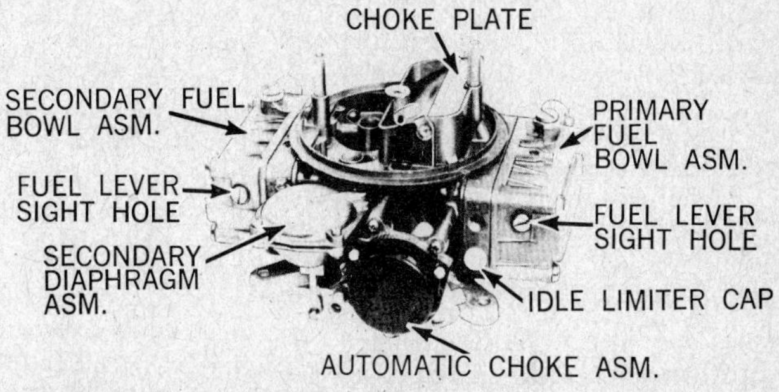

Carburetor model 4150C (© International Harvester Co.)

5. Adjust the carburetor as outlined.

Four-Barrel Holley Model 4150, 4150C, 4150G

1. Remove the air cleaner, throttle linkage and choke linkage, fuel lines, vacuum lines, and other hoses and linkages attached to the carburetor.
2. Remove the nuts or bolts holding the carburetor to the intake manifold.
3. Lift the carburetor from the manifold and remove the gasket from the base of the carburetor and from the manifold surface.
4. To install the carburetor, reverse the removal procedure.
5. Adjust the idle mixture and speed as outlined.

Carter Thermo-Quad Carburetor

1. Remove the air cleaner, throttle linkage, vacuum hoses, fuel lines, and any other hoses and linkages attached to the carburetor.
2. Remove the bolts or nuts holding the carburetor to the manifold, and remove the carburetor from the intake manifold.
3. Discard the base gasket and clean the base and manifold surface of gasket particles.
4. To install the carburetor, reverse the removal procedure, using a new base gasket.
5. Adjust the idle speed and air mixture as outlined.

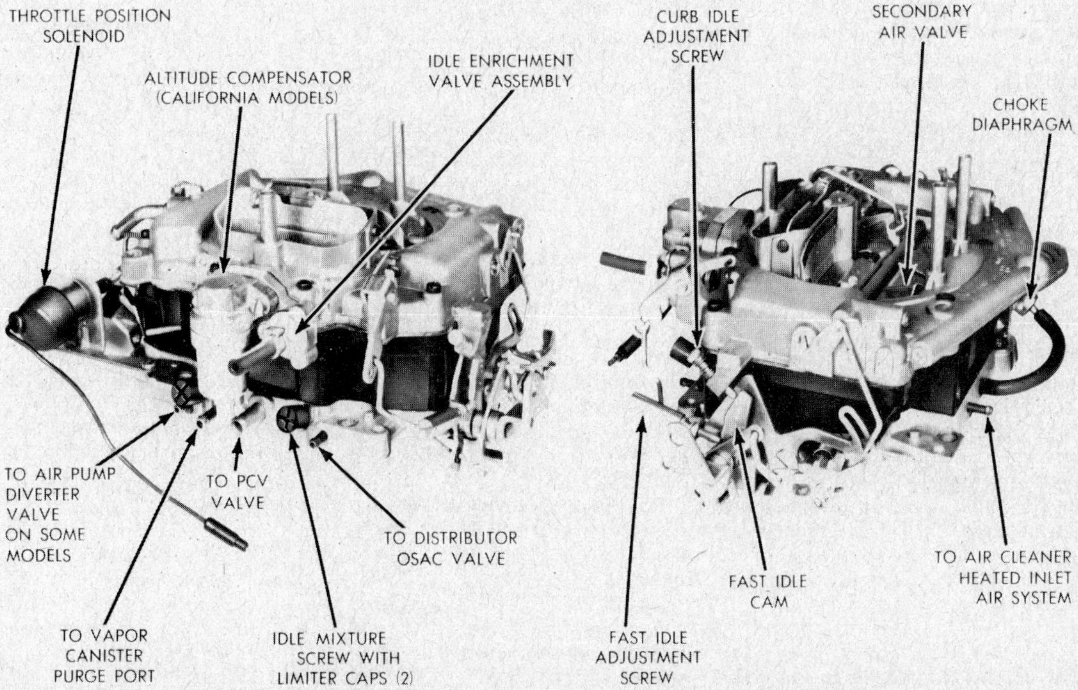

Carburetor model Carter Thermo-Quad (© International Harvester Co.)

Idle Mixture and Speed Adjustment

To comply with the mandated emission control requirements, certain procedures must be followed when adjusting the air/fuel mixture and speed. The engine must be at normal operating temperature, choke open, air cleaner installed, dwell and ignition timing correct, and the parking brake applied. The following procedures apply to all carburetors, with minor deviations possible, depending upon the carburetor used.

Observe the following precautions when adjusting the idle mixture and speed.

1. Do not idle the engine for longer than three minutes at a time.
2. After each three minute interval, increase the engine speed to 2000 RPM for one minute.
3. Continue with the idle adjustment and repeat step 2 as necessary.

Preliminary Idle Setting—(After carburetor overhaul)

1. Connect a calibrated tachometer to the engine.
2. Connect a test vacuum gauge to the engine intake manifold.
3. Operate the engine at a fast idle speed to bring the operating temperature to normal.
4. Adjust the carburetor to the specified idle speed. Refer to the chart at the beginning of this section.
5. Adjust the idle mixture screw(s) and idle speed screw to obtain "lean best idle" at the specified speed. *NOTE: "Lean best idle" is the point at which intake manifold vacuum starts to drop due to leanness.*
6. Install the colored (service) plastic cap(s) with the tab fully turned counterclockwise against the stop.
7. Adjust the idle speed to specifications.
8. Make final idle adjustments to obtain the recommended idle setting.

Idle Adjustment—Lean Drop Method

1. Connect a calibrated tachometer to the engine.
2. Rotate the idle adjusting screw(s) counterclockwise against the stops.
3. Adjust the idle speed to give an engine speed 25 RPM higher than the specified idle speed.
4. Rotate the idle mixture screw(s) clockwise slowly and equally (if two) until the specified speed is obtained.
5. If the engine is rough or the specified idle speed cannot be attained, remove the limiter cap(s) and continue the adjustment as outlined in step 4, until the specified RPM is attained and the engine is smooth.
6. Install new plastic limiter cap(s) with the tab fully counterclockwise against the stop.
7. Readjust as necessary to maintain the specified RPM.

Idle Adjustment—Exhaust Analyzer Method

When exhaust analyzer equipment is used, the following procedure is recommended to be used to adjust the idle mixture and speed. The test equipment must give accurate readings in the 0-5% Carbon Monoxide (CO) range.

1. Connect a calibrated tachometer to the engine and insert the exhaust analyzer into the exhaust pipe. *NOTE: Refer to the manufacturers instructions for complete connection procedures.*
2. Operate the engine for fifteen minutes at fast idle speed (approximately 1000-1200 RPM), to bring engine to normal operating temperature and to stabilize the temperature of the exhaust analyzer.
4. Calibrate the test equipment as per the manufacturers instructions. *NOTE: If the combustion analyzer does not respond to changes in the mixture quality, check for leaks or restrictions in the sample lines. The thermal conductivity instruments used in the analyzer are both temperature and pressure sensitive, and require a definite sample flow. Refer to the manufacturer's instructions as necessary.*
5. Adjust the idle mixture screw(s) counterclockwise against the tab stop.
6. Adjust the idle speed screw to obtain the specified idle speed.
7. Observe the analyzer dial and adjust the idle mixture screw(s) clockwise by 1/16 turn increments to obtain the specified idle mixture setting and readjust the idle speed as necessary.
8. If the idle speed and mixture cannot be obtained, remove the idle limiter cap(s). *NOTE: To prevent damage to the mixture screw(s) or seat, file or grind the side of the plastic cap. Do Not Pry Cap Off.*
9. With the engine operating, adjust the mixture screw(s) to obtain the "lean best idle" at the specified idle speed. *NOTE: "Lean best idle" is the point at which maximum manifold vacuum begins to drop due to leanness.*
10. Install new plastic limiter cap(s) with the tab fully counterclockwise against the stop.
11. Readjust the idle mixture screw(s) to obtain the recommended CO setting.

NOTE: After completing the idle adjustment procedure, if unsatisfactory idle operation still exists, a recheck of the ignition system, crankcase ventilation system, timing advance system, air induction system, exhaust gas recirculation system, or hot idle compensation system should be made.

Fuel Pumps

The fuel pumps used on the gasoline engines are of two types.

a. Mechanical type—This type is mounted on the engine block and is operated by a special eccentric on the camshaft.
b. Electric type—This type is mounted in the fuel tank and is supported by an adjustable hanger assembly, therefore, making it adaptable to all I. H. fuel tank depths. A spring loaded latch is normally used to permit easy motor replacement.

Mechanical Fuel Pump

Removal

1. Remove the fuel inlet pipe or hose and the outlet fuel pipe to the carburetor from the fuel pump fittings.
2. Remove the attaching bolts from the fuel pump housing to engine block and remove the fuel pump.
3. Clean the gasket surfaces of all gasket particles.

Installation

1. Install new gasket on the fuel pump mounting flange and install the fuel pump operating arm into the hole in the block, and into contact with the eccentric lobe on the camshaft.
2. Install the attaching bolts and tighten the pump to the block securely.
3. Install the inlet hose or pipe, and the outlet pipe to the fuel pump and tighten securely to avoid air leaks.

NOTE: An additional hose may be used from the fuel filter to the fuel pump. Install to the proper fitting if so equipped.

Electric Fuel Pump

Removal

1. Remove the electrical connections, the outlet pipe or hose, and the retaining screws holding the assembly to the tank.
2. Withdraw the pump/support assembly from the tank, being

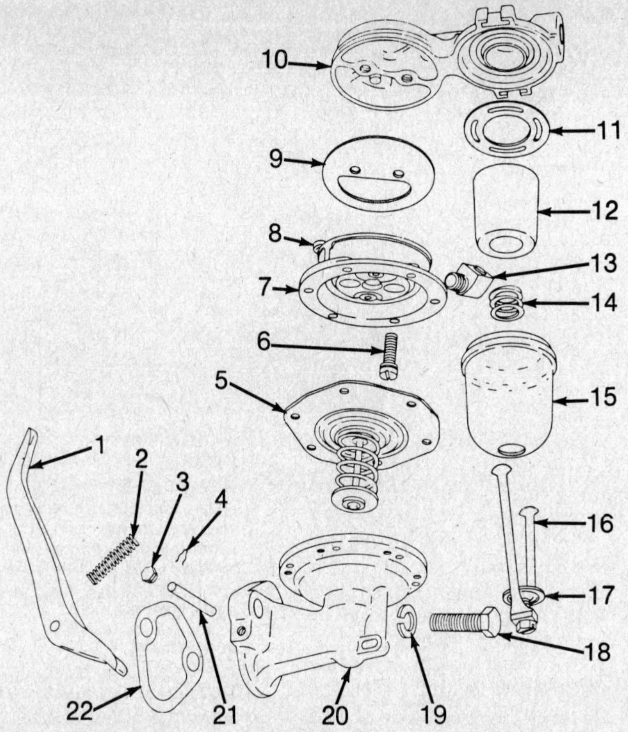

Exploded view mechanical fuel pump typical (© International Harvester Co.)

1 Lever, cam
2 Spring, cam lever return
3 Plug, cam lever shaft seal
4 Pin, spring, cam lever shaft retaining
5 Diaphragm, assembly
6 Screw, with lockwasher, assembly
7 Housing, valve assembly
8 Screw, with lockwasher, assembly
9 Diaphragm, air dome
10 Air dome and filter cover
11 Gasket, filter bowl
12 Filter, glazed ceramic or paper
13 Elbow
14 Spring, filter
15 Bowl, filter
16 Retainer, with screw assembly
17 Washer, Filter bowl retaining
18 Bolt, hex head
19 Lockwasher
20 Pump body
21 Pin, cam lever
22 Gasket, pump-to-crankcase

careful not to allow dirt to enter the tank hole.

3. With the unit out of the tank, remove the pump from the support assembly.
4. Remove the gasket and any particles from the gasket surfaces.

Installation

1. Install the pump assembly into the support arms and retain it securely.
2. Using a new gasket, insert the pump/support assembly into the tank and secure it with the attaching screws. Tighten securely to avoid air or gasoline leaks.
3. Install the outlet pipe or hose, and the electrical connections to the assembly.

Fuel Pump Pressure Test

1. Disconnect fuel line at carburetor inlet and attach pressure gauge between the inlet and disconnected line.
2. Start engine and take reading. Consult Tune-up Specifications at the beginning of this section for correct pump pressure.

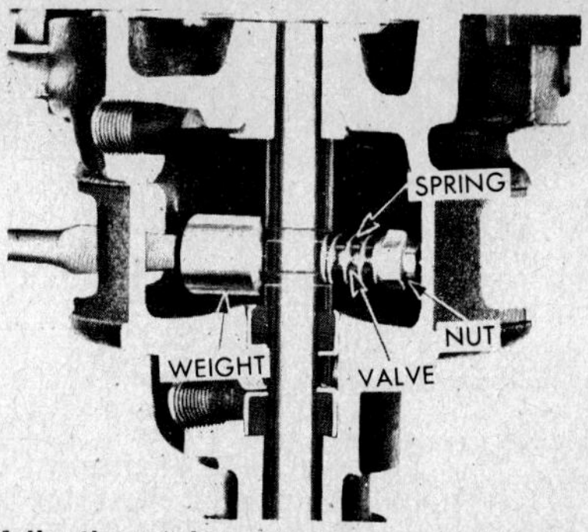

Adjusting spinner governor distributor (© International Harvester Co.)

3. When engine is stopped, the pressure should remain constant or very slowly return to zero.

Fuel Pump Capacity Test

1. Disconnect fuel line from the fuel pump.
2. Connect a piece of hose to the line so that fuel can be directed into a measuring container.
3. Start engine and note time it takes to fill a pint container. Pump should fill one pint within 20-30 seconds.

Governor Speed Adjustments

Excessive engine RPM causes rapid wear and strains on the internal engine parts, and for this reason, many engines are governed at predetermined RPM. The recommended no-load governed RPM for each engine is found in the specification charts at the beginning of the chapter and should be referred to when determining the need for governed RPM changes.

Adjustment of the governed speed is made at the governor spinner valve, located on the distributor, for the RD engines, and in the distributor housing for the V8 engines.

RD Engine Governor Adjusting Procedure

1. Attach a calibrated tachometer to the engine.
2. Accelerate the engine and note

Cutaway view in tank fuel pump mounted on adjustable supports
(© International Harvester Co.)

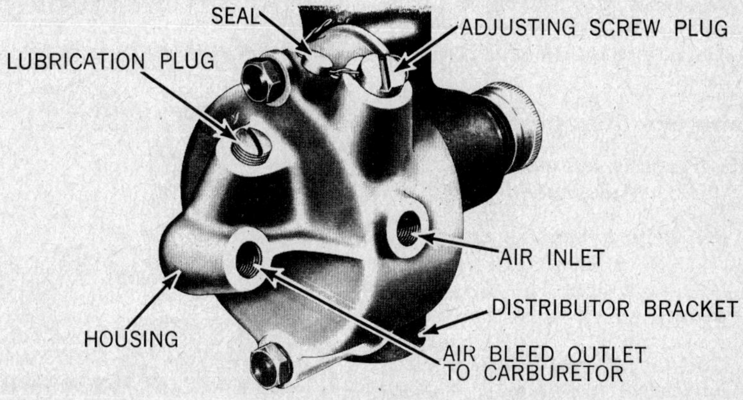

RD engine model governor control housing (© International Harvester Co.)

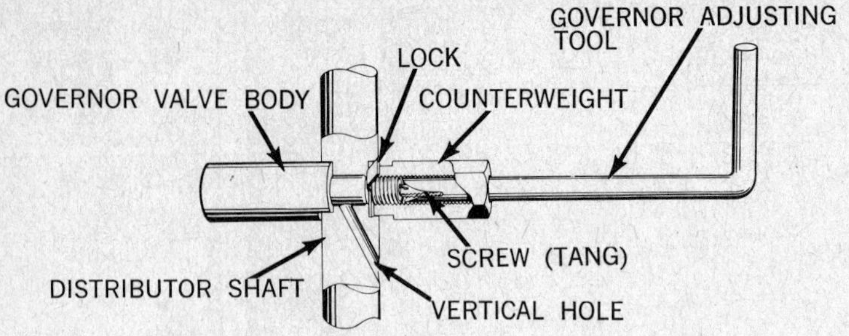

Governor valve adjustment model 1530 distributor
(© International Harvester Co.)

the governed top speed and compare with the specification charts.

3. If necessary to adjust the governor, remove the seal wire and the adjusting hole plug from the governor housing.
4. With the ignition off, rotate the engine until the adjusting screw in the end of the spinner valve appears at the plug hole.
5. Insert a screwdriver and engage the adjusting screw.
6. Turn the adjusting screw clockwise to increase the governed speed, or counterclockwise to decrease governed speed. *NOTE: One turn of the screw will affect governed speed approximately 150 RPM.*
7. Again accelerate the engine, and observe the governed speed. Readjust the governor as needed.
8. Install the adjusting screw hole plug and install a new seal wire.

V8 Engine Governor Adjustment Procedure

1. Connect a calibrated tachometer to the engine.
2. Accelerate the engine and observe the governed speed at no-load. Refer to the specification charts at the beginning of this chapter.
3. If necessary, adjust the governor by removing the seal wire, governor clamp and gasket from the distributor housing.
4. With the ignition off, rotate the engine until the adjusting screw hole appears in the opening of the distributor housing.
5. With a 1/8 Allen wrench, remove the adjusting hole plug from the governor.

Carburetor Adjustment

LPG (Propane-Butane) Carburetor Adjustment

All OHV 6 Engines Except PT 6 & RD 501

1. Loosen locknut on starting adjusting screw and turn screw clockwise until it bottoms, then back it out the required number of turns (see table). Tighten locknut.

until the engine speed starts to drop again, then set in between the two extremes and tighten locknut. For part throttle adjustment, loosen small locknut on economizer cover and turn economizer adjusting screw clockwise the required number of turns from bottom position (see table) and tighten locknut.

2. Turn idle adjusting screw on the regulating unit clockwise until it bottoms gently, then back it out the required number of turns (see table).
3. On BD engines, loosen the large lock nut on the economizer unit and turn load adjusting screw clockwise to extreme position, then turn counterclockwise the required number of turns (see table). Tighten locknut. On BD engines (engine not running),

LPG carburetor
(© International Harvester Co.)

1 Fuelock-strainer, assembly
2 Fuelock, connection to ignition switch
3 Governor, diaphragm housing
4 Governor, spinner box air line
5 Drag, link idle adjusting screw
6 Spacer (insulator)
7 Throttle, control rod
8 Metering, valve lever
9 Throttle, lever

disconnect vacuum line from economizer before setting load adjustment. Then loosen locknut and turn entire economizer assembly clockwise until it bottoms in carburetor, then counterclockwise the specified number of turns (see table). Temporarily plug the vacuum line and start engine. After the engine is warmed up, set hand throttle at about 2/3 governed speed. Screw economizer body in until engine speed starts to drop and then out

LPG Carburetor Adjustment Specifications

Engine	*RD-406*	*RD-450*
Starting Adjusting Screw (number turns off seat)	1	2
Economizer (load adjustment) (number turns off seat)	5 4-11/16	4-3/4 3-3/4

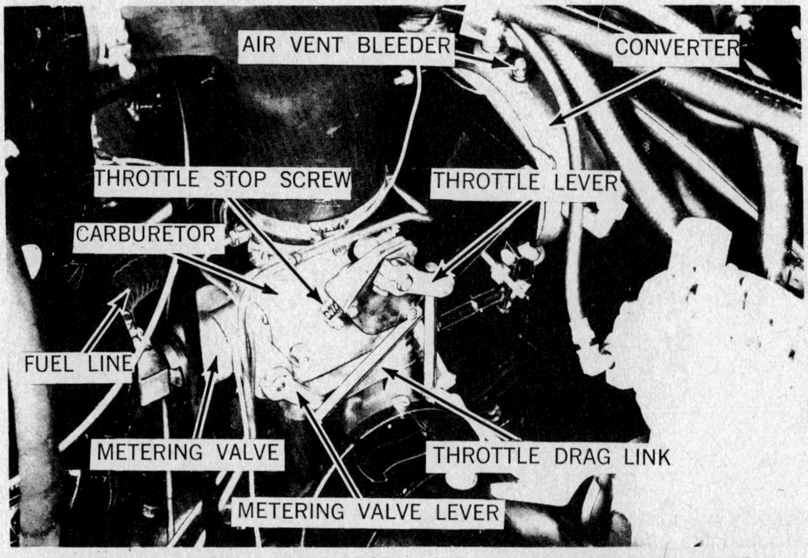

LPG carburetion V401, 461 and 548 engines (© International Harvester Co.)

Carburetor Diagnosis Service

The following diagnosis and troubleshooting chart can be used as a general guide to determine the cause of carburetor related problems. When the problem has been isolated to a particular component and more information is needed, refer to the related chapter within this section, or to the General Repair Section.

1. Rough Idle or Stalling—Engine Hot or Cold

a. Binding linkage, choke valve, or choke piston
b. Disconnected or broken choke control cable
c. Incorrect choke thermostat adjustment
d. Fast idle linkage and cam not properly adjusted
e. Idle mixture screw(s) out of adjustment
f. Idle speed screw out of adjustment
g. Air cleaner air flow restricted
h. Hot idle compensator valve stuck.
i. Secondary throttle plates open (4V carburetors)
j. Clogged air bleed or idle passages
k. Vacuum leakage
l. Improper float level
m. Electrical or emission control systems malfunction

2. Poor low speed operation

a. Clogged idle transfer slots
b. Clogged air bleed or idle passages
c. Air cleaner air flow restricted
d. Improper float level
e. Faulty automatic choke operation
f. Improper use of hand controlled choke
g. Vacuum leakage
h. Electrical or emission control system malfunction

3. Poor Engine Acceleration

a. Improper acceleration pump stroke
b. Inoperative or missing pump discharge check valve, ball, or needle
c. Damaged or worn pump diaphragm or piston
d. Leaking gaskets
e. Defective fuel pump
f. Clogged discharge jets
g. Electrical or emission control systems malfunction

4. Poor High Speed Operation

a. Defective fuel pump or clogged fuel filter
b. Clogged vacuum passages
c. Power valve stuck
d. Metering rods stuck
e. Improper size or obstructions in the main jets
f. Restricted air supply to air cleaner
g. Improper float level
h. Electrical or emission control system malfunction

5. Surging—Cruising Speeds

a. Clogged main jets
b. Undersize main jets
c. Low fuel level
d. Defective fuel pump or clogged fuel filter
e. Blocked air bleeds
f. Restricted air supply to air cleaner
g. Vacuum leakage
h. Metering rods out of adjustment
i. Power valve sticking
j. Electrical or emission control system malfunction

6. Stalling When The Accelerator is Closed Quickly

a. Improperly adjusted or defective throttle modulator or dash pot
b. Clogged air bleed or idle passages
c. Vacuum leakage
d. Throttle plates not closing

7. Governor Not Operating—No Engine Speed Control

a. Seal broken—Governor maladjusted
b. Vacuum leakage or lines broken
c. Modulator diaphragm leaking or broken
d. Sticking governor spinner valve

8. Governor Cuts Off At Low Speeds—Erratic Operation

a. Clogged distributor governor filter
b. Restricted vacuum lines
c. Sticking governor spinner valve
d. Restrictions in the spinner shaft or housing

9. Engine Surges At And Below Governed Speed

a. Vacuum leakage or restriction
b. Carburetor jets or air bleeds clogged
c. Spinner valve sticking
d. Electrical or emission control systems malfunctfion

COOLING SYSTEM

The cooling system is a closed type, utilizing a two valve pressure cap. One valve is used to relieve excessive pressure from the system, and the second valve is used to allow atmospheric air to enter the system during the cooling down period. The engine temperature is controlled in two ways. One method is by a thermostat, located on the front of the engine block or cylinder head. The second method is by a shutter assembly, mounted on the grille of the vehicle, and controlled by heat sensitive switches mounted on the engine and radiator. The coolant is forced through the engine and radiator by the water pump, located on the front of the engine, which is belt driven by the crankshaft pulley.

CAUTION: To avoid personal injury, remove the pressure cap from the radiator in two steps. Loosen the cap to its first notch and allow the pressure to escape through the overflow pipe. After the pressure has been released, press on the cap and continue to turn until the prongs on the cap disengage from the radiator neck.

Heater Core Removal and Installation

Without Air Conditioning Except Scout

Due to the many body styles, a general description of the heater core removal and installation will be outlined. Utilize the operations as necessary for the vehicle being serviced. Use caution when removing the heater box assembly, to avoid breakage to the box due to hidden screws or bolts.

1. Drain the cooling system and remove the negative battery cable.
2. Disconnect the heater hoses at the heater core tubes.
3. Disconnect the heater electrical wiring and the control cables.

   NOTE: Cables may have to be disconnected at the control panel and removed with the heater box.

4. Remove the heater distribution manifold at the heater box.
5. Remove the heater box attaching bolts or nuts from the cab side and from the engine side of the firewall.
6. Remove the heater box assembly from the vehicle.
7. Remove the heater box back cover or the outer door and shaft. Remove the heater core.

8. The installation of the heater assembly is the reverse of removal. Fill the cooling system and check the operation of the heater system.

With Air Conditioning (Blend Air System) Except Scout

NOTE: This air conditioning/heater system unit is located under the passenger seat as a compact unit, for ease in servicing.

1. Close the heater hose shutoff valves at engine, if equipped, or drain the cooling system. Disconnect the negative battery cable.
2. Remove the heater hoses from the heater core tubes.
3. Remove the floor mounted blower motor well cover, and disconnect the wiring at the connectors.
4. Loosen the unit mounting stud nuts. *NOTE: Lower the cab on the CO models before removing the mounting stud nuts.*
5. Remove the floor mat from the passenger side.
6. Remove the floor panel on the passenger side to expose the air duct.
7. Remove the rubber seals from the fresh air duct and treated air duct.
8. Remove the hose connecting the bunk duct to the blower housing (if equipped).
9. Remove the thumb screws securing the passenger seat and heater cover plate assembly. Remove the seat and cover assembly.
10. Disconnect the control cables at the heater assembly.
11. Disconnect the electrical wiring from the heater assembly.
12. Remove the unit mounting stud nuts and washers. Remove the heater assembly from the cab.
13. Remove the sponge rubber seals on the heater tubes and set aside for later installation.
14. The installation is in the reverse of the removal. Replace the coolant lost during removal, and operate the system and check for leakage.

Scout

1. Drain the cooling system and remove the negative battery cable.
2. Remove the heater hoses from the heater core outlets.
3. Remove the windshield washer bottle from the firewall.
4. Remove the cover plate from the heater box and remove the heater core from the housing.
5. Remove the core end cover. *NOTE: Do not damage the core fins during the removal and installation procedure.*
6. Installation is the reverse of removal. Fill the cooling system and check the operation of the heater system.

Water Pump Removal

1. Drain cooling system.
2. If radiator shrouds hinder access they must be removed before proceeding (large V-8's and cab-forward models).
3. Loosen alternator pivot bolts and adjusting bolt on bracket to relieve tension on the fan belt and remove belt from water pump pulley. On V(S)-401, 478, 549, 537, 605 engines all accessories are driven by belts from the water pump pulley and are removed by loosening the alternator and power steering pump adjusting brackets and pivots. The idler pulley on the belts between the crankshaft and water pump pulleys is then loosened so that these belts may be removed.
4. On V(S)-401, 478, 549, 537, 605 engines the fan blades and pulley are removed.
5. Remove all pipes and hoses connected to the water pump.
6. Remove mounting bolts or stud nuts and water pump. On all models except 4-196 and V-304, 345, 392, only the front half of the pump housing is removed for water pump servicing.
7. Installation is the reverse of the above procedure. Be sure to install new gaskets and, if applicable, new O-rings on pipe end fittings.

Water Pump Service

Engine Models 232, 258 MV 404, 446, V537, V605

This water pump is nonadjustable, has a packless seal and must be serviced as a complete unit: in the event of malfunction the whole assembly is replaced.

1. Remove pump as described in the preceding section.
2. Clean impeller cavity before installing new pump.
3. Spin shaft on new pump to be sure it rotates freely.
4. Install as described in preceding section, using a new gasket.

Water Pump Disassembly

Engine Models 4-196 and 4-196E

1. Separate the housing from the pump body. *NOTE: The housing holds the impeller and shaft assembly.*
2. Unless special tools, number SE 1950 and SE 1950-1 installers or their equivalents are used, the following measurements should be taken and recorded for the reassembly of the pump.
   a. Measure the distance from the pump hub to the end of the shaft and record the measurement.
   b. Measure the distance from the impeller hub to the end of the shaft and record the measurement.
3. Remove the snapring from the groove in front of the shaft bearing assembly.
4. Press the shaft and bearing assembly from the housing and from the impeller. *NOTE: The bearing and shaft assembly are replaced as an assembly only.*
5. Remove the seal from the rear of the housing with the aid of a drift and hammer.

Installation

1. Press a new seal into the housing bore.

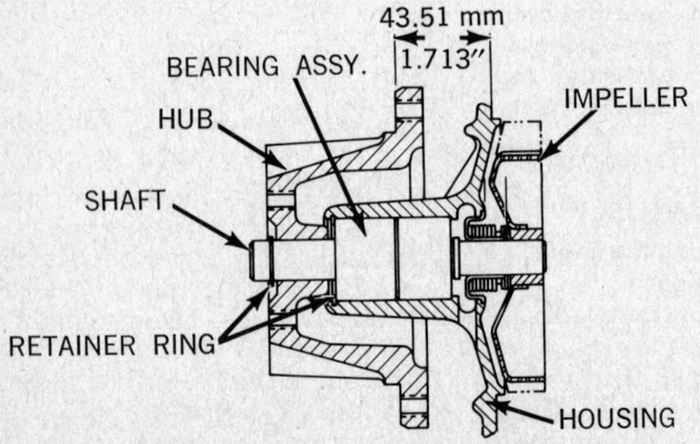

Sectional view of water pump V537 and 605 engines
(© International Harvester Co.)

Water pump location MV404 and 446 engines
(© International Harvester Co.)

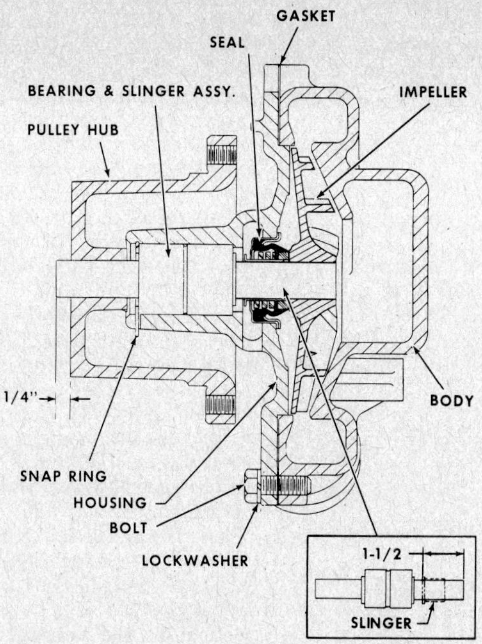

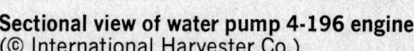

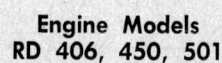

Sectional view of water pump 4-196 engine
(© International Harvester Co.)

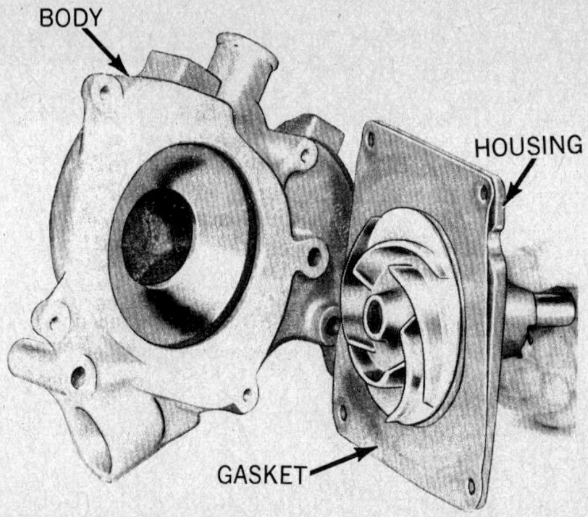

Separation of water pump body and housing 4-196 engine
(© International Harvester Co.)

2. Install new slinger on the bearing shaft, if not equipped, 1½ inch from the rear end of the shaft to the forward edge of the slinger.
3. Press the bearing and shaft assembly into the housing and install the snapring.
4. Using special tool SE 1950 or equivalent, or by using the measurement taken before removal, press the impeller in place on the shaft.
5. Using special tool SE 1950-1 or equivalent, or by using the measurement taken during the removal, press the pulley hub in position on the shaft.
6. Using a new gasket, install the pump housing to the pump body and secure with the attaching bolts.

Engine Models RD 406, 450, 501

1. Remove the nut and washer holding the pulley to the shaft and remove the pulley from the shaft with the aid of a puller.
2. Remove the snapring from the front of the water pump shaft front bearing.
3. Press the shaft and bearing from the impeller and the pump housing.
4. Press the shaft out of the bearing, spacer and slinger. Do not lose the two half-moon lock rings from under the slinger.
5. Remove the seal assembly from the housing through the back of the pump.
6. Use a drift and hammer, and carefully drive the seal from the pump housing and discard.

Installation

1. Install a new pump seal into the housing bore and press into place.
2. Place the slinger on the shaft and press into position 1 33/64 inch on the shaft, measuring from the rear of the shaft. Pack the bearings with short fiber wheel bearing grease and place the rear bearing, spacer, and front bearing onto the shaft.
3. Place the two half-moon lock rings in the groove on the shaft and press the shaft into the bearings and spacer until the rear

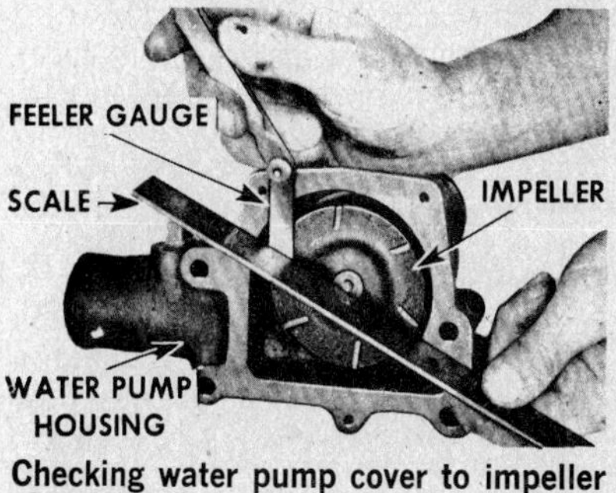

Checking water pump cover to impeller clearance
(© International Harvester Co.)

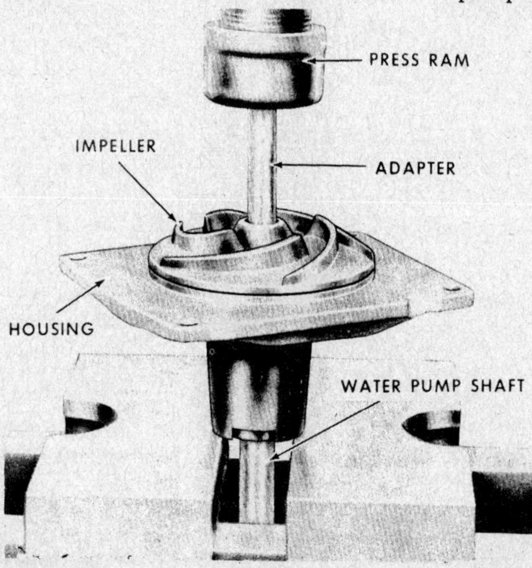

Removal of water pump shaft and bearing assembly from the pump housing (© International Harvester Co.)

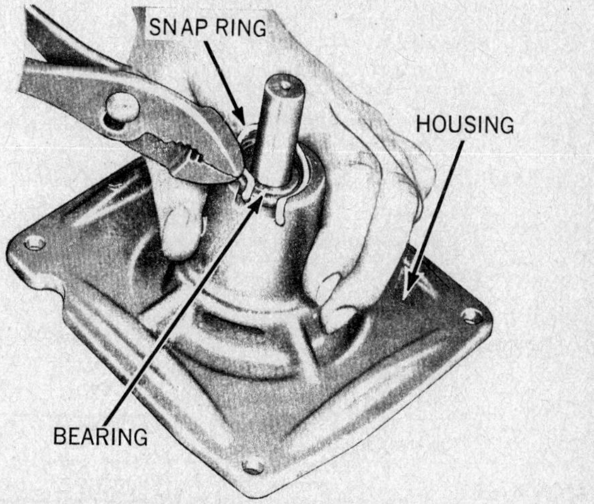

Removing shaft and bearing assembly snap ring from water pump (© International Harvester Co.)

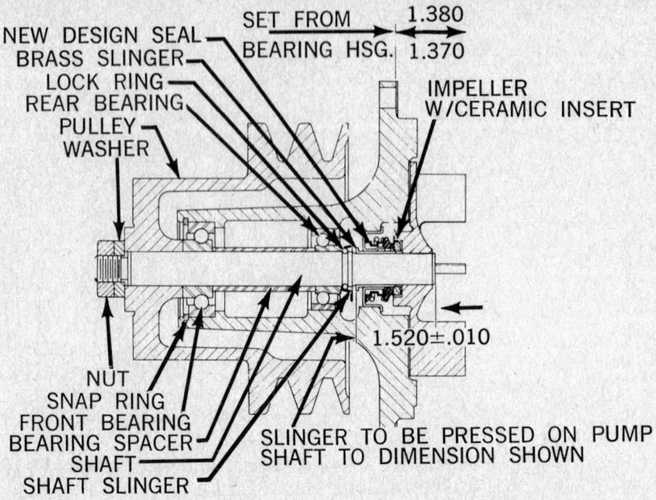

Sectional view of water pump RD406, 450 and 501 engines
(© International Harvester Co.)

bearing rests firmly against the slinger and lock rings.

4. Install the shaft and bearing assembly into the housing of the pump and hold it into place by inserting the snapring in the groove in front of the front bearing. *NOTE: Fill the pump housing with an ounce and one-half of the short fiber grease before installing the shaft and bearing assembly.*
5. Press the pulley onto the front end of the shaft and secure with the washer and nut.
6. Support the shaft at the front end and press the impeller onto the rear of the shaft.
7. Locate the impeller at 1.520 ± .010 inch, measuring from the shaft end to the edge of the impeller vane.
8. Check for freedom of operation and install the pump, using a new gasket.

Engine Models VS 401, 478, 549 series, V 304, 345, 392

1. Remove the pump housing from the pump body on engine models V 304, 345, 392.
2. Remove the pulley from the shaft, and the bearing and shaft snapring.
3. Remove the impeller from the bearing shaft and the shaft from the housing by the use of a press.
4. Using a drift and hammer, remove the seal and discard.
5. Remove the impeller seat and bushing from the housing and discard.

Installation

1. Install new bushing and seat into the housing bore.
2. Install a new seal into the housing.
3. Press the bearing and shaft assembly into the housing until the bearing bottoms into the counterbore. *NOTE: Due to variations in the pump housing, bearings and shaft assembly, and the impeller, the impeller cannot be pressed to the correct location on the shaft during the first press application. The following procedure must be used to achieve the correct location of the impeller.*
4. With the use of SE 2086 special tool kit or its equivalent, select a .060 shim stop and place it on the impeller end of the shaft and press the impeller on the shaft until the press ram bottoms on the shim. *NOTE: The purpose of the shim stop is to limit the travel of the pump shaft in the impeller, so that an interference will exist between the impeller and the pump housing.*
5. Place the pump assembly on the front cover of the engine and install two bolts finger tight.
6. With the use of a feeler gauge, determine the clearance between the housing flange and the front cover.
7. Record the clearance and add to the specification of .015 inch running clearance. Subtract the total of the two from the original .060 shim thickness and record.
8. From the special tool kit SE 2086 or its equivalent, select the shims to provide the thickness of the above recorded figure, and place the shims on the shaft end. Press the impeller further onto the shaft until the ram bottoms on the shim stop. This operation should provide the proper operating clearance for the impeller. *NOTE: If no clearance exists between the housing flange and the front cover, and the impeller*

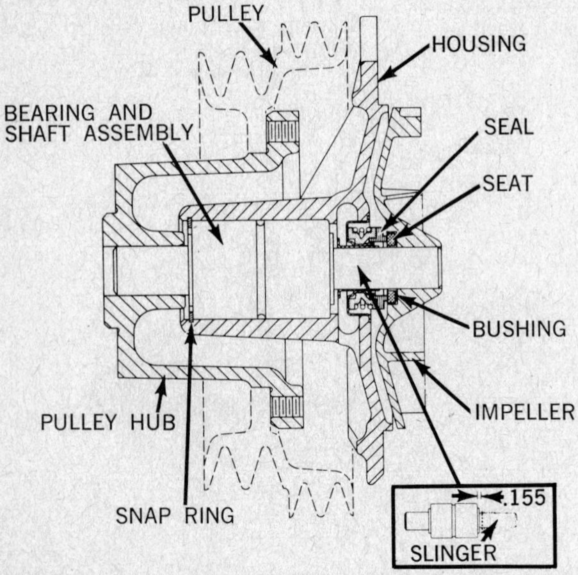

Sectional view water pump VS401, 478 and 549 engines
(© International Harvester Co.)

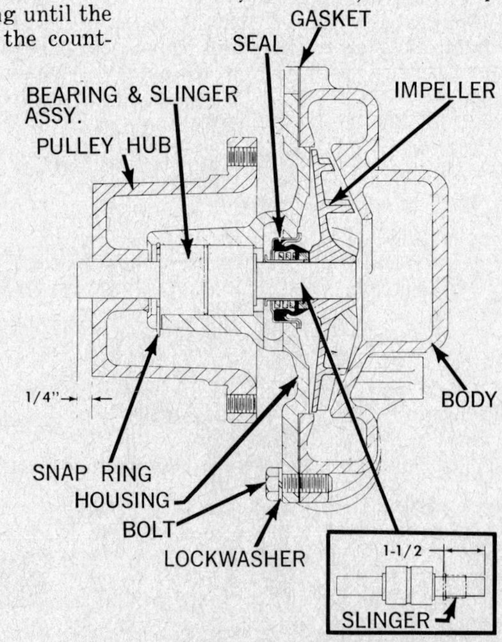

Water pump V266, 304, 345 and 392 engines
(© International Harvester Co.)

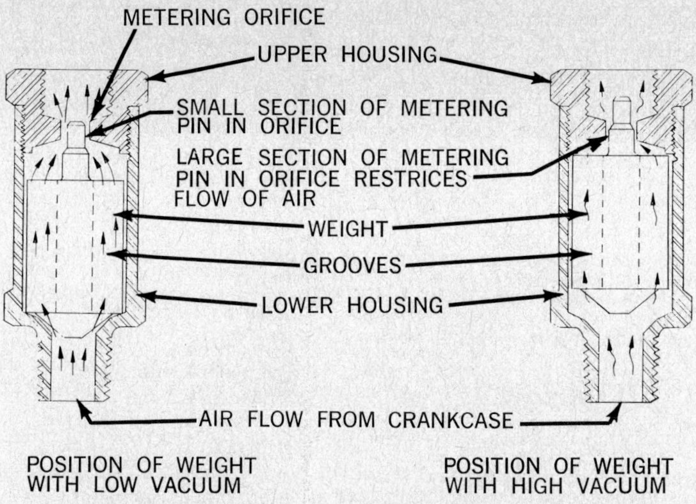

PCV valve RD engines (© International Harvester Co.)

turns free, check the impeller running clearance by the following method.

a. Use molding clay and place on the edges of two of the impeller vanes.
b. Install the pump and torque the mounting bolts. Do not rotate the impeller.
c. Remove the pump and measure the thickness of the moulding clay on the vanes. The thickness should be .015 above the impeller vane edge.
d. If the thickness exceeds the specification, the fan hub and snapring will have to be removed and the impeller relocated on the shaft by following steps 4 through 8.

9. Position the gasket on the pump body and install the pump assembly. Torque the mounting bolts to specified torque.

ENGINE

Emission Control Systems

Emission control systems are designed to control the emissions of Hydrocarbons (HC), Carbon Monoxide (CO), and Oxides of Nitrogen (NOx) at the levels specified by the Federal and State governments. Emission control Systems vary with engine, transmission, and series applications.

Positive Crankcase Ventilation System

The Positive Crankcase ventilation system draws the crankcase vapors into the intake manifold to be burned along with the air-fuel mixture. This is normally a closed system so that the crankcase vapors are not emitted into the atmosphere. The system consists of a valve and hose routings mounted to and operated by engine vacuum from the intake manifold.

Thermostatically Controlled Air Cleaner System

The air cleaner snorkel incorporates a thermostatically controlled valve, which directs air from the exhaust manifold area and from the engine compartment, depending upon the underhood temperature, to insure the carburetor induction air is warm before entry into the engine.

Air Guard System

This system is used to inject air into the exhaust ports to mix with the hot unburned gases, and to further burn the combustion mixture and reduce the emissions of hydrocarbons and carbon monoxide into the atmosphere. The system includes an air pump, a diverter valve, hose routings, and air injector manifolds and tubes.

Exhaust Gas Recirculation System

This system is used to meter exhaust gases into the combustion chambers to dilute the intake charge, thereby reducing the peak temperature of the gases and limit the formation of the oxides of nitrogen that form as the result of the high temperature during the combustion process. The system consists of a exhaust gas recirculating valve which connects the intake manifold to the exhaust manifold, and is operated by vacuum and temperature.

Fuel Tank Vapor Emission Control System

A closed fuel tank vent system is used to prevent fuel vapors from entering the atmosphere. The system consists of a two-way relief valve filler cap, which is closed to the atmosphere under normal operating conditions and opens when pressure exceeds 0.75 to 1.50 PSI, or vacuum exceeds 15 to 25 inches. A liquid check valve is used to route the vapors and collect any liquid before they are drawn into the fuel vapor storage cannister. The vapors are then drawn into the intake manifold through the air cleaner assembly. The amount of vapor drawn from the cannister is relative to the air volicity through the air cleaner snorkel.

Vacuum Throttle Modulating System

This system is used to reduce the emissions of hydrocarbons during rapid throttle closure at high speeds. It consists of a deceleration valve and a throttle modulating diaphragm located on the carburetor base to allow the throttle to remain slightly open and admit more air into the combustion chambers to lean out the overrich mixture. The decel valve and the modulator diaphragm are operated by engine vacuum signals.

Electric Choke

This system is used to assist in maintaining an open choke butterfly during cruising conditions, when vacuum may not be sufficient to draw enough heated air from the manifold to the choke assembly. When the engine cylinder head temperature is below 130 degrees, the electric choke is inoperative and the choke operates in the normal manner. Above the stated temperature, the electric choke is in operation.

Engine Removal

The following is an outline of general engine removal. Removal procedure will vary from truck to truck due to the variety of body models and accessory equipment. Before lifting out engine be certain that everything has been disconnected. Remove anything that might be in the way of the actual lifting.

1. Drain water from radiator and engine block.
2. Drain crankcase oil.

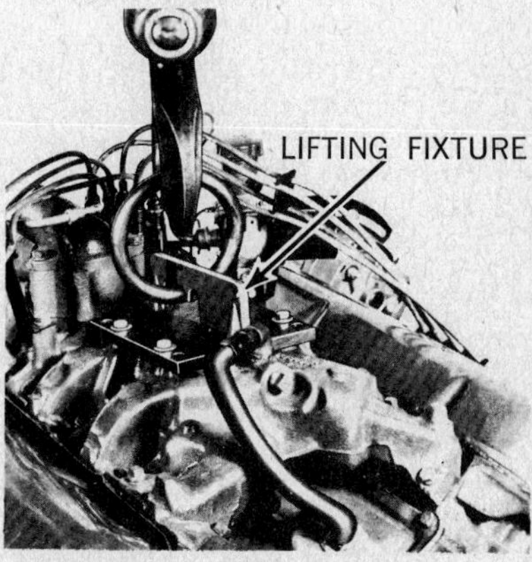

Engine lifting sling V8 engines
(© International Harvester Co.)

3. Disconnect battery ground cable and remove cable clamp from hot terminal of battery.
4. Remove all water hoses to radiator and heater.
5. Remove fan blades and fan shroud.
6. Remove any radiator cross-brace rods or brackets.
7. Remove radiator mounting bolts and lift out radiator. WARNING: On vehicles with LPG fuel systems observe all safety precautions. Be sure shop procedures are in compliance with local fire regulations. Close all tank valves and exhaust fuel from lines before working on fuel system.
8. On conventional chassis, remove hood hinge bracket mounting bolts and remove hood assembly. On CO models, tilt cab forward and prop securely. On cab-forward models, remove all front end sheet metal: bumper, fenders, radiator shell and disconnect any wiring that goes to these parts.
9. Disconnect and remove air filter from engine. Remove breather hose from air cleaner, if applicable.
10. Disconnect fuel pump inlet line.
11. Remove vacuum lines from manifold and all other components, and lines from air compressor, and air pump, if applicable.
12. Disconnect throttle linkage, choke control wire and hand throttle control wire, if applicable. On V-304, 345, 392 engines the carburetor must be removed for the fitting of the lifting fixture.
13. If so equipped, disconnect wire from heater control valve.
14. Disconnect all wiring from engine:
    a. Water temperature gauge sender.
    b. Oil pressure gauge sender.
    c. Generator wires.
    d. Primary ignition wire to resistor.
    e. Starter solenoid wires and battery cable.
15. On V(S)-401, 478, 549 engines, loosen alternator belts and disconnect alternator strap bracket to swing alternator away from thermostat housing. Then remove thermostats and housing.
16. If so equipped, remove tachometer drive at the distributor on the small V-8—or at the rear of the block on the big V-8.
17. Disconnect exhaust pipes at manifolds.
18. If so equipped, remove automatic transmission filler tube, freon compressor lines and disconnect power steering pump line and hose.

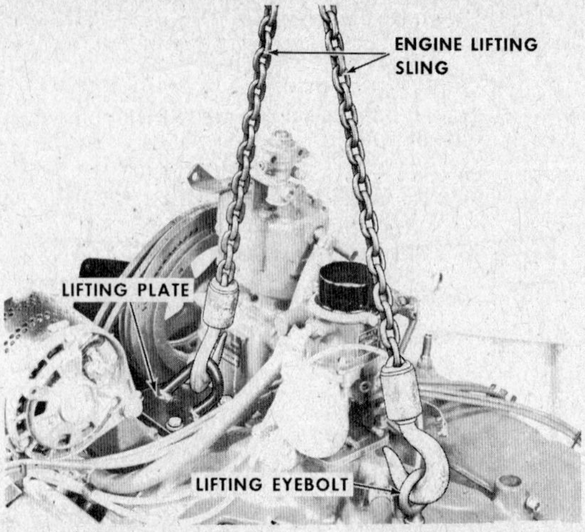

Engine removal using lifting sling (© International Harvester Co.)

19. Install lifting fixtures and suitable sling. On the V(S)-401, 478, 549 engines an eye bolt is installed at rear of intake manifold and a plate where the thermostat was mounted. On V-304, 345, 392 models the lifting fixture is mounted on the intake manifold where the carburetor was removed. On 400 engines, lifting eyes are installed in predrilled holes at front right and left rear of intake manifold. On six cylinder engines two brackets are secured by the two extreme head bolts and sling attached.
20. Connect hoisting equipment to lifting fixture and hoist enough to support engine.
21. Remove bell housing mounting bolts. On the PT-6 and V-8 engines the flywheel housing front cover is removed before the flywheel housing is removed from crankcase. On vehicles with RD engines the floor panel is removed to provide access to the bolts securing bell housing.
22. Disconnect clutch linkage.
23. Remove front engine mounting bolts. On some models it is easier to unbolt the mount from the frame crossmember.
24. Remove side engine mount bolts.
25. In hoisting out engine, first pull engine forward to clear clutch assembly from transmission, then tilt front up and carefully out of the chassis.

CAUTION: **Avoid damaging clutch driven disc.**

26. Installation of the engine is in general the reverse of the above described procedure. Be careful when installing that wires are not pinched between engine and frame. Lower the engine until transmission main drive gear spline can be aligned with the clutch driven disc. The weight of the engine must remain supported until the bell housing is secured to flywheel housing. After engine has been secured to chassis, remove hoisting equipment and lifting fixtures.

Manifolds

Intake Manifold Removal & Installation

4 Cylinder and V8 Engines

1. If engine is in vehicle, remove air cleaner and, if applicable, governor vacuum line.
2. Disconnect throttle linkage, choke cable and fuel line.
3. Remove carburetor.
4. On V-304, 345, 392, 400 engines, disconnect hose from thermostat housing and bracket for spark plug wires.
5. On 4 cylinder models, remove coil, coil mounting bracket and ignition resistor from intake manifold.
6. Remove positive crankcase ventilation pipe and vacuum line.
7. Remove mounting bolts, manifold and gasket.
8. Installation is the reverse of the above procedure. Install new gaskets and tighten the mount-

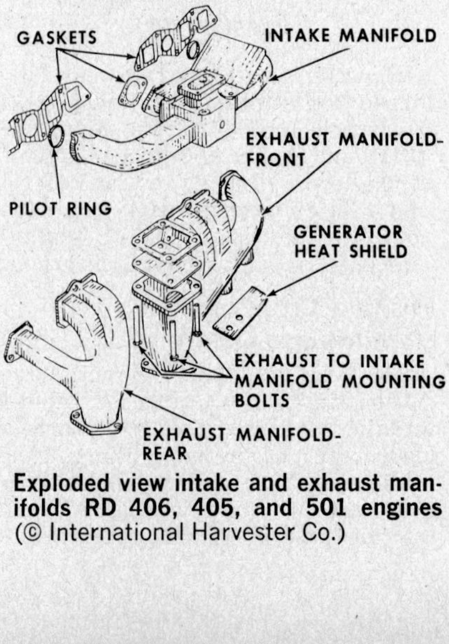

Exploded view intake and exhaust manifolds RD 406, 405, and 501 engines (© International Harvester Co.)

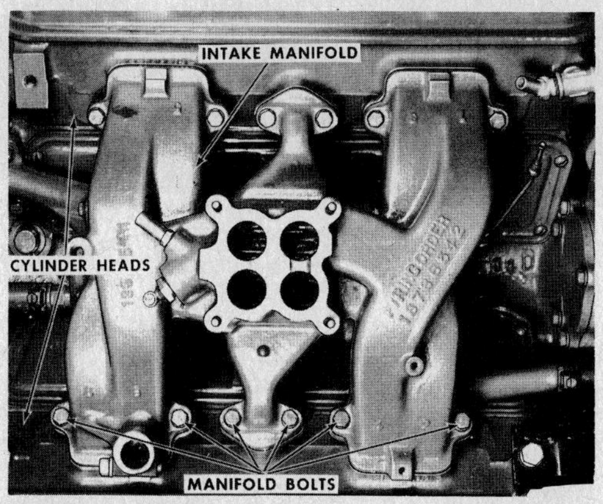

Intake manifold removal V8 engine (© International Harvester Co.)

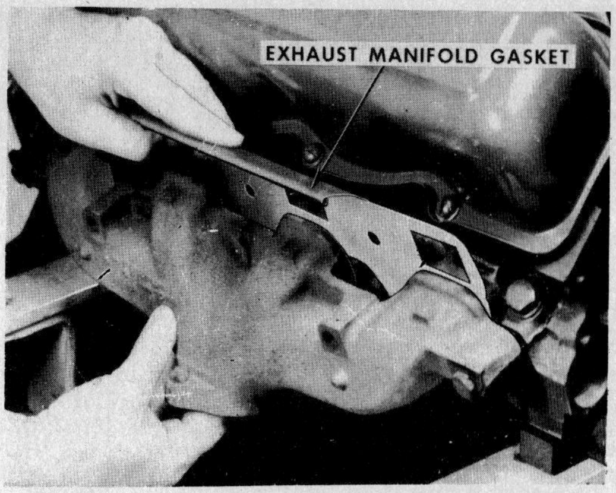

Exhaust manifold removal OHV4 and V8 engines (© International Harvester Co.)

ing bolts from the center out, torquing to 40-45 ft. lbs.

Exhaust Manifold Removal & Installation

4 Cylinder and V8 Engines

1. Disconnect exhaust pipe from manifold.
2. Unbolt exhaust manifold from head.
3. Remove manifold.
4. Installation is the reverse of the above procedure. Install new manifold-to-head gasket and new manifold-to-pipe gasket.
5. Torque manifold-to-head bolts to 25-30 ft.lb.

6 Cylinder Engines

1. Remove exhaust pipe from manifold.
2. Disconnect PCV line and vacuum lines from intake manifold.
3. Disconnect throttle linkage, fuel line and choke cable from carburetor.
4. Remove air filter and carburetor.
5. Remove exhaust/intake manifold unit and gaskets.
6. Separate intake from exhaust manifold.

NOTE: The RD engines use a two piece exhaust manifold and one piece intake manifold, bolted together as a unit, with only the rear half of the exhaust manifold being separate and removable by itself.

7. The PT-6, engines are equipped with a manifold heat control valve in the exhaust manifold. To remove this valve, first note position of counter-weight in relation to valve plate. Remove thermostatic spring from end of shaft. With a hacksaw blade or cutting torch, cut the shaft on both sides of the valve plate and remove plate and shaft pieces, being careful not to ruin bushings. If bushings need replacement, remove and install, spacing them .3120-.3130″. With valve plate in the "heat on" position, insert shaft, hold counterweight in the correct position and secure plate with screw or tack weld. Install thermostatic spring and hook spring over stop pin. Lubricate with a mixture of penetrating oil and graphite.
8. Intake and exhaust manifolds must be assembled properly to insure alignment. Position intake manifold to exhaust manifold using new gasket.
9. Install nuts and bolts holding the two manifolds together but do not tighten.
10. Position manifolds to cylinder head with intake manifold pilot rings in place and install mounting bolts, but do not tighten.
11. Tighten nuts and bolts which hold manifolds together, torquing to 25-28 ft. lbs.
12. Tighten manifold mounting bolts, torquing to 25-28 ft. lbs.

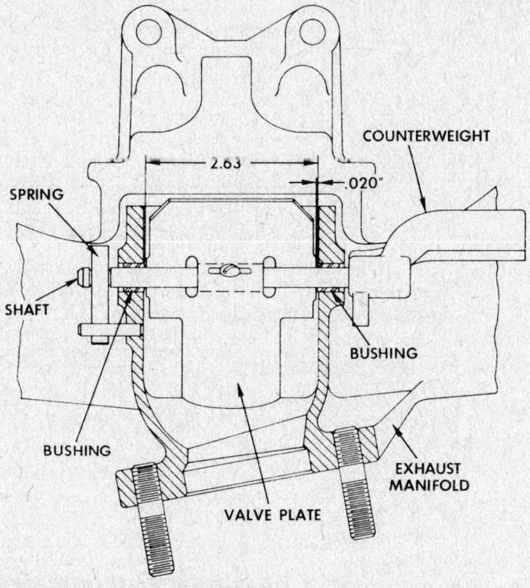

Manifold heat control valve PT6 engines (© International Harvester Co.)

Cylinder Head

Cylinder Head Removal & Installation

6 Cylinder Engines

1. If the engine is to remain in the vehicle, first do the following: Drain cooling system, disconnect water hose(s) and disconnect the fuel line from the carburetor. On the PT-6 engine, positive crankcase ventilation and vacuum advance lines must also be removed. In some cases, depending on the model, various accessory or other equipment may have to be removed.
2. Disconnect spark plug wires and, if applicable, remove wires from bracket on cylinder head. Identify cylinder number of each wire with tags or marks.
3. Disconnect ignition coil wires

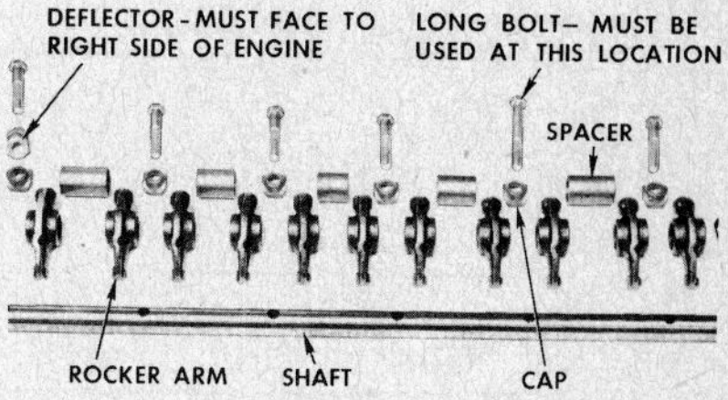

Rocker arm Assembly 1st type P6 engines (© International Harvester Co.)

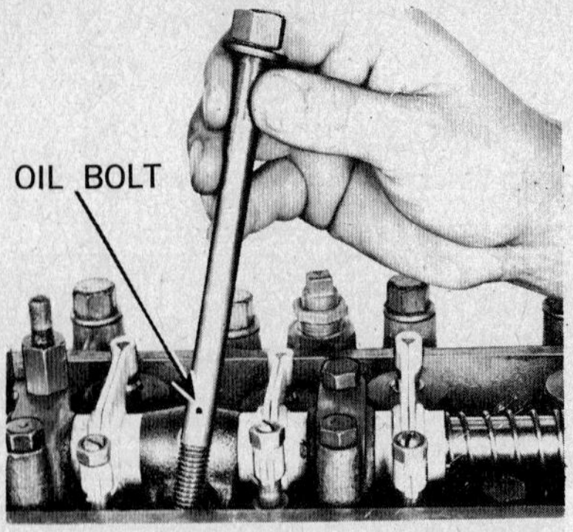

Rocker arm shaft oil feed bolt RD engines (© International Harvester Co.)

and remove coil from cylinder **head.**

4. Remove manifolds as described in preceding section.
5. On BD engines, disconnect water by-pass hose at cylinder head and remove water pump as described in preceding section.
6. Remove rocker arm cover bolts and remove rocker arm cover and gasket. If there are any dowel sleeves in brackets, note their location.
7. Remove push rods and keep them in order so that they may be replaced in the same locations.
8. Remove cylinder head bolts, marking any odd length or oil feed bolts for proper reinstallation.
9. Remove cylinder head and gasket.
10. Installation is the reverse order of the above instructions. Be sure to note the following steps where applicable.
11. Align new head gasket with bolt holes and carefully place cylinder head into position without damaging or shifting gasket.
12. Install all short head bolts and flat washers, but do not tighten.
13. On the PT-6 engine, apply No. 2

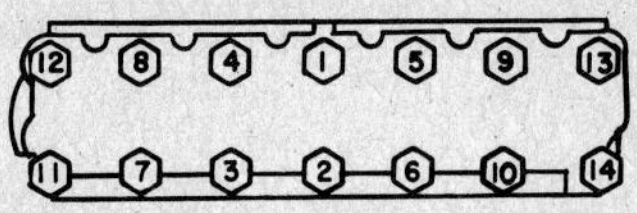

Cylinder head bolt tightening sequence PT6-232 engines
(© International Harvester Co.)

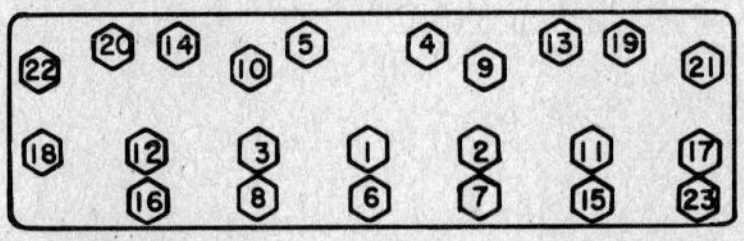

Cylinder head bolt tightening sequence RD engines
(© International Harvester Co.)

Permatex or equivalent sealant to the threads of the long (4¼″) bolt at position "11". On this engine, proceed to tighten the head bolts to 80-85 ft. lbs. torque in the sequence illustrated. Tighten in approximately 20 ft. lb. steps until proper torque readings are obtained.

14. Install push rods into original positions.
15. Install rocker arm assembly, installing any dowel sleeves which were removed. On BD engines, rocker arm bolts serve as head bolts and all should be tightened in the sequence illustrated at this point. Tighten to 85-95 ft. lbs. torque.
16. On RD engines, leave the long oil bolt out and tighten only the short head bolts to 100-110 ft. lbs. torque.
17. On the PT-6 engine, the long rocker arm assembly mounting bolt is placed in the fifth (next to rear) position. Tighten rocker arm assembly mounting bolts to 20-23 ft. lbs. torque, inner first, then outer.

NOTE: On later PT-6 engines, individual rocker arms are used for each valve, with a double bridge used as bearing surface and retainer.

18. On RD engines, insert drilled oil bolt in special oil connector and tighten rocker arm shaft mounting bolts to 25-30 ft. lbs. torque. Be sure to install those bolts with the cover mounting studs in the correct position. Note lock washers which key into end brackets.
19. Adjust rocker to valve clearance. See the following section, "Valve Clearance Adjustment," for correct procedure. The PT-6 engine has hydraulic lifters and cannot be adjusted. See Unit Repair Section for hydraulic lifter service operations.
20. Reinstall any components which were removed and have not yet been put back. Replace rocker cover gasket if necessary.

V8 and 4 Cylinder Engines

1. Remove intake and exhaust manifolds as described in preceding section. On V-8's, this may entail removal of the air compressor and air compressor mounting bracket.
2. Head removal is facilitated by the use of a lifting sling which is attached with bolts in the intake manifold mounting bolt holes.
3. Remove cylinder head covers and gaskets.
4. Loosen rocker arm shaft bracket bolts and remove the rocker arm assembly.

NOTE: Be sure to remove and keep track of the two dowel sleeves on the end brackets of the rocker arm assembly.

5. Remove pushrods, marking them so that they may be installed in their same locations.
6. Remove spark plug wires.
7. Remove cylinder head bolts.
8. When lifting off cylinder, do not lose the two locating dowel sleeves.
9. Installation is basically the reverse of the above procedure,

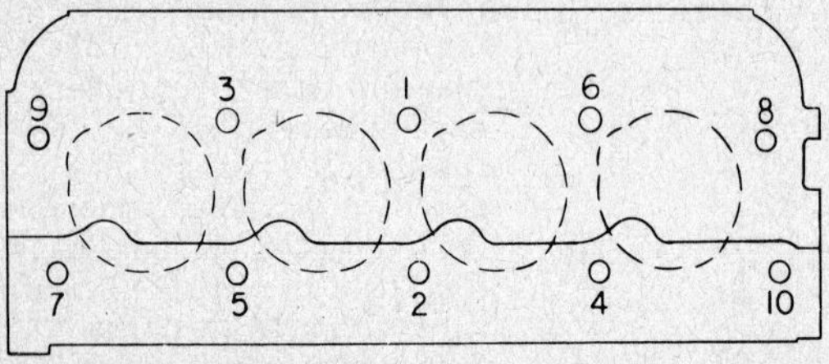

Cylinder head bolt tightening sequence 4-196, V304, 345, 392, MS406, and 446 engines
(© International Harvester Co.)

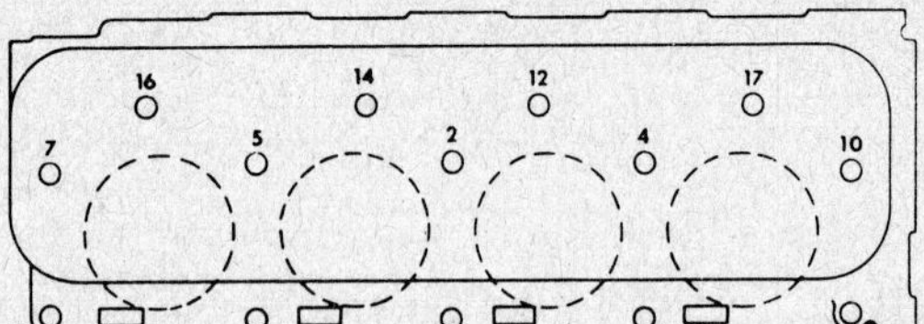

Cylinder head bolt tightening sequence V537 and 605 engine (© International Harvester Co.)

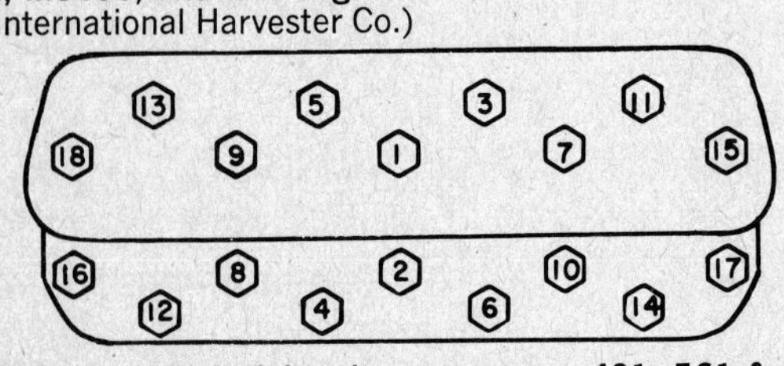

Cylinder head bolt tightening sequence—401, 561 & 549 engines

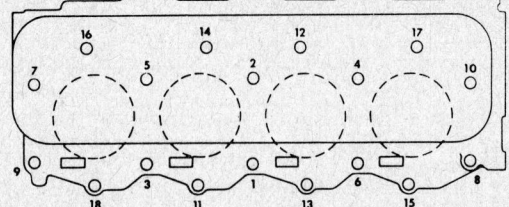

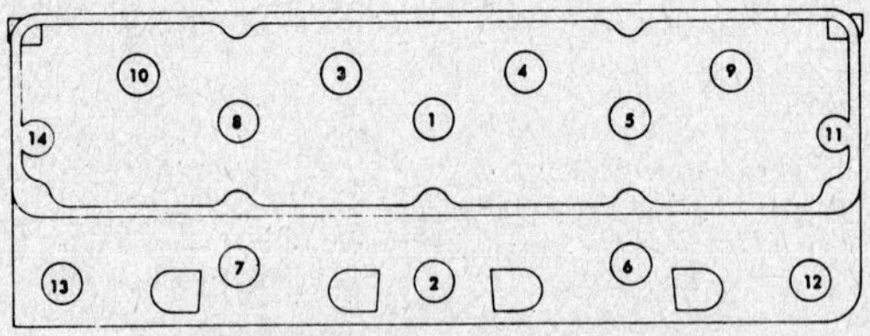

Head bolt torque sequence V8-400
(© Internationai Harvester Co.)

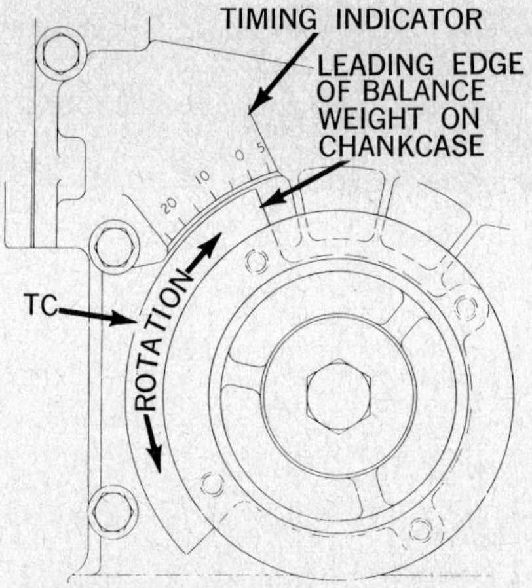

Correct pulley location for installing pushrods OHV-4 and small V8 engines (© International Harvester Co.)

with the exception of the following additional steps.

10. Be sure to use a new head gasket and to reinstall dowel sleeves when positioning the head and mounting the rocker assembly. Reinstall pushrods in their original locations.
11. On 4-196 and V-304, 345, 392, turn engine crankshaft until leading edge of balance weight on crankshaft pulley is aligned with the zero degree mark on the timing indicator before installing rocker arm assembly.
12. On 4-196 engines, be sure to install rocker assembly so that the oil feed shaft bracket is third from the rear.
13. On V-304, 345, 392 engines, install rocker arm assembly so that the notches at the end of the shaft are facing upward. Oil feed brackets are third from the rear on the right (even numbers) bank and third from the front on the left (odd numbers) bank.
14. On the V(S)-401, 478, 549 engines, rocker arm assembly mounting bolts serve as head bolts and are tightened in the head bolt torque sequence. Torque head bolts in the sequence

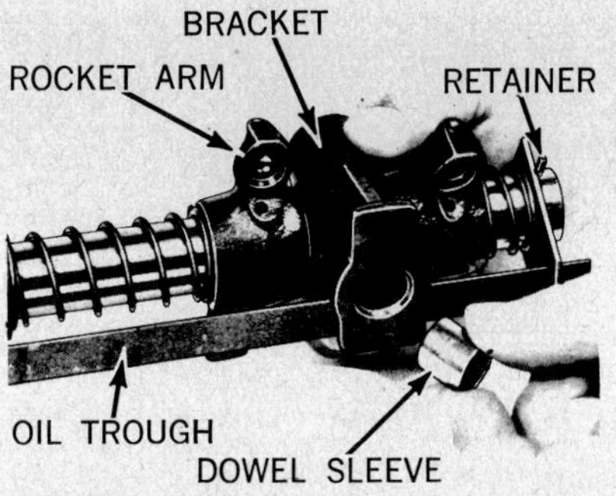

Rocker arm shaft dowel sleeve OHV-4 and V8 engines
(© International Harvester Co.)

pattern illustrated to 80-90 ft. lbs. torque.

CAUTION: Do not use a power wrench on heads of engines with hydraulic lifters. Torque head bolts slowly so that the leakdown of the lifters may relieve strain from the valve train.

15. On 4-196 and V-304, 345, 392, 400 engines, tighten the head bolts in the sequence illustrated to 110 ft. lb. on 400 engines and 90-100 ft. lb. on all others.
16. Retorque head bolts to the specified torque after 1000 miles of operation.
17. Install rocker covers and any other equipment removed for head work. Replace rocker cover gasket if necessary.

Valves

Valve Rotators

RD Engines

Exhaust valves on RD engines have a special stem and valve cap which permit the valve to rotate for an instant during each cycle. The clearance between the valve cap and the valve stem is critical for service life of the valve. The clearance is measured with a special gauge as illustrated. Grind bottom of valve cap to decrease clearance. To increase clearance, grind top of valve stem. If valve keys are removed they must be

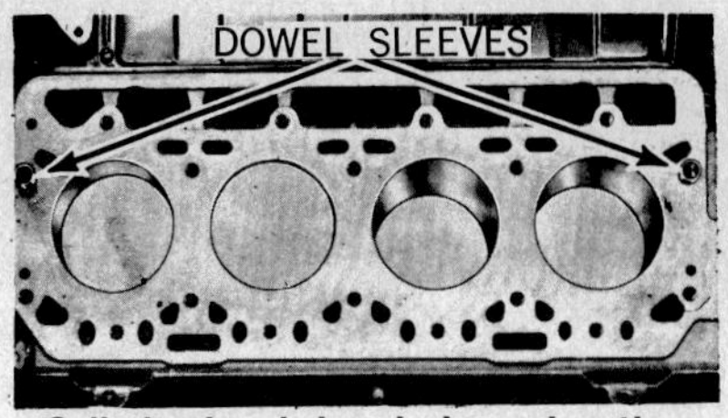

Cylinder head dowel sleeve location OHV-4 and V8 engines
(© International Harvester Co.)

reinstalled with the wear on the top side.

4 Cylinder and V8 Engines

Rotators are used between the valve springs and the cylinder heads on both the intake and exhaust valves on the VS 401, VS 478, VS 549, V 537, and V 605 engines. On the 4-196, MV-404, MV-446, V-304, V-345, V-392 engines, rotators are used between the valve spring and the cylinder head on the exhaust valve only.

NOTE: Keep the valves and their related parts together so they may be reinstalled in their respective positions.

Valve Train Service

The PT-6, 4-196 and V-8 engines utilized hydraulic lifters for which there is no lash adjustment. Excess noise in the valve train of these engines indicates that service is required. Instructions for servicing hydraulic lifters may be found in the General Repair Section.

Valve removal, service, and installation procedures may be found in the Engine Rebuilding Section. See Specifications table at the beginning of this section for valve spring and valve seat angle specifications.

E E E E
I I I I
4-196 Engine

E I I E E I I E E I I E
RD 406, 450, 501, P-6 232, 258 Engines

I E I E I E I E

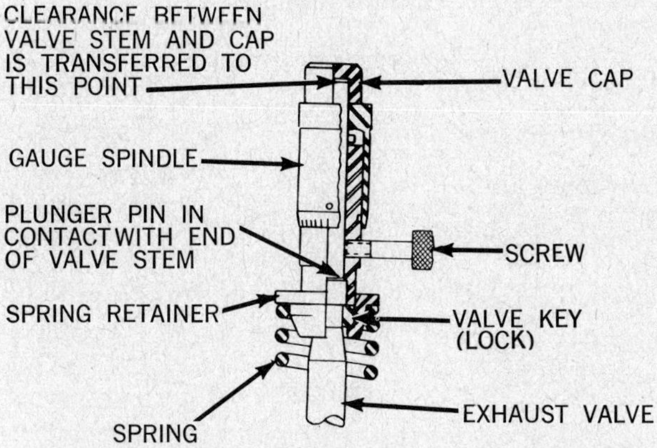

Checking rotatiing valve cap clearance RD engines
(© International Harvester Co.)

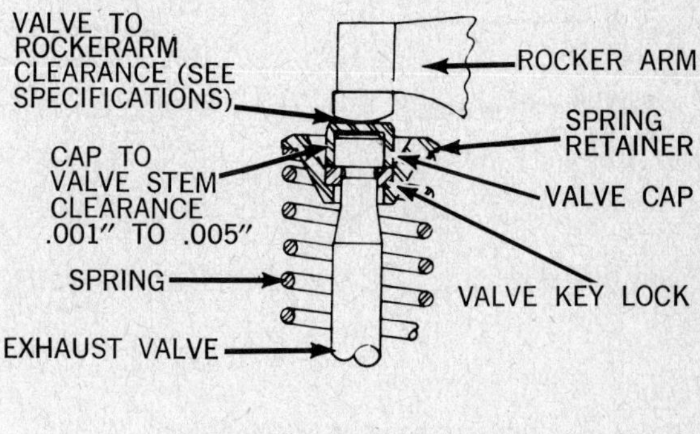

"Sol-Roto" valve rotators RD engines
(© International Harvester Co.)

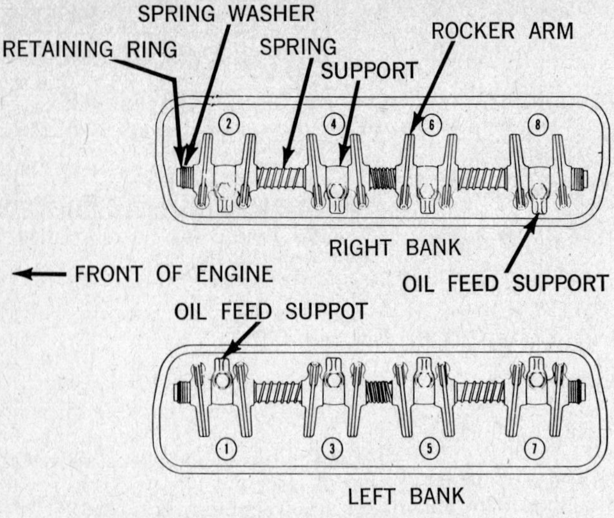

Correct rocker arm installation VS401, 478 and 549 engines (© International Harvester Co.)

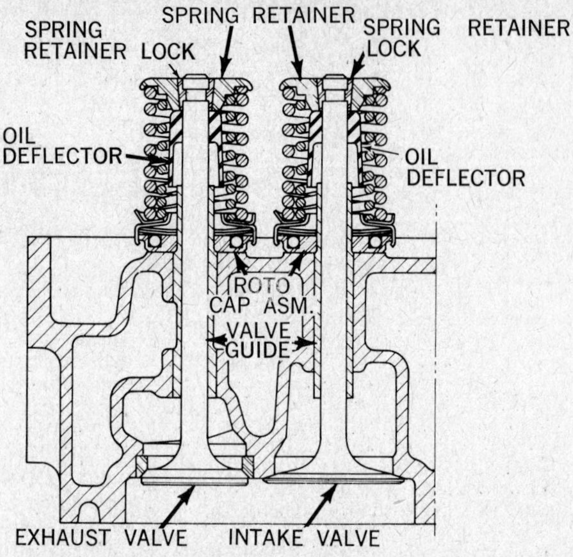

Rotors used under valve springs intake and exhaust valve VS 401, 478, and 549 engines
(© International Harvester Co.)

E I E I E I E I
MV 404, 446, V 537, 605, V 304, 345, 392 Engines

E I I E E I I E
E I I E E I I E
VS 401, 478, 549 Engines

Valve Adjustment

RD Engines

1. Remove valve rocker cover and gasket.
2. Rotate crankshaft until No. 1 cylinder is at top dead center of the compression stroke (both valves closed). Timing marks on the crankshaft pulley of RD engines should be aligned for zero degrees (TDC).
3. Clearance is adjusted on both valves. Loosen lock nut.
4. Holding the proper feeler gauge between adjusting screw on the end of the rocker arm and the valve stem, turn adjusting screw until specified clearance is obtained (feeler gauge just held snugly).
5. While holding adjusting screw, tighten lock nut.
6. Recheck clearance.
7. Rotate crankshaft ⅓ turn so that No. 5 cylinder is at top dead center of compression stroke and repeat Steps 3 to 6.
8. Repeat for each cylinder following the sequence of the firing order.
9. Replace rocker cover, using a new gasket if necessary.
10. Valve clearance should be rechecked with engine at normal running temperature and after 500 miles when new or reground valves have been installed.

Rocker Arm Removal & Installation

1. Remove rocker cover and gasket.
2. Remove rocker arm assembly mounting bolts and flat washers.
3. Remove rocker assembly.
4. If applicable, remove clip-ring and retainer to disassemble rocker components. Be sure to keep all parts in order so that they may be replaced in their original positions.
5. Clean all parts thoroughly, making sure that oil passages are clear. If necessary to remove plugs from ends of shaft, drill a hole in one plug, knock out the other with a steel rod, then knock out the drilled plug.
6. Inspect shaft for wear and warpage. Replace bent or worn shaft.
7. On engines without hydraulic lifters (all 6 cylinder except the PT-6), inspect rocker arm adjusting screws for wear at the contact surface and for damaged threads. Replace any that are defective.
8. Inspect rocker arm shaft bushings for wear. On V(S)-401, 478, 549 and early V-304, 345 engines the rocker arm bushings may be pressed out and new bushings pressed in. On all other engines the bushing is integral with the rocker arm, and if the bushing is worn, the whole rocker arm must be replaced.
9. Inspect valve stem contact pad

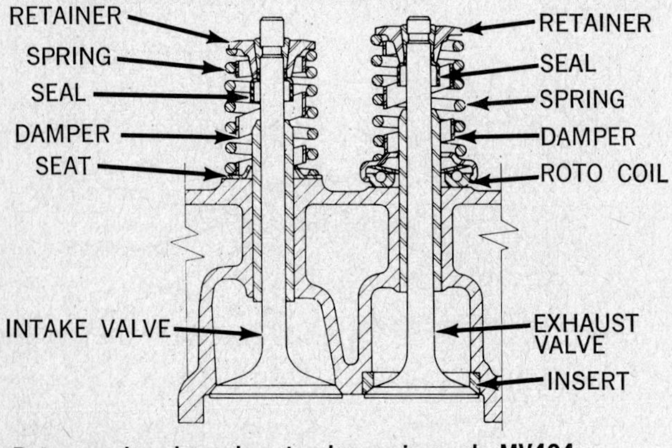

Rotor used under exhaust valve spring only MV404, 446, 4-196, V304, 345 and 392 engines
(© International Harvester Co.)

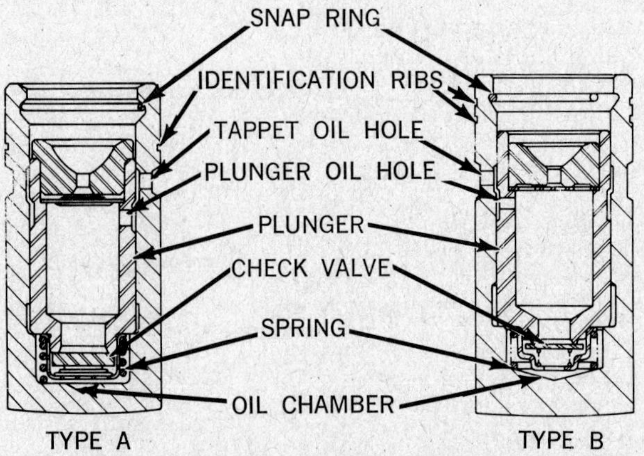

Sectional view of two types of hydraulic valve lifters
(© International Harvester Co.)

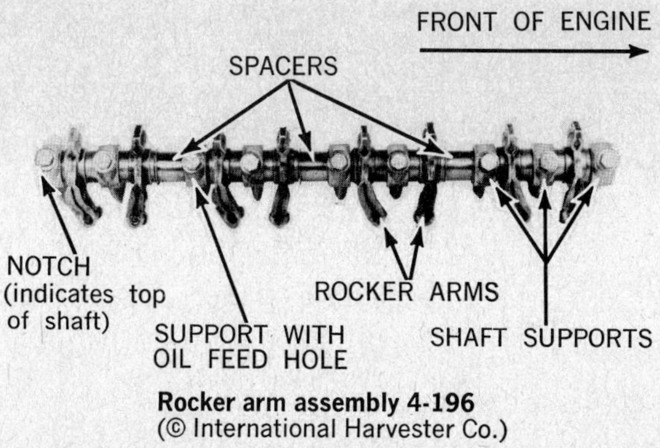

Rocker arm assembly 4-196 (© International Harvester Co.)

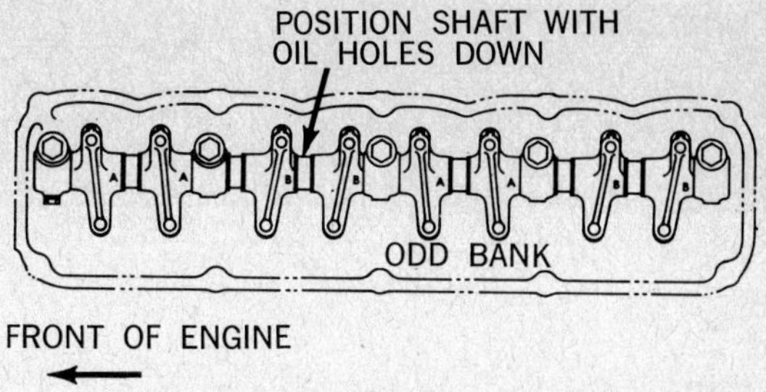

Correct rocker arm positioning V537 and 605 engines (© International Harvester Co.)

surfaces of rocker arm and resurface if wear is excessive. Do not remove more than .010″ of material when resurfacing.

10. If applicable, replace any defective tension springs.
11. Remove and inspect push rods one by one (to insure original position). Roll them on a flat surface to check for straightness. Replace any pushrods that are bent, have loose ends or are worn.
12. Reassemble all rocker arm assembly components in their original order. On RD engines, note that lock washers key into shaft and the end brackets.
13. Install rocker arm assembly, making sure that the oil feed bracket is in the proper position and that dowel sleeves are in place. On 4-196 and V-304, 345, 392 engines turn the crankshaft until leading edge of balance weight on crankshaft pulley is aligned with the zero degree mark on the timing indicator before installing rocker arm assembly.
14. Tighten mounting bolts.
15. Adjust rocker arm to valve stem clearance as described above.
16. Install rocker cover, replacing gasket if necessary.

NOTE: Later P-6, 232, 258 engines use the individual type rocker arms, as do the MV 404, and 446 engines. Inspect the bearing surface of the pivot ball and bridge to determine the extent of wear and need for replacement.

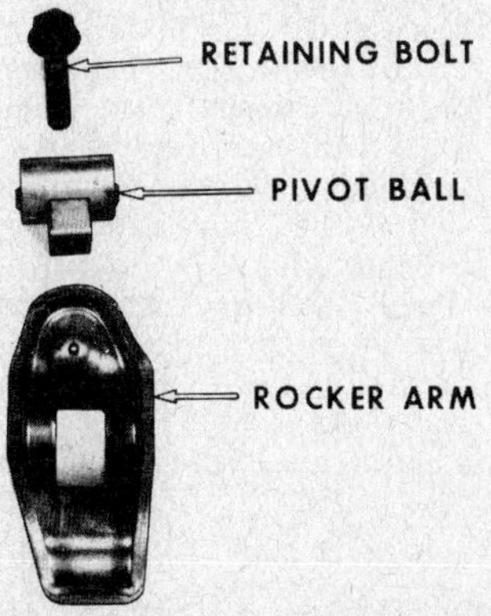

Rocker arm assembly MV404 and 446 engines (© International Harvester Co.)

Timing Case & Gears

Crankshaft Pulley Removal

Accessibility of the crankcase pulley and front (timing) cover will vary according to the model. On some vehicles the timing case will be accessible only if the engine is completely removed. The following instructions are general and apply to most front cover repairs and service.

1. Drain cooling system.
2. Disconnect radiator hoses and remove radiator. In some cases the radiator shroud and truck hood must be removed.
3. Loosen front engine mounts and jack up engine enough to provide access to the crankshaft pulley with a puller.
4. Loosen and remove fan belts and remove fan blades.
5. Remove crankshaft pulley retaining bolt. On V(S)-401, 478, 549 engines, scribe a line alongside the timing indicator and remove the indicator from front cover. The line is for reassembly purposes. The 400 engine has a pulley which is removed simply by removing 4 capscrews. The vibration damper behind the pulley must be removed with a puller.
6. Using a suitable puller, remove the pulley from the crankshaft. On some models the pulley is in two pieces and the pulley must be unbolted from its hub before the hub is removed with a puller.

Front Oil Seal Removal & Installation

1. Remove crankshaft pulley as described in Steps 1 through 6 above.
2. Remove seal. It is preferable to use an appropriate seal puller. Use a new gasket when installing front cover and be sure to align cover before tightening.
3. Install a new seal using a suitable seal installing tool if possible. Lubricate first and be careful not to damage seal or seating surface of cover.
4. Install crankshaft pulley, fan belt and fan blades.
5. Lower engine and tighten mounting bolts.
6. Install radiator, shroud, hoses and whatever else was removed.
7. Fill cooling system.

Timing Gear Removal

Timing gears can be removed without disassembling the engine. In some cases, however, the engine must be removed.

1. Remove crankcase pulley as described in Steps 1 through 6 above.
2. Remove engine front cover.
3. Rotate engine to align timing marks on crankshaft gear and camshaft gear.

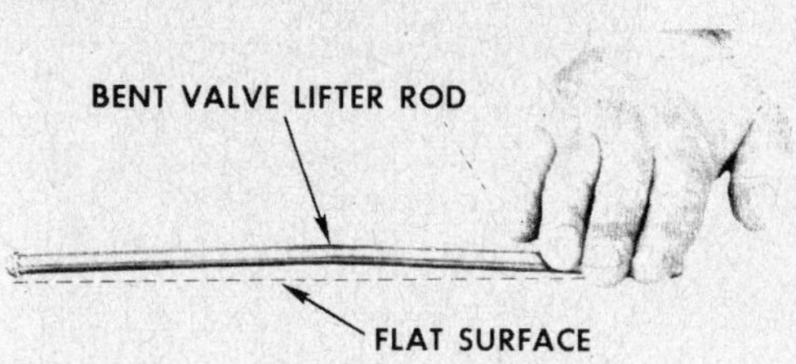

Method of checking for bent push rod (© International Harvester Co.)

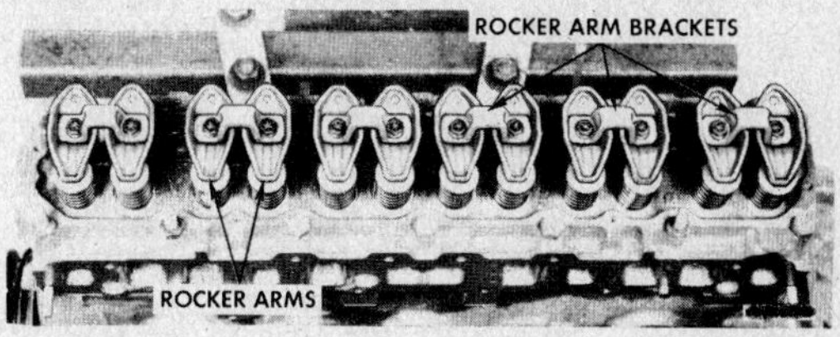

Second type rocker arm assembly 6-232 and 258 engines (© International Harvester Co.)

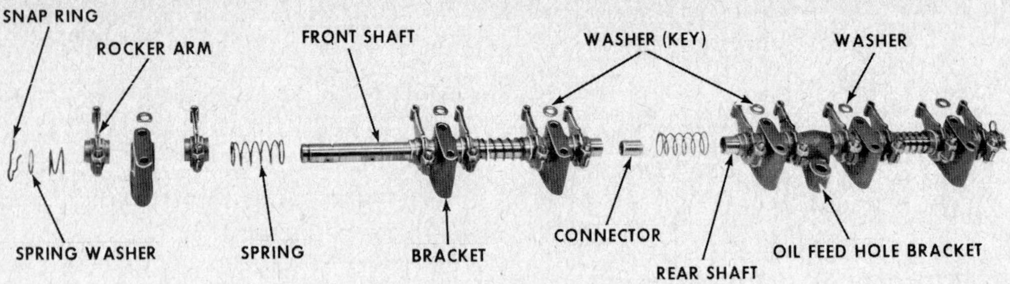

Rocker arm assembly RD engines (© International Harvester Co.)

4. To remove either gear, remove bolt and washer. Use a suitable puller.

NOTE: On the P-6 engines, simultaneously loosen the camshaft gear while pulling the gear from the crankshaft, and remove both gears and the timing chain as an assembly. Normal replacement would include the three parts, due to running wear patterns. On all other engines, replace both the cam gear and crankshaft gear, due to being serviced in matched sets.

5. Use a suitable installing tool to install gears. Lubricate with engine oil and insert key in shaft to align gear. Align timing marks as illustrated. Be careful not to damage threads on shaft. Install and tighten retaining bolt.
6. Rotate engine to check that gears are not binding.
7. Check gear backlash with a dial indicator. It should be within .004-.007" on OHV6 engines and .0005-.0045" on OHV4 and V8 engines.
8. Use a new gasket when installing front cover and be sure to align cover before tightening. On some models there is an oil slinger on the crankshaft.
9. Install crankshaft pulley, belt and fan blades. Tighten retaining bolt.
10. Lower engine and tighten engine mounting bolts.
11. Install radiator and hoses.
12. Fill cooling system.

Camshaft Removal & Installation

On most International truck models, it is possible to remove the camshaft with the engine remaining in the vehicle. However, the body grille work, radiator, A/C condensor (if equipped), hood, bumper, and braces must be removed to allow clearance for the camshaft to be withdrawn from the engine block. In some cases, it would be more advantageous to remove the engine from the vehicle to replace the camshaft. The decision would depend upon the individual mechanic and his shop facilities.

1. Remove the cylinder head on the P-6 engines, and the intake manifolds on the V8 engines, and the rocker covers on all engines.
2. Remove the rocker arms or assemblies, pushrods and tappets.

NOTE: On the RD engines, the tappets are of the mushroom type and must be removed from the bottom. In order for the tappets to be out of the way during camshaft removal, the engine, if out of the vehicle, must be turned upside down. If the engine is in the vehicle the tappets must be raised and held to allow the camshaft to clear when being withdrawn from the block.

Typical timing marks 4-196, V304, 345 and 392 engines
(© International Harvester Co.)

3. Remove the distributor and mechanical fuel pump.
4. Remove the oil pan and oil pump, if necessary.

NOTE: RD Series, VS 401, 478, 549 engines have camshaft driven oil pumps which must be removed before the camshaft is removed.

5. Remove the crankshaft pulley as previously described.
6. Remove the front timing cover, gasket and seal.
7. Remove the two screws securing the camshaft thrust flange to the block.

NOTE: On the P-6 engines, remove the camshaft bolt and washer retaining the gear to the shaft. Remove the crankshaft and camshaft gears and chain as an assembly.

8. Remove the camshaft and gear. To prevent nicking and damaging the camshaft or bearings, use a camshaft removal and installation tool, which is an extension on the front of the camshaft to act as a handle.
9. When installing the camshaft and gear, coat the bearing surfaces and lobes with lubricant and use the installing tool if possible, to aid in the installation of the camshaft. Make sure the

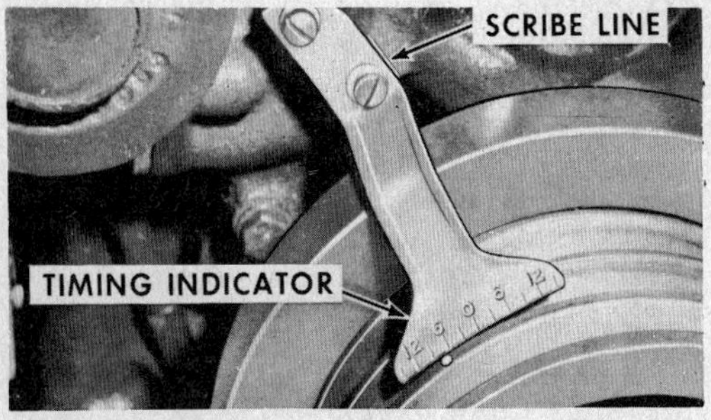

Marking exact position of timing indicator V8 engines
(© International Harvester Co.)

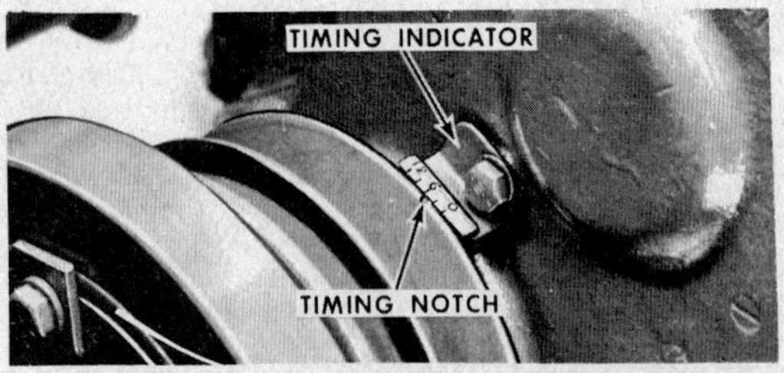

Timing mark alignment for valve adjustment
(© International Harvester Co.)

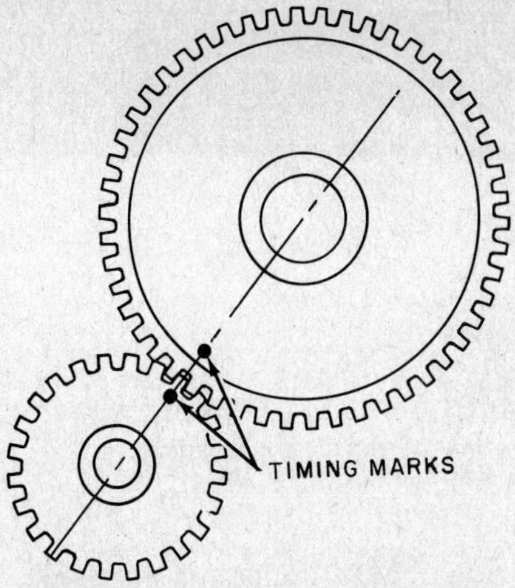

Timing gear alignment marks except PT6 engines
(© International Harvester Co.)

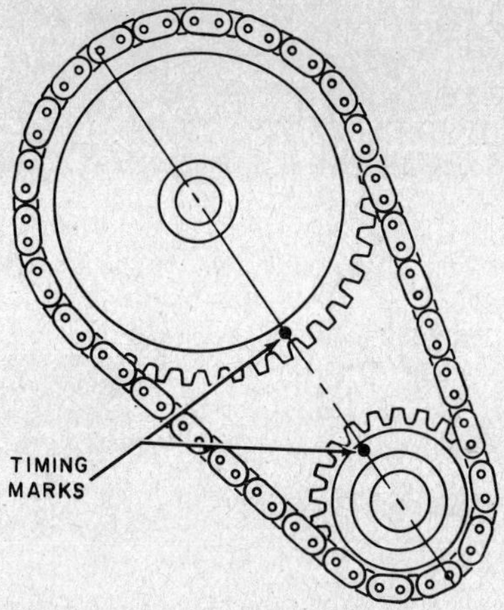

Timing gear alignment marks PT6 engines (© International Harvester Co.)

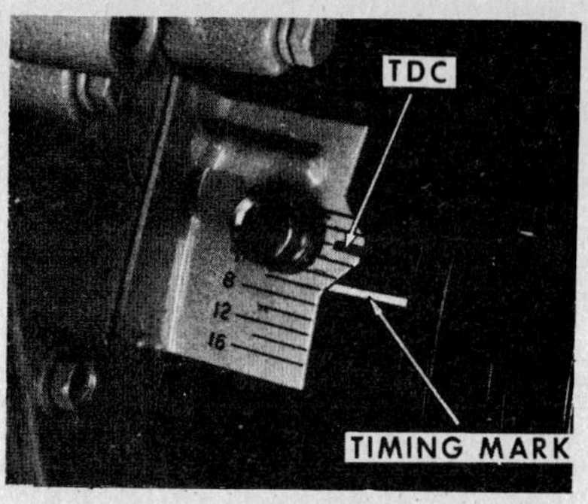

Typical timing marks MV404 and 446 engines (© International Harvester Co.)

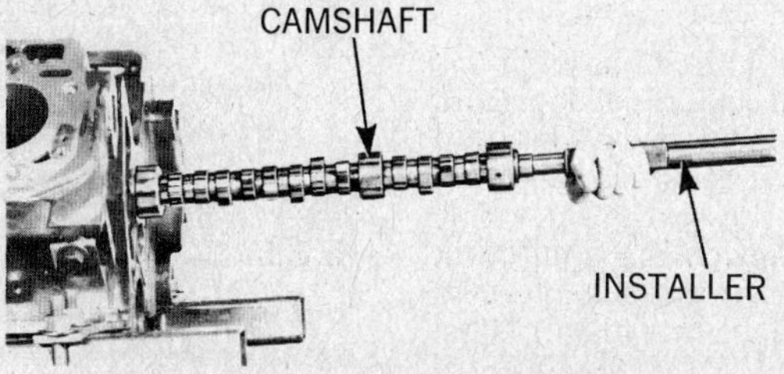

Use of a camshaft remover and installer
(© International Harvester Co.)

gear timing marks align properly.

NOTE: For the P-6 engine chain installation, refer to the timing gear removal and installation procedure.

NOTE: FTVS 549 engines should have the camshaft gear retarded one tooth from normal position.

10. Working through the two large holes in the camshaft gear, install the two thrust flange screws and tighten to proper torque specifications.
11. Check timing gear backlash. If the end play exceeds the allowable limits, replace the thrust flange.
12. Place the oil slinger over the end of the crankshaft.
13. Install the front cover, using a new seal and gasket. Align the cover before tightening the bolts to the specified torque.
14. Install the crankshaft pulley, tightening to the proper torque.
15. Install the cylinder head, if removed, the intake manifold, tappets, pushrods, and rocker arms. Torque all bolts to the specified torque.
16. Install the fan pulley, blades and belts.
17. Install the distributor and fuel pump.
18. Install the oil pump and oil pan.
19. If the engine was raised, lower and tighten the engine mounts.
20. Complete the assembly as necessary for the removed body parts.
21. Start the engine, time it to specifications, and check for proper operation.

Pistons and Connecting Rods

For piston and connecting rod overhaul procedures see Engine Rebuilding General Section.

Piston Removal & Installation

1. Remove oil pan and oil pump. On some models this may require loosening the engine mounts and jacking up the engine until spacer blocks can be installed. When removing oil pump on big V8's turn crank until counter weight is out of the way.
2. Remove cylinder head. See "Cylinder Head R&R" above.
3. Using a ridge reamer, remove the ridge from the top of the cylinders.
4. Rotate the crankshaft until journal is in lowermost position for removal of connecting rod assemblies. Remove the cap and push the connecting rod and piston up through the cylinder bore. Replace the cap and bearing inserts on the rods so the numbered sides match. The numbers indicate position.
5. To install pistons and connecting rods, rotate crankshaft until No. 1 crankpin is at the bottom of its

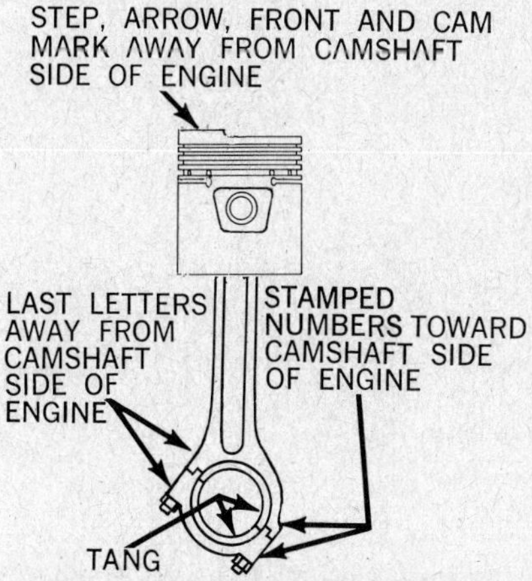

Piston & rod assembly RD engines
(© International Harvester Co.)

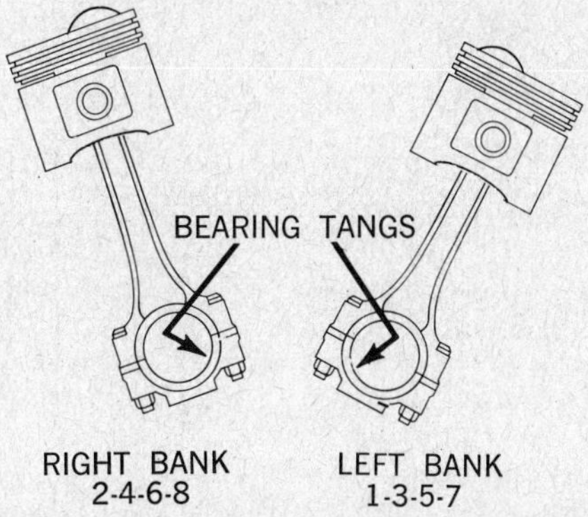

Correct assembly of piston & rods V8 engines (© International Harvester Co.)

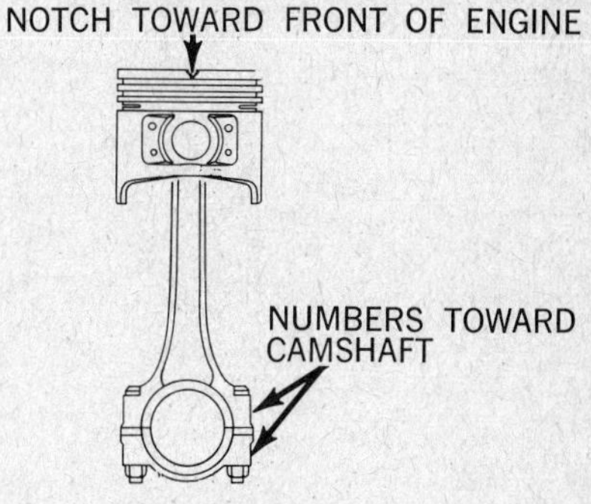

Piston & rod assembly PT-6-232 engines
(© International Harvester Co.)

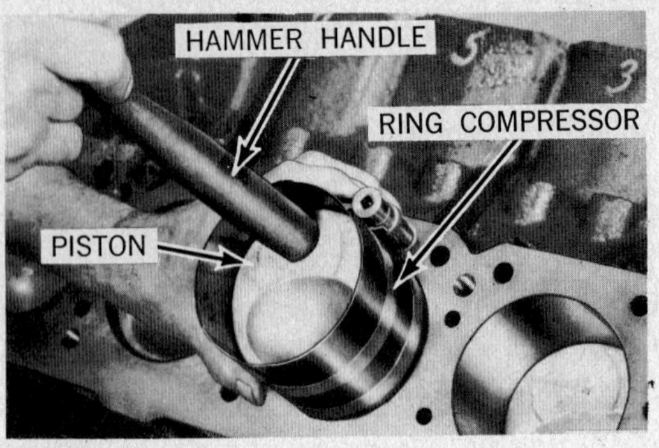

Piston installation (© International Harvester Co.)

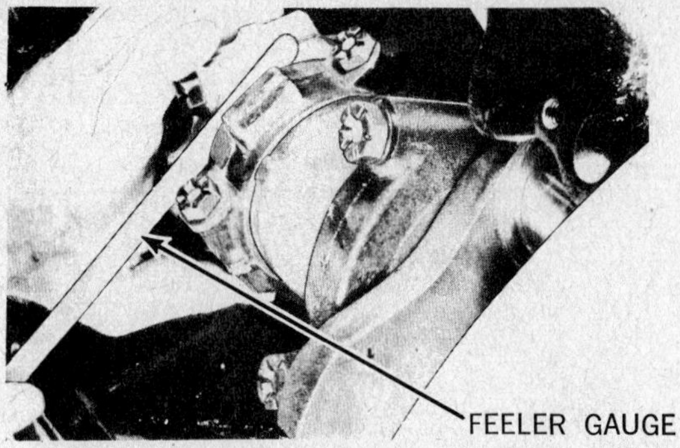

Checking connecting rod end clearance typical (© International Harvester Co.)

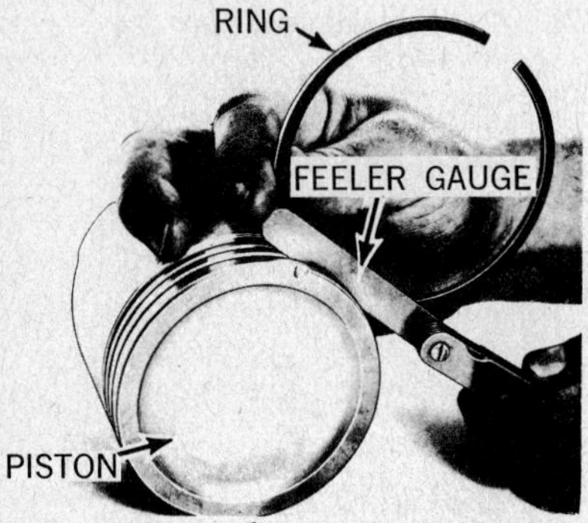

Checking ring groove clearance (© International Harvester Co.)

stroke. Correctly seat rod bearing insert in rod then dip piston assembly in clean oil to lubricate rings. Using a ring compressor, install piston and rod in cylinder. Push piston in, do not strike. On the PT-6 engines, the notch on the top of piston perimeter faces toward the front of the engine (number on connecting rod toward the camshaft). On 4-196 and all V8 engines, except the 400, the piston assembly is installed with the word "UP" toward the top (camshaft) side of the engine block. On the 400, the piston is installed with the notch facing front. On all OVH 6 except the PT-6, install piston assembly with the arrow stamped on piston crown toward camshaft.

6. Place lower half of bearing insert in rod cap and lubricate with oil. Assemble bearing cap to connecting rod with the number side of cap on the same side as the number on the connecting rod. Lubricate threads of bolts with engine oil and install bolts,

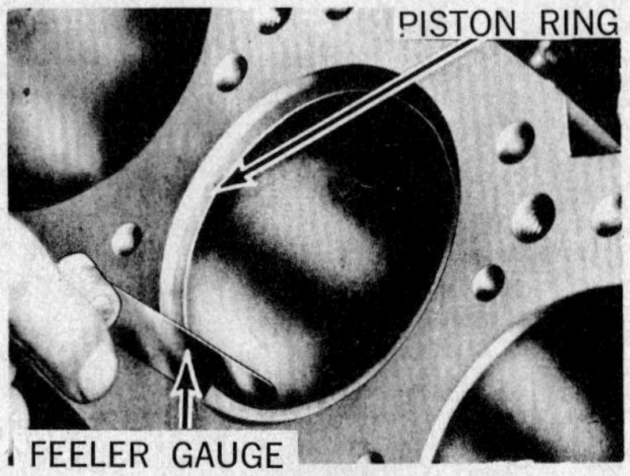

Checking ring groove clearance (© International Harvester Co.)

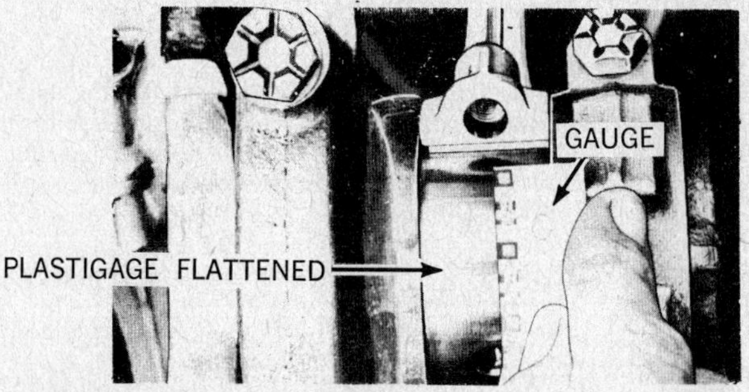

Checking connecting rod bearing clearance with plastigage typical (© International Harvester Co.)

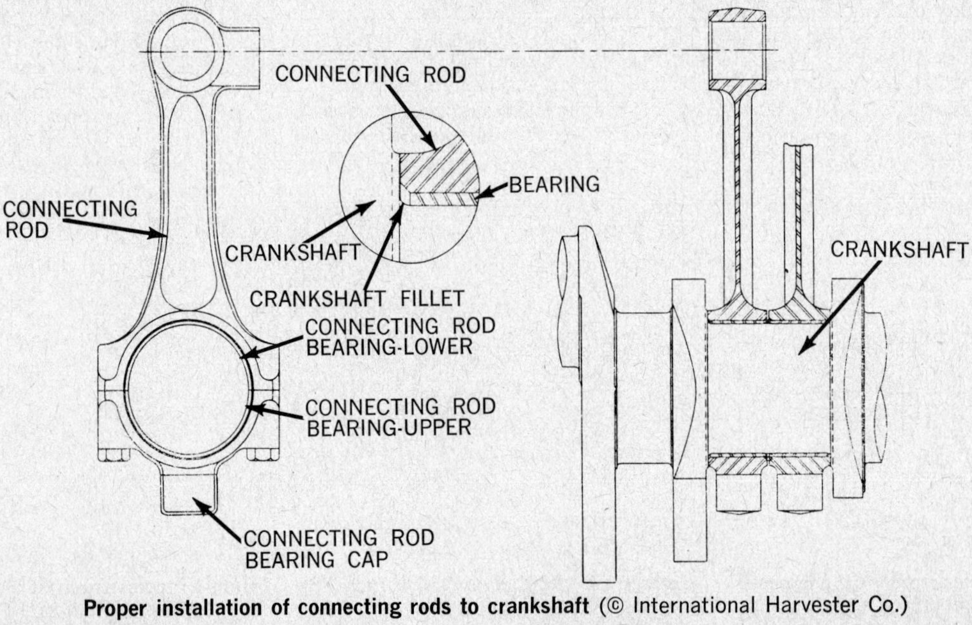

Proper installation of connecting rods to crankshaft (© International Harvester Co.)

tightening to the correct torque (see Specifications at the beginning of this section).

7. Rotate crankshaft and repeat installation procedure with the rest of the pistons and connecting rods.
8. Install oil pump and oil pan, using a new pan gasket if necessary.
9. Install cylinder head as described in "Cylinder Head R&R" above.
10. If engine was raised, remove spacers and lower engine. Tighten engine mount bolts.

Piston Ring Replacement

1. Remove pistons as described above.
2. Remove both compression rings and three-piece oil ring.
3. Using rings which correspond to the piston size (standard or oversize), check rings for gap clearance and ring-to-groove side clearance.
4. Install rings on piston with a suitable ring expander tool.
5. Install piston assembly as described above.

Oil Pan Removal and Installation

The engine and mounts may have to be loosened from the crossmember and lifted, and spacer blocks installed between the mounts and crossmember, to gain clearance to remove the oil pan from the engine. Other engine applications may only require the removal of steering linkage to gain sufficient clearance. Be sure to clean all old gasket material from the oil pan and the block before installing the oil pan and new gasket.

Main Bearing Replacement

On most models it is possible to replace main bearings without removing the engine from the vehicle. However, it is easier to do a better job with the engine removed and, if facilities are available for pulling the engine, this is the preferable method. See "Engine R&R" above. For detailed procedures on main bearing, rod bearing and crankshaft servicing see General Repair Section.

1. Remove crankshaft pulley and front (timing) cover.
2. Remove cylinder head(s) and piston assemblies.
3. If the bell housing and transmission were not removed during engine removal, remove them now.
4. On many engines the clutch plate may be compressed by installing three cap screws (3/8"-16x2½" for RD and V(S)-401, 478, 549 engines or 3/8"-16x2" for V-304, 345, 392 engines). If the clutch plate cannot be compressed in this way, cut three ½"x1"x3" wood blocks and insert them between the clutch fingers and back plate. Loosen backing plate mounting bolts slightly if it is difficult to insert wood blocks. A third alternative procedure for compressing the clutch plate is to insert three retaining clips as illustrated. The clutch plate is compressed during removal and installation of the clutch to prevent warpage.

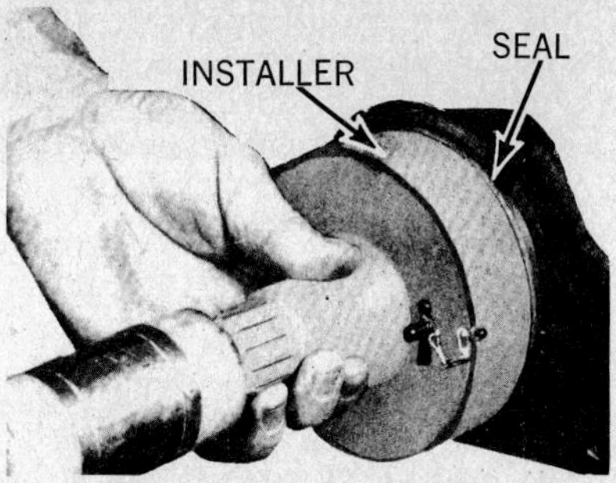

Installing rear main oil seal
(© International Harvester Co.)

5. Remove the backing plate mounting bolts and clutch assembly.
6. Remove flywheel bolts and pull off flywheel.
7. On RD engines remove the upper and lower rear main bearing oil seal retainers.
8. Remove main bearing caps. On OHV4, V-304, 345, 392, engines use a rear main bearing cap puller to remove rear main bearing cap. On RD engines the lower oil seal retainer must be removed before the cap can be unbolted. Note that the caps are numbered and should be reinstalled in their original positions.
9. When installing new main bearings make sure that the oil holes are properly aligned and that bearing tangs are fitted into tang recesses. Thoroughly clean all surfaces and coat lightly with oil. Be sure to align timing marks when positioning crankshaft. On the PT-6 engine main bearing caps have an arrow which indicates front of engine. On the OHV4 and V-304, 345, 392, 400 engines the numbered sides of the main bearing caps face the left side of the engine. On the RD engines the numbered side of the bearing caps face the camshaft side of the engine. On V(S)-401, 478, 549, 537, 605 engines the bearing caps are installed with the numbered side facing to the right side of the engine. When tightening main bearing caps, first tap them lightly into place, then tighten bolts in an alternating manner until the specified torque is reached. See Specifications for correct torque.
10. Install a new rear main bearing oil seal. On OHV4 and V-304, 345, 392, 400 engines the round seal is pressed in after the rear main bearing cap is installed. Rear main bearing cap side oil seals are installed on these engines with an installer tool made from a piece of 1/8" welding rod. Puddle a ball on the end of the rod and file the ball to approximately 5.32" diameter. On RD engines the rear upper seal and retainer are installed before the crankshaft and the lower main bearing lower oil seal is installed after the rear main bearing cap, using new gaskets on each side of the lower seal retainer. On V(S)-401, 478, 549 engines the rear main bearing cap side seals are marked for right and left side. On PT-6, and V(S)-401, 478, 549 engines, the top and bottom rear main bearing oil seals are made of wick type material which fits into slots in the block and bearing

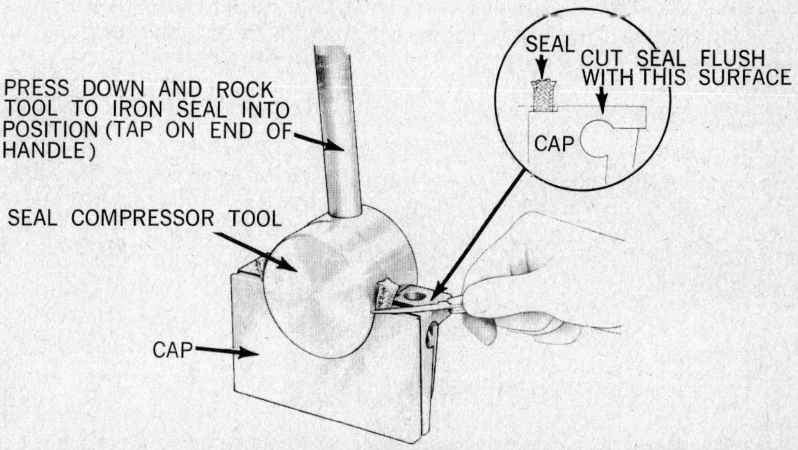

Installation of oil seal in rear main bearing cap (© International Harvester Co.)

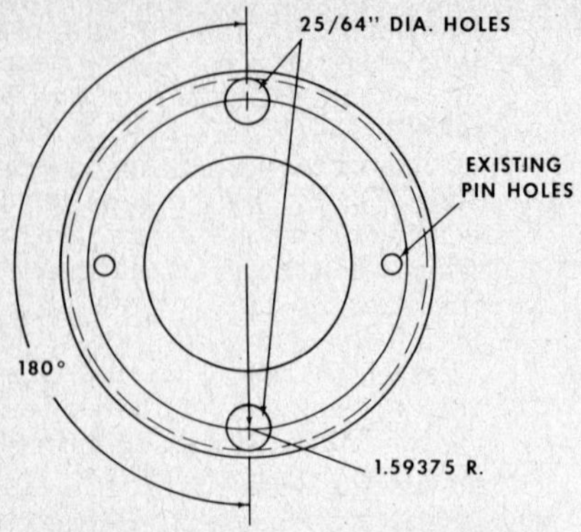

Rework of pilot tool SE1942-2 for MV404 and 446 engine rear main bearing oil seal installation
(© International Harvester Co.)

cap. These must be cut to the correct length while the seal is being held in place with a seal compressing tool as illustrated.

11. Check main bearing clearance and crankshaft endplay and compare to clearance limits listed in Specifications at the beginning of this section. See Engine Rebuilding General Section for clearance measurement and service procedures.
12. Reassemble engine following Steps 1 through 7 in reverse order. Be sure to align clutch driven disc with transmission shaft or clutch aligning tool before tightening clutch plate mounting bolts.

Rear Main Bearing Seal Replacement

OHV 4, V 304, 345, 392, 400, 536, 605 Engines

The rear main bearing cap seal can be replaced with the engine in the chassis, but the transmission, clutch assembly, and flywheel must be removed to gain access to the seal.

1. Remove the transmission, clutch assembly, and the flywheel.
2. Remove the engine oil pan.
3. With a slide hammer with a screw end adapter pierce the seal and remove it from the recess in the cap and block.

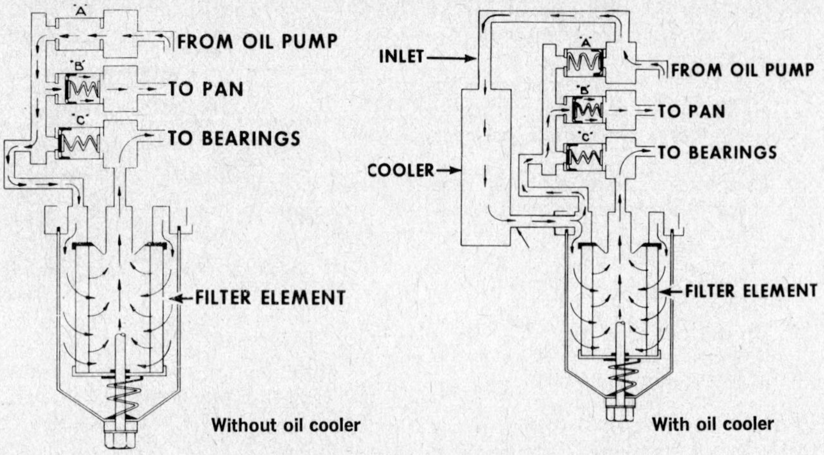

RD engine oil filter circuits with and without oil cooler
(© International Harvester Co.)

4. Lubricate the new seal, seat it squarely with a seal installer tool .085 inch from the rear face of the block.

NOTE: Production installed seals are seated flush with the rear of the block.

5. Install the bearing cap side seals with the use of a ⅛ inch welding rod, 8 inches long, with a 5/32 inch puddled ball on the end. Cut off any excess side seal, flush with the oil pan block surface.
6. Install the oil pan, flywheel, clutch assembly, and transmission.

PT 6, RD, VS 401, 478, 549 Engines

1. Drain crankcase and remove oil pan.
2. Remove rear main bearing cap.
3. Remove oil seal from bearing cap and clean cap thoroughly.
4. Loosen all remaining main bearing cap mounting bolts.
5. Using a brass drift and hammer, tap the upper seal until sufficient seal is protruding on the other side to permit pulling it out with pliers.
6. Wipe crankshaft seal surface clean and coat lightly with oil.
7. Coat crankcase surface of upper seal with soap and the lip of seal with No. 40 engine oil.
8. Install upper seal with lip toward front of engine.
9. Coat mating surfaces of crankcase and cap with No. 2 Permatex or equivalent, back surface of seal with soap and lip of seal with No. 40 engine oil.
10. Seat seal firmly into seal recess of cap and apply No. 2 Permatex or equivalent to both chamfered edges of the rear main bearing cap.
11. Install main bearing halves and cap.
12. Tighten all main bearing cap mounting bolts to specified torque.
13. Install oil pan.

MV 404, 446 Engines

The rear main bearing oil seal is a pressed fit into a retainer plate, which is bolted to the rear of the engine block.

1. Remove the transmission, clutch assembly, and flywheel.
2. Remove the capscrews holding the retainer to the engine block, and remove the retainer.
3. Press out the old seal from the retainer, clean the retainer seal pocket, and press the new seal in place on the retainer.

NOTE: The seal must be installed from the crankcase side of the retai-

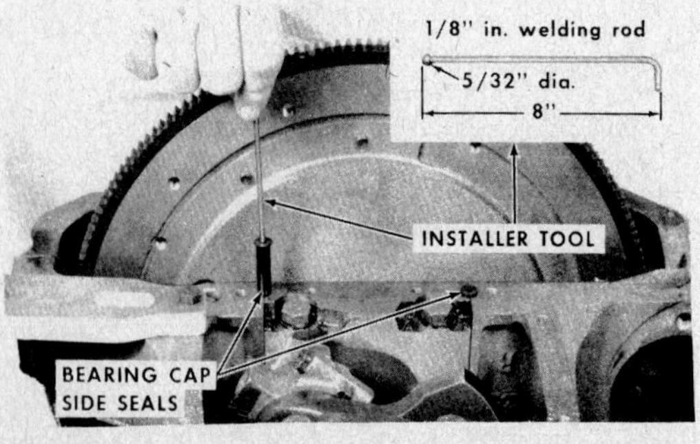

Installation of rear main bearing cap side seals, V304, 345 and 392 engines (© International Harvester Co.)

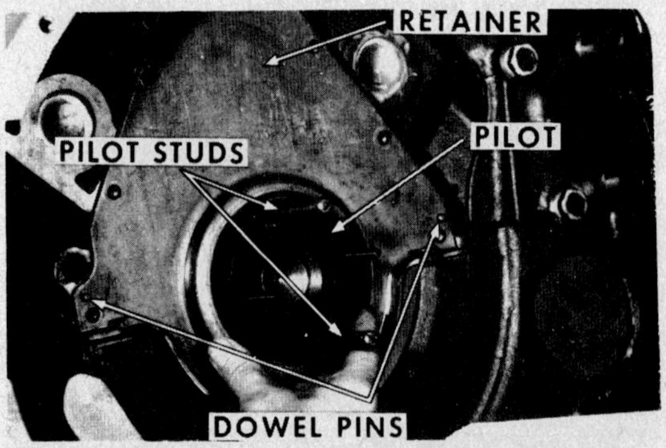

Rear main bearing oil seal installation MV404 and 406 engines (© International Harvester Co.)

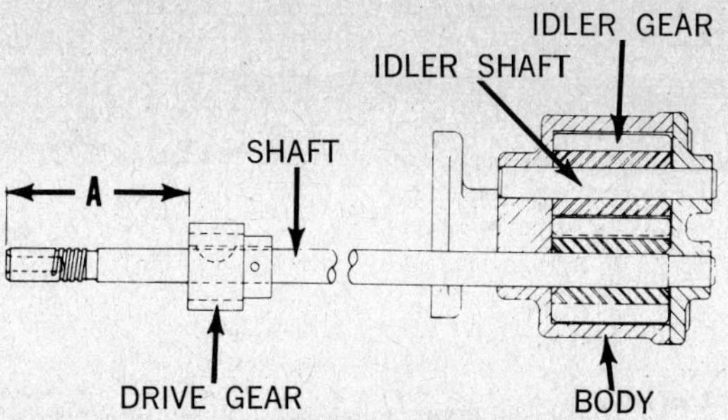

Oil pump drive gear installation VS401, 478 and 548 engines
"A" **2⅞″ Front mounted distributor**
1 15/16″ Rear mounted distributor
(© International Harvester Co.)

ner, flush with the seal bore inner surface.

4. With the use of tool SE-1942-2 pilot, or its equivalent, install the rear oil seal and retainer with gaskets on the engine block.

NOTE: When using the SE-1942-2 pilot tool to install the seal with the engine in the vehicle, drill two 25/64 inch diameter holes in the pilot, 180 degrees apart, 90 degrees from each existing hole. This will allow the use of two ⅜ x 4 inch pilot studs to serve as a safety measure to retain the pilot on the crankshaft.

5. Replace the flywheel, clutch assembly, and transmission.

Oil Filter Replacement

On all models except the RD-6 and the 400 engines, the oil filter unit is on the left side of the engine block. On the PT-6 and 400 engines, the filter is located on the right side of the block. All engines except the RD series and the VS 401, 478, and 549 series, use a spin-on type oil filter, which is replaced as a complete unit, using a strap wrench to remove it from the engine. Follow the instructions printed on the filter assembly to install.

The RD and VS series use a paper type filter, inserted in the filter shell, with the shell bolted to the filter base. To replace the filter, follow this procedure.

1. Remove drain plug from bottom of filter body, drain oil and replace drain plug.
2. Loosen filter body retaining bolt and remove filter body and element. Check condition of body to base gasket and replace if necessary.
3. Wash filter body with cleaning solvent, being sure to remove all sediment.
4. Install new filter element onto filter base with seal end away from base. Be sure element is fully seated onto base.

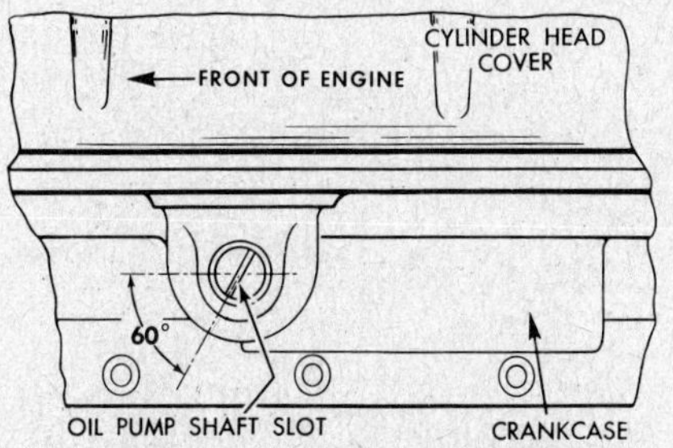

Oil pump installation RD engines
(© International Harvester Co.)

5. Install oil filter body and bolt with spring, making sure body seats evenly on gasket. Tighten filter body retaining bolt to 30-35 ft. lbs. torque on all engines.
6. Start engine and run for at least 5 minutes until oil is warm and check for leaks.
7. Check crankcase oil level. Lubricant capacity of oil filter is about one quart.

Oil Pump Removal and Installation

1. Drain crankcase and remove oil pan.
2. Remove oil pump mounting bolts and pull straight down on pump to remove.
3. When installing oil pump, guide pump shaft into position and rotate shaft until tang of drive gear is engaged. On PT-6 and V(S)-400, 401, 478, 549 engines install a new oil pump gasket when installing. On RD engines the oil pump shaft drives the distributor shaft and must be installed so that it is correctly timed to the crankshaft. Rotate the crankshaft until No. 1 cylinder is in firing position. On RD engines the oil pump is installed so that the slot in the top of the shaft is at a 60-degree angle to the side of the engine.
4. Tighten oil pump mounting bolts to:
   25-30 ft. lb. for all exc. 400.
   400-55 in. lb.
5. Install oil pan and fill crankcase.

Oil Pump Service

1. Thoroughly clean oil pump. Do not disturb or remove pickup tube unless absolutely necessary.
2. Remove pump cover bolts and pump cover.
3. Check gear to body clearance. If it is not within .0025-.0055″ on the OHV6 engines or .0007-

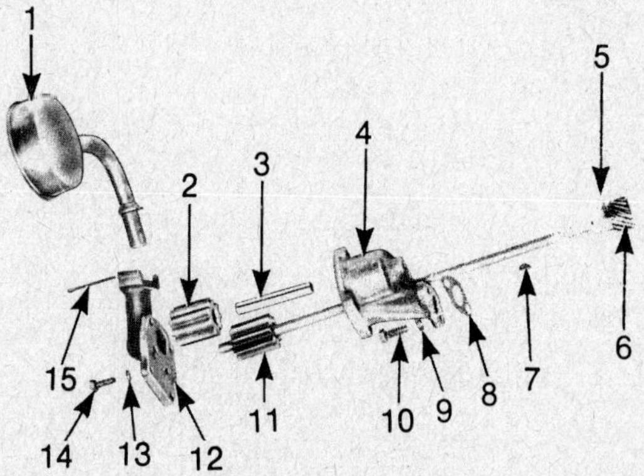

Typical gear type oil pump (© International Harvester Co.)

1 Screen, assy.	6 Gear, drive	11 Shaft, drive
2 Gear, idler	7 Key, Woodruff	12 Cover
3 Shaft, idler	8 Gasket, mounting	13 Washer, lock
4 Body	9 Washer, lock	14 Screw
5 Pin	10 Screw	15 Pin, cotter

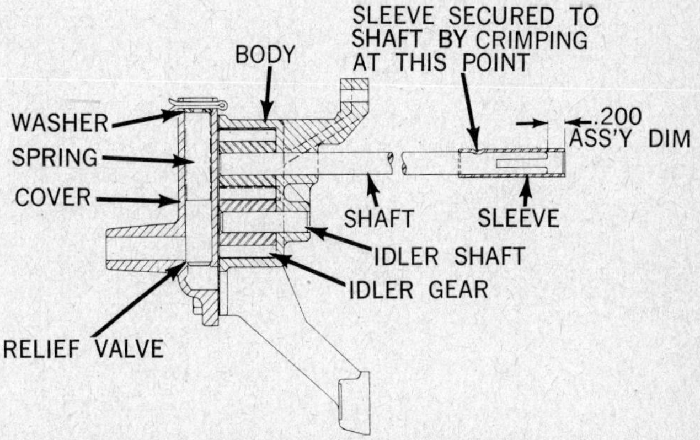

Oil pump shaft sleeve installation OHV4, V266, 304, 345 and 392 engines (© International Harvester Co.)

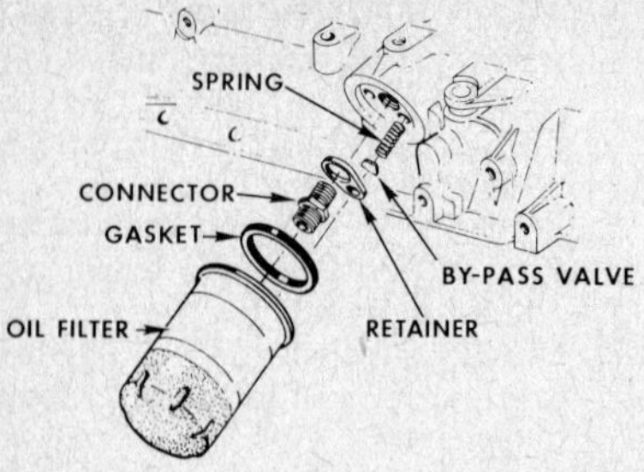

Oil filter bypass valve and spring PT6 engines (© International Harvester Co.)

.0027″ on the OHV4 and V8 engines, obtain new parts.

4. Check gear backlash. If it exceeds .011″ on OHV4 and V8 engines or .006″ on OHV6 engines, replace gears.
5. Check pump shaft clearance in bore. If it exceeds .004″ on OHV6 engines or .003″ on V8 and OHV4 engines, replace the whole pump assembly.
6. Remove relief valve and spring. Remove any burrs and clean. Be sure to install with bevelled or pointed end in seat. Check that valve moves freely in bore.
7. Check body and gear clearance. This is the distance between the pump gears and the pump cover, except on the PT-6 where it is the distance the gears protrude beyond the pump body. Adjustment of this clearance is made by the addition or removal of cover gaskets. On V(S)-401, 478, 549 engine oil pumps the clearance must be .0015-.009″. On the OHV4 and V-304, 345, 392 engines the clearance is .0015-.006″. On all OHV6 except the PT-6 (which is .000-.004″ *above* pump body) the clearance is .0025-.0055″.

   On the V 537, 605 engines, the body to gear clearance is .0007 to .0027 inch, while the clearance on the MV 404, 446 engine oil pumps are 0014 to .0054 inch.
8. When installing drive gears on

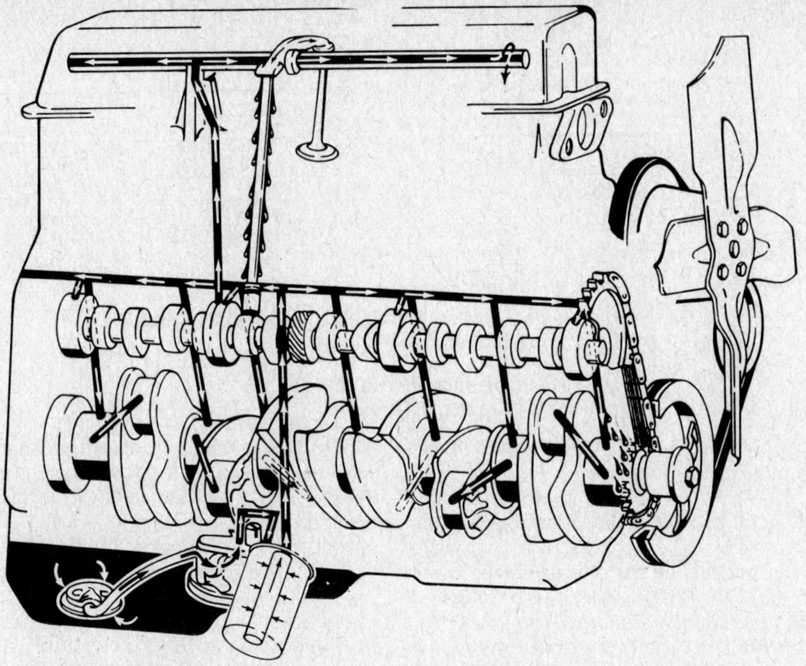

Engine lubrication system PT6 engines (© International Harvester Co.)

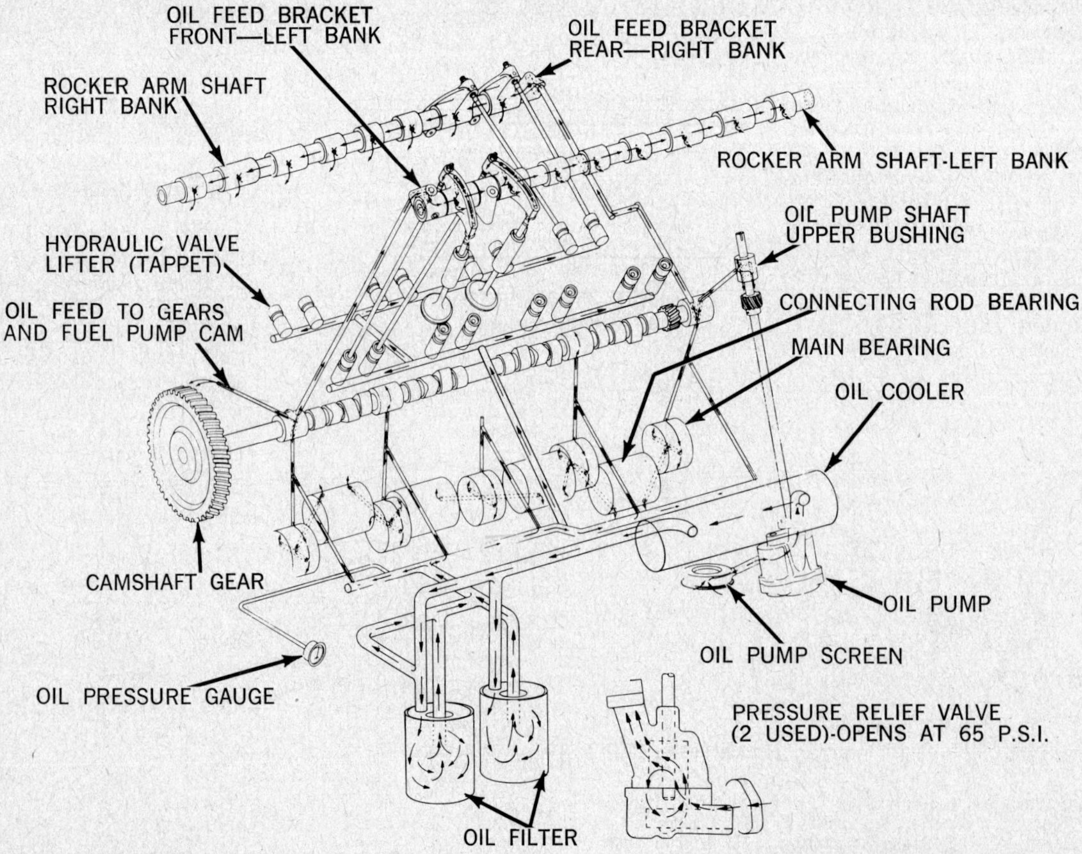

Lubricating system circuits V537 and 605 engines (© International Harvester Co.)

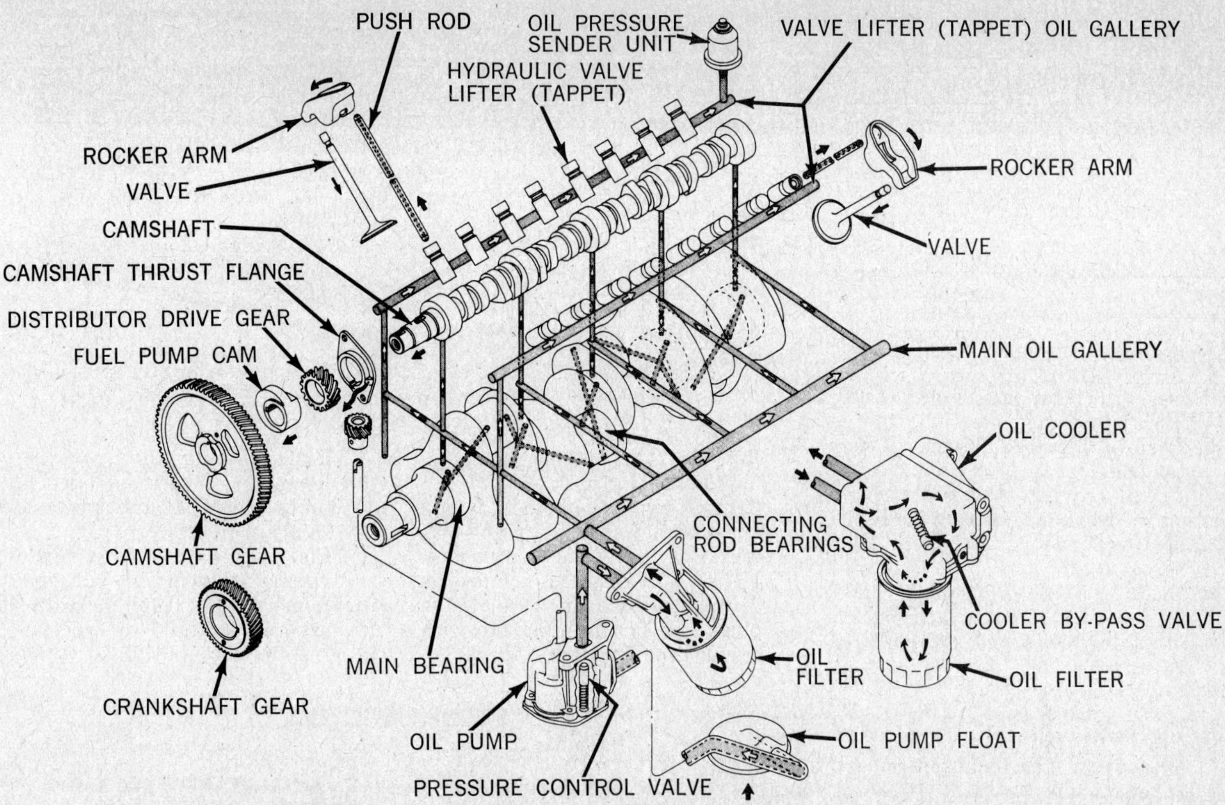

Lubricating system circuits MV 404 and 466 engines (© International Harvester Co.)

pump shaft be sure that the correct drive gear to pump body clearance is obtained. On RD engines the clearance is .025-.035". On OHV4 and V-304, 345, 392 engines the oil pump shaft sleeve is crimped onto the shaft. On the OHV4 the assembly dimension is .200" and on the V-304, 345, 392 engines the assembly dimension is .375". On V(S)-401, 478, 549 engines the distance "A" is 2⅞" for front-mounted distributors, 1-15/16" for rear-mounted distributors.

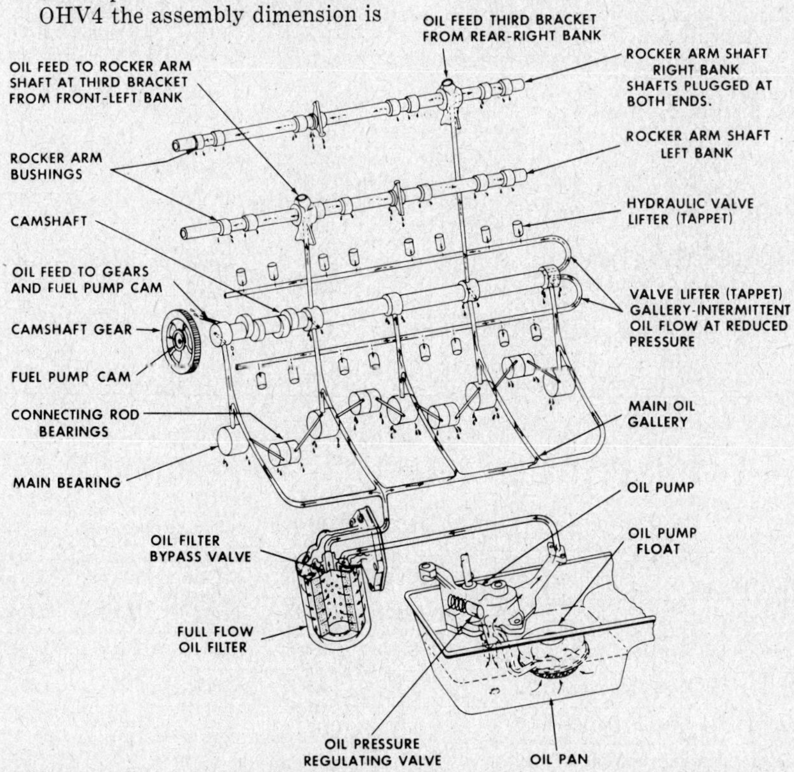

Lubricating system circuits V304, 345 and 392 engines. Typical of MS401, 478 and 549 engines (© International Harvester Co.)

Lubrication System Priming

The recommended procedure to prime the internal parts and the oil pump is to attach a bearing leak detector or similar tool to a suitable fitting on the oil gallery, located on the left side of the engine block. (right side on the PT-6 and 400 engines). Inject enough oil into the engine to fill the oil filter and the various passage ways for the lubrication system. Disconnect the primary coil wire and turn the engine over, while the priming operation is in process. Do not overfill the crankcase when this method is used. This type of priming will minimize the possibility of scuffing or heat build-up in the areas of friction, which could cause premature engine failure.

FRONT AXLE AND SUSPENSION

Front I-Beam Suspension

Shock Absorber Removal And Installation

1. Raise the vehicle and support safely.
2. Remove the retaining nuts and

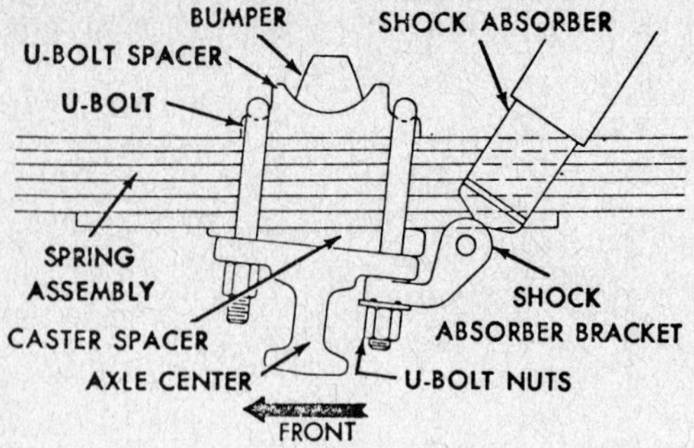

Typical front axle mounting (© International Harvester Co.)

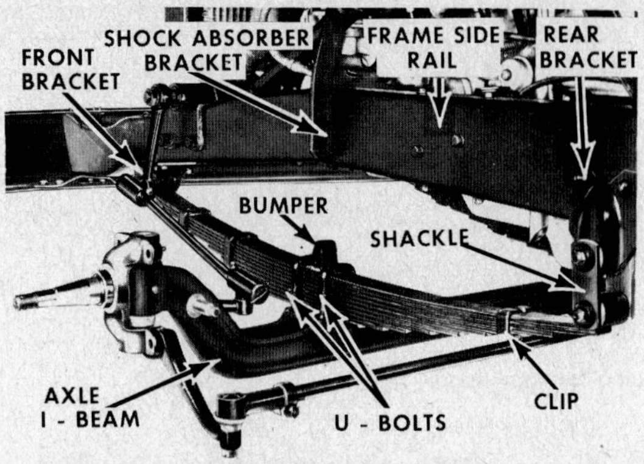

Typical front spring installation (medium duty)
(© International Harvester Co.)

washers from the upper and lower attaching bolts.

3. Remove the shock absorber from the bolts.
4. Install the new shock absorber on the bolts and position the rubber grommets at the shock absorber eyes.
5. Install the retaining nuts and washers on the upper and lower attaching bolts and tighten securely.
6. Lower the vehicle.

Spring Removal

1. Disconnect shock absorber at lower mount.
2. Raise front of vehicle just enough to take weight off spring.
3. Unbolt U-bolts, tapered caster wedge and U-bolt.
4. Remove lube fittings from spring mountings.
5. Remove spring pins and spring.
6. To install, reverse the above procedure, mounting fixed end of spring first.

King Pin and Bushings Replacement

1. Remove spindle nuts and spindle bearing retaining nuts.
2. Remove wheels, inner bearings and grease retainers from spindles.
3. Remove dirt shields.
4. Remove bolts holding backing plates and place backing plate assemblies over ends of axle I-beam.

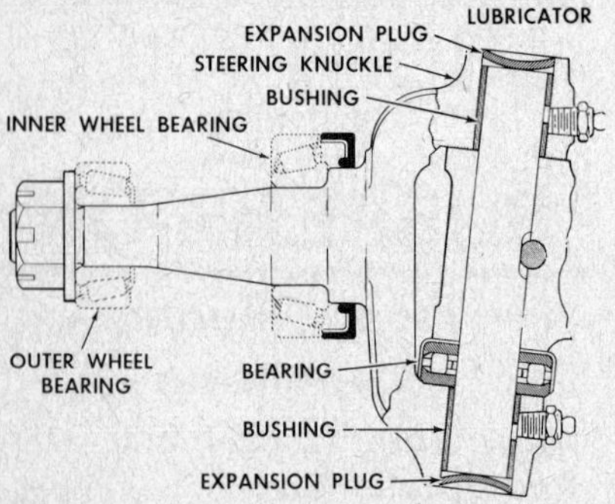

Typical steering knuckle expansion type seal plugs
(© International Harvester Co.)

5. Remove tapered draw keys holding the knuckle pins.
6. Remove expansion plugs or cap and gasket from the top and bottom of steering knuckles. (Remove expansion plugs by drilling a hole in one of the plugs and driving king pin with a punch to remove the other).
7. Drive out king pin.
8. Remove steering knuckles, thrust bearings and any spacer shims present.
9. Clean all parts thoroughly and inspect for wear and damage.
10. Remove old bushings with an arbor or drift.
11. Install new bushings with an

SPECIFICATIONS

IH MODEL	FA1 FA10	FA12 FA28 FA48	FA68 FA72	FA91 FA98 FA99	FA69
IH CODE	02001 02010	02012 02028 02048	02068 02072	02091 02098 02099	02069
Knuckle Pin Bushing Diameter (Inch)	.8625 / .8615	1.111 / 1.110	1.236 / 1.235	1.236 / 1.235	1.236 / 1.235
Knuckle Pin Diameter (Inch)	.861 / .860	1.110 / 1.109	1.234 / 1.233	1.234 / 1.233	1.234 / 1.233
Knuckle Pin Length (Inch)	5-7/16	6-1/4	6-3/4	7-21/32	6-3/4
Steering Knuckle Spindle Diameter At Inner Bearing (Inch)	Early Prod. 1.312 / 1.311 Late Prod. 1.374 / 1.371	Early Prod. 1.562 / 1.561 Late Prod. 1.687 / 1.686	1.749 / 1.748	2.1248 / 2.1240	1.874 / 1.873
At Outer Bearing (Inch)	Early Prod. .812 / .811 Late Prod. .843 / .842	.937* / .936	1.124 / 1.123	1.312 / 1.311	1.124 / 1.123

*FA12 .9998 / .9988

SPECIFICATIONS

IH Model	FA-71	FA-73	FA-74	FA-101	FA-103
IH Code	02071	02073	02074	02101	02103
Knuckle Pin Bushing Diameter (inch)	1.360	1.360	1.360	1.360	1.360
Knuckle Pin Diameter (inch)	1.358	1.358	1.358	1.358	1.358
Knuckle Pin Length (inch)	7.97	7.97	7.97	7.97	7.97
Steering Knuckle Spindle Diameter:					
At Inner Bearing (inch)	1.967	1.967	1.967	2.164	2.164
At Outer Bearing (inch)	1.374	1.374	1.374	1.374	1.374

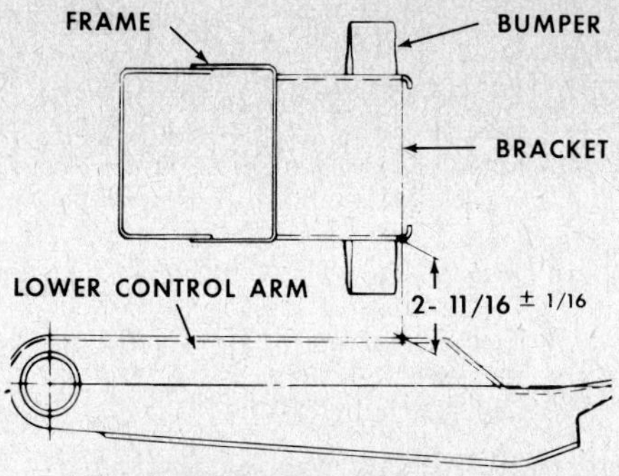

Checking front suspension height
(© International Harvester Co.)

arbor or bushing installing tool, making sure that the grease holes are aligned.

12. Ream or hone bushings to fit king pin with .001-.002″ clearance.
13. Lubricate and install steering knuckle, thrust bearings, spacer shims and king pins.
14. Install draw key (front side of axle) and tighten securely.
15. Insert expansion plugs or cap and gasket seals in the top and bottom of the steering knuckles.
16. Install brake backing plates, tightening bolts securely.
17. Install dirt shields, their retaining screws, cleaned and repacked wheel bearings and new grease seals.
18. Install wheel and spindle nuts, rotating wheel while tightening nut until slight drag is felt. Back off to the first castellation and install new cotter pin.
19. Lubricate and check and align front wheels if necessary.

Torsion Bar Front Suspension

Shock Absorber Removal and Installation

1. Remove the shock absorber upper retaining nut, washer, and rubber grommet from the top of the upper control arm.
2. Raise the vehicle and support it in such a manner so as not to cover the bottom of the lower arm with a floor jack or jack stands.
3. Remove the two shock absorber retaining bolts from the bottom of the lower control arm and withdraw the shock absorber.
4. To install new shock absorber, position the washer and rubber grommet on the extended shock absorber rod, and position the shock absorber up through the lower control arm, and engage the hole in the upper control arm with the extended rod.
5. Install the two bottom retaining bolts and tighten the shock absorber securely to the lower control arm.
6. Carefully lower the vehicle, so as not to lose the shock absorber rod from the upper control arm hole.
7. Install the upper rubber grommet, washer, and nut on the rod and tighten until the rubber grommet squeezes out slightly.

NOTE: Follow the manufacturers recommendation concerning the in-

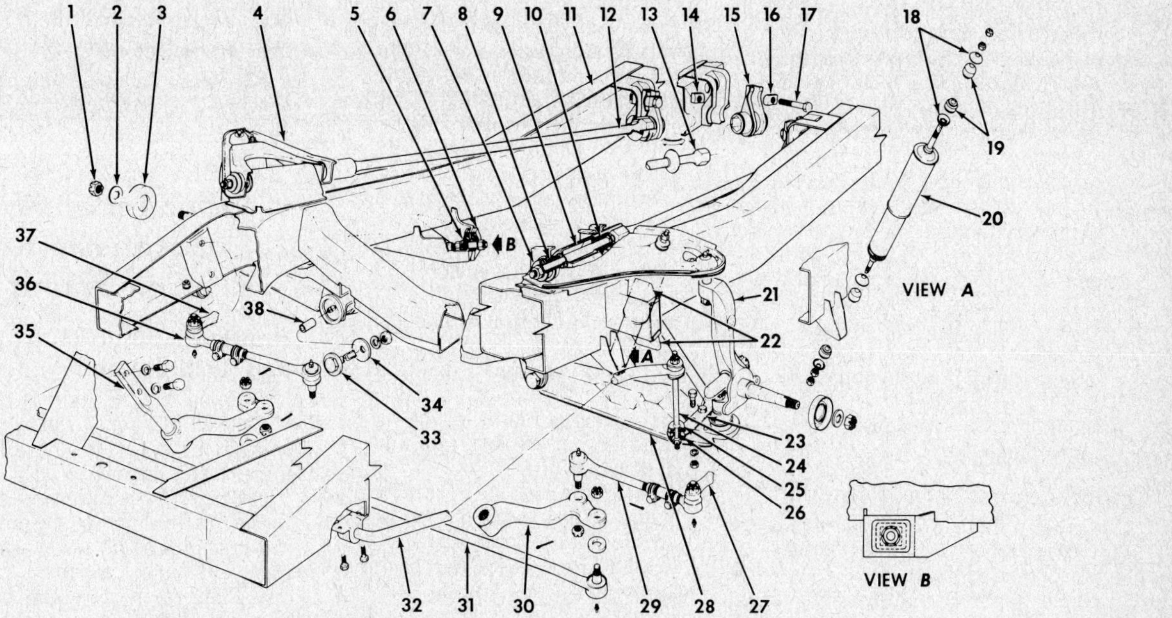

Torsion bar front wheel suspension (© International Harvester Co.)

1 Nut, hex., slotted
2 Washer
3 Seal, oil, front wheel
4 Arm, upper, asm.
5 Cushion, rubber, strut
6 Washer, lower arm strut
7 Washer
8 Bushing, upper control arm, front
9 Spindle, upper control arm
10 Bushing, upper control arm, rear
11 Frame
12 Bar, torsion
13 Seal, torsion bar
14 Nut, adjusting, torsion bar
15 Lever, retainer, torsion bar
16 Washer, adjusting, torsion bar
17 Bolt, hex.-hd.
18 Washer, retaining
19 Cushion, rubber
20 Shock absorber, front
21 Knuckle, steering
22 Bumper, control arm
23 Strut, lower control arm
24 Link, sway bar
25 Retainer, sway bar link cushion
26 Cushion, rubber, sway bar link
27 Arm, steering, left
28 Arm, lower, asm.
29 Link, vertical, left (or tie rod)
30 Arm, pitman
31 Rod, tie, asm.
32 Bar, sway
33 Bolt, hex.-hd.
34 Cam, lower control arm
35 Arm, idler, asm.
36 Link, vertical, right (or tie rod)
37 Arm, steering, right
38 Spacer, lower control arm

stallation of lock nuts or self-locking nuts.

Torsion Bar Removal

Right and left torsion bars are not interchangeable. The bars are marked with an "L" or "R" on one end and the bars should always be installed with the marked end towards the rear of the vehicle. There is an arrow indicating the direction of wind-up on the end of the bar.

1. Jack up the vehicle by the frame crossmember and release the load from the torsion bar by loosening the retainer lever adjusting bolt.
2. Remove retainer lever adjusting bolt and slide retainer lever from end of torsion bar.
3. Remove torsion bar by sliding it rearward. CAUTION: Do not nick or scratch torsion bars—this may create a fracture.
4. To install torsion bar, position torsion bar in upper control arm, observing right and left side and rearward direction as indicated above.
5. Install retainer lever on end of torsion bar and position bar nut in bracket on frame so that torsion bar adjusting bolt may be installed.
6. Insert bolt in bar washer, then through retainer lever and bracket and thread into bar nut.
7. Adjust height by lowering vehicle to ground (check for correct tire pressure), bouncing front end up and down, then turning bolt on torsion bar adjusting lever until correct height is achieved. Measure height between top of lower control arm and lower edge of rubber bumper frame bracket (vehicle unloaded).

Upper Control Arm Removal

1. Jack up vehicle by front frame crossmember until front wheels are off the ground.
2. Remove wheel and torsion bar (see preceding section).
3. Disconnect top mount of shock absorber.
4. Remove cotter pin, nut and dust seal (cut away seal) from lower ball joint.
5. Drive out lower ball joint stud (do not damage threads) or use special ball stud remover and nut.
6. Remove fender splash panel front shield.
7. Remove nut and washers from front end of upper control arm spindle and carefully drive out spindle with hammer.
8. Remove upper control arm.
9. To install, position upper control arm and install spindle through arm and bracket from rear.
10. Install flat washer, lock washer and nut. Tighten securely.
11. Install fender splash panel front shield.
12. Install new dust seal on ball stud, then line up shock absorber with hole in control arm and position ball stud into steering knuckle. Use jack to raise lower control arm until ball stud is well into steering knuckle.
13. Install nut on ball stud. Tighten securely.
14. Install top mounting of shock absorber, tightening just enough to squash rubber cushion slightly.
15. Install torsion bar on upper control arm as described in preceding section.
16. Mount front wheel.
17. Check alignment (see General Repair Section) of steering.

Lower Control Arm Removal

1. Raise vehicle by jacking frame crossmember. Remove wheel.
2. Disconnect sway bar link from strut and remove two bolts which secure strut to lower control arm.
3. Cut away dust seal from lower ball stud and remove cotter pin and nut from lower ball stud.
4. Either drive out ball stud with a soft hammer while supporting control arm or use special ball stud remover and nut.
5. Disconnect tie rod end from either side of vehicle.
6. Remove nut, lockwasher, cam and bolt from lower control arm and frame bracket.
7. Remove control arm and spacer in bushing.
8. To install, place new dust seal on ball stud and position ball stud into steering knuckle.
9. Tighten nut on ball stud and install cotter pin.
10. Position spacer in bushing and, while holding control arm in position, install bolt from front. Install cam, lockwasher, and nut, tightening to 81-135 ft. lbs. torque.
11. Mount strut to lower control arm tightening bolts securely.
12. Connect tie rod end.
13. Position cushion and retainer on sway bar link and place sway bar link into strut with cushion, retainer and nut. Tighten nut until cushion is slightly squished. Insert cotter pin.
14. Mount front wheel.
15. Check alignment (see General Repair Section) and tighten nut on strut to 120-150 ft. lbs. torque and camber adjusting bolt nut to 81-135 ft. lbs. torque.

Ball Joint Inspection

Upper Ball Joint

The upper ball joint is a loose fit when not connected to the steering knuckle.

1. Use a floor jack or position the vehicle on a frame contact lift and raise the vehicle until the wheels fall to the full down position.
2. Grasp the tire at the top and bottom and move the tire in and out. The radial end play should not exceed .180 inch. If so, replace the ball joint.

Lower Ball Joint

The lower ball joint is spring loaded in its socket and this minimizes looseness and compensates for normal wear.

1. Locate a floor jack or position the vehicle on a frame contact lift and raise the vehicle until the wheels fall to the full down position.
2. Grasp the tire at the top and bottom and move the tire in and out. Any movement at the ball joint socket and stud indicates wear and the loss of preload, and the ball joint should be replaced.

Ball Joint Removal and Installation

Refer to "Independent Front Suspension-Coil Spring," for the procedures necessary to remove and install the ball joints.

Independent Front Suspension— Coil Spring

Shock Absorber Removal and Installation

1. Remove the shock absorber upper retaining nut, washer, and rubber grommet from the top of the upper control arm.
2. Raise the vehicle and support it in such a manner so as not to cover the bottom of the lower arm with a floor jack or jack stands.
3. Remove the two shock absorber retaining bolts from the bottom of the lower control arm and withdraw the shock absorber.
4. To install new shock absorber, position the washer and rubber grommet on the extended shock absorber rod, and position the shock absorber up through the lower control arm, and engage the hole in the upper control arm with the extended rod.
5. Install the two bottom retaining bolts and tighten the shock absorber securely to the lower control arm.
6. Carefully lower the vehicle, so as not to lose the shock absorber rod from the upper control arm hole.
7. Install the upper rubber grommet, washer, and nut on the rod and tighten until the rubber grommet squeezes out slightly.

NOTE: Follow the manufacturers recommendation concerning the installation of lock nuts or self-locking nuts.

Ball Joint Inspection—Coil Spring Suspension

Upper Ball Joint

The upper ball joint stud is spring loaded in its socket and this minimizes looseness and compensates for normal wear.

1. Locate a floor jack under the lower control arm on the outboard side and raise the vehicle so that the wheels clear the floor.
2. Grasp the tire at the top and bottom and move the tire in and out. If any perceptible lateral or vertical movement is noted, the ball joint should be replaced.

Lower Ball Joint

The lower ball joints are a loose fit when not connected to the steering knuckle.

1. Locate a floor jack under the lower control arm on the outboard side and raise the vehicle until the wheels clear the floor.
2. Grasp the tire at the top and bottom and move the tire in and out. The radial play should not exceed .250 inch. If so, the ball joint should be replaced.

Coil Spring Removal and Installation

1. Raise the front of the vehicle and support safely on floor stands.
2. Remove the wheels and tires.
3. Remove the caliper from the rotor assembly and support to avoid damage to the brake hose.
4. Remove the hub assembly from the steering knuckle.
5. Remove the brake shield from the knuckle.
6. Disconnect the sway bar link, if equipped.
7. Remove the axle bumper and wheel stop bracket from the lower control arm.

NOTE: This also disconnects the lower control arm rod assembly from the control arm.

8. Remove the shock absorber.
9. Position the spring compressor screw into the shock absorber upper mounting hole in the crossmember. Position the puller hooks under the lower second spring coil and turn the spring compressor screw until coil spring unseats from the lower control arm.
10. Remove the cotter pins from the upper and lower ball joint studs, and loosen the lower nut approximately two turns.

NOTE: The cotter pin is removed from the upper ball joint stud to allow a special tool to be placed over the upper stud and nut.

11. With the aid of special tool SE-2493 (ball joint stud remover) or its equivalent, and by placing it over the upper stud at its hex end, extend the screw to contact the lower ball joint stud.
12. Apply pressure by turning the screw out from the tool. Tap the steering knuckle lightly to loosen the stud from the knuckle.
13. Remove the tool and remove the nut from the lower ball joint stud. Separate the ball joint stud from the knuckle.
14. Loosen the spring compressor and relieve the spring of all tension. Remove the spring from the vehicle.
15. Position new spring into the crossmember and the lower control arm.

Note: Turn the coil spring to line up the bottom coil with the seal groove in the lower control arm.

16. Install the hooks of the spring compressor under the second coil of the spring. Tighten the compressor until the lower ball joint stud can be installed into the steering knuckle.
17. Position a hydraulic jack under the lower control arm and raise the arm until the bottom ball joint stud will enter the steering knuckle. Install the nut and torque to specifications.
18. Install the cotter pins in both the upper and lower ball joint studs. Confirm the position of the spring in the lower arm.
19. Remove the spring compressor tool and install the shock absorber.
20. Install the lower control arm rod assembly and axle bumper and wheel stop bracket to the lower control arm.
21. Install the brake shield on the steering knuckle.
22. Install the rotor-hub assembly.
23. Install the caliper on the rotor assembly.
24. Install the wheel and tire assembly.
25. Remove the floor stands and lower the vehicle to the floor.
26. Depress the brake pedal to force the disc pads against the rotor.

Upper Control Arm and Ball Joint Removal and Installation

Follow the procedure outlined under "Coil Spring Removal And Installation," except that the special tool SE-2493 or its equivalent, is used to apply pressure to the upper ball joint stud after loosening the nut approximately two turns. Follow the procedure as outlined.

1. After removing the ball joint stud from the steering knuckle, remove the upper control arm from the frame rail.
2. Place the upper control arm in a vise and with a ball joint remover socket, remove the ball joint from the upper arm.
3. Lubricate the threads in the arm and place the new ball joint into the arm.
4. With the use of the ball joint socket, tighten the ball joint to specifications in the upper arm.
5. Inner upper arm bushings may be replaced by pressing the old bushings out and pressing the new bushings into the upper arm.
6. Install the upper arm onto the frame rail and tighten securely.
7. Follow the procedure outlined under the "Coil Spring Removal and Installation" to complete the operation.

Lower Control Arm and Ball Joint Removal and Installation

Follow the procedure outlined under "Coil Spring Removal and Installation" to remove the coil spring from the suspension. After the coil spring is removed, follow this procedure to remove the lower control arm and ball joint.

1. After removing the lower ball joint stud from the steering knuckle, remove the lower control arm from the frame bracket.
2. Place the lower control arm in a vise.
3. Remove the ball joint from the lower control arm with the aid of tool SE-2494-2 ball joint remover and installer, or an equivalent tool.
4. Lubricate the threads in the arm and place a new ball joint into the control arm.
5. With the use of tool SE-2494-2 or equivalent, tighten the ball joint into the arm.
6. Inner lower arm bushings may be replaced by pressing the old bushings out and pressing the new bushings into place.
7. Install the lower arm onto the frame rail bracket and tighten securely.
8. Follow the procedure outlined under "Coil Spring Removal and Installation" to complete the operation.

Front Wheel Bearing Adjustment

(All Non-Driving Axles)

1. While rotating the wheel and hub assembly, adjust the spindle nut to 30 ft. lbs. (50 ft. lbs. on Loadstar and Cargostar), then back off nut 1/4 turn.
2. **Series 100, 200**—Finger tighten and insert lock so that cotter pin

can be inserted with out backing off nut.

Loadstar and Cargostar—If the lock or cotter pin can be installed at this position, do so, if not, tighten to the nearest locking position and insert the cotter pin or lock.

NOTE: Bent type lockwashers must have one tab bent over the adjusting nut. With double locknuts, tighten jam nut to 100-200 ft. lbs. and bend one tab of the lockwasher over the jam nut.

All other series—Finger tighten and if possible, insert cotter pin. If not able to install cotter pin, back off the nut to the nearest hole and insert the cotter pin.

NOTE: When using the cotter pin as a lock, the long tang should be bent over the spindle end. Clip the remaining tang, leaving enough stock to bend down against the side of the nut.

Front Drive Axle

For Service on Transfer Case and Differential—see General Repair Section.

Description

The front drive axles incorporate hypoid gears and use both spherical and ball joint wheel-end steering knuckles. The axle shaft assemblies are full floating and may be removed without disassembling the steering knuckles. Two types of axle shafts are used, one, a drive flange arrangement, bolted to the hub, and a second, mated to an internally splined gear, which in turn is splined and mated to the wheel hub, to transmit the driving torque to the front wheels.

Leaf Spring—Removal and Installation

1. Raise the vehicle and support on the frame rails behind the front springs with floor stands.
2. Remove the shock absorber from the spring.
3. Remove the U-bolts, spring bumpers and retainer, or the U-bolt seat.
4. Remove the lubricators, if used.
5. Remove the nuts from the shackles and bracket pins.
6. Slide the spring off the bracket and shackle pins.
7. Remove the spring from the vehicle.
8. Installation is the reverse of removal. Tighten all nuts and bolts securely.

Front Drive Axle Removal

1. Jack up truck until load is removed from springs and block up frame to safely hold weight.
2. Drain lubricant from main housing and, if applicable, from wheel end housings.
3. Disconnect brakes.
4. Disconnect drag link from ball stud bracket.
5. Disconnect drive shaft from pinion shaft yoke.
6. Supporting axle with a portable floor jack, remove spring U-bolts.
7. Roll axle assembly out from under truck.
8. To install, reverse the above procedure.

Front Drive Axle Adjustments

Preload on the knuckle bearings of these front axles must be maintained at all times. Check for looseness each time knuckle is lubricated.

1. Jack up front end of truck until off-center weight of the wheel is relieved (wheel just barely touching ground).
2. Remove wheel and wheel adapter from hub.
3. Disconnect tie rod and drag link.
4. Remove axle shaft.
5. To remove play (check for play by pushing and pulling on top and bottom of knuckle) and increase preload drag, turn adjusting bolt into back of knuckle. Preload should read (spring scale hooked into end of steering arm) 12 lbs.

Front Wheel Bearing Adjustment

1. Remove wheel and adapter from hub.
2. Remove axle shaft or internal gear, and adjusting nut lock plate.
3. Tighten nut until just against bearing.
4. Rotate the wheel forward and backward until a slight drag can be felt. Turn nut back to the first lock hole to obtain about a ½ hole relief.
5. Bearing adjustment is correct when no play can be felt when pushing and pull at top and bottom of wheel.

Reference for overhaul procedures see International Single Reduction Rear Axle in General Repair Section.

Axle Shaft and Universal Joint

(Axles having drive flange)

Removal

1. Raise vehicle, support with floor stands and remove wheel from vehicle.
2. Remove grease cap and snap ring from end of axle shaft.
3. Remove drive flange cap screws, lock-washer, flange and gasket. If equipped with locking hubs, bend up locking tab, take out capscrews and remove clutch body.

NOTE: Lift off clutch body holding it erect so as not to let drive pins fall out of body. If they do fall out, be certain to install them during reassembly.

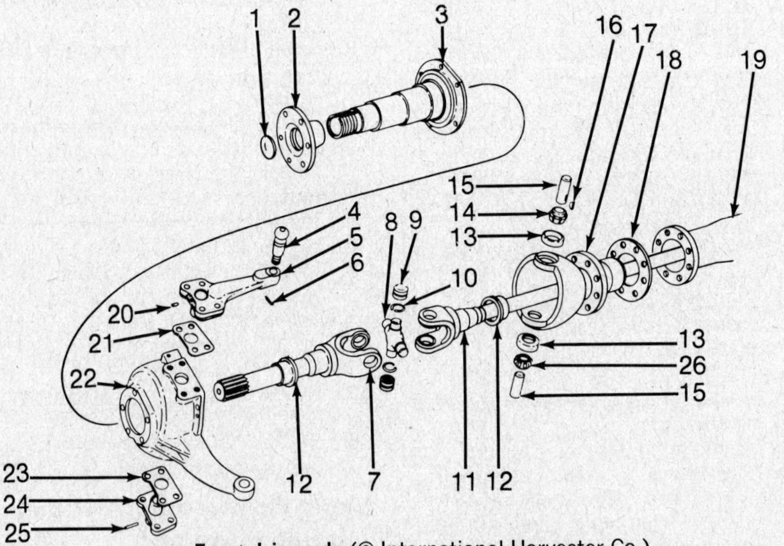

Front drive axle (© International Harvester Co.)

1 Plug, expansion
2 Flange, wheel drive
3 Knuckle, wheel
4 Ball, steering arm
5 Arm, steering
6 Pin, cotter
7 Shaft, axle outer
8 Spider
9 Bearing, trunnion
10 Ring, snap
11 Shaft, axle inner
12 Bushing, knuckle
13 Bearing trunnion
14 Bushing, steering knuckle
15 Pin, king cone
16 Key, woodruff
17 Yoke, trunnion
18 Gasket, yoke mounting
19 Housing, axle
20 Pin
21 Gasket
22 Knuckle, steering
23 Shim
24 Cap, king pin bearing
25 Pin
26 Cone, bearing

Remove hub body. Loosen setscrew and unscrew drag shoe from spindle.

4. Remove brake drum countersunk setscrews, where applicable and remove drum.
5. Bend the lip on the wheel bearing lockwasher away from the outer wheel bearing nut and remove the nut and lockwasher. Remove wheel bearing adjusting nut (inner) and bearing lockwasher.
6. Remove the wheel hub with wheel bearing.
7. Remove backing plate and wheel spindle retaining bolts and lockwashers. Support backing plate to prevent damage to brake hose if hose is not disconnected.
8. Remove wheel bearing spindle with bushing. If spindle bushing requires replacing, press out bushing using an adapter of correct size. An alternate method of bushing removal is the use of a cape chisel or punch to collapse the bushing.
9. Pull axle shaft and universal joint assembly out of axle housing.

Installation

1. Insert axle shaft and universal joint assembly into axle housing. Position splined end of axle shaft into differential pinion gear and push into place.
2. If wheel bearing spindle bushing was removed, press new bushing into spindle using an installer tool or adapter of proper size. Lubricate ID of bushing with chassis lube when installed to provide initial lubrication. Bushing should be pressed in until bushing flange is seated against shoulder in spindle. Assemble wheel spindle and backing plate to steering knuckle. Secure with six (6) bolts and lockwashers and tighten to specifications. Connect hydraulic brake fluid line if disconnected.
3. Pack wheel bearings using a pressure lubricator or by carefully working lubricant into bearing cones by hand. Slide lubricated inner wheel bearing on spindle until it stops against spindle shoulder.
4. Apply thin coating of lubricant specified for wheel bearings to seal lip and install seal into wheel hub using an adapter of correct diameter. Lip of seal should extend towards wheel (away from backing plate assembly).
5. Assemble wheel hub on spindle. Install lubricated outer wheel bearing cone on spindle. Push cone on spindle until it rests against bearing cup.
6. Install wheel bearing lockwasher and adjusting (inner) nut. Tighten adjusting nut until there is a slight drag on the bearings when the hub is turned; then back-off approximately one-sixth turn.

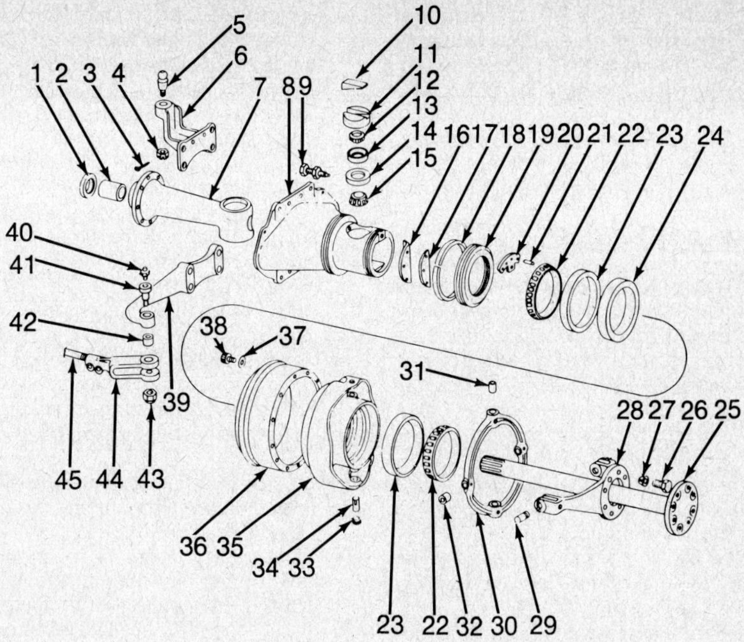

Front drive axle (drive gear type) (© International Harvester Co.)

1 Seal axle shaft	16 Seal	31 Bushing, ring
2 Bushing, axle shaft	17 Plate, retaining	32 Bushing, yoke
3 Pin, cotter	18 Seal, wheel	33 Pin, hub to ring
4 Nut	19 Nut, bearing adjusting	34 Plug, pipe
5 Ball, steering arm	20 Plate lock	35 Hub
6 Bracket, ball stud	21 Pin, lock plate	36 Drum
7 End, stub	22 Bearing	37 Washer, lock
8 Spindle	23 Bearing	38 Bolt, hex-hd.
9 Screw, adjusting	24 Ring, clamp	39 Arm, steering
10 Wedge, adjusting	25 Shaft, left axle	40 Lubricator
11 Cap, upper brg.	26 Bolt, hex-hd.	41 Bolt, tie-rod end
12 Bearing cone	27 Dowel, shaft flange	42 Bushing, steering
13 Bearing cup	28 Yoke, power	43 Nut, tie-rod end bolt
14 Bearing cup	29 Pin, ring to yoke	44 Yoke, tie-rod
15 Bearing cone	30 Ring, compensating	45 Rod, tie

7. Install tang-type lockwasher and lock nut (outer). Tighten nut and bend lockwasher tang over lock nut. If axle is equipped with locking hubs, install drag shoe on spindle and tighten setscrew.
8. Align splines of drive flange with those of axle shaft and secure drive flange and new gasket to wheel hub with capscrews and lockwashers. Tighten capscrews securely. If equipped with locking hubs, lightly lubricate hub body and clutch using a light grade chassis lubricant and install new gasket, hub body, snap ring and hub clutch. Be certain that all drive pins are positioned in locking hub clutch when clutch is installed. Secure hub clutch to wheel hub with capscrews and lock. Tighten to specifications and bend tang over head of capscrew.
9. Install snap ring and grease cup if not equipped with locking hubs.
10. Assemble brake drum and wheels to wheel hub. Bleed and adjust brakes.

CAUTION: **Be certain that master cylinder is full of brake fluid after completing bleeding operation.**

(Axles having drive gear)

Removal

1. Raise and support vehicle with floor stands placed under frame rails. Remove wheel from vehicle.
2. Lightly tap alternately around edge of hub cap with hammer and screwdriver or similar tool until hub cap is removed.
3. If axle is equipped with locking hubs, remove the eight (8) socket-head setscrews securing hub clutch assembly to wheel hub assembly.

NOTE: Drive pins may fall out of hub clutch when separated from wheel hub assembly. Be certain to replace them during installation.

4. Remove retaining ring from wheel hub if equipped with locking hubs.
5. Remove snap ring from axle shaft.
6. Pull drive gear out of wheel hub. If difficulty is encountered in re-

moving drive gear, obtain a screwdriver or similar tool having the end bent approximately 90° with the handle. Insert end of tool into groove in drive gear and withdraw gear. If necessary, move wheel alternately backward and forward to aid removal of gear.
7. Remove retaining ring and locking hub body, if so equipped.
8. Using Wheel Bearing Adjusting Nut Wrench, remove wheel bearing outer nut and slide lock ring off of axle shaft. Again using wrench, remove wheel bearing inner nut.
9. Pull drive gear spacer out of wheel hub.
10. Remove brake drum from wheel hub and slide wheel hub assembly off of spindle.

NOTE: Do not allow tapered roller bearings to drop on floor as bearings may be damaged.

11. Remove screws retaining grease guard to backing plate. Take off grease guard and gasket.
12. Remove the six (6) bolts securing wheel spindle and backing plate to steering knuckle. Pull spindle with bushing off of axle shaft. If spindle bushing requires replacing, press or drive out bushing using an adapter of correct size. An alternate method of bushing removal is the use of a cape chisel or punch to collapse the bushing.
13. Pull axle shaft and universal joint assembly out of axle housing.

Installation

1. Proceed with steps 1 through 5 of *Axle Shaft and Universal Joint Installation* (Axles having drive flange).
2. Insert drive gear spacer over spindle and against outer wheel bearing cup.
3. Position wheel bearing inner adjusting nut Wheel Bearing Adjusting Nut wrench with pin in nut extending toward handle end of wrench. Install nut on spindle and tighten until it is snug against outer wheel bearing; then loosen adjusting nut 1/4 turn. Align tang on adjusting nut lock ring with groove in wheel spindle. Slide ring on spindle and index pin on adjusting nut with hole in lock ring. If pin will not index with hole in lock ring, turn adjusting nut to the left (Loosen) until it will index.

NOTE: When attempting to index pin with hole in lock ring, turn nut very slightly since adjusting nut should be locked with first hole in lock ring past 1/4 turn lose. Position wheel bearing outer nut in adjusting nut wrench and install on spindle. Tighten nut securely.

4. Align splines on axle shaft and splines in wheel hub with those of drive gear. Insert drive gear on axle shaft. Push gear into hub until it rests against drive gear spacer.

NOTE: Groove on side of gear must be toward hub cap.

5. If axle is equipped with locking hubs, lightly lubricate locking hub body using a light grade chassis lubricant. Align splines and insert hub body into wheel hub.
6. Install snap ring on end of axle shaft.
7. Place retaining ring in groove in wheel hub, if equipped with locking hub.
8. If applicable, lightly grease hub clutch assembly using a light grade chassis lubricant. Be sure that all eight (8) drive pins are positioned in the locking hub clutch. Assemble hub clutch to hub body and secure with eight (8) socket head setscrews.
9. Position hub cap on wheel hub and lightly tap alternately around cap until flange is against edge of hub.
10. Assemble brake drum and wheel to wheel hub. Bleed and adjust brakes.

CAUTION: Be certain that the master cylinder is full of brake fluid after bleeding operation.

Steering Knuckle (Spherical)

Removal

1. Remove drag link at steering arm and tie-rod at steering knuckle.
2. Remove oil seal retaining bolts from inner flange of steering knuckle and remove oil seals.
3. Remove bolts and lockwashers securing king pin lower bearing cap. Remove bearing cap and shim pack. Retain shim pack for use during reassembly.
4. Remove capscrews or self-locking nuts, which ever is applicable, securing steering arm or upper bearing cap to steering knuckle.
5. Lift steering arm assembly and knuckle until bronze bearing cone will clear ball yoke. Separate steering knuckle from ball yoke.

NOTE: Do not allow lower tapered roller bearing cone to drop on floor during removal of steering knuckle.

6. Support steering knuckle and with a long brass drift, drive or press king pin out of bronze bearing cone.

NOTE: Be careful not to damage end of king pin during removal of cone.

Installation

1. Assemble steering arm to knuckle using original shim pack. Install self-locking nuts or capscrews and tighten securely.
2. Coat king pin and bronze bearing cone ID and OD with chassis lubricant to prevent galling. Align serrations of new bronze bearing cone with serrations of king pin and press cone on king pin.

NOTE: Make sure the cone is pressed all the way on or against the shoulder.

3. With bronze cone and tapered roller bearing pre-lubricated, place tapered roller bearing cone into cup at lower end of ball yoke. While retaining lower bearing cone in position, assemble steering knuckle to ball yoke. Seat bronze cone into cup at upper end of ball yoke.
4. Lubricate lower king pin with chassis lubricant and using original shim pack, install lower bearing cap to knuckle securing with bolts and lockwasher. Tighten bearing cap bolts securely.
5. Assemble opposite knuckle proceeding with instructions similar to those outlined above.
6. Individually check knuckle bearing preload by placing a torque wrench on any one (1) of the steering arm or bearing cap bolts or nuts. Read the starting torque (not rotating torque). Remove or add shims at the lower bearing cap until the specified preload is obtained. Knuckle bearing preload should be checked without ball joint oil seal, drag link or tie-rod installed.
7. Assemble the knuckle oil seals with the split on top. Knuckle retainer plate must be adjacent to ball yoke; followed by rubber seal, felt seal and metal retainer. Install seal retainer bolts and tighten securely.
8. Connect tie-rod to steering knuckle and tighten nut. Connect drag link to steering arm ball. Install cotter keys.

Cleaning, Inspection

All parts of the wheel end assembly should be thoroughly cleaned and dried with compressed air or a lint-free clean cloth.

Inspect all parts for wear, cracks or other damage. Replace all oil seals, felts and gaskets to prevent lubricant leakage.

Steering Knuckle (Ball Joint)

Removal

1. With the vehicle safely supported, remove the wheel and brake drum.
2. Remove the backing plate and the spindle from the knuckle.

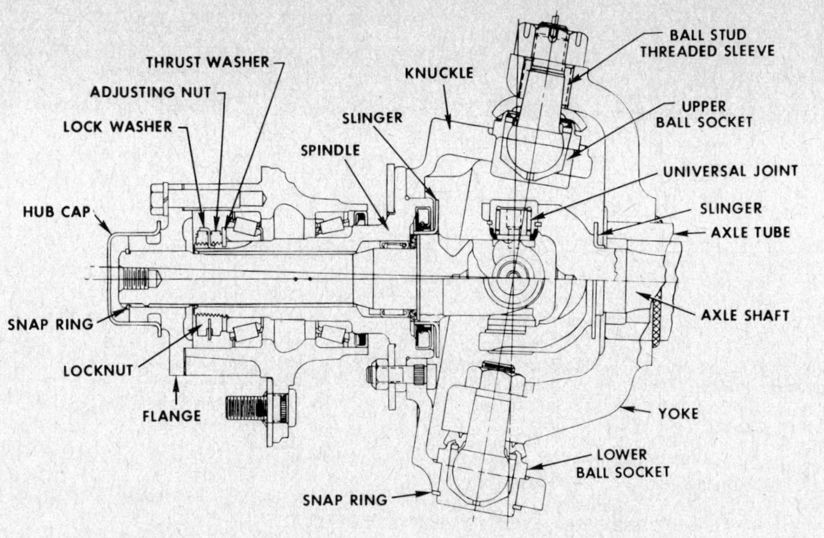

Front drive axle with 40° steer (© International Harvester Co.)

NOTE: If necessary, tap the spindle lightly with a soft hammer to loosen it from the knuckle bolts. The spindle oil seal, needle bearings, and bronze spacer can be removed and replaced at this time.

3. Remove the axle from the housing.

NOTE: The slingers can be removed from the axle by using pullers or tapping the axle through the slingers.

4. Disconnect and remove the tie rod from the steering arm.
5. Remove the cotter pin from the upper ball socket stud and remove the nut.
6. Remove the nut from the lower ball socket stud and discard.

NOTE: This nut is of a special torque design and should only be used one time.

7. Remove the lower ball socket snap ring (used on 4 x 4 applications only), and unseat the upper and lower ball socket studs with a lead hammer or with a puller tool arrangement, to separate the knuckle from the yoke.

NOTE: If the upper ball socket stud remains in the yoke flange, remove it by striking it on the stud with a soft hammer.

8. With the aid of puller tools or a press and ram, remove the bottom ball socket.
9. Reverse the knuckle and remove the upper ball socket.
10. With the aid of a special socket, remove the threaded sleeve in the top flange of the yoke.

Installation

1. Assemble the lower ball socket into the knuckle with a press and ram or a puller tool arrangement, making sure that the ball socket is firmly seated against the knuckle. Install the snap ring on the 4 x 4 application.
2. Assemble the upper ball socket into the knuckle with a press and ram or a puller type tool arrangement, making sure that the ball socket is firmly seated against the knuckle. *NOTE: Use a .0015 inch feeler gauge blade between the socket and knuckle. The blade should not enter at the minimum area of contact.*
3. Install new threaded sleeve into the top flange of the yoke, leaving approximately two threads exposed.
4. Install the knuckle assembly to the yoke, using a new nut on the lower ball socket stud. Torque the lower nut to 80 ft. lbs.
5. With the use of a special socket, torque the threaded sleeve to 50 ft. lbs. in the upper yoke flange.
6. Install the top ball socket stud nut and torque to 100 ft. lbs. Align the cotterpin holes between the stud and the castellated nut. Do not loosen nut to align the holes. Install the cotter pin.
7. Assemble the tie rod to the steering arm.
8. Assure that slingers are properly installed on the axle shaft and install the shaft into the housing.
9. Position the spindle over the axle end with the bronze bushing in place.
10. Install the backing plate and torque the nuts to 30 ft. lbs.
11. Install the hub and wheel assembly, and lower the vehicle.

Checking Ball Sockets For Looseness

To check the ball sockets for excessive looseness, raise the vehicle and attach a dial indicator to the lower yoke or axle tube and set the indicator against the knuckle or lower ball socket, with a loaded pressure so as to read in both directions. Grasp the wheel at the top and bottom and move the wheel inward and outward. If the total indicator reading exceeds .020 inch, both the upper and lower ball sockets should be replaced.

Front Drive Locking Hubs

Two types of locking hubs are used: manual and Lock-O-Matic. Manual locking hubs are either engaged or disengaged, depending on how they are set. Lock-O-Matic hubs, when in "free" position, automatically engage axle and wheel when forward torque is applied by the axle shaft. Thus, whenever front wheel drive is disengaged at the transmis-

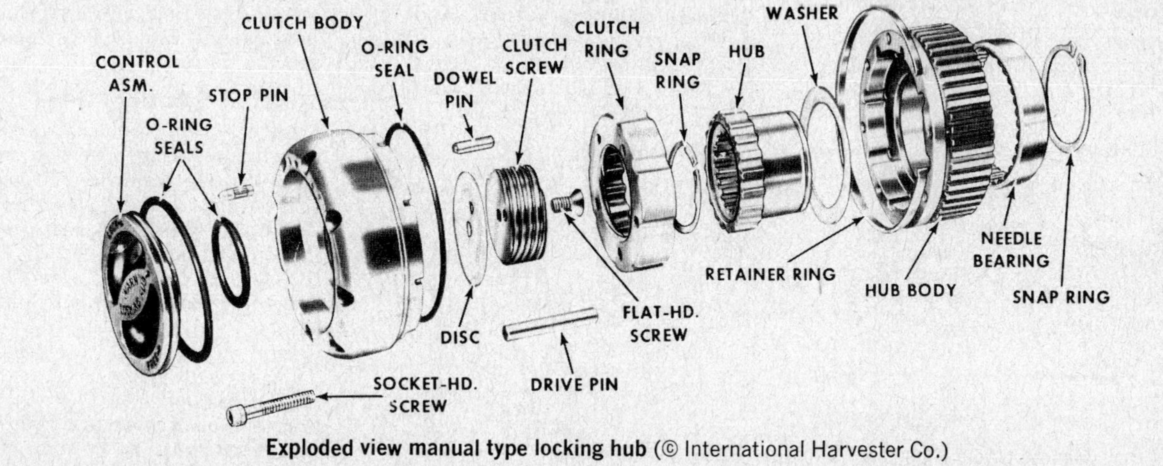

Exploded view manual type locking hub (© International Harvester Co.)

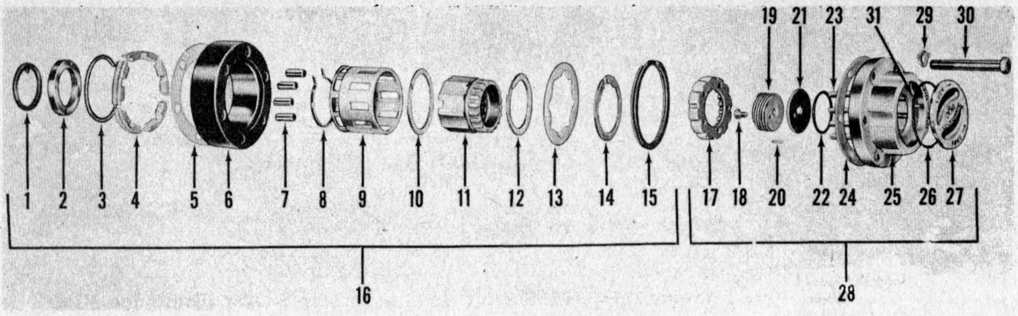

1 Washer, spindle lock
2 Shoe, drag
3 Spring, friction shoe
4 Shoe, friction
5 Gasket
6 Body, hub
7 Roller
8 Spring, centering
9 Cage, roller
10 Ring, lock
11 Hub, axle shaft
12 Ring, lock
13 Washer, thrust
14 Ring, lock
15 Ring, lock
16 Body, hub assembly
17 Ring, clutch
18 Screw, flat head
19 Screw, clutch
20 Pin, dowel
21 Disc
22 "U" ring, oil seal
23 Pin, drive
24 Gasket, clutch
25 Body, clutch
26 "U" ring, oil seal
27 Control, assembly
28 Body, clutch assembly
29 Washer, lock
30 Bolt
31 Pin, stop

Exploded view Lock-O-Matic hub (© International Harvester Co.)

sion, the wheels free wheel. "Lock" position is required only when engine braking control on the front wheel is desired.

Front Locking Hubs Removal

1. Bend up tabs on mounting bolt lock washers.
2. Remove six (eight) mounting bolts using a thin-walled socket or appropriate hex wrench (externally splined type).
3. When clutch body is lifted off, immediately tilt it up so that the drive pins do not fall out.
4. Remove lock ring holding hub body onto axle shaft and pull off hub body.
5. Remove drag shoe (Lock-O-Matic only) from axle spindle by loosening hex-head set screw and unscrew drag shoe.
6. To install, reverse the above procedure.

Steering Linkage

See specifications at the beginning of this section for steering alignment specifications.

Tie Rods

Tie rods are of three-piece construction: rod and two end assemblies. The end assemblies are threaded into the end of the tie rod and adjustment is made by turning them either in or out to shorten or lengthen the tie rod. When tightening the clamp it is important to make sure that the end assembly is threaded in far enough so that the clamping action of the clamp is right over the end pieces. Ball studs are integral in the end assemblies.

When disconnecting ball studs, loosen ball stud nut, then strike the nut with one hammer while another larger hammer is backing up the nut.

STEERING GEAR

For manual steering gear overhaul, see the General Repair Section.

Steering Gear Removal

1. Loosen collar clamp at bottom of steering wheel column.
2. Remove nut or loosen clamp bolt which secures steering arm to lever shaft, removing steering arm from lever shaft using a suitable puller if necessary.
3. Remove mounting bolts and steering gear assembly.
4. To install, reverse the above procedure, taking special care not to bind steering column if there is no universal joint.

Steering Gear Adjustment

Twin Stud Levershaft Type

1. Free steering gear of all load by disconnecting drag link from steering arm and loosening bracket clamp on steering gear jacket tube.
2. To adjust end play on cam (ball thrust bearings), loosen lock nut and adjusting screw, then unscrew four upper cover (steering column) bolts.
3. Remove (cut) or add shims, replacing and tightening down upper cover to test drag. Drag should be just slight enough so that steering wheel can be moved from lock to lock with one finger.
4. To adjust lever shaft cams for backlash, place steering wheel in middle (straight-forward) position and turn adjusting screw until very slight drag is felt through mid-position range.
5. Tighten lock nut and give final test for drag.
6. Install drag link onto levershaft and tighten clamp on steering gear jacket tube.

Triple Roller Steering Gear

1. To check cam preload, disconnect linkage from steering arm and turn steering wheel through entire range, noting lash area.
2. Check the preload in lash area. It should be 7-13 inch-pounds.
3. If adjustment is necessary, drain lubricant and remove four lower cover bolts.
4. Remove top shim with a knife, being careful not to mutilate remaining shims.
5. Replace lower cover and tighten bolts to 13-22 ft. lbs. torque.

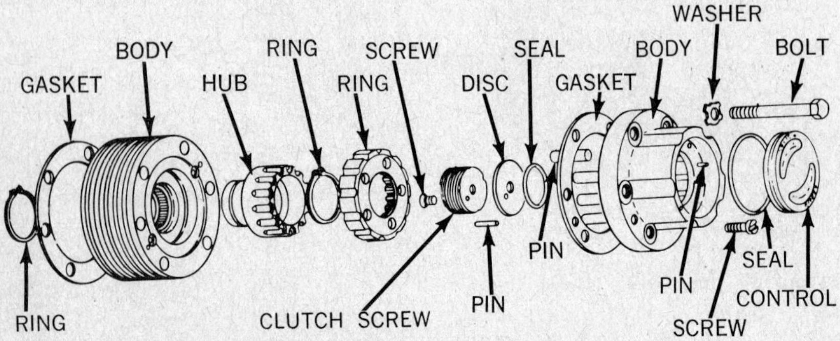

Manual type locking hub (© International Harvester Co.)

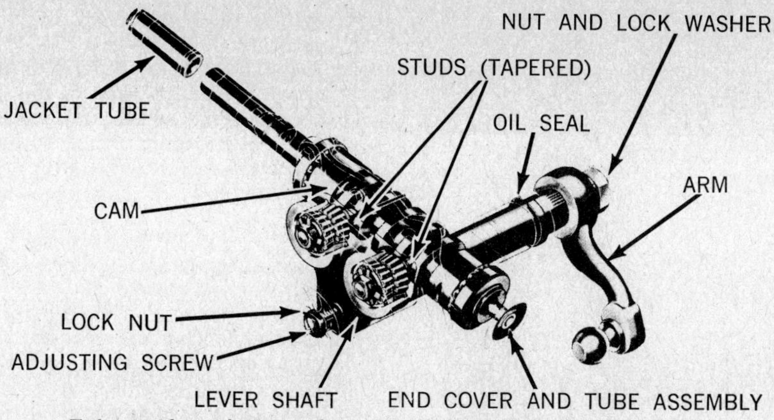

Twin stud levershaft steering gear (© International Harvester Co.)

6. Recheck preload and repeat above procedure if necessary.
7. Refill with SAE multi-purpose type gear lubricant.
8. To adjust levershaft, raise the vehicle and centralize the steering.
9. Rotate the steering 180° through center and check preload:
   S-161: 2-3⅜ lbs.
   S-108, S-165: 1 11/16-3¼ lbs.
   S-109: 2⅝-3⅞ lbs.
10. To adjust:
    a. Loosen lock nut.
    b. Turn slotted adjusting screw clockwise to increase preload; counterclockwise to decrease.
    c. when preload is within specifications, hold adjusting screw and tighten lock nut to 16-20 ft. lb.

Cam (Worm) and Roller Type

1. Disconnect linkage from pitman arm and drain lubricant.
2. Loosen locknut (1) at housing side cover, then turn adjusting screw (6) counterclockwise one turn to assure release of levershaft preload.
3. Turn steering wheel tube to about center of travel and check bearing preload (should register 9/16 to 1⅛ ft. lbs. @ 9″ radius).
4. If preload needs adjustment, drain lubricant and remove four housing cover bolts and housing.
5. Remove one shim.
6. Replace housing cover and bolts, torquing bolts to 18-22 ft. lbs.
7. Check preload and repeat the above procedure if necessary.
8. Adjust levershaft preload by turning adjusting screw (6). Correct levershaft preload is ¾ to 1¼ ft. lbs. @ 9″ radius (over cam preload).
9. Refill with SAE-90 SP type lubricant.

STEERING GEAR IDENTIFICATION CHART

I.H. Code No.	I.H. Designation	Description
05031	S-31	TD-67 Ross, Manual Aluminum Case
05044	S-44	TD-70 Ross, Manual Aluminum Case
05063	S-63	TE-70 Manual
05165	S-165	#378 Gemmer, Manual
05219	S-219	HPS 52 Ross, Power Not Integral
05236	S-236	M-39 Sheppard, Power Vickers Pump, Gear Division
05243	S-243	HPS 70 Ross, Power Not Integral
05261	S-261	HF 64 Ross, Integral Power Gear
05267	S-267	M-39 Sheppard, Power Vickers Pump, Belt Driven
05268	S-268	M-39 Sheppard, Power Eaton Pump, Belt Driven
05270	S-270	M-491 Sheppard, Power Eaton Pump, Belt Driven
05271	S-271	M-59 Sheppard, Power Eaton Pump, Belt Driven
05272	S-272	M-491 Sheppard, Power Vickers Pump, Gear Driven
05273	S-273	M-59 Sheppard, Power Vickers Pump, Gear Driven
05276	S-276	HF 54 Ross, Integral Power Gear
05277	S-277	HF 64 Ross, Integral Power Gear
05283	S-283	M-492 Sheppard, Power Vickers Pump, Belt Driven
05284	S-284	M-492 Sheppard, Power Vickers Pump, Gear Driven
05285	S-285	M-49 Sheppard, Power Vickers Pump, Belt Driven
05286	S-286	M-592 Sheppard, Power Eaton Pump, Belt Driven
05287	S-287	M-592 Sheppard, Power Vickers Pump, Gear Driven
05290	S-290	M-39 Sheppard, Power Dual—Belt Driven Pump
05291	S-291	M-39 Sheppard, Power Dual—Gear Driven Pump
05293	S-293	M-392 Sheppard, Power Eaton Pump, Gear Driven
05296	S-296	M-392 Sheppard, Dual Power Eaton Pump, Belt Driven
05297	S-297	M-392 Sheppard, Dual Power Vickers Pump, Gear Driven
05298	S-298	M-292 Sheppard, Dual Power Vickers Pump, Gear Driven
05299	S-299	HF 54 Ross, Integral Power Gear
05301	S-301	HF 64 Ross, Integral Power Gear
05302	S-302	HF 64 Ross, Integral Power Gear
05311	S-311	M-292 Sheppard, Dual Power Vickers Pump, Belt Driven
05312	S-312	M-392 Sheppard, Dual Power Vickers Pump, Belt Driven
05320	S-320	HF 64 Ross, Power Vickers Pump, Belt Driven
05321	S-321	HF 64 Ross, Power Vickers Pump, Belt Driven
05322	S-322	HF 64 Ross, Power Vickers Pump, Gear Driven
05323	S-323	HF 64, Ross, Power Vickers Pump, Gear Driven
05325	S-325	HF 64 Ross, Dual Power Vickers Pump, Gear Driven
05326	S-326	HF 64 Ross, Power Gear Driven Pump
05327	S-327	M-39 Sheppard, Power Gear Driven Pump
05329	S-329	HF 64 Ross, Power Eaton Pump, Belt Driven

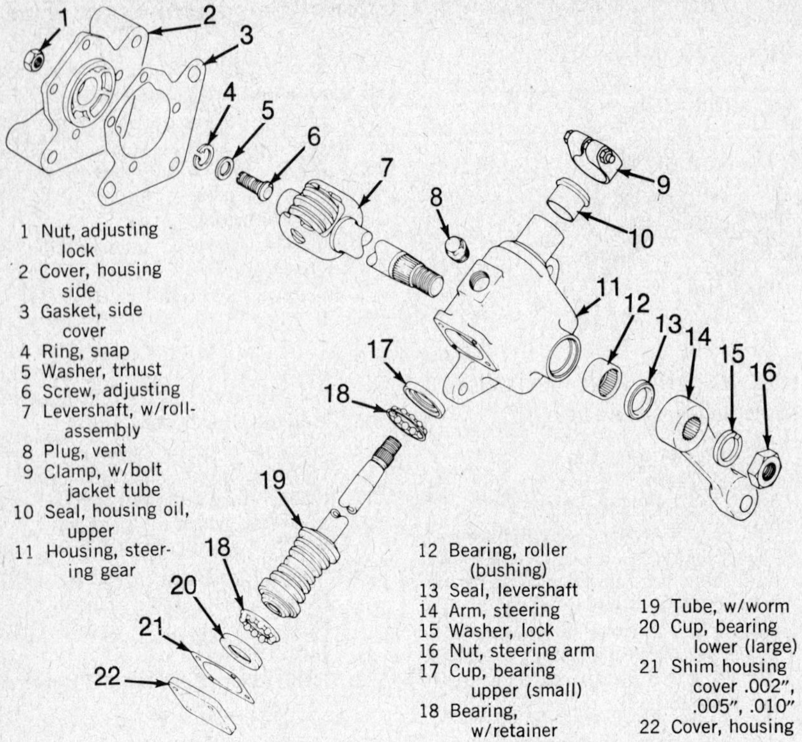

Cam (worm) and roller type steering gear (© International Harvester Co.)

Recirculating Ball Type

Worm Bearing Adjustment

1. Raise the vehicle and disconnect the linkage from the pitman arm.
2. Loosen the adjuster lock nut and turn the worm bearing adjuster plug clockwise.
3. Using a spring scale attached to the steering wheel, pull at a right angle to the wheel spoke, and measure the pull required to keep the wheel moving.
4. Turn the adjuster plug until a pull of 14-18 in. lbs. is obtained on the spring scale.
5. Tighten the adjuster plug lock nut and recheck worm bearing preload. Readjust if necessary.

Pitman Shaft Preload Adjustment

1. Center the steering wheel by turning wheel from the extreme right to the extreme left position, counting the exact number of turns.
2. Return the steering wheel to the exact half-way position and mark the wheel.
3. Loosen the preload adjuster lock nut and turn the adjuster clockwise until all lash between the gears is removed.
4. Tighten the locknut and as outlined previously, with the aid of a spring scale, pull the steering wheel through the center position. The pull pressure should be 24-30 in. lbs.
5. After all adjustments have been made, reconnect the steering linkage to the pitman arm. Lower the vehicle.

Steering Wheel Alignment

1. Set front wheels in a straight-ahead position. This can be checked by driving the vehicle a short distance on a flat surface to determine steering wheel position when vehicle is following a straight path.
2. Raise vehicle and check number of turns required from center point to extreme right and left. The number of turns should be the same in each direction.
3. If step 2 moves wheels off of straight-ahead, loosen adjusting sleeve clamps on both left and right-hand tie rods, then turn both sleeves an equal number of turns in the same direction to bring gear back on high point.

Power Steering Gear

For overhaul of power steering systems, see General Repair Section.

In-Line Booster Removal

1. Disconnect and plug hydraulic lines from valve and cylinder unit.
2. Loosen clamp bolts and disconnect cylinder link from cylinder.
3. Remove nut and lockwasher from piston rod and remove rod from frame bracket.
4. Loosen clamp bolt and unscrew cylinder assembly from pivot on relay.
5. Installation is the reverse of the above procedure. Be sure to center steering wheel and wheels before tightening clamp bolts of cylinder link. Bleed hydraulic system.

Hydraulic Cylinder Removal

1. Disconnect hydraulic lines from cylinder and plug lines.
2. Unbolt piston rod from frame bracket, noting approximate position of clamp.
3. Disconnect cylinder assembly from steering linkage.
4. Installation is the reverse of the above procedure. Approximate original position of clamp on piston rod, center adjusting steering wheel if necessary.

Separate Control Valve Removal

1. Disconnect and plug hydraulic lines from control valve.
2. Loosen clamp bolts at each end of control valve and remove valve.
3. Installation is the reverse of removal. Since the control valve in this type of power steering system serves, in a sense, as a relay arm, it must be adjusted to center the steering wheel for straight-forward running. Tighten clamp bolts after adjustment is made.

Hydraulic Pump Removal

1. Disconnect hydraulic lines at pump. When hoses are disconnected, secure them in a raised position to prevent leakage. Plug fittings of pump.
2. Remove drive pulley attaching nut.
3. Loosen bracket-to-pump mounting bolts, and remove pump belt.
4. Slide pulley from shaft. **CAUTION: Do not hammer pulley off shaft as this will damage the pump.**
5. Remove bracket-to-pump bolts and take off pump assembly.
6. Installation is the reverse of the above removal procedure. Do not tighten mounting bolts or pulley nut until installation is complete. Move pump until belt is tight, then tighten mounting bolts. Tighten pulley attaching nut last, torquing to 35-45 ft. lbs.

Power Steering Gear Adjustments

Semi-Integral Valve Toggle Type Thrust Bearing Adjustment

1. Free steering gear of load by disconnecting drag link.
2. Turn gear off center to free stud in the cam groove.

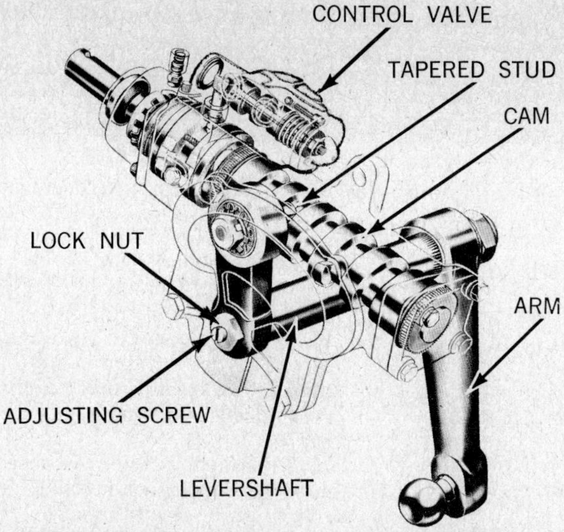

Power steering gear with toggle type integral valve
(© International Harvester Co.)

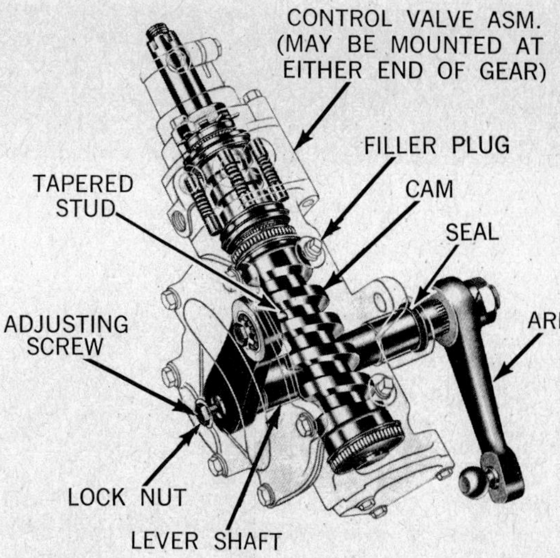

Model S36 power steering gear with integral concentric valve (© International Harvester Co.)

3. Remove yoke and joint assembly from stub shaft.
4. Remove key from stub shaft.
5. Remove upper cover.
6. Reassemble actuator housing screws with a 3/8" thick spacer under each head to hold actuator and cam assembly in the gear.
7. Remove the adjusting nut, lock washer, thrust washer and thrust housing.
8. Clean threads on nut and camshaft so that nut can be run freely by hand.
9. Reassemble nut, washers, and bearing.
10. Tighten nut to 10 ft. lb., then back off 10-20°. Bend locknut.
11. Attach cover and other parts.

Stud in Cam Groove Adjustment

1. Tighten side cover adjusting screw until a very slight drag can be felt when turning through mid-position. If no drag is felt, remove shims until it can be felt. Back off adjusting nut 1/16 turn and lock.
2. If a drag can be felt without removing shims, it will be necessary to add shims, then remove enough shims to reestablish a very slight drag.
3. After adjustment, back off nut 1/16 turn and lock.

Fully Integral Valve Type Adjustment

Sector Shaft

1. Adjust the screw in the side cover to provide a 15-20 in. lb. torque at the input shaft as the gear is moved 90 degrees either side of center.
2. Back out the adjusting screw one turn and note the torque required to move the input shaft through 90 degrees each side of center.
3. Move the adjusting screw in to provide a rise in torque of 2-4 in. lb. at a point 45 degrees off center after the jam nut is locked at 20-25 ft. lbs.

NOTE: Input torque of the completely assembled gear unit less oil, should not exceed 15 in. lbs. over full travel of 95 degrees at the output shaft.

Valve Thrust Bearings

NOTE: The upper housing must be removed for this adjustment procedure.

1. Tighten the adjusting nut until all play is removed from the bearings and zero preload exists.
2. Back off the nut approximately 20 degrees and bend one tang of the lock washer into a matching slot in the adjusting nut.
3. Check for free rotation of the valve on the shaft and for any perceptible end play. The assembly should rotate at 3-5 in. lbs.

Pressure Relief Valve

1. Install a suitable pressure gauge in the line between the pump and the steering valve pressure port.
2. Actuate the steering to provide full travel to the wheel stops and note the pressure reading on the gauge.
3. Adjust the pressure relief screw in a clockwise direction to provide a pressure of at 400 psi below the maximum operating pressure.

NOTE: Care should be exercised not to hold the pressure for more than 15 seconds, while the adjustment is being made or damage to the pump from excess heat can result.

4. Repeat the above procedure for the other direction of steering.

Steering Gear Removal

Full and Semi-Integral Steering Gear

1. Remove horn button from steering wheel. Unscrew retaining screws and remove base plate assembly. Remove steering wheel nut.
2. Using a suitable puller, remove steering wheel.

NOTE: Where the steering column is the jointed type, the steering column and wheel need not be removed. Loosen nut on steering column shaft collar and remove steering column shaft from gear. Retain woodruff key.

3. Using suitable puller, remove pitman arm from levershaft.
4. Identify hydraulic connecting lines by tagging and marking the valve ports to which they are connected. Disconnect hydraulic

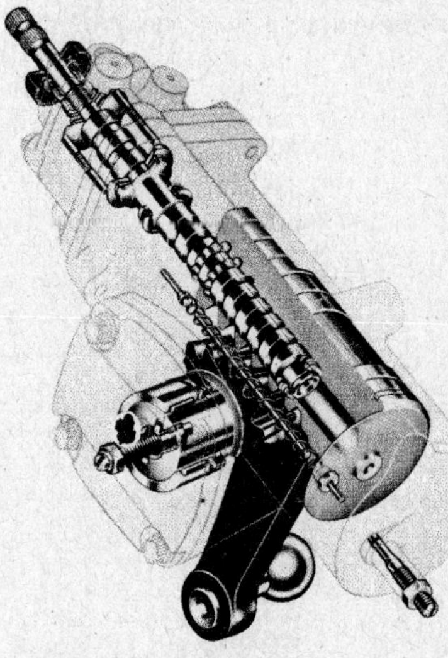

Types S276 and 299 integral power steering gear
(© International Harvester Co.)

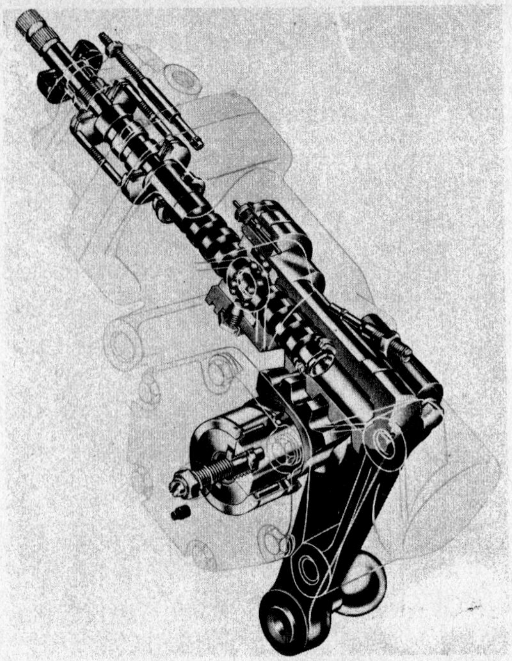

Types S261, 277, 301, 302, 320, 322, 323 and 325 integral power steering gear (© International Harvester Co.)

lines from valve. Plug all openings.

5. Remove mounting flange bolts and remove gear from chassis.
6. To install, mount steering gear in chassis and fasten securely.
7. Place woodruff key in stud end of steering gear and install collar of steering column shaft. Secure with bolt and nut.
8. Center steering gear. Center steering wheel. Set front wheels straight ahead.
9. Connect drag link to ball on steering arm.
10. Install steering arm on levershaft of gear. If arm does not line up with splines of shaft, turn steering wheel to the right or left 1/4 turn until it does.
11. Secure arm to levershaft with lockwasher and nut. Tighten nut to 250 ft. lbs.
12. Install hydraulic lines to control valve.
13. Fill the steering gear housing with the specified lubricant on the semi-integral power steering units.
14. Fill the Power steering reservoir with the recommended fluid and bleed the system.

Output Shaft Preload Adjustment

Integral Rotary Valve Type

1. Position steering in the straight-ahead position. Check for lash by moving steering wheel. If there is steering wheel movement without moving the steering arm, over-center adjustment must be made.
2. Disconnect steering arm and remove horn ring.
3. Position steering wheel at center of travel, then turn 1/2 turn off center.
4. Using an inch pound torque wrench and socket on the steering wheel retaining nut, determine the torque required to rotate the shaft slowly through a 20-degree arc. Turn gear to center and take a second reading. If second torque reading is 4-8 inch pounds in excess of first reading, no preload adjustment is necessary.
5. If adjustment is required, loosen adjuster screw locknut and turn screw until second reading exceeds first reading by 4-8 inch pounds.
6. Tighten locknut while holding adjusting screw in place to 27-37 ft. lbs. torque.
7. Recheck torque reading after adjustment is made.
8. Install steering arm, tightening nut to 120-125 ft. lbs. torque.
9. Install horn ring.

Steering Gear Removal

Horizontal Output Shaft Type

1. Apply parking brake and raise front of vehicle. Place drip pan under steering gear.
2. Position front wheels straight-ahead and tie steering wheel in centered position.
3. Disconnect and plug hydraulic lines from gear. Tag the lines for identification.
4. Remove nut and lockwasher securing steering arm to output shaft and remove arm from shaft with a suitable puller.
5. Remove lower flexible coupling clamp bolt.

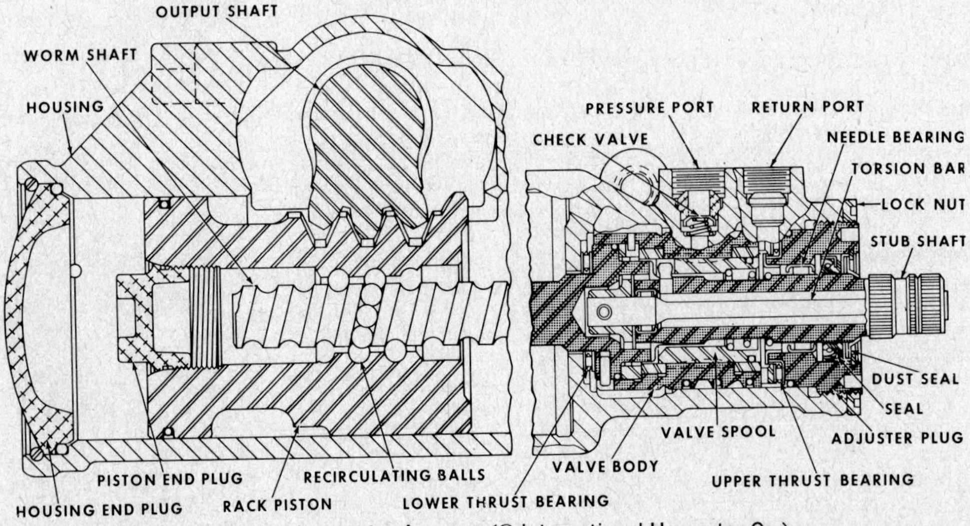

Rotary valve type power steering gear (© International Harvester Co.)

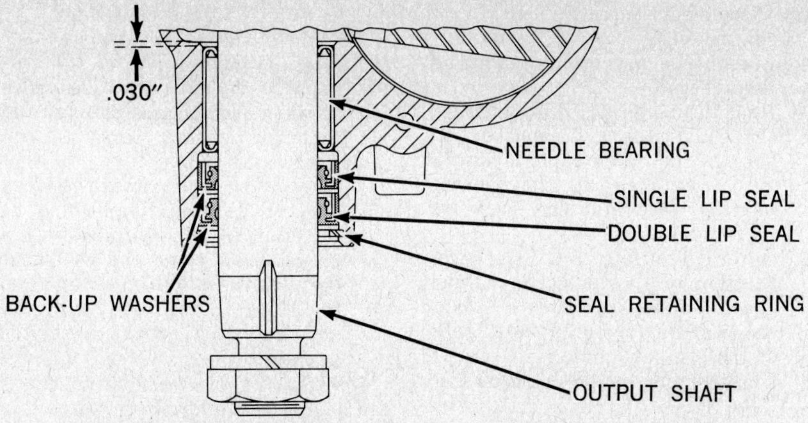

Correct installation of output shaft seal and bearing S281 and 282
(© International Harvester Co.)

6. Remove steering gear mounting bolts and remove gear from chassis.
7. To install, set gear assembly on center and position gear in chassis.
8. Insert gear stub shaft into lower flexible coupling and install and tighten gear mounting bolts to 55-60 ft. lbs. torque.
9. Install and tighten lower flexible coupling bolt clamp to 30-35 ft. lbs. torque.
10. With steering wheel centered and front wheels straight ahead, place steering arm on output shaft by matching master serrations of arm with shaft. Secure arm to shaft with lockwasher and nut, tightening nut to 120-125 ft. lbs. torque. Untie steering wheel.
11. Remove plugs and connect hydraulic lines to proper ports, tightening connections to 20-30 ft. lbs. torque.
12. Fill power steering system with fluid and start engine. Bleed system.
13. Check system for operation and leaks.
14. Remove drip pan and lower vehicle.

Steering Gear Removal

Vertical Output Shaft Type

1. Follow Steps 1 through 6 of the horizontal shaft gear removal above, leaving out Step 2 (centering and tying steering wheel). Disconnect battery cables, remove battery and battery box from chassis to permit gear removal.
2. To install, follow Steps 7 through 11 of horizontal output shaft gear installation described above.
3. Install battery box, battery and cables.
4. Follow Steps 12 through 14 of horizontal output shaft installation described above.

Power System Bleeding

1. Fill pump reservoir to correct level with fluid.
2. Start engine and turn steering wheel through entire travel two or three times. This will permit air to escape and be replaced with fluid.
3. Check fluid level and refill if necessary.

CLUTCH

NOTE: Due to the various medium and heavy duty truck models and different power combinations used, the clutch operating clearances and specifications are given in the owner-operator manual, accompaning each truck. The clutch release bearing may be actuated by mechanical, hydraulic, or a combination of air over hydraulic means, and for this reason the owner-operator manual should be referred to regarding the free travel and pedal height measurement for the particular model being serviced.

Hydraulic Clutch Adjustment

Light Duty Vehicles

1. Check clutch pedal height. If it is not approximately 7¾" from

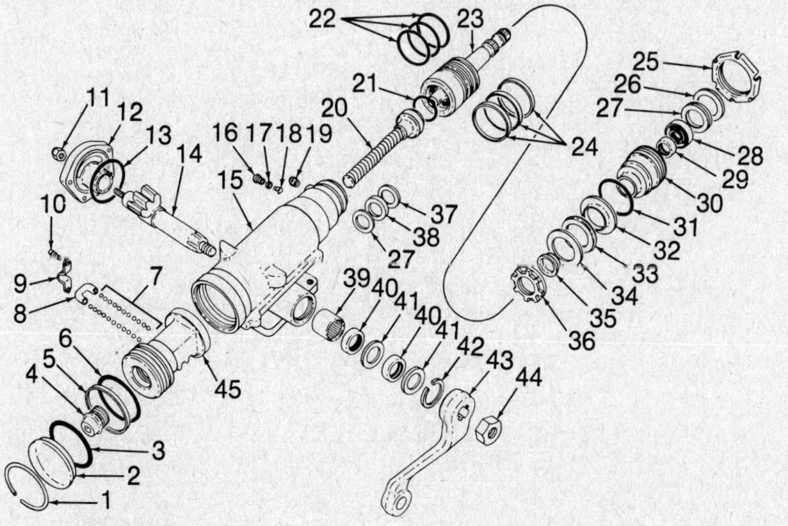

1 Ring, retaining
2 Plug, housing end
3 Seal, O-ring
4 Plug, rack piston end
5 Ring, rack piston
6 O-Ring, rack piston backu-up
7 Ball, recirculating
8 Guide, ball return
9 Clamp, ball return guide
10 Screw, clamp
11 Nut, lock output shaft adjuster
12 Cover, housing side
13 Seal, O-ring side cover
14 Shaft, output
15 Housing, gear
16 Seat, pressure connector
17 Valve, poppet check
18 Spring, poppet check valve
19 Seat, return connector
20 Shaft, worm
21 Seal, O-ring
22 O-Ring, valve body back-up
23 Valve, control
24 Ring, valve body
25 Nut, lock adjuster plug
26 Ring, retainer
27 Seal, dust
28 Seal, oil
29 Bearing, Needle
30 Plug, adjuster
31 Seal, O-ring
32 Race, thrust bearing, upper
33 Bearing, thrust upper
34 Race, thrust bearing, upper
35 Retainer, thrust bearing
36 Spacer, thrust bearing
37 Race, thrust bearing, lower
38 Bearing, thrust lower
39 Bearing, needle
40 Seal, output shaft
41 Washer, back-up
42 Ring, seal retaining
43 Arm, steering
44 Nut, steering arm retaining
45 Rack piston

Integral rotary valve type power steering gear (© International Harvester Co.)

the floorboard (measured at right angles from floorboard), loosen two bolts on the clutch pedal stop bracket and move bracket either way until proper pedal height is achieved. Tighten bracket mounting bolts.

2. Clutch pedal push rod to master cylinder piston clearance is adjusted by loosening the locknut on the pushrod and turning the rod either in or out until 3/16″ pedal stroke is obtained before clutch pedal push rod contacts master cylinder. Tighten locknut on pushrod and recheck pedal stroke.
3. Release bearing to clutch lever (finger) clearance is adjusted at the slave cylinder pushrod. Measure stroke of clutch pedal required to produce contact of clutch release bearing to clutch release levers. If it is not 1⅞″ ± ⅛″, loosen locknut on slave cylinder pushrod and rotate pushrod either in or out until proper pedal travel is obtained. Tighten locknut on pushrod and recheck pedal free travel.

Medium and Heavy Duty Vehicles

1. Clutch pedal pushrod stroke adjustment is made by disconnecting clutch pedal from pushrod (remove yoke pin). Holding master cylinder pushrod out snugly against the stop in the end of the cylinder and making sure that the spring is holding the clutch pedal against its stop, adjust yoke on pushrod until yoke can be connected to pedal. Install yoke pin and cotter pin. Tighten locknut on yoke. A clutch pedal free travel of 5/16″ should result.
2. Clutch finger to bearing clearance is adjusted at the slave cylinder pushrod. Clutch pedal should travel 1½″ before clutch bearing makes contact with release fingers. Loosen locknut on slave cylinder pushrod and turn pushrod to obtain correct pedal travel. Tighten locknut and recheck pedal travel.

Mechanically Controlled Linkage or Cable Adjustment

Light Duty Vehicles

1. Measure and correct the clutch pedal height to approximately 9 inches. *NOTE: On some models it may be necessary to increase the clutch pedal height setting slightly over the amount specified, in order to obtain complete clutch release.*
2. Disconnect the return spring on release fork.
3. Loosen the nut on the cable or linkage rod.
4. Hold the pedal assembly against the pedal stop and lengthen or shorten the rod or cable to obtain zero clearance at the release bearing face and the pressure plate fingers.
5. After obtaining zero clerance, lengthen or shorten cable or linkage to obtain 3/32 inch between the bearing face and the fingers of the pressure plate.
6. Tighten nut on the cable or linkage rod.
7. Reconnect the return spring.

Medium and Heavy Duty Vehicles

External Adjustment

NOTE: Refer to the owner-operator manual for the correct free travel and pedal height for the particular model being serviced.

1. In general, the mechanically controlled clutch should have 1½ inch of free travel before the clutch begins to disengage.
2. Pedal clearance or free travel in the linkage must be sufficient to prevent the clutch from being partially disengaged. A clearance of ⅛ inch should be maintained between the yoke fingers and the release bearing wear pads.
3. Slave cylinder air assist units must have an average of ½ inch clutch release bearing travel for poper release.

Internal Adjustment

1. Remove the clutch housing inspection cover.
2. Inspect the running clearance between the release fork and the bearing housing for ⅛ inch clearance.
3. Inspect the clearance between the release bearing and the clutch brake (if equipped with a clutch brake), or the clearance between the clutch cover hub and the release bearing housing (if not equipped with a clutch brake).

NOTE: Gauges of proper thickness can be fabricated locally.

a. Vehicles with clutch brake—Weld ½ inch stock material to a handle to check the gap between the release bearing and the clutch brake assembly and use a ⅛ inch wire rod to check the release bearing to release lever clearance.
b. Vehicles with out clutch brake — Weld 19/32 inch stock material to a handle to check the gap between the release bearing and the clutch cover hub. The same ⅛ inch rod as used above, can be used to check the clearance between the release bearing and the release lever.

4. If the clearances are more or less than specified, readjust as follows:
   a. Rotate the engine flywheel until the adjusting ring lock is exposed. Remove the lock bolt and pry the lock free of the adjuster ring.

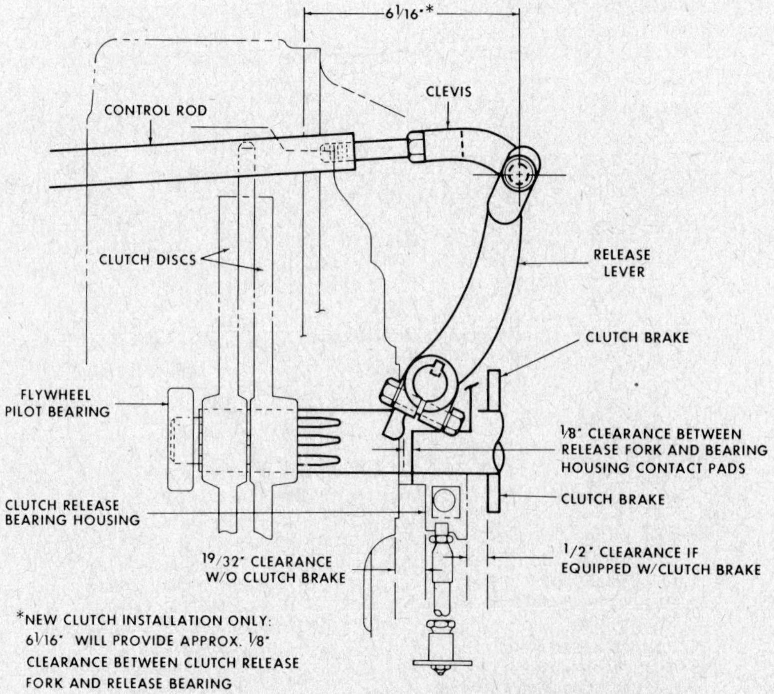

Clutch clearance heavy duty vehicles with two clutch discs
(© International Harvester Co.)

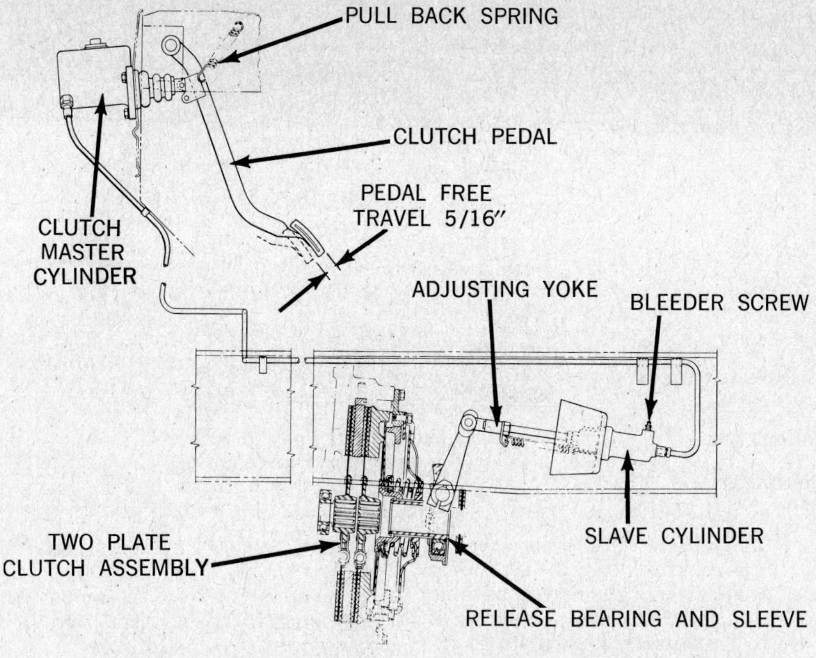

Clutch control diagram (hydraulic) (© International Harvester Co.)

CAUTION: Lock is spring loaded.

b. Release clutch by blocking the pedal in the depressed position.

c. Turn the clutch adjusting ring counterclockwise to move the release bearing housing towards the flywheel and clockwise to move the bearing housing away from the flywheel. *NOTE: Rotation of one lug position will move the release bearing housing approximately 1/32 inch.*

d. Re-engage the clutch and check clearance. Readjust as necessary.

e. Install the lock plate, bolt and washer, and install the clutch housing cover plate.

Clutch Master Cylinder Removal

1. Remove hydraulic line from master cylinder and remove yoke pins connecting pedal to master cylinder pushrod. On models with dual cylinders (brake-/clutch integral unit), disconnect brake hydraulic line, stoplight switch wire and brake pedal. If the fluid reservoir is separate from the cylinder unit, disconnect reservoir fluid line.
2. Remove cylinder assembly mounting bolts and remove cylinder.
3. To install, first mount the cylinder unit, then connect hydraulic lines.
4. Adjust clutch pedal as described above.
5. Bleed hydraulic clutch system.

Slave Cylinder Removal

1. Disconnect slave cylinder pushrod from clutch release lever.
2. Disconnect hydraulic line.
3. Unbolt and remove slave cylinder unit.
4. To install, reverse Steps 1 through 3.
5. Adjust clutch pedal as described above.
6. Bleed hydraulic clutch system.

Bleeding Hydraulic Clutch System

1. Fill fluid reservoir with hydraulic brake fluid.
2. Remove dust cover from bleeder screw on slave cylinder and open bleeder screw approximately ¾ turn.
3. Attach a short bleeder tube to bleeder screw and place the other end in clear container filled with brake fluid.
4. Pump clutch pedal slowly through full stroke repeatedly until only clear (no air bubbles) fluid flows from bleeder hose.
5. Tighten bleeder screw on down stroke of clutch pedal and remove bleeder tube. Replace rubber bleeder screw dust cover.
6. Refill fluid reservoir if necessary.

Clutch Removal

1. Remove transmission. Extreme care should be taken to support the transmission until it is completely removed so that the main shaft splines will clear the driven member. For transmission removal procedures see "Transmission—R&R" immediately following this section.
2. Remove flywheel housing cover.
3. Disconnect clevis yoke from clutch release lever.
4. Compress clutch assembly. On the 13″, 14″, 15″ and 10″ (9 spring) clutches, the pressure plate is drilled and tapped so that three retaining cap screws

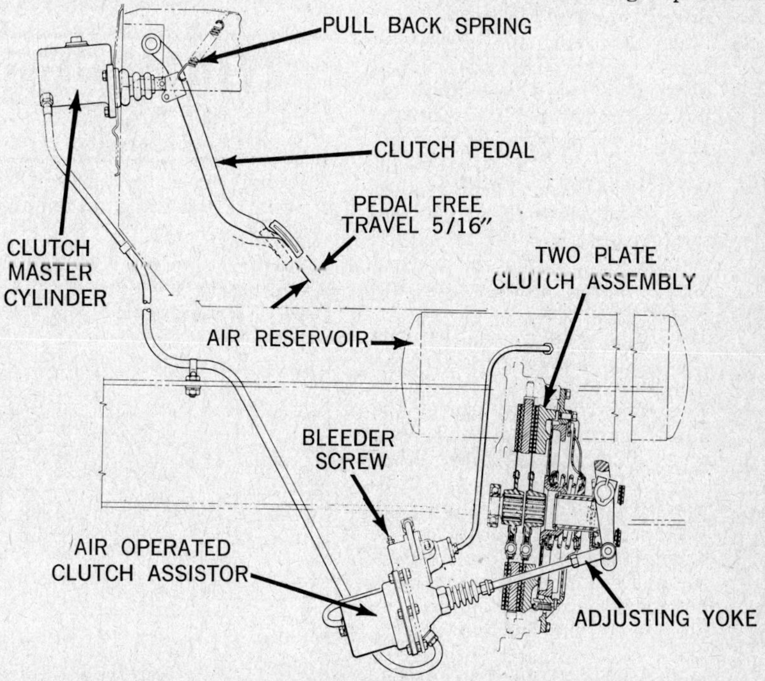

Clutch control diagram (combination hydraulic-air) (© International Harvester Co.)

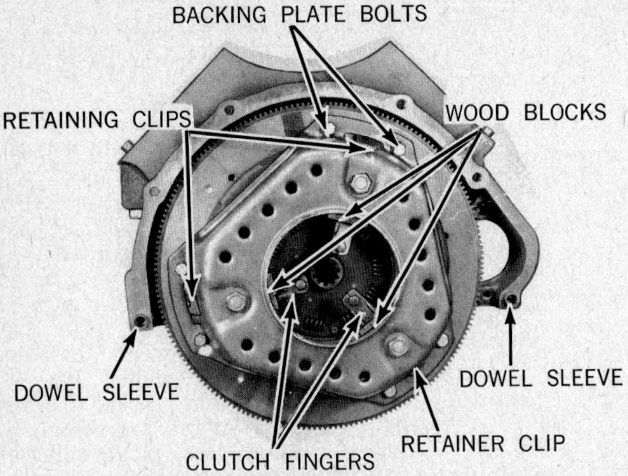

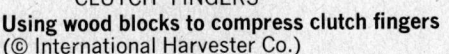

Using wood blocks to compress clutch fingers
(© International Harvester Co.)

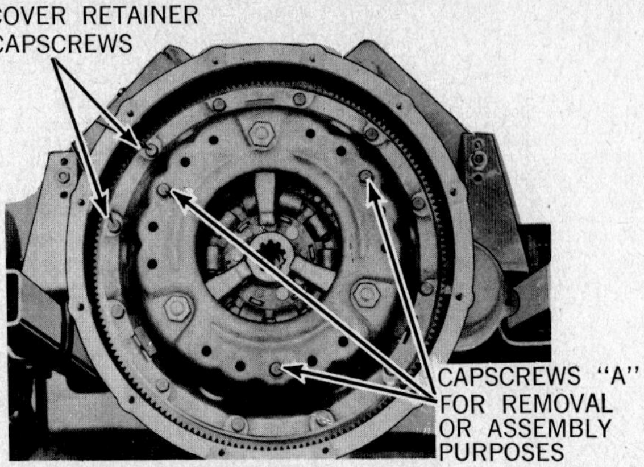

Clutch compressing cap screws
(© International Harvester Co.)

and flat washers may be installed. Tighten the cap screws until flat washers and cap screw heads are seated on the back plate. On the 11″, 12″ and 10″ (6 spring, open back plate type) clutches, three retaining spacers are used to hold the clutch assembly compressed during removal. Slightly loosen the back plate to flywheel mounting screws to wedge the retaining spacers into place. On the 10″ six spring (full back plate type) clutch, three 5/8″x3″x1/4″ hardwood blocks are used to compress the clutch during removal. Loosen back plate to flywheel retaining screws enough to wedge the blocks between the back plate inner flange and release fingers.

5. Remove back plate to flywheel screws and remove back plate assembly and driven disc.
6. When removing the clutch assembly, observe that the balance mark (spot of white paint) on the back plate flange is located as near as possible to the balance mark ("L") stamped on the flywheel face. These balance marks should be located in the same relative position at clutch installation. If there are no marks, scribe a line to indicate correct position.
7. To install clutch, position the clutch driven member so that the long portion of the hub is toward the rear (all except the 10″ 6 spring open back plate type, which may be fitted either way). Clutch must be compressed for correct installation.
8. Place clutch assembly over the driven member on the flywheel so that the balance mark (spot of white paint) is as near as possible to the flywheel balance mark ("L"). Loosely install two or three back plate to flywheel mounting screws.
9. Using a clutch aligning arbor or transmission main drive gear shaft to hold the driven member in place, complete installation of the remaining back plate to flywheel mounting screws and lockwashers. Tighten capscrews alternately and evenly.
10. Remove retaining capscrews, wood blocks or retaining spacers which were used to hold the clutch compressed.
11. Install transmission as described in "Transmission—R&R".
12. Connect linkage to clutch release lever.
13. Install flywheel housing cover.
14. If the vehicle is equipped with a hydraulic system, bleed the system and refill the reservoir with hydraulic fluid.
15. If the vehicle is equipped with the manual type linkage or cable, adjust as outlined.

TRANSFER CASE

Transfer cases may be mounted to the rear of the transmission and connected directly to the output shaft of the transmission by a coupler, or may be mounted to a crossmember and connected to the transmission by a driveshaft.

For transfer case overhaul procedures, see the General Repair Section.

Linkage and Cable Adjustment

Shifter rods connect the shift arms of the transfer case to the shift lever arms. Non-adjustable and adjustable links are used on the various models of vehicles. To insure the proper alignment of the rods to the arms, use the following procedure.

Linkage Adjustment

1. Place the shift lever in the neutral position.
2. Remove the shift control rod at the transfer case.
3. Assure that the shift arm of the transfer case is in the center or neutral position.
4. If the control rod is adjustable, position the trunnion or clevis to align with the hole in the shift arm of the transfer case.
5. If the control rod is non-adjusta-

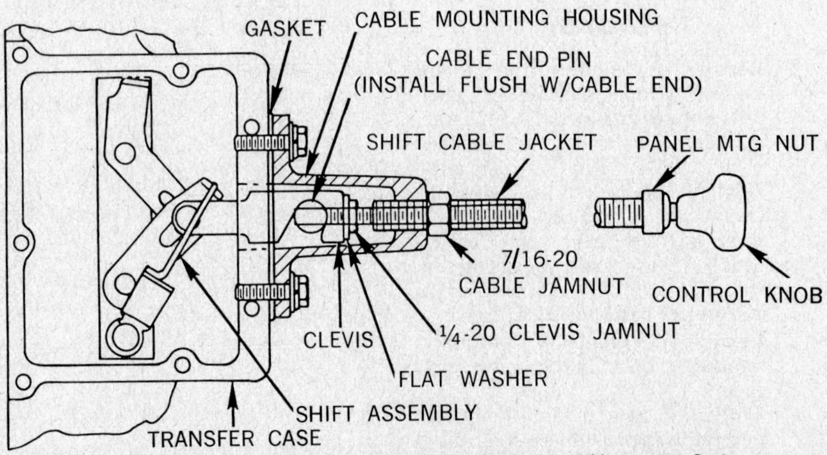

Exploded view shift cable control (© International Harvester Co.)

ble and the rod does not line up with the hole in the shift arm of the transfer case, replacement or bending will be necessary for the control rod.

6. Reconnect the control rod to the transfer case shift arm and check for proper operation.

Cable Adjustment

A pull on the cable will engage the gears. To disengage, merely push the control cable in. To adjust, follow this procedure.

1. Pull the control cable knob out approximately two inches and block in this position.
2. Loosen the cable mounting housing jam nut.
3. Remove the two cable mounting housing bolts.
4. Unscrew the cable mounting housing away from the transfer case housing.
5. Confirm the inner clevis is positioned in the engaged position.
6. Turn the cable housing down the cable jacket to a snug fit against the gasket on the transfer case mounting boss. Install the two retaining screws.
7. Turn the jam nut down the cable jacket and secure against the cable mounting housing.
8. Remove the control cable knob block and operate the cable assembly to check the shifter operation.

Cable Removal and Installation

Removal

1. Leave the control knob pushed in.
2. Loosen the cable jam nut at the cable mounting housing on the transfer case and turn it back to the end of the threads.
3. Remove the two bolts holding the cable mounting housing to the transfer case.
4. Unscrew the housing all the way to the jam nut.
5. Pull the cable mounting housing forward until the inner cable jam nut is clear.
6. Loosen the inner cable jam nut at the shift clevis and unhook the cable end pin from the clevis.
7. Position the shift cable to obtain working clearance.

Installation

1. Turn the jam nut and the cable mounting housing to the bottom of the thread end.
2. With the transfer case shifter assembly in the fully engaged position, install the cable mounting housing gasket to the case. *NOTE: The clevis is pulled out to engage.*
3. Connect the cable end pin to the shifter assembly and secure with the jam nut. *NOTE: Confirm that the pin is installed flush with the cable end.*
4. Block the control knob out approximately two inches.
5. Turn the cable mounting housing down the cable jacket to a snug fit against the gasket on the transfer case mounting boss.
6. Secure the cable mounting housing with the two mounting bolts to the transfer case.
7. Turn the jam nut down the cable jacket and lock against the cable mounting housing.
8. Remove the block from the shift control cable knob and operate the cable to check the shifter operation.

Transfer Case Removal and Installation

Frame Mounted

1. Drain the transfer case and disconnect the rear axle drive shaft at the transfer case.
2. Disconnect the front drive shaft at the transfer case.
3. Disconnect the speedometer cable, and indicator light switch wire, if equipped.
4. Disconnect the shift linkage. If erquipped with a shift cable, refer to the cable removal and installation outlined previously.
5. Place a transmission jack under the transfer case and remove the mounting bolts from the frame to case.
6. Remove the transfer case from the vehicle.
7. The installation of the transfer case is the reverse of removal.

Transmission Mounted

1. Disconnect the rear driveshaft at the transfer case and drain the case assembly.
2. Disconnect the front driveshaft at the transfer case.
3. Disconnect the speedometer cable and the indicator light switch wire, if equipped.
4. Disconnect the shift linkage or cable. If equipped with a shift cable, refer to the removal and installation of the cable outlined previously.
5. Place a transmission jack under the transfer case and remove the flange bolts holding the transfer case to the transmission.
6. Pull the transfer case rearward to disengage the transmission output shaft from the coupler.
7. Lower the transfer case and remove from the vehicle.
8. The installation of the transfer case is the reverse of removal.

MANUAL TRANSMISSION

For manual transmission overhaul procedures see the Manual Transmission General Repair Section.

Frame mounted transfer case typical
(© International Harvester Co.)

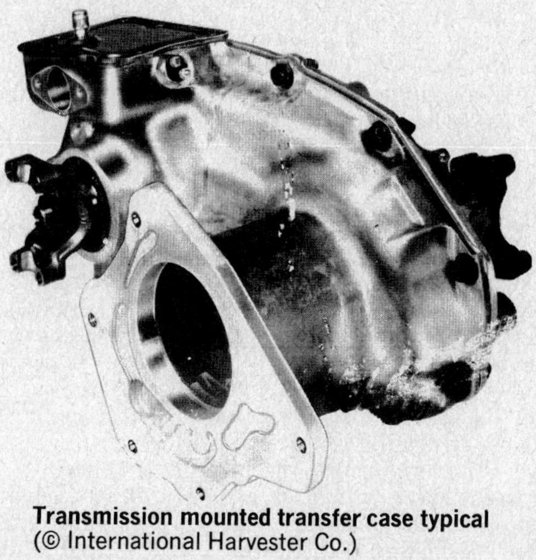

Transmission mounted transfer case typical
(© International Harvester Co.)

Shift Linkage

Different types of transmissions are used which may require the shift linkage to be either mounted in the transmission and controlled by a shift lever, or to have a shift lever mounted remotely with linkage rods connecting the lever to the transmission. No adjustment is provided when the linkage is mounted in the transmission. When the shift lever is remotely mounted, the connecting rods have adjustment provisions. The adjustments are made with the shift control and the transmission arms in the neutral position, and the control rods adjusted to enter either the transmission arms or the shift lever arms with a free fit. Normally the control rods are threaded and trunnions and jam nuts are used to position the rods.

Manual Transmission Removal

Removal and installation of manual transmissions will vary in detail, depending on which vehicle is being serviced. The following general procedure includes the basic steps common to all models.

1. Access to the transmission may be improved by removing cab floor panels.
2. Raise vehicle on a hoist or jack up and support with jack stands.
3. Drain the transmission lubricant.
4. Disconnect drive shaft at the transmission. If the vehicle is equipped with a transfer case which is not mounted directly to the transmission, disconnect the shaft between the transfer case and transmission at the yoke. If the vehicle is equipped with a transfer case which is mounted directly to the transmission, it must be removed with the transmission as a unit and the forward and rear drive shafts must be disconnected. Secure shaft out of the way with wire.
5. Disconnect shift linkage from transmission shift levers. If the vehicle is equipped with a transfer case which is mounted directly to the transmission, disconnect the shift linkage from the transfer case shift levers.
6. If the vehicle is equipped with a transmission mounted handbrake, disconnect the handbrake cable at the relay lever.
7. Disconnect speedometer cable from the transmission.
8. Remove the clutch slave cylinder from its mount. Do not disconnect the hydraulic line from the slave cylinder. Secure the push rod to the slave cylinder to avoid ejection of the internal components. Keeping the hydraulic system sealed eliminates the necessity of bleeding.
9. On some models it may be necessary to remove the starter motor.
10. Support the rear of engine by means of a hydraulic jack.
11. Remove the transmission mounting bolts and insulators at the engine rear crossmember. If possible, remove the rear engine crossmember. Remove gear shift lever and housing from top of transmission if applicable.
12. Attach suitable hoisting equipment or jack to transmission and raise enough to support the transmission assembly.
13. Remove top transmission to clutch housing bolts and install transmission guide pins.
14. Remove remaining transmission to clutch housing bolts.
15. Carefully pull transmission rearward, keeping it in line until the main drive gear shaft is clear of ther clutch. **CAUTION: Extreme care must be exercised to insure that the weight of the transmission does not rest on the hub of the clutch driven disc.**
16. Depending on vehicle model, either lift the transmission up through the floorboard and out the right door or lower it with a jack.
17. Installation is the reverse of the above procedure.
18. Fill transmission with fluid.

Auxiliary Transmission Linkage Adjustment

1. Disconnect the shift rods at the lever assembly.
2. Position the transmission shafts in neutral.
3. Position the shift control lever so that the slots in the rails are exactly opposite each other with the lever inclined to the rear.
4. Adjust each rod clevis until the pins enter the shift control rail and clevis easily.
5. Install the clevis pins and retainers.
6. Check the shift operation.

Auxiliary Transmission Removal and Installation

1. Drain the lubricant from the auxiliary transmission.
2. Remove the pins and retainers from the shift rods and remove the rods from the rails.
3. Disconnect the front drive shaft universal joint and tie out of the way.
4. Disconnect the rear drive shaft universal joint and tie the shaft out of the way.
5. Remove the speedometer cable, if equipped.
6. Remove the parking brake linkage from the output shaft parking brake drum.
7. Place a transmission jack under the auxiliary transmission, remove the mounting bolts, and remove the unit from the vehicle.
8. Installation is the reverse of removal.

AUTOMATIC TRANSMISSION

Identification

Two types of automatic transmissions are used in the I. H. vehicles. The models T-39, T-49 and T-409 use a cast iron case with a removable aluminum converter housing. The transmission model T-407 uses a complete aluminum case and converter housing, cast as a unit. The rear extension housings may differ from one transmission to another, due to the vehicle application of engine and drive train. Some models may use a parking brake mounted on the rear extension housing. All transmissions use a parking pawl type lock, controlled by the shift linkage. The selector lever may be mounted on the floor or on the steering column, along with an indicator quadrant for the gear position.

For automatic transmission overhaul procedures, see Automatic Transmission in the General Repair Section.

Transmision Models T-39, T-49, T-409

Removal

1. Raise the vehicle with a hoist.
2. Disconnect the fluid filler tube at the pan, and drain the fluid. Loosening the tube clip capscrew at the extension on the starting motor will permit rotating filler

Pilot stud location automatic transmission (© International Harvester Co.)

tube for transmission removal.
3. Disconnect the vacuum line at vacuum unit located at rear of transmission.
4. Disconnect the speedometer cable at speedometer adapter on transmission.
5. Disconnect the hand brake cable at drive shaft brake if chassis is so equipped.
6. Disconnect the shift linkage at manual shift lever on transmission.
7. Disconnect the two oil cooler lines on right side of transmission if chassis is so equipped.
8. Disconnect the drive shaft at transmission companion flange.

   NOTE: Wire the end of the drive shaft to the frame to permit transmission removal.
9. Place the hydraulic hoist with a suitable transmission lift cradle in position under the transmission oil pan. Adjust the hoist to align the cradle to the transmission oil pan flange so that the weight of the transmission case is supported by the hoist.
10. Remove the transmission case to converter housing upper capscrews and install two pilot studs into the capscrew holes.
11. Remove the transmission case to converter lower capscrews.
12. With the hydraulic hoist and cradle adjusted so the transmission case is in alignment with the converter housing, pull the transmission rearward with the hydraulic hoist to disengage the transmission from the converter housing and converter assembly. Lower transmission and remove from the vehicle.
13. To install, place two transmission pilot studs in the upper transmission to converter housing mounting screw holes.
14. Mount the transmission on a jack and position it under vehicle.
15. Rotate engine until the front pump drive lugs on the converter are in a vertical position.
16. Rotate the front pump until the slots in the pump drive gear are in a vertical position.
17. Apply lubricant similar to lubriplate to seal the surface of converter impeller cover hub.
18. Being extremely careful to align the turbine shaft splines with the turbine hub splines and the converter impeller lugs with the slots in the front pump drive gear, raise transmission and move it forward into the converter housing and converter.
19. Install the transmission to converter housing lower mounting screws. Remove two pilot studs and install upper mounting screws. Tighten all mounting screws securely.
20. Install oil cooler lines on the right side of the transmission if so equipped.
21. Connect the shift linkage at the manual shift lever on the transmission.
22. Connect the hand brake cable to the drive shaft brake if so equipped.
23. Connect the speedometer cable to the transmission.
24. Connect the vacuum line to the vacuum unit located at the rear of transmission.
25. Connect the fluid filler tube to the oil pan, tightening securely. Also tighten tube clip capscrews at the extension on the starter motor.
26. Connect the drive shaft to the transmission companion flange. Tighten mounting screws securely and lock with lock plates.
27. Lower vehicle to floor and fill transmission with type "A" automatic transmission fluid.
28. Road test vehicle to check performance and shift points.

Torque Converter Removal

1. Remove transmission as described above.
2. Disconnect and remove starter motor.
3. If vehicle has conventional chassis, remove floormat and transmission floor opening cover.
4. Install a rear engine support or support the rear weight of the engine with a jack.
5. Remove converter housing to crossmember mounting bolts, lower insulators and retainers.
6. Unbolt and remove rear engine crossmember.
7. Remove eight capscrews and lockwashers which attach converter housing to crankcase adapter and remove converter housing. On some models it may be necessary to lower the engine to provide clearance for converter removal.
8. Remove six nuts which attach the converter assembly to the flywheel assembly and remove converter.
9. To install, carefully place converter into position (do not damage bolt mounting threads) and install six nuts which attach converter to converter drive plate, but do not tighten nuts at this time.
10. After thoroughly cleaning crankcase converter housing adapter, install converter housing and engage the dowels being careful not to damage the dowels or the converter housing.
11. Install eight converter housing mounting capscrews and lockwashers.
12. Install rear engine crossmember.
13. Install upper and lower insulators and retainers, the converter to crossmember mounting bolts and lockwashers. Lower converter housing and engine. With insulators and retainers firmly seated, hand tighten bolts, then give bolts one-half additional turn and lock.
14. Remove rear engine support or jack.
15. If vehicle has conventional chassis, install floormat and transmission floor opening cover.
16. Install starter motor and wiring.
17. Install transmission as described above.
18. Rotate engine and converter assembly through two complete revolutions to center converter (to rotate, remove spark plugs and pry on drive plate ring gear).
19. Tighten converter to the converter drive plate attaching nuts.
20. Install converter housing adapter cover.

Transmission Fluid

1. Transmission fluid should be changed and band adjusted every 15,000 miles.
2. Remove converter housing front plate.
3. Remove one of the converter drain plugs, then rotate converter 180 degrees and remove other converter drain plug.
4. Disconnect fluid filler tube at the transmission pan.
5. Drain fluid and remove pan. Clean pan.
6. Connect filler tube to pan and tighten securely.
7. Install drain plugs in converter cover and tighten them to 7-10 ft. lbs. torque.
8. Install converter housing front plate.
9. Add five quarts of type "A" automatic transmission fluid through filler tube.
10. Run engine at idle (do not race) for about two minutes, then add five more quarts of fluid. Let engine idle until it reaches normal operating temperature.
11. Move selector lever through all positions, then place it in "P" (park). Check fluid level and add enough fluid to bring level up to the "F" (full) mark on indicator.

Front Band Adjustment

1. Drain fluid from transmission and remove pan (disconnect filler tube from pan).

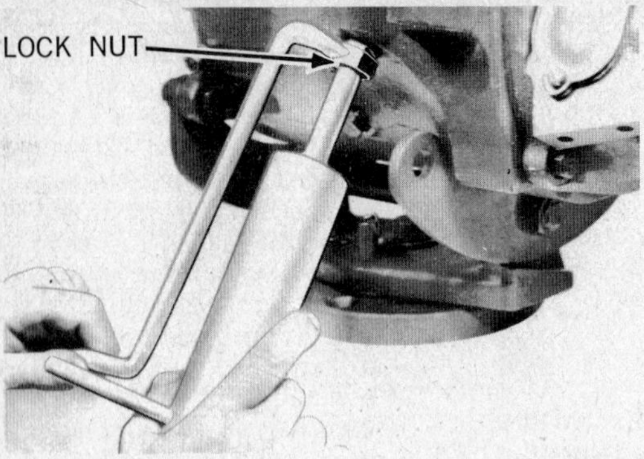

Adjust rear band (© International Harvester Co.)

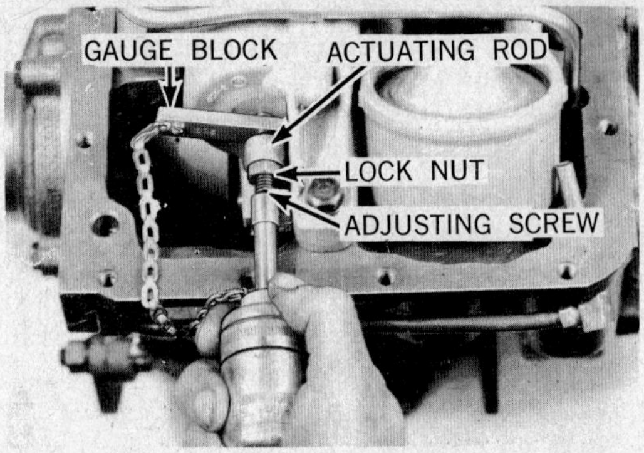

Adjusting front band (© International Harvester Co.)

2. Loosen front servo adjusting screw locknut two full turns and check the adjusting screw for free rotation.
3. Pull back on the actuating rod and insert gauge block of the front band adjusting tool (SE-1910) between the servo piston stem and adjusting screw. Tighten adjusting screw until adjusting tool handle overruns. Holding adjusting screw stationary, tighten locknut to 20-25 ft. lbs. torque. Remove gauge block.
4. Install fluid screen and pan, using a new gasket. Connect filler tube to pan.
5. Refill transmission as described above, adding new fluid if necessary.

Rear Band Adjustment

1. If vehicle is conventional model, remove floor mat and transmission cover plate from floor board.
2. Clean adjusting screw threads thoroughly and oil threads.
3. Loosen rear band adjusting locknut.
4. Using tool SE-1909, tighten adjusting screw until wrench overruns, at 10 ft. lbs. torque. *NOTE: If adjusting screw is tighter than overrun of wrench, loosen screw and retighten.*
5. Back off adjusting screw one and one-half turns, then hold adjusting screw stationary and tighten locknut to 25-40 ft. lbs. torque. CAUTION: **Severe damage may result if the adjusting screw is not backed off exactly one and one-half turns.**
6. Install transmission cover plate and floor mat to floor board.

Shift Linkage Adjustment

1. With engine off, disconnect the manual shift rod from the selector lever on the steering column and the transmission lever on the conventional chassis, or bellcrank on the Metro chassis.
2. Position selector lever in "D" and place transmission manual lever in the "D" detent (second from the top of the transmission).
3. Position the manual shift rod into the ball joint on the steering column. The opposite end of the rod should be installed in the transmission shift lever on the conventional chassis and secured with a washer and cotter pin. On the Metro chassis, the rod yoke should be positioned on the bellcrank and secured with the clevis pin, washer and cotter pin.
4. Tighten ball joint nut at the steering column lever.
5. Move the selector lever through all positions, checking the alignment of the pointer in all positions.

Kickdown Switch Adjustment

1. On the conventional chassis the kickdown switch is located in the toeboard under the throttle pedal. On the Metro chassis it is mounted on a bracket under the toeboard and operated by a pad welded to one of the throttle linkage rods.
2. Loosen two mounting nuts and turn them either direction until a clearance of 1/4" is obtained between switch and throttle pedal on the conventional chassis and between switch and throttle linkage pad on the Metro chassis.

Vacuum Control Adjustment

1. Connect a tachometer to the engine.
2. Remove the 1/8 inch pipe plug located on the left front of the transmission case. Install a pressure gauge line connection at this point, then connect a pressure gauge to the line and place gauge in cab.
3. Start engine and move selector lever to "D" (drive) position. Apply hand brake and accelerate engine until 1000 rpm is reached. Pressure reading on gauge should be 82-88 psi.
4. If correct pressure is not obtained, loosen locknut on vacuum control unit (located at rear of transmission) and turn vacuum unit clockwise to increase pressure or counterclockwise to decrease pressure. Adjust for proper pressure, then tighten locknut. CAUTION: **Do not operate engine over 10 seconds at any one time while performing the above.**

Neutral Safety Switch Adjustment

1. Place the selector lever in the "N" position and loosen the two capscrews securing the switch to the steering jacket tube.
2. Using a 3/32 pin punch as an aligning tool, insert the pin into the hole on the face of the switch. *NOTE: If necessary, rotate the switch until the pin enters freely into the hole in the switch.*
3. Secure the two capscrews holding the switch to the steering jacket tube and remove the pin punch.
4. Attempt to start the vehicle in

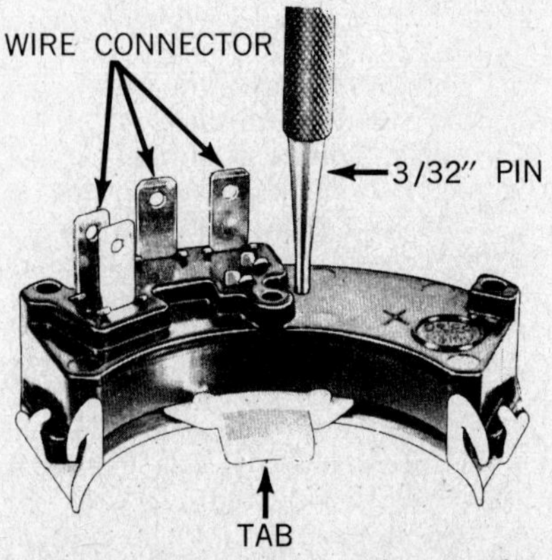

Using a 3/32" pin punch to adjust to safety starter switch
(© International Harvester Co.)

all positions. If the engine will start in the "P" and the "N" positions and not in any of the others, the switch is correctly adjusted.

Caution: Block the wheels before testing the switch adjustment.

Transmission Model T-407

Removal

NOTE: The transmission and converter must be removed as a unit assembly. Damage can result to the converter drive plate, pump bushing, or to the pump seal, if the converter is allowed to remain on the converter drive plate.

1. Connect a remote switch to the starter solenoid so that the engine can be rotated from under the vehicle.
2. Disconnect the coil high tension cable.
3. Raise the vehicle and support safely.
4. Remove the engine rear crossmember on 4 x 4 vehicles, if necessary.
5. Remove the cover plate from the front of the converter housing to provide access to the converter drain plug and mounting bolts.
6. Rotate the engine to bring the drain plug to the six o'clock position. Drain the converter and loosen the pan bolts to drain the transmission.
7. Mark the converter and drive plate to aid in the assembly. Rotate the engine to locate the converter-to-drive plate bolts and remove the bolts.
8. Disconnect the negative battery cable and remove the starter motor assembly.
9. Disconnect the wires from the back-up light and neutral start switch.
10. Disconnect the gearshift cable or rod and bellcrank from the transmission.
11. Disconnect the throttle rod from the left side of the transmission.
12. Disconnect the cooler lines at the transmission and remove the filler tube.
13. Disconnect the speedometer cable, and move cable away from the transmission.
14. Disconnect the front universal joint and secure the shaft out of the way.
15. On vehicles equipped with parking brake mounted on the rear extension, remove the parking brake cable.
16. On vehicles equipped with dual exhaust, the left exhaust system may have to be removed.
17. Install an engine support fixture to hold the rear of the engine.
18. Raise the transmission slightly, and remove the support crossmember holding the rear mount assembly.
19. Remove all bell housing bolts.
20. Carefully move the transmission assembly rearward off the block dowels and disengage the converter hub from the end of the crankshaft. Place a converter holding tool on the bell housing to hold the converter in place.
21. Lower the transmission assembly and remove the transmission from the vehicle.
22. To remove the converter assembly from the transmission, remove the holding tool and carefully slide the converter out of the transmission.

Installation

1. Rotate the pump rotors with tool SE-2402 or its equivalent, so that the lugs on the pump inner rotor are vertical.
2. Position the converter so that the impeller shaft slots are vertical and carefully slide the converter assembly over the input shaft and reaction shaft. Make sure that the converter slots fully engage the pump inner rotor lugs.

   NOTE: The surface of the converter front cover lug should be at least 1/2 inch to the rear of a straightedge, placed on the face of the bell housing, when the converter is pushed all the way into the transmission.
3. Install the converter holding tool to hold the converter in place.
4. Position the transmission on a jack assembly and move the unit under the vehicle.
5. Rotate the converter to align the previously made marks on the drive plate and converter.
6. Raise the transmission and align with the engine. Install a pilot stud to aid in the alignment of the converter to the drive plate. Carefully work the transmission assembly forward over the engine block dowels with the converter hub entering the crankshaft opening.
7. Install the converter housing bolts and tighten to specified torque.
8. Install the crossmember and mount at the rear of the transmission. Remove the engine support fixture.
9. Install the oil filler tube and speedometer cable.
10. Connect the throttle rod and the gear shift rod to the transmission levers.
11. Connect the wires to the neutral start and back-up light switch.
12. Install the drive shaft and front universal joint.
13. Install the starter motor assembly.
14. Remove the pilot stud from the converter and install the bolts to the converter-drive plate assembly.
15. Install the cooler lines to the transmission.
16. Install the converter access plate on the front of the converter housing.
17. If the left exhaust system was removed, replace the pipes and brackets.
18. Install the parking brake cable and adjust, if equipped with the extension housing parking brake assembly.
19. Adjust the shift and throttle linkage.
20. Fill the transmission and connect the negative battery cable, if not done, and start the engine. Recheck the fluid level and refill as necessary.

Transmission Fluid Drain and Refill

1. Raise the vehicle on a jack or hoist. Support safely.
2. Place a large drain container under the transmission oil pan.
3. Loosen the pan bolts and tap one corner of the pan to break it loose, allowing the fluid to drain.
4. Remove the access plate from the front of the converter housing. Remove the converter drain plug and allow the fluid to drain.
5. Remove and clean the pan, remove the fluid filter and discard.
6. Install a new filter assembly on the valve body and tighten the screws securely.
7. Using a new pan gasket, install the pan and tighten the bolts securely.
8. Install and tighten the converter drain plug.
9. Install the converter housing access plate.
10. Install six quarts of transmission fluid into the transmission. Start the engine and allow to run for two minutes. Check the fluid level and add enough oil to bring the level to the "ADD ONE PINT" mark.
11. Recheck the level after moving the selector lever through all the gear positions and after the transmission has reached normal operating temperature. The level should be between the "FULL" mark and the "ADD ONE PINT" mark.

Kickdown Band Adjustment

NOTE: The kickdown band is located on the left side of the transmission case near the throttle lever shaft.

1. Loosen the locknut and back off approximately five turns.

2. Tighten the adjusting screw to 10 ft. lbs.
3. Back off the adjusting screw 2¼ turns with the 6 and 8 cylinder engines. Hold the adjusting screw in position and tighten the lock nut to 29 ft. lbs.

Low and Reverse Band Adjustment

1. Raise the vehicle, support safely, drain the transmission fluid, and remove the pan.
2. Loosen the lock nut on the adjusting screw.
3. Tighten the adjusting screw to 10 ft. lbs.
4. Tighten the lock nut to 30 ft. lbs.
5. Install the pan using a new pan gasket.
6. Fill the transmission with fluid, start the engine and recheck the level. Add as necessary.

Back-up Light and Neutral Start Switch

No provisions are made for any adjustments of the back-up light and neutral start switch. The neutral start circuit is controlled by the inner terminal and the back-up light circuits are controlled by the two outside terminals.

The replacement of the switch is accomplished by unscrewing the switch from the transmission case, and screwing a new switch into the case. Since fluid leakage will occur when removing the switch, fluid must be added after the new switch is installed.

Shift Linkage

Adjustable Cable Control

1. Install cable conduit anchor clamps at both ends.
2. Install swivel on the control lever so that a distance of .55 inch exists from the end of the cable to the opposite side of the trunnion. Tighten the jam nut securely.
3. With the control in PARK position and transmission lever in the full rearward position (PARK detent), adjust the yoke so that the rod end pin installs freely and secure the yoke nut and install the cotter pin.

Column Shift

1. Assemble all linkage parts, but leave the upper control rod bolt loose.
2. Place the selector lever in DRIVE position.
3. Move the shift control lever on the transmission to the DRIVE position.
4. Tighten the upper bolt on the control rod to 14-16 ft. lbs.
5. Check the adjustment as follows.
   a. Shift effort must be free and detents feel crisp. All gate stops must be positive.
   b. Key start must only occur in the PARK or NEUTRAL positions.
   c. Detent positions must be in proper relationship to the transmission lever positions.

Throttle Valve Linkage Adjustment

1. With the engine off and an assistant holding the accelerator pedal to the floor, check for full carburetor throttle plate opening.
2. If necessary, adjust the throttle cable and pedal floor stop to obtain wide open throttle.
3. If necessary, adjust the idle speed of the engine with the use of a tachometer and with the engine at normal operating temperature and the carburetor off the fast idle cam. Adjust the curb idle speed, (throttle stop solenoid activated) with the transmission in neutral and the air conditioning in the OFF position.

NOTE: Be sure that carburetor is not being held open by a deceleration valve dashpot, solenoid valve, or a vacuum throttle modulator valve.

CAUTION: **All components in the throttle control and transmission linkage system must operate freely with absolutely no sticking, excessive friction, or interference from other chassis components.**

6-258 Engine with 1940 Carburetor

1. Hold the throttle valve control rod on the transmission in the forward position while adjusting the length of the throttle push rod.
2. Adjust the link at the upper end of the control rod until the rear end of the slot in the adjusting link contacts the pin in the bellcrank.
3. Tighten the lock nut against the throttle valve control rod link. Position the link on the bellcrank pin and install the washer and cotter pin. Connect the control rod return spring.
4. Check the throttle valve control rod linkage for freedom of movement and for full return to the forward position upon movement of the bellcrank.
5. Road test the vehicle. If no kickdown is present, adjust the throttle valve control rod one turn to move the lever at the transmission farther to the rear.
6. Repeat the road test. If no kickdown is obtainable as yet, repeat the procedure as outlined in paragraph 5 above.

V-304, V-345, V-392 and V-400 Engines With 2210, 2300, and 4150 Holley Carburetors

Two types of throttle linkages are used on these carburetors to transmissions. They are designated as FIRST RELEASE and MODIFIED type linkages. The differences are;

a. FIRST RELEASE—has both the throttle push rod and the throttle valve control rod piloted by guide holes in the throttle valve rod bracket. The throttle push rod is capped by a lock nut and acorn nut.
b. MODIFIED TYPE—has only the throttle valve control rod piloted in the throttle valve rod bracket. The throttle push rod is piloted in the spring clip plate which is welded to the throttle valve control rod.

FIRST RELEASE—Adjustment

1. On the first release type throttle valve linkage, loosen the jam nut of the acorn adjusting nut and turn the acorn nut clockwise until clearance between the acorn nut and the spring clip is obtained.
2. Move the throttle valve linkage control rod to its forward most position. Adjust the acorn nut so it just rides against the spring clip on the throttle valve control rod and tighten the jam nut.
3. Check the throttle linkage for freedom of movement by pushing the linkage to its full rearward position and making sure its complete return to the full forward position.

MODIFIED LINKAGE—Adjustment

1. Loosen the jam nut and turn the adjusting nut clockwise until clearance between adjusting nut and spring clip is obtained.
2. Move the control rod to its forward most position. Adjust the nut so it just rides against the spring clip on the throttle valve control rod and tighten the jam nut.
3. Check the throttle linkage for freedom of movement by pushing the linkage to its full rearward position and making sure of its complete return to the full forward position.

V-345 and V-392 Engines With Carter Thermo-Quad Carburetor

NOTE: Two types of throttle linkages are used as with the V-304, V-345, V-392, and V-400 Carburetors.

FIRST RELEASE—Adjustment

This procedure is the same as for the V-304, V-345, V-392, and V-400.

MODIFIED LINKAGE—Adjustment

1. Loosen the jam nut and turn the adjusting nut clockwise until the adjusting nut just contacts the spring clip.
2. Move the control rod to its forward most position. Adjust the nut so it just rides against the spring clip on the throttle valve control rod and tighten the jam nut.
3. Check the throttle linkage for freedom of movement and return to its full forward position when moved.

DRIVESHAFT

Driveshaft Assembly

It is imperative that all components of the drive train be tight to insure balance. Check companion flanges at the axles and transmission, center bearing mounts and engine mounts.

When assembling drive train, lubricate slip joint (splined) assemblies and universal joint bearings. Make sure that universal joints are kept on parallel planes by observing the arrows stamped on the shaft end and slip yoke.

Removal and Installation

1. Beginning at the front or the rear of the shaft, bend the lock strip tabs, if equipped, away from the bolts in the trunnion flanges of the universal joints. Mark the shaft, universal joint, and yoke for proper reassembly.
2. Remove the bolts from the trunnion flange to yoke and support the ends of the shaft.
3. If equipped with a center bearing assembly, use a floor jack or other means to support the shaft assembly and center bearing during removal. Remove the bolts from the center bearing to crossmember and lower the shaft assembly.

   NOTE: Some drive shafts will have a slip joint or universal joint near the center bearing assembly. Separating the shaft at these points will lighten the weight and control awkwardness of handling the complete shaft assembly during the disassembly and assembly.
4. The installation of the shaft is in the reverse of the removal procedure. Make sure all indexing marks are properly aligned.

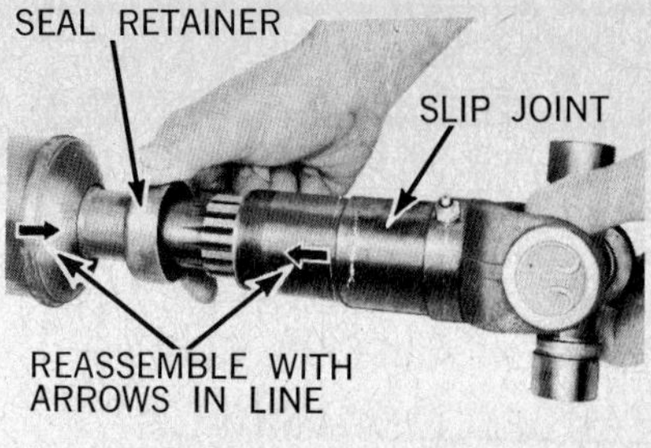

Correct slip joint assembly
(© International Harvester Co.)

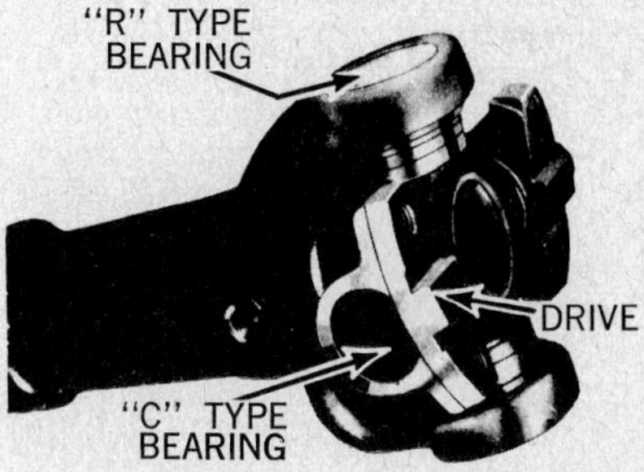

CR type universal joint
(© International Harvester Co.)

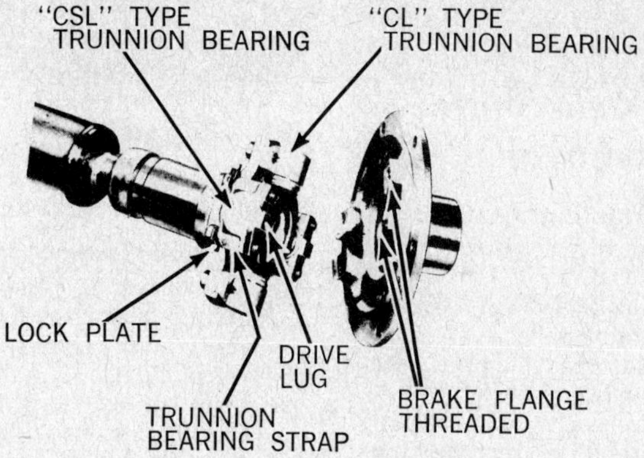

CL type universal joint
(© International Harvester Co.)

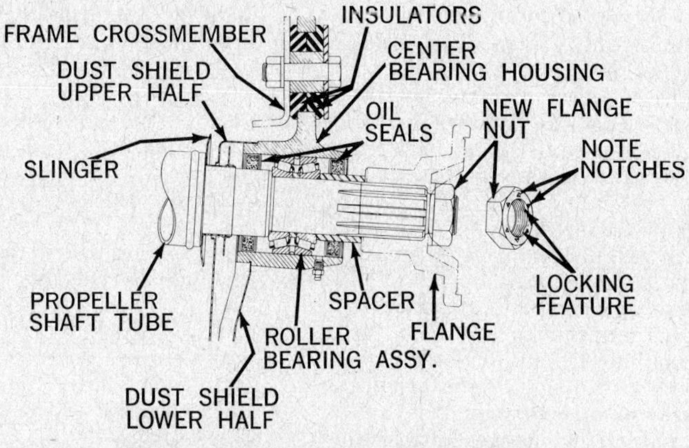

Silent spin type center driveshaft bearing (© International Harvester Co.)

Universal Joints

To remove universal joints, bend down tabs on bearing bolt lock plate and remove four bolts at each universal joint. Joint and shaft assembly must be removed as a unit to service "R" type trunnion bearings. Do not disassemble drive shaft from slip yoke unless these parts are to be replaced. On vehicles equipped with "CL" type trunnion bearings, the universal joint may be unbolted from both the drive shaft and the companion flange and the whole shaft assembly does not have to be removed to service one joint.

When replacing trunnion bearings, remove retaining clips then carefully drive out one, then the other, bearing. Use new packing washers (seals) when reassembling.

REAR AXLE

For overhaul procedures and out of truck adjustments see Rear Axle General Section.

Rear Axle Assembly Removal

1. Jack and block up truck until load is removed from springs and rear wheels are clear of the ground.
2. Drain differential housing.
3. Disconnect brake lines and parking brake cables (where used).
4. On two speed differentials, disconnect control wires or air hoses from the shift mechanism.
5. Disconnect driveshaft at rear axle companion flange.
6. Support differential on portable floor jack and take off U-bolts at springs.
7. Roll out axle from under truck.
8. Installation is the reverse of the above procedure. Be sure to bleed hydraulic brake systems. Remove axle housing breather valve and clean thoroughly with solvent.

Rear Axle Shaft Removal

Semi-Floating Type

1. Remove wheel and nut from axle shaft end.
2. Remove hub and drum assembly with a suitable puller.
3. Unbolt and remove brake backing plate and bearing retainer.
4. Pull axle shaft and bearing using suitable puller. Bearings are pressed on.
5. When installing axle shaft assembly, use new oil seals and be careful not to damage seals.
6. Lightly tap bearing cap into axle housing.
7. Install shims on end of axle housing flange and insert backing plate bolts to retain shims.
8. Install backing plate, bearing retainer and seal retainer. Tighten nuts to specified torque.
9. Install wheel hub. Grasp wheel hub and pull outward to be sure that axle shaft is withdrawn as far as possible.
10. Check axle shaft end play as follows: Mount dial indicator on stationary location at right-hand side of axle assembly. Position indicator against end of axle shaft and check shaft end play. If end play is not within .006″, shims must be added or removed between backing plate and axle housing flange.
11. Place key in axle shaft and install hub and drum assembly on shaft, securing with washer and nut. Tighten nut and install cotter pin.

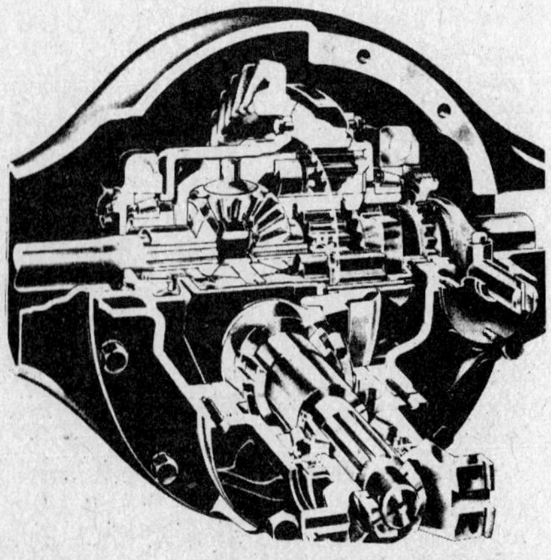

Two speed planetary gear type axle final drive (© International Harvester Co.)

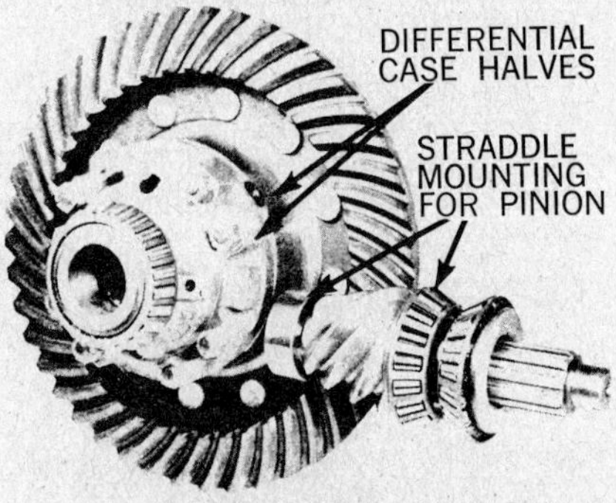

Single reduction type axle final drive (© International Harvester Co.)

Full-Floating Type

1. Axle shaft is removed without taking off wheels. Remove axle shaft nuts from studs in the wheel hub.
2. Install puller screws in the two tapped holes provided in the axle shaft flange.
3. Turn in puller screws until axle shaft is loose, then pull axle.
4. Installation is the reverse of the above procedure. Be sure puller screws are removed.

Full-Floating Type With Tapered Dowel Mounting

1. Remove flange nuts from studs of wheel hub.
2. Using a heavy hammer, strike sharply on the center of the flange of the axle shaft. This will unseat and loosen tapered dowels.
3. Remove tapered dowels.
4. Push axle flange back into position against wheel hub and strike again with a hammer to spring axle shaft away from the wheel hub. Do not pry on flange.
5. When installing axle shaft, make sure there is between the axle shaft driving flange and lockwasher. Dowel must not be "sunken in."

Axle Shaft Bearing and Oil Seal

Removal and Installation

The only axle type that has a bearing mounted on the shaft is the semi-floating axle. Follow the procedure outlined under the Axle Shaft Removal to expose the seals and bearings for replacement.

1. The bearing must be pressed from the axle shaft and a new one pressed back on the shaft to seat against the bearing shoulder on the axle.
2. Lubricate the bearing with wheel bearing grease and fill the roller cavities completely.
3. Remove the axle tube inner seal by the use of a seal puller or by engaging the lip of the seal with the end of the axle shaft and prying outward on the seal.
4. Using a seal installer or its equivalent, seat the seal against the shoulder within the axle tube.
5. During assembly of the brake support plate, install the outer seal.

NOTE: Lubricate the lips of the seals during installation.

Oil Seal Installation and Wheel Bearing Adjustment

Full Floating Axle

1. Raise the rear of the vehicle and support safely. Keep both rear wheels parallel with the floor surface.
2. Remove the axle as outlined under Rear Axle Shaft Removal.
3. Remove the wheel bearing lock nut by bending the lock tab away from the lock nut shoulders. Remove the lock nut and lock.
4. Place a dolly under the rear wheels and maneuver the truck height so that the wheels are neither hanging nor supporting the truck.
5. Remove the adjusting nut and outer wheel bearing. Pull the wheel assembly outward and off the housing tube.
6. Remove the oil seal and inner wheel bearing from the truck side of the hub assembly.
7. Clean the hub of any old grease and replace the bearings and races as necessary. Repack the bearings if they are to be used again. Pack wheel bearing grease in the hub cavity between the inner and outer bearings.
8. Install the wheel hub oil seal and clean the hub and drum of any grease droppings.
9. Install the wheel assembly on the housing tube, keeping the hub

assembly parallel with the housing tube.
10. Install the outer bearing and adjuster nut. Raise the vehicle and wheel assembly upward to clear the dolly.
11. Tighten the adjusting nut to 50 ft. lbs. while rotating the wheels to seat the bearings.
12. Back off the adjusting nut 1/4 turn and install the lock washer and lock nut. Tighten the lock nut to 150 ft. lbs. and bend the lock tabs to secure the nut.

NOTE: Assemblies using doweled adjusting nuts and pierced wheel bearing lock nut, require 200-300 ft. lbs. torque on the outer nut.

13. Install the axle shaft and bolt to the wheel assembly.
14. Lower the vehicle and check the level of lubricant in the differential.

Locking Differentials

For overhaul procedures of differentials with "NoSPIN" and "Powr-Lok" locking units see Rear Axle portion of General Section.

REAR SUSPENSION

Description

The rear springs used on the IH vehicles are classified as leaf, air, and rubber block types. The heavier the vehicle load requirement, the heavier the spring assemblies would be to carry the load. Care should be exercised in the removal and installation of the spring assemblies so that personal injury can be avoided. The suspensions using shock absorbers will normally be found on the light and medium duty vehicles. The removal and installation of the shock absorbers require only the removal and installation of the retaining nuts or bolts, with the possibility of raising the vehicle for working clearance.

The following procedure can be used as a general outline for the removal and installation of leaf springs. The air and rubber block suspension, along with the tandem leaf springs, are outlined in this section.

Rear Spring Removal

1. Place floor jack under truck frame and raise truck sufficiently to relieve weight from spring to be removed.
2. Remove shock absorbers where used.
3. Remove U-bolts, spring bumper and retainer or U-bolt seat.
4. Remove lubricators (not used where springs are equipped with rubber bushings).
5. Remove nuts from spring shackle pins or bracket pins.
6. Slide spring off bracket pin and shackle pin.
7. If spring is rubber bushed, bushing halves may be removed from each side of spring and shackle eye.

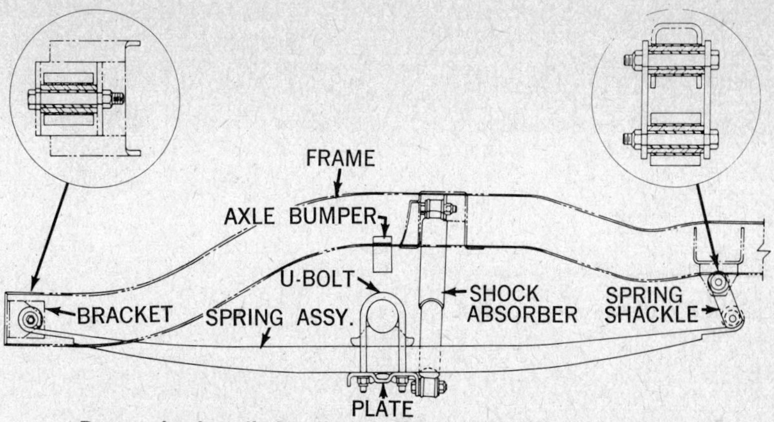

Rear spring installation diagram light and medium duty vehicles
(© International Harvester Co.)

Installation

1. Install pivot end of spring first. Align shackle end to other frame bracket. When installing nuts on spring pins which are welded or pressed in, be sure that washer is tightened against shoulder of pin. Spring pins which are driven in must be installed so that slot for lock bolt is aligned. Spring pins which are threaded in must be installed so that the lubrication hole is facing up. Tighten pin into bracket, then back off one-half turn. Install locknut tightly and install cotter pin. Turn pin out to permit installation of cotter pin.
2. Install lubricators.
3. Install U-bolt seat or retainer and U-bolts. Install U-bolt nuts, but do not tighten.
4. Install shock absorber where used.
5. Lower vehicle.
6. Tighten U-bolt nuts securely.

Air Suspension

The air suspension system was developed to improve the ride characteristics of highway transport vehicles. The major components, whether used on single or tandem axles, are as follows: Trailing arms, frame hanger brackets, shock absorbers, track bars, air springs, axle connections, air leveling valve.

Spring Height Adjustment

1. Start engine, and wait until the air pressure indicates near maximum pressure of 85-90 lbs.
2. Measure the distance from the top of the trailing arm to the bottom of the frame at the rear of the air spring on one side only.
3. If the distance is greater than 12 1/4 inches, (± 3/8 inch), shorten the linkage from the height control valve arm to the axle, wait 15 seconds and remeasure. Repeat the procedure if necessary.
4. If the distance is less than 12 1/4 inches, (± 3/8), lengthen the linkage from the height control valve arm to the axle, wait 15 seconds and remeasure. Repeat the procedure if necessary.
5. Repeat the adjustment procedure on the opposite side of vehicle.

Air Spring Pressure Balance

Air spring pressure imbalance on an unloaded IH air suspension system is a normal condition and causes no harm to the suspension components so long as chassis remains unloaded. If, however, the imbalance continues after the chassis is loaded, do not operate the vehicle until the cause is located and corrected. These causes can be incorrect spring height adjustment, air leaks, plugged or pinched air lines, defective leveling control valve, or loose or broken parts.

Air Spring Removal and Installation

1. Block the vehicle wheels and release the air pressure build-up from the air brake system.
2. Support the vehicle in the raised position to relieve any pressure on the air spring.
3. Remove the front or rear trailing arm, depending upon the air spring affected, by removing the attaching bolts at the front and center of the arm.
4. Lower the arm and the air spring away from the axle.
5. Installation is the reverse of removal.

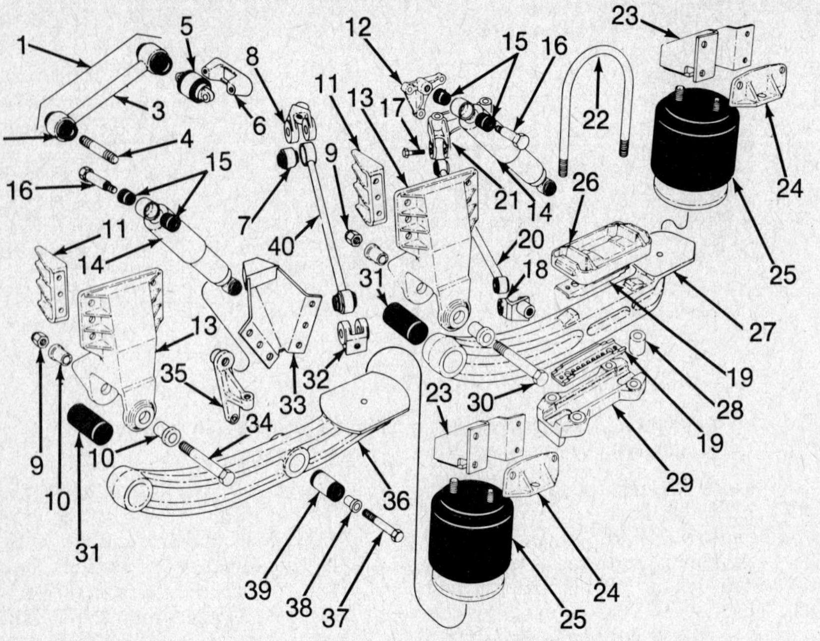

Exploded view air suspension typical (© International Harvester Co.)

1 Rod, torque, assembly
2 Bushing, torque rod
3 Tube, torque rod
4 Stud, torque rod mounting
5 Shaft, torque rod
6 Bracket, torque rod mounting
7 Bushing, trac bar
8 Yoke, right front trac bar mounting
9 Nut, hex lock, 1 NC
10 Adapter, bushing
11 Bracket, crossmember mounting
12 Bracket, rear shock absorber mounting
13 Bracket, trailing arm mounting
14 Absorber, shock, assembly
15 Bushing, shock absorber mounting
16 Bolt, hex head, 3/4 NC x 3
17 Bolt, hex head, 3/4 NC x 4
18 Yoke, left rear trac bar mounting
19 Pad, rear axle mounting
20 Bar, rear trac, assembly
21 Yoke, right rear trac bar mounting
22 U-bolts with nuts
23 Bracket, air spring mounting
24 Bracket, air spring mounting
25 Spring, air ride, assembly
26 Saddle, axle mounting
27 Arm, rear trailing, assembly
28 Spacer, saddle
29 Bracket, saddle
30 Bolt, hex head, 1 NC x 8
31 Bushing, trailing arm
32 Yoke, left front trac bar mounting
33 Bracket, shock absorber mounting
34 Bolt, hex head, 1 NC x 10
35 Bracket, Front, lower, shock absorber mounting
36 Arm, front trailing
37 Bolt, hex head, 3/4 NF x 7 3/4
38 Adapter, bushing
39 Bushing, front trailing arm center
40 Bar, trac, assembly front

Equalizing Beam Suspension (Hendrickson)

Tandem drive axles require a special suspension which permits flexibility between the axles, the equalizing beam suspension. Semi-elliptic springs are used mounted on saddle assemblies above the equalizer beams and pivoted at the front end on spring pins and brackets. The rear end of the springs have no rigid attachment to the spring brackets, but are free to move forward and backward to compensate for spring deflection.

NOTE: As options, airspring assemblies and four point rubber mounted suspensions are available in place of the leaf spring type.

There are two approaches to servicing the suspension system. One is the removal and installation of individual parts. Removal and overhaul of the entire unit can also be done.

CAUTION: When complete removal is performed, be careful when disconnecting the torque rods, springs, or rubber cushions from the frame since the axle assemblies will be free to roll or pivot at the equalizer beam ends. Use jacks and other equipment and block the vehicle securely to prevent injury to personnel and damage to the unit.

Four Spring Suspension (Dayton)

The four spring suspension system is used to distribute the load over a greater area of the frame rail. The six torque rods of the Dayton four spring suspension serve a dual purpose. The rods provide a means of suspension alignment as well as perming the axles to accept complete drive line torque. The torque rods consist of two non-adjustable and four adjustable units.

The removal and installation of parts can be accomplished by the removal of the individual parts or the removal of the complete unit, as with the Equalizing Beam Suspension.

Axle Alignment

1. Clamp a straight edge to the top of the frame rail ahead of the forward rear axle. Use a framing square against the straight-edge and the outside surface of the frame siderail to insure the straightedge is perpendicular to the frame.

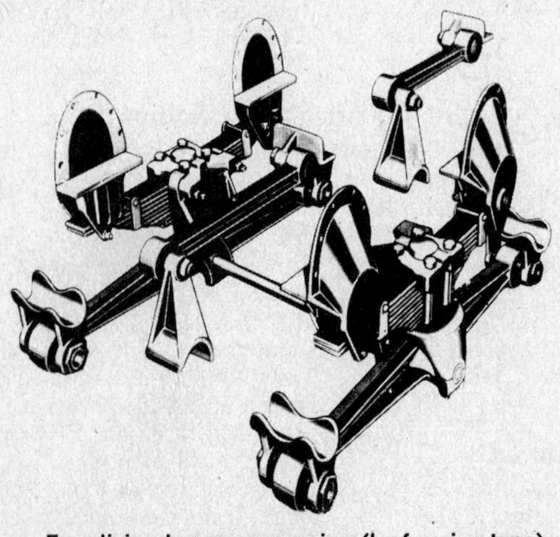

Equalizing beam suspension (leaf spring type) (© International Harvester Co.)

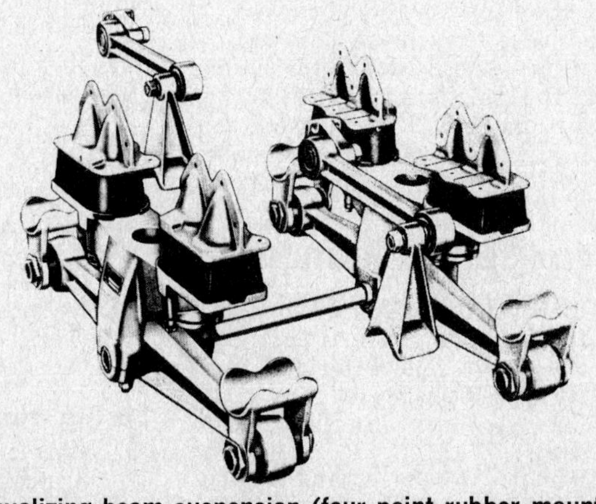

Equalizing beam suspension (four point rubber mounted) (© International Harvester Co.)

2. Suspend a plumb bob from the straightedge in front of the tire and on the outboard side of the forward rear axle.
3. Position a bar with pointers that can be engaged in the center holes of the rear axles.
4. Measure the distance between cord of the plumb bob and the pointer on the forward axle and record (Dimension A).
5. Position the plumb bob and bar on the opposite side of the vehicle and measure as outlined in paragraph 4. Record the result.
6. Any difference in dimensions from side to side must be equalized if the difference exceeds .0625 inch.
7. Equalize the dimensions by loosening the clamp bolts on the lower adjustable torque rod on the forward rear axle and adjusting the length of the torque rod. Tighten the clamp bolts.

   NOTE: Remove one end of the left and right upper torque rods on the forward rear axle to relieve any stresses which may be present due to an improperly adjusted torque rod, before adjusting the lower torque rods.
8. Reposition the bar pointers to the axle centers on each side. If any differences exist in the center to center measurement, (Dimension B), after the forward rear axle has been squared to the frame, the rear rear axle must also be aligned.
9. To align the rear axle, loosen the clamp bolts on the lower adjustable torque rod and adjust to equalize the center to center distance between the axle ends. Tighten the clamp bolts.
10. Reinstall the upper torque rod ends that were removed in step 7. Tighten the mounting bolts.

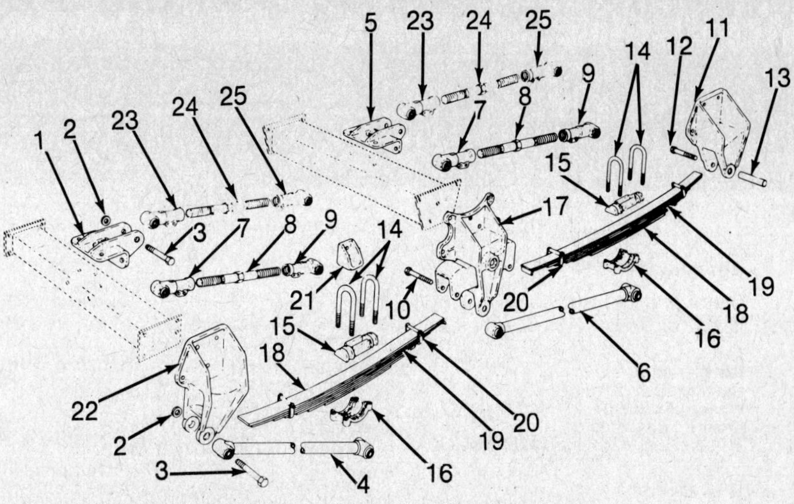

Exploded view Dayton four spring suspension (© International Harvester Co.)

1 Bracket, torque rod
2 Washer, torque rod
3 Bolt and nut, torque rod
4 Rod, torque, lower left front
5 Bracket, torque rod
6 Rod, torque, lower left rear
7 End, torque rod
8 Rod, torque, lower adjustable
9 End, torque rod
10 Bolt, shoulder
11 Bracket, rear spring rear
12 Bolt, shoulder
13 Spacer, spring roller
14 U-bolt, spring
15 Seat, U-bolt
16 Plate, U-bolt
17 Bracket, Equalizer
18 Leaf, spring
19 Spring assembly
20 Clip, spring
21 Stop, axle
22 Bracket, rear spring front
23 End, torque rod
24 Rod, torque upper adjustable
25 End, torque rod

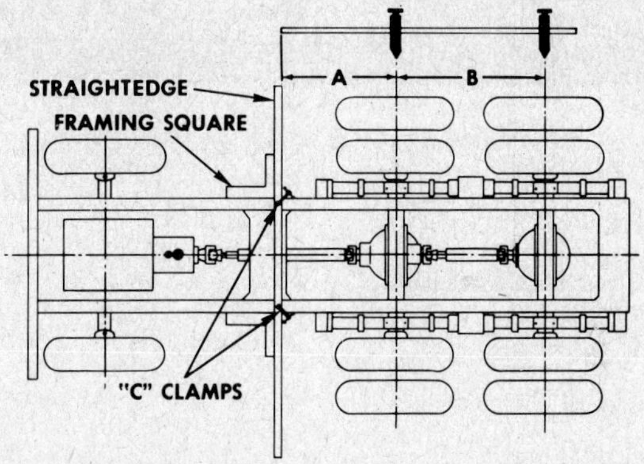

Measurement points of tandem axles for alignment check (© International Harvester Co.)

Axle Load Distribution

The Dayton four spring suspension provides for equal load distribution through the adjustment of the upper torque rod lengths. To adjust, follow this procedure.

1. Disconnect the forward and rear upper torque rods at the frame crossmembers.
2. If the vehicle is equipped with an adjustable fifth wheel, position it in the normal operating location.
3. Apply the maximum rated load on the suspension assembly to obtain the full deflection of the leaf springs when adjusting the torque rods.
4. To settle the suspension to normal operating position, move the vehicle to a level area and bring the vehicle to an easy stop, using the trailer brake, if equipped. Keep the vehicle in a straight ahead position.
5. Loosen the torque clamp bolts and lengthen or shorten the torque rods as required to obtain bolt hole alignment for easy installation of the bolts in the torque rod ends.
6. Tighten the mounting bolts and the torque rod clamp bolts.
7. No further adjustment should be required.

Jeep CJ-5, CJ-6, CJ-7, Wagoneer, Commando, Cherokee, J-10 and J-20

INDEX

GENERAL ENGINE SPECIFICATIONS

Year	Engine Cu In. Displacement	Carburetor Type	Advertised Horsepower @ rpm ■	Advertised Torque @ rpm (ft lbs) ■	Bore and Stroke (in.)	Advertised Compression Ratio	Oil Pressure @ 30 mph (psi)
'73	6-232	1 bbl	100 @ 3600	185 @ 1800	3.895 x 3.500	8.0:1/7.6:1	37
	6-258	1 bbl	110 @ 3500	195 @ 2000	3.750 x 3.500	8.0:1/7.6:1	37
	8-304	2 bbl	150 @ 4200	245 @ 2500	3.750 x 3.440	8.4:1	37
	8-360	2 bbl	175 @ 4000	285 @ 2400	4.080 x 3.440	8.5:1	37
	8-360	4 bbl	195 @ 4400	295 @ 2900	4.080 x 3.440	8.5:1	37
'74-'77	6-232	1 bbl	100 @ 3600①	185 @ 1800②	3.750 x 3.500	8.0:1	37
	6-258	1 bbl	110 @ 3500③	195 @ 2000④	3.750 x 3.900	8.0:1	37
	8-304	2 bbl	150 @ 4200⑤	245 @ 2500⑥	3.750 x 3.440	8.4:1	37
	8-360	2 bbl	175 @ 4000⑦	285 @ 2400⑧	4.080 x 3.440	8.3:1	37
	8-360	4 bbl	195 @ 4400⑨	295 @ 2900⑩	4.080 x 3.440	8.3:1	37
	8-401	4 bbl	215 @ 4200	320 @ 2800	4.165 x 3.680	8.4:1	37
'78	6-232	1 bbl	90 @ 3400	168 @ 1600	3.750 x 3.500	8.0:1	37
	6-258	1 bbl	100 @ 3400	200 @ 1600	3.750 x 3.895	8.0:1	37
	6-258	2 bbl	120 @ 3600	201 @ 1800	3.750 x 3.895	8.0:1	37
	8-304	2 bbl	130 @ 3200	238 @ 2000	3.750 x 3.440	8.40:1	37
	8-360	2 bbl	140 @ 3350	278 @ 2000	4.080 x 3.440	8.25:1	37
	8-360	4 bbl	195 @ 4400	295 @ 2900	4.080 x 3.440	8.25:1	37
	8-401	4 bbl	215 @ 4400	320 @ 2800	4.165 x 3.680	8.25:1	37
'79-'80	6-258	2 bbl	110 @ 3200	210 @ 1800	3.750 x 3.895	8.0:1	37
	8-304	2 bbl	125 @ 3200	220 @ 2400	3.750 x 3.440	8.40:1	37
	8-360	2 bbl	175 @ 4000	285 @ 2900	4.080 x 3.440	8.25:1	37

■ Horsepower and torque are SAE net figures. They are measured at the rear of the transmission with all accessories installed and operating. Since the figures vary when a given engine is installed in different models, some are representative rather than exact.

① 90 @ 3050 1976-77
② 170 @ 2000 1976-77
③ 95 @ 3050 1976-77
④ 180 @ 2100 1976-77
⑤ 120 @ 3200 1976-77
⑥ 220 @ 2200 1976-77
⑦ 140 @ 3300 1976-77
⑧ 251 @ 1600 1976-77
⑨ 180 @ 3600 1976-77
⑩ 280 @ 2800 1976-77

TUNE-UP SPECIFICATIONS

When analyzing compression test results, look for uniformity among cylinders rather than specific pressures.

Year	ENGINE No. Cyl Displacement (cu. in.)	hp	SPARK PLUGS Type	SPARK PLUGS Gap (in.)	DISTRIBUTOR Point Dwell (deg)	DISTRIBUTOR Point Gap (in.)	IGNITION TIMING (deg) ▲	VALVES Intake Opens (deg) ■	Fuel Pump Pressure (psi)	IDLE SPEED (rpm) ● Man Trans	IDLE SPEED (rpm) ● Auto Trans
'73-'74	6—232	100	N-12Y	.035	32	.016	5B⑥	12½	4-5	700⑦	—
	6—258	258	N-12Y	.035	32	.016	3B⑥	12½	4-5	700⑦	550
	8—304	150	N-12Y	.035	30	.016	5B⑥	14¾	5-6½	750	700
	8—360	175	N 12Y	.035	30	.016	5B⑥	14¾	5-6½	750	700
	8—360	195	N-12Y	.035	30	.016	5B⑥	14¾	5-6½	750	700
	8—401	225	N-12Y	.035	30	.016	5B⑥⑧	25½	5-6½	750⑨	700
'75	6—232	100	N-12Y	.035	Electronic		5B	12	4-5	700(600)	—
	6—258	110	N-12Y	.035	Electronic		3B	12	4-5	700⑩(600)	550
	8—304	150	N-12Y	.035	Electronic		5B	14¾	5-6½	750	—
	8—360	175	N-12Y	.035	Electronic		2-5B	14¾	5-6½	750	700
	8—360	195	N-12Y	.035	Electronic		2-5B	14¾	5-6½	750	700
	8—401	215	N-12Y	.035	Electronic		2-5B	25½	5-6½	750	700
'76-'77	6—232	90	N-12Y	.035	Electronic		8B	12	4-5	600	—
	6—258	95	N-12Y	.035	Electronic		6B⑪	12	4-5	600	550(700)
	8—304	120	N-12Y	.035	Electronic		5B⑫	14¾	5-6½	750	700
	8—360	175	N-12Y	.035	Electronic		5B⑬	14¾	5-6½	750	700
	8—401	215	N-12Y	.035	Electronic		5B⑬	25½	5-6½	750	700

TUNE-UP SPECIFICATIONS

When analyzing compression test results, look for uniformity among cylinders rather than specific pressures.

Year	ENGINE No. Cyl Displacement (cu. in.)	hp	SPARK PLUGS Type	Gap (in.)	DISTRIBUTOR Point Dwell (deg)	Point Gap (in.)	IGNITION TIMING (deg) ▲	VALVES Intake Opens (deg) ■	Fuel Pump Pressure (psi)	IDLE SPEED (rpm) • Man Trans	Auto Trans
'78	6—232	90	N-13L	.035	Electronic		5B①	12	4-5	850⑮	—
	6—258	100⑱	N-13L	.035	Electronic		6B②③	14½	4-5	850⑯⑰	550
	8—304	130	N-12Y	.035	Electronic		5B④	14¾	5-6½	750	700
	8—360	140⑲	N-12Y	.035	Electronic		5B	14¾	5-6½	750	700
	8—401	215	N-12Y	.035	Electronic		8B	25½	5-6½	—	700
'79	6—258	110	N-13L	.035	Electronic		8B⑭	14½	4-5	700	600
	8—304	125	N-12Y	.035	Electronic		8B⑤	14¾	5-6½	700(750)	600
	8—360	175	N-12Y	.035	Electronic		8B	14¾	5-6½	800	600
'80	6—258	110	N-14LY⑳	.035	Electronic		8B㉑	14½	4-5	700	600㉒
	8—304	125	N-12Y	.035	Electronic		㉓	14¾	5-6	700	600
	8—360	175	N-12Y	.035	Electronic		8B	14¾	5-6	800	600

NOTE: If the information given in this chart disagrees with the information on the engine tune-up decal, use the specifications on the decal—they are current for the engine in your car.

NOTE: Figures in parentheses are for California engines
▲ With vacuum advance disconnected
■ All figures before TDC (BTDC)
• With manual transmission in Neutral and automatic transmission in Drive
B Before top dead center (BTDC)
① 10B for Altitude
② w/Manual trans.—10B Altitude; 8B Calif.
③ w/Auto. trans.—8B 49 States and Calif.; 10B Altitude
④ w/Auto. trans.—10B 49 States and Calif.
⑤ w/Manual trans.—5B, CJ model only
⑥ At 550 rpm in 1973; 700 rpm in 1974-75
⑦ 700 rpm for CJ, 600 rpm Commando and Wagoneer
⑧ 2.5° B on heavy-duty engine (painted red)
⑨ 650 rpm on heavy-duty engine (painted red)
⑩ 650 rpm w/EGR
⑪ 8B w/Automatic transmission
⑫ 10B w/Automatic transmission; 5B in California
⑬ 8B w/Automatic transmission; 5B in California
⑭ w/Manual trans.—4B, w/Auto. trans.—6B, CJ model only
⑮ 600 RPM Altitude
⑯ w/Manual trans. and 1 bbl. carburetor 600 RPM for Altitude
⑰ w/Manual trans. and 2 bbl. carburetor 650 RPM
⑱ 120 HP—2 bbl. carburetor engine
⑲ 195 HP—4 bbl. carburetor engine
⑳ CJ models with Auto. Trans. and all California CJ's: N-13L
㉑ California CJ's with manual transmission: 6B
All CJ's with auto. trans.: 10B
㉒ Cherokee, Wagoneer and J series: 700
㉓ Manual trans., except Calif. and Hilly Terrain: 8B at 700 RPM
Automatic trans. except Calif.: 10B at 600 RPM
Manual trans. Calif.: 5B at 750 RPM
Manual trans. Hilly Terrain: 12B at 700 RPM
Automatic trans. Calif.: 5B at 600 RPM

FIRING ORDER AND ROTATION

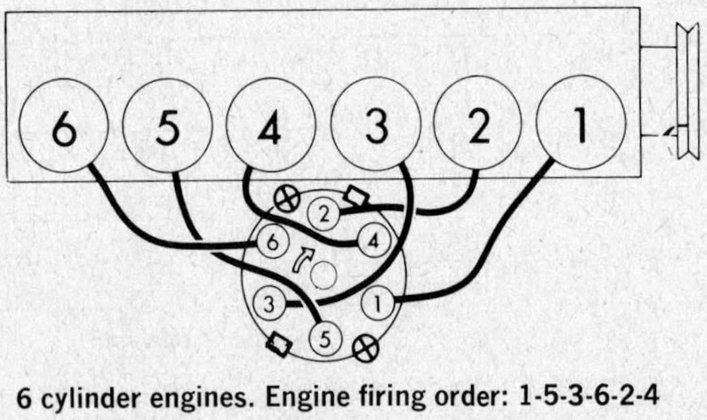

6 cylinder engines. Engine firing order: 1-5-3-6-2-4

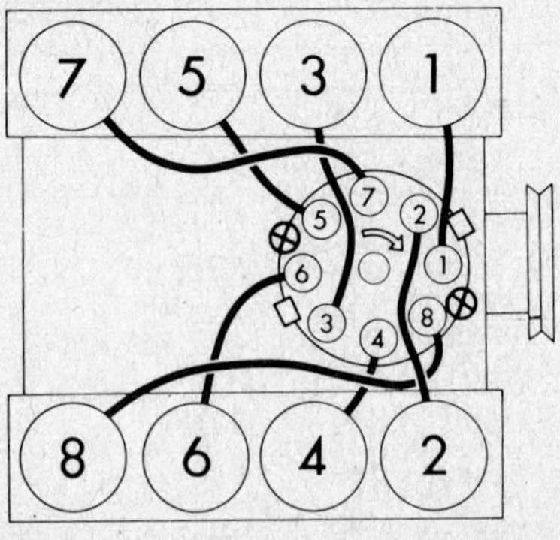

V8 engines. Engine firing order: 1-8-4-3-6-5-7-2

CRANKSHAFT AND CONNECTING ROD SPECIFICATIONS

All measurements are given in inches

Engine No. Cyl. Displacement (cu in.)	CRANKSHAFT Main Brg. Journal Dia	Main Brg. Oil Clearance	Shaft End-Play	Thrust on No.	CONNECTING ROD Journal Diameter	Oil Clearance	Side Clearance
6-232	2.4986-2.5001	.001-.003	.0015-.0065	3	2.0934-2.0955	.001-.003④⑤	.005-.015①
6-258	2.4986-2.5001	.001-.003	.0015-.0065	3	2.0934-2.0955	.001-.003④⑤	.005-.014①

CRANKSHAFT AND CONNECTING ROD SPECIFICATIONS

All measurements are given in inches

Engine No. Cyl. Displacement (cu in.)	CRANKSHAFT				CONNECTING ROD		
	Main Brg. Journal Dia	Main Brg. Oil Clearance	Shaft End-Play	Thrust on No.	Journal Diameter	Oil Clearance	Side Clearance
8-304	2.7474-2.7489②	.001-.003③	.003-.008	3	2.0934-2.0955	.001-.003⑤	.006-.018
8-360	2.7474-2.7489②	.001-.003③	.003-.008	3	2.0934-2.0955	.001-.003⑤	.006-.018
8-401	2.7474-2.7489②	.001-.003③	.003-.008	3	2.2464-2.2485	.001-.003⑤	.006-.018

① .008-.010 1973-only
② Rear main, 2.7464-2.7479
③ Rear main #5—.0020-.003; on 1979-'80 engines—.002-.004
④ 1979-'80—.0010-.0025
⑤ 1973—.001-.002

VALVE SPECIFICATIONS

Year	Engine No. Cyl. Displacement (cu in.)	Seat Angle (deg) •	Face Angle (deg) ■	Spring Test Pressure (lbs @ in.)	Spring Installed Height (in.)	STEM TO GUIDE Clearance (in.)		STEM Diameter (in.)	
						Intake	Exhaust	Intake	Exhaust
'73-'80	6-232	44½	44	100 @ 1 13/16⑨	2 15/64⑦⑧⑥	.0010-.0030	.0010-.0030	.3720	.3720
	6-258	44½	44	100 @ 1 13/16⑨	2 15/64⑦⑧⑥	.0010-.0030	.0010-.0030	.3720	.3720
	8-304	44½	44	84 @ 1 13/16⑨	2 7/32⑦⑧⑥	.0010-.0030	.0010-.0030	.3720	.3720
	8-360	44½	44	84 @ 1 13/16⑨	2 7/32⑦⑧⑥	.0010-.0030	.0010-.0030	.3720	.3720
'74-'78	8-401	44½	44	84 @ 1 13/16⑨	2 7/32⑦⑧⑥	.0010-.0030	.0010-.0030	.3720	.3720

• Exhaust valve seat angle given; all intake valve seat angles are 30° unless otherwise noted
■ Exhaust valve face angle given; all intake valve face angles are 29° unless otherwise noted
⑥ 1978-'80—2"; except 1978—304, 360, 401—2 1/5
⑦ Free length
⑧ 1974 and later only; other years N.A.
⑨ Without rotators

PISTON RING SPECIFICATIONS

	Engine	Ring Gap			Ring Side Clearance			Piston to Bore Clearance
		Top Compression	Bottom Compression	Oil Control	Top Compression	Bottom Compression	Oil Control	
'73-'80	6-232	.010-.020	.010-.020	.010-.025	.0015-.003	.0015-.003	.001-.008	.0009-.0017
	6-258	.010-.020	.010-.020	.010-.025	.0015-.003	.0015-.003	.001-.008	.0009-.0017
	8-304	.010-.020	.010-.020	.010-.025	.0015-.0035	.0015-.003	.0011-.008	.0010-.0018
	8-360	.010-.020	.010-.020	.015-.045	.0015-.0035	.0015-.0035	.000-.007	.0012-.0020
	8-401	.010-.020	.010-.020	.0015-.055	.0015-.003	.0015-.0035	.000-.007	.0010-.0018

TORQUE SPECIFICATIONS

All readings in ft lbs

Engine No. Cyl. Displacement (cu in.)	Cylinder Head Bolts	Rod Bearing Bolts	Main Bearing Bolts	Crankshaft Balancer Bolt	Flywheel to Crankshaft Bolts	MANIFOLD	
						Intake	Exhaust
6-232, 258	95-115	26-30①	75-85	50-64	95-120	37-47②	20-30②
8-304, 360	100-120	26-30①	90-105	48-64	95-120	37-47	20-30⑥③
8-401	100-120	35-40⑥	90-105	48-64	95-120	37-47	20-30⑥

① 30-35 for 1978-1980
② 18-20 for 1974-1980
③ 20-30, center two bolts; 12-18, outer four bolts for 1979-80

WHEEL ALIGNMENT

Model	CASTER Pref. Setting (deg)	CAMBER Pref. Setting (deg)	Toe-In (in.)	King-Pin Inclination (deg)	WHEEL PIVOT RATIO Inner Wheel	WHEEL PIVOT RATIO Outer Wheel
CJ-5, CJ-6, CJ-7, DJ-5, DJ-6, CJ-5A, CJ-6A	3	1°30′	3/64-3/32	7½①	20	20
Commando	3	1°30′	3/64-3/32	7½	31	32
Wagoneer, Cherokee, J-10, J-20	3②	1°30′	3/64-3/32	7½①	37	38

N.A. Not available
① 8½° in 1974-'80
② 4° in 1974-'80

MODEL AND ENGINE APPLICATION

(All Jeep engines are gas engines)

Model	Engine (CID)	Carburetor	Year
CJ-5, CJ-6, CJ-7	232	1 bbl	1973-1978
	258	1 bbl	1973-1978
	304	2 bbl	1973-1980
	258	2 bbl	1979-1980
Wagoneer	258	1 bbl	1973 and 1976
	360	2 bbl	1973-1980
	360	4 bbl	1973-1978
	401	4 bbl	1974-1978
Cherokee	258	1 bbl	1974-1976
	258	2 bbl	1977-1980
	360	2 bbl	1974-1980
	360	4 bbl	1974-1978
	401	4 bbl	1974-1978
Commando	232	1 bbl	1973
	258	1 bbl	1973
	304	2 bbl	1973
J-10, J-20	258	1 bbl	1973-1978
	258	2 bbl	1977-1980
	360	2 bbl	1973-1980
	360	4 bbl	1973-1978
	401	4 bbl	1974-1978

ENGINE IDENTIFICATION SPECIFICATIONS

The Engine Identification Code letter is the 6th character in the vehicle identification number for Jeep vehicles.

Engines	Model Year & Engine Code							
	1973	1974	1975	1976	1977	1978	1979	1980
258-6 cyl.-Reg.	A	A	A	A	A	A	—	—
258-6 cyl.-L/C①	B	—	—	—	—	—	—	—
258-6 cyl. 2bbl.	—	—	—	—	C	C	C	C
232-6 cyl.-Reg.	E	E	E	E	E	E	—	—
232-6 cyl.-L/C①	F	—	—	—	—	—	—	—
304-V8-2bbl.	H	H	H	H	H	H	H	H
360-V8-2bbl.	N	N	N	N	N	N	N	N
360-V8-4bbl.	P	P	P	P	P	P	—	—
401-V8-4bbl.	Z	Z	Z	Z	Z	Z	—	—

① Low compression engine

DISTRIBUTOR

Refer to the Electrical General Repair section for detail procedures on the different distributors.

Starting in the 1975 model year all engines use the American Motors Breakerless Inductive (BID) Ignition System. This system consists of five major components: an electronic ignition control unit, an ignition coil, a distributor, high tension spark plug wires, and spark plugs. This system uses a conventional coil, spark plug wires, and spark plugs. The main difference in components from a conventional system is the points and condensor are eliminated from the distributor and are replaced by a trigger wheel and an electromagnetic sensor, and an electronic control unit is added.

Distributor

Removal and Installation

1. Remove the high-tension wires from the distributor cap terminal towers, noting their positions to assure correct reassembly. For diagrams of firing orders and distributor wiring, refer to the front of this section.
2. Remove the primary lead from the terminal post at the side of the distributor.
3. Disconnect the vacuum tube if there is one.

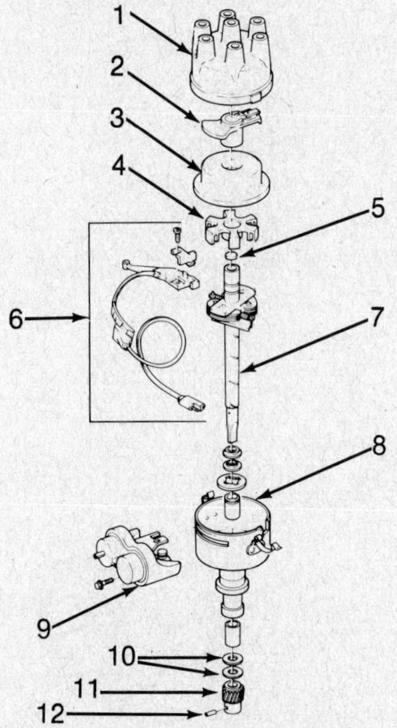

Electronic ignition distributor (BID)—exploded view (© Jeep Corp.)

1 Distributor cap
2 Rotor
3 Dust shield
4 Trigger wheel
5 Felt wick
6 Sensor assembly
7 Shaft assembly
8 Housing
9 Vacuum control
10 Shim
11 Drive gear
12 Pin

4. Unlatch the two distributor cap retaining hooks and remove the distributor cap.
5. Note the position of the rotor in relation to the base. Scribe a mark on the base of the distributor and on the engine block to facilitate reinstallation. Align the marks with the direction the metal tip of the rotor is pointing.
6. Remove the screw that holds the distributor to the engine.
7. Lift the distributor assembly from the engine.

If the engine has not been disturbed, install the distributor as follows:

1. Insert the distributor shaft and assembly into the engine. Line up the mark on the distributor and the one on the engine with the metal tip of the rotor. Make sure that the vacuum advance diaphragm is pointed in the same direction as it was pointed originally. This will be done automatically if the marks on the engine and the distributor are lined up with the rotor.
2. Install the distributor hold-down bolt and clamp. Leave the screw loose enough so that you can move the distributor with heavy hand pressure.
3. Connect the primary wire to the distributor side of the coil. Install the distributor cap on the distributor housing. Secure the distributor cap with the spring clips or the screw type retainers, whichever is used.
4. Install the spark plug wires. Make sure that the wires are pressed all of the way into the top of the distributor cap and firmly onto the spark plugs.
5. Adjust the point cam dwell and set the ignition timing.

If the engine has been turned while the distributor has been removed, or if the marks were not drawn, it will be necessary to initially time the engine. Follow the procedure below:

1. It is necessary to place the No. 1 cylinder in the firing position to correctly install the distributor. To locate this position, some engines have marks placed on the flywheel while other engines have marks placed on the timing gear covers and crankshaft pulleys. The flywheel marks may be viewed through a covered opening directly in back of the starting motor by loosening the hole cover and sliding it to one side.
2. Remove the No. 1 cylinder spark plug. Turn the engine until the piston in No. 1 cylinder is moving up on the compression stroke. This can be determined by placing your thumb over the spark plug hole and feeling the air being forced out of the cylinder.
3. Oil the distributor housing lightly where the distributor bears on the cylinder block.
4. Install the distributor so that the rotor, which is mounted on the shaft, points toward the No. 1 spark plug terminal tower position when the cap is installed. Of course you won't be able to see the direction in which the rotor is pointing if the cap is on the distributor. Lay the cap on the top of the distributor and make a mark on the side of the distributor housing just below the No. 1 spark plug terminal. Make sure that the rotor points toward that mark when you install the distributor.
5. When the distributor shaft has reached the bottom of the hole, move the rotor back and forth slightly until the drive gears of the distributor and cam mesh and until the distributor assembly slides down into place.

On models that have a gear on the end of the distributor shaft and a gear on the end of the oil pump drive, these gears have to mesh with the same teeth as originally installed when the distributor is inserted into the engine. Once again, the marks that were placed on the engine and the base of the distributor housing come into play. If the distributor shaft gear and the oil pump drive gear are but one tooth off from what they are supposed to be, the engine will not run correctly.

6. When the distributor is correctly installed, the breaker points should be in such a position that they are just ready to break contact with each other. This is accomplished by rotating the distributor body after it has been installed in the engine. Once again, line up the marks that you made before the distributor was removed from the engine.
7. Install the distributor hold-down screw and the hold-down bracket. Be sure that the models that have vacuum advance units are free to turn in the mounting socket. Note that the vacuum advance control of some distributors is connected directly to the plate on which the points are mounted. When this is the case, the plate must be free to turn rather than the distributor body.
8. Install the spark plug into the No. 1 spark plug hole and continue from Step 3 of the distributor installation procedure.

Contact Points

Removal and Installation

1. Remove the distributor cap by

releasing the hold-down screws or clamps. Remove the rotor.
2. Release the primary and condenser wire from the point set. Remove the holding screws from the point set and remove the points from the distributor.
3. Clean the breaker plate with a clean cloth, to remove any dirt or oil.
4. Align the pilot pin on the new point set with the pilot hole in the breaker plate and install the point set. Lubricate the cam lobe or the cam wick.
5. Connect the primary and condenser leads to the point set.
6. Rotate the engine until the contact set rubbing block is resting on the high point of a cam lobe.
7. Adjust the point gap to specifications and tighten the locking screw.
8. Replace the rotor and cap, start the engine to check the point dwell and the ignition timing.

Ignition Timing

All Engines

1. Locate the timing marks on the crankshaft pulley and the front of the timing case cover.
2. Clean off the timing marks, so that you can see them.
3. Use chalk or white paint to color the mark on the scale that will indicate the correct timing, when aligned with the mark on the pulley or the pointer. It is also helpful to mark the notch in the pulley or the tip of the pointer with a small dab of color.

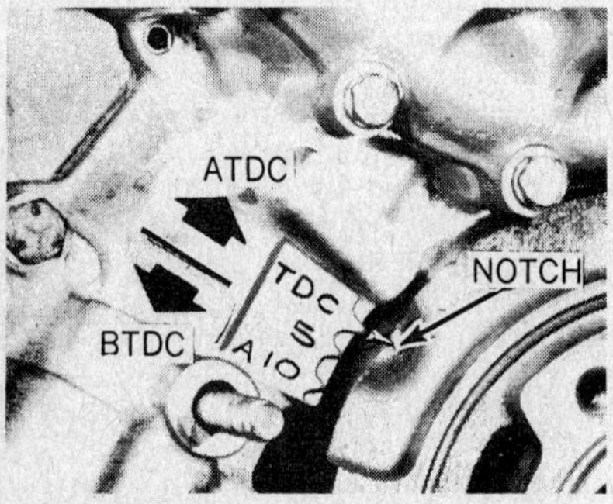

Timing mark location—8 cyl. engines
(© Jeep Corp.)

4. Attach a tachometer to the engine.
5. Attach a timing light to the engine.
6. Disconnect the vacuum lines to the distributor at the distributor and plug the vacuum lines. Disconnect the TCS switch if so equipped. Loosen the distributor lock-bolt just enough so that the distributor can be turned with a little resistance.
7. Check to make sure that all of the wires clear the fan and then start the engine.

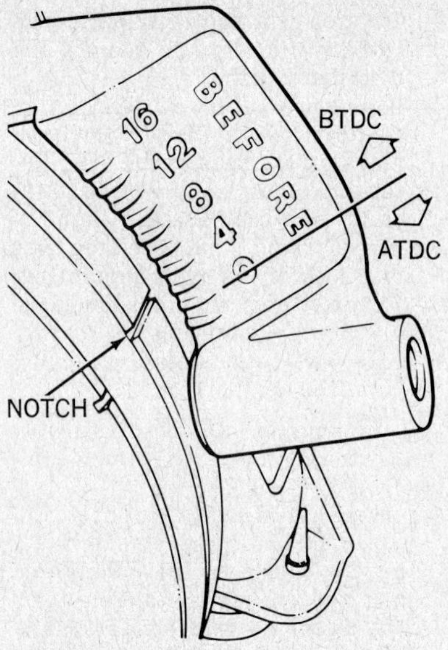

Timing mark location—6 cyl. engine
(© Jeep Corp.)

8. Adjust the idle to the correct specification.
9. With the timing light aimed at the pulley and the marks on the engine, turn the distributor in the direction of rotor rotation to retard the spark, and in the opposite direction of rotor rotation to advance the spark. Align the marks on the pulley and the engine with the flashes of the timing light.

Magnetic Timing Probe

A bracket and hole are cast into the timing case cover on 1974 and later engines for the use of a magnetic timing probe, connected to a special electronic timing meter for precise ignition timing. The probe is inserted into the hole of the bracket until the vibration damper is touched. When the engine is started, the probe is automatically spaced away from the damper by the damper's eccentricity, or being slightly out of center. The probe senses a milled slot on the damper and compensating for the bracket's 9.5° ATDC position, registers the reading on the timing meter. Any necessary corrections can then be made to the ignition timing.

NOTE: Do not use the probe bracket and hole the check the ignition timing, using a conventional timing light.

ALTERNATOR

Refer to the Electrical General Repair Section for detailed alternator test and overhaul procedures.

CAUTION: Since the AC generator and regulator are designed for use on only one polarity system, the following precautions must be observed:

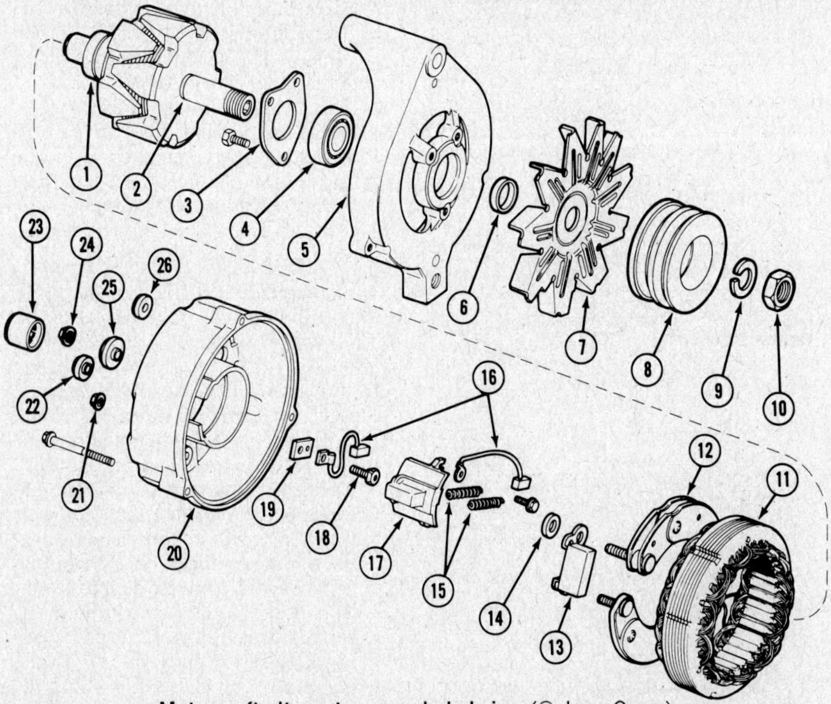
Motorcraft alternator—exploded view (© Jeep Corp.)

1 Rotor
2 Stop ring
3 Front bearing retainer
4 Front bearing
5 Front housing
6 Front bearing spacer
7 Fan
8 Pulley
9 Lockwasher
10 Nut
11 Stator
12 Rectifier assembly
13 Radio noise suppression capacitor
14 Insulator capacitor
15 Brush spring
16 Brush set
17 Brush Holder
18 Brush terminal screw
19 Brush terminal insulator
20 Rear housing
21 GRD terminal nut
22 Field insulator (orange)
23 Rear bearing
24 Bat terminal nut
25 Battery insulator (red)
26 Stator insulator (black)

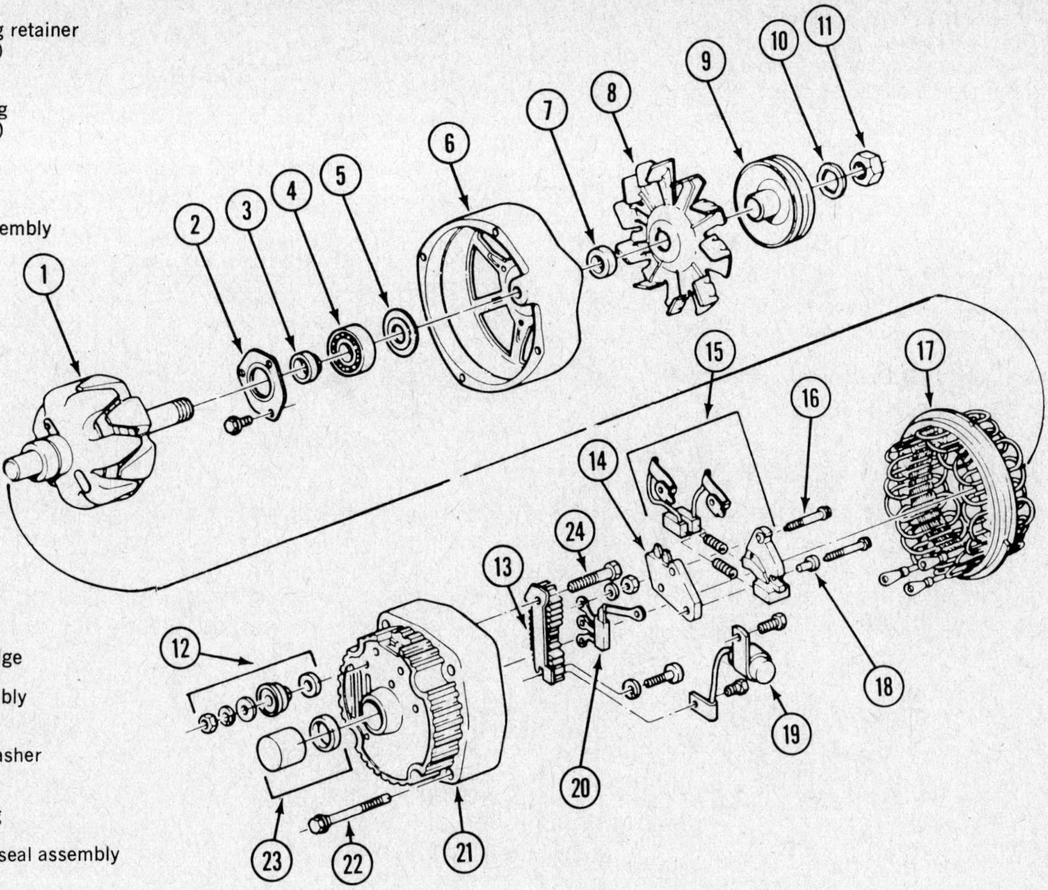

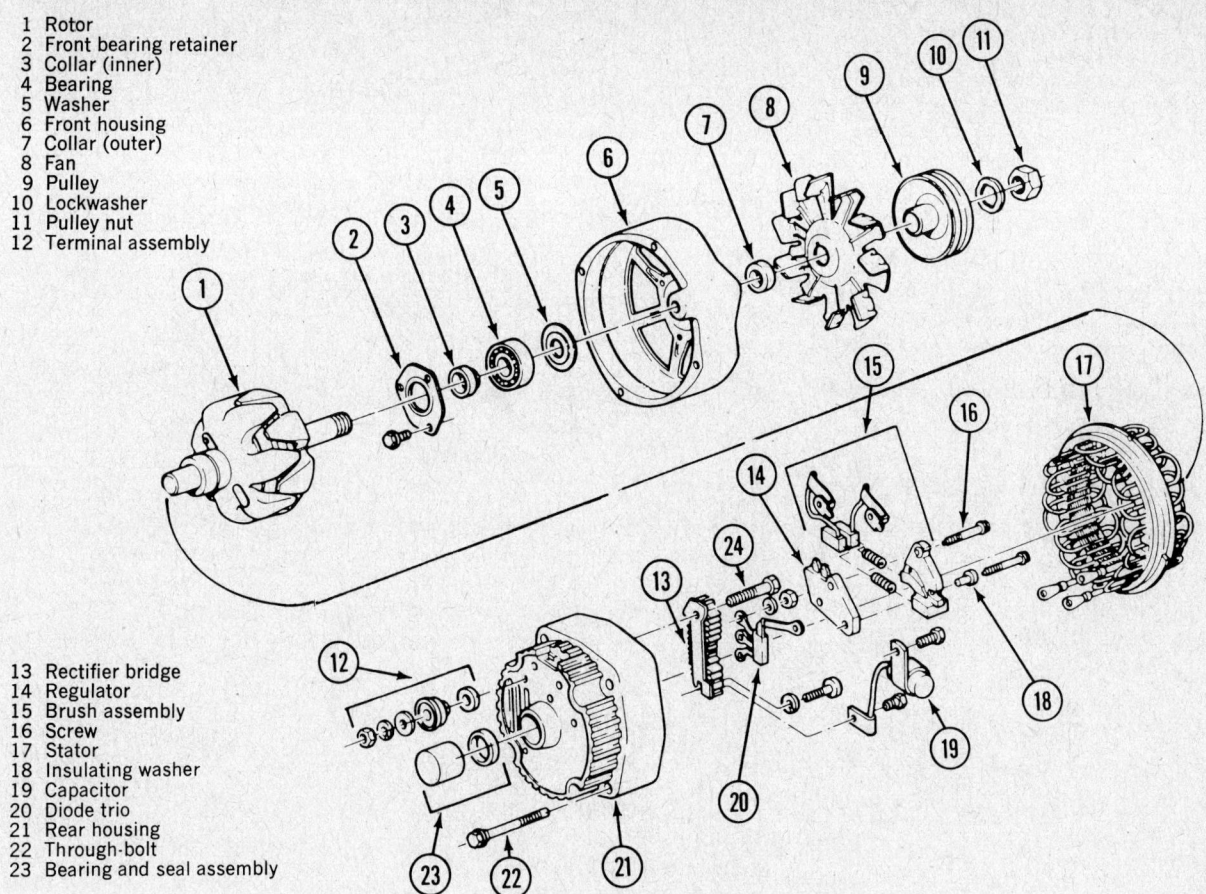

1 Rotor
2 Front bearing retainer
3 Collar (inner)
4 Bearing
5 Washer
6 Front housing
7 Collar (outer)
8 Fan
9 Pulley
10 Lockwasher
11 Pulley nut
12 Terminal assembly
13 Rectifier bridge
14 Regulator
15 Brush assembly
16 Screw
17 Stator
18 Insulating washer
19 Capacitor
20 Diode trio
21 Rear housing
22 Through-bolt
23 Bearing and seal assembly

Delco alternator—exploded view with mini-regulator (© Jeep Corp.)

a. The polarity of the battery, generator and regulator must be matched and considered before making any electrical connections in the system.
b. When connecting a booster battery, be sure to connect the negative battery terminals together and the positive battery terminals together.
c. When connecting a charger to the battery, connect the charger positive lead to the battery positive terminal. Connect the charger negative lead to the battery negative terminal.
d. Never operate the AC generator on open circuit. Be sure that all connections in the circuit are clean and tight.
e. Do not short across or ground any of the terminals on the AC generator.
f. Do not attempt to polarize the AC generator.
g. Do not use test lamps of more than 12 V for checking diode continuity.
h. Avoid long soldering times when replacing diodes or transistors. Prolonged heat is damaging to these units.
i. Disconnect the battery ground terminal when servicing any AC system. This will prevent the possibility of accidentally reversing polarity.

Alternator

Removal and Installation

1. Remove the negative battery cable from the battery.
2. Remove the wire terminals attached to the rear of the alternator.
3. Loosen the bolt holding the adjusting bar and the pivot bolt at the opposite side of the alternator.
4. Move the alternator inward to relieve the belt tension and remove the belt.
5. Remove the adjusting bar and pivot bolts and remove the alternator from the engine.
6. Install the alternator in the reverse procedure of the disassembly.
7. When installing the belt, adjust to allow ½ inch play on the longest run between the pulleys.

Voltage Regulator

Removal and Installation

1. Disconnect the wires from the regulator, either at the wire harness connector or at the regulator frame.
2. Remove the attaching screws and remove the regulator from the vehicle.
3. Install the regulator in the reverse procedure of the removal, and attach all wires.

NOTE: Beginning with the 1975 model year, the voltage regulator is an integral part of the Delco alternator. Refer to the Unit Repair Section for the integral voltage regulator removal and installation procedures.

STARTER

Reference

Refer to the Electrical General Repair Section for detailed starter test and overhaul procedures.

Starter

Removal and Installation

All Models

1. Disconnect the battery ground cable.
2. If necessary, raise the vehicle to gain working clearance.

3. Remove the positive battery lead from the starter or solenoid. Remove remaining wires as necessary.
4. Remove the starter retaining bolts and remove the starter from the vehicle.

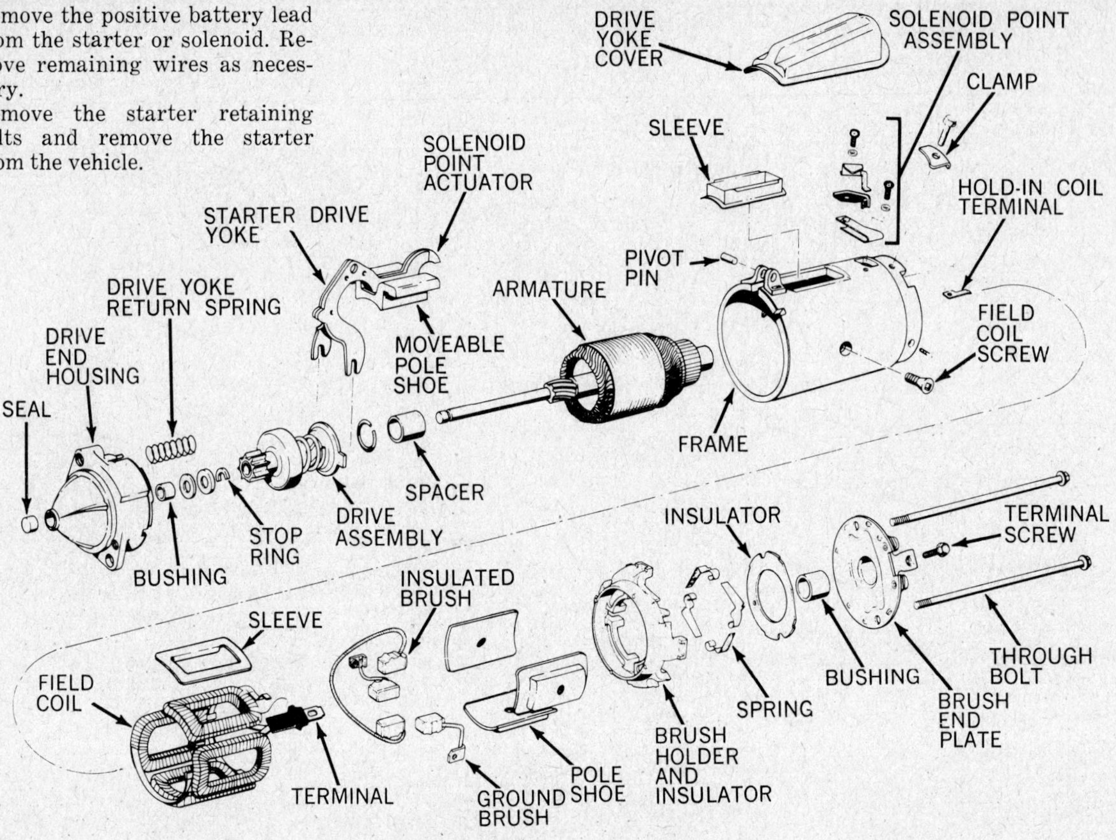

Starter motor (© Jeep Corp.)

5. The installation is in the reverse order of the removal procedure.

NOTE: On some models, the transmission oil filler tube may have to be removed.

BRAKES

Reference

Refer to the Brakes General Repair Section for detail troubleshooting and brake hydraulic system repair procedures.

Master Cylinder

Removal and Installation

1. Disconnect and plug the brake lines at the master cylinder.
2. Disconnect the wires from the stoplight switch.
3. Disconnect the master cylinder push rod at the brake pedal on vehicles with manual brakes.
4. Remove all attaching bolts and nuts and lift the master cylinder from the vehicle.
5. Install the master cylinder in the reverse order of removal and bleed the hydraulic system.

Power Unit 1973-77

Removal and Installation

1. Clean the master cylinder and booster unit.
2. Remove the cotter and clevis pins securing the booster pushrod to the pedal linkage.
3. Disconnect the vacuum hose from the booster check valve.
4. Disconnect the fluid lines from the master cylinder. Plug the ends and catch any escaping fluid. *Do not reuse brake fluid.*
5. Disconnect the stoplight wires from the switch.
6. Remove the attaching nuts, booster unit assembly, and block spacers.
7. Remove the attaching nuts and separate the master cylinder from the booster.

To install the booster unit, reverse the removal procedure and bleed the brakes.

CAUTION: Do not pressure-bleed power-assisted brake systems.

1978-80 Models

1. Disconnect brake pedal pushrod rod at brake pedal.
2. Disconnect vacuum hose from booster check valve.
3. Remove attaching nuts and separate master cylinder from brake booster. Do not disconnect brake lines at master cylinder.
4. On CJ models, remove bolts holding power unit bellcrank to dash panel and remove power unit and bellcrank as one assembly. Remove the bellcrank from the original power unit and lubricate the pivot pins with chassis lubricant before installing it on the replacement unit.
5. On all other models, remove bolts attaching power unit to dash panel and remove the unit.
6. Installation is the reverse of removal.

NOTE: When replacing the power brake unit, use the push rod that is supplied with the new unit, as it has been correctly gauged and preset to the new unit.

Wheel Cylinder

Removal and Installation

1. Raise and support the vehicle and remove the brake drums and brake shoes.
2. Disconnect the brake line. Do not bend the line away from the wheel cylinder. When the cylinder is removed from the support plate, the line will separate from the wheel cylinder easily.
3. Remove the wheel cylinder mounting bolts and remove the wheel cylinder from the brake backing plate.
4. Clean the wheel cylinder mounting surface on the brake support plate. Clean the brake line fitting and threads.
5. Start the brake line fitting into the wheel cylinder and attach the wheel cylinder to the support plate and tighten the brake line

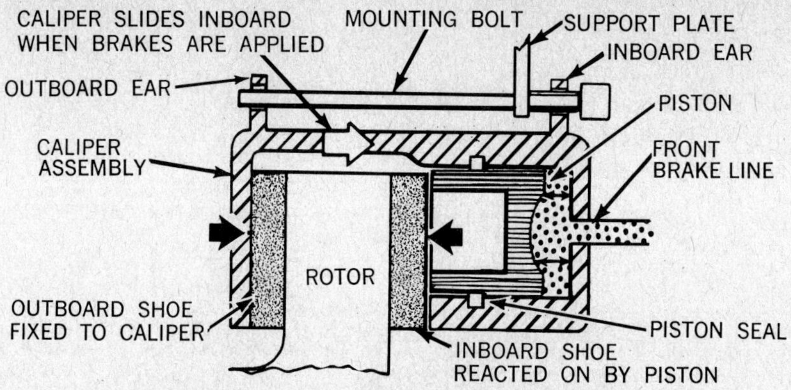

Operation of disc brake—typical (© Jeep Corp.)

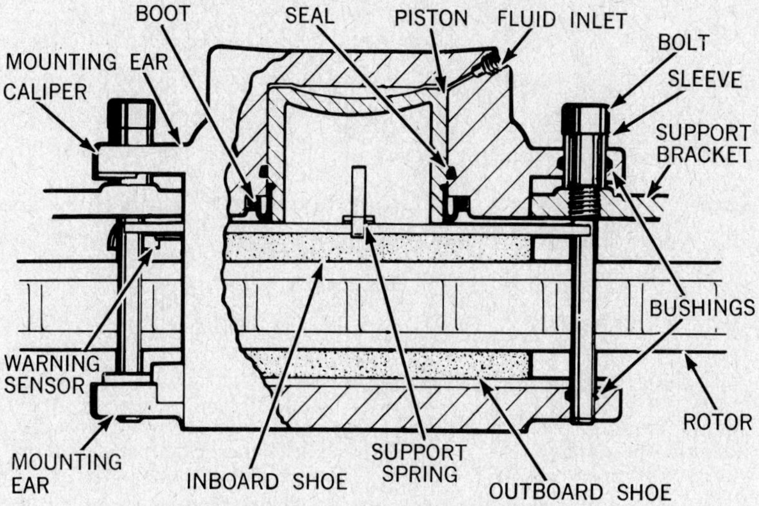

Single piston caliper—exploded view (© Jeep Corp.)

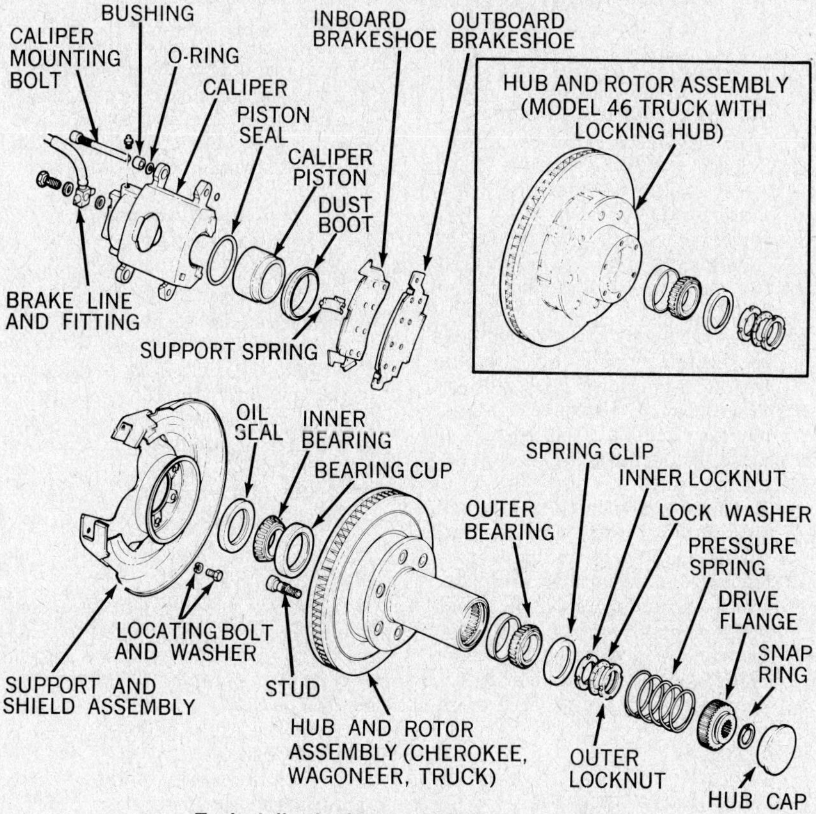

Typical disc brake assembly (© Jeep Corp.)

fitting. Tighten the wheel cylinder mounting bolts to 18 ft lbs.

Disc Brakes

Floating caliper, single piston type disc brakes are used on the front wheels of the Jeep vehicles, and consists of three assemblies, the caliper assembly, the hub and rotor assembly, and the support and shield assembly.

The caliper is attached to the support and shield assembly and upon hydraulic pressure application, the piston within the caliper is forced outward and pushes the inboard shoe against the rotor face. The reaction force moves the caliper body and the outboard shoe against the opposite rotor face, causing a pinching action of the two brake shoes against the rotor and bringing the vehicle to a stop. Brake adjustment is not needed because wear is automatically compensated for by the sliding movement of the caliper and the increased piston extension.

Brake Shoes

Replace the brake shoes when the linings are worn within 1/32 inch of the shoe or rivets.

Removal

1. Remove the wheel and tire assembly.
2. Remove approximately ⅔ of the brake fluid from the front section of the master cylinder.
3. Using a C-clamp, bottom the piston in its bore by placing the solid end of the clamp on the back of the caliper and the screw end contacting the metal part of the out board shoe, and tighten the clamp screw.

   NOTE: This procedure backs the brake shoes off the rotor surface, easing the lining replacement.
4. Remove both allen head mounting screws from the caliper to support, and lift the caliper off the rotor.

   NOTE: Hang the caliper by a wire hook or tie it to the frame, to avoid allowing the brake hose to support the weight of the caliper assembly.
5. Remove both disc brake shoes from the caliper, and note the position of the support spring on the inboard shoe for later installation, and remove the spring from the shoe.
6. Remove the sleeves and rubber bushings from the ears of the calipers.

Cleaning and Inspection

Clean the sliding surfaces of the caliper and clean any dirt from the mounting bolts, clips or keys. Inspect the boot on the piston for signs of

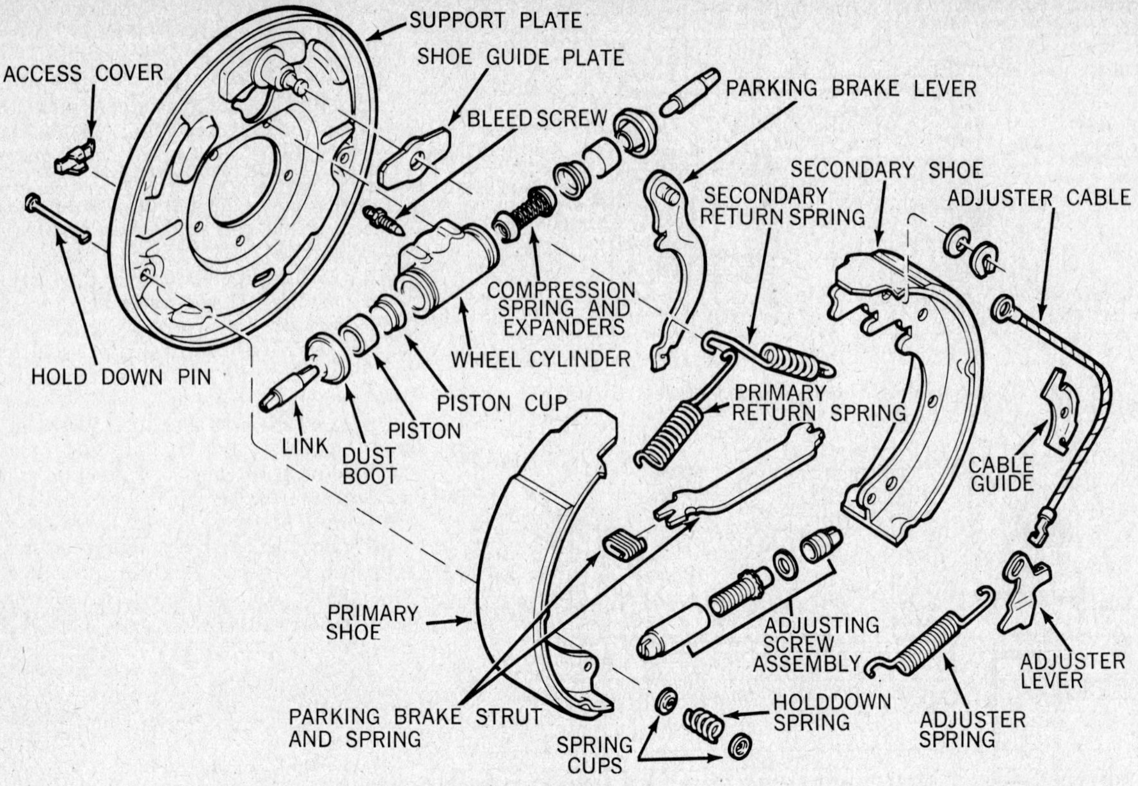

Drum brake assembly—CJ models (© Jeep Corp.)

cracks, cuts of any other damage. Check to see if there is any signs of fluid leakage around the seal on the piston. This will show up in the boot.

If there is any indication of a fluid leak, the entire caliper will have to be overhauled.

NOTE: Refer to the Brake General Repair Section for caliper overhaul procedures.

Installation

1. Clean all mounting holes, bolts, and bushing grooves. Lubricate and install new bushings and sleeves.

   NOTE: Sleeves should be installed in the inboard mounting ears of the caliper, and positioned so the sleeve end facing the shoe and lining, is flush with the mounting ear.
2. Install the support spring on the inboard shoe. Place the single tang end of the spring over the notch in the shoe.
3. Install the two brake shoes into the caliper and assure that both shoes are fully seated by having the ears of the shoes resting on the ears of the caliper.
4. Position the caliper over the rotor and install the mounting bolts. Assure that the bolts pass through the holes of the outboard shoes and caliper ears, and that the retaining ears of the inboard shoes are over the bolts. Torque the bolts to 35 ft. lbs.
5. Fill the master cylinder and pump the brake pedal to seat the shoes to the rotor.
6. Bend the upper ears of the outboard shoe until the radial clearance between the shoe and the caliper is eliminated.

Drum Brakes

Removal and Installation

1. Remove wheel and brake drum.
2. Release parking brake and loosen locknuts at parking brake equalizer.
3. On truck models with model 60 full-floating rear axle, remove the two screws that hold rear drums on hubs.
4. Remove lever tang from hole in secondary shoe by grasping the adjusting lever with a pliers.
5. Place brake cylinder clamp over wheel cylinder to hold pistons in place while brake shoes are removed.
6. Remove brake return springs, secondary return spring, adjuster cable, primary return spring, cable guide, adjuster lever, adjuster springs, holddown springs and brake shoes.
7. Disengage parking brake cable from parking brake lever.
8. Installation is the reverse of removal.

Stop Light Switch

Two types of switches are used on the Jeep vehicles. One type is attached to the brake pedal rod end of the push rod, and cannot be adjusted. The second type is mounted on a flange attached to the brake pedal support bracket and is held in the off position by the brake pedal being in its released position. Upon depressing the brake pedal, the switch plunger is allowed to move outward and contact is made within the switch to allow current to pass and operate the stop lights.

Switch Adjustment

1974-76

1. Release the brake pedal, unhook the retaining fingers of the wire connector from the switch and remove the wire harness.
2. Adjust the switch by turning it in or out of the mounting bracket. The switch should operate after 3/8 to 5/8 inch of brake pedal travel.
3. Connect the wire harness and recheck the switch operation.

1977-80

NOTE: CJ models with air conditioning, remove screws attaching the evaporator housing to the instrument panel and move housing away from the panel.

1. Hold the brake pedal in the applied position.
2. Push the stop light switch through the mounting bracket until it stops against the brake

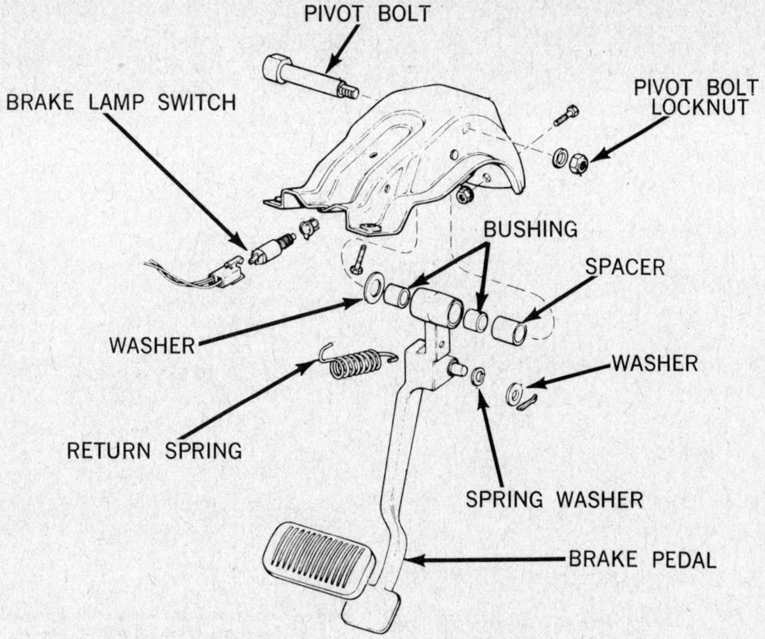

Brake pedal and adjusting switch— typical (© Jeep Corp.)

pedal bracket. Release the pedal to set the switch in the proper position.

3. Check the position of the switch. The switch plunger should be in the ON position and activate the brake lights after a brake pedal travel of 3/8 to 5/8 inch.

Parking Brakes

Adjustments—Typical

1. Make sure that the hydraulic brakes are in satisfactory adjustment.
2. Raise the rear wheels off the ground and disengage the parking brake pedal.
3. Loosen the locknut on the brake cable adjusting rod, located directly behind the frame center crossmember.
4. Spin the wheels and tighten the adjustment until the rear wheels drag slightly. Loosen the adjustment until there is no drag and the wheels spin freely.
5. Tighten the locknut to lock the adjusting nut.

FUEL SYSTEM

Reference

Refer to the Carburetor General Repair Section for exploded views of carburetors and specifications.

Carburetor

Removal and Installation

To remove the carburetor from any engine, first remove the air cleaner from the top of the carburetor. Remove all lines and hoses, noting their positions to facilitate installation. Remove all throttle and choke linkage at the carburetor. Remove the carburetor attaching nuts which hold it to the intake manifold. Lift the carburetor from the engine along with the carburetor base gasket. Discard the gasket. Install the carburetor in the reverse order of removal, using a new base gasket.

Idle Speed and Mixture Adjustments

1973-80

The procedure for adjusting the idle speed and mixture on 1973-80 Jeep vehicles is called the lean drop procedure and is made with the engine operating at normal operating temperature and the air cleaner in place as follows:

1. Turn the mixture screws to the full rich position with the tabs on the limiters against the stops. Note the position of screw head slot inside limiter cap slots.
2. Remove idler limiter caps.
3. Remove limiter caps by threading a sheet metal screw in center of cap and turning clockwise. Discard limiter caps.
4. Reset adjustment screws to same position noted before limiter caps were removed.
5. Start engine and allow it to reach normal operating temperature.
6. Adjust idle speed to 30 rpm above the specified rpm in the Tune-Up Specifications.
   a. On 6 cylinder engines with throttle stop solenoid, turn nut on solenoid plunger in or out to obtain specified rpm. This is done with solenoid wire connected.
   b. On V8 engines with throttle stop solenoid, turn hex screw on throttle stop solenoid carriage to obtain specified rpm. This is done with solenoid wire connected.
   c. Tighten solenoid locknut, if so equipped.
   d. Disconnect solenoid wire and adjust curb idle speed screw to obtain idle speed of 500 rpm.
   e. Re-connect solenoid wire.
7. Starting from the full rich position, as was determined before limiter caps were removed, turn mixture adjusting screws clockwise (leaner) until a loss of engine speed is noticed.
8. Turn screws counterclockwise (richer) until the highest rpm reading is obtained at lean best idle setting. The lean best idle setting is on the lean side of the highest rpm setting without changing rpm.
9. If the idle speed changed more than 30 rpm during the mixture adjustment procedure, reset the idle speed to 30 rpm above the specified rpm with idle speed ad-

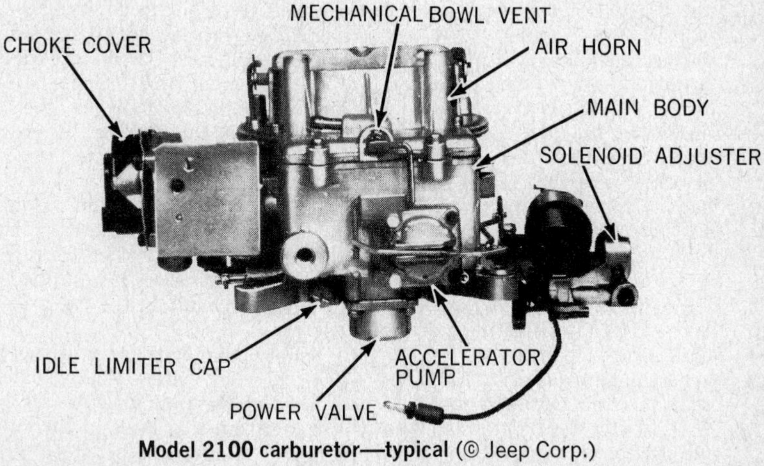

Model 2100 carburetor—typical (© Jeep Corp.)

justing screw or the throttle stop solenoid and repeat the mixture adjustment.

10. The final adjustment is to turn the mixture adjusting screws clockwise until engine rpm drop as follows:

1973-74	
6 Cylinder Automatic	20 rpm
6 Cylinder Manual	35 rpm
V8 All	40 rpm
1975	
6 Cylinder Automatic	25 rpm
6 Cylinder Manual with EGR and Catalytic Converter	35 rpm
6 Cylinder Manual with EGR only	50 rpm
V8 Automatic	20 rpm
V8 Manual	40 rpm
1976-77	
6 Cylinder Automatic	25 rpm
6 Cylinder Manual	50 rpm
V8 Automatic	20 rpm
V8 Manual	100 rpm
1978	
6 Cylinder Automatic	25 rpm
6 Cylinder Manual	50 rpm
V8-304 Automatic	20 rpm
V8-304 Manual	100 rpm
V8-360, 401 All	Lean best idle
1979-80	
6 Cylinder Automatic	25 rpm
6 Cylinder Manual	50 rpm (25 rpm Cherokee)
V8-304 Automatic	40 rpm
V8-304 Manual	20 rpm (100 rpm Calif.)
V8-360 Automatic	20 rpm
V8-360 Manual	50 rpm

11. Install new limiter caps over mixture adjusting screws with tabs positioned against full rich stops. Be careful not to disturb idle mixture setting while installing caps.

Fuel Pump

Removal and Installation

All Engines

1. Disconnect the fuel lines leading to the carburetor and from the fuel tank.
2. Remove the two attaching bolts that hold the fuel pump to the engine and lift the fuel pump off of the engine.
3. Before installing the fuel pump, make sure that all of the mating surfaces are clean.
4. Cement a new gasket to the mating surface of the fuel pump.
5. Position the fuel pump on the cylinder block so that the cam lever of the pump rests on the camshaft.
6. Secure the pump to the engine with the two bolts and lock washers.
7. Connect the fuel lines to the fuel pump.

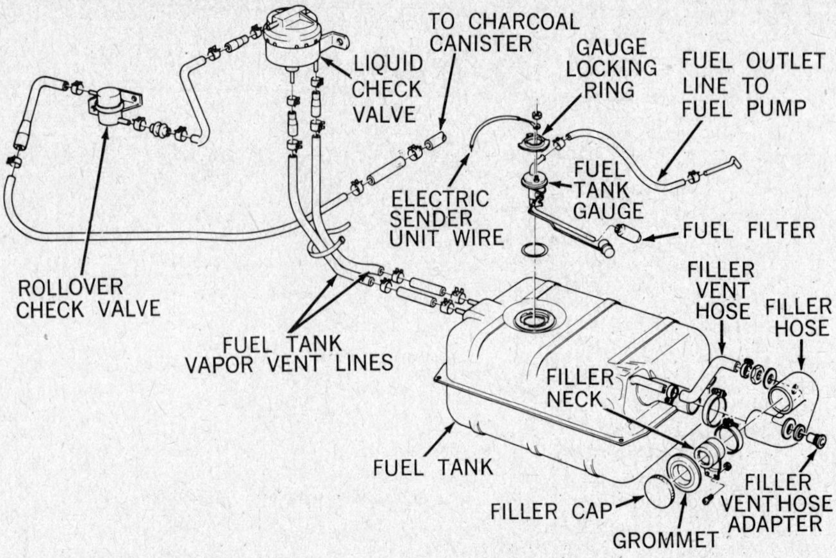

Typical fuel tank and vent lines (© Jeep Corp.)

Fuel Tank

Removal and Installation

All Models

The fuel tank on 1973-80 models is attached to the frame by brackets and bolts. The brackets are attached to the tank at the seam flange.

Before removing the fuel tank, make sure the level of the fuel inside the tank is at least below any of the various hoses connected. It is best to either drain or siphon the majority of fuel out of the tank to make it easier to handle while removing it.

To remove the tank, loosen all of the clamps retaining hoses to the tank and disconnect the hoses from the tank. It may be necessary to remove the fuel tank-to-mounting bracket screws and lower the tank slightly to gain access to some of the connecting hoses. Disconnect the tank from the mounting brackets, if not already done, and lower the tank from under the vehicle. Be careful not to spill any fuel in the tank while removing it.

On some Cherokee and Wagoneer models, it may be necessary to remove the parking brake cable guide clips and skid-plate, if equipped, and to disconnect one brake cable at connector.

Empty the tank of all fuel and flush it with water before soldering or welding the tank.

Install the fuel tank in the reverse order of removal.

COOLING SYSTEM

Water Pump

Removal and Installation
232 and 258 Sixes

1. Drain the cooling system at the radiator.
2. Disconnect the radiator and heater hoses from the water pump.
3. Loosen the alternator adjustment strap screw, upper pivot bolt, and remove the drive belt.
4. If the vehicle is equipped with a radiator shroud, separate the shroud from the radiator to facilitate removal and installation of the cooling fan and hub.
5. Remove the cooling fan and hub assembly.
6. Remove air conditioning intermediate idler pulley and mounting bracket, if so equipped.
7. Remove the power steering pump front mounting bracket, if so equipped.
8. Remove the water pump and gasket from the engine.
9. Clean all the old gasket material from the gasket surface of the engine.
10. Install the new water pump and assemble the engine in the reverse order of removal, tightening the water pump retaining bolts to 13 ft lbs.

V8 All

1. Disconnect the negative battery cable.
2. Drain the radiator and disconnect the upper radiator hose at the radiator.
3. Loosen all the drive belts.

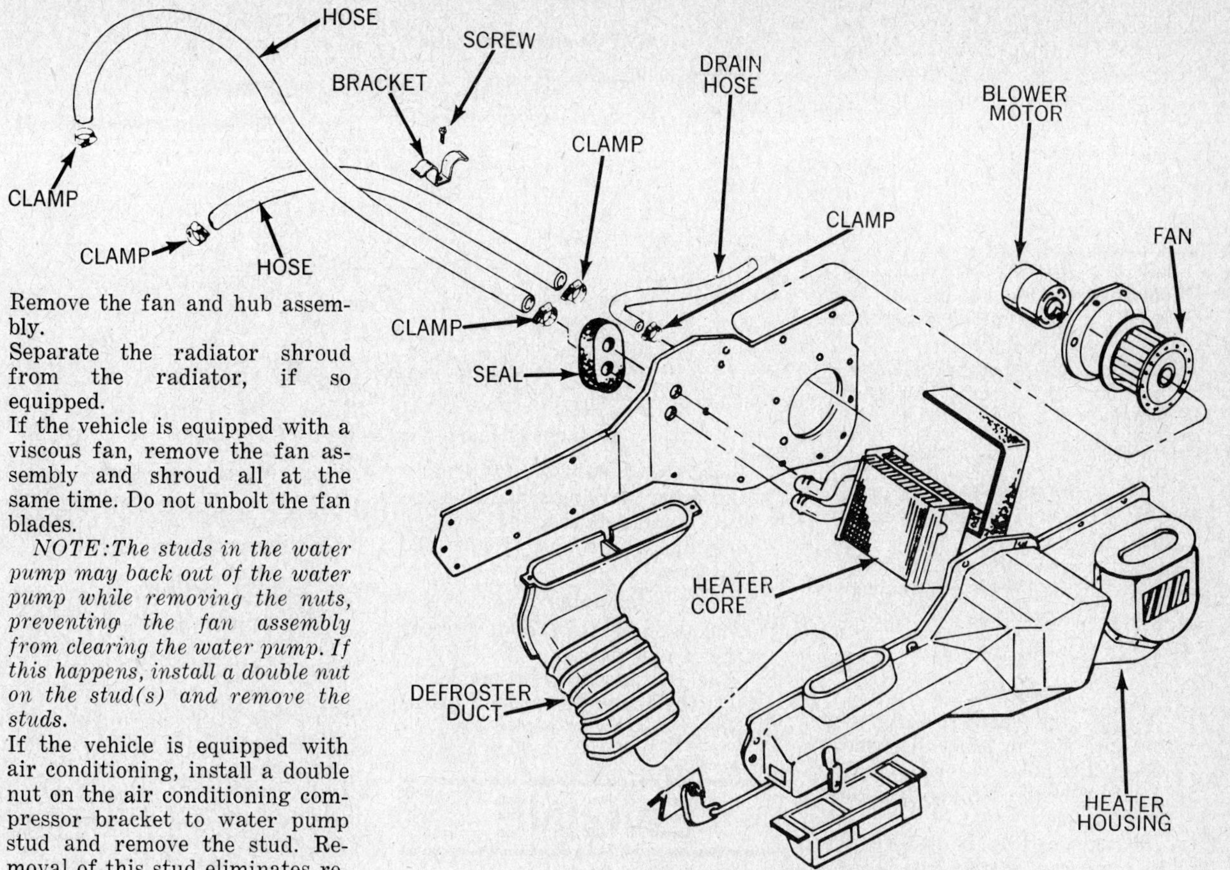

Heater defroster assembly—CJ models (© Jeep Corp.)

4. Remove the fan and hub assembly.
5. Separate the radiator shroud from the radiator, if so equipped.
6. If the vehicle is equipped with a viscous fan, remove the fan assembly and shroud all at the same time. Do not unbolt the fan blades.

   NOTE: The studs in the water pump may back out of the water pump while removing the nuts, preventing the fan assembly from clearing the water pump. If this happens, install a double nut on the stud(s) and remove the studs.
7. If the vehicle is equipped with air conditioning, install a double nut on the air conditioning compressor bracket to water pump stud and remove the stud. Removal of this stud eliminates removing the compressor mounting bracket.
8. Remove the alternator and mounting bracket assembly and place it aside. Do not disconnect the alternator wires.
9. Remove the two nuts attaching the power steering pump to the rear half of the pump mounting bracket, if so equipped.
10. Remove the two bolts attaching the front half of the bracket to the rear half.
11. Remove the remaining upper bolt from the inner air pump support brace, loosen the lower bolt and drop the brace away from the power steering front bracket.
12. Remove the front half of the power steering bracket from the water pump mounting stud.
13. Disconnect the heater hose, bypass hose, and lower radiator hose at the water pump.
14. Remove the water pump and gasket from the timing chain cover and clean all old gasket material from the gasket surface of the timing chain cover.
15. Install the new water pump and assemble the remaining components in the reverse order of removal, tightening the water pump-to-engine block screws to 25 ft lbs and the water pump-to-timing case cover screws to 4 ft lbs (48 in. lbs).

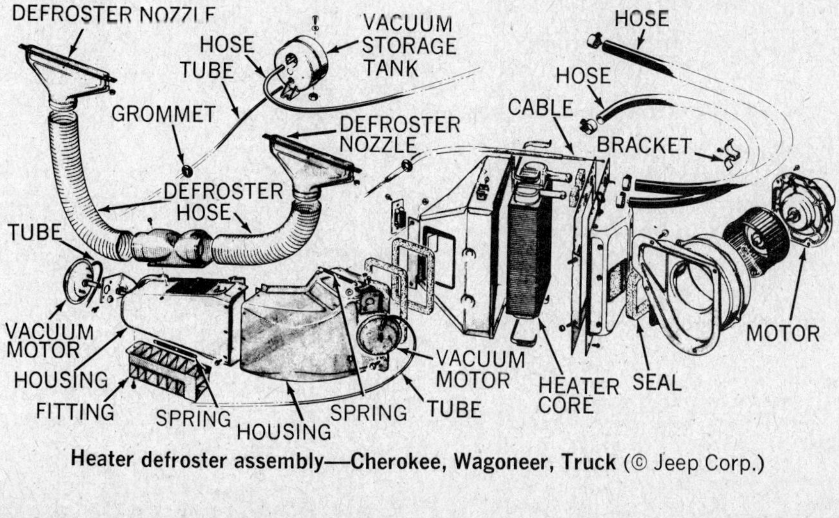

Heater defroster assembly—Cherokee, Wagoneer, Truck (© Jeep Corp.)

Heater Core

NOTE: (All models) If equipped with air conditioning, the unit must be removed from the dash and lowered to gain access to the heater control box for the removal of the heater core.

1973 CJ and Commando

Removal

1. Remove the negative battery cable and drain the cooling system.
2. Mark the duct halves for proper reassembly.
3. Separate the duct halves by removing the four attaching screws.
4. Remove the heater core.

Installation

1. The assembly is in the reverse of the disassembly.
2. When the assembly is complete, test the operation of the heater and controls.

1973 Wagoneer—Truck

Removal

1. Drain the cooling system and disconnect the negative battery cable.

2. Disconnect the temperature control cable at the heater housing.
3. Disconnect the heater hoses and remove the wire plug connector from the heater resistor.
4. Remove the four nuts that retain the heater core and duct to the firewall.
   NOTE: Two of the nuts are located inside the vehicle to the right of the transition duct.
5. Remove the duct assembly and scribe a mark on the two halves for proper assembly.
6. Separate the duct halves by removing the four attaching screws.
7. Remove the heater core.

Installation

1. The assembly is in the reverse of the disassembly.
2. Upon completion of the assembly, test the heater assembly for proper operation.

1974-80 CJ Models

Removal

1. Remove the battery, drain the cooling system, and disconnect the heater hoses.
2. Disconnect the damper door control cable.
3. Disconnect the blower motor wire harness and ground wire at the switch and instrument panel.
4. Remove the glove box; water drain hose and defroster duct hose.
5. Disconnect the heater to air deflector duct at the heater housing.
6. Remove the nuts from the heater housing studs, protruding into the engine compartment.
7. Remove the heater housing assembly from the vehicle and remove the core from the housing.

Installation

1. The assembly is in the reverse of the disassembly.
2. When the assembly is completed, test the heater for proper operation.

1974-80 Cherokee-Wagoneer —Truck

Removal

1. Remove the negative battery cable and drain the cooling system.
2. Disconnect the temperature control cable from the blend air door.
3. Remove the heater hoses and blower motor resistor wires.
4. Remove the heater core housing to dash panel attaching screws or nuts, projecting into the engine compartment.
5. Remove the heater housing assembly from the vehicle.
6. Separate the halves of the housing, after scribing a mark on the two halves, remove the core retaining screws and remove the heater core.

Assembly

1. The assembly is in the reverse of the disassembly.
2. When the assembly is completed, test the heater for proper operation.

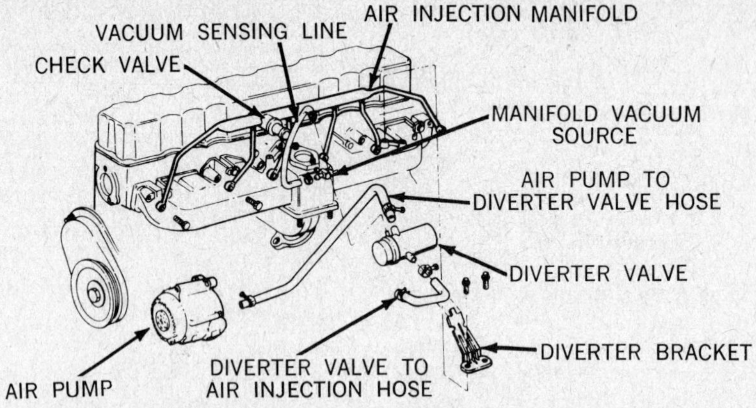

Air guard system—6 cyl.—typical (© Jeep Corp.)

ENGINE

Reference

Refer to the Engine General Repair Section for troubleshooting and rebuilding procedures.

Emission Control Systems

Emission control systems are designed to control the emissions of Hydrocarbons (HC), Carbon monoxide (CO), and Oxides of Nitrogen (NOx), at the levels specified by Federal and State governments. Emission control systems vary in their usage, in relationship to engine, transmission, and series applications.

Overhaul of the units are covered in the General Repair Section.

Air Guard System

This system is used to inject air into the exhaust ports, to mix with the hot unburned gases, and to further burn the combustion mixture and reduce the hydrocarbons and carbon monoxide emissions into the atmosphere. The system consists of a belt driven air pump, a diverter valve, air injector manifolds, air injector tubes, and connecting hoses.

Exhaust Gas Recirculation System (EGR)

This system is used to meter exhaust gases into the combustion chambers to dilute the intake charge, thereby reducing the peak temperature of the gases and limit the formation of the Oxides of Nitrogen that forms as a result of the high temperature during the combustion process.

The exhaust gases introduced is inert and much cooler than the combustion temperature. Since the exhaust gas will not burn, peak combustion temperatures are lowered.

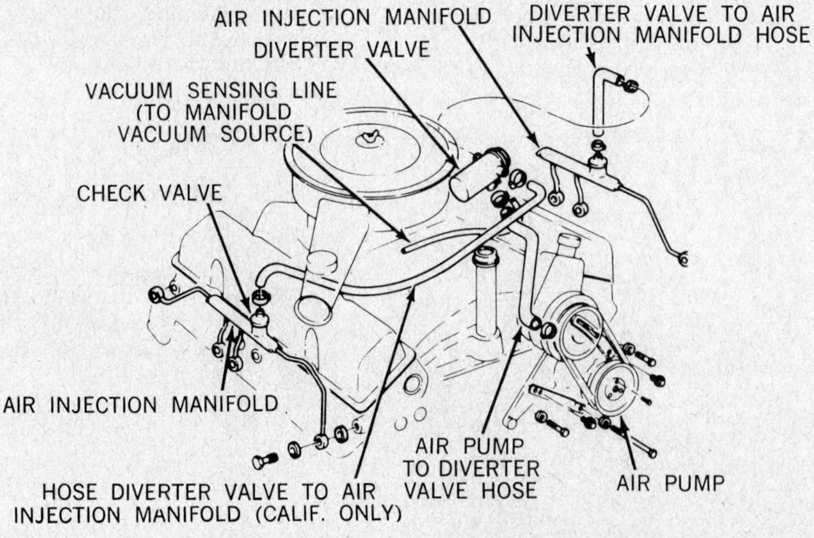

Air guard system—8 cyl.—typical (© Jeep Corp.)

The system consists of a exhaust gas recirculating valve which connects the exhaust manifold to the intake manifold. An exhaust back pressure sensor is used on some models. A coolant override temperature switch and various lengths of vacuum hoses complete the system.

Catalytic Converter

A catalytic converter is used as part of the exhaust system to have the exhaust gases pass through and undergo a chemical reaction which changes the hydrocarbons and carbon monoxide into harmless carbon dioxide and water before it is emitted into the atmosphere. Beads of Alumina, covered with Platinum and Palladium are used as the catalyst. Unleaded gasoline must be used as leaded fuels poisons or spoils the catalyst used in the converter.

Fuel Tank Vapor Emission Control System

A closed fuel tank vent system is used to prevent fuel vapors from entering the atmosphere. The raw vapors are routed into the intake system and is burned along with the fuel-air mixture.

The system consists of a two-way relief valve filler cap, which is closed to the atmosphere pressures under normal operating conditions and opens when pressure exceeds 0.75 to 1.50 PSI, or a vacuum of 15 to 25 inches. A liquid check valve is used to route the vapors and collect any liquid before the vapors are drawn into and stored in the fuel vapor storage cannister, until they are drawn into the intake manifold through the carburetor air cleaner assembly. The amount of vapors drawn from the cannister is relative to the air velocity passing through the air cleaner snorkel.

Positive Crankcase Ventilation System (PCV)

The positive crankcase ventilation system draws the crankcase vapors into the intake manifold, to be burned along with the air-fuel mixture. This is normally a closed system so that the crankcase vapors are not emitted into the atmosphere. The system consists of hose routings, a ventilation valve, connected to and operated by engine vacuum from the intake manifold.

Thermostatically Controlled Air Cleaner System (TAC)

The thermostatically controlled air cleaner system operates to avoid the induction of cold air into the carburetor and intake manifold before the engine reaches normal operating temperature. When the engine is first started, a thermostatically controlled valve in the air cleaner snorkel closes to outside air and exhaust manifold heater air is directed into the air cleaner assembly, carburetor, and intake manifold. As the engine warms, and the surrounding air temperature increases, the valve in the air cleaner snorkel opens and admits air from the engine compartment, while closing off the heated manifold air.

Vacuum Throttle Modulating System (VTM)

The VTM system is used to reduce the emission off hydrocarbons during rapid throttle closure at high speeds and consists of a deceleration valve and a throttle modulating diaphragm located on the carburetor base to allow the throttle to remain slightly open and admit more air into the combustion chambers to lean out the overrich mixture, during the rapid throttle release. The decel valve and modulator diaphragm are operated by engine vacuum signals.

Transmission Controlled Spark System (TCS)

The TCS system is used to reduce the emissions of oxide of nitrogen by lowering the peak combustion temperatures during the power stroke by not allowing vacuum to be routed to the distributor vacuum advance unit during low speed operation, thereby not allowing the advance unit to operate. This system is controlled by switches located and operated by the transmission gear selector, or oil pressure, directed to a switch, at a predetermined speed.

Spark Coolant Temperature Override Switch (Spark CTO)

This system is used to override the TCS system to improve driveability during the warmup period by providing full distributor vacuum advance operation until the temperature reaches 160° F within the cooling system. The system then reverts to the transmission controlled spark system.

Engine Modification

The design of certain engine components are directly related to the approved emission standards. The correct combination of engine components, such as the camshaft, carburetor, ignition distributor, cylinder head, and other internal parts, must be used in service, as prescribed by government certification.

Engine Assembly

Removal and Installation

232, 258 Sixes

NOTE: This operation requires discharging the air conditioning system. This requires special tools and skills for safety reasons. It should not be attempted by untrained persons.

1. Remove the hood after marking the hinge locations. The hood need not be removed on the CJ series.
2. Remove the air cleaner.
3. Drain the coolant. Disconnect the radiator hoses. Disconnect automatic transmission cooler lines from the radiator. If there is a radiator shroud, remove it, then remove the radiator.
4. Remove the fan.
5. Remove and set aside the power steering pump and belt. Do not disconnect the hydraulic lines.
6. Bleed the compressor refrigerant charge. See the note at the start of this procedure. Remove the condenser and receiver assembly.
7. Disconnect all wires, lines, linkage, and hoses from the engine.
8. Drain the oil and remove the filter.
9. Remove both engine front support cushion-to-frame retaining nuts.
10. Disconnect the exhaust pipe at the support bracket and the manifold.
11. Support the engine with the lifting equipment.
12. Remove the front support cushion and bracket assemblies from the engine.
13. Remove the transfer case lever boot, the floor mat, and the transmission access cover.
14. In automatic transmissions, remove the upper bolts holding the bellhousing to the engine adapter plate. On manual transmissions, remove the upper bolts holding the clutch housing to the engine.
15. Remove the starter.
16. On automatics, remove the two adapter plate inspection covers. Mark the relationship of the converter to the flex plate and remove the converter-to-flex plate bolts. Remove the rest of the bolts holding the bellhousing to the adapter plate. On manual transmissions, remove the clutch housing lower cover and the rest of the bolts holding the clutch housing to the engine.
17. Support the transmission with a floor jack and remove the engine by pulling it forward and upward.

To install the engine:

18. Lower the engine into place and align it with the bellhousing or clutch housing. Make sure the manual transmission clutch shaft aligns with the splines of the clutch driven plate.
19. On automatics, install the bellhousing-to-engine adapter plate bolts. On manuals, install the clutch housing-to-engine bolts. Torque the bolts to 25-28 ft lbs

at the top and 40-45 ft lbs at the bottom.
20. Remove the floor jack.
21. Align the marks made in step 16 and install the converter-to-flex plate bolts, torquing them to 21-23 ft lbs.
22. Install the two engine adapter plate inspection covers or the clutch housing lower cover.
23. Replace the starter.
24. Install the front support cushion and bracket assemblies to the engine, torquing the bolts to 25-30 ft lbs. Lower the engine onto the frame supports. Install the front support cushion retaining nuts, torquing them to 25-30 ft lbs.
25. Connect the exhaust pipe at the support bracket and manifold. A new manifold seal is advisable.
26. Install the oil filter.
27. Replace all the items removed in step seven.
28. Replace the air conditioning condenser and receiver assembly and recharge the system.
29. Replace the power steering pump and belt. Install the fan and tighten the bolts to 15-25 ft lbs.
30. Replace and reconnect the radiator. Replace the oil cooler lines. Fill the cooling system.
31. Fill the crankcase and replace the air cleaner. Install the transmission access cover, floor mat, and transfer case lever boot. Replace the hood.

304, 360 and 401 V8

NOTE: This operation requires discharging the air conditioning system. This requires special tools and skills. For safety reasons, it should not be attempted by untrained persons.

The engine is removed without the transmission and bellhousing.

1. On the Commando, Cherokee, Truck, and Wagoneer, the hood must be removed. Mark the hinge locations at the hood panel for alignment during installation. Remove the hood from the hinges.
2. Remove the air cleaner assembly.
3. Drain the cooling system and disconnect the upper and lower radiator hoses. If equipped with automatic transmission, disconnect the cooler lines from the radiator.

   NOTE: If the vehicle is equipped with a radiator shroud, it is necessary to separate the shroud from the radiator to facilitate removal and installation of the radiator and engine fan.
4. Remove the radiator.
5. Remove the engine fan.
6. If equipped with power steering, remove the pump from the engine and lay it aside. Do not disconnect the hoses.
7. If equipped with air conditioning, turn both service valves clockwise to the front seated position. Bleed the compressor refrigerant charge by slowly loosening the service valve fittings. Disconnect the condenser and evaporator lines from the compressor. Disconnect the receiver outlet at the disconnect coupling. Remove the condenser and receiver assembly.
8. Remove the battery and tray.
9. On Wagoneers and Cherokees, (1973-75) remove the heater core housing and charcoal canister from the firewall.
10. If equipped, remove cruise command vacuum servo bellows and mounting bracket as a complete assembly.
11. On CJ models, (1976-80) remove left front support cushion and bracket from cylinder block.
12. Disconnect all wires, lines linkage, and hoses which are connected to the engine.
13. If equipped with automatic transmission, disconnect the transmission filler tube bracket from the right cylinder head. Do not remove the filler tube from the transmission.
14. Remove both engine front support cushion-to-frame retaining nuts.
15. Support the weight of the engine with a lifting device.
16. On CJ and Commando models, remove the transfer case shift lever boot, floor (if so equipped), and transmission access cover.
17. Remove the upper bolts which secure the transmission bellhousing to the engine adapter plate on vehicles equipped with automatic transmission. If equipped with manual transmission, remove the upper bolts which secure the clutch housing to the engine.
18. Disconnect the exhaust pipes at the exhaust manifolds and support bracket.
19. Remove the starter motor.
20. Support the transmission with a floor jack.
21. If equipped with automatic transmission, remove the two engine adapter plate inspection covers. Mark the assembled position of the converter and flex plate and remove the converter-to-flex plate cap screws. Remove the remaining bolts which secure the transmission bellhousing to the engine adapter plate.
22. If equipped with manual transmission, remove the clutch housing lower cover and the remaining bolts which secure the clutch housing to the engine.
23. Remove the engine by pulling upward and forward.

   NOTE: If equipped with power brakes, care must be taken to avoid damaigng the power unit while removing the engine.

To install the engine:

24. Lower the engine slowly into the engine compartment and align with the transmission bellhousing (automatic transmission) or clutch housing (manual transmission). On manual transmissions, make certain the clutch shaft is aligned properly with the splines of the clutch driven plate.
25. Install the transmission bellhousing-to-engine adapter plate bolts (automatic transmission) or the clutch housing to engine bolts (manual transmission). Tighten the bolts to the specified torque. Remove the floor jack which was used to support the transmission.
26. If equipped with automatic transmission, align the marks previously made on the converter and flex plate, install the converter-to-flex plate cap screws and tighten to the specified torque.
27. Install the two engine adapter plate inspection covers (automatic transmission) or the clutch housing lower cover (manual transmission).
28. Install the starter motor.
29. Lower the engine onto the frame supports, remove the lifting device and install the front support cushion retaining nuts. Tighten the nuts to the specified torque.
30. Connect the exhaust pipes at the exhaust manifolds and support bracket.
31. If equipped with automatic transmission, connect the transmission filler tube bracket to the right cylinder head.
32. On Wagoneers and Cherokees, install the heater core housing and charcoal canister to the firewall.
33. If removed, install the battery and tray.
34. Connect all wires, lines, linkage and hoses which were previously disconnected from the engine.
35. If removed, install the air conditioning condenser and receiver assembly. Connect the receiver outlet to the disconnect coupling. Connect the condenser and evaporator lines to the compressor. Purge the compressor of air.

   NOTE: Both service valves must be open before the air conditioning system is operated.
36. If equipped with power steering, connect the power steering, pump to the engine.
37. Install the engine fan and tighten the retaining bolts to the specified torque.

38. Install the radiator and connect the upper and lower hoses. If equipped with automatic transmission, connect the cooler lines.
39. Fill the cooling system to the specified level.
40. Install the air cleaner assembly. Install cruise command vacuum servo bellows and mounting bracket.
41. Start the engine. Check all connections for leaks. Stop the engine.
42. If removed, install the transmission access cover, floor mat and transfer case shift lever boot.
43. If removed, install the transmission access cover, floor mat and transfer case shift level boot.

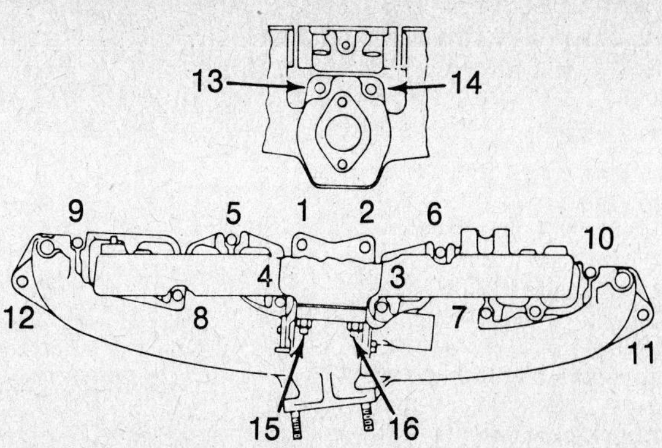

Intake/exhaust manifold torque sequence—6 cyl. (© Jeep Corp.)

Manifolds

Removal and Installation

Intake Manifold

232 and 258 Sixes

The intake and exhaust manifold are mounted externally on the left side of the engine and are attached to the cylinder head. They are removed as a unit. On later engines, an exhaust gas recirculation valve is mounted on the side of the intake manifold.

1. Remove the air cleaner and carburetor.
2. Disconnect the accelerator cable from the accelerator bellcrank.
3. Disconnect the PCV vacuum hose from the intake manifold.
4. Disconnect the distributor vacuum hose and electrical wires at the TCS solenoid vacuum valves.
5. Remove the TCS solenoid vacuum valve and bracket from the intake manifold. In some cases it might not be necessary to remove the TCS unit.
6. If so equipped, disconnect the EGR valve and back pressure sensor hoses.
7. Remove the power steering mounting bracket and pump and set it aside without disconnecting the hoses. Remove Air Pump, if equipped.
8. Remove the EGR valve and backpressure sensor, if so equipped. If equipped, remove air conditioning drive belt idler assembly from cylinder head.
9. Disconnect the exhaust pipe from the manifold flange.
10. Remove the manifold attaching bolts, nuts and clamps.
11. Separate the intake manifold and exhaust manifold from the engine as an assembly, and discard the gasket.
12. If either manifold is to be replaced, they should be separated at the heat riser area.
13. Clean the mating surface of the manifolds and the cylinder head before replacing the manifolds. Replace them in reverse order of the above procedure with new gasket. Tighten the bolts and nuts to the specified torque in the proper sequence.

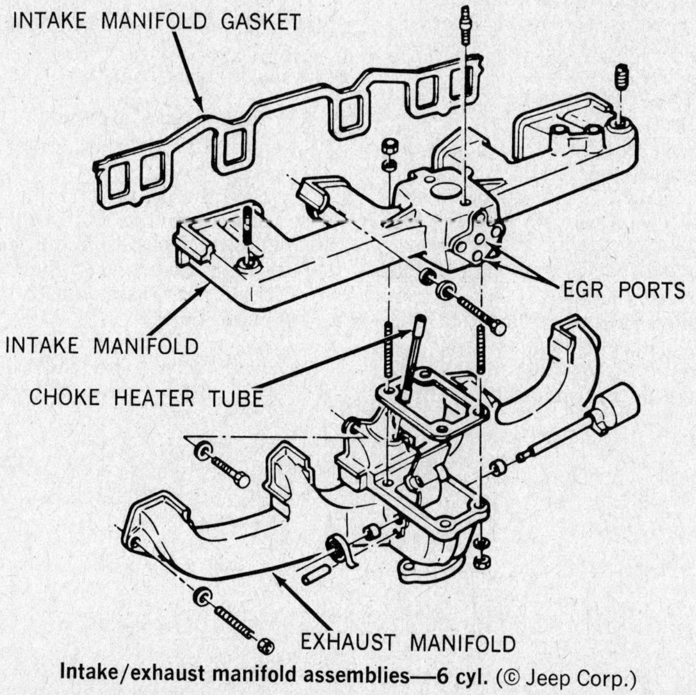

Intake/exhaust manifold assemblies—6 cyl. (© Jeep Corp.)

304, 360 and 401 V8s

1. Drain the coolant from the radiator.
2. Remove the air cleaner assembly.
3. Disconnect the spark plug wires.
4. Disconnect the upper radiator hose and the by-pass hose from the intake manifold. Disconnect the heater hose from the rear of the manifold.
5. Disconnect the ignition coil bracket and lay the coil aside.
6. Disconnect the TCS solenoid vacuum valve from the right side valve cover.
7. Disconnect all lines, hoses, linkages and wires from the carburetor and intake manifold and TCS components as required. Remove carburetor.
8. Disconnect the air delivery hoses at the air distribution manifolds.
9. Disconnect the air pump diverter valve and lay the valve and the bracket assembly, including the hoses, forward of the engine.
10. Remove the intake manifold after removing the cap bolts that hold it in place. Remove and discard the side gaskets and the end seals.
11. Clean the mating surfaces of the intake manifold and the cylinder head before replacing the intake manifold. Use new gaskets and tighten the cap bolts to the correct torque. Install in reverse order of the above procedure.

NOTE: There is no specified tightening sequence for the V8 304, 360 and 401 intake manifold. Begin at the center and work outward.

Exhaust Manifold

232, 258 Sixes

The intake and exhaust manifolds of the 232 and 258 cu in. Sixes must be removed together. See the procedure for removing and installing the intake manifold.

All V8

1. Disconnect the spark plug wires.
2. Disconnect the air delivery hose at the distribution manifold.
3. Remove the air distribution manifold and the injection tubes.
4. Disconnect the exhaust pipe at the manifold.
5. Remove the exhaust manifold attaching bolts and washers along with the spark plug shields.
6. Separate the exhaust manifold from the cylinder head.
7. Install in reverse order of the above procedure. Clean the mating surfaces and tighten the attaching bolts to the correct torque.

Engine Mounts

Removal and Installation

All Engines

Resilient rubber mounting cushions support the engine and transmission at three points. A cushion is located at each side on the center line of the engine, with the rear supported by a cushion between the transmission extension housing and the rear engine support crossmember.

Replacement of the cushion may be accomplished by supporting the weight of the engine or transmission at the area of the cushion.

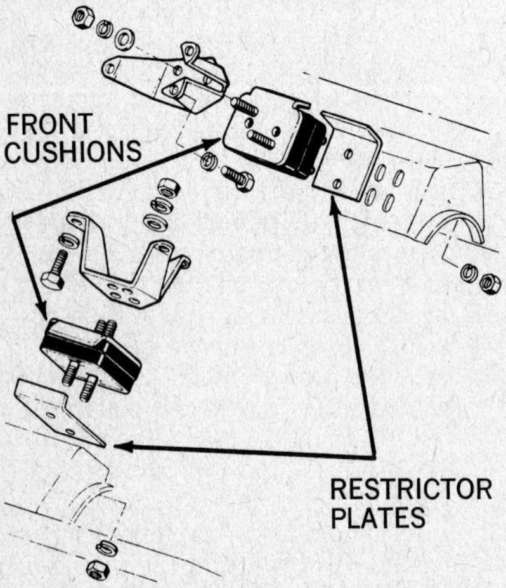

V8 engine mounts typical (© Jeep Corp.)

Cylinder Head

Removal and Installation

232 and 258 Sixes

1. Drain the cooling system and disconnect the hoses at the thermostat housing.
2. Remove the cylinder head cover (valve cover), the gasket, the rocker arm assembly, and the pushrods.

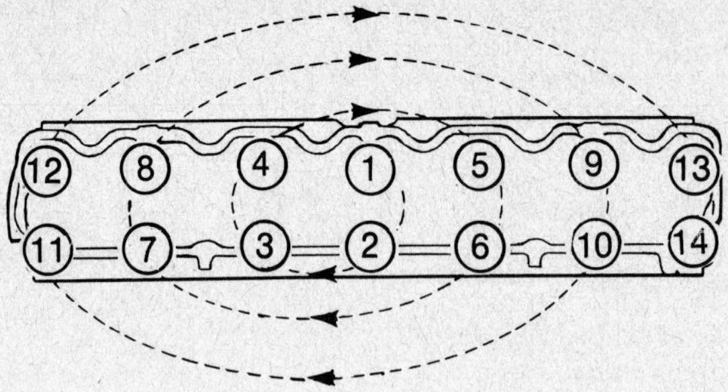

Cylinder head bolt tightening sequence—6 cyl. (© Jeep Corp.)

NOTE: The pushrods and rockers must be replaced in their original positions.

3. Remove the intake and exhaust manifold from the cylinder head.
4. Disconnect the spark plug wires and remove the spark plugs to avoid damaging them.
5. Remove air conditioning drive belt idler bracket from cylinder head. Loosen alternator belt and remove bracket-to-head mounting screw. Remove compressor mounting bracket and set the unit aside.
6. Disconnect the temperature sending unit wire, ignition coil and bracket assembly and battery ground cable from the engine.
7. Remove the cylinder head bolts, the cylinder head and gasket from the block.
8. To install, reverse the above procedure. Tighten the cylinder head bolts to the specified torque, in the proper sequence.

V8 Engines

1. Drain the cooling system and the cylinder block.
2. When removing the right cylinder head, it may be necessary to remove the heater core housing from the firewall.
3. Remove the valve cover(s) and gasket(s).
4. Remove the rocker arm assemblies and push rods.

   NOTE: The valve train components must be replaced in their original positions.
5. Remove the spark plugs to avoid damaging them.
6. Remove the intake manifold with the carburetor still attached.
7. Remove the exhaust pipes at the flange of the exhaust manifold. When replacing the exhaust pipes, it is advisable to install new gaskets at the flange.
8. Loosen all of the drive belts.
9. Disconnect negative battery cable at cylinder head. Remove air conditioning compressor mount bracket and alternator support brace from cylinder head.
10. Disconnect the air pump and power steering pump brackets from the left cylinder head.
11. Remove the cylinder head bolts and lift the head(s) from the cylinder block.
12. Remove the cylinder head gasket(s) from the head(s) or the block.
13. To install, reverse the above procedure.

NOTE: Apply an even coat of sealing compound to both sides of the new head gasket only. Wire brush the cylinder head bolts, then lightly oil them prior to installation. First, tighten all bolts to 80 ft lbs, then tighten them to the specified torque. Follow the correct tightening sequence.

Rocker Arm Assemblies

6 Cylinder Engines

Removal (1st type)

1. Remove the cylinder cover and gasket.
2. Loosen the shaft retaining bolts evenly until the shaft is loose, and then remove all the retaining bolts from the supports and lift the shaft assembly from the cylinder head.
3. Remove the roll pin and spring washer from one end of the shaft, and remove the rocker

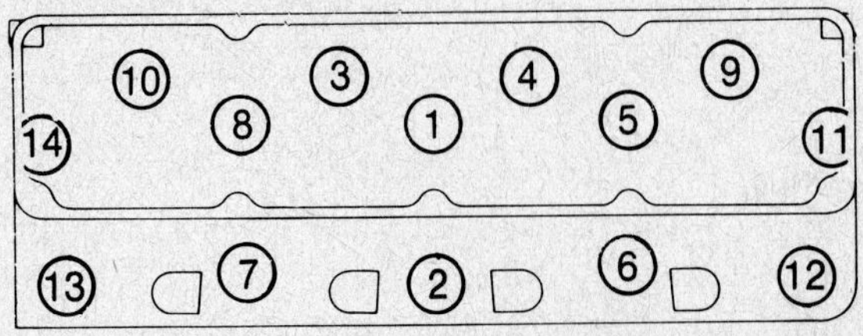

Cylinder head bolt tightening sequence—V8 (© Jeep Corp.)

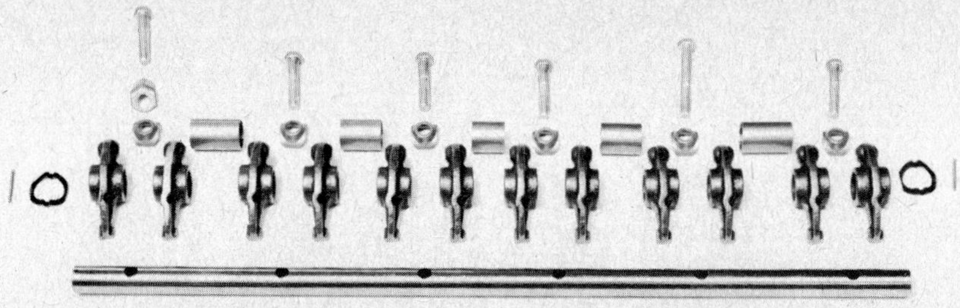

Rocker arm assembly—6 cyl.—1st type (© Jeep Corp.)

arms, spacers, retainers and bolts, and the oil deflector.
4. Maintain the parts in the order of the disassembly.

Installation

1. Assemble the rocker arms, spacers, retainers and bolts, and the oil deflector in the same order as removed.

   NOTE: The oil holes in the rocker arm shaft must face the cylinder head.
2. Install the rocker arm and shaft assembly onto the cylinder head and install the retaining bolts. Align the push rods with the rocker arms and tighten the retaining bolts evenly, by starting at the center and working outward.
3. Torque the bolts to 20-23 ft. lbs.
4. Install the cylinder head cover with a new gasket and torque the bolts to 45-55 in. lbs.

6 Cylinder Engines

Removal (2nd type)

1. Remove the cylinder head cover and gasket.
2. Remove the two capscrews at each bridged pivot, a turn at a time, to avoid cocking and breaking the bridge.
3. Remove the bridge and rocker arm from the cylinder head.

Rocker arm assembly—6 cyl.—2nd type (© Jeep Corp.)

Installation

1. Install the bridge and rocker arms in the same order as the removal, making sure the push rods are aligned to the rocker arms.
2. Install the capscrews and tighten alternately, a turn at a time, to avoid breaking the bridges. Torque the capscrews to 21 ft. lbs.
3. Install the cylinder head cover and a new gasket. Torque the bolts to 44-55 in. lbs.

V8 Engines

Removal (1st type)

NOTE: The removal and installation is described for one side only. Follow the same procedure to remove and install the opposite side.

1. Remove the cylinder head cover and gasket.
2. Remove the retaining nuts from the individually mounted rocker arms, and remove the rocker arm and pivot ball from the rocker arm retaining stud.

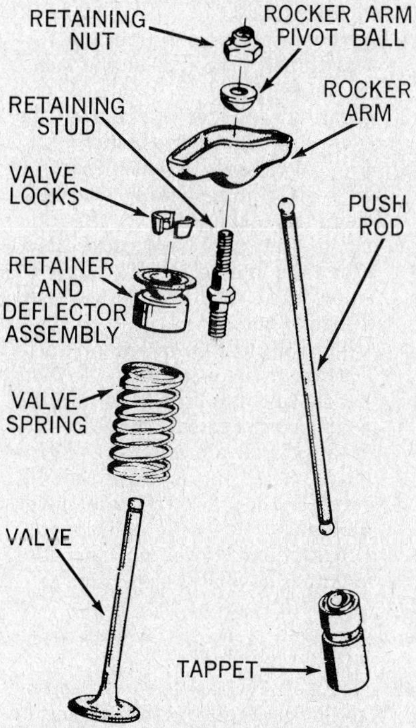

Valve train assembly—V8—1st type (© Jeep Corp.)

Installation

1. Install the rocker arm and pivot ball on the retaining stud.
2. Align the push rod to the rocker arm and torque the retaining nut to 20-25 ft. lbs.
3. Install the cylinder head cover and new gasket. Torque the bolts to 20-30 in. lbs.

V8 Engines

Removal (2nd type)

1. Remove the cylinder head cover and gasket.
2. Loosen the bridged pivot capscrews a turn at a time, so as not to break the bridge.
3. Remove the rocker arm and bridge assembly from the cylinder head.

V8 rocker arm-bridged pivot assembly—2nd type (© Jeep Corp.)

Installation

1. Install the rocker arms and bridge assembly on the cylinder head, and align the push rods.
2. Install the capscrews and tighten each one a turn at a time to avoid breaking the bridge. Tighten the capscrews to 19 ft. lbs. torque.
3. Install the cylinder head cover with a new gasket and torque the cover bolts to 50 in. lbs.

Valve Arrangement

6 Cylinder Engines

E I I E E I I E E I I E → Front

V8 Engines

E I I E E I I E
E I I E E I I E → Front

Crankshaft Pulley Assembly (Vibration Damper)

Removal and Installation

1. Remove drive belts from pulley.
2. Remove the retaining bolts and separate the pulley from the vibration damper.
3. Remove the vibration damper retaining bolt from the crankshaft end.
4. Using a vibration damper puller, remove the damper from the crankshaft.
5. Upon installation, align the key slot of the pulley hub to the crankshaft key. Complete the assembly in the reverse order of removal. Torque the retaining bolts to specifications.

Timing Gear Cover and Oil Seal

Removal and Installation

232, 258 Sixes

1. Remove the drive belts, engine fan and hub assembly, the accessory pulley and vibration damper.
2. Remove the oil pan to timing chain cover screws and the screws that attach the cover to the block.
3. Raise the timing chain cover just high enough to detach the retaining nibs of the oil pan neoprene seal from the bottom side of the cover. This must be done to prevent pulling the seal end tabs away from the tongues of the oil pan gaskets which would cause a leak.
4. Remove the timing chain cover and gasket from the engine.
5. Use a razor blade to cut off the oil pan seal end tabs flush with the front face of the cylinder block and remove the seal. Clean the timing chain cover, oil pan, and cylinder block surfaces.
6. Remove the crankshaft oil seal from the timing chain cover.
7. Install in reverse order of the above procedure. It will be necessary to cut the same amount from the end tabs of a new oil pan seal as was cut from the original seal, before installing the new gasket.

304, 360 and 401 V8

1. Remove the negative battery cable.
2. Drain the cooling system and disconnect the radiator hoses and by-pass hose.
3. Remove all of the drive belts and the fan and spacer assembly. Remove air conditioning compressor and bracket assembly from the engine, if equipped. Do not disconnect air conditioning hoses.
4. Remove the alternator and the front portion of the alternator bracket as an assembly.
5. Disconnect the heater hose.
6. Remove the power steering pump, and/or the air pump, and the mounting bracket as an assembly. Do not disconnect the power steering hoses.

V8 engine timing gear-to-oil pan seal installation (© Jeep Corp.)

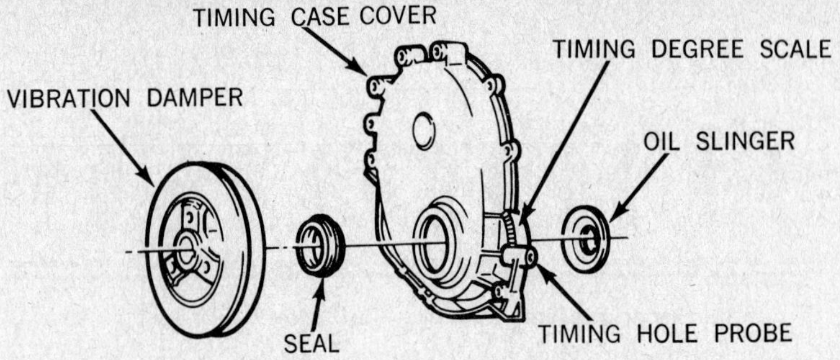

Timing case cover—6 cylinder engine (© Jeep Corp.)

7. Remove the distributor cap and note the position of the rotor. Remove the distributor. (See the Engine Electrical Section.)
8. Remove the fuel pump.
9. Remove the vibration damper and pulley.
10. Remove the two front oil pan bolts and the bolts which secure the timing chain cover to the engine block.

    NOTE: The timing gear cover retaining bolts vary in length and must be installed in the same locations from which they were removed.
11. Remove the cover by pulling forward until it is free of the locating dowel pins.
12. Clean the gasket surface of the cover and the engine block.
13. Pry out the original seal from inside the timing chain cover and clean the seal bore.
14. Drive the new seal into place from the inside with a block of wood until it contacts the outer flange of the cover.
15. Apply a light film of motor oil to the lips of the new seal.
16. Before reinstalling the timing gear cover, remove the lower locating dowel pin from the engine block. The pin is required for correct alignment of the cover and must either be reused or a replacement dowel pin installed after the cover is in position.
17. Cut both sides of the oil pan gasket flush with the engine block with a razor blade.
18. Trim a new gasket to correspond to the amount cut off at the oil pan.
19. Apply seal to both sides of the new gasket and install the gasket on the timing case cover.
20. Install the new front oil pan seal.
21. Align the tongues of the new oil pan gasket pieces with the oil pan seal and cement them into place on the cover.
22. Apply a bead of sealer to the cutoff edges of the original oil pan gaskets.
23. Place the timing case cover into position and install the front oil pan bolts. Tighten the bolts slowly and evenly until the cover aligns with the upper locating dowel.
24. Install the lower dowel through the cover and drive it into the corresponding hole in the engine block.
25. Install the cover retaining bolts in the same locations from which they were removed, tightened to 25 ft lbs.
26. Assemble the remaining components in the reverse order of removal.

Timing Chain or Gears

Removal and Installation

Valve Timing Inspection

1. Disconnect the ignition wires and remove the spark plugs.
2. Remove the cylinder head cover and gasket.
3. Remove the number one cylinder rocker arms and bridged pivots.
4. Rotate the crankshaft until number six piston is at top dead center (TDC) on the compression stroke. The number one piston is now on the exhaust stroke in the valve overlap position.
5. As viewed from the front, rotate the crankshaft counterclockwise 90°.
6. Install a dial indicator on number one intake valve pushrod end and set the dial indicator to zero.
7. As viewed from the front, rotate the crankshaft clockwise until the dial indicator indicates 0.016 inch for the 232, 258 CID six cylinder engines, 0.020 inch for the 304, 360 CID V-8 engines and 0.025 inch for the 401 CID V-8 engines.
8. The timing mark on the vibration damper should be indexed with the TDC mark on the timing case cover. If the timing mark is off more than ½ inch from TDC in either direction, the valve timing is incorrect and disassembly is indicated.

232, 258 Sixes

1. Remove the drive belts, engine fan and hub assembly, accessory pulley, vibration damper and timing chain cover.
2. Remove the oil seal from the timing chain cover.
3. Remove the camshaft sprocket retaining bolt and washer.
4. Rotate the crankshaft until the timing mark on the crankshaft sprocket is closest to and in a center line with the timing pointer of the camshaft sprocket.
5. Remove the crankshaft sprocket, camshaft sprocket and timing chain as an assembly. Disassemble the chain and sprockets.

Installation is as follows:

1. Assemble the timing chain, crankshaft sprocket and camshaft sprocket with the timing marks aligned.
2. Install the assembly to the crankshaft and the camshaft.
3. Install the camshaft sprocket retaining bolt and washer and tighten to 45-55 ft lbs.

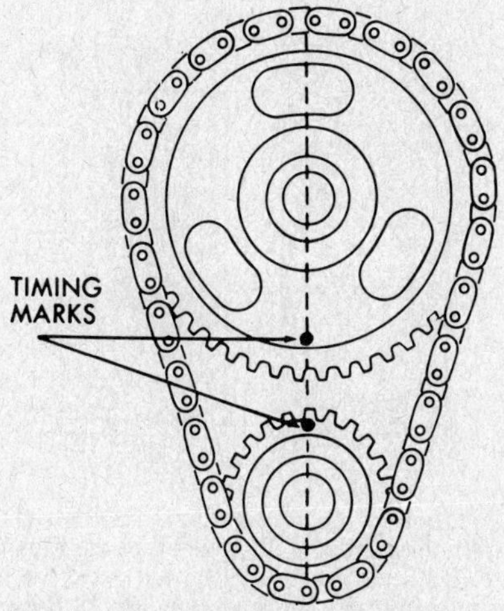

Alignment of timing chain sprockets—6 cyl. (© Jeep Corp.)

4. Install the timing chain cover and in a new oil seal.
5. Install the vibration damper, accessory pulley, engine fan and hub assembly and drive belts. Tighten the belts to the proper tension.

304, 360 and 401 V8s

1. Remove the timing chain cover and gasket.
2. Remove the crankshaft oil slinger.
3. Remove the camshaft sprocket retaining bolt and washer, distributor drive gear and fuel pump eccentric.
4. Rotate the crankshaft until the timing mark on the crankshaft sprocket is adjacent to, and on a center line with, the timing mark on the camshaft sprocket.
5. Remove the crankshaft sprocket, camshaft sprocket and timing

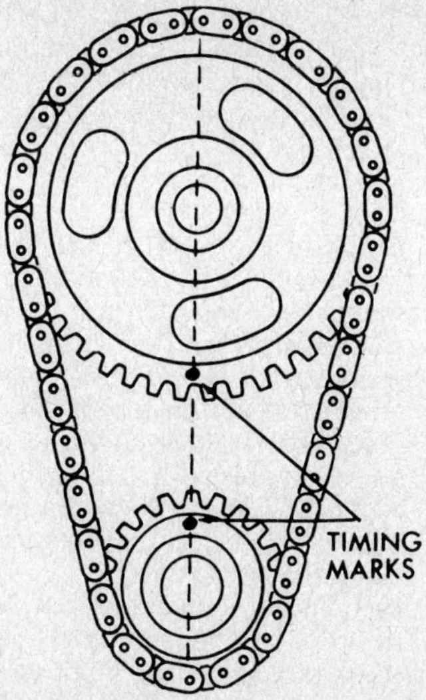

Alignment of timing chain sprockets—V8 (© Jeep Corp.)

chain as an assembly. Disassemble the chain and sprockets.

Installation is as follows:

1. Assemble the timing chain, crankshaft sprocket and camshaft sprocket with the timing marks on both sprockets aligned.
2. Install the assembly to the crankshaft and the camshaft.
3. Install the fuel pump eccentric, distributor drive gear, washer and retaining bolt. Tighten the bolt to 25-35 ft lbs.

   NOTE: The Fuel Pump eccentric must be installed with the stamped word "REAR" facing the camshaft sprocket.
4. Install the crankshaft oil slinger.
5. Install the timing chain cover using a new gasket and oil seal.

Camshaft

Removal and Installation

232, 258 Sixes

1. Drain and remove radiator.
2. If equipped, remove air conditioning condenser and receiver assembly as a charged unit.
3. Remove fuel pump, distributor and ignition wires.
4. Remove cylinder head cover and gasket.
5. Remove rocker arms, bridged pivot assemblies and pushrods. Be sure to replace these parts in the same order as removed.
6. Remove cylinder head and gasket and lifters.
7. Remove timing case cover.
8. Remove timing chain and sprockets as one assembly, being careful to rotate the crankshaft until the timing mark on the crankshaft sprocket is lined up with the timing pointer on the camshaft sprocket.
9. Remove the front bumper or grill as required.
10. Carefully remove the camshaft from the engine.
11. Installation is the reverse of removal.

V8

1. Drain and remove radiator.
2. If equipped, remove air conditioning condenser and receiver assembly as a charged unit.
3. Remove fuel pump, distributor and ignition wires.
4. Remove cylinder head cover and gasket.
5. Remove drive belts, fan, and hub assembly.
6. Remove intake manifold.
7. Remove rocker arms, bridged pivot assemblies and pushrods. Be sure to replace these parts in the same order as removed.
8. Remove cylinder head and gasket and lifters.
9. Remove timing case cover.
10. Remove distributor drive gear and fuel pump eccentric from the camshaft.

    NOTE: The fuel pump eccentric must be installed with the word "REAR" facing the camshaft sprocket.
11. Remove timing chain and sprocket as assembly, being careful to rotate the crankshaft until the timing mark on the crankshaft sprocket is lined up with the timing pointer on the camshaft sprocket.
12. Remove the front bumper or grill, and hood latch support bracket as required.
13. Carefully remove the camshaft from the engine.

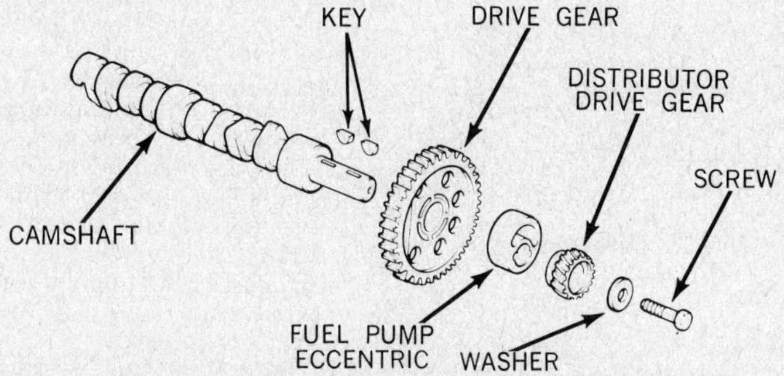

V-8 camshaft and components (© Jeep Corp.)

14. Installation is the reverse of removal.

Pistons and Connecting Rods

Removal and Installation

232 and 258 Sixes

1. Remove the cylinder head cover and gasket.
2. Remove the rocker arm assemblies. If the engine is equipped with the individual bridged pivot type of rockers, back off each capscrew a turn at a time to prevent breaking the bridge.
3. Remove the push rods.
4. Remove the cylinder head and gasket.
5. Position the pistons one at a time near the bottom of their stroke and use a ridge reamer to remove any ridge from the top end of the cylinder walls.
6. Drain the engine oil.
7. Remove the oil pan and gaskets.
8. Remove the connecting rod bearing caps and inserts and retain them in the same order as removed. The connecting rods and caps are stamped with the number of the cylinder when they are installed.
9. Remove the connecting rod and piston assemblies through the top of the cylinder bores.

NOTE: Be careful the connecting rod bolts do not scratch the connecting rod journals or cylinder walls. Short pieces of rubber hose can be slipped over the rod bolts to prevent damage.

10. After thoroughly cleaning the cylinder bores, apply a light film of clean engine oil to the cylinder bores with a clean cloth.
11. Position the piston rings on the pistons with:
    a. Oil ring spacer gap on centerline of piston skirt.
    b. Oil ring rail gaps 180° apart on center line of piston pin.
    c. Second compression ring gap 180° from top oil rail gap.
    d. First compression ring gap 180° from second compression ring gap with at least 30° between each ring gap.

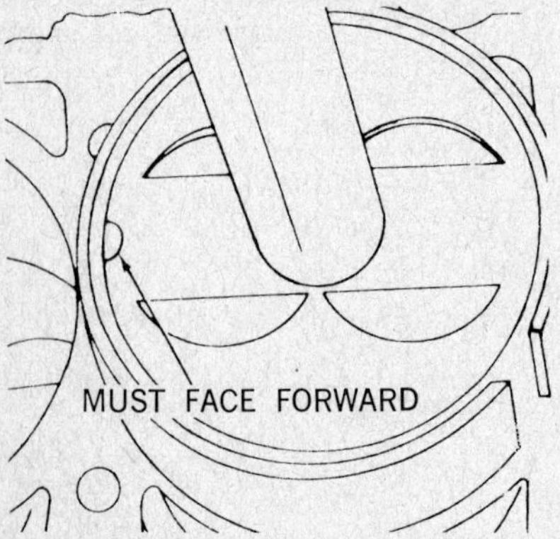

Piston installation—all engines (© Jeep Corp.)

12. Lubricate the piston and rings with clean engine oil.
13. With the notch in the top of the piston facing forward and the oil squirt hole in the connecting rod facing the camshaft, use a piston ring compressor to install the connecting rod and piston assemblies through the top of the cylinder bores. Make sure you have the little pieces of hose over the connecting rod bolts so as not to scratch the cylinder bores or the crankshaft journals.
14. Install the connecting rod bearing caps and inserts in the same order as removed. Tighten the retaining nuts to 28 ft lbs.
15. Install the oil pan with new gaskets.
    Tighten the drain plug.
16. Install a new gasket and the cylinder head.
17. Install push rods.
18. Install the rocker assemblies.
19. Install the cylinder head cover and gasket.
20. Fill the crankcase with new oil.

V8

1. Remove the cylinder head covers.
2. Remove the rocker arms and bridged pivot assemblies, loosening each capscrew one turn at a time to avoid breaking the bridge.
3. Remove the push rods.
4. Remove the intake manifold assembly.
5. Remove the cylinder head and gasket.
6. Position the pistons, one at a time, near the bottom of their stroke and use a ridge reamer to remove any ridge from the top end of the cylinder walls.
7. Drain the engine oil.
8. Remove the oil pan.
9. Remove the connecting rod bearing caps and inserts. Keep these parts in the same order as they are removed. The connecting rods and caps are stamped with the number of the cylinder from which they are removed.
10. Remove the connecting rod and piston assemblies through the top of the cylinder bores. Be careful not to scratch the cylinder bores or the crankshaft connecting rod bearing journals with the connecting rod bolts. Install short pieces of rubber hose over the bolts for protection.
11. After thoroughly cleaning the cylinder bores, apply a light film of clean engine oil to the bores with a clean cloth.
12. Arrange the piston ring gaps around the piston as follows:

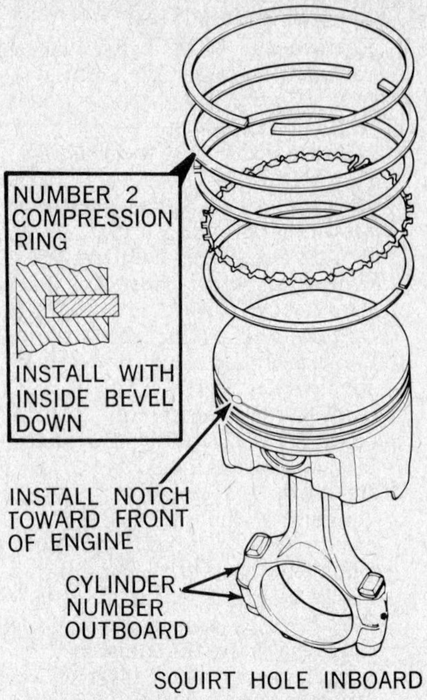

Engine piston and connecting rod assembly—V8 (© Jeep Corp.)

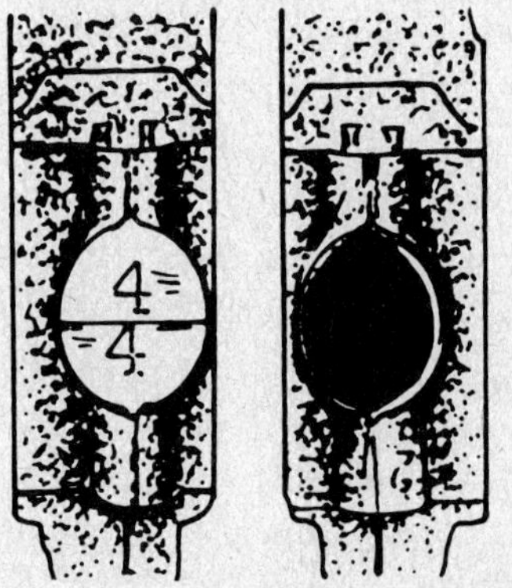

Location of the connecting rod identifying numbers and the oil squirt hole on the AMC V8 engines. The numbers and the squirt hole are on the same side of the connecting rod on the 232 and 258 six cylinder AMC engines. On both cases, the oil squirt hole must face the camshaft when installed in the engine. (© Jeep Corp.)

    a. Oil spacer gap on centerline of either skirt face.
    b. Oil rail gaps 180° apart and in line with piston pin centerline.
    c. Second compression ring gap 180° from top oil rail gap.
    d. First compression ring gap 180° from second compression ring gap.
13. Lubricate piston and ring surfaces with clean engine oil.
14. With the notch on the top of the pistons facing forward and the oil squirt hole in the connecting rod facing the camshaft, use a ring compressor to install the piston assemblies through the top of the cylinder bores. Place the lengths of rubber hose over the connecting rod bolts so to

protect the cylinder bores and crankshaft bearing journals.

15. Install the connecting rod bearing caps and inserts in the same order as removed. Tighten the nuts to the proper torque.
16. Install the oil pan with new gaskets and tighten the drain plug.
17. Install the cylinder heads and gaskets.
18. Install the push rods and rocker assemblies.
19. Install the intake manifold assembly.
20. Install the cylinder head covers with new gaskets.
21. Fill the crankshaft with new oil.

Connecting Rod Bearings

The connecting rod bearings are steel-backed aluminum-alloy, precision type.

Each bearing is selectively fitted to its respective journal to obtain the desired operating clearance. In production, the select fit is obtained by using various sized, color coded bearing inserts. The color code appears on the edge of the insert. Bearing size is not stamped on production inserts.

The rod journal size is identified in production by a color coded paint mark on the adjacent cheek or counterweight toward the rear end of the crankshaft.

When required, different sized upper and lower bearing inserts may be used as a pair, thus reducing clearance by 0.0005 in.

NOTE: Never use a pair of bearing inserts with more than 0.001 in. difference in size.

Service replacement bearing inserts are available as pairs in the following sizes: standard, 0.001, 0.002, 0.010, and 0.012 in. undersize. The bearing size is stamped on the back of the service replacement bearing inserts.

NOTE: The 0.002 and 0.012 in. undersize inserts are not used in production.

Connecting Rod Bearing

Removal and Installation

1. Drain engine oil and remove oil pan.
2. Rotate crankshaft so that two connecting rods at a time are at the bottom of their stroke.
3. Remove bearing caps and lower inserts. Remove upper insert by rotating insert out of connecting rod.

   NOTE: Do not mix bearing caps.
4. Installation is the reverse of removal.

CAUTION: When rotating the crankshaft with the bearing caps removed, be sure the connecting rod screws do not come in contact with the rod journals and scratch the finish.

Crankshaft Main Bearings

232 and 258 Sixes

The crankshaft main bearings are steel-backed, micro-babbit, precision type. Each bearing is selectively fitted to its respective journal to obtain the desired operating clearance. In production, the select fit is obtained by using various sized color coded vearing inserts. The color code appears on the edge of the insert. Bearing size is not stamped on the inserts used in production.

The main bearing journal size is identified in production by a color coded paint mark on the adjacent cheek toward the rear end of the crankshaft, except for the rear main journal which is on the crankshaft rear flange.

When required, different sized upper and lower bearing inserts may be used as a pair. A standard size insert is sometimes used in combination with a 0.001 in. undersize insert to reduce clearance by 0.0005 in.

NOTE: Never use bearing inserts in pairs with greater than 0.001 in. difference in size. When replacing inserts, all the odd size inserts must be either on the top (in the block) or the bottom (in the main bearing cap).

Service replacement bearing inserts are available as pairs in the following sizes: standard, 0.001, 0.002, 0.010, and 0.012 in. undersize. The size on these service replacement bearings is stamped on the back of the inserts.

NOTE: The 0.012 in. undersize insert is not used in production.

304, 360 and 401 V8

The main bearing caps are numbered from front to rear 1 through 5, with an arrow indicating forward.

CONNECTING ROD BEARING FITTING CHART (232 AND 258 SIXES) IN.

Crankshaft Connecting Rod Journal Color and Diameter in Inches (Journal Size)		Bearing Color Code			
		Upper Insert Size		Lower Insert Size	
Yellow	— 2.0955 to 2.0948 (Standard)	Yellow	— Standard	Yellow	— Standard
Orange	— 2.0948 to 2.0941 (0.0007 Undersize)	Yellow	— Standard	Black	— .001 Undersize
Black	— 2.0941 to 2.0934 (0.0014 Undersize)	Black	— .001-Inch Undersize	Black	— .001 Undersize
Red	— 2.0855 to 2.0848 (0.010 Undersize)	Red	— .010-Inch Undersize	Red	— .010 Undersize

CONNECTING ROD BEARING FITTING CHART (304, 360 AND 401 V8) (IN.)

Crankshaft Connecting Rod Journal Color and Diameter in Inches (Journal Size)		Bearing Color Code			
		Upper Insert Size		Lower Insert Size	
		304-360 CID Engines			
Yellow	— 2.0955 to 2.0948 (Standard)	Yellow	— Standard	Yellow	— Standard
Orange	— 2.0948 to 2.0941 (0.0007 Undersize)	Yellow	— Standard	Yellow	— .001 Undersize
Black	— 2.0941 to 2.0934 (0.0014 Undersize)	Black	— .001-inch Undersize	Black	— .001 Undersize
Red	— 2.0855 to 2.0848 (0.010 Undersize)	Red	— .010-inch Undersize	Red	— .010 Undersize
		401 CID Engine			
Yellow	— 2.2485 to 2.2478 (Standard)	Yellow	— Standard	Yellow	— Standard
Orange	— 2.2478 to 2.2471 (0.0007 Undersize)	Yellow	— Standard	Black	— .001 Undersize
Black	— 2.2471 to 2.2464 (0.0014) Undersize)	Black	— .001-inch Undersize	Black	— .001 Undersize
Red	— 2.2385 to 2.2378 (0.010 Undersize)	Red	— .010-inch Undersize	Red	— .010 Undersize

MAIN BEARING FITTING CHART (232 AND 258 SIXES)

Crankshaft Main Bearing Journal Color Code and Diameter in Inches (Journal Size)		Bearing Color Code			
		Upper Insert Size		Lower Insert Size	
Yellow	— 2.5001 to 2.4996 (Standard)	Yellow	— Standard	Yellow	— Standard
Orange	— 2.4996 to 2.4991 (0.0005 Undersize)	Yellow	— Standard	Black	— .001-inch Undersize
Black	— 2.4991 to 2.4986 (0.001 Undersize)	Black	— .001-inch Undersize	Black	— .001-inch Undersize
Green	— 2.4986 to 2.4981 (0.0015 Undersize)	Black	— .001-inch Undersize	Green	— .002-inch Undersize
Red	— 2.4901 to 2.4896 (0.010 Undersize)	Red	— .010-inch Undersize	Red	— .010-inch Undersize

MAIN BEARING FITTING CHART (304, 360 AND 401 V8)

Crankshaft Main Bearing Journal Color Code and Diameter (Journal Size)		Bearing Color Code			
		Upper Insert Size		Lower Insert Size	
Yellow	— 2.7489 to 2.7484 in.	Yellow	— Standard	Yellow	— Standard
Orange	— 2.7484 to 2.7479 in.	Yellow	— Standard	Black	— .001-in. undersize
Black	— 2.7479 to 2.7474 in.	Black	— .001-in. undersize	Black	— .001-in. undersize
Green	— 2.7474 to 2.7469 in.	Black	— .001-in. undersize	Green	— .002-in. undersize
Red	— 2.7389 to 2.7384 in.	Red	— .010-in. undersize	Red	— .010-in. undersize

MAIN BEARING FITTING CHART (232 AND 258 SIXES)

Crankshaft Main Bearing Journal Color Code and Diameter in Inches (Journal Size)		Bearing Color Code			
		Upper Insert Size		Lower Insert Size	
Yellow	— 2.5001 to 2.4996 (Standard)	Yellow	— Standard	Yellow	— Standard
Orange	— 2.4996 to 2.4991 (0.0005 Undersize)	Yellow	— Standard	Black	— .001-inch Undersize
Black	— 2.4991 to 2.4986 (0.001 Undersize)	Black	— .001-inch Undersize	Black	— .001-inch Undersize
Green	— 2.4986 to 2.4981 (0.0015 Undersize)	Black	— .001-inch Undersize	Green	— .002-inch Undersize
Red	— 2.4901 to 2.4896 (0.010 Undersize)	Red	— .010-inch Undersize	Red	— .010-inch Undersize

MAIN BEARING FITTING CHART (304, 360, AND 401 V8)

Crankshaft Main Bearing Journal Color Code and Diameter (Journal Size)		Bearing Color Code			
		Upper Insert Size		Lower Insert Size	
Yellow	— 2.7489 to 2.7484 in.	Yellow	— Standard	Yellow	— Standard
Orange	— 2.7484 to 2.7479 in.	Yellow	— Standard	Black	— .001-in. undersize
Black	— 2.7479 to 2.7474 in.	Black	— .001-in. undersize	Black	— .001-in. undersize
Green	— 2.7474 to 2.7469 in.	Black	— .001-in. undersize	Green	— .002-in. undersize
Red	— 2.7389 to 2.7384 in.	Red	— .010-in. undersize	Red	— .010-in. undersize

The upper inserts are grooved while the lower inserts have a smooth surface on the 304 and 360 V8. The 401 V8 has a groove in both the upper and lower insert.

Each bearing is a select fit to its respective journal to obtain the desired operating clearance. In production the select fit is obtained by using various sized color coded bearing inserts. The bearing code color appears on the edge of the insert. The bearing size is not stamped on production inserts.

The main bearing journal size is identified in production by a color coded paint mark on the adjacent cheek toward the rear end of the crankshaft except for the rear main journal. The paint mark for the rear main journal is on the crankshaft rear flange.

When required, different sized upper and lower bearing inserts may be used as a pair to reduce clearance by 0.0005 in.

NOTE: When using upper and lower inserts of different sizes, install all the same size inserts together either on the top (block) or bottom (bearing cap). Never use bearing inserts with greater than 0.001 in. difference in pairs.

Service replacement bearings are available as pairs in the following sizes: standard, 0.001, 0.002, 0.010, and 0.012 in. undersize. The size on the service replacement inserts is stamped on the back of the inserts.

NOTE: The 0.012 in. undersize inserts are not used in production.

Oil Pan

Removal and Installation

6 Cylinder Models

1. Drain engine oil, and remove starter.
2. On CJ models: place jack under transmission bellhousing. Disconnect right engine support cushion bracket from block and raise engine to allow clearance for the oil pan.
3. Remove oil pan, also remove the front and rear neoprene seals and side gaskets.
4. Installation is the reverse of removal.

V8

1. Drain engine oil and remove starter.
2. On CJ models: remove frame cross bar and automatic transmission lines.
3. If required, cut corner of engine mount on right side to provide clearance for pan removal.
4. If equipped with manual transmission, bend tabs down on dust shield.
5. Remove oil pan bolts and pan.

6. Remove oil pan front and rear neoprene oil seals.
7. Installation is the reverse of removal.

Oil Pump

6 Cylinder Engines

Removal

1. Drain the engine oil and remove the oil pan.
2. Remove the oil pump retaining screws, oil pump, and gasket from the engine block.
3. Remove the cover retaining screws, cover, and gasket from the pump body.
4. Measure the gear end clearance between the gears and the face of the oil pump body.
5. Measure the gear lobe clearance to the pump body sides.
6. Remove the gears and shaft from the body.
7. Remove the cotter pin, spring retainer, spring, and oil pressure relief valve from the pump body.

NOTE: The oil inlet tube must be removed to gain clearance for the removal of the relief valve. A new pick-up tube assembly must be replaced upon installation, to assure an air tight seal.

Installation

1. Install the oil pressure relief valve, spring retainer, and cotter pin.
2. Install new inlet tube into the pump body, making sure that the support bracket is properly lined up.
3. Install the idler shaft, idler gear and drive gear assembly.

NOTE: Fill the pump gear cavity with petroleum jelly prior to the installation of the pump cover, to insure self priming.

4. Install the pump cover and new gasket.
5. Install the oil pump assembly and a new gasket on the engine block.
6. Install the oil pan, using a new gasket and seals.

V8 Engines

Removal

1. Remove the oil pump cover from the timing chain cover and remove the oil pump gears and shaft.
2. Remove the oil pressure relief valve from the body.
3. Inspect the gears for abnormal wear, chips, looseness on the shafts, galling, and scoring.
4. Inspect the cover and cavity for breaks, cracks, distortion, and abnormal wear.
5. Install the gears into the pump cavity, and with the use of a straight edge and feeler gauge, check the gear to housing clearance.
6. If the clearances measure out of the allowable span, the timing chain cover and gears should be replaced.

Installation

1. Install the pressure relief valve, if previously removed.
2. Install the gears into the gear cavity, and pack the cavity with petroleum jelly to insure the self priming of the pump.

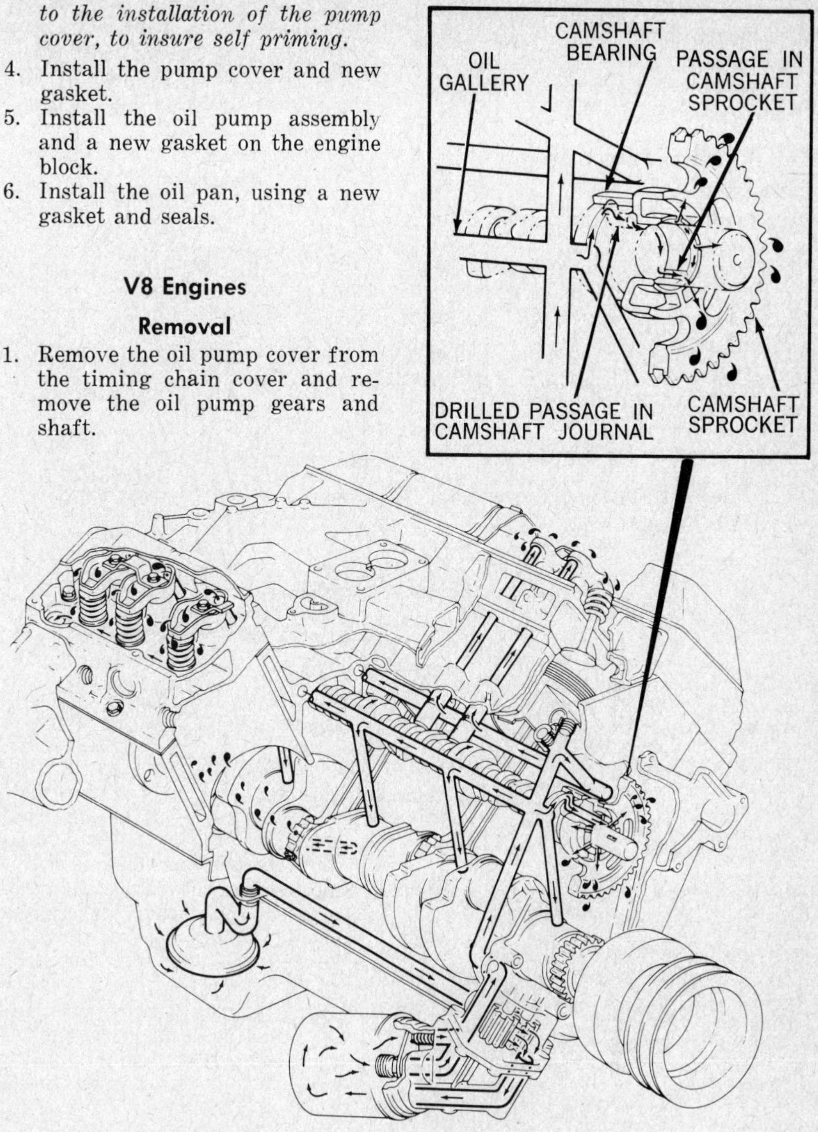

Typical V8 engine lubrication system (© Jeep Corp.)

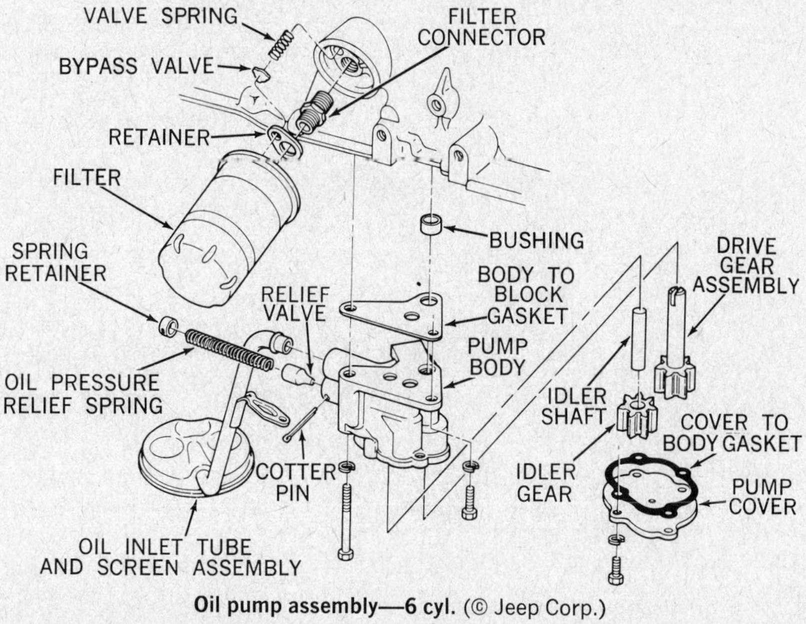

Oil pump assembly—6 cyl. (© Jeep Corp.)

NOTE: Never use chassis or wheel bearing grease to pack the gear cavity.

3. Install the gear cover, using a new gasket.

Oil Pump Clearances—Checking

1. Remove cover and gasket from pump body.
2. Place a strip of plastigage across the full width of each gear.
3. Install pump cover with gasket and tighten.

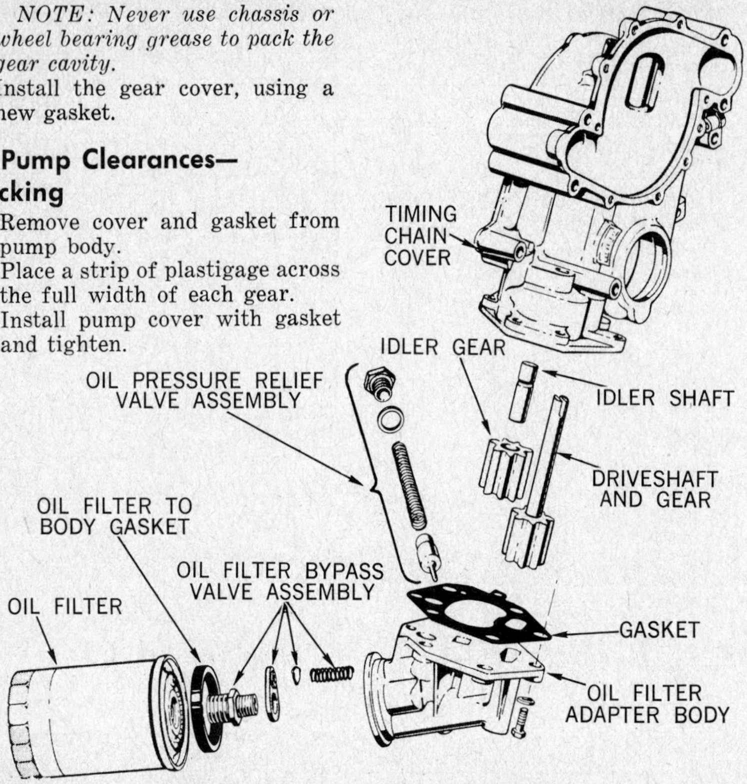

Oil pump assembly—V8 (© Jeep Corp.)

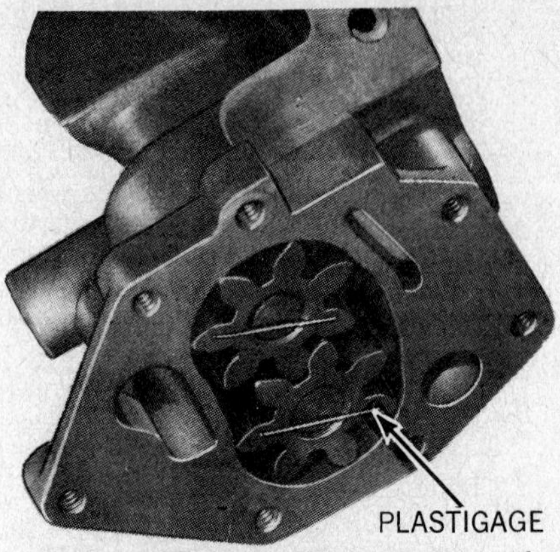

Alternate Method—Oil pump gear end measurement (© Jeep Corp.)

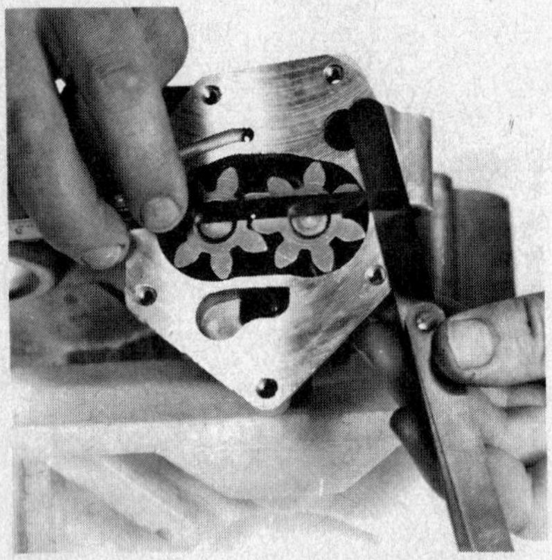

Method of obtaining gear end clearance measurement—typical (© Jeep Corp.)

4. Remove pump cover and determine the amount of clearance by measuring the width of the compressed plastigage. Clearance should be .002-.006 inch for 1973-76 and .002-.008 inch for 1977-80.
5. Measure gear-to-body clearance by inserting a feeler gauge between gear tooth and pump body inner wall directly opposite the point of gear mesh. The reading should be, .0005-.0025 inch for 1973-80.

   NOTE: On the 6 cylinder engine, if gear-to-body clearance is more than specified, replace idler gear, idler shaft, and drive gear assembly. On V8 engines, if gear-to-body clearance is more than specified, measure gear diameter with micrometer. If gear diameter is correct, check gear end clearance and correct. If gear clearance is acceptable and relief valve is functioning properly, replace timing case cover. If gear diameter is incorrect, replace gears and idler shaft.

Rear Main Bearing Oil Seal

Removal and Installation

1. Raise the vehicle and support safely.
2. Drain the engine oil from the oil pan and remove the oil pan from the engine.
3. Remove the oil pan gaskets and neoprene seals. Clean all sealing surfaces.
4. Remove the rear main bearing cap and discard the bottom oil seal.
5. Loosen the remaining main bearing caps to allow the crankshaft to drop slightly.
6. Using a brass drift and hammer, tap the upper oil seal until enough seal is exposed on the opposite

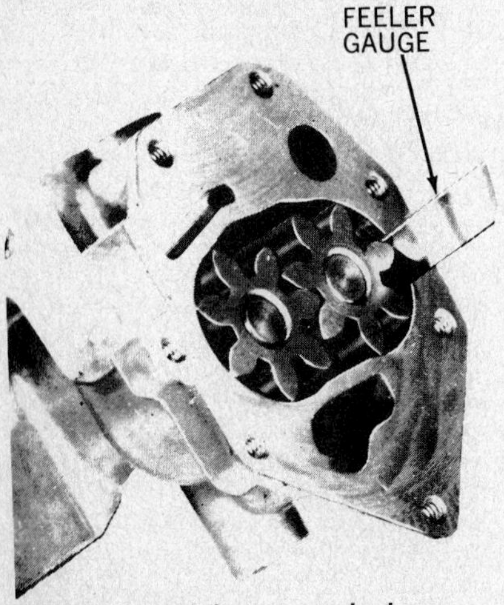

Method of obtaining gear to body clearance measurement (© Jeep Corp.)

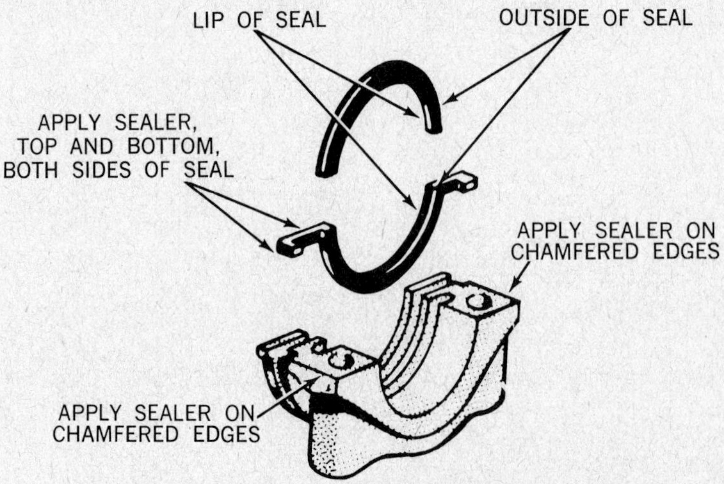

Rear main seal installation—all engines (© Jeep Corp.)

side of the crankshaft to permit pulling the seal from the engine block.

7. Coat the block contacting surface of the seal with soap, and the lip of the seal with engine oil and install the seal into the engine block.

   NOTE: The lip of the seal must face the front of the engine.

8. Coat the lower seal in the same manner as the upper and install in the rear main bearing cap. Install RTV silicone sealer or equivalent to the lower seal end tabs before installation.
9. Install sealer on both chamfered edges of the rear main bearing cap and install to the block.

   NOTE: Do not apply sealer to the mating surface of the bearing cap and the engine block. The main bearing oil clearance could be changed.

10. Tighten all main bearing caps to the proper torque.
11. Install the oil pan using new gaskets and seals. Add the necessary oil to the oil pan, lower the vehicle, start the engine and inspect for oil leaks.

FRONT AXLE AND SUSPENSION

Reference

Refer to the Drive Axles General Repair Section for application, troubleshooting overhaul, and specifications.

Front Axle Assembly

Removal

1. Raise and support the front of the vehicle, supporting the weight at the rear of the front spring.
2. Remove the wheel covers and wheels.
3. Index the propeller shaft to the differential yoke for the proper alignment upon installation.
4. Disconnect the steering linkage from the steering knuckles.
5. On vehicles equipped with sway bar, remove nuts attaching sway bar connecting links to spring tie plates.
6. Disconnect the shock absorbers and breather tube from the axle housing.

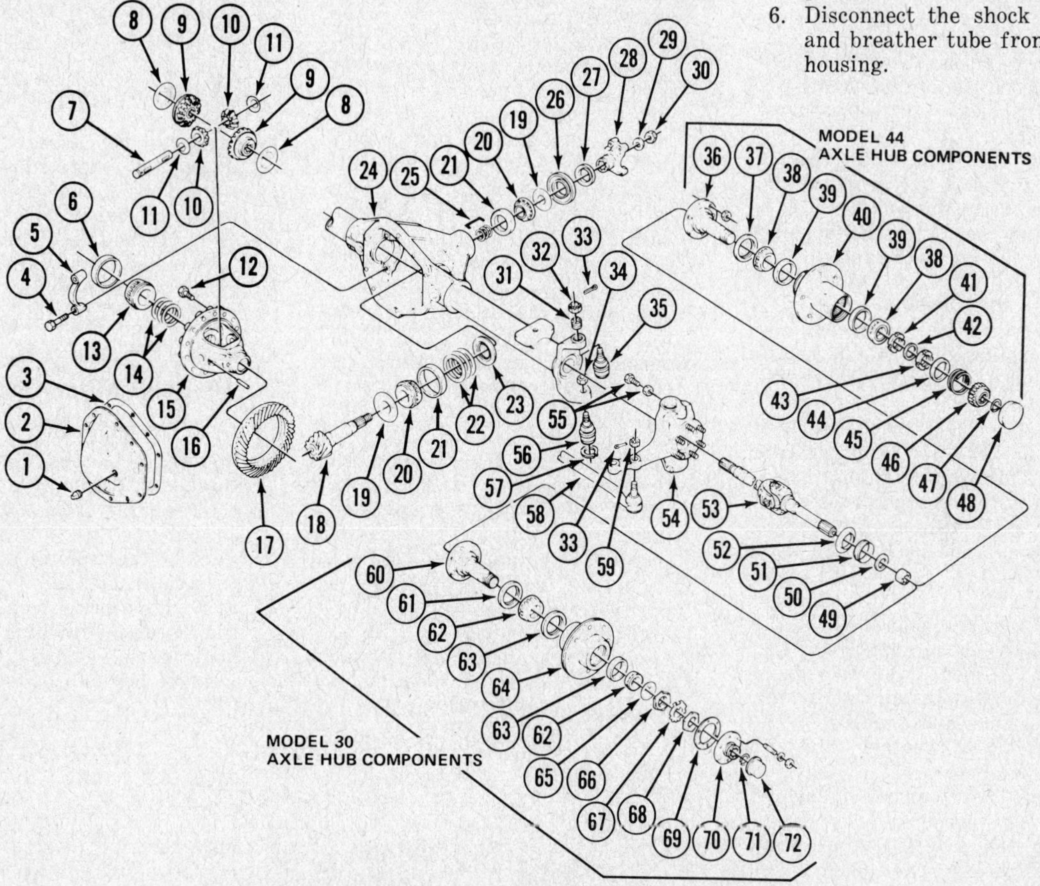

Front drive axle assembly—model 30 & model 44 (© Jeep Corp.)

1 Fill plug
2 Axle housing cover
3 Axle housing cover gasket
4 Differential bearing cap bolt
5 Differential bearing cap
6 Differential bearing cup (2)
7 Pinion mate shaft
8 Thrust washer
9 Differential side gear
10 Differential pinion gear
11 Thrust washer
12 Ring gear mounting bolts
13 Differential bearing (2)
14 Differential bearing preload shims
15 Differential case
16 Pinion mate shaft pin
17 Ring gear
18 Pinion gear
19 Slinger
20 Pinion bearing
21 Pinion bearing cup
22 Pinion depth shims
23 Baffle
24 Axle housing
25 Pinion preload shims
26 Oil seal
27 Dust cap
28 Yoke
29 Washer
30 Pinion nut
31 Upper ball stud split ring seat
32 Upper ball stud nut
33 Cotter pin
34 Lower ball stud jamnut
35 Upper ball stud
36 Spindle
37 Seal
38 Bearing
39 Bearing cup
40 Hub
41 Inner lockout
42 Washer
43 Outer locknut
44 Spring cup
45 Pressure spring
46 Drive gear
47 Snap ring
48 Hub cap
49 Spindle bearing
50 Washer
51 Seal
52 Seal seat
53 Axle shaft
54 Steering knuckle
55 Steering stop bolt
56 Lower ball stud
57 Snap ring
58 Tie rod
59 Tie rod end nut
60 Spindle
61 Seal
62 Bearing
63 Bearing cup
64 Hub
65 Tabbed washer
66 Inner locknut
67 Lock washer
68 Outer locknut
69 Gasket
70 Drive flange
71 Snap ring
72 Hub cap

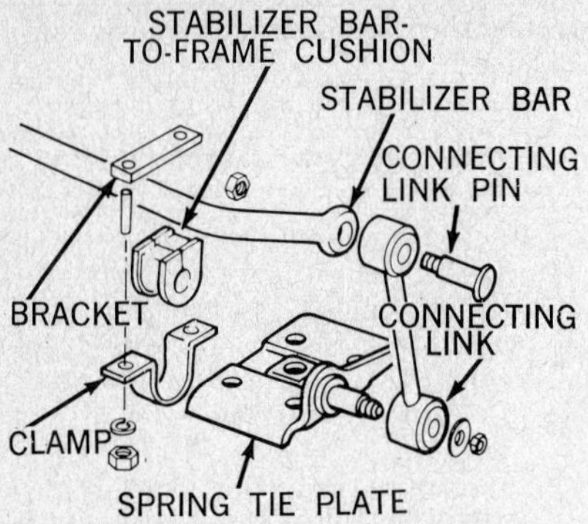

Stabilizer bar mounting—typical (© Jeep Corp.)

7. Remove the brake drums and backing plates, or the brake calipers, hub and rotor, and the brake shield.
8. Remove the spring clips and the spring clip plates.
9. Support the assembly on a jack and loosen the nuts securing the rear shackles, but do not remove the bolts.
10. Remove the front spring shackle bolts and rest the front of the spring on the floor.
11. Pull the jack and axle housing from underneath the vehicle.

Installation

1. Support the axle on a jack and slide the assembly under the vehicle, and position it over the springs.
2. Raise the front of the springs and install the front shackle bolts, but do not tighten.
3. Position the axle on the springs and install the spring clips and spring clip plates.
4. Tighten the front and rear shackle bolts.
5. On disc brake models, install the brake shield, hub and rotor, and brake calipers. On the drum brake models, install the backing plates, hubs and drums.
6. Connect the breather tube and shock absorbers.
7. Connect the steering linkage at the steering knuckles.
8. Align the indexing marks and install the propeller shaft.
9. Install the wheels and tighten. Install the wheel covers.
10. Lower the vehicle and check the wheel alignment and turning angle.

Shock Absorbers

The upper ends of the shock absorbers are attached to the frame side rails with mounting brackets and pins. The lower ends are attached to the axle or to the spring by mounting brackets. The shock absorbers are not refillable or adjustable and must be replaced if defective.

Front Spring

Removal and Installation

1. Raise the vehicle with a jack under the axle. Place a jackstand under the frame side rail. Then lower the axle jack so the load is relieved from the spring and the wheels rest slightly on the floor.
2. Disconnect the shock absorber from the spring clip plate.
3. Remove the nuts which secure the spring clips (U-bolts). Remove the spring plate and spring clips. Free the spring from the axle by raising the axle.
4. Remove the pivot bolt nut and drive out the pivot bolt. Disconnect the shackle from the shackle bracket by removing the lock nut, lock nut and bolt or nut, or lockwasher and bolt.
5. With the spring removed, the spring shackle and/or shackle plate may be removed from the spring by removing the lock nut, lock nut and shackle bolt or nut, or lockwasher and shackle bolt.
6. Inspect the bushings in the eye of the main spring leaf and the bushings of the spring shackle for excessive wear. Replace if necessary.
7. The spring can be disassembled, for replacing an individual spring leaf, by removing the clips and the center bolt.
8. To install the spring on the vehicle with the bushings in place and the spring shackle attached to the springs, position the spring in the pivot hanger and install the pivot bolt and lock nut. Only tighten the lock nut enough to hold the bushings in position until the vehicle is lowered from the jack.
9. Position the spring and install the shackle, shackle bolts, shackle plate if applicable, lockwasher, and nut. Only finger tighten the nuts at this time.
10. Move the axle into position on the spring by lowering the axle jack. Place the spring center bolt in the axle saddle hole. Install the spring clips, spring plate, lockwashers and nuts. Torque the 7 1/6 in. nuts to 36-42 ft lbs and the ½ in. nuts to 45-65 ft lbs.

    NOTE: Be sure that the center bolt is properly centered in the axle saddle.
11. Connect the shock absorber.
12. Remove the axle and allow the weight of the vehicle to seat the bushings in their operating positions. Then torque the 7/16 in. spring pivot bolt nuts and spring shackle nuts to 25-40 ft lbs. Torque the ⅝ in. shackle nuts to 55-75 ft lbs.

Selective Drive Hubs

Selective drive hubs are used to disengage the front axles from the drive train when the vehicle is used in two-wheel drive. When Quadra-Trac is used, the selector hubs are not used. Two different types are used, Automatic and manual.

C J Models, Automatic Hubs

Removal

1. Remove the allen screws from the clutch assembly and remove the assembly from the hub body assembly.
2. Remove the retaining ring from the axle shaft end.
3. Straighten lock tabs and remove the screws attaching the hub body assembly to the front hub. Remove the hub body assembly.

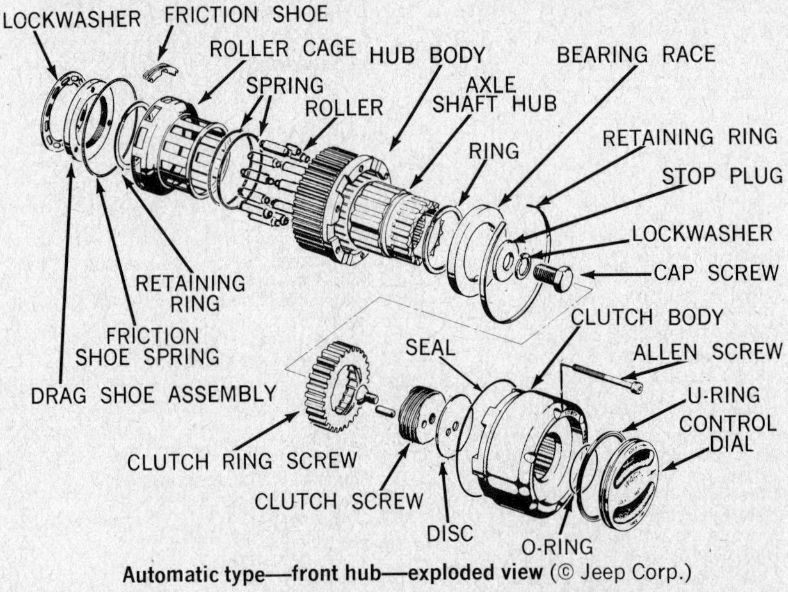

Automatic type—front hub—exploded view (© Jeep Corp.)

Clutch Assembly Overhaul—Automatic Hubs

1. Push out the control dial, turn the unit over and remove the cluster ring and disc.
2. Clean and inspect all parts for damage. Replace "U" ring and "O" ring seals on the control dial.
3. Install the control dial assembly and install the disc.

   NOTE: Lubricate "O" ring and inside of cap.
4. Rotate the control dial to "FREE" position. Install the clutch ring and thread to the bottom.
5. Turn back the clutch ring until the holes align and install in the body assembly.
6. Turn the control from "FREE" to "LOCK" and check the operation.

Body Assembly

Overhaul

1. Remove the friction shoe spring, retaining ring, and separate the hub body from the roller clutch.
2. Remove the centering spring, and spirolock ring. Separate the cage and axle shaft hub.
3. Clean and inspect all parts, coat lightly with grease.
4. Install the friction shoe on the cage, (avoid stretching the shoe) and lubricate the friction shoes liberally, and install.

Installation

1. Position the gasket and body assembly on the wheel hub.
2. Install the tab lock washer and screws. Torque the screws to 40-45 ft. lbs. and secure with the lock washer tabs.
3. Install the retaining ring on the axle shaft end.
4. Place the gasket and cap assembly on the body assembly and torque the allen headed screws to 6-8 ft. lbs.

Cherokee and Truck

Removal

1. Remove the six allen screws and remove the clutch assembly.
2. Remove the capscrews, lock washers, and stop-ring on the axle shaft end.
3. Remove the retaining ring and slide the hub body off the axle end.

Clutch Assembly—Automatic Hubs

Overhaul

1. Remove the taper headed screw from the clutch screw unit.
2. Push out the control dial, turn the assembly over and push out the clutch and clutch screw.
3. Clean and inspect all parts. Replace the "U" ring and "O" ring seals on the control dial.
4. Lubricate the clutch ring and thread the clutch screw into the clutch ring until the ring raises slightly.
5. Install the taper headed screw and stake it in place.

   NOTE: If new parts are used, drill a 3/16 inch hole through the clutch screw into the thick webbing on the control dial 5/8 inch deep. Install a pin and stake into place.
6. Turn the dial from "FREE" to "LOCK" and check the operation.

Hub Body—Automatic Hubs

Overhaul

1. Remove the friction shoe spring and the retaining ring.
2. Clean and inspect all parts.
3. Lubricate the bearing race lightly.
4. Place the cage into the body and pack rollers with chassis lub.
5. Place the body over the axle shaft hub, carefully, and install the retaining ring.

Installation

1. Carefully install the friction shoe spring and lubricate the shoes with chassis lube, and slide the body assembly into the hub.

   NOTE: The body assembly will stop about 1/4 inch from full position. Allow the body to slide to full position by pushing the assembly to expand the friction shoes over the drag shoe nut.
2. Install the retaining ring to hold the body assembly to the hub.
3. Install the screw, lock washer, and stop ring in the axle end and torque to 35-40 ft. lbs.
4. Install the clutch assembly to the body assembly with the allen headed screws, and torque to 4-6 ft. lbs.
5. Rotate the wheel and check for freedom of movement.

Manual Hubs

Removal

1. Remove the allen screws from the cap and remove the cap from the clutch hub.
2. Remove the hub body bolts from the front hub.
3. Remove the retaining ring and pull the clutch ring assembly and axle shaft hub body from the axle.

   NOTE: The clutch ring assembly cannot be disassembled. The control assembly and the clutch screw cannot be separated.

Disassembly

1. Remove the snap ring from the hub bore.
2. Remove the needle bearing and thrust washer from the clutch hub body and the axle shaft hub, noting the side of the hub body from which the axle shaft hub is removed.

Assembly

1. Install the axle shaft hub into the hub body from the same side as it was removed.
2. Install the needle bearings in the hub and install the snap ring.

Installation

1. With a new gasket, install the hub body assembly onto the wheel hub and over the axle shaft, and install the attaching bolts.
2. Install the retaining ring in the groove at the end of the axle shaft hub.
3. Lubricate the bearing side and the grooves of the control assembly and install the new "O" rings.
4. Insert the clutch ring assembly

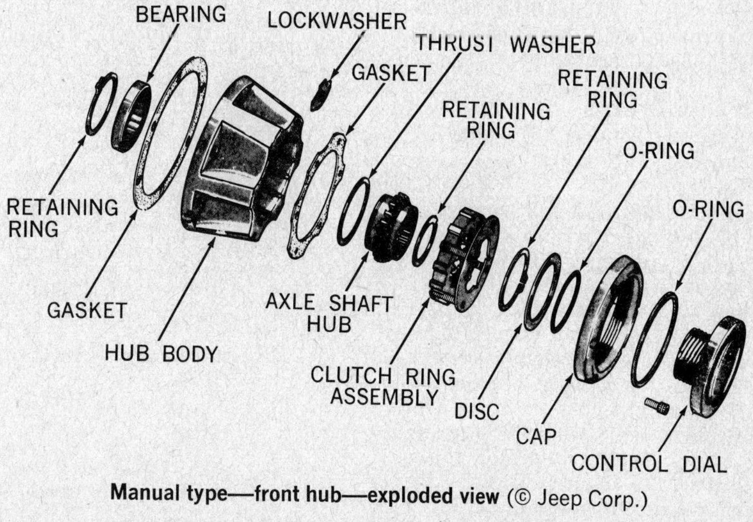

Manual type—front hub—exploded view (© Jeep Corp.)

into the hub body and retain it with the snap ring.

NOTE: Try the clutch ring for a free sliding fit on the drive pins. If a binding occurs, lift the unit out and reposition it. If the binding still exists, remove and examine for damage.

5. Position the control assembly with the dowel pin into the face of the clutch body, so that the arrow stops on the dot marked "FREE".
6. Install the control assembly over the axle end and retain it to the hub body with the allen headed screws. Use a new gasket.
7. Move the control from the "FREE" position to the "LOCK" position and assure that the unit is operating satisfactorily.

Axle Shaft

Removal and Installation

Without Disc Brakes

1. Remove the wheel.
2. Remove the hub dust cap.
3. Remove the axle shaft drive flange snap ring.
4. Remove the axle shaft driving flange bolts.
5. Apply and hold the foot brakes. Remove the axle shaft flange with a puller.
6. Release the lip on the lockwasher, remove the outer nut, lockwasher, adjusting nut, and bearing lockwasher. Use a special wrench for these nuts.
7. Remove the wheel hub and drum assembly with the bearings.
8. Remove the hydraulic brake tube, backing plate screws, and backing plate.
9. Remove the spindle and spindle bearing.
10. Remove the axle shaft and universal joint assembly.
11. Install in reverse order. Tighten the wheel bearing adjusting nut with the special wrench until there is a slight drag on the bearings, then back off about ¼-1/6 of a turn.

With Disc Brakes

1. Raise and support the vehicle.
2. Remove the wheel and dust cover.
3. Remove the axle shaft snap ring, drive flange, pressure spring and spring retainer. If the drive flange is stuck to the shaft, use a pry bar to pry it out.
4. Use the special nut wrench to remove the wheel bearing locknut, lockring, and wheel bearing adjusting nut.
5. Remove the two bolts securing the brake caliper assembly to the disc brake shield and move the caliper assembly aside.
6. Remove the rotor and hub assembly. The spring retainer and outer wheel bearing will slide out as the hub assembly is removed.
7. Remove the nuts and bolts attaching the spindle and disc brake shield.
8. Remove the spindle and disc brake shield. It may be necessary to tap the spindle lightly to free it.
9. Remove the axle shaft.
10. Install the new axle shaft, spindle, and bearing assembly.
11. Install the hub, brake shield, rotor, and the brake caliper assembly.
12. Install the inner wheel bearing adjusting nut. This is the nut with the peg on the side. Tighten the nut to 50 ft lbs with the special wheel bearing nut wrench. Rotate the hub and back off the adjusting nut ¼ turn maximum.
13. Install the lockwasher with the inner tab lined up with the keyway spindle. Turn the inner adjusting nut until the peg engages the nearest hole in the lockwasher. Install the outer locknut and tighten it to 50 ft lbs. Install the spring retainer, pressure spring and drive flange.
14. Push the drive flange inward to provide clearance and install the axle shaft snap ring.
15. Install the wheel and dust cover and lower the vehicle.

Axle Shaft Seal

Removal and Installation

1. Remove axle shaft.
2. Remove seal and bronze thrust washer. If washer is worn it must be replaced.
3. Install seal and washer with washer chamfered side toward the axle shaft seal.
4. Installation is the reverse of removal.

NOTE: Pack wheel bearing grease around thrust face of shaft and seal and fill seal area of spindle with wheel bearing grease.

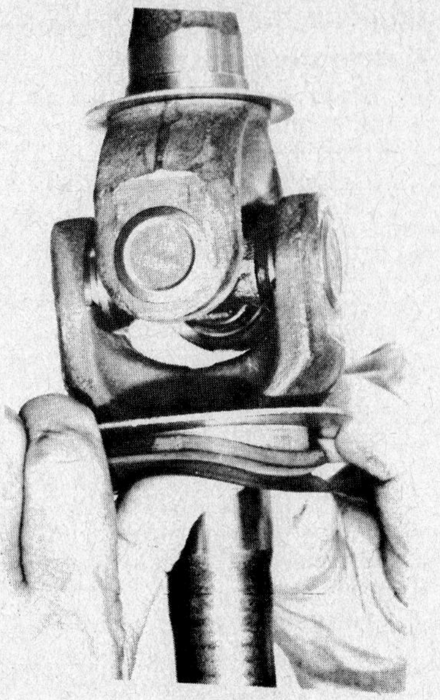

Axle shaft seal installation (© Jeep Corp.)

Wheel Bearing Adjustment

CJ Models

1. With the front of the vehicle raised, remove the hubcaps, snapsprings, capscrews, and washers attaching the drive flange to the hub.
2. Remove the drive flange from the front hub.

   NOTE: A puller may be needed for this operation.
3. Straighten the edge of the lock washer, so that the lock nut and lock washer can be removed.
4. With a special wrench or equivalent, tighten the adjusting nut until the wheel binds, and back off approximately 1/6 turn, so that the wheel turns freely without any lateral shake.
5. Install the lock washer and lock nut on the housing end, tighten the lock nut and crimp the lock washer edge over the lock nut.
6. Assemble the drive flange, bolts, and the hub cap. Assure that the gasket is properly installed between the hub and the flange.

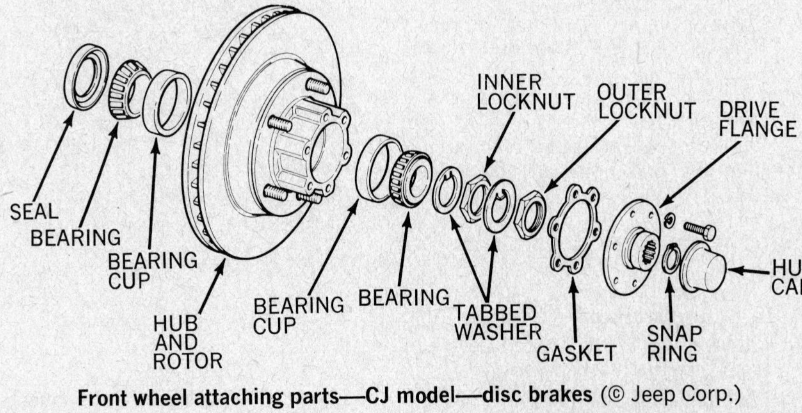

Front wheel attaching parts—CJ model—disc brakes (© Jeep Corp.)

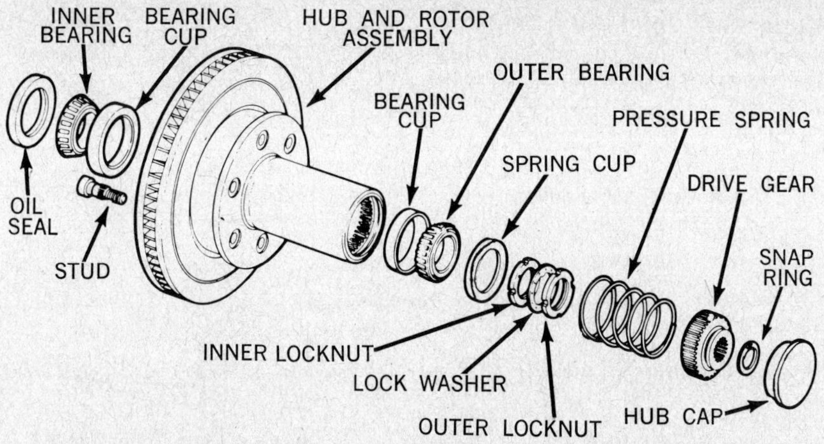

Front wheel attaching parts—Cherokee, Wagoneer, Truck (© Jeep Corp.)

Cherokee, Wagoneer, and Trucks

1. Remove the hub caps, snapring, drive gear pressure spring, outer lock nut, and lock washer.
2. Loosen the inner wheel bearing nut, and then retighten to 50 ft. lbs. torque (inner nut has peg on outer side).
3. Rotate the hub, back off the adjusting nut 1/4 turn maximum.
4. Install the lock washer to have the tab engage the key way in the spindle and move the adjusting nut until the peg engages the nearest hole in the lock washer.
5. Install the outer lock washer and tighten to 50 ft. lbs.

Steering Knuckle Service

The AMC Jeep vehicles were equipped with both the closed knuckle and open knuckle types of front drive units through 1973, and beginning with the 1974 models, only the open knuckle type is used on all vehicle models.

A tubular non-driving axle is used on all two wheel drive vehicles, with the model 30 open knuckle components used.

Models 30 and 44 Axles—Closed Knuckles

Steering Knuckle and Pivot Pins

Removal

NOTE: Replacement of the bearings require the removal of the hub and drum assembly, axle shaft, spindle, steering tie rod, and the steering knuckle. To complete the following procedure , it is assumed that the above have been removed, with the exception of the steering knuckle.

1. Remove the eight screws holding the seal retainer in place.
2. Remove the four screws from the upper bearing cap and the four screws from the lower bearing cap. Remove the caps.
3. Remove the steering knuckle from the axle.
4. The bearings and cups can be replaced with suitable tools. Do not loose the shims from under the top bearing cap.

Installation

1. Position the upper and lower bearings in the cups and place the knuckle on the axle end.
2. Place the old shim pack in position under the upper bearing cap to determine the preload of the knuckle pivot bearings. Tighten the bearing cap screws to 25-40 ft. lbs. torque for the model 30 axle, and 70-90 ft. lbs. torque for the model 44 axle.
3. Without the seal in place, use a spring scale, graduated to 25 lbs., and attach it to the steering arm hole for the tie rod stud, and pull the knuckle through its arc and record the reading on the spring scale.
4. The preload reading should be 12 to 16 lbs. Remove or add shims under the upper bearing cap to obtain the proper preload. *NOTE: Shims are available in .003," .005", .010", and .030"* thicknesses.
5. Install the oil seal and oil seal felt. Install the backing ring assembly wth the two retainer split halves, and tighten the eight screws to 10 to 25 ft. lbs.
6. Assemble the Axle shaft and components as previously outlined.

Models 30 and 44 Axles—Open Knuckles

Steering Knuckle

Removal

1. Follow the Axle Removal procedure as outlined previously.
2. Remove the steering rods from the steering arm.
3. Remove the lower ball stud nut. *NOTE: This nut is a self-locking nut and should be discarded and replaced with a new nut upon assembly.*

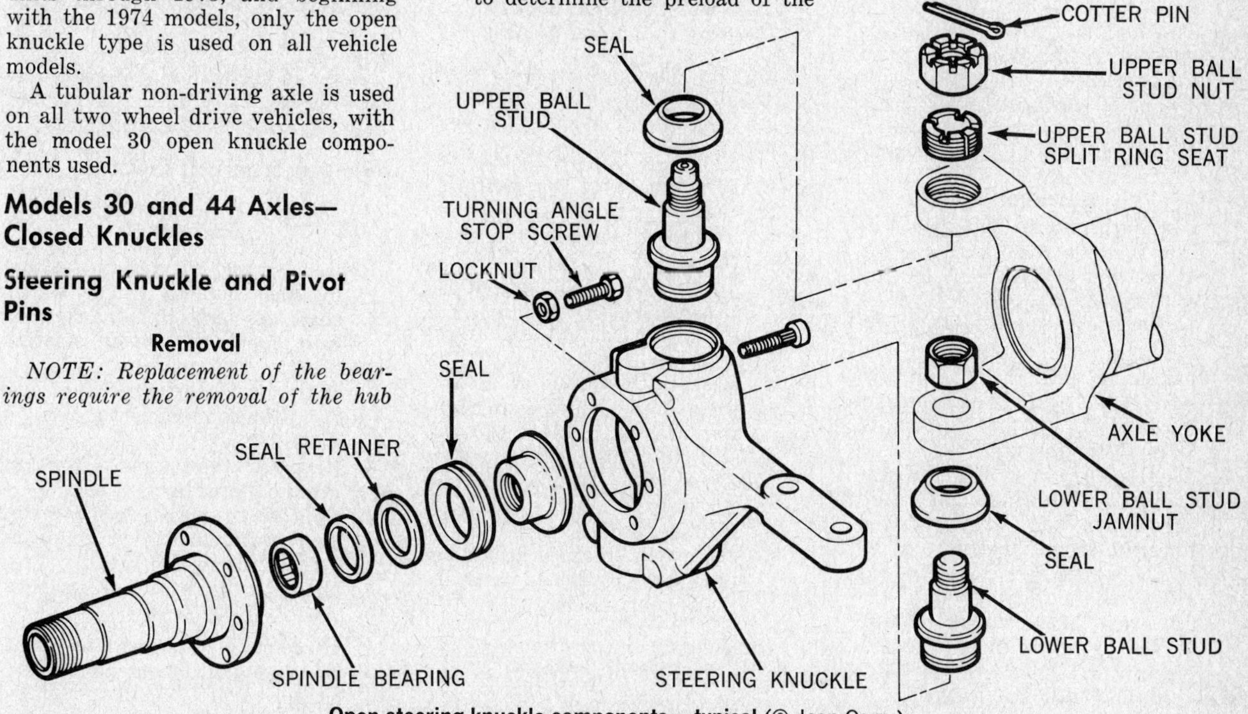

Open steering knuckle components—typical (© Jeep Corp.)

4. Remove the cotter pin from the upper ball stud nut and loosen it to the top of the stud in a flush manner. With the aid of a lead hammer, unseat the upper and lower ball studs from the yoke.
5. Remove the knuckle assembly from the axle.

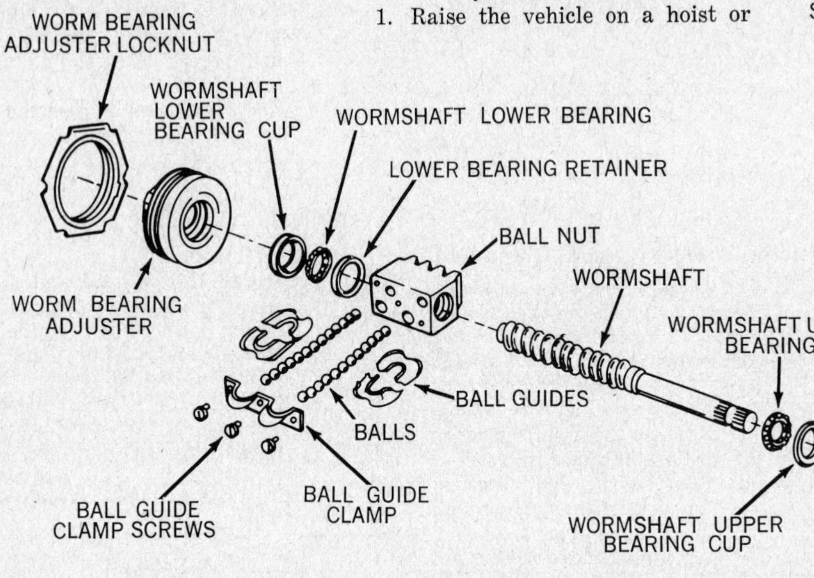
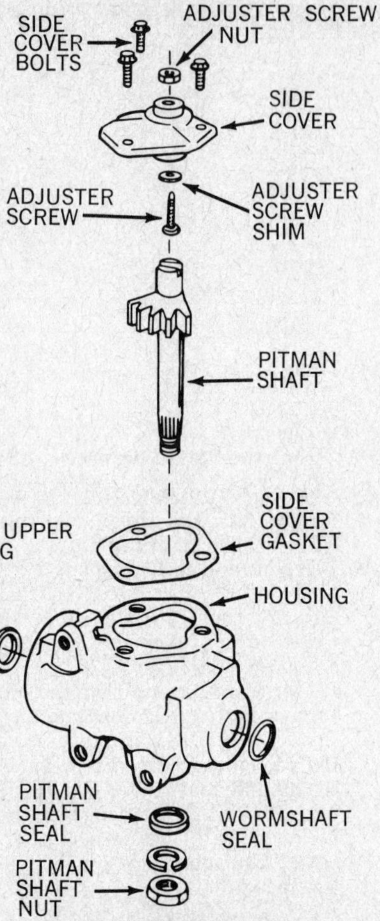

Manual steering gear—typical (© Jeep Corp.)

6. With the use of a suitable tool remove the upper ball stud seat from the axle yoke.

Ball Joints

Removal and Replacement

1. With the aid of a puller or a press, position the tool to force the *lower* ball joint from the knuckle.
2. Position the puller or the press to force the upper ball joint from the knuckle.
3. To install the ball joints, press the *lower* joint into place and follow with the upper ball joint.

Installation

1. Install the upper ball stud seat into the axle yoke, until the top of the seat is flush with the top of the yoke.
2. Install the knuckle assembly onto the axle yoke by inserting the ball studs into their respective holes in the yoke. Install the new lower stud nut and tighten to 70-90 ft. lbs. torque.
3. Tighten the upper ball stud seat to 60 ft. lbs. torque, and install the upper ball stud nut and torque to 100 lbs. torque.
4. If the cotter pin holes do not align, tighten the nut until the pin can be installed. Never loosen the nut to install the cotter pin.
5. Continue with the assembly as previously outlined.

Upper Ball Joint Adjustment

Adjustment of the upper ball joint is necessary only when there is excessive play in the steering, persistent loosening of the steering linkage, or abnormal wear of the tires.

Adjustment Procedure

1. Raise the vehicle on a hoist or jack and support with stands if necessary.
2. Disconnect the steering linkage from the left and right knuckle assemblies.
3. Attach a torque wrench and socket to a steering arm stud and check the torque needed to move the knuckle through its arc.
4. Maximum Torque is:
   12-16 lbs. Model 30 Axle
   15-20 lbs. Model 44 Axle

   NOTE: The knuckle should turn smoothly through the turning arc and have no vertical end play.

5. If the torque is too low, perform the following procedures.
   a. Remove the upper ball stud cotter pin.
   b. Torque the stud adjusting sleeve to 50 ft lbs.
   c. Install the lock nut and a new cotter pin.
   d. Recheck the torque necessary to turn the knuckle through its arc, and if the torque is still too low, retorque the sleeve to 60 ft. lbs. and recheck.
   e. If the torque specifications can not be obtained, it will be necessary to replace parts in the knuckle assembly.

Important: Temperature will affect the turning torque, therefore, allowances in the torque reading should be made.

STEERING GEAR

Manual Steering Gear

Reference

Refer to the Manual Steering Gear General Repair Section for troubleshooting and overhaul procedures.

Manual Steering Gear

Removal and Installation 1973-76

1. Remove the bolt and nut attaching the coupling to the wormshaft, disconnecting the steering gear from the lower steering shaft.
2. Disconnect the steering arm from the connecting rod using a puller.
3. Remove the upper steering gear-to-frame bracket bolt.
4. Remove the two lower steering gear-to-frame bracket bolts and remove the steering gear.
5. Install in the reverse order.

1977-80

1. Disconnect intermediate shaft, by removing intermediate shaft-to-wormshaft coupling clamp bolt.

2. Remove pitman arm nut and lockwasher, and remove arm from steering gear pitman shaft using special puller.
3. On Cherokee, Wagoneer and Truck models, remove bolts attaching steering gear to frame and remove gear.
4. On CJ models, raise left side of vehicle to relieve tension on left front spring and place jack stand under frame. Remove bolts attaching steering gear lower bracket to frame. Remove bolts attaching steering gear upper bracket to frame rail and remove gear. Remove Torx head upper bracket bolt. Remove remaining bolts attaching upper bracket to tie plate and lower bracket to steering gear and remove brackets from gear.
5. Installation is the reverse of removal.

Adjustment

NOTE: Adjustment procedures must be performed exactly as described in this outline. Failure to do so can result in damage to the unit, and improper steering response. Always adjust worm bearing preload first and pitman shaft overcenter drag torque last.

Worm Bearing Preload Adjustment

1. Tighten worm bearing adjuster until it bottoms, then back off 1/4 turn.
2. Install torque wrench on splined end of wormshaft. Rotate wormshaft clockwise to stop; then back off shaft 1/2 turn.
3. Tighten worm bearing adjuster until torque required to rotate wormshaft is 5 to 8 in. pounds. Tighten worm bearing adjuster lock nut to 90 ft. lbs.
4. Record worm bearing preload torque reading.

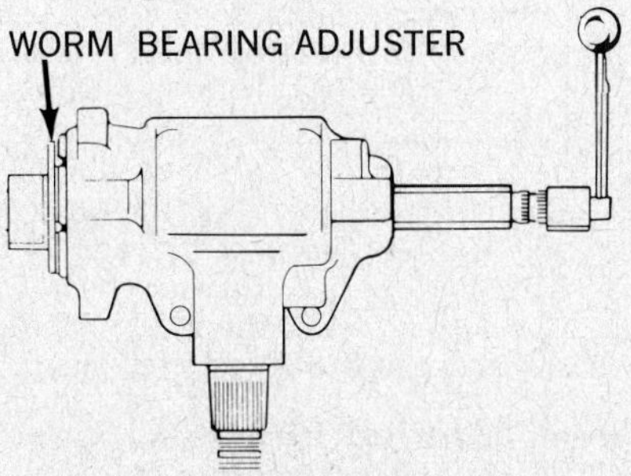

Adjusting worm bearing preload (© Jeep Corp.)

Pitman Shaft Overcenter Drag Torque Adjustment

1. Rotate wormshaft from stop-to-stop and count total number of turns.
2. Turn wormshaft back 1/2 total number of turns to place ball nut and pitman shaft in centered position.
3. Install torque wrench on pitman shaft splines. Tighten pitman shaft adjuster screw (while rotating shaft back and forth over center) until torque required to rotate shaft over center equals worm bearing preload setting.
4. Rotate shaft over center and continue tightening adjuster screw until drag torque is increased by additional 4 to 10 in. lbs. The total amount of overcenter drag torque (worm bearing preload setting plus additional 4 to 10 in. lbs.), must not exceed a combined total of 16 in. lbs.
5. Hold adjuster screw in position and tighten adjuster screw locknut to 23 ft. lbs. Do not allow screw to turn when tightening locknut.

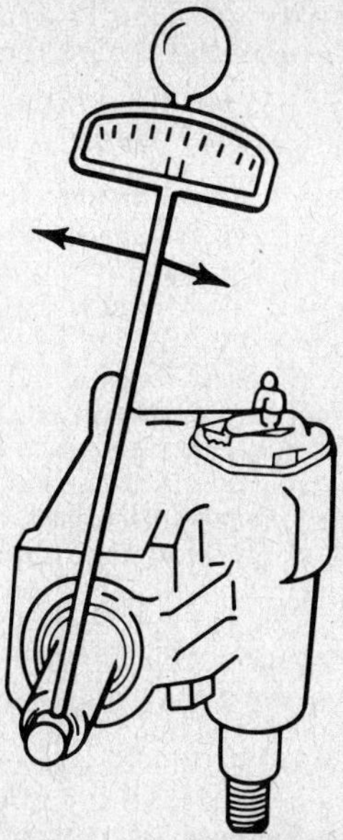

Adjusting pitman shaft overcenter drag (© Jeep Corp.)

Power Steering Gear

References

Refer to the Power Steering Gear General Repair Section for troubleshooting and overhaul procedures.

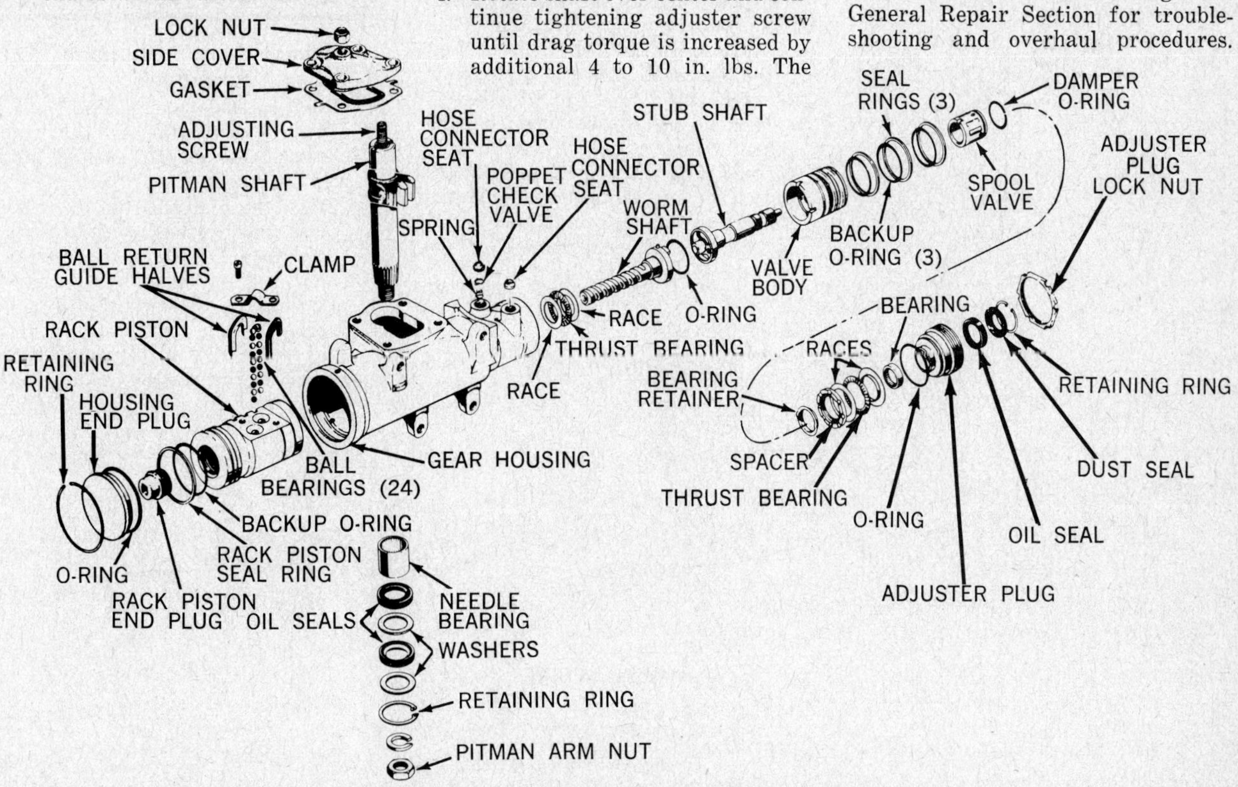

Power steering gear assembly—typical (© Jeep Corp.)

Power steering pump services are also covered in the general repair section.

Power Steering Gear

Removal and Installation

1. Disconnect the hoses from the return port and pressure port. Raise the hoses above the level of the pump to prevent any further lose of power steering fluid.
2. On CJ models, disconnect the intermediate shaft coupling at the steering gear stub shaft. On the other models, disconnect the flexible coupling at the intermediate shaft.
3. Remove the pitman arm nut, lockwasher, and remove the pitman arm using a puller.
4. Remove the mounting bolts attaching the steering gear assembly to the frame, and remove the steering gear assembly.
5. On 1977 and later CJ models, it will be necessary to raise left side of vehicle to relieve tension on the left front spring by placing a jack stand under frame. Remove three lower steering gear mounting bracket-to-frame bolts. Remove two upper steering gear mounting bracket-to-crossmember bolts and remove steering gear and mounting brackets as an assembly.
6. To install the steering gear, mount the steering gear on the frame and install the attaching bolts, tightening them to 65 ft lbs.
7. Install the pitman arm on the pitman shaft and install the lockwasher and pitman arm nut. Tighten the nut to 190 ft lbs.
8. On CJ models, connect the stub shaft to the intermediate shaft. Tighten the clamp bolt to 40 ft lbs.
9. On the other models, install the flexible coupling on the stub shaft, if it was removed, and tighten the clamp to 30 ft lbs. Connect the intermediate shaft to the flexible coupling and tighten the attaching bolts and nuts to 20 ft lbs.
10. Connect the hoses to the gear and tighten the hose fittings to 30 ft lbs.
11. Check the level of the fluid in the reservoir and add as necessary.

Power Steering Pump

Removal and Installation

Before working on the power steering pump, clean the exterior of the pump and the reservoir assembly.

NOTE: The power steering pump need not be removed to service the pressure relief/flow control valve. The valve is located behind a pressure union on all engines.

1. Loosen the drive belt tension adjustment bolt and remove the belt (power steering and air pump, if so equipped).
2. Place a receptacle under the pump/reservoir assembly and disconnect the pressure and return hoses from the pump. Fluid will drain out of the pump and hoses. Lay the ends of the hoses up higher than the steering gear to prevent all of the fluid from draining out. Cover the ends of the hoses to prevent dirt from entering.
3. Remove either the bolts that hold the pump to the mounting bracket or the bolts that hold the bracket and pump to the engine, whichever is easiest. Remove the pump from the engine.
4. Install the pump in the reverse order of removal and install the correct type and amount of fluid.

Bleeding the Power Steering System

1. Fill the reservoir with fluid until the *cold* level on the dipstick is reached.
2. Start the engine and move the steering wheel back and forth. Stop the engine and refill the reservoir again to the *cold* level mark on the dipstick.
3. Repeat the procedure until the fluid level stabilizes. Operate the engine until normal operating temperature is reached. Recheck the fluid level and correct as necessary.
4. Bleed the air from the system by turning the wheel from side to side, without contacting the stops, while the engine is running.

   NOTE: The fluid level must be maintained just above the pump body.
5. After the air has been expelled from the system, recheck the fluid level and correct to the *Hot* mark on the dipstick.
6. Road test the vehicle to check the power steering operation. Recheck the fluid level.

CLUTCH

Removal and Installation All Models

1. Remove the transmission.
2. Remove the starter, throwout bearing and sleeve assembly and clutch housing.
3. Mark the clutch cover, pressure plate and flywheel with a center punch to insure correct alignment during assembly.
4. Loosen the attaching screws in sequence, one or two turns at a time until the spring tension on the cover is released. This is to

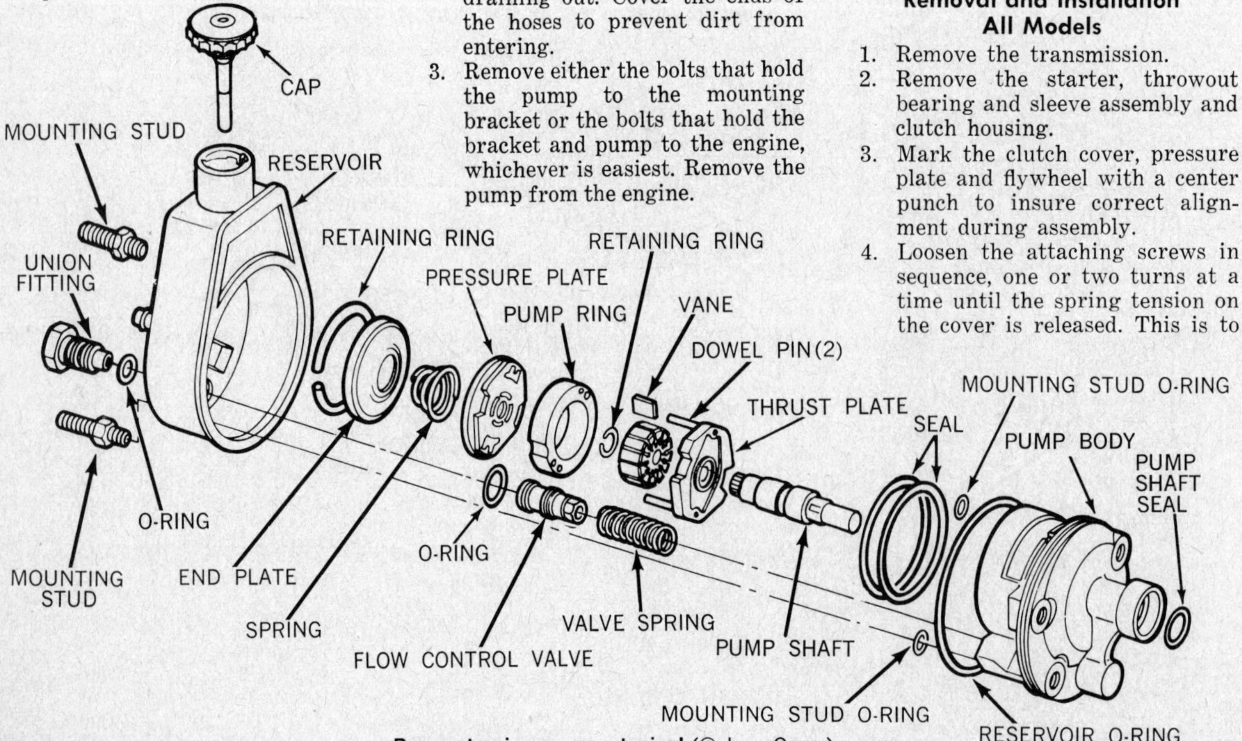

Power steering pump—typical (© Jeep Corp.)

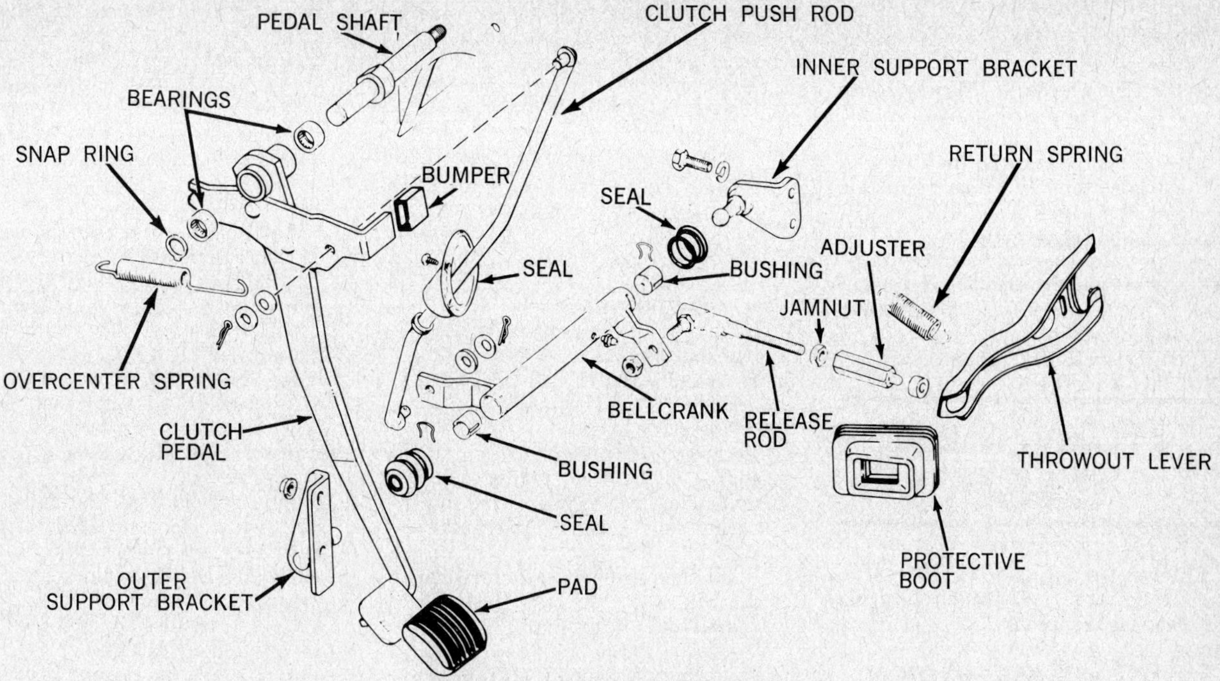

Clutch linkage—CJ model (© Jeep Corp.)

prevent the clutch cover from becoming warped, which could result in clutch chatter when reinstalled.

5. Install the clutch in the reverse order of removal, tighten the attaching bolts of the cover in sequence.

NOTE: The clutch pedal is not to be depressed until the transmission has been installed.

Clutch Pedal Free-Play Adjustment

All Models 1973-75

1. Adjust the bellcrank outer support bracket to provide about 1/8 in. of bellcrank end play.
2. Lift up the clutch pedal against the pedal stop.
3. On the clutch push rod (pedal-to-bellcrank), adjust the lower ball pivot assembly onto or off the rod, as required, to position the bellcrank inner lever parallel to the front face of the clutch housing (slightly forward from vertical).
4. Adjust the clutch fork release rod (bellcrank-to-release fork) to obtain the maximum specified clutch pedal free play.

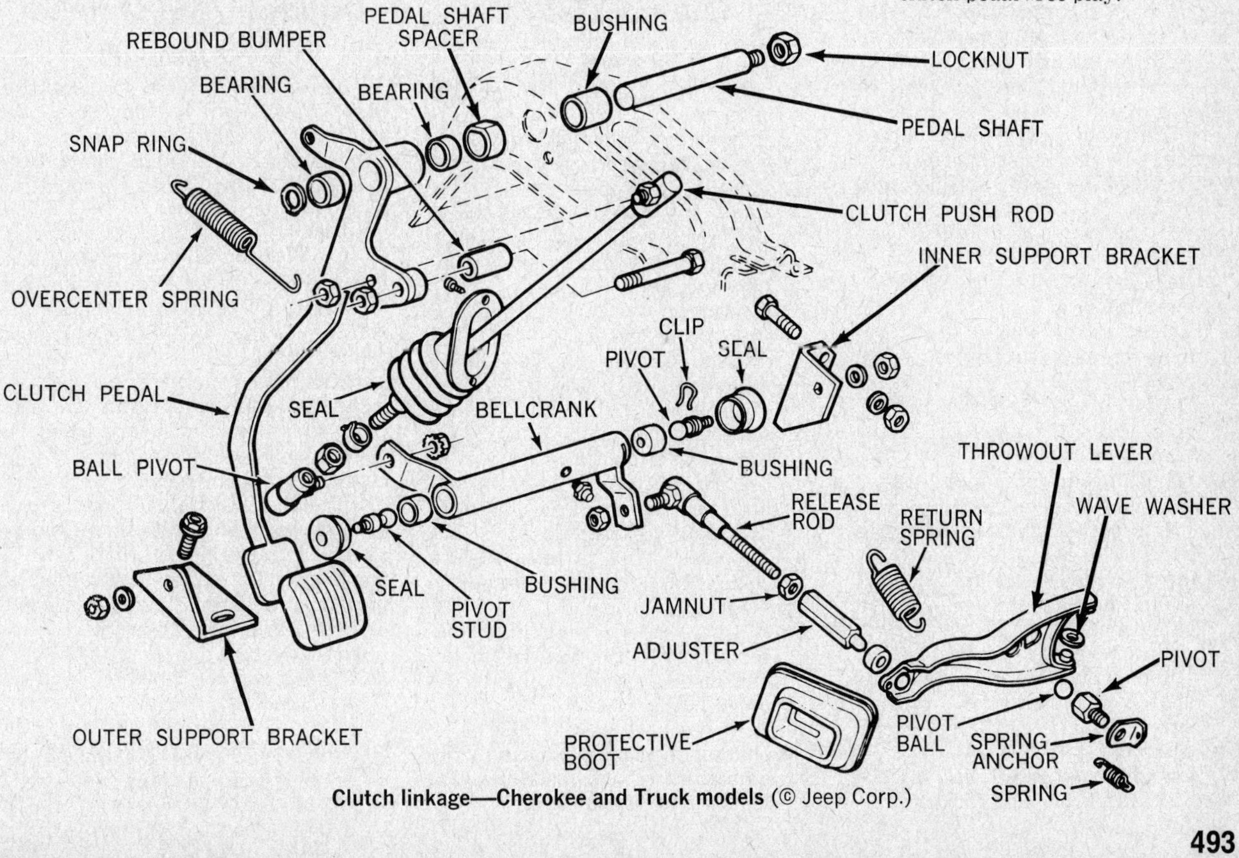

Clutch linkage—Cherokee and Truck models (© Jeep Corp.)

1976-80

1. Lift clutch pedal upward and against pedal stop.
2. On Cherokee and Truck models, adjust clutch push rod lower ball pivot assembly in-or-out on push rod until bellcrank inner lever is parallel to front face of clutch housing. Lever should be slightly forward from vertical.
3. Loosen release rod adjuster jamnut and turn release rod adjuster in or out to obtain clutch pedal free play.
4. Tighten release rod jamnut.

TRANSFER CASE

Reference

Refer to the Transfer Case General Repair Section for troubleshooting and overhaul procedures.

Transfer Case—Spicer Model 20

Removal

1973-75

1. Remove the shift lever knob, boot, and shift lever.
2. Raise and support the vehicle safely.
3. Mark the propeller shafts for reference at assembly and disconnect them from the yokes.
4. Disconnect the parking brake cable at the equalizer bar, and disconnect the speedometer cable from the transfer case.
5. Remove the transfer case to transmission bolts and install a guide bolt on each side to aid in the removal and installation.
6. Remove the transfer case and gasket.

1976-80

1. Remove shift lever knob, boot, and shift lever.
2. Remove floor covering and remove transmission access cover from floorpan.
3. Drain lubricant from transfer case. On CJ models drain the transmission also.
4. If equipped, disconnect torque reaction bracket from crossmember. Disconnect speedometer at transfer case.
5. On CJ models, place support stand under clutch housing to support engine and transmission, and remove rear crossmember.
6. Disconnect front and rear driveshafts at transfer case, making sure to mark shaft yokes for assembly.
7. On Cherokee and Truck models, disconnect parking brake cable at equalizer and exhaust pipe support bracket at transfer case.
8. Remove bolts attaching transfer case to transmission and remove transfer case.

NOTE: One transfer case attaching bolt must be removed from front end of the case. This bolt is located at the bottom right right corner of the transmission.

Installation—All

1. Install a new gasket on the transmission.
2. Shift the transfer case into 4WD low and install the case assembly on the guide bolts.
3. Rotate the transfer case output shaft until the transmission main shaft gear engages the rear output shaft gear of the transfer case.
4. Slide the transfer case forward until the two units mate flush.
5. Install one upper bolt, remove the dowel guide bolts and install the remaining bolts. Torque to 30 ft. lbs.
6. Connect the speedometer cable and parking brake cable.
7. Install the propeller shafts after aligning the indexing marks.
8. Fill the unit with gear lube, and lower the vehicle.
9. Install the transfer case shift lever, boot, and knob.

Transfer Case—Quadra-Trac

Removal

1. Lift and support the vehicle safely.
2. Remove reduction unit on Cherokee, Wagoneer, and Truck models, if equipped.
3. Index the marks on the front and rear yokes and propeller shafts for proper alignment during assembly.
4. Disconnect both the front and rear propeller shafts. On CJ-7 models, place support stand under transmission and remove crossmember.
5. Mark the vacuum diaphragm control for identification during the assembly, and then disconnect the vacuum hoses, wiring, and speedometer cable.
6. Disconnect the parking brake cable guide from the pivot on the right frame side.
7. Remove the two front side transfer case to transmission bolts, and install a guide bolt into the upper hole.
8. Remove the two rear side bolts, holding the transfer case to the transmission, and install a guide bolt into the upper hole.
9. Move the transfer case rearward until the unit is free of the transmission output shaft and guide pins. Lower the assembly to the floor.
10. Remove all gsaket material from the rear of the transmission.

Installation

1. Install a new gasket on the rear of the transmission.
2. Install the guide bolts in the upper transmission adapter and transfer case, if they were removed.
3. Raise the transfer case, engage the guide bolts, and move the case assembly forward to the transmission. Make sure a flush fit is achieved.
4. If necessary, rotate the transfer case rear output shaft yoke until the drive hub splines align with the transmission output shaft.
5. Install front and rear attaching bolts, and remove the guide bolts during this operation.
6. Attach the exhaust pipe bracket support, if removed.
7. Align the propeller shaft and indexing marks on the yokes and attach the propeller shafts.
8. Connect the speedometer cable, wiring, and vacuum hoses.
9. Connect the parking brake cable guide to the pivot bracket on the right frame side.
10. Install the specified lubricant, and lower the vehicle.

Linkage Adjustments

Spicer Model 20

The shifter rails of the transfer case lever assembly connect to the shifter rails of the transfer case either directly or through non-adjustable links. The linkage should be lubricated periodically.

Warner Quadra-Trac

Since the Quadra-Trac system is a "full time 4WD" system, and is constantly engaged in 4WD, there is no "shift linkage" as such. There are two features which can be operated manually concerning the transfer case: the "Lock-Out" feature and the engagement of the optional "Low Range Reduction Unit."

Since the "Lock-Out" feature is a vacuum actuated unit, there are no external adjustments that can be made other than making sure that all vacuum lines are in place, connected and not damaged in any way.

The reduction unit is actuated by a shift cable and can be adjusted in the following manner:

1. Loosen the nut which clamps the cable to the shift lever pivot. Be sure that the cable can move freely in the pivot.

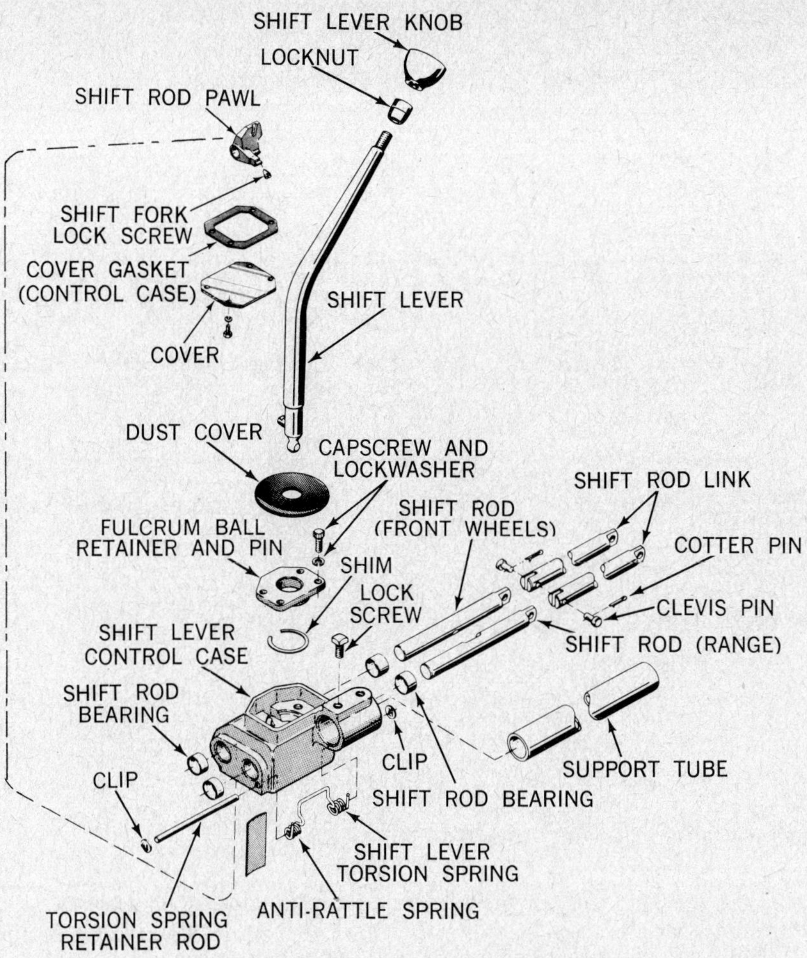

Transfer case shift controls—Cherokee, Wagoneer, Truck (© Jeep Corp.)

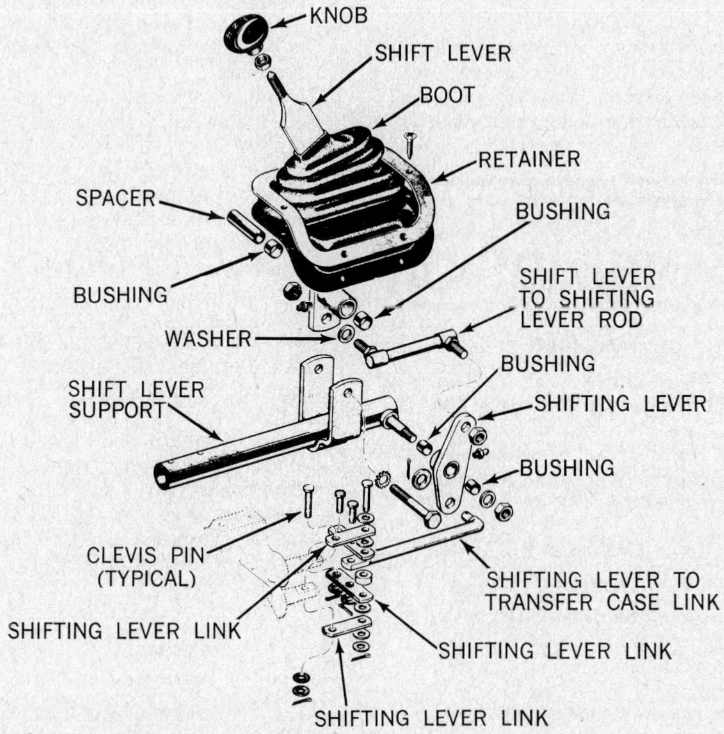

Transfer case shift controls—CJ models (© Jeep Corp.)

2. Move the reduction shift lever to the most rearward detent position (Hi-Range position).
3. Push the Low Range lever inward until it stops. Pull the Low Range lever out slightly, no more than 1/16 in.
4. Tighten the cable clamp nut at the reduction unit shift lever.

NOTE: This procedure only applies to the Quadra-Trac transfer case equipped with a reduction unit.

MANUAL TRANSMISSION

Reference

Refer to the Manual Transmission General Repair Section for application, troubleshooting and overhaul.

Transmission

Removal and Installation

The transmission and transfer case can be removed as a unit. These instructions apply to both three and four-speed transmissions.

All Models

1. Remove the shift level knobs, trim rings, and boots.
2. On three-speed floorshift models, remove the floor covering. Remove the floor pan section from above the transmission. Remove the shift control and level assembly. On four-speed models, remove the shift control housing cap, washer, spring, shift lever, and pin.
3. Remove the transfer case shift lever and bracket.
4. Raise the vehicle on a lift.
5. Disconnect the column shift rods.
6. Remove the front driveshaft and disconnect the front of the rear driveshaft. Disconnect the vacuum line and electrical lead on a Quadra-Trac unit.
7. Disconnect the clutch cable, if so equipped and remove the cable mounting bracket from the transfer case.
8. Disconnect the speedometer cable, TCS switch, and back-up light switch. Disconnect the parking brake cable if it is connected to the crossmember.
9. On models equipped with V8 engines, disconnect and lower the exhaust pipes from the exhaust manifolds, and catalytic converter, if equipped.
10. Support the transmission with a floor jack.
11. Unbolt the crossmember from the frame. Unbolt the transmission from the clutch housing.

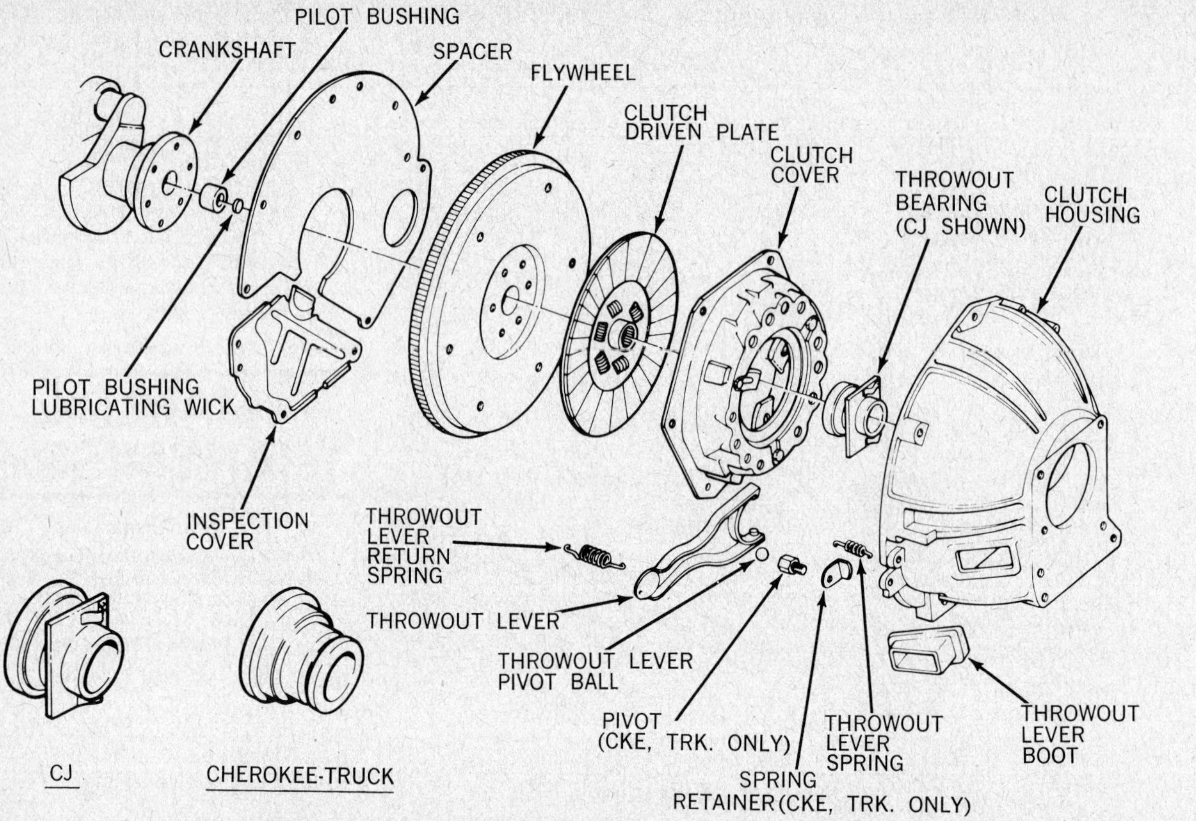

Clutch assembly and throw out bearing—typical (© Jeep Corp.)

12. Lower the transmission slightly and move it to the rear to disengage the clutch shaft. Remove the unit.

To replace the transmission:

13. Place the wave washer and throw-out bearing and sleeve assembly in the fork. Center the bearing over the release levers.
14. Slide the transmission into place, being careful to align the transmission splines with those on the clutch plate. Bolt the transmission to the clutch housing and torque the bolts.
15. Bolt the crossmember to the frame. Remove the jack.
16. On models equipped with V8 engines, connect the exhaust pipes to the exhaust manifolds, and catalytic converter, if equipped.
17. Connect the speedometer cable, back-up light switch, TCS switch, parking brake cable, clutch cable and cable mounting bracket.
18. Install the driveshafts. Flange bolts should be torqued to 25-45 ft lbs.
19. Replace the column shift linkage.
20. Lower the vehicle.
21. Replace the transfer case shift lever and bracket.
22. On four-speeds, install the lever pivot pin, shift lever, spring, washer, and control housing cap. On three-speeds, install the shift control and lever assembly. Set the gears and the cover in the neutral position. Install the cover, placing the shift forks into the sleeves.
23. Replace the floor covering, boots, trim rings, and shift lever knobs.

Linkage Adjustments

All Models

The shift lever is connected to the transfer case shift rails through rods and nonadjustable links, therefore external adjustments are not possible.

AUTOMATIC TRANSMISSION

Reference

All Jeep vehicles use the General Motors Turbo-Hydramatic 400 3-speed automatic transmission. Refer to the Automatic Transmission General Repair Section for troubleshooting and overhaul procedures.

Removal

1973-75

1. Remove the dipstick tube attaching bolt at the engine block.
2. Remove the carpet trim ring (if equipped).
3. If equipped with the Spicer Model 20 transfer case, remove the top cover and lever.
4. Mark and remove the rear propeller shaft.
5. Remove the exhaust pipe clamp bolt, shift lever, detent solenoid wire and speedometer cable.
6. Support the transmission and remove the rear cross member.
7. Remove the exhaust pipes.
8. Mark and remove the front propeller shaft from the transfer case end.
9. Remove the vacuum lines and the oil cooler lines from the transmission.
10. When equipped with the Quadra-Trac transfer case, remove the lockout signal wire and the diaphragm control hoses.
11. Disconnect the low range cable (if equipped), and the converter housing splash pan.
12. Mark the converter and flywheel for alignment at assembly and remove the converter to flywheel bolts.
13. Remove the converter housing to engine bolts and remove the transmission.
14. Installation is the reverse of removal. Torque the converter-to-flywheel bolts to 33 ft.

Removal

1976-80

1. Remove transmission dipstick.
2. If vehicle is equipped with radiator shroud, remove bolts attach-

ing shroud to core support. Raise vehicle and support safely.

3. Mark front and rear universal joints and axle yokes.
4. On Cherokee, Wagoneer, and Truck models, remove parking brake cable jamnut and adjuster nut, remove clip attaching parking brake cable to crossmember and pull out of crossmember.
5. On CJ, and Truck models, with low range reduction unit, disconnect shift rod at reduction unit shift lever and remove reduction unit. On all other models, remove reduction unit shift lever from shift shaft and remove reduction unit.
6. Disconnect speedometer cable. Disconnect and mark emergency drive control vacuum lines and indicator lamp wire. Remove bolt attaching vacuum line routing bracket to rear of transfer case.
7. Disconnect detent solenoid wire at transmission case connector. Remove starter. Remove converter housing inspection cover and mark the torque converter. Remove converter-to-drive plate attaching bolts.
8. Support the transmission and remove the rear crossmember. Disconnect exhaust system components where necessary.
9. Remove spring clip and flat washer attaching transmission gearshift rod trunnion to outer range selector lever. Do not loosen trunnion locknut. Disengage gearshift rod and trunnion from outer range selector lever. Remove spring clip and spring attaching outer range selector lever to transmission selector lever. Remove bolts attaching outer range selector lever bracket and bushing to frame and remove bracket, lever, and bushing as an assembly.
10. Disconnect front propeller shaft at transfer case yoke and secure shaft. Disconnect transmission oil cooler lines. Disconnect engine-to-modulator vacuum hose, and remove transmission filler tube.
11. Position a support stand under the engine. Remove the transmission filler tube.
12. Remove the converter housing to engine attaching bolts and move the transmission assembly rearward with a supporting jack until it clears the crankshaft.
13. Hold the converter in place and lower the transmission from the vehicle.
14. The installation of the transmission is in the reverse of the removal procedure. Be sure the converter is properly aligned to the drive plate during installation.

Linkage Adjustment

1. Place the steering column gearshift lever in the Neutral position.
2. Raise the vehicle on a hoist.
3. Loosen the locknut on the gearshift rod trunnion just enough to permit movement of the gearshift rod in the trunnion.
4. Place the outer range selector lever at the transmission, fully into the Neutral detent position and tighten the locknut at the trunnion to 9 ft lbs.
5. Lower the car and operate the steering column gearshift in all ranges. The car should start in Park and Neutral only and the column gearshift lever engage properly in all detent positions.

Band Adjustment

No provisions are made for the external band adjustments of this transmission. Only during the assembly, can a different sized pin be installed in the rear band apply system, to compensate for lining wear.

Detent Adjustment

An electrical detent solenoid is located on the control valve assembly of the transmission and is activated by an electrical switch, located either on the carburetor or under the accelerator pedal, and is energized by depressing the pedal to the bottom of its travel, which causes the transmission to downshift at speeds below 70 MPH. The only adjustment needed is to insure the switch contacts engage when the pedal is depressed. This can be accomplished by movement of the switch or of the throttle linkage.

Neutral Switch Adjustment

1. Apply the parking brake.
2. Check and adjust the manual linkage, if necessary.
3. Remove the Neutral switch from the steering column.
4. Place the selector lever in Park and lock the steering column.
5. Move the switch actuating lever until it is aligned with the letter "P" stamped on the back of the switch.
6. Insert a 3/32 in. drill in the hole located below the letter "N" stamped on the back of the switch.
7. Move the switch actuating lever until it stops against the drill.
8. Position the switch on the steering column, install the attaching screws and remove the drill.
9. Check the operation of the switch. The engine should start in Park and Neutral only. The backup light should glow only in the Reverse position.

Transmission Oil Pan

Removal

1. Raise the vehicle and support safely.
2. Position a drain pan under the transmission and remove the oil pan bolts, except the four corner ones.
3. Loosen the corner bolts and pry the oil pan loose from the transmission case.
4. Allow the oil to drain from the corners of the oil pan, while tilting the pan to remove as much oil as possible.
5. Carefully remove the corner bolts and the oil pan from the transmission case.
6. Remove the oil filter, oil pan gasket, and intake tube "O" ring seal.

Installation

1. Place a new "O" ring on the intake tube, and install the tube in place.
2. Install a new filter and retain it to the control valve assembly with the attaching bolt.
3. Install the oil pan and gasket. Torque the pan bolts to 12 ft. lbs.
4. Lower the vehicle and fill the transmission with the specified fluid. (Dexron or equivalent).

DRIVESHAFT

Removal and Installation

In order to remove the front and rear driveshafts, unscrew the attaching nuts from the universal joint's U-bolts, remove the U-bolts and slide the shaft forward or backward toward the slip-joint. The shaft can then be removed from the end yokes and removed from under the vehicle. Install the driveshaft in the reverse order.

NOTE: Some driveshafts are marked at the slip-joints with arrows on the spline and sleeve yoke. When installing the driveshaft, align the arrows to have the yokes at the front and rear of the shaft in the same parallel plane.

U-Joint Overhaul

Snap-Ring Type Disassembly and Repair

1. Remove the snap-rings.

2. Press on the end of one bearing until the opposite bearing is pushed from the yoke arm.
3. Turn the joint over. Press the first bearing back out of the arm by pressing on the exposed end of the journal shaft. Repeat this operation for the other two bearings, then lift out the journal assembly by sliding it to one side.
4. Wash all parts in solvent and inspect for wear. Replace all worn parts.
5. Install new gaskets on the journal assembly. Make certain that the grease channel in each journal trunnion is open.
6. Pack the bearing cones one-third full of grease and install the rollers.
7. Assemble in the reverse order of disassembly. If the joint binds when assembled, tap the arms lightly to relieve any pressure on the bearings at the end of the journal.

U-Bolt Type Disassembly and Repair

Remove the attaching U-bolts to release one set of bearing races. Slide the driveshaft into the yoke flange to remove the races. The rest of the disassembly and repair procedure is the same as that given above for the snap-ring type of cross and roller joint. The correct U-bolt torque is 15-20 ft lbs.

Ball and Trunnion Disassembly and Repair

1. Clamp the shaft firmly in a vise.
2. Bend the grease cover lugs away from the universal joint body. Remove the cover and gasket.
3. Remove the two clamps from the dust cover. Push the joint body toward the driveshaft tube. Remove two each; centering buttons, spring washers, ball and roller bearings, and thrust washers, from the trunnion pin.
4. Press the trunnion pin from ballhead.
5. If the ballhead is bent out of alignment or if the trunnion pin bore is worn or damaged, replace the driveshaft.

To reassemble:

6. Secure the larger end of the dust cover to the joint body with the larger of two clamps. Install the smaller clamp. Fit the cover over the ballhead shaft.
7. Push the universal joint cover toward the driveshaft tube. Press the trunnion pin into the centered position. If the trunnion pin is not centered, imbalance will result.
8. Install the thrust washers, ball and roller bearings, spring washer, and centering buttons on the trunnion pin. Compress the centering buttons. Move the joint body to hold the buttons in place.
9. Insert the breather between the dust cover and the ballhead shaft, along the length of the shaft. The breather must extend no more than ½ in. beyond the dust cover. Tighten the clamp screw to secure the cover to the shaft. Cut away any portion of dust cover protruding under the clamps.
10. Pack the raceways around the ball and roller bearings with about 2 oz of universal joint grease.
11. Position the gasket and grease cover on the body. Bend the lugs of the cover into the notches of the body. Move the body back and forth to distribute grease in the raceways.

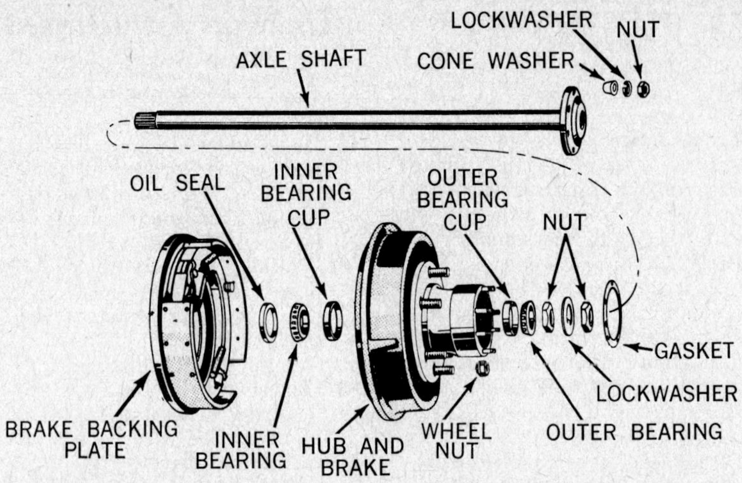

Axle shaft and wheel attaching parts—full floating axle (© Jeep Corp.)

REAR AXLE

Refer to the Drive Axle General Repair Section for application, troubleshooting, and overhaul procedures.

Rear Axle Assembly

Removal

1. Raise the vehicle and place jack stands forward of the rear springs.
2. Remove the rear wheels.
3. Place an indexing mark on the rear yoke and propeller shaft, and disconnect the shaft.
4. Disconnect the shock absorbers from the axle tubes.
5. Disconnect the brake hose from the tee fitting on the axle housing.
6. Disconnect the parking brake cable at the frame mounting.

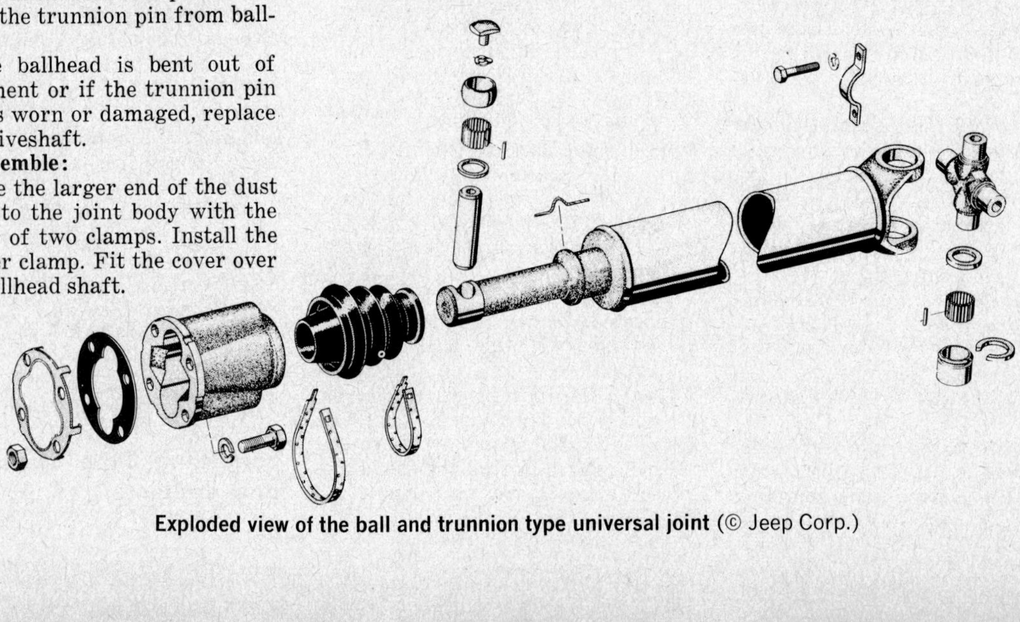

Exploded view of the ball and trunnion type universal joint (© Jeep Corp.)

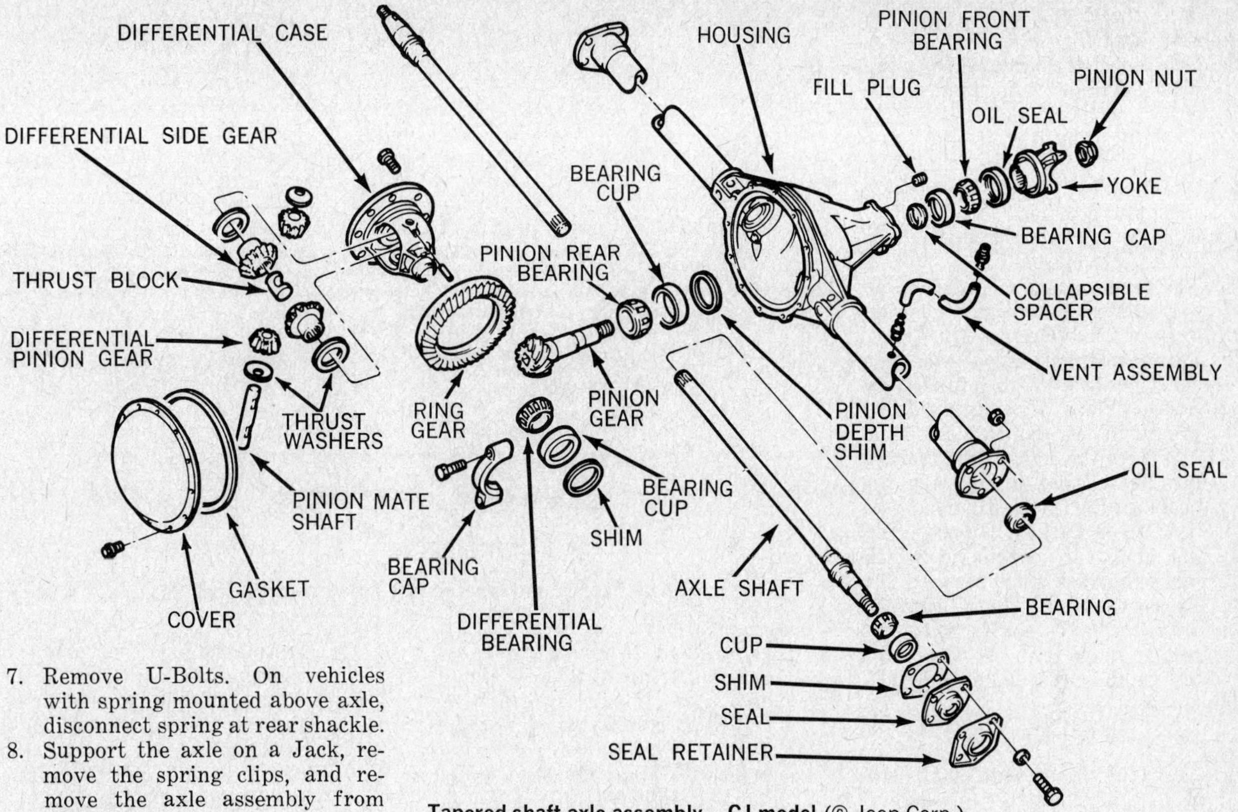

Tapered shaft axle assembly—CJ model (© Jeep Corp.)

7. Remove U-Bolts. On vehicles with spring mounted above axle, disconnect spring at rear shackle.
8. Support the axle on a Jack, remove the spring clips, and remove the axle assembly from under the vehicle.
9. Installation is the reverse of removal.

NOTE: Bleed and adjust brakes accordingly.

Axle Shaft

Removal and Installation

Tapered Shaft

1. Jack up the vehicle and remove the hub cap.
2. Remove the wheel.
3. Remove the axle nut dust cap.
4. Remove the axle shaft cotter pin, castle nut and flat washer.
5. Back-off the brake adjustment.
6. Use a puller to remove the wheel hub.
7. Remove the screws attaching the brake dust protector, grease and bearing retainers, brake assembly and shim to the housing.
8. Remove the hydaulic line from the brake assembly.
9. Remove the dust shield and oil seal.
10. Use a puller to remove the axle shaft.
11. Install the axle shaft in the reverse order of removal, using a new grease seal and installing the hub assembly before the woodruff key.

NOTE: Should the axle shaft be broken, the inner end can usually be drawn out of the housing with a wire loop after the outer oil seal is removed. However, if the broken end is less than 8 in. long, it usually is necessary to remove the differential assembly.

Axle Shaft Bearing

Removal and Installation (Axle Out)

1. With the aid of a combination puller, remove the bearing from the axle shaft.

   NOTE: If a puller is not available, place the threaded end of the axle on a heavy block of wood and with the aid of an assistant, drive the bearing from the axle shaft with a punch and hammer. Contact the inner race only with the punch.
2. The new bearing can be installed with the use of a combination puller, or with the use of a length of pipe, fitted to the diameter of the inner bearing race, and slipped over the axle end to contact and drive the bearing to its seat on the axle shaft.
3. Lubricate the bearing with wheel bearing grease, making sure the grease fills the cavities between the bearing rollers.

Inner Oil Seal

Removal and Installation (Axle Out)

1. Insert the splined end of the axle shaft into the inner seal, hooking the axle end to the seal, and prying downward. The seal will move outward from the housing tube.
2. Install a new seal into the housing tube with the aid of a seal installer or its equivalent.
4. Seat the seal and lubricate the lip.

   NOTE: The lip of the seal should point towards the center of the axle housing.
5. The outer seal is installed during the assembly of the brake support plate.

CJ Models Only, 1976 and Later

1. With the wheel on the ground, remove the axle shaft cotter pin and nut. Loosen the wheel nuts.
2. Raise and support the rear of the car, preferably with jackstands under the axle housing.
3. Remove the wheel.
4. Remove the drum retaining screws, 3 per drum.
5. Remove the drum from the hub. If the brake shoes hold the drum, the brake adjustment will have to be backed off slightly.
6. Attach a puller to the wheel bolts and pull off the hub.

   CAUTION: Don't use a knock-out type puller. It could damage the rear wheel bearings or the differential.
7. Disconnect the parking brake cable at the equalizer. The equalizer is where the single cable from the parking brake pedal

joins the double cable from the rear wheels.

8. Disconnect the brake tube at the wheel cylinder and remove the brake support plate assembly (backing plate), oil seal, and shims (left-side only).
9. Use a puller to remove the axle shaft and bearing.
10. Remove and discard the axle shaft inner oil seal.
11. The bearing cone is pressed onto the shaft. A hydraulic press must be used to remove it.
12. Before installation, pack the axle shaft bearings with high quality grease. Place a healthy glob of grease in the palm of one hand and force the edge of the bearing into it so that grease fills the bearing. Do this until the whole bearing is packed. Grease packing tools are available which make this task much easier.
13. Press the axle shaft bearings onto the axle shafts with the small diameter of the cone toward the outer end of the shaft.

CAUTION: Always press on the inner bearing race.

14. Coat the inner axle shaft seal with light oil.
15. Coat the outer surface of the metal seal retainer with sealant.
16. Use a seal driver to install the inner oil seal in the axle housing.
17. Install the axle shaft(s), turning them as necessary to fit the splines into the differential.
18. Install the outer bearing cup.
19. Apply sealant to the axle housing flange and brake support plate mounting areas. Install the original shims in their original locations, oil seal assembly, and brake support plate. Tighten the retaining bolts to 35 ft lbs.

NOTE: The oil seal and retainer go on the outside of the brake support plate.

20. Axle shaft end-play can be measured by installing the hub retaining nut on the shaft so it can be pushed and pulled with relative ease. Strike the end of each axle shaft with a lead hammer to seat the bearing cups against the support plate. Mount a dial indicator on the left side support plate with the stylus resting on the end of the axle shaft. Check the end-play while pushing and pulling on the axle shaft. End play should be within 0.004-0.008 in., with 0.006 in. ideal. Add shims to increase end play and subtract whims to decrease end-play. Remove the hub retaining nut when finished checking end-play.

NOTE: When a new axle shaft is installed, a new hub must also be installed. However, a new hub can be installed on an original axle shaft if the serrations on the shaft are not worn or damaged. The procedures for installing an original hub and a new hub are different.

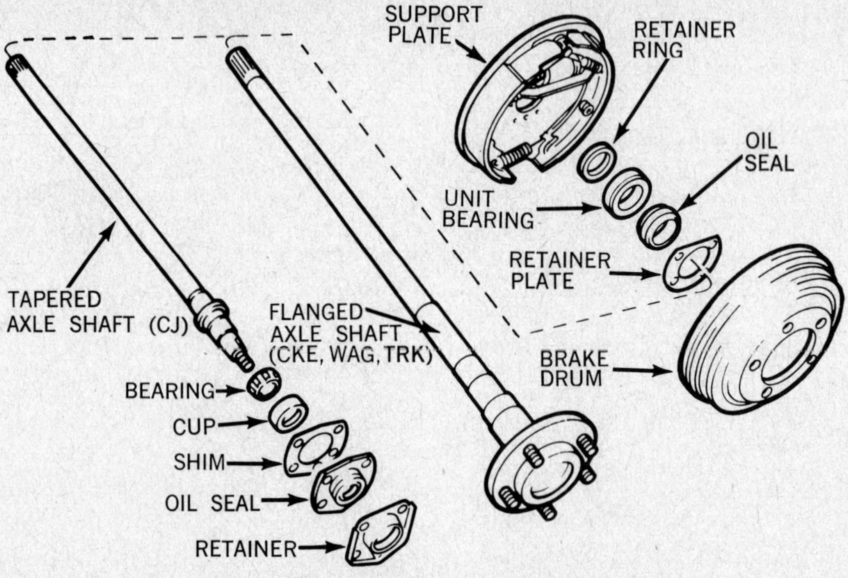

Typical flanged and tapered axle assemblies (© Jeep Corp.)

21. Install an original hub in the following manner:
    a. Align the keyway in the hub with the axle shaft key.
    b. Slide the hub onto the axle shaft as far as possible.
    c. Install the axle shaft nut and washer.
    d. Install the drum, drum retaining screws, and wheel.
    e. Lower the vehicle onto its wheels and tighten the axle shaft nut to 250 ft lbs. If the cotter pin hole is not aligned, tighten the nut to the next castellation and install the pin. Do not loosen the nut to align the cotter pin hole.
22. Install a new hub in the following manner:
    a. Align the keyway in the hub with the axle shaft key.
    b. Slide the hub onto the axle shaft as far as possible.
    c. Install two well-lubricated thrust washers and the axle shaft nut.
    d. Install the brake drum, drum retaining screws, and wheel.
    e. Lower the vehicle onto its wheels.
    f. Tighten the axle shaft nut until the distance from the outer face of the hub to the outer end of the axle shaft is 1-5/16 in. Pressing the hub onto the axle to the specified distance is necessary to form the hub serrations properly.
    g. Remove the axle shaft nut and one thrust washer.
    h. Install the axle shaft nut and tighten it to 250 ft lbs. If the cotter pin hole is not aligned, tighten the nut to the next castellation and install the pin. Do not loosen the nut to install the cotter pin.
23. Connect the brake line to the wheel cylinder and bleed the brake hydraulic system and adjust the brake shoes.

Flanged Shaft

Removal and Installation

1. Raise the vehicle and support safely. Remove the wheel.
2. Remove the brake drum spring lock nuts and remove the drum.
3. Remove the axle shaft flange cup plug by piercing the center with a sharp tool and prying it out.
4. Using the access hole in the axle shaft flange, remove the nuts which attach the brake support plate and retainer to the axle tube flange.
5. Remove the axle shaft from the housing with an axle puller.
6. Remove the inner oil seal from the axle housing tube. Install a new seal in the tube.

NOTE: Lip of seal must be facing towards the center of the differential.

7. Mount the axle in a vise, and with a chisel, cut the bearing retaining ring, and drive the ring off the axle shaft.
8. Using a hacksaw, cut through the oil seal and remove from the axle shaft. Do not damage the seal contact surface while cutting.
9. With the aid of a puller or its equivalent, remove the bearing from the shaft.

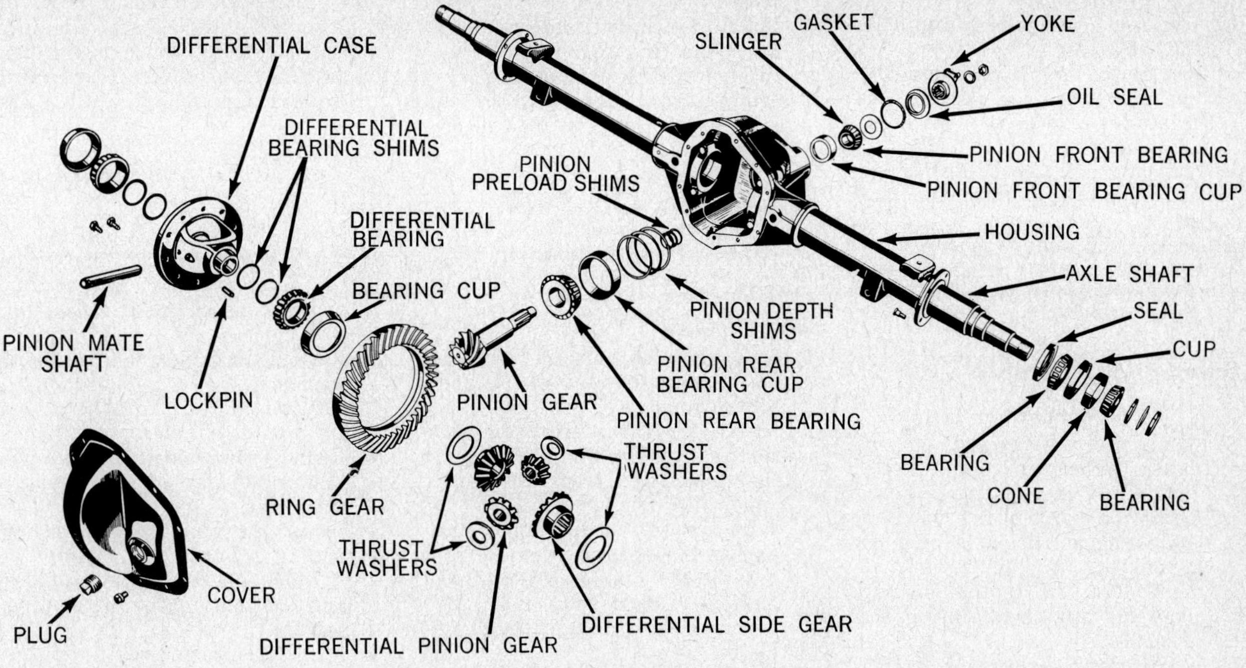

Full-floating rear axle assembly (© Jeep Corp.)

10. Install the retainer plate on the axle shaft.
11. Apply wheeel bearing grease to the oil seal cavity and between the seal lips and install seal on the axle shaft seal seat.
    NOTE: Outer face of seal must face the axle flange.
12. Pack wheel bearing with grease and install on the axle shaft.
    NOTE: Cup rib ring should be facing the axle flange.
13. Install the retainer ring on the axle shaft, and press both the retainer and the bearing on the shaft at the same time, until both are seated against the shaft shoulder.
14. Install the axle shaft into the housing bore, being careful not to damage the inner seal.
15. Lubricate the outer surface of the bearing cup before installing into the bearing bore.
16. Tap the flanged end of the axle to position it into the bearing bore.
17. Attach the axle shaft retainer and brake support plate to the axle tube flange, and secure with the nuts and lockwashers.
18. Install the brake drum, spring type locknuts, and rear wheels.
19. Remove the safety stands and lower the vehicle.

Full-Floating Axle Shaft—

It is not necessary to raise the rear wheels in order to remove the rear axle shaft on full-floating rear axles.

1. Remove the axle flange nuts, lock washers, and split washers retaining the axle shaft flange.
2. Remove the axle shaft from the axle housing.
3. Clean the axle flange mating area on the hub and axle, removing all old gasket material.

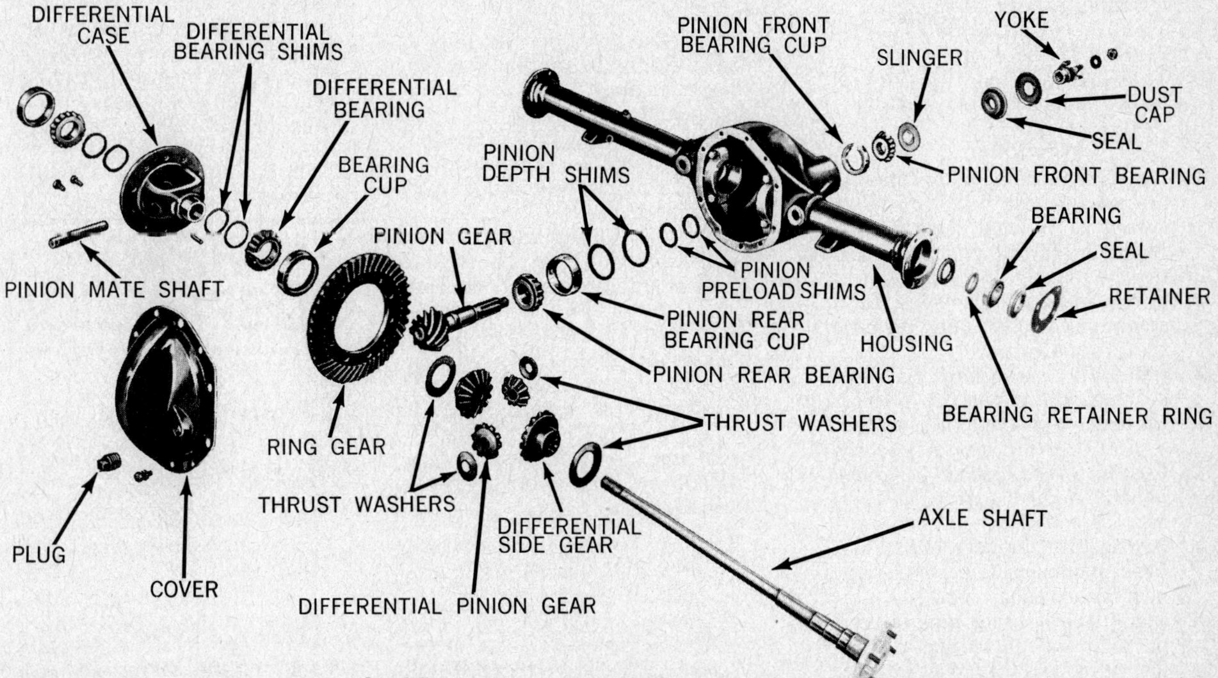

Semi-floating rear axle assembly (© Jeep Corp.)

4. Install a new flange gasket onto the hub studs.
5. Insert the axle shaft into the housing. It may be necessary to rotate the axle shaft to align the shaft splines with the differential gear splines and the flange attaching holes with the hub studs.
6. Install the split washers, lockwashers, and flange nuts. Tighten the nuts securely.

Differential Assembly

Removal

1. Raise the vehicle and support safely. Remove the wheels, drums and axle shafts.
2. Drain the axle housing lubricant and remove the axle housing cover.
3. Mark the differential bearing caps for alignment during the assembly.
4. Loosen the bearing cap bolts, but do not remove.
5. Install an axle housing spreader tool on the axle housing and secure with the hold-down clamps.
6. Mount a dial indicator on the axle housing to measure the amount of spread. Zero the indicator dial.
7. Spread the axle housing no more than 0.020 inch.
8. Remove the differential bearing caps and the dial indicator from the housing.
9. Using two pry bars, remove the differential carrier from the axle housing.
10. Remove the spreader tool from the housing as soon as the differential carrier is removed to avoid the possibility of the axle housing taking a set.
11. The differential housing can now be overhauled or replaced.

Installation

1. Install the axle housing spreader tool on the axle housing and secure with the hold down clamps. Install a dial indicator and center the dial.
2. Spread the axle housing to a maximum of 0.020 inch. Remove the dial indicator.
3. Lubricate the differential side bearings and install the differential carrier in the axle housing.

   NOTE: Prior shim fitting and bearing preload should be accomplished before differential carrier installation.
4. Tap the unit in place with a soft faced hammer. Remove the axle housing spreader tool.
5. Install the bearing caps in their proper place and torque to 40 ft. lbs. on model 30 rear axle and to 80 ft. lbs. on models 44 and 60.
6. Install a dial indicator and recheck the ring gear backlash at two points. Correct as necessary.
7. Complete the assembly in the reverse of the removal, add lubricant and road test.

Pinion Oil Seal

Removal and Installation

Semi-Floating Axle with Tapered Shaft

1. Raise and support the vehicle and remove the rear wheels and brake drums.
2. Mark the driveshaft and yoke for reassembly and disconnect the driveshaft from the rear yoke.
3. With a socket on the pinion nut and an in. lb torque wrench, rotate the drive pinion several revolutions. Check and record the torque required to turn the drive pinion.
4. Remove the pinion nut. Use a flange holding tool to hold the flange while removing the pinion nut. Discard the pinion nut.
5. Mark the yoke and thee drive pinion shaft for reassembly reference.
6. Remove the rear yoke with a puller.
7. Inspect the seal surface of the yoke and replace it with a new one if the seal surface is pitted, grooved, or otherwise damaged.
8. Remove the pinion oil seal.
9. Before installing the new seal, coat the lip of the seal with rear axle lubricant.
10. Install the seal, driving it into place with the proper driving tool.
11. Install the yoke on the pinion shaft. Align the marks made on the pinion shaft and yoke during disassembly.
12. Install a new pinion nut. Tighten nut until end play is removed from the pinion bearing. Do not overtighten.
13. Check the torque required to turn the drive pinion. The pinion must be turned several revolutions to obtain an accurate reading.
14. Tighten the pinion nut to obtain the torque reading observed during disassembly (step 3) plus 5 in. lbs. Tighten the nut minutely each time, to avoid overtightening. Do not loosen and then retighten the nut.

NOTE: If the desired torque is exceeded a new collapsible pinion spacer sleeve must be installed and the pinion gear preload reset. Refer to the General Repair Section and Overhaul procedures for this operation.

15. Install the driveshaft, aligning the index marks made during disassembly. Install the rear brake drums and wheels.

Semi-Floating and Full-Floating Axles with Flange Shaft

1. Raise and support the vehicle.
2. Mark the driveshaft and yoke for reference during assembly and disconnect the driveshaft at the yoke.
3. Remove the pinion shaft nut and washer.
4. Remove the yoke from the pinion shaft, using a puller.
5. Remove the pinion shaft oil seal.
6. Install the new seal with a suitable driver.
7. Install the pinion shaft washer and nut. Tighten the nut to 210 ft lbs on the semi-floating axles and 260 ft lbs on the full-floating axles.
8. Align the index marks on the driveshaft and yoke and install the driveshaft. Tighten the attaching bolts or nuts to 16 ft lbs.
9. Remove the supports and lower the vehicle.

Wheel Bearing Adjustment

Full Floating Axle

1. Raise the vehicle so that the wheel can be rotated. Support the vehicle safely.
2. Remove the axle shaft.
3. Straighten the lip of the lock washer and remove the lock washer and lock nut.
4. Tighten the adjusting nut and rotate the wheel until binding exists. Back off the adjusting nut 1/6 turn until the wheel rotates freely without any lateral shake.
5. Replace the lock washer and tighten the lock nut, bending the lip of the lock washer over the lock nut.
6. Install the axle with a new gasket and tighten the axle nuts securely.

REAR SUSPENSION

Spring

Removal and Installation

Mounted Below the Axle

1. Raise the vehicle and support the axle.
2. Disconnect the shock absorber and stabilizer bar, if so equipped.
3. Remove the U-bolts and tie plates.
4. Disconnect the front and rear ends of the spring and remove the spring.

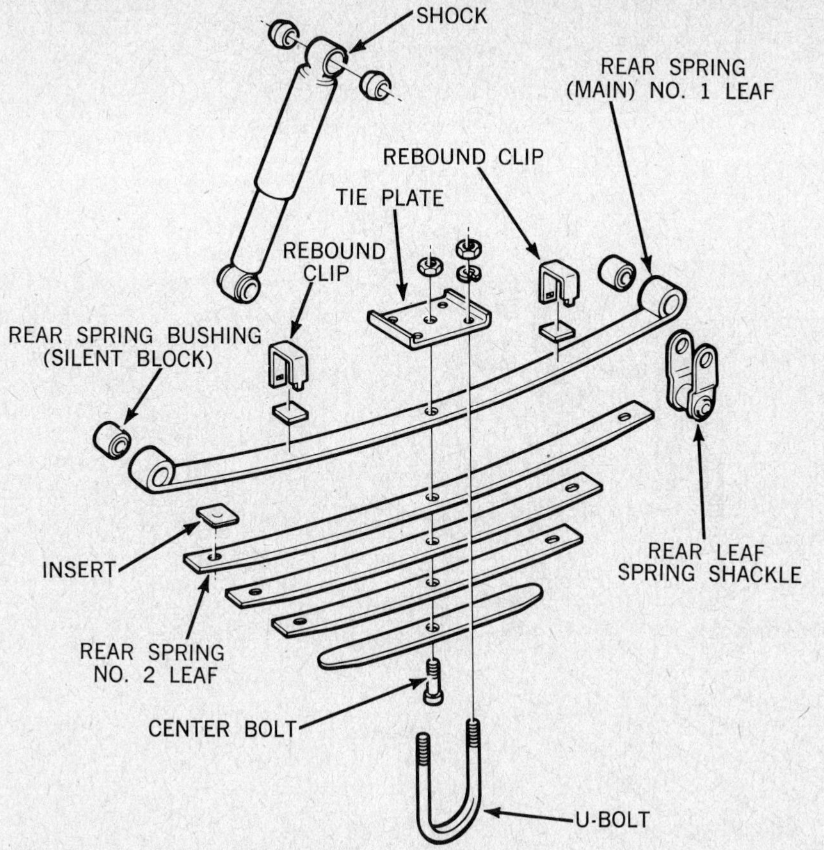

Typical rear suspension components—Cherokee, Wagoneer, Truck (© Jeep Corp.)

5. The spring can be disassembled by removing the spring rebound clips and the center bolt.
6. Mount the spring in the vehicle, but do not tighten the pivot bolts.
7. Align the spring center bolt and install the tie plate and U-bolts.
8. Connect the shock absorber and stabilizer bar, if so equipped.
9. Remove the axle support and lower the vehicle.
10. Tighten the pivot bolts with the weight of the vehicle on the springs to 45 ft lbs on CJ models and 75 ft lbs on all other models. Tighten 9/16 in. U-bolt nuts to 100 ft lbs, $\frac{1}{2}$ in. nuts to 55 ft lbs and 7/16 in. U-bolt nuts to 40 ft lbs.

NOTE: If left-side spring is to be serviced, remove fuel tank skid plate.

Mounted Above the Axle

1. Raise the vehicle and support the frame ahead of the axle.
2. Remove the U-bolts.
3. Unclip the axle vent hose from the frame.
4. Disconnect the shock absorber.
5. Remove the spring pivot bolts.
6. Lower the axle enough so the spring can be turned over and remove the spring. The spring can be disassembled by removing the rebound clips and center bolt.
7. Mount the spring in the vehicle and install the pivot bolts and nuts.
8. Raise the axle, align the spring center bolt, and install the U-bolts.
9. Connect the shock absorber, vent hose, and remove the supports and lower the vehicle.
10. Tighten the spring pivot bolts with the weight of the vehicle on the springs. Tighten the pivot bolts to 75 ft lbs. Tighten 9/16 in. U-bolt nuts to 100 ft lbs, $\frac{1}{2}$ in. nuts to 55 ft lbs, and 7/16 in. U-bolt nuts to 40 ft lbs.

Spring Bushing

Removal and Installation

Small Bushing

1. Install an 8 in. length of threaded rod halfway through the bushing and place a $1\frac{1}{8}$ in. socket with the open end toward the bushing, one $\frac{1}{2}$ in. flat washer, and one $\frac{3}{8}$ in. hex nut on one end of the rod.
2. Place a 2 in. section of $1\frac{5}{8}$ in. or $1\frac{3}{8}$ in. ID pipe, one $\frac{3}{4}$ in. flat washer, or $\frac{1}{2}$ in. flat washer and on $\frac{3}{8}$ in. hex nut on the opposite end of the threaded rod.
3. Tighten both of the $\frac{3}{8}$ in. nuts finger-tight and align all of the components. Make sure the socket is positioned in the eye of the spring and aligns with the bushing. The pipe section must butt against the spring eye so the bushing can pass through it. The socket will act as a press and will press the bushing out of the spring eye.
4. Tighten the nut at the socket end of the rod until the bushing is pressed out of the spring eye. Remove the tools and the bushing.
5. Install the replacement bushing on the threaded rod and assemble the bushing tools as outlined in steps 1 and 2, and press the bushing into the spring eye. Make sure the bushing is centered in the spring eye.

Large Bushing

1. Place $\frac{1}{2}\times 11$ in. length of threaded rod half-way through the bushing and install 1-1/16 in. deep socket with the open end toward the bushing, one $\frac{1}{2}$ in. flat washer, and one $\frac{1}{2}$ in. nut on the end of the rod.
2. Install a 3 in. length of $1\frac{1}{2}$ in. ID pipe, one $\frac{1}{2}$ in. flat washer and one $\frac{1}{2}$ in. nut on the opposite end of the threaded rod.
3. Tighten both nuts finger tight and align all of the components. Make sure the socket is positioned in the eye of the spring and aligns with the bushing. The pipe section must butt against the spring eye so the bushing can pass through it. The socket will act as a press ram and press the bushing out of the spring eye.
4. Tighten the nut at the socket and press the bushing out of the spring eye.
5. Install the new bushing on the threaded rod and assemble the bushing tools as outlined in steps 1 and 2. Press the bushing into the spring eye until it is centered in the eye.

Shock Absorber

Removal and Installation

1. Raise the vehicle for working ing clearance and support safely.
2. Place a jack under the axle assembly and raise to relieve the springs of axle weight and to place the shock absorber in its mid stroke.
3. Remove the retaining nuts or bolts and remove the shock absorber from the vehicle.
4. Install the new shock absorber and tighten the attaching nuts or bolts.
5. Lower the vehicle to the ground.

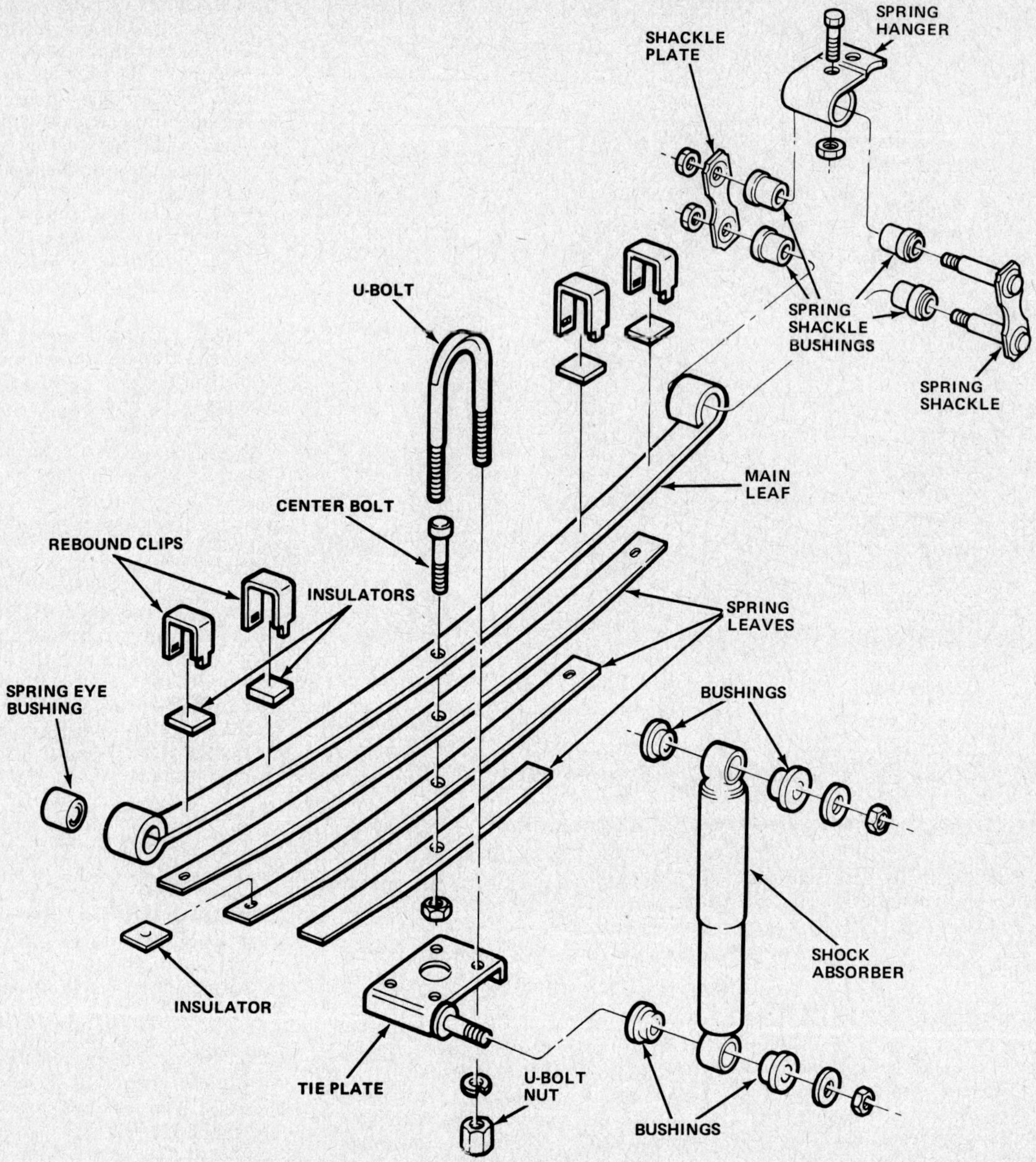

Typical rear suspension components—CJ models (© Jeep Corp.)

DOMESTIC TRUCK GENERAL REPAIR SECTION

INDEX

EMISSION CONTROL

Gasoline Engines

Introduction

The Emission Control devices required by law on trucks are determined by weight classification and were considered either "Light Duty" or "Heavy Duty" applications, with the Gross Vehicle Weight (GVW) of 6000 lbs. as the dividing line. State and Federal Government regulations have now mandated a new weight standard from the 6000 lbs. GVW to a new GVW of 8500 lbs. or less as "Light Duty" and a GVW of 8500 lbs. or more as "Heavy Duty" applications.

The "Light Duty" emission devices are normally the same as used on the passenger cars.

During certain model years, passenger carrying vehicles, such as window vans with greater GVW of 6000 lbs. were also considered to be "Light Duty" models and must comply with the "Light Duty" emission control requirements.

"Heavy Duty" truck models use less emission control devices than the "Light Duty" models, although more emission controls are being required in each succeeding year to comply with the changing emission control regulations and requirements.

The State of California remains stringent in their emission control standards and through out this section, reference will be made to either the California, High Altitude or to the Federal engines. (Federal referring to the remaining 49 states, High Altitude referring to areas above 4000 ft. (1,219 meters)).

Engine Modifications

Internal engine modifications have been made from year to year by redesigning the following;

1. Lowering the compression ratios to allow the use of low or non-leaded fuels.
2. Combustion chambers and piston modifications for a more efficient air/fuel flow rate and burning time.
3. Cam shaft modification to improve valve timing and to increase valve overlap periods.
4. Higher engine operating temperatures and increased cooling areas.
5. Balanced fuel induction manifolds to properly balance the air/fuel flow to the cylinders.
6. Other modifications include changes in metals used in the construction of the engines and components to allow the operation of the engine with non-leaded, non-lubricating fuels.

External engine modifications have been made to the carburetors and distributors to provide the proper air/fuel mixture and to provide the proper timing of the ignition spark to insure the engine emission levels remain within the legislated limits, while providing the best engine performance and fuel economy at varying speeds and loads.

Emission Control Systems

In order to control the engine crankcase, fuel and exhaust emissions, three major systems have been designated.

1. Crankcase controls—are used to provide a more complete scavenging of the crankcase vapors and to route the vapors to the engine

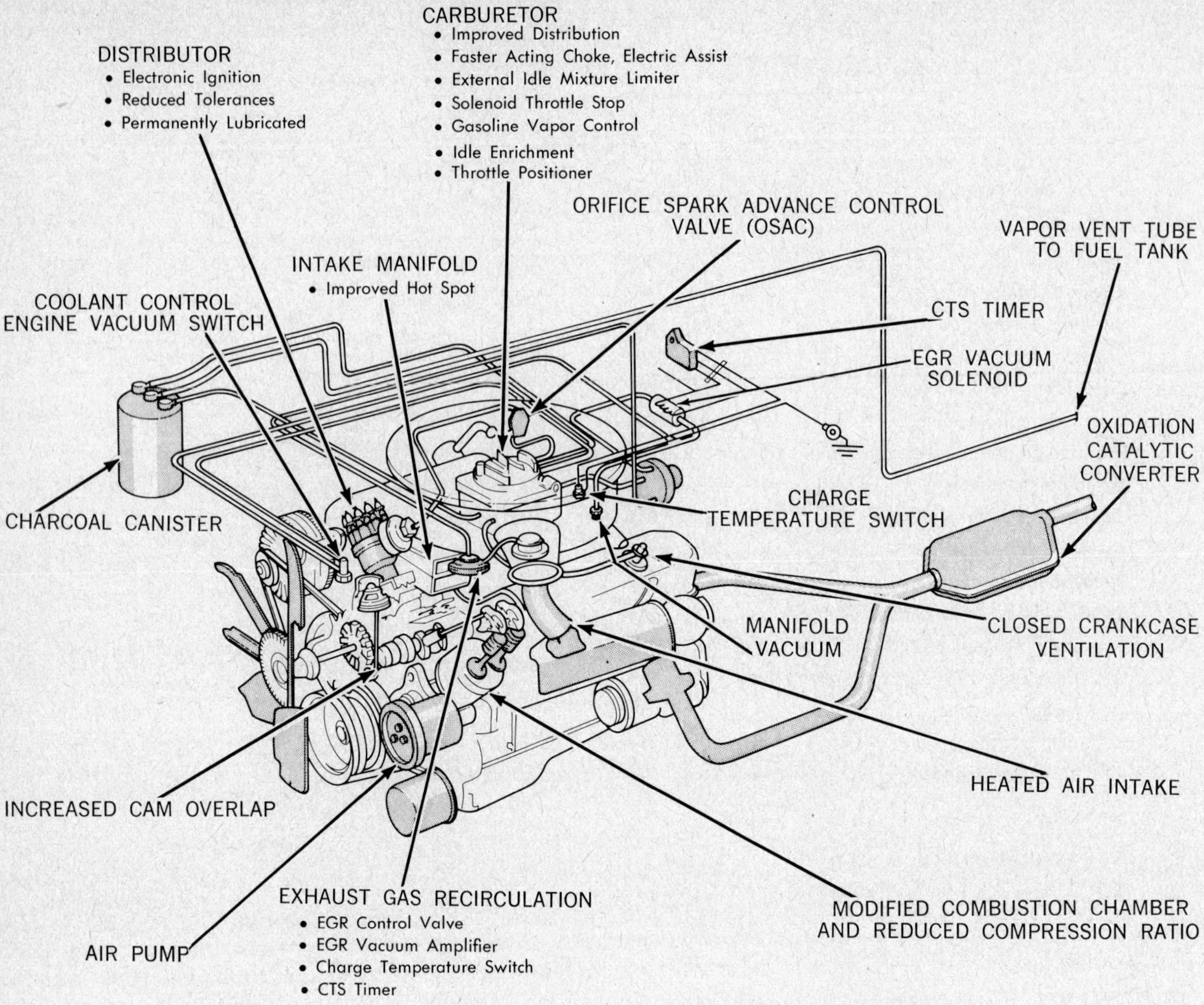

Emission Control System—typical of "Light Duty" emission operation (© Chrysler Corp.)

fuel induction system for burning with the air/fuel mixture.

2. Evaporation controls—are used to prevent the emission of gasoline vapors from the fuel tank and carburetor, into the atmosphere. Charcoal canisters are used to store the gasoline vapors during periods of engine shutdown and during periods of engine operation, the gasoline vapors are drawn into the fuel induction system and burned with the air/fuel mixture.

3. Exhaust controls—are used to limit the emission of Carbon Monoxide (CO), Hydrocarbons (HC) and Oxides of Nitrogen (NOx) from the engine exhaust. Numerous controls are used on the engines and the exhaust systems to perform this removal of pollutants.

LIGHT AND HEAVY DUTY EMISSION CLASS VEHICLES

All States Except California	
Light Duty Emission	**Heavy Duty Emission**
C-10 Pick-Up (Except over 6000 Lbs. GVW)	C-10 Pick-Up & Cab Chassis (Over 6000 Lbs. GVW) C-K 10 Blazer, Jimmy C-K 10-20 Suburban C-20-30 Pick-Up & Cab Chassis K-10-20-30 Pick-Up & Cab Chassis P-10-20-30 Van & F/C Chassis
California	
C-K 10-20 Pick-Up & Cab Chassis C-K 10-20 Suburban C-K 10 Blazer, Jimmy P-20 Van & F/C Chassis	C-K 30 Pick-Up & Cab Chassis P-30 Van & F/C Chassis

NOTE: Calif. vehicles 8500 Lbs. GVW or less will be Light Duty Emission Vehicles; over 8500 Lbs. will be Heavy Duty Emission.

Emission Certification Label—typical (© General Motors Corp.)

Maintenance

In order for the emission controls to function properly, maintenance must be performed at regular intervals, either by time or mileage increments. Owner manuals will normally contain a maintenance schedule for services to be done and should be followed for longer emission systems and vehicle life.

Emission Certification Label

An Emission Certification label is attached to either the engine or engine compartment sheet metal and should be consulted before any adjustments are made to the engine.

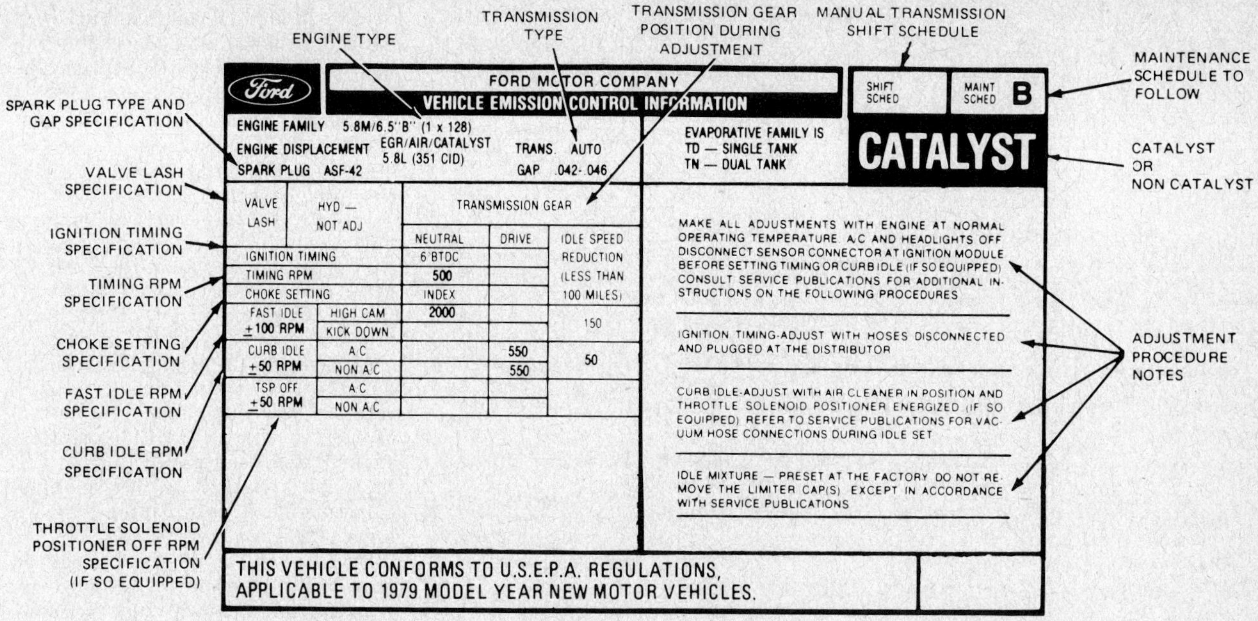

Emission Certification Label—typical—other manufacturers similar (© Ford Motor Co.)

NOTE: It is a good practice to copy the information from the Emission Certification label and keep with the owners manual, in case the label becomes mutilated or lost.

Emission Control Systems and Components Crankcase Control System

Postive Crankcase Ventilation (PCV)

With the engine operating, crankcase ventilation air is drawn through an air cleaner mounted filter assembly, through a hose to the crankcase air inlet, down into the crankcase and up to the rocker arm chamber, out through a flow control valve and into a hose connected to the base of the carburetor or to the intake manifold. The crankcase vapors are then mixed with the air/fuel mixture and burned through the normal combustion process. The purpose of the flow control valve is to restrict the flow of crankcase vapors when the intake manifold is high (such as idle or coast modes), to avoid upsetting the air/fuel mixture at idle and causing roughness of the engine at low speeds or while idling.

With the flow control valve open at times of low engine vacuum and high air flow through the carburetor (such as having the throttle valves open as in the drive mode), the added crankcase vapor flow has no noticable effect on the engine operation.

Crankcase Control Testing

Checking crankcase vacuum is the most effective way to test any PCV system. If there is vacuum in the crankcase, then the major part of the system has to be working.

On all models, use a piece of paper or a PCV tester to measure the crank-

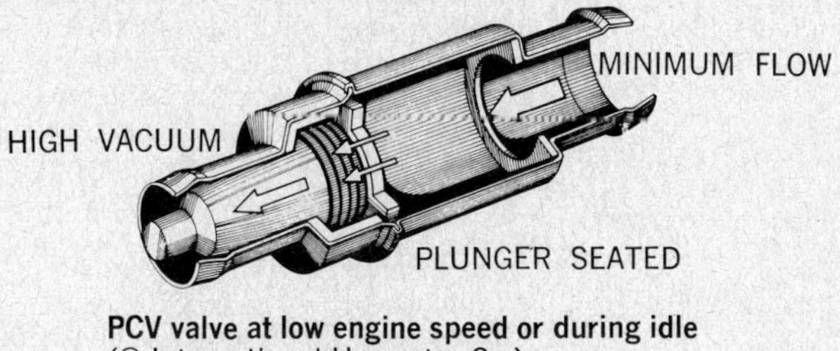

PCV valve at low engine speed or during idle
(© International Harvester Co.)

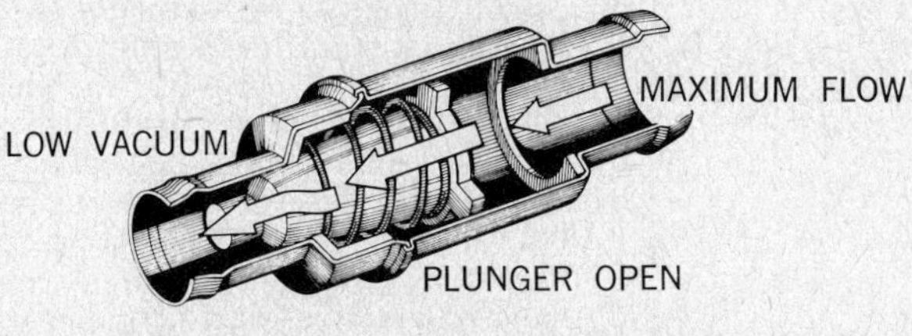

PCV valve operation at high engine speed
(© International Harvester Co.)

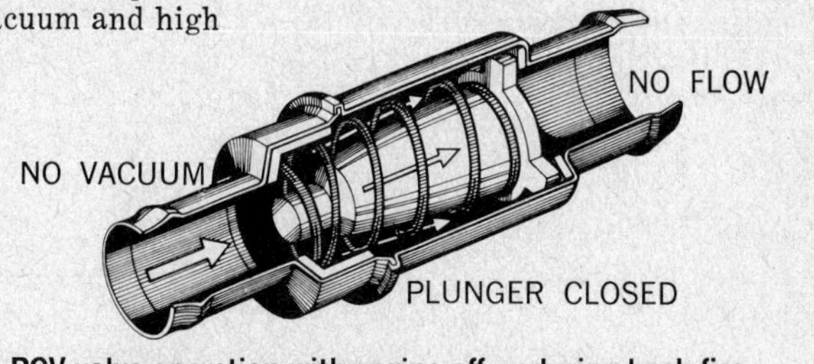

PCV valve operation with engine off or during back fire
(© International Harvester Co.)

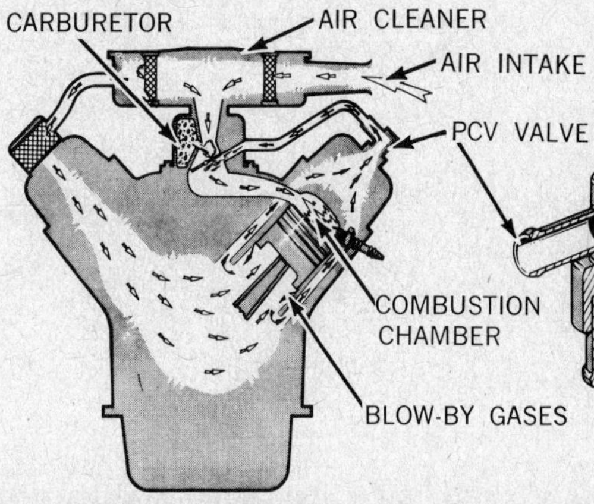

Closed Crankcase Ventilation System (© Chrysler Corp.)

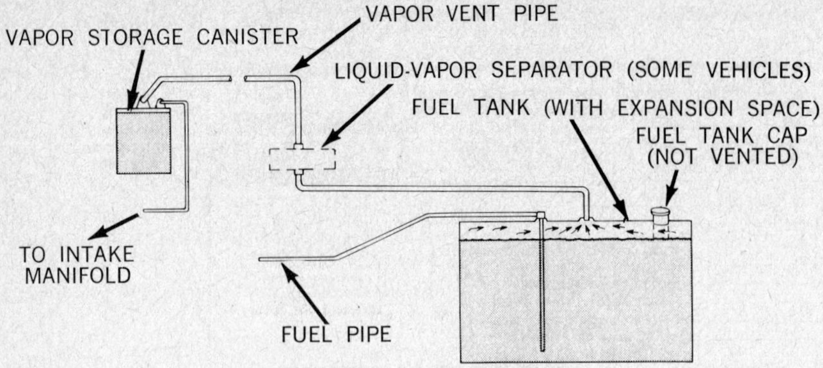

Schematic view of Gasoline Evaporation System (© International Harvester Co.)

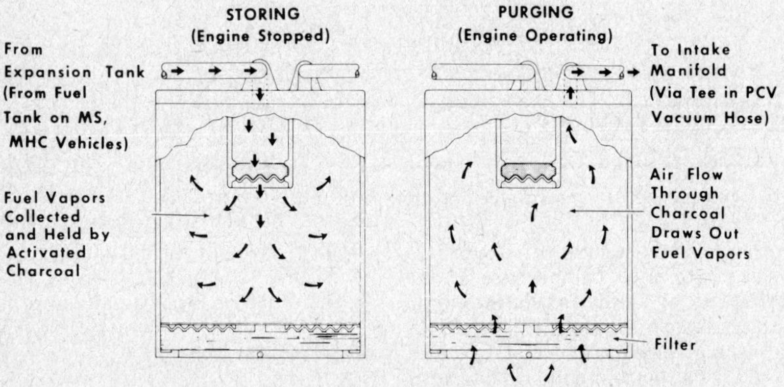

Vapor storage—engine off and during operation (© International Harvester Co.)

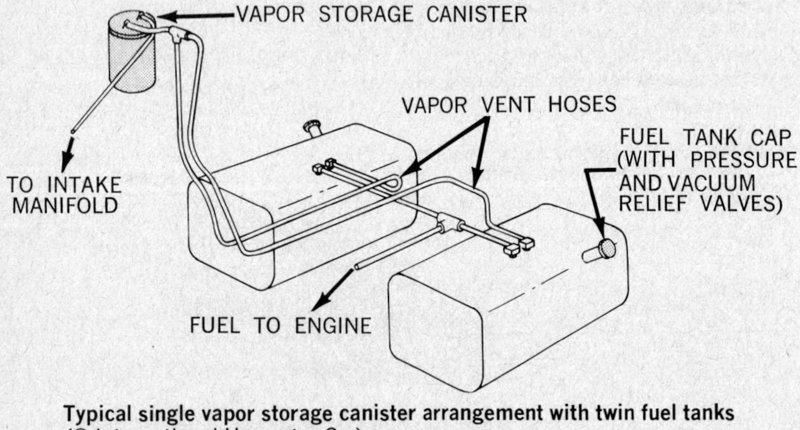

Typical single vapor storage canister arrangement with twin fuel tanks (© International Harvester Co.)

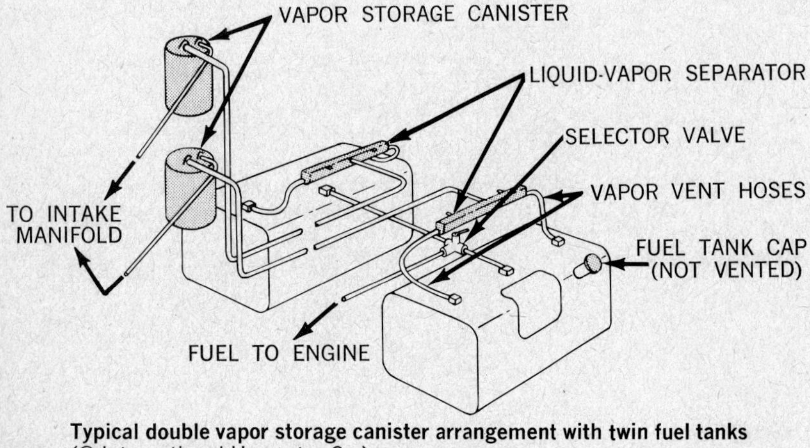

Typical double vapor storage canister arrangement with twin fuel tanks (© International Harvester Co.)

case vacuum at the oil filler cap, with the cap removed, and the engine idling in Park or Neutral. It may take a few seconds for the vacuum to build up enough to suck the piece of paper against the oil filler hole. If the vacuum does not build up, check to be sure you have plugged the fresh air entry. An alternate method on some models is to use the piece of paper or PCV tester on the end of the fresh air entry hose. When you do it that way, the oil filler cap must be the solid type and you must leave it in place.

If there is no crankcase vacuum, pull the PCV valve from the crankcase and hold your finger over the end of it. You should feel full manifold vacuum with the engine idling. If not, the valve is plugged or there is an obstruction in a hose or passageway. On some designs the valve may be screwed into its mounting, with a hose leading to the rocker cover or crankcase. If the valve has good suction, but there is no crankcase vacuum, check the hose to be sure it is open. PCV valves that are restricted or plugged must be replaced, unless they are the type that will come apart for cleaning. Lack of crankcase vacuum can also be caused by vacuum leaks at rocker cover, oil pan, or other engine gaskets. Usually, tightening the bolts will stop the leak.

Evaporation Control System

To prevent the emission of gasoline vapors into the atmosphere from the gasoline tank and carburetor vents, vapors are routed by hoses to one or more charcoal filled canisters for storage while the engine is stopped and are routed from and/or through the canister(s) to the engine fuel induction system, when the engine is operating.

On single canister arrangements, the throttle valve is normally used as purge valve, with the vapor hoses routed to the intake manifold or to the carburetor base. On some vehicle models, the purging of the canister is accomplished by air movement through the air cleaner snorkle and into the engine, by having the purge hose connected from the canister to the snorkel.

On dual canister arrangements, the purging action of the secondary canister is triggered by a vacuum signal from the distributor vacuum hose to open the canister purge switch, which allows the vapors to purge through the PC system and into the engine.

Fuel filler caps that are used with the vapor Emmission Control System, normally have a pressure-vacuum valve assembly as part of the cap, to allow air to enter the tank as the fuel is consumed to avoid fuel tank collapse, when the vacuum is between 15 to 25 in. Hg. When the fuel tank internal pressure builds up from .75 to 2.0 psi (nominal) over atmospheric pressure, the pressure valve opens to relieve the excess internal pressures.

Larger trucks will normally have fuel caps with anti-surge mechanisms built into the caps to prevent fuel spillage during truck operation or will have non-vented caps with the fuel tanks vented through vapor storage canisters.

Vapor separators and anti-rollover valves are used with the vapor control systems, to avoid having raw fuel collect in the charcoal canister or to have fuel leakage in case of a vehicle rollover.

Evaporation Control System Inspection

The system inspection consists of examining the fuel resistance hoses, connections, metal lines, nylon lines, valves, separators and canisters. The only needed replacement is the canister air filter.

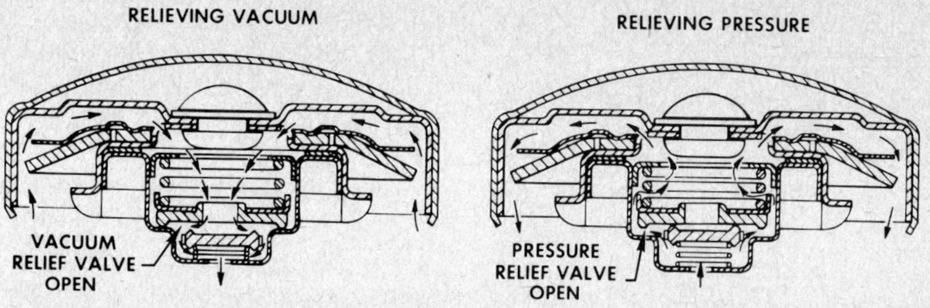

Pressure-vacuum type fuel filler cap operation (© International Harvester Co.)

Exhaust Control System

Exhaust controls vary considerably in design. There are many different systems or devices used on the domestic makes to control exhaust emissions. Following are basic descriptions of the common systems.

Thermostatic Air Cleaner

Fresh air supplied to the air cleaner comes either from the normal snorkel, or from a tube connected to an exhaust manifold stove. A door in

EVAPORATION CONTROL SYSTEM DIAGNOSIS CHART

Problem	Cause	Remedy
Persistent Odor of Fuel Vapors	Canister saturated due to extend parking of vehicle.	Operate (idle) engine for several minutes to purge canister.
	Fuel tank cap not sealing.	Replace cap.
	Canister not purging:	
	a. Vacuum hose to intake manifold or tee obstructed or leaking.	Check for vacuum at canister end of hose. Blow through hose with compressed air. Replace hose if cracked, deteriorated or obstruction cannot be removed.
	b. Vacuum orifice in manifold fitting or tee obstructed.	Remove manifold fitting or tee and blow orally through fitting to check for obstruction. If orifice is plugged, soak fitting in solvent and blow out with compressed air.
	Loose vent hose connections or loose filler neck connections.	Pressure test vapor vent system for leakage. If leakage is indicated, visually inspect for damaged hoses or tubes, loose, damaged or missing clamps. Repair as needed.
Fuel Leakage:		
a. From Fuel Tank Cap	Fuel tank cap seal faulty.	Replace cap,
	Pressure relief valve in fuel tank cap faulty.	Test operation of pressure relief valve. If valve is faulty, replace cap.
	Valve vent hoses obstructed.	Remove fuel tank cap and blow hoses with compressed air. Replace hoses if necessary.
b. From Fuel Tank, Liquid/Vapor Separator or Connecting Tubes and Hoses	Loose connections, cracked or broke tube or hose.	Pressure test vapor vent system for leakage. If leakage is Indicated, repair as needed.
	Cracked or damaged fuel tank or liquid/vapor separator.	Replace damaged components.
c. From Vapor Storage Canister (Through Air Flow Filter)	Pressure relief valve in fuel tank cap faulty.	Test operation of valve. If faulty, replace cap.
Noisy Fuel Tank—Wall Fluctuation ("Oilcanning")	Vacuum buildup in tank:	
	Vacuum relief valve in fuel tank cap faulty.	Test operation of valve. If faulty, replace cap.
	Pressure buildup in tank:	
	a. Pressure relief valve in fuel tank cap faulty.	Test operation of valve. If faulty, replace cap.
	b. Vapor vent hoses obstructed.	Remove fuel tank cap and blow out hoses with compressed air. Replace hoses if necessary.

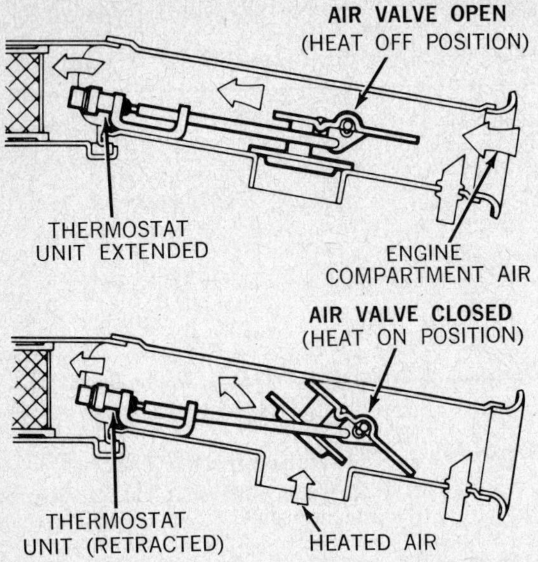

Thermostatic Controlled air cleaner operation—typical (© Jeep Corp.)

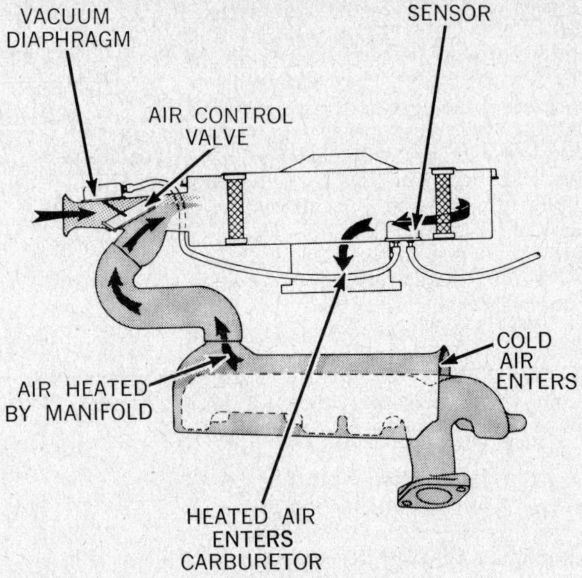

Vacuum operated air cleaner operation (© Chrysler Corp.)

the snorkel regulates the source of incoming air so that a warm engine always takes in warm air, approximately 100°F. The door may be controlled by a thermostatic spring or expansion bulb, or it may be vacuum operated. The vacuum operated designs use a thermostatic bimetal switch inside the air cleaner that bleeds off vacuum as the engine warms up, and regulates the position of the air door. On all late models, the snorkel is connected to a long tube so it takes in cooler air from outside the engine compartment. In hot climates the cool air tube is necessary because underhood air can easily reach 200°F.

Vacuum operated air doors are all designed so that the air cleaner takes in cold air when there is no vacuum. This means that an air door in the hot air position will switch to the cold position at wide open throttle because of the loss of manifold vacuum. The sudden switching of the door from hot to cold may cause a stumble or misfire in the engine, so some designs include a modulator valve mounted on the side of the air cleaner to block the vacuum and hold the door in the hot air position. A small thermostat inside the modulator opens it when the underhood temperatures reach normal. Other designs use a delay valve that allows the air door to move to the cold position slowly, to prevent stumble.

Testing Air Cleaners, Non-Vacuum Type

To test the non-vacuum type of heated air cleaner, start with an engine that is cold enough to have the air door in the hot air position. Remove the top of the air cleaner and put a thermometer inside the cleaner, then replace the cover without the nuts. Start the engine and watch the air door through the end of the air cleaner. You may have to remove some air ducting to be able to see the air door. As soon as the air door starts to move from the hot air position, lift the top off the air cleaner and read the temperature. If the temperature is between 130 and 150°F. the thermostat is working correctly. If not, replace the thermostat.

CAUTION: Do not replace the thermostat if the temperature is off by only a few degrees. It must be considerably out of specification, or perhaps not opening at all, to affect the running of the vehicle.

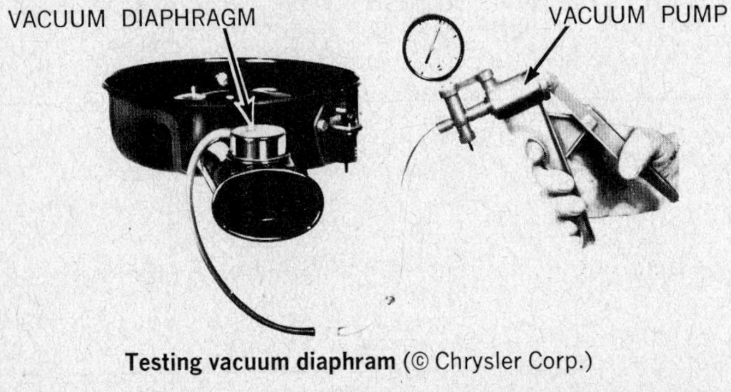

Testing vacuum diaphram (© Chrysler Corp.)

Testing Air Cleaners, Vacuum Type

To test the vacuum type of heated air cleaner, inspect the air door with the engine off. It should be in the cold air position. Start the engine. If the engine is cold, the air door should move to the hot air position. As the engine warms up, the air door should move to a mid position, depending on the outside air temperature.

If the outside air is extremely cold, the air door may stay in the hot air position indefinitely. On a warm day, after the engine warms up the air door should move to the cold air position. If it doesn't, the temperature sensor inside the air cleaner might be faulty, or the air door itself might be hanging up. Check the air door by running a hose from manifold vacuum to the vacuum motor. Connect and disconnect the hose to see if the air door moves freely. If the air door is free, check out the hoses for leaks or blockage. If the hoses are okay, the trouble must be in the temperature sensor, and it should be replaced.

Modulators are used in the air cleaner vacuum line on some engines. The modulator mounts on the side of the air cleaner and has two hose connections, one to the air cleaner temperature sensor, and the other to the vacuum motor. Below 50-80°F. the modulator is a one-way check valve, which allows vacuum to move the air door to the hot air position, but traps the vacuum so the door will not jump back to the cold air position during acceleration. This prevents a stumble.

After the modulator warms up, the check valve unseats so that the vacuum can pass freely in either direction, and the air door then operates normally. The connections for the modulator are important. The

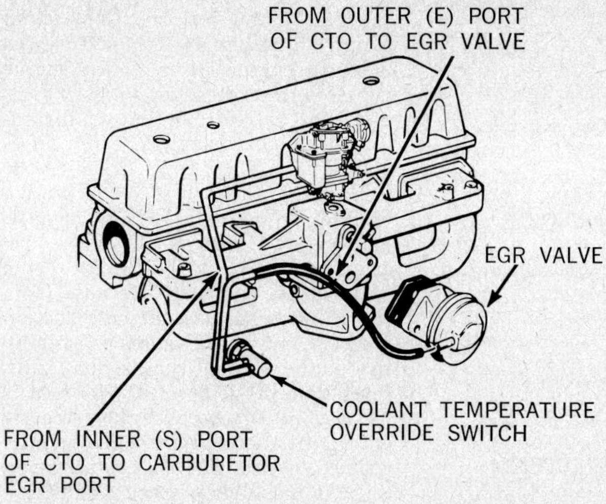

EGR system—6 cylinder engine—typical (© Jeep Corp.)

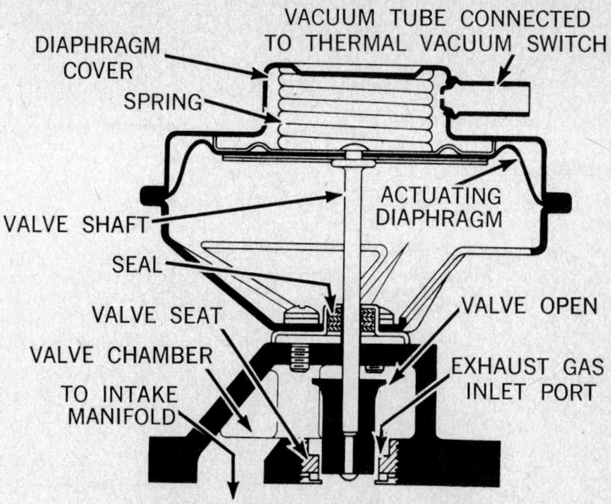

Cross section of ported vacuum signal EGR valve (© General Motors Corp.)

connection in the center goes to the vacuum motor, and the connection on the edge goes to the vacuum source, which is the temperature sensor.

To test the modulator on a cold engine, apply enough vacuum to the edge port to move the air door to the hot position. Then remove the hose from the port, and the air door should stay in the hot position. Make the same test when the engine is warmed up, and the air door should move to the cold position when you pull off the hose.

Exhaust Gas Recirculation

NOx (oxides of nitrogen) is a tailpipe emission caused by the oxidation of nitrogen in the combustion chamber. When the peak combustion temperatures go over 2500°F. NOx is formed in excessive amounts. To keep the combustion temperatures down, exhaust gas is recirculated.

Recirculation of the exhaust gases is accomplished by having a movable valve between the exhaust and intake manifolds, and upon a predetermined demand, route engine vacuum to the valve and open the connecting port to allow the exhaust gases to flow into the intake manifold and mix with the air/fuel mixture.

Three types of EGR valves are used, with the major differences in the method used to control the valve opening. The three types are as follows;

1. An EGR valve with no back pressure sensor and is controlled by ported vacuum.
2. An EGR valve with an integral back pressure sensor and is controlled by ported vacuum and exhaust gas back pressure. Both positive and negative type transducers are used to react to either high or low exhaust gas back pressures.
3. An EGR valve with an external, non-integral back pressure sensor and is controlled by ported vacuum and exhaust gas back pressure.

   NOTE: Venturi vacuum is used as a triggering agent when a vacuum amplifier is used in the EGR system.

Several different types of controls are used to turn the vacuum to the EGR valve on and off. Most of them have to do with engine temperature, as described later.

When the EGR valve hose is connected to the base of the carburetor, without a separate amplifier, the system is operated by ported vacuum. The hose may not run directly from the EGR valve to the carburetor, but may go through a temperature control valve of some sort. In a ported

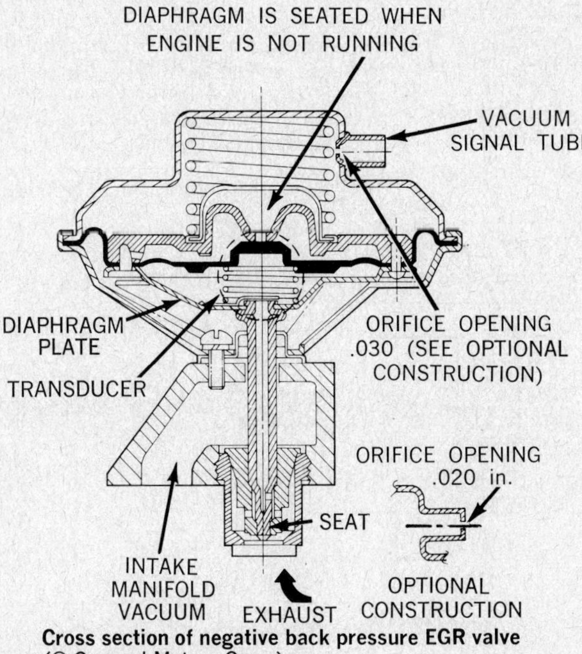

Cross section of negative back pressure EGR valve (© General Motors Corp.)

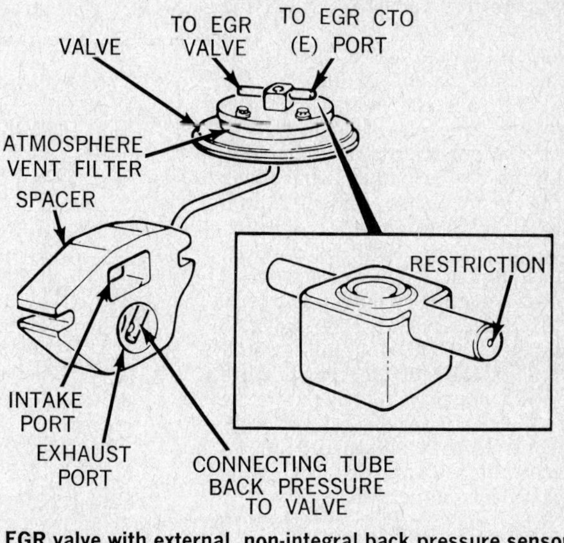

EGR valve with external, non-integral back pressure sensor (© Jeep Corp.)

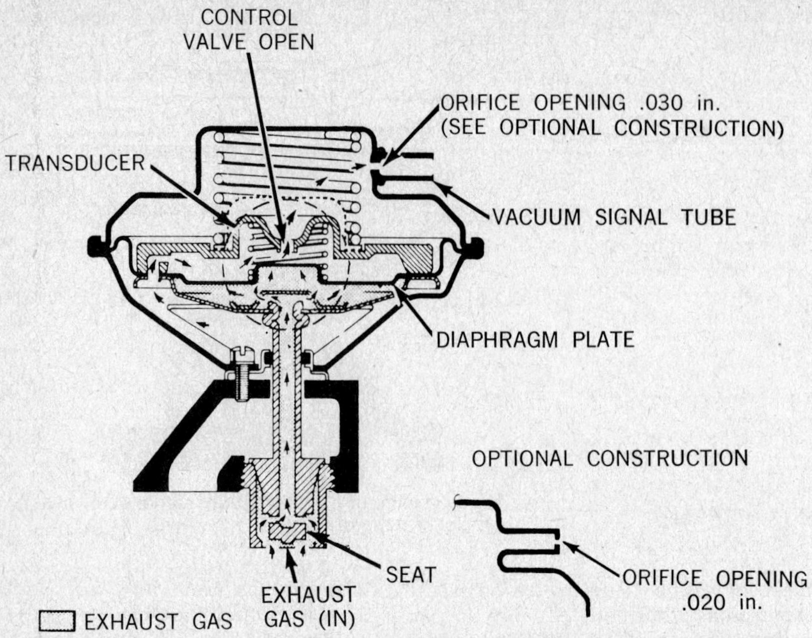

Cross section of positive back pressure EGR valve (© General Motors Corp.)

vacuum system, the vacuum to operate the EGR valve is taken from a port that is above the throttle plate at idle, and thus not subject to vacuum. Because there is no vacuum, the spring in the EGR valve closes it, and the exhaust gas does not recirculate. As the throttle is opened, the port is exposed to vacuum, and the EGR valve opens.

Vacuum systems, with an amplifier, are the most complicated, because of the number of hoses. Manifold vacuum is connected to the amplifier by a hose, and then connects to the EGR valve. The amplifier also connects to venturi vacuum. At idle there is no venturi vacuum, but above idle the air moves through the carburetor venturi fast enough to create a vacuum. This slight amount of vacuum opens the amplifier, which then allows manifold vacuum to open the EGR valve.

Temperature controls for EGR systems come in many different designs. They are all made so that the EGR valve stays closed when the engine or the outside air is cold. After the engine or the outside air warms up, the temperature control allows the EGR valve to operate normally. Before March 15, 1973, many EGR systems used a temperature control that was sensitive to outside air temperature. Even with a fully warmed up engine, the EGR system would stay off if the outside temperature was cold enough. On vehicles made after March 15, 1973, the temperature controls were all sensitive to engine coolant temperature, or engine compartment temperature.

Testing EGR Systems

Testing of EGR systems should verify that the EGR valve is closed at idle, open above idle, and that the exhaust gas is actually recirculating. If the EGR valve sticks open at idle, the engine will run very rough, or may not even start. If this happens the valve should be removed and cleaned, or replaced. To check for valve opening above idle, check with a mirror or your fingers to see if the diaphragm or stem moves when the engine is at a fast idle in Park or Neutral. If the diaphragm does not move when the throttle is opened, there is either a problem with vacuum, or the valve is stuck closed. With a vacuum gauge connected to the EGR port, you should see vacuum on the gauge when the throttle is opened. EGR valves should not leak when tested with a hand vacuum pump. If they do they must be replaced.

To find out if the exhaust gas is actually recirculating, use a hand vacuum pump or mouth suction through a hose to open the EGR valve with the engine idling. If the engine runs rough or dies, you know the exhaust gas is recirculating. If the engine does not run rough, make a second test at 2500 rpm. Opening the EGR valve at that rpm should cause a change in engine speed. If it does, you know the exhaust gas is recirculating. To make the 2500 rpm test, remove and plug the hose from the EGR port. Attach your suction hose to the EGR valve before running the engine at 2500 rpm. Simply pulling off the EGR hose at 2500 rpm is not a valid test, because the extra air entering the engine through the hose could cause a speed change all by itself. On most engines you won't have to go this far, because opening the EGR valve at idle will prove that the exhaust is recirculating.

If the exhaust is not recirculating, it means that a passageway or the valve itself is clogged up. The only way to fix it is to scrape out the clogging as best you can, or replace the valve.

The back-pressure sensor is a pressure-operated bleed that disables the EGR valve and keeps it closed when there is no exhaust pressure. This type of valve cannot be tested with a hand vacuum pump with the engine off because the bleed is open. The only practical way to test these new valves is by substitution of a known good valve. If a valve is not available, the suspected valve can be removed, and the holes temporarily taped shut. If this corrects the problem, then a new valve should be installed.

EGR delay systems are used on some vehicles to prevent the recirculation of the exhaust gases for approximately 60 seconds after the ignition switch is turned on by an electrical timer, connected to an engine mounted solenoid switch. The solenoid is connected in the vacuum line between the carburetor venturi nipple and the vacuum amplifier.

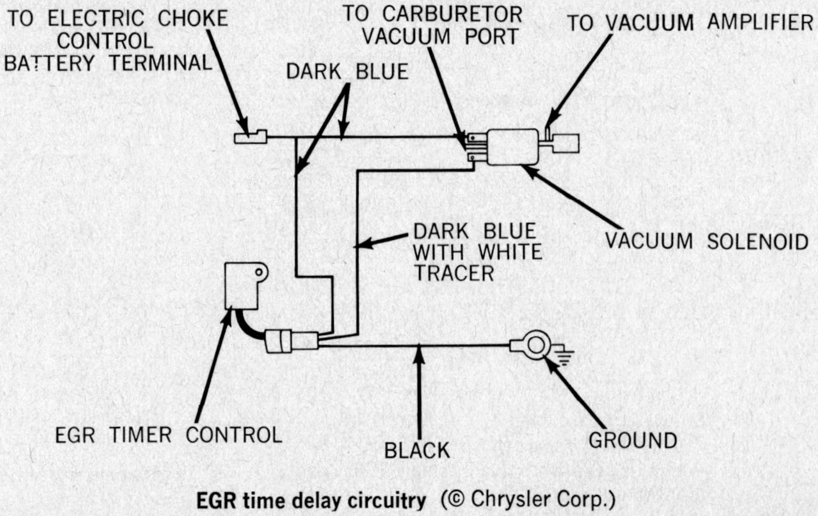

EGR time delay circuitry (© Chrysler Corp.)

A charge temperature switch is used on some models by being installed in the intake manifold on the number 6 branch, 6 cyl., and on the number 8 branch on the V8 engine. No EGR timer on EGR valve operation is permitted when the air/fuel mixture temperature is below 60°F. (16°C).

Catalytic Converter

A catalytic converter is a chamber in the exhaust system that contains a catalyst. When hydrocarbons or carbon monoxide pass over the catalyst they react with the oxygen in the exhaust and are converted into harmless water and carbon dioxide. The catalyst inside the converter is made in two forms. General Motors, and Jeep use the pellet form, in which loose pellets are packaged into the converter and can be emptied out and changed, if necessary. Ford, International and Chrysler use the honeycomb catalyst, which is built into the converter shell and is not replaceable. On Ford, International and Chrysler products the entire converter must be replaced if it goes bad.

There is no way to test a converter in the field to see if it is actually working. Tailpipe readings may be used to set carburetor idle mixtures, when the car maker requires it, but taking a tailpipe reading to determine if the converter is working is not possible.

The one field check that is recom-

EXHAUST GAS RECIRCULATION SYSTEM DIAGNOSIS CHART

Condition	Possible Cause	Correction
Engine idles abnormally rough and/or stalls.	EGR valve vacuum hoses misrouted.	Check EGR valve vacuum hose routing. Correct as required.
	Leaking EGR valve.	Check EGR valve for correct operation.
	EGR valve gasket failed or loose EGR attaching bolts.	Check EGR attaching bolts for tightness. Tighten as required. If not loose, remove EGR valve and inspect gasket. Replace as required.
	EGR thermal control valve and/or EGR-TVS.	Check vacuum into valve from carburetor EGR port with engine at normal operating temperature and at curb idle speed. Then check the vacuum out of the EGR thermal control valve to EGR valve. If the two vacuum readings are not equal within ± ½ in. Hg. (1.7 kPa), then proceed to EGR vacuum control diagnosis.
	Improper vacuum to EGR valve at idle.	Check vacuum from carburetor EGR port with engine at stabilized operating temperature and at curb idle speed. If vacuum is more than 1.0 in. Hg., refer to carburetor idle diagnosis.
Engine runs rough on light throttle acceleration, poor part load performance and poor fuel economy.	EGR valve vacuum hose misrouted.	Check EGR valve vacuum hose routing. Correct as required.
	Failed EGR vacuum control valve.	Same as listing in "Engine Idles Rough" condition.
	EGR flow unbalanced due to deposit accumulation in EGR passages or under carburetor.	Clean EGR passages of all deposits.
	Sticky or binding EGR valve.	Remove EGR valve and inspect. Clean or replace as required.
	Wrong or no EGR gaskets.	Check and correct as required.
(Vehicle with back pressure EGR valve.)	Control valve blocked or air flow restricted.	Check internal control valve function per service procedure.
Engine stalls on decelerations.	Restriction in EGR vacuum line.	Check EGR vacuum lines for kinks, bends, etc. Remove or replace hoses at required. Check EGR vacuum control valve funtion.
		Check EGR valve for excessive deposits causing sticky or binding operation. Clean or repair as required.
	Sticking or binding EGR valve.	Remove EGR valve and inspect, clean or repair as required.
(Vehicle with a back pressure EGR valve.)	Control valve blocked or air flow restricted.	Check internal control valve function per service procedure.
Part throttle engine detonation.	Insufficient exhaust gas recirculation flow during part throttle accelerations.	Check EGR valve hose routing. Check EGR valve operation. Repair or replace as required. Check EGR thermal control valve and/or EGR-TVS as listed in "Engine Idles Rough" section. Replace valve as required. Check EGR passage and valve for excessive deposit. Clean as required.
(Vehicle with a back pressure EGR valve.)	Control valve blocked or air flow restricted.	Check internal control valve function per service procedure.
(NOTE: Detonation can be caused by several other engine variables. Perform ignition and carburetor related diagnosis.)		
Engine starts but immediately stalls when cold.	EGR valve hoses misrouted.	Check EGR valve hose routing.
	EGR system malfunctioning when engine is cold.	Perform check to determine if the EGR thermal control valve and/or EGR-TVS are operational. Replace as required.
(Vehicle with a back pressure EGR valve.)	Control valve blocked or air flow restricted.	Check internal control valve function per service procedure.

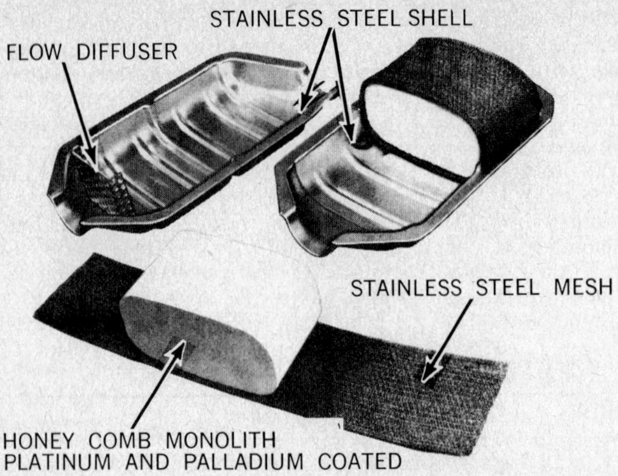

Cut-away view of Catalytic Converter using honeycomb monolith catalyst (© Chrysler Corp.)

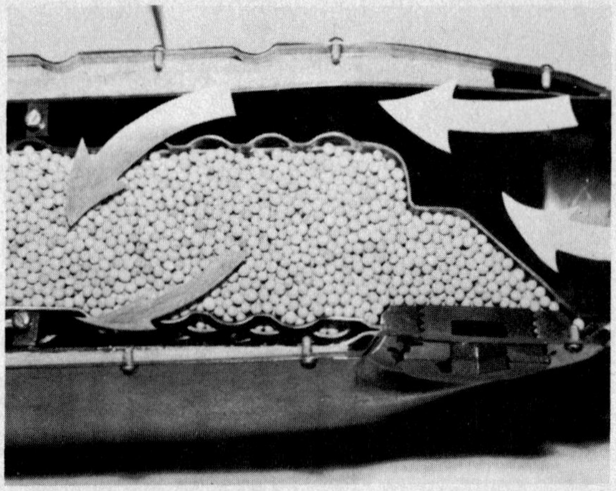

Cut-away view of pellet type Catalytic Converter with exhaust flow shown (© General Motors Corp.)

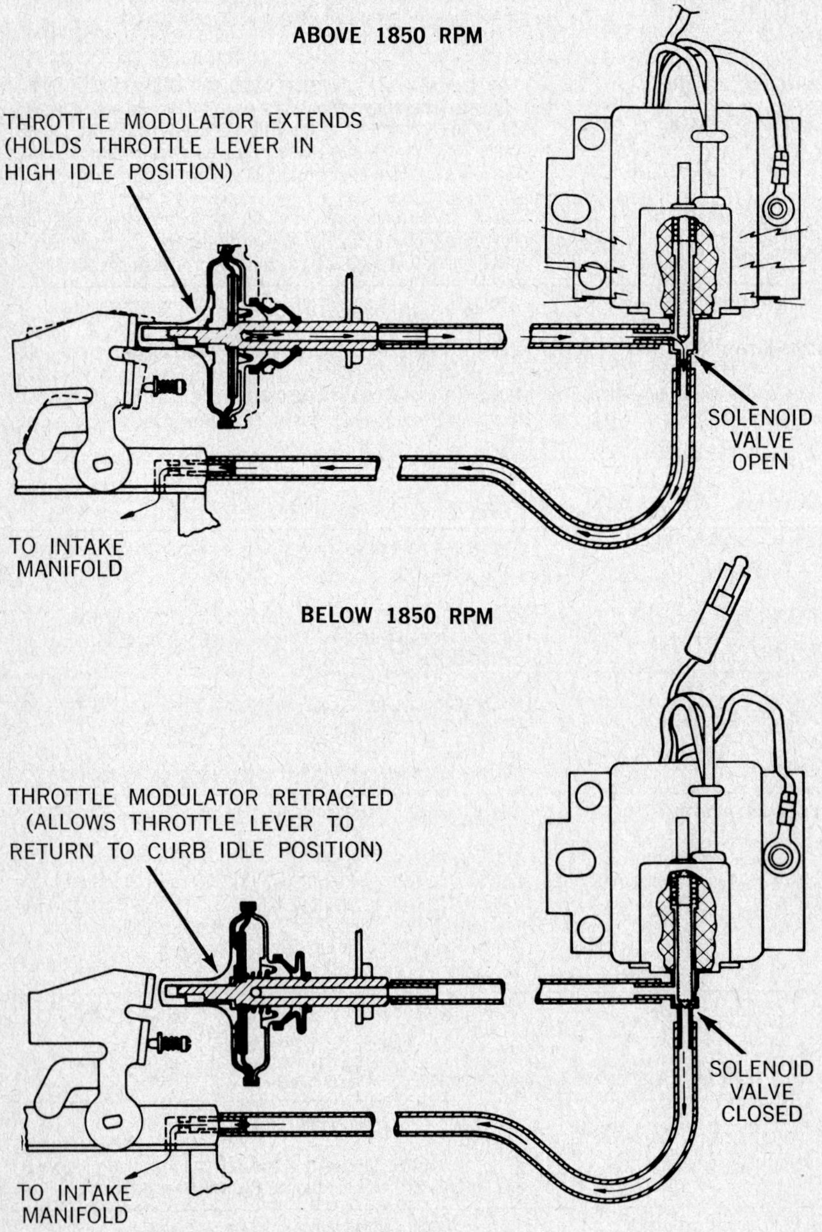

Typical throttle modulator operation used on I. H. vehicles (© International Harvester Co.)

mended in all cases is to inspect for mechanical damage. If a converter gets overheated, the catalyst can melt and block the exhaust. Pellets or pieces of the catalyst may even come flying out the tailpipe while the engine is running. If this happens, the pellets or the entire converter must be changed.

Checking for a melted converter that restricts the exhaust can be done with a vacuum gauge connected to the engine. Run the engine at about 2500 rpm in Park or Neutral. If the vacuum reading is steady, the exhaust is okay. If the vacuum reading slowly drops, it indicates a buildup of pressure in the exhaust.

The use of leaded fuel will slowly destroy the efficiency of the catalyst until finally, after several tanks full, it won't do its job any more. If used long enough, leaded fuel can even cause catalyst plugging to the point that the engine will not run. If you know that a vehicle has been run on several tanks of leaded fuel, then you can be sure that the catalyst has lost its ability to convert. But there is no way to test for this condition in the field.

Do not change the catalyst if the vehicle has been run on only one tank or less of leaded fuel. Switching back to lead free fuel will allow the catalyst to recover and be almost as efficient as it was.

Converter Overheat Protection

Engine controls are used to prevent the converter from being damaged by overheating due to overly rich fuel mixtures during periods of deceleration.

The controls are named differently by the manufacturers, but are all designed to accomplish the same purpose and to operate basically in the same manner. To prevent the engine from operating at a rich mode when the throttle plates are closed during deceleration, electrical and/or me-

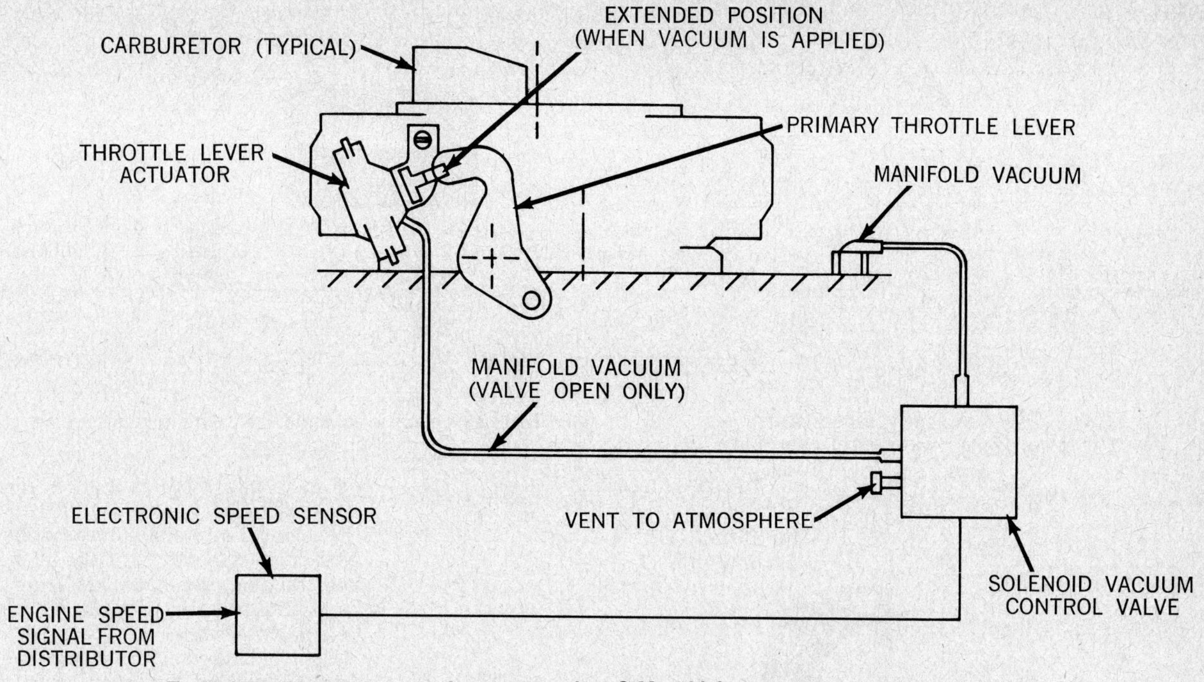

Typical throttle return control system used on G.M. vehicles (© General Motors Corp.)

chanical means are provided to hold the throttle plates open at predetermined engine speeds, in order to lean the air/fuel mixture as necessary to control the exhaust emissions. The engine control should be inoperative under engine speeds of 1800 to 2000 RPMs to avoid engine overrun or vehicle overspeed in slow traffic.

The various parts are as follows;

1. The throttle level actuator is mounted as part of the carburetor assembly and operates when vacuum is applied to it from a separate solenoid vacuum control valve.
2. The solenoid vacuum control valve is controlled by a signal from the electronic speed sensor or a throttle modulator deceleration valve vacuum signal to

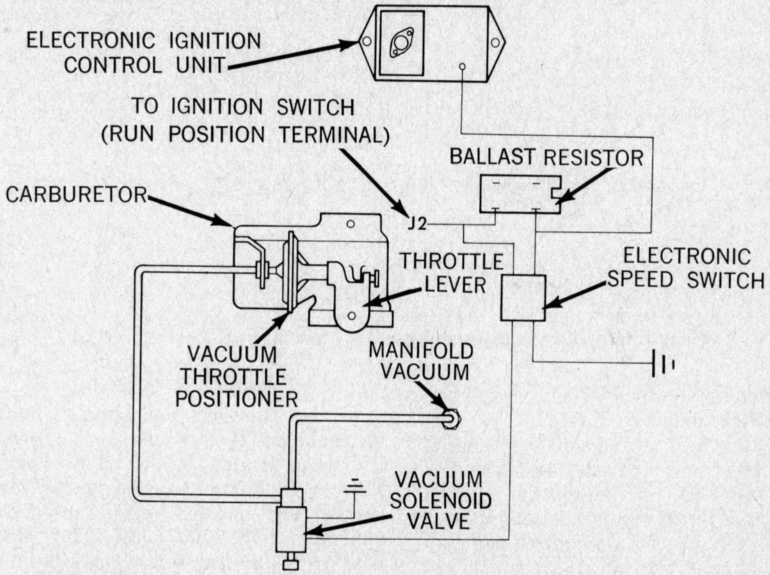

Typical throttle positioner system used on Chrysler Corp. vehicles having California Emission requirements (© Chrysler Corp.)

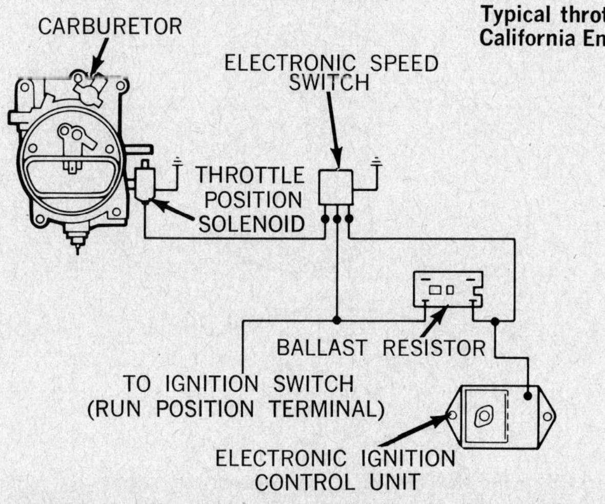

Typical throttle positioner electrical circuitry used on Chrysler Corp. vehicles (© Chrysler Corp.)

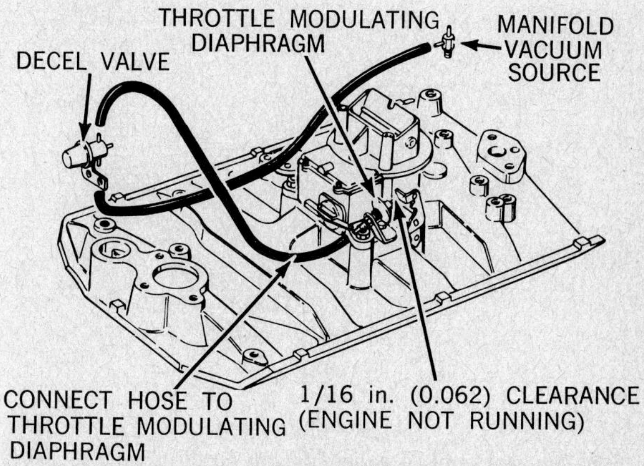

Typical Vacuum throttle modulating system (© Jeep Corp.)

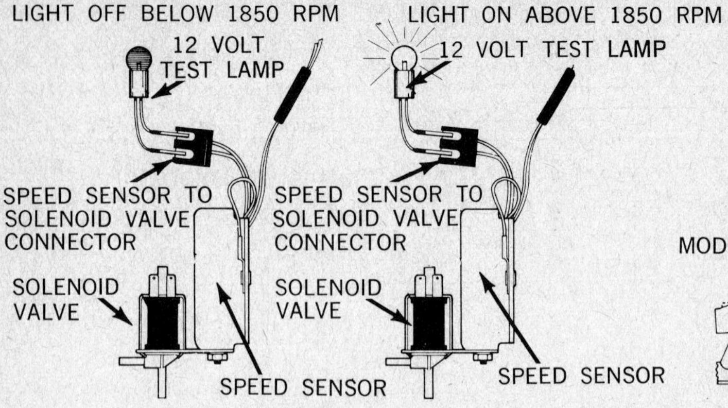

Testing of electric speed sensor switch
(© International Harvester Co.)

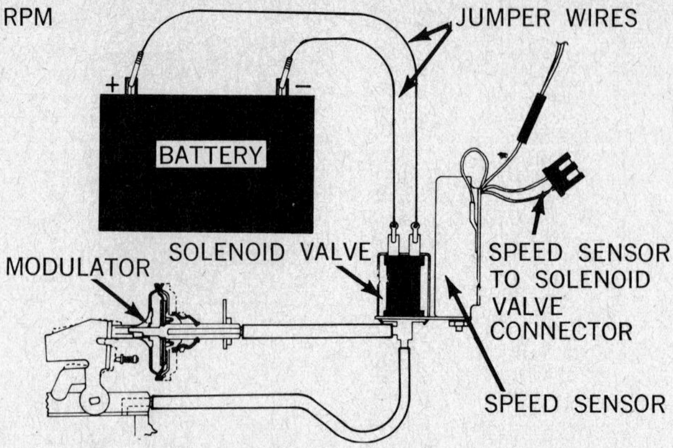

Testing of electric solenoid valve with engine running
(© International Harvester Co.)

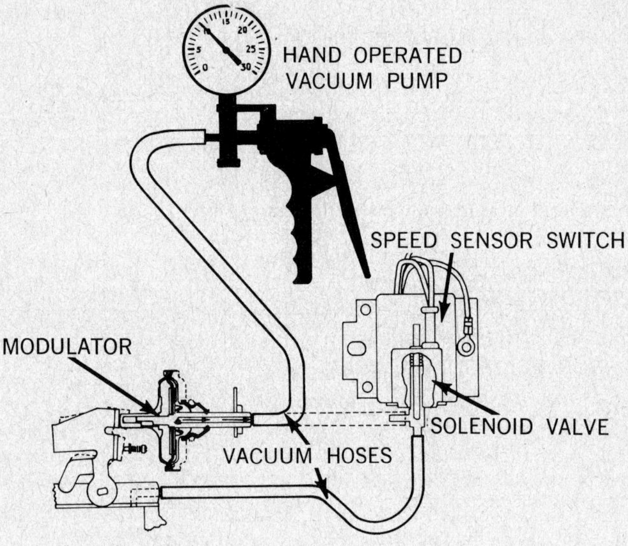

Typical testing of vacuum modulator (© International Harvester Co.)

allow vacuum to be routed to the throttle lever actuator.

3. Electronic speed sensor is mounted near or included with the distributor and senses the engine speed and sends a signal to the solenoid vacuum control valve as long as the preset speed is exceeded.

Testing the System

To test the electrical speed sensor system, place the transmission in neutral or park and set the hand brake. With a tachometer attached to the engine, increase the engine speed to approximately 2000 RPM. The solenoid or modulator stem should extend to hold the carburetor throttle lever off curb idle setting. As the engine speed is reduced to below 1800 RPM, the solenoid or modulator stem should retract to the off position. A hand held vacuum pump and test lamp can be used to test the individual components of the system.

To test the vacuum operated system, without an electrical sensor, 21 to 22 in. Hg. must be directed to the decel valve to open the port to direct vacuum to the throttle modulating diaphragm, located on the carburetor base. With the vacuum present, the stem of the modulating diaphragm will be extended. Release of the vacuum should allow the stem of the modulating diaphragm to retract.

Vacuum Operated Exhaust Heat Riser Valves

Exhaust heat riser valves have been used for many years to force part of the engine exhaust through a passageway under the intake manifold and preheat the fuel mixture. The heat valve was spring loaded into the closed position, but heat would make the spring relax so that during high speed operation or after warm-up the exhaust would push it open.

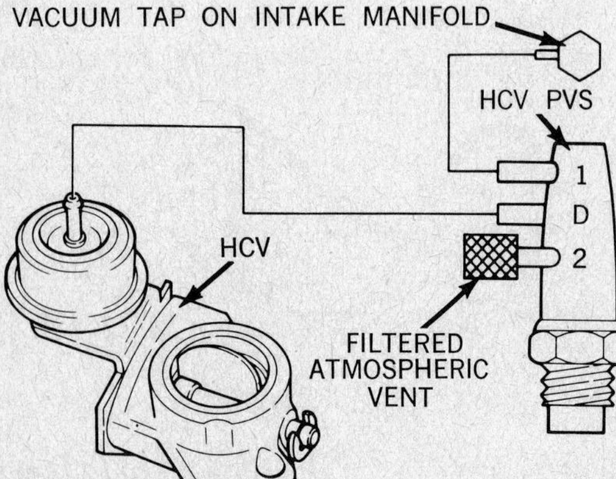

Exhaust heat control valve vacuum circuit using a ported vacuum coolant switch—typical (© Ford Motor Co.)

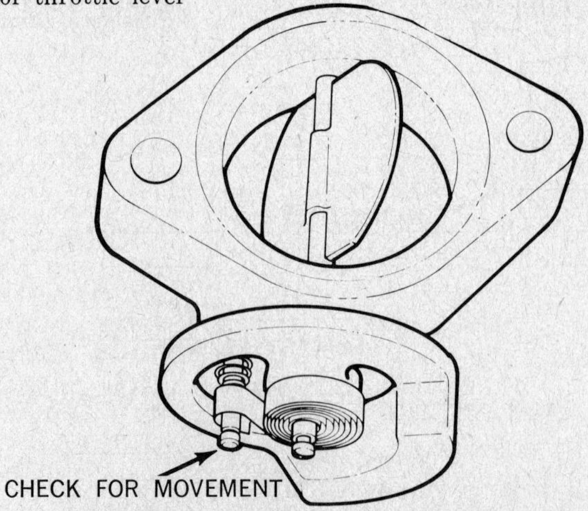

Spring controlled exhaust heat control valve—typical
(© Ford Motor Co.)

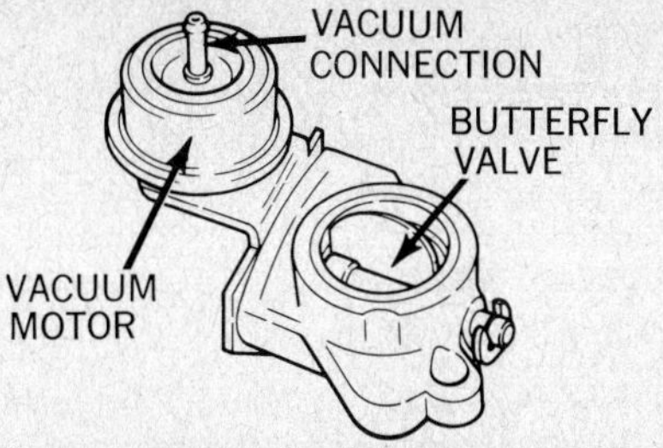

Vacuum operated exhaust heat control valve—typical (© Ford Motor Co.)

Now, many engines use vacuum operated heat valves, controlled by a vacuum switch that is sensitive to engine temperature.

On these systems, manifold vacuum is used to close the valve, and force the exhaust gases through the crossover passage in the intake manifold. All the systems have a temperature valve that shuts the vacuum off when the engine warms up.

A simple coolant temperature-sensitive vacuum switch is mounted on the intake manifold coolant passage and has two hose connections. It actually does triple duty because it also controls the vacuum supply to the idle enrichment system and the air switching valve.

A second type vacuum switch has three hose connections, but one of them is a vent with a filter to keep the dirt out.

A third control uses either a coolant vacuum switch, or a vacuum solenoid connected to an oil temperature switch. The coolant vacuum switch has two hose connections and a vent when it controls the heat valve only. When it is tied into other emission control systems, it can have as many as five hose connections, and a vent. Some models also have a check valve in the hose so that vacuum will be trapped in the heat valve actuator when the engine is accelerated. This keeps the heat valve in the closed position and prevents a rattle.

Testing Vacuum Operated Exhaust Heat Riser Valves

Testing the vacuum operated heat riser valve is a matter of making sure it closes and opens freely. You can move it to see if it works, on a warm engine. On a cold engine, the valve should be closed, and disconnecting the hose should allow it to open. On a cold engine, there should be vacuum at the vacuum actuator, and on a warm engine the vacuum should be shut off.

Air Injection Systems

A belt-driven air pump supplies air to small tubes positioned in the exhaust port near each exhaust valve. The air mixes with unburned hydrocarbons in the exhaust and the hydrocarbons actually burn up in the exhaust system. Air injection systems are used on engines with catalytic converters, so that the converter gets enough air to keep the reaction going.

Plumbing on air injection systems varies considerably.

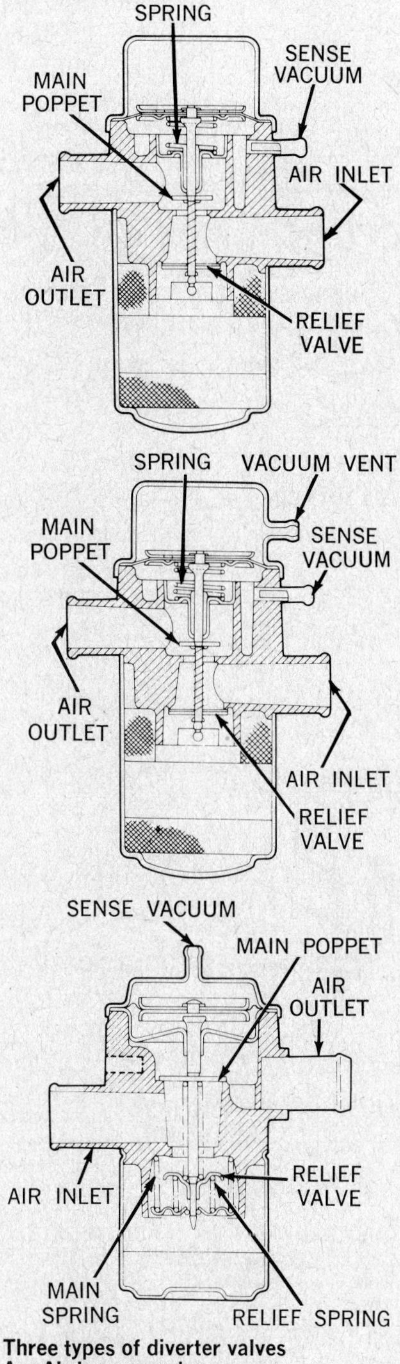

Three types of diverter valves
A—Air by-pass valve
B—Closed air by-pass valve
C—Timed air by-pass valve with vacuum vent (© Ford Motor Co.)

A check valve is used between the pump and the exhaust port nozzle to keep hot exhaust gases from traveling up the plumbing and destroying the pump. V8s use two check valves.

An anti-backfire valve, also called bypass valve or diverter valve, is used between the pump and the check valve. Usually, the diverter valve is mounted on the pump or near it. A small sensing hose connects the diverter valve to intake manifold vacuum. When the vacuum rises during deceleration, the diverter valve opens, and sends the pump air into the atmosphere. This prevents the overrich deceleration mixture in the exhaust system from exploding or backfiring out the tailpipe.

Some models started using a diverter valve that has the small hose connection on the end instead of the side. The older diverter valve was normally in the running position, but the new one is normally in the dump position. In other words, the old valve allowed the air to pass through the engine exhaust ports regardless of whether the small sensing line was hooked up. The new valve, being normally in the dump position, must have the small sensing line hooked up to manifold vacuum, which pulls the valve mechanism from the dump position into the normal running position.

Unfortunately, the new style valve will not go into the dump position automatically during deceleration. To get the valve to dump, a vacuum differential valve (VDV) is connected in the sensing line. Manifold vacuum goes through the VDV and then to the diverter valve. When the manifold vacuum increases during deceleration, the VDV closes the sensing line. This shuts off the vacuum to the diverter valve, and the valve goes into the dump position.

A further refinement of this, is to connect the sensing line to ported (above the throttle plates) vacuum instead of manifold vacuum and eliminate the VDV. In this situation, the diverter valve only receives vacuum above idle, because the vacuum port in the carburetor throat is above the throttle plate at idle. So whenever the engine idles, the diverter valve goes to the dump position. It also dumps during deceleration, because the throttle at that time is in the idle position.

Some systems have a delay valve, similar to a spark delay valve, in the sensing hose. This delays for a few seconds the drop in vacuum when the throttle closes, so that the air is not dumped every time the driver takes his foot off the throttle in traffic.

Temperature controls are also used in the sensing hose hookup. Usually, the temperature valve shuts the vacuum off when the engine is cold, so that the pump air doesn't go to the engine exhaust ports until the engine warms up.

A idle vacuum valve is used to operate in conjunction with the vacuum delay valve, to provide backfire control, full time idle dumping of secondary air during cold engine operation, deceleration or extended idle periods of ½ to 2 minutes or more.

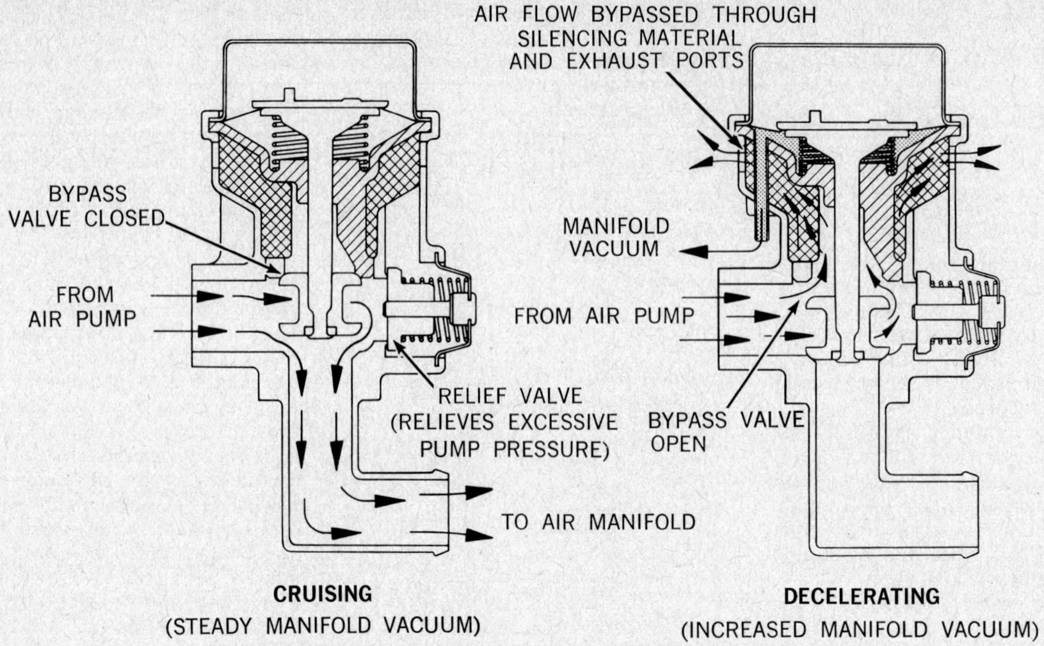

Diverter valve operation (© International Harvester Co.)

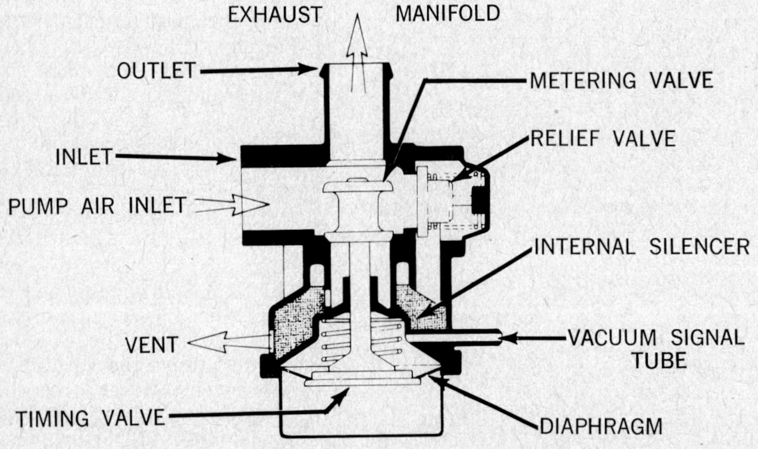

Diverter valve with internal muffler (© General Motors Corp.)

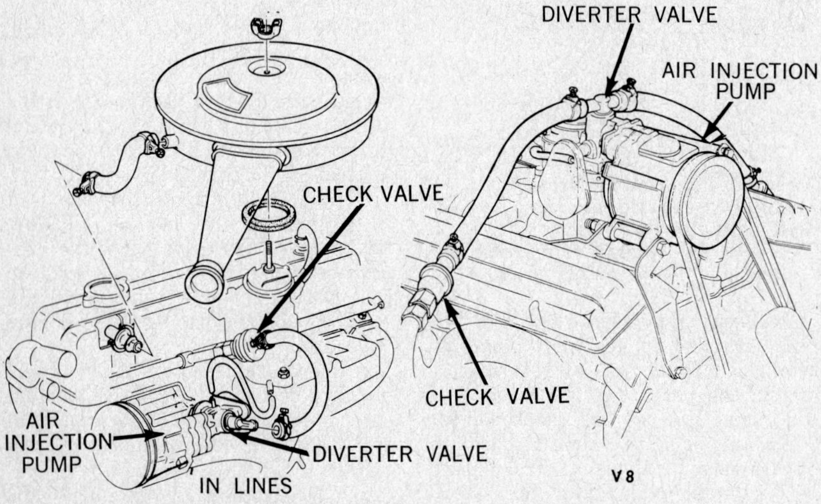

Air Injection System —typical (© General Motors Corp.)

The valve also provides cold temperature protection for the catalyst and a cold EGR valve lockout.

Air Pump Tests

CAUTION: Do not hammer on, pry or bend the pump housing while tightening the drive belt or testing the pump.

Before proceeding with the tests, check the pump drive belt tension.

If the belt squeals when the engine is running, the pump may be dragging or seized. Remove the belt and turn the pump by hand to check for seizure. Disregard any chirping, squealing, or rolling sounds from inside the pump when turning it by hand, as these are normal.

Check the hoses and connections for leaks. Hissing or a blast of air is indicative of a leak. Soapy water, applied lightly around the area in question, is a good method for detecting leaks.

To test air output, disconnect the air hose from the pump wherever it is convenient. If you disconnect it from one check valve on a V8, the other hose should also be disconnected and plugged for the test. Run the engine at idle and feel the blast of air from the hose with your hand. Increase the engine speed to 1500 rpm and feel the blast of air again. If the blast increases, and is steady, the pump is okay.

Pump Noise Diagnosis

The air pump is normally noisy; as engine speed increases, the noise of the pump will rise in pitch. The rolling sound the pump bearings make is normal. However, if this sound be-

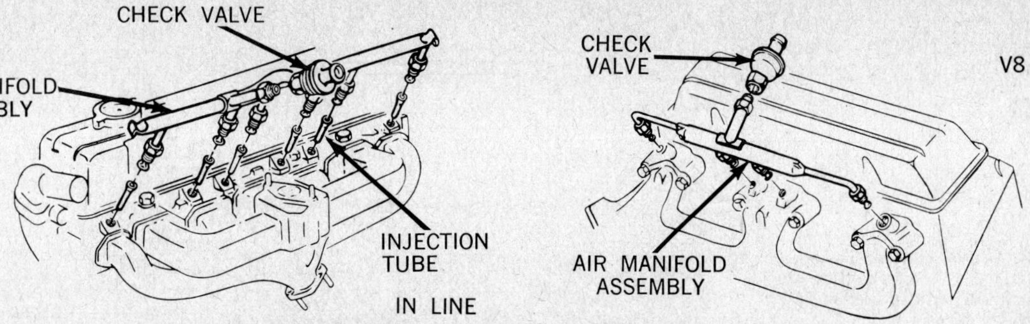

Air Injection tubes (© General Motors Corp.)

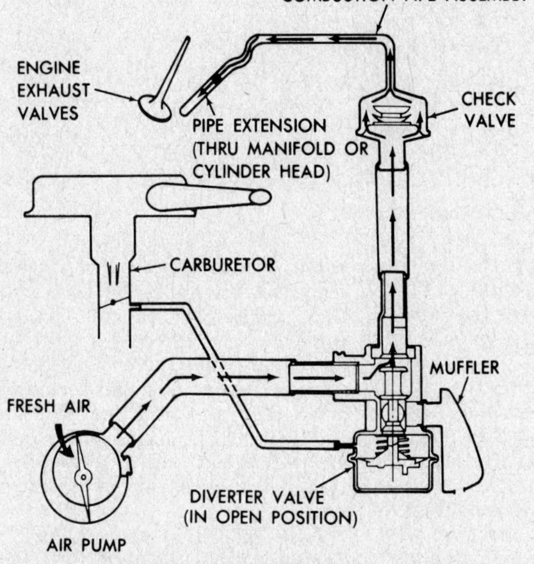

Air Injection System operation—typical
(© General Motors Corp.)

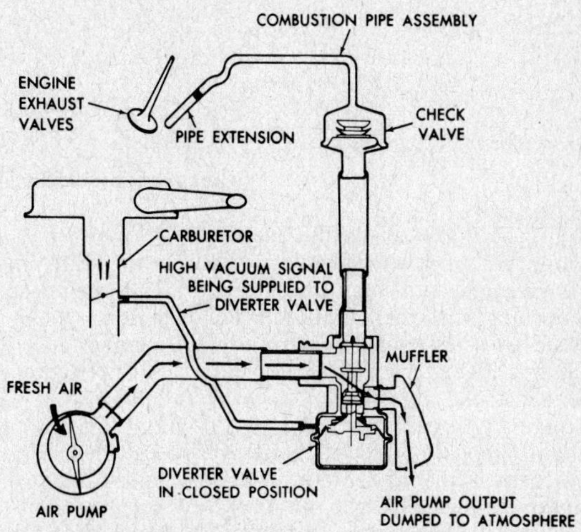

Diverter valve operation—air exhausted—typical
(© General Motors Corp.)

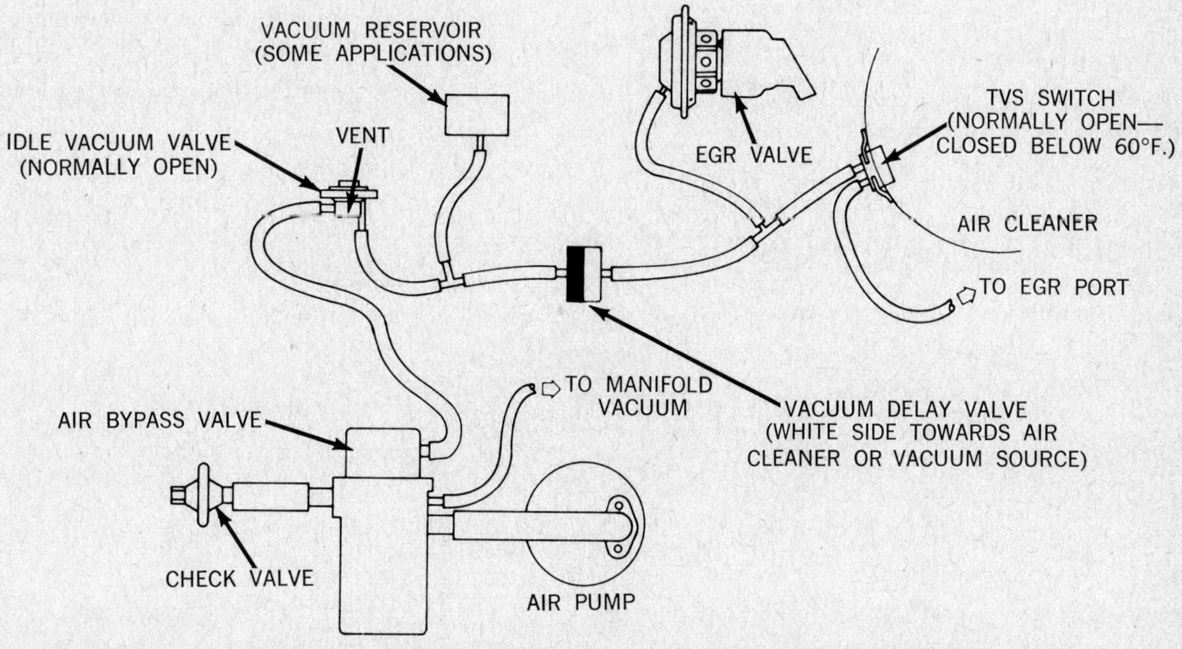

Air Injection System with an idle vacuum valve used to control converter overheating (© Ford Motor Co.)

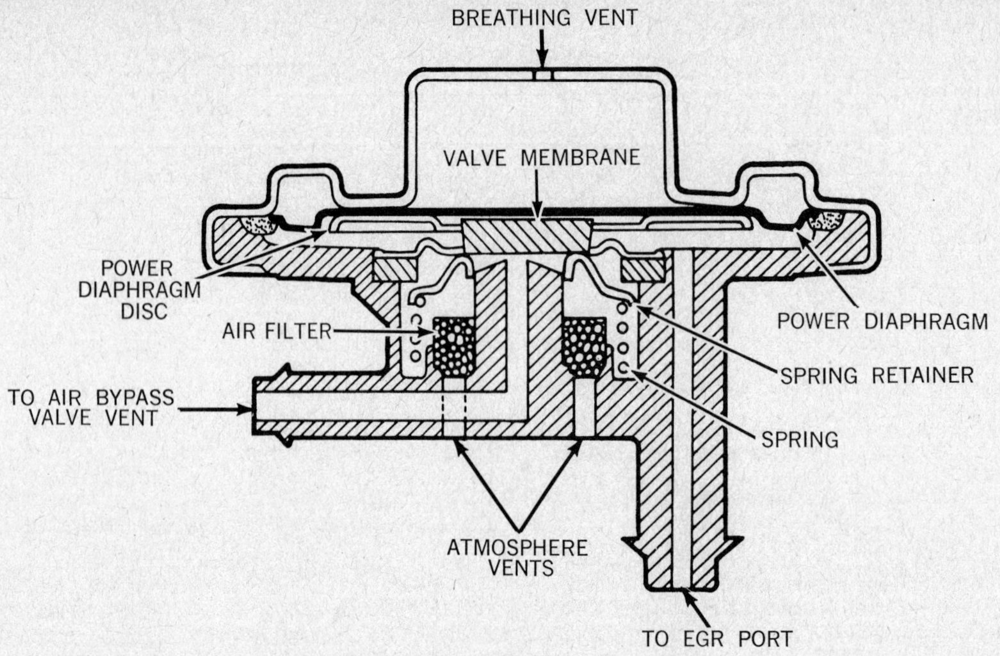

Cross section of idle vacuum valve (© Ford Motor Co.)

comes objectionable at certain speeds, the pump may be defective and will have to be replaced.

A continual hissing sound from the air pump pressure relief valve at idle indicates a defective valve. Replace the relief valve.

If the pump rear bearing fails, a continual knocking sound will be heard. Since the rear bearing is not separately replaceable, the pump will have to be replaced as an assembly.

Anti-backfire Valve Tests

Detach the hose, which runs from the bypass valve to the check valve.

Connect a tachometer to the engine. With the engine running at normal idle speed, check to see that air is flowing from the bypass valve hose connection.

Speed the engine up, so that it is running at 1,500-2,000 rpm. Allow the throttle to snap shut. The flow of air from the bypass valve at the check valve hose connection should stop momentarily and air should then flow from the exhaust port on the valve body or the silencer assembly.

Let the throttle snap shut several times. If the flow of air is not diverted into the atmosphere from the valve exhaust port or if it fails to stop flowing from the hose connection, check the vacuum lines and connections. If these are tight, either the bypass valve or one of the accessory valves in the small sensing hose is defective and must be replaced.

A leaking diaphragm will cause the air to flow out both the hose connection and the exhaust port at the same valve.

Late model, systems should stop flowing at idle, as described earlier. If not, the bypass valve or accessory valve is defective.

Check Valve Test

Remove the hose from the check valve. With the engine running at 1,500 rpm in Park or Neutral, hold the back of your hand near the check valve to test for exhaust gas leakage.

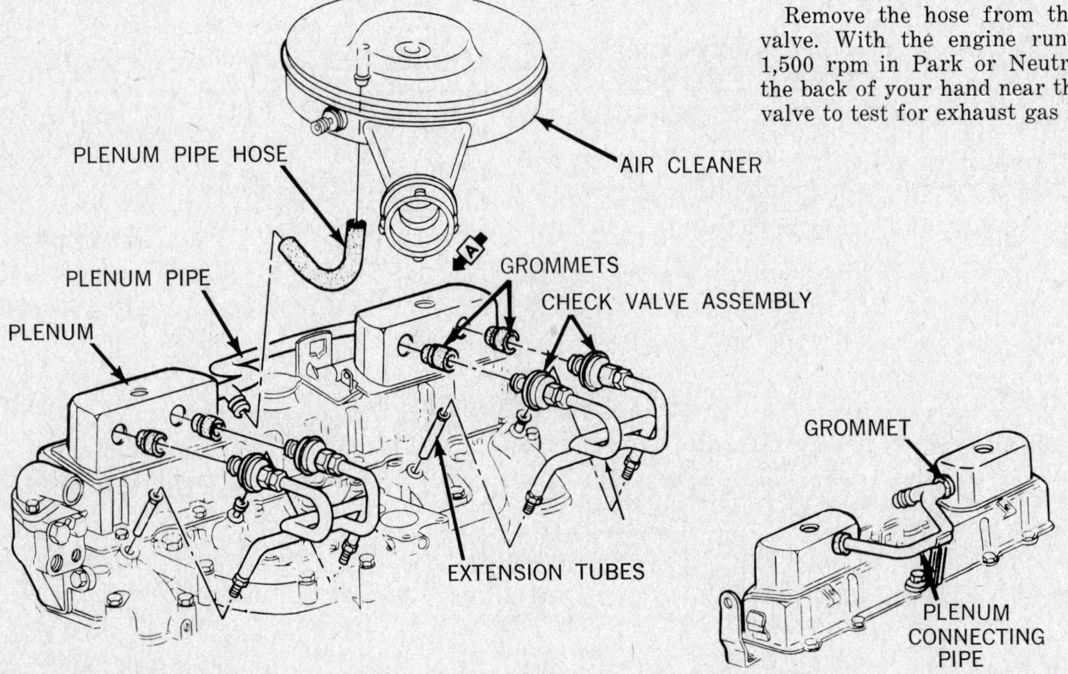

Pulse Air Injection System (PAIR) (© General Motors Corp.)

If the valve leaks, it must be replaced.

NOTE: Vibration and flutter of the valve at idle is a normal condition caused by exhaust pulsations. It does not mean that the valve is defective.

Vacuum Differential Valve Test

Disconnect the small sensing hose at the bypass valve and connect a vacuum gauge to the hose. With the engine idling in Park or Neutral, the gauge should read full manifold vacuum.

Run the engine at a steady 2500 rpm in Park or Neutral, and release the throttle. As the engine decelerates, the vacuum gauge should drop close to zero, then return to full manifold vacuum as the engine speed drops to idle. If not, the VDV is defective and must be replaced.

NOTE: The small hose nozzle should be connected to manifold vacuum.

Pulse Air Injection System

The Pulse Air Injection System is installed on the small inline 6 cylinder engine, used in General Motors light duty trucks, beginning in 1979. The Pulse Air system uses no air pump, but relies on the negative and positive exhaust gas impulses to draw fresh air into the exhaust manifold to assist in the further burning of the Hydrocarbons (HC) before leaving the tailpipe.

Four individual check valves are used to prevent the exhaust gases from entering the fresh air intake chamber plenums. Two sets of pipes are used, one set in the front section of the exhaust manifold and the second set in the rear section of the exhaust manifold.

Two sets of plenum chambers are used and connected to the carburetor air cleaner by a common hose, for the fresh air intake.

During periods of high engine RPM the check valves will remain closed to prevent the flow of exhaust gases to the engine air cleaner.

Failure Diagnosis

1. Inspect the Pulse Air valve and pipes for leakages or defective operation, if a hissing noise is heard.

AIR INJECTION REACTOR SYSTEM DIAGNOSIS CHART

Condition	Possible Cause	Correction
No air supply—accelerate engine to 1500 rpm and observe air flow from hoses. If the flow increases as the rpm's increase, the pump is functioning normally. If not, check possible cause.	1. Loose drive belt.	1. Tighten to specifications.
	2. Leaks in supply hose.	2. Locate leak and repair.
	3. Leak at fittings.	3. Tighten or replace clamps.
	4. Air expelled through by-pass valve	
	4a. Connect a vacuum line directly from engine manifold vacuum to by-pass valve.	4a. If this corrects the problem go to step b. If not, replace air by-pass valve.
	4b. Connect vacuum line from engine manifold vacuum source to by-pass valve through vacuum differential valve directly, by passing the differential vacuum delay and separator valve.	4b. If this corrects the problem, check differential vacuum, delay and separator valve and vacuum source line for plugging. Replace as required. It it doesn't, replace vacuum differential valve.
	5. Check valve inoperative.	5. Disconnect hose and blow through hose toward check valve. If air passes, function is normal. If air can be sucked from check valve, replace check valve.
	6. Pump failure.	6. Replace pump.
Excessive pump noise, chirping, rumbling, knocking, loss of engine performance.	1. Leak in hose.	1. Locate source of leak using soap solution and correct.
	2. Loose hose	2. Reassemble and replace or tighten hose clamp.
	3. Hose touching other engine parts.	3. Adjust hose position.
	4. Vacuum differential valve inoperative.	4. Replace vacuum differential valve.
	5. By-pass valve inoperative.	5. Replace by-pass valve.
	6. Pump mounting fasteners loose.	6. Tighten mounting screws as specified.
	7. Pump failure.	7. Replace pump.
	8. Check valve inoperative.	8. Replace check valve.
Excessive belt noise.	1. Loose belt.	1. Tighten to spec.
	2. Seized pump.	2. Replace pump.
Excessive pump noise. Chirping.	1. Insufficient break-in.	1. Run vehicle 10-15 miles at interstate speeds—recheck.
Centrifugal filter fan damaged or broken.	1. Mechanical damage.	1. Replace centrifugal filter fan.
Exhaust tube bent or damaged.	1. Mechanical damage.	1. Replace exhaust tube.
Poor idle or driveability.	1. A defective A.I.R. system cannot cause poor idle or driveability,	1. Do not replace A.I.R. system.

2. If one or more of the check valves are defective, exhaust gases will enter the carburetor area and cause poor driveability such as stalling, surge, or poor performance.

Inspection of Pulse Air System

1. Burned off paint on the rocker arm plenum chambers indicates a defective pulse air valve. Rubber grommets and hoses will deteriorate and can cause a hissing noise.
2. Inspect the carburetor for pieces of rubber hoses or grommets, indicating an overheating of the components.
3. Inspect the operation of the pulse air valve by applying at least 17 in. Hg at the grommet end of the valve. A drop of 6 in. Hg in two seconds is allowed.

Distributor Systems

Electronic Ignition System

A change has been made through the model years from the conventional distributors to the Electronic Ignition systems for more precise ignition control.

Different types are available from the manufacturers, but the operation of the systems are basically the same. Greater dependability, higher secondary voltages and less need for adjustments are the important factors considered in using this system for emission control.

Refer to the individual truck sections and to the Electrical Section for expanded information.

Distributor Controls

All distributor controls act in some way to change or eliminate vacuum advance during certain operating conditions. Usually, the control cuts down on the amount of vacuum advance, in effect retarding the spark, so that the exhaust will get hotter and burn up hydrocarbon and carbon monoxide emissions before they go out the tailpipe.

The distributor vacuum advance unit might be connected, according to factory design, to either manifold vacuum or ported (above the throttle plates) carburetor vacuum. Either way, the vacuum spark advance curve is approximately the same for all running conditions above idle. At idle, however, the manifold vacuum hookup results in full advance, while the ported hookup gives zero advance. If the hoses are hooked up the wrong way, the addition or lack of advance will affect idle speed, requiring a readjustment of the throttle position to bring the idle speed back to specifications. When this is done, emissions will usually be high, so it is important to keep the hoses hooked up correctly.

Dual Diaphragm Distributors

These distributors have two hose connections, one in the normal position, and the other closer to the distributor body. The hose fitting next to the body is for the retard diaphragm, and is connected to manifold vacuum. The retard diaphragm affects the spark only at idle, when there is no vacuum on the advance diaphragm. In effect, the retard diaphragm provides a movable resting place for the advance diaphragm. When ported vacuum is not acting on the advance diaphragm, it returns to the neutral or no-advance position against the retard diaphragm. At idle, manifold vacuum pulls the retard diaphragm to the retard position, and the advance diaphragm follows along to retard the spark.

Testing Dual Diaphragm Distributors

To test a dual diaphragm distributor, connect a timing light to the engine. Remove the retard hose from the distributor and plug the hose. With the engine running, increase the speed to a fast idle and watch the timing marks. The timing should advance. If not, either the vacuum unit is faulty, the vacuum port is plugged, or there is a temperature control device that is shutting off the vacuum. Apply hand pump or mouth suction vacuum to the advance diaphragm and the timing should advance. If not, the distributor or advance unit must be repaired or replaced. Failure

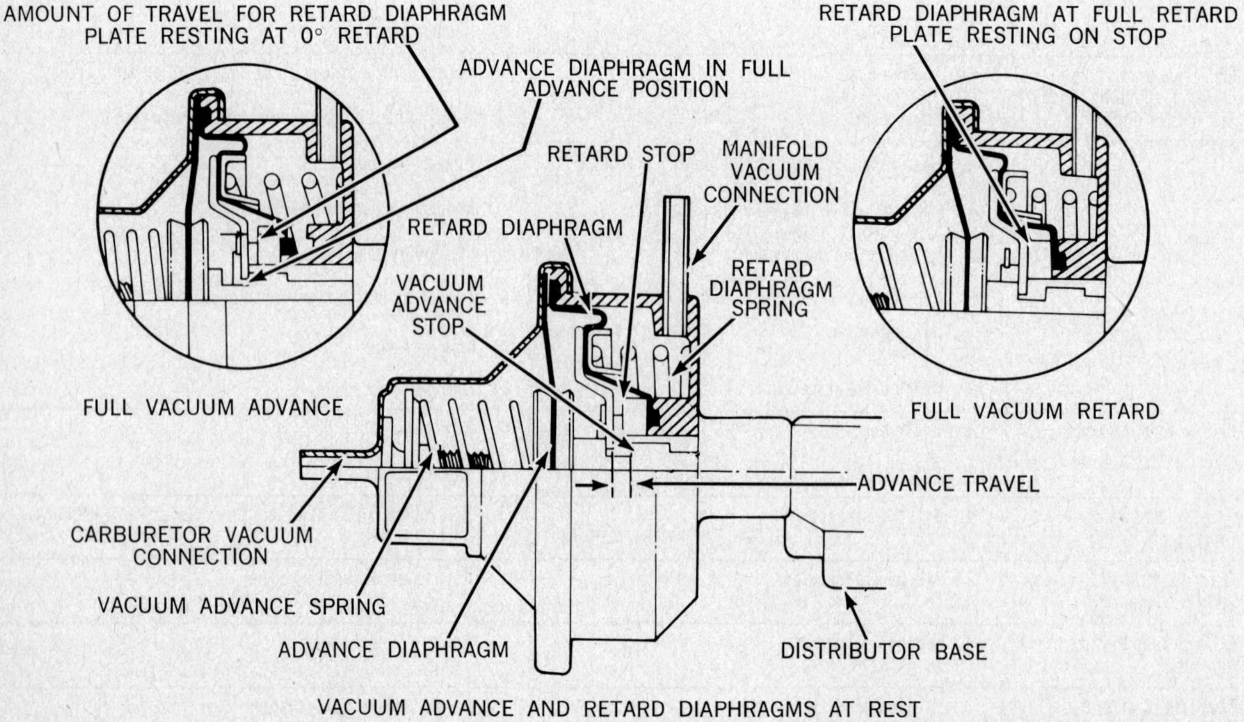

Dual diaphragm vacuum advance mechanism (© Ford Motor Co.)

to advance could be caused by a faulty diaphragm or a sticky advance plate.

Remove the advance hose from the vacuum unit and read the timing at normal idle speed. Remove the plug that was inserted in the retard hose, and check for full manifold vacuum at the end of it. If there is no vacuum, temperature controls may be shutting it off.

Connect the hose to the retard diaphragm, or apply vacuum from another source. The timing should immediately retard several degrees. If not, the diaphragm is not working, and the unit must be replaced. Reconnect all hoses as they were originally.

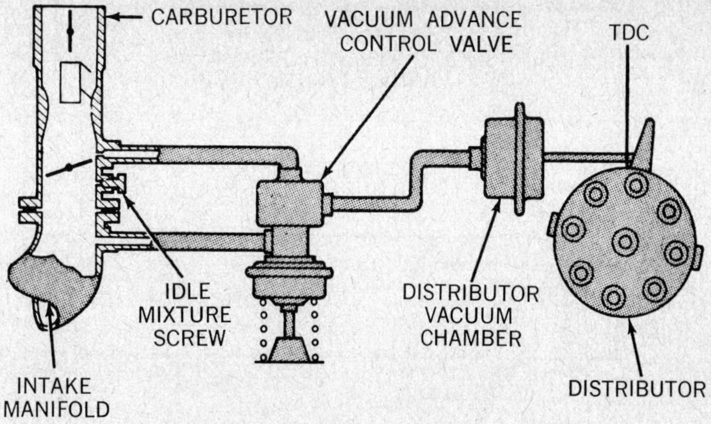

Carburetor—control valve—distributor relationship (© Ford Motor Co.)

Distributor Vacuum Deceleration Valve

Its purpose is to advance the spark during deceleration, by sending full manifold vacuum to the vacuum advance unit. At all other times the vacuum advance unit receives ported (above the throttle plates) carburetor vacuum.

Three checks should be made on the valve: the amount of vacuum at the distributor, any valve leaks, and the adjustment. To check the amount of vacuum at the distributor, use a T-fitting and a short length of vacuum hose to connect a vacuum gauge into the distributor vacuum line near the distributor. At idle, with the engine fully warmed up, the vacuum on the gauge should be less than 1 Hg. If the gauge shows more than 1 Hg. the idle speed is too fast, or the valve is leaking. To check for a leak, remove the large manifold vacuum hose on the side of the valve. If the vacuum drops, the valve is leaking and must be replaced. If the vacuum stays high, reduce the engine idle speed so that the port in the carburetor is covered.

To check the valve adjustment, connect the manifold vacuum hose and run the engine at 2000 rpm for 5 seconds. Then release the throttle. The distributor vacuum should go over 16 in. Hg. and stay there for about one second. Within about three seconds after you release the throttle, the distributor vacuum should drop to below 6 in. Hg. If the carburetor is equipped with a dashpot to make the throttle close slowly, the time may be about one second longer. If the time is too long, remove the cover on the valve and turn the screw clockwise to reduce the time. To increase the time, turn the screw counterclockwise. If the valve will not adjust properly, it must be replaced, and the new valve adjusted to specifications.

Spark Delay Valve

This small valve is connected between the carburetor and the distributor vacuum advance, so that the ported (above the throttle plates) vacuum to the distributor must pass through the valve. A restriction in the valve delays the vacuum applied to the vacuum advance unit so that the advance comes in slowly. When there is no vacuum at the carburetor port, as during idle or wide open throttle a check valve inside the spark delay valve opens and dumps the vacuum so that the vacuum advance unit returns to the no-advance position without any delay.

Spark delay valves can be tested for correct operation and leaks with a source of vacuum such as a hand vacuum pump or a running engine, and a vacuum gauge. Connect the vacuum gauge to the distributor side of the valve, and the vacuum source to the other side. The gauge should rise slowly until it reads the amount of vacuum available. The time to rise to the maximum reading should be from one to 28 seconds. If the vacuum gauge does not read anything, the valve is plugged. If the vacuum reads instantly, without any delay, the valve is open. In either case, the spark delay valve must be replaced. To test the check valve part of the spark delay valve, remove the vacuum source and the vacuum gauge should drop instantly to zero without any delay. If there is any delay,the spark delay valve is defective and must be replaced.

Transmission Controlled Spark

The purpose of the transmission controlled spark is to eliminate vacuum spark advance in the lower gears. When the transmission is in high gear, vacuum spark advance is allowed for better gasoline milage and part throttle response. This system was used during the 1973-1974 model years on most "Light Duty" models and continued on some California and High Altitude vehicles in later years.

Testing TCS Systems

Testing the system is done by connecting a vacuum gauge to the distributor vacuum line with a long hose so you can put it through the window into the front seat and see it while driving. There should be no vacuum in the lower gears on a warm engine, but after the transmission shifts into a gear that allows vacuum advance, you should see vacuum on the gauge. Engines that run their distributors on manifold vacuum will show vacuum at all times when in the proper gear. Engines that use ported (above the throttle plates) vacuum will show vacuum in the proper gear only when the throttle is open. If you don't get vacuum when you should, test the individual units in the system.

Vacuum solenoids can be tested by disconnecting all wiring and connecting hot and ground wires to the solenoid terminals, to make it open or close. You should be able to blow through the solenoid when it is open, but not when it's closed. Because solenoids exist in both normally open and

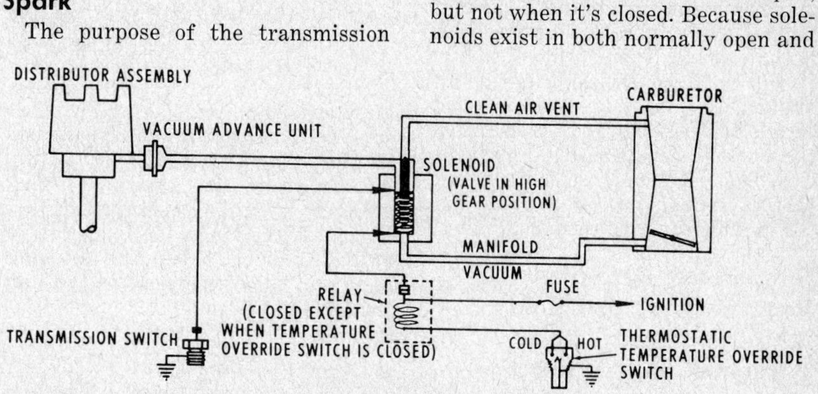

A typical transmission controlled spark system (© General Motors Corp.)

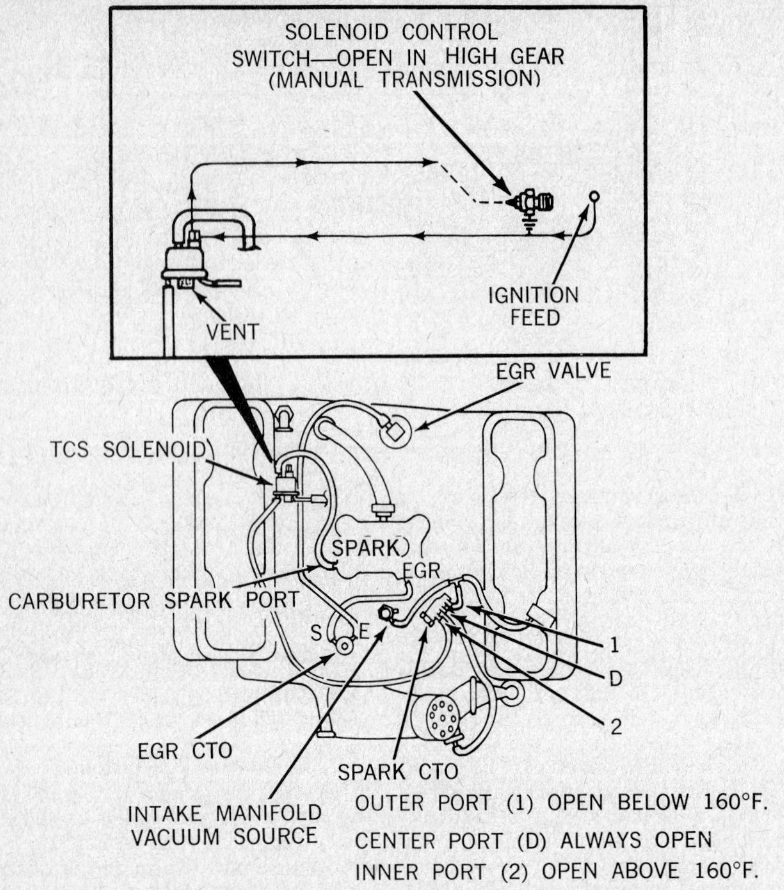

Transmission Controlled Spark System—V8 engine shown (© Jeep Corp.)

normally closed designs, it is important to use the right solenoid. If the wrong solenoid is used, the system will work backwards, giving advance in the lower gears but not in high. The same goes for the transmission switch, which exists in both normally open and normally closed designs. The term "normally open" means that the solenoid or switch is open when it is not energized or activated. In the case of a vacuum solenoid, normally open means that if you were holding the solenoid in your hand without any wires connected to it, the vacuum passages would be open, allowing vacuum to pass. In the case of a transmission switch, the term "normally open" refers to the electrical path, which is "open" or "off" so that it will not conduct electricity. Normally closed, of course, means that the electric contacts are closed so that the current can pass. But normally closed on a vacuum solenoid means that the vacuum passage is blocked so the vacuum can't get through.

Temperature Activated Vacuum (TAV) and Cold Temperature Activated Vacuum (CTAV) Systems

This system switches the vacuum source back and forth between the carburetor spark port and EGR port, according to the air temperature. A 3-nozzle vacuum solenoid is used. Below approximately 55°F. outside air temperature, the temperature switch is open, and the solenoid is not energized. In this position, the solenoid connects the spark port to the vacuum advance unit. Above 55°F. the temperature switch closes, and energizes the solenoid. In this position, the solenoid connects the EGR port to the vacuum advance unit.

The temperature switch is located in the air cleaner, and a latching relay is on the firewall. Once the temperature switch has closed, the relay latches so that any sudden rush of cold air through the air cleaner will not cycle the solenoid on and off. The latching relay keeps the solenoid energized as long as the ignition switch is on. When the ignition switch is turned off, the relay unlatches and the system is ready for the next start, whether the air temperature is hot or cold. If the air at the temperature switch is over 55°F. the latching relay will come on when the ignition switch is turned on.

Testing

Test the system with a vacuum gauge connected to the vacuum advance hose at the distributor. With the temperature above 65°F. (to be sure the temperature switch has closed) you should be getting vacuum from the EGR port. If you disconnect the EGR port hose and the vacuum drops, you know the system is working. When making a cold test, the vacuum should come from the spark port hose, so disconnecting that hose should make the vacuum drop. Because both ports are above the throttle plate, the throttle must be opened slightly to get vacuum at the hose.

Identifying the spark port and EGR ports on the carburetor is easy if they are marked. If there is no marking on the carburetor, connect two vacuum gauges, one to each port. At idle you should not have any vacuum. If you do have vacuum, it usually means the engine is idling too fast. Close the throttle slightly to slow down the idle and the vacuum should drop to almost zero.

When you open the throttle, you will see vacuum on one gauge before the other. The gauge that gets vacuum first is connected to the spark port.

Orifice Spark Advance Control (OSAC)

It is a mechanism that delays the application of vacuum to the distributor vacuum advance unit. When the throttle is opened, the carburetor port is exposed to vacuum. This vacuum goes through a hose to the OSAC valve, and then to the distributor vacuum advance. The OSAC valve is sometimes mounted on the firewall, and sometimes on the air cleaner. Inside the OSAC valve is a calibrated orifice that delays the vacuum as much as 27 seconds, depending on the calibration of the valve.

Some OSAC valves have temperature control that senses the temperature inside the air cleaner or inside the plenum chamber behind the firewall, depending on where the valve is mounted. If the valve contains temperature control, it will be wide open below 60°F. bypassing the orifice and allowing vacuum advance without any delay. Above 60°F. the bypass closes and the delay takes over.

Testing

To test the valve, connect a vacuum gauge to the DIST connection on the valve. With the engine idling, you should have no reading on the gauge. If there is a reading, the engine is idling too fast. With the engine idling, open the throttle to a fast idle, and hold it steady. The vacuum on the gauge will rise slowly until it reaches a maximum reading. If not, there is something wrong with the system, and you should check out the hoses and the carburetor port, or replace the valve if necessary.

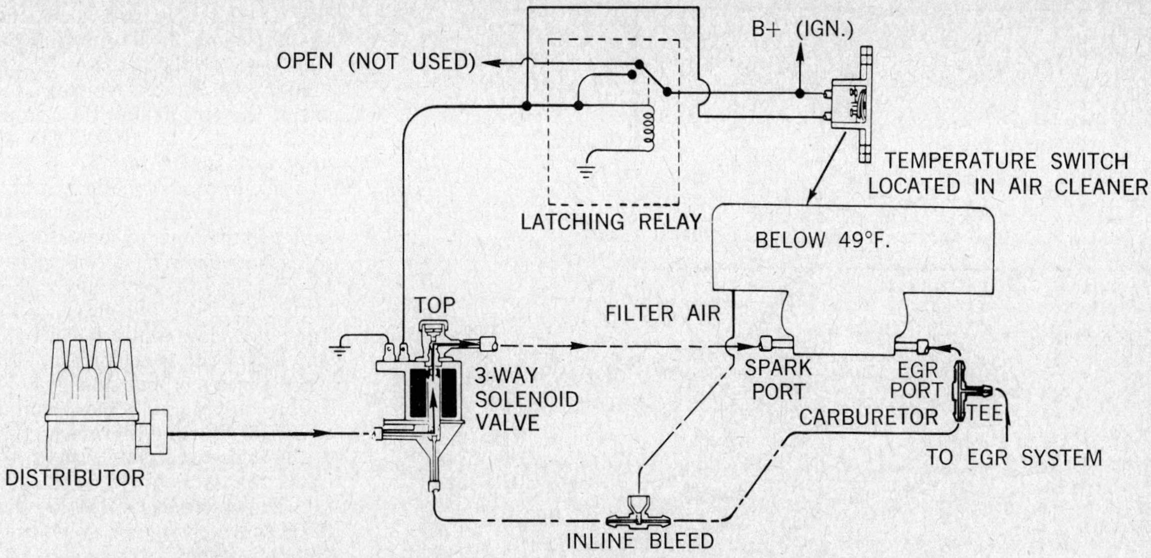

Schematic of Cold Temperature Activated Vacuum System (CTAV) below 49° F. Used on some California Engines (© Ford Motor Co.)

Vacuum Reducer Valve

Inserted between the manifold vacuum source and the distributor, this valve reduces the vacuum acting on the advance diaphragm by about 3 in. Hg. This valve is always used on a system that includes a distributor thermal vacuum switch. The vacuum advance unit operates on ported (above the throttle plates) vacuum, except when the engine overheats above 225°F. This opens the thermal vacuum switch and sends full manifold vacuum through the vacuum reducer valve to the advance unit. Thus, the vacuum reducer valve is only operating when the engine is overheated.

To test the valve, connect a vacuum gauge to the TVS nozzle, and a hand vacuum pump to the MAN nozzle. When you pump up 15 in. Hg. vacuum on the hand pump, the vacuum on the separate gauge should be 3 to 4 in. Hg. lower. Both gauges should hold the vacuum without leakdown. If not, the valve is defective and must be replaced.

Retard Delay Valve

When the throttle is suddenly opened, engine vacuum drops immediately, and this causes the vacuum advance to move quickly from the advance position to the neutral or no-advance position. A retard delay valve is a restriction with a one-way check valve. It allows the vacuum to act on the vacuum advance unit normally, but when the vacuum drops, the delay valve traps the vacuum in the advance unit and lets it out slowly. It takes several seconds for the advance unit to return to the neutral position.

Some models have the retard delay valve hooked up so that it only operates when the engine is cold. At normal operating temperature the delay is bypassed.

Testing of the delay valve can be done with a hand vacuum pump. Connect the pump to the MAN side of the valve, or the side that connects to the vacuum source on the engine. Connect a separate vacuum gauge to the other side of the valve. When the hand pump is operated, the vacuum will rise on both the pump gauge and the separate gauge equally. When the release is pulled, the pump gauge will drop to zero immediately, but the separate gauge will take several seconds to drop to zero. If it doesn't work that way, the delay valve is defective, and must be replaced.

Cold Start Spark Advance

A coolant sensitive vacuum switch (PVS) is combined with a delay valve (Distributor Retard Control Valve) to provide retard delay when the engine coolant is below 128°F. The hose routing is set up so that the vacuum advance unit operates on manifold vacuum through the retard delay valve when the engine is cold, and on ported vacuum through a spark delay valve when the engine is warm. The system also has an overheat PVS that switches the vacuum advance over to manifold vacuum (through the spark delay valve) when the engine coolant gets over 235°F.

Testing the spark delay valve is covered in this section under Spark Delay Valve. Testing for the Distributor Retard Control Valve is the same as for the Retard Delay Valve in this section.

When the 128° PVS is cold, connection No. 2 is blocked and D and 1 are connected. When it is over 128°F No. 1 is blocked and D and 2 are connected.

Carburetor Choke Controls

Non-Electric Choke

A non-electric choke uses a "stove" on the exhaust manifold or a well on the intake manifold to provide heat. When the well is used, the choke coil is surrounded by the warm intake manifold, heated by the exhaust crossover passage. When the stove is used, the choke housing is connected to engine vacuum, and a long tube pulls the heated air from the stove into the choke housing to heat up the choke coil and cause the choke to open as the engine warms up. When an electric choke is used, it can be in addition to all the above, or it can be the only source of choke heat, depending on the design.

Electric Choke

The electric choke has a small heater next to the choke coil. This heater receives its current from different sources, depending on the car maker.

Ford Motor Company and Jeep chokes are powered from the alternator "center tap," which produces about 7 volts. As the alternator is only putting out voltage when the engine is running, the electric choke is automatically shut off when the engine is off. It is important that the choke is connected only to the special "center tap" provided on the alternator. The description "center tap" refers to the construction of the alternator wiring, and not to the location of the connection.

Inside is a thermostatic switch that turns on the heating element at approximately 80°F. Above that, the elements stays on as long as the engine is running. The 80°F. figure was se-

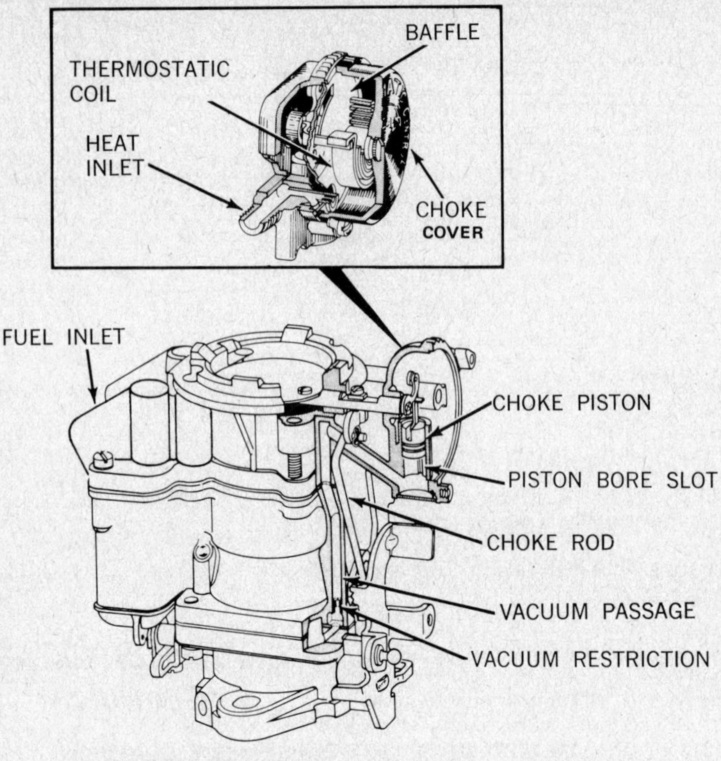

Non-electric choke assembly used with choke stove in the exhaust manifold—typical (© Jeep Corp.)

lected because the engine is warm enough at that temperature to keep running without the choke. When the heater comes on, the choke opens very quickly. When the engine is shut off and cools down, the choke switch may stay on to as low as 65°F. at the choke housing. On a warm restart, where the choke switch was still on, the heating element would heat up the choke and open it shortly after the engine started.

Chrysler Corporation vehicles with an electric choke use a well type choke, which receives heat both from the intake manifold and the electric choke heater. A separate choke control unit is mounted on top of the intake manifold and connected to the heater with a wire. This wire disconnects at the choke control unit only, not at the heater.

Choke control units may be single and double stage. The double stage is recognized by the external resistor alongside the unit. The single stage unit turns on the choke heater at approximately 60°F. and off at 110°F. The double stage unit keeps the heater on below 60°F. but the current runs through the resistor. At approximately 60°F. the resistor is taken out of the circuit and the heater gets full current. At 110°F. the control unit turns the heater off.

Testing can be done with a non-powered test light on the choke terminal to find out if the heater is on or off. The ignition switch must be on. If the light glows, you know the control unit is on. On two-stage units, the light will glow dimly when the resistor is in the circuit, and brightly when the resistor is out. The current to the control unit comes from the ignition switch, and there is no fuse.

Chevrolet and GMC use an electric choke that is mounted on the carburetor. The choke has a dual element behind the coil spring. Whenever the engine is running, the choke heater is in operation. Below 50-70°F. a bimetal snap disc in the choke cover turns off the large section of the heating element so that only the small section gives off heat. Above 50-70°F. the disc switches on the large heating element for faster choke opening.

Current to the choke is controlled by a three-terminal oil pressure switch. One of the terminals is a ground for the red oil pressure light on the instrument panel. The other two terminals are a switch in series between the ignition switch and the choke heater. Oil pressure operates the switch so that the choke gets current only when the engine is running. The circuit is fused through the backup light or transmission fuse in the fuse block.

NOTE: Failure of the choke heater circuit will cause the oil pressure light to go on.

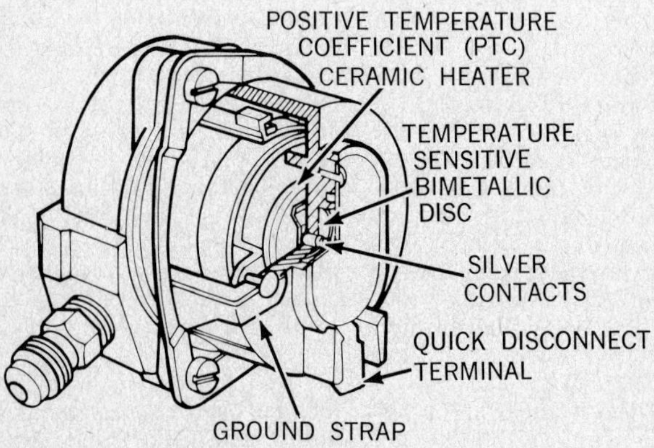

Electric choke assembly—Used with choke stove (© Ford Motor Co.)

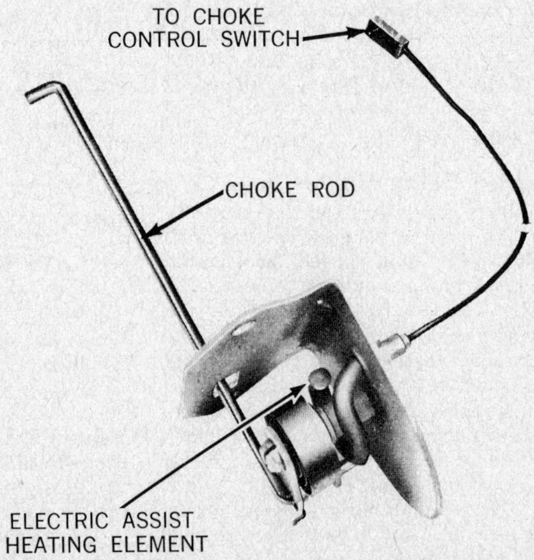

Manifold well type choke assembly—electric assembly illustrated—both electric and non-electric types used (© Chrysler Corp.)

INDEX

Gasoline Engines Rebuilding

ENGINE TROUBLESHOOTING

Possible Cause	Correction
LOSS OF OIL PRESSURE	
1. Low oil level.	Add oil to correct level.
2. Clogged oil filter element.	Change filter element.
3. Oil pressure indicator defective.	Repair or replace as needed.
4. Oil leaks.	Check for leaks and correct as needed.
5. Oil pump screen clogged.	Clean pump screen and oil pan.
6. Oil pressure relief valve sticking on broken relief valve spring.	Clean valve or replace spring.
7. Oil pump worn.	Repair or replace.
8. Worn main connecting rod or camshaft bearings.	Replace worn bearings.
EXCESSIVE OIL CONSUMPTION	
1. Oil leaks.	Check for leaks and correct as needed.
2. Incorrect grade of lubricating oil.	Use grade of oil specified in "Operator's Manual".
3. Engine overheated.	Refer to "Engine Overheated".
4. Excessive oil in crankcase.	Drain to correct level.
5. Stuck oil control rings, worn valve guides, pistons, rings and cylinder walls.	Replace worn parts. Rebore cylinder block if necessary.
LOSS OF COMPRESSION	
1. Valves sticking.	Clean valve guides and stems. Replace worn parts.
2. Valve mechanism parts worn or broken.	Replace worn or damaged parts.
3. Cylinder heads not bolted down tight.	Tighten cylinder head bolts to specified torque following correct bolt tightening sequence:
4. Damaged cylinder head gaskets.	Replace gaskets.
5. Worn or damaged pistons, rings and cylinder walls.	Replace worn parts. Rebore cylinder block if necessary.
ENGINE OVERHEATED	
1. Coolant level low.	Add coolant to correct level. Check for cause of coolant loss.
(a) Radiator cap loose or missing.	Tighten or replace cap.
(b) Leaks in cooling system.	Correct as necessary.
(c) Leaking cylinder head gaskets or cracked heads or cylinder block.	Replace cylinder head gasket. Check for cracks. Replace heads or block if necessary.
2. Engine overloaded.	Reduce load on engine. Use lower gear.
3. Dirt and trash on outside of radiator.	Clean radiator fins with air or water pressure.
4. Fan belt slipping.	Replace fan belts.
5. Cooling system clogged.	Drain and flush cooling system.
6. Thermostats or radiator shutters inoperative.	Replace thermostats or repair shutters as needed.
7. Water pump defective.	Repair or replace.
8. Low oil pressure.	Refer to "Loss of Oil Pressure".

ENGINE NOISES

Possible Cause	Correction
NOISY VALVES	
Constant loud clacking, light clicking or intermittent noise indicates faulty hydraulic valve lifters (tappets).	
1. High or low oil level in crankcase.	Check for correct oil level.
2. Low oil pressure.	Check engine oil level.
3. Dirt in tappets.	Clean tappets.
4. Bend push rods.	Install new push rods.
5. Worn rocker arms.	Inspect oil supply to rockers.
6. Worn tappets.	Install new tappets.
7. Worn valve guides.	Replace guides if removable or ream and install new valves.
8. Excessive run-out of valve seats or valve faces.	Grind valve seats and valves.
9. Incorrect tappet lash.	Adjust to specifications.
CONNECTING ROD NOISE	
A metallic knock when idling or retarding engine speed, which disappears under load indicates worn or loose connecting rod bearings. The bearing at fault can be found by shorting out the spark plugs one at a time. The noise will disappear when the cylinder with the faulty bearing is shorted out.	
1. Insufficient oil supply	Check engine oil level.
2. Low oil pressure.	Check engine oil level.
3. Thin or diluted oil.	Change oil to correct viscosity.
4. Excessive bearing clearance.	Measure bearings for correct clearance or failures.
5. Connecting rod journals out-of-round.	Remove crankshaft and regrind journals.
6. Misaligned connecting rods.	Remove bent connecting rods.

ENGINE NOISES

MAIN BEARING NOISE

A main bearing knock is more of a bump than a knock, and it can be located by shorting out the plugs near it. The noise is loudest when the engine is "lugging" (pulling hard at slow speed). The sound is heavier and more dull than a connecting rod knock.

1. Insufficient oil supply.	Check engine oil level. Inspect oil pump relief valve, damper and spring.
2. Low oil pressure.	Check engine oil level.
3. Thin or diluted oil.	Change the oil to correct viscosity.
4. Excessive bearing clearance.	Check the bearings for correct clearances or failures.
5. Excessive end play.	Check thrust main bearing for wear on flanges.
6. Crankshaft journals out-of-round or worn.	Remove crankshaft and regrind journals.
7. Loose flywheel.	Tighten correctly.

OTHER ENGINE NOISES

1. A sharp rap at idle speed indicates a loose piston pin. The pin at fault can be found by shorting out the spark plugs one at a time. The noise will disappear when the cylinder with the faulty pin is shorted out.	Replace piston pin.
2. A flat slap, when advancing engine speed under load, indicates a loose piston.	Replace piston and rebore cylinder block if necessary.

This section describes in detail, the procedures involved in rebuilding a typical gasoline engine. A rebuilt engine can be expected to give many miles of dependable service only if the proper reconditioning procedures are performed and clearances are kept within the manufacturers recommended specifications.

The following systems of the gasoline engine should be checked to determine to what degree the rebuilding should be accomplished.

Engine Oil Pressure

The engine oil pressure developed, should be compared to the manufacturers recommended pressure, necessary to provide lubricating oil to the engine oil circuits. If the pressure is below specifications, the cause must be located and repaired.

The following wear points should be considered during this determination.

- Oil Pump—Check Gear clearances (A new oil pump is a good investment).

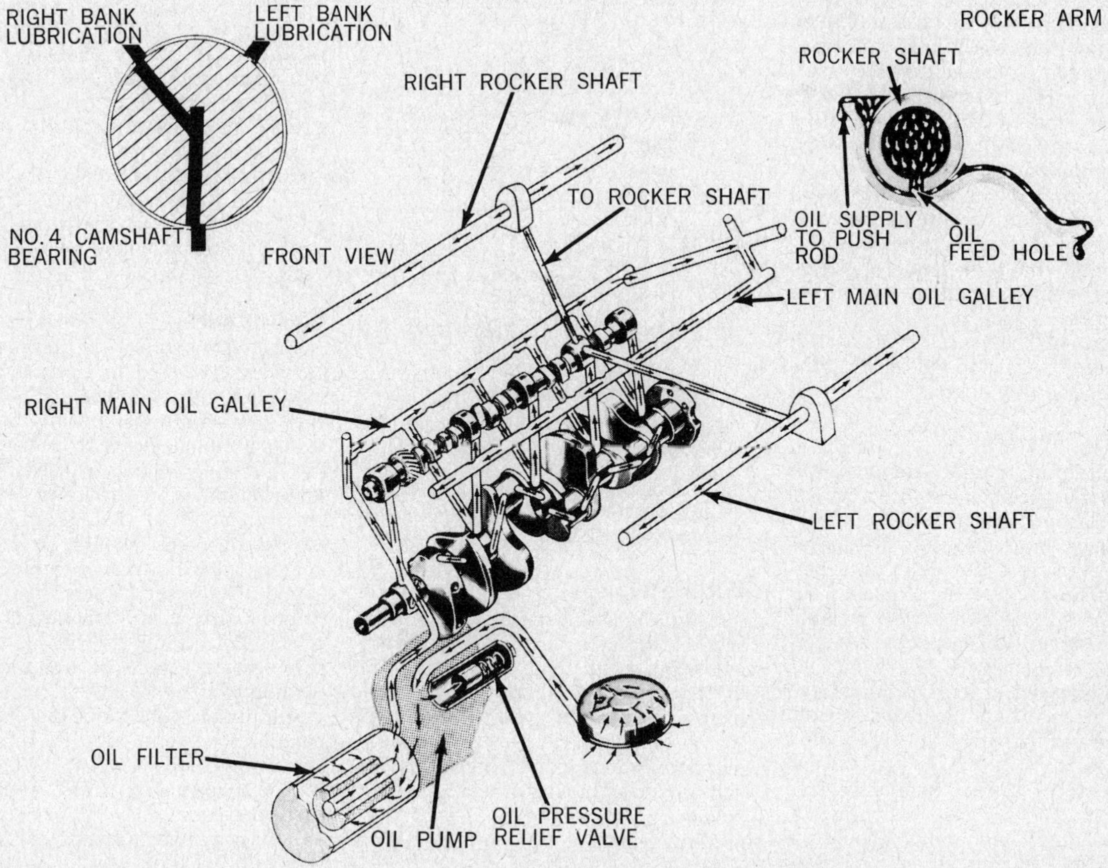

Typical oiling system—V8 engine (© Chrysler Corp.)

- Main Bearings and Journals—Check clearances, taper and roundness.
- Connecting Rod Bearings and Journals—Check clearances, taper and roundness.
- Camshaft and bearings—Check clearances, taper and roundness.
- Rocker Arms, Rocker Arm Shafts —Check arm and shaft wear, ball and seat wear.
- Tappets—Check clearances between tappet and bore and for excessive leakdown of hydraulic tappets.
- Leakage of oil pressure along external or internal oil gallerys or gaskets.
- Dilution of the oil by gasoline leakage through failures of the carburetor or mechanical fuel pump.
- External damage to the oil pan, causing blockage or movement of the oil pick-up tube, resulting in loss of oil pick-up to the pump.

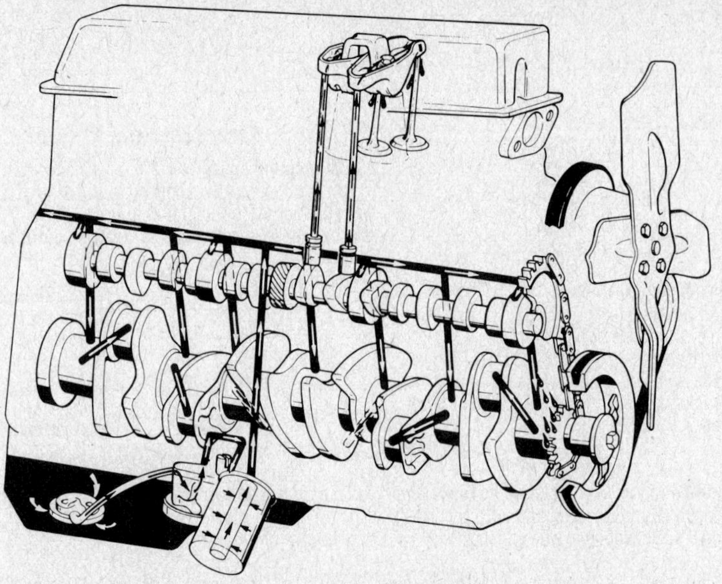

Typical oiling system—6 cylinder engine (© American Motors Corp.)

Compression

Compression in an engine is determined by the correct fit and sealing efficiency of the piston and rings against the cylinder walls, the quality of the seal between the valve and its seat, and the seal between the cylinder head, head gasket and block. Here are some important check points.

- Valve, seat and face—Machine face and seat to original specifications.
- Valve guides—The reconditioned seat and face won't hold up long if the valve stem clearance isn't within specifications.
- Valve seals—Oil reaching the valve seat will become a solid when it combines with the heat in the combustion chamber. This solid (carbon) will build up and eventually keep the valve from seating.
- Cylinder walls—Check for taper, out-of-round and hone to proper cross hatch pattern.
- Pistons—Check all dimensions. A poorly fitted piston will shorten the life of the new rings.

Cooling System

Maintaining engine temperatures within the specified range is critical to the life of a rebuilt engine. Until new parts mate properly with each other, excessive heat can cause permanent damage or substantially reduce the service life of the reconditioned engine. If the engine is operated at temperatures below normal, the oil may not properly lubricate all of the parts. Some parts that should be checked during the rebuilding process are:

- Coolant passages—Should be free of rust and corrosion deposits.
- Core plugs—all plugs should be replaced during the rebuilding process.
- Hoses—Should be free of cracks, hard spots, and oil softened spots.
- Thermostat—Check for opening and closing at the specfied temperature.
- Radiator—Check for leaks, and rust or corrosion deposits.
- Pressure cap—Should hold specified pressure, also check the gasket and vent valve operation.

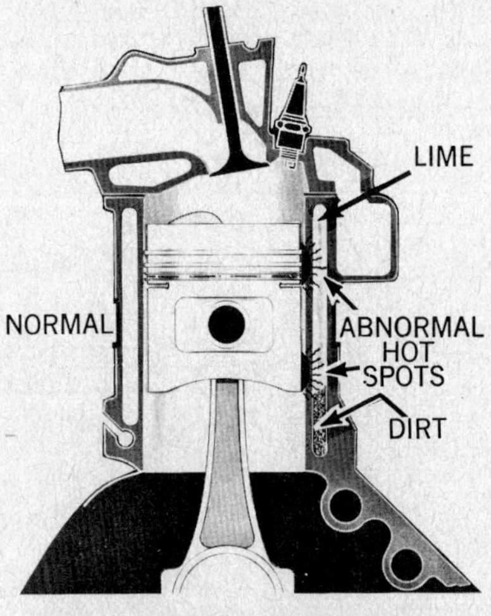

Illustration of cooling system passages being restricted, causing internal engine problems

Engine Noises

Engine noises are not only annoying, but indicate conditions inside the engine that can limit the service life of the engine or shut it down completely. Generally, noises are caused by too much clearance between parts or loss of oil supply. Engine noises can be caused by any of the following parts.

- Main bearings
- Connecting rod bearings
- Piston and/or rings
- Wrist pins
- Rocker arms, shaft, ball and seat
- Push rods
- Tappets and camshaft
- Timing chain and gears
- Oil pump failure
- Valves and valve springs
- Head gasket failure
- Cylinder head or block face warpage

Tools

The tools required for the basic rebuilding procedure should, with minor exception, be those included in a mechanics tool kit. Accurate torque wrench, micrometers and dial indicators should readily be available to the repairman. Special tools are available from the major tool suppliers. The services of a competent automotive machine shop must also be available.

Precautions

When assembling the engine, any parts that will be in frictional contact must be pre-lubricated, to provide protection on initial start-up. Any product specifically formulated for this purpose may be used. Where semipermanent locked but removable) installation of bolts or nuts is desired, threads should be cleaned and coated with a liquid locking compound. Studs may be permanently installed using a stud mounting compound. Bolts and nuts with no torque specification should be tightened according to size (see chart).

Aluminum has become increasingly popular for use in engines, due to its low weight and excellent heat transfer characteristics. The following precautions must be observed when handling aluminum engine parts:

—Never hot-tank aluminum parts.
—Remove all aluminum parts (iden-

STANDARD TORQUE SPECIFICATIONS AND CAPSCREW MARKINGS

Note: Newton-Metre has been designated as the world standard for measuring torque and will gradually replace the foot-pound and kilogram-meter torque measuring standard. Torquing tools are still being manufactured with foot-pounds and kilogram-meter scales, along with the new Newton-Metre standard. To assist the repairman, foot-pounds, kilogram-meter and Newton-Metre are listed in the following charts, and should be followed as applicable.

U. S. BOLTS

SAE Grade Number	1 or 2			5			6 or 7			8		
Capscrew Head Markings Manufacturer's marks may vary. Three-line markings on heads shown below, for example. Indicate SAE Grade 5. 	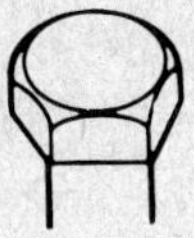						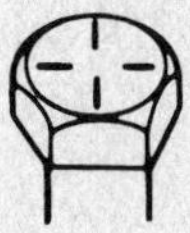					
Usage	Used Frequently			Used Frequently			Used at Times			Used at Times		
Quality of Material	Indeterminate			Minimum Commercial			Medium Commercial			Best Commercial		
Capacity Body Size (inches)—(Thread)	Torque			Torque			Torque			Torque		
	Ft-Lb	kgm	Nm	Ft-Lb	kgm	Nm	Ft-Lb	kgm	Nm	Ft-Lb	kgm	Nm
1/4-20	5	0.6915	6.7791	8	1.1064	10.8465	10	1.3630	13.5582	12	1.6596	16.2698
-28	6	0.8298	8.1349	10	1.3830	13.5582				14	1.9362	18.9815
5/16-18	11	1.5213	14.9140	17	2.3511	23.0489	19	2.6277	25.7605	24	3.3192	32.5396
-24	13	1.7979	17.6256	19	2.6277	25.7605				27	3.7341	36.6071
3/8-16	18	2.4894	24.4047	31	4.2873	42.0304	34	4.7022	46.0978	44	6.0852	59.6560
-24	20	2.7660	27.1164	35	4.8405	47.4536				49	6.7767	66.4351
7/16-14	28	3.8132	37.9629	49	6.7767	66.4351	55	7.6065	74.5700	70	9.6810	94.9073
-20	30	4.1490	40.6745	55	7.6065	74.5700				18	10.7874	105.7538
1/2-13	39	5.3937	52.8769	75	10.3725	101.6863	85	11.7555	115.2445	105	14.5215	142.3609
-20	41	5.6703	55.5885	85	11.7555	115.2445				120	16.5860	162.6960
9/16-12	51	7.0533	69.1467	110	15.2130	149.1380	120	16.5960	162.6960	155	21.4365	210.1490
-18	55	7.6065	74.5700	120	16.5960	162.6960				170	23.5110	230.4860
5/8-11	83	11.4789	112.5329	150	20.7450	203.3700	167	23.0961	226.4186	210	29.0430	284.7180
-18	95	13.1385	128.8027	170	23.5110	230.4860				240	33.1920	325.3920
3/4-10	105	14.5215	142.3609	270	37.3410	366.0660	280	38.7240	379.6240	375	51.8625	508.4250
-16	115	15.9045	155.9170	295	40.7985	399.9610				420	58.0860	568.4360
7/8- 9	160	22.1280	216.9280	395	54.6285	535.5410	440	60.8520	596.5520	605	83.6715	820.2590
-14	175	24.2025	237.2650	435	60.1605	589.7730				675	93.3525	915.1650
1- 8	236	32.5005	318.6130	590	81.5970	799.9220	660	91.2780	894.8280	910	125.8530	1233.7780
-14	250	34.5750	338.9500	660	91.2780	849.8280				990	136.9170	1342.2420

METRIC BOLTS

Description	Torque ft-lbs. (Nm)			
Thread for general purposes (size x pitch (mm))	Head mark		Head mark	
6 x 1.0	2.2 to 2.9	(3.0 to 3.9)	3.6 to 5.8	(4.9 to 7.8)
8 x 1.25	5.8 to 8.7	(7.9 to 12)	9.4 to 14	(13 to 19)
10 x 1.25	12 to 17	(16 to 23)	20 to 29	(27 to 39)
12 x 1.25	21 to 32	(29 to 43)	35 to 53	(47 to 72)
14 x 1.5	35 to 52	(48 to 70)	57 to 85	(77 to 110)
16 x 1.5	51 to 77	(67 to 100)	90 to 120	(130 to 160)
18 x 1.5	74 to 110	(100 to 150)	130 to 170	(180 to 230)
20 x 1.5	110 to 140	(150 to 190)	190 to 240	(160 to 320)
22 x 1.5	150 to 190	(200 to 260)	250 to 320	(340 to 430)
24 x 1.5	190 to 240	(260 to 320)	310 to 410	(420 to 550)

CAUTION: Bolts threaded into aluminum require much less torque.

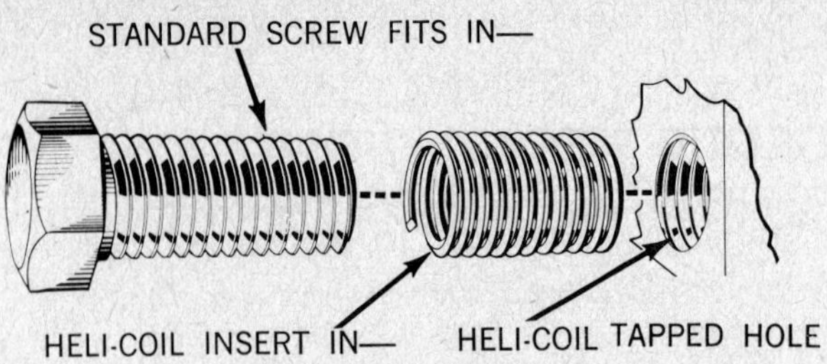

Helicoil installation

tification tags, etc.) from engine parts before hot-tanking (otherwise they will be removed during the process).
—Always coat threads lightly with engine oil or anti-seize compounds before installation, to prevent seizure.

Heli-coil

Never over-torque bolts or spark plugs in aluminum threads. Should stripping occur, threads can be restored according to the following procedure, using Heli-Coil thread inserts:

Tap drill the hole with the stripped threads to the specified size (see chart). Using the specified tap (NOTE: *Heli-Coil tap sizes refer to the size thread being replaced, rather than the actual tap size*), tap the hole for the Heli-Coil. Place the insert on the proper installation tool (see chart). Apply pressure on the insert while winding it clockwise into the hole, until the top of the insert is one turn below the surface. Remove the installation tool, and break the installation tang from the bottom of the insert by moving it up and down. If the Heli-Coil must be removed, tap the removal tool firmly into the hole, so that it engages the top thread, and turn the tool counter-clockwise to extract the insert.

Broken Bolts or Studs

Snapped bolts or studs may be removed, using a stud extractor (unthreaded) or locking pliers (threaded). Penetrating oil will often aid in breaking frozen threads. In cases where the stud or bolt is flush with, or below the surface, proceed as follows:

Drill a hole in the broken stud or bolt, approximately ½ its diameter. Select a screw extractor of the proper size, and tap it into the stud or bolt. Turn the extractor counter-clockwise to remove the stud or bolt.

Locating Metal Flaws and Cracks

Magnaflux® and Zyglo® are inspection techniques used to locate material flaws, such as stress cracks. Magnafluxing® coats the part with fine magnetic particles, and subjects the part to a magnetic field. Cracks cause breaks in the magnetic field, which are outlined by the particles.

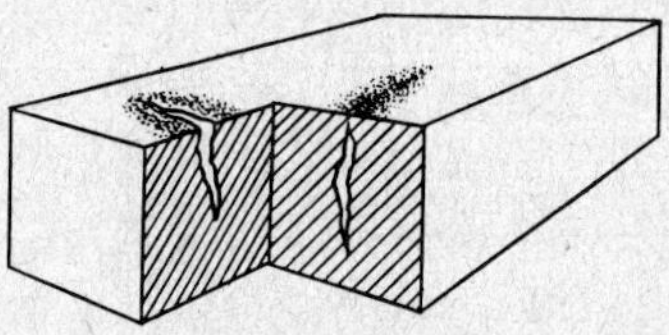

Magnaflux® indication of cracks

Since Magnaflux® is a magnetic process, it is applicable only to ferrous materials. The Zyglo® process coats the material with a fluorescent dye penetrant, and then subjects it to blacklight inspection, under which cracks glow brightly. Parts made of any material may be tested using Zyglo®. Whlie Magnaflux® and Zyglo® are excellent for general inspection, and locating hidden defects, specific checks of suspected cracks may be made at lower cost and more readily using spot check dye. The dye is sprayed onto the suspected area, wiped off, and the area is then sprayed with a developer. Cracks then will show up brightly. Spot check dyes will only indicate surface cracks; therefore, structural cracks below the surface may escape detection. When questionable, the part should be tested using Magnaflux® or Zyglo®.

Overhaul Procedures

The section is divided into two parts. The first, Cylinder Head Reconditioning, assumes that the cylinder head is removed from the engine, all manifolds are removed, and the cylinder head is on a workbench. The camshaft should be removed from overhead cam cylinder heads. The second section, Cylinder Block Reconditioning, covers the block, pistons, con--necting rods and crankshaft. It is assumed that the engine is mounted on a work stand, and the cylinder head and all accessories are removed.

In many cases, a choice of methods is provided. The choice of method for a procedure is at the discretion of the user.

Many makes and types of special tools are available to the rebuilder for the express purpose of doing a specific rebuilding operation, easier and quicker. It is the choice of the rebuilder as to the tool desired and obtained.

Cylinder Head Reconditioning

Identify the Valves

Invert the cylinder head and clean the carbon from the valve heads. Number the valve heads from front to rear with touch-up paint or a felt tip marking pencil. Upon removal of the valves from the cylinder head, place them in a holder, made from cardboard, wood or metal, in their respective order.

Remove the Rocker Arms

Remove the rocker arms and shaft or balls and nuts, if not done during the cylinder head removal. Wire the sets of rockers, balls and nuts together, and identify according to the corresponding valve.

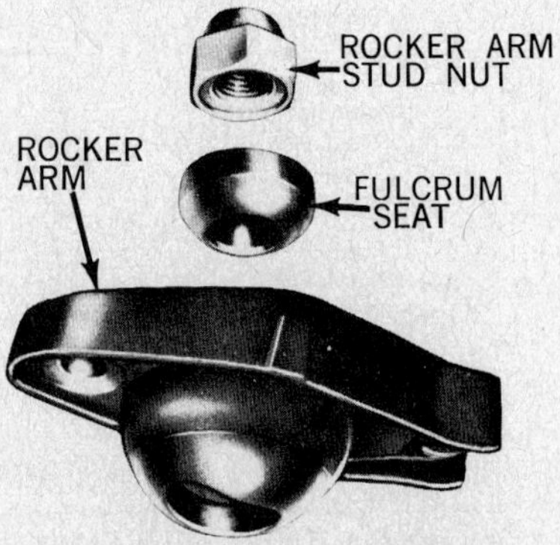

Individual rocker arm assembly
(© Ford Motor Co.)

HELI-COIL SPECIFICATIONS

Thread Size	Heli-Coil Part No.	Insert Length	Drill Size	Tap Part No. (Aluminum)	Tap Part No. Steel & Iron	Inserting Tool Part No.	Extracting Tool Part No.
10-24	1185-3CN	9/32"	13/64"	3 CPB	1187-3	2288-3	1227-6
1/4-20	1185-4CN	3/8"	17/64"	4 CPB	1187-4	2288-4	1227-6
5/16-18	1185-5CN	15/32"	21/64"	5 CPB	42187-5	2288-5	1227-6
3/8-16	1185-6CN	9/16"	25/64"	6 CPB	42187-6	2288-6	1227-6
7/16-14	1185-7CN	21/32"	29/64"	7 CPB	42187-7	2288-7	1227-16
1/2-13	1185-8CN	3/4"	33/64"* 17/32"**	8 CPB	42-187-8	2288-8	1227-16

* In Aluminum
** In Case Iron or Steel

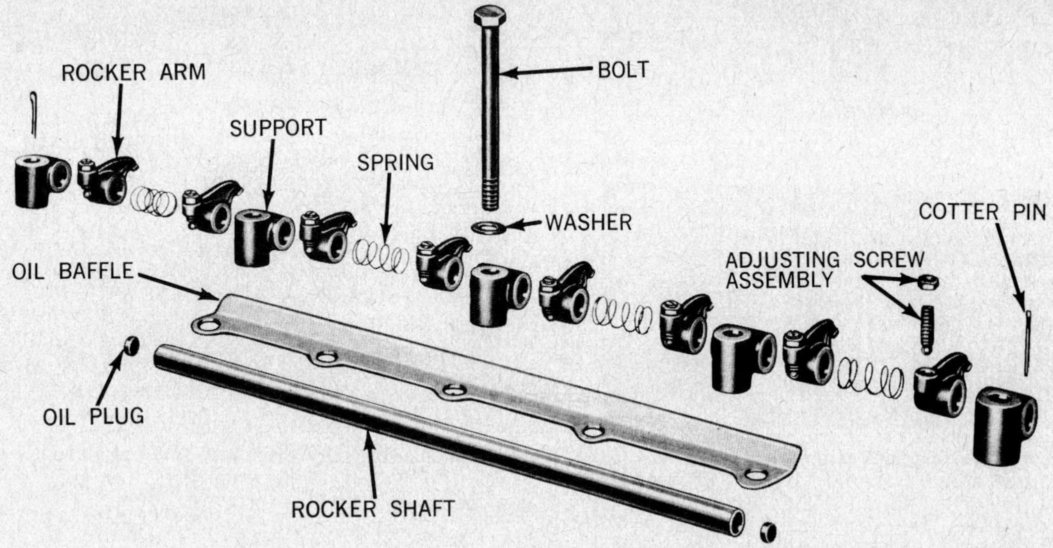

Rocker arm and shaft assembly—typical (© Ford Motor Co.)

Remove the Valves and Springs

Using an appropriate valve spring compressor, compress the valve springs and remove the keepers with needlenose pliers or a magnet. Release the compressor and remove the valve spring, retainer and oil seal from the valve stem. Remove the valve from the cylinder head and keep in order.

NOTE: Rotor units are used on numerous valve assemblies. Replace the rotor if any doubt exists on its performance.

De-carbon the Cylinder Head and Valves

Carbon is removed from the cylinder head combustion chamber, valves and valve ports by various methods. The most common is a wire brush tool, chucked to an electric drill. A hand held wire brush, a chisel made from hard wood or a special carbon removing tool, supplied by a tool company, is used to complete the carbon removal procedure.

CAUTION: When using a motorized wire brush, safety glasses must be worn to avoid personal injury.

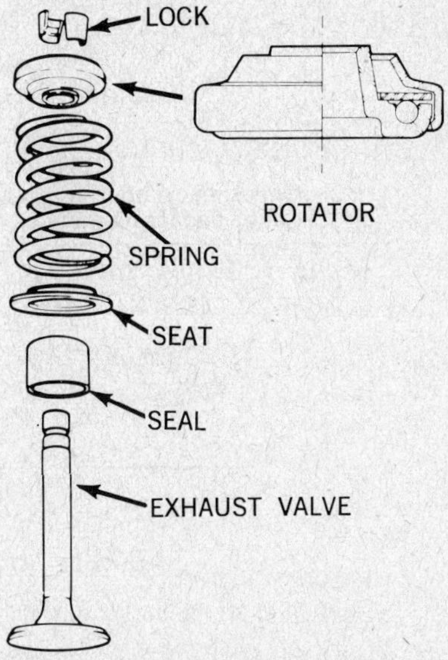

Valve assembly using rotator on top of the valve spring (© Jeep Corp.)

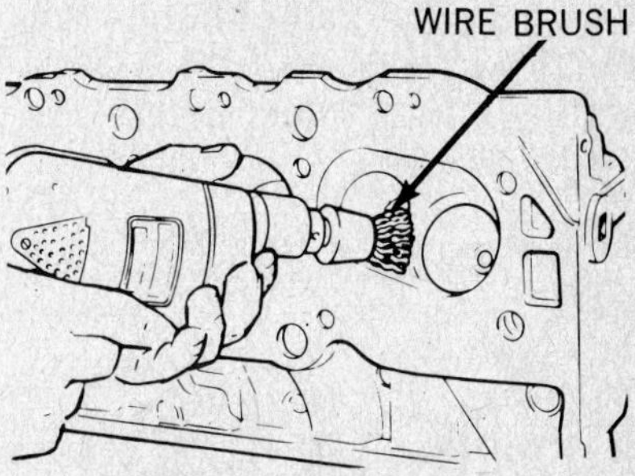

Removing carbon from the cylinder head

Cleaning the Cylinder Head

The cylinder head and certain components can be cleaned of grease, corrosion and scale by immersing

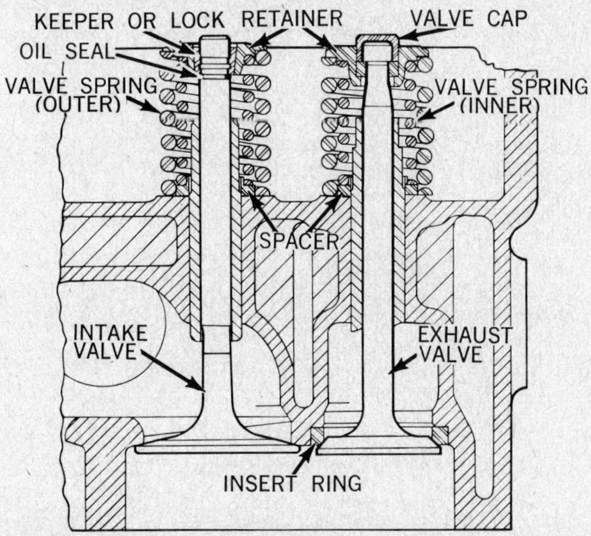

Cross section of valve assemblies with valve rotor cap on exhaust valve stem (© International Harvester Co.)

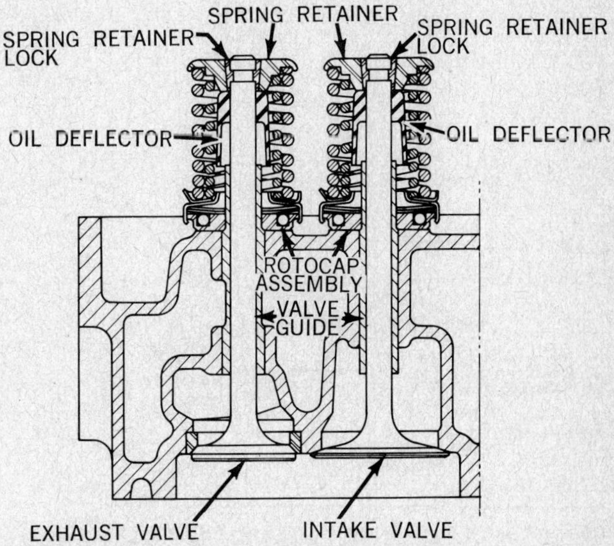

Cross section of valve assemblies with roto-cap assembly under the spring (© International Harvester Co.)

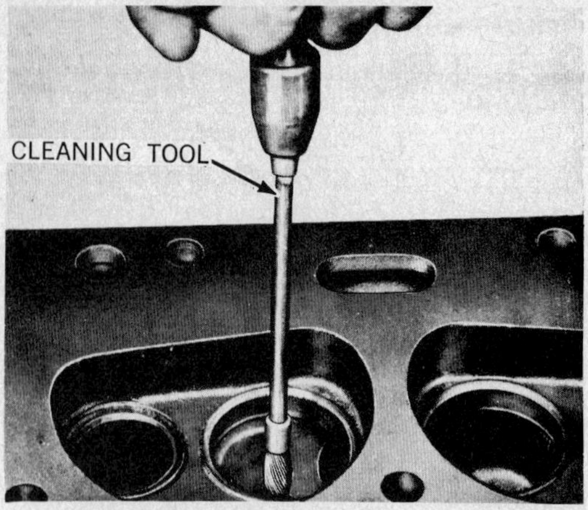

Cleaning valve guides with wire type cleaner
(© International Harvester Co.)

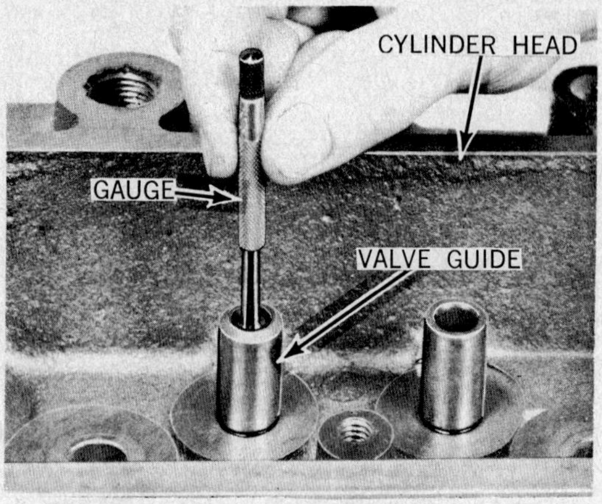

Measuring valve guide with small hole gauge
(© International Harvester Co.)

them in a "Hot Tank" solution. Generally, an automotive machine shop will have this type of equipment.

CAUTION: Consult with the "Hot Tank" operator to determine if overhead cam bearings of an OHC cylinder head will be damaged by the solution. If necessary to remove the bearings, replace them with new bearings.

Cleaning the Remaining Cylinder Head Parts

Using solvent, clean the rocker arm assemblies, (or rocker balls and

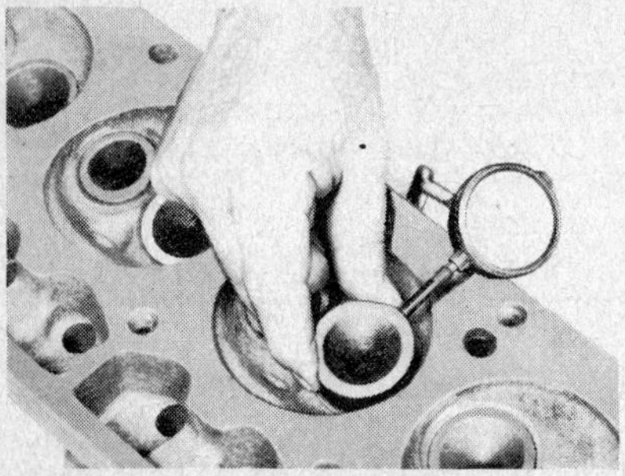

Measuring valve guide wear at valve head
(© Chrysler Corp.)

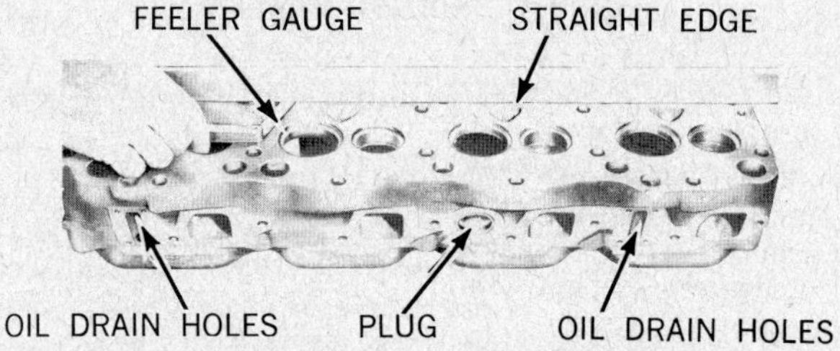

Checking cylinder head surface for flatness with feeler gauge and straight edge (© General Motors Corp.)

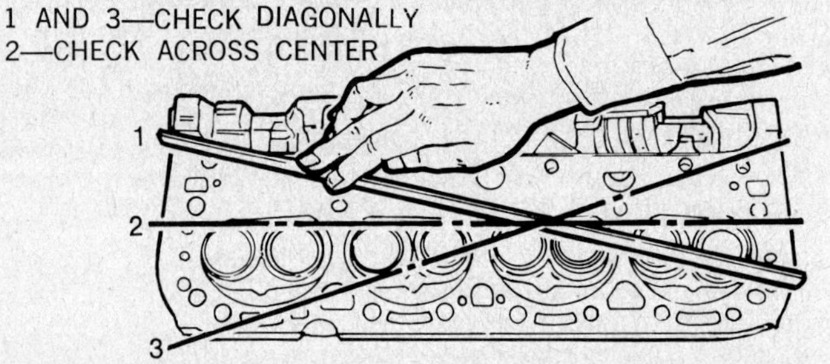

Location of straight edge to check cylinder head surface for flatness

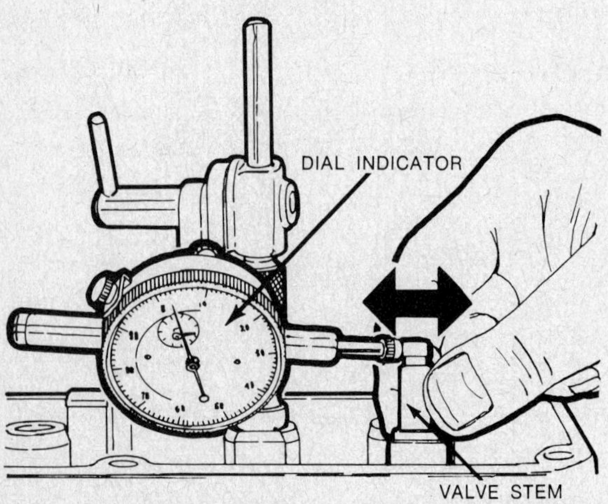

Measuring valve guide wear at valve stem
(© American Motors Corp.)

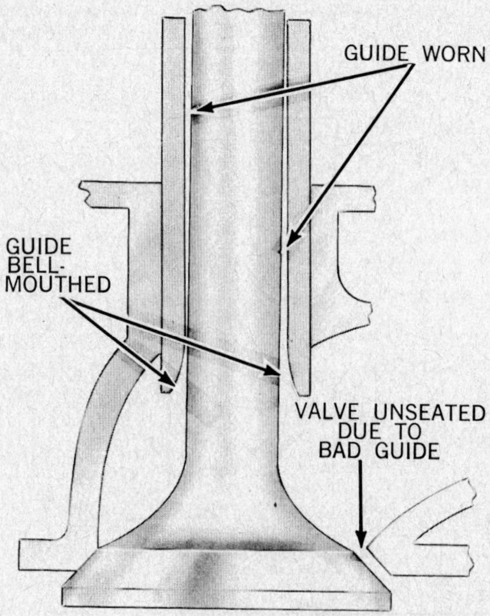

Effects of worn and bellmouthed guides on valve head seating (© International Harvester Co.)

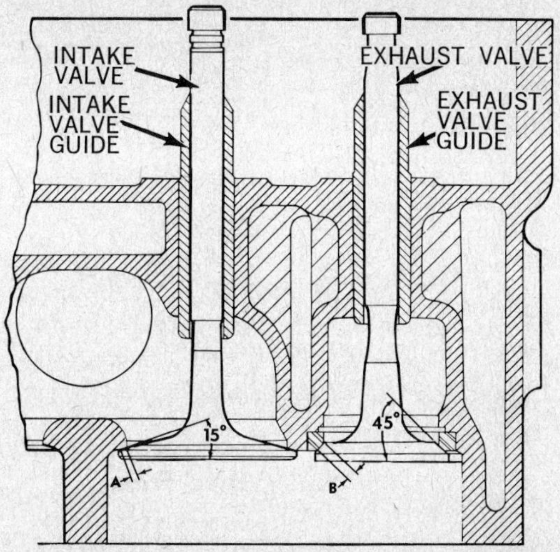

Cross section of valves showing exhaust valve seat insert and intake valve seat with out insert. Method of measuring seat angle is illustrated (© International Harvester Co.)

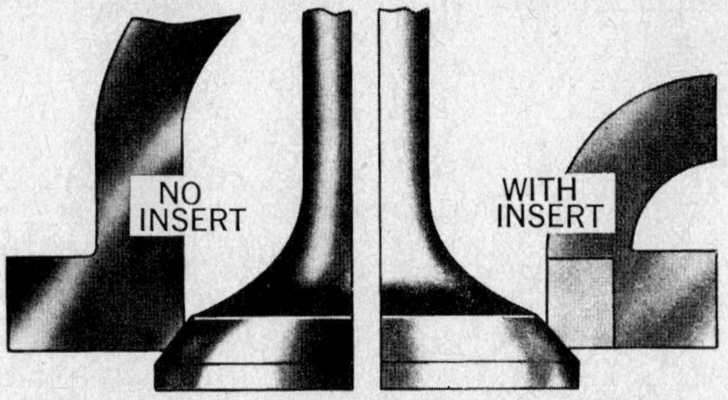

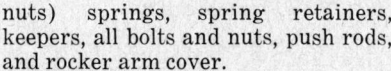

Correct seat installation and grinding in relation to the valve head (© International Harvester Co.)

Seat installation tool—typical (© International Harvester Co.)

nuts) springs, spring retainers, keepers, all bolts and nuts, push rods, and rocker arm cover.

Check the Cylinder Head for Warpage

Place a straight-edge across the gasket surface of the cylinder head. Using feeler gauges, determine the clearance at the center of the straight-edge. Measure across both diagonals, along the longitudinal centerline, and across the cylinder head at several points. If warpage exceeds .003″ in a 6″ span, or .006″ over the total length, the cylinder head must be resurfaced. *NOTE: If warpage exceeds the manufacturers maximum tolerance for material removal, the cylinder head must be replaced.* When milling the cylinder heads of V-type engines, the intake manifold mounting position is altered, and must be corrected by milling the manifold flange a proportionate amount.

Check the Valve Stem to Guide Clearance

Clean the valve stem with a solvent to remove all gum and varnish. Clean the valve guides with a solvent and/or a wire type expanding valve guide cleaner tool. Insert the proper valve into its guide and hold the valve head to the valve seat tightly. Mount a dial indicator on the spring side of the cylinder head so that the dial indicator foot is against the valve stem, protruding from the guide, at a 90° angle. Move the valve off its seat and measure the valve guide to stem clearance by moving the stem back and forth to actuate the dial indicator. Measure the valve stems using a micrometer and compare to specifications to determine if the valve stem or valve guide is responsible for the excessive wear clearance.

An alternate method of checking the valve stem to guide clearance is to mount a dial indicator on the combustion side of the cylinder head, with the foot of the indicator to contact the side of the valve head. The valve head is moved away from its seat a predetermined distance, either by a special collar tool, placed on the valve stem between the head of the valve and the guide, or by measuring the height of the valve head above the seat with the use of a scale. The valve head is moved back and forth to actuate the dial indicator. Measure the valve stems, using a micrometer, and compare to specifications. Determination of wear from either the valve guide or valve stem can be made.

Other types of measuring methods are available to the rebuilder. Go and No-Go gauge, Inside caliper type small hole gauges or shim stock can be used to determine the wear of the guides.

Careful inspection will detect bell-mouthing or elliptical wear of the guides, normally at the port end of the guide.

Replacing Valve Seat Inserts

Most exhaust and some intake valve seats are of the insert type and can be replaced if found to be loose, burned or cracked.

The valve seat insert can be removed by either pulling it from its counterbore with a puller, or by drilling a small hole into the seat insert on two sides and cracking it with a chisel. Care must be exercised to avoid drilling into the cylinder head. The insert counterbore in the cylinder head, should be machined prior to the insert installation, with special emphasis on having the bottom of the counterbore square to insure proper seating of the valve insert. Most inserts are supplied in standard, .015 in. and .030 in. oversizes.

After installation of the valve seat insert, grinding by a refacing machine should be made to insure the seat is angled to specification and in proper relationship to the valve guide.

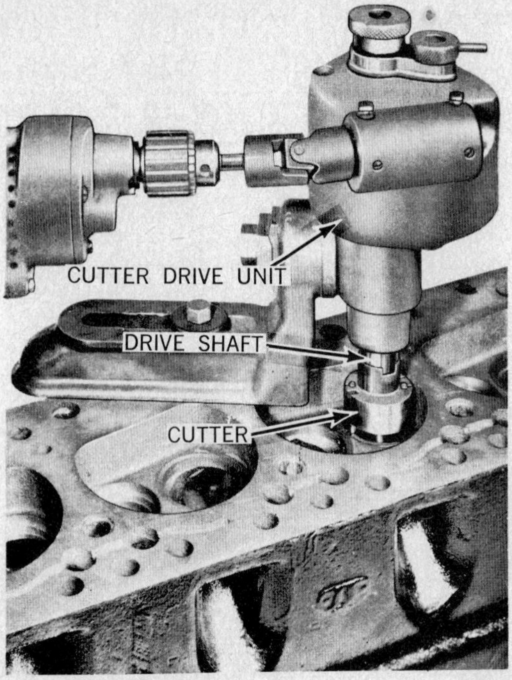

Machining cylinder head for valve seat insert installation —typical (© International Harvester Co.)

Replacing Valve Guides

Integral Guide Type

This type of cylinder heads do not have removable guides, but have the guide holes bored directly in the cylinder head material. When the clearances become excessive between the valve and guide, the guides can be reamed to an oversize deminsion, and oversize valves used. The "knurling" process may be used to recondition the inside of the guide surface, is the valve to guide clearance is not excessive.

A machining operation can be used to drill out the non-replaceable guide holes and have a standard type guide installed. This operation should be done by an automotive machine shop, equipped with the special boring machine.

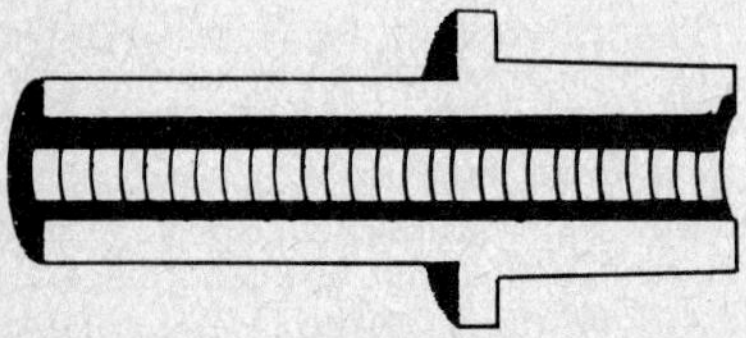

Cross section of knurled valve guide

Replaceable Guide Type

Depending on the type of cylinder head, valve guides may be pressed, hammered, or shrunk in. In cases where the guides are shrunk into the head, replacement should be left to an equipped machine shop. In other cases, the guides are replaced as follows: Press or tap the valve guides out of the head using a stepped drift. Determine the height above the boss

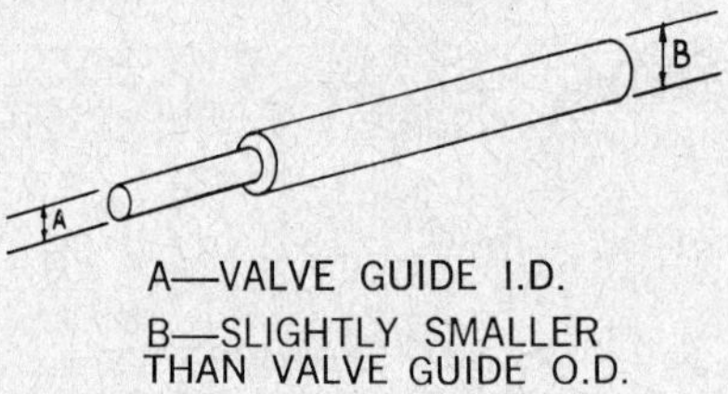

Valve guide removing tool

that the guide must extend, and obtain a stack of washers, their I.D. similar to the guide's O.D., of that height. Place the stack of washers on the guide, and insert the guide into the boss.

NOTE: Valve guides are often tapered or beveled for installation.

Using the stepped installation tool (see illustration), press or tap the guides into position. Ream the guides according to the size of the valve stem.

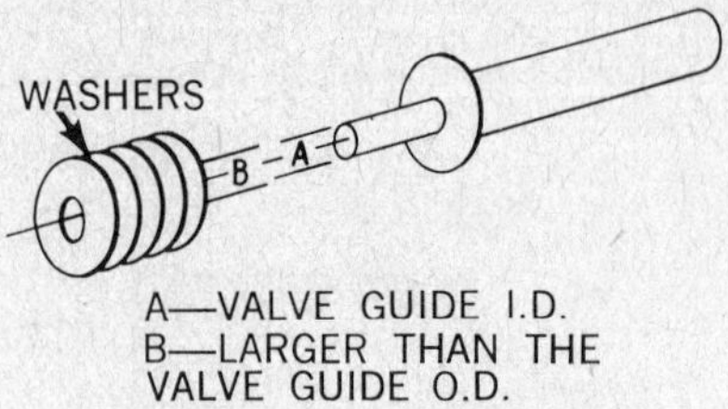

Valve guide installation tool with washer stack

Resurfacing (grinding) the Valve Face

Using a valve grinder, resurface the valves according to specifications.

CAUTION: Valve face angle is not always identical to valve seat angle.

A minimum margin of 3/64" should remain after grinding the valve. The valve stem tip should also be squared and resurfaced, by placing the stem in the V-block of the grinder, and turning it while pressing lightly against the grinding wheel.

Resurfacing the Valve Seats Using a Grinder

Select a pilot of the correct size, and a coarse stone of the correct seat angle. Lubricate the pilot if necessary, and install the tool in the valve guide. Move the stone on and off the seat at approximately two cycles per

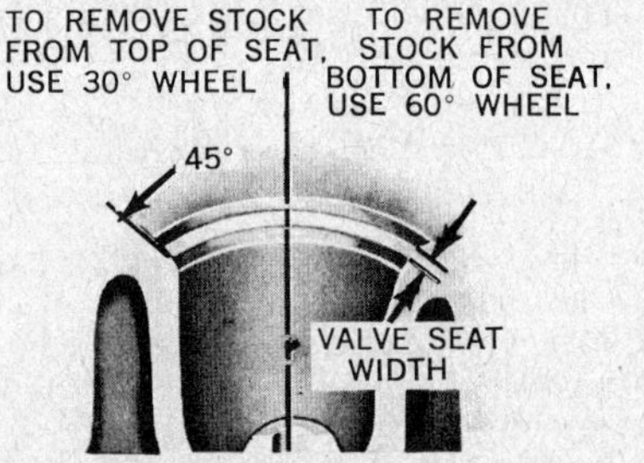

Centering and narrowing valve seat with correction stone (© Ford Motor Co.)

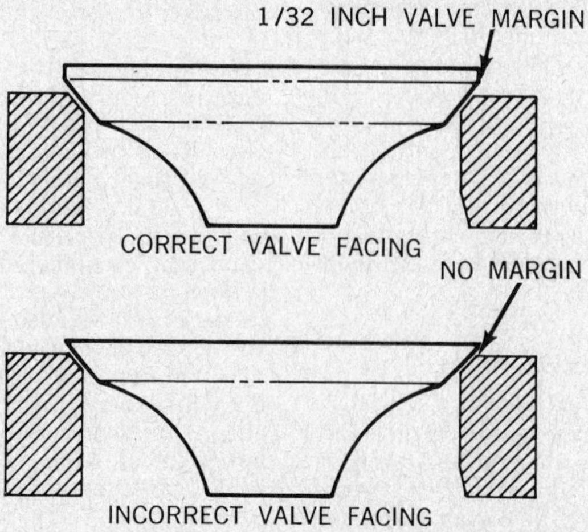

Correct and incorrect grinding of the valve face with proper margin indicated (© American Motors Corp.)

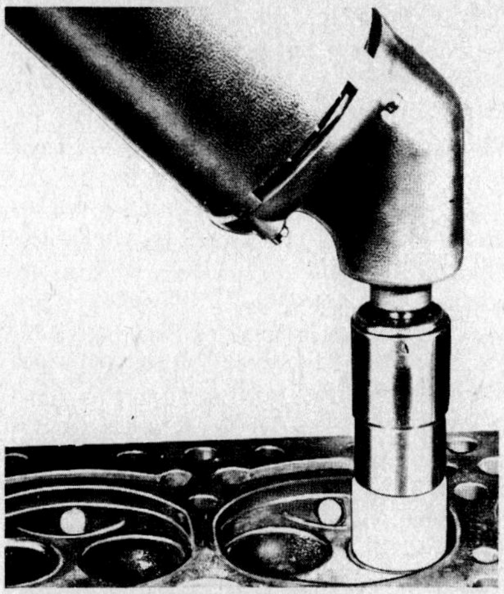

Grinding valve seats
(© International Harvester Co.)

second, until all flaws are removed from the seat. Install a fine stone, and finish the seat. Center and narrow the seat using correction stones. Intake seat width—1/16 to 5/64 in. Exhaust seat width—3/64 to 1/16 in.

Checking the Valve Seat Concentricity

a. Coat the valve face with Prussian blue dye, install the valve, and

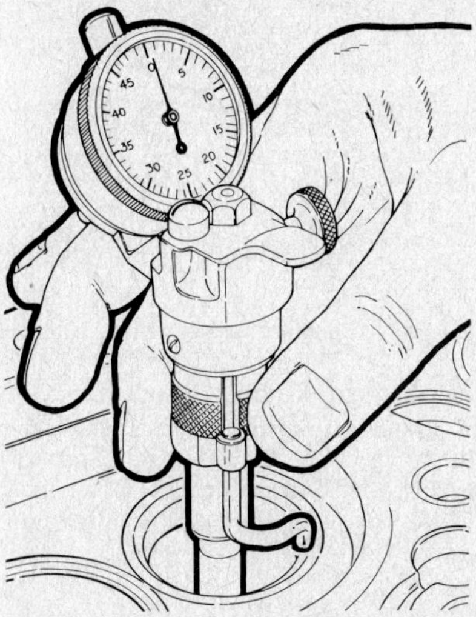

Checking valve seat run-out with a dial gauge (© International Harvester Co.)

rotate it on the valve seat. If the entire seat becomes coated, and the valve is known to be concentric, the seat is concentric.

b. Install a dial gauge pilot into the guide, and rest the arm on the valve seat. Zero the gauge, and rotate the arm around the seat. Run-out should not exceed .002″.

Lapping the Valves

NOTE: Valve lapping is done to ensure efficient sealing of resurfaced valves and seats. Valve lapping alone is not recommended for use as a resurfacing procedure.

a. Invert the cylinder head, lightly lubricate the valve stems, and install the valves in the head as numbered.

Hand lapping the valve to the seat

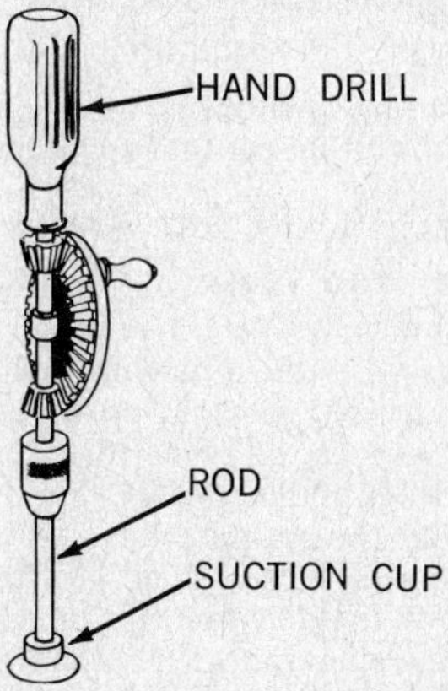

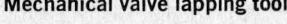

Mechanical valve lapping tool

Coat valve seats with fine grinding compound, and attack the lapping tool suction cup to a valve head.

NOTE: Moisten the suction cup.

Rotate the tool between the palms, changing position and lifting the tool often to prevent grooving. Lap the valve until a smooth, polished seat is evident. Remove the valve and tool, and rinse away all traces of grinding compound.

b. Fasten a suction cup to a piece of drill rod, and mount the rod in a hand drill. Proceed as above, using the hand drill as a lapping tool.

CAUTION: Due to the higher speeds involved when using the hand drill, care must be exercised to avoid grooving the seat.

Lift the tool and change direction of rotation often.

NOTE: Many manufacturers do not recommend the lapping of valves to the seats after each has been reground. However, for the rebuilder to be certain a perfect seal exists between the valve and the seat, lapping is suggested.

Check the Valve Springs

Test the spring pressure at the installed and compressed (installed height minus valve lift) height using a valve spring tester. Springs used on small displacement engines (up to 3 liters) should be ± 1 lb. of all other springs in either position. A tolerance of ± 5 lbs. is permissible on larger engines.

Install Valve Stem Seals

Due to the pressure differential that exists at the ends of the intake valve guides (atmospheric pressure above, manifold vacuum below), oil is drawn through the valve guides into the intake port. This has been alleviated somewhat since the addition of positive crankcase ventilation, which lowers the pressure above the guides. Several types of valve stem seals are available to reduce blow-by.

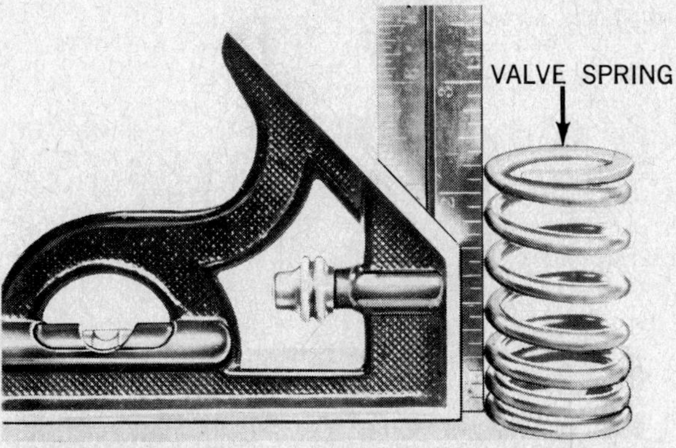

Checking valve spring for free length and squareness
(© Chrysler Corp.)

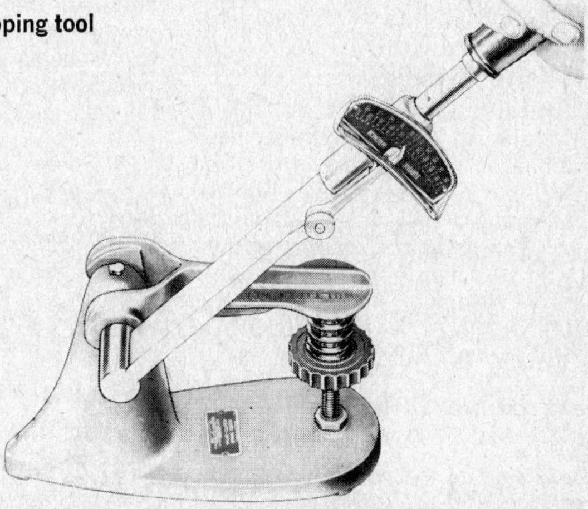

Testing valve spring compressed height (© Chrysler Corp.)

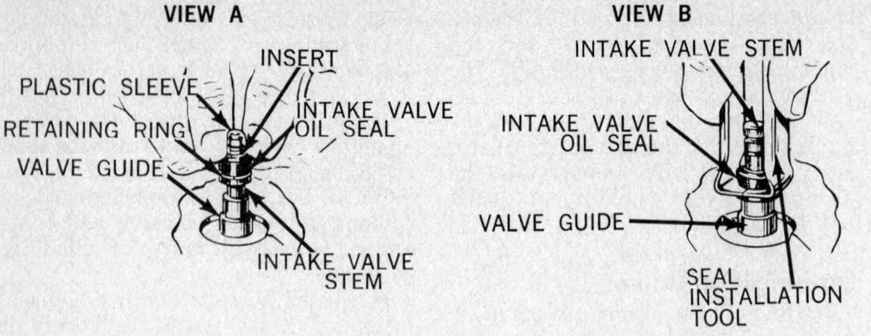

Installing intake valve oil seals, Perfect Circle type, using plastic sleeve and special installation tool (© General Motors Corp.)

Certain seals simply slip over the stem and guide boss, while others require that the boss be machined. Recently, Teflon guide seals have become popular. Consult a parts supplier or machinist concerning availability and suggested usages.

NOTE: When installing seals, ensure that a small amount of oil is able to pass the seal to lubricate the valve guides; otherwise, excessive wear may result.

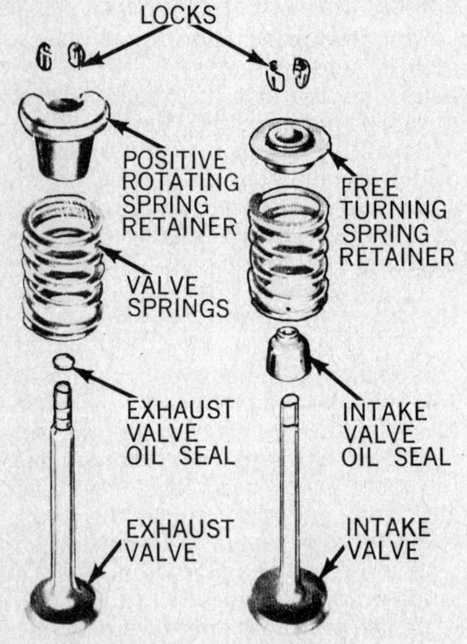

Oil seal installation on exhaust and intake valves, using "umbrella" and "O" ring type seals (© Ford Motor Co.)

Install the Valves

Lubricate the valve stems, and install the valves in the cylinder head as numbered. Lubricate and position the seals (if used, see above) and the valve springs. Install the spring retainers, compress the springs, and insert the keys using needlenose pliers or a tool designed for this purpose.

NOTE: Retain the keys with wheel bearing grease during installation.

Check Valve Spring Installed Height

Measure the distance between the spring pad and the lower edge of the spring retainer, and compare to specifications. If the installed height is incorrect, add shim washers between the spring pad and the spring.

CAUTION: Use only washers designed for this purpose.

Measuring valve spring assembled height with caliper (© Ford Motor Co.)

Inspect the Rocker Arms, Balls, Studs, and Nuts

Visually inspect the rocker arms, balls, studs, and nuts for cracks, galling, burning, scoring, or wear. If all parts are intact, liberally lubricate the rocker arms and balls, and install them on the cylinder head. If wear is noted on a rocker arm at the point of valve contact, grind it smooth and square, removing as little material as possible. Replace the rocker arm if excessively worn. If a rocker stud shows signs of wear, it must be replaced. If a rocker nut shows stress cracks, replace it.

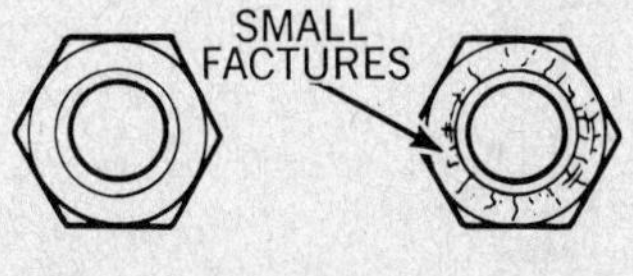

Stress cracks in rocker arm nut (© Ford Motor Co.)

Inspect the Rocker Shaft(s) and Rocker Arms

Remove rocker arms, springs and washers from rocker shaft.

NOTE: Lay out parts in the order in which they are removed.

Inspect rocker arms for pitting or wear on the valve contact point, or excessive bushing wear. Bushings need only be replaced if wear is excessive, because the rocker arm normally contacts the shaft at one point only. Grind the valve contact point of rocker arm smooth if necessary, removing as little material as possible. If excessive material must be removed to smooth and square the arm, it should be replaced. Clean out all oil holes and passages in rocker shaft. If shaft is grooved or worn, replace it. Lubricate and assemble the rocker shaft.

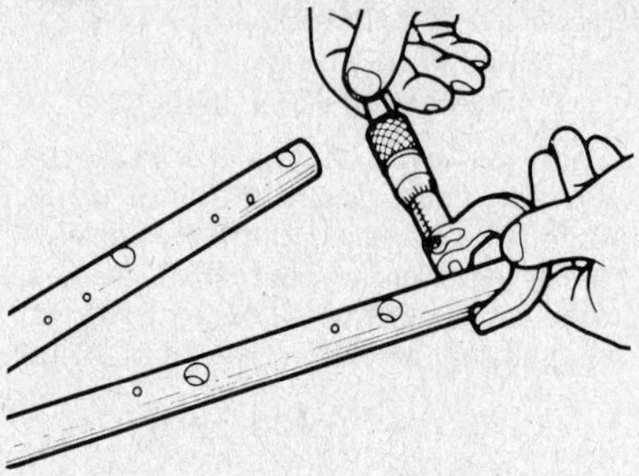

Checking rocker arm shaft O.D. with micrometer (© Chrysler Corp.)

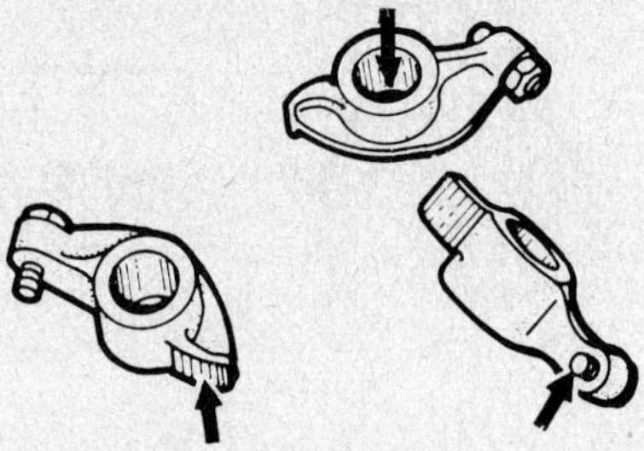

Checking rocker arms

Replacing Rocker Studs

In order to remove a threaded stud, lock two nuts on the stud, and unscrew the stud using the lower nut. Coat the lower threads of the new stud with Loctite, and install.

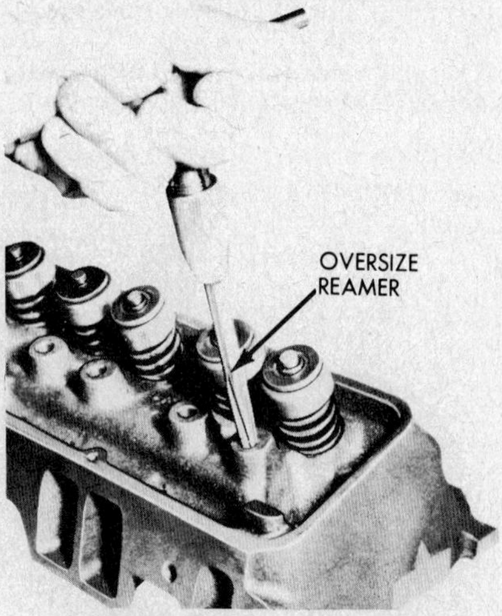

Reaming the stud bore for oversize rocker studs (© General Motors Corp.)

Removing a pressed in rocker stud
(© General Motors Corp.)

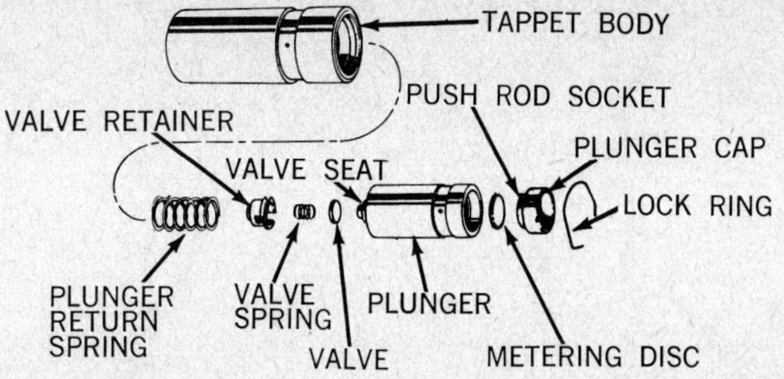

Exploded view of hydraulic lifter—typical (© American Motors Corp.)

Two alternative methods are available for replacing pressed in studs. Remove the damaged stud using a stack of washers and a nut or use a stud puller. In the first, the boss is reamed .005-006" oversize, and an oversize stud pressed in. Control the stud extension over the boss using washers, in the same manner as valve guides. Before installing the stud, coat it with white lead and grease. To retain the stud more positively, drill a hole through the stud and boss, and install a roll pin. In the second method, the boss is tapped, and a threaded stud installed. Retain the stud using a locking compound.

Inspect the Pushrods

Remove the pushrods, and, if hollow, clean out the oil passages using fine wire. Roll each pushrod over a piece of clean glass. If a distinct clicking sound is heard as the pushrod rolls, the rod is bent, and must be replaced.

The length of all pushrods must be equal. Measure the length of the pushrods, compare to specifications, and replace as necessary.

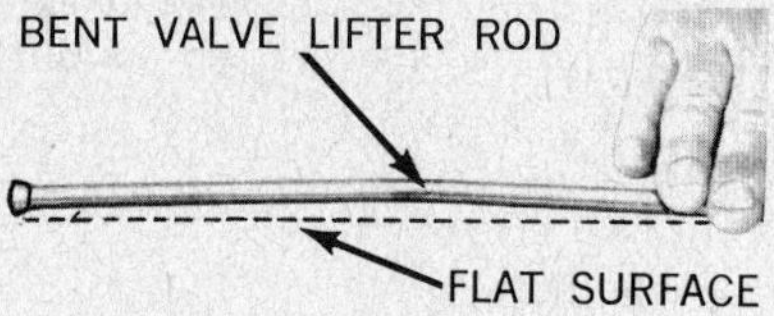

Checking for bent push rod
(© International Harvester Co.)

Inspect the Valve Lifters, (Mechanical or Hydraulic)

Remove lifters from their bores, and remove gum and varnish, using solvent. Clean walls of lifter bores. Check lifters for concave wear as illustrated. If face is worn concave, replace lifter, and carefully inspect the camshaft. Lightly lubricate lifter and insert it into its bore. If play is excessive, an oversize lifter must be installed (where possible). Consult a machinist concerning feasibility. If play is satisfactory, remove, lubricate, and reinstall the lifter.

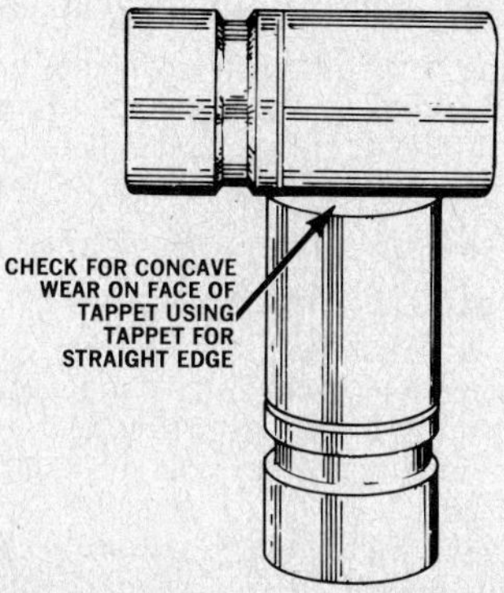

Checking the tappet for concave wear on its base, using second tappet for a straight edge (© American Motors Co.)

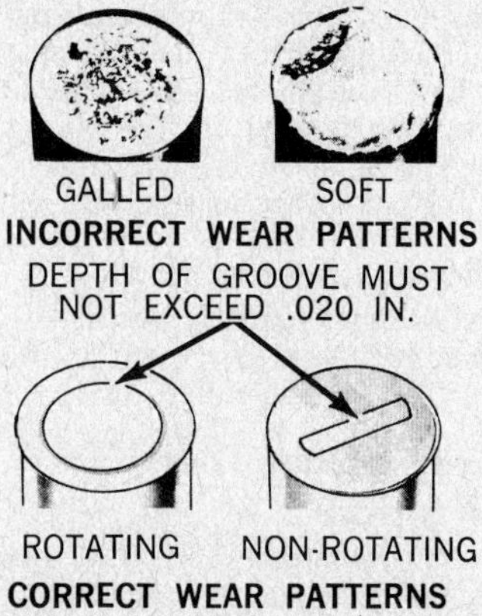

Wear patterns on base of lifter bodies
(© General Motors Corp.)

Testing Hydraulic Lifter Leak Down Rate

Special testers are available for the checking of the hydraulic lifter leak down rate. Special instructions accompanying the testers should be followed by the rebuilder. If the tester is not available, the following alternate method can be used.

Submerge lifter in a container of kerosene. Chuck a used pushrod or its equivalent into a drill press. Position container of kerosene so pushrod acts on the lifter plunger. Pump lifter with the drill press, until resistance increases. Pump several more times to bleed any air out of lifter. Apply very firm, constant pressure to the lifter, and observe rate at which fluid bleeds out of lifter. If the fluid bleeds very quickly (less than 15 seconds), lifter is defective. If the time exceeds 60 seconds, lifter is sticking. In either case, recondition or replace lifter. If lifter is operating properly (leak down time 15-60 seconds), lubricate and install it.

Hydraulic lifter leakdown tester—typical
(© Jeep Corp.)

Engine Block Reconditioning

Marking Main and Correcting Rod Caps

Using a punch, mark the corresponding main bearing caps and saddles according to position (i.e., one punch on the front main cap and saddle, two on the second, three on the third, etc.). Using number stamps, identify the corresponding connecting

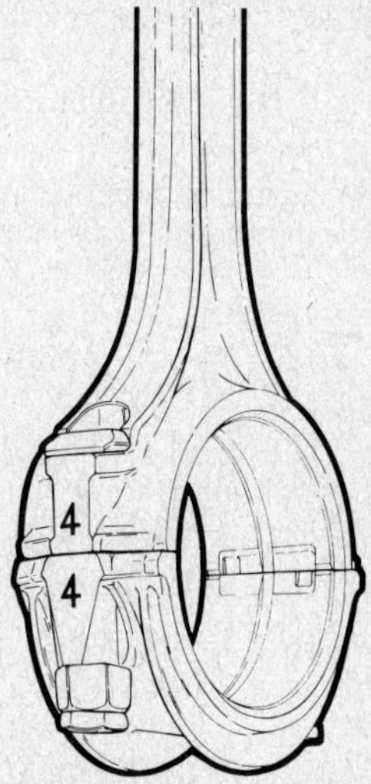

Connecting rod matched to cylinder with a number stamp

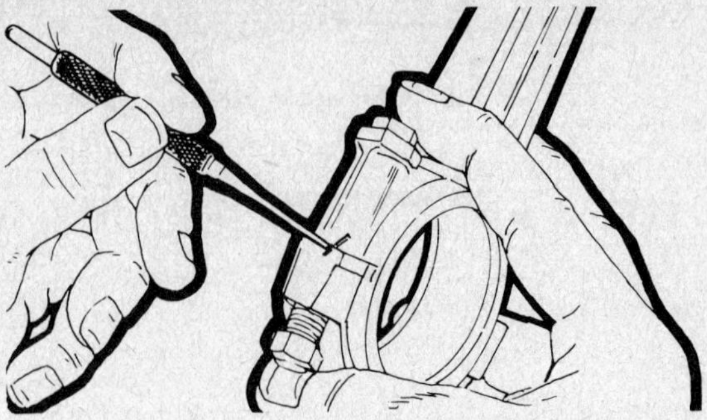

Scribe connecting rod matchmarks

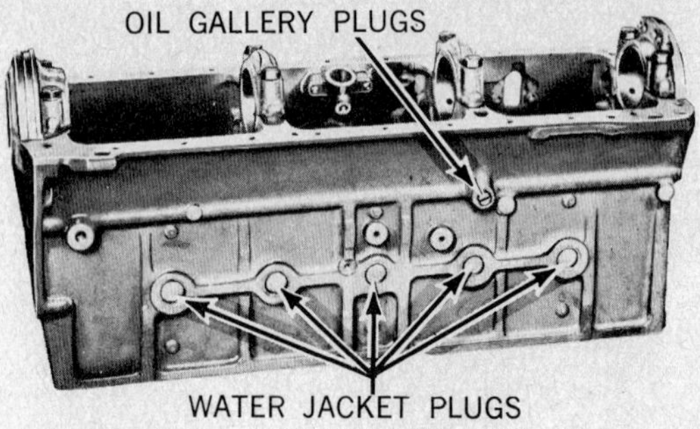

Location of oil galley and water jacket plugs—6 cylinder engine—typical (© General Motors Corp.)

rods and caps, according to cylinder (if no numbers are present). Remove the main and connecting rod caps, and place sleeves of plastic tubing over the connecting rod bolts, to protect the journals as the crankshaft is removed.

Remove the Ridge

In order to facilitate removal of the piston and connecting rod, the ridge at the top of the cylinder (unworn area; see illustration) must be removed. Place the piston at the bottom of the bore, and cover it with a rag. Cut the ridge away using a ridge reamer, exercising extreme care to avoid cutting too deeply. Remove the rag, and remove cuttings that remain at the piston.

CAUTION: If the ridge is not removed, and new rings are installed, damage to rings will result.

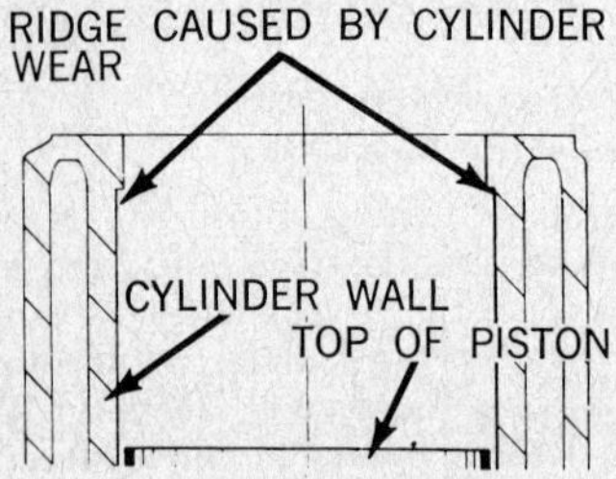

Cylinder bore ridge

Removing the Piston and Connecting Rod

Invert the engine, and push the pistons and connecting rods out of the cylinders. If necessary, tap the connecting rod boss with a wooden hammer handle, to force the piston out.

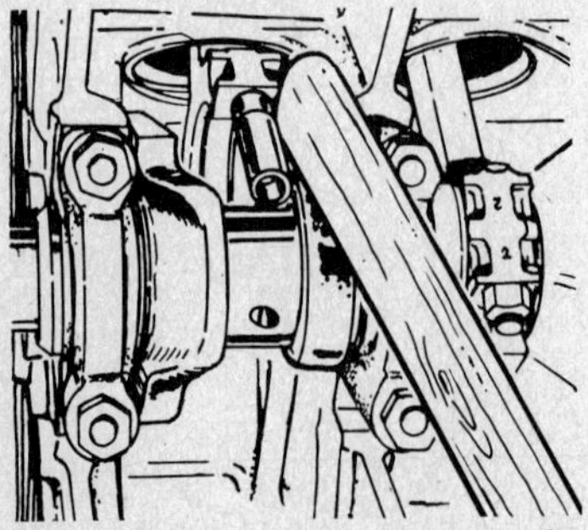

Removing the piston and connecting rod assembly

CAUTION: Do not attempt to force the piston past the uncut cylinder ridge.

Inspect the Timing Chain

Visually inspect the timing chain for broken or loose links, and replace the chain if any are found. If the chain will flex sideways, it must be replaced.

NOTE: If the original timing chain is to be reused, install it in its original position.

Remove the Oil Gallery Plugs

Threaded plugs should be removed using an appropriate (usually square) wrench. To remove soft, pressed in plugs, drill a hole in the plug, and thread in a sheet metal screw. Pull the plug out by the screw using pliers.

Removing Freeze Plugs

Drill a hole in the center of the freeze plugs, and pry them out using a drift or special puller.

Check the Bore Diameter and Surface

Visually inspect the cylinder bores for roughness, scoring, or scuffing. If evident, the cylinder bore must be bored or honed oversize to eliminate imperfections, and the smallest possible oversize piston used. The new pistons should be given to the machinist with the block, so that the cylinders can be bored or honed exactly to the piston size (plus clearance). If no flaws are evident, measure the bore diameter using a telescope gauge and micrometer, or dial gauge, parallel

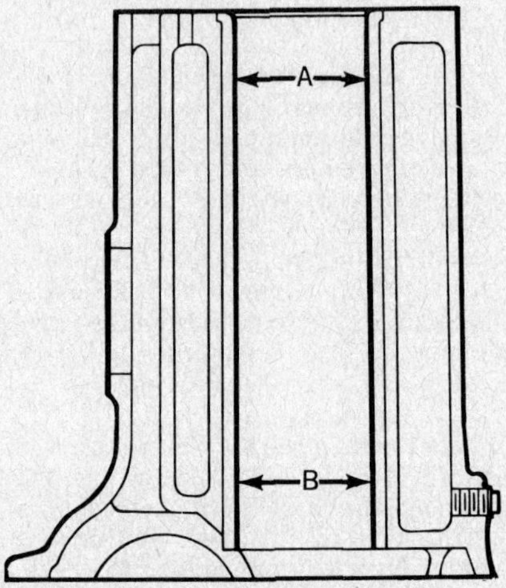

Checking points for cylinder bore taper measurement. Taper is difference between measurement A and B (© International Harvester Co.)

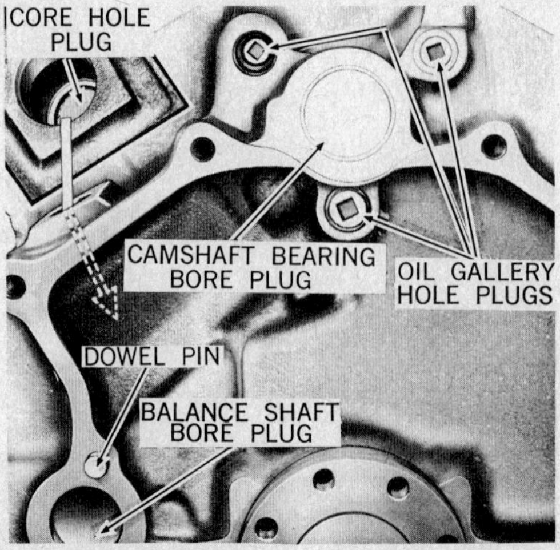

Location of oil gallery plugs, core plugs and camshaft bearing bore plug—V8 engine (some engines may be equipped with a balance shaft) (© General Motors Corp.)

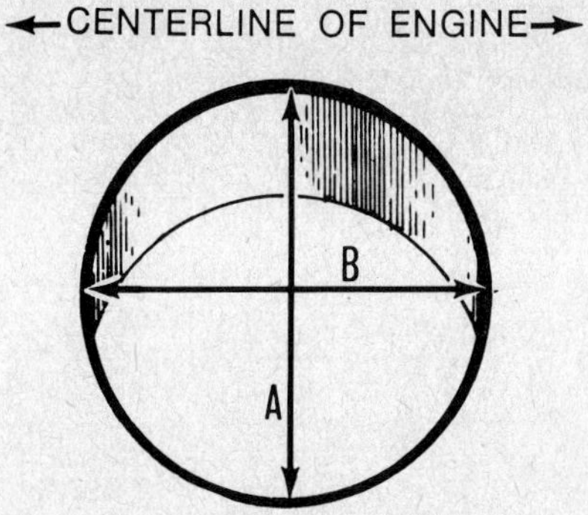

Checking points for cylinder bore out-of-round measurement. Out-of-round is difference between measurement A and B (© International Harvester Co.)

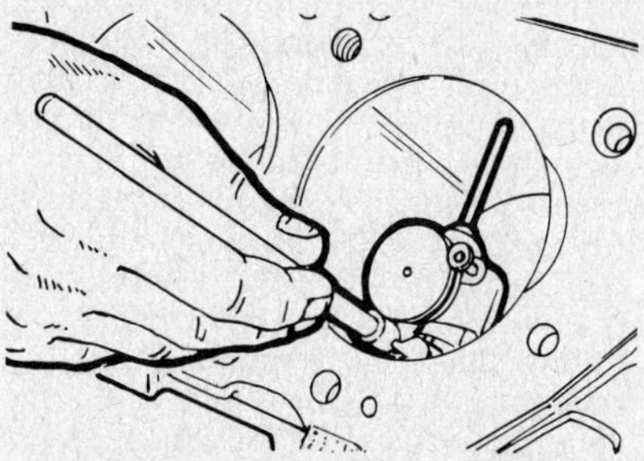

Checking cylinder bore taper and out-of-round using dial indicator cylinder bore gauge (© International Harvester Co.)

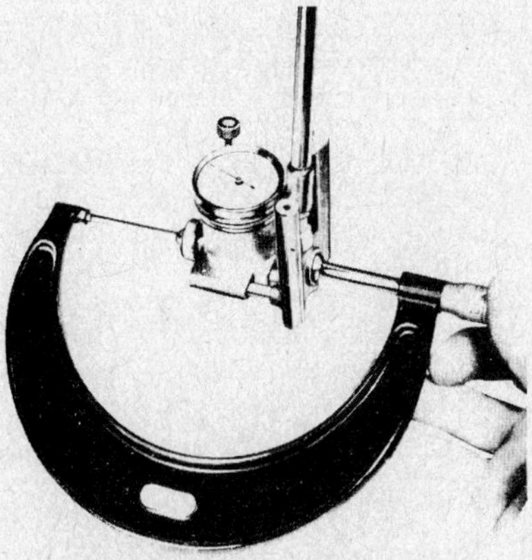

Measuring cylinder gauge to determine bore size (© General Motors Corp.)

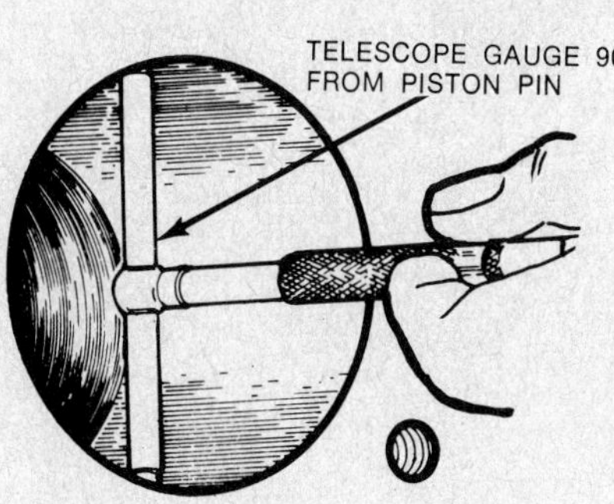

Measuring cylinder bore with telescope gauge (© General Motors Corp.)

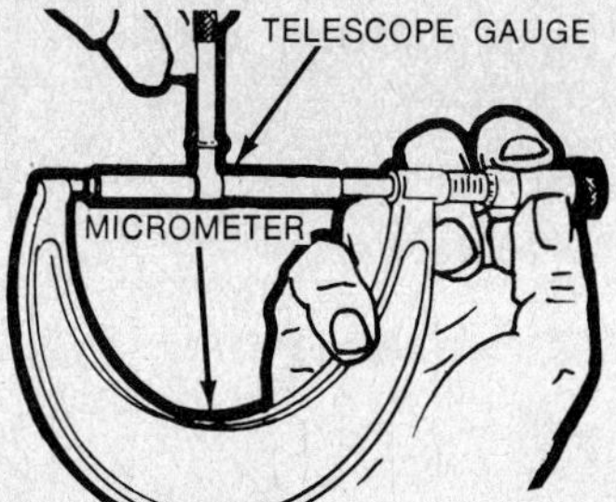

Measuring telescope gauge to determine bore size (© General Motors Corp.)

and perpendicular to the engine centerline, at the top (below the ridge) and bottom of the bore. Subtract the bottom measurements from the top to determine taper, and the parallel to the centerline measurements from the perpendicular measurements to determine eccentricity. If the measurements are not within specifications, the cylinder must be bored or honed, and an oversize piston installed. If the measurements are within specifications the cylinder may be used as is, with only finish honing.

Cylinder Sleeve Liners

Various engines are fitted with dry type cylinder liners at the time of manufacture. This type of liner can be replaced with the use of special pulling tools at the time of engine overhaul.

When the cylinder bore is part of the block assembly and if only one or two cylinder bores are damaged, sleeves can be installed in the damaged bores to avoid reboring all cylinders to an oversize condition.

The services of a competent automotive machine shop should be used for the boring of the cylinders and the installation of the liners.

Cylinder reboring machine (© International Harvester Co.)

Cylinder honing tool (© International Harvester Co.)

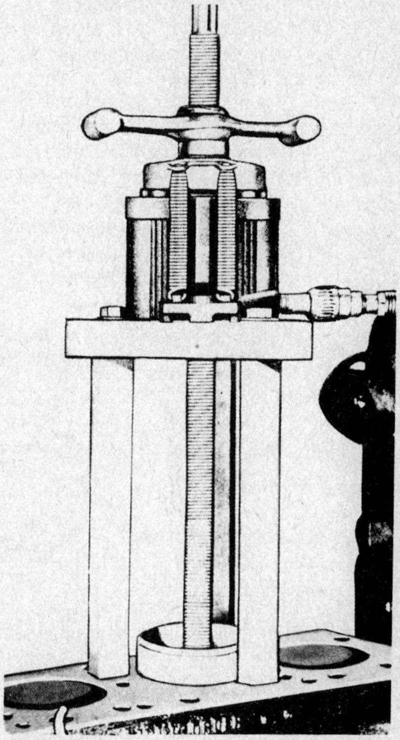

Removing cylinder sleeve with the use of hydraulic tool (© International Harvester Co.)

Check the Cylinder Block Bearing Alignment

Remove the upper bearing inserts. Place a straightedge in the bearing saddles along the centerline of the

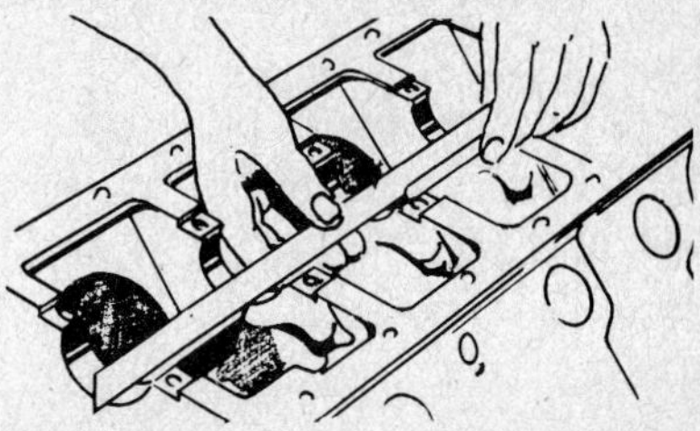

Checking main bearing saddle alignment

crankshaft. If clearance exists between the straightedge and the center saddle, the block must be alignbored.

Hot-tank the Block

Have the block hot-tanked to remove grease, corrosion, and scale from the water jackets.

NOTE: Consult the operator to determine whether the camshaft bearings will be damaged during the hot-tank process.

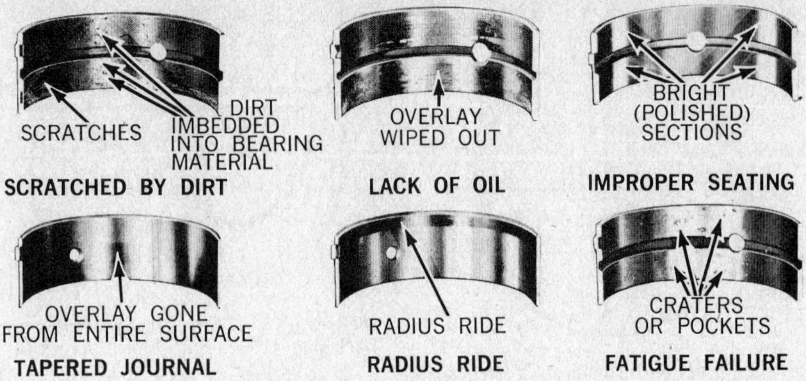

Causes of crankshaft bearing failures (© Ford Motor Co.)

Service the Crankshaft

Ensure that all oil holes and passages in the crankshaft are open and free of sludge. If necessary, have the crankshaft ground to the largest possible undersize.

Have the crankshaft Magnafluxed, to locate stress cracks. Consult a machinist concerning additional service procedures, such as surface hardening (e.g., Nitriding, Tuftriding) to improve wear characteristics, cross drilling and chamfering the oil holes to improve lubrication, and balancing.

Measure the main bearing journals at each end twice (90° apart) using a micrometer, to determine diameter, journal taper and eccentricity. If journals are within tolerances, reinstall bearing caps at their specified torque. Using a telescope gauge and micrometer, measure bearing I.D. parallel to piston axis and at 30° on each side of piston axis. Subtract journal O.D. from bearing I.D. to determine oil clearance. If crankshaft journals appear defective, or do not meet tolerances, there is no need to measure bearings; for the crankshaft will require grinding and/or undersize bearings will be required. If bearing appears defective, cause for failure should be determined prior to replacement. Refer to the failure diagnosis section to help you determine the cause of the failure.

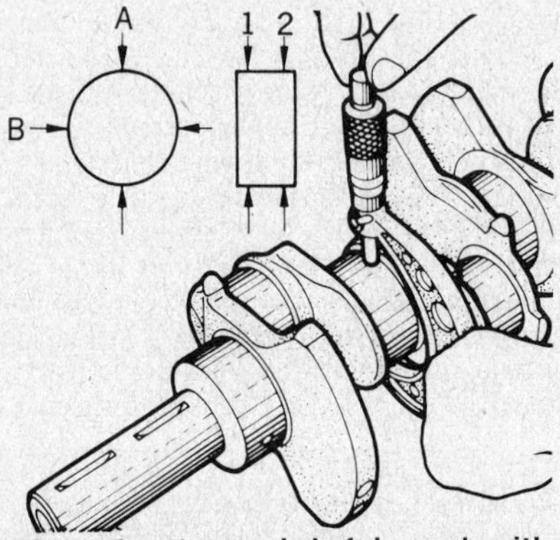

Measuring the crankshaft journals with a micrometer

Check the Block for Cracks

Visually inspect the block for cracks or chips. The most common locations are as follows:

- Adjacent to freeze plugs.
- Between the cylinders and water jackets.
- Adjacent to the main bearing saddles.
- At the extreme bottom of the cylinders.

Check only suspected cracks using spot check dye (see introduction). If a crack is located, consult a machinist concerning possible repairs.

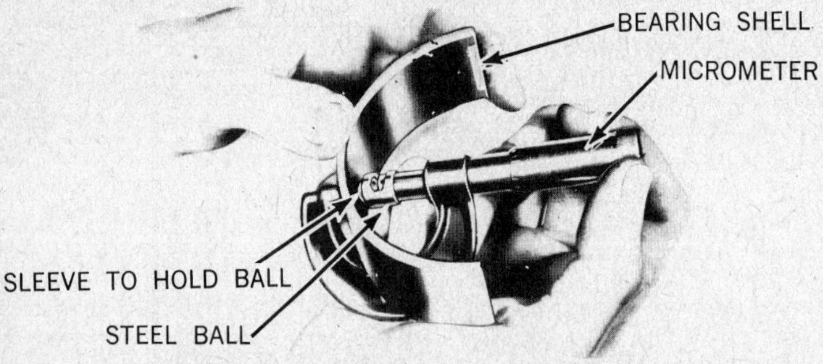

Measuring bearing insert thickness with special ball adapter on micrometer (© General Motors Corp.)

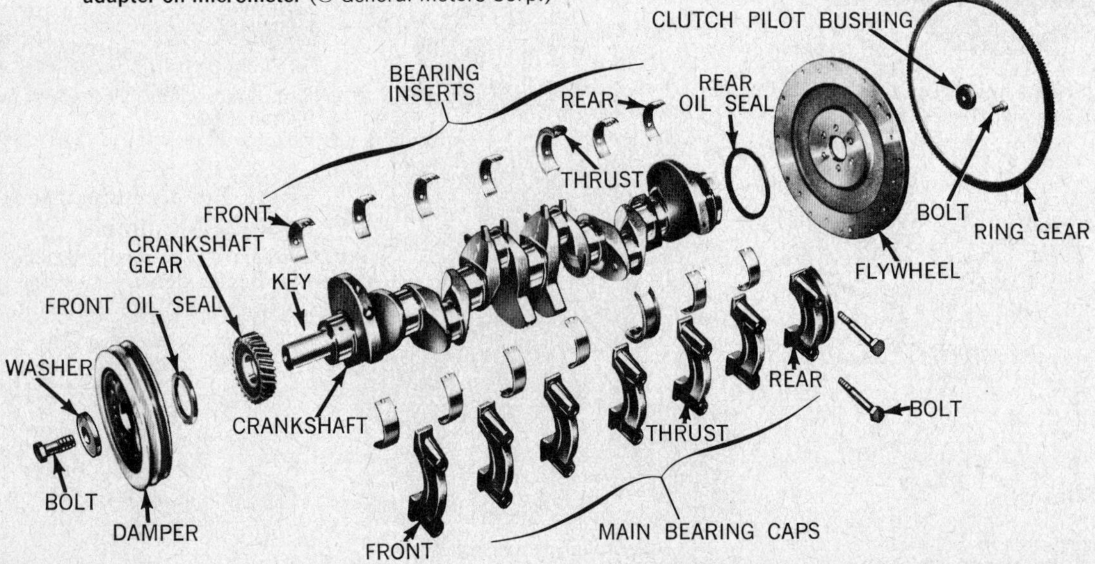

Crankshaft assembly—typical (© Ford Motor Co.)

Magnaflux the block to locate hidden cracks. If cracks are located, consult a machinist about feasibility of repair.

NOTE: Engine blocks that are porous or have sand holes, can be repaired with metallic plastic where coolant or oil pressure does not exist. Do not attempt to repair cracked blocks with the metallic plastic.

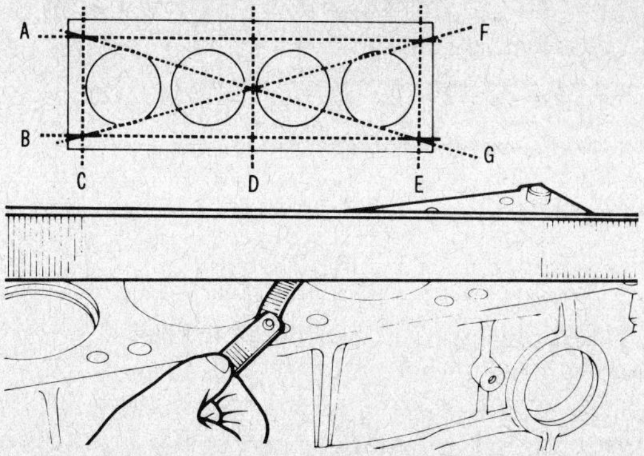

Checking the cylinder block for distortion (© Chrysler Corp.)

Check the Block Deck for Warpage

Using a straightedge and feeler gauges, check the block deck for warpage in the same manner that the cylinder head is checked (see Cylinder Head Reconditioning). If warpage exceeds specifications, have the deck resurfaced.

NOTE: In certain cases a specification for total material removal (Cylinder head and block deck) is provided. This specification must not be exceeded.

Check the Deck Height

The deck height is the distance from the crankshaft centerline to the block deck. To measure, invert the engine, and install the crankshaft, retaining it with the center main cap. Measure the distance from the crankshaft journal to the block deck, parallel to the cylinder centerline. Measure the diameter of the end (front and rear) main journals, parallel to the centerline of the cylinders, divide the diameter in half, and subtract it from the previous measurement. The results of the front and rear measurements should be identical. If the difference exceeds .005″, the deck height should be corrected.

NOTE: Block deck height and warpage should be corrected together.

Install the Oil Gallery Plugs and Freeze Plugs

Coat freeze plugs with sealer and tap into position using a piece of pipe, slightly smaller than the plug, as a driver. To ensure retention, stake the edges of the plugs. Coat threaded oil gallery plugs with sealer and install. Drive replacement soft plugs into block using a large drift as a driver.

Rather than reinstalling lead plugs, drill and tap the holes, and install threaded plugs, where possible.

Clean and Inspect the Camshaft

Degrease the camshaft, using solvent, and clean out all oil holes. Visually inspect cam lobes and bearing journals for excessive wear. If a lobe

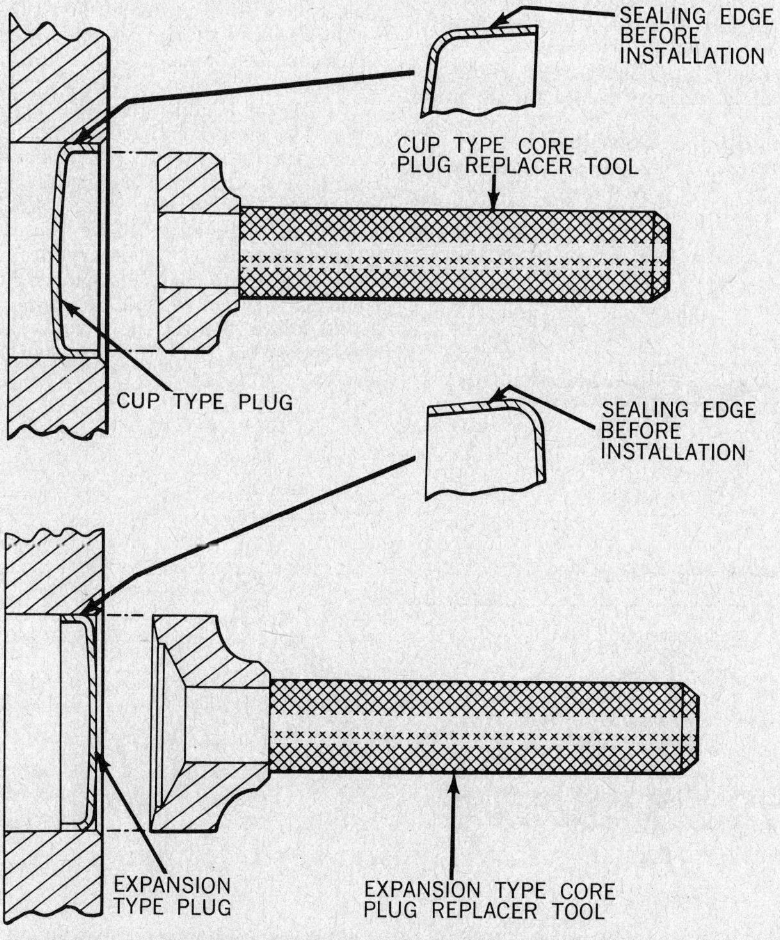

Installation of cup type and expansion type core plugs with special tools (© Ford Motor Co.)

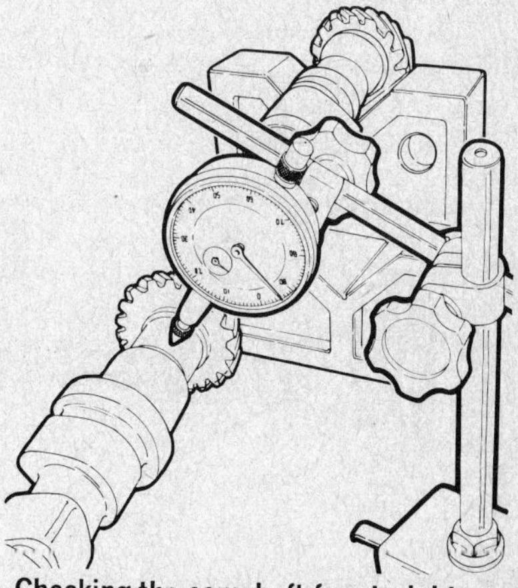
Checking the camshaft for straightness

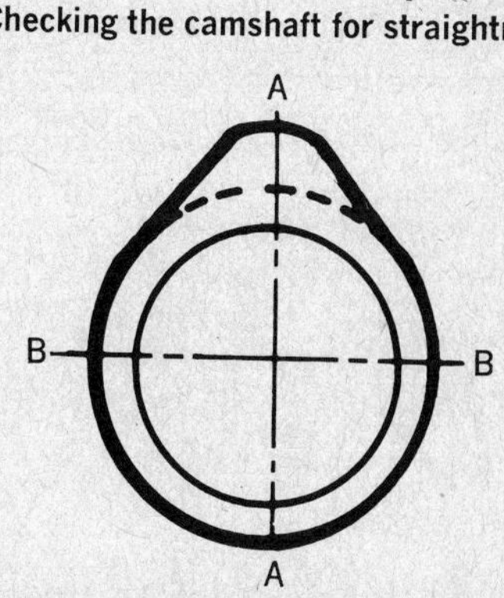

Camshaft lobe measurement—Lift is difference between A and B measurements

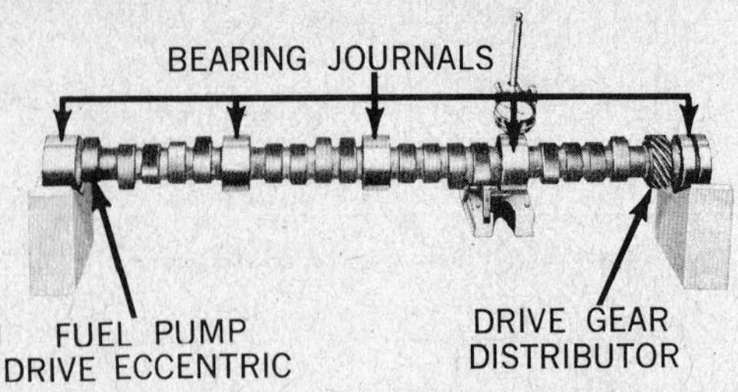

Checking camshaft alignment with Vee blocks and dial indicator (© General Motors Corp.)

Removing and installing cam bearings with special puller tool—typical (© Chrysler Corp.)

is questionable, check all lobes as indicated below. If a journal or lobe is worn, the camshaft must be reground or replaced.

NOTE: If a journal is worn, there is a good chance that the bushings are worn.

If lobes and journals appear intact, place the front and rear journals in V-blocks, and rest a dial indicator on the center journal. Rotate the camshaft to check straightness. If deviation exceeds .001″, replace the camshaft.

Check the camshaft lobes with a micrometer, by measuring the lobes from the nose to base and again at 90° (see illustration). The lift is determined by subtracting the second measurement from the first. If all exhaust lobes and all intake lobes are not identical with specs, the camshaft must be reground or replaced.

Replace the Camshaft Bearings

If excessive wear is indicated, or if the engine is being completely rebuilt, camshaft bearings should be replaced as follows: Drive the camshaft rear plug from the block. Assemble the removal puller with its shoulder on the bearing to be removed. Gradually tighten the puller nut until bearing is removed. Remove remaining bearings, leaving the front and rear for last. To remove front and rear bearings, reverse position of the tool, so as to pull the bearings in toward the center of the block. Leave the tool in this position, pilot the new front and rear bearings on the installer, and pull them into position. Return the tool to its original position and pull remaining bearings into position.

NOTE: Ensure that oil holes align when installing bearings.

Replace camshaft rear plug, and stake it into position to aid retention.

Install the Camshaft

Liberally lubricate the camshaft lobes and journals, and slide the camshaft into the block.

CAUTION: Exercise extreme care to avoid damaging the bearings when inserting the camshaft.

Be careful not to force the shaft towards the rear of the engine block as this can unseat the welch plugs in some engines. Install and tighten the camshaft thrust plate retaining bolts.

Check Camshaft End-Play

a. Using feeler gauges, determine whether the clearance between the camshaft boss (or gear) and backing plate is within specifications. Install shims behind the thrust plate, or reposition the camshaft gear and retest end-play.

b. Mount a dial indicator stand so that the stem of the dial indicator rests on the nose of the camshaft, parallel to the camshaft axis. Push the camshaft as far in as possible and zero the gauge. Move the camshaft outward to determine the amount of camshaft end-play. If the end-play is not within tolerance, install shims behind the thrust plate, or reposition the camshaft gear and retest.

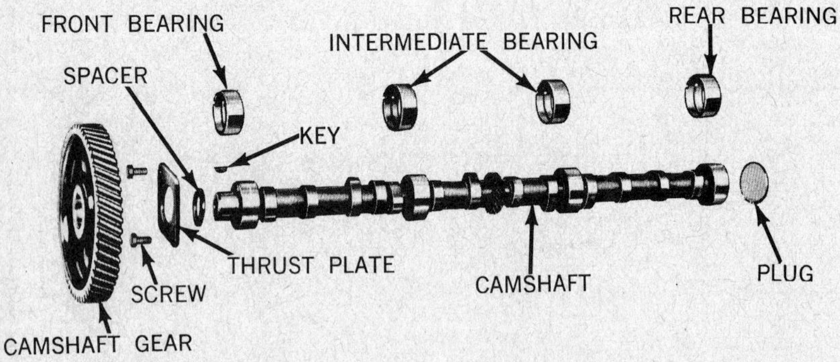

Gear driven camshaft assembly—typical (© Ford Motor Co.)

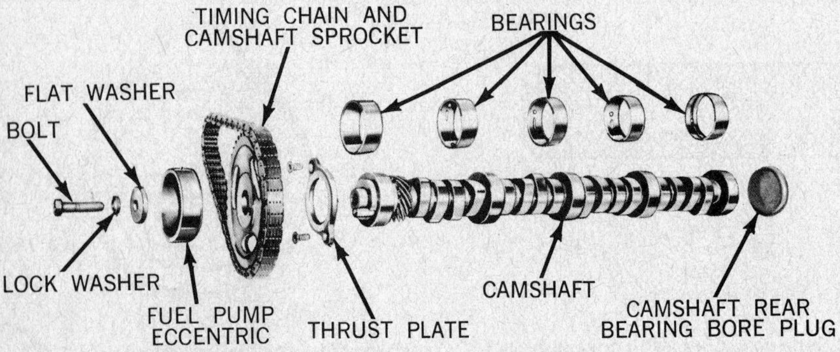

Chain driven camshaft assembly—typical (© Ford Motor Co.)

Checking clearance between timing gear and thrust plate with feeler gauge (© General Motors Corp.)

1. PUSH CAM TO REAR OF ENGINE
2. SET DIAL ON ZERO
3. PULL CAM FORWARD AND RELEASE

Checking camshaft end play with dial indicator (© Ford Motor Co.)

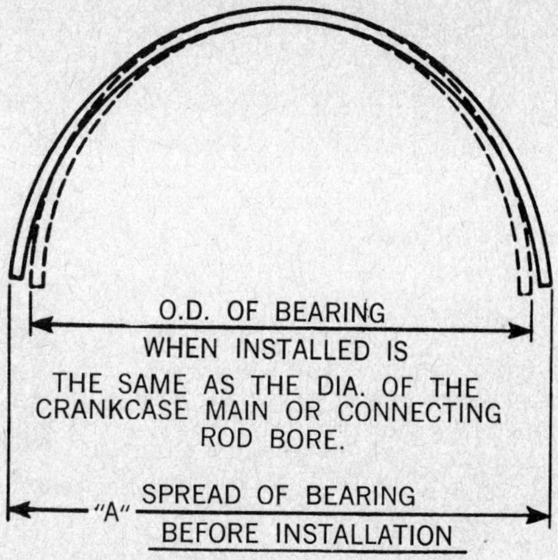
O.D. OF BEARING
WHEN INSTALLED IS
THE SAME AS THE DIA. OF THE CRANKCASE MAIN OR CONNECTING ROD BORE.
"A"
SPREAD OF BEARING
BEFORE INSTALLATION

Illustration of bearing insert spread (© International Harvester Co.)

Installing Bearing Inserts in Block or Connecting Rod Bores

The bearing inserts must fit tightly in the connecting rod or main bearing bores. The bearing inserts are made slightly larger than the actual diameter of the bore into which they are to be used. As the bearing caps are drawn tight, the bearing inserts are compressed, assuring a positive contact between the bearing insert and the bore. This is necessary to relieve the heat and to give the bearing insert a firm support for the loads placed on them during engine operation. This increased diameter of the bearing insert is referred to as bearing "crush". Because of this, the bearing caps, connecting rods and engine block must not be filed, lapped or reworked in any manner and all attaching bolts must be properly torqued.

Main and connecting rod bearing inserts are made with the width across the open and slightly larger than the main bearing or connecting rod bearing bore, so that the bearing inserts must be snapped or lightly forced into its seat. A spread of .025 in. is normally minimum on most engines, but will vary from engine to engine. (Some bearing kits will have instruction for the proper installation of the inserts).

To adjust the bearing spread of the thick wall bearings, such as main bearing inserts, place one end of the bearing insert on a wood block and strike the other end with a soft mallet to decrease the spread. To increase the spread, place the bearing insert ends on a wood block and strike the back of the insert with a soft mallet, squarely and lightly. The bearing spread on the thin walled bearing inserts, such as connecting rod bearing inserts, can be adjusted by hand, either spreading with the thumbs and

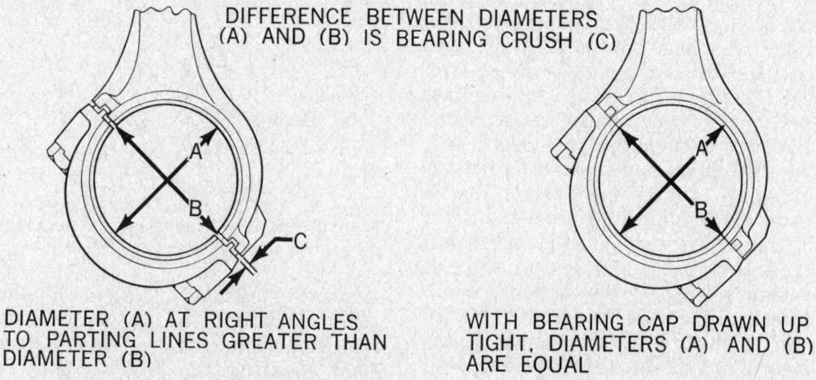
DIFFERENCE BETWEEN DIAMETERS (A) AND (B) IS BEARING CRUSH (C)
A
B
C
DIAMETER (A) AT RIGHT ANGLES TO PARTING LINES GREATER THAN DIAMETER (B)
WITH BEARING CAP DRAWN UP TIGHT, DIAMETERS (A) AND (B) ARE EQUAL

Bearing crush in connecting rod bore (© International Harvester Co.)

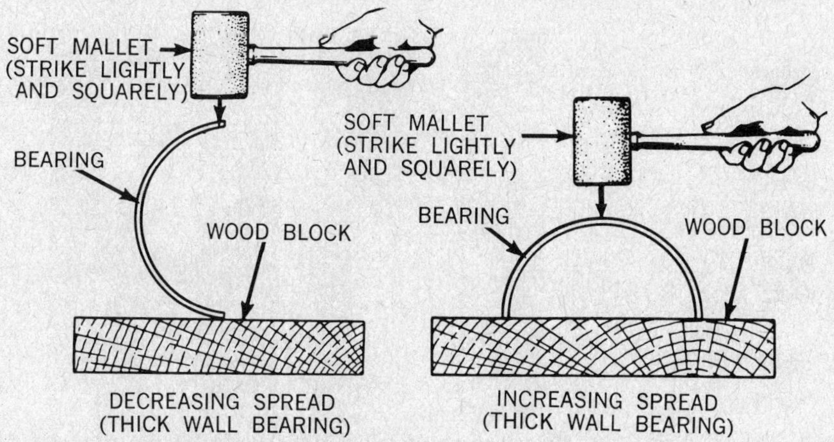
SOFT MALLET (STRIKE LIGHTLY AND SQUARELY)
BEARING
WOOD BLOCK
DECREASING SPREAD (THICK WALL BEARING)
SOFT MALLET (STRIKE LIGHTLY AND SQUARELY)
BEARING
WOOD BLOCK
INCREASING SPREAD (THICK WALL BEARING)

Increasing and decreasing thick walled bearing spread (© International Harvester Co.)

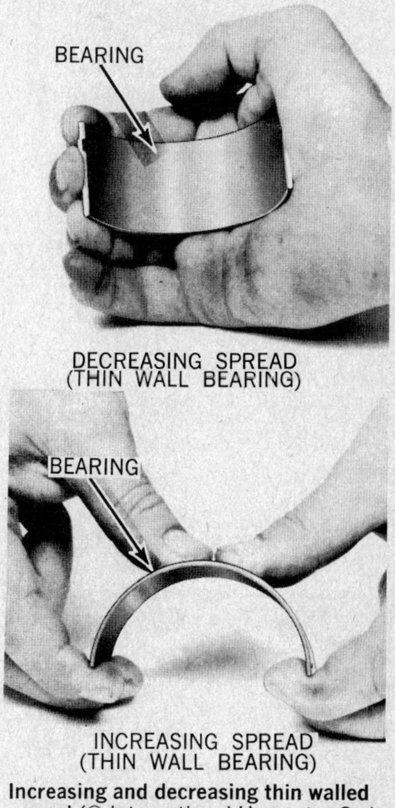
BEARING
DECREASING SPREAD (THIN WALL BEARING)
BEARING
INCREASING SPREAD (THIN WALL BEARING)

Increasing and decreasing thin walled spread (© International Harvester Co.)

forefingers of both hands, or by squeezing the bearing insert by the palm of the hand to decrease the spread. Check the spread distance often during the adjustment procedure.

Install the Rear Main Seal (Where Applicable)

Position the block with the bearing saddles facing upward. Lay the rear main seal in its groove and press it lightly into its seat. Place a piece of pipe the same diameter as the crankshaft journal into the saddle, and firmly seat the seal. Hold the pipe in position, and trim the ends of the seal flush if required.

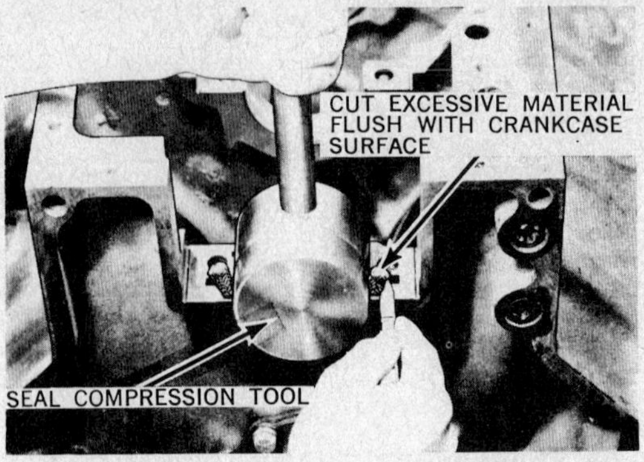

Seating rear main bearing seal—wix type (© International Harvester Co.)

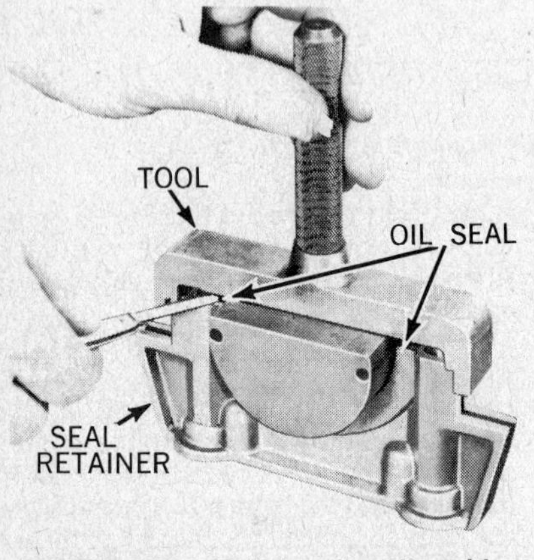

Installing rear main bearing oil seal in bearing cap (© Chrysler Corp.)

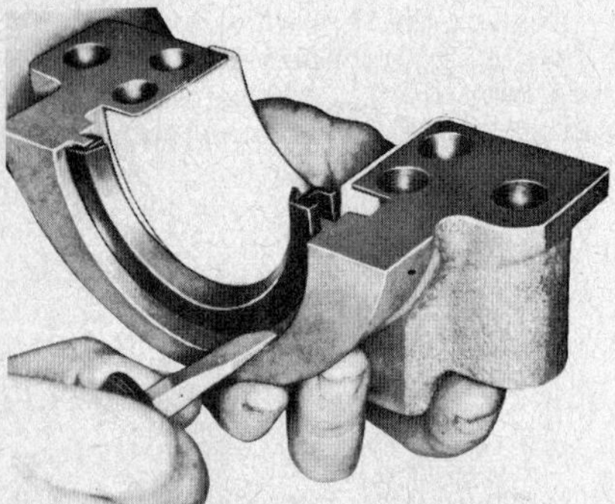

Removing rear main bearing oil seal from the bearing cap—performed seal type (© General Motors Corp.)

Install the Crankshaft

Thoroughly clean the main bearing saddles and caps. Place the upper halves of the bearing inserts on the saddles and press into position.

NOTE: Ensure that the oil holes align.

Press the corresponding bearing inserts into the main bearing caps. Lubricate the upper main bearings, and lay the crankshaft in position. Place a strip of Plastigage on each of the crankshaft journals, install the main caps, and torque to specifications. Remove the main caps, and compare the Plastigage to the scale on the Plastigage envelope. If clearances are within tolerances, remove the Plastigage, turn the crankshaft 90°, wipe off all oil and retest. If all clearances are correct, remove all Plastigage, thoroughly lubricate the main caps and bearing journals, and install the main caps. If clearances are not within tolerance, the upper bearing inserts may be removed, without removing the crankshaft, using a bearing roll out pin (see illustration). Roll in a bearing that will provide proper clearance, and retest. Torque all main caps, excluding the thrust bearing cap, to specifications. Tighten the thrust bearing cap finger tight. To properly align the thrust bearing, pry

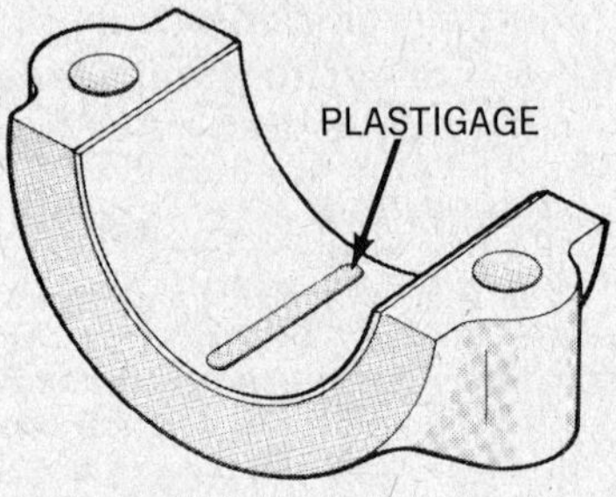

Laying Plastigage in cap for measurement (© Chrysler Corp.)

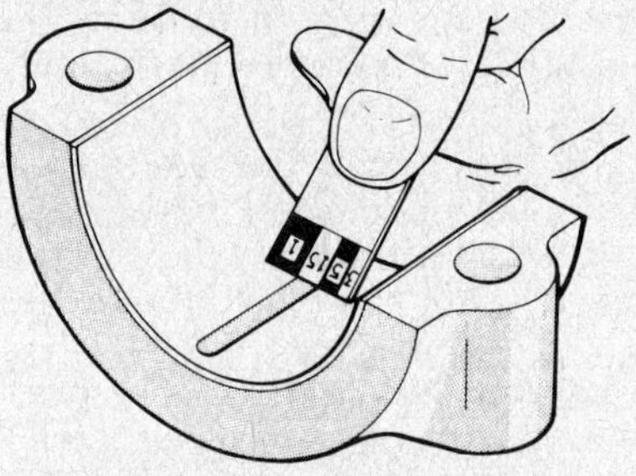

Measurement of Plastigage for bearing clearance (© Chrysler Corp.)

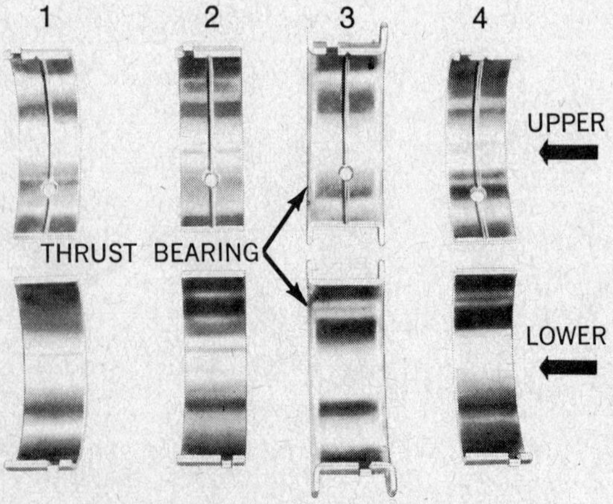

Main bearing insert identification—typical (© Ford Motor Co.)

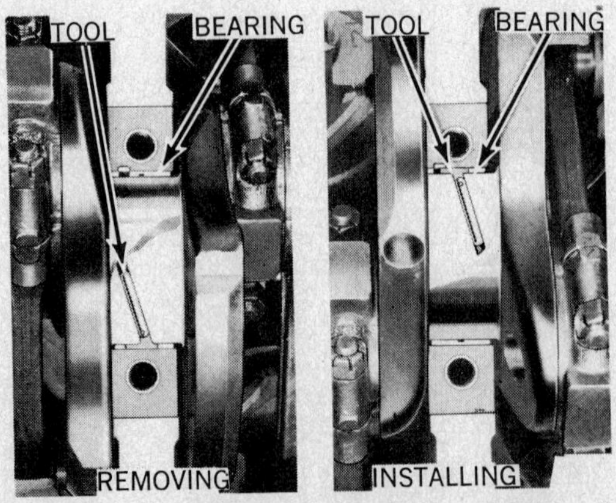

Removing and installing main bearing inserts with roll-out pins (cross section of crankshaft journal) (© Chrysler Corp.)

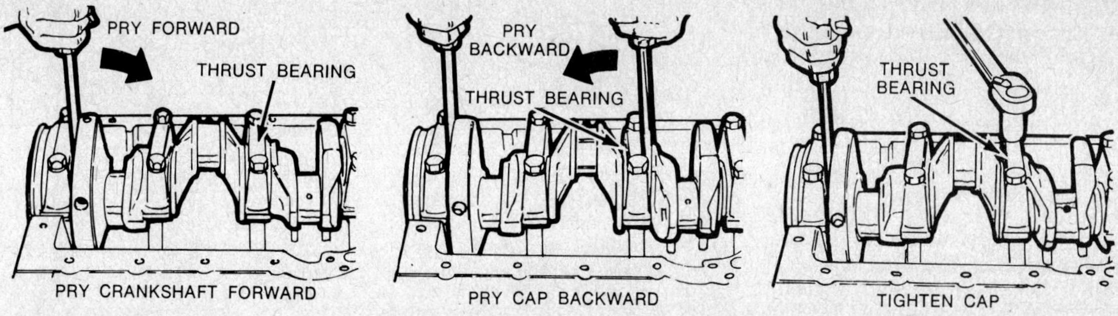

Alignment and torquing of thrust bearing (© Ford Motor Co.)

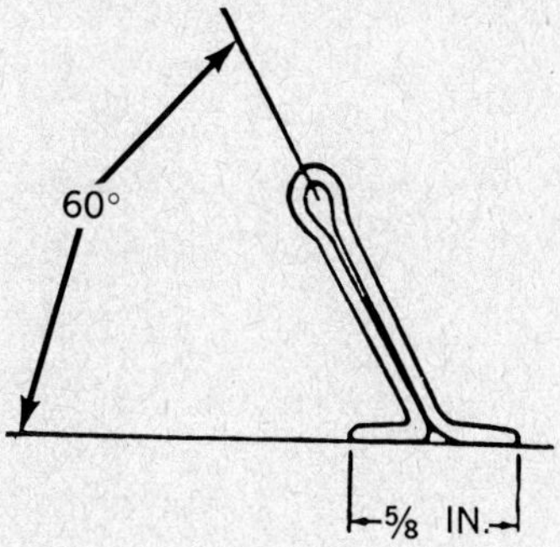

Bearing insert roll-out pin made from cotter pin

the crankshaft the extent of its axial travel several times, the last movement held toward the front of the engine, and torque the thrust bearing cap to specifications. Determine the crankshaft end-play (see below), and bring within tolerance with thrust washers.

Measure Crankshaft End-Play

Mount a dial indicator stand on the block, with the dial indicator stem resting on the crankshaft, parallel to the crankshaft axis. Pry the crankshaft rearward to the full extent of its travel, and zero the indicator. Pry the crankshaft forward and record crankshaft end-play.

NOTE: Crankshaft end-play also may be measured at the thrust bearing, using feeler gauges.

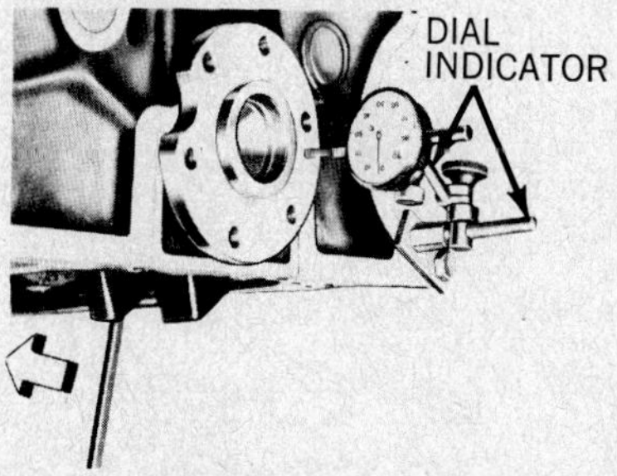

Checking crankshaft end play—typical (© Ford Motor Co.)

Clean and Inspect the Pistons and Connecting Rods

Using a ring expander, remove the rings from the piston. Remove the retaining rings (if so equipped) and remove piston pin.

CAUTION: If the piston pin must be pressed out, determine the proper method and use the proper tools; otherwise the piston will distort.

Clean the ring grooves using an appropriate tool, exercising care to avoid cutting too deeply. Thoroughly clean all carbon and varnish from the piston with solvent.

CAUTION: Do not use a wire brush or caustic solvent on pistons.

Inspect the pistons for scuffing, scoring, cracks, pitting, or excessive ring groove wear. If wear is evident, the piston must be replaced. Check the connecting rod length by measuring the rod from the inside of the large end to the inside of the small end using calipers (see illustration). All connecting rods should be equal length. Replace any rod that differs from the others in the engine.

Have the connecting rod alignment checked in an alignment fixture by a machinist. Replace any twisted or bent rods.

Magnaflux the connecting rods to locate stress cracks. If cracks are found, replace the connecting rod.

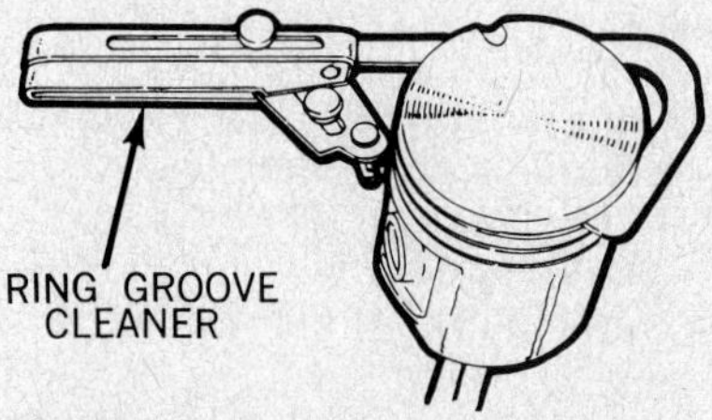

Clearing piston ring grooves—typical (© Ford Motor Co.)

Finish Hone the Cylinders

Chuck a flexible drive hone into a power drill, and insert it into the cylinder. Start the hone, and move it up and down in the cylinder at a rate which will produce approximately a 60° cross-hatch pattern (see illustration).

NOTE: Do not extend the hone below the cylinder bore.

After developing the pattern, remove the hone and recheck piston fit. Wash the cylinders with a detergent and water solution to remove abrasive dust, dry, and wipe several times with a rag soaked in engine oil.

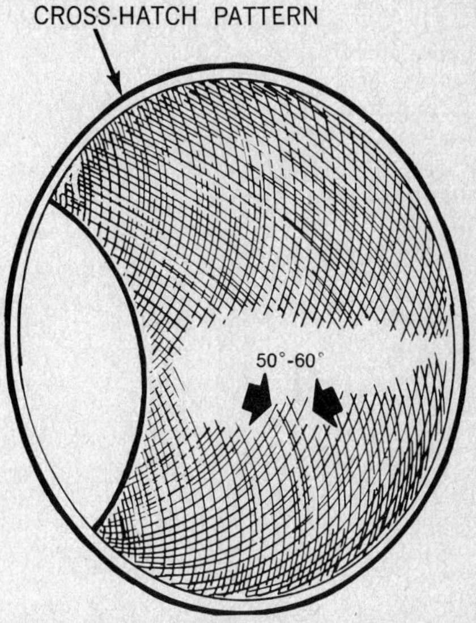

Cross hatching of cylinder bore by finish honing (© International Harvester Co.)

Check Piston Ring End-Gap

Compress the piston rings to be used in a cylinder, one at a time, into that cylinder, and press them approximately 1" below the deck with an inverted piston. Using feeler guages, measure the ring end-gap, and compare to specifications. Pull the ring out of the cylinder and file the ends with a fine file to obtain proper clearance.

CAUTION: If inadequate ring end-gap exists, ring breakage could result.

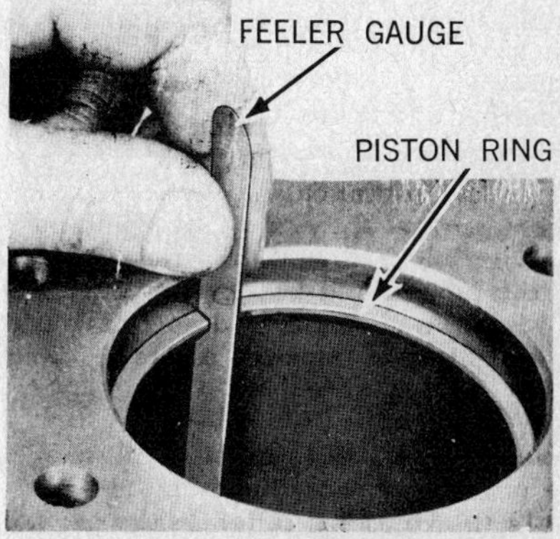

Checking ring gap in cylinder bore (© International Harvester Co.)

Fit the Pistons to the Cylinders

Using a telescope gauge and micrometer, or a dial gauge, measure the cylinder bore diameter perpendicular to the piston pin, 2½″ below the deck. Measure the piston perpendicular to its pin on the skirt. The difference between the two measurements is the piston clearance. If the clearance is within specifications or slightly below (after boring or honing), finish honing is all that is required. If the clearance is excessive, try to obtain a slightly larger piston to bring clearance within specifications. Where this is not possible, obtain the first oversize piston, and hone (or if necessary, bore) the cylinder to size.

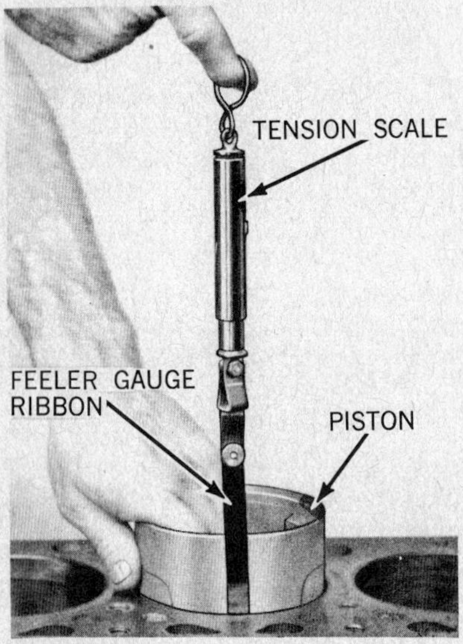

Checking piston to cylinder bore clearance
(© International Harvester Co.)

Assemble the Pistons and Connecting Rods

Inspect piston pin, connecting rod small end bushing, and piston bore for galling, scoring, or excessive wear. If evident, replace defective part(s). Measure the I.D. of the piston boss and connecting rod small end, and the O.D. of the piston pin. If within specifications, assemble piston pin and rod.

CAUTION: If piston pin must be pressed in, determine the proper method and use the proper tools; otherwise the piston will distort.

Install the lock rings; ensure that they seat properly. If the parts are not within specifications, determine the service method for the type of engine. In some cases, piston and pin are serviced as an assembly when either is defective. Others specify reaming the piston and connecting rods for an oversize pin. If the connecting rod bushing is worn, it may in many cases be replaced. Reaming the piston and replacing the rod bushing are machine shop operations.

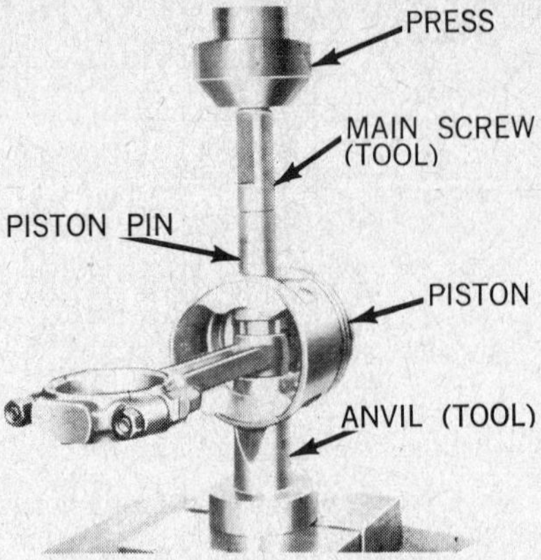

Removing or installing piston pin
(© Chrysler Corp.)

Install the Piston Rings

Inspect the ring grooves in the piston for excessive wear or taper. If necessary, recut the groove(s) for use with an overwidth ring or a standard ring and spacer. If the groove is worn uniformly, overwidth rings, or standard rings and spacers may be installed without recutting. Roll the outside of the ring around the groove to check for burrs or deposits. If any are found, remove with a fine file. Hold the ring in the groove, and measure side clearance. If necessary, correct as indicated above.

NOTE: Always install any additional spacers above the piston ring.

The ring groove must be deep enough to allow the ring to seat below the lands. In many cases, a "go-no-go" depth gauge will be provided with the piston rings. Shallow grooves may be corrected by recutting, while deep grooves require some type of filler or expander behind the piston. Consult the piston ring supplier concerning the suggested method. Install the rings on the piston, lowest ring first, using a ring expander.

NOTE: Position the ring markings as specified by the manufacturer.

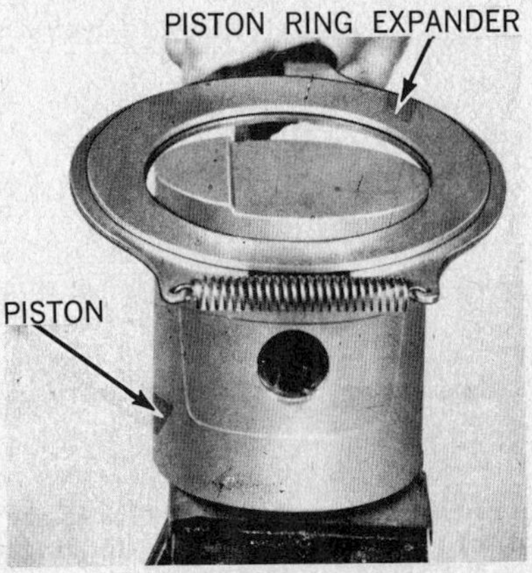

Installing rings on piston with the use of an expander tool
(© International Harvester Co.)

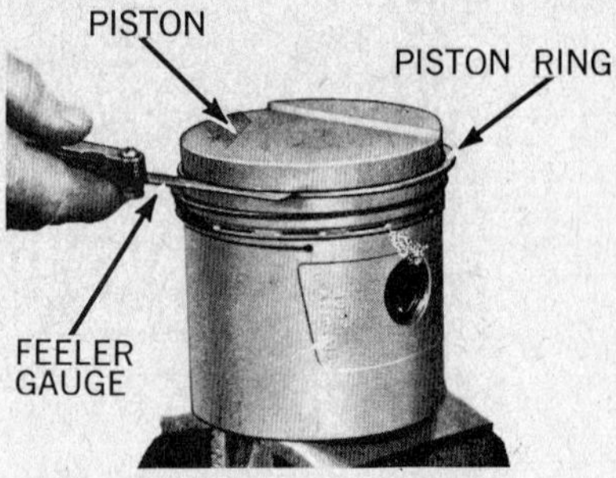

Checking ring to groove side clearance
(© International Harvester Co.)

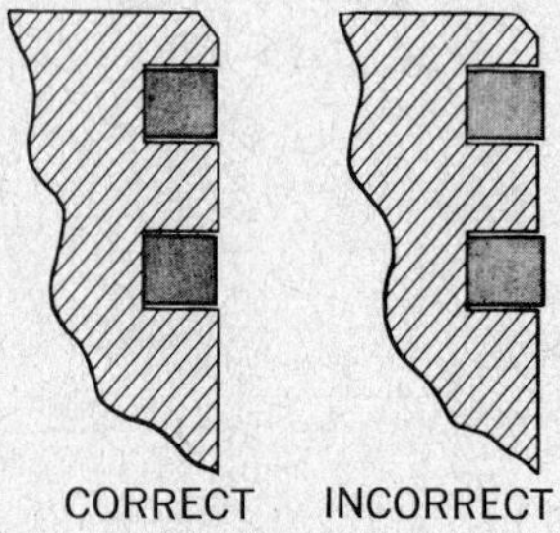

Ring groove depth

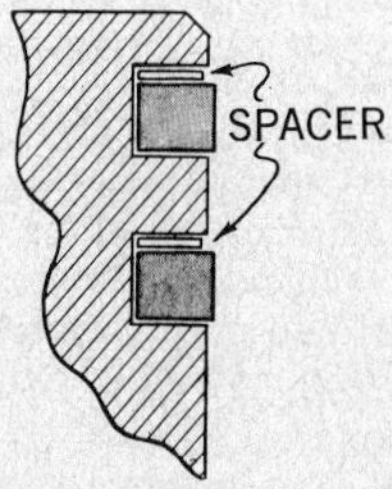

Correct ring spacer installation

Install the Pistons

Press the upper connecting rod bearing halves into the connecting rods, and the lower halves into the connecting rod caps. Position the piston ring gaps according to specifications (see car section), and lubricate the pistons. Install a ring compresser on the piston, and press two long (8″) pieces of plastic tubing over the rod bolts. Using the plastic tubes as a guide, press the piston into the bore

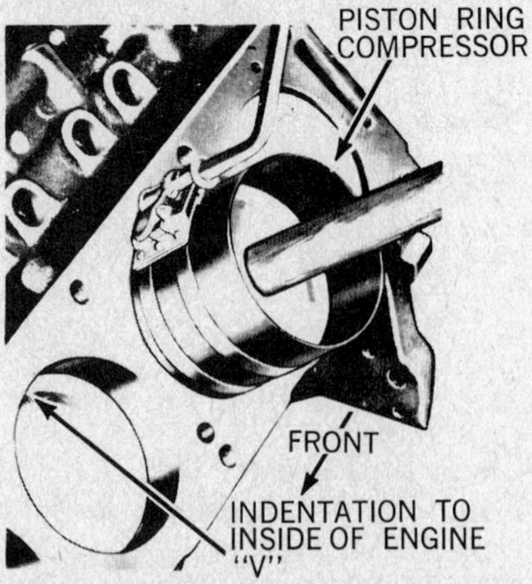

Installing piston assembly with straight sided ring compressor tool
(© Ford Motor Co.)

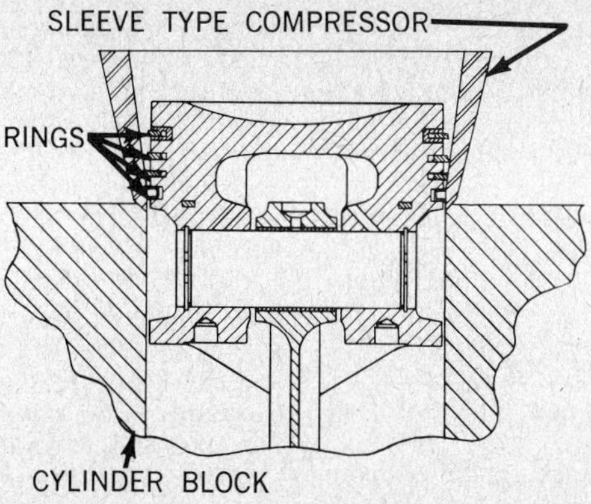

Installing piston assembly with a tapered sleeve type ring compressor tool (© General Motors Corp.)

and onto the crankshaft with a wooden hammer handle. After seating the rod on the crankshaft journal, remove the tubes and install the cap nuts finger tight. Install the remaining pistons in the same manner. Invert the engine and check the bearing clearance at two points (90° apart) on each journal with Plastigage.

NOTE: Do not turn the crankshaft with Plastigage installed.

If clearance is within tolerances, remove *all* Plastigage, thoroughly lubricate the journals, and torque the rod caps to specifications. If clearance is not within specifications, install different thickness bearing inserts and recheck.

CAUTION: Never shim or file the connecting rods or caps.

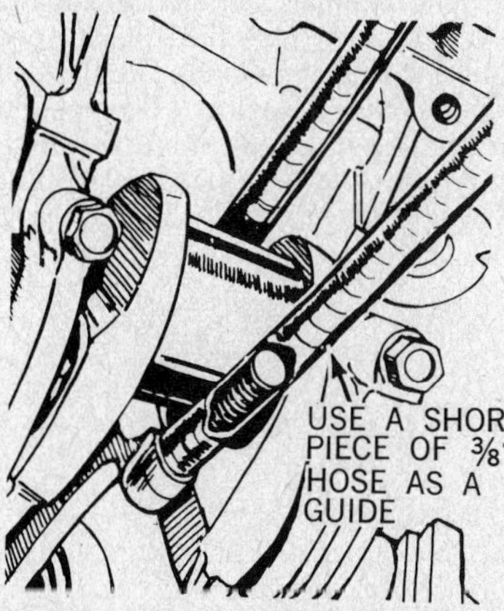

Tubing used as a guide during piston-connecting rod installation

Always install plastic tube sleeves over the rod bolts when the caps are not installed, to protect the crankshaft journals.

Check Connecting Rod Side Clearance

Determine the clearance between the sides of the connecting rods and the crankshaft, using feeler gauges. If clearance is below the minimum tolerance, the rod may be machined to provide adequate clearance. If clearance is excessive, substitute an unworn rod, and recheck. If clearance is still outside specifications, the crankshaft must be welded and reground, or replaced.

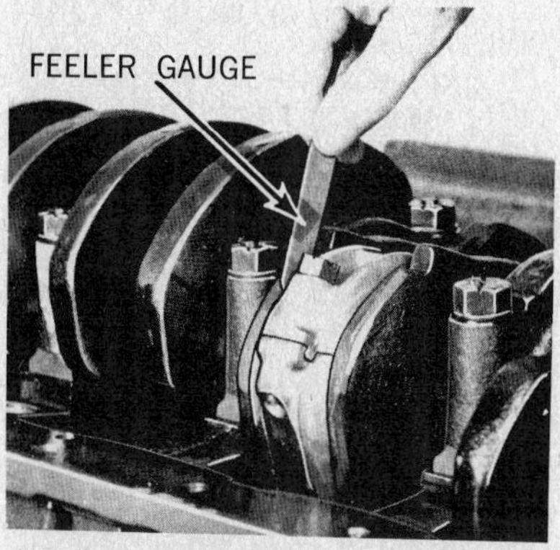

Checking connecting rod end clearance with feeler gauge blade
(© International Harvester Co.)

Inspect the Timing Chain Deflection

Different methods are used by the engine manufacturers to measure the timing chain deflection, and to determine the condition of the chain. Two such methods are as follows:

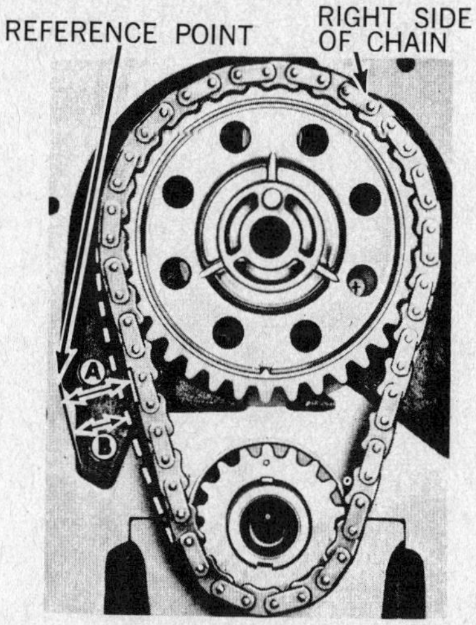

Checking timing chain deflection using point on engine block as reference point
(© Ford Motor Co.)

a. Rotate the crankshaft in a counterclockwise direction to remove the slack on the left side of the chain. Make a reference mark on the block and measure from the mark to the outside of the chain, halfway between the camshaft and crankshaft sprockets. Rotate the crankshaft in the opposite direction and remove the slack from the right side of the chain. Force the chain outward on the left side and measure from the original reference mark to the chain. The difference between the first and second measurements is the amount of chain deflection. The allowable deflection can be from 1/4 to 1/2 inch, depending upon the manufacturer.

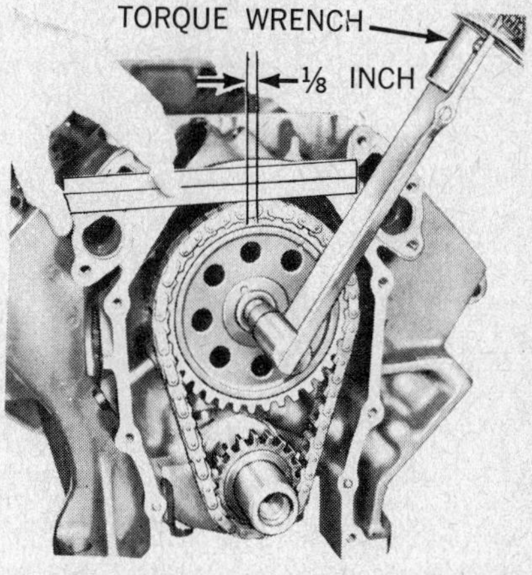

Using torque wrench to measure timing chain deflection (© Chrysler Corp.)

b. The second method of chain deflection measurement is to block the crankshaft to prevent movement. Using a torque wrench and socket on the camshaft sprocket bolt and placing a scale even with the edge of a chain link, apply 30 ft. lbs. (w/cylinder head on block) or 15 ft. lbs. (w/cylinder head off block) in the direction of engine rotation and obtain a reference point on the scale to link. Apply 30 ft. lbs. (w/cylinder head on block) or 15 ft. lbs. (w/cylinder head off block) in the opposite direction and measure the chain movement on the scale. The measurement should not exceed 1/8 inch.

Check Timing Gear Backlash and Runout

Mount a dial indicator with its stem resting on a tooth of the camshaft gear (as illustrated). Rotate the gear until all slack is removed, and zero the indicator. Rotate the gear in the opposite direction until slack is removed, and record gear backlash. Mount the indicator with its stem resting on the edge of the camshaft gear, parallel to the axis of the camshaft. Zero the indicator, and turn the camshaft gear one full turn, recording the runout. If either backlash or runout exceed specifications, replace the worn gear(s).

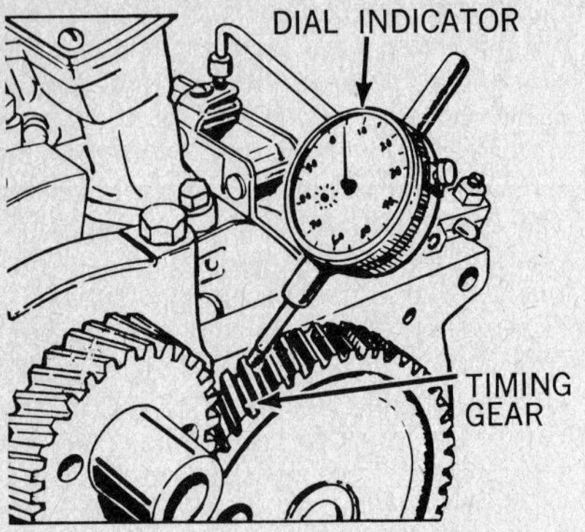

Checking timing gear backlash
(© Ford Motor Co.)

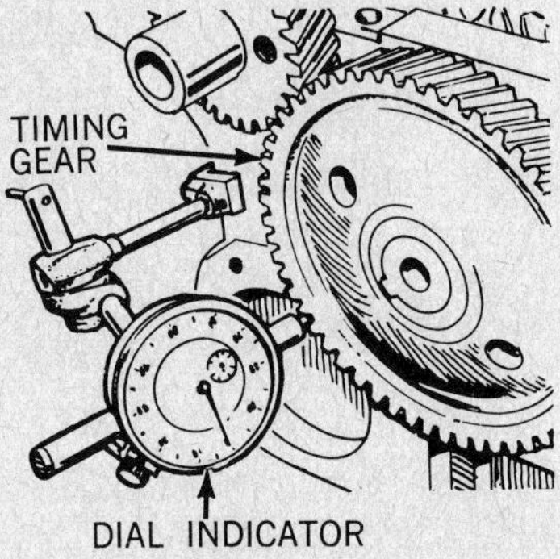

Checking timing gear runout
(© Ford Motor Co.)

Completing the Rebuilding Process

Following the above procedures, complete the rebuilding process as follows:

Fill the oil pump with oil, or petroleum jelly, to prevent cavitating (sucking air) on initial engine start up. Install the oil pump and the pickup tube on the engine. Coat the oil pan gasket as necessary, and install the gasket and the oil pan. Mount the flywheel and the crankshaft vibrational damper or pulley on the crankshaft.

NOTE: Always use new bolts when installing the flywheel.

Inspect the clutch shaft pilot bushing in the crankshaft. If the bushing is excessively worn, remove it with an expanding puller and a slide hammer, and tap a new bushing into place.

Position the engine, cylinder head side up. Lubricate the lifters, and install them into their bores. Install the cylinder head, and torque it as specified in the car section. Insert the pushrods (where applicable), and install the rocker shaft(s) (if so equipped) or position the rocker arms on the pushrods. If solid lifters are utilized, adjust the valves to the "cold" specifications.

Mount the intake and exhaust manifolds, the carburetor(s), the distributor and spark plugs. Adjust the point gap and the static ignition timing. Mount all accessories and install the engine in the car. Fill the radiator with coolant, and the crankcase with high quality engine oil.

Break-in Procedure

Before starting the engine, be sure all coolant hoses are attached and tight, the coolant level is correct, a new oil filter is installed and the crankcase filled with the proper level of oil.

The oil pump should be primed and if possible, the engine lubrication system should be charged with a pressure tank. Adjust the tappets (if required), the timing and carburetor as accurately as possible.

Start the engine and adjust the throttle to an approximate engine speed of 1000 to 2000 RPM, until the engine reaches normal operating temperature, normally within 20 to 30 minutes.

CAUTION: **Do not leave the vehicle unattended during the warm-up period. Observe the engine operation and check for any oil or coolant leaks. Stop the engine immediately if a problem exists, to avoid engine damage.**

After the engine has "run-in", lower the idle speed and stop the engine. Retorque the cylinder head bolts as required.

NOTE: Engines with aluminum heads or blocks must be allowed to cool to room temperature before any bolts are retorqued.

After rechecking the coolant and oil levels, make any further adjustments as necessary.

Follow the manufacturers recommended driving break-in procedure or as a general rule, the following procedures may be used.

Drive the vehicle on the highway and accelerate from 30 to 50 MPH, approximately 10 to 15 times, traffic flow permitting, to properly seat the piston rings to the cylinder walls. If traffic flow does not permit this procedure, accelerate the engine rapidly during shifting through the intermediate gears. The vehicle should be put in light duty service for the first 50 miles and sustained high speed should be avoided during the first 100 miles. Most important: Do not Lug the engine. (Lugging exists when the engine does not respond to further opening of the throttle).

INDEX

MANUAL STEERING

POWER STEERING

STEERING TROUBLE DIAGNOSIS

MANUAL STEERING

Condition	Possible Cause	Correction
Excessive Play or Looseness in the Steering	(1) Steering gear shaft adjusted too loose or shaft and/or bushing badly worn. (2) Excessive steering gear worm end play due to bearing adustment. (3) Steering linkage loose or worn. (4) Front wheel bearings improperly adjusted. (5) Steering arm loose on steering gear shaft. (6) Steering gear housing attaching bolts loose. (7) Steering arms loose at steering knuckles. (8) Working pins or bushings. (9) Loose spring shackles.	(1) Replace worn parts and adjust according to instructions. (2) Adjust according to instructions. (3) Replace worn parts. (4) Adjust wheel bearings. (5) Inspect for damage to the gear shaft and steering arm, replace parts as necessary. (6) Tighten the attaching bolts to specifications. (7) Tighten according to specifications. (8) Replace king pins and bushings. (9) Adjust or replace parts as necessary.
Hard Steering	(1) Low or uneven tire pressure. (2) Insufficient lubricant in the steering gear housing or in steering linkage. (3) Steering gear shaft adjusted too tight. (4) Improper caster or toe-in. (5) Steering column misaligned.	(1) Inflate the tires to recommended pressures. (2) Lubricate as necessary. (3) Adjust according to instructions. (4) Align the wheels. (5) See "Steering Gear Alignment."
Wheel Tramp (Excessive Vertical Motion of Wheels)	(1) Incorrect tire pressure. (2) Improper balance of wheels, tires and brake drums. (3) Loose tie rod ends or steering connections. (4) Worn or inoperative shock absorbers. (5) Excessive run-out of brake drums, wheels or tires.	(1) Inflate the tires to recommended pressures. (2) Balance as necessary. (3) Inspect and repair as necessary. (4) Replace the shock absorbers. (5) Repair or replace as required.
Shimmy	(1) Badly worn and/or unevenly worn tires. (2) Wheels and tires out of balance. (3) Worn or loose steering linkage parts. (4) Worn king pins and bushings. (5) Loose steering gear adjustments. (6) Loose wheel bearings. (7) Improper caster setting. (8) Weak or broken springs. (9) Incorrect tire pressure or tire sies not uniform. (10) Faulty shock absorbers.	(1) Rotate tires or replace if necessary. (2) Balance wheel and tire assemblies. (3) Replace parts as required. (4) Replace king pins and bushings. (5) Adjust steering gear as necessary. (6) Adjust wheel bearings. (7) Adjust caster to specifications. (8) Replace as required. (9) Check tire sizes and inflate tires to recommended pressure. (10) Replace as necessary.
Pull to One Side (Tendency of the Vehicle to Veer in one Direction Only)	(1) Incorrect tire pressue or tires not uniform. (2) Wheel bearings improperly adjusted. (3) Dragging brakes. (4) Improper caster, camber or toe-in. (5) Grease, dirt, oil or brake fluid on brake linings. (6) Broken or sagging rear springs. (7) Bent front axle, linkage or steering knuckle. (8) Worn or tight king pin bushings.	(1) Check tire sizes and inflate the tires to recommended pressures. (2) Adjust wheel bearings. (3) Inspect for weak, or broken brake shoe spring, binding pedal. (4) Adjust to specifications. (5) Inspect, replace and adjust as necessary. (6) Replace the rear springs. (7) Replace the parts as necessary. (8) Lubricate or replace as necessary.
Wander or Weave	(1) Improper caster, camber or toe-in. (2) Worn king pin and bushings. (3) Worn or improperly adjusted front wheel bearings. (4) Loose spring shackles. (5) Incorrect tire pressure or tire sizes not uniform. (6) Loose steering gear mounting bolts. (7) Tight king pin bushings. (8) Tight king pin thrust bearings.	(1) Adjust to specifications. (2) Replace parts as required. (3) Adjust or replace parts as necessary. (4) Adjust or replace parts as necessary. (5) Check tire sizes and inflate tires to recommended pressure. (6) Tighten to specifications. (7) Lubricate or ream to proper fit. (8) Adjust to .001 to .005 inch clearance.

Manual Steering Gear

Manual Steering Gear Service

Steering Gear Alignment

Before any steering gear adjustments are made, it is recommended that the front end of the truck be raised and a thorough inspection be made for stiffness or lost motion in the steering gear, steering linkage and front suspension. Worn or damaged parts should be replaced, since a satisfactory adjustment of the steering gear cannot be obtained if bent or badly worn parts exist.

It is also very important that the steering gear be properly aligned in the truck. Misalignment of the gear places a stress on the steering worm shaft, therefore a proper adjustment is impossible. To align the steering gear, loosen the steering gear-to-frame mounting bolts to permit the gear to align itself. Check the steering gear to frame mounting seat. If there is a gap at any of the mounting bolts, proper alignment

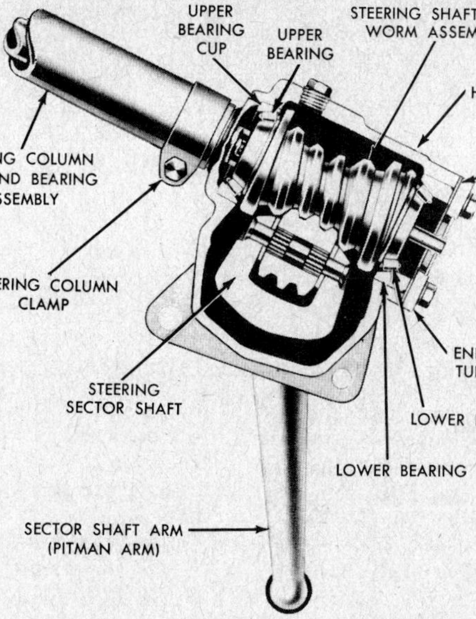

Worm and roller type steering gear (© Ford Motor Co.)

may be obtained by placing shims where excessive gap appears. Tighten the steering gear-to-frame bolts. Alignment of the gear in the truck is very important and should be done carefully so that a satisfactory, trouble-free gear adjustment may be obtained.

Gemmer Worm and Double Roller Tooth Type

With Screw Adjusted Mesh

The steering gear is of the worm and roller type with a 24 to 1 gear ratio. The cross shaft is straddle mounted with a bearing surface at the top and bottom points of the shaft mounting areas. The three tooth cross shaft roller is mounted in ball bearings. The proper lubricant used in the gear box is S.A.E. 90 Extreme Pressure Lubricant.

The external adjustments given below will properly adjust the steering gear.

Worm Bearing Adjustment

1. Turn the steering wheel about one full turn from straight ahead and secure it so it doesn't move.
2. Determine if there is any worm gear end-play by shaking the front wheel sideways and noting if there is any end movement that may be felt between the steering wheel hub and the steering jacket tube. (Be sure any movement noted is not looseness in the steering jacket tube.)
3. If end play is present, adjust the worm bearings by loosening the four cover cap screws about 1/8″. Separate the top shim, using a knife blade, and remove it. Do not damage the remaining shims or gaskets.
4. Replace the cover and recheck the end-play again. If necessary, repeat steps 2 and 3 until the end-play movement is as small as possible without tightening the steering gear too much.

NOTE: Adjustment may be done with the Pitman arm disconnected. With the steering wheel turned about one full turn from straight ahead and using a spring scale tool, adjust with the shims as given above until the spring scale pull is between 1/4 and 5/8 ft. lbs.

Cross Shaft Roller and Worm Mesh Adjustment

1. Turn the steering wheel to the middle of its turning limits with the Pitman arm disconnected. The steering gear roller should be on the worm high spot.
2. Shake the Pitman arm sideways to determine the amount of clearance between the worm cross shaft roller. Movement of more than 1/32″ indicates that the roller and worm mesh must be adjusted.
3. Loosen the adjusting screw lock nut and tighten the external cross shaft adjusting screw a small amount. Recheck the clearance by shaking the Pitman arm. Repeat until the clearance is correct. (Do not overtighten.)

   NOTE: The cross shaft roller and worm mesh adjustment may be done, using a spring scale tool, by measuring the amount of wheel pull as the external cross shaft adjusting screw is tightened. When the spring scale pull is between 7/8 and 1 1/8 ft. lbs., the adjustment is correct.
4. Tighten the Pitman arm attaching nut to 100-125 ft. lbs. The steering wheel nut (if loosened) should be tightened to 15-20 ft. lbs. torque.

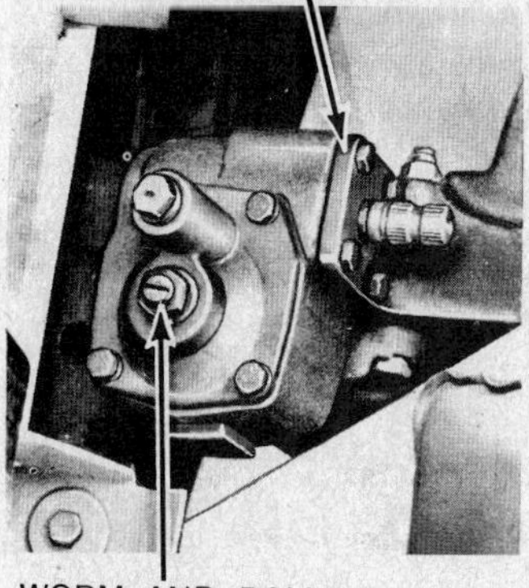

Steering gear adjustments (© Ford Motor Co.)

Disassembly

1. Remove steering gear oil seal, using a suitable puller.
2. Remove cross shaft, using an arbor to prevent bearings from dropping out.
3. Remove cover, shims and cover gasket.
4. Remove worm gear, thrust bearings and bearing cups.

Assembly

1. Clean and inspect all parts, replace as necessary.

   NOTE: If either thrust bearing is excessively worn, replace them both.
2. Reassemble steering gear, using new oil seal.
3. Perform worm bearing and cross shaft roller and worm mesh adjustments.
4. Lubricate to specifications.

Ford Steering Gear—Recirculating Ball Type

Steering Worm and Sector Gear Adjustments

The ball nut assembly and the sector gear must be adjusted properly to maintain a minimum amount of steering shaft end play and a minimum amount of backlash between the sector gear and the ball nut. There are only two adjustments that may be done on this steering gear and they should be done as given below:

1. Remove the steering gear from the vehicle.
2. Loosen the locknut on the sector shaft adjustment screw and turn the adjusting screw counterclockwise about three turns.
3. Measure the worm bearing pre-

load by attaching an in. lbs. torque wrench to the input shaft. Note the reading required to rotate input shaft about 1½ turns either side of center. If the torque reading is not about 4-5 in. lbs., adjust the gear as given in the next step.

4. Loosen the steering shaft bearing adjuster lock nut and tighten or back off the bearing adjusting screw until the preload is within the specified limits.
5. Tighten the steering shaft bearing adjuster lock nut, and recheck the preload torque.
6. Turn the input shaft slowly to either stop. Turn gently against the stop to avoid possible damage to the ball return guides. Then rotate the shaft three turns to center the ball nut.
7. Turn the sector adjusting screw clockwise until the proper torque (9-10 in. lbs.) is obtained that is necessary to rotate the worm gear past its center (high spot).
8. With the input shaft centered, hold the sector shaft and check the lash between the ball nuts, balls, and worm shaft by applying 15 lbs. torque to the steering input shaft in both right and left turn directions. The total travel of the wrench should not exceed 1¼″.
9. Tighten the sector adjusting screw locknut, and recheck the backlash. Install the steering gear.

Disassembly

1. Rotate the steering shaft three turns from either stop.
2. Remove the sector shaft adjusting screw locknut and loosen the screw one turn. Remove the steering shaft bearing adjuster, and the housing cover bolts and remove the sector shaft. Remove the shaft by turning the screw clockwise. Keep the shim with the screw.
3. Remove the sector shaft from the housing.
4. Carefully pull the steering shaft and ball nut from the housing, and remove the steering shaft lower bearing. Do not run the ball nut to either end of the worm gear to prevent damaging the ball return guides. Disassemble the ball nut only if there are signs of binding or tightness.
5. To disassemble the ball nut, remove the ball return guide clamp and the ball return guides from the ball nut. Keep ball nut clamp side up until ready to remove the ball bearings.
6. Turn the ball nut over and rotate the worm shaft from side to side until all 50 balls have dropped out into a clean pan. With all balls removed, the nut will slide off the wormshaft.
7. Remove the upper bearing cup from the bearing adjuster and the lower cup from the housing. It may be necessary to tap the housing or the adjuster on a wooden block to jar the bearing cups loose.

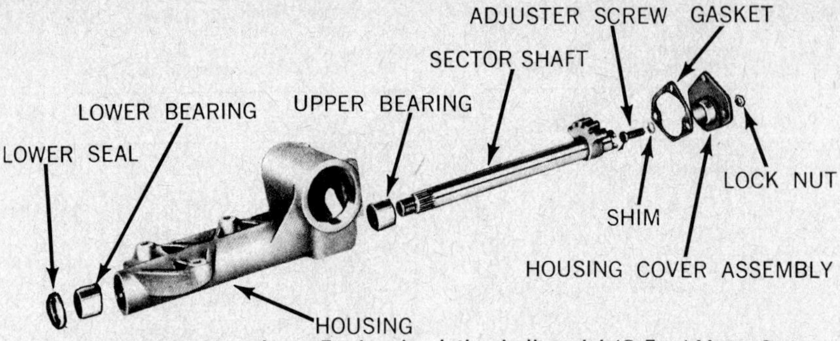

Sector shaft and housing—Ford recirculating ball model (© Ford Motor Co.)

Inspection

1. Carefully clean and inspect all parts. If the inspection shows bearing damage, the sector shaft bearing and the oil seal should be pressed out.
2. If the sector shaft bearing and oil seals were removed, press new bearings and oil seals into the housing. Do not clean, wash, or soak seals in cleaning solvent.
3. Apply the recommended steering gear lubricant to the housing and seals, filling the pocket between sector shaft bearings.

Assembly

1. Install the bearing cup in the lower end of the housing and a bearing cup in the adjuster nut. Install a new seal in the bearing adjuster if the old seal was removed.
2. Apply gear lube to the outside of the worm shaft and the inside of the ball nut. Lay the steering shaft down, and position the ball nut on the shaft with the guide holes upward and the shallow end of the teeth to the left of the steering wheel position. Align the grooves in worm and ball nut by sighting through the guide holes.
3. Insert the ball guides into the holes in the ball nut, lightly tapping them, if necessary, to seat them.
4. Insert 25 balls into the hole in the top of each ball guide. If necessary, rotate the shaft slightly to distribute the balls evenly in the circuit.
5. Install the ball guide clamp, tightening the screws to the proper torque. Check that the worm shaft rotates freely.
6. Coat the threads of the steering shaft bearing adjuster, the housing cover bolts, and the sector adjusting screw with a suitable oil-resistant sealing compound. Do not apply sealer to female threads and do not get sealer on the steering shaft bearings.
7. Coat the worm bearings, sector shaft bearings, and gear teeth with steering gear lubricant.
8. Clamp the housing in a vise, with the sector shaft axis horizontal, and place the steering shaft lower bearing in its cup. Place the steering shaft and ball nut assemblies in the housing.
9. Position the steering shaft upper bearing on top of the worm gear and install the steering shaft bearing adjuster, adjuster nut, and the bearing cup. Leave the nut loose.
10. Adjust the worm bearing preload according to the instructions given earlier.
11. Position the sector adjusting screw and adjuster shim, and check for a clearance of not more than 0.002″ between the screw head and the end of the

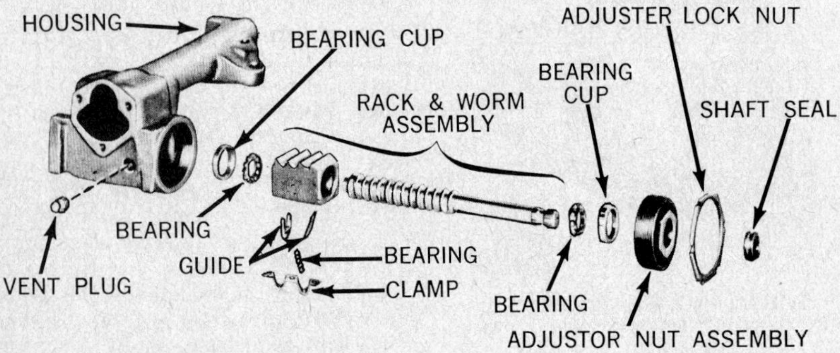

Steering shaft and related parts—Ford recirculating ball model (© Ford Motor Co.)

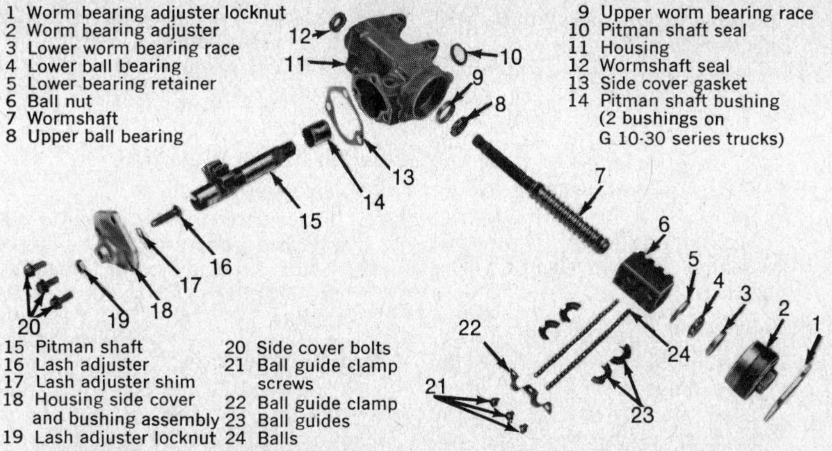

Exploded view—Saginaw recirculating ball model (© General Motors Corp.)

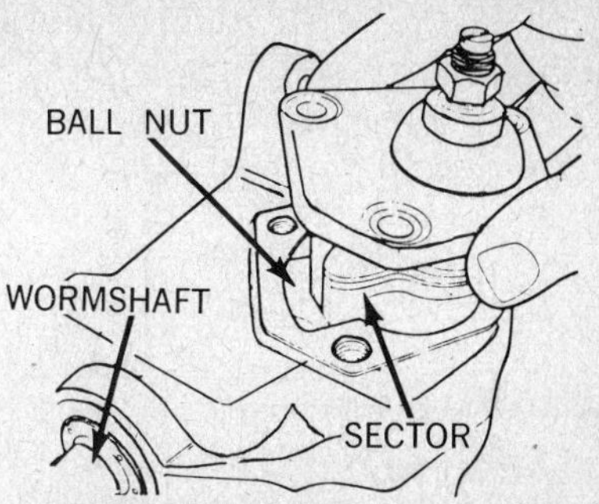

Removing sector shaft assembly—Saginaw recirculating ball model
(© Ford Motor Co.)

sector shaft. If the clearance exceeds 0.002″, add enough shims to reduce the clearance to under 0.002″ clearance.

12. Start the sector shaft adjusting screw into the housing cover. Install a new gasket on the cover.
13. Rotate the steering shaft until the ball nut teeth mesh with the sector gear teeth, tilting the housing so the ball will tip toward the housing cover opening.
14. Lubricate the sector shaft journal and install the sector shaft and cover. With the cover moved to one side, fill the gear with lubricant (about 0.97 lb.). Push the cover and the sector shaft into place, and install the two top housing bolts. Do not tighten the bolts until checking to see that there is some lash between the ball nut and the sector gear teeth. Hold or push the cover away from the ball nut and tighten the bolts to the proper torque (30-40 ft. lbs.).
15. Loosely install the sector shaft adjusting screw lock nut and adjust the sector shaft mesh load as given earlier. Tighten the adjusting screw lock nut.

Saginaw Recirculating Ball Type

The steering gear is of the recirculating ball nut type. The ball nut, mounted on the worm gear, is driven by means of steel balls which circulate in helical grooves in both the worm and nut. Ball return guides attached to the nut serve to recirculate the two sets of balls in the grooves. As the steering wheel is turned to the right, the ball nut moves upward. When the wheel is turned to the left, the ball nut moves downward.

The sector teeth on the pinion shaft and the ball nut are designed so that they fit the tightest when the steering wheel is straight ahead. This mesh action is adjusted by an adjusting screw which moves the pinion shaft endwise until the teeth mesh properly. The worm bearing adjuster provides proper preloading of the upper and lower bearings.

Before doing the adjustment procedures given below, ensure that the steering problem is not caused by faulty suspension components, bad front end alignment, etc. Then, proceed with the following adjustments.

Steering Worm and Sector Adjustment

1. Tighten the worm bearing adjuster plug until all end play has been removed, then loosen ¼ turn.
2. Use an 11/16 in. 12 point socket to carefully turn the wormshaft all the way into the right corner then turn back about ½ turn.
3. Tighten the adjuster plug until the proper thrust bearing preload is obtained (5-8 in. lbs.). Tighten the adjuster plug locknut to 85 ft. lbs.
4. Turn the wormshaft from one stop to the other counting the number of turns. Then turn the shaft back exactly half the number of turns to the center position.
5. Turn the lash (sector shaft) adjuster screw clockwise to remove all lash between the ball nut and sector teeth. Tighten the locknut to 25 ft. lbs.
6. Using an 11/16 in. 12 point socket and an in. lb. torque wrench, observe the highest reading while the gear is turned through the center position. It should be 16 in. lbs. or less.
7. If necessary repeat steps 5 and 6.

Disassembly

1. Place the steering gear in a vise, clamping onto one of the mounting tabs. The wormshaft should be in a horizontal position.
2. Rotate the wormshaft from stop to stop and count the total number of turns. Turn back exactly halfway, placing the gear on center.
3. Remove the three self locking bolts which attach the sector cover to the housing.
4. Using a plastic hammer, tap lightly on the end of the sector

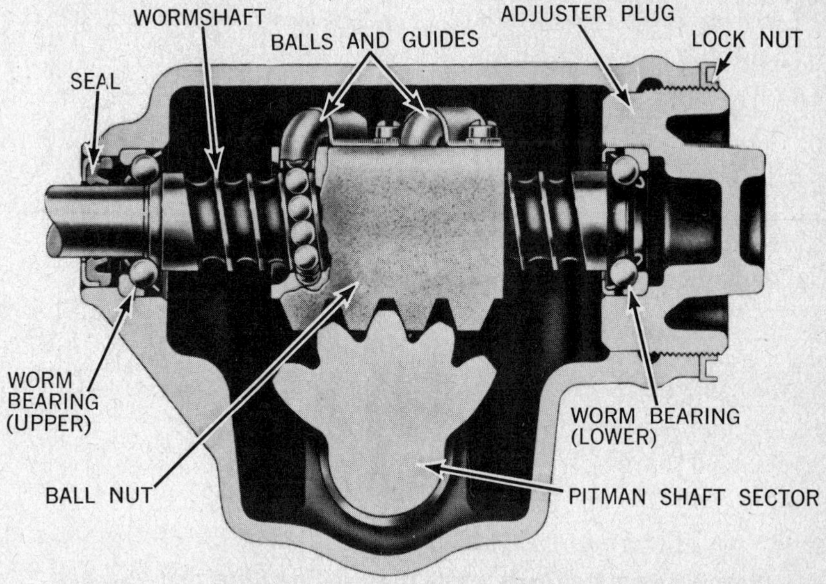

Cross section—Saginaw recirculating ball model (© General Motors Corp.)

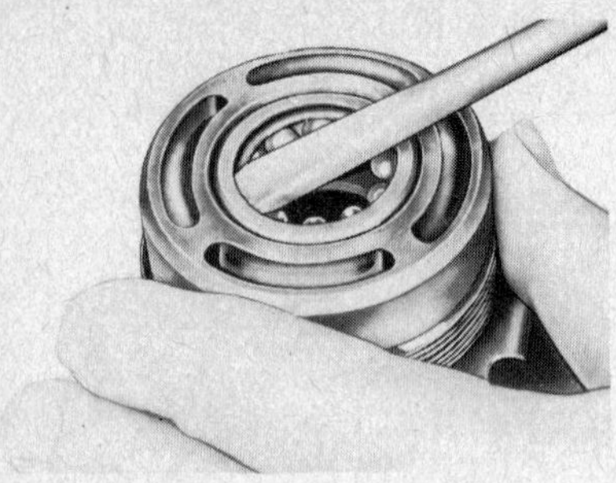

Removing the bearing retainer from the worm bearing adjuster—Saginaw recirculating ball model
(© General Motors Corp.)

shaft and lift the sector cover and sector and sector shaft assembly from the gear housing.

NOTE: It may be necessary to turn the wormshaft by hand until the sector will pass through the opening in the housing.

5. Remove the locknut from the adjuster plug and remove the adjuster plug assembly.
6. Pull the wormshaft and ball nut assembly from the housing.
   NOTE: Damage may be done to the ends of the ball guides if the ball nut is allowed to rotate to the end of the worm.
7. Remove the worm shaft upper bearing from inside the gear housing.
8. Pry the wormshaft lower bearing retainer from the adjuster plug housing and remove the bearing.
9. Remove the locknut from the lash adjuster screw in the sector cover. Turn the lash adjuster screw clockwise and remove it from the sector cover. Slide the adjuster screw and shim out of the slot in the end of the sector shaft.
10. Pry out and discard both the sector shaft and wormshaft seals.

Inspection

1. Wash all parts in cleaning solvent and blow dry with an air hose.
2. Use a magnifying glass and inspect the bearings and bearing caps for signs of indentation, or chipping. Replace any parts that show signs of damage.
3. Check the fit of the sector shaft in the bushings in the sector cover and housing. If these bushings are worn, a new sector cover and bushing assembly or housing bushing should be installed.
4. Check steering gear wormshaft assembly for being bent or damaged.

Shaft Seal Replacement

1. Remove the old seal from the pump body.
2. Install the new seal by pressing the outer diameter of the seal with a suitable size socket.

NOTE: Make sure the socket is large enough to avoid damaging the external lip of the seal.

Sector Shaft Bushing Replacement

1. Place the steering gear housing in an arbor press.

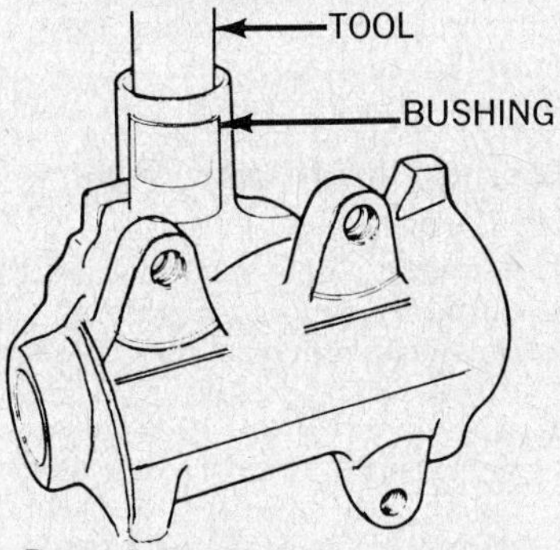

Removing sector shaft bushing—Saginaw recirculating ball model
(© Ford Motor Co.)

2. Press the sector shaft bushing from the housing.

NOTE: Service bushings are bored to size and require no further reaming.

Sector Cover Bushing Replacement

1. The sector cover bushing is not serviced separately. The entire sector cover assembly including the bushing must be replaced as a unit.

Ball Nut Service

If there is any indication of binding or tightness when the ball nut is rotated on the worm the unit should be disassembled, cleaned and inspected as follows:

Ball Nut Disassembly

1. Remove the screws and clamp retaining the ball guides in the ball nut. Pull the guides out of the ball nut.
2. Turn the ball nut upside down and rotate the wormshaft back and forth until all the balls have dropped out of the ball nut. The ball nut can now be pulled endwise off the worm.
3. Wash all parts in solvent and dry them with air. Use a magnifying glass and inspect the worm and nut grooves and the surface of all balls for signs of indentation. Check all ball guides for damage at the ends. Replace any damaged parts.

Ball Nut Assembly

1. Slip the ball nut over the worm with the ball guide holes up and the shallow end of the ball nut teeth to the left from the steering wheel position. Sight through the ball guide to align the grooves in the worm.
2. Place two ball guide halves together and insert them in the upper circuit in the ball nut. Place the two remaining guides together and insert them in the lower circuit.
3. Count out 25 balls and place them in a suitable container. This is the proper number of balls for one circuit.

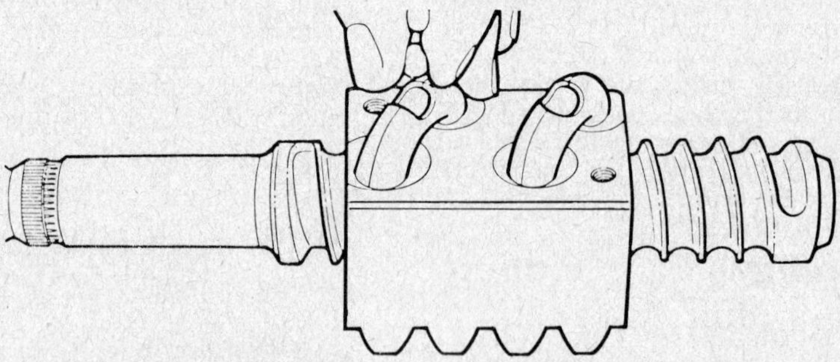

Filling the ball circuits—Saginaw recirculating ball model (© Ford Motor Co.)

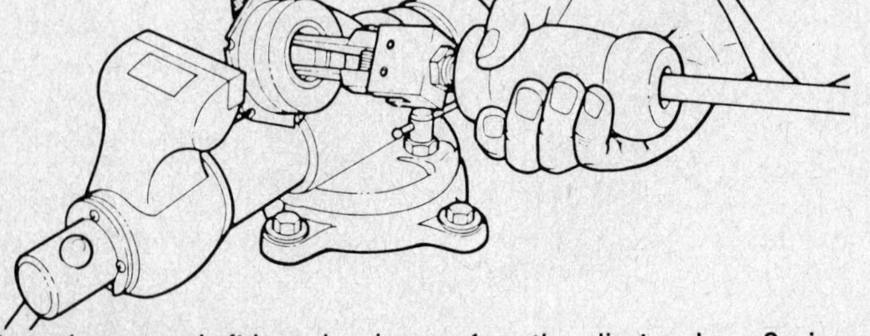

Removing worm shaft lower bearing cup from the adjuster plug—Saginaw recirculating ball model (© Ford Motor Co.)

4. Load the 25 balls into one of the guide holes while turning the wormshaft gradually away from that hole.
5. Fill the remaining ball circuit in the same manner.
6. Assemble the ball guide clamp to the ball nut and tighten the screws to 18-24 in. lbs.
7. Check the assembly by rotating the ball nut on the worm to see that it moves freely.
   NOTE: Do not rotate the ball nut to the end of the worm threads as this may damage the ball guides.

Assembly

1. Coat the threads of the adjuster plug, sector cover bolts and lash adjuster with a non-drying oil resistant sealing compound.
   NOTE: Do not apply compound to the female threads. Use extreme care when applying compound to the bearing adjuster so that it does not come in contact with the wormshaft bearing.
2. Place the steering gear housing in a vise with the wormshaft bore horizontal and the sector cover opening up.
3. Make sure that all seals, bushings and bearing cups are installed in the gear housing and that the ball nut is installed on the wormshaft.
4. Slip the wormshaft upper bearing assembly over the wormshaft and insert the wormshaft and ball nut assembly into the housing, feeding the end of the shaft through the upper ball bearing cup and seal.
5. Place the wormshaft lower bearing assembly in the adjuster plug bearing cup and press the stamped retainer into place with a suitable size socket.
6. Install the adjuster plug and locknut into the lower end of the housing while carefully guiding the end of the wormshaft into the bearing until nearly all end play has been removed from the wormshaft.
7. Position the lash adjuster including the shim in the slotted end of the sector shaft.

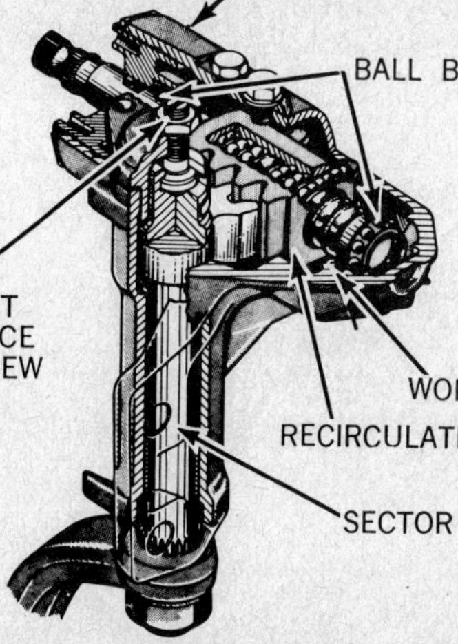

Chrysler recirculating ball type steering gear (© Chrysler Corp.)

NOTE: End clearance should not be greater than .002. If the end clearance is greater than .002 a shim package is available with thicknesses of .063, .065, .067, .069.

8. Lubricate the steering gear with 11 oz. of steering gear grease. Rotate the wormshaft until the ball nut is at the other end of its travel and then pack as much new lubricant into the housing as possible without losing out the sector shaft opening. Rotate the wormshaft until the ball nut is at the other end of its travel and pack as much lubricant into the opposite end as possible.
9. Rotate the wormshaft until the ball nut is in the center of travel. This is to make sure that the sector shaft and ball nut will engage properly with the center tooth of the sector entering the center tooth space in the ball nut.
10. Insert the sector shaft assembly including lash adjuster screw and shim into the housing so that the center tooth of the sector enters the center tooth space in the ball nut.
11. Pack the remaining portion of the lubricant into the housing and also place some in the sector cover bushing hole.
12. Place the sector cover gasket on the housing.
13. Install the sector cover onto the sector shaft by reaching through the sector cover with a screwdriver and turning the lash adjuster screw counterclockwise until the screw bottoms, then back the screw off one-half turn. Loosely install a new lock nut onto the adjuster screw.
14. Install and tighten the sector cover bolt to 30 ft. lbs.

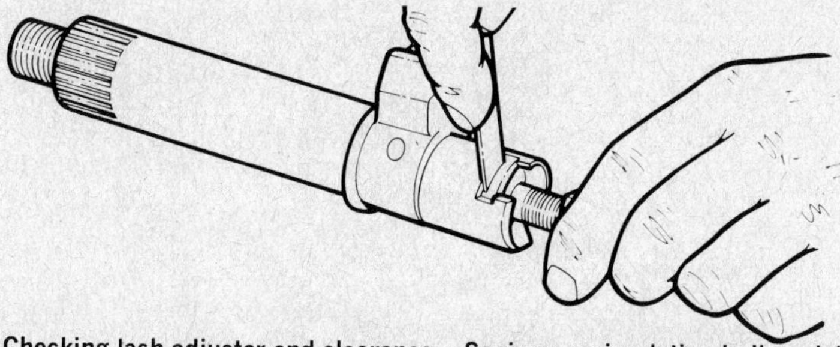

Checking lash adjuster end clearance—Saginaw recirculating ball model (© Ford Motor Co.)

Chrysler Recirculating Ball Type

The steering gear is of the recirculating ball nut type. The ball nut, mounted on the worm gear, is driven by means of steel balls which circulate in helical grooves in both the worm and nut. Ball return guides attached to the nut serve to recirculate the two sets of balls in the grooves. As the steering wheel is turned to the right, the ball nut moves upward. When the wheel is turned to the left, the ball nut moves downward.

The sector teeth on the pinion shaft and the ball nut are designed so that they fit the tightest when the steering wheel is straight ahead. This mesh action is adjusted by an adjusting screw which moves the pinion shaft endwise until the teeth mesh properly. The worm bearing adjuster provides proper preloading of the upper and lower bearings.

Worm Bearing Pre-load Adjustment

1. Remove the steering gear arm and lockwasher from the sector shaft, using a suitable gear puller.
2. Remove the horn button or horn ring.
3. Loosen the sector-shaft adjusting screw locknut, and back out the adjusting screw about two turns.
4. Turn the steering wheel two

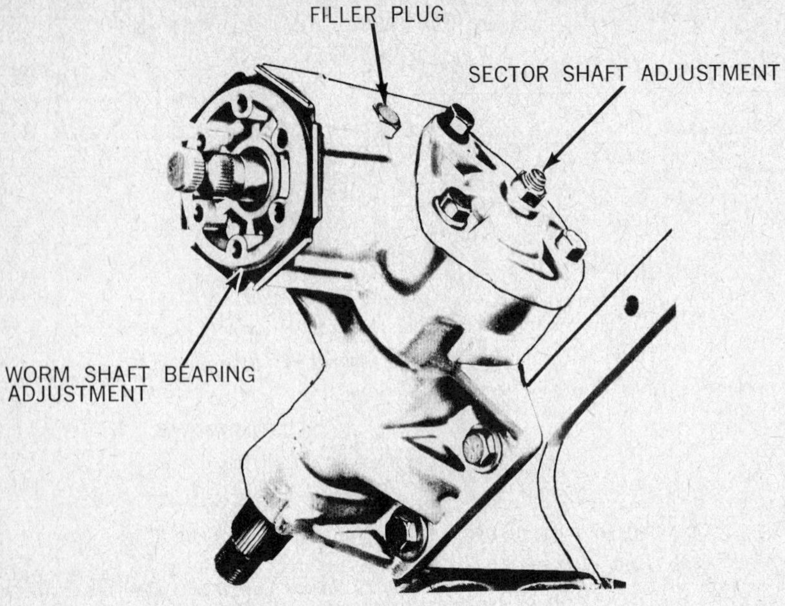

Steering gear adjustment locations (© Chrysler Corp.)

complete turns from the straight ahead position, and place an in. lb torque wrench on the steering shaft nut.

5. Rotate the steering shaft at least one turn toward the straight ahead position while measuring the torque on the torque wrench. The torque should be between 1⅛ and 4½ in. lbs. to move the steering wheel. If torque is not within these limits, loosen the worm shaft bearing adjuster locknut and turn the adjuster clockwise to increase the preload or counterclockwise to decrease the preload. When the preload is correct, hold the adjuster screw steady and tighten the locknut. Recheck preload.

Ball Nut Rack and Sector Mesh Adjustment

NOTE: this adjustment can be accurately made only after proper preloading of worm bearing.

1. Turn steering wheel gently from one stop to the other, counting the number of turns. Turn the steering wheel back exactly half way, to the center position.
2. Turn the sector-shaft adjusting screw clockwise to remove all lash between ball nut rack and the sector gear teeth, then tighten adjusting screw locknut to 35 ft. lbs.
3. Turn the steering wheel about ¼ turn away from the center or high spot position. With the torque wrench on the steering wheel nut measure the torque required to turn the steering wheel through the high spot at the center position. The reading should be between 8 and 11 in. lbs. This is the total of the worm shaft bearing preload and the ball nut rack and sector gear mesh load. Readjust the sector-shaft adjustment screw if necessary to obtain a correct torque reading.
4. After completing the adjustments, place the front wheels in a straight ahead position, and with the steering wheel and steering gear centered, install the steering arm on sector-shaft. Tighten the steering arm retaining nut to 180 ft. lbs.

Steering Gear Disassembly and Assembly

1. Attach the steering gear assembly to a holding fixture and put the holding fixture in a bench vise. Thoroughly clean the outside surface before disassembly.
2. Loosen the sector-shaft adjusting screw locknut, and back out the adjusting screw about two turns to relieve the mesh load between the ball nut rack and the sector gear teeth.
3. Position the steering gear worm shaft in a straight ahead position.
4. Remove the attaching bolts from the sector-shaft cover and slowly remove the sector-shaft while sliding an arbor tool into the housing. Remove the locknut from the adjusting screw and remove the screw from the cover by turning it clockwise. Slide the adjustment screw and its shim out of the slot in the end of the sector-shaft.
5. Loosen the worm shaft bearing adjuster locknut with a brass drift (punch) and remove the locknut. Hold the worm shaft steady while unscrewing the adjuster. Slide the worm adjuster off the shaft.

   CAUTION: Handle the adjuster carefully to avoid damaging the aluminum threads. Also, do not run the ball nut down to either end of the worm shaft to avoid damaging the ball guides.

6. Carefully remove the worm and ball nut assembly. This assembly is serviced as a complete assembly only and is not to be disassembled or the ball return guides removed or disturbed.

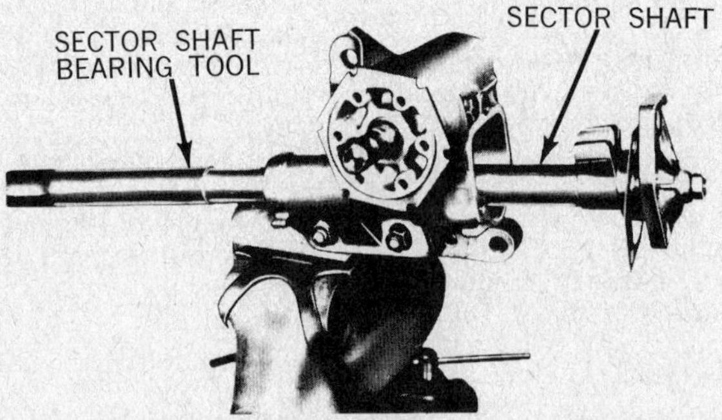

Removing the sector shaft (© Chrysler Corp.)

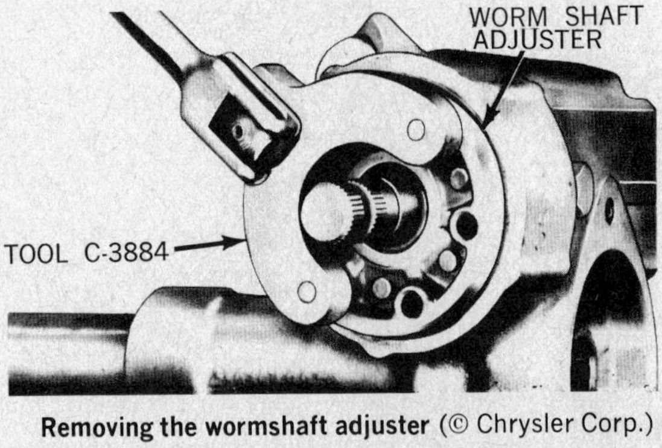

Removing the wormshaft adjuster (© Chrysler Corp.)

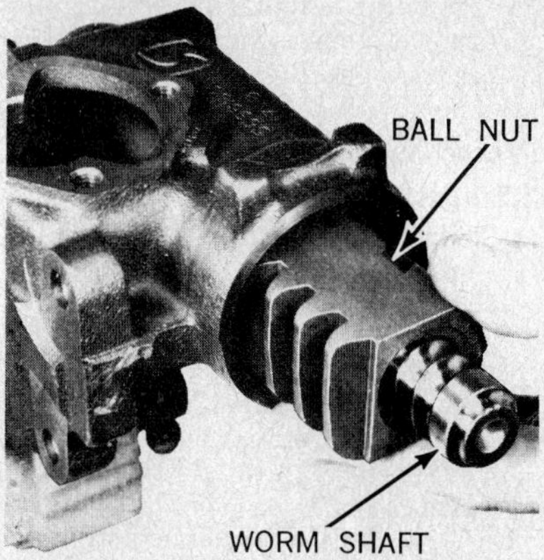

Removing the wormshaft and ballnut assembly (© Chrysler Corp.)

7. Remove the sector-shaft needle bearing by placing the gear housing in an arbor press; insert a tool in the lower end of the housing and press both bearings through the housing.
   The sector-shaft cover assembly, including a needle bearing or bushing, is serviced as an assembly.
8. Remove the worm shaft oil seal from the worm shaft bearing adjuster by inserting a blunt punch behind the seal and tapping alternately on each side of the seal until it is driven out of the adjuster.
9. Remove the worm shaft in the same manner as that given in step 8. *Be careful not to cock the bearing cup and distort the adjuster counter bore.*
10. Remove the lower cup if necessary. Pull the bearing cup out.
11. Wash all parts in clean solvent and dry thoroughly. Inspect all parts for wear, scoring, pitting, etc. Test operation of the worm shaft and ball nut assembly. If

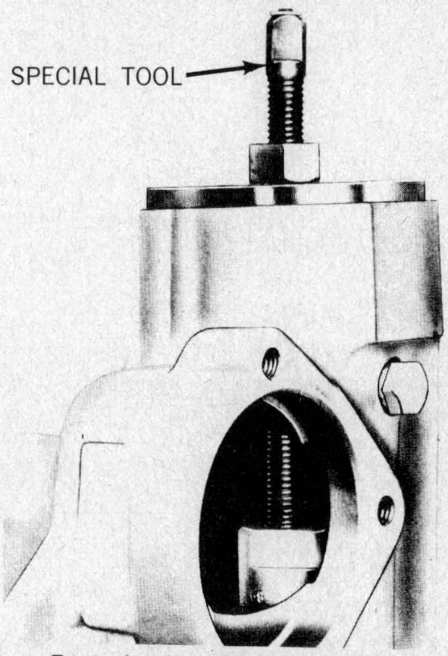

Removing the lower bearing cup (© Chrysler Corp.)

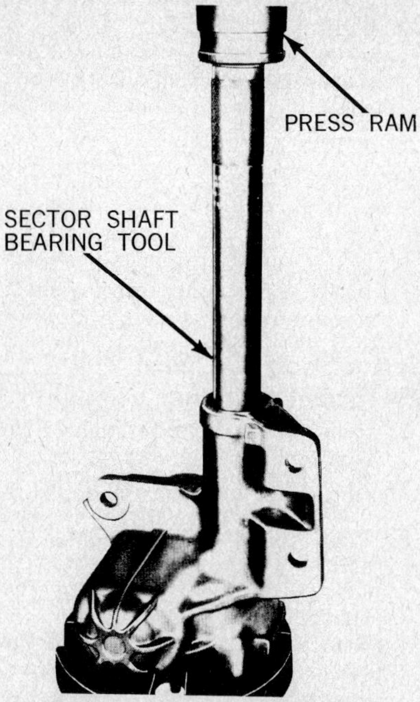

Removing the sector shaft inner and outer bearings (© Chrysler Corp.)

ball nut does not travel smoothly and freely on the worm shaft or if there is binding, replace the assembly.

NOTE: Extreme care must be taken when handling the aluminum worm bearing adjuster to avoid thread damage. Also, be careful not to damage the threads in the gear housing. Always lubricate the worm bearing adjuster before screwing it into the housing.

12. Inspect the sector-shaft for wear and check the fit of the shaft in the housing bearings. Inspect the fit of the shaft pilot bearing in the housing. Be sure the worm shaft is not bent or damaged.

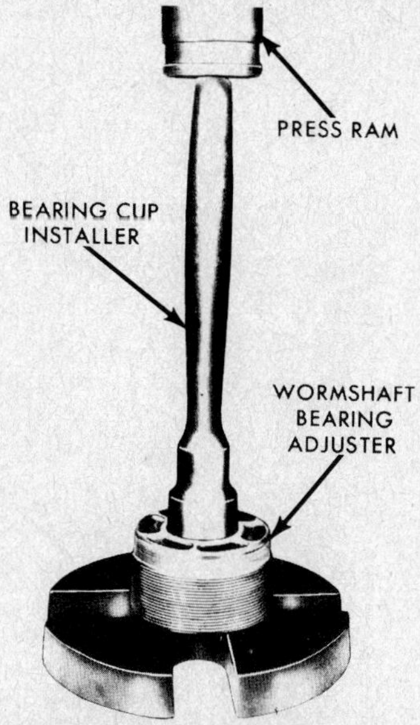

Installing the wormshaft upper bearing cup (© Chrysler Corp.)

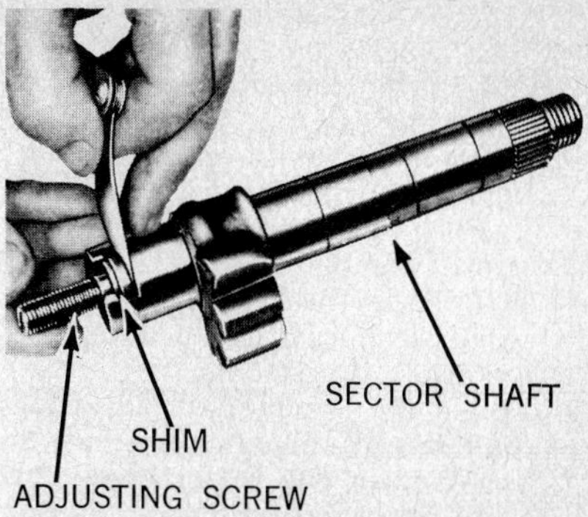

Measuring the sector shaft adjusting screw end clearance (© Chrysler Corp.)

13. Install the sector-shaft lower needle bearing. Press the bearing into the housing about 7/16 in. below the end of the bore to leave space for the new oil seal.
14. Install the upper needle bearing in the same manner and press it into the inside end of the housing bore flush with the inside end of the bore surface.
15. Install the worm shaft bearing cups (upper and lower) by placing them and their spacers in the adjuster nut and press them into place.
16. Install the worm shaft oil seal by placing the seal in the worm shaft adjuster with the metal seal retainer up. Drive the seal into place with a suitable sleeve until it is just below the end of the bore in the adjuster.

    NOTE: Apply a coating of steering gear lubricant to all moving parts during assembly. Also, put lubricant on and around oil seal lips.
17. Clamp the holding fixture and housing in a bench vise with the bearing adjuster opening upward. Place a thrust bearing in the lower cup in the housing.
18. Hold the ball nut from turning and insert the worm shaft and ball nut assembly into the housing with the end of the worm shaft resting in the thrust bearing. Place the upper thrust bearing on the worm shaft. Thoroughly lubricate the threads on the adjuster and the threads in the housing.
19. Place a protective sleeve of tape over the splines on the worm shaft to avoid damaging the seal. Slide the adjuster assembly over the shaft.
20. Thread the adjuster into the housing and tighten the adjuster to 50 ft. lbs. while rotating the worm shaft to seat the bearings.
21. Loosen the adjuster so no bearing preload exists. Tighten the adjuster for a worm shaft bearing preload of $1\frac{1}{8}$ to $4\frac{1}{2}$ in. lbs. Tighten the bearing adjuster locknut and recheck the preload.

22. Before installing the sector-shaft, pack the worm shaft cavities in the housing above and below the ball nut with steering gear lubricant. A good grade of multi-purpose lubricant may be used if steering gear lubricant is not available. *Do not use gear oil.* Pack enough lubricant into the worm cavities to cover the worm.
23. Slide the sector-shaft adjusting screw and shim into the slot in the end of the shaft. Check the end clearance for no more than 0.004 in. clearance. If the clearance is not within the limit, remove old shim and install a new shim, available in three different thicknesses, to get the proper clearance.
24. Start the sector-shaft and adjuster screw into the bearing in the housing cover. Using a screwdriver through the hole in the cover, turn the screw counterclockwise to pull the shaft into the cover. Install the adjusting screw locknut, but do not tighten at this time.
25. Rotate the worm shaft to center the ball nut.
26. Place a new gasket on the housing cover and install the sector-shaft and cover assembly into the steering gear housing. *Be sure to coat the sector-shaft and sector teeth with steering gear lubricant before installing the sector-shaft in the housing.* Allow some lash between the sector-shaft sector teeth and the ball nut rack. Install and tighten the cover bolts to 25 ft. lbs.
27. Place the sector-shaft seal on the cross-shaft with the lip of the seal facing the housing. Press the seal in place.
28. Turn the worm shaft about ¼ turn away from the center of the high spot position. Using a torque wrench and a ¾ in. socket on the worm shaft spline, check the torque needed to rotate the shaft through the high spot. The reading should be between 8 and 11 in. lbs. Readjust the sector-shaft adjusting screw until the proper reading is obtained. Tighten the locknut to 35 ft. lbs. and recheck sector-shaft torque.

Sector-Shaft Oil Seal Replacement

1. Remove the steering gear arm retaining nut and lockwasher.
2. Remove seal with a seal puller or other appropriate tool.
3. Place a new oil seal onto the splines of the sector-shaft with the lip of the seal facing the housing.
4. Remove the tool, and install the steering gear arm, lockwasher, and retaining nut. Tighten the nut to 180 ft. lbs. torque.

Ross Worm and Roller Steering Gear

The steering gear is of the worm and roller type, with shim adjustments provided for the worm gear bearings and an adjusting screw for the sector shaft adjustment.

Bearing Preload Adjustment

1. Loosen the four capscrews which fasten the end cover to the steering gear housing.
2. Alternately tighten the capscrews evenly and rotate the worm gear shaft. Tighten the screws to 18 to 22 ft. lbs.
3. If necessary, remove the end cover and either add or subtract from the number of shims, and repeat steps 1 and 2 to obtain the correct bearing preload.

Worm Gear and Roller Gear Backlash Adjustment

1. Loosen the locknut and turn the adjustment at the side cover counterclockwise until the worm gear shaft turns freely through its entire range of travel.
2. Count the number of turns necessary to rotate the worm gear shaft through its entire range of travel.
3. Turn the shaft back exactly half the number of turns to the center position.
4. Turn the shaft back and forth through its center of travel and tighten the adjustment screw to obtain a rolling torque requirement of 7 to 12 inch lbs.
5. Hold the adjustment screw in position and torque the locknut to 16-20 ft. lbs.
6. Recheck the rolling torque and repeat the above procedure if necessary.

Disassembly

1. Drain the lubricant from the gear.
2. Make index marks on the roller gear and shaft assembly and on the steering arm to assure correct alignment during reassembly.
3. Remove the nut and lockwasher from the shaft.
4. Using a puller remove the arm from the shaft.

   NOTE: Do not use a hammer or wedge to remove the steering arm or damage to the gear and shaft assembly may result.
5. Remove the four side cover attaching screws and remove the

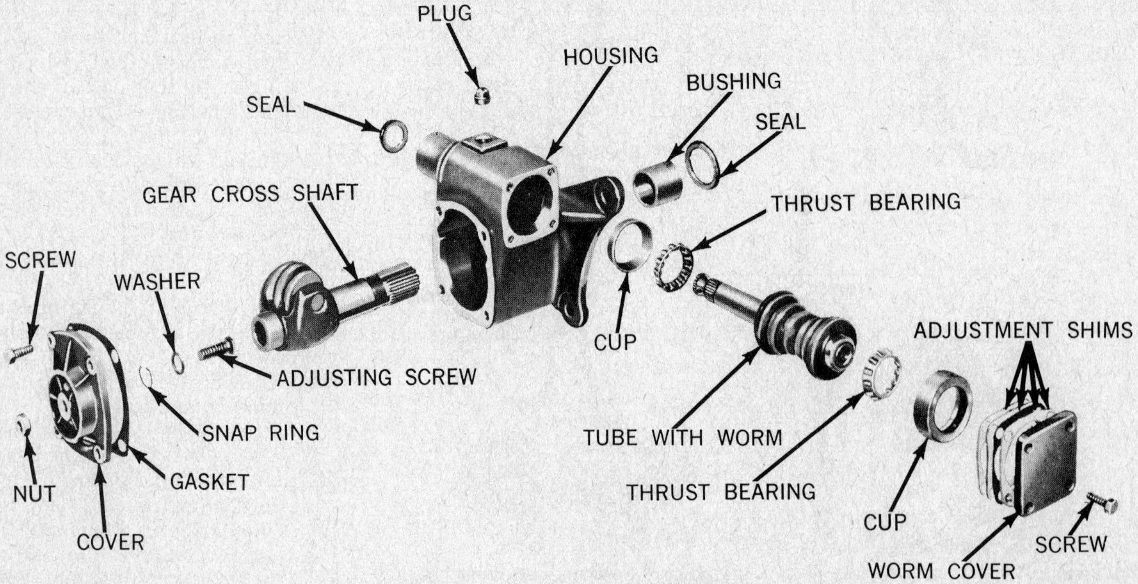

Ross worm and roller steering gear (© Chrysler Corp.)

cover and roller gear and shaft assembly as a unit.

6. Remove the locknut from the adjustment screw and turn the screw clockwise until it is completely unthreaded from the side cover, then remove the roller gear and shaft assembly from the cover.
7. Remove the four end cover attaching screws and remove the cover from the housing.
8. Withdraw the worm gear and shaft assembly from the housing.
9. Remove the lower and upper bearing cups and ball bearings from the shaft.
10. Remove and discard both the worm gear shaft and roller gear shaft housing oil seals.

Inspection

1. Clean all parts with a suitable cleaning solvent and blow dry with an air hose.
2. Check the steering gear housing for cracks, leaks or breaks and replace if damaged.
3. Examine the roller gear to assure that it has proper freedom of movement and does not have excessive lash or roughness. Replace if necessary.
4. Check the adjustment screw of the roller gear and shaft assembly for excessive end play. If end play exceeds 0.015 inch, remove the retaining ring, thrust washer and screw from the gear and shaft assembly and replace with new parts.
5. Inspect the roller gear and shaft needle bearings for wear or damage. Insert a shaft through each bearing and check for clearance. If clearance exceeds 0.010 inch, replace the bearings. Either needle bearing may be removed by pressing out with a piloted mandrel. When pressing in a new bearing make sure that the face of the bearing is flush with the bearing boss of the cover or housing.
6. Inspect the worm gear and shaft assembly for wear, scoring or pitting. Polish the assembly with a fine abrasive cloth or replace if necessary.
7. Check the upper and lower ball bearings and cups of the worm gear and shaft assembly for wear and damage. Replace the ball bearings as a full set if worn or damaged.

Assembly

1. Press new oil seals into the worm gear shaft and roller gear shaft oil seal bores of the housing with the longer lip of each seal facing into the housing.
2. Lubricate the worm gear and shaft assembly and upper ball bearing and cup with SAE 80 gear lubricant.
3. Install the bearing and cup on the shaft.
4. Carefully install the shaft assembly into the steering gear housing.
5. Lubricate the lower end of the worm gear and shaft assembly and lower ball bearing and cup with SAE 80 gear lubricant.
6. Install the bearing, cups and spacer on the shaft.
7. Position the shims and end cover on the steering gear housing and install the four capscrews loosely.
8. Adjust the bearing preload.
9. Position the tapped hole of the side cover to the adjustment screw of the roller gear and shaft assembly and thread the adjustment screw counterclockwise into the cover until the end of the shaft just touches the inner face of the cover.
10. Install a locknut loosely on the adjustment screw.
11. Install a new side cover gasket.
12. Lubricate the roller gear with SAE 80 gear lubricant.
13. Carefully insert the gear and shaft assembly into the steering gear housing. The roller gear and worm gear must mesh to seat the side cover to the housing.
14. Tighten the side cover capscrews to 18-22 ft. lbs.
15. Make a worm gear and roller gear backlash adjustment.
16. Clamp the exposed section of the roller gear and shaft assembly firmly into a soft jaw vise.
17. Align the index marks made during disassembly and position the steering arm to the splined end of the shaft.
18. Install the lockwasher and nut on the shaft threads and tighten the nut to draw the arm into position on the splines.
19. Fill the steering gear housing to the required level with SAE 80 gear lubricant.

Power Steering Gear

General Information

The procedures for maintaining, adjusting, and repairing the power steering systems and components discussed in this chapter are to be done only after determining that the steering linkages and front suspension systems are correctly aligned and in good condition. All worn or damaged parts should be replaced before attempting to service the power steering system. After correcting any condition that could affect the power steering, do the preliminary tests of the steering system components.

Preliminary Tests

Lubrication

Proper lubrication of the steering linkage and the front suspension components is very important for the proper operation of the steering systems of trucks equipped with power steering. Most all power steering systems use the same lubricant in the steering gear box as in the power steering pump reservoir, and the fluid level is maintaned at the pump reservoir.

With power cylinder-assist power steering, the steering gear is of the standard mechanical type and the lubricating oil is self contained within the gear box and the level is maintained by the removal of a filler plug on the gear box housing. The control valve assembly is mounted on the gear box and is lubricated by power steering oil from the power steering pump reservoir, where the level is maintained.

Air Bleeding

Air bubbles in the power steering system must be removed from the fluid. Be sure the reservoir is filled to the proper level and the fluid is warmed up to operating temperature. Then, turn the steering wheel through its full travel three or four times until all the air bubbles are removed. Do not hold the steering wheel against its stops. Recheck the fluid level.

Fluid Level Check

1. Run the engine until the fluid is at the normal operating temperature. Then, turn the steering wheel through its full travel three or four times, and shut off the engine.
2. Check the fluid level in the steering reservoir. If the fluid level is low, add enough fluid to raise the level to the Full mark on the dipstick or filler tube.

Pump Belt Check

1. Inspect the pump belt for cracks, glazing, or worn places. Using a belt tension gauge, check the belt tension for the proper range of adjustment. The amount of tension varies with the make of truck and the condition of the belt. New belts (those belts used

less than 15 minutes) require a higher figure. The belt deflection method of adjustment may be used only if a belt tension gauge is not available. The belt should be adjusted for a deflection of 3/8″ to 1/2″.

Fluid Leaks

Check all possible leakage points (hoses, power steering pump, or steering gear) for loss of fluid. Turn engine on and rotate the steering wheel from stop to stop several times. Tighten all loose fittings and replace any defective lines or valve seats.

Turning Effort

Check the turning effort required to turn the steering wheel after aligning the front wheels and inflating the tires to the proper pressure.

1. With the vehicle on dry pavement and the front wheel straight ahead, set the parking brake and turn the engine on.
2. After a short warm-up period for the engine, turn the steering wheel back and forth several times to warm the steering fluid.
3. Attach a spring scale to the steering wheel rim and measure the pull required to turn the steering wheel one complete revolution in each direction. The

POWER STEERING

Condition	Possible Cause	Correction
Hard Steering	(1) Low or uneven tire pressure. (2) Insufficient lubricant in the steering gear housing or in steering linkage. (3) Steering gear shaft adjusted too tight. (4) Improper caster or toe-in. (5) Steering column misaligned. (6) Loose, worn or broken pump belt. (7) Air in system. (8) Low fluid level in the pump reservoir. (9) Pump output pressure low. (10) Leakage at power cylinder piston rings. (Linkage type). (11) Binding or bent cylinder linkage. (Linkage type). (12) Valve spool and/or sleeve sticking. (Linkage type).	(1) Inflate the tires to recommended pressures. (2) Lubricate as necessary. (3) Adjust according to instructions. (4) Align the wheels. (5) See "Steering Gear Alignment." (6) Adjust or replace belt. (7) Bleed air from system. (8) Fill to correct level. (9) See "Pressure Test." (10) Replace piston rings and repair as required. (11) Replace or repair as required. (12) Free-up or replace as required.
Intermittent or No Power Assist	(1) Belt slipping and/or low fluid level. (2) Piston or rod binding in power cylinder. (Linkage type). (3) Sliding sleeve stuck in control valve. (Linkage type). (4) Improper pump operation.	(1) Adjust or replace belt. Add fluid as necessary. (2) Repair or replace piston and rod. (3) Free-up or replace sleeve. (4) Refer to "Power Steering Pump."
Poor or No Recovery from Turns	(1) Improper caster setting. (2) Steering gear adustments too tight. (3) Improper spool nut adjustment. (Linkage type). (4) Valve spool installed backwards. (Linkage type). (5) Low tire pressure. (6) Tight steering linkage. (7) King pins frozen.	(1) Adjust to specifications. (2) Adjust according to instructions. (3) Adjust according to instructions. (4) Install valve spool correctly. (5) Inflate tires to recommended pressure. (6) Lubricate as necessary. (7) Lubricate as necessary.
Lack of Effort (Both Turns)	(1) Improper sector shaft adjustment. (2) Pressure plates on wrong side of reaction rings.	(1) Adjust Sector Shaft. (2) Gear Recondition.
Lack of Effort (Left Turn Only)	(1) Left turn reaction seal "O" ring worn, damaged or missing. (2) Left turn reaction oil passageway not drilled in housing or cylinder head. (3) Left turn reaction ring sticking in cylinder head.	(1) Gear Recondition. (2) Replace parts as required. (3) Replace parts as required.
Lack of Effort (Right Turn Only)	(1) Right turn U-shaped reaction seal worn, damaged, or missing. (2) Right turn reaction oil passageway not drilled in housing head, or ferrule pin. (3) Right turn reaction ring sticking in housing head.	(1) Gear Recondition. (2) Replace parts as required. (3) Replace parts as required.
Lack of Assist (Left Turn Only)	(1) Left turn reaction seal "O" ring worn, damaged, or missing.	(1) Gear Recondition.
Lack of Assist (Right Turn Only)	(1) Right turn U-shaped reaction seal worn, damaged, or missing. (2) Worm sealing ring (teflon) worm sleeve seal, ferrule pin "O" ring damaged or worn. (3) Excessive internal leakage thru piston end plug and/or side plugs.	(1) Gear Recondition. (2) Gear Recondition. (3) Replace worm-piston assembly.
Lack of Assist (Both Turns)	(1) Low oil level in pump reservoir (usually accompanied by pump noise). (2) Loose pump belt. (3) Pump output low. (4) Engine idle too low. (5) Excessive internal leakage thru piston end plug and/or side plugs.	(1) Fill to proper level. (2) Adjust belts. (3) Pressure test pump. (4) Adjust engine idle. (5) Replace worm-piston assembly.

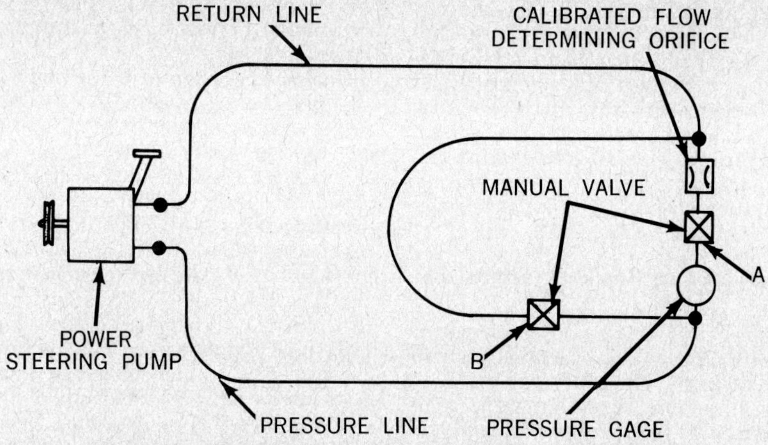

Power steering pump test circuit diagram (© Ford Motor Co.)

effort needed to turn the steering wheel should not exceed the limits specified.

NOTE: This test may be done with the steering wheel removed and a torque wrench applied on the steering wheel nut.

Power Steering Pump Flow

Since the power steering pump provides all the power assist in a power steering system, the pump must operate properly at all times for the system to work. After performing all the checks given above, the power steering pump may be tested for proper flow by the following procedures:

Two Gauges and Flow Meter

1. Disconnect the pressure and return lines at the power steering pump and connect the test pressure and return lines. The test lines are connected to a pressure gauge and two manual valves.
2. Open the two manual valves, connect a tachometer to the engine, and start the engine. Run the engine at idle speed until the reservoir fluid temperature reaches about 165-175 degrees Fahrenheit. This temperature must be maintained during the test. Manual valve B may be partially opened to create a back pressure of no more than 350 psi to aid the temperature rise. Reservoir fluid must be at the proper level.
3. After the engine and the reservoir fluid are sufficiently warmed up, close the manual valve B. Note the pressure gauge reading. It must be a minimum of 620 psi.
4. If the pressure reading is below the minimum acceptable pressure, the pump is defective and must be repaired. If the pressure reading is at or above the minimum value, the pump is normal. Open manual valve B and proceed to the pump fluid pressure test.

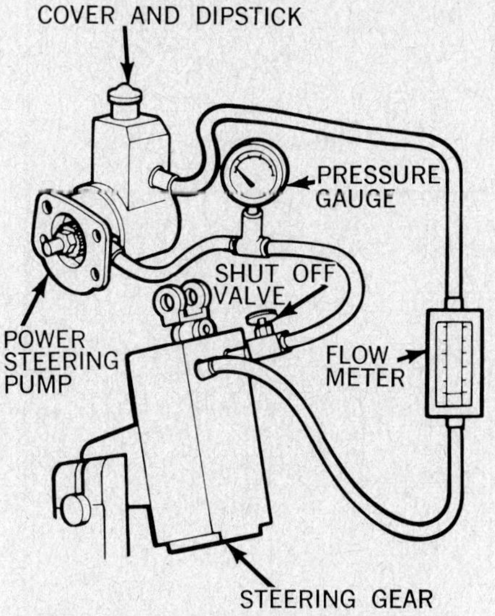

Testing power steering hydraulic system for internal leakage using a pressure gauge, shut-off valve and flow meter—typical (© Ford Motor Co.)

Power Steering Pump Fluid Pressure Test

1. Keep the lines and pressure gauge connected as in the Pump Flow Test.
2. With manual valve A and B opened fully, run the engine at the proper idle speed. Then, close manual valve A and manual valve B, in that order.

CAUTION: Do not keep both valves closed for more than 5 seconds since the fluid temperature will increase abnormally and cause unnecessary wear to the pump.

3. With both manual valves closed, the pressure reading should be as given in the specifications. If the pressure is below the minimum reading, the pump is defective and must be repaired. If the pressure reading is at or above the minimum reading, the pump is normal and the power steering gear or power assist control valve must be checked.

Checking the Oil Flow and Pressure Relief Valve in the Pump Assembly

When the wheels are turned hard right, or hard left, against the stops, the oil flow and pressure relief valves come into action. If these valves are working and are not stuck there should be a slight buzzing noise.

CAUTION: Do not hold the wheels in the extreme position for over three or four seconds because, if the pressure relief valve is not working, the pressure could get high enough to damage the system.

Single Gauge

1. Install the test pressure gauge (0-2000 psi) between the power steering pump and the control valve.
2. With the fluid at a temperature of 170 to 190°F, the engine running above idle and the shut-off valve open, observe the pressure reading while moving the wheels to the end of their right and left travel.
3. If the gauge registers the correct relief valve pressure, the hydraulic system should be satisfactory. If pressure cannot be built up on either side of the gear, internal pump or gear problems exist.

   NOTE: A shuttle valve equipped power cylinder may register a sharp drop-off in pressure at the end of the wheel travel and is considered normal.
4. To check the pump, close the shut-off valve and observe the pressure gauge. The pressure reading should be at relief valve pressure.

   NOTE: Do not keep the shut-off valve closed longer than 15 seconds as damage to the pump could occur.
5. Repeat the closing of the shut-off valve twice more and record the highest pressure reading each time.
6. If the pressure readings are

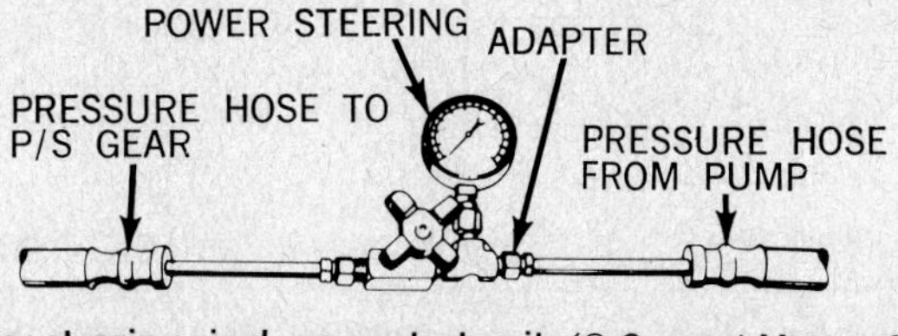

Power steering single gauge test unit (© General Motors Corp.)

within 50 lbs. of each other and with-in the pump relief valve specifications, the pump operation is normal.
Example: Pump specifications—900 to 1500 psi.
Readings: 1st—1310 psi
2nd—1290 psi
3rd—1320 psi

7. If the readings are high but do not repeat within-in 50 lbs of each other, the flow control valve can be sticking. If 100 lbs difference is noted below the low listed specification, replace the flow valve and recheck the system.

Relief Valve Pressure

Relief valve pressures normally range between 800 to 2000 psi, depending upon the requirements of the power steering system and the axle application used on the vehicle. The lighter the truck, the less pressure is needed to operate the steering system, while the opposite is true of the heavier vehicles.

The minimum pressures with the wheels straight ahead and at engine idle should be in the 80 to 120 psi range.

Power Steering Hose Inspection

1. Inspect both the input and output hoses of the power steering pump for worn spots, cracks, or signs of leakage. Replace hose if defective, being sure to reconnect the replacement hose properly. Many power steering hoses are identified as to where they are to be connected by special means, such as fittings that will only fit on the correct pump fitting, or hoses of special lengths.

Test Driving Truck to Check the Power Steering

When test driving to check power steering, drive at a speed between 15 and 20 mph. Make several turns in each direction. When a turn is completed, the front wheels should return to the straight ahead position with very little help from the driver.

If the front wheels fail to return as they should and yet the steering linkage is free, well oiled and properly adjusted, the trouble is probably due to misalignment of the power cylinder or improper adjustment of the spool valve.

The power steering pump supplies all the power assist used in power steering systems of all designs. There are various designs of pumps used by the truck manufacturers but all pumps supply power to operate the steering systems with the least effort. All power steering pumps have a reservoir tank built onto the oil pump. These pumps are driven by belts turned by pulleys on the engine, normally on the front of the crankshaft.

During operation of the engine at idle speed, there is provision for the power steering pump to supply more fluid pressure. During driving speeds or when the truck is moving straight ahead, less pressure is needed and the excess is relieved through a pressure relief and flow control valve. The pressure relief part of the valve is inside the flow control and is basically the same for all pumps. The flow control valve regulates, or controls, the constant flow of fluid from the pump as it varies with the demands of the steering gear. The pressure relief valve limits the hydraulic pressure built up when the steering gear is turned against its stops.

During pump disassembly, make sure all work is done on a clean surface. Clean the outside of the pump thoroughly and do not allow dirt of any kind to get inside. Do not immerse the shaft oil seal in solvent.

If replacing the rotor shaft seal, be extremely careful not to scratch sealing surfaces with tools.

Pump Overhaul

Vane Type Power Steering Pump

The vane type power steering pump is used in Saginaw steering

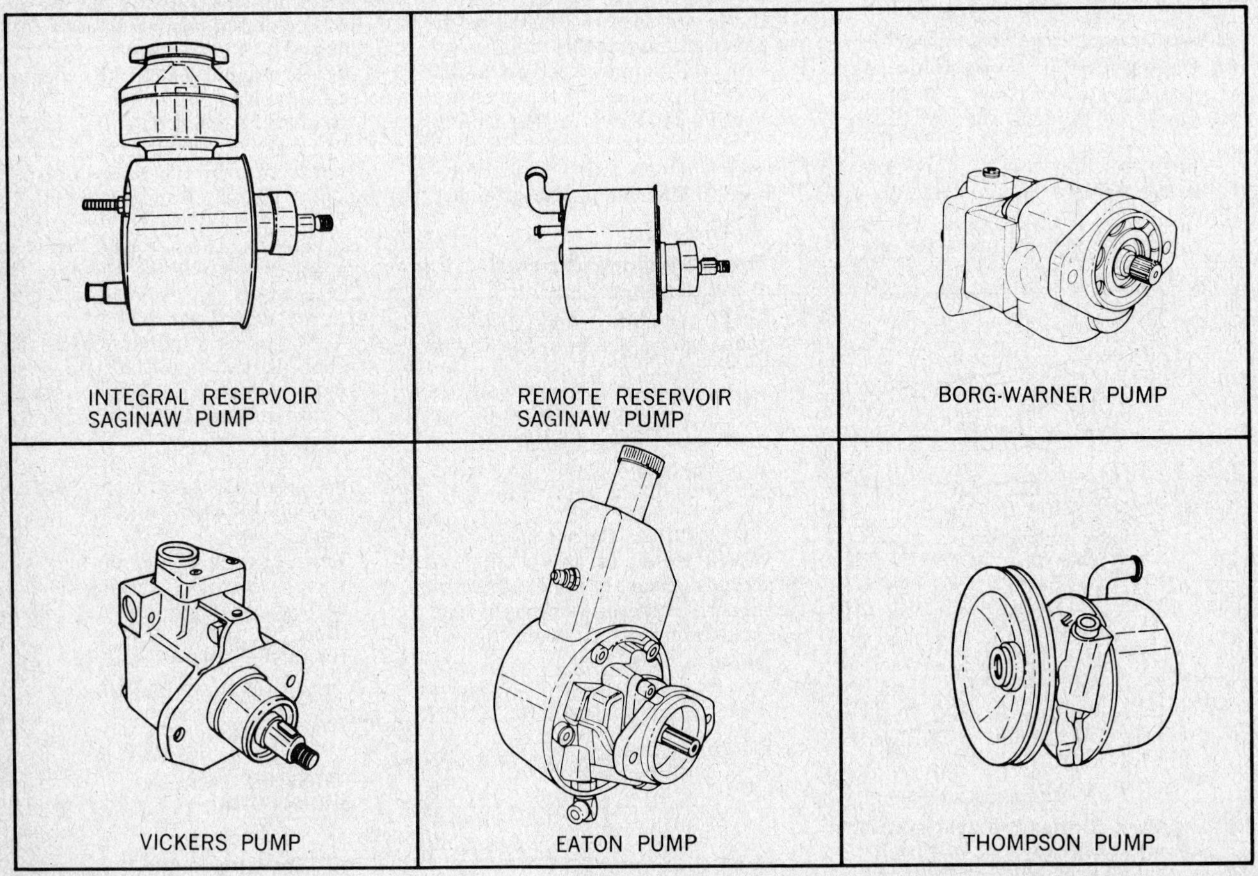

Identification of power steering pumps used on General Motors trucks—typical (© General Motors Corp.)

POWER STEERING PUMP

Condition	Possible Cause	Correction
Intermittent Assist	(1) Flow control valve sticking. (2) Slipping belt. (3) Low fluid level. (4) Low pump efficiency.	(1) Pressure test pump and service as necessary. (2) Adjust belt. (3) Inspect and correct fluid level. (4) Pressure test pump and service as necessary.
No Assist	(1) Pump seizure. (2) Broken slipper spring(s). (3) Flow control bore plug ring not in place. (4) Flow control valve sticking.	(1) Replace pump. (2) Recondition pump or replace as necessary. (3) Replace snap ring. Inspect groove for depth. (4) Pressure test pump and service as necessary.
No Assist When Parking Only	(1) Wrong pressure relief valve. (2) Broken "O" ring on flow control bore plug. (3) Loose pressure relief valve. (4) Low pump efficiency.	(1) Install proper relief valve. (2) Replace "O" ring. (3) Tighten valve. DO NOT ADJUST. (4) Pressure test pump and service as necessary.
Noisy Pump	(1) Low fluid level. (2) Belt noise. (3) Foreign material blocking pump housing oil inlet hole.	(1) Inspect and correct fluid level. (2) Inspect for pulley alignment, paint or grease on pulley and correct. Adjust belt. (3) Remove reservoir, visually check inlet oil hole and service as necessary.
Pump Vibration	(1) Pump hose interference with sheet metal or brake lines. (2) Belt loose. (3) Pulley loose or out of round. (4) Crankshaft pulley loose or damaged. (5) Bracket pivot bolts loose.	(1) Reroute hoses. (2) Adjust belt. (3) Replace pulley. (4) Replace crankshaft pulley. (5) If unable to tighten, replace bracket.
Pump Leaks	(1) Cap or filler neck leaks. (2) Reservoir solder joints leak. (3) Reservoir "O" ring leaking. (4) Shaft seal leaking. (5) Loose rear bracket bolts. (6) Loose or faulty high pressure ferrule. (7) Rear bolt holes stripped or casting cracked.	(1) Correct fluid level. (2) Resolder or replace reservoir as necessary. (3) Inspect sealing area of reservoir. Replace "O" ring or reservoir as necessary. (4) Replace seal. 5) Tighten bolts. (6) Tighten fitting to 24 foot-pounds or replace as necessary. (7) Repair, if possible, or replace pump.

systems. The operation is basically the same as that of the roller type pumps. Centrifugal force moves a number of vanes outward against the pump ring, causing a pumping action of the fluid to the control valve.

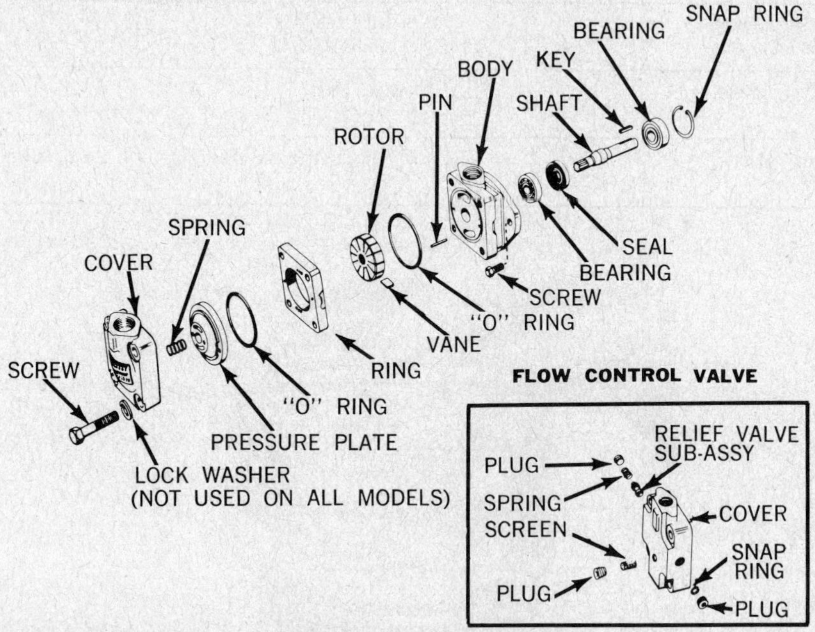

Exploded view of vane type pump—Vickers (© International Harvester Co.)

Removal

1. Disconnect hoses at the pump, securing them in a raised position to prevent oil drainage. Cap or cover the ends of the hoses to keep dirt out.
2. Install two caps on the pump fittings to prevent oil drainage.
3. Loosen the bracket-to-pump mounting nuts, move pump toward engine slightly, and remove the pump drive belt.
4. Remove the bracket-to-pump bolts and remove the pump from the truck.
5. While holding the drive pulley steady, loosen and remove the pulley attaching nut. Slide the pulley off the shaft.

   NOTE: Do not hammer the pulley off the shaft.

Installation

1. To install the pump on the truck, reverse the removal procedure. Always use a new pulley nut, tightening it to 35-45 ft. lbs. torque.
2. After reconnecting the hoses to the pump, fill the reservoir with fluid and bleed the pump of air by turning the drive pulley counterclockwise (as viewed from the front) until air bubbles do not appear.
3. Install the pump drive belt over the pulley, move the pump against the belt until tight enough, then tighten the mounting bolts and nuts.

POWER STEERING NOISE

Condition	Possible Cause	Correction
Objectionable "Hiss"	(1) Noisy valve.	(1) Do not replace valve unless "hiss" is extremely objectionable. A replacement valve will also exhibit sight noise and is not always a cure for the objection.
Rattle or Chuckle Noise in Steering Gear	(1) Gear loose on frame. (2) Steering linkages looseness. (3) Pressure hose touching other parts of truck. (4) Loose Pitman shaft over center adjustment. **NOTE:** A slight rattle may occur on turns because of increased clearance off the "high point". This is normal and clearance must not be reduced below specified limits to eliminate this slight rattle. (5) Loose Pitman arm.	(1) Check gear mounting bolts. Torque bolts to specifications. (2) Check linkage pivot points for wear. Replace if necessary. (3) Adjust hose position. Do not bend tubing by hand. (4) Adust (5) Torque Pitman arm pinch bolt.
Squawk Noise in Steering Gear When Turning or Recovering From a Turn	(1) Dampener O-ring on valve spool cut. (2) Loose or worn valve.	(1) Replace dampener O-Ring. (2) Replace valve.
Chirp Noise in Steering Gear	(1) Gear relief valve.	(1) Replace relief valve.
Chirp Noise in Steering Pump	(1) Loose belt.	(1) Adjust belt tension.
Belt Squeal (Particularly Noticeable at Full Wheel Travel and Standstill Parking)	(1) Loose belt.	(1) Adjust belt tension.
Growl Noise in Steering Pump	(1) Excessive back pressure in hoses or steering gear caused by restriction.	(1) Locate restriction and correct. Replace part if necessary.
Growl Noise in Steering Pump (Particularly Noticeable at Standstill Parking)	(1) Scored pressure plates, thrust plate or rotor. (2) Extreme wear of cam ring.	(1) Replace parts and flush system. (2) Replace parts.
Groan Noise in Steering Pump	(1) Low oil level. (2) Air in the oil. Poor pressure hose connection.	(1) Fill reservoir to proper level. (2) Torque connector. Bleed system.
Rattle or Knock Noise in Steering Pump	(1) Loose pump pulley nut.	(1) Torque nut.
Rattle Noise in Steering Pump	(1) Vanes not installed properly. (2) Vanes sticking in rotor slots.	(1) Install properly. (2) Repair or replace.
Swish Noise in Steering Pump	(1) Defective flow control valve.	(1) Replace part.
Whine Noise in Steering Pump	(1) Pump shaft bearing scored.	(1) Replace housing and shaft. Flush and bleed system.

4. Bleed the air from the system.

Disassembly

1. Clean the outside of the pump in a non-toxic solvent before disassembling.
2. Mount the pump in a vise, being careful not to squeeze the front hub too tight.
3. Remove the union and seal.
4. Remove the reservoir retaining studs and separate the reservoir from the housing.
5. Remove the mounting bolt and union O-rings.

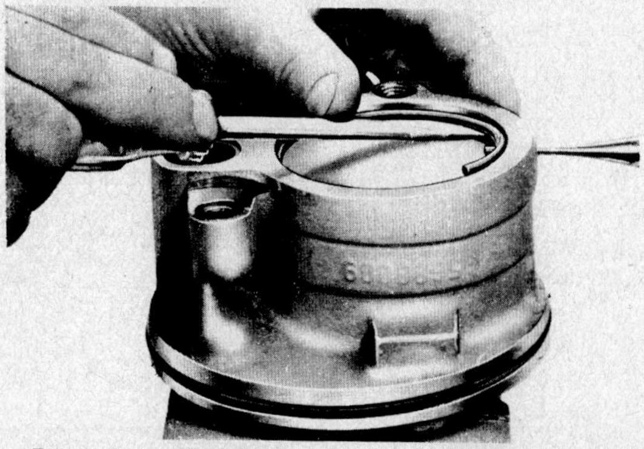

Removing end plate ring (© General Motors Corp.)

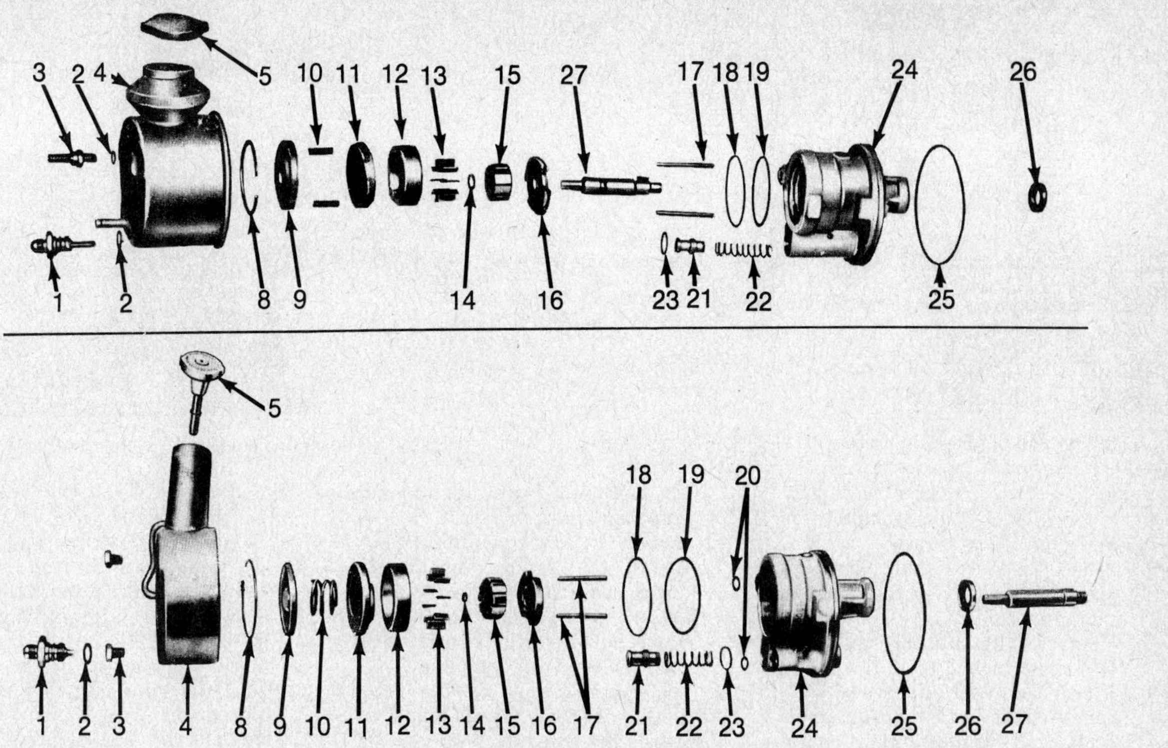

Vane type power steering pumps (© General Motors Corp.)

1 Union
2 Union "O" ring seal
3 Mounting studs
4 Reservoir
5 Dip stick and cover
8 End plate retaining ring
9 End plate
10 Spring
11 Pressure plate
12 Pump ring
13 Vanes
14 Drive shaft retaining ring
15 Rotor
16 Thrust plate
17 Dowel pins
18 End plate "O" ring
19 Pressure plate "O" ring
20 Mounting stud square ring
21 Flow control valve
22 Flow control valve spring
23 Flow control valve square ring seal
24 Pump housing
25 Reservoir "O" ring seal
26 Shaft seal
27 Shaft

6. Remove the filter and filter cage; discard the element.
7. Remove the end plate retaining ring by compressing the retaining ring and then prying it out with a removal tool. The retaining ring may be compressed by inserting a small punch in the ⅛" diameter hole in the housing and pushing in until the ring clears the groove.
8. Remove the end plate. The end plate is spring-loaded and should rise above the housing level. If it is stuck inside the housing, a slight rocking or gentle tapping should free the plate.
9. Remove the shaft woodruff key and tap the end of the shaft gently to free the pressure plate, pump ring, rotor assembly, and thrust plate. Remove these parts as one unit.
10. Remove the end plate O-ring. Separate the pressure plate, pump ring, rotor assembly, and thrust plate.

Inspection

Clean all metal parts in a non-toxic solvent and inspect them as given below:

1. Check the flow control valve for free movement in the housing bore. If the valve is sticking, see if there is dirt or a rough spot in the bore.
2. Check the cap screw in the end of the flow control valve for looseness. Tighten if necessary being careful not to damage the machined surfaces.
3. Inspect the pressure plate and the pump plate surfaces for flatness and check that there are no cracks or scores in the parts. Do not mistake the normal wear marks for scoring.
4. Check the vanes in the rotor assembly for free movement and that they were installed with the radiused edge toward the pump ring.
5. If the flow control valve plunger

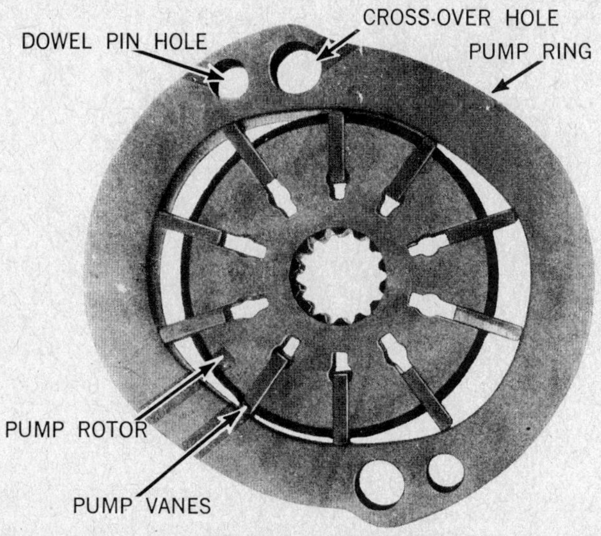

Correct vane assembly (© General Motors Corp.)

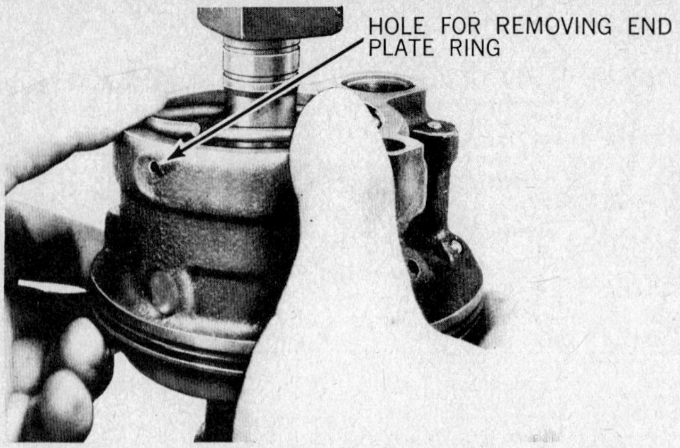

Installing end plate retaining ring (© General Motors Corp.)

Installing flow control valve (© General Motors Corp.)

is defective, install a new part. The valve is factory calibrated and supplied as a unit.

6. Check the drive shaft for worn splines, breaks, bushing material pick-up, etc.
7. Replace all rubber seals and O-rings removed from the pump.
8. Check the reservoir, studs, casting, etc. for burrs and other defects that would impair operation.

Assembly

1. Install a new shaft seal in the housing and insert the shaft at the hub end of housing, splined end entering mounting face side.
2. Install the thrust plate on the dowel pins with the ported side facing the rear of the pump housing.
3. Install the rotor on the pump shaft over the splined end. Be sure the rotor moves freely on the splines. Countersunk side must be toward the shaft.
4. Install the shaft retaining ring. Install the pump ring on the dowel pins with the rotation arrow toward the rear of the pump housing. Rotation is clockwise as seen from the pulley.
5. Install the vanes in the rotor slots with the radius edge towards the outside.
6. Lubricate the outside diameter and chamfer of the pressure plate with petroleum jelly so as not to damage the O-ring and install the plate on the dowel pins with the ported face toward the pump ring. Seat the pressure plate by placing a large socket on top of the plate and pushing down with the hand.
7. Install the pressure plate spring in the center groove of the plate.
8. Install the end plate O-ring. Lubricate the outside diameter and chamfer of the end plate with petroleum jelly so as not to damage the O-ring and install the end plate in the housing, using an arbor press. Install the end plate retaining ring while pump is in the arbor press. Be sure the ring is in the groove and the ring gap is positioned properly.
9. Install the flow control spring and plunger, hex head screw end in bore first. Install the filter cage, new filter stud seals and union seal.
10. Place the reservoir in the normal position and press down until the reservoir seats on the housing. Check the position of the stud seals and the union seal.
11. Install the studs, union, and drive shaft woodruff key. Support the shaft on the opposite side of the key when tapping the key into place.

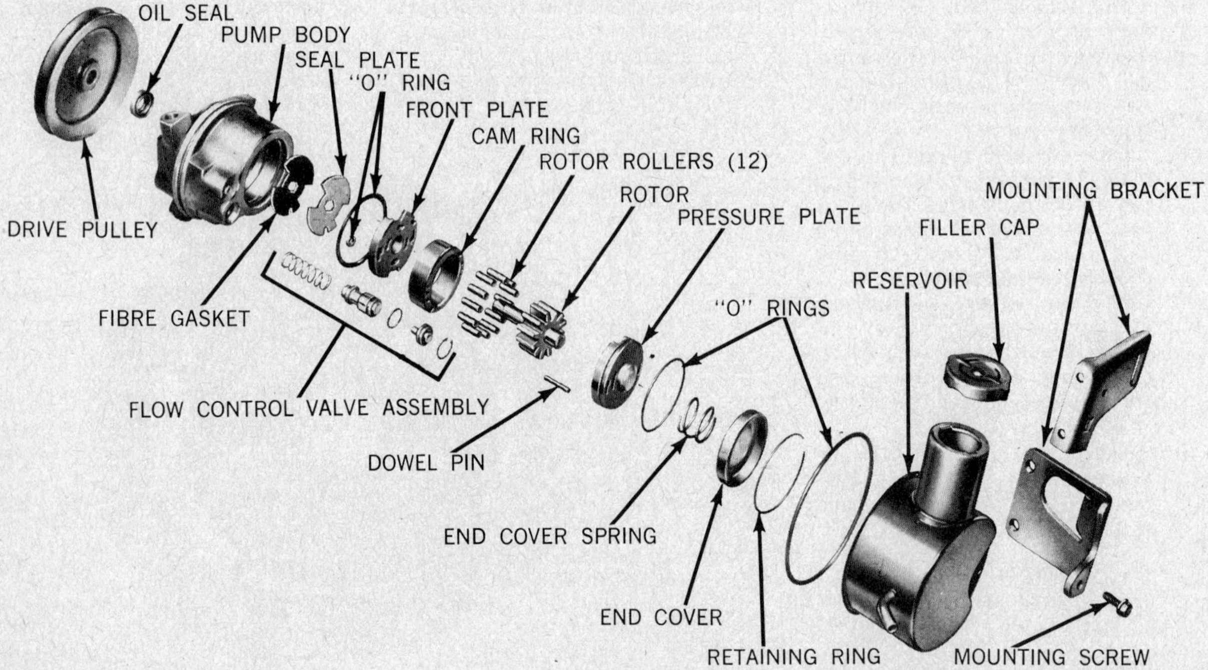

Roller type power steering pump (© Chrysler Corp.)

Roller Type Power Steering Pump

The roller type power steering pump is designed similar to other constant flow centrifugal force pumps. A star-shaped rotor forces 12 steel rollers against the inside surface of a cam ring. As the rollers follow the eccentric pattern of the cam ring, oil is drawn into the inlet ports and exhausted through the discharge ports while the rollers are moved into vee shaped cavities of the rotor, forcing oil into the high pressure circuit. A flow control valve permits a regulated amount of fluid to return to the intake side of the pump when excess output is produced during high speed operation. This reduces the power needs to drive the pump and minimizes temperature build-up.

The flow control valve used in one make of pump is a two-stage valve. Fluid under high pressure passes through two holes into a metering circuit located in a sealed passage. At low speed, about 2.7 gpm. passes to the gear. As speed increases and the valve moves, excess fluid is bypassed to the inlet and the valve blocks flow through one hole. This drops the flow to about 1.6 gpm. at high speeds.

When steering conditions produce excessive pressure needs (such as turning the wheels against the stops), the pressure built up in the steering gear exerts force on the spring end of the flow control valve.

This end of the valve contains the pressure relief valve. High pressure lifts the relief valve ball from its seat, allowing fluid to flow through a trigger orifice located in the front land of the flow control valve. This reduces pressure on the spring end of the valve which then opens and allows the fluid to return to the intake side of the pump. This action limits the maximum pressure output of the pump to a safe level. Normally, the pressure needs of the pump are below the maximum limits, causing the pressure relief ball and the flow control valve to remain closed.

Removal

1. Loosen the pump mounting and locking bolts and remove the belt.
2. Disconnect both hoses at the pump. Cap and tie the hoses out of the way. Cap the hose fittings on the pump.
3. Remove the mounting and locking bolts, the pump and brackets from the truck.

Installation

1. Position the pump and brackets on the engine and install the mounting and locking bolts.
2. Install the drive belt and adjust for the proper tension.
3. Connect the pressure and return hoses, using a new pressure hose O-ring.
4. Fill the pump reservoir to the top of the filler neck with power steering fluid.
5. Start the engine and turn the steering wheel several times from stop to stop to bleed the pump of air. Check the level and add fluid if necessary.

NOTE: When checking the level, see that the level is as follows: engine cold–bottom of filler tube; engine hot–half way up filler tube.

Disassembly

1. Remove pump from engine, drain reservoir, and clean outside of pump. Clamp the pump in a vise at the mounting bracket.
2. Remove the drive pulley.
3. Remove the shaft seal by installing the seal remover adapter over the end of the drive shaft with the large end toward the pump. Place the seal remover tool over the shaft and through the adapter. Then, screw the tapered thread well into the metal portion of the seal. Tighten the large drive nut and remove the seal.
4. Remove the pump from the vise and remove the bracket mounting bolts. Remove the bracket.
5. Remove the reservoir and place the pump in a soft-faced vise with the shaft down. Discard the mounting bolt and the reservoir O-rings.
6. Move the end cover retaining ring around until one end of the ring lines up with the hole in the pump body. Insert a small punch in the hole and push it in far enough to bend the ring so a screwdriver can be inserted between the ring and the housing. Remove the ring.
7. Remove the end cover and spring from the housing. It may be necessary to tap the cover gently to loosen it in the housing.

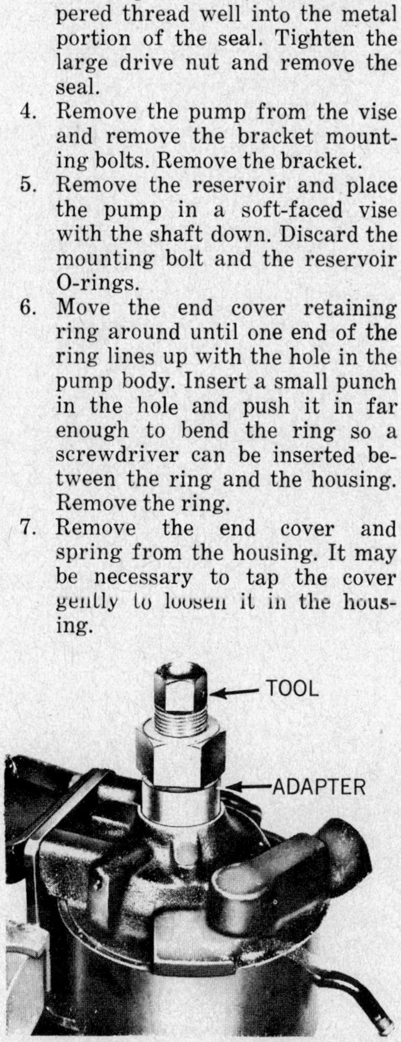

Removing shaft seal (© Chrysler Corp.)

8. Remove the pump from the vise and turn the pump over so the rotating group may come out of the housing. Tap the end of the drive shaft to loosen these parts. Lift the pump body off the rotating group. Check that the seal plate is removed from the bottom of the housing bore.
9. Discard the O-rings from the pressure plate and end cover.
10. Remove the snap-ring, bore plug, flow control valve and spring from the housing. Discard the O-ring. If necessary to dismantle the flow control valve for cleaning, see the procedure for disassembly.

Inspection

1. Remove the clean out plug with an Allen wrench.
2. Wash all metal parts in clean, non-toxic solvent. Blow out all passages with compressed air and air dry all cleaned parts.
3. Inspect the drive shaft for excessive wear and the seal area for nicks or scoring. Replace if necessary.
4. Inspect the end plates, rollers, rotor and cam ring for nicks, burrs, or scratches. If any of the components are damaged enough to cause poor operation of the pump, all the interior parts may have to be replaced to prevent later failures.
5. Inspect the pump body drive shaft bushing for excessive wear. Replace the pump body and bushing as one assembly.

Assembly

1. Install the 1/8" pipe clean out plug, tightening it to 80 in. lbs. torque.
2. Place the pump body on a clean flat surface and install a new shaft seal into the bore.
3. Install a new end cover O-ring into the groove in the pump bore. Be sure to lubricate the O-ring with power steering fluid before installing it.
4. Lubricate and install a new O-ring in the groove on the pump body where the reservoir fits snugly.
5. Install the brass seal plate to the bottom of the housing bore. Align the notch in the seal plate with the dowel pin hole in the housing.
6. Carefully install the front plate with the chamfered edge down in the pump bore. Align the index notch in the plate with the dowel pin hole in the housing.

CAUTION: Be extremely careful to align the dowel pin hole properly. Pump can be completely assembled with the dowel pin not seated properly in the hole.

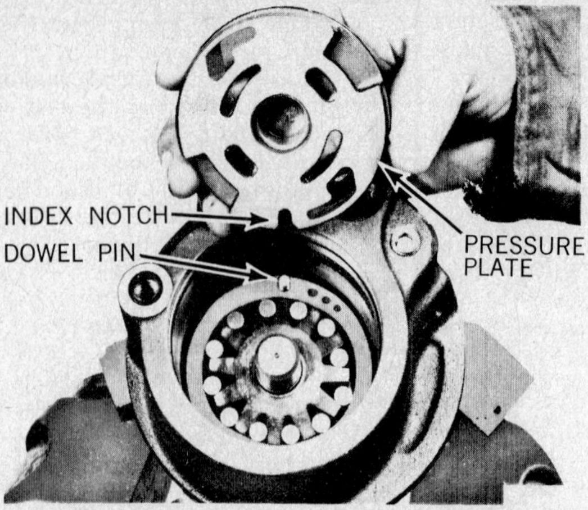

Installing pressure plate (© Chrysler Corp.)

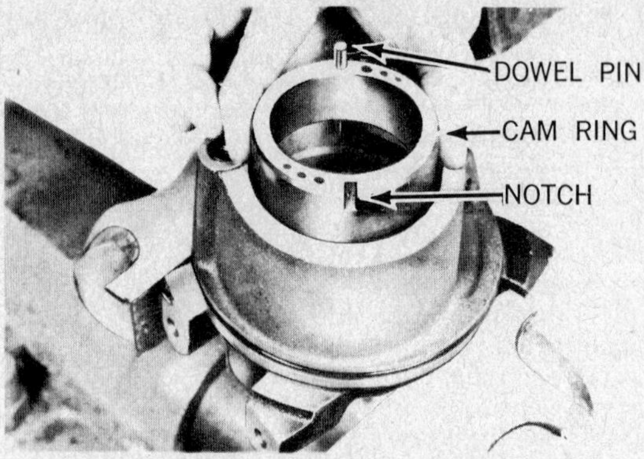

Installing cam ring (© Chrysler Corp.)

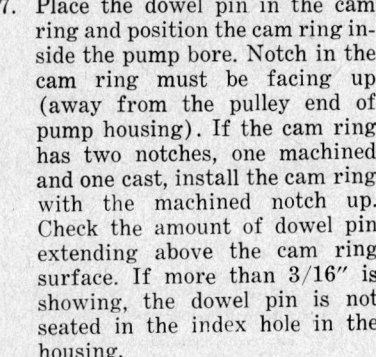

7. Place the dowel pin in the cam ring and position the cam ring inside the pump bore. Notch in the cam ring must be facing up (away from the pulley end of pump housing). If the cam ring has two notches, one machined and one cast, install the cam ring with the machined notch up. Check the amount of dowel pin extending above the cam ring surface. If more than 3/16" is showing, the dowel pin is not seated in the index hole in the housing.
8. Install the rotor and shaft in the cam ring and carefully install the 12 steel rollers in the cavities of the rotor. Lubricate the rotor, rollers, and the inside surface of the cam ring with power steering fluid. Rotate the shaft by hand to be sure all the rollers are seated parallel with the shaft and are not sticking or binding.
9. Position the pressure plate by carefully aligning the index notch on the plate with the dowel pin and inserting a clean drill (number 13 to 16) in the cam ring oil hole next to the dowel pin notch until it bottoms on the housing floor.
10. Lubricate and install a new O-ring on the pressure plate. Position the pressure plate in the pump bore so that the dowel pin is in the index notch on the plate and the drill extends through the oil passage in the pressure plate. Seat the pressure plate on the cam ring using a clean 1⅛" socket and a soft-faced hammer to tap it gently. Remove the drill and inspect the plate at both oil passage slots to be sure that the plate is squarely seated on the cam ring.
11. Place the large coil spring over the raised portion of the installed pressure plate.
12. Place the end cover, lip edge facing up, over the spring. Press the end cover down below the retaining ring groove. Install the retaining ring in the groove. Be sure the end cover chamfer is squarely seated against the snap-ring.
13. Replace the reservoir mounting bolt seal.
14. Lubricate the flow control valve assembly with power steering fluid and insert the valve spring and valve in the bore. Install a new O-ring on the bore plug, lubricate with fluid, and carefully install in the bore. Install the snap-ring with the sharp edge up. Do not depress the bore plug more than 1/16" below the snap-ring groove.
15. Place the reservoir on the pump body and visually align the mounting bolt hole. Tap the reservoir down on the pump with a plastic-faced hammer.
16. Remove the pump from the vise and install the mounting brackets with the mounting bolts on the pump. Tighten the bolts to 18 ft. lbs. torque.

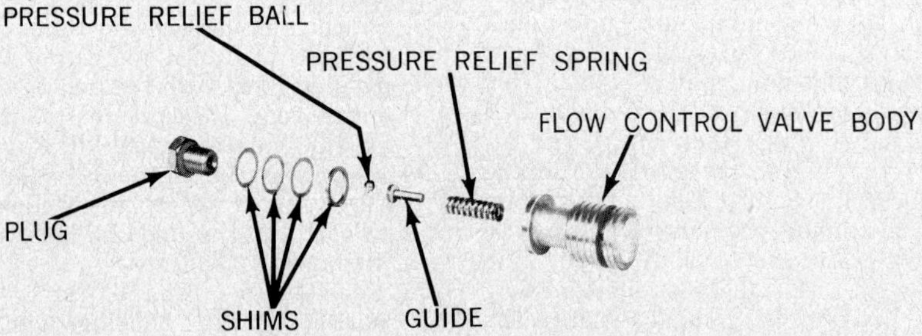

Flow control valve (© Chrysler Corp.)

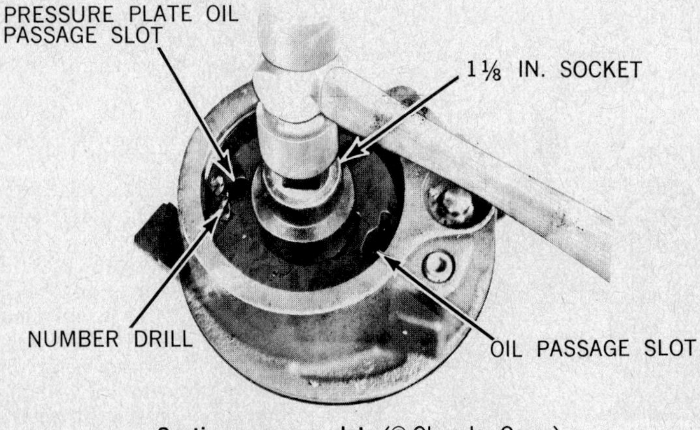

Seating pressure plate (© Chrysler Corp.)

17. Install the drive pulley by using the installer tool as follows: place the pulley on the end of the shaft and thread the installer tool into the ⅜" threaded hole in the end of the shaft. Put the installer shaft in a vise and tighten the drive nut against the thrust bearing, pressing the pulley on the shaft until it is flush. Do not try to press the pulley on the shaft without the special installer tool since the pump interior will be damaged by any other installation procedure. A small amount of drive shaft end play will be seen when the pulley is installed. This end play is nec-

essary and will be minimized by a thin coat of oil between the rotor and the end plates when the pump is operating.

18. Install the pump assembly on the engine, install the drive belt and hoses (use new O-ring on pressure hose), and check for leaks.

Flow Control Valve Disassembly

1. After removing the pump from the engine and the reservoir from the pump, remove the snap-ring and plug from the flow bore. Discard the O-ring.
2. Depress the control valve against the spring pressure and allow the valve to spring out of the bore. If the valve is stuck in the bore or it did not come out of the bore far enough, it may be necessary to tap the housing lightly to remove it.
3. If the valve has dirt or foreign particles on it or in its bore, the rest of the pump needs cleaning. The hoses should be flushed and the steering gear valve body reconditioned. If the valve bore is badly scored, replace the pump body and the flow control valve.
4. Remove any nicks or burrs by gently rubbing the valve with crocus cloth. Clamp the valve land in a vise with soft-jaws and remove the hex head ball seat and shims. Note the number and gauge (thickness) of the shims on the ball seat. They must be re-installed for the same shim thickness to keep the same value of relief pressure.
5. Remove the valve from the vise and remove the pressure relief ball, guide, and spring.

Flow Control Valve Assembly

1. Insert the spring, guide and pressure relief ball in the end of the flow control valve.
2. Install the hex head plug using the exact number and thickness shims that were removed. Tighten the plug to 80 in. lbs. torque.
3. Lubricate the valve with power steering fluid and insert the flow control valve spring and valve in the housing bore. Install a new O-ring on the bore plug, lubricate with fluid and carefully install into the bore. Install the snap-ring. Do not depress the bore plug more than 1/16″ beyond the snap-ring groove.

Slipper Type Power Steering Pump

The slipper type power steering pump is a belt-driven constant displacement assembly that uses a number of spring-loaded slippers in the pump rotor to force fluid from the inlet side to the flow control valve. Openings in the metering pin allow a flow of about two gpm. of fluid to the steering gear before the flow control valve directs the excess fluid to the inlet side of the pump again. Maximum pressure in the pump is limited by the pressure relief valve which opens when the pressure exceeds the maximum limits.

The slipper type power steering pump discussed in this section is used on Ford trucks and is called the Ford-Thompson power steering pump.

Removal

1. Drain the fluid from the pump reservoir by disconnecting the fluid return hose at the pump. Then, disconnect the pressure hose from the pump.
2. Remove the mounting bolts from the front of the pump. On eight cylinder engines, there is a nut on the rear of the pump that must be removed. After removing all the mounting bolts and nuts from the pump, move the unit inward to loosen the belt tension and remove the belt from the pulley. Then remove the pump from the engine.

Installation

1. Position the pump on the mounting bracket and loosely install the mounting bolts and nuts. Put the drive belt over the pulley and move the pump outward against the belt until the proper belt tension is obtained. Measure the belt tension with a gauge for the proper adjustment. Only in cases where a belt tension gauge is not available should the belt deflection method be used. If the belt deflection method is used, be sure to check the belt with a tension gauge at the earliest time since the deflection method is not accurate.

2\. Tighten the mounting bolts and nuts to the specified torque limits.

5\. Tighten the pressure hose fitting hex nut to the proper torque. Then connect the pressure hose to the pump and tighten the hose nut to the proper torque.

4\. Connect the fluid return hose to the pump and tighten the clamp.

5\. Fill the pump reservoir with power steering fluid and bleed the air bubbles from the system.

6\. Check for leaks and recheck the fluid level. If necessary, add fluid to raise the level properly.

Disassembly

1. Drain as much fluid from the pump as possible after removing the pump from the truck.
2. Install a 3/8-16″ capscrew in the end of the pump shaft to avoid damaging the shaft end with the pulley remover tool. Install the pulley remover tool on the pulley hub and place the pump and remover tool in a vise. Hold the pump steady and turn the tool nut counterclockwise to draw the pulley off the shaft. The pulley must be removed without in and out pressure on the pump shaft to avoid damaging the internal thrust washers.
3. Remove the pump reservoir by installing the pump in a holding fixture with an adapter plate in a vise with the reservoir facing up.
4. Remove the outlet fitting hex nut and any other attaching parts from the reservoir case.
5. Invert the pump so the reservoir is now facing down. Using a wooden block, remove the reservoir by tapping around the

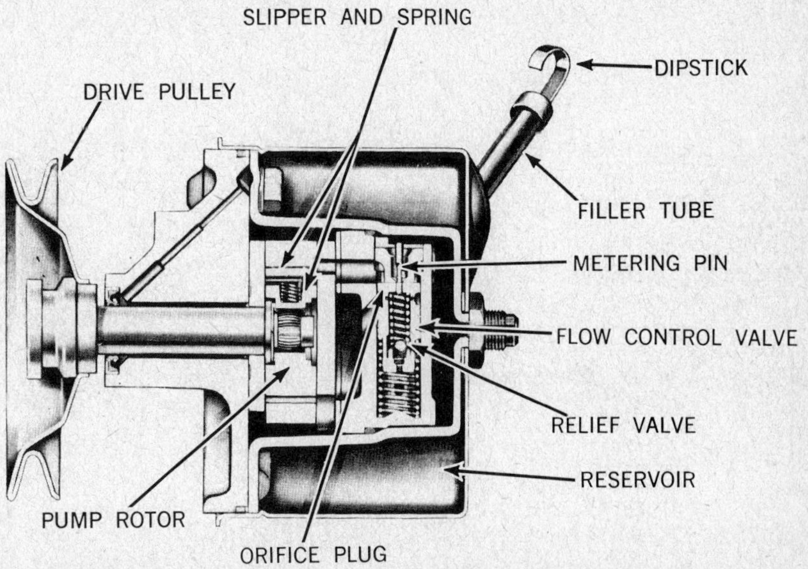

Ford Thompson power steering pump—Sectional view (© Ford Motor Co.)

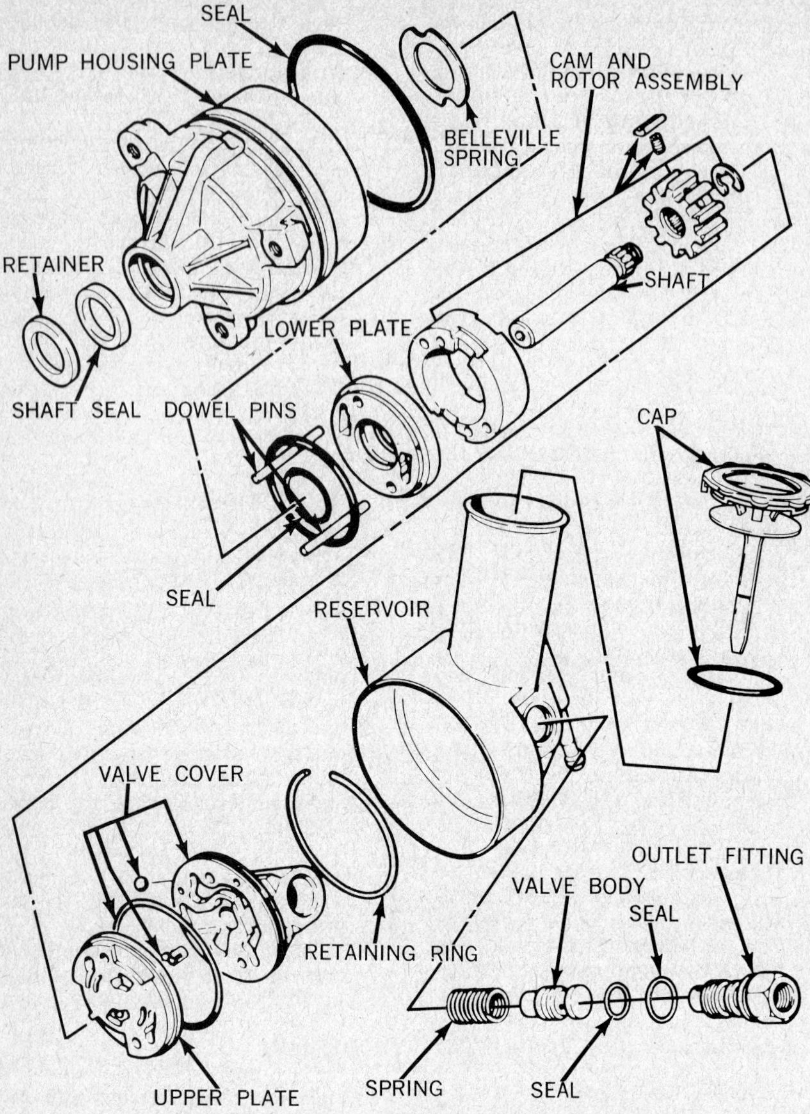

Exploded view—model C-11 slipper type pump (© Ford Motor Co.)

flange until the reservoir is loose. Remove the reservoir O-ring seal and the outlet fitting gasket from the pump.

6. Again invert the pump assembly in the vise, remove the pump housing holding bolts and the pump housing.
7. Remove the housing cover, the O-ring seal and the pressure springs from inside the pump housing. Remove the pump cover gasket and discard it.
8. Remove the retainer end plate and upper pressure plate. In some pumps, the end plate and the upper pressure plate are made as one unit.
9. Remove the loose fitting dowel pin. Be careful not to bend the fixed dowel pin which remains in the housing plate assembly.
10. Remove the rotor assembly being careful not to let the slippers and springs fall out of the rotor. It may not be necessary to disassemble the rotor assembly unless the lower pressure plate, housing plate, rotor shaft and/or seal is to be replaced. However, the rotor assembly may be disassembled by removing the slippers and springs from the cam ring.
11. Remove any rust, dirt, burrs, or scoring from the pulley end of the rotor shaft before removing the shaft from the housing plate. The shaft must come out without restrictions to avoid scoring or damaging the bushing. Remove the pump rotor shaft.
12. Remove the lower pressure plate.
13. Remove the rotor shaft seal after first wrapping a piece of

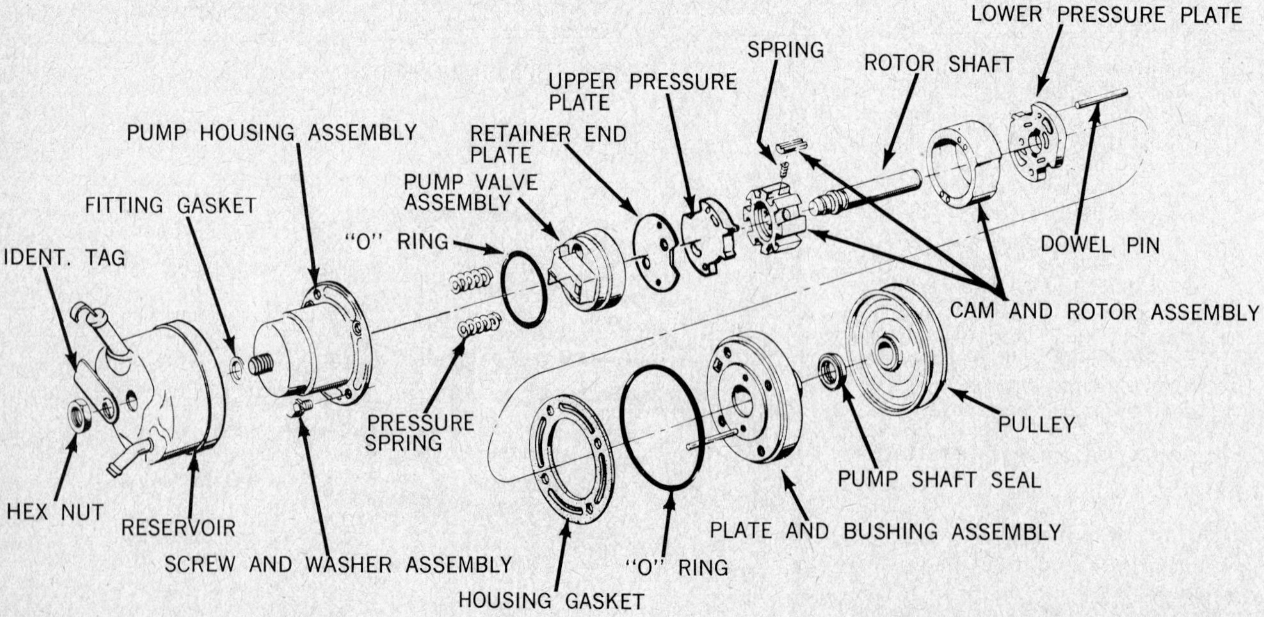

Ford Thompson power steering pump—exploded view (© Ford Motor Co.)

0.005″ shim stock around the shaft and pushing it into the inside of the seal until it touches the bushing. With a sharp tool, pierce the seal body and pry the seal out. Do not damage the bushing, housing, or the shaft. Install a new seal using a soft-faced hammer.

14. If the pump has a flow control valve, disassemble according to instructions given in the section on the roller type power steering pump.

Inspection

1. Wash all metal parts in clean, non-toxic solvent. Blow out all oil passages with compressed air and air dry all cleaned parts.
2. Inspect the drive shaft for excessive wear and seal area for nicks or scoring. Replace if necessary.
3. Inspect the pressure plates, slippers, rotor, and cam ring for nicks, burrs, or scratches. If any of the parts are damaged enough to cause poor operation or binding of the pump, replace the defective part.
4. Inspect the pump body drive shaft bushing for excessive wear. Replace if necessary.

Assembly

1. With the pump assembly positioned on the adapter plate in the holding fixture, install the lower pressure plate on the anchor pin with the chamfered slots at the center hole facing up.
2. Lubricate the rotor shaft with power steering fluid and insert the shaft into the lower pressure and housing plates.
3. Assemble the rotor, slippers, and springs by wrapping a piece of wire around the rotor, installing the springs, and sliding a slipper in each groove of the rotor over the springs. Then, insert the assembly into the cam ring. Be sure the flat side of the slippers are toward the left side. Be sure

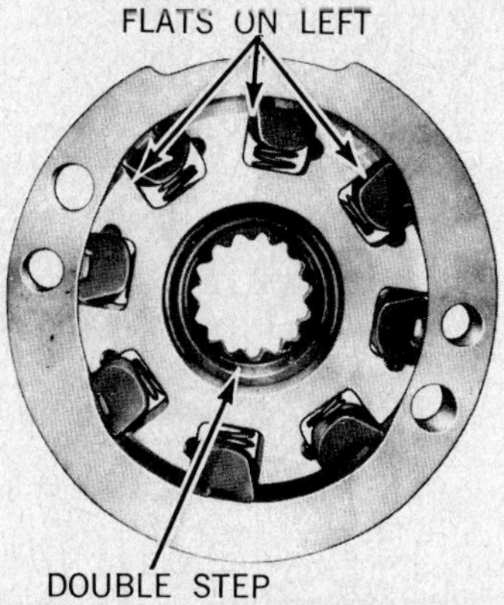

Correct slipper installation—Ford models (© Ford Motor Co.)

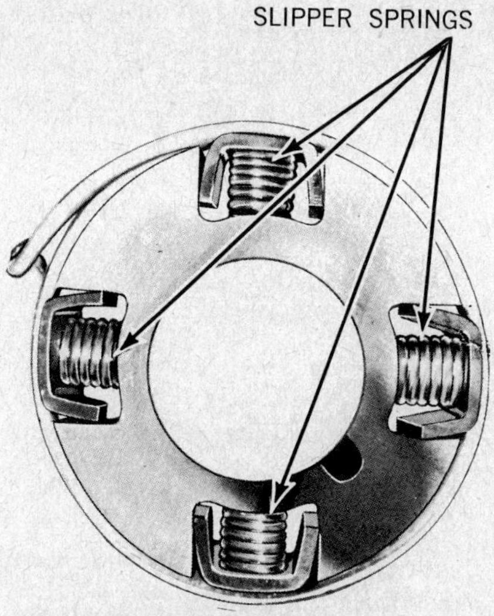

Correct slipper installation—Chrysler models (© Chrysler Corp.)

that the springs are installed straight and are not cocked to one side under the slippers.

4. Install the cam ring and rotor assembly on the drive shaft with the fixed dowel passing through the first hole to the left of the cam notch when the arrow on the cam outside diameter is pointing toward the lower pressure plate. If the cam and rotor assembly does not seat properly, turn the rotor shaft slightly until the spline teeth mesh, allowing the cam and rotor to drop into position.

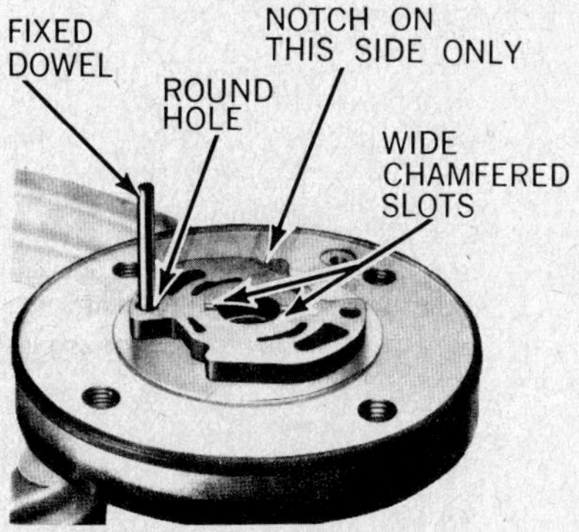

Lower pressure plate installed (© Ford Motor Co.)

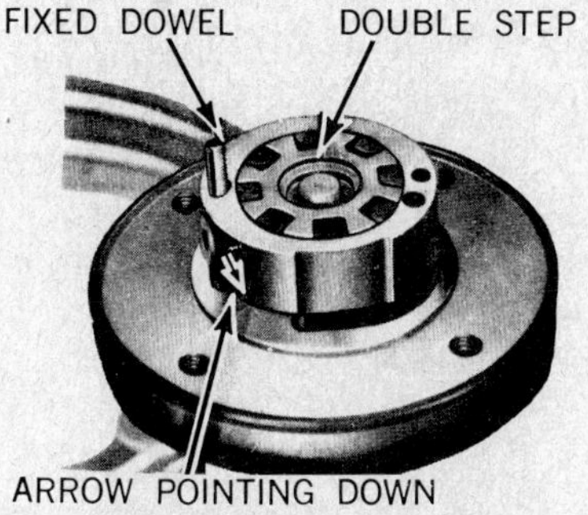

Cam and rotor installation (© Ford Motor Co.)

5. Insert the loose fitting dowel through the cam insert and lower pressure plate into the hole in the housing plate assembly. When both dowels are installed properly, they will be the same height.
6. Install the upper pressure plate so the tapered notch is facing down against the cam insert. The fixed dowel should pass through the round dowel hole and the loose dowel through the long hole. The slot between the ears on the outside of the pressure plate should match the notch on the cam insert.

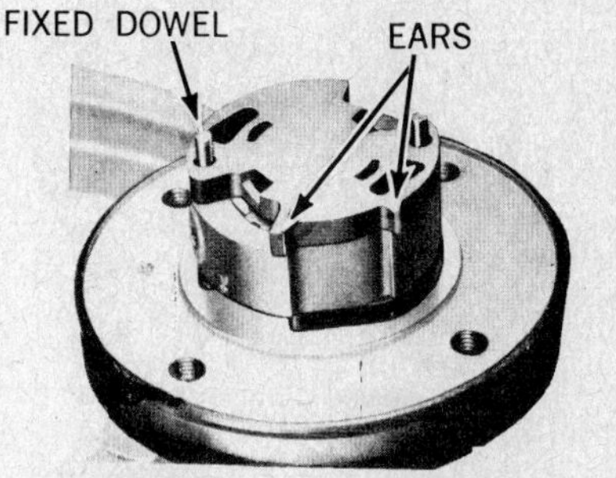

Upper pressure plate installation (© Ford Motor Co.)

7. Install the retainer end plate so the slot on the end plate matches the notches on the upper pressure plate and the cam insert.
8. Install the pump valve assembly O-ring seal on the pump valve assembly. Do not twist the seal.
9. Place the pump valve assembly on top of the retainer end plate with the large exhaust slot on the pump valve in line with the outside notches of the cam, upper pressure plate, and retainer end plate. All parts must be fully seated. If correctly installed, the relief valve stem will be in line with the lube return hole in the pump housing plate.
10. Put small amounts of vaseline on the pump housing plate to hold the cover gasket in place. Install the cover gasket in place.
11. Insert the pressure plate springs into the pockets in the pump valve assembly.
12. Plug the intake hole in the housing.
13. Lubricate the inside of the housing and the housing cover seal with power steering fluid. Install two studs for use as positioning guides, one in the bolt hole nearest the drain hole and the other in the bolt hole on the opposite side of the housing plate.
14. Align the small lube hole in the housing rim and the lube hole in the housing plate. Install the housing, using a steady, even, downward pressure. Do not jar the pressure spring out of position. Remove the guide studs and

loosely install the housing retaining bolts finger tight.

15. Tighten the retaining bolts evenly to 28-32 ft. lbs. until the housing flange contacts the gasket.
16. Install a 3/8-16 hex head screw into the end of the rotor shaft and put a torque wrench on it. Check the amount of torque needed to rotate the rotor shaft. If the torque is more than 15 in. lbs., loosen the retaining bolts

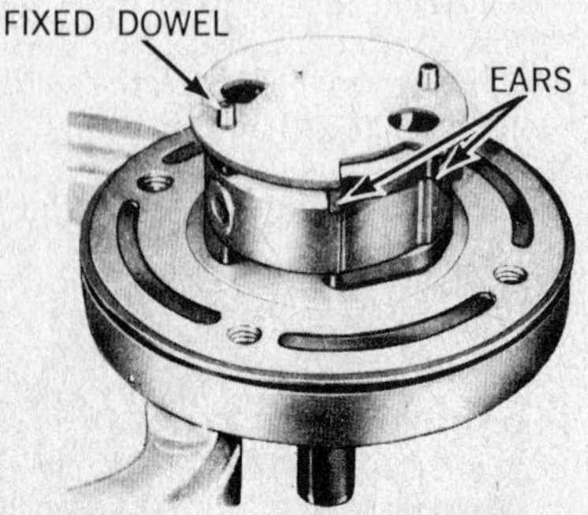

Retainer end plate installation
(© Ford Motor Co.)

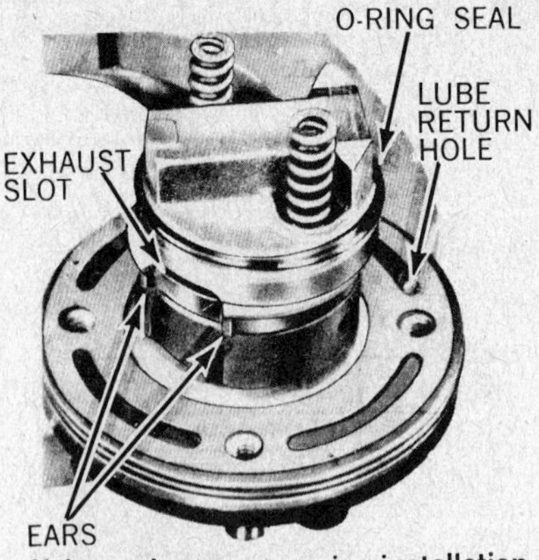

Valve and pressure spring installation
(© Ford Motor Co.)

slightly and rotate the rotor shaft. Then, retighten the retaining bolts evenly. Do not use the pump if the shaft torque exceeds 15 in. lbs.

17. Release the pin in the bench holding fixture and shake the pump assembly back and forth. If there is a rattle, the pressure springs have fallen out of their seats and must be reinstalled.
18. Install the reservoir O-ring seal on the housing plate without twisting it. Lubricate the seal and install the reservoir, aligning the notch in the reservoir flange with the notch in the outside edge of the pump housing plate and bushing assembly. Using only a soft-faced hammer, tap at the rear outer corners of the reservoir. Inspect the assembly to be sure the reservoir is fully seated on the housing plate.
19. Install the identification tag (if one was removed) on the outlet valve fitting. Install the outlet valve fitting nut and tighten to 43-45 ft. lbs. torque.
20. Turn the pump assembly over and install the pulley using the tool used to remove the pulley. Turn the tool nut clockwise to draw the pulley on the shaft until it is flush with the shaft end. Do not exert inward and outward pressures on the shaft to avoid damaging the internal thrust areas. Remove the tool.

Bendix Linkage—Type Power Steering System

The Bendix linkage-type power steering is a hydraulically controlled system composed of an integral pump and fluid reservoir, a control valve, a power cylinder, connecting fluid lines, and the steering linkage. The hydraulic pump, which is driven by a belt turned by the engine, draws fluid from the reservoir and provides pressure through hoses to the control valve and the power cylinder. There is a pressure relief valve to limit the pressures within the steering system to a safe level. After the fluid has passed from the pump to the control valve and the power cylinder, it returns to the reservoir.

Control Valve Centering Spring

Adjustment

1. Raise the truck and remove the spring cap attaching screws and remove the spring cap.

CAUTION: **Be very careful not to position the hoist adapters of two post hoists under the suspension and/or steering components. Place the hoist adapters under the front suspension lower arms.**

2. Tighten the adjusting nut snug (about 90-100 in. lbs.); then, loosen the nut 1/4 turn (90 degrees). Do not turn the adjusting nut too tight.
3. Place the spring cap on the valve housing. Lubricate and install the attaching screws and washers. Tighten the screws to 72-100 in. lbs. torque.
4. Lower the truck and start the engine. Check the steering effort using a spring scale attached to the steering wheel rim for a pull of no more than 12 lbs.

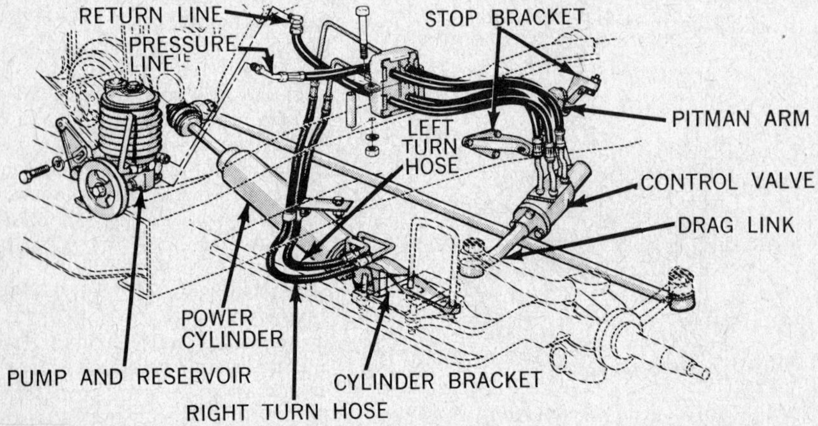

Linkage type power steering installation—typical (© Ford Motor Co.)

Power Steering Control Valve

Removal

1. Raise the truck. If a two post hoist is used, be sure to place the hoist adapters under the front suspension steering arms. Do not allow the hoist adapters to contact the steering linkage.
2. Disconnect the four fluid line fittings at the control valve and drain the fluid from the lines. Turn the front wheels back and forth to force all the fluid from the system.
3. Loosen the clamping nut and bolt at the right end of the sleeve.
4. Remove the roll pin from the steering arm-to-idler arm rod through the slot in the sleeve.
5. Remove the control valve ball stud nut.
6. Remove the ball stud from the sector shaft arm.
7. After turning the front wheels fully to the left, unthread the control valve from the center link steering arm-to-idler arm rod.

Installation

1. Thread the valve on the center link until about four threads are still visible.
2. Position the ball stud in the sector shaft arm.
3. Measure the distance between

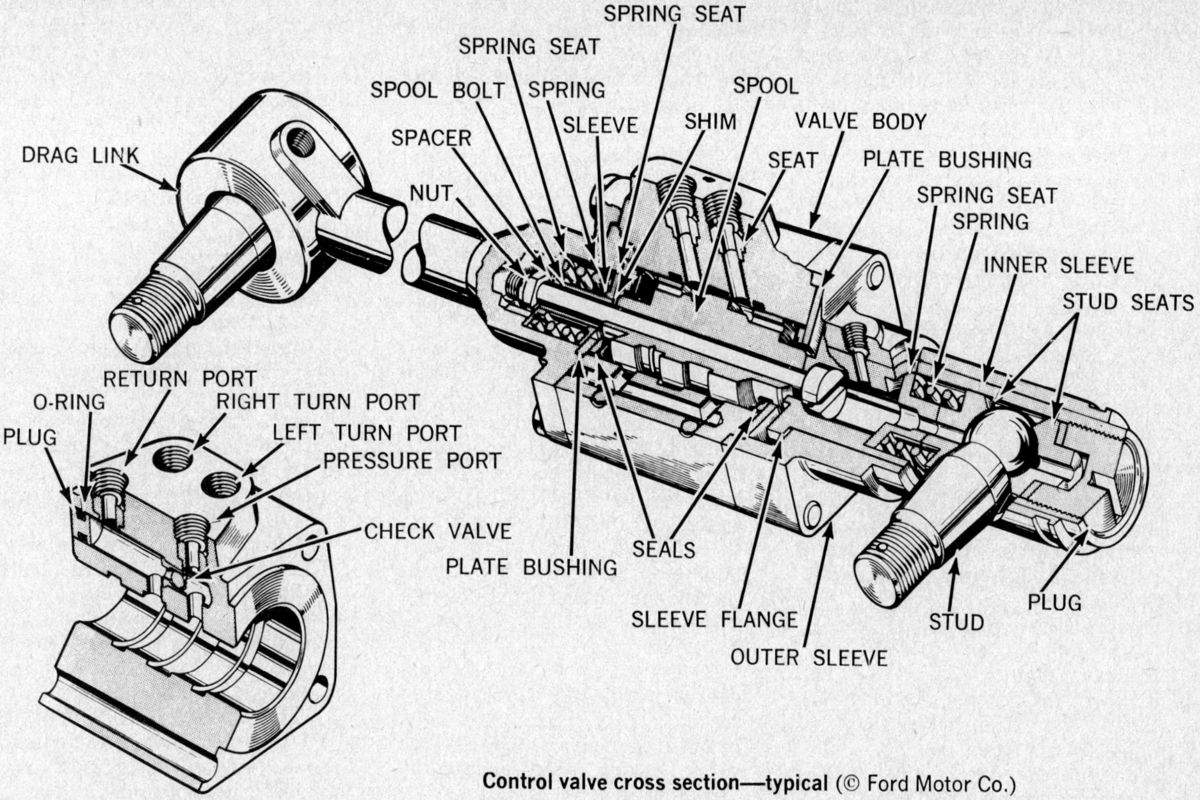

Control valve cross section—typical (© Ford Motor Co.)

the grease plug in the sleeve and the stud at the inner end of the left spindle connecting rod. If the distance is not correct, disconnect the ball stud from the sector shaft arm and turn the valve on the center link until the correct distance is obtained.

4. When the distance is correct and the ball stud is positioned in the sector shaft arm, align the hole in the steering arm-to-idler arm rod with the slot near the end of the valve sleeve. Install the roll pin in the rod hole to lock the valve in place on the rod.
5. Tighten the valve sleeve clamp bolt to the proper torque.
6. Install the ball stud nut and tighten to the proper torque. Install a new cotter pin.
7. Connect all fluid lines to the control valve and tighten all fittings securely. Do not over-tighten.
8. Fill the fluid reservoir with power steering fluid to the full mark on the dipstick.
9. Start the engine and run it for a few minutes to warm the fluid in the power steering system. Turn the steering wheel back and forth to the stops and check the system for leaks.
10. Increase the engine idle speed to about 1000 rpm. Turn the steering wheel back and forth several times, then stop the engine. Check the control valve and hose connections for leaks.
11. Recheck the fluid level and add fluid if necessary.
12. Start the engine again, and check the position of the steering wheel when the front wheels are straight ahead. Do not make any adjustments until toe-in is checked.
13. With engine running, check front wheel toe-in.
14. Check steering wheel turning effort which should be equal in both directions.

Power Steering Power Cylinder

Removal and Installation

1. Disconnect the two fluid lines from the power cylinder and drain the fluid.
2. Remove the pal nut, attaching nut, washer and the insulator from the end of the power cylinder rod. Remove the cotter pin and castellated nut holding the power cylinder stud to the center link.
3. Disconnect the power cylinder stud from the center link.
4. Remove the insulator sleeve and washer from the end of the power cylinder.
5. Inspect the tube fittings and seats in the power cylinder for nicks, burrs, or other damage. Replace the seats or tubes if damaged.
6. Install the washer, sleeve and the insulator on the end of the power cylinder rod.
7. While extending the rod as far as possible, insert the rod in the bracket on the frame and then, compress the rod so the stud may be inserted in the center link. Secure the stud with the castellated nut and a new cotter pin.
8. Install the insulater, washer, nut, and a pal nut on the power cylinder rod.
9. Connect the two fluid lines to their proper ports on the power cylinder.
10. Fill the reservoir with power steering fluid to the full mark on the dipstick. Start the engine and run for a few minutes to warm the fluid. Turn the steering wheel back and forth to the stops to fill the system. Stop the engine.
11. Recheck the fluid level and add fluid if necessary. Check for fluid leaks.
12. Start the engine again, turn the steering wheel back and forth, and check for leaks while the engine is running.

Control Valve

Disassembly

1. Clean the outside of the control valve of dirt and fluid.
2. Remove the centering spring cap from the valve housing. The control valve should be put in a soft-faced bench vise during disassembly. Clamp the control valve around the sleeve flange only to avoid damaging the valve housing, spool, or sleeve.
3. Remove the nut from the end of

the valve spool bolt. Remove the washers, spacer, centering spring, adapter, and the bushing from the bolt and valve housing.

4. Remove the two bolts holding the valve housing and the sleeve together. Separate the valve housing and the sleeve.
5. Remove the plug from the sleeve. Push the valve spool out of the centering spring end of the valve housing, and remove the seal from the spool.
6. Remove the spacer, bushing and valve housing.
7. Drive the pin out of the travel regulator stop with a punch and hammer. Pull the head of the valve spool bolt tightly against the travel regulator stop before driving the pin out of the stop.
8. Turn the travel regulator stop counterclockwise in the valve sleeve to remove the stop from the sleeve.
9. Remove the valve spool bolt, spacer, and rubber washer from the travel regulator stop.
10. Remove the rubber boot and clamp from the valve sleeve. Slide the bumper, spring, and ball stud seat out of the valve sleeve and remove the ball stud socket from the sleeve.
11. Remove the return port hose seat and the return port relief valve.
12. Remove the spring plug and O-ring. Then remove the reaction limiting valve.
13. Replace all worn or damaged hose seats by using an Easy-Out screw extractor or a bolt of proper size as a puller. Tap the existing hole in the hose seat, using a starting tap of the correct size. Remove all metal chips from the hose seat after tapping. Place a nut and washer on a bolt of the same size as the tapped hole. The washer must be large enough to cover the hose seat port. Insert the bolt in the tapped hole and remove the hose seat by turning the nut clockwise and drawing the bolt out. Install a new hose seal in the port, and thread a bolt of the correct size in the port. Tighten the bolt enough to bottom the seal in the port.

Assembly

1. Coat all parts of the control valve assembly with power steering fluid. Seals should be coated with lubricant before installation.
2. Install the reaction limiting valve, spring and plug. Install the return port relief valve and the hose seat.
3. Insert one of the ball stud seats (flat end first) into the ball stud socket, and insert the threaded end of the ball stud into the socket.
4. Place the socket in the control valve sleeve so that the threaded end of the ball stud can be pulled out through the slot.
5. Place the other ball stud seat, spring, and bumper in the socket. Install and securely tighten the travel regulator stop.
6. Loosen the stop just enough to align the nearest hole in the stop with the slot in the ball stud socket and install the stop pin in the ball stud socket, travel regulator stop, and valve spool bolt.
7. Install the rubber boot, clamp, and the plug on the control valve sleeve. Be sure the lubrication fitting is turned on tightly and does not bind on the ball stud socket.
8. Insert the valve spool in the valve housing, rotating it while installing it.
9. Move the spool toward the centering spring end of the housing, and place the small seal bushing and spacer in the sleeve end of the housing.
10. Press the valve spool against the inner lip of the seal and, at the same time, guide the lip of the seal over the spool with a small screwdriver. Do not nick or scratch the seal or the spool during installation.
11. Place the sleeve end of the housing on a flat surface so that the seal, bushing and spacer are at the bottom end; then push down the valve spool until it stops.
12. Carefully install the spool seal and bushing in the centering spring end of the housing. Press the seal against the end of the spool, guiding the seal over the spool with a small flat tool. Do not nick or scratch the seal or the spool during installation.
13. Pick up the housing, and slide the spool back and forth in the housing to check for free movement.
14. Place the valve sleeve on the housing so that the ball stud is on the same side of the housing as the ports for the two power cylinder lines. Install the two bolts in the sleeve, and torque them to the proper torque.
15. Place the adapter on the centering spring end of the housing, and install the bushing, washers, spacers and centering spring on the valve spool bolt.
16. Compress the centering spring and install the nut on the bolt. Tighten the nut snug (about 90-100 in. lbs.); then, loosen it not more than 1/4 turn. Do not over-tighten to avoid breaking the stop pin at the travel regulator stop.
17. Move the ball stud back and forth to check for free movement.
18. Lubricate the two cap attaching bolts. Install the centering spring cap on the valve housing, and tighten the two cap bolts to the proper torque.
19. Install the nut on the ball stud so that the valve can be put in a vise. Then, push forward on the cap end of the valve to check the valve spool for free movement.
20. Turn the valve around in the vise, and push forward on the sleeve end to check for free movement.

Power Cylinder Seal

Removal

1. Clamp the power cylinder in a vise and remove the snap-ring from the end of the cylinder. Do not distort or crack the cylinder in the vise.
2. Pull the piston rod out all the way to remove the scraper, bushing, and seals. If the seals cannot be removed in this manner, remove them by carefully prying them out of the cylinder with a sharp pick. Do not damage the shaft or seal seat.

Installation

1. Coat the new seals with power steering fluid and place the parts on the piston rod. Coat with grease or lubricant.
2. Push the rod in all the way, and install the parts in the cylinder with a deep socket slightly smaller than the cylinder opening.

Power Steering Pump

Removal and Replacement

To remove or install the power steering pump, see the section on the slipper type pump.

Saginaw Linkage—Type Power Steering System

Control Valve

Removal

1. Raise front of vehicle and place on stands.
2. Remove relay rod to control valve clamp bolt.
3. Disconnect two pump to control valve hose connections and allow fluid to drain into a container, then disconnect the valve to power cylinder hoses.
4. Remove ball stud to pitman arm retaining nut and disconnect control valve.

5. Turn steering gear so that pitman arm is away from valve, to allow working room, and unscrew control valve from relay rod.
6. Remove control valve from vehicle.

Disassembly

1. Place valve assembly in vise with dust cap end up, then remove dust cap.
2. Remove adjusting nut.
3. Remove valve to adapter bolts then remove housing and spool from adapter.
4. Remove spool from housing.
5. Remove spring, reaction spool, washer, reaction spring and seal. O-ring may now be removed from reaction spool.
6. Remove annulus spacer, valve shaft washer and plug-to-sleeve key.
7. Carefully turn adjuster plug out of sleeve. Use care not to nick the top surface.
8. If necessary to replace a connector seat, tap threads in center hole using a 5/16-18 tap. Thread a bolt with a nut and a flat washer into the tapped hole so the washer is against the face of the port boss and the nut is against the washer. Hold the bolt from turning while backing the nut off the bolt. This will force the washer against the port boss face and back out the bolt, drawing the connector seat from the top cover housing. Discard the old connector seat and clean the housing out thoroughly to remove any metal tapping chips. Drive a new connector seat against the housing seat, being careful not to damage either seat.
9. Remove adapter from vise and turn over to allow spring and one of the two ball seats to drop out.

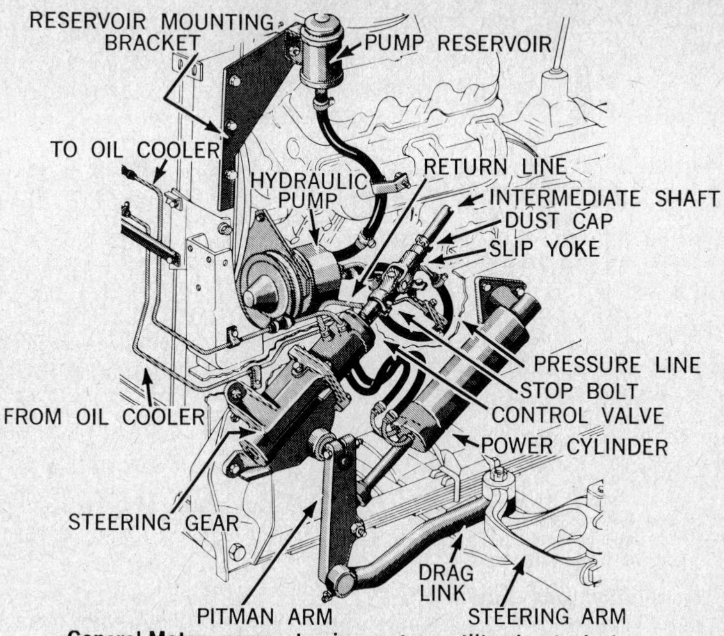

General Motors power steering system—tilt cab—typical (© General Motors Corp.)

10. Remove ball stud with other ball seat and allow sleeve to fall free.

Inspection

1. Wash all parts in non-toxic solvent and blow dry with air.
2. Inspect all parts for scratches, burrs, distortion, excessive wear and replace all worn or damaged parts.
3. Replace all seals and gaskets.

Assembly

1. Install sleeve and ball seat in adapter, then the ball stud and then the other ball seat and spring (small end down).
2. Place adapter in vise. Put the shaft through the seat in the adjuster plug and screw adjuster plug into sleeve.
3. Turn plug in until tight, then back off until slot lines up with notches in sleeve.
4. Insert key. Be sure small tangs on end of key fit into notches in sleeve.
5. Install valve shaft washer, annulus spacer, reaction seal (lip up), spring retainer, reaction spring and spool, then washer and adjustment spring. Install O-ring seal on reaction spool before installing spool on shaft. Install washer with chamfer up.
6. Install seal on valve spool with lip down. Then install spool, being careful not to jam spool in housing.
7. Install housing with spool onto adapter. The side ports should be on the same side as the ball stud. Bolt the housing to the adapter.
8. Depress the valve spool and turn the locknut into the shaft about four turns. Use a clean wrench or socket.

NOTE: Always use a new nut.

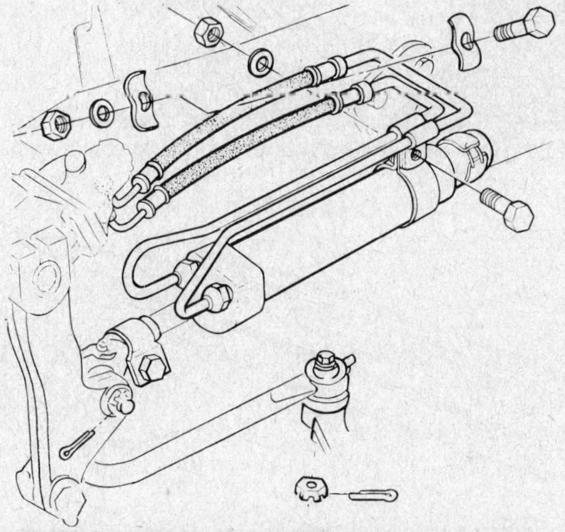

General Motors side mounted power cylinder (© General Motors Corp.)

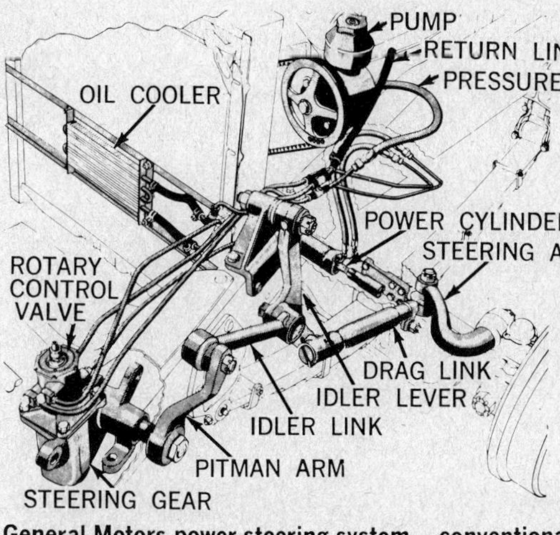

General Motors power steering system—conventional cab—typical (© General Motors Corp.)

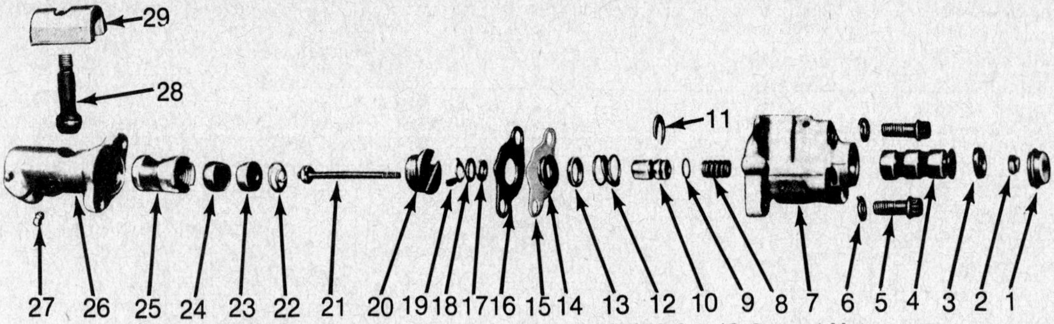

General Motors power steering control valve—exploded view (© General Motors Corp.)

1 Dust cover
2 Adjusting nut
3 Vee block seal
4 Valve spool
5 Valve mounting bolts
6 Lock washer
7 Valve housing
8 Valve adjustment spring
9 "O" ring seal
10 Valve reaction spool
11 Spring thrust washer
12 Valve spring
13 Spring retainer
14 Annulus seal
15 Annulus spacer
16 Gasket
17 Valve shaft washer
18 "O" ring seal
19 Plug to sleeve key
20 Ball adjuster nut
21 Valve shaft
22 Ball seat spring
23 Ball seat
24 Ball seat
25 Sleeve bearing
26 Adapter housing
27 Lubrication fitting
28 Ball stud
29 Cover

Installation and Balancing

1. Install the control valve on the relay rod so that control valve bottoms, then back off enough (if necessary) to install the clamp bolt. Do not back off more than two turns. There should be approximately 1/16-1/8" gap.
2. Tighten control valve clamping-bolt and install ball stud to pitman arm.
3. Reconnect the four hoses to the valve.
4. Fill system with type A fluid and bleed air by running engine, then slowly turning wheels from lock to lock with engine idling. Be sure to keep reservoir full during this process. Do not replace dust cover before the following balancing procedure is completed.
5. Disconnect the piston rod from frame bracket if not already separated.
6. If piston rod is retracted, turn adjusting nut clockwise until rod begins to move out. Then turn nut counterclockwise until rod just begins to move in. Now, turn the nut clockwise exactly half the rotation needed to change the direction of piston rod movement. If piston rod is extended before starting, reverse the above to get the midpoint in piston movement.

   CAUTION: **Do not turn the nut back and forth more than is absolutely necessary to balance the valve.**
7. With valve properly balanced it should be possible to move the rod in and out manually.
8. Shut off engine and connect piston rod to frame bracket.
9. Restart engine with front wheels still off ground. If the wheels do not turn in either direction from center, the valve has been properly balanced. Correct the condition by rebalancing the valve if necessary.
10. After proper adjustment, grease the end of valve and install dust cap.

Power Cylinder

Removal

1. Remove the two hoses which are connected to the cylinder and drain fluid into a container.
2. Remove power cylinder from frame bracket.
3. Remove cotter pin and nut and pull stud out of relay rod.
4. Remove cylinder from vehicle.

Inspection

1. Check seals for leaks around cyl-

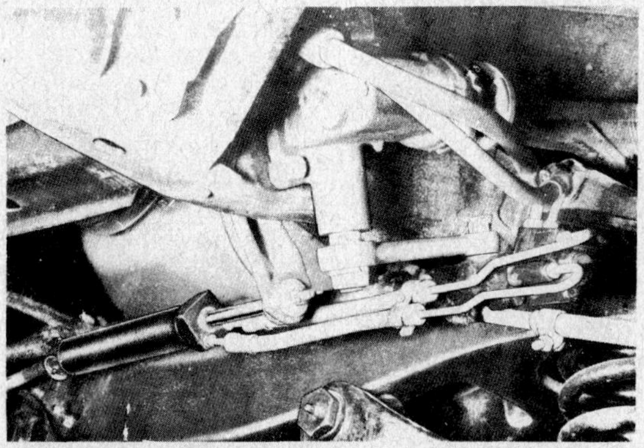

Typical light duty power cylinder (© General Motors Corp.)

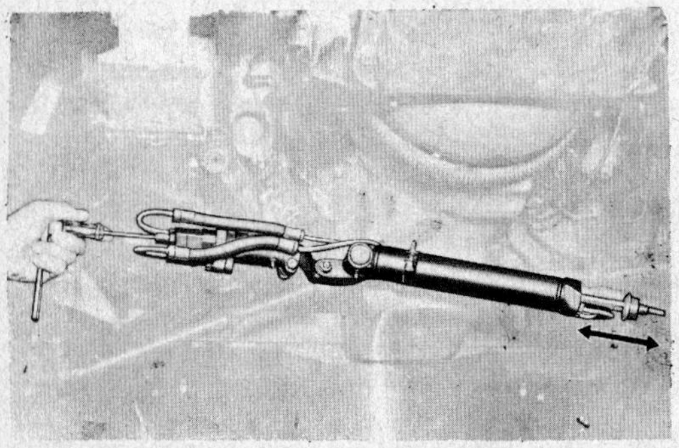

Balancing control valve (© General Motors Corp.)

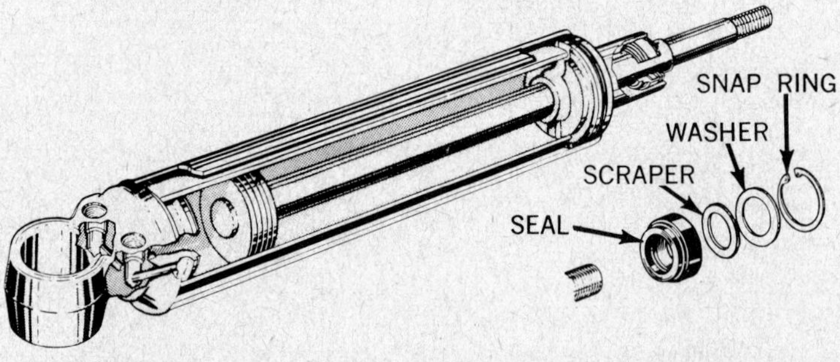

Phantom view of power cylinder—typical (© Ford Motor Co.)

inder rod. If leaks are found, replace seals.

2. Check hose connection seats for damage and replace if necessary.
3. For service other than seat or seal replacement, it is necessary to replace the power cylinder.
4. The ball stud may be replaced by removing snap-ring.

Disassembly and Assembly

1. To remove piston rod seal, remove snap-ring and pull out on rod. Remove back-up washer, piston rod scraper and piston rod seal from rod.
2. To remove the ball stud, depress the end plug and remove the snap-ring. Push on the end of the ball stud and the end plug, spring, spring seat, ball stud and seal may be removed. If the ball seat is to be replaced, it must be pressed out.
3. Reverse disassembly procedure. Be sure snap-ring is properly seated.

Installation

1. Install power cylinder on vehicle in reverse of removal procedure.
2. Reconnect the hydraulic lines, fill system and bleed out air as described in the installation and balancing section of control valve servicing.

Power Steering Hoses

Carefully inspect the hoses. When installing, be sure to place in such a position as to avoid all chafing or other abuse when making sharp turns.

Saginaw Rotary Type Power Steering

The rotary type power steering gear is designed with all components in one housing.

The power cylinder is an integral part of the gear housing. A double-acting type piston allows oil pressure to be applied to either side of the piston. The one-piece piston and power rack is meshed to the sector shaft.

The hydraulic control valve is composed of a sleeve and valve spool. The spool is held in the neutral position by the torsion bar and spool actuator. Twisting of the torsion bar moves the valve spool, allowing oil pressure to be directed to either side of the power piston, depending upon the directional rotation of the steering wheel, to give power assist.

On many trucks of the General Motors Corporation, a modified version of the rotary valve power steering system provides variable ratio steering to assist the driver to steer the truck easier and safer. The steering gear ratio will vary from a high ratio of about 16:1 while steering straight ahead to a lower gear ratio of about 12.1:1 while making a full turn to either side.

Roller Pump

Removal

Remove the reservoir cover and use a suction gun to empty the reservoir. Disconnect the hoses from the pump and tie them in a raised position to prevent oil drainage. Loosen the pump adjusting screw and remove the pump belt, then take out the retaining bolts and remove the pump and reservoir.

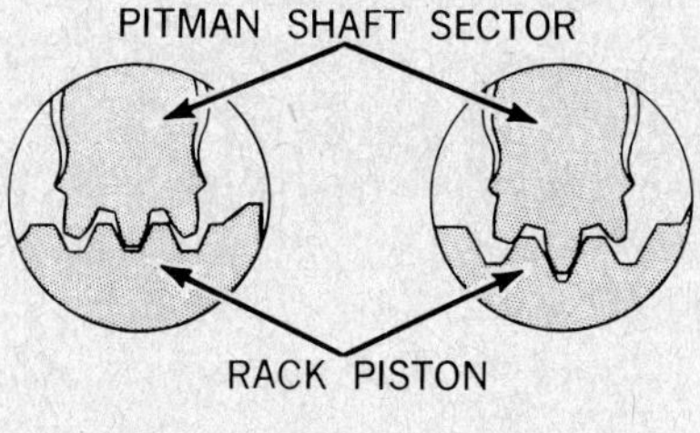

Comparison of constant ratio and variable ratio steering sector shaft teeth (© General Motors Corp.)

Installation

Position the pump assembly and install the retaining bolts. Be sure there is clearance between the pump bracket and the engine front support bracket. Install the hoses and place the pump belt on the pulley. Adjust the belt to ½" deflection, then tighten the adjusting screw.

Connect the hoses to the pump assembly.

Fill the reservoir to within ½" of the top with automatic transmission fluid type A.

Start the engine and rotate the steering wheel several times to the right and left to expel air from the system, then recheck the oil level and install the reservoir cover.

Power Steering Unit

Fluid Used

This unit uses automatic transmission fluid type A. The fluid capacity is 4½ pints.

Bleeding the System

Fill the pump reservoir to within ½" of the top. Start and run the engine to attain normal operating temperatures. Now, turn the steering wheel through its entire travel three or four times to expel air from the system, then recheck the fluid level.

Checking Steering Effort

Run the engine to attain normal operating temperatures. With the wheels on a dry floor, hook a pull scale to the spoke of the steering wheel at the outer edge. The effort required to turn the steering wheel should be 3½-5 lbs. If the pull is not within these limits, check the hydraulic pressure.

Pressure Test

To check the hydraulic pressure, disconnect the pressure hose from the gear. Now connect the pressure gauge between the pressure hose from the pump and the steering gear housing. Run the engine to attain normal operating temperatures, then turn the wheel to a full right and a full left turn to the wheel stops.

Hold the wheel in this position only long enough to obtain an accurate reading.

The pressure gauge reading should be within the limits specified. If the pressure reading is less than the minimum needed for proper operation, close the valve at the gauge and see if the reading increases. If the pressure is still low, the pump is defective and needs repair. If the pressure reading is at or near the minimum reading, the pump is normal and needs only an adjustment of the power steering gear or power assist control valve.

Worm Bearing Preload and Sector Mesh Adjustments

Disconnect the pitman arm from the sector shaft, then back off on the sector shaft adjusting screw on the sector shaft cover.

Center the steering on the high point, then attach a pull scale to the spoke of the steering wheel at the outer edge. The pull required to keep the wheel moving for one complete turn should be ½-⅔ lbs.

If the pull is not within these limits, loosen the thrust bearing locknut and tighten or back off on the valve sleeve adjuster locknut to bring the preload within limits. Tighten the thrust bearing locknut and recheck the preload.

Slowly rotate the steering wheel several times, then center the steering on the high point. Now, turn the sector shaft adjusting screw until a steering wheel pull of 1-1½ lbs. is required to move the worm through the center point. Tighten the sector shaft adjusting screw locknut and recheck the sector mesh adjustment.

Install the pitman arm and draw the arm in position with the nut.

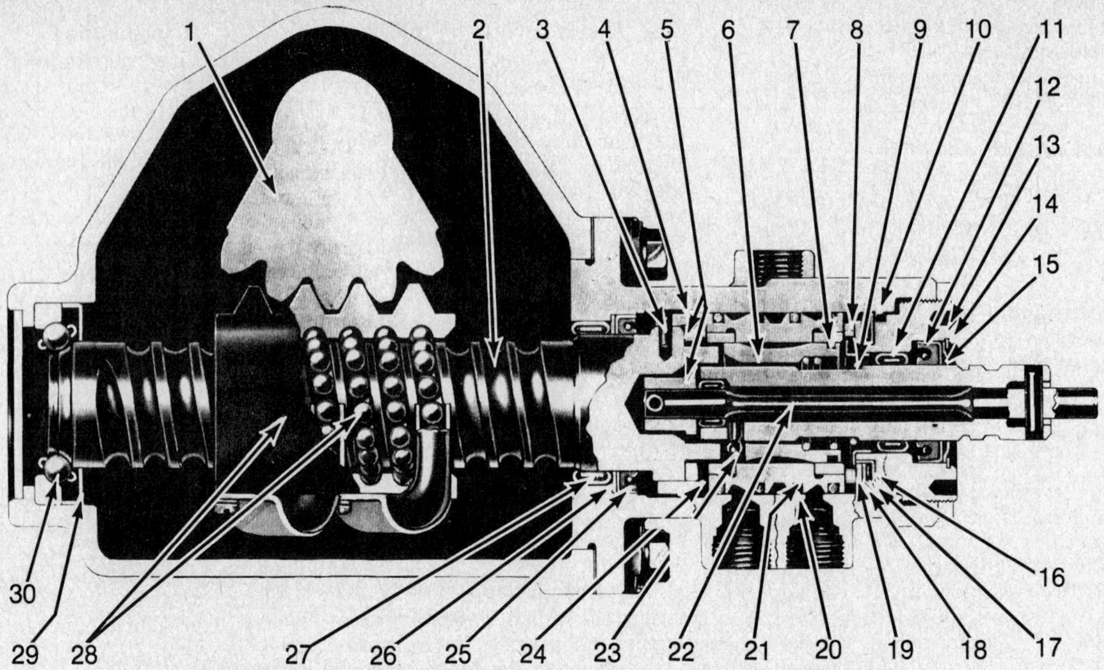

Cross section—Saginaw power steering gear used on medium duty trucks
(© General Motors Corp.)

1 Sector
2 Wormshaft
3 Body drive pin
4 Valve body
5 Cap assembly
6 Valve spool
7 Spool dampener "O" ring
8 Thrust bearing spacer
9 Spool spring
10 Adjuster plug "O" ring seal
11 Adjuster plug needle bearing
12 Adjuster plug shaft seal
13 Adjuster plug
14 Adjuster plug snap ring
15 Adjuster plug dust seal
16 Bearing race
17 Upper thrust bearing
18 Bearing race
19 Spacer
20 Valve body ring
21 Ring back-up seal
22 Torsion bar
23 Spool valve pin
24 Valve body pin
25 Top cover (valve) seal
26 Back-up washer
27 Top cover (valve) bearing
28 Ball nut and balls
29 Bearing retainer
30 Lower thrust bearing

Service Operations

Adjuster Plug and Rotary Valve

Removal

1. Thoroughly clean exterior of gear assembly. Drain by holding valve ports down and rotating worm back and forth through entire travel.
2. Place gear in vise.
3. Loosen adjuster plug locknut with punch. Remove adjuster plug with spanner.
4. Remove rotary valve assembly by grasping stub shaft and pulling it out.

Adjuster Plug

Disassembly & Assembly

1. Remove upper thrust bearing retainer with screwdriver. Be

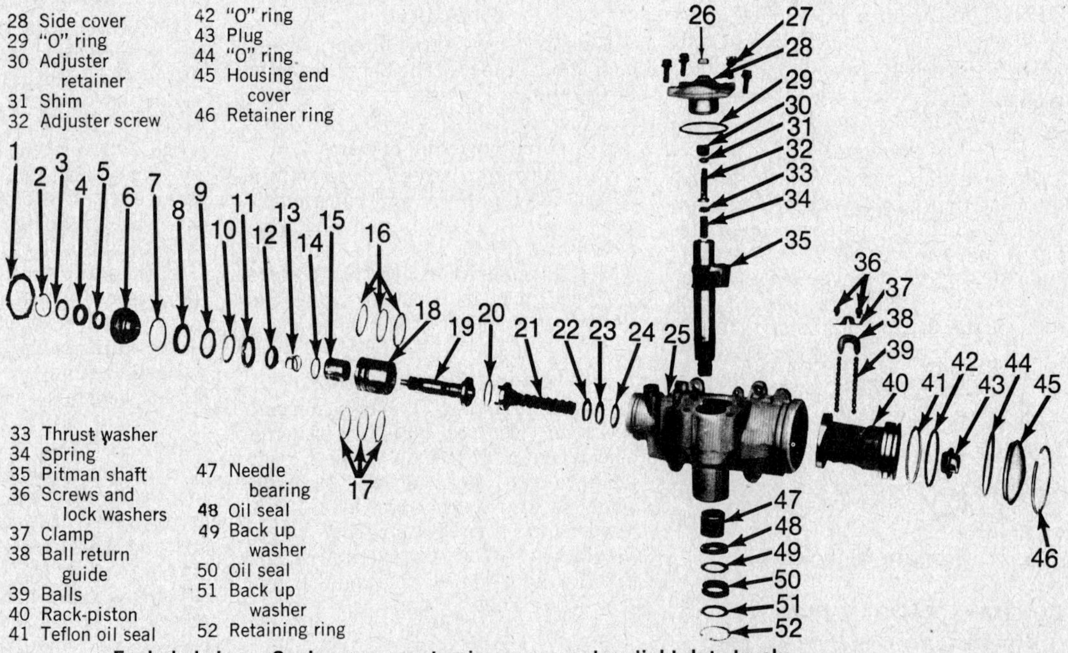

1 Locknut
2 Retaining ring
3 Dust seal
4 Oil seal
5 Bearing
6 Adjuster plug
7 "O" ring
8 Thrust washer (large)
9 Thrust bearing
10 Thrust washer (small)
11 Spacer
12 Retainer
13 Spool valve spring
14 "O" ring
15 Spool valve
16 Teflon oil rings
17 "O" rings
18 Valve body
19 Stub shaft
20 "O" ring
21 Wormshaft
22 Thrust washer
23 Thrust bearing
24 Thrust washer
25 Housing
26 Locknut
27 Attaching bolts and washers
28 Side cover
29 "O" ring
30 Adjuster retainer
31 Shim
32 Adjuster screw
33 Thrust washer
34 Spring
35 Pitman shaft
36 Screws and lock washers
37 Clamp
38 Ball return guide
39 Balls
40 Rack-piston
41 Teflon oil seal
42 "O" ring
43 Plug
44 "O" ring
45 Housing end cover
46 Retainer ring
47 Needle bearing
48 Oil seal
49 Back up washer
50 Oil seal
51 Back up washer
52 Retaining ring

Exploded view—Saginaw power steering gear used on light duty trucks
(© General Motors Corp.)

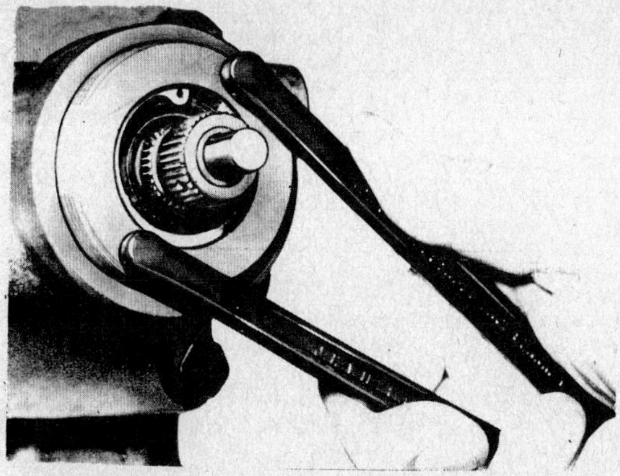

Removing adjuster plug (© General Motors Corp.)

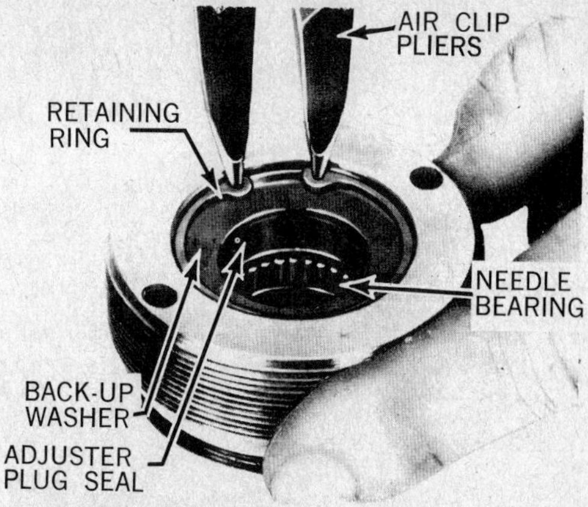

Removing adjuster plug seal retaining ring (© General Motors Corp.)

careful not to damage bearing bore. Discard retainer. Remove spacer, upper bearing and races.

2. Remove and discard adjuster plug O-ring.
3. Remove stub shaft seal retaining ring (Truarc pliers will help) and remove and discard dust seal.
4. Remove stub shaft seal by prying out and discard.
5. Examine needle bearing and, if required, remove same by pressing from thrust bearing end.
6. Inspect thrust bearing spacer, bearing rollers and races.
7. Reassemble in reverse of above.

Rotary Valve

Disassembly

Repairs are seldom needed. Do not disassemble unless absolutely necessary. If the O-ring seal on valve spool dampener needs replacement, perform this portion of operation only.

1. Remove cap-to-worm O-ring seal and discard.
2. Remove valve spool spring by prying on small coil with a small tool to work spring onto bearing surface of stub shaft. Slide spring off shaft. Be careful not to damage shaft surface.
3. Remove valve spool by holding the valve assembly in one hand with the stub shaft pointing down. Insert the end of pencil or wood rod through opening in valve body cap and push spool until it is out far enough to be removed. In this procedure, rotate to prevent jamming. If spool becomes jammed it may be necessary to remove stub shaft, torsion bar and cap assembly.

Assembly

CAUTION: **All parts must be free and clear of dirt, chips, etc., before assembly and must be protected after.**

1. Lubricate three new back-up O-ring seals with automatic transmission oil and reassemble in the ring grooves of valve body. Assemble three new valve body rings in the grooves over the O-ring seals by carefully slipping over the valve body.

   NOTE: If the valve body rings seem loose or twisted in the grooves, the heat of the oil during operation will cause them to straighten.
2. Lubricate a new dampener O-ring with automatic transmission oil and install in valve spool groove.
3. Assemble stub shaft torsion bar and cap assembly in the valve body, aligning the groove in the valve cap with the pin in the valve body. Tap lightly with soft remainder of assembly. Valve body pin must be in the cap groove. Hold parts together during the remainder of assembly.
4. Lubricate spool. With notch in spool toward valve body, slide the spool over the stub shaft. Align the notch on the spool with the spool drive pin on stub shaft and carefully engage spool in valve body bore. Push spool evenly and with slight rotating motion until it reaches the drive pin. Rotate slowly, with some pressure, until notch engages pin. Be sure dampener O-ring seal is evenly distributed in the spool groove.

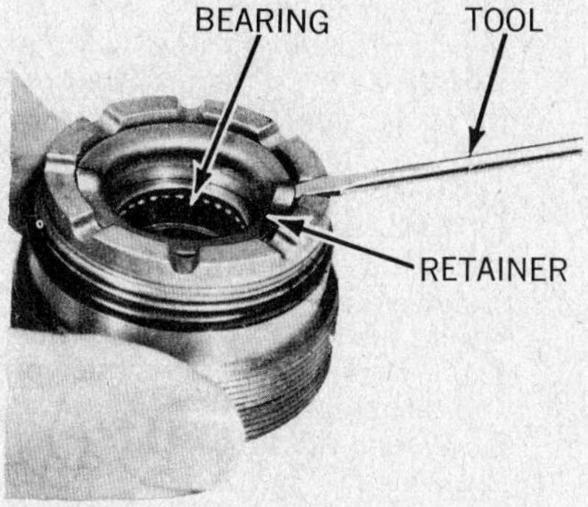

Exploded view of adjuster plug assembly (© General Motors Corp.)

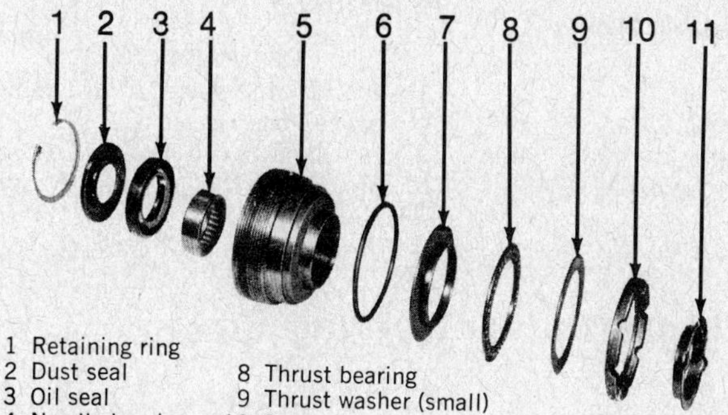

1 Retaining ring
2 Dust seal
3 Oil seal
4 Needle bearing
5 Adjuster plug
6 "O" ring
7 Thrust washer (large)
8 Thrust bearing
9 Thrust washer (small)
10 Spacer
11 Retainer

Removing thrust bearing retainer (© General Motors Corp.)

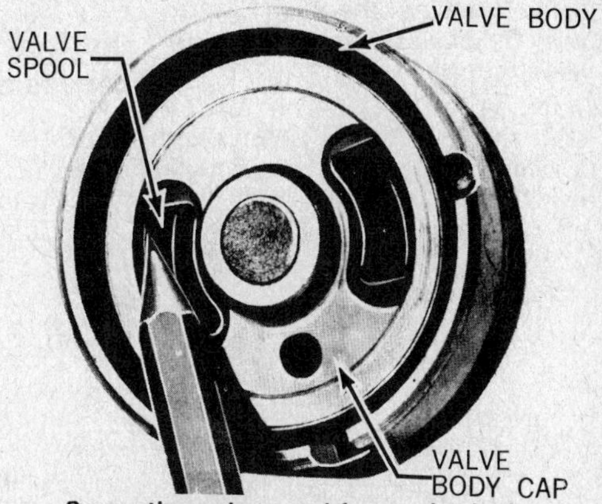

Separating valve spool from valve body (© General Motors Corp.)

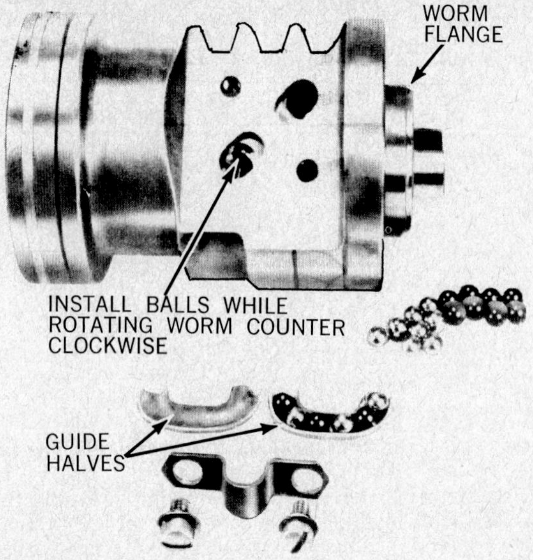

Installing balls in rack piston (© General Motors Corp.)

CAUTION: Use extreme care because spool to valve body clearance is very small. Damage is easily caused.

5. With seal protector over stub shaft, slide valve spool spring over shaft, with small diameter of spring going over shaft last. Work spring onto shaft until small coil is located in stub shaft groove.
6. Lubricate a new cap to O-ring seal and install in valve body.

Adjuster Plug and Rotary Valve

Installation

1. Align narrow pin slot on valve body with valve body drive pin on the worm. Insert the valve assembly into gear housing by pressing against valve body with finger tips. Do not press on stub shaft or torsion bar. The return hole in the gear housing should be fully visible when properly assembled.

   CAUTION: Do not press on stub shaft as this may cause shaft and cap to pull out of valve body, allowing the spool dampener O-ring seal to slip into valve body oil grooves.

2. With seal protector over end of stub shaft, install adjuster plug assembly into gear housing snugly with spanner, then back plug off approximately one-eighth turn. Install plug locknut but do not tighten. Adjust preload as described in the adjustment section.
3. After adjustment, tighten locknut.

Pitman Shaft

Removal and Installation

1. Completely drain the gear assembly and thoroughly clean the outside.
2. Place gear in vise.
3. Rotate stub shaft until pitman shaft gear is in center position. Remove side cover retaining bolts.
4. Tap end of pitman shaft with soft hammer and slide shaft out of housing.
5. Remove and discard side cover O-ring seal.
6. The seals, washers, retainers and bearings may now be removed and examined.
7. Examine all parts for wear or damage and replace as required.
8. Install in reverse of above. Make proper adjustment as described in adjustment section.

Rack-Piston Nut and Worm Assembly

Removal

1. Completely drain the gear assembly and thoroughly clean the outside.
2. Remove pitman shaft assembly as previously described.
3. Rotate housing end plug retaining ring so that one end of ring is over hole in gear housing. Spring one end of ring so pin punch can be inserted to lift it out.
4. Rotate stub shaft to full left turn position to force end plug out of housing.
5. Remove and discard housing end plug O-ring seal.
6. Remove rack-piston nut end plug with ½″ square drive.
7. Insert special tool in end of worm. Turn stub shaft so that rack-piston nut will go into tool and then remove rack-piston nut from gear housing.
8. Remove adjuster plug and rotary valve assemblies as previously described.
9. Remove worm and lower thrust bearing and races.
10. Remove cap O-ring seal and discard.

Rack-Piston Nut and Worm

Disassembly and Assembly

1. Remove and discard piston ring and back-up O-ring on rack piston nut.
2. Remove ball guide clamp and return guide.
3. Place nut on clean cloth and remove ball retaining tool. Make sure all balls are removed.
4. Inspect all parts for wear, nicks, scoring or burrs. If worm or rack-pinion nut need replacing, both must be replaced as a matched pair.
5. In reassembling reverse the above.

NOTE: When assembling, alternate black and white balls, and install guide and clamp. Packing with grease helps in holding during assembly. When new balls are used, various sizes are available and a selection must be made to secure proper torque when making the high point adjustment.

Rack-Piston Nut and Worm Assembly

Installation

1. Install in reverse of removal procedure.
2. In all cases use new O-ring seals.
3. Make adjustments as previously described.

Saginaw Model 170, 170-D Integral Power Steering Gear

The model 170, 170-D power steering gear unit is used in conjunction with the heavier pitman and steering arms, and eliminates the need for power cylinder assist units attached to the axle and to the steering linkage.

The unit uses a remote mounted, belt driven, vane type hydraulic pump for fluid pressure and directs the fluid to and from the gear unit by the use of pressure and return hoses.

As the vehicle operator turns the steering wheel, the control valve is moved within the gear housing, and closes the pressure relief port and directs fluid pressure to the opposite ends of the primary and secondary pistons. The pressure assists the movement of the pistons as they rotate the pitman shaft, which in turn, moves the steering linkage to turn the wheels. The greater the turning effort, the more pressure is applied to the piston ends, therefore assuring the operator a smooth hydraulic assist in turning at all times.

As the steering effort to the steering wheel is stopped, the control valve is returned to its neutral position, the fluid pressure to the piston ends are equalized on both sides, the pressure is directed to the relief port and returned to the pump reservoir, and the steering gear is returned to the neutral or straight ahead position.

Adjustments

There are no on-the-vehicle adjustments of the integral type steering gear.

Removal

1. Center the steering gear and remove the pitman arm bolt.
2. Spread the pitman arm clamp boss slightly to remove the arm. Do not spread the arm clamp boss over .004 inch.
3. Remove the pot joint to stub shaft clamp bolt, loosen the steering column assembly and pull upward until the shaft coupling clears the stub shaft.
4. Disconnect the hydraulic lines and plug them. Remove the steering gear attaching bolts and with the aid of an assistant, turn the gear in a vertical position and lower the gear between the frame and the inner fender panel.

Installation

1. Install adapter plate to the gear assembly, if removed. (Install the lower forward bolt through the adapter plate before attaching it to the gear housing.)
2. With the gear in a vertical position, (stub shaft up), move the gear upward between the fender panel and the frame. Loosely install the bolts.
3. Unplug the hydraulic lines and install them into the fittings of the gear housing.
4. Tighten the gear to frame bolts and torque to specifications.
5. With the aid of one or more assistants, center and push the steering shaft over the stub equivalent into the bore of the rack piston. Turn the stub shaft counterclockwise while holding the tool firmly against the worm, forcing the rack piston over the shaft until the coupling lines up with the cross groove in the stub shaft.
6. Install the clamp bolt in the cross groove clamp and tighten. Tighten the steering column assembly.
7. Install the pitman arm, install the bolt and torque to specifications.
8. Fill the reservoir and bleed the system as outlined previously.

Gear Unit

Disassembly

1. Place the steering gear box in a holding fixture or a vise. With a small pin punch, dislodge the end cover retaining rings from their grooves in the primary and secondary piston housings and pry them out.
2. Turn the stub shaft counterclockwise to force the cover from the primary cylinder. Remove the cover and "O" ring seal.
3. Remove the rack piston end plug, the sector preload adjuster nut, and the four side cover bolts.
4. Using a ¼ in. Allen wrench, turn the preload adjusting nut clockwise until the side cover separates from the sector shaft and remove the cover.
5. Turn the stub shaft counterclockwise until the sector shaft teeth are out of engagement with the teeth of the rack piston.

   NOTE: If the secondary piston end cover is stuck, turn the stub shaft counterclockwise until the rack piston bottoms in the housing, then engage the sector end tooth in the center tooth spacing on the primary rack piston. Turn the stub shaft counterclockwise until the secondary rack piston forces the end cover from the housing.
6. Remove the secondary rack piston from the bore in the gear housing. Do not remove the end plug unless it is to be replaced.
7. Rotate the stub shaft clockwise until the teeth of the sector and the rack piston clear each other and the rack piston can move freely.
8. Insert a ball retainer tool or its tool and retaining the recirculating balls in place. Remove the rack piston from the housing.
9. Rotate the sector shaft teeth to clear the housing and remove the shaft from the gear housing.
10. Remove the adjuster plug lock nut and with the aid of a spanner wrench, remove the adjuster plug from the stub shaft end of the gear housing.
11. Remove the valve and worm as an assembly with the thrust bearings and races and separate the worm from the valve assembly.

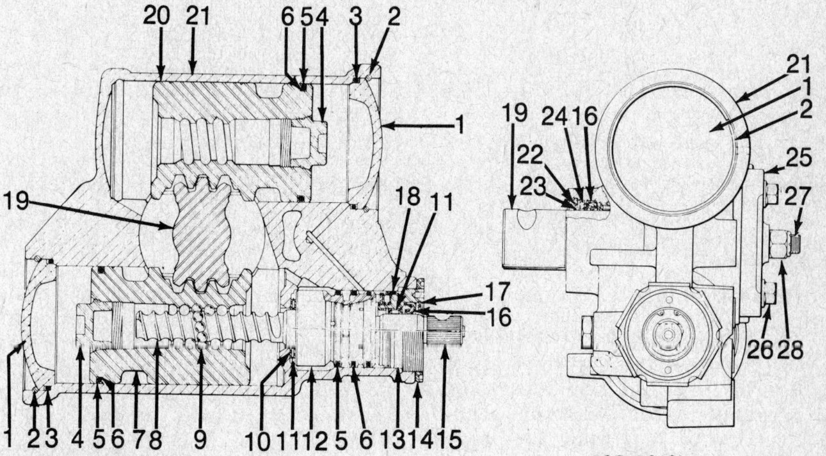

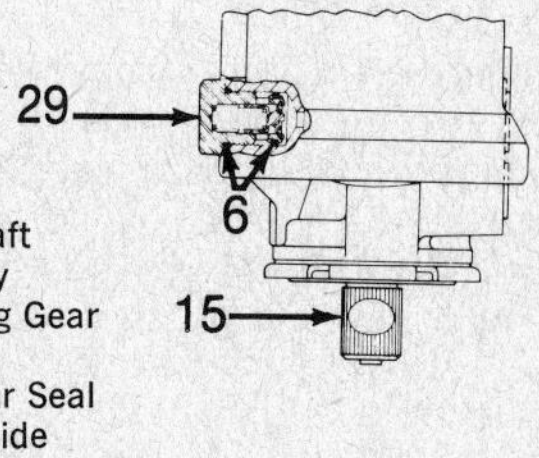

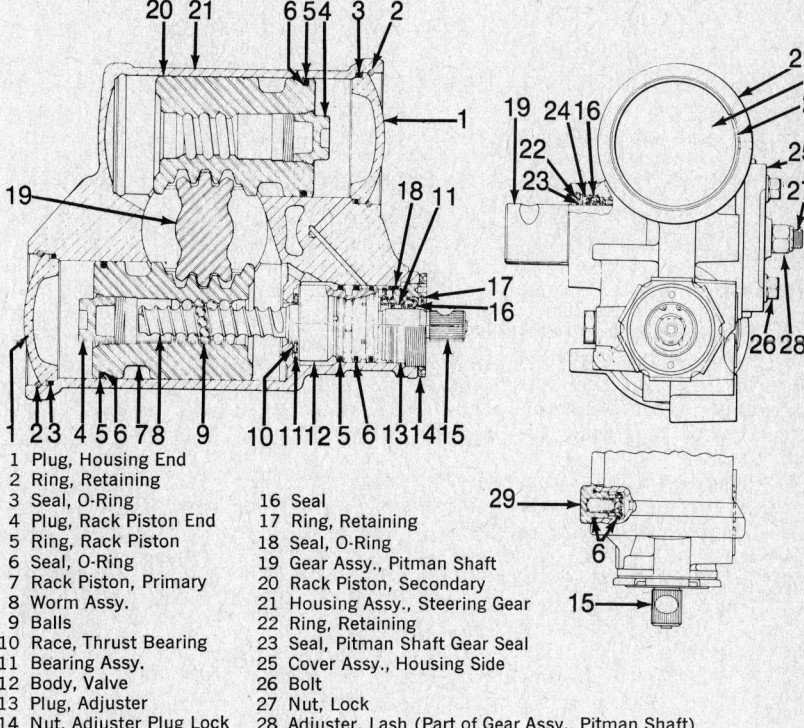

1 Plug, Housing End
2 Ring, Retaining
3 Seal, O-Ring
4 Plug, Rack Piston End
5 Ring, Rack Piston
6 Seal, O-Ring
7 Rack Piston, Primary
8 Worm Assy.
9 Balls
10 Race, Thrust Bearing
11 Bearing Assy.
12 Body, Valve
13 Plug, Adjuster
14 Nut, Adjuster Plug Lock
15 Shaft, Stub
16 Seal
17 Ring, Retaining
18 Seal, O-Ring
19 Gear Assy., Pitman Shaft
20 Rack Piston, Secondary
21 Housing Assy., Steering Gear
22 Ring, Retaining
23 Seal, Pitman Shaft Gear Seal
25 Cover Assy., Housing Side
26 Bolt
27 Nut, Lock
28 Adjuster, Lash (Part of Gear Assy., Pitman Shaft)
29 Valve Assy., Relief

Integral power steering gear and control unit—models 170-170D
(© General Motors Corp.)

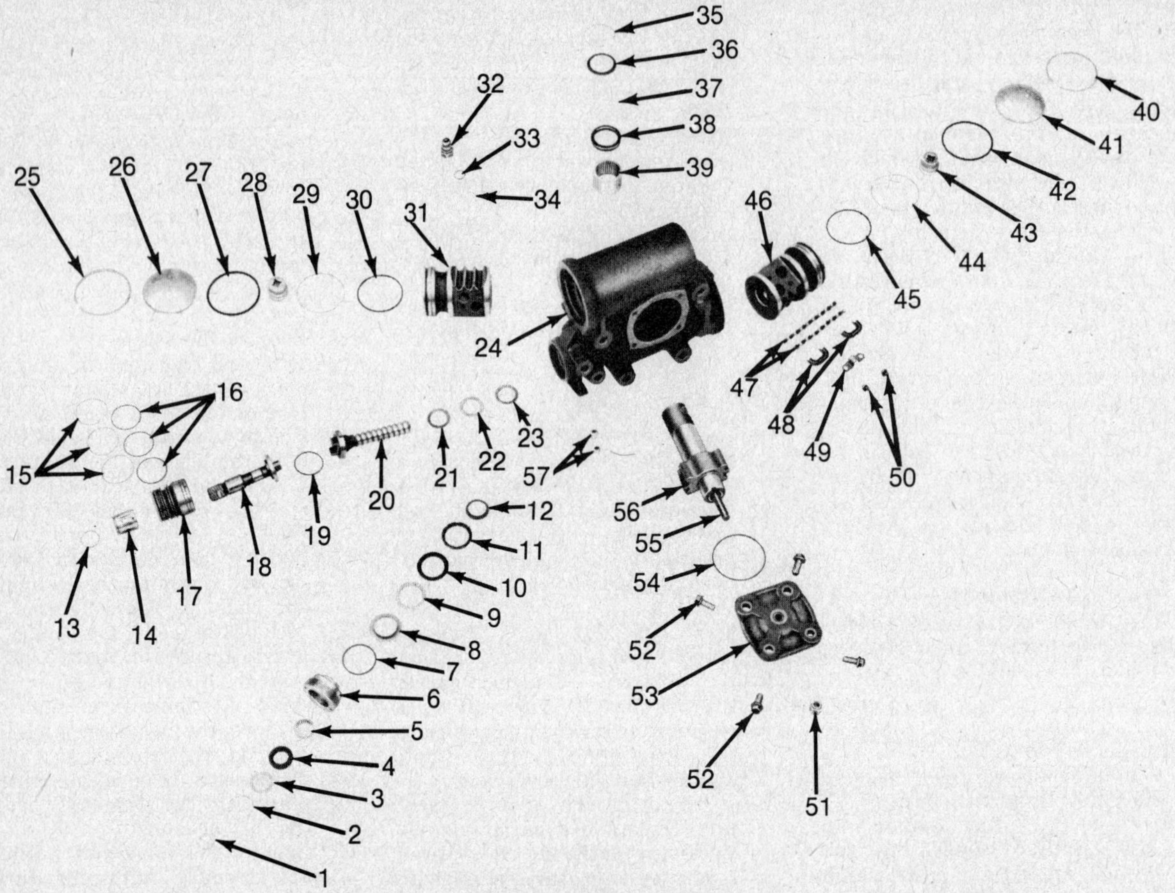

Exploded view—models 170-170D steering gear (© Chrysler Corp.)

1 Locknut
2 Retaining ring
3 Back-up washer
4 Stub shaft seal
5 Needle bearing
6 Adjuster plug
7 "O" ring
8 Thrust race (upper)
9 Thrust bearing
10 Thrust race
11 Spacer
12 Retainer
13 Dampener "O" ring
14 Valve spool
15 Teflon "O" rings
16 Back-up "O" rings
17 Valve body
18 Stub shaft
19 Cap to body "O" ring
20 Steering worm
21 Thrust bearing race
22 Thrust bearing
23 Thrust bearing race
24 Housing
25 Retaining ring
26 Housing end plug
27 End plug "O" ring
28 Rack piston end plug
29 Teflon "O" ring
30 Back-up "O" ring
31 Rack piston
32 Relief valve
33 "O" ring
34 "O" ring
35 Retaining ring
36 Dust seal
37 Back-up washer
38 Oil seal
39 Needle bearing
40 Retaining ring
41 Housing end plug
42 End plug "O" ring
43 Rack piston end plug
44 Teflon "O" ring
45 Back-up "O" ring
46 Rack piston
47 Balls
48 Ball return guides
49 Clamp
50 Lockwasher & screw assemblies
51 Lock-nut
52 Side cover bolts
53 Side cover
54 Side cover "O" ring
55 Preload adjuster screw
56 Sector shaft
57 Connectors

Adjuster Plug

Disassembly and Assembly

1. Reinstall the adjuster plug into the gear housing and snug it finger tight. Remove the snap retaining ring and the back-up washer.
2. Remove the seal from the plug by prying the seal outward, being careful not to damage the bore.
3. Pry the thrust bearing retainer from the bore. Remove the spacer, washer, bearing and second washer.
4. The needle bearing assembly can be removed from the plug by driving it out.
5. The assembly of the plug can be accomplished by the reversal of the disassembly procedure. Install new "O" rings, seals, and bearings as needed and lubricate the parts with power steering fluid.

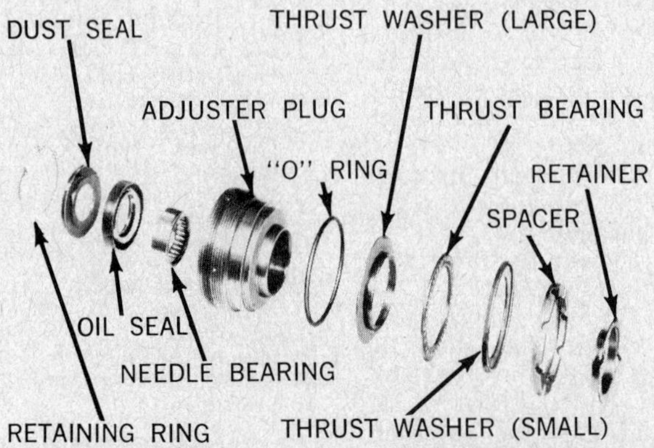

Exploded view of adjuster plug (© Chrysler Corp.)

Valve and Stub Shaft

Disassembly and Assembly

1. Hold the valve assembly by hand

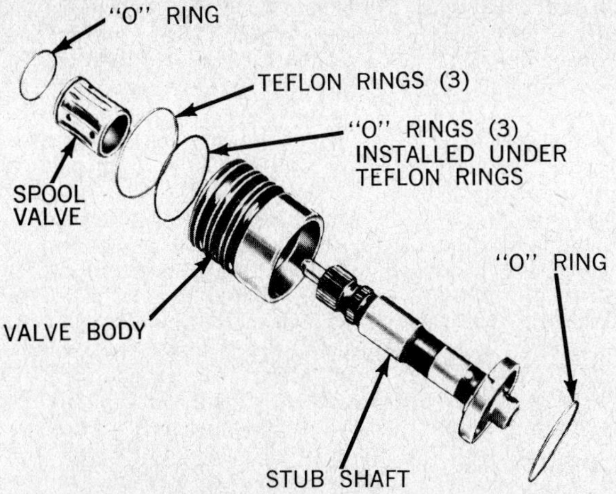

Exploded view of valve body and stub shaft (© Chrysler Corp.)

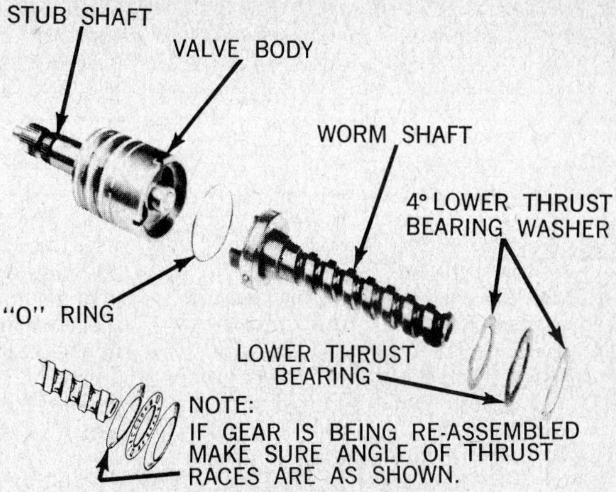

Exploded view of worm shaft and valve body (© Chrysler Corp.)

with the stub shaft down. Lightly tap the stub shaft against a wood block until the cap is raised from the valve body approximately ¼ inch.

2. Remove the shaft assembly from the spool by disengaging the shaft pin, and remove the spool from the valve body by rotating it.
3. Remove and discard the "O" rings and replace the teflon rings if needed.
4. The assembly is in the reverse of disassembly. All parts should be lubricated with power steering fluid.

NOTE: The valve body pin must mate with the cap notch before the valve body is assembled into the gear assembly, and a new "O" ring placed in the shaft end of the valve body assembly.

ing with the guide clamps and screws.

5. Install the ball retaining tool in place of the worm shaft, being careful not to allow any balls to drop.

NOTE: When installing the teflon rings, looseness will be noticed. The teflon rings will heat-shrink when the gear is operated. Therefore, care must be exercised when assembling the internal parts into the housing, to insure that all parts are lubricated with power steering fluid and not forced during the reassembly. The seals and "O" rings may be damaged if this is allowed to happen.

Secondary Rack Piston

No disassembly is necessary on this unit unless the teflon and "O" rings are to be replaced.

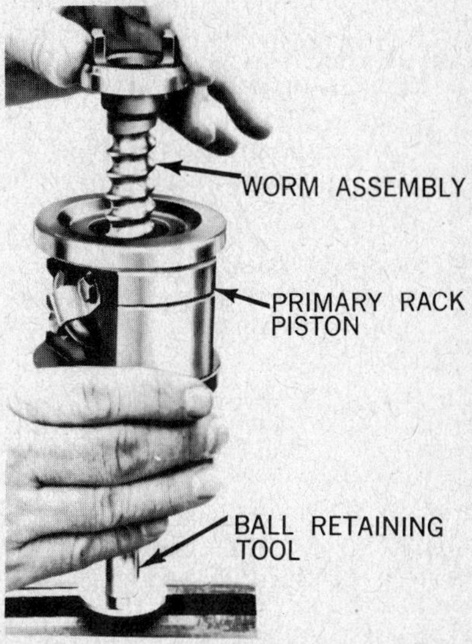

Removing worm shaft while installing a ball retaining tool (© Chrysler Corp.)

Primary Rack Piston

Disassembly

1. Remove the two screws from the ball return clamp. Remove the guide, retaining tool and the recirculating balls.
2. Remove the teflon ring and "O" ring from the rack piston.

Assembly

1. Install the teflon and "O" rings.
2. Slide the worm into the rack piston and rotate the worm to align the grooves with the ball return guide hole nearest the piston ring.
3. While turning the worm shaft, feed 28 balls into the rack piston.

   NOTE: The silver and black balls must be alternately installed as the black balls are .0005 inch smaller than the silver balls.

4. Place the remaining 6 balls alternately into the ball return guide, holding the balls in place with grease. Install the guide into the holes of the rack piston, retain-

Gear Unit

Assembly and Adjustment

1. Install the thrust washer, bearing and second thrust washer over the end of the worm and lubricate with power steering fluid.

NOTE: The tapered surfaces of the washers should be parallel to each other and the cupped side towards the stub shaft.

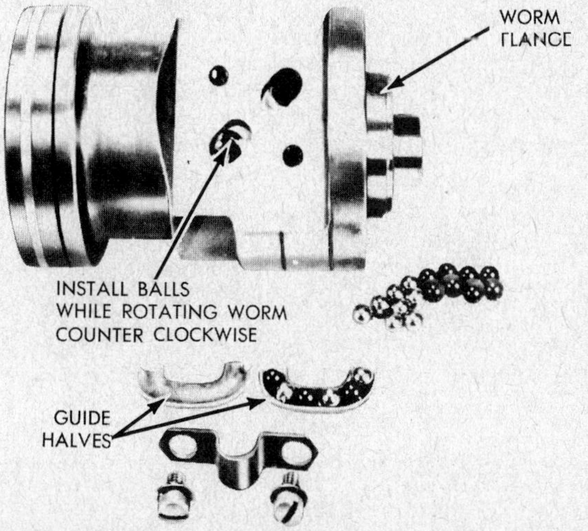

Exploded view of primary rack piston (© Chrysler Corp.)

2. Install the "O" ring in the valve body so that it is seated against the lower shaft cap and lubricate the valve body, rings and seals with power steering fluid.
3. Align the narrow notch in the valve body with the pin in the worm and install the unit into the gear housing, by exerting pressure on the valve body and not the stub shaft.
4. The return hole in the gear housing should be fully uncovered when the valve body is fully seated. Screw in the adjuster plug assembly and seat it against the valve body.
5. Adjust the thrust bearing preload by torquing the adjuster plug to 20 ft. lbs. to seat the thrust bearings.
6. Mark the steering housing in line with one of the tool hole locations on the adjuster plug. Measure counterclockwise 3/16 to ¼ inch and remark the housing.
7. Loosen the adjuster until the tool hole is in line with the second mark on the steering housing and install the lock nut and tighten while maintaining the alignment of the adjuster tool hole with the mark on the housing.
8. With the aid of a torque wrench, turn the stub shaft evenly and observe the torque reading. The reading should be from 4 to 10 inch pounds.
9. Continue the adjustment as necessary to obtain the specified torque reading.
10. With the ball retaining tool in position, lubricate and install the primary rack piston into the gear housing until the retaining tool bottoms against the center of the worm.
11. Turn the stub shaft clockwise to thread the rack piston onto the worm. Keep the retaining tool tight against the worm while turning the stub shaft.
12. Remove the ball retainer tool when the rack piston is completely threaded onto the worm. Center the rack teeth in the sector shaft opening.
13. Install the secondary rack piston in the gear housing and line up the center tooth space with the teeth of the primary rack piston.
14. Slide the sector shaft into the gear housing with the tapered teeth engaging the primary rack piston.
15. Install a new "O" ring on the side cover and push the cover into the housing until contact is made with the preload adjuster screw. With the aid of a ¼ inch Allen wrench inserted through the cover, turn the adjusting screw counterclockwise until the cover bottoms on the housing.
16. Install the side cover bolts and torque to 45 ft. lbs. Install the rack piston plug and torque to 75 ft. lbs.
17. Install the primary and secondary end covers, "O" rings, and install the retainer rings.
18. With the steering gear on center, tighten the sector adjusting screw. Install and tighten the lock nut and check the overcenter torque while rotating the stub shaft through an arc of 180 degrees, with a torque wrench. Adjust the sector shaft accordingly until the correct torque is obtained.

    New gears—4 to 8 in. lbs., but not over 18 in. lbs. combined torque.

    Used gears—4 to 5 in. lbs., but not over 14 in. lbs. combined torque.

NOTE: Combined torque includes the thrust bearing adjustment reading, over-center and internal friction.

Chrysler Full-Time Power Steering (Constant Control Type)

The Chrysler Corporation Constant Control Type Power Steering Gear System consists of a hydraulic pressure pump, a power steering gear and connecting hoses.

The power steering gear housing contains a gear shaft and sector gear, a power piston with gear teeth milled into the side of the piston which is in constant mesh with the gear shaft sector teeth, a worm shaft which connects the steering wheel to the power piston through a coupling. The worm shaft is geared to the piston through recirculating ball contact.

A pivot lever is fitted into the spool valve at the upper end and into a drilled hole in the center thrust bearing race at the lower end. The center thrust bearing race is held firmly against the shoulder of the worm shaft by two thrust bearings, bearing races and an adjusting nut. The pivot lever pivots in the spacer which is held in place by the pressure plate.

When the steering wheel is turned to the left the worm shaft moves out of the power piston a few thousandths of an inch, the center thrust bearing race moves the same distance since it is clamped to the worm shaft. The race thus tips the pivot lever and moves the spool valve down, allowing oil under pressure to flow into the left-turn power chamber and force the power piston down. As the power piston moves, it rotates the cross-shaft sector gear and, through the steering linkage, turns the front wheels.

On a right turn the worm shaft

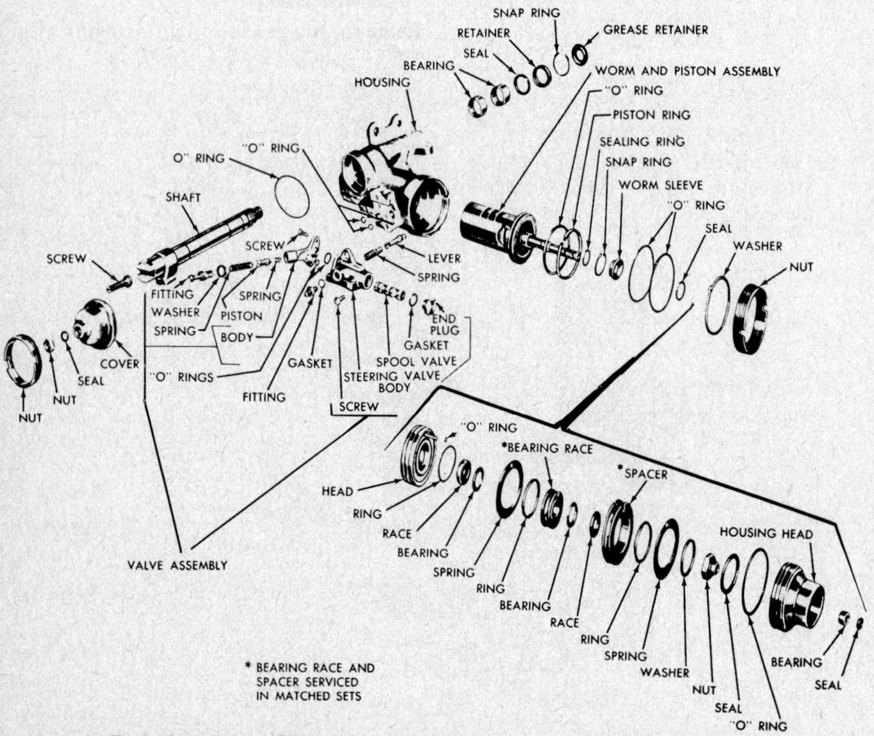

Exploded view of Chrysler power steering gear unit (© Chrysler Corp.)

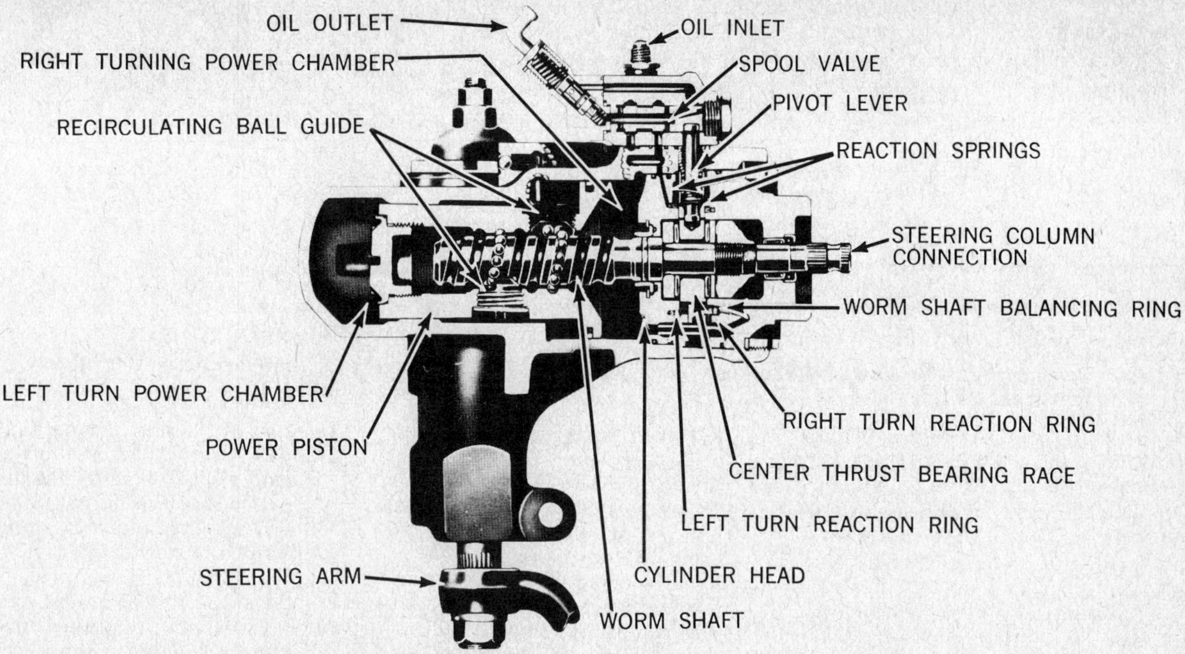

Chrysler power steering gear—cross section (© Chrysler Corp.)

moves into the power piston, the center thrust bearing race thus tips the pivot lever and moves the spool valve up, allowing oil under pressure to flow into the right power chamber and force the power piston up.

Pressure Test

Connect the pressure test hoses with the pressure gauge installed between the pump and steering gear.

Now, fill the reservoir to the level mark, then start the engine and bleed the system. Allow the engine to idle until the fluid in the reservoir is between 150° F. and 170° F. Now turn the steering wheel to the extreme right and check the pressure reading, then turn to the extreme left and check the reading again. The gauge reading should be equal in each direction. If not, it indicates excessive internal leakage in the unit.

The pressure should agree with the specifications in Pump Section for satisfactory power steering operation.

Reconditioning

1. Drain gear by turning worm shaft from limit to limit with oil connections held downward. Thoroughly clean outside.
2. Remove valve body attaching screws, body and three O-rings.
3. Remove pivot lever and spring. Pry under spherical head with a small bar.

   CAUTION: Use care not to collapse slotted end of valve lever as this will destroy bearing tolerances of the spherical head.
4. Remove steering gear arm from sector shaft.
5. Remove snap-ring and seal back-up washer.
6. Remove seal, using proper tool to prevent damage to relative parts.
7. Loosen gear shaft adjusting screw locknut and remove gear shaft cover nut.
8. Rotate wormshaft to position sector teeth at center of piston travel. Loosen power train retaining nut.
9. Insert tools into housing until both tool and shaft are engaged with bearings.
10. Turn worm shaft either to full left or full right (depending on car application) to compress power train parts. Then remove power train retaining nut as mentioned above.
11. Remove housing head tang washer.
12. While holding power train completely compressed, pry on piston teeth with a small bar, using shaft as a fulcrum, and remove complete power train.

    CAUTION: Maintain close contact between cylinder head, center race and spacer assembly and the housing head. This will eliminate the possibility of reactor rings becoming disengaged from their grooves in cylinder and housing head. It will prohibit center spacer from separating from center race and cocking in the housing. This could make it impossible to remove the power train without damaging involved parts.
13. Place power train in soft-jawed vise in vertical position. The worm bearing rollers will fall

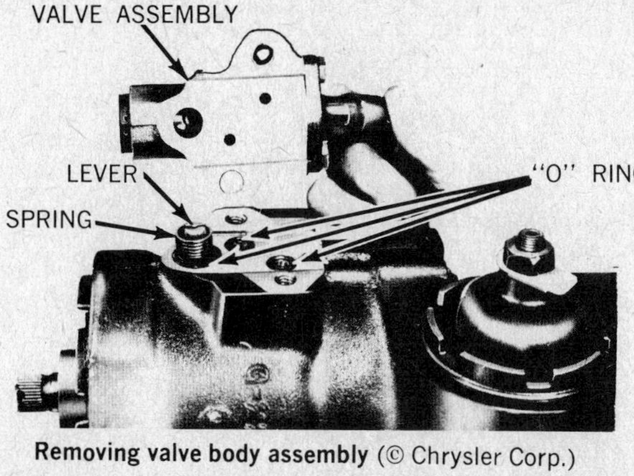

Removing valve body assembly (© Chrysler Corp.)

Removing pilot lever (© Chrysler Corp.)

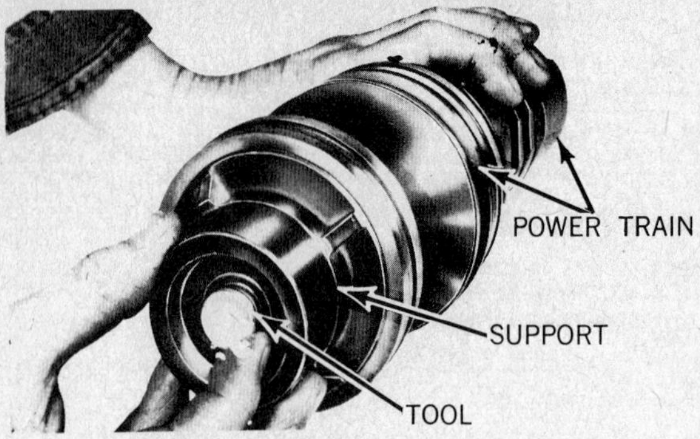

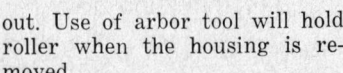

Retaining bearing rollers with arbor tool
(© Chrysler Corp.)

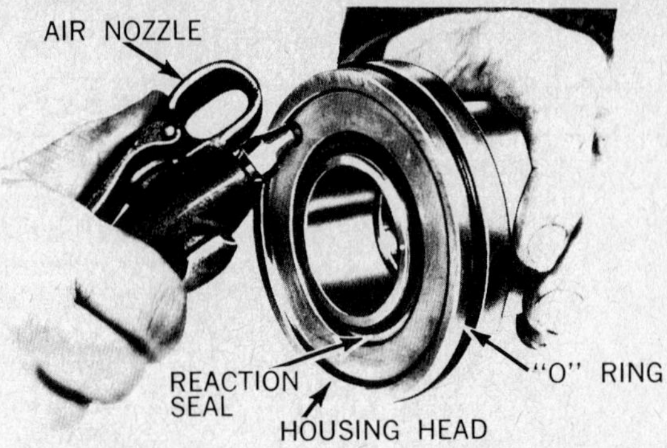

Removing reaction seal from wormshaft support
(© Chrysler Corp.)

out. Use of arbor tool will hold roller when the housing is removed.

14. Raising housing head until wormshaft oil shaft just clears the top of wormshaft and position arbor tool on top of shaft and into seal. With arbor in position, pull up on housing head until arbor is positioned in bearing. Remove when the housing is removed.
15. Remove large O-ring from housing head groove.
16. Remove reaction seal from groove in face of head with air pressure directed into ferrule chamber.
17. Remove reactor spring, reactor ring, worm balancing ring and spacer.
18. While holding wormshaft from turning, turn nut with enough force to release staked portions from knurled section and remove nut.

    NOTE: Pay strict attention to cleanliness.
19. Remove upper thrust bearing race (thin) and upper thrust bearing.
20. Remove center bearing race.
21. Remove lower thrust bearing and lower thrust bearing race (thick).
22. Remove lower reaction ring and reaction spring.
23. Remove cylinder head assembly.
24. Remove O-rings from outer grooves in head.
25. Remove reaction O-ring from groove in face of cylinder head. Use air pressure in oil hole located between O-ring grooves.
26. Remove snap-ring, sleeve and rectangular oil seal from cylinder head counterbore.
27. Test wormshaft operation. Not more than 2 in. lbs. should be required to turn it through its entire travel, and with a 15 ft. lb. side load.

    NOTE: The worm and piston is serviced as a complete assembly and should not be disassembled.
28. Shaft side play should not exceed 0.008 in. under light pull applied 2 5/16 in. from piston flange.
29. Assemble in reverse of above, noting proper adjustments and preload requirements following.
30. When cover nut is installed, tighten to 20 ft-lbs. torque.
31. Valve mounting screws should be tightened to 200 in.-lbs. torque.
32. With hoses connected, system bled, and engine idling roughly, center valve unit until not self-steering. Tap on head of valve body attaching screws to move valve body up, and tap on end plug to move valve body down.
33. With steering gear on center, tighten gear shaft adjusting screw until lash just disappears.
34. Continue to tighten $3/8$ to $1/2$ turn and tighten locknut to 50 ft. lbs.

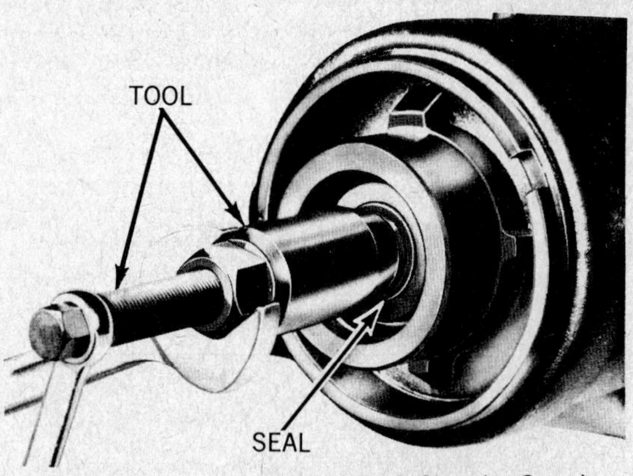

Removing worm shaft oil seal (© Chrysler Corp.)

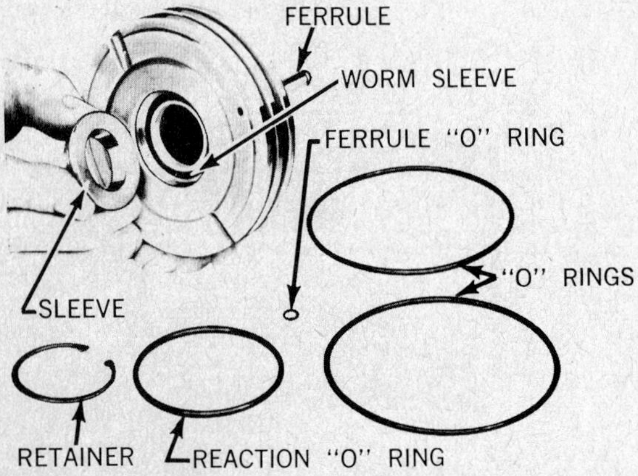

Removing cylinder head oil seal (© Chrysler Corp.)

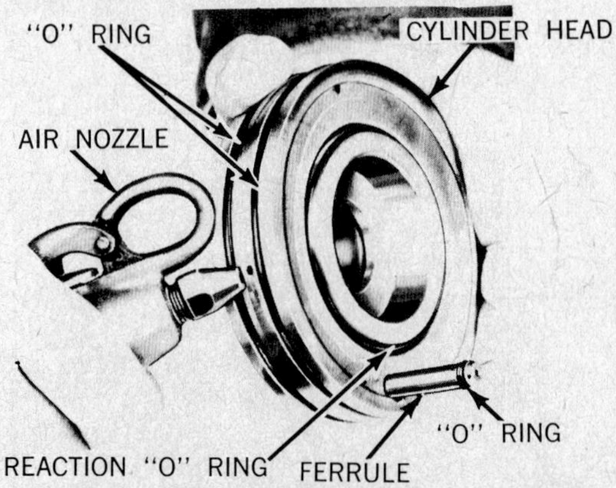

Removing reaction seal from cylinder head
(© Chrysler Corp.)

Ford Integral Power Steering Gear

The Ford integral power steering unit is a torsion-bar type.

The torsion bar power steering unit includes a worm and one-piece rack piston, which is meshed to the gear teeth on the steering sector shaft. The unit also includes a hydraulic valve, valve actuator, input shaft and torsion bar assembly which are mounted on the end of the worm shaft and operated by the twisting action of the torsion bar.

The torsion-bar type of power steering gear is designed with the one piece rack-piston, worm and sector shaft in one housing and the valve spool in an attaching housing. This makes possible internal fluid passages between the valve and cylinder, thus eliminating all external lines and hoses, except the pressure and return hoses between the pump and gear assembly.

The power cylinder is an integral part of the gear housing. The piston is double acting, in that fluid pressure may be applied to either side of the piston.

A selective metal shim, located in the valve housing of the gear is for the purpose of tailoring steering gear efforts. If efforts are not within specifications they can be changed by increasing or decreasing shim thickness as follows:

Efforts heavy to the left—Increase shim thickness.

Efforts light to the left—Decrease shim thickness.

Adjustments

The only adjustment which can be performed is the total over center position load, to eliminate excessive lash between the sector and rack teeth.

1. Disconnect the Pitman arm from the sector shaft.
2. Disconnect the fluid return line at the reservoir, at the same time cap the reservoir return line pipe.
3. Place the end of the return line in a clean container and cycle the steering wheel in both directions as required, to discharge the fluid from the gear.
4. Turn the steering wheel to 45 degrees from the left stop.
5. Using an in-lb torque wrench on the steering wheel nut, determine the torque required to rotate the shaft slowly through an approximately $\frac{1}{8}$ turn from the 45 degree position.
6. Turn the steering gear back to center, then determine the torque required to rotate the shaft back and forth across the center position. Loosen the adjuster nut, and turn the adjuster screw until the reading is 11-12 in-lb greater than the torque 45 degrees from the stop. Tighten the lock nut while holding the screw in place.
7. Recheck the readings and replace the Pitman arm and the steering wheel hub cover.
8. Correct the fluid return line to the reservoir and fill the reservoir with specified lubricant to the proper level.

Valve Centering Shim

Removal and Installation

1. Hold the steering gear over a drain pan in an inverted position and cycle the input shaft several times to drain the remaining fluid from the gear.
2. Mount the gear in a soft-jawed vise.
3. Turn the input shaft to either stop then, turn it back approximately $1\frac{3}{4}$ turns to center the gear.
4. Remove the two sector shaft cover attaching screws, the brake line bracket and the identification tag.
5. Tap the lower end of the sector shaft with a soft-faced hammer to loosen it, then lift the cover and shaft from the housing as an assembly. Discard the O-ring.
6. Remove the four valve housing attaching bolts. Lift the valve housing from the steering gear housing while holding the piston to prevent it from rotating off the worm shaft.
7. Remove the valve housing and the lube passage O-rings and discard them.
8. Place the valve housing, worm and piston assembly in the bench mounted holding fixture with the piston on the top.
9. Rotate the piston upward (back off) $3\frac{1}{2}$ turns.
10. Insert Tool T66P-3553-C or equivalent (with the arm facing away from the piston) into a bolt hole in the valve housing. Rotate the arm into position under the piston.
11. Loosen the Allen head race nut set screw from the valve housing.
12. Using Tool T66P-3553-B or equivalent, loosen the worm bearing race nut.
13. Lift the piston-worm assembly from the valve housing. During removal hold the piston to prevent it from spinning off at the shaft.

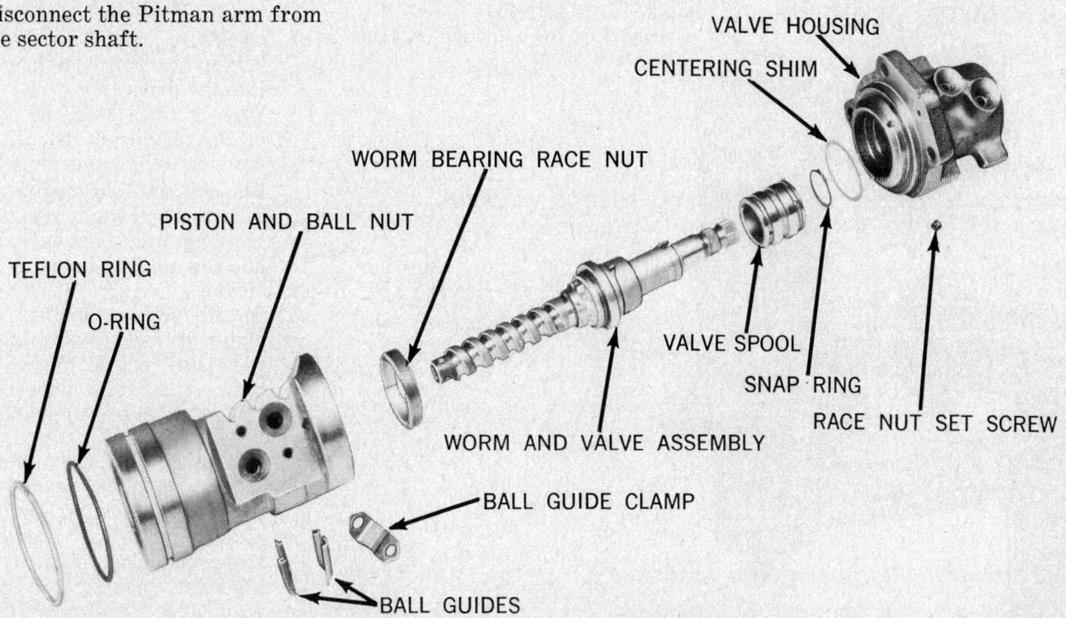

Ball nut and valve housing (© Ford Motor Co.)

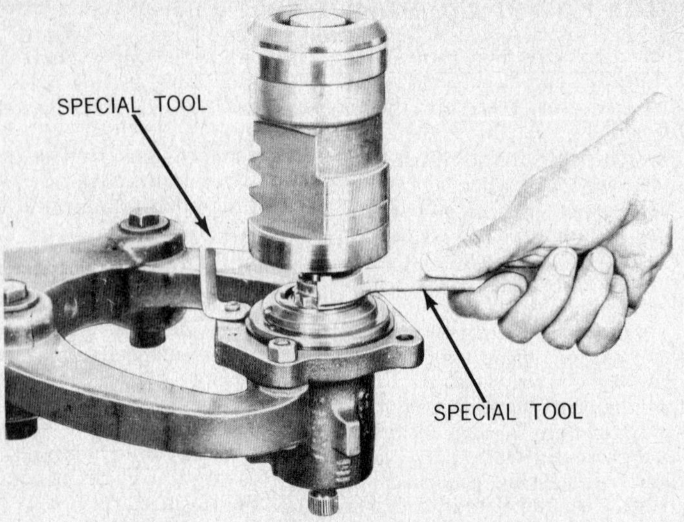

Removing worm bearing race nut (© Ford Motor Co.)

14. Change the power steering valve centering shim.
15. Install the piston-worm assembly into the valve housing. Hold the piston worm to prevent it from spinning off of the shaft.
16. Install the worm bearing race nut and torque to 2-8 in-lbs using Tool T66P-3553-B or equivalent.
17. Install the race nut set screw (Allen head) through the valve housing.
18. Rotate the piston upward (back off) ½ turn and remove Tool T66P-3553-C or equivalent.
19. Remove the valve housing, worm, and piston assembly from the holding fixture.
20. Position a new lube passage O-ring in the counterbore of the gear housing.
21. Apply vaseline to the teflon seal on the piston.
22. Place a new O-ring on the valve housing.
23. Slide the piston and valve into the gear housing being careful not to damage the teflon seal.
24. Align the lube passage in the valve housing with the one in the gear housing, and install but do not tighten the attaching bolts.
25. Rotate the ball nut so that the teeth are in the same place as the sector teeth. Tighten the four valve housing attaching bolts to 35-45 ft-lbs.
26. Position the sector shaft cover O-ring in the steering gear housing. Turn the input shaft as required to center the piston.
27. Apply vaseline to the sector shaft journal; then, position the sector shaft and cover assembly in the gear housing. Install the brake line bracket, steering gear identification tag and the two sector shaft cover attaching studs.
28. Position an in-lb torque wrench on the gear input shaft and adjust the meshload to approximately 4 in-lbs. Then, torque the sector shaft cover attaching studs to 55-70 ft-lbs.
29. After the cover attaching bolts have been tightened to specification, adjust the mesh load to 17 in-lbs with an in-lb torque wrench.

Steering Gear Disassembly

1. Hold the steering gear over a drain pan in an inverted position and cycle the input shaft several times to drain the remaining fluid from the gear.
2. Mount the gear in a soft-jawed vise.
3. Remove the lock nut from the adjusting screw.
4. Turn the input shaft to either stop then, turn it back approximately 1¾ turns to center the gear.
5. Remove the two sector shaft cover attaching studs, the brake line bracket and the identification tag.
6. Tap the lower end of the sector shaft with a soft-hammer to loosen it, then lift the cover and shaft from the housing as an assembly. Discard the O-ring.
7. Turn the sector shaft cover counterclockwise off the adjuster screw.
8. Remove the four valve housing attaching bolts. Lift the valve housing from the steering gear housing while holding the piston to prevent it from rotating off the worm shaft. Remove the valve housing and the lube passage O-rings and discard them.
9. Stand the valve body and piston on end with the piston end down. Rotate the input shaft counterclockwise out of the piston allowing the ball bearings to drop into the piston.
10. Place a cloth over the open end of the piston and turn it upside down to remove the balls.
11. Remove the two screws that attach the ball guide clamp to the ball nut and remove the clamp and the guides.
12. Install the valve body assembly in the holding fixture (do not clamp in a vise) and loosen the race nut screw (Allen head) from the valve housing and remove the worm bearing race nut.
13. Carefully slide the input shaft, worm and valve assembly out of the valve housing. Due to the close diametrical clearance between the spool and housing, the slightest cocking of the spool may cause it to jam in the housing.

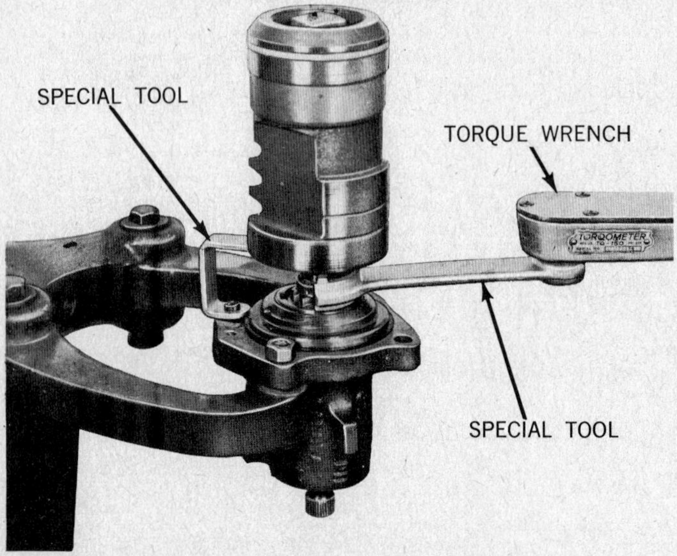

Installing worm bearing race nut (© Ford Motor Co.)

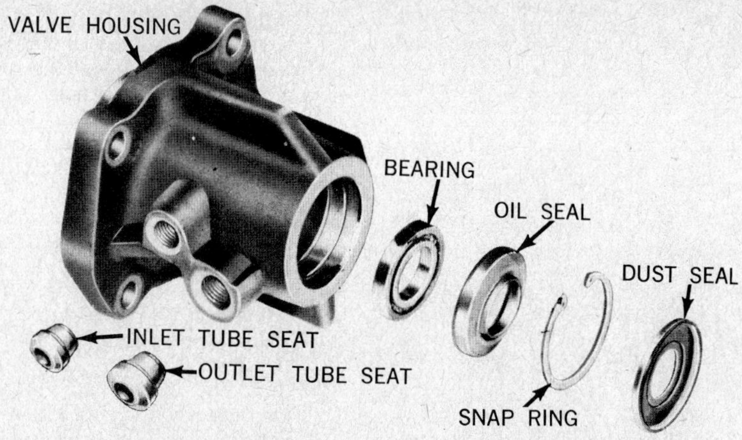

Valve housing disassembled (© Ford Motor Co.)

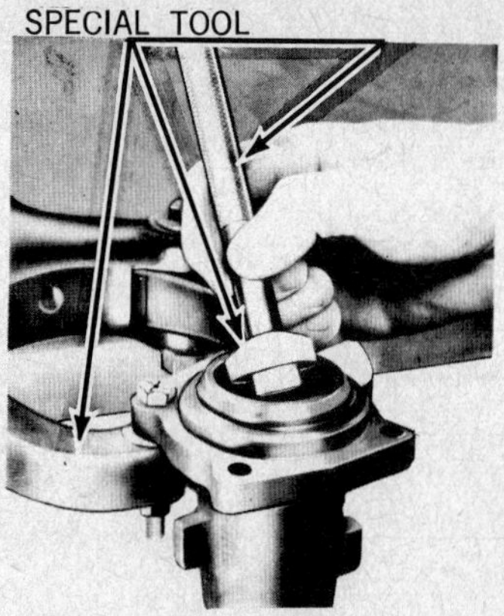

Removing bearing and oil seal (© Ford Motor Co.)

14. Remove the shim from the valve housing bore.

Valve Housing

1. Remove the dust seal from the rear of the valve housing and discard the seal.
2. Remove the snap-ring from the valve housing.
3. Turn the fixture to place the valve housing in an inverted position.
4. Insert special tool in the valve body assembly opposite the seal end and gently tap the bearing and seal out of the housing. Discard the seal. Caution must be exercised when inserting and removing the tool to prevent damage to the valve bore in the housing.
5. Remove the fluid inlet and outlet tube seats with an EZ-out if they are damaged.
6. Coat the fluid inlet and outlet tube seats with vaseline and position them in the housing. Install and tighten the tube nuts to press the seats to the proper location.
7. Coat the bearing and seal surface of the housing with a film of vaseline.
8. Seat the bearing in the valve housing. Make sure that the bearing is free to rotate.
9. Dip the new oil seal in gear lubricant; then, place it in the housing with the metal side of the seal facing outward. Drive the seal into the housing until the outer edge of seal does not quite clear the snap-ring groove.
10. Place the snap-ring in the housing; then, drive on the ring until the snap-ring seats in its groove to properly locate the seal.
11. Place the dust seal in the housing with the dished side (rubber side) facing out. Drive the dust seal into place. The seal must be located behind the undercut in the input shaft when it is installed.

Worm and Valve

1. Remove the snap-ring from the end of the actuator.
2. Slide the control valve spool off the actuator.
3. Install the valve spool evenly and slowly with a slight oscillating motion into the flanged end of valve housing with the valve identification groove between the valve spool lands outward, checking for freedom of valve movement within the housing working area. The valve spool should enter the housing bore freely and fall by its own weight.
4. If the valve spool is not free, check for burrs at the outward edges of the working lands in the housing and remove with a hard stone.
5. Check the valve for burrs and if burrs are found, stone the valve in a radial direction only. Check for freedom of the valve again.
6. Remove the valve spool from the housing.
7. Slide the spool onto the actuator making sure that the groove in the spool annulus is toward the worm.
8. Install the snap-ring to retain the spool. The beveled ID of the snap-ring must be assembled toward the spool.
9. Check the clearance between the spool and the snap-ring. The clearance should be between .0005-.035 inch. If the clearance is not within these limits, select a snap-ring that will allow a clearance of .002 inch.

Piston and Ball Nut

1. Remove the teflon ring and the O-ring from the piston and ball nut.
2. Dip a new O-ring in gear lubricant and install it on the piston and ball nut.
3. Install a new teflon ring on the piston and ball nut being careful not to stretch it any more than necessary.

Steering Gear Housing

1. Remove the snap-ring and the spacer washer from the lower end of the steering gear housing.
2. Remove the lower seal from the housing. Lift the spacer washer from the housing.
3. Remove the upper seal in the same manner as the lower seal. Some housings require only one seal and one spacer.
4. Dip both sector shaft seals in gear lubricant.
5. Apply lubricant to the sector shaft seal bore of the housing and position the sector shaft inner seal into the housing with the lip facing inward. Press the

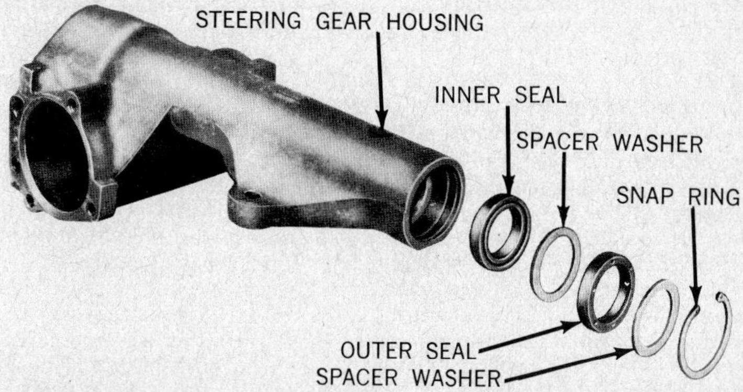

Steering gear housing and sector shaft seal assembly (© Ford Motor Co.)

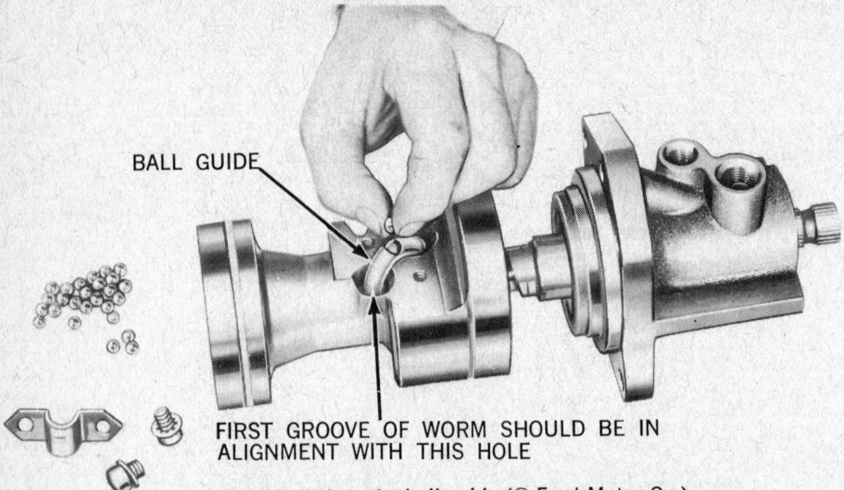

Loading balls into the ball guide (© Ford Motor Co.)

the seal and apply more lubricant to the housing bore.

6. Place the outer seal in the housing with the lip facing inward and press it into place. Then, place a 0.090 inch spacer washer on top of the seal.
7. Position the snap-ring in the housing. Press the snap-ring into the housing to properly locate the seals and engage the snap-ring in the groove.

Steering Gear Assembly

Do not clean, wash, or soak seals in cleaning solvent.

1. Mount the valve housing in the holding fixture with the flanged end up.
2. Place the required thickness valve spool centering shim in the housing.
3. Carefully install the worm and valve in the housing.
4. Install the race nut in the housing and torque it to 42 ft-lbs.
5. Install the race nut set screw (Allen head) through the valve housing and torque to 20-25 in-lbs.
6. Place the piston on the bench with the ball guide holes facing up. Insert the worm shaft into the piston so that the first groove is in alignment with the hole nearest to the center of the piston.
7. Place the ball guide in the piston. Place the 27 to 29 balls, depending on the piston design, in the ball guide turning the worm in a clockwise direction as viewed from the input end of the shaft. If all of the balls have not been fed into the guide upon reaching the right stop, rotate the input shaft in one direction and then in the other while installing the balls. After the balls have been installed, do not rotate the input shaft or the piston more than 3½ turns off the right stop to prevent the balls from falling out of the circuit.
8. Secure the guides in the ball nut with the clamp.
9. Position a new lube passage O-ring in the counterbore of the gear housing.
10. Apply petroleum jelly to the teflon seal on the piston.
11. Place a new O-ring on the valve housing.
12. Slide the piston and valve into the gear housing being careful not to damage the teflon seal.

the gear housing and install but

13. Align the lube passage in the valve housing with the one in do not tighten the attaching bolts.
14. Rotate the ball nut so that the teeth are in the same plane as the sector teeth. Tighten the four valve housing attaching bolts to 35-45 ft-lbs.
15. Position the sector shaft cover O-ring in the steering gear housing. Turn the input shaft as required to center the piston.
16. Apply vaseline to the sector shaft journal then position the sector shaft and cover assembly in the gear housing. Install the brake line bracket, the steering identification tag and two sector shaft cover attaching bolts. Torque the bolts to 55-70 ft-lbs.
17. Attach an in-lb torque wrench to the input shaft. Adjust the mesh load to 17 in-lbs.

seal into place. Place a spacer washer (0.090 inch) on top of

Ross HF-54 and HF-64 Integral Power Steering Gear

The Ross Model HF-54, HF-64 integral power steering gears have a hydraulically operated control valve, a power cylinder (piston rack and housing) and a mechanical means of steering control, all incorporated in a main housing with oil pressure supplied by an engine driven pump.

Adjustments

Unloader Valve Adjustment

This unloader valve adjustment is for right turn only on HF-54 Model gears and for both turns on HF-64 Model gears. Prior to performing the following procedure, obtain the vehicle's straight ahead position by driving the vehicle with hands off the steering wheel thus allowing the unit to find its own center. Now mark the steering column to steering wheel with chalk or masking tape.

1. Check the front wheel turning angles and adjust as required with the wheels off the ground.
2. Position the wheels straight ahead and lower the vehicle.
3. RIGHT TURN—HF-54 OR HF-64 GEARS: With the engine at idle, the vehicle standing still and the fluid at normal operating temperature, rotate the steering wheel to the right the prescribed number of turns.

   H-54 .... 1¾
   H-64 - 2 port 1¼
   H-64 - 4 port 1½

   Hold in this position.
4. Loosen the locknut and turn the unloader valve pressure adjusting screw until an audible hiss is heard. Tighten the locknut.
5. Return the wheel to a straight ahead position while the vehicle is moving. With the vehicle standing still, again rotate the steering wheel the prescribed turns; then, check for the audible hiss. Readjust if necessary as in Step 4 and check once more as in this step. It is important to remember that the HF-64 gear has a pitman arm stop for the right turn cast on the gear housing. The pitman arm must not contact this stop prior to contacting the unloader valve. When the hiss is heard during the adjustment, the clearance between the pitman arm and the cast stop should be 1/16 to ⅛-inch minimum.
6. *Left turn—HF-64 gear only:* Repeat Steps 3, 4, and 5 while rotating the steering wheel to the left 1¾ turns.

Sector Shaft Adjustment

1. Disconnect the drag link from the Pitman arm.

2. Center the steering wheel. Grasp the Pitman arm and check it for free movement (lash) between the sector shaft and the rack piston.
3. If free movement is noted (lash), remove the steering gear from the vehicle.
4. Loosen the sector shaft adjustment screw locknut on the side cover.
5. After rotating the input shaft through its full travel for a minimum of five cycles, adjust the sector shaft adjusting screw to provide 15-20 in-lb torque as the input shaft is rotated 90 degrees each side of center.
6. Back out the adjusting screw one turn and note the torque required to move the input shaft 90 degrees each side of the center position. Move the adjusting screw in to provide an increase in torque of 2-4 in-lb at a point within 45 degrees each side of center after the adjusting screw jam nut is first tightened snug. Now torque to a final 20-25 ft-lb. The input torque of the completely assembled gear, minus hydraulic oil, should not exceed 15 in-lb for the full travel of the output shaft.
7. Install the steering gear in the vehicle.
8. Connect the drag link to the Pitman arm.
9. Connect the pump lines and refill the system with the specified fluid.

Disassembly

1. Rotate the input shaft so the index mark on the end of the sector shaft is perpendicular to the center-line of the gear (straight-ahead position).
2. Remove the side cover attaching screws and washers.
3. Tap lightly on the end of the sector shaft with a soft hammer to disengage the side cover seal and allow the housing to drain.
4. Remove all nicks, burrs, rust and paint before removing the shaft. Lift the side cover and sector shaft from the housing as an assembly.
5. Remove the sector shaft seal adapter attaching screws and remove the adapter from the housing.
6. Remove the four screws that attach the control valve adapter to the housing.
7. Remove the control valve and rack piston from the housing as an assembly.
8. Remove the sector shaft adjustment screw lock nut. Turn the adjustment clockwise until free of the side cover.

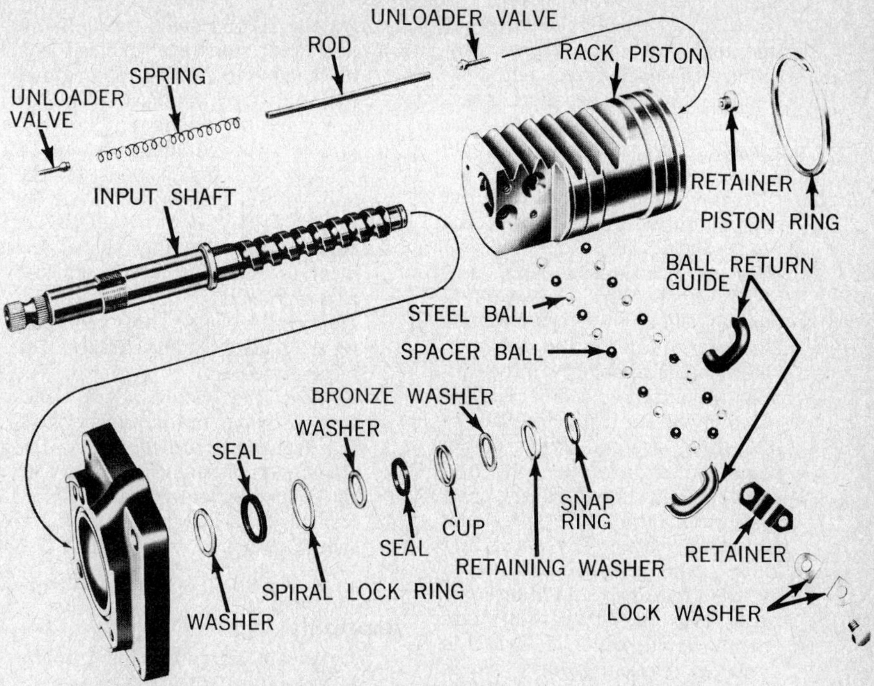

Input shaft seals and retainers—models HF-54 (model HF-64 similar) (© Ford Motor Co.)

9. Remove the unloader valve retainer, unloader valves, rod and the spring from the rack piston.
10. If all parts appear undamaged, do not disassemble the rack piston assembly. If there is evidence of damage, place the rack piston on a clean surface with the ball return guides facing upward. Remove the two ball return guide retainer attaching screws, lock washers, guide retainer, guide and balls. It may be necessary to tilt the rack piston over a clean pan and oscillate the worm shaft to empty the rack of all the balls. Lift the worm shaft from the rack after all the balls have been removed.
11. Carefully hold the input shaft in a vise equipped with soft jaws. Remove the snap-ring, washer, bronze washer, cup, seal and washer. It may be necessary to cut the teflon cup off the shaft.
12. Remove the valve cover dirt and water seal.
13. Remove the four valve cover attaching screws. Lift the cover from the control valve.

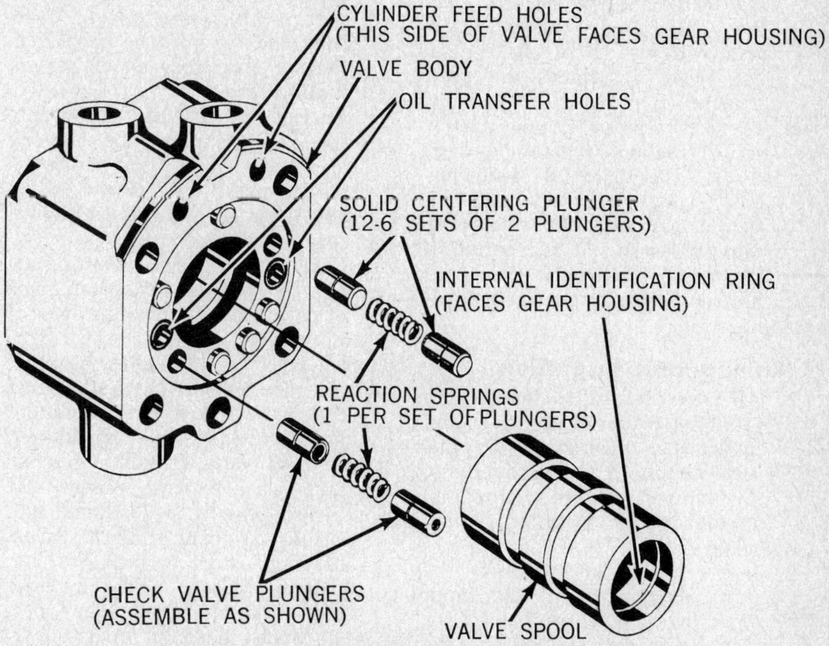

Hydraulic control valve assembly (© Ford Motor Co.)

14. Unstake the thrust bearing adjustment nut lock washer and remove the adjustment nut.
15. Remove the lock washer, internal tang washer, bearing race (small), thrust bearing and the large bearing race.
16. Lift the control valve and the control valve adapter from the input shaft.
17. Remove spiral lock ring, seal and washer from the counterbore of the valve cover adapter. Discard the washer and seal.
18. Do not disassemble the valve unless absolutely necessary. The valve is the control center of the hydraulic system. The major parts, which are the body and spool, are machined to very close tolerances and with precision machined edges. The spool and valve body are selectively fitted at the factory, and therefore these two parts are not separately replaceable. If either is damaged or excessively worn, the complete valve assembly should be replaced. Good performance of power steering is not assured if a mismatched valve spool and body are used. Care should be exercised in the handling of these parts to prevent damage. Sealing edges of the valve bore and the spool should not be broken. This will result in excessive leakage and reduced hydraulic power. If valve parts should drop out during gear disassembly, reassemble the valve as follows:
    a. Clean all parts with a clean petroleum base solvent and blow dry with clean, dry air.
    b. Insert the valve spool in the control valve making certain that the machined identification groove in the ID of one end of the spool is toward the gear housing.
    c. There are 7 sets of plungers, each set having one reaction spring. Insert the 6 solid centering plunger sets first along with one spring per set. The remaining plunger set should be inserted in the valve body with the small hole on each plunger facing outboard.

Cleaning and Inspection

1. All parts should be cleaned in a clean petroleum base solvent and blown dry with clean dry air. Avoid wiping parts with a cloth, since lint may cause binding and sticking of closely fitted components.
2. Inspect the worm grooves in the rack piston and on the input shaft for wear scores. Inspect the OD of the rack piston and the ring or teeth for wear or scores. On the HF-64 gear, the ball nut and input shaft are serviced as a matched assembly. Therefore, both must be replaced if either are worn or damaged. The rack piston is not matched.
3. Inspect the inside ends of the ball return guides for wear or damage.
4. Inspect the housing bore for wear or scores or being cracked and replace as required.
5. Inspect the sector shaft teeth for wear or the bearing surfaces for wear or scores.
6. Replace the sector shaft bearings if worn or damaged. Note the sector shaft bearing in the side cover is replaced as part of the side cover assembly.
7. Replace all seals at time of disassembly.

Assembly

1. Lubricate all rubber parts prior to assembly.
2. If the sector shaft bearing was removed from the steering gear housing, install the snap-ring in the outboard side of the housing (HF-54 gear only).
3. Place the steering gear housing in a press with the side cover area on a wood block to prevent damage to the machined area.
4. Position the bearing on the housing with the numbered end facing up. Carefully press the bearing into the housing until the outer surface is flush. Use a tool that pilots in the ID of the bearing and contacts the bearing end surface.
5. Coat the unloader valve pressure adjusting screw O-ring liberally with clean grease or oil. Carefully slide it into the groove on the non-threaded end of the adjusting screw.
6. Thread the adjusting screw into the lower end of the housing leaving 7/8 inch of the screw exposed. Install the lock nut on the adjusting screw and tighten it securely.
7. Carefully secure the input shaft in a vise equipped with soft jaws to permit access to both ends of the shaft.
8. On HF-54 gears, slide the bearing race (large) thrust bearing, control valve (with cylinder ports toward the shoulder), bearing race (small), internal tang washer, lock washer and thrust bearing adjustment nut. On HF-64 gears, slide the thrust bearing race washer, spacer, control valve (with cylinder ports toward the shoulder), needle thrust bearing, thrust bearing race washer, tang washer, lock washer and thrust bearing adjustment nut.
9. Tighten the adjustment nut to 20 ft-lbs, then back it off 1/2-1 lock washer tangs. Bend one tang of the lock washer into the slot provided on the adjustment nut. When adjusted in this manner, the control valve should rotate freely on the shaft with a torque of 2-3 1/2 in-lbs and have no perceptible end play.
10. Assemble a new washer seal and the spiral lock ring in the counterbore of the valve cover adapter. Make sure that the lip of seal is facing toward the spiral lock ring.
11. Coat a new valve cover seal and two new cylinder port seals with grease to retain them in place. Position the seals in the recesses provided in the control valve cover adapter on the surface adjacent to the control valve.
12. Reposition the input shaft in the vise securing the serrated end.
13. Slip the adapter over the worn groove end of the input shaft. Align the cylinder port seals with the ports in the control valve. Install one of the attaching bolts finger tight to facilitate assembly.
14. Assemble the washer (steel), a new rubber seal, new teflon cup with the lip toward the seal, bronze washer and retaining washer. Compress the washer and seal, then install the snap-ring on the end of the input shaft. Make sure that the snap-ring is fully seated in the groove and the recessed area of the retaining washer.
15. Secure the rack piston in a soft-jawed vise with the ball guide holes facing upward.
16. Carefully expand the piston ring and install it in the piston groove.
17. Place the two unloader valves, spring, and rod in the rack piston. Apply a drop of sealer to the threads of the retainer. Install and torque the retainer to 25 ft-lbs.
18. Coat the input shaft seal at the end of worm with grease and place it in the rack piston bore.
19. Assemble sixteen balls while rotating the input shaft counterclockwise. The black spacer balls and the polished steel balls must be installed alternately. Coat the ball return guides with grease to retain the balls, then install the six remaining balls in the guides making sure that the balls in the guide alternate with the last balls installed in the rack piston. If a ball is lost, no more than three black spacer balls may be

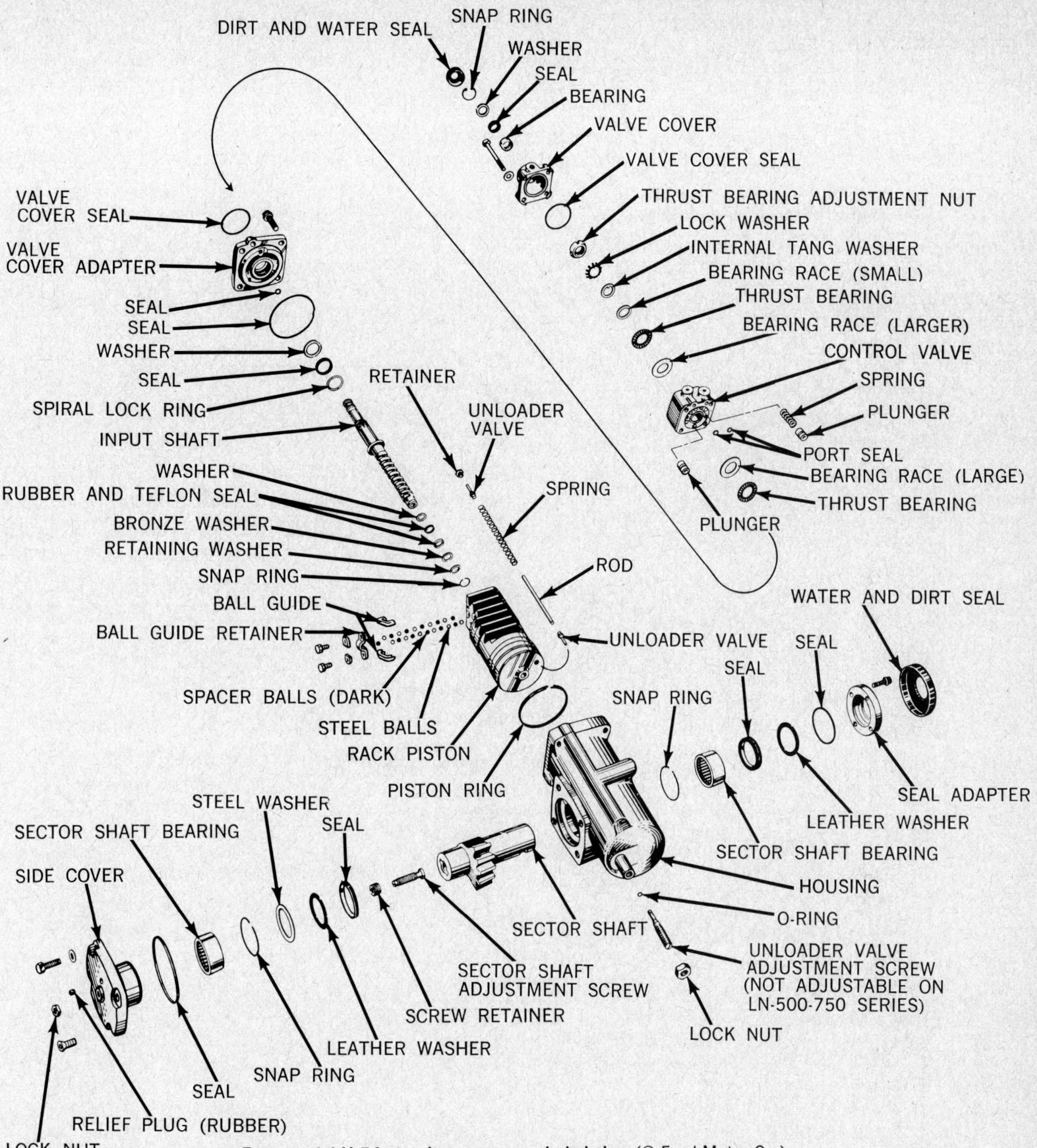

Ross model H-54 steering gear—exploded view (© Ford Motor Co.)

used for replacement. Secure the guide retaining clip to the rack piston with two screws and washers. Torque the screws to 30-35 ft-lbs and bend the tab of the locking washer against the flat.

20. Grip the serrated end of the sector shaft in a soft-jawed vise.
21. Coat the head of the sector shaft adjusting screw with grease. Position the head of adjusting screw into the slot in the end of sector shaft.
22. Install a new sector shaft adjustment screw retainer in the end of shaft. Tighten the retainer to permit free rotation of screw without perceptible end play. Stake the retainer in the two slots provided and recheck the rotation effort.
23. If the pressure relief plug has been removed or ruptured, press a new one into the side cover until it is flush with the surface.
24. Assemble the snap-ring, steel washer (with taper toward the snap-ring), leather washer and the two piece seal into the side cover. The seal has "Oil Side" molded into one side and must be visible after installation.
25. Coat the end of sector shaft with lubricant. Rotate the sector shaft adjusting screw counterclockwise to thread it into the side cover. Rotate the screw until a firm stop is reached. Make sure that the shaft seal has not fallen out of position.
26. Place the outer seal in the seal adapter. Then install the leather washer and inner seal making sure that the side having the mold "Oil Side" is visible after installation.
27. If the input shaft needle bearing has been removed from the control valve cover it must be in-

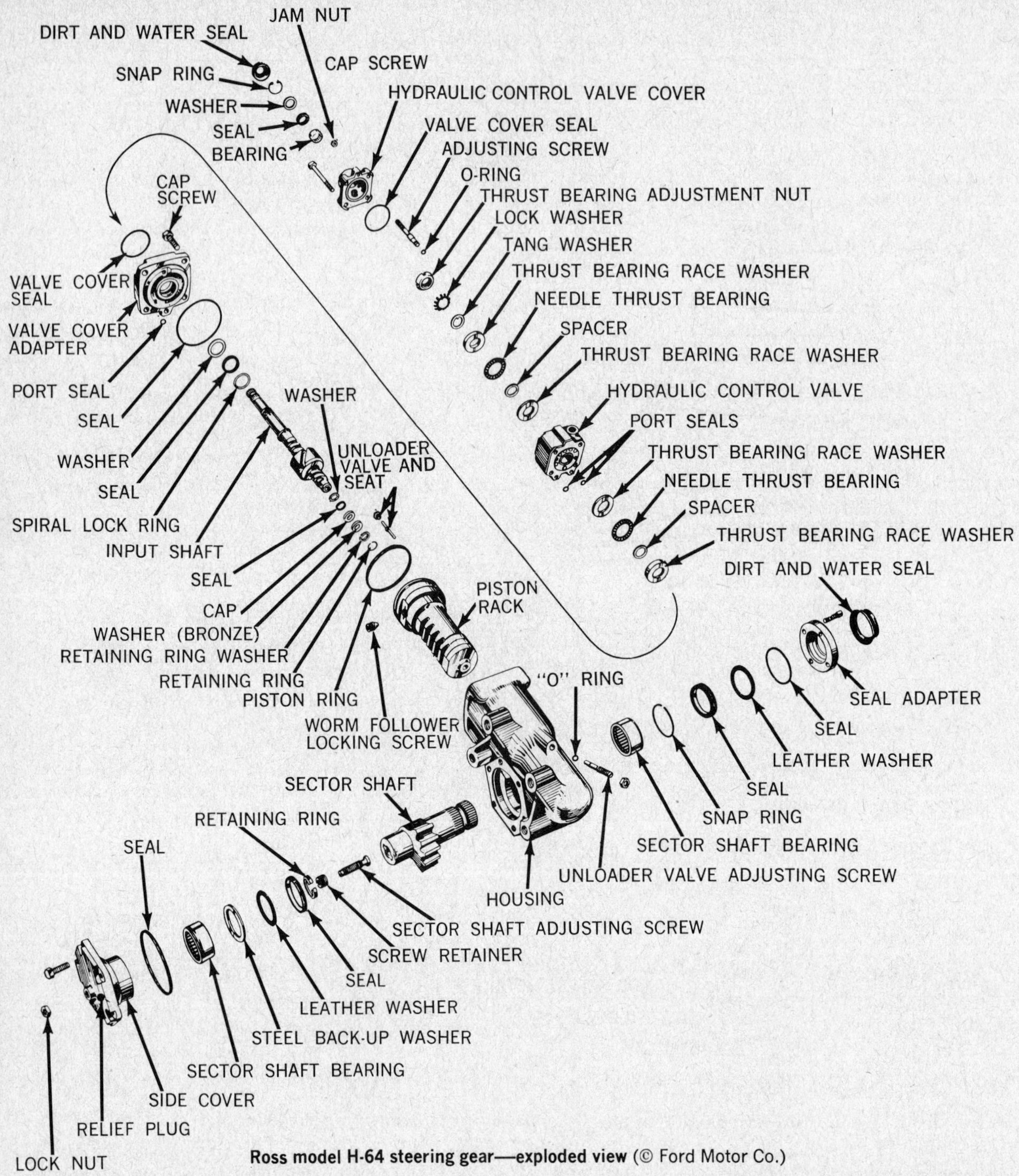

Ross model H-64 steering gear—exploded view (© Ford Motor Co.)

stalled with a tool that will pilot in the bearing and have clearance in the cover bore. The bearing must be pressed from the part number end, and to a depth of $1\frac{1}{8}$ inches from the face of the valve cover. After installation of the bearing, make sure that all rollers rotate freely.

28. Install the seal on the control valve cover with the lip facing toward the needle bearing. Coat the washer with grease and install it on the cover. Install the snap-ring to secure the seal and washer.
29. Pack the new dirt and water seal with grease and install it on the control valve cover.
30. Secure the steering gear housing in a vise equipped with soft jaws.
31. Lubricate the steering gear housing bore. Start the rack piston into the bore, then compress the ring and move the piston into position so that the teeth are visible through the side cover opening. Install the four adapter - to - housing attaching bolts. Remove the one bolt that was previously installed.
32. Lubricate a new valve cover seal with grease and position it in the recess of the valve cover.
33. Slide the valve cover onto the input shaft and install the four cover-to-control valve attaching bolts.
34. Rotate the input shaft as required to align the center tooth of the rack piston (marked tooth) with the side cover opening.
35. Lubricate a new side cover O-ring and position it on the side cover.
36. Position the sector shaft and

side cover to the steering gear housing making sure that the center tooth (marked tooth) engages the center space (marked space).

37. Install the four side cover attaching bolts and lock washers. Torque the bolts to 45-55 ft-lbs.
38. Adjust sector shaft adjustment screw as outlined in the Sector Shaft Adjustment.
39. Cover the sector shaft serrations with a layer of scotch tape to prevent damage to the seal in the adapter.
40. Position the adapter over the sector shaft and on the housing. Install and tighten the attaching bolts.
41. Pack the seal adapter outer seal with grease, then install it on the adapter to prevent water entry.

Final Checks

1. After rotating the input shaft through its full travel for a minimum of five cycles, recheck the sector shaft adjustment. No rotational lash or bind of the sector shaft in center position is permissible.
2. If the gear is properly assembled and adjusted, the input torque of the empty gear should not exceed 15 in-lbs over full travel of 95 degrees at the output shaft.
3. Reverse-torque applied to output shaft for full gear travel should not exceed 50 ft-lbs.

Ross Model HFB-52 Integral Power Steering Gear

The model HFB-52 power steering gear is a fully integral unit, consisting of a hydraulic control valve, a power cylinder and a manual steering mechanism in a single housing. The control valve is of the rotory type.

Adjustments

When adjustments are made to the steering gear while on the vehicle, disconnect the pitman arm or drag link and the input coupling. Leave the plumbing attached and allow the engine to idle while preforming the adjustments.

Sector Shaft Adjustment

1. Loosen the locknut and adjust the screw to provide a torque at the worm gear of 23-28 in. lbs. as the steering gear is moved 90 degrees from each side of center.
2. Back out the adjusting screw one turn and note the torque necessary to move the worm shaft 90 degrees from each side of center.
3. Rotate the adjusting screw to provide a rise in torque of 2 to 4 in. lbs. at a point within 45 degrees from each side of center. Tighten the locknut to 40-45 ft. lbs.
4. The torque to rotate the worm shaft must not exceed 26 in. lbs. at any point of steering gear travel.

Worm Preload Adjustment

1. Loosen the adjustment screw jam nut and tighten the adjusting screw to 25-30 in. lbs.
2. Tighten the jam nut to 40-50 ft. lbs. while holding the adjusting screw so that it does not rotate.
3. The purpose of the adjustment is to put a light preload on the worm thrust bearing assembly. The input shaft must rotate smoothly and without binding through the full steering gear travel with a maximum torque of 26 in. lbs.

Poppet Adjusting Screws

The steering gear must be in the vehicle for this adjustment. The purpose of the adjustment is to set the poppet adjusting screw so the poppet contacts the adjusting screw just before full wheel cut is reached. When at full wheel cut (steering against axle stops), the poppet should be fully tripped and the pressure shown

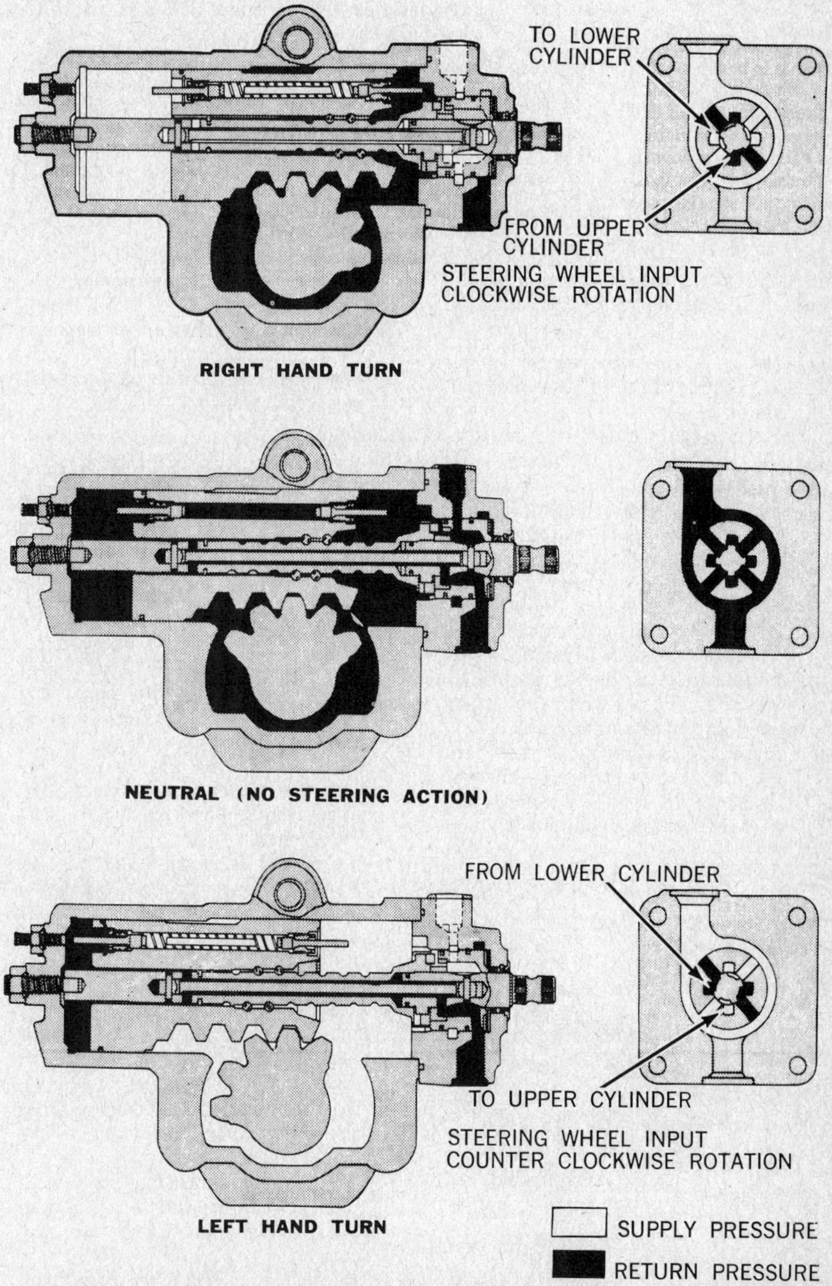

Oil flow through turns and centered—Ross model HFB-52 (© Ford Motor Co.)

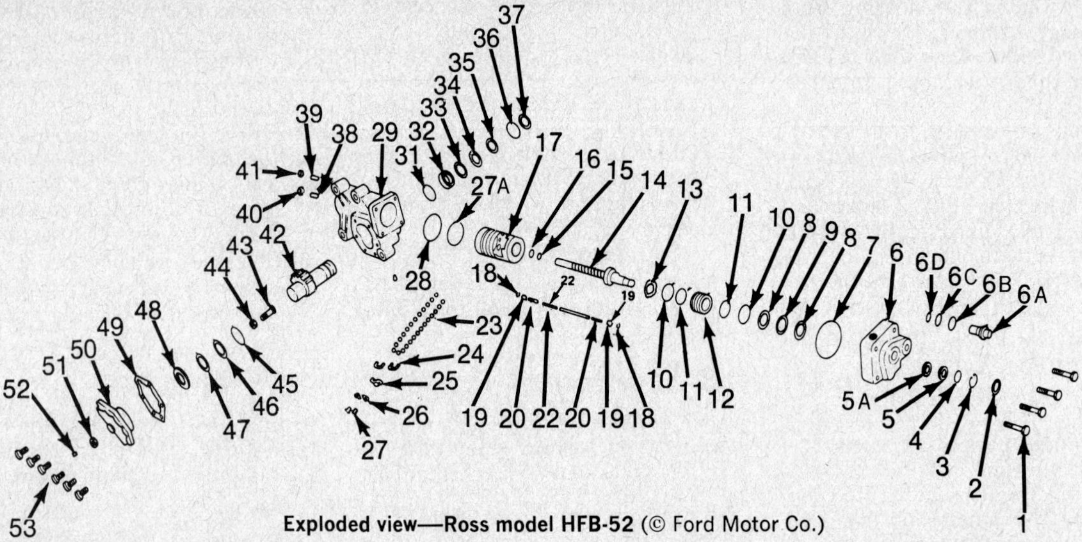

Exploded view—Ross model HFB-52 (© Ford Motor Co.)

1 Hexagon head bolt
2 Seal
3 Retaining ring
4 Back-up washer (steel)
5 Seal (two-piece)
6 Valve housing
6A Relief valve
7 "O" ring
8 Thrust washer (2)
9 Thrust bearing
10 Seal ring (2) (plastic)
11 "O" ring (2)
12 Valve sleeve
13 Drive ring
14 Worm shaft
15 "O" ring
16 Seal ring (plastic)
17 Rack piston
18 Retaining ring (2)
19 Poppet seat (2)
20 Poppet (2)
21 Spring
22 Rod
23 Ball (25)
24 Ball return guide (2)
25 Clip
26 Lock washer (2)
27 Screw (2)
27A "O" ring
28 Seal ring (plastic)
29 Housing
30 Bleed screw
31 Retaining ring
32 Bearing
33 Seal
34 Back-up washer (plastic)
35 Back-up washer (metal)
36 Retaining ring
37 Seal
38 Adjusting screw (1.250 long)
39 Sealing nut
40 Adjusting screw (1.500 long)
41 Sealing nut
42 Sector shaft
43 Adjusting screw
44 Retainer
45 Retaining ring
46 Seal
47 Back-up washer (plastic)
48 Washer
49 Side cover gasket
50 Side cover
51 Nut
52 Vent plug
53 Special bolt (6)

on a pressure gauge in the supply line should be between 200 and 500 psi.

1. Install a pressure gauge in the oil supply line to the steering gear.
2. Note the oil pressure when turning the wheels against the axle stops.
3. If the pressure reading is less than the pressure relief setting, back the poppet adjusting screw out until the system is operating at relief pressure when the wheels are against the axle stops.
4. Turn the poppet adjusting screw in until the pressure reading is less than 500 psi when the wheels are against the axle stops.
5. Lock the adjusting screw jam nut and tighten the sealing nut to 12 to 18 ft. lbs. Remove the pressure guage from the system.

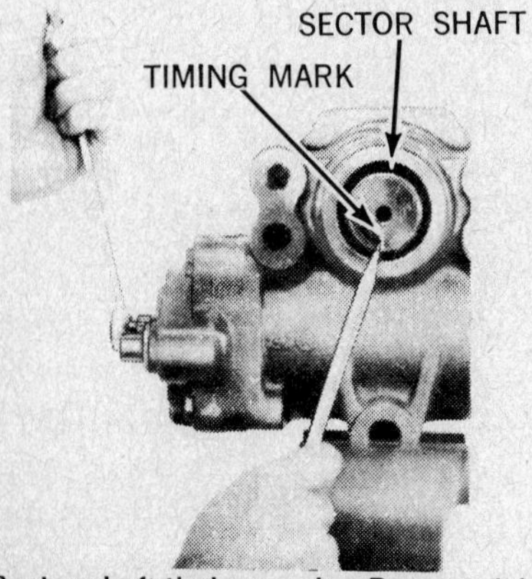

Sector shaft timing mark—Ross model HFB-52 (© Ford Motor Co.)

CAUTION: **Do not operate the steering system at relief pressure for more than a few seconds at a time or damage to the system may result due to excessive heat generation.**

Steering Gear

Disassembly

1. Place the steering gear in a vise in a horizontal position. Note the timing mark on the end of the sector shaft. Position this mark in a vertical position with the steering gear in the center of its travel.
2. Remove the sector shaft seal from the housing and loosen the sector shaft adjusting screw jamnut.
3. Place a drain pan under the steering unit and remove the six special ring head bolts from the side cover.

   NOTE: If these bolts are replaced for any reason, the same special type and length of bolt must be used.
4. Remove the side cover and the sector shaft, while applying a generous amount of wheel bearing grease to the housing roller bearings to avoid having them drop out.
5. Remove the adjuster screw from the side cover and remove the sector shaft.
6. Remove the retaining ring, seal, plastic back-up washer and steel back-up washer from the side cover.
7. Remove the bearing rolls from the side cover.

   NOTE: The bearing and bearing rolls cannot be replaced with-out replacing the side cover.
8. Remove the retaining ring, metal and plastic back-up washers, and seal from the housing.
9. Loosen the poppet and worm preload adjusting screw locknuts and loosen the adjusting screws approximately two turns.
10. Remove the relief valve from the valve housing, the "O" rings and the sealing rings from the relief valve.
11. Remove the four bolts from the valve housing and remove the housing from the steering housing.

    NOTE: Timing marks have been added to the valve sleeve and worm shaft so that they may be reassembled in their original position.

    CAUTION: **Do not attempt to unbend tangs that hold the drive ring to the worm shaft or to separate the drive ring and worm shaft.**
12. Remove the valve sleeve, "O" ring, thrust washers, thrust bearing, seal, retaining ring, back-up washer and seal cup from the valve housing.
13. Remove the seal rings and "O" rings from the valve sleeve.
14. Remove the rack piston and worm shaft from the housing.
15. Remove the worm shaft from the rack piston while catching the balls as they come out, after removing the ball return guides.

    NOTE: A complete new set of twenty-five matched balls will be required if any of the balls are lost.

16. No further need of disassembly is needed unless there is evidence of damage to the remaining parts.

Inspection

1. Inspect the rack piston teeth and worm groove for excessive wear.
2. Inspect the worm shaft helical groove for brinelling. (Surface indentations.)
3. Inspect the housing bore for abnormal wear or marks that would affect sealing and cause the steering gear to leak internally.
4. Inspect all bearings and contact surfaces.
5. Wash all parts in clean solvent and blow dry with air.

Assembly

1. Install all hard parts as necessary and use new seals, gaskets and sealing rings.
2. Assemble all sealing rings onto rack piston.
3. Apply clean wheel bearing grease to the housing bearing rolls to retain them.
4. Assemble poppet seat, retaining ring into the rack piston and tighten the poppet seat to 20-25 ft. lbs.
5. Assemble the "O" ring and sealing ring onto the worm shaft, using special installation and compression tools to avoid damage.
6. Lubricate the seal ring area and assemble the worm shaft into the rack piston.
7. Assemble the ball return guides into the rack piston and assemble the balls into the ball return guides and rack piston, by dropping the balls through the hole provided in the ball return guides.
8. Rotate the worm shaft as the twenty-five balls are being assembled to pull the balls into the groove.

   CAUTION: **Be sure the ball return guides remain in place while assembling the balls.**

   Complete the assembly of the rack piston as necessary.
9. Lubricate the seal ring area of the rack piston and assemble the rack piston and worm shaft assembly into the housing.
10. Install the "O" ring into the groove on the valve housing and lubricate with clean grease to hold the "O" ring in place.
11. Install the thrust washer and thrust bearing into the valve housing.
12. A tapered mandrel and seal pusher tool should be used to install the seal into the valve sleeve groove

    CAUTION: **This operation should be done in one short smooth time period to avoid permanent deformation of the seal.**
13. Remove the mandrel and pusher tool, install one spacer and reinstall the special tools and repeat the operation to install the remaining seal and "O" ring.

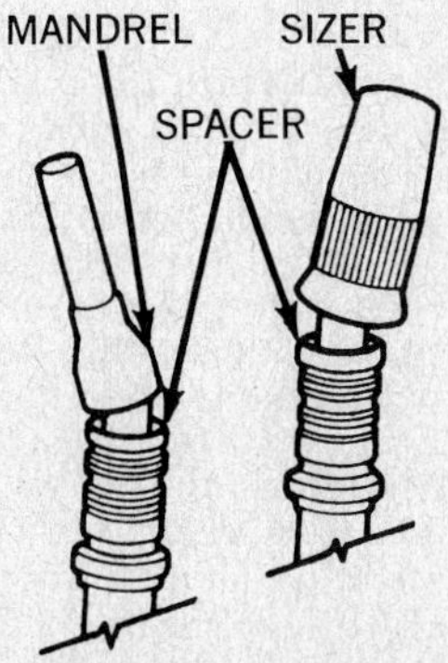

Mandrel for installation of seals (view A), and sizer tool for seals (view B)—Ross model HFB-52 (© Ford Motor Co.)

14. After the seals are positioned in their grooves on the valve, they must be compressed or sized, before installing the worm and valve sleeve assembly into the gear housing. A special compression (sizer) tool is used for this operation.
15. Apply a light coat of lubricant to the valve sleeve and seals. Slowly push the sizer tool over the valve sleeve until it bottoms.

    NOTE: Be careful that the seals are not being bent over when the sizer slides over them.
16. Keep the sizer tool over the seals for a minimum of one minute and then remove the sizer tool.
17. Apply lubricant to the seal ring areas of the valve sleeve.
18. Assemble the thrust washer to the end of the valve sleeve and hold the washer with grease. Install the valve sleeve into the valve housing. The distance from the face of the valve housing to the face of the valve sleeve should be approximately .400 inch.
19. Align the timing marks on the valve sleeve and the worm shaft. Assemble the valve housing onto the worm shaft.

    CAUTION: **The drive ring teeth must engage the notches in the valve sleeve.**
20. Use a 13/16–12 point box end wrench to rotate the worm shaft, in order to pull the valve housing against the steering housing. Install the four bolts into the housing and torque to 45-50 ft. lbs.
21. Locate the rack piston near the center of the steering gear travel

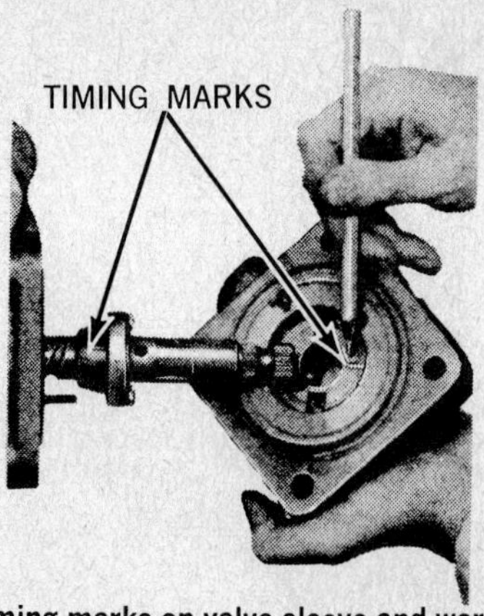

Timing marks on valve sleeve and worm shaft—Ross model HFB-52
(© Ford Motor Co.)

and turn the adjusting screw in, no more than 10 ft. lbs., and back the adjusting screw out one turn.
22. Measure the torque required to rotate the worm shaft through 90 degrees from each side of center. The torque should not exceed 15 in. lbs. Tighten the lock nut to 40-50 ft. lbs.
23. *Important:* After tightening the lock nut, the rotating torque for the worm shaft must rise 4 to 7 in. lbs. above the previously checked torque.
24. Assemble the forty bearing rolls to the bearing race inside the side cover, using grease to hold the rolls in place.
25. Assemble the steel and plastic back-up washers, seal and retaining ring into the side cover and install the seal in the side cover with the flat side towards the bearing.
26. Lubricate the short bearing area of the sector shaft and install in the side cover. Screw the adjusting screw in to the side cover until it bottoms. The side cover should rotate freely on the sector shaft with no appreciable axle movement.
27. Press the vent plug into the side

Valve housing installation—Ross model HFB-52 (© Ford Motor Co.)

Sector shaft seal assembly positioning —Ross model HFB-52 (© Ford Motor Co.)

cover until flush. Put locknut on the adjusting screw.

28. Position rack piston in the center of the steering gear travel. Align the center tooth on the sector shaft with the third notch from the sealing ring end on the rack piston and using a new side cover gasket, install the sector shaft and side cover assembly, into the steering housing.

    CAUTION: Do not dislodge the bearing rolls while installing the sector shaft into the steering housing.

29. Install the six special bolts and torque them to 150 to 170 ft. lbs.
30. Adjust the side cover adjusting screw to provide a 23 to 28 in. lbs. torque at the worm shaft as the steering gear is moved 90 degrees from each side of center. Back out the adjusting screw one turn and note the torque required to move the worm shaft through 90 degrees of center. Move the adjusting screw in to provide a rise in torque of 2 to 4 in. lbs. at a point 45 degrees of center. Tighten the locknut to 40-45 ft. lbs. and recheck the rotating torque. It should not exceed 26 in. lbs. at any point of steering gear travel.
31. Cover the serrations of the sector shaft with a seal protector or tape. Place seal, plastic and metal back-up washers and retaining ring on the sector shaft and use a seal installation tool to press into place. Lock with the retaining ring.
32. Place the "O" ring, seal ring, and "O" ring onto the relief valve and asemble into the housing. Tighten to 25-35 ft. lbs.
33. Install "O" ring onto the seal cup and install both parts into the the valve housing. With the aid of a seal driver, push the steel back-up washer into the valve housing.
34. Install the seal into the valve housing and seat with a seal driver or soft punch and hammer.
35. Install the bleed screw and torque to 27-33 in. lbs.
36. Install the unit on the vehicle and bleed the hydraulic system.

Semi Integral Power Steering Gear

This gear is a semi-integral hydraulic steering gear which incorporates a hydraulic control valve on a single stud cam and lever mechanical steering gear. When the steering wheel is turned it actuates the control valve. The valve then directs fluid from a pump to a power cylinder located in the linkage.

Adjustments

The following are the two principal adjustments on this type gear:

1. Adjustment of the needle thrust bearings on the cam shaft on each side of the centering washer assembly.
2. Adjustment of the tapered stud in the cam groove for backlash.

If adjustments are made with the steering gear mounted in the vehicle, free the steering gear of all load by disconnecting the drag link from the steering gear arm. Disconnect the coupling if the gear is the stub shaft type.

Thrust Bearing Adjustment

If the gear is mounted in the vehicle it may be necessary to remove any parts restricting the removal of the actuator housing.

1. Remove the four screws retaining the valve to the actuator housing and remove the valve.
2. Pull out the actuator lever.
3. Remove the four actuator housing mounting screws and remove the actuator housing.
4. Remove the adjusting nut, tongued washer, upper thrust washer and needle bearing. Wash all parts in solvent and coat with a light oil.
5. Reassemble the thrust bearing parts, tongued washer and adjusting nut.
6. Turn the steering gear off its center position to free the lever-shaft stud in the cam groove.
7. Torque the nut to 10 ft. lbs. Back the nut off 10°-20° and restake the lip of the adjusting nut in the slot of the cam shaft.
8. Position the actuator housing to the gear housing. Make sure that the pin engages in the hole of the actuator housing.
9. Position the actuator lever in the actuator housing making sure that the slotted end of the lever straddles the centering washer assembly and position on the slot

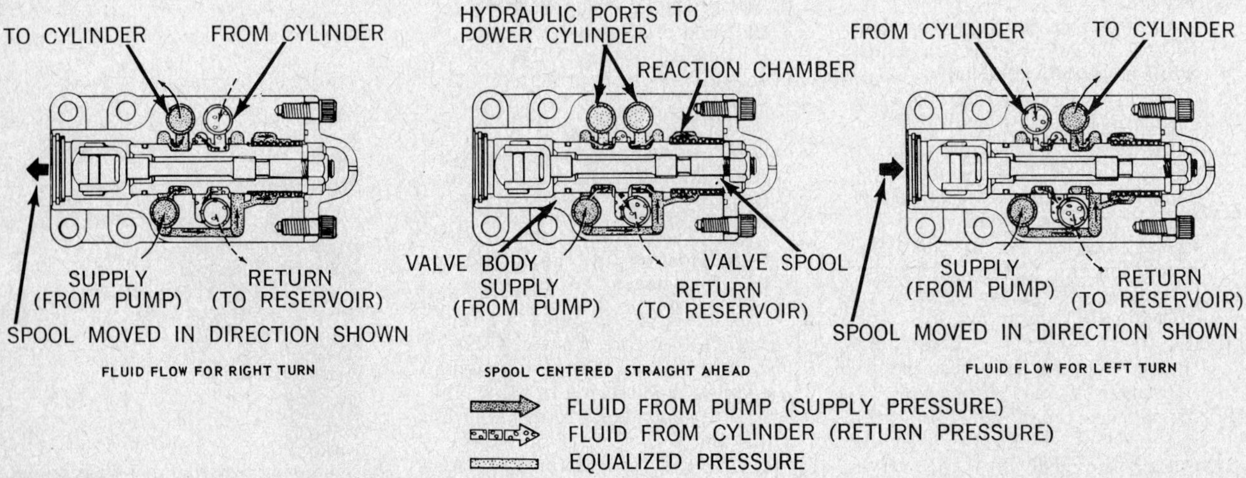

Semi-Integral power steering gear valve power flow (© Ford Motor Co.)

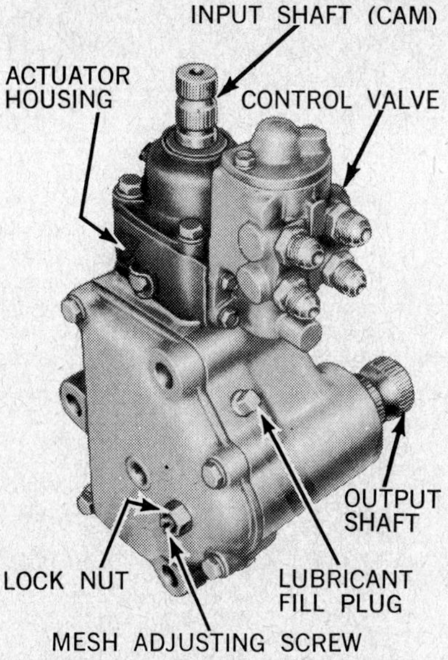

Semi-Integral power steering gear assembly—Ross HPS-70
(© Ford Motor Co.)

in the other end of the lever so that the pin in the clevis of the valve fixture rod will fit freely into it when mounting the valve.

10. Mount the valve and gasket on the actuator housing making sure the valve spool clevis pin fits freely into the slot of the actuator lever. Install all four mounting screws and tighten lightly in rotation, then torque to 10-15 ft. lbs.

NOTE: Careless tightening may cause the valve spool to be pulled off center by actuator lever interference with the clevis pin.

Backlash adjustment (stud in cam groove)

1. Turn the adjusting screw clockwise in the side cover until a very slight drag is felt when turning the gear through the mid position.
2. Lock the adjusting screw with the locknut and turn the gear from the extreme left to the extreme right and back again to check adjustment.

Steering Gear

Disassembly

1. Unscrew the locknut and adjusting screw.
2. Slide the sub-assembly of the side cover and the levershaft from the housing and remove the gasket.
3. Remove the four screws retaining the valve to the actuator housing and remove the valve.
4. Pull out the actuator lever.
5. Remove the four actuator housing mounting screws and remove the actuator housing.
6. Remove the cam and wheel tube and centering washer assembly as a unit from the housing.
7. Remove the adjusting nut then remove the tongued spacer washer and upper thrust washer and needle bearing.
8. Remove the centering washer assembly and bearing and without losing any springs remove the spring retainer.

Inspection

1. Clean all parts with solvent and blow dry with compressed air.
2. Examine all parts for chips, wear or pitting.

NOTE: The cam is copper plated. The operation of the stud in the cam groove will wear away the copper plating. This is a normal condition.

Assembly

1. Use new gaskets and seals.
2. Replace any needle bearings in the ends of the housing that were removed.
3. Install the valve spring retainer over the wheel tube and then assemble in the following order: Springs into retainer, bearing, centering washer assembly, bearing, thrust washer, tongued washer, adjusting nut.
4. Adjust the bearings (See "Thrust Bearing Adjustment").
5. Assemble the cam in the housing making sure it rotates freely.
6. Use a new gasket and install the actuator housing and pin to the gear housing. Make sure the pin engages in the hole of the actuator housing.
7. Assemble the retainer, screw and seal washer to the actuator housing. Screw the retainer in far enough to eliminate play between the adjusting screw and levershaft but the screw must be free to rotate.
8. Assemble the side cover to the adjusting screw. Position the gasket and install the side cover and levershaft in the housing.
9. Install the locknut to the adjusting screw and adjust the screw properly (see "Backlash Adjustment").

NOTE: On stub shaft type gears, assemble the lubricated oil seal with the lip out, into the counterbore of the actuator housing.

Control Valve

Disassembly

1. Remove the retainer ring, cover plate and O-ring seal.
2. Remove the end cover from the valve body.
3. Remove the elastic stop nut and washer from the end of the fixture rod and pull the fixture rod out of the spool.
4. Push the spool out in the same direction to permit removal of the centering washers, O-ring and centering spring from the valve body.
5. Remove the O-ring from the spool.
6. Remove the by-pass valve parts, plug assembly and spring and ball.

NOTE: The spool and valve body are selectively fitted at the factory and should not be replaced separately. A "mis-matched" spool and body could result in a loss of good performance of the power steering.

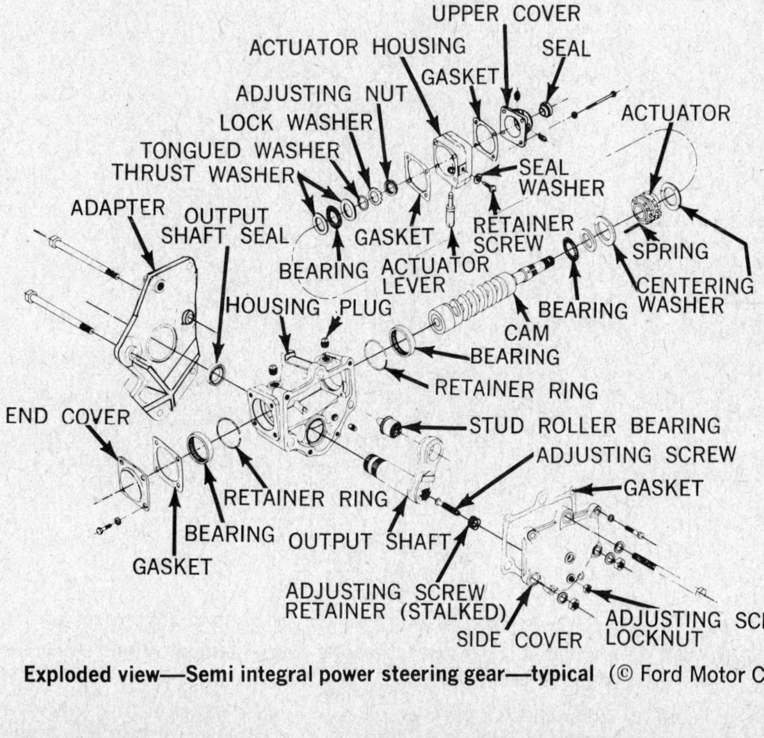

Exploded view—Semi integral power steering gear—typical (© Ford Motor Co.)

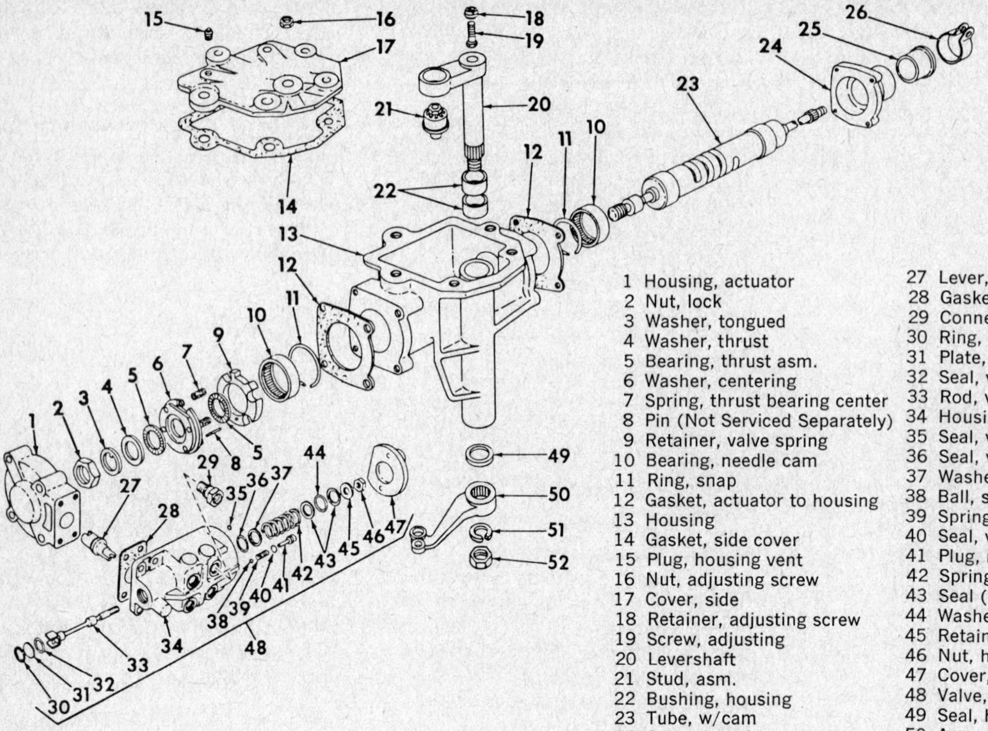

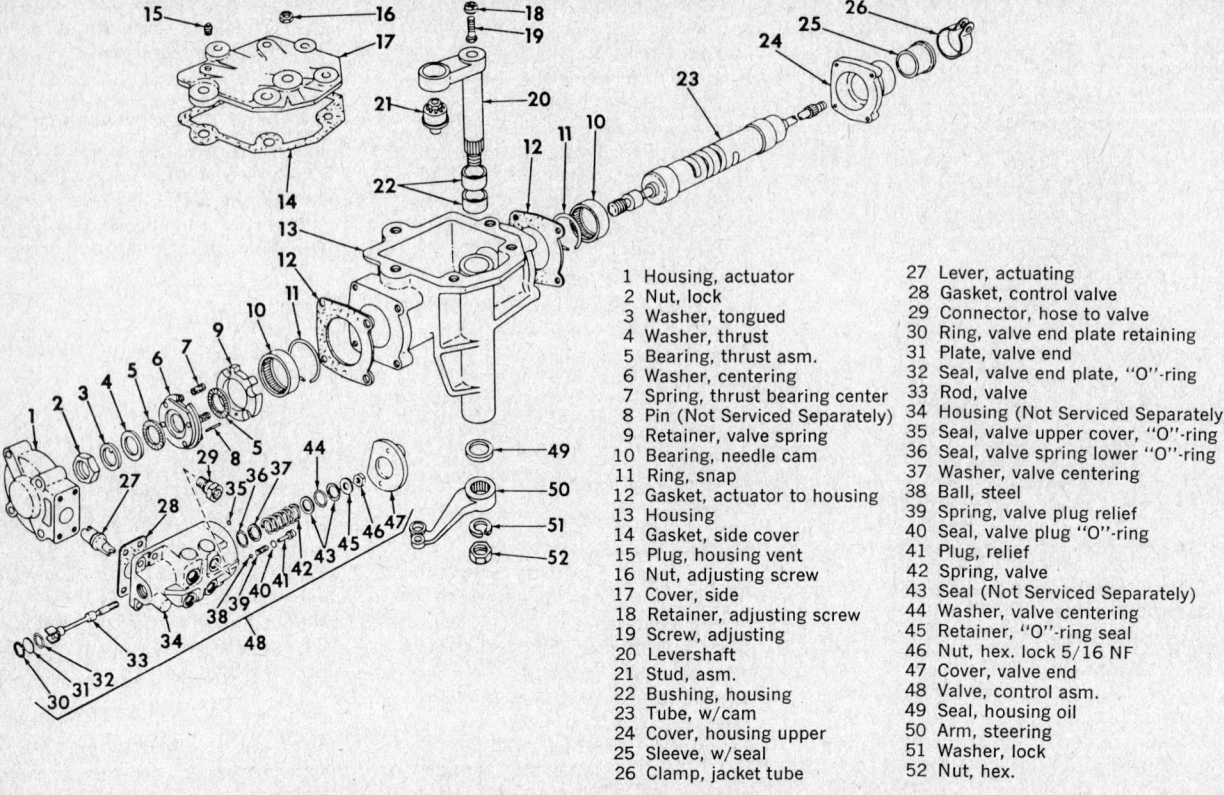

1 Housing, actuator
2 Nut, lock
3 Washer, tongued
4 Washer, thrust
5 Bearing, thrust asm.
6 Washer, centering
7 Spring, thrust bearing center
8 Pin (Not Serviced Separately)
9 Retainer, valve spring
10 Bearing, needle cam
11 Ring, snap
12 Gasket, actuator to housing
13 Housing
14 Gasket, side cover
15 Plug, housing vent
16 Nut, adjusting screw
17 Cover, side
18 Retainer, adjusting screw
19 Screw, adjusting
20 Levershaft
21 Stud, asm.
22 Bushing, housing
23 Tube, w/cam
24 Cover, housing upper
25 Sleeve, w/seal
26 Clamp, jacket tube
27 Lever, actuating
28 Gasket, control valve
29 Connector, hose to valve
30 Ring, valve end plate retaining
31 Plate, valve end
32 Seal, valve end plate, "O"-ring
33 Rod, valve
34 Housing (Not Serviced Separately)
35 Seal, valve upper cover, "O"-ring
36 Seal, valve spring lower "O"-ring
37 Washer, valve centering
38 Ball, steel
39 Spring, valve plug relief
40 Seal, valve plug "O"-ring
41 Plug, relief
42 Spring, valve
43 Seal (Not Serviced Separately)
44 Washer, valve centering
45 Retainer, "O"-ring seal
46 Nut, hex. lock 5/16 NF
47 Cover, valve end
48 Valve, control asm.
49 Seal, housing oil
50 Arm, steering
51 Washer, lock
52 Nut, hex.

Semi-integral power steering gear—solid column type (© International Harvester Co.)

1 Reinforcement, steering gear
2 Nut, adjusting screw
3 Cover, side
4 Gasket, side cover
5 Retainer, adjusting screw
6 Nut, levershaft stud
7 Washer, lock
8 Washer, roller
9 Screw, adjusting
10 Levershaft
11 Bearing, roller
12 Stud, cover to housing
13 Stud, levershaft
14 Plug, housing vent
15 Cover, lower housing
16 Gasket, lower housing cover
17 Bearing, needle cam
18 Ring, snap
19 Housing
20 Arm, steering
21 Seal, housing oil
22 Bushing, housing
23 Gasket, actuator to housing
24 Tube, w/cam
25 Retainer, valve spring
26 Bearing, thrust, assy.
27 Spring, thrust bearing center
28 Pin, (Not Serviced Separately)
29 Washer, centering
30 Washer, thrust
31 Washer, tongued
32 Nut, lock
33 Plug, sq-hd 1/8 pipe
34 Seal, oil
35 Housing, actuator
36 Lever, actuating
37 Gasket, control valve
38 Connector, hose to valve
39 Ring, valve end plate retaining
40 Plate, valve end
41 Seal, valve end plate, O-ring
42 Rod, valve
43 Housing, (Not Serviced Separately)
44 Seal, valve upper cover O-ring
45 Seal, valve spring lower O-ring
46 Washer, valve centering
47 Ball, steel
48 Spring, valve plug relief
49 Seal, valve plug O-ring
50 Plug, relief
51 Spring, valve
52 Seal, (Not Serviced Separately)
53 Retainer, O-ring seal
54 Nut, hex, lock 5/16 NF
55 Cover, valve end
56 Valve, control, assy.

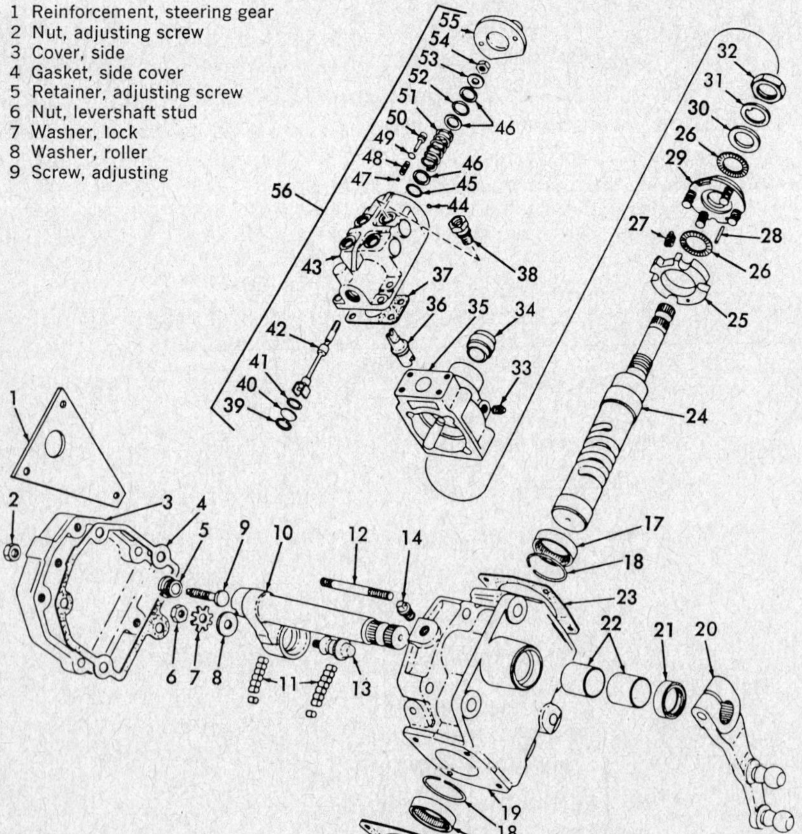

Exploded view—semi-integral power steering gear—jointed column type (© International Harvester Co.)

Assembly

1. Install the O-ring on the spool.
2. Apply a light coat of lubricating oil to the spool and O-rings and position the spool in the valve body with the O-ring toward the clevis end of the valve.

NOTE: Easily twist the spool into place: do not force it.

3. Assemble the centering washer, spring, centering washer, O-ring, centering washer into the valve body.
4. Assemble the flexure rod into the spool.
5. Install the washer and nut to the flexure rod and torque to 125-150 in. lbs.
6. If the by-pass valve parts were removed replace the O-ring on the plug before reassembly in the body. Assemble the ball, spring and plug into the body.
7. Position the actuator lever in the actuator housing making sure that the slotted end of the lever straddles the centering washer assembly and position on the slot in the other end of the lever so that the pin in the clevis of the valve fixture rod will fit freely into it when mounting the valve.
8. Mount the valve and gasket on the actuator housing making sure the valve spool clevis pin fits freely into the slot of the actuator lever. Install all four mounting screws and tighten lightly in rotation then torque to 10-15 ft. lbs.

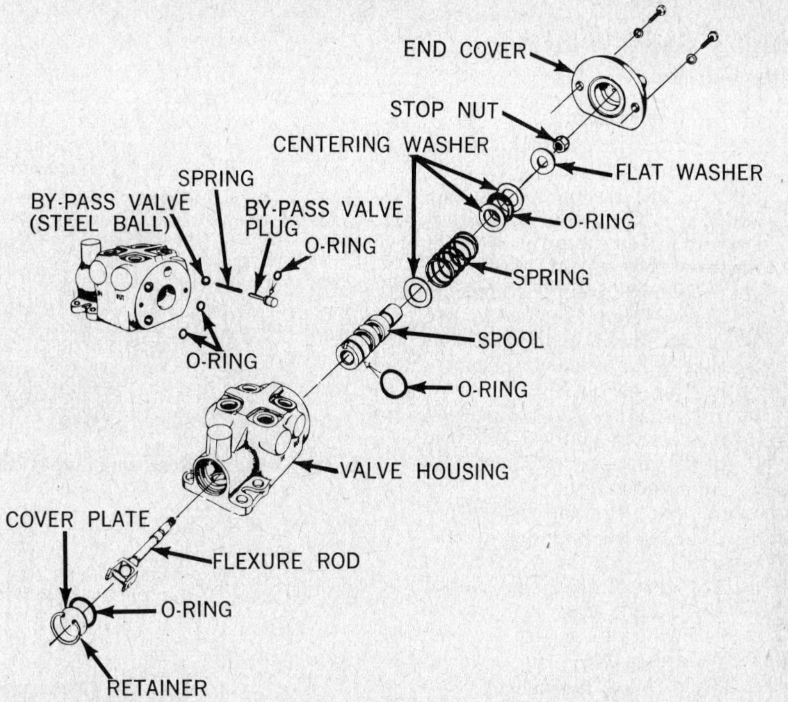

Exploded view—semi-integral power steering gear control valve—typical (© Ford Motor Co.)

NOTE: Careless tightening may cause the valve spool to be pulled off center by actuator lever interference with the clevis pin.

9. Make sure the valve spool actuates before assembling the end covers.

NOTE: Valve spool travel should be a minimum of .065 in. each direction for full flow.

10. Position the O-rings on the end of the valve body and install the end cover.
11. Install the O-ring, cover plate, and retaining ring to the clevis end of the valve.

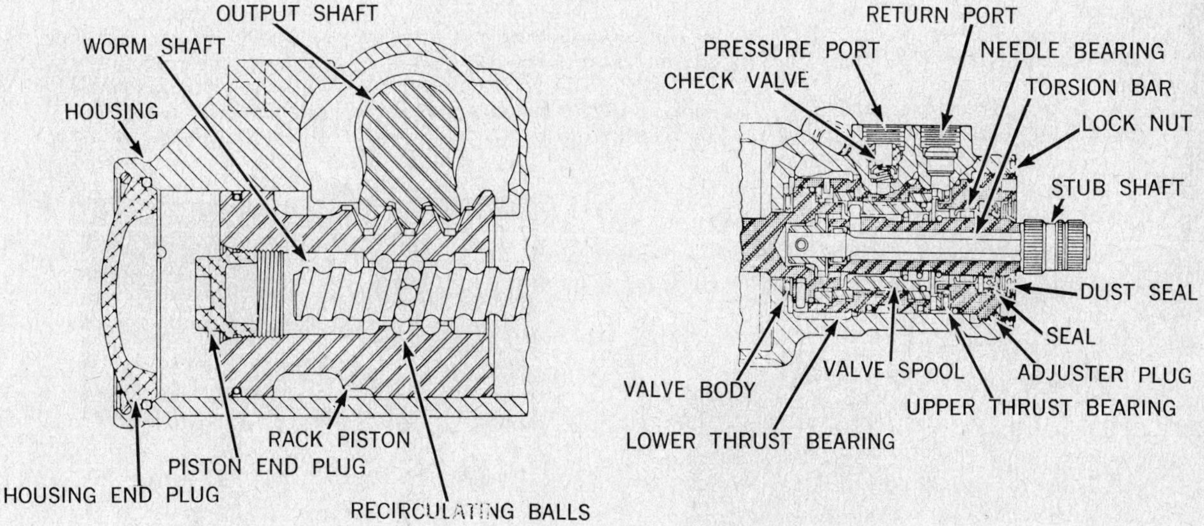

Cross section of rotary valve power steering gear—typical (© International Harvester Co.)

Sheppard Integral Type System

Steering Gear—Without Miter Gearbox

Disassembly

1. Loosen the plunger locknut and remove the relief valve plungers.
2. Remove the housing cover bolts and tap on the end of the output shaft to loosen the cover.
3. Remove the output shaft and gear assembly from the housing.
   a. Before moving, check the scribe marks on the rack and gear for alignment purposes during reassembly.
   b. If the marks can not be seen make your own so that the parts can be easily timed during reassembly.
4. Leave the gear on the output shaft unless replacement is necessary.
   a. To disassemble the output shaft and gear, remove the screws which secure the gear retaining nut.
   b. Turn the retaining nut counterclockwise and remove the nut.
   c. Press the output shaft out of the gear.
5. Mark the cylinder head and housing for reassembly and remove the cylinder head and gasket.
6. Mark the bearing cap and housing for reassembly and remove the bearing cap attaching bolts.
7. Turn the bearing cap and actuating shaft out of the actuating valve.
8. Disassemble the bearing and actuating shaft only if a defect is suspected.
   a. To disassemble, remove the lock-pin from the retaining nut.
   b. Use a spanner wrench and remove the retaining nut.
   c. Tap or press the actuating shaft out of the bearing cap. *NOTE: The bearing and actuating shaft is serviced as a unit and should not be disassembled after removing from the bearing cap.*
   d. Pry the dirt seal from the bearing cap.
   e. Drive the oil seal from the bearing cap.
9. Pull the piston assembly out of the housing.
10. Mark the piston and valve ad-

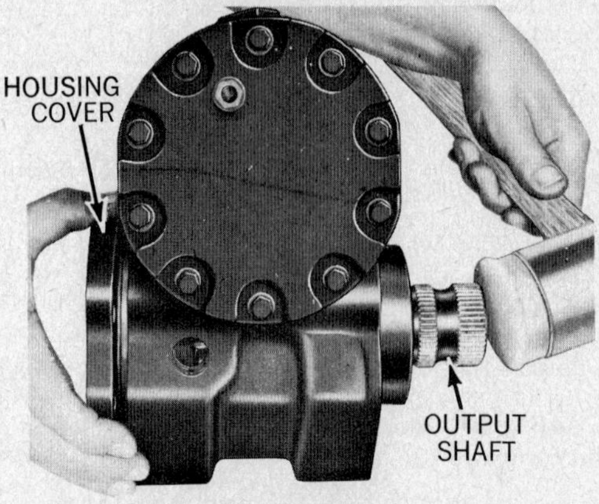

Removing output shaft (© Mack Trucks Inc.)

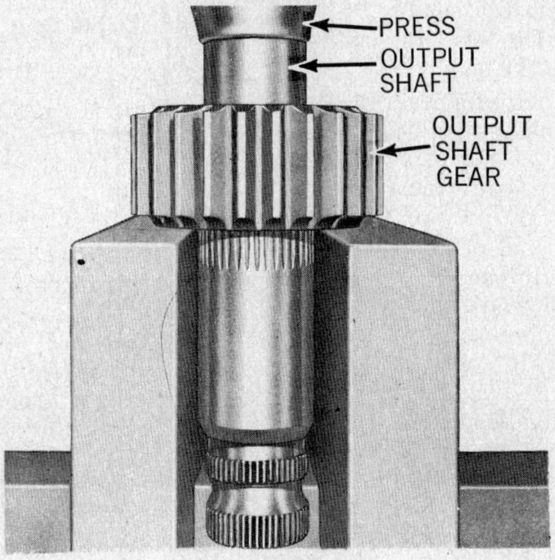

Removing output gear from shaft (© Mack Trucks Inc.)

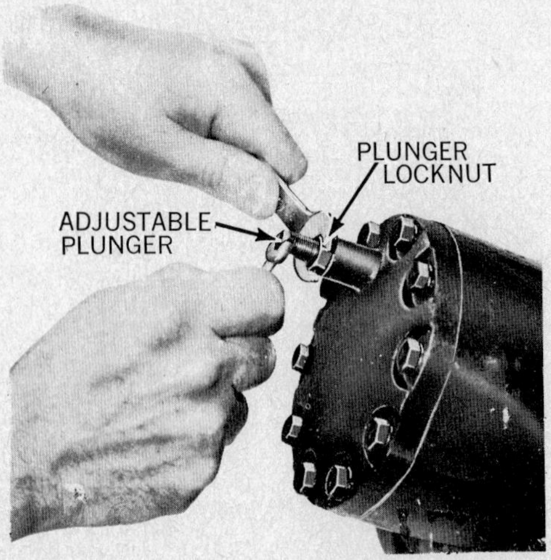

Removing relief valve plunger (© Mack Trucks Inc.)

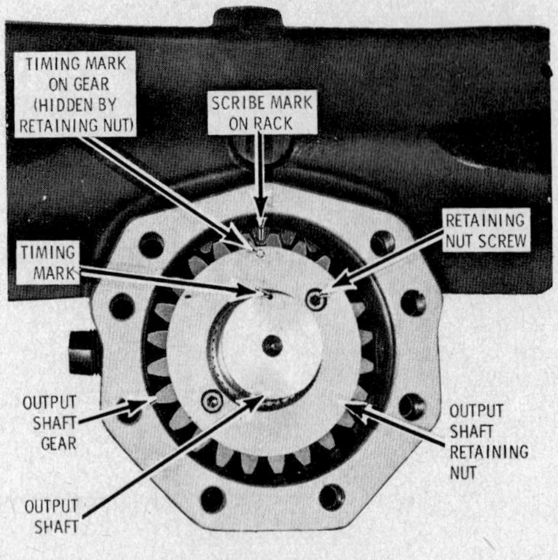

Output shaft and gear alignment marks (© Mack Trucks Inc.)

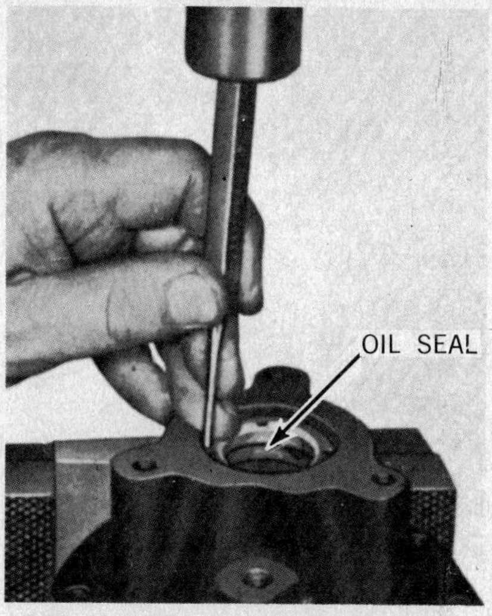

Removing oil seal from bearing cap
(© Mack Trucks Inc.)

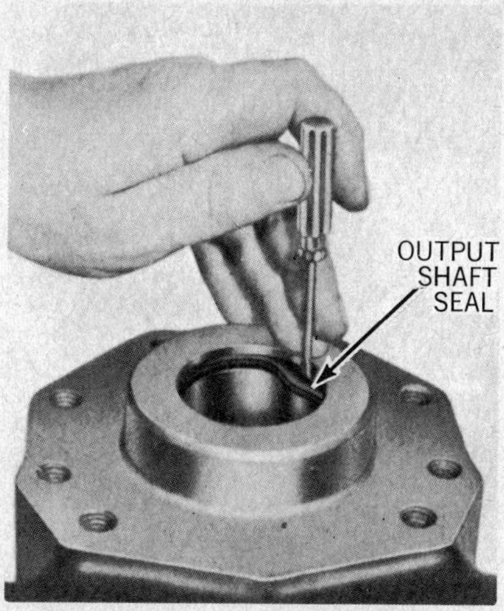

Removing output shaft seal
(© Mack Trucks Inc.)

Removing bearing cap and actuating shaft
(© Mack Trucks Inc.)

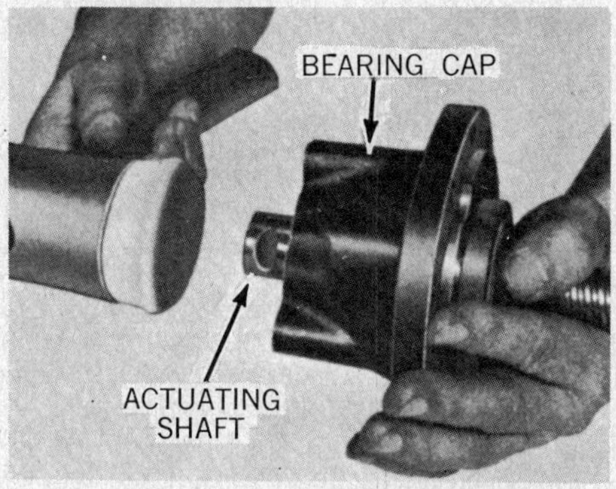

Removing actuating shaft and bearing assembly from bearing cap
(© Mack Trucks Inc.)

Removing dirt seal from bearing cap
(© Mack Trucks Inc.)

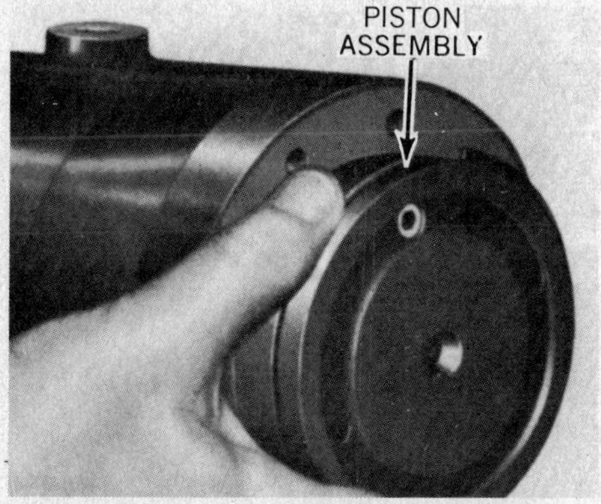

Removing piston assembly from housing
(© Mack Trucks Inc.)

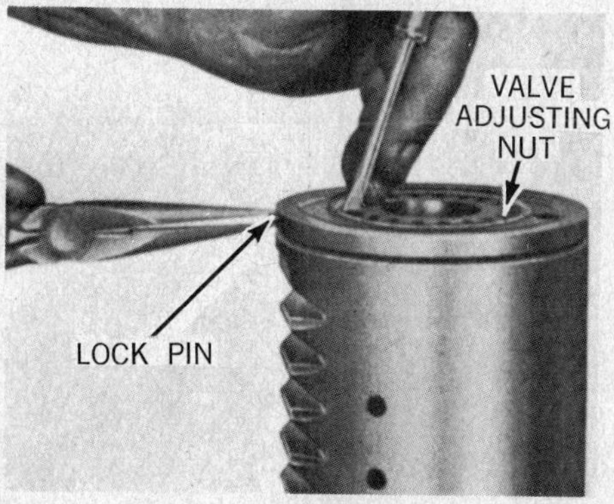

Removing valve positioning pin (© Mack Trucks Inc.)

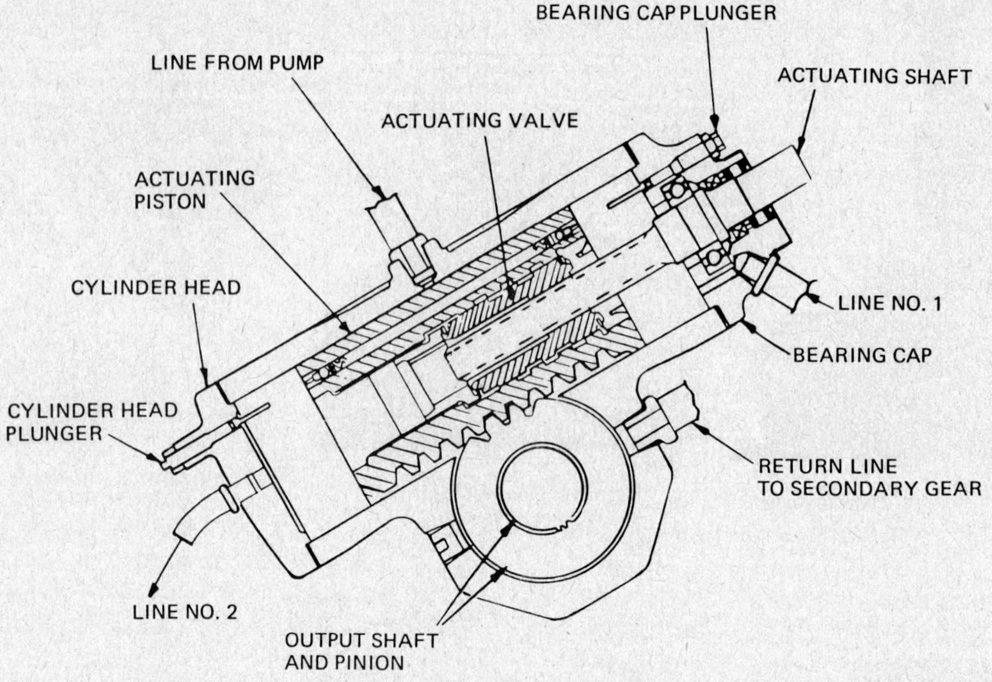

Main gear assembly (© Mack Trucks Inc.)

justing nut for reassembly. Remove the lock pin from the nut, then remove the nut.

11. Remove the reversing spring and without forcing, remove the actuator valve from the piston.
12. Remove the valve positioning pin.
13. Remove the second reversing spring from the piston.
14. Remove the piston rings.
15. Remove the valve seats, balls and spring from the piston. **CAUTION: Be careful when removing the valve seats as the balls are spring loaded.**
16. Remove the output shaft seal.
17. If it necessary to replace the output shaft bushings in either the housing or cover, use a puller.

Assembly

1. Clean all parts individually in a solvent and replace any parts that are worn or broken.
2. If removed, press new cover or housing bushings flush with the inside face.
3. Install a new output shaft seal.
4. Insert a valve spring, ball and seat into each bore.
   NOTE: Be sure the valve seats are flush with or below the surface of the piston.
5. Place one of the reversing springs on the bottom of the actuating valve bore and center so the actuating valve end will enter into the spring.
6. Install the valve positioning pin in the piston.
   a. Turn the pin into the piston until it protrudes ¼ inch into the actuating valve bore.
   b. Make sure the flats on the pin are parallel to the axis of the piston so the pin will enter the slot.

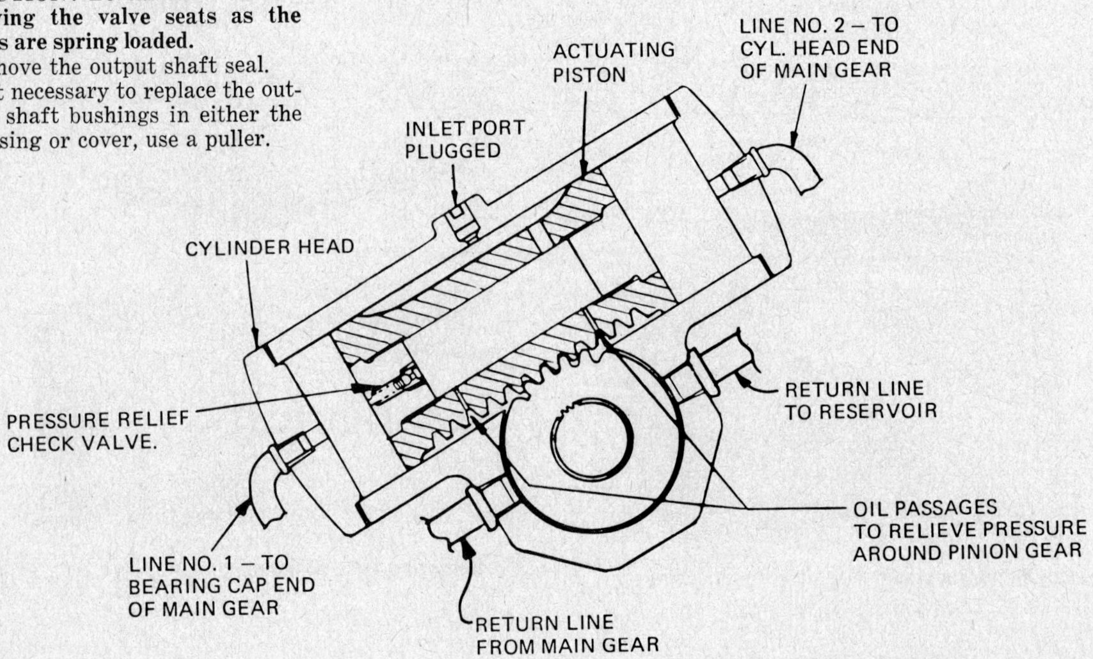

Secondary gear assembly (© Mack Trucks Inc.)

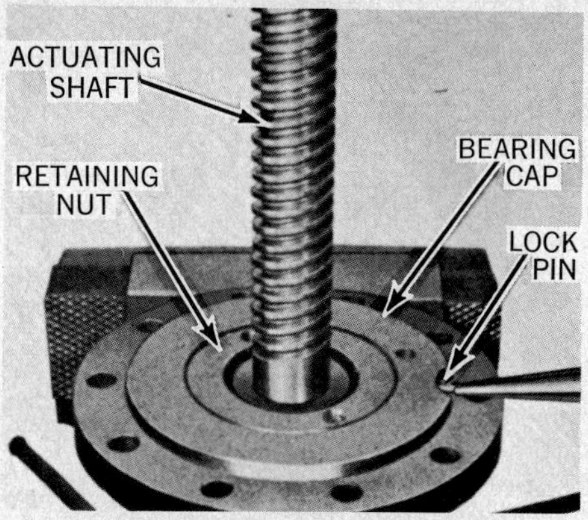

Disassembling bearing cap and actuating shaft (© Mack Trucks Inc.)

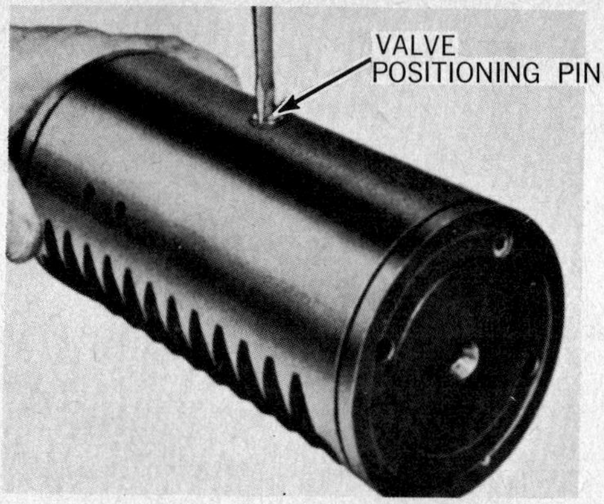

Removing valve adjusting nut lockpin (© Mack Trucks Inc)

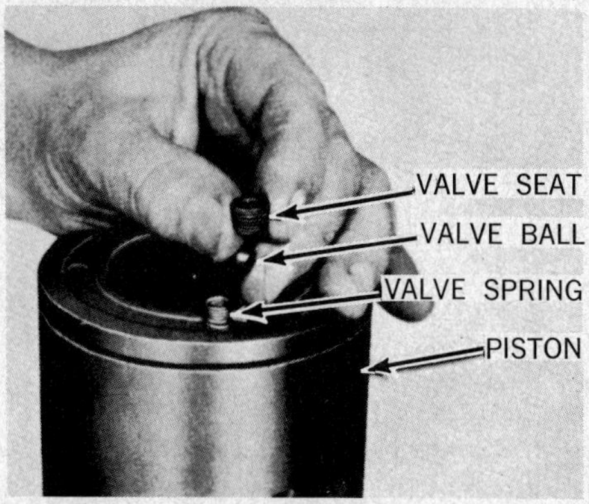

Removing relief valve from piston (© Mack Trucks Inc.)

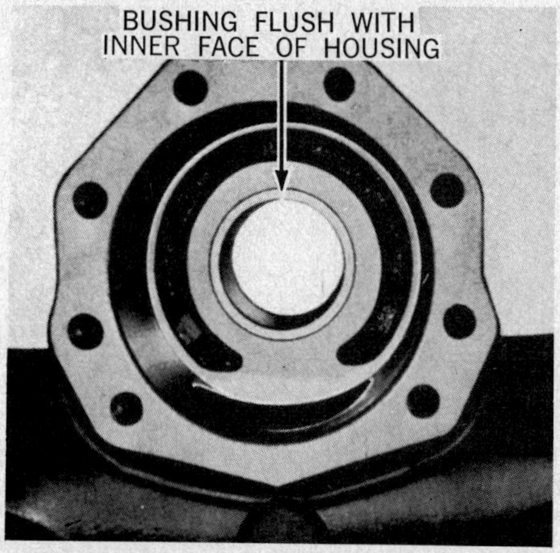

Installing housing bushing (© Mack Trucks Inc.)

7. Insert the actuating valve into the piston with the slot for the positioning pin first. Place the second reversing spring on the valve.
8. Install the valve adjusting nut into the piston and turn it clockwise until it makes contact with the reversing spring.
9. Align the marks previously made on the nut and piston and drive the lock-pin into place. Make sure the pin is below the surface of the piston.
   NOTE: It is recommended that the piston rings not be reinstalled on the piston assembly of the Sheppard Power Steering Gear during an overhaul. The unit will operate properly without the rings. Production steering gears will have the rings omitted, and may be encountered upon disassembly of the steering gear.
10. Coat the piston and housing bore with oil.
11. Install the piston into the housing with the actuating valve end towards the bearing cap end of the housing.
12. Install the cylinder head and use a new gasket.
    a. Align the marks so the head will be in the correct position and the relief valve plunger

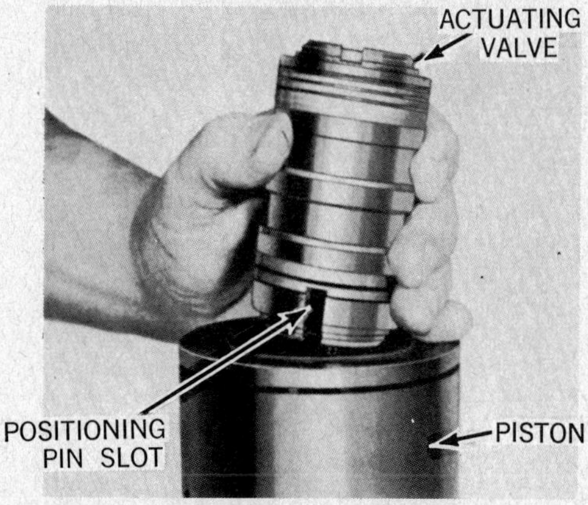

Installing actuating valve (© Mack Trucks Inc.)

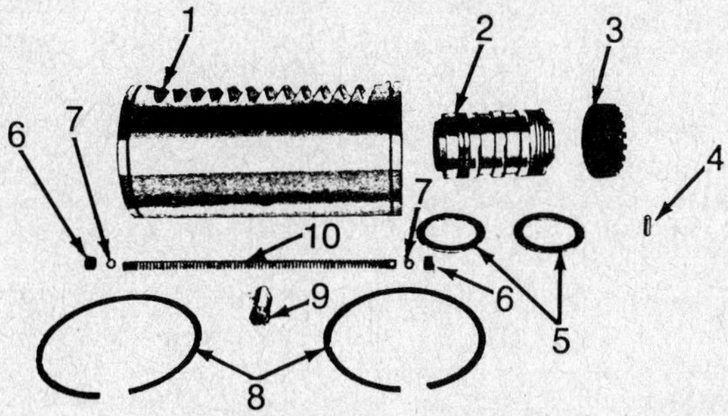

1 Piston
2 Actuating valve
3 Actuating valve Adjusting nut
4 Actuating valve Adjusting nut lockpin
5 Reversing spring
6 Relief valve seat
7 Relief valve ball
8 Piston ring*
9 Actuating valve Positioning pin
10 Relief valve spring
* Not used in current production

Exploded view of piston assembly (© Mack Trucks Inc.)

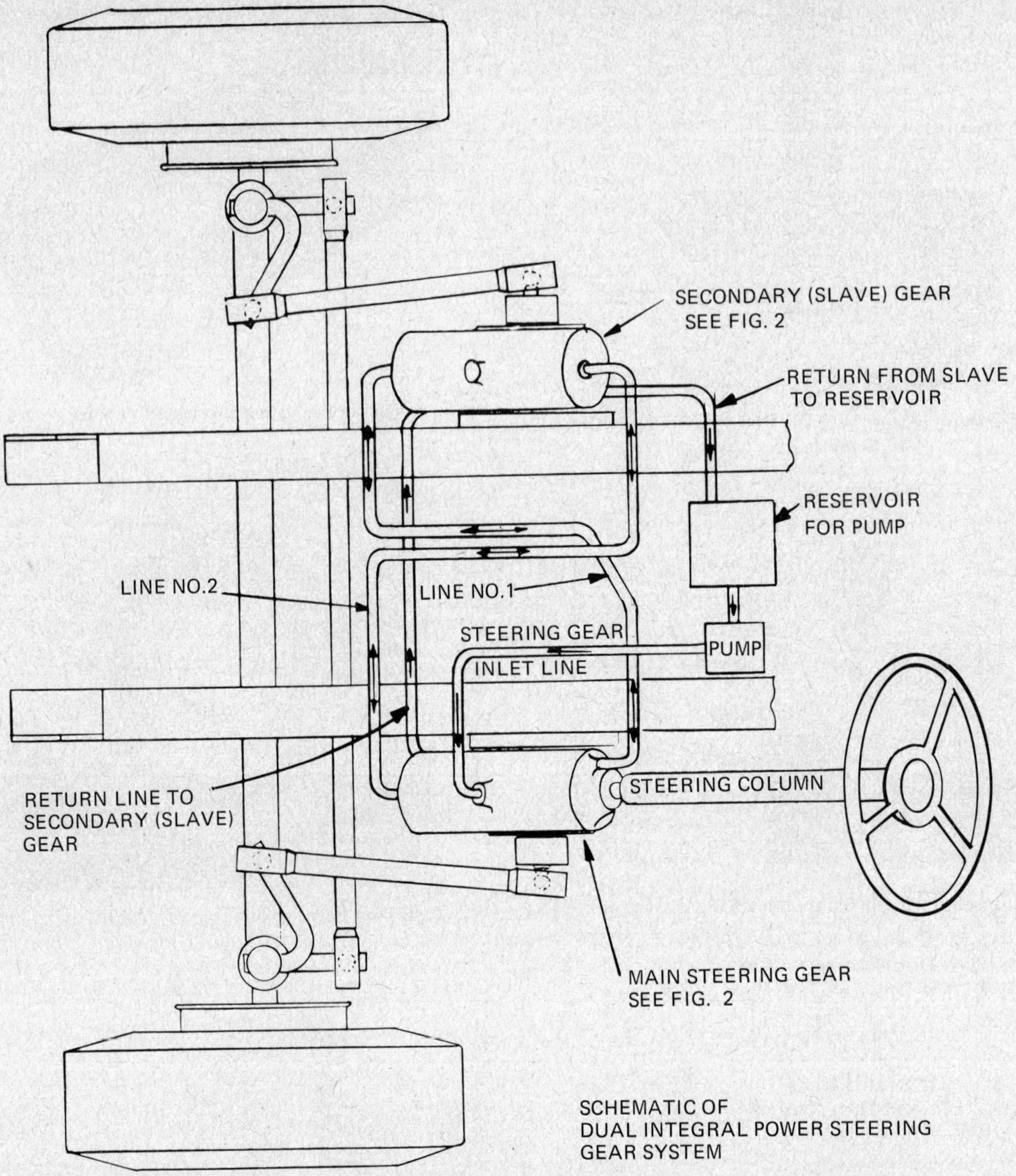

SCHEMATIC OF
DUAL INTEGRAL POWER STEERING
GEAR SYSTEM

will line up with the relief valve in the piston.

b. Torque the attaching bolt. (5/16 bolts to 20 ft.lbs.; 3/8 bolts to 33 ft.lbs.)

13. Press a new oil and dirt seal into the bearing cap.
14. If removed previously, press the actuating shaft and bearing assembly into the bearing cap.
15. Install the actuating shaft bearing retaining nut and insert the locking pin.

NOTE: When using a new retaining nut the hole for the lockpin must be drilled after the nut is seated. Use a 3/32 inch drill and drill the nut 3/16 inch deep through the hole in the bearing cap.

16. Thread the actuating shaft into the actuating valve and install the bearing cap with a new gasket.

a. Align the marks on the cap and housing to insure the plunger lining up with the relief valve.

b. Hold the bearing cap in the proper position and turn the actuating shaft until the bearing cap is seated.

c. Torque the attaching bolts (5/16 bolts to 20 ft.lbs.; 3/8 bolts to 33 ft.lbs.).

17. Install the output shaft on the gear if it was previously disassembled.

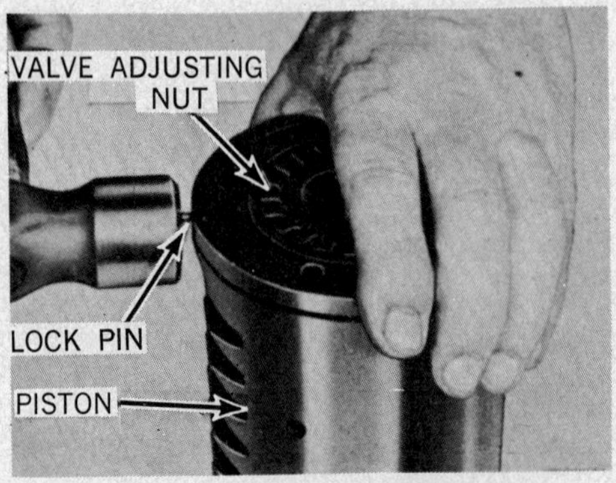

Installing valve adjusting nut and lock pin (© Mack Trucks Inc.)

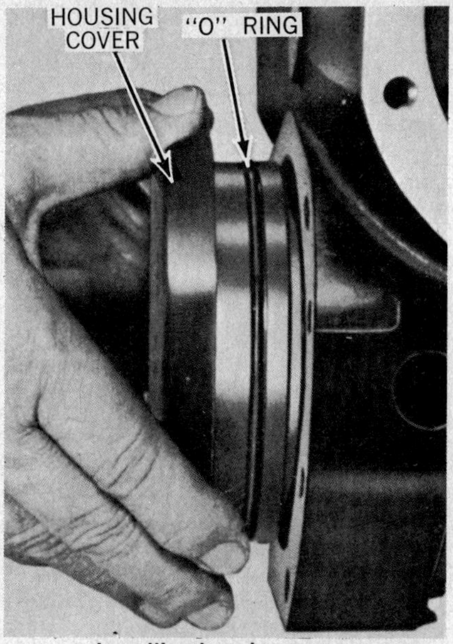

Installing housing cover
(© Mack Trucks Inc.)

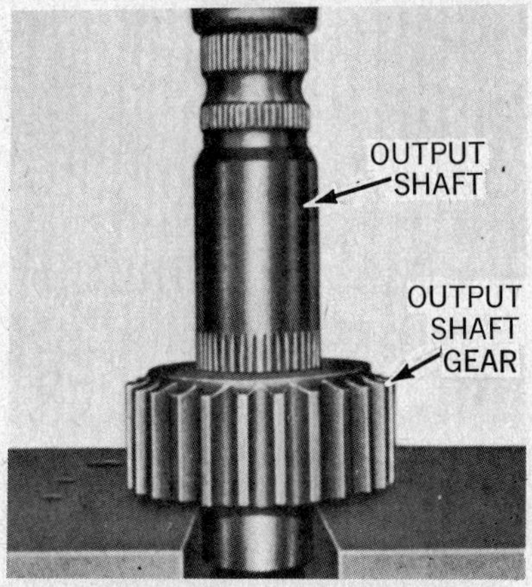

Pressing gears on output shaft
(© Mack Trucks Inc.)

Align the marks on the output shaft and the gear and press the gear on the shaft.

18. Insert the output shaft and gear assembly into the gear housing and make sure the timing mark on the gear is aligned with the mark on the rack.
    NOTE: It may be necessary to make another scribe mark on the rack if the original mark is difficult to see when the output shaft gear is in place. It is important that the rack and gear are correctly timed.
19. Install the output shaft gear retaining nut and tighten against the gear while aligning the holes in the nut and the gear.
    Install and tighten the two retaining nut screws.
20. Place a new O-ring in the groove and install the housing cover.
    a. Tap the cover with a soft hammer to seat it properly.
    b. Install the attaching bolts and tighten (7/16 bolts to 20-36 ft.lbs.; 5/8 bolts to 100 ft.lbs.).
21. Use new O-rings and install the relief valve plungers.
    Turn into the bearing cap or cylinder head approximately six turns.
22. Install the gear in the vehicle and make the final relief valve plunger adjustments.
    See the "Relief Valve Plunger Adjustment" for procedures.

Steering Gear—With Miter Gearbox

Disassembly

1. Loosen the locknut and remove the relief valve plunger in the cylinder head.
2. Remove the housing cover bolts and tap on the end of the output shaft to loosen the cover.
3. Remove the output shaft and gear assembly from the housing.
    a. Before removing, check the scribe marks on the rack and gear for alignment purposes during reassembly.
    b. If the marks cannot be seen, make your own so that the parts can be easily timed during reassembly.
4. Leave the gear on the output shaft unless replacement is necessary.
    a. To disassemble the output shaft and gear, remove the screws which secure the gear retaining nut.
    b. Turn the retaining nut counterclockwise and remove the nut.
    c. Press the output shaft out of the gear.
5. Mark the cylinder head and housing for reassembly and remove the cylinder head and gasket.
6. Mark the bearing cap and housing for reassembly and remove the bearing cap attaching bolts.
7. Turn the bearing cap and actuating shaft out of the actuating valve.
8. Remove the cover attaching bolts and remove the cover with the input shaft and bearing assembly. Check for the shaft and gear timing marks.
9. Remove the input gear by driving out the retaining pin.
10. Pull the bearing retaining nut lock-pin from the gear box cover.
11. Use a spanner wrench and turn the bearing retainer nut counterclockwise and remove it from the gearbox cover.
12. Remove the bearing and input shaft assembly from the cover using a soft hammer.
13. If necessary, the shaft can be

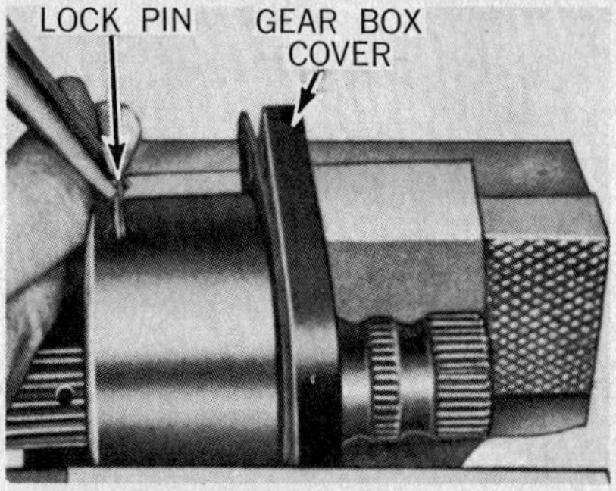

Removing bearing retaining nut lockpin
(© Mack Trucks Inc.)

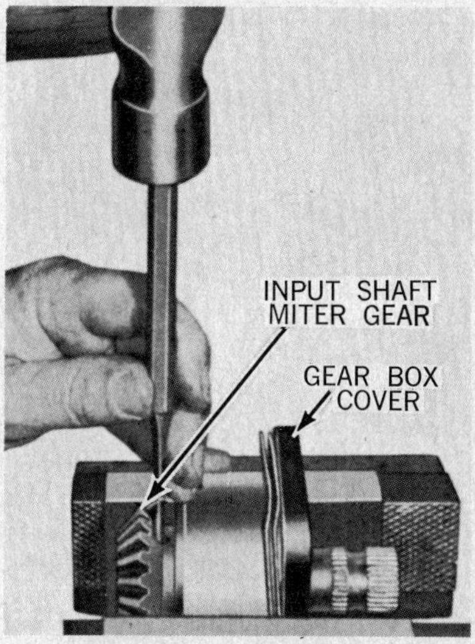

Removing miter gear retaining pin
(© Mack Trucks Inc.)

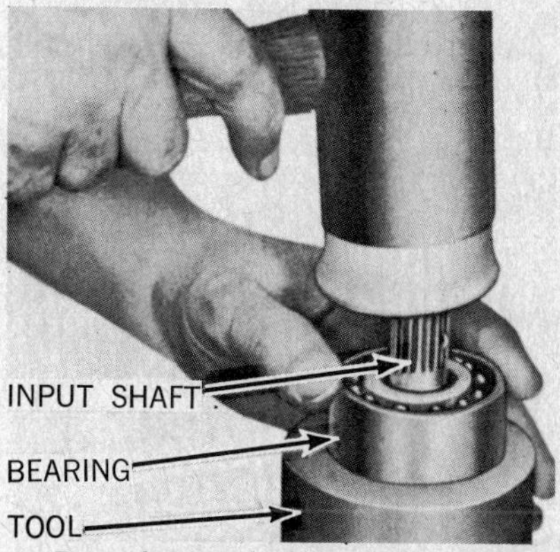

Removing bearing from input shaft
(© Mack Trucks Inc.)

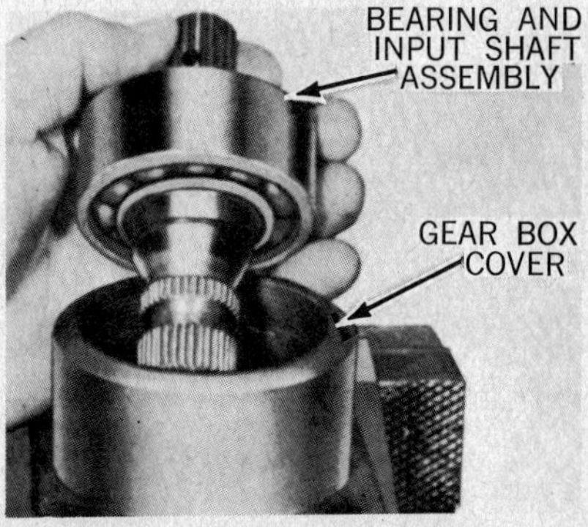

Removing bearing and input shaft assembly

Removing hidden capscrew holding gearbox housing (© Mack Trucks Inc.)

driven or pressed out of the bearing.

14. Remove the seal from the cover.
15. Remove the bolts, including the one hidden inside the housing, that attaches the gearbox housing to the bearing cap. Tap the gearbox with a soft hammer to loosen it, then lift it from the bearing cap.
16. Remove the bearing cap O-ring.
17. Remove the gear retaining nut and washer from the shaft and pull the gear off the shaft.
18. Mark the bearing retaining nut at the pin hole location for reassembly.
19. Remove the lock pin from the bearing cap and remove the bearing retaining nut.
20. Remove the shims located next to the bearing and save for reassembly.
21. Remove the bearing cap to housing screws.
22. Note the timing marks on the actuating shaft and valve for reassembly then turn and unscrew the bearing cap and shaft assembly out of the valve.
23. Remove the actuating shaft and bearing from the bearing cap by tapping easily with a soft hammer.
24. If necessary, remove the fixed plunger from the bearing cap. Pry the plunger lock-pin out far enough from the cap to be gripped with pliers then withdraw the pin completely.
    NOTE: Do not remove the fixed plunger unless damaged.
25. Remove the oil seal from the bearing cap.
    a. On non-current models pry the seal from the bearing cap.
    b. On current models, holes in the cap are provided so that the seal may be driven out with a punch.

Assembly

1. Clean all parts individually in a solvent and replace any parts that are worn or broken.
2. Position a new seal in the bearing cap so that the lip faces the piston side and press into place.
3. If the fixed plunger was removed insert it in the bearing cap and install the retaining pin. Make sure the pin is below the surface of the bearing cap.
4. Press the bearing on the actuating shaft.
5. Press the shaft and bearing assembly into the bearing cap without damaging the seal.
6. Screw the actuating shaft into the actuating valve and align the timing marks.
7. Install the bearing cap attaching bolts and tighten. (5/16 bolts to 20 ft.lbs.; 3/8 bolts to 33 ft.lbs.)
8. Place the shims over the bearing and install the bearing retaining nut.
    a. Tighten the nut against the bearing while aligning the mark on the nut with the lock-pin hole.
    b. Install the lock-pin.
9. Position the gear on the actuating shaft and install the washer and nut.
10. Install a new O-ring in the groove in the bearing cap.
11. Position the gearbox housing on the bearing cap and tap into place using a soft hammer.
12. Install the gearbox housing to bearing cap retaining bolts and washers including the bolt inside the housing.
13. Install a new cover seal.
14. Press or drive the input shaft into the bearing.
15. Install the bearing and shaft assembly into the cover.
16. Install the bearing retaining nut and turn clockwise into the cover.
17. Install the bearing retaining nut lock-pin.
18. Install the miter gear on the input shaft and align the timing marks.
19. Install the retaining pin.
20. Install the cover assembly and shim on the gearbox housing.
21. Fill the gearbox housing with the correct grade of grease through the grease fitting.

Relief Valve Plunger Adjustment

This adjustment should be made periodically and any time the gears, springs, axle, etc. are disturbed. The adjustment is important because it protects the pump, steering gear, and steering linkage from overloading when the wheels are at full turn. Steering gears using the miter gearbox do not have an adjustable plunger at the gearbox end.

With Miter Gearbox

1. With the power off check the right and left steering angles (See the steering angle procedures in the General Repair Section.)
2. Turn the adjustable plunger in the cylinder head inward until it bottoms.
3. Return the wheels to the straight forward position and start the engine to operate the power steering.
4. For the right turn adjustment, proceed as follows:
    a. Slowly turn the steering wheel to the right until the hydraulic assist is stopped (resistance in the wheel is felt). The wheel should not be forced beyond this point.
    b. Hold the wheel at this position and measure the clearance between the axle turn circle stop screw and boss or stop-nut on the back of the knuckle.
    c. Set clearance by adjusting the drag link.
    d. Loosen the drag link clamp and lengthen the link to decrease clearance and shorten then length to increase the clearance.
    e. After the adjustment has been made, measure the clearance again.
5. For left turn adjustment, proceed as follows:
    a. Slowly turn the steering wheel to the left until the hydraulic assist is stopped (resistance in the wheel is felt). The wheel should not be forced beyond this point.
    b. Hold the wheel at this position and measure the clearance between the axle turn circle stop-screw and boss or stop-nut.
    c. The clearance should be 1/8 inch. If the clearance is incorrect, adjust the relief valve plunger at the lower end of the cylinder.
    d. Turn the valve in to increase clearance and out to decrease clearance.
    NOTE: If it is impossible to obtain accurate adjustments in the previous steps, check to see that the arrow stamped on the output shaft is indexed with the notched mark on the steering lever. The spline groove marked with a zero is not the index point.
6. Tighten all clamps and lock-nuts and shut down the engine.

Without Miter Gearbox

1. With the power off, check the right and left steering angles (see the steering angle procedures in the General Repair Section).

2. Turn the adjustable plungers all the way in.
3. Start the engine and run at a fast idle so the power steering operates.
4. For the left turn adjustment, proceed as follows:
   a. Turn the steering wheel to the left until the relief valve contacts the plunger. This can be felt by an increased steering effort.
   b. Hold the wheel at this position and do not force the wheel beyond this point.
   c. Check the clearance between the axle stop-screw and the boss.
   d. Turn the bearing cap upper plunger outward until the clearance is 1/8 inch between the stop-screw and boss.
   e. Tighten the lock-nut.
5. For the right turn adjustment, proceed as follows:
   a. Turn the steering wheel to the right until an increased steering effort is felt.
   b. Hold the wheel at this position and do not force the wheel beyond this point.
   c. Turn the cylinder head plunger outward until there is a clearance of 1/8 inch between the stop-screw and boss.
   d. Tighten the locknut.

Vickers Power Steering Pump

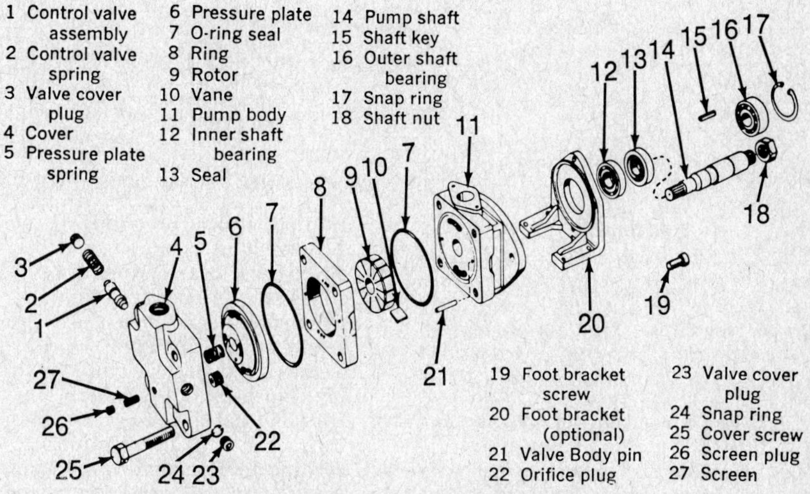

Vickers V200 series pumps (© Mack Trucks Inc.)

V-200 Series

Disassembly

1. Clamp pump in vise with cover end up and remove cover screws. Lift off cover and remove O-ring.
2. If pump is equipped with flow control valve, remove plug spring and valve subassembly.
3. Remove pressure plate and spring.
4. Mark position of ring and remove it along with locating pin.
5. Separate vanes from rotor and slide rotor from shaft.
6. Turn pump body over and remove shaft key and outer bearing snap ring. Tap on splined end of shaft with a soft hammer to force it out of housing.
7. If bearing is to be removed, support the inner race and press shaft out of bearing.
8. Pull shaft seal out of body.
9. Press inner bearing out of body.

Assembly

1. Coat all parts with hydraulic fluid before assembly.
2. If flow control valve is used, assemble components into cover. If cover has a blind bore, install spring first, then valve. Install snap ring and plug. Install screen and retaining plug.
3. Press shaft into outer bearing while supporting inner race. Press inner bearing into body using a driver on the outer race.
4. Install seal. Seals should be assembled with holes facing the shaft end of the pump. Lube lip with petroleum jelly.
5. Slide driveshaft in place until outer bearing is sealed. Install bearing retaining snap ring in body.
6. Install new O-ring in body. Insert ring locating pins in body and assemble ring so that arrow points in direction of rotation.
7. Install rotor on shaft and insert vanes in rotor slots. Be sure radiused edge of vanes is toward the ring.
8. Place pressure plate over locating pins and flat against ring.
9. Insert pressure plate spring in pressure plate recess, then install cover using new O-ring. Be sure outlet port in cover is in correct position with respect to inlet port in body. Tighten attaching bolts to specified torque. Check binding.

VTM 27 and VTM 42 Series

Disassembly

NOTE: Two versions of the VTM 27 are in use. The noncurrent production pump uses needle bearings on the shaft; the current models use ball bearings and dispense with the thrust spacers.

1. If the pump has an attached reservoir, remove it before working by removing wing nut, washer, cover and gasket. Lift washer, filter retainer, spring and filter element from stud. Remove reservoir stud and nut, two reservoir retaining screws, baffle and reinforcing plate. Separate reservoir from pump. Discard O-rings.
2. If pump has manifold instead of reservoir, remove it along with attaching capscrews, copper washer and O-rings.
3. Clamp pump mounting flange in a vise with soft jaws. Remove cover attaching bolts and separate cover from body.
4. Remove pressure plate spring and pressure plate.
5. Remove ring, locating pins and rotor and vane assembly. Remove and discard O-rings found between body and cover.
6. Mount cover in a vise and drive relief valve retaining pin out. Do not allow relief valve plug and subassembly to fall from bore. Remove plug, valve and spring from bore.
7. Non-current VTM 27: support shaft outer end of pump body on a two inch pipe coupling and using an arbor press, remove the shaft assembly, shaft thrust spacers, outer needle bearing and shaft seal.
8. Current VTM 27 and all VTM 42: remove large snap ring retaining ball bearing in body. Press shaft and bearing assembly from body. Remove snap ring that retains bearing on shaft and remove bearing if unserviceable.
9. Inner bearing, if used, and seal in current production pumps, can be driven from body using a pin punch.

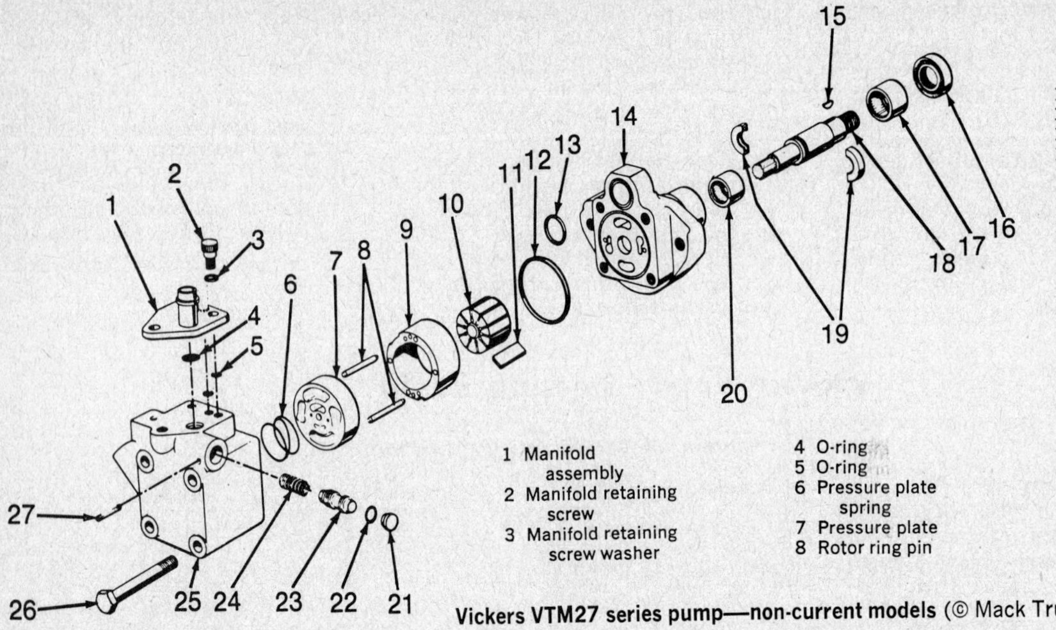

1 Manifold assembly
2 Manifold retaining screw
3 Manifold retaining screw washer
4 O-ring
5 O-ring
6 Pressure plate spring
7 Pressure plate
8 Rotor ring pin
9 Ring
10 Rotor
11 Vane
12 Body O-ring
13 O-ring
14 Body
15 Key
16 Oil seal
17 Shaft outer bearing
18 Shaft
19 Thrust spacer
20 Shaft inner bearing
21 Control valve plug
22 O-ring
23 Control valve assembly
24 Control valve spring
25 Cover
26 Cover screw
27 Control valve retaining pin

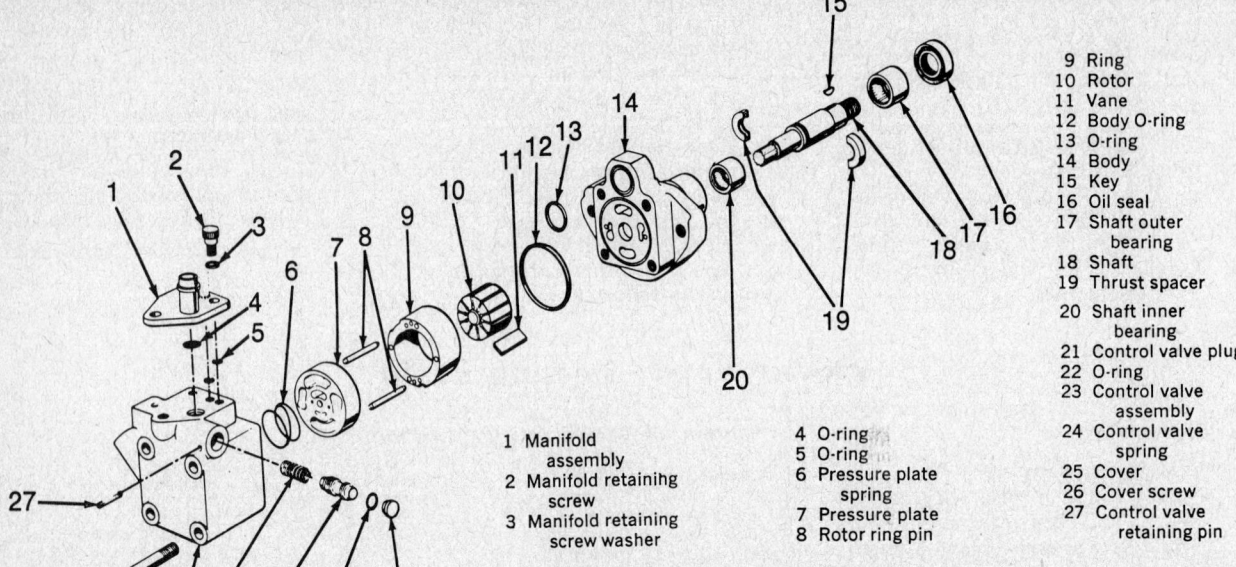

Vickers VTM27 series pump—non-current models (© Mack Trucks Inc.)

Assembly

NOTE: Lubricate all parts in hydraulic fluid before assembly. For non-current production VTM 27 pump, use steps 1 thru 4 and steps 9 thru 15. For current production VTM 27 and 42 pumps use steps 5-15.

1. Install inner bearing by pressing into body with an arbor press.
2. Assemble thrust spacers on shaft and install shaft in pump body.
3. Press outer needle bearing over shaft and into pump body to 1/64" past seal shoulder. This gives .010 - .015" end play.
4. Position seal on body and press into place until it contacts locating shoulder.
5. Press inner bearing into body.
6. Press seal into body.
7. Press ball bearing on shaft and secure with snap ring.
8. Install shaft and bearing assembly into body. Install snap ring.
9. Install locating pins in pump body. Install ring over pins according to direction of rotation.
10. Install rotor with chamfered edge towards inner ring contour.
11. Install vanes with radiused edge towards inner ring contour.
12. Install pressure plate.
13. Insert O-ring in body, then install pressure plate spring and cover. Tighten cover screws to torque.
14. Place spring and valve assembly in relief bore. Position valve with hex towards spring. Insert plug, with O-ring, in bore and hold in place while driving in new retaining pin.
15. Install reservoir or manifold as required. Place new O-rings over reservoir outlet tube and use copper washer on screw which enters oil passage if manifold is used. Assemble reservoir.

Mack-Scania Pump

Disassembly

1. Remove cover retaining capscrews.
2. Tap cover with soft mallet to separate from housing.
3. Remove housing O-ring from groove in pump housing.
4. Remove lock ring from shaft and lift rotor assembly out of housing.
5. Remove key from shaft and tap shaft out of housing.
6. Remove oil seal.
7. Remove connector from valve body.
   CAUTION: Take care when removing connector as it compresses the flow control spring and could cause injury if not restrained when unscrewed.
8. Remove flow control spring.
9. Turn cover assembly over and tap lightly to remove valve assembly.
10. Use suitable pliers and remove snap ring.
11. Remove piston and spring from valve body.

Assembly

1. Install spring and piston in flow control valve body and secure with snap ring.
2. Position valve body into pump cover and install spring.
3. Position new O-ring on connector and install in cover.

1 Connector
2 O-ring
3 Flow control valve spring
4 Lock ring
5 Pressure regulator piston
6 Pressure regulator spring
7 Flow control valve
8 Dowel
9 Housing O-ring
10 Valve plug
11 Gasket
12 Spring
13 Valve ball
14 Housing
15 Oil seal
16 Gasket
17 Pump shaft
18 Key
19 Rubber bushing
20 Connector
21 Connector gasket
22 Rotor assembly
23 Pump shaft lock ring
24 Cover
25 Cover screws

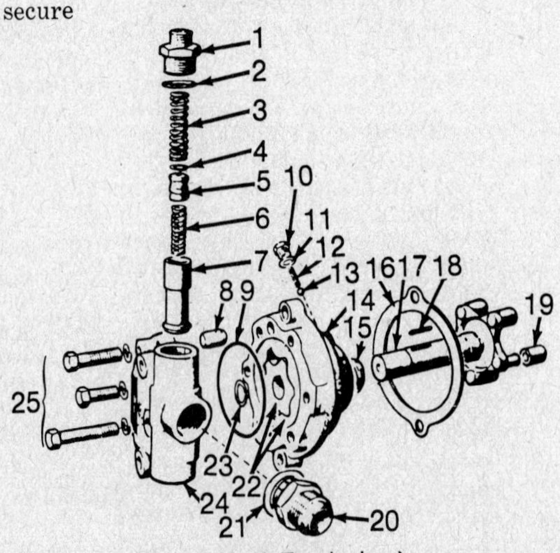

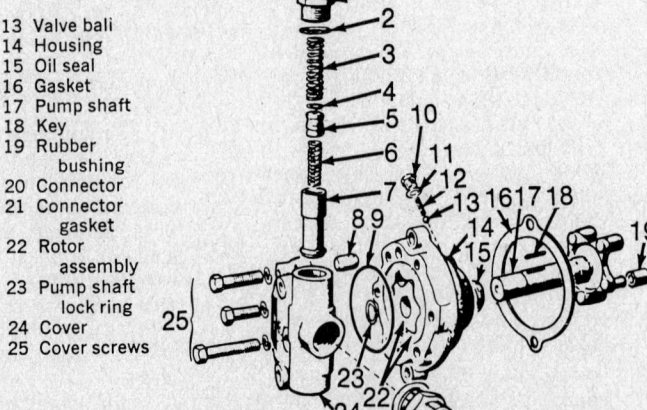

Exploded view of Mack-Scania pump (© Mack Trucks Inc.)

4. Install new oil seal in housing.
5. Position rotor assembly in housing and install shaft, aligning keyway in shaft with key slot in rotor.
6. Install key in shaft and rotor.
7. Install lockring on shaft and position new O-ring on housing.
8. Install cover-to-housing aligning dowelpins.
9. Install cover.
10. Turn shaft to be sure pump rotates freely with no binding.

Eaton Pump

Disassembly

1. Remove coupling assembly from pump shaft.
2. Place pumps in soft jawed vise and remove cover attaching screws. Separate cover from body.
3. Remove cover and O-ring seal. Do not lose O-ring retainer.
4. Mark rotors for reference. Remove pump shaft, key, snap ring and inner rotor from pump body.
5. Remove outer rotor by turning body over and tapping on a soft surface.
6. Slide rotor and key off pump shaft.
7. Remove oil seal from body.
8. Disassemble flow control relief valve by:
   a. Remove connector, O-ring and flow control valve spring.
   b. Tap cover on soft surface to dislodge valve assembly.
   c. Remove relief valve by pushing valve into flow control valve and removing snap ring. Remove valve and spring.

Assembly

NOTE: Lubricate all parts before assembly.

1. Install new oil seal in pump body. Press seal in place using a driver on outer edge of seal.
2. Install inner rotor and key on shaft and insert shaft and rotor assembly into body, coupling end front.
3. Place outer rotor in body. Be sure rotors are aligned according to marks made during disassembly.
4. Locate O-rings in body and insert thrust washer in cover. Place cover in position on body and tighten to torque.
5. Reassemble flow control relief valve by:
   a. Insert spring and relief valve into flow control valve, small end first.
   b. Push relief valve into flow control valve far enough to allow installation of snap ring.
   c. Install valve assembly into pump body, narrow land first, insert spring and install connector using new O-ring.

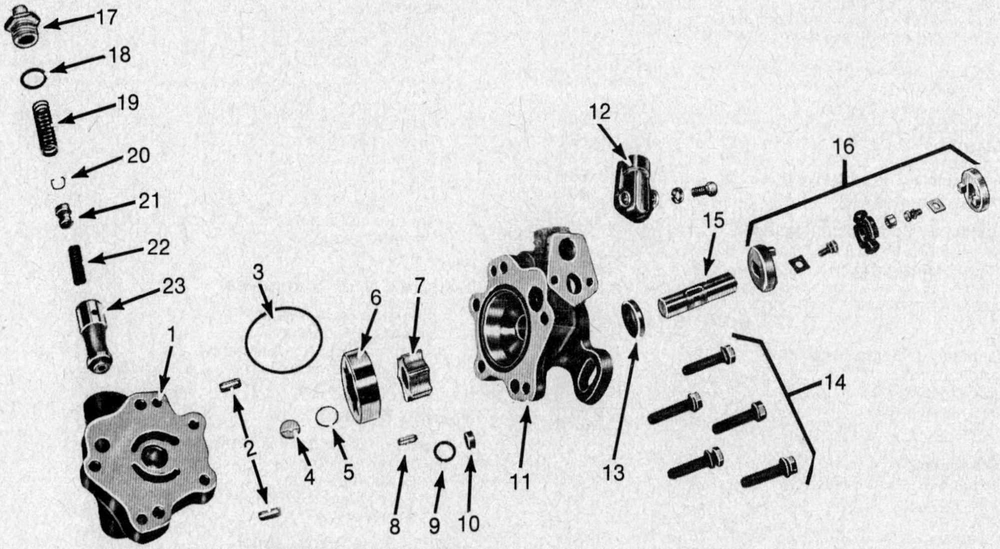

Exploded view—Eaton pump (© Mack Trucks Inc.)

1 Cover
2 Cover dowel
3 Body O-ring
4 Thrust washer
5 Snap ring
6 Outer rotor
7 Inner rotor
8 Drive pin
9 Bypass O-ring
10 Bypass O-ring retainer
11 Body
12 Outlet adapter
13 Oil seal
14 Cover screws
15 Pump shaft
16 Coupling assembly
17 Hose connector
18 Connector O-ring
19 Flow control valve spring
20 Valve retainer snap ring
21 Relief valve
22 Relief valve spring
23 Flow control valve

Electrical Section

INDEX

Electrical Diagnosis

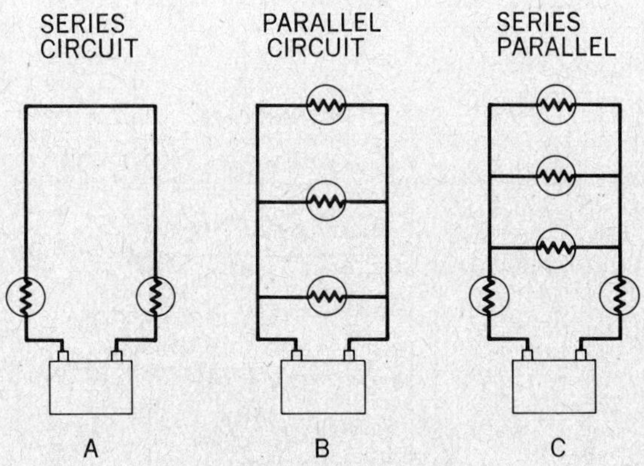

Basic electrical circuits

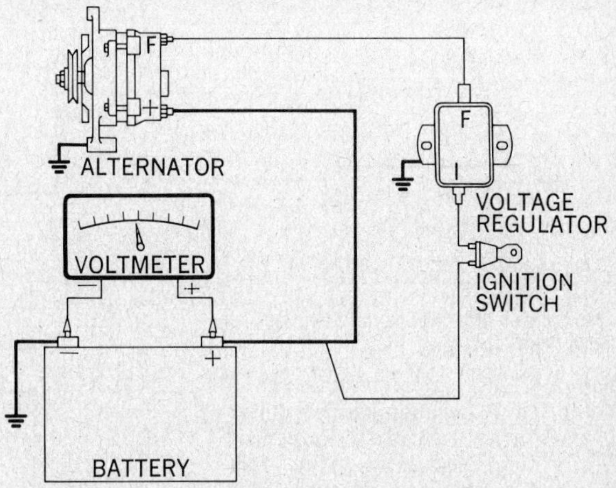

Voltmeter connected in parallel circuit—typical

To satisfy the growing trend toward organized engine diagnosis and tune-up, the following gauge and meter hook-ups, as well as diagnosis procedures are covered. The most sophisticated tune-up and diagnostic facilities are no more than a complex of the basic gauges and meters in common, everyday use. Therefore, to understand gauge and meter hook-ups, their applications and procedures, is to be equipped with the know-how to perform the most exacting diagnosis.

Know Your Instruments

Ohmmeter

An ohmmeter is used to measure electrical resistance in a unit or circuit. The ohmmeter has a self-contained power supply. In use, it is connected across (or in parallel with) the terminals of the unit being tested.

Ammeter

An ammeter is used to measure current (amount of electricity) flowing through a unit, or circuit. Ammeters are always connected in the line (in series) with the unit or circuit being tested.

Voltmeter

A voltmeter is used to measure voltage (electrical pressure) pushing the current through a unit, or circuit. The meter is connected across the terminals of the unit being tested. The meter reading will be the difference in pressure (voltage drop) between the two sides of the unit.

Testing the Starting Motor

Testing the Starter Circuit

The starter circuit should be divided and tested in four separate phases:

1. Cranking voltage check.
2. Amperage draw.
3. Voltage drop—grounded side.
4. Voltage drop—battery side.

NOTE: The battery must be in good condition for this test to have significance. To accurately check battery condition, use equipment designed to measure its capacity under a load. Instructions accompanying the equipment should be followed.

Cranking Voltage

Connect voltmeter leads to prods tapped into the battery posts (observe polarity and reverse meter leads if necessary). Remove the high tension wire from the distributor cap and ground it to prevent starting. With electronic ignition, disconnect the control box harness from the distributor. Now, turn the key. Observe both voltmeter reading and cranking speed. The cranking speed should be even, and at a satisfactory rate of speed, with a voltmeter reading of at least 9.6 volts for 12-volt systems.

Amperage Draw

The amount of current the starter motor draws is usually (but not always) associated with the mechanical problems involved in cranking the engine. (Mechanical trouble in the engine, frozen or worn starter parts,

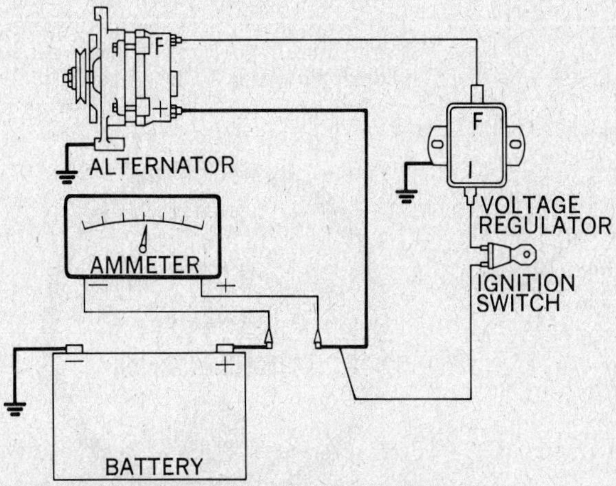

Ammeter connected to test wire—typical
(Ammeter has self containing power supply)

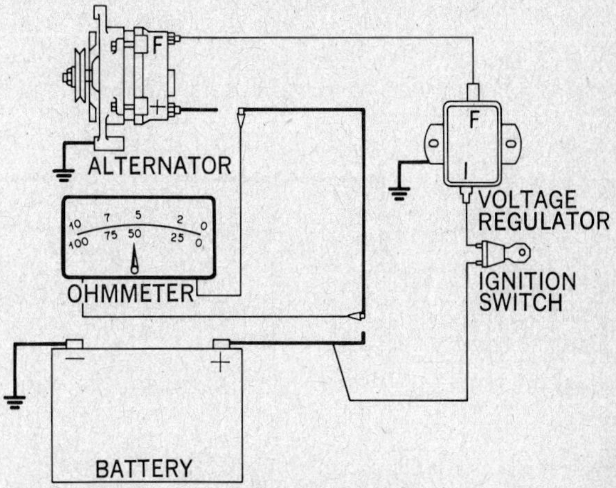

Ohmmeter connected to test wire resistance—typical
(Ohmmeter has self-contained power supply)

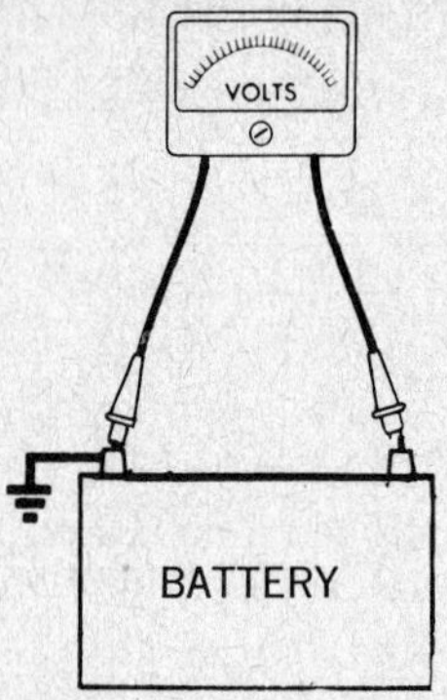

Voltmeter attached to battery for cranking voltage test

misaligned starter or starter components, etc.) Because starter motor amperage draw is directly influenced by anything restricting the free turning of the engine, or starter, it is important that the engine and all components be at operating temperatures.

To measure starter current draw, remove the high tension wire from the center of the distributor cap and ground it. With electronic ignition, disconnect the control box harness from the distributor. A very simple and inexpensive starter current indicator is available at auto stores. This indicator is an induction type gauge and shows, without disconnecting any wires, starter current draw.

Place the yoke of the meter directly over the insulated starter supply cable (cable must be straight for a minimum of 2 in.). Close the starter switch for about 20 seconds, watch the meter dial and record the average reading. If the indicator swings in the wrong direction, reverse the position of the meter.

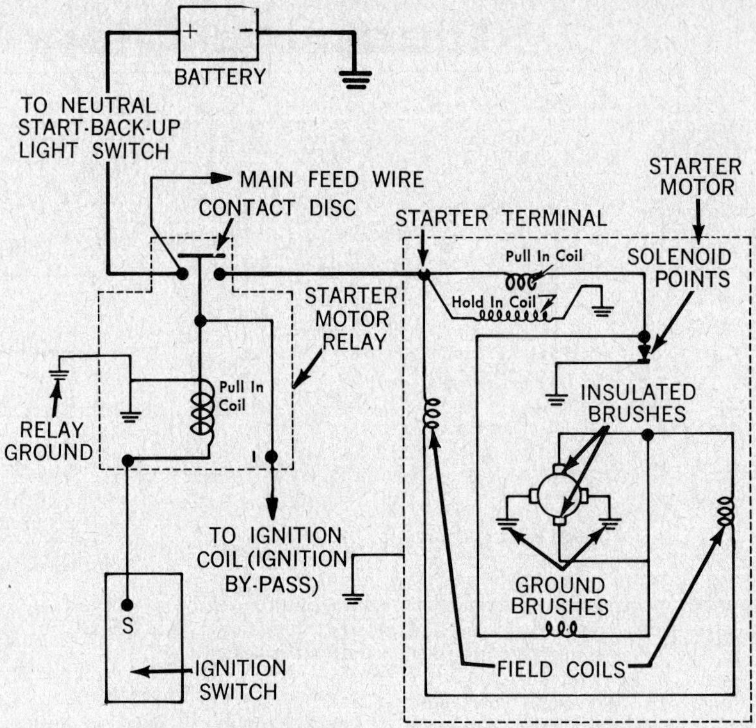

Positive engagement starter circuits (© Jeep Corp.)

The cranking amperage draw can vary from 150 to 400 amperes, depending on the engine size, engine compression, and starter type.

NOTE: When starter specifications are not available, average starter draw amperage can be derived from testing a like starter unit, known to be operating satisfactorily.

More accurate but complex equipment is available from many manufacturers. This equipment consists of a combination voltmeter, ammeter, and carbon pile rheostat. When using this equipment, follow the equipment manufacturer's procedures and recommendations.

High amperage and lazy performance would suggest an excessively tight engine, friction in the starter or starter drive, grounded starter field or armature.

Normal amperage and lazy performance suggest high resistance, or possibly poor connections somewhere in the starter circuit.

Low amperage and lazy or no performance suggest battery condition poor, bad cables or connections along the line.

Voltage Drop—Grounded Side

With a voltmeter on the 3-volt scale, without disconnecting any wires, connect negative test lead of the voltmeter to a prod secured in the grounded battery post. The positive test lead is connected to a cleaned, bare metal portion of the starter motor housing. Close the starter switch and note the voltmeter read-

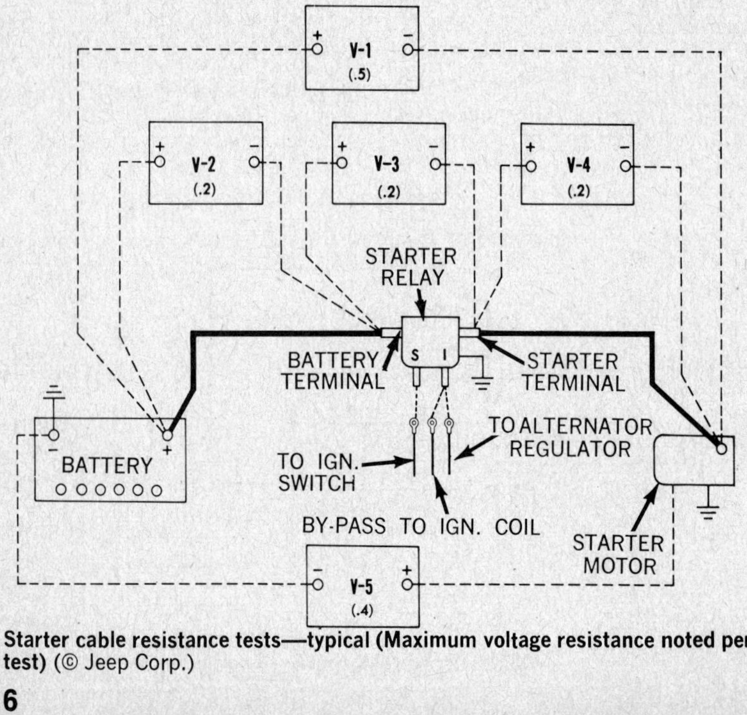

Starter cable resistance tests—typical (Maximum voltage resistance noted per test) (© Jeep Corp.)

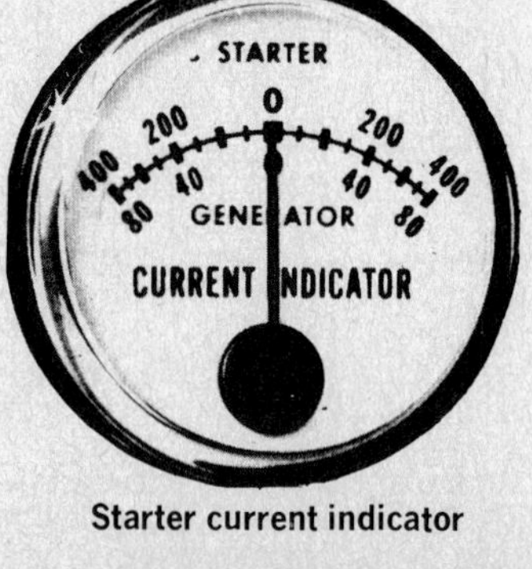

Starter current indicator

ing. If the reading is the same as battery reading, the ground circuit is open somewhere between the battery and the starter. In many cases the reading will be very small. The reading shown will indicate voltage drop (loss) between battery ground post and starter housing. The drop should not exceed 0.2 volt. If the voltage drop is above the specified amount, the next step is to isolate and correct the cause. It can be a bad cable or connection anywhere in the battery-to-starter ground circuit. A check of this type should progress along the various points of possible trouble, between the battery ground post and the starter motor housing, until the trouble spot has been located.

NOTE: due to the design of the Chrysler reduction gear starter, testing is limited to measuring voltage drop to starter cable connection.

Voltage Drop—Battery Side

Bad starter cranking may result from poor connections or faulty components of the battery or hot phase of the starter motor circuit. To check this phase of the circuit, without disconnecting any wires, connect one lead of a voltmeter to a prod secured in the hot post of the battery and the other voltmeter lead to the field terminal of the starting motor. The meter should be set to the 16-20 volt scale. Before closing the starter switch, the voltmeter reading will be that of the battery. After closing the starter switch, change the selector on the voltmeter to the 3-volt scale. With a jumper wire between the relay battery terminal and the relay starter switch terminal, crank the engine. If the starting motor cranks the engine, the relay (solenoid) is operating.

While the engine is being cranked, watch the voltmeter. It should not register more than 0.5 volt. If more than this, check each part of the circuit for voltage drop to isolate the trouble, (high resistance).

Without disturbing the voltmeter-to-battery hook-up, move the free voltmeter lead to the battery terminal of the relay (solenoid), and crank the engine. The voltmeter should show no more than 0.1 volt.

If this reading is correct, move the same voltmeter lead to the starting motor terminal of the relay (solenoid). While the engine is being cranked, the voltmeter should show no more than 0.3 volt. If it does, the trouble lies in the relay.

If the reading is correct, the trouble is in the cable or connections between the relay and the starting motor.

Diagnosis

Starter Won't Crank the Engine

1. Dead battery.
2. Open starter circuit, such as:
   a. Broken or loose battery cables.
   b. Inoperative starter motor solenoid.
   c. Broken or loose wire from starter switch to solenoid.
   d. Poor solenoid or starter ground.
   e. Bad starter switch.
3. Defective starter internal circuit, such as:
   a. Dirty or burnt commutator.
   b. Stuck, worn or broken brushes.
   c. Open or shorted armature.
   d. Open or grounded fields.
4. Starter motor mechanical faults, such as:
   a. Jammed armature end bearings.
   b. Bad bearing, allowing armature to rub fields.
   c. Bent shaft.
   d. Broken starter housing.
   e. Bad starter worm or drive mechanism.
   f. Bad starter drive or flywheel driven gear.
5. Engine hard or impossible to crank such as:
   a. Hydrostatic lock, water in combustion chamber.
   b. Crankshaft seizing in bearings.
   c. Piston or ring seizing.
   d. Bent or broken connecting rod.
   e. Seizing of connecting rod bearing.
   f. Flywheel jammed or broken.

Starter Spins Free, Won't Engage

1. Sticking or broken drive mechanism.

Alternators and Regulators

Is it the Alternator or the Voltage Regulator?

The first step in diagnosing troubles of the charging system, is to identify the source of failure. Does the fault lie in the alternator or the regulator? The next move depends upon preference or necessity; either repair or replace the offending unit.

It is just as easy to separate an alternator, electrically, from the AC regulator as it is to separate its counterpart, the DC generator from its regulator.

AC generator output is controlled by the amount of current supplied to the field circuit of the system.

Unlike the DC generator, an AC generator is capable of producing substantial current at idle speed. Higher maximum output is also a possibility. This presents a potential danger when testing. As a precaution, a field rheostat should be used in the field circuit when making the following isolation test. The field rheostat permits positive control of the amount of current allowed to pass through the field circuit during the isolation test. Unregulated alternator capacity could ruin the unit.

NOTE: most manufacturers of precision gauges offer special test connectors, in sets, that will adapt to the leads and connections of any AC charging system.

CAUTION: Before attempting the isolation test, disconnect the field wire from the regulator. Failure to take this precaution can cause instant burning and permanent damage to the regulator.

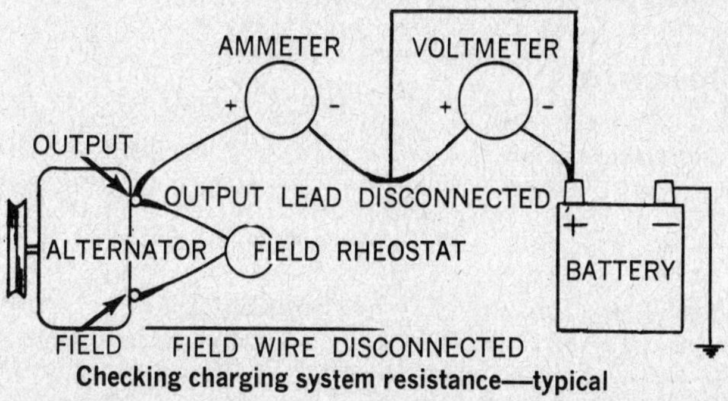

Checking charging system resistance—typical

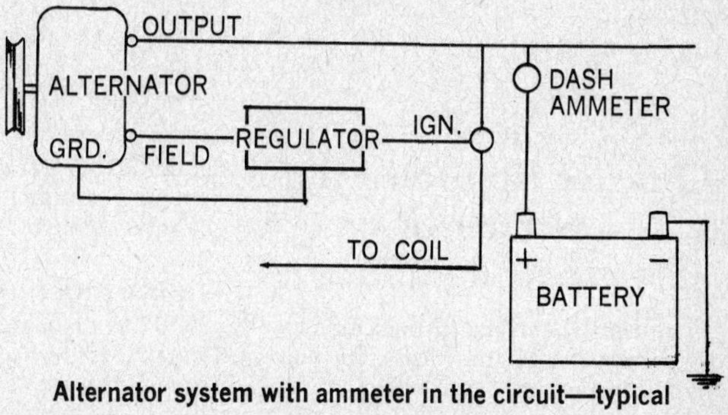

Alternator system with ammeter in the circuit—typical

Isolation Test

(By-passing the Regulator)

1. Connect voltmeter leads to two prods driven into the battery posts.
2. Disconnect field wire from the FLD terminal of the voltage regulator.
3. Connect one lead of a field rheostat to the undisturbed IGN terminal of the regulator, and the other field rheostat lead to the wire that was removed from the FLD terminal of the regulator.
4. With field rheostat turned to the low side of the scale, (high resistance) start the engine and adjust throttle to about 2,000 rpm.
5. Slowly move field rheostat control knob to decrease resistance, (allowing more current to flow through the field circuit) until voltmeter reading slightly exceeds manufacturers' specifications.

NOTE: under load conditions, observe the alternator for arcing or any other evidence of malfunction.

6. If alternator performs satisfactorily, repair or replace the regulator. Conversely, if the voltmeter reading is zero, or below specifications, repair or replace the alternator.

Alternator Test Plans

The following is a procedure pattern for testing the various alternators and their control systems.

There are certain precautionary measures that apply to alternator tests in general. These items are listed in detail to avoid repetition when testing each make of alternator, and to encourage a habit of good test procedure.

1. Check alternator drive belt for condition and tension.
2. Disconnect battery cables, check physical, chemical, and electrical condition of battery.
3. Be absolutely sure of polarity before connecting any battery in the circuit. Reversed polarity will ruin the diodes.
4. Never use a battery charger to start the engine.
5. Disconnect both battery cables when making a battery recharge hook-up.
6. Be sure of polarity hook-up when using a booster battery for starting.
7. Never ground the alternator output or battery terminal.
8. Never ground the field circuit between alternator and regulator.
9. Never run any alternator on an open circuit with the field energized.
10. Never try to polarize an alternator.
11. Do not attempt to motor an alternator.
12. The regulator cover must be in place when taking voltage limiter readings.
13. The ignition switch must be in off position when removing or installing the regulator cover.
14. Use insulated tools only to make adjustments to the regulator.
15. When making engine idle speed adjustments, always consider potential load factors that influence engine rpm. To compensate for electrical load, switch on the lights, radio, heater, air conditioner, etc.

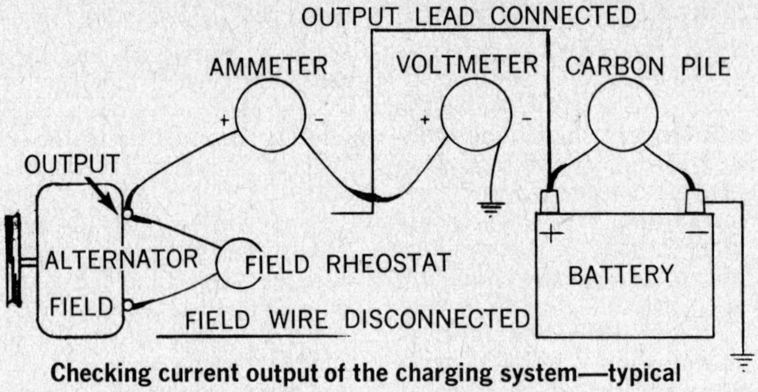

Checking current output of the charging system—typical

Diagnosis

Low or No Charging

1. Blown fuse.
2. Broken or loose fan belt.
3. Voltage regulator not working.
4. Brushes sticking.
5. Slip ring dirty.
6. Open circuit.
7. Bad wiring connections.
8. Bad diode rectifier.
9. High resistance in charging circuit.
10. Voltage regulator needs adjusting.
11. Grounded stator.
12. May be open rectifiers (check all three phases).
13. If rectifiers are found blown or open, check capacitor.

Noisy Unit

1. Damaged rotor bearings.
2. Poor alignment of unit.
3. Broken or loose belt.
4. Open diode rectifiers.

Regulator Points Burnt or Stuck

1. Regulator set too high.
2. Poor ground connections.
3. Shorted generator field.
4. Regulator air gap incorrect.

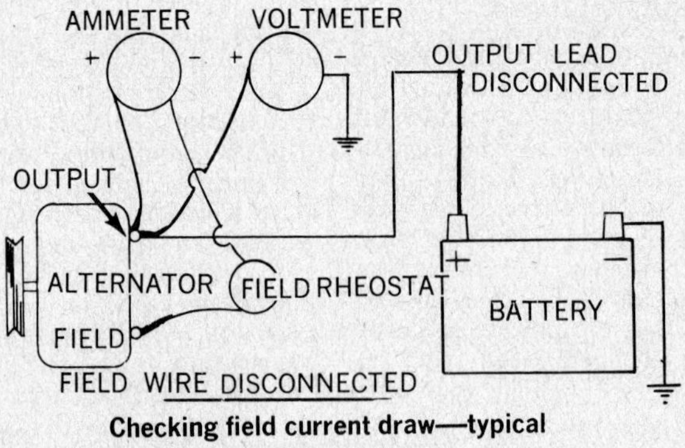

Checking field current draw—typical

Chrysler Alternators

Chrysler Isolated Field Alternator (Electronic Regulator)

The Chrysler isolated field alternator derives its name from its construction. Both of the brushes are insulated from ground and there is no heat sink connection, thereby isolating the internal field.

Troubleshooting

NOTE: see the "Alternator Test Plans" section before proceeding further. Make sure that the continuous running blower, if equipped, is disconnected. This blower will run with the key turned on even if the blower controls are off unless disconnected.

Fusible Links

Chrysler Corporation trucks have a single fusible link which is connected

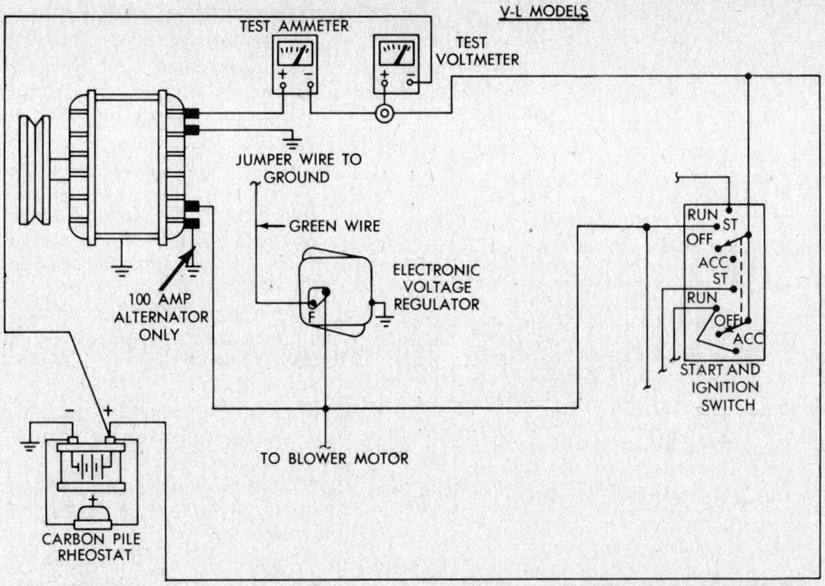

Typical resistance test connections—Chrysler charging system (© Chrysler Corp.)

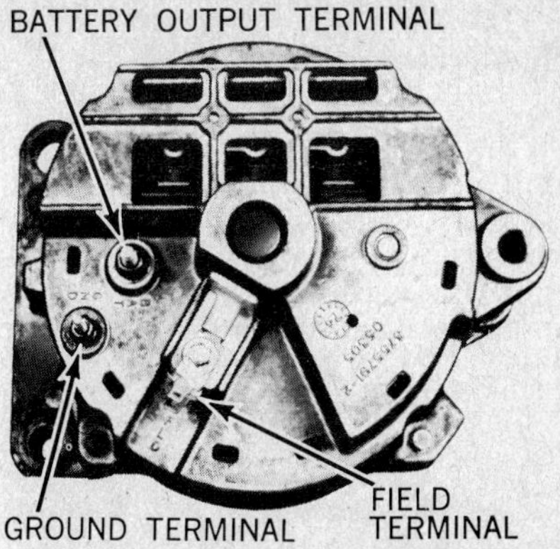

View of rear housing—100 ampere Chrysler alternator (© Chrysler Corp.)

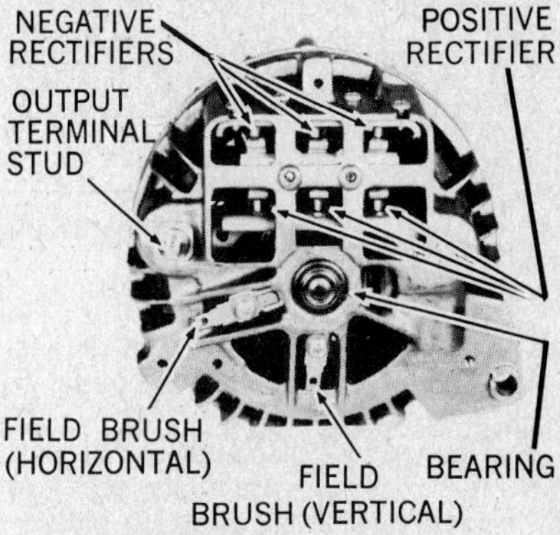

View of rear housing (except 100 ampere)—Chrysler alternator (© Chrysler Corp.)

between the starter relay and the junction block. Failure of this link will cause all electrical systems to stop functioning.

Charging System Operation

NOTE: if the current indicator is to give an accurate reading, the battery cables must be of the same gauge and length as the original equipment.

1. With the engine running and all electrical systems off, place a current indicator over the positive battery cable.
2. If a charge of about 5 amps is recorded, the charging system is working. If a draw of about 5 amps is recorded the system is not working. The needle moves toward the battery when a charge condition is indicated and away from the battery when a draw condition is indicated. If a draw is indicated, proceed to the next testing procedure. If an overcharge of 10-15 amps is indicated, check for a faulty regulator.

Ignition Switch-to-Regulator Circuit Check

1. Disconnect the regulator wires at the regulator.
2. Turn the key on but do not start the engine.
3. Using a voltmeter or test light, check for voltage across the I and F terminals. If there is current present, the circuit is good. If there is no current, check for bad connections, a bad ballast resistor, a bad ammeter, broken wires, or bad ground at the alternator or voltage regulator. Also, check for voltage from the I wire to ground; current should be present. Check for voltage from the F terminal to ground; current should not be present.

Isolation Test

This test determines whether the regulator or alternator is bad if everything else in the circuit was OK.

1. Disconnect, at the alternator, the wire that runs between one of the alternator field connections and the voltage regulator.

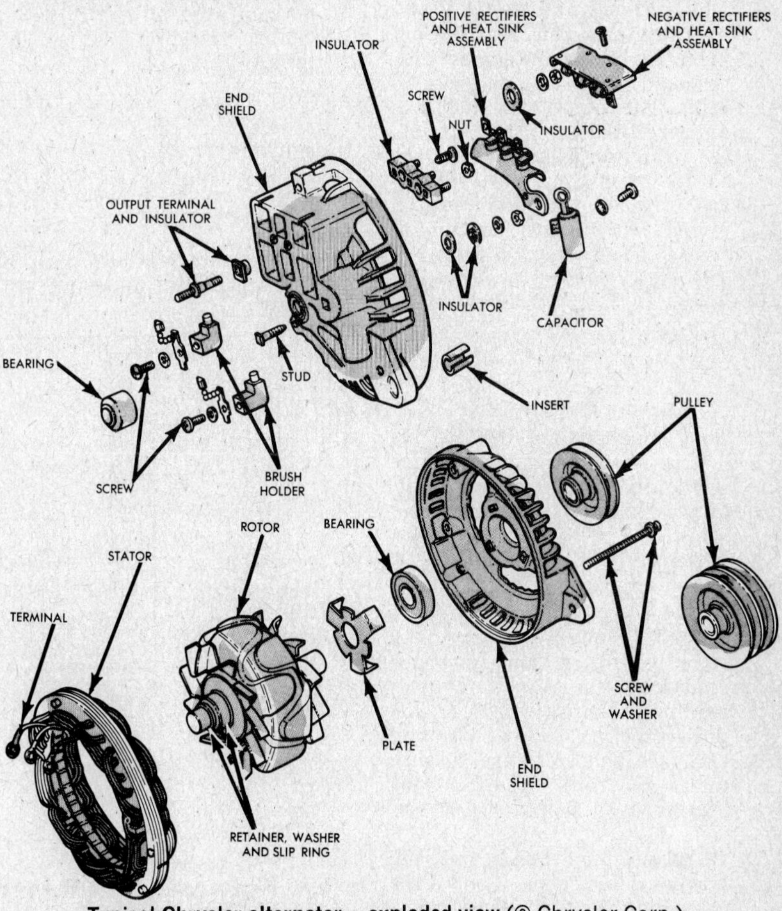

Typical Chrysler alternator—exploded view (© Chrysler Corp.)

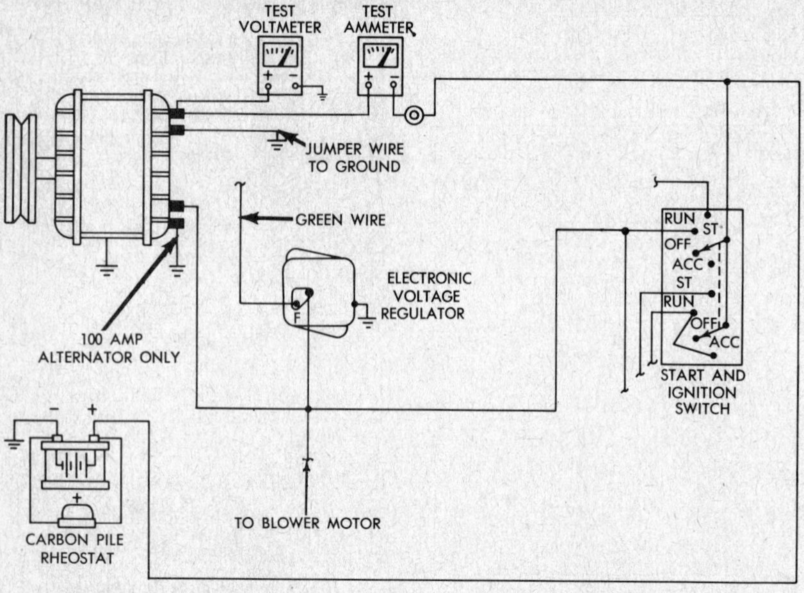

Typical current output test connections—Chrysler charging systems
(© Chrysler Corp.)

2. Run a jumper wire from the disconnected alternator terminal to ground.
3. Connect a voltmeter to the battery. The positive voltmeter lead connects to the positive battery terminal, and the negative lead goes to the negative terminal. Record the reading.
4. Make sure that all electrical systems are turned off. Start the engine. Do not race the engine.
5. Gradually raise engine speed to 1500-2000 rpm. There should be an increase of one to two volts on the voltmeter. If this is true, the alternator is good and the voltage regulator should be repaired. If there is no voltage increase, the alternator is faulty.

NOTE: the following tests require the use of a carbon pile and an ammeter.

Current Output Test

1. The ammeter and carbon pile hookup should remain the same as for the circuit resistance test.
2. Connect the voltmeter negative lead to the battery negative post.
3. Move the positive voltmeter lead to the alternator "BATT" post.
4. Start the engine and adjust speed to 1250 rpm.
5. Note voltmeter and ammeter readings. Maintain a 15 volt reading by adjusting the carbon pile control.
6. Compare ammeter reading with manufacturer's specifications The reading should be no less than specified, 3 amps.
7. If below specifications, internal trouble is indicated. Remove the alternator for further testing.

Electronic Voltage Regulator Test

1. Make sure battery terminals are clean and battery is charged.
2. Connect the positive lead of a test voltmeter to ignition Terminal No. 1 of the ballast resistor.
3. Connect the negative voltmeter lead to a good *body* ground.
4. Start engine and allow it to idle at 1250 rpm, all lights and accessories turned off. Voltage should be as follows:

Ambient Temp. ¼ in. from Regulator	*Voltage*
-20°F.	14.3-15.3
80°F.	13.8-14.4
140°F.	13.3-14.0

5. If the voltage is *below* specifications, check the following:
   a. Voltage regulator ground—check voltage drop between regulator cover and ground.
   b. Harness wiring—disconnect regulator plug (ign. switch off), then turn on ign. switch and check for battery voltage at the ternimal having the blue and green leads. *Wiring harness must be disconnected from the regulator when checking individual leads.* If no voltage is present in either lead, the problem is in the truck wiring or alternator field.
6. If Step 5 tests showed no malfunctions, install a new regulator and repeat Step 4.
7. If voltage is *above* specifications (Step 4), or fluctuates, check the following:
   a. Ground between regulator and body, and between body and engine.
   b. Ignition switch circuit between switch and regulator.
8. If voltage is still more than ½ volt above specifications, install a new regulator and repeat Step 4.

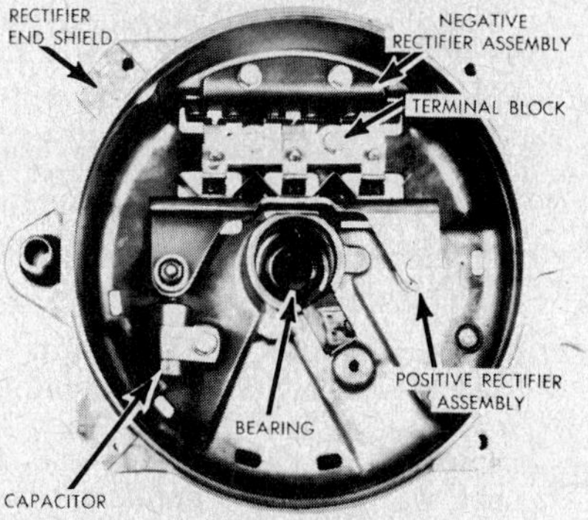

Typical rear housing assembly—Chrysler charging system
(© Chrysler Corp.)

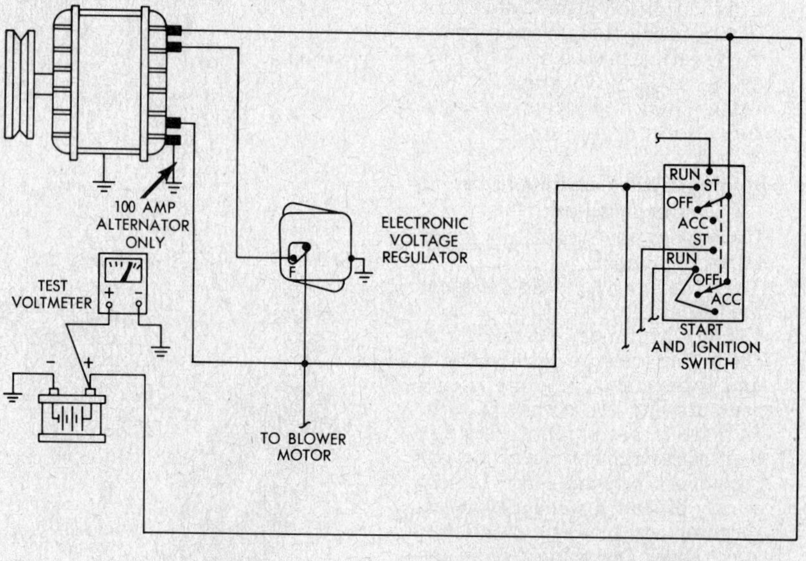

Typical voltage regulator test connection—Chrysler charging system
(© Chrysler Corp.)

Chrysler Overhaul and Internal Testing

Alternator disassembly, repair and assembly procedures are basically the same for all Chrysler alternators. Certain variations in design, or in-production modifications, could require slightly different procedures that should be obvious upon inspection of the unit being serviced.

Disassembly

To prevent damage to the brush assemblies they should be removed before proceeding with the disassembly of the alternator. The insulated brush is mounted in a plastic holder that positions the brush vertically against one of the slip rings.

1. Remove the retaining screw, flat washer, nylon washer and field terminal and carefully lift the plastic holder containing the spring and brush assembly from the end housing.
2. The ground brush is positioned horizontally against the remaining slip ring and is retained in the holder that is integral with the end housing. Remove the retaining screw and lift the clip, spring and brush assembly from the end housing.

CAUTION: The stator is laminated, don't burr the stator or end housings.

3. Remove the through bolts and pry between the stator and drive end housing with a thin blade screwdriver. Carefully separate the drive end housing, pulley and rotor assembly from the stator and rectifier housing assembly.
4. The pulley is an interference fit on the rotor shaft. Remove with a puller and special adapters.
5. Remove the three nuts and washers and, while supporting the end frame, tap the rotor shaft with a plastic hammer and separate the rotor and end housing.
6. The drive end ball bearing is an interference fit with the rotor shaft. Remove the bearing with puller and adapters.

NOTE: further dismantling of the rotor is not advisable, as the remainder of the rotor assembly is not serviced separately.

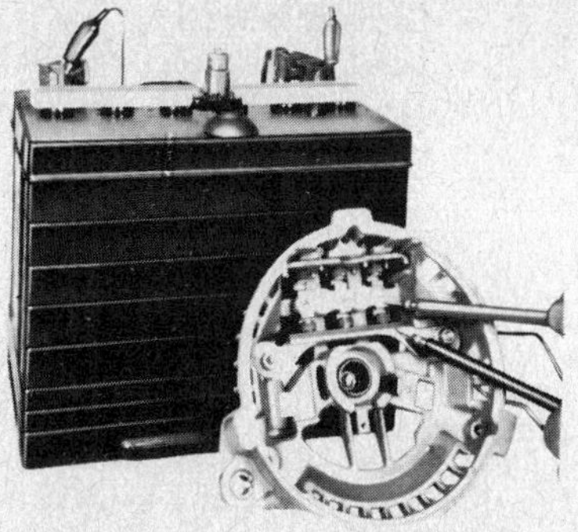

Rectifier test with test light and 12 volt battery (© Chrysler Corp.)

7. Remove the DC output terminal nuts and washers and remove terminal screw and inside capacitor (on units so equipped).
8. Remove the insulator.

NOTE: three positive rectifiers are pressed into the heat sink and three negative rectifiers in the end housing. When removing the rectifiers, it is necessary to support the end housing and/or heat sink to prevent damage to these castings. Another caution is in order relative to the diode rectifiers. Don't subject them to unnecessary jolting. Heavy vibration or shock may ruin them.

a. Cut rectifier wire at point of crimp.
b. Support rectifier housing.

NOTE: the factory tool is cut away and slotted to fit over the wires and around the bosses in the housing. Be sure that the bore of the tool completely surrounds the rectifier, then press the rectifier out of the housing.

NOTE: the roller bearing in the rectifier end frame is a press fit. To protect the end housing it is necessary to support the housing with a tool when pressing out the bearing.

Bench Tests

Testing Silicon Diode Rectifiers With Ohmmeter

Preferred method—rectifiers open in all three phases.

Disassemble the alternator and separate the wires at the Y-connection of the stator.

There are six diode rectifiers mounted in the back of the alternator. Three of them are marked with a plus (+), and three are marked with a minus (—). These marks indicate diode case polarity.

NOTE: The 100 ampere alternator has twelve silicone diodes. Six positive and six negative.

To test, set ohmmeter to its lowest range. If case is marked positive (+), place positive meter probe to case and negative probe to the diode lead. Meter should read between 4 and 10 ohms. Now, reverse leads of ohmmeter, connecting negative meter probe to positive case and positive meter probe to wire of rectifier. Set meter on a high range. Meter needle should move very little, if any (infinite reading). Do this to all three positive diode rectifiers.

The three with minus (—) marks on their cases are checked the same way as above. Only now the negative ohmmeter probe is connected to the case for a reading of 4 to 10 ohms. Reverse leads as above for the other part to test.

If a reading of 4 to 10 ohms is obtained in one direction and no reading (infinity) is read on the ohmmeter in the other direction, diode rectifiers are good. If either infinity or a low resistance is obtained in both directions on a rectifier, it must be replaced.

If meter reads more than 10 ohms when ohmmeter positive probe is connected to positive on diode, and negative probe to negative, replace diode rectifier.

NOTE: with this test, it is necessary to determine the polarity of the ohmmeter probes. This can be done by connecting the ohmmeter to a DC voltmeter. The voltmeter will read up-scale when the positive probe of the ohmmeter is connected to the positive side of the voltmeter and the negative probe of the ohmmeter is connected to the negative side of the voltmeter.

Alternate method—test light.

Make up a tester as shown in the sketch. Be sure that the lead from the center of the diode rectifiers is disconnected.

To test rectifiers with plus (+) case, touch positive probe of tester to case and minus (—) probe to lead wire of rectifier. Bulb should light if rectifier is good. If bulb does not light, replace rectifier.

Now reverse tester probe connections to rectifier. Bulb should not light. If bulb does light, replace rectifier.

For testing minus (—) marked cases, follow above procedure, except that now bulb should light with negative probe of tester touching rectifier case and positive probe touching lead wire.

Rectifier is good if the bulb lights when tester probes are connected one

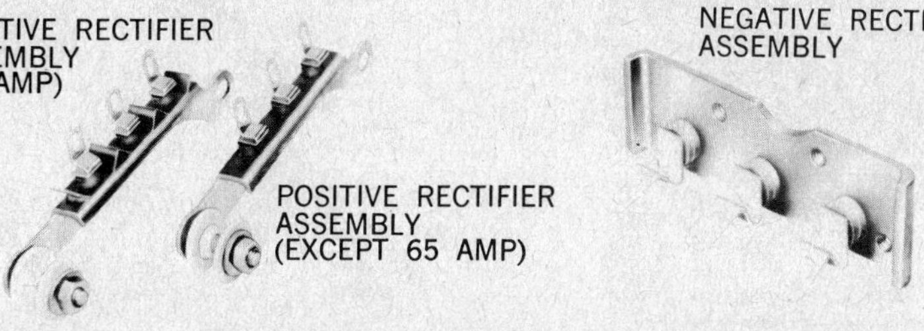

Positive and negative rectifier identification—Chrysler charging system (© Chrysler Corp.)

way, and does not light when tester connections are reversed.

Rectifier must be replaced if the bulb does not light either way. Also, replace rectifier if bulb lights both ways.

NOTE: the usual cause of an open or blown diode or rectifier is a defective capacitor or a battery that has been installed in reverse polarity. If the battery is installed properly and the diodes are open, test the capacitor.

Capacitor capacity:
(int. installed)
...........158 microfarad, min.
(ext. installed) ....5 microfarad

Alternator Bench Tests

Field Coil Draw

1. Connect a jumper between one FLD terminal and the positive terminal of a fully charged 12 volt battery.
2. Connect the positive lead of a test ammeter to the other field (FLD) terminal and the negative test lead to the negative battery terminal.
3. Slowly rotate the rotor by hand and observe the ammeter. The proper field coil draw is 2.3-2.7 amps at 12 volts.

NOTE: Field coil draw for the 100 ampere alternator should be 4.75 amperes to 6.0 amperes at 12 volts.

Field Circuit Ground Test

1. Touch one test lead of a 110 volt AC test bulb to one of the alternator brush (field) terminals and the other test lead to the end shield.
2. If the lamp lights, remove the field brush assemblies and separate the end housing by removing the three thru-bolts.
3. Place one test lead on a slip ring and the other on the end shield.
4. If the lamp lights, the rotor assembly is grounded internally and must be replaced.
5. If the lamp does not light, the cause of the problem was a grounded brush.

Grounded Stator

1. Disconnect the diode rectifiers from the stator leads.
2. Test from stator leads to stator core, using a 110-volt test lamp. Test lamp should not light. If it does, stator is grounded and must be replaced.

Low Output

(About 50% output accompanied with a growl-hum caused by a shorted phase or a shorted rectifier.)

Perform Steps 1, 2 and 3 (rectifier open in all three phases). If the rectifiers are found to be within specifications, replace the stator assembly.

Current Output Too High (No Control) Caused by Open Rectifier or Open Phase

Perform Steps 1, 2 and 3 (rectifier open in all three phases). If the rectifier tests satisfactorily, inspect the stator connections before replacing the stator.

Assembly

1. Support the heat sink or rectifier end housing on circular plate.
2. Check rectifier identification to be sure the correct rectifier is being used. The part numbers are stamped on the case of the rectifier. They are also marked, red for positive and black for negative.
3. Start the new rectifier into the casting and press it in squarely.

CAUTION: Do not start rectifier with a hammer or it will be ruined.

4. Crimp the new rectifier wire to the wires disconnected at removal, or solder (using a heat sink with rosin core solder).
5. Support the end housing on tool so that the notch in the support tool will clear the raised section of the heat sink, then press the bearing into position with tool SP-3381, or equivalent.

NOTE: new bearings are pre-lubricated, additional lubrication is not required.

6. Insert the drive end bearing in the drive end housing and install the bearing plate, washers and nuts to hold the bearing in place.
7. Position the bearing and drive end housing on the rotor shaft and, while supporting the base of the rotor shaft, press the bearing and housing in position on the rotor shaft with an arbor press and arbor tool.

CAUTION: Be careful that there is no cocking of the bearing at installation; or damage will result. Press the bearing on the rotor shaft until the bearing contacts the shoulder on the rotor shaft.

8. Install pulley on rotor shaft. Shaft of rotor must be supported so that all pressing force is on the pulley hub and rotor shaft.

NOTE: Do not exceed 6,800 lbs. pressure. Pulley hub should just contact bearing inner race.

9. Some alternators will be found to have the capacitor mounted internally. Be sure the heat sink insulator is in place.
10. Install the output terminal screw with the capacitor attached through the heat sink and end housing.
11. Install insulating washers, lockwashers and locknuts.
12. Make sure the heat sink and insulator are in place and tighten the locknut.
13. Position the stator on the rectifier end housing. Be sure that all of the rectifier connectors and phase leads are free of interference with the rotor fan blades and that the capacitor (internally mounted) lead has clearance.
14. Position the rotor assembly in the rectifier end housing. Align the through bolt holes in the stator with both end housings.
15. Enter stator shaft in the rectifier end housing bearing, compress stator and both end housings manually and install through bolts, washers and nuts.
16. Install the insulated brush and terminal attaching screw.
17. Install the ground screw and attaching screw.
18. Rotate pulley slowly to be sure the rotor fan blades do not hit the rectifier and stator connectors.

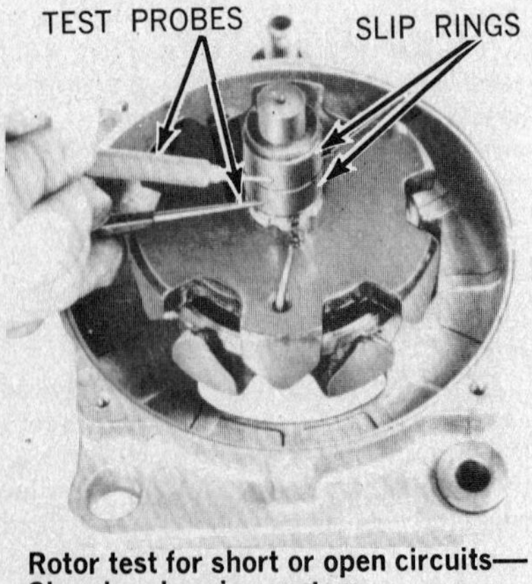

Rotor test for short or open circuits—Chrysler charging system
(© Chrysler Corp.)

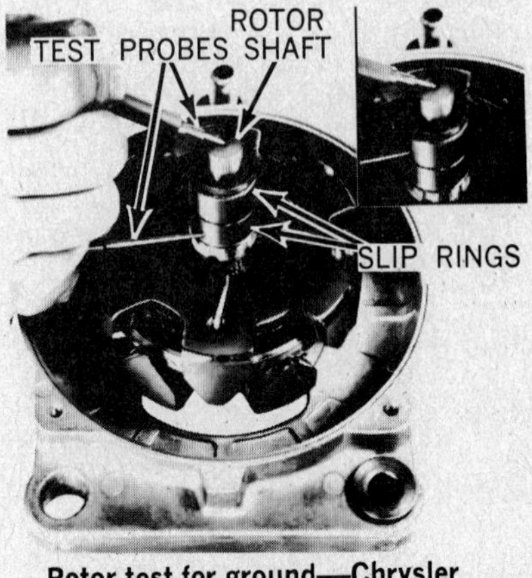

Rotor test for ground—Chrysler charging system (© Chrysler Corp.)

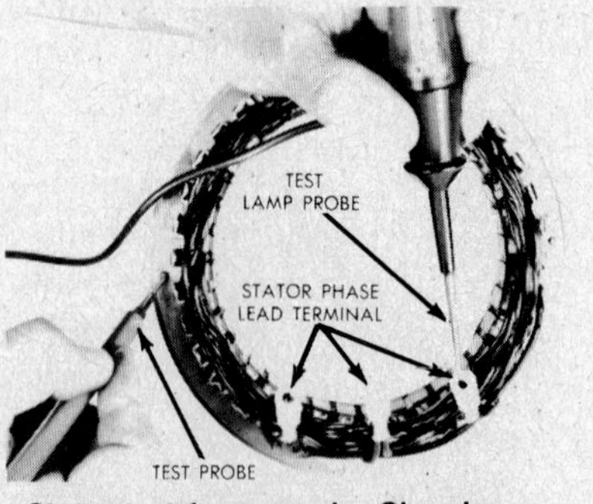

Stator test for ground—Chrysler charging system (© Chrysler Corp.)

General Motors Alternators

Delcotron 5.5 Series 1D and 6.2 Series 2D (General Motors Corporation)

Description

The Delcotron continuous output AC generator consists of two major parts—the stator and the rotor. The stator is composed of many turns of wire on the inside of a laminated core that is attached to the generator frame. The rotor is mounted on bearings at each end. Two brushes carry current through slip rings to the field coils, which are wound on the rotor shaft.

The 5.5 Series 1D Delcotron is similar in operation to the 6.2 Series 2D perforated Stator Delcotron. Where differences exist, the two units are mentioned separately.

Six diodes, mounted on internal heat sinks, change the AC current output into DC current. This current is controlled by the regulator. The regulator is a double-contact unit combined with a field relay or a triple-contact unit containing an indicator lamp relay as well as the field relay and voltage relay. Transistor regulators were also used in production intermittently.

On high-output Delcotron units, the regulator incorporates a field discharge diode.

Troubleshooting

NOTE: see the "Preliminary Charging System Inspection" section before proceeding further. Make sure that the continuous running blower, if equipped, is disconnected. This blower will run with the key on and even if the blower control is off, it is not disconnected.

Fusible Links

There are four fusible links on all GM trucks.

1. The 14 gauge wire that runs from the junction block to the positive battery terminal serves as a fusible link.
2. There is a second link in the circuit between the horn relay and the ignition switch.
3. A third link is in the wire running to the No. 3 voltage regulator terminal. Its purpose is to protect the regulator contacts and the alternator field circuit.
4. The fourth link is connected between the main junction block and the horn relay.

These links must be inspected before proceeding with troubleshooting

Charging System Operation

NOTE: if the current indicator is to give an accurate reading, the battery cables must be the same gauge and length as the original equipment.

1. With the engine running and all electrical systems turned off, place a current indicator over the positive battery cable.
2. If a charge of about 5 amps is recorded, the charging system is working. If a draw of about 5 amps is recorded, the system is not working. The needle moves toward the battery when a charge condition is indicated, and away from the battery when a draw condition is indicated. If a draw is indicated, proceed with further testing. If an excessive charge (10-15 amps) is indicated, check for an overcharge, caused by a faulty regulator.

Indicator Light Circuit Testing

The indicator lights is important in AC charging systems, for it provides initial field excitation current to the alternator. The light goes out when the field relay closes, which applies battery current to both sides of the bulb. If the light does not go on when key is turned, the bulb could be faulty, there could be an open circuit in the wiring or a positive diode in the alternator could be shorted to ground.

1. Disconnect plug from regulator and connect a test light between terminal No. 4 (in plug) and ground. Turn on ignition switch and observe the light. If light does not go on, check bulb, socket or wiring between switch and regulator plug. If light goes on, check regulator, wiring between regulator F terminal and alternator, or Delcotron itself.
2. Disconnect jumper wire at ground end and reconnect to F terminal in plug. Turn on ignition for a second and note light. If light goes on, problem is in regulator. If light does not go on, problem is in wire between F terminals (regulator and alternator).
3. Disconnect light at plug F terminal and reconnect the free end to F terminal at alternator. Turn on ignition switch for a second and note light. If light goes on, the problem is an open circuit in the wire connecting the regulator and alternator F terminals. If light does not go on, the alternator field windings are defective.

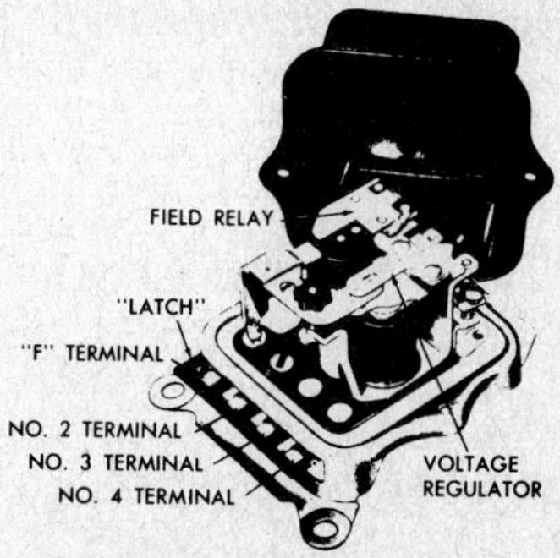

Mechanical voltage regulator (© Chevrolet Div., G.M. Corp.)

If the indicator light does not extinguish when engine is started, check for a loose drive belt, faulty field relay, faulty alternator, open parallel resistance wire (usually shows up at idle). If the light stays on with the key turned off, an alternator positive diode is shorted to ground.

Isolation Test

1. Disconnect the wiring harness from the voltage regulator. With a jumper wire connect the F

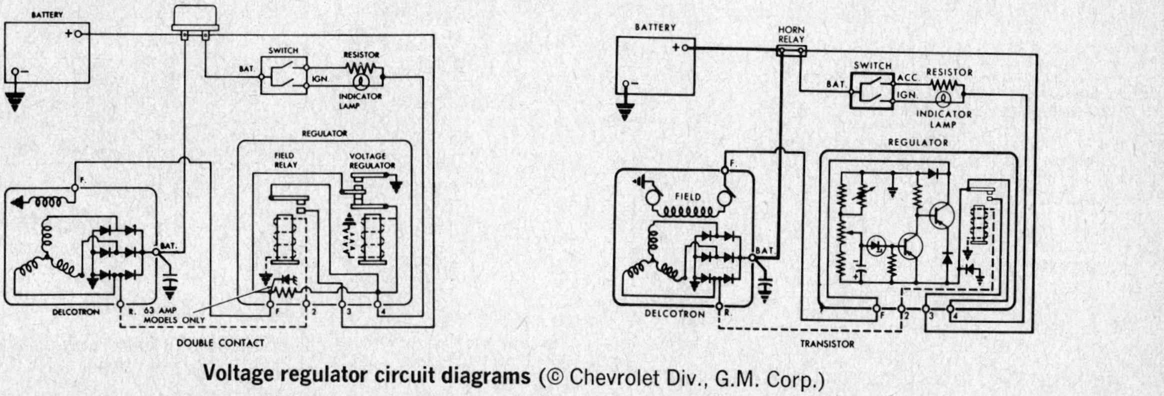

Voltage regulator circuit diagrams (© Chevrolet Div., G.M. Corp.)

wire to the no. 3 wire in the wire harness plug.

2. Connect a voltmeter across the battery terminals, the positive voltmeter lead to the positive battery terminal, and the negative lead to the negative terminal. Record the reading.
3. Start the engine. Do not race the engine.
4. Gradually raise engine speed to 1500-2000 rpm. The reading on the voltmeter should increase one to two volts over the initial reading. If there is no increase in the reading, repair the alternator. If there is an increase in the voltmeter reading, replace the regulator.

Field Relay Test

1. Connect a voltmeter between the No. 2 terminal and the ground on the regulator.
2. Turn ignition switch on; do not start the engine. Voltmeter should read battery voltage.
3. If voltmeter reads zero, check circuit connecting regulator terminal No. 2 and Delcotron R terminal.
4. Start engine and run at 1,500-2,000 rpm. If voltage exceeds closing voltage (field relay), and light remains on, field relay is faulty and must be checked.

Field Relay Adjustment

1. Connect a voltmeter between No. 2 regulator terminal and ground.
2. To adjust, connect a 50 ohm rheostat between wiring harness terminal No. 3 and regulator terminal No. 2, after disconnecting the spade lug on the end of the No. 2 regulator terminal wire. Connect a voltmeter between regulator terminal No. 2 and ground, then turn the resistor to "open" position, turn off ignition switch and slowly decrease resistance until relay closes (noting voltage at this point). Voltage can be adjusted by bending heel iron.

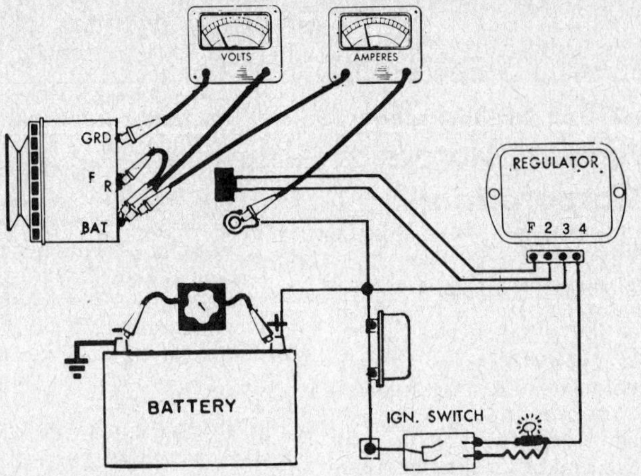

Delcotron output test connections (© Chevrolet Div., G.M. Corp.)

Field Circuit Resistance Testing

The resistance wire is an integral part of the ignition wiring harness. The wire cannot be soldered; any connections must be made using crimp-type connectors. Resistance is 10 ohms, 6¼ watts.

1. Connect a voltmeter between the wiring harness terminal No. 4 and ground.
2. Turn on ignition switch, needle must indicate or resistor is open.

Delcotron Current Output Test

NOTE: disconnect battery ground cable while making test connections, then reconnect cable after completing Step 5. Disconnect battery ground cable again before removing test set-up. This test yields the same information as the isolation test but requires the use of an ammeter and a carbon pile.

1. Disconnect lead from BAT. terminal of Delcotron.
2. Hook an ammeter to the lead just disconnected, and to the BAT. terminal of the Delcotron.
3. Hook up the voltmeter leads to the BAT. terminal and a good ground on the alternator.
4. Disconnect the lead from the FR. terminal of the Delcotron.
5. Hook up a jumper wire between BAT. and F terminals of the Delcotron.
6. With a carbon pile load control hooked up to the battery posts, start the engine and set engine to 1,500 rpm, while adjusting carbon pile to obtain 14 volts. With a 6.2 in. alternator, only 600-800 rpm is required.

CAUTION: Be careful not to exceed the recommended regulator voltage setting. This is controlled by the carbon pile load.

7. Ammeter should read within 10% of rated output, as stamped on frame of each unit.

Alternator Overhaul (5.5 and 6.2 Delcotron)

Disassembly—5.5 Series 1D

1. Remove four bolts.
2. Separate drive end frame and rotor from stator assembly by prying with screwdriver. Note that separation is between stator frame and drive end frame.
3. Place tape over slip ring end frame bearing to seal dirt.
4. Lightly clamp rotor in vise to remove shaft nut.

CAUTION: Do not distort rotor by overtightening vise.

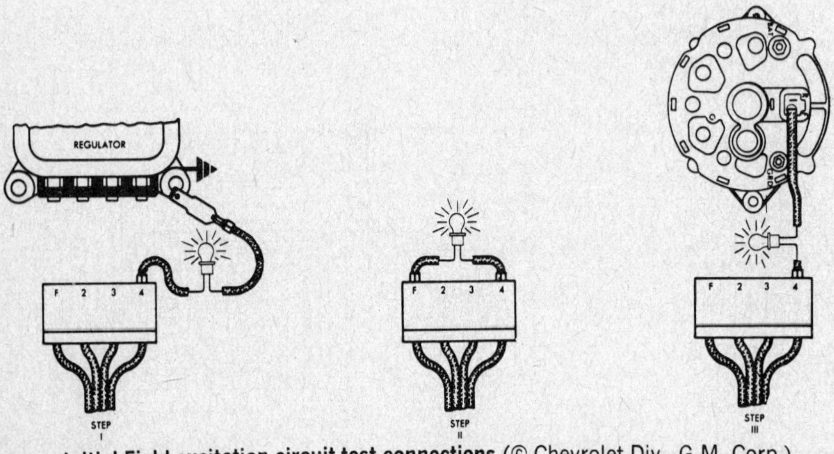

Initial Field excitation circuit test connections (© Chevrolet Div., G.M. Corp.)

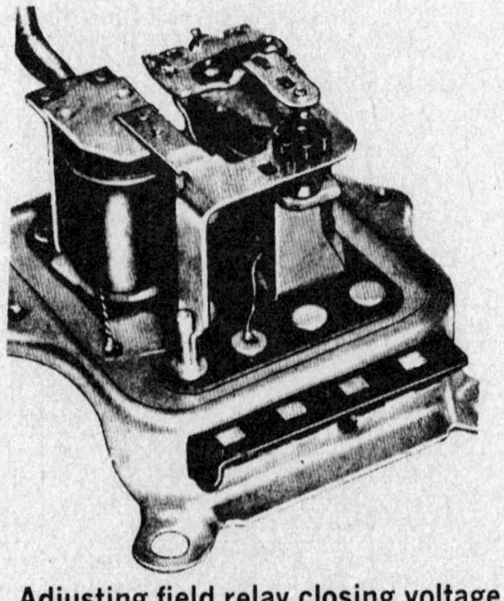

Adjusting field relay closing voltage (© Chevrolet Div., G.M. Corp.)

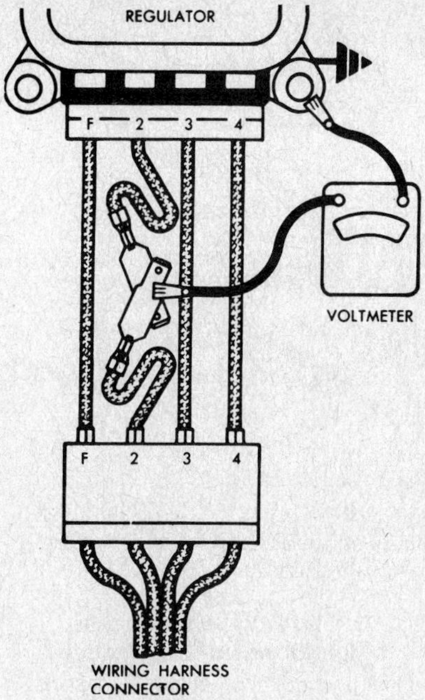

Testing field relay
(© Chevrolet Div., G.M. Corp.)

5. After nut removal, take off washer, pulley, fan and collar.
6. Separate drive end frame from rotor shaft.
7. Remove three stator lead attaching nuts and separate stator from end frame.
8. Remove screws, brushes and holder assembly.
9. Remove BAT., GND., and attaching screw terminals, then remove heat sink.

Disassembly—6.2 Series 2D

1. Clamp drive end mounting flange in a vise, remove the two screws that secure the cover to the brush holder and remove the cover.
2. Remove the nut that holds the indicator light wire to the blade connector post; disconnect wire lead from post.
3. Remove the two screws that hold the condenser and brush holder to rear end frame, then remove brush holder. Allow condenser to remain with alternator.
4. Remove three slip ring end frame bolts and tab nuts, then carefully pry end frame and case apart, working evenly around the circumference.
5. Remove the three drive end frame bolts and tab nuts, then remove end frame, rotor and pulley as an assembly.
6. Remove shaft nut, washer, pulley and Woodruff key from rotor shaft, then slide rotor from end frame.
7. Remove drive end frame bearing retainer plate and bearing from end frame.
8. Bearing can be removed, if necessary, at this time. Use puller to prevent damage.
9. Disconnect the three stator leads by cutting between coils and diodes.

NOTE: diode leads can be cleaned and unsoldered, if proper heat sinks are used to prevent diode damage.

10. Remove heat sink-to-case retaining screws, then remove heat sinks. Insulated heat sink (BATT. terminal) holds positive diode.

Diode Tests

All diodes are marked with either a + or — on the head or are marked with *red* paint for + diodes, *black* paint for — diodes to identify the polarity of the case. On a generator to be used with a negative ground system, the negative case diodes are mounted into the slip ring end frame and the positive case diodes are mounted into the insulated heat sink. Diodes with a negative case have positive polarity leads, whereas positive case diodes have negative polarity leads.

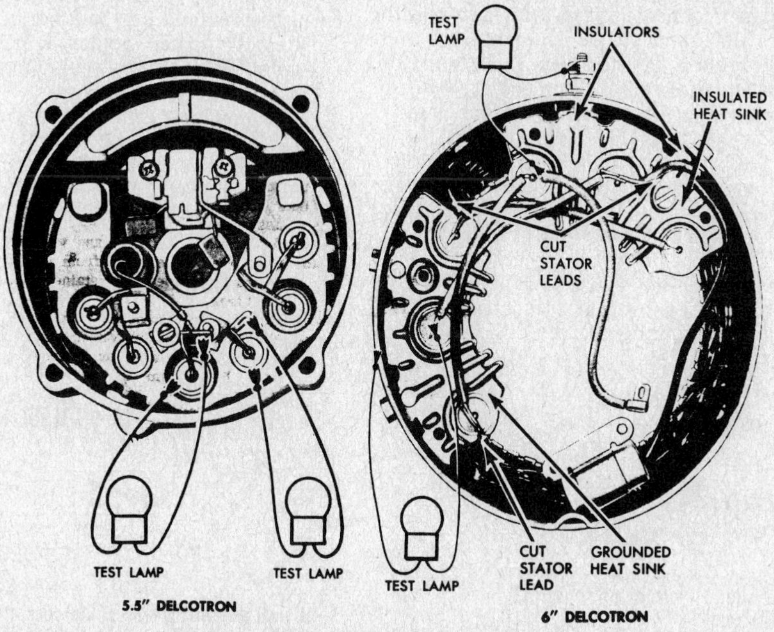

Testing diodes (© Chevrolet Div., G.M. Corp.)

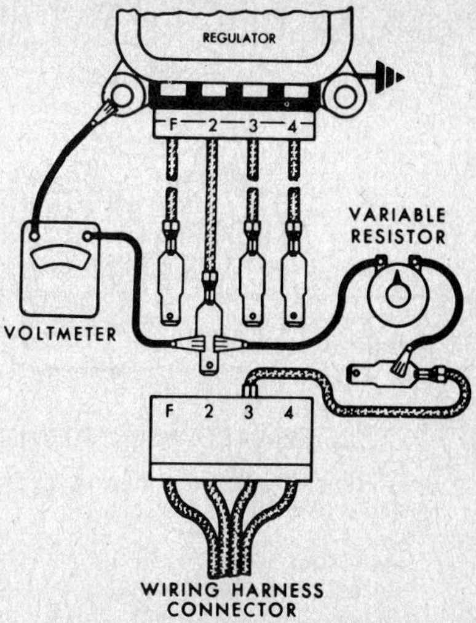

Testing field relay closing voltage
(© Chevrolet Div., G.M. Corp.)

Diodes can be checked for shorts or opens with an ohmmeter.

With the stator leads disconnected, connect one ohmmeter test prod to the diode lead and the other test prod to the heat sink. Reverse the test prods and note the ohmmeter readings. The meter should read high ohms in one direction, low ohms in the other. If both readings are the same, either both high or both low, the diode is faulty and must be replaced. A $1\frac{1}{2}$ volt test light also will indicate a faulty diode. It will light in one direction and not in the other if the diode is good. If it lights in both directions, or in neither direction, the diode is bad.

Diode Replacement

Early Delcotrons had screwed-in diodes, as does the extremely heavy-duty 6.6 Series 4D Delcotron. Models covered here use pressed-in diodes exclusively. If there is any doubt about the year and model of the Delcotron being serviced, not the diode construction—screwed-in diodes have hexagonal heads and the later, pressed-in, units have straight sides with no hex head. Old-style, screwed-in diodes have both right-and left-hand threads. Plus (+) diodes have left-hand and minus (—) have right-hand threads.

5.5 Series 1D

1. Support end frame on a deep socket with a larger inside diameter than the diode outside diameter.
2. Carefully *press* out the diode with a brass drift and an arbor press, or a large bench vise. Be

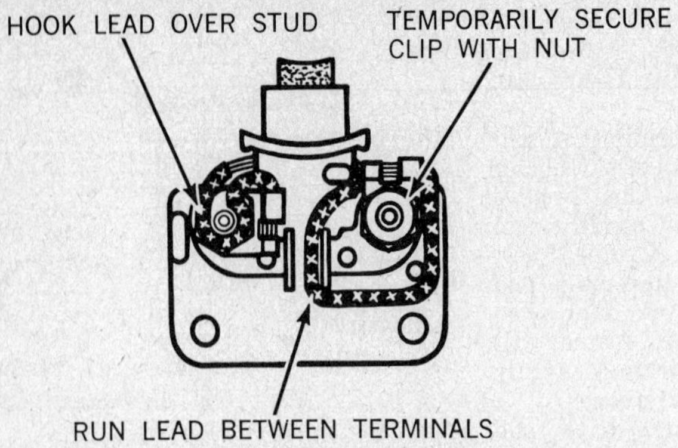

Brush lead arrangement during assembly—6.2 Delcotron
(© Chevrolet Div., G.M. Corp.)

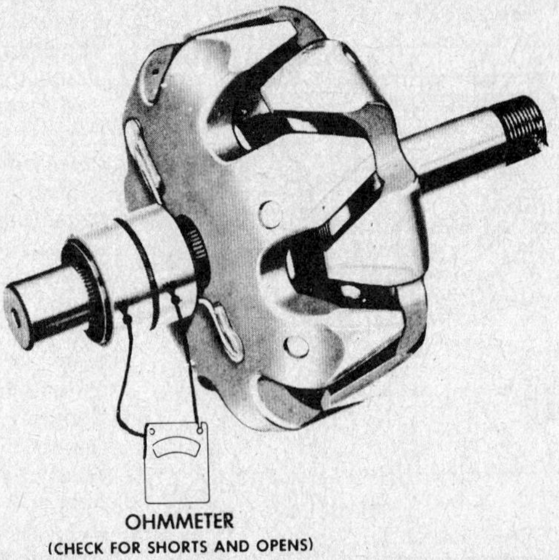

Checking rotor for grounds or open circuits—all Delcotron models (© Chevrolet Div., G.M. Corp.)

extremely careful so as not to distort the end frame.

3. Select a new diode (red or black), noting that the red (+) diodes go into the heat sink and the black (−) diodes into the end frame.
4. Support end frame on a flat, smooth surface around diode hole and carefully *press* the new diode into position. Diode must be square when starting or both diode and frame will be ruined.

6.2 Series 2D

1. Cut leads connected to diode stem as close as possible to stem, then support end frame as for 5.5 Delcotron and press out diode.
2. Select diode with proper color marking (same as for 5.5 Delcotron), then press new diode into position.
3. Scrape enough insulation from diode stem and leads to ensure good contact, then install a sleeve over diode and place the T-clip from diode package over diode stem.
4. Place the flexible lead and stator lead (if applicable) into the T-clip, crimp clip and solder with rosin core solder only, using heat sinks (pliers) to avoid destroying diode.
5. Tape the leads together to prevent vibration damage.

Rotor Checks—All Models

The rotor may be checked electrically for grounded, open, or shorted field coils.

To check for grounds, connect a 110-volt test light from either slip ring to the rotor shaft or to the laminations. If the lamp lights, the field windings are grounded.

To check for opens, connect the leads of a 110-volt test light to each slip ring. If the lamp fails to light, the windings are open.

The windings are checked for short-circuits by connecting a battery and ammeter in series with the two slip rings. Note the ammeter reading.

An ammeter reading greater than that specified indicates shorted windings.

Since the field windings are not serviced separately, the rotor assembly must be replaced if the windings are defective.

Stator Checks—All Models

Stator windings may be checked for grounded, open, or shorted windings. If a 110-volt test lamp lights when connected from any stator lead to the stator frame, the windings are grounded. If the lamp fails to light when successively connected between each pair of stator leads, the windings are open.

A short circuit in the stator windings is difficult to locate without laboratory equipment, due to the low resistance of the windings. However, if all other electrical checks are normal and the generator fails to supply the rated output, shorted stator windings are indicated.

Slip Ring Servicing and Replacement—All Models

Slip rings which are rough or out of round should be trued in a lathe to .001 in. maximum indicator reading. Remove only enough material to make the rings smooth and round. Finish with 400 grit or finer polishing cloth and blow away all dust.

Slip rings which must be replaced can be removed from the shaft with a gear puller, after the leads have been unsoldered. The new assembly should be pressed on with a sleeve which just fits over the shaft; this will apply all the pressure to the inner slip ring collar and prevent damage to the outer slip ring. Only pure tin solder should be used when reconnecting field leads.

Brush Replacement—All Models

The extent of brush wear can be determined by comparison with a new brush. If brushes are one-half worn, they should be replaced.

1. Remove brush holder assembly from end frame by removing two holder assembly screws.
2. Place springs and brushes in the holder and insert straight wire or pin into holes at bottom of holder to retain brushes.
3. Attach holder assembly onto end frame.

Assembly—5.5 Series 1D

1. Install stator assembly into slip ring end frame and locate diode

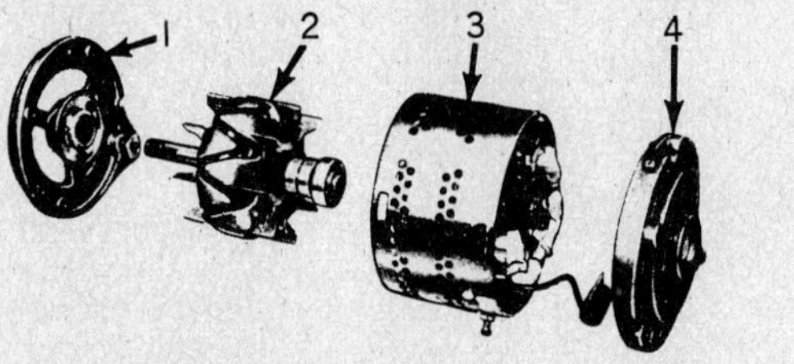

6.2 Delcotron assembly sequence: 1—drive end frame, 2—rotor, 3—stator, 4—end frame
(© Chevrolet Div., G.M. Corp.)

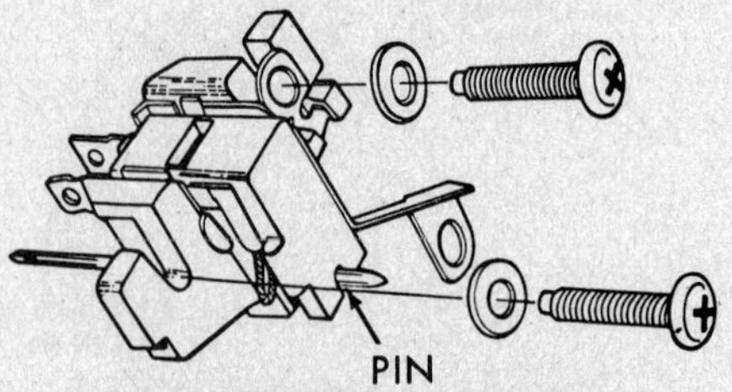

Brush assembly—5.5 Delcotron
(© Chevrolet Div., G.M. Corp.)

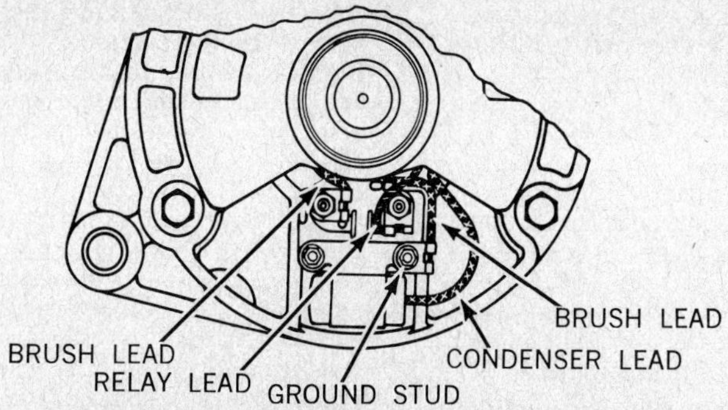

Brush lead arrangement after assembly—6.2 Delcotron
(© Chevrolet Div., G.M. Corp.)

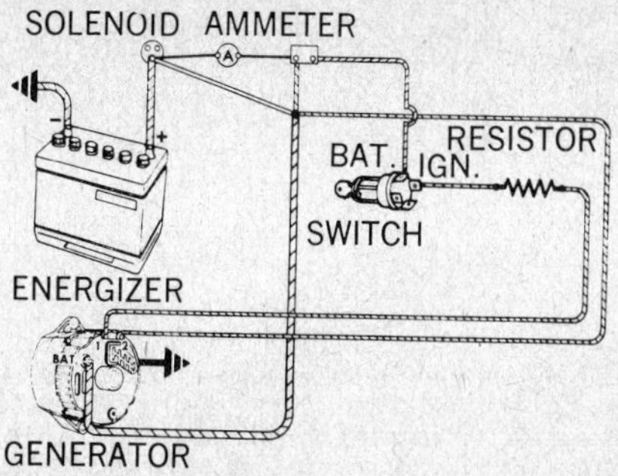

10-S1 Basic wiring diagram (© Chevrolet Div., G.M. Corp.)

connectors over the relay, diode and stator leads. Tighten terminal nuts.

2. Install rotor into drive end frame.
3. Install fan, spacer, pulley washer and nut.
4. Install Allen wrench (5/16 in.) into end of shaft to hold drive shaft, then tighten pulley nut to 40-50 ft. lbs. using a crowsfoot wrench (15/16 in.) and torque wrench.
5. Assemble slip ring end frame and stator assembly to drive end frame and rotor.
6. Install four through bolts and tighten securely.

Assembly—6.2 Series 2D

1. Install stator assembly into slip ring end frame and locate diode connectors over the relay, diode and stator leads. Tighten terminal nuts.
2. Install the front frame over the rotor.
3. Install the front frame over the key, pulley, washer and nut.
4. Clamp pulley in a padded-jaw vise and tighten shaft nut to 50-60 ft. lbs.

CAUTION: Do not clamp rotor, or segments will be distorted.

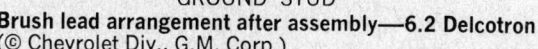

5. Position rotor and drive end frame assembly into slip ring end frame and stator. Install through bolts and tighten securely.
6. Push the brushes into the holder and secure the leads.
7. Attach brush assembly and condenser to the end frame with left-hand hex stud only.
8. Arrange the leads with the right-hand brush lead connected under the right-hand hex stud.
9. Attach terminal cover with two screws, making sure not to pinch the leads.

Delcotron 10-SI Series 100 (General Motors Corp.)

This system is an integrated AC generating system containing a built-in voltage regulator. Removal and replacement is essentially the same as for the standard AC generator.

The regulator is mounted inside the slip ring end frame. All regulator components are enclosed in an epoxy molding, and the regulator cannot be adjusted. Rotor and stator tests are the same as for the 5.5 Delcotron, covered previously.

Troubleshooting

NOTE: see the "Alternator Test Plans" section before proceeding fur-

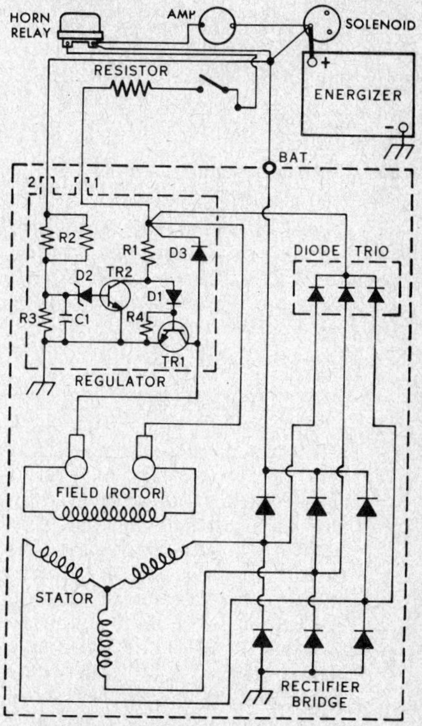

10-S1 charging circuit schematic
(© Chevrolet Div., G.M. Corp.)

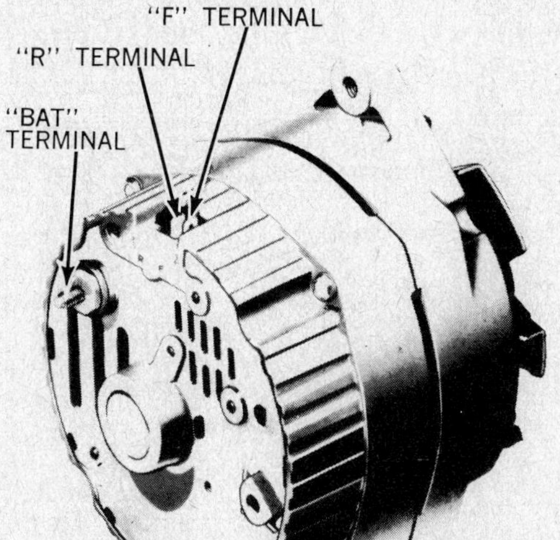

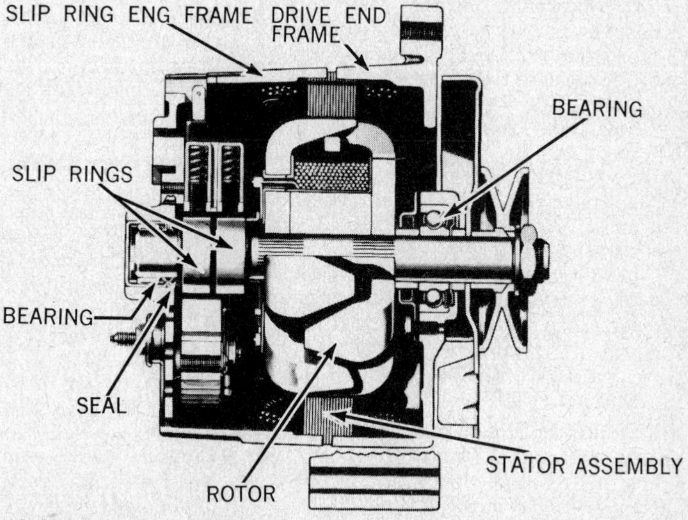

10-S1 Delcotron (© Chevrolet Div., G.M. Corp.)

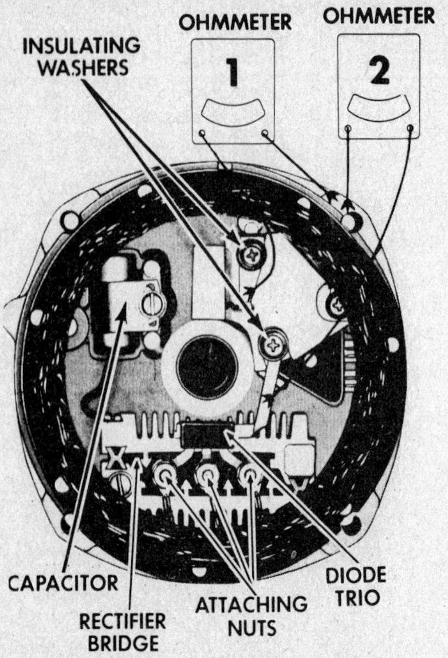

Brush lead clip ground test—10-S1 Delcotron (© Chevrolet Div., G.M. Corp.)

ther. Make sure that the continuous running blower, if equipped, is disconnected. This blower will run with the key on even if the blower control is off, unless disconnected.

Charging System Test—Low Charging Rate

1. After battery condition, drive belt tension, and wiring terminals and connections have been checked, charge the battery fully and perform the following test:
2. Connect a test voltmeter between the alternator BAT. terminal and ground, ignition switch on. Connect the voltmeter in turn to alternator terminals No. 1 and No. 2, the other voltmeter lead being grounded as before. A zero reading indicates an open circuit between the battery and each connection at the alternator. If this test discloses no faults in the wiring, proceed to Step 3.
3. Connect the test voltmeter to the alternator BAT. terminal (the other test lead to ground), start the engine and run at 1,500-2,000 rpm with all lights and electrical accessories turned on. If the voltmeter reads 12.8 volts or greater, the alternator is good and no further checks need be made. If the voltmeter reads less than 12.8 volts, ground the field winding by inserting a screwdriver into the test hole in the end frame.

CAUTION: **Do not force tab more than ¾ in. into end frame.**

a. If voltage increases to 13 volts or more, the regulator unit is defective.
b. If voltage does not increase significantly, alternator is defective.

Alternator Output Test

1. Connect a test voltmeter, ammeter and 10 ohm 6 watt resistor into the charging circuit. Do not connect the carbon pile to the battery posts at this time.
2. Increase alternator speed and observe voltmeter—if voltage is uncontrolled with speed and increases to 16 volts or more, check for a grounded brush lead clip as covered previously. If brush lead clip is not grounded, the voltage regulator is faulty and must be replaced.
3. Connect the carbon pile load to the battery terminals.
4. Operate the alternator at moderate speed and adjust the carbon pile to obtain maximum alternator output as indicated on the ammeter. If output is within 10% of rated output as stamped on the alternator frame, alternator is O.K. If ouput is not within specifications, ground the alternator field by inserting a screwdriver into the test hole in the end frame. If output now is within 10% of rating, replace the voltage regulator; if still not within specifications, check field winding, diode trio, rectifier bridge and stator, as described later. Disassembly of alternator up to and including Step 6 is necessary.

Disassembly and Assembly

1. Place alternator in a vise, clamped by the mounting flange only.
2. Remove the four through bolts and separate the slip ring end frame and stator assembly from the drive end and rotor assembly, using a screwdriver to pry the two sections apart. Use the slots provided for the purpose.
3. Place a piece of tape over the slip ring end frame bearing to prevent entry of dirt; also tape shaft at slip ring end to prevent scratches.
4. Clean brushes, if they are to be reused, with trichloroethylene or carbon tetrachloride solvent. Use these solvents only in an adequately ventilated area.
5. Remove the stator lead nuts and separate the stator from the end frame.
6. Remove the screw that secures the diode trio and remove diode trio.

NOTE: at this point, test the rotor, rectifier bridge, stator and diode trio if these tests are necessary.

7. Remove the rectifier bridge hold-down screw and the BAT. terminal screw, then disconnect condenser lead. Remove rectifier bridge from end frame.
8. Remove the two securing screws and brush holder and regulator assemblies. Note the insulating sleeves over the screws.
9. Remove the retaining screw and condenser from the end frame.
10. Remove the slip ring end frame bearing, if it is to be replaced, using the procedure given later in this section.
11. Remove the pulley nut, washer, pulley, fan and spacer from the rotor shaft, using a 5/16 in. Allen key to hold the shaft while loosening the nut.
12. Remove rotor and spacers from drive end frame assembly.
13. Remove drive end frame bearing retainer plate, screws, plate, bearing, and slinger from end frame, if necessary.
14. To assemble, reverse order of disassembly. Pulley nut must be tightened to 40-50 ft. lbs.

Cleaning and Inspection

1. Clean all metal parts, except stator and rotor assemblies, in solvent.
2. Wipe off bearings and inspect them for pitting or roughness.
3. Inspect rotor slip rings for scoring. They may be cleaned with 400 grit sandpaper (not emery), rotating the rotor to make the rings concentric. Maximum out-of-true is 0.001 in. If slip rings are deeply scored, the entire rotor must be replaced as a unit.
4. Inspect brushes for wear; minimum length is ¼ in.

Charging System Test—High Charging Rate

1. With the battery fully charged,

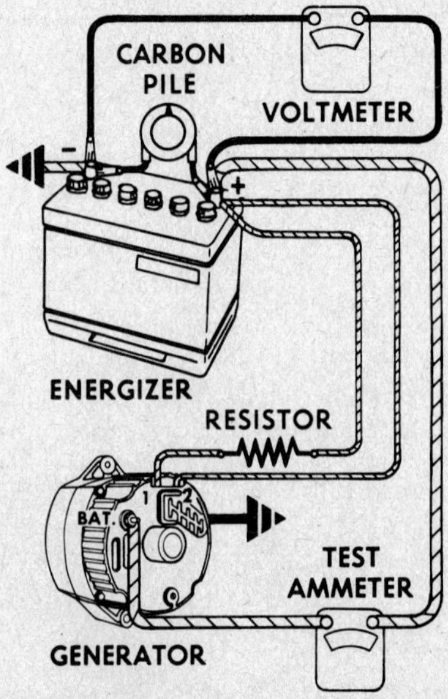

10-S1 Delcotron output test connections (© Chevrolet Div., G.M. Corp.)

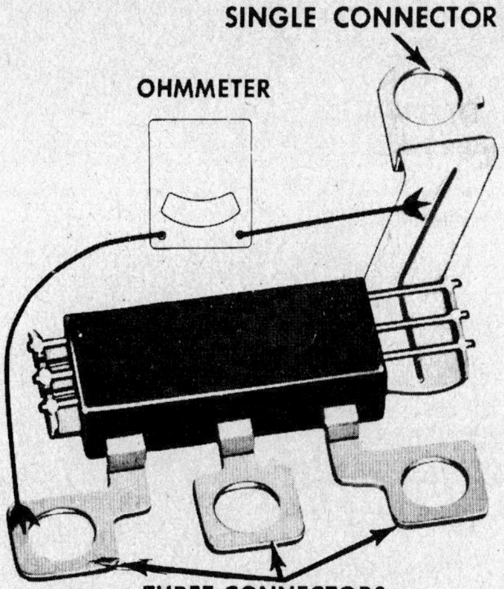

Testing diode trio—10-S1 Delcotron
(© Chevrolet Div., G.M. Corp.)

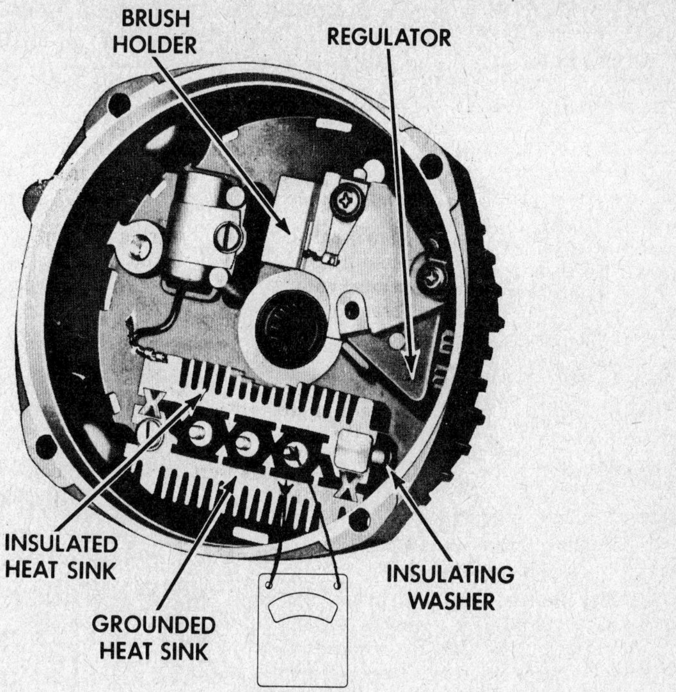

Rectifier Bridge testing—10-S1 Delcotron (© Chevrolet Div., G.M. Corp.)

connect a voltmeter between alternator terminal no. 2 and ground. If the reading is zero, no. 2 circuit from the battery is open.

2. If no. 2 circuit is OK, but an obvious overcharging condition still exists, proceed as follows:
   a. Remove the alternator and separate the end frames.
   b. Connect a low-range ohmmeter between the brush lead clip and the end frame, as illustrated (test no. 1), then reverse the lead connections. If both readings are zero, either the brush lead clip is grounded or the regulator is defective. A grounded brush lead clip can be due to a damaged insulating sleeve or omission of the insulating washer.

Diode Trio Initial Testing

1. Before removing this unit, connect an ohmmeter between the brush lead clip and the end frame. The lowest reading scale should be used for this test.
2. After taking a reading, reverse the lead connections. If the meter reads zero, the brush lead clip is probably grounded, due to omission of the insulating sleeve or insulating washer.

Diode Trio Removal

1. Remove the three nuts which secure the stator.

Brush holder—10-S1 Delcotron
(© Chevrolet Div., G.M. Corp.)

2. Remove stator.
3. Remove the screw which secures the diode trio lead clip, then remove diode trio.

NOTE: The position of the insulating washer on the screw is critical; make sure it is returned to the same position on reassembly.

Diode Trio Testing

1. Connect an ohmmeter, on lowest range, between the single brush connector and one stator lead connector.
2. Observe the reading, then reverse the meter leads. Repeat this test with each of the other two stator lead connectors. The readings on each of these tests should NOT be identical, there should be one low and one high reading for each test. If this is not the case, replace the diode trio.

CAUTION: Do not use high voltage on the diode trio.

Rectifier Bridge Testing

1. Connect an ohmmeter between the heat sink (ground) and the base of one of the three terminals. Then, reverse the meter leads and take a reading. If both readings are identical, the bridge is defective and must be replaced.
2. Repeat this test with the remaining two terminals, then between the INSULATED heat sink (as opposed to the GROUNDED heat sink in previous test) and each of the three terminals. As before, if any two readings are identical, on reversing the meter leads, the rectifier bridge must be replaced.

Rectifier Bridge Removal

1. Remove the attaching screw and the BAT. terminal screw.
2. Disconnect the condenser lead.
3. Remove the rectifier bridge.

NOTE: The insulator between the insulated heat sink and the end frame is extremely important to the operation of the unit. It must be replaced in exactly the same position on reassembly.

Brush and/or Voltage Regulator R & R

1. Remove two brush holder screws and stator lead to strap nut and washer, brush holder screws and one of the diode trio lead strap attaching screws.

NOTE: The insulating washers must be replaced in the same position on reassembly.

2. Remove brush holder and brushes. The voltage regulator may also be removed at this time, if desired.
3. Brushes and brush spring must be free of corrosion and must be undamaged and completely free of oil or grease.
4. Insert spring and brushes into holder, noting whether they slide freely without binding. Insert wooden or plastic toothpick into bottom hole in holder to retain brushes.

NOTE: The brush holder is serviced as a unit; individual parts are not available.

5. Reassemble in reverse order of disassembly.

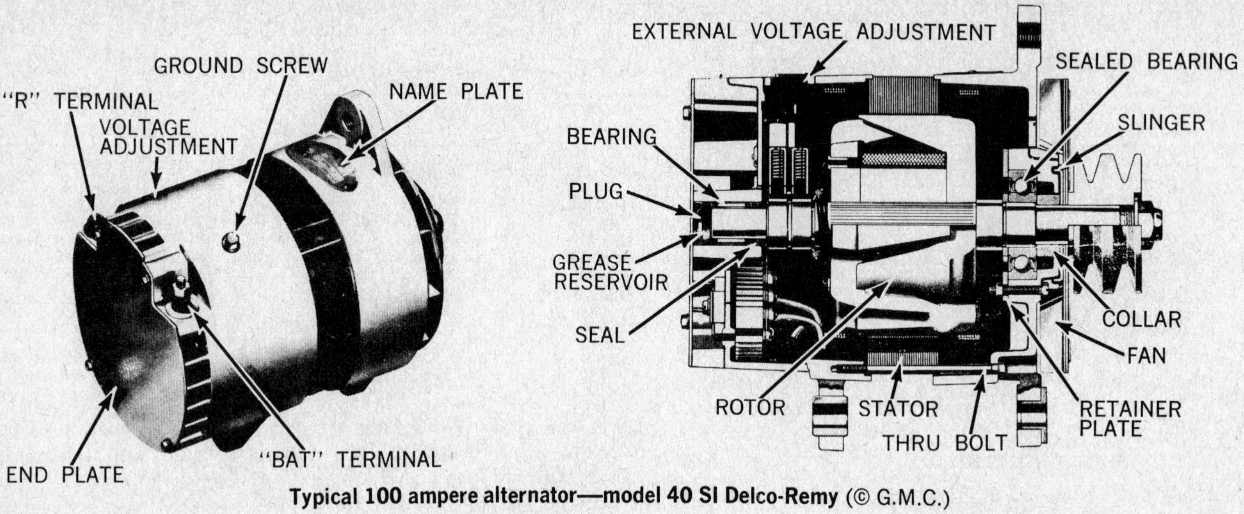

Typical 100 ampere alternator—model 40 SI Delco-Remy (© G.M.C.)

Slip Ring End Frame Bearing and Seal R & R

1. With stator removed, press out bearing and seal, using a socket or similar tool that fits inside the end frame housing. Press from outside to inside, supporting the frame inside with a hollow cylinder (large, deep socket) to allow the seal and bearing to pass.
2. The bearings are sealed for life and permanently lubricated. If a bearing is dry, do not attempt to repack it, as it will throw off the grease and contaminate the inside of the generator.
3. Using a flat plate, press the new bearing from the outside toward the inside. A large vise is a handy press, but care must be exercised so that end frame is not distorted or cracked. Again, use a deep socket to support the inside of the end frame.
4. From inside the end frame, insert seal and press flush with housing.
5. Install stator and reconnect leads.

Alternators 40 SI (100 ampere) 2600 JB (105 ampere) 2700 JB (130 ampere) (General Motors Corp.)

These alternators feature a fully adjustable built-in, solid state voltage regulator and six silicone diodes mounted in heat sinks, to convert the alternating current, produced in the Delta wound stator, to direct current. These units use a capacitor to assist in suppressing transient voltage which could effect diode operation. A diode trio is used to supply field current to the rotor.

Troubleshooting

NOTE: refer to the "Alternator test plans" section before proceeding with any alternator tests. Because of the high output of amperage that can be produced, extreme care must be exercised in the testing and handling of these units.

40 SL Alternator

Charging System Tests—High and Low Rated Output

1. After checking the battery condition drive belt tension, and wiring terminals, charge the battery fully and perform the following tests.
2. Disconnect the negative battery cable and connect an ammeter between the positive battery post and the Battery terminal of the alternator. Connect a voltmeter between the battery terminal of the alternator and to ground. Reconnect the negative battery cable. The voltmeter should register battery voltage.
3. Connect a carbon pile control across the battery posts. Start the engine and operate at approximately 2000 RPMs. Turn on the vehicles' accessories and adjust the carbon pile control to obtain maximum current output.
4. If the amperage reading is within 10% of the rated output, the alternator is not defective. If the amperage is not within

2600 JB and 2700 JB alternators—typical (© Chevrolet Div., G.M. Corp.)

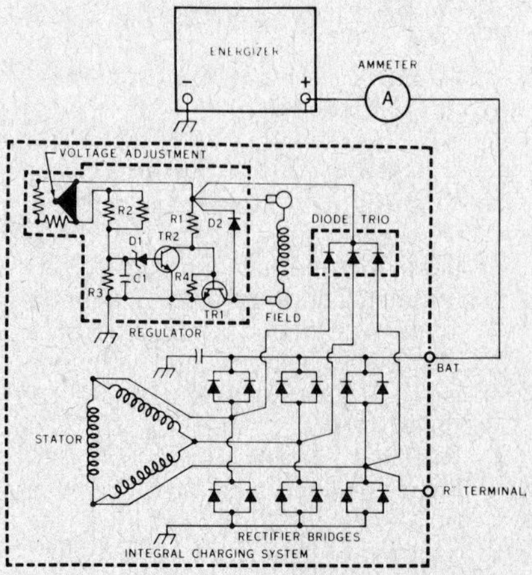

Charging circuit—model 40 SI Delco-Remy (© G.M. Corp.)

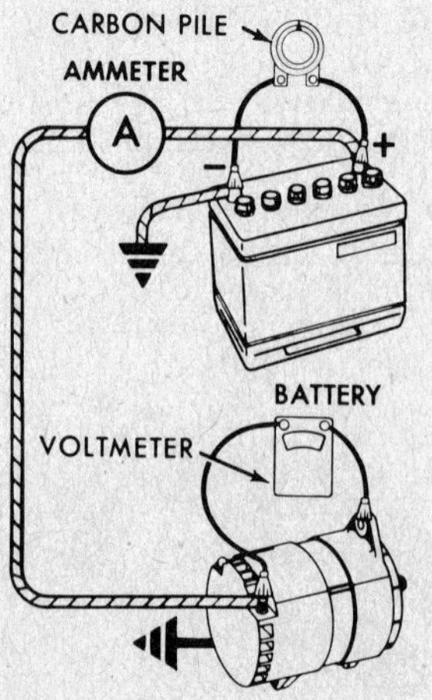

Test connections for 40 SI Delco-Remy (© G.M. Corp.)

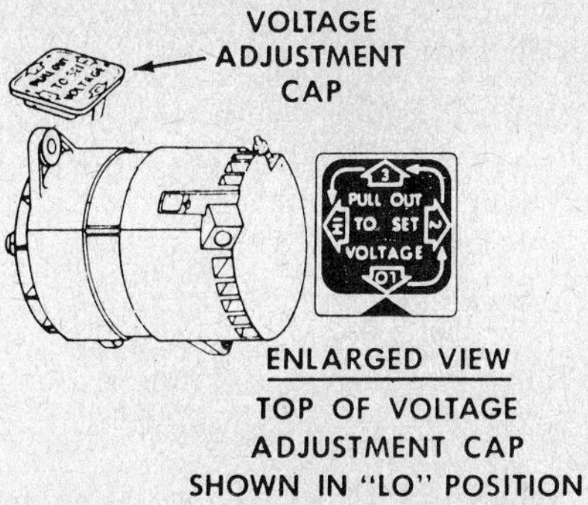

Voltage adjustment cap—model 40 SI Delco-Remy (© G.M. Corp.)

the 10% range, the alternator should be removed for testing and repairs.

NOTE: With the carbon pile control in the off position, and the engine operating at 2000 RPMs, the voltage reading should increase to 15 volts. If needed, the voltage can be adjusted up or down scale by raising the voltage regulator cap and relocating it in one of the new positions, which are indicated by; LO (low), 2 (med. low), 3 (med. high), and HI (high). Recheck the voltage reading after movement of the cap.

Disassembly

1. Remove the cover plate from the rear housing.
2. Remove the pulley nut, pulley, fan, slinger, and spacer collar.
3. Remove the four through bolts. Separate the rear housing from the stator and drive end frame by inserting a screw driver in the stator slots.

NOTE: Expect the brushes to fall from their holders. Do not break them.

4. Disconnect the stator leads from the rectifier bridge and remove the stator from the frame.

Testing

Follow the procedure for testing the diode trio, rectifiers, stator, and rotor as outlined under the 10SL alternator section.

The field current specifications are 4.0 to 4.5 amperes at 12 volts.

Assembly

1. Install brushes into their holders and insert a wire to hold them in place.
2. Assemble the three stator wire leads to the rectifier bridges.
3. Assemble the drive end frame and rotor into the stator and rectifier end frame assembly carefully so as not to damage the seal. Install the four through bolts and tighten.
4. Assemble the collar spacer, slinger, fan, and pulley. While holding the rotor shaft, torque the pully nut to 72 ft. lbs.
5. Relase the brushes by removing the wire from the holder. Install the end plate cover. Rotate the rotor assembly to insure that no windings or wires contact the rotor surface.

2600 JB and 2700 JB Alternators

Charging System Tests

Voltage Regulator Test and Adjustment

1. Connect a voltmeter across the battery. Observe the voltage and start the engine.
2. Increase the engine speed to 1000 to 1500 RPMs and note the voltage reading. An increase to 13.6 to 14.2 volts should occur.
3. If the voltage reading is out of specifications, attempt to bring the voltage within the OK range by rotating the regulator adjusting screw back and forth.
4. If the voltage cannot be lowered by adjustment, the voltage regulator may be defective and should be replaced.
5. If the voltage cannot be raised by the adjustment, the alternator, regulator, or diode trio may be at fault and the alternator must be removed for testing and repairs.

Alternator, Regulator or Diode Trio Fault Determination

1. Connect a voltmeter across the battery and start the engine.
2. Insert a paper clip type wire into the small hole located on the regulator housing, so that it firmly contacts the outer brush holder.
3. Connect a jumper wire from the negative output terminal to the stiff wire inserted in the regulator housing.
4. With the engine operating between 1500 to 2000 RPMs the voltmeter reading should rise above battery voltage. This indicates the alternator is good and the fault lies with the voltage regulator and /or the diode trio.
5. If the voltage reading does not increase above battery voltage, the alternator must be removed for testing and repairs.

Checking Output—Alternate Method

An alternate method used to check current output from each phase is to construct a test lamp from a two filament sealed beam bulb, connected in such a manner that the two filaments are in parallel.

The lamp should light with equal brilliancy when each phase is tested. If a dimmer light is observed between two phases, a defective diode, stator, or power diode is indicated and further testing would have to be done.

NOTE: Point to point resistance checks with an ohmmeter on the circuit board of the voltage regulator can be misleading and inconclusive, due to the circuitry in parallel of the

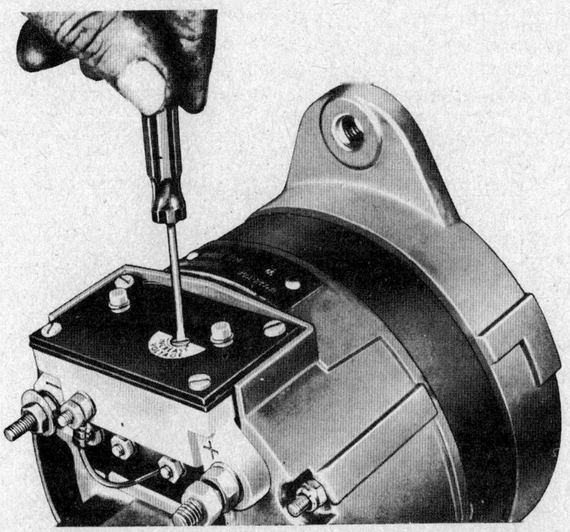

Voltage regulator adjustment (© Chevrolet Div., G.M. Corp.)

Testing alternator with jumper wire (© Chevrolet Div., G.M. Corp.)

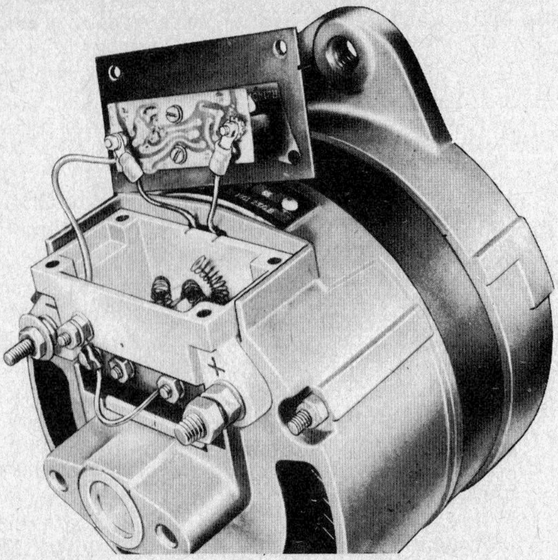

Voltage regulator panel—underside shown (© Chevrolet Div., G.M. Corp.)

Removal of diode trio (© Chevrolet Div., G.M. Corp.)

capacitors, resistors, diodes and transistors. To check a regulator, it is advisable to install it on an alternator known to be good, if possible. If in doubt, replace the regulator with a new unit.

Disassembly

1. Remove the voltage regulator panel from the regulator housing carefully, so as not to loose the brush springs.
2. Remove the red and black wire leads from the regulator panel. Note their positions.
3. Remove the blue lead from the diode trio assembly within the regulator housing and remove the regulator panel.
4. Remove the pulley nut, pulley, fan and spacer. Remove the through bolts and nuts and separate the rear stator housing from the front drive housing assembly.
5. Upon separation, the rotor can be removed from the front housing, and the stator leads removed from the rectifier bridges for further testing of the diodes and the stator windings. The diode trio can be removed from the outside of the regulator housing by the removal of the three retaining nuts.

Testing

Follow the procedure for testing the diode trio, rectifiers, stator, and rotor as outlined under the 10 SI alternator section.

The field current specifications are 2.8 amperes at 12 volts for the 2600 JB alternator, and 5.0 to 6.0 amperes at 12 volts for the 2700 JB alternator.

Assembly

1. Assemble the rotor into the front drive housing.
2. Connect the stator leads to the rectifier bridges and assemble the front drive housing and rotor into the stator and rear housing assembly.
3. Install the three through bolts and nuts and tighten. Rotate the rotor to insure free movement.
4. Install the diode trio to the regulator housing and secure with attaching nuts.
5. Install the brushes and springs. Compress the springs and retain them with a stiff 1/16 inch wire, placed through the hole in the regulator housing.
6. Attach the red and black leads to the regulator panel and position it on the housing and secure it loosely with the four attaching screws.

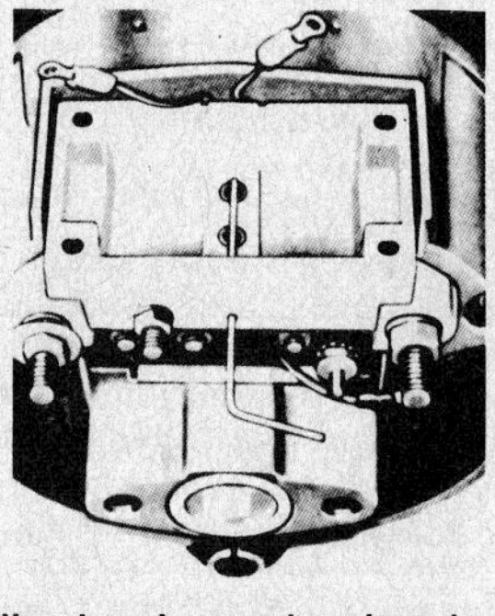

Holding brushes and springs in place with a 1/16 wire tool
(© Chevrolet Div., G.M. Corp.)

7. Remove the wire retainer from the brush springs, and tighten the regulator retaining screws.
8. Attach the blue regulator leads to the diode terminal.
9. Assemble the pulley, fan, and spacer to the rotor shaft. Torque the pulley nut to 70-80 ft. lbs.

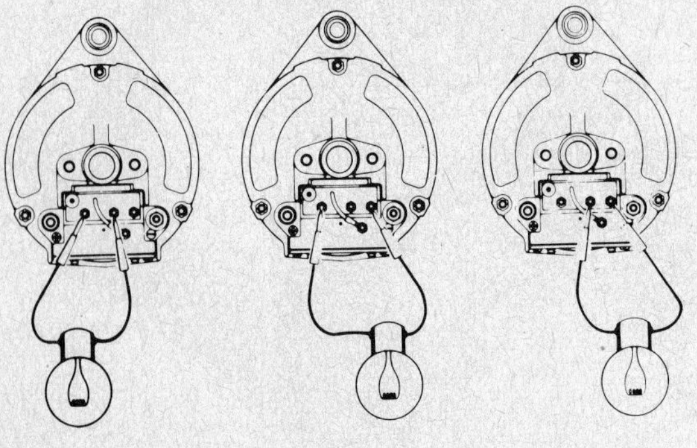

Alternate method of testing alternator output with the use of a test lamp tool (© Chevrolet Div., G.M. Corp.)

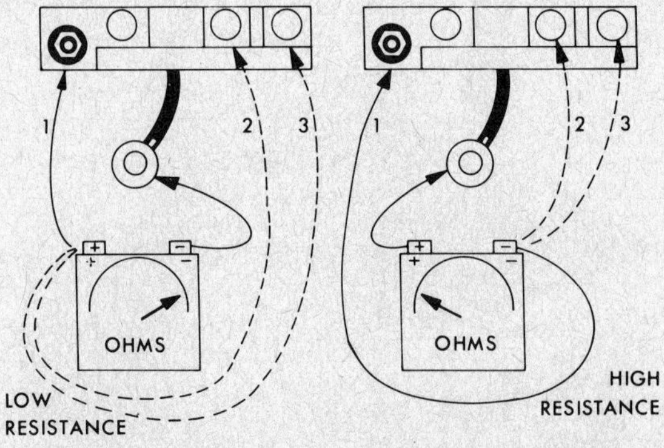

Method of testing diode trio (© Chevrolet Div., G.M. Corp.)

Ford Alternators

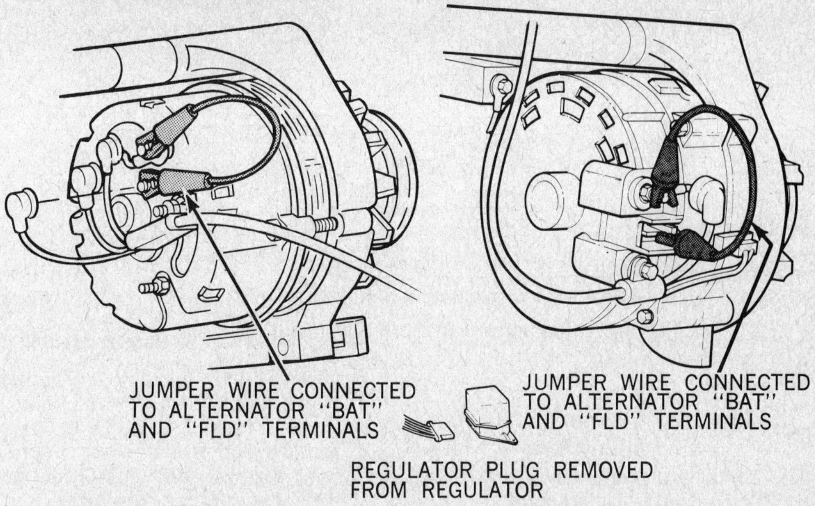

Location of jumper wire for circuit tests—rear and side terminal alternators shown (© Ford Motor Co.)

Ford-Autolite (Ford Motor Co.) with Electro-Mechanical Regulator

The Ford-Autolite charging system is a negative ground system. It includes an alternator, an electro-mechanical regulator, a charge indicator, and a storge battery.

NOTE: Late model Ford systems have replaced the electro-mechanical regulator with either a non-adjustable transistorized regulator or an adjustable transistorized regulator. The adjustable transistorized unit used with high output systems has a single, voltage limit adjusting screw under the cover. Do not use a metal screwdriver for adjustment.

Troubleshooting

NOTE: see the "Alternator Test Plans" section before proceeding further.

Fusible Links

1. Check the fusible link located between the starter relay and the alternator. Replace the link if it is burned or open.

Charging System Operation

NOTE: if the current indicator is to give an accurate reading, the battery cables must be of the same gauge and length as the original equipment.

1. With the engine running, and all electrical systems turned off, place a current indicator over the positive battery cable.
2. If a charge of about 5 amps is recorded, the charging system is working. If a draw of about 5 amps is recorded, the system is not working. The needle moves toward the battery when a charge condition is indicated, and away from the battery when a draw condition is indicated. If a draw is indicated, continue to the next testing procedure. If an overcharge of 10-15 amps is indicated, check for a faulty regulator or a bad ground at the regulator or the alternator.

Testing the Ignition Switch to Regulator Circuit

1. Disconnect the regulator wiring harness from the regulator.
2. Turn on the key. Using a test light or voltmeter, check for voltage between the I wire and ground. Check for voltage between the A wire and ground. If voltage is present at this part of the system, the circuit is OK. If there is no voltage at the I wire, check for a burned-out charge indicator bulb, a burned-out resistor, or a break or short in the wiring. If there is no voltage present at the A wire, check for a bad connection at the starter relay or a break or short in the wire.

Isolation Test

This test determines whether the regulator or the alternator is faulty, after the rest of the circuit is found to be in good working order.

1. Disconnect the regulator wiring harness from the regulator.
2. Connect a jumper wire from the A wire to the F wire in the wiring harness plug.
3. Connect a voltmeter to the battery. The positive voltmeter lead goes to the positive terminal and the negative lead to the negative terminal. Record the reading on the voltmeter.
4. Turn off all of the electrical systems and start the engine. Do not race the engine.
5. Gradually increase engine speed to 1500-2000 rpm. The voltmeter reading should increase above the previously recorded battery voltage reading by at least one to two volts. If there is no increase, the alternator is not working correctly. If there is an increase, the voltage regulator needs to be replaced.

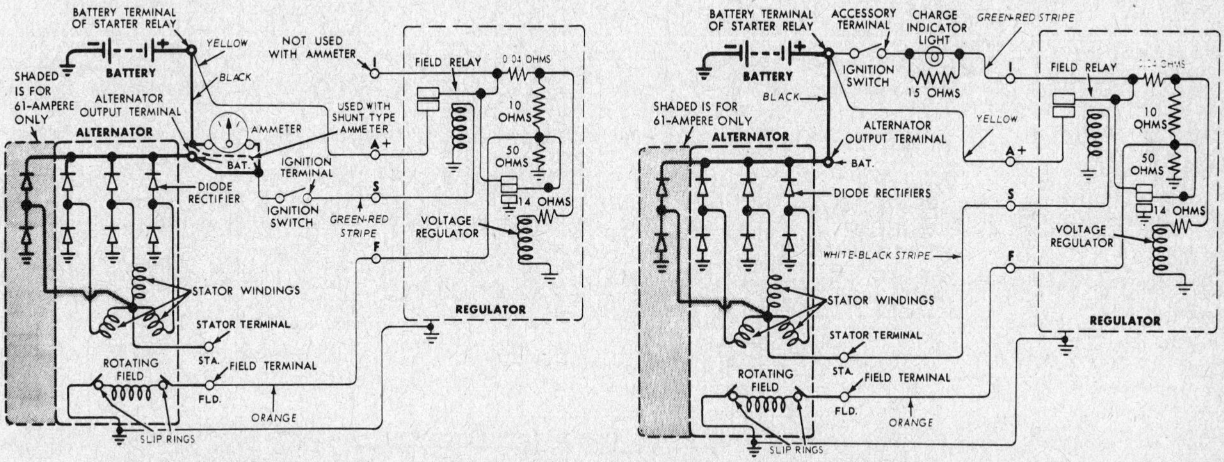

Charging system schematic with electro-mechanical regulator and charging light (© Ford Motor Co.)

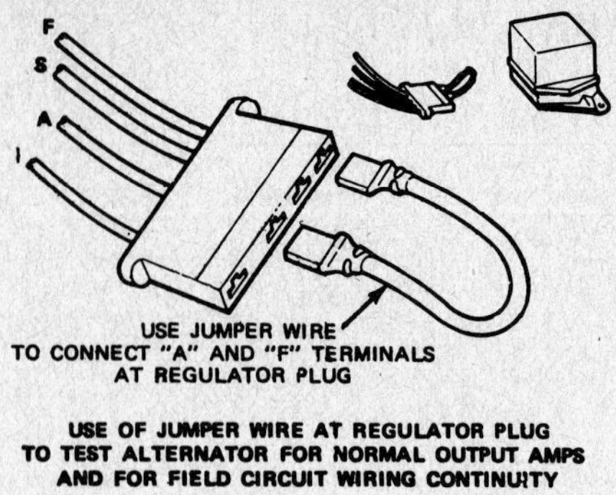

Isolation test jumper wire (© Ford Motor Co.)

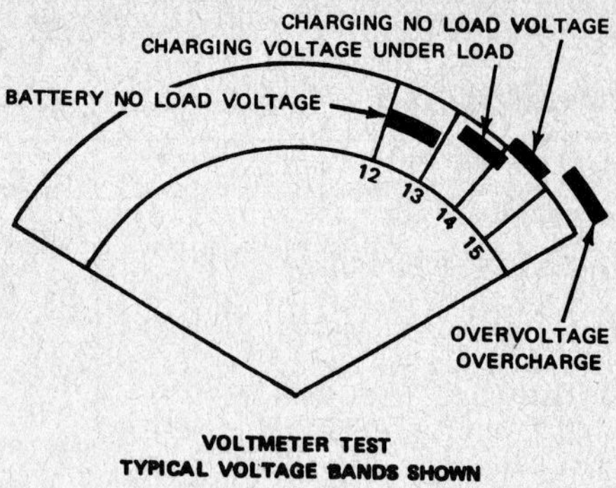

Voltmeter reading during isolation test (© Ford Motor Co.)

Overhaul

Disassembly—Except 65, 70, 90 Amp Alternators

1. Mark both end housings with a scribe mark for assembly.
2. Remove the three housing through bolts.
3. Separate the front housing and rotor from the stator and rear housing.
4. Remove the nuts from the rectifier to rear housing mounting studs, and remove the rear housing.
5. Remove the brush holder mounting screws and the holder, brushes, springs, insulator, and terminal.
6. If replacement is necessary, press the bearing from the rear end housing, support housing on inner boss.
7. If rectifiers are to be replaced, carefully unsolder the leads from the terminals.

CAUTION: Use only a 100-watt soldering iron. Leave the soldering iron in contact with the diode terminals only long enough to remove the wires. Use pliers as temporary heat sinks in order to protect the diodes.

8. There are various types of rectifier assembly circuit boards installed in production. One type has the circuit board spaced

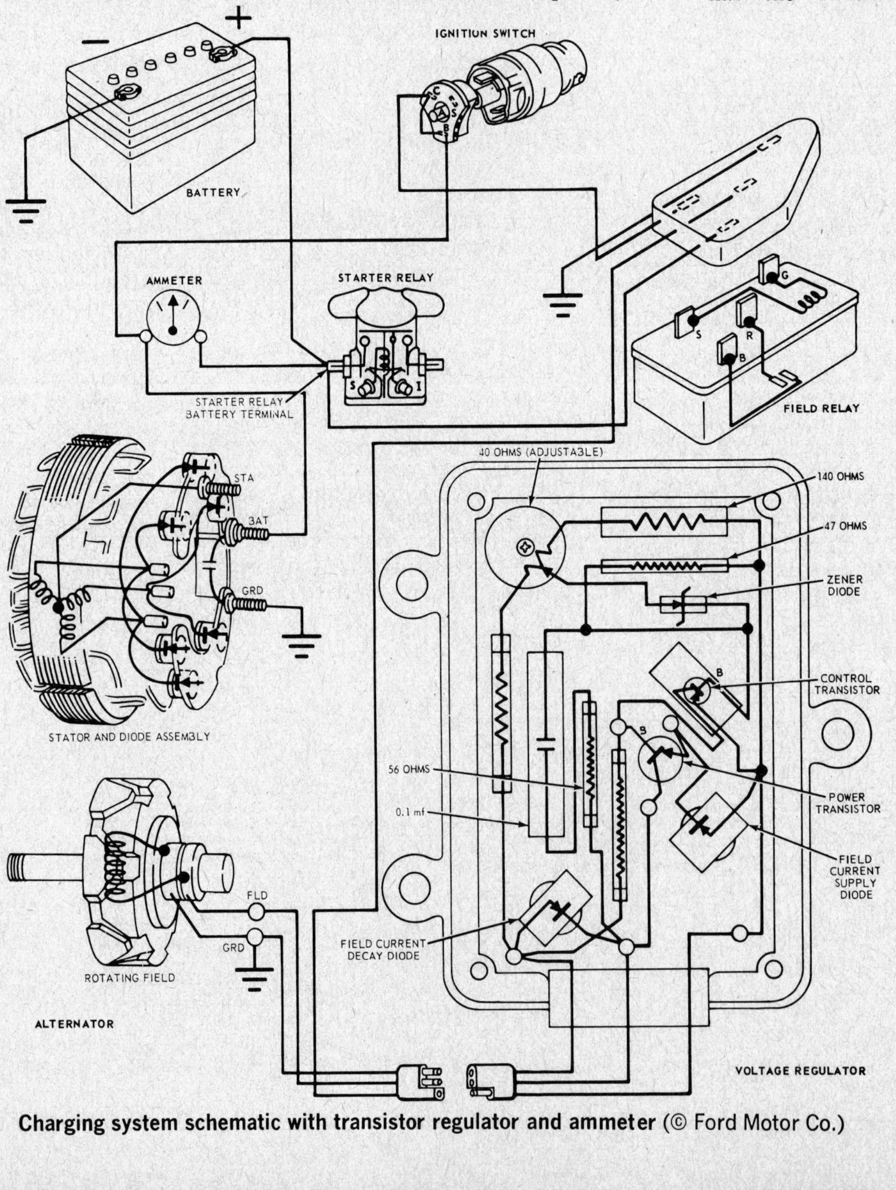

Charging system schematic with transistor regulator and ammeter (© Ford Motor Co.)

away from the diode plates and the diodes are exposed. Another type consists of a single circuit board with integral diodes; and still another has integral diodes with an additional booster diode plate containing two diodes. This last type is used only on the eight-diode, 61-amp. Autolite alternator. To disassemble, use the following procedures:

a. Exposed Diodes—remove the screws from the rectifier by rotating bolt heads ¼ turn clockwise to unlock, then unscrewing.
b. Integral Diodes—press out the stator terminal screw, making sure not to twist it while doing this. Do not remove grounded screw.
c. Booster Diodes—press out the stator terminal screw about ¼ in., then remove the nut from the end of the screw and lift screw from circuit board, making sure not to twist it as it comes out.

9. Remove the drive pulley and fan. On alternator pulleys with threaded holes in the outer end of the pulley, use a standard puller for removal.
10. Remove the three screws that hold the front bearing retainer, and remove the front housing.
11. If the bearing is to be replaced, press from housing.

Cleaning and Inspection

1. The rotor, stator, diode rectifier assemblies, and bearings are not to be cleaned with solvent. These parts are to be wiped off with a clean cloth. Cleaning solvent may cause damage to the electrical parts or contaminate the bearing internal lubricant. Wash all other parts in solvent and dry them.
2. Rotate the front bearing on the driveshaft. Check for any scraping noise, looseness or roughness that indicates that the bearing is excessively worn. As the bearing is being rotated, look for excessive lubricant leakage. If any of these conditions exist, replace the bearing. Check rear bearing and rotor shaft.
3. Place the rear end housing on the slip ring end of the shaft and rotate the bearing on the shaft. Make a similar check for noise, looseness or roughness. Inspect the rollers and cage for damage. Replace the bearing if these conditions exist, or if the lubricant is missing or contaminated.
4. Check both the front and rear housings for cracks.
5. Check all wire leads on both the stator and rotor assemblies for loose soldered connections, and for burned insulation. Solder all poor connections. Replace parts that show burned insulation.
6. Check the slip rings for damaged insulation and runout. If the slip rings are more than 0.0005 in. out of round, take a light cut (minimum diameter limit 1.22 in.) from the face of the rings to true them. If the slip rings are badly damaged, the entire rotor will have to be replaced, as they are serviced as a complete assembly.
7. Replace any parts that are burned or cracked. Replace brushes that are worn to less than 5/16 in. in length. Replace the brush spring if it had less than 7-12 oz. tension.

Field Current Draw Test

NOTE: alternator must be removed from the truck.

1. Connect a test ammeter between the alternator frame and the positive post of a 12-volt test battery.
2. Connect a jumper wire between the negative test battery post and the alternator field terminal.
3. Observe the ammeter:
   a. Little or no current flow indicates high brush resistance, open field windings, or high winding resistance.
   b. Current in excess of specifications (approximately 2.9 amps. for most models) indicates shorted or grounded field windings, or brush leads touching.

NOTE: sometimes the alternator produces current output at low engine speeds, but ceases to put out at higher speeds. This can be caused by certrifugal force expanding the rotor windings to the point where they short to ground. Place in a test stand and check field current draw while spinning alternator.

Diode Tests

Disassemble the alternator. Disconnect diode assembly from stator and make tests. To test one set of diodes, contact one ohmmeter probe to the diode plate and contact each of the three stator lead terminals with the

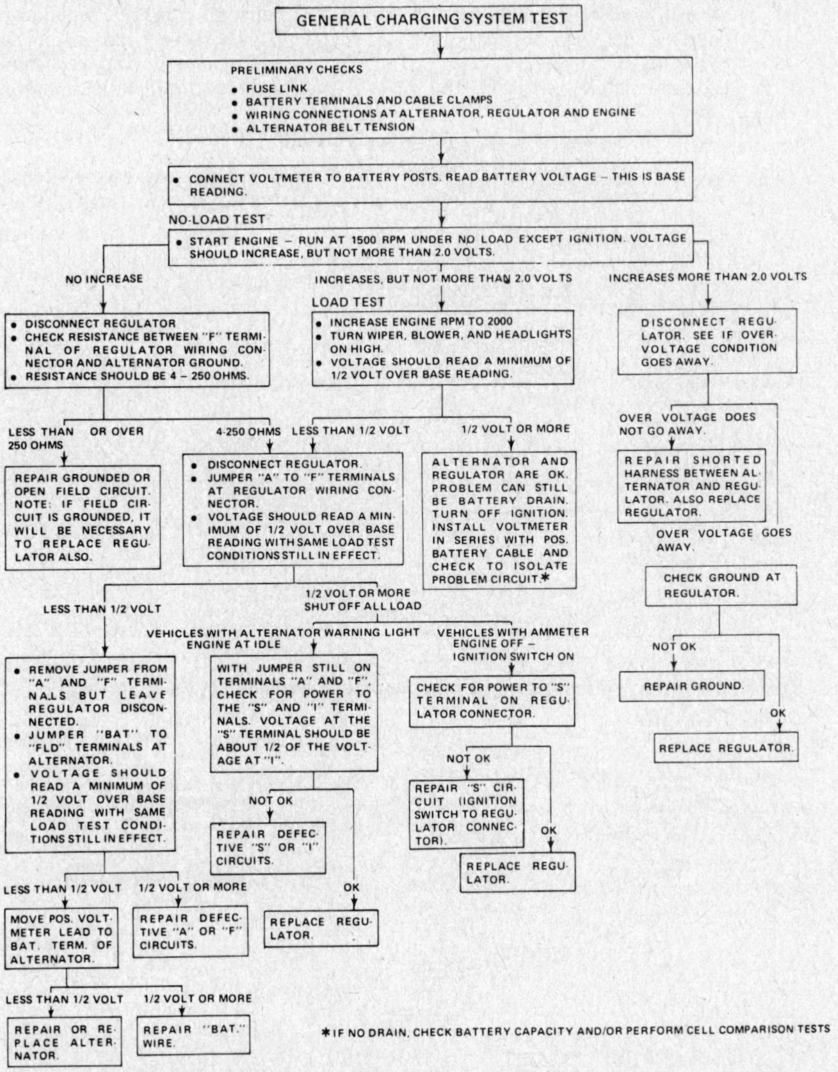

General charging system tests—with ohmmeter and voltmeter (© Ford Motor Co.)

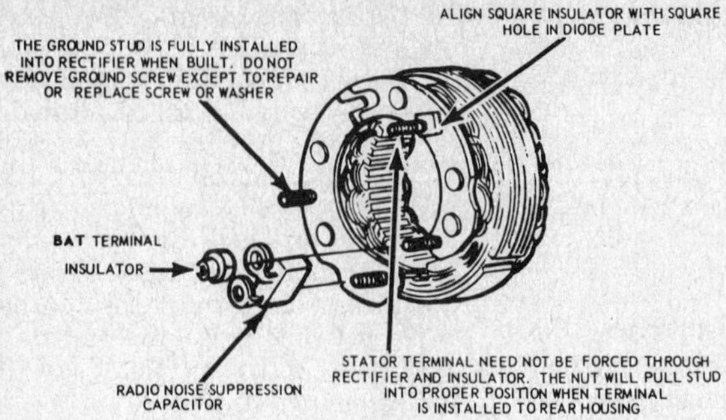

Terminal insulators—fiber circuit board (© Ford Motor Co.)

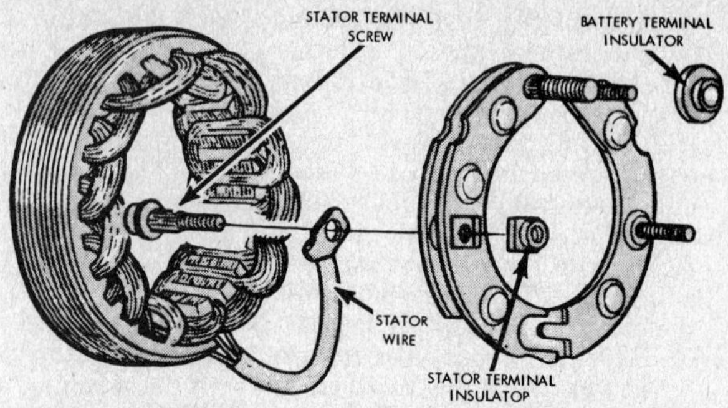

Stator and rectifier assembly—61 amp. booster diode model (© Ford Motor Co.)

other probe. Reverse the probes and repeat the test. All six tests (eight for 61 amp. Autolite eight-diode models) should show a reading of about 60 ohms in one direction and infinite ohms in the other. If two high readings, or two low readings, are obtained after reversing probes the diode is faulty and must be replaced.

Stator Tests

Disassemble the stator from the alternator assembly and rectifiers. Connect test ohmmeter probes between each pair of stator leads. If the ohmmeter does not indicate equally between each pair of leads, the stator coil is open and must be replaced.

Connect test ohmmeter probes between one of the stator leads and the stator core. The ohmmeter should not show any reading. If it does show continuity, the stator winding is grounded and must be replaced.

Assembly—Except 65, 70, 90 Amp Alternators

1. Press the front bearing into the front housing boss, putting pressure on outer race only. Install bearing retainer.
2. If the stop ring on the driveshaft was damaged, install a new stop ring. Push the new ring onto the shaft and into the groove.
3. Position the front bearing spacer on the driveshaft against the stop ring.
4. Place the front housing over the shaft, with the bearing positioned in the front housing cavity.
5. Install fan spacer, fan, pulley, lockwasher and retaining nut and tighten nut to 60-100 ft. lbs. holding the drive shaft with an Allen key.
6. If rear bearing was removed, press a new one into rear housing.
7. Assemble brushes, springs, terminal and insulator in the brush holder, retract the brushes and insert a short length of 1/8 in. rod or stiff wire through the hole in the holder to hold the brushes in the retracted position.
8. Position the brush holder assembly in the rear housing and install mounting screws. Position brush leads to prevent shorting.
9. Wrap the three stator winding leads around the circuit board terminals and solder them using only rosin core solder and a 100-watt iron. Position the stator neutral lead eyelet on the stator terminal screw and install the screw in the rectifier assembly.
10. A. Exposed Diodes—insert the special screws through the wire lug, dished washers and circuit board. Turn 1/4 turn counterclockwise to lock in place.

    B. Integral Diodes—insert the screws straight through the holes.

    NOTE: the dished washers are to be used on the molded circuit boards only. Using these washers on a fiber board will result in a serious short circuit, as only a flat insulating washer between the stator terminal and the board is used on fiber circuit boards.

    C. Booster Diodes—position the stator wire terminal on the stator terminal screw, then position screw on rectifier. Position square insulator over the screw and into the square hole in the rectifier, rotate terminal screw until it

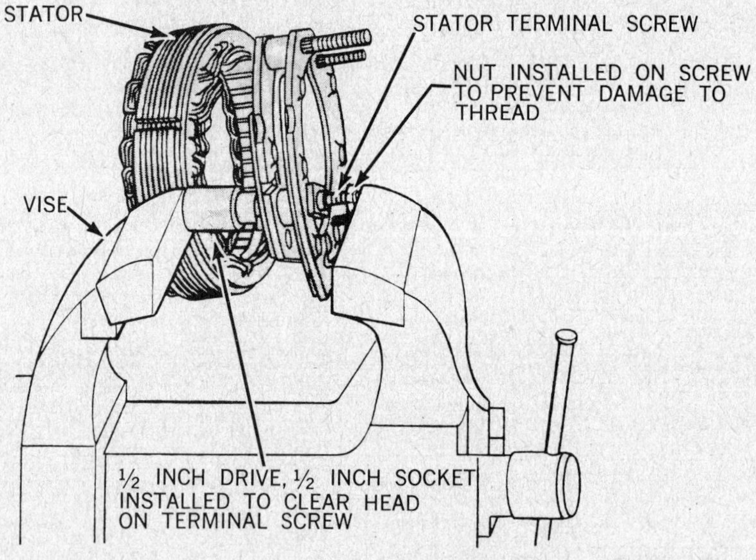

Stator terminal screw removal—61 amp. booster diode model (© Ford Motor Co.)

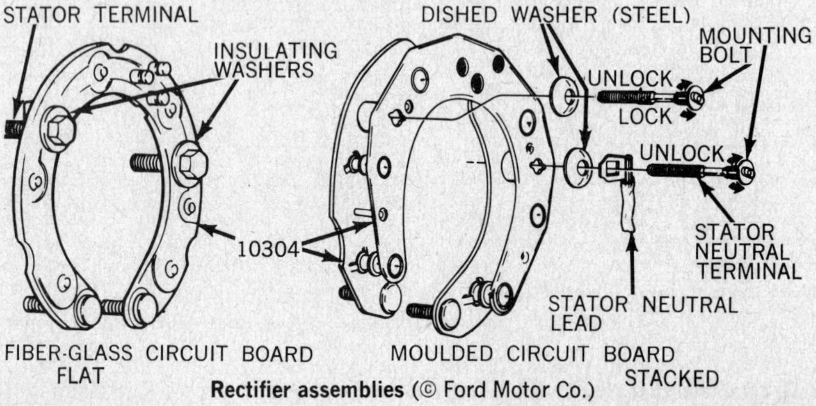

Rectifier assemblies (© Ford Motor Co.)

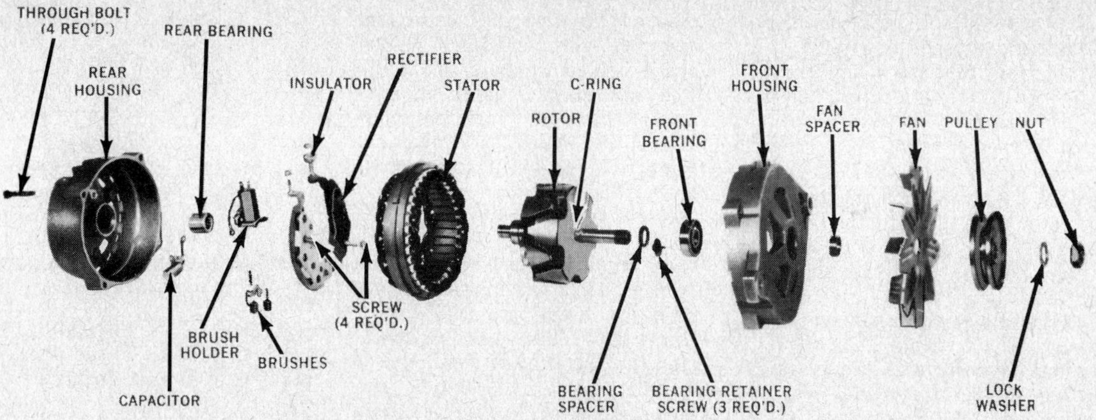

Exploded view—side terminal alternator (© Ford Motor Co.)

locks, then press it in finger-tight. Position the stator wire, then press the terminal screw into the rectifier and insulator with a vise.

11. Place the radio noise suppression condenser on the rectifier terminals. With molded circuit board, install the STA and BAT terminal insulators. With fiber circuit board, place the square stator terminal insulator in the square hole in the rectifier assembly, then position BAT terminal insulator.

    Position the stator and rectifier assembly in the rear housing, making sure that all terminal insulators are seated properly in the recesses. Position STA, BAT and FLD insulators on terminal bolts; install nuts.
12. Clean the rear bearing surface of the rotor shaft with a rag, then position rear housing and stator assembly over rotor. Align matchmarks made during disassembly and install through bolts. *Remove brush retracting wire and place a dab of silicone sealer over the hole.*

Disassembly (typical) 65, 70, 90 Ampere Alternators

NOTE: When disassembling the side terminal alternator, the brush holder would be removed after the rectifier is removed. During the assembly, the brush holder would be installed in the reverse order.

1. Remove the brush holder and cover assembly from the rear housing.
2. Mark both end housings and the stator.
3. Remove the three housing through bolts.
4. Separate the front housing and rotor from the stator and rear housing.
5. Remove the drive pulley nut, lockwasher, flat washer, pulley, fan, fan spacer and rotor from the front housing.
6. Remove the three screws that hold the front bearing retainer and remove the retainer. If the bearing is damaged or has lost its lubricant, support the housing close to the bearing boss and press out the bearing.
7. Remove all the nut and washer assemblies and insulators from the rear housing and remove the rear housing from the stator and rectifier assembly.
8. If necessary, press the rear bearing from the housing, supporting the housing on the inner boss.
9. Unsolder the three stator leads from the rectifier assembly, and separate the stator from the assembly. Use a 200-watt soldering iron.
10. Perform a diode test and an open and grounded stator coil test.

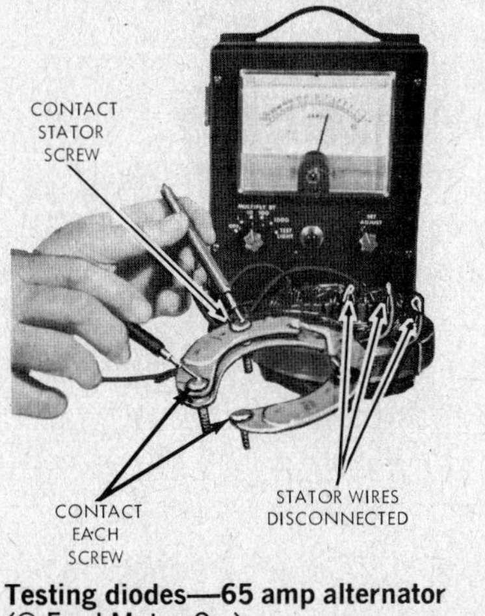

Testing diodes—65 amp alternator (© Ford Motor Co.)

Cleaning and Inspection

Nicks and scratches may be removed from the rotor slip rings by turning down the slip rings. Do not go beyond the minimum diameter limit of 1.22 in. If the slip rings are badly damaged, the entire rotor must be replaced. The rectifier also is serviced as an assembly. See Lower Ampere Alternator Section for test procedures.

Assembly—65, 70, 90 AMP

1. If the front bearing is being replaced, press the new bearing into the bearing boss, putting pressure on the outer race only. Install the bearing retainer and tighten the retainer screws until the tips of the retainer touch the housing.
2. Position the rectifier assembly to the stator, wrap the three stator leads around the diode plate terminals and solder them using a 200-watt soldering iron.
3. If the rear housing bearing was removed, press in a new bearing from the inside of the housing, putting pressure on the outer race only.
4. Install the BAT-GRD insulator, and position the stator and rectifier assembly in the rear housing.
5. Install the STA (purple) and BAT (red) terminal insulators

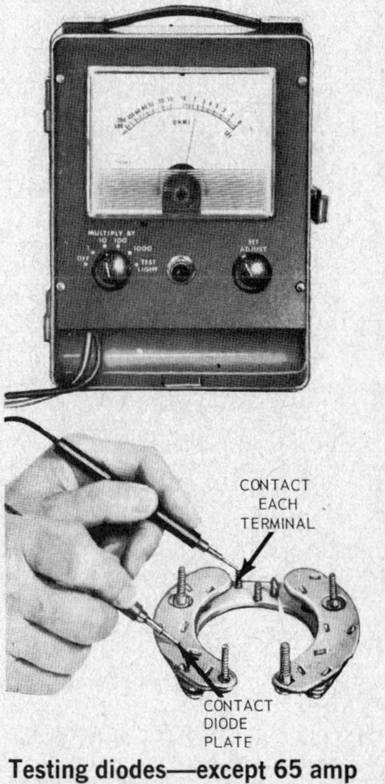

Testing diodes—except 65 amp alternator (© Ford Motor Co.)

on the terminal bolts and install the nut and washer assemblies. *Make certain that the shoulders on all insulators, both inside and outside of the housing, are seated properly before tightening the nuts.*

6. Position the front housing over the rotor and install the fan spacer, fan, pulley, flat and lockwasher and nut on the rotor shaft.
7. Wipe the rear bearing surface of the rotor shaft with a clean rag.
8. Position the rotor with the front housing into the stator and near housing assembly, and align the matchmarks made during disassembly. Seat the machined portion of the stator core into the step in both housings and install the through bolts.
9. If the field brushes have worn to less than 3/8 in., replace both brushes. Hold the brushes in position by inserting a stiff wire into the brush holder.
10. Position the brush holder assembly into the rear housing and install the three mounting screws. Remove the brush retracting wire and put a dab of silicone cement over the hole.

Brush Replacement—65, 70, 90 AMP

1. Remove the brush holder and cover assembly from the rear housing.
2. Remove the terminal bolts from the brush holder and cover assembly, then remove the brush assemblies.
3. Position the new brush terminals on the terminal bolts and assemble the terminals, bolts, brush holder washers and nuts. The insulating washer mounts under the FLD terminal nut. The entire brush and cover assembly also is available for service.
4. Depress the brush springs in the brush holder cavities and insert the brushes on top of the springs. Hold the brushes in position by inserting a stiff wire in the brush holder as shown. Position the brush leads as shown.
5. Install the brush holder and cover assembly into the rear housing. Remove the brush retracting wire and put a dab of silicone cement over the hole.

Autolite Alternator with Integral Regulator

Description

Some vehicles are equipped with an Autolite alternator having an integral regulator mounted to the rear end housing. The regulator is a hybrid unit featuring use of solid state integrated circuits. These circuits may consist of transistors, diodes and resistors. The unusual feature of this type of micro-electronic circuit is that the entire circuit is within a silicone crystal approximately 1/8 in. square. Because of the small size of the circuit, it is not repairable or adjustable and must be replaced as a unit if found to be defective. It should be noted that the size of the regulator housing is dictated only by the fact that some means of connecting the regulator to the alternator is necessary. Overhaul is the same as for other Autolite alternators.

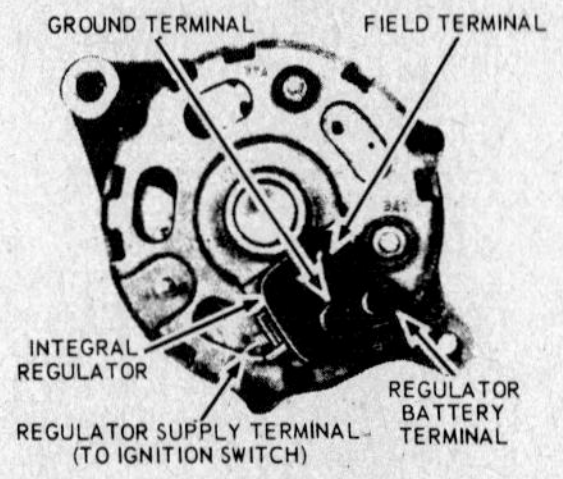

Alternator with integral regulator (© Ford Motor Co.)

Troubleshooting

NOTE: see the "Alternator Test Plans" section before proceeding further.

Fusible Links

1. Check the fusible link located between the starter relay and the alternator. Replace the link if it is burned or open.

Output Test

1. Place transmission in Neutral or Park.
2. Remove the positive battery cable and install a battery adapter switch in the line.
3. Attach one lead of a test voltmeter to the negative battery post and the other test lead to the circuit side of the adapter switch.
4. Connect a test ammeter to each side of the adapter switch, so that charging current will go through the ammeter when the switch is opened.
5. Connect a jumper wire between the alternator frame and the in-

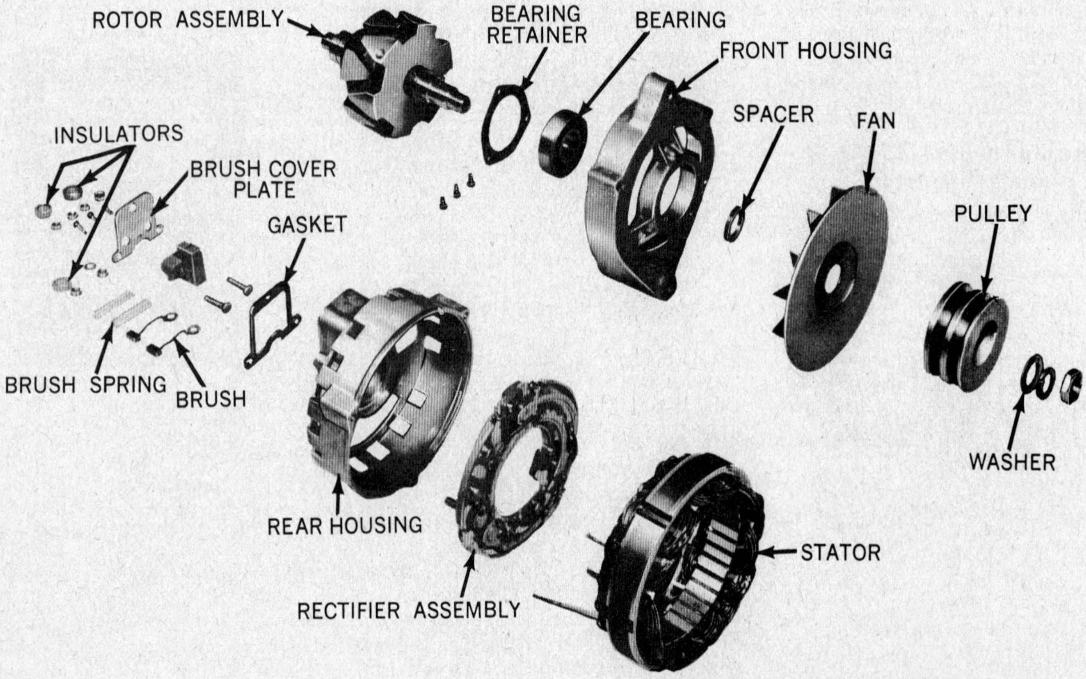

Exploded view—70 ampere rear terminal alternator—typical 90 ampere alternator (© Ford Motor Co.)

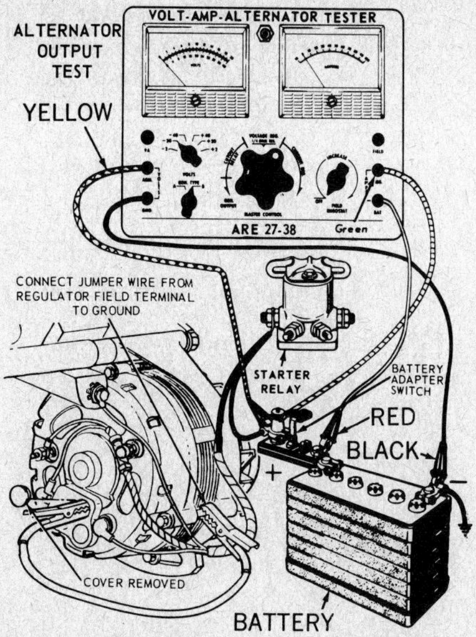

Voltmeter connection for field test—integral regulator equipped alternator (© Ford Motor Co.)

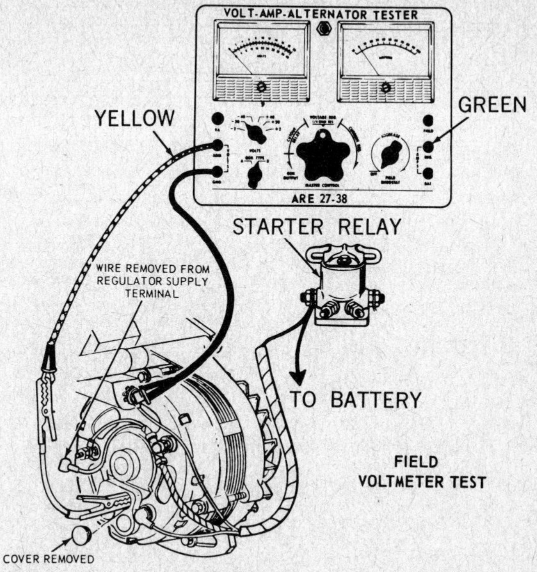

Output test connection—integral regulator equipped alternator (© Ford Motor Co.)

tegral regulator field terminal (cover plug removed).

6. Close adapter switch, start engine and open adapter switch.
7. Running engine at 2,000 rpm, observe voltmeter and ammeter. At 15 volts indicated, the ammeter should read 50-57 amps. If so, and there is still a no-charge condition, the regulator is probably faulty and must be replaced. An output 2-8 amps. below 50 amps. usually indicates an open diode rectifier, while an output 10-15 amps. below minimum specifications usually indicates a shorted diode. An alternator with a shorted diode usually will whine at idle speed.

Field Test (Voltmeter)

1. Turn ignition switch to OFF position.
2. Remove wire from regulator supply terminal.
3. Remove cover plug from regulator field terminal and connect one test voltmeter lead to this terminal. A ¼ ohm resistor should be in the circuit.
4. Connect the other test voltmeter lead to a good engine ground.
5. The voltmeter should read 12 volts. If *no* voltage is present, the field circuit is open or grounded.
6. If voltmeter reads more than I volt, but still less than battery voltage, there is probably a partial ground in the alternator field circuit and the circuit should be checked with an ohmmeter.

Field Test (Ohmmeter)

1. Disconnect battery ground cable; remove alternator from truck.
2. Remove the regulator from the alternator (covered later).
3. Make the ohmmeter tests as illustrated. If any of the tests indicates a field circuit problem, disassemble the alternator to further isolate the trouble.
   a. Contact each ohmmeter probe to a slip ring. Resistance should be 4-5 ohms. A higher reading indicates a damaged slip ring soldered connection or a broken wire. A lower reading indicates a shorted wire or slip ring assembly.
   b. Contact one ohmmeter probe to a slip ring and the other probe to the rotor shaft. Any reading other than infinite ohms indicates a short to ground. If neither of these tests (A and B) isolates the trouble, the brushes or brush assembly are the probable cause.

Voltage Limiter Test

1. Check the battery specific gravity. If it is not at least 1.230, charge the battery or install a charged battery for the test.
2. Make sure all lights and accessories are turned off, including such items as dome lights.
3. Make the test connections as illustrated.
4. Place transmission in Neutral or Park, close battery adapter switch and start the engine.
5. Open the battery adapter switch and operate engine at 2,000 rpm for 5 minutes. The voltmeter should read 13.3-15.3 volts.
6. If voltage does not rise above 12 volts, perform a regulator supply voltage test to determine whether or not the regulator is getting voltage from the battery. Before replacing a regulator, check the wiring of the entire charging system for shorts, opens, or high resistance connections.

Regulator Supply Voltage Test

The regulator is "turned on" by

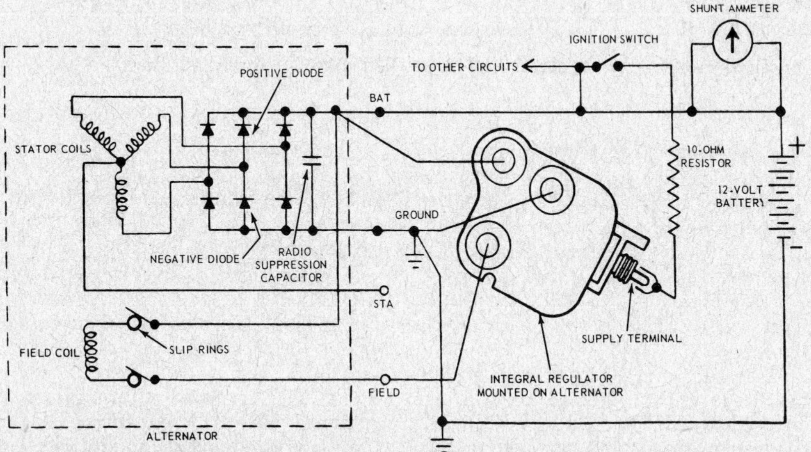

Charging system schematic with integral regulator (© Ford Motor Co.)

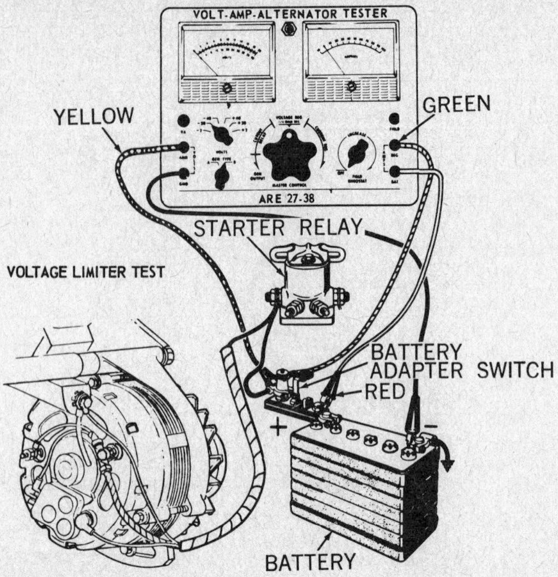

Voltage limiter test connections—integral regulator equipped alternator (© Ford Motor Co.)

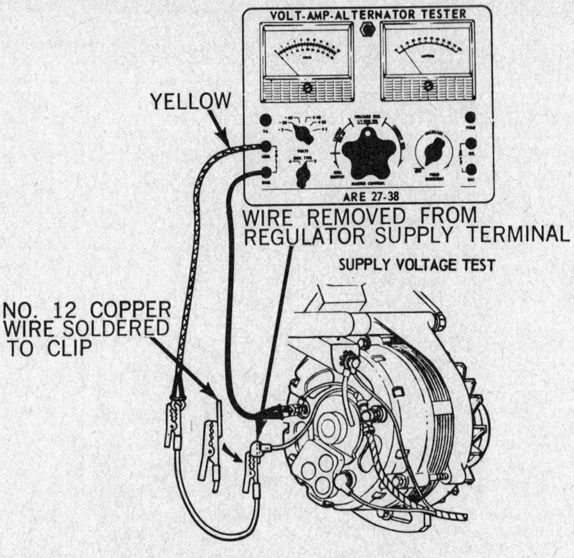

Supply voltage test connections—integral regulator equipped alternator (© Ford Motor Co.)

the application of battery voltage through a 10 ohm resistor wire. If the supply circuit is defective, the regulator will not function and the alternator will not put out current.

1. Connect a 12-volt test light or voltmeter between the regulator supply lead and ground.
2. Turn on the ignition switch. The test light should glow or the voltmeter indicate. If not, the supply circuit should be checked back to the battery, especially the resistance wire.

Overhaul

The overhaul procedures for the alternator are the same as for the Ford Autolite electro-mechanical alternator.

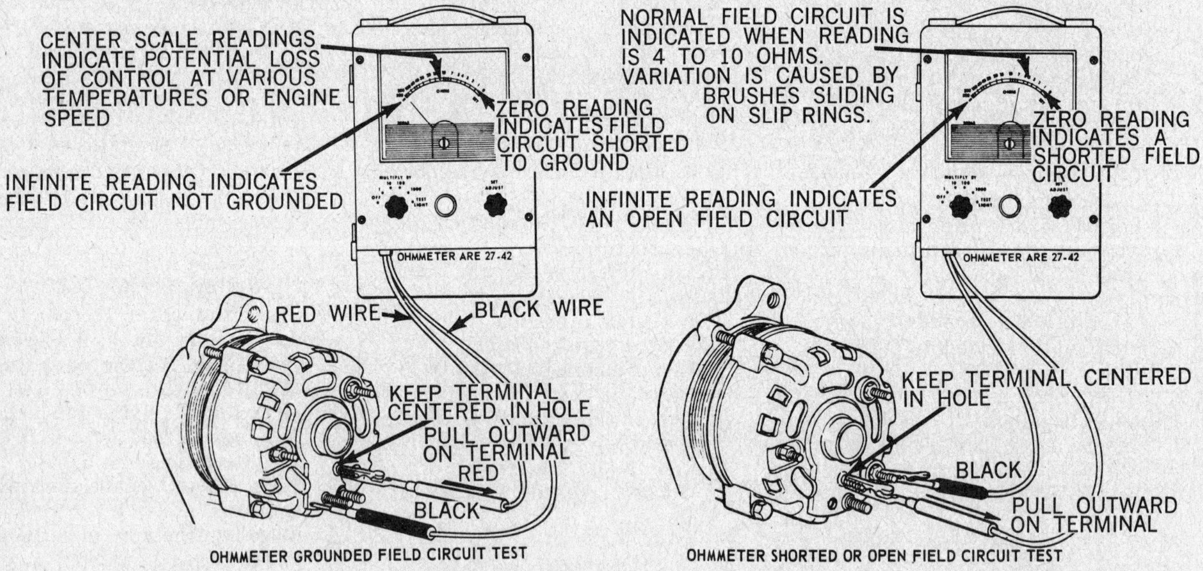

Field circuit test connection with ohmmeter—integral regulator equipped alternator (© Ford Motor Co.)

Motorola System

The Motorola alternator is an electro-mechanical device producing alternating current, which is changed to direct current by the rectifier diodes, accomplished by the characteristics of the diodes to allow current to flow in one direction only.

A three phase stator winding is used, a "Wye" type for the 37 ampere rated alternator, and a "Delta" type for the 51 and 55 ampere rated alternators.

A field diode assembly is used to provide the excitation current to the rotor (field) windings when the alternator is operating and is sensed and regulated by the voltage regulator to control the output of the alternator.

The field diode assembly is either mounted on a circuit board or encased within a epoxy "pot" with the leads attached in parallel to the positive rectifier diodes. If one or more of the field diodes become open, shorted, or downgraded, the alternator output will be affected.

NOTE: Do not use the regulator terminal for a source of current for any reason. To do so would adversely affect the operation of the voltage regulator.

CAUTION: Some alternators are equipped with a 7 volt terminal for the supply of current to the electric automatic choke. This terminal is

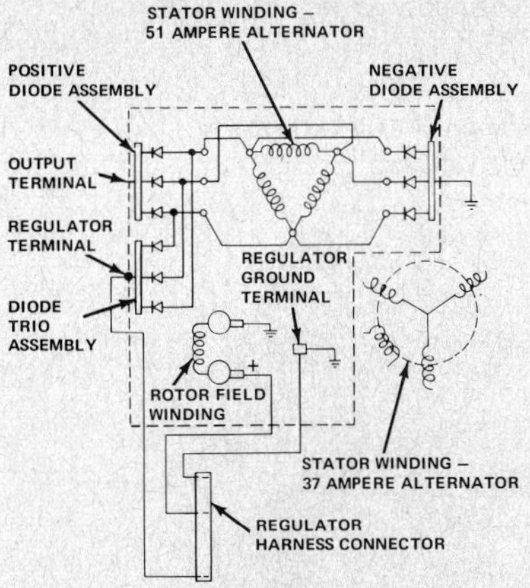

Motorola alternator internal circuits
(© Jeep Corp.)—**51 and 55**

located on the negative rectifier assembly. Do not interchange the wires between the regulator terminal and this terminal.

The voltage regulator is a sealed unit and requires no adjustment. Replacement of the unit is required if the regulator becomes defective.

Troubleshooting

NOTE: see the "Alternator Test Plans" section before proceeding further.

Fusible Link Test

There are many fuse links in the truck however the fuse link located in the wiring between the battery terminal of the horn relay to the main wire harness is the only one that concerns the charging system. This link protects the entire wiring harness. If it fails, all the electrical systems will fail to function.

Testing the Ignition Switch to Regulator Circuit

1. Disconnect the regulator wires from the regulator.
2. Turn on the key. Using a test light or voltmeter, check for current between the voltage supply wire and ground. This wire is usually orange and has another wire connected to it, usually blue or orange with a tracer.
3. If current is present, this part of the system is OK. If no voltage is present, check for broken or shorted wiring, a bad indicator bulb, a bad fuse in the fuse panel, or a bad connection at the ignition switch or on the battery side of the starter relay.

Alternator Tests (In vehicle)

NOTE: Various types of charging system testers are available to perform the tests necessary to determine if the system or components are defective. Follow the manufactures instructions for the tester being used, as the following charging system tests are generalized.

CAUTION: Do not disconnect the output lead or the voltage regulator, other than as directed, while the alternator is being operated. Do not ground the field terminal. Severe charging system damage could result.

Alternator Output Test

1. Connect voltmeter to battery, observing proper polarity.
2. Start the engine and operate at 1000 RPMs for two minutes with the headlamps on low beam.
3. Observe the voltage reading. If the voltage remains above 13 volts and below 15 volts, the alternator and the regulator are working satisfactory.
4. If the voltage is registering out of the above range, further testing will have to be done.

Field Draw Test

1. Loosen the alternator belt so that the rotor can be turned by hand.
2. Connect ammeter leads between the positive battery post and the positive brush post on the alternator.
3. The ammeter should register a reading within a range of 1½ to 3 amperes and if by turning the rotor by hand, the reading varies within the scale, the brushes and the slip rings require cleaning or repairs.
4. If the readings are too high or too low, the alternator should be removed and disassembled for further tests and repairs.

Regulator Bypass Test

1. Connect a volt meter to the battery, observing the proper polarity. Disconnect the voltage regulator.
2. Start the engine and allow to idle.
3. Connect an ammeter lead between the positive battery post to the alternator positive brush terminal.

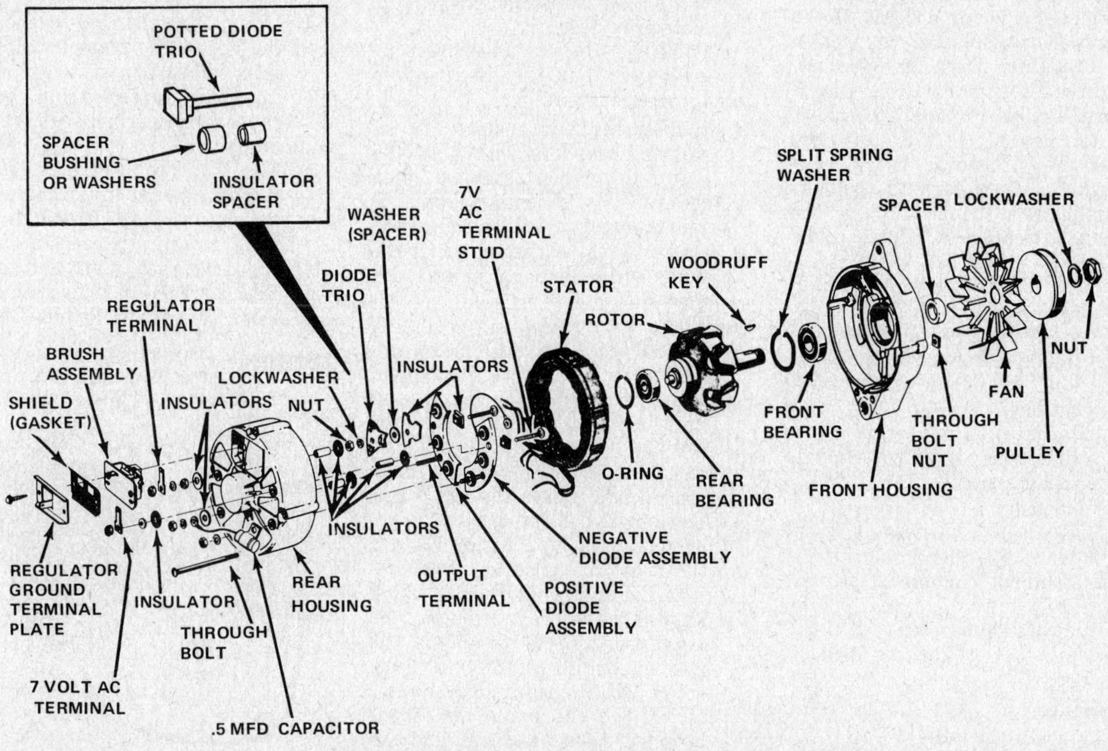

Motorola alternator—exploded view (© Jeep Corp.)

4. Increase the engine speed while observing the voltage reading. A reading of 16 volts should be obtained, if the alternator is not defective.

NOTE: Do not allow the voltage to increase over 16 volts, as damage to the charging system can result.

Field Diode Assembly Test

NOTE: A shorted or open field diode assembly will cause reduced alternator output and require unit disassembly and removal of the diode assembly for testing. A downgrading of one or more of the diodes will cause the dash indicator bulb to glow dimly, but will normally not effect the alternator output.

1. Start the engine and operate at idle speed.
2. With the voltmeter adjusted to the low scale, connect the leads to the alternator output terminal and the negative lead to the regulator terminal.
3. Turn the blower motor to the high position and turn the headlamps to the high beam position for approximately two minutes of operation. This causes the diode assembly to heat up due to the electrical load.
4. Observe the reading on the voltmeter. A range of 0 to 0.2 volts indicates the diode assembly is good. A reading above 0.2 volts indicates the downgrading of the diode assembly although it is not necessary to replace the assembly unless the reading is over 0.6 volts.
5. A pulsating reading on the meter indicates a positive diode of the rectifier or a soldered connection is breaking down under heat, and the alternator will have to be disassembled for testing repairs.
6. If the reading is over 0.6 volts and the alternator output was deemed satisfactory in the earlier tests, a bench test of the diode assembly will have to be made.
7. If the dash indicator bulb remains on dimly after a satisfactory diode assembly test has been made, inspect the following locations for loose or corroded connections.
   a. alternator output terminal
   b. starter relay battery terminal
   c. ignition switch
   d. fuse panel
   e. instrument harness connections
   f. instrument cluster printed circuits
   g. indicator bulb socket
   h. main wiring harness connectors

Alternator

Disassembly

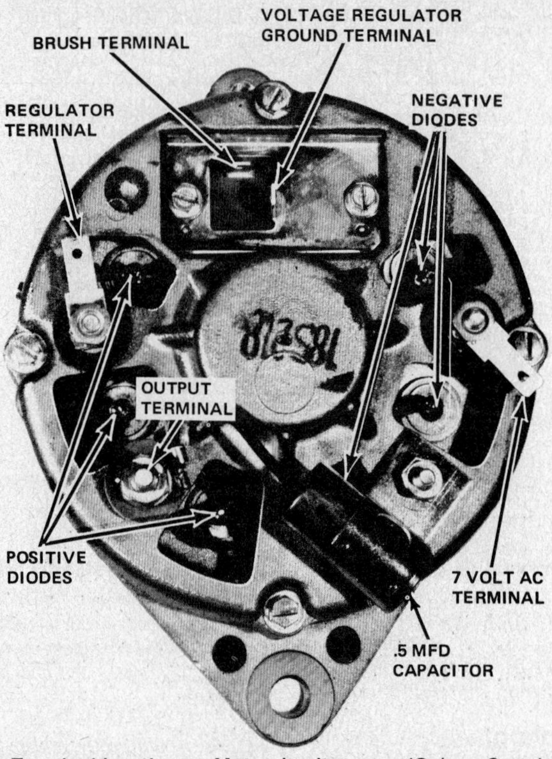

Terminal locations—Motorola alternator (© Jeep Corp.)

1. Remove the two self-tapping screws and the cover. Pull the brush assembly straight up to clear the locating pins, then lift out the brush assembly.
2. Scribe a matchmark across the front housing, stator, and rear housing. Remove the four thru-bolts and nuts, then carefully separate the rear housing and stator from the front housing using two screwdrivers in the slots provided.

CAUTION: Do not insert screwdrivers deeper than 1/16 in., to avoid damaging stator winding.

3. Remove the four locknuts and insulating washers that hold the stator and diode assembly, then separate the assembly from the rear housing. Avoid bending the stator wires—do not unsolder the wires without using pliers as a heat sink.
4. There is no reason to remove the rotor from the front housing upless there is a defect in the field coil or front bearing. Front and rear bearings are lubricated for life and sealed and, as a rule, do has been adjusted with too much not go bad unless the drive belt tension. If the rotor must be removed, use a puller to remove the front drive pulley, then unseat the split-ring washer using long-nose pliers through the front housing to compress the washer while pulling on the rotor. Tap the rotor shaft lightly to remove the rotor and front bearing, then reach in and remove the split-ring washer. Bearings must be removed using a puller and new bearings must be pressed into place.

Assembly

1. Clean the bearing and the inside of the bearing hub in the front housing, then gently seat the bearing using a socket of appropriate size and a small hammer.
2. Insert the split-ring washer into the hub of the front housing and seat the washer in its groove. Be extremely careful doing this, because the bearing seal is easily damaged.
3. The front bearing now must be seated against the shoulder on the rotor shaft. Install the fan and pulley spacer, then the Woodruff key, fan and pulley. Using a 7/16 in. socket or equivalent tool to fit inside the rear

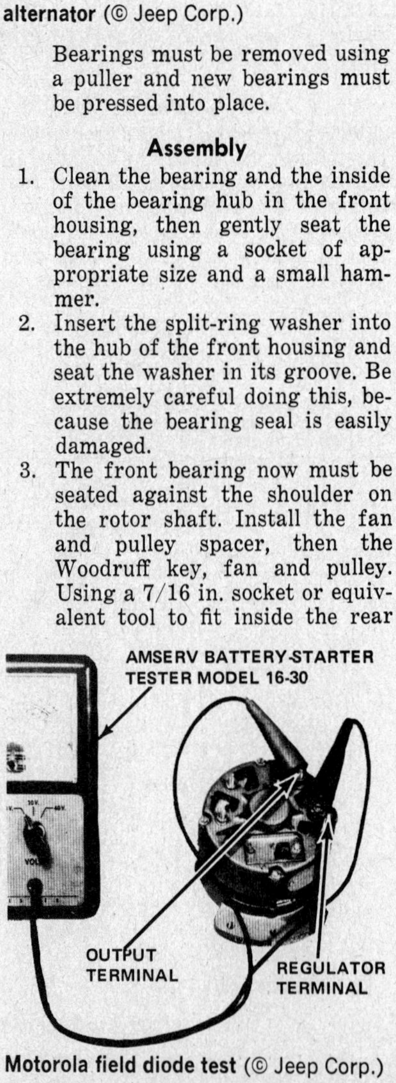

Motorola field diode test (© Jeep Corp.)

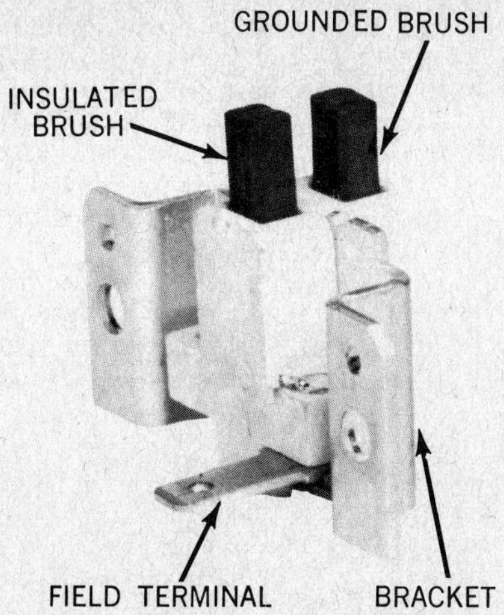

Motorola brush assembly—typical (© Jeep Corp.)

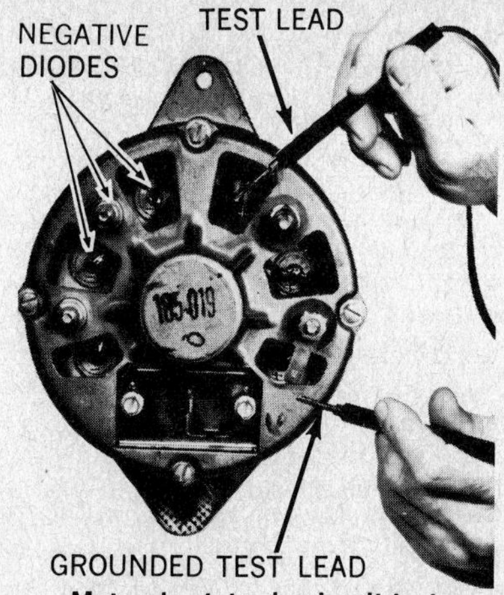

Motorola stator in-circuit test (© Jeep Corp.)

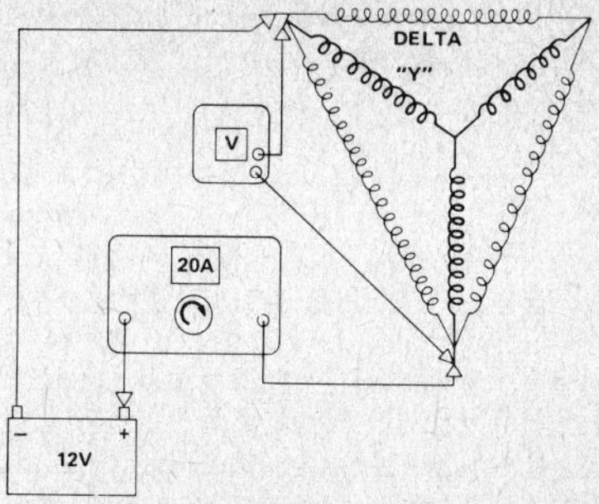

ALTERNATOR	LOAD	MAXIMUM VOLTAGE DROP	MAXIMUM VARIANCE BETWEEN WINDINGS
37	20A	7.2 – 8.2	.7
51	20A	5.5 – 6.5	.6

Motorola stator load test (© Jeep Corp.) **—51 and 55**

bearing race, apply pressure to drive the bearing against the shoulder of the rotor shaft.
4. Assemble the front and rear housing assemblies by hand, making certain that the rear bearing is properly seated in the rear housing hub and that the diode wires are not touching the rotor at any point.
5. Align the matchmarks made during disassembly, then spin the rotor to make sure sufficient clearance exists between it and the diode wires. Install the through bolts and tighten them evenly, using only a hand wrench. Continue assembly in reverse of disassembly.

Stator

In-Circuit Test

NOTE: When making the in-circuit test, consideration must be given to the rectifier diodes, which are connected to the stator windings. When properly polarized, the diode will conduct current in one direction only. A shorted diode would make the stator appear to be shorted also, so if during this test, a defect is noted, the stator windings and the rectifier diodes must be tested individually. Do not use a 120 volt test lamp as the diodes will be damaged.

1. With the use of a diode continuity light tool or a dc test lamp, connect one test lead to a diode terminal and the second lead to ground. Observe the test lamp and reverse the test leads.
2. The test lamp should light in one direction and not in the other with the leads reversed.
   a. If the test lamp lights in both directions, the stator windings are shorted or one of the negative diodes are shorted. Disassemble, unsolder, and test.
   b. If the test lamp does not light in either direction, all three rectifiers in the negative assembly are indicated to be open. Disassemble, unsolder, and test.

Out of Circuit Tests

To prepare for out of the circuit tests, the stator and diode assemble must be removed from the rear housing. Unsolder the stator leads from the diode stems. Upon reassemble, be certain that the same leads are soldered to the diodes in the same location as removed.

Stator Short Test

1. With the use of a test lamp or ohmmeter, test the windings of the stator by attaching one lead to the stator core and probing the stator leads with the other test lead.
2. The test lamp will light and the ohmmeter will register if a short circuit exists between the windings and the core. The short circuit must be found or the stator unit be replaced.

Stator Load Test

To test the stator coil windings for short circuits or high resistance, the following tools are needed. A fully charged 12 volt battery, a voltmeter, an ammeter, and a variable load control.

1. Connect the negative battery lead to any one of the three stator leads.
2. Connect the positive battery lead to one lead of the variable load control.

NOTE: If the load control has a built-in ammeter, the other load control lead would be connected to either of the two remaining stator leads. If the ammeter is a separate unit, the remaining load control lead would be connected to the positive ammeter lead and the negative ammeter lead

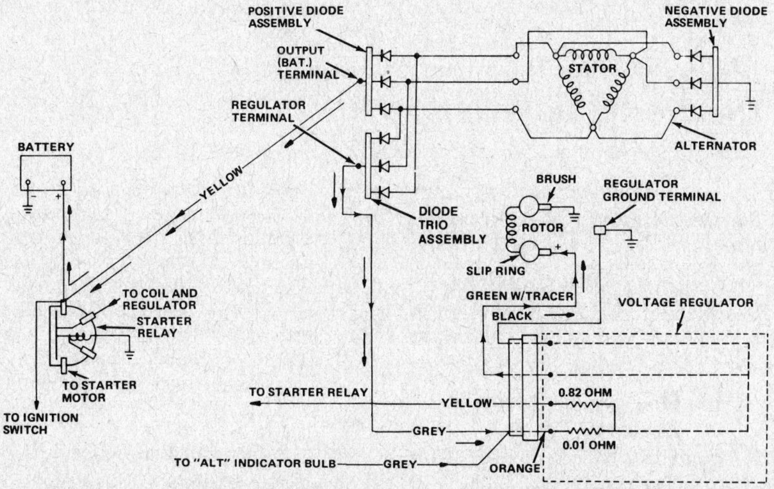

Motorola charging system (© Jeep Corp.)

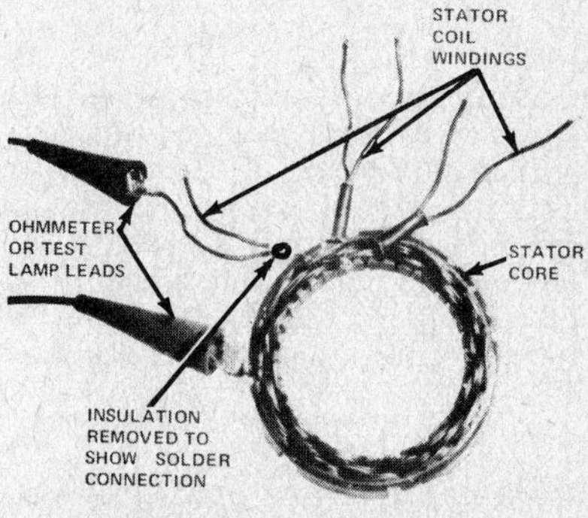

Motorola stator winding short test (© Jeep Corp.)

would be connected to one of the two remaining stator leads. (series connection)

3. Connect the voltmeter leads between the two stator leads being tested, (parallel connection) and adjust the variable load control to draw 20 amperes. Allow the windings to warm up for 15 seconds and note the reading on the voltmeter scale. The reading should not exceed 8.2 volts for a 37 ampere rated alternator, or exceed 6.5 volts for the 51 and 55 ampere rated alternators.
4. Stop the current flow to the coil and disconnect the test leads from the stator leads and reconnect them to the remaining stator leads and test the circuits as outlined in paragraph 3. Continue with the test for the third set of windings.
5. Note the variance between the windings. It should not exceed 0.7 volt for the 37 ampere alternator or 0.6 volt for the 51 and 55 ampere alternator.

Rectifier Diode Test

1. With diodes unsoldered, use a commercial type tester and follow the manufacturer's test procedure or make up a heavy load tester as illustrated.

NOTE: A 15 ampere load is necessary to properly test the rectifier diodes for heat related defects.

2. With the use of the heavy load tester probes, connect them to the diode so the test bulb is lighted.
3. Maintain the test load on the diode for 1 to 3 minutes. If the light flickers or goes out, the diode is defective.
4. If the light remains on after three minutes, immediately reverse the test leads. If the test bulb lights, the diode is defective.
5. Test the remaining diodes in the same manner.

NOTE: The diodes are normally not replaced separately, but are replaced as a positive or negative rectifier bridge assembly.

CAUTION: When soldering the stator wires to the diodes, it is advisable to use a set of needle nose pliers attached to the diode stem, to act as a heat sink to avoid heat damage to the diodes.

Field Diode Assembly (Diode Trio)

Two types of diode assemblies are used. The board and the potted type and both are tested with the same procedure.

1. With the diode assembly removed, use a commercial type tester and follow the manufacturer's test procedures or make a load tester as illustrated.
2. Connect the test leads to one of the diodes so that the test bulb is lighted.

NOTE: A one ampere load is needed to properly test the field diode assembly for heat related defects.

3. Maintain a load on the diode for approximately one minute to detect any heat failure.
4. Reverse the test leads and if the test bulb would light, the diode is defective. Test the remaining diodes as outlined.

Rotor Winding Tests

With the rotor removed, use a test probe connected in series with a 110 volt test lamp. Place one probe on a slip ring and the other probe on the rotor core. The rotor is shorted if the test bulb lights.

To test for shorted windings, use a fully charged 12 volt battery, an ammeter, a voltmeter, a variable rheostat, and test probes.

With the use of the test probe leads, place the rheostat and ammeter in series with the battery. Connect one test probe to one slip ring and the other test probe to the other slip ring. Place the voltmeter in parallel with the slip rings.

Slowly reduce the resistance of the rheostat to zero and with full battery voltage, (12.6 ± 0.2 volt), applied to the rotor coil, the field current should register between 1.8 to 2.5 amperes. Excessive ampere draw would indicate shorted windings and low ampere draw would indicate open windings of the rotor.

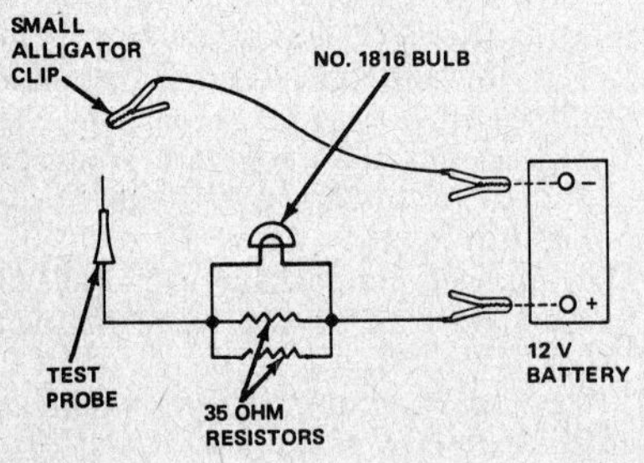

Rectifier diode tester (produces 15 AMP load)

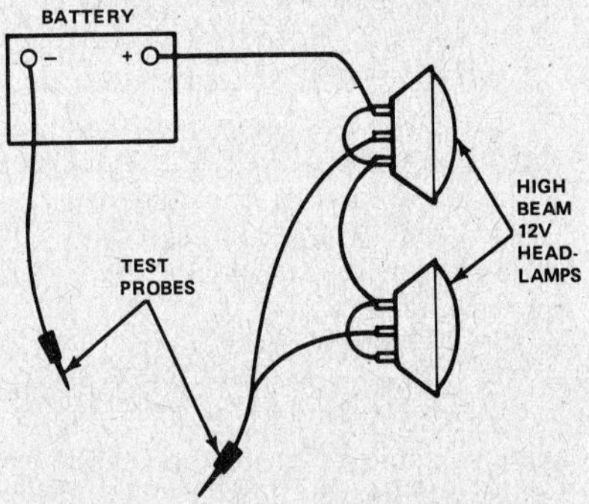

Field diode tester (produces 1 AMP load)

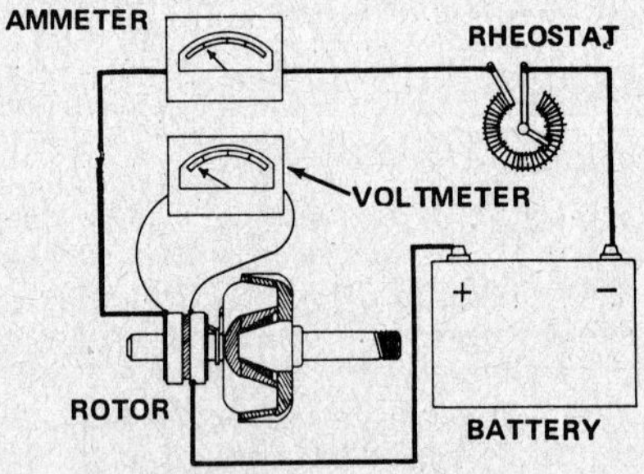

Motorola rotor winding test
(© Jeep Corp.)

The Prestolite System

Prestolite alternators incorporate an *isolation diode,* mounted as a component part of the internal positive heat sink assembly. Such alternators are almost identical to late model Motorola units in operation. Test procedures for the Motorola alternator also apply to the diode-equipped Prestolite.

Troubleshooting

NOTE: see the "Alternator Test Plans" section before proceeding further.

Fusible Link Test

See the Motorola system section for the fuse link test.

Charging System Operation

See the Motorola system section for the "Charging System Operation" tests.

Testing the Ignition Switch-to-Regulator Circuit

1. Disconnect the regulator wires from the regulator.
2. Turn on the key. Using a test light or voltmeter, check for current between the I terminal and ground and the L terminal ground. If voltage is present, this part of the system is OK. If no voltage is present, check for broken or shorted wires, a bad indicator bulb, a bad ammeter (if so equipped), or bad connections.

Alternator Disassembly

1. Remove the two brush mounting screws and cover, then tip the

brush assembly away from the alternator and remove.
2. Matchmark the rear housing, stator and drive end housing, then remove the four retaining screws. The stator and rear housing are removed as a unit by tapping lightly with a fiber hammer to separate them from the front housing.
3. The rotor should not be removed unless it or the front bearing is defective. To remove the rotor under these conditions, first remove the pulley nut and pulley (using a two-jaw puller), then remove the fan, Woodruff key and spacer. The rotor is removed from the front housing using a three-paw puller.
4. The front bearing is easily removed, after taking out the retaining ring, by pressing it out in a large vise using sockets to support the housing from the rear.

Stator Coil Test—Diode Type

1. Using a No. 57 bulb, connected in series with a 12-volt battery, as a test light, touch one test lead to the connection of the three stator windings and the other test lead to each stator lead that is connected to the diodes. If the bulb does not light, the winding is open.
2. To test for a grounded stator, use a 110-volt test lamp. First disconnect the diodes from the stator leads, then touch one test lead to the stator core and the other test lead to each of the three stator leads. If the test lamp lights, the winding is grounded.

NOTE: if all other components are O.K. and alternator still does not work, it can be assumed that the stator windings are internally shorted. This type of short is impossible to detect by using the previous test. Diode tests are the same as for the Motorola alternator.

Alternator Assembly

1. Press the front bearing into the front housing, making sure the dust seal faces the rotor. Install the bearing retaining snap-ring, then press the shoulder of the shaft against the inner bearing race using a tool that fits over the shaft and against the race. Install the spacer, Woodruff key, fan and pulley, then install lockwasher and pulley nut.
2. Install the diode heat sink, negative diodes and stator. Solder any stator to diode connections that were unsoldered, using pliers as a heat sink to prevent overheating.
3. Install the rotor and front drive housing to stator and rear housing, aligning matchmarks made during disassembly. Install the four retaining screws, then the brush holder assembly and retaining screws.
4. Make sure the stator leads and brush holder assembly clear the rotor and that the rotor can be spun by hand without binding.

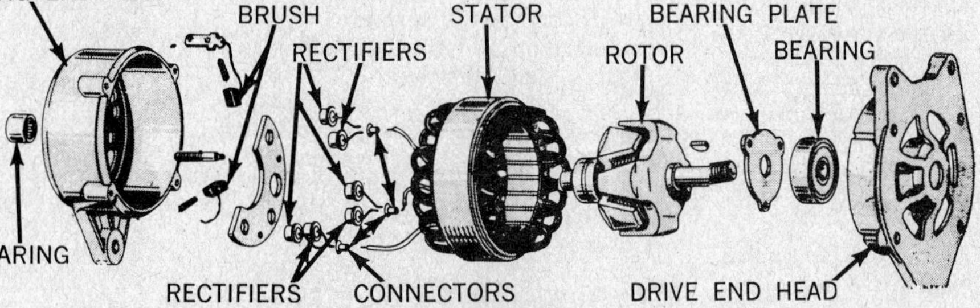

Exploded view—Prestolite alternator (© Prestolite Co.)

C.S.I. AC Generator

The C.S.I. system is an integrated AC generating system containing a built-in voltage regulator. Removal and replacement is essentially the same as for the standard AC generator. Specialized service procedures are as follows:

Diode Trio Initial Testing

1. Before removing this unit, easily identified in the illustration, connect an ohmmeter between the brush lead clip and the end frame. The lowest reading scale should be used for this test.
2. After taking a reading, reverse the lead connections. If the meter reads zero, the brush lead clip is probably grounded, due to omission of the insulating sleeve or insulating washer.

Diode Trio Removal

1. Remove the three nuts which secure the stator.
2. Remove stator.
3. Remove the screw which secures the diode trio lead clip, then remove diode trio.

NOTE: The position of the insulating washer on the screw is critical; make sure it is returned to the same position on reassembly.

Diode Trio Testing

1. Connect an ohmmeter, on lowest range, between the single brush connector and one stator lead connector.

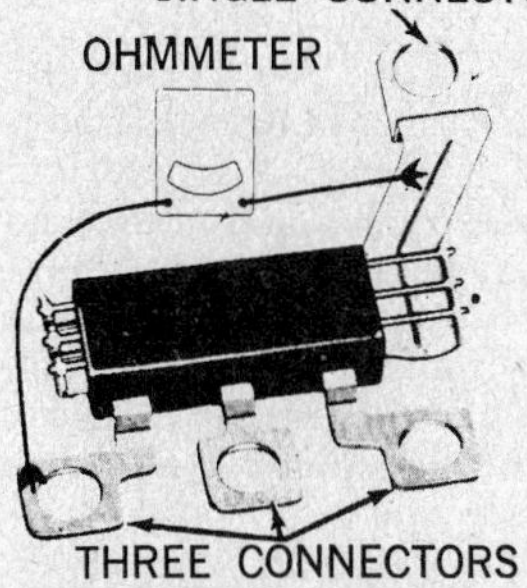

Testing diode trio—C.S.I. Alternator (© G.M. Corp.)

2. Observe the reading, then reverse the meter leads. Repeat this test with each of the other two stator lead connectors. The readings on each of these tests should NOT be identical, there should be one low and one high reading for each test. If this is not the case, replace the diode trio.

CAUTION: **Do not use high voltage on the diode trio.**

Rectifier Bridge Testing

1. Connect an ohmmeter between the heat sink (ground) and the base of one of the three terminals. Then, reverse the meter leads and take a reading. If both readings are identical, the bridge is defective and must be replaced.
2. Repeat this test with the remaining two terminals, then between the INSULATED heat sink (as opposed to the GROUNDED heat sink in previous test) and each

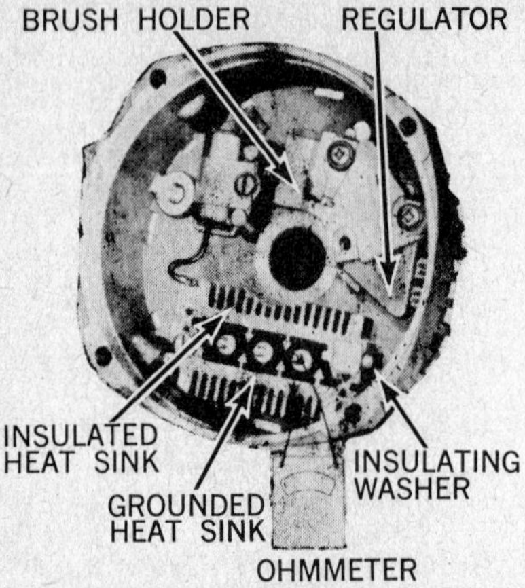

Testing rectifier bridge diodes—C.S.I. alternator (© G.M. Corp.)

of the three terminals. As before, if any two readings are identical, on reversing the meter leads, the rectifier bridge must be replaced.

Rectified Bridge Removal

1. Remove the attaching screw and the BAT. terminal screw.
2. Disconnect the condenser lead.
3. Remove the rectifier bridge.

NOTE: The insulator between the insulated heat sink and the end frame is extremely important to the operation of the unit. It must be replaced in exactly the same position on reassembly.

Brush and/or Voltage Regulator R & R

1. Remove two brush holder screws and stator lead to strap nut and washer, brush holder screws and one of the diode trio lead strap attaching screws.

NOTE: The insulating washers must be replaced in the same position on reassembly.

2. Remove brush holder and brushes. The voltage regulator may also be removed at this time, if desired.
3. Brushes and brush springs must be free of corrosion and must be undamaged and completely free of oil or grease.
4. Insert spring and brushes into holder, noting whether they slide freely without binding. Insert wooden or plastic toothpick into bottom hole in holder to retain brushes.

Brush holder—C.S.I. alternator (© G.M. Corp.)

NOTE: The brush holder is serviced as a unit; individual parts are not available.

5. Reassemble in reverse order of disassembly.

Voltage Regulator Testing

NOTE: The voltage regulator must be tested with the C.S.I. unit still in place.

1. Disconnect battery ground strap.
2. Connect an ammeter in series with the BAT. terminal of the generator and the lead removed from that terminal.
3. Reconnect battery ground strap, then turn on all accessoris to place a load on the system.
4. Connect a carbon pile across the battery terminals.

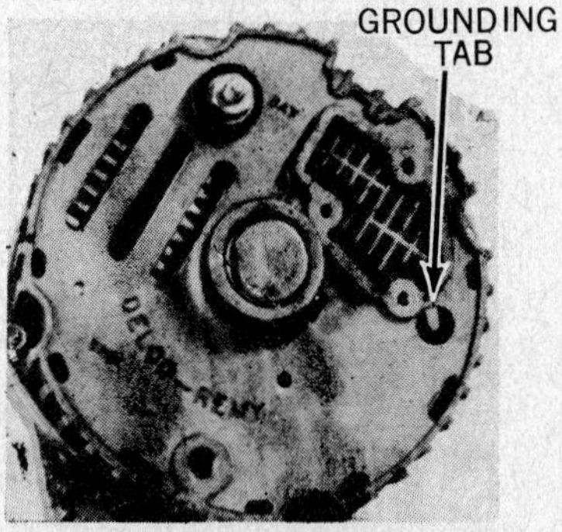

Grounding tab for voltage regulator test —C.S.I. alternator (© G.M. Corp.)

5. Ground the field winding by inserting an insulated screwdriver into the test hole in the alternator frame and depressing the tab. Do not push the tab into the generator more than 1 in.
6. Run the engine at moderate rpm, equivalent to 30-40 mph in high gear, and adjust the carbon pile to obtain maximum current output.
7. If the output is within 10% of the rated output of the alternator and the system does not charge properly, the voltage regulator is defective and must be replaced.

Generator—C.S.I.
Amps.—cold rating 55
Output @ rpm ....30 @ 2000
Output @ rpm ....55 @ 5000
Field current draw 4.0-4.5
Regulator—C.S.I.
Model 1116368
Normal range .....13.5-16.0 volts

Slip Ring End Frame Bearing and Seal R & R

1. With stator removed, press out bearing and seal, using a socket or similar tool that fits inside the end frame housing. Press from outside to inside, supporting the frame inside with a hollow cylinder (large, deep socket) to allow the seal and bearing to pass.
2. The bearings are sealed for life and permanently lubricated. If a bearing is dry, do not attempt to repack it, as it will throw off the grease and contaminate the inside of the generator.
3. Using a flat plate, press the new bearing from the outside toward the inside. A large vise is a handy press, but care must be exercised so that end frame is not distorted or cracked. Again, use a deep socket to support the inside of the end frame.
4. From inside the end frame, insert seal and press flush with housing.
5. Install stator and reconnect leads.

The Leece-Neville System

The Leece-Neville charging systems use varied types of alternator housings and controls. The types most commonly encountered on light and medium trucks and vans will be illustrated and described.

105 Ampere Alternator (early type)

With the use of an adjustable carbon pile load control, field rheostat control, and voltamp tester, the rated ampere output and field current draw can be tested with the alternator mounted on the engine. If any indication of malfunction is determined, the alternator should be removed and the internal circuits tested.

Upon disassembly, the testing procedure for the internal circuits follows the outline described in the Autolite (Ford) type alternator section.

Rated Output Test

1. With battery disconnected, ignition switch in off position, and the wire disconnected at the alternator B+ terminal, hook an ammeter between the alternator B+ terminal and the wire that was just disconnected from this terminal.
2. Disconnect wire from the alternator F terminal.
3. With the field rheostat adjusted to open position, connect its leads to the alternator F terminal and the alternator B+ terminal.
4. Hook up a voltmeter between the

alternator B+ terminal and ground.
5. Reconnect battery cables.
6. Connect a carbon pile load control between the battery posts.
7. With a tachometer connected to the engine, start the engine and set its speed at the recommended rpm.
8. While watching both ammeter and voltmeter, adjust the carbon pile load control to maintain 15 volts. When field rheostat control is fully closed, note voltmeter and ammeter readings.
9. Adjust field rheostat to open position and carbon pile control to off.
10. Compare readings with specifications. Readings should be at least equal to rated output specified by the manufacturer. If output complies with specifications, proceed to the voltage regulator test. If readings are below rated output, it indicates possible internal troubles.

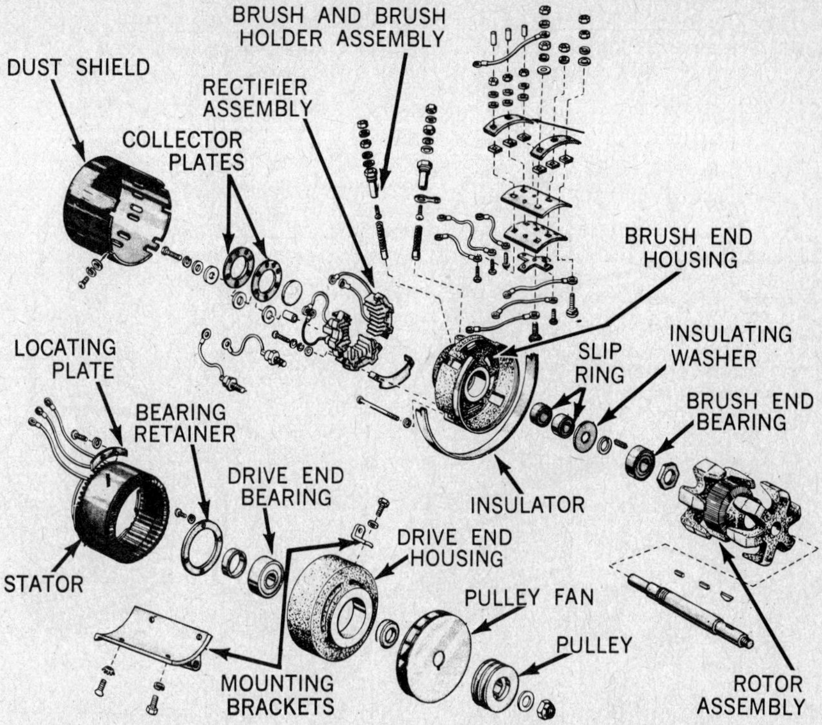

Leece-Neville 105 Ampere alternator exploded view (early model) (© Ford Motor Co.)

Field Current Draw Test

1. Disconnect battery ground cable.
2. Disconnect carbon pile, voltmeter, ammeter and field rheostat from the previous check.
3. Reconnect the regular circuit wire to the alternator B+ terminal.
4. With the field rheostat adjusted to the open position, connect one of its leads to the alternator B+ terminal and the other lead to a test ammeter lead.
5. Connect the remaining ammeter lead to the alternator F terminal.
6. Connect one voltmeter lead to the alternator F terminal and the remaining voltmeter lead to ground.
7. Reconnect battery ground cable, start the engine, and run it at about 1,000 rpm.
8. With field rheostat in closed position, read the ammeter and voltmeter for a very brief period.
9. Compare these readings with specifications.
10. If readings are low, it indicates trouble in slip rings or brushes.
11. If readings are too high, it indicates trouble in the rotor field windings.
12. If readings are as specified on an alternator which did not deliver its rated output, look for trouble in the stator or diodes.

Disassembly

1. Remove the mounting brackets. Remove the pulley nut, pulley, fan, key, and spacer from rotor shaft.
2. Remove the dust shield. Remove three screws holding the six stator and terminal board wire leads to the rectifier assemblies.
3. Remove the three screws holding the terminal board to the brush end housing.
4. Remove the field lead from the brush holder and remove the brush assembly from the housing.
5. Remove the four through bolts and separate the drive end housing and rotor from the stator and brush end housing. Remove the stator from the brush end housing.
6. The bearings can be pressed from the rotor shaft and replaced. The slip rings can be pressed from the rotor after removal of the field wire.
7. Remove the two circular copper collector plates from the brush end housing.

NOTE: The retaining screws hold the diode lead wires and terminal board output leads. Tag the wires for identification during assembly.

8. Remove the terminal board and the rectifier assemblies from the brush end housing.
9. Testing of the internal circuits can now be accomplished.

Assembly

1. Replace any necessary parts and assemble the terminal board and wires.
2. Position the two stator winding insulators in the brush end housing.
3. Install the rectifier assemblies

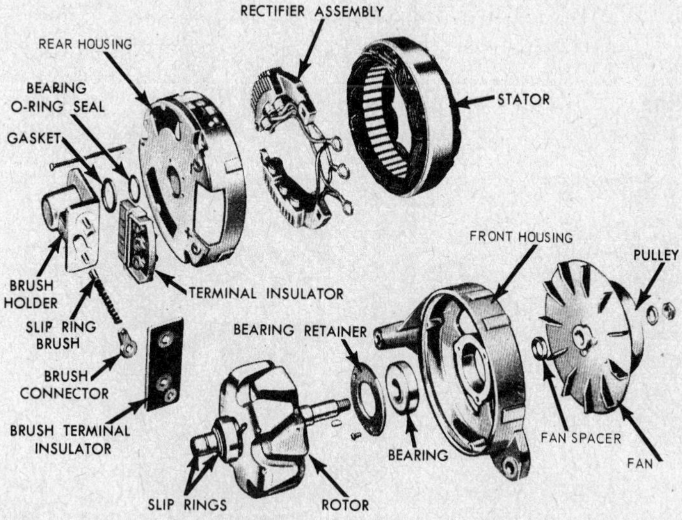

Exploded view 65, 70, 105 Leece-Neville alternator (© Ford Motor Co.)

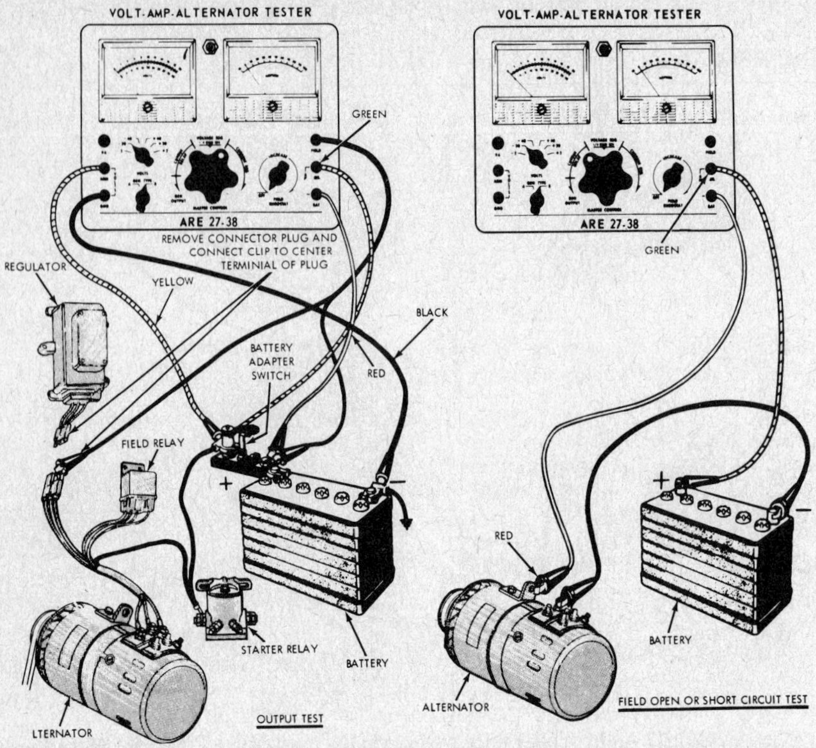

Alternator tests—105 ampere alternator (early model) (© Ford Motor Co.)

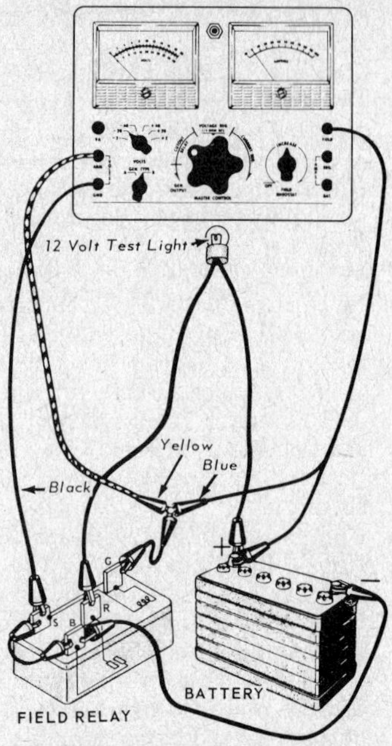

Testing field relay—Leece-Neville system (early model)
(© Ford Motor Co.)

and insulators into the brush end housing.
4. Position the terminal board and wire assembly, the two circular collector plates, insulators, and washers into the brush end housing and install the retaining screws with the diode leads and output leads in their respective locations as previously tagged.
5. Position the stator to the brush end housing and connect the assembly to the rotor and drive end housing. Install the four through bolts and tighten.
6. Install the brushes, springs, and brush holders into the housing and connect the field wire to the brush holder.
7. Position the terminal board leads and stator leads to their respective rectifiers as previously tagged.
8. Install the dust shield. Install the rotor spacer, fan, key, and pulley. Torque the pulley nut to 45-50 ft. lbs.
9. Install the mounting brackets to the alternator housing.

65, 70, 105 Ampere Alternators

These differently rated units utilize the same type housing assembly with the internal wiring circuits being responsible for the varied current output. The disassembly and assembly will follow the same procedures. The testing of the internal circuits

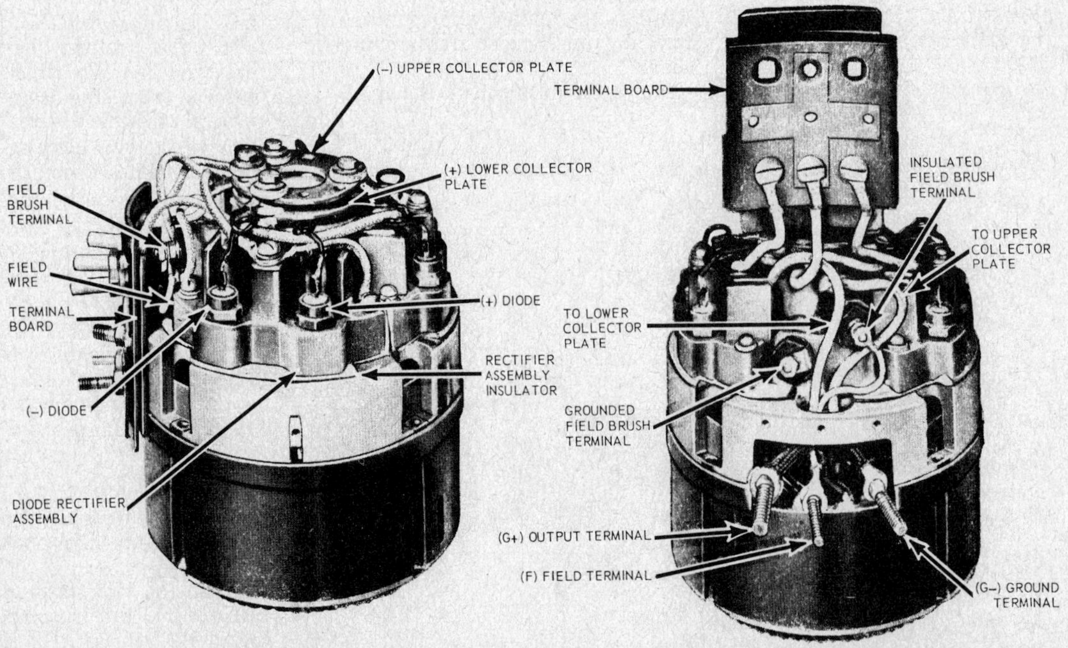

Collector plates and wire lead assembly—Leece-Neville 105 ampere (© Ford Motor Co.)

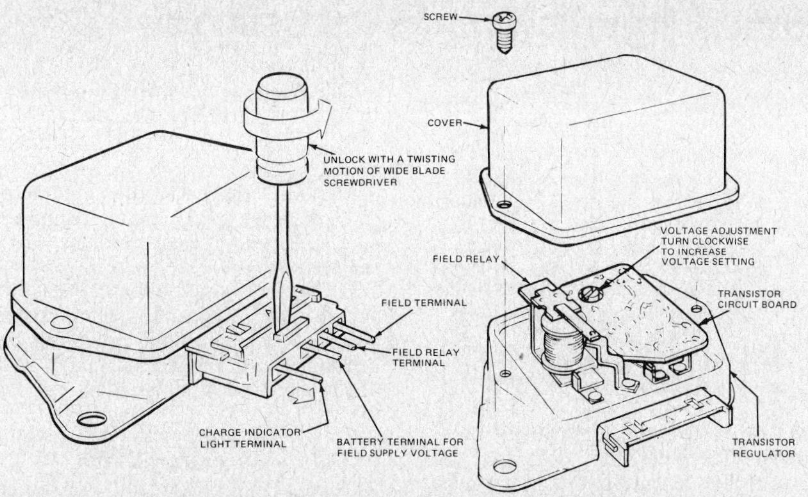

Transistorized voltage regulator (© Ford Motor Co.)

will follow the procedures outlined in the Autolite (Ford) alternator section.

An adjustable transistorized regulator is used to control the current output.

For the testing of the alternator circuits with the unit on the vehicle, refer to the Autolite (Ford) alternator section.

Disassembly

1. Scribe a mark on the housings for proper assembly.
2. Remove the pulley nut, pulley, fan, key, and spacer from the rotor shaft.
3. Remove the brush terminal insulator, springs, and brushes. Remove the brush holder assembly.
4. Remove the through bolts and separate the brush end housing from the drive end housing.
5. Remove the stator lead retaining nuts and remove the stator from the brush end housing.
6. Remove the rectifier assemblies and stator terminal insulators.
7. Testing and replacement of necessary parts can now be accomplished.

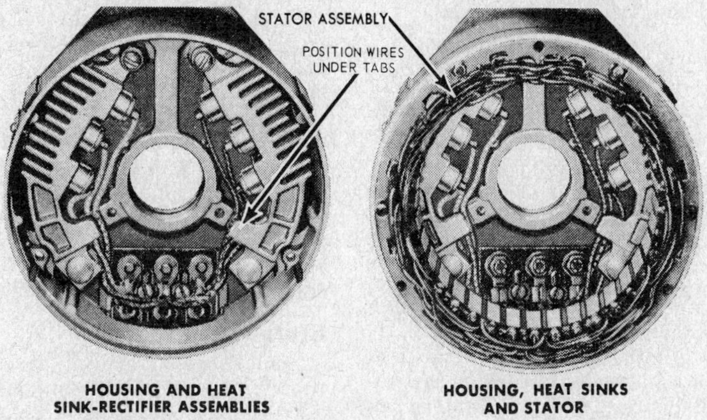

Brush end housing, rectifier and stator assembly—65,70,105 Leece-Neville (© Ford Motor Co.)

Assembly

1. Install the stator insulators and position the rectifier insulators.
2. Install the rectifier assemblies in the housing and install the mounting screws and terminals.

NOTE: Be certain that the rectifier assemblies are insulated from the end frame.

3. Position the three rectifier terminals to the studs and route the wire leads under the tabs of the rectifier heat sinks.
4. Place the stator in position and connect the stator terminals.
5. Assemble the stator and brush end housing to the rotor and drive end housing, while aligning the previously scribed marks.
6. Install the brush holder assembly and assemble the brushes and springs. Hold the brush connectors in position with a machinist steel scale until the terminal insulator is installed.
7. Install the spacer, key, fan, and pulley on the rotor shaft and torque the pulley nut to 40 50 ft. lbs.

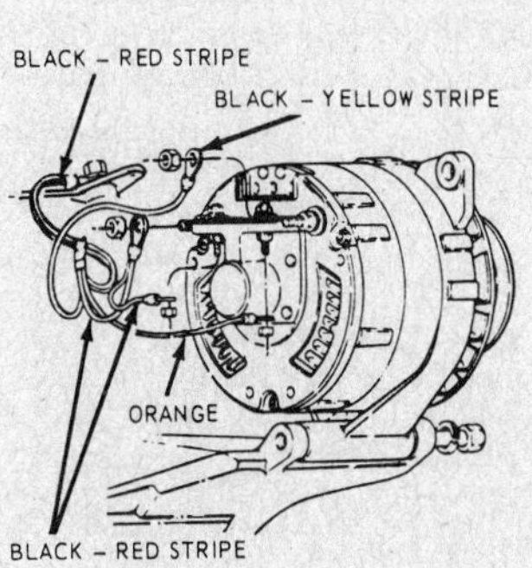

Typical Leece Neville Alternator wiring connections (© Ford Motor Co.)

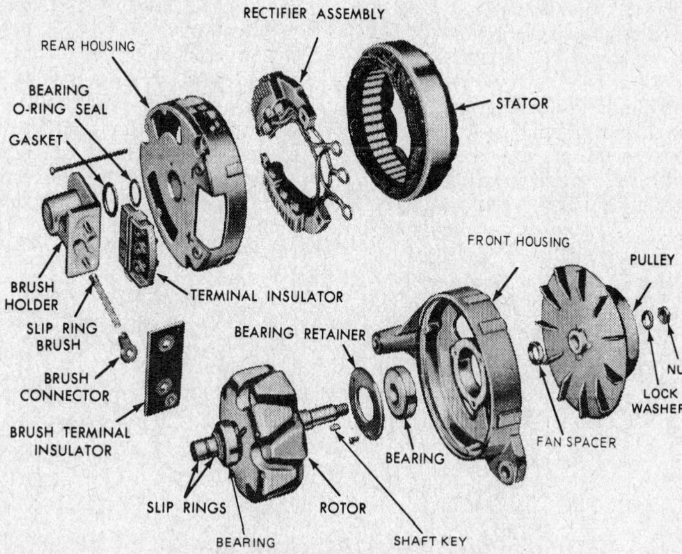

Disassembled 70 and 105-ampere Leece Neville alternator (© Ford Motor Co.)

Conventional Ignition Systems

The Ignition System is divided into two circuits; a low voltage or primary circuit, and a high voltage or secondary circuit.

The primary circuit carries current, (usually modified for ignition by a resistor, on 12-volt systems) at battery voltage. It includes the battery, ignition-starter switch, starter relay, ignition ballast resistor, primary winding of the coil, condenser, contact points, and ground.

The secondary circuit begins with the ignition coil. Secondary voltage is a product of the coil and emerges from the secondary terminal and flows through a cable to the distributor cap. It is distributed by the rotor, through the distributor cap and cables, to the spark plugs, and to ground.

CAUTION: Secondary circuit pressure could reach as high as 30,000 volts.

Coil Polarity

Coil polarity is predetermined and must match the circuit polarity of the system being tested. It is an established fact that the electron flow through the spark plug is better from the hotter center plug electrode-to-ground than by the opposite route, from ground-to-center electrode. Therefore, negative ground polarity has been established as standard. There is about a 14% difference in required voltage of the two polarity designs at idling speed. This differential increases with engine speed.

Correct coil polarity can be checked on the truck by connecting a voltmeter negative lead to the ignition coil secondary wire, and the positive voltmeter lead to engine ground. If the voltmeter reading is up-scale, polarity is correct: if voltmeter reading is down-scale, polarity is reversed.

Lately, automotive batteries are designed with the battery posts on the same side of the battery, opposed to the earlier diagonal post design. Therefore, terminal size and cable length will discourage improper battery installation. This results in the battery and distributor terminals of

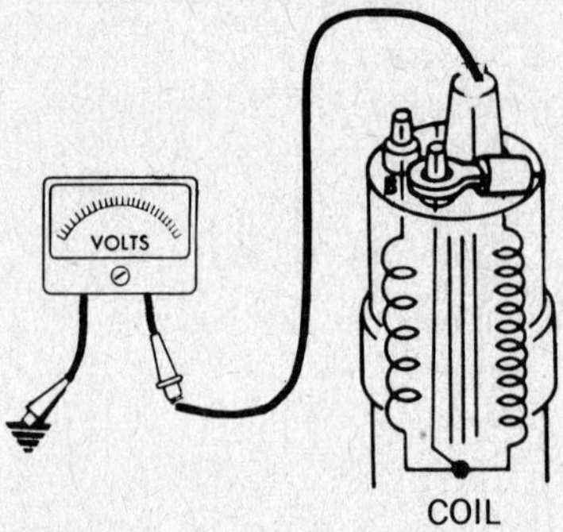

the coil being the most likely points of possible reversal of polarity.

Another tentative, but less precise, method is to hold a regular carbon-cored wooden lead pencil in the gap between a disconnected spark plug wire and ground. It is possible to observe the direction of spark flow, from wire-to-pencil-to-ground when polarity is correct.

CAUTION: Hold the pencil with a heavy glove or you may observe the spark flow along your fingers.

Primary Circuit Test

A quick, tentative check of the 12 volt ignition primary circuit (including ballast resistor) can be made with a simple voltmeter, as follows:

1. With engine at operating temperature, but stopped, and the distributor side of the ignition coil grounded with a jumper wire, hook up a voltmeter between the ignition coil (switch side) and a good ground.
2. Jiggle the ignition switch (switch on) and watch the meter. An unstable needle will indicate a defective ignition switch.
3. With ignition switch on (engine stopped) the voltmeter should read 5.5 to 7 volts for 12-volt systems.
4. Crank the engine. Voltmeter should read at least 9 volts during cranking period.
5. Now remove the jumper wire from the coil. Start the engine. Voltmeter should read from 9.0 volts to 11.5 volts (depending upon generator output) while running.

Coil Resistance, with Ohmmeter —Primary Circuit

To check ignition coil resistance, primary side, switch ohmmeter to low scale. Connect the ohmmeter leads across the primary terminals of the coil and read the low ohms scale.

Coils requiring ballast resistors should read about 1.0 ohm resistance. 12-volt coils, not requiring external ballast resistors, should read about 4.0 ohms resistance.

Coil Resistance, with Ohmmeter —Secondary Circuit

To check ignition coil resistance, secondary side, switch ohmmeter to high scale. Connect one test lead to the distributor cap end of the coil secondary cable. Connect the other test lead to the distributor terminal of the coil. A coil in satisfactory condition should show between 4 K and 8 K on the scale. Some special coils (Mallory, etc.) may show a resistance as high as 13 K. If the reading is much lower than 4 K, the coil probably has shorted secondary turns. If the reading is extremely high (40 K or more) the secondary winding is either open, there is a bad connection at the coil terminal, or resistance is high in the cable.

If both primary and secondary windings of the coil test good, but the ignition system is still unsatisfactory, check the system further.

Ballast Resistor

Some sort of ballast resistor is used with most trucks equipped with 12-volt ignition systems. This resistance may be built into the ignition coil, or it may be a special wire of specific resistance, comprising the primary ignition circuit.

To provide a greater safety margin of sufficient voltage for high speed operation, a special ignition coil is used with whatever type of ballast resistance is used. Other reasons for

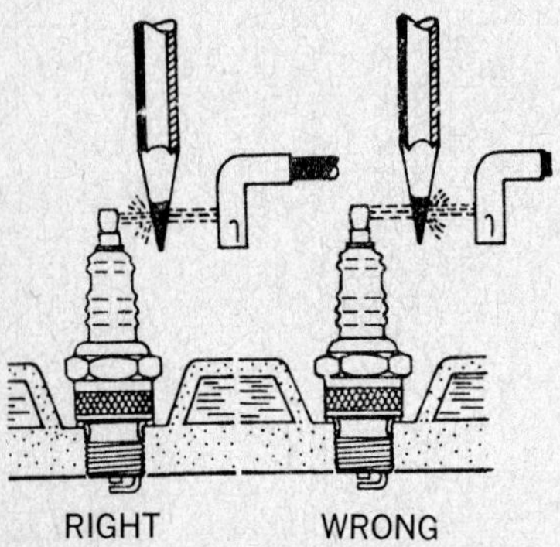

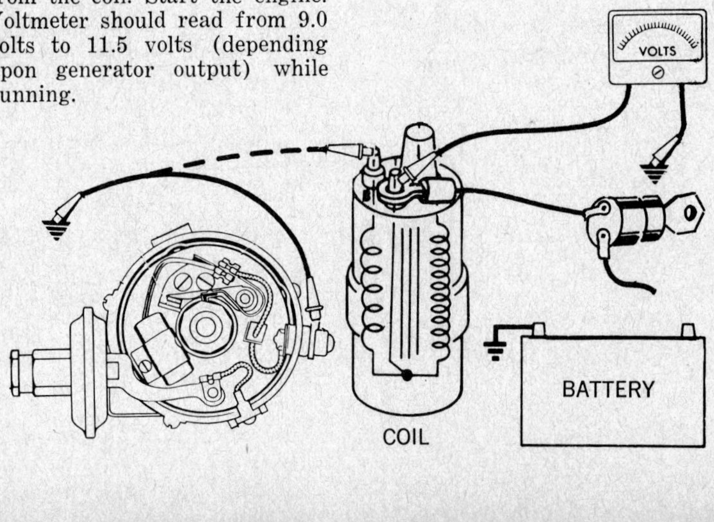

ballast resistance are to limit to a safe maximum the primary current flow through the coil and through the distributor contact points. This helps protect the contact points at slow engine speed when they are closed for a longer period of time. The resistor also protects against excessive build-up of primary current when the ignition switch is on with the engine stopped and ignition points closed.

On some systems, the resistor is removed from the ignition circuit during engine cranking, then with the ignition connected directly to battery voltage. This keeps ignition voltage as high as possible while cranking. The by-pass type system can have the by-pass factor built into the ignition switch, or it may be part of the starter solenoid.

Primary Circuit—Distributor Side

With the voltmeter on the 16-20 volt scale, connect one voltmeter lead to ground. Connect the other voltmeter lead to the distributor side of the coil. Remove the high tension wire from the coil and ground it. Close ignition switch and slowly bump the starter switch to open and close the points. When the distributor contacts make and break during cranking, the voltmeter reading should be from one-third to one-half battery voltage. Normally, with engine stopped and with points open, the reading will be the same as battery voltage. Furthermore, with the engine stopped and the points closed and in good condition, the reading will be close to zero.

If while cranking, the voltmeter reading remains zero or close to it, the trouble may be one or more of the following:

A. No current at distributor. Disconnect the distributor primary wire from the top of the coil. Now, take a

Ballast resistor

voltmeter reading from the distributor terminal of the coil to make sure that the current is going through the circuit.

B. Points are not opening because of mechanical (points or cam) failure or maladjustment. Dual points in parallel, one set not opening.

C. The movable point, the stud at the primary distributor wire terminal, or the pigtail wire is grounded.

D. The condenser has a dead short. An ohmmeter check of the condenser will show this condition. Connect one test lead of an ohmmeter to the body of the condenser and the other test lead to the pigtail. If the meter shows the slightest reading, the condenser is shorted. With a few exceptions, a visual inspection of the distributor contact points will generally indicate the condition of the condenser. An open, or shorted condenser will not function. A condenser of too great capacity will cause metal to transfer from the movable distributor point to the stationary point. This will cause a pit on the movable point. An under-capacity condenser, causes metal to leave the stationary point and build up on the movable point.

Any excessive resistance in either the primary or secondary circuits will upset the sensitive balance of the ignition system and cause the ignition points to pit.

Ignition Point Dwell

It is very important that point

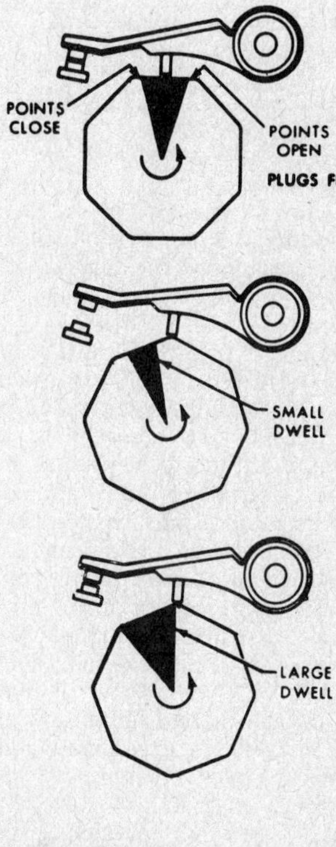

dwell be adjusted to exact specifications before any attempt is made to time the engine.

Point dwell (cam angle) is the degree value for the closed attitude of ignition points for each make-and-break period of a distributor cycle. It is that phase of ignition system functioning during which the coil becomes saturated (builds up to voltage capacity) for its next discharge at the moment of point opening.

Some current production truck engines demand in excess of 23,000 spark plug firings per minute to fire their cylinders. This places a tremen-

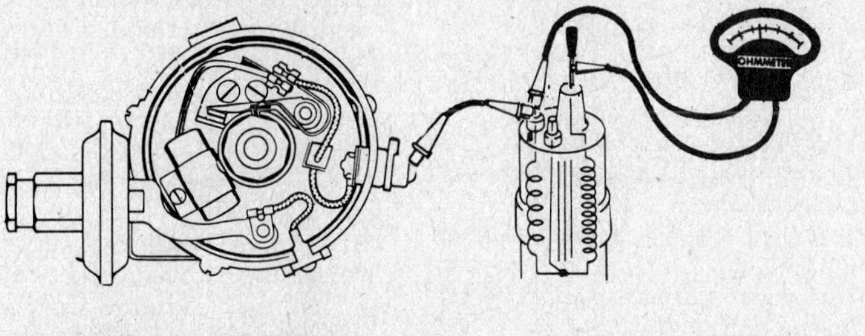

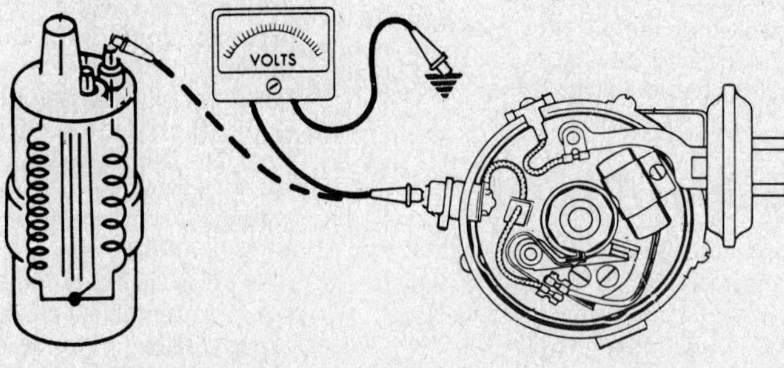

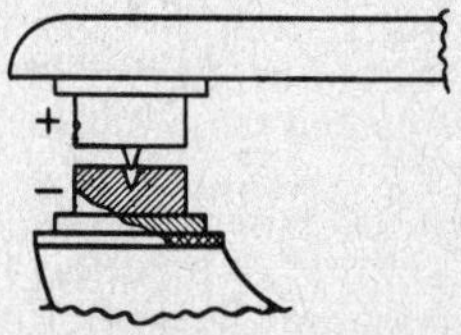

Pitting caused by low capacity

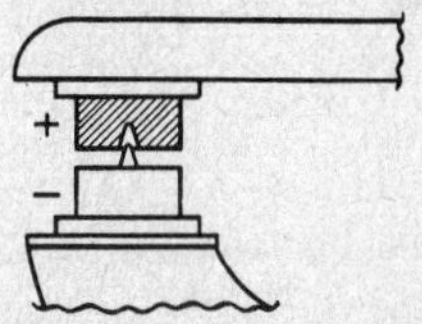

Pitting caused by high capacity

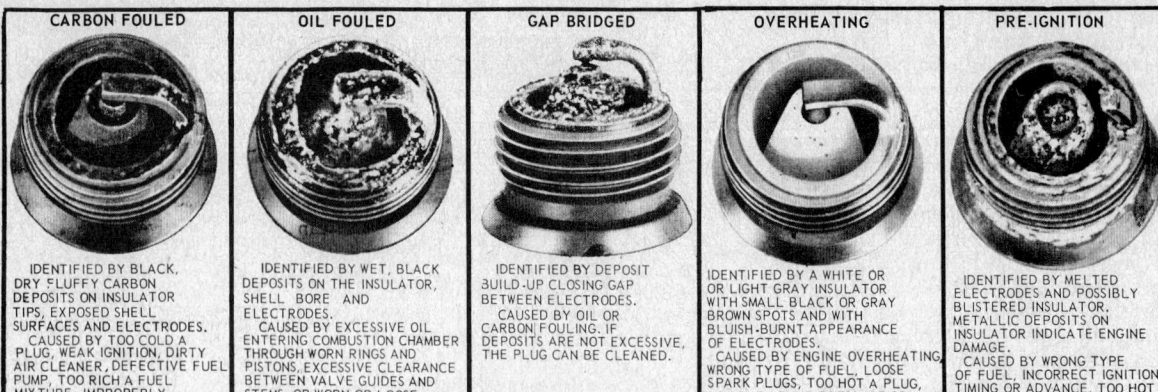

CARBON FOULED

IDENTIFIED BY BLACK, DRY FLUFFY CARBON DEPOSITS ON INSULATOR TIPS, EXPOSED SHELL SURFACES AND ELECTRODES.
CAUSED BY TOO COLD A PLUG, WEAK IGNITION, DIRTY AIR CLEANER, DEFECTIVE FUEL PUMP, TOO RICH A FUEL MIXTURE, IMPROPERLY OPERATING HEAT RISER OR EXCESSIVE IDLING. CAN BE CLEANED.

OIL FOULED

IDENTIFIED BY WET, BLACK DEPOSITS ON THE INSULATOR, SHELL BORE AND ELECTRODES.
CAUSED BY EXCESSIVE OIL ENTERING COMBUSTION CHAMBER THROUGH WORN RINGS AND PISTONS, EXCESSIVE CLEARANCE BETWEEN VALVE GUIDES AND STEMS, OR WORN OR LOOSE BEARINGS. CAN BE CLEANED.

GAP BRIDGED

IDENTIFIED BY DEPOSIT BUILD-UP CLOSING GAP BETWEEN ELECTRODES.
CAUSED BY OIL OR CARBON FOULING. IF DEPOSITS ARE NOT EXCESSIVE, THE PLUG CAN BE CLEANED.

OVERHEATING

IDENTIFIED BY A WHITE OR OR LIGHT GRAY INSULATOR WITH SMALL BLACK OR GRAY BROWN SPOTS AND WITH BLUISH-BURNT APPEARANCE OF ELECTRODES.
CAUSED BY ENGINE OVERHEATING, WRONG TYPE OF FUEL, LOOSE SPARK PLUGS, TOO HOT A PLUG, LOW FUEL PUMP PRESSURE OR INCORRECT IGNITION TIMING.

PRE-IGNITION

IDENTIFIED BY MELTED ELECTRODES AND POSSIBLY BLISTERED INSULATOR. METALLIC DEPOSITS ON INSULATOR INDICATE ENGINE DAMAGE.
CAUSED BY WRONG TYPE OF FUEL, INCORRECT IGNITION TIMING OR ADVANCE, TOO HOT A PLUG, BURNT VALVES OR ENGINE OVERHEATING. REPLACE THE PLUG.

Spark plug inspection

dous demand upon the ignition system, particularly the aspect of coil build up (saturation) and discharge time.

While it is true that ignition points can be adjusted by using a thickness gauge, the results, even when using new points, are sometimes inconclusive. Point gap is incidental to particular distributor cam shape and could be misleading. This is one reason for the use of a dwell meter.

Another point in favor of the dwell meter is its ability to detect high resistance, (oxidized points, poor connections, etc.). The dwell meter, a modified voltmeter, often includes a band on the extreme high end of the scale to indicate excessive point resistance. Follow instrument manufacturer's instructions to get the most out of your particular equipment.

The most informative procedure is to use both methods (dwell meter and point gap) then compare the two. Many times the comparison is surprising, and leads to the location of previously unnoticed distributor troubles.

Using the Dwell Meter

1. With distributor vacuum control line disconnected and plugged, turn the meter selector switch to the eight lobe position (eight cylinder engines) or the six lobe position (six cylinder engines). On four cylinder engines, follow instrument makers' instructions, or select the eight lobe position and double the reading for eight cylinder engines.
2. Connect one tach-dwell meter lead to the coil terminal of the distributor and the other meter lead to ground.
3. Start the engine and operate it at idle speed. Note reading on dwell meter. On eight cylinder engines, (single contacts) dwell should read 26°-32°. Double contacts should read 26°-32° (each set), or 34°-40° combined. Six cylinder engines should show a

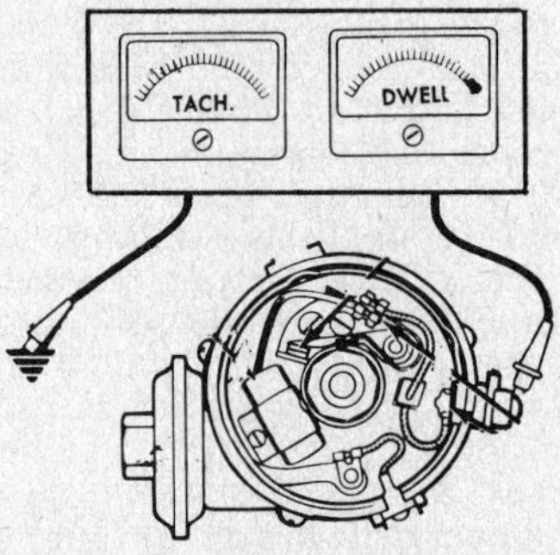

dwell of 36°-45° and four cylinder engines, a dwell in the area of 40°. These are tentative figures and cover a wide latitude. It is therefore, urgent that manufacturers' specifications be followed without exception.

An excessive variation in dwell, (over 3°) as engine speed is increased usually indicates a worn distributor shaft, bushing, breaker plate or secondary circuits.

NOTE: on some Auto-Lite or Ford distributors, a pivoted, movable type breaker plate is used. This pivoted plate, operated by the vacuum control unit, carries the contacts and rotates on its own center, independent of the distributor cam center. This design affects a running dwell variation of as much as 12°. To check this type distributor, hook up the distributor vacuum control line. Increase engine rpm and observe dwell changes at various engine rpm and throttle attitudes.

NOTE: experience dictates that all distributor adjustments are best performed with the use of a good off-car distributor tester.

Dwell information at idle speed is given for each engine in the Tune-up Specification Table in the truck Section.

Ignition Timing

Ignition timing is a term applied to the relationship of piston travel and moment of spark in a gas engine.

Due to the many variables involved, such as compression ratio, temperature, humidity, elevation, fuel octane value, engine condition, work load, etc. published timing data must be considered approximate; some tolerance permitted.

Ignition timing consists of basic (prime) timing and dynamic (variable) timing.

It is very important that point dwell be correct before setting timing.

Basic Timing

Basic timing can be checked quite accurately by using one of the many timing lights, (strobe-flashers) available. A timing light, when properly connected to No. 1 spark wire, (or the exact opposite cylinder in firing sequence of any multiple cylinder, four stroke cycle automotive engine) will indicate the moment of ignition for that cylinder.

NOTE: Some International Harvester engines are timed on No. 8 cylinder.

Index markings may be on either the rotating member of the crankshaft, (vibration damper or flywheel) with the pointer stationary, or the index may be on an engine stationary member, with the pointer or scribe mark rotating.

NOTE: because ignition timing is directly affected by distributor contact spacing, points should be adjusted to specifications before timing is attempted.

1. Unless otherwise stated by the manufacturer, the distributor control vacuum line should be disconnected, and plugged, to prevent fuel induction disturbance.
2. Hook up the timing light, (power or otherwise) according to the equipment instructions.
3. With engine at operating temperature and adjusted to function smoothly, run engine at low idle. Use a tachometer and be sure the rpm is below the speed of governor advance influence.

4. Shine the timing light on the indexing area (balancer or flywheel) and note the degree value indicated by the pointer.
5. Rotate the distributor body one way or the other until the pointer appears to correspond with the index value published.

CAUTION: Power timing (on the road adjusting for ping cannot be tolerated, especially on engines equipped with exhaust emission control devices.

Possible Indications and Causes

If The Flash Is Intermittent:

A. The test light is defective.
B. The test light has a bad connection.
C. Distributor points are bad or badly out of adjustment.
D. Distributor grounding is poor.
E. Distributor cap is cracked or tracking.
F. Spark plug gaps too small.
G. Broken or badly worn rotor.

If Pointer Appears To Move On The Index Scale (Unfixed At Constant Engine Speed):

A. Distributor governor weights loose or with broken springs.
B. Distributor shaft or bushing worn.
C. Rotor loose or broken.
D. Distributor base plate loose.
E. Cam lobes worn.

Dynamic Timing

To accurately check and calibrate dynamic timing through all attitudes of engine operation, more sophisticated equipment than the common strobe-light is needed. A distributor tester, an oscillograph, or one of the more complex timing lights equipped with an advance value index is needed.

It is possible, however, to determine to some degree, the action of both governor advance and vacuum control mechanisms with a tachometer and a timing light.

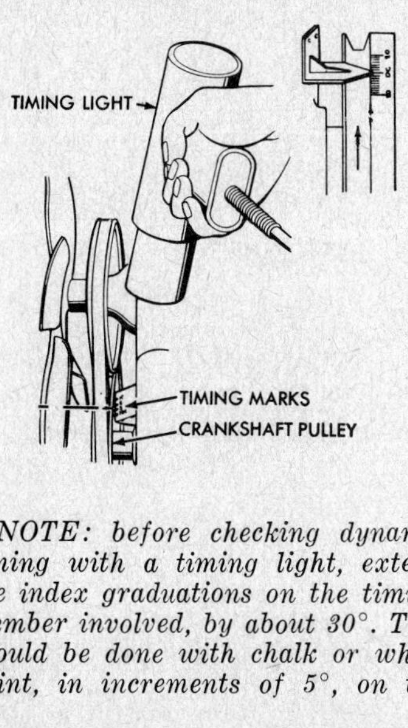

NOTE: before checking dynamic timing with a timing light, extend the index graduations on the timing member involved, by about 30°. This should be done with chalk or white paint, in increments of 5°, on the rotating member, whether that member carries the index or the pointer. Some measurements and extreme care will be necessary in making this extension.

Governor Control

1. Repeat Steps 1 through 4 of basic timing procedures.
2. By watching the timing light flash on the timing index, determine the exact engine rpm that starts the distributor to advance. Compare this with published specifications.

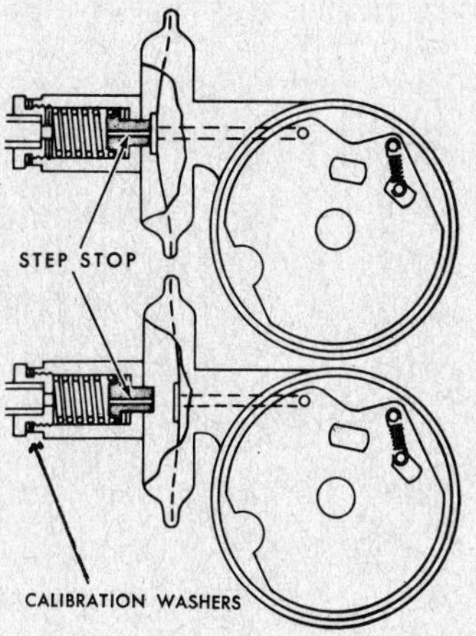

3. It is equally important that distributor advance progresses steadily with engine speed. It is just as important that a decrease in engine speed will smoothly and gradually return the index pointer to its original position.
4. After checking the indications against specifications, turn the engine off and make corrections, if necessary.

NOTE: dynamic timing cannot be accurately checked using the above method; therefore it is recommended that no attempt be made to modify advance curves (especially on exhaust emission equipped engines) unless the proper distributor test facilities are available.

Vacuum Control

Vacuum control action can be observed and evaluated by using a tachometer and a timing light.

This type of spark control, whether used as the only means of control or used in conjunction with a governor type mechanism, operates through a spring loaded vacuum chamber. This chamber is attached to the side of the distributor, then, through linkage, to the breaker plate (or pick-up assembly of transistorized distributors).

Carefully metered vacuum is piped to one side of the spring loaded diaphragm of the vacuum unit. Vacuum

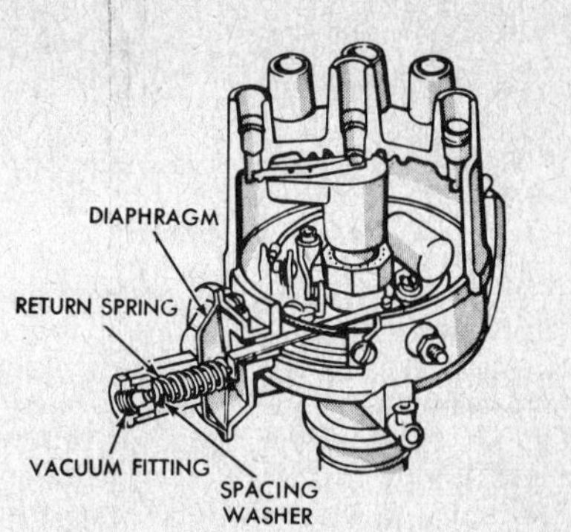

controlled timing is then the result of differential (vacuum-spring) pressures.

In the case of vacuum-only controls, (Ford Loadmatic, etc.) metering is more critical; therefore, a manometer or a very accurately calibrated vacuum gauge is required, in conjunction with the tachometer and timing light.

To Check Vacuum Control:

1. Hook up a tachometer and the timing light in the conventional manner.
2. Connect a good vacuum gauge or a manometer into the vacuum line between the carburetor and distributor.
3. With engine at operating temperature and adjusted to function smoothly, run engine at low idle.
4. Shine timing light on the indexing area and observe the vacuum reading and timing light index relationship.
5. Compare these readings with published vacuum advance data.

Indications and Causes

If timing is not within degree range as specified vacuum reading, a faulty vacuum or mechanical control mechanism, or Loadmatic control mechanism is defective.

If all parts are good, adjustments in control valve can sometimes be made by changing the calibration washers between the vacuum chamber spring and the spring retaining nut. Adding washers will decrease the amount of advance. Removing washers will increase the advance. After one vacuum setting has been adjusted, the others should be checked. Do not change original rpm setting when going to a different vacuum setting.

If other settings are not within limits, there is incorrect spring tension, leakage in the vacuum chamber and/or the line, or the wrong stop has been used in the vacuum chamber of the diaphragm housing.

Electronic Ignition Systems

Ford-Autolite Breaker Point System

This transistorized system uses conventional breaker points, but does not use a condenser. The only external components that serve to distinguish this system from a conventional ignition are an external ballast resistor, a tachometer connecting block, a cold-start relay and an amplifier (transistor switching device).

The major hurdle to increasing primary ignition circuit voltage in point-type is that the points burn very easily. This system uses a transistor to by-pass that weakness.

The design of the main transistor in this system allows it to conduct current from the wire running into it to the wire running out of it—if it is connected to a complete electrical circuit. However, as the current passes through the transistor, it breaks that current down into two paths, one of high voltage and one of low voltage. This transistor is called a PNP transistor because of its three component parts. The top part of the transistor is called a collector (C), the middle part the base (B), and lower part the emitter (E). The two currents that form inside the transistor are the high current one, or power current, which runs from E to C and the low current, or the switching current, which runs from B to E.

The power current is connected to the primary side of the ignition coil and the switching current is connected to the ignition points. This allows high current to energize the primary circuit in the coil while permitting a much smaller current to pass through the points.

In order for the transistor to pass current, both the power circuit and the switching circuit must make a complete circuit. This has made adaptation of this transistor system to an automotive ignition system relatively simple.

When the ignition key is turned on and the breaker points are closed, current passes from the battery, through the ignition switch, to the amplifier which contains the PNP transistor. As the current from the battery passes through the transistor, the two transistor circuits are connected as follows: the power current is connected to the coil, and the switching current is connected to the points. Since the points are closed, both transistor circuits are complete and the primary side of the ignition

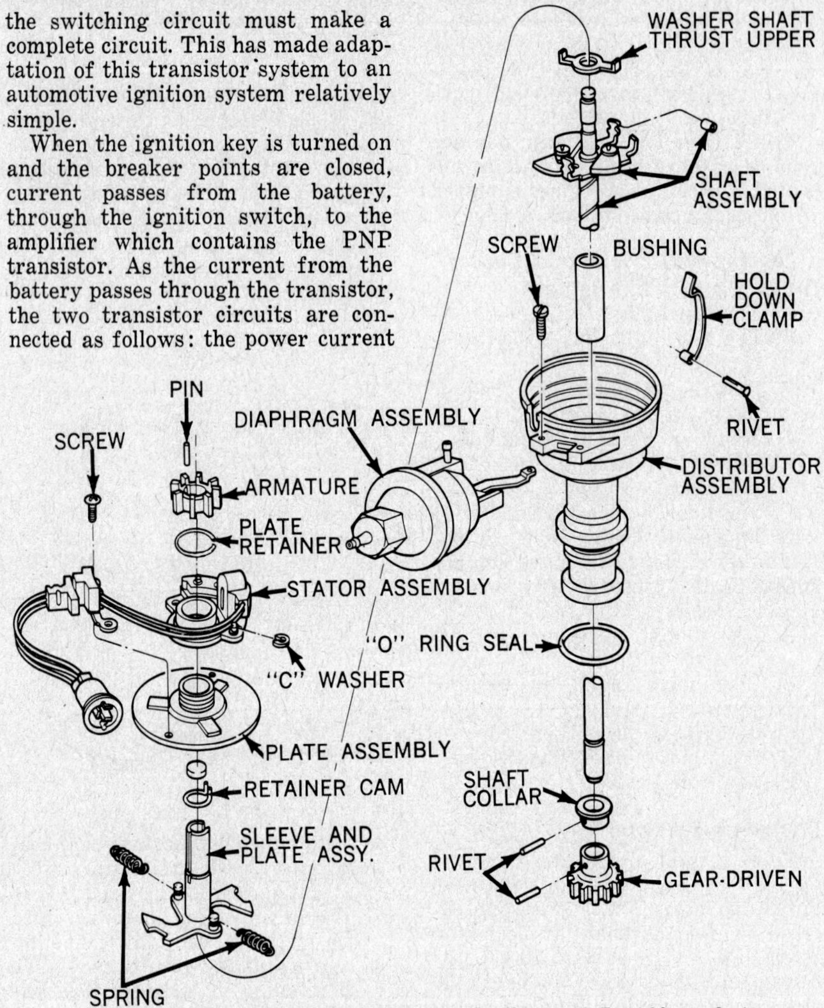

Exploded view—8 cylinder breakerless distributor (© Ford Motor Co.)

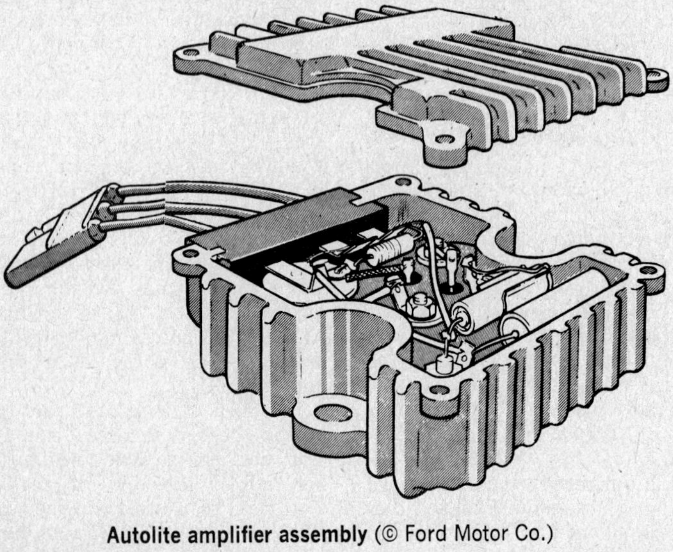
Autolite amplifier assembly (© Ford Motor Co.)

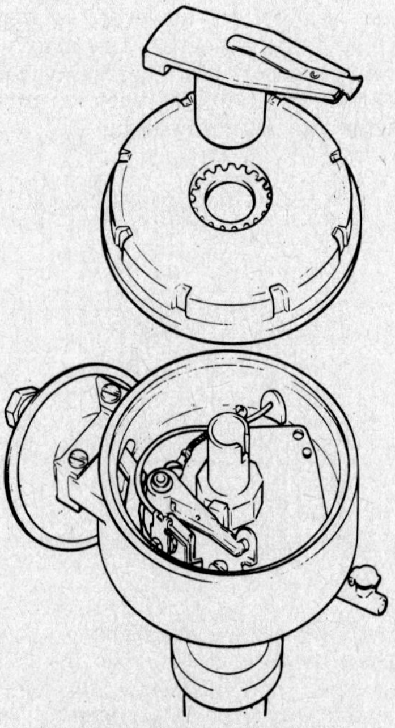
Autolite transistor distributor (© Ford Motor Co.)

coil builds up a magnetic field. When the ignition points open, the switching circuit in the transistor (B to E) opens causing the transistor to stop passing current. When the transistor stops passing current, the primary ignition circuit breaks down, and the induction of the magnetic field from the primary circuit in the coil into the secondary circuit in the coil takes place. However, since the initial voltage in the primary circuit in the coil was much higher than in a conventional system, the voltage buildup in the coil will be much quicker and will rise to a higher level than in a conventional ignition system.

The other components of the system, all of which are contained in the amplifier housing with the PNP transistor, are a condenser, a zener diode, a toroid, a base-to-emitter resistor, and a collector resistor.

The base reisstor is similar to the conventional ignition resistor wire and is located between the distributor and the transistor (heat sink). It provides an 8.0 ohm resistance which is necessary for current limitation and it should not be replaced with any other wire, resistance or otherwise. To do so would result in immediate transistor destruction.

The collector and emitter resistors both are located in a ballast resistor block made of white ceramic for electrical and thermal insulation. Both resistors serve the same purpose—limiting system current and control of voltages within their respective circuits. The two resistors are in series in the collector-emitter circuit, together with the ignition coil, toroid and transistor. The emitter resistor also is in series with the base resistor, the toroid, and the transistor, in the base-emitter circuit. The transistor and emitter resistance therefore are common to both circuits. The combined resistances in each circuit permit a base current of approximately 1.0 amp. and a collector current of approximately 12 amps.

A tach block is included in the circuit for attaching tachometer and dwellmeter leads. In the conventional system, these leads are connected to the distributor primary lead and ground, but in the transistorized circuit, the connection of the leads in this manner would jump the contact gap, contributing to a current buildup in the base circuit and in the collector circuit which would overheat and burn out the transistor. The area surrounding the collector terminal is colored *red* for the meter red lead while the area surrounding the emitter terminal is colored *black* for the meter black lead.

A cold start relay is incorporated into the circuit at the starter relay, interrupting the conventional battery-to-coil lead. The purpose of this is to furnish additional current to the coil primary windings during situations when the starter draw is excessive. The cold start relay contacts normally are closed; only opening during the cranking cycle. However, when the available battery voltage drops below a predetermined value during the cranking cycle, they again close, bypassing the ignition resistor and furnishing full battery current to the system.

The distributor differs from the conventional distributor only in the absence of the condenser and in the highly polished breaker cam. Because one of the big advantages of the transistor ignition is long breaker point life, wear on the rubbing block must be reduced to a minimum. Because the current at the breaker points is so small, the amount of pitting that occurs during normal operation is hardly measurable and point life should be indefinite. The points should be set to .020 in. gap and high-temperature grease used for cam lubrication.

When testing the transistor ignition distributor in a test machine, in-

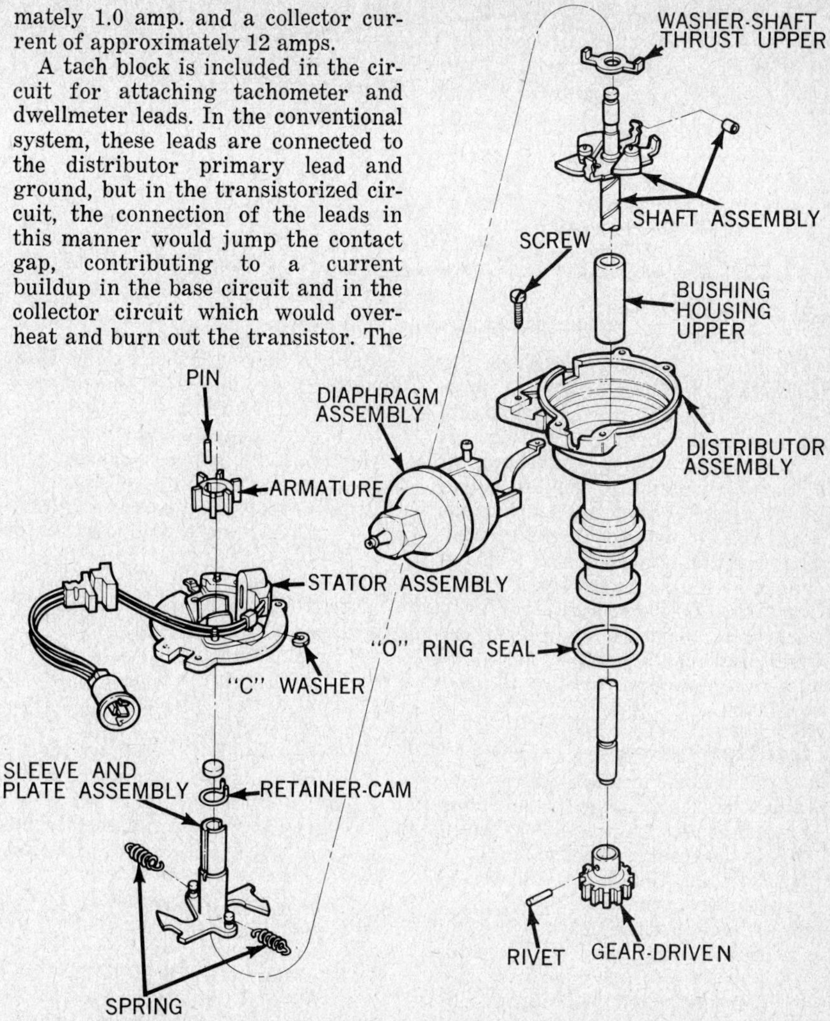

Exploded view—6 cylinder breakerless distributor (© Ford Motor Co.)

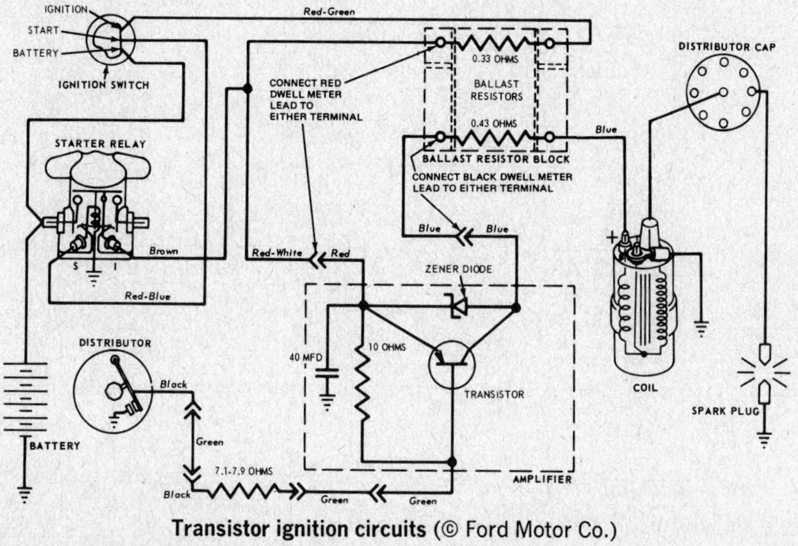

Transistor ignition circuits (© Ford Motor Co.)

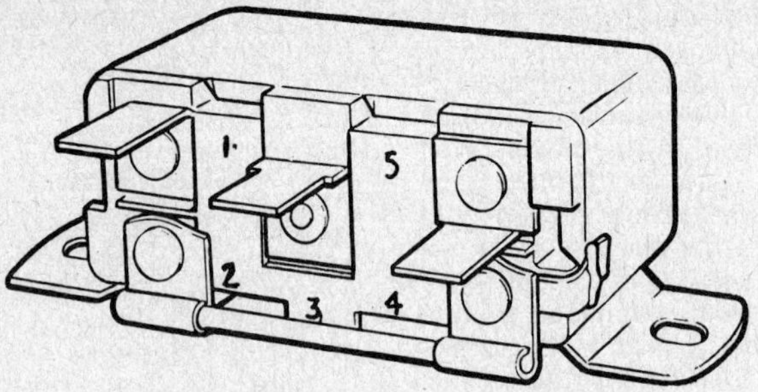

Autolite cold start relay (© Ford Motor Co.)

corporate a condenser into the primary-to-ground circuit using a jumper wire. This will prevent point pitting or oxidation during testing.

CAUTION: **When connecting an in-car tachometer to the Ford System, always shunt the tachometer leads that go to the coil IGN terminal and ignition switch with a 10 in. length of Ford ignition resistor wire, part No. COLF-12250-A, to prevent tachometer damage. The higher current draw of the transistor system can ruin a tach if this precaution is not taken.**

Troubleshooting

Ignition problems are caused by a failure in the primary or secondary circuit, or incorrect ignition timing. Isolate the trouble as follows:

1. Remove the coil high tension lead from the distributor cap.
2. Disconnect the brown wire from the starter relay "I" terminal and the red and blue wire from the starter relay "S" terminal.
3. Turn the ignition switch on.
4. While holding the high tension lead approximately 1/4 in. from the engine block, crank the engine by using a remote starter switch between the starter relay "S" and battery terminals.

If the spark is good, the trouble lies in the secondary (high voltage) circuit. If there is no spark or a weak spark, the trouble is in the primary (low voltage) circuit.

A breakdown or energy loss in the primary circuit can be caused by:

1. Defective primary wiring.
2. Improperly adjusted, contaminated or defective distributor points.
3. Defective amplifier assembly.

The trouble can be isolated by performing a primary circuit test.

A breakdown or enery loss in the secondary circuit can be caused by:

1. Fouled or improperly adjusted spark plugs.
2. Defective high voltage wiring.
3. High voltage leakage across the coil, distributor cap, or rotor.

To isolate a problem in the secondary circuit, turn the ignition switch off, remove the remote starter switch from the starter relay, install the coil high tension lead in the distributor cap, the red and blue wire to the starter relay (this goes on the "S" terminal) and the brown wire to the starter relay (this goes on the "I" terminal) and perform a secondary circuit test.

Primary Circuit Tests

CAUTION: **Do not use any other procedure, conventional short-cut, or connect test equipment in any other manner than described, or extensive damage can be caused to the transistor ignition system.**

Connect a dwell meter to the tachometer block. Connect the black lead to the black (large) terminal and the red lead to the red (small) terminal.

With the remote starter switch installed and the ignition switch on, ground the coil high tension wire and crank the engine and observe the dwell reading.

0° Dwell

1. The distributor points are contaminated or are not closing.
2. An open circuit in the distributor lead to the amplifier.

To determine which item listed is causing the trouble, proceed as follows:

Disconnect the distributor lead at the bullet connector and connect a voltmeter red lead to the red (small) tach block terminal and the voltmeter black lead to the distributor lead from the distributor. *Do not connect the voltmeter to the lead from the amplifier.* Crank the engine and note the voltmeter reading.

If a steady indication of voltage is obtained, the trouble is in the distributor lead to the amplifier. Absence of any voltage indication on the voltmeter shows that there is an open circuit between the distributor lead and the breaker point ground.

0-45° Dwell

1. The transistor and the primary circuit are functioning properly.
2. The trouble could be in the secondary circuit.

45° Dwell

1. No power from the ignition switch.

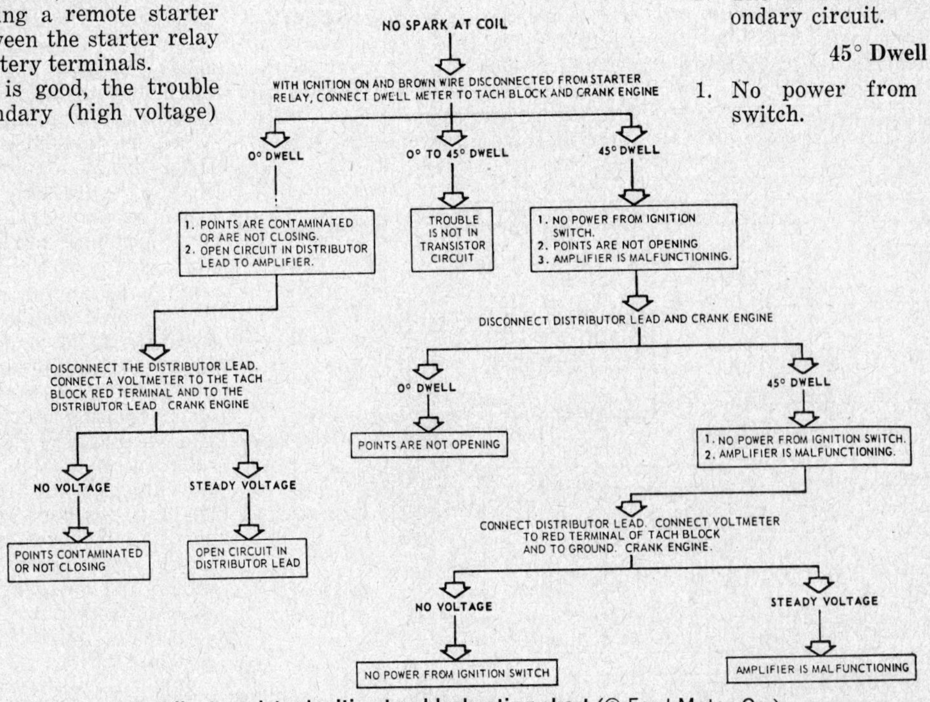

Autolite transistor ignition troubleshooting chart (© Ford Motor Co.)

2. The distributor points are closed and not opening.
3. Defective amplifier assembly.

To determine which of the three items listed is causing the trouble, proceed as follows:

Disconnect the distributor lead at the bullet connector, and crank the engine. If the dwellmeter indicates 0° dwell, the distributor points are not opening. If 45° dwell is indicated, the amplifier is malfunctioning or there is no power from the ignition switch.

Use a voltmeter or test light to determine if the transistor (amplifier assembly) is at fault. Connect the voltmeter to the red-green lead terminal of the ballast resistor and to ground. Crank the engine.

Absence of any voltage indication on the voltmeter shows there is an open circuit, or no power between the ignition switch and the amplifier. The ballast resistor could be defective. Replace it with a good ballast resistor, and repeat the test.

A steady indication of voltage on the voltmeter indicates either a defective amplifier or the coil to amplifier lead is defective or improperly connected to the ballast resistor. Proceed as follows:

1. Disconnect the amplifier at the quick disconnect.
2. Connect an ohmmeter across the outside terminals of the amplifier side of the quick disconnect.
3. Reverse the ohmmeter leads.

If a very high resistance is obtained one way and a very low or *zero* resistance is obtained the other way, the amplifier is not defective. Check the coil to amplifier wiring for a loose connection or defective wiring.

After a repair has been made, run through the test again to check for any other malfunctions.

Secondary Circuit Tests

Use conventional system test procedures.

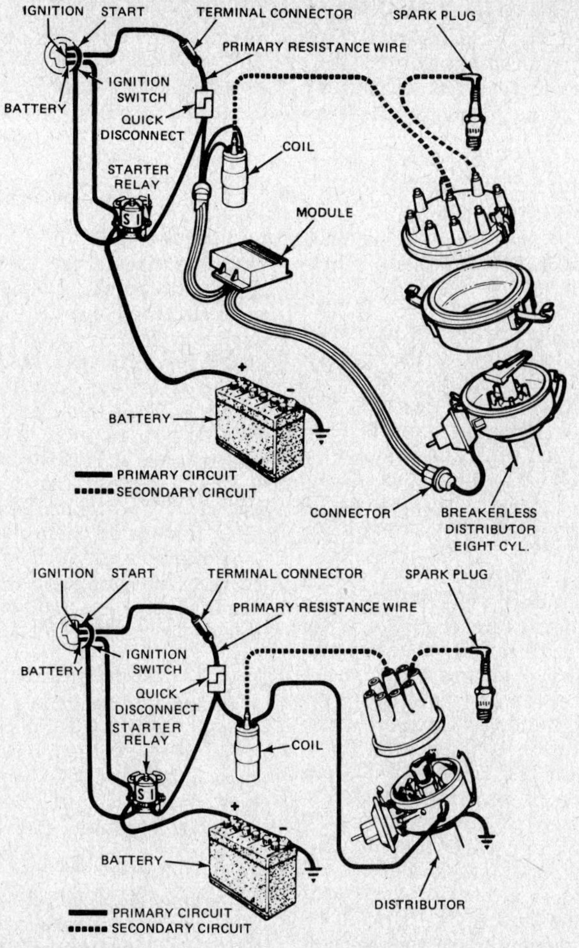

Circuit routings for conventional and breakerless ignition systems (© Ford Motor Co.)

Ford-Motorcraft Solid-State Ignition System

The Ford-Motorcraft Solid-State Ignition System is a pulse triggered, breakerless, transistor controlled ignition system. The system utilizes most of the standard ignition components, but substitutes an amplifier module and magnetic pickup assembly for the conventional ignition contact points.

Operation

With the ignition switch "on", the primary circuit is on and the ignition coil is energized. When the armature "spokes" approach the magnetic pickup coil assembly, they induce a voltage which tells the amplifier to turn the coil primary current off. A timing circuit in the amplifier module will turn the current on again after the coil field has collapsed. When the current is "on", it flows from the battery through the ignition switch, the primary windings of the ignition coil, and through the amplifier module circuits to ground. When the current is off, the magnetic field built up in the ignition coil is allowed to collapse, inducing a high voltage into the secondary windings of the coil. High voltage is produced each time the field is thus built up and collapsed.

The high voltage flows through the coil high tension lead to the distributor cap where the rotor distributes it to one of the spark plug terminals in the distributor cap. This process is repeated for every power stroke of the engine.

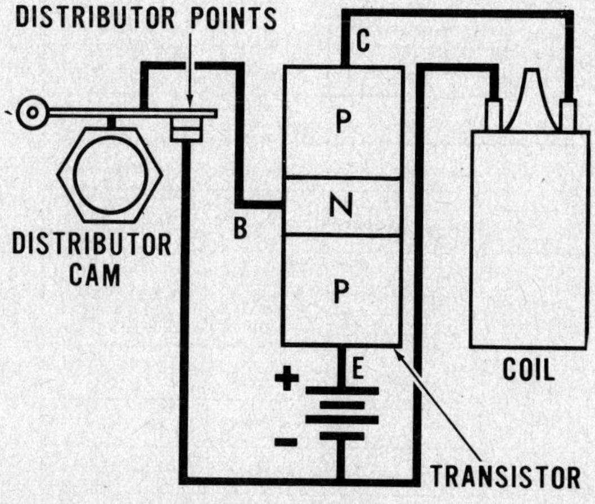

Primary circuit connected to PNP transistor (© Ford Motor Co.)

Ignition system troubles are caused by a failure in the primary and/or the secondary circuit; incorrect ignition timing; or incorrect distributor advance. Circuit failures may be caused by shorts, corroded or dirty terminals, loose connections, defective wire insulation, cracked distributor cap or rotor, defective pick-up coil assembly or amplifier module, defective distributor points, fouled spark plugs, or by improper dwell angle.

If an engine starting or operating trouble is attributed to the ignition system, start the engine and verify the complaint. On engines that will not start, be sure that there is gasoline in the fuel tank and that fuel is reaching the carburetor. Then locate the ignition system problem by an oscilloscope test or by a spark intensity test.

Primary Circuit Testing

A breakdown or energy loss in the primary circuit can be caused by: defective primary wiring, loose or corroded connections, inoperative or defective magnetic pick-up coil assembly, or defective amplifier module.

A complete test of the primary circuit consists of checking the circuits in the ignition coil, the magnetic pick-up coil assembly and the amplifier module. Wiring harness checks will be included as a part of basic component circuit tests.

Always inspect connectors for dirt, corrosion or poor fit before assuming you have spotted a possible problem.

Troubleshooting

Make sure that the battery is fully charged before beginning tests. Perform a Spark Intensity Test. If no spark is observed, make sure that the high tension coil wire is good. Disconnect the three-way and four-way connectors at the electronic module.

The first trouble isolation test will be conducted on the harness terminals, with the electronic module disconnected from the circuit. The pin numbers shown in the schematic correspond to those shown in the trouble isolation test table.

Make the following tests using a sensitive volt-ohmmeter. These tests will direct you to the proper follow-up test to determine the actual problem.

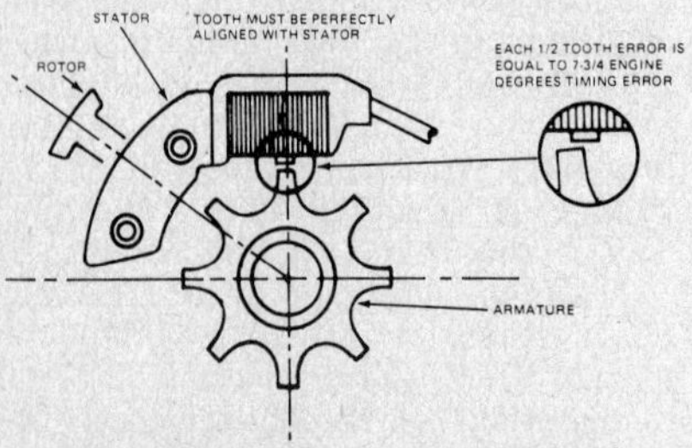

Breakerless armature alignment in relationship with ignition timing (© Ford Motor Co.)

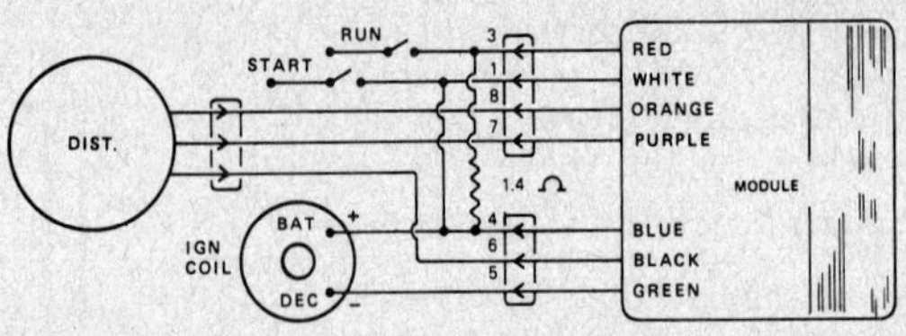

Electronic module schematic—solid state ignition (© Ford Motor Co.)

If the circuit checks good at all these test points, connect a known good electronic module in place of the vehicle module and again perform the spark intensity test. If the substitution corrects the malfunction again reconnect the vehicle module and perform the spark intensity test. If the malfunction still exists, the problem is in the module and it must be replaced. If the problem is gone, it may be in the wiring connectors.

If the substitute module does not correct the problem, reconnect the original module and make repairs elsewhere in the system.

Module Bias Test

Measure the voltage at Pin 3 to engine ground with the ignition key "on". If the voltage observed is less than battery voltage, repair the voltage feed wiring to the module for running conditions (re-wire).

Battery Source Test

1. Connect the voltmeter leads from the battery terminal at the coil to engine ground, without disconnecting the coil from the circuit.
2. Install a jumper wire from the DEC terminal of the coil to a good engine ground.
3. Turn the lights and all accessories off.
4. Turn the ignition switch "on".
5. If the voltmeter reading is between 4.9 and 7.9 volts, the primary circuit from the battery is satisfactory.
6. If the voltmeter reading is less than 4.9 volts, check the following:
   a. The primary wiring for worn insulation, broken strands, and loose or corroded terminals.
   b. The resistance wiring for defects.
7. If the voltmeter reading is greater than 7.9 volts, the resistance wire should be replaced after verifying a defect.

Cranking Test

Measure the voltage at Pin 1 to engine ground with the engine cranking. If the voltage observed is not 8 to 12 volts, repair the voltage feed to the module for starting conditions (white wire).

Starting Circuit Test

If the reading is not between 8 and 12 volts, the ignition by-pass circuit is open or grounded from either the starter solenoid or the ignition switch to Pin 5. Check the primary connections at the coil.

Distributor Hardware Test

1. Disconnect the three-wire weatherproof connector at the distributor pigtail.
2. Connect a D.C. voltmeter on a 2.5 volt scale to the two parallel

TROUBLE ISOLATION TESTS

	TEST VOLTAGE BETWEEN	SHOULD BE	IF NOT, CONDUCT
KEY ON	Pin # 3 and Engine Ground	Battery Voltage	Module Bias Test
	Pin # 5 and Engine Ground	Battery Voltage	Battery Source Test
CRANKING	Pin # 1 and Engine Ground	8 to 12 volts	Cranking Test
	Pin # 5 and Engine Ground	8 to 12 volts	Starting Circuit Test
	Pin # 7 and Pin # 8	½ volt A.C. or D.C. volt wiggle	Distributor Hardware Test

	TEST RESISTANCE BETWEEN	SHOULD BE	IF NOT, CONDUCT
KEY OFF	Pin # 7 and Pin # 8 Pin # 6 and Engine Ground Pin # 7 and Engine Ground Pin # 8 and Engine Ground	400 to 800 ohms 0 ohms more than 70,000 ohms more than 70,000 ohms	Magnetic Pick-up (Stator) Test
	Pin # 3 and Coil Tower Pin # 5 and Pin # 4	7000 to 13000 ohms 1.0 to 2.0 ohms	Coil Test
	Pin # 5 and Engine Ground	more than 10.0 ohms	Short Test
	Pin # 3 and Pin # 4	1.0 to 2.0 ohms	Resistance Wire

Solid state ignition diagnosis (© Ford Motor Co.)

blades. With the engine cranking, the meter needle should oscillate.

3. Remove the distributor cap and check for visual damage or misassembly.
   a. Sintered iron armature (6 or 8-toothed wheel) must be tight on the sleeve, and the roll pin aligning the armature must be in position.
   b. Sintered iron stator must not be broken.
   c. Armature must rotate when the engine is cranked.
4. If the hardware is alright, but the meter doesn't oscillate, replace the magnetic pick-up assembly.

Magnetic Pick-up Tests

1. Resistance of pick-up coil measured between two parallel pins in the distributor connector must be 400-800 ohms.
2. Resistance between the third blade (ground) and the distributor bowl must be zero ohms.
3. Resistance between either parallel blade and engine ground must be greater than 70,000 ohms.
4. If any test fails, the distributor stator assembly is defective and must be replaced.
5. If the above readings are not the same as measured in the original test, check for a defective harness. If the readings are the same, proceed.
6. If these tests check alright, the signal generator portion of the distributor is working properly.

Ignition Coil Test

The breakerless ignition coil must be diagnosed separately from the rest of the ignition system.

1. Primary resistance must be 1.0-2.0 ohms, measured from the BAT to the DEC terminals.
2. Secondary resistance must be 7,000-13,000 ohms, measured from the BAT or DEC terminal to the center tower of the coil.
3. If resistance tests are alright, but the coil is still suspected, test the coil on a coil tester by following the test equipment manufacturer's instructions for a standard coil. If the reading differs from the original test, check for a defective harness.

Module Test 1975 and later

1. Unplug the electronic module connector, but don't remove the existing module from the car.
2. Connect a module which is known to be good to the connector. There is no need to attach the module to the car in order to have it work.
3. Start the engine; if it starts and operates correctly go on to the next step. If it won't start and run the trouble is somewhere else. Check and repair the wiring and other systems, as required.
4. If the engine started in step 3, reconnect the original module and try to start the engine again. If the engine won't start, replace the module.
5. If the engine starts in step 4, the original module is not defective. Check all the wiring and connections in the ignition system.

Short Test

If the resistance from Pin 5 to ground is less than 10 ohms, check for a short to ground at the DEC terminal of the ignition coil or in the connection wiring to that terminal.

Resistance Wire Test

Replace the resistance wire if it is out of specifications (See "Ignition Resistor Wire").

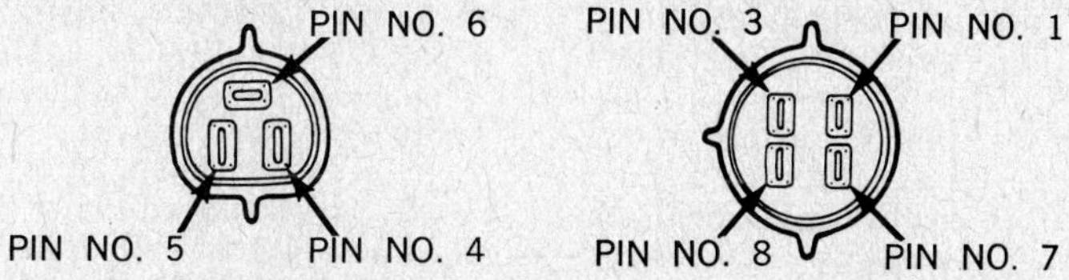

Electronic module connectors—harness side (© Ford Motor Co.)

Adjustments

The air gap between the armature and magnetic pick-up coil in the distributor is not adjustable, nor are there any adjustments for the amplifier module. Inoperative components are simply replaced. Any attempt to connect components outside the vehicle may result in component failure.

Component Replacement

Magnetic Pick-up Assembly Removal and Installation

1. Remove the distributor cap and rotor and disconnect the distributor harness plug.
2. Using a small gear puller or two screwdrivers, lift or pry the armature from the advance plate sleeve. Remove the roll pin.
3. Remove the large wire retaining clip from the base plate annular groove.
4. Remove the snap-ring which secures the vacuum advance link to the pick-up assembly.
5. Remove the magnetic pick-up assembly ground screw and lift the assembly from the distributor.
6. Lift the vacuum advance arm off the post on the pick-up assembly and move it out against the distributor housing.
7. Place the new pick-up assembly in position over the fixed base plate and slide the wiring in position through the slot in the side of the distributor housing.
8. Install the fine wire snap-ring securing the pick-up assembly to the fixed base plate.
9. Position the vacuum advance arm over the post on the pick-up assembly and install the snap-ring.
10. Install the grounding screw through the tab on the wiring harness and into the fixed base plate.
11. Install the armature on the advance plate sleeve making sure that the roll pin is engaged in the matching slots.
12. Install the distributor rotor cap.
13. Connect the distributor wiring plug to the vehicle harness.

Delco Remy Electronic Ignition Systems

Delco-Remy Magnetic Pulse System

Components

The Delco-Remy magnetic pulse, fully transistorized ignition system uses a magnetic pulse distributor having no breaker points. This system switches power electronically rather than with ignition contact points. Instead of the familiar cam and breaker plate assembly, this distributor uses a rotating iron timer core and a magnetic pickup assembly. The magnetic pickup assembly consists of a bearing plate on which are sandwiched a ceramic ring-type permanent magnet, two pole pieces and a pick-up coil. The pole pieces are doughnut shaped steel plates with accurately spaced internal teeth, one tooth for each cylinder of the engine.

A critically important part is the iron timer core. It has a number of equally spaced projections or vanes and is attached to, and rotates with, the distributor shaft.

The transistor control unit, the switchbox of the system, is mounted

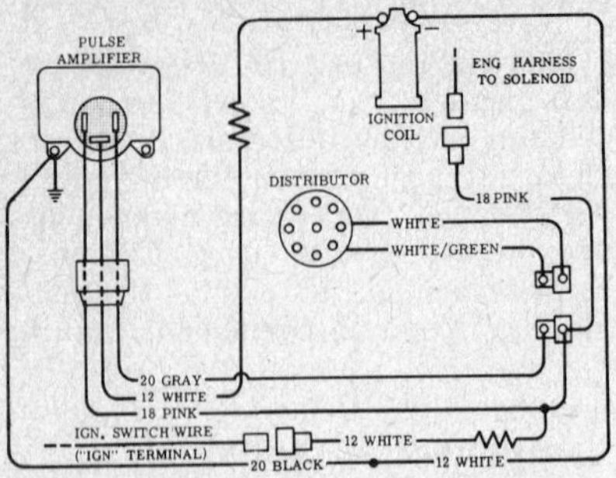

Magnetic pulse system circuit diagram
(© Chevrolet Div., G.M. Corp.)

in an aluminum case and contains three transistors, a zener diode, a condenser and five small resistors. The zener diode is a circuit protection device. Remaining components control and switch ignition-coil current electronically; there are no moving parts in the control unit.

The ignition coil is of standard design except for a special winding. The external primary resistor is a ceramic type, similar to those used on various conventional systems.

Operation

The ignition primary circuit is connected from the battery, through the ignition switch, through the ignition pulse amplifier assembly, through the primary side of the ignition coil, and back to the amplifier housing where it is grounded externally. The secondary circuit is the same as in conventional ignition systems: the secondary side of the coil, the coil wire to the distributor, the rotor, the spark plug wires and the spark-plugs.

The magnetic pulse distributor is also connected to the ignition pulse amplifier. As the distributor shaft rotates, the distributor rotating pole piece turns inside the stationary pole piece. As the rotating pole piece turns inside the stationary pole piece, the eight teeth on the rotating pole piece align with the eight teeth on the stationary pole piece eight times during each distributor revolution (two crankshaft revolutions since the distributor runs at one-half crankshaft speed). As the rotating pole piece teeth move close to, and align with, the teeth on the stationary pole piece, the magnetic rotating pole piece induces voltage into the magnetic pole piece through the stationary pole piece. This voltage pulse is sent to the ignition pulse amplifier from the magnetic pole piece. When the pulse enters the amplifier, it signals the ignition pulse amplifier to interrupt the ignition primary circuit. This causes the primary circuit to collapse and begins the induction of the magnetic lines of force from the primary side of the coil into the secondary side of the coil. This induction provides the required voltage to fire the spark plugs.

The advantages of this system are that the transistors in the ignition pulse amplifier can make and break the primary ignition circuit much faster than conventional ignition points, and higher primary voltage can be utilized since this system can be made to handle higher voltage without adverse effects, whereas ignition breaker points cannot. The shorter switching time of this system allows longer coil primary circuit saturation time and longer induction time when the primary circuit collapses. This increased time allows the primary circuit to build up more current and the secondary circuit to discharge more current.

Troubleshooting

Cautions

1. Don't use 18 volts or 24 volts for emergency starting.
2. Never crank engine with coil high-tension lead or more than three spark plug leads disconnected.
3. Don't short circuit between coil positive terminal and ground.
4. On any repair that necessitates replacement of control unit or ignition resistor, perform complete charging system check before releasing the unit. Basic cause of trouble may be high or uncontrolled charging rate.

Engine Surge or Intermittent Miss

Since there are so many possible causes for this problem, all other possible defects must be ruled out before the specialized components of the electronic ignition system are judged defective.

As a general rule, a miss or surge that is caused by an ignition problem will be much more pronounced than a similiar problem that is caused by carburetion. Also, carburetion is usually affected by temperature more than the ignition system is. A carburetor or intake manifold vacuum leak is often compensated for by the choke when the engine is cold. When the engine warms up and the choke is released, the engine surge will show up.

If the ignition system is found to be the source of the problem, first check all connections in the system to make sure that they are *clean and tight*. Check the coil and spark plug high-tension wires with an ohmmeter to be sure they have the correct resistance. Check the inside and outside of the distributor cap and the tower on the ignition coil for cracks which would allow the high voltage intended for the spark plugs to short to ground.

If none of the above checks uncovers a defective component, the distributor pick-up coil leads may be reversed in the connector, or the pickup coil itself may have an intermittent open.

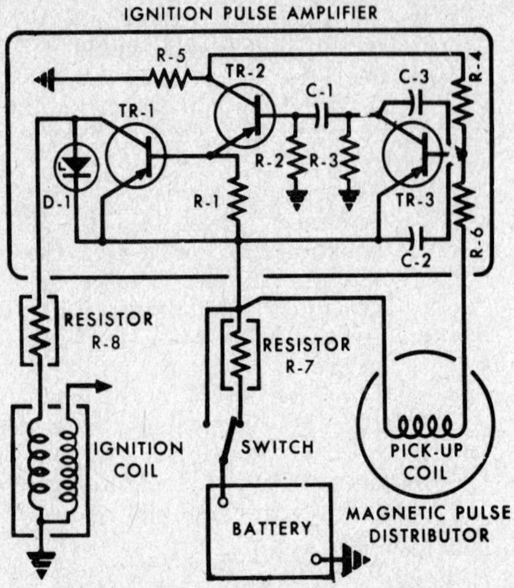

Magnetic pulse amplifier schematic
(© Chevrolet Div., G.M. Corp.)

Engine Will Not Start or Is Hard to Start

1. Disconnect a spark plug wire from one spark plug and hold the wire ¼ in. from a good ground with a pair of insulated pliers.
2. Crank the engine over and observe whether a spark jumps from the plug wire to ground.
3. *If spark occurs,* the problem is not in the ignition system.
4. *If spark does not occur,* reconnect the spark plug wire that was disconnected and connect a tachometer between the positive (+) coil primary terminal and the pink wire in the three-wire connector to the ignition pulse amplifier.
5. Crank the engine over and observe the tachometer.
6. *If the tachometer needle deflects* while cranking the engine, perform "Ignition Distributor Test" to locate the problem.
7. *If the tachometer needle does not deflect* while cranking the engine, perform "Circuit Resistance Test" to pinpoint the problem.

Circuit Resistance Test Ignition Distributor Check

1. Disconnect the distributor leads from the engine wiring harness.
2. Connect the two leads of an ohmmeter to the distributor leads at the connector.
3. Rotate the magnetic pick-up assembly in the distributor through full vacuum advance travel and read the ohmmeter. If the reading is not within a range of 500-700 ohms, replace the magnetic pick-up assembly.

4. If the reading is within the 500-700 ohms range, disconnect one ohmmeter lead from the distributor connector and connect it to a good ground. If the reading is less than infinity (needle moves to end of scale), replace the magnetic pick-up assembly.
5. If the reading is infinite, and there was no spark when the spark plug wire was disconnected from the plug, the amplifier is defective.

Delco-Remy High Energy Ignition (HEI) System

Components

The Delco-Remy High Energy Ignition (HEI) System is a breakerless, pulse triggered, transistor controlled, inductive discharge ignition system.

It is similar in operation to the Magnetic Pulse System. There are only nine external electrical connections; the ignition switch feed wire, and the eight spark plug leads. On V8 engines, the ignition coil is located within the distributor cap, connecting directly to the rotor.

Operation

The magnetic pick-up assembly located inside the distributor contains a permanent magnet, a pole piece with internal teeth, and a pick-up coil. When the teeth of the rotating timer core and pole piece align, an induced voltage in the pick-up coil signals the electronic module to open the coil primary circuit. As the primary current decreases, a high voltage is induced in the secondary windings of the ignition coil, directing a spark through the rotor and high voltage leads to fire the spark plugs. The dwell period is automatically controlled by the electronic module and is increased with increasing engine rpm. The HEI System features a longer spark duration which is instrumental in firing lean and EGR diluted fuel/air mixtures. The condenser (capacitor) located within the HEI distributor is provided for noise (static) suppression purposes only and is not a regularly replaced ignition system component.

Major Repair Operations (Distributor in Engine)

Ignition Coil Replacement V8 Engines

1. Disconnect the feed and module wire terminal connectors from the distributor cap.
2. Remove the ignition set retainer.
3. Remove the 4 coil cover-to-distributor cap screws and the coil cover.
4. Remove the 4 coil-to-distributor cap screws.
5. Using a blunt drift, press the coil wire spade terminals up out of distributor cap.
6. Lift the coil up out of the distributor cap.
7. Remove and clean the coil spring, rubber seal washer and coil cavity of the distributor cap.
8. Coat the rubber seal with a dielectric lubricant furnished in the replacement ignition coil package.
9. Reverse the above procedures to install.

Six Cylinder Engines

On 6 cylinder engines, a separate ignition coil is used. To remove and install it, proceed as follows:

1. Remove the ignition switch-to-coil lead from the coil.
2. Unfasten the distributor leads from the coil.
3. Remove the screws which secure the coil to the engine and lift it off.

Installation is the reverse of removal.

Distributor Cap Replacement

1. Remove the feed and module wire terminal connectors from the distributor cap.
2. Remove the retainer and spark plug wires from the cap.
3. Depress and release the 4 distributor cap-to-housing retainers and lift off the cap assembly.
4. Remove the 4 coil cover screws and cover (V8 only).
5. Using a finger or a blunt drift, push the spade terminals up out of the distributor cap (V8 only).
6. Remove all 4 coil screws and lift the coil, coil spring and rubber seal washer out of the cap coil cavity (V8 only).
7. Using a new distributor cap, reverse the above procedures to assemble being sure to clean and lubricate the rubber seal washer with dielectric lubricant.

Rotor Replacement

1. Disconnect the feed and module wire connectors from the distributor.
2. Depress and release the 4 distributor cap to housing retainers and lift off the cap assembly.
3. Remove the two rotor attaching screws and rotor.

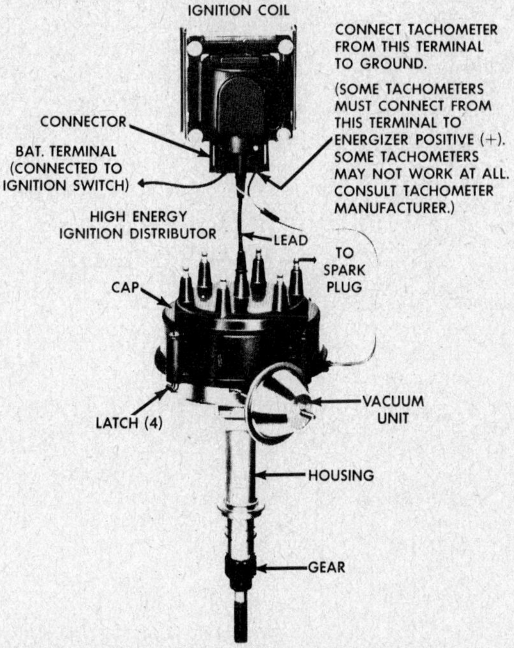

Connector details for inline six cylinder HEI system (© Chevrolet Div., G.M. Corp.)

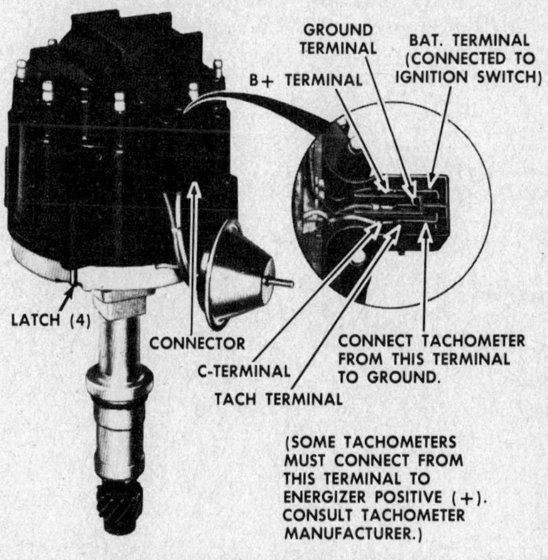

Connector details for V8 HEI system (© Chevrolet Div., G.M. Corp.)

4. Reverse the above procedure to install.

Vacuum Advance Unit Replacement

1. Remove the distributor cap and rotor as previously described.
2. Disconnect the vacuum hose from the vacuum advance unit. Remove the module.
3. Remove the two vacuum advance retaining screws, pull the advance unit outward, rotate and disengage the operating rod from its tang.
4. Reverse the above procedure to install.

Module Replacement

1. Remove the distributor cap and rotor as previously described.
2. Disconnect the harness connector and pick-up coil spade connectors from the module (note their positions).
3. Remove the two screws and module from the distributor housing.
4. Coat the bottom of the new module with dielectric lubricant. Reverse the above procedure to install. Be sure that the leads are installed correctly.

Distributor Removal

1. Disconnect the ground cable from the battery.
2. Disconnect the feed and module terminal connectors from the distributor cap. (Don't use a screwdriver).
3. Disconnect the hose at the vacuum advance.
4. Depress and release the 4 distributor cap-to-housing retainers and lift off the cap assembly.
5. Using crayon or chalk, make locating marks on the rotor and module and on the distributor housing and engine for installation purposes.
6. Loosen and remove the distributor clamp bolt and clamp, and lift distributor out of the engine. Noting the relative position of the rotor and module alignment marks, make a second mark on the rotor to align it with the one mark on the module.

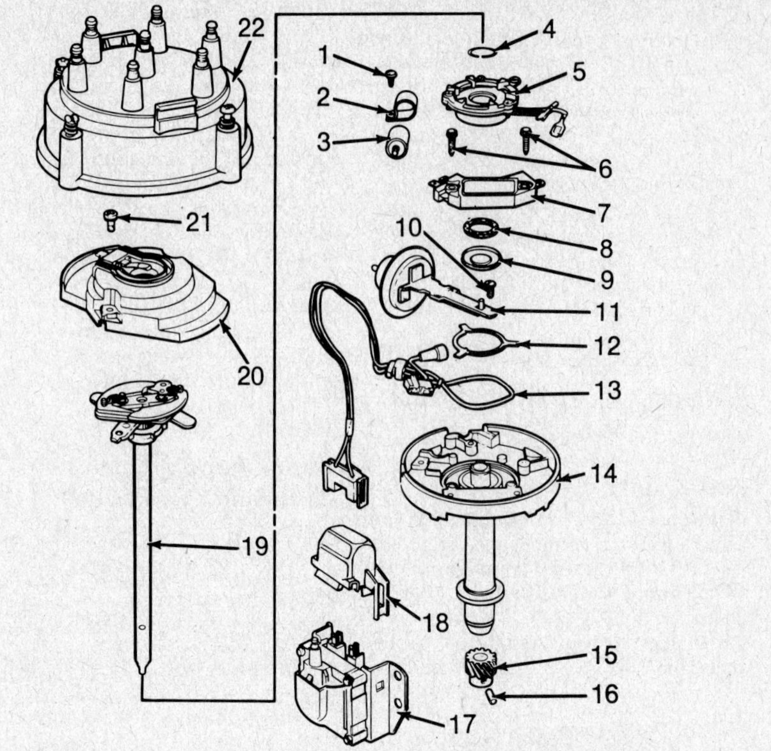

1 Screw
2 Bracket
3 Capacitor
4 Thin c-washer (retainer)
5 Pole piece and plate assembly (pick up coil)
6 Screw
7 Module assembly
8 Felt washer
9 Plastic grease retainer seal
10 Screw
11 Vacuum control assembly
12 Retainer (wire harness)
13 Wire harness assembly
14 Housing assembly
15 Gear
16 Roll pin
17 Ignition coil
18 Cover
19 Distributor shaft assembly
20 Rotor
21 Screw
22 Distributor cap

H E I distributor—6 cylinder (© Chevrolet Div., G.M. Corp.)

Distributor Installation

1. With a new O-ring on the distributor housing and the second mark on the rotor aligned with the mark on the module, install the distributor, taking care to align the mark on the housing with the one on the engine. It may be necessary to lift the dis-

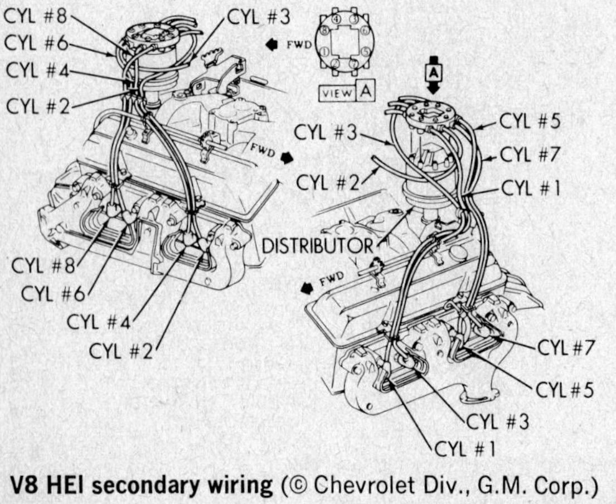

V8 HEI secondary wiring (© Chevrolet Div., G.M. Corp.)

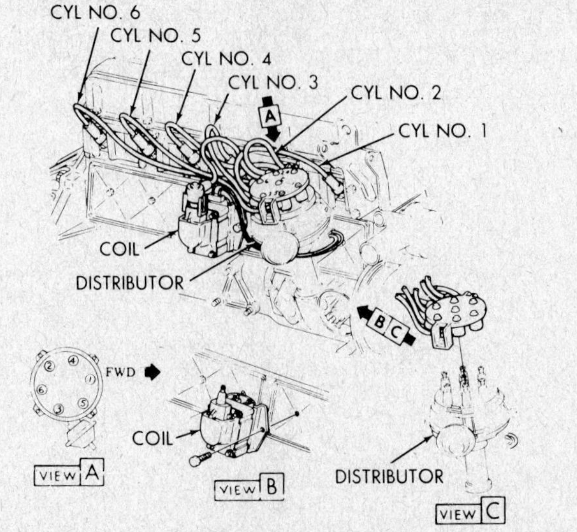

Inline six cylinder HEI secondary wiring (© Chevrolet Div., G.M. Corp.)

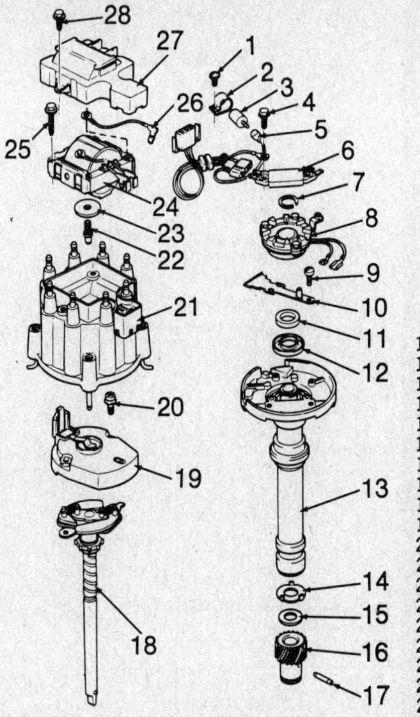

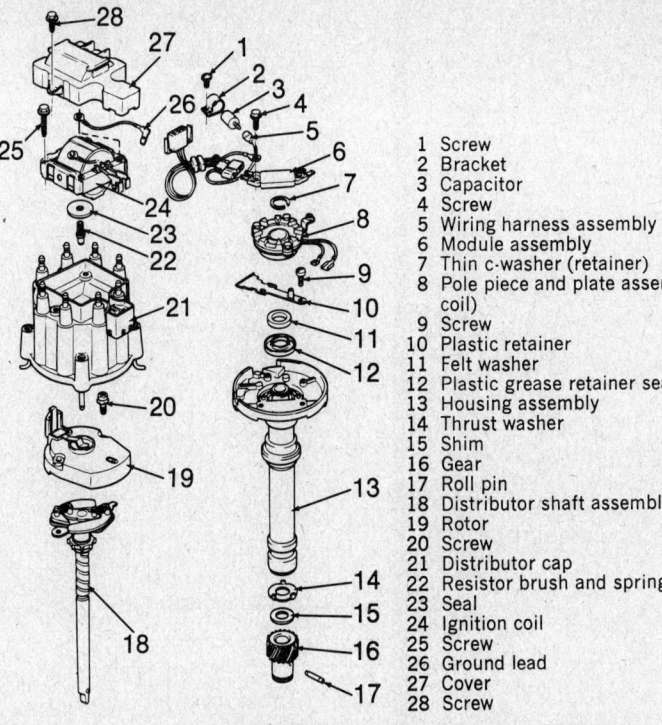

1 Screw
2 Bracket
3 Capacitor
4 Screw
5 Wiring harness assembly
6 Module assembly
7 Thin c-washer (retainer)
8 Pole piece and plate assembly (pick up coil)
9 Screw
10 Plastic retainer
11 Felt washer
12 Plastic grease retainer seal
13 Housing assembly
14 Thrust washer
15 Shim
16 Gear
17 Roll pin
18 Distributor shaft assembly
19 Rotor
20 Screw
21 Distributor cap
22 Resistor brush and spring
23 Seal
24 Ignition coil
25 Screw
26 Ground lead
27 Cover
28 Screw

H E I distributor—V8 (© Chevrolet Div., G.M. Corp.)

tributor and turn the rotor slightly to align the gears and the oil pump driveshaft.

2. With the respective marks aligned, install the clamp and bolt finger-tight.
3. Install and secure the distributor cap.
4. Connect the feed and module connectors to the distributor cap.
5. Connect a timing light to the engine and plug the vacuum hose.
6. Connect the ground cable to the battery.
7. Start the engine and set the timing.
8. Turn the engine off and tighten the distributor clamp bolt. Disconnect the timing light and unplug and connect the hose to the vacuum advance.

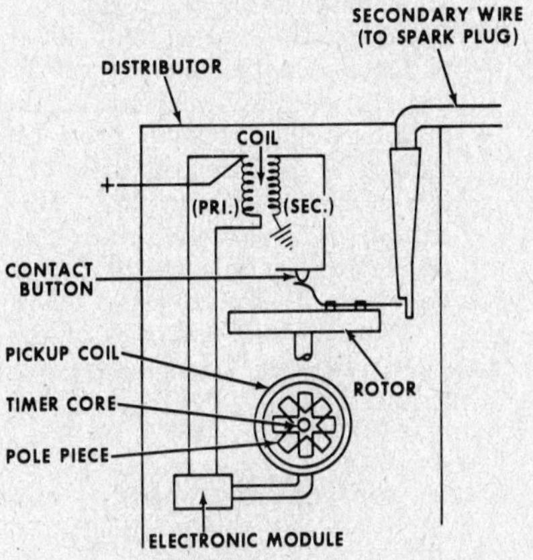

H E I schemitic
(© Chevrolet Div., G.M. Corp.)

Service Procedures (Distributor Removed)

Driven Gear Replacement

1. With the distributor removed, use a $\frac{1}{8}$ in. pin punch and tap out the driven gear roll pin.
2. Hold the rotor end of shaft and rotate the driven gear to shear any burrs in the roll pin hole.
3. Remove the driven gear from the shaft.
4. Reverse the above procedure to install.

Terminals on distributor cap assembly
(© Chevrolet Div., G.M. Corp.)

Mainshaft Replacement

1. With the driven gear and rotor removed, gently pull the mainshaft out of the housing.
2. Remove the advance springs, weights and slide the weight base plate off the mainshaft.
3. Reverse the above procedure to install.

Pole Piece, Magnet or Pick-up Coil Replacement

1. With the mainshaft out of its housing, remove the 3 retaining screws, pole piece and magnet and/or pick-up coil.
2. Reverse the removal procedure to install making sure that the pole piece teeth do not contact the timer core teeth by installing and rotating the mainshaft. Loosen the 3 screws and realign the pole piece as necessary.

Chrysler Electronic Ignition

Components

This system consists of a special pulse-sending distributor, an electronic control unit, a two-element ballast resistor, and a special ignition coil.

The distributor does not contain breaker points or a condenser, these parts being replaced by a distributor reluctor and a pick-up unit.

Operation

The ignition primary circuit is connected from the battery, through the ignition switch, through the primary side of the ignition coil, to the control unit where it is grounded. The secondary circuit is the same as in conventional ignition systems: the secondary side of the coil, the coil wire to the distributor, the rotor, the spark plug wires, and the spark plugs.

The magnetic pulse distributor is also connected to the control unit. As the distributor shaft rotates, the distributor reluctor turns past the pick-up unit. As the reluctor turns past the pick-up unit, each of the eight teeth on the reluctor pass near the pick-up unit once during each distributor revolution (two crankshaft revolutions since the distributor runs at one-half crankshaft speed). As the reluctor teeth move close to the pick-up unit, the magentic rotating reluctor induces voltage into the magnetic pick-up unit. This voltage pulse is sent to the ignition control unit from the magnetic pick-up unit. When the pulse enters the control unit, it signals the control unit to interrupt the

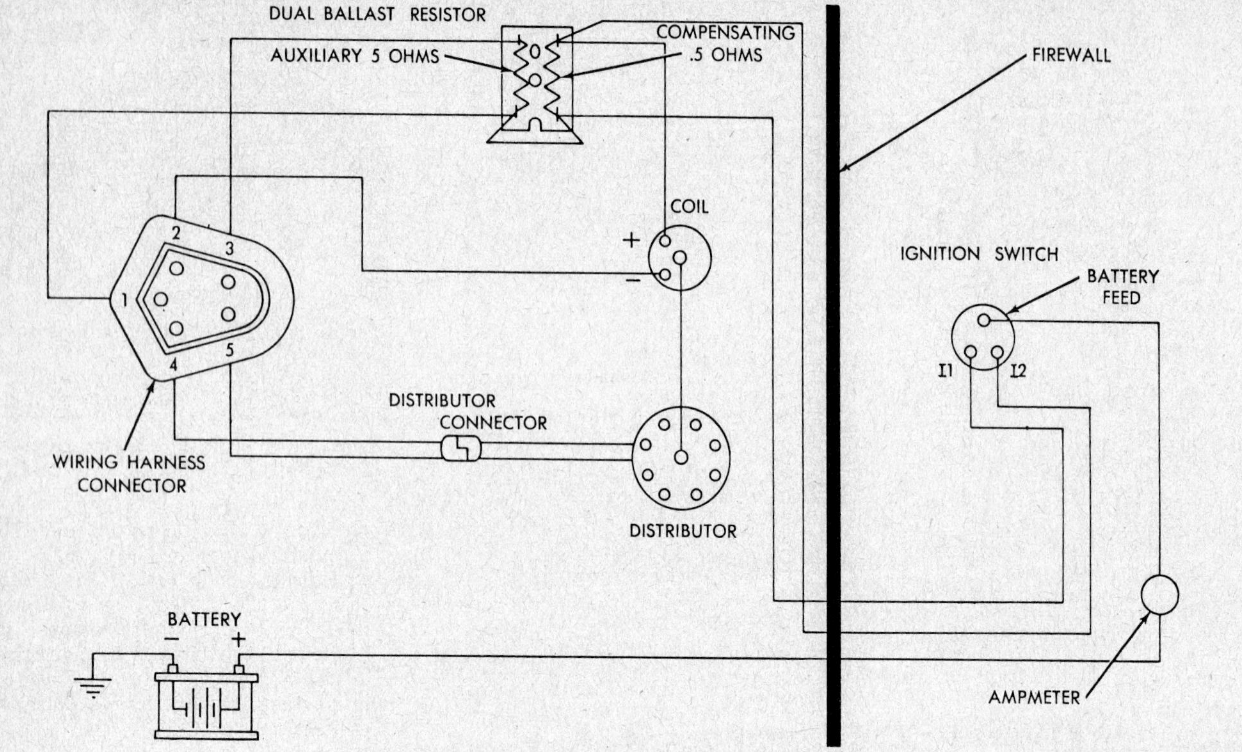

Chrysler electronic ignition schematic (© Chrysler Corp.)

ignition primary circuit. This causes the primary circuit to collapse and begins the induction of the magnetic lines of force from the primary side of the coil into the secondary side of the coil. This induction provides the required voltage to fire the spark plugs.

The advantages of this system are that the transistors in the control unit can make and break the primary ignition circuit much faster than conventional ignition points can, and higher primary voltage can be utilized, since this system can be made to handle higher voltage without adverse effects, whereas ignition breaker points cannot. The quicker switching time of this system allows longer coil primary circuit saturation time and longer induction time when the primary circuit collapses. This increased time allows the primary circuit to build up more current and the secondary circuit to discharge more current.

Pick-up Coil Replacement

1973-74

1. Remove the distributor.
2. Remove the pick-up coil mounting screw.
3. Remove the wires from the retainers on the upper plate and distributor housing.
4. Remove pick-up coil from the upper plate.
5. Position the pick-up coil on the pivot of the upper plate and install the mounting screw. Do not tighten.
6. Insert the wires into the appropriate retainers in the distributor.
7. Install the distributor.
8. Set the air gap.

1975 and later

1. Remove the distributor from the engine.
2. Using two small pry-bars or screwdrivers (maximum 7/16 in. wide), pry the reluctor off the shaft from the bottom.

CAUTION: Do not damage the teeth on the reluctor.

3. Unfasten the vacuum advance-to-distributor housing screws. Remove the vacuum unit, after disconnecting the arm from the upper plate.
4. Unfasten the pick-up coil wires from the distributor housing.
5. Unfasten the two screws which secure the lower plate to the distributor housing. Lift out the lower plate together with the upper plate and pick-up coil.
6. Separate the upper and lower plates by depressing the retaining clip on the underside of the plate and slide it away from the stud. The pick-up coil will come off with the upper plate; they cannot be separated; they must be serviced as an assembly.

Installation is the reverse of removal. Place a small amount of distributor grease on the support pins on the lower plate.

Air Gap Adjustment

1. Align one reluctor tooth with the pick-up coil tooth.
2. Loosen the pick-up coil hold-down screw.
3. Insert a 0.008 in. nonmagnetic feeler gauge between the reluc-

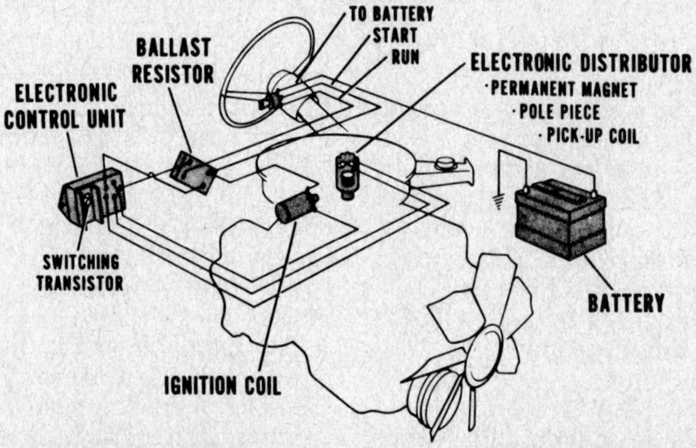

Chrysler electronic ignition system (© Chrysler Corp.)

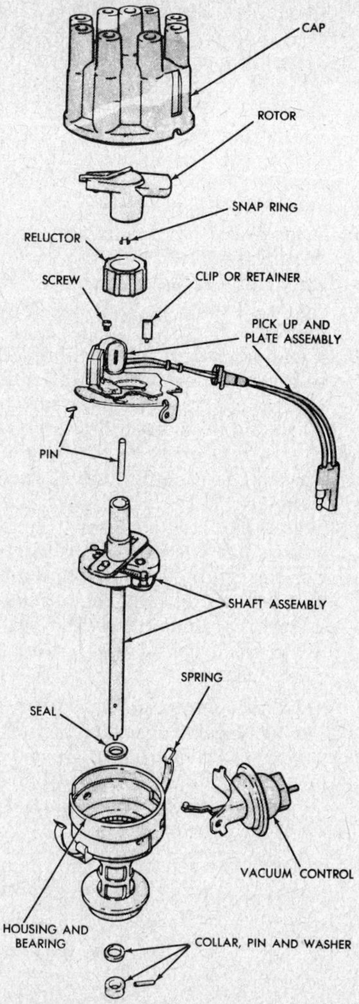

Exploded view of V8 electronic ignition distributor (© Chrysler Corp.)

tor tooth and the pick-up coil tooth.

4. Adjust the air gap so that contact is made between the reluctor tooth, the feeler gauge, and the pick-up coil tooth.
5. Tighten the hold-down screw.
6. Remove the feeler gauge.

NOTE: No force should be required in removing the feeler gauge.

7. Check the air gap with a 0.010 in. feeler gauge. A 0.010 in. feeler gauge should not fit into the air gap.

CAUTION: A 0.010 in. feeler gauge can be forced into the air gap. DO NOT FORCE THE GAUGE INTO THE AIR GAP.

8. Apply vacuum to the vacuum unit and rotate the governor shaft. The pick-up pole should not hit the reluctor teeth. The gap was not properly adjusted if any hitting occurs. If hitting occurs on only one side of the reluctor, the distributor shaft is probably bent, and the governor and shaft assembly should be replaced.

TROUBLESHOOTING CHRYSLER ELECTRONIC IGNITION

Condition	*Possible Cause*	*Correction*
ENGINE WILL NOT START (Fuel and carburetion known to be OK)	a) Dual Ballast	Check resistance of each section: Compensating resistance: .50-.60 ohms @ 70°-80°F Auxiliary Ballast: 4.75-5.75 ohms Replace if faulty. Check wire positions.
	b) Faulty Ignition Coil	Check for carbonized tower. Check primary and secondary resistances: Primary: 1.41-1.79 ohms @ 70°-80°F Secondary: 9,200-11,700 ohms @ 70°-80°F Check in coil tester.
	c) Faulty Pickup or Improper Pickup Air Gap	Check pickup coil resistance: 400-600 ohms Check pickup gap: .010 in. feeler gauge should not slip between pickup coil core and an aligned reluctor blade. No evidence of pickup core striking reluctor blades should be visible. To reset gap, tighten pickup adjustment screw with a .008 in. feeler gauge held between pickup core and an aligned reluctor blade. After resetting gap, run distributor on test stand and apply vacuum advance, making sure that the pickup core does not strike the reluctor blades.
	d) Faulty Wiring	Visually inspect wiring for brittle insulation. Inspect connectors. Molded connectors should be inspected for rubber inside female terminals.
	e) Faulty Control Unit	Replace if all of the above checks are negative. Whenever the control unit or dual ballast is replaced, make sure the dual ballast wires are correctly inserted in the keyed molded connector.
ENGINE SURGES	a) Wiring	Inspect for loose connection and/or broken conductors in harness.
SEVERELY (Not Lean	b) Faulty Pickup Leads	Disconnect vacuum advance. If surging stops, replace pickup.
Carburetor)	c) Ignition Coil	Check for intermittent primary.
ENGINE MISSES (Carburetion OK)	a) Spark Plugs	Check plugs. Clean and regap if necessary.
	b) Secondary Cable	Check cables with an ohmmeter, or observe secondary circuit performance with an oscilloscope.
	c) Ignition Coil	Check for cabonized tower. Check in coil tester.
	d) Wiring	Check for loose or dirty connections.
	e) Faulty Pickup Lead	Disconnect vacuum advance. If miss stops, replace pickup.
	f) Control Unit	Replace if the above checks are negative.

AMC Breakerless Inductive Discharge (BID) Ignition

Components

The AMC breakerless inductive discharge (BID) ignition system consists of five components:

Control unit
Coil
Breakerless distributor
Ignition cables
Spark plugs

The control unit is a solid-state, epoxy-sealed module with waterproof connectors. The control unit has a built-in current regulator, so no separate ballast resistor or resistance wire is needed in the primary circuit. Battery voltage is supplied to the ignition coil positive (+) terminal when the ignition key is turned to the "ON" or "START" position; low voltage is also supplied by the control unit.

The coil used with the BID system requires no special service. It works just like the coil in a conventional ignition system.

The distributor is conventional, except for the lack of points, condenser and cam. Advance is supplied by both a vacuum unit and a centrifugal advance mechanism. A standard cap, rotor, and dust shield are used.

In place of the points, cam, and condensor, the distributor has a sensor and trigger wheel. The sensor is a small coil which generates an electromagnetic field when excited by the oscillator in the control unit.

Standard spark plugs and ignition cables are used.

Operation

When the ignition switch is turned on, the control unit is activated. The control unit then sends an oscillating signal to the sensor which causes the sensor to generate a magnetic field. When one of the trigger wheel teeth enters this field, the strength of the oscillation in the sensor is reduced. Once the strength drops to a predetermined level, a demodulator circuit operates the control unit's switching transistor. The switching transistor is wired in series with the coil primary circuit; it switches the circuit off when it gets the demodulator signal.

From this point on, the BID ignition system works in the same manner as a conventional ignition system.

Troubleshooting

1. Check all of the BID ignition system electrical connections.
2. Disconnect the coil-to-distributor high tension lead.
3. Hold the end of the lead ½ in. away from a ground. Crank the engine. If there is a spark, the trouble is not in the ignition system.
4. If there was no spark in step 3, connect a test light with a No. 57 bulb between the positive coil terminal (+) and a good ground. Have an assistant turn the ignition switch to "ON" and "START" (Do not start the engine). The bulb should light in both positions; if it doesn't, the fault lies in the battery-to-coil circuit. Check the ignition switch and related wiring.
5. If the test light lit in step 4, disconnect the coil-to-distributor leads at the connector and connect the test light between the positive (+) and negative (—) coil terminals.
6. Turn the ignition switch on. If the test light doesn't come on, check the control unit's ground lead. If the ground lead is in good condition, replace the control unit.
7. If the bulb lights in step 6, leave the test light in place and short the terminals on the coil-to-distributor connector together with a jumper lead, (connector separated) at the coil side of the connector. If the light stays on, replace the control unit.
8. If the test light goes out, remove it. Check for a spark, as in step 2, each time that the coil-to-distributor connector terminals are shorted together with the jumper lead. If there is a spark, replace the control unit; if there is no spark, replace the coil.

Coil Testing

Test the coil with a conventional coil checker or an ohmmeter. Primary resistance should be 1-2 ohms and secondary resistance should be 8-12 kilohms. The open output circuit should be more than 20 kilovolts. Replace the coil if it doesn't meet specifications.

Sensor Testing

Check the sensor resistance by connecting an ohmmeter to its leads. Resistance should be 1.8 ohms (±10%) at 77° F. Replace the sensor if it doesn't meet these specifications.

Distributor Overhaul

NOTE: If you must remove the sensor from the distributor for any reason, it will be necessary to have the special sensor positioning gauge in order to align it properly during installation.

1. Scribe matchmarks on the distributor housing, rotor, and engine block. Disconnect the leads and vacuum lines from the distributor. Remove the distributor. Unless the cap is to be replaced, leave it connected to the spark plug cables and position it out of the way.
2. Remove the rotor and dust cap.
3. Place a small gear puller over the trigger wheel, so that its jaws grip the inner shoulders of the wheel and not its arms. Place a thick washer between the gear puller and the distributor shaft to act as a spacer; do not press against the smaller inner shaft.
4. Loosen the sensor hold-down screw with a small pair of needle-nosed pliers; it has a tamper-proof head. Pull the sensor lead grommet out of the distributor body and pull out the leads from around the spring pivot pin.
5. Release the sensor securing spring by lifting it. Make sure that it clears the leads. Slide the sensor off the bracket. *Remember, a special gauge is required for sensor installation.*
6. Remove the vacuum advance unit securing screw. Slide the vacuum unit out of the distributor. Remove it only if it is to be replaced.
7. Clean and dry the vacuum unit and sensor brackets. Lubrication of these parts is not necessary.

BID distributor assembly is as follows:

1. Install the vacuum unit, if it was removed.
2. Assemble the sensor, sensor guide, flat washer, and retaining screw. Tighten the screw only far enough to keep the assembly together; don't allow the screw to project below the bottom of the sensor.

NOTE: Replacement sensors come with a slotted-head screw to aid in assembly. If the original sensor is being used, replace the tamper-proof screw with a conventional one. Use the original washer.

3. Secure the sensor on the vacuum advance unit bracket, making

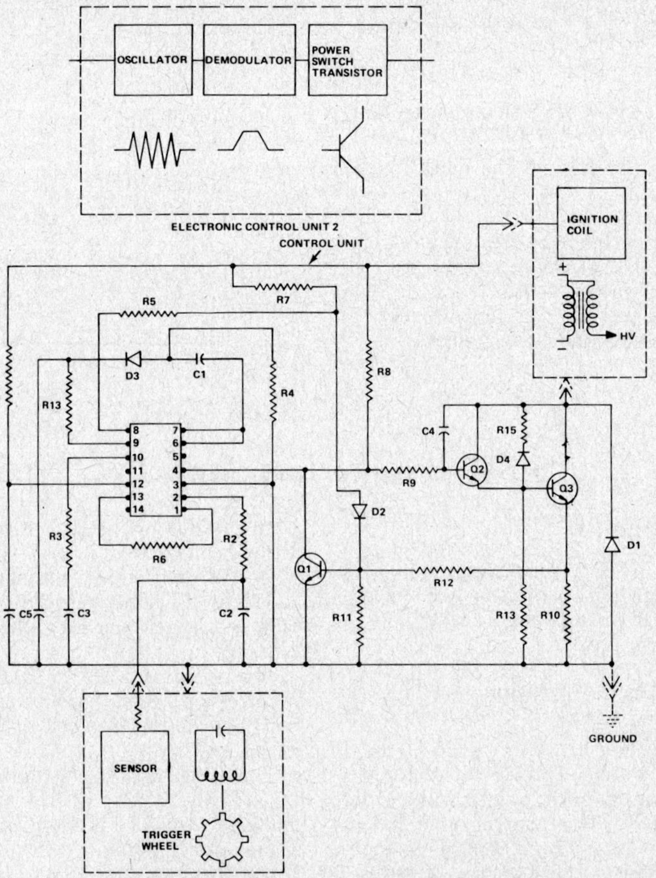

BID system schematic (© Jeep Corp.)

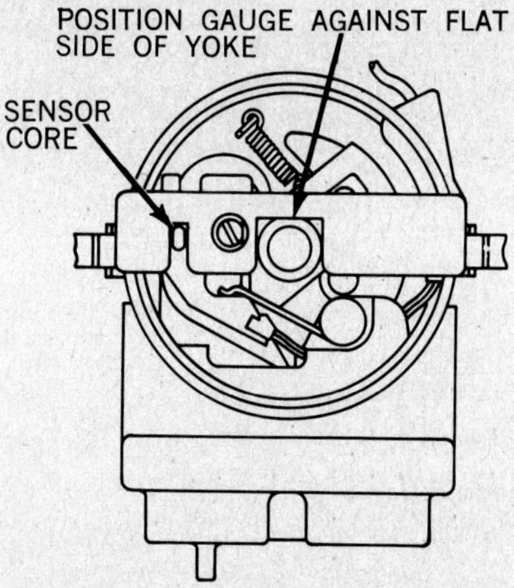

Usinging the special gauge to align the BID sensor coil (© Jeep Corp.)

sure that the tip of the sensor is placed in the notch on the summing bar.

4. Position the spring on the sensor and route the leads around the spring pivot pin. Fit the sensor lead grommet into the slot on the distributor body. Be sure that the lead can't get caught in the trigger wheel.
5. Place the special sensor positioning gauge over the distributor shaft, so that the flat on the shaft is against the large notch on the gauge. Move the sensor until the sensor core fits into the small notch on the gauge. Tighten the sensor securing screw with the gauge in place (through the round hole in the gauge).
6. It should be possible to remove

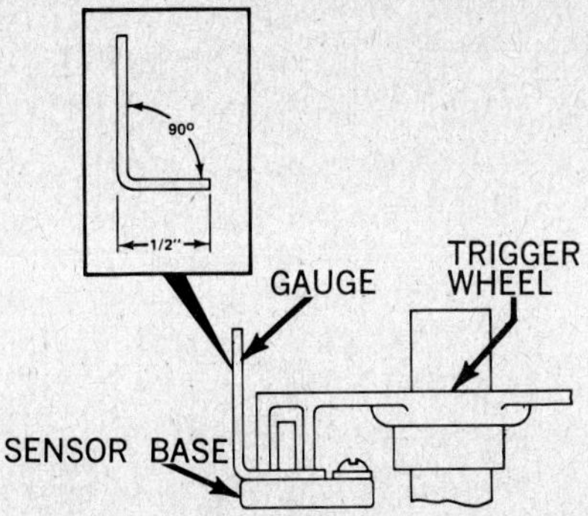

Fabricating BID trigger wheel clearance gauge (© Jeep Corp.)

and install the gauge without any side movement of the sensor. Check this and remove the gauge.

7. Position the trigger wheel on the shaft. Check to see that the sensor core is centered between the trigger wheel legs and that the legs don't touch the core.
8. Bend a piece of 0.050 in. gauge wire, so that it has a 90° angle and one leg ½ in. long. Use the gauge to measure the clearance between the trigger wheel legs and the sensor boss. Press the trigger wheel on the shaft until it just touches the gauge. Support the shaft during this operation.
9. Place 3 to 5 drops of SAE 20 oil on the felt lubricator wick.
10. Install the dust shield and rotor on the shaft.
11. Install the distributor on the engine using the matchmarks made during removal and adjust the timing. Use a new distributor mounting gasket.

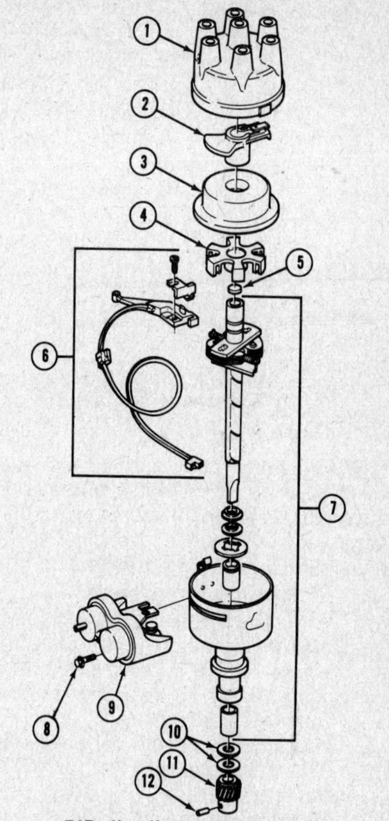

BID distributor components (© Jeep Corp.)

1 Cap
2 Rotor
3 Dust shield
4 Trigger wheel
5 Felt lubricator
6 Sensor assembly
7 Distributor body
8 Vacuum unit screw
9 Vacuum advance unit
10 Shim
11 Drive gear
12 Pin

IH Electronic Ignition

There are two versions of the system. The first, with a black control box, was used on 1974 V8 models, while the second, with a gold control box, was introduced in 1975 on four-cylinder and V8 models. The two versions of the system are very similar in appearance; the main external difference is that the gold control box combines all wiring into a single plug.

The system uses a standard ignition coil with no ballast resistor or resistance wire, since the control box regulates the primary, low-voltage, current. The distributor part of the system consists of a metal detecting sensor and a toothed trigger wheel in place of the distributor cam. The only adjustment is for sensor to trigger wheel air gap. The control box components are permanently sealed in a waterproof and vibration resistant compound. Most of these systems use vacuum spark advance in addition to mechanical advance.

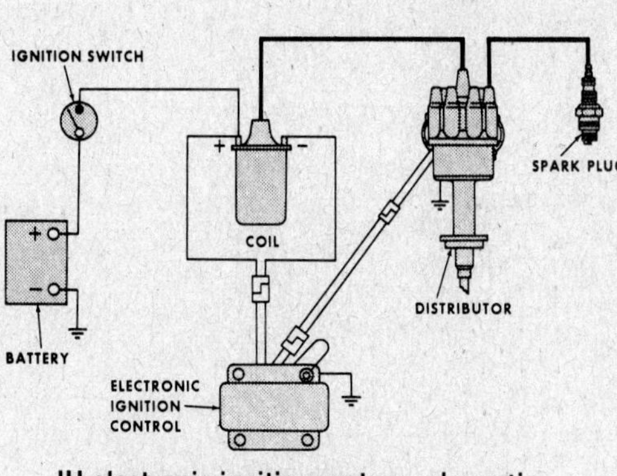

IH electronic ignition system schematic (© International Harvester Co.)

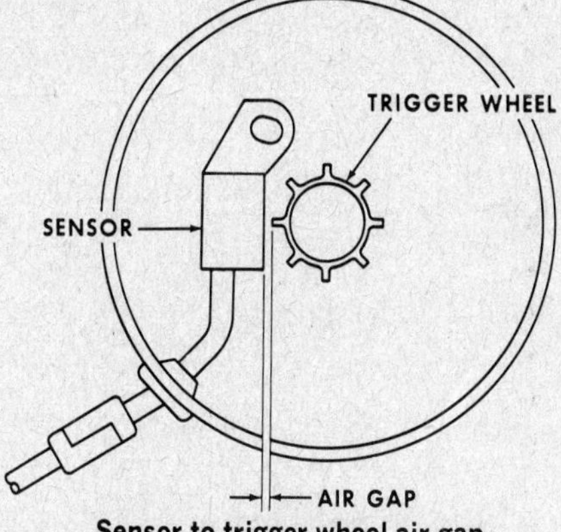

Sensor to trigger wheel air gap (© International Harvester Co.)

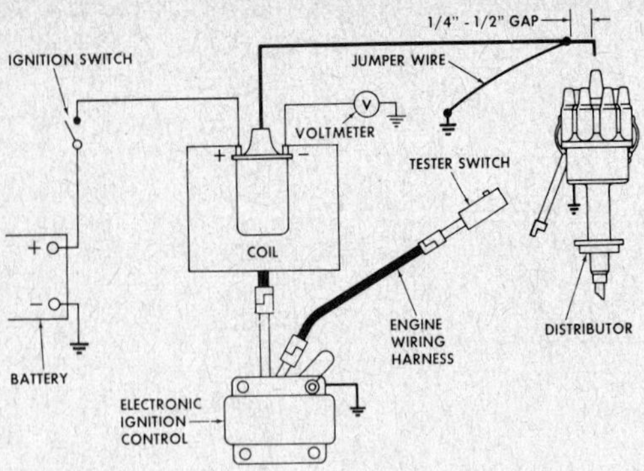

Voltmeter connected to coil negative terminal
(© International Harvester Co.)

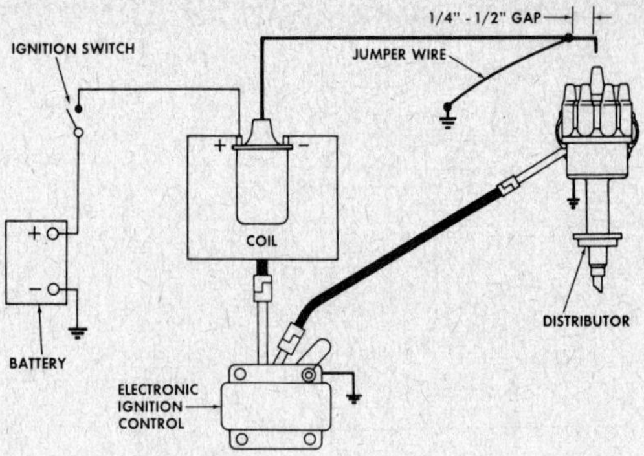

Spark gap for testing electronic ignition system
(© International Harvester Co.)

Disassembly and overhaul of the distributor is very similar to that for International V8 point-type distributors.

Sensor to Trigger Wheel Air Gap Adjustment

1. Align the trigger wheel so that one tooth is aligned with the centerline of the sensor. The tooth should be at right angles to the flat side of the sensor.
2. The gap should be .014 in. for 1974 units and .008 in. for 1975 and later models.
3. A distributor machine or a dwell/tachometer calibrated for electronic ignition systems can be used to measure dwell.

NOTE: Most ordinary dwell/tachometers will give a reading, but this will not be accurate.

On 1974 models, dwell should be 27-30 degrees at curb idle; on a distributor machine the reading will be 22-28 degrees at 2000 distributor rpm with 12-13 volts primary input. On 1975 and later models, dwell should be 26-32 degrees at curb idle and also at 300 distributor rpm with 12-13 volts primary input.

4. Adjust the gap and dwell by moving the sensor. Move the sensor toward the trigger wheel to decrease dwell or away to increase dwell. .001 in. of sensor movement equals about ½ degree of dwell change.

Troubleshooting

1. Make sure that the battery is fully charged, delivering 12-13 volts. Make sure that all wiring, connections, and mounting bolts are in good condition.
2. Disconnect one spark plug wire and insert an extension of some sort into the boot. Hold the wire with insulated pliers and a heavy glove so that there is a gap of about ¼-½ in. between the extension and a ground. If the spark jumps the gap when the engine is cranked with the starter, the system is in good condition. If not, replace the wire and go on.
3. Detach the coil wire from the center of the distributor cap. Attach one end of a jumper wire to a ground and the other around the coil wire (don't pierce the insulation) ¼-½ in. from the metal tip. If there is a spark when the engine is cranked, the distributor cap, rotor, or spark plug and coil wires may be faulty. If not, keep the jumper in place and go on.
4. Disconnect the primary wiring plug near the distributor and plug a tester switch, part no. SE-2503, into the wiring harness. The switch replaces the distributor sensor in the circuit. Turn the ignition switch on and press the tester switch button. If there is a spark at the jumper, the sensor is defective and must be replaced. If not, go on.
5. Disconnect the primary wiring plug near the control box and install the tester switch. Turn the ignition switch on and press the tester switch button. If there is a spark at the jumper now, the primary wiring harness is defective. If not, go on.
6. Connect a voltmeter between the coil negative terminal and a ground. Voltage should be 12-13 volts. A low reading indicates high resistance between the battery and the coil, probably due to defective wires or ignition switch.
7. Connect the voltmeter between the coil negative terminal and a ground. With the ignition switch on, voltage should be 5-8 volts. A lower or higher reading indicates a bad coil. Press the tester switch button; voltage should go up to 12-13 volts and go back down when the button is released. If the voltage doesn't go up and down, the control box is faulty and must be replaced. If the voltage goes up and down but there is no spark at the jumper, the coil is defective.
8. Reconnect the system and make a final check for spark at the plug wire, as in Step 2.

Switches and Solenoids

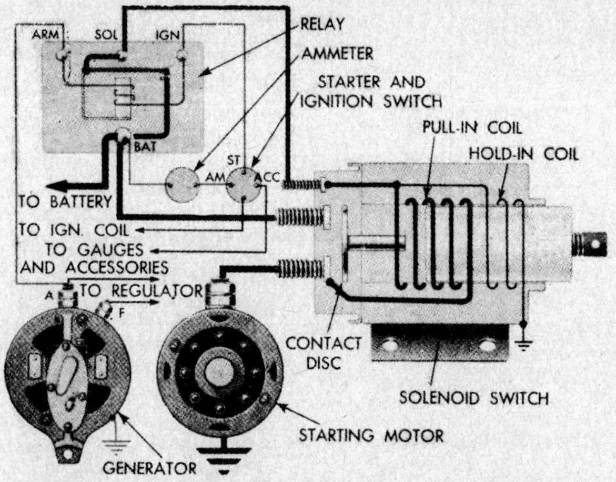

Pictorial drawing of solenoid with a separate relay

Magnetic Switches

Magnetic switches serve only to make contact for the starter motor. Usually, such switches are located on the inner fender panel, although they are found mounted on the starter in a few cases.

Magnetic Switches with Two Control Terminals

On this type of magnetic switch current is supplied from the ignition switch or transmission neutral button to one of the magnetic switch control terminals. The other control terminal is connected to the transmission neutral safety switch (on the transmission) where it is grounded.

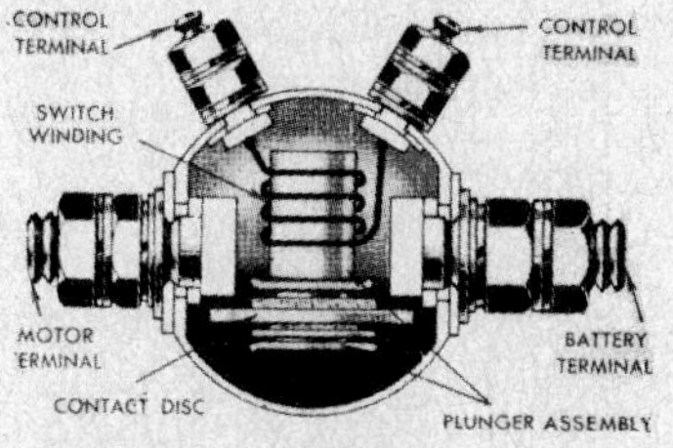

Schematic diagram of a magnetic switch with two control terminals

Magnetic Switches with Ignition Resistor By-Pass Terminals

All normally use a magnetic switch with a single control terminal. The second terminal is an ignition resistor by-pass terminal.

Solenoids Without Relays

This type of starter solenoid is always mounted on the starter. Makes electrical contact for the starter and pulls the starter and drive clutch into mesh with the flywheel. The Chrysler reduction gear starter has this solenoid embodied in the starter housing.

There is only one control terminal on the solenoid.

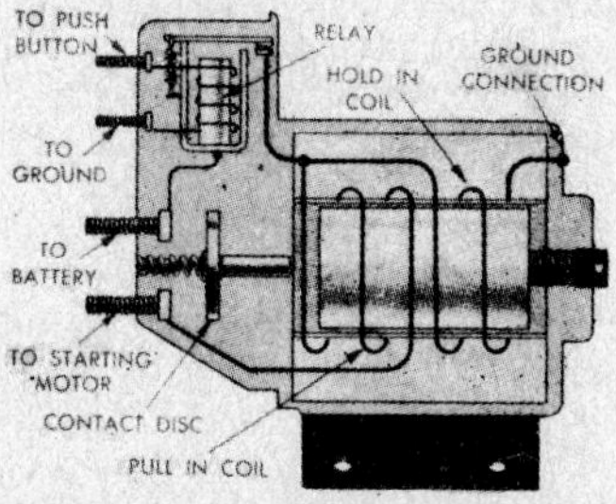

Pictorial drawing of solenoid with a built-in relay

The ignition by-pass terminal is usually marked R or IGN, if it is used.

Solenoids With Separate Relays

The solenoid itself is always mounted on the starter. In addition to making contact for the starter, it also pulls the starter drive clutch gear into mesh with the flywheel. A single control terminal is used on the solenoid itself. The relay is usually found mounted to the inner fender panel or on the firewall.

Solenoids With Built-In Relays

These units are always mounted on the starter and are connected, through linkage, to the starter drive clutch. The relay portion is a square box built into and integral with the front end of the solenoid assembly.

Neutral Safety Switches

The purpose of the neutral safety switch is to prevent the starter from cranking the engine except when the transmission is in neutral or park.

On some trucks the neutral safety switch is located on the transmission. It serves to ground the solenoid or magnetic switch, whichever is used.

On other trucks the neutral safety switch is located either at the bottom of the steering column, where it contacts the shift mechanism, on the steering column, underneath the dash, or on the shift linkage (console).

Some manual transmission models have a clutch linkage safety switch to prevent starter operation unless the clutch pedal is depressed.

On most trucks the neutral safety switch and the backup light switch are combined into a single switch mechanism.

Troubleshooting Neutral Safety Switches—Quick Test

If the starter fails to function and the neutral safety switch is to be checked, a jumper can be placed across its terminals. If the starter then functions the safety switch is defective.

In the case of neutral safety switches with one wire, this wire must be grounded for testing purposes. If the starter works with the wire grounded, the switch is defective.

Neutral Safety Switch—Back-Up Light Switch

When the neutral safety switch is built in combination with the back-up light switch, the easiest way to tell which terminals are for the back-up lights is to take a jumper and cross every pair of wires. The pair of wires which light the back-up lamps should be ignored when testing the neutral safety switch. Once the back-up light wires have been located, jump the other pair of wires to test the neutral safety switch. If the starter functions only when the jumper is placed across these two wires, the neutral safety switch is defective or requires adjustment.

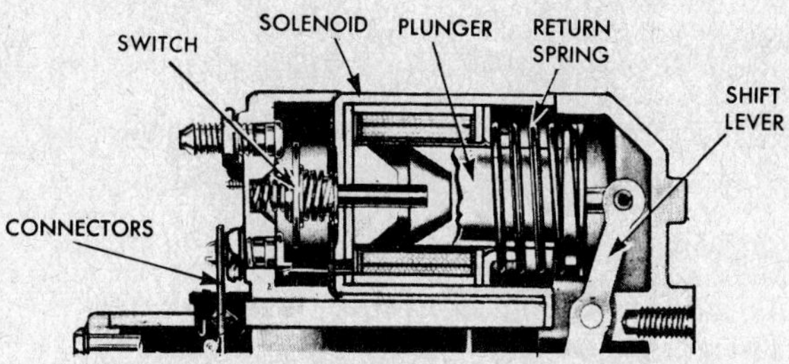

Starter solenoid mounted on starter motor

Starting Systems

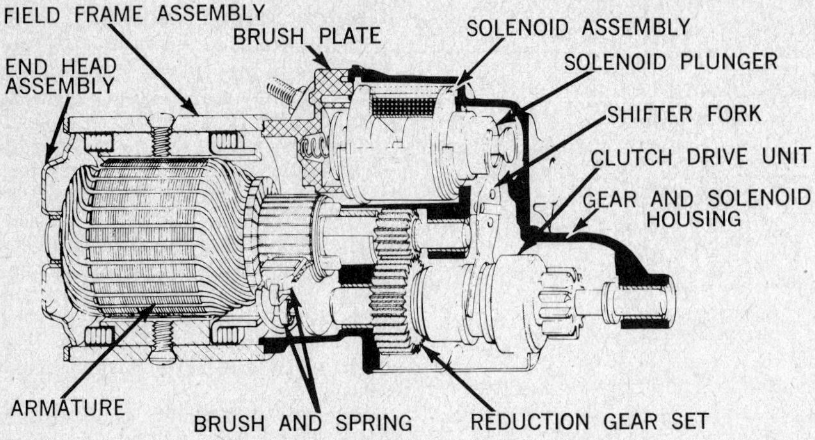

Reduction gear starter motor (© Chrysler Corp.)

Reduction-Gear Starter Motor

(Chrysler Corporation)

The housing is die-cast aluminum. A 3.5 to 1 reduction, combined with the starter to ring gear ratio, results in a total gear reduction of about 45 to 1.

NOTE: the high-pitched sound is caused by the higher starter speed.

The positive shift solenoid is enclosed in the starter housing and is energized through the ignition switch When ignition switch is turned to start, the solenoid plunger engages drive gear through a shifting fork. At the completion of travel, the plunger closes a switch to revolve the starter.

The tension of the spring-type shifting prevents a butt-tooth lock up and motor will not start before total shift.

An overrunning clutch prevents motor damage if key is held on after engine starts.

No lubrication is required due to Oilite bearings.

Disassembly

1. Support assembly in a vise equipped with soft jaws. Do not clamp. Care must be used not to distort or damage the die cast aluminum.
2. Remove the thru-bolts and the end housing.
3. Carefully pull the armature up and out of the gear housing, and the starter frame and field assembly. Remove the steel and fiber thrust washer.

NOTE: on eight cylinder engines the starting motors have the wire of the shunt field coil soldered to the brush terminal. Six cylinder engines have the four coils in series and do not have a wire soldered to the brush terminal. One pair of brushes is connected to this terminal. The other pair of brushes is attached to the series field coils by means of a terminal screw. Carefully pull the frame and field assembly up just enough to expose the terminal screw and the solder connection of the shunt field at the brush terminal. Place two wood blocks between the starter frame and starter gear housing to facilitate removal of the terminal screw and unsoldering of the shunt field wire at the brush terminal.

4. Support the brush terminal with a finger behind terminal and remove screw.
5. On eight cylinder engine starters unsolder the shunt field coil lead from the brush terminal and housing.
6. The brush holder plate with terminal, contact and brushes is serviced as an assembly.
7. Clean all old sealer from around plate and housing.
8. Remove the brush holder attaching screw.
9. On the shunt type, unsolder the solenoid winding from the brush terminal.
10. Remove 11/32 in. nut, washer and insulator from solenoid terminal.
11. Remove brush holder plate with brushes as an assembly.
12. Remove gear housing ground screw.
13. The solenoid assembly can be removed from the well.
14. Remove nut, washer and seal from starter battery terminal and remove terminal from plate.
15. Remove solenoid contact and plunger from solenoid and remove the coil sleeve.
16. Remove the solenoid return spring, coil retaining washer, retainer and the dust cover from the gear housing.
17. Release the snap-ring that locates the driven gear on pinion shaft.
18. Release front retaining ring.
19. Push pinion shaft toward the rear and remove snap-ring, thrust washers, clutch and pinion, and two shift fork nylon actuators.
20. Remove driven gear and friction washer.
21. Pull shifting fork forward and remove moving core.
22. Remove fork retainer pin and shifting fork assembly. The gear housing with bushings is serviced as an assembly.

Replacement of Brushes

1. Brushes that are worn more than one-half the length of new brushes, or are oil-soaked, should be replaced.

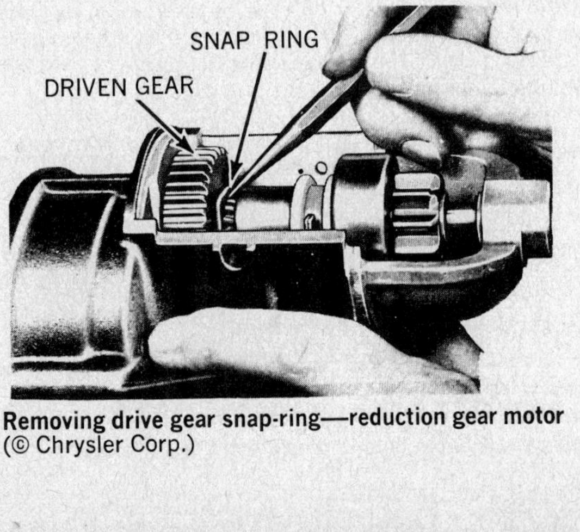

Removing drive gear snap-ring—reduction gear motor (© Chrysler Corp.)

Removing terminal screw—reduction gear motor (© Chrysler Corp.)

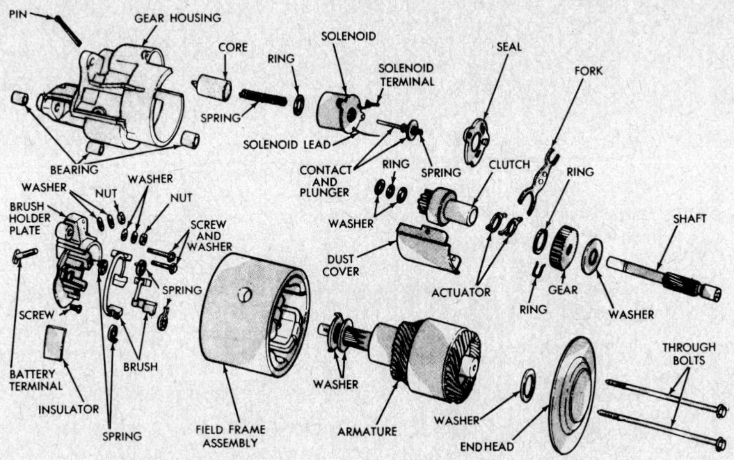

Reduction gear motor—exploded view (© Chrysler Corp.)

2. When resoldering the shunt field and solenoid lead, make a strong, low-resistance connection using a high-temperature solder and resin flux. Do not use acid or acid-core solder. Do not break the shunt field wire units when removing and installing the brushes.

Starter Clutch and Pinion Gear Inspection

1. Do not immerse the starter clutch unit in a cleaning solvent. The outside of the clutch and pinion must be cleaned with a cloth so as not to wash the lubricant from the inside of the clutch.
2. Rotate the pinion. The pinion gear should rotate smoothly and in one direction only. If the starter clutch unit does not function properly, or if the pinion is worn, chipped, or burred, replace the starter clutch unit.

Commutator Inspection

1. Inspect the commutator and the surface contacted by the brushes when the starter is assembled, for flat spots, out-of-roundness, or excessive wear.
2. Reface the commutator if necessary, removing only a sufficient amount of metal to provide a smooth, even surface.
3. Using light pressure, clean the grooves of the face of the commutator with a pointed tool. Neither remove any metal or widen the grooves.

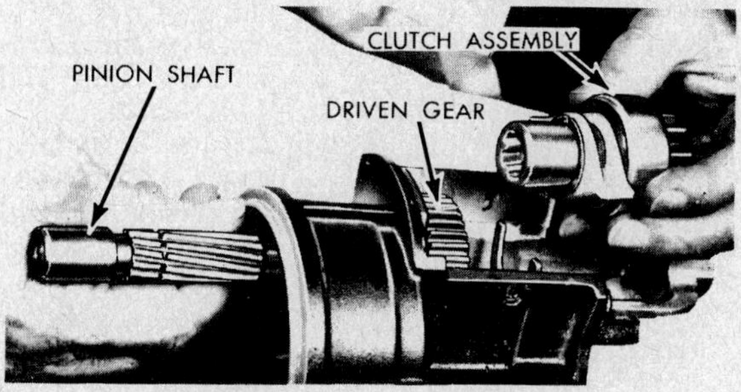

Removing clutch assembly—reduction gear motor (© Chrysler Corp.)

Assembly

1. The shifter fork consists of two spring steel plates held together by two rivets. Before assembling the starter, check the plates for side movement. After lubricating between the plates with a small amount of SAE 10 engine oil, they should have about 1/16 in. side movement to insure proper pinion gear engagement.
2. Position the shift fork in the drive housing and install the shifting fork retainer pin. One tip of the pin should be straight and the other bent at a 15 degree angle away from the housing. The fork and retainer pin should operate freely after bending the tip of the pin.
3. Install the solenoid moving core and engage the shifting fork.
4. Place the pinion shaft into the drive housing and install the friction washer and drive gear.
5. Install the clutch and pinion assembly, thrust washer, and retaining washer.
6. Engage the shifting fork with the clutch actuators.

CAUTION: **The friction washer must be positioned on the shoulder of the splines of the pinion shaft before the driven gear is positioned.**

7. Install the driven gear snap ring.
8. Install the pinion shaft retaining ring.
9. The starter solenoid return spring can now be inserted in the moveable core.
10. Install the solenoid contact plunger assembly into the solenoid and reform the double wires so they can be curved around the contactor. This will allow the terminal stud to enter the brush holder properly.

CAUTION: **The contactor must not touch these double wires after assembly is complete.**

11. Assemble the battery terminal stud in the brush holder.
12. Position the seal on the brush holder plate.
13. Run the solenoid lead wire

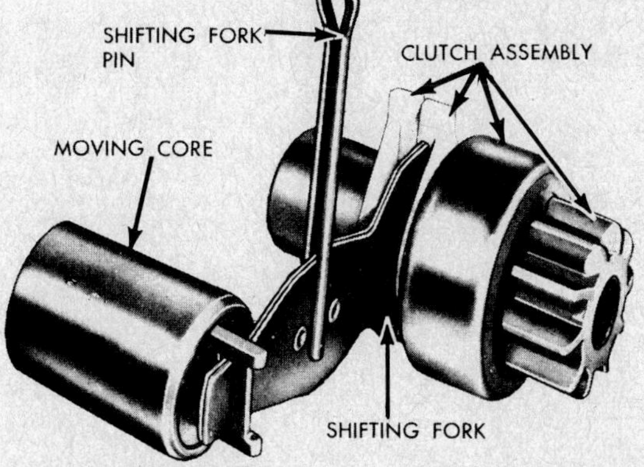

Shift fork and clutch arrangement—reduction gear motor (© Chrysler Corp.)

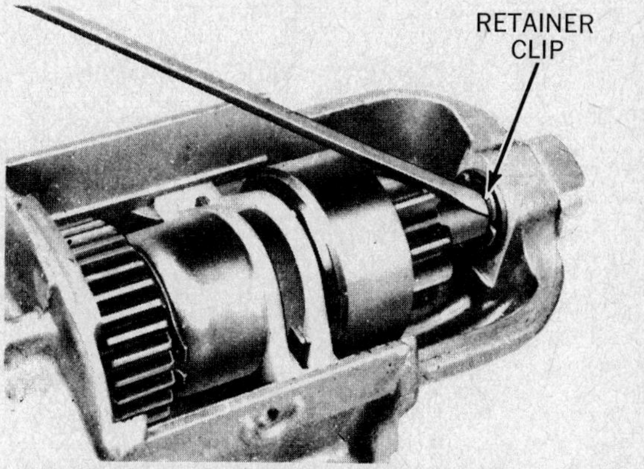

Removing retaining ring—reduction gear motor (© Chrysler Corp.)

through the hole in the brush holder and attach the solenoid stud, insulating washers, flat washer, and nut.
14. Wrap the solenoid lead wire tightly around the brush terminal post and solder it.
15. Fix the brush holder to the solenoid attaching screws.
16. Gently lower the solenoid coil and brush plate into the gear housing.
17. Position the brush plate assembly into the starter gear housing, install the nuts, and tighten.
18. Solder the shunt coil lead wire to the starter brush terminal.
19. Install the brush terminal screw.
20. Position the field frame on the gear housing and start the armature into the housing, carefully engaging the splines on the shaft with the reduction gear by rotating the armature.
21. Install the fiber thrush washer and the steel washer on the armature shaft.
22. Replace the starter end housing and starter through bolts; tighten securely.

Direct Drive Starter Motor

(Chrysler Corporation)

This starter can be identified by the externally mounted solenoid bolted to the case.

Disassembly

1. Remove through bolts and tap commutator end head from frame.
2. Remove thrust washers from armature shaft.
3. Lift brush holder springs and remove brushes from holders.
4. Remove brush holder plate.
5. Disconnect the field coil wires at the solenoid connector, and remove the solenoid screws.
6. Remove solenoid and boot.
7. Drive out shift fork pivot pin.
8. Remove drive end pinion housing and spacer washer.
9. Remove shift fork from starter drive.

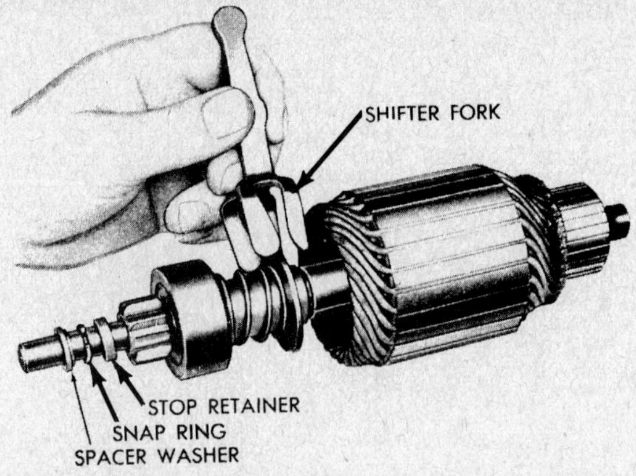

Removing shift fork—direct drive motor (© Chrysler Corp.)

10. Slide overrunning clutch pinion gear toward commutator, drive stop retainer toward clutch pinion gear and remove the now-exposed snap-ring.
11. Remove overrunning clutch drive from armature shaft.
12. If field coils are good, stop disassembly at this point. If field coils must be replaced, remove ground brushes terminal screw and remove brushes, terminal and shunt wire. Remove pole shoe screws, using a ratchet-type impact driver and special wide screwdriver blade, then remove field coils.
13. Replacement of the brushes, inspection of the starter clutch and pinion, and inspection of the commutator procedures are the same as the reduction-gear starter procedures.

Assembly

1. Install field coils into frame, if removed.
2. Lubricate armature shaft and splines with engine oil.
3. Install starter drive, stop retainer, lock ring and spacer washer.
4. Install shift fork, with *narrow* leg of fork toward commutator.
5. Install pinion housing onto armature shaft, indexing shift fork with slot in housing.
6. Install shift fork pivot pin.
7. With clutch drive, shift fork, and pinion housing assembled onto the armature, slide armature into frame until pinion housing indexes with slot.
8. Install solenoid and boot, tightening bolts to 60-70 in. lbs.
9. Conect field coil wires to solenoid connector, making sure they do not touch frame.
10. Install brush holder plate, indexing tang in frame hole.
11. Place brushes in holders, making sure field coil wires do not interfere.
12. Install thrust washers on commutator end of armature shaft to obtain a maximum of 0.010 in. end-play.
13. Install commutator end head and through bolts. Tighten bolts to 40-50 in. lbs.
14. Measure drive gear pinion clearance; it should be ⅛ in. Adjust by moving solenoid fore and aft as required.

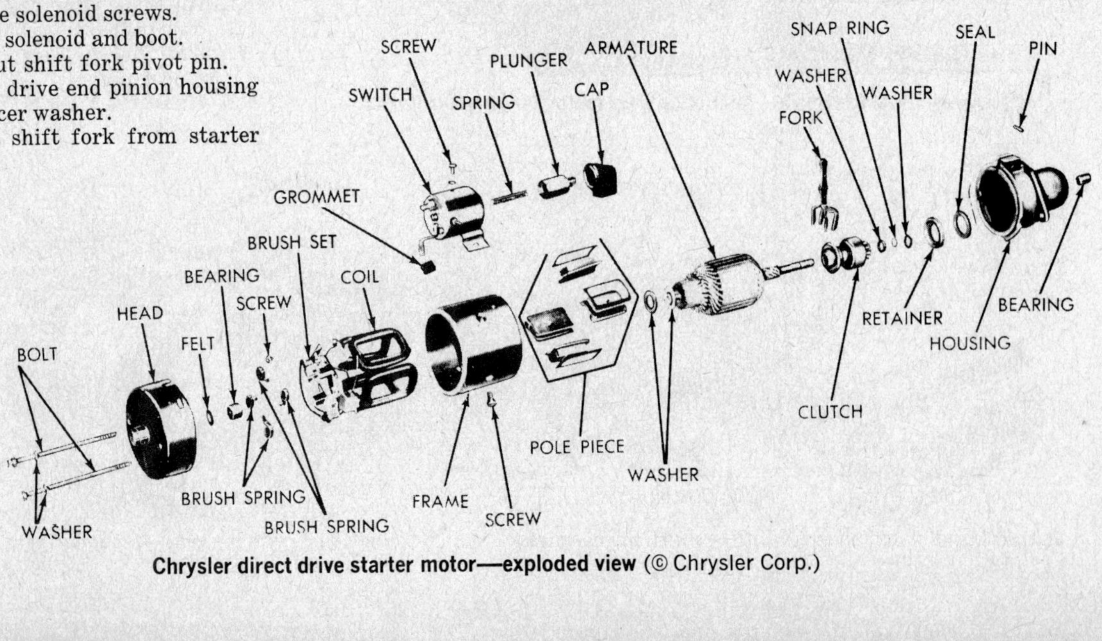

Chrysler direct drive starter motor—exploded view (© Chrysler Corp.)

Motorcraft Positive Engagement Starter Motor

(Ford Motor Co.)

This starting motor is a series-parallel wound, four pole, four brush unit. It is equipped with an overrunning clutch drive pinion, which is engaged with the flywheel ring gear by an actuating lever, operated by a movable pole piece. This pole piece is hinged to the starter frame and can drop into position through an opening in the frame.

Three conventional field coils are located at three pole piece positions. The fourth field coil is designed to serve also as an engaging coil and a hold-in coil for the operation of the drive pinion.

When the ignition switch is turned to the start position, the starter relay is energized and current flows from the battery to the starter motor terminal. This prime surge of current first flows through the starter engaging coil, creating a very strong magnetic field. This magnetism draws the movable pole piece down toward the starter frame, which then causes the lever attached to it to move the starter pinion into engagement with the flywheel ring gear.

When the movable pole shoe is fully seated, it opens the field coil, grounding contacts, and the starter is then in normal operation. A holding coil is used to hold the movable pole shoe in the fully seated position during the engine cranking operation.

Trucks, equipped with automatic transmissions have a starter neutral switch circuit control. This is to prevent operation of the starter if the selector lever is not in Neutral or Park.

Disassembly

1. Remove brush cover band and starter drive gear actuating lever cover. Observe the brush lead locations for reassembly, then remove the brushes from their holders.

NOTE: factory brush length is ½ in.; wear limit is ¼ in.

2. Remove the through bolts, starter drive gear housing and the drive gear actuating lever return spring.
3. Remove the pivot pin retaining the starter gear actuating lever and remove the lever and the armature.
4. Remove the stop ring retainer. Remove and discard the stop ring holding the drive gear to the armature shaft; then remove the drive gear assembly.
5. Remove the brush end plate.
6. Remove the two screws holding the ground brushes to the frame.
7. On the field coil that operates the starter drive gear actuating lever, bend the tab up on the field retainer and remove the field coil retainer.
8. Remove the three coil retaining screws. Unsolder the field coil leads from the terminal screw, then remove the pole shoes and coils from the frame (use a 300 watt iron).
9. Remove the starter terminal nut, washer, insulator and terminal from the starter frame.
10. Check the commutator for runout. If the commutator is rough, has flat spots, or is more than 0.005 in. out of round, reface the commutator. Clean the grooves in the commutator face.
11. Inspect the armature shaft and the two bearings for scoring and excessive wear. Replace if necessary.
12. Inspect the starter drive. If the gear teeth are pitted, broken, or excessively worn, replace the starter drive.

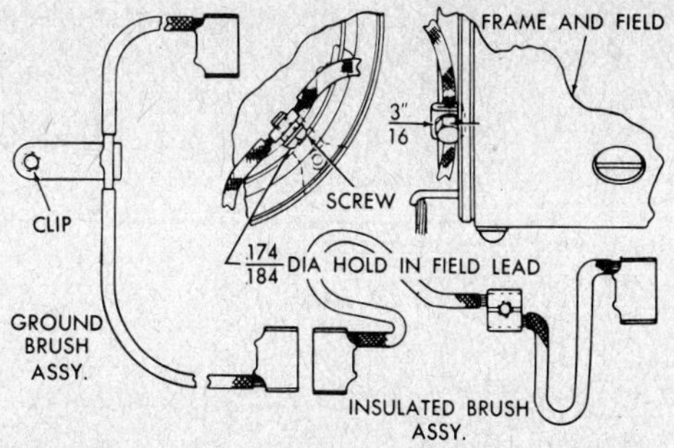

Brush lead arrangement—Chrysler direct drive starter (© Chrysler Corp.)

Assembly

1. Install starter terminal, insulator, washers and retaining nut in the frame. (Be sure to position the slot in the screw perpendicular to the frame end surface.)
2. Position coils and pole pieces, with the coil leads in the terminal screw slot, then install the retaining screws. As the pole screws are tightened, strike the frame several sharp hammer blows to align the pole shoes. Tighten, then stake the screws.
3. Install solenoid coil and retainer and bend the tabs to hold the coils to the frame.
4. Solder the field coils and solenoid wire to the starter terminal, using rosin-core solder and a 300 watt iron.
5. Check for continuity and ground connections in the assembled coils.
6. Position the solenoid coil ground terminal over the nearest ground screw hole.
7. Position the ground brushes to the starter frame and install retaining screws.

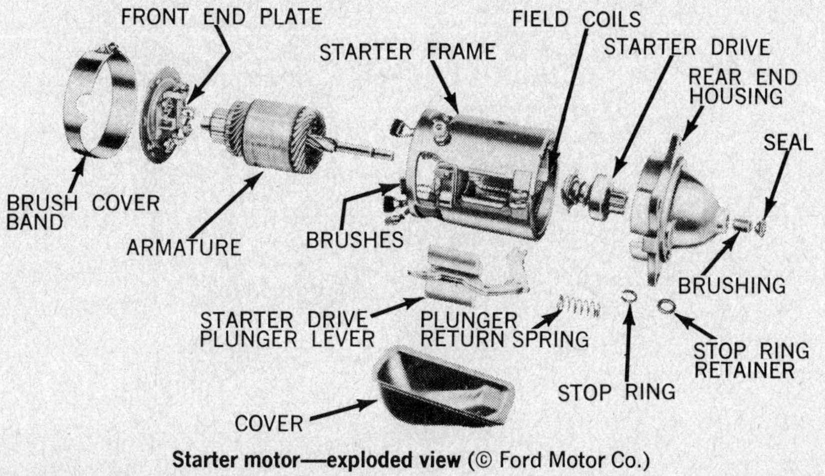

Starter motor—exploded view (© Ford Motor Co.)

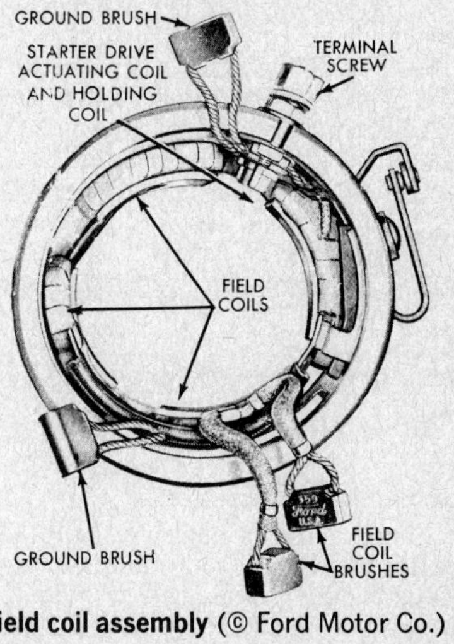

Field coil assembly (© Ford Motor Co.)

Starter cranks engine slowly

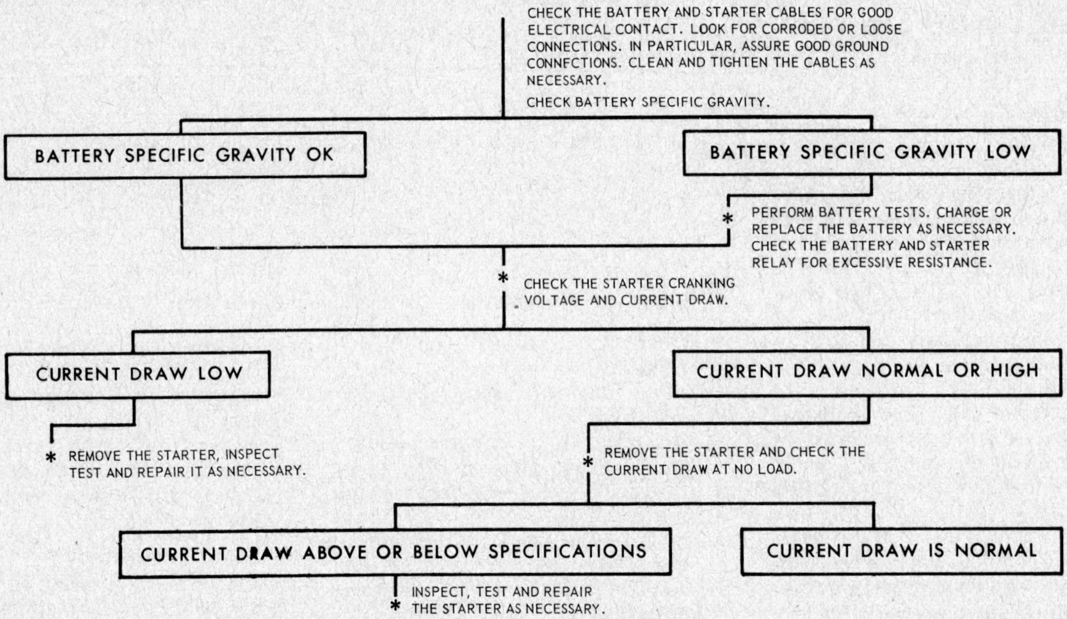
CHECK THE BATTERY AND STARTER CABLES FOR GOOD ELECTRICAL CONTACT. LOOK FOR CORRODED OR LOOSE CONNECTIONS. IN PARTICULAR, ASSURE GOOD GROUND CONNFCTIONS. CLEAN AND TIGHTEN THE CABLES AS NECESSARY.
CHECK BATTERY SPECIFIC GRAVITY.
BATTERY SPECIFIC GRAVITY OK
BATTERY SPECIFIC GRAVITY LOW
* PERFORM BATTERY TESTS. CHARGE OR REPLACE THE BATTERY AS NECESSARY. CHECK THE BATTERY AND STARTER RELAY FOR EXCESSIVE RESISTANCE.
* CHECK THE STARTER CRANKING VOLTAGE AND CURRENT DRAW.
CURRENT DRAW LOW
CURRENT DRAW NORMAL OR HIGH
* REMOVE THE STARTER, INSPECT TEST AND REPAIR IT AS NECESSARY.
* REMOVE THE STARTER AND CHECK THE CURRENT DRAW AT NO LOAD.
CURRENT DRAW ABOVE OR BELOW SPECIFICATIONS
CURRENT DRAW IS NORMAL
* INSPECT, TEST AND REPAIR THE STARTER AS NECESSARY.

8. Position the brush end plate to the frame, with the end plate boss in the frame slot.
9. Lightly Lubriplate the armature shaft splines and install the starter drive gear assembly in the shaft. Install a new retaining stop ring and stop ring retainer.
10. Position the fiber thrust washer on the commutator end of the armature shaft, then position the armature in the starter frame.
11. Position the starter drive gear actuating lever to the frame and starter drive assembly, and install the pivot pin.

NOTE: fill drive gear housing bore ¼ full of grease.

12. Position the drive actuating lever return spring and the drive gear housing to the frame, then install and tighten the through bolts. Do not pinch brush leads between brush plate and frame. Be sure that the stop ring retainer is properly seated in the drive housing.
13. Install the brushes in the brush holders and center the brush springs on the brushes.
14. Position the drive gear actuating lever cover on the starter and install the brush cover band with a new gasket.
15. Check starter no-load amperage draw.

Motorcraft Solenoid Actuated Starter Motor

(Ford Motor Co.)

This starter motor, usually used with late-model 460 engines, is a four-brush, four-field, four-pole wound unit. The frame encloses a wound armature, which is supported at the drive end by caged needle bearings and at the commutator end by a sintered copper bushing. The four pole shoes are retained to the frame by one pole screw apiece, and on each pole shoe is wound a ribbon-type field coil connected in series-parallel.

The solenoid is mounted to a flange on the starter drive housing, which encloses the entire shift mechanism and solenoid plunger. The solenoid utilizes two windings—a pull-in winding and a hold-in winding.

Disassembly

1. Disconnect the copper strap from the solenoid starter terminal, remove the remaining screws and remove the solenoid.
2. Loosen the retaining screw and slide the brush cover band back far enough to gain access to the brushes.
3. Remove the brushes from their holders, then remove the through bolts and separate the drive end housing from the frame and brush end plate.

NOTE: factory brush length is ½ in., wear limit ¼ in.

4. Remove the solenoid plunger and shift fork. These two items can be separated from each other by removing the roll pin.
5. Remove the armature and drive assembly from the frame. Remove the drive stop ring and slide the drive off the armature shaft.
6. Remove the drive stop ring retainer from the drive housing.
7. Inspection of the commutator, armature and bearings, and pinion gear procedures is the same as the positive engagement starter procedures.

Assembly

1. Lubricate the armature shaft

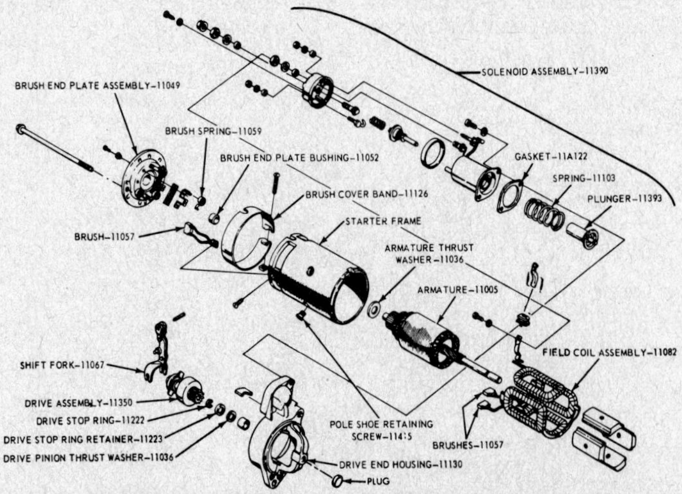

Ford Solenoid starter motor (© Ford Motor Co.)

splines with Lubriplate, then install drive assembly and a new stop ring.

2. Lubricate shift lever pivot pin with Lubriplate, then position solenoid plunger and shift lever assembly in the drive housing.
3. Place a new retainer in the drive housing. Apply a small amount of Lubriplate to the drive end of the armature shaft, then place armature and drive assembly into the drive housing, indexing the shift lever tangs with the drive assembly.
4. Apply a small amount of Lubriplate to the commutator end of the armature shaft, then position the frame and field assembly to the drive housing.
5. Position the brush plate assembly to the frame, making sure it properly indexes. Install through bolts and tighten to 45-85 in. lbs.
6. Install brushes into their holders and make sure leads are not touching any interior starter components.
7. Place the rubber gasket between the solenoid mount and the frame surface.
8. Place the starter solenoid in position with metal gasket and spring, install heat shield (if so equipped) and install solenoid screws.
9. Connect copper strap and install cover band.

Delco-Remy Starter Motor

(General Motors Corp.)

There are many different versions of the Delco-Remy starter, depending upon application. In general, six-cylinder engines use a unit having four field coils in series between the terminal and armature. Standard V8 engines use, depending on displacement, one of three types: one has two field coils in series with the armature and parallel to each other; another has two field coils in parallel between the field terminal and ground, and another has three field coils in series with the armature and one field connected between the motor terminal and ground. Heavy-duty starter motors, such as used on some of the largest G.M. high-output engines (over 400 cu. in.) have series compound windings.

In spite of these differences, all Delco-Remy starters are disassembled and assembled in essentially the same manner.

Disassembly

1. Disconnect the field coil connectors from the motor solenoid terminal.

NOTE: on models so equipped, remove solenoid mounting screws.

2. Remove the through bolts.
3. Remove commutator end frame, field frame and armature assembly from drive housing.
4. Remove the overruning clutch from the armature shaft as follows:
   a. Slide the two-piece thrust collar off the end of the armature shaft.
   b. Slide a standard ½ in. pipe coupling or other spacer onto the shaft so that the end of the coupling butts against the edge of the retainer.
   c. Tap the end of the coupling with a hammer, driving retainer towards armature end of snap-ring.
   d. Remove snap-ring from its groove in the shaft using pliers. Slide retainer and clutch from armature shaft.
5. Disassemble brush assembly from field frame by releasing the V-spring and removing the support pin. The brush holders, brushes and springs now can be pulled out as a unit and the leads disconnected.
6. On models so equipped, separate solenoid from lever housing.

Cleaning and Inspection

1. Clean parts with a rag, but do not immerse the parts in a solvent. Immersion in a solvent will dissolve the grease that is packed in the clutch mechanism and damage the armature and field coil insulation.
2. Test overrunning clutch action. The pinion should turn freely in the overrunning direction and must not slip in the cranking direction. Check pinion teeth to see that they have not been chipped, cracked, or excessively worn. Replace the unit if necessary.
3. Inspect the armature commutator. If the commutator is rough or out of round, it should be turned down and undercut.

CAUTION: Undercut the insulation between the commutator bars by 1/32 in.

This undercut must be the full width of the insulation and flat at the bottom; a triangular groove will not be satisfactory. Some starter motor models use a molded armature commutator design and no attempt to undercut the insulation should be made or serious damage may result to the commutator.

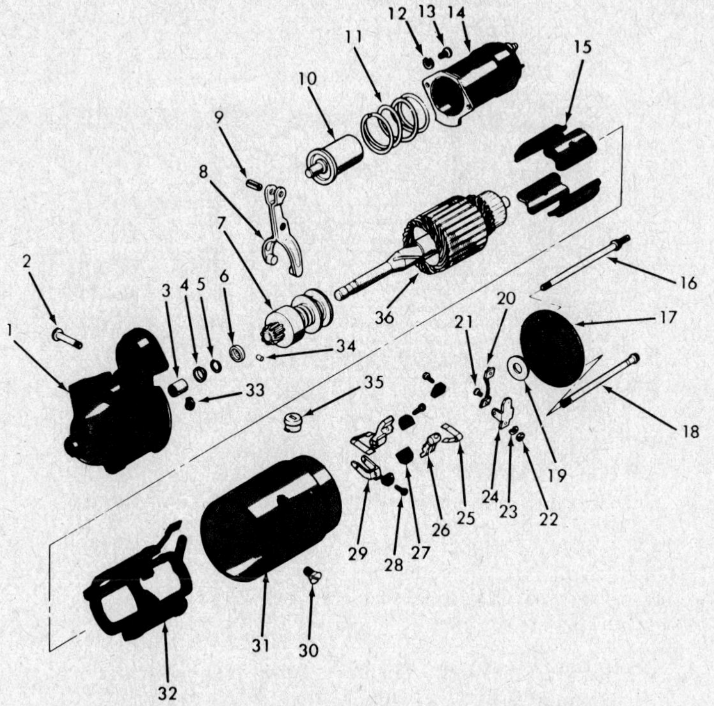

Typical Delco-Remy starter motor—exploded view
(© Chevrolet Div., G.M. Corp.)

1 Starter drive housing
2 Shift lever shaft
3 Drive end bushing
4 Drive end washer
5 Pinion ring stop
6 Armature shaft collar
7 Starter drive assembly
8 Shift lever
9 Pin
10 Solenoid plunger
11 Solenoid return spring
12 Washer
13 Screw
14 Solenoid switch assembly
15 Pole shoes
16 Through bolt
17 End frame
18 Through bolt
19 Washer
20 Brush lead
21 Screw
22 Nut
23 Washer
24 Brush support pin
25 Brush spring
26 Brush holder
27 Brush
28 Screw
29 Ground brush holder
30 Screw
31 Field frame
32 Field coil assembly
33 Ring
34 Pin
35 Field frame grommet
36 Armature

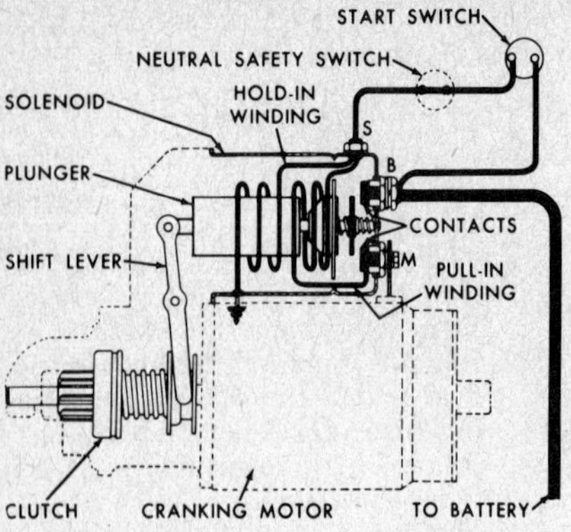

Delco-Remy solenoid windings
(© G.M. Corp.)

Assembly

1. Install brushes into holders. Install solenoid, if so equipped.
2. Assemble insulated and grounded brush holder together using the V-spring and position the assembled unit on the support pin. Push holders and spring to bottom of support and rotate spring to engage the slot in support. Attach ground wire to grounded brush and field lead wire to insulated brush, then repeat for other brush sets.
3. Assemble overruning clutch to armature shaft as follows:
   a. Lubricate drive end of shaft with silicone lubricant.
   b. Slide clutch assembly onto shaft with pinion outward.
   c. Slide retainer onto shaft with cupped surface facing away from pinion.
   d. Stand armature up on a wood surface, commutator downwards. Position snap-ring on upper end of shaft and drive it onto shaft with a small block of wood and a hammer. Slide snap-ring into groove.
   e. Install thrust collar onto shaft with shoulder next to snap-ring.
   f. With retainer on one side of snap-ring and thrust collar on the other side, squeeze together with two sets of pliers until ring seats in retainer.

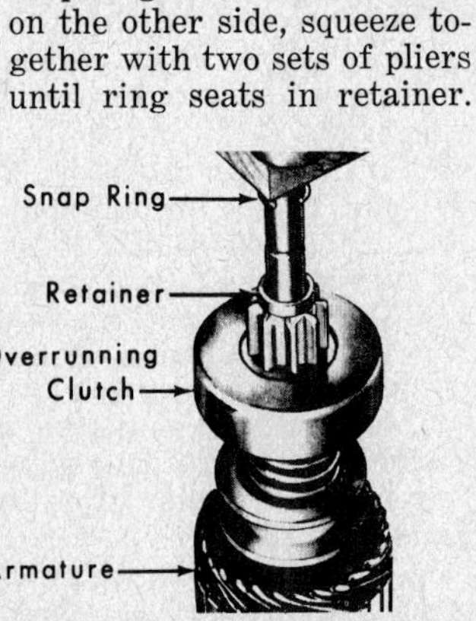

Forcing snap-ring over armature shaft—Delco-Remy starter motor
(© Chevrolet Div., G.M. Corp.)

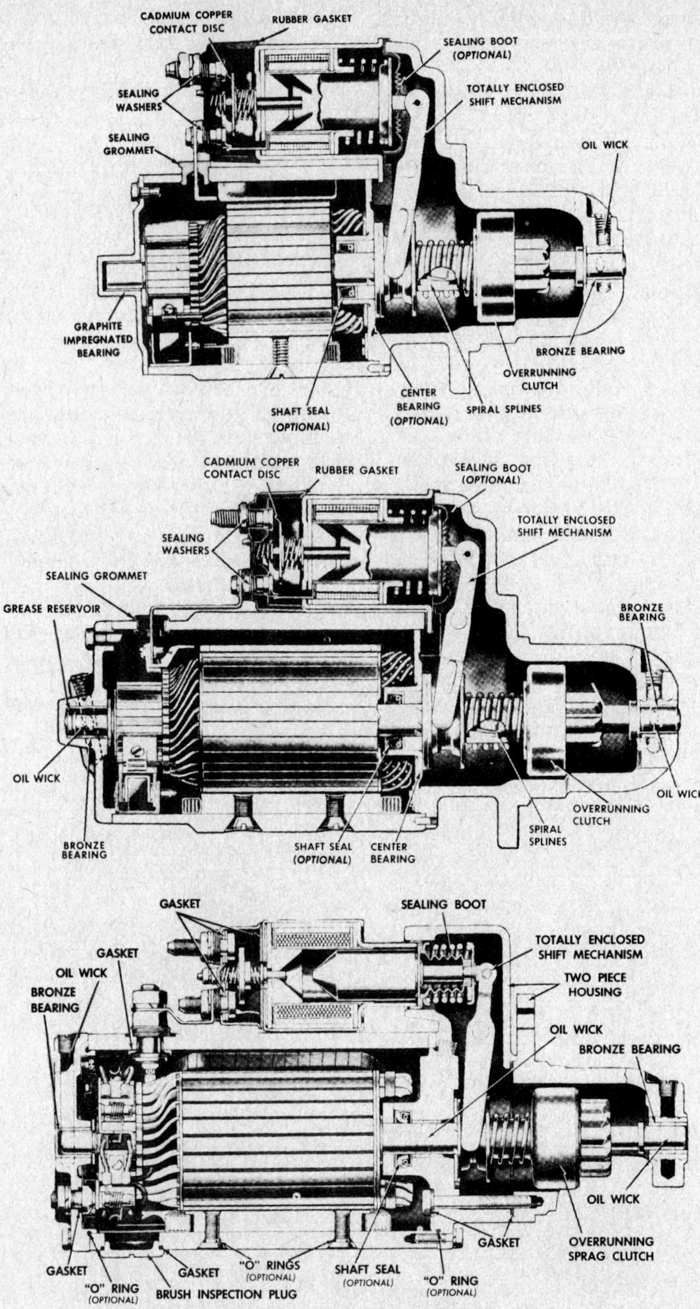

Three types of Delco-Remy starter motors (© G.M. Corp.)

On models without thrust collar, use a washer. Remember to remove washer before continuing.

4. Lubricate drive end bushing with silicone lubricant, then slide armature and clutch assembly into place, at the same time engaging shift lever with clutch.
5. Position field frame over armature and apply sealer (silicone) between frame and solenoid case. Position frame against drive housing, making sure brushes are not damaged in the process.
6. Lubricate commutator end bushing with silicone lubricant, place a leather brake washer on the armature shaft and slide commutator end frame onto shaft. Install through bolts and tighten to 65 in. lbs.
7. Reconnect field coil connector/s to the solenoid motor terminal. Install solenoid mounting screws, if so equipped.
8. Check pinion clearance; it should be 0.010-0.140 in. on all models.

Prestolite Starter Motor

Disassembly

1. Remove the cover band and remove the brushes from their holders.
2. Remove the brush end plate

mounting screws and the two through bolts.

3. Remove the drive housing, end brush plate, and armature from the starter frame.
4. Compress the starter drive spring on the armature side of the shaft and remove the lock screw and remove the starter drive, center bearing plate and thrust washers.
5. Remove the four field pole shoes and remove the field coils from the frame.

NOTE: The positive brushes can be replaced on the field coils by soldering, and the negative brushes replaced on the brush end plate by riveting.

Assembly

1. Assemble the field coils and pole shoes into the frame and secure with screws.
2. Assemble the center bearing plate, thrust washers, and starter drive on the armature shaft and secure with the locking screw.
3. Place the armature assembly into the drive housing aligning the slot in the shaft center bearing support with the pin in the drive housing.
4. Install the end frame to the frame housing and install the six mounting screws.
5. Position the armature assembly into the frame housing and engage the frame dowel with the bolt of the drive frame. Install the two through bolts and secure.
6. Install the brushes into the holders. Center the brush springs on the brushes and locate the insulated brush leads clear of the armature. Install the cover band.

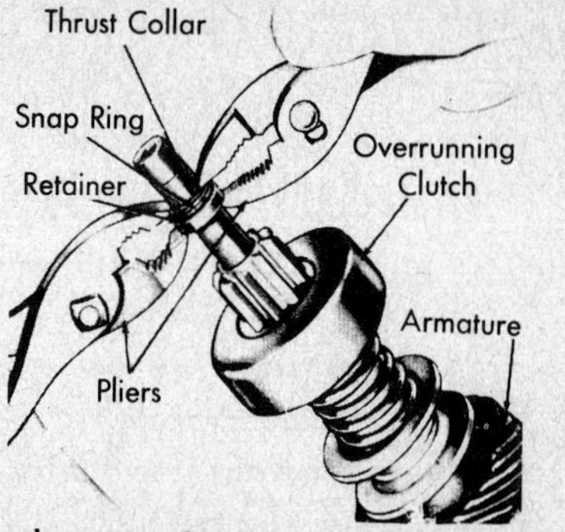

Forcing snap-ring into retainer—Delco-Remy starter motor (© Chevrolet Div., G.M. Corp.)

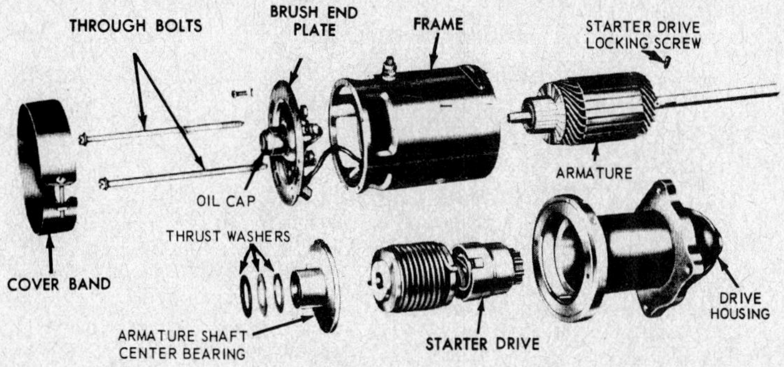

Exploded view—Prestolite heavy duty starter (© Ford Motor Co.)

SPECIFICATIONS

PRESTOLITE STARTER

Vendor	Current Draw Under Normal Load (Amperes)	Minimum Stall Torque (Ft-Lbs)	Minimum Stall Torque (Volts)	Maximum Load (Amperes)	No-Load (Amperes)	Brushes: Mfg. Length (Inches)	Brushes: Wear Limit (Inches)	Brushes: Brush Spring Tension (Ounces)	Through Bolt Torque (In-Lbs)	Mounting Bolt Torque (Ft-Lbs)
Prestolite	200	17.2	5	525	60	0.46–0.48	0.25	45–53	72–96	23–28

Maximum commutator runout in inches is 0.005. Maximum starting circuit voltage drop (battery + terminal to starter terminal) at normal engine temperature 0.5 volt.

Carburetors

INDEX

Carburetor Identification

All carburetors are identified by code numbers, either stamped on the attaching flange side, the main body or on a metal tag, retained by a bowl cover screw. This identifying number is most important to the repairman in order to obtain the correct carburetor replacement or parts and to properly adjust the carburetor when matched to a specific engine.

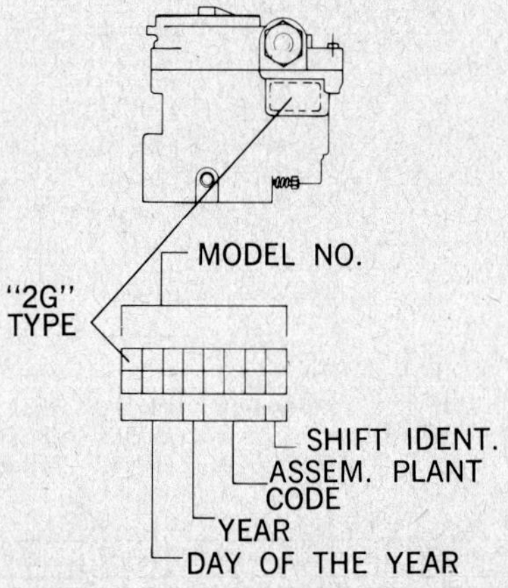

Rochester two barrel models—typical
(© General Motors Corp.)

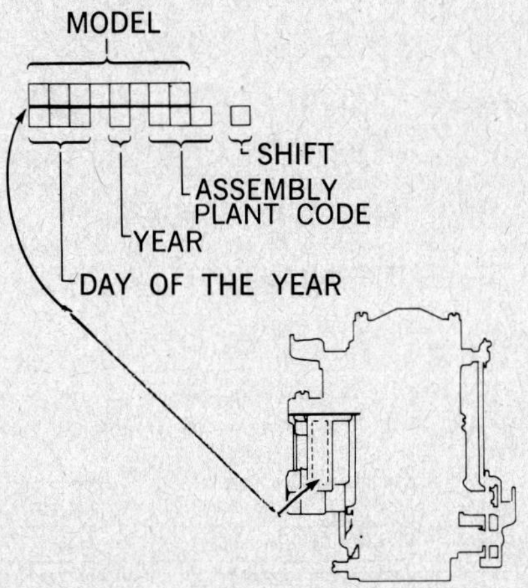

Rochester one barrel models—typical
(© General Motors Corp.)

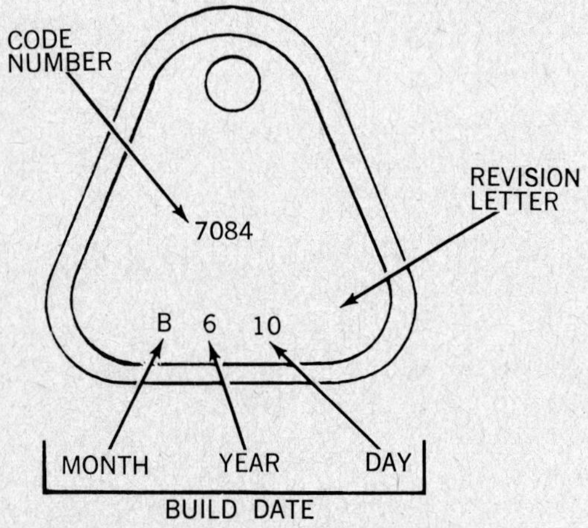

Carter carburetors for Jeep usage—typical
(© Jeep Corp.)

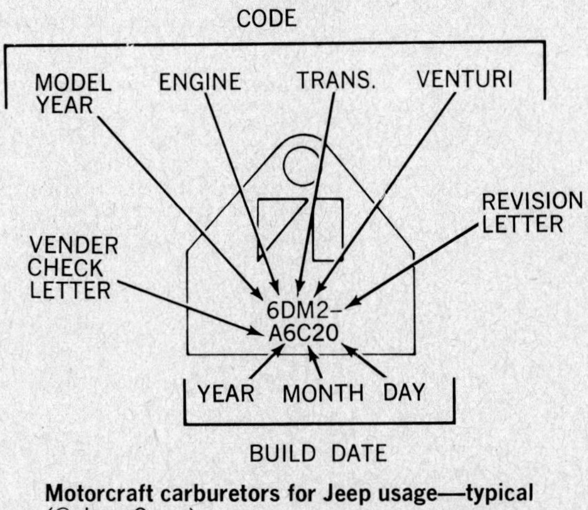

Motorcraft carburetors for Jeep usage—typical
(© Jeep Corp.)

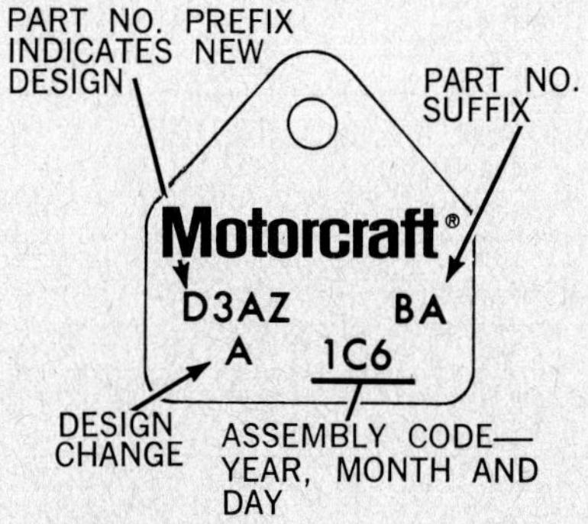

Motorcraft carburetors for Ford usage—typical (© Ford Motor Co.)

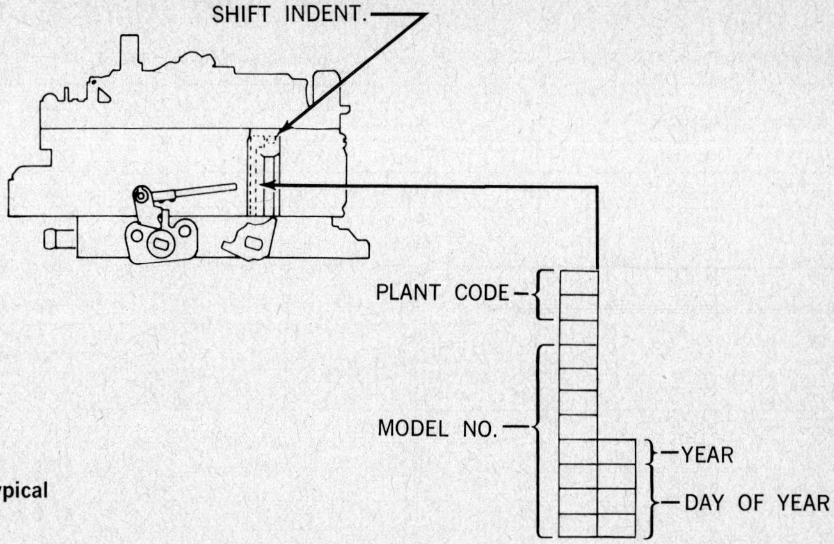

Rochester four barrel models—typical (© General Motors Corp.)

CARTER CARBURETORS

MODEL BBS

Dodge/Plymouth

(All measurements in inches)

Year	Carburetor List Number	Float Level①	Choke Unloader	Fast Idle Cam Setting	Choke Valve Initial Opening w/Vacuum Kick	Fast Idle Speed (RPM)	Choke Setting	Accelerator Pump Setting	Step-up Piston Gap
1973	6219S	.250	.190	.075	.110	2000	Fixed	—	—
	6218S	.250	.190	.075	.075	1800	Fixed	—	—

① Carburetor bowl invented

MODEL BBD

Dodge/Plymouth

(All measurements in inches)

Year	Carburetor List Number	Float Level①	Choke Unloader	Fast Idle Cam Setting	Choke Valve Initial Opening w/Vacuum Kick	Fast Idle Speed (RPM)	Choke Setting	Accelerator Pump Setting	Step-up Piston Gap
1973	6316S	.250	.250	.095	.150	1700	Fixed	.280	—
	6317S	.250	.250	.095	.130	1700	Fixed	.280	—
	6343S	.250	.250	.095	.150	1700	Fixed	.280	—
	6444S	.250	.250	.095	.150	1700	Fixed	.280	—
	6221S	.250	.250	.095	.160	1600	Fixed	.310	—
	6222S	.250	.250	.095	.160	1900	Fixed	.310	—
	6363S	.250	.250	.095	.160	1600	Fixed	.310	—
	6364S	.250	.250	.095	.130	1700	Fixed	.310	—
1974	6610S	.250	.280	.095	.150	1700	Fixed	.500	.030
	6611S	.250	.280	.095	.110	1500	Fixed	.500	.030
	8008S	.250	.280	.095	.150	1700	Fixed	.500	.030
	6613S	.250	.280	.095	.150	1600	Fixed	.500	.030
1975	8019S	.250	.280	.070	.130	1500	Fixed	.500	.035
	8020S	.250	.280	.070	.130	1500	Fixed	.500	.035
	8022S	.250	.310	.070	.070	1500	Fixed	.500	.035
	8024S	.250	.280	.070	.130	1500	Fixed	.500	.035
	8025S	.250	.310	.070	.070	1500	Fixed	.500	.035
	6536S	.250	.280	.095	.150	1700	Fixed	.500	.035
	6537S	.250	.310	.095	.110	1500	Fixed	.500	.035
	8013S	.250	.310	.070	.130	1500	Fixed	.500	.035
	8014S	.250	.310	.070	.110	1500	Fixed	.500	.035

MODEL BBD (Cont'd)

Dodge/Plymouth, Continued

(All measurements in inches)

Year	Carburetor List Number	Float Level①	Choke Unloader	Fast Idle Cam Setting	Choke Valve Initial Opening w/Vacuum Kick	Fast Idle Speed (RPM)	Choke Setting	Accelerator Pump Setting	Step-up Piston Gap
1976	8081S	.250	.310	.070	.150	1500	Fixed	.500	—
	8108S	.250	.310	.070	.150	1500	Fixed	.500	—
	8082S	.250	.280	.070	.130	1500	Fixed	.500	—
	8085S	.250	.280	.070	.130	1500	Fixed	.500	—
	6536S	.250	.280	.095	.150	1700	Fixed	.500	—
	6537S	.250	.280	.095	.110	1500	Fixed	.500	—
	8013S	.250	.310	.070	.130	1500	Fixed	.500	—
	8014S	.250	.310	.070	.110	1500	Fixed	.500	—
1977	8081S	.250	.280	.070	.150	1500	Fixed	.500	—
	8082S	.250	.280	.070	.130	1500	Fixed	.500	—
	8085S	.250	.280	.070	.130	1500	Fixed	.500	—
	8147S	.250	.310	.070	.070	1500	Fixed	.500	—
	8146S	.250	.280	.070	.070	1600	Fixed	.500	—
	8113S	.250	.310	.070	.130	1500	Fixed	.500	—
	8110S	.250	.280	.070	.095	1500	Fixed	.500	—
1978	8149S	.250	.280	.070	.130	1500	Fixed	.500	.035
	8151S	.250	.280	.070	.130	1500	Fixed	.500	.035
	8180S	.250	.280	.070	.150	1600	Fixed	.500	.035
	8152S	.250	.280	.070	.130	1500	Fixed	.500	.035
	8147S	.250	.310	.070	.070	1500	Fixed	.500	.035
	8154S	.250	.310	.070	.130	1500	Fixed	.500	.035
	8156S	.250	.310	.070	.110	1500	Fixed	.500	.035
	8146S	.250	.280	.070	.070	1500	Fixed	.500	.035
1979	8214S	.250	.280	.070	.110	1400	Fixed	.500	—
	8215S	.250	.280	.070	.110	1600	Fixed	.500	—
	8249S	.250	.280	.070	.110	1400	Fixed	.500	—
	8232S	.250	.280	.070	.110	1500	Fixed	500	—
	8210S	.250	.280	.070	.110	1400	Fixed	.500	—
	8211S	.250	.280	.070	.110	1500	Fixed	500	—

① Carburetor bowl inverted

MODEL TQ

Dodge/Plymouth

(All measurements in inches)

Year	Carburetor List Number	Float Level	Fast Idle Speed (RPM)	Auto Choke Setting	Fuel Bowl Vent Adjustment	Accelerator Pump Stroke Adjustment ②	Secondary Throttle Lock-Out Adjustment	Metering Rod Adjustment	Vacuum Kick Adjustment	Vacuum Choke Pull-off Adjustment	Fast Idle Cam and Linkage Adjustment	Choke Unloader Adjustment
1973	6446	1.0	1700	Fixed	.815	31/64 (23/64)	.060-.090	—	.160	.040	.110	.190
	6518	1.0	1700	Fixed	.815	31/64 (23/64)	.060-.090	—	.160	.040	.110	.190
1974	9022S	1.0①	1800	Fixed	13/16	35/64	.060-.090	—	.210	.040	.100	.310
	9025S	1.0①	1700	Fixed	13/16	31/64 (23/64)	.060-.090	—	.160	.040	.100	.310
	9017S	1.0①	1700	Fixed	13/16	31/64 (23/64)	.060-.090	—	.160	.040	.100	.310
	6545S	29/32	1700	Fixed	—	31/64 (23/64)	.060-.090	—	.160	.040	.100	.310
1975	9034S	1.0	—	—	—	—	—	—	—	—	—	—
	9035S	1.0	—	—	—	—	—	—	—	—	—	—
	6545S	29/32	1700	Fixed	—	31/64 (23/64)	.060-.090	—	.160	.040	.100	.310
	9036S	29/32	1700	Fixed	—	31/64 (23/64)	.060-.090	—	.160	.040	.100	.310
1976	6545S	29/32	1700	Fixed	—	31/64 (23/64)	.060-.090	—	.160	.040	.100	.310
	9036S	29/32	1700	Fixed	—	31/64 (23/64)	.060-.090	—	.160	.040	.100	.310
1977	6545S	27/32	1700	Fixed	—	1/2 (5/16)	.060-.090	—	.160	.040	.100	.310
	9096S	27/32	1700	Fixed	—	1/2 (5/16)	.060-.090	—	.160	.040	.100	.310

MODEL TQ (Cont'd)

Dodge/Plymouth, Continued

(All measurements in inches)

Year	Carburetor List Number	Float Level	Fast Idle Speed (RPM)	Auto Choke Setting	Fuel Bowl Vent Adjustment	Accelerator Pump Stroke Adjustment ②	Secondary Throttle Lock-Out Adjustment	Metering Rod Adjustment	Vacuum Kick Adjustment	Vacuum Choke Pull-off Adjust-ment	Fast Idle Cam and Linkage Adjust-ment	Choke Unloader Adjustment
1978	9118S	27/32	1700	Fixed	—	1/2 (5/16)	.060-.090	—	.160	.040	.100	.310
	9151S	27/32	1700	Fixed	—	1/2 (5/16)	.060-.090	—	.160	.040	.100	.310
	9116S	29/32	1600	Fixed	—	11/32 (9/64)	.060-.090	—	.100	.040	.100	1/2
	9149S	29/32	1600	Fixed	—	11/32 (9/64)	.060-.090	—	.100	.040	.100	1/2
	9117S	27/32	1700	Fixed	—	1/2 (5/16)	.060-.090	—	.100	.040	.100	.310
	9150S	27/32	1700	Fixed	—	1/2 (5/16)	.060-.090	—	.100	.040	.100	.310
	9173S	29/32	1500	Fixed	—	5/16 (3/16)	.060-.090	—	.150	.040	.100	.310
	9123S	29/32	1600	Fixed	—	33/64 (5/16)	.060-.090	—	.150	.040	.100	1/2
	9124S	29/32	1600	Fixed	—	33/64 (5/16)	.060-.090	—	.100	.040	.100	1/2
	9152S	29/32	1600	Fixed	—	33/64 (5/16)	.060-.090	—	.100	.040	.100	1/2
	9175S	29/32	1700	Fixed	—	33/64 (5/16)	.060-.090	—	.150	.040	.100	1/2
	9126S	29/32	1600	Fixed	—	33/64 (5/16)	.060-.090	—	.100	.040	.100	1/2
	9151S	29/32	1400	Fixed	—	33/64 (5/16)	.060-.090	—	.160	.040	.100	1/2
	9150S	29/32	1400	Fixed	—	33/64 (5/16)	.060-.090	—	.100	.040	.100	1/2
1979	9228S	29/32	1600	Fixed	—	11/32 (9/64)	.060-.090	—	.100	.040	.100	.500
	9229S	29/32	1600	Fixed	—	11/32 (9/64)	.060-.090	—	.100	.040	.100	.500
	9223S	29/32	1600	Fixed	—	11/32 (9/64)	.060-.090	—	.100	.040	.100	.500
	9227S	29/32	1600	Fixed	—	11/32 (9/64)	.060-.090	—	.100	.040	.100	.500
	9224S	29/32	1600	Fixed	—	5/16 (3/16)	.060-.090	—	.100	.040	.100	.500
	9225S	29/32	1600	Fixed	—	5/16 (3/16)	.060-.090	—	.100	.040	.100	.500
	9207S	29/32	1600	Fixed	—	31/64 (23/64)	.060-.090	—	.150	.040	.100	.310
	9208S	29/32	1600	Fixed	—	31/64 (23/64)	.060-.090	—	.150	.040	.100	.310
	9209S	29/32	1600	Fixed	—	31/64 (23/64)	.060-.090	—	.150	.040	.100	.310
	9210S	29/32	1600	Fixed	—	31/64 (23/64)	.060-.090	—	.150	.040	.100	.310
	9211S	29/32	1400	Fixed	—	31/64 (23/64)	.060-.090	—	.100	.040	.100	.500
	9212S	29/32	1400	Fixed	—	31/64 (23/64)	.060-.090	—	.100	.040	.100	.500
	9247S	29/32	1400	Fixed	—	31/64 (23/64)	.060-.090	—	.100	.040	.100	.500
	9248S	29/32	1400	Fixed	—	31/64 (23/64)	.060-.090	—	.100	.040	.100	.500

① Brass Float, 29/32 in. For Plastic Float
② Stage I (Stage II)

MODEL YF

Ford

(All measurements in inches)

Year	Carburetor List Number	Float Level	Float Drop	Choke Unloader Setting	Choke Setting	Dash Pot Plunger	Initial Choke Opening
1973	D3TF						
	JA	3/8	—	.250	Index	—	.230
	TA	3/8	1 1/4	.280	Index	—	—
	KA	3/8	1 1/4	.280	1 Lean	—	—
	AAA	3/8	1 1/4	.280	1 Lean	—	—
	ACA	3/8	1 1/4	.280	Index	—	—
	ABA	3/8	1 1/4	.280	Index	—	—
	LA	3/8	1 1/4	.280	1 Rich	—	—
	D5PE						
	ANA	3/8	—	.280	—	—	—
	AZA	3/8	—	.280	—	—	—
	ALA	3/8	—	.280	—	—	—
	AKA	3/8	—	.280	—	—	—
	D3UF						
	HA	3/8	—	.250	1 Lean	—	.230
	LA	3/8	—	.280	—	—	—
	NA	3/8	—	.280	—	—	—

MODEL YF (Cont'd)

(All measurements in inches)

Ford, Continued

Year	Carburetor List Number	Float Level	Float Drop	Choke Unloader Setting	Choke Setting	Dash Pot Plunger	Initial Choke Opening
	MA	3/8	—	.280	—	—	—
	PA	3/8	—	.280	—	—	—
	UA	3/8	—	.280	—	—	—
	VA	3/8	—	.280	—	—	—
	XA	3/8	—	.280	—	—	—
	D3HF						
	HA	3/8	—	.280	—	—	—
1974	D4TE						
	ABA	3/8	—	.120	Index	.100	.260
	LA	3/8	—	.280	1 Lean	—	.230
	ZA	3/8	—	.280	1 Lean	—	.230
	AAA	3/8	—	.280	1 Lean	—	—
	NA	3/8	—	.280	Index	—	.230
	YC	3/8	—	.280	Index	—	.290
	ACA	3/8	—	.120	Index	—	.260
	KB	3/8	—	.280	Index	—	.290
	AVA	3/8	—	—	—	—	—
	D5PE						
	ANA	3/8	—	.280	—	—	—
	AGA	3/8	—	—	—	—	—
	ALA	3/8	—	.280	—	—	—
	D4HE						
	AA	3/8	—	—	Manual	—	—
	D5UE						
	HA	23/32	—	—	—	—	—
	HB	23/32	—	—	—	—	—
	GA	23/32	—	—	—	—	—
	GB	23/32	—	.280	Index	—	.290
	EA	23/32	—	.280	Index	—	.290
	EB	23/32	—	—	—	—	—
	FA	23/32	—	.280	Index	—	.290
	FB	23/32	—	.280	Index	—	.290
	RA	23/32	—	—	—	—	—
	RB	23/32	—	—	—	—	—
	AAA	23/32	—	—	—	—	—
	AAB	23/32	—	—	—	—	—
1975	D4TE						
	ACA	3/8	—	—	Manual	—	—
	AGA	3/8	—	—	Manual	—	—
	AVA	3/8	—	—	Manual	—	—
	AUA	3/8	—	—	Manual	—	—
	D5TE						
	ADA	3/8	—	.280	Index	—	.290
	ADB	3/8	—	.280	Index	—	.290
	AKA	3/8	—	.280	Index	—	.290
	AKB	3/8	—	.280	Index	—	.290
	AMA	3/8	—	.280	1 Rich	—	.230
	AGA	3/8	—	.280	1 Rich	—	.230
	AGB	3/8	—	.280	1 Rich	—	.230
	ANA	3/8	—	.280	1 Rich	—	.230
	AHA	3/8	—	.280	Index	—	.290
	APA	3/8	—	.280	Index	—	.290
	APB	23/32	—	.280	Index	—	.290
	AJA	3/8	—	—	Manual	—	—
	AJB	3/8	—	—	Manual	—	—
	AFA	3/8	—	—	Manual	—	—

MODEL YF (Cont'd)

(All measurements in inches)

Ford, Continued

Year	Carburetor List Number	Float Level	Float Drop	Choke Unloader Setting	Choke Setting	Dash Pot Plunger	Initial Choke Opening
	AFB	3/8	—	—	Manual	—	—
	ALA	3/8	—	.280	Index	—	.290
	ALB	3/8	—	.280	Index	—	.290
	CAA	3/8	—	.280	Index	—	.290
	CAB	23/32	—	.280	Index	—	.290
	CBA	3/8	—	.280	Index	—	.290
	D5PE						
	ANA	3/8	—	.280	—	—	—
	AVA	3/8	—	—	—	—	—
	D4HE						
	AA	3/8	—	—	Manual	—	—
	D5UE						
	HA	23/32	—	.280	Index	—	.290
	HB	23/32	—	—	—	—	—
	GA	23/32	—	—	—	—	—
	GB	23/32	—	.280	Index	—	.290
	EA	23/32	—	.280	Index	—	.290
	EB	23/32	—	—	—	—	—
	FA	23/32	—	.280	Index	—	.290
	FB	23/32	—	.280	Index	—	.290
	RA	23/32	—	—	—	—	—
	RB	23/32	—	—	—	—	—
	AAA	23/32	—	.280	Index	—	.290
	AAB	23/32	—	.280	Index	—	.290
1976	D5TE						
	AGA	3/8	—	.280	1 Rich	—	.230
	APA	3/8	—	.280	Index	—	.290
	APB	23/32	—	.280	Index	—	.290
	AJA	3/8	—	—	Manual	—	—
	AJB	3/8	—	—	Manual	—	—
	AFA	3/8	—	—	Manual	—	—
	AFB	3/8	—	—	Manual	—	—
	CAA	3/8	—	.280	Index	—	.290
	CAB	23/32	—	.280	Index	—	.290
	CBA	3/8	—	.280	Index	—	.290
	CBB	3/8	—	.280	Index	—	.290
	D5PE						
	ANA	3/8	—	.280	Index	—	.290
	D6UE						
	FA	23/32	—	.280	Index	—	.290
	MA	23/32	—	.280	Index	—	.290
	D6TE						
	ZA	23/32	—	.280	Index	—	.290
	KA	23/32	—	.280	Index	—	.290
	DA	23/32	—	.280	Index	—	.290
	HA	23/32	—	.280	Index	—	.290
	D5UE						
	EA	3/8	—	.280	Index	—	.290
	EB	23/32	—	.280	Index	—	.290
	FA	3/8	—	.280	Index	—	.290
	FB	23/32	—	.280	Index	—	.290
	RA	23/32	—	—	—	—	—
	RB	23/32	—	—	—	—	—
	AAA	23/32	—	—	—	—	—
	AAB	23/32	—	.280	Index	—	.290

MODEL YF (Cont'd)

(All measurements in inches)

Ford Continued

Year	Carburetor List Number	Float Level	Float Drop	Choke Unloader Setting	Choke Setting	Dash Pot Plunger	Initial Choke Opening
1977	D5TE						
	AGA	3/8	—	280	1 Rich	—	.230
	AGB	23/32	—	280	1 Rich	—	.230
	AJA	3/8	—	—	Manual	—	—
	AJB	3/8	—	—	Manual	—	—
	AFA	3/8	—	—	Manual	—	—
	AFB	3/8	—	—	Manual	—	—
	D5PF						
	ANA	3/8	—	.280	—	—	—
	D7PE						
	LA	3/8	—	—	—	—	—
	KA	3/8	—	—	—	—	—
	SA	3/8	—	—	—	—	—
	RA	3/8	—	—	—	—	—
	NA	3/8	—	—	—	—	—
	D7TE						
	CAA	25/32	—	—	—	—	—
	CBA	25/32	—	—	—	—	—
	CCA	25/32	—	—	—	—	—
	PA	25/32	—	.280	Index	—	.290
	CFA	25/32	—	—	—	—	—
	CFB	25/32	—	—	—	—	—
	MA	25/32	—	.280	Index	—	.290
	CDA	25/32	—	—	—	—	—
	CEA	25/32	—	—	—	—	—
	D6TE						
	ZA	23/32	—	.280	Index	—	.290
	HA	23/32	—	.280	Index	—	.290
	D6UE						
	MA	23/32	—	.280	Index	—	.290
1978	D8TE						
	BVA	25/32	1 19/32	.280	Index	—	.230
	CKB	25/32	1 19/32	.280	Index	.070	.230
	BWA	25/32	1 19/32	.280	Index	.070	.230
	BUA	25/32	1 19/32	.280	Index	.070	.230
	BUB	25/32	—	—	—	—	—
	CNA	25/32	1 19/32	.280	Index	.070	.230
	AAA	25/32	1 19/32	.280	Index	.070	.230
	UA	23/32	1 1/2	—	Manual	—	—
	CDA	23/32	1 1/2	—	Manual	—	—
	D8UE						
	AAA	—	—	—	—	—	—
	ZA	25/32	1 19/32	.280	Index	.070	.230
	D6TE						
	ZA	23/32	—	.280	Index	—	.290
	D6UE						
	MA	23/32	—	.280	Index	—	.290
	D2UE						
	EA	25/32	1 19/32	—	—	—	—

MODEL BBD-2

(All measurements in inches)

Jeep

Year	Carburetor Number	Float Level (in.)	Step-up Piston Gap (in.)	Initial Choke Clearance (in.)	Fast Idle Cam Setting (in.)	Choke Cover Setting	Choke Unloader (Min.) (in.)	Fast Idle Speed (RPM)①
1977	8107	.250	.040	.128	.095	2 Rich	.280	1700

MODEL BBD-2

Jeep

(All measurements in inches)

Year	Carburetor Number	Float Level (in.)	Step-up Piston Gap (in.)	Initial Choke Clearance (in.)	Fast Idle Cam Setting (in.)	Choke Cover Setting	Choke Unloader (Min.) (in.)	Fast Idle Speed (RPM)①
1978	8107	.250	.040	.128	.095	2 Rich	.280	1700
1979	8185	.250	.035	.140	.110	1 Rich	.280	1600
	8186	.250	.035	.150	.110	1 Rich	.280	1500
	8187	.250	.035	.140	.110	1 Rich	.280	1600
	8188	.250	.035	.150	.110	1 Rich	.280	1500
	8195	.250	.035	.140	.110	1 Rich	.280	1500(M) 1600(A)
	8229	.250	.035	.128	.095	1 Rich	.280	1500

① On second step of fast idle cam with TCS solenoid and EGR disconnected.

MODEL TQ

International

(All measurements in inches)

Year	Carburetor List Number	Float Level	Fast Idle Speed (RPM)	Auto Choke Setting	Fuel Bowl Vent Clearance	Accelerator Pump Stroke Adjustment	Secondary Throttle Lock-Out Adjustment	Metering Rod Adjustment	Vacuum Kick Adjustment	Vacuum Pull-off Choke Adjustment	Fast Idle Cam and Linkage Adjustment	Choke Unloader Adjustment
1979	TQ91285	.91 ± .030 (Old Needles) .88 ± .030 (New Needles)	1600	¼ Rod	.800-.830	Primary① .328-.358 Secondary① .120-.260	.060-.090	.468 ± .031	Vac. High .440-.460 Vac. Low .235-.255	.840-.880	.089-.109	.280-.320
	TQ6591S, 6550S	1.06	1550-1600	1 Rich	.800-.830	Primary .328-.358 Secondary .120-.260	.060-.090	15/32	Vac. High .335-.355 Vac. Low .250-.270	.840-.880 (6550S only)	.089-.109	.280-.320
	TQ6590S, 6552S, 6551S	1.06	1550-1600	1 Rich	.800-.830	Primary .328-.358	.060-.090	15/32	Vac. High .335-.355 Vac. Low .250-.270	.840-.880 (6551S only)	.089-.109	.280-.320

① Rod in inner hole

MODEL YF

Jeep

(All measurements in inches)

Year	Carburetor Number	Float Level	Float Drop	Initial Choke Clearance	Fast Idle Cam Setting	Choke Cover Setting	Choke Unloader (Min.)	Fast Idle Speed (RPM)①	Dash Pot
1973	6299S	.450	1¼	.215	Index Mark	1 Rich	.275	1600	.095
	6300S	.450	1¼	.215	Index Mark	1 Rich	.275	1600	.095
	6401S	.450	1¼	.215	Index Mark	1 Rich	.275	1600	.095
1974	6431	.476	1.38	.215	190	1 Rich	.275	1600	.095②
	6511	.476	1.38	.215	190	1 Rich	.275	1600	.095
	7001	.476	1.38	.215	190	1 Rich	.275	1600	—
	7029②	.476	1.38	.215	190	1 Rich	.275	1600	.095
1975	7043	.476	1.38	.215	190	1 Rich	.275	1600	—
	7041	.476	1.38	.215	190	1 Rich	.275	1600	.075
	7040	.476	1.38	.215	190	1 Rich	.275	1600	.075
1976	7088	.476	1⅜	.215	.195	1 Rich	.275	1600	.075
	7084	.476	1⅜	.215	.195	2 Rich	.275	1600	.075
	7109	.476	1⅜	.215	.195	2 Rich	.275	1600	.075
	7083	.476	1⅜	.215	.195	1 Rich	.275	1600	.075
	7085	.476	1⅜	.215	.195	1 Rich	.275	1600	.075
1977	7154	.476	1⅜	.215	.195	1 Rich	.275	1600	—
	7151	.476	1⅜	.215	.195	1 Rich	.275	1600	—
	7153	.476	1⅜	.215	.195	1 Rich	.275	1600	—
	7110, 7111 (Alt.)	.476	1⅜	.221	.201	2 Rich	.275	1800	—

MODEL YF

(All measurements in inches)

Jeep

Year	Carburetor Number	Float Level	Float Drop	Initial Choke Clearance	Fast Idle Cam Setting	Choke Cover Setting	Choke Unloader (Min.)	Fast Idle Speed (RPM)①	Dash Pot
1978	7201	.476	1⅜	.215	.195	Index	.275	1600	—
	7228	.476	1⅜	.215	.195	1 Rich	.275	1600	—
	7230	.476	1⅜	.215	.195	1 Rich	.275	1600	—
	7231 (Alt.)	.476	1⅜	.221	.201	2 Rich	.275	1500	—

① On 2nd step of fast idle cam with TCS solenoid and EGR disconnected
② Without Air Guard

SINGLE BARREL—YF TYPE

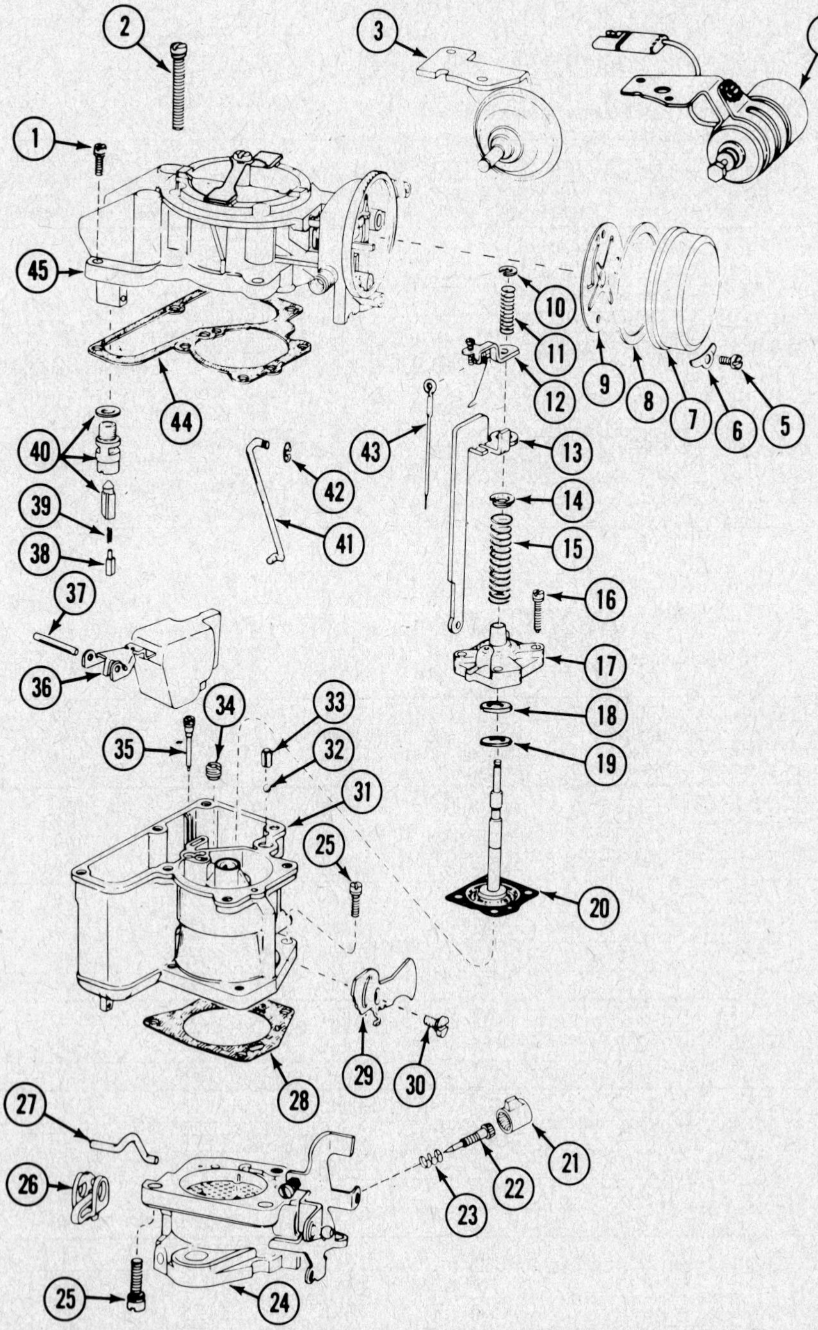

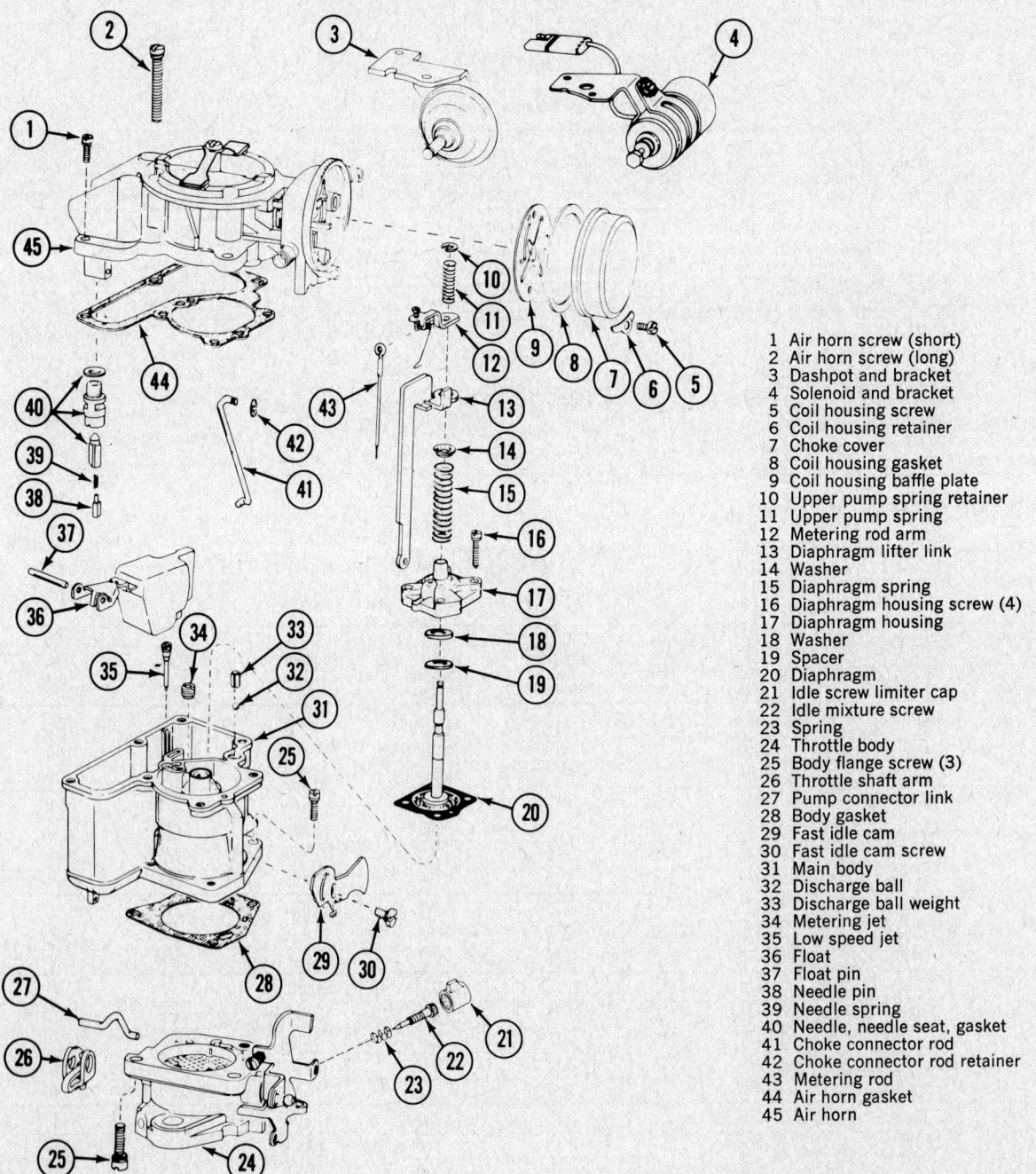

1 Air horn screw (short)
2 Air horn screw (long)
3 Dashpot and bracket
4 Solenoid and bracket
5 Coil housing screw
6 Coil housing retainer
7 Choke cover
8 Coil housing gasket
9 Coil housing baffle plate
10 Upper pump spring retainer
11 Upper pump spring
12 Metering rod arm
13 Diaphragm lifter link
14 Washer
15 Diaphragm spring
16 Diaphragm housing screw (4)
17 Diaphragm housing
18 Washer
19 Spacer
20 Diaphragm
21 Idle screw limiter cap
22 Idle mixture screw
23 Spring
24 Throttle body
25 Body flange screw (3)
26 Throttle shaft arm
27 Pump connector link
28 Body gasket
29 Fast idle cam
30 Fast idle cam screw
31 Main body
32 Discharge ball
33 Discharge ball weight
34 Metering jet
35 Low speed jet
36 Float
37 Float pin
38 Needle pin
39 Needle spring
40 Needle, needle seat, gasket
41 Choke connector rod
42 Choke connector rod retainer
43 Metering rod
44 Air horn gasket
45 Air horn

Exploded view of YF carburetor—Typical (© Jeep Corp.)

MODEL YF (Cont'd)

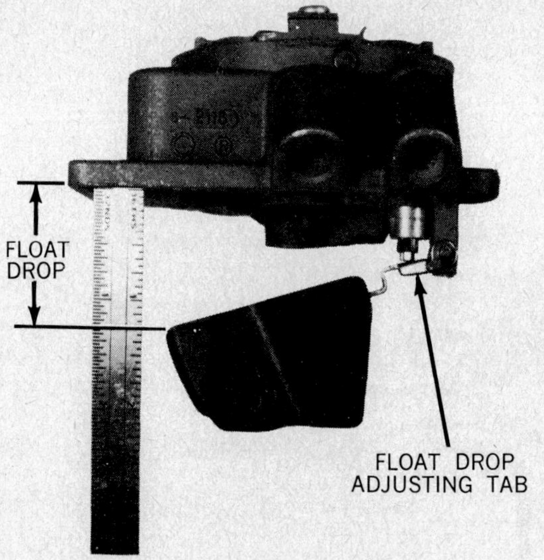

Measurement of float drop—YF carburetor (© Jeep Corp.)

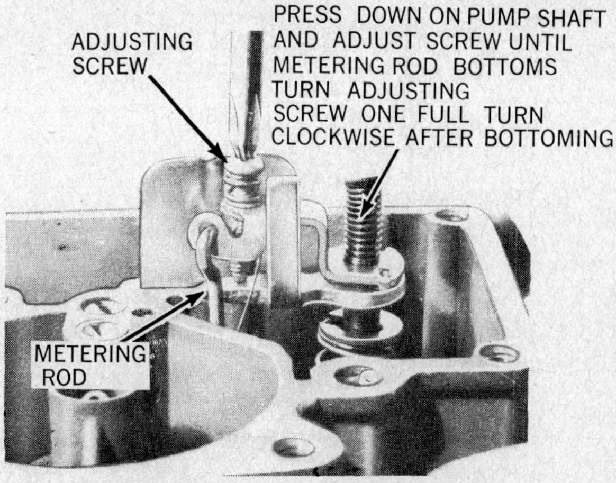

Metering rod adjustment—YF carburetor (© Jeep Corp.)

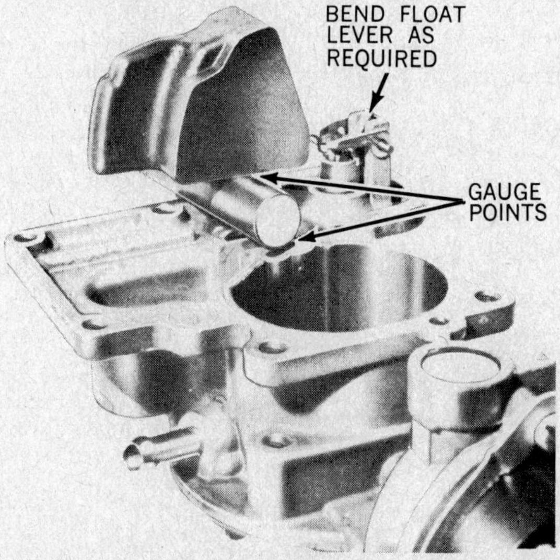

Float level measurement—YF carburetor (© Jeep Corp.)

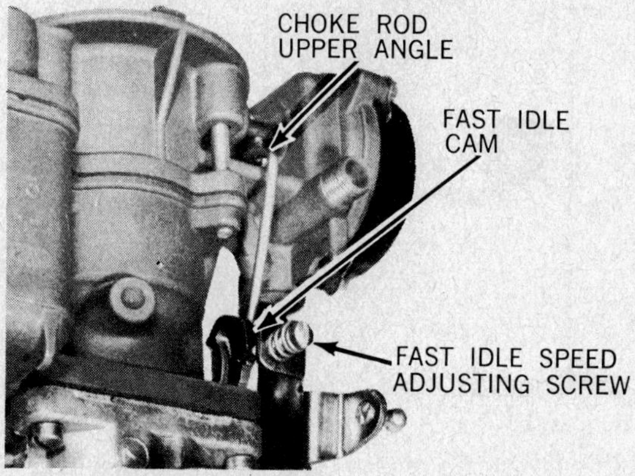

Fast idle cam and linkage adjustment points—YF carburetor (© Jeep Corp.)

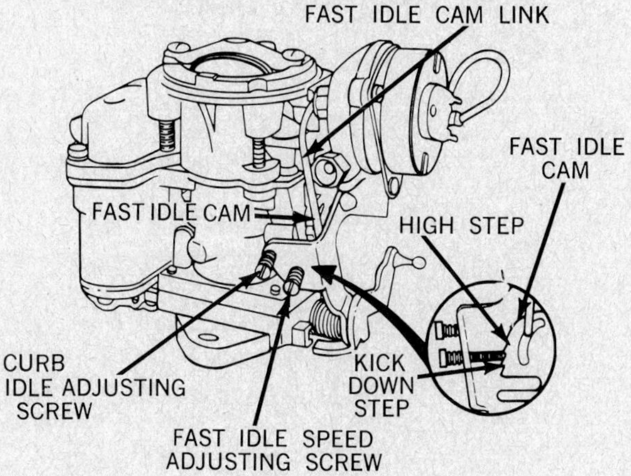

Typical adjustment points—YF carburetor with electric choke (© Ford Motor Co.)

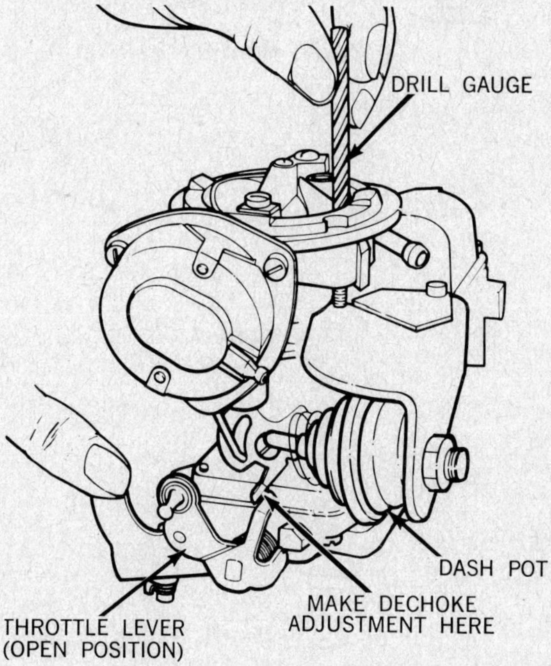

Choke plate unloader (Dechoke) adjustment—typical —YFA carburetor (© Ford Motor Co.)

MODEL BBS

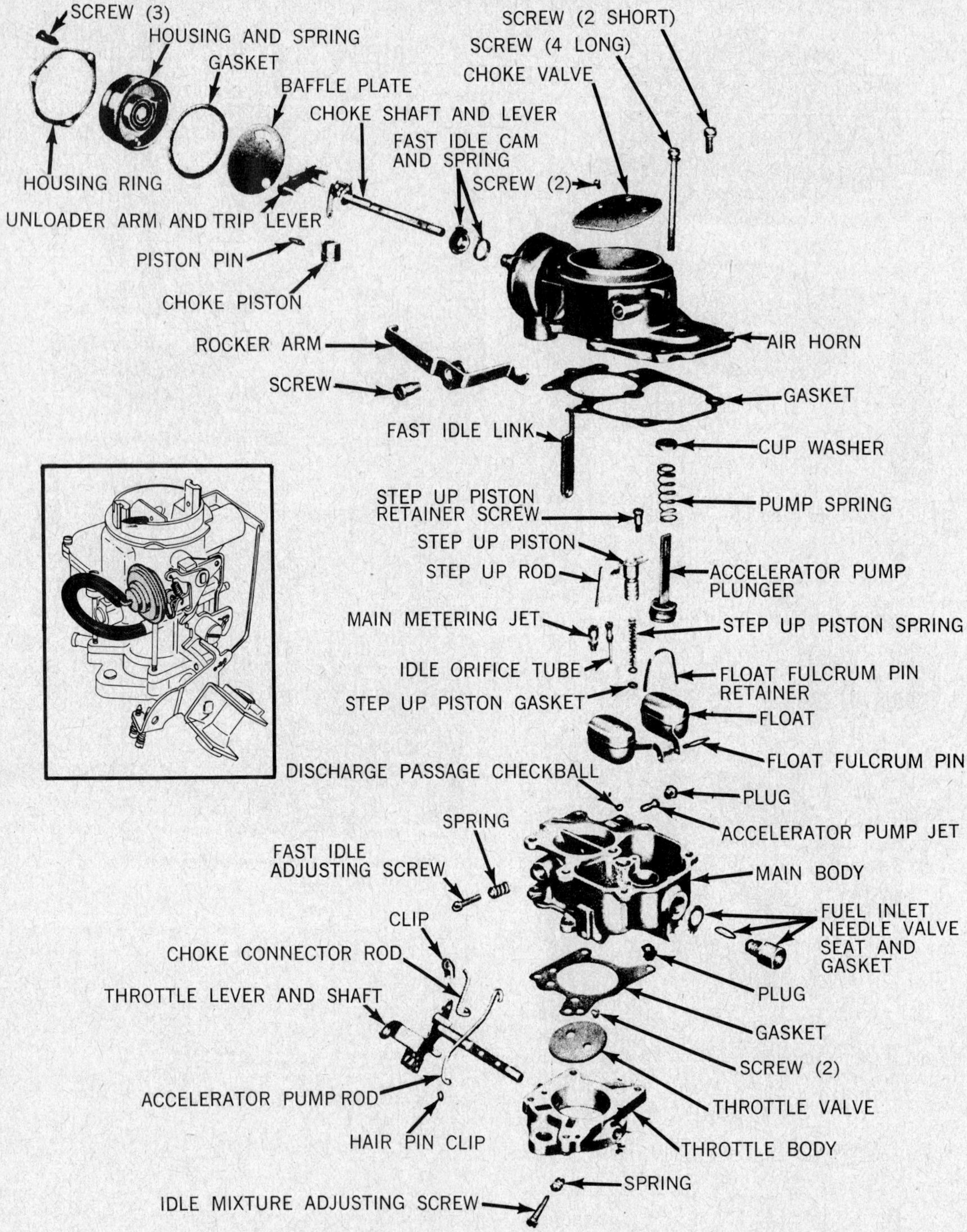
SCREW (3)
HOUSING AND SPRING
GASKET
BAFFLE PLATE
CHOKE SHAFT AND LEVER
FAST IDLE CAM AND SPRING
SCREW (2)
SCREW (2 SHORT)
SCREW (4 LONG)
CHOKE VALVE
HOUSING RING
UNLOADER ARM AND TRIP LEVER
PISTON PIN
CHOKE PISTON
ROCKER ARM
AIR HORN
SCREW
GASKET
FAST IDLE LINK
CUP WASHER
STEP UP PISTON RETAINER SCREW
PUMP SPRING
STEP UP PISTON
STEP UP ROD
ACCELERATOR PUMP PLUNGER
MAIN METERING JET
STEP UP PISTON SPRING
IDLE ORIFICE TUBE
FLOAT FULCRUM PIN RETAINER
STEP UP PISTON GASKET
FLOAT
FLOAT FULCRUM PIN
DISCHARGE PASSAGE CHECKBALL
PLUG
SPRING
ACCELERATOR PUMP JET
FAST IDLE ADJUSTING SCREW
MAIN BODY
FUEL INLET NEEDLE VALVE SEAT AND GASKET
CLIP
CHOKE CONNECTOR ROD
PLUG
THROTTLE LEVER AND SHAFT
GASKET
SCREW (2)
ACCELERATOR PUMP ROD
THROTTLE VALVE
HAIR PIN CLIP
THROTTLE BODY
SPRING
IDLE MIXTURE ADJUSTING SCREW

Carter BBS single barrel—typical

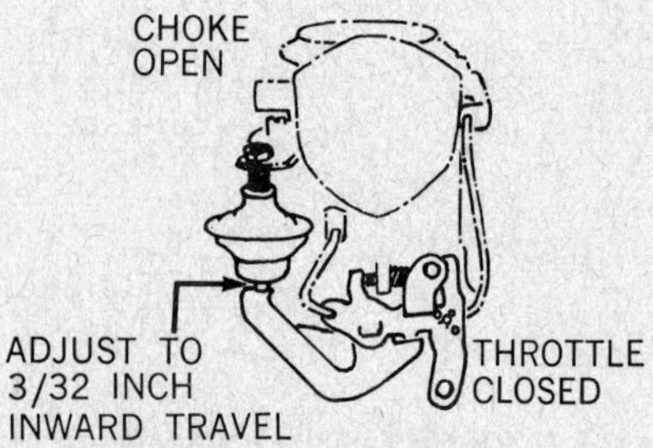
CHOKE OPEN
ADJUST TO 3/32 INCH INWARD TRAVEL
THROTTLE CLOSED

BBS dashpot adjustment

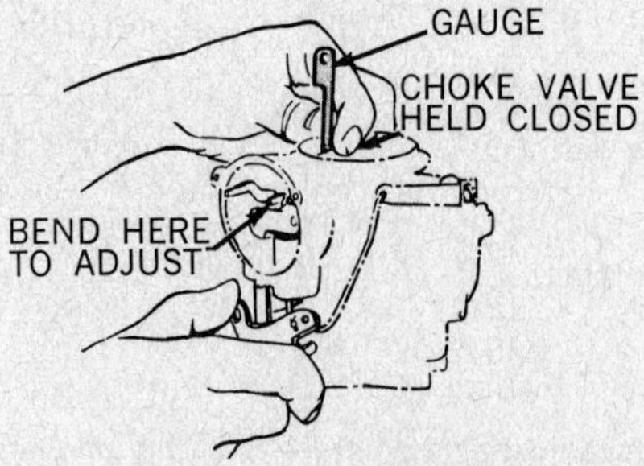
GAUGE
CHOKE VALVE HELD CLOSED
BEND HERE TO ADJUST

BBS unloader adjustment

MODEL BBS

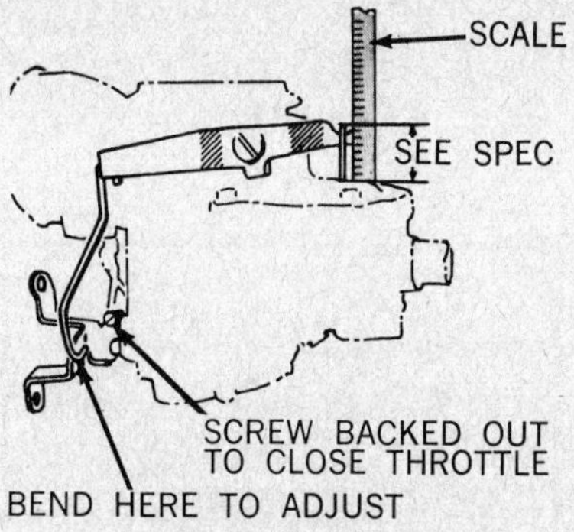

BBS pump adjustment

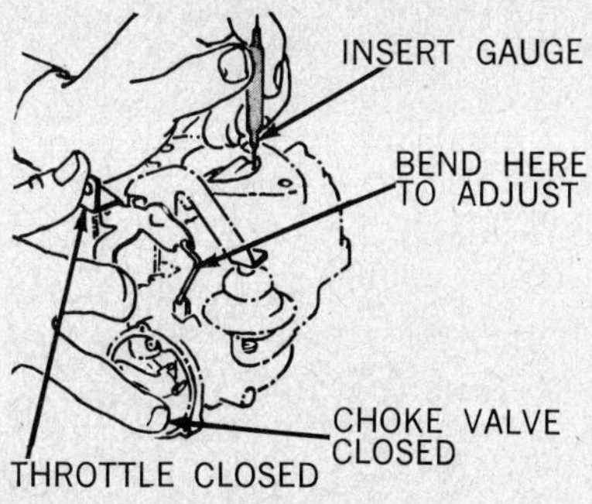

BBS fast idle adjustment

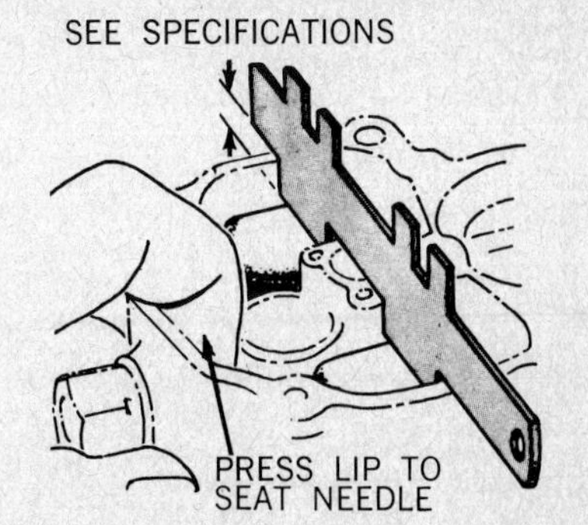

BBS float adjustment (invert fuel bowl)

MODEL BBD

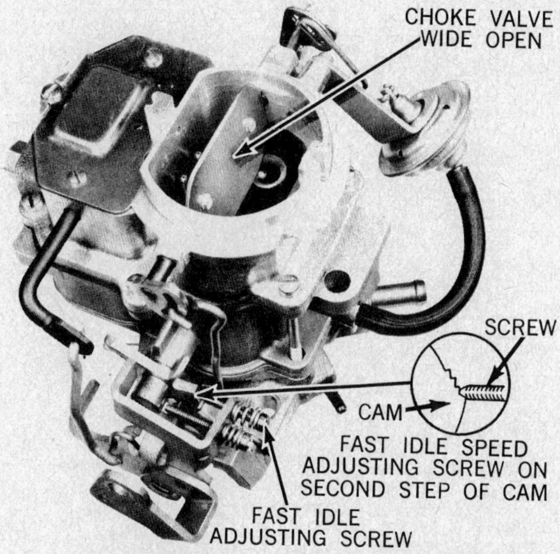

Adjustment of fast idle speed—BBD carburetor
(© Chrysler Corp.)

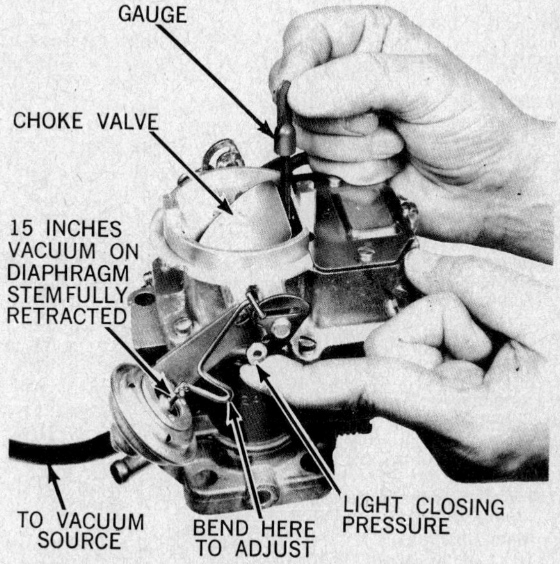

Adjustment of initial choke opening (vacuum kick)—BBD carburetor (© Chrysler Corp.)

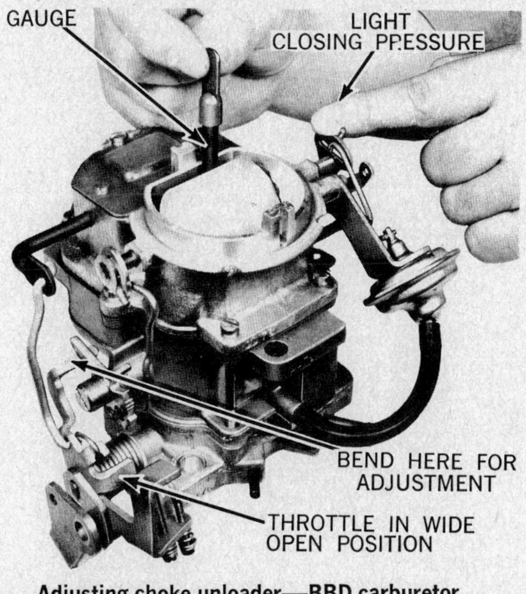

Adjusting choke unloader—BBD carburetor
(© Chrysler Corp.)

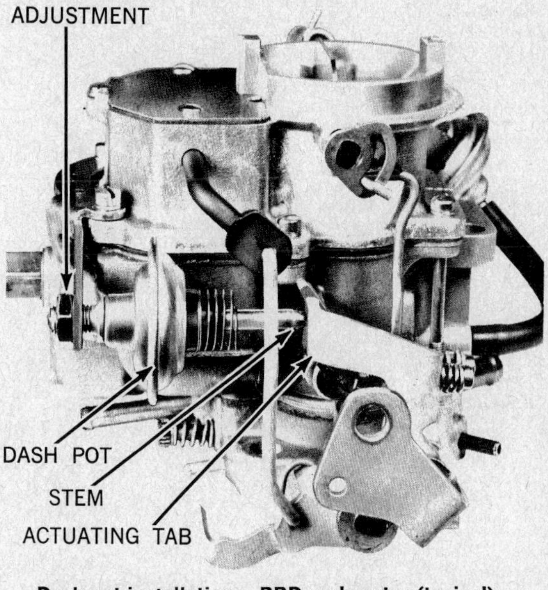

Dash pot installation—BBD carburetor (typical)
(© Chrysler Corp.)

MODEL BBD (Cont'd)

1 Diaphragm connector link
2 Screw
3 Choke vacuum diaphragm
4 Hose
5 Valve
6 Metering rod
7 S-Link
8 Pump arm
9 Gasket
10 Rollover check valve
11 Screw
12 Lock
13 Rod lifter
14 Bracket
15 Nut
16 Solenoid
17 Screw
18 Air horn retaining screw (short)
19 Air horn retaining screw (long)
20 Pump lever
21 Venturi cluster screw
22 Idle fuel pick-up tube
23 Gasket
24 Venturi cluster
25 Gasket
26 Check ball (small)
27 Float
28 Fulcrum pin
29 Baffle
30 Clip
31 Choke link
32 Screw
33 Fast idle cam
34 Gasket
35 Thermostatic choke shaft
36 Spring
37 Screw
38 Pump link
39 Clip
40 Gasket
41 Limiter cap
42 Screw
43 Throttle body
44 Choke housing
45 Baffle
46 Gasket
47 Retainer
48 Choke coil
49 Lever
50 Choke rod
51 Clip
52 Needle and seat assembly
53 Main body
54 Main metering jet
55 Check ball (large)
56 Accelerator pump plunger
57 Fulcrum pin retainer
58 Gasket
59 Spring
60 Air horn
61 Lever

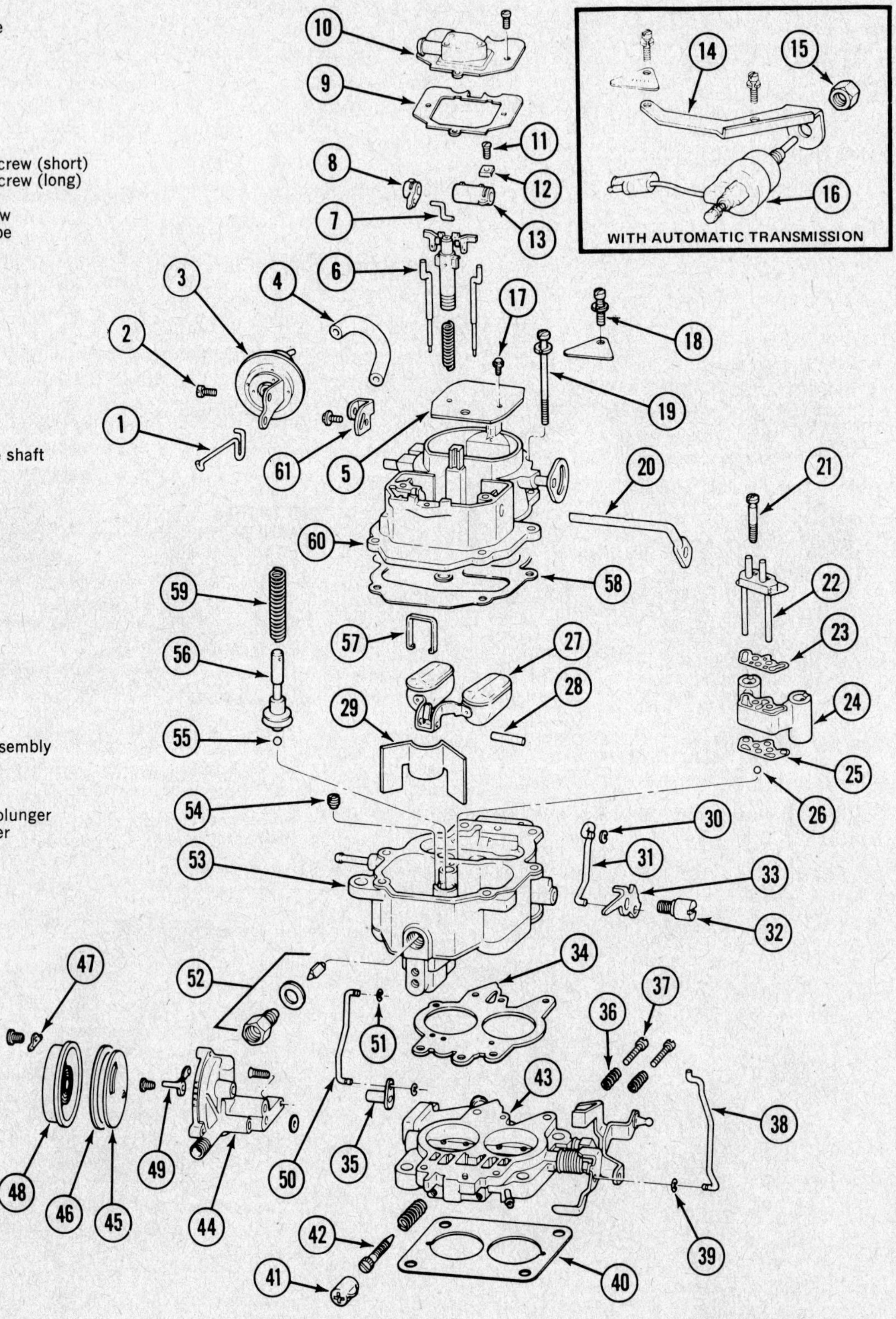

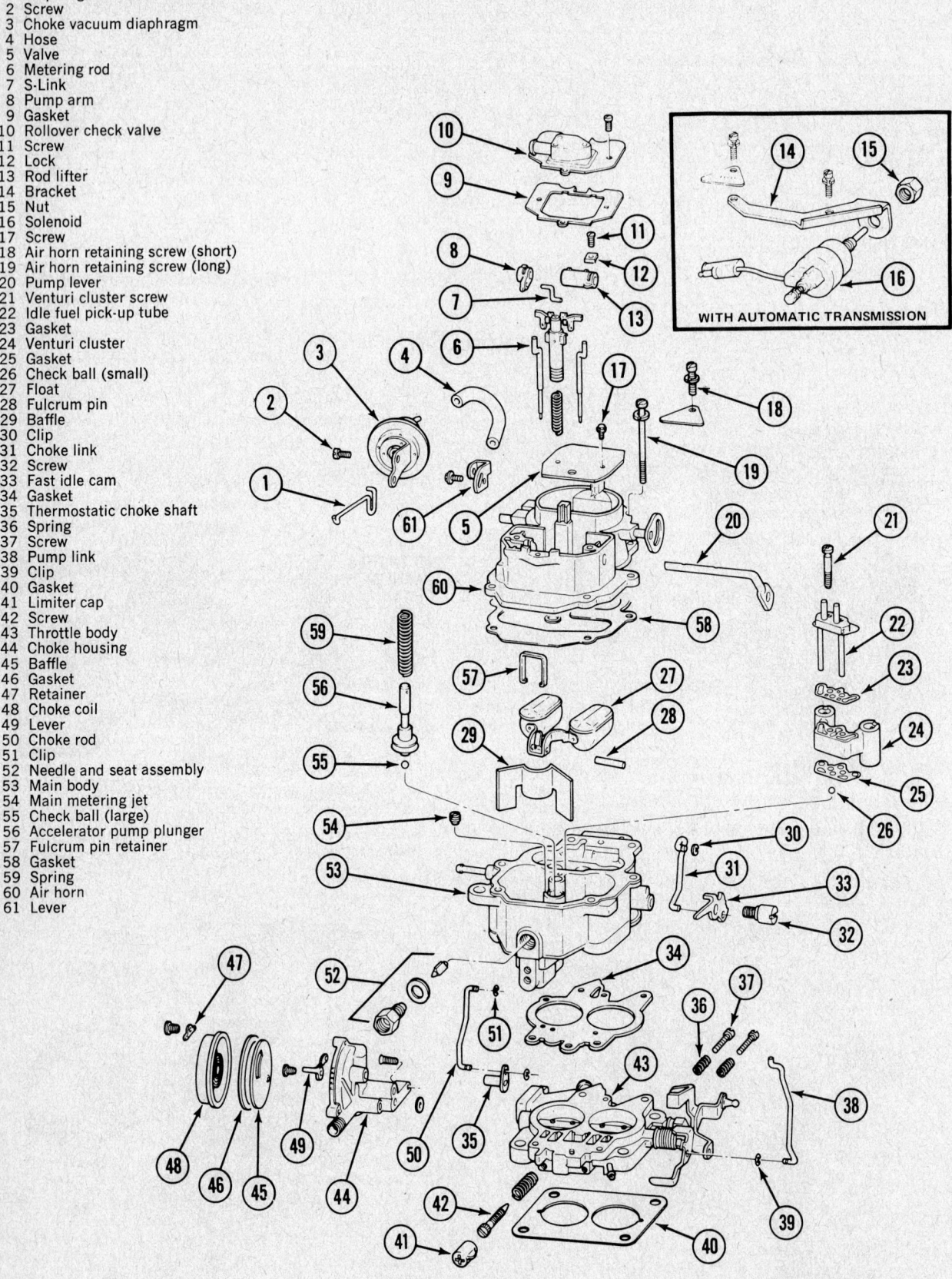

Carter BBD two barrel—typical

MODEL BBD (Cont'd)

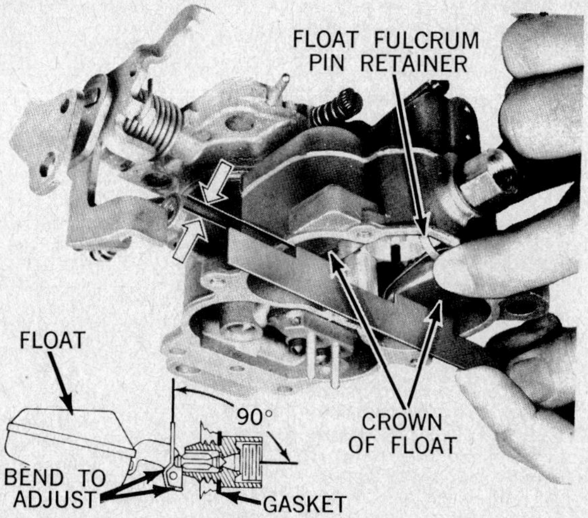

Adjusting float level with the bowl inverted—BBD carburetor (© Chrysler Corp.)

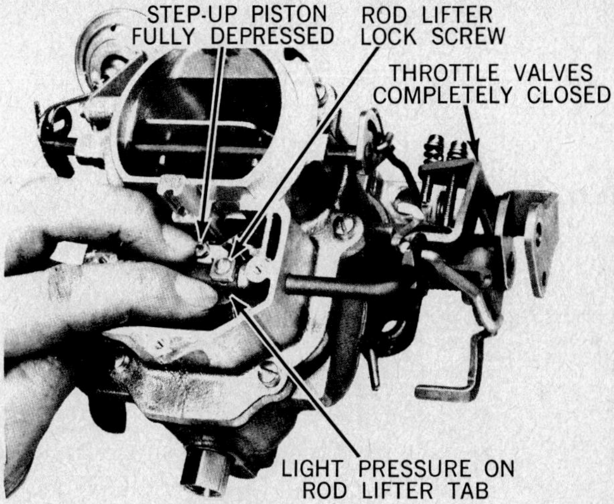

Step-up piston qualification—BBD carburetor (© Chrysler Corp.)

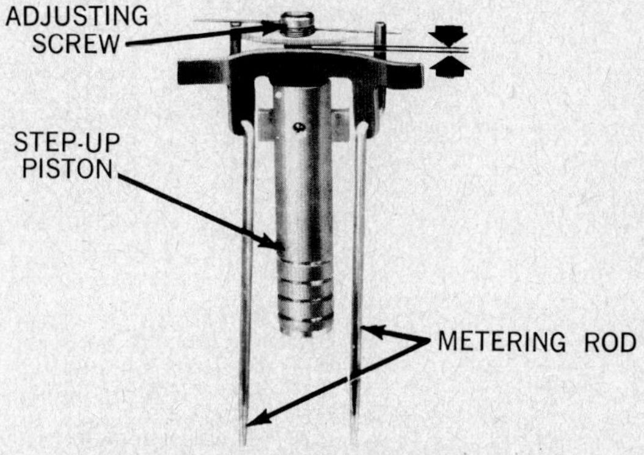

Step-up piston clearance adjustment—BBD carburetor (© Chrysler Corp.)

MODEL TQ

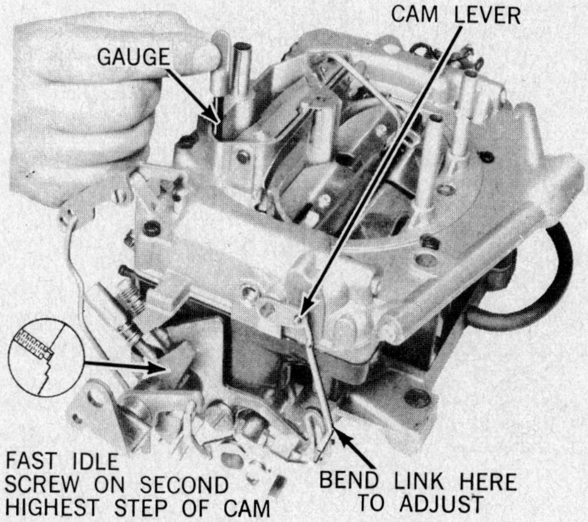

Adjustment of fast idle cam setting—Thermo Quad carburetor (© Chrysler Corp.)

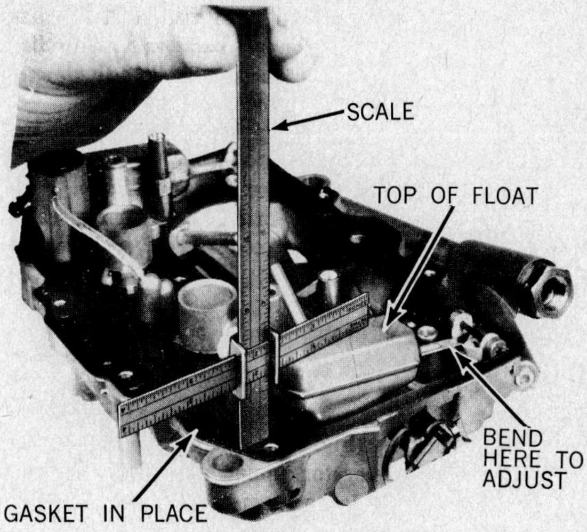

Carter TQ float height measurement

MODEL TQ (Cont'd)

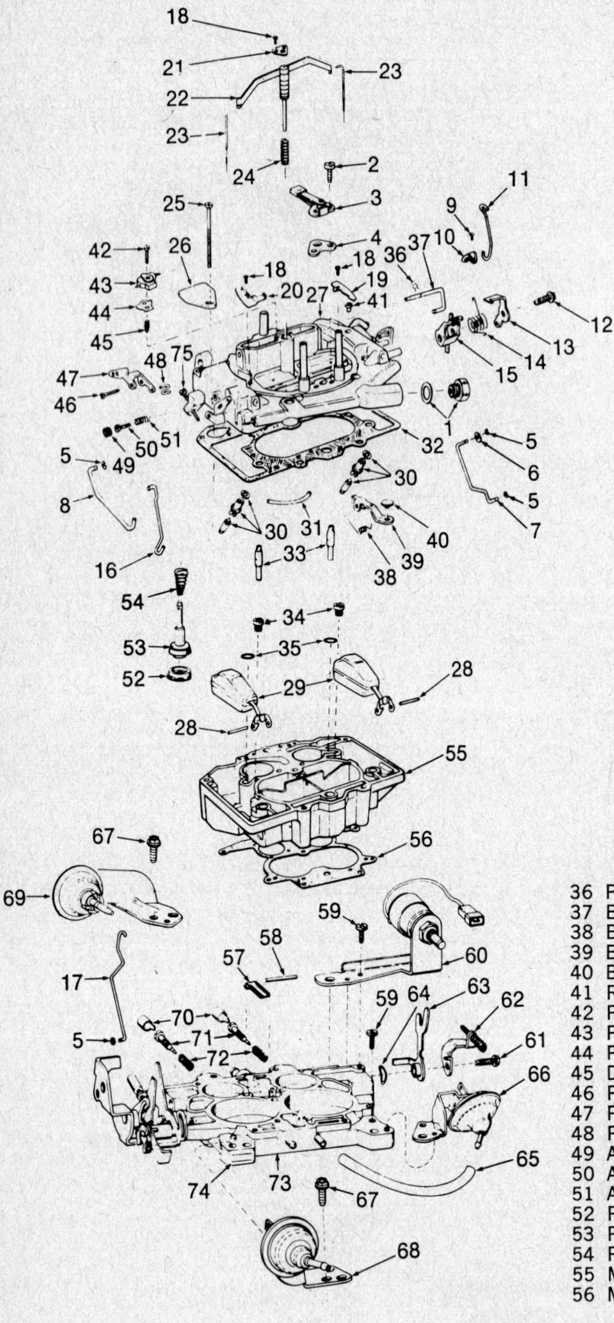

1 Fuel inlet nut and gasket
2 Idle compensator screw
3 Idle compensator
4 Idle compensator gasket
5 "E" retainer
6 Primary diaphragm choke pull-off rod washer
7 Primary diaphragm choke pull-off rod
8 Auxiliary diaphragm choke pull-off rod (if equipped)
9 Choke lever screw
10 Choke lever
11 Choke connector rod
12 Countershaft lever screw
13 Countershaft, lever, outer
14 Countershaft lever spring
15 Countershaft lever, inner
16 Fast idle cam rod
17 Throttle connector rod
18 Cover plate screw
19 Metering rod cover plate (opposite pump)
20 Metering rod cover plate (pump side)
21 Step-up piston cover plate
22 Step-up piston & hanger assembly
23 Metering rod
24 Step-up piston spring
25 Bowl cover screw
26 IH part number location
27 Bowl cover assembly
28 Float pin
29 Float assembly
30 Needle, seat, and gasket
31 Pump passage tube
32 Bowl cover gasket
33 Secondary metering jet
34 Primary metering jet
35 Quad rings
36 Pin spring retainer
37 Bowl vent valve lever, upper
38 Bowl vent valve lever spring
39 Bowl vent valve arm
40 Bowl vent valve grommet
41 Rivet plug
42 Pump housing screw
43 Pump housing
44 Pump housing gasket
45 Discharge check needle
46 Pump arm screw
47 Pump arm
48 Pump "S" link
49 Air valve lock plug
50 Air valve adjustment plug
51 Air valve spring
52 Pump intake check assembly
53 Plunger assembly
54 Plunger spring
55 Main body
56 Main body gasket
57 Step-up piston lifter
58 Step-up piston lifter lever pin
59 Solenoid & diaphragm choke pull-off bracket screw
60 Solenoid
61 Solenoid operating lever screw
62 Curb idle speed screw & lever
63 Bowl vent lever, lower
64 Throttle shaft washer
65 Hose
66 Primary diaphragm choke pull-off bracket
67 Auxiliary choke pull-off and dashpot
68 Auxiliary choke pull-off and bracket (if equipped)
69 Dashpot and bracket
70 Limiter cap
71 Idle mixture screw
72 Idle mixture screw spring
73 Throttle body assembly
74 Carter part number location
75 Low idle speed screw

Exploded view of typical Carter Thermo-Quad

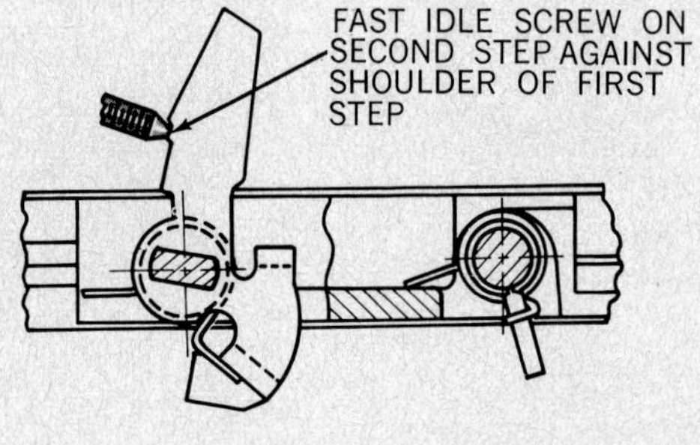

Carter TQ fast idle speed adjustment cam position

MODEL TQ (Cont'd)

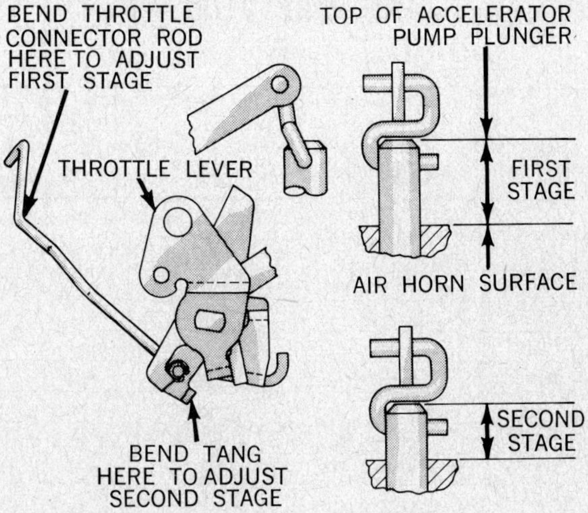

Adjustment of the primary and secondary accelerator pump (© Chrysler Corp.)

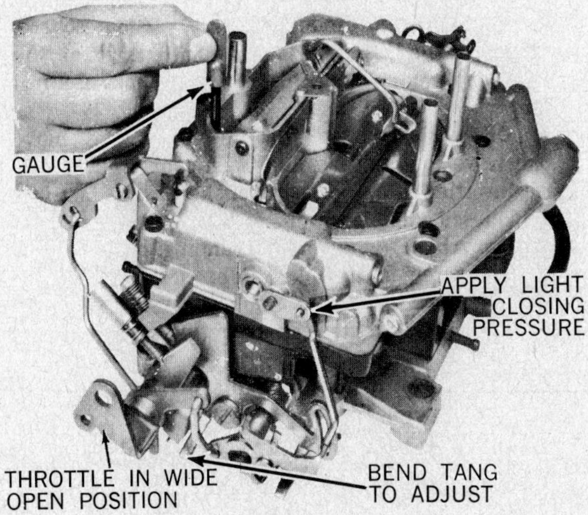

Carter TQ choke unloader adjustment

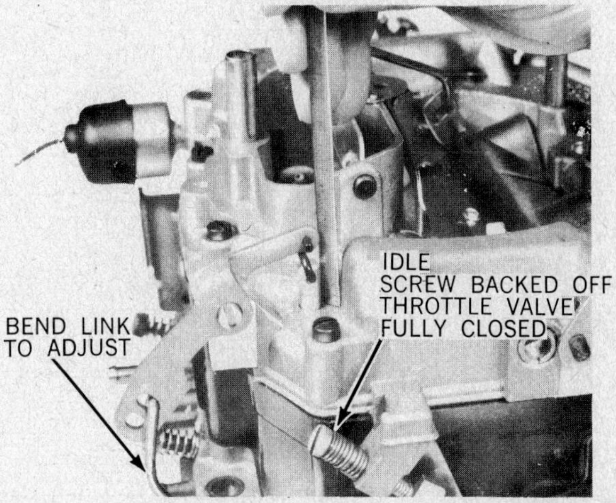

Carter TQ accelerator pump stroke adjustment

Ford/Autolite/Motorcraft Carburetors

MODEL 2100

(All measurements in inches)

Ford

Year	Carburetor List Number	Float Level (Dry)	Choke Unloader Setting	Choke Setting	Accelerator Pump Rod Location	Fuel Level (Wet)	Initial Choke Valve Setting (Min)
1973	D3TF						
	BC	7/16	—	—	—	—	—
	CC	7/16	—	—	—	—	—
	BD	31/64	—	2 Rich	—	29/32	.160
	BE	31/64	—	—	—	13/16	.160
	CD	7/16	—	2 Rich	—	—	—
	SA	7/16	—	—	—	—	—
	UA	13/16	—	Index	3	—	.160
	VA	7/8	—	Index	3	—	.160
	XA	13/16	—	1 Lean	3	—	.160
	AB	7/16	—	Manual	—	—	—
	HC	7/16	—	Index	4	13/16	.160
	CE	7/16	—	—	—	—	—
	DC	31/64	—	2 Rich	3	13/16	.160
	GC	7/16	—	Index	4	7/8	.160
	NA	7/16	—	2 Rich	—	13/16	.160
	YA	7/16	—	—	—	—	—
	DD	7/8	—	Index	3	—	.160
	DE	7/8	—	Index	3	—	.160
	MC	13/16	—	Index	3	—	.160
	D3UF						
	DC	7/16	—	2 Rich	3	13/16	—
	EC	7/16	—	2 Rich	3	13/16	—
	FC	7/16	—	2 Rich	2	13/16	—
	AD	7/16	—	2 Rich	3	13/16	—
	CD	7/16	—	2 Rich	2	13/16	—
	D4BE						
	FA	1/2	—	2 Rich	3	29/32	—
1974	D4TF						
	AA	1/2	—	2 Rich	3	29/32	—
	KA	1/2	—	2 Rich	3	29/32	—
	DA	1/2	—	2 Rich	3	29/32	—
	D4UF						
	AA	7/16	—	2 Rich	3	13/16	—
	BA	7/16	—	2 Rich	3	13/16	—
	D4TE						
	EA	7/16	—	2 Rich	2	13/16	—
	GA	31/64	—	1 Lean	3	7/8	—
	LA	7/16	—	2 Rich	2	13/16	—
	VA	7/16	—	2 Rich	2	13/16	—
	TA	31/64	—	Index	3	7/8	—
	AZA	7/16	—	2 Rich	2	13/16	—
	CAA	7/16	—	2 Rich	2	13/16	—
	BAA	31/64	—	1 Rich	3	7/8	—
	D4UE						
	UA	7/16	—	2 Rich	2	13/16	—
	BA	7/16	—	2 Rich	2	13/16	—
	FA	7/16	—	3 Rich	3	13/16	—
	GA	7/16	—	2 Rich	2	13/16	—
	HA	7/16	—	2 Rich	2	13/16	—
	JA	7/16	—	2 Rich	2	13/16	—

MODEL 2100 (Cont'd)

Ford, Continued

(All measurements in inches)

Year	Carburetor List Number	Float Level (Dry)	Choke Unloader Setting	Choke Setting	Accelerator Pump Rod Location	Fuel Level (Wet)	Initial Choke Valve Setting (Min)
1975	D5TE						
	ABA	7/16	—	Manual	4	.810	—
	ASA	31/64	—	Index	4	.875	—
	ATA	31/64	—	Index	4	.875	—
1976	D5TE						
	ABA	7/16	—	Manual	4	.810	—
	ASA	31/64	—	Index	4	7/8	.179
	ATA	31/64	—	Index	4	7/8	.179

MODEL 2150

Ford

(All measurements in inches)

Year	Carburetor List Number	Float Level (Dry)	Choke Unloader Setting	Choke Setting	Accelerator Pump Rod Location	Fuel Level (Wet)	Initial Choke Valve Setting (Min)
1975	D5TE						
	BHA	31/64	—	Index	2	7/8	.135
	BJA	31/64	—	2 Rich	2	7/8	.160
	LA	31/64	—	Index	2	7/8	.135
	PA	31/64	—	3 Rich	2	7/8	.160
	AAD	31/64	—	3 Rich	3	.875	.179
	ACB	7/16	—	Manual	4	.810	—
	YD	31/64	—	3 Rich	3	.875	.179
	BCA	31/64	—	2 Rich	2	7/8	.179
	BCB	31/64	—	2 Rich	2	7/8	.179
	BFA	31/64	—	2 Rich	3	7/8	.179
	BFB	31/64	—	2 Rich	3	7/8	.179
	AUB	31/64	—	2 Rich	3	7/8	.179
	BGA	31/64	—	3 Rich	3	7/8	.179
	VA	31/64	—	2 Rich	3	7/8	.179
	ZA	31/64	—	3 Rich	4	7/8	.179
	BDA	31/64	—	2 Rich	2	7/8	.179
	BDB	31/64	—	2 Rich	2	7/8	.179
	BEA	31/64	—	2 Rich	3	7/8	.179
	D5UE						
	BA	31/64	—	1 Rich	3	.875	.153
	CA	1/2	—	3 Rich	2	.875	.145-.175
	DC	31/64	—	3 Rich	3	.875	.153
	JD	31/64	—	3 Rich	3	.875	.160
	KD	31/64	—	3 Rich	3	.875	.160
	ZA	31/64	—	1 Rich	3	.875	.153
1976	D5TE						
	BMA	31/64	—	Index	2	7/8	.140
	PA	31/64	—	2 Rich	2	7/8	.160
	AAF	31/64	—	3 Rich	3	7/8	.140
	AUB	31/64	—	2 Rich	3	7/8	.179
	BCA	31/64	—	2 Rich	2	7/8	.179
	BCB	31/64	—	2 Rich	2	7/8	.179
	BFA	31/64	—	2 Rich	3	7/8	.179
	BFB	31/64	—	2 Rich	3	7/8	.179

MODEL 2150 (Cont'd)

(All measurements in inches)

Ford, Continued

Year	Carburetor List Number	Float Level (Dry)	Choke Unloader Setting	Choke Setting	Accelerator Pump Rod Location	Fuel Level (Wet)	Initial Choke Valve Setting (Min)
	BGA	31/64	——	3 Rich	3	7/8	.179
	BYA	31/64	——	2 Rich	3	7/8	.140
	VA	31/64	——	2 Rich	3	7/8	.179
	YF	31/64	——	2 Rich	3	7/8	.140
	ZA	31/64	——	3 Rich	3	7/8	——
	ZB	31/64	——	2 Rich	3	7/8	——
	BEA	31/64	——	2 Rich	3	7/8	——
	BEB	31/64	——	2 Rich	3	7/8	——
	BDA	31/64	——	2 Rich	2	7/8	——
	BDB	31/64	——	2 Rich	2	7/8	——
	ACB	7/16	——	Manual	4	.810	——
	D5UE						
	AA	31/64	——	3 Rich	2	7/8	.160
	CA	1/2	——	3 Rich	2	7/8	145-.175
	LA	31/64	——	3 Rich	2	7/8	.160
	MA	31/64	——	3 Rich	2	7/8	.160
	BA	31/64	——	1 Rich	3	7/8	.153
	DC	31/64	——	3 Rich	3	7/8	.153
	JD	31/64	——	3 Rich	3	7/8	.160
	KD	31/64	——	3 Rich	3	7/8	.160
	ZA	31/64	——	1 Rich	3	7/8	.153
	D6TE						
	FA	31/64		Index	2	7/8	.140
	GA	31/64	——	3 Rich	2	7/8	.140
	JA	31/64	——	3 Rich	2	7/8	.135
	MA	31/64	——	3 Rich	2	7/8	.135
	VA	31/64	——	2 Rich	2	7/8	.135
	YB, YA	31/64	——	3 Rich	2	7/8	.135
	RA	31/64	——	2 Rich	2	7/8	.179
	SA, TA	31/64	——	2 Rich	3	7/8	.179
	AAC	31/64	——	3 Rich	4	7/8	.160
	D6UE						
	JA	31/64	——	3 Rich	2	7/8	.180
1977	D7TE						
	AHA	31/64	——	Index	3	7/8	.160
	ALA	31/64	——	Index	3	7/8	.160
	AKA	31/64	——	Index	3	7/8	.160
	BEA	31/64	——	Index	3	7/8	.160
	BZA	31/64	——	Index	3	7/8	.160
	BZB	31/64	——	Index	3	7/8	.160
	ANA	31/64	——	3 Rich	4	7/8	.160
	CJA	31/64	——	3 Rich	4	7/8	.160
	CZA	31/64	——	3 Rich	4	7/8	.160
	AMA	31/64	——	3 Rich	4	7/8	.160
	DBA	31/64	——	3 Rich	4	7/8	.160
	ARA	31/64	——	3 Rich	4	7/8	.160
	AUA, CKA	31/64	——	3 Rich	4	7/8	.160
	AYA, DAA	31/64	——	3 Rich	4	7/8	.160
	AZA, APA	31/64	——	3 Rich	4	7/8	.160
	CUA	31/64	——	3 Rich	4	7/8	.160
	D7PE						
	AGA	31/64	——	2 Rich	3	7/8	.145

MODEL 2150 (Cont'd)

(All measurements in inches)

Ford, Continued

Year	Carburetor List Number	Float Level (Dry)	Choke Unloader Setting	Choke Setting	Accelerator Pump Rod Location	Fuel Level (Wet)	Initial Choke Valve Setting (Min)
	D7UE						
	ADA	31/64	—	2 Rich	4	7/8	.170
	TA	7/16	—	3 Rich	3	13/16	.170
	ZC	7/16	—	Index	3	13/16	.170
	YA	7/16	—	3 Rich	2	13/16	.170
	AAA	31/64	—	1 Rich	2	13/16	.170
	ACA	31/64	—	1 Rich	3	7/8	.170
	AEA	31/64	—	1 Rich	4	7/8	.170
	ABA	31/64	—	1 Rich	4	7/8	.170
	ARB	31/64	—	1 Rich	4	7/8	.170
	ANA	31/64	—	2 Rich	3	7/8	.170
	APA	31/64	—	2 Rich	3	7/8	.170
1978	D8TE						
	LA	31/64	—	Index	3	7/8	.130
	ARA	31/64	—	Index	3	7/8	.145
	DA	31/64	—	Index	4	7/8	.130
	CTA	31/64	—	Index	4	7/8	.130
	DBA	31/64	—	2 Rich	4	7/8	.130
	BLA	31/64	—	2 Rich	4	7/8	.180
	CRA	31/64	—	2 Rich	4	7/8	.130
	BJA	31/64	—	3 Rich	3	7/8	.175
	ATA	31/64	—	2 Rich	3	7/8	.145
	BEA	31/64	—	3 Rich	2	7/8	.200
	BA	31/64	—	Index	3	7/8	.140
	D7PE						
	AGA	31/64	—	2 Rich	3	7/8	.145
	D7UE						
	APA	31/64	—	2 Rich	3	7/8	.170
	D8UE						
	VA	31/64	—	Index	4	7/8	.145
	DA	31/64	—	3 Rich	3	7/8	.185
	KA	7/16	—	Index	3	13/16	.185
	GA	31/64	—	1 Rich	2	7/8	.205
	HA	31/64	—	Index	2	7/8	.215
	MA	31/64	—	Index	2	7/8	.215
	MB	31/64	—	Index	2	7/8	.215
	SA	31/64	—	3 Rich	3	7/8	.180

MODEL 4300

(All measurements in inches)

Ford

Year	Carburetor List Number	Float Level (Dry)	Choke Unloader Setting	Choke Setting	Accelerator Pump Rod Location	Fuel Level (Wet)	Initial Choke Valve Setting (Min)
1974	D4TE						
	BB	3/4	—	Index	1	—	.220

MODEL 4350

Ford, Continued

(All measurements in inches)

Year	Carburetor List Number	Float Level (Dry)	Choke Unloader Setting	Choke Setting	Accelerator Pump Rod Location	Fuel Level (Wet)	Initial Choke Valve Setting (Min)
1975	D5TE						
	ARC	15/16	.300	Index	3	—	.160
	ARD	1.0	.300	Index	3	—	.160
	BBA	15/16	—	Index	3	—	.160
	BBB	.92	.300	Index	3	—	.160
	BBC	1.0	.300	Index	3	—	.160
	D5UE						
	SA	15/16	.300	Index	3	—	.160
	SB	1.0	.300	Index	3	—	.160
	NA	15/16	.300	Index	3	—	.160
	NB	.92	.300	Index	3	—	.160
	NC	1.00	.300	Index	3	—	.160
1976	D5TE						
	ARC	15/16	.300	Index	3	—	.160
	ARD	1.0	.300	Index	3	—	.160
	BBA	15/16	.300	Index	3	—	.160
	BBB	.92	.300	Index	3	—	.160
	BBC	1.0	.300	Index	3	—	.160
	D6TE						
	NA	1.0	.300	Index	3	—	.160
	UA	1.0	.300	Index	3	—	.160
	D5UE						
	NA	15/16	.300	Index	3	—	.160
	NB	.92	.300	Index	3	—	.160
	NC	1.0	.300	Index	3	—	.160
	SA	15/16	.300	Index	3	—	.160
	SB	1.0	.300	Index	3	—	.160
	D6UE						
	KA	1.0	.300	Index	3	—	.160
	LA	1.0	.300	Index	3	—	.160
1977	D7TE						
	BLA	1.0	.300	Index	3	—	.160
	BJA	.1.0	.300	Index	3	—	.160
	D7UE						
	AGA	1.0	.300	Index	3	—	.160
	AFA	1.0	.300	Index	3	—	.160
1978	D8TE						
	AKA	1.0	.300	Index	3	①	.160
	AMA	1.0	.300	Index	3	①	.160
	D7UE			Index	3	①	.160
	ASA	1.0	.300				
	D8UE						
	AA	1.0	.300	Index	3	①	.160
	CA	1.0	.300	Index	3	①	.160

① Fuel Level Between 4 and 6 on Special Gauge

MODEL 2100

Jeep

(All measurements in inches)

Year	Carburetor List Number	Float Level (Dry)	Fuel Level (Wet)	Initial Choke Valve Clearance	Fast Idle Cam Setting ②	Choke Cover Setting	Choke Unloader Valve Clearance	Fast Idle Speed ①	Dash Pot Clearance	Bowl Vent Clearance	Rod Pump Location Hole
1973	3DM2	⅜	¾	.130	.130	1 Rich	.250	1600	.140	—	3
	3DA2	⅜	¾	.120	.110	2 Rich	.250	1600	—	—	3
	3RA2	⅜	¾	.120	.110	2 Rich	.250	1600	—	—	3
	3RHD2	⅜	¾	.120	.110	2 Rich	.250	1600	—	—	3
1974	4DMJ2	.400	.780	.140	.130	2 Rich	.250	1600	—	—	3
	4RHD2	.375	.750	.140	.130	2 Rich	.250	1600	—	—	3
	4DM2	.400	.780	.130	.130	2 Rich	.250	1600	.140	—	3
	4RA2	.400	.780	.140	.130	2 Rich	.250	1600	—	—	3
1975	5RHM2	.555	.930	.140	.130	2 Rich	.250	1600	—	—	3
	5RHA2	.555	.930	.140	.130	2 Rich	.250	1600	—	—	3
	5DM2	.400	.780	.130	.130	2 Rich	.250	1600	.095	—	3
	5DM2J	.400	.780	.130	.130	2 Rich	.250	1600	.095	—	3
1976	6RHM2	.555	.930	.136	.115	2 Rich	.250	1600	—	—	—
	6RHA2	.555	.930	.136	.115	2 Rich	.250	1600	—	—	—
	6DM2	.555	.930	.132	.120	2 Rich	.250	1600	.075	—	—
	6DA2J	.555	.930	.136	.126	1 Rich	.250	1600	.075	—	—
	6DM2J	.555	.930	.136	.126	1 Rich	.250	1600	.075	—	—
1977	6RHM2	.555	.930	.136	.115	2 Rich	.250	1600	—	—	3
	6RHA2	.555	.930	.136	.115	2 Rich	.250	1600	—	—	3
	6DM2	.555	.930	.132	.120	2 Rich	.250	1600	.093	—	3
	6DA2J	.555	.930	.136	.120	1 Rich	.250	1600	—	—	3
	6DM2J	.555	.930	.132	.126	1 Rich	.250	1600	.093	—	3
1978	8DM2	.555	.930	.132	.120	2 Rich	.250	1500	—	.120	3
	8DM2C	.555	.930	.132	.120	1 Rich	.250	1500	—	.120	3
	8DA2J	.555	.930	.136	.126	1 Rich	.250	1600	—	.120	3
	8DA2JC	.555	.930	.136	.126	1 Rich	.250	1600	—	.120	3
	6RHA2	.555	.930	.136	.115	2 Rich	.250	1600	—	.120	3
	6RHM2	.555	.930	.136	.115	2 Rich	.250	1600	—	.120	3
1979	9DM2	.555	.930	.125	.120	2 Rich	.250	1500	—	.120	—
	9DM2C	.555	.930	.132	.120	1 Rich	.250	1500	—	.120	—
	9DA2J	.555	.930	.128	.113	1 Rich	.250	1600	—	.120	—
	9DM2H	.555	.930	.140	.125	Index	.250	1500	—	.120	—

① TCS solenoid and EGR disconnected, fast idle screw on 2nd cam step.
② Measured between choke valve and air horn, fast idle screw on 2nd cam step.

MODEL 2150

Jeep

(All measurements in inches)

Year	Carburetor List Number	Float Level (Dry)	Fuel Level (Wet)	Initial Choke Valve Clearance	Fast Idle Cam Setting ②	Choke Cover Setting	Choke Unloader Valve Clearance	Fast Idle Speed ①	Dash Pot Clearance	Bowl Vent Clearance	Rod Pump Location Hole
1977	7DM2A	.555	.930	.110	.089	2 Rich	.290	1600	—	—	3
	7DA2A	.555	.930	.104	.089	1 Rich	.290	1600	—	—	3
1978	8DA2A	.555	.930	.089	.078	2 Rich	.290	1600	—	—	3
	8DM2A	.555	.930	.093	.078	2 Rich	.290	1600	—	—	3
1979	9RHM2	.555	.930	.104	.086	2 Rich	.348	1500	—	—	3
	9RHA2	.555	.930	.113	.093	2 Rich	.350	1600	—	—	3

① TCS solenoid and EGR disconnected, fast idle screw on 2nd cam step
② Measured between choke valve and air horn, fast idle screw on 2nd cam step

MODEL 4300

Jeep

(All measurements in inches)

Year	Carburetor List Number	Float Level (Dry)	Fuel Level (Wet)	Initial Choke Valve Clearance	Fast Idle Cam Setting ②	Choke Cover Setting	Choke Unloader Valve Clearance	Fast Idle Speed ①	Dash Pot Clearance	Bowl Vent Clearance	Rod Pump Location Hole
1973	3TM4	13/16	—	.190	.160	2 Rich	.275	1600	.140	—	Center
	3TA4	13/16	—	.190	.160	2 Rich	.275	—	—	—	Center

① TCS solenoid and EGR disconnected, fast idle screw on 2nd cam step.
② Measured between choke valve and air horn, fast idle screw on 2nd cam step.

MODEL 4350

Jeep

(All measurements in inches)

Year	Carburetor List Number	Float Level (Dry)	Fuel Level (Wet)	Initial Choke Valve Clearance	Fast Idle Cam Setting ②	Choke Cover Setting	Choke Unloader Valve Clearance	Fast Idle Speed ①	Dash Pot Clearance	Bowl Vent Clearance	Rod Pump Location Hole
1974	4TA4	.820	—	.170	.160	2 Rich	.325	1600	.140	—	Center
	4THD4	.820	—	.170	.160	2 Rich	.325	1600	—	—	—
1975	5THA4	.900	—	.140	.160	2 Rich	.325	1600	—	—	—
	5THM4	.900	—	.140	.160	2 Rich	.325	1600	—	—	Lower
1976	6THA4	.900	—	.135	.135	2 Rich	.325	1600	—	—	Lower
	6THMA	.900	—	.135	.135	2 Rich	.325	1600	—	—	—
	6THA4C	.900	—	.135	.135	2 Rich	.325	1600	—	—	—
1977	6THA4	.900	—	.135	.135	2 Rich	.325	1600	—	—	—
	6THM4	.900	—	.135	.135	2 Rich	.325	1600	—	—	—
	6THA4C	.900	—	.135	.135	2 Rich	.325	1600	—	—	—
1978	6THA4	.900	—	.135	.135	2 Rich	.325	1600	—	—	—
	6THM4	.900	—	.135	.135	2 Rich	.325	1600	—	—	—

① TCS solenoid and EGR disconnected, fast idle screw on 2nd cam step.
② Measured between choke valve and air horn, fast idle screw on 2nd cam step.

MODEL 2100 MODEL 2150

TWO BARREL

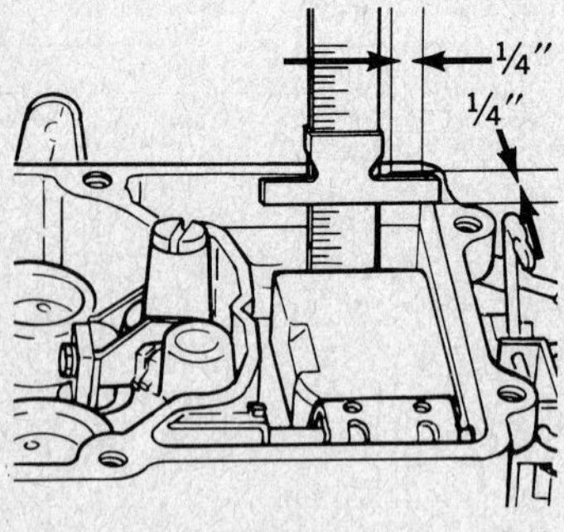

Fuel level adjustment (wet)—Model 2100, 2150 carburetors
(© Ford Motor Co.)

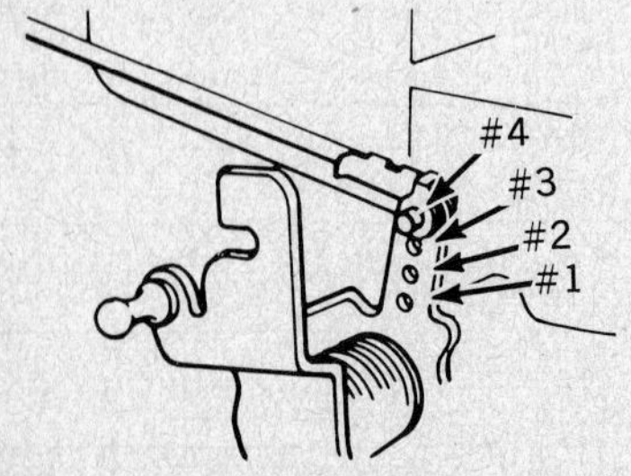

Accelerator pump stroke hole location—typical—Model 2100, 2150 carburetors
(© Ford Motor Co.)

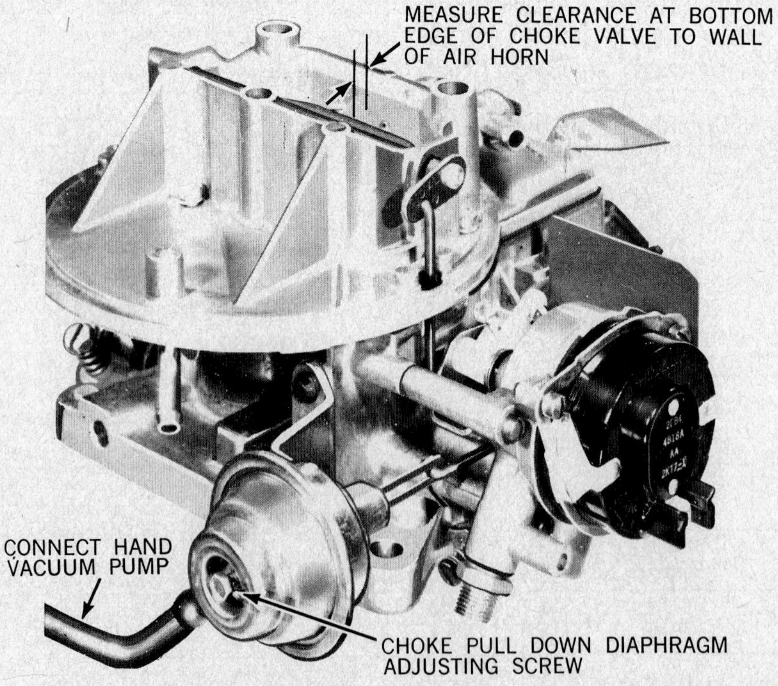

Adjustment of choke plate initial setting—typical—Model 2100, 2150 carburetors (© Ford Motor Co.)

MODEL 2100 MODEL 2150

TWO BARREL

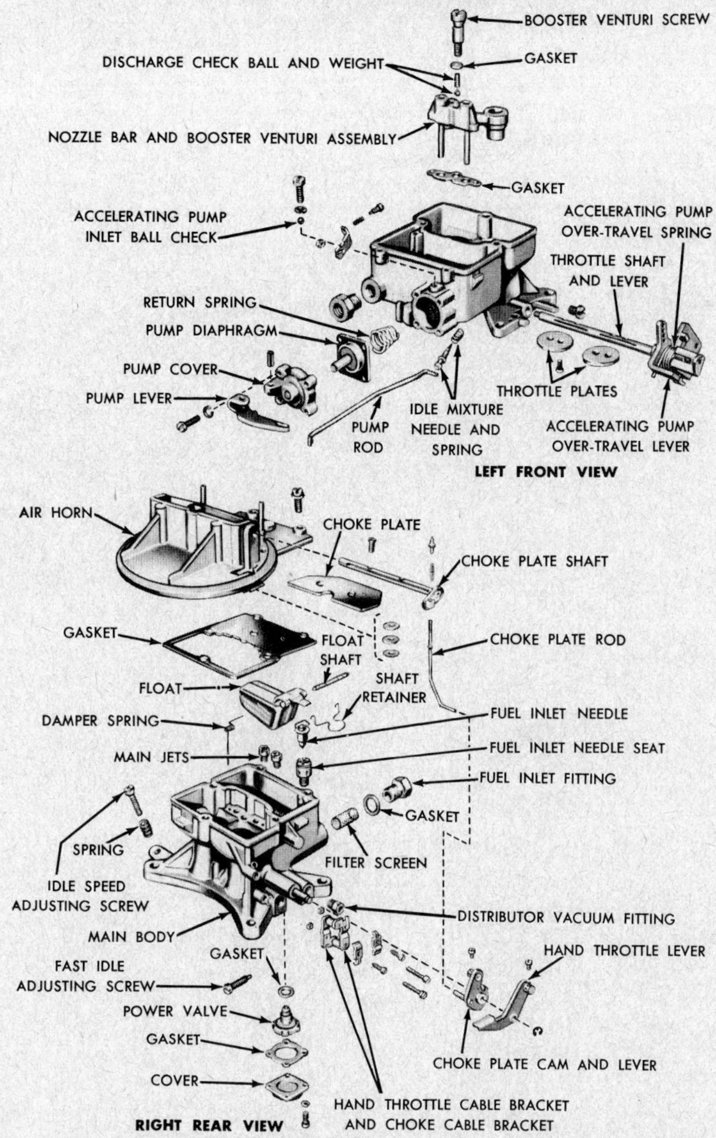

Exploded view—model 2100 carburetor (with manual choke, manual throttle and automatic choke mechanisms shown) (© Ford Motor Co.)

Indexing marks for automatic choke thermostatic spring housing and choke housing—typical Model 2100, 2150 carburetors (© Ford Motor Co.)

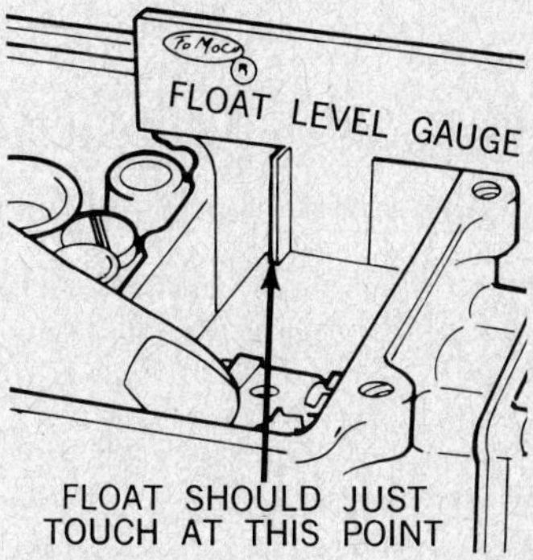

Float adjustment (dry)—Model 2100, 2150 carburetors (© Ford Motor Co.)

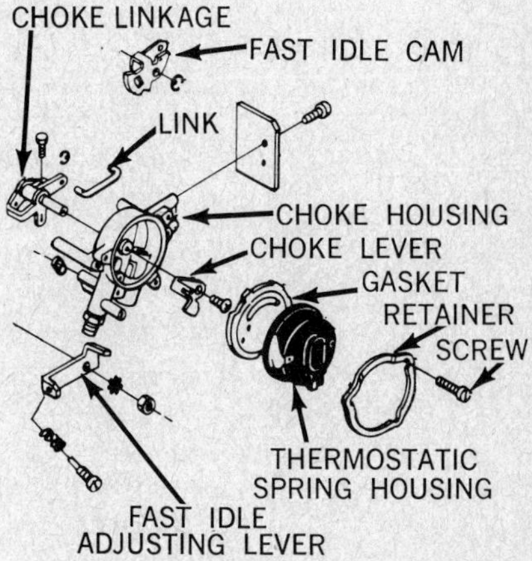

Automatic choke assembly—typical—Model 2100 carburetor (© Ford Motor Co.)

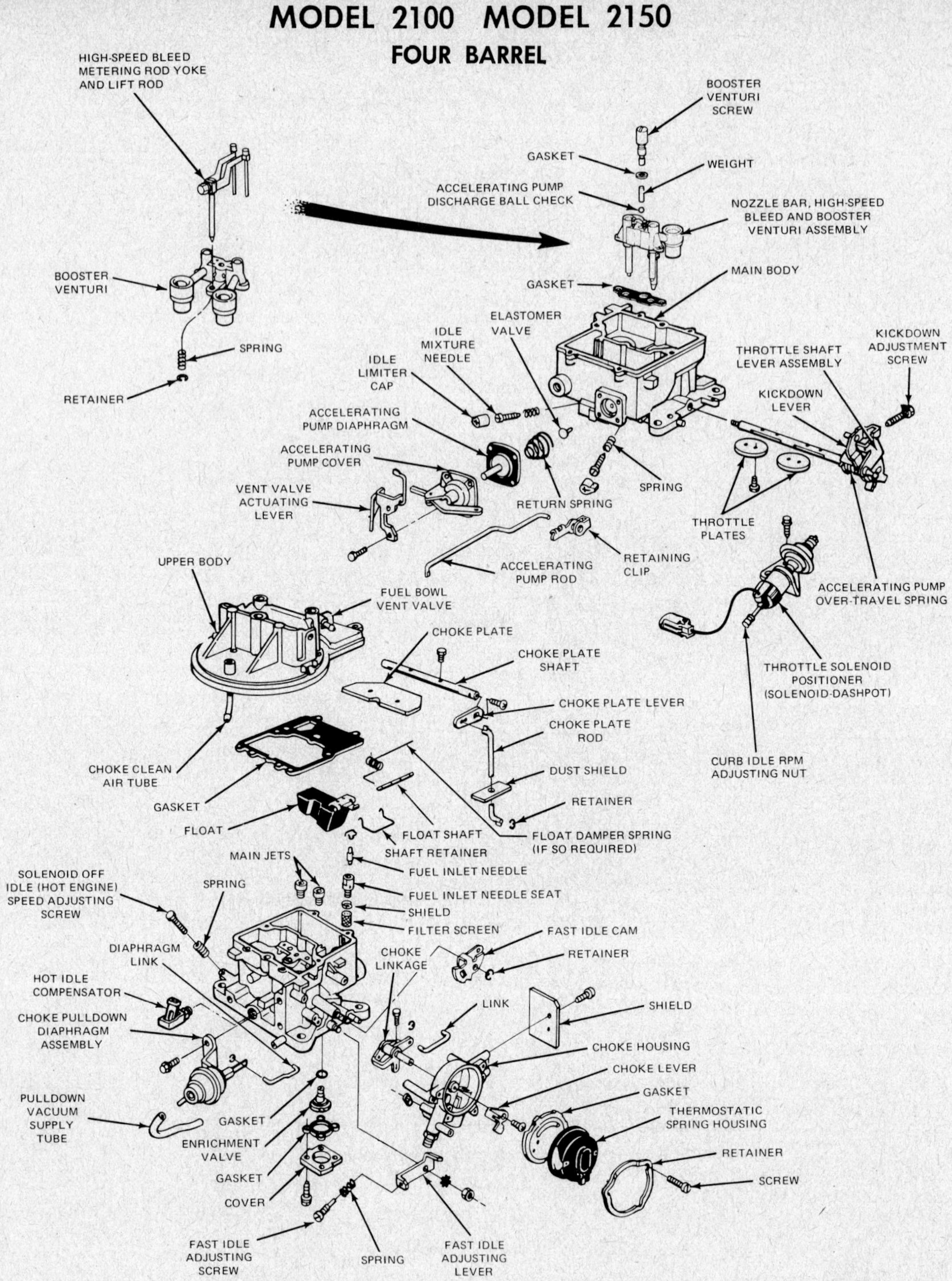

Motorcraft 2150 carburetor, typical exploded view

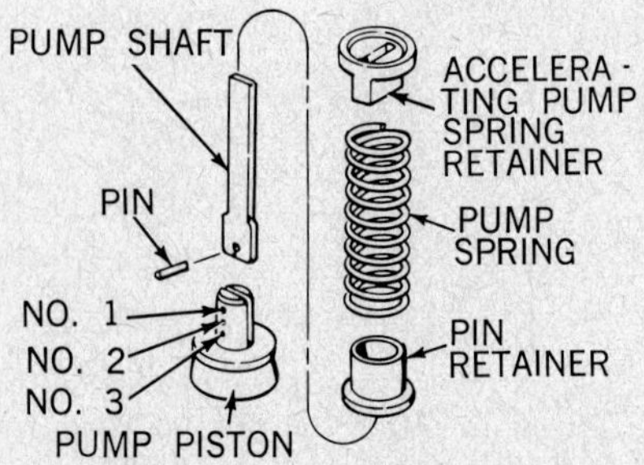

Setting accelerator pump stroke, Motorcraft 4350

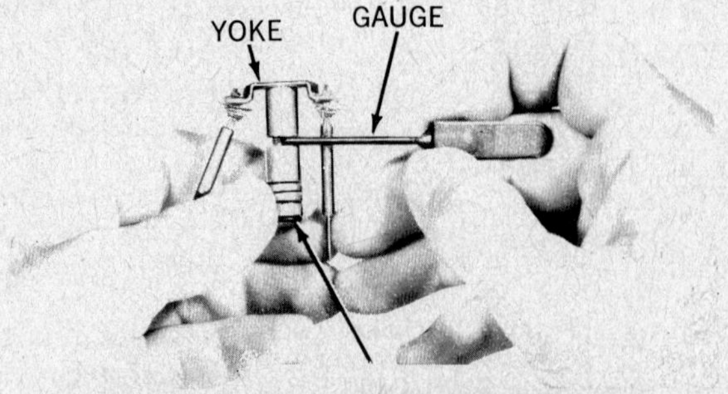

Metering rod vacuum piston adjustment to a clearance of .120 inches (© Jeep Corp.)

MODEL 4300 MODEL 4350

FOUR BARREL

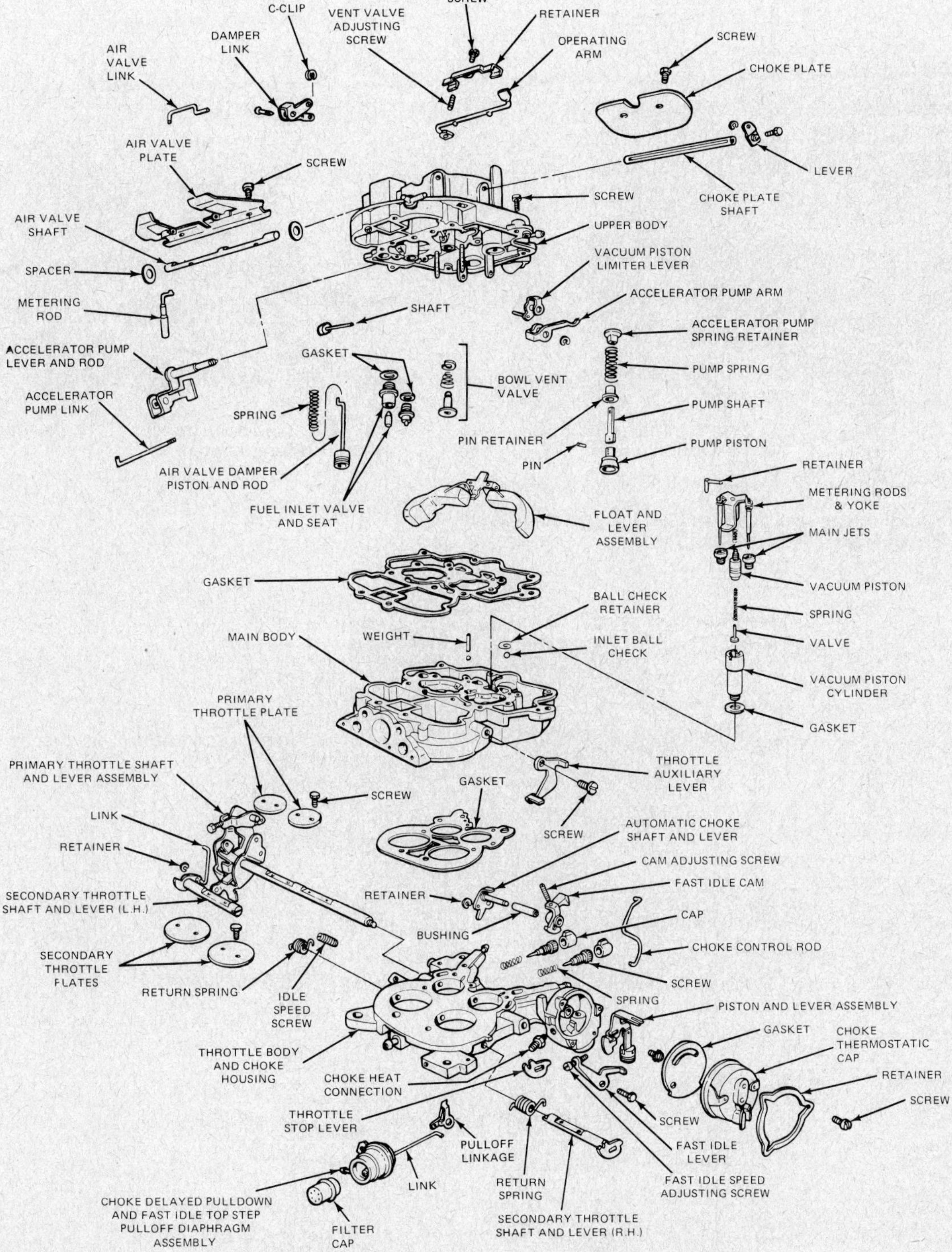

Exploded view model 4350, typical of model 4300 carburetors

MODEL 4300 MODEL 4350

FOUR BARREL

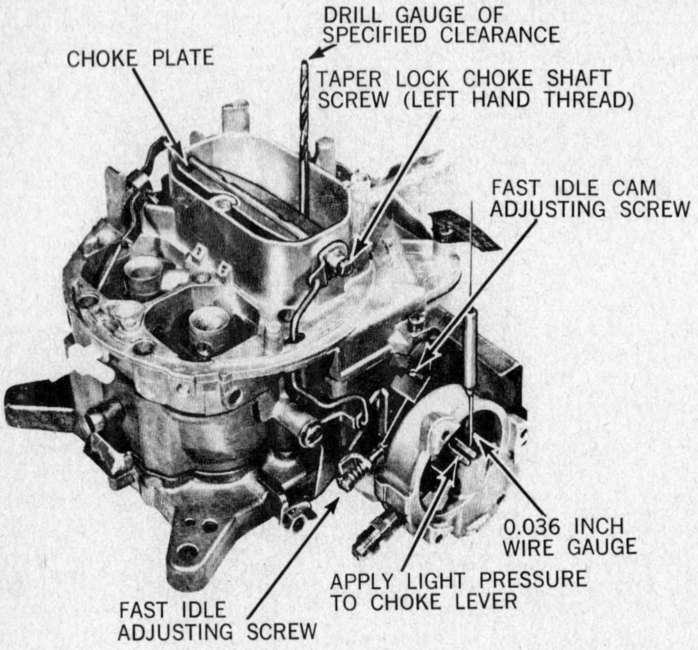

Choke plate initial setting (pull down) and fast idle cam adjustment—model 43300, 4350 carburetors (© Ford Motor Co.)

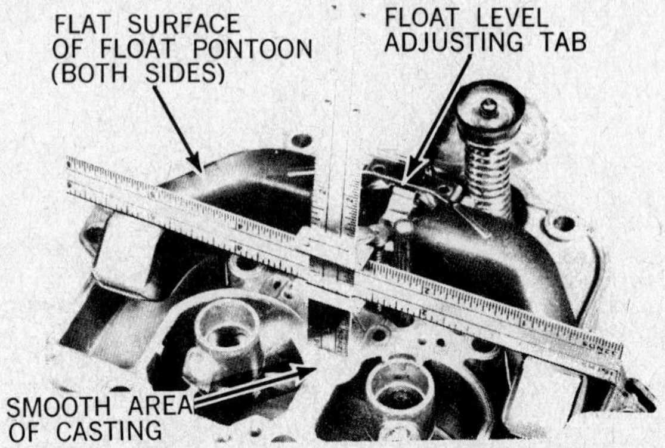

Adjustment of float level with "T" scale—Model 4300, 4350 carburetors (© Ford Motor Co.)

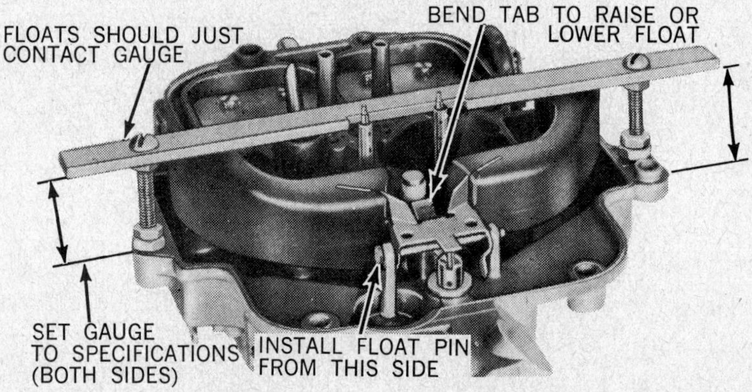

Checking float level with fabricated gauge—models 4300, 4350 carburetors

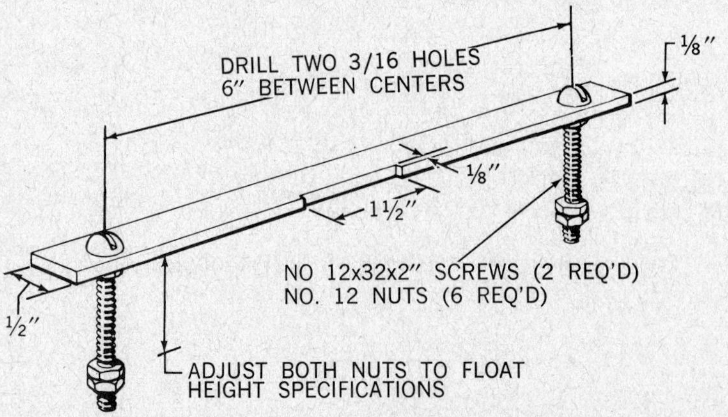

Fabricating float gauge—models 4300, 4350 carburetors

Holley Carburetors

MODEL 4150G

Chevrolet

(All measurements in inches)

Year	Carburetor List No.	Float Level (Dry)	Fuel Level (Wet)	Accelerator Pump (Min.)	Fast Idle (RPM)	Air Vent Clearance	Fast Idle Mechanical Clearance
1973	R6510	—	①	.015	1800-2400	.060	.035
	R6521A	—	①	.015	1800-2400	—	.035
	R6511A	—	①	.015	1800-2400	.060	.035
	R6522A	—	①	.015	1800-2400	—	.035
1974	R6742A	②	①	.015	2200	.045-.075	.038
	R6743A	②	①	.015	2200	.045-.075	.038
	R6744A	②	①	.015	2200	—	.038
	R6745A	②	①	.015	2200	—	.038
1975-76	R6928A	③	—	.015	2200	.045-.075	.038
	R6929A	③	—	.015	2200	.045-.075	.038
	R6930A	③	—	.015	2200	—	.031
	R6931A	③	—	.015	2200	—	.031
	R7264A	③	—	.015	2200	.045-.075	.038
	R7266A	③	—	.015	2200	.045-.075	.038
1977	R7703A	④	—	.015	2200	.045-.075	.038
	R7704A	④	—	.015	2200	.045-.075	.031

MODEL 4150EG

Chevrolet

Year	Carburetor List No.	Float Level (Dry)	Fuel Level (Wet)	Accelerator Pump (Min.)	Fast Idle (RPM)	Air Vent Clearance	Fast Idle Mechanical Clearance
1978	R7923A	④	—	.015	2200	.045-.075	.031
	R7927A	④	—	.015	2200	.045-.075	.031
	R7925A	④	—	.015	2200	—	.031
	R7928A	④	—	.015	2200	—	.031
	R7924A	④	—	.015	2200	.045-.075	.031
	R7926A	④	—	.015	2200	—	.031
1979	R8278A	④	—	.015	2200	.045-.075	.031
	R8280A	④	—	.015	2200	.045-.075	.031
	R8282A	④	—	.015	2200	.045-.075	.031
	R8283A	④	—	.015	2200	.045-.075	.031
	R8444A	④	—	.015	2200	.045-.075	.031
	R8279A	④	—	.015	2200	.045-.075	.031
	R8281A	④	—	.015	2200	.045-.075	.031

① Fuel Level at bottom of Sight Plug.
② Adjust Float Parallel to Inner Surface of Fuel Bowl.
③ Primary Bowl—.197
Secondary Bowl—.166
④ Primary Bowl—.194
Secondary Bowl—.213

MODEL 1920 1-bbl

Dodge/Plymouth

(All measurements in inches)

Year	Carburetor List No.	Float Level (Dry)	Vacuum Kick Choke (Unloader)	Choke Setting	Pump Rod Adjustment (Hole)	Fast Idle Cam Position	Fast Idle Speed	Vacuum Kick (Initial Choke Opening)
1973	6593A	.260	①	②	—	.065	2000	.100
	6594A	.260	①	②	—	.065	1700	.100
	6595A	.260	①	②	—	.065	2000	.100
	6596A	.260	①	②	—	.065	1700	.100

MODEL 1945 1-bbl

(All measurements in inches)

Dodge/Plymouth

Year	Carburetor List No.	Float Level (Dry)	Vacuum Kick Choke (Unloader)	Choke Setting	Pump Rod Location	Fast Idle Cam Position	Fast Idle Speed	Vacuum Kick (Initial Choke Opening)
1975	R7074A	3/64	.250	②	2 7/32	.080	1600	.110
	R7209A	3/64	.250	②	2 7/32	.080	1600	.130
	R7076A	3/64	.250	②	2 21/64	.080	1700	.090
	R7210A	3/64	.250	②	2 21/64	.080	1700	.090
	R7078A	3/64	.250	②	2 7/32	.080	1600	.110
	R7079A	3/64	.250	②	2 21/64	.080	1700	.090
	R7080A	3/64	.250	②	2 7/32	.080	1600	.110
	R7081A	3/64	.250	②	2 21/64	.080	1700	.090
	R7082A	3/64	.250	②	2 7/32	.080	1600	.110
	R7083A	3/64	.250	②	2 21/64	.080	1700	.090
1976	R7428A	③	.250	②	2 7/32 (2)	.080	1600	.110
	R7429A	③	.250	②	2 21/64 (3)	.080	1700	.110
	R7401A	③	.250	②	2 7/32 (2)	.080	1600	.110
	R7080A	③	.250	②	2 7/32 (2)	.080	1600	.110
	R7081A	③	.250	②	2 21/64 (3)	.080	1700	.090
	R7082A	③	.250	②	2 7/32 (2)	.080	1600	.110
	R7083A	③	.250	②	2 21/64 (3)	.080	1700	.090
1977	R7815A	③	.250	②	2 21/64 (3)	.080	1600	.110
	R7816A	③	.250	②	2 21/64 (3)	.080	1700	.110
	R7847A	③	.250	②	2 7/32 (2)	.080	1600	.110
	R7848A	③	.250	②	2 21/64 (3)	.080	1700	.110
1978	—	—	—	—	—	—	—	—
1979	R8593A	③	.250	②	2 7/32 (1)	.080	1600	.100
	R8594A	③	.250	②	2 21/64 (2)	.080	1600	.100
	R8799A	③	.250	②	2 7/32 (1)	.080	1600	.100
	R8800A	③	.250	②	2 21/64 (2)	.080	1600	.100

① Automatically set with fast idle cam adjustment
② Fixed setting
③ Flush with top of bowl cover gasket, carb inverted

MODEL 2210 2-bbl

Dodge/Plymouth

1973	R6484A	.180	.250	①	3	.110	1900	.160
	R6452A	.180	.170	①	3	.110	1900	.150
	R6575A	.180	.170	①	3	.110	1900	.150
	R6485A	.180	.170	①	3	.110	1900	.160
	R6486A	.180	.170	①	3	.110	1800	.110
	R6454A	.180	.170	①	3	.110	1800	.150
	R6472A	.180	.170	①	3	.110	1800	.150
	R6487A	.180	.170	①	1	.110	1800	.160
	R6488A	.180	.170	①	3	.110	1800	.110
1974	—	—	—	—	—	—	—	—
1975	R6764A	.180	.170	①	②	.110	1700	.150
	R6765A	.180	.170	①	②	.110	1800	.150
1976	R6764A	.180	.170	①	②	.110	1700	.150
	R6765A	.180	.170	①	②	.110	1800	.150
	R6886-1A	.180	.170	①	②	.110	1400	.150
1977	R7676A	3/16③	.170	①	⑤	.110	1700	.150
	R7870A	3/16③	.170	①	④	.110	1800	.150
	R6886-1A	3/16③	.170	①	④	.110	1600	.90

① Fixed setting
② Accelerator pump setting
At curb idle—.260 in. (R6764A—.270)
At closed throttle—.310 in.
③ Bottom of float to be parallel with air horn bottom
④ At curb idle—slot #1—.310 in.
⑤ At curb idle—slot #2—.320 in.

MODEL 2245

Dodge/Plymouth

(All measurements in inches)

Year	Carburetor List No.	Float Level (Dry)	Vacuum Kick Choke (Unloader)	Choke Setting	Pump Rod Location (Hole)	Fast Idle Cam Position	Fast Idle Speed (RPM)	Vacuum Kick (Initial Choke Opening)
1974	R6762-1A	.180	.220	①	Slot 1	.110	1700	.150
	R6860A	.180	.170	①	Slot 1	.110	1800	.150
1975	R7187A	.180	.170	①	②	.110	1600	.150
	R7188A	.180	.170	①	②	.110	1600	.150
1976	R7403A	.180	.170	①	②	.110	1600	.150
	R7188A	.180	.170	①	②	.110	1600	.150
1977	R7697A	3/16③	.170	①	④	.110	1600	.150
	R7871A	3/16③	.170	①	⑤	.110	1600	.150
	R8036A	3/16③	.170	①	④	.110	1600	.150
	R8182A	3/16③	.170	①	④	.110	1600	.150
1978	R8453A	.180	.170	①	⑥	.110	1600	.150
	R8135A	.180	.170	①	⑦	.110	1600	.90
	R6886A	.180	.170	①	⑦	.110	1600	.150
	R7756A	.180	.170	①	⑦	.110	1600	.150
	R8484A	.180	.170	①	⑥	.110	1600	.150
	R7088A	.180	.170	①	⑦	.110	1600	.150
	R8028A	.180	.170	①	⑥	.110	1600	.150
	R7871A	.180	.170	①	⑥	.110	1600	.130
	R8026A	.180	.170	①	⑥	.110	1600	.150
1979	R8597A	.200③	.170	①	.290 (1)	.110	1600	.110
	R8598A	.200③	.170	①	.290 (1)	.110	1600	.110
	R8925A	.200③	.170	①	.290 (1)	.110	1600	.110

① Fixed setting
② Accelerator pump setting
Curb idle—.260 in.
Closed throttle—.310 in.
#1 Slot
③ Float drop—Bottom of float to be parallel with air horn bottom
④ At idle—Slot #1—.310 in.
⑤ At idle—Slot #2—.320 in.
⑥ At idle—Slot #2—.260 in.
⑦ At idle—Slot #2—.260 in.

MODEL 2300G 2-bbl

Dodge/Plymouth

(All measurements in inches)

Year	Carburetor List No.	Float Level (Dry)	Vacuum Kick Choke (Unloader)	Choke Setting	Pump Rod Location	Fast Idle Cam Position	Fast Idle Speed	Vacuum Kick (Initial Choke Opening)
1973	R6277A	① ②	—	Manual	—	.035	—	—
	R6278A	① ②	—	Manual	—	.035	—	—

① Float parting line parallel with bowl floor
② Fuel level with bottom of sight plug hole

MODEL 4150 4-bbl

1974	R6771A	① ②	—	Manual	#1 Hole	.066	—	—

① Primary and secondary—Float level parallel with bowl floor
② Fuel level with bottom of sight plug hole

MODEL 2140G 4-bbl

1973	R6456	¼	—	Manual	Center	—	—	—

MODELS 2300, 2300G

(All measurements in inches)

Ford

Year	Carburetor List No.	Float Level	Choke Unloader Setting	Choke Setting	Accelerator Pump Rod Location	Fuel Level (Wet)	Initial Choke Valve Setting
1973	D3HF						
	AA	②	—	Manual	#2 hole	①	—
	BA	②	—	Manual	#2 hole	①	—
	JA	②	—	Manual	#2 hole	①	—
	JB	②	—	Manual	#2 hole	①	—
	CA	②	—	Manual	#2 hole	①	—
1974-76	D4TE						
	AKA	②	—	Manual	#2 hole	①	—
	AKA	②	—	Manual	#2 hole	①	—
	AMA	②	—	Manual	#2 hole	①	—
	ALA	②	—	Manual	#2 hole	①	—
1974-78	D4TE						
	AJA	②	—	Manual	#2 hole	①	—
1978	D8TE						
	BPA	②	—	Manual	#2 hole	①	—
	CEA	②	—	Manual	#2 hole	①	—
	AJA	②	—	Manual	#2 hole	①	—

MODEL 4150G

1974-78	D5TE						
	CB	②	—	Manual	#2 hole	①	—
	CA	②	—	Manual	#1 hole	①	—
	CB	②	—	Manual	#2 hole	①	—
1975-77	D5TE						
	BA	②	—	Manual	#2 hole	①	—
	AA	②	—	Manual	#2 hole	①	—
1975-78	D5TE						
	BRA	②	—	Manual	#2 hole	①	—
1975	D5TE						
	AA	②	—	Manual	#2 hole	①	—
1976	D5TE						
	BA	②	—	Manual	#2 hole	①	—
	BRA	②	—	Manual	#2 hole	①	—
1978	D8TE						
	AHA	②	—	Manual	—	①	—
	BZA	②	—	Manual	—	①	—
	AGA	②	—	Manual	—	①	—
	BRA	②	—	Manual	—	①	—
	CBA	②	—	Manual	—	①	—
	BSA	②	—	Manual	—	①	—

MODEL 4150MG

1973	D3HF						
	DA	②	—	Manual	#1 hole	①	—
	DB	②	—	Manual	#1 hole	①	—
	EA	②	—	Manual	#1 hole	①	—
	EB	②	—	Manual	#1 hole	①	—
	FA	②	—	Manual	#1 hole	①	—
	FB	②	—	Manual	#1 hole	①	—
	GA	②	—	Manual	#1 hole	①	—
	GB	②	—	Manual	#1 hole	①	—

MODEL 4150MG

Ford

(All measurements in inches)

Year	Carburetor List No.		Float Level	Choke Unloader Setting	Choke Setting	Accelerator Pump Rod Location	Fuel Level (Wet)	Initial Choke Valve Setting
1974	D4HE							
		BA	②	——	Manual	#1 hole	①	——
1975	D4HE							
		CA	②	——	Manual	#1 hole	①	——
		DA	②	——	Manual	#1 hole	①	——
1975-77	D5HE							
		CA	②	——	Manual	#1 hole	①	——
		BA	②	——	Manual	#1 hole	①	——
1976	D4HE							
		CA	②	——	Manual	#1 hole	①	——
		DA	②	——	Manual	#1 hole	①	——
1976	D5HE							
		CA	②	——	Manual	#1 hole	①	——
		BA	②	——	Manual	#1 hole	①	——
1976	D6HE							
		CB	②	——	Manual	#1 hole	①	——
		DB	②	——	Manual	#1 hole	①	——
1977	D7HE							
		AA	②	——	Manual	#1 hole	①	——
		CA	②	——	Manual	#1 hole	①	——
1978	D8HE							
		AA	②	——	Manual	#1 hole	①	——
		EA	②	——	Manual	#1 hole	①	——
		CA	②	——	Manual	#1 hole	①	——
		BA	②	——	Manual	#1 hole	①	——
		FA	②	——	Manual	#1 hole	①	——
		DA	②	——	Manual	#1 hole	①	——

MODEL 4160C

Ford

Year	Carburetor List No.		Float Level	Choke Unloader Setting	Choke Setting	Accelerator Pump Rod Location	Fuel Level (Wet)	Initial Choke Valve Setting
1974-75	D4TE							
		ARA	②	.315	Index	#1 hole	①	.180
		ASA	②	.315	Index	#1 hole	①	.180
		ANA	②	.315	Index	#1 hole	①	.180
		EAA	②	.315	Index	#1 hole	①	.180
1975	D5TE							
		DA	②	.315	Index	#1 hole	①	.180
		EA	②	.315	Index	#1 hole	①	.180
		FA	②	.315	Index	#1 hole	①	.180
		GA	②	.315	Index	#1 hole	①	.180
		DB	②	.315	Index	#1 hole	①	.180
1976	D5TE							
		EA	②	.315	Index	#1 hole	①	.180
		DA	②	.315	Index	#1 hole	①	.180
		AB	②	.315	Index	#1 hole	①	.180
		GA	②	.315	Index	#1 hole	①	.180
		GB	②	.315	2 Lean	#1 hole	①	.190
		FA	②	.315	Index	#1 hole	①	.180
		FB	②	.315	2 Lean	#1 hole	①	.200
		DB	②	.315	Index	#1 hole	①	.180

① Fuel Level to Lower Edge of Sight Plug Hole.
② With Fuel Bowl Inverted, Float Should be Parallel with Float Bowl Floor.

MODEL 4150G

GMC

(All measurements in inches)

Year	Carburetor List No.	Float Level (Dry)	Fuel Level (Wet)	Accelerator Pump (Min.)	Fast Idle (RPM)	Air Vent Clearance	Fast Idle Mechanical Clearance
1973	R6510	—	①	.015	1800-2400	.060	.035
	R6521A	—	①	.015	1800-2400	—	.035
	R6511A	—	①	.015	1800-2400	.060	.035
	R6522A	—	①	.015	1800-2400	—	.035
1974	R6742A	②	①	.015	2200	.045-.075	.038
	R6743A	②	①	.015	2200	.045-.075	.038
	R6744A	②	①	.015	2200	—	.038
	R6745A	②	②	.015	2200	—	.038
1975-76	R6928A	③	—	.015	2200	.045-.075	.038
	R6929A	③	—	.015	2200	.045-.075	.038
	R6930A	③	—	.015	2200	—	.031
	R6931A	③	—	.015	2200	—	.031
	R7264A	③	—	.015	2200	.045-.075	.038
	R7266A	④	—	.015	2200	.045-.075	.038
1977	R7703A	④	—	.015	2200	.045-.075	.038
	R7704A	④	—	.015	2200	.045-.075	.031

MODEL 4150EG

GMC

1978	R7923A	④	—	.015	2200	.045-.075	.031
	R7927A	④	—	.015	2200	.045-.075	.031
	R7925A	④	—	.015	2200	—	.031
	R7928A	④	—	.015	2200	—	.031
	R7924A	④	—	.015	2200	.045-.075	.031
	R7926A	④	—	.015	2200	—	.031
1979	R8278A	④	—	.015	2200	.045-.075	.031
	R8280A	④	—	.015	2200	.045-.075	.031
	R8282A	④	—	.015	2200	.045-.075	.031
	R8283A	④	—	.015	2200	.045-.075	.031
	R8444A	④	—	.015	2200	.045-.075	.031
	R8279A	④	—	.015	2200	.045-.075	.031
	R8281A	④	—	.015	2200	.045-.075	.031

① Fuel Level at bottom of Sight Plug.
② Adust Float Parallel to Inner Surface of Fuel Bowl.
③ Primary Bowl—.197
Secondary Bowl—.166
④ Primary Bowl—.194
Secondary Bowl—.213

MODEL 1920

International

(All measurements in inches)

Year	Carburetor List No. (49 States)	Carburetor List No. (Calif.)	Float Level	Fuel Level	Fast Idle Speed (RPM)	Auto Choke Setting	Dash-Post Setting	Fuel Bowl Vent Clearance	Pump Piston Stroke Adjustment	Fast Idle Cam Pos. Adjustment (Top Step—Hot)	Choke Vac. Pulldown (Kick) Adjustment	Choke Unloader Adjustment	Choke Qualification Adjustment
1973	6442, 6831, 6442-1	6775, 6832, 6775-1	①	$11/16 \pm 1/32$	2000	1 Rich	.070-.090	.153-.159	$25/32$	.115-.145	.125-.155	.235-.295	—
1974 (Light Duty)	6831	6800	①	$11/16 \pm 1/32$	2000	1 Rich	.070-.090	.130-.150	$25/32$	—	—	.235-.295	.125-.155
1974 (Heavy Duty)	6832	6832	①	$11/16 \pm 1/32$	2000	1 Rich	—	—	$25/32$	—	—	.235-.295	.140-.170
1975-76	7161	7161	①	$11/16 \pm 1/32$	2000	1 Rich	—	—	$25/32$	—	—	.235-.295	.100-.130
1977-78	7161, 7161-1	7576 8238	①	$11/16 \pm 1/32$	2000	1 Rich	—	—	$25/32$	—	—	.235-.295	.100-.130
1979-80	7771	7771	①	$11/16 \pm 1/32$	2200	1 Lean	—	—	$25/32$	—	—	.235-.295	.150-.180

① Flush with top edge of bowl and with fuel inlet valve held closed

MODEL 1920

International

(All measurements in inches)

Year	Carburetor List No.	Fuel Valve Seat	Fuel Level	Float Level	Dash-Pot Setting	Accelerator Pump Stroke Hole	Throttle Modulator Setting (RPM)	Curb Idle Speed (RPM)
1973-74	4405	.082	27/32①	②	.105-.135	Center	—	700④
	4542-1	.082	27/32①	②	—	Center	1150-1250	700④
	6286	.096	27/32①	③	.050-.080	Center	—	700④
	6266	.096	27/32①	③	.105-.135	Center	—	700④

① Measured through economizer diaphragm opening (Fuel pump pressure—4.5 psi)
② Use gauge number SE-1772-9F or equivalent
③ Use gauge number SE-1772-9G or equivalent
④ With auto transmission—550 RPM in drive

MODELS 2140G, 2140SG

International

(All measurements in inches)

Year	Carburetor List No.	Fuel Level	Float Level	Accelerator Pump Link Location	Governor Speed No-Load (RPM)	Governor Speed Full-Load (RPM)	Curb Idle Speed (RPM)	Idle Mixture Setting % CO
1973-74	w/Std. Trans. 4334, 864-1 w/Auto. Trans. 4335, 4344, 977	1/2①	1/4②	No. 2 Hole	2800	2650	500-550	3.0
1973-74	w/Std. Trans. 4337, 4338, 4339, 4636, 4635 w/Auto. Trans. 4340, 4341, 4636, 4635	1/2①	1/4②	No. 2 Hole	3350-3400	3200	500-550	3.0
1973-74	w/Std. Trans. 4342, 4343, 4634, 4633 w/Auto. Trans. 4634, 4633	1/2①	1/4②	No. 2 Hole	3350-3400	3200	500-550	3.0

① @ 4.5 PSI ② Top of float to top of bowl

MODEL 2210C

International

(All measurements in inches)

Year	Carb. List No. (48 States)	Carb. List No. (Calif.)	Float Level	Fuel Level	Fast Idle Speed	Auto Choke Setting	Dash Pot Setting	Fuel Bowl Vent Clear-ance	Pump Piston Stroke Adjust-ment	Fast Idle Cam Position Adjust-ment (Top Step—Hot)	Choke Vac. Pulldown (Kick) Adjust-ment	Choke Unloader Adjust-ment	Choke Qualifi-cation Adjust-ment
1973	6443	6443	.200①	1/2	2200	Index②	.070-.090	.010-.020	.700	.116 ± .015	.115-.145	.228 ± .030	—
(Light	6443-1	6443-1	.200①	1/2	2200	Index②	.070-.090	.010-.020	.700	.116 ± .015	.120-.140	.228 ± .030	—
Duty)	6776	6776	.200①	1/2	2200	Index	.070-.090	.010-.020	.700	.116 ± .015	.120-.140	.228 ± .030	—
1974	6828	—	.200①	1/2	2200	Index	.070-.090	.015 ± .010	.650	—	—	.228 ± .030	.120-.140
(Light Duty)	6674-1	—	.200①	1/2	2000	Preset③	.070-.090	.015 ± .010	.650	—	—	.228 ± .030	.159-.179
1974-80	6620-1 7309	—	.180	1/2④	2000	⑤	—	—	—	—	—	.198-.258	.040-.070
	7214, 7214-1	—	.180	1/2④	1800	Preset	—	—	—	—	—	.228 ± .030	.135 ± .015
	—	7309, 6620-2, 7133, 7940 8241	.180	1/2④	2200	⑤	—	—	—	—	—	.198-.258	.040-.070
	—	7657, 7217, 8244	.180	1/2④	1800	Preset	—	—	—	—	—	.198-.258	.120-.150

① Measure between Top of Float and Float Stop with Air Horn Inverted
② 2 Notches Rich in Winter
③ 1 1/4 Rod Diameter Preload
④ @ 5.5 PSI
⑤ Choke with Index Marks—1 Notch Lean (Restrained)
Choke Without Index Marks—Preset (Unrestrained)

MODELS 2300, 2300C, 2300G

International

(All measurements in inches)

Year	Carburtor List No.	Fuel Level①	Fast Idle Setting (in. or RPM)	Auto Choke Setting	Dash Pot Setting	Governor Speed No-Load (RPM)	Governor Speed Full Load (RPM)	High Idle Speed (RPM)③	Curb Idle Speed (RPM)	Idle Setting % CO
1973	6391-1	3/8	.110②	—	—					
(Federal	6393-1	3/8	2000 RPM	1 Lean	—	—	—	—	700	—
Only	6394-1	3/8	2000 RPM	1 Lean	.090-.120	—	—	—	700	—
	4310-2	3/8	.018-.020②	—	—	4000	3800	—	700	—
1973	6623	3/8	.018-.020②	—	—	4000	3800	1300-1400	650-700	2.0 Max
(Calif. Only)	6624-1	3/8	.018-.020②	—	—	4000	3800	1300-1400	650-700	1.5 Max
1974	6801-1	3/8	.018-.020②	—	—	4000	3800	1300-1400	650-700	2.0 Max
(50 States)	6802	3/8	.018-.020②	—	—	4000	3800	1300-1400	650-700	1.5 Max
1975-77	6801	3/8	2200	—	—	4000	3800	1300-1400	650-700	④
(Federal)	7213	3/8	2400	—	—	3800	3600	1300± 50	525-575	0.5-2.5
	6908	3/8	2000	—	—	3400	3200	1300± 50	500-550	1.5-3.0
1975-76	6899	3/8	2000	—	—	4000	3800	1450± 50	625-675	0.5-1.5
(Calif)	7216	3/8	2400	—	—	3800	3600	1350± 50	525-575	0.5-2.5
	7198	3/8	2000	—	—	3400	3200	1300-1400	500-550	1.0-2.0
1977-80	7656	3/8	2000	—	—	4000	3800	1450± 50	625-675	1.0-3.0
(Calif)	7216	3/8	2400	—	—	3800	3600	1350± 50	525-575	0.5-2.0
	7198	3/8	2000	—	—	3400	3200	1300-1400	500-550	1.0-2.0

① @ 5.5 PSI
② Clearance between Stopscrew and Fast Idle Cam with Choke Valve Open
③ Throttle Modulator Extended
④ V-304 = 2.0 Max., V-345 = 1.5 Max.

MODELS 4150G, 4150EG

International

(All measurements in inches)

Year	Carburetor List No.	Fuel Valve Seal	Fuel Level	Fast Idle Setting (in. or RPM)	Governor Speed No-Load (RPM)	Governor Speed Full-Load (RPM)	Curb Idle Speed (RPM)	Idle Mixture Setting % CO
1973-74	4323-5, 6	①	②	.010-.015	3800	3600	700	2.0 Max
	4323-7	①	②	.010-.015	3800	3600	700	2.0 Max
	6803	①	②	.010-.015	3800	3600	700	2.0 Max
	6803-1	①	②	.010-.015	3800	3600	700	2.0 Max
1975-80	6803-3	—	②	2000	3800	3600	650-700	2.0 Max
(Federal)	7215	—	②	2400	3800	3600	525-575	0.5-2.5
	7251	—	②	2400	3800	3600	525-575	0.5-2.5
	6911	—	②	2000	3400	3200	500-550	1.5-3.0
1975-80	7028, 7529	—	②	.015-.020	3800	3600	625-675	0.5-1.5
(Calif)	7218, 7218-1	—	②	2400	3800	3600	525-575	0.5-2.5
	7581	—	②	2400	3800	3600	525-575	0.5-2.5
	7921	—	②	2400	3800± 50	—	525-575	0.5-2.5
1975-80	7029, 7029-1	—	②	2400	3800	3600	525-575	0.5-2.5
(50 States)	6974	—	②	2000	3400	3200	500-550	1.0-2.0

① Primary = .097, Secondary = .097
② Primary 3/8 in., Secondary 5/8 in.

MODEL 4150C

International

(All measurements in inches)

Year	Carburetor List No.	Fuel Valve Seat	Fuel Level①	Fast Idle Setting②	Auto Choke Setting	Governor Speed No-Load (RPM)	Governor Speed Full-Load (RPM)	Dash Pot Setting	Choke Qualification Setting③	Curb Idle Speed (RPM)	Idle Mixture Setting % CO
1973-74	4312-2, 4313-2, 4313-3	Primary .097 Secondary .097	Primary 1/2 Secondary 1/2	2000	2-Lean	—	—	.060-.090	.185-.215	700	2.0 Max

① @ 5 PSI
② Top Step of Cam—Carburetor Hot
③ Measured on Downstream Side of Choke Valve

MODEL 852-FFG

International

(All measurements in inches)

Year	Carburetor List No.	Fuel Level①	Float Level	Governor Speed No-Load (RPM)	Governor Speed Full-Load (RPM)	Curb Idle Speed (RPM)	Idle Mixture Setting % CO
1973-74	4329	5/8	1¼	2800	2600	500	3.0
	6398, 6398-1, 6438	5/8	1¼	2800	2600	500-550	3.5 Max
1973-74	4438, 4679, 4378	5/8	1¼	3600	3400	600	3.0
1973-74	4331, 4338, 4377, 4332	5/8	1¼	3600	3400	500	3.0

① @ 4.5 PSI

MODEL 885-FFG

International

(All measurements in inches)

Year	Carburetor List No.	Fuel Valve Seat	Fuel Level	Governor Speed No-Load (RPM)	Governor Speed Full-Load (RPM)	Accelerator Linkage Position	High Idle Speed (RPM)	Curb Idle Speed (RPM)	Idle Mixture Setting % CO
1973-74	4327	.098	½	2950	2800	Center Hole	—	450-500	3.0
	4328, 6397, 6397-1	.098	½	2950	2800	Center Hole	—	450-500	3.0
	6337	.098	½	2950	2750	Center Hole	—	500-550	3.0
	6625	.098	½	2950	2750	Center Hole	1300-1400	500-550	3.0

MODEL 1920 1-bbl

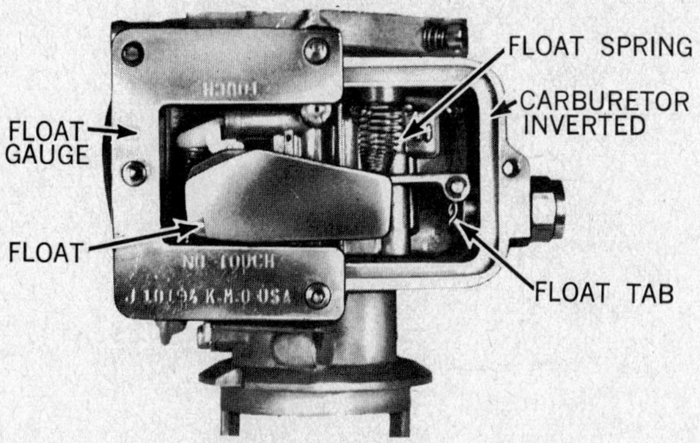

Checking float setting

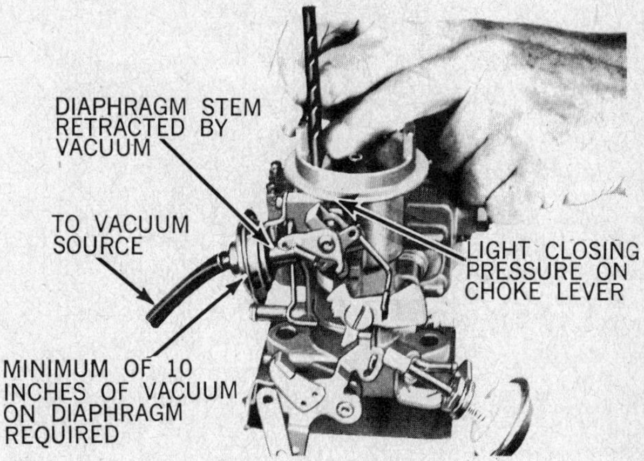

Choke vacuum kick setting

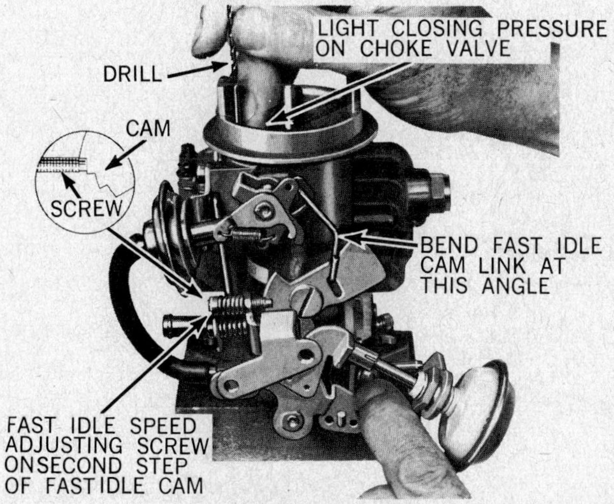

Fast idle cam adjustment

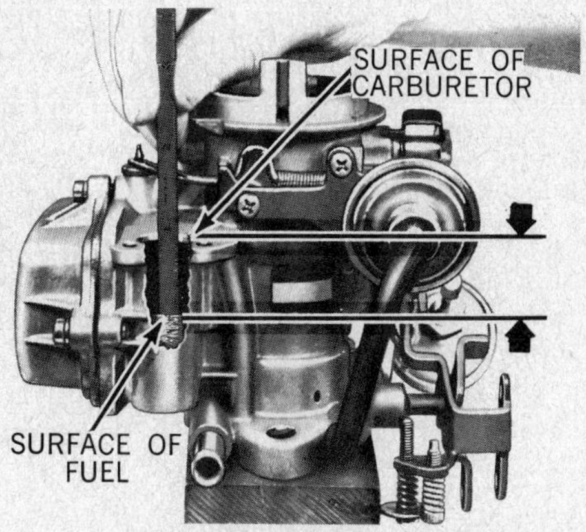

Measuring wet fuel level

MODEL 1945 1-bbl

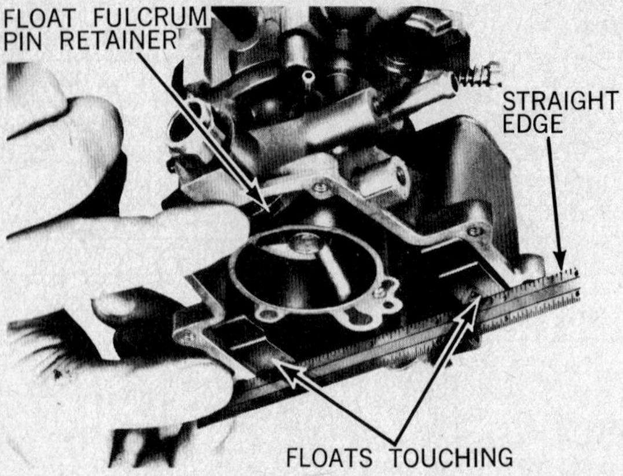

Adjusting float level with fuel bowl inverted—model 1945 carburetor (© Chrysler Corp.)

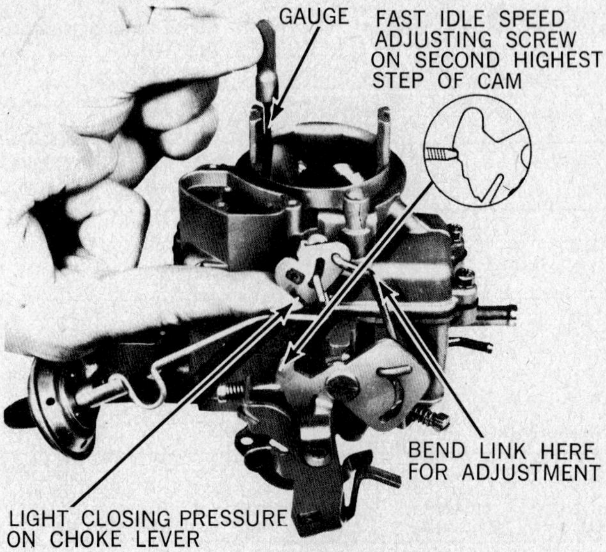

Fast idle cam to choke valve adjustment—model 1945 carburetor (© Chrysler Corp.)

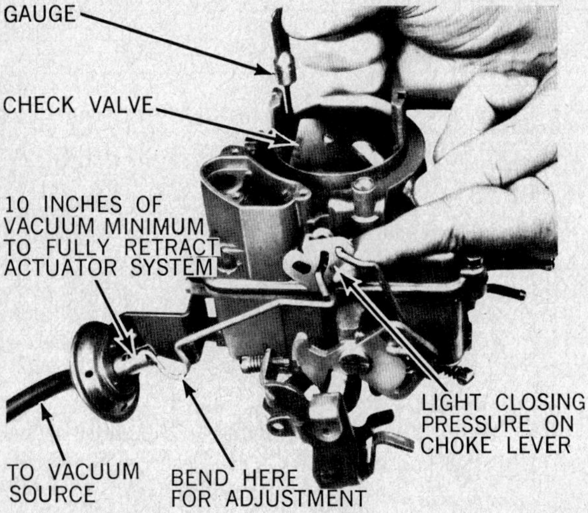

Choke valve initial setting (vacuum kick)—model 1945 (© Chrysler Corp.)

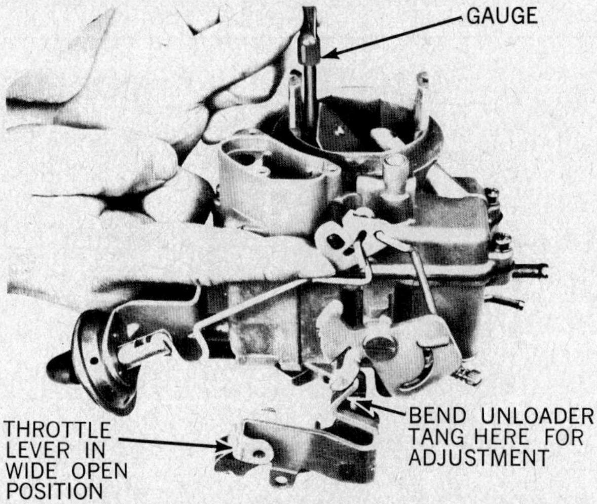

Choke valve unloader adjustment—model 1945 carburetor (© Chrysler Corp.)

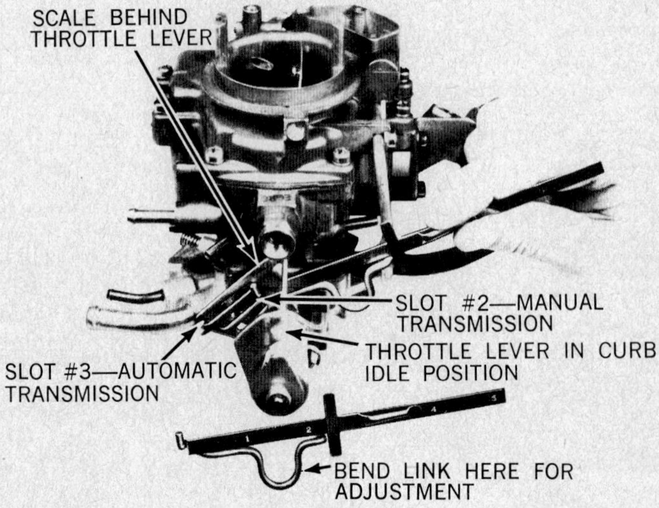

Accelerator pump piston stroke adjustment—model 1945 carburetor (© Chrysler Corp.)

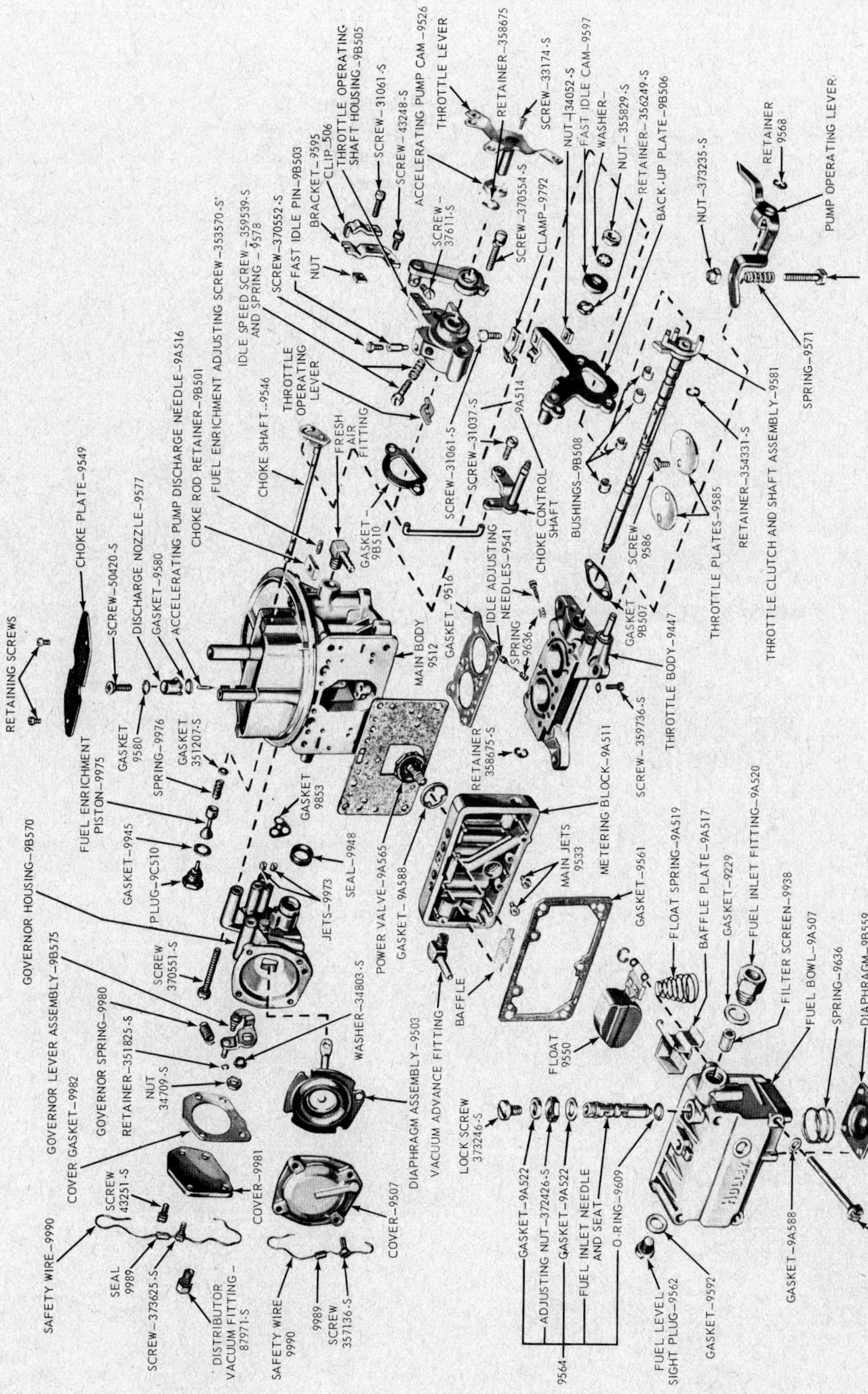

Holley two barrel—typical

MODEL 2210 MODEL 2210C MODEL 2245 2-bbl

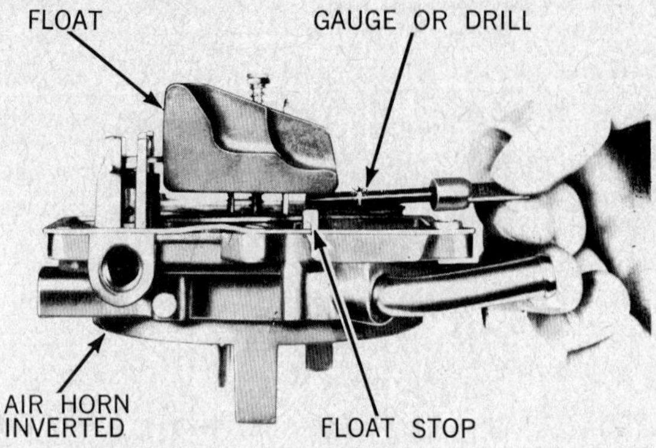

Adjusting float level—models 2210, 2210C, 2245 carburetors (© Chrysler Corp.)

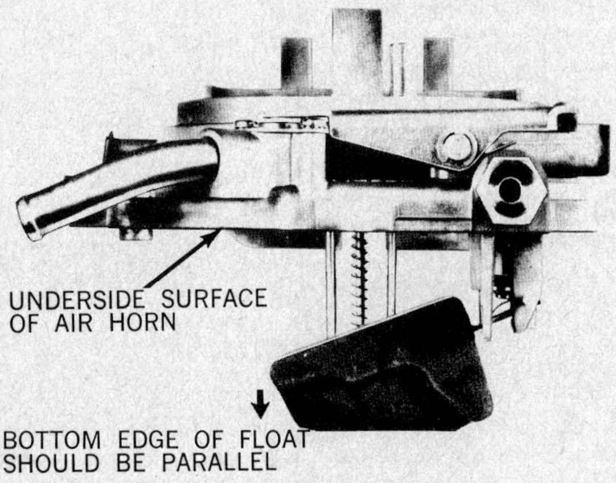

Adjusting float drop—models 2210, 2210C, 2245 carburetors (© Chrysler Corp.)

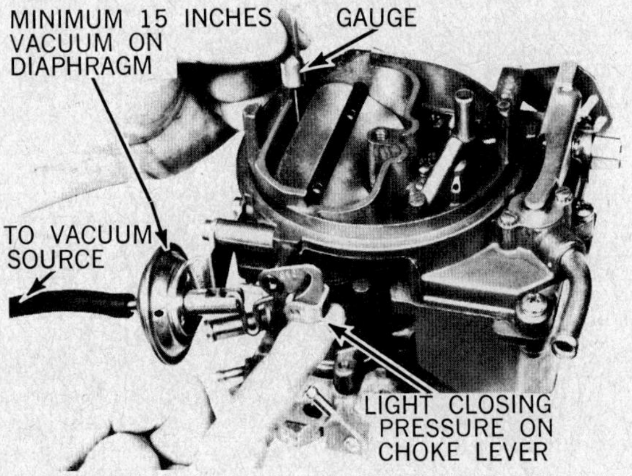

Adjusting initial choke valve setting—models 2210, 2210c, 2245 carburetors (© Chrysler Corp.)

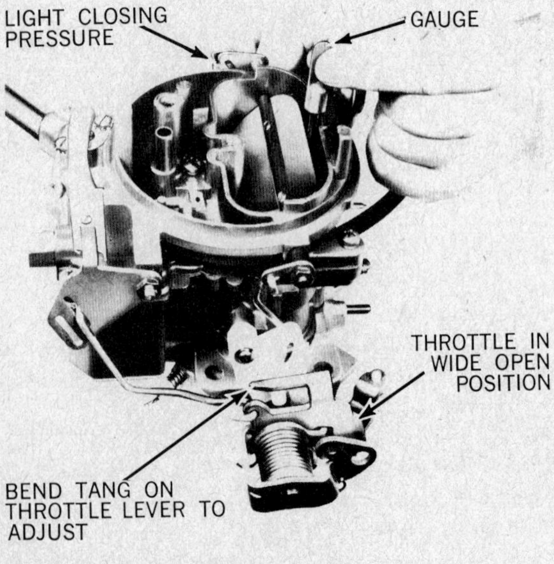

Choke unloader adjustment—models 2210, 2210C, 2245 carburetors (© Chrysler Corp.)

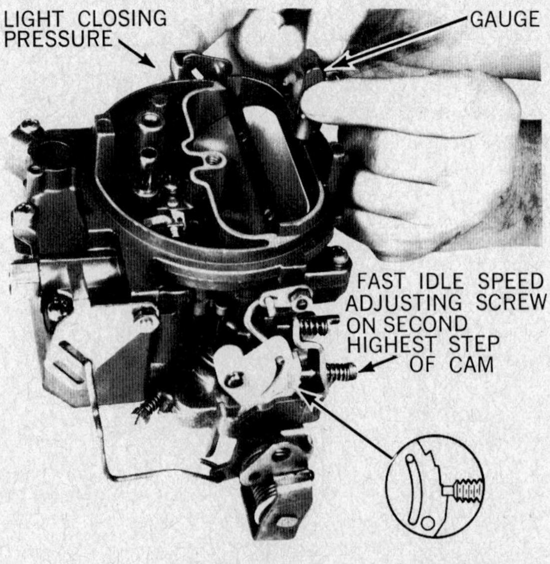

Fast idle cam position—models 2210, 2210C, 2245 carburetors (© Chrysler Corp.)

MODEL 2300 2-bbl

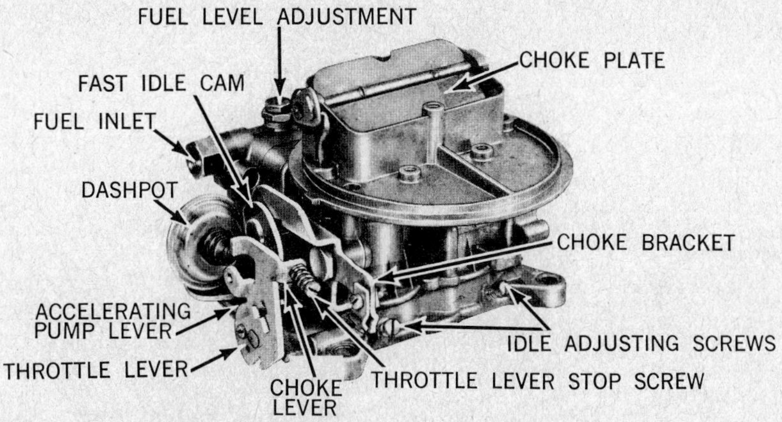

Adjustment locations—model 2300 carburetor

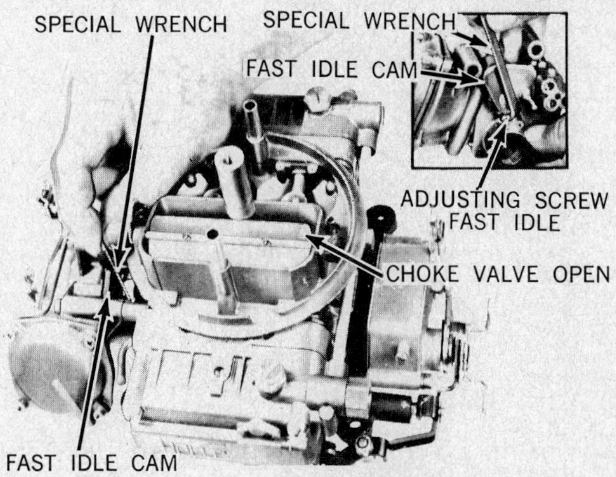

Fast idle speed adjustment

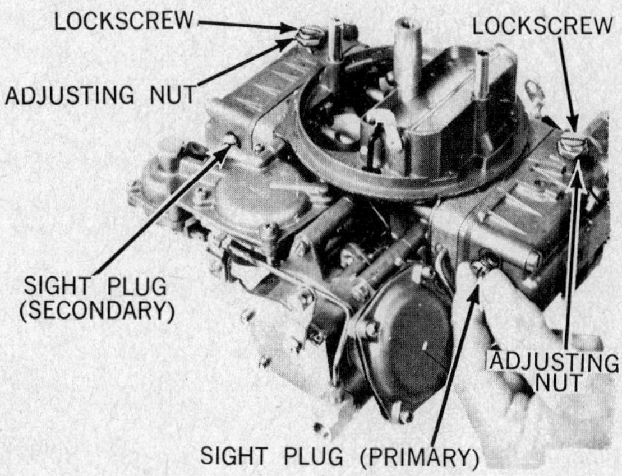

Fuel level sight plug location

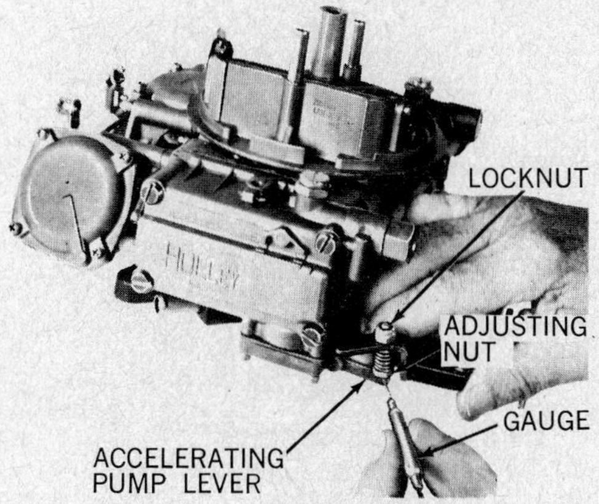

Checking accelerating pump lever clearance

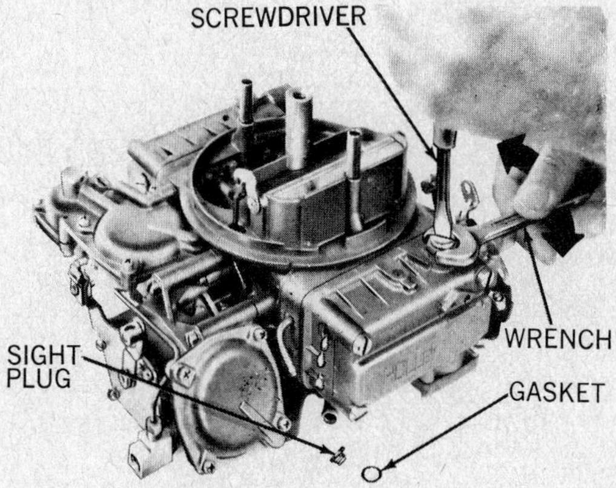

Adjusting fuel level

MODEL 2300 2-bbl

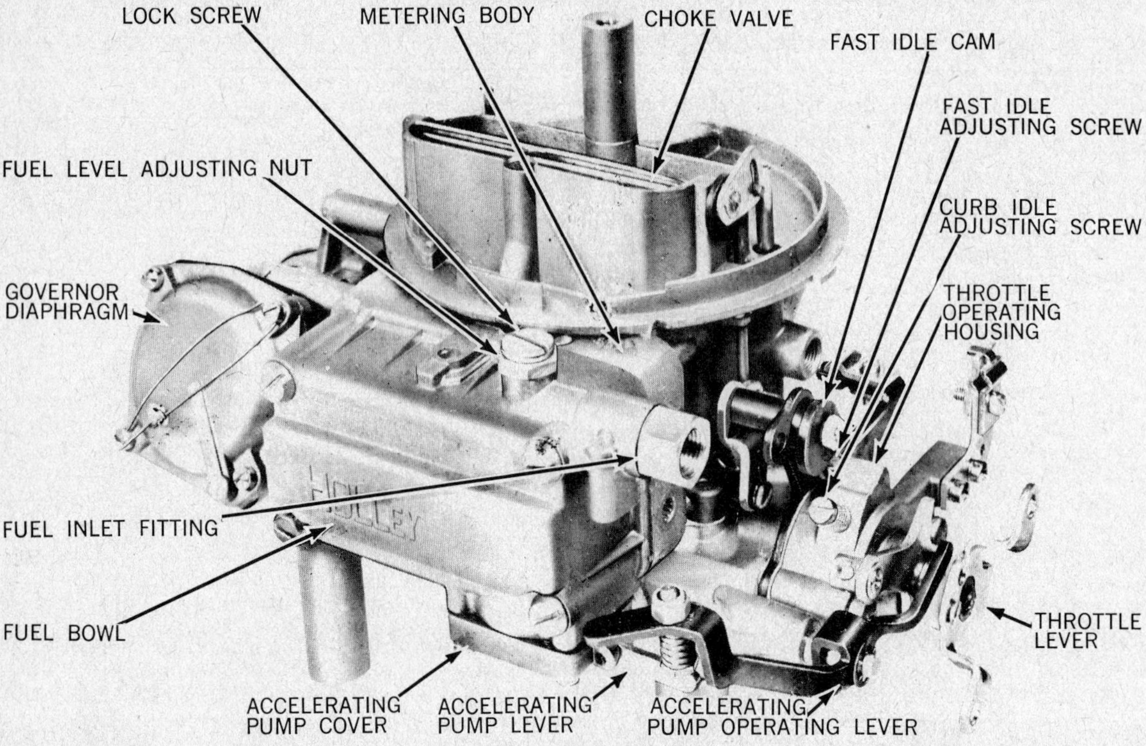

Model 2300 carburetor-typical

MODEL 4150 2-bbl

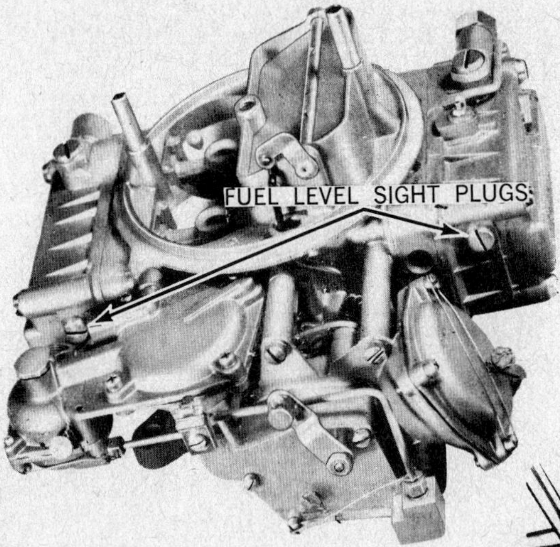

Model 4150 carburetor—typical

Adjusting float level (dry)—model 4150 carburetor (© Ford Motor Co.)

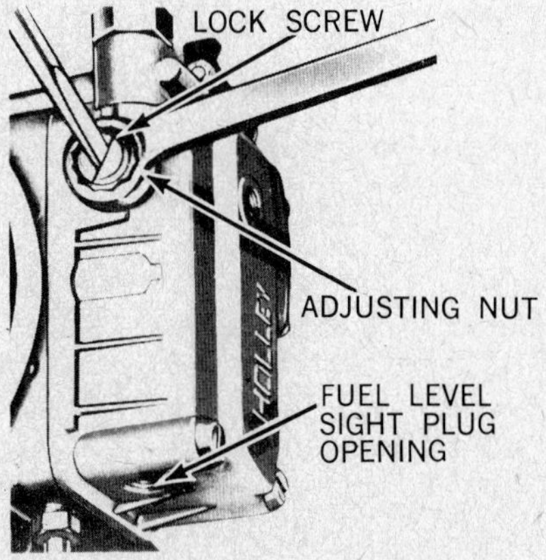

Adjusting fuel level (wet)—model 4150 carburetor (© Ford Motor Co.)

MODEL 4160C 4-bbl

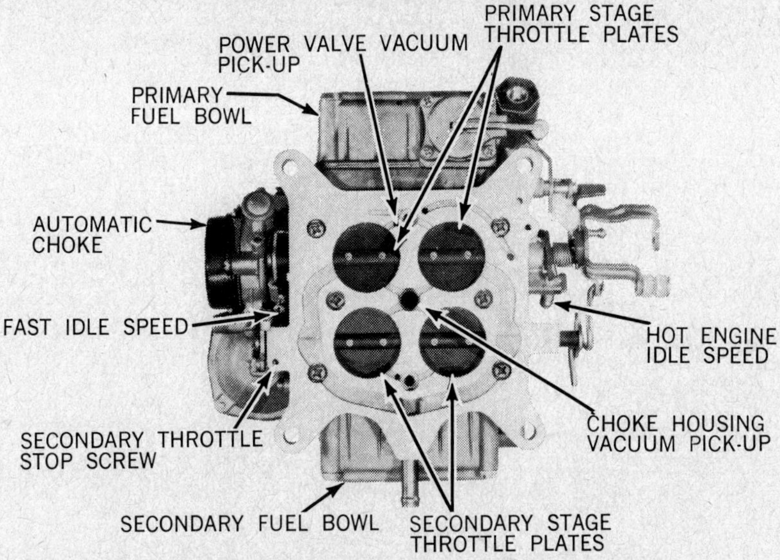

Bottom view—model 4160C carburetor (© Ford Motor Co.)

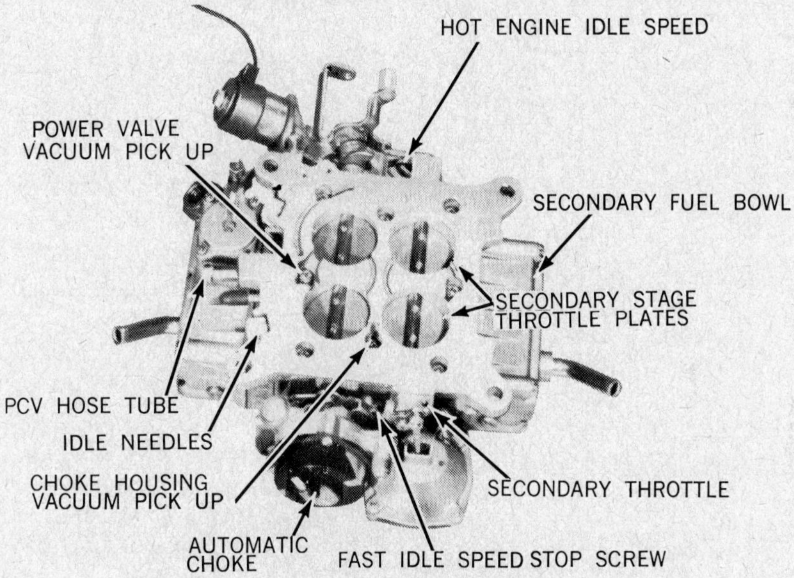

Bottom view—model 4180C carburetor (© Ford Motor Co.)

MODELS 2140G, 2140SG

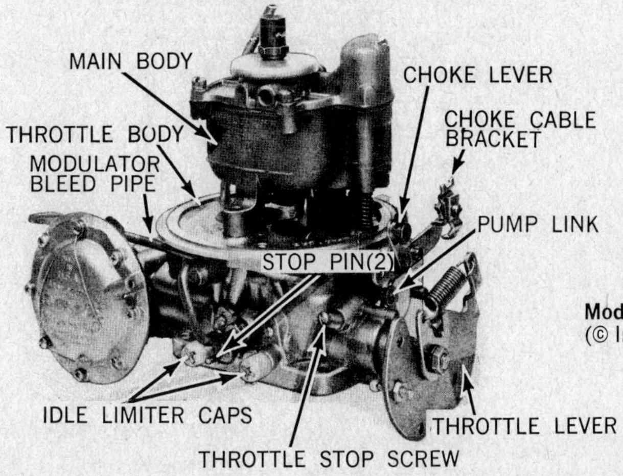

Models 2140C, 2140SG carburetors
(© International Harvester Co.)

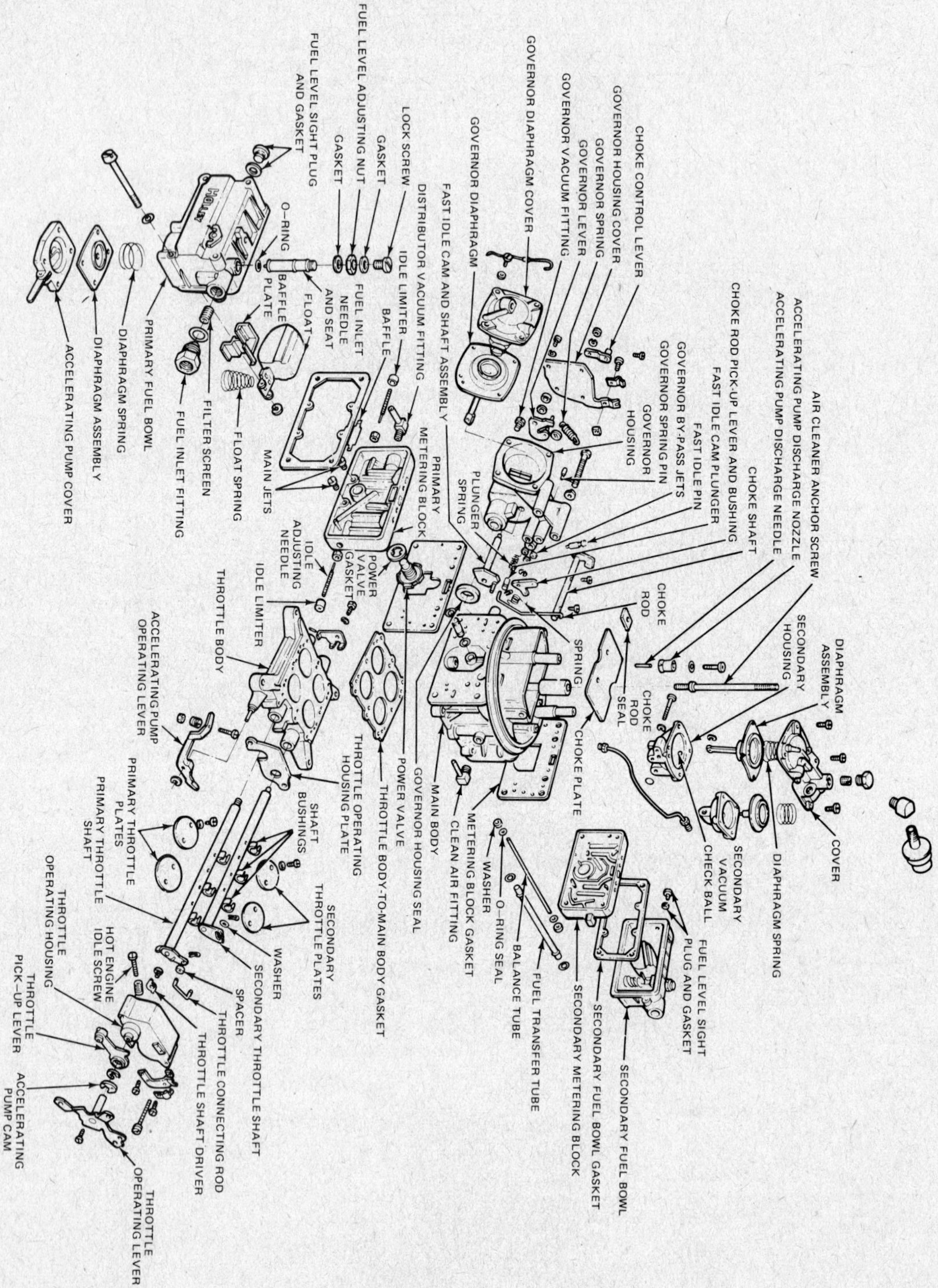
CHOKE CONTROL LEVER
GOVERNOR HOUSING COVER
GOVERNOR SPRING
GOVERNOR LEVER
GOVERNOR VACUUM FITTING
GOVERNOR DIAPHRAGM COVER
GOVERNOR DIAPHRAGM
FAST IDLE CAM AND SHAFT ASSEMBLY
DISTRIBUTOR VACUUM FITTING
IDLE LIMITER
LOCK SCREW
GASKET
FUEL LEVEL ADJUSTING NUT
GASKET
FUEL LEVEL SIGHT PLUG AND GASKET
O-RING
BAFFLE PLATE
FLOAT
FUEL INLET NEEDLE AND SEAT
BAFFLE
PRIMARY FUEL BOWL
DIAPHRAGM SPRING
DIAPHRAGM ASSEMBLY
ACCELERATING PUMP COVER
FUEL INLET FITTING
FILTER SCREEN
FLOAT SPRING
MAIN JETS
PRIMARY METERING BLOCK
IDLE ADJUSTING NEEDLE
POWER VALVE GASKET
IDLE LIMITER
THROTTLE BODY
ACCELERATING PUMP OPERATING LEVER
PLUNGER SPRING
AIR CLEANER ANCHOR SCREW
ACCELERATING PUMP DISCHARGE NOZZLE
ACCELERATING PUMP DISCHARGE NEEDLE
CHOKE SHAFT
CHOKE ROD PICK-UP LEVER AND BUSHING
FAST IDLE CAM PLUNGER
FAST IDLE PIN
GOVERNOR BY-PASS JETS
GOVERNOR SPRING PIN
GOVERNOR HOUSING
CHOKE ROD
SPRING
CHOKE ROD SEAL
CHOKE PLATE
SECONDARY HOUSING
DIAPHRAGM ASSEMBLY
COVER
DIAPHRAGM SPRING
SECONDARY VACUUM CHECK BALL
FUEL LEVEL SIGHT PLUG AND GASKET
SECONDARY FUEL BOWL
SECONDARY FUEL BOWL GASKET
SECONDARY METERING BLOCK
FUEL TRANSFER TUBE
BALANCE TUBE
O-RING SEAL
WASHER
METERING BLOCK GASKET
CLEAN AIR FITTING
MAIN BODY
GOVERNOR HOUSING SEAL
THROTTLE BODY-TO-MAIN BODY GASKET
POWER VALVE
THROTTLE OPERATING HOUSING PLATE
SHAFT BUSHINGS
SECONDARY THROTTLE PLATES
WASHER
SECONDARY THROTTLE SHAFT
SPACER
THROTTLE CONNECTING ROD
THROTTLE SHAFT DRIVER
PRIMARY THROTTLE PLATES
PRIMARY THROTTLE SHAFT
HOT ENGINE IDLE SCREW
THROTTLE OPERATING HOUSING
THROTTLE PICK-UP LEVER
ACCELERATING PUMP CAM
THROTTLE OPERATING LEVER

Holley four barrel—typical

MODEL 852-FFG

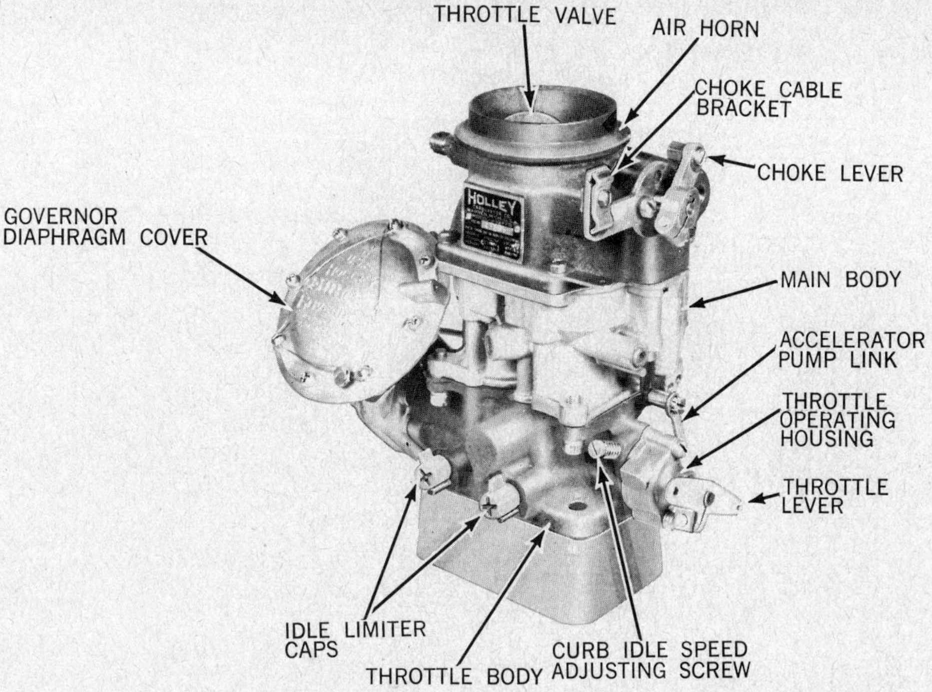

Model 852 FFG carburetor

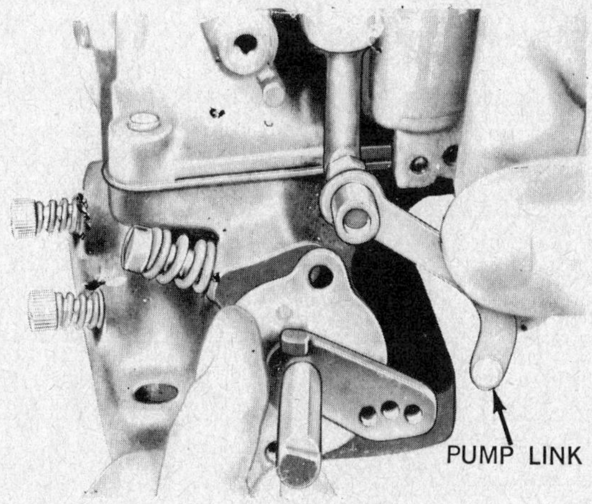

Accelerator pump link

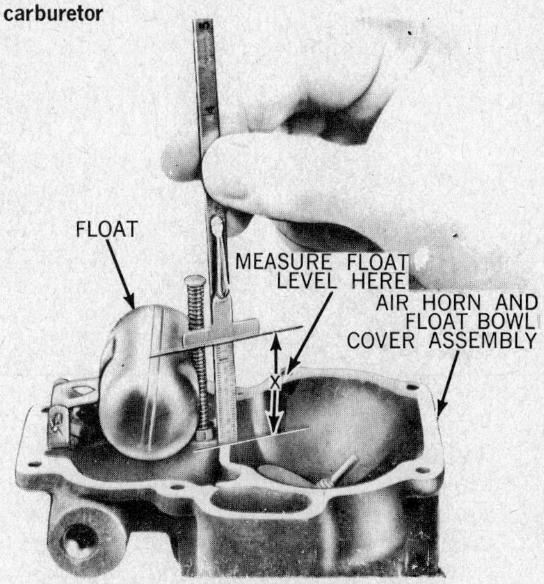

Setting float level

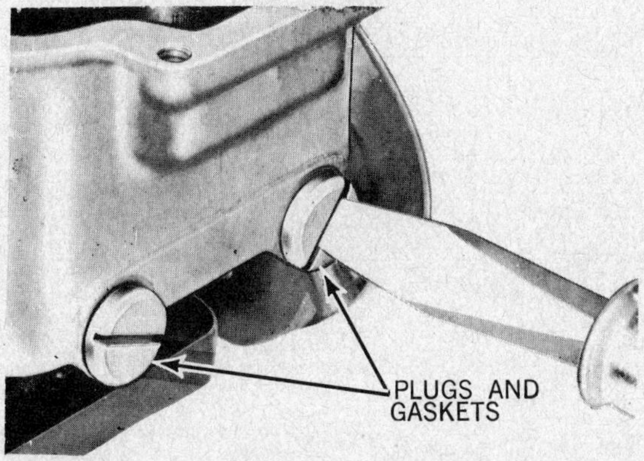

Main jet passage plugs

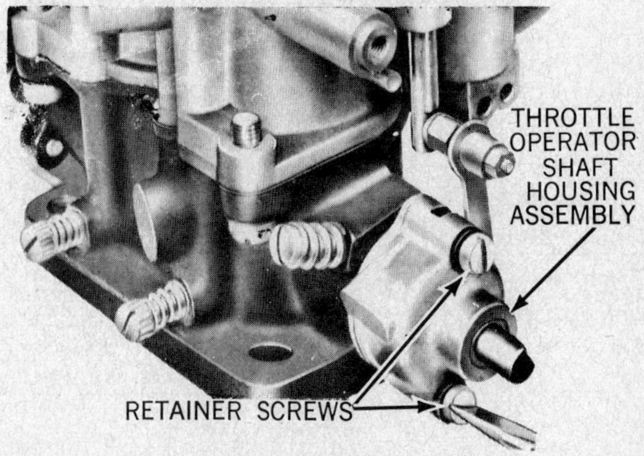

Throttle operating housing—removal

MODEL 852-FFG

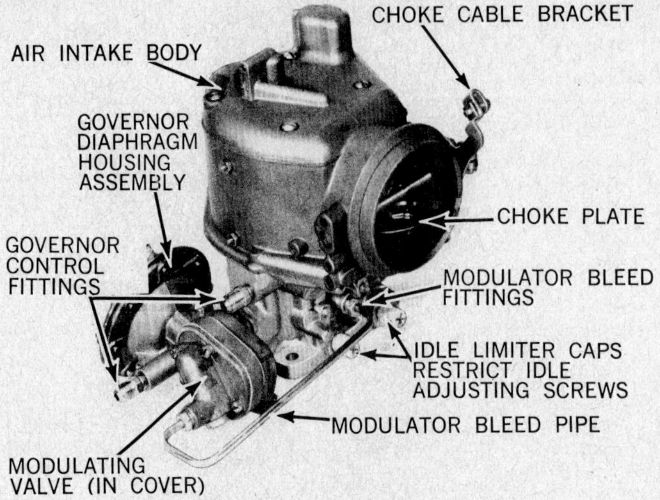

Side view of model 885 FFG carburetor
(© International Harvester Co.)

Rochester Carburetors

MODEL 2GV

(All measurements in inches)

Chevrolet

Year	Carburetor Number	Float Level	Float Drop	Choke Unloader Setting	Choke Setting	Pump Rod Location	Fast Idle Speed (RPM)	Metering Rod Setting	Fast Idle Cam 2nd Step	Choke Vacuum Break
1973	7043105	21/32	1 9/32	.215	Fixed	1 5/16	—	—	.150	.080
	7043103	21/32	1 9/32	.215	Fixed	1 5/16	—	—	.150	.080
	7043108	25/32	1 9/32	.250	Fixed	1 5/16	—	—	.150	.140
	7043123	23/32	1 9/32	—	Fixed	1 7/16	—	—	—	—
	7043124	23/32	1 9/32	—	Fixed	1 7/16	—	—	—	—
	7043424	23/32	1 9/32	—	Fixed	1 7/16	—	—	—	—
	7047796	23/32	1 9/32	—	Fixed	1 7/16	—	—	—	—
1974	7044011	1/4	—	—	Fixed	—	1600	.070	.150	—
	7044012	1/4	—	—	Fixed	—	1600	.070	.150	—
	7044133	19/32	1 9/32	—	Fixed	1 9/16	1600	—	—	—
	7044134	19/32	1 9/32	—	Fixed	1 7/16	1600	—	—	—
	7044434	19/32	1 9/32	—	Fixed	1 7/16	1600	—	—	—
	7044113	19/32	1 9/32	.250	Fixed	1 9/32	1600	.200	—	.140
	7044114	19/32	1 9/32	.325	Fixed	1 3/16	1600	.245	—	.130
	7044123	19/32	1 9/32	.250	Fixed	1 9/32	1600	.200	—	.140
	7044124	19/32	1 9/32	.325	Fixed	1 3/16	1600	.245	—	.130
1975	7045115	21/32	31/32	.350	Index	1 5/8	—	—	.400	.130
	7045116	21/32	31/32	.350	Index	1 5/8	—	—	.400	.130
	7045123	21/32	31/32	.350	Index	1 5/8	—	—	.400	.130
	7045124	21/32	31/32	.350	Index	1 5/8	—	—	.400	.130
	7044133	19/32	1 9/32	—	Manual	1 9/16	—	—	—	—
	7044134	19/32	1 9/32	—	Manual	1 7/16	—	—	—	—
	7044434	19/32	1 9/32	—	Manual	1 7/16	—	—	—	—

MODEL 2GV

Chevrolet

(All measurements in inches)

Year	Carburetor Number	Float Level	Float Drop	Choke Unloader Setting	Choke Setting	Pump Rod Location	Fast Idle Speed (RPM)	Metering Rod Setting	Fast Idle Cam 2nd Step	Choke Vacuum Break
1976	7044133	19/32	1 9/32	—	—	1 9/16	—	—	—	—
	7044134	19/32	1 9/32	—	—	1 7/16	—	—	—	—
	704434	19/32	1 9/32	—	—	1 7/16	—	—	—	—
	17056115	21/32	1 9/32	.325	Index	1 11/16	—	—	.260	.130
	17056116	21/32	1 9/32	.325	1 Rich	1 11/16	—	—	.260	.130
	17056123	21/32	1 9/32	.325	Index	1 11/16	—	—	.260	.130
	17056124	21/32	1 9/32	.325	1 Rich	1 11/16	—	—	.260	.130
1977	7044133	19/32	1 9/32	.325	Index	1 21/32	—	—	.260	.130
	7044134	19/32	1 9/32	.325	Index	1 21/32	—	—	.260	.130
	17056433	19/32	1 9/32	.325	Index	1 21/32	—	—	.260	.130
	17056434	19/32	1 9/32	.325	Index	1 21/32	—	—	.260	.130
	17056137	19/32	1 9/32	.325	Index	1 21/32	—	—	.260	.190

MODEL 2G

Chevrolet

(All measurements in inches)

Year	Carburetor Number	Float Level	Float Drop	Choke Unloader Setting	Choke Setting	Pump Rod Location	Fast Idle Speed (RPM)	Metering Rod Setting	Fast Idle Cam 2nd Step	Choke Break Vacuum
1978	7044133	19/32	19/32	—	—	1 9/16	—	—	—	—
	7044134	19/32	19/32	—	—	1 7/16	—	—	—	—
	17058423	19/32	19/32	—	—	1 7/16	—	—	—	—
	17058423	19/32	19/32	—	—	1 7/16	—	—	—	—
1979	17059126	5/8	1 9/32	—	—	1 15/32	—	—	—	—
	17059127	17/32	1 9/32	—	—	1 15/32	—	—	—	—
	17059120	17/32	1 9/32	—	—	1 15/32	—	—	—	—
	17059423	5/8	1 9/32	—	—	1 21/32	—	—	—	—
	17059424	17/32	1 9/32	—	—	1 15/32	—	—	—	—
	17059420	17/32	1 9/32	—	—	1 15/32	—	—	—	—

MODEL MV

Chevrolet

(All measurements in inches)

Year	Carburetor Number	Float Level	Float Drop	Choke Unloader Setting	Choke Setting	Pump Rod Location	Fast Idle Speed (RPM)	Metering Rod Setting	Fast Idle Cam 2nd Step	Choke Vacuum Break
1973	7043022	1/4	—	.500	Fixed	—	—	.080	.245	.300
	7043021	1/4	—	.500	Fixed	—	—	.080	.275	.350
	7043025	1/4	—	.500	Fixed	—	—	.070	.250	.430
	7043026	1/4	—	.500	Fixed	—	—	.070	.375	.430
	7043326	1/4	—	.500	Fixed	—	—	.070	.375	.430
	7043009	1/4	—	—	—	—	1800-2400	.070	—	—
	7043012	1/4	—	—	—	—	1800-2400	.070	—	—
	7043312	1/4	—	—	—	—	1800-2400	.070	—	—
1974	7044021	.295	—	.500	Fixed	—	1800	.080	.275	.350
	7044022	.295	—	.500	Fixed	—	1800	.080	.245	.300
	7044321	.295	—	.500	Fixed	—	1800	.080	.300	.375
	7044025	1/4	—	.521	Fixed	—	2400	.070	.245	.300
	7044026	1/4	—	.521	Fixed	—	2400	.070	.275	.350

MODEL IMV

Chevrolet

(All measurements in inches)

Year	Carburetor Number	Float Level	Float Drop	Choke Unloader Setting	Choke Setting	Pump Rod Location	Fast Idle Speed (RPM)	Metering Rod Setting	Fast Idle Cam 2nd Step	Choke Vacuum Break
1975	7045002	11/32	—	.325	Fixed	—	1800	.080	.260	①
	7045003	11/32	—	.325	Fixed	—	1800	.080	.275	①
	7045004	11/32	—	.325	Fixed	—	1800	.080	.245	①
	7045005	11/32	—	.325	Fixed	—	1800	.080	.275	②
	7045302	11/32	—	.275	Fixed	—	1800	.080	.245	①
	7045303	11/32	—	.275	Fixed	—	1800	.080	.275	②
	7045304	11/32	—	.325	Fixed	—	1800	.080	.245	①
	7045305	11/32	—	.325	Fixed	—	1800	.080	.275	②
1976	17056002	11/32	—	.335	Fixed	—	2100	.080	.130	③
	17056003	11/32	—	.335	Fixed	—	2100	.080	.145	.180
	17056004	11/32	—	.335	Fixed	—	2100	.080	.130	③
	17056006	1/4	—	.270	Fixed	—	2100	.080	.130	.165
	17056007	1/4	—	.275	Fixed	—	2100	.070	.130	.165
	17056008	1/4	—	.275	Fixed	—	2100	.070	.150	.190
	17056009	1/4	—	.275	Fixed	—	2100	.080	.150	.190
	17056302	11/32	—	.325	Fixed	—	2100	.080	.155	.190
	17056303	11/32	—	.325	Fixed	—	2100	.080	.180	.225
	17056308	1/4	—	.275	Fixed	—	2100	.070	.150	.190
	17056309	1/4	—	.275	Fixed	—	2100	.070	.150	.190

① Primary—.300
Secondary—.325

② Primary—.350
Secondary—.325

③ Primary—.165
Auxiliary—.265

MODEL IME

Chevrolet

(All measurements in inches)

Year	Carburetor Number	Float Level	Float Drop	Choke Unloader Setting	Choke Setting	Pump Rod Location	Fast Idle Speed (RPM)	Metering Rod Setting	Fast Idle Cam 2nd Step	Choke Vacuum Break
1977	17057001	3/8	—	.325	Index	—	2100	.080	.125	.150
	17057002	3/8	—	.325	Index	—	2100	.080	.110	.135
	17057004	3/8	—	.325	Index	—	2100	.080	.110	.135
	17057005	3/8	—	.325	Index	—	2100	.080	.125	.180
	17057010	3/8	—	.325	Index	—	2100	.080	.110	.180
	17057302	3/8	—	.325	Index	—	2100	.080	.150	.135
	17057303	3/8	—	.325	Index	—	2100	.090	.125	.150
	17057006	5/16	—	.275	Index	—	2400	.070	.150	.180
	17057007	5/16	—	.275	Index	—	2400	.070	.150	.180
	17057008	5/16	—	.275	Index	—	2400	.065	.150	.180
	17057009	5/16	—	.275	Index	—	2400	.065	.150	.180
	17057308	5/16	—	.275	Index	—	2400	.065	.150	.180
	17057309	5/16	—	.275	Index	—	2400	.065	.150	.180

MODEL ME, M

Chevrolet

(All measurements in inches)

Year	Carburetor Number	Float Level	Float Drop	Choke Unloader Setting	Choke Setting	Pump Rod Location	Fast Idle Speed (RPM)	Metering Rod Setting	Fast Idle Cam 2nd Step	Choke Vacuum Break
1978	17058009	1/4	—	—	—	—	2400	.065	.150	—
	17058011	1/4	—	—	—	—	2400	.065	.150	—
1979	17059009	5/16	—	.520	2 Rich	—	2400	.090	.275	.400

MODEL M4MC/4MV QUADRAJET FOUR BARREL

(All measurements in inches)

Chevrolet

Year	Model or Type	Float Level	Air Valve Dashpot	PUMP ROD Adj.	PUMP ROD Hole	Initial Choke Valve Opening	Vacuum Break	Choke Unloader	Air Valve Spring Wind-up
1973	7043202	7/32	—	13/32	—	—	.215	.450	1/2
	7043203	7/32	—	13/32	—	—	.215	.450	1/2
	7043210	7/32	—	13/32	—	—	.215	.450	1/2
	7043211	7/32	—	13/32	—	—	.215	.450	1/2
	7043208	5/16	—	13/32	—	—	.215	.450	1/2
	7043215	5/16	—	13/32	—	—	.215	.450	1/2
	7043200	1/4	—	13/32	—	—	.250	.450	11/16
	7043216	1/4	—	13/32	—	—	.250	.450	11/16
	7043207	1/4	—	13/32	—	—	.250	.450	11/16
	7043507	1/4	—	13/32	—	—	.275	.450	11/16
1974	7044202, 7044502	1/4	—	13/32	—	.430	.230	.450	7/8
	7044203, 7044503	1/4	—	13/32	—	.430	.230	.450	7/8
	7044218, 7044518	1/4	—	13/32	—	.430	.215	.450	7/8
	7044219, 7044519	1/4	—	13/32	—	.430	.215	.450	7/8
	7044213, 7044513	11/32	—	13/32	—	.430	.215	.450	7/8
	7044223, 7044227	.675	—	13/32	—	.430	.220	.450	7/16
	7044212, 7044217	.675	—	13/32	—	.430	.230	.450	7/16
	7044512, 7044517	.675	—	13/32	—	.430	.230	.450	7/16
	7044500, 7044520	.675	—	13/32	—	.430	.250	.450	7/16
	7044224	11/32	—	13/32	—	.430	.215	.450	7/8
	7044214, 7044514	11/32	—	13/32	—	.430	.215	.450	7/8
	7044215, 7044515	11/32	—	13/32	—	.430	.215	.450	7/8
	7044216, 7044516	11/32	—	13/32	—	.430	.215	.450	7/8
1975	7045212	3/8	.015	.275	Inner	.430	.225	.450	7/16
	7045213	11/32	.015	.275	Inner	.430	.210	.450	7/8
	7045214	11/32	.015	.275	Inner	.430	.215	.450	7/8
	7045215	11/32	.015	.275	Inner	.430	.215	.450	7/8
	7045216	11/32	.015	.275	Inner	.430	.210	.450	7/8
	7045217	3/8	.015	.275	Inner	.430	.225	.450	7/16
	7045225	11/32	.015	.275	Inner	.430	.200	.450	3/4
	7045229	15/32	.015	.275	Inner	.430	.200	.450	3/4
	7045583	11/32	.015	.275	Inner	.430	.230	.450	7/8
	7045584	11/32	.015	.275	Inner	.430	.230	.450	7/8
	7045585	11/32	.015	.275	Inner	.430	.230	.450	7/8
	7045586	11/32	.015	.275	Inner	.430	.230	.450	7/8
	7045588	11/32	.015	.275	Inner	.430	.230	.450	3/4
	7045589	11/32	.015	.275	Inner	.430	.230	.450	3/4
	7045202	15/32	.015	.275	Inner	.300	.180/.170	.325	7/8
	7045203	15/32	.015	.275	Inner	.300	.180/.170	.325	7/8
	7045218	15/32	.015	.275	Inner	.325	.180/.170	.352	3/4
	7045219	15/32	.015	.275	Inner	.325	.180/.170	.352	3/4
	7045220	17/32	.015	.275	Inner	.300	.200/.550	.325	9/16
	7045512	17/32	.015	.275	Inner	.300	.180/.550	.325	9/16
	7045517	17/32	.015	.275	Inner	.300	.180/.550	.325	9/16

MODEL M4MC/4MV
QUADRAJET FOUR BARREL (Cont'd)

(All measurements in inches)

Chevrolet

Year	Model or Type	Float Level	Air Valve Dashpot	PUMP ROD Adj.	PUMP ROD Hole	Initial Choke Valve Opening	Vacuum Break	Choke Unloader	Air Valve Spring Wind-up
1976	7045213	11/32	.015	9/32	Inner	.290	.145	.295	7/8
	7045214	11/32	.015	9/32	Inner	.290	.145	.295	7/8
	7045215	11/32	.015	9/32	Inner	.290	.145	.295	7/8
	7045216	11/32	.015	9/32	Inner	.290	.145	.295	7/8
	7045225	11/32	.015	9/32	Inner	.290	.138	.295	3/4
	7045229	11/32	.015	9/32	Inner	.290	.138	.295	3/4
	7045583	11/32	.015	9/32	Inner	.290	.155	.295	7/8
	7045584	11/32	.015	9/32	Inner	.290	.155	.295	7/8
	7045585	11/32	.015	9/32	Inner	.290	.155	.295	7/8
	7045586	11/32	.015	9/32	Inner	.290	.155	.295	7/8
	7045588	11/32	.015	9/32	Inner	.290	.155	.295	3/4
	7045589	11/32	.015	9/32	Inner	.290	.155	.295	3/4
	17056212	3/8	.015	9/32	Inner	.290	.155	.295	7/16
	17056217	3/8	.015	9/32	Inner	.290	.155	.295	7/16
	17056208	3	.015	9/32	Inner	.325	.185	.325	7/8
	17056209	3	.015	9/32	Inner	.325	.185	.325	7/8
	17056218	5/16	.015	9/32	Inner	.325	.185	.325	7/8
	17056219	5/16	.015	9/32	Inner	.325	.185	.325	7/8
	17056508	3	.015	9/32	Inner	.325	.185	.325	7/8
	17056509	3	.015	9/32	Inner	.325	.185	.325	7/8
	17056512	7/16	.015	9/32	Inner	.325	.185	.275	7/8
	17056517	7/16	.015	9/32	Inner	.325	.185	.275	7/8
	17056518	5/16	.015	9/32	Inner	.325	.185	.325	7/8
	17056519	5/16	.015	9/32	Inner	.325	.185	.325	7/8
1977	17057202	15/32	.015	9/32	Inner	.325	.160	.280	7/8
	17057204	15/32	.015	9/32	Inner	.325	.160	.280	7/8
	17057502	15/32	.015	9/32	Inner	.325	.165	.280	7/8
	17057582	15/32	.015	3/8	Outer	.325	.182	.280	7/8
	17057584	15/32	.015	3/8	Outer	.325	.180	.280	7/8
	17057503	15/32	.015	9/32	Inner	.325	.165	.280	7/8
	17057504	15/32	.015	9/32	Inner	.325	.165	.280	7/8
	17057209	7/16	.015	9/32	Inner	.325	——	.325	7/8
	17057218	7/16	.015	9/32	Inner	.325	.160	.280	7/8
	17057222	7/16	.015	9/32	Inner	.325	.160	.280	7/8
	17057518	7/16	.015	9/32	Inner	.325	.165	.280	7/8
	17057522	7/16	.015	9/32	Inner	.325	.165	.280	7/8
	17057586	7/16	.015	3/8	Outer	.325	.180	.295	7/8
	17057588	7/16	.015	3/8	Outer	.325	.180	.280	7/8
	17057219	7/16	.015	9/32	Inner	.325	.165	.280	7/8
	17057519	7/16	.015	9/32	Inner	.325	.165	.280	7/8
	17057512	7/16	.015	9/32	Inner	.325	.165	.240	7/8
	17057517	7/16	.015	9/32	Inner	.325	.165	.240	7/16
	17056212	3/8	.015	9/32	Inner	.290	.120	.295	7/16
	17057221	3/8	.015	9/32	Inner	.325	——/.160	.325	7/8
	17056217	3/8	.015	9/32	Inner	.290	.120	.295	7/16
	17057213	11/32	.015	9/32	Inner	.285	.115	.205	7/8
	17057215	11/32	.015	9/32	Inner	.285	.115	.205	7/8
	17057216	11/32	.015	9/32	Inner	.285	.115	.205	7/8
	17057525	11/32	.015	9/32	Inner	.285	.120	.225	3/4
	17057514	11/32	.015	9/32	Inner	.285	.120	.280	7/8
	17507529	11/32	.015	9/32	Inner	.285	.110	.205	7/8
	17057229	11/32	.015	9/32	Inner	.285	.110	.205	7/8
	7045583	11/32	.015	9/32	Inner	.285	.120	.295	7/8
	7045585	11/32	.015	9/32	Inner	.285	.120	.295	7/8
	7045586	11/32	.015	3/8	Outer	.285	.120	.295	7/8

MODEL M4MC/4MV
QUADRAJET FOUR BARREL (Cont'd)

Chevrolet

(All measurements in inches)

Year	Model or Type	Float Level	Air Valve Dashpot	PUMP ROD Adj.	PUMP ROD Hole	Initial Choke Valve Opening	Vacuum Break	Choke Unloader	Air Valve Spring Wind-up
1978	17058201	15/32	.015	9/32	Inner	.314	.168	.277	7/8
	17058213	15/32	.015	9/32	Inner	.217	.095	.204	7/8
	17058215	15/32	.015	9/32	Inner	.217	.095	.204	7/8
	17058229	15/32	.015	9/32	Inner	.217	.095	.204	7/8
	17058503	15/32	.015	9/32	Inner	.217	.179	.277	7/8
	17058506	15/32	.015	9/32	Inner	.314	.179	.277	7/8
	17058508	15/32	.015	9/32	Inner	.314	.179	.277	7/8
	17058509	15/32	.015	11/32	Outer	.314	.179	.277	7/8
	17058510	15/32	.015	11/32	Outer	.314	.179	.277	7/8
	17058513	15/32	.015	9/32	Inner	.314	.120	.225	7/8
	17058514	15/32	.015	9/32	Inner	.217	.120	.225	7/8
	17058515	15/32	.015	9/32	Inner	.217	.120	.225	7/8
	17058518	15/32	.015	9/32	Inner	.217	.179	.277	7/8
	17058519	15/32	.015	9/32	Inner	.314	.179	.277	7/8
	17058522	15/32	.015	9/32	Inner	.314	.179	.277	7/8
	17058523	15/32	.015	9/32	Inner	.314	.179	.277	7/8
	17058524	15/32	.015	9/32	Inner	.314	.179	.277	7/8
	17058527	15/32	.015	9/32	Inner	.314	.179	.277	7/8
	17058528	15/32	.015	9/32	Inner	.314	.179	.277	7/8
	17058529	15/32	.015	9/32	Inner	.314	.112	.277	7/8
	17058586	15/32	.015	11/32	Outer	.314	.179	.277	7/8
	17058588	15/32	.015	11/32	Outer	.314	.179	.277	7/8
	17058212	7/16	.015	9/32	Inner	.217	.120	.225	7/8
	17058218	7/16	.015	9/32	Inner	.314	.157	.277	7/8
	17058219	7/16	.015	9/32	Inner	.314	.168	.277	7/8
	17058222	7/16	.015	9/32	Inner	.314	.157	.277	7/8
	17058525	7/16	.015	9/32	Inner	.314	.120	.277	3/4
	17058501	3/8	.015	9/32	Inner	.314	.164	.277	7/8
	17058520	3/8	.015	9/32	Inner	.314	.164	.277	7/8
	17058521	3/8	.015	9/32	Inner	.314	.164	.277	7/8
	17058512	13/32	.015	9/32	Index	.314	.168	.260	7/8
1979	17059212	7/16	.015	9/32	Inner	.314	.136	.260	3/4
	17059512	13/32	.015	9/32	Inner	.314	.136	.260	3/4
	17059061	15/32	.015	13/32	Inner	.314	.129	.277	7/8
	17059201	15/32	.015	13/32	Inner	.314	.129	.277	7/8
	17059065	15/32	.015	13/32	Inner	.314	.129	.277	7/8
	17059205	15/32	.015	13/32	Inner	.314	.129	.277	7/8
	17059066	15/32	.015	13/32	Inner	.314	.129	.277	7/8
	17059206	15/32	.015	13/32	Inner	.314	.129	.277	7/8
	17059068	15/32	.015	13/32	Inner	.314	.129	.277	7/8
	17059208	15/32	.015	13/32	Inner	.314	.129	.277	7/8
	17059069	15/32	.015	13/32	Inner	.314	.129	.277	7/8
	17059209	15/32	.015	13/32	Inner	.314	.129	.277	7/8
	17059076	15/32	.015	13/32	Inner	.314	.129	.277	7/8
	17059226	15/32	.015	13/32	Inner	.314	.129	.277	7/8
	17059077	15/32	.015	13/32	Inner	.314	.129	.277	7/8
	17059227	15/32	.015	13/32	Inner	.314	.129	.277	7/8
	17059213	15/32	.015	9/32	Inner	.234	.129	.260	1
	17059215	15/32	.015	9/32	Inner	.234	.129	.260	1
	17059363	15/32	.015	13/32	Inner	.314	.149	.277	7/8
	17059503	15/32	.015	13/32	Inner	.314	.149	.277	7/8
	17059506	15/32	.015	13/32	Inner	.314	.149	.277	7/8
	17059506	15/32	.015	13/32	Inner	.314	.149	.277	7/8
	17059368	15/32	.015	13/32	Inner	.314	.149	.277	7/8

QUADRAJET FOUR BARREL (Cont'd)

(All measurements in inches)

Chevrolet

Year	Model or Type	Float Level	Air Valve Dashpot	Pump Rod Adj.	Pump Rod Hole	Initial Choke Valve Opening	Vacuum Break	Choke Unloader	Air Valve Spring Wind-up
	17059508	15/32	.015	13/32	Inner	.314	.149	.277	7/8
	17059377	15/32	.015	9/32	Outer	.314	.149	.277	7/8
	17059527	15/32	.015	9/32	Outer	.314	.149	.277	7/8
	17059378	15/32	.015	9/32	Outer	.314	.149	.277	7/8
	17059528	15/32	.015	9/32	Outer	.314	.149	.277	7/8
	17059509	15/32	.015	13/32	Inner	.314	.179	.277	7/8
	17059515	15/32	.015	9/32	Inner	.234	.129	.260	1
	17059510	15/32	.015	9/32	Inner	.314	.179	.277	7/8
	17059529	15/32	.015	9/32	Inner	.234	.129	.260	1
	17059513	15/32	.015	9/32	Inner	.234	.129	.260	1
	17059586	15/32	.015	13/32	Inner	.314	.179	.277	7/8
	17059588	15/32	.015	13/32	Inner	.314	.179	.277	7/8
	17059229	15/32	.015	9/32	Inner	.234	.129	.260	1
	17059520	3/8	.015	9/32	Inner	.324	.164	.277	7/8
	17059521	3/8	.015	9/32	Inner	.314	.164	.277	7/8

MODEL 2GV

(All measurements in inches)

GMC

Year	Carburetor Number	Float Level	Float Drop	Choke Unloader Setting	Choke Setting	Pump Rod Location	Fast Idle Speed (RPM)	Metering Rod Setting	Fast Idle Cam 2nd Step	Choke Vacuum Break
1973	7043105	21/32	1 9/32	.215	Fixed	1 5/16	—	—	.150	.080
	7043103	21/32	1 9/32	.215	Fixed	1 5/16	—	—	.150	.080
	7043108	25/32	1 9/32	.250	Fixed	1 5/16	—	—	.150	.140
	7043123	23/32	1 9/32	—	Fixed	1 7/16	—	—	—	—
	7043124	23/32	1 9/32	—	Fixed	1 7/16	—	—	—	—
	7043424	23/32	1 9/32	—	Fixed	1 7/16	—	—	—	—
	7047796	23/32	1 9/32	—	Fixed	1 7/16	—	—	—	—
1974	7044011	1/4	—	—	Fixed	—	1600	.070	.150	—
	7044012	1/4	—	—	Fixed	—	1600	.070	.150	—
	7044133	19/32	1 9/32	—	Fixed	1 9/16	1600	—	—	—
	7044134	19/32	1 9/32	—	Fixed	1 7/16	1600	—	—	—
	7044434	19/32	1 9/32	—	Fixed	1 7/16	1600	—	—	—
	7044113	19/32	1 9/32	.250	Fixed	1 9/32	1600	.200	—	.140
	7044114	19/32	1 9/32	.325	Fixed	1 3/16	1600	.245	—	.130
	7044123	19/32	1 9/32	.250	Fixed	1 9/32	1600	.200	—	.140
	7044124	19/32	1 9/32	.325	Fixed	1 3/16	1600	.245	—	.130
1975	7045115	21/32	31/32	.350	Index	1 5/8	—	—	.400	.130
	7045116	21/32	31/32	.350	Index	1 5/8	—	—	.400	.130
	7045123	21/32	31/32	.350	Index	1 5/8	—	—	.400	.130
	7045124	21/32	31/32	.350	Index	1 5/8	—	—	.400	.130
	7044133	19/32	1 9/32	—	Manual	1 9/16	—	—	—	—
	7044134	19/32	1 9/32	—	Manual	1 7/16	—	—	—	—
	7044434	19/32	1 9/32	—	Manual	1 7/16	—	—	—	—
1976	7044133	19/32	1 9/32	—	—	1 9/16	—	—	—	—
	7044134	19/32	1 9/32	—	—	1 7/16	—	—	—	—
	704434	19/32	1 9/32	—	—	1 7/16	—	—	—	—
	17056115	21/32	1 9/32	.325	Index	1 11/16	—	—	.260	.130
	17056116	21/32	1 9/32	.325	1 Rich	1 11/16	—	—	.260	.130
	17056123	21/32	1 9/32	.325	Index	1 11/16	—	—	.260	.130
	17056124	21/32	1 9/32	.325	1 Rich	1 11/16	—	—	.260	.130
1977	7044133	19/32	1 9/32	.325	Index	1 21/32	—	—	.260	.130
	7044134	19/32	1 9/32	.325	Index	1 21/32	—	—	.260	.130
	17056433	19/32	1 9/32	.325	Index	1 21/32	—	—	.260	.130
	17056434	19/32	1 9/32	.325	Index	1 21/32	—	—	.260	.130
	17056137	19/32	1 9/32	.325	Index	1 21/32	—	—	.260	.190

MODEL 2G

(All measurements in inches)

GMC, Continued

Year	Carburetor Number	Float Level	Float Drop	Choke Unloader Setting	Choke Setting	Pump Rod Location	Fast Idle Speed (RPM)	Metering Rod Setting	Fast Idle Cam 2nd Step	Choke Vacuum Break
1978	7044133	19/32	1 9/32	—	—	1 9/16	—	—	—	—
	7044134	19/32	1 9/32	—	—	1 7/16	—	—	—	—
	17058423	19/32	1 9/32	—	—	1 7/16	—	—	—	—
	17058434	19/32	1 9/32	—	—	1 7/16	—	—	—	—
1979	17059126	5/8	1 9/32	—	—	1 15/32	—	—	—	—
	17059127	17/32	1 9/32	—	—	1 15/32	—	—	—	—
	17059120	17/32	1 9/32	—	—	1 15/32	—	—	—	—
	17059423	5/8	1 9/32	—	—	1 21/32	—	—	—	—
	17059424	17/32	1 9/32	—	—	1 15/32	—	—	—	—
	17059420	17/32	1 9/32	—	—	1 15/32	—	—	—	—

MODEL MV

(All measurements in inches)

GMC

Year	Carburetor Number	Float Level	Float Drop	Choke Unloader Setting	Choke Setting	Pump Rod Location	Fast Idle Speed (RPM)	Metering Rod Setting	Fast Idle Cam 2nd Step	Choke Vacuum Break
1973	7043022	1/4	—	.500	Fixed	—	—	.080	.245	.300
	7043021	1/4	—	.500	Fixed	—	—	.080	.275	.350
	7043025	1/4	—	.500	Fixed	—	—	.070	.250	.430
	7043026	1/4	—	.500	Fixed	—	—	.070	.375	.430
	7043326	1/4	—	.500	Fixed	—	—	.070	.375	.430
	7043009	1/4	—	—	—	—	1800-2400	.070	—	—
	7043012	1/4	—	—	—	—	1800-2400	.070	—	—
	7043312	1/4	—	—	—	—	1800-2400	.070	—	—
1974	7044021	.295	—	.500	Fixed	—	1800	.080	.275	.350
	7044022	.295	—	.500	Fixed	—	1800	.080	.245	.300
	7044321	.295	—	.500	Fixed	—	1800	.080	.300	.375
	7044025	1/4	—	.521	Fixer	—	2400	.070	.245	.300
	7044026	1/4	—	.521	Fixed	—	2400	.070	.275	.350

MODEL IMV

(All measurements in inches)

GMC

Year	Carburetor Number	Float Level	Float Drop	Choke Unloader Setting	Choke Setting	Pump Rod Location	Fast Idle Speed (RPM)	Metering Rod Setting	Fast Idle Cam 2nd Step	Choke Vacuum Break
1975	7045002	11/32	—	.325	Fixed	—	1800	.080	.260	①
	7045003	11/32	—	.325	Fixed	—	1800	.080	.275	①
	7045004	11/32	—	.325	Fixed	—	1800	.080	.245	①
	7045005	11/32	—	.325	Fixed	—	1800	.080	.275	②
	7045302	11/32	—	.275	Fixed	—	1800	.080	.245	①
	7045303	11/32	—	.275	Fixed	—	1800	.080	.275	②
	7045304	11/32	—	.325	Fixed	—	1800	.080	.245	①
	7045305	11/32	—	.325	Fixed	—	1800	.080	.275	②

MODEL IMV

(All measurements in inches)

GMC, Continued

Year	Carburetor Number	Float Level	Float Drop	Choke Unloader Setting	Choke Setting	Pump Rod Location	Fast Idle Speed (RPM)	Metering Rod Setting	Fast Idle Cam 2nd Step	Choke Vacuum Break
1976	17056002	11/32	—	.335	Fixed	—	2100	.080	.130	③
	17056003	11/32	—	.335	Fixed	—	2100	.080	.145	.180
	17056004	11/32	—	.335	Fixed	—	2100	.080	.130	③
	17056006	1/4	—	.270	Fixed	—	2100	.080	.130	.165
	17056007	1/4	—	.275	Fixed	—	2100	.070	.130	.165
	17056008	1/4	—	.275	Fixed	—	2100	.070	.150	.190
	17056009	1/4	—	.275	Fixed	—	2100	.080	.150	.190
	17056302	11/32	—	.325	Fixed	—	2100	.080	.155	.190
	17056303	11/32	—	.325	Fixed	—	2100	.080	.150	.225
	17056308	1/4	—	.275	Fixed	—	2100	.070	.150	.190
	17056309	1/4	—	.275	Fixed	—	2100	.070	.150	.190

① Primary—.300
Secondary—.325
② Primary—.350
Secondary—.325
③ Primary—.165
Auxiliary—.265

MODEL IME

(All measurements in inches)

GMC

Year	Carburetor Number	Float Level	Float Drop	Choke Unloader Setting	Choke Setting	Pump Rod Location	Fast Idle Speed (RPM)	Metering Rod Setting	Fast Idle Cam 2nd Step	Choke Vacuum Break
1977	17057001	3/8	—	.325	Index	—	2100	.080	.125	.150
	17057002	3/8	—	.325	Index	—	2100	.080	.110	.135
	17057004	3/8	—	.325	Index	—	2100	.080	.110	.135
	17057005	3/8	—	.325	Index	—	2100	.080	.125	.180
	17057010	3/8	—	.325	Index	—	2100	.080	.110	.180
	17057302	3/8	—	.325	Index	—	2100	.080	.150	.135
	17057303	3/8	—	.325	Index	—	2100	.090	.125	.150
	17057006	5/16	—	.275	Index	—	2400	.070	.150	.180
	17057007	5/16	—	.275	Index	—	2400	.070	.150	.180
	17057008	5/16	—	.275	Index	—	2400	.065	.150	.180
	17057009	5/16	—	.275	Index	—	2400	.065	.150	.180
	17057308	5/16	—	.275	Index	—	2400	.065	.150	.180
	17057309	5/16	—	.275	Index	—	2400	.065	.150	.180

MODEL ME, M

(All measurements in inches)

GMC

Year	Carburetor Number	Float Level	Float Drop	Choke Unloader Setting	Choke Setting	Pump Rod Location	Fast Idle Speed (RPM)	Metering Rod Setting	Fast Idle Cam 2nd Step	Choke Vacuum Break
1978	17058009	1/4	—	—	—	—	2400	.065	.150	—
	17058011	1/4	—	—	—	—	2400	.065	.150	—
1979	17059009	5/16	—	.520	2 Rich	—	2400	.090	.275	.400

MODEL M4MC/4MV
QUADRAJET FOUR BARREL

GMC

(All measurements in inches)

Year	Model or Type	Float Level	Air Valve Dashpot	PUMP ROD Adj.	PUMP ROD Hole	Initial Choke Valve Opening	Vacuum Break	Choke Unloader	Air Valve Spring Wind-up
1973	7043202	7/32	—	13/32	—	—	.215	.450	1/2
	7043203	7/32	—	13/32	—	—	.215	.450	1/2
	7043210	7/32	—	13/32	—	—	.215	.450	1/2
	7043211	7/32	—	13/32	—	—	.215	.450	1/2
	7043208	5/16	—	13/32	—	—	.215	.450	1/2
	7043215	5/16	—	13/32	—	—	.215	.450	1/2
	7043200	1/4	—	13/32	—	—	.250	.450	11/16
	7043216	1/4	—	13/32	—	—	.250	.450	11/16
	7043207	1/4	—	13/32	—	—	.250	.450	11/16
	7043507	1/4	—	13/32	—	—	.275	.450	11/16
1974	7044202, 7044502	1/4	—	13/32	—	.430	.230	.450	7/8
	7044203, 7044503	1/4	—	13/32	—	.430	.230	.450	7/8
	7044218, 7044518	1/4	—	13/32	—	.430	.215	.450	7/8
	7044219, 7044519	1/4	—	13/32	—	.430	.215	.450	7/8
	7044213, 7044513	11/32	—	13/32	—	.430	.215	.450	7/8
	7044223, 7044227	.675	—	13/32	—	.430	.220	.450	7/16
	7044212, 7044217	.675	—	13/32	—	.430	.230	.450	7/16
	7044512, 7044517	.675	—	13/32	—	.430	.230	.450	7/16
	7044500, 7044520	.675	—	13/32	—	.430	.250	.450	7/16
	7044224	11/32	—	13/32	—	.430	.215	.450	7/8
	7044214 7044514	11/32	—	13/32	—	.430	.215	.450	7/8
	7044215, 7044515	11/32	—	13/32	—	.430	.215	.450	7/8
	7044216, 7044516	11/32	—	13/32	—	.430	.215	.450	7/8
1975	7045212	3/8	.015	.275	Inner	.430	.225	.450	7/16
	7045213	11/32	.015	.275	Inner	.430	.210	.450	7/8
	7045214	11/32	.015	.275	Inner	.430	.215	.450	7/8
	7045215	11/32	.015	.275	Inner	.430	.215	.450	7/8
	7045216	11/32	.015	.275	Inner	.430	.210	.450	7/8
	7045217	3/8	.015	.275	Inner	.430	.225	.450	7/16
	7045225	11/32	.015	.275	Inner	.430	.200	.450	3/4
	7045229	15/32	.015	.275	Inner	.430	.200	.450	3/4
	7045583	11/32	.015	.275	Inner	.430	.230	.450	7/8
	7045584	11/32	.015	.275	Inner	.430	.230	.450	7/8
	7045585	11/32	.015	.275	Inner	.430	.230	.450	7/8
	7045586	11/32	.015	.275	Inner	.430	.230	.450	7/8
	7045588	11/32	.015	.275	Inner	.430	.230	.450	3/4
	7045589	11/32	.015	.275	Inner	.430	.230	.450	3/4
	7045202	15/32	.015	.275	Inner	.300	.180/.170[2]	.325	7/8
	7045203	15/32	.015	.275	Inner	.300	.180/.170[2]	.325	7/8
	7045218	15/32	.015	.275	Inner	.325	.180/.170[2]	.325	3/4
	7045219	15/32	.015	.275	Inner	.325	.180/.170[2]	.325	3/4
	7045220	17/32	.015	.275	Inner	.300	.200/.550[2]	.325	9/16
	7045512	17/32	.015	.275	Inner	.300	.180/.550[2]	.325	9/16
	7045517	17/32	.015	.275	Inner	.300	.180/.550[2]	.325	9/16

MODEL M4MC/4MV
QUADRAJET FOUR BARREL (Cont'd)

GMC, Continued

(All measurements in inches)

Year	Model or Type	Float Level	Air Valve Dashpot	PUMP ROD Adj.	PUMP ROD Hole	Initial Choke Valve Opening	Vacuum Break	Choke Unloader	Air Valve Spring Wind-up
1976	7045213	11/32	.015	9/32	Inner	.290	.145	.295	7/8
	7045214	11/32	.015	9/32	Inner	.290	.145	.295	7/8
	7045215	11/32	.015	9/32	Inner	.290	.145	.295	7/8
	7045216	11/32	.015	9/32	Inner	.290	.145	.295	7/8
	7045225	11/32	.015	9/32	Inner	.290	.138	.295	3/4
	7045229	11/32	.015	9/32	Inner	.290	.138	.295	3/4
	7045583	11/32	.015	9/32	Inner	.290	.155	.295	7/8
	7045584	11/32	.015	9/32	Inner	.290	.155	.295	7/8
	7045585	11/32	.015	9/32	Inner	.290	.155	.295	7/8
	7045586	11/32	.015	9/32	Inner	.290	.155	.295	7/8
	7045588	11/32	.015	9/32	Inner	.290	.155	.295	3/4
	7045589	11/32	.015	9/32	Inner	.290	.155	.295	3/4
	17056212	3/8	.015	9/32	Inner	.290	.155	.295	7/16
	17056217	3/8	.015	9/32	Inner	.290	.155	.295	7/16
	17056208	3	.015	9/32	Inner	.325	.185	.325	7/8
	17056209	3	.015	9/32	Inner	.325	.185	.325	7/8
	17056218	5/16	.015	9/32	Inner	.325	.185	.325	7/8
	17056219	5/16	.015	9/32	Inner	.325	.185	.325	7/8
	17056508	3	.015	9/32	Inner	.325	.185	.325	7/8
	17056509	3	.015	9/32	Inner	.325	.185	.325	7/8
	17056512	7/16	.015	9/32	Inner	.325	.185	.275	7/8
	17056517	7/16	.015	9/32	Inner	.325	.185	.275	7/8
	17056518	5/16	.015	9/32	Inner	.325	.185	.325	7/8
	17056519	5/16	.015	9/32	Inner	.325	.185	.325	7/8
1977-78	17057202	15/32	.015	9/32	Inner	.325	.160	.280	7/8
	17057204	15/32	.015	9/32	Inner	.325	.160	.280	7/8
	17057502	15/32	.015	9/32	Inner	.325	.165	.280	7/8
	17057582	15/32	.015	3/8	Outer	.325	.182	.280	7/8
	17057584	15/32	.015	3/8	Outer	.325	.180	.280	7/8
	17057503	15/32	.015	9/32	Inner	.325	.165	.280	7/8
	17057504	15/32	.015	9/32	Inner	.325	.165	.280	7/8
	17057209	7/16	.015	9/32	Inner	.325	—	.335	7/8
	17057218	7/16	.015	9/32	Inner	.325	.160	.280	7/8
	17057222	7/16	.015	9/32	Inner	.325	.160	.280	7/8
	17057518	7/16	.015	9/32	Inner	.325	.165	.280	7/8
	17057522	7/16	.015	9/32	Inner	.325	.165	.280	7/8
	17057586	7/16	.015	3/8	Outer	.325	.180	.295	7/8
	17057588	7/16	.015	3/8	Outer	.325	.180	.280	7/8
	17057219	7/16	.015	9/32	Inner	.325	.165	.280	7/8
	17057519	7/16	.015	9/32	Inner	.325	.165	.280	7/8
	17057512	7/16	.015	9/32	Inner	.325	.165	.240	7/8
	17057517	7/16	.015	9/32	Inner	.325	.165	.240	7/16
	17056212	3/8	.015	9/32	Inner	.290	.120	.295	7/16
	17057221	3/8	.015	9/32	Inner	.325	—/.160	.325	7/8
	17056217	3/8	.015	9/32	Inner	.290	.120	.295	7/16
	17057213	11/32	.015	9/32	Inner	.285	.115	.205	7/8
	17057215	11/32	.015	9/32	Inner	.285	.115	.205	7/8
	17057216	11/32	.015	9/32	Inner	.285	.115	.205	7/8
	17057525	11/32	.015	9/32	Inner	.285	.120	.225	3/4
	17057514	11/32	.015	9/32	Inner	.285	.120	.280	7/8
	17057529	11/32	.015	9/32	Inner	.285	.110	.205	7/8
	17057229	11/32	.015	9/32	Inner	.285	.110	.205	7/8
	7045583	11/32	.015	9/32	Inner	.285	.120	.295	7/8
	7045585	11/32	.015	9/32	Inner	.285	.120	.295	7/8
	7045586	11/32	.015	3/8	Outer	.285	.120	.295	7/8

MODEL M4MC/4MV
QUADRAJET FOUR BARREL (Cont'd)

GMC, Continued

(All measurements in inches)

Year	Model or Type	Float Level	Air Valve Dashpot	PUMP ROD Adj.	PUMP ROD Hole	Initial Choke Valve Opening	Vacuum Break	Choke Unloader	Air Valve Spring Wind-up
1978	17058201	15/32	.015	9/32	Inner	.314	.168	.277	7/8
	17058213	15/32	.015	9/32	Inner	.217	.095	.204	7/8
	17058215	15/32	.015	9/32	Inner	.217	.095	.204	7/8
	17058229	15/32	.015	9/32	Inner	.217	.095	.204	7/8
	17058503	15/32	.015	9/32	Inner	.217	.179	.277	7/8
	17058506	15/32	.015	9/32	Inner	.314	.179	.277	7/8
	17058508	15/32	.015	9/32	Inner	.314	.179	.277	7/8
	17058509	15/32	.015	11/32	Outer	.314	.179	.277	7/8
	17058510	15/32	.015	11/32	Outer	.314	.179	.277	7/8
	17058513	15/32	.015	9/32	Inner	.314	.120	.225	7/8
	17058514	15/32	.015	9/32	Inner	.217	.120	.225	7/8
	17058515	15/32	.015	9/32	Inner	.217	.120	.225	7/8
	17058518	15/32	.015	9/32	Inner	.217	.179	.277	7/8
	17058519	15/32	.015	9/32	Inner	.314	.179	.277	7/8
	17058522	15/32	.015	9/32	Inner	.314	.179	.277	7/8
	17058523	15/32	.015	9/32	Inner	.314	.179	.277	7/8
	17058524	15/32	.015	9/32	Inner	.314	.179	.277	7/8
	17058527	15/32	.015	9/32	Inner	.314	.179	.277	7/8
	17058528	15/32	.015	9/32	Inner	.314	.179	.277	7/8
	17058529	15/32	.015	9/32	Inner	.314	.112	.277	7/8
	17058586	15/32	.015	11/32	Outer	.314	.179	.277	7/8
	17058588	15/32	.015	11/32	Outer	.314	.179	.277	7/8
	17058212	7/16	.015	9/32	Inner	.217	.120	.225	7/8
	17058218	7/16	.015	9/32	Inner	.314	.157	.277	7/8
	17058219	7/16	.015	9/32	Inner	.314	.168	.277	7/8
	17058222	7/16	.015	9/32	Inner	.314	.157	.277	7/8
	17058525	7/16	.015	9/32	Inner	.314	.120	.277	3/4
	17058501	3/8	.015	9/32	Inner	.314	.164	.277	7/8
	17058520	3/8	.015	9/32	Inner	.314	.164	.277	7/8
	17058521	3/8	.015	9/32	Inner	.314	.164	.277	7/8
	17058512	13/32	.015	9/32	Inner	.314	.168	.260	7/8
1979	17059212	7/16	.015	9/32	Inner	.314	.136	.260	3/4
	17059512	13/32	.015	9/32	Inner	.314	.136	.260	3/4
	17059061	15/32	.015	13/32	Inner	.314	.129	.277	7/8
	17059201	15/32	.015	13/32	Inner	.314	.129	.277	7/8
	17059065	15/32	.015	13/32	Inner	.314	.129	.277	7/8
	17059205	15/32	.015	13/32	Inner	.314	.129	.277	7/8
	17059066	15/32	.015	13/32	Inner	.314	.129	.277	7/8
	17059206	15/32	.015	13/32	Inner	.314	.129	.277	7/8
	17059068	15/32	.015	13/32	Inner	.314	.129	.277	7/8
	17059208	15/32	.015	13/32	Inner	.314	.129	.277	7/8
	17059069	15/32	.015	13/32	Inner	.314	.129	.277	7/8
	17059209	15/32	.015	13/32	Inner	.314	.129	.277	7/8
	17059076	15/32	.015	13/32	Inner	.314	.129	.277	7/8
	17059226	15/32	.015	13/32	Inner	.314	.129	.277	7/8
	17059077	15/32	.015	13/32	Inner	.314	.129	.277	7/8
	17059227	15/32	.015	13/32	Inner	.314	.129	.277	7/8
	17059213	15/32	.015	9/32	Inner	.234	.129	.260	1
	17059215	15/32	.015	9/32	Inner	.234	.129	.260	1
	17059363	15/32	.015	13/32	Inner	.314	.149	.277	7/8
	17059503	15/32	.015	13/32	Inner	.314	.149	.277	7/8
	17059366	15/32	.015	13/32	Inner	.314	.149	.277	7/8
	17059506	15/32	.015	13/32	Inner	.314	.149	.277	7/8
	17059368	15/32	.015	13/32	Inner	.314	.149	.277	7/8

MODEL M4MC/4MV
QUADRAJET FOUR BARREL (Cont'd)

(All measurements in inches)

GMC, Continued

Year	Model or Type	Float Level	Air Valve Dashpot	Pump Rod Adj.	Pump Rod Hole	Initial Choke Valve Opening	Vacuum Break	Choke Unloader	Air Valve Spring Wind-up
	17059508	15/32	.015	13/32	Inner	.314	.149	.277	7/8
	17059377	15/32	.015	9/32	Outer	.314	.149	.277	7/8
	17059527	15/32	.015	9/32	Outer	.314	.149	.277	7/8
	17059378	15/32	.015	9/32	Outer	.314	.149	.277	7/8
	17059528	15/32	.015	9/32	Outer	.314	.149	.277	7/8
	17059509	15/32	.015	13/32	Inner	.314	.179	.277	7/8
	17059515	15/32	.015	9/32	Inner	.234	.129	.260	1
	17059510	15/32	.015	9/32	Inner	.314	.179	.277	7/8
	17059529	15/32	.015	9/32	Inner	.234	.129	.260	1
	17059513	15/32	.015	9/32	Inner	.234	.129	.260	1
	17059586	15/32	.015	13/32	Inner	.314	.179	.277	7/8
	17059588	15/32	.015	13/32	Inner	.314	.179	.277	7/8
	17059229	15/32	.015	9/32	Inner	.234	.129	.260	1
	17059520	3/8	.015	9/32	Inner	.314	.164	.277	7/8
	17059521	3/8	.015	9/32	Inner	.314	.164	.277	7/8

MODEL 2G

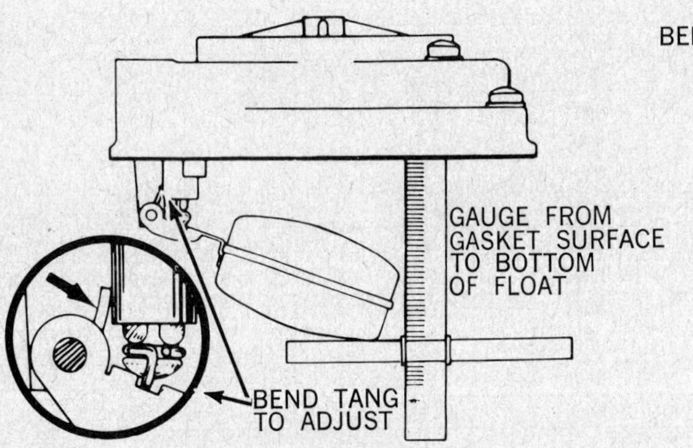

Float drop adjustment

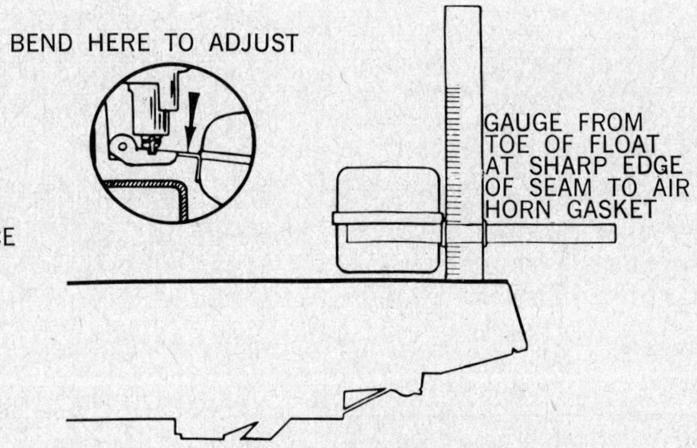

Float level adjustment

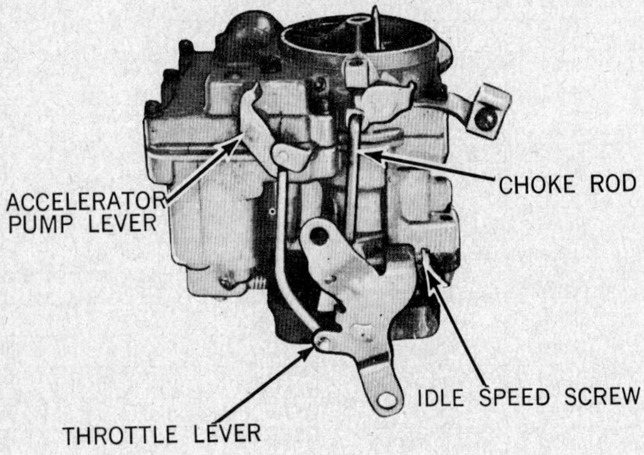

Rochester model 2G carburetor

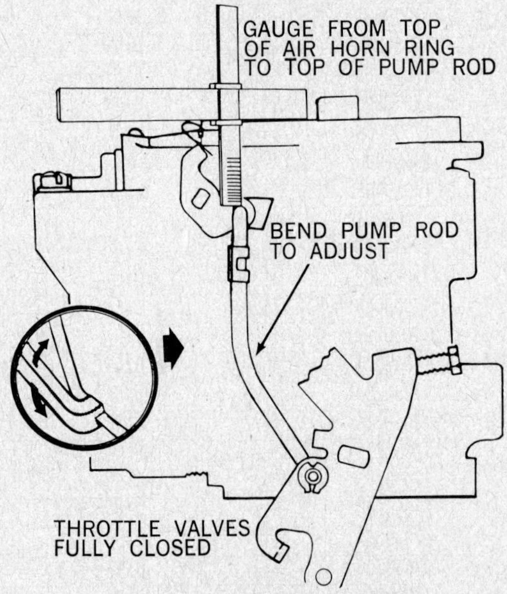

Accelerator pump rod adjustment

ROCHESTER MODELS M AND MV

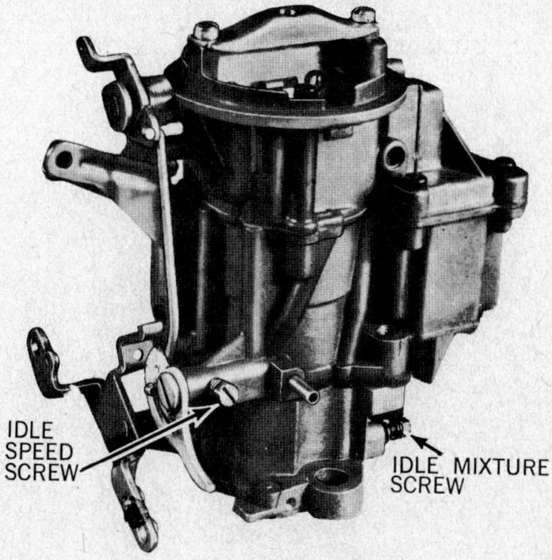

Rochester monojet carburetor

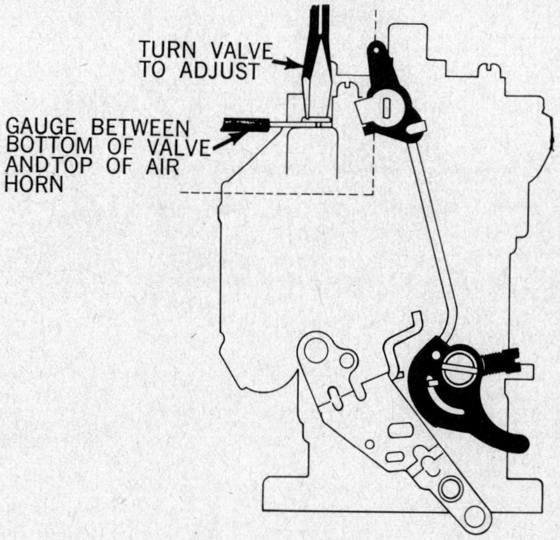

Idle vent adjustment

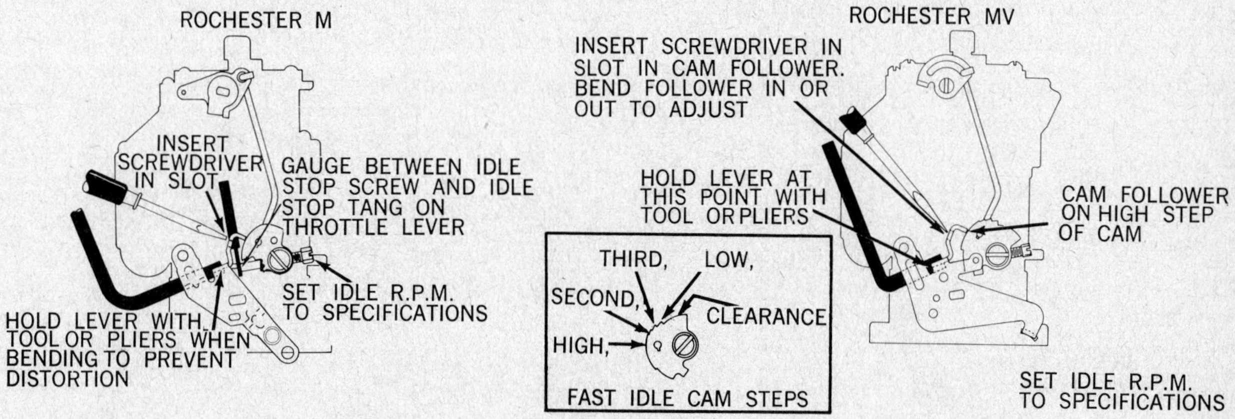

Fast idle adjustment

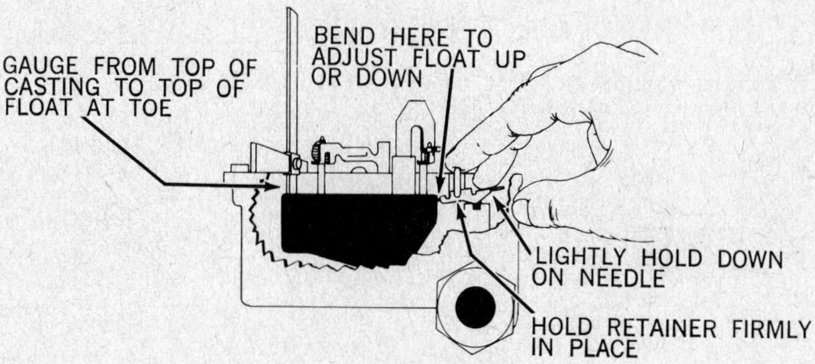

Float level adjustment

ROCHESTER MODEL 4MV

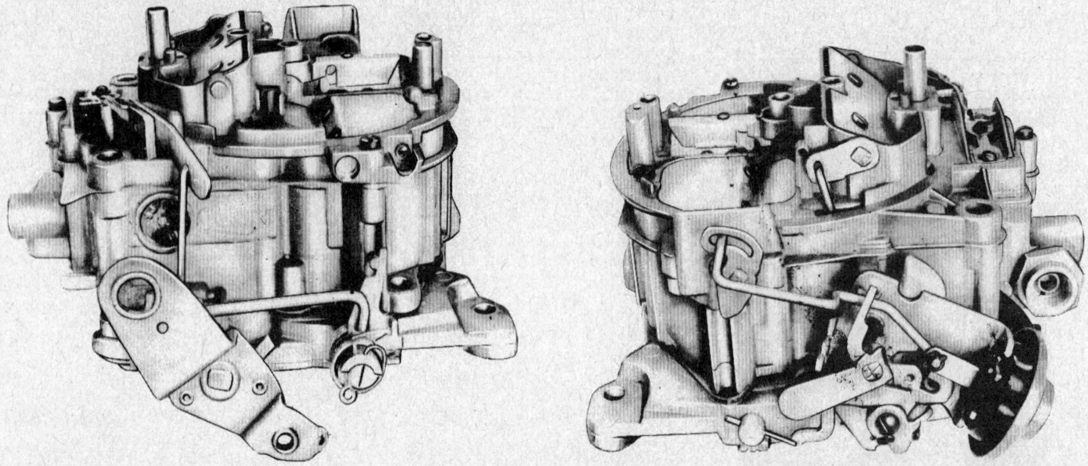

Rochester 4MV carburetor

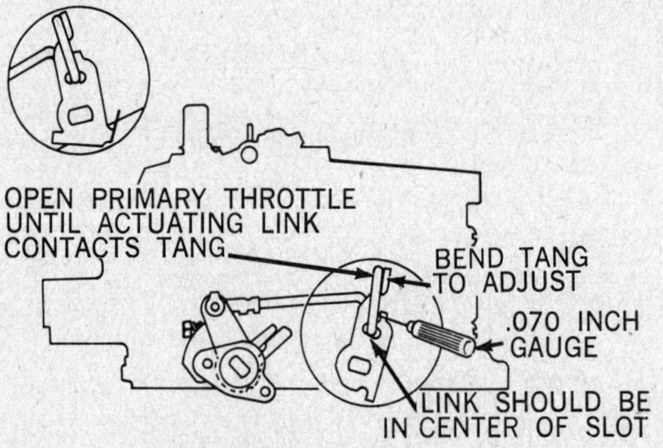

Secondary opening adjustment

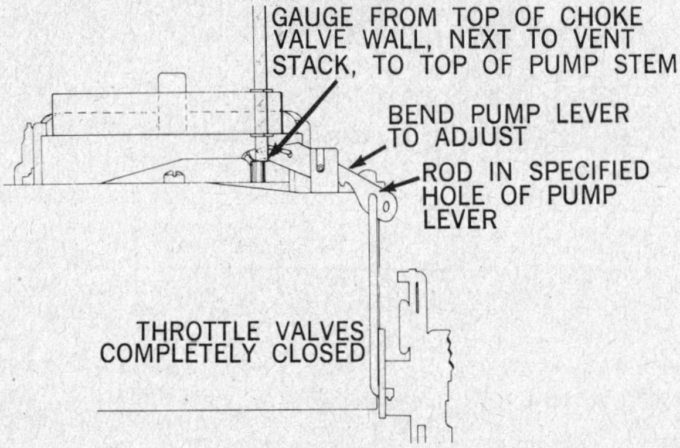

Pump rod adjustment

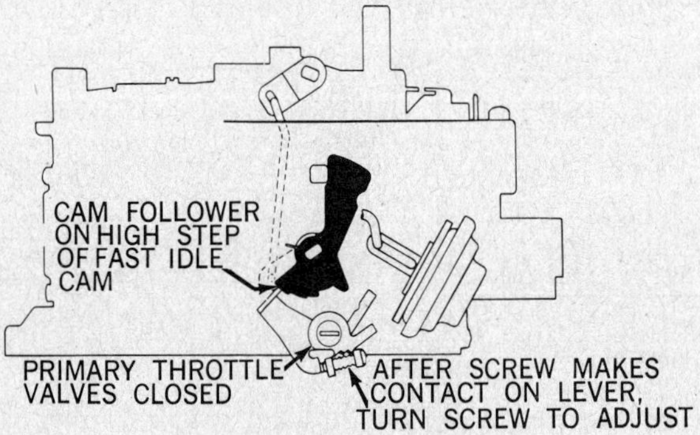

Fast idle adjustment

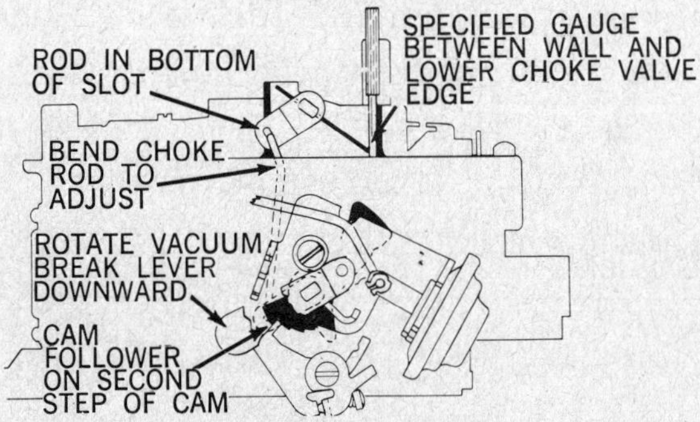

Choke rod adjustment

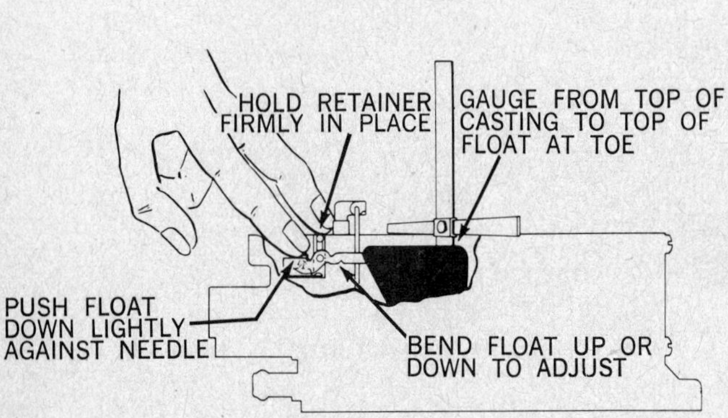

Float level adjustment

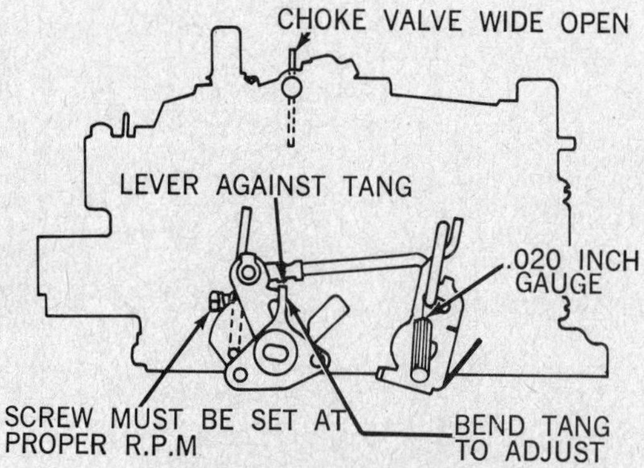

Secondary closing adjustment

ROCHESTER MODEL 4MV

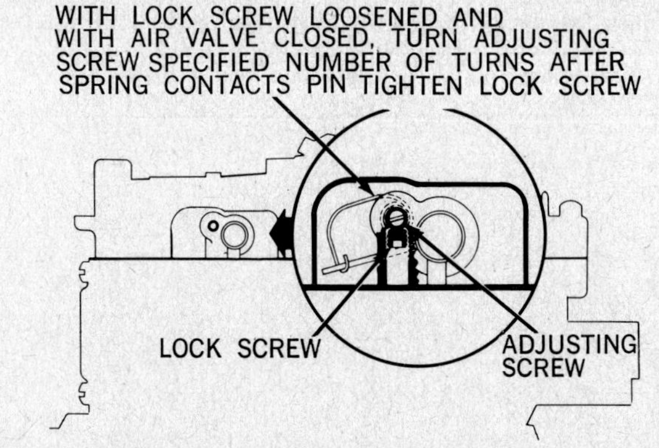

Air valve spring adjustment

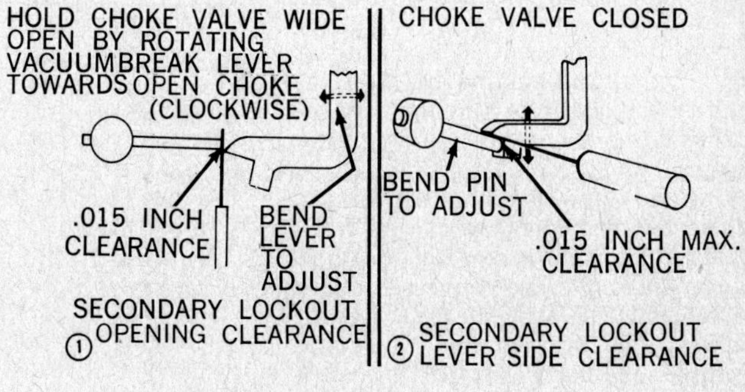

Secondary lockout adjustment

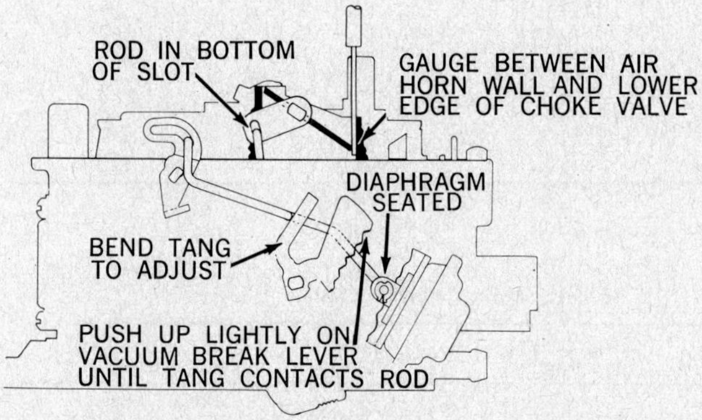

Vacuum break adjustment

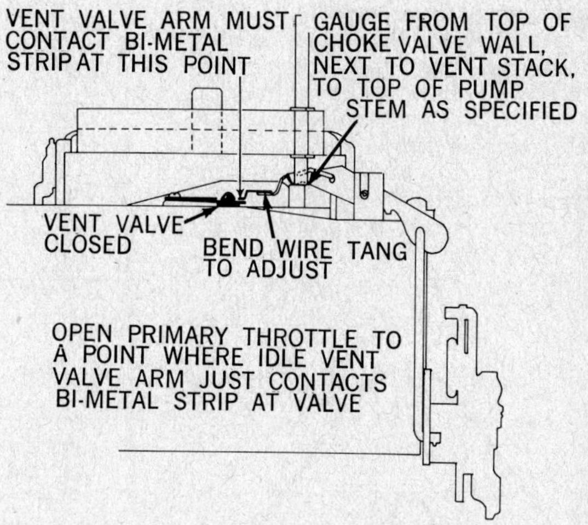

Idle vent adjustment

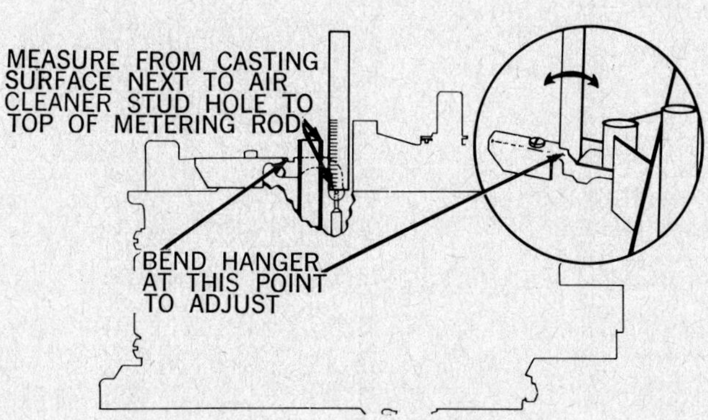

Secondary metering adjustment

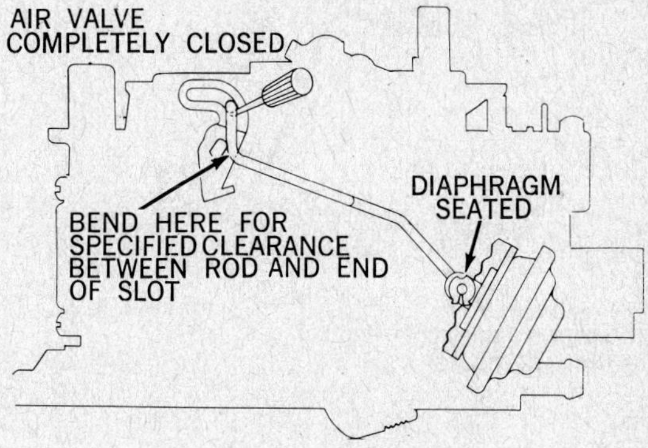

Air valve dashpot adjustment

Angle Degree Tool

An angle degree tool is recommended by Rochester Products Division, for use to confirm adjustments to the choke valve and related linkages on their late model two and four barrel carburetors, in place of the plug type gauges.

Decimal and degree conversion charts are provided for use by technicans who have access to an angle gauge and not plug gauges. It must be remembered that the relationship between the decimal and the angle readings are not exact, due to manufacturers tolerances.

To use the angle gauge, rotate the degree scale until zero (0) is opposite the pointer. With the choke valve completely closed, place the gauge magnet squarely on top of the choke valve and rotate the bubble until it is centered. Make the necessary adjustments to have the choke valve at the specified degree angle opening as read from the degree angle tool.

NOTE: The carburetor may be off the engine for adjustments. Be sure the carburetor is held firmly during the use of the angle gauge.

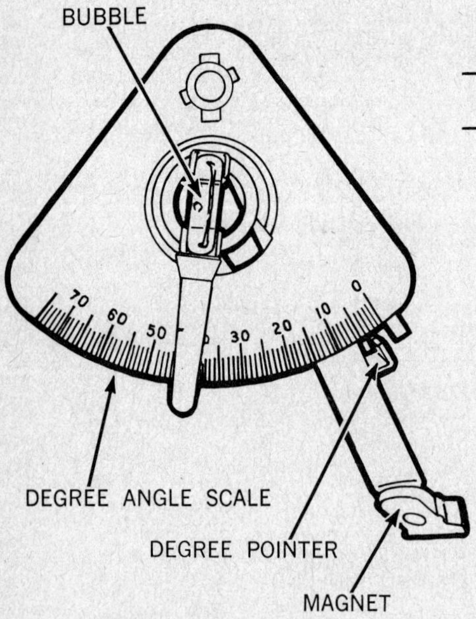

Degree angle tool—typical
(© Kent-Moore)

ANGLE DEGREE TO DECIMAL CONVERSION

MODEL M2MC, M2ME AND M4MC CARBURETOR

Angle Degrees	Decimal Equiv. Top of Valve	Angle Degrees	Decimal Equiv. Top of Valve
5	.023	33	.203
6	.028	34	.211
7	.033	35	.220
8	.038	36	.227
9	.043	37	.234
10	.049	38	.243
11	.054	39	.251
12	.060	40	.260
13	.066	41	.269
14	.071	42	.277
15	.077	43	.287
16	.083	44	.295
17	.090	45	.304
18	.096	46	.314
19	.103	47	.322
20	.110	48	.332
21	.117	49	.341
22	.123	50	.350
23	.129	51	.360
24	.136	52	.370
25	.142	53	.379
26	.149	54	.388
27	.157	55	.400
28	.164	56	.408
29	.171	57	.418
30	.179	58	.428
31	.187	59	.439
32	.195	60	.449

MODEL 4MV CARBURETOR

Angle Degrees	Decimal Equiv. Top of Valve	Angle Degrees	Decimal Equiv. Top of Valve
5	.019	33	.158
6	.022	34	.164
7	.026	35	.171
8	.030	36	.178
9	.034	37	.184
10	.038	38	.190
11	.042	39	.197
12	.047	40	.204
13	.051	41	.211
14	.056	42	.217
15	.060	43	.225
16	.065	44	.231
17	.070	45	.239
18	.075	46	.246
19	.080	47	.253
20	.085	48	.260
21	.090	49	.268
22	.095	50	.275
23	.101	51	.283
24	.106	52	.291
25	.112	53	.299
26	.117	54	.306
27	.123	55	.314
28	.128	56	.322
29	.134	57	.329
30	.140	58	.337
31	.146	59	.345
32	.152	60	.353

Stromberg Carburetors

YEAR	Carb. Model	Fuel Level (Wet)	Float Level (Dry)	Float Drop	Hot Idle Speed (RPM)	Pump Setting	Idle Mix. Screw Setting	Idle Vent Setting	Choke Setting
Chevrolet									
				MODEL WW, WWC					
1973	23-257	—	3/16	—	—	.97	—	—	—
	23-258	—	3/16	—	—	.97	—	—	—
	23-259	—	7/32	—	—	.28	—	—	—
	23-260	—	7/32	—	—	.28	—	—	—
1974	23-264	—	.22	—	—	.97	—	—	—
	23-265	—	.22	—	—	.68	—	—	—
GMC									
				MODEL WW					
1973	23-257	—	3/16	—	—	.97	—	—	—
	23-258	—	3/16	—	—	.97	—	—	—
1974	23-264	—	.22	—	—	.97	—	—	—
				MODEL WWC					
1973	23-259	—	7/32	—	—	.28	—	—	—
	23-260	—	7/32	—	—	.28	—	—	—
1974	23-265	—	.22	—	—	.68	—	—	—

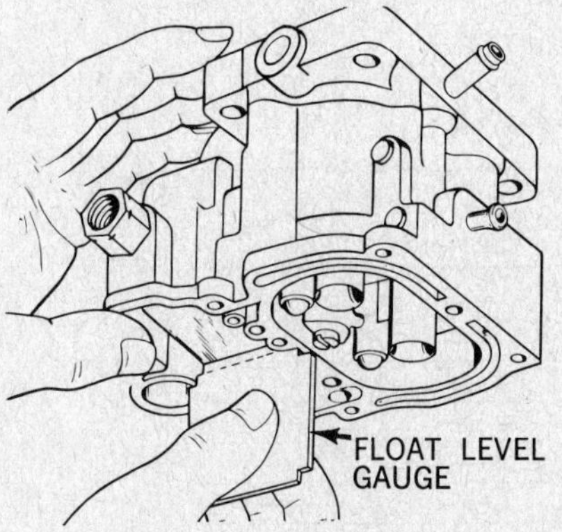

Checking float setting

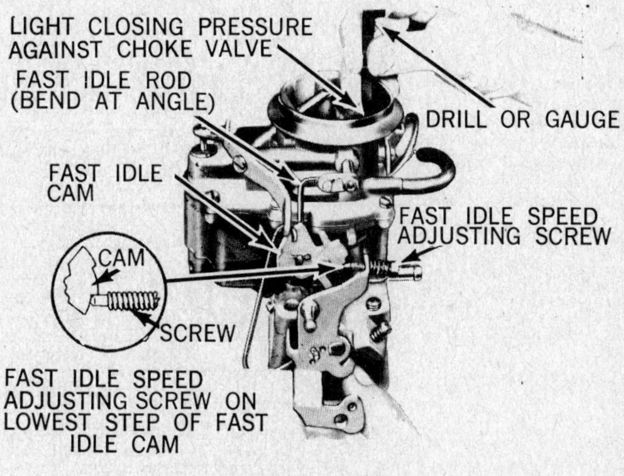

Fast idle cam adjustment

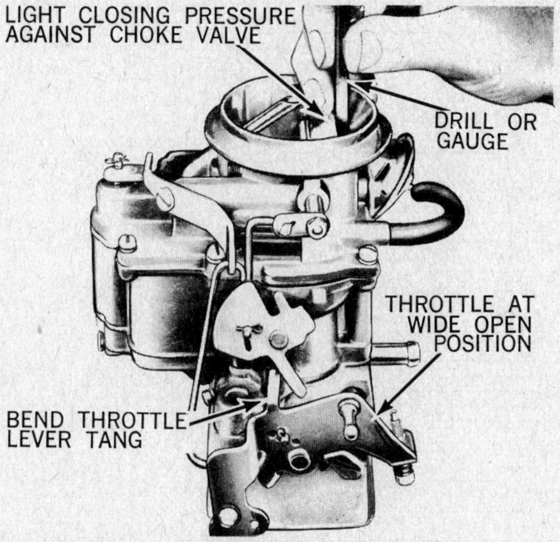

Unloader adjustment (wide open kick)

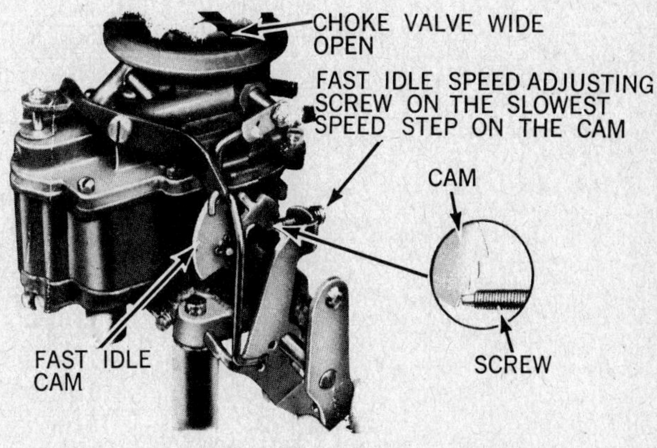

Fast idle speed adjustment (on vehicle)

Emission Calibration Numbers

Emission calibration numbers are used by Ford Motor Company to provide the technician with the necessary specifications to adjust a specific engine to the proper emission control levels.

The calibration numbers are listed on the lower right of the Vehicle Emission Control Information label, which is attached to the engine valve cover.

The information on the decal must be used when differences exist between the decal and other specification tables, unless otherwise noted by Ford Motor Company.

LIGHT TRUCK ONLY

Year	Emission Calibration Number	Choke Setting	Fast Idle (RPM) High Cam	Fast Idle (RPM) Kick Down①	Choke Valve Pull Down
1977	7-53G-RO	3 Rich	2000	—	—
	7-53H-RO	3 Rich	2000	—	—
	7-53S-RO	3 Rich	2000	—	—
	7-54K-RO	3 Rich	2100	—	—
	7-54S-RO	3 Rich	2100	—	—
	7-54T-RO	3 Rich	2100	—	—
	7-59G-RO	Index	1900	—	—
	7-60G-RO	Index	1900	—	—
	7-62G-RO	Index	1900	—	—
	7-64U-RO	3 Rich	—	1500	—
	7-65G-RO	3 Rich	—	1500	—
	7-65H-RO	3 Rich	—	1500	—
	7-65U-RO	Index	—	1500	—
	7-71-RO	3 Rich	—	1250	—
	7-71J-RO	3 Rich	—	1250	—
	7-72-RO	3 Rich	—	1500	—
	7-72J-RO	3 Rich	—	1500	—
	7-73-RO	3 Rich	—	1200	—
	7-74-RO	3 Rich	—	1500	—

① Kickdown—2nd step of fast idle cam

LIGHT and HEAVY TRUCKS

Year	Emission Calibration Number	Choke Setting	Fast Idle (RPM) High Cam	Fast Idle (RPM) Kick Down①	Choke Valve Pull Down
1978	5-81A-RO	None	—	—	—
	5-81B-RO	None	2200	—	—
	5-82-RO	None	2200	—	—
	5-82A-RO	None	2200	—	—
	5-85A-R1	None	2200	—	—
	5-85J-R6	None	—	—	—
	5-86A-RO	None	2200	—	—
	5-86J-R3	None	2500	—	—
	5-89-R2	None	2000	—	—
	5-89J-R3	None	2200	—	—
	5-90A-R1	None	2200	—	—
	5-90B-R1	None	2200	—	—
	5-90J-R3	None	2200	—	—
	6-51A-RO	Index	—	1600	—
	6-51E-RO	Index	—	1600	—
	6-93-R7	None	2500	—	—
	6-94-R4	None	2500	—	—
	6-95-R6	None	2500	—	—
	6-95-95	None	2500	—	—
	7-60E-R11	Index	1900	—	—
	7-71-R10	2 Rich	—	1250	—
	7-71J-R10	2 Rich	—	1450	—
	7-72-R11	3 Rich	—	1500	—
	7-72J-R11	3 Rich	—	1500	—
	7-73-R10	2 Rich	—	1250	—
	7-74-R10	3 Rich	—	1500	—
	7-74J-R11	3 Rich	—	1500	—
	7-75A-R16	1 Rich	—	1250	—

LIGHT and HEAVY TRUCKS (Cont'd)

Year	Emission Calibration Number	Choke Setting	Fast Idle (RPM) High Cam	Fast Idle (RPM) Kick Down①	Choke Valve Pull Down
	7-76A-R10	2 Rich	—	1500	—
	7-76J-R11	3 Rich	—	1700	—
	7-77-R10	1 Rich	—	1500	—
	7-77A-R10	None	—	1500	—
	7-77J-R10	1 Rich	—	1500	—
	7-77M-R10	None	—	1500	—
	7-78-R10	1 Rich	—	1500	—
	7-78J-R10	1 Rich	—	1500	—
	7-79-R1	3 Rich	—	1250	—
	7-80-RO	3 Rich	—	1500	—
	7-81K-RO	None	1400	—	—
	7-93J-RO	None	2500	—	—
	7-95J-RO	None	2500	—	—
	7-96J-90	None	2500	—	—
	8-51J-RO	Index	—	1600	—
	8-51K-RO	Index	—	1600	—
	8-51L-RO	Index	—	1600	—
	8-51M-RO	Index	—	1600	—
	8-51S-RO	Index	—	1600	—
	8-51T-RO	Index	—	1600	—
	8-52K-RO	Index	—	1600	—
	8-52L-R10	Index	—	1600	—
	8-52U-RO	Index	—	1600	—
	8-53A-RO	1 Rich	2000	—	—
	8-53G-RO	3 Rich	2000	—	—
	8-53S-RO	3 Rich	2000	—	—
	8-54A-RO	3 Rich	2000	—	—
	8-54G-RO	3 Rich	2000	—	—
	8-54S-RO	3 Rich	2100	—	—
	8-54T-R10	3 Rich	2100	—	—
	8-59G-RO	Index	2100	—	—
	8-59T-R2	Index	2100	—	—
	8-60A-RO	2 Rich	2200	—	—
	8-60J-RO	Index	2100	—	—
	8-60S-R11	Index	1900	—	—
	8-60S-R12	Index	1900	—	—
	8-62T-RO	—	—	—	—
	8-62J-RO	Index	2100	—	—
	8-64G-RO	3 Rich	—	1750	—
	8-64S-RO	Index	—	1500	—
	8-65A-RO	Index	2100	—	—
	8-65G-RO	1 Rich	2000	—	—
	8-65S-RO	Index	—	1500	—
	8-65U-RO	Index	—	1500	—
	R-66U-RO	Index	—	1500	—
	8-97-RO	Index	—	1200	—
	7-97J-RO	Index	—	1200	—
1979	9-51G-RO	Index	—	1600	.230
	9-51J-RO	Index	—	1600	.230
	9-51K-RO	Index	—	1600	.230
	9-51L-RO	Index	—	1600	.230
	9-51M-RO	Index	—	1600	.230

LIGHT and HEAVY TRUCKS (Cont'd)

Year	Emission Calibration Number	Choke Setting	Fast Idle (RPM) High Cam	Fast Idle (RPM) Kick Down①	Choke Valve Pull Down
	9-51S-RO	Index	—	1600	.230
	9-51T-RO	Index	—	1600	.230
	9-52G-RO	Index	—	1600	.230
	9-52J-RO	Index	—	1600	.230
	9-52L-RO	Index	—	1600	.230
	9-52M-RO	Index	—	1600	.230
	9-53G-RO	3 Rich	2000	—	.140
	9-53H-RO	3 Rich	2000	—	.140
	9-54A-RO	—	—	—	.145
	9-54G-RO	3 Rich	2000	—	.145
	9-54H-RO	3 Rich	2000	—	.145
	9-54J-RO	2 Rich	2000	—	.145
	9-54R-RO	3 Rich	2000	—	.145
	9-54S-RO	1 Rich	2400	—	.136
	9-54T-RO	3 Rich	2000	—	.145
	9-54U-RO	1 Rich	2400	—	.136
	9-59H-RO	Index	2000	—	.135
	9-59J-RO	Index	2000	—	.145
	9-59K-RO	Index	2000	—	.145
	9-59S-RO	Index	2000	—	.135
	9-60T-RO	—	—	—	.150
	9-60G-RO	Index	2000	—	.145
	9-60H-RO	Index	2000	—	.150
	9-60J-RO	Index	2000	—	.140
	9-60L-RO	Index	2000	—	.150
	9-60M-RO	Index	2000	—	.150
	9-60S-RO	3 Rich	2100	—	.150
	9-61G-RO	Index	2000	—	.145
	9-61H-RO	Index	2000	—	.135
	9-62A-RO	—	—	—	.145
	9-62B-RO	—	—	—	.145
	9-62J-RO	Index	1900	—	.145
	9-62M-RO	Index	1900	—	.145
	9-63H-RO	Index	—	1500	.190
	9-64G-RO	Index	2200	—	.200
	9-64H-RO	Index	2200	—	.200
	9-64S-RO	Index	2200	—	.200
	9-66G-RO	5 Rich	—	1600	.210
	9-72J-RO	3 Rich	2000	—	.150
	9-77J-RO	Index	—	1600	.290
	9-77M-RO	Manual	2550	—	—
	9-78J-RO	Index	—	1600	.290
	9-83G-RO	Manual	2200	—	—
	9-83H-RO2	Manual	2500	—	—
	9-87G-RO	Manual	2700	—	—
	9-97J-RO	5 Rich	—	1600	.210
	7-76J-R11	3 Rich	—	1700	.180
	7-93J-RO	Manual	2500	—	—
	7-95J-RO	Manual	2500	—	—
	9-71J-RO	3 Rich	1750	—	—
	9-73J-RO	2 Rich	1750	—	—
	9-74J-RO	3 Rich	2000	—	—
	9-97J-R11	5 Rich	—	1600	—

① Kickdown—2nd Step of Fast Idle Cam

INDEX

Dodge/Plymouth Loadflite

New Process A-345

Ford C-4

Ford C-6

Ford FMX

GM Turbo Hydra-Matic 250

GM Turbo Hydra-Matic 350

GM Turbo Hydra-Matic 400/475

Dodge/Plymouth Loadflite

The LoadFlite Transmission, Model 727, is a fully automatic, three speed unit, utilizing a torque converter, coupled to the engine by a flexible drive plate. The transmission internal parts consists of two multiple disc clutches, an over running clutch, two servos and bands and two planetary gear sets to provide the three forward and one reverse ratios.

The torque converter is a sealed unit and cannot be serviced. A lock-up clutch is incorporated in some converter assemblies for use in certain engine/transmission combinations.

The lock-up is activated in the direct drive mode only and at a preset minimum vehicle speed.

NOTE: The lock-up shift will occur immediately after the 2-3 shift, when the 2-3 upshift occurs above the minimum lock-up speed because of a wider throttle opening.

The lock-up converter became available during the 1978 model year, so care must be exercised during the repairs to the transmission that proper parts are installed in the right transmission model.

DIAGNOSIS

This guide covers the most common symptoms and is an aid to careful diagnosis. The items to check are listed in sequence to be followed for quickest results. Follow the checks in the order given for the particular transmission type.

LOADFLITE

CONDITION	POSSIBLE CAUSE 1	2	3	4	5	6	7	8	9	10	11	12	13	14	15	16	17	18	19	20	21	22	23	24	25	26	27	28	29	30	31	32	33	34	35
Harsh Engagement From Neutral to D or R			X			X																				X				X					X
Delayed Engagement From Neutral to D or R				X		X	X	X	X	X	X	X	X	X						X			X							X					
Runaway Upshift				X		X		X		X			X		X					X		X	X												
No Upshift				X		X		X	X						X				X	X	X	X	X												
3-2 Kickdown Runaway				X		X		X					X		X	X				X		X	X												
No Knockdown or Normal Downshift						X									X						X	X													
Shifts Erratic				X		X		X	X	X	X		X		X				X	X	X	X	X												
Slips in Forward Drive Positions				X		X		X	X	X	X	X	X		X		X													X			X		
Slips in Reverse Only				X	X	X	X	X	X		X		X							X			X												
Slips in All Positions				X		X		X		X	X	X	X																						
No Drive in Any Position				X		X		X		X	X																					X			
No Drive in Forward Drive Positions				X		X		X				X					X													X		X	X		
No Drive in Reverse				X	X	X	X		X											X			X							X		X			
Drives in Neutral						X			X																				X	X	X				
Drags or Locks		X			X																						X					X	X		
Grating, Scraping Growling Noise					X											X		X														X	X		
Buzzing Noise						X		X					X																					X	
Hard to Fill, Oil Blows Out Filter Tube										X			X											X	X										
Transmission Overheats	X		X	X				X	X		X																X	X	X						
Harsh Upshift				X											X	X										X									X
Delayed Upshift															X	X			X	X	X	X	X												
Slips in Reverse or Manual Low					X						X																								

POSSIBLE CAUSE

1. Stuck switch valve
2. Stuck lock-up valve
3. Engine idle speed too high
4. Hydraulic pressures too low
5. Low-Reverse band out of adjustment
6. Valve body malfunction or leakage
7. Low-Reverse servo, band or linkage malfunction
8. Low fluid level
9. Incorrect gearshift control linkage adjustment
10. Oil filter clogged
11. Faulty oil pump
12. Worn or broken input shaft seal rings
13. Aerated fluid
14. Engine idle speed too low
15. Incorrect throttle linkage adjustment
16. Kickdown band out of adjustment
17. Overrunning clutch not holding
18. Output shaft bearing and/or bushing damaged
19. Governor support seal rings broken or worn
20. Worn or broken reaction shaft support seal rings
21. Governor malfunction
22. Kickdown servo band or linkage malfunction
23. Worn or faulty front clutch
24. High fluid level
25. Breather clogged
26. Hydraulic pressure too high
27. Kickdown band adjustment too tight
28. Faulty cooling system
29. Insufficient clutch plate clearance
30. Worn or faulty rear clutch
31. Rear clutch dragging
32. Planetary gear sets broken or seized
33. Overrunning clutch worn, broken or seized
34. Overrunning clutch inner race damaged
35. Faulty lock-up clutch

LOCK-UP TORQUE CONVERTER

CONDITION	15	14	13	12	11	10	9	8	7	6	5	4	3	2	1
No Lock-up		X				X		X	X	X	X				X
Will Not Unlock									X	X	X	X		X	
Stays Locked Up to Too Low a Speed in Direct									X	X				X	
Locks Up or Drags in Low or Second									X						X
Stalls or Is Sluggish in Reverse												X	X		X
Loud Chatter During Lock-up Engagement—(Cold)					X			X							
Vibration or Shudder During Lock-up Engagement			X					X							
Vibrations After Lock-up Engagement	X		X	X										X	
Vibration when "Revved" in Neutral							X								
Overheating; Oil Blowing Out Dipstick or Pump Seal											X		X		

(Column numbers refer to POSSIBLE CAUSE.)

POSSIBLE CAUSE

1. Faulty Oil Pump
2. Sticking Governor Valve
3. Plugged Cooler, Lines or Fittings
4. Valve Body Malfunction
5. Stuck Switch Valve
6. Stuck Lock-up Valve
7. Stuck Fail-Safe Valve
8. Faulty Torque Converter
9. Out of Balance
10. Failed Locking Clutch
11. Leaking Turbine Hub Seal
12. Align Exhaust System
13. Tune Engine
14. Faulty Input Shaft or Seal Ring
15. Throttle Linkage Misadjusted

CLUTCH AND BAND APPLICATION CHART

WITHOUT LOCK-UP CONVERTER

Lever Position Drive-Ratio	Front Clutch	Rear Clutch	Front (Kickdown) Band	Rear (Low-Rev) Band	Overrunning Clutch
N-NEUTRAL					NO MOVEMENT
D-DRIVE					
(Breakaway)		X			HOLDS
(Second)		X	X		OVERRUNS
(Direct)	X	X			OVERRUNS
KICKDOWN					
(To Second)		X	X		OVERRUNS
(To Low)		X			HOLDS
2-Second		X	X		OVERRUNS
1-Low		X		X	PARTIAL HOLD
R-REVERSE	X			X	NO MOVEMENT

X=Applied

WITH LOCK-UP CONVERTER

Lever Position	Start Safety	Parking Sprag	Clutches Front	Clutches Rear	Clutches Over-running	Lock-up	Bands (Kickdown) Front	Bands (Low-Rev.) Rear
P—PARK	X	X						
R—REVERSE			X					
N—NEUTRAL	X							X
D—DRIVE								
First				X	X			
Second				X			X	
Direct			X	X		X		
2—SECOND								
First				X	X			
Second				X			X	
—LOW First)				X				X

X=Applied

AUTOMATIC SHIFT SPEEDS AND GOVERNOR PRESSURE CHART

(APPROXIMATE MILES PER HOUR)

TYPICAL

Engine	225			318/360			400/440	
Model	100	200	300	100	200	300	200	300
Axle Ratio	3.55	3.55	4.10	3.20	3.20	4.10	3.20	4.10
Tire Size	E78x15	G78x15	8.00x16.5	E78x15	G78x15	8.00x16.5	G78x15	8.00x16.5
Throttle Closed								
1-2 Upshift	9-11	9-11	8-10	9-11	9-11	7-9	9-11	7-9
2-3 Upshift	12-15	12-15	10-13	12-15	12-15	10-12	12-15	10-12
3-1 Downshift	7-11	7-11	6-10	7-11	7-11	6-9	7-11	6-9
Throttle Wide Open								
1-2 Upshift	28-34	28-34	25-30	34-42	34-42	27-33	34-42	27-33
2-3 Upshift	56-62	56-62	49-54	67-75	67-75	53-59	67-75	53-59
Kickdown Range								
3-2 Downshift	53-60	53-60	47-53	64-72	64-72	51-57	64-72	51-57
3-1 Downshift	24-28	24-28	21-24	25-33	25-33	20-26	25-33	20-26
Governor Pressure*								
15 PSI	17-19	17-19	15-17	17-19	17-19	14-15	17-19	14-15
50 PSI	41-45	41-45	36-39	49-54	49-54	39-43	49-54	39-43
75 PSI	56-61	56-61	50-54	68-73	68-73	54-58	69-73	54-58

*Governor pressure should be from zero to 1.5 psi at stand-still or downshift may not occur.
NOTE: Figures given are typical for other models. Changes in tire size or axle ratio will cause shift points to occur at corresponding higher or lower vehicle speeds.

GENERAL SPECIFICATIONS AND FLUID CAPACITY

Type	Three speed—fully automatic
Oil capacity (dry)	16½ pints "Dexron"
Cooling	Air and water cooled
Lubrication	Pump—rotor type
Gear train end play	.010 to .025 inch
Input shaft end	.036 to .082 inch
Band adjustment	See automatic transmission chapter under appropriate truck section

Tests

Air Pressure Tests

The front clutch, rear clutch, kickdown servo and low and reverse servo may be checked with air pressure, after the valve body assembly has been removed.

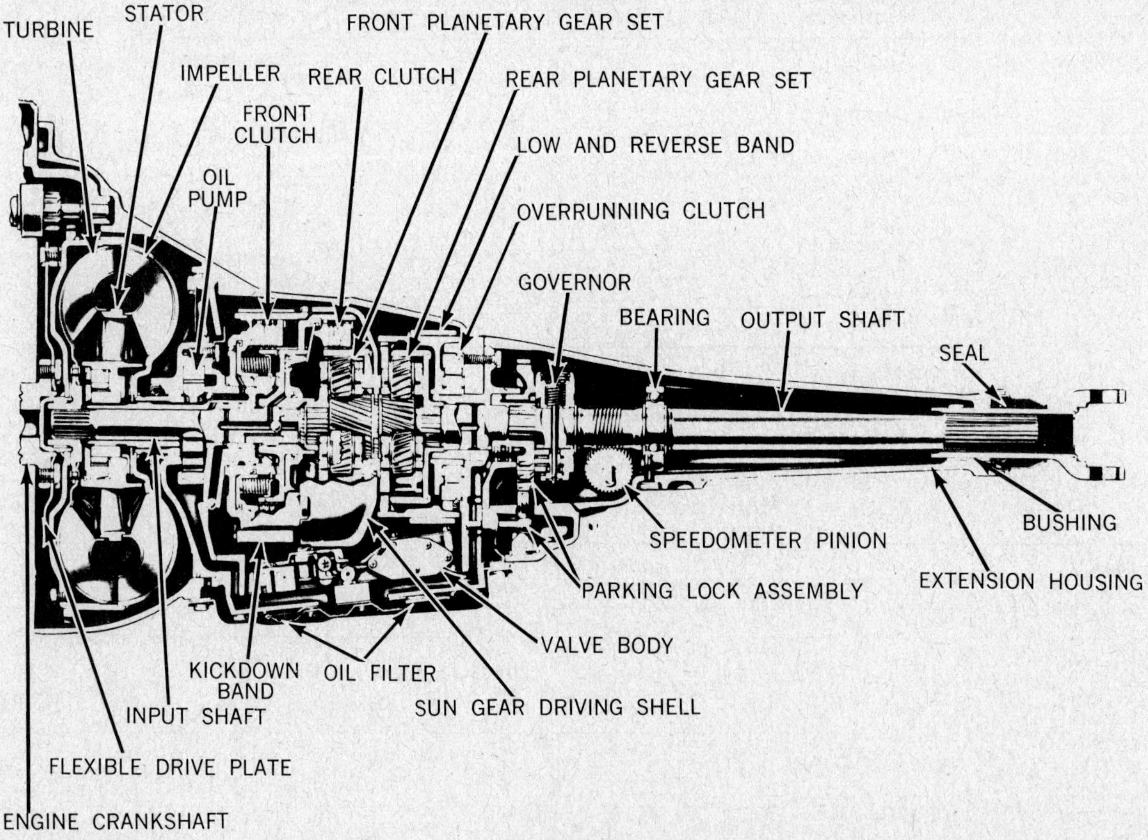

Dodge/Plymouth LoadFlite Transmission—727 model with out lock-up converter (© Chrysler Corp.)

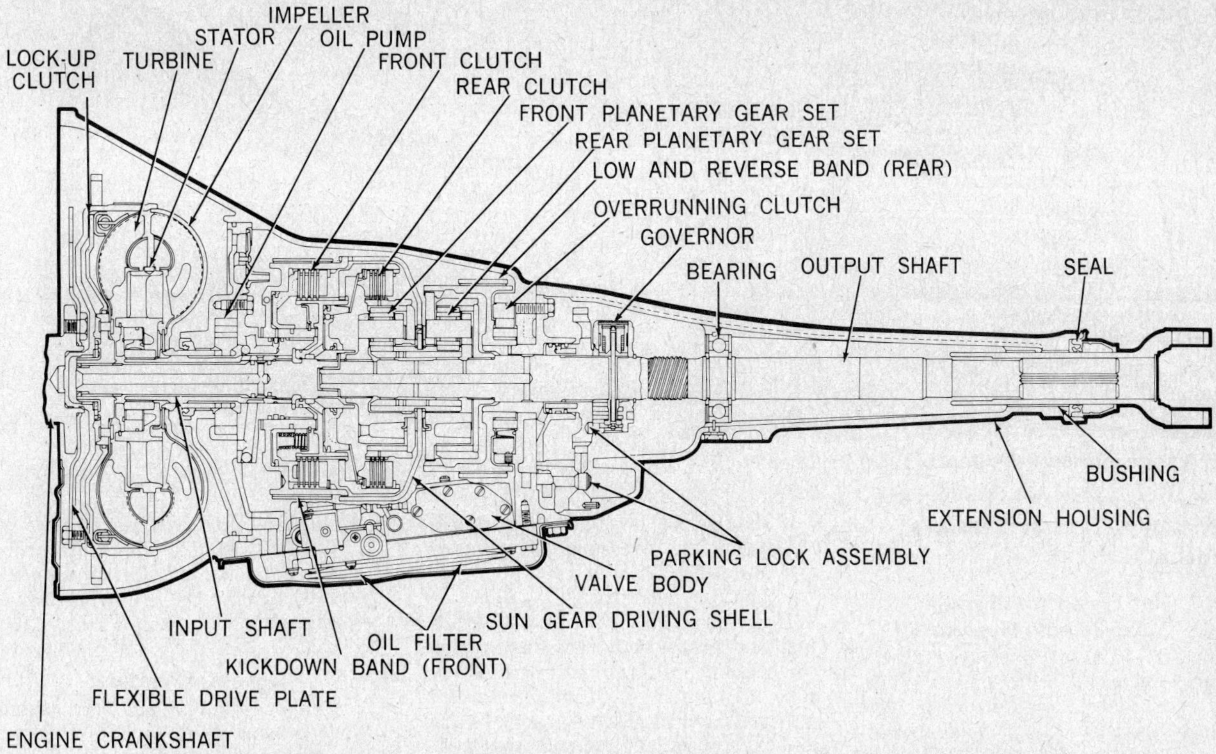

Dodge/Plymouth LoadFlite Transmission—727 model with lock-up converter (© Chrysler Corp.)

To make air pressure tests, proceed as follows:

CAUTION: Compressed air must be free of dirt and moisture. Use pressure of 30-100 psi.

Front Clutch

Apply air pressure to the front clutch apply passage and listen for a dull thud. This will indicate operation of the front clutch. Hold the air pressure at this point for a few seconds and check for excessive oil leaks.

NOTE: If a dull thud cannot be heard in the clutch, place finger tips on clutch housing and again apply air pressure. Movement of piston can be felt as clutch is applied.

Rear Clutch

Apply air pressure to the rear clutch apply passage and proceed in an identical manner as that described in the previous paragraph.

Kickdown Servo

Air pressure applied to the kickdown servo apply passage should tighten the front band. Spring tension should be sufficient to release the band.

Low and Reverse Servo

Direct air pressure into the low and reverse servo apply passage. Response of the servo will result in a tightening of the rear band. Spring tension should be enough to release the band.

If clutches and servos operate properly, no upshift or erratic shift conditions existing, trouble exists in the control valve body assembly.

Governor

Governor troubles can usually be found during a road or pressure test.

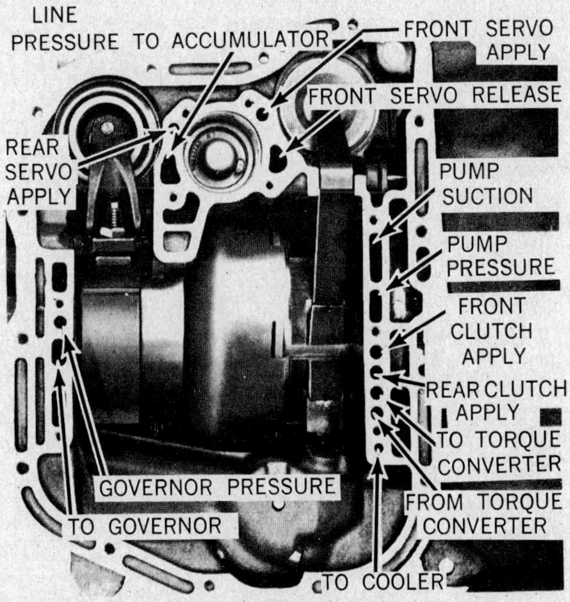

Air pressure test points (© Chrysler Corp.)

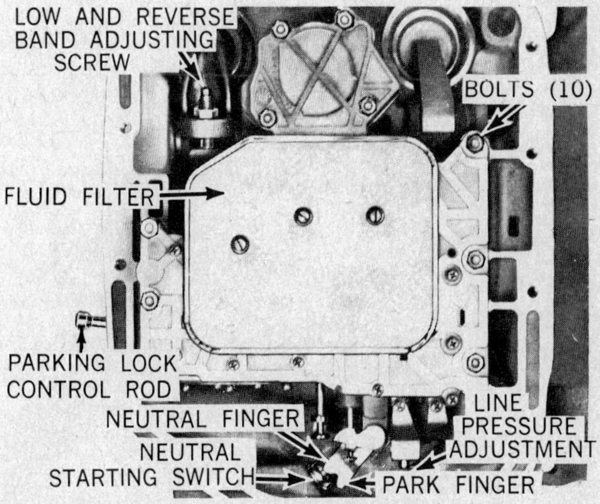

Bottom view of transmission (pan removed) (© Chrysler Corp.)

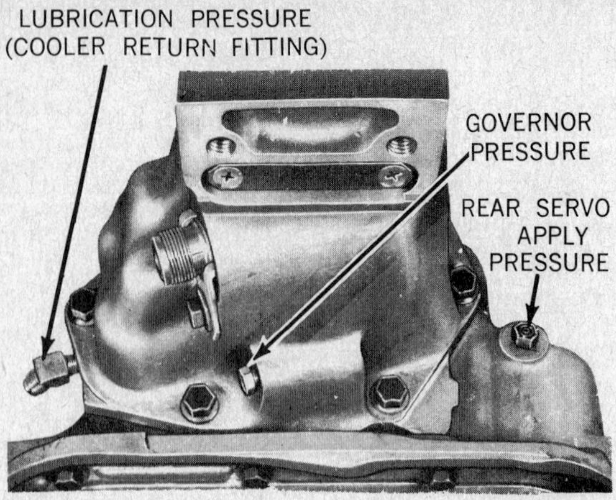

Pressure test locations (rear of case) (© Chrysler Corp.)

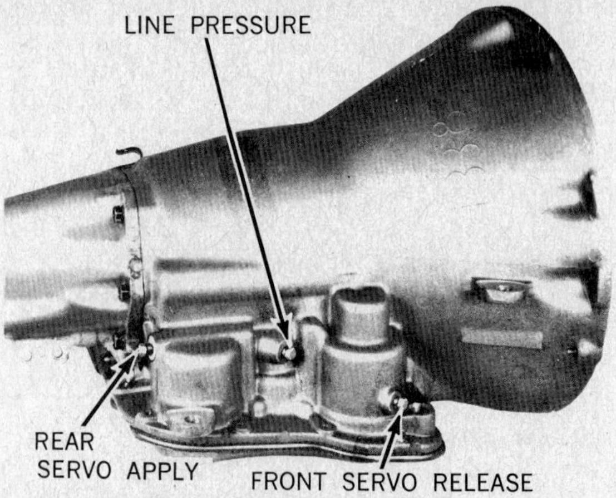

Pressure test locations (right side of case) (© Chrysler Corp.)

Hydraulic Control Pressure Checks

Line Pressure and Front Servo Release Pressure

NOTE: These pressure checks must be made in the D position with the rear wheels free to turn. The transmission fluid must be at operating temperature (150°-200°F).

1. Install an engine tachometer, then, raise the truck on a hoist and locate the tachometer so it can be read from under the truck.
2. Connect two 0-100 psi pressure gauges to pressure takeoff points at the top of the accumulator and at the front servo release on the outside of the transmission case.
3. With the selector in D position, increase engine speed gradually until the transmission shifts into High. Reduce engine speed slowly to 100 rpm. The line pressure must be 54-60 psi with front servo release having no more than a 3 psi drop.
4. Disconnect throttle linkage from transmission throttle lever and more throttle lever gradually to full throttle position. Line pressure must rise to maximum of 90-96 psi just before or at kickdown into low gear. Front servo pressure must follow line pressure up to kickdown point and should not be more than 3 psi below line pressure. If pressure is not 54-60 psi at 1000 rpm, adjust line pressure.

If line pressure is not as above, adjust the pressure as outlined under the heading: Hydraulic Control Pressure Adjustments—"Line Pressure."

If front servo release pressures are less than specified, and line pressures are within limits, there is excessive leakage in the front clutch and/or front servo circuits.

Lubrication Pressures

A lubrication pressure check should be made when line pressure and front servo release pressures are checked.

1. Install a T fitting between the cooler return line fitting and the fitting hole in the transmission case at the rear left side of the transmission. Connect a 0-100 psi pressure gauge to the T-fitting.
2. At 1000 engine rpm, with throttle closed and transmission in selector "2" position, lubrication pressure should be 5-15 psi. Lubrication pressure will approximately double as throttle is opened to maximum line pressure.

Rear Servo Apply Pressure

1. Connect a 0-300 psi pressure gauge, to the apply pressure take off point at the rear servo.
2. With the control in the R position, and the engine running at 1600 rpm, the reverse servo apply pressure should be 230-260 psi.

Governor Pressure

1. Connect a 0-100 psi gauge (same as the one used for line pressure and front servo release pressure) to the governor pressure takeoff point. This location is at the lower left rear corner of the extension mounting flange.
2. The governor pressure should respond smoothly during the changes in speed and should return to 0 to 1½ PSI, when the vehicle is stopped. A pressure reading above 2 PSI, at standstill, will prevent the transmission from downshifting. If the governor pressure is erratic during the upshifting of the transmission, the governor valve and/or weights are probably sticking.

Hydraulic Control Pressure Adjustments

Line Pressure

An incorrect throttle pressure setting will cause incorrect line pressure even though line pressure adjustment is correct. Always inspect and correct throttle pressure adjustment before adjusting line pressure.

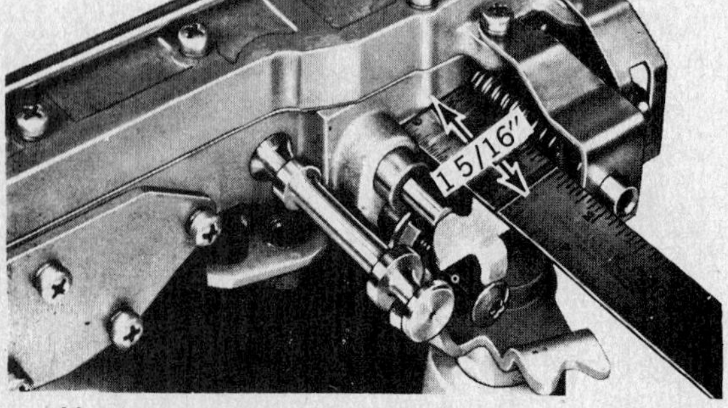

Line pressure adjustment (© Chrysler Corp.)

Measuring spring retainer location (© Chrysler Corp.)

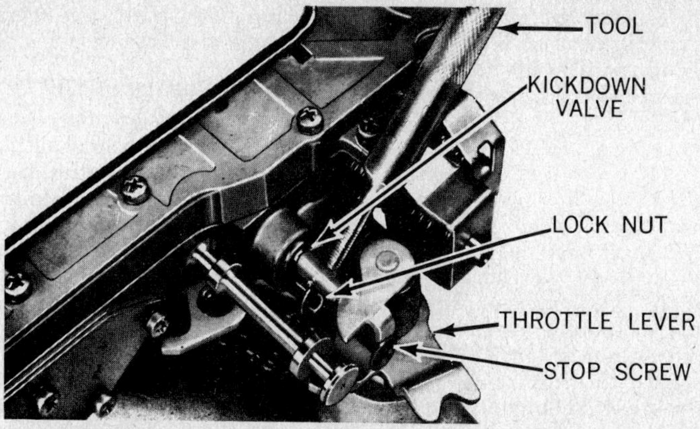

Throttle pressure adjustment (© Chrysler Corp.)

NOTE: Before adjusting line pressure, measure distance between manual valve (valve in 1-low position and line pressure adjusting screw. This measurement must be 1⅞ in. Correct by loosening spring retainer screws and repositioning spring retainer. The regulator valve may cock and hang up in its bore if spring retainer is out of position.

If line pressure is not correct remove valve body assembly to adjust. The correct adjustment is 1-5/16 in. measured from valve body to inner edge of adjusting nut. Vary adjustment slightly to obtain specified line pressure.

One complete turn of the adjusting screw (Allen head) changes closed throttle line pressure about 1.66 psi. Turning the screw counterclockwise increases pressure, clockwise decreases pressure.

Throttle Pressure

Because throttle pressures cannot be checked, exact adjustments should be checked and made correct whenever the valve body is disturbed.

1. Remove the valve body assembly, as outlined in a succeeding coverage entitled, Valve Body Assembly and Accumulator Piston.
2. Loosen throttle lever stop screw locknut and back off the screw about five turns.
3. Insert gauge pin between the throttle lever cam and the kickdown valve.
4. Push on the tool and compress the kickdown valve against its spring, so that the throttle valve is completely bottomed inside the valve body.
5. As the spring is being compressed, finger tighten the throttle lever stop screw against the throttle lever tang, with the lever cam touching the tool and the throttle valve bottomed. (Be sure the adjustment is made with the spring fully compressed and the valve bottomed in the valve body.)
6. Remove the tool and secure the stop screw locknut.

Stall Test

The purpose of the stall test is to check the torque converter stator clutch operation and the holding abilities of the transmission internal clutches, by determining the engine speed obtained at full throttle with the transmission in "D" position.

The transmission fluid level must be checked, the engine/transmission assembly brought to normal operating temperature, the front wheels blocked and both the parking and service brakes fully applied, before the stall test can be made.

CAUTION: Do not allow anyone to stand in front of the vehicle during the stall test. Personal injury can result.

Do not hold the throttle open any longer than 5 seconds at a time during the test. If more than one test is needed, operate the engine/transmission assembly at 1000-1500 RPM for at least 20 seconds, with the transmission in neutral, to cool the fluid and internal transmission parts before proceeding with any further tests.

If the engine speed exceeds the maximum specified RPM, transmission clutch slippage is indicated and further tests, both oil pressure and air pressure, will have to be made to determine the failure.

Low stall speeds can indicate torque converter stator clutch problems or a poorly tuned engine. When the engine is known to be in proper tune and the stall speed is 250-350 RPM below specifications, and the vehicle operates satisfactorily at highway speeds, but has poor through gear acceleration, stator clutch slippage is indicated.

If the stall speed and acceleration are normal but abnormally high throttle opening is required to maintain highway speed, a seized stator clutch is indicated.

NOTE: Refer to the individual truck section for stall speed specifications.

Service Operations in Truck

Some sub-assemblies can be removed for repairs without removing the transmission from the truck. Detailed reconditioning of sub-assemblies is covered further in the text.

Band Adjustments

Because of the varied engine applications, the kickdown and low-reverse band adjustment specifications will be found in the separate truck sections. Refer to the appropriate section.

Speedometer Pinion

Removal and Installation

Rear axle gear ratio and tire size determine pinion gear size.

1. Remove bolt and retainer securing speedometer pinion adapter in extension housing.
2. With cable housing connected, carefully work adapter and pinion out of extension housing.
3. If transmission fluid is found in

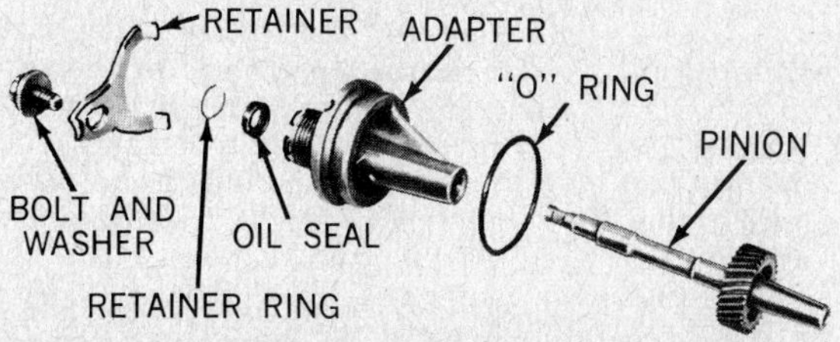

Speedometer driven gear assembly (© Chrysler Corp.)

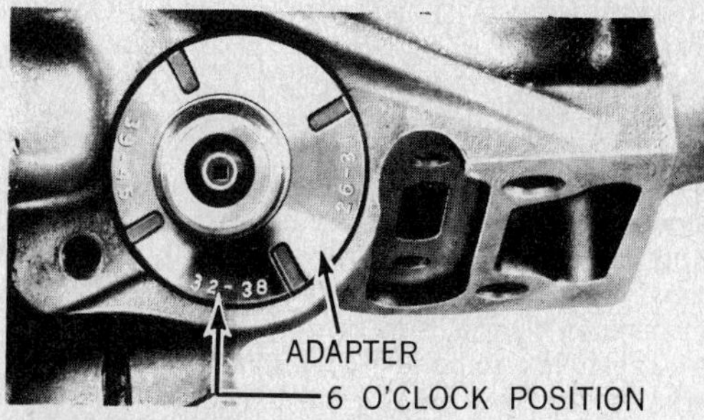

Speedometer pinion and adapter installed in extension case (© Chrysler Corp.)

cable housing, replace seal in adapter. Start seal and retainer ring in adapter, then push them into adapter until tool bottoms. **CAUTION: Before installing pinion and adapted assembly make sure adapter flange and mating area on extension housing are perfectly clean. Dirt or sand will cause misalignment and speedometer pinion gear noise.**

4. Note number of gear teeth and install pinion gear into adapter.
5. Rotate pinion gear and adapter assembly so that number on adapter corresponding to number of teeth on gear is in six o'clock position as assembly is installed.
6. Install retainer and bolt with retainer tangs in adapter position ing slots. Tap adapter firmly into extension housing and tighten retainer bolt to 100 in. lbs.

Output Shaft Oil Seal

Replacement

1. Mark parts for reassembly. Disconnect driveshaft at rear universal joint. Carefully pull shaft yoke out of transmission extension housing. Be careful not to scratch or nick ground surface of sliding spline yoke.
2. Remove extension housing yoke seal by gently tapping out around circumference of seal with slide hammer.
3. To install new seal, place seal in opening of extension housing and drive it into housing with suitable drift.
4. Carefully guide front universal joint yoke into extension housing and onto the mainshaft splines. Align marks made at removal and connect driveshaft to pinion shaft yoke.

Short Extension Housing

Removal

1. Mark parts for reassembly. Disconnect driveshaft at rear universal joint. Carefully pull shaft out of extension housing.
2. Remove speedometer pinion and adapted asembly. Drain approximately two quarts of fluid from transmission.
3. Remove bolts securing extension housing to crossmember. Raise transmission slightly with service jack and remove center crossmember and support assembly.
4. Remove extension housing to transmission bolts. On console shifts, remove two bolts securing gearshift torque shaft lower bracket to extension housing. Swing bracket out of way.

   NOTE: Gearshift lever must be in 1-low position so that parking lock control rod can be engaged or disengaged with parking lock sprag.
5. Remove two screws, plate, and gasket from bottom of extension housing mounting pad.
6. Spread large snap ring from output shaft bearing.
7. With snap ring spread as far as possible tap extension housing gently off output shaft bearing.
8. Carefully pull extension housing rearward to bring parking lock control rod knob past parking sprag and remove housing.

Long Extension Housing Bushing and Output Shaft Bearing

Removal

1. Mark drive shaft components for reassembly then disconnect drive shaft at rear universal joint. Carefully, pull the drive shaft assembly out of the extension housing.
2. Remove the speedometer pinion and adapter assembly. Drain two quarts of fluid from the transmission.
3. Remove the bolts securing the extension housing to the crossmember. Raise the transmission slightly with a service jack, then remove the crossmember and support assembly.
4. Remove the extension housing to transmission bolts.

   NOTE: When removing or installing the extension housing the gearshift lever must be in the 'l' (low) position. This positions the parking lock control rod rearward so it can be disengaged or engaged with the parking lock sprag.
5. Remove the access plate gasket from the extension housing. Spread the large snap ring from the output shaft bearing. When the snap ring is spread as far as possible, carefully tap the extension housing off the output shaft bearing. Carefully pull the extension housing rearward to remove parking lock rod control rod knob past the parking sprag, then remove the extension housing.

Bushing Replacement

1. Remove the oil seal with special Chrysler tool.
2. Press or drive out the bushing.
3. Slide a new bushing on installation tool. Align the oil hole in the bushing with the oil slot in the housing, then press or drive the bushing into place.
4. Position a new seal in the opening of the extension housing and drive it into the housing.

Bearing Replacement

1. Using a heavy duty snap ring pliers, remove the output shaft bearing rear snap ring and remove the bearing from the shaft.
2. Install a new bearing on the shaft with the outer race ring groove toward the front. Install the rear snap ring.

Installation

1. Place a new extension housing gasket on the transmission case. Position output shaft bearing retaining snap ring in the extension housing. Slide the extension housing on the output shaft, guiding the parking lock control rod knob past the parking sprag. While spreading the large snapring in the housing, carefully tap the housing into place. Release the snap ring. Make sure that the snap ring is fully seated in the bearing outer race ring groove.
2. Install and tighten the extension housing bolts to 24 foot-pounds.
3. Install the gasket and access plate on the extension housing.
4. Install the center crossmember and the rear mount assembly. Tighten the retaining bolts. Lower the transmission, install the extension housing and torque bolts to 40 foot-pounds.
5. Install the speedometer pinion and adapter.
6. Carefully guide the front universal joint yoke into the extension housing and on the output shaft splines. Align the marks made during removal and connect the drive shaft to the rear axle pinion shaft yoke.
7. Add fluid to the transmission to bring it up to proper operating level.

Governor

Removal

1. Remove extension housing. *NOTE: Remove output shaft, support bearing if so equipped.*
2. With a screwdriver, carefully pry the snapring from the weight end of governor valve shaft. Slide the valve and shaft assembly out of the governor housing.
3. Remove the large snap-ring from the weight end of the governor housing and lift out the governor weight assembly.
4. Remove snap-ring from inside governor weight, remove inner weight and spring from the outer weight.
5. Remove the snap-ring from behind the governor housing, then

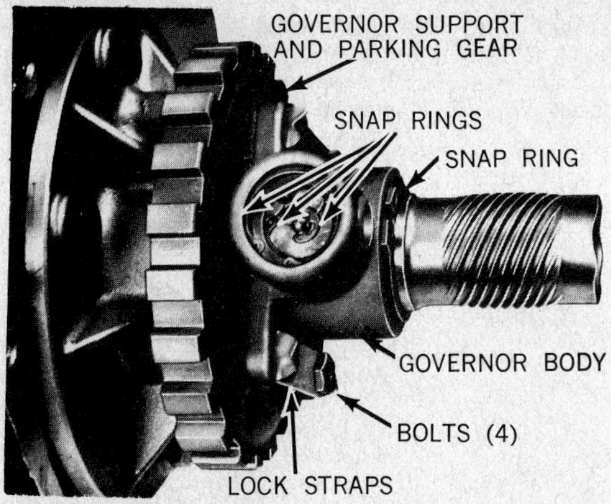

Governor shaft and weight snap-rings (© Chrysler Corp.)

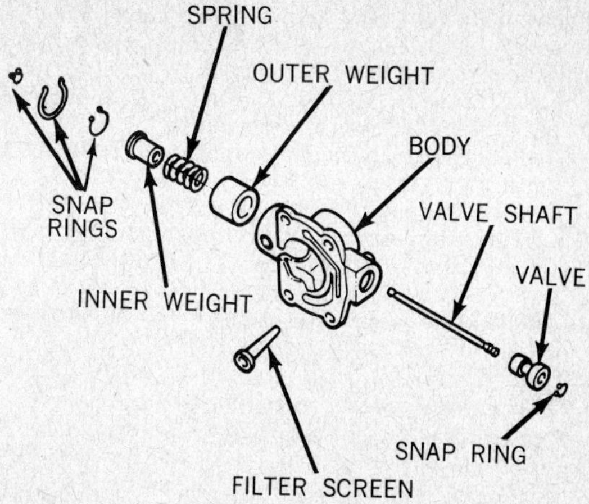

Exploded view—governor assembly (© Chrysler Corp.)

slide the governor housing and support assembly from the output shaft. If necessary, remove the four screws and separate the governor housing from the support.

Cleaning and Inspection

The primary cause of governor operating trouble is sticking of the valve or weights. This is brought about by dirt or rough surfaces. Thoroughly clean and blow dry all of the governor parts, crocus cloth any burrs or rough bearing surfaces and clean again. If all moving parts are clean and operating freely, the governor may be reassembled.

Installation

1. Assemble governor body and screen to the support, if disassembled, and tighten the bolts finger tight. Make sure the oil passages of the governor body aligns with the passage in the support.
2. Position the support and the governor on the output shaft. Align the assembly so that the valve shaft hole in the governor body alighs with the hole in the output shaft, then slide the assembly in place. Torque the body support bolts to 100 inch-pounds. Bend the ends of the lock straps over the bolt heads.
3. Assemble the governor weights and spring, and secure with the snap ring inside of the large governor weight. Place the weight assembly in the governor body and install the snap ring.
4. Place the governor valve on the valve shaft, insert the assembly into the body and through the governor weights. Install the valve shaft retaining snap ring. Inspect the valve and weight assembly for free-movement after installation.
5. Install the output shaft bearing and the extension housing.

Parking Lock Components

Removal

1. Remove the extension housing.
2. Slide the shaft out of the extension housing to remove the parking sprag and spring. Remove the snap ring and slide the reaction plug and pin assembly out of the housing.
3. To replace the parking lock rod, refer to "Valve Body-Removal and Installation".

Assembly

1. Install the reaction plug and pin assembly in the housing and secure with a snap ring.
2. Position the sprag and spring in the housing and insert the shaft. Make sure that the square lug on the sprag is toward the parking gear, and the spring is positioned so it moves the sprag away from the gear.
3. Install the extension housing.

Valve Body

Removal

1. Raise vehicle on hoist and loosen oil pan bolts, tap pan to break it loose, allowing fluid to drain.
2. Remove pan and gasket.
3. Disconnect throttle and gear shift linkage from levers on transmission. Loosen clamp bolts and remove levers.
4. Remove E clip securing parking lock rod to valve body manual lever.
5. Remove backup light and neutral start switch.
6. Place drain pan under transmission, remove ten hex head valve body to transmission

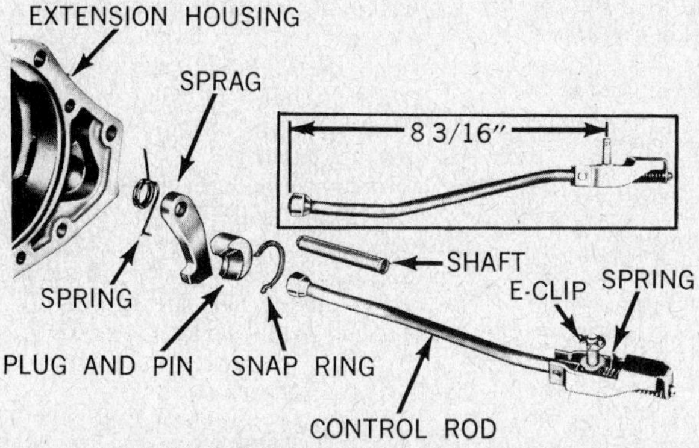

Parking lock components (© Chrysler Corp.)

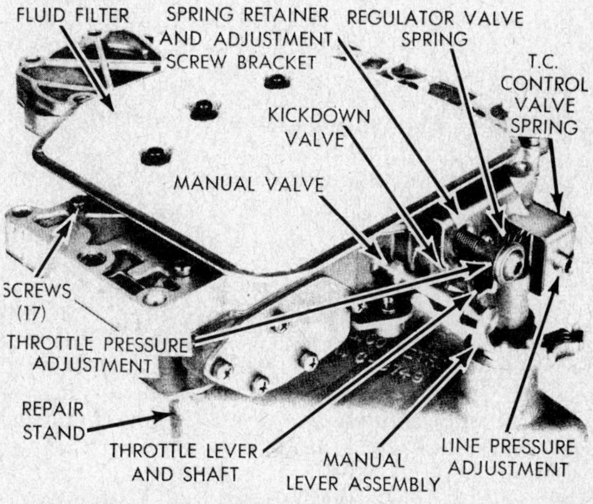

Control valve assembly (© Chrysler Corp.)

case bolts. Hold valve body in position while removing bolts.
7. While lowering valve body down out of transmission case, disconnect parking lock rod from lever. To remove rod pull if forward out of case. If necessary rotate driveshaft to align parking gear and sprag to permit knob on end of control rod to pass sprag.
8. Withdraw accumulator piston from transmission case. Inspect piston for scoring, and rings for wear or breakage.
9. If valve body manual lever shaft seal requires replacement, drive it out of case with punch.
10. Drive new seal into case with 15/16 in. socket and hammer.

Installation

1. If parking lock rod was removed, insert it through opening in rear of case with knob positioned against plug and sprag. Move front end of rod toward center of transmission while exerting rearward pressure on rod to force it past sprag. Rotate driveshaft if necessary.
2. Install accumulator piston in transmission case.
3. Place accumulator spring on valve body.
4. Place valve body manual lever in low position. Lift valve body into its approximate position, connect parking lock rod to manual lever and secure with E clip. Place valve body in case, install retaining bolts finger tight.
5. With neutral start switch installed, place manual lever in neutral position. Shift valve body if necessary to center neutral finger over neutral switch plunger. Snug bolts down evenly. Torque to 100 in. lbs.
6. Install gearshift lever and tighten clamp bolt. Check lever shaft for binding by moving lever through all detends. If lever binds, loosen valve body bolts and re-align.
7. Make sure throttle shaft seal is in place, install flat washer and lever and tighten clamp bolt. Connect throttle and gearshift linkage and adjust as required.
8. Install oil pan using new gasket. Add transmission fluid to proper level.

Detailed Unit Reconditioning

The following reconditioning data covers the removal, disassembly, inspection, repair, assembly and installation procedures for each subassembly in detail.

NOTE: In the event that any part has failed in the transmission, the converter should be thoroughly flushed to insure the removal of fine particles that may cause damage to the reconditioned transmission.

Oil Pan

Removal

1. Secure transmission in a repair stand.
2. Unscrew attaching bolts and remove oil pan and gasket.

Valve Body

Removal

1. Loosen clamp bolts and remove throttle and gearshift levers from transmission.
2. Remove backup light and neutral start switch.
3. Remove ten hex head valve body to transmission bolts. Remove E clip securing parking lock rod to valve body manual lever.
4. While lifting valve body upward out of transmission case, disconnect parking lock rod from lever.

Accumulator Piston and Spring

Removal

Lift the spring from the accumulator piston and withdraw the piston from the case.

Checking Drive Train End-Play

1. Attach a dial indicator to the extension housing and seat the plunger on the end of the output shaft.
2. Pry the output shaft out and tap it in to register the extreme shaft end-play.
3. Record this reading for possible future use. Correct end play is found at front of section.

Governor and Support

Removal

1. Remove the snap-ring from the weight end of the governor valve shaft. Slide the valve and shaft assembly from the governor housing.
2. Remove the snap-ring from behind the governor housing, then slide the governor housing and support from the output shaft.

Oil Pump and Reaction Shaft Support

Shaft Support Removal

1. Tighten the front band on the front clutch retainer.
2. Remove front pump housing retaining bolts.
3. Attach slide hammers to the pump housing flange, using the eleven and four o'clock hole locations.
4. Bump outward, evenly. with tool to withdraw oil pump and reaction shaft support assembly from the case.

Front Band and Front Clutch

Removal

1. Loosen the front band adjuster, remove the head strut and slide the band from the case.
2. Slide the front clutch assembly from the case.

Input Shaft and Rear Clutch

Removal

Grasp the input shaft and slide the shaft and rear clutch assembly out of the case.

NOTE: Don't lose the thrust washer located between the rear end of the input shaft and the front end of the output shaft.

Planetary Gear Assemblies, Sun Gear, Driving Shell, Low and Reverse Drum

Removal

While hand-supporting the output shaft and driving shell, carefully slide the assembly forward and out of the case.

Rear Band and Low-Reverse Drum

Removal

Remove low-reverse drum, loosen rear band adjuster, remove band strut and link, and remove band from case.

Overrunning Clutch

Removal

1. Notice the established position of the overrunning clutch rollers and springs before disassembly.
2. Slide out the clutch hub and remove rollers and springs.

Kickdown Servo

Removal

1. Compress kickdown servo spring using engine valve spring compressor. Then remove snap ring.
2. Remove the rod guide, spring and piston rod from the case. Don't damage the piston rod or guide during removal.
3. Withdraw piston from the transmission case.
4. If so equipped, disassemble the "controlled load" servo piston assembly by removing small snap-ring from servo piston then remove the washer, spring and piston rod from servo piston.

Low and Reverse Servo

Removal

1. Using a suitable tool, depress the

piston spring retainer and remove the snap ring.
2. Remove the spring retainer, spring, servo piston and plug assembly from the case.

Flushing the Torque Converter

1. The torque converter must be removed in order to flush it.
2. Place the converter in a horizontal position and pour two quarts of new clean solvent into the converter through the impeller hub.
3. Turn and shake the converter, swirling the solvent through the internal parts. Turn the turbine and stator with the input and reaction shafts to dislodge foriegn material.
4. Position the converter in its normal position with the drain plug at its lowest point. Drain the solvent. At the same time, rotate the turbine and stator and shake the converter, to prevent dirt particles from settling.
5. Repeat the flushing operation at least once, until the solvent or kerosene is clear.
6. After flushing, shake and rotate the converter several times, with the drain plug removed, to drain out any residual solvent or dirt.
7. Flush any remaining solvent or dirt with two quarts of new transmission fluid. Tighten the drain plug to 110 in. lbs.
8. Flush and blow out the oil cooler and lines.

Before removing any of the transmission sub-assemblies, thoroughly clean the exterior of the unit, preferably by steam. When disassembling, each part should be washed in a suitable solvent, and either set aside to drain or dried with compressed air. Do not wipe with shop towels. All of the transmission parts require extremely careful handling to avoid nicks and other damage to the accurately machined surfaces.

Sub-Assembly Reconditioning

The following procedures cover the disassembly, inspection, repair and assembly of each sub-assembly as removed from the transmission.

The use of crocus cloth is permissible but not encouraged as extreme care must be used to avoid rounding off sharp edges of valves. The edge portion of valve body and valves is very important to proper functioning.

NOTE: Use all new seals and gaskets, and coat each part with automatic transmission fluid, type A, suffix A, during assembly.

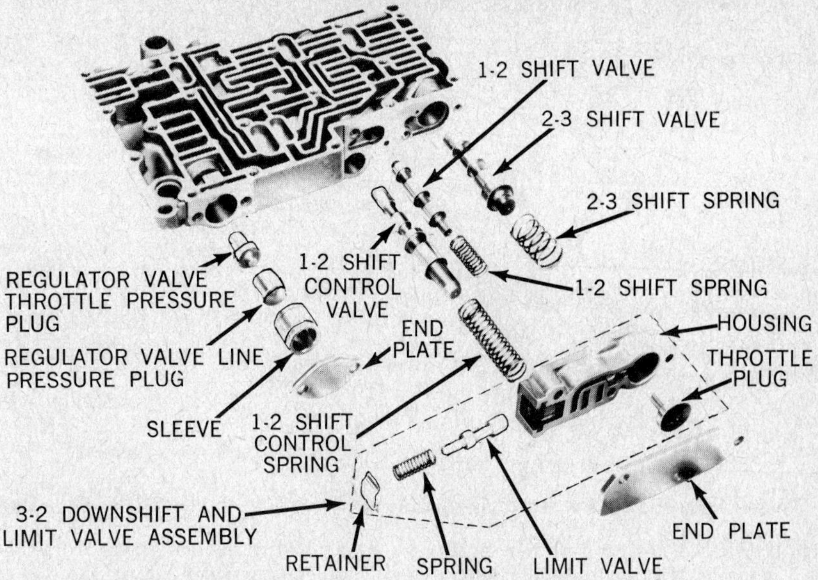

Exploded view—shift valves and pressure regulator valves (© Chrysler Corp.)

Valve Body

Disassembly

NOTE: This area is extremely critical, and sensitive to distortion. Never clamp any portion of the valve body or transfer plate in a vise. Clean with new solvent and dry with compressed air. Start all valves into their respective chambers with a twisting motion, seeing that they are well lubricated with automatic transmission fluid.

Disassembly 1973-74

1. Place the valve body on a clean repair stand. Never place any part of the valve body or transfer plate in a vise, since distortion can cause sticking valves and excessive leakage.
2. Remove the three screws from the fluid filter and remove the filter.
3. Remove the transfer plate retaining screws and 2 of the spring retainer mounting screws.
4. Lift off the transfer plate assembly. Separate the stiffener and separator plate for cleaning.
5. Remove the seven balls and spring from the valve body. Tag all springs as they are removed, for identification.
6. Turn the valve body over and remove the shuttle valve cover plate.
7. Remove the governor plug end plate and slide out the shuttle valve, throttle valve and spring, 1-2 shift valve governor plug and the 2-3 shift valve governor plug.
8. Remove the shuttle valve E-clip and remove the shuttle valve. If equipped, also remove the secondary spring and guides which are held by the clip.

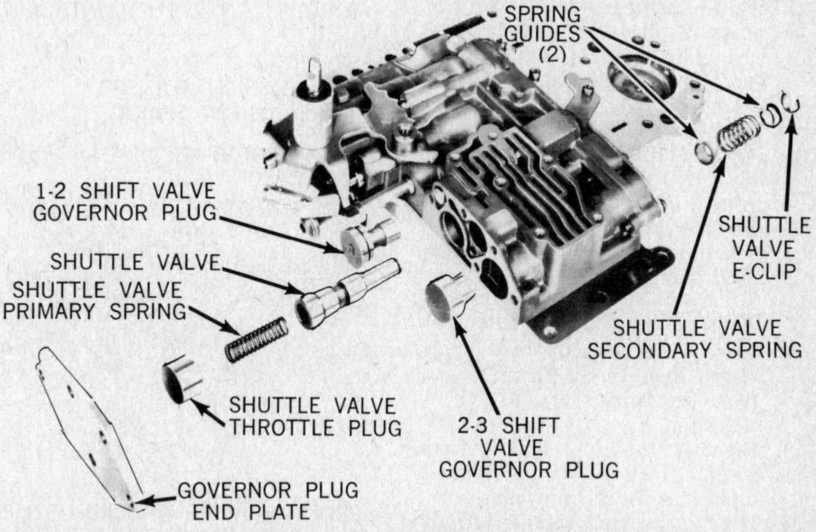

Exploded view—shuttle valve and governor plugs (© Chrysler Corp.)

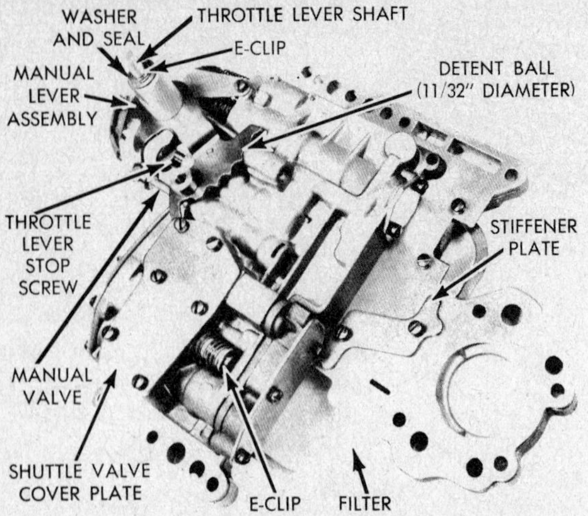

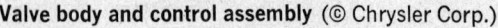

Valve body and control assembly (© Chrysler Corp.)

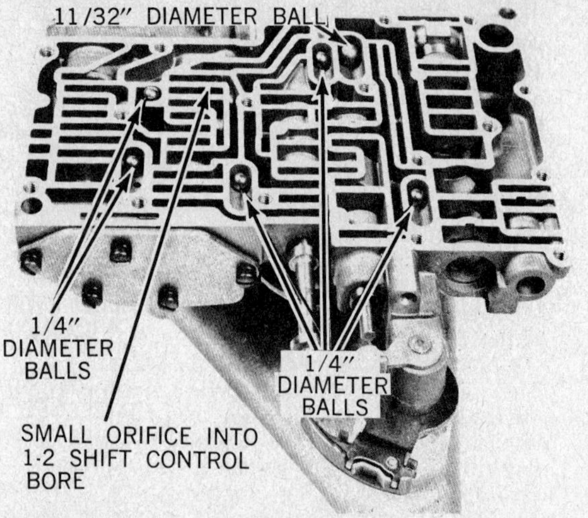

Valve body steel check valve locations (© Chrysler Corp.)

9. Hold the spring retainer firmly against the spring and remove the last screw from the valve body.
10. Remove the spring retainer, line pressure adjusting screw (do not disturb the setting), and the line pressure and torque converter regulator springs.
11. Slide the torque converter and line pressure valves out of their bores.
12. Remove the E-clip and washer from the throttle lever shaft. Remove any burrs from the shaft, and, while holding the manual lever detent ball and spring in their bore, slide the manual lever from the throttle shaft. Remove detent ball and spring.
13. Slide the manual valve from its bore.
14. Remove the throttle lever stop screw assembly from the valve body and slide out the kickdown detent, kickdown valve, throttle valve spring and throttle valve.
15. Remove the line pressure regulator valve end plate and slide out the regulator valve sleeve, line pressure plug and throttle pressure plug. If equipped, remove end plate and downshift housing assembly.
16. Remove the throttle plug housing and slide the throttle plug out. If equipped, remove retainer. limit valve, and spring.
17. Remove the shift valve springs and slide both shift valves from their bores.

Disassembly 1975 and Later

1. Place the valve body on a repair stand. Remove the three screws from the fluid filter and lift off the filter.
2. Remove the top and bottom screws from the spring retainer and adjustment screw basket.
3. Hold the spring retainer firmly against the spring force while removing the last screw from the side of the valve body.
4. Remove the spring retainer, with the line and throttle pressure adjusting screws (do not disturb the setting). Remove the line pressure and torque converter regulator springs.
5. Slide the torque converter and line pressure valves out of their bores.
6. Remove the transfer plate retaining screws and lift off the transfer plate and separator plate assembly.
7. Remove the screws from the stiffener and separate parts for cleaning.
8. Remove the rear clutch ball check valve from the transfer plate and regulator valve screen from the separator plate for cleaning.
9. Remove the seven balls and spring from valve body.

NOTE: Tag all springs as they are removed for reassembly identification.

10. Turn the valve body over and remove the shuttle valve and cover plate.
11. Remove the governor plug end plate and slide out the shuttle valve throttle plug and spring, the 1-2 shift valve governor plug and the 2-3 shift valve governor plug.

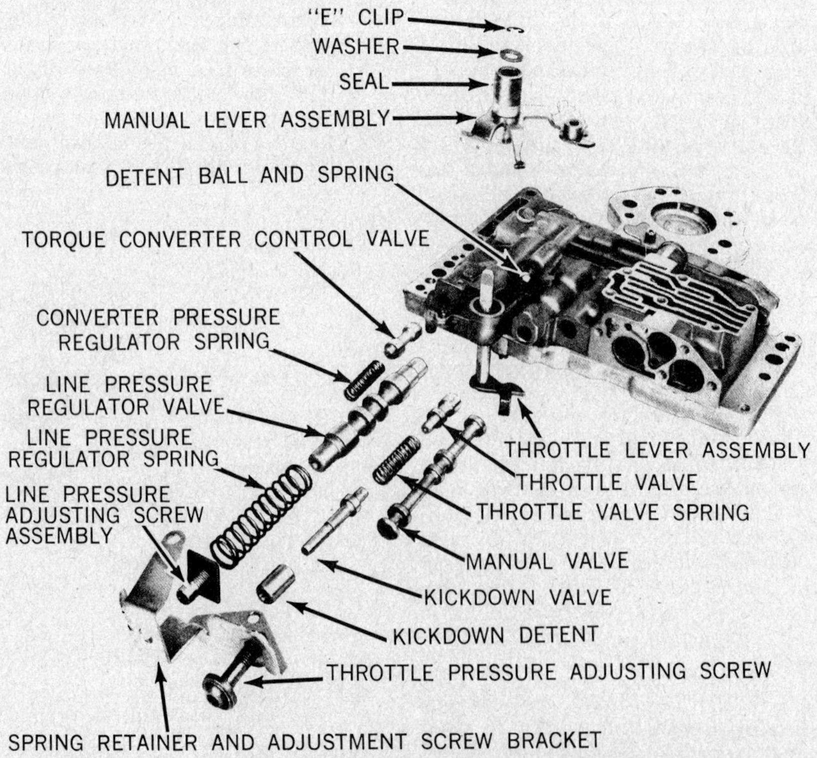

Exploded view—pressure regulator and manual control (© Chrysler Corp.)

12. Remove the shuttle valve "E" clip and slide the shuttle valve out of its bore. Also remove the secondary spring and guides which were retained by the "E" clip.
13. Remove the "E" clip and the park control rod from the manual lever.
14. Remove the "E" clip and washer from the throttle lever shaft. Remove any burrs from the shaft, then while holding the manual their bore, slide the manual lever off the throttle shaft. Remove the detent ball and spring.
15. Slide the manual valve out of its bore.
16. Slide out the kickdown detent, kickdown valve, throttle valve spring and throttle valve.
17. Remove the line pressure regulator valve end plate and slide out the regulator valve sleeve, line pressure plug, and the throttle pressure plug.
18. Remove the end plate and the downshift housing assembly.
19. Remove the throttle plug from the housing.
20. Slide the retainer plug from the housing and remove the limit valve and spring.
21. Remove the three springs and shift valves from the valve body.

Cleaning and Inspection

Inspect all components for scores, loose or bent levers, burrs and warping. Don't straighten bent levers; renew them. Loose levers may be silver soldered at the shaft. Burrs and minor nicks may be carefully removed with crocus cloth. Check for valve body warpage or distortion with a surface plate (plate glass will do) and a feeler gauge. Do not attempt to service a distorted plate or valve body, since this is a very critical area. Check all springs for distortion or fatigue. Check valves for scores and freedom of movement in the bores, they should fall of their own weight, in and out of the bore.

Assembly 1973-74

1. Slide the shift valves and springs into the proper valve body bores.
2. If so equipped, assemble the downshifts housing. Insert the limit valve and spring into the housing. Slide the spring retainer into the groove.
3. Insert the throttle plug into the housing bore and install the housing on the valve body. Torque the screws to 28 in. lbs.
4. Install the throttle pressure plug, line pressure plug and sleeve, fastening the end plate. Torque to 28 in. lbs.
5. Install the throttle valve, throttle valve spring, kickdown valve, kickdown detent and throttle lever stop screw with the locknut (do not adjust yet).
6. Slide the manual valve into its bore.
7. Install the throttle lever and shaft on the valve body. Insert the detent ball and spring into its bore in the valve body. Depress the ball and spring and slide the manual lever over the throttle shaft. Be sure that it engages the manual valve and detent ball. Install the seal, retaining washer and E-clip on the throttle shaft.
8. Insert the torque converter control valve and spring into the valve body.
9. Insert the line pressure regulator and spring into the valve body.
10. Install the line pressure adjusting screw assembly and spring retainer on the springs temporarily with one screw.
11. Place the 1-2 and 2-3 shift valve governor plugs in their proper bores.
12. Install the shuttle valve, spring, and shuttle valve throttle plug. If so equipped, install the secondary spring with two guides and clip on the other end.
13. Install the governor plug end plate and torque the screws to 28 in. lbs.
14. On those valve bodies not having a secondary spring, install the E-clip on the end of the shuttle valve.
15. Install the shuttle valve cover plate and torque screws to 28 in. lbs.
16. Install the spring and seven balls in the valve body. The seven include: five $\frac{1}{4}$ in. balls, one $\frac{3}{8}$ in. diameter ball in the corner and one 11/32 in. diameter ball in the large chamber.
17. Place the separator plate on the transfer plate. Make sure all bolt holes are aligned and torque the two transfer plate screws and two stiffener plate screws to 28 in. lbs.
18. Place the transfer plate assembly on the valve body. Align the spring loaded ball as the 17 shorter screws are installed. Start at the center and work outward, tightening the screws to 35 in. lbs.
19. Install the oil filter and torque to 35 in. lbs.
20. Check spring engagement with the tang and adjusting nut. Install the remaining spring retainer screws. Check alignment and torque to 28 in. lbs.
21. After valve body has been serviced and completely assembled, adjust throttle and line pressures. If pressures were satisfactory prior to disassembly, use the original settings.

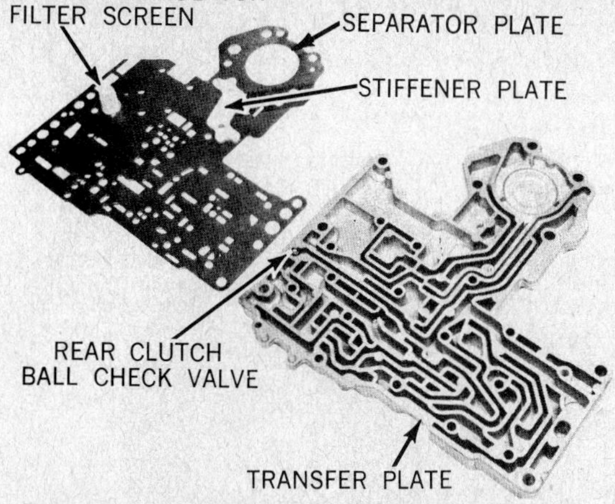

Transfer and separator plates (© Chrysler Corp.)

Assembly 1975 and Later

1. Slide the shift valves and springs into their proper valve body bores.
2. Assemble the downshift housing as follows:
   a. Insert the limit valve and spring into the housing.
   b. Slide the spring retainer into the groove in the housing.
   c. Insert the throttle plug in the housing bore. Position the assembly against the shift valve springs.
3. Install the end plate and tighten the screws to 28 inch-pounds.
4. Install the throttle pressure plug, line pressure plug and sleeve, then fasten the end plate to the valve body. Tighten to 28-inch pounds torque.
5. Install the throttle valve, throttle valve spring, kickdown valve, and the kickdown detent.
6. Slide the manual valve into its bore.
7. Install the throttle lever and shaft on the valve body. Insert the detent spring and ball in its bore in the valve body. Depress

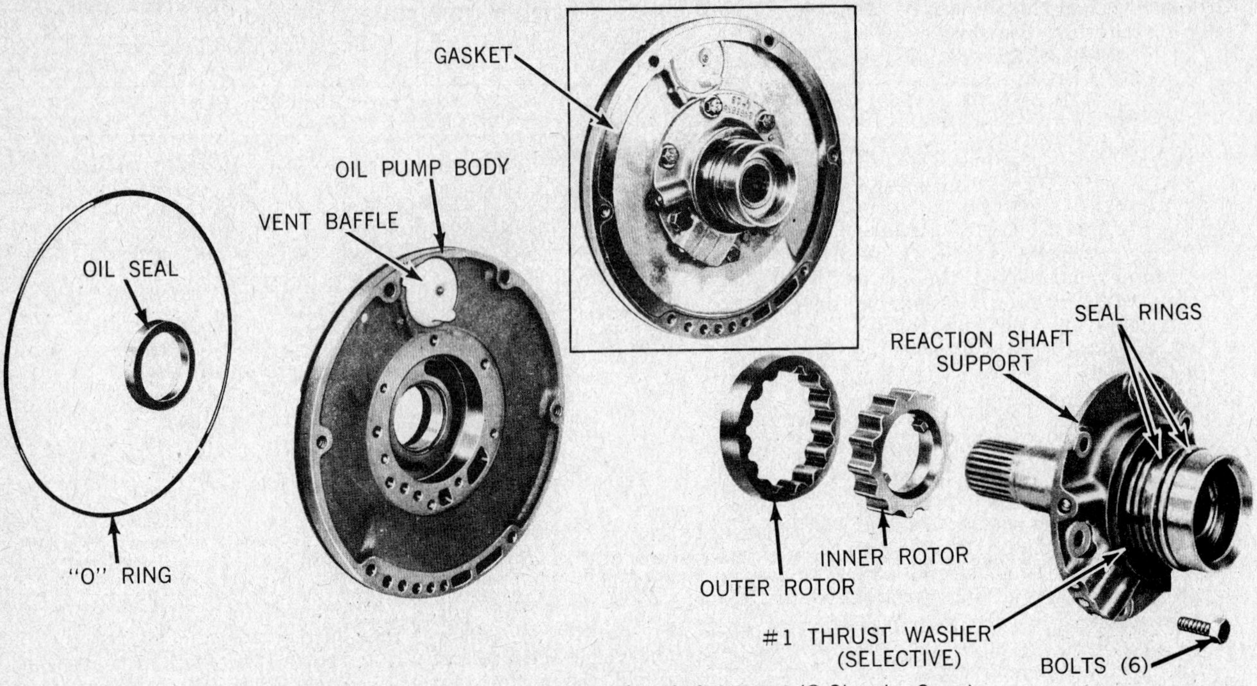

Exploded view—oil pump and reaction shaft support (© Chrysler Corp.)

the ball and spring and slide the manual lever over the throttle shaft so that it engages the manual valve and detent ball. Install the seal, retaining washer, and "E" clip on the throttle shaft.

8. Install the torque converter control valve and spring into the valve body.
9. Insert the line pressure regulator valve and spring into the valve body.
10. Install the pressure adjusting screw and bracket assembly on the springs and fasten it with the screw which goes into the side of the valve body. Start the screws on the top and bottom, do not tighten, and then tighten the screw on the side of the valve body.
11. Place the 1-2 and 2-3 shift valve governor plugs in their respective bores.
12. Install the shuttle valve and hold it in the bore with your index finger, while installing on the other end of it the secondary spring with the guides and retaining "E" clip.
13. Install the primary shuttle valve spring and the throttle plug.
14. Install the governor plug end plate and tighten the five retaining screws to 28 inch-pounds.
15. Install the shuttle valve cover plate and tighten the six retaining screws to 28 inch-pounds.
16. Install the spring and seven balls in the valve body in their respective locations.
17. Place the separator plate on the transfer plate. Install the stiffener plate and retaining screws in their original positions.
18. Make sure that all the bolt holes are aligned, then tighten two transfer plate screws and two stiffener plate screws to 28 inch pounds.
19. Place the transfer plate assembly on the valve body. Be careful to align the spring loaded ball as the 17 shorter screws are installed, the three longer screws are for the oil filter.
20. Starting in the center and working outward tighten the screws to 35 inch-pounds.
21. Check the spring engagement and install the remaining top and bottom screws in the adjusting screw bracket. Tighten the side screw first to 28 inch pounds, then tighten the top and bottom screws.
22. Install the oil filter and tighten to 35 inch-pounds.
23. After the valve body has been serviced and completely assembled, adjust the throttle and line pressures. If pressures were satisfactory prior to disassembly, use oirginal settings.

Accumulator Piston and Spring

Inspect both seal rings for wear and freedom in the piston grooves. Check the piston for scores, burrs, nicks and wear. Check the piston bore for corresponding damage and check piston spring for distortion and fatigue. Replace parts as required.

Governor

Disassembly

1. Carefully remove the snap-ring from weight end of governor valve shaft and pull out valve and shaft. Remove the large snap-ring from the weight end of governor housing and lift out the governor weight assembly.
2. Remove the snap-ring from inside the governor weight, remove the inner weight and spring from the outer weight.

NOTE: throughly clean all parts in a suitable and clean solvent. Check for damage and free movement before assembly.

3. If lugs on support gear are damaged, remove four bolts and separate support from governor body.

Assembly

1. If support was separated from governor body, assemble and tighten bolts finger-tight. Make sure the oil passage of the body aligns with passage in the support. Position support and governor on output shaft so that the valve shaft hole in the governor aligns with the hole in the output shaft. Install a snap-ring behind the governor body and tighten the bolts to 100 in. lbs.
2. Assemble the governor weights and spring, then secure with snap-ring inside large governor weight.
3. Place the weight assembly in the governor housing and install snap-ring.

Oil Pump and Reaction Shaft Support

Disassembly

1. Remove the bolts from the rear side of the reaction shaft sup-

port and lift the support off the pump.
2. Remove the rubber seal ring from the pump body flange.
3. Drive the oil seal out with a blunt punch.

Inspection

1. Inspect the interlocking steel rings on the reaction shaft for wear or broken locks, make sure they turn freely in the grooves.
2. Inspect the machined surfaces on the pump body and the reaction shaft support for nicks and burrs.
3. Inspect the pump body and reaction shaft support bushings for wear or scores.
4. Inspect the pump rotors for scoring or pitting.
5. With the rotors cleaned and installed in the pump body, place a straight edge across the face of the rotors and pump body. Use a feeler gauge to measure the clearance between the straight edge and the face of the rotors. Clearance limits are 0.0015-0.003 inch. Also measure the rotor tip clearance between the inner and outer teeth. Clearance limits are 0.005-0.010 inch. Clearance between outer rotor and its bore in the oil pump body should be from 0.004-0.008 inch.

Oil Pump Bushing

Replacement

1. Place the pump housing on a clean smooth surface with the rotor cavity down.
2. Place the removing head of the special bushing tool in the bushing, and install the tool handle.
3. Drive the bushing straight down and out of the bore. Be careful not to cock the tool in the bore.
4. Place a new bushing on the installation tool.
5. With the pump housing on a smooth clean surface, hub end down, start the bushing and installation head in the bushing bore. Install the tool handle in the installation head.
6. Drive the bushing into the housing until the tool bottoms in the pump cavity. Be careful not to cock the tool during installation.
7. Stake the bushing in place using a blunt punch or similar tool. A gentle tap at each stake slot location will suffice.
8. Using a narrow bladed knife, remove high points of burrs around the staked area. Do not use a file that will remove more metal than is necessary.
9. Thoroughly clean the pump housing before installation.

Reaction Shaft Bushing

Replacement

CAUTION: Do not clamp any part of the reaction shaft or support in a vise.

1. Assemble the special bushing removal tool which consists of: cup, hex nut and removal tool.
2. With the cup held firmly against the reaction shaft, thread the remover into the bushing as far as possible by hand.
3. Using a wrench to screw remover into the bushing 3 to 4 additional turns to firmly engage the threads in the bushing.
4. Turn the hex nut down against the cup to pull the bushing out of the reaction shaft. Throughly clean the reaction shaft to remove chips made by the remover threads.
5. Lightly grip the bushing in a vise or with pliers and back the tool out of the bushing. Be careful not to damage the threads on the bushing remover.
6. Slide a new bushing (chamfered end first) on the installing head of the special tool and start them in the bore of the reaction shaft.
7. Support the reaction shaft upright on a clean smooth surface and install the installation tool handle. Drive the bushing into the shaft until the tool bottoms.
8. Thoroughly clean the reaction shaft support assembly before installation.

Assembly

1. Assemble the pup rotors and 'O' ring in the pump housing.
2. Install the reaction shaft support. Install the retaining bolts and torque to 160 inch-pounds.
3. Place a new oil seal in the opening of the pump housing, lip of the seal facing inward, and drive the seal into the housing until it bottoms.

Front Clutch

Disassembly

1. With screwdriver or pick, remove large snap-ring, which holds the pressure plate in the clutch piston retainer. Lift pressure plate and clutch plates out of the retainer.
2. Install spring compresison tool or similar tool, over piston spring retainer. Compress spring and remove snap-ring, then, slowly release tool until the spring retainer is free of the hub. Remove the compressor, retainer and spring.
3. Turn the clutch retainer upside down and bump on a wooden block to remove the piston.

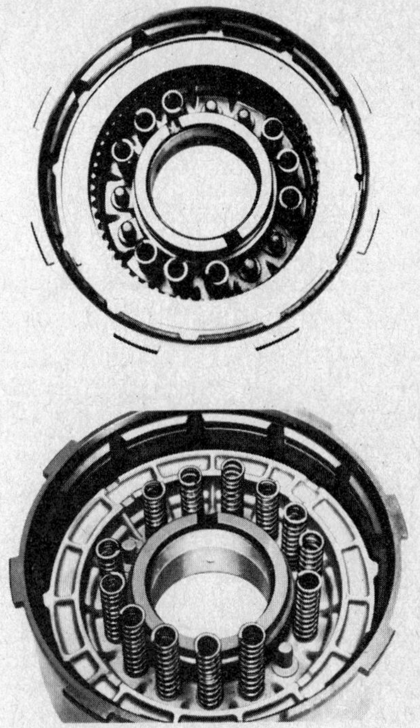

Location of front clutch springs—two types—9 and 13 springs
(© Chrysler Corp.)

Remove seal rings from the piston and clutch retainer hub.

Inspection

Inspect clutch discs for evidence of burning, glazing and flaking. A general method of determining clutch plate breakdown is to scratch the lined surface of the plate with a finger nail. If material collects under the nail, replace all driving discs. Check driving splines for wear or burrs. Inspect steel plates and pressure plate surfaces for discoloration, scuffing or damaged driving lugs. Replace if necessary.

Check steel plate lug grooves in clutch retainer for smooth surfaces. Plate travel must be free. Inspect band contacting surface of clutch re-

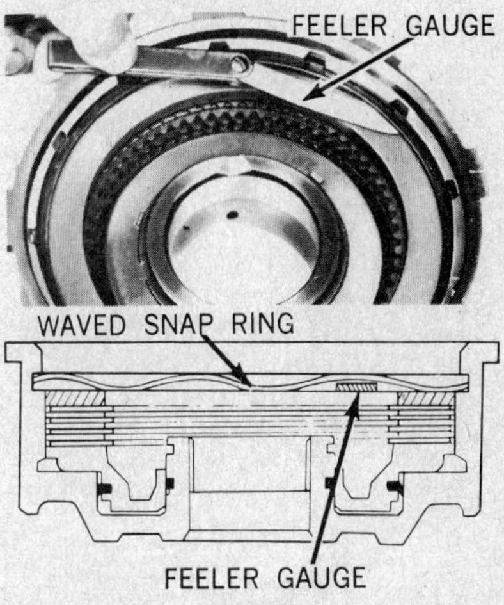

Measuring front clutch plate clearance
(© Chrysler Corp.)

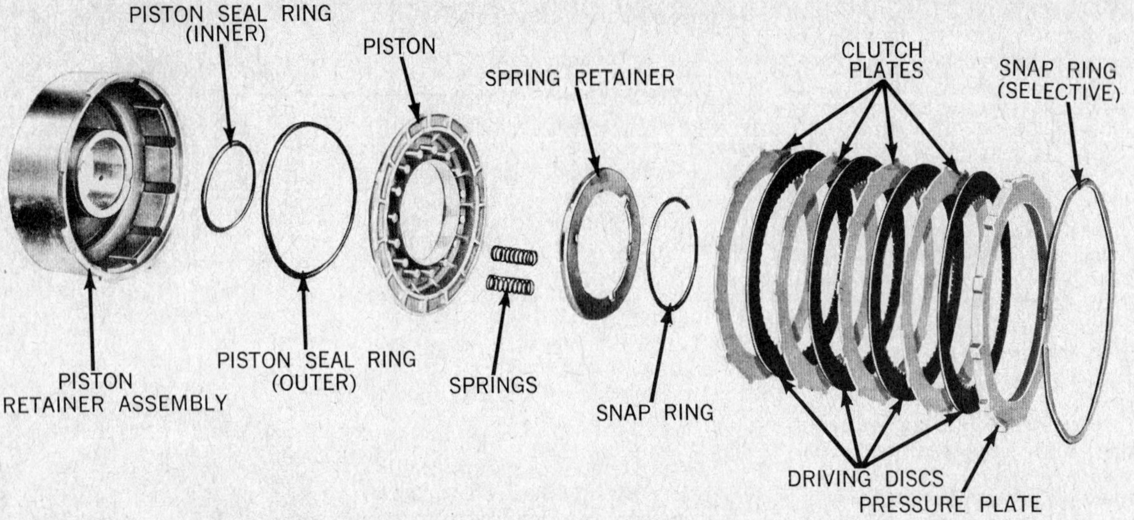

Exploded view—front clutch assembly (© Chrysler Corp.)

tainer, being sure the ball moves freely. Check seal ring surfaces in clutch retainer for scratches or nicks, light annular scratches will not interfere with the sealing of neoprene rings.

Inspect inside bore of piston for score marks. If light marks exist, polish with crocus cloth. Check seal ring grooves for nicks and burrs. Inspect neoprene seal rings for deterioration, wear and hardness. Check piston spring, retainer, and snap-ring for distortion and fatigue.

Front Clutch Retainer Bushing

Replacement

1. Lay clutch retainer (open end down) on a clean smooth surface and place removing head in the bushing. Install the bushing removal tool handle.
2. Drive the bushing straight down and out of clutch retainer bore. Be careful not to cock the tool in the bore.
3. Lay the clutch retainer (open end up) on a clean smooth surface. Slide a new bushing on the installation head tool, and start them in the clutch retainer bore.
4. Install the bushing installation tool handle and drive the bushing into the clutch retainer until the tool bottons.
5. Thoroughly clean the clutch retainer before assembly and installation.

Assembly

1. Lubricate and install inner seal ring onto hub of clutch retainer. Be sure that lip of seal faces down and is properly seated in the groove.
2. Lubricate and install outer seal ring onto clutch piston, with lip of seal toward the bottom of the clutch retainer. Place piston assembly in retainer and, with a twisting motion, seat the piston in the bottom of the retainer.
3. Place spring on the piston hub and position spring retainer and snap-ring on spring. Compress spring with tool, or suitable ring compressor, and seat snap-ring in the hub groove. Remove compressor.
4. Lubricate all clutch plates, then, install a steel plate, followed by a lined plate, until all plates are installed. Install the pressure plate and snap-ring. Be sure the snap-ring is correctly seated.
5. With front clutch assembled, insert a feeler gauge between the pressure plate and snap-ring. The clearance should be to specification. If not, install a snap-ring of proper thickness.

Rear Clutch

Disassembly

1. With a small screwdriver or

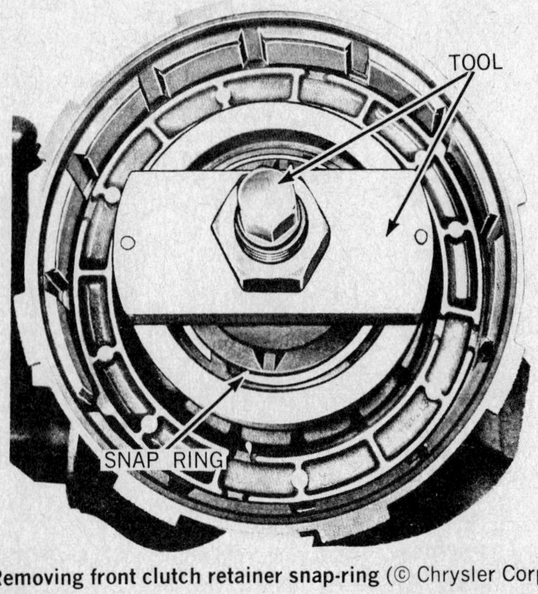

Removing front clutch retainer snap-ring (© Chrysler Corp.)

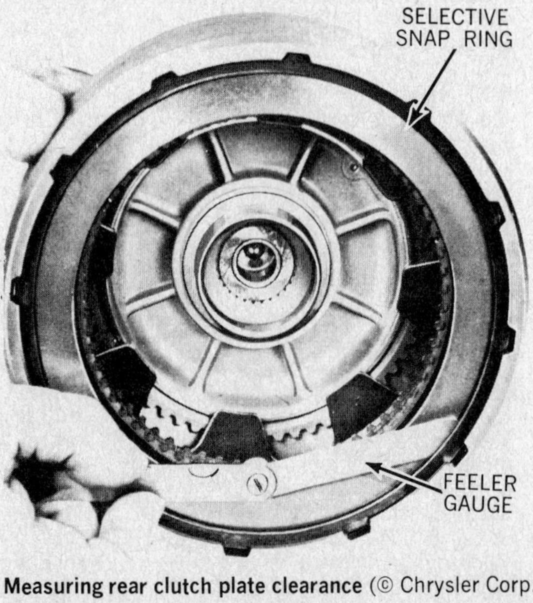

Measuring rear clutch plate clearance (© Chrysler Corp.)

pick, remove the large snap-ring that secures the pressure plate in the clutch piston retainer. Lift the pressure plate, clutch plates, and inner pressure plate from the retainer.

2. Carefully pry one end of wave spring out of its groove in clutch retainer and remove wave spring, spacer ring and clutch piston spring.
3. Turn clutch retainer assembly upside down and bump on a wood block to remove the piston. Remove seal rings from the piston.
4. If necessary, remove snap-ring and press the input shaft from the clutch piston retainer.

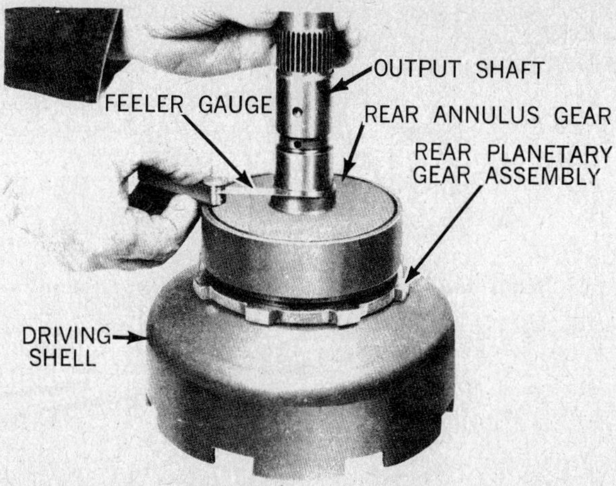

Measuring end play of planetary gear assembly (© Chrysler Corp.)

Inspection

Inspect driving discs for indication of damage; handle as previously outlined under front clutch inspection.

Input Shaft Bushing

Replacement

1. Clamp the input shaft in a vise with soft faced jaws, being careful not to clamp on the seal ring lands or bearing journals.
2. Assemble the remover tool, cup tool and hex nut
3. With the cup held firmly against the clutch piston retainer, thread the remover into the bushing as far as possible by hand.
4. Using a wrench, screw the remover into the bushing as far as possible by hand.
5. Turn the hex nut down against the cup to pull the bushing from the input shaft.
6. Thoroughly clean the input shaft to remove the chips made by the remover threads. Make sure that the small lubrication hole next to the ball in the end of the shaft is not plugged. Make certain that no chips have lodged next to the steel ball.
7. Slide a new bushing on the installation head of the bushing tool and start them in the bore of the input shaft.
8. Stand the input shaft upright on a clean surface and position the handle on the installation tool. Drive the bushing into the shaft until the tool bottoms.
9. Thoroughly clean the input shaft and clutch piston retainer before assembly and installation.

Assembly

1. If removed, press input shaft into the piston retainer and install snap ring
2. Lubricate, then install inner and outer seal rings onto the clutch piston. Be sure the seal lips face toward the head of the clutch retainer and seals are properly seated in the piston grooves.
3. Place piston assembly in retainer and, with a twisting motion, seat piston in bottom of retainer.
4. Place spring over piston with outer edge of spring positioned below snap ring groove. Start one end of snap ring in groove. Make sure spring is exactly centered on piston. Progressively tap snap ring into groove. Be sure snap ring is fully seated in groove.
5. Install inner pressure plate into clutch retainer, with raised portion of plate resting on the spring.
6. Lubricate all clutch plates, then install one lined plate, followed by a steel plate, until all plates are installed. Install outer pressure plate and snap-ring.
7. With rear clutch completely assembled, insert a feeler gauge between the pressure plate and snap-ring. The clearance should be to specification. If not, install snap-ring of proper thickness to obtain the required clearance.

NOTE: Rear clutch plate clearance is very important to obtaining satisfactory clutch performance. Clearance is influenced by the use of various thickness outer snap-rings.

Planetary Gear Train End Play

NOTE: Before removal of the planetary gear assemblies, sun gear and drive shell parts from the output shaft, measure the end play as follows:

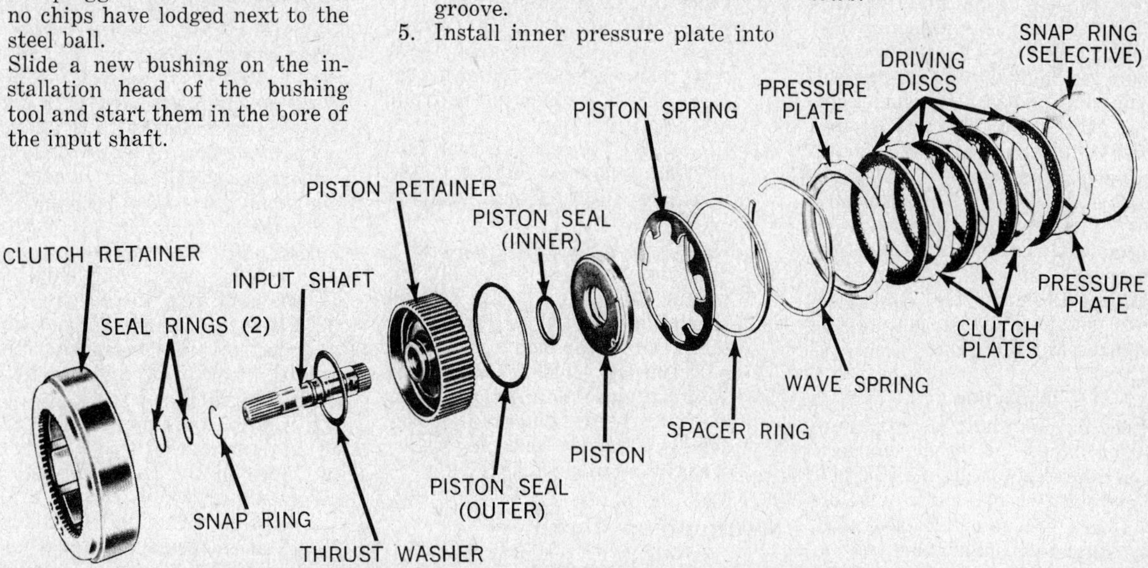

Exploded view—rear clutch assembly (© Chrysler Corp.)

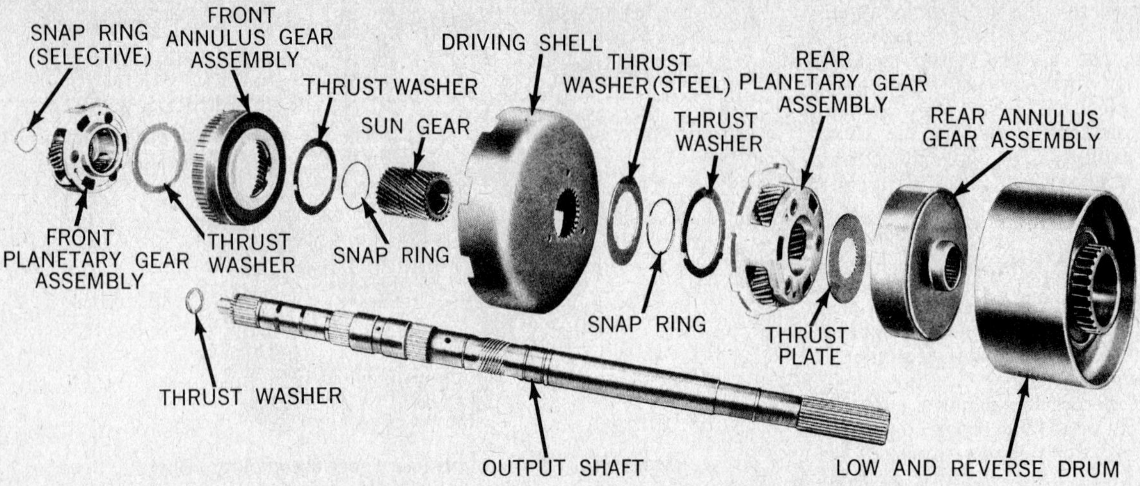

Exploded view—planetary gear train and output shaft assembly (© Chrysler Corp.)

1. With the assembly in an upright position, push the rear annulus gear support downward on the output shaft.
2. Insert a feeler gauge between the rear annulus gear support hub and sholder on the output shaft.
3. The clearance should be 0.010-0.025 inch. If the clearance is not within limits, replace thrust washer and/or necessary parts.

Disassembly

1. Remove thrust washer from forward end of output shaft.
2. Remove snap-ring from forward end of output shaft, then, slide front planetary assembly from the shaft.
3. Slide front annulus gear off planetary gear set. Remove thrust washer from rear side of planetary gear set.
4. Slide the sun gear, driving shell, and rear planetary assembly, from the output shaft.
5. Remove sun gear and driving shell from the rear planetary assembly, remove thrust washer from inside driving shell, remove snap-ring and steel washer from sun gear (rear side of driving shell). Slide sun gear out of driving shell, then remove snap-ring and steel washer from opposite end of sun gear, if necessary.
6. Remove thrust washer from forward side of rear planetary assembly. Remove the planetary gear set and thrust plate from the rear annulus gear.

Inspection

Inspect output shaft bearing surfaces for burrs or other damage. Light scratches or burrs may be polished out with crocus cloth or a fine stone. Check speedometer drive gear for damage, and make sure all oil passages are clear.

Check bushings in the sun gear for wear or scores. Replace sun gear assembly if bushings show wear or other damage. Inspect all thrust washers for wear and scores. Replace if necessary. Check lockrings for distortion and fatigue. Inspect annulus gear and driving gear teeth for damage. Inspect planetary gear carrier for cracks and the pinions for broken or worn gear teeth.

Assembly

1. Install rear annulus gear on output shaft. Apply thin coat of grease on thrut plate, place it on shaft, and in annulus gear making sure teeth are over shaft splines.
2. Position rear planetary gear assembly in rear annulus gear. Place thrust washer on front side of planetary gear assembly.
3. Install snap-ring in front groove of sun gear (long end of gear). Insert sun gear through front side of driving shell. Install rear steel washer and snap-ring.
4. Carefully slide driving shell and sun gear assembly on output shaft, engaging sun gear teeth with rear planetary pinion teeth. Place thrust washer inside front driving shell.
5. Place thrust washer on rear hub of front planetary gear set. Slide assembly into front annulus gear.
6. Carefully work front planetary and annulus gear assembly on output shaft, meshing planetary pinions with sun gear teeth.
7. With all components properly positioned, install selective snap ring on front end of output shaft. Measure end-play of assembly. Adjust end-play with selective snap rings.

Overrunning Clutch

Inspection

Inspect clutch rollers for smooth round surfaces, they must be free of flat spots, chipped edges and flaking. Inspect roller contacting surfaces on both cam and race for pock marks and roller wear-marks. Check springs for distortion and fatigue and inspect low and reverse drum thrust. Inspect cam set screw for tightness. If loose, tighten and restake the case.

Overrunning Clutch Cam

Replacement

If the overrunning clutch cam or roller spring retainer are found to be defective, replace the cam and spring in the following manner:

1. Remove the set screw from the case below the clutch cam.
2. Remove the four bolts securing the output shaft support to the rear transmission case. Insert a punch through the bolt holes and drive the cam from the case. Alternately, punch from one bolt hole to another so the cam will be driven evenly from the case.

NOTE: The output shaft support must be in the case to install the overrunning clutch cam. If the support requires replacement, drive it rearward out of the case with a wood block and hammer. To install, screw two pilot studs into the case. Chill the support with dry ice. Quickly position the support over the pilot studs, and drive it firmly into the case with a wood block and hammer.

3. Clean all burrs and chips from the cam area in the case.
4. Place the spring retainer on the cam, making sure the retainer lugs snap firmly into the notches on the cam.
5. Position the cam in the case with the cam serrations aligned with those in the case. Tap the cam evenly into the case as far as possible with a soft faced mallet.
6. Position the cam installation tool on the cam and tighten the hex nut on the tool to seat the cam in

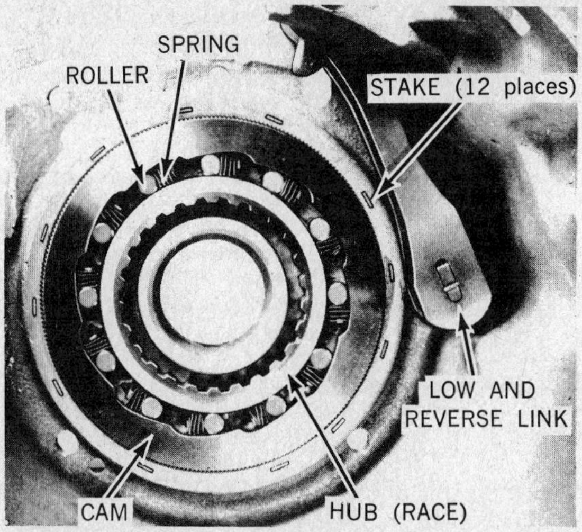

Overrunning clutch installation—with low-reserve band link in position (© Chrysler Corp.)

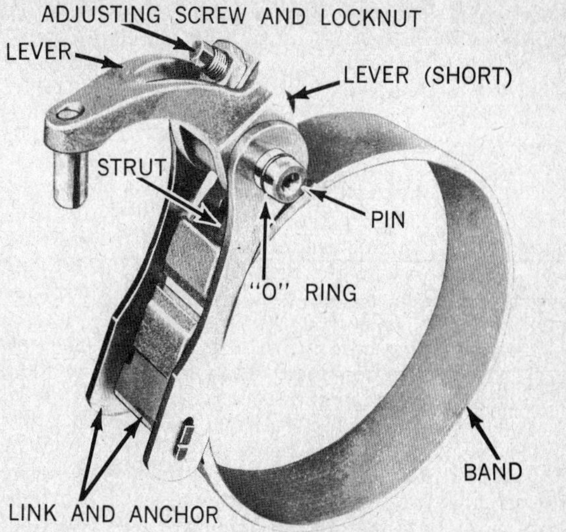

Low and reverse band and linkage (© Chrysler Corp.)

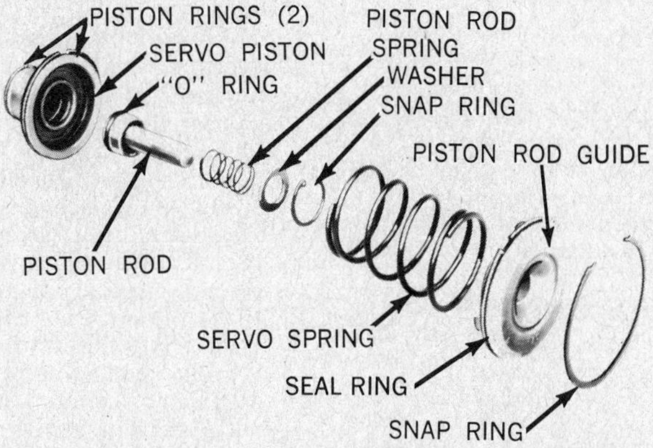

Exploded view—"Controlled Load" type kickdown servo piston assembly (© Chrysler Corp.)

the case. Make sure that the cam is firmly seated. Install the cam retaining set screw and stake the case around the set screw to prevent it coming loose.

7. Remove the cam installation tool. Install the support retaining screws and tighten to 140 inch-pounds torque. Stake the case around the cam in twelve places with a blunt chisel.

Kickdown Servo and Band

Two kick down servo designs are used. One for standard engine applications and one for heavy duty engine applications, called "Controlled Load". The removal and installation is basically the same with the "Controlled Load" servo piston requiring further disassembly after removal from the servo.

Disassembly

Disassemble the controlled load servo piston by removing the small snap ring from the servo piston. Remove the washer, spring and piston rod from the servo piston.

Inspection

Inspect piston and guide seal rings for wear, and be sure of their freedom in grooves. It is not necessary to remove seal rings, unless circumstances warrant. Inspect piston for scores, burrs or other damage. Check fit of guide on piston rod. Check piston for distortion and fatigue. Inspect band lining for wear and fit of lining material to the metal band. This lining is grooved; if grooves are not still visible at the ends or any part of the band, replace the band. Inspect band for distortion or cracked ends.

Assembly

Assemble the controlled load servo piston as follows:

1. Grease the "O" ring and install on the piston rod.
2. Install the piston rod into the servo piston.
3. Install the spring, flat washer and snap ring to complete the assembly.

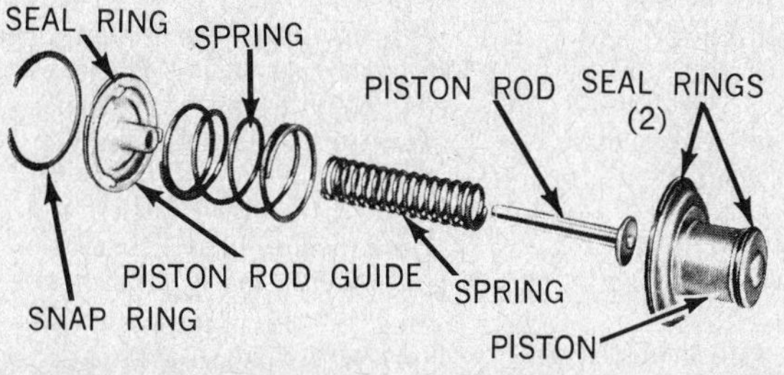

Exploded view—standard type kickdown servo piston assembly (© Chrysler Corp.)

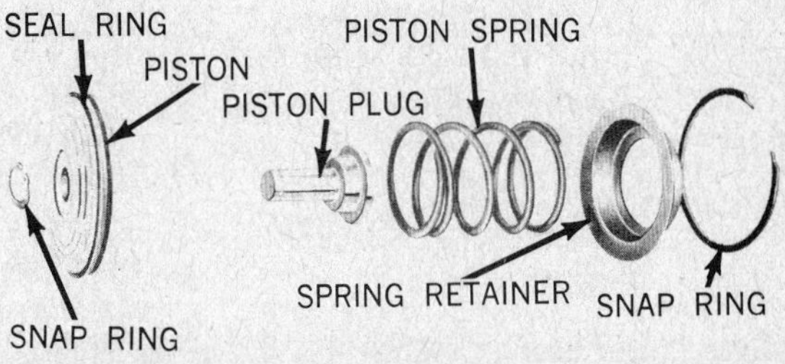

Exploded view—low and reverse servo piston assembly (© Chrysler Corp.)

Low and Reverse Servo and Band

Disassembly

Remove snap-ring from piston and remove the piston plug and spring.

Inspection

Inspect neoprene seal ring for damage, rot, or hardness. Check piston and piston plug for nicks, burrs, scores and wear. The piston plug must operate freely in the piston. Check the piston bore in the case for scores or other damage. Examine springs for distortion and fatigue.

Check band lining for wear and the fit of the lining to the metal band. This lining has a grooved surface; if the grooves are worn away at the ends or at any part of the band, replace the band. Inspect the band for distortion or cracked ends.

Assembly

Lubricate and insert the piston plug and spring into the piston, and secure with the snap-ring.

Sub-Assemblies Installation

The following assembly procedures include the installation of sub-assemblies into the transmission case and adjustment of the drive train end-play. Do not use force to assemble any of the mating parts. Always use new gaskets during the assembly operations.

NOTE: use only automatic transmission fluid, type A, suffix A, or fluid of equivalent chemical structure, to lubricate automatic transmission parts during, or after, assembly.

Band Adjustments

Because of the varied engine applications, the kickdown and low-reverse band adjustment specifications will be found in the separate truck sections. Refer to the appropriate section.

Overrunning Clutch

With transmission case in upright position, insert clutch race inside cam. Install overrunning clutch rollers and springs.

Low and Reverse Servo and Band

1. Carefully work servo piston assembly into the case with a twisting motion. Place spring, retainer and snap-ring over the piston.
2. Using a valve spring compressor, compress the spring and install the snap-ring.
3. Position rear band in the case, install the short strut, then connect the long lever and strut to the band. Screw in band adjuster just enough to hold struts in place. Install low-reverse drum. Be sure long link and anchor assembly is installed to provide running clearance for low-reverse drum.

Kickdown Servo

1. If equipped with a controlled load servo piston, sub-assemble the unit as follows: grease the O ring and install on the piston rod; install the piston rod into the servo piston; install the spring, flat washer and snapring.
2. Carefully insert servo piston into case bore. Install piston rod, two springs and guide.
3. Compress the kickdown servo springs by using a engine valve spring compressor. Install the snapring.

Planetary Gear Assemblies, Sun Gear, Driving Shell, Low and Reverse Drum

1. While supporting the assembly in the case, insert the output shaft through the rear support. Carefully work the assembly rearward, engaging the carrier lugs with low-reverse drum slots.

CAUTION: Be careful not to damage the ground surfaces of the output shaft during installation.

Front and Rear Clutch

1. The following method may be used to support the transmission; cut a 3½" hole in a bench, small drum or box, strong enough to support the transmission; file notches at the edge so the output shaft support will lie flat; insert the output shaft into the hole and support the transmission upright.
2. Apply a coat of grease to the input shaft to output shaft thrust washer and install the thrust washer on the front end of the output shaft.
3. Align the front clutch plate inner splines, and place the assembly in position on the rear clutch. Be sure the clutch plate splines are fully engaged.
4. Align the rear clutch plate inner splines and lower the two clutch assemblies in to the case.
5. Carefully, work the clutch assemblies in a circular motion to engage the rear clutch splines over the front annulus gear splines. Make sure the front clutch drive lugs are fully engaged in the driving shell.

Front Band

1. Slide the band over the front clutch assembly.
2. Install band strut, screw in the adjuster just enough to hold the band in place.

Oil Pump and Reaction Shaft Support

1. If drive train end-play was not within specifications, replace the thrust washer on the reaction shaft support hub, with one of proper thickness (see specifications).
2. Screw (two) pilot studs into front pump opening in the case.
3. Place a new rubber seal ring in groove on outer flange of pump. Be sure the seal ring is not twisted.
4. Install the assembly into the case, tap lightly with a soft mallet if necessary. Install four bolts, remove pilot studs, install remaining bolts and pull down evenly.
5. Rotate the input and output shafts to see if any binding exists. Tighten bolts to 175 inch-pounds. Check shafts again for free roattion. Adjust both bands.

Governor and Support

1. Place the governor and support on the output shaft. Position it so that the governor valve shaft hole aligns with the hole in the output shaft, then slide the assembly into place. Install snapring behind the governor housing. Torque housing-to-support screws to specification.
2. Place the governor valve on the valve shaft, insert the assembly into the housing and through the governor weights. Install the valve shaft retaining snap-ring.

Extension Housing-Short

1. Position a new gasket on the extension housing. Carefully slide the extension housing into place. Install the remaining bolts and washers and tighten to 24 foot-pounds torque.
2. Install the transmission yoke. Install the nut with its three projections toward the washer. Hold the yoke and tighten to 175 foot-pounds.
3. Install the speedometer pinion and adapter assembly.

Extension Housing-Long

1. Install the snap ring in the front groove on the output shaft. Install the bearing on the shaft with its outer race ring groove toward the front. Press or tap the bearing tight against the front snap ring. Install the rear snap ring.
2. Position a new gasket on the transmission case. Place the output shaft bearing retaining snap ring in the extension housing. Spread the snap ring as far as possible. Carefully, tap the extension housing into place. Make

sure that the snap ring is fully seated in the bearing groove.

3. Install and tighten the extension housing bolts to 24 foot-pounds.
4. Install the access plate and gasket on the side of bottom of the extension housing mounting pad.
5. Install the speedometer pinion and adapter assembly.
6. Measure the input shaft end play, correct if necessary.

Valve Body Assembly and Accumulator Piston

1. Clean the mating surfaces and inspect for burrs on both the transmission case and the valve body steel plate.
2. Install the accumulator piston in the transmission case and place the piston spring on the accumulator piston.

NOTE: There is no spring used with the 440 cu. in. engine.

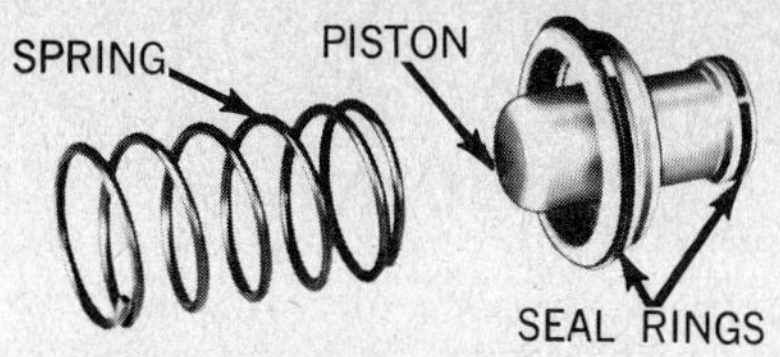

Accumulator piston and spring assembly (© Chrysler Corp.)

3. Make sure that the back-up light and neutral start switches have been removed.
4. Insert the parking lock rod through the opening in the rear of the case with the knob positioned against the reaction plug and sprag. Move the front end of the rod toward the center of the transmission while exerting rearward pressure on the rod, to force it past the sprag, rotate the output shaft if necessary.
5. Place the valve body manual lever in the low position. Place the valve body in its approximate position in the case. Connect the parking lock rod to the manual lever and secure with an "E" clip. Align the valve body in the case, install the retaining bolts finger tight.
6. With the neutral start switch installed, place the manual valve in the neutral position. Shift the valve body if necessary to the center neutral finger over the neutral switch plunger. Snug the bolts down evenly, and torque to 100 inch-pounds.
7. Install the gearshift lever and tighten the clamp bolt. Check the lever shaft for binding in the case by moving the lever through all detent positions. If binding exists, loosen the valve body bolts and realign.
8. Install the flat washer and throttle lever, then tighten the lever clamp bolt.
9. Adjust the kickdown and low-reverse bands.
10. Install the oil pan, using a new gasket. Tighten the pan bolts to 150 inch-pounds.

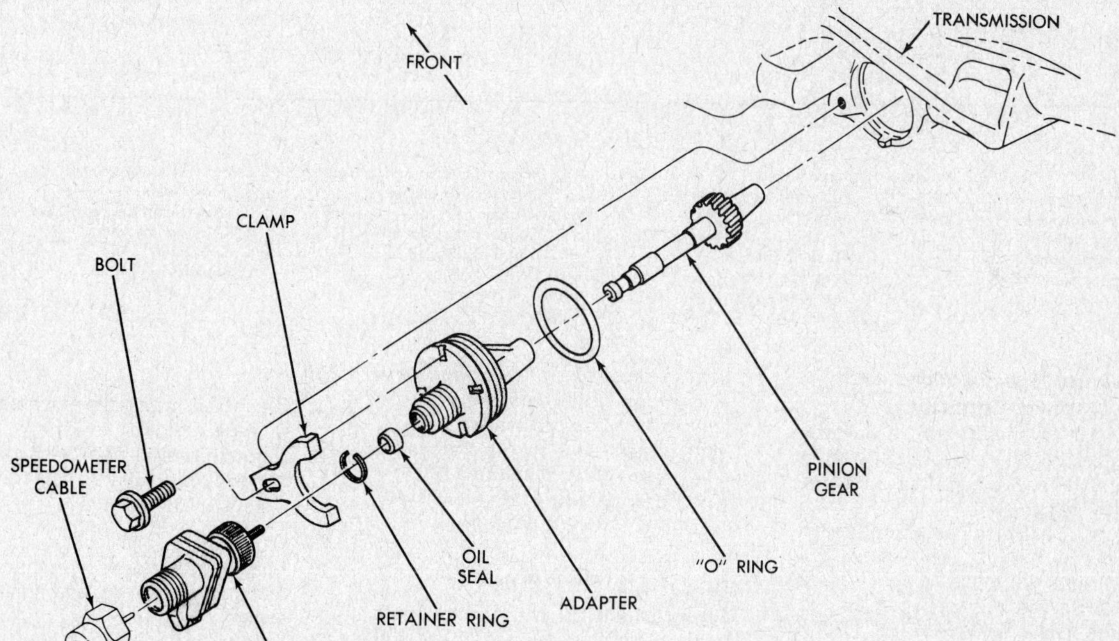

Speedometer drive disassembled (© Chrysler Corp.)

DIAGNOSIS

This guide covers the most common symptoms and is an aid to careful diagnosis. The items to check are listed in sequence to be followed for quickest results. Follow the checks in the order given for the particular transmission type.

TROUBLE SYMPTOMS	ITEMS TO CHECK IN TRUCK	OUT OF TRUCK
Harsh N to D or N to R shift	CDEFGIJ	ab
Delayed Shift—N to D	ACIHKJ	ca
Runaway on upshift and 3-2 kickdown	ABCDLIHK	b
Harsh upshift and 3-2 kickdown	BCDLIHJ	b
No upshift	ABCDLIHKM	b
No kickdown on normal downshift	ABNCDLIHKM	d
Erratic shifts	ABNCFOPQ IKMJ	c
Slips in forward drive positions	ACIHK	abd
Slips in reverse only	CEGIK	
Slips in all positions	ACOIK	e
No drive in any position	ACOQIKJ	ca
No drive in forward positions	CDOLIHK	abd
No drive in reverse	CEGKMI	b
Drives in neutral	NIJ	a
Drags or locks	DELG	abfd
Noises	AORPMIJ	a
Hard to fill or blows out	AORSTQI	
Transmission overheats	ADEORTMI	abe

Key to Checks

A. Oil level
B. Control linkage
C. Oil pressure check
D. Kickdown band
E. Low-reverse band
F. Improper engine idle
G. Servo linkage
H. Accumulator
I. Valve body assembly
J. Manual valve lever
K. Air pressure check
L. K-D servo link
M. Governor
N. Gear shift cable
O. Regulator valve and/or spring
P. Output shaft bushing
Q. Strainer
R. Converter control valve
S. Breather clogged
T. Cooler or lines
a. Front-kickdown clutch
b. Rear clutch
c. Front pump and/or sleeve
d. Overrunning clutch
e. Converter
f. Planetary

General Specifications and Fluid Capacity

Type ......4 speed fully automatic
Oil Capacity (Dry) .....28½ pints
Cooling ....Water
Oil Filter Type
...........Bottom suction screen
Clutches 4
Overrunning Clutches 2
Bands & Servos 2
Planetary Gear Sets 3

Band Adjustment

See automatic transmission chapter under appropriate truck section.

Sub-Assembly Removal

NOTE: Before removing any transmission sub-assemblies, plug all openings and thoroughly clean the exterior of the unit with steam. Cleanliness during the entire disassembly and assembly cannot be over-emphasized. When disassembling, each part should be washed in a suitable solvent, then dried by compressed air. Do not wipe parts with shop towels. All mating surfaces in the transmission are accurately machined; therefore, careful handling of parts must be exercised to avoid damage.

Input Shaft End Play

Measurement of the input shaft end play before disassembly will usually indicate when a thrust washer should be changed. The thrust washer is located between the reaction shaft support and the front clutch retainer.

1. Attach a dial indicator to the transmission bell housing with its plunger seated against the end of the input shaft. Move the input shaft in and out to obtain the end play reading. End play should be 0.018-0.062 inch.
2. Record the indicator reading for reference during reassembly.

Oil Pan

1. Place the transmission assembly in repair stand.
2. Remove the oil pan bolts and remove the oil pan. Discard the gasket.

Valve Body

1. Loosen the clamp bolts and remove the throttle and gearshift levers.
2. Remove the back-up light and neutral safety switches.
3. Remove the bolts securing the valve body to the transmission case, remove the valve body.

Accumulator Piston and Spring

1. Remove the accumulator piston from the case and lift the spring from the case.

Transmission Compounder

Disassembly

NOTE: Before removing the com-

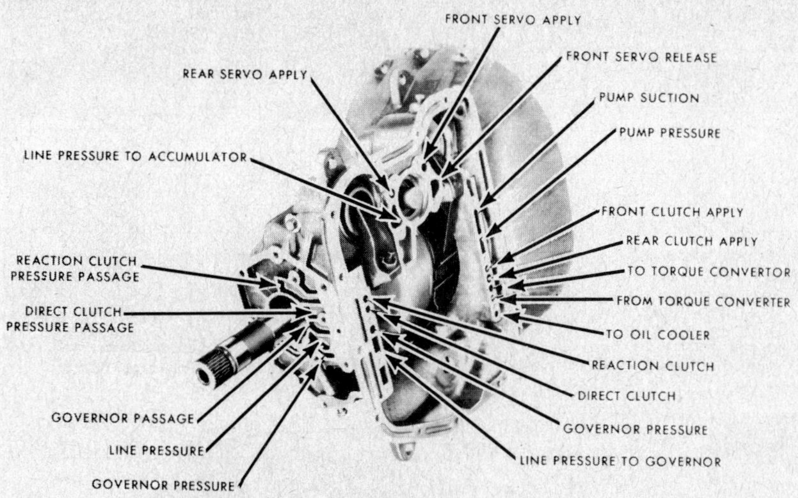

Passages for air pressure tests (© Ford Motor Co.)

pounder, reduce the input shaft end play to zero by inserting and wedging a flat screw driver between the low-reverse drum and the transmission case. When the low-reverse drum is as far forward as possible, tighten the rear band until the band is tight on the low-reverse drum. Remove the screw driver. This prevents the #2 thrust washer or one of the clutches from coming out of position.

1. Remove the propeller shaft companion flange and yoke retaining nut and washer from the output shaft and remove the drum and yoke. Carefully pull the shaft yoke out of the transmission extension housing. Remove the parking brake assembly.
2. Remove the speedometer pinion and governor cover and gasket.
3. Remove the governor assembly from the extension housing.
4. Remove the compounder extension to compounder adapter screws and remove the compounder extension for further disassembly on work bench.
5. Remove the snap ring retaining the compounder annulus gear to intermediate shaft and remove the annulus gear and fiber washer and direct clutch.
6. Remove the two seal rings from the adapter. Unlock the seal ring hooks by compressing the rings.
7. Spring the seal rings just enough so that they can be removed without scratching the adapter hub.

NOTE: The two seal rings for the direct clutch are different metal than the two seal rings for the reaction clutch. Do not mix these seal rings.

8. Remove the snap ring retaining the reaction clutch to the adapter clutch hub using snap ring tool.
9. Remove the reaction clutch assembly.
10. *DO NOT remove the reaction clutch seal rings unelss they are worn or damaged.*
11. Remove the snap ring retaining the compounder planetary gear assembly to the output shaft.
12. Remove the planetary gear assembly.
13. Remove the driving shell and the sun gear assembly.
14. Remove the overrunning clutch hub rollers and springs. Note the position of the overrunning clutch rollers and springs before disassembly to assist during assembly.
15. Remove the output shaft oil seal with a suitable hook type slide hammer. *Place the puller hooks between the output shaft and under the side of the seal so that the hooks do not damage the housing bore.*
16. Remove the output shaft bearing snap ring with special tool.
17. Remove the output shaft from the rear of the compounder extension.

NOTE: The output shaft bearing is a sliding fit in the housing bore and an interference fit on the output

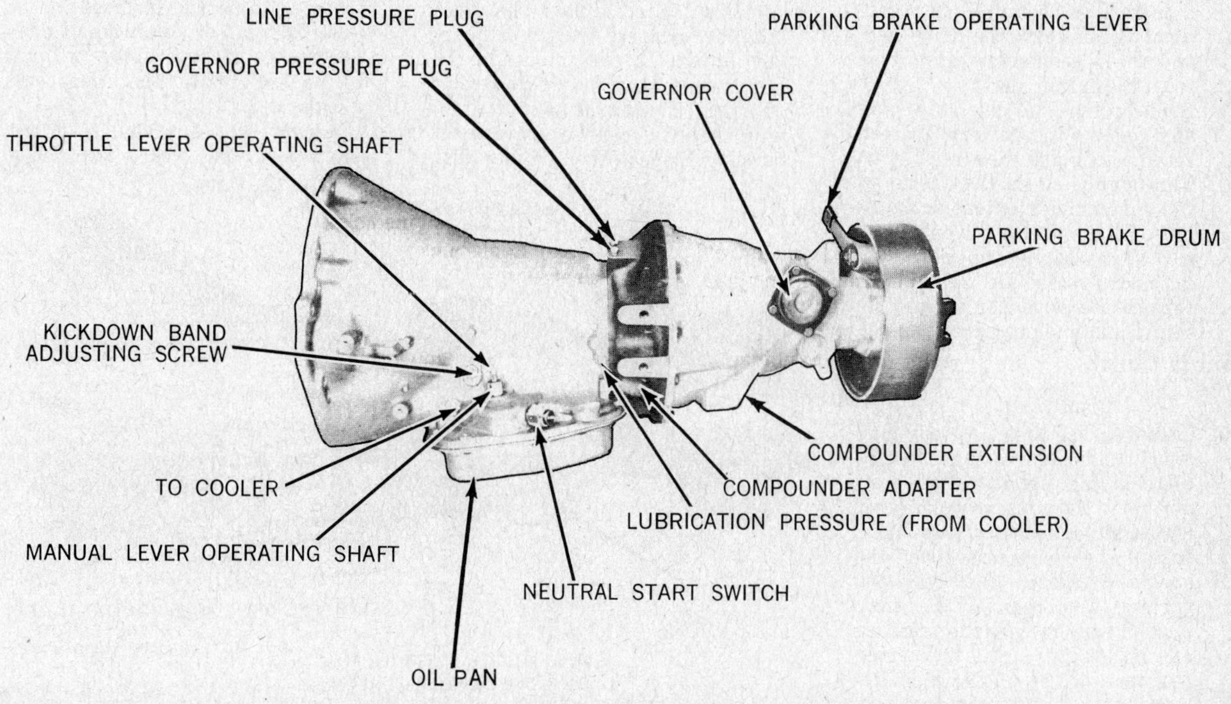

New process model A-345 transmission (© Ford Motor Co.)

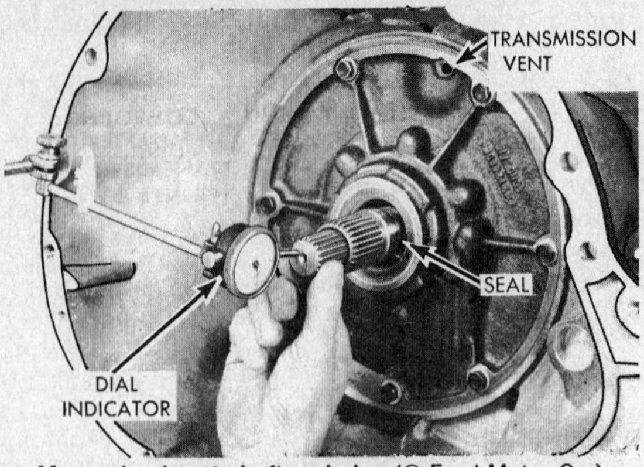

Measuring input shaft end play (© Ford Motor Co.)

Removing or installing direct clutch seal rings (© Ford Motor Co.)

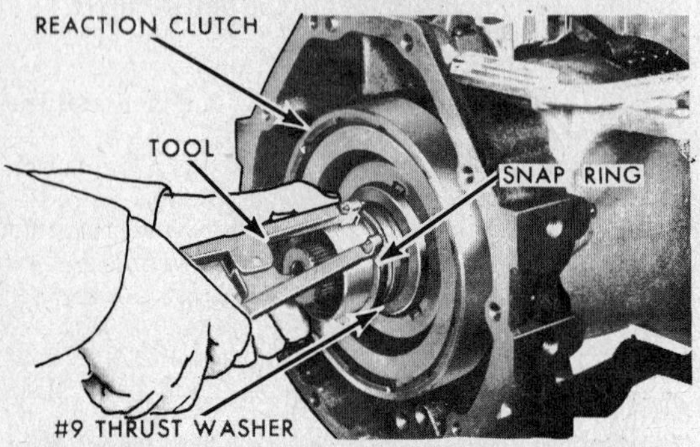

Removing or installing the reaction clutch snap ring (© Ford Motor Co.)

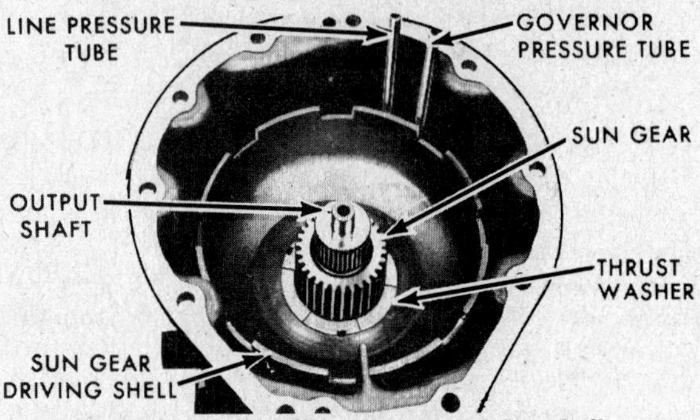

Removing or installing the rear driving shell (© Ford Motor Co.)

shaft. The overrunning clutch cam and spring retainer cannot be removed from the extension housing. If the clutch cam or roller spring retainer is damaged, it will be necessary to replace the extension housing with the cam and retainer as an assembly.

18. Remove the output shaft bearing by tapping the threaded end of the output shaft on a hard wood block or press. Note the position, then remove the snap ring, governor drive gear, the drive ball, and the speedometer drive gear from the output shaft.
19. Remove the line pressure plug and remove the governor screen retainer clip and the screen.
20. Thoroughly clean the inside of the compounder extension housing with a suitable solvent. Blow out all passages and blow dry with compressed air. Reinstall or replace the governor screen, retainer and line pressure plug.

Direct Clutch

Disassembly

1. Remove the large waved snap ring which secures the pressure plate in the clutch piston retainer. Lift the pressure plate and clutch plates out of the retainer.
2. Install the compressor over the spring retainer. Compress the springs and remove the snap ring. Slowly release the pressure on the springs until the spring retainer is free of the hub. Remove the compressor tool, retainer, and springs.
3. Invert the clutch retainer assembly and bump it on a wood block to remove the piston. Remove the seals from the piston and the clutch retainer hub.

Inspection

1. Inspect the clutch plates and discs for flatness. They must not be warped or cone shaped.
2. Inspect the facing mateiral on driving discs. Replace the discs that are charred, glazed or heavily pitted. Discs should also be replaced if they show evidence of material flaking off or if the facing material can be scraped off easily. Inspect the driving disc splines for wear or damage. Inspect the steel plate and pressure plate surfaces for burning, scoring of damaged driving lugs. Replace if necessary.
3. Inspect the steel plate lug grooves in the clutch retainer for smooth surfaecs, the plates must travel freely in the grooves. Note the ball check in the retainer, make sure the ball moves freely.
4. Inspect the seal surfaces in the clutch retainer for nicks of deep scratches, light scratches will not interfere with the neopreme seals.
5. Inspect the neopreme seals for deterioration, wear, and hard-

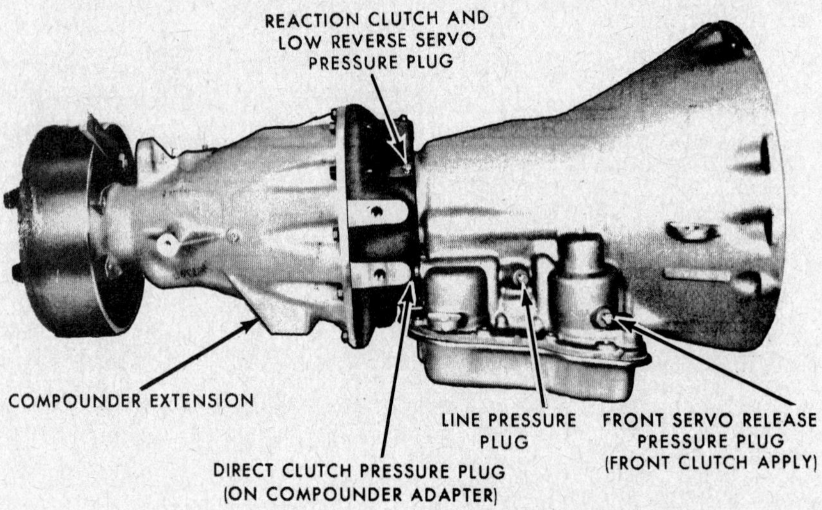

Pressure test locations (right side of case) (© Ford Motor Co.)

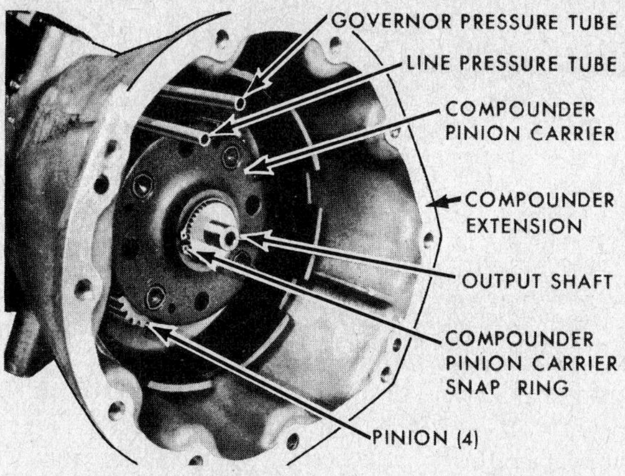

Compounder pinion carrier snap ring (© Ford Motor Co.)

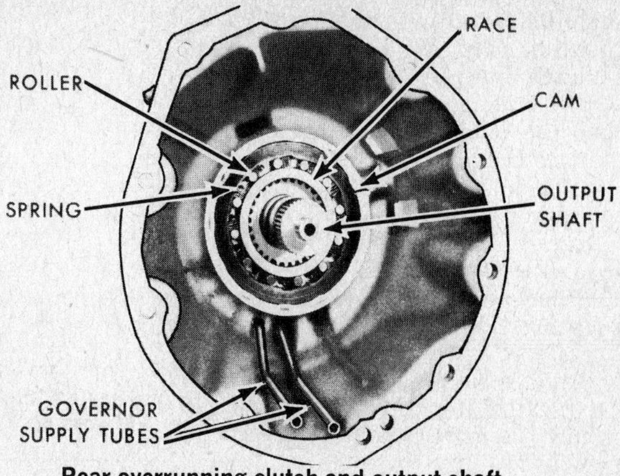

Rear overrunning clutch and output shaft (© Ford Motor Co.)

ness.

6. Inspect the piston springs, wave spring, and spacer for distortion or breakage.

Assembly

1. Lubricate and install the inner seal on the clutch retainer hub. Make sure the lip of the seal faces down and is properly seated in the groove.
2. Install the outer seal in the clutch piston and with the lip of the seal toward the bottom of the clutch retainer, apply a coating of wax type lubricant (Door Ease) to the outer edge of the seals. Place the piston assembly in the retainer and carefully seat the piston in the retainer.
3. Install the eight springs on the piston. Position the spring retainer and snap ring over the springs. Compress the springs with special tool and seat the snap ring in the hub groove. Remove the compressor tool.
4. Lubricate all the clutch plates. Install one steel plate by a friction plate (wa e type) until the four discs are installed. Install the pressure plate and snap ring. Make sure that the snap ring is completely seated in the groove.
5. Push downward on the pressure plate and insert a feeler gauge between the pressure plate and the waved snap ring to measure the maximum clearance where the snap ring is waved way from the pressure plate. Clearance should be 0.088-0.145 inch.

Reaction Clutch

Disassembly

1. Remove the large waved snap ring that secures the pressure palte in the clutch retainer. Lift the pressure plate and the clutch plates out of the retainer.
2. Install the spring compressor tool over the piston spring retainer. Compress the springs and remove the snap ring. Slowly release the tool until the spring retainer is free of the hub. Remove the tool, the retainer, and springs.
3. Invert the clutch retainer assembly and bump it on a wood block to remove the piston. Remove the seals from the piston and the clutch retainer hub.

Inspection

1. Inspect the plates and discs for flatness. They must not be warped or cone shaped.
2. Inspect the facing material on all driving discs. Replace any discs that are charred, glazed, or show heavy pitting. Discs should also be replaced if they show evidence of material flaking off or if the facing material can be scraped off easily. Inspect the driving disc splines for wear or damage. Inspect the steel plate and pressure plate for burning, scoring, or damaged driving lugs.
3. Inspect the steel plate lug grooves in the clutch retainer for smooth surfaces, plates must travel freely in the grooves. Inspect the seal surfaces in the clutch retainer for nicks or deep scratches. Light scratches will not interfere with the neoprene seals. Inspect the neoprene seals for deterioration, wear and hardness.
4. Inspect the pitson spring, wave spring and spacer for distortion or breakage.

Assembly

1. Lubricate and install the inner seal on the hub of the clutch retainer. Make sure that the lip faces down and is properly seated in the groove.
2. Install the outer seal on the

CLUTCH AND BAND APPLICATION CHART

A-345 AUTOMATIC TRANSMISSION

LEVER POSITION	FRONT CLUTCH	REAR CLUTCH	REACTION CLUTCH	DIRECT CLUTCH	FRONT (KICKDOWN) BAND	REAR (LOW-REV.) BAND	FRONT OVERRUNNING CLUTCH	REAR OVERRUNNING CLUTCH
Neutral							NO MOVEMENT	
"D" Drive								
Breakaway		X					HOLDS	HOLDS
Second		X			X		OVERRUNS	HOLDS
Third	X	X					OVERRUNS	HOLDS
Fourth	X	X		X			OVERRUNS	OVERRUNS
"3" Third	X	X	X				OVERRUNS	PARTIAL HOLD
"2" Second		X	X		X		OVERRUNS	PARTIAL HOLD
"1" First		X	X			X	PARTIAL HOLD	PARTIAL HOLD
Reverse	X		X			X	NO MOVEMENT	

X=Applied

clutch piston with the lip of the seal toward the bottom of the clutch retainer. Apply a coat of a wax type lubricant (Door Ease) to the outer edge of the seals. Place the piston assembly in the retainer and carefully seat the piston.

3. Install the eight springs on the piston. Position the spring retainer and snap ring over the springs. Install the spring compressor tool and compress the piston spring until the snap ring is seated in the groove on the hub. Remove the compressor tool.
4. Lubricate all the clutch plates. Install one steel plate by a friction plate (plain gray) until four discs are installed. Install the pressure plate and snap ring. Make sure that the snap ring is properly seated.
5. Push downward on the pressure plate and insert a feeler gauge between the pressure plate and the waved snap ring. Clearance should be 0.088-0.145 inch.

Governor Bushing

Installation

1. Loosely bolt the reamer fixture to the compounder extension.
2. Place the alignment arbor into the reamer fixture and down into the governor bore.
3. Righten the screws on the reamer fixture to 8-12 foot pounds.

CAUTION: **Do not over-torque and strip the threads.**

NOTE: Be sure the alignment arbor rotates freely after the screws are properly tightened.

4. Remove the alignment arbor.
5. Working with the proper reamer and drive ratchet, hand ream the governor bore in the following manner:
   a. Oil the reamer, reamer fixture, and governor bore.
   b. Using a 5-10 pound feeding force on the reamer, ream until the reamer bottoms in the extension and then continue to rotate the reamer 10 (ten) complete revolutions.
   c. Remove the reamer using a *clockwise rotation* and 5-10 pounds force upward.

CAUTION: **Pulling the reamer out without using a rotating motion may score the governor bore and cause a leak between the extension and the bushing.**

6. Remove the reamer fixture from the extension.
7. Thoroughly clean the chips from the extension. Visually check the governor feed holes to insure that they are free of chips.
8. Install the bushing using the following operation:
   a. Note the position of the two (2) notches at one end of the bushing.
   b. Position the notches so that one notch is at the 11 o'clock position and the other is at the 2 o'clock position, viewing the extension in its normal installed, parallel position.
   c. Use the alignment arbor and the bushing installation tool to drive the bushing into the extension. A brass hammer should be used to strike the hardened steel bushing installation tool.
   d. Drive the bushing until it is flush with the top of the bore.
9. Oil a new governor and insert it into the installed bushing .The governor should spin freely. If slight honing on the bushing is required, use crocus cloth around your ringer and rotate the cloth within the new bushing.

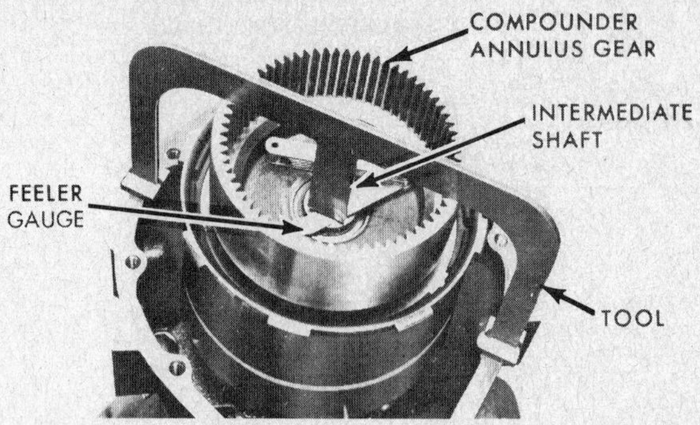

Selecting the proper thrust washer thickness with special tool and feeler gauge (© Ford Motor Co.)

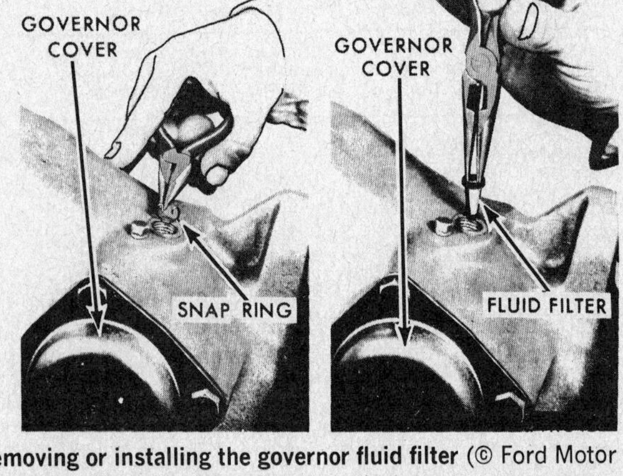

Removing or installing the governor fluid filter (© Ford Motor Co.)

Transmission Compounder

Assembly

NOTE: Be sure the #2 thrust washer, front clutch discs, and rear clutch discs are in their proper position.

1. Push the intermediate shaft forward to reduce the input shaft end play to zero.
2. Insert and wedge a flat screw driver between the low-reverse drum and the transmission case, moving the low-reverse drum as far forward as possible.
3. Tighten the rear (low-reverse) band adjusting screw until the band is tight on the low-reverse drum. Remove the screw driver.
4. Install the two seal rings on the forward grooves on the adapter hub.
5. Inspect the seal rings for wear or broken locks. Be sure that the rings move freely in the grooves.
6. Install the reaction clutch assembly on the adapter hub.
7. Install the fiber thrust washer. Install the snap ring.
8. Install the two seal rings on the rear grooves of the adapter hub. Inspect for wear or broken hock locks. Be sure that the rings turn freely in the groves.
9. Install the direct clutch assembly on the adapter with the direct clutch drum gear teeth engaging all the clutch discs in the reaction clutch.
10. Use the thrust washer selection tool and a feeler gauge to select the proper thrust washer thickness.
11. Assemble the compounder annulus gear to the annulus gear support and retain with a snap ring.
12. Install the selective fiber thrus washer on the compounder annulus gear support.
13. Install the annulus gear assembly into the direct clutch, engaging all the clutch discs in the di-

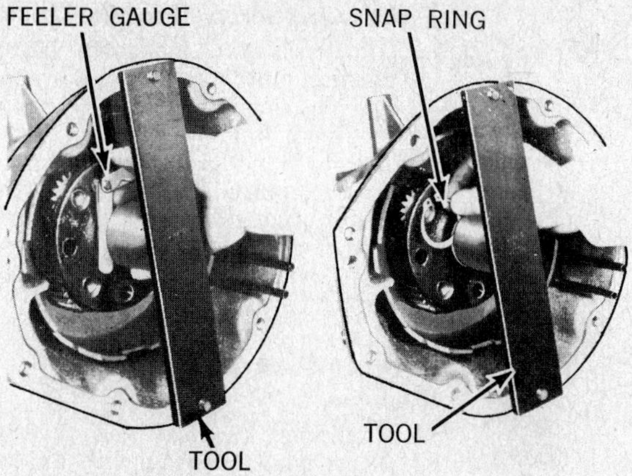

Selecting snap ring with special tool and feeler gauge (© Ford Motor Co.)

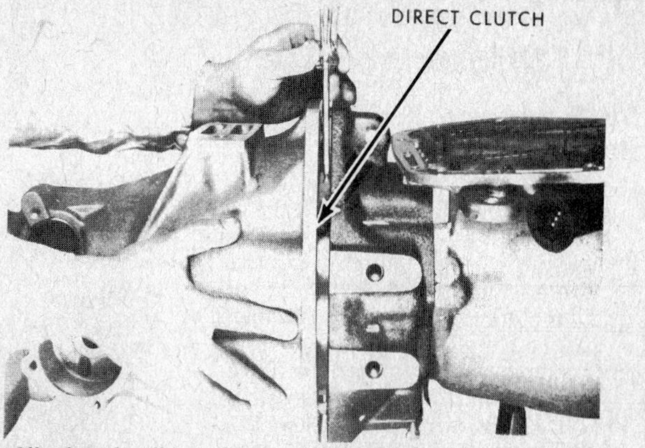

Aligning the direct clutch with the driving shell, and the annulus gear with the compounder plantetary pinions (© Ford Motor Co.)

rect clutch. Install the snap ring in the groove on the intermediate shaft.

14. Install the speedometer drive gear, drive ball, governor drive gear, and snap ring on the output shaft.
15. Assemble the bearing to the output shaft. Install the output shaft and bearing into the extension housing.
16. Install the bearing retainer snap ring. Avoid scoring the housing bore.
17. Install a new output shaft oil seal.
18. Place the extension housing in an upright position, insert the overrunning clutch hub (race) inside the clutch cam.
19. Install the overrunning clutch rollers and spring.
20. Install the governor pressure and line pressure tubes in the extension.
21. Assemble the sun gear and the overrunning clutch roller retainer to the driving shell. Install the snap ring.
22. Install the driving shell and sun gear assembly on the output shaft.
23. Install the bronze thrust washer in the driving shell. Install the planetary carrier assembly and install the selective snap ring.

NOTE: Use the snap ring selector tool and a feeler gauge to measure the clearance between the pinion carrier and selector tool hub. Position the feeler gauge in the output shaft snap ring groove. Do not rest the extension housing assembly on the output shaft.

24. Install the speedometer gear and the governor assembly in the extension housing. Install the governor cover with a new gasket. Tighten the cover screws to 12 foot-pounds torque.
25. Install the gasket and position the extension housing assembly on the compounder adapter using pilot studs. Carefully align the pressure tubes with the matching holes in the adapter.

With light pressure against the extension housing, use a 3/16 inch diameter phillips head screw driver in the hole in the direct clutch drum, rotate the drum to align the tangs of the drum with the slots in the driving shell and the compounder annulus gear with the compounder planetarp gear pinions.

26. Install the compounder extension housing to the compounder adapter. Tighten the retaining bolts to 30 foot-pounds.
27. Install the parking brake assembly, drum and yoke on the compounder extension housing. Tighten the output shaft nut to 175 foot-pounds.

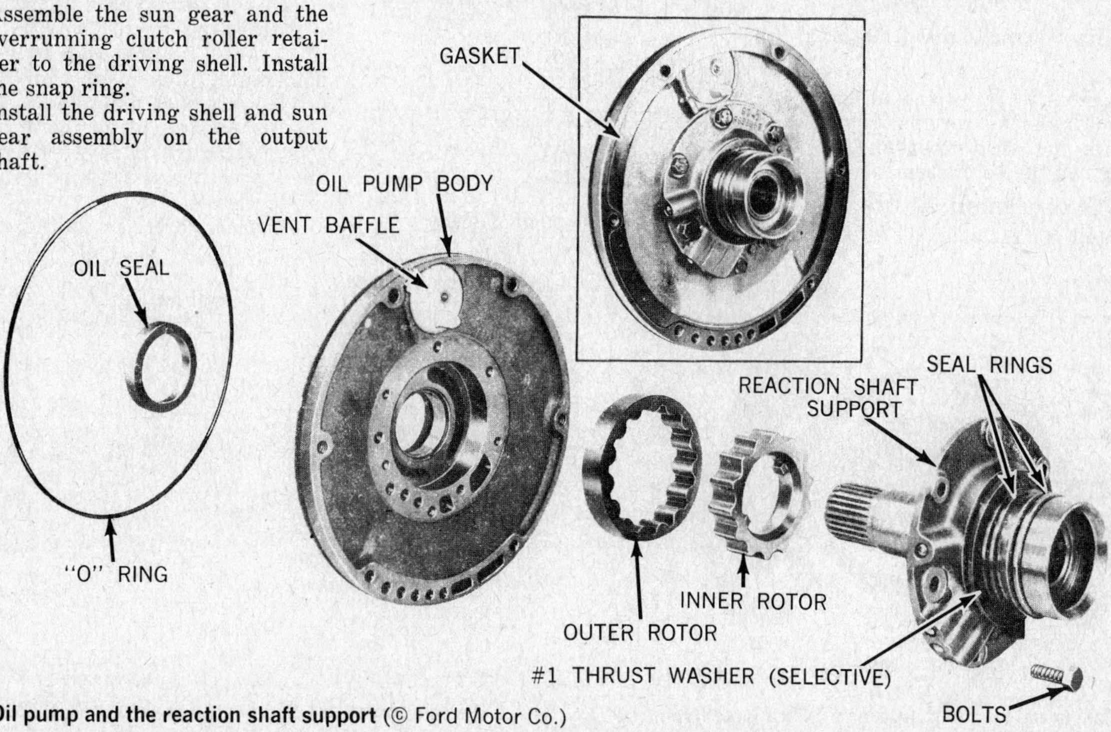

Oil pump and the reaction shaft support (© Ford Motor Co.)

Transmission Disassembly

Oil Pump and Reaction Shaft Support

1. Tighten the front band adjusting screw until the band is tight on the front clutch retainer. This prevents the clutch retainer from coming out with the oil pump which might cause damage to the clutches.
2. Remove the oil pump housing retaining bolts.
3. Install the two slide hammers on the pump housing flange.
4. Move the slide hammer weights outward evenly to remove the pump and reaction shaft from the case.

Front Band and Front Clutch

1. Loosen the front band adjuster remove the band strut and slide the band out of the transmission case.
2. Slide the front clutch assembly out of the transmission case.

Input Shaft and Rear Clutch

1. Grasp the input shaft and slide the input shaft and rear clutch assembly out of the transmission acse. *Be careful not to lose the thrust washer located between and the forward end of the intermediage shaft.*

Planetary Gear Assemblies, Sun Gear and Driving Shell

1. While supporting the intermediate shaft and drive shell, carefully slide the assembly forward and out through the case.

Rear Band and Low-Reverse Drum

1. Loosen the rear band adjuster, remove the low-reverse drum, remove the band strut and link. Remove the band from the case.

Front Overrunning Clutch

1. Note the position of the overrunning clutch rollers and springs before disassembly to assist during reassembly.
2. Carefully slide the clutch hub out of the case and remove the rollers and springs. *If the overrunning clutch cam and roller spring retainer are found to be damaged or worn, refer to replacement procedures later in this section.*

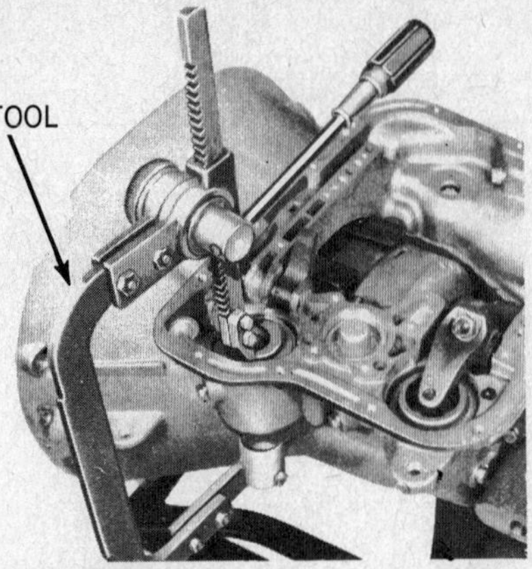

Compressing the kickdown servo spring (© Ford Motor Co.)

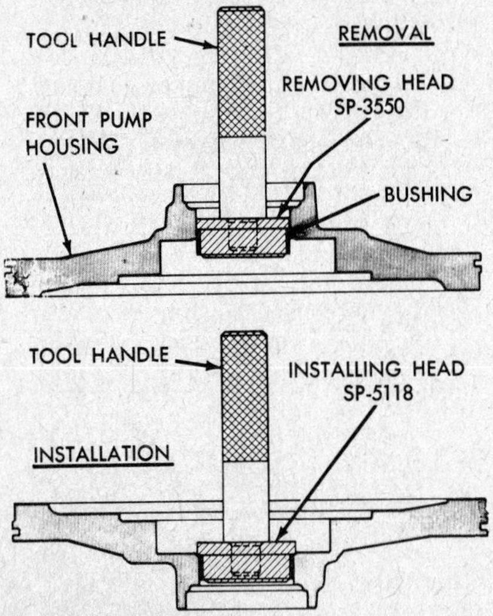

Replacing the oil pump bushing (© Ford Motor Co.)

Kickdown Servo (Front)

1. Compress the kickdown servo spring with an engine valve spring compressor and remove the snap ring.
2. Remove the rod guide, springs and piston rod from the case. Be careful not to damage the piston rod or guide during removal.
3. Withdraw the piston from the transmission case.

Low and Reverse Servo (Rear)

1. Compress the low and reverse servo piston spring with an engine valve spring compressor and remove the snap ring.
2. Remove the spring retainer, spring, and servo piston and plug asesmbly from the transmission case.

Compounder Adapter

1. Remove the ten compounder to transmission case bolts. Remove the adapter and discard the gasket.,
2. Inspect the intermediate shaft bushings and replace if necessary.

Sub-Assemblies Reconditioning

Accumulator Piston and Springs

Inspection

1. Inspect the seal rings for wear and make sure they turn freely in the piston grooves. It is not necessary to remove the rings unless conditions warrant.
2. Inspect the piston for nicks, burrs, scores, and wear.
3. Inspect the piston bore in the case for scores or other damage.
4. Inspect the piston spring for distortion.
5. Replace parts as required.

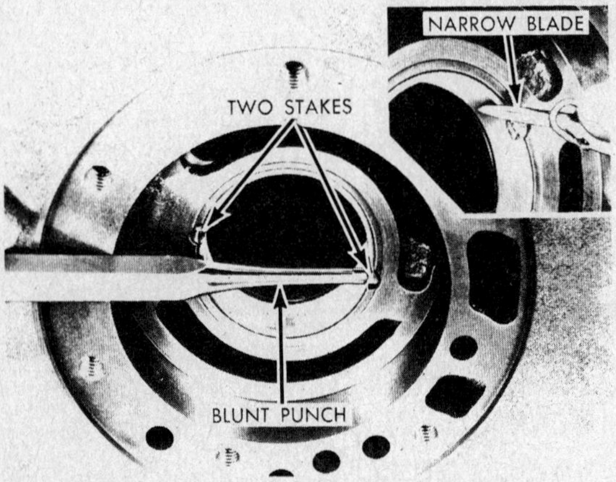

Staking the oil pump bushing (© Ford Motor Co.)

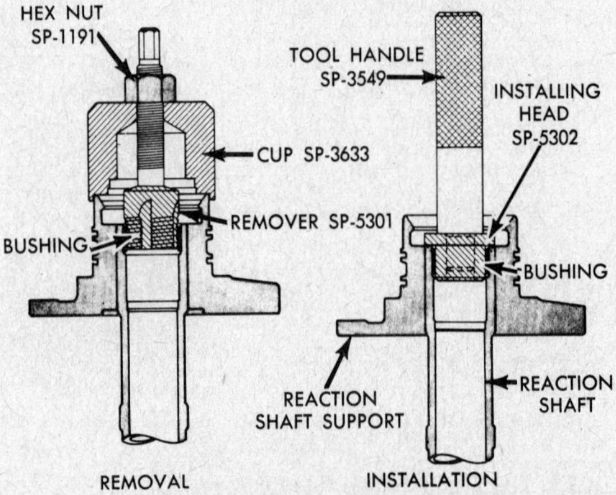

Replacing the reaction shaft bushing (© Ford Motor Co.)

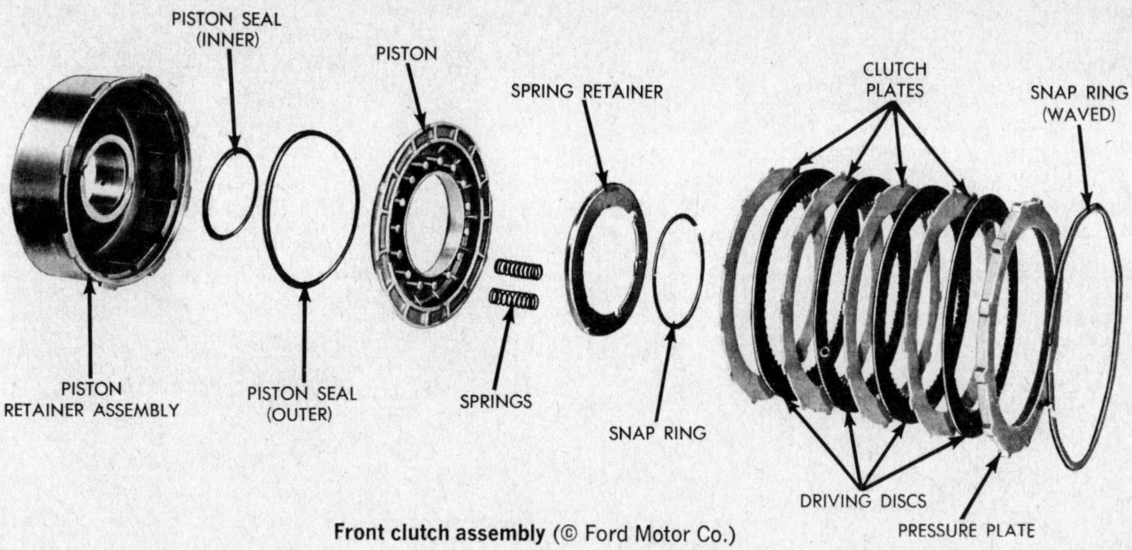

Front clutch assembly (© Ford Motor Co.)

Oil Pump and Reaction Shaft Support

Disassembly

1. Remove the bolts from the rear side of the reaction shaft support, and lift the support off the pump.
2. Remove the rubber seal ring from the pump body flange.
3. Drive the oil seal out with a blunt punch.

Inspection

1. Inspect the interlocking steel rings on the reaction shaft support for wear or broken locks Make sure the rings turn freely in the grooves.
2. Inspect the machined surfaces on the pump body and reaction shaft support for nicks and burrs.
3. Inspect the pump body and reaction shaft support bushings for wear or scoring.
4. Inspect the pump rotors for scoring or pitting.
5. Clean the rotors and install them in the pump body. Place a straight edge across the face of the rotors and pup body. Use a feeler gauge to measure the clearance between the straight edge and the face of the rotors. Clearance limits are 0.0015 0.003 inch.
6. Measure the rotor tip clearance between the inner and outer teeth. Clearance limits are 0.005-0.010 inch.
7. Measure the clearance between the outer rotor and its bore in the oil pump body. Clearance limits are 0.004-0.008 inch.

Oil Pump Bushing

Replacement

1. Place the oil pump housing on a clean smooth surface with the rotor cavity down.
2. Place the bushing removal tool head in the bushing and install the handle on the tool.
3. Drive the bushing straight down and out of the bore. Be careful not to cock the tool in the bore.
4. Place a new bushing on the installation tool head.
5. With the pump housing on a clean smooth surface, hub end down, start the bushing and installation head in the bushing bore. Install the tool handle.
6. Drive the bushing into the housing until the tool bottoms in the pump cavity. Be careful not to cock the tool during installation. Remove the installation tool.
7. Stake the bushing in place by using a blunt punch. A gentle tap at each stake slot should be sufficient.
8. Working with a narrow-bladed knife, remove the high points or burrs around the staked area. Do not use a file that will remove more metal than necessary.
9. Thoroughly clean the pump housing before installation.

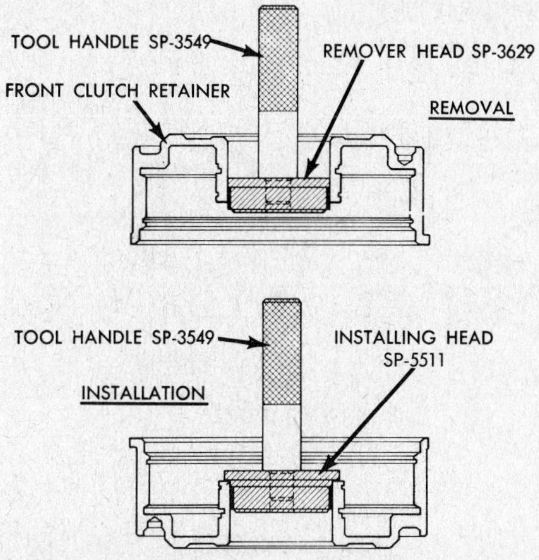

Replacing the front clutch retainer bushing (© Ford Motor Co.)

Reaction Shaft Bushing

Replacement

1. Assemble the removal tool complete with the cup and hex nuts. *Do not clamp any part of the reaction shaft or support in a vise.*
2. With the cup held firmly against the reaction shaft, thread the remover into the bushing as far as possible by hand.
3. Screw the remover three or four additional turns into the bushing with a wrench to firmly engage the threads in the bushing.
4. Turn the hex nut down against the cup to pull the bushing from the reaction shaft. Thoroughly clean the reaction shaft to reove any chips made by the remover threads.
5. Lightly grip the bushing in a vise or pair of pliers and back the removal tool out of the old bushing. Be careful not to dam-

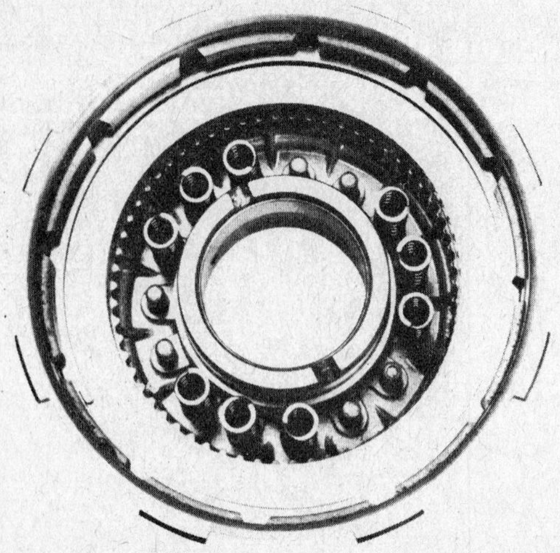

Front spring location—9 springs (© Ford Motor Co.)

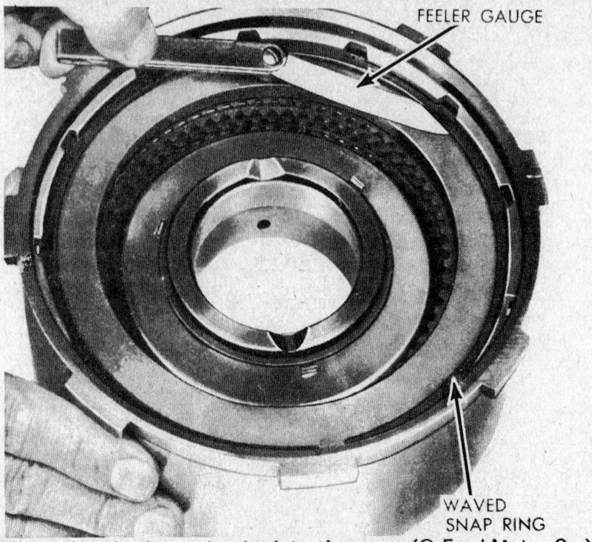

Measuring the front clutch plate clearance (© Ford Motor Co.)

age the threads on the bushing remover.

6. Slide a new bushing (chamfered end first) on the installation head of bushing tool and start the bushing and tool into the reaction shaft bore.
7. Support the reaction shaft in an upright position on a clean smooth surface and install the installation tool handle. Drive the bushing into the shaft until the installation head bottoms. Remove the bushing installation tool.
8. Thoroughly clean the reaction shaft support assembly before installation.

Assembly

1. Assemble the pump rotor and "O" ring in the pump housing.
2. Install the reaction shaft support. Install the retaining bolts and tighten to 160 inch-pounds.
3. Place a new oil seal in the opening of the pump housing (lip of the seal facing inward) using a suitable drift.

Front Clutch

Dissassembly

1. Remove the large waved snap ring that secures the pressure plate in the clutch piston retainer. Lift the clutch plates out of the retainer.
2. Install the piston spring compressor over the piston spring retainer. Compress the springs and remove the snap ring. Slowly release the tool until the spring retainer is free of the hub. Remove the tool, the spring retainer and the springs.
3. Invert the clutch retainer assembly and tap it on a wood block to remove the piston. Remove the seals from the piston and the clutch retainer hub.

Inspection

1. Inspect the facing material on all the driving plates. Replace any plates that are charred, glazed or heavily pitted. Plates should also be replaced if they show evidence of material flaking off or if the facing material can be scraped off easily.
2. Inspect the driving plate splines for wear or other damage.
3. Inspect the steel plate and pressure plate surfaces for burring, scoring or damaged driving lugs.
4. Inspect the steel plate lug grooves in the clutch retainer for smooth surfaces, plates must travel freely in the grooves.
5. Inspect the band contacting surface on the clutch retainer for scores.
6. Note the ball check in the clutch retainer, make sure that the ball moves freely.
7. Inspect the seal surfaces in the clutch retainer for nicks or deep scratches, light scratches will not interfere with the neoprene seals.
8. Inspect the clutch retainer bushing for wear or scoring.
9. Inspect the inside bore of the piston for score marks, if light remove with crocus cloth.
10. Inspect the neoprene seals for deterioration, wear, and hardness.
11. Inspect the piston springs, retainer and snap ring for distortion.

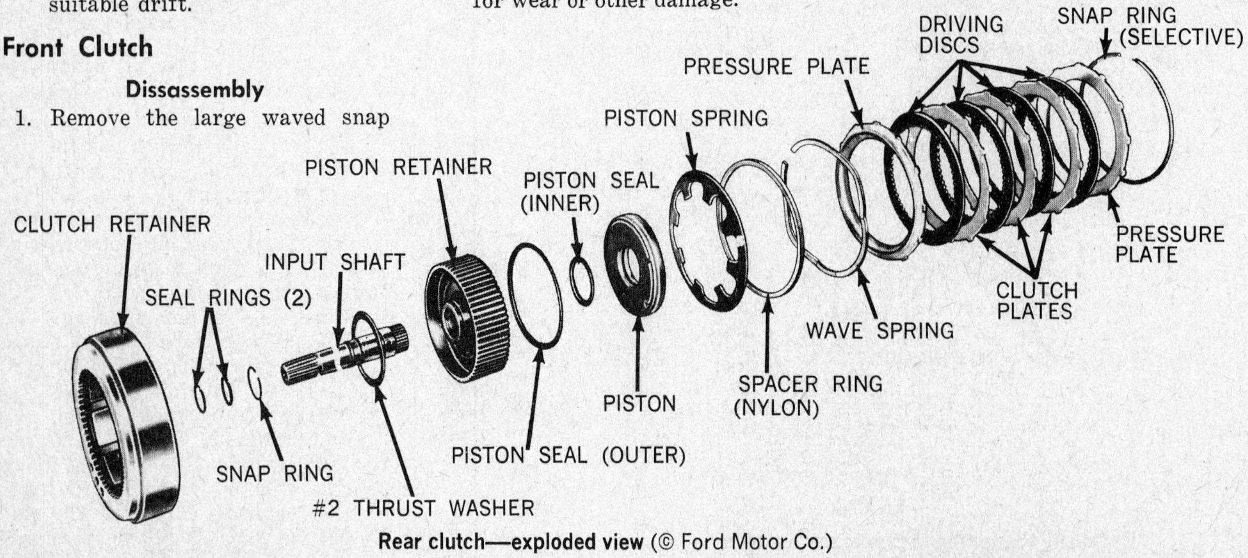

Rear clutch—exploded view (© Ford Motor Co.)

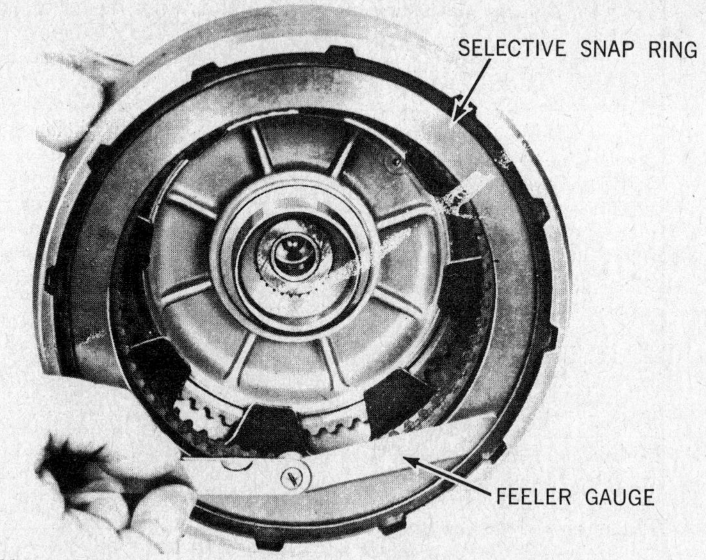

Measuring the rear clutch plate clearance (© Ford Motor Co.)

Front Clutch Retainer Bushing

Replacement

1. Place the clutch retainer (open end down) on a clean smooth surface. Install the removing head of bushing tool in the bushing. Install the bushing tool handle.
2. Drive the bushing straight down and out of the clutch retainer bore. Be careful not to cock the tool in the bore.
3. Lay the clutch retainer (open end up) on a clean smooth surface. Slide a new bushing on the installation head of the bushing tool. Start the tool and bushing in the clutch retainer bore.
4. Install the bushing tool handle. Drive the bushing into the clutch retainer until the tool bottoms.
5. Thoroughly clean the clutch retainer before assembly and installation.

Assembly

1. Lubricate and install the inner seal on the clutch retainer hub. Make sure that the lip of the seal faces down and is properly seated in the groove.
2. Install the outer seal on the clutch piston, with the lip toward the bottom of the clutch retainer. Apply a coating of wax type lubricant (Door Ease) to outer edges of the seals. Place the piston assembly in the retainer and carefully seat the piston in the bottom of the retainer.
3. Install the clutch piston springs on the piston exactly as they were removed.
4. Place the spring retainer and snap ring over the springs. Install the spring compressor tool. Compress the springs and seat the snap ring in its groove. Remove the compressor tool.
5. Lubricate all clutch plates. Install one steel plate followed by a lined (driving) plate until all the plates are installed. Install the pressure plate and snap ring. Make sure that the snap ring is correctly seated in the groove.
6. When the front clutch is completely assembled, push downward on the pressure plate and insert a feeler gauge between the pressure plate and the snap ring. Clearance should be 0.088-0.145 inch.

Rear Clutch

Disassembly

1. Remove the large selective snap ring that secures the pressure plate in the clutch retainer. Lift the pressure plate, clutch plates and the inner pressure plate out of the clutch retainer.
2. Carefully pry one end of the wave spring out of its groove in the clutch retainer. Remove the wave spring, spacer ring, and the clutch piston spring.
3. Invert the clutch piston retainer assembly and tap it on a wood block to remove the piston. Remove the seals from the piston.
4. If necessary, remove the snap ring and press the input shaft from the clutch retainer.

Inspection

1. Inspect the facing material on all the driving plates. Replace any plates that are charred, glazed or heavily pitted. Plates should also be replaced if they show evidence of material flaking off or if the facing material can be scraped off easily.
2. Inspect the driving plate splines for wear or other damage.
3. Inspect the steel plate and the pressure plates surfaces for burring, scoring or damaged driving lugs.
4. Inspect the steel plate lug grooves in the clutch retainer for smooth surfaces, plates must travel freely in the grooves.
5. Inspect the band contacting surface on the clutch retainer for scores.
6. Note the ball check in the clutch retainer, make sure that the ball moves freely.
7. Inspect the seal surfaces in the clutch retainer for nicks or deep scratches, light scratches will not interfere with the neoprene seals.

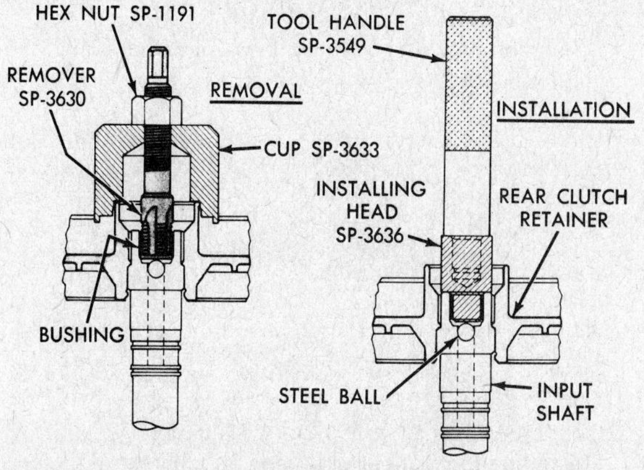

Replacing the input shaft bushing (© Ford Motor Co.)

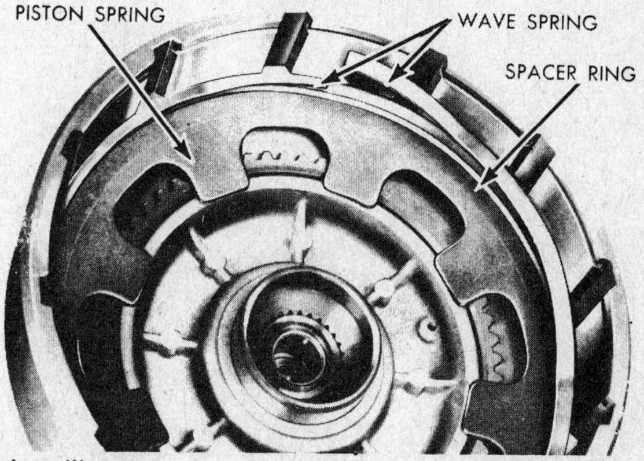

Installing the rear clutch springs, spacer ring, and wave spring (© Ford Motor Co.)

8. Inspect the neoprene seals for deterioration, wear, and hardness.
9. Inspect the piston springs, wave spring, and spacer for distortion or breakage.
10. Inspect the interlocking seal rings on the input shaft for wear or broken locks. Make sure that they turn freely in the grooves. Do not remove the seal rings unless necessary.
11. Inspect the bushing in the input shaft for wear or scores.
12. Inspect the rear clutch to front clutch thrust washer for wear. Washes thickness should be 0.061-0.063 inch, replace if necessary.

Input Shaft Bushing

Replacement

NOTE: Perform this operation only if necessary.

1. Clamp the input shaft in a vise with soft faced jaws. Be careful not to clamp on the seal ring lands or the bearing journals.
2. Assemble the removal tool, cup and hex nut.
3. Hold the cup firmly against the clutch piston retainer and thread the remover into the bushing as far as possible by hand.
4. Working with a wrench, screw the remover into the bushing three or four additional turns to firmly engage the threads in the bushing.
5. Turn the hex nut down against the cup to pull the bushing out of the input shaft.
6. Thoroughly clean the input shaft to remove any chips made by the remover threads. Make sure that the smapp lubrication hole next to the ball in the end of the shaft is not plugged. Be sure no chips have lodged next to the steel ball.
7. Place a new bushing on the installation head of the bushing tool and start them into the input shaft bore.
8. Stand the input shaft on a clean smooth surface and install the installation tool handle. Drive the bushing into the shaft until the tool bottoms.
9. Thoroughly clean the input shaft and the clutch piston retainer before installation.

Assembly

1. If removed, press the input shaft into the clutch piston retainer, and install the snap ring.
2. Lubricate and install the inner and outer seal rings on the clutch piston. Be sure that the lip of the seals face toward the head of the clutch retainer, and that they are properly seated in the piston grooves.
3. Place the piston assembly in the retainer and with a twisting action, seat the piston in the bottom of the retainer.
4. Place the clutch retainer over the piston retainer splines and support the assembly so that the clutch retainer remains in position.
5. Place the clutch piston spring and the spacer ring on the top of the piston in the clutch retainer. Make sure that the spring and the spacer ring are positioned in the retainer recess. Start one end of the waved spring in the retainer groove, then progressively push or tap the spring into place. Make sure that the waved spring is fully seated in its groove.
6. Install the inner pressure plate in the clutch retainer with the raised position of the plate resting on the spring.
7. Lubricate all the clutch plates, install one lined plate followed by a steel plate until all the plates are installed. Install the outer pressure plate and secure with the selective snap ring.
8. Measure the rear clutch plate clearance by having an assistant press downward firmly on the outer pressure plate, then insert a feeler gauge between the plate and the snap ring. Clearance should be 0.025-0.045 inch. If clearance is not within limits, install a snap ring of the proper thickness to obtain the proper

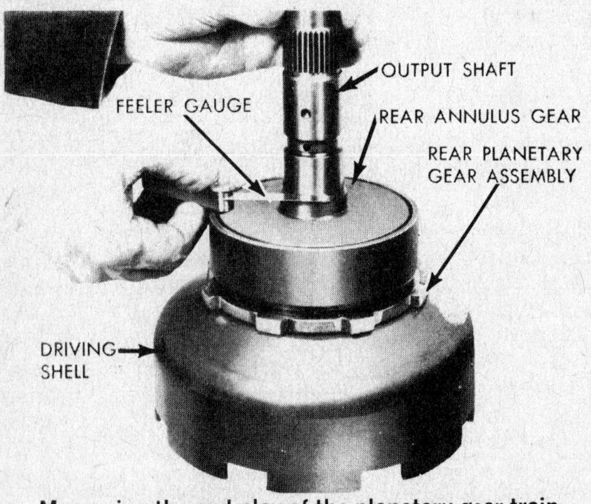

Measuring the end play of the planetary gear train
(© Ford Motor Co.)

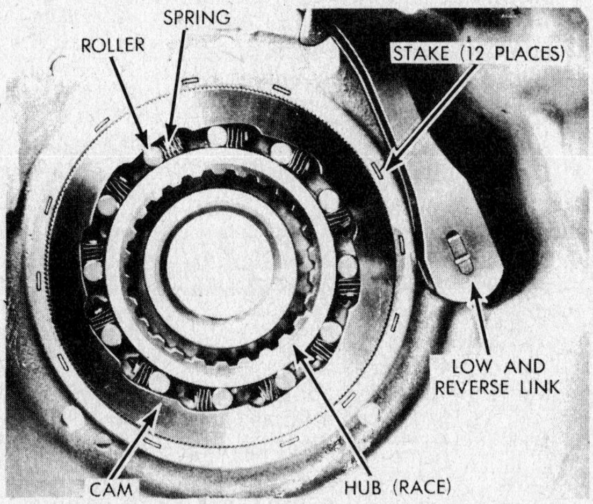

Overrunning clutch and the low-reverse band link
(© Ford Motor Co.)

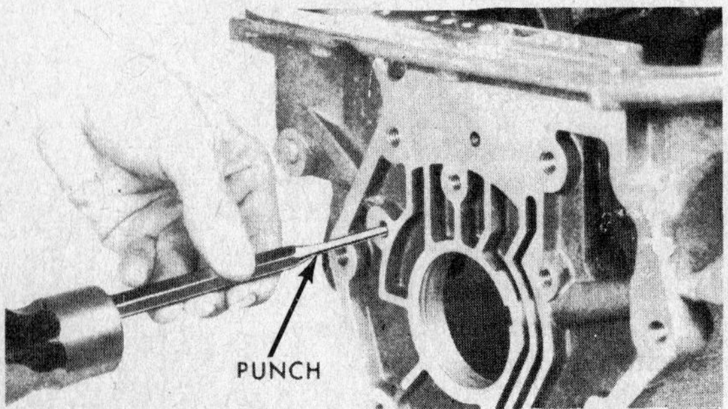

Removing the front overrunning clutch cam
(© Ford Motor Co.)

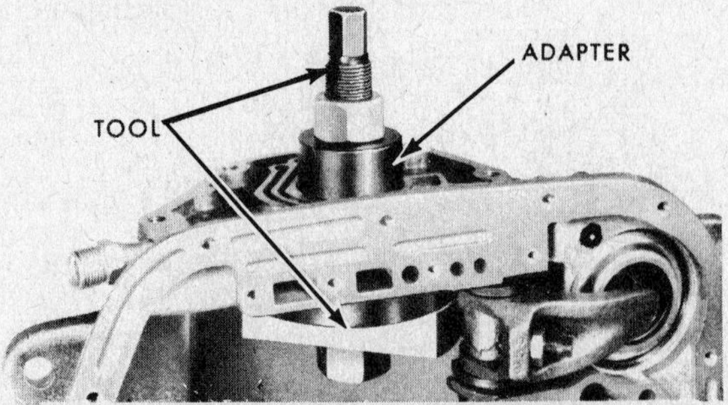

Installing the front overrunning clutch cam
(© Ford Motor Co.)

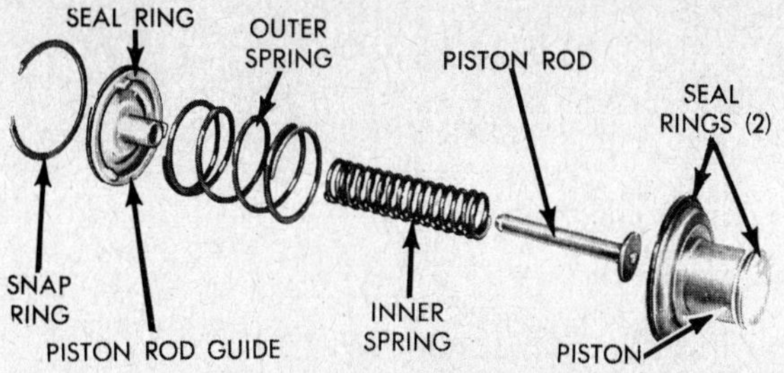

Kickdown servo—exploded view (© Ford Motor Co.)

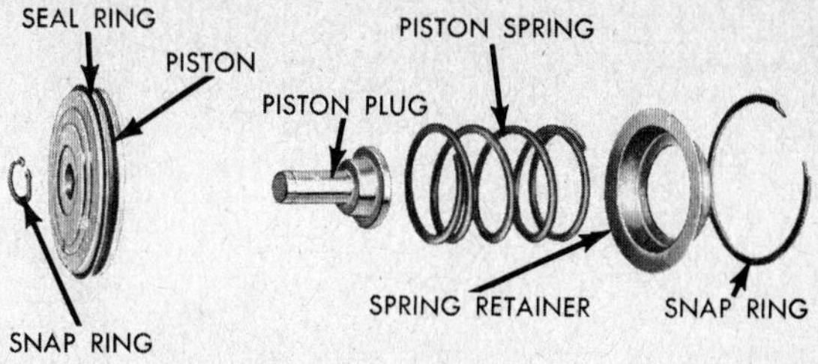

Low-reverse servo—exploded view (© Ford Motor Co.)

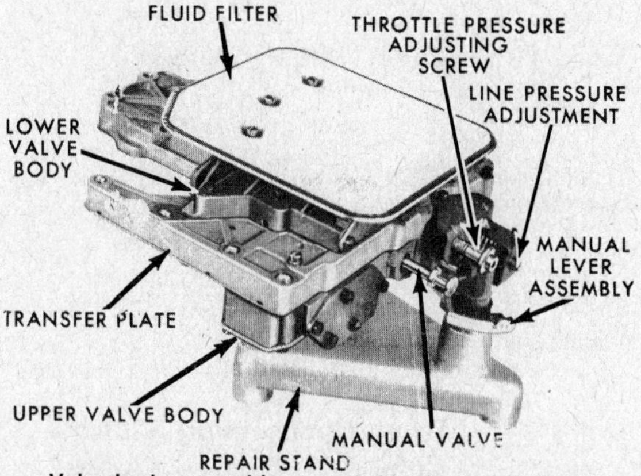

Valve body assembly mounted in the repair stand (© Ford Motor Co.)

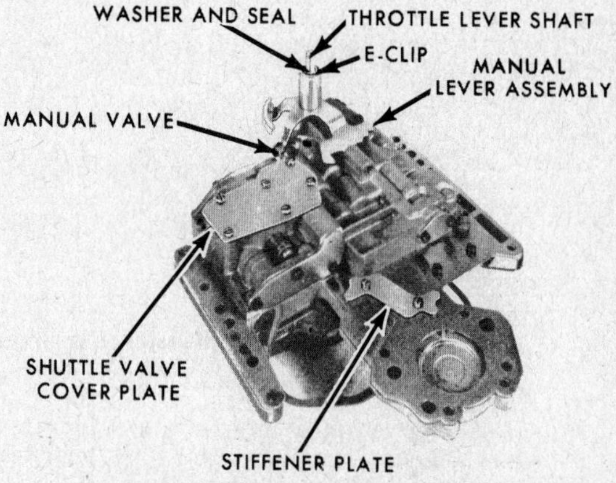

Valve body controls (© Ford Motor Co.)

clearance. Low limit clearance is desirable. *Rear clutch plate clearance is very important in obtaining the proper clutch operation. The clearance can be adjusted by the use of various thickness outer snap rings. Snap rings are available in .060, .074, .088, and .106 inch thickness.*

Planetary Gear Train End Play

1. Place the planetary gear assembly in an upright position, push the rear annulus gear support downward on the intermediate shaft.
2. Insert a feeler gauge between the rear annulus gear support hub and the shoulder on the intermediate shaft.
3. The clearance should be 0.010 to 0.025 inch. If the clearance is excessive, replace the thrust washers and/or necessary parts.

Disassembly

1. Remove the thrust washer from the forward end of the intermediate shaft.
2. Remove the selective snap ring from the forward end of the intermediate shaft, then slide the front planetary assembly off the shaft.
3. Slide the front annulus gear off the planetary gear set. Remove the thrust washer from the rear side of the planetary gear set.
4. Slide the sun gear, driving shell and the rear planetary assembly off the intermdiate shaft.
5. Lift the sun gear and the driving shell off the rear planetary gear assembly. Remove the thrust washer from the inside of the driving shell. Remove the snap ring and the steel washer from the sun gear (rear side of the driving shell) and slide the sun gear out of the shell. Remove the front snap ring from the sun gear if necessary. Note that the front end of the sun gear is longer than the rear.
6. Remove the thrust washer from the forward side of the rear planetary gear assembly. Remove the planetary gear set and the thrust plate from the rear annulus gear.

Inspection

1. Inspect the bearing surface on the output shaft for nicks, burrs, scores or other damage. Light srcatches can be removed with crocus cloth or a fine stone. Be sure that all oil passages in the shaft are open and clean.
2. Inspect the bushings in the sun gear for wear or scores. Replace the sun gear assembly if the bushings are damaged.
3. Inspect all the thrust washers for wear and scores. Replace any washer that is in questionable condition.

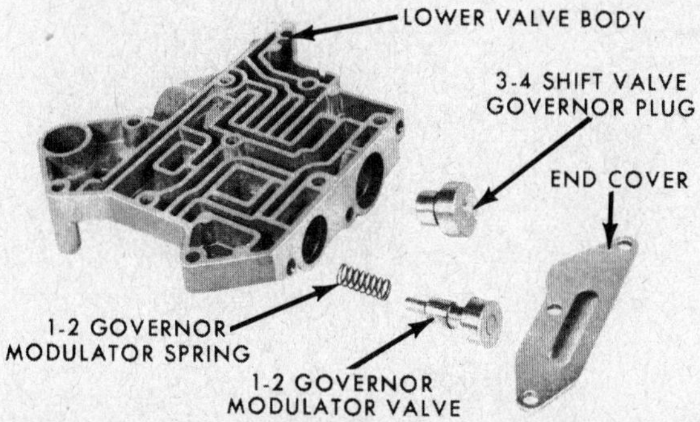

Governor modulator and the 3-4 governor plug (© Ford Motor Co.)

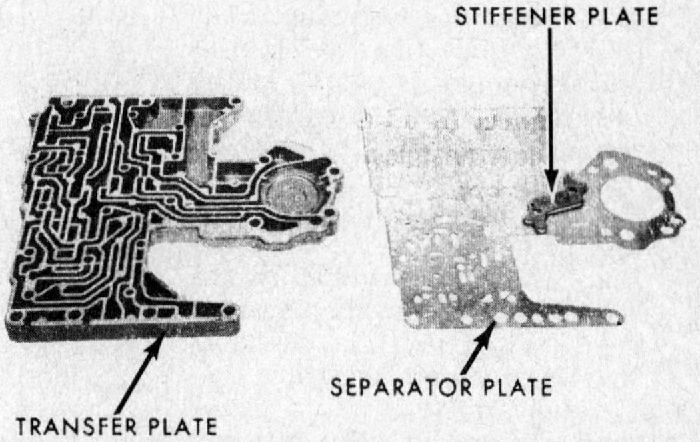

Transfer and separate plates (© Ford Motor Co.)

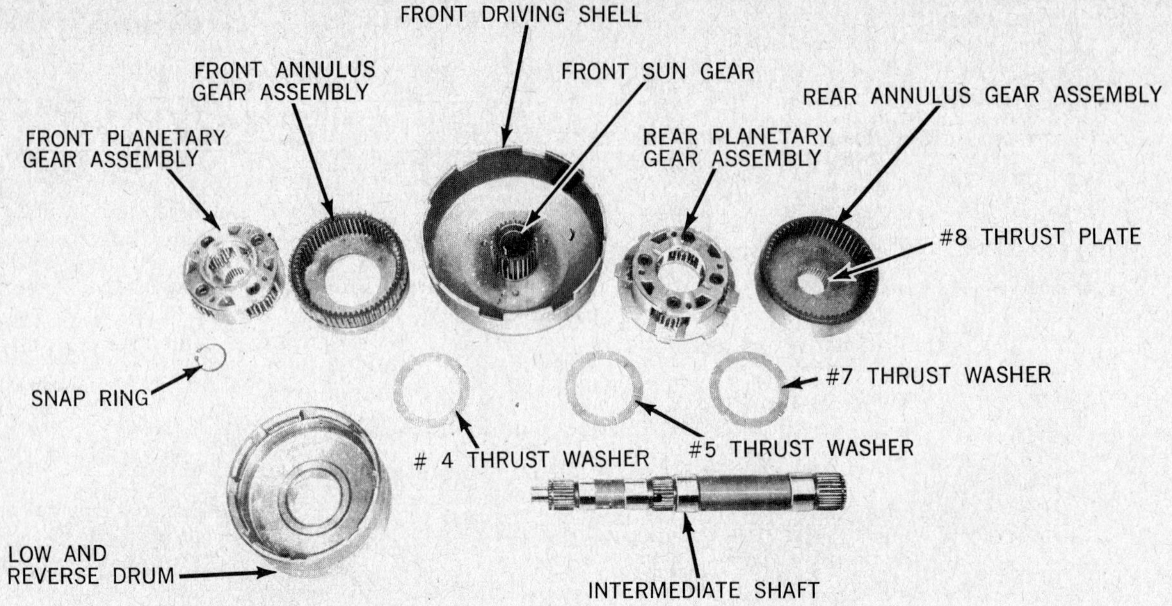

Front planetary gear train and the intermediate shaft—exploded view (© Ford Motor Co.)

4. Inspect the thrust faces of the planetary gear carriers for wear, scoring or other damage. Replace as necessary.
5. Inspect the planetary gear carriers for cracks and pinions with broken teeth or ware. Check the pinion shaft for broken lock pins.
6. Inspect the annulus gear and the driving gear teeth for damage. Replace distorted lock rings.

Assembly

1. Install the rear annulus gear on the intermediate shaft. Apply a thin coat of petroleum jelly on the thrust plate, place it on the shaft and in the annulus gear making sure that the teeth are over the shaft splines.
2. Position the rear planetary gear assembly in the rear annulus gear. Place the thrust washer on the front side of the planetary gear assembly.
3. Install the snap ring in the front groove of the sun gear (long end of the gear). Insert the sun gear through the front side of the driving shell, install the rear steel washer and snap ring.
4. Carefully slide the driving shell and the sun gear assembly on the intermediate shaft, engaging the sun gear teeth with the rear planetary pinion teeth. Place the thrust washer inside the front driving shell.
5. Place the thrust washer on the rear hub on the front planetary gear set and slide the assembly into the front annulus gear.
6. Carefully work the front planetary and annulus gear assembly on the output shaft, meshing the planetary pinions with the sun gear teeth.
7. With all components properly positioned, install the selective snap ring on the front end of the intermediate shaft. Remeasure the end play of the assembly.

The clearance can be adjusted by use of various thickness snap rings. Snap rings are available in .048, .055, and .062 inch thickness.

Front Overrunning Clutch

Inspection

1. Inspect the clutch rollers for smooth round surfaces, they must be free of flat spots and chipped edges.
2. Inspect the roller contacting surfaces in the cam and race for brinnelling.
3. Inspect the roller springs for distortion, wear or other damage.
4. Inspect the cam set screw for tightness. If loose, tighten and restake the case around the screw.

Front Overrunning Clutch Cam

Replacement

NOTE: If the overrunning clutch cam or the roller spring retainer are damaged, replace the cam and spring retainer in the following manner:

1. Remove the set screw from the case below the clutch cam.
2. Insert a blunt punch through the bolt holes and drive the cam from the case. Alternate the punch from one hole to another so that the cam will be driven evenly from the case.
3. Clean all burrs and chips from the cam area in the case.
4. Place the spring retainer on the cam, making sure that the retainer lugs snap firmly into the notches on the cam.
5. Position the cam in the case with the cam serrations aligned with those in the case. Tap the cam *evenly* into the case as far as possible, use a soft faced mallet.
6. Install the cam replacement tool and adapter, tighten the nut on the tool to seat the cam in the

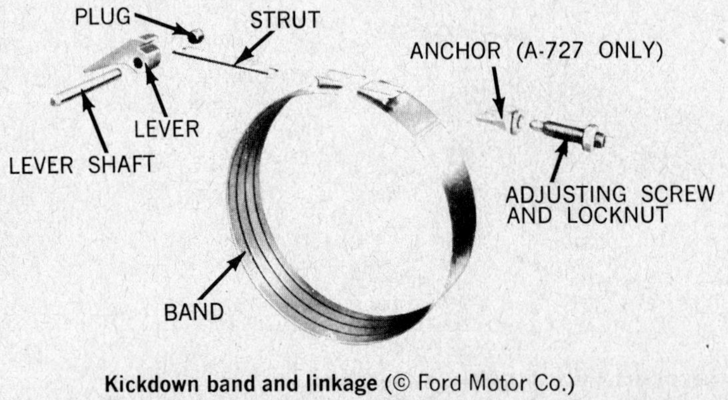

Kickdown band and linkage (© Ford Motor Co.)

case. Make sure that the cam is firmly bottomed, then install the cam retaining set screw. Stake the case around the set screw to prevent it from coming loose.
7. Remove the cam installation tool. Stake the case around the cam in twelve places with a blunt chisel.

Kickdown Servo and Band

Inspection

1. Inspect the piston and the guide seal rings for wear, and make sure that they turn freely in the grooves. It is not necessary to remove the seal rings unless they are worn or damaged.
2. Inspect the piston for nicks, burrs, scores, and wear.
3. Inspect the piston bore in the case for scores or other damage.
4. Inspect the fit of the guide on the piston rod.
5. Inspect the piston spring for distortion.
6. Inspect the band lining for wear and the bond of the lining to the band. Check the lining for burn marks, glazing, non-uniform wear patterns and flaking. If the lining is worn so that the grooves are not visible at the ends or any portion of the bands, replace the band.
7. Inspect the band for distortion or cracked ends.

Low-Reverse Servo and Band

Disassembly

Remove the snap ring from the piston and remove the piston plug.

Inspection

1. Inspect the seal for deterioration, wear and hardness.
2. Inspect the piston and the piston plug for nicks, burrs, scores and wear; the piston plug must operate freely in the piston.
3. Inspect the piston bore in the case for scores or other damage.
4. Inspect the spring for distortion.
5. Inspect the band lining for wear and the bond of the lining to the band. If the lining is worn so that the grooves are not visible at the ends or any portion of the bands, replace the band.
6. Inspect the band for distortion or cracked ends.

Assembly

Lubricate and insert the piston plug in the piston and secure with the snap ring.

Valve Body

NOTE: Do not clamp any portion of the valve body or transfer plate in a vise. Any distortion on the aluminum body or transfer plate will result in sticking valves excessive leakage or both. When removing or installing the valves or plugs, slide them in or out carefully. Do not use force.

Disassembly

1. Place the valve body assembly on the special repair stand. Remove the three screws from the fluid filter and lift off the filter.
2. Remove the lower valve body and the steel plate from the transfer plate. Observe the two steel balls in the transfer plate for proper location.

NOTE: Tag all springs as they are removed for assembly identification.

3. Remove the flat end plate, 3-4 shaft valve governor plug, 1-2 governor modulator valve spring.
4. Remove the end cover from the opposite side of the lower valve body.
5. Remove the part throttle downshift plug, the 3-4 shift valve.
6. Remove the remaining transfer plate screws and the top and bottom spring retainer mounting screws.
7. Lift off the transfer plate and the separator plate assembly. Remove the four screws from the stiffener and separator plates and separate the parts for cleaning.
8. Observe the location of the seven balls and springs in the valve body. Remove the balls and springs.
9. Turn the valve body over and remove the shuttle valve cover plate.
10. Remove the governor plug end plate and slide the shuttle valve throttle plug and spring, the 1-2 shift valve thrtotle plug and spring, the 1-2 shift valve governor plug, and the 2-3 shift valve governor, out of the valve body.
11. Remove the shuttle valve "E" clip and slide the shuttle valve out of its bore. Remove the secondary guides and spring which are retained by an "E" clip.
12. Hold the spring retainer firmly against the spring force while removing the last retaining screw from the side of the valve body.
13. Remove the spring retainer, with the line and the throttle pressure adjusting screws (do not disturb the settings) and the line pressure and torque converter regulator springs.
14. Slide the torque converter and line pressure valves out of their bores.
15. Remove the "E" clip and washer from the throttle lever shaft. Remove any burrs from the shaft. While holding the manual lever detent ball and spring in their

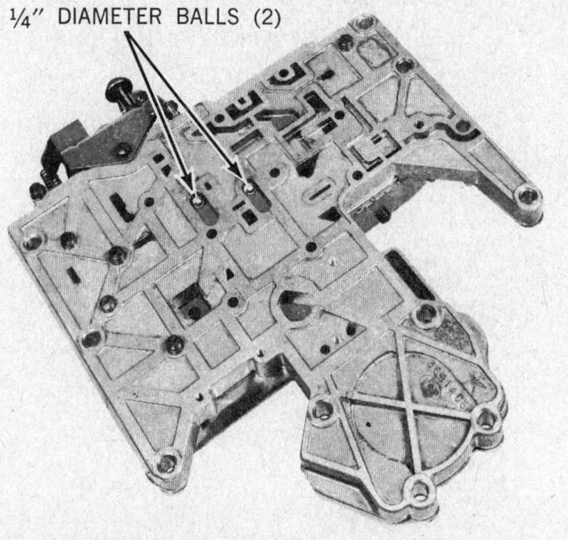

Steel ball locations (two) (© Ford Motor Co.)

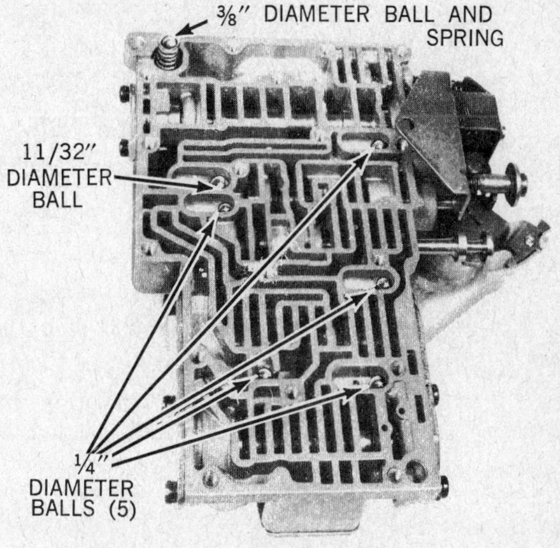

Steel ball locations (seven) (© Ford Motor Co.)

bore with a suitable tool, slide the manual lever off of the throttle shaft. Remove the detent ball and spring.

16. Slide the manual valve out of its bore.
17. Slide the kickdown detent, kickdown valve, throttle valve spring and the throttle valve out of their bores in the valve body.
18. Remove the line pressure regulator valve end plate. Slide the pressure regulator valve sleeve, line perssure plug, and the throttle pressure plug out of the valve body.
19. Remove the shift valve end plate.
20. Remove the three springs, two shift valves and the 1-2 shift control valve from the valve body.

Cleaning and Inspection

1. Soak all parts in a suitable solvent for a few minutes. Wash thoroughly and blow dry with filtered compressed air. Make sure that all passages are clean and free of obstructions.
2. Inspect the manual valve operating levers and shafts for distortion or wear. If a lever is loose on its shaft, it may be *silver soldered* only, or replace the shaft assembly. *Do not attempt to straighten a bent lever.*
3. Inspect all mating surfaces for burrs, nicks and scratches. Minor defects can be removed with crocus colth, *use very light pressure.*
4. Inspect all mating surfaces for warpage or distortion with a straight edge. Slight distortion can be corrected with a surface plane.

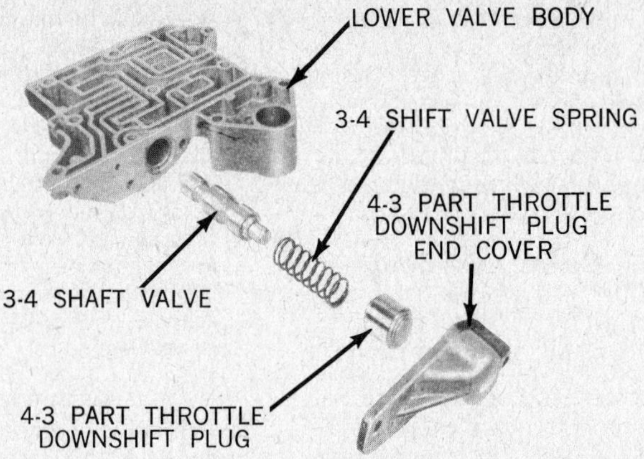

The 3-4 shift valve and the downshift plug (© Ford Motor Co.)

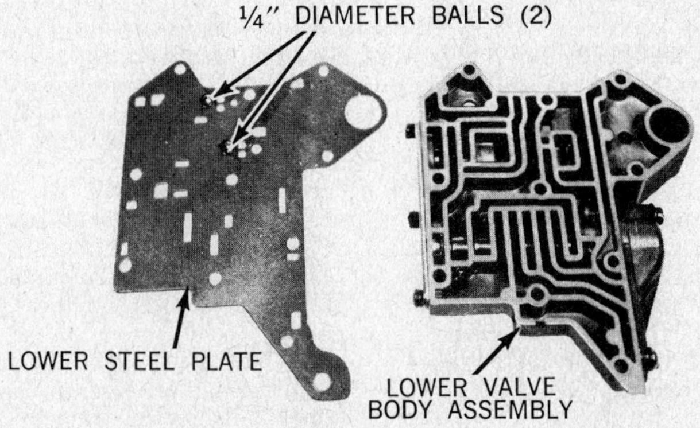

Lower valve body and steel plate (© Ford Motor Co.)

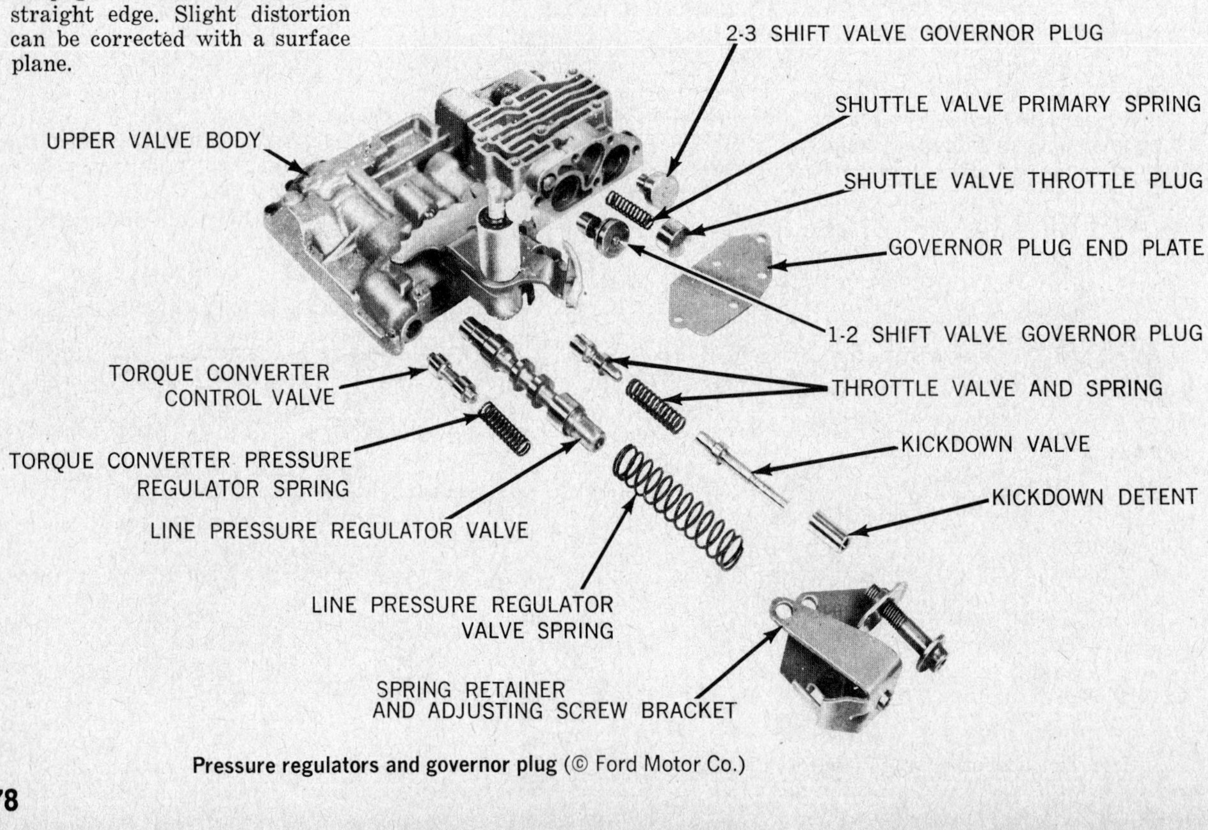

Pressure regulators and governor plug (© Ford Motor Co.)

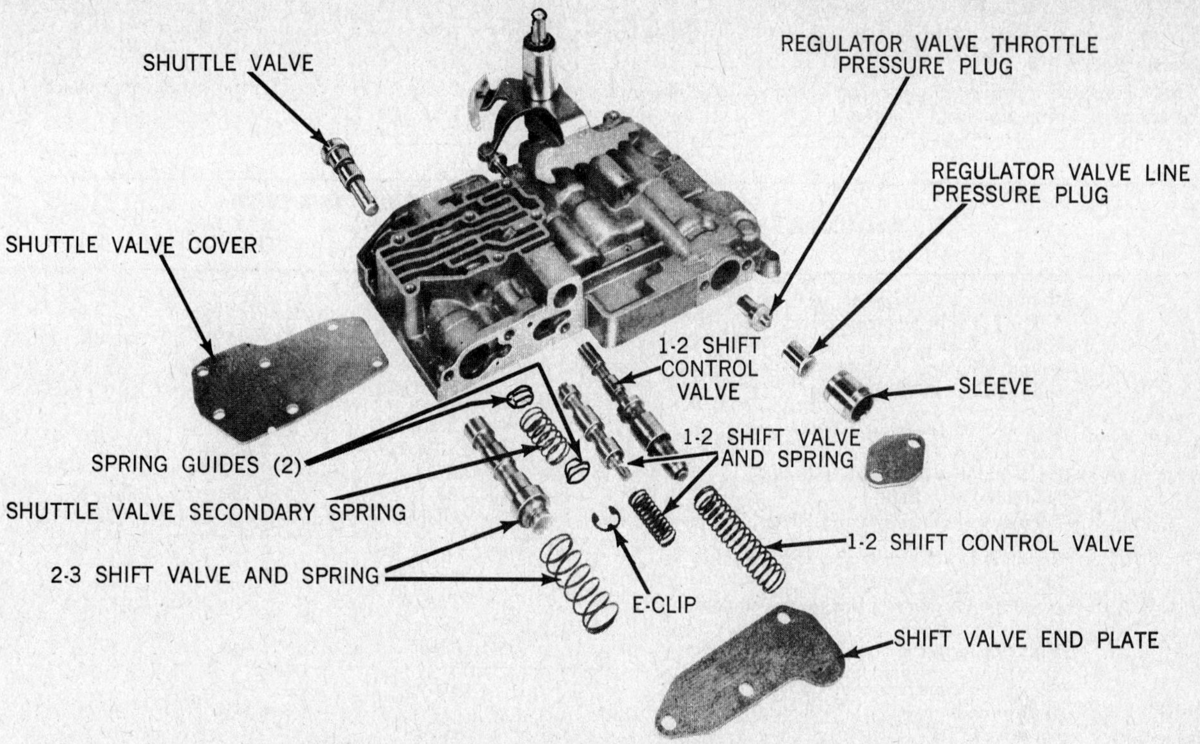

Shift valve and pressure regulator valve plugs (© Ford Motor Co.)

5. Inspect all metering holes in the steel plate and the valve body to make sure that they are open.
6. Inspect the bores in the valve body for scores, scratches, pits and irregularities with a pen light.
7. Inspect all valve springs for distortion and collapsed coils.
8. Inspect all valves and plugs for burrs, nicks or scoring. Small nicks and scores may be removed with crocus cloth using *extreme* care not to round off sharp edges. The sharpness of these edges is vitally important because it prevents foreign matter from lodging between the valve and the valve body.
9. Inspect all valves and plugs for freedom of operation in the valve body bores.

NOTE: The valve body bores do not change dimensionally with use. Therefore, a valve body that was functioning properly when the truck was new, will operate correctly if it is properly and thoroughly cleaned. There is no need to replace the valve body unless it is damaged in handling.

Assembly

1. Slide the shift valves, 1-2 shift control valve and springs into their bores in the valve body.
2. Install the end plate and tighten the screws to 28-inch-pounds.
3. Install the throttle pressure plug, the line pressure plug and sleeve. Attach the end plate for the valve body and tighten the screws to 28 inch-pounds.
4. Install the throttle valve, throttle valve spring, kickdown valve, and the kickdown detent.
5. Slide the manual valve into the bore in the valve body.
6. Install the throttle lever and shaft on the vavle body. Insert the detent spring and ball in the bore of the valve body. Depress the ball and spring with a suitable tool and slide the manual lever over the throttle shaft so that it engages the manual valve and the detent ball. Install the seal, retaining washer and the "E" clip on the throttle shaft.
7. Install the torque converter control valve and spring in the valve body.
8. Install the line pressure regulator valve and spring in the valve body.
8. Install the line pressure regulator valve and spring in the valve body.
9. Install the pressure adjusting screw and bracket assembly on the springs and fasten, finger tight, with the screw which goes on the side of the valve bodv.
10. Install the 1-2 and the 2-3 shift valve governor plugs into their bores in the valve body.
11. Install the shuttle valve and hold it in the bore with your index finger while instalilng the secondary spring, with guides, on the other end. Retain the shuttle valve components with an "E" clip.
12. Install the primary shuttle valve spring and throttle plug in the valve body.

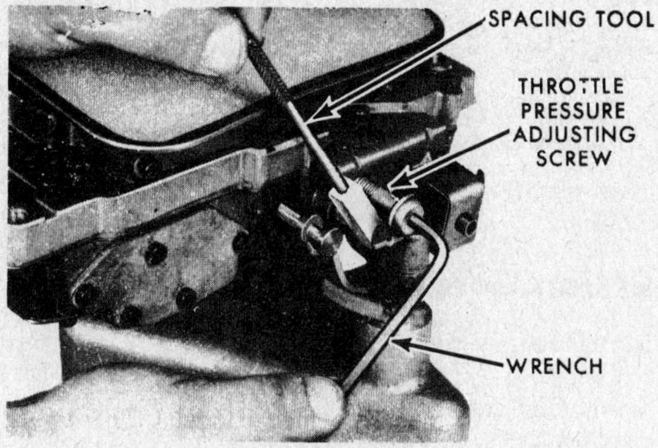

Adjusting the throttle pressure (© Ford Motor Co.)

Ford C-4 (Dual Range)

DIAGNOSIS

This diagnosis guide covers the most common symptoms and is an aid to careful diagnosis. The items to check are listed in the sequence to be followed for quickest results. Thus, follow the checks in the order given for the particular transmission type.

TROUBLE SYMPTOMS	ITEMS TO CHECK IN TRUCK	ITEMS TO CHECK OUT OF TRUCK
Rough initial engagement in D1 or D2	KBUFEG	a
1-2 or 2-3 shift points incorrect or erratic	ABLCDUER	
Rough 1-2 shifts	BJGUEF	
Rough 2-3 shifts	BJUFGER	bl
Dragged out 1-2 shift	ABJUGEFR	c
Engine overspeeds on 2-3 shift	CABJUEFG	bl
No 1-2 or 2-3 upshift	CLBDUEGJ	bc
No 3-1 shift in D1 or 3-2 shift in D2	DE	
No forced downshift	LEB	
Runaway engine on forced downshift	UJGFEB	c
Rough 3-2 or 3-1 shift at closed throttle	KBJEF	
Shifts 1-3 in D1 and D2	GJBEDR	
No engine braking in first gear—manual low	CHIEDR	
Creeps excessively	KW	
Slips or chatters in first gear, D1	ABUFE	acg
Slips or chatters in second gear	ABJGUFER	ac
Slips or chatters in R	ABHUIFER	bcl
No drive in D1	ACUER	g
No drive in D2	ACUJER	cg
No drive in L	ACUEIR	cg
No drive in R	ACHUIER	bcl
No drive in any selector position	ACUFER	cd
Lockup in D1		bec
Lockup in D2	HI	becg
Lockup in L	GJ	bec
Lockup in R	GJ	aec
Parking lock binds or does not hold	C	e
Transmission overheats	OFBU	i
Maximum speed too low, poor acceleration	VW	i
Transmission noisy in N and P	AF	df
Transmission noisy in any drive position	AF	fadg
Fluid leaks	AMNOPQ STBIJX	hik
Car moves forward in N	C	a

Key to Checks

A. Fluid level
B. Vacuum diaphragm unit or tube
C. Manual linkage
D. Governor
E. Valve body
F. Pressure regulator
G. Intermediate band
H. Reverse band
I. Reverse servo
J. Intermediate servo
K. Engine idle speed
L. Downshift linkage—inner lever position
M. Converter drain plug
N. Oil pan and/or filler tube gaskets/seals
O. Oil cooler and/or connections
P. Manual or downshift lever shaft seal
Q. Pipe plug, side of case
R. Perform air pressure checks
S. Extension housing-to-case gasket or washers
T. Extension housing rear oil seal
U. Make control pressure test
V. Engine performance
W. Vehicle brakes
X. Speedometer driven gear adaptor seal

a. Forward clutch
b. Reverse—high clutch
c. Hydraulic system leakage
d. Front pump
e. Parking brake linkage
f. Planetary assembly
g. Planetary one-way clutch
h. Engine rear oil seal
i. Front oil pump seal
j. Converter oneway clutch
k. Front pump-to-case seal or gasket
l. Reverse—high clutch piston air bleed valve

Transmission Checks

Transmission Fluid Leakage Checks

Make the following checks if a leakage is suspected from the transmission case:

1. Clean all dirt and grease from the transmission case.
2. Inspect the speedometer cable connection at the extension housing of the transmission. If fluid is leaking here, disconnect the cable and replace the rubber seal.
3. Inspect the oil pan gasket and attaching bolts for leaks. Tighten any bolts that appear loose to the proper torque (10-13 ft-lbs) Recheck for signs of leakage. If necessary, remove the pan attaching bolts and old pan gasket and install new gasket and reinstall the pan and its attaching bolts.
4. Check filler tube connection at the transmission for signs of

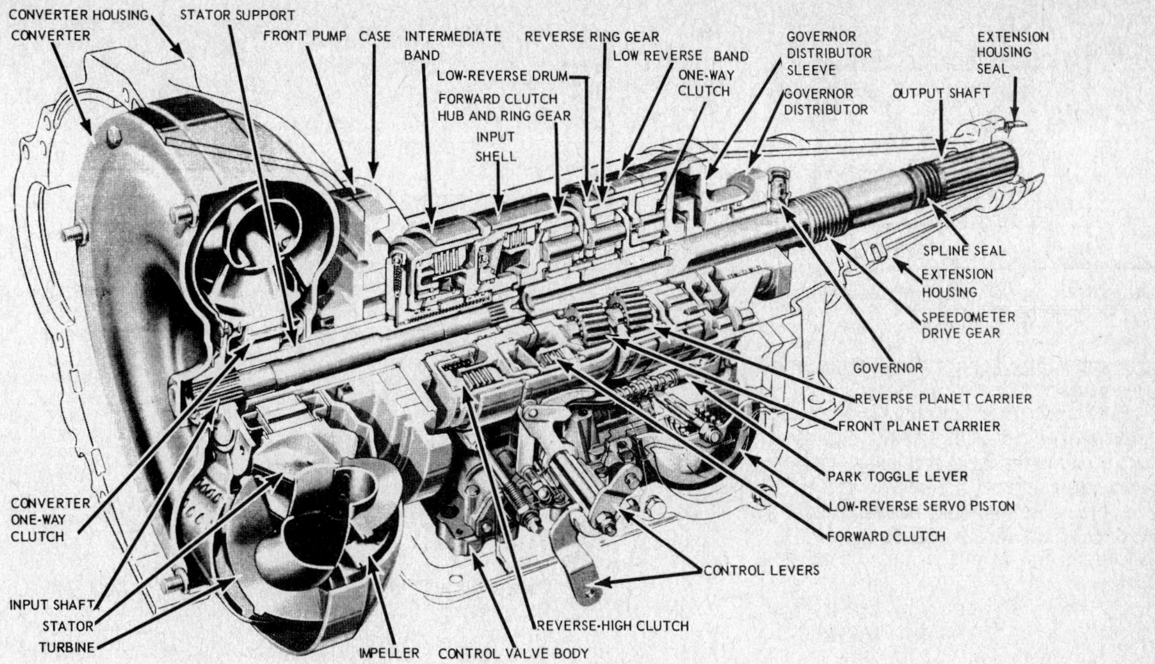

C-4 automatic transmission (© Ford Motor Co.)

leakage. If tube is leaking, tighten the connection to stop the leak. If necessary, disconnect the filler tube, replace the O-ring, and reinstall the filler tube.

5. Inspect all fluid lines between the transmission and the cooler core in the lower radiator tank. Replace any lines or fittings that appear to be worn or damaged. Tighten all fittings to the proper torque.
6. Inspect the engine coolant for signs of transmission fluid in the radiator. If there is transmission fluid in the engine coolant, the oil cooler core is probably leaking. The oil cooler core may be tested further by disconnecting all lines to it and applying 50-75 psi air pressure through the fittings. Remove the radiator cap to relieve any pressure buildup outside the cooler core. If air bubbles appear in the coolant or if the cooler core will not hold pressure, the oil cooler core is leaking and must be replaced. Oil cooler core repair and replacement is discussed in the section on Cooling Systems in this manual.
7. Inspect the openings in the case where the downshift control lever shaft and the manual lever shaft are located for leaks. If necessary, replace the defective seal.
8. Inspect all plugs or cable connections in the transmission for signs of leakage. Tighten any loose plugs or connectors to the proper torque according to the specifications.
9. Remove the lower cover from the front of the bellhousing and inspect the converter drainplugs for signs of leakage. If there is a leak around the drainplugs, loosen the plug and coat the threads with a sealing compound and tighten the plug to the proper torque.

NOTE: Fluid leaks from around the converter area may be caused by the converter drain plug, oil pump seal, and/or gaskets, engine oil leakage past the rear main bearing seal, oil gallery plugs loose, valve cover gaskets, or the power steering system. To determine the exact cause of the leak before beginning repair procedures, an oil-soluble Aniline or flourescent dye may be added to the leak detection process. When using the dye, a black light must be used to detect the dye within the oil.

If further converter checks are necessary, remove the transmission from the truck and the converter from the transmission. The converter cannot be disassembled for cleaning or repair. If the converter is leaking, it must be replaced with a new unit. To further check the converter for leaks, assemble and install the converter leak checking tool shown and fill the converter with 20 psi air pressure. Then, place the converter in a tank of water and watch for air bubbles. If no air bubbles are seen, the converter is not leaking.

CLUTCH AND BAND APPLICATION CHART—C-4 AUTOMATIC TRANSMISSION

GEAR	FORWARD CLUTCH	REVERSE HIGH CLUTCH	INTER-MEDIATE BAND	LOW REVERSE BAND	ONE-WAY CLUTCH
1-st*	on	off	off	off	holding
2-nd*	on	off	on	off	over-running
3-rd*	on	on	off	off	over-running
Low(1)	on	off	off	on	holding
Reverse	off	on	off	on	not affected

* Transmission selector in "D" position

Control Pressure Check for Automatic Transmissions (C4)

When the vacuum diaphragm unit operates properly and the downshift linkage is adjusted correctly, all transmission shifts (automatic and kickdown) should occur within the specified road speed limits. If these shifts do not occur within the limits or if the transmission slips during a shift point, perform the following procedure to locate the problem:

1. Connect the Automatic Transmission Tester (see illustration) as follows:
   a. Tachometer cable to engine
   b. Vacuum gauge hose to the

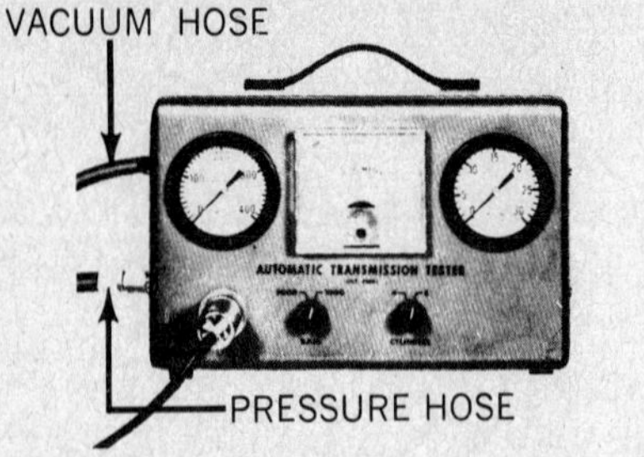

Automatic transmission tester—typical (© Ford Motor Co.)

transmission vacuum diaphragm unit (see illustration)

2. Apply the parking brake and start the engine. On a truck equipped with a vacuum brake release, disconnect the vacuum line or use the service brake since the parking brake will release automatically when the transmission is put in any Drive position.

3. Check engine idle speed and throttle and downshift linkage for correct operation. Check the transmission diaphragm unit for leaks.

Vacuum Diaphragm Check (Off Truck)

With the use of a vacuum pump, set the vacuum to read 18 inches, with the end of the hose blocked off. On single area diaphragms, connect the vacuum hose to the manifold vacuum hose port. On the dual area diaphragms, connect the vacuum hose to the EGR port, leaving the manifold vacuum port open to the atmosphere. If the gauge holds at 18 inches, the vacuum unit diaphragm is not leaking. A second check can be made by holding the control rod end by a finger, with the other end inserted into the unit. Install the vacuum hose from the vacuum pump onto the diaphragm port. The control rod should move inward and when the vacuum supply is cut off by the removal of the hose, the rod should move outward.

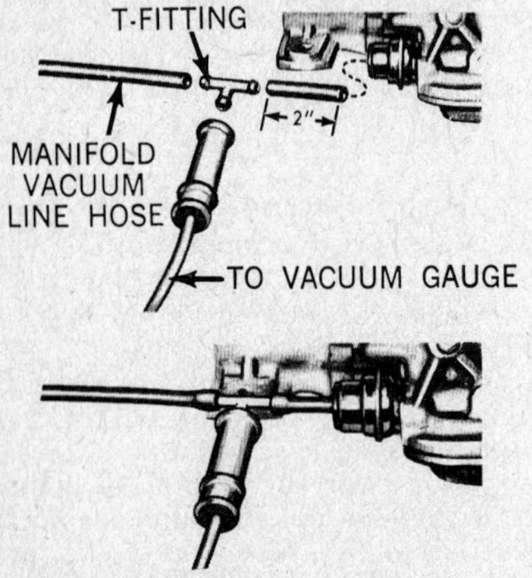

Typical vacuum test line connections at modulator (© Ford Motor Co.)

Air Pressure Checks

If the truck will not move in one or more ranges, or, if it shifts erratically, the items at fault can be determined by using air pressure at the indicated passages.

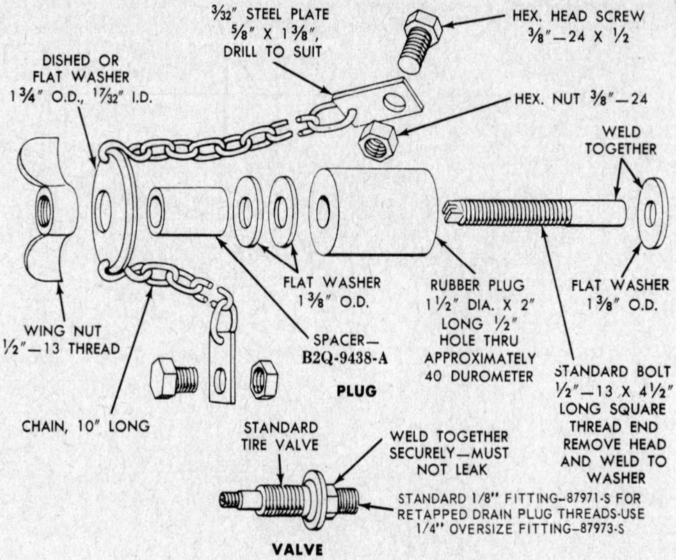

Converter leak checking tool (© Ford Motor Co.)

Drain the transmission and remove the oil pan and the control valve assembly.

NOTE: Oil will spray profusely during this operation.

Front Clutch

Apply sufficient air pressure to the front clutch input passage. (See illustration.) A dull thud can be heard when the clutch piston moves. Check also, for leaks.

Governor

Remove the governor inspection cover from the extension housing. Apply air to the front clutch input passage. (See illustration). Listen for a sharp click and watch to see if the governor valve snaps inward as it should.

Rear Clutch

Apply air to the rear clutch passage (See illustration) and listen for the dull thud that will indicate that the rear clutch piston has moved. Listen also for leaks.

Front Servo

Apply air pressure to the front servo apply tube (See illustration.) and note if front band tightens. Shift the air to the front servo release tube, which is next to the apply tube, and watch band release.

Rear Servo

Apply air pressure to the rear servo apply passage. The rear band should tighten around the drum.

Conclusions

If the operation of the servos and clutches is normal with air pressure, the no-drive condition is due to the control valve and pressure regulator valve assemblies, which should be disassembled, cleaned and inspected.

If operation of the clutches is not normal; that is, if both clutches apply from one passage or if one fails to move, the aluminum sleeve (bushing) in the output shaft is out of position or badly worn. (See illustration.)

Use air pressure to check the passages in the sleeve and shaft, and also check the passages in the primary sun gear shaft.

If the passages in the two shafts and the sleeve are clean, remove the clutch assmblies, clean and inspect the parts.

Erratic operation can also be caused by loose valve body screws. When reinstalling the valve body be careful to tighten the control valve body screws as specified in the Torque Limits table.

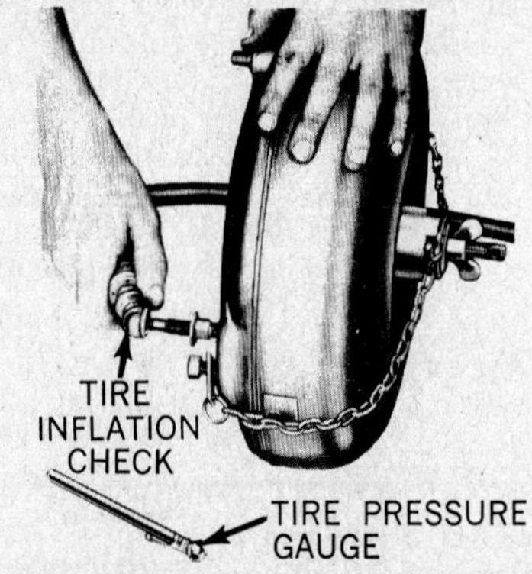

Converter leak checking tool installed (© Ford Motor Co.)

In-Vehicle Adjustments and Repairs

The adjustments and repairs presented in this part of the section on transmissions may be done without removing the entire transmission from the truck. Some of these procedures will require the use of special tools and instruments.

Band Adjustments

Intermediate Band

1. Clean all the dirt from the adjusting screw and remove and discard the locknut.
2. Install a new locknut on the adjusting screw. Using the tool shown in the illustration, tighten the adjusting screw until the wrench clicks and breaks at 10 ft-lbs. torque.
3. Back off the adjusting screw *Exactly* $1\frac{3}{4}$ turns.
4. Hold the adjusting screw steady and tighten the locknut to the proper torque.

Low-Reverse Band

1. Clean all dirt from around the band adjusting screw, and remove and discard the locknut.
2. Install a new locknut on the adjusting screw. Using the tool shown in the illustration, tighten the adjusting screw until the wrench clicks and breaks at 10 ft-lbs torque.
3. Back off the adjusting screw *Exactly 3 full turns.*
4. Hold the adjusting screw steady and tighten the locknut to the proper torque.

Transmission Component

Removal and Installation

The components that may be removed from and installed in the transmission while it is in the truck are discussed in this part of the C4 transmission section. Only procedures for removing and installing these components are given here. Disassembly and repair of the units is given in a later part.

To avoid repetition, the following tasks should be done before proceeding with the removal and installation of components.

1. Raise the truck so the transmission is accessible from under the truck.

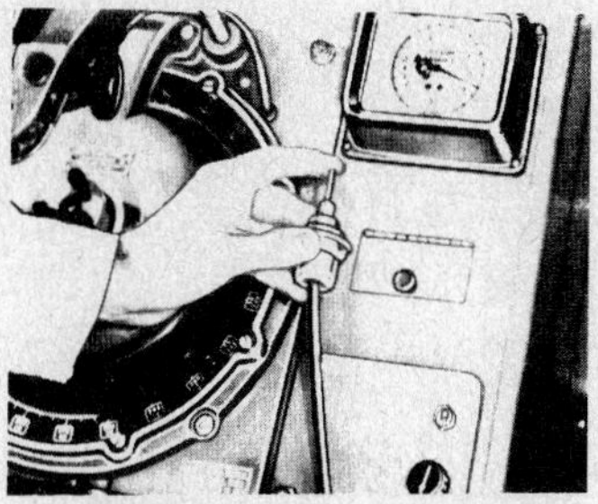

Testing transmission vacuum for leakage (© Ford Motor Co.)

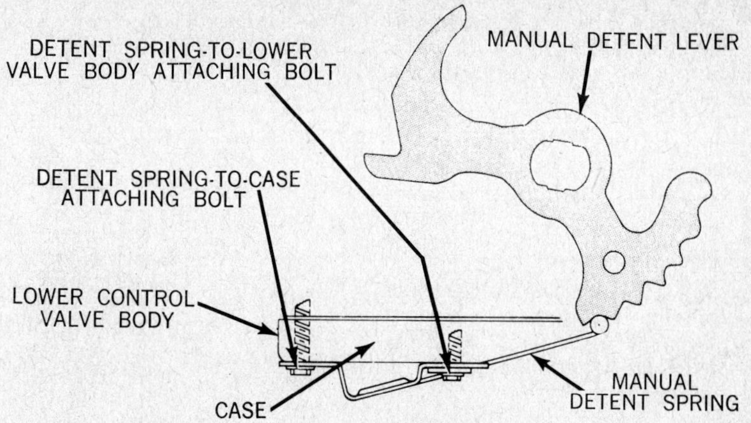

Control valve body detent spring installed (© Ford Motor Co.)

2. Drain the fluid from the transmission. Some models are drained by removing the filler tube from the transmission oil pan. Others are drained by removing the oil pan attaching bolts gradually from the rear of the pan. If the same fluid is to be reused, filter it through a 100 mesh screen. Reuse the fluid only if it is in good condition.
3. Remove the oil pan attaching bolts, the oil pan, and the old gasket. Discard gasket.
4. Be sure to have a good transmission jack available and a holding device for the transmission if it is removed from the truck later.

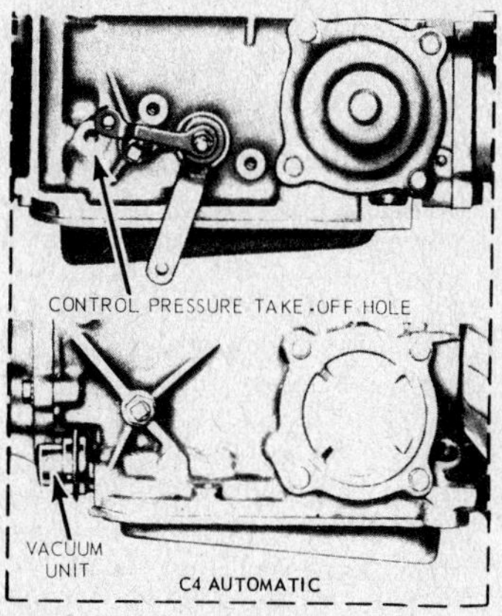

Typical vacuum diaphragm and control pressure connecting point. (© Ford Motor Co.)

Oil Pan and Control Valve

Removal

1. Do all the preliminary operations given at the beginning of this section.
2. Shift the transmission to Park position and remove the two bolts holding the manual detent spring to the control valve body and case.
3. Remove all the valve body-to-case attaching bolts. Hold the manual valve in place and remove the valve body from the case.

   CAUTION: If the manual valve is not held in place, it could be bent or damaged.
4. Refer to the Component Disassembly and repair section for control valve body repair procedures.

   NOTE: The oil filter screen and gasket retain the throttle pressure limit valve and spring on the C4. These parts will drop out when the screen and gasket are removed. The valve is installed with the large end toward the valve body in the transmission; the spring fits over the valve stem.
5. Thoroughly clean the old gasket material from the case and remove the nylon shipping plug from the oil filler tube hold. This nylon plug is installed before shipment and should be discarded when the transmission oil pan is removed.

Installation

1. Be sure the transmission is in the Park position (manual detent lever is in P detent position). Install the valve body in the case. Position the inner downshift lever between the downshift lever stop and the downshift valve. Be sure the two lands on the end of the manual valve engage the actuating pin on the manual detent lever.
2. Install seven valve body attaching bolts but do not tighten them.
3. Place the detent spring on the lower valve body and install the spring-to-case bolt finger tight.
4. While holding the detent spring roller in the center of the manual detent lever, install the detent spring-to-lower valve body bolt and tighten it to 80-120 in-lbs. torque.
5. Tighten the remainder of the

control valve body attaching bolts to 80-120 in-lbs. torque.

6. Put a new gasket on the oil pan, install pan in place, and install and tighten all the pan attaching bolts to the proper torque.
7. If the filler tube was removed, reinstall it and tighten securely. If necessary, replace the oil seal around the filler tube to prevent leakage.
8. Lower the car and fill the transmission with enough fluid to bring the level up to the FULL mark on the dipstick. Check for fluid leaks at this time.

Intermediate Servo

Removal and Installation

1. Raise the truck and remove the four servo cover attaching bolts (right-hand side of case). Remove the cover and identification tag (*do not lose tag*).
2. Remove the gasket, piston, and piston return spring.
3. Install the piston return spring in the case. Place a new gasket on the cover. Install the piston and cover in the transmission case, using two 51/6-18 x 1¼ bolts 180 degrees apart to align the cover against the case.
4. Install the transmission identification tag and two attaching bolts. Remove the two 1¼ bolts and install the other two cover attaching bolts. Tighten all cover attaching bolts to the proper torque.
5. Adjust the intermediate band. Lower the truck and fill the transmission with enough fluid to raise the fluid level to the FULL mark on the dipstick.
6. If the intermediate band cannot be adjusted correctly, remove the oil pan and control valve body and see if the struts are installed correctly. Adjust the struts and reinstall the control valve body and oil pan with a new gasket. Refill the transmission with fluid.

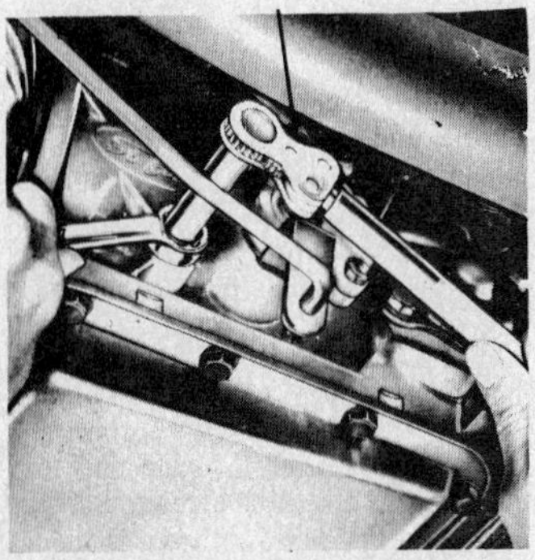

Adjusting intermediate band
(© Ford Motor Co.)

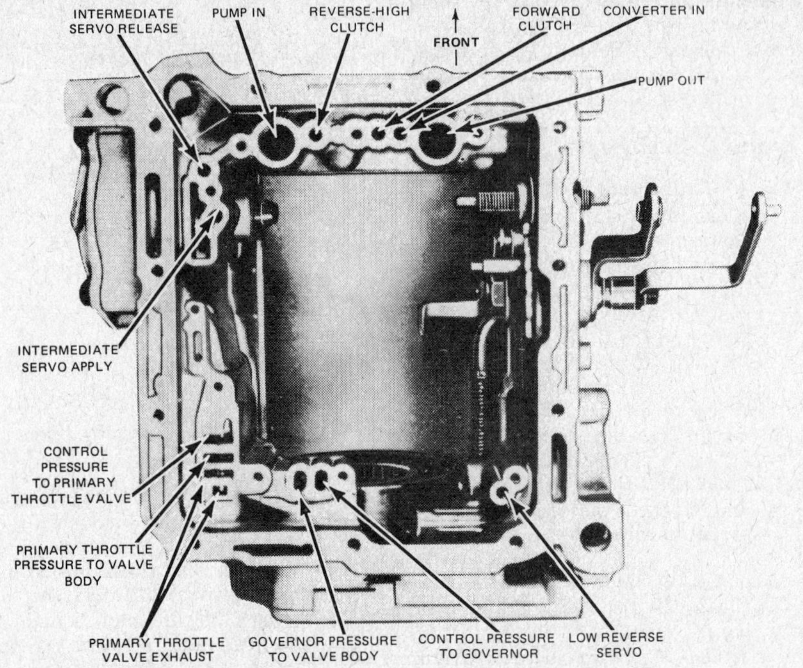

Case fluid passage hole identification (© Ford Motor Co.)

Low-Reverse Servo Piston

Removal and Installation

1. Raise the truck on a hoist.
2. Loosen the reverse band adjusting screw locknut and tighten the adjusting screw to 10 ft-lbs torque. This operation will hold the band strut against the case and prevent it from falling when the reverse servo piston is removed.
3. Remove the four servo cover attaching bolts and remove the servo cover and seal from the case.
4. Remove the servo piston from the case. *The piston and piston seal are bonded together and must be replaced together.*
5. Install the servo piston assembly into the case. Place a new cover seal on the cover and position them by installing two 51/6-18 bolts, 1¼ in. long, at 180 degrees apart on the case. Install two cover attaching bolts with the identification tag.
6. Remove the two positioning bolts and install the other two cover bolts. Tighten all the cover attaching bolts to the proper torque.
7. Adjust the low-reverse band. Lower the truck and fill the transmission with enough fluid to raise the fluid level to the FULL mark on the dipstick.
8. If the low-reverse band cannot be adjusted properly, the transmission must be drained and the oil pan and valve body removed. Check the alignment of the band struts. Reinstall the valve body and the oil pan with a new gasket, and refill the transmission with fluid.

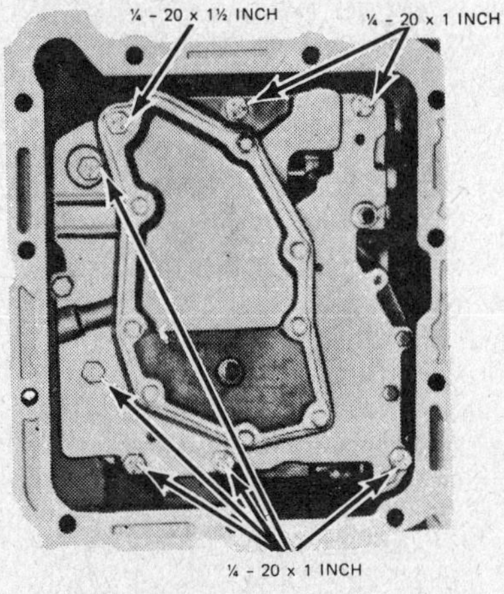

Control valve body attaching bolts
(© Ford Motor Co.)

Adjusting low-reverse band
(© Ford Motor Co.)

Extension Housing Bushing and Rear Seal

Removal and Installation

1. Disconnect the drive shaft from the transmission.
2. If only the rear seal needs replacing, carefully remove it with a tapered chisel or use the tools shown in the illustration. Remove the bushing as shown. Be careful not to damage the spline seal with the bushing remover.
3. Install the new bushing, using the special tool shown.
4. Before installing a new rear seal, inspect the sealing surface of the universal joint yoke for scores. If the universal joint yoke is scored, replace the yoke.
5. Inspect the housing counterbore for burrs and remove them with crocus cloth if necessary.
6. Install the new rear seal into the housing, using the tool shown in the illustration. The seal should be firmly seated in the housing. Coat the inside diameter of the fiber portion of the seal with lubricant.
7. Coat the front universal joint spline with lubricant and install the drive shaft.

Extension Housing

Removal and Installation

1. Raise the truck on a hoist.
2. Remove the drive shaft. Place a transmission jack under the transmission for support.
3. Remove the speedometer cable from the extension housing.

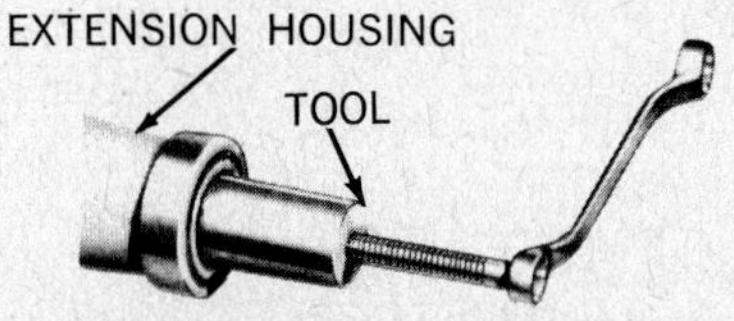

Removing extension housing bushing (© Ford Motor Co.)

4. Remove the extension housing-to-crossmember mount attaching bolts. Raise the transmission and remove the mounting pad between the extension housing and the crossmember.
5. Loosen the extension housing attaching bolts to drain the transmission fluid.

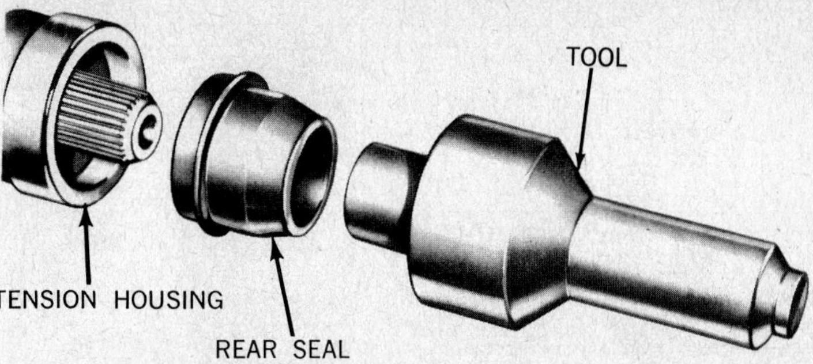

Installing extension housing seal (© Ford Motor Co.)

6. Remove the six extension housing attaching bolts and remove the extension housing.
7. To install the extension housing, reverse the above removal instructions. Install a new extension housing gasket. When the extension housing has been installed and all parts have been secured, lower the truck and fill the transmission with the correct amount of fluid. Check for fluid leaks around the extension housing area.

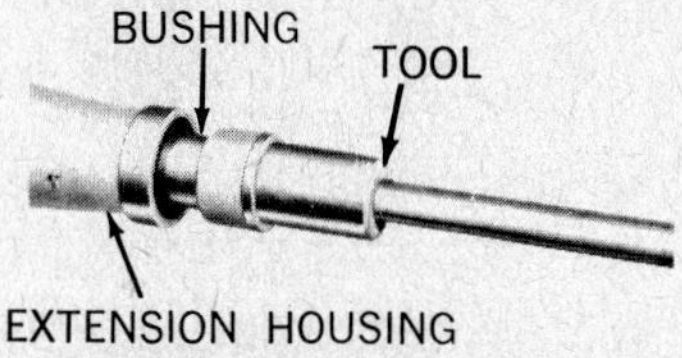

Installing extension housing bushing (© Ford Motor Co.)

Governor

Removal and Installation

1. After removing the extension housing according to the instructions above, remove the governor housing-to-governor distributor attaching bolts. Remove the governor housing from the distributor.
2. Refer to the Component Disassembly and Repair section for instructions on repairing the governor assembly.
3. Install the governor housing on the governor distributor and tighten the attaching bolts to the proper torque.
4. Install the extension housing with a new gasket according to the instructions above.

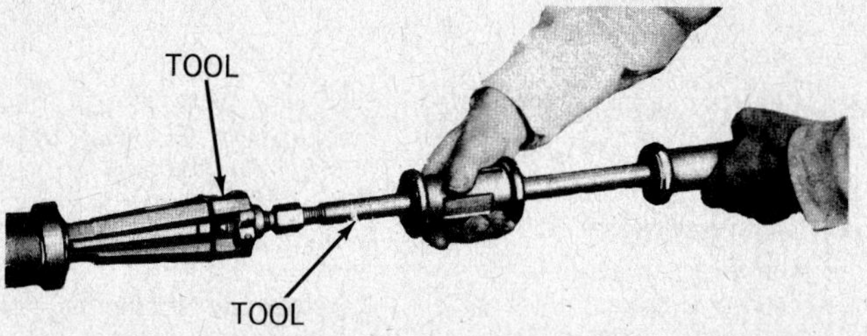

Removing extension housing seal (© Ford Motor Co.)

5. When the extension housing has been installed and all bolts have been tightened to the proper torque, lower the truck and fill the transmission with fluid to the proper level. Check around the extension housing area for leaks.

Transmission Overhaul Procedures

The transmission overhaul procedures presented here are the checks and repairs that must be done with the transmission out of the truck. Disassembly of each transmission subassembly is illustrated by exploded views of the subassembly showing how the individual parts fit together. Reassembly of the subassembly is often the reverse of the disassembly procedure except for alignment, special tolerances, etc.

Procedures for removing the transmission from the truck and reinstalling it back in the truck are given in the Truck Section.

During the transmission disassembly and reassembly operations, ten thrust washers that are installed between the subassemblies of the gear train must be removed and reinstalled correctly. Since it is very important that these thrust washers be installed correctly, they are shown in their positions and they are numbered for further identification. The No. 1 thrust washer is located at the front pump, and the No. 10 thrust washer is located at the packing pawl ring gear.

During all repairs to the transmission subassemblies, the following instructions must be followed:

1. Be sure that no dirt or grease gets in the transmission. All parts must be clean. *Remember—a little dirt can disable a transmission completely if it gets in a fluid passage.*
2. Handle all transmission parts carefully to avoid burring or nicking bearing or mating surfaces.
3. Lubricate all internal parts of the transmission with clean transmission fluid before assem-

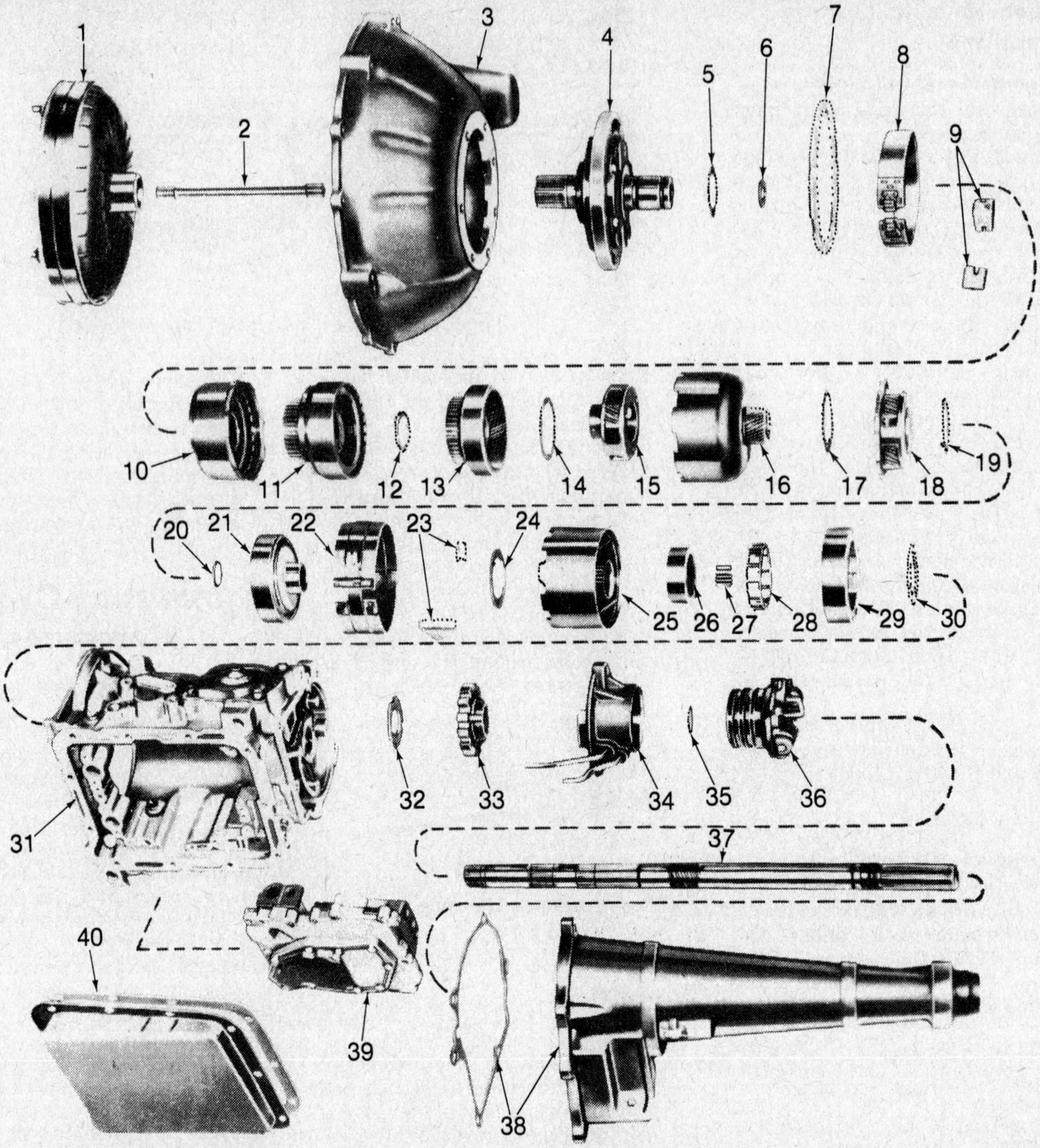

Transmission subassemblies—typical—C-4 (© Ford Motor Co.)

1 Converter
2 Input shaft
3 Converter housing
4 Front pump
5 Thrust washer no. 1
6 Thrust washer no. 2
7 Front pump gasket
8 Intermediate band
9 Band struts
10 Reverse and high clutch drum
11 Forward clutch and cylinder
12 Thrust washer no. 3
13 Forward clutch hub and ring gear
14 Thrust washer no. 4
15 Front planet carrier
16 Input shell, sun gear and thrust washer no. 5
17 Thrust washer no. 6
18 Reverse planet carrier
19 Thrust washer no. 7
20 Snap ring
21 Reverse ring gear and hub
22 Low and reverse band
23 Band struts
24 Thrust washer no. 8
25 Low and reverse drum
26 One-way clutch inner race
27 Roller (12) and spring (12)
28 Spring and roller cage
29 One-way clutch outer race
30 Thrust washer no. 9
31 Case
32 Thrust washer no. 10
33 Parking gear
34 Governor distributor sleeve
35 Snap ring
36 Governor and distributor assy. (automatic only)
37 Output shaft
38 Extension housing and gasket
39 Control valve body
40 Oil pan and gasket

bling. *Do not use any other lubricants except on gaskets or thrust washers which may be coated lightly with vaseline to ease assembly.*

4. Always use new gaskets when assembling the parts of the transmission.
5. Tighten all bolts and screws to the recommended torque limits using a torque wrench.

Transmission Disassembly

Disassemble the transmission by following the procedures below:

1 Thoroughly clean the outside of the transmission to prevent dirt or grease from getting inside the mechanism. *Do this before removing any subassembly.*
2. Place the transmission in the transmission holder. See illustration.
3. Remove the converter from the transmission front pump and converter housing.

4. On a C4 automatic transmission, remove the transmission vacuum unit with the tool shown in the illustration. Remove the vacuum unit gasket and the control rod.
5. On a C4 automatic transmission, remove the primary throttle valve from the opening at the rear of the case.
6. Remove the transmission pan attaching bolts, oil pan, and gasket.
7. Remove the control valve body attaching bolts and then lift the control valve body from the case.
8. Loosen the intermediate band adjusting screw and remove the intermediate band struts from the case. Loosen the low-reverse band adjusting screw and remove the low-reverse band struts.

Transmission End-Play Check

1. Remove one of the converter housing attaching bolts and mount the dial indicator support tool in the hole. Mount a dial indicator on the support so that a contact rests on the end of the input shaft. See illustration.
2. Install the extension housing seal replacer tool on the output shaft to provide support and alignment for the shaft.
3. Using a screwdriver, move the input shaft and the gear train to the rear of the case as far as possible. Set the dial indicator at zero while holding a slight pressure on the screwdriver.

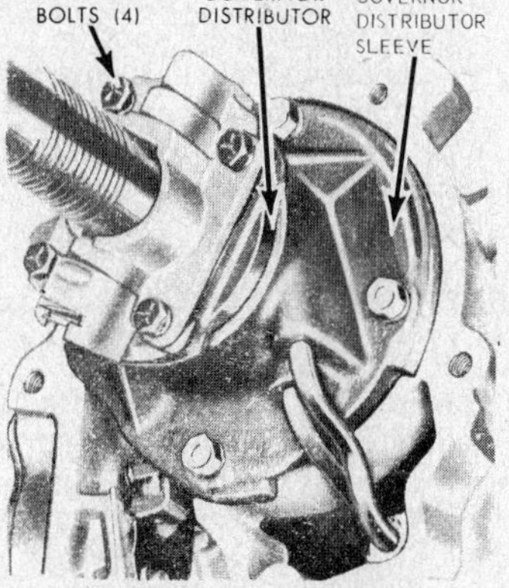

Governor location (© Ford Motor Co.)

4. Remove the screwdriver and insert it behind the input shell. Move the input shell and the front part of the gear train forward.
5. Record the dial reading for later reference during transmission reassembly. The end play reading should be from 0.008 to 0.042 in. If the end play reading is not within this range, selective thrust washers must be used to obtain the proper reading.

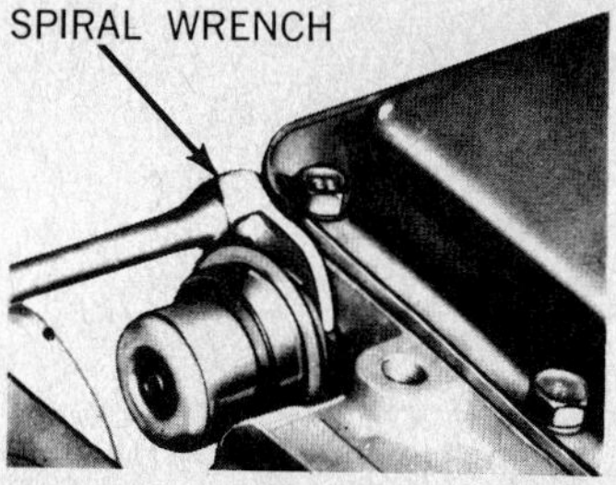

Removing or installing vacuum unit (© Ford Motor Co.)

The selective thrust washers to be used are listed in the table shown.

6. Remove the dial indicator, its support bar, and the extension housing seal replacer tool.

Removal of Case and Extension Parts

1. Rotate the transmission in the holding fixture until it is in a vertical position with the converter housing up.
2. Remove the five converter housing attaching bolts and remove the converter housing from the transmission case.
3. Remove the seven front pump attaching bolts. Remove the front pump by inserting a screwdriver behind the input shell and pushing it forward until the front pump seal is above the edge of the case. Remove the front pump and gasket from the case. If the selective thrust washer No. 1 did not come out with the front pump, lift it from the top of the reverse-high clutch.
4. Remove the intermediate and low-reverse adjusting screws from the case. Rotate the intermediate band to align the band ends with the clearance hole in the case. Remove the intermediate band from the case.
5. Using a screwdriver between the input shell and the rear planet carrier (see illustration), lift the input shell upward and remove the forward part of the gear train as an assembly.

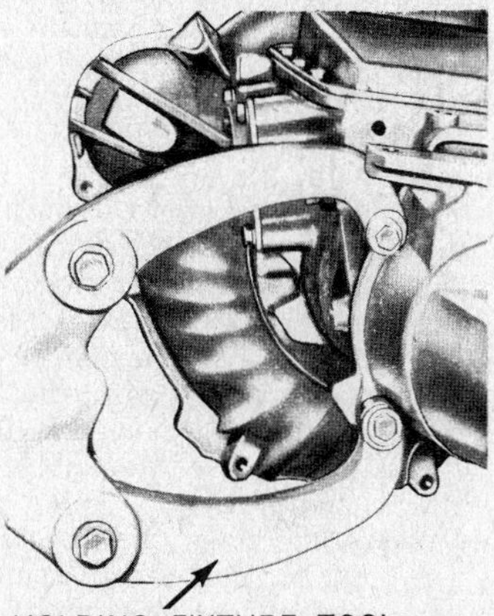

Transmission mounted in holding fixture (© Ford Motor Co.)

6. Place the forward part of the gear train in the holding fixture shown.
7. With the gear train in the holding fixture, remove the reverse-high clutch and drum from the forward clutch. If thrust washer No. 2 did not come out with the front pump, remove the thrust washer from the forward clutch cylinder. If a selective spacer was used, remove the spacer. Remove the forward clutch from the forward clutch hub and ring gear.

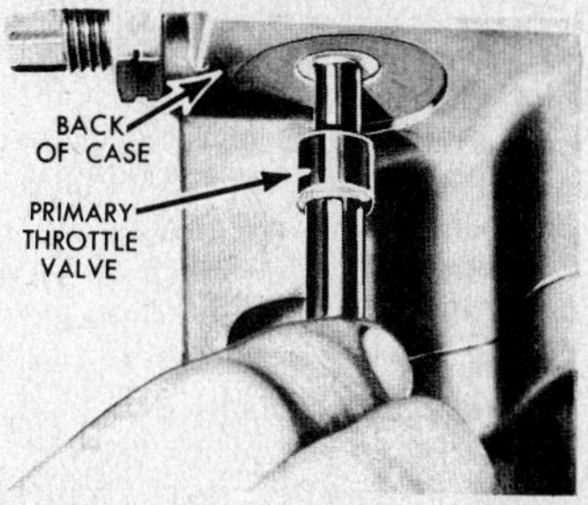

Removing or installing primary throttle valve (© Ford Motor Co.)

8. If the thrust washer No. 3 did not come out with the forward clutch, remove the thrust washer from the forward clutch hub and lift the forward clutch hub and ring gear from the front planet carrier.
9. Remove thrust washer No. 4 and the front planet carrier from the input shell.
10. Remove the input shell, sun gear and thrust washer No. 5 from the holding fixture.
11. From inside the transmission case, remove thrust washer No. 6 from the top of the reverse planet carrier. Remove the reverse planet carrier and thrust washer No. 7 from the reverse ring gear and hub.

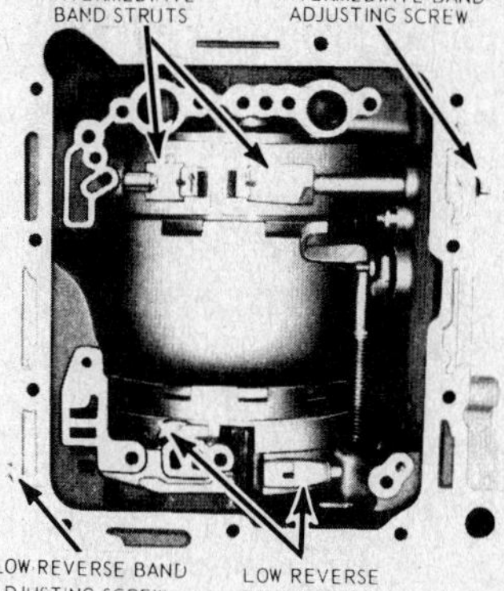

Layout of band struts (© Ford Motor Co.)

12. Move the output shaft forward and, with the tool shown in the illustration, remove the reverse ring gear and hub from the output shaft. Remove the thrust washer No. 8 from the low and reverse drum.
13. Remove the low-reverse band from the case. Remove the one-way clutch inner race by rotating the race clockwise as it is removed.
14. Remove the 12 one-way clutch rollers, springs and the spring retainer from the outer race. *Do not lose or damage any of the 12 springs or rollers. The outer race of the one-way clutch cannot be removed from the case until the extension housing, output shaft and governor distributor sleeve are removed.*
15. Remove the transmission from the holding fixture. Place the transmission on the bench in a vertical position with the extension housing up. Remove the four extension housing attaching bolts, the extension housing, and the gasket from the case.
16. Pull outward on the output shaft and remove the output shaft and governor distributor assembly (if so equipped) from the governor distributor sleeve.
17. Remove the governor distributor lock ring from the output shaft. Remove the governor distributor from the output shaft.
18. Remove the four distributor sleeve attaching bolts and the distributor sleeve from the case. *Do not bend or distort the fluid tubes as the tubes are removed from the case with the distributor sleeve.*
19. Remove the parking pawl return spring, pawl, and pawl retaining pin from the case.
20. Remove the parking gear and thrust washer No. 10 from the case.
21. Remove the six one-way clutch outer race attaching bolts with the tool shown. As the bolts are removed, hold the outer race that is located inside the case in position. Then, remove the outer race and thrust washer No. 9 from the case.

Component Disassembly and Assembly

Downshift and Manual Linkage

Removal

1. Loosen the outer downshift lever nut with penetrating oil. Remove the nut and the inner and outer downshift levers.

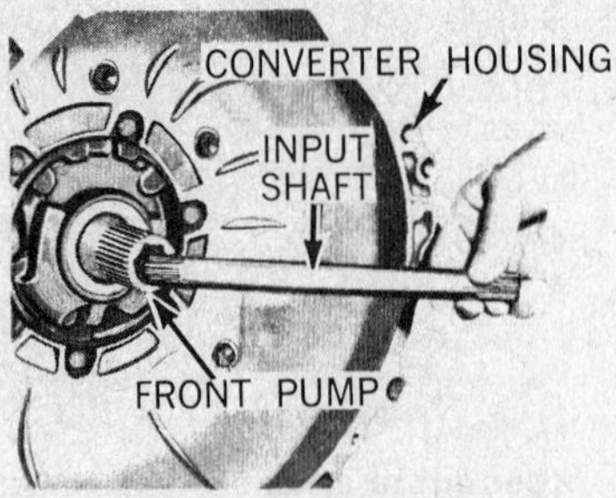

Removing or installing input shaft
(© Ford Motor Co.)

Checking gear train and play
(© Ford Motor Co.)

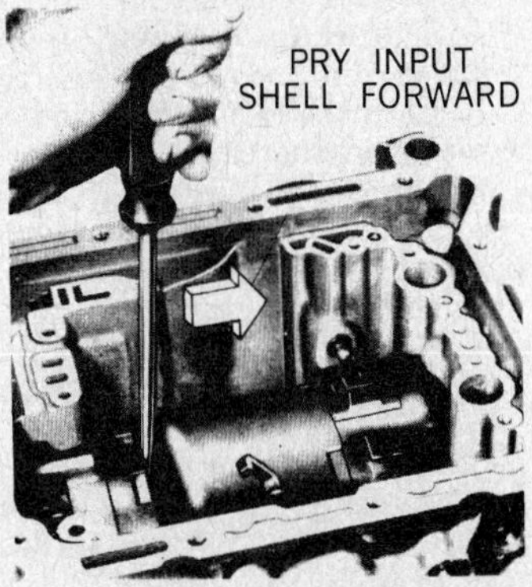

Removing front pump
(© Ford Motor Co.)

From inside the case, remove the upper retaining ring and the flat washer from the manual lever link. Remove the upper end of the lever link from the case retaining pin.

2. From the back of the transmission case, remove the upper retaining clip and flat washer from the parking pawl link. Remove the pawl link and spacer from the case retaining pin, and remove the parking pawl link, toggle rod, and the manual lever link as an assembly.
3. Remove the inner manual lever retaining nut and lever. Remove the outer manual lever from the case. Remove manual lever seal, and drive a new seal into the case with an appropriate driver.

Install outer manual lever into the case. Install inner manual lever and retaining nut. Torque nut to specifications.

4. From back of the transmission case, install parking toggle rod and link into the case. Install parking pawl link spacer onto the case retaining pin. Dimpled side of the spacer should be facing the link.
5. Install the parking pawl link onto the case retaining pin. Install flat washer and retaining ring.
6. Position inner manual lever behind the manual lever link, with the cam on the lever contacting the lower link pin.
7. Install the upper end of the manual lever link onto the case retaining pin. Install flat washer and retaining ring.
8. Operate the manual lever and check for correct linkage operation.

Control Valve Body

Removal

1. Remove the screws attaching the oil screen to the valve body and remove the oil screen. Be careful not to lose the throttle pressure limit valve and spring when separating the oil screen from the valve body.
2. Remove the attaching screws from the lower valve body and separate the upper and lower valve bodies, the gasket, separator plate and the hold-down plate. Be careful not to lose the upper valve body shuttle valve and check valve when separating the upper and lower valve bodies.
3. Slide the manual valve out of the body.

Control Valve Body

Disassembly

1. Remove the screws attaching the oil screen to the valve body and

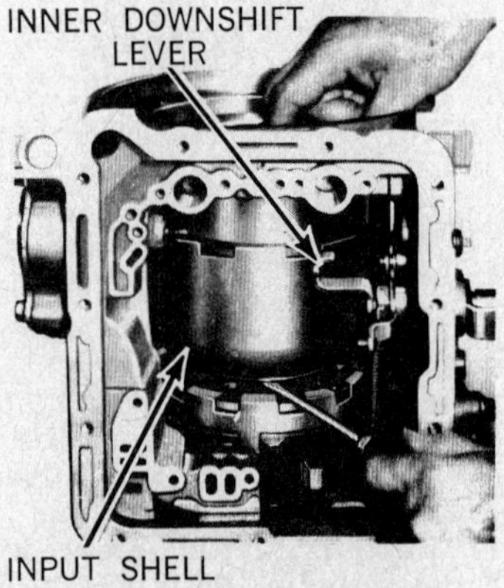

Lifting input shell and gear train
(© Ford Motor Co.)

Position of intermediate band for removal or installation (© Ford Motor Co.)

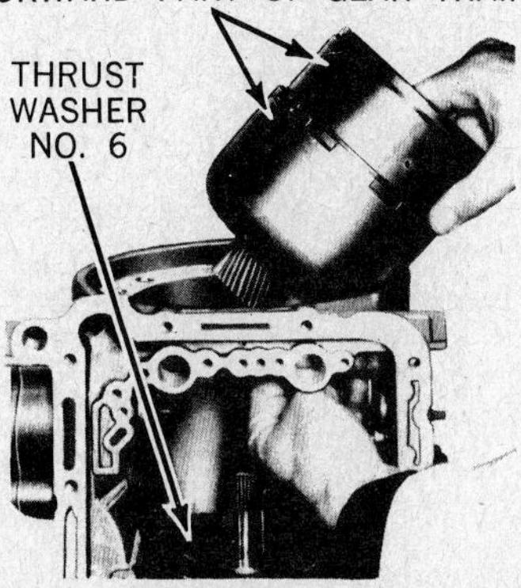

Removing or installing forward part of gear train (© Ford Motor Co.)

remove the oil screen. Be careful not to lose the throttle pressure limit valve and spring when separating the oil screen from the valve body.

2. Remove the attaching screws from the lower valve body and separate the upper and lower valve bodies, the gasket, separator plate and the hold-down plate. Be careful not to lose the upper valve body shuttle valve and check valve when separating the upper and lower valve bodies.
3. Slide the manual valve out of the body.
4. Pry the low servo modulator valve retainer from the body and remove the retainer plug, spring, and valve from the valve body. While working in the same bore, pry the retainer, spring, and the downshift valve from the valve body (see illustration).
5. Depress the throttle booster plug and remove the retaining pin. Then, remove the plug, valve, and spring from the valve body.
6. Remove the cover over the cut-back valve and the transition valve from the valve body.
7. Remove the cut-back valve and the transition valve spring, transition valve, 2-3 back-out valve, and spring from the valve body.
8. Remove the cover from over the 1-2 shift valve and the 2-3 shift valve. Remove the 2-3 shift valve, spring, and the throttle modulator valve from the valve body. Remove the 1-2 shift valve, D-2 valve, and spring from the valve body.
9. Remove the retaining pin from the retainer after depressing the intermediate servo accumulator valve. Remove the retainer, intermediate servo accumulator valve, and spring from the valve body.
10. Depress the main oil pressure booster valve and remove the retaining pin. Remove the main oil pressure booster valve, sleeve, springs, retainer, and main oil pressure regulator valve from the valve body.
11. Remove the line coasting boost valve retaining clip, the spring, and line coasting boost valve from the valve body.

Front Pump

Disassembly

1. Remove the four seal rings from the stator support.
2. Remove the five bolts that secure the stator support to the front pump housing. Remove stator support from pump housing.
3. Replace the stator bushings if they are worn or damaged. Use a cape chisel to cut the bushing through. Then, pry up the loose

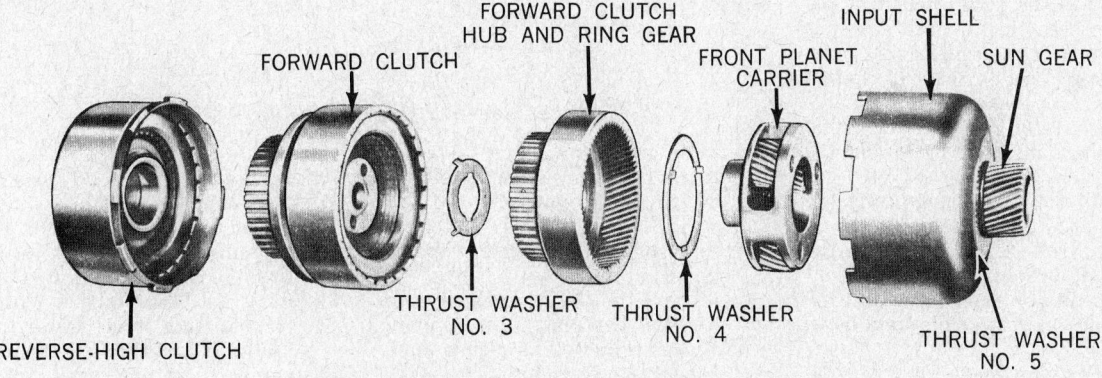

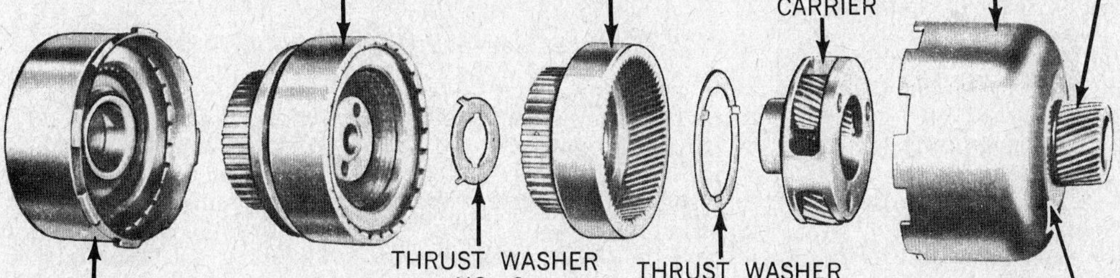

Forward part of gear train disassembled (© Ford Motor Co.)

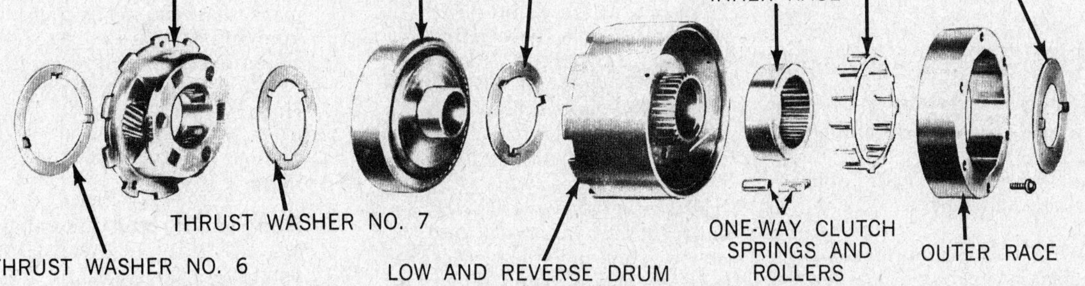

Lower part of gear train disassembled (© Ford Motor Co.)

Forward part of gear train in holding fixture (© Ford Motor Co.)

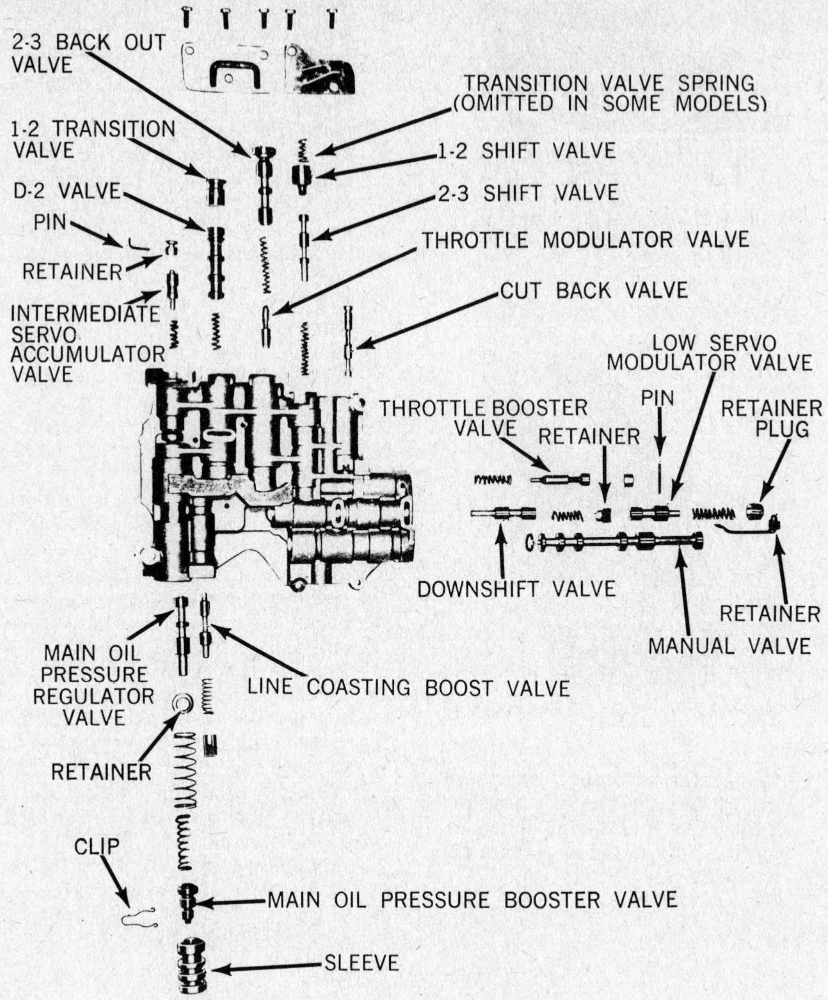

Exploded view—upper valve body (© Ford Motor Co.)

ends of the bushing with an awl and remove the bushing. Press a new bushing into the stator support.

NOTE: Ensure that the oil hole in the bushing lines up with the hole in the stator support.

4. Remove drive and driven gears from the front pump housing.
5. Replace the bushing in the pump housing with the tools shown, making sure the slot and groove are toward the rear of the body and 60° below the horizontal centerline of the pump.
6. Install the drive and driven gears in the pump housing. The chamfered side of each gear has an identification mark that must be positioned downward, against the face of the pump housing.
7. Place stator support in pump housing. Install and torque the five retaining bolts.
8. Install four seal rings onto the stator support. The two large oil rings are assembled first, in the oil ring grooves toward the front of the stator support. Install the O-ring seal onto the pump housing.
9. Check pump gears for free rotation by placing pump on the converter drive hub and turning pump housing.
10. If the front pump seal must be replaced, mount the pump in the transmission case and remove the seal with a seal removing tool.

Reverse-High Clutch

Disassembly and Assembly

1. Remove pressure plate retaining snap-ring.
2. Remove the pressure plate, and the drive and driven clutch plates.
   CAUTION: Use no detergent or other cleaning solution on the lined clutch plates. Wipe the plates with a lint-free cloth.
3. Remove piston spring retainer by applying pressure to the clutch hub. Compress piston return springs, and remove the retainer.
4. Remove the piston return spring.
5. Remove the piston by applying air pressure to the piston apply hole of the clutch hub.
6. Remove piston outer seal from the piston and the piston inner seal from the clutch drum.
7. Remove the drum bushing if it is worn or damaged. Use a cape chisel to cut the bushing seam until it is broken. Pry up the loose ends of the bushing with an awl and remove the bushing. *To prevent leakage at the stator support O-rings, do not nick or damage the hub surface with the chisel.*
8. Position the drum and a new bushing in a press and install the bushing with the tool shown.
9. Install a new inner seal into the clutch drum and a new outer seal onto the clutch piston. Lubricate and install the piston into the clutch drum.
10. Locate the piston return spring on the piston. Place retainer on top of the springs. Compress the assembly with a press, and install the retainer snap-ring.
11. Soak new composition plates in transmission fluid before installation. Install clutch plates, alternately, starting with a steel plate. The last plate installed is the pressure plate with the internally-chamfered side up.
12. Install the pressure plate retaining snap-ring.
13. Using feeler gauges, check the clearance between the pressure plate and the snap-ring while applying pressure to the plate. If clearance is not within specifications, selective thickness snap-rings are available.

Forward Clutch

Disassembly and Assembly

1. Remove the clutch pressure plate retaining snap ring.
2. Remove the pressure plate, drive and driven plates from the hub.

3. Remove the disc spring retaining snap-ring.
4. Apply air pressure to the clutch piston pressure hole to remove the piston from the hub.
5. Remove piston outer seal and the inner seal from the clutch hub.
6. Install new piston seals onto the clutch piston and drum.
7. Lubricate and insert the piston into the clutch hub. Install the disc spring and retaining snap-ring.
8. Install the lower pressure plate, with the flat side up and the radiused side downward. Install one composition clutch plate and alternately install the drive and driven plates. Install the pressure plate with the internally chamfered side up.
9. Install pressure plate retaining snap-ring.
10. With a feeler gauge, check clearance between the snap ring and the pressure plate. Downward pressure on the plate should be used when making this check. If clearance is not within specifications, selective snap-rings are available.

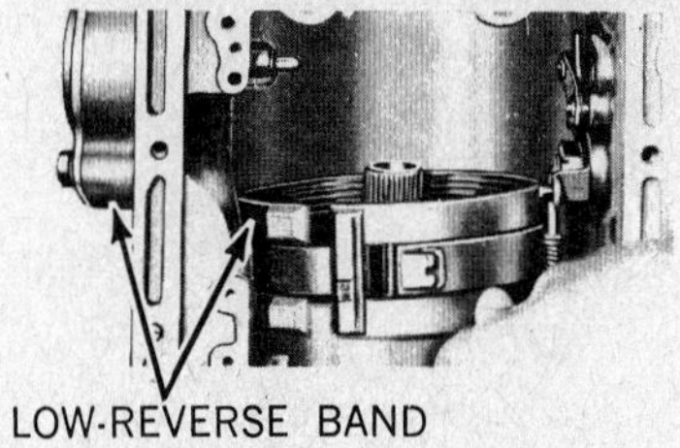

Removing low-reverse band (© Ford Motor Co.)

Forward Clutch Hub and Ring Gear

Disassembly and Assembly

1. Remove forward clutch hub retaining snap-ring.
2. Separate clutch hub from ring gear.
3. Press the bushing from the clutch hub.
4. Install a new bushing into the clutch hub as shown.
5. Install clutch hub into ring gear.
6. Install hub retaining snap-ring.

Input Shell and Sun Gear

Disassembly and Assembly

1. Remove external snap-ring from sun gear.
2. Remove thrust washer No. 5 from input shell and sun gear.
2. From inside the shell, remove the sun gear. Remove internal snap-ring from sun gear.
4. If the sun gear bushings are to be replaced use the tool shown in the illustration and press both bushings through the gear.

Removing one way clutch outer race retaining bolts (© Ford Motor Co.)

5. Press a new bushing into each end of the sun gear.
6. Install internal snap-ring onto sun gear. Install sun gear into the input shell.
7. Install thrust washer No. 5 onto sun gear and input shell.
8. Install external snap-ring onto sun gear.

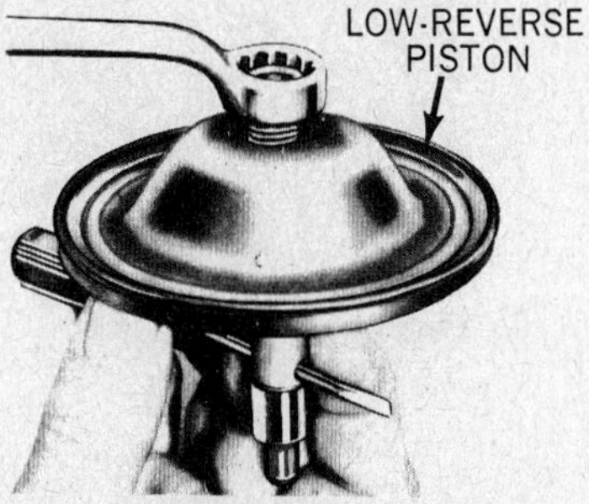

Low-reverse servo piston—removal (© Ford Motor Co.)

Reverse ring gear retaining ring—removal (© Ford Motor Co.)

Governor and Oil Distributor

Disassembly

1. Remove the oil rings from the governor oil distributor.
2. Remove the governor housing attaching bolts and remove the governor assembly from the distributor. Remove the governor oil screen.

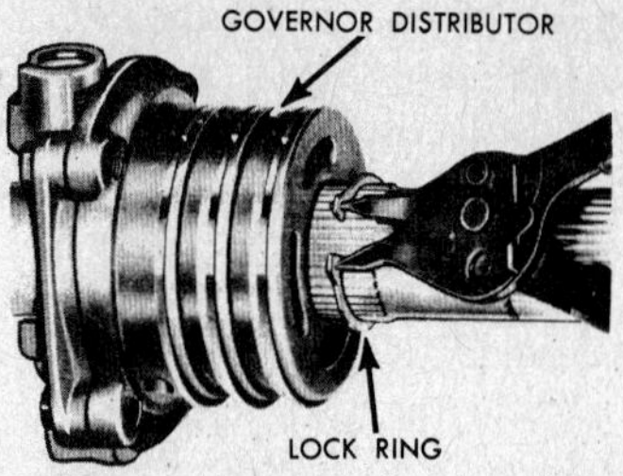

Removing governor snap-ring (© Ford Motor Co.)

3. Remove the primary governor valve retaining ring. Remove the washer, spring, and primary governor valve from the housing.
4. Remove the secondary governor valve retaining clip, spring, and governor valve from the housing.
5. After cleaning and inspecting all governor parts, install the secondary governor valve in its housing. Install the spring and spring retaining clip with its small concave area facing downward.
6. Install the primary governor valve in the housing. Install the spring, washer, and retaining clip. Be sure the washer is centered in the housing on the spring and the retaining ring is fully seated in the ring groove in the housing.
7. Install the oil rings on the governor distributor. Install the governor oil screen and mount the governor assembly on the distributor, tightening the attaching bolts to the proper torque.

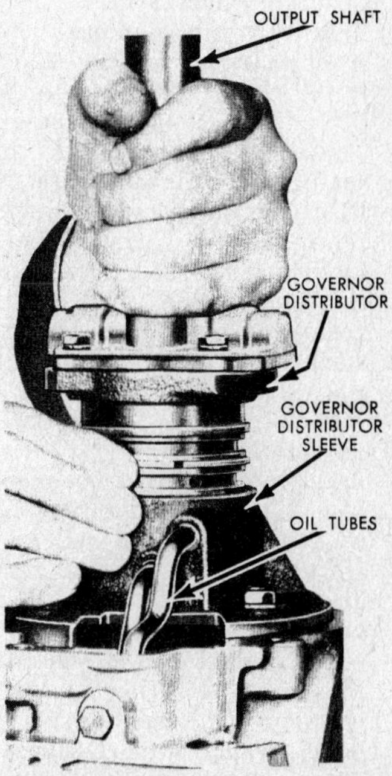

Removing or installing output shaft and governor distributor (© Ford Motor Co.)

Ford C-4 (Dual Range)

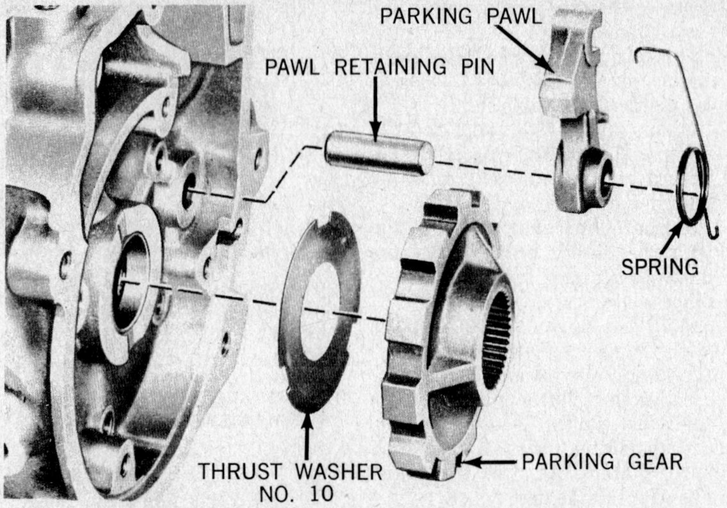

Parking pawl, disassembled (© Ford Motor Co.)

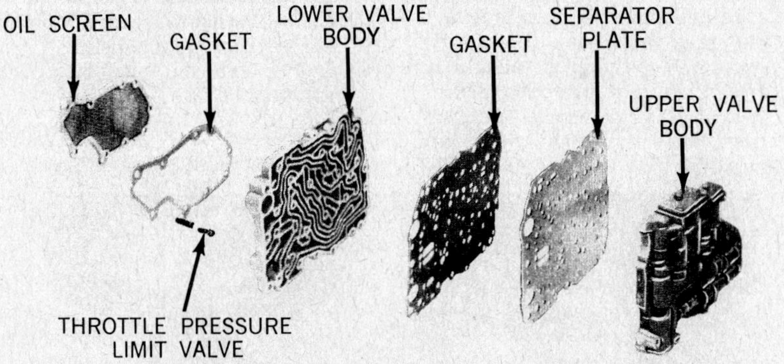

Upper & lower valve bodies C-4 (© Ford Motor Co.)

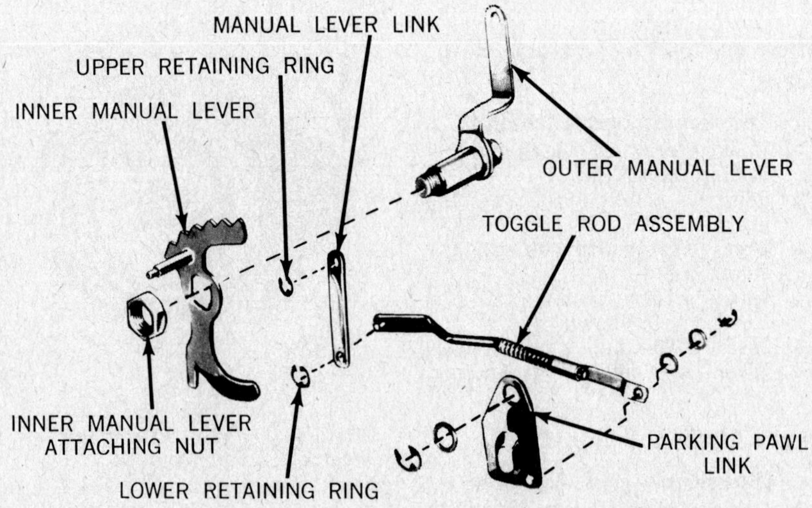

Transmission case internal linkage (© Ford Motor Co.)

Transmission Assembly

1. Install thrust washer No. 9 inside the transmission case.
2. Place the one-way clutch outer race inside the case. From the rear of the case, install the six outer race-to-case retaining bolts. Torque to specifications.
3. Stand the transmission case on end (rear end up). Install parking pawl retaining pin.
4. Install parking pawl on the case retaining pin. Install pawl return spring.
5. Install thrust washer No. 10 onto the parking pawl gear. Place gear and thrust washer on back face of case.
6. Place two oil distributor tubes in the governor distributor sleeve. Install the sleeve onto the case. As the distributor sleeve is installed, the oil tubes have to be inserted into the two holes in the case and the parking pawl retaining pin has to be inserted in the alignment hole in the distributor.
7. Install the four governor distributor sleeve-to-case retaining bolts and torque to specifications.
8. Install governor distributor assembly onto the output shaft. Install the distributor retaining snap-ring.
9. Check oil rings in the governor distributor for free rotation. Install the output shaft and governor distributor into the distributor sleeve.
10. With a new gasket in place on the extension housing, install the extension housing, vacuum tube clip and the extension housing to case retaining bolts. Torque bolts to specifications.
11. Rotate transmission case so that front end is up, making sure that thrust washer No. 9 is in position at the bottom of the case.
12. Install the 12 one-way clutch springs onto the spring retainer.
13. Place the one-way clutch spring retainer, with springs installed, into the outer race, located inside the transmission.
14. Install the inner race inside the spring retainer and 12 springs.
15. Starting at the back of the one-way clutch outer race, install the 12 clutch rollers.
16. After the clutch has been assembled, rotate the inner race clockwise to center the rollers and springs. Install low and reverse drum. The splines of the drum must engage the splines of the one-way clutch inner race. Check the clutch operation by rotating the low and reverse drum. The drum should rotate clockwise but not counterclockwise.
17. Install thrust washer No. 8 on top of the low and reverse drum. Install the low and reverse band into the case, with the small strut end facing the low-reverse servo.
18. Install the reverse ring gear and hub onto the output shaft.
19. Move the output shaft forward and install the reverse ring gear hub-to-output shaft retaining ring.
20. Place thrust washers Nos. 6 and 7 on the reverse planet carrier. Install planet carrier into the reverse ring gear and engage the tabs of the carrier with the slots in the low-reverse drum.

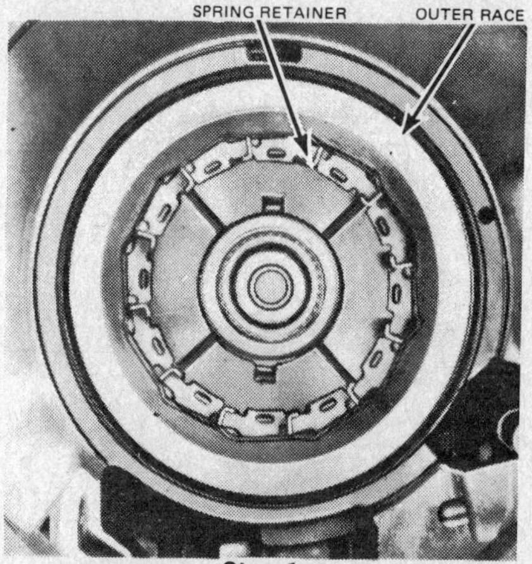

Step 1
Install spring retainer into outer race

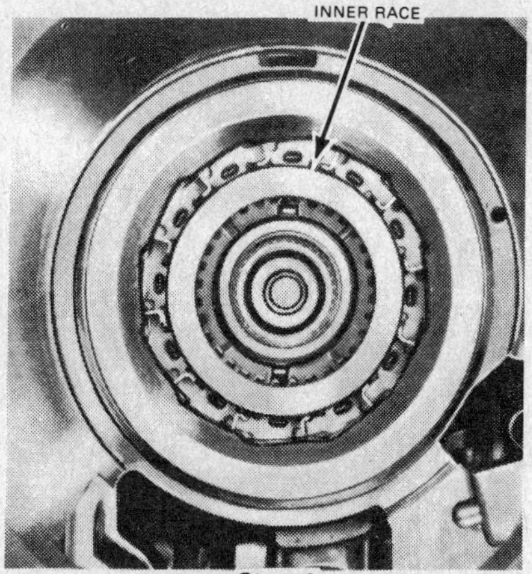

Step 2
Install inner race

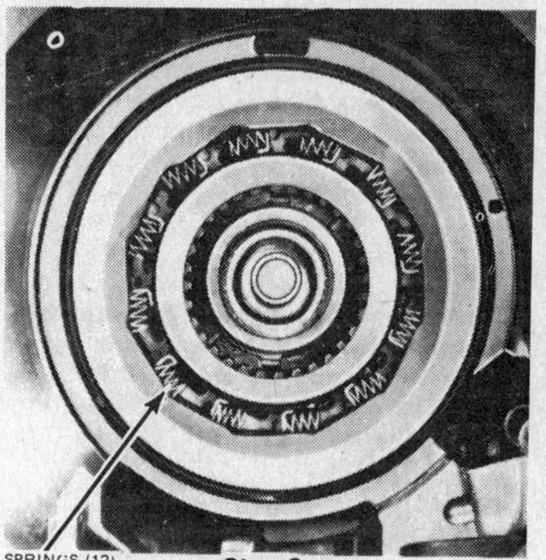

Step 3
Install 12 springs

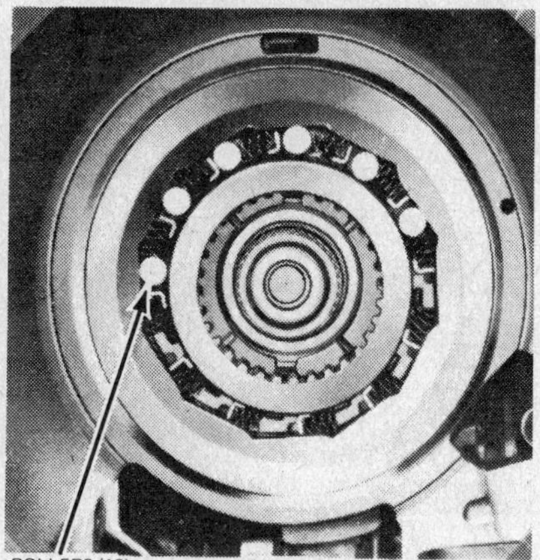

Step 4
Install 12 rollers

Installing one-way clutch (© Ford Motor Co.)

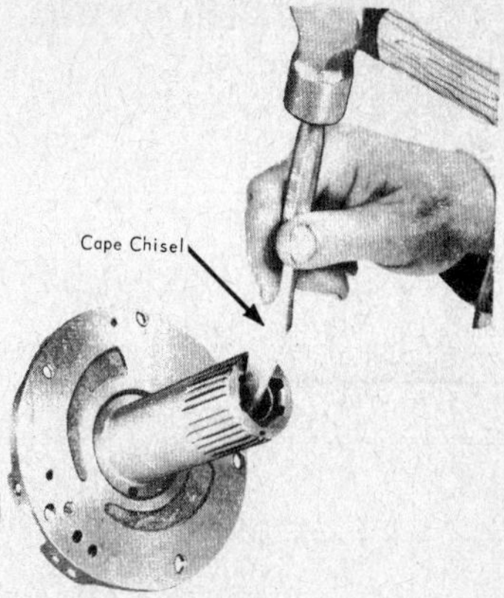

Removing stator support bushings (© Ford Motor Co.)

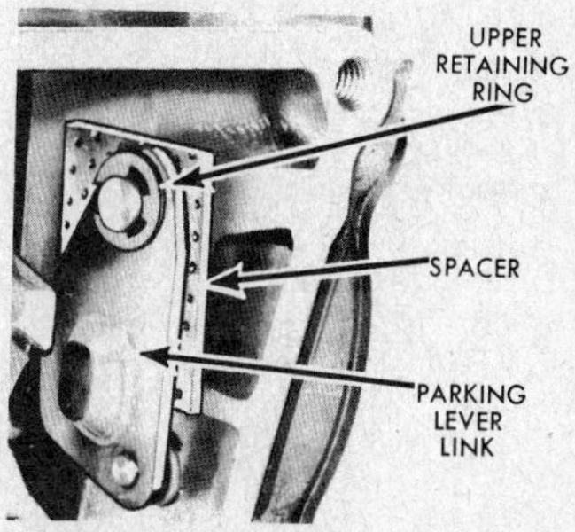

Parking lever pawl link and spacer (© Ford Motor Co.)

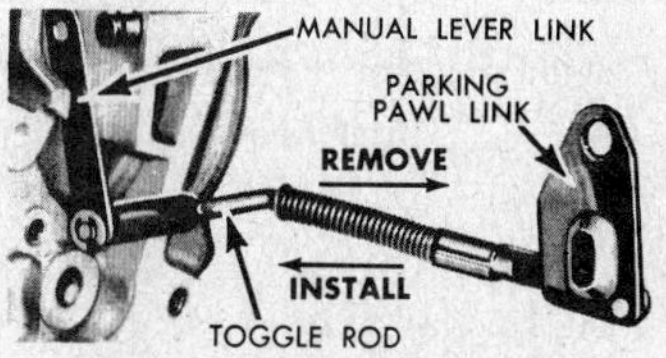

Parking pawl toggle rod (© Ford Motor Co.)

21. From inside the transmission case, install the inner downshift lever.
22. Install the forward clutch into the reverse-high clutch by meshing the reverse-high clutch plates with the splines of the forward clutch. Using the end-play check reading obtained during the transmission disassembly, determine which No. 2 thrust washer is necessary to get the proper

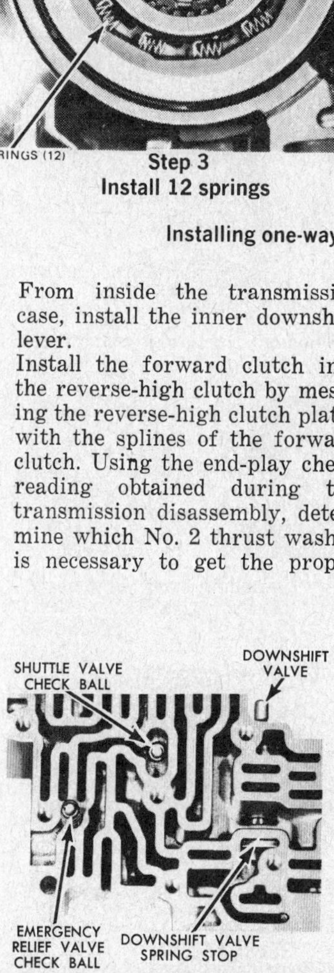

Upper valve check ball and spring location (© Ford Motor Co.)

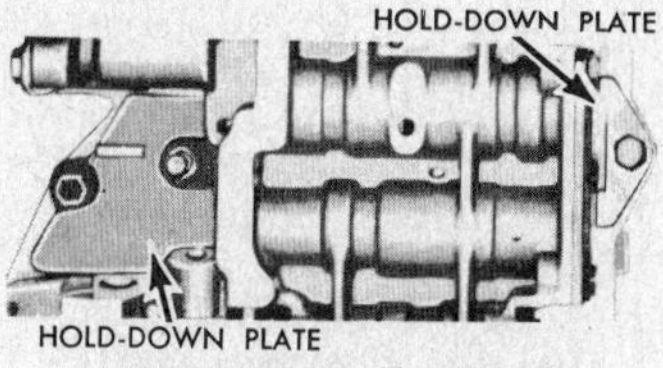

Hold down plate location (© Ford Motor Co.)

end-play reading and proceed as follows:

a. Place the stator support vertically on the bench and install the correct No. 2 thrust washer or washer and spacer as required to bring the end-play within the correct range.
b. Install the reverse-high clutch and the forward clutch on the stator support.
c. Invert the complete assembly making sure the intermediate brake drum bushing is seated on the forward clutch mating surface. Select the thickest fiber washer (No. 1) that can be inserted between the stator support and the intermediate brake drum thrust surfaces and still maintain a slight clearance. Do not select a washer that must be forced between the stator support and the intermediate brake drum.
d. Remove the intermediate brake drum and forward clutch unit from the stator support.
e. Install the selected No. 1 and No. 2 thrust washers on the front pump stator support using vaseline to hold the thrust washers in place while installing the front pump.

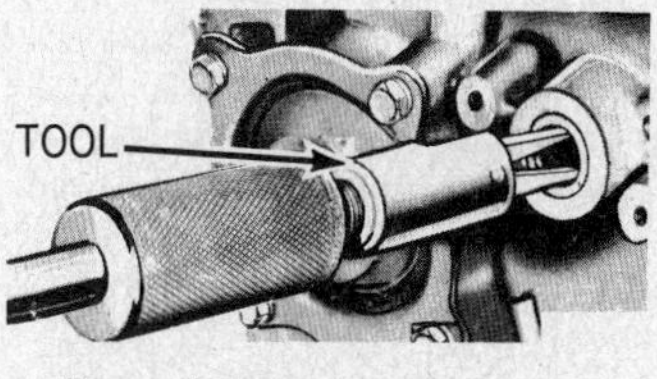

Removing manual lever seal (© Ford Motor Co.)

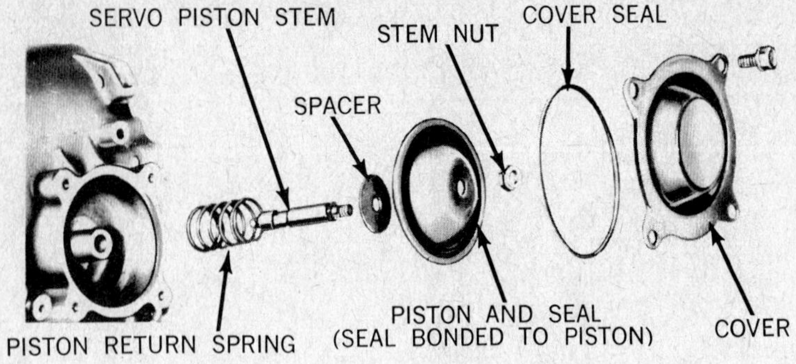

Low-reverse servo—disassembled (© Ford Motor Co.)

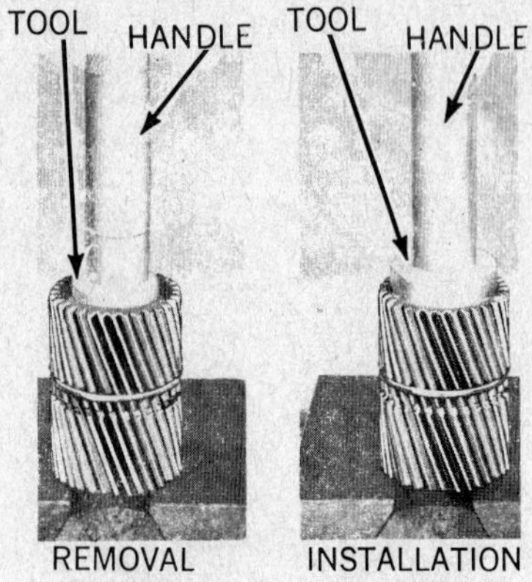

Replacing sun gear bushing
(© Ford Motor Co.)

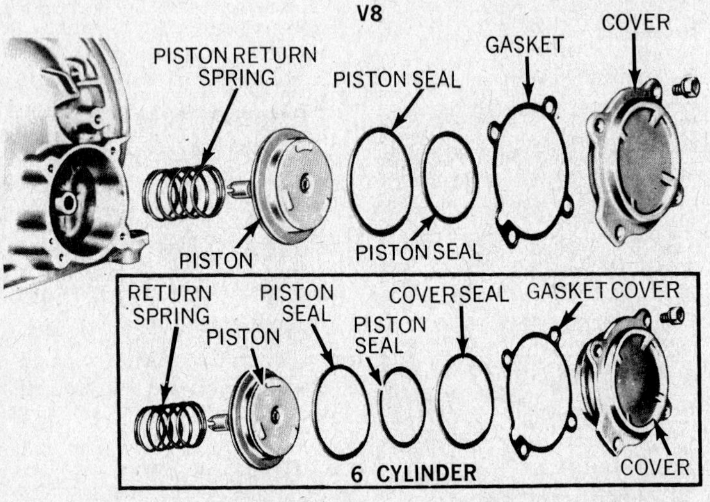

Intermediate servo—disassembled (© Ford Motor Co.)

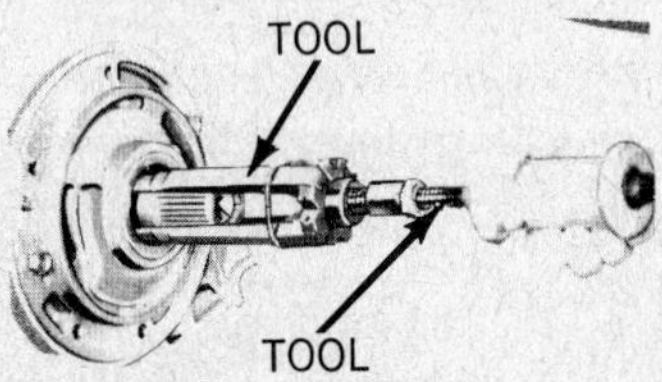

Front pump seal removal
(© Ford Motor Co.)

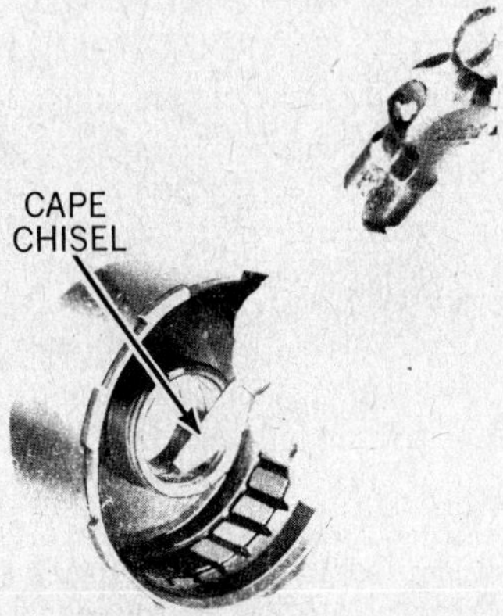

Removing reverse-high clutch bushing
(© Ford Motor Co.)

23. Install thrust washer No. 3 onto the forward clutch.
24. Install forward clutch hub and ring in the forward clutch by rotating the units to mesh the forward clutch plates with the splines on the forward clutch hub.
25. Install thrust washer No. 4 on the front planet carrier, and install the planet carrier into the forward clutch hub and ring gear.
26. Install input shell and sun gear onto the gear train. Rotate the input shell to engage the drive lugs of the reverse-high clutch. If the drive lugs will not engage, the outer race inside the forward planet carrier is not centered in the end of the sun gear inside the input shell. Center the thrust bearing race and install the input shell.
27. Hold the gear train together and install the forward part of the gear train assembly into the case. The input shell sun gear must mesh with the reverse pinion gears. The front planet car-

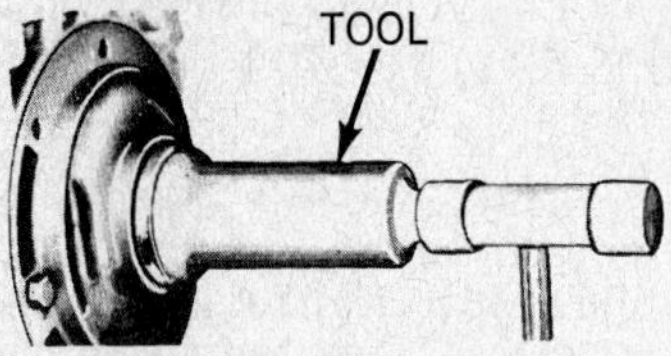

Installing front pump seal
(© Ford Motor Co.)

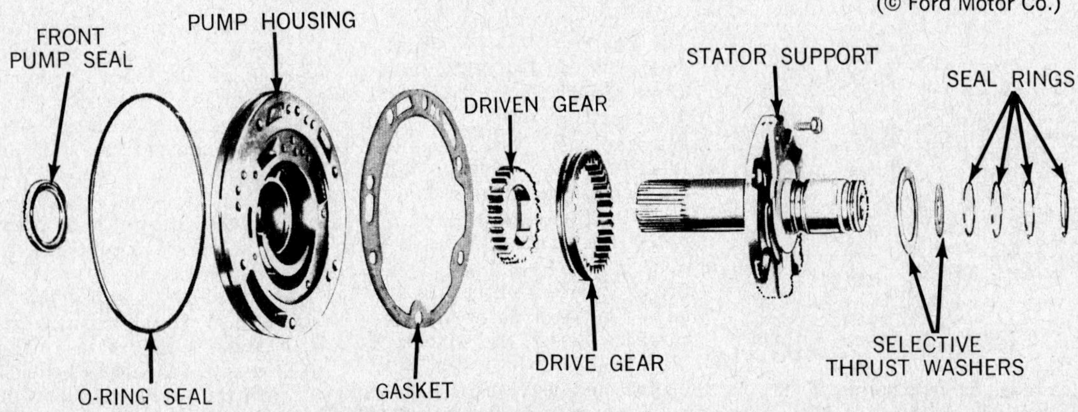

Typical front pump and stator support (© Ford Motor Co.)

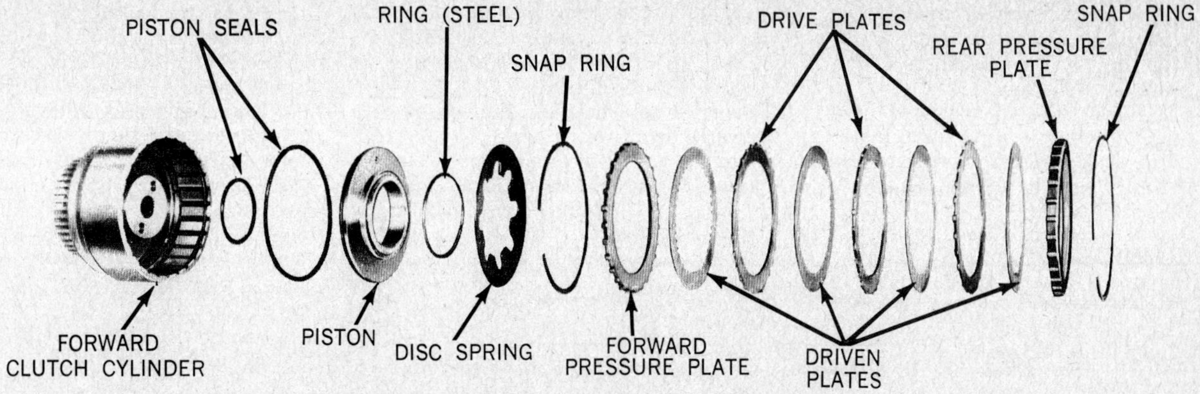

Forward clutch—disassembled (© Ford Motor Co.)

rier internal splines must mesh with the splines of the output shaft.

28. Install intermediate band through front of case. The side of the band with the anchor tabs faces the back of the transmission. If using a new band, soak it in transmission fluid prior to installation.
29. Install a new front pump gasket onto the case. Install selective thrust washers No. 1 and 2 onto the front pump stator support. Use vaseline to hold the washers in place.
30. Lubricate the front pump O-ring with transmission fluid, and install the front pump stator support into the reverse-high clutch.

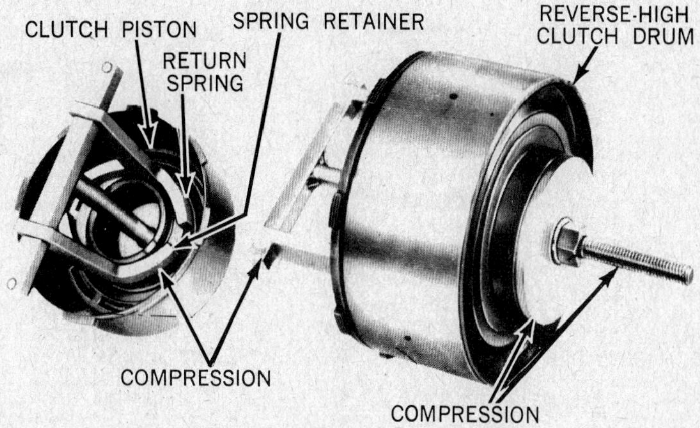

Removing or installing clutch piston retainer snap-ring (© Ford Motor Co.)

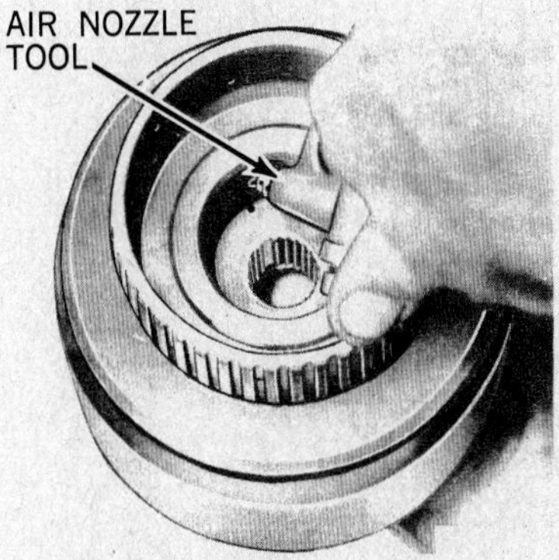

Removing forward clutch piston (© Ford Motor Co.)

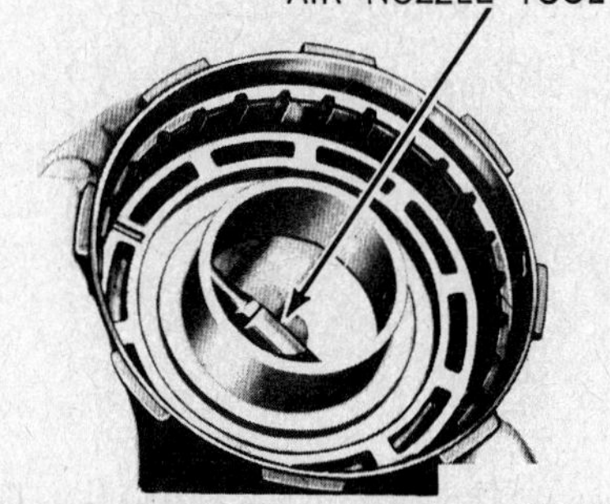

Removing reverse-high clutch piston (© Ford Motor Co.)

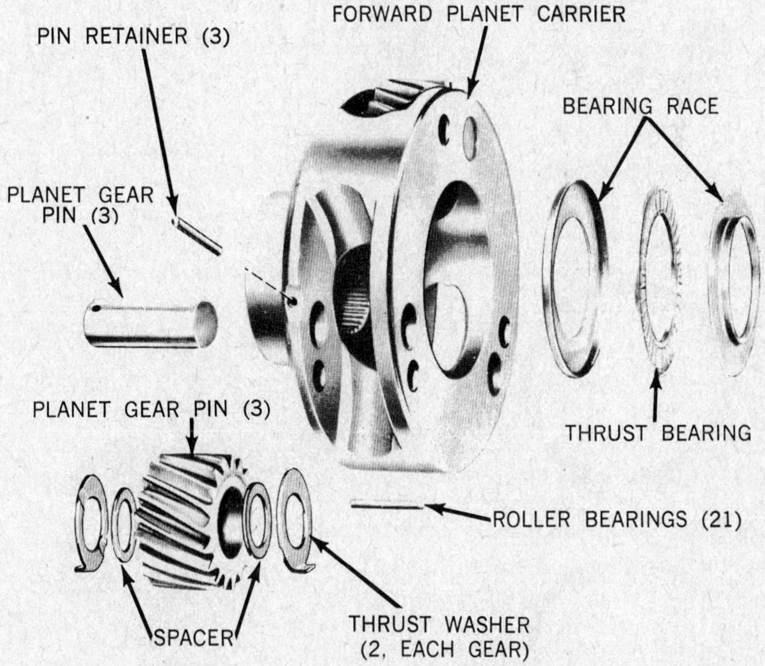

Forward planet carrier—disassembled (© Ford Motor Co.)

Align the pump to the case and install the front pump to case retaining bolts.

31. Install the converter housing onto the front pump and case. Install the six converter housing to case retaining bolts. Torque bolts to specifications.
32. Install input shaft. Place transmission in horizontal position, then check transmission end play. If end-play is not within

limits, either the wrong selective thrust washers were used, or one of the 10 thrust washers is improperly positioned.

33. Remove the dial indicator used for checking end play and install the one converter housing to case retaining bolt. Torque the bolt to specifications.

34. Install the intermediate and low-reverse band adjusting screws into the case. Install the struts for each band.

35. Adjust intermediate and low-reverse band.

36. Install a universal joint yoke onto the output shaft. Rotate the input and output shafts in both directions to check for free rotation of the gear train.

37. Install control valve body. As the valve body is installed, engage the manual and down-shift valves with the inner control levers. Torque the eight control valve body-to-case bolts to specifications.

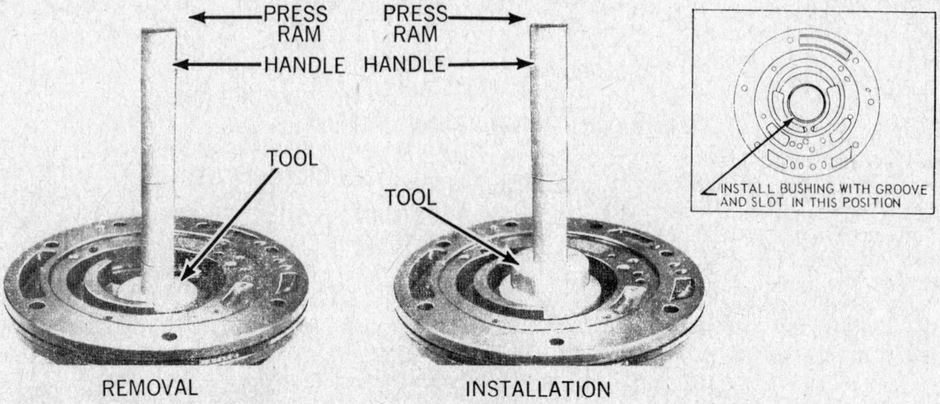

Removing front pump housing bushing (© Ford Motor Co.)

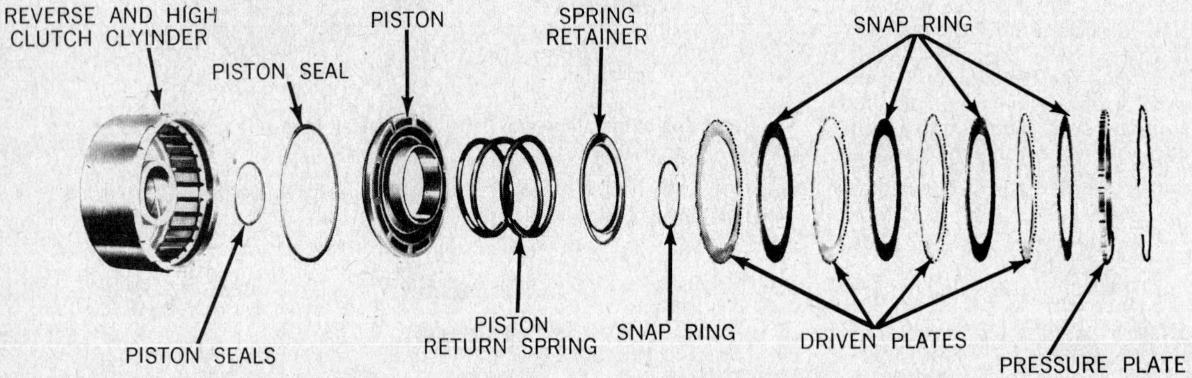

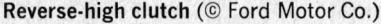

Reverse-high clutch (© Ford Motor Co.)

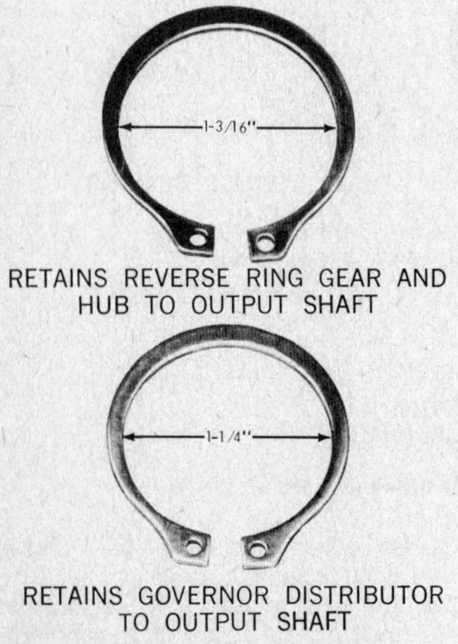

Governor and reverse ring gear and hub identification (© Ford Motor Co.)

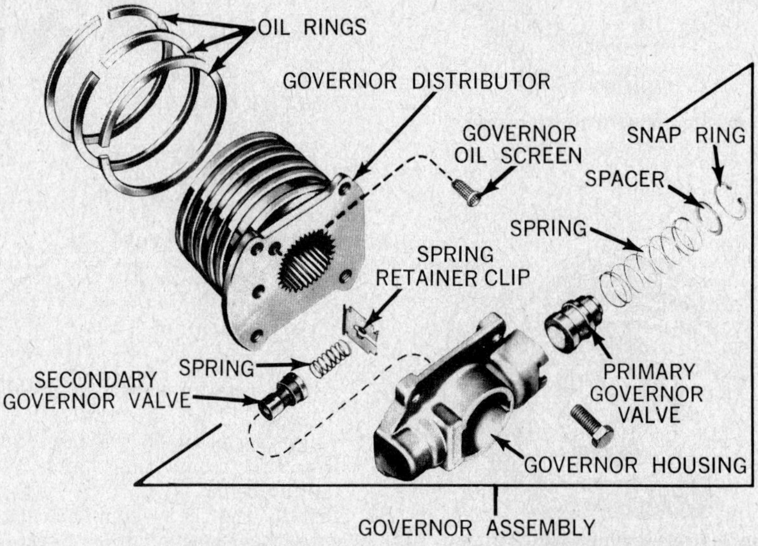

Governor and oil distributor (© Ford Motor Co.)

38. With a new oil pan gasket in place, install the oil pan and torque the bolts to specifications.
39. Install primary throttle valve into the transmission case.
40. Install vacuum unit, gasket and control rod into the case.
41. Make sure the input shaft is properly installed in the front pump, stator support and gear train. Install the converter into the front pump and the converter housing.

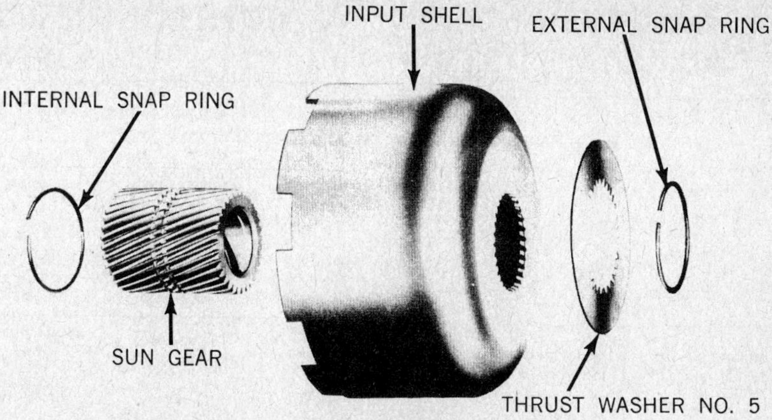

Input shell and sun gear disassembly (© Ford Motor Co.)

FORD C4 TORQUE SPECIFICATIONS

	Foot Pounds
Converter to flywheel	20-30
Converter housing to transmission case	28-40
Front pump to transmission case	28-40
Overrunning clutch face to case	13-20
Oil pan to case	12-16
Rear servo cover to case	12-20
Stator support to pump	12-20
Converter cover to converter housing	12-16
Intermediate servo cover to case	16-22
Diaphragm assembly to case	15-23
Extension assembly to transmission case	28-40
Engine to transmission	23-33
Starter attaching bolts	20-30
Engine support-to-crossmember	40-60
Pressure gauge tap	6-12
Band adjusting screw locknut to case	35-45
Yoke to output shaft	60-120
Reverse servo piston to rod	12-20
Converter drain plug	20-30
Manual valve inner lever to shaft	30-40
Downshift lever to shaft	12-16
Filler tube to engine	23-33
Filler tube to pan	32-42
Transmission to engine	40-50
Distributor sleeve to case	12-20
T.R.S. switch to case	4-8
Transfer case to transmission	21-30
Crossmember attaching bolts	14-24

	Inch Pounds
Lower to upper valve body	40-55
Reinforcement plate to body	40-55
Screen and lower to upper valve body	40-55
Neutral switch to case (Econoline)	55-75
Neutral Switch to column	20
Seperator plate to lower valve body	40-55
Control Assembly to case	80-120
Governor assembly to collector body	80-120
Cooler line fittings	80-120
Detent spring to lower valve body	80-120
Upper valve body to lower valve body	80-120
Oil tube connector	80-120
End plates to body	20-35

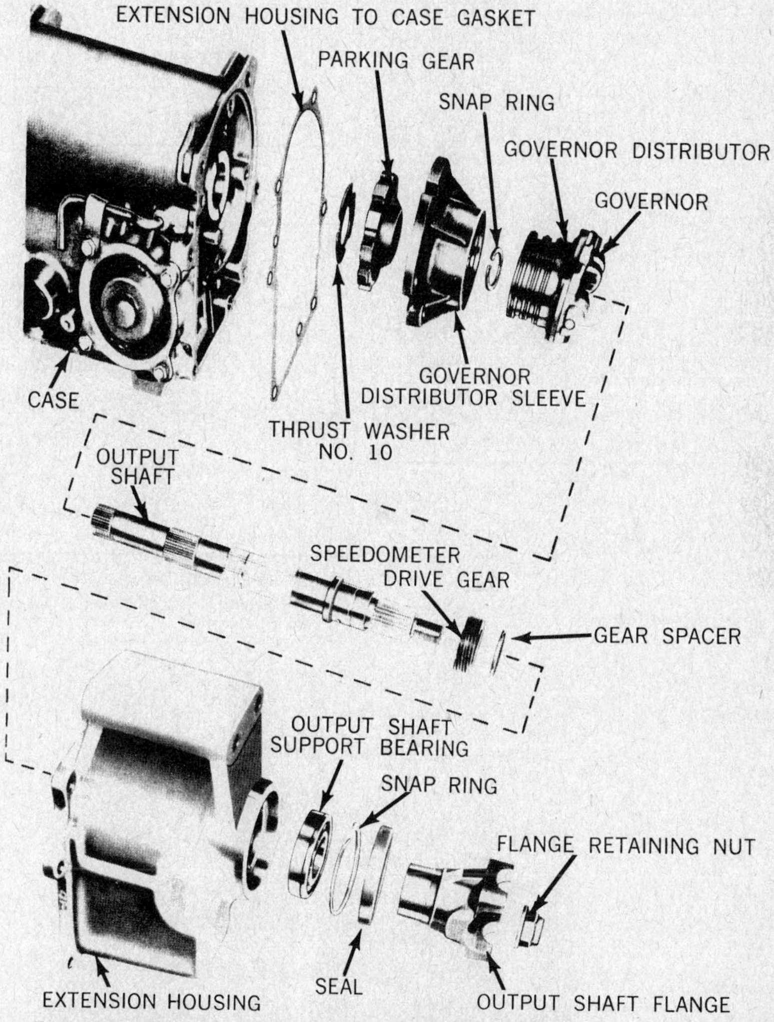

Extension housing and output shaft related parts (© Ford Motor Co.)

SELECTIVE THRUST WASHERS

Thrust washer No. 1		Thrust Washer No. 2	
Nylon Thrust Washer W/Tangs	*Color of Washer*	*No. Stamped On Washer*	*Metal Thrust Washer*
.053-.0575	Red	1	.041-.043
.070-.074	Green	2	.056-.058
.087-.091	Natural (White)	3	.073-.075
.104-.108	Black	Spacer	.032-.036①
.121-.125	Yellow		

① This is a selective spacer. The spacer must be installed next to the stator support to obtain correct end play.

CHECKS AND ADJUSTMENTS C4

Operation	Specification
Transmission end play	0.008-0.042 inch (selective thrust washers available)
Turbine and stator end play	Model PEE, PEA, PEF—New or rebuilt 0.023 max. Used 0.C40 max.
Intermediate band adjustment	Remove and discard lock nut. Adjust screw to 10 ft-lbs torque, then back off 1¾ turns. Install new lock nut and torque to specification.
Low-reverse band adjustment	Remove and discard lock nut. Adjust screw to 10 ft-lbs torque, then back off 3 turns. Install new lock nut and torque to specification.
Forward clutch pressure plate to snap ring clearance	0.025-0.050 Selective snap ring thicknesses 0.082-0.078, 0.068-0.064, 0.054-0.050
Reverse-high clutch pressure plate to snap ring clearance	0.050-0.071 Selective snap ring thicknesses 0.096-0.092, 0.082-0.078, 0.068-0.064, 0.054-0.050

CONTROL PRESSURE AT ZERO GOVERNOR RPM-FORD C4

Year	Engine Speed	Throttle	Manifold Vac. Ins. Hg.	Range	P.S.I.
1971-72	As Required	As Required	15 and Above	P, N, D 2, 1 R	52-85 52-115 52-180
	As Required	As Required	10	P, N, D	96-110
	Stall	Thur Detent	Below 1.0	D, 2, 1 R	143-160 230-260
1973	As Required	As Required	12 and Above	P, N, D 2, 1 R	55-86 55-122 55-197
	As Required	As Required	10	P, N, D	98-110
	Stall	Thru Detent	Below 1.0	D, 2, 1 R	143-164 239-272
1974-78	Idle	As Required	15 and Above	P, N, D 2, 1 R	55-86 55-122 55-197
	As Required	As Required	10	D 2, 1	98-110 90-115
	Stall	Thru Detent	Below 1.0	D, 2, 1 R	143-164 239-272

STALL SPEEDS

1977

TRANS.	ENGINE	CONVERTER IDENT. ON COVER	CONVERTER SIZE	STALL RATIO	STALL SPEED RPM ①
C-4	300-1V	DC/DD	12	2.04	1490-1760 1460-1710
	302-2V	DC/DD	12	2.04	1350-1630

1978-79

TRANS.	ENGINE	CONVERTER IDENT. ON COVER	CONVERTER SIZE	STALL RATIO	STALL SPEED RPM ①
C-4	300-1V	DC/DD	12	2.04	1490-1760 1460-1710

① Stall speed shown above are for vehicles operating in areas at or near sea level.
Stall speeds at higher altitudes may be slightly lower because of changes in engine output.

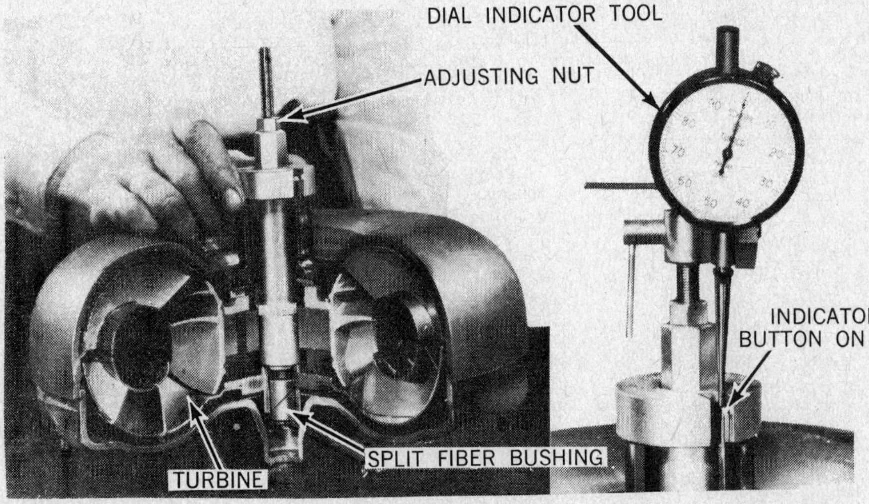

Checking turbine and stator end play (© Ford Motor Co.)

DIAGNOSIS

This diagnosis guide covers the most common symptoms and is an aid to careful diagnosis. The items to check are listed in the sequence to be followed for quickest results. Thus, follow the checks in the order given for the particular transmission type

TROUBLE SYMPTOMS	ITEMS TO CHECK IN TRUCK	OUT OF TRUCK
No drive in D, 2 and 1	CWER	ac
Rough initial engagement in D or 2	KBWFE	a
1-2 or 2-3 shift points incorrect or erratic	ABLCDWER	
Rough 1-2 upshifts	BJGWEF	
Rough 2-3 shifts	BJWFGER	br
Dragged out 1-2 shift	ABJWGEFR	c
Engine overspeeds on 2-3 shift	CABJWEFG	br
No 1-2 or 2-3 shift	CLBDWEGJ	bc
No 3-1 shift in D	DE	
No forced downshifts	LEB	
Runaway engine on forced 3-2 downshift	WJGFEB	c
Rough 3-2 or 3-1 shift at closed throttle	KBJEF	
Shifts 1-3 in D	GJBEDR	
No engine braking in first gear—1 range	CHEDR	
Creeps excessively	K	
Slips or chatters in first gear, D	ABWFE	aci
Slips or chatters in second gear	ABJGWFER	ac
Slips or chatters in R	ABHWFER	bcr
No drive in D only	CWE	i
No drive in 2 only	ACWJER	c
No drive in 1 only	ACWER	c
No drive in R only	ACHWER	bcr
No drive in any selector lever position	ACWFER	cd
Lockup in D only		gc
Lockup in 2 only	H	bgci
Lockup in 1 only		gc
Lockup in R only		agc
Parking lock binds or does not hold	C	g
Transmission overheats	OFBW	ns
Maximum speed too low, poor acceleration	YZ	n
Transmission noisy in N and P	AF	d
Transmission noisy in first, second, third or reverse gear	AF	hadi
Fluid leak	AMNOPQS UXBJ	jmp
Car moves forward in N	C	a

Key to Checks

Fluid level	N.	Oil pan gasket, filler tube or	b.	Reverse-high clutch	F.
Vacuum diaphragm unit or tubes		seal	c.	Leakage in hydraulic system	
restricted—leaking—adjust-	O.	Oil cooler and connections	d.	Front pump	L.
ment	P.	Manual or downshift lever shaft	g.	Parking linkage	B.
Manual linkage		seal	h.	Planetary assembly	G.
Governor	Q	⅛ inch pipe plugs in case	i.	Planetary one-way clutch	K.
Valve body	R.	Perform air pressure check	j.	Engine rear oil seal	C.
Pressure regulator	S.	Extension housing-to-case gasket	m.	Front pump oil seal	H.
Intermediate band	U.	Extension housing rear oil seal	n.	Converter one-way clutch	M.
Low-reverse clutch	W.	Perform control pressure check	p.	Front pump to case gasket or	E.
Intermediate servo	X.	Speedometer driven gear		seal	A.
Engine idle speed		adapter seal	r.	Reverse-high clutch piston air	
Downshift linkage—including	Y.	Engine performance		bleed valve	
inner level position	Z.	Vehicle brakes	s.	Converter pressure check valves	J.
Converter drain plugs	a.	Forward clutch			D.

General Information

The C6 automatic transmission is very similar to the C4 automatic transmission, and most of the maintenance and overhaul procedures given for the C4 transmission will apply to the C6 transmission. One important difference between the C6 and the C4 transmissions is that the C6 transmission uses a low-reverse clutch in place of the low-reverse band. Otherwise, the gear trains are the same as are the clutch combinations. The hydraulic control systems are very similar, except for minor differences in design. All components which are different from the C4 components are illustrated and the procedures to repair them are given.

Transmission Checks

Vacuum Diaphragm Check (Off Truck)

With the use of a vacuum pump, set the vacuum to read 18 inches, with the end of the hose blocked off. On single area diaphragms, connect the vacuum hose to the manifold vacuum hose port. On the dual area diaphragms, connect the vacuum hose to the EGR port, leaving the manifold vacuum port open to the atmosphere. If the gauge holds at 18 inches, the vacuum unit diaphragm is not leaking. A second check can be made by holding the control rod end by a finger, with the other end inserted into the unit. Install the vacuum hose from the vacuum pump onto the diaphragm port. The control rod should move inward and when the vacuum supply is cut off by the removal of the hose, the rod should move outward.

Vacuum Diaphragm

A screw is provided in the inlet tube of the vacuum diaphragm assembly, to permit small adjustments in control pressure. If control pressure is uniformly high or low, in all ranges, it may be brought within specifications by turning this screw. Control pressure may also be varied to alter shift feel, but in no case should it go beyond the specified minimum or maximum.

Control pressure is increased by turning the adjusting screw clockwise, and reduced by turning counterclockwise. One full turn will change control pressure approximately 2-3 psi.

Adjustments

Intermediate Band

1. Raise the truck on a hoist or place on jack stands.
2. Clean threads of the intermediate band adjusting screw.
3. Loosen adjustment screw locknut.
4. Tighten the adjusting screw to 10 ft. lbs., and back the screw off exactly 1½ turns. Tighten the adjusting screw locknut.

Transmission Disassembly

1. Thoroughly clean outside of transmission.

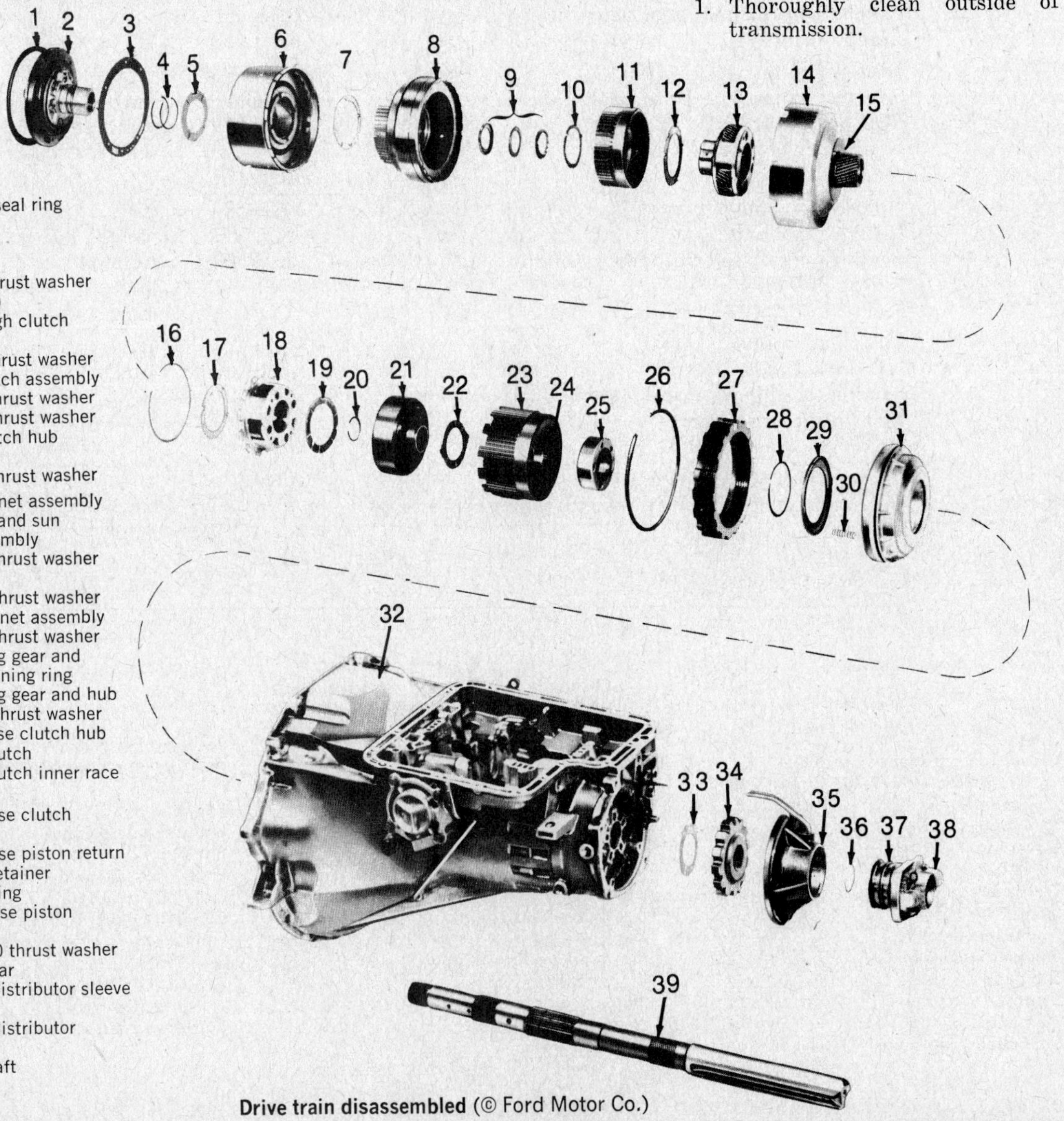

1 Front pump seal ring
2 Front pump
3 Gasket
4 Seal
5 Number 1 thrust washer (selective)
6 Reverse—high clutch assembly
7 Number 2 thrust washer
8 Forward clutch assembly
9 Number 3 thrust washer
10 Number 4 thrust washer
11 Forward clutch hub assembly
12 Number 5 thrust washer
13 Forward planet assembly
14 Input shell and sun gear assembly
15 Number 6 thrust washer
16 Snap ring
17 Number 7 thrust washer
18 Reverse planet assembly
19 Number 8 thrust washer
20 Reverse ring gear and hub retaining ring
21 Reverse ring gear and hub
22 Number 9 thrust washer
23 Low—reverse clutch hub
24 One-way clutch
25 One-way clutch inner race
26 Snap ring
27 Low—reverse clutch
28 Snap ring
29 Low—reverse piston return spring retainer
30 Return spring
31 Low—reverse piston
32 Case
33 Number 10 thrust washer
34 Parking gear
35 Governor distributor sleeve
36 Snap ring
37 Governor distributor
38 Governor
39 Output shaft

Drive train disassembled (© Ford Motor Co.)

2. Secure the unit in a repair stand, and drain the oil.
3. Remove converter from the unit.
4. Unbolt and remove the valve body from the case.
5. Check and record gear train end-play.
6. Slip the input shaft out of the front pump. Remove the vacuum diaphragm, rod and primary throttle valve from the case.
7. Remove the front pump attaching bolts. Pry the gear train forward to remove the pump.
8. Loosen the band adjusting screw and remove the two struts. Rotate the band 90° counterclockwise, to align the ends with the slot in the case. Slide the band off the reverse-high clutch drum.
9. Remove the forward part of the gear train as an assembly. Remove the large snap-ring that holds the reverse planet carrier in the low-reverse clutch hub. Lift the planet carrier from the drum.
10. Remove the snap-ring that holds the reverse ring gear and hub on the output shaft. Slide the ring gear and hub from the shaft.
11. Rotate the low-reverse clutch hub clockwise, and withdraw it from the case.
12. Remove the low-reverse snap-ring from the case, then remove the clutch discs, plates and pressure plate from the case.
13. Remove the extension housing bolts and vent tube from the case. Remove the extension housing and gasket.
14. Slide the output shaft assembly from the transmission case.
15. Remove the distributor sleeve attaching bolts and remove the sleeve, parking gear, and the thrust washer.
16. Compress the low-reverse clutch piston release spring. Remove the snap-ring. Remove the tool and spring retainer.
17. Remove the one-way clutch inner race attaching bolts from the rear of the case. Remove the inner race from the inside of the case.
18. Remove the low-reverse clutch piston from the case.

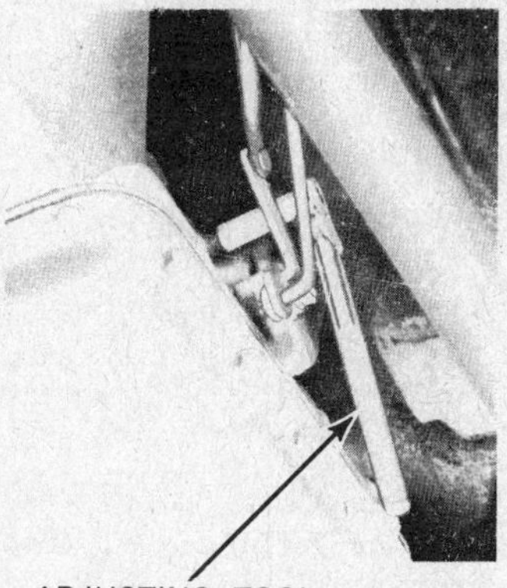

Adjusting intermediate band
(© Ford Motor Co.)

CLUTCH AND BAND APPLICATION CHART— C-6 AUTOMATIC TRANSMISSION

GEAR	INTERMEDIATE BAND	DIRECT CLUTCH	FORWARD CLUTCH	REVERSE CLUTCH	ONE-WAY CLUTCH
1-st*	off	off	on	off	holding
2-nd*	on	off	on	off	overrunning
3-rd*	off	on	on	off	overrunning
Low(1)	off	off	on	on	holding
Reverse	off	on	off	on	not affected

* Transmission selector in "D" position

Component Disassembly and Assembly

NOTE: For most component services, see Component Disassembly and Assembly, in the C4 Section. The exceptions are as follows.

One-Way Clutch

1. Remove the snap-ring and rear bushing from the rear of the low-reverse clutch hub.
2. Remove the springs and rollers from the spring retainer and lift the spring retainer from the hub.
3. Remove the remaining bushing and snap-ring from the hub.
4. Install the snap-ring in the forward snap-ring groove of the low-reverse clutch hub.
5. Place the forward clutch bushing against the snap-ring with the flat side up. Install the one-way clutch spring retainer on top of the bushing. Install the retainer in the hub so that the springs load the rollers in a counterclockwise direction.
6. Install a spring and roller into each of the spring retainer compartments by slightly compressing each spring and placing the roller between the spring and the spring retainer.
7. Install the rear bushing on top of the retainer with the flat side down.
8. Install the remaining snap-ring at the rear of the low-reverse clutch hub.

Servo

1. Apply air pressure to the port in the servo cover in order to remove the piston and stem.
2. Remove the seals from the piston.
3. Dip the new seals in transmission fluid.
4. Install the new seals onto the piston and cover.
5. Dip the piston in transmission

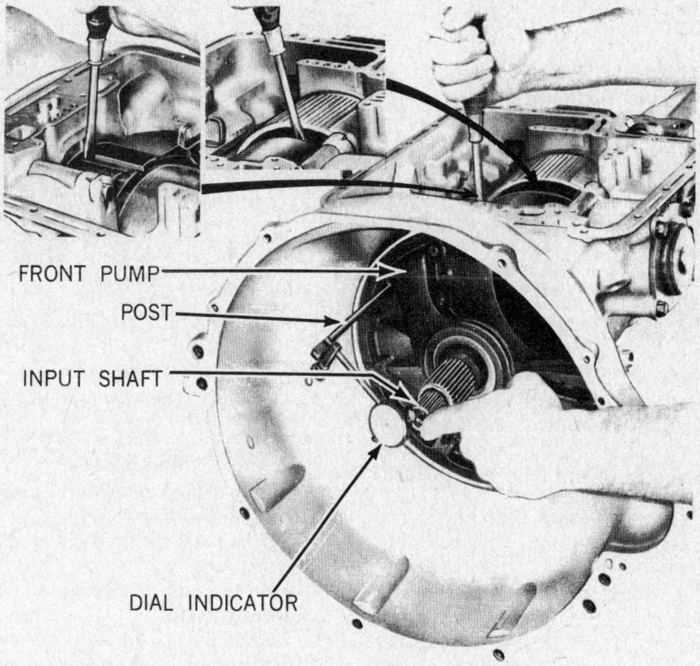

Checking gear train end play (© Ford Motor Co.)

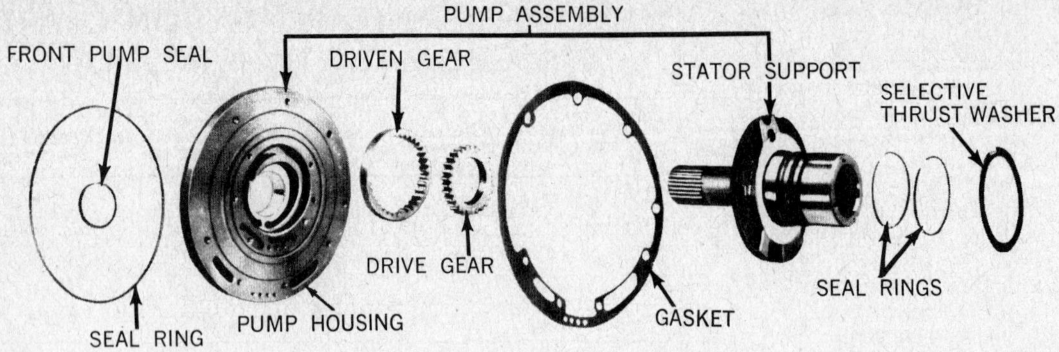

Front pump disassembled (© Ford Motor Co.)

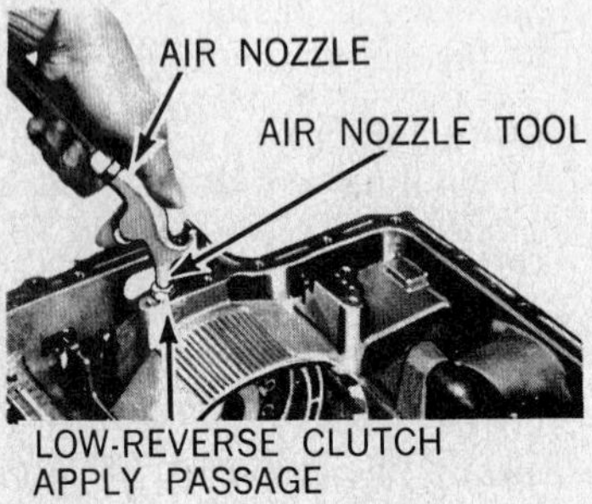

Removing reverse clutch piston (© Ford Motor Co.)

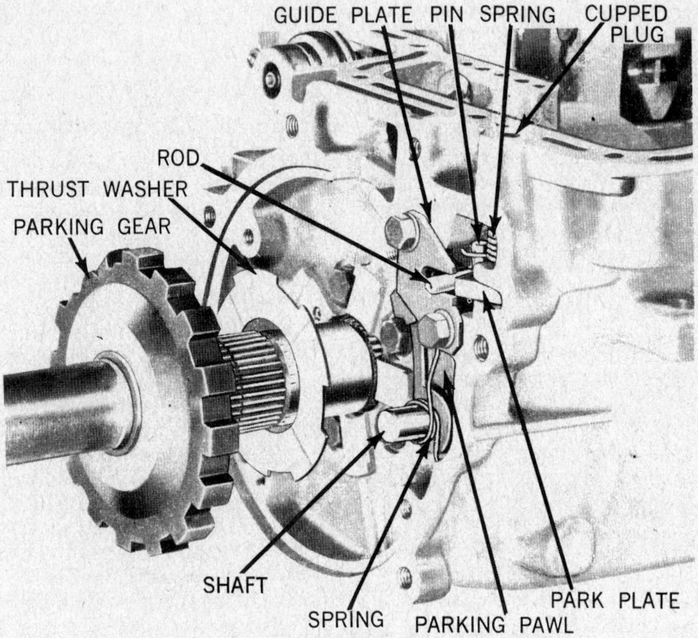

Parking pawl mechanism (© Ford Motor Co.)

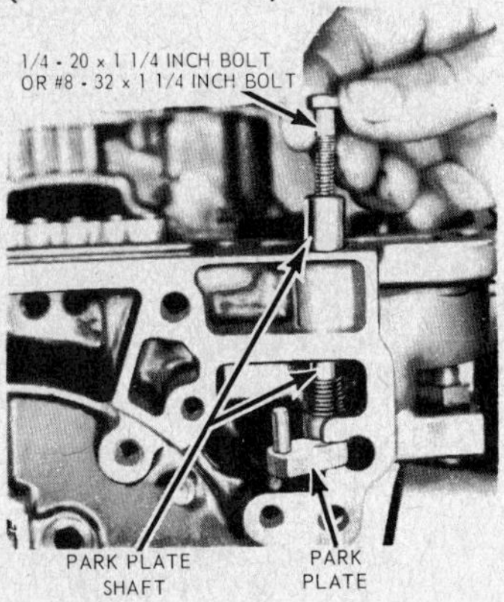

Removing park plate shaft (© Ford Motor Co.)

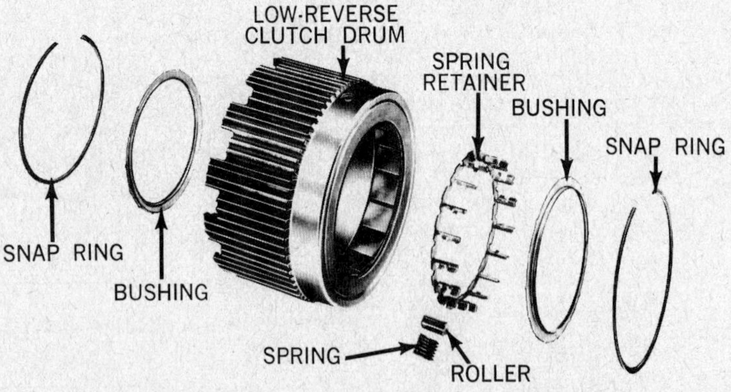

One-way clutch—disassembled (© Ford Motor Co.)

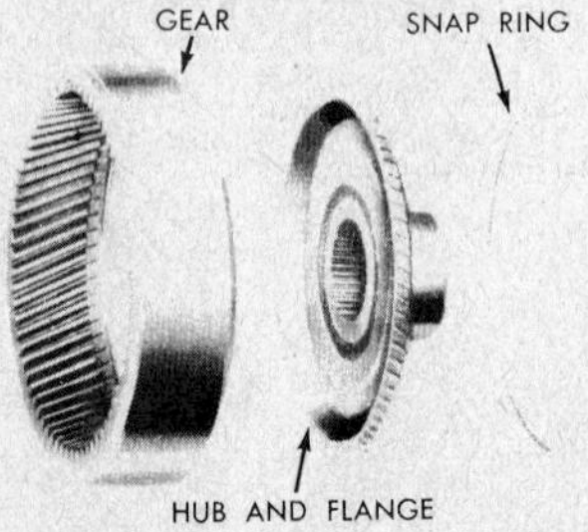

Output shaft hub and ring gear (© Ford Motor Co.)

fluid and install it into the cover.

Reverse-High Clutch

Reverse-high clutch disassembly and assembly is similar to the procedure described for the C4, with the exception that, during disassembly the *exact* position of the piston return spring must be noted, and that they must be installed in the same position.

Output Shaft

1. Remove the governor attaching bolts and the governor.
2. Remove the snap-ring that secures the governor distributor onto the output shaft and slide it off of the shaft.
3. Remove the seal rings from the distributor.
4. Carefully install new seal rings onto the distributor.
5. Slide the governor distributor into place on the shaft, and install the snap-ring to secure it. Make sure the snap-ring is seated in the groove.
6. Position the governor on the distributor and secure with attaching screws.

Parking Pawl Linkage

1. Unbolt and remove the parking

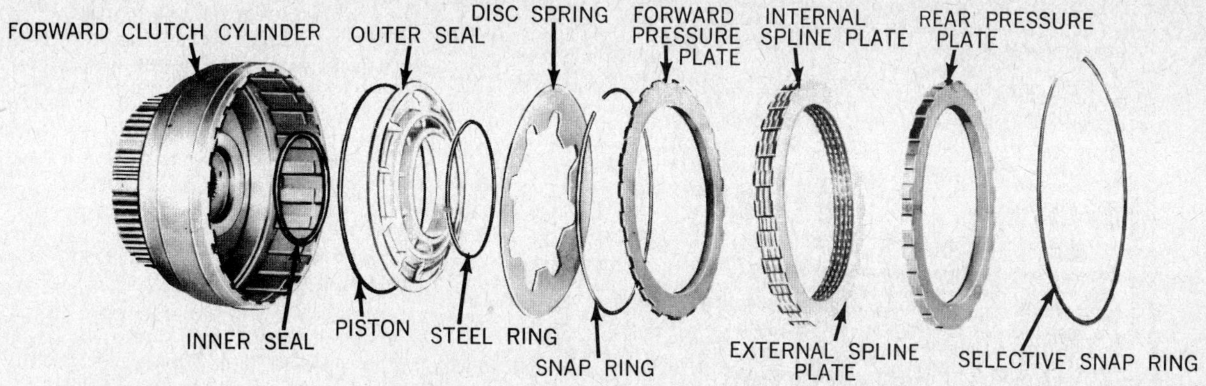

Forward clutch disassembled (© Ford Motor Co.)

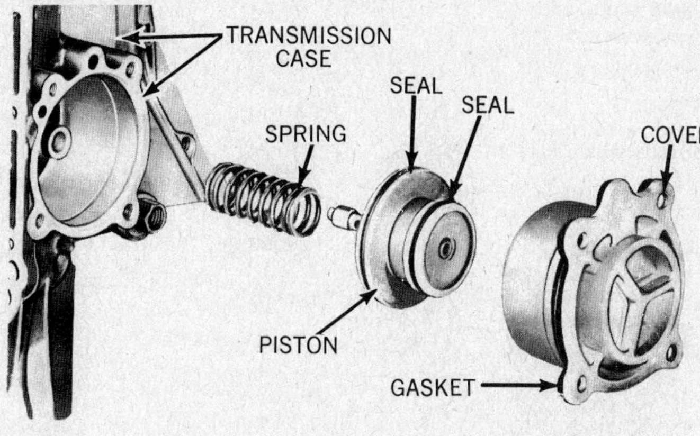

Servo—disassembled (© Ford Motor Co.)

pawl guide plate from the case.
2. Remove the spring, parking pawl, and shaft from the case.
3. Drill a ⅛ in. hole in the park plate shaft retainer plug, and pull the plug out with a wire hook. Unhook the spring from the park plate.
4. Thread a bolt into the park plate shaft, and pull the shaft from the case. Remove the park plate and spring.
5. Position the spring and park plate in the case and install the shaft. Hook the spring on the park plate.
6. Install a new retainer plug.
7. Install the parking pawl shaft in the case, and slip the parking pawls and spring onto the shaft.
8. Bolt the guide plate to the case, making sure that the actuating rod is seated in the slot of the plate.

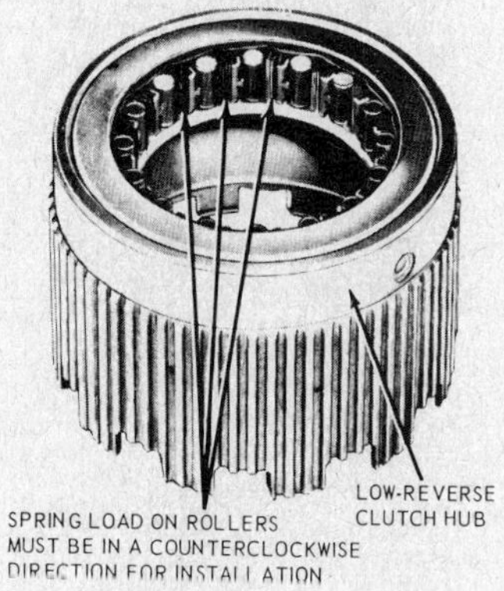

Installing one-way clutch (© Ford Motor Co.)

Transmission Assembly

1. Place transmission case in a holding fixture.
2. Tap the reverse clutch piston into place with a rubber hammer.
3. Hold the one-way clutch inner race in position, install and torque attaching bolts.
4. Install a low-reverse clutch return spring into each pocket of the reverse clutch piston. Press the springs firmly into the piston to prevent their falling out.
5. Position the spring retainer over the springs and position the retainer snap-ring in place on the one-way inner race.
6. Install the compressing tool and compress the springs just enough to install the low-reverse clutch piston retainer snap-ring.
7. Place the transmission case on the bench, bellhousing facing downward.
8. Position the parking gear thrust washer and gear on the case.
9. Position the oil distributor sleeve and tubes in place on the rear of the case. Install and torque the

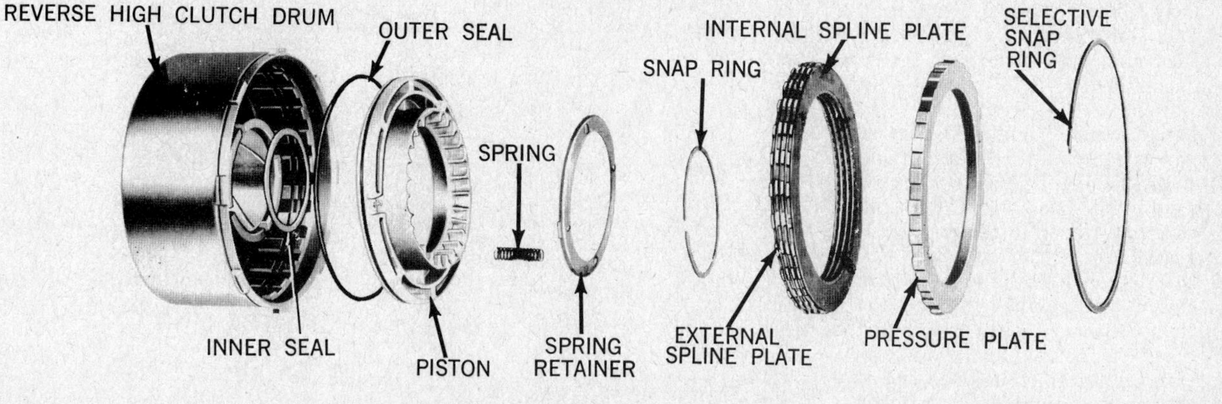

Reverse high clutch disassembled (© Ford Motor Co.)

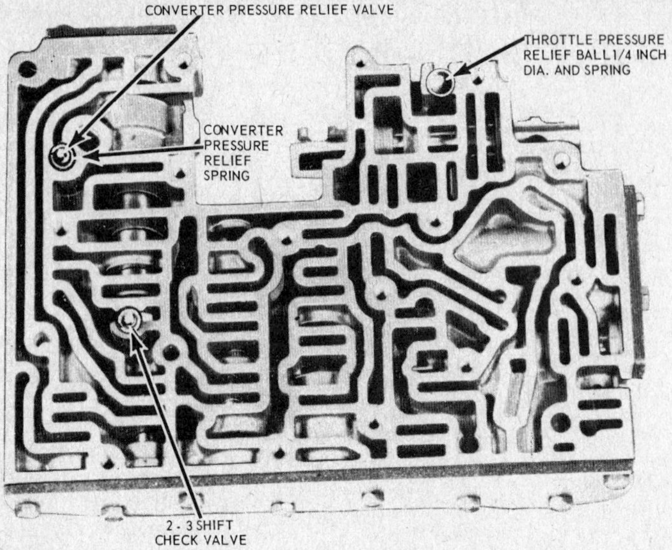

Converter pressure relief valve, throttle pressure relief valve and 2-3 shift check valve locations (© Ford Motor Co.)

attaching bolts.

10. Install the output shaft and as an assembly.
11. Place a new gasket on the rear of the transmission case. Position the extension housing on the case and install attaching bolts. Return the case to the holding fixture.
12. Align the low-reverse clutch hub and one-way clutch with the inner race at the rear of the case. Rotate the low-reverse clutch hub clockwise, while applying pressure to seat it.
13. Install the low-reverse clutch plates. Start with a steel plate and follow with friction and steel plates, alternately. If new composition (friction) plates are being used, soak them in transmission fluid for 15 minutes before installation. Install the pressure plate and snap-ring. Test the operation of the low-reverse clutch by applying air pressure at the clutch pressure apply hole in the case.
14. Install the reverse planet ring gear thrust washer, ring gear and hub assembly. Insert the snap-ring onto its groove in the output shaft.
15. Assemble the front and rear thrust washers onto the reverse planet assembly. Retain them with vaseline, then insert the assembly into the ring gear. Install the snap-ring into the ring gear.
16. Install the thrust washer onto the rear end of the reverse-high clutch assembly. Retain the thrust washer with vaseline and insert the splined end of the forward clutch into the open end of the reverse-high clutch so that the splines engage the reverse-high clutch friction plates.
17. Install the thrust washer onto the front end of the planet ring gear and hub. Insert the ring gear into the forward clutch.
18. Install the thrust washer onto the front end of the forward planet assembly. Retain the washer with vaseline and insert the assembly into the ring gear. Install the input shell and sun gear assembly.
19. Install the reverse-high clutch, forward clutch, forward planet assembly and input shell and sun gear, as an assembly, into the transmission case.
20. Insert the intermediate band into the case around the reverse and high clutch cylinder, with the narrow band end facing the servo apply lever. Install the struts and tighten the band adjusting screw just enough to retain the band.
21. Place a selective thickness bronze thrust washer on the rear shoulder of the stator support

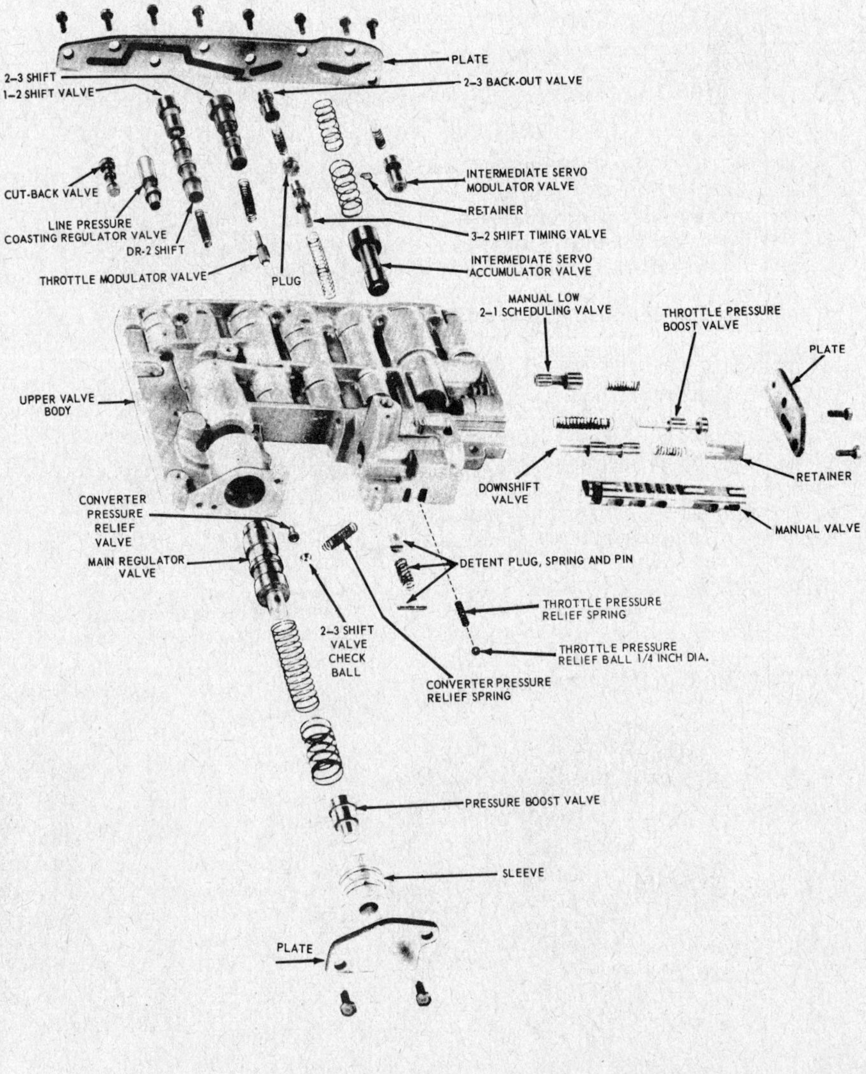

Upper control valve body—disassembled (© Ford Motor Co.)

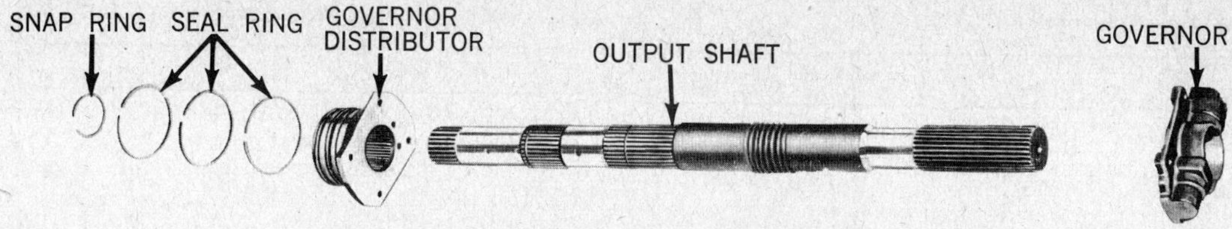

Output shaft disassembled (© Ford Motor Co.)

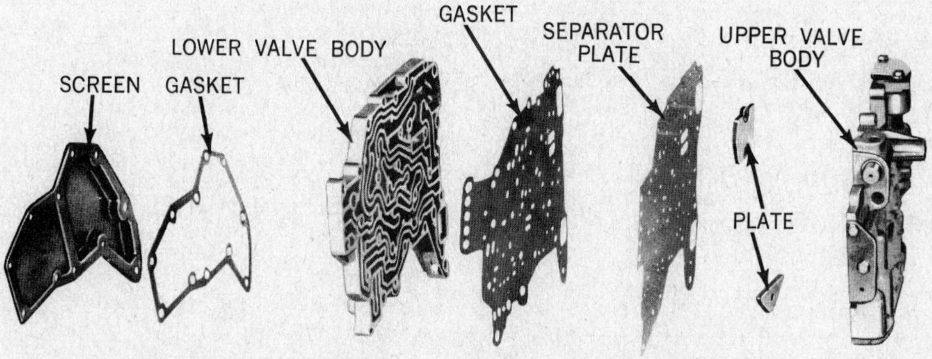

Upper and lower valve bodies—disassembled (© Ford Motor Co.)

and retain it with vaseline. Lay a new gasket on the rear mounting face of the pump and position it on the case, being careful not to damage the O-ring. Install six of the seven mounting bolts. Adjust the intermediate band as previously described. Then, install the input shaft.

22. Install a dial indicator stand in place of the seventh mounting bolt, and check the transmission end-play. Remove the tool, and install the remaining bolt.

23. Install the control valve into the case, making sure that the levers engage the valves properly.

24. Install the primary throttle valve, rod, and the vacuum diaphragm into the case.

25. Install a new oil pan gasket, and the oil pan.

26. Install the converter assembly.

CONTROL PRESSURE AT ZERO GOVERNOR RPM

Year	*Engine Speed*	*Throttle*	*Manifold Vac. In. Hg.*	*Range*	*Psi*
1971	Idle	As Required	Above 15	P, N, D, 2, 1 R	56-62 71-86
	As Required	As Required	10	D, 2, 1	100-115
	Stall	Thru Detent	Below 1.0	D, 2, 1	160-190
1972	Idle	As Required	Above 15	D, 2, 1 R	56-94 78-132
	As Required	As Required	10	D, 2, 1	100-125
	Stall	Thru Detent	Below 1.0	D, 2, 1 R	160-190 240-300
1973-78	Idle			D, 2, 1, P, N R	56-112 78-161
	As Required	As Required	10	D, 2, 1	100-125
	Stall	Thru Detent	Below 1.0	D, 2, 1 R	160-190 240-300

① It may not be possible to obtain 18 inches of engine vacuum at idle. For idle vacuum of less than 18 inches, the following chart provides idle speed pressure specifications in the "D" range:

Vac.	Psi	Vac.	Psi
17	56-69	13	56-98
16	56-75	12	56-105
15	56-84	11	56-111
14	56-92		

Ford C-6 (3 speed)

Checks and Adjustments—

Operation	*Specification*
Transmission end play	0.008-0.044 (selective thrust washers available)
Turbine and stator end play	New or rebuilt 0.021 in .max. Used 0.030 in. max. ①
Intermediate band adjustment	Remove and discard locknut. Adjust screw to 10 ft-lbs torque, then back off 1 turn ,install new lock nut and tighten locknut to specification. ②
Forward clutch pressure plate-to-snap ring clearance	0.031-0.044
Selective snap ring thicknesses	0.056-0.060 in., 0.065-0.069 in., 0.074-0.078 in., 0.083-0.87 in., 0.092-0.096 in.
Reverse-high clutch pressure plate-to-snap ring clearance	*Transmission Models*
	PGA, PJA, PJB (1973-74) 0.022-0.036 in.
	PGB-AF2, F3, G3, PJB, PJC-A, B, E, F, PJD ③ 0.027-0.043 in.
Selective snap ring thicknesses	0.065-0.069 in., 0.074-0.078 in, 0.083-0.087 in. ④

① To check end play, exert force on checking tool to compress turbine to cover thrust washer wear plate. Set indicator at zero.
② 1971-74 models: back off adjusting screw 1½ turns.
③ PJB only to 1972.
④ For 1973-4 add 0.056-0.060; 0.092-0.096.

Selective Thrust Washers—

Identification No.	*Thrust Washer Thickness—Inch*	*Identification No.*	*Thrust Washer Thickness—Inch*
1	0.056-0.058	4	0.103-0.105
2	0.073-0.075	5	0.118-0.120
3	0.088-0.090		

Torque Limits—

	Ft-Lbs
Converter to flywheel	20-30
Front pump to trans. case	12-20
Overrunning clutch race to case	18-25
Oil pan to case	12-16
Stator support to pump	12-16
Converter cover to converter hsg.	12-16
Guide plate to case	12-16
Intermediate servo cover to case	10-14
Diaphragm assy to case	15-23
Distributor sleeve to case	12-16
Extension assy. to trans. case	25-30
Pressure gauge tap	9-15
Band adj. screw locknut to case	35-45
Cooler tube connector lock	25-35②
Converter drain plug	14-28
Manual valve inner lever to shaft	30-40
Downshift lever to shaft	12-16
Filler tube to engine	20-25
Transmission to engine	40-50
Steering col. lock rod adj. nut	10-20
Neutral start switch actuator lever bolt	6-10
T.R.S. switch-to-case	4-8

	In-Lbs
End plates to body	20-30
Inner downshift lever stop	20-30
Reinforcement plate to body	20-30
Screen and lower to upper valve body	50-60
Neutral switch to case	55-75
Neutral switch-to column	20
Control assy. to case	90-125
Gov. body to collector body	80-120
Oil tube connector	80-145①

① 1972 torque limits—80-120 in. lbs.; 1973-75 torque limits—60-120 in. lbs.
② 1972-75 torque limits—20-35 in. lbs.

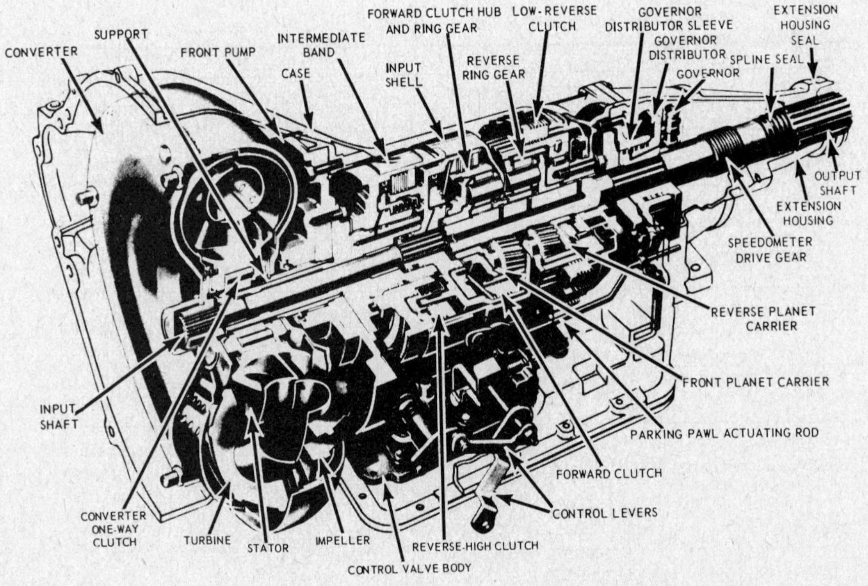

C-6 automatic transmission (© Ford Motor Co.)

DIAGNOSIS

This diagnosis guide covers the most common symptoms and is an aid to careful diagnosis. The items to check are listed in the sequence to be followed for quickest results. Thus, follow the checks in the order given for the particular transmission type.

TROUBLE SYMPTOMS	ITEMS TO CHECK IN TRUCK	ITEMS TO CHECK OUT OF TRUCK
Rough initial engagement in D1 or D2	KBWFEG	
1-2 or 2-3 shift points incorrect or erratic	ABCDWEL	
Rough 2-3 shifts	BGFEJ	
Engine overspeeds on 2-3 shift	BGEF	m
No 1-2 or 2-3 upshift	DECJG	bcf
No 3-1 shift	KBE	
No forced downshift	LWE	
Runaway engine on forced downshift	GFEJB	c
Rough 3-2 or 3-1 shift at closed throttle	KBE	
Creeps excessively	KZ	
Slips or chatters in first gear, D1	ABWFE	acfi
Slips or chatters in second gear	ABGWFEJ	ac
Slips or chatters in R	AHWFEIB	bcf
No drive in D1	CE	i
No drive in D2	ERC	acf
No drive in L	CER	acf
No drive in R	HIERC	bef
No drive in any selector position	ACWFER	cd
Lockup in D1	CIJ	bgc
Lockup in D2	CHI	bgci
Lockup in L	GJE	bjc
Lockup in R	GJ	agc
Parking lock binds or does not hold	C	g
Transmission overheats	OFG	l
Engine will not push-start	ACFE	ec
Maximum speed to low, poor acceleration	Y	l
Transmisison noisy in N and P	F	ad
Noisy transmission during coast 30-20 mph with engine stopped		e
Transmission noisy in any drive position	F	hbad
Fluid leaks	MNOPQSTUX	jkl

Key to Checks

A. Fluid level
B. Vacuum diaphragm unit or tubes
C. Manual linkage
D. Governor
E. Valve body
F. Pressure regulator
G. Front band
H. Rear band
I. Rear servo
J. Front servo
K. Engine idle speed
L. Downshift linkage
M. Converter drain plug
N. Oil pan, filler tube and/or seals
O. Oil cooler and/or connections
P. Manual or throttle shaft seals
Q. Pipe plug, side of case
R. Perform air pressure checks
S. Extension housing-to-case gasket or washer
T. Center support bolt lock washer
U. Extension housing rear oil seal
W. Make control pressure check
X. Speedometer drive gear adaptor seal
Y. Engine performance
Z. Vehicle brakes

a. Front clutch
b. Rear clutch
c. Hydraulic system leakage
d. Front pump
e. Rear pump
f. Fluid distributor sleeve—output shaft
g. Parking linkage
h. Planetary assembly
i. Planetary oneway clutch
j. Engine rear oil seal
k. Front oil pump seal
l. Front pump-to-case seal or gasket
m. Rear clutch piston air bleed valve

General Information

This section provides procedures for testing, inspection, adjustment, and repair of the FMX 3-speed automatic transmission. Where there are differences in procedures or specifications for various model changes, these differences will be outlined.

The Ford FMX 3-speed automatic transmission is a three-speed unit that provides automatic upshifts and downshifts through three forward gear ratios and also provides manual selection of first and second gears. The transmission consists of a torque converter, planetary gear assembly, two multiple disc clutches, and a hydraulic control system.

The FMX transmission cools its transmission fluid through a cooler

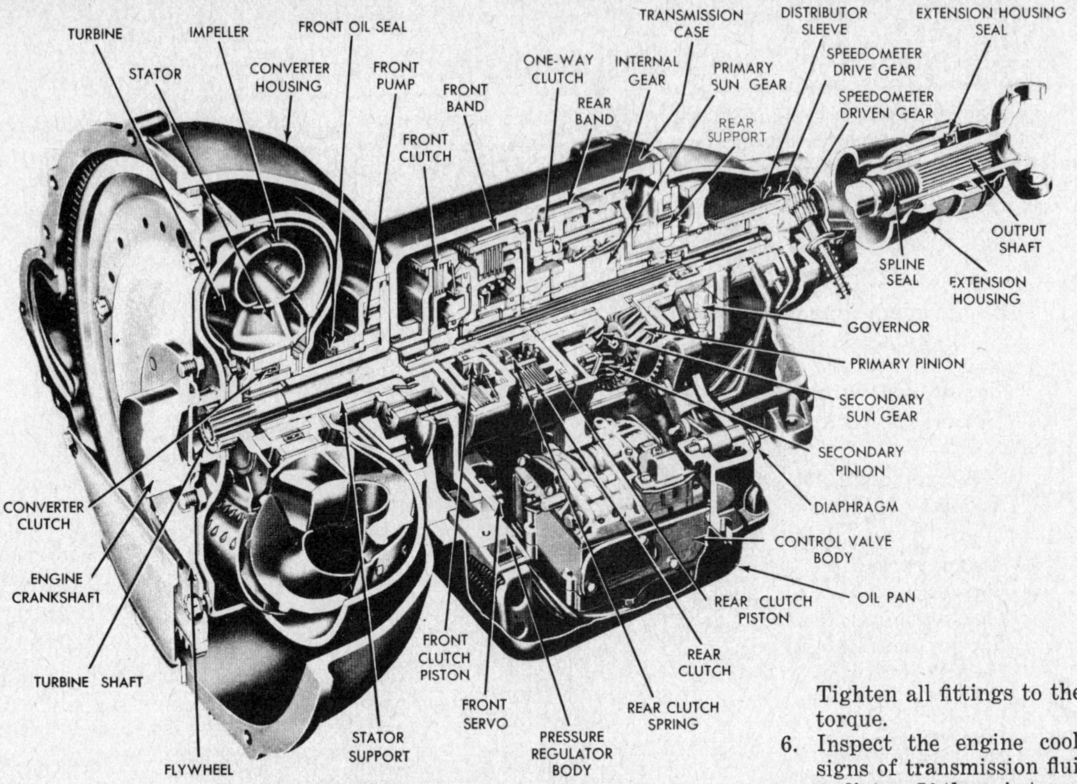

Typical MX—H. D. transmission (© Ford Motor Co.)

core in the radiator lower tank when a steel converter is used. If an aluminum converter is used, the transmission fluid is air-cooled.

Transmission Checks

Prior to performing any of the tests or adjustments described below, engine idle speed, manual linkage adjustment, and transmission fluid level must be checked.

If fluid level is excessively low, check for leakage as follows.

Transmission Fluid Leakage Checks

Make the following checks if leakage is suspected from the transmission:

1. Clean all dirt and grease from the transmission case.
2. Inspect the speedometer cable connection at the extension housing of the transmission. If fluid is leaking here, disconnect the cable and replace the rubber seal.
3. Inspect the oil pan gasket and attaching bolts for leaks. Tighten any bolts that appear loose to the proper torque (10-13 ft. lbs.). Recheck for signs of leakage. If necessary, remove the pan attaching bolts and old pan gasket and install new gasket. Reinstall the pan and its attaching bolts.
4. Check filler tube connection at the transmission for signs of leakage. If tube is leaking, tighten the connection to stop the leak. If necessary, disconnect the filler tube, replace the O-ring, and reinstall the filler tube.

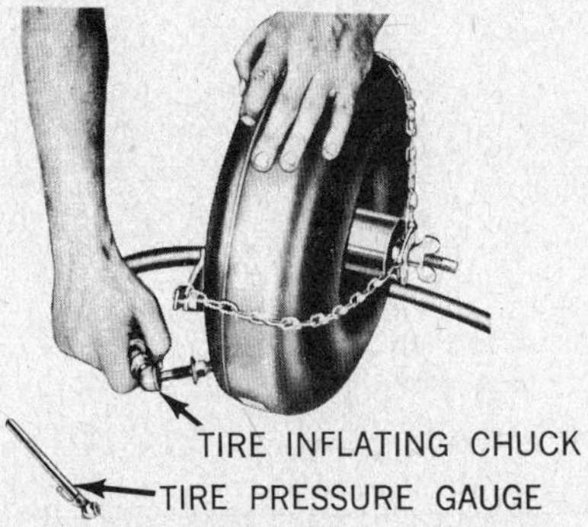

Typical converter leak checking tool (© Ford Motor Co.)

5. Inspect all fluid lines between the transmission and the cooler core in the lower radiator tank. Replace any lines or fittings that appear to be worn or damaged. Tighten all fittings to the proper torque.
6. Inspect the engine coolant for signs of transmission fluid in the radiator. If there is transmission fluid in the engine coolant, the oil cooler core is probably leaking. *NOTE: The oil cooler core may be tested further by disconnecting all lines to it and applying 50-75 psi air pressure through the fittings. Remove the radiator cap to relieve any pressure build-up outside the cooler core. If air bubbles appear in the coolant or if the cooler core will not hold pressure, the oil cooler core is leaking and must be replaced.*
7. Inspect the openings in the case where the downshift control lever shaft and the manual lever shaft are located. If necessary, replace the defective seal.
8. Inspect all plugs or cable connections in the transmission for signs of leakage. Tighten any loose plugs or connectors to the proper torque (see torque chart at end of this section).
9. Remove the lower cover from the front of the bellhousing and in-

CLUTCH AND BAND APPLICATION CHART—FMX AUTOMATIC TRANSMISSION

GEAR	FORWARD CLUTCH	REAR CLUTCH	FRONT BAND	REAR BAND	OVERRUNNING CLUTCH
1st*	on	off	off	off	holding
2nd*	on	off	on	off	overrunning
3rd*	on	on	off	off	overrunning
Low(1)	on	off	off	on	overrunning
Reverse	off	on	off	on	not affected

* Transmission selector lever in "D" position

spect the converter drainplugs for signs of leakage. If there is a leak around the drainplugs, loosen the plug and coat the threads with sealing compound. Tighten the plug to the proper torque.

NOTE: Fluid leaks from around the converter drainplug may be caused by engine oil leaking past the rear main bearing or from the oil gallery plugs. To determine the exact cause of the leak before beginning repair procedures, an oil-soluble aniline or fluorescent dye may be added to the transmission fluid to find the source of the leak and whether the transmission is leaking. If a fluorescent dye is used, a black light must be used to detect the dye.

If further converter checks are necessary, remove the transmission from the truck and the converter from the transmission. The converter cannot be disassembled for cleaning or repair. If the converter is leaking, it must be replaced with a new unit. To check the converter for leaks, assemble and install the converter leak checking tool and fill the converter with 20 psi air pressure. Then, place the converter in a tank of water and watch for air bubbles. If no air bubbles are seen, the converter is not leaking.

Control Pressure Check

When the vacuum diaphragm unit operates properly and the downshift linkage is adjusted correctly, all transmission shifts (automatic and kickdown) should occur within the specified road speed limits. If these shifts do not occur within the limits or if the transmission slips during a shift point, perform the following procedure to locate the problem:

1. Connect the Automatic Transmission Tester (see illustration) as follows:
   a. Tachometer cable to engine.
   b. Vacuum gauge hose with a T-fitting between the vacuum hose and vacuum diaphragm (see illustration).
   NOTE: On vehicles equipped with a dual area diaphragm (DAD), check the control pressure at 10 in. of vacuum by removing the exhaust gas recirculation (EGR) control hose from the diaphragm and plugging the hose. Do not plug the EGR port in the diaphragm; this port must be left open to atmospheric pressure. When checking the control pressure at stall and idle, keep the hose connected.
   c. Pressure gauge to the control pressure outlet on the transmission (see illustration).
2. Apply the parking brake and start the engine. On a truck equipped with a vacuum brake release, use the service brakes since the parking brake will release automatically when the transmission is put in any Drive position.
3. Check the transmission diaphragm unit for leaks (see below).
4. Check control pressure in all selector lever positions at specified manifold vacuum (see specifications). Record readings and compare to specifications.

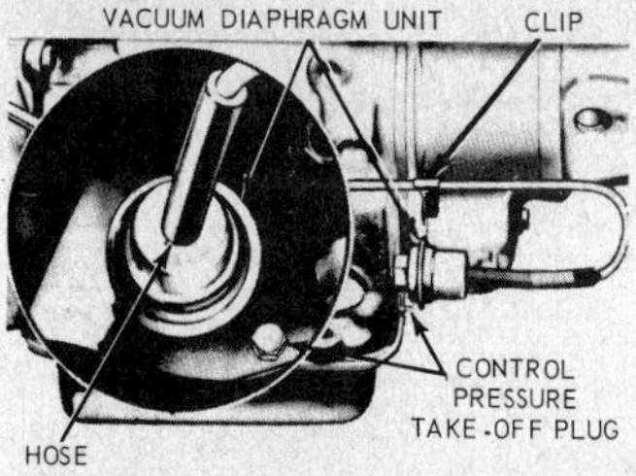

Typical control pressure connecting points (© Ford Motor Co.)

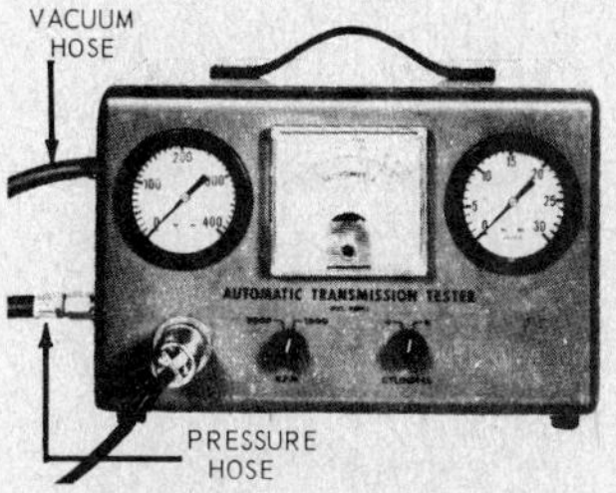

Automatic transmission tester (© Ford Motor Co.)

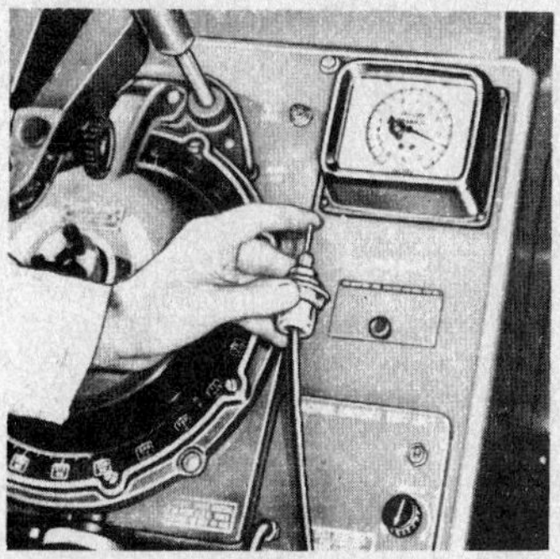

Testing transmission vacuum unit for leakage (© Ford Motor Co.)

Vacuum Diaphragm Unit Check

1. Remove the vacuum diaphragm unit from the transmission using crowfoot wrench, after disconnecting the vacuum hose (see illustration).
2. Adjust a vacuum pump until the vacuum gauge shows 18 in/Hg. with the vacuum hose blocked.
3. Connect the vacuum hose to the vacuum diaphragm unit and note the reading on the vacuum gauge. If the reading is 18 inches of vacuum, the vacuum diaphragm unit is good. While removing the vacuum hose from the vacuum diaphragm unit, hold a finger over the end of the control rod. As the vacuum is released, the internal spring of the vacuum diaphragm unit will push the control rod out.

Air Pressure Checks

If the truck will not move in one or more ranges, or, if it shifts erratically, the items at fault can be determined by using air pressure at the indicated passages.

Drain the transmission and remove the oil pan and the control valve assembly.

NOTE: Oil will spray profusely during this operation.

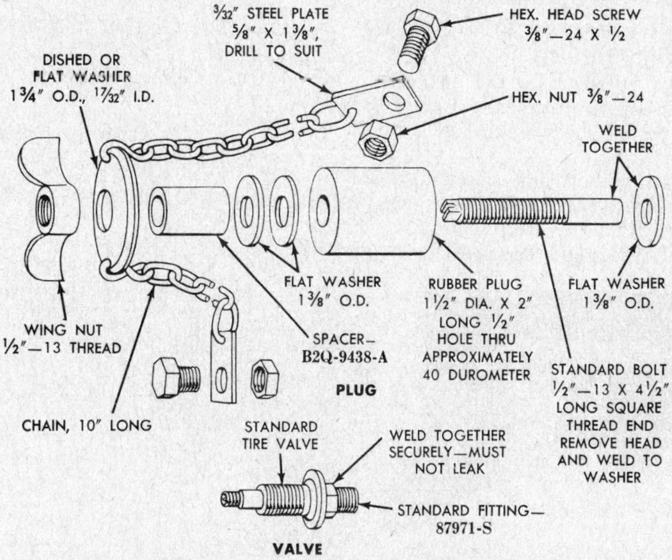

Converter leak checking tool (© Ford Motor Co.)

Front Clutch

Apply sufficient air pressure to the front clutch input passage. A dull thud can be heard when the clutch piston moves. Check also, for leaks.

Governor

Remove the governor inspection cover from the extension housing. Apply air to the front clutch input passage. (See illustration). Listen for a sharp click and watch to see if the governor valve snaps inward as it should.

Rear Clutch

Apply air to the rear clutch passage (See illustration) and listen for the dull thud that will indicate that the rear clutch piston has moved. Listen also for leaks.

Front Servo

Apply air pressure to the front servo apply tube and note if front band tightens. Shift the air to the front servo release tube, which is next to the apply tube, and watch band release.

Rear Servo

Apply air pressure to the rear servo apply passage. The rear band should tighten around the drum.

Conclusions

If the operation of the servos and clutch is normal with air pressure, the no-drive condition is due to the control valve and pressure regulator valve assemblies, which should be disassembled, cleaned and inspected.

If operation of the clutches is not normal; that is, if both clutches apply from one passage or if one fails to move, the aluminum sleeve (bushing) in the output shaft is out of position or badly worn. (See illustration.)

Use air pressure to check the passages in the sleeve and shaft, and also check the passages in the primary sun gear shaft.

If the passages in the two shafts and the sleeve are clean, remove the clutch assemblies, clean and inspect the parts.

Erratic operation can also be caused by loose valve body screws. When reinstalling the valve body be careful to tighten: the pressure regulator valve to case bolts to 17-22 ft. lbs., the pressure regulator valve cover screws to 20-30 in. lbs., the control valve body screws to 20-30 in. lbs., the 1/4-20 capscrew (lower to upper valve body) to 4-6 ft. lbs., and the control valve body to case bolts to 8-10 ft. lbs.

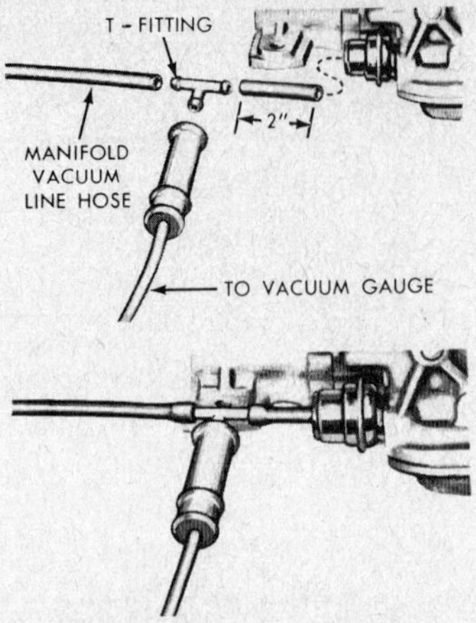

Typical vacuum test line connections (© Ford Motor Co.)

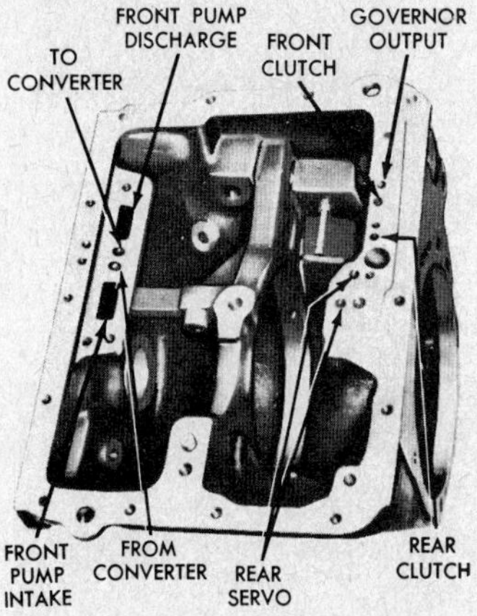

Case fluid hole identification (© Ford Motor Co.)

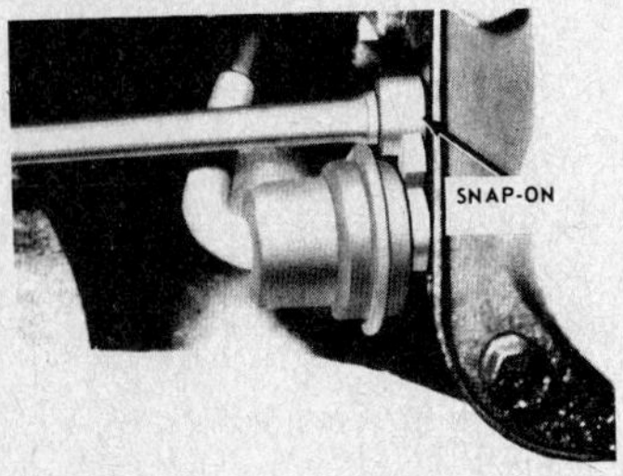

Removing or installing vacuum diaphragm (© Ford Motor Co.)

Shift Point Checks for Automatic Transmissions

To determine if the transmission is shifting at the proper road speeds, use the following procedure:

1. Check the minimum throttle upshifts by placing the transmission selector lever in the Drive position and noting the road speeds at which the transmission shifts from first gear to second gear to third gear. All shifts should occur within the specified limits.
2. While driving in third gear, depress the accelerator pedal past the detent (to the floor). Depending on vehicle speed, the transmission should downshift from third gear to second gear or from second gear to first gear.
3. Check the closed-throttle downshift from third gear to first gear by coasting down from about 30 mph in third gear. This downshift should occur at the specified road speed.
4. With the transmission in third gear and the truck moving at a road speed of 35 mph, the transmission should downshift to second gear when the selector lever

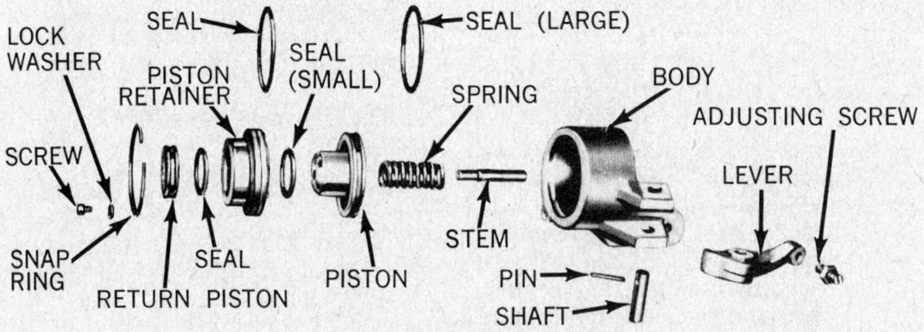

Front servo disassembled (© Ford Motor Co.)

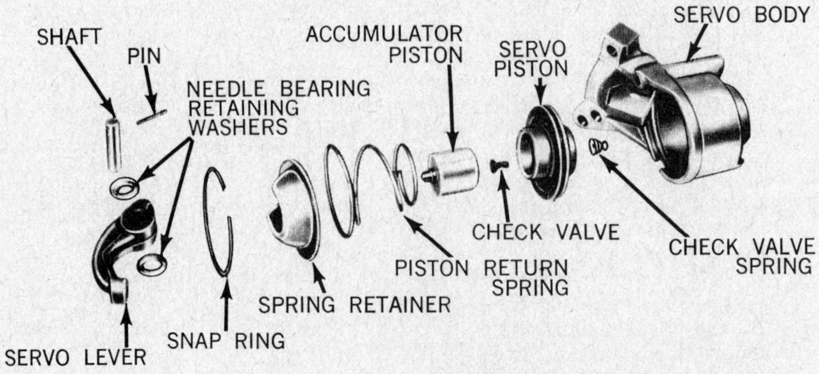

Rear servo disassembled (© Ford Motor Co.)

is moved from D to 2 to 1. This check will determine if the governor pressure and shift control valves are operating properly. If the transmission does not shift within the specified limits or certain gears cannot be obtained, refer to the Trouble Diagnosis chart at the beginning of this section.

In-Vehicle Adjustments and Repairs

The following adjustments and repairs may be performed without removing the transmission.

Band Adjustments

Front Band Adjustment

When it is necessary to adjust the front band of the transmission, perform the following procedure:

1. Drain the transmission fluid and remove the oil pan, fluid filter screen, and clip. The same transmission fluid may be reused if it is filtered before being installed. Only transmission fluid in good condition should be used.
2. Clean the pan and filter screen and remove the old gasket.
3. Loosen the front servo adjusting screw locknut.
   NOTE: Special band adjusting wrenches are recommended to do this operation correctly and quickly.
4. Pull back the actuating rod and insert a 1/4 in. spacer bar between the adjusting screw and the servo piston stem. Tighten the adjusting screw to 10 in. lbs. torque. Remove the spacer bar and tighten the adjusting screw an additional 3/4 turn. Hold the adjusting scew and tighten the locknut securely (20-25 ft. lbs.).
5. Install the transmission fluid filter screen and clip. Install the pan with a new pan gasket.
6. Refill the transmission to the FULL mark on the Dipstick. Start the engine, run for a few minutes, shift the selector lever through all positions, and place it in Park. Recheck the fluid level again and add fluid to proper level is necessary.

Rear Band Adjustments

The rear band of the FMX transmission may be adjusted by any of the methods given below. On most trucks the basic external band adjustment is satisfactory. The internal adjustment may be performed in cases where the adjustment required is outside the range of the external adjustment.

Rear Band External Adjustment

The procedure for adjusting the rear band externally is as follows:

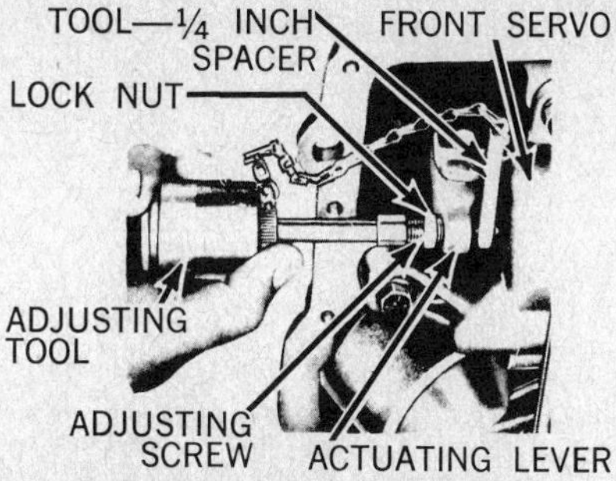

Front band adjustment—typical (© Ford Motor Co.)

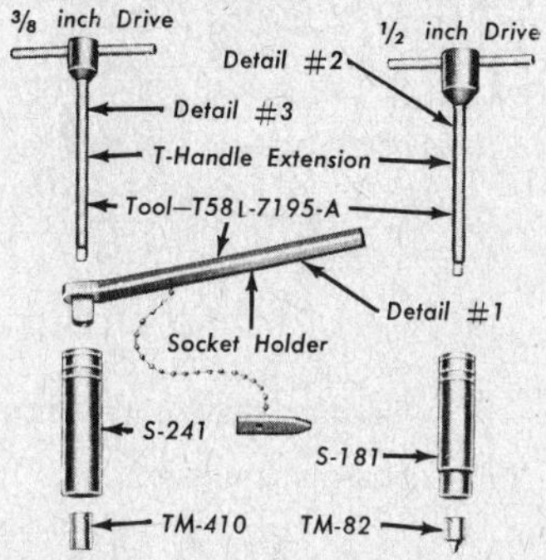

Front and rear band adjusting tools (© Ford Motor Co.)

1. Locate the external rear band adjusting screw on the transmission case, clean all dirt from the threads, and coat the threads with light oil.
   NOTE: The adjusting screw is located on the upper right side of the transmission case. Access is often through a hole in the front floor to the right of center under the carpet.
2. Loosen the locknut on the rear band external adjusting screw.
3. Using the special preset torque wrench shown, tighten the adjusting screw until the handle clicks at 10 ft. lbs. torque. If the adjusting screw is tighter than 10 ft. lbs. torque, loosen the adjusting screw and retighten to the proper torque.
4. Back off the adjusting screw 1½ turns. Hold the adjusting screw steady while tightening the locknut to the proper torque (35-40 ft. lbs.).
   CAUTION: Severe damage may result if adjusting screw is not backed off exactly 1½ turns.

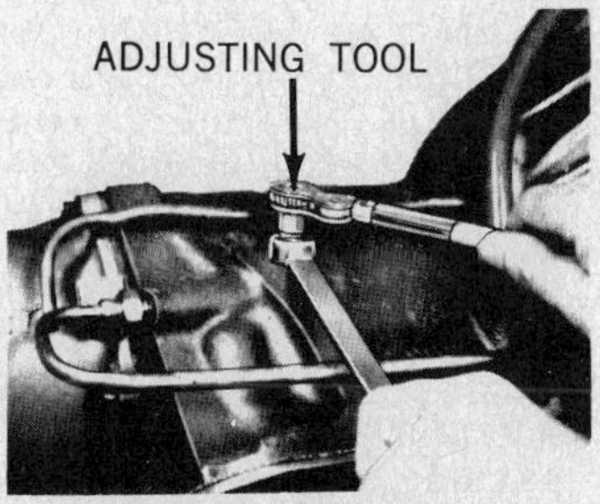

Rear band adjustment (© Ford Motor Co.)

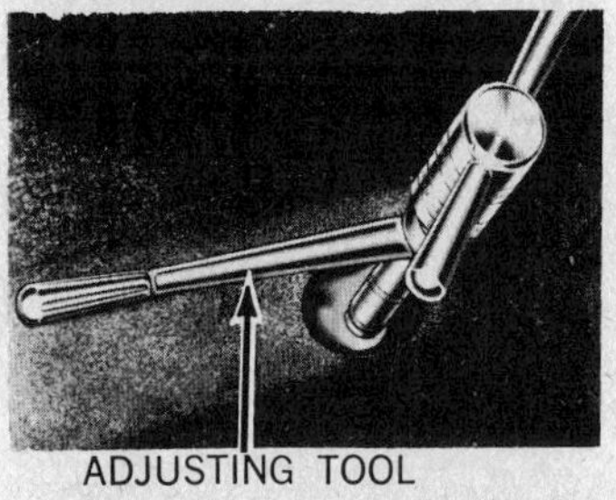

Adjusting rear band through floor boards (© Ford Motor Co.)

Rear Band Internal Adjustment

The rear band is adjusted internally as follows:

1. Drain the transmission fluid. If it is to be resued, filter it as it drains from the transmission. Reuse the transmission fluid only if it is in good condition.
2. Remove and clean the pan, fluid filter, and clip.
3. Loosen the rear servo adjusting locknut.
4. Pull the adjusting screw end of the actuating lever away from the servo body and insert the spacer tool (see illustration) between the servo accumulator piston and the adjusting screw. Be sure the flat surfaces of the tool are placed squarely between the adjusting screw and the accumulator piston. Tool must not touch servo piston and the handle must not touch the servo piston spring retainer.
5. Using a torque wrench with an allen head socket adapter tighten the adjusting screw to 24 in. lbs.
6. Back off the adjusting screw exactly 1½ turns. Hold adjusting screw steady and tighten the locknut securely. Remove the spacer tool.
7. Install the fluid filter, clip, and pan with a new gasket.
8. Fill the transmission with the correct amount of fluid.

Transmission Component

Removal and Installation

Various components of the FMX transmission may be removed while the transmission is in the truck. Installation is often the reverse of the removal instructions except for adjustment and alignment. Repair of the individual components is given in the overhaul section.

Governor Assembly

Removal

1. Raise the truck so that the transmission extension housing is accessible.

2. Remove the governor inspection cover from the extension housing.
3. Rotate the drive shaft until the governor is in line with the inspection hole.
4. Remove the governor valve body from the counterweight.
CAUTION: Do not drop the attaching bolts of the valve parts into the extension housing.

Installation

1. Lubricate the new governor valve parts with clean transmission fluid.
NOTE: The valve must move freely in the valve body bore.
2. Install the governor body on the counterweight so that the valve body cover is facing the rear. Tighten the attaching bolts.
3. Install the governor inspection cover with a new gasket on the extenison housing. Tighten the attaching bolts to proper torque specifications. (Torque specifications are at the end of this section).

Extension Housing Bushing and Rear Seal

Removal

1. Raise the truck and remove the drive shaft. Remove the parking brake drum if so equipped. Remove the transmission output shaft and attaching nut with special tool.
2. Working with a sharp chisel, remove the seal from the extension housing.
CAUTION: Do not allow any metal chips to enter the output shaft bearing.
3. To remove the output shaft bearing, remove the snap ring securing the bearing to the extension housing.
4. Remove the bearing from the extension housing.

Installation

1. Position a new bearing in the extension housing and secure with a snap ring.
2. Install a new extension housing seal with the proper seal replacement tool. Install the output shaft yoke and retaining nut. Torque the attaching nut to specifications. Install the parking brake drum, if so equipped.
3. Install the drive shaft and torque bolts to specifications.
4. Lower the truck and check the transmission fluid level.

Control Valve Body and Oil Pan

Removal

1. Raise the truck on a hoist or jackstands and place a drain pan under the transmission.
2. Drain the transmission.
3. Remove the oil pan, fluid filter screen, and clip and clean them thoroughly. Discard the old pan gasket.
4. Remove the vacuum diaphragm assembly using a crowfoot wrench. *Do not use pliers, pipe wrenches, etc. to remove the vacuum diaphragm unit. Do not let any solvents enter the vacuum diaphragm unit.* Remove the push rod, the fluid screen and its retaining clip.
5. Remove the small compensator pressure tube.
6. Disconnect the main pressure oil tube by carefully loosening the end connected to the control valve body first and then removing the tube from the pressure regulator unit.
CAUTION: Be sure to remove the tube in this manner. Otherwise, the tube could be kinked or bent causing improper fluid pressures and possible damage to the transmission.
7. Loosen the front servo attaching bolts about three turns.
8. Remove the three control valve body attaching bolts and carefully lower the valve body, sliding it off the front servo tubes. *Do not damage the valve body or the tubes.*

Installation

1. When installing the control valve body, align the front servo tubes with the holes in the valve body. Shift the manual lever to the 1 detent and place the inner downshift lever between the downshift lever stop and the downshift valve. Be sure the manual lever engages the actuating pin in the manual detent lever.
2. Loosely install the control valve body attaching bolts and move the control valve body toward the center of the transmission case until there is a clearance of 0.050 in. between the manual valve and the actuating pin on the manual detent lever.
3. Tighten the attaching bolts to 8-10 ft. lbs. torque. Ensure that the rear fluid filter retaining clip is installed under the valve body.
4. Install the main pressure oil tube, connecting the end to the pressure regulator unit first and then connecting the other end to the main control valve assembly

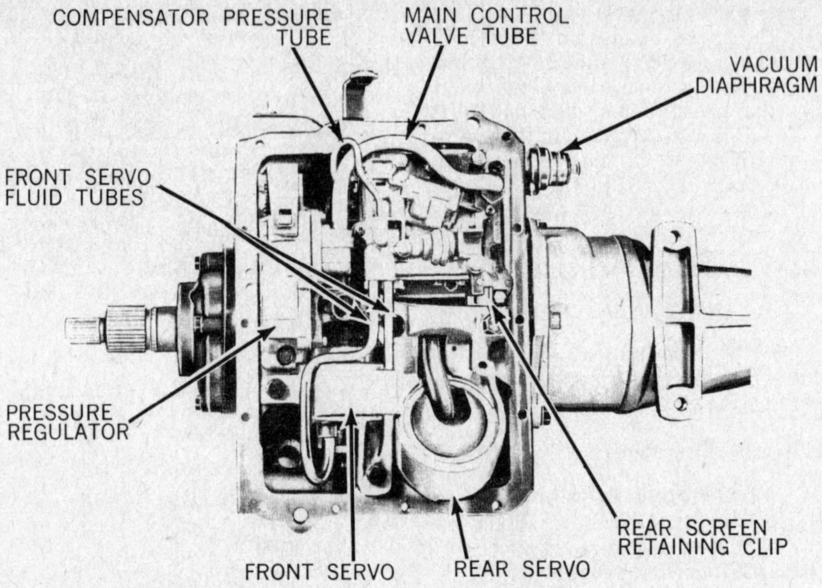

Typical hydraulic control system (© Ford Motor Co.)

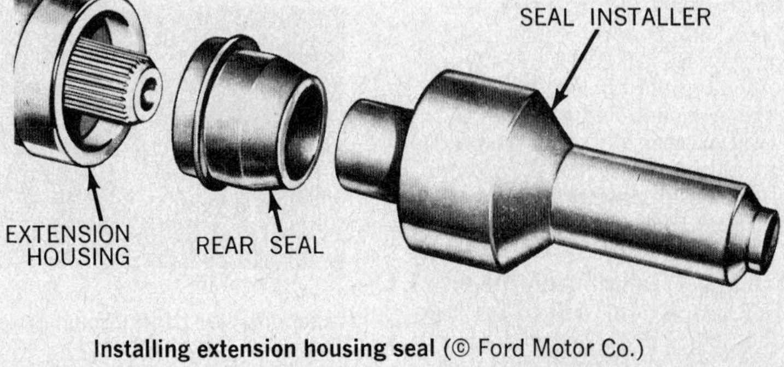

Installing extension housing seal (© Ford Motor Co.)

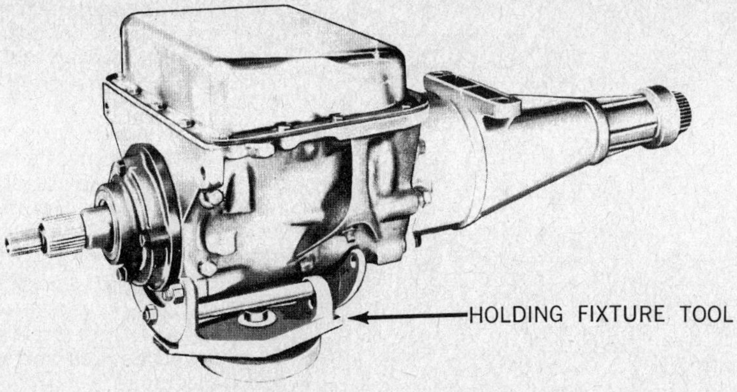

Transmission mounted in holding fixture (© Ford Motor Co.)

by gently tapping it with a soft-faced hammer.

5. Install the compensator pressure tube on the pressure regulator and control valve body.
6. Check the manual lever for free motion in each detent position by rotating it one full turn. If the manual lever binds in any detent position, loosen the valve body attaching bolts and move the valve body away from the center of the transmission case until the binding is relieved. Retighten the attaching bolts according to step 3.
7. Place the pushrod in the bore of the vacuum diaphragm unit and install the vacuum diaphragm unit.
8. Tighten the front servo attaching bolts.
9. Adjust the front band.
10. Install the fluid filter and its retaining clip.
11. Adjust the rear band.
12. Install the oil pan with a new, pan gasket.
13. Fill transmission with fluid. Start and run engine for a few minutes and check the fluid level after shifting the transmission through all positions. *Do not overfill the transmission.*
14. Check the adjustment of the transmission control linkage.

Pressure Regulator

Removal

1. Drain the transmission of fluid and remove the pan, fluid filter screen, and its retaining clip. Discard the used pan gasket.
2. Remove the compensator pressure tube from between the control valve body and the pressure regulator.
3. Remove the main pressure oil tube by gently prying off the end connected to the control valve first and then disconnect the other end from the pressure regulator. *Be sure to remove the tube in this order to prevent kinking or bending it.*
4. Loosen the spring retainer clip and carefully release the spring tension on the pressure springs. Remove the valve springs, retainer and valve stop, and the valves from the pressure regulator body.
5. Remove the pressure regulator attaching bolts and washers and take the regulator body out of the transmission case.

Installation

1. Place the replacement regulator body on the transmission case and install the two securing bolts, tighten the bolts to specifications.
2. Check the converter pressure and the control pressure valves to be sure that the valves are operating freely in the bores.
3. Install the valve springs, spacer and retainer.
4. Install the main pressure oil tube.

   NOTE: Be sure to install the end of the tube that connects to the pressure regulator assembly first. Then, install the other end of the tube into the main control assembly by tapping it gently with a soft faced hammer.
5. Install the small compensator pressure tube.
6. Install the fluid screen and the oil pan. Fill the transmission to the correct level with the specified fluid.

Front Servo

Removal

1. Drain the transmission fluid from the transmission and remove the pan, fluid filter screen, and its retaining clip.
2. Remove the vacuum diaphragm unit.
3. Loosen the three control valve body attaching bolts.
4. Remove the front servo attaching bolts, hold the band strut steady, and remove the front servo unit.

Installation

1. After repairing the front servo unit, install it by first positioning the front band forward in the transmission case with the end of the band facing downward. Be sure the front servo anchor pin is placed in the case web. Align the large end of the servo strut with the servo actuating lever, and align the small end with the band end.
2. Rotate the band, strut, and servo to align the anchor end of the band with the anchor in the case. Push the servo unit onto the control valve body tubes.
3. Install the attaching bolts and tighten them to 30-35 ft. lbs. torque.
4. Tighten the control valve body attaching bolts to 8-10 ft. lbs. torque. Check the clearance (0.050 in.) between the manual valve and the manual lever actuating pin.
5. Adjust the front band.
6. Install the vacuum diaphragm unit and its pushrod.
7. Install the fluid filter screen, its retaining clip, and the pan with a new pan gasket.
8. Fill the transmission with fluid.
9. Adjust the downshift and manual shift linkage.

Rear Servo

Removal

1. Drain the transmission fluid from the transmission, and remove the pan, fluid filter screen, and its retaining clip.
2. Remove the vacuum diaphragm unit.
3. Remove the control valve body and the two front servo tubes.
4. Remove the rear servo attaching bolts, hold the actuating and anchor struts, and remove the rear servo unit.

Installation

1. Before installing the rear servo unit, position the servo anchor strut on the servo band and rotate the band to engage the strut.
2. While holding the servo anchor strut in place, position the actuating lever strut and install the rear servo unit in place.
3. Loosely install the rear servo attaching bolts, with the longer bolt in the inner bolt hole.
4. Move the rear servo unit toward the center of the transmission case against the attaching bolts. While holding the servo in this position, tighten the attaching bolts.
5. Install the two front servo tubes and the control valve body. Check for proper clearance (0.050 in.) between the manual

valve and the manual actuating pin.
6. Adjust the rear band.
7. Install the fluid filter screen, its retaining clip, and the oil pan with a new gasket. Fill the transmission with fluid.

Transmission Overhaul Procedures

The transmission overhaul procedures presented here are the checks and repairs that must be done with the transmission out of the truck. Each transmission subassembly is illustrated by exploded views of the subassembly showing how the individual parts fit together. Assembly is often the reverse of the disassembly procedure except for alignment, special tolerances, etc.

During all repairs to the transmission subassemblies, the following instructions must be followed:

1. Be sure that no dirt or grease gets in the transmission. All parts must be clean. *Remember—a little dirt can disable a transmission completely if it gets in a fluid passage.*
2. Handle all transmission parts carefully to avoid burring or nicking bearing or mating surfaces.
3. Lubricate all internal parts of the transmission with clean transmission fluid before assembling. *Do not use any other lubricants except on gaskets or thrust washers which may be coated lightly with vaseline to ease assembly.*
4. Always use new gaskets when assembling the transmission.
5. Tighten all bolts and screws to the recommended torque limits using a torque wrench.

Transmission Disassembly

1. Thoroughly clean the outside of the transmission to prevent dirt or grease from getting inside. *Do this before removing any subassembly.*
2. Place the transmission in the transmission holder or stand.
3. Remove the transmission oil pan, gasket, and fluid filter retaining clip.
4. Lift the fluid filter screen off the forward tube, and then off the rear tube.
5. Remove the spring seat from the pressure regulator. *Maintain constant pressure on the spring seat and release slowly to prevent spring distortion and personal injury.*
6. Remove the pressure regulator springs and pilots, but do not remove the valves yet.
7. Loosen but do not remove the

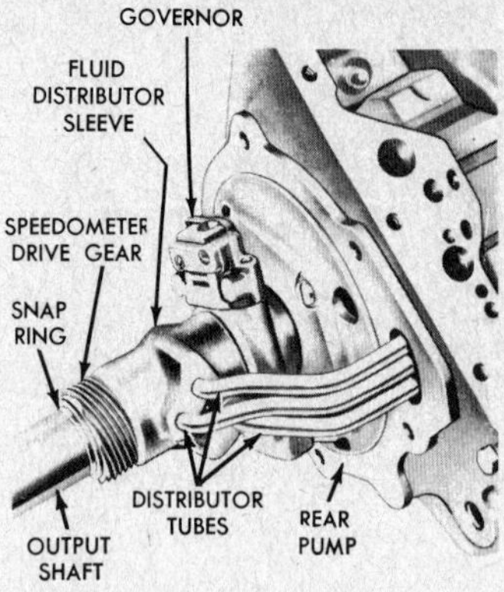

Output shaft and rear pump installed (© Ford Motor Co.)

pressure regulator attaching bolts.
8. Remove the small compensator pressure tube from the pressure regulator and the control valve body.
9. Remove the main pressure oil tube from the pressure regulator and the main control valve body assembly. Gently pry off the end connected to the main control valve body first and then remove the tube from the pressure regulator. *Failure to do this may kink or bend the tube causing damage to the transmission.*
10. Loosen the front and rear band adjusting screws five turns. Loosen the front servo attaching bolts three turns.
11. Remove the vacuum diaphragm unit and pushrod.
12. Remove the control valve body attaching bolts and align the levers to allow removal of the valve body. Lift the valve body up and pull it off the servo tubes. Place the valve body on a clean surface.
13. Remove the pressure regulator from the case. Keep the control pressure valve and the converter pressure valve in the regulator body to avoid damaging the valves.
14. Remove the front servo supply and release tubes by twisting and pulling at the same time. Remove the front servo attaching bolts. While holding the front servo strut, lift the front servo from the case.
15. Remove the rear servo attaching bolts. While holding the actuating and anchor struts, lift the rear servo from the case.

Transmission End-Play Check

The transmission end-play is checked as follows:

1. Remove one of the front pump attaching bolts and mount the dial indicator support tool in the hole. Mount a dial indicator on the support so that the stem rests on the end of the turbine shaft.
2. Install the extension housing seal replacer on the output shaft to provide support for the shaft.
3. Using a screwdriver, move the front clutch cylinder to the rear of the transmission case as far as possible. Set the dial indicator to zero while holding a slight pressure on the screwdriver.
4. Remove the screwdriver. Insert it between the large internal gear and the case and move the front clutch cylinder to the front of the case.
5. Record the indicator reading for later use during transmission reassembly. The end-play reading should be between 0.010-0.029 in. If the reading is not within these limits, a new selective thrust washer must be used when reassembling the transmission.

Extension Housing Parts and Case

Removal

1. Remove the front pump attaching bolts. Remove the front pump and gasket. It may be necessary to tap the screw bosses with a soft faced hammer to loosen the pump from the case. *NOTE: If the parking brake drum is mounted on the transmission, remove the drum and yoke from the output shaft.*

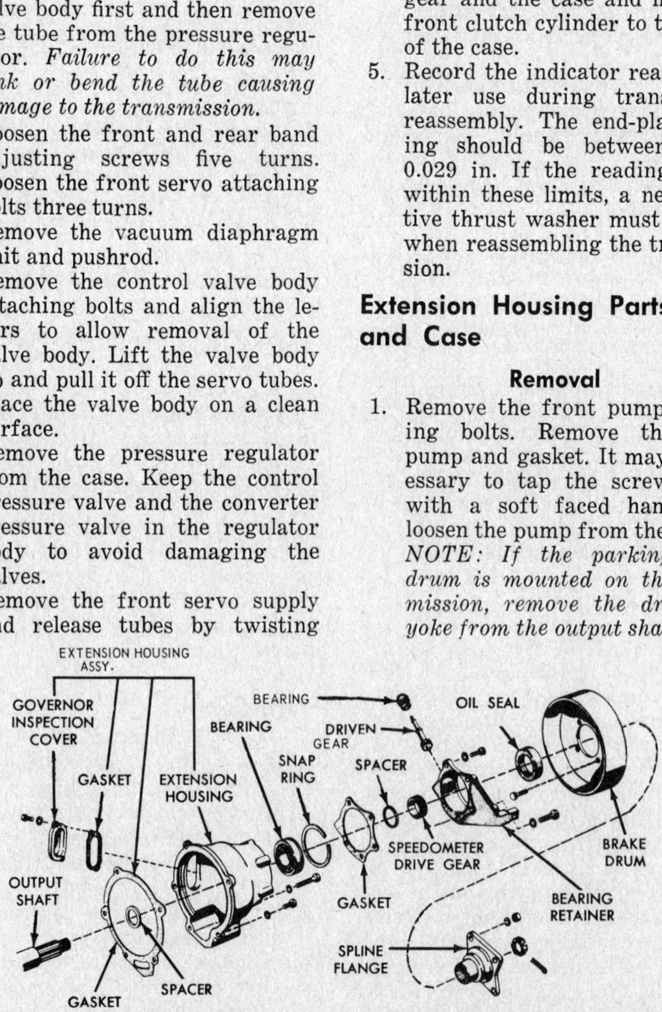

Parking brake drum and extension housing components—Ford FMX (© Ford Motor Co.)

2. Remove the extension housing seal. Remove the lubrication tube from the case. Remove the transmission-to-extension housing bolts and the extension housing. These bolts also secure the rear support to the case.
3. Remove the output shaft assembly. Be sure not to bend the pressure tubes between the distributor sleeve and case, as the tubes are being removed from the case.
4. Place the output shaft assembly on the bench and remove the oil distributor tubes from the sleeve.
5. Slide the speedometer drive gear ball off the shaft.
6. If the drive gear ball does not fall out as the speedometer gear is removed, remove the ball from the seat in the output shaft.
7. Remove the distributor sleeve. Remove the four seal rings from the output, be careful not to break the rings.
8. Remove the governor snap ring from the output shaft. Slide the governor assembly off the output shaft. Remove the governor drive ball. Remove the extension housing and pump gaskets.
9. Remove the rear pump drive key from the output shaft. Remove the bronze thrust washer from the output shaft.
10. Remove the selective thrust washer from the rear pinion carrier.
11. Remove the two seal rings from the primary gear shaft. Remove the pinion carrier.
12. Remove the primary sun gear rear thrust bearing and race from the pinion carrier.
    NOTE: Record the rear band position for reference during assembly.
13. The end of the band next to the adjusting screw has a depression in the center of the boss. Squeeze the ends of the rear band together, tilt the band to the rear, and remove the rear band from the case.
14. Remove the two center support outer bolts from the transmission case.
15. Hold the clutch units together on the input shaft. Remove the center support and the front and rear clutches as a unit.
16. Place the clutch assemblies in a holding fixture.
17. Remove the thrust washers from the front of the input shaft.
18. Position the front band ends between the case webbing and tilt the bottom of the band rearward. Squeeze the ends of the band together and remove the front band from the rear of the case.
19. Lift the front clutch assembly from the primary sun gear shaft.

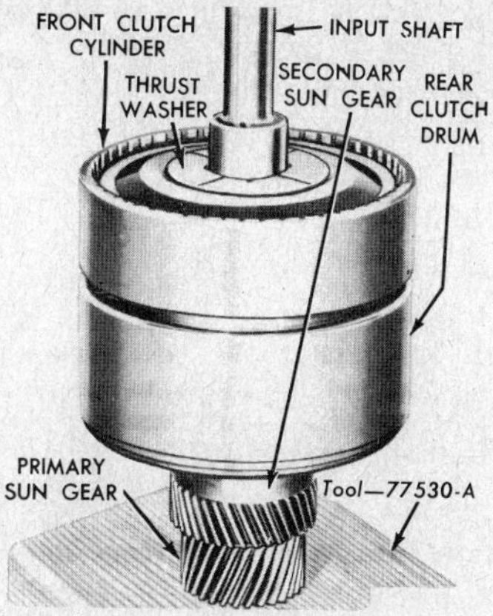

Input shaft and clutch mounted in holding fixture (© Ford Motor Co.)

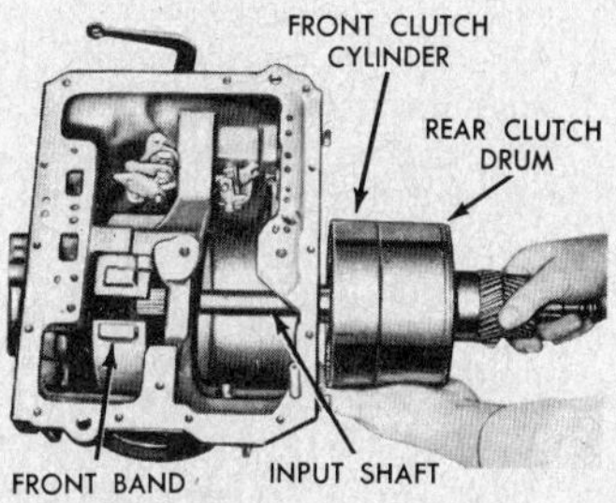

Removing input shaft and clutch (© Ford Motor Co.)

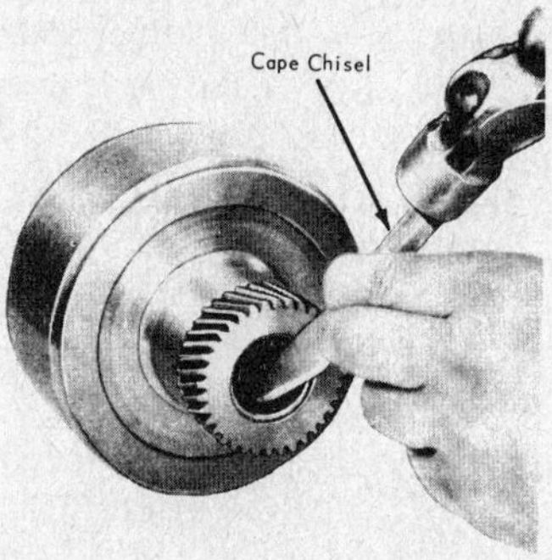

Removing rear clutch sun gear bushing (© Ford Motor Co.)

20. Remove the bronze and the steel thrust washers from the rear clutch assembly, wire the thrust washers together to be sure of correct assembly.
21. Remove the front clutch seal rings from the primary sun gear shaft. Lift the rear clutch assembly from the primary sun gear shaft and remove the rear clutch seal rings from the primary sun gear shaft.
    CAUTION: Do not break the rear clutch seal rings.
    Remove the primary sun gear front thrust washer.
    NOTE: If the transmission case bushing is worn or damaged, replace the bushing.
22. If the rear brake drum support bushing is worn or damaged, replace it.
23. Remove the output shaft bushing if it is worn or damaged. Use a chisel and cut along the bushing seam until the chisel breaks through the bushing wall. Pry the loose ends of the bushing up with an awl and remove the bushing.
24. Install a new bushing with its proper installation tool. The bushing must be pressed into position.

Assembly

NOTE: Do not use force to assemble mating parts. If the parts do not go together easily, examine them for the cause of the problem. Always use new gaskets and seals during assembly operations.

1. Install the front band in the transmission case with the anchor end aligned with the anchor in the case.
2. Make sure the thrust washer is in place on the input shaft. Lift the clutch assemblies out of the holding fixture.
   CAUTION: Do not allow the clutches to separate.
3. Install the clutch sub-assemblies

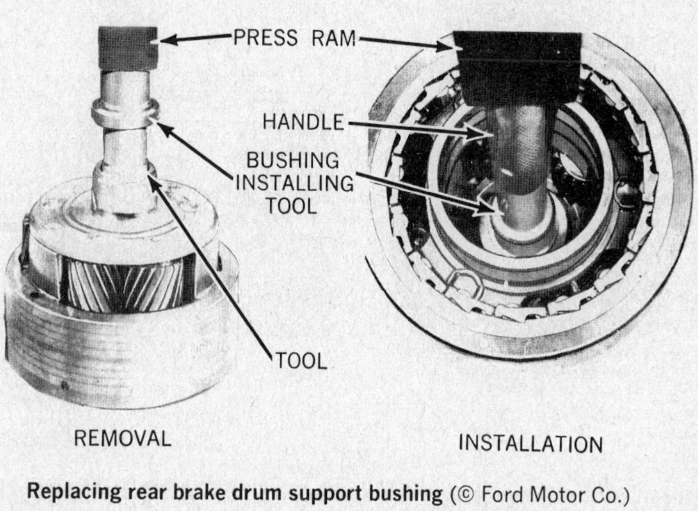

Replacing rear brake drum support bushing (© Ford Motor Co.)

in the transmission case while positioning the servo band on the drum. Hold the units together while installing them.

4. Assemble and install the center support assembly as follows:
   a. Install the center support and the rear band in the case.
   b. Install the one piece needle bearing and race assembly in the planet carrier, be sure that the black oxide coated race is facing the front of the transmission.
   c. Lubricate the bearing surface on the center support, the rollers of the planetary clutch, and the cam race in the carrier with petroleum jelly.
   d. Install the planetary clutch in the carrier.
   e. Carefully, position the planet carrier on the center support. Move the carrier forward until the clutch rollers are felt to contact the bearing surface on the center support.
   f. While applying forward pressure on the planet carrier, rotate it counterclockwise, as viewed from the rear. The clutch rollers will roll towards the large opening end of the cams in the race, compressing the spring slightly and the rollers will ride up

Installing output shaft bushing (© Ford Motor Co.)

the chamber on the planetary support onto the inner race.
   g. Push the planet carrier all the way forward.
   h. Check the operation of the planetary clutch by rotating the carrier counterclockwise, viewed from the rear, with a slight drag, and should lock up when attempting to rotate in the clockwise direction.
   i. Install the selective thrust washer on the pinion carrier rear pilot. If the end play was not within specifications when checked prior to disassembly, replace the washer with one of proper thickness. Refer to the specifications at the end of this section.
   j. Install the output shaft, carefully meshing the internal gear with the pinions.
5. With the center support properly assembled, position the rear pump drive key in the keyway on the output shaft.
6. Position the new front and rear gaskets on the pump body. Retain the gaskets with clean transmission fluid. Then install the rear pump. Be sure that the key is aligned with the keyway in the pump drive gear.
7. Position the governor drive ball in the pocket in the output shaft. Retain the ball with clean transmission fluid.
8. Install the governor assembly aligning the groove with the ball in the output shaft.
9. Install the governor with the governor body plate facing towards the rear of the transmission. Install the governor snap ring.
10. Place the four seal rings in the distributor seleves, and check the ring gap.
11. Check the fit of the grooves in the output shaft. The rings should rotate freely. Install the rings in the grooves of the output shaft.
12. Install the three tubes in the distributor sleeve.
13. Install the distributor sleeve on the output shaft, with the chamfer facing forward. Lubricate the parts with clean transmission fluid to facilitate assembly. Slide the sleeve over the four rings and at the same time start the tubes into the case. The distributor sleeve is located between the governor snap ring and the speedometer drive gear.
14. Make sure that the speedometer drive gear lock ball is in place, then install the speedometer drive gear.
15. Install the output shaft ball bearing front spacer and the ball bearing with the snap ring toward the rear.
16. Install the output shaft rear spacer and the speedometer drive gear.
17. Install the rear bearing retainer gasket and the retainer. Torque the bolts to specification.
18. Install the parking brake drum, if so equipped, and/or the u-joint yoke. Torque the nut to specification. Tighten the nut to the nearest cotter pin hole, and install a new cotter pin.
19. Install the front pump gasket in the counter bore of the transmission case.
20. Install the front pump, aligning the pump bolt holes with the holes in the case. Install the

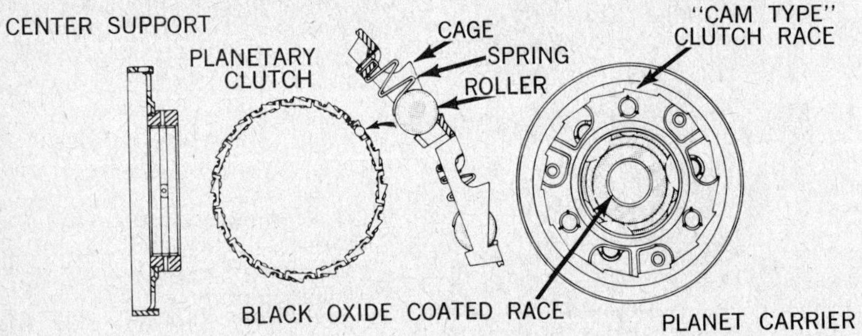

Planetary clutch, planet carrier and center support—Ford FMX (© Ford Motor Co.)

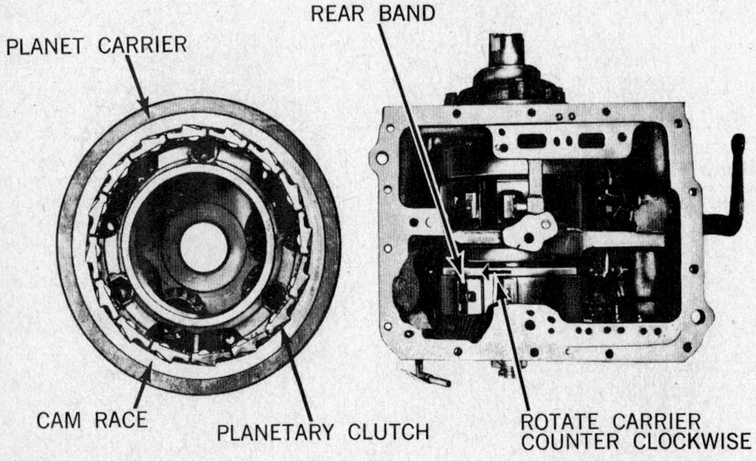

Installation of planetary clutch in carrier—Ford FMX (© Ford Motor Co.)

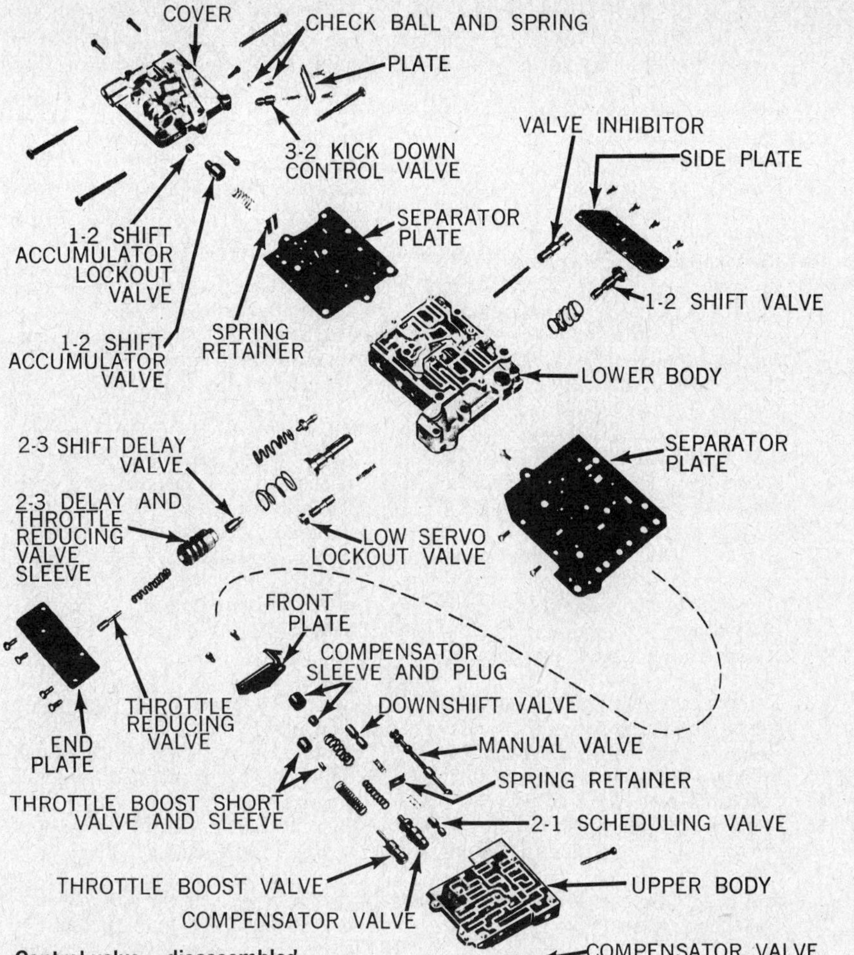

Control valve—disassembled
(© Ford Motor Co.)

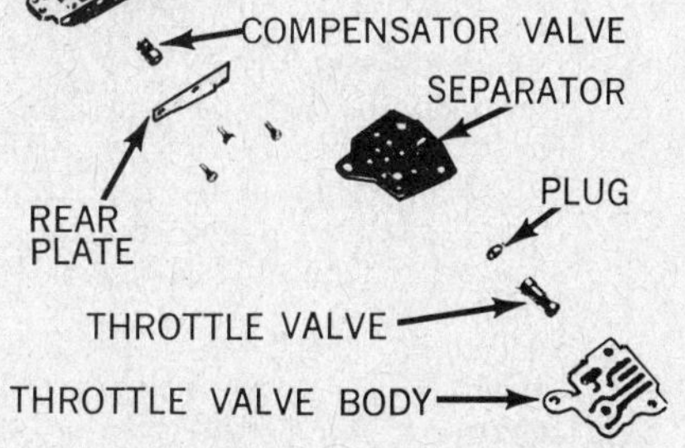

front pump attaching bolts and torque to specifications.

21. Mount a dial indicator support in a front pump bolt hole. Mount a dial indicator on the support so that the contact rests on the end of the turbine shaft.
22. Pry the output shaft all the way forward by using a screw driver between the large internal gear and the case.
23. Lightly block the output shaft in the forward position to eliminate all output shaft end play.
24. Inserting a screwdriver between the planet carrier and the large internal gear move the pinion carrier all the way forward. Maintain slight forward pressure, and set the dial indicator at zero.
25. Measure and record the end play between the front of the case and the large internal gear by prying between the front clutch cylinder and the case. This end play should be 0.010-0.029 inch. Total end play including the output shaft must not exceed 0.044 inch. If the end play is not within limits, a new selective thrust washer must be used.
26. Remove the dial indicator and install the remaining pump retaining bolt, tighten to specifications.
27. Position the front band forward in the case with the band end up.
28. Position the servo strut with the slotted end aligned with the servo actuating lever, and the small end aligned with the band end. Rotate the band, strut and servo into position, engaging the anchor end of the band with the anchor pin in the case.
29. Locate the servo on the case, and install the attaching bolts. Tighten the attaching bolts only 2 or 3 threads.
30. Install the servo tubes.
31. Position the servo anchor strut, and rotate the rear band to engage the strut.
32. Position the servo actuating lever strut with a finger, and then install the servo and attaching bolts. Move the servo toward the centerline of the case, against the attaching bolts. While holding the servo in this position, torque the attaching bolts to specification.
33. Install the pressure regulator body and attaching bolts. Torque the bolts to specifications.
34. Install the control and converter valve guides and springs. Install the spring retainer.
35. Install the control valve assembly, carefully alining the servo tubes with the control valve. Align the inner downshaft lever between the stop and the downshift valve. Shift the manual lever to the #1 position. Align the manual valve with the actuating pin in the manual detent lever. Do not tighten the attaching bolts.
36. Install the main pressure oil tube. Be sure to install the end of the tube that connects to the pressure regulator assembly first. Then, install the other end of the tube into the main control assembly, by tapping gently with a soft faced hammer.
37. Install the small control pressure compensator tube in the valve body and regulator.
38. Move the control valve body toward the center of the case, until the clearance is less than 0.050 inch between the manual valve and the actuating pin on the manual detent lever.
39. Torque the attaching bolts to specifications. Be sure that the rear fluid screen retaining clip is installed under the valve body bolt.
40. Turn the manual valve one full turn in each manual lever detent position. If the manual valve binds against the actuating pin in any detent position, loosen the valve body attaching bolts and move the body away from the center of the case. Move the body only enough to relieve the binding. Torque the attaching bolts to specifications. Recheck the manual valve for binding.
41. Torque the front servo attaching bolts to specifications.
42. Adjust the front and rear bands as outlined in the "Adjustment" section.
43. Position the control rod in the bore of the vacuum diaphragm unit and install the diaphragm unit. Make sure that the control rod enters the throttle valve as the vacuum unit is installed, torque the retaining bolts to specifications.
44. Position the fluid screen under the rear clip and over the front pump inlet tube. Press the screen

down firmly. Install the screen retaining clip.

45. Place a new gasket on the transmission case and install the pan. Install the attaching bolts and lock washers. Tighten the bolts to specifications.
46. If the converter and converter housing were removed from the transmission, install these components. Position the transmission assembly on a transmission jack and install in the vehicle.

Control Valve Body

Disassembly

NOTE: During disassembly of the control valve assembly, avoid damage to the valve parts and keep the valve parts clean. Place the valve assembly on a clean shop towel while performing the disassembly operations. Do not separate the upper and lower valve bodies and cover until after the valves have been removed.

1. Remove the manual valve.
2. Remove the throttle valve body and the separator plate. Be careful not to lose the check valve when removing the separator plate from the valve body. Remove the throttle valve and plug.
3. Remove one screw attaching the separator plate to the lower valve body. Remove the upper body front plate. The plate is spring-loaded. Apply pressure to the plate while removing the attaching screws.
4. Remove the compensator sleeve and plug, remove the compensator valve springs. Remove the compensator valve.
5. Remove the throttle boost short valve and sleeve. Remove the throttle boost spring and valve.
6. Remove the downshift valve and spring.
7. Remove the upper valve body rear plate.
8. Remove the compensator cut back valve.
9. Remove the lower body side plate. The plate is spring-loaded. Apply pressure to the plate while removing the attaching screws.
10. Remove the 1-2 shift valve and spring. Remove the inhibitor valve and spring.
11. Remove the two screws attaching the separator plate to the cover. Remove the lower valve body end plate. The end plate is spring-loaded. Apply pressure to the plate while removing the attaching screws.
12. Remove the low servo lockout valve, low servo modulator valve and spring.
13. Remove the 2-3 delay and throttle reducing valve sleeve, the throttle reducing valve, spring, and the 2-3 shift delay valve. The reducing valve sleeve is lightly staked in the valve body bore. To remove the sleeve, use a blunt instrument against the end of the 2-3 shift valve and push the sleeve from its bore. Remove the 2-3 shift valve spring, spring retainer and the valve.
14. Remove the transition valve spring and valve.
15. Remove the plate from the valve body cover.
16. Remove the check ball spring and the check ball.
17. Remove the 1-2 shift accumulator valve spring from the cover. Remove the spring, the 1-2 accumulator valve and the 1-2 shift accumulator lockout valve.
18. Remove the through bolts and screws. Then separate the upper and lower control valve bodies and cover. Be careful not to lose the check valves.

Assembly

1. Arrange all the parts in their correct positions. Rotate the valves and plugs when inserting them in their bores, to avoid shearing off the soft body castings.
2. Place the check valve in the upper body, then position the separator plate on the body.
3. Position the lower body on the upper body, and start, but do not tighten the attaching bolts.
4. Position the cover and separator plate on the lower body. Start the four through bolts.
5. Align the separator with the upper and lower valve body attaching bolt holes. Install and torque the four valve body bolts to specifications.

CAUTION: Excessive tightening of these bolts will distort the valve bodies and cause the valves and plugs to bind.

6. Install the check ball and spring in the cover. Install the plate.
7. Insert the 1-2 shift accumulator lockout valve, 1-2 shift accumulator valve, and the spring in the cover. Install the valve spring retainer.
8. Install the transition valve and spring in the lower valve body.
9. Install the 2-3 shift valve, spring retainer and spring. Install the 2-3 shift delay valve, spring and throttle reducing valve in the sleeve. Slide the assembly into position in the lower body. Do not restake the sleeve.
10. Install the low servo lockout valve and spring. Install the low servo modulator and the low servo lockout valves. Install the lower body end plate.
11. Install the inhibitor valve spring and valve in the lower body.
12. Install the 1-2 shift valve spring and valve. Install the lower body side plate.
13. Install the compensator cutback valve in the upper body. Install the upper body rear plate.
14. Install the downshift valve and spring in the body.
15. Install the throttle boost valve and spring. Install the throttle boost short valve and spring.
16. Install the compensator valve, inner and outer compensator springs, and the compensator sleeve and plug.
17. Position the front plate. Apply pressure to the plate while installing the two attaching screws.
18. Install the throttle valve, plug, and check valve in the throttle valve body. Position the separator on the upper body and install the throttle valve body. Install the three attaching screws.
19. Install the four screws attaching the cover to the lower body, two screws attaching the separator plate to the lower body. Torque the cover and body screws to specifications.
20. Install the manual valve.

Front Servo

Disassembly

1. Remove the servo piston retainer snap ring. The servo piston is spring loaded. Apply pressure to the piston when removing the snap ring.
2. Remove the servo piston retainer, and the servo piston from the servo body. If necessary, tap the piston stem lightly with a soft-faced hammer to separate the piston retainer from the servo body.

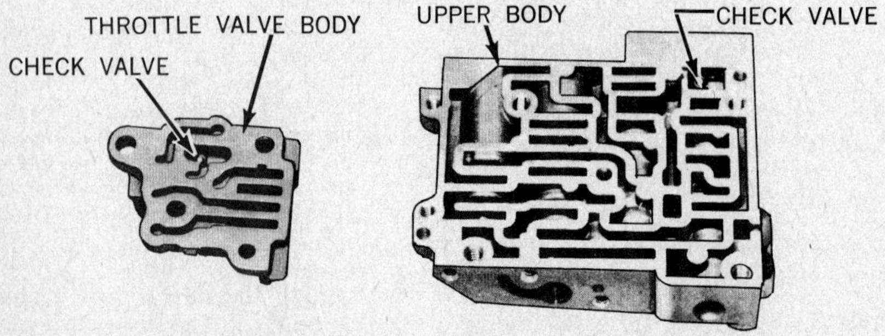

Check valve locations—Ford FMX (© Ford Motor Co.)

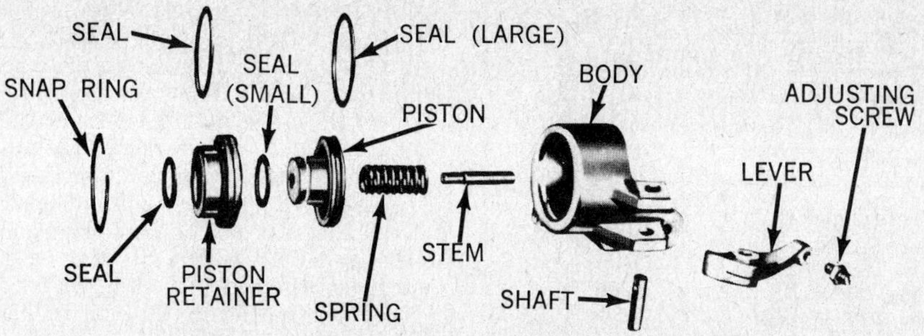

Front servo disassembled—Ford FMX (© Ford Motor Co.)

3. Remove all the seal rings, and remove the spring from the servo body.
4. Inspect the servo body for cracks, and the piston bore and the servo piston stem for scores. Check the fluid passages for obstructions.
5. Check the actuating lever for free movement and inspect it for wear. To replace the actuating lever shaft, it will be necessary to press the shaft out of the bracket. The shaft is retained in the body by serrations on one end of the shaft. These serrations cause a press fit at the end. To remove the shaft, press on the end opposite the serrations. Inspect the adjusting screw threads and the threads in the lever.
6. Check the servo spring and the servo band strut for distortion.
7. Inspect the servo band lining for excessive wear and bonding of the metal. The band should be replaced if worn to a point where the grooves are not clearly evident.
8. Inspect the band ends for cracks and check for band distortion.

Assembly

1. Lubricate all parts of the front servo with clean transmission fluid before starting assembly.
2. Install the inner and outer 'O' rings on the piston retainer. Install a new 'O' ring on the return piston and on the servo piston.
3. Position the servo piston release spring in the servo body. Install the servo piston, retainer, and return piston in the servo body. Compress the assembly into the body and secure it with the snap ring. Make sure that the snap ring is fully seated in the groove.
4. Install the adjusting screw and lock nut in the actuating lever if they were removed.

Rear Servo

Disassembly

1. Remove the servo actuating lever shaft retaining pin with a $1/8$ inch punch.
2. Press down on the servo spring retainer, and remove the snap ring. Release the pressure on the retainer slowly to prevent the spring from flying out.
3. Remove the retainer and servo spring.
4. Force the piston out of the servo body with air pressure. Hold one hand over the piston to prevent damage.
5. Remove the piston seal ring.

Assembly

1. Install a new piston seal ring on the servo piston.
2. Install the piston in the servo body. Lubrication of the parts with clean transmission fluid will facilitate assembly. Install the servo spring with the small coiled end against the servo piston.
3. Install the spring retainer. Compress the spring with a C-clamp. Then, install the snap ring. The snap ring must be fully seated in the groove.
4. Install the actuating lever with the socket in the lever bearing on the piston stem. Install. the actuating lever shaft, aligning the retaining pin holes, and install the pin.
5. Check the actuating lever for free movement.

Governor

Disassembly

1. Remove the governor valve body cover.
2. Remove the valve body from the counterweight.
3. Remove the plug, sleeve, and the valve and spring from the governor body.
4. Remove the screen from its bore in the valve body.

Assembly

1. Install the governor valve and spring assembly in the bore of the valve body. Install the sleeve and plug.
2. Install the screen.
3. Install the body counterweight. Make sure that the fluid passages in the body and counterweight are aligned.
4. Position the valve body cover on the body, and install the screws.

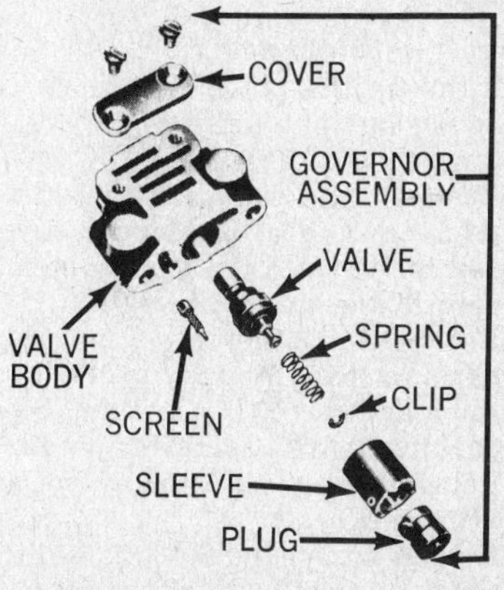

Governor disassembled—Ford FMX (© Ford Motor Co.)

Pressure Regulator

Disassembly

1. Remove the valves from the regulator body.
2. Remove the regulator body cover attaching screws, and remove the cover.
3. Remove the separator plate.
4. Wash all parts thoroughly in a clean solvent and blow dry with moisture-free compressed air.
5. Inspect the regulator body and cover mating surfaces for burrs.
6. Check all fluid passages for obstructions.
7. Inspect the control pressure converter pressure valves and bores for burrs and scoring. Remove all burrs with crocus cloth.
8. Check the free movement of the valve in their bores. Each valve

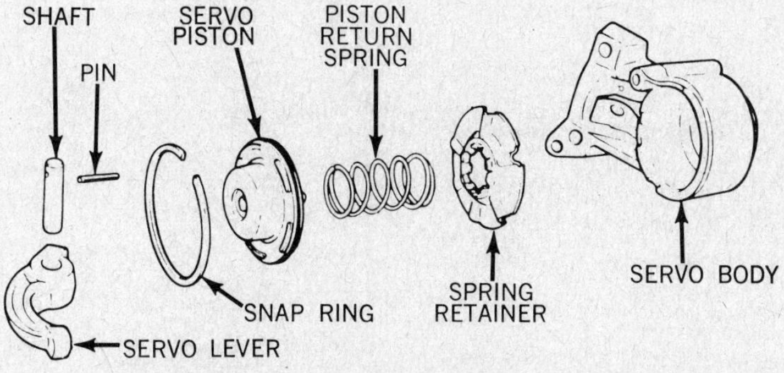

Rear servo disassembled—Ford FMX (© Ford Motor Co.)

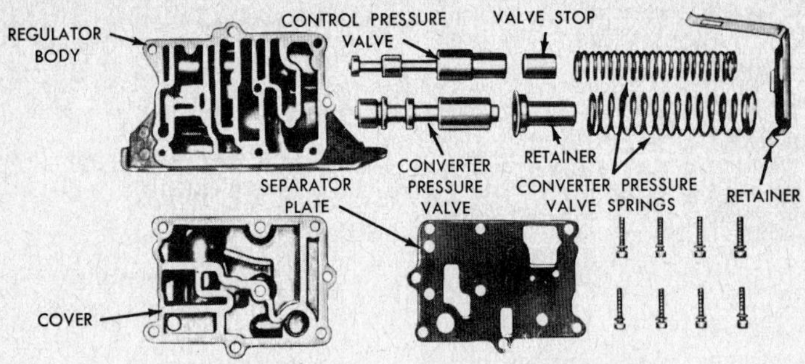

Pressure regulator assembly (© Ford Motor Co.)

should fall freely into its bore when both the valve and bore are dry.

9. Inspect the valve springs for distortion.

Assembly

1. Position the separator plate on the regulator cover.
2. Position the regulator cover and separator plate on the regulator body and install the attaching screws. Tighten to specifications.
3. Insert the valves in the pressure regulator body.

Downshift and Manual Linkage

Disassembly

1. Remove the inner downshift lever shaft nut. Then remove the inner downshift lever.
2. Remove the outer downshift lever and shaft. Remove the downshift seal from the counterbore in the manual lever shaft.
3. Remove the cotter pin from the parking pawl toggle operating rod and remove the clip from the parking pawl operating lever. Remove the parking pawl operating rod.
4. Rotate the manual shaft until the detent lever clears the detent plunger. Then, remove the detent plunger and spring. Do not allow the detent plunger to fly out of the case.
5. Remove the manual lever shaft nut and remove the detent lever. Remove the outer manual lever and shaft from the transmission case.
6. Tap the toggle lever sharply toward the rear of the case to remove the plug and pin.
7. Remove the pawl pin by working the pawl back and forth. Remove the pawl and toggle lever assembly and then disassemble.
8. Remove the manual shaft seal and the case vent tube.

Assembly

1. Coat the outer diameter of a new manual shaft seal with sealer and install the seal in the transmission case with a driver.
2. Install the vent tube in the transmission case.
3. Assemble the link to the pawl with the pawl link pin, washer, and pawl return spring. Assemble the toggle lever to the link with the toggle link pin. Position the pawl return spring over the toggle link pin and secure in place with the washer and small retainer clip. Position the pawl assembly in the transmission case and install the pawl pin, and the toggle lever pin. Press the retaining plug tightly against the toggle lever pin. Install the torsion lever assembly. Position the spring on the torsion lever with a screwdriver. Make sure that the short side of the toggle lift lever does not extend beyond the largest diameter of the ball on the toggle link. Tap the toggle lift lever in or out as necessary to center the lever on the ball.
4. Install the manual lever and shaft in the transmission case. Position the detent lever on the shaft, and secure with the nut. Tighten the nut to 20-30 ft-lbs of torque. Rotate the manual lever to the rear of the case. Position the detent spring in the case. Hold the detent plug on the spring with a 3/16 inch socket wrench, then depress the spring until the plug is flush with the case. Carefully rotate the manual lever to the front of the case to secure the plug. A piece of thin walled tubing may be used to depress the plug if a small socket wrench is not available.
5. Position the ends of the parking pawl operating rod in the detent lever and toggle lift lever, secure with the two small retaining pins.
6. Install a new seal on the downshift lever shaft, then install the lever and shaft in the transmission case. Position the inner end of the shaft with the mark "O" racing toward the center of the case. Install the lock washer and nut, then tighten the nut to 17-20 ft-lbs torque.
7. Check the operation of the linkage. The linkage should operate freely without binding.

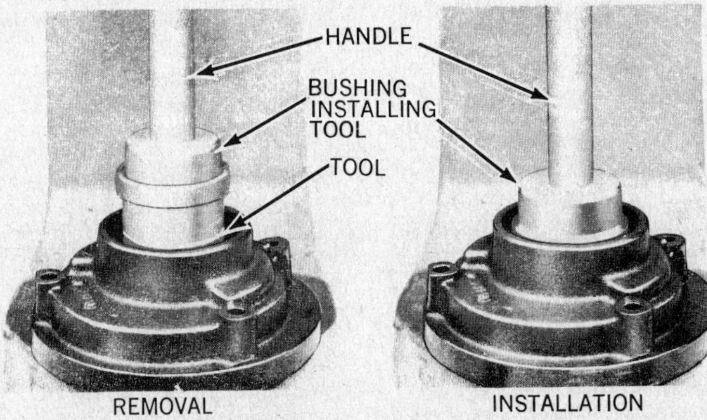

Replacing front pump housing bushing (© Ford Motor Co.)

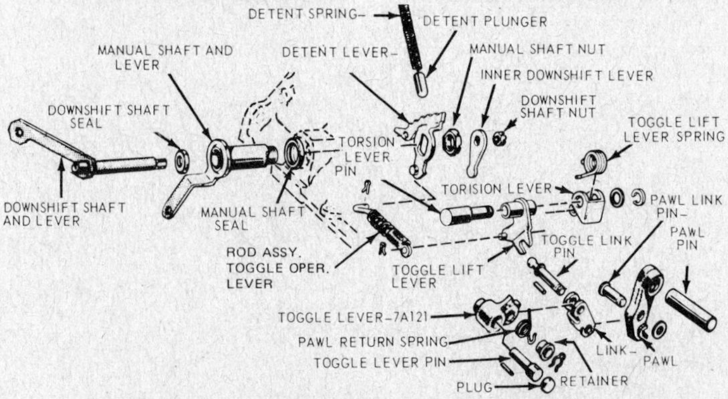

Transmission case control linkage—Ford FMX (© Ford Motor Co.)

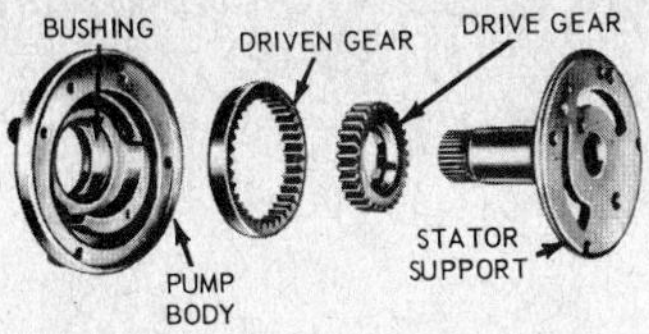

Front pump disassembled
(© Ford Motor Co.)

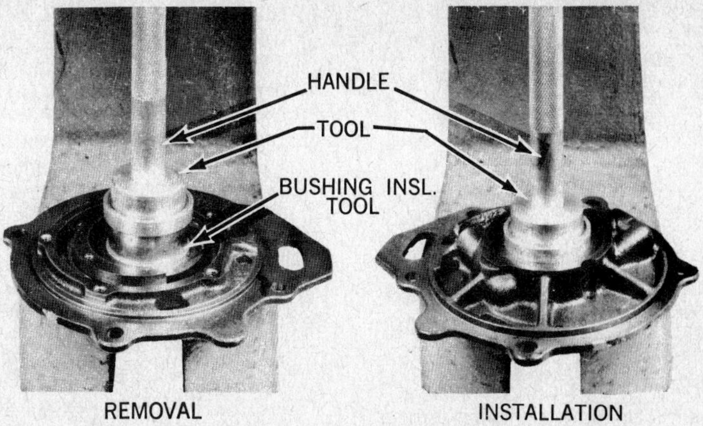

Replacing rear support housing bushing (© Ford Motor Co.)

Front Pump

Disassembly

1. Remove the stator support attaching screws and remove the stator support. Mark the top surface of the pump driven gear with Prussian blue to assure correct assembly. Do not scratch the pump gears.
2. Remove the drive and driven gears from the pump body.
3. Inspect the pump body housing, gear pockets and crescent for signs of wear or damage.
4. If the pump housing bushing is worn or damaged, replace the bushing with the proper tool.
5. If any parts other than the stator support, bushings of oil seal are found to be defective, replace the pump as a unit. Minor burrs and scores may be removed with crocus cloth. The stator support is serviced separately.
6. If the oil seal requires replacement, bolt the front pump to the transmission case. Install the seal removing tool and pull the seal from the body.
7. Clean the pump body counterbore. Inspect the bore for rough spots. Smooth up the counterbore with crocus cloth.
8. Remove the pump body from the transmission case.

Assembly

1. If the oil seal was removed, coat the outer diameter with sealing compound. Position the seal in the pump body and drive the new seal into the pump body with the proper tool. Be sure that the seal is firmly seated.
2. Place the pump driven gear in the pump body with the mark on the gear or tooth gear chamfer facing down. Install the drive gear in the pump body with the chamfered side of the flats facing down.
3. Install the stator support and the attaching screws. Check the pump gears for free rotation.

Rear Pump

Disassembly

1. Remove the screws and lock washers securing the pump cover to the pump body and remove the cover.
2. Remove the drive gear from the pump body.
3. If the pump housing bushing is worn or damaged, replace the bushing with the proper installation and removal tool.

Assembly

1. Install the drive gear in the pump body.
2. Install the pump cover, attaching screws, and lock washers. Torque the screws to specifications.

Rear Clutch

Disassembly

1. Remove the clutch pressure plate snap ring and remove the plate from the drum. Remove the waved cushion spring. Remove the composition and steel plates.
2. Compress the spring with the special spring compression tool, and remove the snap ring.
3. Guide the spring retainer while releasing the pressure, this will prevent retainer from locking in the snap ring grooves.
4. Position the primary sun gear shaft in the rear clutch. Place an air hose nozzle in one of the holes in the shaft, and place one finger over the other hole. Force the clutch piston out of the clutch drum with air pressure. Hold one hand over the piston to prevent damage to the piston during removal.
5. Remove the inner and outer seal rings from the clutch piston.
6. Remove the rear clutch sun gear bushing if it is worn or damaged. Use a cape chisel and cut along the bushing seam until the chisel breaks through the bushing wall. Pry the loose ends of

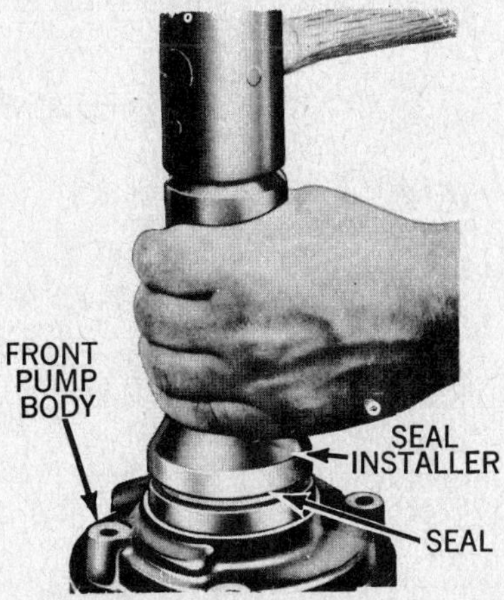

Installing front pump seal
(© Ford Motor Co.)

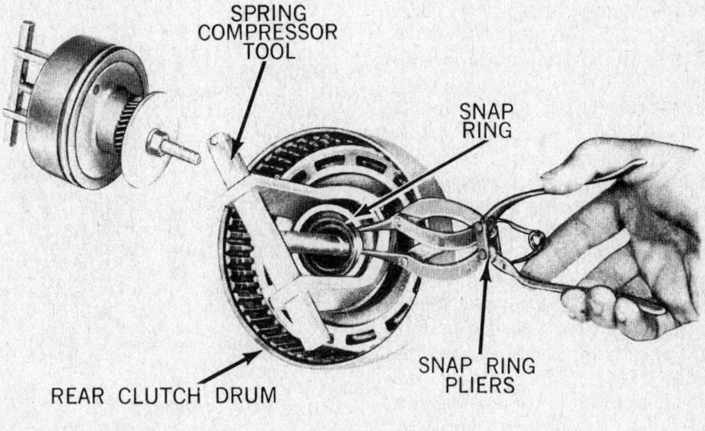

Removing rear clutch spring snap-ring (© Ford Motor Co.)

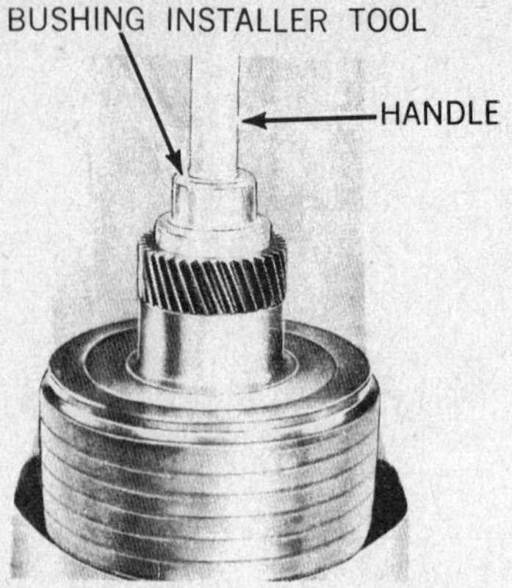

Installing rear clutch sun gear bushing
(© Ford Motor Co.)

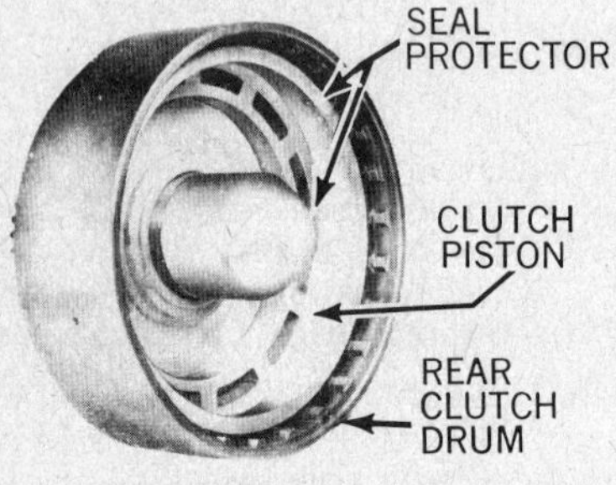

Installing rear clutch piston
(© Ford Motor Co.)

the bushing up with an awl and remove the bushing.

Assembly

1. If the rear sun gear bushing was removed, press a new bushing into the rear clutch sun gear.
2. Install a new inner and outer seal ring on the piston.
3. Lubricate the piston seals and tools with clean transmission fluid. Push the small fixture over the cylinder hub. Insert the piston into the large fixture with the seal toward the thin walled end. Hold the piston and large fixture and insert as unit into the cylinder. Push down over the small fixture until the large tool stops against the shoulder in the cylinder; then push the piston down, out of the tool until it bottoms in the cylinder. Remove the tool.
4. Install the clutch release spring, and position the retainer on the spring.
5. Install the tool on the spring retainer. Compress the clutch spring and install the snap ring. While compressing the spring, guide the retainer to avoid interference of the retainer with the snap ring grooves. Make sure that the snap ring is fully seated in the groove. When a new composition clutch plate is used, soak the plates in clean transmission fluid for 15 minutes before assembly.
6. Install the external tabbed waved cushion spring. Install the composition and the steel clutch plates alternately, starting with a steel plate.
7. Install the clutch pressure plate with the bearing surface down. Install the clutch pressure plate snap ring. Make sure that the snap ring is fully seated in the groove.
8. Check the free pack clearance between the pressure plate and the first internal plate with a feeler gauge. The clearance should be 0.030-0.055 inch. If the clearance is not within limits, selective snap rings are available in the following thicknesses; 0.060-0.064, 0.074-0.078, 0.088-0.092 and 0.102-0.106 inch. Insert the correct size snap ring and recheck the clearance.
9. Install the thrust washer on the primary sun gear shaft. Be sure the thrust washer is installed with the tabs of the washer away from the sun gear thrust face. Lubricate all parts with clean transmission fluid or with petroleum jelly. Install the two center seal rings.
10. Install the rear clutch on the primary sun gear shaft. Be sure all of the needles are in the hub if the unit is equipped with loose needles. Install the two seal rings in the front grooves.
11. Install the steel and the bronze thrust washers on the front of the secondary sun gear assembly. If the steel washer is chamfered, place the chamfered side down.

Front Clutch

Disassembly

1. Remove the clutch cover snap rings with a screwdriver, and remove the input shaft from the front clutch drum.
2. Remove the thrust washer from the thrust surface on the clutch hub. Place one finger in the clutch hub and lift the hub

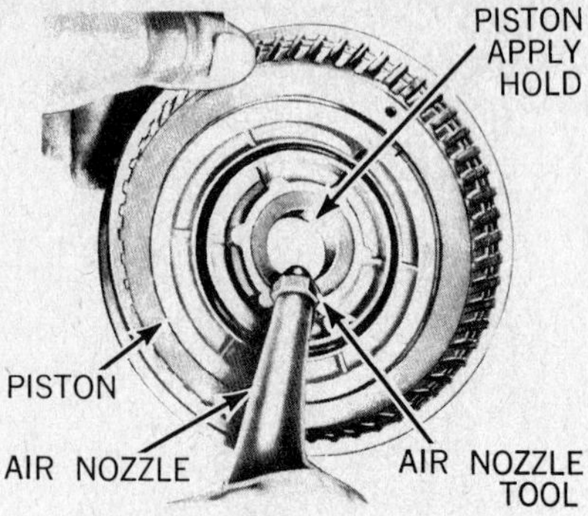

Removing front clutch piston
(© Ford Motor Co.)

straight up to remove the hub from the clutch drum.

3. Remove the composition and the steel pressure plates, and then remove the pressure plate from the clutch drum.
4. Place the front clutch spring compressor on the release spring, position the clutch drum on the bed of an arbor press, and compress the release spring with the arbor press until the release spring snap ring can be removed.
5. Remove the clutch release spring from the clutch drum.
6. Install the special air nozzle on an air line. Place the nozzle against the clutch apply hole in the front clutch housing and force the piston out of the housing.
7. Remove the piston inner seal from the clutch housing. Remove the piston outer seal from the groove in the piston.
8. Remove the input shaft bushing if it is worn or damaged. Use a cape chisel and cut along the bushing seam until the chisel breaks through the bushing wall. Pry the loose ends of the bushing up with an awl and remove the bushing.

Assembly

1. If the input shaft bushing was removed, slip a new bushing over the end of the bushing installa-

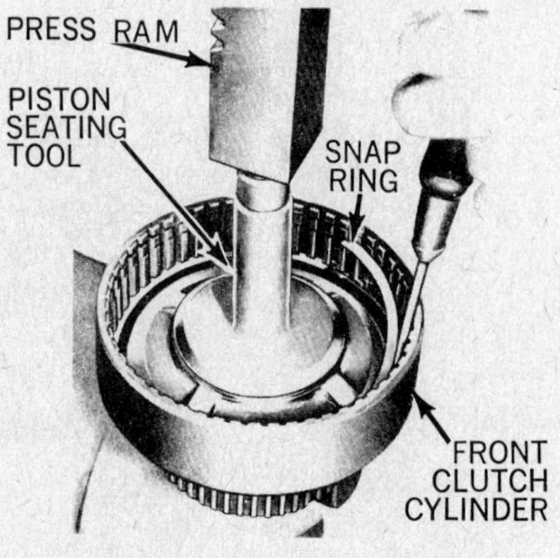

Removing front clutch snap-ring
(© Ford Motor Co.)

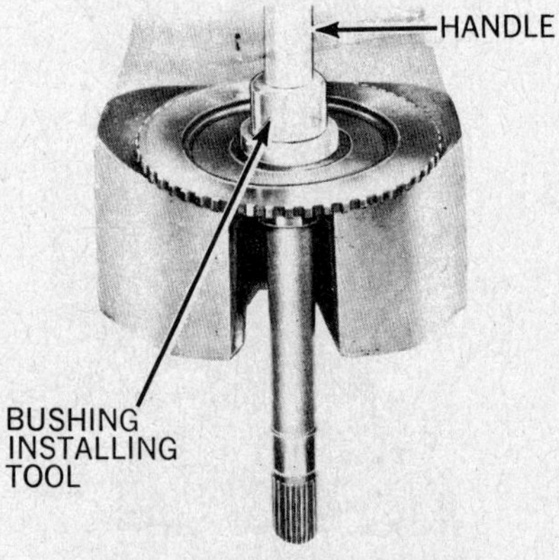

Installing input shaft bushing
(© Ford Motor Co.)

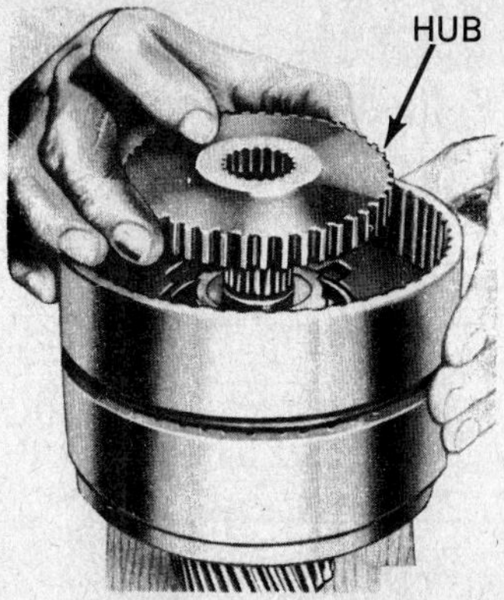

Installing front clutch hub
(© Ford Motor Co.)

tion tool and place the tool and bushing on the bushing hole. Press the bushing into the input shaft.

2. Lubricate all parts with clean transmission fluid. Install a new piston inner seal ring in the clutch cylinder. Install a new piston outer seal in the groove in the piston.
3. Install the piston in the clutch housing. Make sure that the steel bearing ring is in place on the piston.
4. Position the release spring in the clutch cylinder with the concave side up. Place the release spring compressor on the spring and compress the spring with an arbor press. Install the snap ring. Make sure that the snap ring is firmly seated in the groove.
5. Install the front clutch housing on the primary sun gear shaft. Rotate the clutch units to mesh the rear clutch plates with the serrations on the clutch hub. Do not break the seal rings.
6. Install the clutch hub in the clutch cylinder with the deep counterbore down. Install the thrust washer on the clutch hub.
7. Install the pressure plate in the clutch cylinder with the bearing surface up. Install the composi-

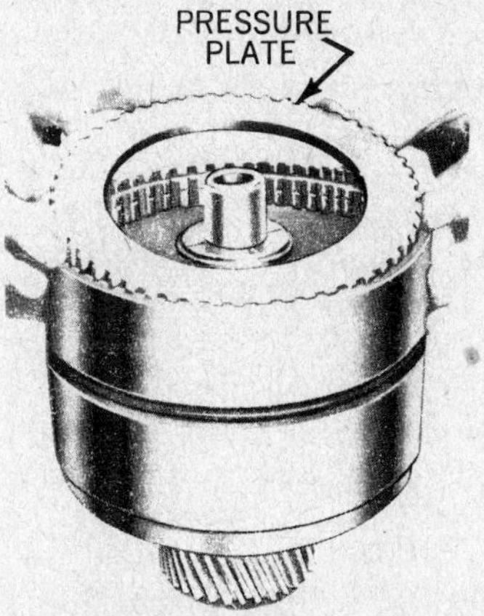

Installing pressure plate
(© Ford Motor Co.)

Installing clutch plates
(© Ford Motor Co.)

tion and steel clutch plates alternately, starting with a composition plate. When new composition clutch plates are used, soak them in clean transmission fluid for 15 minutes before assembly.

8. The finial friction plate to be installed is selective. Install the thickest plate what will be a minimum of 0.010 inch below the input shaft shoulder in the cylinder. For all other plates, use the thinnest available (see specifications at end of section).
9. Install the turbine shaft in the clutch cylinder, and secure with the snap ring. Make sure that the snap ring is firmly seated in the groove.
10. Install the thrust washer on the turbine shaft.

Primary Sun Gear Shaft

1. Position the primary sun gear shaft in the clutch bench fixture.
2. Check the fit of the seal rings in their bores. A clearance of 0.002-0.009 inch should exist between the ends of the rings.
3. Replace the seal rings, and check for free movement in the grooves.

TORQUE LIMITS FOR FMX AUTOMATIC TRANSMISSION

	Ft. Lbs.
Converter to flywheel	23-28
Converter hsg. to trans. case	40-50
Front pump to trans. case	17-22
Front servo to trans. case	30-35
Rear servo to trans. case	40-45
Upper valve body to lower valve body	4-6
Oil pan to case	10-13
Converter cover to converter hsg.	12-16
Regulator to case	17-22
Planetary support to trans. case	20-25
Control valve body to trans. case	8-10
Diaphragm assy. to case	20-30
Cooler return check valve	9-12
Extension assy. to trans. case	30-40
Pressure gauge tap	7-15
Converter drain plug	15-28
Rear band adjusting screw to case	35-40
Front band adjusting screw locknut	20-25
Manual valve inner lever to shaft	20-30
Downshift lever to shaft	17-20
Filler tube to engine	20-25
Transmission to engine	40-50
Neutral start switch actuator lever bolt	6-10
Steering col. lock rod adj. nut	10-20
T.R.S. switch to case	4-8
	In Lbs.
Governor to counterweight	50-60
Governor valve body cover screws	20-30
Pressure regulator cover screws	20-30
Pressure regulator cover screws	20-30
Control valve body screws (10-24)	20-30
Front servo release piston	20-30
End plates to body	20-30
Stator support to pump	25-35
Lower body and cover plate to valve body	20-30
T.V. body to valve body	20-30
Lower valve body cover and plate to valve body	48-72

SPECIFICATIONS

Checks and Adjustments Operation	*Specification*
Transmission end play	0.010-0.029 plus end play between output shaft ball bearing and retainer. Not to exceed a total of .044 inch.
Turbine and stator end play check	New or rebuilt 0.023 maximum. Used 0.040 maximum.
Front band adjustment (Use ¼ inch spacer between adjustment screw and servo stop piston stem)	Adjust screw to 10 in-lbs torque. Remove spacer, then tighten screw an additional ¾ turn. Hold screw and tighten lock nut.
Rear band adjustment	Adjust screw to 10 ft-lbs torque, and back off 1½ turns. Hold screw and tighten lock nut.
Primary sun gear shaft ring end gap check	0.002-0.009

FRONT CLUTCH SELECTIVE CLUTCH PLATE-FMX

Thickness (in.)	*Identification*
0.0565-0.0605	No Stripe
0.0705-0.0745	One Stripe
0.0845-0.0885	Two Stripes
0.0985-0.1025	Three Stripes

SELECTIVE THRUST WASHERS-FMX

Thickness (in.)	*Identification*
0.061-0.063	by thickness
0.067-0.069	by thickness
0.074-0.076	by thickness
0.081-0.083	by thickness
0.092-0.094	by thickness
0.105-0.107	by thickness

CAPACITY

Model	*Refill (qt.)*
All ①	11

① F-100 with 302 engine-9¼ qts.

CONTROL PRESSURE AT ZERO GOVERNOR RPM

Year	*Range*	*Control Pressure (psi) Manifold Vacuum (in. Hg)*		
		① 18 and Above	*10*	*Below 1.0*
		12 and Above		
1973	P, N, D, 2, 1	61-107	75-120	—
	R	90-156	—	185-225
	D, 2, 1	—	—	154-188
1974-78	D, 2, 1	58-80	75-120	143-188
	R	64-124	—	185-225
	P, N	56-80	—	—

① 15 and above 1974-76; 12 and above 1973

DIAGNOSIS

This diagnosis guide covers the most common symptoms and is an aid to careful diagnosis. The items to check are listed in the sequence to be followed for quickest results. Thus, follow the checks in the order given for the particular transmission type.

TROUBLE SYMPTOMS	ITEMS TO CHECK	
	IN TRUCK	OUT OF TRUCK
All ranges—slips	ACDFGHOP	abc
Drive slips—no first gear	ACDFGHOP	abcdei
Line pressure—all low	ADEFGOP	abcd
Line pressure—all high	BCEGL	a
1-2 intermediate pressure low	ADFGHINP	abcdg
2-3 direct clutch pressure high	BG	a
2-3 direct clutch pressure low	ADFGJ	abcf
No 1-2 upshift	BEFGIP	acg
1-2 upshift—early/late	BEFHI	a
1-2 upshift—with wide open throttle	BIL	a
Slips—1-2 upshifts	ACFGHINP	abcdg
Rough—1-2 upshifts	BCGP	a
No 2-3 upshift	FK	acf
2-3 upshift—early/late	BCEFHJL	a
Slips—2-3 upshift	ACFGHJ	abcf
Rough—2-3 upshift	BCGJN	a
No part throttle downshift	JL	—
No full throttle downshift	L	—
No wide open throttle 1-2 upshift	M	a
2-3 upshift—wide open throttle only	L	—
Harsh downshift	H	—
L-1 range—no engine brake	GIKO	aceh
L-2 range—no engine brake	GO	acde
Neutral—drives in neutral	—	e
Reverse—no reverse	GHO	acefh
Slips in reverse	ACDFGHJO	acfh
Spews fluid out of breather	A	j
Hunts between 2 and 3, 3 and 2 shifts	L	—

A. Low fluid level/water in fluid
B. Vacuum leak
C. Modulator and/or valve
D. Strainer and/or gasket
E. Governor—valve or screen
F. Valve body—gasket or plate
G. Pressure regulator and/or boost valve
H. Valve body check balls
I. 1-2 shift valve
J. 2-3 shift valve
K. Manual low control valve
L. Detent valve and linkage
M. Detent regulator valve
N. 2-3 accumulator
O. Manual valve and linkage
P. L-2 accumulator

a. Porosity check-case, passageways
b. Pumps—gears
c. Clutch seal rings
d. Intermediate servo
e. Forward clutch assembly
f. Forward clutch assembly
g. Intermediate band assembly
h. Low and reverse clutch assembly
i. Low and reverse roller clutch assembly
j. Converter assembly

CAPACITY AND GENERAL SPECIFICATIONS

Oil capacity (dry)	20 pints
Cooling	Water
Oil filter type	Suction screen
Clutch units	Three
Roller clutch	One
Band (adjustable)	One
Planetary gear sets	Two

Description

The Turbo Hydra-Matic 250 transmission is a fully automatic unit, consisting of a three element torque converter, two planetary gear sets, three multiple-disc clutches, one roller clutch, and an adjustable intermediate band. A radiator cooler is used to assist in the cooling of the transmission oil.

Transmission Disassembly

Converter and Modulator Valve

Removal

1. Clean the outside of the transmission case throughly, to prevent dirt from entering the unit during disassembly.
2. Install the transmission in a holding fixture or other suitable tool arrangement, and remove the converter assembly.
3. Remove the vacuum modulator assembly retainer and bolt, and remove the valve unit frm the transmission case. Discard the "O" ring from the modulator sleeve.

Rear Extension Housing and Components, Oil Pan and Screen

Removal

1. Remove four extension housing bolts, remove the housing from the case, and remove the square cut "O" ring seal from the extension housing.
2. With the aid of a puller, remove the speedometer drive gear and retaining clip.
3. Remove the governor cover, retained by a press fit into the case, by gently tapping along the cover lip, with the use of a screwdriver blade and light hammer.
4. Pull the governor assembly from the case, and inspect the case bore and governor sleeve for

scoring.

5. Remove the oil pan attaching screws, oil pan, and gasket.
6. Remove the oil pump suction screen attaching screws and remove the screen and gasket.

Valve Body and Linkage

Removal

1. Remove the detent spring and roller assembly from the valve body, and remove the body to case attaching bolts.
2. Remove the control wire by removing the actuator pin from the detent actuator valve lever.
3. Remove the manual control link and remove the valve body from the case.
4. Remove the intermediate servo return spring.
5. Remove the transfer support plate and bolts. Remove the upper gasket, transfer plate, and lower gasket.
6. Locate, mark, and remove the four check balls from the case.
7. Remove the oil pressure screen, and the governor feed screen from the holes in the case.
8. Remove the retainer for the manual control shaft with a screwdriver blade.
9. Loosen and remove the nut holding the range selector inner lever to the manual shaft.
10. Remove the range selector lever and parking pawl actuator rod from the case. Disengage the actuator rod from the inner lever.
11. Remove the parking lock, and lock bracket from the case.
12. Remove the parking pawl disengaging spring, parking pawl shaft retaining plug, shaft, and pawl.

CLUTCH AND BAND APPLICATION— TURBO HYDRA-MATIC 250 TRANSMISSION

GEAR	DIRECT	FORWARD	LOW AND REVERSE CLUTCH	LOW AND REVERSE ROLLER CLUTCH	INTERMEDIATE BAND
1st*	off	on	off	locked	off
2nd*	off	on	off	freewheeling	on
3rd*	on	on	off	freewheeling	off
low	off	on	on	freewheeling	off
reverse	on	off	on	freewheeling	off

* Transmission lever in "D" position

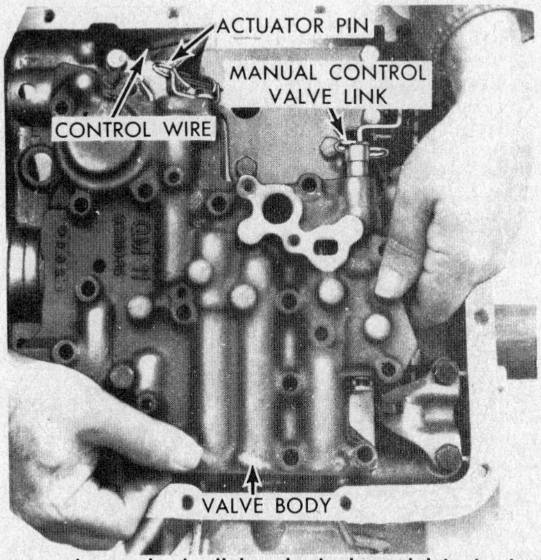

Removing manual control valve link, valve body, and detent actuating lever (© G.M. Corp.)

Internal Case Components and Oil Pump

Removal

1. Remove the front oil pump retaining bolts and washers.
2. By using two slide hammers, threaded into the pump body, remove the pump from the case.
3. Loosen the intermediate band anchor bolt and remove the band.
4. Remove the intermediate servo from the case, and disassembly can be accomplished by the re-

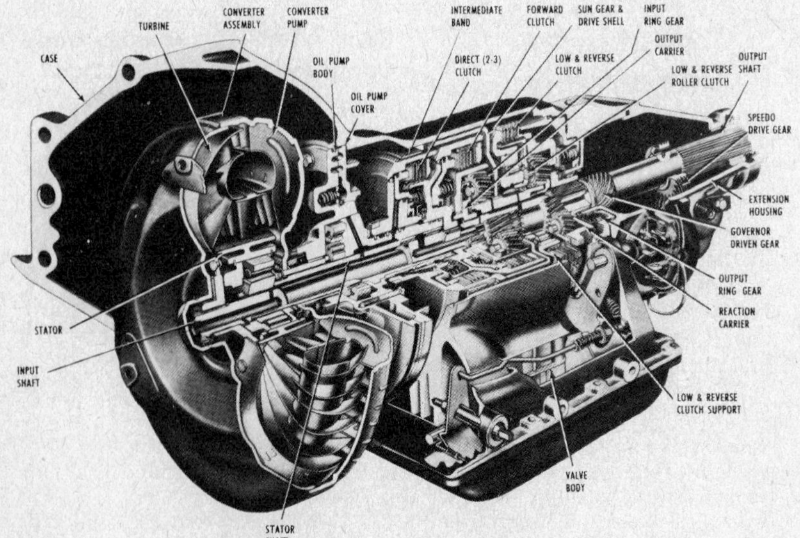

Sectional view—250 Turbo Hydra-Matic (© G.M. Corp.)

Governor cover removal (© G.M. Corp.)

Location of detent roller and spring (© G.M. Corp.)

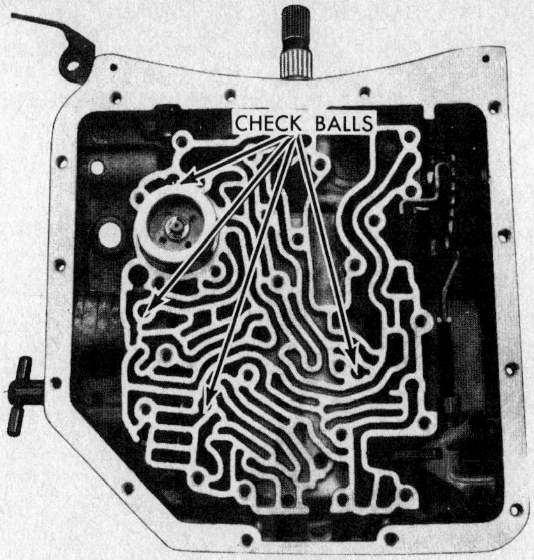

Check ball location in case pockets (© G.M. Corp.)

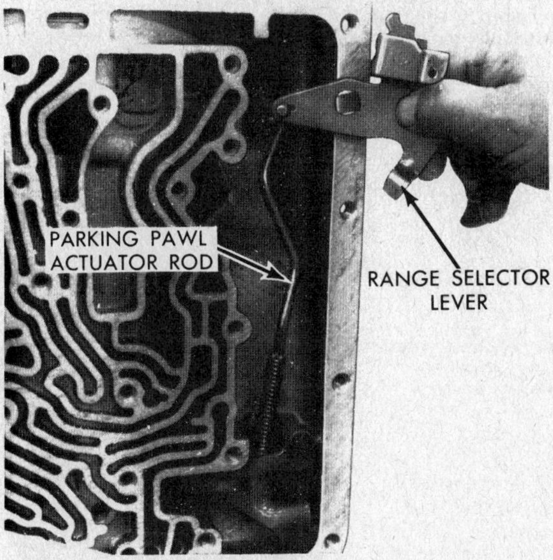

Removal of parking pawl actuator rod and range selector lever from case (© G.M. Corp.)

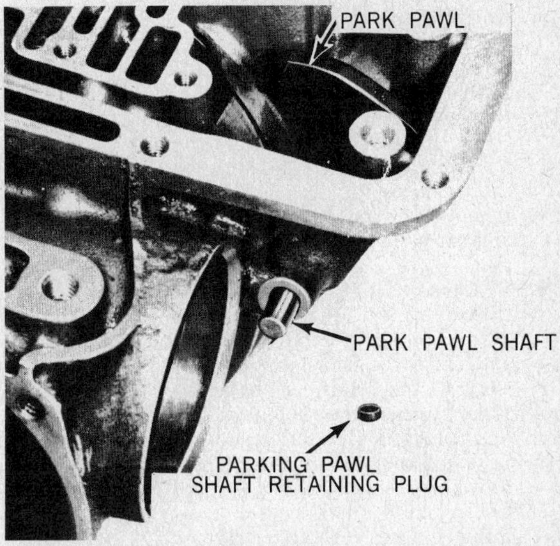

Parking pawl, shaft, and retaining plug (© G.M. Corp.)

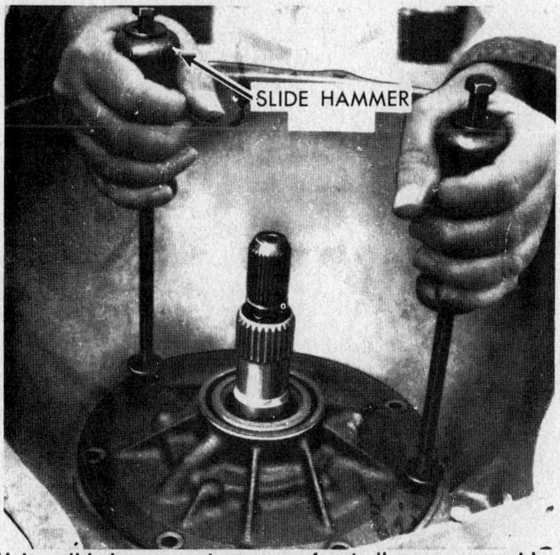

Using slide hammers to remove front oil pump assembly (© G.M. Corp.)

Intermediate band and anchor bolt (© G.M. Corp.)

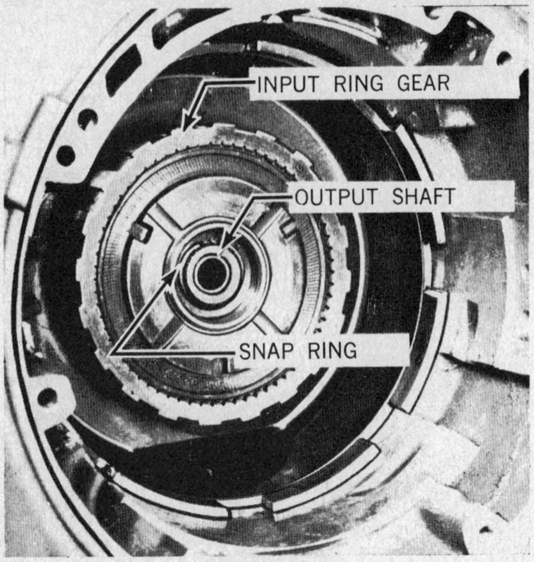

Removal of snap ring—retaining input ring gear to output shaft (© G.M. Corp.)

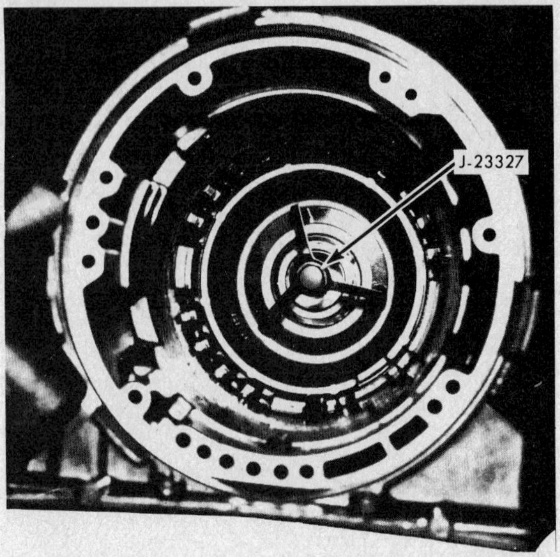

Compressing low and reverse clutch spring retainer with special tool usage (© G.M. Corp.)

moval of the snap rings at each end of the apply rod.

5. Remove the direct and forward clutch assemblies from the case.
6. Remove the input ring gear front thrust washer, noting the positions of the three tangs on the washer.
7. Remove the output shaft snap ring and remove the input ring gear.
8. Remove the input ring gear rear thrust washer and remove the output carrier assembly and the sungear drive shell assembly.
9. Remove the retaining snap ring from the case that holds the low and reverse roller clutch support in place, and remove the support assembly, the race assembly, and the anticlunk spring.
10. Remove the low and reverse clutch pack. (Steel and faced plates).
11. Separate the reaction carrier assembly from the output ring gear and shaft assembly.
12. Remove the tanged thrust washer and the output ring gear to case needle bearing assembly.
13. Compress the low and reverse clutch piston spring retainer and remove the nap ring and retainer. Remove the seventeen piston springs from the piston.
14. With air pressure applied to the low and reverse clutch piston apply passage, remove the piston from the case.
15. Remove the seals from the piston and inspect piston and bore for scoring.

Accumulator Valve

Removal

1. With the aid of a suitable tool, compress the accumulator piston cover inward, and remove the

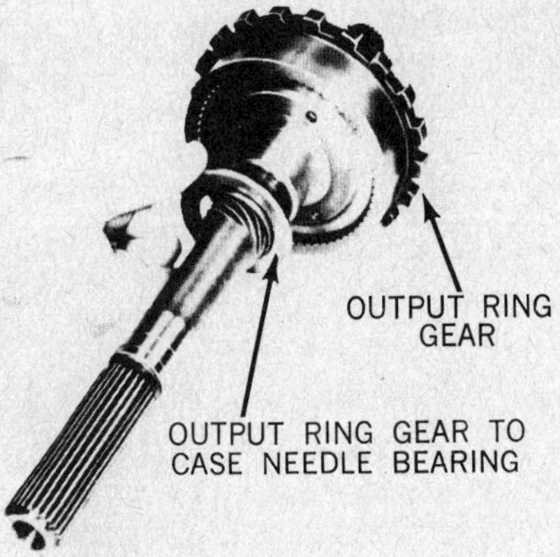

Output shaft, ring gear, and needle bearing assembly (© G.M. Corp.)

snap ring retainer.

2. Remove the cover, and piston spring.
3. Remove the 1-2 accumulator piston with the inner and outer hook type seals.

Location of apply passageway for low and reverse clutch piston (© G.M. Corp.)

Disassembly, Inspection, and Reassembly of Individual Components

Valve Body

Disassembly

1. Position the valve body with the core face up and the direct clutch accumulator piston pocket positioned to the upper left. *NOTE: The use of a multi-channelled steel or wood block assists in keeping the valves and springs in their proper order during the disassembly and assembly of the valve body.*
2. Remove the manual control valve, lower left.
3. From the lower right hand bore, remove the pressure regulator valve train, consisting of the retaining pin, boost valve sleeve, intermediate boost valve, reverse and modulator boost valve, pressure regulator valve and spring.
4. From the second right hand bore from the bottom, remove the 2-3 shift valve retaining pin, sleeve, control valve spring, 2-3 shift control valve, shift valve spring, and the 2-3 shift valve.
5. From the third bore, remove the retaining pin, sleeve, shift control valve spring, 1-2 control valve, and the 1-2 shift valve.
6. From the fourth bore, remove the retaining pin, plug, manual low control valve spring, and the manual low control valve.
7. From the fifth bore, remove the retaining pin, spring, seal, and detent regulator valve.
8. From the upper left bore, remove the detent actuating lever bracket bolt, bracket stop, spring

Exploded view—1-2 accumulator (© G.M. Corp.)

Removal and replacement of 1-2 accumulator piston cover retaining ring with special usage (© G.M. Corp.)

retainer, seat, outer and inner spring washers, and the detent valve.

Inspection

1. Inspect all the valves for scoring, cracks, distortion, and free movement in their respective bores.
2. Inspect all springs for distortion of the coils or being collapsed in length.
3. Inspect the valve body for cracks, scores in the bores, interconnected passageways, and flatness of the body.

Assembly

1. Reverse the disassembly procedures for the assembly of the valve body.
2. Lubricate the bores and valves with automatic transmission fluid during the assembly.

Oil Pump

Disassembly

1. Remove the pump cover to body attaching bolts.
2. Remove the two forward clutch oil seal rings and the three direct clutch oil seal rings from the pump hub.
3. Remove the selective thrust washer from the pump cover.
4. Separate the pump cover and stator shaft assembly from the pump body.
5. Remove the oil pump gears and "O" ring seal.

Inspection

1. Inspect the gears for nicks and abnormal wear patterns.
2. Inspect the pump body and cover for nicks and scoring.
3. Remove the outer seal and inspect the bushing for galling or scoring.
4. Install the pump gears into the body and measure the pump body to gear face clearance. The clearance should be .0005 to .0015 inch.
5. Check the oil passages in the body to insure of no restrictions.

Assembly

1. Replace the hub seal, using a non-harding sealer on the outer diameter of the seal, and seat it

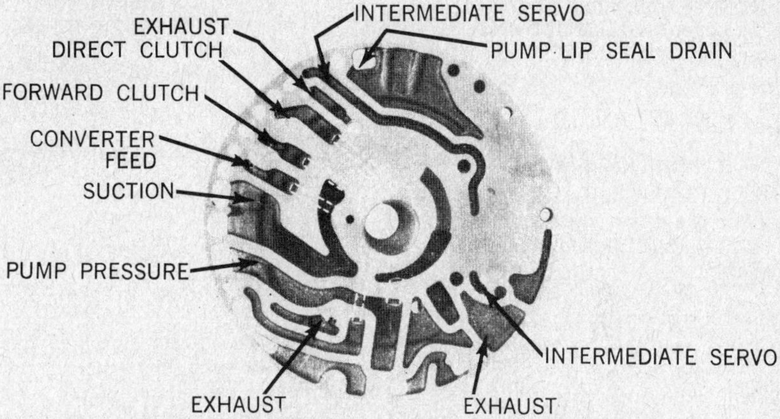

Oil passage locations in oil pump cover (© G.M. Corp.)

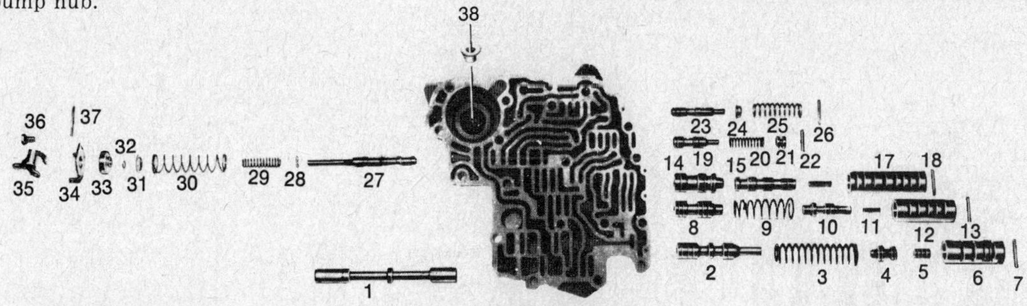

1 Manual valve
2 Pressure regulator valve
3 Pressure regulator valve spring
4 Reverse and modulator boost valve
5 Intermediate boost valve
6 Boost valve sleeve
7 Retaining pin
8 2-3 shift valve
9 2-3 shift valve spring
10 2-3 shift control valve
11 2-3 shift control valve spring
12 2-3 shift control valve sleeve
13 Retaining pin
14 1-2 shift valve
15 1-2 shift control valve
16 1-2 Shift control valve spring
17 1-2 shift control valve sleeve
18 Retaining pin
19 Manual low control valve
20 Manual low control valve spring
21 Plug
22 Retaining pin
23 Detent regulator valve
24 Detent regulator valve spring seat
25 Detent regulator valve spring
26 Retaining pin
27 Detent valve
28 Washer
29 Detent valve inner spring
30 Detent valve outer spring
31 Detent valve outer spring seat
32 Detent valve spring retainer
33 Detent valve stop
34 Detent valve actuating lever bracket
35 Detent valve actuating lever
36 Retaining bolt
37 Retaining pin
38 Cap

Exploded view—valve body—typical (© G.M. Corp.)

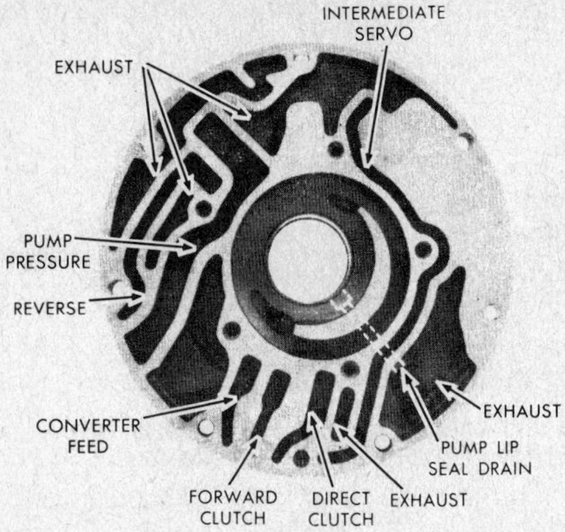

Oil passage locations in oil pump body (© G.M. Corp.)

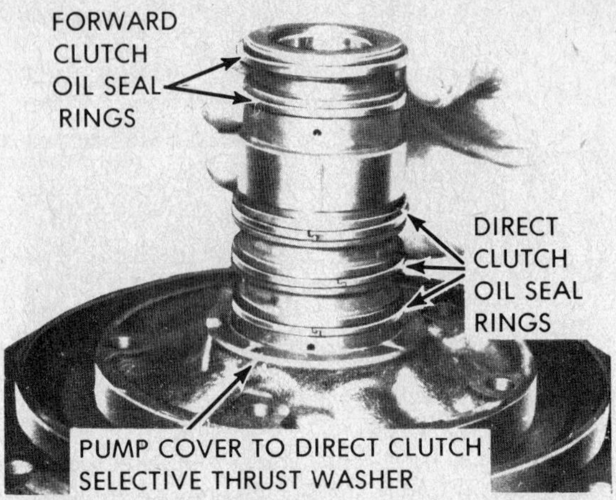

Location of hub oil seal rings and selective thrust washer (© G.M. Corp.)

firmly into the counter bore.

2. Install the drive and driven gears, and align the marks on the gears.
3. Install the pump cover thrust washer, the three direct clutch oil seal rings, and the two forward clutch oil seal ring.
4. Install the pump outside diameter "O" ring, align the body to the cover, and install the five attaching bolts, torquing them to 18 ft. lbs.

Direct Clutch

Disassembly

1. Remove retaining snap ring from the direct clutch drum and remove the direct clutch pressure plate.
2. Remove the clutch pack, consisting of three lined and three steel plates, and the cushion spring.
3. With the aid of a compression tool, remove the direct clutch retaining ring, spring seat, and seventeen clutch return coil springs.
4. Remove the direct clutch piston from the direct clutch drum.
5. Remove the piston outer and inner seals.

Alignment of oil pump gears (© G.M. Corp.)

Inspection

1. Inspect the drive and driven clutch plates for signs of overheating, scoring, or wear.
2. Inspect the seventeen springs for being collapsed or distorted.

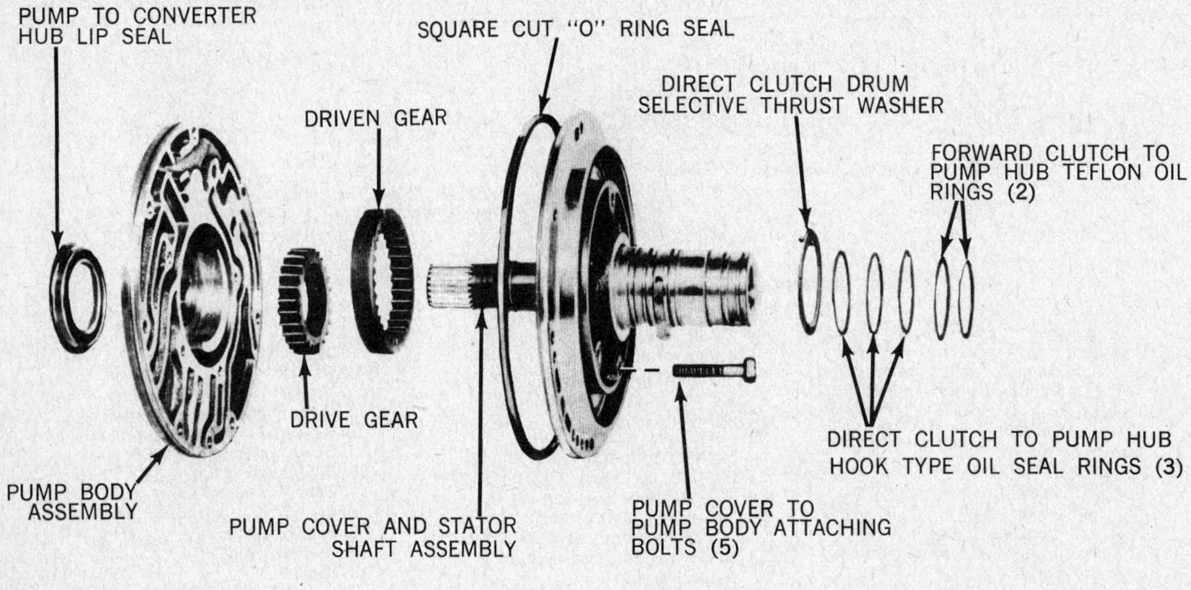

Exploder view—oil pump assembly (© G.M. Corp.)

Checking gear face to pump body clearance (© G.M. Corp.)

3. Inspect piston for cracks or scoring, ad the direct clutch drum piston seal mating surfaces for scores, wear, oil passages open, and free operation of the check ball.

Assembly

1. Install new inner and outer seals on the direct clutch piston and install it into the drum housing. *NOTE: Lubricate the seals with automatic transmission fluid and aid in the installation of the seals with the use of a feeler gauge blade or a .020 inch piano wire, crimped into a copper tubing.*

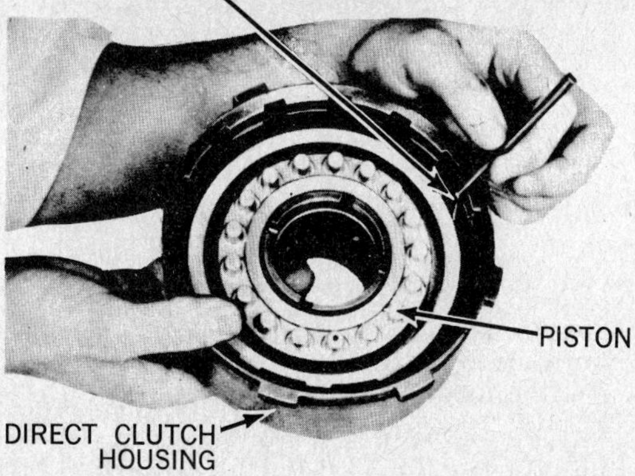

Use of piano wire to assist in the installation of piston seals—typical (© G.M. Corp.)

2. Install the seventeen clutch return springs.
3. Install the return spring seat, compress with a compression type tool, and install the retaining snap ring.
4. Install the clutch pack, beginning with the cushion spring, and alternating with the steel plates and the lined plates.
5. Install the direct clutch pressure plate and retaining rings.

Forward Clutch

Disassembly

1. Remove the needle roller bearing from the forward clutch housing.
2. Remove the retaining ring and pressure plate from the forward clutch drum.
3. Remove the clutch pack from the drum.
4. With the aid of a compression tool, remove the retaining ring and the piston return seat.
5. Remove the twenty-one clutch return springs.

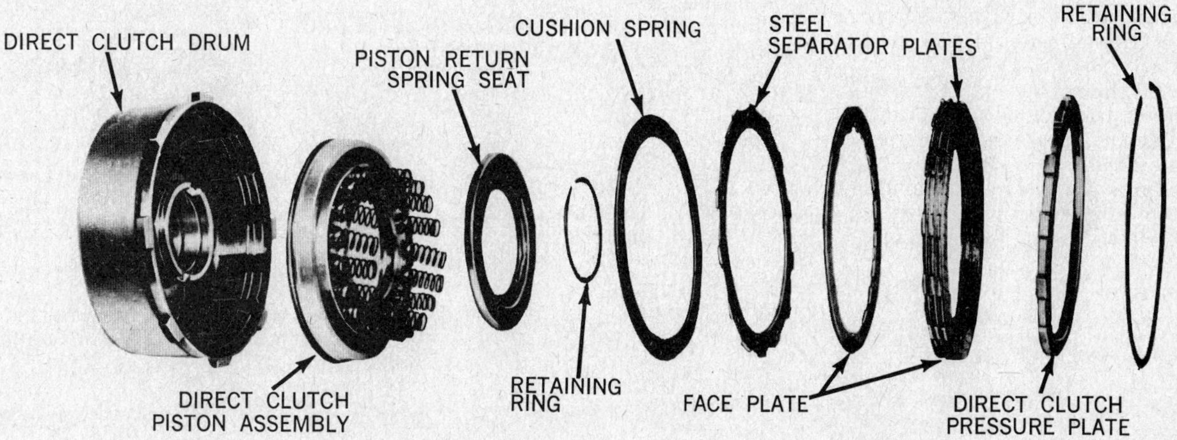

Exploded view—direct clutch assembly (© G.M. Corp.)

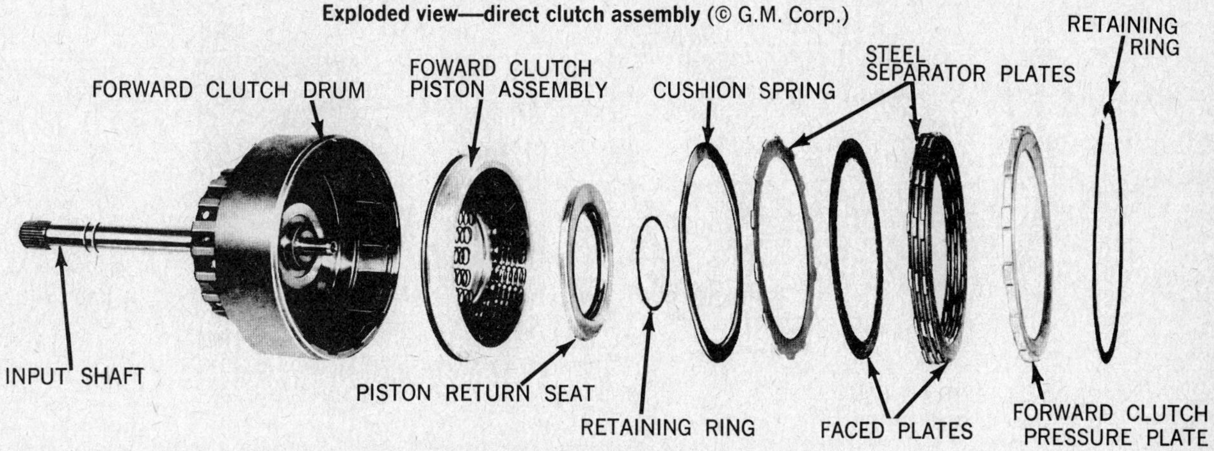

Exploded view—forward clutch assembly (© G.M. Corp.)

6. Remove the forward clutch piston assembly and remove the inner and outer piston seal.

Inspection

1. Inspect the clutch pack for signs of wear, scoring, or overheating.
2. Inspect the twenty-one springs for distortion, or having collapsed coils.
3. Inspect the piston for cracked or scored surfaces, and the forward clutch drum piston seal mating surface for scores, wear, oil passages open, and free operation of the ball check.

Assembly

1. Install new inner and outer seals on the piston and install it into the forward clutch drum housing.
   NOTE: Lubricate the seals with automatic transmission fluid and aid in the installation of the seals with the use of a feeler gauge blade or a .020 inch piano wire, crimped into a copper tubing.
2. Install the twenty-one clutch return springs.
3. Install the spring retainer and compress, and install the snap ring.
4. Install the cushion spring face plate and steel separator plates, starting with the cushion spring and alternating steel and lined plates.
5. Install the pressure plate and retaining ring and determine, by measuring, the proper presure plate needed.
6. Measure the distance from the top of clutch pack to the top of the clutch drum, (A). Measure the distance from the lower edge of the notch on the inner surface of the drum end of the drum (B). Subtract B from A to obtain dimension C.
7. Obtain the proper thickness pressure plate from the following chart.

When dimension C is:	Use (or equivalent)
.0160-.0520	6261072 (GM #)
.0520-.0830	6261349 (GM #)
.0830-.1218	6261350 (GM #)

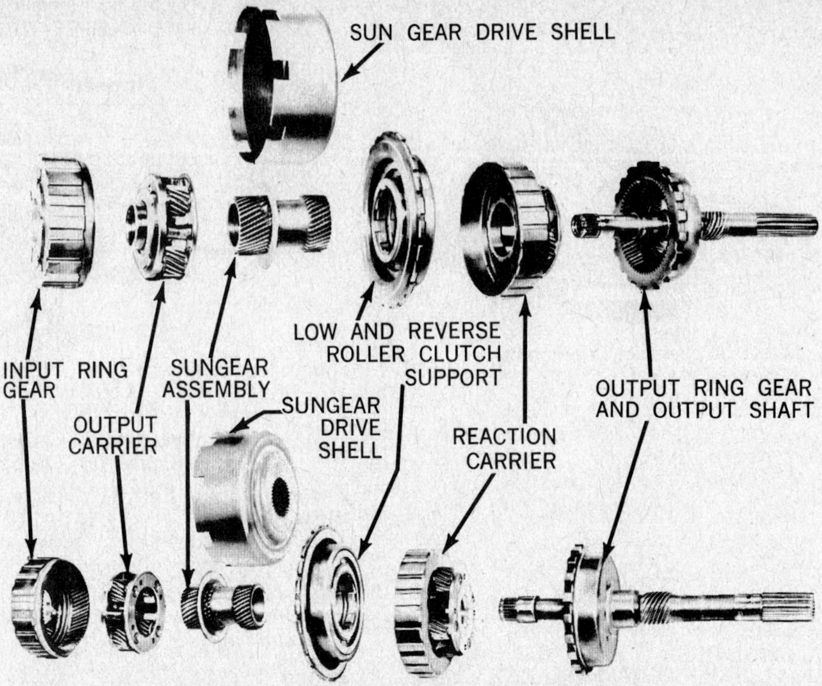

Exploded view—planetary gear train (© G.M. Corp.)

WHEN DIM. C IS	USE (OR EQUIVALENT)
.0160— .0520	6261072
.0520— .0830	6261349
.0830— .1218	6261350

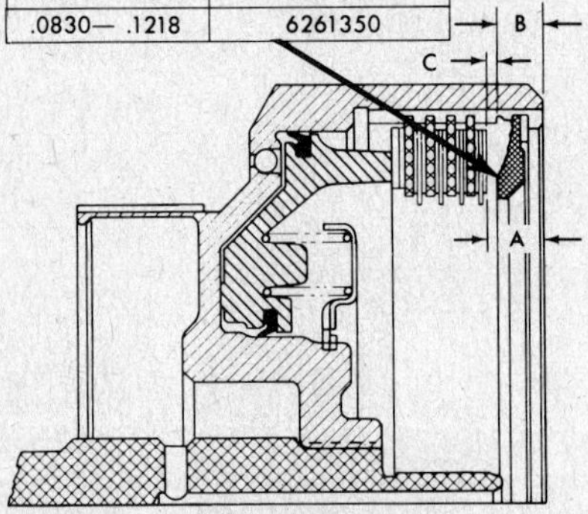

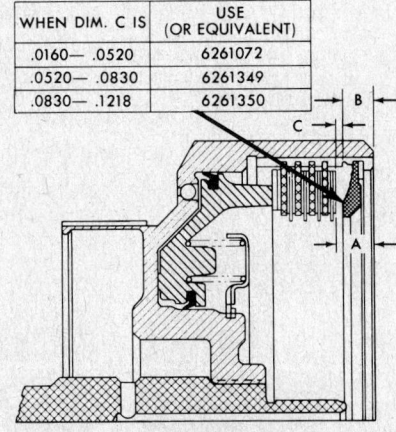

Selecting forward clutch pressure plate —through measurement (© G.M. Corp.)

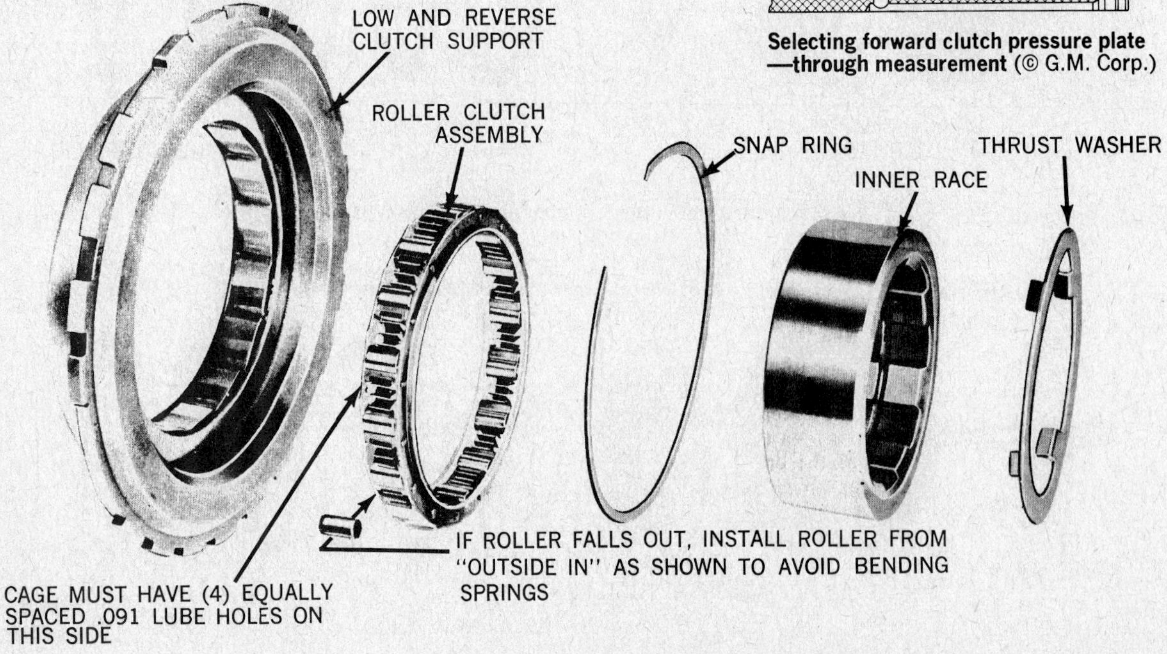

Exploded view—low and reverse clutch assembly (© G.M. Corp.)

Sun Gear and Sun Gear Drive Shaft

Disassembly

1. Remove the retaining snap ring from the sun gear hub, and remove the flat thrust washer.
2. Remove the sun gear assembly from the drive shell.
3. Remove the sun gear to drive shell front retaining snap ring and discard.

Inspection

1. Inspect the shell and sun gear for wear or damage.

Assembly

1. Install new sun gear to drive shell front retaining snap ring.
2. Install the sun gear assembly into the drive shell.
3. Install the flat steel thrust washer and retaining snap ring on the sun gear hub.

Low and Reverse Roller Clutch Support

Disassembly

1. Remove the thrust washer from the inner race and remove the race from the support.
2. Remove the low and reverse clutch roller retaining ring.
3. Remove the roller clutch from the support.

Inspection

1. Inspect the rollers, races, for scratches, indentations, wear and distortion of the roller springs.

Assembly

1. Install the roller clutch assembly into the inner race with the oil holes towards the rear of the transmission.
2. Install the outer race and the retaining snap ring into the groove on the clutch support. *NOTE: The low and reverse overrun clutch inner race should free wheel in the clockwise direction only.*

Governor Assembly

NOTE: The components of the governor assembly, except the driven gear, are a select fit and each assembly is calibrated and is serviced as a complete assembly. The driven gear can be serviced separately, but the governor assembly must be disassembled to replace it. A repair kit is available, which consists of a gear, gear retainer pin, and two governor weight retaining pins.

The following procedure involves the replacement of the driven gear.

Disassembly

1. Cut off one end of each governor weight pin and remove the pins.
2. Remove the governor valve from the sleeve and carrier assembly.
3. Drive out the driven gear retaining split pin.
4. With the aid of a press, force the driven gear out of the sleeve.
5. Press the new gear into the sleeve and carrier assembly, cleaning any chips from the gear hub before bottoming it on the sleeve shoulder.
6. Locate a new pin hole, 90 degrees from the existing hole, and drill through the sleeve and gear, using a 1/8 inch drill bit.
7. Install the new split pin and clean the governor of any chips that may have collected.

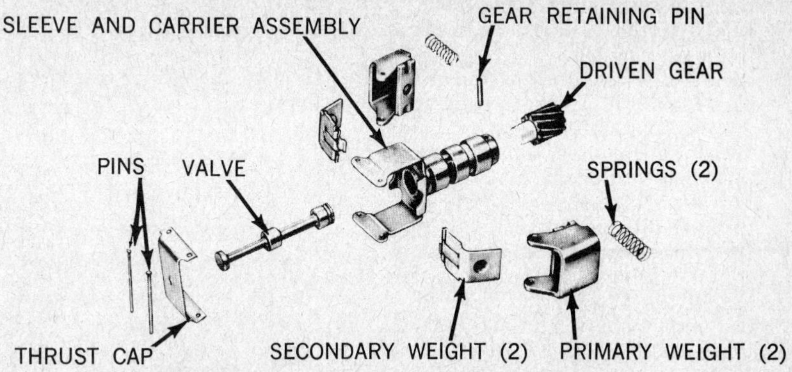

Exploded view—governor assembly—typical (© G.M. Corp.)

Inspection

While the governor is out of its bore and disassembled, it should be inspected for the following defects:

1. Inspect the sleeve and carrier assembly, and the governor valve for nicks, burrs, scoring, or galling.
2. Inspect the governor valve for free operation in the bore of the governor sleeve.
3. Inspect the governor weights and springs for freedom of operation, distortion, and looseness.

Assembly

1. Install the governor valve into the bore of the sleeve and carrier assembly.
2. Install the governor weights and springs, along with the thrust caps, on the sleeve assembly.
3. Align the holes of the thrust caps, governor sleeve, and weight assemblies, and install the new pins. Crimp the ends of the pins to prevent them from coming out.
4. Check the weights and governor valve for free movement.

Bushing Replacement

Most internal bushings are replaceable, and the use of the proper removal and installation tools are most important when replacement is needed, to insure proper alignment, and to avoid installation damage to the bushings by using improper tools. It is advisable to match the installed bushing to its operating surface before the transmission is assembled to insure proper bushing fit.

Transmission Assembly

Transmission Internal Components

Assembly

1. Install the low and reverse clutch

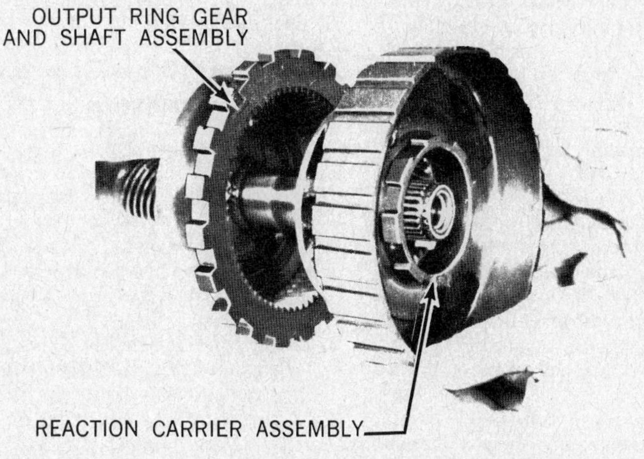

Reaction carrier assembly (© G.M. Corp.)

piston assembly, with the notch in the piston installed adjacent to the parking pawl.

2. Install the seventeen piston return springs, spring retainer, and retainer ring.
3. With the use of a compressing tool, compress the return seat so the retaining snap ring can be installed into its groove.
4. Install the output ring gear rear thrust bearing in the case.
5. Install the output ring gear on the output shaft, and the reaction carrier to output ring gear front thrust washer, (three tanged), into the output ring gear support.
6. Install the output shaft into the case and install the reaction carrier assembly into the output ring gear and shaft assembly.
7. Starting with a steel plate, and alternating with a lined plate, install the low and reverse clutch pack. Install the clutch support retainer, (anti-clunk), spring. *NOTE: Notch in the steel separator plates should be placed towards the bottom of the case.*
8. Align the splines on the inner race of the roller clutch with the splines on the reaction carrier, and install the low and reverse support assembly with the notch aligned with the support retainer (anti-clunk) spring.
9. Install the thrust washer on the low and reverse roller clutch inner race.
10. Install the retainer snap ring for the low and reverse clutch support into the case groove, with the anti-clunk spring between the gap.
11. Install the rear thrust washer and the sun gear drive shell assembly, and install the output carrier assembly.
12. Install the input ring gear rear thrust washer and install the input ring gear and retain it with a snap ring.
13. Install the input gear front thrust washer, direct clutch assembly, and special thrust washer to forward clutch assembly.
14. Install the forward and direct clutch assemblies into the case. *NOTE: Assure that forward clutch face plates are positioned over the input ring gear and the tangs on the direct clutch housing are installed into the slots on the sun gear drive shell.*
15. Install the intermedidate servo and intermediate band. Tighten the adjusting screw enough to engage the slot in the band lug.
16. Temporarily install the oil pump with the selective thrust washer and gasket in place, using two guide bolts to position pump.

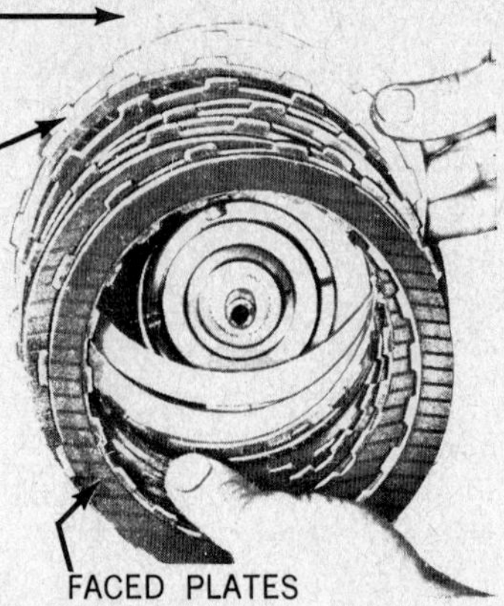

Typical clutch pack (© G.M. Corp.)

17. Install two pump to case bolts and tighten snugly.
18. Position the transmission so that the input shaft points down, and install a dial indicator to contact the input shaft and zero the indicator.
19. Lift upward on the input shaft and note the total indicator movement. The proper limits are from .032 to .064 inch. If the readings are not correct, the pump must be removed and thicker or thinner selective washers must be obtained *NOTE: Selective fit Thrust washers are available in the following thicknesses.*
   .065-.067
   .082-.084
   .099-.101
21. Install the pump assembly with a new gasket and "O" ring.

   CAUTION: If the input shaft cannot be rotated as the pump is placed into the case, the direct and forward clutch housing and clutches have not been properly installed. Correct the condition before continuing.
22. Adjust the intermedidate band by adjusting the screw to 30 in. lbs. and backing off three complete turns, and tightening the lock nut to 15 ft lbs.

Speedometer Drive Gear and Extension Housing

Assembly

1. Install the speedometer gear retaining clip on to the output shaft.
2. Heat a new gear with a heat lamp or another suitable source. *NOTE: Do not use a torch or open flame.*
3. Align the slot in the drive gear with the retainer clip and install the gear on the output shaft.
4. Install the "O" ring seal on the extension housing, install the housing to the case, and torque the attaching bolts to 25 ft lbs.
5. Install a new extension housing seal.

Manual Linkage

Assembly

1. Install the parking pawl, tooth towards the inside of the case, install the pawl shaft into the case and through the parking pawl, and install the shaft retainer plug, staking in three places to retain it in the case.
2. Install the parking pawl disengaging spring, square end hooked on the pawl.
3. Install the park lock bracket and torque the bolts to 29 ft lbs.
4. Install the range selector inner lever to the parking pawl actuator rod, and position it under the park lock bracket and parking pawl.
5. Install the manual shaft through the case and range selector inner lever, and install the retaining nut on the manual shaft.
6. Install the manual shaft to case spacer clip.

Valve Body, Oil Pan, and Gasket Assembly

Assembly

1. Install the governor feed screen and oil pump pressure screen.
2. Install the four check balls into their respective case pockets.
3. Install the lower gasket and transfer plate, followed by the upper valve gasket.
4. Install the intermediate servo return spring.
5. Install the valve body and connect the manual control valve link to the range selector inner lever. Torque the bolts to 130 in. lbs.
6. Install the transfer support plate and torque the bolts to 130 in. lbs.
7. Connect the detent control valve wire to the detent valve actuating lever, and attach the lever to the valve body.

Location of oil pump pressure screen (© G.M. Corp.)

Location of governor feed screen (© G.M. Corp.)

8. Install the detent roller and spring assembly to the valve body.
9. Install the suction screen and gasket.
10. Install the oil pan and gasket, and torque the bolts to 130 in. lbs.

Governor and Vacuum Modulator

Assembly

1. Install the governor assembly, cover and seal. Tap the cover into place on the case.
2. Install the vacuum modulator valve, modulator and retainer clip. Torque bolt to 130 in. lbs.

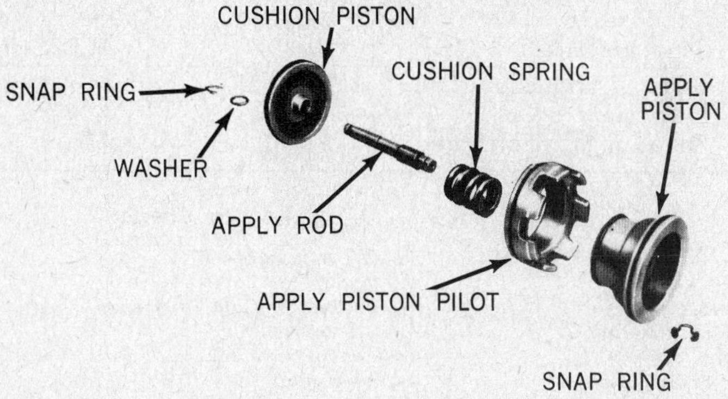

Exploded view—intermediate servo (© G.M. Corp.)

Accumulator

Assembly

1. Install the 1-2 accumulator piston assembly and spring.
2. Install new "O" ring in the case groove and install the cover.
3. Compress the cover and install the retaining snap ring.

Converter

Assembly

1. Engage the converter to the splines of the input shaft and the stator shaft assembly.
2. Install a holding bracket to the converter from the case, so as not to lose the converter during the installation into the vehicle.

Removing 1-2 accumulator piston cover retaining ring (© G.M. Corp.)

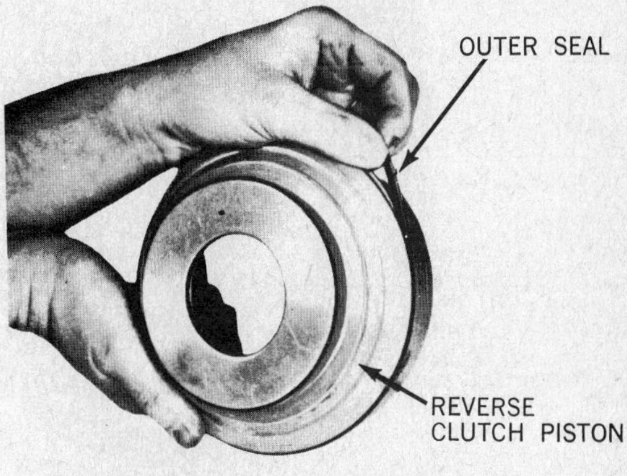

Removing low and reverse clutch outer seal (© G.M. Corp.)

DIAGNOSIS

This diagnosis guide is a list of the most common troubles and their causes. The items to check are listed in the sequence to be followed.

TROUBLE SYMPTOMS	Items to Check: In Truck	Items to Check: Out of Truck
Slips in all ranges	ACDFGMO	N
Drive slips—no 1st gear	ACDFGMO	NQV
No 1-2 upshift	BEFGH	SU
1-2 upshift, early or late	BEFH	
Slips, 1-2 upshift	ACFGHL	NSU
Harsh 1-2 upshift	BCG	
No 2-3 upshift	FI	R
2-3 upshift, early/late	BCEFIK	
Slips, 2-3 upshift	ACFGI	NR
Harsh 2-3 upshift	BCGIL	
No full throttle downshift	K	
2-3 upshift, wide open throttle only	BK	
L_1 gear—no engine braking	GHJM	PQU
Car drives in neutral	K	Q
Slips in reverse	ACDFGHMO	RT
1-2, 2-3 shift noisy	A	RSY
Noisy in all ranges	ADFO	NXYW
Spews oil out of breather	AD	

Key to Checks

A. Low oil level/water in oil
B. Vacuum leak
C. Modulator and/or valve
D. Strainer and/or gasket leak
E. Governor valve/screen
F. Valve body gasket/plate
G. Pressure regulator and/or boost valve
H. 1-2 shift valve
I. 2-3 shift valve
J. Manual low control valve
K. Detent valve and linkage
L. 2-3 accumulator
M. Manual valve linkage
N. Pump gears
O. Gasket screen-pressure
P. Band—intermediate overrun roller clutch
Q. Forward clutch assembly
R. Direct clutch assembly
S. Intermediate clutch assembly
T. Low & reverse clutch assembly
U. Intermediate roller clutch
V. Low & reverse roller clutch
W. Parking pawl/linkage
X. Converter assembly
Y. Gear set and bearings

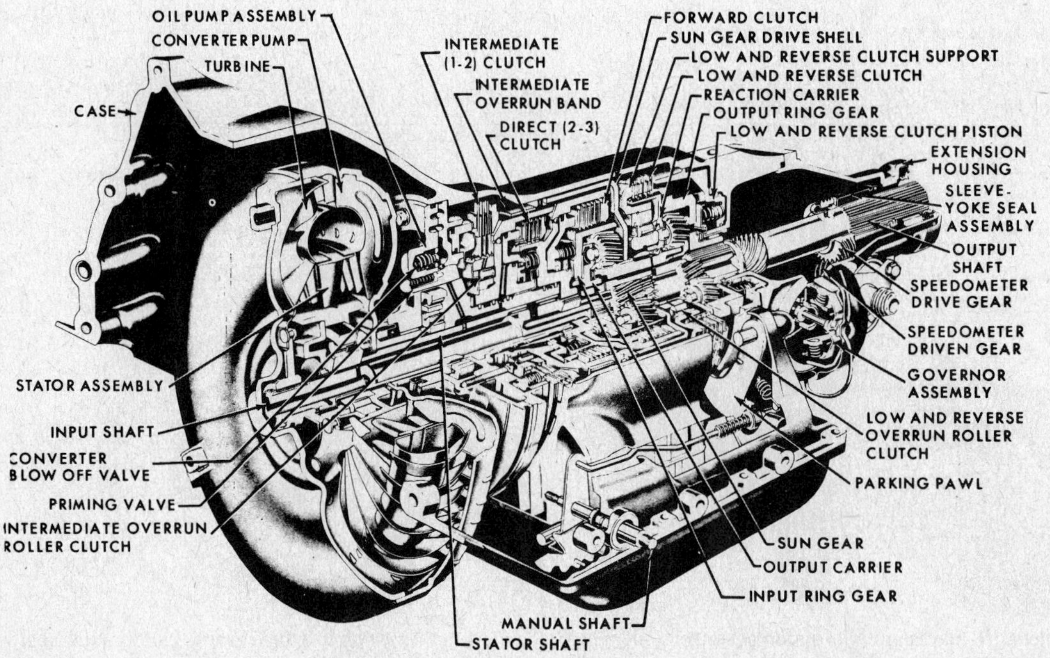

Sectional view of the General Motors Turbo Hydra-Matic 350 (© General Motors)

General Description

The 350 Turbo Hydra-Matic transmission is a fully automatic unit, consisting of a three element torque converter, two planetary gear sets, four multiple-disc clutches, two roller clutches, and an non-adjustable intermediate band. A radiator cooler is used to assist in the cooling of the transmission oil.

CAPACITY AND GENERAL SPECIFICATIONS

Oil Capacity (dry) ....20 Pints
Cooling ....Water
Oil Filter Type
..........Bottom Suction Screen
Clutches 4
Roller Clutches 2
Band (non-adjustable) 1

Check ball locations (© G.M. Corp.)

Transmission Disassembly

Clean outside of transmission thoroughly to prevent dirt from entering the unit.

1. With transmission in a holding fixture, lift off torque converter assembly.
2. Remove vacuum modulator assembly attaching bolt and retainer.
3. Remove vacuum modulator assembly, O-ring seal and modulator valve from the case.
4. Remove four extension housing-to-case attaching bolts.
5. Remove extension housing and the square cut O-ring seal.
6. Remove extension housing lip seal from output end of housing, using a screwdriver.
7. Remove extension housing bushing, using chisel to collapse bushing.
8. Drive in new extension housing bushing.
9. Install extension housing lip seal.
10. Depress speedometer drive gear retaining clip, then slide speedometer drive gear off output shaft.
11. Remove governor cover retainer wire with a screwdriver.
12. Remove governor cover and O-ring seal from case, then remove O-ring seal from governor cover.
13. Remove governor assembly from case.

    NOTE: Check governor bore and sleeve for scoring.
14. Remove oil pan attaching screws, pan, and gasket.
15. Remove two oil pump suction screen (strainer) to valve body attaching screws.
16. Remove oil pump screen (strainer) and gasket from valve body.
17. Remove detent roller and spring assembly from valve body. Remove valve body-to-case attaching bolts.
18. Remove manual control valve link from range selector inner lever. Remove valve body. Remove detent control valve link from detent actuating lever.

    NOTE: Refer to later text for valve body disassembly and passage identification.

    NOTE: At this time, when handling valve body assembly, do not touch sleeves, because retaining pins may fall into the transmission.
19. Remove valve body-to-spacer plate gasket.
20. Remove spacer support plate gasket. Remove spacer support plate.
21. Remove valve body spacer plate and plate-to-case gasket.
22. Remove four check balls from passages in case face.

    NOTE: If, during assembly, any of the balls are omitted or installed in the wrong locations, transmission failure will result.
23. Remove oil pump pressure screen from oil pump pressure hole in the case.
24. Remove governor feed screen from governor feed passage in case. Remove the manual control valve link from the range selector inner lever.
25. Remove manual shaft to case retainer with a screwdriver.
26. Remove jam nut holding range selector inner lever to manual shaft. Remove manual shaft.
27. Disconnect parking pawl actuating rod from range selector inner lever. Remove both from case.
28. Remove manual shaft to case lip oil seal, using a screwdriver.

CLUTCH AND BAND APPLICATION— 350 TURBO HYDRA-MATIC TRANSMISSION

GEAR	INTER-MEDIATE CLUTCH	DIRECT CLUTCH	FORWARD CLUTCH	LOW AND REVERSE CLUTCH	INTER-MEDIATE OVERRUN BAND	LOW AND REVERSE ROLLER CLUTCH	INTER-MEDIATE OVERRUN ROLLER CLUTCH
1st*	off	off	on	off	off	Locked	Locked
2nd*	on	off	on	off	off	Freewheel	Locked
3rd*	on	on	on	off	off	Freewheel	Freewheel
Low	off	off	on	on	off	Locked	Locked
Reverse	off	on	off	on	off	Freewheel	Freewheel

* Gear shift lever in "D" position

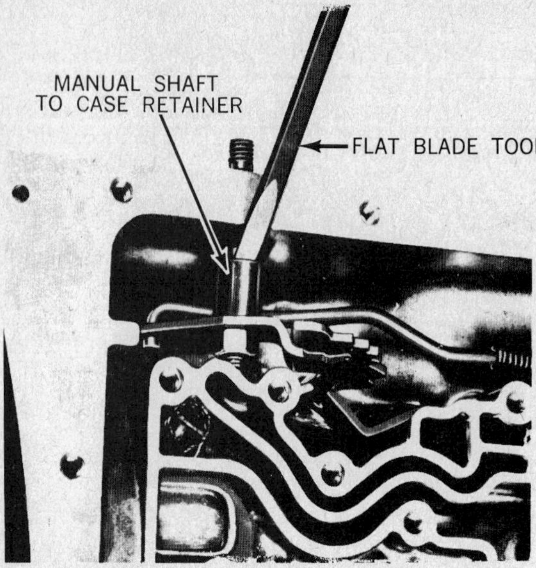

Removing the manual shift to case retainer (© G.M. Corp.)

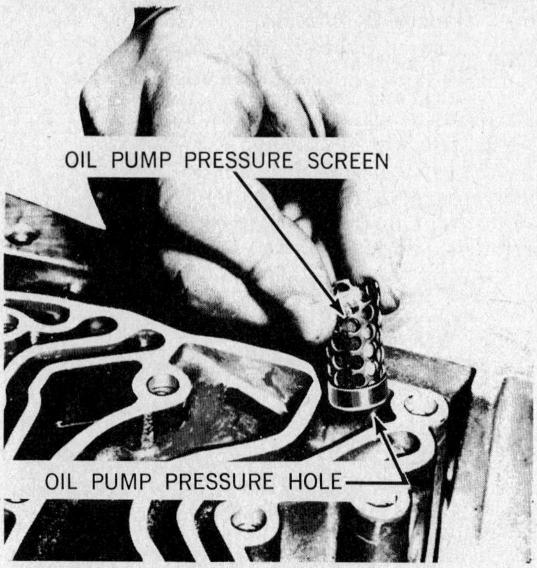

Removing the oil pump pressure screen (© G.M. Corp.)

29. Remove parking lock bracket.
30. Disconnect and remove parking pawl disengaging spring.
31. Remove parking pawl shaft retaining plug with a bolt extractor. Cock parking pawl on shaft. Using drift and hammer, tap on drift to force the parking pawl shaft from the case. Remove the parking pawl.
32. Remove intermediate servo piston and metal oil seal ring. Remove washer, spring seat, and apply pin.
33. Remove eight pump attaching bolts with washer-type seals. Discard seals.
34. Install two threaded slide hammers into threaded holes in pump body. Tighten jam nuts and remove pump assembly from the case.
35. Remove pump assembly to case gasket and discard.
36. Remove intermediate clutch cushion spring.
37. Remove intermediate clutch faced plates and steel separator plates. Inspect lined plates for pitting, flaking, wear, glazing, cracking and chips or metal particles imbedded in lining. Replace any lined plates showing any of these conditions. Inspect steel plates for heat spot discoloration or surface scuffing. If the surface is smooth and has an even color smear, the steel plates may be re-used.
38. Remove intermediate clutch pressure plate.
39. Remove intermediate overrun brake band.
40. Remove direct and forward clutch assemblies.
41. Remove forward clutch housing-to-input ring gear front thrust washer.

NOTE: Washer has three tangs.

42. Remove output carrier-to-output shaft snap-ring.
43. Remove input ring gear.
44. Remove input ring gear to output carrier thrust washer.
45. Remove output carrier assembly.
46. Remove sun gear drive shell assembly.
47. Remove low and reverse roller clutch support to case retaining ring.
48. Remove low and reverse roller clutch, support assembly, and retaining spring.
49. Remove low and reverse clutch faced plates and steel separator plates.
50. Remove reaction carrier assembly from output ring gear and shaft assembly.
51. Remove output ring gear and shaft assembly from case.
52. Remove reaction carrier to output ring gear tanged thrust washer.
53. Remove output ring gear-to-case needle bearing assembly.
54. Compress low and reverse clutch piston spring retainer and remove piston retaining ring and spring retainer.
55. Remove 17 piston return coil springs from piston.
56. Remove low and reverse clutch piston by application of air pressure.
57. Remove low and reverse clutch piston outer seal.
58. Remove low and reverse clutch piston center and inner seal.
59. Install suitable tool to compress intermediate clutch accumulator cover and remove retaining ring.
60. Remove intermediate clutch accumulator piston cover. Remove cover O-ring seal from case.
61. Remove intermediate clutch accumulator piston spring.
62. Remove intermediate clutch accumulator piston assembly. Remove inner and outer hook-type oil seal rings if required.

Component Disassembly

Valve Body

Disassembly

1. Position valve body assembly with cored face up and direct clutch accumulator piston pocket located as illustrated in valve body assembly illustration.
2. Remove manual valve from lower left-hand bore, A.
3. From lower right-hand bore, B, remove the pressure regulator valve train retaining pin, boost valve sleeve, intermediate boost valve, reverse and modulator boost valve, pressure regulator valve spring, and the pressure regulator valve.
4. From the next bore, C, remove the second-third shift valve train retaining pin, sleeve, control valve spring, second-third shift control valve, shift valve spring, and the second-third shift valve.
5. From the next bore, D, remove the first-second shift valve train retaining pin, sleeve, shift control valve spring, first-second shift control valve, and the first-second shift valve.
6. From the next bore, E, remove retaining pin, plug, manual low control valve spring, and the manual low control valve.
7. From the next bore, F, remove retaining pin, spring seat and the detent regulator valve.

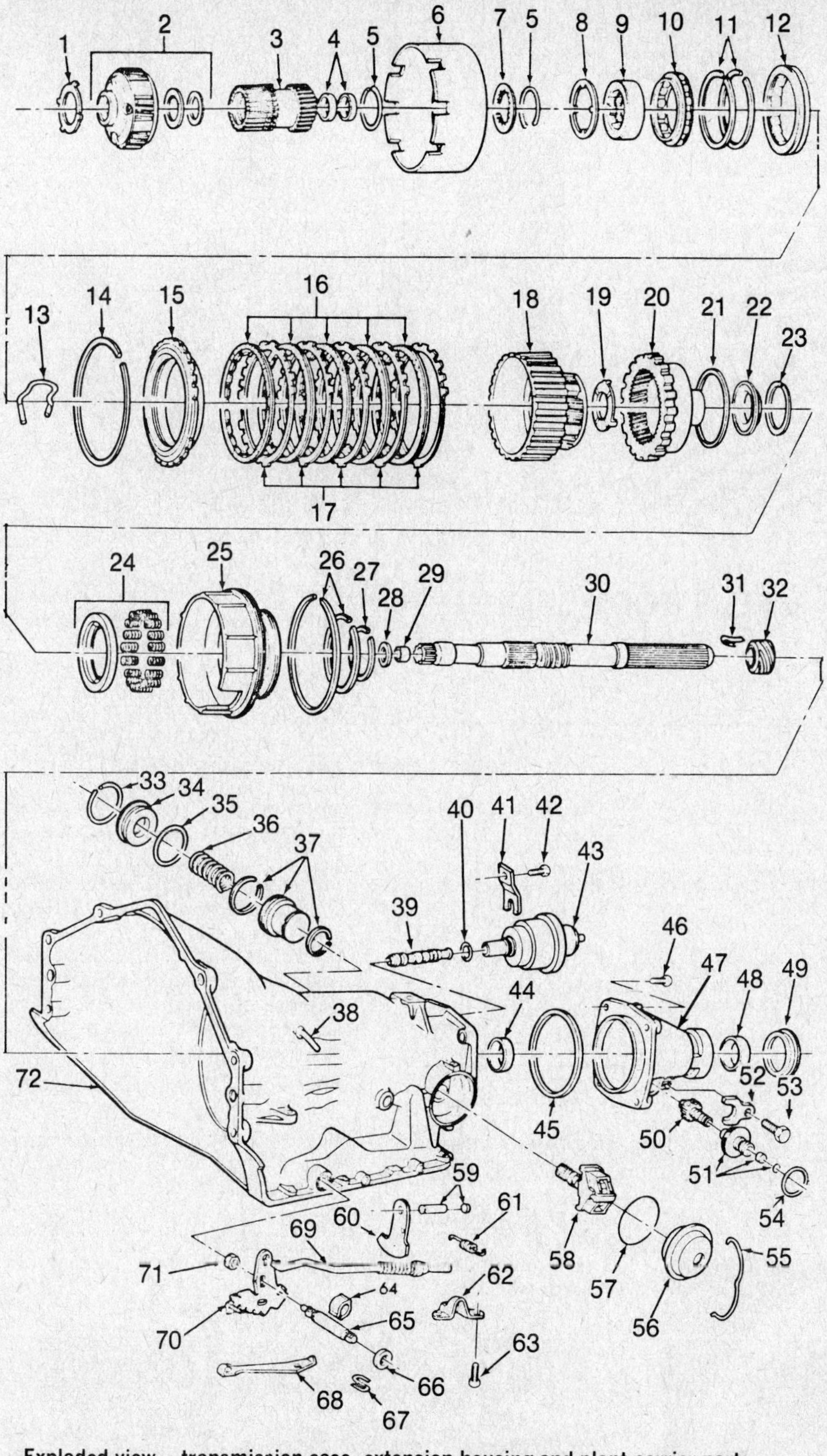

Exploded view—transmission case, extension housing and plant carrier parts
(© G.M. Corp.)

1 Input ring gear thrust washer
2 Output planet carrier assembly
3 Sun gear assembly
4 Sun gear bushings
5 Sun gear drive shell retaining ring
6 Sun gear drive shell
7 Sun gear thrust washer
8 Sun gear rear thrust washer
9. Low and reverse clutch race
10 Low and reverse clutch assembly
11 Low and recerse clutch ring
12 Low and reverse clutch cam (part of support assembly)
13 Low and reverse clutch support spring
14 Low and reverse clutch support spring retainer
15 Low and reverse clutch support assembly
16 Low and reverse reaction plate
17 Low and reverse clutch drive plate assy
18 Reaction planet carrier assembly
19 Output ring gear front thrust washer
20 Output ring gear
21 Output ring
22 Output ring gear rear thrust bearing
23 Output ring gear support to output shaft ring
24 Low and reverse clutch seat assembly with springs
25 Low and reverse clutch piston
26 Low and reverse clutch piston seal unit
27 Low and reverse clutch piston return spring seat retainer
28 Reaction planet carrier bushing
29 Output shaft bushing
30 Output shaft assembly
31 Drive gear retaining clip
32 Speedometer drive gear
33 Intermediate clutch accumulator piston retainer
34 Intermediate clutch accumulator piston cover
35 Intermediate clutch piston accumulator cover seal
36 Intermediate clutch accumulator piston spring
37 Intermediate clutch accumulator piston assembly with seals
38 Case vent assembly
39 Vacuum modulator valve assembly
40 Vacuum modulator to transmission case seal
41 Vacuum modulator retainer
42 Vacuum modulator to transmission bolt
43 Vacuum modulator
44 Transmission case bushing
45 Extension housing to case seal
46 Extension housing to transmission case bolt
47 Extension housing assembly
48 Extension housing bushing
49 Extension housing oil seal assembly
50 Speedometer driven gear
51 Speedometer drive fitting assy with seal
52 Speedometer drive fitting retainer
53 Speedometer drive fitting retainer to case bolt
54 Speedometer drive fitting seal
55 Governor cover retainer
56 Governor cover
57 Governor cover seal
58 Governor assembly
59 Shaft assembly with parking pawl plug
60 Parking lock pawl
61 Parking lock spring
62 Parking lock reaction bracket
63 Parking lock bracket bolt
64 Parking lock and range selector shaft retaining ring
65 Parking lock and range selector shaft (outer)
66 Manual shift seal assembly
67 Manual valve control link
68 Detent spring assembly
69 Parking lock actuator assembly
70 Parking lock and range selector lever (inner)
71 Selector shaft to lever nut
72 Transmission case assembly

8. Install spring compressor onto direct clutch accumulator piston and remove retaining E-ring at H.
9. At location H, remove direct clutch accumulator piston, then metal oil seal ring and spring.
10. From the upper left hand bore, G, remove the detent actuating lever bracket bolt, bracket, actuating lever and retaining pin, stop, spring retainer, seat, outer spring, and the detent valve.

Inspection

1. Wash all parts in solvent. Air dry. Blow out all passages.
2. Inspect all valves for scoring, cracks, and free movement in their bores.
3. Inspect sleeves for cracks,

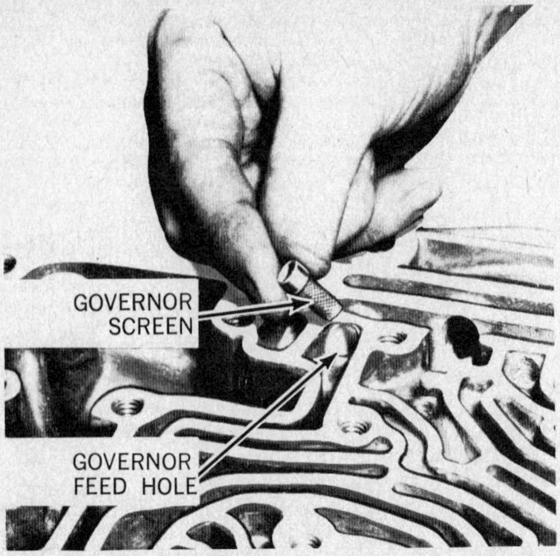

Removing the governor feed screen (© G.M. Corp.)

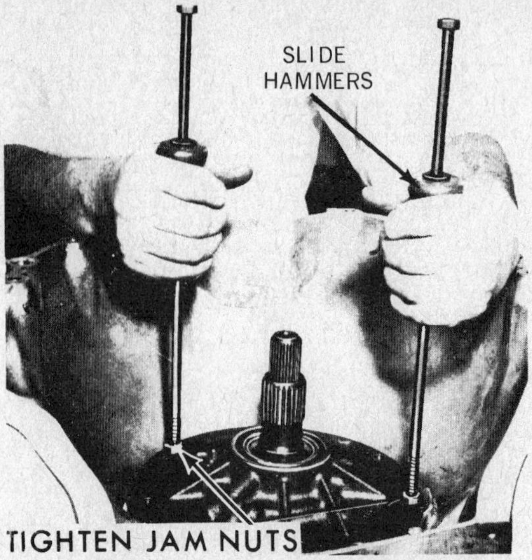

Removing the oil pump from the transmission case (© G.M. Corp.)

scratches, or distortion.

4. Inspect valve body for cracks, scored bores, interconnected oil passages, and flatness of mounting face.
5. Check all springs for distortion or collapsed coils.

Assembly

1. Reverse disassembly procedures for assembly. Refer to Valve Body Springs chart for identification of springs.

Oil Pump

Disassembly

1. Remove five pump cover-to-body attaching bolts. Remove spring seat retainer.
2. Remove the intermediate clutch spring seat retainer, intermediate clutch return springs, and the intermediate clutch piston assembly.
3. Remove intermediate clutch piston inner and outer seals.

VALVE BODY SPRINGS

Valve	*Free Length of Spring (in.)*	*Diameter (in.)*
Detent regulator	1⅞	9/16
Manual low control valve	1½	7/16
1-2 shift control valve	1 15/16	¼
2-3 shift valve	2 1/16	⅞
2-3 shift control valve	11/16	3/16
Pressure regulator valve	1 11/16	17/32
Direct clutch accumulator	1¾	1½
Detent valve	1⅞	¾

4. Remove two forward clutch-to-pump hub hook-type oil seal rings. Remove three direct clutch-to-pump hub hook type oil rings.
5. Remove pump cover-to-direct clutch drum selective thrust washer.
6. Remove pump cover and stator shaft assembly from pump body.
7. Remove pump drive gear and driven gear from pump body.
8. Remove pump outside diameter-to-case square cut O-ring seal.
9. Pry out pump body to converter hub lip seal, using a screwdriver. Place pump on wood blocks to prevent damage to surface finish.
10. Install pump-to-converter hub lip seal, using seal driver. Examine after installation to be sure the sealing surface is not damaged.
11. Remove oil pump priming valve and spring.

    NOTE: The valve and spring have been deleted from all transmissions built after Feb. 1971.

12. Remove cooler by-pass valve seat. Pack cooler by-pass passage with grease. Insert 5/16 in. dia.

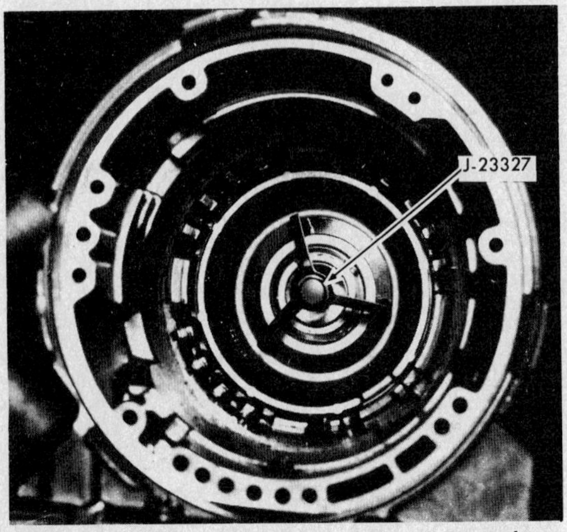

Compressing the low and reverse clutch piston spring retainer (© G.M. Corp.)

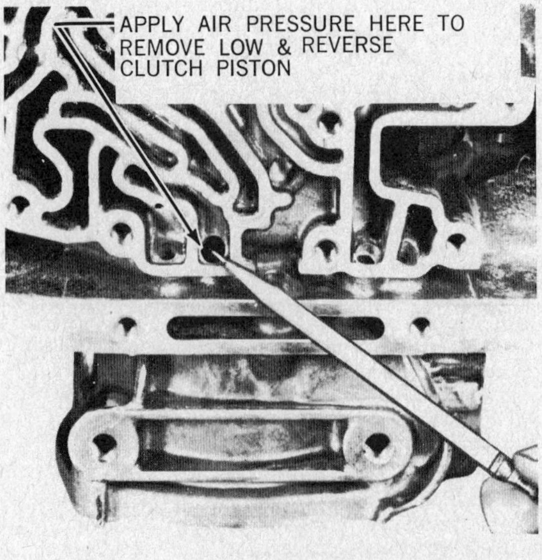

Removing low and reverse clutch piston (© G.M. Corp.)

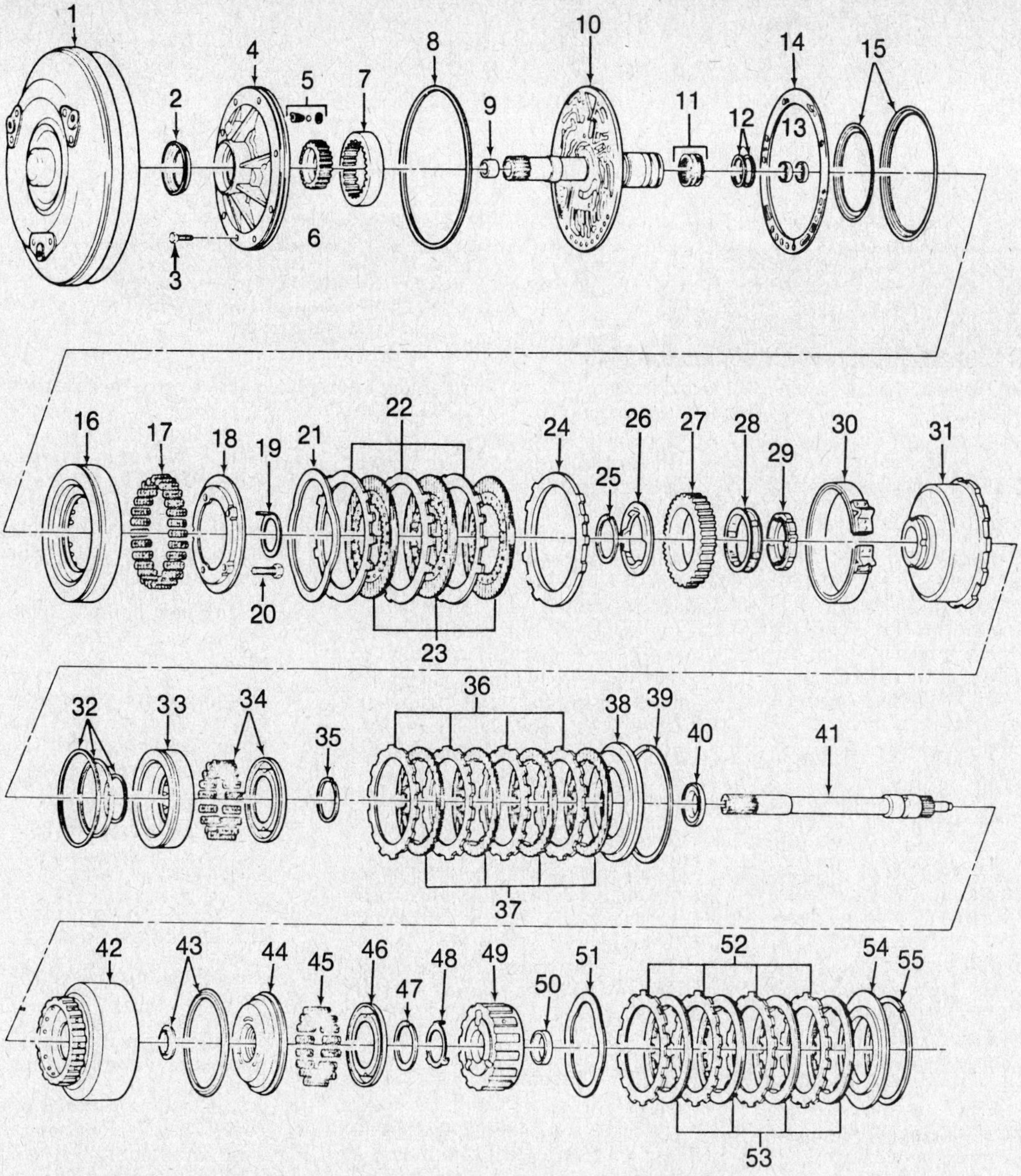

Exploded view—pump, central support, forward, direct and intermediate clutches (© G.M. Corp.)

1 Torque converter assembly
2 Front oil pump seal
3 Oil pump to case screw
4 Oil pump body assembly
5 Oil cooler bypass valve
6 Oil pump drive gear
7 Oil pump driven gear
8 Oil pump to case seal
9 Startor shaft front bushing
10 Oil pump cover assembly
11 Direct clutch drum oil seal
12 Forward clutch housing oil seal
13 Stator shaft rear bushing
14 Oil pump to case gasket
15 Intermediate clutch piston seal
16 Intermediate clutch piston
17 Intermediate clutch piston return spring
18 Intermediate clutch piston return spring seat
19 Direct clutch drum front thrust washer
20 Oil pump to cover bolt
21 Intermediate clutch piston cushion spring
22 Intermediate clutch reaction plate
23 Intermediate clutch drive plate assembly
24 Intermediate clutch pressure plate assembly
25 Intermediate overrunning clutch retainer
26 Intermediate overrunning clutch outer race
27 Intermediate overrunning clutch inner race
28 Intermediate overrunning clutch assembly
29 Intermediate overrunning brake band assembly
30 Intermediate overrunning brake and band assembly
31 Direct clutch drum assembly
32 Direct clutch piston seal
33 Direct clutch piston
34 Direct clutch piston return spring and seat assembly
35 Direct clutch piston return spring seat retainer ring
36 Direct clutch drive plate
37 Direct clutch drive plate assembly
38 Direct clutch pressure plate assembly
39 Direct clutch pressure plate retaining ring
40 Direct clutch drum rear thrust bearing
41 Imput shaft
42 Forward clutch housing assembly
43 Forward clutch piston seal unit (inner and outer)
44 Forward clutch piston
45 Forward clutch piston return spring
46 Forward clutch piston return spring seat
47 Forward clutch piston return spring seat retaining ring
48 Input ring gear front thrust washer
49 Input ring gear assembly with support
50 Input ring gear bushing
51 Forward clutch piston cushion spring
52 Forward clutch driven plate
53 Forward clutch drive plate assembly
54 Forward clutch pressure plate
55 Forward clutch pressure plate retaining ring

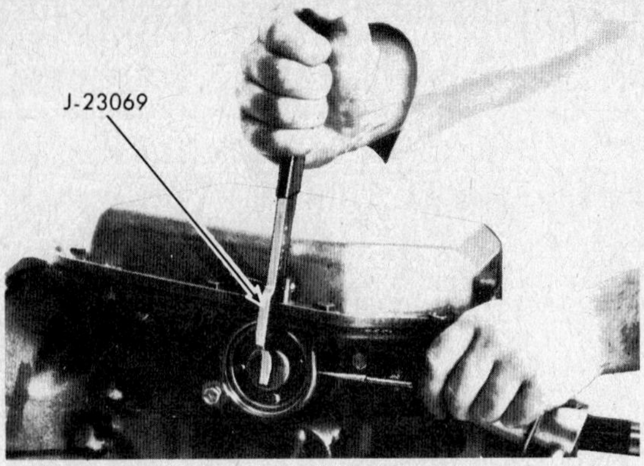

Removing the accumulator piston cover retaining ring (© G.M. Corp.)

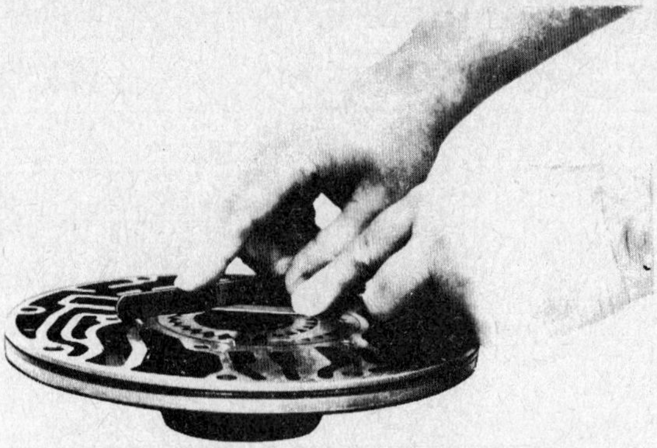

Checking the oil pump body to gear face clearance (© G.M. Corp.)

rod and tap with hammer to lift seat. Remove check ball and spring.

Inspection

1. Wash all parts in solvent. Air dry. Blow out all passages.
2. Inspect drive and driven gears, gear pocket, and crescent for nicks, galling or other damage.
3. Inspect pump body and cover for nicks or scoring.
4. Check pump cover outer diameter for nicks or burrs.
5. Inspect pump body bushing for galling or scoring. Check clearance between pump body bushing and converter hub. It must be no more than .005 in. If bushing is damaged, replace pump body.
6. Install pump gears in body and check pump body face to gear face clearance. It should be from .0005-.0015 in.
7. Inspect pump body to converter hub lip oil seal. Inspect converter hub for nicks or burrs which might have damaged pump lip oil seal or pump body bushing.
8. Check priming valve for free operation. Replace if necessary.
9. Check condition of cooler bypass valve. Replace valve if it leaks excessively.
10. Check all springs for distortion or collapsed coils.
11. Check oil passages in pump body and in pump cover.
12. Inspect three pump cover stator shaft bushings for galling or scoring. If they are damaged, remove using a slide hammer. Drive the new bushings into place. The front stator shaft bushing must be .250 in. below the front face of the pump body. The center bushing should be 11/32 in. below the face of the pump cover hub. The rear bushing should be flush or up to .010 in. below the face of the pump cover hub.
13. Check three pump cover and hub lubrication holes to make certain they are not restricted.

Assembly

1. Install cooler by-pass valve spring, check ball and seat. Press seat into bore until top of seat is flush to .010 in. with face of pump body.
2. Install oil pump priming valve and spring. The priming valve is used on all pump bodies having a reamed hole in the priming valve area and on all replacement pump assemblies.
3. Install new pump outside diameter to case square cut O-ring seal.
4. Install pump drive and driven gears. If drive gear has offset tangs, assemble with tangs face up to prevent damage by converter.
5. Install selective thrust washer and five oil seal rings on pump cover hub.
6. Install intermediate clutch piston inner and outer seals.
7. Install pump cover on pump body.
8. Install intermediate clutch piston and clutch return springs.
9. Install spring retainer and pump cover bolts. Position aligning strap over pump body and cover. Tighten strap. Torque pump bolts to 18 ft. lbs.

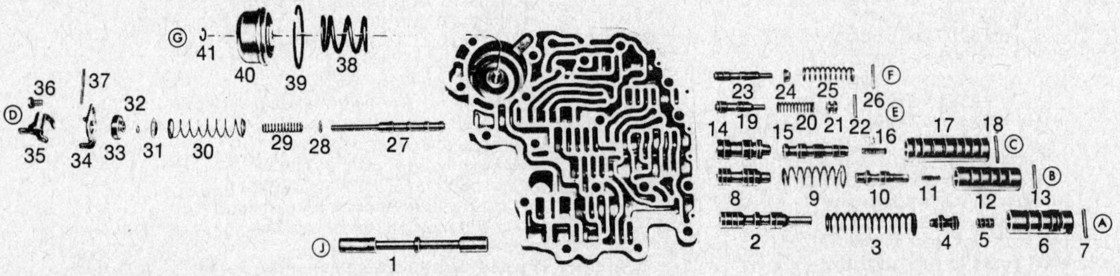

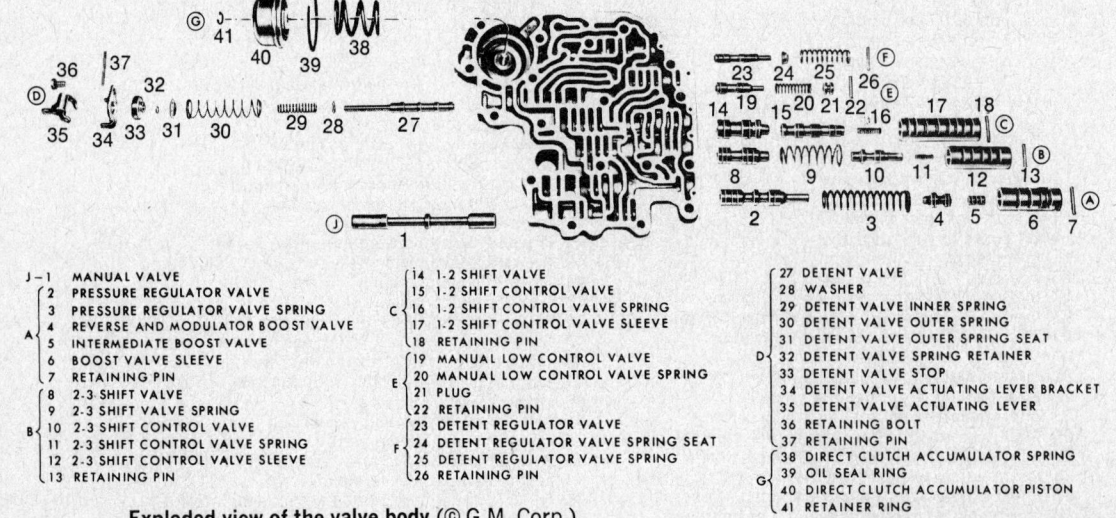

J–1 MANUAL VALVE
A: 2 PRESSURE REGULATOR VALVE
3 PRESSURE REGULATOR VALVE SPRING
4 REVERSE AND MODULATOR BOOST VALVE
5 INTERMEDIATE BOOST VALVE
6 BOOST VALVE SLEEVE
7 RETAINING PIN
B: 8 2-3 SHIFT VALVE
9 2-3 SHIFT VALVE SPRING
10 2-3 SHIFT CONTROL VALVE
11 2-3 SHIFT CONTROL VALVE SPRING
12 2-3 SHIFT CONTROL VALVE SLEEVE
13 RETAINING PIN
C: 14 1-2 SHIFT VALVE
15 1-2 SHIFT CONTROL VALVE
16 1-2 SHIFT CONTROL VALVE SPRING
17 1-2 SHIFT CONTROL VALVE SLEEVE
18 RETAINING PIN
E: 19 MANUAL LOW CONTROL VALVE
20 MANUAL LOW CONTROL VALVE SPRING
21 PLUG
22 RETAINING PIN
F: 23 DETENT REGULATOR VALVE
24 DETENT REGULATOR VALVE SPRING SEAT
25 DETENT REGULATOR VALVE SPRING
26 RETAINING PIN
D: 27 DETENT VALVE
28 WASHER
29 DETENT VALVE INNER SPRING
30 DETENT VALVE OUTER SPRING
31 DETENT VALVE OUTER SPRING SEAT
32 DETENT VALVE SPRING RETAINER
33 DETENT VALVE STOP
34 DETENT VALVE ACTUATING LEVER BRACKET
35 DETENT VALVE ACTUATING LEVER
36 RETAINING BOLT
37 RETAINING PIN
G: 38 DIRECT CLUTCH ACCUMULATOR SPRING
39 OIL SEAL RING
40 DIRECT CLUTCH ACCUMULATOR PISTON
41 RETAINER RING

Exploded view of the valve body (© G.M. Corp.)

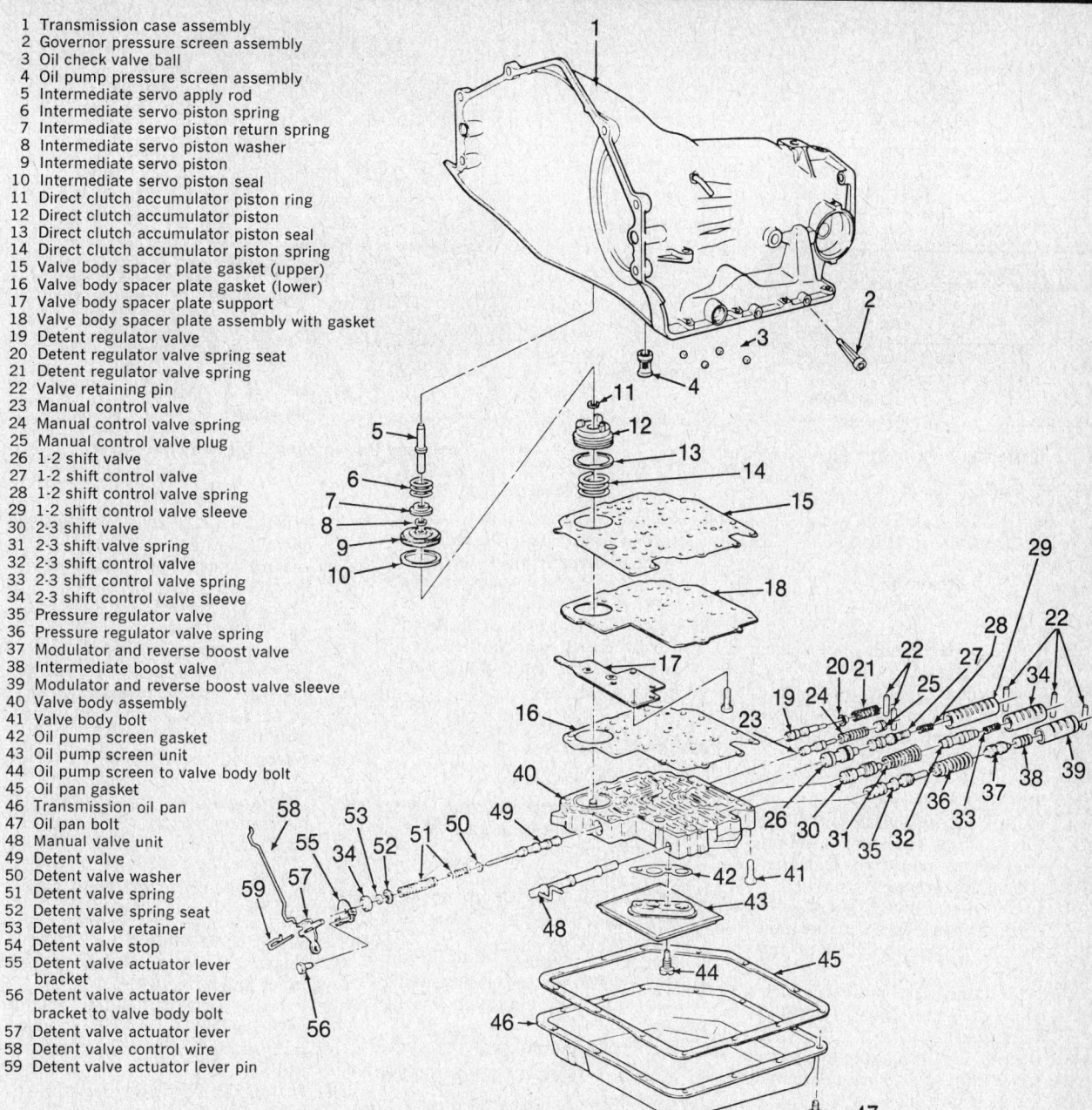

1 Transmission case assembly
2 Governor pressure screen assembly
3 Oil check valve ball
4 Oil pump pressure screen assembly
5 Intermediate servo apply rod
6 Intermediate servo piston spring
7 Intermediate servo piston return spring
8 Intermediate servo piston washer
9 Intermediate servo piston
10 Intermediate servo piston seal
11 Direct clutch accumulator piston ring
12 Direct clutch accumulator piston
13 Direct clutch accumulator piston seal
14 Direct clutch accumulator piston spring
15 Valve body spacer plate gasket (upper)
16 Valve body spacer plate gasket (lower)
17 Valve body spacer plate support
18 Valve body spacer plate assembly with gasket
19 Detent regulator valve
20 Detent regulator valve spring seat
21 Detent regulator valve spring
22 Valve retaining pin
23 Manual control valve
24 Manual control valve spring
25 Manual control valve plug
26 1-2 shift valve
27 1-2 shift control valve
28 1-2 shift control valve spring
29 1-2 shift control valve sleeve
30 2-3 shift valve
31 2-3 shift valve spring
32 2-3 shift control valve
33 2-3 shift control valve spring
34 2-3 shift control valve sleeve
35 Pressure regulator valve
36 Pressure regulator valve spring
37 Modulator and reverse boost valve
38 Intermediate boost valve
39 Modulator and reverse boost valve sleeve
40 Valve body assembly
41 Valve body bolt
42 Oil pump screen gasket
43 Oil pump screen unit
44 Oil pump screen to valve body bolt
45 Oil pan gasket
46 Transmission oil pan
47 Oil pan bolt
48 Manual valve unit
49 Detent valve
50 Detent valve washer
51 Detent valve spring
52 Detent valve spring seat
53 Detent valve retainer
54 Detent valve stop
55 Detent valve actuator lever bracket
56 Detent valve actuator lever bracket to valve body bolt
57 Detent valve actuator lever
58 Detent valve control wire
59 Detent valve actuator lever pin

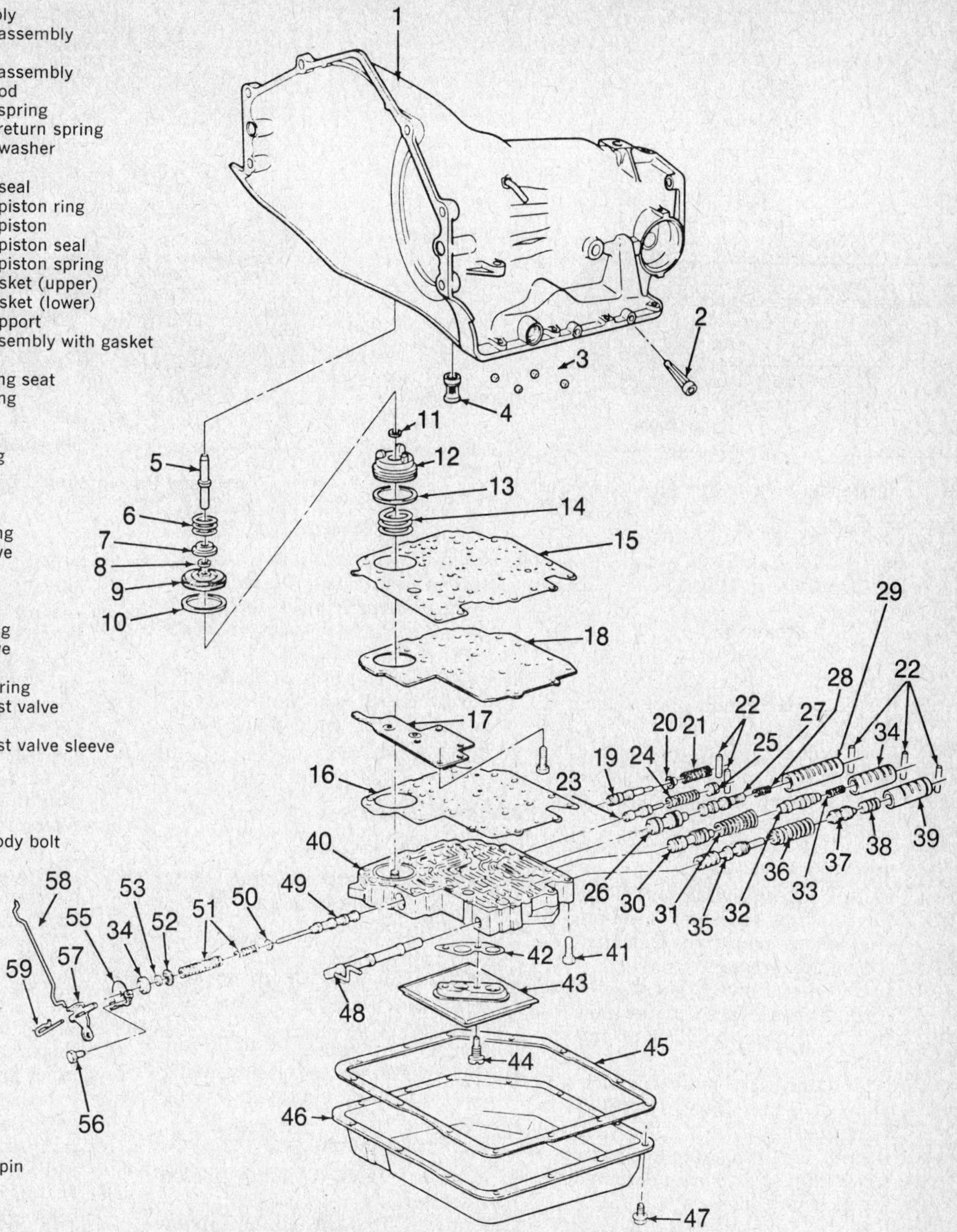

Exploded view—front and rear servos, and control valve body (© G.M. Corp.)

Direct Clutch and Intermediate Overrun Roller Clutch

Disassembly

1. Remove intermediate overrun clutch front retainer ring and retainer.
2. Remove intermediate overrun clutch outer race.
   NOTE: Before removal, check for correct assembly. The outer race should free wheel counterclockwise only.
3. Remove intermediate overrun roller clutch assembly.
4. Remove intermediate overrun roller clutch cam.
5. Remove direct clutch drum to forward clutch housing special needle bearing.
6. Remove direct clutch pressure plate to clutch drum retaining ring and pressure plate.
7. Remove direct clutch lined and steel plates.
8. Remove direct clutch piston return spring seat retaining ring and spring seat.
9. Remove 17 clutch return coil springs and piston.
10. Remove direct clutch piston inner and outer seals.
11. Remove direct clutch piston center seal.

Inspection

1. Wash all parts in solvent. Blow out all passages. Air dry.
2. Inspect clutch plates for burning, scoring, or wear.
3. Check all springs for collapsed coils or distortion.
4. Inspect piston for cracks and free operation of ball check. Ball should be loose enough to rattle but not to fall out.
5. Check overrun clutch inner cam and outer race for scratches, wear, or indentations.
6. Inspect overrun roller clutch assembly rollers for wear. Check springs for distortion.
7. Inspect clutch drum for wear, scoring, cracks, proper opening of oil passages, wear on clutch plate drive lugs, and free operation of ball check.
8. Check direct clutch drum bushing for galling or scoring. When replacing bushing, drive the new

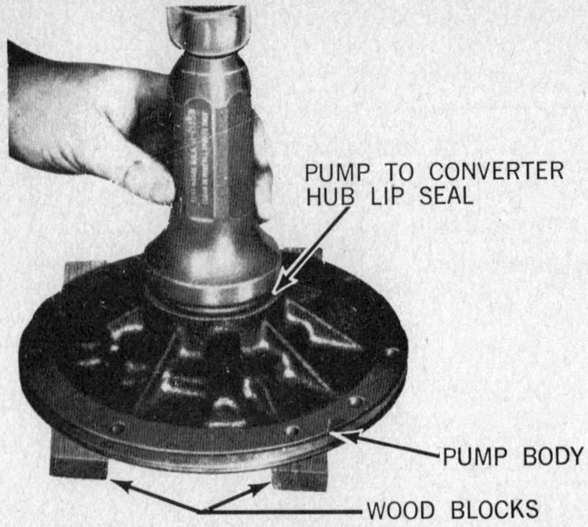

Installing the hub lip seal (© G.M. Corp.)

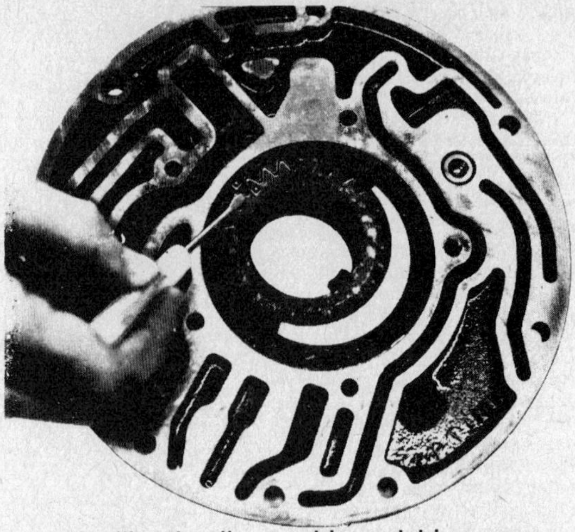

Installing the oil pump drive and driven gears (© G.M. Corp.)

bushing 9/32 in. below clutch plate side of hub face and .010 in. below slot in hub face.

Assembly

1. Install direct clutch drum center seal.
2. Install direct clutch piston inner and outer seals.
3. Install direct clutch piston into housing with a loop of .020 in. wire crimped into a length of copper tubing.
4. Install 17 clutch return springs on piston.
5. Install direct clutch piston return spring seat and retaining ring using snap-ring pliers and spring compressor.
6. Install direct clutch housing. Install steel and faced plates alternately, beginning with a steel plate.
7. Install direct clutch pressure plate in clutch drum. Install retaining ring.
8. Install intermediate overrun roller clutch inner cam on hub of direct clutch drum.
9. Replace intermediate overrun roller clutch assembly.
10. Install intermediate overrun clutch outer race. The outer race must free-wheel in the counterclockwise direction only.
11. Replace intermediate overrun clutch retainer and retainer ring. If the retainer ring is dished, install the ring so that it compresses the retainer.
12. Install direct clutch drum to forward clutch housing needle thrust washer on hub of roller clutch inner race.

Forward Clutch

Disassembly

1. Remove forward clutch drum to pressure plate retaining ring.
2. Remove forward clutch pressure plate.
3. Remove forward clutch housing faced plates, steel plates and cushion spring.
4. Compress springs. Remove forward clutch piston return spring seat retaining ring and spring seat.
5. Remove 21 clutch return springs.
6. Remove forward clutch piston assembly.
7. Remove forward clutch piston inner and outer seals.
8. Be sure the ball check exhaust in the drum is operable and free of dirt.

Inspection

1. Wash all parts in solvent. Blow out all passages. Air dry.
2. Inspect clutch plates for burning, scoring, or wear.
3. Check all springs for distortion or collapsed coils.
4. Inspect piston for cracks.
5. Inspect clutch drum for wear, scoring, cracks, proper opening of oil passages, and free operation of ball check.
6. Check input shaft for:
   a. Open lubrication passages at each end.
   b. Damage to splines or shaft.
   c. Damage to ground bushing journals.
   d. Cracks or distortion of shaft.

Assembly

1. Install forward clutch piston inner and outer seals.
2. Install forward clutch piston with a loop of .020 in. wire crimped into a length of copper tubing.
3. Install the 21 forward clutch return springs. These springs are identical to those used in the direct clutch. Install spring seat.
4. Compress springs and replace spring seat retaining ring.

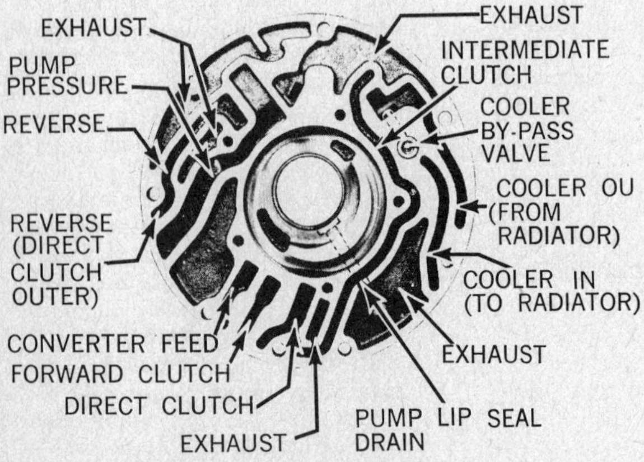

Oil pump oil passages (© G.M. Corp.)

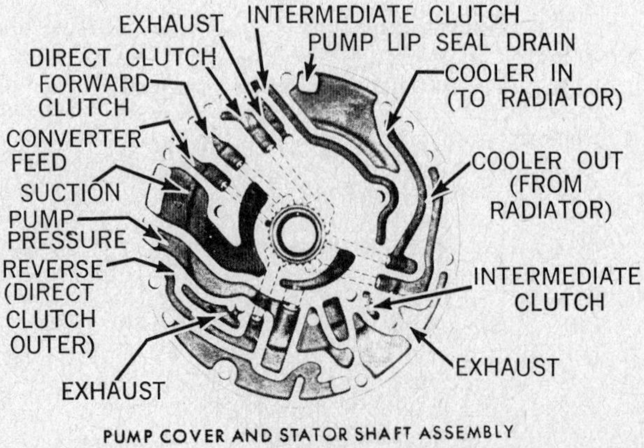

Oil pump cover oil passages (© G.M. Corp.)

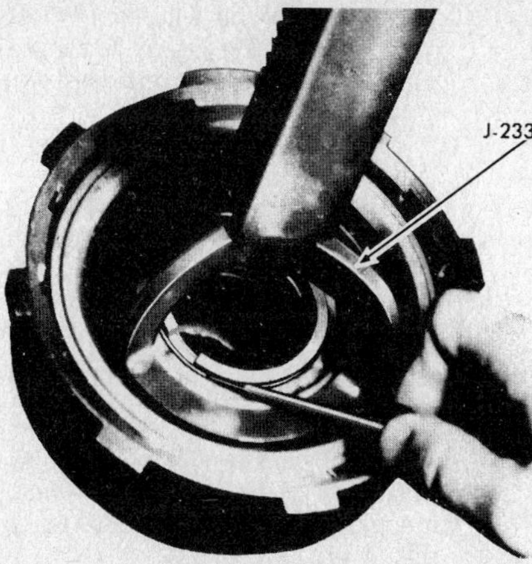

Compressing the direct clutch spring seat (© G.M. Corp.)

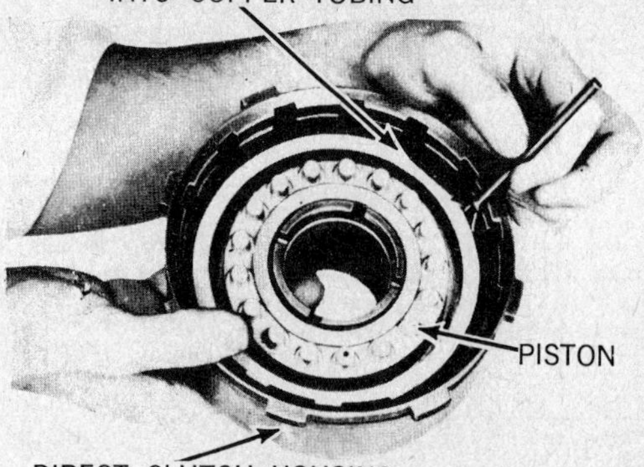

Install the direct clutch piston (© G.M. Corp.)

5. Replace forward clutch housing cushion spring. Replace steel and faced plates alternately, starting with a steel plate.
6. Install forward clutch pressure plate and retaining ring.
7. Use a feeler gauge to check the clearance between the top of the clutch pack to the top of the clutch; dimension A, (use the chart that follows to select the correct pressure plate). Measure the distance between the lower edge of the notch on the inner surface of the drum and the end of the drum; dimension B. Subtract dimension B from dimenison A to get dimension C.

Subtract dim. B from C to obtain dim. A

When dim. A is:	*use plate number*
.016-.052 in.	6261072
.052-.083 in.	6261349
.083-.122 in.	6261350

8. Install direct clutch drum on input shaft and align faced plates with splines on forward clutch housing.

Sun Gear and Sun Gear Drive Shell

Disassembly

1. Remove sun gear to sun gear drive shell rear retaining ring.
2. Remove sun gear to drive shell flat rear thrust washer.
3. Remove sun gear and front retaining ring from drive shell.
4. Remove front retaining ring from sun gear.

Inspection

1. Wash all parts in solvent. Air dry.
2. Inspect sun gear and sun gear drive shell for wear or damage.
3. Inspect sun gear bushings for galling or scoring. Drive out damaged bushings. Install new bushings flush to .010 in. below surface of counterbore.

Assembly

1. Install new front retaining ring on sun gear. Be careful not to over-stress this ring.
2. Install sun gear and retaining ring in drive shell.
3. Install sun gear to drive shell flat rear thrust washer.
4. Install new sun gear to sun gear drive shell retaining ring.

Low and Reverse Roller Clutch Support

Disassembly

1. Remove low and reverse clutch to sun gear shell thrust washer.
2. Remove low and reverse overrun clutch inner race.
3. Remove low and reverse roller clutch retaining ring.
4. Remove low and reverse roller clutch assembly.

Inspection

1. Wash all parts in solvent. Air dry.
2. Inspect roller clutch inner and outer races for scratches, wear, or indentations.
3. Inspect roller clutch assembly rollers for wear and roller springs for distortion. If rollers are removed from assembly, install rollers from outside in to avoid bending springs.

Assembly

1. Install low and reverse roller clutch assembly.
2. Install low and reverse roller clutch retaining ring.
3. Install low and reverse overrun clutch inner race. Inner race must free-wheel in the clockwise direction only.

Governor

NOTE: All components of the governor, with the exception of the driven gear, are a select fit and each assembly is calibrated. The governor, including the driven gear, is serviced as a complete assembly. It is necessary to disassemble the governor to replace the driven gear. Disassembly, may also be necessary due to improper operation of the governor.

Disassembly & Inspection

1. Cut off one end of each governor weight pin and remove pins, governor thrust cap, governor weights and springs. Governor weights are interchangeable from side to side and need not be identified.
2. Remove the governor valve from the governor sleeve. Be careful not to damage the valve.
3. Wash all parts in clean solvent, air dry and blow out all passages with filtered compressed air.
4. Inspect the governor sleeve for nicks, burrs, scoring or galling.
5. Check the governor sleeve for free operation in the bore of the transmission case.
6. Inspect the governor valve for nicks, burrs or galling.
7. Check governor valve for free operation in the bore of the governor sleeve.
8. Inspect the governor driven gear for nicks, burrs or damage.

CLUTCH PLATES

Year	*Model*	*Intermediate Clutch*		*Direct Clutch*		*Forward Clutch*		*Low-Reverse Clutch*	
		Driven Plates	*Drive Plates*	*Driven Plates*	*Drive Plates*	*Driven Plates*	*Drive Plates*	*Driven Plates*	*Drive Plates*
1973-80	All	3	3	4	4	5	5	5	5

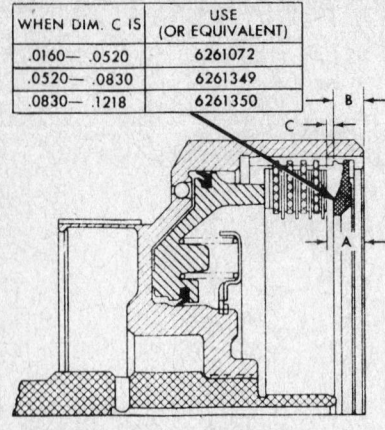

WHEN DIM. C IS	USE (OR EQUIVALENT)
.0160— .0520	6261072
.0520— .0830	6261349
.0830— .1218	6261350

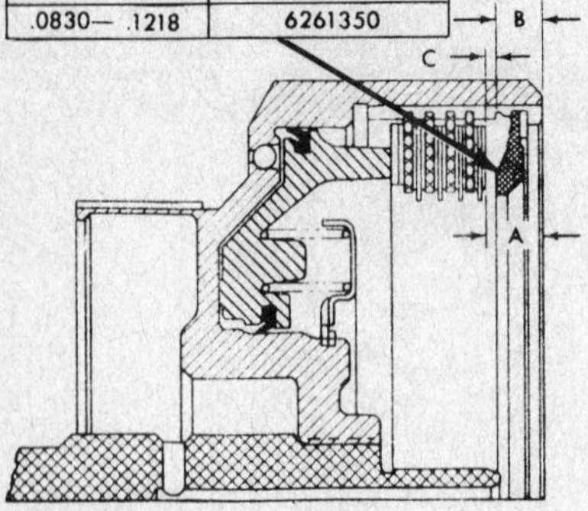

Determining the selective fit for the forward clutch pressure plate
(© G.M. Corp.)

9. Check the driven gear for excessive play on the governor sleeve.
10. Inspect the governor weight springs for distortion or damage.
11. Check governor weights for free operation in their retainers.
12. Check the valve opening at the entry and exhaust, 0.020 inch minimum.

Governor Driven Gear

Replacement

1. Using a small punch, drive out the governor gear retaining split pin.
2. Support the governor on 3/16 inch plates installed in the exhaust slots of the governor sleeve, place in an arbor press, and with a long punch, press the driven gear out of the sleeve.
3. Carefully, clean the governor sleeve of chips that remain from original rear installation.
4. Support the governor on 3/16 inch plates installed in the exhaust slots of the sleeve, position the new gear in the sleeve and, with a suitable socket, press the gear into the sleeve until nearly seated. Carefully, remove any chips that may have shaved off the gear hub, and press the gear in until it bottoms on the shoulder.
5. A new pin must be drilled through the sleeve and gear. Locate the hole position 90 degrees away from the existing hole, center punch and while supporting the governor in press, drill the new hole through the sleeve and gear using a standard 1/8 inch drill.
6. Install new split retaining pin.
7. Wash governor assembly thoroughly to remove any chips that may have collected.

Assembly

1. Install the governor valve in bore of sleeve, large land first.
2. Install the governor weights and springs, and the thrust cap on the governor sleeve.
3. Align the holes in the thrust cap, governor weight assemblies and governor sleeve, install new pins. Crimp both ends of the pins to prevent them from falling out.
4. Check the operation of the governor weight assemblies. Pins should operate freely.
5. Check the governor valve for free movement in the governor sleeve.

Transmission Assembly

NOTE: During assembly of transmission, use only clean transmission fluid or petroleum jelly to lubricate or retain parts. Lubricate all bearings, seals rings, and clutch plates before assembly.

Internal Components

1. Install the low and reverse clutch piston assembly with the piston installed next to the parking pawl.
2. Install the piston return springs, there are seventeen.
3. Install the spring retainer and retaining ring. Use the special spring compressing tool. Compress the return seat so the spring retainer retaining ring can be installed. Install the output ring gear thrust bearing in the transmission case.
4. Install the output ring gear on the output shaft.
5. Position the reaction carrier on the output ring gear front tanged washer, and install in the output ring gear support.
6. Install the output shaft assembly in the transmission case.
7. Place the reaction carrier in the output ring gear and shaft assembly.
8. Lubricate (with clean transmission fluid) and install the low and reverse clutch steel reaction and face plates. Starting with a steel plate and alternating with a face plate, assemble the clutch. Install the low and reverse clutch support retainer spring, the notch in the steel separator plate must be placed toward the bottom of the transmission case.
9. Install the low and reverse clutch support assembly. The notch must be aligned so that the retainer spring is in proper contact.
10. Install the low and reverse roller clutch inner race to the sun gear shell thrust washer.
11. Install the low and reverse clutch support to case snap ring with retainer spring between gap.
12. Install thrust rear thrust washer and sun gear drive shell assembly.
13. Install output carrier assembly.
14. Install the input ring gear rear thrust washer.
15. Install the ring gear.
16. Install the new input ring gear

CAUTION: Do not over stress the snap ring.

17. Install the input gear front thrust washer.
18. Install the direct clutch assembly, and the special thrust washer to the forward clutch assembly.
19. Install the clutch assemblies in the transmission case.

CAUTION: Be sure the forward clutch face plates are positioned over the input ring gear. Make certain that the tangs on the direct clutch housing are installed in the slots on the sun gear drive shell.

20. Install the intermediate clutch overrun brake band.
21. Install the intermediate clutch pressure plate.
22. Lubricate (with clean transmis-

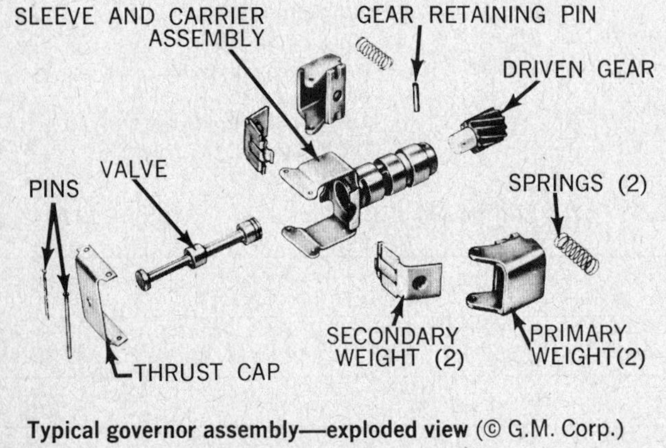

Typical governor assembly—exploded view (© G.M. Corp.)

Checking the end play for proper thrust washer selection
(© G.M. Corp.)

sion fluid) and install the steel and face plates of the intermediate clutch. Starting with a face plate and alternating with a steel plate, assemble the clutch pack. The steel reaction plates are installed toward the selector lever inner bracket.

23. Install the intermediate clutch cushion spring.
24. Use the following procedure to check for the proper thickness of the selective thrust washer used between the oil pump cover and the direct clutch assembly.
    a. Install the selective fit thrust washer, oil pump gasket. Install the oil pump with two slide hammer bolts and two pump to case bolts.
    b. Move the transmission so that the output shaft points down. Mount a dial indicator on one of the slide hammer bolts so that the indicator plunger is resting on the end of the input shaft. Zero the indicator.
    c. Push the transmission output shaft upward and observe the total indicator movement.
    d. The indicator should read .032-.064 inch. If the reading is within these limits, the proper washer is being used. If the reading is not within the limits, it will be necessary to remove the pump and change the selective fit thrust washer to obtain the proper clearance. Selective fit thrust washers are available in thickness of; 0.066, 0.083, and 0.100 inch.
25. Install a new pump to case gasket.
26. Install a new pump to case square cut oil seal ring.
27. Install the guide pins in the case
28. Install the pump assembly in the transmission case. Install attaching bolts and new washer type seals.

NOTE: If the input shaft can not be rotated as the pump is being pulled into place, the direct and forward clutch housings have not been properly installed to index the faced plates with their respective parts. This condition must be corrected before the pump is pulled into place.

Extension and Speedometer Drive Gear

Installation

1. Place the speedometer drive gear retaining clip in the hole on the output shaft.
2. Heat a new speedometer drive gear using a suitable heat source.
3. Align the slot in the speedometer drive gear with the retaining clip and install the gear.

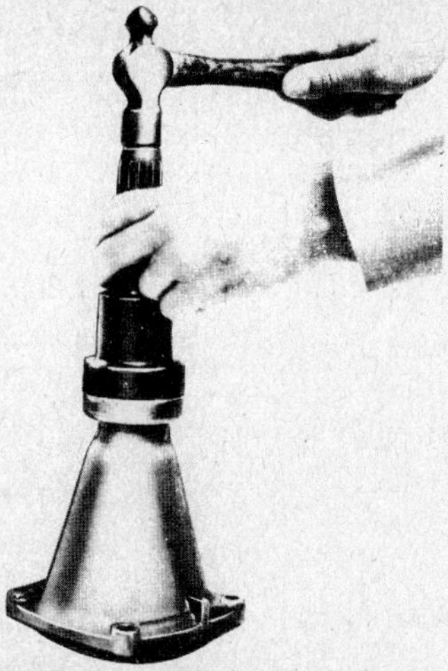

Installing the extension housing seal
(© G.M. Corp.)

4. Install the extension housing to case square cut 'O' ring.
5. Install the extension housing on the transmission case with the attaching bolts and tighten to 25 foot pounds torque.
6. Install a new extension housing rear seal, if necessary, with the proper size drift.

Manual Linkage Assembly

Installation

1. Install a new manual shift shaft seal using ¾ inch rod, be sure the seal seats in the trassmission case.
2. Install the parking pawl, tooth toward the inside, in the transmission case.
3. Install the parking pawl shaft in the case through the parking pawl.
4. Install the parking pawl shaft retaining plug. Drive the retaining plug into the transmission case with a ⅜ inch rod, until the retaining plug is 0.1330-0.170 inch below the face of the transmission case. Stake the retaining plug in three places.
5. Install the parking pawl disengaging spring, with the square end hocked on the parking pawl.
6. Install the park lock bracket and tighten the bolts to 29 foot pounds torque.

CAUTION: **These bolts are type 290 M and have six marks on their heads.**

7. Install the actuating rods between the range selector inner lever and parking pawl.
8. Install the actuating rod under the park lock bracket and parking pawl.
9. Install the manual shift shaft through the transmission case and the range selector inner lever.
10. Install the retaining nut on the manual shift shaft and tighten to 30 foot pounds of torque.
11. Install the manual shift shaft to transmission case spacer clip.

Intermediate Servo Piston, Valve Body, Oil Pan, and Gasket

Installation

1. Install the intermediate servo piston, apply pin, spring, and spring seat.
2. Install the intermediate servo piston and the metal oil seal ring.
3. Install the four check balls into the proper transmission case pockets.
4. Install the oil pump pressure screen and governor feed screen.
5. Install the valve body transfer plate and the gasket.
6. Install the valve body to the transfer plate.
7. Install the valve body. Connect the manual control valve link to the range selector inner lever. Torque the retaining bolts in a random sequence to 130 inch pounds.
8. Install the spacer support plate, tighten the bolts to 130 inch pounds torque.
9. Connect the detent control valve wire to the detent valve actuating lever, attach the lever to the valve body.
10. Attach the roller and spring assembly to the valve body.
11. Align the lube holes in the strainer with the holes in the valve body and install the strainer assembly gasket and strainer.
12. Install the oil pan with a new gasket. Tighten the bolts to 130 inch pounds torque.

Governor and Vacuum Modulator

Installation

1. Install the governor assembly, cover and retainer wire.
2. Install the vacuum modulator valve.
3. Install the vacuum modulator retaining clip and tighten the retaining bolts to 130 inch pounds.

NOTE: Position the retainer with the tangs pointing toward the modulator.

Intermediate Clutch Accumulator

Installation

1. Install the intermediate clutch accumulator piston assembly.
2. Install the intermediate clutch accumulator spring.

3. Install a new 'O' ring in the groove of the transmission case before installing cover.
4. Install the intermediate clutch accumulator cover and retaining ring.

TRANSMISSION CLUTCH PLATES DIAGNOSIS

1. Lined Drive Plates.
   a. Dry plates with compressed air and inspect the lined surface for:
      1. pitting and flaking
      2. wear
      3. glazing
      4. cracking
      5. charring
      6. chips or metal particles imbedded in lining.

      If a lined drive plate exhibits any of the above conditions, replacement is required. Do not diagnose drive plates by color.
2. Steel Driven Plates

   Wipe plates dry and check for heat discoloration. If the surface is smooth and an even color smear is indicated, the plate should be reused. If severe heat spot discoloration or surface scuffing is indicated, the plate must be replaced.
3. Clutch Release Springs

   Evidence of extreme heat or burning in the area of the clutch may have caused the springs to take a heat set and would justify replacement of the springs.

CAUSES OF BURNED CLUTCH PLATES

1. FORWARD CLUTCH
   a. Check ball in clutch housing damaged, stuck or missing.
   b. Clutch piston cracked, seals damaged or missing.
   c. Low line pressure.
   d. Pump cover oil seal rings missing, broken or undersize; ring groove oversize.
   e. Case valve body face not flat or porosity between channels.
2. INTERMEDIATE CLUTCH
   a. Intermediate clutch piston seals damaged or missing.
   b. Low line pressure.
   c. Case valve body face not flat or porosity between channels.
3. DIRECT CLUTCH
   a. Restricted orifice in vacuum line to modulator (poor vacuum response).
   b. Check ball in direct clutch piston damaged, stuck or missing.
   c. Defective modulator bellows.
   d. Clutch piston seals damaged or missing.
   e. Case valve body face not flat or porosity between channels.
   f. Clutch installed backwards.

   NOTE: Burned clutch plates can be caused by incorrect usage of clutch plates. Also, anti-freeze in transmission fluid can cause severe damage, such as large pieces of composition clutch plate material peeling off.

OIL PRESSURE CHECK

		Oil Pressure (psi) @ Altitude (± 5 psi) ①								
Year	*Engine*	*Sea Level*			*2,000 ft.*			*8,000 ft.*		
		D, P, N	*L1, L2*	*R*	*D, P, N*	*L1, L2*	*R*	*D, P, N*	*L1, L2*	*R*
1971	L6 & V8	168	166	254	158	159	240	133	141	202
1972-73	L6 & V8	150	150	244	150	150	233	126	150	194
1974-78	L6	173	166	262	163	159	248	138	141	210
	V8	167	166	254	158	159	240	133	140	202

① Pressures are at 0 (zero) output speed, 1,200 engine rpm and vacuum line disconnected and plugged.

TORQUE SPECIFICATIONS

	Foot pounds	*Inch Pounds*
Pump cover to pump body	17	—
Pump assembly to case	18½	—
Valve body and support plate	—	130
Parking lock bracket	29	—
Oil suction screen	—	40
Oil pan to case	—	130
Extension to case	25	—
Modulator retainer to case	—	130
Inner selector lever to shaft	25	—
Detent valve actuating bracket	—	52

	Foot pounds	*Inch Pounds*
Converter to flywheel bolts	32	—
Upper pan to transmission case	—	110
Transmission case to engine	35	—
Oil cooler pipe connection to transmission case or radiator	—	125
Oil cooler pipe to connections	10	—
Detent cable to transmission	—	75
Detent cable to carburetor	—	112

DIAGNOSIS

This diagnosis guide covers the most common symptoms and is an aid to careful diagnosis. The items to check are listed in the sequence to be followed for quickest results. Thus, follow the checks in the order given for the particular transmission type.

TROUBLE SYMPTOMS	Items to Check	
	In Truck	Out of Truck
No drive in D range	ABCD	abc
No drive in R or slips in reverse	ABCEGHIJL	efa
Drive in neutral	B	a
First speed only—no 1-2 shift	KG	g
1-2 shift at full throttle only	MNG	
First and second speeds only—no 2-3 shift	MNG	f
Slips in all ranges	ACEFG	dfahc
Slips—1-2 shift	ACELGO	gh
Rough 1-2 shift	CELGJOGJ	hi
Slips 2-3 shift	ACELG	fh
Rough 2-3 shift	CELO	
Shifts occur—too high or too low car speed	CKEMGL	
No detent downshifts	NMG	
No part throttle downshift (heavy-duty model "OE" only)	CEG	
No engine braking—super range—second speed	O	i
No engine braking—low range—first speed	GJ	ik
Park will not hold	BPQ	
Poor performance or rough idle—stator not functioning	RS	lo
Noisy transmission	TF	dafgn

Key to Checks

A. Oil level
B. Manual linkage (external)
C. Check oil pressure
D. Manual control disconnected inside
E. Modulator and/or lines
F. Clogged strainer or intake leaks
G. Valves, body and/or leaks
H. Reverse feed passages
I. Valve check balls
J. Rear servo and accumulator
K. Governor and/or feed line seals
L. Pump regulator and boost valve
M. Detent solenoid
N. Detent switch
O. Front servo and accumulator
P. Internal linkage
Q. Parking pawl and/or link
R. Stator switch
S. Valve body-stator section
T. Cooler or lines
a. Front clutch
b. Clutch feed seals and gaskets
c. Low sprags
d. Front pump
e. Rear band
f. Direct clutch
g. Intermediate clutch
h. Pump-to-case gasket
i. Intermediate check valve ball in case
j. Front band
k. Rear band
l. Turbine shaft
m. Converter assembly
n. Planetary assembly

General Information

The Turbo Hydra-Matic Transmission is a fully automatic unit, consisting of a three stage torque converter, three multiple-disc clutches, one gear unit, two roller clutches, and two non-adjustable bands. An electrical operated detent valve is used for forced 3-2 downshifts. While the design and repair procedures are similar, components vary with truck applications and should not be considered interchangeable.

Transmission Disassembly

Clean outside of the unit thoroughly to prevent dirt from entering the unit.

1. With transmission in a work cradle or on a clean bench, lift the converter straight off the transmission input shaft.
2. With transmission bottom-up, remove modulator assembly attaching screw and retainer, then remove the modulator assembly and O-ring seal.

Governor, Speedometer Driven Gear, Oil Pan, Strainer and Intake Pipe

Removal

1. Remove attaching screws, governor cover and gasket, then withdraw governor from the case.
2. Remove speedometer driven gear attaching screw and retainer, then withdraw the driven gear assembly.
3. Remove oil pan attaching screws, then the oil pan. Discard gasket.
4. Remove pump intake pipe and strainer assembly, then the pipe-to-case O-ring seal.

Control Valve Assembly, Governor Pipes and Detent Spring Assembly

Removal

1. Remove the control valve body attaching screws and detent roller and spring assembly.
2. Remove the control valve assembly and the governor pipes. *NOTE: Do not remove the solenoid attaching screws.*
CAUTION: The front servo parts may fall from the transmission when the unit is still in the ve-

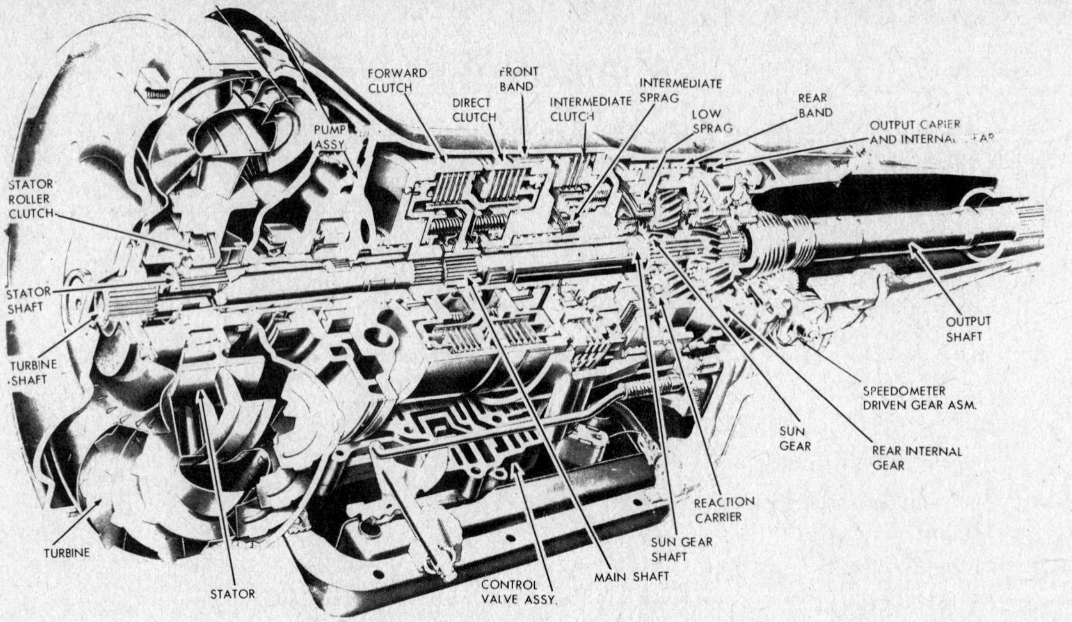

General Motors type turbo hydramatic transmission (© G.M. Corp.)

hicle. Do not drop the manual valve from the valve body.

3. Remove the governor screen from the governor feed pipe hole in the case or from the end of the governor feed pipe.
4. Remove the governor pipes from the control valve assembly.
5. Disconnect the lead wire of the solenoid from the connector terminal.

Rear Servo, Solenoid, Valve Body Spacer, Front Servo, Manual Detent and Parking Linkage

Removal

1. Remove rear servo cover attaching screws, the cover and gasket, then the rear servo assembly from the case.
2. Remove servo accumulator springs.
3. Disconnect the solenoid leads from connector terminal. Withdraw connector and O-ring seal.
4. Make the band apply pin selection check to determine the possible cause of malfunction, proceed as follows:
   a. Attach the band apply pin selection gauge to the transmission case with attaching screws. Make sure that the gauge pin does not bind in the servo pin hole.

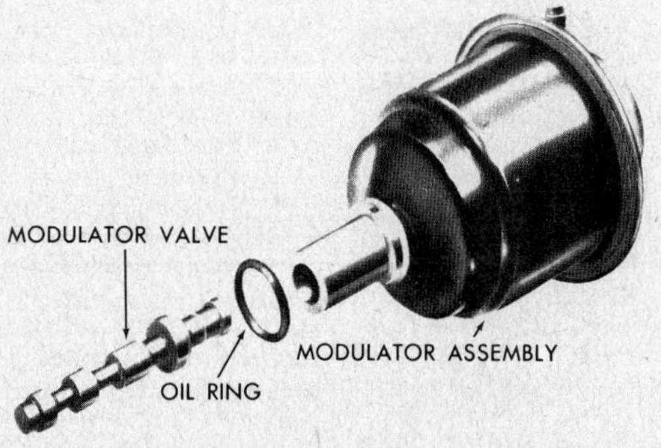

Modulator unit, seal, and valve (© G.M. Corp.)

FLUID SPECIFICATIONS

Oil capacity, transmission and converter
Approx. 22 pints
Capacity between marks on dip stick
1 pint
Type of oil
Automatic transmission fluid Type A
Drain and refill
24,000

BAND AND CLUTCH APPLICATION—400/475 TURBO HYDRA-MATIC TRANSMISSION

GEAR	FORWARD CLUTCH	DIRECT CLUTCH	FRONT BAND	REAR BAND	INTER-MEDIATE CLUTCH	INTER-MEDIATE ROLLER CLUTCH	LOW ROLLER CLUTCH
1st*	on	off	off	off	off	off	locked
2nd*	on	off	off	off	on	locked	off
3rd*	on	on	off	off	on	off	off
Low(L1)	on	off	off	on	off	off	on
L2	on	off	on	off	on	on	off
Reverse	off	on	off	on	off	off	off

* Shift lever in "D" position

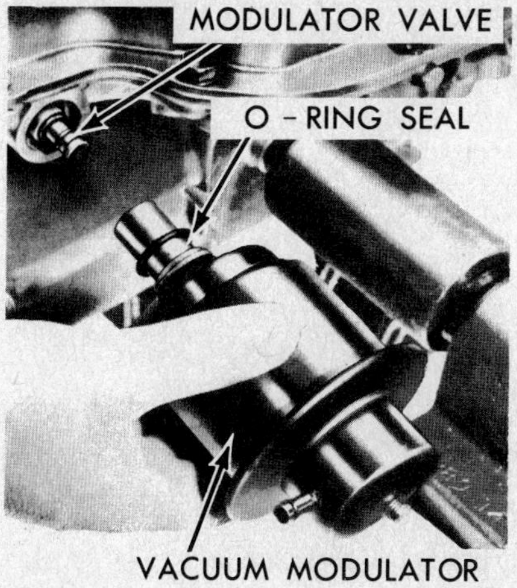

Removing vacuum modulator and valve (© G.M. Corp.)

b. Apply 25 foot pounds torque and select the proper pin to be used during reassembly of the transmission.

Selection of the proper length pin is equivalent to adjusting the band. The band lug end of each selection apply pin bears an identification in the form of one, two or three rings.

c. If both steps of the gauge lever are below the gauge surface, the long pin, identified by three rings must be used.

d. If the gauge surface is between the steps, the medium pin, identified by 2 rings, should be used.

e. If both steps are above the gauge surface, the short pin identified by 1 ring, should be used.

NOTE: If the transmission is in the vehicle, be careful when the detent solenoid is removed as it prevents the spacer plate, gasket, and check balls from dropping down.

5. Remove the detent solenoid attaching screws, detent solenoid and gasket.
6. Remove the electrical connector and 'O' ring seal.
7. Remove valve body spacer plate and gasket.
8. Remove six check balls from cored passages in transmission case.
9. Remove the front servo assembly.
10. Loosen the jam nut which holds the detent lever to the manual shaft. Then remove detent lever from manual shaft and remove manual shaft.
11. Remove the parking actuator rod and detent lever assembly. Then remove detent lever E-ring and the detent lever.
12. Remove attaching screws and park bracket; then the parking pawl return spring.
13. Remove parking pawl shaft retainer, then the parking pawl shaft, O-ring and pawl.

Rear Oil Seal and Extension Housing

Removal

1. Pry rear oil seal from extension housing.
2. Remove housing attaching bolts, then remove extension housing and housing-to-case oil seal.
3. Check the front unit end play as follows:
   a. Remove one front pump bolt and install a 3/8"-16 threaded slide hammer bolt.
   b. Mount a dial indicator on the slide hammer bolt and index the indicator to register with the end of the turbine shaft.
   c. Push the turbine shaft rearward and the output shaft forward.
   d. Set the dial indicator to Zero.
   e. Pull the turbine shaft forward and read the resulting travel or end play. Indicator readings should be .003-.024 inch.

   The selective thrust washer that controls the end play is located between the pump cover and the forward clutch housing. If end play is not within specifications, select a washer thickness from the following chart for use during reassembly.

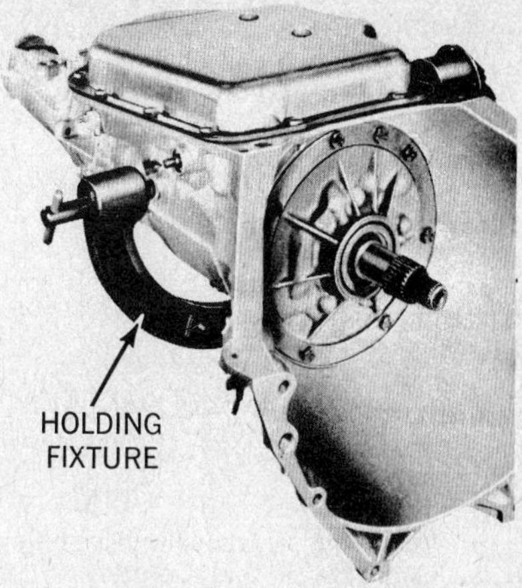

Transmission in holding fixture (© G.M. Corp.)

Thickness (inch)	*Color*
0.060-0.064	Yellow
0.071-0.075	Blue
0.082-0.086	Red
0.093-0.097	Brown
0.104-0.108	Green
0.115-0.119	Black
0.126-0.130	Purple

NOTE: An oil soaked washer may tend to discolor, so it may be necessary to measure the washer for its actual thickness.

Oil Pump, Forward Clutch and Gear Unit

Removal

1. Pry front seal from the pump. Then remove pump attaching bolts.
2. With slide hammers attached, remove pump from transmission

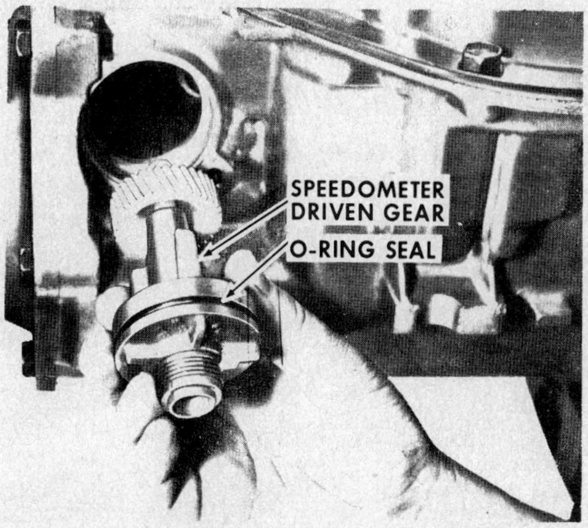

Removing speedometer drive gear and sleeve (© G.M. Corp.)

Removing rear servo (© G.M. Corp.)

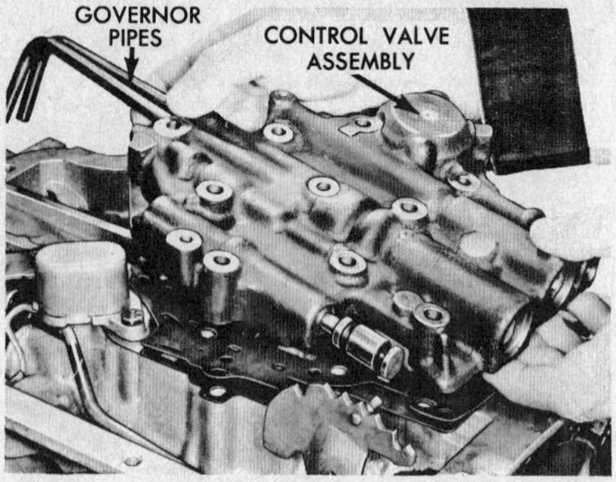

Removing control valve assembly and governor pipes from case (© G.M. Corp.)

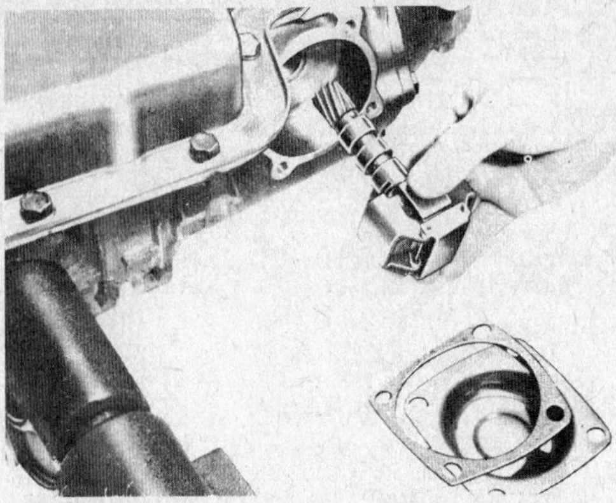
Removing governor (© G.M. Corp.)

case. Discard pump-to-case seal ring. Discard pump-to-case gasket.

3. Remove turbine shaft from transmission.
4. Remove forward clutch assembly. Be sure that the bronze thrust washer came out with the clutch housing assembly.
5. Remove the direct clutch assembly. Remove front band and sun gear shaft.
6. Check the rear end play as follows:
   a. Install a 3/8″ threaded bolt into one of the extension housing bolt holes. Mount a dial indicator on the bolt end and index with the end of the shaft.
   b. Move the output shaft in and out to read the end play. End play should be between 0.007-0.019 inch. The selective thrust washer controlling this end play is composed of steel having three lugs and is located between the output shaft thrust washer and the rear face of the transmission case.

If the end play readings are not within limits, select one from the following chart and install during reassembly.

Thickness (inch)	*Identification* Notches	Numeral
0.074-0.078	None	1
0.082-0.086	1-tab side	2
0.090-0.094	2-tab side	3
0.098-0.102	1-tab O.D.	4
0.106-0.110	2 tabs O.D.	5
0.114-0.118	3-tabs O.D.	6

7. Remove the case center support-to-case bolt using a 3/8″ 12-point thin wall deep socket.
8. Remove intermediate clutch backing plate-to-case snap-ring. Then remove the backing plate, three composition, and three steel clutch plates.
9. Remove the center support-to-case retaining snap-ring.
10. Remove the entire gear unit assembly.
11. Remove the output shaft-to-case thrust washer from the rear of the output shaft, or from inside the case.
12. Remove rear unit selective washer from transmission case.
13. Remove rear band assembly.
14. Remove support to case spacer from inside case.
15. Remove rear band assembly.

Component Disassembly, Inspection, and Assembly

Governor

All components of the governor, except the driven gear, are a select fit and so calibrated. Therefore, service this unit as an assembly.

Clean and inspect all parts for wear or other damage. Check valve opening at feed port with a feeler gauge, holding the governor with the weights extended completly outward. Check valve opening at exhaust port, holding governor with weights completely inward. If either opening is less than .020 in., replace governor assembly.

If a new governor drive gear is installed, a new pin hole must be drilled 90 degrees from the original hole.

Front Servo Inspection

1. Inspect servo pin for damage.
2. Inspect servo piston for damaged oil ring groove, cracks, or porosity. Check freedom of oil seal ring in groove.
3. Check fit of servo pin in piston.

Rear Servo

Disassembly

1. Remove E-ring which holds the servo piston to band apply pin.
2. Remove servo piston and seal from band apply pin. Remove second washer from band apply pin.
3. Remove washer, spring, and retainer.

Inspection

1. Check freedom of accumulator rings in piston.
2. Check fit of band apply pin in servo piston. Inspect pin for scores or cracks.
3. Inspect accumulator and servo pistons for cracks or porosity.

Assembly

1. Install spring retainer, spring,

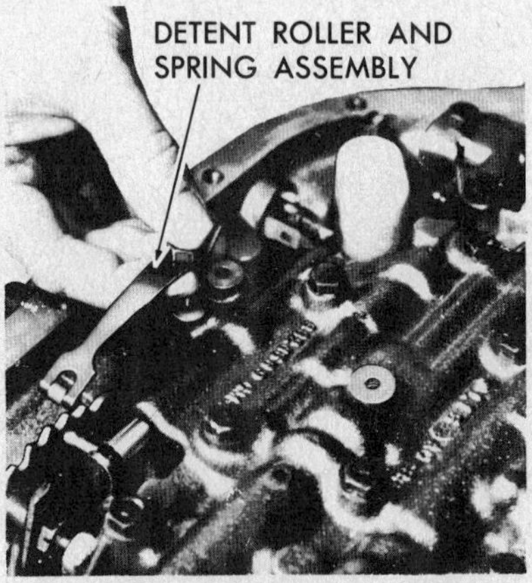

Removing detent roller and spring assembly (© G.M. Corp.)

Removing detent solenoid and gasket (© G.M. Corp.)

and washer on band apply pin.

2. Install band apply pin, retainer, spring, and washer into bore of servo piston and secure with E-ring.
3. Install oil seal on servo piston. Install outer and inner oil seal rings on accumulator piston and assembly into bore of servo piston.

Control Valve Body

Disassembly

When disassembling control valve body, be careful to identify springs so that they can be replaced in their proper locations.

1. Position valve assembly with cored face up and accumulator pocket on bottom.
2. Remove manual valve from upper bore.
3. Compress accumulator piston spring and remove E-ring retainer. Remove accumulator piston and spring.
4. Press out retaining pin from upper right bore. Remove 1-2 modulator bushing, 1-2 regulator valve and spring, 1-2 detent valve, and 1-2 shift valve. 1-2 regulator valve and spring may be inside of 1-2 modulator bushing.
5. Press out retaining pin from center right bore. Remove 2-3 modulator bushing, 2-3 shift valve spring, 2-3 modulator valve, 3-2 intermediate spring, and 2-3 shift valve. 2-3 modulator valve will be inside of 2-3 modulator bushing.
6. Press out retaining pin from lower right bore. Hold hand over bore, as plug may pop out. Remove plug, 3-2 valve spring, spacer, and 3-2 valve.
7. Holding hand over bore, press out retainer pin from upper left bore. Remove bore plug, detent valve, detent regulator valve, spacer, and detent regulator valve spring.
8. Pry out grooved retainer ring from lower left bore with long nose pliers. Remove bore plug, 1-2 accumulator bushing, 1-2 accumulator valve, secondary spring, primary 1-2 accumulator valve, and spring.
9. Remove governor oil feed screen from oil feed hole in valve body.

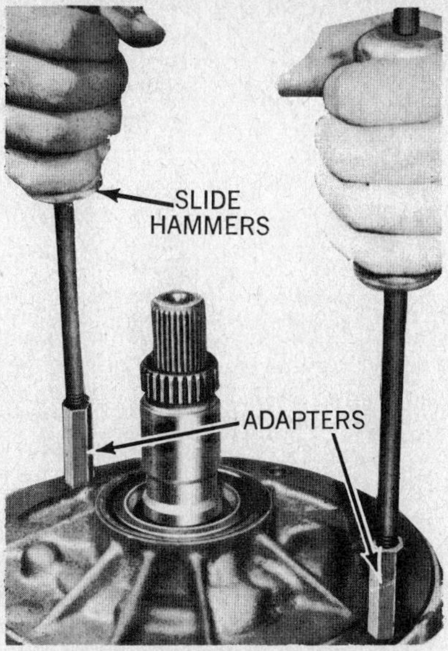

Removing front pump using slide hammers (© G.M. Corp.)

Inspection

1. Wash control valve body, valves and other parts in solvent. Do not allow valves to bump together. Air dry parts and blow out all passages.
2. Inspect all valves and bushings carefully. Burrs may be removed with a fine stone or fine crocus cloth and light oil. Be careful not to round off shoulders of valves.
3. Test all valves and bushings for free movement in their bores. All valves should fall freely of their own weight.
4. The manual valve is the only valve that can be serviced separately. If any of the other valves are defective or damaged, install a new control valve assembly.
5. Inspect body for cracks or scored bores. Check all springs for distortion or collapsed coils.

Assembly

1. Replace front accumulator spring and piston into valve body. Compress spring and piston, assuring that piston pin is correctly aligned with hole in piston and that oil seal ring does not catch on lip of bore when installing piston. Secure piston and spring with E-ring retainer.
2. Install 1-2 accumulator primary spring, 1-2 primary valve, and 1-2 accumulator bushing into lower left bore. Place 1-2 accumulator secondary valve, stem end out, into the 1-2 accumulator bushing. Place 1-2 accumulator secondary spring over stem end of valve. Replace bore plug and retaining pin.

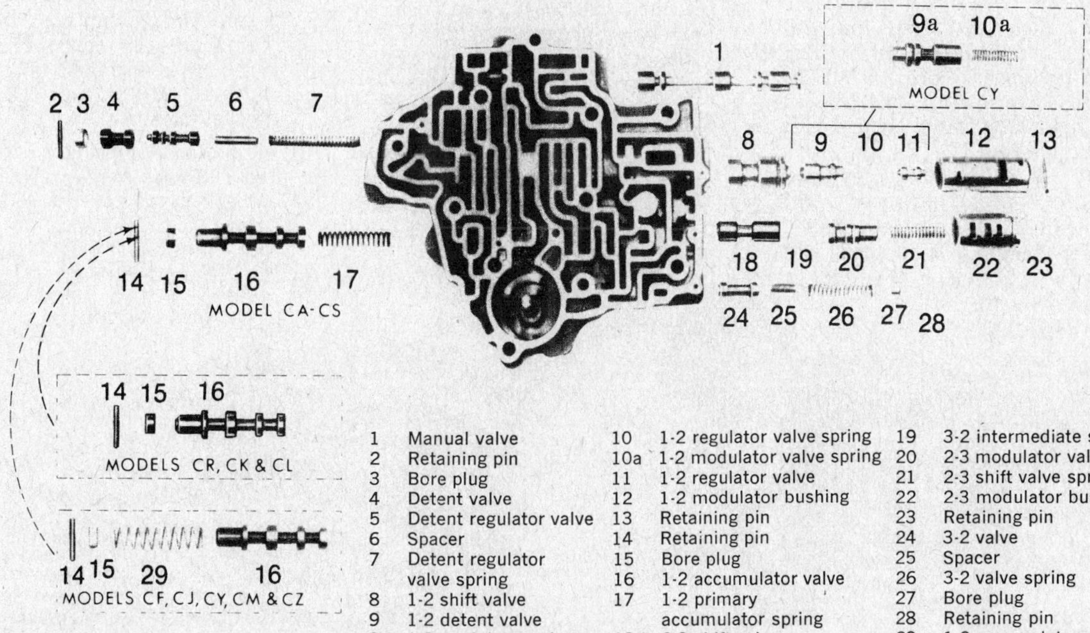

1 Manual valve
2 Retaining pin
3 Bore plug
4 Detent valve
5 Detent regulator valve
6 Spacer
7 Detent regulator valve spring
8 1-2 shift valve
9 1-2 detent valve
9a 1-2 modulator valve
10 1-2 regulator valve spring
10a 1-2 modulator valve spring
11 1-2 regulator valve
12 1-2 modulator bushing
13 Retaining pin
14 Retaining pin
15 Bore plug
16 1-2 accumulator valve
17 1-2 primary accumulator spring
18 2-3 shift valve
19 3-2 intermediate spring
20 2-3 modulator valve
21 2-3 shift valve spring
22 2-3 modulator bushing
23 Retaining pin
24 3-2 valve
25 Spacer
26 3-2 valve spring
27 Bore plug
28 Retaining pin
29 1-2 accumulator valve sec. spring

Exploded view—valve body assembly (© G.M. Corp.)

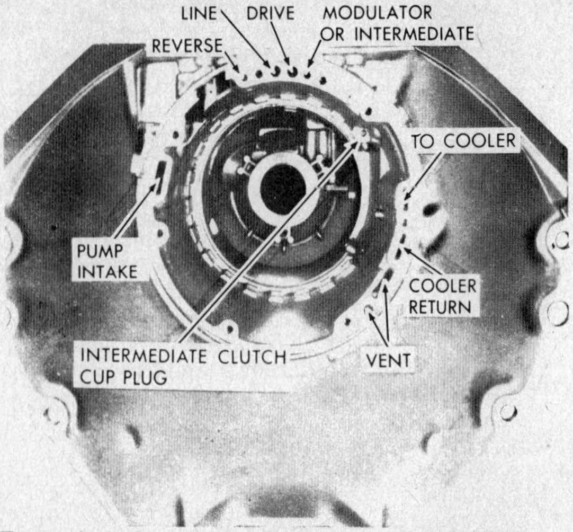

Transmission front view—oil passage identification (© G.M. Corp.)

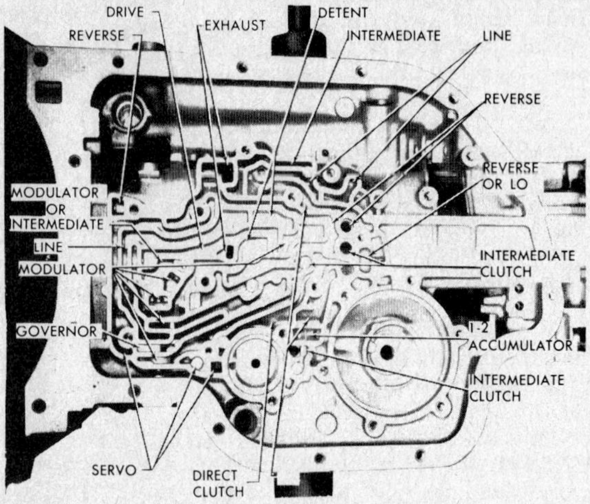

Transmission oil passage identification (© G.M. Corp.)

3. Install detent regulator valve spring and spacer into upper left bore, making certain that spring seats in bottom of bore. Compress spring and hold with a small screwdriver between end of spring and wall on cored side of valve body. Insert detent regulator valve, stem end out, and detent valve, small land first. Insert bore plug, press inward, remove screwdriver, and install retaining pin.
4. Insert 3-2 valve in bottom right bore. Place spacer inside 3-2 valve spring and insert spacer and spring in bore. Install bore plug and retaining pin.
5. Install 3-2 intermediate spring on stem end of 2-3 shift valve. Install valve and spring, valve first, into center right bore. Be sure that valve seats in bottom of bore. Place 2-3 modulator valve, hole end first, into 2-3 modulator bushing. Install valve and bushing in bore. Install 2-3 shift valve spring into hole in 2-3 modulator valve. Secure with retaining pin.
6. Seat 1-2 shift valve, stem end out, in bottom of upper right bore. Install 1-2 regulator valve, larger stem first, and spring and 1-2 detent valve, hole end first, into 1-2 modulator bushing. Align spring in bore of 1-2 detent valve. Install assembly into upper right bore of control valve body. Install retaining pin.
7. Replace governor oil feed screen assembly in governor oil feed hole.
8. Install manual valve with detent pin groove to the right.

Oil Pump

Disassembly

1. Place the pump over a hole in the bench, shaft down, cover up.
2. Compress regulator boost valve bushing against the pressure regulator spring and remove the snap-ring.
   CAUTION: Presure regulator spring is under extreme pressure.
3. Remove the boost valve bushing and valve, then the spring.
4. Remove valve spring retainer and spacer/s, if present, and regulator valve.
5. Remove pump cover to body attaching bolts, then remove the cover.
6. Remove the retaining pin and bore plug from the pressure regulator bore.
7. Remove the two hook-type oil rings from the pump cover.
8. Remove pump to forward clutch housing selective washer.
9. Mark drive and driven gears for reassembly, then remove the gears.

Inspection

1. Inspect drive gear, driven gear, gear pocket, and crescent for scoring, galling, or other damage.
2. Replace pump gears in pump and check pump body face to face gear clearance. The clearance should be .0008-.0035 in.
3. Check pump body face for scoring or nicks. Check oil passages in pump body for roughness or obstructions. Check condition of cover bolt attaching threads. Check for flatness of pump body face. Check pump body bushing, for scores or nicks. If a new bushing is installed, drive it in flush to .010 in. below the gear pocket face.
4. Replace pump attaching bolt seals if necessary.
5. Check pump cover face for flatness. Check for scoring or chips in pressure regulator bore.

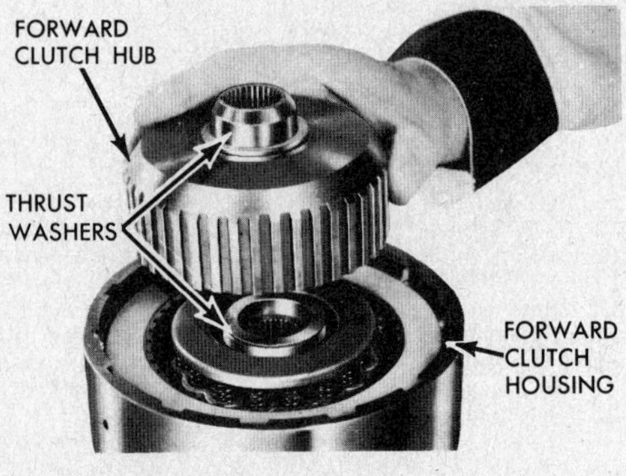

Removing forward clutch (© G.M. Corp.)

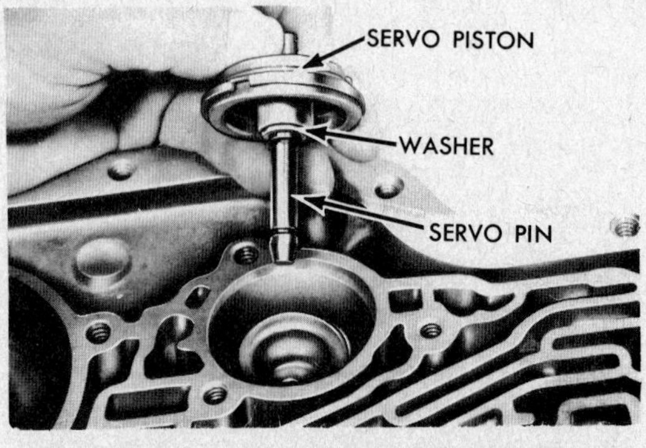

Removing front servo piston, washer and pin (© G.M. Corp.)

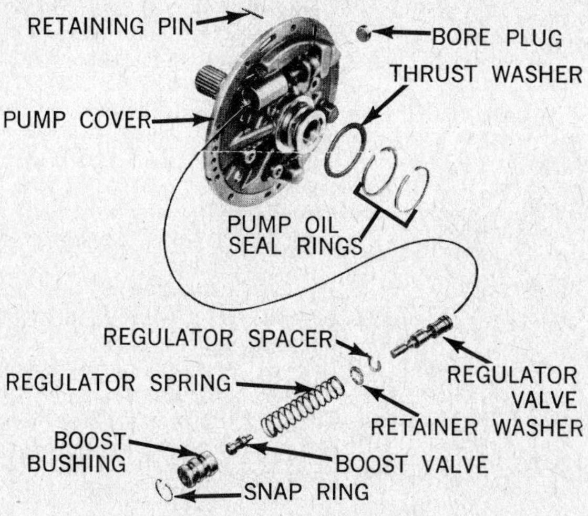

Exploded view of pump cover (© G.M. Corp.)

Installing pump drive gear (© G.M. Corp.)

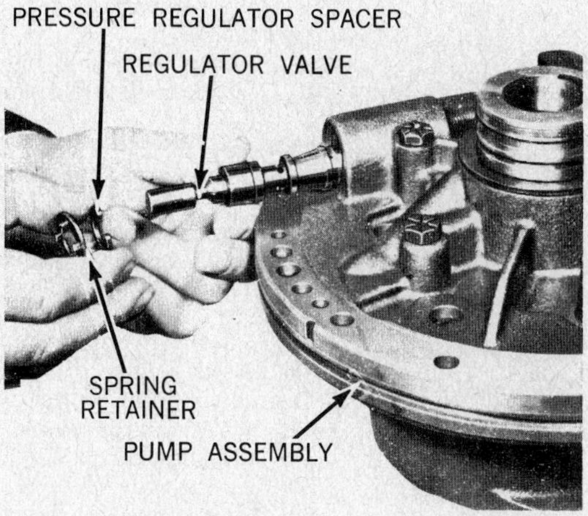

Removing pressure regulator valve (© G.M. Corp.)

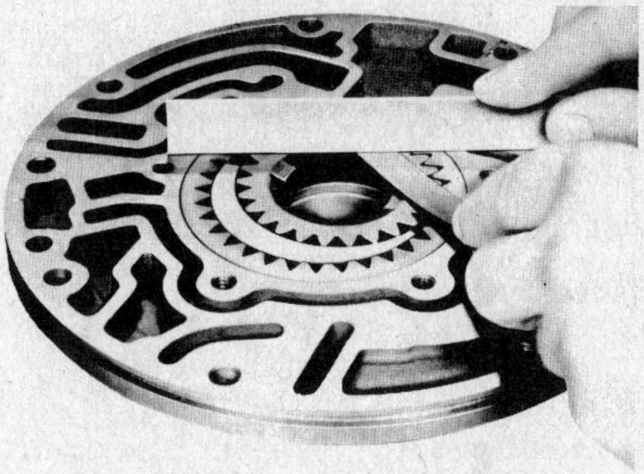

Check pump body face to gear clearance (© G.M. Corp.)

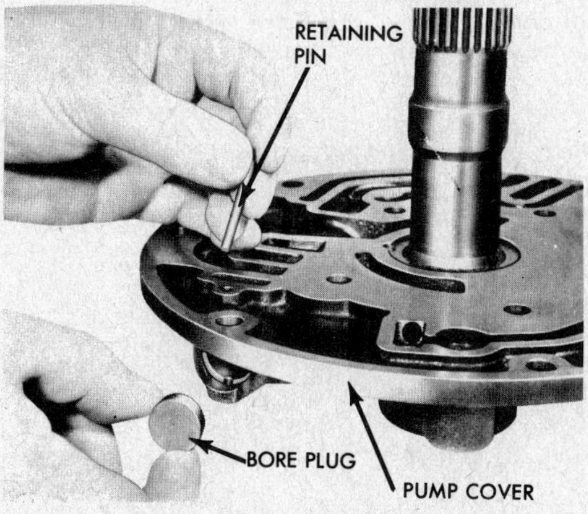

Installing pressure regulator retaining pin and bore, lug (© G.M. Corp.)

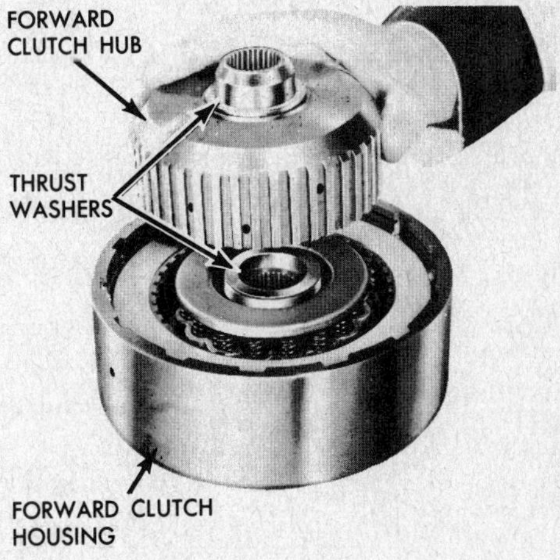

Removing forward clutch hub and thrust washers (© G.M. Corp.)

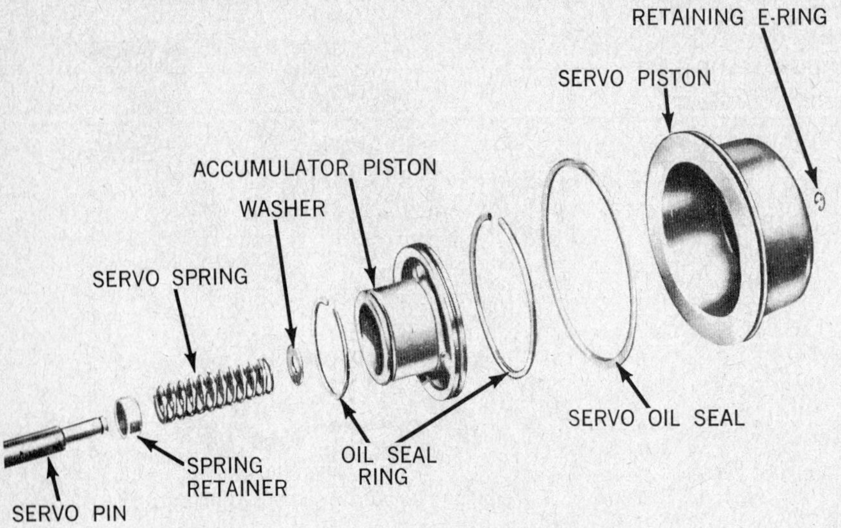

Exploded view of rear servo and accumulator (© G.M. Corp.)

Check that all passages are unobstructed. Check for scoring or damage at pump gear face. Check that breather hole in pump cover is open.

6. Check condition of stator shaft splines and bushings.
7. Check oil ring grooves for damage or wear. Check selective thrust washer for wear.
8. Make sure that pressure regulator valve and boost valve operate freely.

Assembly

1. Install drive and driven gears into the pump body, alignment marks up and in proper index, (drive gear with drive tangs up).
2. Install pressure regulator spring spacer/s if required, retainer and spring into the pressure regulator bore.
3. Install pressure regulator valve from the opposite end of the bore, stem end first.
4. Install boost valve into bushing, stem end out, and install both parts into the pump cover by compressing the bushing against the spring. Install the snap-ring.
5. Install the regulator valve bore plug and retaining pin into opposite end of bore.
6. Install the front unit selective thrust washer over the pump cover delivery sleeve.
7. Install two hook-type oil seal rings.
8. Assemble pump cover to pump body with attaching bolts. (Leave bolts one turn loose at this time.)
9. Place pump aligning strap over pump body and cover, then tighten tool.
10. Install pump cover bolts. pump-to-case O-ring seal and gasket.

Forward Clutch

Disassembly

1. Remove forward clutch housing-to-direct clutch hub snap-ring.
2. Remove direct clutch hub. Remove clamp and install
3. Remove forward clutch hub and thrust washers.
4. Remove five composition and five steel clutch plates. Press out the turbine shaft.
5. Compress the spring retainer and remove the snap-ring.
6. Remove the compressor, snap-ring, spring retainer and 16 release springs, then lift out the piston.
7. Remove inner and outer piston seals.
8. Remove center piston seal from the forward clutch housing.

Inspection

1. Inspect clutch plates for burning, scoring, or wear.
2. Inspect springs for collapsed coils or distortion.
3. Check clutch hubs for worn splines, thrust faces, and open lubrication holes.
4. Check piston for cracks.
5. Check clutch housing for wear, scoring, open oil passages, and free operation of ball check.
6. Inspect turbine shaft for:
   a. Open lubrication passages at each end.
   b. Spline damage.
   journals.
   c. Damage to ground bushing
   d. Cracks or distortion of shaft.

Assembly

1. Place new inner and outer oil seals on clutch piston, lips away from spring pockets.
2. Place a new center seal on the clutch housing, lip faces up.
3. Place a seal protector (thimble) tool into clutch drum and install the piston.
4. Install 16 clutch release springs into pockets in the piston.
5. Lay the spring retainer and the snap-ring on the springs.
6. Compress springs using compressor, and install snap-ring. Press in turbine shaft.
7. Install the direct clutch hub washers; retain with petroleum jelly.
8. Place forward clutch hub into forward clutch housing.
9. Lubricate with transmission oil and install the clutch pack, five

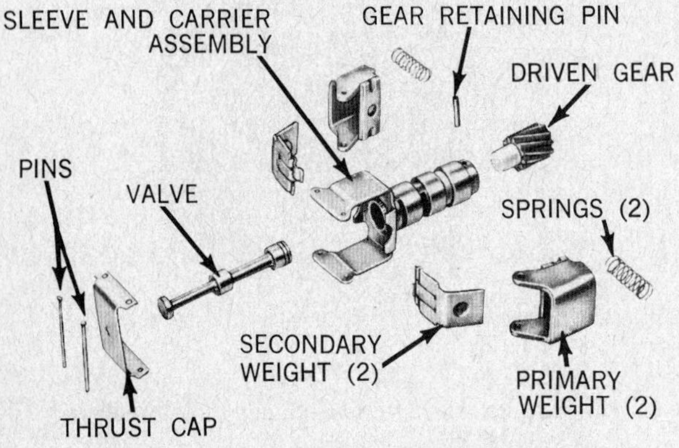

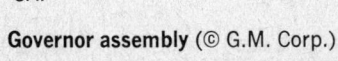

Governor assembly (© G.M. Corp.)

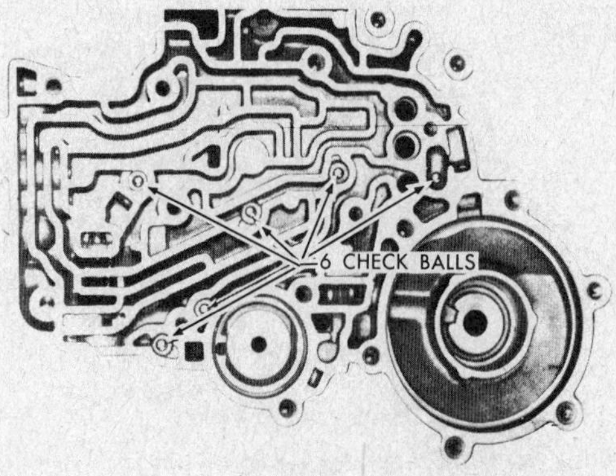

Location of check balls (© G.M. Corp.)

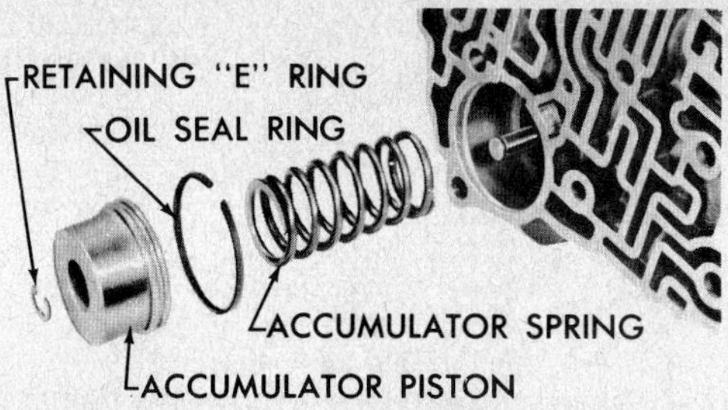

Removing front accumulator piston and spring (© G.M. Corp.)

composition, and five steel plates, starting with steel and alternating steel and composition.

10. Install clutch hub and retaining snap-ring.
11. Place forward clutch housing on pump delivery sleeve and air-check clutch operation.

Direct Clutch and Intermediate Sprag

Disassembly

1. Remove intermediate clutch retainer snap-ring, then the retainer.
2. Remove clutch outer race, bushings and sprag assembly.
3. Invert the unit and remove backing plate to clutch housing snap-ring.
4. Remove direct clutch backing plate, five composition, and five steel plates.
5. Using clutch compressor tool compress the spring retainer and remove the snap-ring.
6. Remove retainer and 16 piston release springs.
7. Remove direct clutch piston, then remove the outer and inner seals from the piston.
8. Remove center piston seal from the direct clutch housing.

Inspection

1. Check for popped or loose sprags.
2. Check sprag bushings for distortion or wear.
3. Inspect inner and outer races for scratches or wear.
4. Check clutch housing for cracks, wear, proper opening of oil passages, and wear on clutch plate drive lugs.
5. Check clutch plates for wear or burning.
6. Check backing plate for scratches or damage.
7. Check clutch piston for cracks and free operation of ball check.

Assembly

1. Install a new clutch piston seal onto the piston, lips facing away from spring pockets. Apply transmission fluid to oil seals.
2. Install a new outer piston seal, and a new center seal onto the clutch housing, lip of seal facing up.
3. Place seal protectors over hub and clutch housing, then install piston.
4. Install 16 springs into piston, place retainer and snap-ring on retainer.
5. With clutch compressor, compress the clutch and install snap-ring.
6. Install five composition and five steel clutch plates, starting with steel and alternating composition and steel.
7. Install clutch backing plate, then install the backing plate snap-ring.
8. Invert the unit and install one sprag bushing, cup side up, over the inner race.
9. Install sprag assembly into outer race.
10. With ridge on inner cage facing down, start sprag and outer race over inner race with clockwise turning motion. NOTE: outer race should not turn counterclockwise.
11. Install sprag bushing over sprag cup side down.
12 Install clutch retainer and snap-ring.
13. Place direct clutch assembly over center support and air check operation of direct clutch.

NOTE: it is normal for air applied to reverse passage to escape from direct clutch passage. Air applied to direct clutch passage should move direct clutch.

Center Support

Disassembly

1. Remove four hook-type oil rings from center support.

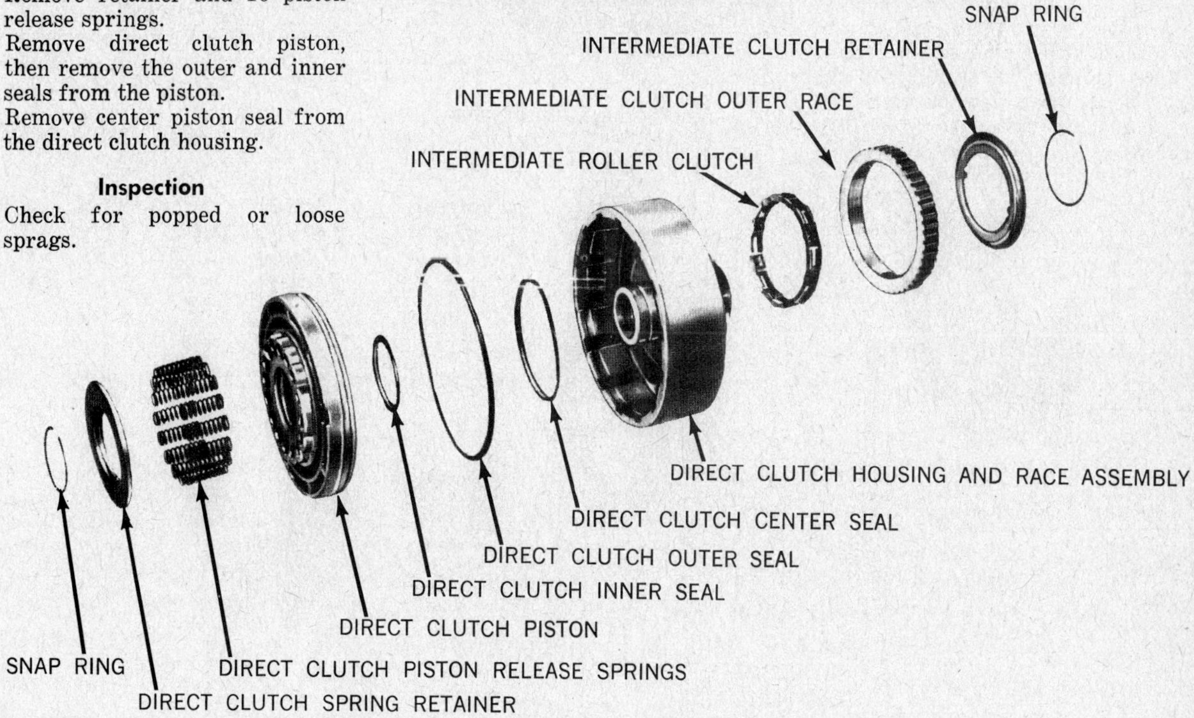

Exploded view—direct clutch and intermediate roller assembly (© G.M. Corp.)

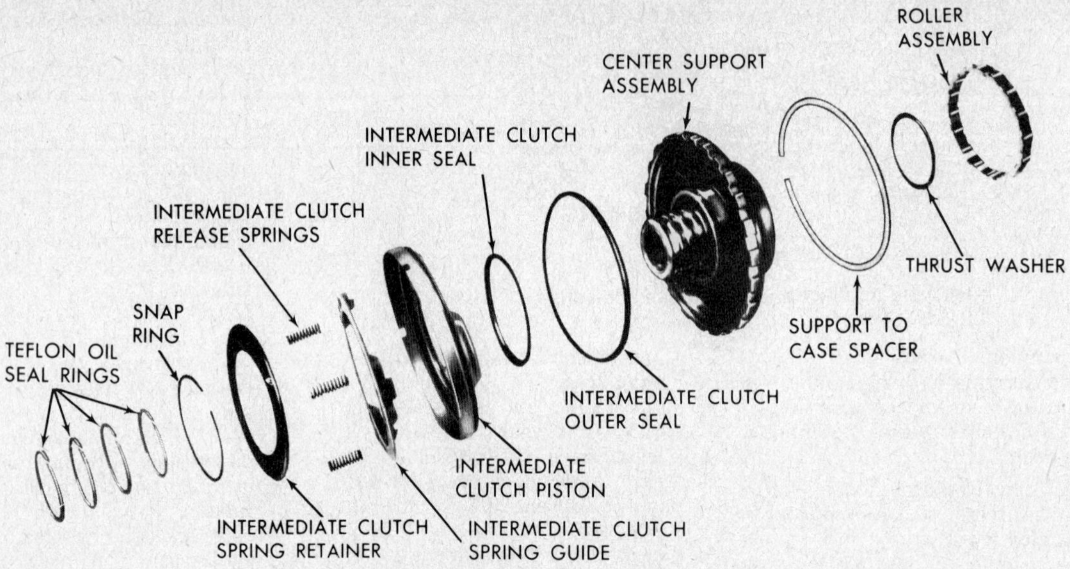

Exploded view—center support assembly (© G.M. Corp.)

2. Using clutch fingers, compress the spring retainer and remove the snap-ring.
3. Remove spring retainer and 12 clutch release springs.
4. Remove intermediate clutch piston.
5. Remove inner piston seal. *NOTE: do not remove the three screws holding the roller clutch inner race to the center support.*
6. Remove outer piston seal.

Inspection

1. Inspect roller clutch inner race for scratches or identations. Check that lubrication hole is open.
2. Check bushing for scoring, wear, or galling. If bushing is replaced, drive new bushing into bore until it is flush to .010 in. below the top of the oil delivery

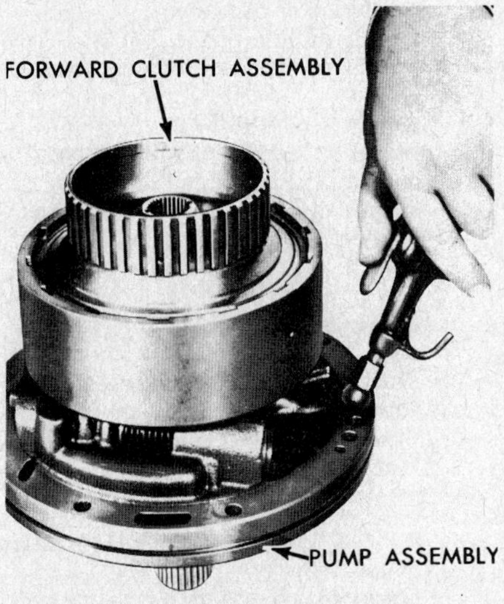

Air checking forward clutch (© G.M. Corp.)

sleeve.

3. Check oil seal rings and ring grooves in the center support tower for damage.
4. Make air pressure check of oil passages to be sure they are not interconnected.
5. Inspect piston sealing surfaces for scratches. Inspect piston seal grooves for damage. Check piston for cracks or porosity.
6. Check release springs for distortion or collapsed coils.
7. Check support to case spacer for burrs or raised edges. Repair with a stone or fine sand paper.

Assembly

1. Install new inner and outer seals on the piston, lip on inner seal facing away from the spring pocket.
2. Install inner spring protector

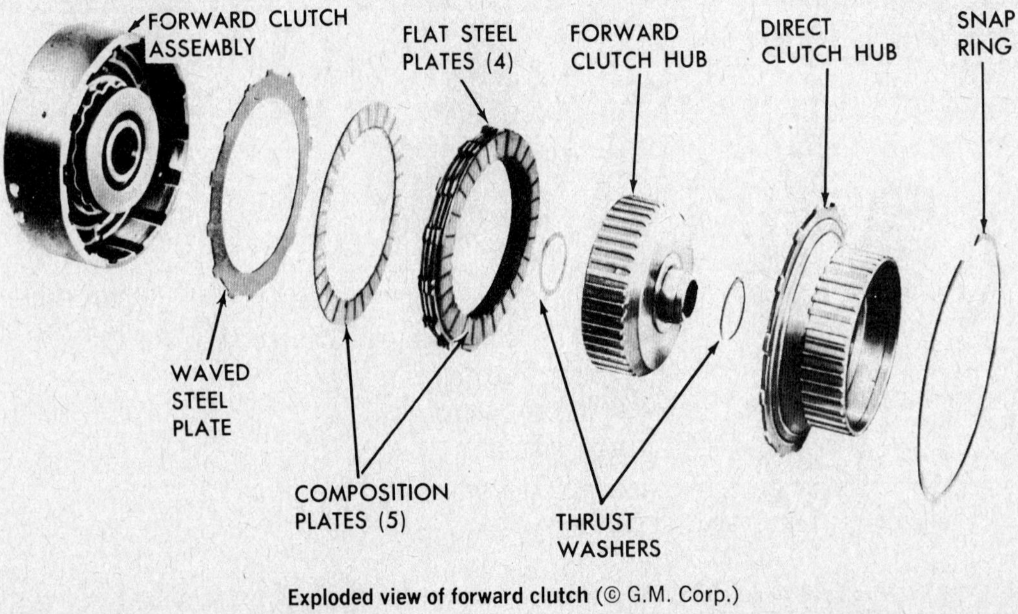

Exploded view of forward clutch (© G.M. Corp.)

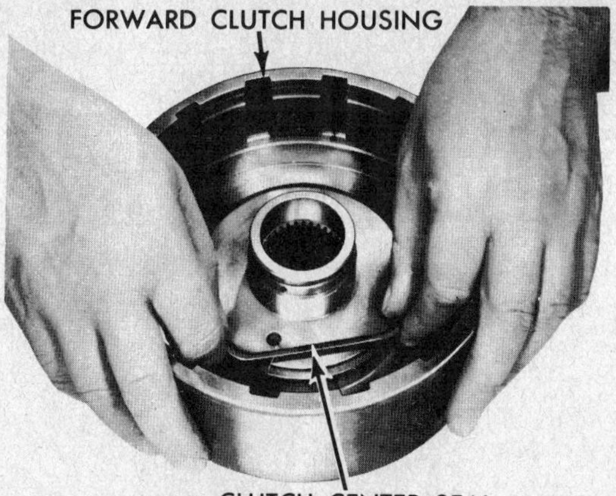

Removing forward clutch center seal (© G.M. Corp.)

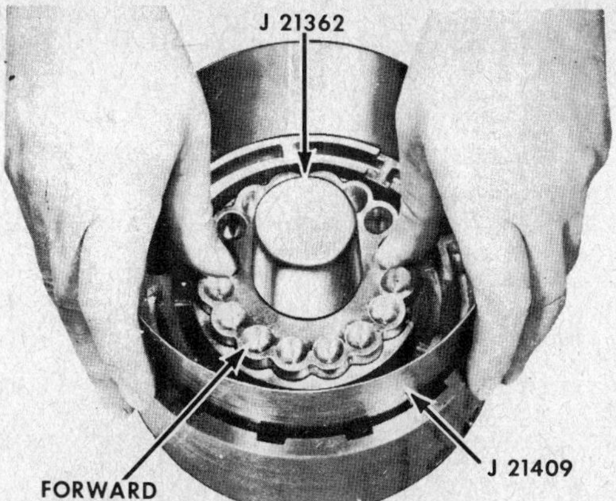

Installing forward clutch piston (© G.M. Corp.)

tool onto the center support hub; lubricate the seal and install the piston.

3. Install 12 release springs into the piston.
4. Place spring retainer and snap-ring over the springs.
5. Using the clutch spring compressor, compress the springs and install the snap-ring.
6. Install four hook-type oil rings.
7. Air check the operation of intermediate clutch piston.

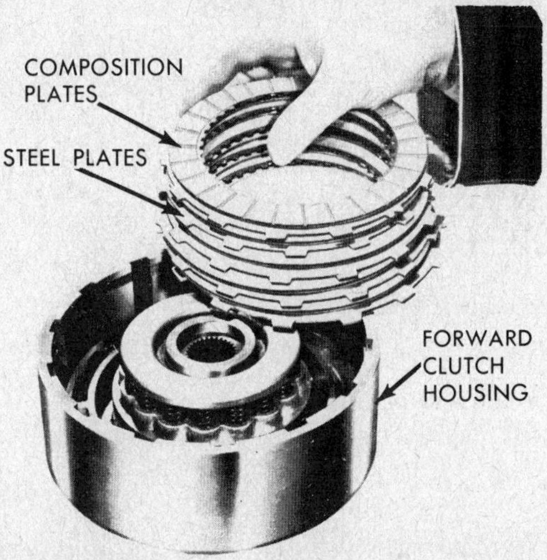

Installing forward clutch composition and steel plates (© G.M. Corp.)

Torque Converter Inspection

The torque converter is a welded assembly and must be serviced as a unit. If converter output shaft has more than .050 in. end-play, renew the unit.

Check for leaks as follows:

A. Install converter leak test fixture and tighten.
B. Fill converter with air, 80 psi.
C. Submerge in water and check for bubbles.

Planetary Gear Unit

Disassembly

1. Remove center support assembly.
2. Remove center support to reaction carrier thrust washer.
3. Remove center support to sun gear races and thrust bearing. One race may already have been removed with the center support.
4. Remove reaction carrier and roller clutch assembly.
5. Remove front internal gear ring from output carrier assembly.
6. Remove sun gear.
7. Take off reaction carrier to output carrier thrust washer.
8. Turn carrier assembly over. Remove output shaft to output carrier snap ring.
9. Output shaft may now be removed.
10. Measure to determine speedometer drive gear location with relation to the end of the shaft for reassembly. Remove nylon speedometer drive gear by depressing retaining clip and sliding gear off output shaft. Remove steel speedometer drive gear with a suitable puller.
11. Remove output shaft to rear internal gear thrust bearing and two races.
12. Remove rear internal gear and mainshaft. Remove rear internal gear to sun gear thrust bearing and two races. Remove rear internal gear to mainshaft snap ring. Remove mainsahft.

Inspection of Reaction Carrier, Roller Clutch, and Output Carrier Assembly

1. Insert band surface reaction carrier for burring or scoring.
2. Check roller clutch outer race for scoring or wear. Check thrust washer for wear.
3. Check bushing for damage. If bushing is damaged, replace reaction carrier.
4. Check reaction carrier pinions for damage, rough bearings, or excessive tilt. Check pinion end play. It should be .009-.024 in. Pinions may be replaced if necessary.
5. Check roller clutch for damaged members. Check roller clutch cage for damage.
6. Inspect front internal gear (out-put carrier) for damaged teeth. Inspect output carrier pinions, for damage, rough bearings, and excessive tilt. Check pinion end play. It should be .009-.024 in.
7. Inspect parking pawl lugs for cracks or damage. Inspect output locating splines for damage.
8. Check front internal gear ring for flaking.

Assembly

1. Install rear internal gear onto end of mainshaft, then install the snap-ring.
2. Install sun gear to internal gear thrust races and bearings against inner face of rear internal gear as follows:

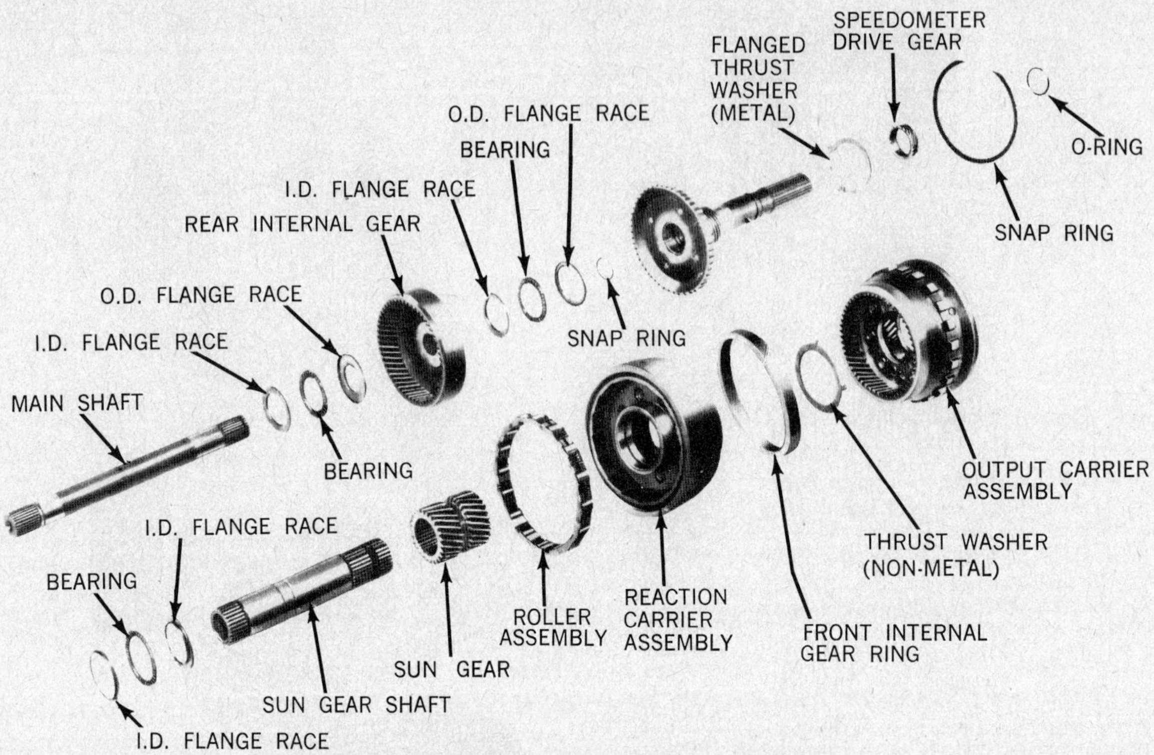

Exploded view—planetary gear unit assembly (© G.M. Corp.)

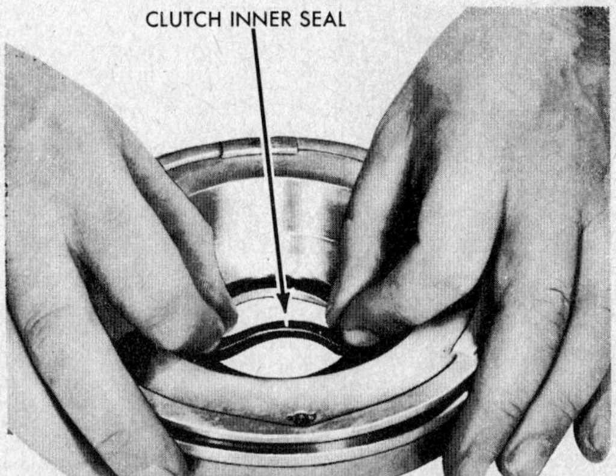

Installing direct clutch inner seal (© G.M. Corp.)

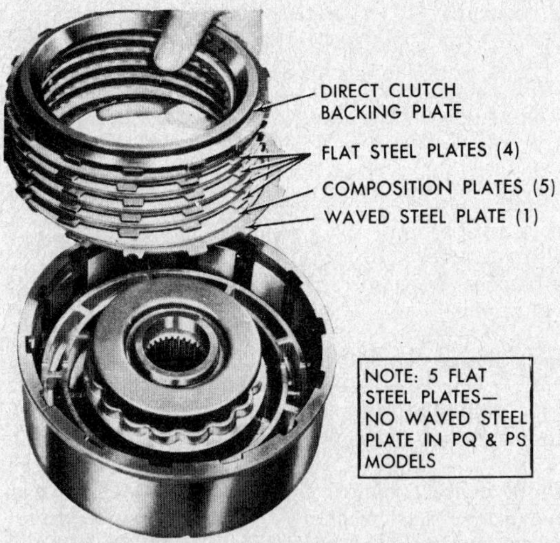

Installing direct clutch backing plate and clutches (© G.M. Corp.)

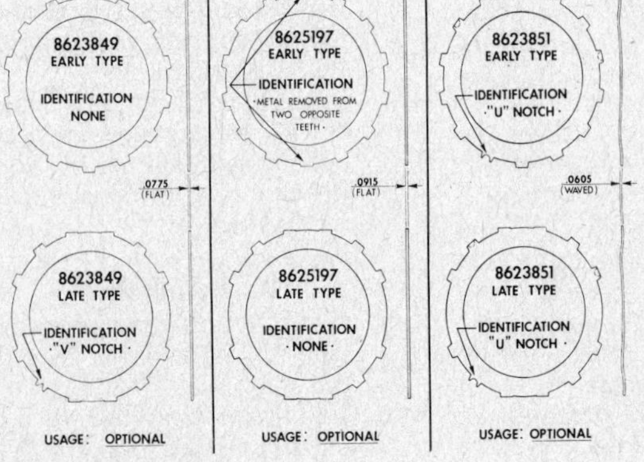

Clutch plate identification (© G.M. Corp.)

Removing direct clutch assembly (© G.M. Corp.)

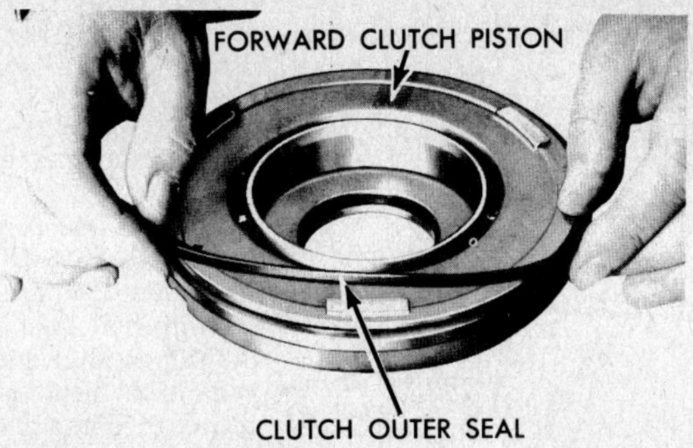

Removing or installing forward clutch piston outer seal (© G.M. Corp.)

a. Place large race against the internal gear, with flange facnig up.
b. Place thrust bearing against race.
c. Place small race against the bearing, with inner flange facing the bearing, or down.

3. Install the output carrier over the mainshaft so that the pinions mesh with the rear internal gear.
4. Place the above portion of the assembly through a hole in the bench so that the mainshaft hangs downward.
5. Install the rear internal gear to output shaft thrust races and bearings as follows:
   a. Small diamete race against internal gear, center flange facing up.
   b. Bearing onto the race.
   c. Second race onto the bearing, outer flange cupped over the bearing.
6. Install output shaft into the output carrier assembly.
7. Install output shaft to output carrier snap-ring.
8. Turn assembly over and support it so that the output shaft hangs downward.
9. Install the reaction carrier to output carrier thrust washer, tabs facing down and in their pockets.
10. Install sun gear, splines, chamfer down. Install gear ring over output carrier.
11. Install sun gear shaft, then the reaction carrier.
12. Install the center support to sun gear thrust races and bearing as follows:
   A. Install the large race, center flange up over the sun gear shaft.
   B. Install thrust bearing.
   C. Install the second race, center flange up.
13. Install roller clutch to reaction carrier outer race. Install the center support to reaction carrier thrust washer into the recess in the support. Retain with petroleum jelly.

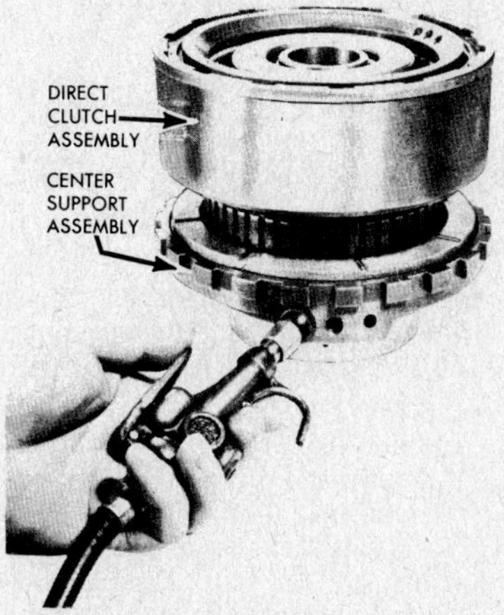

Air checking direct clutch assembly (© G.M. Corp.)

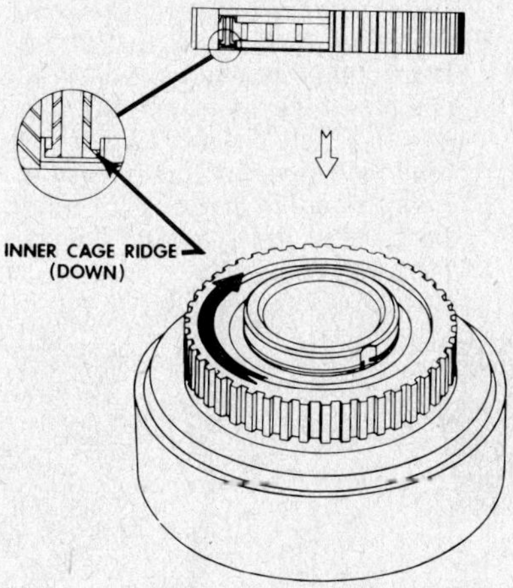

Correct sprag rotation (© G.M. Corp.)

14. Install center support into reaction carrier and roller clutch assembly. With reaction carrier held, center support should only turn counterclockwise.
15. Install a gear unit assembly holding tool to hold units in place. Install output shaft to case thrust washer tabs in pockets and retain with petroleum jelly.

Transmission Assembly

Parking Mechanism, Rear Band and the Complete Gear Assembly

Installation

1. Install O-ring seal onto parking pawl shaft, then install parking pawl, tooth toward inside of case.
2. Install the pawl shaft retaining clip and the return spring, square-end hooked on the pawl.
3. Install parking brake bracket guides over pawl, using two attaching bolts.
4. Install rear band assembly so that the two lugs index with the two anchor pins. Install support to case spacer with ring gap adjacent to band anchor pin.
5. Install rear selective washer into slots provided inside rear of transmission case. Dip washer in transmission fluid.
6. Install the complete gear unit assembly into the case.
7. Lubricate and install center support to case snap-ring. Install bevel side up. *NOTE: The support to case spacer is .040 in. thick and is flat on both sides.* The center support to case snap-ring has one side beveled. The intermediate clutch backing plate to case snap ring is .093 in. thick and is flat on both sides.
8. Lubricate and install case to center support bolt and torque to 22 ft. lbs. Remove the locating screw.
9. Install three steel and three composition clutch plates. Alternate the plates, starting with steel.
10. Install the backing plate, ridge up, then the snap-ring. Locate snap-ring gap opposite band anchor pin.
11. Check rear end-play as follows:
   A. Install a threaded rod or a long bolt into an extension hous-attaching bolt hole.
   B. Mount dial indicator on the rod and index it with the end of the output shaft.
   c. Move the output shaft in and out. Read the end-play. End-play should be .007-.019 in. The selective washer controlling the end-play is the steel washer, having three lugs, that is located between the thrust washer and the rear face of the transmission case.

If a different washer thickness is required to obtain proper end-play, it can be selected from the following chart.

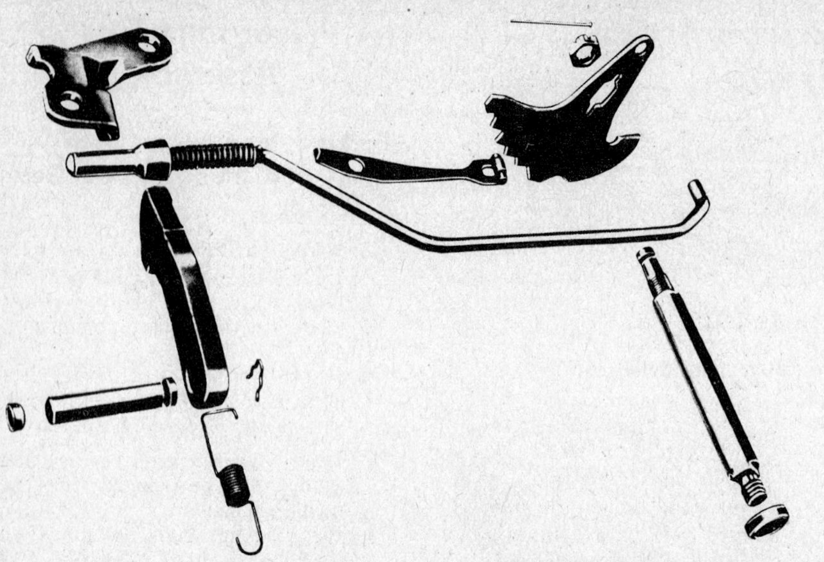

Exploded view—manual and parking linkage (© G. M. Corp.)

Thickness	*Notches and/or Numeral*	
.074—.078 in.	None	1
.082—.086 in.	1 Tab Side	2
.090—.094 in.	2 Tabs Side	3
.098—.102 in.	1 Tab O.D.	4
.106—.110 in.	2 Tabs O.D.	5
.114—.118 in.	3 Tabs O.D.	6

Front Band, Direct Clutch and Forward Clutch

Installation

1. Install front band, with band anchor hole placed over the band anchor pin, and apply lug facing the servo hole.
2. Install the direct clutch and intermediate sprag assembly. (Removal of direct clutch plates may help.)
3. Install forward clutch hub to direct housing bronze thrust washer onto the forward clutch hub. Retain with petroleum jelly.
4. Install forward clutch assembly, indexing the direct clutch hub so the end of the mainshaft will be flush with the end of the forward clutch hub. Use turbine shaft as a tool.
5. Install turbine shaft; end with the short spline goes into the forward clutch housing.
6. Install pump-to-case gasket onto the case face and install the front pump assembly and all but one attaching bolt and seal. Torque to 18 ft. lbs. *NOTE: If turbine shaft cannot be rotated as pump is being pulled into place, forward or direct clutch housing has not been properly installed to index with all clutch plates. This condition must be corrected before pump is fully pulled into place.*
7. Drive in a new front seal.
8. Check front unit end-play as follows:
   A. Install one rod of slide hammer, with 5/16-18 in. thread, into the empty pump assembly attaching bolt hole.
   B. Mount dial indicator on the rod and adjust the indicator probe to contact end of turbine shaft.
   C. Hold output shaft forward while pushing turbine shaft rearward to its stop.
   D. Set dial indicator to zero.
   E. Pull turbine
   F. Read end-play, as registered on dial. The reading should be .003-.024 in.

The selective washer controlling this end-play is located between the pump cover and the forward clutch housing. If more, or less, washer thickness is required to bring end-play within specifications, make selection from the thickness-color chart.

Thickness	*Color*
.060-.064 in.	Yellow
.071-.075 in.	Blue
.082-.086 in.	Red
.093-.097 in.	Brown
.104-.108 in.	Green
.115-.119 in.	Black
.126-.130 in.	Purple

9. Remove dial indicator and install the remaining front pump attaching bolt and seal. Torque to 18 ft. lbs.

Rear Extension Housing Assembly

Installation

1. Install extension housing-to-case

Installing output shaft (© G.M. Corp.)

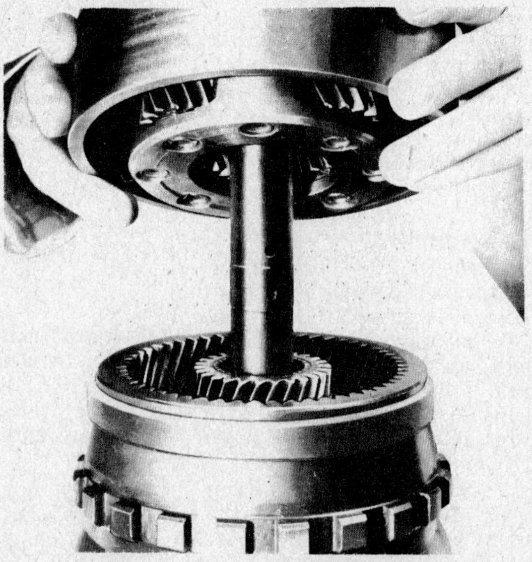

Installing reaction carrier and roller assembly (© G.M. Corp.)

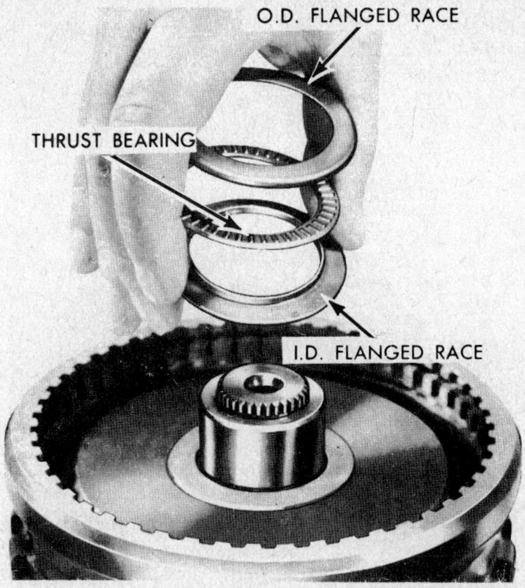

Installing rear internal gear to output shaft bearing and races (© G.M. Corp.)

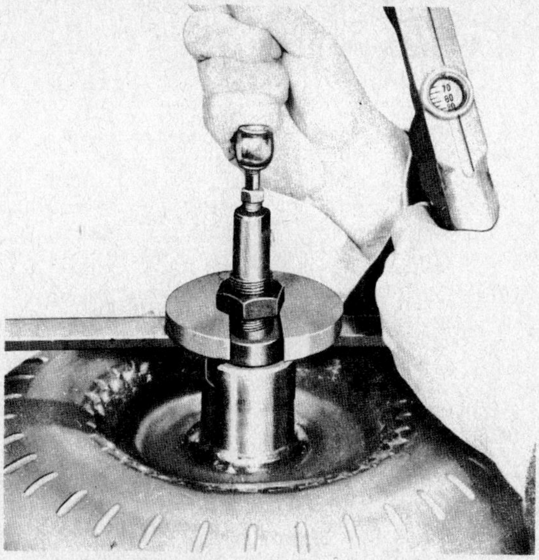

Air checking converter (© G.M. Corp.)

Installing direct clutch assembly (© G.M. Corp.)

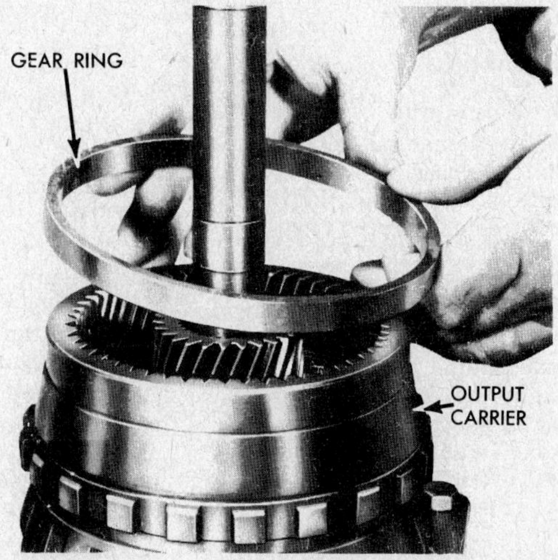

Installing front internal gear ring to output carrier (© G.M. Corp.)

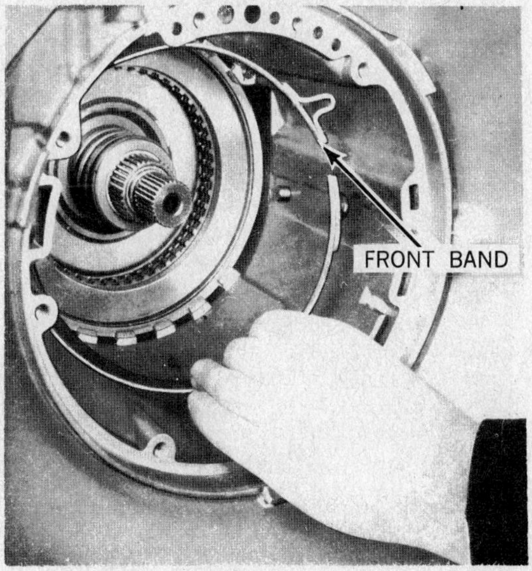

Installing front band (© G.M. Corp.)

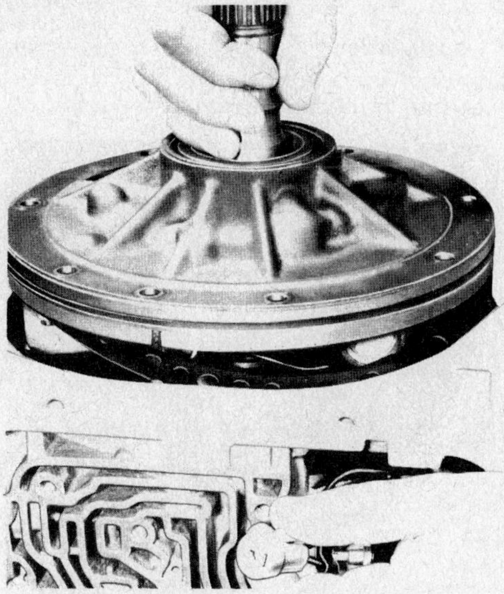

Installing pump assembly (© G.M. Corp.)

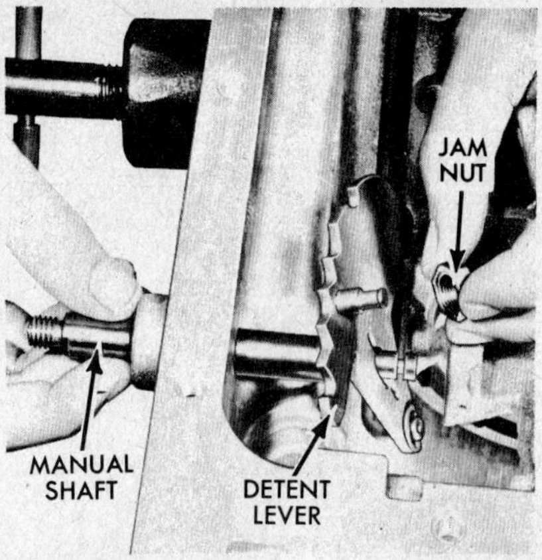

Installing dent lever and jam nut to manual shaft (© G.M. Corp.)

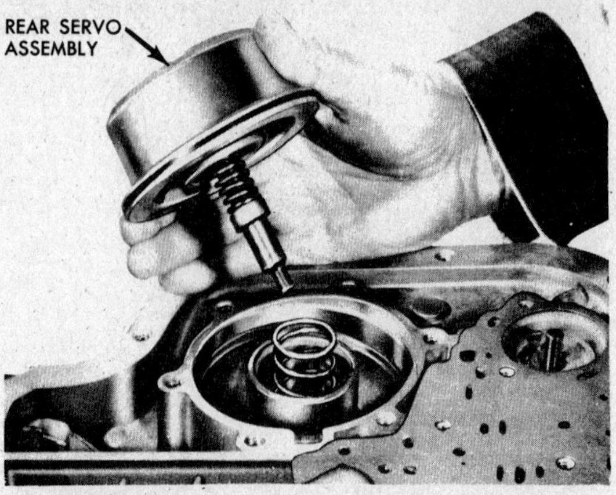

Installing rear servo assembly (© G.M. Corp.)

O-ring seal onto extension housing.
2. Attach extension housing to transmission case. Torque to 22 ft. lbs.
3. Drive in a new extension housing rear seal.

Manual Linkage

Installation

1. Install new manual shift shaft seal into the case.
2. Insert actuator rod into the manual detent lever from the side opposite the pin.
3. Install actuator rod plunger under the parking bracket and over the pawl.
4. Install manual lever and shaft through the case and detent lever, then lock with hex nut on the manual shift shaft. (Be sure detent retaining nut is tight.) Install retaining pin.

Check Balls, Front Servo Gaskets, Spacer and Solenoid

Installation

1. Install front servo spring and retainer into transmission case.

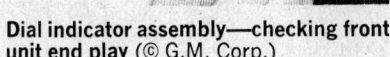

Dial indicator assembly—checking front unit end play (© G.M. Corp.)

2. Install flat washer on front servo pin, on end opposite taper. Install pin and washer into case so that tapered end of pin is contacting band.
3. Install oil seal ring on front servo piston, and install on apply pin so that identification numbers on shoulders are exposed. Check freeness of piston in bore.
4. Install six check balls into transmission case pockets.
5. Install valve body spacer to case gasket and spacer plate. Install detent solenoid and gasket, with connector facing outer edge of case. Do not tighten bolts at this time.
6. Install O-ring seal on electrical connector. Lubricate and install electrical connector with locator tab in notch on side of case. Connect detent wire and lead wire to electrical connector. Be sure to install electrical wire clip.

Rear Servo

Installation

1. Before installing the rear servo assembly, check the band apply pin, using rear band apply fixture as follows:
   A. Attach band apply pin selection gauge, to the transmission case with attaching screws.
   B. Apply 25 ft. lbs. torque and select proper servo pin to be used from scale on the tool.
   C. Remove tool and make note of proper pin to be used during assembly.

There are three selective pins:

The identification consists of a ring located on the band lug end of the pin. Selecting the proper pin is equivalent to adjusting the band.

2. Install rear accumulator spring.
3. Install servo assembly, then the gasket and cover. Torque bolts to 18 ft. lbs.

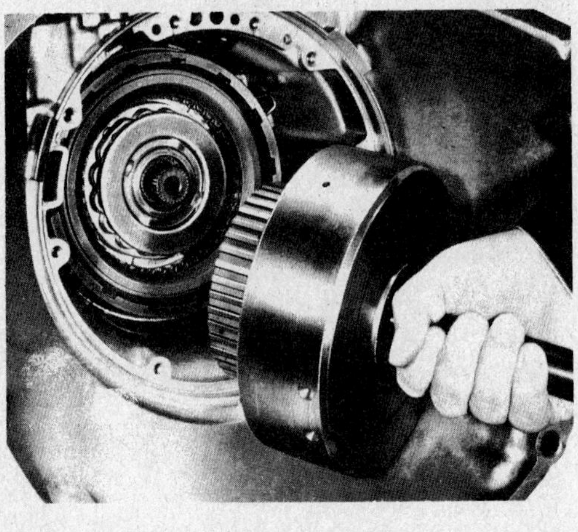

Installing forward clutch assembly (© G.M. Corp.)

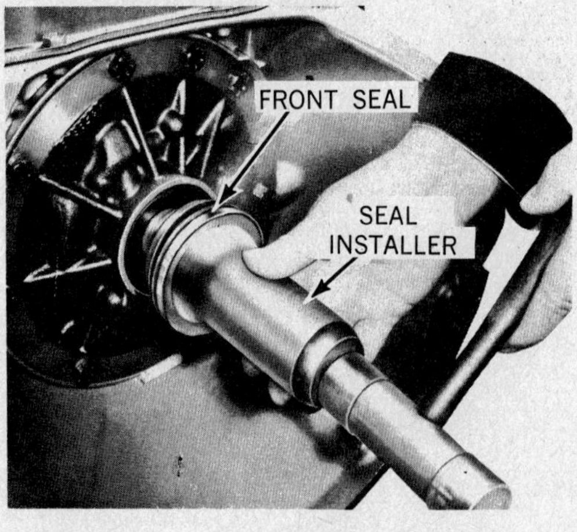

Installing front pump oil seal (© G.M. Corp.)

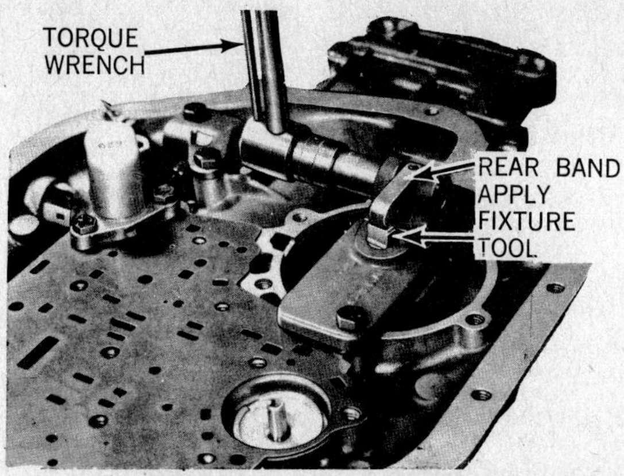

Checking rear band pin (© G.M. Corp.)

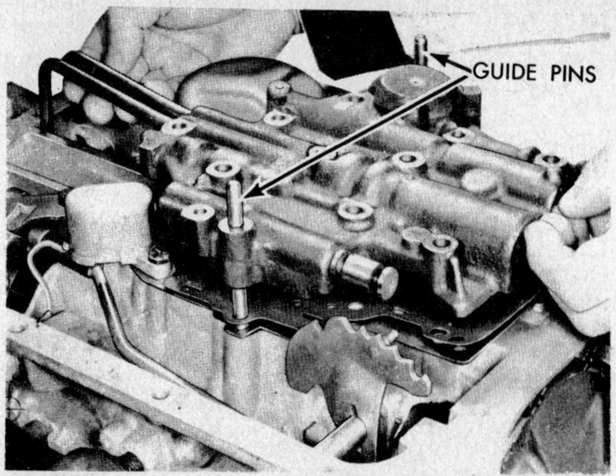

Installing control valve assembly and governor pipes (© G.M. Corp.)

Control Valve and Governor Pipe

Installation

1. Install control valve-to-spacer gasket, then install governor pipes into the control valve body assembly.
2. Install two guide pins, then install the control valve body and governor pipe assembly into the transmission. *NOTE: be sure the manual valve is properly indexed with the pin on the manual detent lever.*
3. Remove guide pins and install valve assembly attaching bolts and manual detent and roller assembly.
4. Tighten detent solenoid and control valve attaching bolts to 8 ft. lbs. torque.

Strainer and Intake Pipe

Installation

1. Install case-to-intake pipe O-ring onto strainer and intake pipe assembly.
2. Install strainer and pipe assembly. Install new filter on models so equipped.
3. Install new pan gasket, then install the pan. Torque to 12 ft. lbs.
4. Install modulator shield and all pan attaching screws. Torque pan attaching screws.

Modulator Assembly

Installation

1. Install modulator valve into the case, stem end out.
2. Install O-ring seal onto the vacuum modulator, then install assembly into the case.
3. Install modulator retainer and attaching bolt. Torque to 18 ft. lbs.

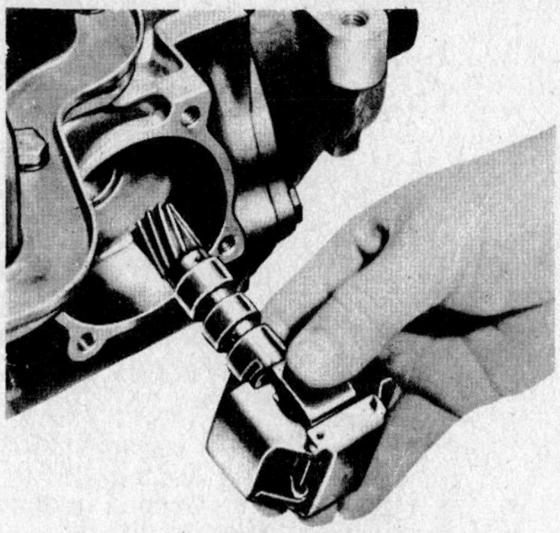

Installing governor assembly (© G.M. Corp.)

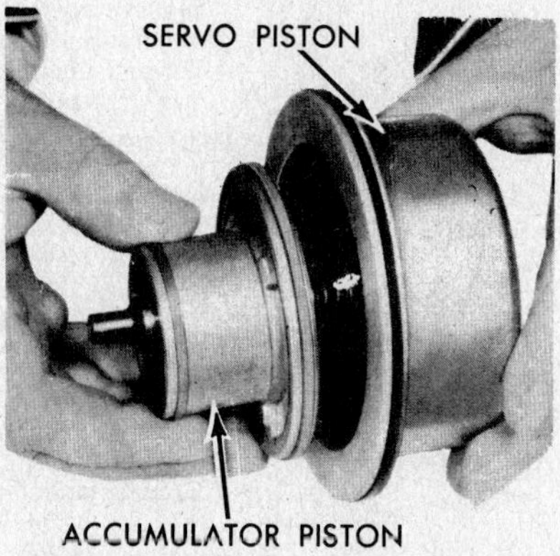

Removing servo accumulator piston (© G.M. Corp.)

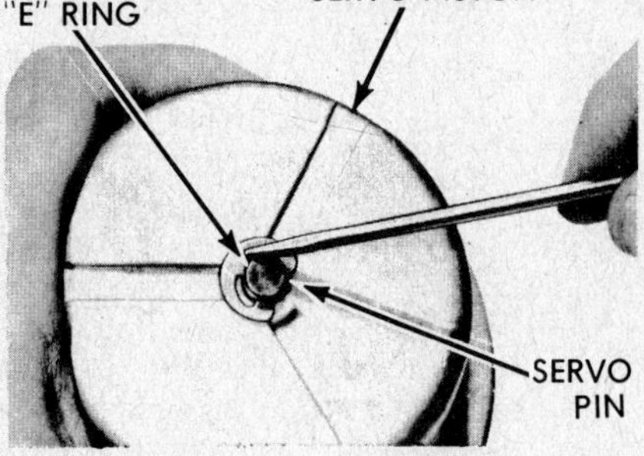

Removing servo "E" clip (© G.M. Corp.)

Governor and Speedometer Driven Gear

Installation

1. Install governor assembly.
2. Attach governor cover and gasket with four bolts. Torque to 18 ft. lbs.
3. Install speedometer driven gear assembly. Install retainer and attaching bolt.

Converter

Installation

1. Place transmission in cradle or portable jack.
2. Install converter assembly to pump assembly, making certain that the converter hub drive slots are fully engaged with the pump drive gear tangs and that the converter is installed all the way toward the rear of the transmission.

TORQUE SPECIFICATIONS

Foot-Pounds

Pump cover bolts	18
Parking pawl bracket bolts	18
Center support bolt	22
Pump-to-case attaching bolts	18
Extension-to-case attaching bolts	22
Rear servo cover bolts	18
Detent solenoid bolts	8
Control valve body bolts	8
Bottom pan attaching screws	12
Modulator retainer bolt	18
Governor cover bolts	18
Manual lever-to-manual shaft nut	20
Linkage swivel clamp screw	20
Transmission-to-engine mounting bolts	40
Rear mount-to-transmission bolts	40
Oil cooler line	16
Filter retainer bolt	10
Pressure switch assembly	8

Manual Transmissions

INDEX

Diagnosis

Jumping out of High Gear

1. Misalignment of transmission case or clutch housing.
2. Worn pilot bearing in crankshaft.
3. Bent transmission shaft.
4. Worn high speed sliding gear.
5. Worn teeth in clutch shaft.
6. Insufficient spring tension on shifter rail plunger.
7. Bent or loose shifter fork.
8. End-play in clutch shaft.
9. Gears not engaging completely.
10. Loose or worn bearings on clutch shaft or mainshaft.

Sticking in High Gear

1. Clutch not releasing fully.
2. Burred or battered teeth on clutch shaft.
3. Burred or battered transmission main-shaft.
4. Frozen synchronizing clutch.
5. Stuck shifter rail plunger.
6. Gearshift lever twisting and binding shifter rail.
7. Battered teeth on high speed sliding gear or on sleeve.
8. Lack of lubrication.
9. Improper lubrication.
10. Corroded transmission parts.
11. Defective mainshaft pilot bearing.

Jumping out of Second Gear

1. Insufficient spring tension on shifter rail plunger.
2. Bent or loose shifter fork.
3. Gears not engaging completely.
4. End-play in transmission mainshaft.
5. Loose transmission gear bearing.
6. Defective mainshaft pilot bearing.
7. Bent transmission shaft.
8. Worn teeth on second speed sliding gear or sleeve.
9. Loose or worn bearings on transmission mainshaft.
10. End-play in countershaft.

Sticking in Second Gear

1. Clutch not releasing fully.
2. Burred or battered teeth on sliding sleeve.
3. Burred or battered transmission main-shaft.
4. Frozen synchronizing clutch.
5. Stuck shifter rail plunger.
6. Gearshift lever twisting and binding shifter rail.
7. Lack of lubrication.
8. Second speed transmission gear bearings locked will give same effect as gears stuck in second.
9. Improper lubrication.
10. Corroded transmission parts.

Jumping out of Low Gear

1. Gears not engaging completely.
2. Bent or loose shifter fork.
3. End-play in transmission mainshaft.
4. End-play in countershaft.
5. Loose or worn bearings on transmission mainshaft.
6. Loose or worn bearings in countershaft.
7. Defective mainshaft pilot bearing.

Sticking in Low Gear

1. Clutch not releasing fully.
2. Burred or battered transmission main-shaft.
3. Stuck shifter rail plunger.
4. Gearshift lever twisting and binding shifter rail.
5. Lack of lubrication.
6. Improper lubrication.
7. Corroded transmission parts.

Jumping out of Reverse Gear

1. Insufficient spring tension on shifter rail plunger.
2. Bent or loose shifter fork.
3. Badly worn gear teeth.
4. Gears not engaging completely.
5. End-play in transmission mainshaft.
6. Idler gear bushings loose or worn.
7. Loose or worn bearings on transmission mainshaft.
8. Defective mainshaft pilot bearing.

Sticking in Reverse Gear

1. Clutch not releasing fully.
2. Burred or battered transmission main-shaft.
3. Stuck shifter rail plunger.
4. Gearshift lever twisting and binding shifter rail.
5. Lack of lubrication.
6. Improper lubrication.
7. Corroded transmission parts.

Failure of Gears to Synchronize

1. Binding pilot bearing on mainshaft, will synchronize in high gear only.
2. Clutch not releasing fully.
3. Detent springs weak or broken.
4. Weak or broken springs under balls in sliding gear sleeve.
5. Binding bearing on clutch shaft.
6. Binding countershaft.
7. Binding pilot bearing in crankshaft.
8. Badly worn gear teeth.
9. Scored or worn cones.
10. Improper lubrication.
11. Constant mesh gear not turning freely on transmission mainshaft. Will synchronize in that gear only.

Gears Spinning When Shifting into Gear from Neutral

1. Clutch not releasing fully.
2. In some cases an extremely light lubricant in transmission will cause gears to continue to spin for a short time after clutch is released.
3. Binding pilot bearing in crankshaft.

Cleaning of Transmission Components

Cleanliness of parts, tools, and work area is of the utmost importance. All transmission components (except bearing assemblies) should be cleaned in cleaning solvent and dried with compressed air before any inspection or work is begun. Great care should be taken when cleaning bearings. Bearings should always be cleaned separately from other parts in clean cleaning solvent and not gasoline. They must never be cleaned in a hot solution tank. It is advisable that they be soaked in cleaning fluid and then tapped against a block of wood in order to free any solidified lubricant that may be trapped inside. Rinse bearings thoroughly in clean solvent and then dry them with moisture-free compressed air being careful not to spin the bearings with the air stream. Rotate each bearing slowly and inspect rollers or balls for any signs of excessive wear, roughness, or damage. Those bearings not in excellent condition must be replaced. If they pass this inspection, they should be dipped in clean oil and wrapped in clean lintless cloth to protect them until installation.

Inspection of Transmission Components

All parts must be completely and carefully inspected for any signs of wear, stress, discoloration or warpage due to excessive heat. Whenever available, the magna flux process should be used on all parts except roller and ball bearings, to detect small cracks unseen by the eye. Inspect the breather assembly to see that it is not clogged or damaged and check all threaded parts for stripped or cross threads. Oil passages must be cleared of obstructions by the use of air pressure or brass rods and all gaskets, oil seals, lock wires, cotter pins, and snap rings are to be replaced. Small nicks or burrs in gears or splines can be removed with a fine abrasive stone. It is important that any housings or covers having cracks or other damage should be replaced and not welded. Synchronizers, not in excellent condition, must be replaced. The bronze synchronizer cone should be checked for wear or for any steel chips that may have become imbedded in it. Springs must be inspected for free length, compressed length, distortion, or collapsed coils.

IMPORTANT: The splines on many clutch gears, mainshafts, etc., are equipped with a machined relief called a "hopping guard". With the clutch gear engaged, the mating gear is free to slip into this notch, preventing the two gears from separating or "walking out of gear" under various load conditions. This is not a worn or chipped gear. Do not grind or discard the gear.

Check all shafts for spline wear or damage. If the mainshaft 1st and reverse sliding gear or clutch hub have worn into the sides of the splines, the shaft should be replaced. Shift forks, shift rods, interlock balls and pins must be replaced if scored, worn, distorted or damaged.

Dodge/Plymouth A-230 3 Speed

Description

The Dodge A-230 is a three-speed transmission equipped with two synchonizer units to assist in the engagement of all forward gears. Lubricant capacity is 5 pints.

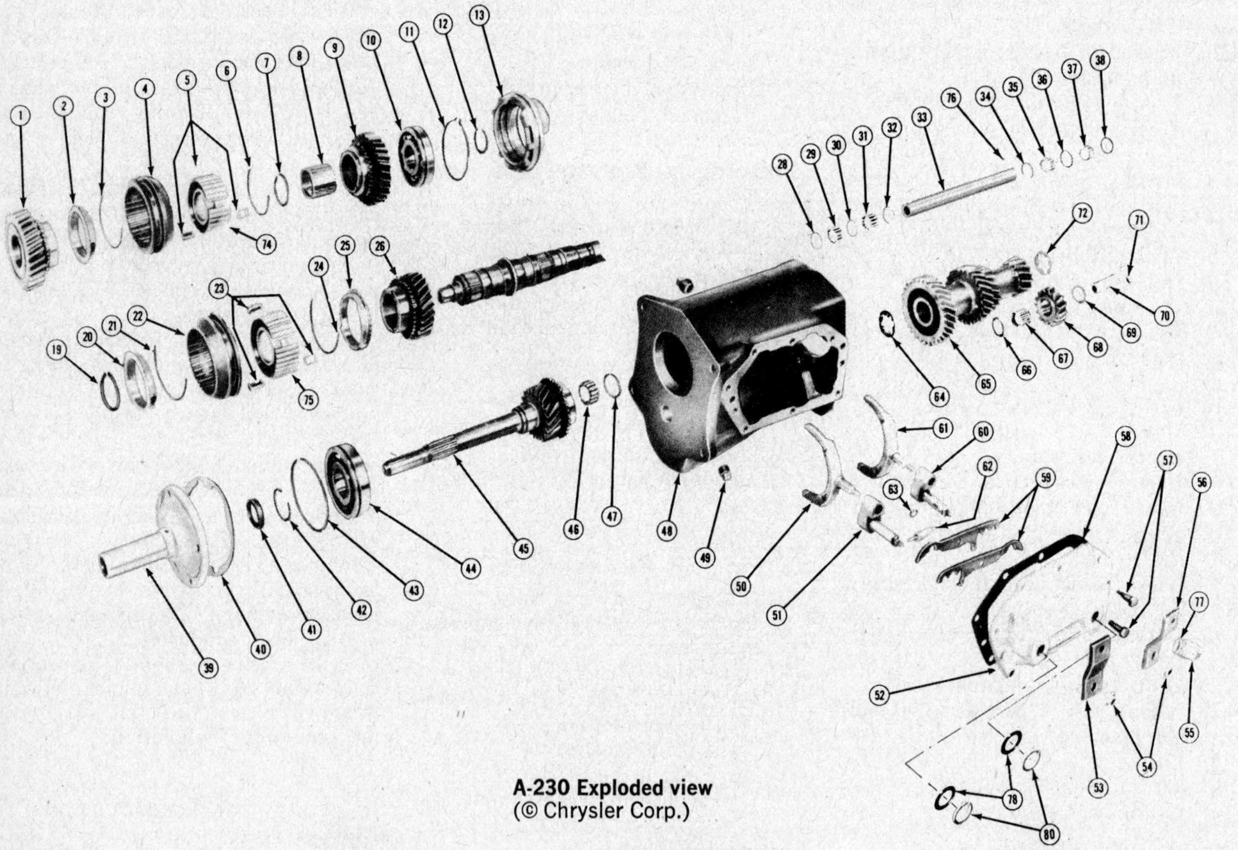

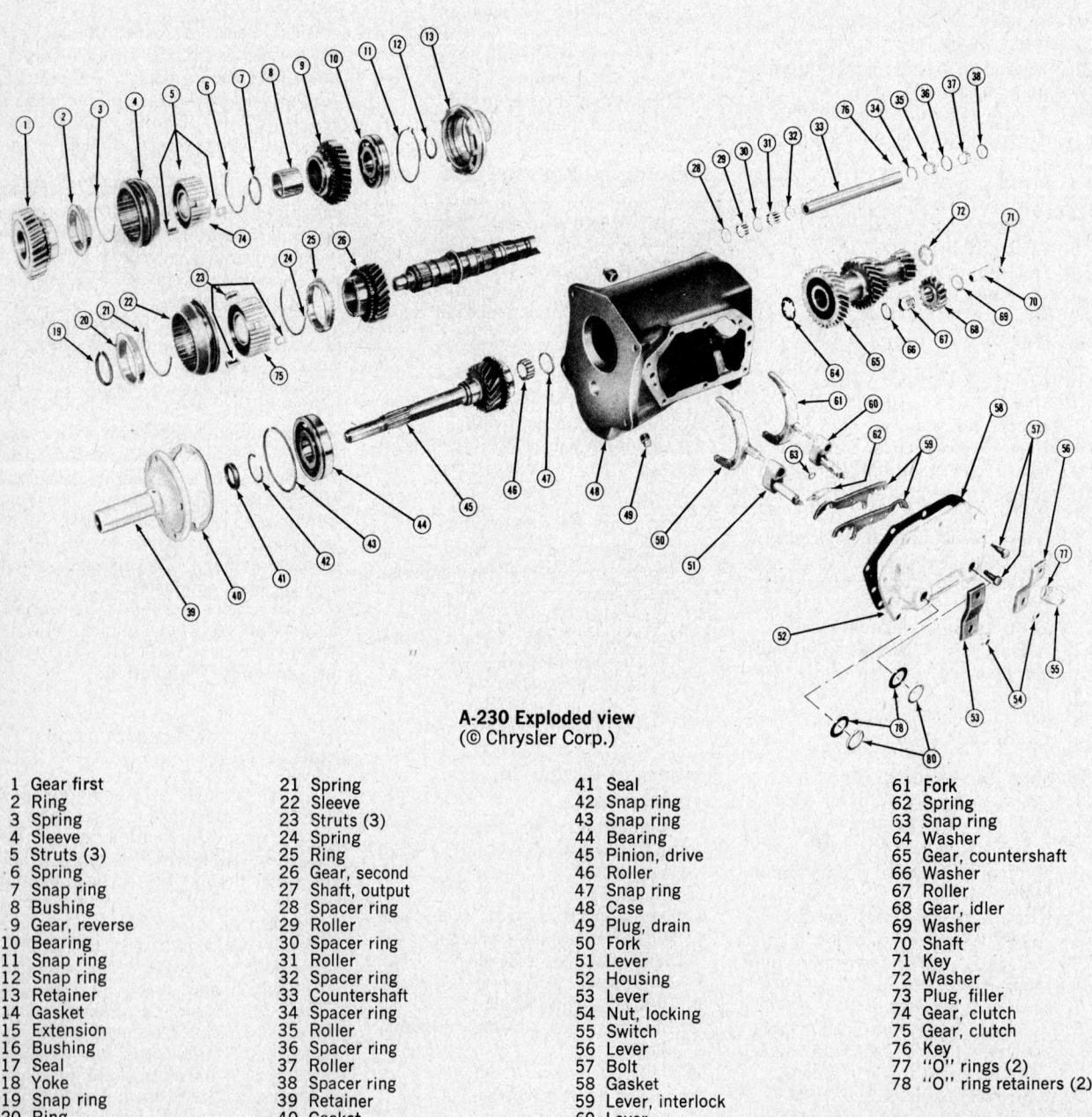

A-230 Exploded view
(© Chrysler Corp.)

1 Gear first
2 Ring
3 Spring
4 Sleeve
5 Struts (3)
6 Spring
7 Snap ring
8 Bushing
9 Gear, reverse
10 Bearing
11 Snap ring
12 Snap ring
13 Retainer
14 Gasket
15 Extension
16 Bushing
17 Seal
18 Yoke
19 Snap ring
20 Ring
21 Spring
22 Sleeve
23 Struts (3)
24 Spring
25 Ring
26 Gear, second
27 Shaft, output
28 Spacer ring
29 Roller
30 Spacer ring
31 Roller
32 Spacer ring
33 Countershaft
34 Spacer ring
35 Roller
36 Spacer ring
37 Roller
38 Spacer ring
39 Retainer
40 Gasket
41 Seal
42 Snap ring
43 Snap ring
44 Bearing
45 Pinion, drive
46 Roller
47 Snap ring
48 Case
49 Plug, drain
50 Fork
51 Lever
52 Housing
53 Lever
54 Nut, locking
55 Switch
56 Lever
57 Bolt
58 Gasket
59 Lever, interlock
60 Lever
61 Fork
62 Spring
63 Snap ring
64 Washer
65 Gear, countershaft
66 Washer
67 Roller
68 Gear, idler
69 Washer
70 Shaft
71 Key
72 Washer
73 Plug, filler
74 Gear, clutch
75 Gear, clutch
76 Key
77 "O" rings (2)
78 "O" ring retainers (2)

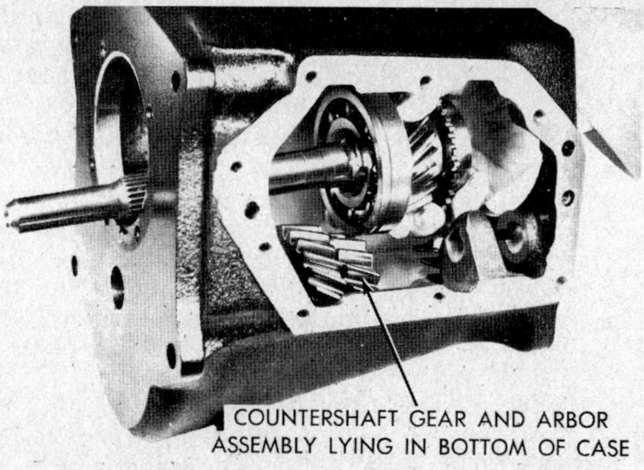

Drive pinion and bearing assembly removal
(© Chrysler Corp.)

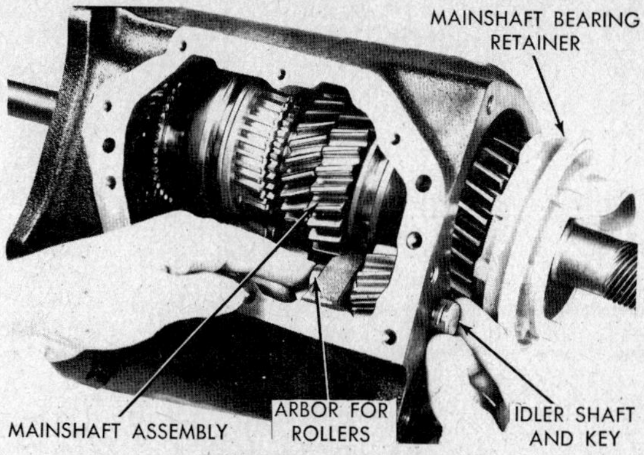

Reverse idler gear removal
(© Chrysler Corp.)

Disassembly of Transmission

Shift Housing and Mechanism

1. Shift to second gear.
2. Remove side cover. If shaft O-ring seals need replacement:
   a. Pull shift-forks out of shafts.
   b. Remove nuts and operating levers from shafts.
   c. Deburr shafts. Remove shafts.

Drive Pinion Retainer and Extension Housing

1. Remove pinion bearing retainer from front of transmission case. Pry off retainer oil seal. For clearance:
   a. With a brass drift, tap drive pinion as far forward as possible. Rotate cut away part of second gear next to countershaft gear. Shift second-third synchronizer sleeve forward.
   b. Remove speedometer pinion adapter retainer. Work adapter and pinion out of extension housing.
   c. Unbolt extension housing. Break housing loose with plastic hammer and carefully remove.

Idler Gear and Mainshaft

1. Insert dummy shaft in case to push reverse idler shaft and key out of case.
2. Remove dummy shaft and idler rollers.
3. Remove both tanged idler gear thrust washers.
4. Remove mainshaft assembly through rear of case.

Countershaft Gear and Drive Pinion

1. Using a mallet and dummy shaft, tap the countershaft rearward enough to remove key. Drive countershaft out of case, being careful not to drop the washers.
2. Lower countershaft gear to bottom of case.
3. Remove snap-ring from pinion bearing outer race (outside front of case).
4. Drive pinion shaft into case with plastic hammer. Remove assembly through rear of case.
5. If bearing is to be replaced, remove snap-ring and press off bearing.
6. Lift counter shaft gear and dummy shaft out through rear of case.

Mainshaft

1. Remove snap-ring from front end of mainshaft along with second gear stop ring and second gear.
2. Spread snap-ring in mainshaft bearing retainer. Slide retainer back off the bearing race.
3. Remove snap-ring at rear of mainshaft. Support front side of reverse gear. Press bearing off mainshaft.
4. Remove from press. Remove mainshaft bearing and reverse gear from shaft.
5. Remove snap-ring and first-reverse synchronizer assembly from shaft. Remove stop ring and first gear rearward.

Cleaning and Inspection

See "Cleaning and Inspection" instructions at front of Transmission Section.

Assembly of Transmission

Countershaft Gear

1. Slide dummy shaft into countershaft gear.
2. Slide one roller thrust washer over dummy shaft and into gear, followed by 22 greased rollers.
3. Repeat Step 2, adding one roller thrust washer on end.
4. Repeat steps 2 and 3 at other end of countershaft gear. There is a total of 88 rollers and 6 thrust washers.
5. Place greased front thrust

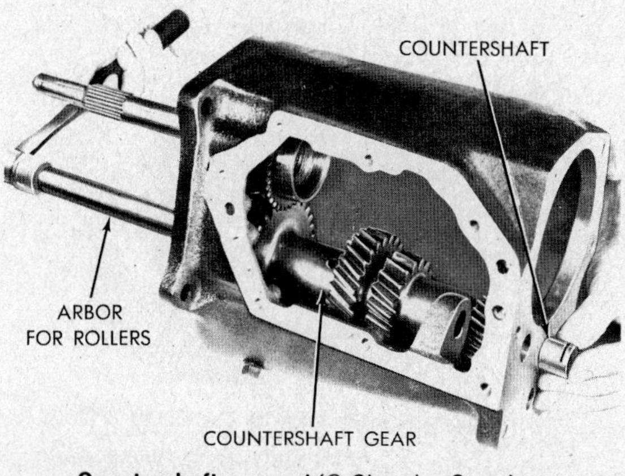

Countershaft removal (© Chrysler Corp.)

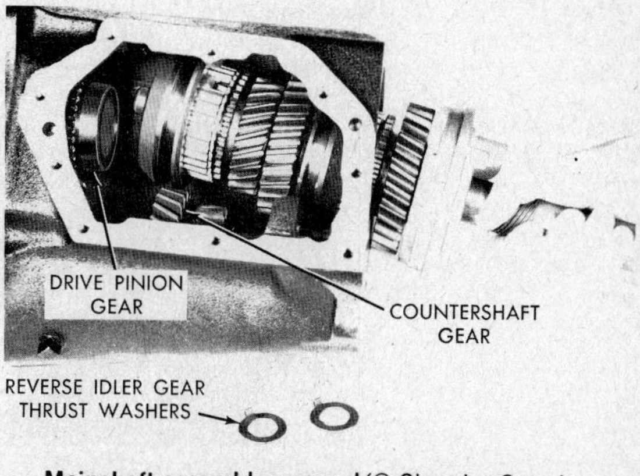

Mainshaft assembly removal (© Chrysler Corp.)

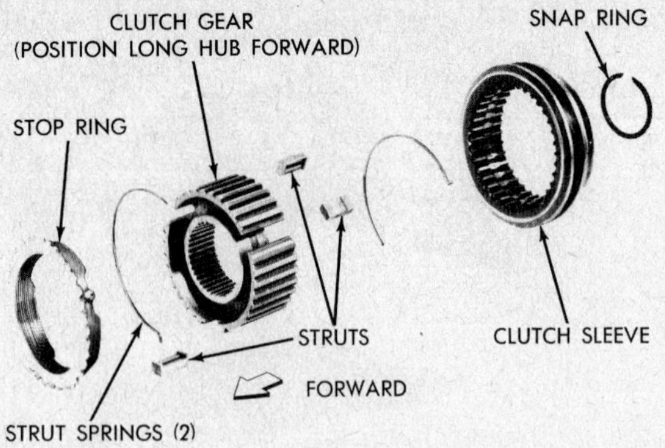

1st-reverse synchronizer disassembled (© Chrysler Corp.)

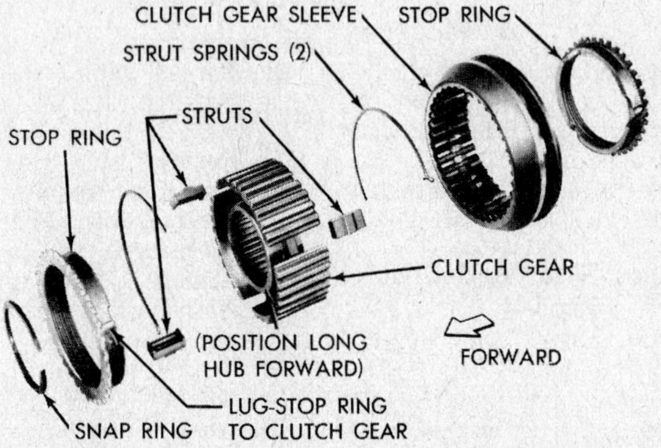

2nd-3rd gear synchronizer (© Chrysler Corp.)

washer on dummy shaft against gear with tangs forward.

6. Grease rear thrust washer and stick it in place in the case, with tangs rearward. Place countershaft gear assembly in bottom of transmission case until drive pinion is installed.

Pinion Gear

1. Press new bearing on pinion shaft with snap-ring groove forward. Install new snap-ring.
2. Install 15 rollers and retaining ring in drive pinion gear.
3. Install drive pinion and bearing assembly into case.
4. Position countershaft gear assembly by positioning it and thrust washers so countershaft can be tapped into position. Be careful to keep the countershaft against the dummy shaft to keep parts from falling between them. Install key in countershaft.
5. Tap drive pinion forward for clearance.

Mainshaft

1. Place a stop ring flat on the bench. Place a clutch gear and a sleeve on top. Drop the struts in their slots and insert a strut spring with the tang inside on strut. Turn the assembly over and install second strut spring, tang in a different strut.
2. Slide first gear and stop ring over rear of mainshaft and against thrust flange between assembly over rear of mainshaft, first and second gears on shaft.
3. Slide first-reverse synchronizer indexing hub slots to first gear stop ring lugs.
4. Install first-reverse synchronizer clutch gear snap-ring on mainshaft.
5. Slide reverse gear and mainshaft bearing in place. Press bearing on shaft, supporting inner race of bearing. Be sure snap-ring groove on outer race is forward.
6. Install bearing retaining snap-ring on mainshaft. Slide snap-

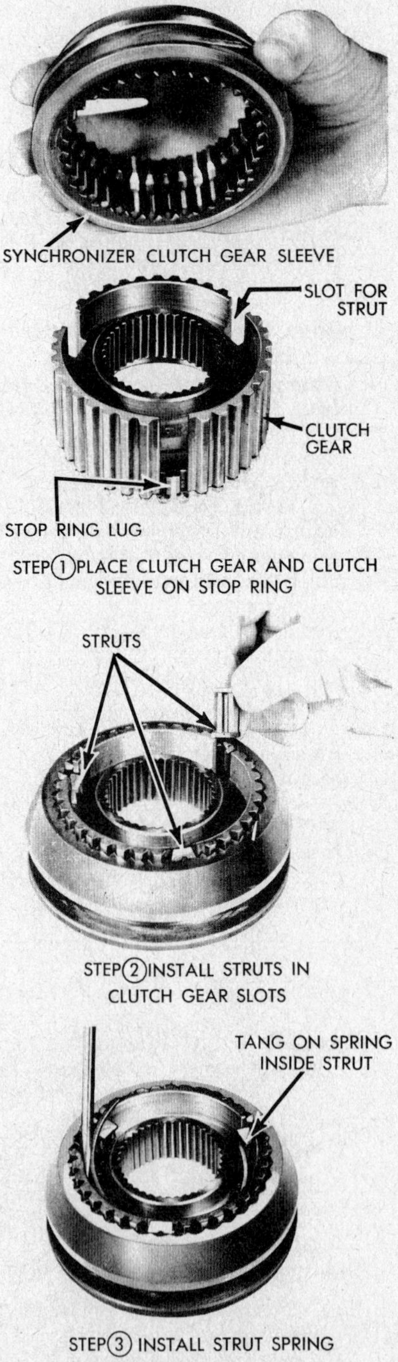

Assembling synchronizer parts (© Chrysler Corp.)

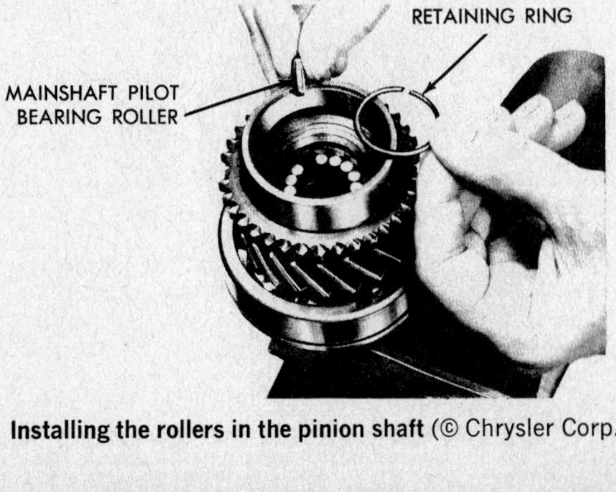

Installing the rollers in the pinion shaft (© Chrysler Corp.)

Countershaft gear roller bearing assembly (© Chrysler Corp.)

Installing the seal, drive pinion bearing retainer (© Chrysler Corp.)

ring over the bearing and seat it in groove.

7. Place second gear over front of mainshaft with thrust surface against flange.
8. Install stop ring and second-third synchronizer assembly against second gear. Install second-third synchronizer clutch gear snap-ring on shaft.
9. Move second-third synchronizer sleeve forward as far as possible. Install front stop ring inside sleeve with lugs indexed to struts.
10. Rotate cut out on second gear toward countershaft gear for clearance.
11. Insert mainshaft assembly into case. Tilt assembly to clear cluster gears and insert pilot rollers in drive pinion gear. If assembly is correct, the bearing retainer will bottom to the case without force. If not, check for a misplaced strut, pinion roller, or stop ring.

Reverse Idler Gear

1. Place dummy shaft into idler gear. Insert 22 greased rollers.
2. Position reverse idler thrust washers in case with grease.
3. Position idler gear and dummy shaft in case. Install idler shaft and key.

Extension Housing

1. Remove extension housing yoke seal. Drive bushing out from inside housing.
2. Align oil hole in bushing with oil slot in housing. Drive bushing into place. Drive new seal into housing.
3. Install extension housing and gasket to hold mainshaft and bearing retainer in place.

Drive Pinion Bearing Retainer

1. Install outer snap-ring on drive pinion bearing. Tap assembly back until snap-ring contacts case.

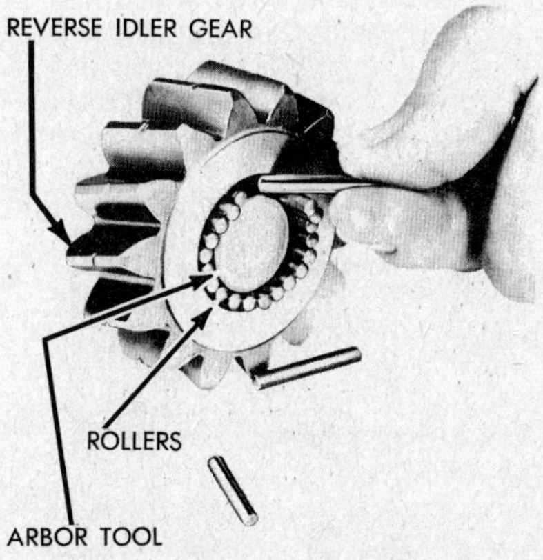

Reverse Idler gear, roller and arbor assembly (© Chrysler Corp.)

2. Using seal installer tool or equivalent, install a new seal in retainer bore.
3. Position main drive pinion bearing retainer and gasket on front of case. Coat threads with sealing compound, install bolts, torque to 30 ft. lbs.

Gearshift Mechanism and Housing

1. If removed, place two interlock levers in pivot pin with spring hangers offset toward each other, so that spring installs in a straight line. Place E-clip on pivot pin.
2. Grease and install new O-ring seals on both shift shafts. Grease housing bores and insert shafts.
3. Install spring on interlock lever hangers.
4. Rotate each shift shaft fork bore to straight up position. Install shift forks through bores and under both interlock levers.
5. Position second-third synchronizer sleeve to rear, in second gear position. Position first-reverse synchronizer sleeve to middle of travel, in neutral position. Place shift forks in the same positions.
6. Install gasket and gearshift mechanism. The bolt with the extra long shoulder must be in-

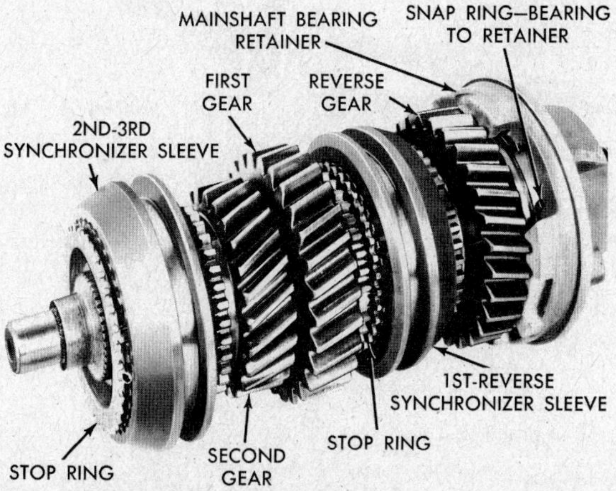

Mainshaft assembled (© Chrysler Corp.)

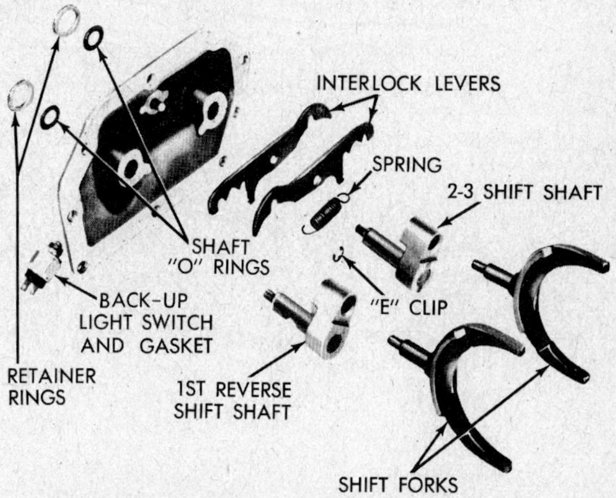

Gearshift mechanism and housing disassembled (© Chrysler Corp.)

stalled at the center rear of the case. Torque bolts to 15 ft. lbs.

7. Install speedometer drive pinion gear and adapter. Range number on adapter, which represents the number of teeth on the gear, should be in 6 o'clock position.

TORQUE CHART

Manual A-203 3-Speed	*Foot-Pounds*		
Back up light switch	15	Gearshift operating lever nuts	18
Extension housing bolts	50	Transmission to clutch housing bolts	50
Drive pinion bearing retainer bolts	30	Transmission cover retaining bolts	12
		Transmission drain plug	25

Dodge/Plymouth A-250 3 Speed

Description

The Dodge A-250 is a three speed transmission equipped with a synchronizer between second and third gears. Lubricant capacity is 4½ pints.

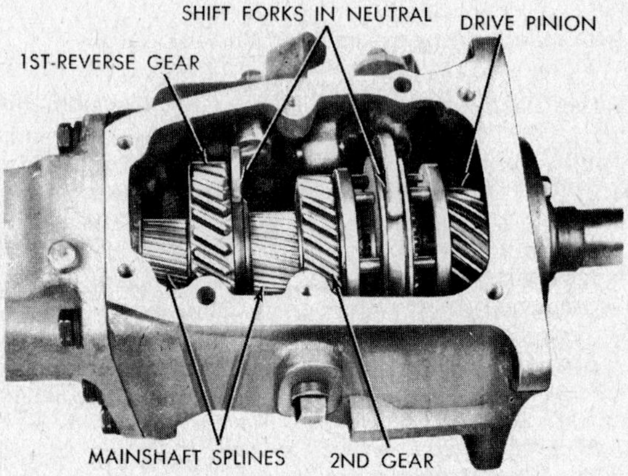

Cover removal—Dodge A-250

Disassembly of Transmission

1. Remove case cover and gasket.
2. Measure the synchronizer "float" with a pair of feeler gauges. Measurement is made between the synchronizer outer ring pin and the opposite synchronizer outer ring. This measurement must be made on two pins 180 degrees apart with equal gap on both ends for "float" determination. The measurement should be between 0.060-0.117 inch. A snug fit should be maintained between feeler gauge and pins.
3. Remove the bolt and retainer holding the speedometer pinion adapter in the extension housing. Carefully work the adapter and pinion out of the extension housing.
4. Remove extension housing bolts and extension housing.
5. Remove the bolts that attach the drive pinion bearing retainer to case, then slide the retainer off the pinion. Pry the seal out of retainer using a screwdriver. Be cautious not to nick or scratch the bore.
6. Rotate the drive pinion so that the blank clutch tooth area is opposite the countershaft for removal clearance.
7. Slide drive pinion assembly slightly out of case. Move the synchronizer front inner stop ring from the short splines on the pinion shaft. Slowly remove drive pinion assembly.
8. Remove snap ring that holds

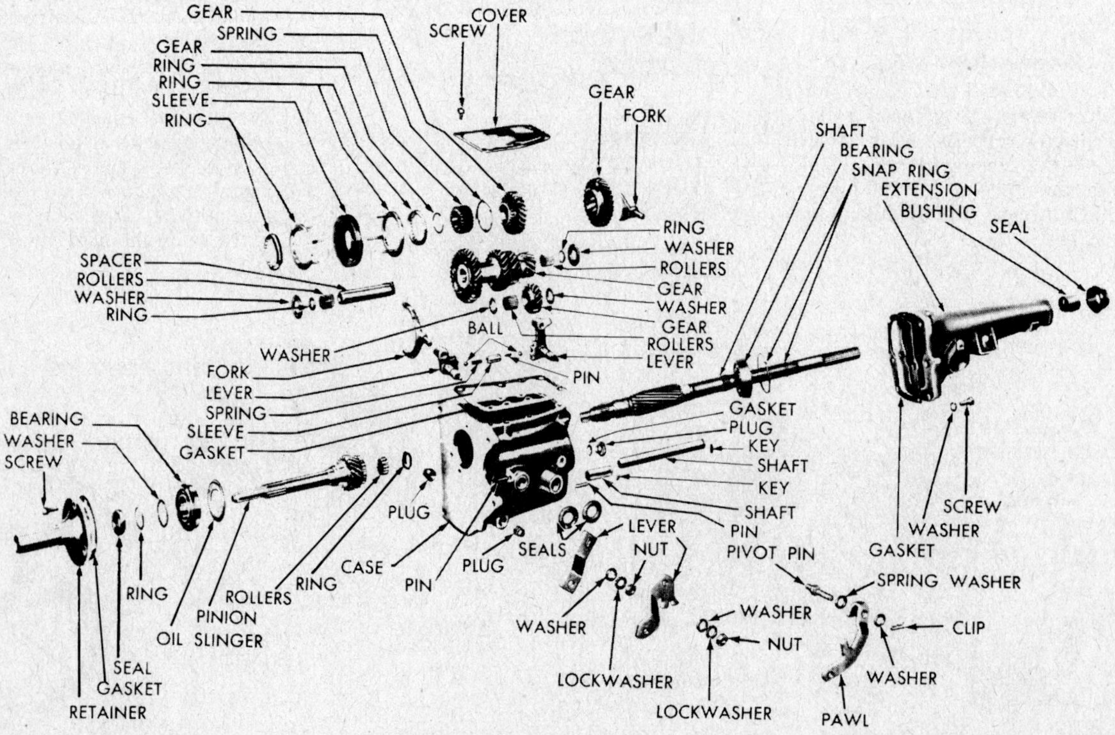

Dodge A-250 transmission—exploded view

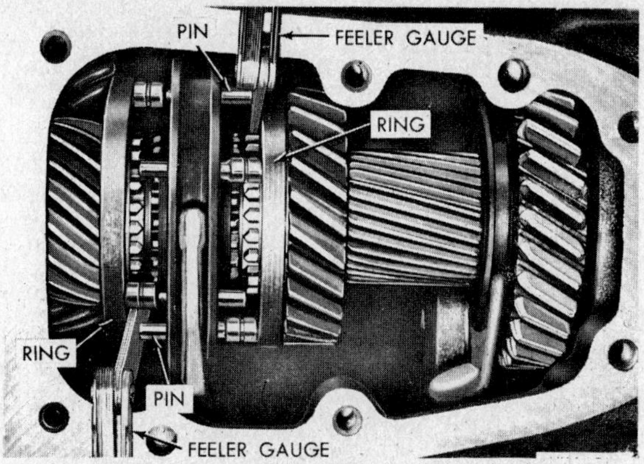

Measuring synchronizer "float"—Dodge A-250

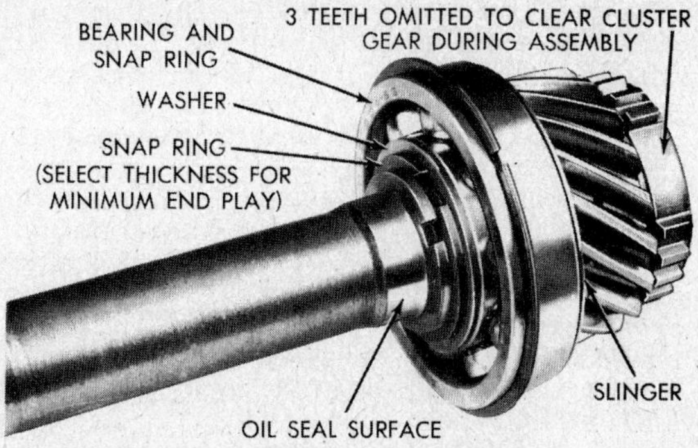

Drive pinion assembly—Dodge A-250

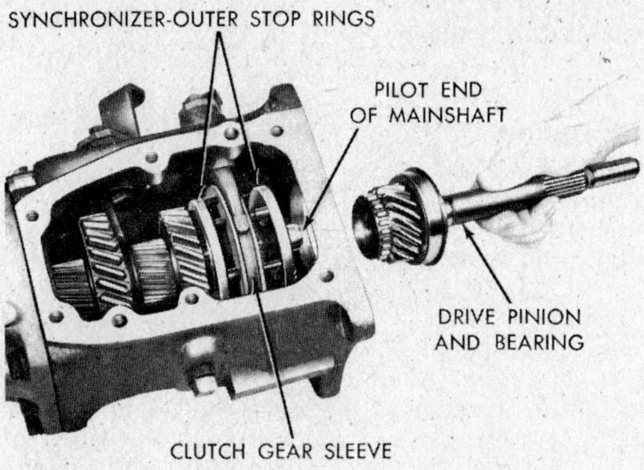

Removing or Installing drive pinion—Dodge A-250

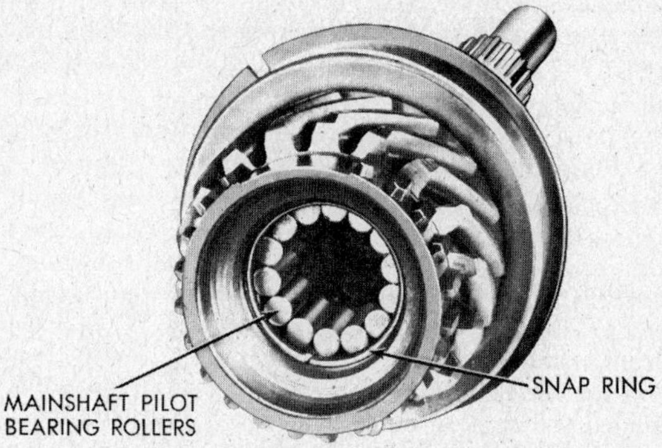

Mainshaft pilot bearings in the end of the drive pinion—Dodge A-250

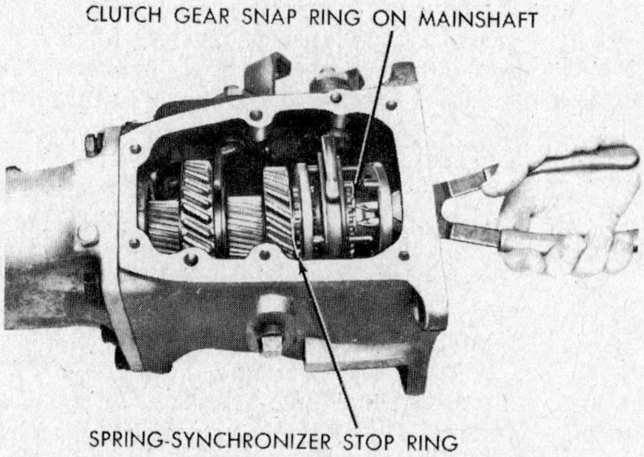

Removing or installing clutch gear snap ring—Dodge A-250

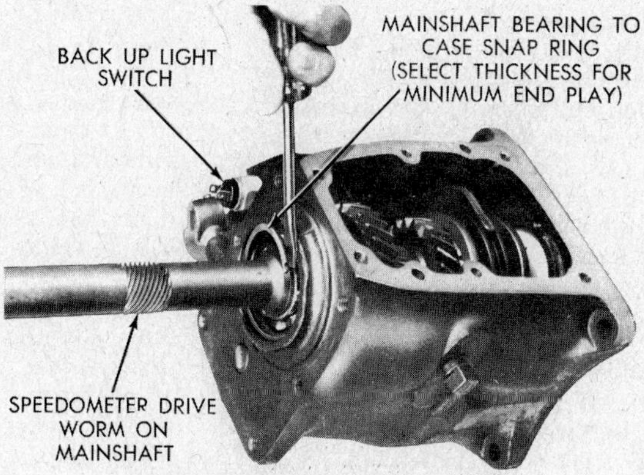

Removing mainshaft-to-case snap ring

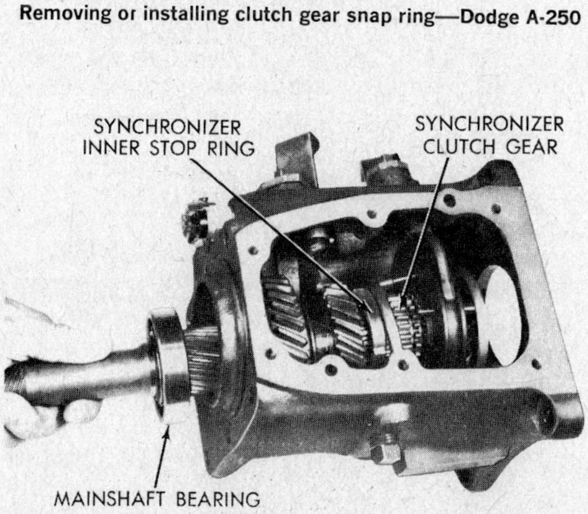

Removing mainshaft from case and gear—Dodge A-250

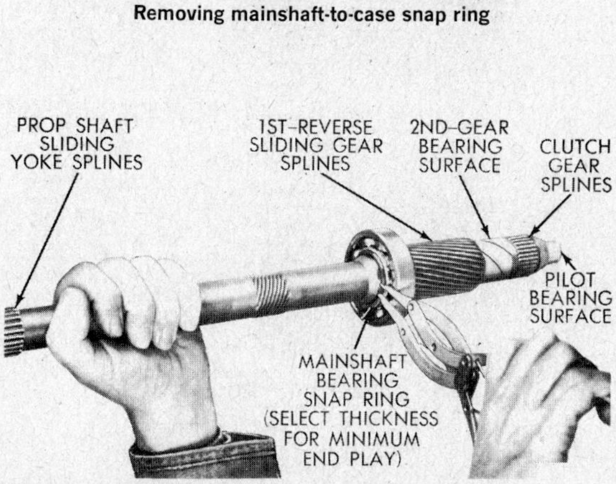

Mainshaft and bearing assembly—Dodge A-250

bearing on pinion shaft. Remove pinion bearing washer. Using an arbor press, press pinion shaft out of bearing. Remove oil slinger.

9. Remove snap ring and bearing rollers from the end of the drive pinion.
10. Remove clutch gear retaining snap ring from the mainshaft.
11. Remove the mainshaft bearing securing snap ring from case.
12. Slide mainshaft and bearing rearward out of case while holding the gears as they drop free.
13. Remove the snap ring from mainshaft and press the bearing off of mainshaft.
14. Remove the synchronizer components, second gear, first-reverse gear and shift forks from case.

NOTE: Steps 15 thru 18 need only be performed if gear shift lever seals are leaking.

15. Remove the shift levers from the shift shafts.
16. Drive out the tapered retaining pin from the first-reverse shift shaft. Remove the shift shaft from inside the case.
    As the detent balls are spring loaded, when the shafts are removed the balls will drop to the bottom of the transmission case.
17. Remove the interlock sleeve, spring and both detent balls from case. Drive tapered retaining pin out of second-third shaft and remove shaft from case.
18. Drive shift shaft seals out of case with a suitable drift.
19. Check end play of countershaft gear with a feeler gauge. The end play should be between 0.005--0.022 inch. This measurement is used to determine if a new thrust washer is necessary during reassembly.
20. Using a countershaft bearing arbor, drive the countershaft towards the rear of the case until the small key can be removed from the countershaft.
21. Drive the countershaft the rest of the way out of the case, keeping the arbor tight against the end of the countershaft. This will prevent loss of roller bearings.
22. Remove the countershaft gear, front thrust washer and rear thrust washer from the case.
23. Remove the bearing rollers, spacer ring and center spacer from the countershaft gear.
24. Drive the reverse idler gear shaft out of the transmission case using a suitable drift. Remove the woodruff key from the end of the reverse idler shaft.
25. Remove the reverse idler gear and thrust washers out of the case. Remove the bearing rollers from the gear.

Cleaning and Inspection

See "Cleaning and Inspection" instructions at the front of the transmission section.

Assembly of Transmission

1. Slide the countershaft gear bearing roller spacer over arbor tool. Coat the bore of gear with lubricant and slide tool and spacer into gear bore.
2. Lubricate the bearing rollers with heavy grease and install two rows of 22 rollers each in both ends of gear in area around arbor. Cover with heavy grease and install bearing spacer rings in each end of gear and between roller rows.
3. If countershaft gear end play was found to be excessive during disassembly, install new thrust washers. Cover with heavy grease and install thrust washer and thrust needle bearing and cap at each end of countershaft gear and over arbor. Install gear and arbor in the case, and make sure that tabs on rear thrust washer slide into grooves in the case.
4. Drive the arbor forward out of the countershaft gear and through the bore in the front of the case using the countershaft and a soft faced hammer. When the countershaft is almost in place, make certain the keyway in the countershaft is aligned with the key slot in the rear of the case. Insert the shaft key and continue to drive the countershaft into the case until the key is bottomed in the slot.

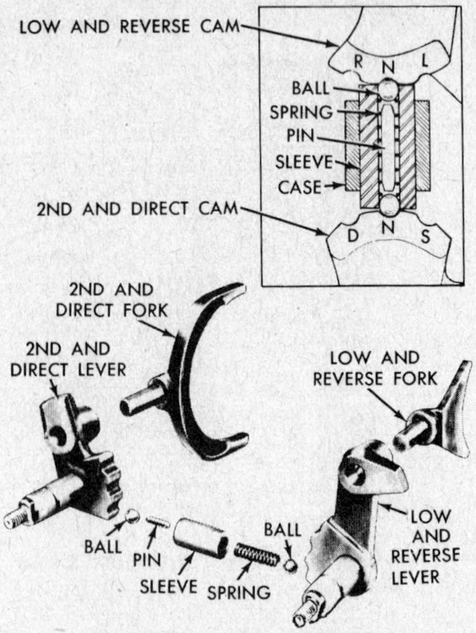

Shift forks and levers—Dodge A-250

5. Position special arbor tool in the reverse idler gear and install the 22 roller bearings using a heavy grease.
6. Place the front and rear thrust washers at each end of the reverse idler gear. Position the assembly in the transmission case with the chamfered end of the gear teeth towards the front. Make sure that the thrust washer tabs engage the slots in case.
7. Insert reverse idler shaft into the bore at rear of case with keyway to the rear, pushing the arbor towards the front of the case.
8. When the keyway is aligned with the slot in the case, insert the key in the keyway. Drive the shaft forward until the key is seated in the recess.

NOTE: Steps 9 thru 14 need only be performed if the shift levers have been disassembled.

9. Place new shift shaft seals in the case and drive it into position with suitable drift.
10. Carefully slide the first-reverse shift shaft into the case and lock

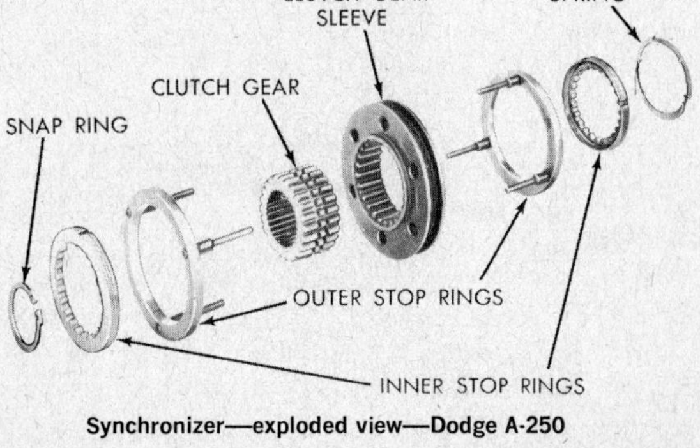

Synchronizer—exploded view—Dodge A-250

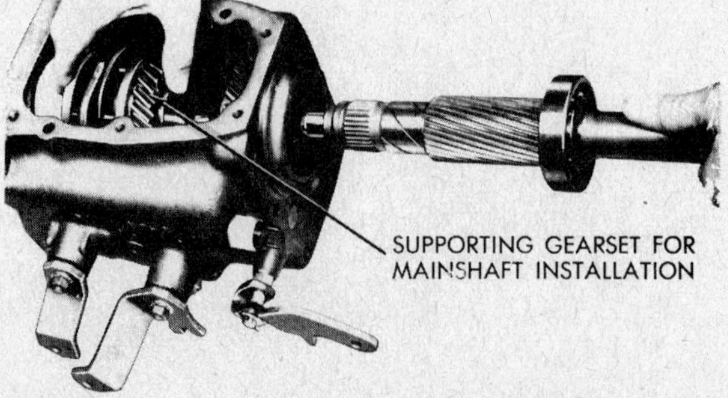

Installing mainshaft into the gears and case—Dodge A-250

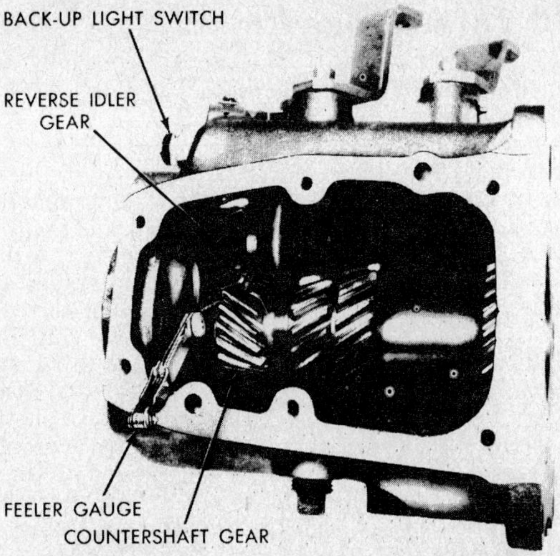

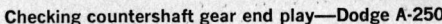

Checking countershaft gear end play—Dodge A-250

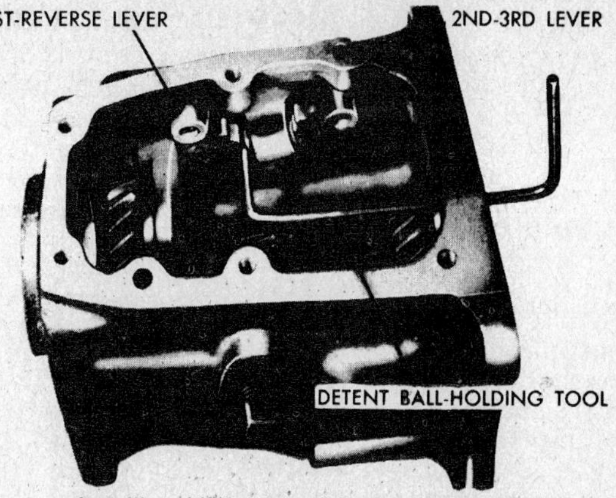

Installing shift levers and detent—Dodge A-250

into place with a tapered retaining pin. Position the lever so that the center detent is aligned with the interlock bore.

11. Install the interlock sleeve into the bore followed by a detent ball, spring and pin.
12. Install remaining detent ball and hold in place with detent ball holding tool.
13. Depress the detent ball and carefully install the second-third shift shaft. Align center detent with detent ball and secure lever with tapered retaining pin.
14. Install shift levers and tighten retaining nuts to 18 foot-pounds.
15. Press the bearing on the mainshaft and select and install snap ring that gives minimum end play.
16. Move shift lever to reverse position, and then place the first-reverse gear and shift fork in the case.

NOTE: Both shift forks are offset toward the rear of the transmission case.

17. Assemble the synchronizer parts with shift fork and second gear.
18. Place the second gear assembly in the transmission case and insert the shift fork into its lever.
19. Install the mainshaft carefully through the gear assembly until it bottoms in rear of case.
20. Install synchronizer clutch gear snap ring on mainshaft.
21. Select and install mainshaft bearing snap ring in case.
22. If "float" measurement was found to be outside specifications, install or remove shims to place "float" within range.
23. Install oil slinger on drive pinion shaft and slide against the gear.
24. Slide the bearing over the pinion shaft with snap ring groove away from gear, then seat bearing on shaft using an arbor press.
25. Install keyed washer between bearing and retaining snap ring groove.
26. Secure bearing and washer with selected thickness snap ring. If large snap ring around bearing was removed, install it at this time.
27. Place drive pinion shaft in a vise with soft faced jaws and install the 14 roller bearings in the shaft cavity. Coat the roller bearings with a heavy grease and install retaining ring in groove.
28. Rotate the drive pinion so that the blank clutch tooth area is next to the countershaft. Guide the drive pinion through the front of case and engage the inner stop ring with the clutch teeth. Then seat pinion bearing. The pinion shaft is fully seated when the snap ring is in full contact with the case.
29. Install a new seal in the pinion bearing retainer.
30. Position retainer assembly and new gasket on the case. Use sealing compound on bolts and tighten to 30 foot-pounds.
31. Slide the extension housing and a new gasket over mainshaft. Guide shaft through bushing and oil seal. Use sealing compound on the bolt used in the hole tapped through the transmission case. Install remaining bolts and tighten all to 50 foot-pounds.
32. Install the transmission cover and gasket and tighten cover bolts to 12 foot-pounds.
33. Rotate the speedometer pinion gear and adapter assembly so that the number on the adapter corresponding to the number of teeth on the gear is in the 6 o'clock position as the assembly is installed.
34. Fill the transmission with the proper lubricant and install the drain plug and tighten to 25 ft.-lbs. Install the back-up light switch and tighten to 15 ft.-lbs.
35. Rotate the drive pinion shaft and check operation of transmission by running the transmission through all gear ranges.

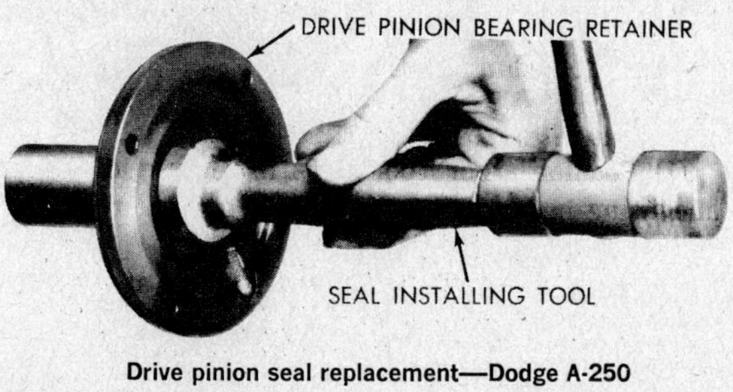

Drive pinion seal replacement—Dodge A-250

Synchronizer shim location—Dodge A-250

Dodge/Plymouth A-390 Three Speed

Description

The A-390 is a three speed synchromesh transmission. Lubricant capacity is 4½ pints.

Disassembly of Transmission

1. Remove the bolts that attach the cover to the case. Remove the cover and gasket.
2. Remove the long spring that retains the detent plug in the case. Remove the detent plug with a small magnet.
3. Remove the bolt and retainer securing the speedometer pinion adapter to the transmission case. Carefully work the adapter and pinion out of the extension housing.
4. Remove the bolts that attach the extension housing to the transmission case. Slide the extension housing off the output shaft.
5. Remove the bolts that attach the input shaft bearing retainer to the case. Slide the retainer off the shaft. Using a suitable tool, pry the seal out of the retainer. Be careful not to nick or scratch the bore in which the seal is pressed of the surface on which the seal is bottomed.
6. Remove the lubricant fill plug from the right side of the case. Working through the fill plug opening, drive the roll pin out of the countershaft with a ¼ inch punch.
7. Working with the countershaft bearing arbor and a soft faced hammer, tap the countershaft toward the front of the case with the arbor tool to remove the expansion plug from the countershaft bore at the front of the case. The countershaft is a loose fit in the case and will slide easily.
8. Insert the arbor tool through the front of the case and push the countershaft out of the rear of the case so the roll pin hole in the countershaft does not travel through the roller bearings. The countershaft gear will drop to the bottom of the case. Remove the countershaft from the rear of the case.
9. Place both shift levers in neutral (center) position.
10. Remove the input shaft assembly and stop ring from the front of the case.
11. Remove the set screw that secures the first-reverse shift fork to the shift rail. Slide the first-reverse shift rail out through the rear of the case.
12. Move the second-third shift fork rearward for access to the set screw. Remove the setscrew from the fork. Using a suitable tool, rotate the shift rail one quarter (¼) turn.
13. Lift the interlock plug from the case with a magnet.
14. Tap on the inner end of the second-third shift rail to remove the expansion plug from the front of the case. Remove the shift rail through the front of the case.
15. Remove the second-third shift rail detent plug and spring from the detent bore with a magnet.
16. Tap the output shaft assembly rearward until the output shaft bearing clears the case. Remove both shift forks. Remove the snap ring that retains the output shaft bearing to the output shaft.
17. Assemble the output shaft bearing removal tool over the output shaft and bearing. Remove the output shaft bearing.
18. Remove the output shaft assembly through top of the case.
19. Using a suitable drift, drive the reverse idler gear shaft toward the rear, and out of the transmission case.
20. Lift the reverse idler gear and thrust washer out of the case.
21. Remove the countershaft gear, arbor assembly, and thrust washers from the bottom of the case.
22. Remove the countershaft roll pin from the bottom of the case.
23. Remove the snap ring that retains the second-third synchronizer clutch gear and sleeve assembly on the output shaft. Slide the second-third synchronizer assembly off the end of the output shaft.

NOTE: Do not separate the second-third synchronizer clutch gear, sleeve, struts, or spring unless inspection reveals that a replacement is necssary.

24. Slide the second gear and stop ring off the output shaft.
25. Remove the snap ring and thrust washer retaining the first gear. Slide the first gear and stop ring off the output shaft.
26. Remove the snap ring that retains the first-reverse synchronizer hub on the output shaft. The first-reverse synchronizer hub is a press fit on the output shaft. To avoid damage to the synchronizer, remove the synchronizer hub using an arbor press. *Do not attempt to remove or install the hub by hammering or prying.*

Sub-Assembly Overhaul

Shift Levers and Seals

1. Remove the operating levers from their respective shafts. Remove any burrs from the shafts to avoid damage to the case.
2. Push the shift levers out of the transmission case. Remove and discard the "O" ring seal from each shaft.
3. Lubricate the new seals with

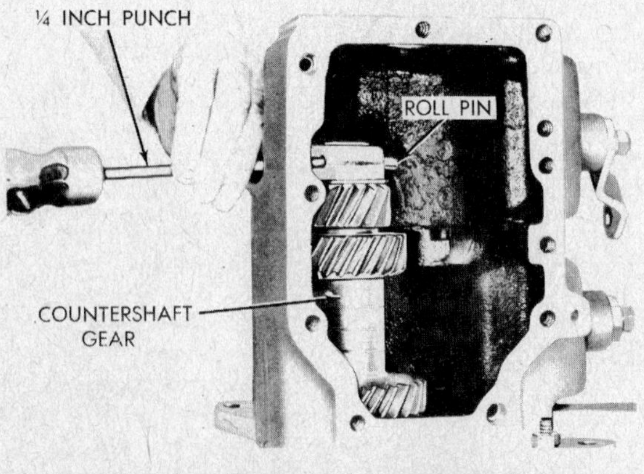

Removing the roll pin from the countershaft—A-390 (© Chrysler Corp.)

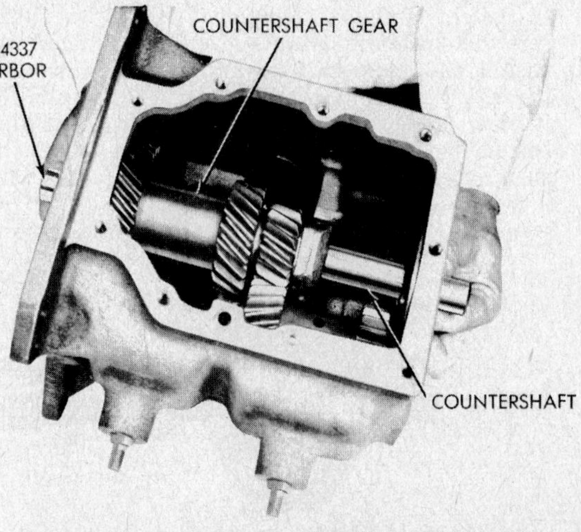

Removing the countershaft—A-390 (© Chrysler Corp.)

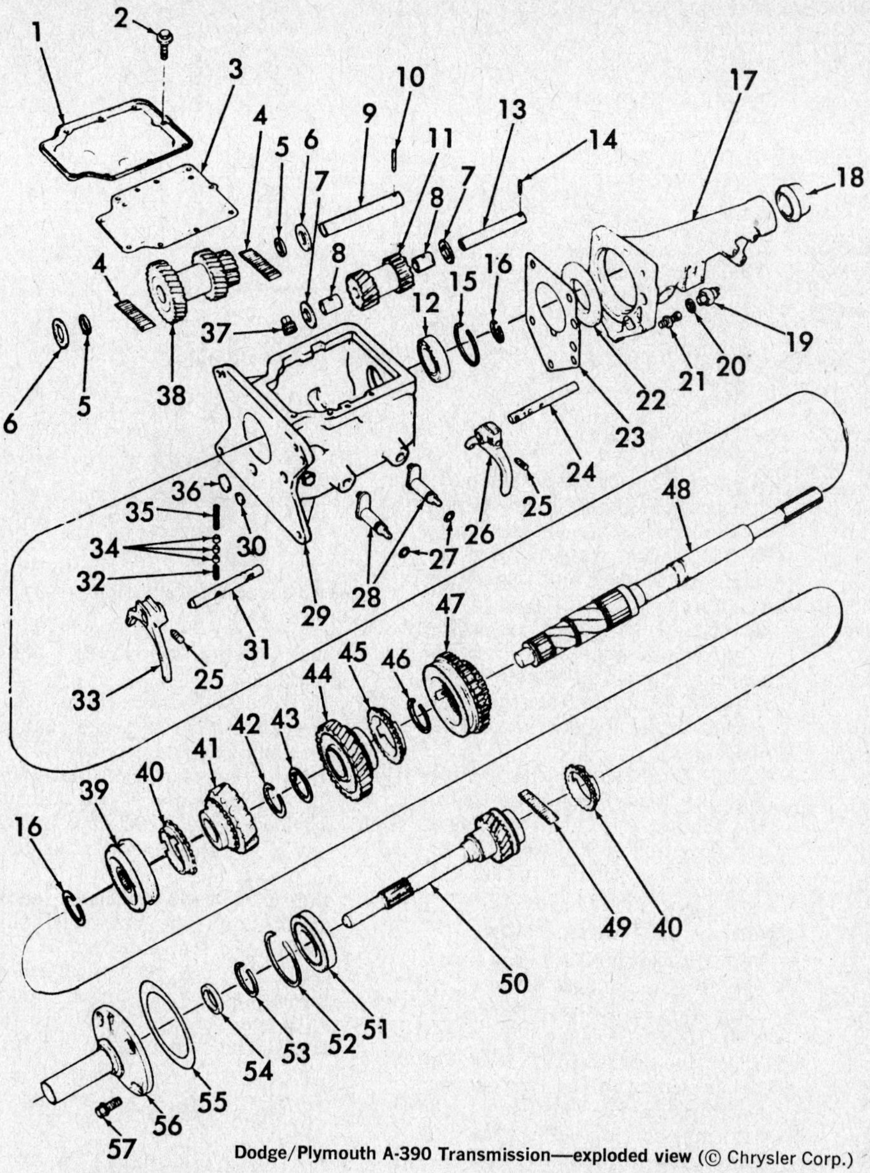

1 Transmission case cover
2 Transmission case cover screw
3 Transmission case cover gasket
4 Countershaft roller bearing
5 Countershaft bearing washer
6 Countershaft thrust washer
7 Reverse idler thrust washer
8 Reverse idler bushing
9 Countershaft
10 Countershaft roll pin
11 Reverse idler gear
12 Output shaft bearing
13 Reverse idler shaft
14 Reverse idler stop pin
15 Output shaft bearing outer snap ring
16 Output shaft inner snap ring
17 Extension
18 Extension seal
19 Back-up light switch
20 Back-up lamp switch gasket
21 Extension screw and lockwasher
22 Output shaft bearing retainer
23 Extension gasket
24 First-reverse shift rail
25 Shift fork set screw
26 First-reverse shift fork
27 Shift lever oil seal
28 Gearshift lever
29 Transmission case
30 Plug
31 Second-third shift rail
32 Shift detent spring pin
33 Second-third shift fork
34 Shift detent pin
35 Shift detent pin spring
36 Plug
37 Transmission case filler plug
38 Countershaft gear
39 Second-third synchronizer assembly
40 Second-third synchronizer stop ring
41 Second gear
42 Low speed gear thrust washer snap ring
43 Low speed gear thrust washer
44 Low speed gear
45 First-reverse synchronizer stop ring
46 First-reverse synchronizer clutch gear snap ring
47 First-reverse synchronizer assembly
48 Output shaft
49 Output shaft pilot roller bearing
50 Input shaft
51 Input shaft bearing
52 Bearing outer snap ring
53 Bearing inner snap ring
54 Bearing retainer oil seal
55 Bearing retainer snap ring
56 Bearing retainer
57 Bearing retainer screw

Dodge/Plymouth A-390 Transmission—exploded view (© Chrysler Corp.)

transmission oil and install them on the shafts.

4. Install the shift levers in the case.
5. Install the operating levers and tighten the retaining nuts to 18 ft-lbs.

Input Shaft Bearing and Rollers

1. Remove the snap ring securing the bearing on the input shaft. Carefully press the input shaft out of the bearing with an arbor press.
2. Remove the fifteen bearing rollers from the cavity in the end of the input shaft.
3. Install the 15 bearing rollers in the cavity of the input shaft. Coat the rollers with a thin film of grease to retain them during installation.
4. Slide the input shaft bearing over the input shaft, snap ring groove away from the gear end. Seat the bearing assembly on the input shaft with an arbor press.
5. Secure the bearing with the snap ring. Be sure the snap ring is properly seated. If a large snap ring around the bearing was removed, be sure to install it at this time.

Synchronizers

NOTE: If either synchronizer is to be disassembled, mark all parts so that they will be reassembled in the same position. Do not mix parts from the two synchronizers.

1. Push the synchronizer hub off each synchronizer sleeve.
2. Separate the struts and springs from the hubs.
3. Install the spring on the front side of the first-reverse synchronizer hub, making sure that all three strut slots are fully cov-

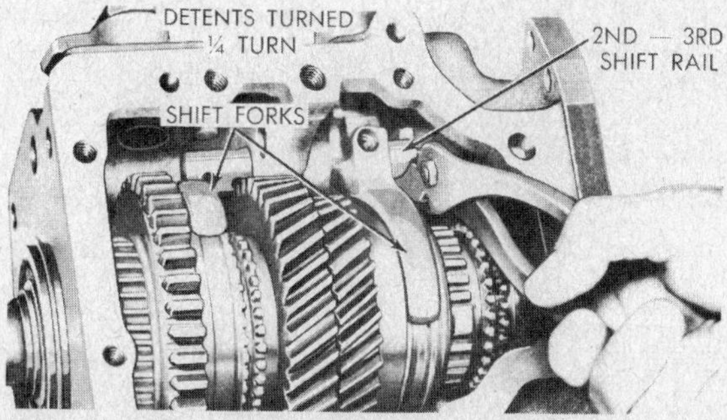

Rotating the second-third shift rail $1/4$ turn—A-390 (© Chrysler Corp.)

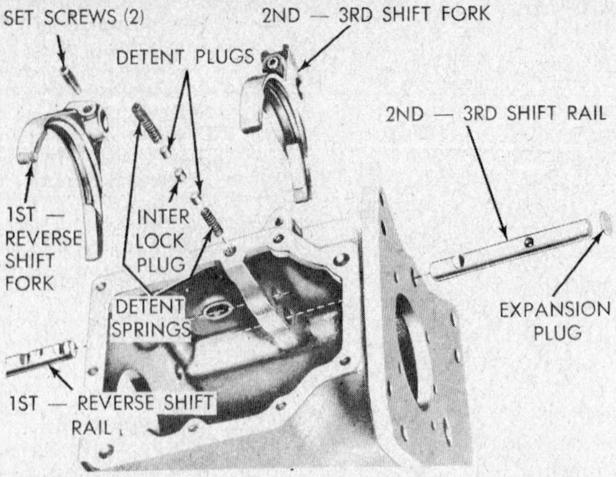

Shift rails and forks—exploded view—A-390 (© Chrysler Corp.)

ered. Hang the three struts on the spring and in the slots with the wide end of the strut inside the hub.

4. With the alignment marks on the hub and sleeve aligned, push the sleeve down on the hub until the struts are in the neutral detent. Place the stop ring on top of the synchronizer assembly.
5. With the alignment marks on the second-third synchronizer sleeve and hub aligned, slide the sleeve on the hub. Drop in the three struts in the strut slots. Install the spring with the hump in the center, into the hollow of the strut. Turn the assembly over and install the other spring so that the hump in the center of the spring is inserted in the same strut. Place the stop ring on each end of the synchronizer assembly.

Countershaft Gear and Bearing

1. Remove the countershaft bearing arbor, the roller bearings and the two bearing retainers from the countershaft gear.
2. Coat the bore in each end of the countershaft gear with grease.
3. Insert the countershaft arbor and install twenty five roller bearings and the retainer washer in each end of the countershaft gear.
4. Position the countershaft gear and arbor assembly in the transmission case. Align the gear bore and the thrust washers with the bores in the case and install the countershaft.
5. Using a feeler gauge, check the countershaft gear end play. The end play should be within 0.004-0.018 inch. If the clearance is not within limits, replace the thrust washers.
6. After establishing the correct end play, install the arbor tool in the countershaft gear and lower the gear and tool out of the bottom of the transmission case.

Assembly of Transmission

1. Coat the countershaft gear thrust surfaces in the case with a thin film of grease and position the two thrust washers in place. Place the countershaft gear and arbor assembly in the proper position in the bottom of the transmission case. The countershaft gear will remain in the bottom of the case until the output and input shafts are installed.
2. Coat the reverse idler gear thrust surfaces in the case with a thin film of grease and position the two thrust washers in place. Install the reverse idler gear in the case and align the gear bore with the thrust washers in the case

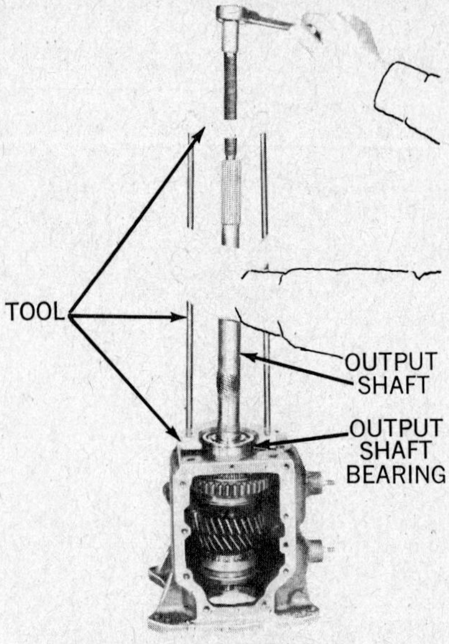

Removing the output shaft bearing—A-390 (© Chrysler Corp.)

bore. Install the reverse idler shaft.

3. Measure the reverse idler gear end play with a feeler gauge. End play should be 0.004-0.018 inch. If the clearance is not within limits, replace the thrust washers. If the end play is correct, leave the reverse idler gear in place.
4. Lubricate the output shaft splines and the machined surfaces with transmission oil.
5. Slide the first reverse synchronizer onto the output shaft with the fork groove toward the front. The first-reverse synchro-

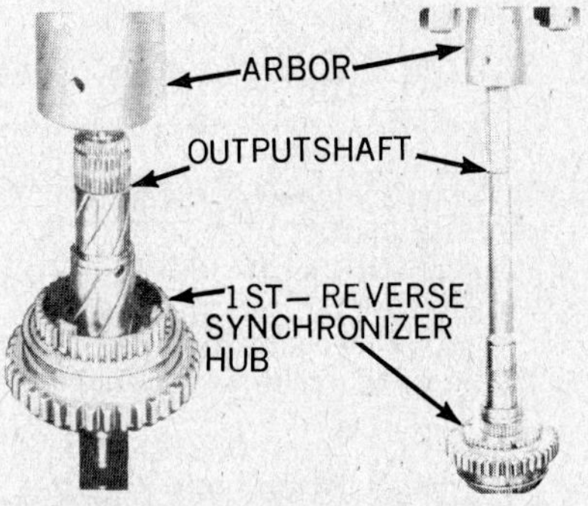

Removing and installing the first-reverse synchronizer hub—A-390 (© Chrysler Corp.)

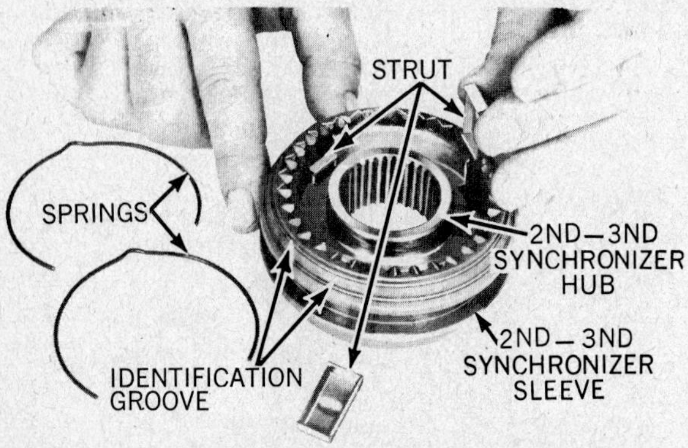

Assembling the second-third synchronizer—A-390 (© Chrysler Corp.)

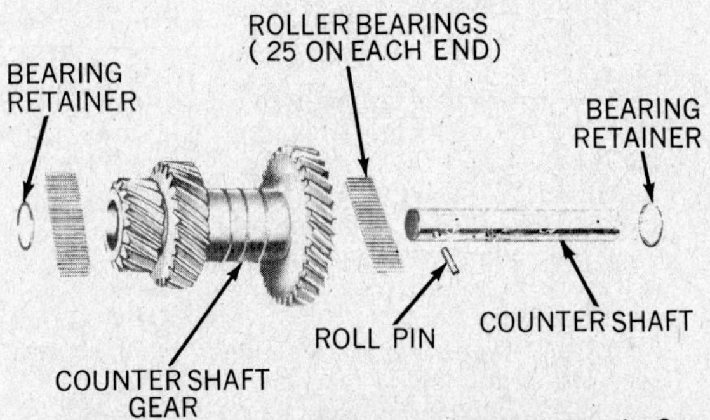

Countershaft and gear—exploded view—A-390 (© Chrysler Corp.)

nizer hub is a press fit on the output shaft. To eliminate the possibility of damage to the hub, install the hub using an arbor press. *Do not attempt to install the hub by hammering or driving.* Secure the hub on the output shaft with the snap ring.

6. Slide the first gear and stop ring onto the output shaft, aligning the slots in the stop ring with the struts. Install the thrust washer and snap ring.
7. Slide the second gear and stop ring on the output shaft.
8. Install the second-third synchronizer assembly on the output shaft. Rotate the second gear to index the struts with the slots in the stop ring. Secure the synchronizer with a snap ring.
9. Position the output shaft assembly in the transmission case. Place the transmission in a vertical position with the front of the case flat on the work bench. Place a 1¼ inch block of wood under the end of the output shaft. The block of wood will hold the output shaft assembly up during installation of the output shaft bearing.
10. Install the large snap ring on the output shaft bearing. Place the bearing on the output shaft with the large snap ring up. Drive the bearing on the shaft until it is seated on the shaft. Secure the bearing on the output shaft with the snap ring. Return the transmission to a horizontal position.
11. Insert both shift forks in the case and in their proper sleeves. Push the output shaft assembly into position and tap it forward until the output shaft bearing is seated in the transmission case.
12. Install the *shortest* detent spring followed by a detent plug into the case. Place the second-third synchronizer assembly in the second gear position.
13. Align the second-third shift fork and install the second-third shift rail. The second-third shift rail is the shortest of the two shift rails. It will be necessary to depress the detent plug to enter the shift rail in the bore. Move the rail inward until the detent plug engages the forward notch (second gear position).
14. Secure the fork to the rail with the set screw. Move the synchronizer to the neutral position.
15. Install a new expansion plug in the transmission case.
16. Install the interlock plug in the transmission case with a magnet. If the second-third shift rail is in the neutral position, the top of the interlock plug will be slightly lower than the surface of the first-reverse shift rail bore.
17. Align the first reverse fork and install the first-reverse shift rail. Move the rail inward until the center notch (neutral) is aligned with the detent bore. Secure the fork to the rail with the set screw.
18. Using a suitable tool, install a new oil seal in the input shaft bearing retainer bore.
19. Coat the bore of the input shaft gear with a thin film of grease. *A thick, heavy grease will plug the lubricant holes and prevent lubrication of the roller bearings.* Install the fifteen roller bearings in the bore.
20. Place the stop ring, slots aligned

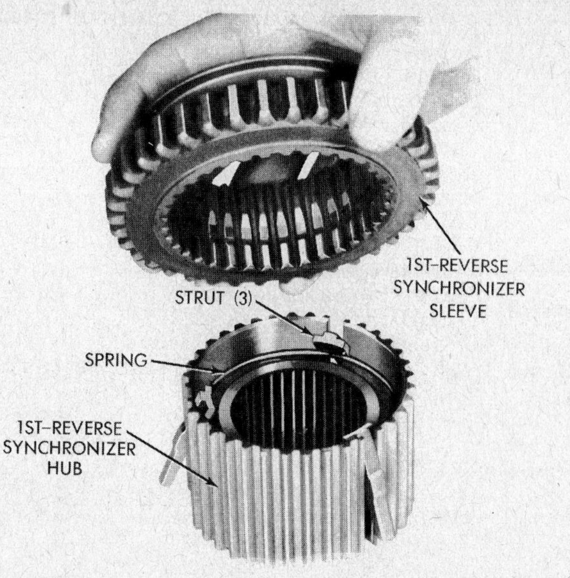

Assembling the first-reverse synchronizer—A-390 (© Chrysler Corp.)

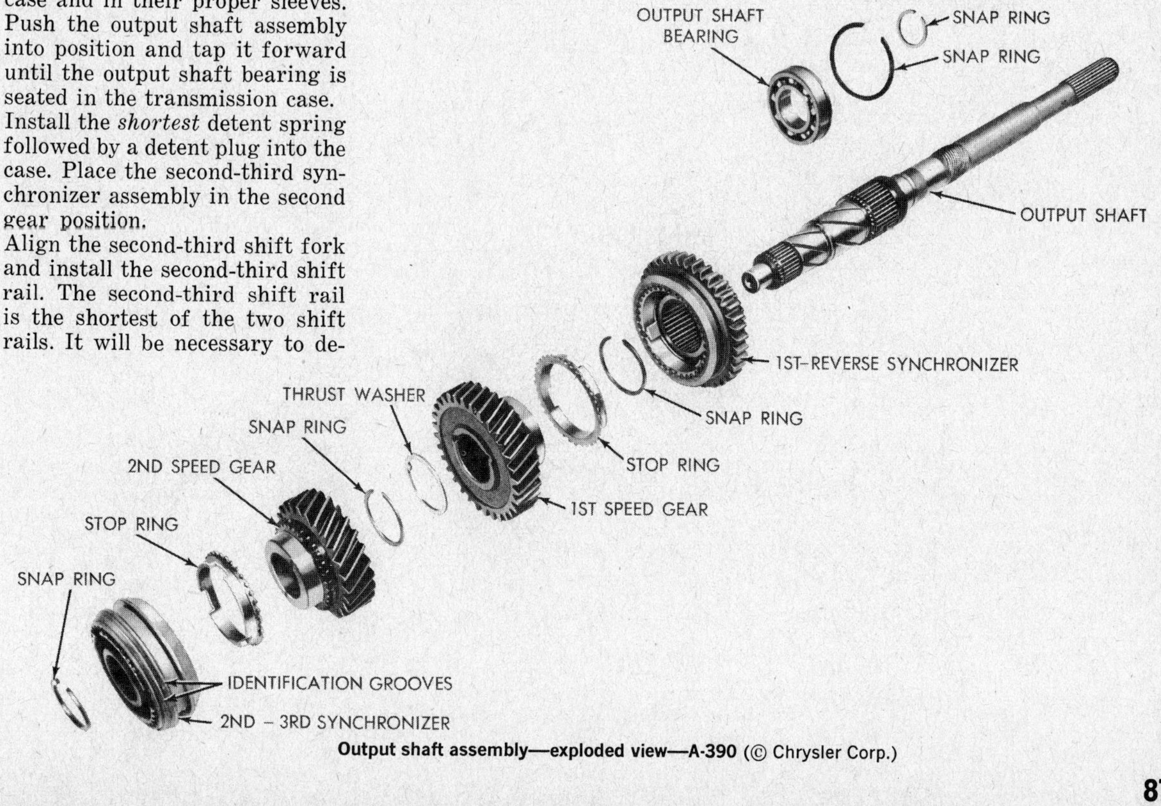

Output shaft assembly—exploded view—A-390 (© Chrysler Corp.)

TORQUE CHART

Gearshift rod and swivel assembly nuts	5/16-24	70 (in.-lbs.)
Backup light switch hole plug	9/16-18	15
Case drain plug	3/8	20
Case filler plug	1/2	30
Cast to clutch housing bolt	7/16-18	50
Drive pinion bearing retainer bolt	5/16-18	15
Extension bolt	3/8-16	30
Gearshift fork lock bolt	3/8-24	30
Gearshift housing lower bolt	5/16-18	15
Gearshift housing upper bolt	5/16-18	20
Gearshift operating lever nut	3/8-24	35
Gearshift selector ball spring bolt	1/2-20	25
Gearshift selector lever washer nut	5/16-24	20
Manual remote gearshift lever shaft bolt	1/4-20	10
Shaft flange nut	3/4-16	175

Dodge/Plymouth 4-Speed Overdrive

The identification numbers are stamped on a pad on the right side of the case.

Disassembly

1. Drain the unit and remove the reverse shift operating lever from the shaft. Remove the bolts that attach the gearshift hous-

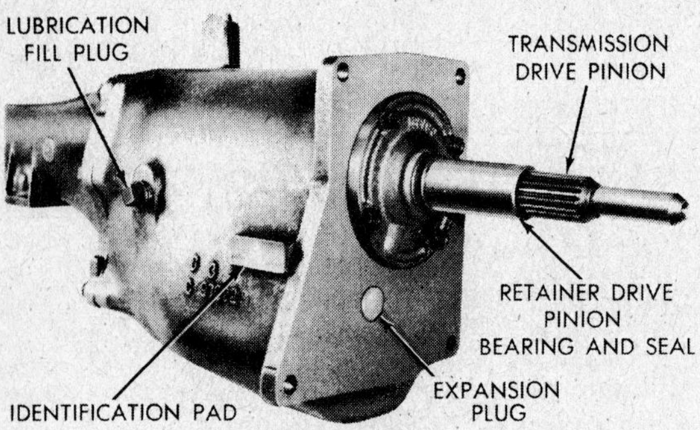

Four speed overdrive right side
(© Chrysler Corp.)

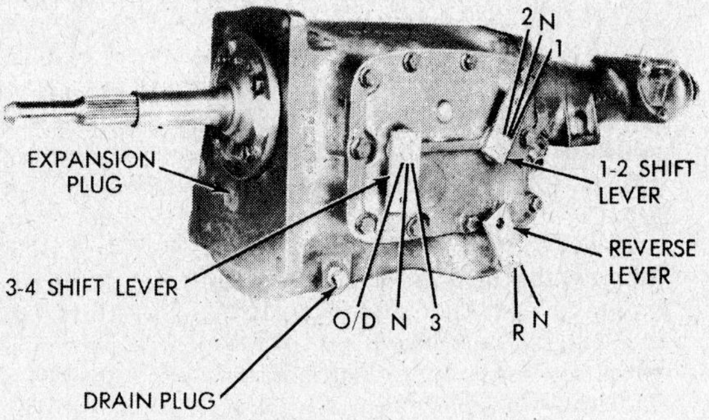

Four speed overdrive left side
(© Chrysler Corp.)

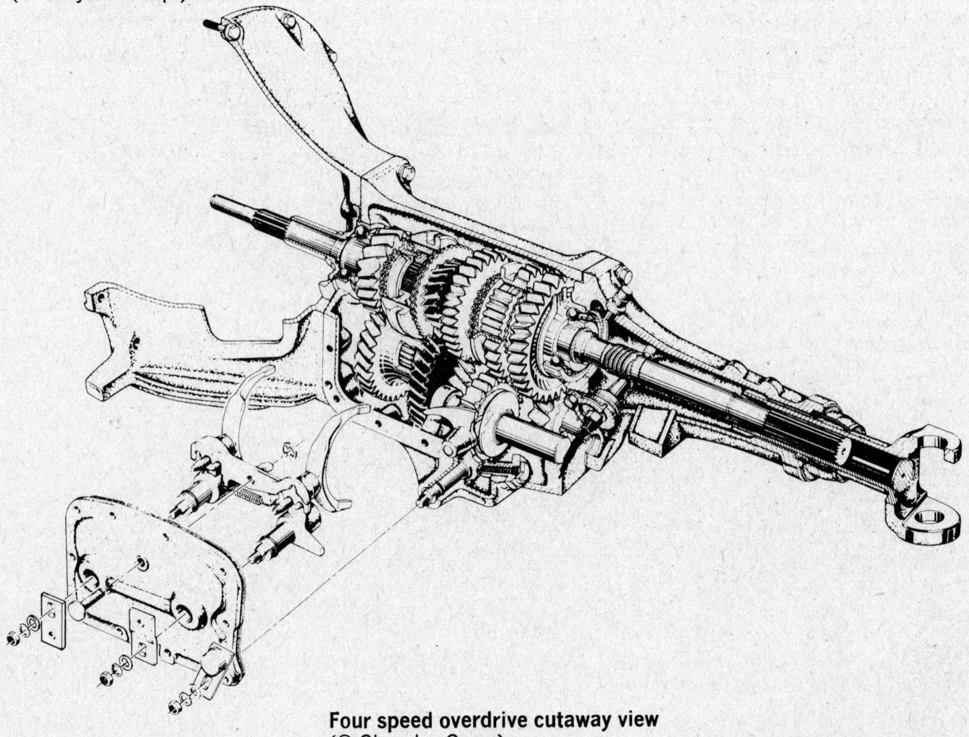

Four speed overdrive cutaway view
(© Chrysler Corp.)

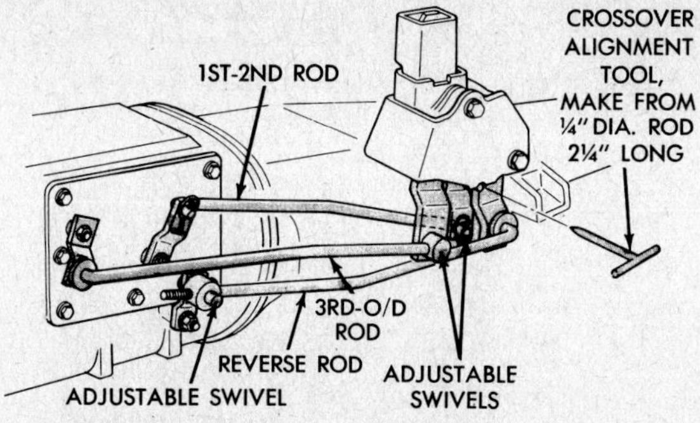

Gearshift linkage adjustment (© Chrysler Corp.)

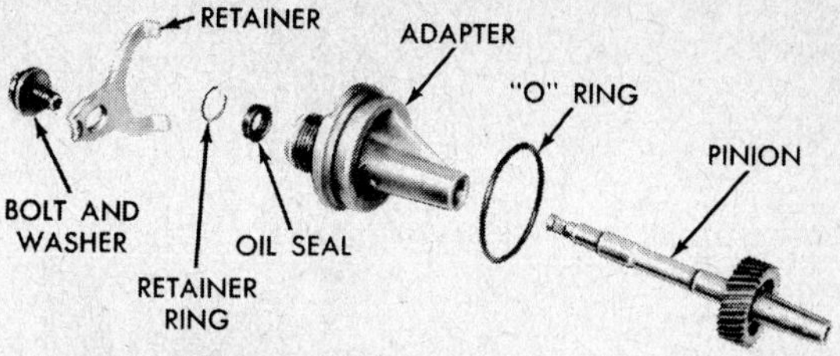

Speedometer pinion and adapter disassembled (© Chrysler Corp.)

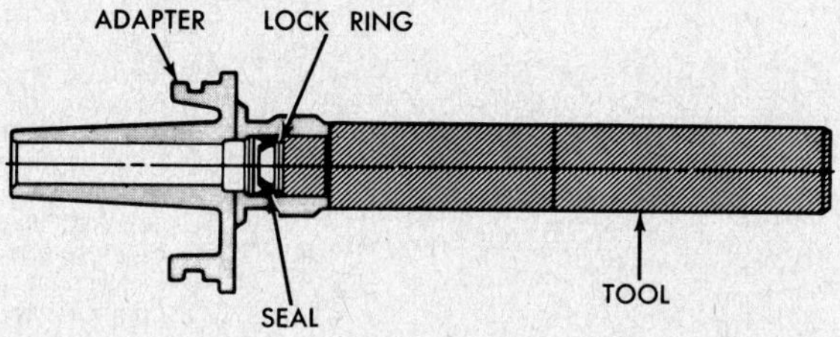

Installing speedometer pinion seal (© Chrysler Corp.)

ing to the case.

2. Put the operating levers in neutral and pull the gearshift housing away from the case. Work the shift forks out of the sleeves and remove them from the case.
3. Remove the speedometer pinion adapter from the extension housing.
4. Remove the extension housing-to-case bolts.
5. Rotate the extension housing on rear of the countershaft. Clearance has been provided on the extension flange to allow one bolt to be reinstalled to hold the extension in the inverted position with access to the countershaft.
6. With a center punch or drill make a hole in the countershaft expansion plug at the front of the case.
7. Reaching through this hole, push the countershaft rearward until the key is exposed. Remove the key. Push the countershaft forward against the expansion plug. Using a brass drift, tap the countershaft forward until the expansion plug is forced out.
8. Using a countershaft arbor, such as C-3938, push the countershaft out of the rear of the case, taking care that the countershaft washers don't fall out of position. Lower the gear to the bottom of the case.
9. Rotate the extension back to the normal position.
10. Remove the drive pinion bearing retainer attaching bolts. Slide the retainer and gasket from the pinion shaft. Pry the pinion or seal from the retainer.
11. Using a brass drift, tap the pinion and bearing assembly forward and through the front of the case.
12. Slide the third and overdrive synchronizer sleeve forward slightly, slide the reverse idler gear to the center of its shaft, then, us- a soft-faced hammer tap the extension housing rearward. Slide the housing and mainshaft assembly, away from the case.
13. Remove the snap ring that retains the 3rd and OD synchronizer clutch gear and sleeve assembly to the mainshaft, then slide the 3rd and OD synchronizer assembly off the end of the mainshaft.
14. Slide the OD gear and stop ring off the mainshaft. Using long nosed pliers, compress the snap ring that retains the mainshaft ball bearing in the extension housing.
15. Holding the snap ring compressed, pull the mainshaft assembly and bearing out of the extension housing.
16. Remove the snap ring that retains the mainshaft bearing on the shaft.
17. Remove the bearing from the mainshaft by inserting steel plates on the front side of the first speed gear, then press or drive the mainshaft through the bearing. Remove the bearing, retainer ring, 1st speed gear and stop ring from the shaft.
18. Remove the 1st and 2nd clutch gear and sleeve snap ring.
19. Slide the 1st and 2nd clutch gear and sleeve assembly from the mainshaft.
20. Remove the pinion bearing inner snap ring and, using a press, remove the bearing from the pinion.
21. Remove the snap ring and 16 bearing rollers from the cavity in the pinion.
22. Remove the countershaft gear from the bottom of the case.
23. Remove the arbor and 76 needle bearings, and the thrust washers and spacers from the center of the countershaft gear.
24. Remove the reverse gearshift

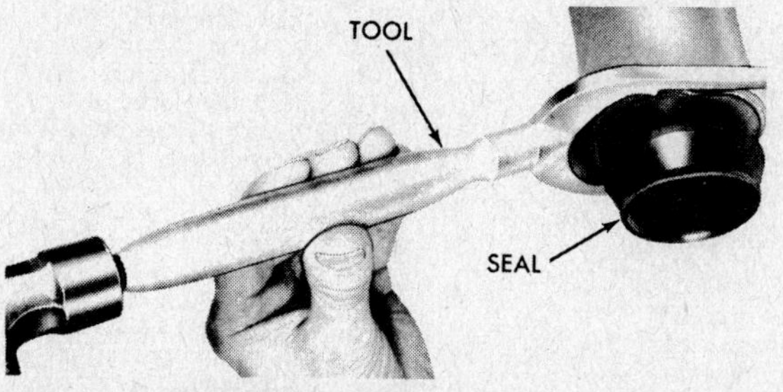

Removing extension housing yoke seal (© Chrysler Corp.)

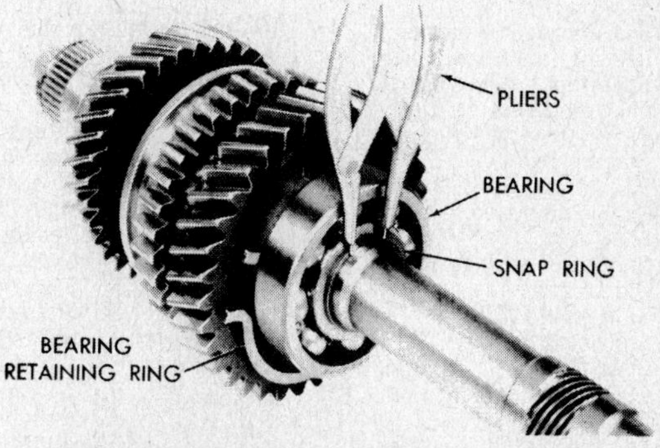

Removing rear mainshaft bearing snap ring (© Chrysler Corp.)

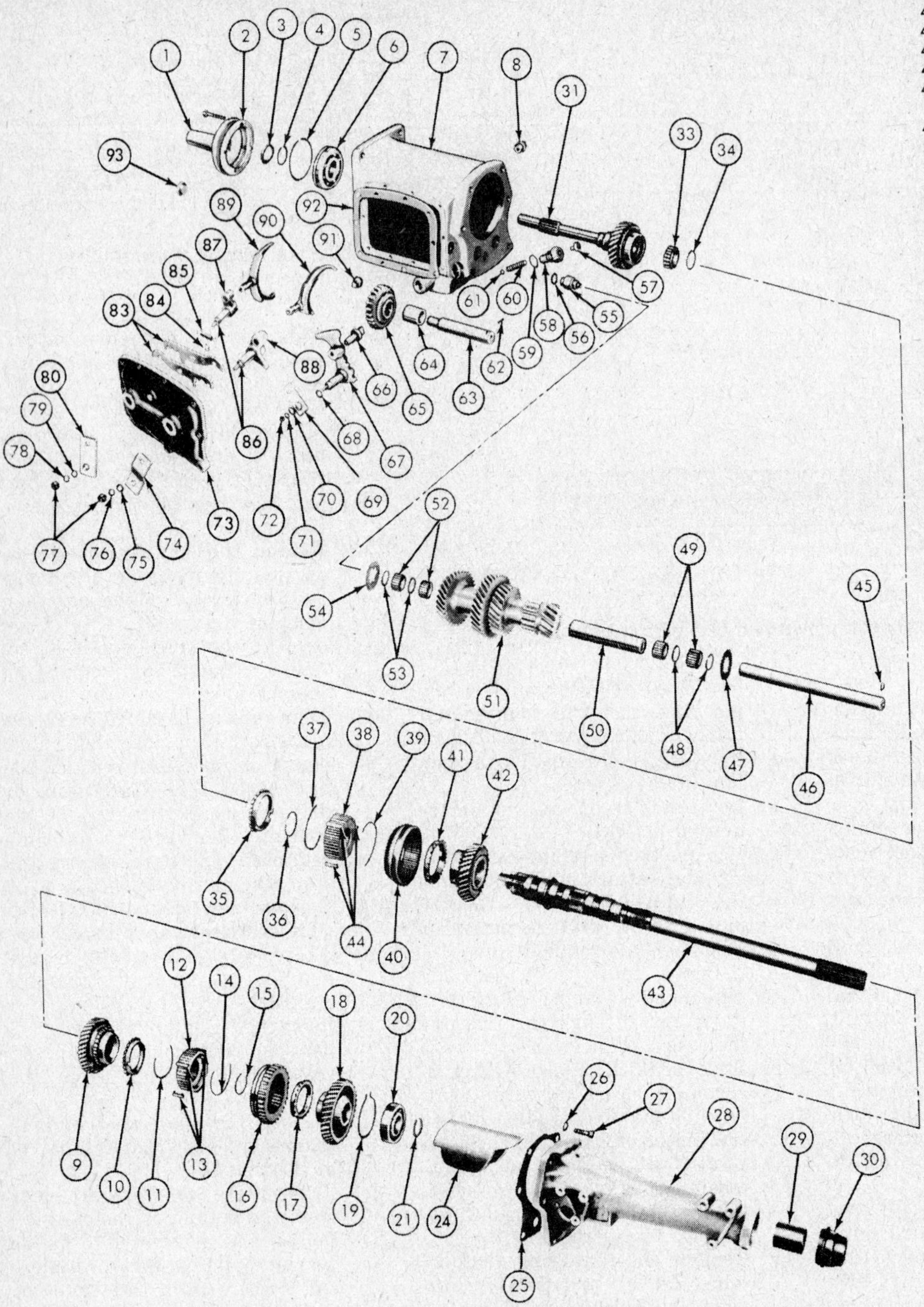

44 Shift struts (3)
45 Woodruff key
46 Countershaft
47 Thrustwasher, gear (1)
48 Spacer ring needle roller bearing
49 Needle bearing rollers
50 Bearing spacer
51 Countershaft gear (cluster)
52 Needle bearing rollers
53 Spacer ring needle roller bearing
54 Thrustwasher, gear (1)
55 Backup light switch
56 Backup light switch gasket
57 Plug
58 Retainer, reverse detent ball spring
59 Gasket
60 Spring, reverse detent ball
61 Ball, reverse detent
62 Woodruff key
63 Reverse idler gear shaft
64 Bushing, reverse idler gear
65 Gear, reverse idler
66 Fork, reverse shifter
67 Reverse lever
68 Oil seal, reverse lever shaft
69 Reverse operating lever
70 Flatwasher
71 Lockwasher

Four speed overdrive disassembled (© Chrysler Corp.)

1 Bearing retainer
2 Bearing retainer gasket
3 Bearing retainer oil seal
4 Snap ring gearing (inner)
5 Snap ring bearing (outer)
6 Pinion bearing
7 Transmission case
8 Filler plug
9 Gear, 2nd speed
10 Snap ring
11 Shift strut springs
12 Clutch gear
13 Shift struts (3)
14 Shift strut spring
15 Snap ring
16 1st and 2nd clutch sleeve gear
17 Stop ring
18 1st speed gear
19 Bearing retainer ring
20 Rear bearing
21 Snap ring
24 Baffle
25 Gasket, case to extension housing
26 Lockwasher
27 Bolt
28 Extension housing
29 Mainshaft yoke bushing
30 Oil seal
31 Main drive pinion
33 Needle bearing rollers
34 Snap ring
35 Stop ring
36 Snap ring
37 Shift strut spring
38 Clutch gear
39 Shift strut spring
40 Clutch sleeve
41 Stop ring
42 OD gear
43 Mainshaft (output)
72 Nut
73 Gearshift control housing
74 1st and 2nd operating lever
75 Flatwasher
76 Lockwasher lever
77 Nut, lever
78 Lockwasher, lever
79 Flatwasher, lever
80 3rd and OD operating lever
83 Interlock lever (2)
84 "E" ring
85 Spring
86 Oil seal (2)
87 3rd and OD lever
88 1st and 2nd lever
89 3rd and OD speed fork
90 1st and 2nd speed fork
91 Drain plug
92 Gasket, shift control housing
93 Expansion plug

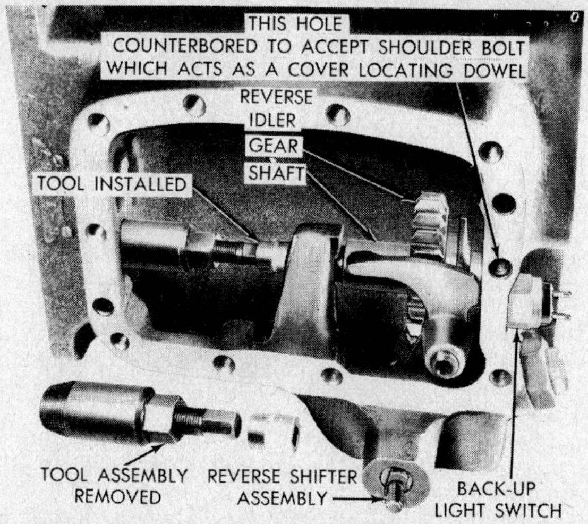

Removing reverse idler gearshaft (© Chrysler Corp.)

Removing reverse shift fork and lever (© Chrysler Corp.)

lever detent spring retainer, gasket, plug and detent ball and spring from the rear of the case.

25. The reverse idler gearshaft is very tight in the case. To remove it, place a $\frac{7}{16}$ inch socket, either $\frac{1}{4}$ or $\frac{3}{8}$ inch drive, on the end of a C-3638 power steering wormshaft remover, or something of its equivalent. Place the tool in the case with the socket against the end of the shaft and the other end of the tool against the case. Turn the screw on the tool to press the shaft out of the case. Remove the key from the shaft. In some cases a $\frac{7}{16}$ inch deep socket and/or a 3 inch extension may be required to press the shaft completely out of the case.

Assembly

1. Install the reverse detent spring retainer and gasket. Torque to 50 ft-lb. Insert the ball and spring. Install the plug and gasket. Torque to 24 ft-lb.
2. Place the reverse idler gearshaft into position in the end of the case, and drive it in far enough to position the reverse idler gear on the protruding end of the shaft with the fork slot toward the rear. At the same time, engage the slot with the shift fork.
3. With the reverse idler gear correctly positioned, drive the reverse gear shaft into the case far enough to install the woodruff key. Drive the shaft in flush with the end of the case.
4. Install the backup light switch and gasket. Torque to 15 ft-lb.
5. Coat the inside bore of the countershaft gear at each end with a thin film of grease and install the roller bearing spacer with an arbor tool. Center the spacer and arbor.
6. Install 19 rollers, followed by a spacer ring and 19 more rollers and another spacer ring into each end of the gear.
7. If the countershaft thrust washers are worn or scored, install new thrust washers. Coat the thrust washers with grease and install them over the arbor with the tang side toward the case boss.
8. Install the countershaft gear assembly into the case. Let the gear rest on the case bottom. Be sure the thrust washers stay in position.
9. Press the drive bearing on the pinion shaft. Be sure the outer snap ring groove is toward the front. Seat the bearing fully against the shoulder on the gear.
10. Install a new snap ring on the shaft to retain the bearing. Be sure the snap ring is seated. This snap ring comes in differ-

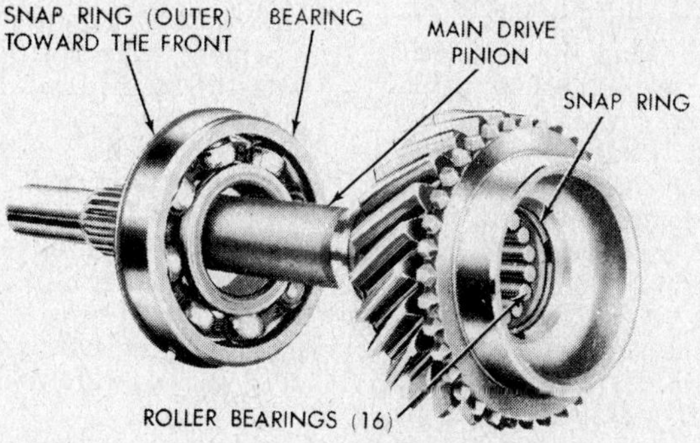

Drive pinion and bearing assembly (© Chrysler Corp.)

Removing reverse idler gear (© Chrysler Corp.)

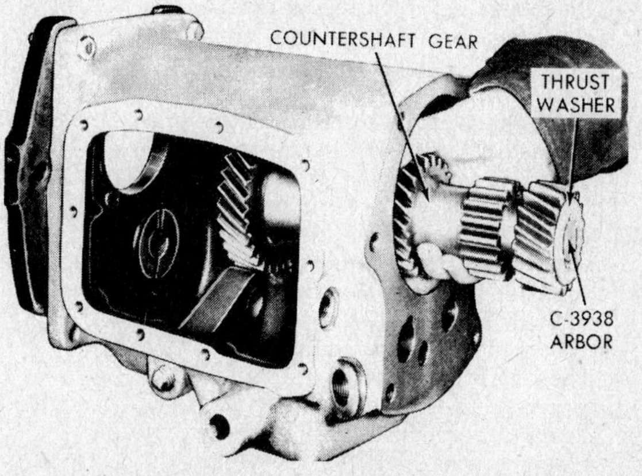

Removing countershaft gear and arbor (© Chrysler Corp.)

ent thicknesses for minimum end play.

11. Place the pinion shaft in a soft-jawed vise. Install 16 rollers in the shaft cavity. Coat the rollers with grease, then install the snap ring in its groove.
12. Install a new oil seal in the retainer bore.
13. Reassemble the synchronizer in the following order: place a stop ring flat on the workbench followed by the clutch gear and sleeve. Drop the struts in their slots and snap in a strut spring, placing the tang inside one strut. Turn the assembly over on the stop ring and install the second strut spring tang in a different strut.
14. Slide the second speed gear over the mainshaft, with the synchronizer cone toward the rear, and down against the shoulder on the shaft.
15. Slide the 1st-2nd synchronizer assembly (including the stop ring with the lugs indexed in the hub slots) over the mainshaft, down against the second gear cone and secure it with a snap ring. Slide the next stop ring over the shaft and index the lugs into the hub.
16. Slide the first speed gear, with the synchronizer cone toward the clutch sleeve gear, just installed, over the mainshaft and into position against the clutch sleeve gear.
17. Install the mainshaft bearing retaining ring and the mainshaft rear bearing. Using an arbor and driver, drive the bearing down into position. Secure it with a snap ring. The snap ring used here comes in various thicknesses for minimum end play.
18. Install the partially assembled mainshaft into the extension housing far enough to engage the bearing retaining ring in the slot in the extension housing. Compress the ring with pliers so that the mainshaft ball bearing can move in and bottom against its thrust shoulder in the extension housing. Release the ring and seat it all around in its groove in the extension housing.
19. Slide the overdrive gear over the mainshaft, with the synchronizer cone toward the front, followed by the OD stop ring.
20. Slide the 3rd-OD synchronizer clutch gear assembly on the mainshaft, with the shift fork slot toward the rear, against the OD gear. Be sure to index the rear stop ring with the clutch gear struts.
21. Install the retaining snap ring. Using grease, position the front stop ring over the clutch gear again indexing the ring lugs with the struts.
22. Coat a new extension housing gasket with grease and place it on the extension.
23. Slide the reverse idler gear to the center of its shaft and move the 3rd-OD synchronizer sleeve as far as practical toward the front. Do not lose the struts.
24. Slowly insert the mainshaft assembly into the case, tilting it as required to clear the idler and countershaft gears.
25. Place the 3rd-OD synchronizer sleeve in the neutral position.
26. Rotate the extension on the mainshaft to expose the rear of the countershaft. Install one extension bolt at the top of the case to hold the extension in the inverted position and prevent it from moving rearward.
27. Install the drive pinion and bearing assembly through the front of the case and position it in the front bore. Install the outer snap ring in the bearing groove. Tap it lightly into place with a soft hammer. If everything is in the right place, the bearing outer snap ring will bottom onto the case face without excessive effort. If not, check to see if a strut, pinion roller, or stop ring is out of position.
28. Turn the transmission assembly upsidedown, holding the countergear assembly to avoid disengaging it.
29. Lower the countershaft gear assembly into position with the teeth meshed with the drive pinion gear. Make sure that the thrust washers remain in position on the ends of the arbor and the tangs are aligned with the slots in the case.
30. Start the countershaft into the bore at the rear of the case and push it forward until the shaft is approximately half way into the case and gear. Install the woodruff key. Push the shaft forward until the end is flush with the rear case face. Remove the arbor.
31. Rotate the extension into alignment with the case.
32. Install the extension housing bolts and torque to 50 ft-lb.
33. Turn the transmission assembly upright.
34. Install the drive pinion bearing retainer and gasket. Coat the threads with sealing compound and install the bolts. Torque them to 30 ft-lb.
35. Install a new expansion plug in the countershaft bore in the front of the case.
36. Install the interlock levers on the pivot pin and fasten with an E ring. Use pliers to install the spring on the interlock lever hangers.
37. Grease and install new O ring seals on both shift shafts. Grease the housing bores and push each shaft into its proper bore.
38. Install the operating levers and tighten the retaining nuts to 18 ft-lb. Be sure that the 3rd-OD operating lever points downward.
39. Rotate each shift shaft fork bore to the neutral position and install the 3rd-OD shift fork in its bore and under both interlock levers.
40. Position both synchronizer sleeves in neutral. Place the 1-2 shift fork in the groove of the 1-2 synchronizer sleeve.
41. Lay the transmission on its right side, coat the gasket with grease and position it on the case.
42. As the shift housing is lowered in place, guide the 3rd-OD shift fork into its synchronizer groove, then lead the shaft of the 1-2 shift fork into its bore in the 1-2 shift lever. Using a screwdriver, raise the interlock lever against

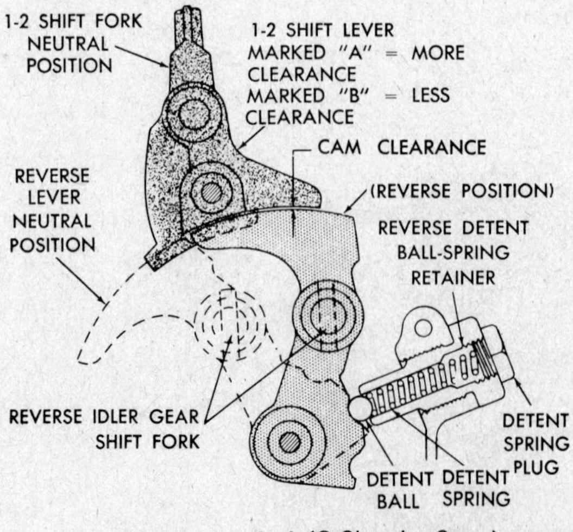

Reverse interlock (© Chrysler Corp.)

its spring tension to allow the 1-2 shift fork shaft to slip under the levers. The shift housing will now seat against the case.

43. Install the housing retaining bolts finger tight and shift through all the gears to check operation.

44. Eight of the housing retaining bolts are shoulder bolts for accurately locating the mechanism on the case. One bolt shoulder is longer and acts as a dowel, passing through the cover and into the case at the center of the rear flange. The two standard bolts are located at the rear lower part of the cover. Torque all bolts in a criss-cross pattern to 15 ft-lb.

45. Place the transmission in reverse and while turning the input shaft, move the 1-2 lever in each direction. If the input shaft locks or becomes hard to turn, the synchronizer is partly engaging caused by too much cam clearance. Select a new 1-2 shift lever, marked A or B as required. An A lever gives more clearance, a B lever, less.

46. Grease the reverse shaft and install the operating lever and nut. Torque to 18 ft-lb.

47. Install the speedometer drive pinion gear and adapter being sure the range number, representing the number of teeth on the gear, is in the 6 o'clock position.

Ford 3.03 3 Speed

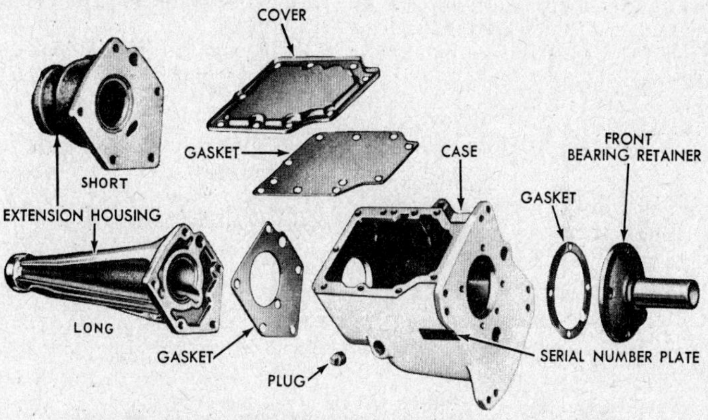

Transmission case and exterior parts—Ford 3.03 (© Ford Motor Co.)

Description

The Ford 3.03 is a fully synchronized three speed transmission. All gears except reverse are in constant mesh. Forward speed gear changes are accomplished with synchronizer sleeves.

Disassembly of Transmission

1. Drain the lubricant by removing the lower extension housing bolt.
2. Remove the case cover and gasket.
3. Remove the long spring that holds the detent plug in the case and remove the detent plug with a small magnet.
4. Remove the extension housing and gasket.
5. Remove the front bearing retainer and gasket.
6. Remove the filler plug on the right side of the transmission case. Working through the plug opening, drive the roll pin out of the case and countershaft with a ¼ inch punch.
7. Hold the countershaft gear with a hook. Install dummy shaft and push the countershaft out of the rear of the case. As the countershaft comes out, lower the gear cluster to the bottom of the case. Remove the countershaft.
8. Remove the snap ring that holds the speedometer drive gear on the output shaft. Slip the gear off the shaft and remove the gear lock ball.
9. Remove the snap ring that holds the output shaft bearing. Using a special bearing puller, remove the output shaft bearing.
10. Place both shift levers in the neutral (center) position.
11. Remove the set screw that holds the first-reverse shift fork to the shift rail. Slip the first-reverse shift rail out through the rear of the case.
12. Move the first-reverse synchronizer forward as far as possible. Rotate the first-reverse shift fork upwards and lift it out of the case.
13. Place the second-third shift fork in the second position. Remove the set screw. Rotate the shift rail 90 degrees.
14. Lift the interlock plug out of the case with a magnet.
15. Remove the expansion plug from the second-third shift rail by lightly tapping the end of the rail. Remove the second-third shift rail.
16. Remove the second-third shift rail detent plug and spring from detent bore.
17. Remove the input gear and shaft from the case.
18. Rotate the second-third shift

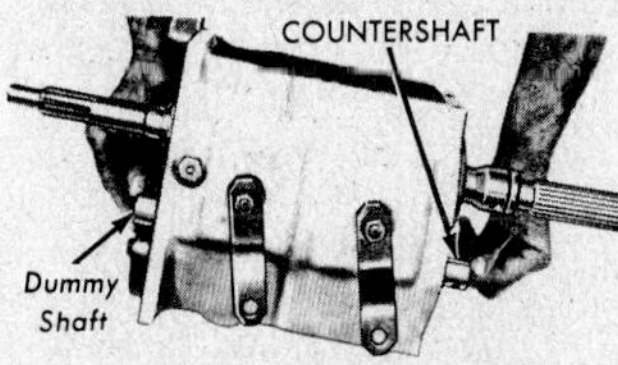

Removing countershaft—Ford 3.03 (© Ford Motor Co.)

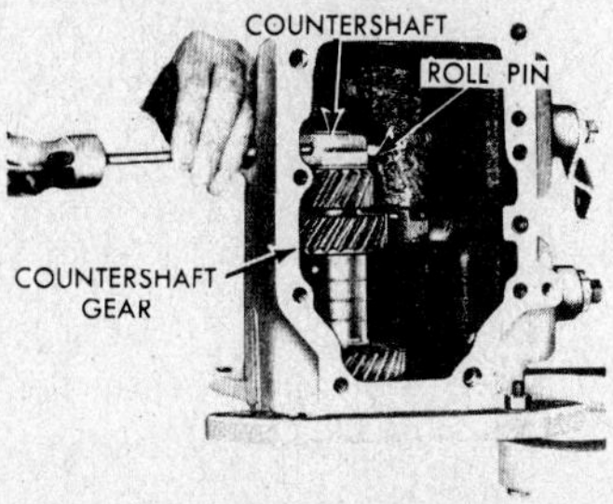

Removing countershaft roll pin—Ford 3.03 (© Ford Motor Co.)

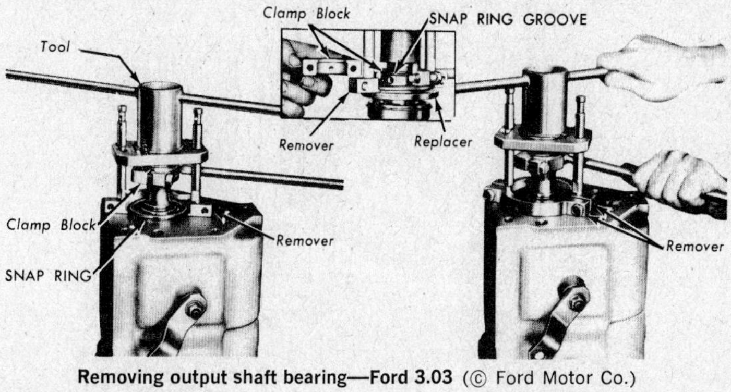

Removing output shaft bearing—Ford 3.03 (© Ford Motor Co.)

fork upwards and remove from case.

19. Using caution, lift the output shaft assembly out through top of case.
20. Lift the reverse idler gear and thrust washers out of case. Remove the countershaft gear, thrust washer and dummy shaft from case.
21. Remove the snap ring from the front of the output shaft. Slip the synchronizer and second gear off shaft.
22. Remove the second snap ring from output shaft and remove the thrust washer, first gear and blocking ring.
23. Remove the third snap ring from the output shaft. The first reverse synchronizer hub is a press fit on the output shaft. Remove the synchronizer hub with an arbor press.

CAUTION: Do not attempt to remove or install the synchronizer hub by prying or hammering.

Disassembly and Assembly of Sub-Assemblies

Shift Levers and Seals

1. Remove shift levers from the shafts. Slip the levers out of case. Discard shaft sealing O-rings.
2. Lubricate and install new O-rings on shift shafts.
3. Install the shift shafts in the case and secure shift levers.

Input Shaft Bearings

1. Remove the snap ring securing the input shaft bearing. Using an arbor press, remove the bearing.
2. Press the input shaft bearing onto shaft using correct tool.

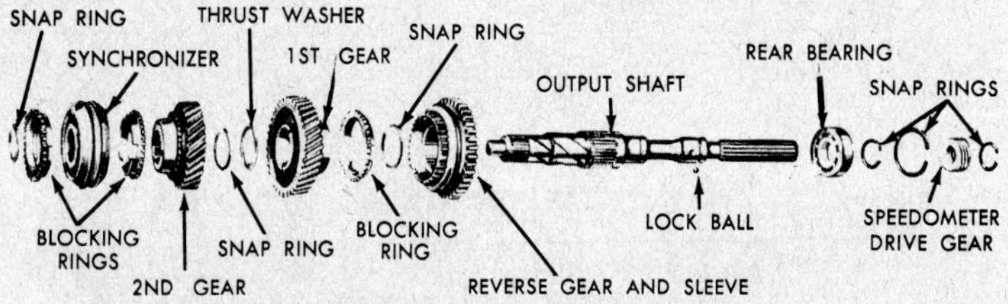

Output shaft—exploded view—Ford 3.03 (© Ford Motor Co.)

Rotating second-third shift rail—Ford 3.03 (© Ford Motor Co.)

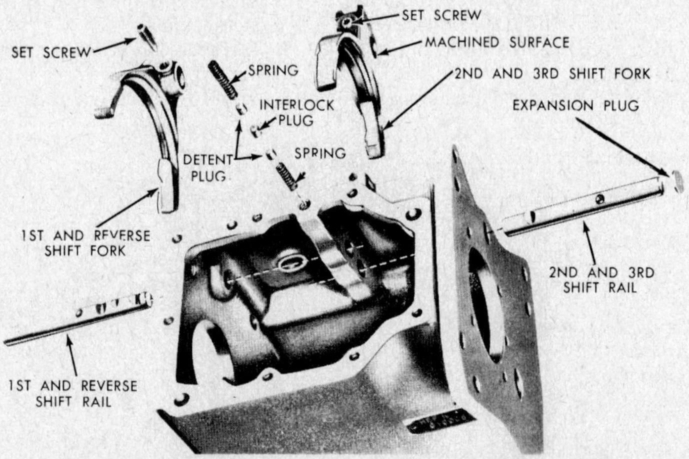

Shift rails and forks—exploded view—Ford 3.03 (© Ford Motor Co.)

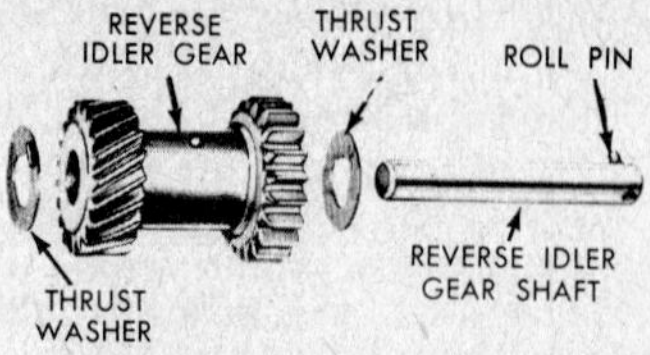

Reverse idler shaft—exploded view—Ford 3.03 (© Ford Motor Co.)

Synchronizers

1. Scribe alignment marks on synchronizer hubs before disassembly. Remove each synchronizer hub from the synchronizer sleeves.
2. Separate the inserts and insert springs from the hubs.

CAUTION: Do not mix parts from the separate synchronizer assemblies.

3. Install the insert spring in the hub of the first-reverse synchronizer. Be sure that the spring covers all the insert grooves. Start the hub on the sleeve making certain that the scribed marks are properly aligned. Place the three inserts in the hub, small ends on the inside. Slide the sleeve and reverse gear onto hub.
4. Install one insert spring into a groove on the second-third synchronizer hub. Be sure that all three insert slots are covered. Align the scribed marks on the hub and sleeve and start the hub into the sleeve. Position the three inserts on the top of the retaining spring and push the assembly together. Install the remaining retainer spring so that the spring ends cover the same slots as the first spring. Do not stagger the springs. Place a synchronizer blocking ring on the ends of the synchronizer sleeve.

Countershaft Gear Bearings

1. Remove the dummy shaft, needle bearings and bearing retainers from the countershaft gear.
2. Coat the bore in each end of the countershaft gear with grease.
3. Hold the dummy shaft in the gear and install the needle bearings in the case.
4. Place the countershaft gear, dummy shaft, and needle bearings in the case.
5. Place the case in a vertical position. Align the gear bore and the thrust washers with the bores in the case and install the countershaft.
6. Place the case in a horizontal position. Check the countershaft gear end play with a feeler gauge. Clearance should be between 0.004-0.018 inch. If clearance does not come within specifications, replace the thrust washers.
7. Install the dummy shaft in the countershaft gear and leave the

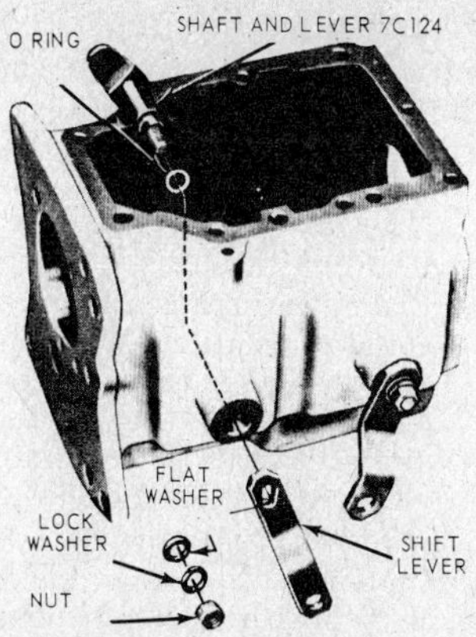

Shift lever and shaft—exploded view—Ford 3.03 (© Ford Motor Co.)

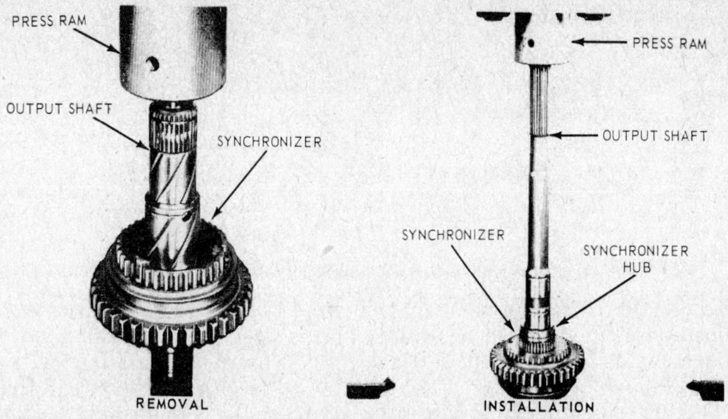

Removing and installing first-reverse synchronizer—Ford 3.03 (© Ford Motor Co.)

gear at the bottom of the transmission case.

Assembly of Transmission

1. Cover the reverse idler gear thrust surfaces in the case with a thin film of lubricant, and install the two thrust washers in the case.
2. Install the reverse idler gear and shaft in the case. Align the case bore and thrust washers with gear bore and install the reverse idler shaft.
3. Measure the reverse idler gear end play with a feeler gauge; clearance should be between 0.004-0.018 inch. If end play is not within specifications, replace the thrust washers. If clearance is correct, leave the reverse idler gear in case.
4. Lubricate the output shaft splines and machined surfaces with transmission oil.
5. The first-reverse synchronizer hub is a press fit on the output shaft. Hub must be installed in an arbor press. Install the synchronizer hub with the teeth-end of the gear facing towards the rear of the shaft.

CAUTION: Do not attempt to install the first-reverse synchronizer with a hammer.

6. Place the blocking ring on the tapered surface of the first gear.
7. Slide the first gear on the output shaft with the blocking ring toward the rear of the shaft. Rotate the gear as necessary to

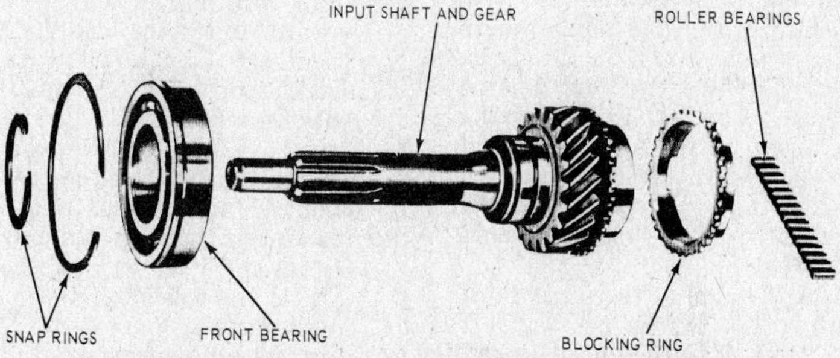

Input shaft gear—exploded view—Ford 3.03 (© Ford Motor Co.)

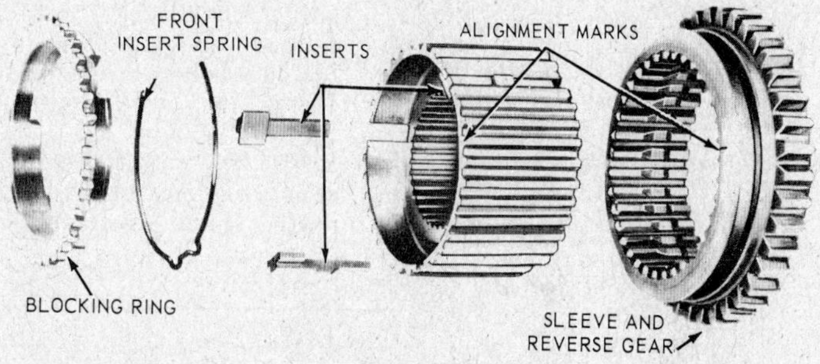

First-reverse synchronizer—exploded view—Ford 3.03 (© Ford Motor Co.)

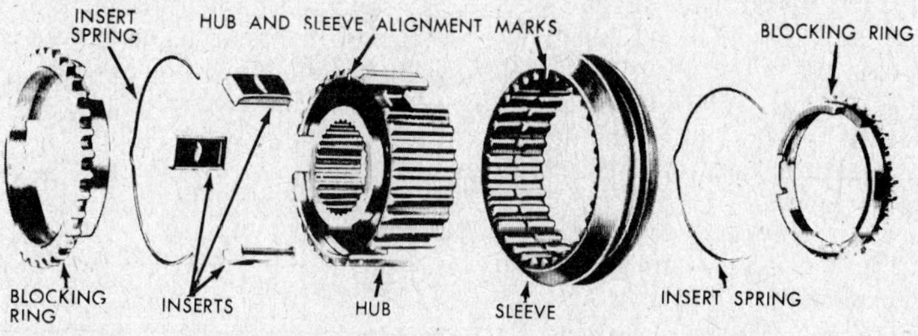

Second-third synchronizer—exploded view—Ford 3.03 (© Ford Motor Co.)

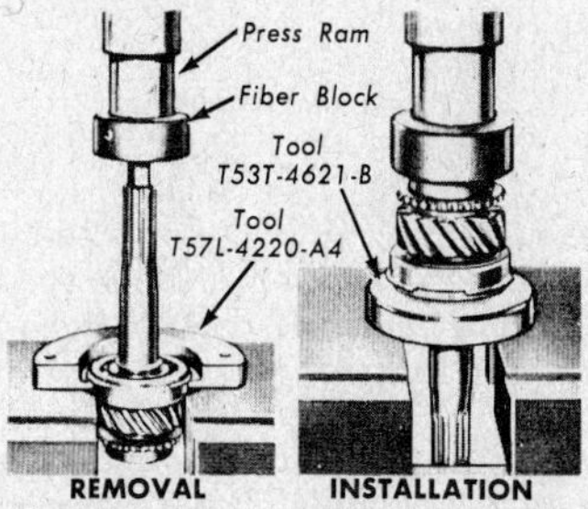

Replacing input shaft bearing—Ford 3.03 (© Ford Motor Co.)

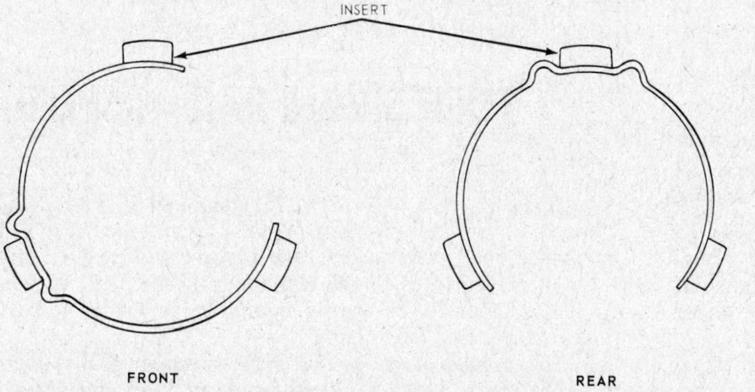

First-reverse synchronizer insert spring installation—Ford 3.03 (© Ford Motor Co.)

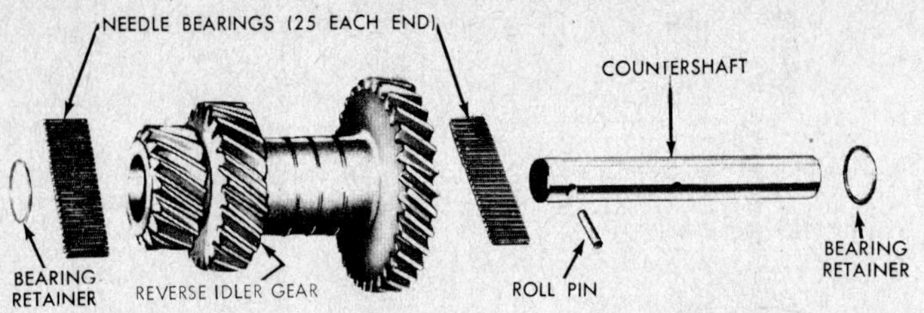

Countershaft gear—exploded view—Ford 3.03 (© Ford Motor Co.)

engage the three notches in the blocking ring with the synchronizer inserts. Install the thrust washer and snap ring.

8. Slide the blocking ring onto the tapered surface of the second gear. Slide the second gear with blocking ring and the second-third synchronizer on the mainshaft. Be sure that the tapered surface of second gear is facing the front of the shaft and that the notches in the blocking ring engage the synchronizer inserts. Install the snap ring and secure assembly.
9. Cover the core of the input shaft with a thin coat of grease.

CAUTION: A thick film of grease will plug lubricant holes and cause damage to bearings.

Install bearings.

10. Install the input shaft through the front of the case and insert snap ring in the bearing groove.
11. Install the output shaft assembly in the case. Position the second-third shift fork on the second-third synchronizer.
12. Place a detent plug spring and a plug in the case. Place the second-third synchronizer in the second gear position (toward the rear of the case). Align the fork and install the second-third shift rail. It will be necessary to depress the detent plug to install the shift rail in the bore. Move the rail forward until the detent plug enters the forward notch (second gear).
13. Secure the fork to the shift rail with a set screw and place the synchronizer in neutral.
14. Install the interlock plug in the case.
15. Place the first-reverse synchronizer in the first gear position (towards the front of the case). Place the shift fork in the groove of the synchronizer. Rotate the fork into position and install the shift rail. Move the shift rail inward until the center notch (neutral) is aligned with the detent bore. Secure shift fork with set screw.
16. Install a new shift rail expansion plug in the front of the case.
17. Hold the input shaft and blocking ring in position and move the output shaft forward to seat the pilot in the roller bearings on the input gear.
18. Tap the input gear bearing into place while holding the output shaft. Install the front bearing retainer and gasket. Torque attaching bolts to specifications.
19. Install the large snap ring on the rear bearing. Place the bearing on the output shaft with the snap ring end toward the rear of the shaft. Press the bearing into place using a special tool. Secure the bearing to the shaft with the snap ring.
20. Hold the speedometer drive gear lock ball in the detent and slide the speedometer drive gear into position. Secure with snap ring.
21. Place the transmission in the vertical position. Working with a screwdriver through the drain hole in the bottom of the case, align the bore of the countershaft gear and the thrust washer with the bore in the case.
22. Working from the rear of the case, push the dummy shaft out of the countershaft gear with the countershaft. Align the roll pin hole in the countershaft with the matching hole in the case. Drive the shaft into place and install the roll pin.
23. Position the new extension housing gasket on the case with sealer. Install the extension housing and torque to specification.
24. Place the transmission in gear and pour gear oil over entire gear train while rotating the input shaft.
25. Install the remaining detent plug and long spring in case.
26. Position cover gasket on case with sealer and install cover. Torque cover bolts to specifications.
27. Check operation of transmission in all gear positions.

TORQUE SPECIFICATIONS	*Foot-Lb.*
Input shaft gear bearing retainer to transmission case	30-36
Transmission to flywheel housing	37-42
Transmission cover to transmission case	14-19
Speedometer cable retainer to transmission extension	3-4.5
Transmission extension to transmission case	42-50
Flywheel housing to engine	40-50
Gear shift lever to cam and shaft assembly lock nuts	18-23
U-Joint flange to output shaft	60-80
Filler plug	10-20
Shifter fork set screws	10-18
T.R.S. switch to case	15-20

Lubricant Refill Capacity (Pints)	U.S.	Imp.
Ford Type 3.03	3.5	3.0

FORD SINGLE RAIL 4-SPEED OVERDRIVE

Description

The Single rail 4-speed overdrive transmission (SROD) is of the fully synchronized type with all gears except the reverse sliding gear being in constant mesh. All forward-speed changes are accomplished with synchronizer sleeves.

All forward-speed gears in the transmission are helical-type. However, the reverse sliding gear and the external teeth of the first- and second-speed synchronizer sleeve are spur-type.

The shift pattern for the control unit is imprinted on the shift lever knob. An automatically adjusted back-up lamp switch is installed in an indexing retainer at the lower rear portion of the shift control assembly.

A transmission service identification tag is located on the right side of the case at the front. The first line on the tag will show the transmission model and service identification code when required. The second line will

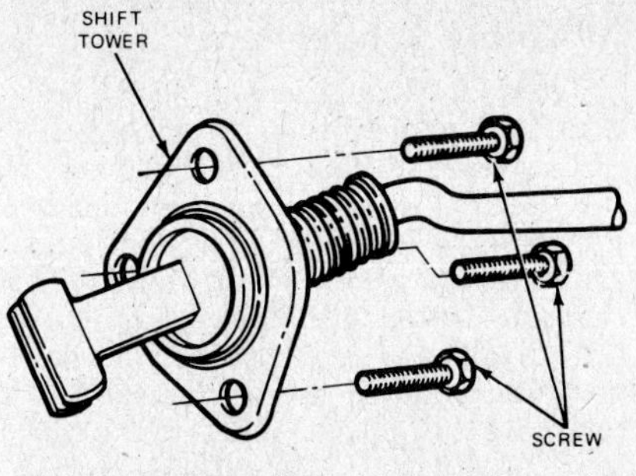

Shift tower (© Chrysler Corp.)

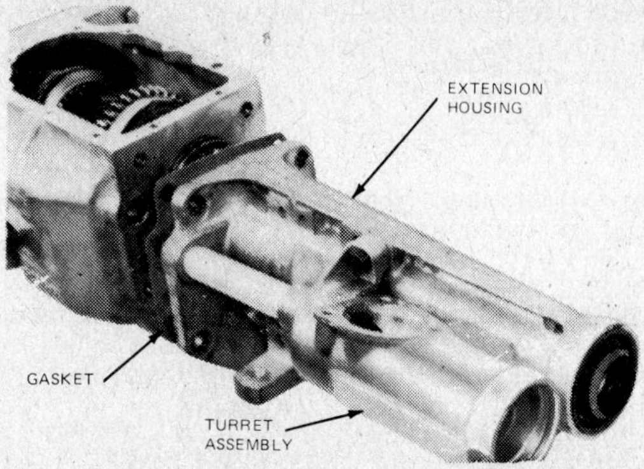

Extension housing removal and installation (© Chrysler Corp.)

show the transmission serial number. Additionally, a serial number is stamped on the top side of the flange on the case for further identification.

Disassembly

1. Mount transmission in a holding fixture and drain the lubricant by removing the lower extension to case screw and washer.
2. Remove the transmission cover attaching screws from the case. Lift the cover and gasket from the case (discard gasket).
3. Remove the screw, detent spring and detent plug from the case. A magnetized rod may have to be used to remove spring and detent plug.
4. Drive roll pin from shifter shaft.
5. Remove back-up lamp switch assembly, snap ring and dust cover from rear of extension housing.
6. Remove shifter shaft from turret assembly.
7. Remove the extension housing attaching screws and lockwashers. Remove the housing and gasket (discard gasket).
8. Remove the snap ring that secures the speedometer drive gear to the output shaft. Slide the gear off the shaft, then remove the speedometer gear drive ball.
9. Remove the snap ring that secures the output shaft bearing to the shaft and remove the output shaft bearing (slip fit) from the output shaft and transmission case.
10. Working from the front of the case push the countershaft out the rear of the case with a dummy shaft. Lower the countershaft to the bottom of the case.
11. Remove the input shaft bearing retainer attaching bolts. Slide the retainer and gasket off the input shaft. Discard gasket.
12. Remove the snap ring that secures the input shaft bearing to the input shaft. Remove the input shaft bearing from the input shaft and transmission case (slip fit).
13. Remove the input shaft and the blocking ring from the case including roller bearings.
14. Remove the overdrive shift pawl, gear selector and interlock plate.
15. Remove 1-2 gearshift selector arm plate.
16. Remove roll pin from 3rd/overdrive shift fork.
17. Remove the 3rd overdrive shift rail and expansion plug (Drive from the rear of case).
18. Remove the first and second speed shift fork. Remove the third overdrive speed shift fork.
19. Remove the output shaft assembly through the top of the case.
20. Remove the snap ring from the front of the output shaft. Slide the third and overdrive synchronizer blocking ring and the gear off the shaft.
21. Remove the next snap ring, thrust washer, and second gear. Remove first speed gear and blocking ring from the rear of the shaft.
22. Lift the countershaft gear thrust washers and roller bearings from the case. Be careful not to drop the bearings or the dummy shaft from the countershaft gear.
23. Remove the roll pin from the reverse fork, slide the reverse shifter rail through the rear of case. Remove reverse fork spacer and remove reverse gearshift fork.
24. From the front of the case drive the reverse gear shaft out the rear of case.
25. Remove the reverse idler gear, thrust washers and roller bearings, being careful not to drop bearing.
26. Remove retaining clip, reverse

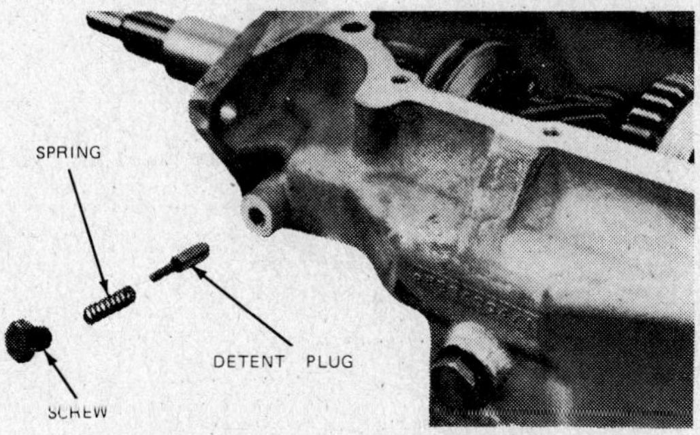

Detent removal and installation (© Chrysler Corp.)

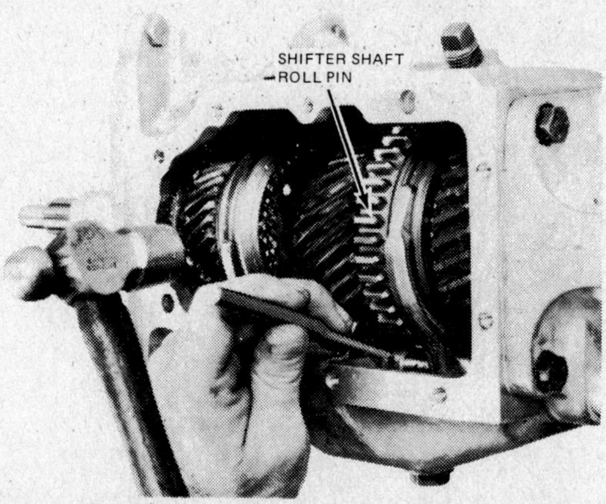

Shifter shaft roll pin removal (© Chrysler Corp.)

gearshift relay lever and reverse gear selector fork pivot pin.

27. Remove the overdrive shift control link assembly.
28. Remove shift shaft seal from rear of case.
29. Remove expansion plug from front of case (shift shaft rail hole).

Assembly

Reverse the disassembly procedure for assembly of the transmission following the lubrication requirement below.

NOTE: Extension housing bolts must be tightened in the following manner:

1. Start all bolts a minimum of two full turns.
2. Tighten bolt number 1 to 42-50 ft-lbs.
3. Tighten remaining bolts to 42-50 ft-lbs.

Assembly Lubrication

These lubricants are to be applied prior to completion of assembly.

The transmission mainshaft bearing rollers, extension housing bushing, reverse idle bearing rollers, and countershaft gear bearing rollers are to be lubricated with ESW-M1C109-A or equivalent at each location. The low gear and 2nd and overdrive gear formals on the output shaft are to be lubricated with ESP-M2C83-G transmission oil or equivalent. All other in-

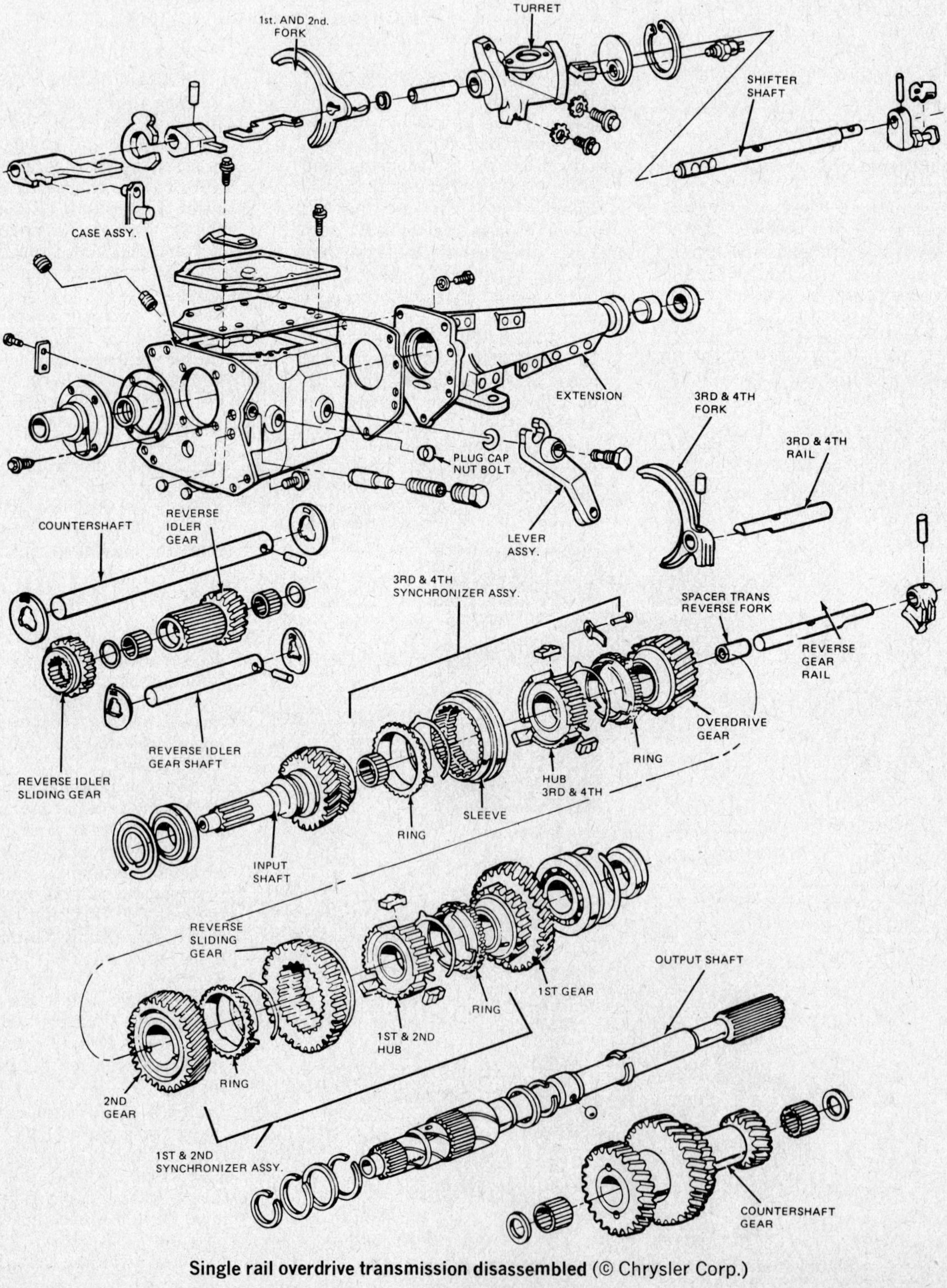

Single rail overdrive transmission disassembled (© Chrysler Corp.)

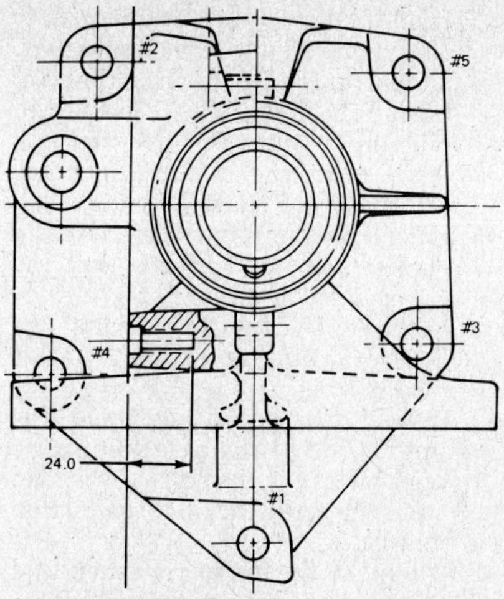

Extension housing torque sequence
(© Chrysler Corp.)

ternal components of the transmission are to be thoroughly flush lubricated with ¼ litre (½ pint) of ESP-M2C83-C transmission oil or equivalent.

Functional Lubrication

Prior to functional operation of the transmission under load, fill with 2.1 litres (4.5 pints) (US) of ESP-M2C83-C lubricant or equivalent at initial installation of transmission.

The transmission shifter shaft and the transmission gear shift damper bushing are to be lubricated with ESA-M1C175-A material or equivalent prior to assembly into the transmission.

Supplemental Sealing Requirements

The transmission gear shift shaft sleeve (both ends) and the turret cover assembly are to be sealed with ESE-M4G132-A or equivalent to prevent intrusion of road contaminates.

Shift Rail Plug

Intermediate and high rail welch plug must be seated firmly and must not protrude above the front face of case or more than 1.52mm (0.06 inch) maximum below front face of case.

Gear End Plays

The end play of the 1st, 2nd and OD (overdrive) gears after their as-

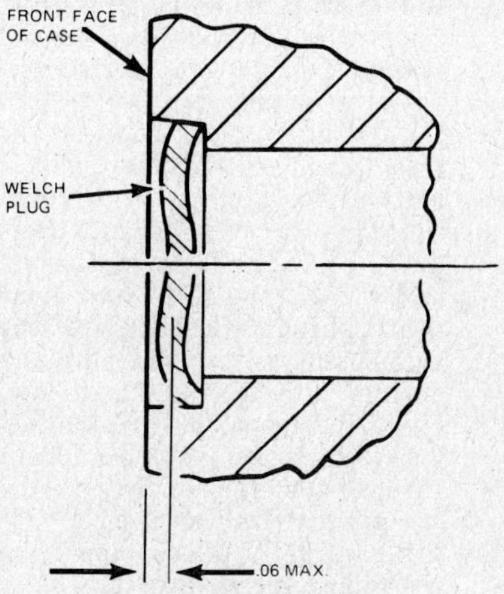

Welch plug installation
(© Chrysler Corp.)

sembly on the output shaft must be checked using a suitable gauge and pass the following specifications:

1. With the 1st gear thrust washer clamped tight against the shoulder on the output shaft the 1st gear end play is 0.127-0.609 mm (0.005-0.024 inch.)
2. 2nd gear end play must be 0.076-0.533 mm (0.003-0.021 inch).
3. OD (overdrive) gear end play must be 0.228-0.584 mm (0.009-0.023 inch).

The end play of the countershaft gear after its assembly into the case between the thrust washers must be checked using a suitable gauge and must pass the countershaft gear end play must be 0.101-0.457 mm (0.004-0.018 inch).

Rebuild with new components if dimensions exceed the limits.

TORQUE LIMITS

Application	Bolt	Nut	Tightening Torque Ft-Lbs (N•m)
Input Shaft Bearing Retainer	5/16	Case	11-25 (15-33)
Extension Assembly	7/16-14	Case	42-50 (54-67)
Case Access Cover	5/16-18	Case	20-25 (28-33)
Filler Plug	½-14 U.S. Pipe Tread	Case	10-20 (14-27)
Back Up Lamp Switch	9/16-18	Turret Cover Assy.	8-12 (11-16)
Pin—Reverse Gear Fork Pivot	M16-1.5	Case	15-25 (21-33)
Turret Assembly	M8-1.25	Extension	8-12 (11-16)
Service I.D.	#6-32	Case	Seat Firmly
Tag Screw	Self-Tapping		
Detent Bolt	3/8-16	Case	10-15 (14-20)

EXTERNAL LINKAGE FORD 4-SPEED OVERDRIVE

Description

The 4-speed overdrive transmission is of the fully synchronized type with all gears except the reverse sliding gear being in constant mesh. All forward-speed changes are accomplished with synchronizer sleeves.

All forward-speed gears in the transmission are helical-type. However, the reverse sliding gear and the external teeth of the first- and second-speed synchronizer sleeve are spur-type.

A transmission service identification tag is located on the right side of the case at the front. The first line on the tag will show the transmission model and service identification code when required. The second line will show the transmission serial number. Additionally, a serial number is stamped on the top side of the flange on the case for further identification.

The 4-speed shift control unit is serviced as a unit only. The shift control is not to be disassembled. The only parts to be removed from the shifter assembly are the 3 shift rods, the in-cab shift lever, back-up switch bracket, and the back-up light switch. The shift pattern for the control unit is imprinted on the shift knob. The automatically adjusted back-up light switch is assembled to the backside of the shift control unit.

Disassembly

1. Mount the transmission in a holding fixture and drain the lubricant by removing the lower extension to case screw and washer.
2. Remove the cover attaching screws from the case. Lift the cover and gasket from the case.
3. Remove the long spring that retains the detent plug in the case. Remove the detent plug with a small magnet.
4. Remove the extension housing attaching screws and lockwashers. Remove the housing and the gasket. Discard gasket.
5. Remove the input shaft bearing retainer attaching screws. Slide the retainer off the input shaft.
6. Support the countershaft gear with a wire hook. Working from the front of the case, push the countershaft out the rear of the case. Lower the countershaft to the bottom of the case with the wire hook. Remove the hook.
7. Remove the set screw from the first and second-speed shift fork. Slide the first and second-speed shift rail out the rear of the case.
8. Using a magnet, remove the interlock detent from between the first-second and third-overdrive shift rails.
9. Shift the transmission into overdrive position. Remove the set screw from the third and overdrive shift fork. Remove the side detent bolt, detent plug and spring. Rotate the third and overdrive speed shift rail 90 degrees clockwise and tap it out through the front of the case using a punch and hammer.
10. Remove the interlock plug from the top of the case with a magnet.
11. Remove the snap ring that secures the speedometer drive gear to the output shaft. Slide the gear off the shaft, then remove the speedometer gear drive ball.
12. Remove the snap ring that secures the output shaft bearing to the shaft. Remove the snap ring from the outside diameter of the output shaft bearing.
13. Assemble the special service tools and remove the output shaft bearing from the output shaft.
14. Remove the snap ring that secures the input shaft bearing to the input shaft. Remove the snap ring from the outside diameter of the input shaft bearing.
15. Remove the input shaft bearing from the input shaft and the transmission case.
16. Remove the input shaft and the blocking ring from the front of the case.
17. Move the output shaft to the right side of the case to provide clearance for the shift forks. Rotate the forks then lift them from the case.
18. Support the thrust washer and first-speed gear to prevent them from sliding off the shaft, then lift the output shaft assembly from the case.
19. Remove the reverse gear shift fork set screw. Rotate the reverse shift rail 90 degrees. Slide the shift rail out of the rear of the case. Lift the reverse shift fork from the case.
20. Remove the reverse detent plug and spring from the case with a magnet.
21. Remove the reverse idler gear shaft from the case.
22. Lift the countershaft gear and

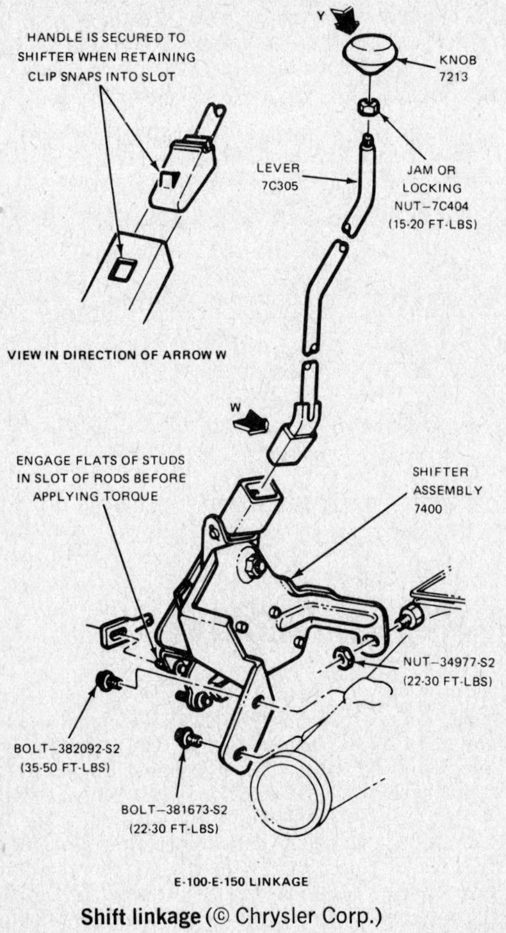

Shift linkage (© Chrysler Corp.)

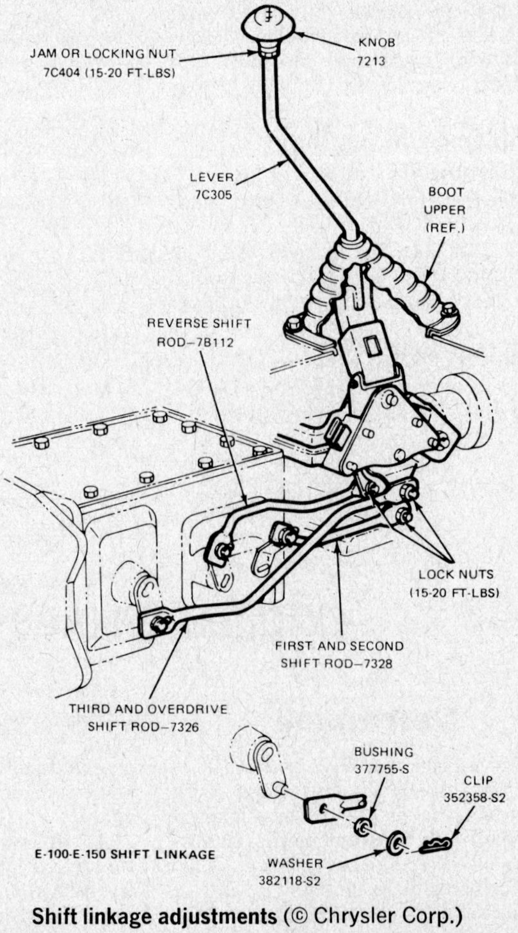

Shift linkage adjustments (© Chrysler Corp.)

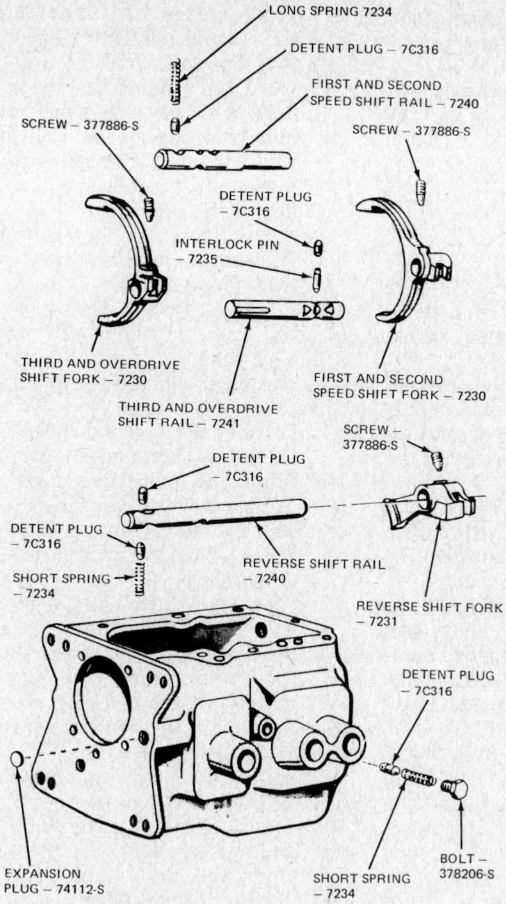

Shift rails and forks disassembled
(© Chrysler Corp.)

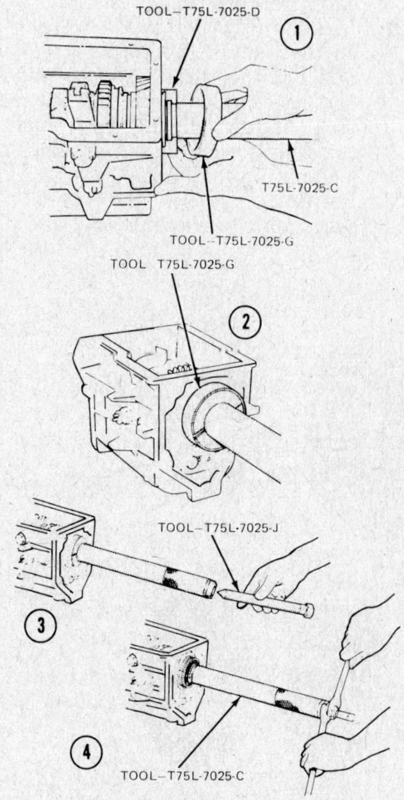

Output shaft bearing removal
(© Chrysler Corp.)

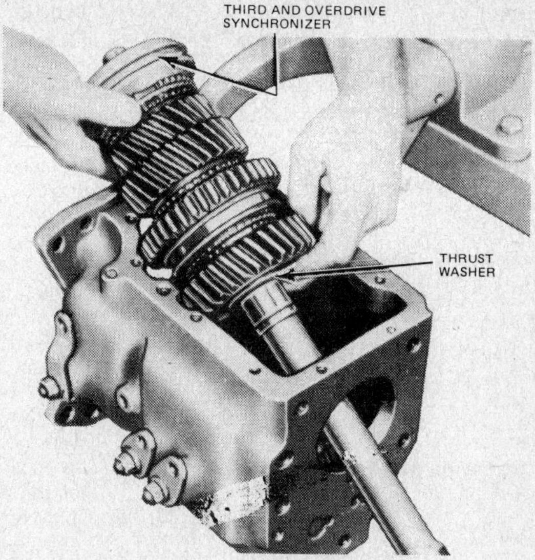

Removing output shaft assembly
(© Chrysler Corp.)

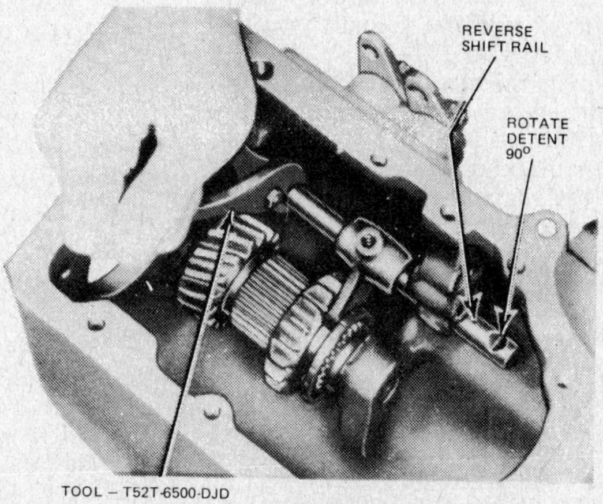

Rotating reverse shift rail
(© Chrysler Corp.)

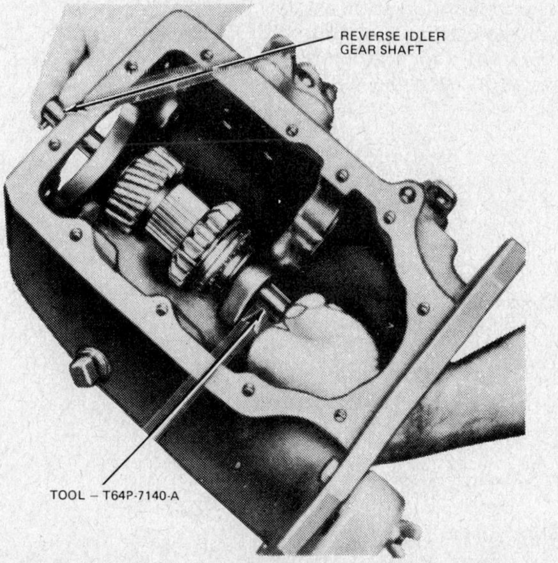

Removing reverse idler gearshaft (© Chrysler Corp.)

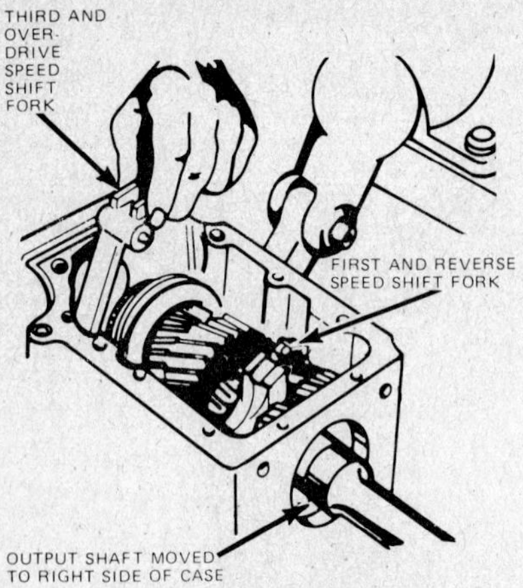

Removing shift fork from case
(© Chrysler Corp.)

the thrust washers from the case. Be careful not to drop the bearings or the dummy shaft from the countershaft gear.

23. Lift the reverse idler gear and the thrust washers from the case. Be careful not to drop the bearings and the dummy shaft from the gear.
24. Remove the snap ring from the front of the output shaft. Slide the third and overdrive synchronizer blocking ring and the gear off the shaft.
25. Remove the next snap ring and the second-speed gear thrust washer from the shaft. Slide the second-speed gear and the blocking ring off the shaft.
26. Remove the next snap ring.
27. Remove the thrust washer, first speed gear and blocking ring from the rear of the shaft. The first and second synchronizer hub is a slip fit on the output shaft.

Assembly

1. Coat the countershaft gear thrust surfaces in the case with a thin film of lubricant and position a thrust washer at each end of the case.
2. Position the countershaft gear, dummy shaft, and roller bearings in the case.
3. Place the case in a vertical position. Align the gear bore and the thrust washers with the bores in the case and install the countershaft.
4. Place the case in a horizontal position and check the countershaft gear end play with a feeler gauge. The end play should be within specification. If not within limits, replace the thrust washers.
5. After establishing the correct end play, install the dummy shaft in the countershaft gear and allow the gear to remain at the bottom of the case.
6. Coat the reverse idler gear thrust surfaces in the case with a thin film of lubricant and position the two thrust washers in place.
7. Position the reverse idler gear, sliding gear, dummy shaft and the roller bearings in place making sure that the shift fork grooves in the sliding gear is toward the front of the case.
8. Align the gear bore and thrust washers with the case bores and install the reverse idler shaft.
9. Measure the reverse idle gear end play with a feeler gauge. End play should be within specification. If the end play is not within limits, replace the thrust washers. If the end play is within limits, leave the reverse idler gear installed.
10. Position the reverse gear shift rail detent spring and detent plug in the case. Hold the reverse shift fork in place on the reverse idler sliding gear and install the shift rail from the rear of the case. Secure the fork to the rail with the Allen head set screw.
11. Install the first and second-speed synchronizer into the front of the output shaft, making sure that the shift fork groove is toward the rear of the shaft. The first and reverse synchronizer hub is a slip fit on the output shaft. Install the synchronizer hub with the teeth end of the gear facing toward the rear of the shaft.
12. Position the blocking ring on the second-speed gear.
13. Slide the second-speed gear onto the front of the shaft, making sure that the inserts in the synchronizer engage the notches in the blocker ring.
14. Install the second-speed gear thrust washer and snap ring.
15. Slide the overdrive gear onto the shaft with the synchronizer coned surface toward the front.
16. Place a blocking ring on the overdrive gear.
17. Slide the third and overdrive gear synchronizer onto the shaft making sure that the inserts in the synchronizer engage the notches in the blocking ring and the thrust surface is toward the overdrive gear.
18. Install the snap ring on the front of the output shaft.
19. Position the blocking ring on the first-speed gear.
20. Slide the first-speed gear onto the rear of the output shaft making sure that the notches in the blocking ring engage the synchronizer inserts.
21. Install the heavy thrust washer on the rear of the output shaft.
22. Support the thrust washer and first-speed gear to prevent them from sliding off the shaft and carefully lower the output shaft assembly into the case.
23. Position the first and second-speed shift fork and the third

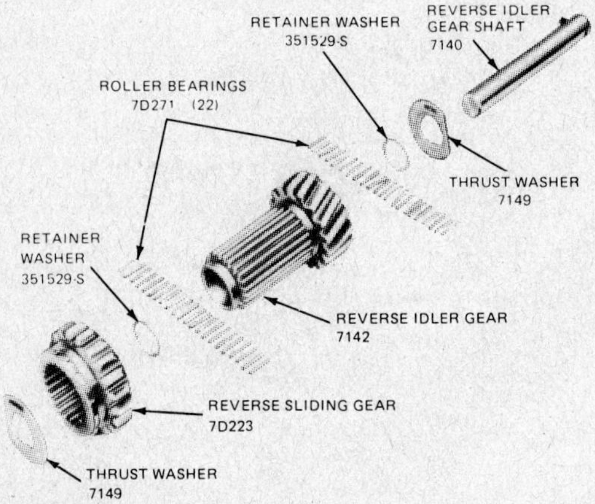

Reverse idler gear disassembled (© Chrysler Corp.)

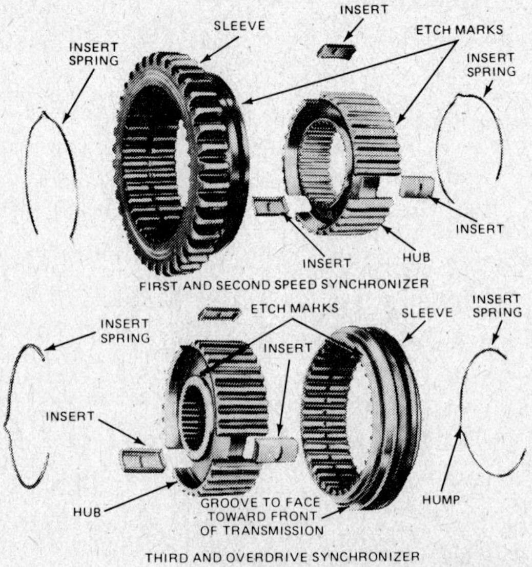

Synchronizers disassembled (© Chrysler Corp.)

and overdrive shift fork in place on their respective gears and rotate them into place.

24. Place a spring and a detent plug in the detent bore. Place the reverse shift rail into neutral position.
25. Coat the third and overdrive shift rail interlock pin (tapered ends) with grease and position it in the shift rail.
26. Align the third and overdrive shift fork with the shift rail bores and slide the shift rail into place making sure that the three detents are facing toward the outside of the case. Place the front synchronizer into overdrive position and install the set screw in the third and overdrive shift fork. Move the synchronizer to the neutral position. Install the third and overdrive shift rail detent plug, spring and bolt in the left side of the transmission case. Place the detent plug (tapered ends) in the detent bore in the case.
27. Align the first and second-speed shift fork with the case bores and slide the shift rail into place. Secure the fork with the set screw.
28. Coat the input gear bore with a thin film of grease, then install the 15 roller bearings in the bore. A thick film of grease could plug the lubricant holes and restrict lubrication of the bearings.
29. Position the front blocking ring in the third and overdrive synchronizer.
30. Position the dummy bearing, Tool T77L-7025B, or equivalent on the output shaft to support and align the shaft assembly in the case.
31. Place the input shaft gear into the transmission case, making sure that the output shaft pilot enters the roller bearings in the input gear pocket.
32. Position the input shaft bearing on the input shaft along with the Clamp Tool T77L-7025-D or equivalent, the Sleeve Tool T75L-7025-K or equivalent, and the bearing Replacer Tube T77L-7025-C or equivalent. Press the bearing onto the shaft and into the transmission case.
33. Remove the special service tools and install the snap rings on the input shaft and the input shaft bearing.
34. Place a new gasket on the input shaft bearing retainer. Dip the attaching bolts in sealer and install and tighten to 19-25 ft-lbs.
35. Remove the dummy bearing from the output shaft. Assemble the special service tools to the output shaft. **Before pressing the bearing onto the output shaft, be sure that the output shaft bearing is aligned with the transmission case bore and that the countershaft is not interfering with the output shaft assembly.**

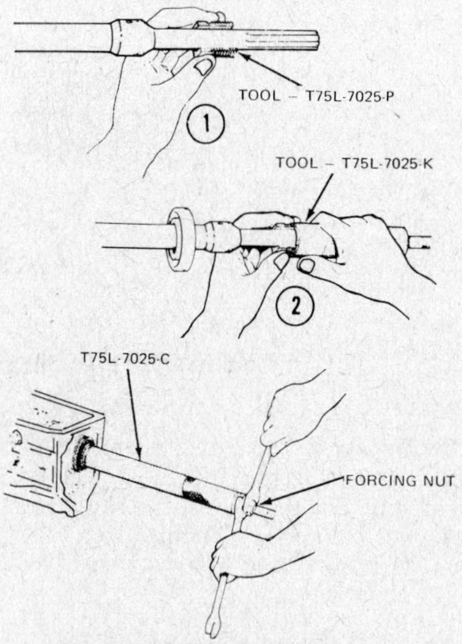

Installing output shaft bearing (© Chrysler Corp.)

36. Install the output shaft bearing onto the output shaft and into the transmission case using the special service tools. Remove the special service tools and install the snap rings on the output shaft and the output shaft bearing.
37. Place the transmission in a vertical position. Align the countershaft gear bore and thrust washers with the bore and thrust washers with the bore in the case. Install the countershaft.

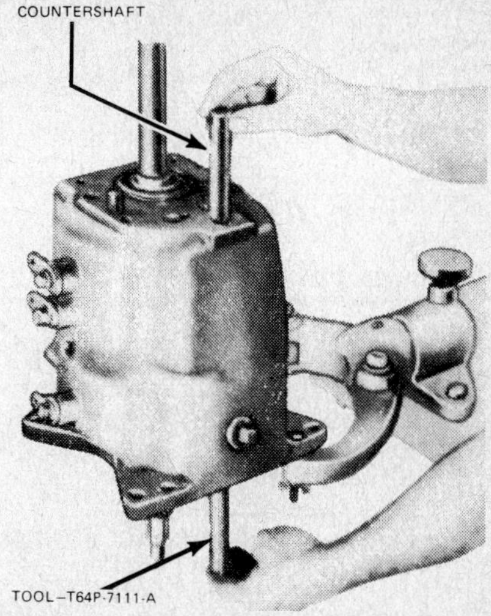

Installing countershaft (© Chrysler Corp.)

38. Use a new gasket and secure the extension housing to the case with the attaching bolts. Use a sealer on the extension housing attaching bolts. Tighten to 42-50 ft-lbs.
39. Install the filler plug in the case if it was removed.
40. Pour the specified lubricant over the entire gear train while rotating the input shaft.
41. Place each shift fork in all positions to make sure that it operates properly.
42. Install the remaining detent plug in the case. Install the long spring (which is retained by the case) to secure the detent plug.
43. Use a new cover gasket and install the cover. Coat the cover attaching screws with sealer and

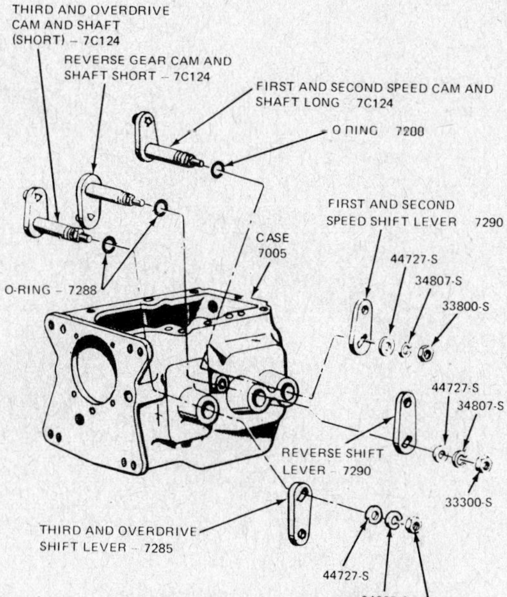

Cam, shafts and shift levers (© Chrysler Corp.)

install and tighten them to 20-25 ft-lbs.

44. Coat the third and overdrive shift rail plug bore with a sealer and install a new expansion plug.

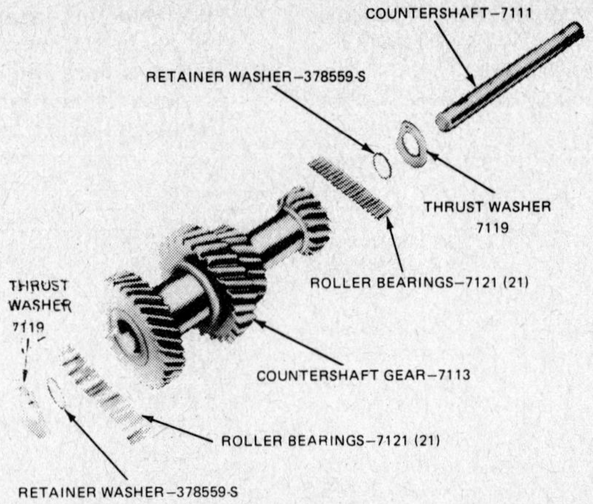

Countershaft gear disassembled (© Chrysler Corp.)

Sub-Assemblies

Cam and Shaft Seals

Removal

1. Remove the attaching nut, lockwasher and the flat washer from each shift lever and remove the three levers.
2. Remove the three cam and shafts from inside the case.
3. Remove and discard the O-ring from each cam and shaft.

Installation

1. Dip the new O-rings in gear lubricant and install them on the cam and shafts.
2. Slide each cam and shaft into its respective bore in the transmission case.
3. Secure each shaft lever with a flat washer, lockwasher and nut.

Synchronizers

Removal

1. Punch or etch alignment marks on the hub and sleeve of the synchronizer before disassembly.
2. Separate the inserts and insert springs from the hubs. Do not mix the parts of the first and second-speed synchronizer with the third and fourth-speed synchronizer.

Installation

1. Position the hub in the sleeve, making sure that the alignment marks are properly indexed.
2. Place the three inserts into place on the hub. Install the insert springs making sure that the irregular surface (hump) is seated in one of the inserts. Do not stagger the springs.

Countershaft Gear Bearings

Removal

Remove the dummy-shaft, two bearing retainer washers and the 21 roller bearings from each end of the countershaft gear.

Installation

1. Coat the bore in each end of the countershaft gear with grease.
2. Hold the dummy shaft in the gear and install the 21 roller bearings and a retainer washer in each end of the gear.

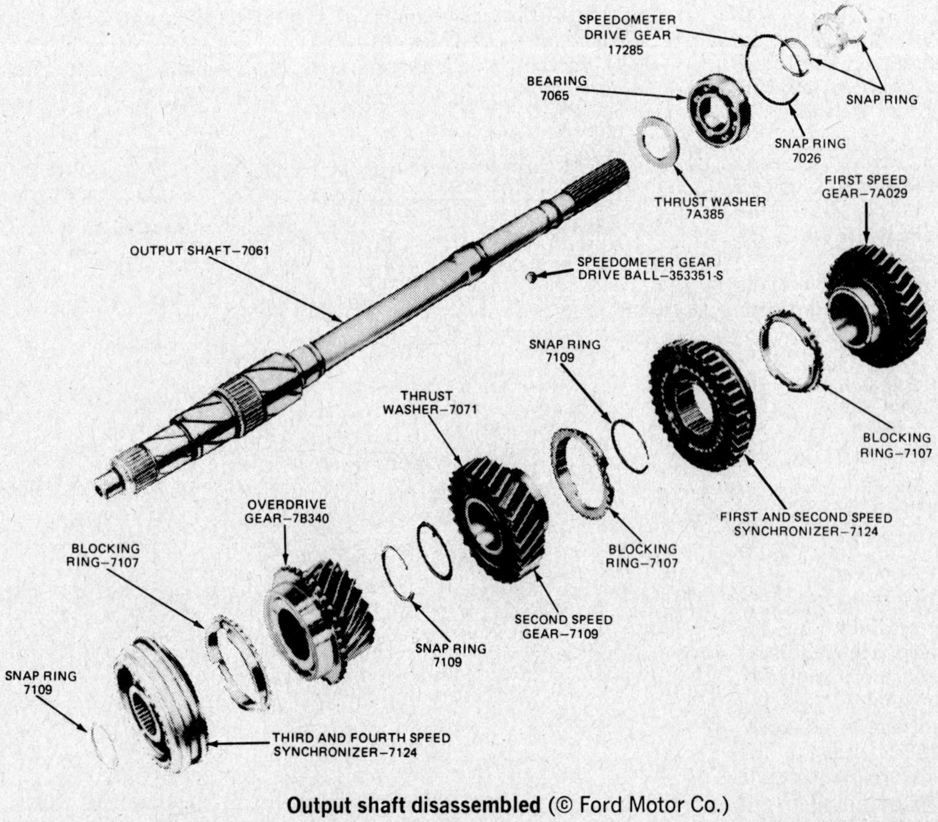

Output shaft disassembled (© Ford Motor Co.)

Reverse Idler Gear Bearings

Removal

1. Slip the reverse idler sliding gear off the reverse idler gear.
2. Remove the dummy shaft, two bearing retainer washers and the 44 roller bearings from the reverse idler gear.

Installation

1. Coat the bore in each end of the reverse idler gear with grease.
2. Hold the dummy shaft in the gear and install the 22 roller bearings and the retainer washer in each end of the gear.
3. Install the reverse idler sliding gear on the reverse idler gear making sure that the shift fork groove is toward the front.

Input Shaft Seal

Removal

Remove the seal from the input shaft bearing retainer using a slide hammer and internal puller.

Installation

1. Coat the sealing surface with lubricant.
2. Install the seal.

TORQUE SPECIFICATIONS

Application	Torque—4-Speed (ft-lbs)	Torque—4-Speed N•m
Input Shaft Bearing Retainer to Case Bolt	19-25	26-33
Extension Housing to Case Bolt	42-50	57-67
Access Cover to Case Screw	20-25	28-33
Outer Gear Shift Levers to Cam and Shaft Nut	18-23	25-31
Filler Plug to Case	10-20	14-27
Detent Bolt to Case	10-15	14-20

Muncie Model SM330 3 Speed

Description

The G.M. Corporation Model SM 330 (Muncie) is a three-speed transmission using helical constant mesh gears. The engagement of all gears except reverse is assisted by synchronizers.

General Data

Type	3-Speed
Synchromesh gears	1st, 2nd, and 3rd
Model	SM330
Gear Ratios	
1st Speed	3.03:1
2nd Speed	1.75:1
3rd Speed	1.00:1
Reverse	3.02:1

Transmission Disassembly

1. Remove side cover and shift forks.
2. Unbolt extension and rotate to line up groove in extension flange with reverse idler shaft. Drive reverse idler shaft and key out of case with a brass drift.
3. Move second-third synchronizer sleeve forward. Remove extension housing and mainshaft assembly.
4. Remove reverse idler gear from case.
5. Remove third speed blocker ring from clutch gear.
6. Expand snap-ring which holds mainshaft rear bearing. Tap gently on end of mainshaft to remove extension.
7. Remove clutch gear bearing retainer and gasket.
8. Remove snap-ring. Remove clutch gear from inside case by gently tapping on end of clutch gear.
9. Remove oil slinger and 16 mainshaft pilot bearings from clutch gear cavity.
10. Slip clutch gear bearing out front of case. Aid removal with a screwdriver between case and bearing outer snap-ring.
11. Drive countershaft and key out to rear.
12. Remove countergear and two tanged thrust washers.

Mainshaft Disassembly

1. Remove speedometer drive gear. Some speedometer drive gears, made of metal, must be pulled off.
2. Remove rear bearing snap-ring.
3. Support reverse gear. Press on rear of mainshaft to remove reverse gear, thrust washer, and rear bearing. Be careful not to cock the bearing on the shaft.
4. Remove first and reverse sliding clutch hub snap-ring.
5. Support first gear. Press on rear of mainshaft to remove clutch assembly, blocker ring, and first gear.
6. Remove second and third speed sliding clutch hub snap-ring.
7. Support second gear. Press on front of mainshaft to remove clutch assembly, second speed blocker ring, and second gear from shaft.

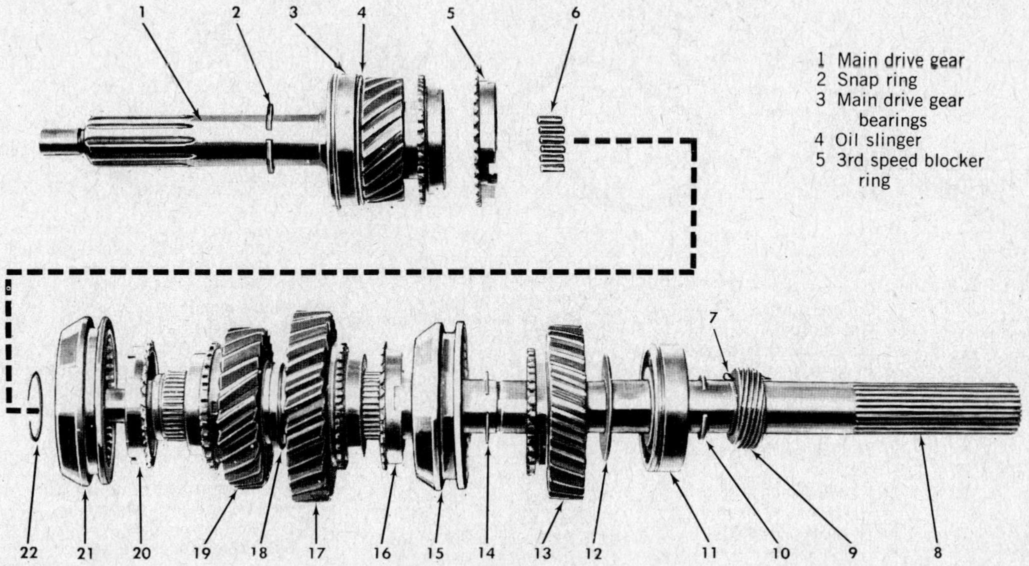

1 Main drive gear
2 Snap ring
3 Main drive gear bearings
4 Oil slinger
5 3rd speed blocker ring
6 Mainshaft pilot bearings
7 Speedometer retainer clip
8 Mainshaft
9 Speedometer drive gear
10 Snap ring
11 Rear bearing
12 Reverse gear thrust washer
13 Reverse gear
14 Snap ring
15 1st & reverse synchronizer assembly
16 First speed blocker ring
17 First speed gear
18 Shoulder (part of mainshaft)
19 Second speed gear
20 Second speed blocker ring
21 2nd and 3rd synchronizer assembly
22 Snap ring

Main drive gear and mainshaft assembly (© G.M.C.)

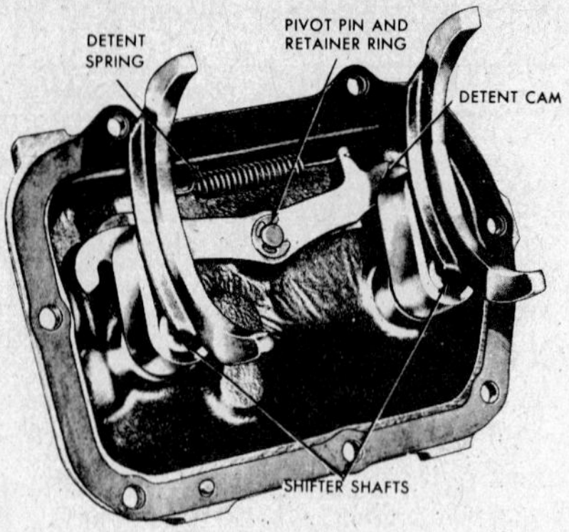

Side cover assembly
(© G.M.C.)

blocker ring, and second gear from shaft.

Cleaning and Inspection

For more detailed information, see the "Cleaning and Inspection" instructions at front of transmission section.

1. Wash all parts in solvent.
2. Air dry.

Clutch Keys and Springs

Keys and sprnigs may be replaced if worn or broken, but the hubs and sleeves must be kept together as originally assembled.

1. Mark hub and sleeve for reassembly.
2. Push hub from sleeve. Remove keys and springs.
3. Place three keys and two springs, one on each side of hub, so all three keys are engaged by both springs. The tanged end of the springs should not be installed into the same key.
4. Slide the sleeve onto the hub, aligning the marks.

Extension Oil Seal and Bushing

1. Remove seal.
2. Using bushing remover and installer, or other suitable tool, drive bushing into extension housing.
3. Drive new bushing in from rear. Lubricate inside of bushing and seal. Install new oil seal with extension seal installer or suitable tool.

Clutch Bearing Retainer Oil Seal

1. Pry old seal out.
2. Install new seal using seal installer or suitable tool. Seat seal in bore.

Mainshaft Assembly

1. Lift front of mainshaft.
2. Install second gear with clutching teeth up; the rear face of the gear butts against the mainshaft flange.

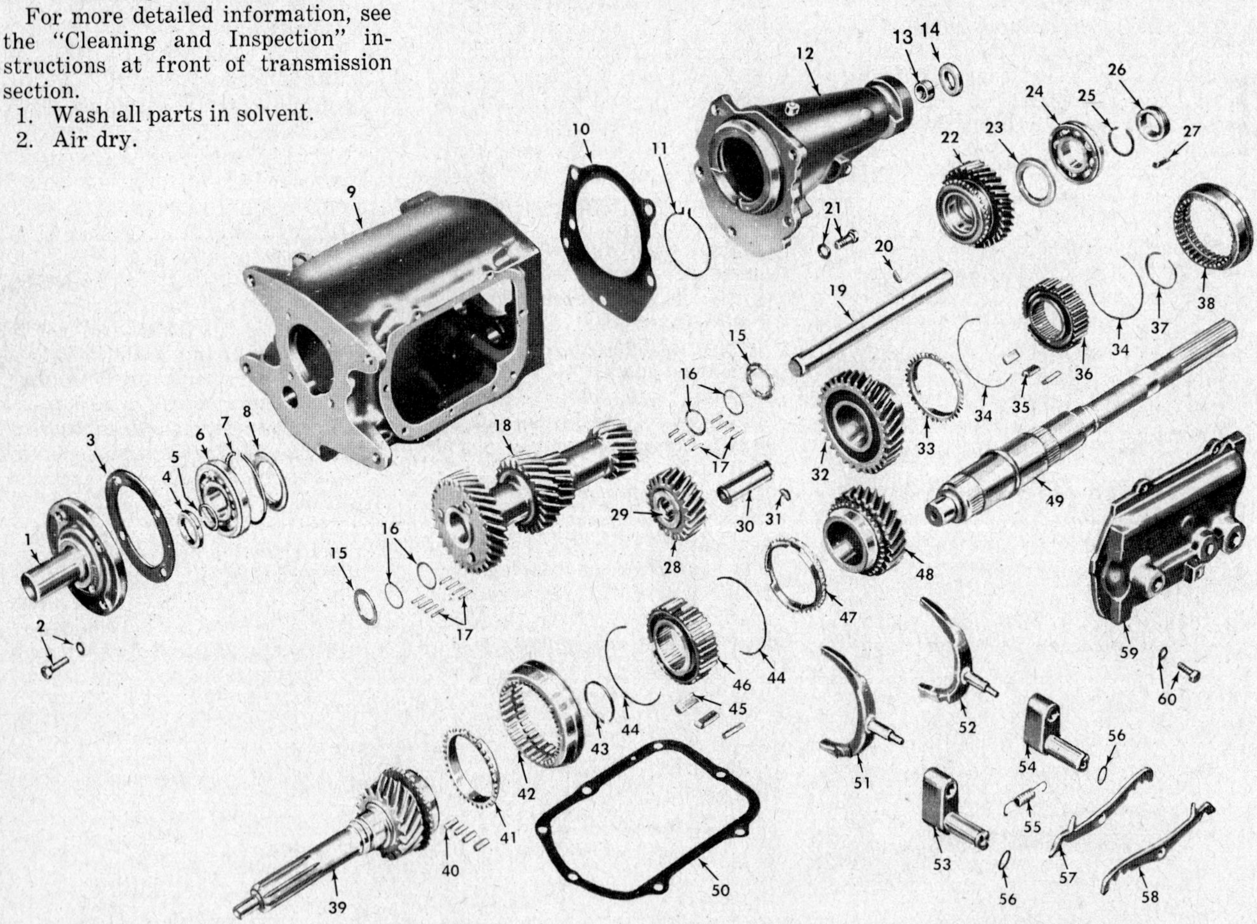

1 Bearing retainer
2 Bolt and lock washer
3 Gasket
4 Oil seal
5 Snap ring (bearing-to-main drive gear)
6 Main drive gear bearing
7 Snap ring bearing
8 Oil slinger
9 Case
10 Gasket
11 Snap ring (rear bearing-to-extension)
12 Extension
13 Extension bushing
14 Oil seal
15 Thrust washer
16 Bearing washer
17 Needle bearings
18 Countergear
19 Countershaft
20 Woodruff key
21 Bolt (extension-to-case)
22 Reverse gear
23 Thrust washer
24 Rear bearing
25 Snap ring
26 Speedometer drive gear
27 Retainer clip
28 Reverse idler gear
29 Reverse idler bushing
30 Reverse idler shaft
31 Woodruff key
32 1st speed gear
33 1st speed blocker ring
34 Synchronizer key spring
35 Synchronizer keys
36 1st and reverse synchronizer hub assembly
37 Snap ring
38 1st and reverse synchronizer collar
39 Main drive gear
40 Pilot bearings
41 3rd speed blocker ring
42 2nd and 3rd synchronizer collar
43 Snap ring
44 Synchronizer key spring
45 Synchronizer keys
46 2nd and 3rd synchronizer hub
47 2nd speed blocker ring
48 2nd speed gear
49 Mainshaft
50 Gasket
51 2nd and 3rd shifter fork
52 1st and reverse shifter fork
53 2-3 shifter shaft assembly
54 1st and reverse shifter shaft assembly
55 Spring
56 O-ring seal
57 1st and reverse detent cam
58 2nd and 3rd detent cam
59 Side cover
60 Bolt and lock washer

SM330 transmission components (© G.M.C.)

3. Install a blocking ring with clutching teeth downward. All three blocking rings are the same.
4. Install second and third synchronizer assembly with fork slot down. Press it onto mainshaft splines. Both synchronizer assemblies are identical but are assembled differently. The second-third speed hub and sleeve is assembled with the sleeve fork slot toward the thrust face of the hub; the first-reverse hub and sleeve, with the fork slot opposite the thrust face. Be sure that the blocker ring notches align with the synchronizer assembly keys.
5. Install synchronizer snap-ring. Both synchronizer snap-rings are the same.
6. Turn rear of shaft up.
7. Install first gear with clutching teeth upward; the front face of the gear butts against the flange on the mainshaft.
8. Install a blocker ring with clutching teeth down.
9. Install first and reverse synchronizer assembly with fork slot down. Press it onto mainshaft splines. Be sure blocker ring notches align with synchronizer assembly keys and synchronizer sleeves face front of mainshaft.
10. Install snap-ring.
11. Install reverse gear with clutching teeth down.
12. Install steel reverse gear thrust washer with flats aligned.
13. Press rear ball bearing onto shaft with snap-ring slot down.
14. Install snap-ring.
15. Install speedometer drive gear and retaining clip.

Transmission Assembly

1. Place a row of 29 roller bearings, a bearing washer, a second row of 29 bearings, and a second bearing washer at each end of the countergear. Hold in place with grease.
2. Place countergear assembly through rear case opening with a tanged thrust washer, tang away from gear, at each end. Install countershaft and key from rear of case. Be sure that thrust washer tangs are aligned with notches in case.
3. Place reverse idler gear in case. Do not install reverse idler shaft yet. *NOTE: The reverse idler gear bushing may not be replaced separately—only as a unit.*
4. Expand snap-ring in extension. Assemble extension over mainshaft and onto rear bearing. Seat snap-ring.
5. Load 16 mainshaft pilot bearings into clutch gear cavity. Assemble third speed blocker ring onto clutch gear clutching surface with teeth toward gear.
6. Place clutch gear assembly, without front bearing, over front of mainshaft. Make sure that blocker ring notches align with keys in second-third synchronizer assembly.
7. Stick gasket onto extension housing with grease. Assemble clutch gear, mainshaft, and extension to case together. Make sure that clutch gear teeth engage teeth of countergear antilash plate.
8. Rotate extension housing. Install reverse idler shaft and key.
9. Torque extension bolts to 45 ft. lbs.
10. Install oil slinger with inner lip facing forward. Install front bearing outer snap-ring and slide bearing into case bore.
11. Install snap-ring to clutch gear stem. Install bearing retainer and gasket and torque to 20 ft. lbs. Retainer oil return hole must be at 6 o'clock.
12. Shift both synchronizer sleeves to neutral positions. Install side cover, inserting shifter forks in synchronizer sleeve grooves.
13. Torque side cover bolts to 20 ft. lbs.

TORQUE SPECIFICATIONS

	Foot-Pounds
Extension to case attaching	45
Drain plug	30
Filler plug	15
Side cover attaching bolts	22
Main drive gear retainer bolts	22
Transmission case to clutch Housing bolts	45

Muncie Model SM465 4 Speed

Description

Muncie model CH 465-SM465 transmission is a four speed transmission using helical gears. The action of all gears except reverse is aided by synchronizers.

Disassembly of Transmission

1. Remove transmission cover assembly. *NOTE: Move reverse shifter fork so that reverse idler gear is partially engaged before attempting to remove cover. Forks must be positioned so rear edge of the slot in the reverse fork is in line with the front edge of the slot in the forward forks as viewed through tower opening.*
2. Lock transmission into two gears. Remove the universal joint flange nut, universal joint front flange and brake drum assembly. *NOTE: On 4-wheel drive models, use a special tool to remove mainshaft rear lock nut.*
3. Remove parking brake and brake flange plate assembly on those vehicles having a driveshaft parking brake.
4. Remove rear bearing retainer and gasket.
5. Slide speedometer drive gear off mainshaft.
6. Remove clutch gear bearing retainers and gasket.
7. Remove countergear front bearing cap and gasket.
8. Using a screwdriver, pry off countershaft front bearing.
9. Remove countergear rear bearing snap-rings from shaft and bearing. Using special tool, remove countergear rear bearings.
10. Remove clutch gear bearing outer race to case retaining ring.
11. Remove clutch gear and bearing by tapping gently on bottom side of clutch gear shaft and prying directly opposite against the case and bearing snap-ring groove at the same time. Remove 4th gear synchronizer ring. **CAUTION: Index cut out section of clutch gear in down position with countergear to obtain clearance for removing clutch gear.**
12. Remove rear mainshaft bearing snap-ring and, using special tools, remove bearing from case. Slide 1st speed gear thrust washer off mainshaft.
13. Lift mainshaft assembly from case. Remove synchronizer cone from shaft.
14. Slide reverse idler gear rearward and move countergear rearward, then lift to remove from case.
15. To remove reverse idler gear, drive reverse idler gear shaft out of case from front to rear using a drift. Remove reverse idler gear from case.

Disassembly of Subassemblies

Transmission Cover Disassembly

1. Remove shifter fork retaining pins and drive out expansion plugs. NOTE: The third and fourth shifter fork must be removed before the reverse shifter head pin can be removed.

2. With shifter shafts in neutral position, remove shafts. CAUTION: Care should be taken when removing the detent balls and springs since removal of the shifter shafts will cause these parts to be forcibly ejected.
3. Remove retaining pin and drive out reverse shifter shaft.

Assembly

1. In reassembling the cover, care should be taken to install the shifter shafts in order—reverse, 3rd.-4th, and 1st.-2nd.
2. Place fork detent ball springs and balls in cover.
3. Start shifter shafts into cover and, while depressing the detent balls, push the shafts over the balls. Push reverse shaft through the yoke.
4. With the 3rd -4th shaft in neutral, line up the retaining holes in the fork and shaft. *NOTE: Detent balls should line up with detents in shaft.*
5. After 1st and 2nd fork is installed, place two inner-lock balls between the low speed shifter shaft and the high speed shifter shaft in the crossbore of

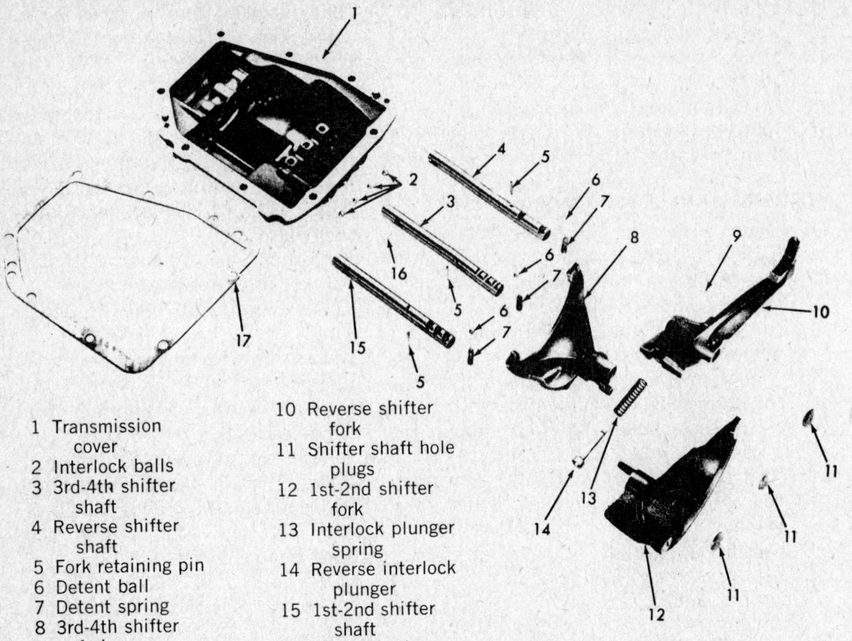

1 Transmission cover
2 Interlock balls
3 3rd-4th shifter shaft
4 Reverse shifter shaft
5 Fork retaining pin
6 Detent ball
7 Detent spring
8 3rd-4th shifter fork
9 "C" ring lock clip
10 Reverse shifter fork
11 Shifter shaft hole plugs
12 1st-2nd shifter fork
13 Interlock plunger spring
14 Reverse interlock plunger
15 1st-2nd shifter shaft
16 Interlock pin
17 Cover gasket

Shift cover assembly components (© G.M.C.)

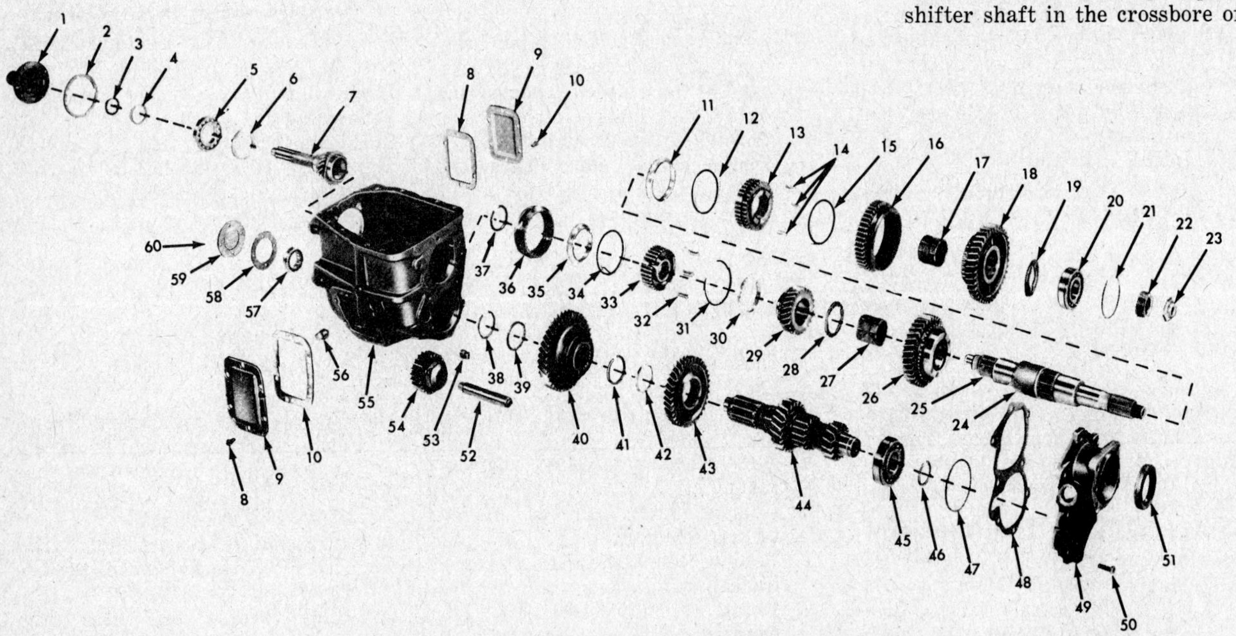

1 Clutch gear bearing retainer
2 Retainer gasket
3 Lip seal
4 Snap ring
5 Clutch gear bearing
6 Oil slinger
7 Clutch gear and pilot bearings
8 Power take-off cover gasket
9 Power take-off cover
10 Retaining screws
11 1st-2nd speed blocker ring
12 Synchronizer spring
13 1st-2nd speed synchronizer hub
14 Synchronizer keys
15 Synchronizer spring
16 Reverse driven gear
17 1st gear bushing
18 1st gear
19 Thrust washer
20 Rear main bearing
21 Bearing snap ring
22 Speedometer gear
23 Rear mainshaft lock nut
24 2nd speed bushing (on shaft)
25 Mainshaft
26 2nd speed gear
27 3rd gear bushing
28 Thrust washer
29 3rd speed gear
30 3rd speed blocker ring
31 Synchronizer spring
32 Synchronizer keys
33 3rd-4th synchronizer hub
34 Synchronizer spring
35 3rd-4th speed blocker ring
36 3rd-4th speed synchronizer sleeve
37 Snap ring
38 Snap ring
39 Thrust washer
40 Clutch countergear
41 Snap ring
42 Snap ring
43 3rd speed countergear
44 Countergear shaft
45 Countergear rear bearing
46 Snap ring
47 Bearing outer snap ring
48 Rear retainer gasket
49 Rear retainer
50 Retainer bolts
51 Retainer lip seal
52 Reverse idler shaft
53 Drain plug
54 Reverse idler gear
55 Case
56 Fill plug
57 Countergear front bearing
58 Gasket
59 Front cover
60 Cover screws

Transmission components (© G.M.C.)

the front support boss. Grease the interlock pin and insert it in the 3rd-4th shifter shaft hole. Continue pushing this shaft through cover bore and fork until retainer hole in fork lines up with hole in shaft.

6. Place two interlock balls in crossbore in front support boss between reverse, and 3rd and 4th shifter shaft. Then push remaining shaft through fork and cover bore, keeping both balls in position between shafts until retaining holes line up in fork and shaft. Install retaining pin.
7. Install 1st/2nd fork and reverse fork retaining pins. Install new shifter shaft hole expansion plugs.

Clutch Gear and Shaft Disassembly

1. Remove mainshaft pilot bearing rollers from clutch gear if not already removed, and remove roller retainer. Do not remove snap-ring on inside of clutch gear.
2. Remove snap-ring securing bearing on stem of clutch gear.
3. To remove bearing, position a special tool to the bearing and, with an arbor press, press gear and shaft out of bearing.

Assembly

1. Press bearing and new oil slinger onto clutch gear shaft using a special tool. Slinger should be located flush with bearing shoulder on clutch gear. CAUTION: Be careful not to distort oil slinger.
2. Install bearing snap-ring on clutch gear shaft.
3. Install bearing retainer ring in groove on O.D. of bearing. **CAUTION: The bearing must turn freely on the shaft.**
4. Install snap-ring on I.D. of mainshaft pilot bearing bore in clutch gear.
5. Lightly grease bearing surface in shaft recess, install transmission mainshaft pilot roller bearings and install roller bearing retainer.

NOTE: This roller bearing retainer holds bearings in position, and, in final transmission assembly, is pushed forward into recess by mainshaft pilot. Clutch Gear Bearing Retainer Oil Seal.

Bearing Retainer Oil Seal Replacement

1. Remove retainer and oil seal assembly and gasket.
2. Pry out oil seal.
3. Install new seal with lip of seal toward flange of tool.
4. Support front surface of retainer in press and drive seal into retainer.
5. Install retainer and gasket on case.

Mainshaft Disassembly

1. Remove first speed gear.
2. Remove reverse driven gear.
3. Press behind second speed gear to remove 3rd-4th synchronizer assembly, 3rd speed gear and 2nd speed gear along with 3rd speed gear bushing and thrust washer.
4. Remove 2nd speed synchronizer ring and keys.
5. Using a press, remove 1st speed gear bushing and 2nd speed synchronizer hub.
6. Without damaging the mainshaft, chisel out the 2nd speed gear bushing.

Inspection

Wash all parts in cleaning solvent and inspect them for excessive wear or scoring.

NOTE: Third and fourth speed clutch sleeve should slide freely on clutch hub but clutch hub should fit snugly on shaft splines.

Third speed gear must be running fit on mainshaft bushing and mainshaft bushing should be press fit on shaft.

First and reverse sliding gear must be sliding fit on synchronizer hub and must not have excessive radial or circumferential play. If sliding gear is not free on hub, inspect for burrs which may have rolled up on front end of half-tooth internal splines and remove by honing as necessary.

Assembly

1. Lubricate with E.P. oil and press onto mainshaft. **CAUTION: 1st, 2nd and 3rd speed gear bushings are sintered iron, exercise care when installing.**
2. Press 1st and 2nd speed synchronizer hub onto mainshaft with annulus toward rear of shaft.
3. Install 1st and 2nd synchronizer keys and springs.
4. Press 1st speed gear bushing onto mainshaft until it bottoms against hub. *NOTE: Lubricate all bushings with E.P. oil before installation of gears.*
5. Install synchronizer blocker ring and 2nd speed gear onto mainshaft and against synchronize hub. Align synchronizer key slots with keys in synchronizer hub.
6. Install 3rd speed gear thrust washer onto mainshaft inserting washer tang in slotted shaft. Then press 3rd speed gear bushing onto mainshaft against thrust washer.
7. Install 3rd speed gear and synchronizer blocker ring against 3rd speed gear thrust washer.
8. Align synchronizer key ring slots with synchronizer assembly keys and drive 3rd and 4th synchronizer assembly onto mainshaft. Secure assembly with snap-ring.
9. Install reverse driven gear with fork groove toward rear.
10. Install 1st speed gear against 1st

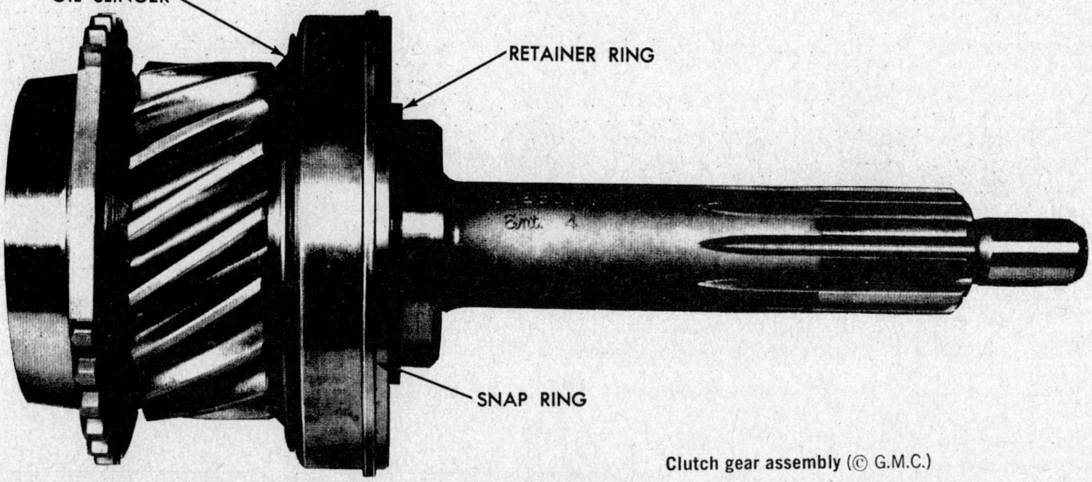

Clutch gear assembly (© G.M.C.)

and 2nd synchronizer hub. Install 1st speed gear thrust washer.

Countershaft Disassembly

1. Remove front countergear retaining ring and thrust washer. Do not re-use this snap-ring or any others.
2. Press countershaft out of clutch countergear assembly.
3. Remove clutch countergear and 3rd speed countergear retaining rings.
4. Press shaft from 3rd speed countergear.

Countershaft Assembly

1. Press the 3rd speed countergear onto the shaft. NOTE: Install gear with marked surface toward front of shaft.
2. Using snap-ring pliers, install new 3rd speed countergear retaining ring.
3. Install new clutch countergear rear retaining ring. CAUTION: **Do not over stress snap-ring. Ring should fit tightly in groove with no side play.**
4. Press countergear onto shaft against snap-ring.
5. Install clutch countergear thrust washer and front retaining ring.

Transmission Assembly

1. Lower the countergear into the case.
2. Place reverse idler gear in transmission case with gear teeth toward the front. Install idler gear shaft from rear to front, being careful to have slot in end of shaft facing down and flush with case.
3. Install mainshaft assembly into case with rear of shaft protruding out rear bearing hole in case. Rotate case onto front end. *NOTE: Install 1st speed gear thrust washer on shaft, if not previously installed.*
4. Install snap-ring on bearing O.D. and place rear mainshaft bearing on shaft. Drive bearing onto shaft and into case.
5. Install synchronizer cone on mainshaft and slide rearward to clutch hub. **CAUTION: Make sure three cut-out sections of 4th speed synchronizer cone align with three clutch keys in clutch assembly.**
6. Install snap-ring on clutch gear bearing O.D. Index cut out portion of clutch gear teeth to obtain clearance over countershaft drive gear teeth, and install into case.
7. Install clutch gear bearing retainer and gasket and torque to 15-18 ft. lbs.
8. Rotate case onto front end.
9. Install snap-ring on countergear rear bearing O.D., and drive bearing into place. Install snap-ring on countershaft at rear bearing.
10. Tap countergear front bearing assembly into case.
11. Install countergear front bearing cap and new gasket and torque to 20-30 in. lbs.
12. Slide speedometer drive gear over mainshaft to bearing.
13. Install rear bearing retainer with new gasket. Be sure snap-ring ends are in lube slot and cut out in bearing retainer. Install bolts and tighten to 15-18 ft. lbs. Install brake backing plate assembly on those models having driveshaft brake. *NOTE: On models equipped with 4-wheel drive, install rear lock nut and washer and torque to 120 ft. lbs. and bend washer tangs to fit slots in nut.*
14. Install parking brake drum and/or universal joint flange. *NOTE: Lightly oil seal surface.*
15. Lock transmission in two gears at once. Install universal joint flange locknut and tighten to 90-120 ft. lbs.
16. Move all transmission gears to neutral except the reverse idler gear which should be engaged approximately 3/8 of an inch (leading edge of reverse idler gear taper lines up with the front edge of the 1st speed gear). Install cover assembly and gasket. Shifting forks must slide into their proper positions on clutch sleeves and reverse idler gear. Forks must be positioned as in removal.
17. Install cover attaching bolts and gearshift lever and check operation of transmission.

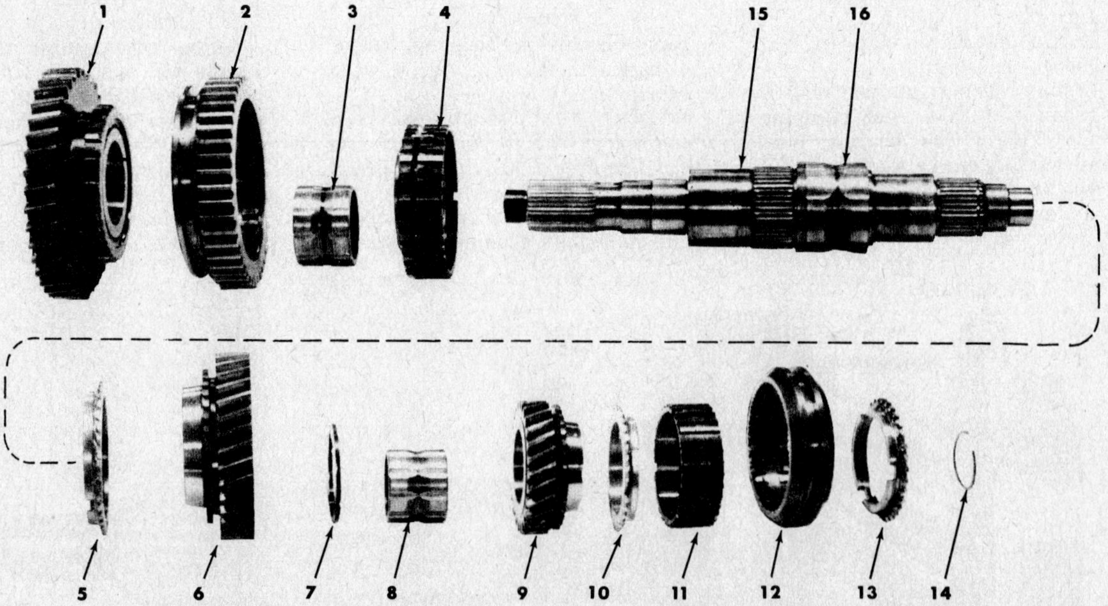

1 1st speed gear
2 Reverse driven gear
3 1st gear bushing
4 1st-2nd gear synchronizer hub assembly
5 2nd speed blocker ring
6 2nd speed gear
7 Thrust washer
8 3rd speed bushing
9 3rd speed gear
10 3rd speed blocker ring
11 3rd-4th speed synchronizer hub assembly
12 3rd-4th speed synchronizer sleeve
13 4th speed blocker ring
14 Snap ring
15 Mainshaft
16 2nd speed gear bushing

Mainshaft assembly (© G.M.C.)

TORQUE CHART

	Foot-Pounds		Foot-Pounds
Rear bearing retainer	18	Universal joint front flange nut	95
Cover bolts	25	Power take off cover bolts	18
Filler plug	35	Parking brake	22
Drain plug	35	Countergear front cover screws	25
Clutch gear bearing retainer bolts	18	Rear mainshaft lock nut (4 wheel drive models)	95

New Process 435 Four Speed Transmission

Disassembly of Transmission

1. Mount the transmission in a holding fixture. Remove the parking brake assembly, if one is installed.
2. Shift the gears into neutral by replacing the gear shift lever temporarily, or by using a bar or screw driver.
3. Remove the cover screws, the second screw from the front on each side is shouldered with a split washer for installation alignment.
4. While lifting the cover, rotate slightly counterclockwise to provide clearance for the shift levers. Remove the cover.
5. Lock the transmission in two gears and remove the output flange nut, the yoke, and the parking brake drum as a unit assembly. *The drum and yoke are balanced and unless replacement of parts are required, it is recommended that the drum and yoke be removed as a assembly.*
6. Remove the speedometer drive gear pinion and the mainshaft rear bearing retainer.
7. Before removal and disassembly of the drive pinion and mainshaft, measure the end play between the synchronizer stop ring and the third gear. *Record this reading for reference during assembly.* Clearance should be within 0.050-0.070 inch. If necessary, add corrective shims during assembly.
8. Remove the drive pinion bearing retainer.
9. Rotate the drive pinion gear to align the space in the pinion gear clutch teeth with the countershaft drive gear teeth. Remove the drive pinion gear and the tapered roller bearing from the transmission by pulling on the pinion shaft, and rapping the face of the case lightly with a brass hammer.
10. Remove the snap ring, washer, and the pilot roller bearings from the recess in the drive pinion gear.
11. Place a brass drift in the front center of the mainshaft and drive the shaft rearward.
12. When the mainshaft rear bearing has cleared the case, remove

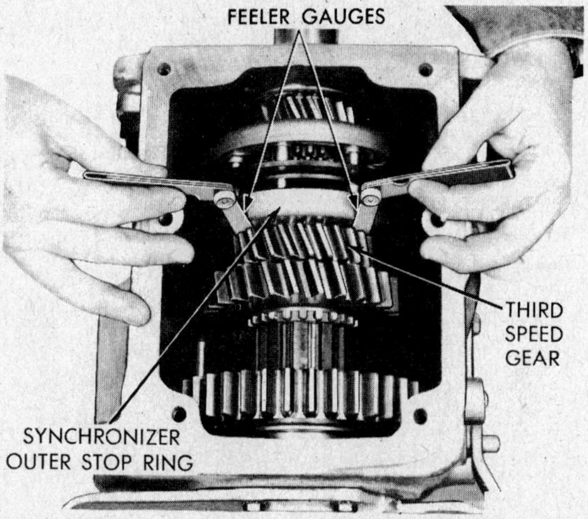

Measuring the synchronizer end-play—New Process 435 (© Chrysler Corp.)

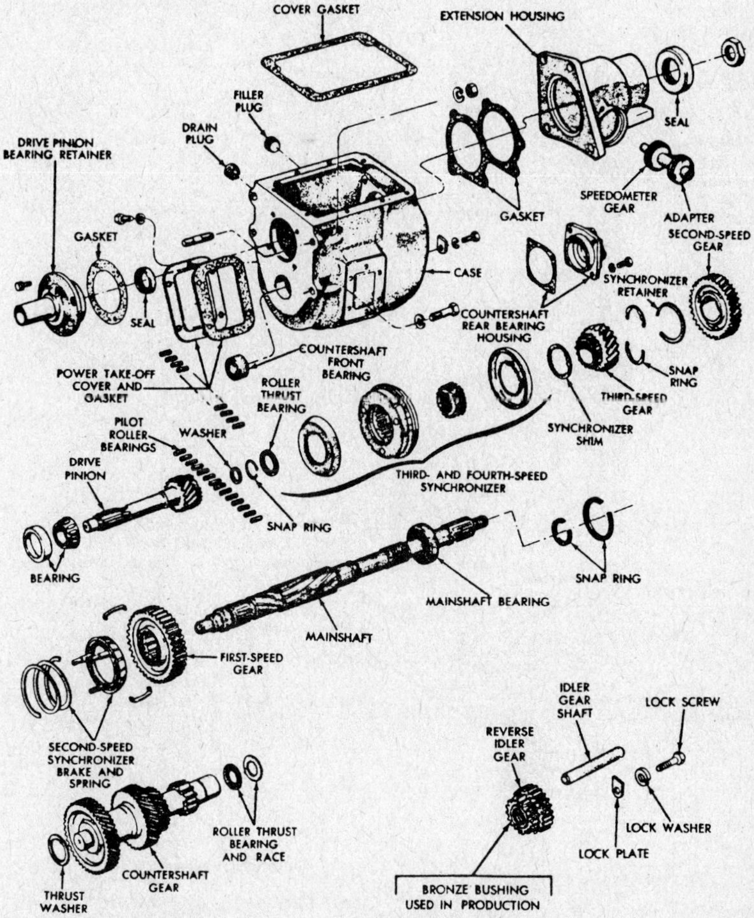

New Process 435 Transmission—exploded view (© Chrysler Corp.)

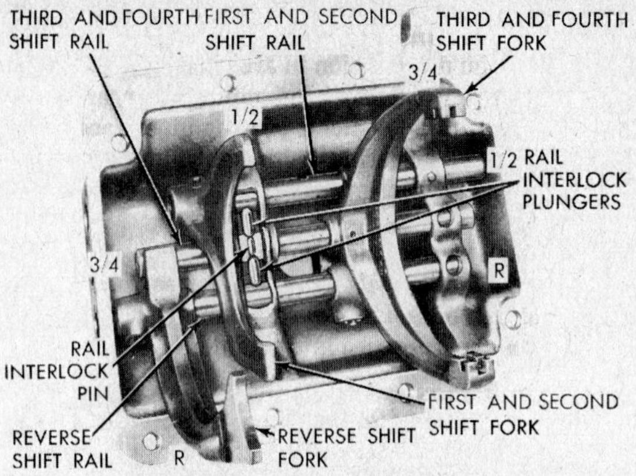

Cover and shift fork assembly—New Process 435 (© Chrysler Corp.)

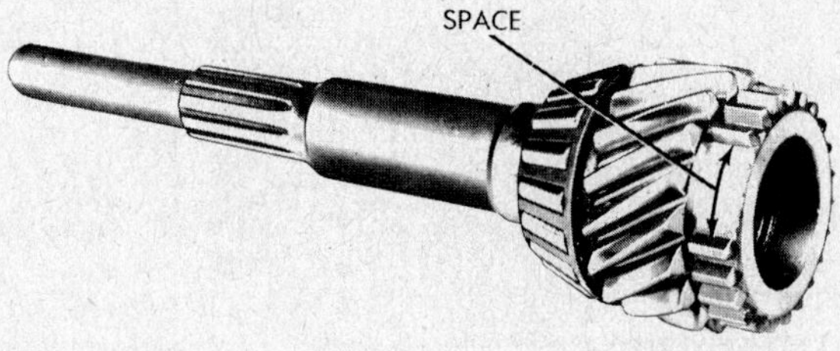

Drive pinion gear showing the teeth removed—New Process 435 (© Chrysler Corp.)

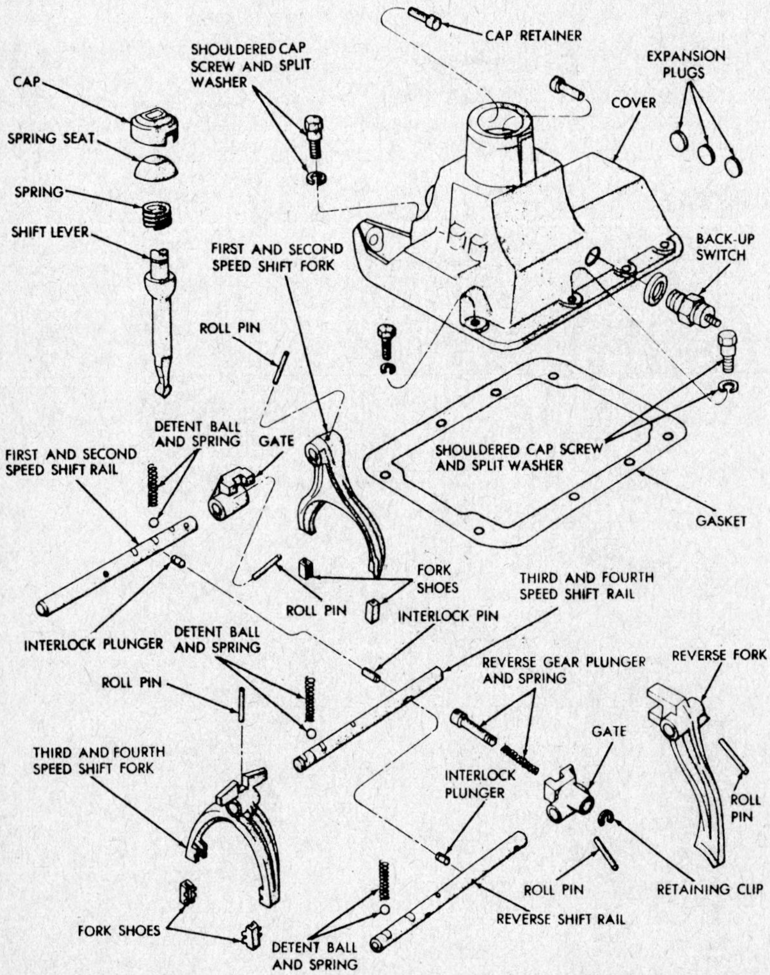

Cover and shift fork assembly—exploded view—New Process 435 (© Chrysler Corp.)

the rear bearing and the speedometer drive gear with a suitable gear puller.

13. Move the mainshaft assembly to the rear of the case and tilt the front of the mainshaft upward.
14. Remove the roller type thrust washer.
15. Remove the synchronizer and stop rings separately.
16. Remove the mainshaft assembly.
17. Remove the reverse idler lock screw and lock plate.
18. Using a brass drift held at an angle, drive the idler shaft to the rear while pulling.
19. Lift the reverse idler gear out of the case.

NOTE: If the countershaft gear does not show signs of excessive side play or end play and the teeth are not badly worn or chipped, it may not be necessary to replace the countershaft gear.

20. Remove the bearing retainer at the rear end of the countershaft. The bearing assembly will remain with the retainer.
21. Tilt the cluster gear assembly and work it out of the transmission case.
22. Remove the front bearings from the case with a suitable driver.

Overhaul of Sub-Assemblies

Mainshaft

Disassembly

1. Remove the clutch gear snap ring.
2. Remove the clutch gear, the synchronizer outer stop ring to third gear shim, and the third gear.
3. Remove the special split lock ring with two screw drivers. Remove the second gear and synchronizer.
4. Remove the first-reverve sliding gear.
5. Drive the old seal out of the bearing retainer.

Assembly

1. Place the mainshaft in a soft-jawed vise with the rear end up.
2. Install the first-reverse gear. Be sure the two spline springs, if used, are in place inside the gear as the gear is installed on the shaft.
3. Place the mainshaft in a soft-jawed vise with the front end up.
4. Assemble the second speed synchronizer spring and synchronizer brake on the second gear. Secure the brake with a snap ring making sure that the snap ring tangs are away from the gear.
5. Slide the second gear on the front of the mainshaft. Make sure that the synchronizer brake is toward the rear. Secure the gear to the shaft with the two piece lock ring. Install the third gear.
6. Install the shim between the third

gear and the third-fourth synchronizer stop ring. Refer to the measurements of end play made during disassembly to determine if additional shims are needed.

NOTE: The exact determination of end-play must be made after the complete assembly of the mainshaft and the main drive pinion is installed in the transmission case.

Reverse Idler Gear

DO NOT disassemble the reverse idler gear. If it is no longer serviceable, replace the assembly complete with the integral bearings.

Cover and Shift Fork Assembly

NOTE: The cover and shift fork assembly should be disassembled ONLY if inspection shows worn or damaged parts, or if the assembly is not working properly.

Disassembly

1. Remove the roll pin from the first-second shift fork and the shift gate with an "easy out".

NOTE: A square type or a closely wound spiral "easy out" mounted in a tap is preferable for this operation.

2. Move the first-second shift rail forward and force the expansion plug out of the cover. Cover the detent ball access hole in the cover with a cloth to prevent it from flying out. Remove the rail, fork, and gate from the cover.
3. Remove the third-fourth shift rail, then the reverse rail in the manner outlined in steps 1 and 2 above.
4. Compress the reverse gear plunger and remove the retaining clip. Remove the plunger and spring from the gate.

Assembly

1. Install the spring on the reverse gear plunger and hold it in the reverse shift gate. Compress the spring in the shift gate and install the retaining clip.
2. Insert the reverse shift rail in the cover and place the detent ball and spring in position. Depress the ball and slide the shift rail over it.
3. Install the shift gate and fork on the reverse shift rail. Install a new roll pin in the gate and the fork.
4. Place the reverse fork in the neutral position.
5. Install the two interlock plungers in their bores.
6. Insert the interlock pin in the third-fourth shift rail. Install the shift rail in the same manner as the reverse shift rail.
7. Install the first-second shift rail in the same manner as outlined above. Make sure the interlock plunger is in place.
8. Check the interlocks by shifting the reverse shift rail into the "Reverse" position. It should be impossible to shift the other rails with the reverse rail in this position.
9. If the shift lever is to be installed at this point, lubricate the spherical ball seat and place the cap in place.
10. Install the back-up light switch.
11. Install new expansion plugs in the bores of the shift rail holes in the cover. Install the rail interlock hole plug.

Drive Pinion and Bearing Retainer Disassembly

1. Remove the tapered roller bearing from the pinion shaft with a suitable tool.
2. Remove the snap ring, washer, and the pilot rollers from the gear bore, if they have not been previously removed.
3. Pull the bearing race from the front bearing retainer with a suitable puller.
4. Remove the pinion shaft seal with a suitable tool.

Assembly

1. Position the drive pinion in an arbor press.
2. Place a wood block on the pinion gear and press it into the bearing until it contacts the bearing inner race.
3. Coat the roller bearings with a light film of grease to hold the bearings in place, and insert them in the pocket of the drive pinion gear.
4. Install the washer and snap ring.
5. Press a new seal into the bearing retainer. Make sure that the lip of the seal is toward the mounting surface.
6. Press the bearing race into the retainer.

Assembly of Transmission

1. Press the front countershaft roller bearings into the case until the cage is flush with the front of the transmission case. Coat the bearings with a light film of grease.
2. Place the transmission with the front of the case facing down. If uncaged bearings are used, hold the loose rollers in place in the cap with a light film of grease.
3. Lower the countershaft assembly into the case placing the thrust washer tangs in the slots in the case, and inserting the front end of the shaft into the bearing.
4. Place the roller thrust bearing and race on the rear end of the countershaft. Hold the bearing in place with a light film of grease.
5. While holding the gear assembly in alignment, install the rear bearing retainer gasket, retainer, and bearing assembly. Install and tighten the cap screws.

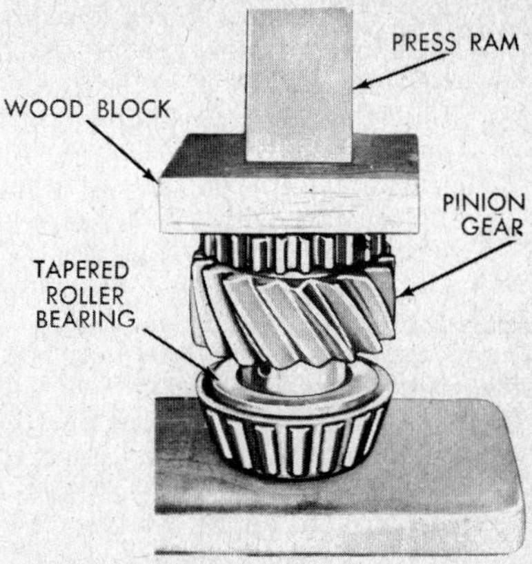

Installing the pinion bearing—New Process 435 (© Chrysler Corp.)

6. Position the reverse idler gear and bearing assembly in the case.
7. Align the idler shaft so that the lock plate groove in the shaft is in position to install the lock plate.
8. Install the lock plate, washer, and cap screw.
9. Make sure the reverse idler gear turns freely.
10. Lower the rear end of the mainshaft assembly into the case, holding the first gear on the shaft. Maneuver the shaft through the rear bearing opening.

NOTE: With the mainshaft assembly moved to the rear of the case, be sure the third-fourth synchronizer and shims remain in position.

11. Install the roller type thrust bearing.
12. Place a wood block in-between the front of the case and the front of the mainshaft.
13. Install the rear bearing on the mainshaft by carefully driving the bearing onto the shaft and into the case, snap ring flush against the case.
14. Install the drive pinion shaft and bearing assembly. Make sure that the pilot rollers remain in place.
15. Install the spacer and speedometer drive gear.
16. Install the rear bearing retainer and gasket.

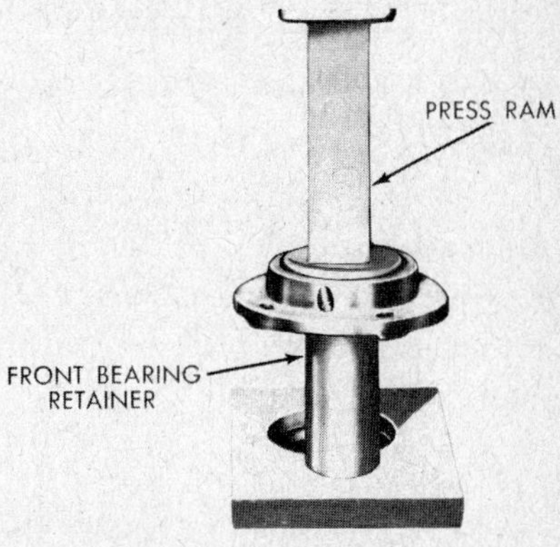

Installing the seal in the bearing retainer—New Process 435 (© Chrysler Corp.)

17. Place the drive pinion bearing retainer over the pinion shaft, without the gasket.
18. Hold the retainer tight aginst the bearing and measure the clearance between the retainer and the case with a feeler gauge.

NOTE: End play in steps 19 and 20 below allows for normal expansion of parts during operation, preventing seizure and damage to bearings, gears, synchronizers, and shafts.

19. Install a gasket shim pack 0.010-0.015 inch thicker than measured clearance between the retainer and case to obtain the required 0.007-0.017 inch pinion shaft end play. Tighten the front retainer bolts and recheck the end play.
20, Check the synchronizer end play clearance (0.050-0.070 inch) after all mainshaft components are in position and properly tightened. Two sets of feeler gauges are used to measure the clearance. Care should be used to keep both gauges as close as possible to both sides of the mainshaft for best results.

NOTE: In some cases, it may be necessary to disassemble the mainshaft and change the thickness of the shims to keep the end play clearance within the specified limits, 0.050-0.070 inch. Shims are available in two thicknesses.

21. Install the speedometer drive pinion.
22. Install the yoke flange, drum, and drum assembly.
23. Place the transmission in two gears at once, and tighten the yoke flange nut.
24. Shift the gears and/or synchronizers into all gear positions and and check for free rotation.
25. Cover all transmissions components with a film of transmission oil to prevent damage during start up after initial lubricant fill-up.
26. Move the gears to the neutral position.
27. Place a new cover gasket on the transmission case, and lower the cover over the transmission.
28. Carefully, engage the shift forks into their poper gears. Align the cover.
29. Install a shouldered alignment screw with split washer in the screw hole second from the front of the cover. Try out gear operation by shifting through all ranges. Make sure everything moves freely.
30. Install the remaining cover screws.

TORQUE SPECIFICATIONS

	Foot-Pounds
Cover screws	20-40
Drive gear retaining screw	15-25
Front countershaft retainer screw	15-25
Front countershaft bearing washer screw	12-22
Flange nut	125
Mainshaft rear retainer screw	15-25
Rear countershaft retainer screw	15-25
PTO cover screws	8-12
Filler and drain plugs	25-45
Reverse idler shaft lock screw	20-40
Brake link shoulder screw	20-40

LUBRICANT CAPACITY

New Process 435	7 pt.

New Process Model 445 Four Speed Transmission

Disassembly of Transmission

1. Place the transmission in a holding fixture and drain the lubricant.
2. Shift the transmission gears into neutral. Remove the gearshift cover attaching bolts. Note that the two bolts opposite the tower are shouldered to properly position the cover. Lift the cover straight up and remove.
3. Lock the transmission in two gears at once and remove the mainshaft nut and yoke.
4. Loosen and remove the extension housing bolts. Remove the main-

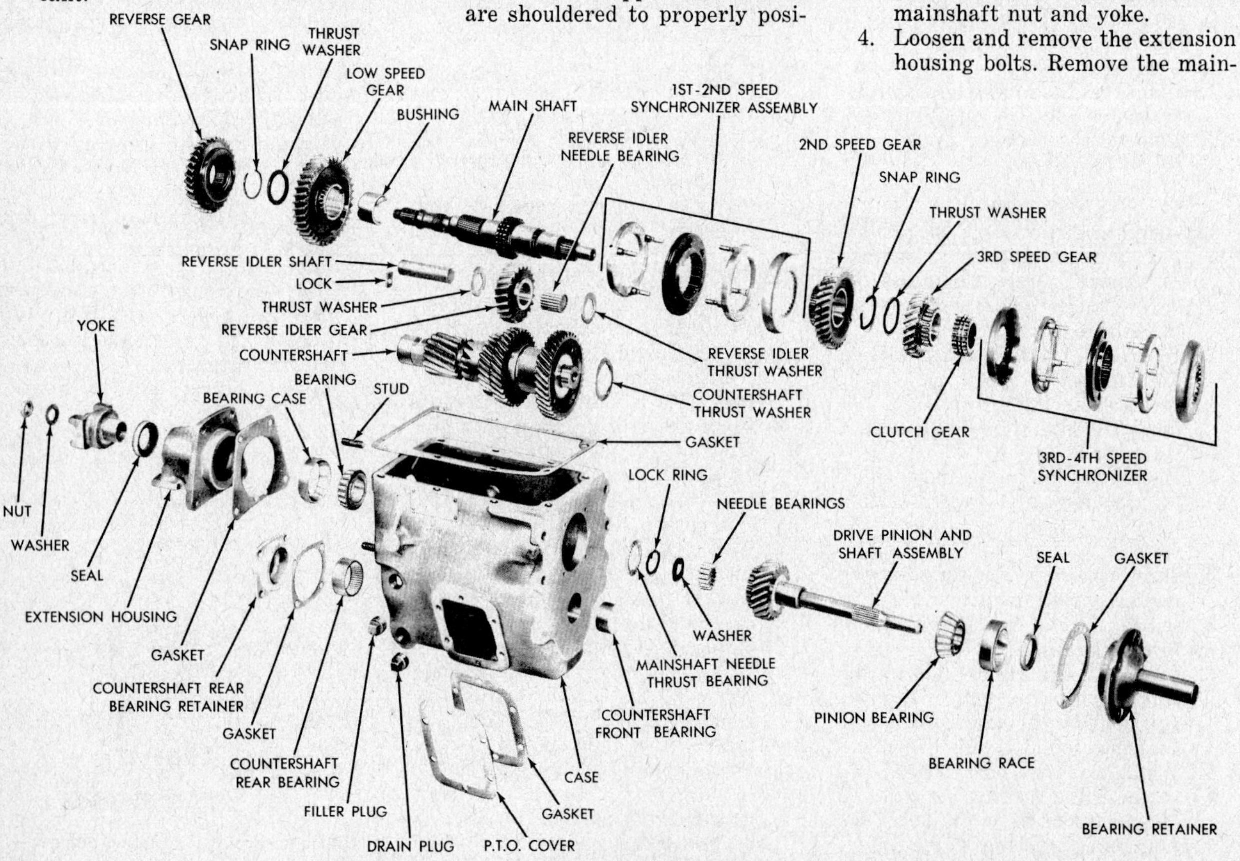

New Process 445 transmission—exploded view (© Chrysler Corp.)

shaft extension housing and the speedometer drive pinion.

5. Remove the bolts from the drive pinion front bearing retainer and pull the bearing retainer and gasket off.
6. Rotate the drive pinion gear to align the pinion gear flat with the countershaft drive gear teeth. Remove the drive pinion gear and the tapered roller bearing from the transmission.
7. Remove the mainshaft thrust bearing.
8. Push the mainshaft assembly to the rear of the transmission and tilt the front of the mainshaft up.
9. Remove the mainshaft assembly from the transmission case.
10. Remove the reverse idler lock screw and lock plate.
11. Using a suitable size brass drift, carefully drive the reverse idler shaft out the REAR of the case.

NOTE: DO NOT ATTEMPT TO DRIVE THE REVERSE IDLER SHAFT FORWARD! This will damage the transmission case and the reverse idler shaft.

12. Remove the countershaft rear bearing retainer.
13. Slide the countershaft to the rear, then up and out of the case.
14. Drive the countershaft forward, out of the bearing and the case.

Overhaul of Sub-Assemblies

Mainshaft
Disassembly

1. Place the mainshaft in a soft-jawed vise with the front end up.
2. Lift the third-fourth synchronizer and high speed clutch off the mainshaft.
3. Remove the third gear.
4. Remove the second gear snap ring. Lift off the thrust washer.
5. Remove the second gear.
6. Remove the first-reverse synchronizer and clutch gear.
7. Install the mainshaft in the vise rear end up.
8. Remove the tapered bearing from the shaft with a suitable gear puller.
9. Remove the first gear snap ring and thrust washer.
10. Remove the first gear.

Assembly

1. Lubricate all parts with transmission lubricant prior to assembly.
2. Place the mainshaft in a soft-jawed vise with the rear end up.
3. Slide the first gear over the mainshaft, with the clutch gear facing down. Install the thrust washer and snap ring.
4. Install the revese gear over the end of the mainshaft with the fork groove facing down.
5. Install the mainshaft rear bearing on the mainshaft with a sleeve of suitable size. Press the bearing on its inner race.
6. Install the mainshaft in the vise with the front end facing up.
7. Install the first-reverse synchronizer.
8. Install the second gear on the mainshaft.
9. Install the keyed thrust washer, ground side toward the second gear and secure with the snap ring.
10. Install the third gear and one shim on the mainshaft.
11. Install the third fourth synchronizer over the mainshaft. Make sure that the slotted end of the clutch gear is positioned toward the third gear.

Cover and Shift Fork Assembly
Disassembly

NOTE: The cover and shift fork assembly should be disassembled ONLY if inspection shows worn or damaged parts, or if the assembly is not working properly.

1. Remove the roll pin from the first-second shift fork and the shift gate. Use a square-type or spirial wound "easy-out" mounted in a tap handle for these operations.
2. Move the first-second shift rail rearward and force the expansion plug out of the cover. Cover the detent ball access hole in the cover with a cloth to prevent it from flying out. Remove the rail, fork, and gate from the cover.
3. Remove the third-fourth shift rail, then the reverse rail in the manner outlined in steps 1 and 2 above.
4. Compress the reverse gear plunger and remove the retaining clip. Remove the plunger and spring from the gate.

Assembly

1. Apply a thin film of grease on the interlock slugs and slide them into the openings in the shift rail supports.
2. Install the reverse shift rail through the reverse shift fork plate and the reverse shift fork.
3. Secure the reverse shift plate and the shift fork with the roll pins. Install the interlock pin in the third-fourth shift rail. Hold in place with a thin film of grease.
4. Slide the third-fourth shift rail into the rail support from the rear of the cover. Slide the rail through the third-fourth shift fork and poppet ball and spring. Secure the third-fourth shift fork with the roll pin.
5. Install the interlock pin in the first-second shift rail and secure with a light coat of grease. Slide the first-second shift rail into the case, through the shift fork and shift gate. Hold the poppet ball and spring down until the shaft rail passes.
6. Secure the first-second shift rail and gate with the roll pins.

Assembly of Transmission

1. Install the countershaft front bearing in the case using a 1⅜ inch socket as a driver. Grease the needle bearings prior to installation. Hold the bearings in place with a socket of suitable size while seating the bearing retainer. Drive the retainer in until it is flush with the case.
2. Install the tanged thrust washer on the countershaft with the

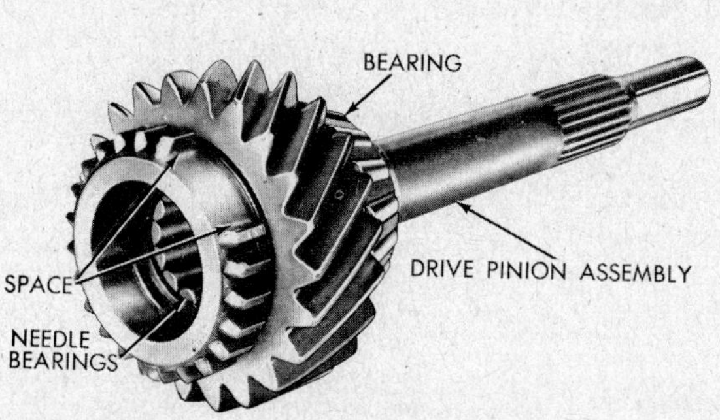

Drive pinion gear—New Process 445 (© Chrysler Corp.)

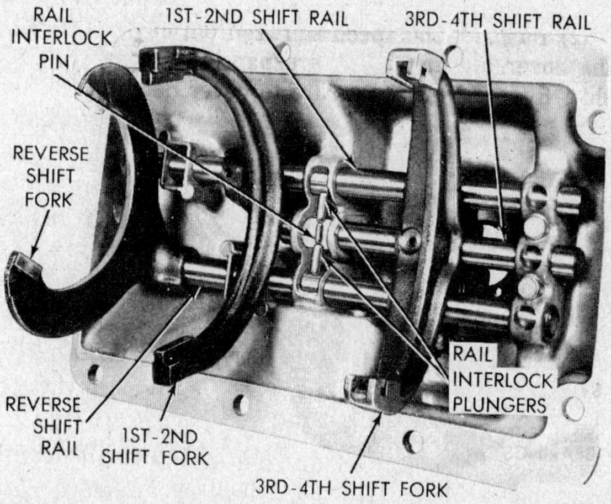

Cover and shift fork assembly—New Process 445 (© Chrysler Corp.)

tangs facing out. Install the countershaft in the transmission case.
3. Install the countershaft rear bearing retainer over the rear bearing. Use a new washer and position the retainer with the curved segment toward the bottom of the case.
4. Install the reverse idler gear into the case with the chamfered section facing the rear. Hold the thrust washer and needle bearings in position.
5. Slide the reverse idler shaft into the case, from the rear, and through the reverse idler gear. Make sure that the lock notch is down and at the rear of the case.
6. Install the reverse idler shaft lock and bolt.
7. Place the mainshaft in a soft-jawed vise with the front end facing up.
8. Install the drive gear on top of the mainshaft.
9. Measure the clearance between the high-speed synchronizer and the drive gear with two feeler gauges.
   If the clearance is greater than 0.043-0.053 inch, install synchronizer shims between the third gear and the synchronizer brake drum. After the required shims have been installed, remove the drive gear from the mainshaft.
10. Install the mainshaft into the transmission case. Place the thrust washer over the pilot end of the mainshaft.
11. Position the drive gear so that the cutaway portion of the gear is facing down. Slide the drive gear into the front of the case and engage the mainshaft pilot in the pocket of the drive gear.
12. Slip the drive gear front bearing retainer over the shaft on gasket, and do not secure with bolts.
13. Install the mainshaft rear bearing retainer. Tighten the screws to specifications.
14. Hold the retainer against the front of the transmission case and measure the clearance between the front bearing retainer and the front of the case with a feeler gauge. Record the measurement and remove the bearing retainer.

Measuring end play float
(© Chrysler Corp.)

15. Install a gasket pack on the front bearing retainer which is 0.010-0.015 inch thicker than the clearance measured in step 14. Install the front bearing retainer and torque attaching screws to specification.
16. The end play float of the front synchronizer must be checked before installation of the transmission cover assembly. Measure the end play "float" by inserting two feeler gauges opposite one another between the third gear and the synchronizer stop ring. Accurate measurement can be made only after all mainshaft parts are in place and torqued to specification.
17. If the front synchronizer end play "float" does not fall between 0.050-0.070 inch, shims should be added or removed as required, from between the third gear and the synchronizer stop ring.
18. Install the yoke retaining nut on the rear of the mainshaft. Shift the transmission into two gears at the same time and torque the yoke nut to 125 ft.-lbs.
19. Shift the transmission into neutral.
20. Install the cover gasket.
21. Shift the transmission into second gear. Shift the cover into second.
22. Carefully lower the cover into position. It may be necessary to position the reverse gear to permit the fork to engage its groove.
23. Install the cover aligning screws (shouldered) and tighten with fingers only.
24. Install the remaining cover screws and tighten to specifications.

TORQUE SPECIFICATIONS

	Foot-Pounds
Cover screws	20-40
Drive gear retaining screw	15-25
Front countershaft retaining screw	15-25
Front countershaft bearing washer screw	12-22
Flange nut	125
Mainshaft rear retainer screw	15-25
Rear countershaft retainer screw	15-25
PTO cover screws	8-12
Filler and drain plugs	25-45
Reverse idler shaft lock screw	20-40
Brake link shoulder screw	20-40

LUBRICANT CAPACITY

New Process 445	7½ pts.

Saginaw Three Speed (GM-SM326)

Description

The G.M. Corporation Model SM326 (Saginaw) is a synchromesh three-speed transmission using helical constant mesh gears. The engagement of all gears except reverse is assisted by synchronizers.

General Data

Type 3-Speed
Synchromesh Gears 1st, 2nd, and 3rd
Model SM326 and SM326 w/Overdrive

Gear Ratios

1st Speed	2.85:1
2nd Speed	1.68:1
3rd Speed	1.00:1
Reverse	2.95:1

Transmission Disassembly

1. Remove side cover assembly and shift forks.
2. Remove clutch gear bearing retainer.
3. Remove clutch gear bearing to gear stem snap-ring. Pull clutch gear outward until a screwdriver can be inserted between bearing and case. Remove clutch gear bearing.
4. Remove speedometer driven gear and extension bolts.
5. Remove reverse idler shaft snap-ring. Slide reverse idler

gear forward on shaft.
6. Remove mainshaft and extension assembly.
7. Remove clutch gear and third-speed blocker ring from inside case. Remove 14 roller bearings from clutch gear.
8. Expand the snap-ring which retains the mainshaft rear bearing. Remove the extension.
9. Usnig a dummy shaft, drive the countershaft and key out the rear of the case. Remove the gear, two tanged thrust washers, and dummy shaft. Remove bearing washer and 27 roller bearings from each end of countergear.
10. Use a long drift to drive the reverse idler shaft and key through the rear of the case.
11. Remove reverse idler gear and tanged steel thrust washer.

Mainshaft Disassembly

1. Remove second and third speed sliding clutch hug snap-ring from mainshaft. Remove clutch assembly, second speed blocker ring, and second speed gear from front of mainshaft.
2. Depress speedometer drive gear retaining clip. Remove gear. Some units have a metal speedometer drive gear which must be pulled off.
3. Remove rear bearing snap-ring.
4. Support reverse gear. Press on rear of mainshaft. Remove reverse gear, thrust washer, spring washer, rear bearing, and snap-ring. When pressing off the rear bearing, be careful not to cock the bearing on the shaft.
5. Remove first and reverse sliding clutch hub snap-ring. Remove clutch assembly, first speed blocker ring, and first gear.

Cleaning and Inspection

See "Cleaning and Inspection" instructions at front of transmission section.

Clutch Keys and Springs

Keys and springs may be replaced if worn or broken, but the hubs and sleeves are matched pairs and must be kept together.

1. Mark hub and sleeve for reassembly.
2. Push hub from sleeve. Remove keys and springs.
3. Place three keys and two springs, one on each side of hub, in position, so all three keys are engaged by both springs. The tanged end of the springs should not be installed into the same key.
4. Slide the sleeve onto the hub, aligning the marks.

NOTE: A groove around the outside of the synchronizer hub marks the end that must be opposite the fork slot in the sleeve when assembled.

Extension Oil Seal and Bushing

1. Remove seal.
2. Using bushing remover and installer tool, or other suitable tool, drive bushing into extension housing.
3. Drive new bushing in from the rear. Lubricate inside of bushing and seal. Install new oil seal with extension seal installer tool or other suitable tool.

Clutch Bearing Retainer Oil Seal

1. Pry old seal out.

1 Thrust washer—front
2 Bearing washer
3 Needle bearings
4 Countergear
5 Needle bearings
6 Bearing washer
7 Thrust washer—rear
8 Countershaft
9 Woodruff key
10 Bearing retainer
11 Gasket
12 Oil seal
13 Snap ring—bearing to case
14 Snap ring—bearing to gear
15 Clutch gear bearing
16 Case
17 Clutch gear
18 Pilot bearings
19 3rd speed blocker ring
20 Retainer E-Ring
21 Reverse idler gear
22 Reverse idler gear bushing (not serviced separately)
23 Reverse idler shaft
24 Woodruff key
25 Snap ring—hub to shaft
26 2-3 synchronizer sleeve
27 Synchronizer key spring
28 2-3 Synchronizer hub assy.
29 2nd speed blocker ring
30 2nd speed gear
31 Mainshaft
32 1st speed gear
33 1st speed blocker ring
34 1st and reverse synchronizer hub assembly
35 1st and reverse synchronizer sleeve
36 Snap ring—hub to shaft
37 Reverse gear assy.
38 Thrust washer
39 Thrust washer
40 Rear bearing
41 Snap ring—bearing to shaft
42 Speedometer drive gear
43 Gasket
44 Snap ring—rear bearing to extension
45 Extension

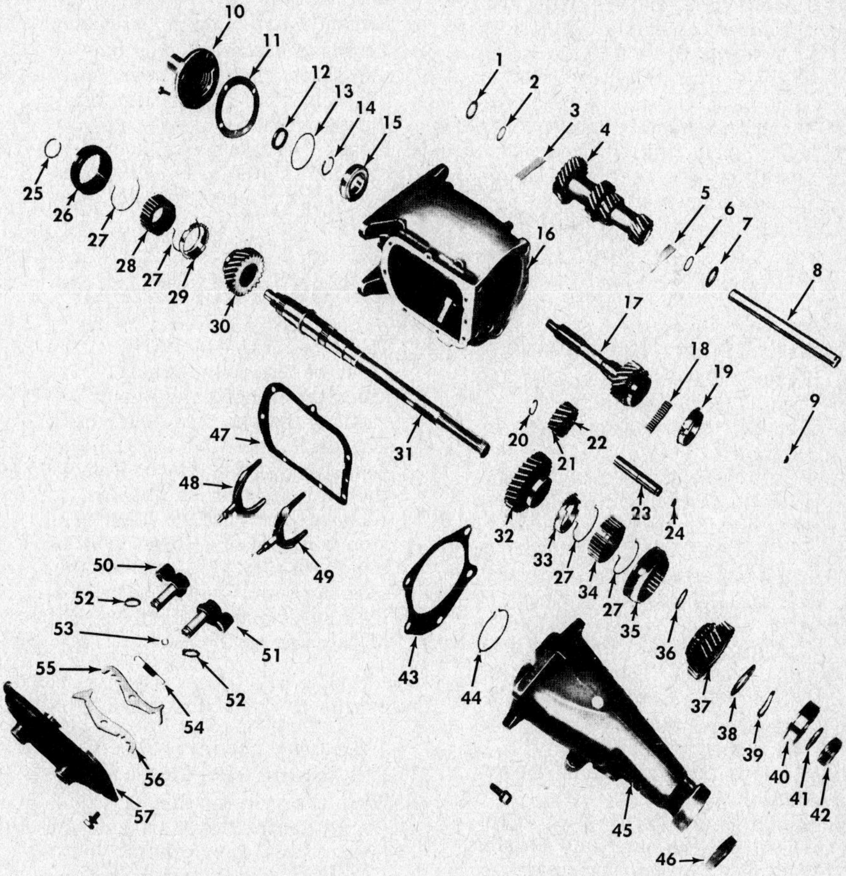

46 Oil seal
47 Gasket
48 2-3 shift fork
49 1st and reverse shift fork
50 2-3 shifter shaft assembly
51 1st and reverse shifter shaft assembly
52 O-ring seal
53 Detent cam retainer ring
54 Spring
55 2nd and 3rd detent cam
56 1st and reverse detent cam
57 Side cover

SM326 transmission components (© G.M.C.)

2. Install new seal using seal installer or suitable tool. Seat seal in bore.

Mainshaft Assembly

1. Turn front of mainshaft up.
2. Install second gear with clutching teeth up; the rear face of the gear butts against the flange on the mainshaft.
3. Install a blocker ring with clutching teeth down. All three blocker rings are the same.
4. Install second and third speed synchronizer assembly with fork slot down. Press it onto mainshaft splines. Both synchronizer assemblies are the same. Be sure that blocker ring notches align with synchronizer assembly keys.
5. Install synchronizer snap-ring. Both synchronizer snap-rings are the same.
6. Turn rear of shaft up.
7. Install first gear with clutching teeth up; the front face of the gear butts against the flange on the mainshaft.
8. Install a blocker ring with clutching teeth down.
9. Install first and reverse synchronizer assembly with fork slot down. Press it onto mainshaft splines. Be sure blocker ring notches align with synchronizer assembly keys.
10. Install snap-ring.
11. Install reverse gear with clutching teeth down.
12. Install steel reverse gear thrust washer and spring washer.
13. Press rear ball bearing onto shaft with snap-ring slot down.
14. Install snap-ring.
15. Install speedometer drive gear and retaining clip. Press on metal speedometer drive gear.

Transmission Assembly

1. Using dummy shaft load a row of 27 roller bearings and a thrust washer at each end of countergear. Hold in place with grease.
2. Place countergear assembly into case through rear. Place a tanged thrust washer, tang away from gear at each end. Install countershaft and key, making sure that tangs align with notches in case.
3. Install reverse idler gear thrust washer, gear, and shaft with key from rear of case. Be sure thrust washer is between gear and rear of case with tang toward notch in case. *NOTE: The reverse idler gear bushing may not be replaced separately—only as a unit with the gear.*
4. Expand snap-ring in extension. Assemble extension over rear of mainshaft and onto rear bearing. Seat snap-ring in rear bearing groove.
5. Install 14 mainshaft pilot bearings into clutch gear cavity. Assemble third speed blocker ring onto clutch gear clutching surface with teeth toward gear.
6. Place clutch gear, pilot bearings, and third speed blocker ring assembly over front of mainshaft assembly. Be sure blocker rings align with keys in second-third synchronizer assembly.
7. Stick extension gasket to case with grease. Install clutch gear, mainshaft, and extension together. Be sure clutch gear engages teeth of countergear anti-lash plate. Torque extension bolts to 45 ft. lbs.
8. Place bearing over stem of clutch gear and into front case bore. Install front bearing to clutch gear snap-ring.
9. Install clutch gear bearing retainer and gasket. The retainer oil return hole must be at the bottom. Torque to 10 ft. lbs.
10. Install reverse idler gear shaft E-ring.
11. Shift synchronizer sleeves to neutral positions. Install cover, gasket, and forks, aligning forks with synchronizer sleeve grooves. Torque side cover bolts to 10 ft. lbs.
12. Install speedometer driven gear.

TORQUE SPECIFICATIONS

	Foot-Pounds
Extension to case attaching bolts	35-55
Drain and filler plugs	10-15
Side cover attaching bolts	18-24
Clutch gear retainer bolts	18-24

Saginaw Four Speed

Disassembly of Transmission

1. Remove the side cover bolts and the side cover assembly.
2. Remove the drive gear bearing retainer.
3. Remove the drive gear to gear stem snap ring. Remove the drive gear bearing by pulling outward on the gear until a screwdriver can be inserted between the bearing and the large snap ring. The drive gear bearing is a slip fit on the gear and into the case bore. This provides clearance between the case bore and the shaft for removal of the drive gear and the mainshaft assembly.
4. Remove the extension housing bolts.
5. Remove the drive gear, mainshaft and the extension housing assembly through the rear case opening. Remove the drive gear and bearing from the mainshaft.
6. Using snap ring pliers, expand the snap ring in the extension housing which holds the mainshaft rear bearing and remove the housing.
7. Using a suitable size drift at the front of the countershaft, drive the countershaft and the woodruff key out the rear of the case. The drift will hold the countergear bearings in place. Remove the gear and thrust washers.
8. Remove the reverse idler gear stop ring. Use a long drift or punch through the front bearing case bore and drive the reverse idler shaft and woodruff key out of the rear of the case.

Overhaul of Sub-Assemblies

Cleaning and Inspection Transmission Case

1. Wash the transmission case thoroughly with clean solvent. Inspect the case for cracks.
2. Check the front and rear faces for burrs. If burrs are present, dress them off with a mill file.

Front and Rear Bearings

1. Wash the front and rear bearings with clean solvent.
2. Blow the bearings out with compressed air.

NOTE: Do not allow the bearings to spin. Turn them slowly by hand. Spinning bearings will damage the race and balls.

3. Make sure that the bearings are clean. Lubricate the bearings with light engine oil and check them for roughness by turning the race slowly by hand.

Bearing Rollers

All clutch gear and countergear bearing rollers should be closely inspected and replaced if they show signs of wear. Inspect the countershaft and the reverse idler shaft, replace if damaged. Replace all worn washers.

Gears

1. Inspect all gears for excessive wear, chips, or cracks. Replace as necessary.
2. Check both clutch sleeves to see that they slide freely on their hubs.

Mainshaft Disassembly

1. Using snap ring pliers, remove the third-fourth sliding clutch hub snap ring from the mainshaft. Remove the clutch assembly, third gear blocking ring, and the third gear from the mainshaft.
2. Depress the speedometer retaining clip and slide the gear from the shaft.
3. Remove the rear bearing snap ring from the shaft groove.
4. Support the first gear with press plates and press on the shaft to remove the first gear, thrust washer, and rear bearing.
5. Remove the first-second sliding clutch hub snap ring from the shaft and remove the clutch assembly, the second gear blocking ring, and the second gear.

Assembly

1. Position the mainshaft with the front end facing upward.
2. Install the third gear with the clutching teeth upward, the rear face of the gear will butt against the flange of the mainshaft.
3. Install the blocking ring with the clutching teeth downward over the synchronizing surface of the third gear.

NOTE: All four blocking rings used in the transmission are identical.

4. Install the third-fourth synchronizer assembly with the fork slot facing downward. Push the assembly onto the splines on the mainshaft until it bottoms against the flange.

CAUTION: Be sure that the notches of the blocking ring align with the keys on the synchronizer assembly.

5. Install the synchronizer hub retaining snap ring on the mainshaft.
6. Position the mainshaft with the rear end facing uward.

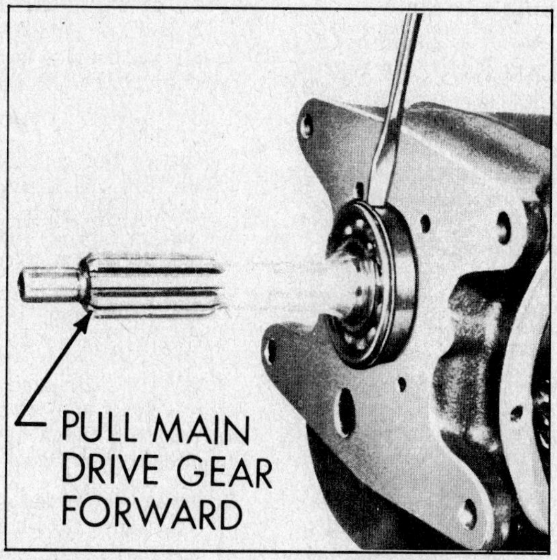

Removing the drive gear bearing—Saginaw Four Speed (© GM Corp.)

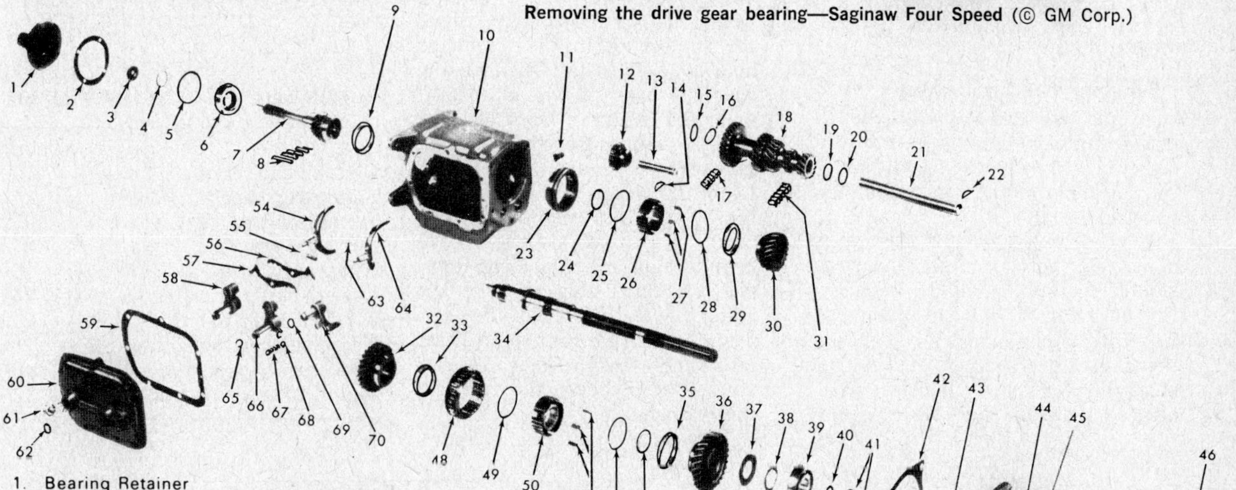

1. Bearing Retainer
2. Gasket-Retainer to Case
3. Oil Seal
4. Snap Ring-Bearing to Shaft
5. Snap Ring-Bearing to Case
6. Drive Gear Bearing
7. Drive Gear
8. Mainshaft Pilot Bearings
9. 4th Speed Blocker Ring
10. Case
11. Filler Plug
12. Reverse Idler Gear
13. Reverse Idler Shaft
14. Woodruff Key
15. Thrust Washer-Front Gear
16. Needle Retainer Washer
17. Needle Bearings
18. Countergear
19. Needle Retainer Washer
20. Thrust Washer-Rear Gear
21. Countershaft
22. Woodruff Key
23. Synchronizer Sleeve
24. Snap Ring-Hub to Shaft
25. Key Retainer
26. 3-4 Synchronizer Hub
27. Clutch Keys
28. Key Retainer
29. 3rd Speed Blocker Ring
30. 3rd Speed Gear
31. Needle Bearings
32. Second Speed Gear
33. 2nd Speed Blocker Ring
34. Mainshaft
35. 1st Speed Blocker Ring
36. First Speed Gear
37. Thrust Washer
38. Wave Washer
39. Rear Bearing
40. Snap Ring-Bearing to Shaft
41. Speedo Drive Gear and Clip
42. Gasket-Extension to Case
43. Snap Ring-Extension to Rear Bearing
44. Extension
45. Vent
46. Bushing
47. Oil Seal
48. 1-2 Synchronizer Sleeve and Reverse Gear
49. Key Retainer
50. 1-2 Synchronizer Hub
51. Clutch Keys
52. Key Retainer
53. Snap Ring-Hub to Shaft
54. 3-4 Shift Fork
55. Detent Spring
56. 3-4 Detent Cam
57. 1-2 Detent Cam
58. 3-4 Shifter Shaft
59. Gasket-Cover to Case
60. Cover
61. TCS Switch and Gasket
62. Lipseal
63. Detent Cam Retainer
64. 1-2 Shift Fork
65. "O" Ring
66. 1-2 Shift Shaft
67. Spring
68. Ball
69. "O" Ring
70. Reverse Shifter Shaft and Fork

Saginaw Four Speed Transmission—exploded view (© GM Corp.)

7. Install the second gear with the clutching teeth facing upward. The front face of the gear will butt against the flange of the mainshaft.
8. Install the blocker ring with the clutching teeth downward over the synchronizing surface of the second speed gear.
9. Install the first-second synchronizer assembly with the fork slot facing downward.

NOTE: Be sure the notches of the blocking ring align with the keys of the synchronizer assembly.

10. Install the synchronizer retaining snap ring on the mainshaft.
11. Install a blocker ring with the notches downward so that they align with the keys on the first-second synchronizer assembly.
12. Install the first gear with the clutching teeth facing downward.
13. Install the first gear steel thrust washer.
14. Install the first gear spring washer.
15. Install the rear ball bearing with the snap ring slot facing downward. Press the bearing onto the shaft.
16. Install the rear bearing snap ring.
17. Install the speedometer drive gear and clip.

Synchronizer Assemblies

1. Mark the hub and sleeve so they can be matched during assembly.
2. Push the hub from the sliding sleeve, the keys and springs may be easily removed.
3. Place the three keys and the two springs in position, one on each side of the hub, so all three keys are engaged with both springs. The tanged end of each synchronizer spring should be installed into different key cavities on either side. Slide the sleeve onto the hub, aligning the marks made before disassembly.

NOTE: A groove around the outside of the synchronizer hub identifies the end that must be opposite the fork slot in the sleeve when assembled. This groove indicates the end of the hub with the greatest recess depth.

Assembly of Transmission

1. Using a suitable size drift, load a row of roller bearings (27) and a bearing washer at each end of the countergear. Use heavy grease to hold the bearings in place.
2. Install the countergear ssembly through the rear opening in the case, along with a tanged thrust washer, tang away from the gear, at each end of the gear. Install the countershaft and woodruff key from the rear of the case.

CAUTION: Be sure that the countershaft picks up both thrust washers and that the tangs are aligned with the notches in the case.

3. Install the reverse idler gear and shaft with its woodruff key from the rear of the case.
4. Using snap ring pliers, expand the snap ring in the extension housing and install the housing over the rear of the mainshaft and onto the rear bearing. Seat the snap ring in the rear bearing groove.
5. Load the mainshaft pilot bearings (14) into the drive gear cavity and assemble the fourth gear blocker ring onto the drive gear clutching surface, with the clutching teeth toward the gear.
6. Install the drive gear, pilot bearings and fourth gear blocker ring assembly over the front of the mainshaft.

NOTE: Be sure that the notches in the blocker ring align with the keys in the third-fourth synchronizer assembly.

7. Place the extension housing gasket on the rear of the case, hold in place with grease. From the rear of the case, install the mainshaft and extension housing assembly.
8. Install the extension housing retaining bolts. Use a sealing compound on the bottom bolt only. Tighten to specification.
9. Install the front bearing outer snap ring and position the bearing over the stem of the drive gear and into the front of the case.
10. Install the snap ring on the drive gear stem. Install the bearing retainer and gasket on the case.

    Make sure that the bearing retainer oil hole is at the bottom.
11. Shift the synchronizer sleeves to the neutral position and install the cover, gasket and fork assembly on the transmission. Make sure that the forks align with the synchronizer sleeve grooves.
12. Tighten all bolts to specification.

TORQUE SPECIFICATIONS

	Foot-Pounds
Clutch gear retainer to case	15
Side cover to case	15
Extension to case	45
Shift lever to shaft bolts	25
Filler plug	18
Case to clutch housing	75
Crossmember to frame	25
Crossmember to mount—mount to extension	40
Mount to transmission	32

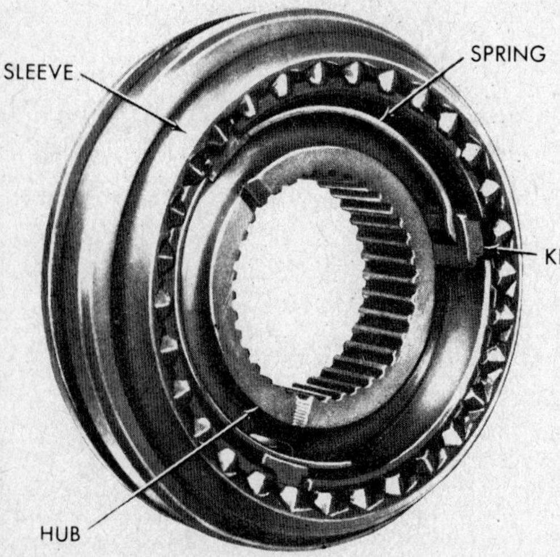

Synchronizer assembly (third-fourth)—Saginaw Four Speed (© GM Corp.)

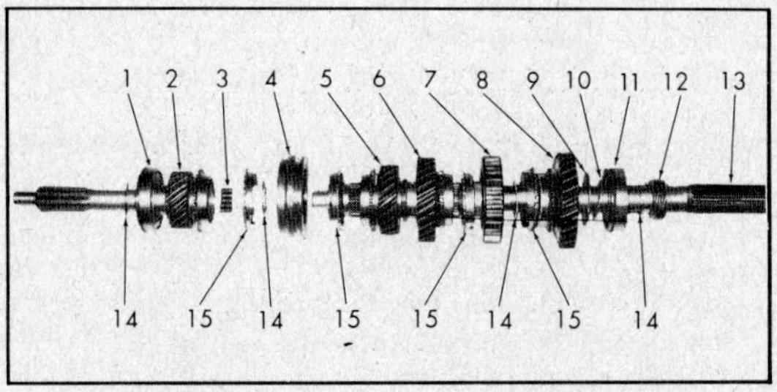

1. Clutch Gear Bearing
2. Clutch Gear
3. Mainshaft Pilot Bearings
4. 3-4 Synchronizer Assembly
5. Third Speed Gear
6. Second Speed Gear
7. 1-2 Synchronizer and Reverse Gear Assembly
8. First Speed Gear
9. Thrust Washer
10. Spring Washer
11. Rear Bearing
12. Speedo Drive Gear
13. Mainshaft
14. Snap Ring
15. Synchronizing "Blocker" Ring

Mainshaft and clutch gear—exploded view—Saginaw Four Speed (© GM Corp.)

Loading countergear bearings (© Chrysler Corp.)

Loading mainshaft pilot bearings (© Chrysler Corp.)

Warner T-14A, T-15A 3 Speed

Description

The Warner T-14A, T-15A are fully synchronized three-speed transmissions having helical drive gears throughout. Lubricant capacity is 2½ pints.

Disassembly of Transmission

1. Separate transfer case from transmission by removing five capscrews.
2. Remove gearshift housing and disassembly by removing shift rails, poppet balls, springs, and shift forks.
3. Remove nut, flat washer, transfer case drive gear, adapter, and spacer.
4. Remove main drive gear bearing retainer gasket.
5. Remove main drive gear and mainshaft bearing snap-rings and bearings.
6. Remove main drive gear and mainshaft assembly. NOTE: The T-15A transmission must be shifted into second gear to allow removal of the mainshaft and gear assembly.
7. On remote shift models, remove roll pins from lever shafts and housing. From inside case, slide levers and interlock assembly out. Remove forks and lever assemblies.
8. Remove lock plate from reverse idler shaft and countershaft.
9. Drive countershaft out to rear with dummy shaft. Remove countergear and two thrust washers. Remove spacer washers, rollers, and spacer from gear.
10. Drive reverse idler shaft out to rear. Remove gear, washers, and roller bearings.
11. Remove clutch hub snap-ring and second-third synchronizer assembly.
12. Remove second and reverse gears.
13. Remove clutch hub snap-ring and low synchronizer assembly.
14. Remove low gear.

Low synchronizer assembly (© Borg Warner Corp.)

Synchronizer

Disassembly and Assembly

1. Remove springs. Low synchronizer has only one spring; second-third, two.
2. Mark sleeve and hub before separating.
3. Remove hub.
4. Remove three shifter plates from hub.
5. Inspect all parts for wear.
6. Assembly in reverse order of disassembly. On second-third unit, make sure that spring openings are 120 degrees from each other, with spring tension opposed.

NOTE: If a synchronized assembly is replaced on a floor shift unit, the shift fork operating the syn-

1 Reverse gear
2 Low synchronizer assembly
3 Low gear
4 Second gear
5 Second-Third synchronizer assembly
6 Main drive gear

Mainshaft assembly
(© Borg Warner Corp.)

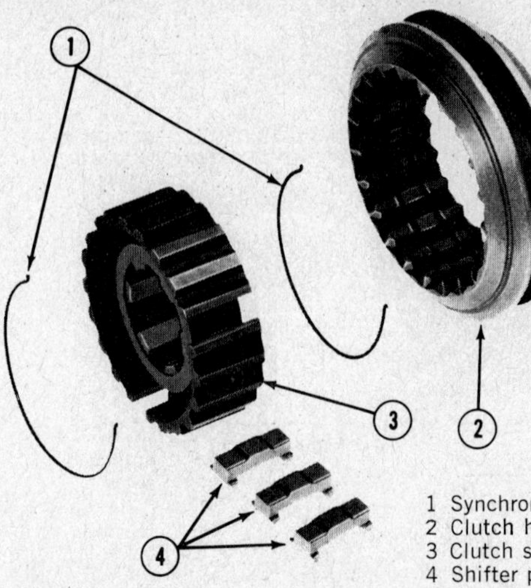

1 Synchronizer spring (2)
2 Clutch hub
3 Clutch sleeve
4 Shifter plate

Second—third synchronizer assembly (© Borg Warner Corp.)

chronizer being replaced must have the letter A just under the shaft hole on the side opposite the pin.

Inspection

1. Wash all parts in solvent.
2. Air dry but do not spin bearings with air pressure.
3. Check case bearing and shaft bores for cracks or burrs.
4. Check all gears and bronze blocking rings for cracks, and chipped, worn, or cracked teeth. If any gears are replaced, also replace the meshing gears.
5. Check all bearings and bushings for wear or damage.
6. Check that synchronizer sleeves slide freely on clutch hubs.

Assembly of Transmission

1. Place reverse idler gear with dummy shaft, roller bearing, and thrust washers in case. Install reverse idler shaft.
2. Assembly countershaft center spacer, four bearing spacers, and bearing rollers in countershaft gear.
3. Install large countergear thrust washer in front of case. Position small thrust washer on countergear hub with lip facing groove in case. Holding countergear in position, push in countershaft from rear.
4. Install lock plate in slots of reverse idler shaft and countershaft.
5. Install to mainshaft:
   a. Low gear.
   b. Bronze blocking ring.
   c. Low synchronizer assembly.
   d. Largest snap-ring that fits in groove.
   e. Second gear.
   f. Bronze blocking ring.
   g. Second-third synchronizer assembly.

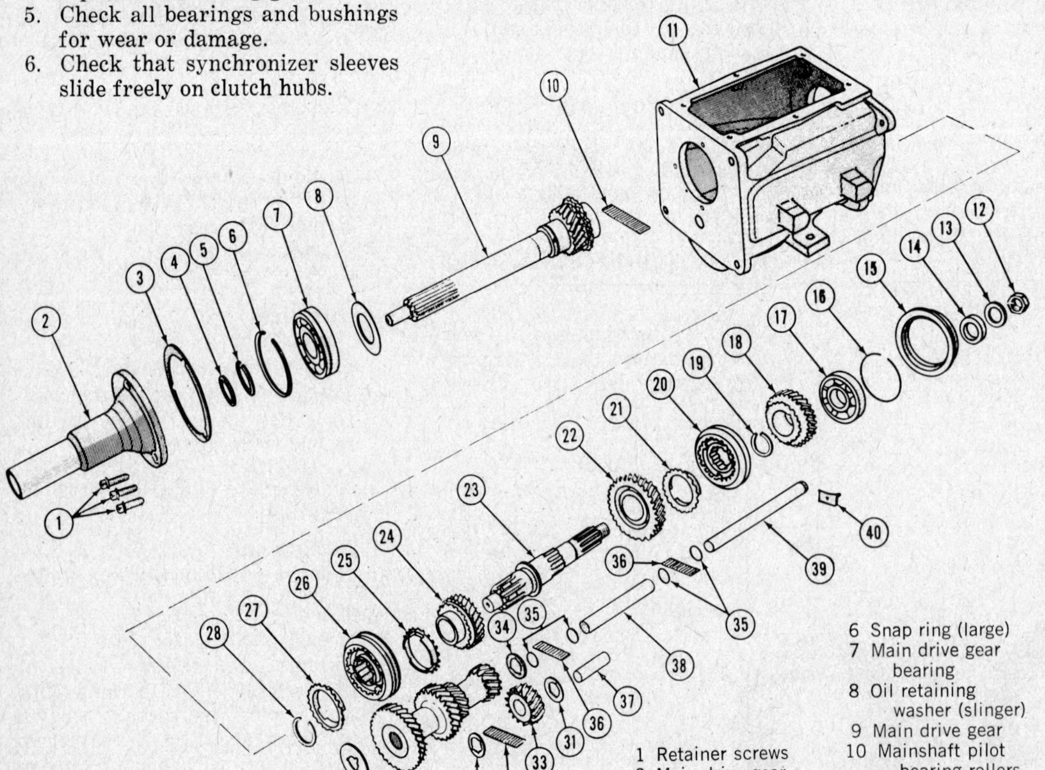

1 Retainer screws
2 Main drive gear bearing retainer
3 Retainer gasket
4 Oil seal
5 Snap ring (small)
6 Snap ring (large)
7 Main drive gear bearing
8 Oil retaining washer (slinger)
9 Main drive gear
10 Mainshaft pilot bearing rollers
11 Case
12 Nut
13 Flatwasher
14 Spacer
15 Bearing adapter
16 Snap ring
17 Mainshaft bearing
18 Reverse gear
19 Snap ring
20 Low synchronizer assembly
21 Synchronizer blocking ring
22 Low gear
23 Mainshaft
24 Second gear
25 Synchronizer blocking ring
26 Second-third synchronizer assembly
27 Synchronizer blocking ring
28 Snap ring
29 Countershaft front thrust washer (large)
30 Countershaft gear
31 Reverse idler gear bearing washer
32 Reverse idler gear roller bearings
33 Reverse idler gear
34 Countershaft rear thrust washer (small)
35 Countershaft bearing spacer washer
36 Countershaft roller bearings
37 Reverse idler shaft
38 Spacer
39 Countershaft
40 Lockplate

T-14A, T-15A three-speed transmission (© Borg Warner Corp.)

h. Largest snap-ring that fits in groove.
i. Reverse gear.
6. Install mainshaft assembly through top of case.
7. Install bronze blocking ring to second-third synchronizer assembly.
8. On remote shift units, install shifter shafts, with new O-rings, into case. NOTE: T-15 interlock levers are marked as to location. T-14 levers have no marks and are interchangeable.
9. Depress interlock lever while installing shift fork into shift lever and synchronizer clutch sleeve. Install poppet spring. Install tapered pins securing shafts in case.
10. Install main drive gear roller bearings.
11. Install main drive gear and oil slinger into case with cutaway portion of gear toward countergear. Install main drive gear to mainshaft.
12. Using bearing installer and thrust yoke tool, install main drive gear and mainshaft bearings and drive into position. The thrust yoke is needed to prevent damage to the synchronizer clutch.
13. Install main drive gear and mainshaft bearing snap-rings. The mainshaft bearing snap-ring is .010 thicker than main drive gear bearing snap-ring.
14. Install mainshaft rear bearing adapter, spacer, transfer case drive gear, flat washer, and nut. Torque nut to 130-170 ft. lbs.
15. Install main drive gear bearing retainer (with new oil seal) and gasket. Align oil drain holes in retainer and gasket.
16. Install case cover gasket. On remote shift units, install cover gasket with vent holes to left side.
17. Position gear train and floorshift assembly in neutral. Insert shifter forks into clutch sleeves and torque to 8-15 ft. lbs.

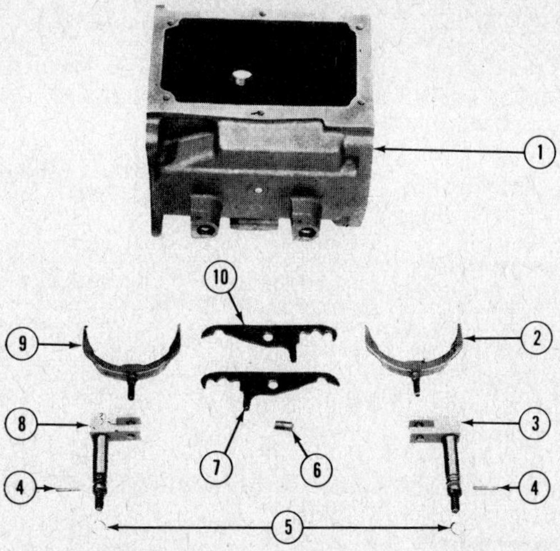

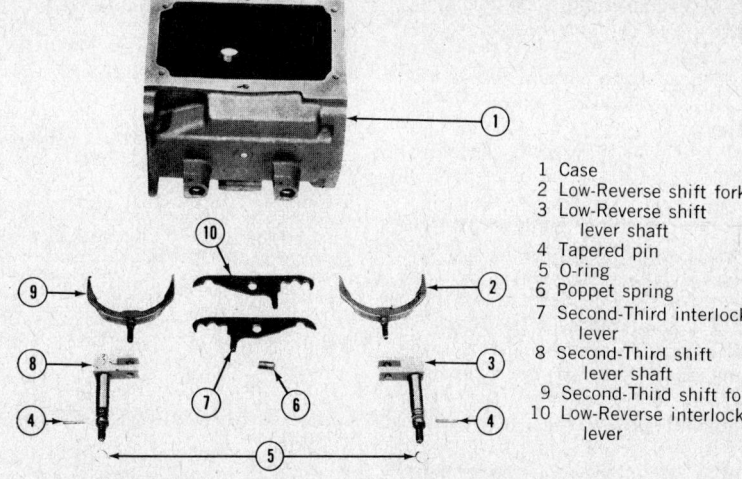

1 Case
2 Low-Reverse shift fork
3 Low-Reverse shift lever shaft
4 Tapered pin
5 O-ring
6 Poppet spring
7 Second-Third interlock lever
8 Second-Third shift lever shaft
9 Second-Third shift fork
10 Low-Reverse interlock lever

Shift bar housing components—remote control (© Borg Warner Corp.)

GENERAL INFORMATION

Model	T14A
Make	Warner
Ratios:	
Low	3.100:1
Second	1.612:1
High	1.000:1
Reverse	3.100:1

1 Low-Reverse shift fork
2 Screwdriver
3 Second-Third interlock lever
4 Second-Third shift fork

Installing shifter forks
(© Borg Warner Corp.)

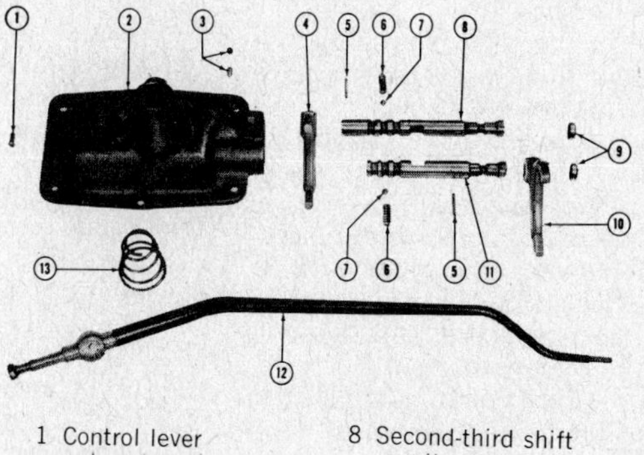

1 Control lever housing pin
2 Control housing
3 Interlock plunger and plug
4 Second-third shift fork
5 Shift fork pin
6 Poppet spring
7 Poppet ball
8 Second-third shift rail
9 Shift rail caps
10 Low-Reverse shift fork
11 Low-reverse shift rail
12 Shift lever
13 Shift lever support spring

Shift control assembly components
(© Borg Warner Corp.)

Warner T-85N 3 Speed W/O.D.

Description

The Warner T-85N overdrive is a synchronized 3 speed transmission with a 2 speed planetary gear transmission attached to the rear of the housing. An electrical control system automatically controls the overdrive shifts. Lubricant capacity is 4 pints.

Disassembly of Transmission

1. Mount the transmission in a vise.
2. Remove the gearshift housing assembly and gasket from the transmission.
3. Remove the shaft levers from the camshafts. Pull the shifter forks and cams out of the gearshift housing. With the cams removed, the interlock balls, sleeve, and spring will fall out of the housing.
4. Pull the shifter forks out of the cam and shaft assembly. Remove the oil seals from the camshafts.

5. Pull the solenoid body about 1/4 turn, and remove it. Remove the governor.
6. With a sharp punch, pierce the snap-ring hole cover and remove the cover.
7. Remove the overdrive housing bolts, and the overdrive control shaft and lever pin.
8. Pull out the manual control shaft and lever as far as possible. Spread the snap-ring that retains the overdrive main shaft front bearing, and then remove the overdrive housing. It may be necessary to tap the overdrive main shaft to free the main shaft bearing from the housing.
9. Remove the overdrive main shaft from the assembly and the free-wheel unit rollers.
10. Remove the speedometer gear and drive ball. To install the main shaft bearing, press on the new bearing, and then install the thickest snap-ring that will fit. Snap-rings are available in the following sizes: 0.086-0.088, 0.0890-0.091, 0.092-0.094, and 0.095-0.097 inch.
11. Remove the free-wheel unit retainers. The free-wheel unit, planetary gear, sun gear, and shaft rail can now be removed.
12. Remove the snap-ring from the adapter, and then remove the plate and trough, balk ring and gear, and pawl.
13. Remove the input shaft bearing retainer and gasket and replace seal if necessary.
14. Rotate the overdrive adapter to expose the countershaft lock, and remove the lock.
15. With a drift, drive the countershaft toward the rear until it just clears the front case bore, and then push the countershaft out the rear with the tool shown.
16. Tap the input shaft and bearing out of the front of the case.
17. If the input shaft bearing is to be replaced, press off the bearing. The bearing baffle acts as a slinger, and must be installed so that it does not rub the bearing outer race as the shaft turns.
18. Remove the overdrive adapter and transmission output shaft as an assembly.
19. Remove the snap-ring at the front of the transmission output shaft, and then slide the synchronizer assembly, intermediate gear, and the sliding low and reverse gear off the shaft.
20. Disassemble the synchronizer unit by sliding the intermediate and high sleeve off the hub. Remove the three inserts and two springs from the hub.
21. Remove the snap-ring that holds the output shaft in the adapter and tap the bearing and shaft out of the adapter. Remove the baffle from the adapter.
22. If the output shaft or bearing is to be replaced, press the old bearing off and the new bearing on and install the thickest snap-ring that will fit. Snap-rings are available in the following thicknesses: 0.0890-0.091, 0.092-0.094, 0.095-0.097, and 0.100-0.0102 inch.
23. While holding the washers and bearing retainer tool at the small end of the cluster gear to prevent the roller bearings and bearing retainer tool from falling out, lift the cluster gear assembly from the case.
24. Drive the reverse idler gear shaft out of the rear of the case.

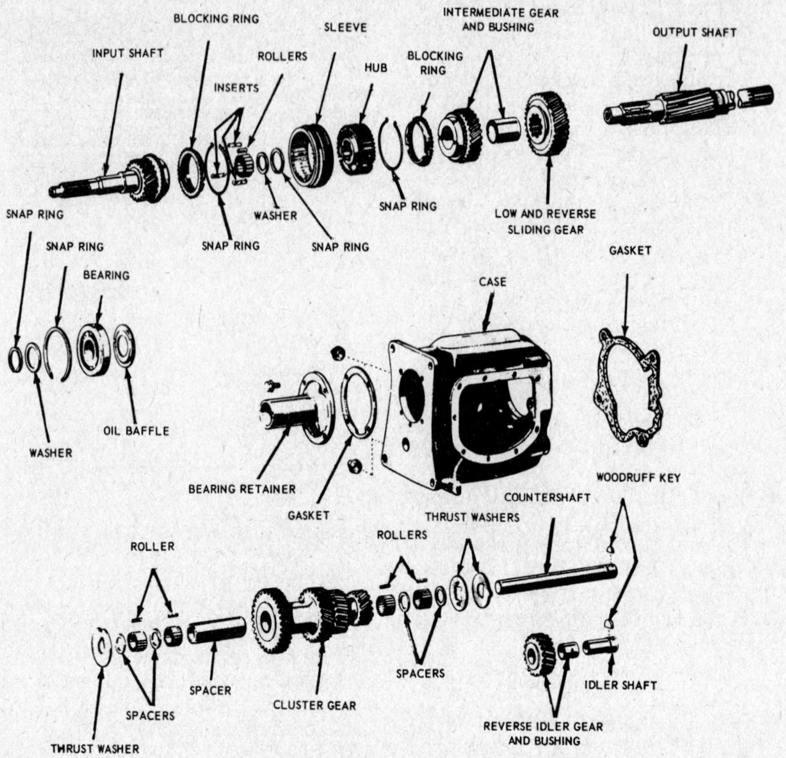

Warner 3-speed transmission
(© Borg Warner Corp.)

Assembly of Transmission

NOTE: Always use new gaskets and gasket cement during assembly. Put a thin coating of lubricant on all parts before installation.

1. Install new oil seals in the camshaft grooves. Place one cam and shaft assembly in position in the gearshift housing, and install the flat washer, lockwasher, and nut. Tighten the nut to specifications.
2. Assemble the interlock pin and balls in the interlock sleeve, and install the interlock assembly in the gearshift housing.

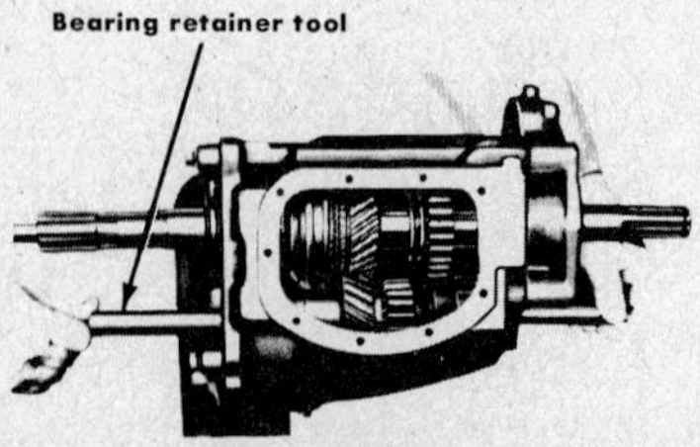

Removing countershaft—typical
(© Borg Warner Corp.)

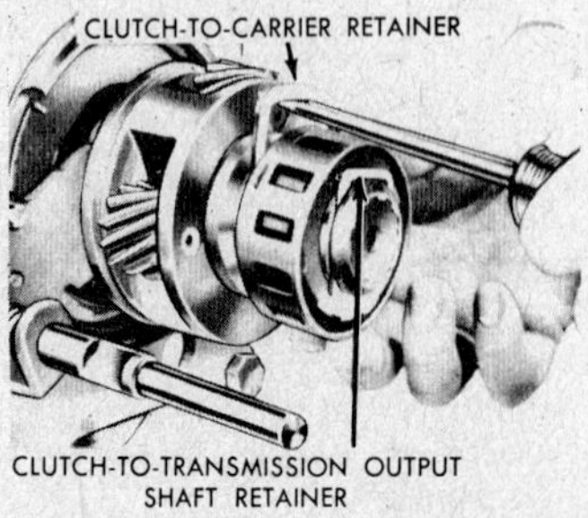

Removing free wheel unit retainer
(© Borg Warner Corp.)

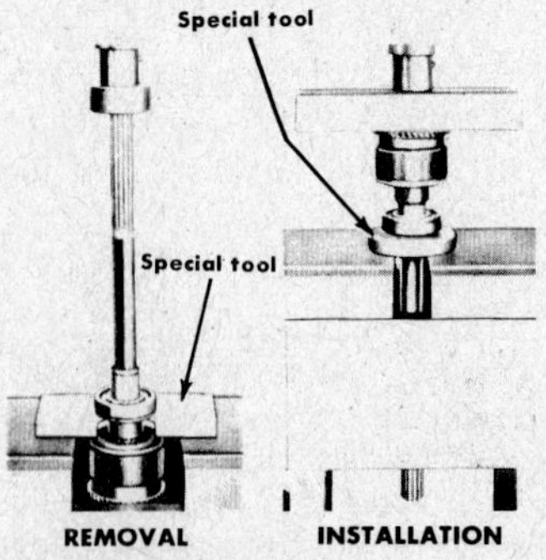

Mainshaft bearing removal or installation
(© Borg Warner Corp.)

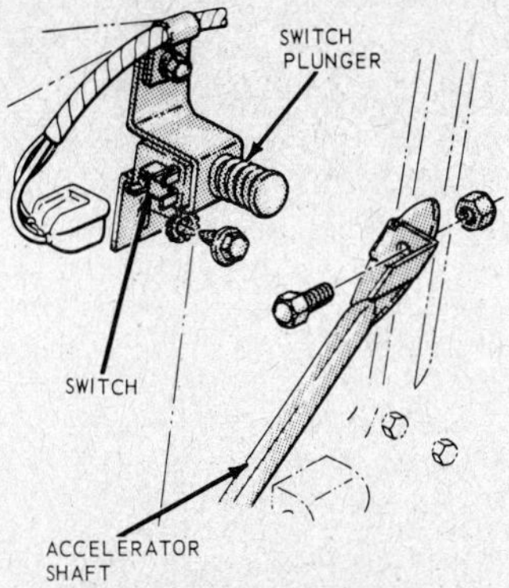

Kickdown switch adjustment
(© Borg Warner Corp.)

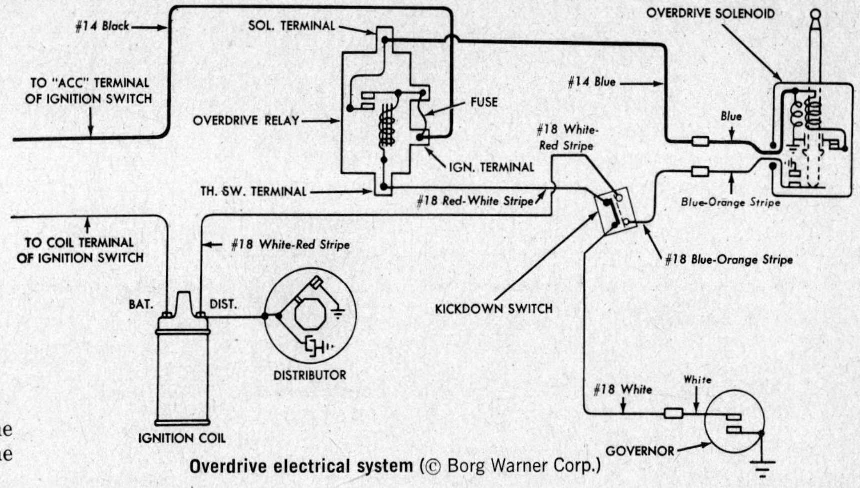

Overdrive electrical system (© Borg Warner Corp.)

44. Install the retaining pin in the overdrive housing to hold the control shaft in place.
45. If necessary, replace the overdrive housing bushing.
46. Thread the governor into the overdrive housing.
47. With the cap drain hole at the bottom, rotate the solenoid ¼ turn from normal position, so that the half ball on the solenoid stem can engage the pawl. Install the two solenoid cap screws.
48. If the solenoid stem is properly engaged, the solenoid cannot be removed from the overdrive in its normal position. Any attempt to pull it out will merely compress the engaging spring in the solenoid.
49. Install a new gasket and the gearshift housing on the transmission. Be sure the shifter forks enter the grooves in the synchronizer and low and reverse sliding gear. Torque gearshift housing to transmission bolts to specifications.
50. Install the drain plugs in the transmission case and the overdrive housing.
51. Fill the transmission with the specified lubricant. This transmission should not be filled through the speedometer cable attachment opening like all other manual transmissions. Instead, pour ½ pint of lubricant in the speedometer cable attachment opening, one pint into the fill plug opening of the overdrive unit and, finally, 3 pints into the fill plug opening of the transmission case.

TORQUE CHART

Nomenclature	*Torque Limits*
Bolt-input shaft bearing retainer to trans. case	5/16-18 25-30 3/8-16 25-30 7/16—14 40-45
Bolt-countershaft front bearing retainer	5/16—18 25-30 3/8—16 25-35 7/16—14 50-55
Bolt-reverse lockout plunger retainer	11/16—16 90-100
Bolt-clutch housing to engine block	7/16—14 24-32 33-45
Nut-drum parking brake to companion flange	3/8—24 37-50 7/16—20 40-55 1/2—20 74-86
Bolt-lever assy. to trans.	3/8—16 20-25
Bolt-clutch housing to trans. case	7/16—14 30-38 5/8—11 96-120 9/16—12 70-90 5/8—18C 115-140 9/16—18C 81-102

Nomenclature	*Torque Limits*
Nut-U-joint flange to trans. output shaft	1.00—20 90-125 1 1/4—18 225-275 1 1/2—18 275-350
Bolt-bellcrank to trans.	3/8—16 20-25
Bolt-countershaft rear bearing retainer	5/16—18 25-30 3/8—16 35-40 7/16—14 45-55 1/2—13 60-70
Nut-bellcrank to trans.	9/16—18 70-90 3/8—16C 20-25
Bolt-countershaft & reverse idler shaft retainer	1/2—13 60-70 5/16—18 25-30 3/8—16 25-37 3/8—16 18-25 7/16—14 40-45 1/2—13 80-85
Bolt-gear shaft housing trans. case	5/16—18 20-25 3/8—16 35-40

Warner T86 Three Speed

Description

The Warner T-86 is a synchronized three-speed transmission having either a floor-mounted or a column shift lever.

Disassembly of Transmission

Except Jeep Models

1. Remove cover.
2. Remove front bearing cap, clutch shaft snap-ring and bearing lock-ring.
3. Remove the front bearing, using a bearing puller and a thrust yoke to prevent damaging synchronizer clutches.

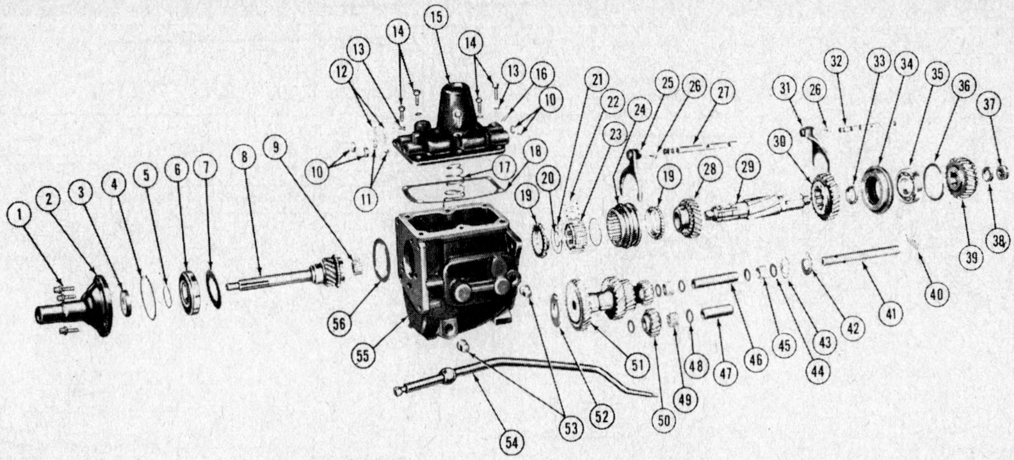

1 Bearing retainer screws
2 Main drive gear bearing retainer
3 Bearing retainer oil seal
4 Bearing snap ring
5 Main drive gear snap ring
6 Main drive gear bearing
7 Front bearing oil retaining washer
8 Main drive gear
9 Pilot roller bearing
10 Shift rail cap
11 Poppet ball
12 Poppet spring
13 Lock washer
14 Shift housing bolt
15 Control housing
16 Interlock plunger
17 Shift lever spring
18 Shift tower gasket
19 Blocking ring
20 Clutch hub snap ring
21 Synchronizer spring
22 Synchronizer plate
23 Clutch hub
24 Clutch sleeve
25 High and intermediate clutch fork
26 Shift fork pin
27 High and intermediate shift rail
28 Second speed gear
29 Main shaft
30 Low and reverse sliding gear
31 Low and reverse shift fork
32 Low and reverse shift rail
33 Bearing spacer
34 Rear bearing adapter
35 Rear bearing
36 Rear bearing snap ring
37 Nut
38 Washer
39 Transfer case drive gear
40 Lock plate
41 Countershaft
42 Rear Countershaft thrust washer (steel)
43 Rear countershaft thrust washer (bronze)
44 Countershaft bearing washer
45 Countershaft bearing
46 Countershaft center bearing spacer
47 Reverse idler gear shaft
48 Reverse idler gear bearing washer
49 Reverse idler gear roller bearings
50 Reverse idler gear
51 Countershaft gear
52 Countershaft front thrust washer
53 Plug
54 Shift lever
55 Transmission case
56 Retainer gasket

T-86 three-speed transmission—floor shift (© Borg Warner Corp.)

4. Remove extension housing. Drive out seal from inside housing with oil seal remover and installer tool. Use bushing remover and installer tool to replace bushing.
5. Move mainshaft assembly back about ¾ in. Lower front end of clutch shaft, move mainshaft assembly over countergear and out of shift forks. Remove clutch shaft from front of case.
6. Check clutch shaft roller bearings for wear or damage.
7. Remove snap-ring speedometer drive gear, and key.
8. Remove snap-ring, synchro-clutch assembly, second gear, friction ring, and low-reverse sliding gear. Press off rear bearing.

Transfer case driving gear
(© Borg Warner Corp.)

9. Remove shifter forks.
10. Remove shaft lock plate from rear of case.
11. Drive countershaft out to rear, using dummy shaft. Lower countergear to bottom of case.
12. Drive out reverse idler shaft. Remove reverse idler gear and countergear.
13. Remove outer shift levers and shifter shaft lock pins. Remove shifter shafts, two interlock ball bearings, sleeve and spring. Remove shaft oil seals from case.

Assembly of Transmission

1. Install new shift shaft oil seals.
2. Install low-reverse shift shaft, interlock sleeve, ball bearing, pin, and spring. Install second-high shift shaft and second ball bearing.
3. Shift mechanism into any gear position with one end of interlock sleeve against shift shaft quadrant, clearance between opposite end of sleeve and quadrant on other shaft should be .001-.007 in. Interlock sleeves are available in several sizes for adjustment.
4. Install lock pins and shift levers.
5. Install dummy shaft and bearings in countergear. Install thrust washers; the bronze front washer must index with the case.
6. Place countergear and dummy shaft in bottom of case.
7. Install reverse idler gear with chamfered side of teeth to front of case. Drive in shaft from rear.
8. Align slots in countershaft and reverse idler shaft. Position countergear and drive in countershaft. Install lock plate.
9. Install shifter forks.
10. Press rear bearing onto mainshaft. Install key, speedometer drive gear, and snap-ring.
11. Install low-reverse sliding gear on mainshaft with sliding collar to front. Gear should slide easily. Install second gear with tapered cone to front.
12. Install rear bearing snap-ring—the thickest possible.
13. Install synchro-clutch assembly and front snap-ring.
14. When synchro-clutch hub is pressed against snap-ring, there should be .003-.010 in. clearance between second gear and shoulder on mainshaft.
15. Install 14 greased rollers in clutch shaft.
16. Install front friction ring on clutch shaft and insert through top of case. Install mainshaft assembly through rear of case,

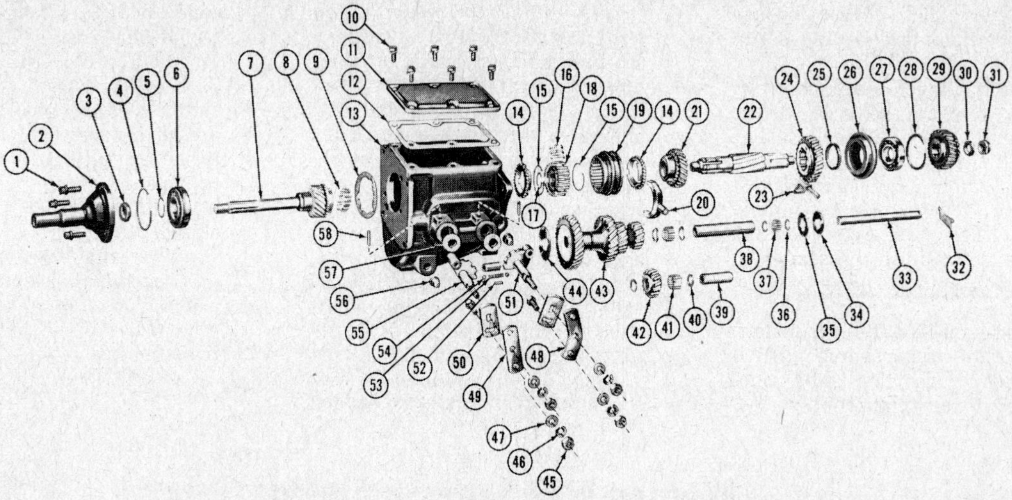

1 Retainer screws
2 Main drive gear retainer
3 Oil seal
4 Snap ring (large)
5 Snap ring (small)
6 Main drive gear bearing
7 Main drive gear
8 Main shaft bearing rollers
9 Retainer gasket
10 Cover bolt and lock washer
11 Case cover
12 Case cover gasket
13 Case
14 Blocking ring
15 Synchronizer spring
16 Shifting plate
17 Snap ring
18 Clutch hub
19 Clutch sleeve
20 Shift fork
21 Second speed gear
22 Main shaft
23 Shifting shoe
24 Sliding gear
25 Seal
26 Bearing adapter
27 Bearing
28 Snap ring
29 Transfer case drive gear
30 Washer
31 Nut
32 Locking plate
33 Countershaft
34 Washer (steel)
35 Washer (bronze)
36 Spacer
37 Needle bearings
38 Spacer washer
39 Reverse idler gear shaft
40 Spacer washer
41 Reverse idler gear roller bearings
42 Reverse idler gear
43 Countershaft gear
44 Countershaft front thrust washer
45 Nut
46 Lock washer
47 Control lever washer
48 Low and Reverse control lever (outer)
49 Intermediate and high control lever (outer)
50 Control lever (inner)
51 Low and reverse shift lever
52 Spacer
53 Spring
54 Ball
55 Intermediate and high shift lever
56 Plug
57 Oil seal
58 Taper pin

T-86 three-speed transmission—remote control (© Borg Warner Corp.)

moving to right to engage shifter forks in synchro-clutch collar and low-reverse sliding gear. Guide clutch shaft onto main shaft.

17. Install extension housing oil seal.
18. Install extension housing.
19. Install oil slinger, concave side to rear. Drive in front bearing using thrust yoke to prevent synchronizer damage.
20. Install thickest clutch shaft snap-ring that will fit in groove.
21. Install front bearing cap with new gasket. Choose thickness of gasket to give zero clutch shaft end play.
22. Clearance of friction rings should be .056-145 in.
23. Install cover end gasket.

Disassembly of Transmission

Jeep Models

1. Drain lubricant and flush out the case.
2. If a transfer case is involved, remove its rear cover.
3. If a power take-off is involved, remove the shift unit which replaces the cover.
4. Remove cotter pin, nut and washer and remove the transfer case main drive gear.
5. Remove the transmission shift cover.
6. Loop a piece of wire around the mainshaft just back of second-speed gear. Twist the wire and attach one end to the right front cover screw, the other end to the left cover screw. Tighten the wire to prevent the mainshaft from pulling out of the case when the transfer case is removed. Should the mainshaft come out, the synchronizer parts will drop into the bottom of the case.
7. Remove transfer case screws then tap lightly on the end of the transmission mainshaft to separate the two units. The transmission mainshaft bearing should slide out of the transfer case and stay with the transmission.
8. Remove front main drive gear bearing retainer and gasket.
9. Remove the oil collector hollow-head screws.
10. Remove lock plate from the reverse idler shaft and countershaft, at the rear of the case.
11. Drive the countershaft out the rear of the case with a dummy shaft and a brass drift.
12. Remove the mainshaft assembly through the case rear opening. Remove main drive gear.
13. Remove the countershaft gear set and three thrust washers from the bottom of the case, then dismantle the countershaft gear assembly.
14. Remove the reverse idler shaft and gear using a brass drift.
15. On column shift models, check clearance between ends of interlock sleeve and notched surface of each shift lever. The correct clearance is .001-.007 in. Several sizes of interlock sleeves are available for adjustment.

Assembly of Transmission

To assemble, reverse the disassembly procedures, giving the following points particular attention:

1. The countershaft gear set, when assembled in the case, should have from .012-.018 in. end-play controlled by the thickness of the rear steel thrust washer.

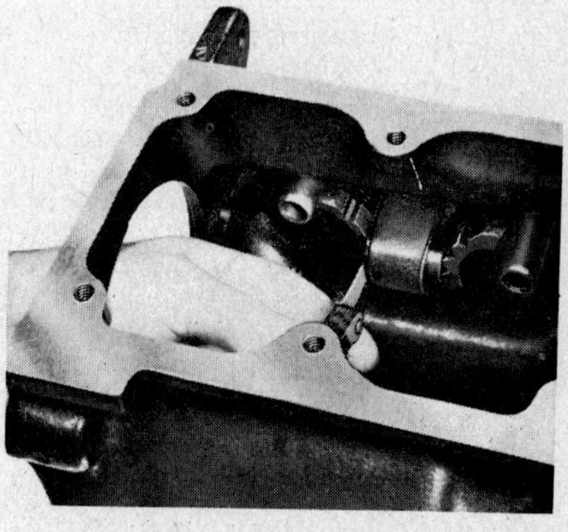

Interlock sleeve clearance
(© Borg Warner Corp.)

2. Assemble the large bronze with the lip entered in the slot in the case.
3. The bronze-faced steel washer is placed next to the gear at the rear end, and the steel washer next to the case.
4. To assemble the countershaft bearing rollers, use a dummy shaft. Use grease and a loading sleeve to facilitate reassembly of the countershaft gear components.
5. In assembling the mainshaft gears, low and reverse gear is installed with the shift shoe groove toward the front.
6. In assembling the synchronizer unit, install the two springs in the high and intermediate clutch hub with spring tension opposed. Place the right lipped end of a spring in the hub slot and place the spring in the hub. Turn the hub around and make the same installation with the other spring, starting with the same slot. Install the three synchronizer shifting plates into the three slots in the hub, wih the smooth sides of the plates out. Hold the plate in position and slip the second and direct clutch sleeve over the hub, with the long beveled edge toward the long part of the clutch hub. Install the completed assembly onto the mainshaft with the beveled edge of the clutch sleeve toward the front end of the shaft.
7. When installing the mainshaft, be sure the bearing rollers are in place in the pilot bore of the clutch gear.
8. Be sure that the countershaft and reverse idler shaft lock plate are in position and completely recessed into the indents of the transfer case.

Warner T-89 Series 3 Speed

Description

The Warner T-89 is a fully synchronized three-speed transmission controlled by a column mounted shift lever.

Disassembly of Transmission

1. Install the transmission in a work stand.
2. Remove the gear shift housing.
3. Shift the transmission into two gears. Remove the output shaft nut and remove the parking brake assembly.
4. Remove the input shaft bearing retainer. Tap the input shaft and bearing toward the front as far as it will go.
5. Remove the output shaft bearing retainer bolts. Turn the retainer to expose the end of the countershaft.
6. Drive the countershaft toward the rear until it just clears the hole at the front of the case. Push the counter shaft out of the rear of the case. Remove the Woodruff key from the countershaft.
7. Remove the output shaft assem-

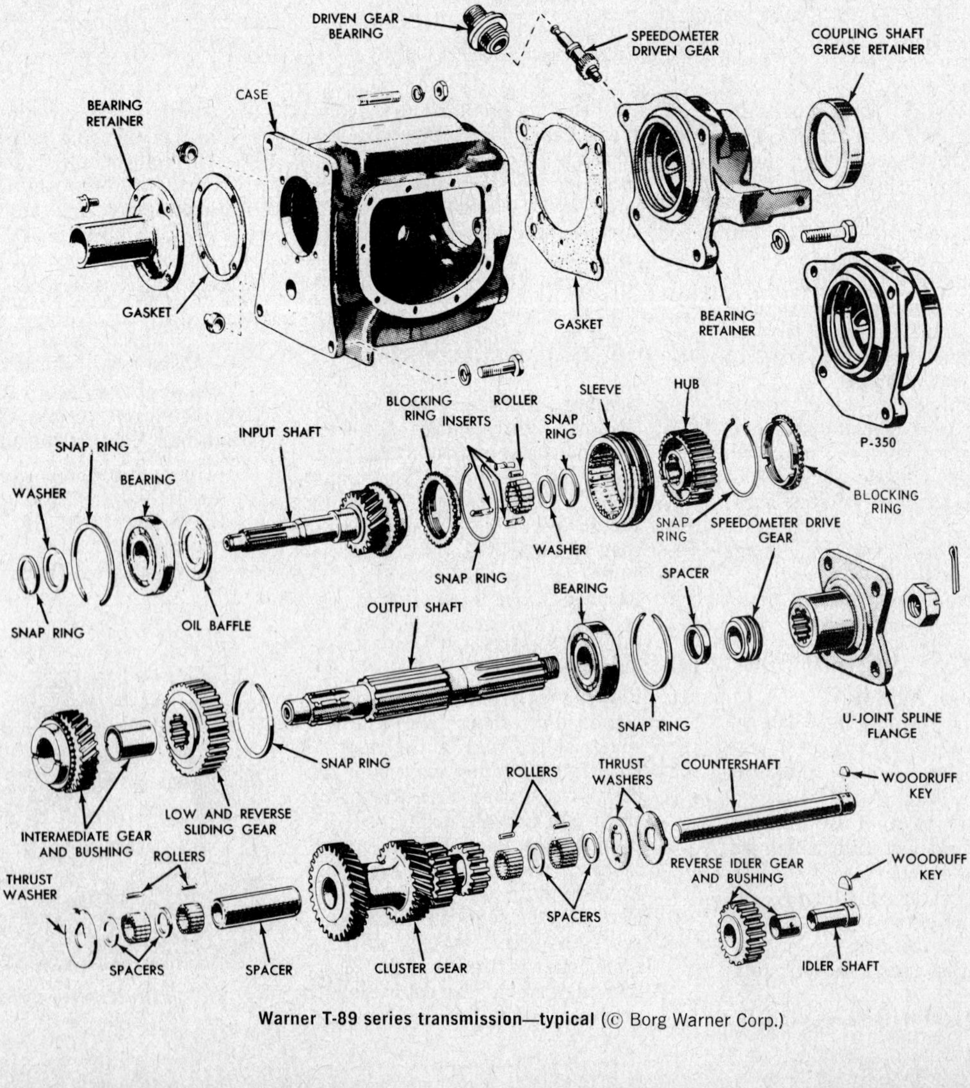

Warner T-89 series transmission—typical (© Borg Warner Corp.)

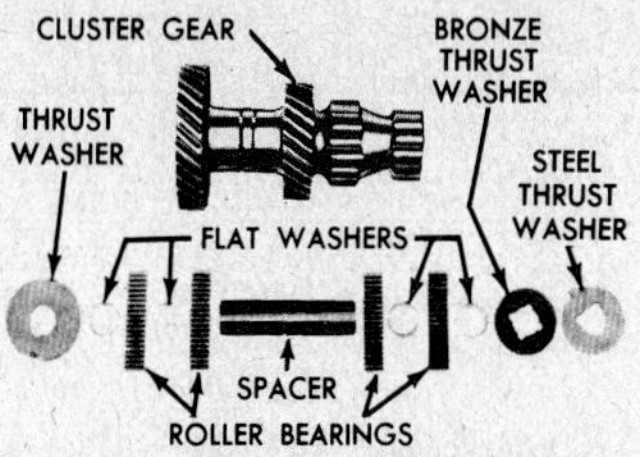

Cluster gear and components
(© Borg Warner Corp.)

bly. Remove the pilot rollers from the rear of the input shaft.

8. Remove the bearing snap-ring and spacer washer from the input shaft. Drive the input shaft through the bearing. Remove the input shaft and bearing from the case.
9. Drive the reverse idler shaft out of the rear of the case.
10. Remove the cluster gear roller bearings and washers.
11. Remove the snap-ring at the front of the output shaft, and slide the synchronizer, intermediate gear, and low and reverse sliding gear off the shaft.
12. Remove the snap-ring that holds the outer race, and tap the output shaft bearing and shaft out of the bearing retainer casting and replace the bearing if worn.

Parts Repair or Replacement

Synchronizer

1. Slide the clutch sleeve off the hub and remove the three inserts and springs.
2. To assemble the synchronizer, align the index mark on the hub with the one on the sleeve.
3. Position the insert on the hub and slide the sleeve into place.
4. Install the insert springs. cover.

Shift Cover

Check the condition of the shift levers and forks. If there is any binding or clashing of gears when the lever is operated, disassemble the cover.

Assembly

1. Install new seal rings in the shifter cam grooves.
2. Position one cam assembly in the gear shift cover.
3. Assemble the interlock spring and balls in the interlock, install the interlock assembly in the gear shift cover, and position the other cam assembly.
4. Install the gear shift levers and forks on the cams.

Assembly of Transmission

1. Position the cluster gear bearings and washers.
2. Position the cluster gear assembly in the case. The tang on the front thrust washer must be fitted into the slot in the case thrust surface. The tab on the rear steel washer must be up. Install the countershaft, and check the cluster gear end play (0.006-0.020 inch).
3. Place the reverse idler gear in the case with the chamfered teeth ends toward the front. Drive the reverse idler shaft through the gear from the rear of the case. When the end of the shaft is nearly flush with the case install the Woodruff key.
4. Tap the input shaft bearing into the case until the snap-ring bottoms on the case. Install the input shaft bearing retainer without a gasket. Install the retainer and barely tighten the cap screws.
5. Position the baffle on the input shaft and hold it there with a light coat of grease. It must be installed at the rear of the bearing with the dished side away from the bearing so that the baffle does not rub the bearing outer race.
6. Place the input shaft (with baffle) in the case and drive the shaft into the bearing with a hardwood block.
7. Remove the input shaft bearing retainer, and install the spacer washer and snap-ring on the shaft. Install the thickest snap-ring that will fit. Snap-rings vary from 0.086-0.103 inch. Tap the input shaft and bearing as far to the front as they will go. Place the pilot bearing rollers in the input shaft and hold them with grease.
8. Install the output shaft and bearing in the bearing retainer casting. Install the thickest snap-ring that will fit. Assemble the low and reverse gear, intermediate gear and synchronizer assembly on the output shaft. Install the snap-ring at the front of the output shaft, and place the pilot bearing flat washer on the shaft.
9. Place a new gasket on the output shaft bearing retainer casting and install assembly in the case. Position the bearing retainer casting so that the countershaft hole is exposed.
10. Tap the input shaft bearing toward the rear until the bearing outer race snap-ring hits the case.
11. Raise the cluster gear assembly and install the countershaft. When the end of the countershaft is nearly flush with the case, install the Woodruff key.
12. Turn the output shaft bearing retainer to a normal position, and torque the retainer bolts to specification.

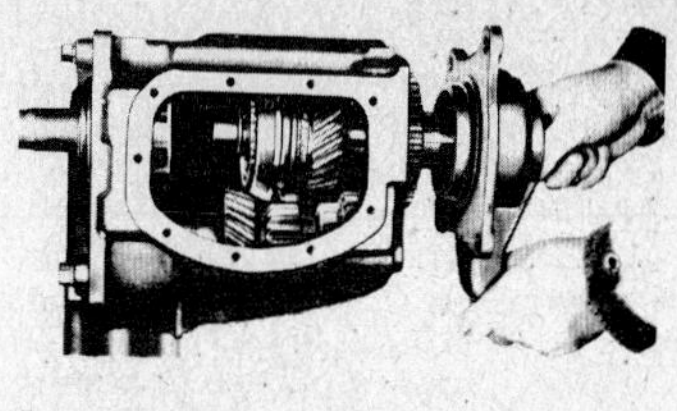
Removing or installing output shaft
(© Borg Warner Corp.)

13. Install a new grease retainer, if necessary, and apply lubricant to the seal lips and cavity.
14. Install the input shaft bearing retainer and gasket. Torque the bolts to specification. Select a gasket that will seal and prevent end play. Gaskets are available in the following thicknesses: 0.010, 0.015, 0.020, 0.025 inch.
15. Install the spacer and speedometer driving gear on the output shaft. Install the parking brake assembly.
16. Shift the transmission into two gears and install the output shaft nut.
17. Pour the specified lubricant over the entire gear train to prevent scoring when the transmission is initially operated.
18. Shift the transmission into neutral. Install the shift cover and gasket and torque the bolts to specification.
19. Fill the transmission with the proper lubricant through the speedometer cable attachment opening.

TORQUE CHART

Nomenclature	*Nuts and/or Bolts and Torque Limits*		
Bolt—gear shift lever tower to gearshift housing	3/8-16 20-25		7/16-14 30-35
Bolt—clutch housing to trans. case	7/16-14 30-38 5/8-11 96-120		9/16-12 70-90
Nut-U-joint flange to trans. output shaft	1.00-20 90-125	1 1/2-18 275-350	1 1/4-18 225-275
Nut—drum parking brake to companion flange	3/8 24 35-45		7/16-20 50-70
Nut—bellcrank to trans.	9/16-18 70-90		
Bolt—lever assy. to trans.	3/8-16 20-25		
Nut—handbrake anchor bar to trans. case (5-speed extra-heavy duty only)	9/16-18 120-130		
Bolt—bellcrank to trans.	3/8-16 20-25		
Bolt—reverse lockout plunger retainer	11/16-16 80-100		

TORQUE CHART

Nomenclature	Nuts and/or Bolts and Torque Limits	
Bolt—countershaft rear bearing retainer	5/16-18 25-30 3/8-16 35-40	7/16-14 45-55 1/2-13 60-70
Bolt—countershaft & reverse idler shaft retainer	5/16-18 25-30 3/8-16 25-37 3/8-16† 18-25†	7/16-14 40-45 1/2-13 80-85
Bolt—gear shift housing to trans. case	5/16-18 20-25 3/8-16 35-40	3/8-16†† 30-35†† 7/16-14 45-50

Nomenclature	Nuts and/or Bolts and Torque Limits
Bolt—power take off cover to trans. case	3/8-16 20-30
Nut—countershaft bearing lock (5-speed extra H.D. & 5-speed exclusive)	1 1/4-18 350-450
Nut—countershaft bearing lock (5-speed exclusive H.D.)	1 1/2-18 350-450

Nomenclature	Nuts and/or Bolts and Torque Limits	
Bolt—input shaft bearing retainer to trans. case	5/16-18 25-30 3/8-16 25-30	7/16-14 40-45
Bolt—countershaft front bearing retainer	5/16-18 25-30 3/8-16 25-35	7/16-14 50-55

Warner T-10 4 Speed

Description

The Warner T-10 is a fully synchronized four-speed transmission having a floor mounted shift lever. Lubricant capacity is 2½ pints.

Disassembly of Transmission

1. Drain transmission, mount in stand and remove side cover and shift controls.
2. Remove front bearing retainer and gasket.
3. Remove output shaft companion flange.
4. Drive out lock pin and pull reverse shift shaft out about ⅛ in. to disengage shifter fork from reverse gear.
5. Remove bolts and tap the case extension (with soft hammer) rearward. When idler gear shaft is out as far as it will go, move extension to the left so the reverse fork clears the reverse gear. Remove extension and gasket.
6. Remove rear bearing snap-ring from mainshaft.
7. Remove case extension oil seal.
8. Using a puller, remove speedometer drive gear.
9. Remove the reverse gear, reverse idler gear and tanged thrust washer.
10. Remove self-locking bolt holding the rear bearing retainer to transmission case.
11. Remove the entire mainshaft assembly.
12. Unload bearing rollers from main drive gear and remove fourth-speed synchronizer blocking ring.
13. Lift the front half of reverse idler gear and its thrust washer from the case.
14. Remove the main drive gear snap-ring and spacer washer.
15. With soft hammer, tap main drive gear out of front bearing.
16. From inside the case, tap out front bearing and snap-ring.
17. From the front of the case, tap out the countershaft with a dummy shaft.
18. Then lift out the countergear assembly with both tanged washers.
19. Dismantle the countergear, consisting of 80 rollers, six .050 in. spacers and a roller tubular spacer.
20. Remove mainshaft front snap-ring and slide third and fourth-speed clutch assembly, third-speed gear and synchronizer ring, second and third-speed gear thrust bearing, second-speed gear and second-speed synchronizer ring from front of mainshaft.
21. Press mainshaft out of retainer.
22. Remove the mainshaft rear snap-ring.
23. Support first and second-speed clutch assembly and press on rear of mainshaft to remove shaft from rear bearing, first-speed gear, and synchromesh ring, first and second-speed clutch sliding sleeve and first-speed gear bushing.

Assembly of Transmission

Mainshaft

1. From the rear of the mainshaft, assemble first and second-speed clutch assembly to mainshaft (sliding clutch sleeve taper toward the rear, hub to the front) and press the first-speed gear bushing onto the shaft.
2. Install first speed gear synchronizing ring aligning notches in ring with keys in hub.
3. Install first-speed gear (hub toward front) and thrust washer with the washer grooves facing first-speed gear.
4. Press on the rear bearing, with the snap-ring groove toward the front of the transmission. Be sure the bearing is firmly seated against the shoulder on the mainshaft.
5. Install the selective fit snap-ring onto the mainshaft behind the rear bearing. Use the thickest ring that will fit between the rear face of the bearing and the front face of the snap-ring.
6. From the front of the mainshaft, install the second-speed gear synchronizing ring so that the ring notches correspond with the hub keys.
7. Install the second-speed gear (hub toward the back) and the second and third-speed gear thrust bearing.
8. Install third-speed gear (hub to front) and third-speed gear synchronizing ring (notches front).
9. Install third and fourth-speed gear clutch assembly (hub and sliding sleeve) with taper front, being sure keys in the hub correspond with notches in third-speed gear synchronizing ring.
10. Install snap-ring (.086-.088 in. thickness) into mainshaft groove in front of the third and fourth-speed clutch assembly.
11. Install rear bearing retainer plate. Spread the snap-ring on the plate to allow the snap-ring to drop around the rear bearing and press on the end of the mainshaft until the snap-ring

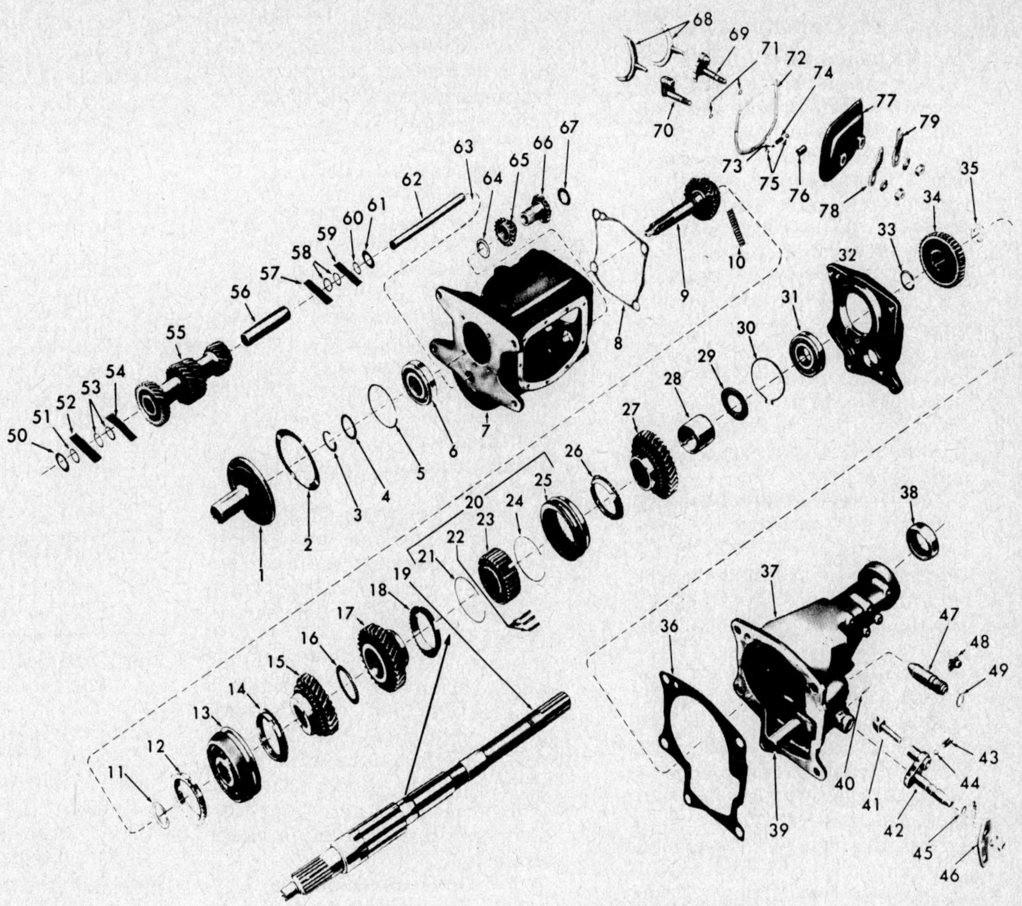

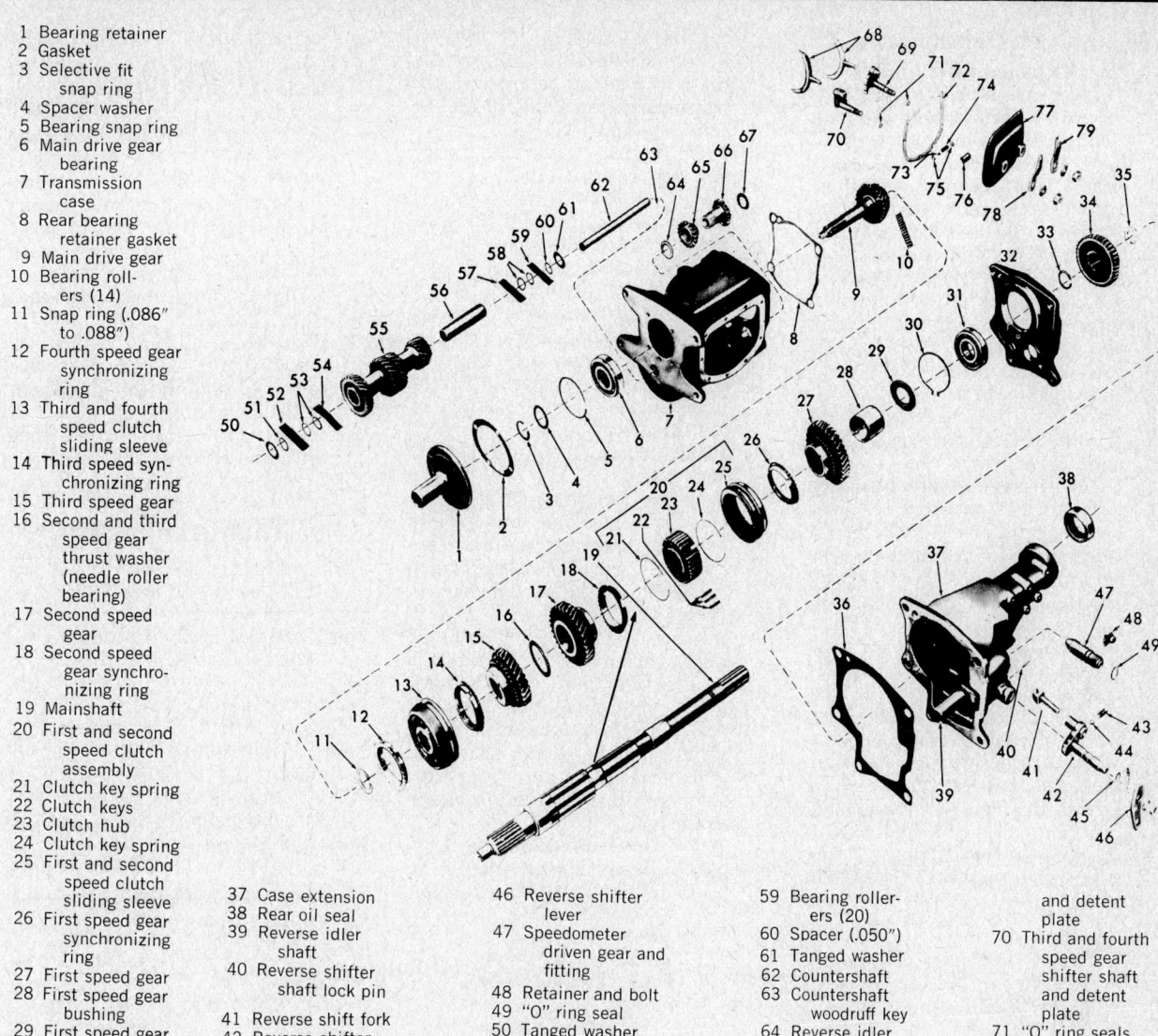

1 Bearing retainer
2 Gasket
3 Selective fit snap ring
4 Spacer washer
5 Bearing snap ring
6 Main drive gear bearing
7 Transmission case
8 Rear bearing retainer gasket
9 Main drive gear
10 Bearing rollers (14)
11 Snap ring (.086" to .088")
12 Fourth speed gear synchronizing ring
13 Third and fourth speed clutch sliding sleeve
14 Third speed synchronizing ring
15 Third speed gear
16 Second and third speed gear thrust washer (needle roller bearing)
17 Second speed gear
18 Second speed gear synchronizing ring
19 Mainshaft
20 First and second speed clutch assembly
21 Clutch key spring
22 Clutch keys
23 Clutch hub
24 Clutch key spring
25 First and second speed clutch sliding sleeve
26 First speed gear synchronizing ring
27 First speed gear
28 First speed gear bushing
29 First speed gear thrust washer
30 Rear bearing snap ring
31 Rear bearing
32 Rear bearing retainer
33 Selective fit snap ring
34 Reverse gear
35 Speedometer drive gear
36 Rear bearing retainer to case extension gasket
37 Case extension
38 Rear oil seal
39 Reverse idler shaft
40 Reverse shifter shaft lock pin
41 Reverse shift fork
42 Reverse shifter shaft and detent plate
43 Reverse shifter shaft ball detent spring
44 Reverse shifter shaft detent ball
45 Reverse shifter shaft "O" ring seal
46 Reverse shifter lever
47 Speedometer driven gear and fitting
48 Retainer and bolt
49 "O" ring seal
50 Tanged washer
51 Spacer (.050")
52 Bearing rollers (20)
53 Spacer (2—.050")
54 Bearing rollers (20)
55 Countergear
56 Countergear roller spacer
57 Bearing rollers (20)
58 Spacers (2—.050")
59 Bearing rollers (20)
60 Spacer (.050")
61 Tanged washer
62 Countershaft
63 Countershaft woodruff key
64 Reverse idler front thrust washer (flat)
65 Reverse idler gear (front)
66 Reverse idler gear (rear)
67 Tanged thrust washer
68 Forward speed shift forks
69 First and second speed gear shifter shaft and detent plate
70 Third and fourth speed gear shifter shaft and detent plate
71 "O" ring seals
72 Gasket
73 Interlock pin
74 Poppet spring
75 Detent balls
76 Interlock sleeve
77 Transmission side cover
78 Third and fourth speed shifter lever
79 First and second speed shifter lever

The Warner T-10 4-speed transmission—typical (© Borg Warner Corp.)

12. Install reverse gear (shift collar to the rear).
13. Press speedometer drive gear onto the mainshaft so that there is a measurement of 4½ in. from the center of the gear to the flat surface of the rear bearing retainer.
14. Install special snap-ring into the groove at the rear of the mainshaft.

Countergear

1. Install countergear dummy and tubular roller bearing spacer into the countergear.
2. Using heavy grease to hold the rollers, install 20 bearing rollers in either end of the countergear, two spacers, 20 more rollers, then one spacer. Install the same combination of rollers and spacers in the other end of the countergear.
3. Set the countergear assembly in the bottom of the transmission case making sure the tanged thrust washers are in their proper position.

Main Drive Gear

1. Press bearing (snap-ring groove front) onto main drive gear until the bearing fully seats against the shoulder on the gear.
2. Install spacer washer and selective fit snap-ring in the groove in the main drive gear shaft.

NOTE: Variable thickness snap-rings are available to obtain a prescribed clearance of .000-.005 in. between the rear face of the snap-ring and the front face of the spacer washer.

Assembly of Transmission

1. Install main drive gear and bearing assembly through the side cover opening and into position in the transmission front bore. After assembly is in place, install front bearing snap-ring.
2. Lift countergear and thrust washers into place. Install Woodruff key into end of countershaft, then from the rear of the case, press the countershaft in until flush with rear of case and the dummy shaft is displaced. Maximum countergear end play is .025 in.
3. Install the 14 bearing rollers into the grease-coated end of the main drive gear.
4. Using heavy grease, position gasket on front face of rear bearing retainer. Install the fourth-speed synchronizing ring onto main drive gear with clutch key notches toward rear of transmission.
5. Position the reverse idler gear thrust washer on the machined face of the ear cast in the case for the reverse idler shaft. Position the front reverse idler gear on top of the thrust washer, hub facing toward rear of case.
6. Lower the mainshaft assembly into the case, with the fourth-speed synchronizing ring notches aligning with the keys in the clutch assembly.
7. Install self-locking bolt, attach the rear bearing retainer to the transmission case and torque the bolt to 20-30 ft. lbs.
8. From the rear of the case, insert the rear reverse idler gear, engaging the splines with the portion of the gear within the case.
9. Place a greased gasket on the rear face of the rear bearing retainer.
10. Install remaining tanged thrust washer into place on reverse idler shaft, being sure the tang on the thrust washer is in the notch in the idler thrust face of the extension.
11. Place the two clutches in neutral position.
12. Pull reverse shifter shaft to left side of extension and rotate shaft to bring reverse fork to extreme forward position in the extension. Align forward and reverse idler gears.
13. Position the extension onto the transmission case by uniting the reverse idler shaft with the idler gears and engaging the shift fork with the reverse shift collar by turning the shifter shaft, the reverse gear will move rearward thus enabling installation of the extension.
14. Install three extension and retainer to case attaching bolts at 35-45 ft. lbs. and two extension to retainer attaching bolts (20-30 ft. lbs.). Use sealer on the lower, right bolt.
15. Align groove in reverse shift shaft with hole in boss and drive in lock pin.
16. Install the main drive gear bearing retainer and gasket aligning the oil well with the oil outlet hole and torque the sealer-coated bolts to 15-20 ft. lbs.
17. Install a shift fork into each clutch sleeve.
18. With both clutches in neutral, install side cover and gasket and torque to 10-20 ft. lbs. Use sealer on the lower right bolt.
19. Install first and second, and third and fourth shift levers.

TORQUE CHART

Part	*Location*	*Thread Size*	*Torque Ft. Lbs.*
Bolt	Front bearing retainer to transmission case	5/16-18	15-20
Bolt	Side cover bolts	5/16-18	15-20
Nut	Shift lever to shaft	5/16-18	12-18
Bolt	Transmission to flywheel housing	1/2-13	45-60
Bolt	Flywheel housing to engine	3/8-16	30-35

Warner T-18, T-19 Series 4 Speed

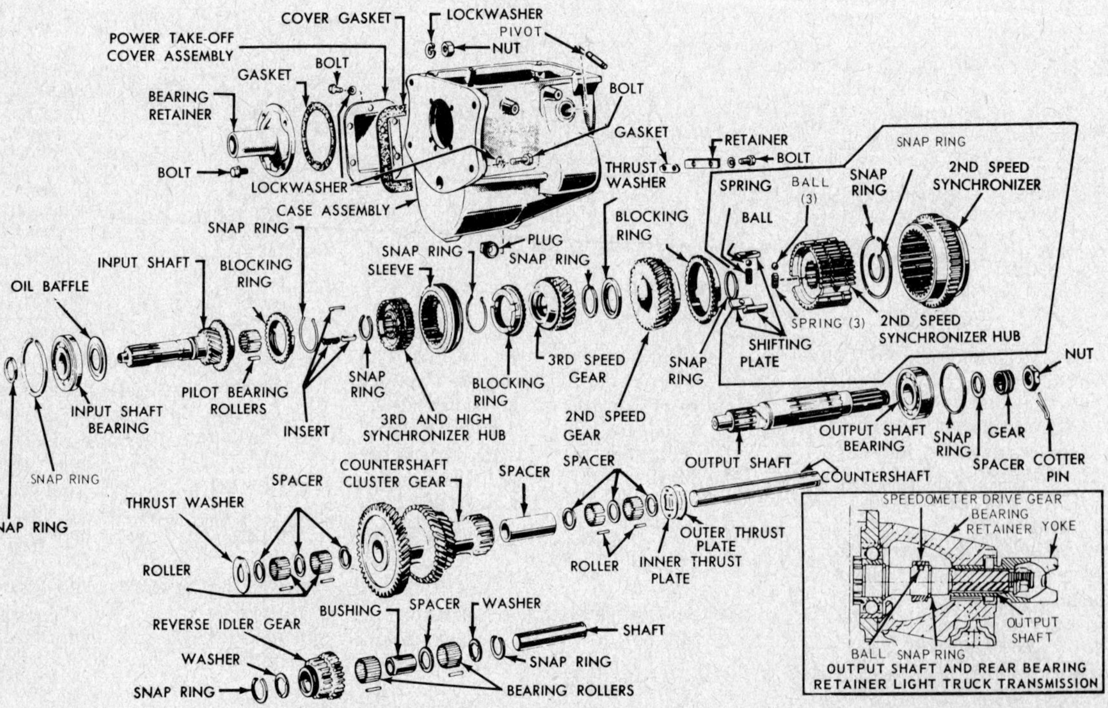

4-speed Warner T-18 transmission (© Borg Warner Corp.)

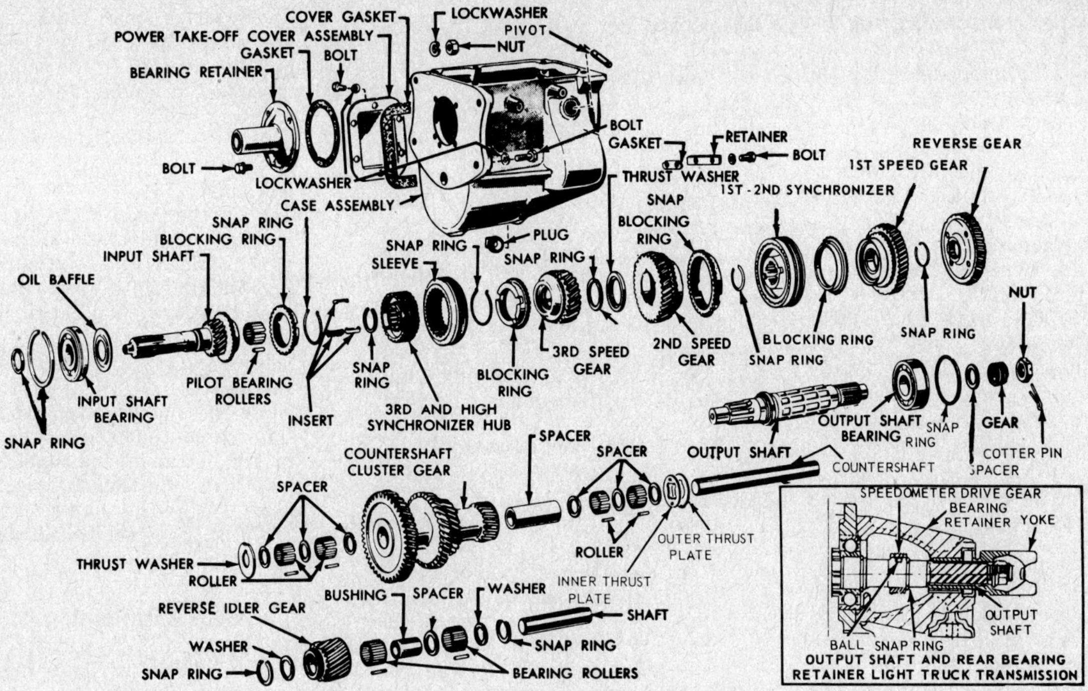

4-speed Warner T-19 transmission (© Borg Warner Corp.)

Description

The Warner T-18, T-19 are four-speed fully synchronized transmissions having a floor-mounted shift lever and a power take-off opening on the right side of the case. The T-18 first and reverse gears are spur gears while the others are helical. The T-19 has all helical gears.

Disassembly of Transmission

1. After draining the transmission and removing the parking break drum (or shoe assembly), lock the transmission in two gears and remove the U-joint flange, oil seal, speedometer driven gear and bearing assembly. Lubricant capacity is 6½ pints.
2. Remove the output shaft bearing retainer and the speedometer drive gear and spacer.
3. Remove the output shaft bearing snap-ring, and remove the bearing.
4. Remove the countershaft and idler shaft retainer and the power take-off cover.
5. After removing the input shaft bearing retainer, remove the

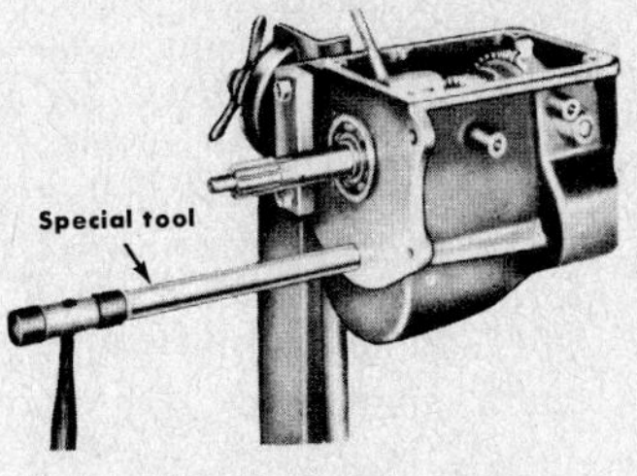

Removing countershaft
(© Borg Warner Corp.)

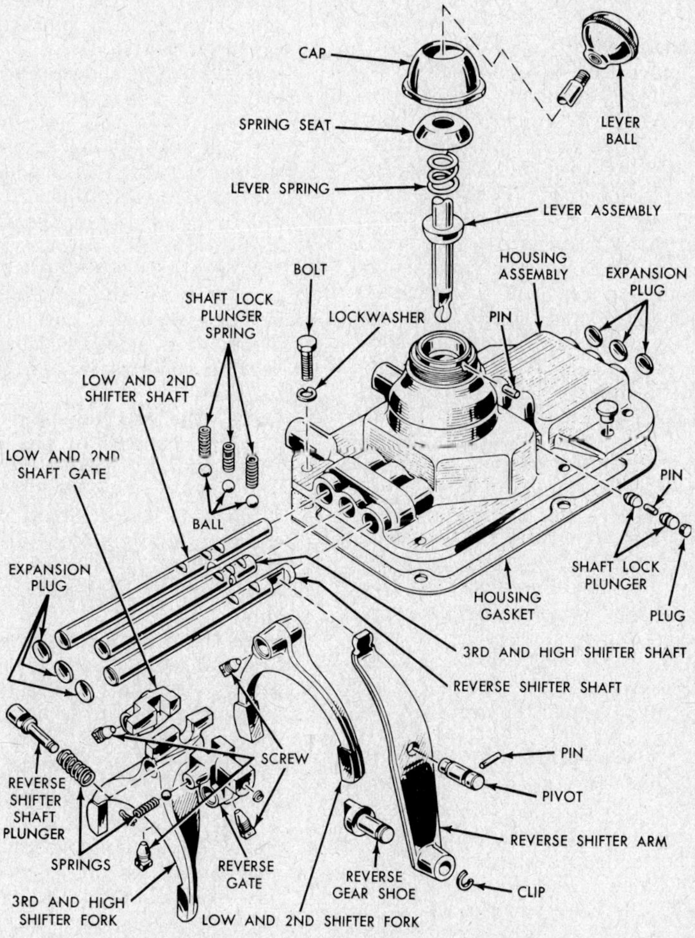

Conventional cab shift linkage (© Borg Warner Corp.)

snap-rings from the bearing and the shaft.
6. Remove the input shaft bearing and oil baffle.
7. Drive out the countershaft (from the front). Keep the dummy shaft in contact with the countershaft to avoid dropping any rollers.
8. After removing the input shaft and the synchronizer blocking ring, pull the idler shaft.
9. Remove the reverse gear shifter arm, the output shaft assembly, the idler gear, and the cluster gear. When removing the cluster, do not lose any of the rollers.

Disassembly of Sub-Assemblies

Output Shaft

1. Remove the third- and high-speed synchronizer hub snap-ring from the output shaft, and slide the third- and high-speed synchronizer assembly and the third-speed gear off the shaft. Remove the synchronizer sleeve and the inserts from the hub. Before removing the two snap-rings from the ends of the hub, check the end play of the second-speed gear (0.005-0.024 inch).
2. Remove the second-speed synchronizer snap-ring. Slide the second-speed synchronizer hub gear off the hub. Do not lose any of the balls, springs, or plates. Pull the hub off the shaft, and remove the second-speed synchronizer from the second-speed gear. Remove the snap-ring from the rear of the second-speed gear, and remove the gear, spacer, roller bearings, and thrust washer from the output shaft. Remove the remaining snap-ring from the shaft.

Cluster Gear

Remove the dummy shaft, pilot bearing rollers, bearing spacers, and center spacer from the cluster gear.

Reverse Idler Gear

Rotate the reverse idler gear on the shaft, and if it turns freely and smoothly, disassembly of the unit is not necessary. If any roughness is noticed, disassemble the unit.

Gear Shift Housing

1. Remove the housing cap and lever. Be sure all shafts are in neutral before disassembly.
2. Tap the shifter shafts out of the housing while holding one hand over the holes in the housing to prevent loss of the springs and balls. Remove the two shaft lock plungers from the housing.

Assembly of Sub-Assemblies

Cluster Gear Assembly

Slide the long bearing spacer into the cluster gear bore, and insert the dummy shaft in the spacer. Hold the cluster gear in a vertical position, and install one of the bearing spacers. Position the 22 pilot bearing rollers in the cluster gear bore. Place a spacer on the rollers, and install 22 more rollers and another spacer. Hold a large thrust washer against the end of cluster gear and turn the assembly over. Install the rollers and spacers in the other end of the gear.

Reverse Idler Gear Assembly

1. Install a snap-ring in one end of the idler gear, and set the gear on end, wtih the snap-ring at the bottom.
2. Position a thrust washer in the gear on top of the snap-ring. Install the bushing on top of the washer, insert the 37 bearing rollers, and then a spacer followed by 37 more rollers. Place the remaining thrust washer on the rollers, and install the other snap-ring.

Output Shaft Assembly

1. Install the second speed gear thrust washer and snap-ring on the output shaft. Hold the shaft vertically, and slide on the second-speed gear. Insert the bearing rollers in the second-speed gear, and slide the spacer into the gear. (The T-18 model does not contain second speed gear rollers or spacer). Install the snap-ring on the output shaft at the rear of the second-speed gear. Position the blocking ring on the second-speed gear. Do not invert the shaft because the bearing rollers will slide out of the gear.
2. Press the second-speed synchronizer hub onto the shaft, and install the snap-ring. Position the shaft vertically in a soft-jawed vise. Position the springs and plates in the second-speed synchronizer hub, and place the hub gear on the hub.
3. With the T-19 model, press the first and second speed synchronizer onto the shaft and install the snap-ring. Install the first speed gear and snap-ring on the shaft and press on the reverse gear.

   For the T-19, ignore steps 2 and 4.
4. Hold the gear above the hub spring and ball holes, and position one ball at a time in the hub, and slide the hub gear downward to hold the ball in place. Push the plate upward, and insert a small block to hold the plate in position, thereby holding the ball in the hub. Follow these procedures for the remaining balls.
5. Install the third speed gear and synchronizer blocking ring on the shaft.
6. Install the snap-rings at both ends of the third and high-speed synchronizer hub. Stagger the openings of the snap-rings so that they are not aligned. Place the inserts in the synchronizer sleeve, and position the sleeve on the hub.
7. Slide the synchronizer assembly onto the output shaft. The slots in the blocking ring must be in line with the synchronizer inserts. Install the snap-ring at the front of the synchronizer assembly.

Gear Shift Housing

1. Place the spring on the reverse gear shifter shaft gate plunger, and install the spring and plunger in the reverse gate. Press the plunger through the gate, and fasten it with the clip. Place the spring and ball in the reverse gate poppet hole. Compress the spring and install the cotter pin.
2. Place the spring and ball in the reverse shifter shaft hole in the gear shift housing. Press down on the ball, and position the reverse shifter shaft so that the reverse shifter arm notch does not slide over the ball. Insert the shaft part way into the housing.
3. Slide the reverse gate onto the shaft, and drive the shaft into the housing until the ball snaps into the groove of the shaft. Install the lock screw lock wire to the gate.
4. Insert the two interlocking plungers in the pockets between the shifter shaft holes. Place the spring and ball in the low and second shifter shaft hole. Press down on the ball, and insert the shifter shaft part way into the housing.
5. Slide the low and second shifter shaft gate onto the shaft, and install the corresponding shifter fork on the shaft so that the offset of the fork is toward the rear of the housing. Push the shaft all the way into the housing until the ball engages the shaft groove. Install the lock screw and wire that fastens the fork to the shaft. Install the third and high shifter shaft in the same manner. Check the interlocking system. Install new expansion plugs in the shaft bores.

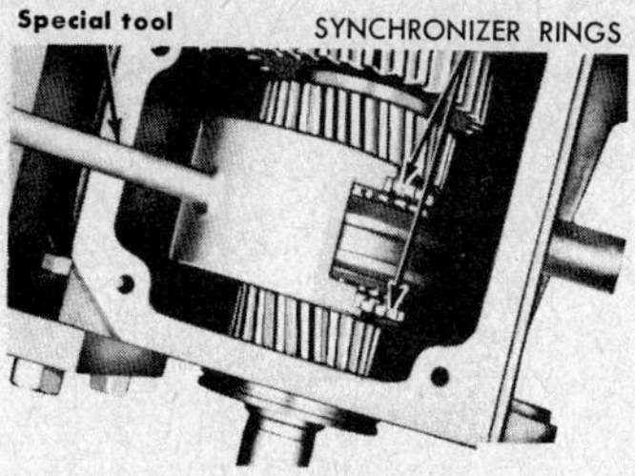

Stop yoke tool
(© Borg Warner Corp.)

Assembly of Transmission

1. Coat all parts, especially the bearings, with transmission lubricant to prevent scoring during initial operation.
2. Position the cluster gear assembly in the case. Do not lose any rollers.
3. Place the idler gear assembly in the case, and install the idler shaft. Position the slot in the rear of the shaft so that it can engage the retainer. Install the reverse shifter arm.
4. Drive out the cluster gear dummy shaft by installing the countershaft from the rear. Position the slot in the rear of the shaft so that it can engage the retainer. Use thrust washers as required to get 0.006 to 0.020 inch cluster gear end play. Install the countershaft and idler shaft retainer.
5. Position the input shaft pilot rollers and the oil baffle, so that the baffle will not rub the bearing race. Install the input shaft and the blocking ring in the case.
6. Install the output shaft assembly in the case, and use a special tool to prevent jamming the blocking ring when the input shaft bearing is installed.
7. Drive the input shaft bearing onto the shaft. Install the thickest select-fit snap-ring that will fit on the bearing. Install the input shaft snap-ring.
8. Install the output shaft bearing.
9. Install the input shaft bearing without a gasket, and tighten the bolts only enough to bottom the retainer on the bearing snap-ring. Measure the clearance between the retainer and the case, and select a gasket (or gaskets) that will seal in the oil and prevent end play between the retainer and the snap-ring. Torque the bolts to specification.
10. Position the speedometer drive gear and spacer, and install a new output shaft bearing retainer seal.
11. Install the output shaft bearing retainer. Torque the bolts to specification, and install safety wire.
12. Install the brake shoe (or drum), and torque the bolts to specification. Install the U-joint flange. Lock the transmission in two gears and torque the nut to specification.
13. Install the power take-off cover plates with new gaskets. Fill the transmission according to specifications.

TORQUE CHART

Nomenclature	*Nuts and/or Bolts and Torque Limits*		
Bolt—gear shift lever tower to gearshift housing	3/8-16 20-25	7/16-14 30-35	
Bolt—clutch housing to trans. case	7/16-14 30-38 5/8-11 96-120	9/16-12 70-90	
Nut—U-joint flange to trans. output shaft	1.00-20 90-125	1 1/2-18 275-350	1 1/4-18 225-275

TORQUE CHART

Nomenclature	*Nuts and/or Bolts and Torque Limits*	
Nut—drum parking brake to companion flange	3/8-24 35-45	7/16-20 50-70
Nut—bellcrank to trans.	9/16-18 70-90	
Bolt—lever assy. to trans.	3/8-16 20-25	
Nut—handbrake anchor bar to trans. case (5-speed extra-heavy duty only)	9/16-18 120-130	
Bolt—belcrank to trans.	3/8-16 20-25	
Bolt—reverse lock-out plunger retainer	11/16-16 80-100	
Bolt—countershaft rear bearing retainer	5/16-18 25-30 3/8-16 35-40	7/16-14 45-55 1/2-13 60-70
Bolt—countershaft & reverse idler shaft retainer	5/16-18 25-30 3/8-16 25-37 3/8-16† 18-25†	7/16 14 40-45 1/2-13 80-85

TORQUE CHART

Nomenclature	*Nuts and/or Bolts and Torque Limits*	
Bolt—gear shift housing to trans. case	5/16-18 20-25 3/8-16 35-40	3/8-16†† 30-35†† 7/16-14 45-50
Bolt—power take off cover to trans. case	3/8-16 20-30	
Nut—countershaft bearing lock (5-speed extra h.d. & 5-speed exclusive)	1 1/4-18 350-450	
Nut—countershaft bearing lock (5-speed exclusive h.d.)	1 1/2-18 350-450	
Bolt—input shaft bearing retainer to trans. case	5/16-18 25-30 3/8-16 25-30	7/16-14 40-45
Bolt—countershaft front bearing retainer	5/16-18 25-30 3/8-16 25-35	7/16-14 50-55

Tremec T-150 Three Speed Transmission

Disassembly of Transmission

1. Remove the bolts securing the transfer case to the transmission. Remove the transfer case.
2. Remove the transfer case drive gear locknut, flat washer, and drive gear. Remove the large fiber washer from the rear bearing adapter. Move the second-third clutch sleeve forward and the first-reverse sleeve to the rear before removing the locknut.
3. Remove the transmission oil plug and drive the countershaft out of the case with a suitable size drift. *Do not lose the countershaft access plug when removing the countershaft.* With the countershaft removed the countershaft gear will lie at the bottom of the case, leave it there until the mainshaft is removed.
4. Punch alignment marks in the front bearing cap and the transmission case for assembly reference.
5. Remove the front bearing cap and gasket.
6. Remove the large lock ring from the front bearing.
7. Remove the clutch shaft, front bearing, and the second-third synchronizer assembly. *A special*

tool is required for this operation, see illustration.

8. Remove the rear bearing and adapter assembly with a brass drift and hammer. Drive the adapter out the rear of the case with light blows from the hammer.
9. Remove the mainshaft assembly. Tilt the spline end of the shaft downward and lift the front end up and out of the case.
10. Remove the countershaft tool and arbor as an assembly. Remove the countershaft thrust washers, countershaft roll pin, and any pilot roller bearings that may have fallen into the case.
11. Remove the reverse idler shaft. Insert a brass drift through the clutch shaft bore in the front of the case and tap the shaft until the end with the roll pin clears the counter bore in the rear of the case. Remove the shaft.
12. Remove the reverse idler gear and thrust washers from the case.
13. Remove the retaining snap ring from the front of the mainshaft. Remove the second-third synchronizer assembly and second gear. Mark the hub and sleeve for reference during assembly.

NOTE: Observe the position of the insert springs and the inserts during removal for correct assembly.

14. Remove the insert springs from the second-third synchronizer, remove the three inserts, and separate the sleeve from the synchronizer hub retaining snap ring.
15. Remove the snap ring and the tabbed thrust washer from the mainshaft and remove the first gear blocking ring.
16. Remove the first-reverse synchronizer hub snap ring.

NOTE: Observe the position of the insert springs and the inserts during removal for correct assembly.

17. Remove the first-reverse sleeve, insert spring and the three insert from the hub. Remove the spacer from the rear of the mainshaft.

CAUTION: Do not attempt to remove the press fit hub by hammering. Hammer blows will damage the hub and mainshaft.

18. Remove the front bearing retaining snap ring and any remaining roller bearings from the clutch shaft.
19. Press the front bearing off the clutch shaft with an arbor press.

CAUTION: Do not attempt to remove the bearing by hammering. Hammer blows will damage the bearing and the clutch shaft.

20. Clamp the rear bearing adapter in a soft-jawed vise. *Do not overtighten.*
21. Remove the rear bearing retaining snap ring. Remove the bearing adapter from the vise.
22. Press the rear bearing out of the adapter with an arbor press. clean solvent and dry with compressed air.

Cleaning and Inspection

1. Thoroughly wash all parts in clean solvent and dry with compressed air.

NOTE: Do not dry the bearings with compressed air, use a clean shop cloth.

2. Clean the needle and clutch shaft bearings by placing them in a shallow parts cleaning tray and covering them with solvent. Allow the bearings to air dry on a clean shop cloth.
3. Check the case for the following:
   a. Cracks in the bores, bosses, or bolt holes.
   b. Stripped threads in bolt holes.
   c. Nicks, burrs, rough surfaces in the shaft bores or on the gasket surfaces.
4. Check the gear and synchronizer assemblies for the following:
   a. Broken, chipped, or worn gear teeth.
   b. Damaged splines on the synchronizer hubs or sleeves.
   c. Bent or damaged inserts.
   d. Damaged needle bearings or bearing bores in the countershaft gear.

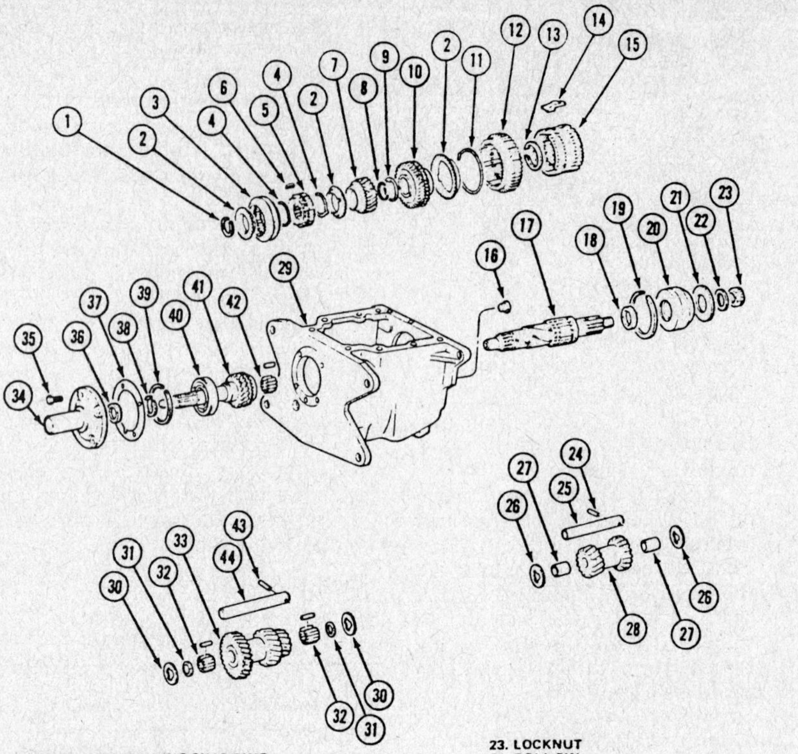

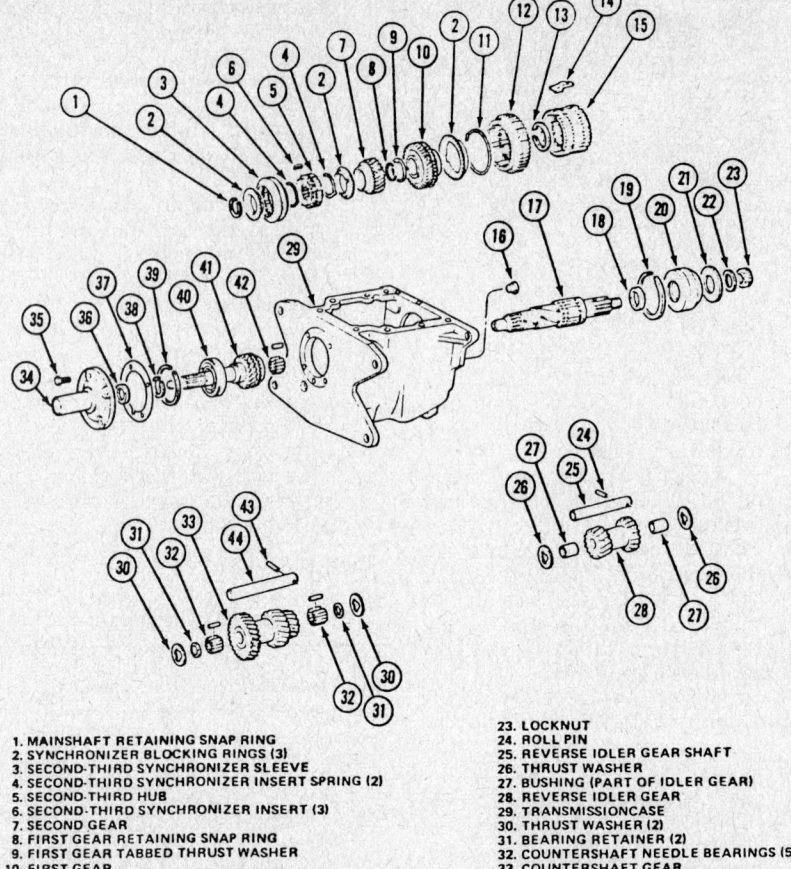

1. MAINSHAFT RETAINING SNAP RING
2. SYNCHRONIZER BLOCKING RINGS (3)
3. SECOND-THIRD SYNCHRONIZER SLEEVE
4. SECOND-THIRD SYNCHRONIZER INSERT SPRING (2)
5. SECOND-THIRD HUB
6. SECOND-THIRD SYNCHRONIZER INSERT (3)
7. SECOND GEAR
8. FIRST GEAR RETAINING SNAP RING
9. FIRST GEAR TABBED THRUST WASHER
10. FIRST GEAR
11. FIRST-REVERSE SYNCHRONIZER INSERT SPRING
12. FIRST-REVERSE SLEEVE AND GEAR
13. FIRST-REVERSE HUB RETAINING SNAP RING
14. FIRST-REVERSE SYNCHRONIZER INSERT (3)
15. FIRST-REVERSE HUB
16. COUNTERSHAFT ACCESS PLUG
17. MAINSHAFT
18. MAINSHAFT SPACER
19. REAR BEARING ADAPTER LOCK RING
20. REAR BEARING AND ADAPTER ASSEMBLY
21. FIBER WASHER
22. FLAT WASHER
23. LOCKNUT
24. ROLL PIN
25. REVERSE IDLER GEAR SHAFT
26. THRUST WASHER
27. BUSHING (PART OF IDLER GEAR)
28. REVERSE IDLER GEAR
29. TRANSMISSIONCASE
30. THRUST WASHER (2)
31. BEARING RETAINER (2)
32. COUNTERSHAFT NEEDLE BEARINGS (50)
33. COUNTERSHAFT GEAR
34. FRONT BEARING CAP
35. BOLT (4)
36. FRONT BEARING CAP OIL SEAL
37. GASKET
38. FRONT BEARING RETAINER SNAP RING
39. FRONT BEARING LOCKRING
40. FRONT BEARING
41. CLUTCH SHAFT
42. MAINSHAFT PILOT ROLLER BEARINGS
43. ROLL PIN
44. COUNTERSHAFT

T-150 Transmission—exploded view (© American Motors)

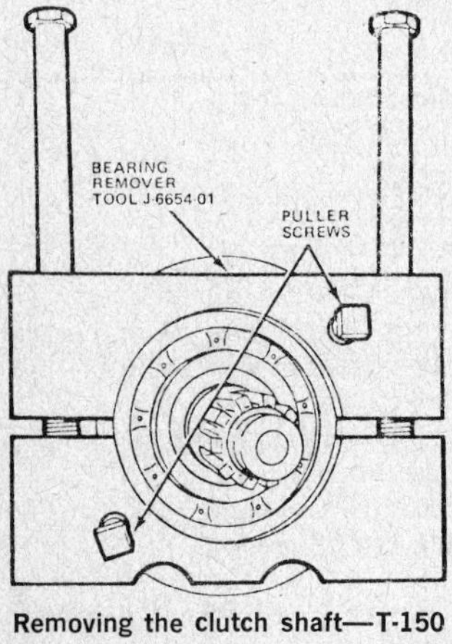

Removing the clutch shaft—T-150
(© American Motors)

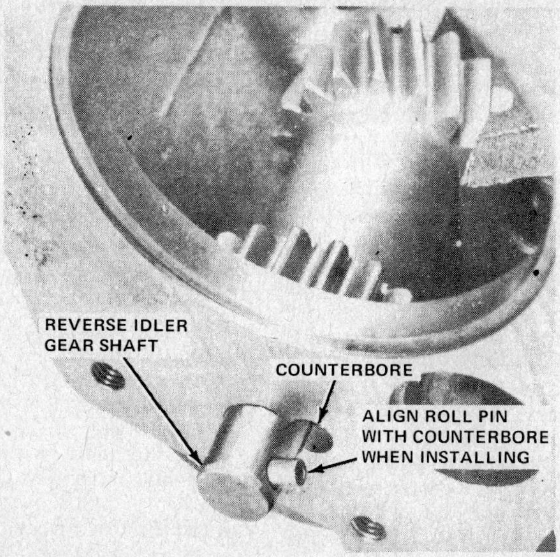

Removing or installing the reverse idler shaft— T-150 (© American Motors)

e. Broken or worn teeth or excessive wear of the blocking rings.
f. Wear of galling of the countershaft, clutch shaft, or reverse idler shaft.
g. Worn thrust washers.
h. Nicked, broken, or worn mainshaft or clutch shaft splines.
i. Bent, distorted, or weak snap rings.
j. Worn bushings in the reverse idler gear. Replace the gear if the bushings are worn.
k. Rough, galled, or broken front or rear bearings.

Assembly of Transmission

1. Lubricate the reverse idler shaft bore and bushings with transmission oil.
2. Coat the transmission case reverse idler gear thrust washer surfaces with petroleum jelly and install the thrust washers in the case.

NOTE: Make sure the locating tangs on the thrust washers are aligned in the slots in the case.

3. Install the reverse idler gear. Align the gear bore, thrust washers, and case bore. Install the reverse idler shaft from the rear of the transmission case. Be sure to align and seat the roll pin in the shaft into the counter bore in the rear of the case.
4. Measure the reverse idler gear end-play by inserting a feeler gauge between the thrust washer and the gear. End-play should be 0.004-0.018 inch. If end play exceeds 0.018 inch, remove the reverse idler gear and replace the thrust washers.
5. Coat the needle bearing bores in the countershaft gear with petroleum jelly. Insert the arbor tool in the bore of the gear and install the twenty-five (25) needle bearings and the retainer washers at each end of the countershaft gear.
6. Coat the countershaft gear thrust washer surface with petroleum jelly and position the thrust washers in the case.

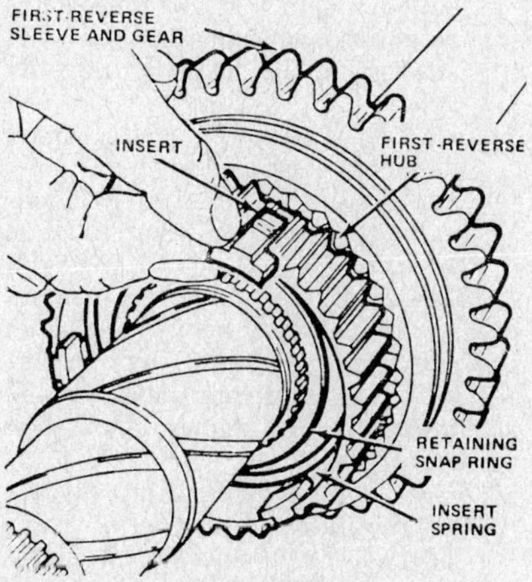

Installing the inserts in the first-reverse synchronizer hub-T-150 (© American Motors)

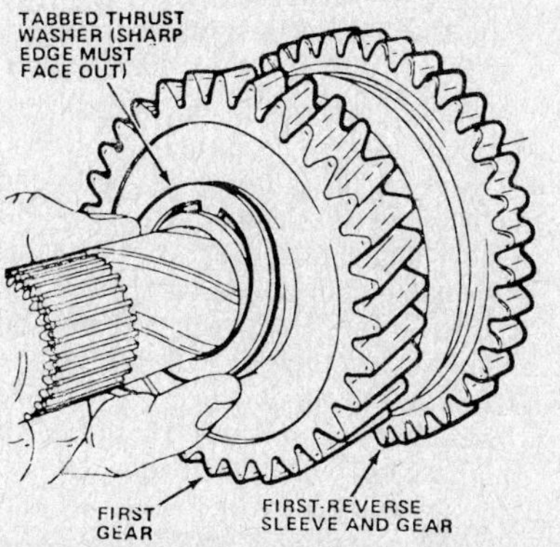

Installing the first gear thrust washer on the mainshaft— T-150 (© American Motors)

NOTE: Make sure the locating tangs on the thrust washers are aligned in the slots in the case.

7. Insert the countershaft into the bore at the rear of the case just far enough to hold the thrust washer in place.
8. Install the countershaft gear in the case. *Do not install the roll pin at this time.* Align the gear bore, thrust washers, the bores in the case, and install the countershaft.

NOTE: Do not remove the arbor tool completely.

9. Measure the countershaft gear end-play by inserting a feeler gauge between the washer and the countershaft gear. End-play should be 0.004-0.018 inch. If the end-play exceeds 0.018 inch, remove the gear and replace the thrust washer.
10. When the correct countershaft gear end-play has been obtained, install the countershaft arbor and remove the countershaft. Allow the countershaft gear to remain at the bottom of the case, leave the countershaft in the case enough to hold the thrust washer in place.
11. Coat the splines and machined surfaces on the mainshaft with transmission oil. Install the first-reverse synchronizer on the output shaft spines by hand. The end of the hub with the slots should face the front of the shaft. Use an arbor press to complete the hub installation. Install the retaining snap ring in the groove farthest to the rear.

CAUTION: Do not attempt to drive the hub on the shaft with a hammer.

12. Coat the splines of the first-reverse hub with transmission oil and install the first reverse sleeve and gear halfway onto the hub, with the gear end of the sleeve facing the rear of the shaft. Align the marks made during disassembly.
13. Install the insert spring in the first-reverse hub. Make sure the spring bottoms in the hub and

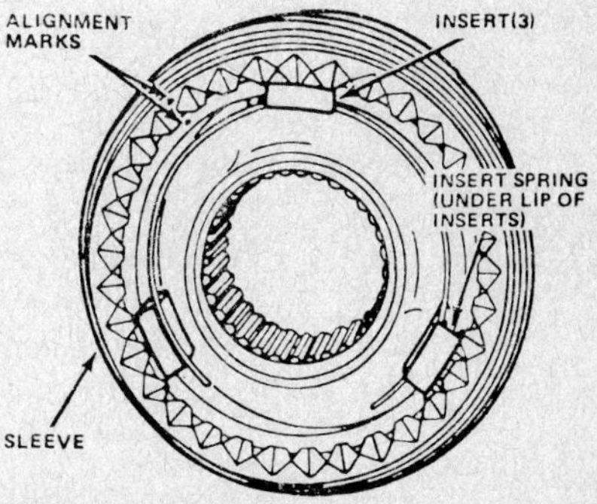

Installing the second gear on the mainshaft— T-150 (© American Motors)

covers all three insert slots. Position the three "T" shaped inserts in the hub with the small ends in the hub slots and the large ends inside the hub. Push the inserts fully into the hub so they seat on the insert spring, slide the first-reverse sleeve and gear over the inserts until the inserts engage in the sleeve.

14. Coat the bore and the blocking ring surface of first gear with transmission oil and place blocking ring on the tapered surface of the gear.
15. Install the first gear on the output shaft. Rotate the gear until the notches in the blocking ring engage the inserts in the first-reverse synchronizer assembly. Install the tanged thrust washer, sharp end facing out, and retaining snap ring on the mainshaft.
16. Coat the bore and blocking ring surface of the second gear with transmission oil. Place the second gear blocking ring on the tapered surface of second gear.
17. Install the second gear on the output shaft with the tapered surface of the gear facing the front of the mainshaft.
18. Install one insert spring into the second-third synchronizer hub. Be sure that the spring covers all three insert slots in the hub. Align the second-third sleeve with the hub using the marks made during disassembly. Start the sleeve onto the hub.
19. Place the three inserts into the hub slots and on top of the insert spring. Push the sleeve fully onto the hub to engage the inserts in the sleeve. Install the remaining insert spring in the exact position as the first spring. The ends of both springs must cover the same slot in the hub and not be staggered.

NOTE: The inserts have a small lip on each end. When they are correctly installed, this lip will fit over the insert spring.

20. Install the second-third synchronizer assembly on the mainshaft.

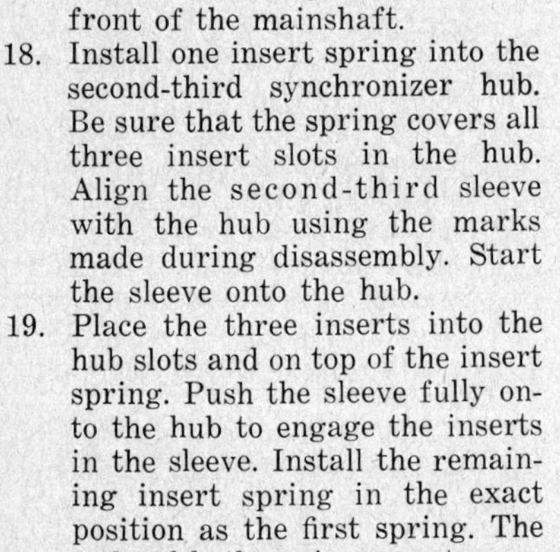

Measuring the mainshaft end-play—T-150
(© American Motors)

Rotate the second gear until the notches in the blocking ring engage the inserts in the second-third synchronizer assembly.

21. Install the retaining snap ring on the mainshaft and measure the end-play between the snap ring and the second-third synchronizer hub. The end-play should be 0.040-0.014 inch. If the end-play exceeds the limit, replace the thrust washer and all the snap rings on the mainshaft assembly. Install the spacer on the rear of the mainshaft.
22. Install the mainshaft assembly in the case. Be sure that the first-reverse sleeve and gear is in the neutral (centered) position.
23. Press the rear bearing into the rear bearing adapter with an arbor press. Install the rear bearing retaining ring and the bearing adapter lockring.
24. Support the mainshaft assembly and install the rear bearing and adapter assembly in the case. Use a soft faced hammer to seat the adapter in the case.
25. Install the large fiber washer in the rear bearing adapter. Install the transfer drive gear, flat washer, and locknut. Tighten the locknut to 150 ft-lbs. torque.
26. Press the front bearing onto the clutch shaft. Install the bearing retaining snap ring on the clutch shaft and the lockring into its groove.
27. Coat the bore of the clutch shaft assembly with petroleum jelly and install the fifteen (15) roller bearings in the clutch shaft bore.

CAUTION: Do not use chassis grease or a similar heavy grease in the clutch shaft bore. Heavy grease will plug the lubricant holes in the shaft and prevent proper lubrication of the roller bearings.

28. Coat the blocking ring surface of the clutch shaft with transmission oil. Position the blocking ring on the clutch shaft.
29. Support the mainshaft assembly and insert the clutch shaft through the front bearing bore in the case. Seat the mainshaft pilot in the clutch shaft roller bearings. Tap the bearings into place with a shoft faced hammer.
30. Apply a thin film of sealer to the front bearing cap gasket and position the gasket on the case. Be sure the cutout in the gasket is aligned with the oil return hole in the case.
31. Remove the front bearing cap oil seal with a suitable tool. Install a new seal with a suitable driver.
32. Install the front bearing cap and tighten the bolts to 33 ft-lbs. Be sure that the marks on the cap and the transmission case are aligned and the oil return slot in the cap lines up with the oil return hole in the case.
33. Make a wire loop about 18-20 inches long and pass the wire under the countershaft gear assembly. The wire loop should raise and support the countershaft gear assembly when it is pulled upward.
34. Raise the countershaft gear with the wire. Align the bore in the countershaft gear with the front thrust washer and the countershaft. Start the countershaft into the gear with a soft faced hammer.
35. Align the roll pin hole in the countershaft with the roll pin holes in the case and complete the installation of the countershaft. Install the countershaft access plug in the rear of the case and seat with a soft faced hammer.
36. Install the countershaft roll pin in the case. Use a magnet or needle nose pliers to insert and start the pin in the case. Use a ½ inch punch to seat the pin. Install the transmission filler plug.
37. Shift the synchronizer sleeves through all gear ranges and check their operation. If the clutch shaft and mainshaft appear to bind in the neutral position, check for blocking rings sticking on the first or second gear tapers.
38. Install the transfer case on the transmission. Tighten the attaching bolts to 30 ft-lbs.

Shift Control Housing

Disassembly

1. Remove the back-up light switch and the transmission controlled spark switch (TCS) if so equipped.
2. Remove the shift control housing cap, gasket, spring retainer, and the shift lever spring as an assembly.
3. Invert the housing and mount in a soft-jawed vise.
4. Move the second-third shift rail to the rear of the housing, rotate the shift fork toward the first-reverse rail until the roll pin is accessible. Drive the roll pin out of the fork and rail with a pin punch. Remove the shift fork and the roll pin.

NOTE: The roll pin hole in the shift fork is offset. Mark the position of the shift fork for assembly reference.

5. Remove the second-third shift rail using a brass drift or hammer. Catch the shift rail plug as the rail drives it out of the housing. Cover the shift and poppet

ball holes in the cover to prevent the poppet ball from flying out. Mark the location of the shift rail for assembly reference.

6. Rotate the first-reverse shift fork away from the notch in the housing until the roll pin is accessible. Drive the role pin out of the fork and rail using a pin punch. Remove the shift fork and roll pin.

NOTE: The roll pin hole in the shift fork is offset. Mark the position of the shift fork for assembly reference.

7. Remove the first-reverse shift rail using a brass drift or hammer. Catch the shift rail plug as the rail drives it out of the housing. Cover the shift and poppet ball holes in the cover to prevent the poppet ball from flying out. Mark the location of the shift rail for assembly reference.
8. Remove the poppet balls, springs, and the interlock plunger from the housing.

Assembly

1. Install the poppet springs and the detent plug in the housing.
2. Insert the first-reverse shift rail into the housing, and install the shift fork on the shift rail.
3. Install the poppet ball on the top of the spring in the first-reverse rail.
4. Using a punch or wooden dowel, push the poppet ball and spring downward into the housing bore and install the first-reverse shift rail.
5. Align the roll pin holes in the first-reverse shift fork and install the roll pin. Move the shift rail to the neutral (center) detent.
6. Insert the second-third shift rail into the housing and install the poppet ball on top of the spring in the shift rail bore.
7. Using a punch or wooden dowel, push the poppet ball and spring downward into the housing bore and install the second-third shift rail.

TORQUE SPECIFICATIONS

	Foot-Pounds
Back-up light switch	15-20
Fill and drain plugs	10-20
Front bearing cap bolt	30-36
Shift control housing bolts	20-25
Transfer case drive gear locknut	150
Transfer case to transmission bolts	30
TCS switch	18

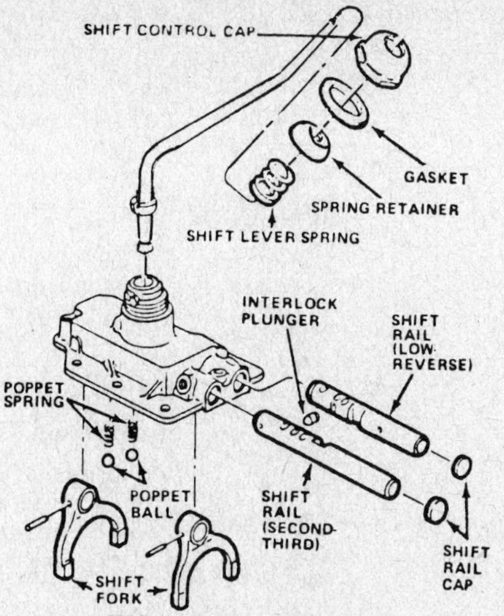

Shift control housing–T-150
(© American Motors)

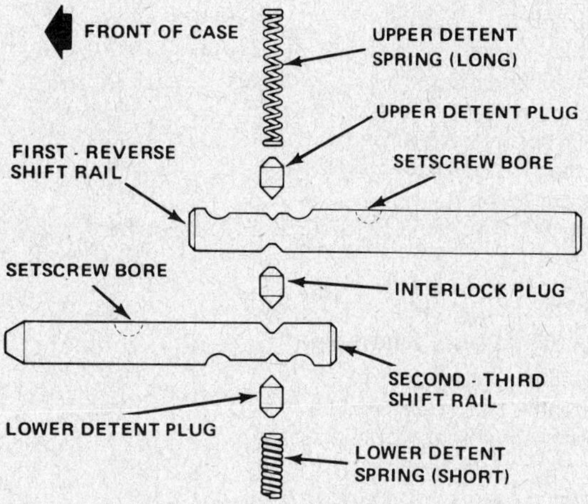

Installation Sequence—Interlock and Detent Plugs and Springs

8. Align the roll pin holes in the second-third shift rail and the shift fork and install the roll pin. Move the shift rail to the neutral (center) position.
9. Install the shift rail plugs in the housing, and remove the shift control cover from the vise.
10. Install the shift lever, shift lever spring, spring retainer, gasket, and the shift control housing cap as an assembly. Tighten the cap securely.
11. Install the back-up light switch and the TCS switch if so equipped.

LUBRICANT CAPACITY

SAE 80-90 Gear Lube	3 pts.

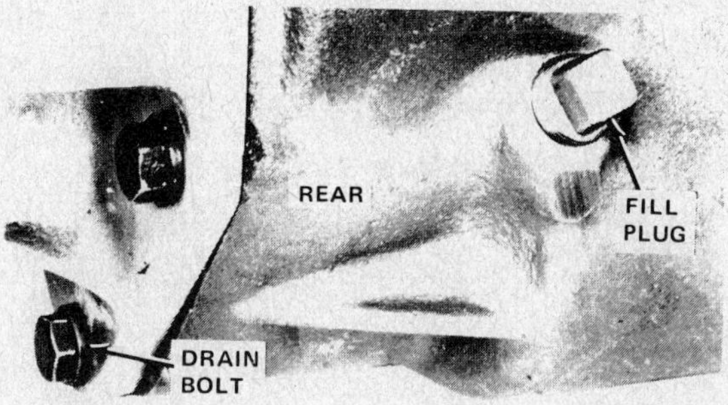

INDEX

DRIVE AXLE SERVICE DIAGNOSIS

Condition	Possible Cause	Correction
Rear Wheel Noise	(1) Wheel loose.	(1) Tighten loose nuts.
	(2) Faulty, brinelled wheel bearing.	(2) Faulty or brinelled bearings must be replaced. Check rear axle shaft end play.
	(3) Excessive axle shaft end play.	(3) Readjust axle shaft end play.
Rear Axle Drive Shaft Noise	(1) Misaligned axle housing.	(1) Inspect rear axle housing, alignment. Correct as necessary.
	(2) Bent or sprung axle shaft.	(2) Replace bent or sprung axle shaft.
	(3) End play in drive pinion bearings.	(3) Refer to Pinion Bearing Pre-load.
	(4) Excessive gear lash between ring gear and pinion.	(4) Check adjustment of ring gear and pinion. Correct as necessary.
	(5) Improper adjustment of drive pinion shaft bearings.	(5) Adjust pinion bearings.
	(6) Loose drive pinion companion flange nut.	(6) Tighten drive pinion flange nut to torque specified.
	(7) Improper wheel bearing adjustment.	(7) Check axle shaft end play. Readjust as necessary.
	(8) Scuffed gear tooth contact surfaces.	(8) If necessary, replace scuffed gears.
Rear Axle Drive Shaft Breakage	(1) Improperly adjusted wheel bearings.	(1) Replace broken shaft and readjust end play.
	(2) Misaligned axle housing.	(2) Replace broken shaft after correcting rear axle housing alignment.
	(3) Vehicle overloaded.	(3) Replace broken shaft. Avoid excessive weight on vehicle.
	(4) Abnormal clutch operation.	(4) Replace broken shaft, after checking for other possible causes. Avoid erratic use of clutch.
	(5) Grabbing clutch.	(5) Replace broken shaft. Inspect clutch and make necessary repairs or adjustments.
	(6) Normal fatigue.	(6) Replace broken shaft. Inspect to determine causes or damage.
Differential Case Breakage	(1) Improper adjustment of differential bearings.	(1) Replace broken case; examine gears and bearings for possible damage. At reassembly, adjust differential bearings.
	(2) Excessive ring gear clearance.	(2) Replace broken case; examine gears and bearings for possible damage. At reassembly, adjust ring gear and pinion backlash.
	(3) Vehicle overloaded.	(3) Replace broken case; examine gears and bearings for possible damage. Avoid excessive weight on vehicle.
	(4) Erratic clutch operation.	(4) Replace broken case. After checking for other possible causes, examine gears and bearings for possible damage. Avoid erratic use of clutch.
Differential Side Gear Broken at Hub	(1) Excessive axle housing deflection.	(1) Replace damaged gears. Examine other gears and bearings for possible damage. Check rear axle housing alignment.
	(2) Misaligned or bent axle shaft.	(2) Replace damaged gears. Check axle shafts or alignment. Examine other gears and bearings for possible damage.
	(3) Worn thrust washers.	(3) Replace damaged gears. Examine other gears and bearings for possible damage. Replace thrust washers that are badly worn.
Scoring of Differential Gears	(1) Insufficient lubrication.	(1) Replace scored gears. Scoring marks on the pressure face of gear teeth or in the bore are caused by instantaneous fusing of the mating surfaces. Scored gears should be replaced. Fill rear axle to required capacity with proper lubricant.
	(2) Improper grade of lubricant.	(2) Replace scored gears. Inspect all gears and bearings for possible damage. Clean out and refill axle to required capacity with proper lubricant.
	(3) Excessive spinning of one wheel.	(3) Replace scored gears. Inspect all gears, pinion bores and shaft for scoring, or bearings for possible damage. Service as necessary.
Tooth Breakage (Ring Gear and Pinion)	(1) Overloading.	(1) Replace gears. Examine other gears and bearings for possible damage. Replace parts as needed. Avoid overloading of vehicle.
	(2) Erratic clutch operation.	(2) Replace gears, and examine remaining parts for possible damage. Avoid erratic clutch operation.
	(3) Ice-spotted pavements.	(3) Replace gears. Examine remaining parts for possible damage. Replace parts as required.
	(4) Normal fatigue.	(4) Replace gears. Examine broken parts to determine cause of normal fatigue.
	(5) Improper adjustment.	(5) Replace gears. Examine other parts for possible damage. Make sure ring gear and pinion backlash is correct.

DRIVE AXLE SERVICE DIAGNOSIS

Condition	*Possible Cause*	*Correction*
Rear Axle Noise	(1) Insufficient lubricant.	(1) Refill rear axle with correct amount of the proper lubricant. Also check for leaks and correct as necessary.
	(2) Improper ring gear and pinion adjustment.	(2) Check ring gear and pinion tooth contact.
	(3) Unmatched ring gear and pinion.	(3) Remove unmatched ring gear and pinion. Replace with a new matched gear and pinion set.
	(4) Worn teeth on ring gear or pinion.	(4) Check teeth on ring gear and pinion for contact. If necessary, replace with new matched set.
	(5) Loose drive pinion bearings.	(5) Adjust drive pinion bearings.
	(6) Loose differential gear bearings.	(6) Adjust differential gear bearings.
	(7) Misaligned or sprung ring gear.	(7) Check ring gear for runout.
	(8) Loose carrier housing bolts.	(8) Tighten carrier housing nuts to Specifications. Also, check for oil leaks and correct as necessary.
Loss of Lubricant	(1) Lubricant level too high.	(1) Drain excess lubricant by removing filler plug and allow lubricant to level at lower edge of filler plug hole.
	(2) Worn axle shaft oil seals.	(2) Replace worn oil seals with new ones. Prepare new seals before replacement.
	(3) Cracked rear axle housing.	(3) Repair or replace housing as required.
	(4) Worn drive pinion oil seal.	(4) Replace worn drive pinion oil seal with a new one.
	(5) Scored and worn companion flange.	(5) Replace worn or scored companion flange and oil seal.
Overheating of Unit	(1) Lubricant level too low.	(1) Refill rear axle.
	(2) Incorrect grade of lubricant.	(2) Drain, flush and refill rear axle with correct amount of the proper lubricant.
	(3) Bearings adjusted too tightly.	(3) Readjust bearings.
	(4) Excessive wear in gears.	(4) Check gears for excessive wear or scoring. Replace as necessary.
	(5) Insufficient ring gear to pinion clearance.	(5) Readjust ring gear and pinion backlash and check gears for possible scoring.

Differential Component Failure Diagnosis

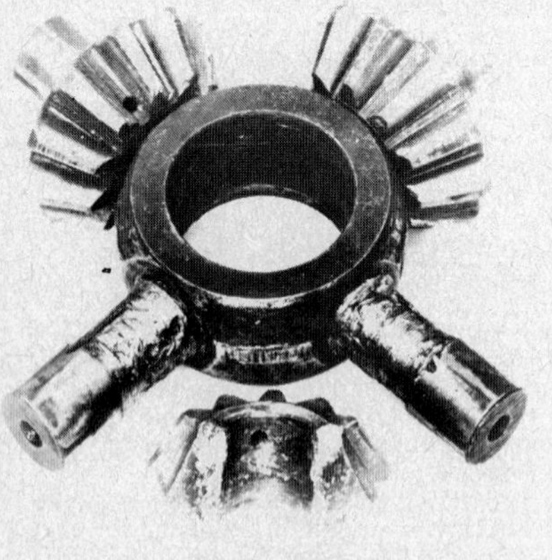

Scoring and seizure of spider and pinion gears

The spider arms and pinion gears were badly discolored by heat, caused by the unit operating for a long time after the initial scoring took place. The most probable cause of this type of failure is excessive wheelspin, particularly in off-road or icy road conditions. Other possible causes are inadequate lubrication or overstress. Friction causes the hardened areas to overheat, score, and eventually to seize. The best way to prevent this problem is to avoid wheelspin and overloading under rough terrain or poor traction conditions.

Shock fracture

These differential pinion and side gears show a grainy structure which indicates a shock fracture. This type of damage occurs instantaneously. The usual cause is a sudden excessive load, as might be caused by sudden clutch engagement at high engine speed. Another cause is a rapidly spinning wheel suddenly reaching a good traction area. This failure can be prevented by proper clutch operation, and by avoiding wheelspin and overloading under rough terrain or poor traction conditions.

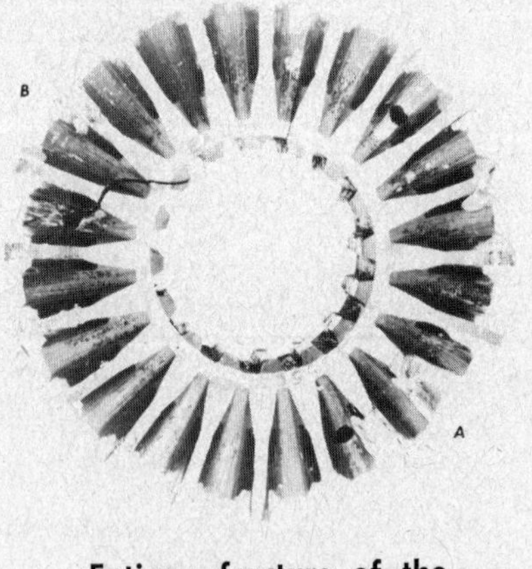

Fatigue fracture of the differential side gears

This damage occurs in stages. An initial stress caused a crack, and repeated stresses caused complete failure. Some of the gear teeth were broken off in the later stages. The failures can be seen best at points A and B. All differential gears should be checked when this type of failure is found, very often the other gears will be in the initial stages of failure and must be replaced. This is most often caused by abuse such as sudden clutch engagement or incorrect two-speed axle operation, combined with overloading.

Differential Component Failure Diagnosis

SCORED AND SCUFFED GEAR TEETH

This wear pattern is a result of the gear running without enough lubrication between the tooth surfaces. Either poor quality gear lube or low lubrication level can cause this condition. Excessive torque input to the rear can also cause this wear since it will break down even the best of gear lube. Changing gear lube at regular recommended intervals and keeping excessive torque input to a minimum will usually prevent this problem.

FATIGUE FRACTURED PINION GEAR

This type of fracture develops over a period of time. The fracture works through the gear tooth until the tooth is not strong enough to support the load applied. Failure happens and a section of the tooth breaks away. Continued use of pitted gears is the usual cause of this type of gear failure. As the gear pits, the support area is reduced and must carry the entire load of the gear tooth. As this continues the gear tooth fatigues and the final result is failure of the gear. To prevent this problem the ring and pinion must be replaced if there is any pitting on the gears.

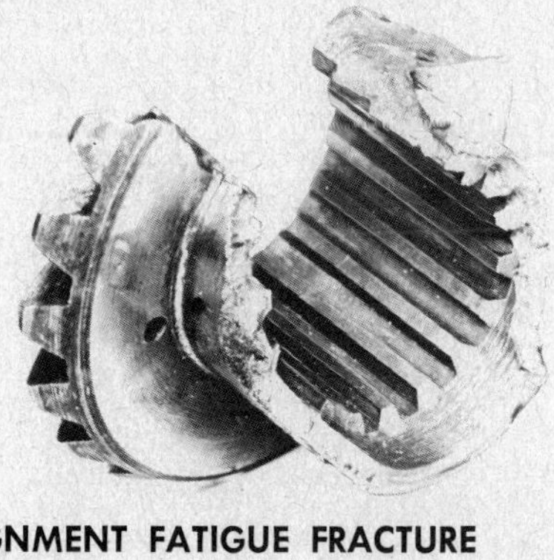

MISALIGNMENT FATIGUE FRACTURE

This problem comes from misalignment in the axle shaft. This kind of failure can also happen when the axle shaft breaks. If twisted, bent or sprung axle shaft are not replaced after they are damaged, this kind of failure to the side gears can occur. Bent axle housing can also cause this to happen. In most cases, this type of failure is not instantaneous. It tends to happen over a period of time. The usual cause of this type of failure is abusive operation of the vehicle and severe overloading.

OVERHEATED GEAR SET

This problem can be caused by one of three, or any combination of the following circumstances. The causes are low gear lubricant level; improper gear lubricant; or infrequent lubricant change. When one or more of these conditions is present in the rear, it causes the lubricant to break down and allows the gear surface to build up heat because of increased friction. In the failure shown, the gears became so hot the pinion bearing fused to the pinion gear and the pinion gear teeth became distorted. To prevent this problem a good quality gear lubricant must be used in the rear to prevent the breakdown of lubricant under a heavy load.

FRACTURED GEAR TEETH

This problem is caused by improper gear adjustment. The picture on the left shows the result of excessive backlash between the ring and pinion gear. Such backlash allows overloading of the heel section of the gear; gear fracture will follow. The picture on the right shows the result of too little backlash thus allowing the toe section of the gear to overload and become fractured. The best way to eliminate this problem is to correctly adjust the ring and piston gears, when necessary, according to specifications.

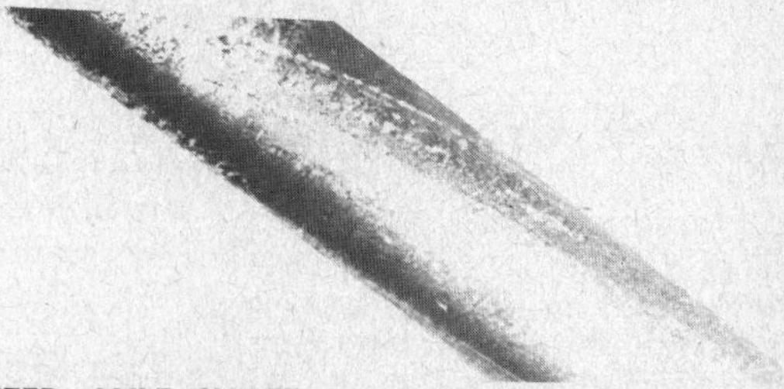

TWISTED AXLE SHAFT

This problem with the axle comes from abusive and/or extremely severe operation of the vehicle. This is only the first stage of failure where the axle shaft has only twisted, but has not yet started to crack. At this stage the shaft should be replaced. If it is not, the shaft will continue to twist and eventually will break. When this happens it will almost certainly damage other axle parts. To eliminate this problem, the shaft should be replaced if found to be twisted. The driver of the vehicle should be informed to adopt better driving procedures.

Differential Component Failure Diagnosis

PITTED PINION TEETH

This problem is the result of extremely high pressure on the gear teeth due to severe use. The pitting located at the hell end of the pinion gear teeth happens when overloading of the pinion moves the pinion out of its proper position relative to the ring gear. The result is a concentrated area of contact on the heel part of the gear teeth which will break down the oil film, and thus allow the pinion teeth to pit. Sometimes the ring gear will appear to be undamaged. This is because ring gear damage might not be visible to the naked eye; but the contour of the gear teeth will have changed. The ring and pinion gears must be replaced as a pair, or early failure will occur. The best way to eliminate this problem is to use good quality gear lube. The more severely the vehicle is used the better quality the gear lube should be.

SCUFFED GEAR TEETH ON THE COAST SIDE ONLY

This wear can be caused by two different things. The first is worn pinion bearing which allows excessive end play in the pinion gear. The result is incorrect contact between the ring and pinion gear teeth on the coast side. This allows excessive pressure to build up on the gear teeth and will break down the oil film. resulting in scoring of the teeth. The second cause is hard, abusive driving in vehicles equipped with a manual transmission. This usually happens when going down a steep grade at high speed and slowing the vehicle by using the clutch to break the speed. The best way to eliminate this problem is to replace the pinion bearing if worn and recommend good driving procedures.

General Axle Service Section

Types of Drive Axles

Full Floating Axles

Support of the vehicle and the payload weight is by the axle housing. The wheels are driven by splined shafts which "float" within the axle housing.

Semi-Floating Axle

This axle design provides for the support of the payload and vehicle weight to be carried by the axle shaft through the wheel bearings to the axle housing.

Single Reduction Axle

Final drive ratio is obtained by the use of a single ring gear and pinion set. This type is used for most light and medium duty applications.

Axle Service and Inspection

Cleaning Bearings

Proper bearing cleaning is important. Bearings should always be cleaned separately from other rear axle parts.

1. Soak all bearings in clean kerosene or Diesel fuel oil. CAUTION: **Gasoline should not be used. Bearings should not be cleaned in hot solution tank.**
2. Slush bearings in cleaning solution until all oil lubricant is loosened. Brush bearings with soft bristled brush until ALL dirt has been removed. Remove loose particles of dirt by striking flat against a wood block.
3. Rinse bearings in clean fluid. While holding races to prevent rotation, blow dry with compressed air. CAUTION: **Do not spin bearings while drying.**
4. After bearings have been inspected, lubricate thoroughly with regular axle lubricant; then wrap each bearing in clean cloth until ready to use.

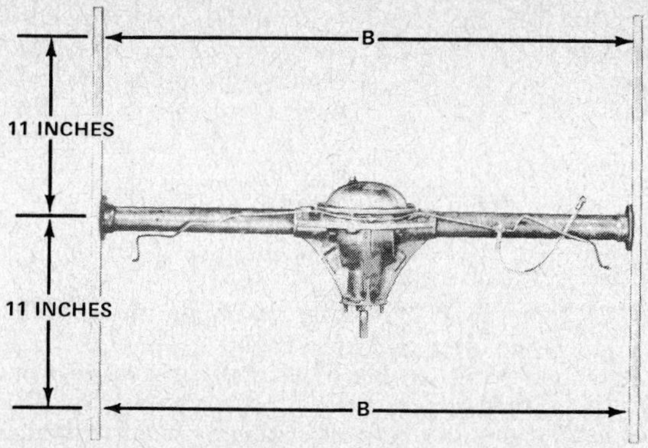

Checking housing alignment with straight edge bars
(© American Motors Corp.)

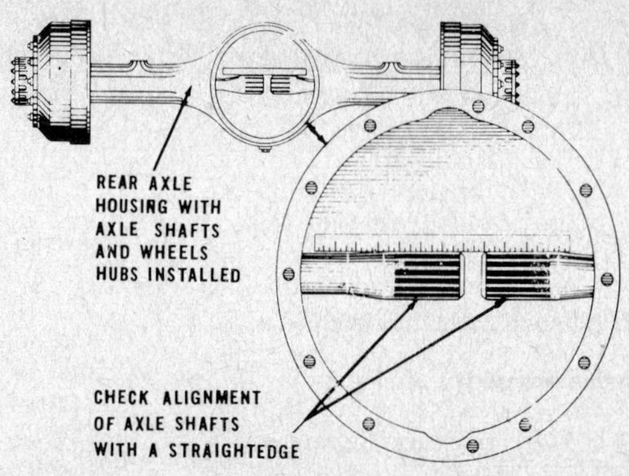

Method of checking axle housing alignment—with full floating axles (© International Harvester Co.)

Cleaning Parts

Immerse all parts in suitable cleaning fluid and clean thoroughly. Use a stiff bristle brush as required to remove foreign deposits. Clean all lubricant passages or channels in pinion cage, carrier, caps and retainers. Make certain that interior of housing is thoroughly cleaned. Clean vent plugs and breathers.

Small parts such as cap screws, bolts, studs, nuts etc., should be cleaned thoroughly.

Inspection

Magna Flux all steel parts, except ball and roller bearings, to detect presence of wear and cracks.

Bearings

Rotate each bearing and check to see if the rollers are worn, chipped, rough or in any other way damaged. Check the cage to see if it is in any way damaged. If either the bearing rollers or the cage are damaged the bearing must be replaced.

Gears

Examine drive gear and drive pinion, differential pinions and differential side gears carefully, for damaged teeth, worn spots in surface hardening, distortion and where drive gear is attached to differential case with rivets, inspect rivets for looseness, replace loose rivets. Check radial clearances between differential side gears and differential case. Check fit of differential pinions on spider.

Checking drive gear run-out
(© G.M. Corp.)

Differential Case

Inspect case for cracks, distortion or damage, if in good condition, thoroughly clean case and cover; then assemble case with bolts and mount in lathe centers of "V" block stand. If lathe is not available, install differential side bearings and mount case in differential carrier. Install dial indicator and check differential case run out.

Differential case with drive gear installed is checked in the same manner, except that dial indicator reading must be taken at gear instead of at case flange.

Whenever run-out exceeds limits, it may be corrected as later described under "Repair" in this section. However, the support case used in the 2-speed axle cannot be repaired and should be replaced with new case.

Axle Shafts

Examine splined end of axle shaft for twisted or cracked splines, twisted shaft, and worn dowel holes in flange. Install new shafts if necessary.

Install axle shaft assembly in lathe centers and check shaft run-out with dial indicator, if run-out exceeds limits, replace shaft. Place dial indicator so that indicator shaft end contacts inner surface of flange near outer edge of flange and check flange run-out.

Shims

Carefully inspect shims for uniform thickness. Where various thickness of shims are used in a pack, it is recommended that the thickest shims be used between the thin shims.

Thrust Washers

Replace all thrust washers.

Spider

Carefully inspect spider arms for wear or defects.

Differential Pinion Bushings

Examine bushings (when used) for excessive wear, looseness, or damage. Check fit of gears on spider for excessive clearance. See "repair" paragraph for directions on bushing replacement.

Axle Housing Sleeves

Sleeves showing damaged threads, wear, or other damage should be replaced if hydraulic press is available, otherwise replace housing.

Housing Check

Before Removal

A check for bent axle housing can be made with unit in vehicle; however, conventional alignment instruments can be used if available.

1. Raise rear axle with a jack until wheels clear floor. Block up axle under each spring seat.
2. Check wheel bearing adjustment and adjust if necessary, then check wheels for looseness and tighten wheel nuts if necessary.
3. Place a chalk mark on outer side wall of tires at bottom. Measure across tires at chalk marks with a toe-in gauge.
4. Turn wheels half-way around so that chalk marks are positioned at top of wheel. Measure across tires again. If measurement at top is 1/8" or more, smaller than measurement at bottom of wheels, axle housing has sagged and is bent. If measurement at top exceeds bottom dimension by 1/8" or more, axle housing is bent at ends.
5. Turn chalk marks on both wheels so that marks are level with axle and at rear of vehicle. Take measurement with toe-in gauge at chalk marks; then turn both chalk marks to front and level with axle and take another measurement. If measurement at front exceeds rear dimension by 1/8" or more, axle is bent to the rear. If the measurement condition is the reverse, the axle is bent forward.

After Removal

Place two straightedges across the housing flanges and measure the distance between the ends of the straightedges at a point 11 inches from the tube center. Relocate the straightedge 180 degrees and remeasure. If the straightedges are parallel in both measurements within 3/32 inch, the housing is serviceable.

General Repair

Oil Seal Contact Surfaces

Surface of parts, contacted by oil seals must be free of corrosion, pits and grooves. When abrasive cleaning fails to clean up the seal contact surface and restore smooth finish, a new part must be installed.

Oil Seal

Removal

Oil seals can be removed with a drift pin. When removing a seal, be careful that it does not become cocked and result in damage to the retainer. Clean surface of retainer carefully, so that seal will seat properly in retainer.

Installation

Coat outer surface of seal retainer with a light coat of sealer, to prevent lubricant leaks. Carefully start seal in retainer. Cutting, scratching, or curling of lip of seal seriously impairs its efficiency and usually results in premature replacement. Lip of seal should be coated with a high temperature grease containing zinc oxide to help prevent scoring and damage to parts during installation.

Seals must always be installed so that seal lip is toward the lubricant.

Pinion Bearing Adjustments (Pre-Load)

Pinion bearing must be adjusted for pre-load before assembly is installed in carrier.

Do not install oil seal until after adjustment is made—installation of seal would produce false rotating torque.

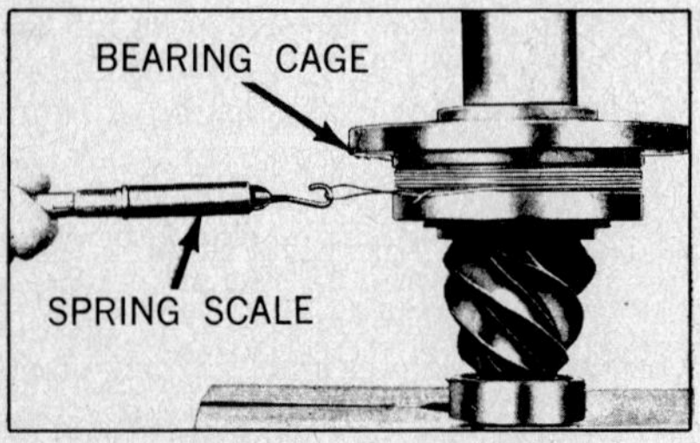

Checking pinion bearing pre-load (© G.M. Corp.)

Cage Type

1. With pinion bearings, and adjusting spacers (or shims) installed in cage, check bearing contact by rotating cage.
2. Using a press, apply pressure (approx. 20,000 lbs.) to outer bearing.
3. Wrap soft wire around cage and pull on horizontal line with spring scale. Rotating (not starting) torque should be within limits recommended by manufacturer. *NOTE: Method of determining inch-pounds torque with scale is to determine radius of cage. Multiply radius in inches by pounds pull required to rotate cage to determine inch-pounds torque. Example: An 8-inch diameter divided by 2 equals 4-inch radius. Multiply 4-inch (radius) by 5 pounds (pull) equals 20 inch pounds torque.*
4. If press is not available, check preload torque by installing propeller shaft yoke, washer, and nut and torque to specifications; then check as previously explained. Remove yoke after correct adjustment is obtained.

Bevel Gear Shaft Bearing Adjustment

Bevel gear shaft bearings must be adjusted for pre-load before pinion and cage assembly and differential assembly are installed in carrier.

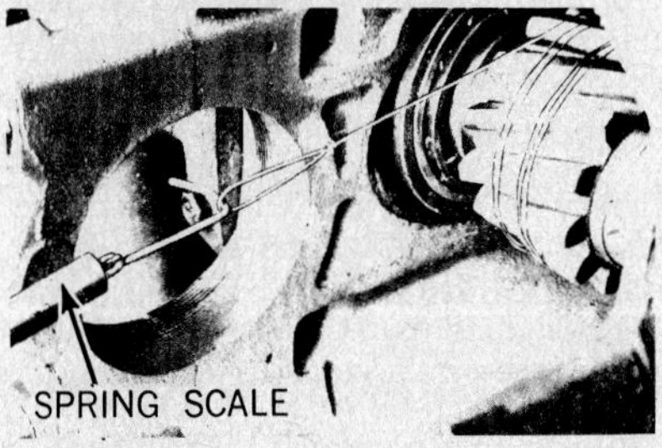

Checking pre-load on bevel gear cross shaft (© G.M. Corp.)

1. Wrap several turns of soft wire around gear teeth on cross shaft, then pull on a horizontal line with spring scale. Rotating (not starting) torque should be used. *NOTE: Method of determining inch-pounds torque with scale is to determine radius. Multiply radius in inches by pounds pull required to rotate shaft to determine inch-pounds torque. Example: An 8-inch diameter divided by 2 equals 4-inch radius times 5 pounds (pull) equals 20 inch-pounds torque.*
2. Remove or add shims from under cage or cap opposite bevel gear to obtain specified bearing pre-load.
3. When making bevel gear and pinion tooth contact or backlash adjustments it is sometimes necessary to remove or add shims from one side. *Always remove or add an equal thickness to the opposite side so to maintain correct pre-load.*

Gear Tooth Contact and Backlash

Pinion Depth Measurement Methods

Methods of adjusting pinions to obtain the proper depths will vary with the axle type and the manufactures recommendations. Pinion depth settings and gear teeth contact may be determined by the use of pinion setting gauges or by the use of marking dye on the gear teeth.

When using the gauge method, backlash is established after the pinion has been properly set. With the dye method, backlash is obtained first, then the proper pinion tooth contact is established.

The pinion gauge method can be a direct reading micrometer, mounted on or through an arbor bar, set in adapter discs and located in the side carrier bearing cup locations on the differential housing and held in place by the bearing cup caps. The arbor bar coincides and represents the center line of the axle shafts. A reading is taken by the mounted micrometer, from the arbor bar to the head of the pinion to determine the need to add to or remove shims from the shim pack total, to adjust the pinion to the proper nominal assembly dimension or standard pinion depth.

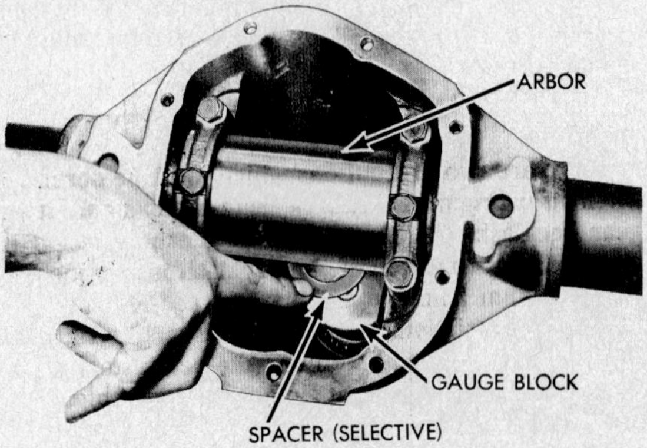

Determining proper shim pack thickness for drive pinion depth of mesh (© Chrysler Corp.)

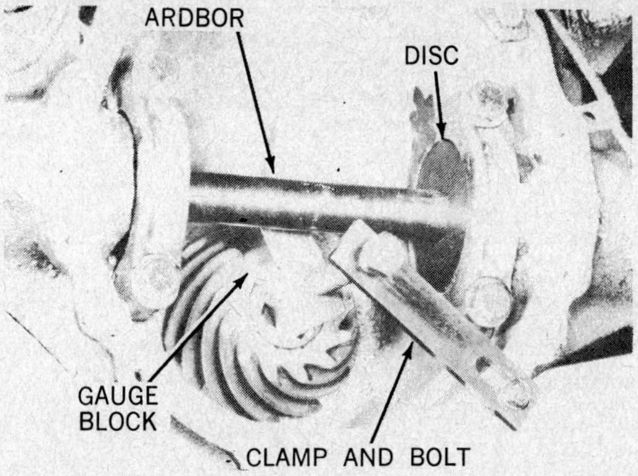

Placement of arbor and gauge block for pinion depth measurement (© Jeep Corp.)

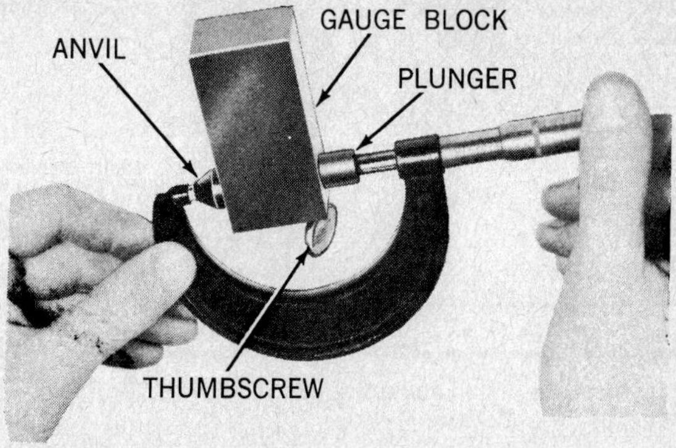

Method of measurement of the gauge block (© Jeep Corp.)

Another method using the arbor bar and discs, is the use of a gauge block with a spring loaded plunger and a thumb screw to lock the plunger upon expansion. A micrometer is used to measure the gauge block after the plunger has been allowed to expand between the arbor bar and the pinion head. As in the mounted micrometer procedure, the shim pack thickness is determined by the reading obtained.

A third method is the use of a gauge block tool, installed in the housing in place of the pinion gear, and a large arbor bar placed in the axle housing differential bearing seats and tightened securely. A measurement is taken between the arbor bar and the pinion tool by either a feeler gauge or the use of individual shims from the shim pack. This measurement represents the shim pack needed for a zero marked pinion.

Setting New Pinion (Without Gauge)

Whenever a pinion setting gauge is not available, the approximate thickness of the pinion shim pack at the rear pinion bearing cup, change the sign of the marking (individual variation distance) on the *new* pinion (plus to minus or minus to plus), then add the variation of the old pinion (sign unchanged) which will determine the amount the original shim pack must be changed when installing a new pinion.

On those types of axles where the shims are located between the pinion cage and differential carrier, change the sign of the marking (individual variation distance) on the *old* pionion (plus to minus or minus to plus), then add variation of the new pinion (sign unchanged) which will determine how much the original shim pack must be altered when installing a new pinion.

When the approximate thickness of shim pack has been determined, final check of gear tooth contact must be made using dye method.

Gear Tooth Contact (dye)

Gear tooth contact cannot be successfully accomplished until pinion and bevel gear bearings are in proper adjustment and gear backlash is within specified limits.

Check for proper tooth contact by painting a few teeth of bevel gear with marking dye. Turn pinion in direction of normal rotation, then check tooth impression on bevel gear.

Gear Backlash

Gears that have been in extended service, form running contacts due to wear of teeth; therefore the original shim pack (between pinion cage and carrier) should be maintained when checking backlash. If backlash exceeds maximum tolerance, reduce backlash only in the amount that will avoid overlap of worn tooth section. Smoothness and roughness can be noted by rotating bevel gear.

If a slight overlap is present at worn tooth section, rotation will be rough.

If new gears are installed, check backlash with dial indicator.

Backlash is increased by moving bevel gear away from pinion, and

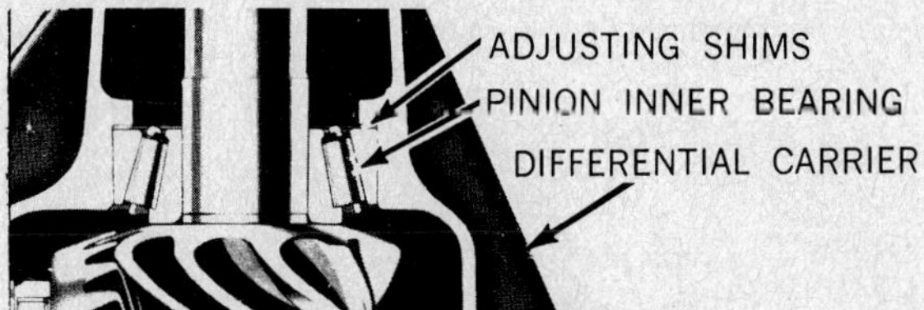

Pinion Markings Old Pinion	Pinion Markings New Pinion	Difference Between Markings
+5	+8	−3 Remove .003″ Shim
+8	+5	+3 Add .003″ Shim
−3	−5	+2 Add .002″ Shim
−5	−3	−2 Remove .002″ Shim
−3	+4	−7 Remove .007″ Shim
+2	−4	+6 Add .006″ Shim

The sign of the new pinion is changed and then added algebraically to the old pinion sign.

Determining pinion shim pack thickness (if shim pack is located at rear pinion bearing cup) (© G.M. Corp.)

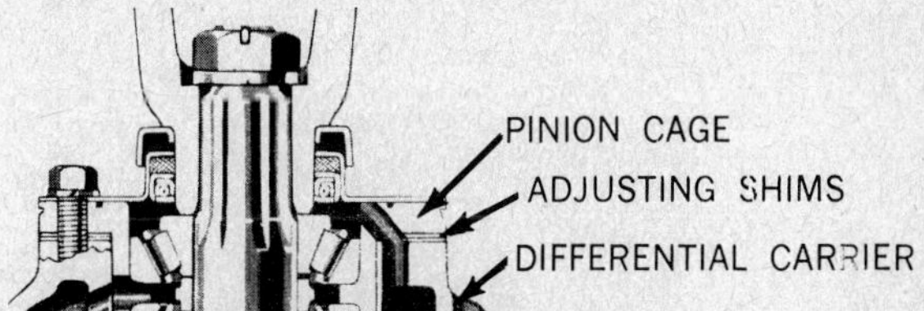

Pinion Markings Old Pinion	Pinion Markings New Pinion	Difference Between Markings
+8	+6	−2 Remove .002″ Shims
+6	−2	−8 Remove .008″ Shims
−4	+4	+8 Add .008″ Shims
+2	+6	+4 Add .004″ Shims
−7	−4	+3 Add .003″ Shims
−2	−6	−4 Remove .004″ Shims

The sign of the old pinion is changed and then added algebraically to the new pinion sign.

Determining pinion shim pack thickness (if shims are located between pinion cage and differential carrier) (© G.M. Corp.)

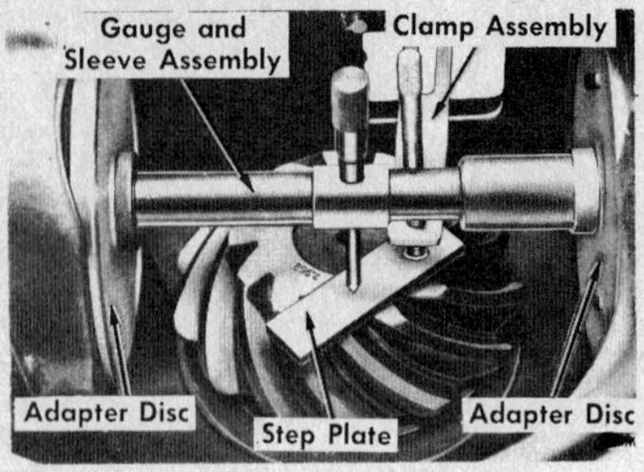

Installment of pinion gauge (Timken 2-speed) (© G.M. Corp.)

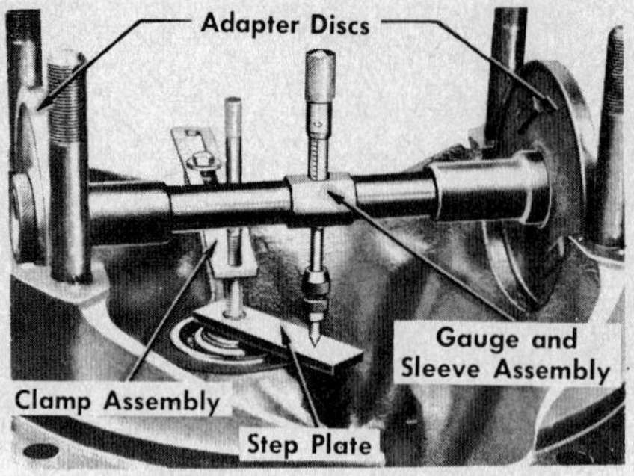

Position of pinion setting gauge (© G.M. Corp.)

Checking gear backlash (bevel gear) (© G.M. Corp.)

PAINTING GEAR TEETH

CORRECT TYPE TOOTH CONTACT

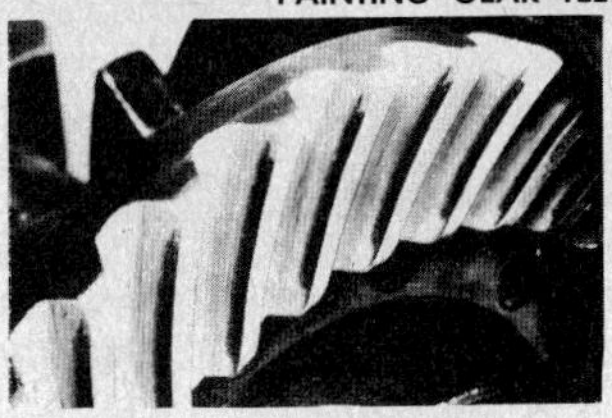

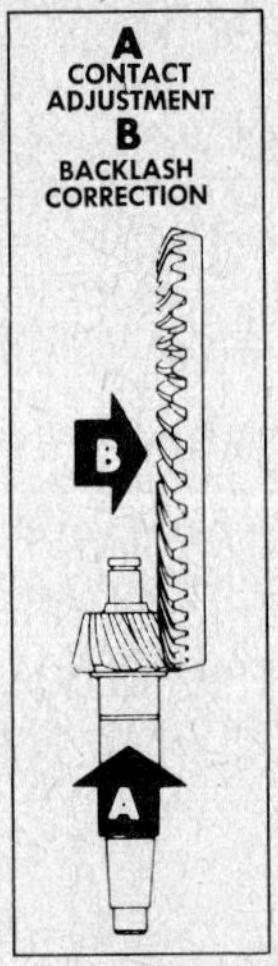

A HIGH NARROW CONTACT is not desirable. If gears are permitted to operate with an adjustment of this kind, noise, galling and rolling over of top edge of teeth will result. To obtain correct contact, move pinion toward bevel gear. This lowers contact area to proper location. This adjustment will decrease the backlash which may be corrected by moving bevel gear away from pinion.

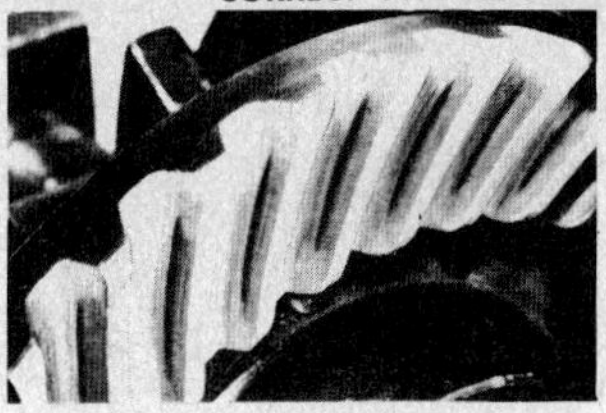

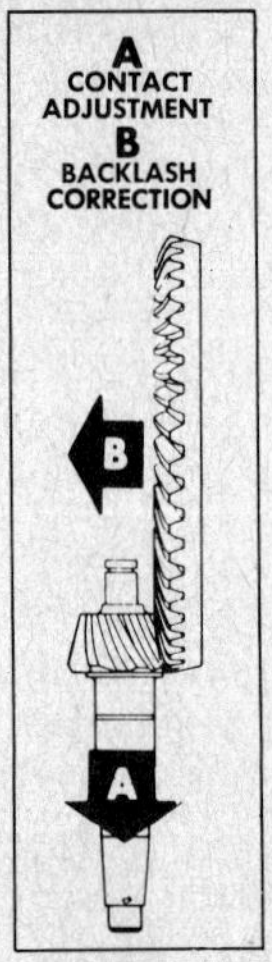

A LOW NARROW CONTACT is not desirable. If gears are permitted to operate with an adjustment of this type, galling, noise and grooving of teeth will result. To obtain correct cc itact, move pinion away from drive gear. This will raise contact area to proper location. A correct backlash is obtained by moving bevel gear toward pinion.

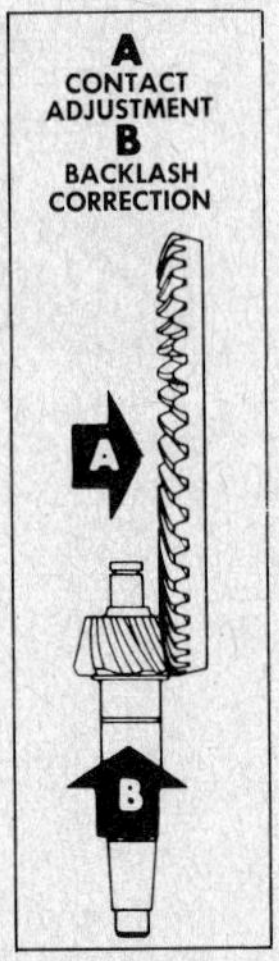

A SHORT TOE CONTACT is not desirable. If gears are permitted to operate with an adjustment of this type, chipping at tooth edges and excessive wear due to small contact area will result. To obtain correct contact, move drive gear from pinion. This will increase the lengthwise contact and move contact toward heel of tooth. Correct backlash is obtained by moving pinion toward bevel gear.

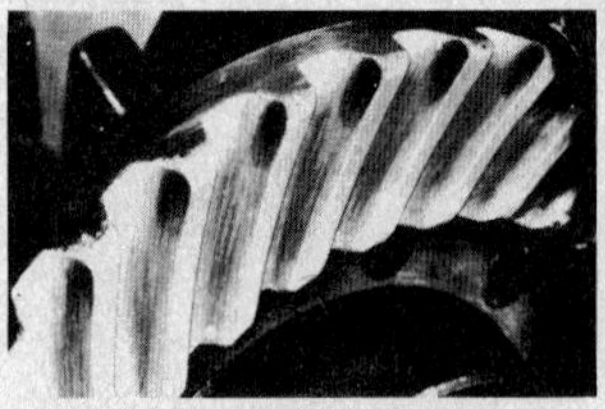

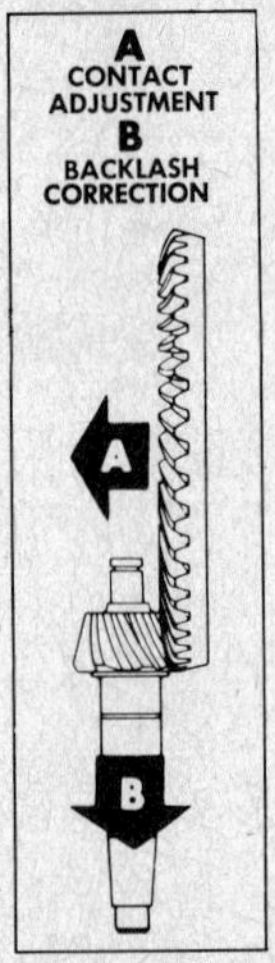

A SHORT HEEL CONTACT is not desirable. If gears are permitted to operate with an adjustment of this type, chipping, excessive wear and noise will result. To obtain correct contact, move drive gear toward pinion to increase lengthwise contact and move contact toward toe. A correct backlash is obtained by moving pinion away from drive gear.

Gear tooth contact chart (© G.M. Corp.)

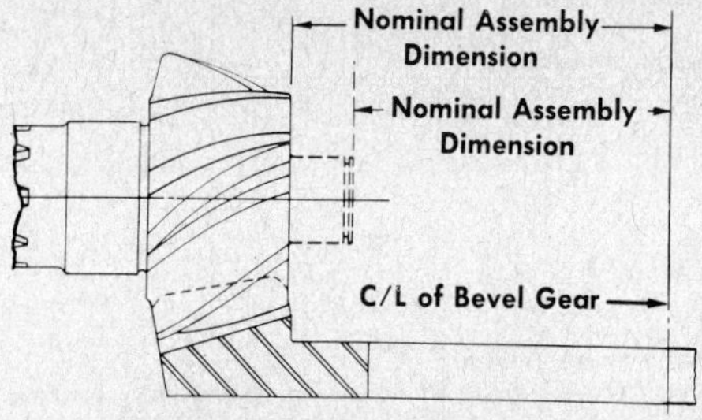

Nominal assembly dimension
(© G.M. Corp.)

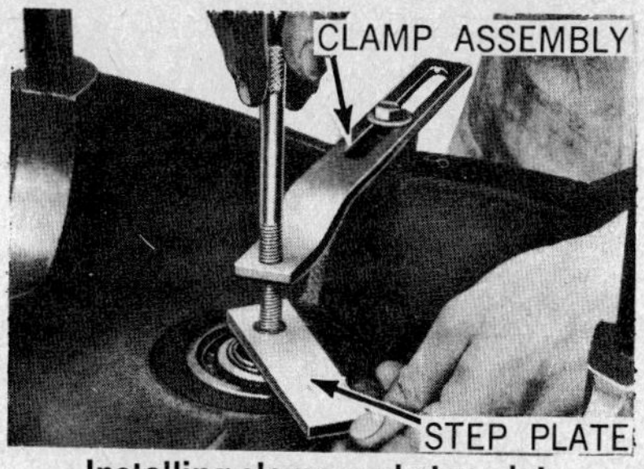

Installing clamp and step plate
(© G.M. Corp.)

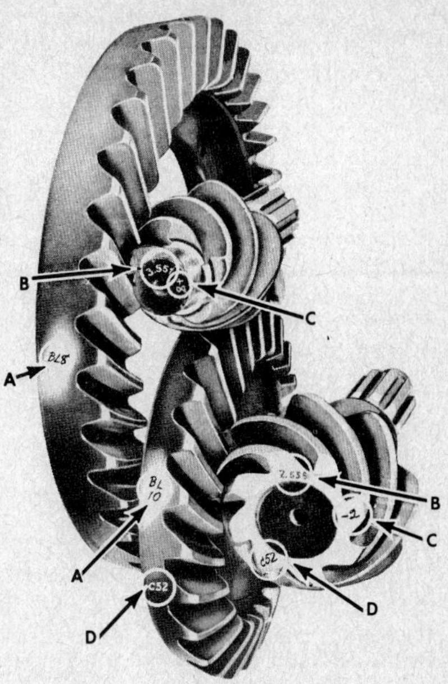

A Backlash
B Nominal assembly dimension
C Individual variation distance
D Gear and pinion matching number

Pinion and bevel gear markings—typical (© G.M. Corp.)

may be decreased by moving bevel gear toward pinion.

When the drive gear is attached to the differential, backlash is accomplished at differential bearing adjusting rings. It should be remembered that when one ring is tightened, the opposite ring must be loosened an equal amount to maintain previously established bearing adjustment.

On axles where the bevel gear is supported by cross shaft, backlash is accomplished by adding or removing shims under bearing cages.

Terms Used

Certain dimensions must be determined when using the pinion setting gauge:

1. *Nominal Assembly Dimension.* (Standard Pinion depth) This dimension (varying with axle model) is the distance between the center line of the drive gear (or differential carrier bore) and the end of the drive pinion. This dimension may be marked on the pinion or listed on the "Nominal Assembly Dimension and Adapter Disc" chart.
2. *Individual Variation Distance,* (Pinion depth variance) This dimension is a plus or minus variation of the *Nominal Assembly*
3. *Corrected Nominal Dimension* (Desired Pinion depth) This dimension is the *Nominal Assembly Dimension* plus or minus the *Individual Variation Distance.*
4. *Corrected Micrometer Distance* is the *Corrected Nominal Dimension* less the thickness of the gauge set step plate (0.400″) mounted on end of pinion.
5. *Initial Micrometer Reading* is the dimension taken by micrometer to the gauge step plate.
6. *Shim Pack Correction* is deter-

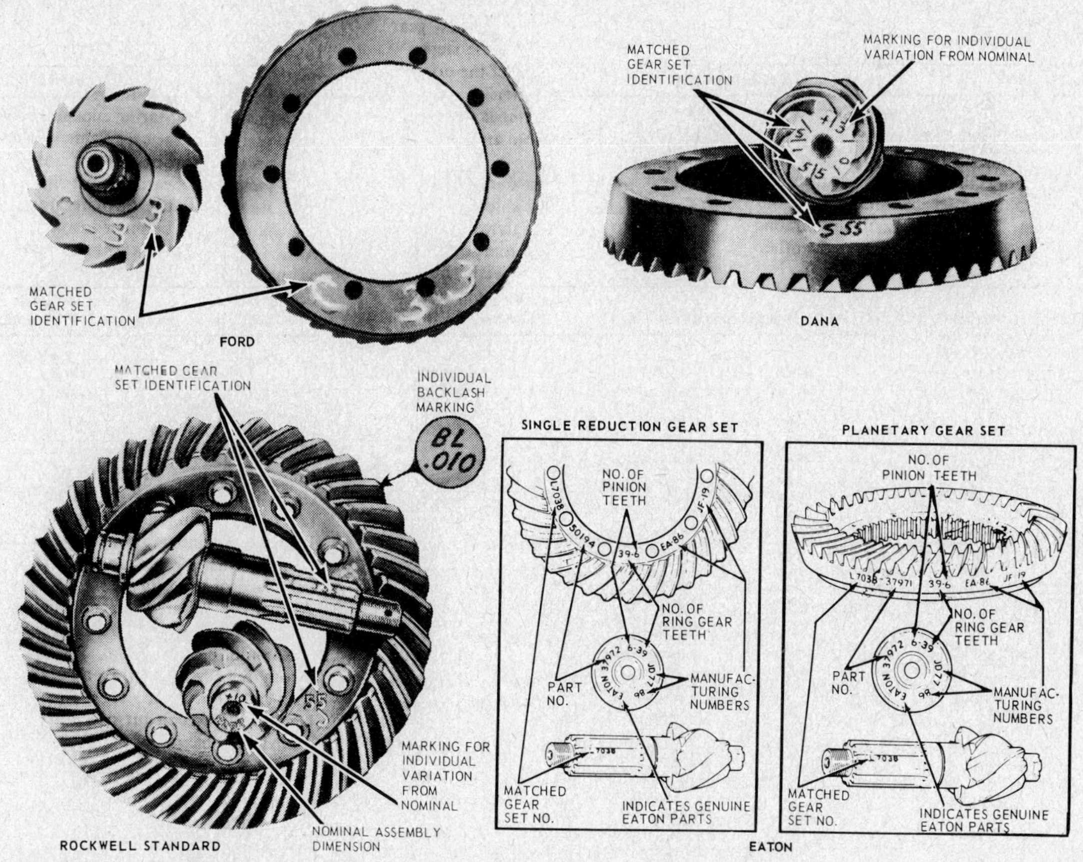

Typical gear set marking codes (© Ford Motor Co.)

Dimension on each individual pinion which may be caused by manufacturing variations.
mined by the difference between the *Corrected Micrometer Distance* and the *Initial Micrometer Reading,* and represents the amount of shim pack to be added or removed as later explained.

7. *Measured Pinion Depth.* This measurement is the distance between the axle center line and the top of the pinion gear. If a step plate or other type gauge tool is used, this measurement is included in the total.

Markings on the Pinion and Drive Gears

Drive gears and pinions are tested at the time of manufacture to detect machining variances and to obtain desirable tooth contact and quietness.

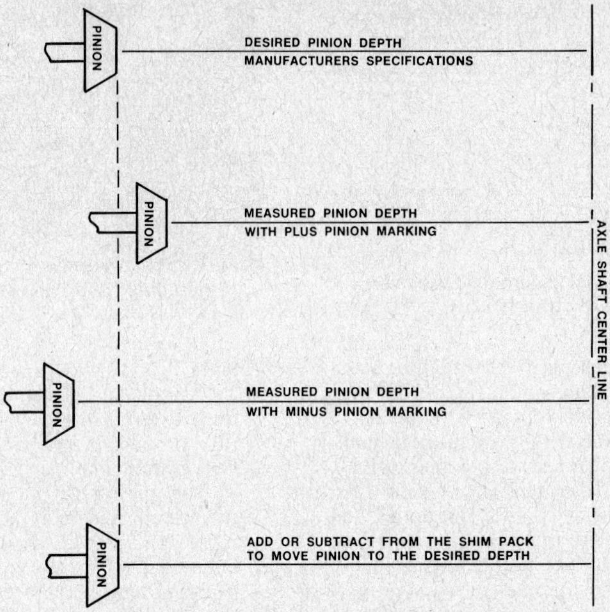

Movement of pinion to obtain desired pinion depth

BOLT TORQUE SPECIFICATIONS

SAE Grade Number	1 or 2	5	6 or 7	8
Capscrew Head Markings Manufacturer's marks may vary. Three-line markings on heads shown below, for example, indicate SAE Grade 5. 	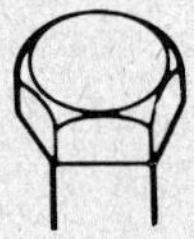		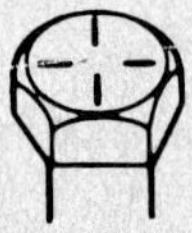	
Usage	Used Frequently	Used Frequently	Used at Times	Used at Times
Capscrew Diameter and Minimum Tensile Strength psi (Kg/sq cm)	To ½-69,000 (4850.7000) To ¾-64,000 (4499.2000) To 1 -55,000 (3866.5000)	To ¾-120,000 (8436.0000) To 1 -115,000 (8084.5000)	To ⅝-140,000 (9842.0000) To ¾-133,000 (9349.9000)	150,000 (10545.0000)
Quality of Matelial	Indeterminate	Minimum Commercial	Medium Commercial	Best Commercial

Capscrew Body Size (Inches) — (Thread)	Torque Ft-Lb	kg m	Torque Ft-Lb	kg m	Torque Ft-Lb	kg m	Torque Ft-Lb	kg m
¼-20	5	0.6915	8	1.1064	10	1.3830	12	1.6596
-28	6	0.8298	10	1.3830			14	1.9362
5/16-18	11	1.5213	17	2.3511	19	2.6277	24	3.3192
-24	13	1.7979	19	2.6277			27	3.7341
⅜-16	18	2.4894	31	4.2873	34	4.7022	44	6.0852
-24	20	2.7660	35	4.8405			49	6.7767
7/16-14	28	3.8132	49	6.7767	55	7.6065	70	9.6810
-20	30	4.1490	55	7.6065			78	10.7874
½-13	39	5.3937	75	10.3725	85	11.7555	105	14.5215
-20	41	5.6703	85	11.7555			120	16.5960
9/16-12	51	7.0533	110	15.2130	120	16.5960	155	21.4365
-18	55	7.6065	120	16.5960			170	23.5110
⅝-11	83	11.4789	150	20.7450	167	23.0961	210	29.0430
-18	95	13.1385	170	23.5110			240	33.1920
¾-10	105	14.5215	270	37.3410	280	38.7240	375	51.8625
-16	115	15.9045	295	40.7985			420	58.0860
⅞- 9	160	22.1280	395	54.6285	440	60.8520	605	83.6715
-14	175	24.2025	435	60.1605			675	93.3525
1- 8	235	32.5005	590	81.5970	660	91.2780	910	125.8530
-14	250	34.5750	660	91.2780			990	136.9170

When the correct setting is achieved, the gears are considered matched and a set of numbers, along with other identifying marks are etched on the gear set.

A + (plus) or — (minus) sign is used, followed by a digit to represent the factory setting where the tooth contact and quietness were the best. This is called the *Pinion Depth Variance* or *Individual Variation Distance.*

If the pinion is marked + 5 for example, this means the distance from the pinion gear rear face to the axle shaft center line is .005 in. more then the standard setting, and if the pinion gear is marked — 5, this means that the distance is .005 in. less than the standard setting. To move the pinion to the standard setting, compensating for the variation, shims must be either added to or subtracted from the total shim pack, located under the rear pinion bearing cup, between the pinion cage and the differential carrier, or under the rear pinion bearing, depending upon the differential model being serviced.

The procedures to follow in the adjustment of the pinion and drive gears are outlined in the respective differential model disassembly and assembly chapters.

As a rule of thumb on the addition or removal of shims for the pinion depth adjustment, draw a diagram as shown and determine which way the pinion must be moved to obtain the desired pinion depth.

Standard Torque Specifications and Capscrew Markings

Because of the varied bolt sizes used in the many models of differentials, the torque specifications are not always available to the technician for a specific bolt. By determining the grade of bolt, size, and thread, the proper torque limit can be found in the following chart.

Chevrolet Full Floating Single Speed

This is a full floating axle design using special hypoid type drive and pinion gears. The pinion gear is supported by three bearings, two in front of the pinion gears and one behind. The differential assembly has either two or four pinions depending upon the application.

Rear Axle Conversion

$8\frac{1}{2}$, $8\frac{7}{8}$ in.—3300 to 3600 lbs.
$9\frac{3}{4}$, $10\frac{1}{2}$ in.—5500 lbs. (Dana)
$10\frac{1}{2}$ in.—5200 to 7200 lbs.

Differential Carrier Removal

1. With vehicle raised and supported securely, drain the lubricant.
2. Remove the axle shafts from the axle.
3. Remove the two drive shaft "U" bolts from the rear yoke and separate the rear universal joint from the yoke. *NOTE: The bearing can be left in place in the trunnion and can be secured with tape.*
4. Push the drive shaft to one side and secure it in place to the frame side rail.
5. Place a jack under the carrier assembly and remove the bolts and lock washers that hold the carrier to the axle housing and supporting the carrier with the jack roll it from under the truck.

Differential Carrier

Disassembly

1. Mount the carrier assembly in a bench vise or holding fixture.
2. On axles so equipped, loosen the ring gear thrust pad lock nut and remove the thrust pad.
3. Remove the differential adjusting nut locks and bearing cap bolts and lockwashers.
4. Mark the bearing caps and carrier for reassembly in the same position. Remove the bearing caps and adjusting nuts by tapping on the bosses of the caps until free from the dowels.
5. Remove the differential and ring gear assembly from the carrier.
6. Remove the bolts which attach the pinion bearing retainer to the carrier.
7. Remove the pinion and bearing assembly from the carrier.

   NOTE: It may be necessary to drive this unit from the carrier. Use a brass drift against the pilot end of the pinion.
8. On all axles except the 11,000 lb. remove shims from inside the carrier housing making note of

1 Universal joint yoke
2 Pinion bearing retainer and oil seal
3 Oil seal packing
4 Oil seal
5 Front pinion bearing
6 Drive pinion
7 Pinion bearing shim
8 Rear pinion bearing
9 Ring gear
10 Differential spider

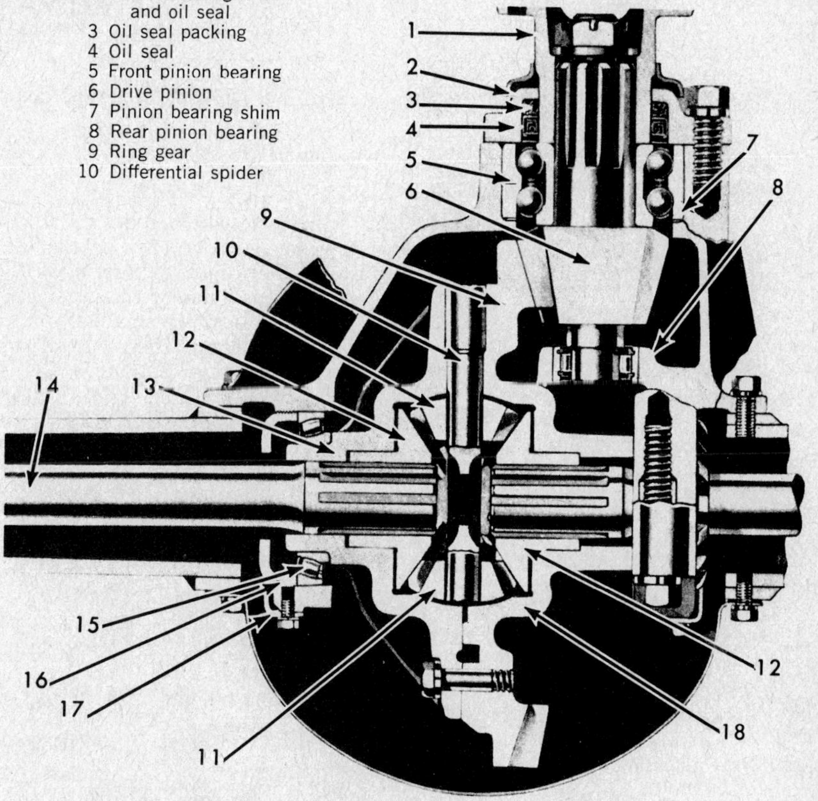

5200 and 7200 lb. axle—cross section (© Chevrolet Div., G.M. Corp.)

11 Differential pinion (spider) gear
12 Differential side gear
13 Differential case—left half
14 Axle shaft
15 Differential bearing
16 Differential bearing adjusting nut
17 Adjusting nut lock
18 Differential case—right half

the number and total thickness of shims removed.

9. On all axles except the 11,000 lb., the pinion rear bearing outer race and roller assembly is pressed into the carrier. Remove the assembly by driving it from its seat using a soft drift or punch.

Pinion and/or Bearing

Replacement

1. Clamp the pinion drive flange in a bench vise.
2. Remove the cotter pin, nut and washer from the end of the pinion.
3. Remove the drive flange and bearing retainer assembly.
4. Drive the oil seal, and packing if present, from the retainer.
5. On the 11,000 lb. axle, remove the pinion rear bearing snap ring and press the bearing from the pinion.
6. On the 13,500, 15,000 and 17,000 lb. axles press the inner race of the rear bearing from the pinion.
7. On the 5200 and 7200 lb. axles press the pinion from the bearing.
8. On the 11,000 lb. axle, press the front bearing from the pinion.

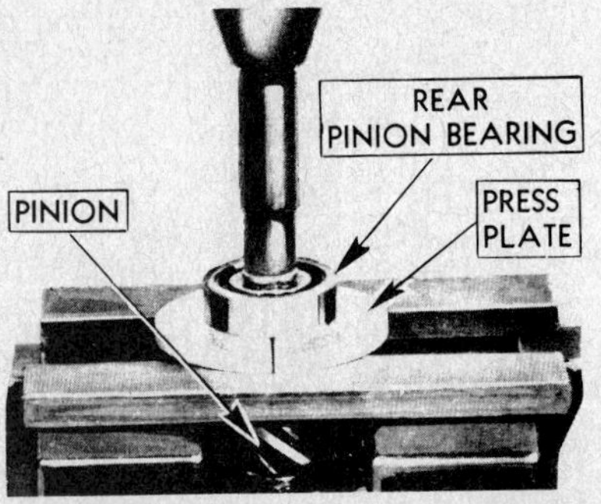

Pinion rear bearing removal (11,000 lb. axle) (© Chevrolet Div., G.M. Corp.)

9. On the 13,500, 15,000 and 17,000 lb. axles press the front bearing from the pinion. Wash all the parts in solvent and inspect the pinion gear for signs of wear, chipping, pitting or scoring. Check the splines on the pinion shaft for signs of wear or distortion. Check the bearings for signs of wear, roughness or defects.
10. Soak the new oil seal (and packing) in engine oil. Install the felt packing, if so equipped, in the bottom of the retainer. Press the oil seal into the retainer.
11. On the 5200, 7200, 13,500, 15,000 and 17,000 lb. axles, lubricate the pinion rear bearing and press it into the carrier. Then install the inner race on the 13,500, 15,000 and 17,000 lb. axle pinion shaft.

1 Universal joint yoke
2 Pinion bearing and oil seal retainer
3 Oil seal
4 Gasket
5 Front pinion bearing
6 Drive pinion
7 Pinion Bearing shim
8 Rear pinion bearing
9 Ring gear thrust pad
10 Ring gear
11 Differential spider
12 Differential pinion (spider) gear

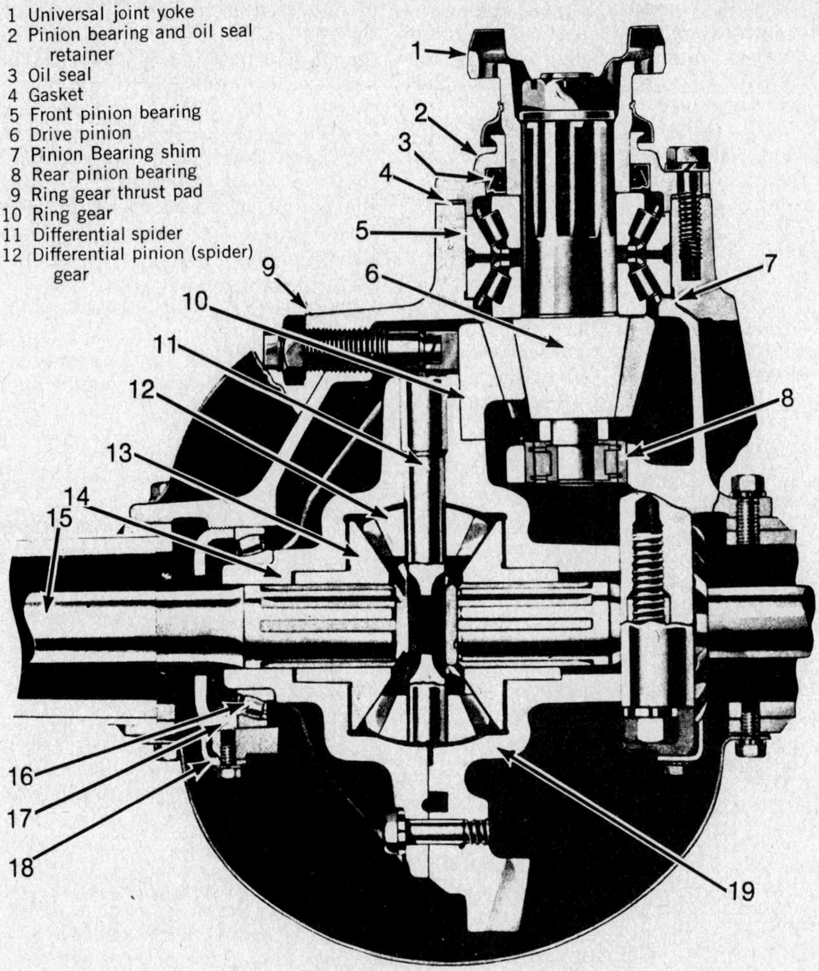

5200 and 7200 lb. axle—with adjusting screw (© Chevrolet Div., G.M. Corp.)

13 Differential side gear
14 Differential case—left half
15 Axle shaft
16 Differential bearing
17 Differential bearing
adjusting nut
18 Adjusting nut lock
19 Differential case—right half

12. On the 11,000 lb. axle, install the pinion rear bearing on the pinion shaft making sure that the chamfered side of the inner race seats against the shoulder on the pinion shaft. Then install the pinon bearing lock ring.
13. On the 11,000 lb. axle, position the one piece double row ball bearing on the pinion shaft so that the extended portion of the inner race is toward the pinion head. Press the bearing onto the shaft until it seats against the pinion head.
14. On the 5200, 7200, 13,500, 15,000 and 17,000 lb. axles, place one cone and roller assembly on the pinion shaft so that the large end of bearing is toward the pinion. Then position the outer race, spacer and cone and roller

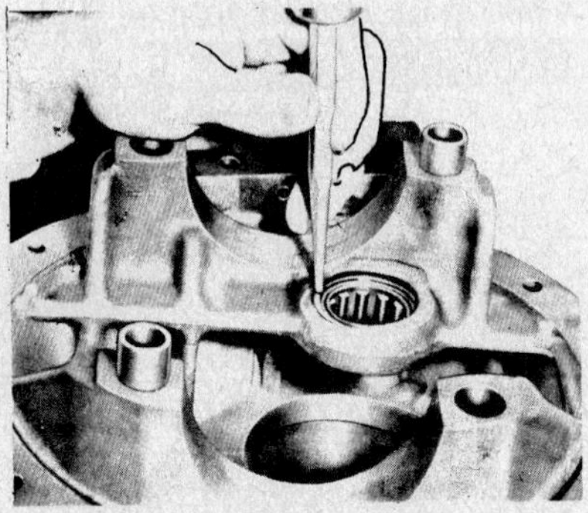

Pinion rear bearing removal—exc. 11,000 lb. axle
(© Chevrolet Div., G.M. Corp.)

Drive pinion front bearing removal—typical (© Chevrolet Div., G.M. Corp.)

Pinion rear bearing inner race installation (13,500-15,000 and 17,000 lb. axles)
(© Chevrolet Div., G.M. Corp.)

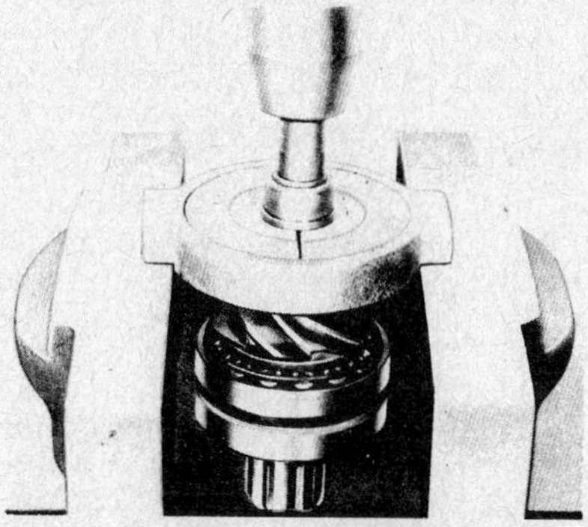

Pinion inner bearing inner race removal (13,500-15,000 and 17,000 lb. axles)
(© Chevrolet Div., G.M. Corp.)

assembly on the pinion shaft. Press the bearing until it seats against the pinion head.

15. Slide the oil seal retainer on the pinion shaft, then tap the flange onto the splines.
16. Clamp the drive flange in a bench vise and install the flange washer and nut. Torque the nut to 220 ft. lbs. and install the cotter pin without backing off on the nut.

Differential

Disassembly

1. Check the differential case to make sure that the two halves are marked so they may be reassembled in the same relation.
2. Remove the bolts holding the case and cover together.
3. Separate the cover from the case and remove the differential side gears and thrust washers, pinion gears with thrust washers and differential spider.
4. Remove the ring gear from the case by tapping the back of the gear with a soft faced hammer.

Assembly

1. Install two guide pins (made from cap screws with the heads cut off and ends slotted) to the new gear opposite each other.
2. Start the guide pins through the case flange and tap the ring gear on the case.

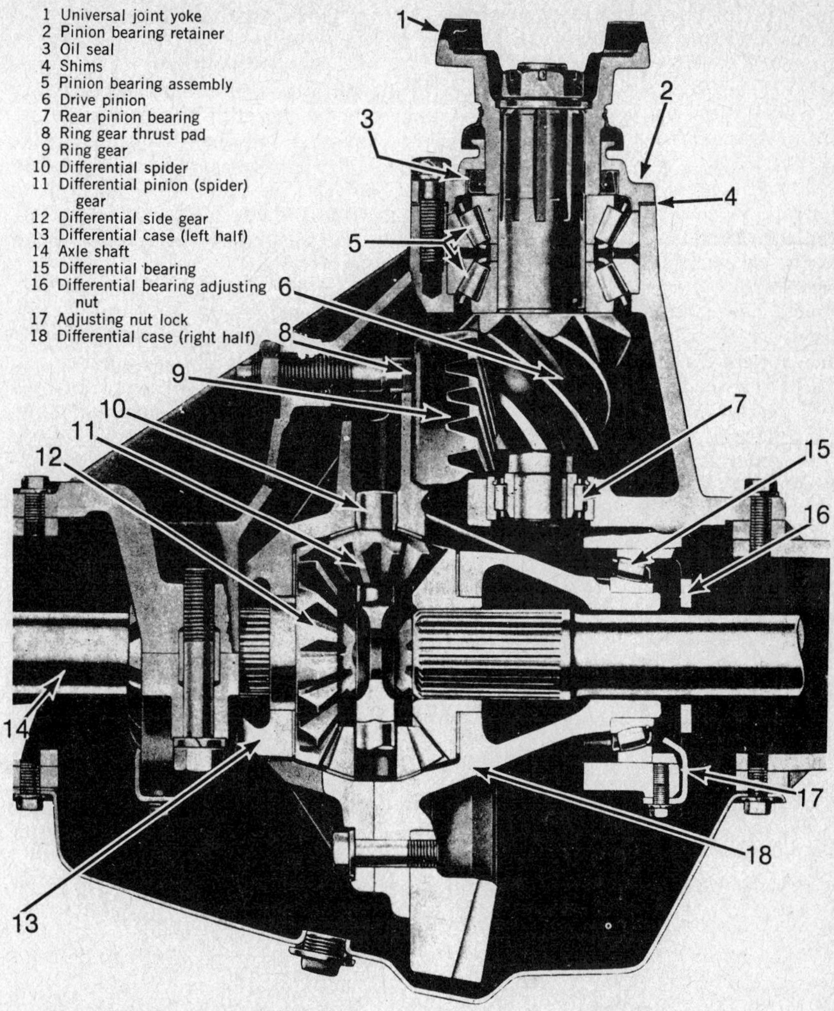

13,500, 15,000 and 17,000 lb. axle—cross section (© Chevrolet Div., G.M. Corp.)

3. Lubricate the differential side gears, pinions and thrust washers.
4. Place the differential pinions and thrust washers on the spider.
5. Assemble the side gears and pinions and thrust washers to the left half of the case.

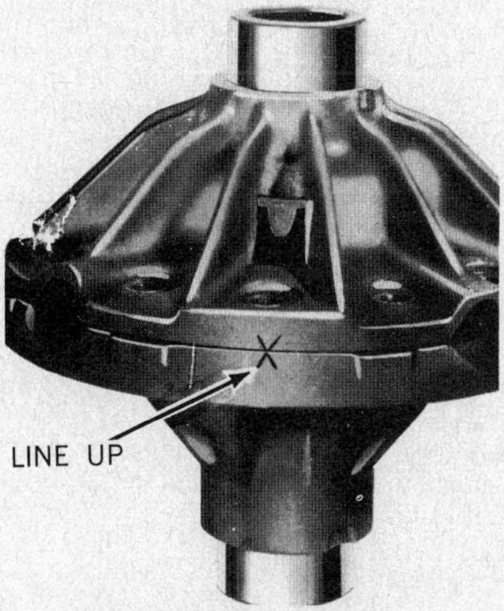

Differential case line up marks
(© Chevrolet Div., G.M. Corp.)

6. Assemble the case halves being sure to line up the marks on the two halves.
7. Install the differential to ring gear bolts and lock washers and tighten evenly until the ring gear is flush with the case flange.
8. Remove the two guide pins and install the remaining two bolts.
9. Torque all bolts to specifications:
   Except below—110 ft. lbs.
   15,000 lb. and 17,000 lb. axles—160 ft. lbs.

Differential Bearing

Replacement

1. Using a bearing puller, remove the bearings from the case.
2. Place the new bearing on the hub of the case, thick side of inner race toward case. Using a bearing driver, drive the bearing into place.

Differential Carrier

Assembly

To facilitate adjusting the pinion

depth in the ring gear, there are five shims available for service use. They are .012″, .015″, .018″, .021″ and .024″.

NOTE: Pinion depth adjustment shims are not required for the 11,000 lb. axle.

If the original ring gear and pinion are to be used it is advisable to replace the same thickness of shims in the carrier counter bore that were removed.

If a new ring gear and pinion are used, one .021″ shim should be used as a standard starting set up.

1. Place the shim in the bore in the carrier.
2. Place a new pinion bearing retainer gasket on the retainer and install the pinion assembly in the carrier.
3. Install and tighten the pinion bearing retainer bolts and lock ing rollers with engine oil and washers.
4. Lubricate the differential bear-place the outer races over them.
5. Install the differential assembly in the carrier and install the adjusting nuts.
6. Install the differential bearing caps making sure the marks on the caps line up with the marks on the carrier.
7. Install the bearing cap bolts and lock washers and tighten until the lock washers just flatten out.

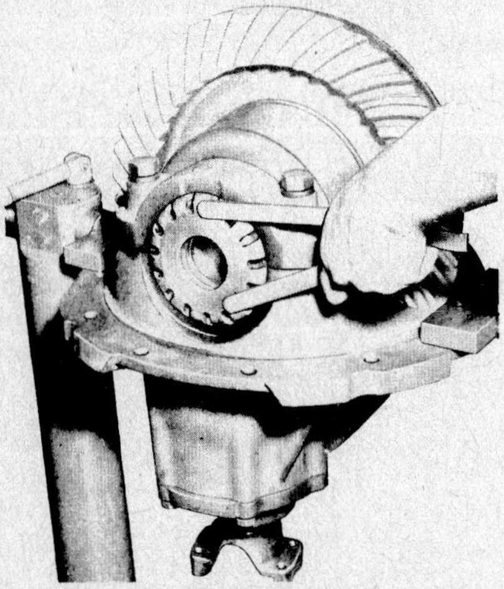

Ring gear and pinion adjustment
(© Chevrolet Div., G.M. Corp.)

Ring Gear and Pinion

Adjustment

1. With the differential bearing cap bolts loosened just enough to permit turning the bearing adjusting nuts, remove all lash between the ring gear and pinion.
2. Back off the left hand adjusting nut one or two notches to a locking position.
3. Tighten the right hand adjusting nut firmly to force the differential in solid contact with the left hand adjusting nut.
4. Back off the right hand adjusting nut and again tighten snugly against the bearing.
5. Tighten the right hand adjusting nut from one to two additional notches to a locking position. *NOTE: This method of adjustment provides for proper preload of the bearings.*
6. Mount a dial indicator on the carrier and check the backlash between the ring gear and pinion Backlash should be .003″ to .012″ (.005″ to .008″ preferred). If the backlash is more than .012″ loosen the right hand adjusting nut one notch and tighten the left hand adjusting nut one notch. If the backlash is less than .003″ loosen the left hand adjusting nut one notch and tighten the right hand adjusting nut one notch.
7. Tighten the bearing cap bolts to specifications.
   Except below—205 ft. lbs.
   5200 and 7200 lb. axles—
   100 ft. lbs.
8. Install the side bearing adjusting nut locks and torque to 15 ft. lbs.

Checking Pinion Depth

1. Coat the ring gear teeth lightly and evenly with a mixture of red lead and oil to produce a contact pattern. Then turn the pinion shaft several revolutions in both directions.
2. Examine the pattern on the ring gear teeth. If the pinion depth is correct, the tooth pattern will be centered on the pitch line and toward the toe of the ring gear. (See Illustration in this section).
3. If the pattern is below the pitch line on the ring gear teeth, the pinion is too deep and it will be necessary to remove the pinion assembly and increase the shim thickness between the pinion bearing and the carrier.
4. If the pattern is above the pitch line on the ring gear teeth, the pinion is too shallow and it will be necessary to decrease the shim thickness.
5. Changing the pinion depth will make some change in the backlash; therefore, it will be necessary to readjust the backlash.

Ring Gear Thrust Pad

Adjustment

On axles equipped with a thrust pad, inspect the bronze tip of the thrust pad and if worn install a new one.

1. Install the thrust pad and tighten the screw until the bronze tip engages the back face of the ring gear while rotating the gear.
2. Back off the screw one-twelfth (1/12) turn and tighten the lock-nut.

Differential Assembly

Installation

1. Clean out any dirt or sludge that may be in the axle housing or on the cover.
2. Install a new gasket on the axle housing and install the differential carrier to the housing securing it in place with the lock-washers and nuts. Torque the nuts to 70 ft. lbs.
3. Install the housing cover, if it was removed, using a new gasket.
4. Reconnect the drive shaft to the yoke on the differential and torque the "U" bolts to 20 ft. lbs.
5. Install the axle shafts in the axle.
6. Fill the axle with gear lubricant until the level is even with the bottom of the filler hole.
7. Road test the vehicle to check for noise and proper operation.

Chevrolet-Full Floating Single Speed 5200 Through 8400 lb. Axle, Non-Removable Carrier Type

This axle is a full floating type that uses special Hypoid type drive and pinion gears. The pinion gear is supported by three bearings, two in front of the pinion gear and one behind. The differential assembly has either two or four pinions depending on the application of the axle. This axle assembly must be removed from the vehicle to remove and service the differential.

Differential

Removal

1. With the axle assembly removed from the vehicle, place the axle assembly in a vise or holding fixture.
2. Remove the bolts that retain the cover assembly and remove the cover, allowing the gear lubricant to drain into a pan.
3. Remove the axle shafts from the

axle assembly. *NOTE: Before going any further, check the pinion backlash and record the measurement so that if the same gears are reused they may be installed at the same backlash to avoid changing the gear tooth pattern.*

4. From the bearing caps, remove the adjusting nut lock retainers.
5. Mark the bearing caps so they may be reinstalled in the same position and remove the bearing caps.
6. Loosen the side bearing adjusting nut and remove the differential carrier from the axle housing.

Pinion Assembly

Removal

1. Remove the differential assembly from the axle.
2. Check the pinion bearing for the proper preload. The force required to turn the pinion should be 25-35 in. lbs. for new bearings and 5-15 in. lbs. for used bearings. If there is no reading, shake the companion flange to check for any looseness in the bearing. If there is any looseness present the bearing should be replaced.
3. Remove the retaining bolts for the pinion bearing from the axle housing.
4. Remove the bearing retainer and pinion assembly from the axle housing. It may be necessary to tap the pilot end of the pinion shaft to help remove the pinion assembly from the carrier.
5. Record the thickness of the shims that are removed from between the carrier assembly and the bearing retainer assembly.

Drive Pinion

Disassembly

1. With the pinion assembly clamped in a vise, install a holder assembly on the flange.
2. Using the proper size socket, remove the pinion nut and washer from the pinion. When reassembling the pinion use a new nut and washer assembly.
3. With the holder assembly still in place, use a puller to remove the flange from the pinion.
4. With the bearing retainer supported in a press, press the pinion out of the retainer assembly. Be careful not to allow the pinion gear to fall onto the floor because this can damage the gear.
5. Separate the pinion flange, oil seal, front bearing and the bearing retainer. If the oil seal needs to be replaced it may have to be driven from the retainer.
6. Using a drift, drive the front and rear bearing cups from the bearing retainer.
7. Support the pinion assembly in a press, with the bearing supported, Press the bearing from the pinion gear.
8. Using a drift, drive the straddle bearing from the carrier assembly.

Cleaning and Inspection

1. Clean off all the parts in solvent and blow dry.
2. Check the pinion gear for signs of wear, chips, cracks or any other imperfections. Check the splines for signs of wear or distortion.
3. Check the bearings for signs of wear or pitting on the rollers and races and check the bearing cage for dents and bends. Check the bearing retainer for any cracks, pits, grooves or corrosion.
4. Check the pinion flange splines for any signs of wear or distortion.
5. Replace parts that show any of the signs mentioned above.

Differential Case

Disassembly

1. Scribe a line across the two halves of the differential case so they may be reassembled in the same position, and with the ring gear removed, separate the two halves. To remove the ring gear, remove the ring gear bolts and washers, and using a soft hammer tap the ring gear from the case.
2. Remove the internal parts from the inside of the case and set them aside in order that they may be reassembled in the same position.

Cleaning and Inspection

1. Check the differential gears, pinions, thrust washers and spider for any signs of unusual wear, chips, cracks or pitting.
2. Check all mating surfaces for signs of wear.
3. Replace parts that show any of the signs mentioned above.

Differential Case

Assembly

1. Using a good quality gear lubricant coat all of the parts.
2. Assemble the differential pinions and thrust washers onto the

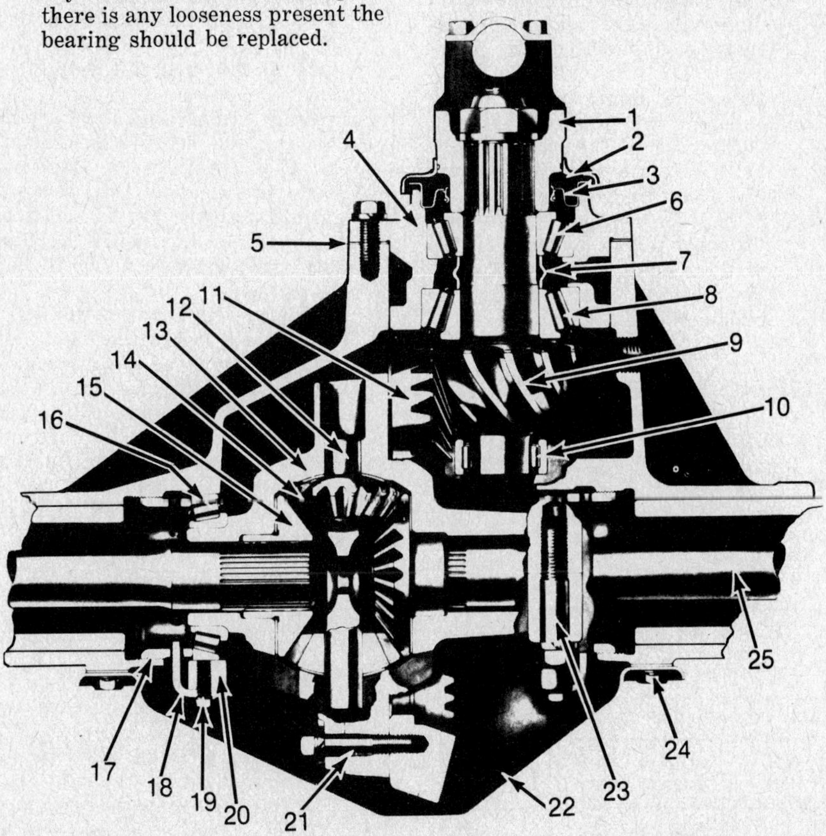

1. Companion Flange
2. Oil Deflector
3. Oil Seal
4. Bearing Retainer
5. Shim
6. Pinion Front Bearing
7. Collapsible Spacer
8. Pinion Rear Bearing
9. Drive Pinion
10. Straddle Bearing
11. Ring Gear
12. Differential Spider
13. Differential Case
14. Differential Pinion
15. Differential Side Gear
16. Side Bearing
17. Side Bearing Adjusting Nut
18. Adjusting Nut Retainer
19. Retainer Screw
20. Bearing Cap
21. Case-to-Ring Gear Bolt
22. Differential Cover
23. Bearing Cap Bolt
24. Cover Screw
25. Axle Shaft

Chevrolet 5,200-17,000 lb. axle cross section (© Chevrolet Div., G.M. Corp.)

spider and install the assembly into the differential case.

3. Line up the scribe marks on the two halves of the differential case and install the ring gear. Install the ring gear washers and bolts and torque the bolts to approx. 110 ft. lbs.

Side Bearing

Replacement

1. Install a bearing puller on the bearing and remove the bearing assembly from the differential case.
2. Check the bearings for any signs of wear on distortion.
3. Install the new bearing by setting it in place on the differential case and, using a bearing driver, drive the bearing onto the case assembly until it seats against the shoulder on the case.

Drive Pinion

Assembly and Adjustment

1. Coat all of the parts with a good quality gear lubricant.
2. With the pinion gear in a press, press the rear bearings onto the pinion assembly.
3. In the bearing retainer, install the front and rear bearing cups using a driver of the proper size.
4. In the axle housing, install the straddle bearing assembly using the proper size driver.
5. Install the bearing retainer with the bearing cups in place on the pinion gear and install a new collapsible spacer.
6. Press the front bearing onto the pinion gear.
7. Lubricate the oil seal with a good quality high pressure grease and install the seal into the retainer bore. Be sure to press the seal down until it rests against the internal shoulder.
8. Install the pinion flange and oil deflector onto the splines of the pinion gear and install a new lock washer and pinion nut.
9. With the pinion flange clamped in a vise and a holder assembly installed on the flange, tighten the nut to obtain the proper preload. Measure the amount of torque required to turn the pinion gear. For a new bearing the torque required is 25-35 in. lbs. and for an old bearing it is 5-15 in. lbs. To preload the bearing, tighten the pinion nut to approx. 350 ft. lbs. and take a reading of the torque required to turn the pinion. Continue tightening the nut until the proper preload is obtained.

CAUTION: **Do not tighten the nut too tightly because it will collapse the spacer too much. This will make replacement necessary.**

Drive Pinion Assembly

Installation

1. If installing a new pinion gear, check the top of the new gear for the depth code number.
2. Compare the new number with the old number on top of the old pinion and check the pinion depth chart for preliminary setting of the pinion depth.
3. Check the thickness of the original shims removed from the pinion and either add or subtract from the shims according to the chart.
4. Place the shim on the carrier assembly and line the holes up with those in the axle housing. Make sure the surfaces are clean of all dirt and grease.
5. Install the retainer and pinion assembly in the housing making sure the holes line up and install the retaining bolts. Torque the bolts to approx. 45 ft. lbs.

		CODE NUMBER ON ORIGINAL PINION				
		+2	+1	0	-1	-2
CODE NUMBER ON SERVICE PINION	+2	–	ADD .001	ADD .002	ADD .003	ADD .004
	+1	SUBT. .001	–	ADD .001	ADD .002	ADD .003
	0	SUBT. .002	SUBT. .001	–	ADD .001	ADD .002
	-1	SUBT. .003	SUBT. .002	SUBT. .001	–	ADD .001
	-2	SUBT. .004	SUBT. .003	SUBT. .002	SUBT. .001	–

Pinion depth codes and corresponding shim thickness

Differential Case

Installation and Adjustments

1. Place the bearing cups over the side bearings on the differential assembly and place the unit into the carrier in the axle housing.
2. Install the bearing caps making sure the marks are lined up and install the bolts. Tighten the bearing retaining bolts.
3. Loosen the right side nut and tighten the left side nut until the ring gear comes in contact with the pinion gear. Do not force the gears together. This brings the gears to zero lash.
4. Back off the left side adjusting nut about two slots and install the lock fingers into the nut.
5. In this order tighten the right side adjusting nut firmly to force the case assembly into tight contact with the left side adjusting nut and then loosen the right side nut until it is free from the bearing.
6. Again retighten the right side adjusting nut until it comes in contact with the bearing. Tighten the right adjusting nut about two slots if it is an old bearing or three slots if it is a new bearing.
7. Install the lock retainers into the slots and torque the bearing cap bolts to 100 ft.-lbs. This procedure now insures that the bearings are preloaded properly. If more adjustments are made, make sure the preload stays the same. To do this, one adjusting nut must be loosened the same amount the other nut is tightened.
8. Install a dial indicator on the housing and measure the amount of backlash between the ring and pinion gear. The backlash should measure between .003 to .012 of an inch with the best figure being between .005 to .008 of an inch.
9. If the backlash is more than .012 of an inch, loosen the right side adjusting nut one slot and tighten the left side one slot. If the backlash is less than .003 of an inch, loosen the left side nut one slot and tighten the right side one slot. These adjustments should bring the backlash measurement into an acceptable range.

Pattern Check

1. Clean all the oil off the ring gear and using a gear marking compound, coat all of the teeth of the ring gear.
2. Make sure the bearing caps are torqued to 110 ft. lbs. and apply load to the gears while rotating the pinion. Rotate the ring gear one full turn in both directions. *NOTE: Load must be applied to the assembly while rotating or the pattern will not show completely.*
3. Check the pattern on the ring gear and following the chart, adjust the assembly to get the contact pattern located centrally on the face of the ring gear teeth.

Chevrolet-Semifloating Single Speed, Non-Removable Carrier Type 2400 to 3500 lb. Axle

This axle assembly is the semi-floating type with Hypoid type drive pinion and ring gears. The drive pinion gear is supported by two bearings. The differential case contains two pinion gears. The carrier assembly is not removable since it is part of the axle assembly but the design allows for the differential assembly to be serviced while the axle is still in the vehicle. The ring gear is bolted to a one piece differential case that is supported by two preloaded roller bearings.

Differential Case

Removal

1. Remove the inspection cover from the axle housing and drain the gear lubricant into a pan.
2. Remove the screw or pin that holds the pinion shaft in place and remove the shaft.
3. Push the axle shafts in a little and remove the "C" locks from the ends of the shafts. Remove the axle shafts from the housing.
4. Before going any further, the backlash should be measured and recorded. This will allow the old gears to be reassembled at the same amount of lash to avoid changing the gear tooth pattern. It also helps to indicate if there is gear or bearing wear, and if there is any error in the original backlash setting.
5. Roll the differential pinions and thrust washers out of the case and also remove the side gears and thrust washers. Make sure to mark the pinions and side gears so they can be reassembled in their original position.
6. Mark the bearing caps and housing and loosen the retaining bolts. Tap the caps lightly to loosen them. When the caps are loose, take the bolts all the way out and then reinstall the bolts just a few turns. This will keep the case from falling out of the housing when it is pried loose.
7. With a pry bar, very carefully pry the case assembly loose. Be careful not to damage the gasket surface on the housing when prying. The case assembly may suddenly come free if the bearings were preloaded, so pry very slowly.
8. When the case assembly is loose, remove the bolts for the bearing caps and remove the caps. Place the caps so they may be reinstalled in the same position. Place any shims that are removed with the cap they were removed from.

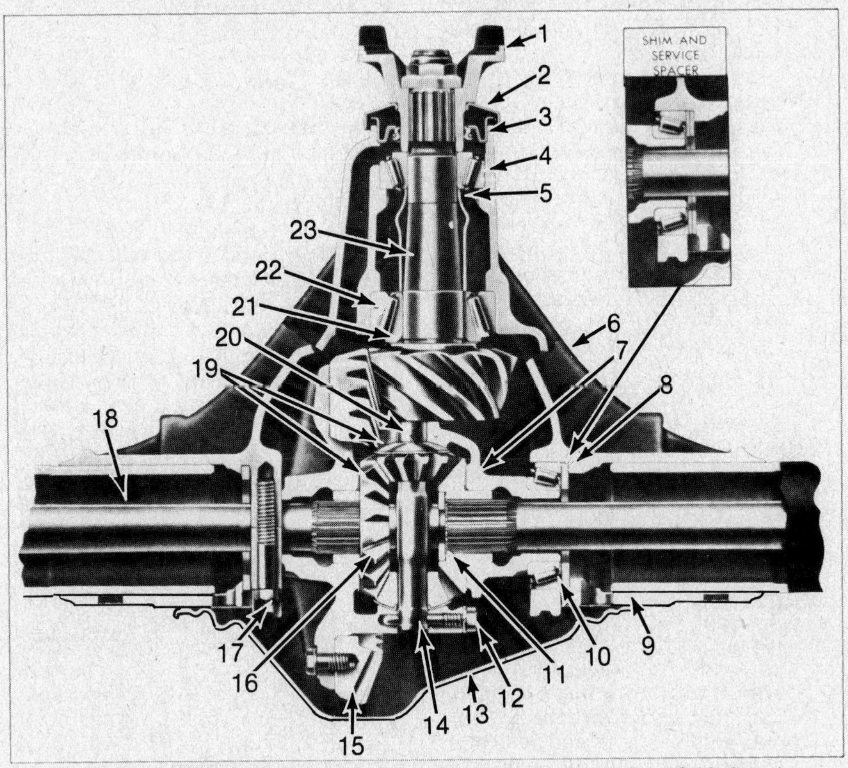

Chevrolet 2,400-3,600 lb. axle cross section (© Chevrolet Div., G.M. Corp.)

1. Companion Flange
2. Deflector
3. Pinion Oil Seal
4. Pinion Front Bearing
5. Pinion Bearing Spacer
6. Differential Carrier
7. Differential Case
8. Shim (A) with Service Shim
9. Gasket
10. Differential Bearing
11. "C" Lock
12. Pinion Shaft Lock Bolt
13. Cover
14. Pinion Shaft
15. Ring Gear
16. Side Gear
17. Bearing Cap
18. Axle Shaft
19. Thrust Washer
20. Differential Pinion
21. Shim
22. Pinion Rear Bearing
23. Drive Pinion

Drive Pinion

Removal

1. With the differential removed, check the pinion preload. Do this by checking the amount of torque needed to turn the pinion gear. For a new bearing, it should be 20-25 in. lbs., and for a used bearing it should be 10-15 in. lbs. If there is no preload reading check the pinion for looseness. If there is any looseness the bearing should be replaced.
2. With a holder assembly installed on the flange, use a socket of the proper size and remove the flange nut and washer.
3. Remove the flange by using a puller assembly and drawing the flange off the pinion splines.
4. Thread the pinion nut a few turns onto the pinion shaft. Using a brass drift and hammer, lightly tap the end of the pinion shaft to remove the pinion from the carrier. Be careful not to allow the pinion to fall out of the carrier after it breaks loose.
5. With the pinion removed from the carrier, discard the old seal, pinion nut and collapsible spacer and install new ones when reassembling.

Cleaning and Inspection

1. Clean all parts in solvent and blow dry.
2. Check all of the parts for any signs of wear, chips, cracks or distortion. Replace any parts that are defective.
3. Check the fit of the differential side gears in the case and the fit of the side gear and axle shaft splines.

Differential Bearing

Replacement

1. With a bearing puller attached to the bearing, pull the bearing from the case.
2. Place the new bearing on the case hub with the thick side of the inner race toward the case. Using a bearing driver, drive the bearing onto the case until it seats against the shoulder on the case.

Drive Pinion Bearing

Replacement and Adjustment

1. Depending on the bearing that is being replaced, remove the front or rear bearing cup from the carrier assembly.
2. With the pinion gear mounted in a press, press the rear bearing from the pinion shaft. Be sure to record the thickness of the shims that are removed from between the bearing and the gear.
3. Using a bearing driver of the proper size, install a new bearing cup for each one that was removed. Make sure the cups are seated fully against the shoulder in the housing.
4. The pinion depth must now be checked to determine the nominal setting. This allows for machining variations in the housing and enables you to select the proper shim so that the pinion depth can be set for the best gear tooth contact.
5. Clean the housing and carrier assemblies to insure accurate measurement of the pinion depth.
6. Lubricate the front and rear pinion bearings with gear lubricant and install them in their races in the carrier assembly.
7. Using a Pinion Setting Gauge, select the proper clover leaf plate, and install it on the preload stud.
8. Insert the stud through the rear bearing, with the proper size pilot on the stud, and through the front bearing using the proper pilot. Install the hex nut and tighten it until it is just snug.
9. Holding the preload stud with a wrench, tighten the hex nut until 20 in. lbs. of torque are required to rotate the bearings.
10. Install the side bearing discs on the ends of the arbor assembly, using the step of the disc that fits the bore of the carrier.
11. Install the arbor and plunger assembly into the carrier. Make sure the side bearing discs fit properly.
12. Install the bearing caps in the carrier assembly finger tight to make sure the discs do not move.
13. Mount a dial indicator on the mounting post of the arbor. Have the contact button resting on the top surface of the plunger.
14. Preload the dial indicator by turning it one-half revolution and tightening it in this position.
15. Use the button on the gauge plate that corresponds to the ring gear size and turn the plate so the plunger rests on top of it.
16. Rock the plunger rod back and forth across the top of the button until the dial indicator reads the greatest amount of variation. Set the dial indicator to zero at the point of most variation. Repeat the rocking of the plunger several times to check the setting.
17. Turn the plunger until it is removed from the gauging plate button. The dial indicator will now read the pinion shim thickness required to set the "nominal pinion depth." Make a note of the reading.
18. Check for the pinion code number on the rear face of the pinion gear being used. This number will indicate the necessary change to the pinion shim thickness. If the pinion is marked with a plus (+) and a number, add that much to the reading you got from the dial indicator. If the pinion has no mark, use the reading from the dial indicator as the correct shim thickness. If the pinion is marked with a minus (—) and a number, subtract that much from the reading on the dial indicator.
19. Remove the depth gauging tools from the carrier assembly and install the proper size shim on the pinion gear.
20. Lubricate the bearing with gear lubricant and using a press, press the bearing into place on the pinion shaft.

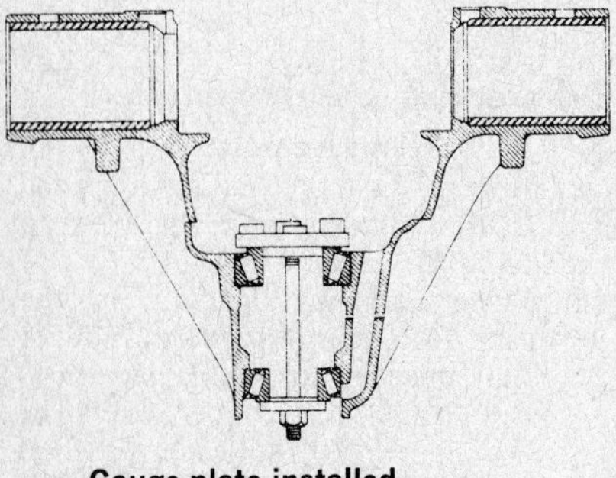

Gauge plate installed
(© Chevrolet Div., G.M. Corp.)

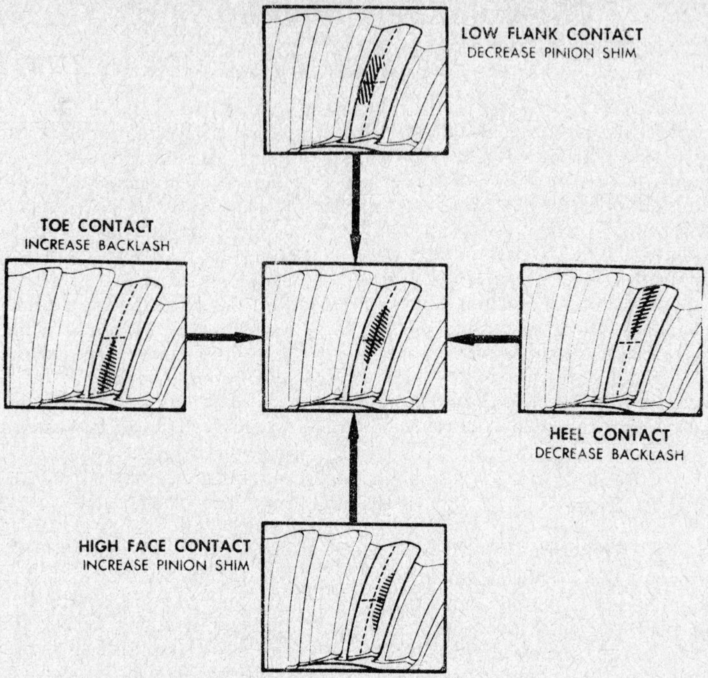

Gear tooth contact check (© Chevrolet Div., G.M. Corp.)

Pinion Gear

Installation and Adjustment

1. Lubricate the front bearing with gear lubricant and install it in the front cup.
2. Install the pinion seal in the bore. Using a seal driver and the proper size gauge plate, drive the seal in until the gauge plate is flush with the shoulder of the carrier.
3. Coat the seal lips with gear lubricant and install a new bearing spacer on the pinion gear.
4. Install the pinion gear in the carrier assembly and using a large washer and nut, draw the pinion gear in through the front

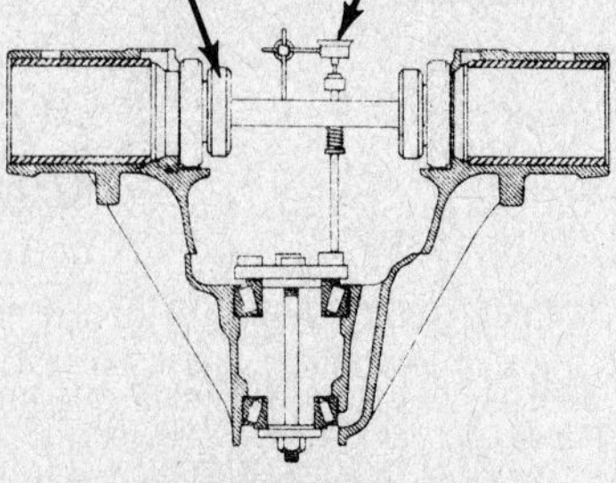

Gauge tools installed in carrier
(© Chevrolet Div., G.M. Corp.)

bearing far enough to get companion flange in place.

5. With the companion flange installed on the pinion shaft, use a holder assembly and tighten the pinion nut until all of the end play is removed from the drive pinion.
6. When there is no more end play the preload should be checked. The preload of the bearing is the amount of torque required to turn the pinion gear. The preload should be 20-25 inch. lbs. on new bearings and 10-15 inch. lbs. on reused bearings. Tighten the pinion nut until these figures are reached. *Do Not* over tighten the pinion. This will collapse the spacer too much and make it necessary to replace it.
7. Turn the pinion gear several times to make sure the bearings are seated and recheck the preload.

Ring Gear

Replacement

1. Remove all of the bolts that hold the ring gear to the differential case and with a soft hammer, tap the ring gear off the case.

NOTE: Do not try to pry the ring gear off the case. This will damage the machined surfaces.

2. Clean all dirt from the case assembly and lubricate the case with gear lube. Align the ring gear bolt holes with the holes in the carrier and lightly press the ring gear onto the case assembly. Install all of the bolts and tighten them all evenly, using a criss-cross pattern to avoid cocking the ring gear.
3. When the ring gear is firmly seated against the case, tighten the bolts to 60 ft. lbs.

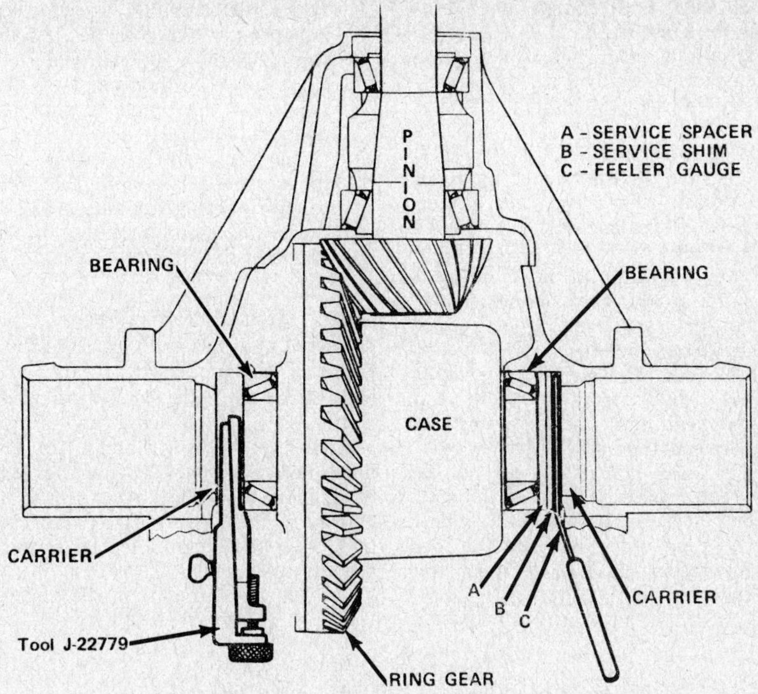

EXAMPLE

	RING GEAR SIDE	OPPOSITE SIDE	
.250"	Thickness of Tool J-22779 required to force ring gear into contact with pinion	Combined total of: Service Spacer (A) Service Shim (B) Feeler Gauge (C)	.265"
-.010" .240"	TO MAINTAIN PROPER BACKLASH (.005" - .008"), ring gear is moved away from pinion by subtracting .010" shims from ring gear side and adding .010" shims to other side		+.010" .275"
+.004"	TO OBTAIN PROPER PRELOAD on side bearings, add .004" shims to each side.		+.004"
.244"	Shim dimension required for ring gear side	Shim dimension required for opposite side	.279"

Shim pack selection chart (© Chevrolet Div., G.M. Corp.)

Differential Case Assembly

Installation and Adjustment

1. Install the thrust washers and side gears into the case assembly. If the original parts are being used, be sure to place them in their original position.
2. Place the pinions in the case so they are 180 degrees apart as they engage the side gears.
3. Turn the pinion gears so the hole in the case lines up with the holes in the gears. When the holes are aligned, install the pinion shaft and lock screw. Do not tighten the lock screw too tightly at this time.
4. Check the bearings, bearing cups, cup seat and carrier caps to make sure they are in good condition.
5. Lubricate the bearings with gear lube. Install the cups on the proper bearings and install the differential assembly in the carrier. Support the carrier assembly to keep it from falling.
6. Install a support strap on the left side bearing and tighten the bearing bolts to an even, snug fit.
7. With the ring gear tight against the pinion gear, insert a gauging tool between the left side bearing cup and the carrier housing.
8. While lightly shaking the tool back and forth, turn the adjusting wheel until a slight drag is felt. Tighten the lock nut.
9. Between the right side bearing and carrier, install a service spacer, .170 of an inch thick, a service shim and a feeler gauge. The feeler gauge must be thick enough so a light drag is felt when it is moved between the carrier and the shim.
10. Add the total of the service spacer, service shim and the feeler gauge. Remove the gauging tool from the left side of the carrier and using a micrometer, measure the thickness in at least three places. Average the readings and record the result.
11. Refer to the chart to determine the proper thickness of the shim packs.
12. Install the left side shim first, then install the right side shim between the bearing cup and spacer. Position the shim so the chamfered side is outward or next to the spacer. If there is not enough chamfer around the outside of the shim, file or grind the chamfer a little to allow for easy installation.
13. If there is difficulty in installing the shim, partially remove the case from the carrier and slide both the shim and case back into place.
14. Install the bearing caps and torque them to 60 ft. lbs. Tighten the pinion shaft lock screw.

NOTE: The differential side bearings are now preloaded. If any adjustments are made in later procedures, make sure not to change the preload. Do Not change the total thickness of the shim packs.

15. Mount a dial indicator on the carrier assembly with the indicator button perpendicular to the tooth angle and in line with the gear rotation.
16. Measure the amount of backlash between the ring and pinion gears. The backlash should be between .005-.008 of an inch. Take readings at four different spots on the gear. There should not be variations greater than .002 of an inch.
17. If there are variations greater than .002 of an inch between the readings, check the runout between the case and ring gear. The gear runout should not be greater than .003 in. If the runout does exceed .003 in. check the case and ring gear for deformation or dirt between the case and gear.
18. If the gear backlash exceeds .008 in., increase the thickness of the shims on the ring gear side and decrease the thickness of the shims on the opposite side, an equal amount.
19. If the backlash is less than .005 in., decrease the shim thickness on the ring gear side and increase the shim thickness on the opposite side an equal amount.

Gear Pattern Check

Before final assembly of the differential, a pattern check of the gear teeth must be made. This determines if the teeth of the ring and pinion gears are meshing properly, for low noise level and long life of the gear teeth. The most important thing to note is if the pattern is located centrally up and down on the face of the ring gear.

1. Wipe any oil out of the carrier and wipe all dirt and oil from the teeth of the ring gear.
2. Coat the teeth of the ring gear with a gear marking compound.
3. With the bearing caps torqued to 55 ft.-lbs., expand the brake shoes until it takes 20-30 ft. lbs. of torque to turn the pinion gear.
4. Turn the companion flange so the ring gear makes one full rotation in one direction, then turn it one full rotation in the opposite direction.
5. Check the pattern on the teeth and refer to the chart for any adjustments necessary.
6. With the gear tooth pattern checked and properly adjusted, install the axle housing cover gasket and cover and tighten securely. Fill the axle with gear lube to the correct level.
7. Road test the vehicle to check for any noise and proper operation of the rear.

Dodge/Plymouth 8¾ in. Removeable Carrier Axle

See the Dodge/Plymouth truck section for external identification and axle shaft service.

Differential

Removal

1. Raise and support vehicle under rear axle housing.
2. Remove wheels, drums and rear axle shafts, as described in truck section. Drain lubricant.
3. Disconnect rear universal joint and place out of way.
4. Remove attaching bolts and remove carrier assembly to bench.

Reconditioning

NOTE: Before disassembling the differential, check and record the side bearing play and ring gear run-out. Also, make a gear tooth contact pattern test, and measure pinion bearing preload.

1. Mount carrier in holding tool, with pinion flange up.
2. Remove pinion shaft nut and washer. Remove flange with puller.
3. With puller screwed into oil seal, pull seal from housing.
4. Rotate assembly with holding tool to allow oil slinger, shim pack and spacer (where used), to drop from the carrier.
5. Matchmark the differential pedestals, adjusting nuts, and bearing caps for reassembly identification.
6. Remove the bearing lockscrews and locks.
7. Remove the cap bolts, caps and back off bearing adjusting nuts slightly.
8. Remove the differential assem-

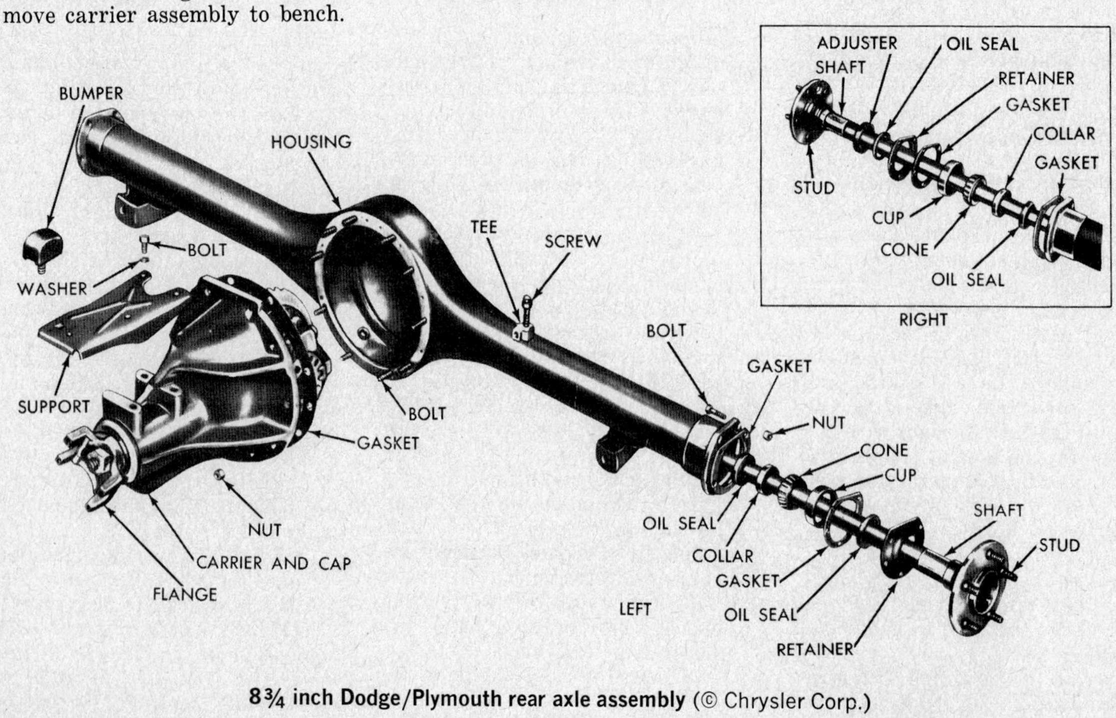

8¾ inch Dodge/Plymouth rear axle assembly (© Chrysler Corp.)

bly, being sure to keep each bearing cup with the proper bearing.
9. Remove the pinion and rear bearing cone from the carrier.
10. The bearing cone and pinion locating washer may now be removed from the shaft.
11. Remove the bearing cups from the carrier housing.

Differential Case

Disassembly

1. Mount the differential case and ring gear in vise with soft jaws. Remove and discard the ring gear bolts.

NOTE: the ring gear bolts have left-hand threads.

2. Tap the ring gear loose, using a non-metallic hammer.
3. If the ring gear runout exceeds .005 in., when previously measured, recheck the case as follows:
   a. Install the cap bolts, bearing caps and bearing adjusters.
   b. Tighten the cap bolts and adjusters sufficiently to prevent any sideplay in the bearings.
   c. Mount a dial indicator so that the pointer contacts the ring gear surface of the differential case flange. Measure the runout, which should not exceed .003 in. If the runout exceeds .003 in., the case must be replaced.
4. With a hammer and drift, remove the differential pinion shaft lockpin from the rear side of the ring gear flange. The hole is reamed only part way through, making it necessary to remove the pin from the proper side.
5. Remove the pinion shaft and axle shaft thrust block.
6. Rotate differential side gears until the pinions and thrust washers can be removed.
7. Remove both differential side gears and thrust washers.

Assembly

1. Lubricate all parts before assembly, with rear axle lubricant.
2. Install the thrust washers on the differential side gears and install the side gears into the case.
3. Place thrust washers on both differential pinions and, working through the large access window, mesh the pinion gears with the side gears. The pinions should be exactly 180° apart.
4. Rotate the side gears 90° to align the pinions and thrust washers with the pinion shaft holes.
5. From the pinion shaft lockpin hole side of the case, insert the slotted end of the pinion shaft through the case, conical thrust washer and just through one of the pinion gears.
6. Install the thrust block through the side gear hub, so that the slot is centered between the side gears.
7. Hold all these parts in alignment, and align the lockpin holes in the pinion shaft and case. Install the lockpin from the pinion shaft side of the ring gear flange.
8. With a stone, relieve the edge of the chamfer on the inside diameter of the ring gear.
9. Heat the ring gear (fluid bath or heat lamp) to a temperature not exceeding 300° F.

NOTE: do not heat ring gear with a torch.

10. Align the ring gear with the case. Insert new ring gear screws through the case flange and into the ring gear.
11. Alternately tighten each cap screw to 55 ft lbs.
12. Position each differential bearing cone on the hub of the differential case (taper away from ring gear) and install the bearing cones with an arbor press.
13. Install the pinion bearing cups squarely in the bores of the carrier.

Differential Assembly, Pinion Bearing Preload and Depth of Mesh

This type axle uses two types of pinions. Pinion depth of mesh and bearing preload are determined in the same manner for small and large stem pinions; only the sequence of adjustments varies. Small stem pinions require bearing preload adjustment first, while large stem pinions require pinion depth of mesh adjustment first. The position of the drive pinion, relative to the position of the ring gear (depth of mesh) is determined by the location of the bearing cup shoulders in the carrier and by the portion of the pinion behind the rear bearing.

NOTE: factory service procedures recommend the use of very specialized tools to assure proper adjustment of the rear axle without duplicating labor. However, the special tools are not readily available. The following procedures are substituted in place of special factory tools.

Assembly

1. Assembly procedures, excluding adjustments and selection of shims, are the reverse of disassembly.

NOTE: some rear axles of this type use a collapsible spacer. Once this spacer has been collapsed or the pinion bearing preload exceeded, the collapsible spacer must be replaced with a new one. Before assembly, gather together shims of several sizes and several spacers in case the assembly is not properly adjusted the first time.

If the differential assembly was satisfactory when disassembled, the drive pinion may be assembled with the original components, excepting the pinion front bearing and collapsible spacer (if used). If any replacement parts are installed, a complete

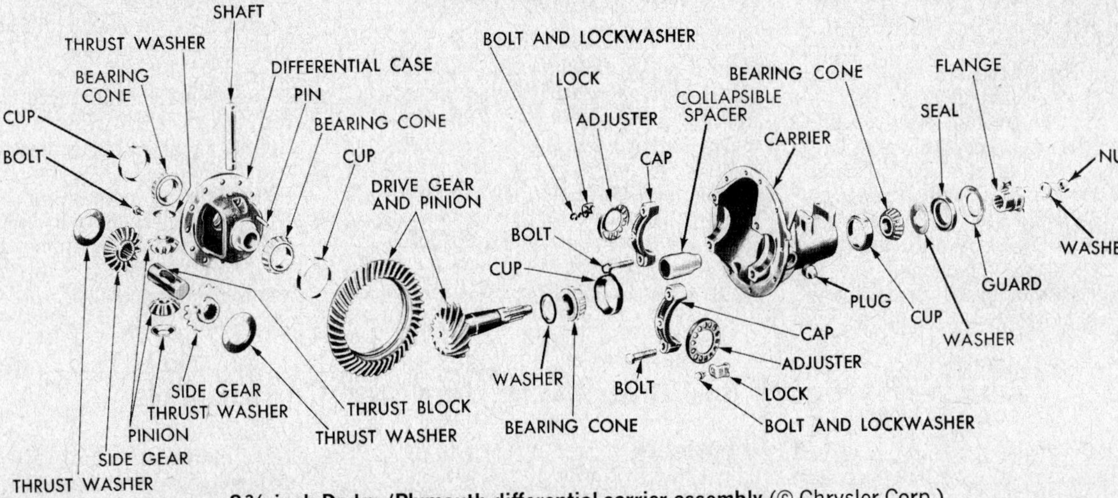

8¾ inch Dodge/Plymouth differential carrier assembly (© Chrysler Corp.)

adjustment will be necessary. Ring gears and pinions are available in matched sets only, and the adjustment position for best tooth contact is marked on the end of the pinion head.

Proper pinion setting, relative to the ring gear is determined by a shim, selected before the pinion is installed in the carrier. Pinion bearing shims are available in .002 in. increments (small stem) and in .001 in. increments (large stem with collapsible spacer).

Depth of Mesh

The head of the pinion is marked with a (+) or (−) followed by a number ranging from 0 to 4. If the old and new pinion have the same marking and the old bearing is being installed, use a shim of the original thickness. But, if the old pinion is marked (0), for example, and the new pinion is marked +2, try a .002 in. thinner shim. If the new pinion is marked −2, try a .002 in. thicker shim. The exact size of the pinion shim cannot be determined exactly without special equipment. This method provides a starting point. When the unit is assembled, check the ring gear teeth contact pattern and adjust the shim size accordingly. The entire unit must be disassembled to change the shim size.

Pinion Bearing Preload (Small Stem)

1. If the bearings are being replaced, place the bearings in the carrier and drive into place with a drift.
2. Assemble the pinion shim (chamfered side toward the gear) onto the pinion stem. Install the tubular spacer if equipped, and the preload shims on the pinion stem.
3. Insert the pinion assembly into the carrier .
4. Install the front pinion bearing cone, U joint flange, Belleville washer (convex side up) and nut. Do not install the oil seal.
5. Tighten the flange nut to 240 ft lbs. (210 ft.lbs. in 1973 and later).
   Rotate the pinion to properly seat the bearing rollers. The preload torque required to turn the pinion with the bearings oiled, should be 20-30 in. lbs. with new bearings and 0-15 in. lbs. for used bearings. Use a thinner shim pack to increase preload and a thicker shim pack to decrease preload.
6. After the correct pinion depth has been established and the preload obtained, remove the drive pinion flange.
7. Lubricate and install the drive pinion oil seal.
8. Install the pinion flange, washer and nut. Torque the nut to 240 ft.lbs. (210 ft.lbs. in 1973 and later).

Pinion Bearing Preload (Large Stem)

1. Place the rear pinion bearing cone on the pinion stem (small side away from pinion head).
2. Lubricate front and rear bearing cones and install the rear pinion bearing cone onto the pinion stem with an arbor press.
3. Insert the pinion bearing and collapsible spacer assembly through the carrier and install the front bearing cone. Install the companion flange.

NOTE: during installation of pinion bearing, do not collapse the spacer.

4. Install the drive pinion oil seal into the carrier .Use tool C-3890 to insure proper seal depth.
5. Support the pinion in the carrier and install the anti-rattle washer.
6. Install the Belleville washer (convex side up) and pinion nut.
7. Hold the companion flange and tighten the pinion nut to remove all end-play, while rotating the pinion to insure proper bearing seating. Remove the tools and rotate the pinion several revolutions.
8. Torque the pinion nut to 170 ft. lbs. (210 ft.lbs. in 1973 and later). With an in. lb. torque wrench, measure the pinion bearing preload, which should be 20-30 in.lbs. for new bearings or 10 in.lbs. over the original figure if the old pinion bearing is used.

NOTE: the correct preload reading can only be obtained with the carrier nose upright. The final assembly is incorrect if the final pinion nut torque is below 170 ft.lbs. (210 ft.lbs. in 1973 and later) or if the pinion bearing preload is not within specifications. Under no circumstances should the pinion nut be backed off to reduce the pinion bearing preload. If this is done, a new collapsible spacer will have to be installed and the unit adjusted again until proper preload is obtained.

9. Check the ring gear teeth contact pattern.

Carrier Assembly

1. Install the differential bearing cups onto their respective bearings and position assembly in the carrier.
2. Install the caps and bolts and tighten bolts finger tight. Be sure all identification markings are properly aligned and positioned.
3. Tighten the adjusters enough to square the bearing cups with the bearings and eliminate end-play. Allow some backlash to remain.
4. Tighten one corresponding bolt on each cap to 85-90 ft lbs.
5. Set dial gauge to contact outer end of ring gear tooth and take readings at 90° intervals to find the spot with the least clearance. Do not rotate ring gear after this position is found.
6. Turn both adjusters equally until backlash is between .005 and .0015 in.
7. Install adjuster lock into adjuster at rear face of ring gear. If holes do not align, tighten to next hole. Never back off to meet hole.
8. Turn the adjuster, on tooth side of ring gear, a notch at a time until the backlash is a minimum of .006 in. and a maximum of .008 in. This will establish proper bearing preload and correct backlash. Tighten the bearing cap bolts to 85-90 ft. lbs.
9. Install the remaining adjuster lock and tighten cap screws to 15-20 ft.lbs.

Final Installation

1. Thoroughly clean the gasket surfaces of the carrier and housing.
2. Install the carrier on the housing using a new gasket. Tighten the nuts to 45 ft.lbs.
3. Install the axle shafts and adjust the axle shaft end-play if necessary.
4. Install the driveshaft and torque the screws to 15 ft.lbs.
5. Install the backing plates, hubs and drums and bleed and adjust the brakes (if necessary).
6. Fill the differential with SAE 90 lubricant to the bottom of the filler plug opening. Lower and road-test the vehicle.

Dodge/Plymouth 8⅜ and 9¼ in. Integral Carrier Axle

See the Dodge/Plymouth truck section for external identification and axle shaft service.

Differential

Removal

1. Keep a pencil and paper handy to record data.
2. Jack up the rear of the vehicle and remove the wheels, drums, and axle shafts.

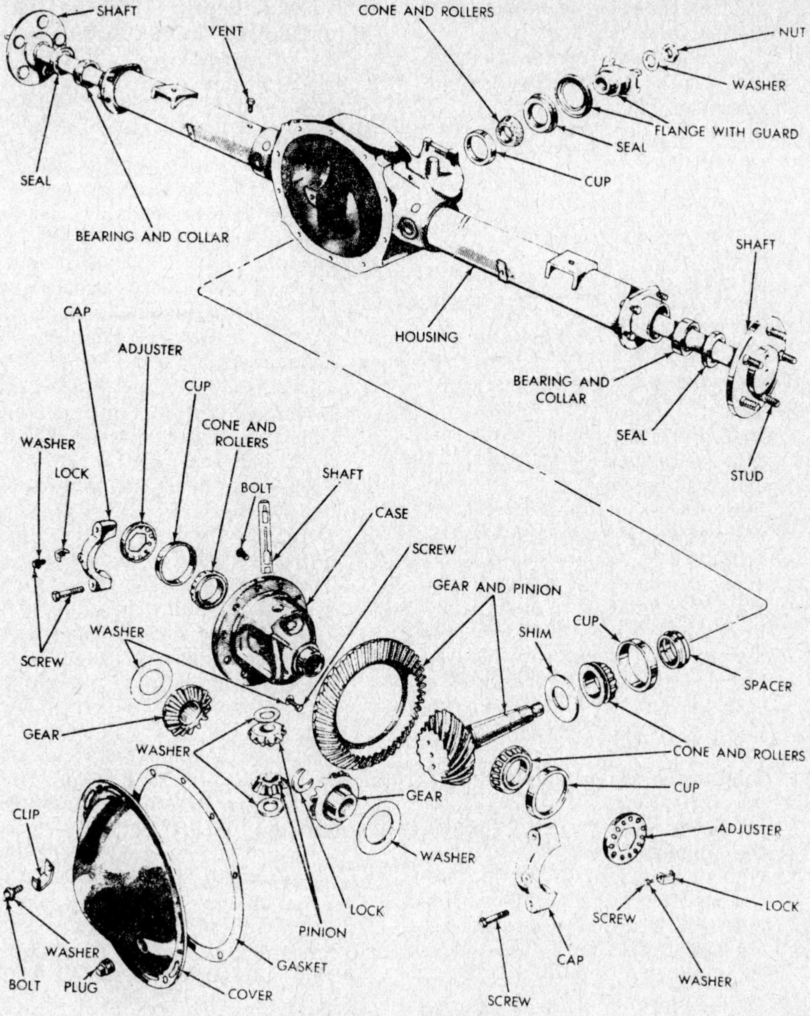

9¼ inch integral carrier Dodge/Plymouth axle (© Chrysler Corp.)

3. Loosen the housing cover screws and drain the lubricant from the rear axle.
4. Remove the cover.
5. Clean the inside of the differential case with solvent and blow dry with compressed air.
6. Check for differential side-play by inserting a large screwdriver between the left side of the axle housing and the differential case flange. Using a prying motion, determine whether side-play exists. There should be no side-play.
7. Paint the ring gear teeth and make a gear tooth contact pattern. Determine if proper depth of mesh can be obtained.
8. If side-play was found in step six, proceed to step nine. If no side-play was found in step six, check the drive gear run-out. Mount a dial indicator and index the indicator stem at right angles to the rear face of the ring gear. Rotate the ring gear and mark the ring gear and case at the point of greatest run-out. Total indicator reading should not exceed 0.005 in. If it does, the possibility exists that the case must be replaced.
9. Measure and record the pinion bearing preload. Use an in. lb. torque wrench to measure the preload.
10. Remove the pinion nut, washer and pinion flange.
11. Remove and discard the pinion oil seal.
12. Match-mark the axle housing and the differential bearing caps.
13. Remove the threaded adjusters and the differential bearing caps. There is a special wrench to do this through the axle tube on late models.
14. Remove the differential case from the housing. The differential bearing cups and threaded adjusters must be kept together so they can be installed in their original position.

Disassembly

1. To remove the drive pinion or front bearing cone, drive the pinion rearward out of the bearing. This will result in damage to the bearing and cup. The bearing cone and cup must be replaced with new parts. Discard the collapsible spacer.
2. Drive the front and rear bearing cups from the housing with a brass drift. Remove the shim from behind the rear bearing cup and record the thickness. Discard the shim.
3. Remove the rear bearing cone from the pinion stem with a puller.
4. Clamp the differential case and ring gear in a vise with soft jaws.
5. Remove the ring gear bolts (left-hand thread). Tap the ring gear loose with a soft-faced mallet.
6. If the ring gear run-out exceeded 0.005 in., recheck the case as follows. Install the differential case, cups, caps, and adjusters in the housing. Turn the adjusters to eliminate all side-play and tighten the differential cap bolts snugly. Measure the run-out at the ring gear flange face. Total indicator reading should not exceed 0.003 in. It is often possible to reduce run-out by removing the ring gear and remounting 180° from its original position. Remove the differential case from the housing.
7. Remove the pinion shaft lock-screw and remove the pinion shaft.
8. Rotate the differential side gears until the differential pinion shafts can be removed through the opening in the case.
9. Remove the differential side gears and thrust washers.
10. Using a puller or a press and press plates, remove the differential side bearings.

Assembly

1. Lubricate all parts, before assembly, with rear axle lubricant.
2. Install the thrust washers on the differential side gears and install the side gears into the case.
3. Place thrust washers on both differential pinions and, working through the large access window mesh the pinion gears with the side gears. The pinions should be exactly 180° apart.
4. Rotate the side gears 90° to align the pinions and thrust washers with the pinion shaft holes.
5. From the pinion shaft lockpin hole side of the case, insert the slotted end of the pinion shaft through the case, conical thrust washer and just through one of the pinion gears.
6. Install a thrust block through

the side gear hub, so that the slot is centered between the side gears.

7. Hold all these parts in alignment, and align the lockpin holes in the pinion shaft and case. Install the lockpin from the pinion shaft side of the ring gear flange.
8. With a stone, relieve the edge of the chamfer on the inside diameter of the ring gear.
9. Heat the ring gear (fluid bath or heat lamp) to a temperature not exceeding 300° F.

NOTE: do not heat ring gear with a torch.

10. Align the ring gear with the case. Insert the ring gear screws through the case flange and into the ring gear.
11. Alternately tighten each cap screw to 55 ft. lbs.
12. Position each differential bearing cone on the hub of the differential case (taper away from ring gear) and install the bearing cones. An arbor press may be helpful.

Pinion Depth of Mesh

1. The proper pinion setting (relative to the ring gear) is determined by a shim which has been selected before the pinion is to be installed in the carrier. Pinion bearing shims are available in 0.001 in. increments.
2. The head of the pinion is marked with a "plus" (+) or a "minus" (—) mark that is followed by a number ranging from zero to four. If the old and new pinions have the same marking and the old bearing is being installed, use a shim of the original thickness. If the old pinion is marked zero (0), however, and the new pinion is marked plus two (+2), try a shim that is 0.002 in. thinner. If the new pinion is marked axle housing cup bore and install minus two (—2), try a shim that is 0.002 in. thicker.
3. Position the selected shim in the the rear bearing cup.
4. Place the rear pinion bearing cone on the pinion stem (small side away from pinion head).
5. Lubricate the front and rear bearing cones and install the rear pinion bearing cone onto the pinion stem with an arbor press.
6. Insert the pinion bearing and collapsible spacer assembly through the carrier and install the front bearing cone. Install the companion flange.

NOTE: during installation of the pinion bearing do not collapse the spacer.

7. Install the drive pinion oil seal into the carrier. Be sure to properly seat the seal.
8. Support the pinion in the carrier and install the anti-clang washer.
9. Install the Belleville washer (convex side up) and pinion nut.
10. Hold the companion flange and tighten the pinion nut to remove all end-play, while rotating the pinion to ensure proper bearing seating. Remove the tools and rotate the pinion several revolutions.
11. Torque the pinion nut to 170 ft. lbs. (210 from 1972 on). With an in. lbs torque wrench, measure the pinion bearing preload, which should be 20-30 in. lbs. for new bearings or 10 in. lbs. over the original figure if the old pinion bearing is used.

NOTE: The correct preload reading can only be obtained with the carrier nose upright. The final assembly is incorrect if the final pinion nut torque is below 170 ft.lbs. (210 from 1972 on) or if the pinion bearing preload is not within specifications. Under no circumstances should the pinion nut be backed off to reduce the pinion bearing preload; if this is done, a new collapsible spacer will have to be installed and the unit adjusted again until proper preload is obtained.

Differential Bearing Preload and Ring Gear-to-Pinion Backlash—First Type

NOTE: for later axles see Side Bearing Preload Adjustment following.

1. With the pinion bearings installed and preload set, install the differential case and ring gear in the housing with the respective bearing caps and adjusters. The adjusters should be flush with the caps. Tighten the bolts on each cap to 10 in. lbs.
2. Turn the right adjuster until the assembly has approximately 0.005 in. spread, measured with a dial indicator.
3. Tighten all four cap bolts to 60 ft.lbs.
4. Turn the adjuster on the right until all spread is removed.
5. Turn the adjusters in until all bearing free-play is eliminated and there is some backlash between the ring and pinion gear. Turn the ring gear and pinion several times to seat the bearings.
6. Install a dial indicator to register on the rear face of any ring gear tooth. Measure the backlash at four points equally spaced around the ring gear. Turn the ring gear to position it at the point of least backlash.
7. Turn both adjusters in, the same amount and in the same direction until backlash is 0.001-0.002 in.
8. Turn the bearing adjuster on the right side in until 0.006-0.008 in. minimum backlash is obtained. Setting the required backlash will also obtain the proper preload.
9. Make a ring gear contact pattern test and evaluate the results. If the unit must be disassembled to put in a new shim behind the pinion, the entire assembly operation must be repeated.

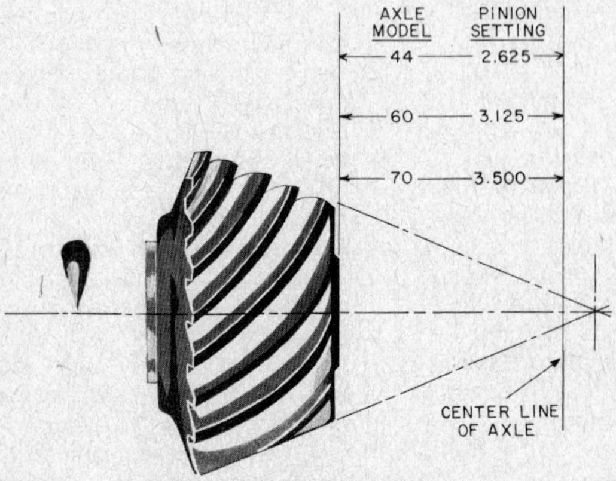

Pinion setting depth measurement (© Chrysler Corp.)

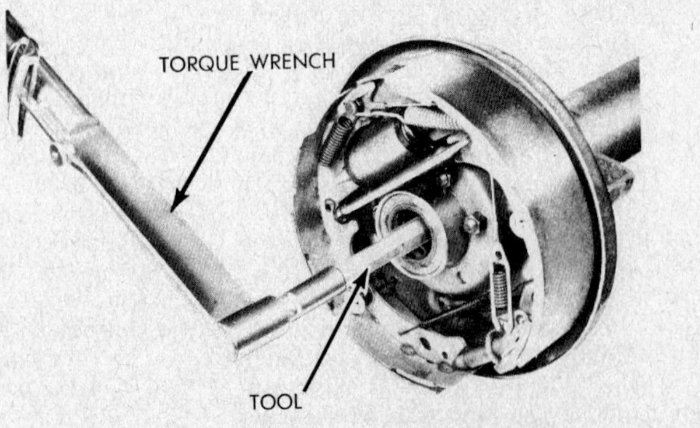

Use of long bar tool with hex end to adjust differential bearing preload and gear backlash (© Chrysler Corp.)

10. Install the axle shafts, drums, and wheels.
11. Install a new cover gasket and the differential cover. Refill the unit with the specified lubricant.
12. Lower and road-test the car.

Side Bearing Preload—Second Type

A number of changes have been incorporated into these axles. The new type of axles still use threaded adjusters to control side bearing preload. The threaded adjuster uses a hex drive hole, and requires special tool C-4164 to adjust the side bearing preload through the axle tube. An adjuster lock with two pointed teeth which engage in the exposed adjuster thread when the lock is tightened is provided. Previously, spacers were used from 0.084-0.100 in. The new shims will range from 0.020-0.038 in. and will be equipped with internal centering tabs. The new shims, marked with a number which represents its thickness in thousandths of an inch, can be installed with either side against the pinion head. To accommodate the new adjuster locks, a new axle cover is used.

The axle pinion has been redesigned to use a short collapsible spacer The short collapsible gear sets are interchangeable with the previous gearsets the only precaution being to ensure that the proper spacer is used.

1. Index the gears so that the same gear teeth are in contact throughout the adjustment.
2. The differential bearing cups will not always move with the adjusters. It is important to seat the bearings by rotating them 5-10 times in each direction, each time the adjusters are moved.
3. With the pinion bearings installed and the preload set, install the differential with adjusters, caps and bearings. Lubricate the bearings and adjuster threads. Check to be sure that there are no crossed threads. Tighten the cap screws on the right and left to 10 ft. lbs. Tighten the bottom cap screws finger-tight until the head is just seated on the bearing cap.
4. Using the tool, check to be sure that the adjuster rotates freely. Turn both adjusters in until bearing play is eliminated with some drive gear backlash (0.010 in.). Seat the bearing rollers.
5. Install and register a dial indicator against the drive side of a gear tooth. Check the backlash at four positions to find the point of minimum backlash. Rotate the gear to the position of least backlash and mark the tooth so that all readings will be taken at the same point.
6. Loosen the right adjuster and turn the right adjuster until the backlash is 0.003-0.004 in. with each adjuster tightened to 10 ft. lbs. Seat the bearings rollers.
7. Tighten the differential bearing cap screws to 100 ft. lbs.
8. Tighten the right adjuster to 70 ft. lbs. and seat the rollers, until the torque remains constant at 70 ft. lbs. Measure the backlash. If the backlash is not 0.006-0.008 in. increase the torque on the right adjusters and seat the rollers until the correct backlash is obtained. Tighten the left adjuster to 70 ft. lbs. and seat the bearings until the torque remains constant.
9. If the assembly is properly done, the initial reading on the left adjuster will be approximately 70 ft. lbs. If it is substantially less, the entire procedure should be repeated.
10. After adjustments are complete, install the adjuster locks. Be sure the teeth are engaged in the adjuster threads. Torque the lockscrews to 90 in. lbs.

Final Assembly

1. Install the axle shafts.
2. Install the cover on the differential housing, using a new gasket.
3. Refill the rear axle housing with SAE 90 lubricant. On 8$^3/_8$ in. axles, fill to $^1/_4$ below the plug opening through 1971, and $^1/_2$ in. below from 1972 on. Fill 9$^1/_4$ in. axles to the bottom of the plug opening.

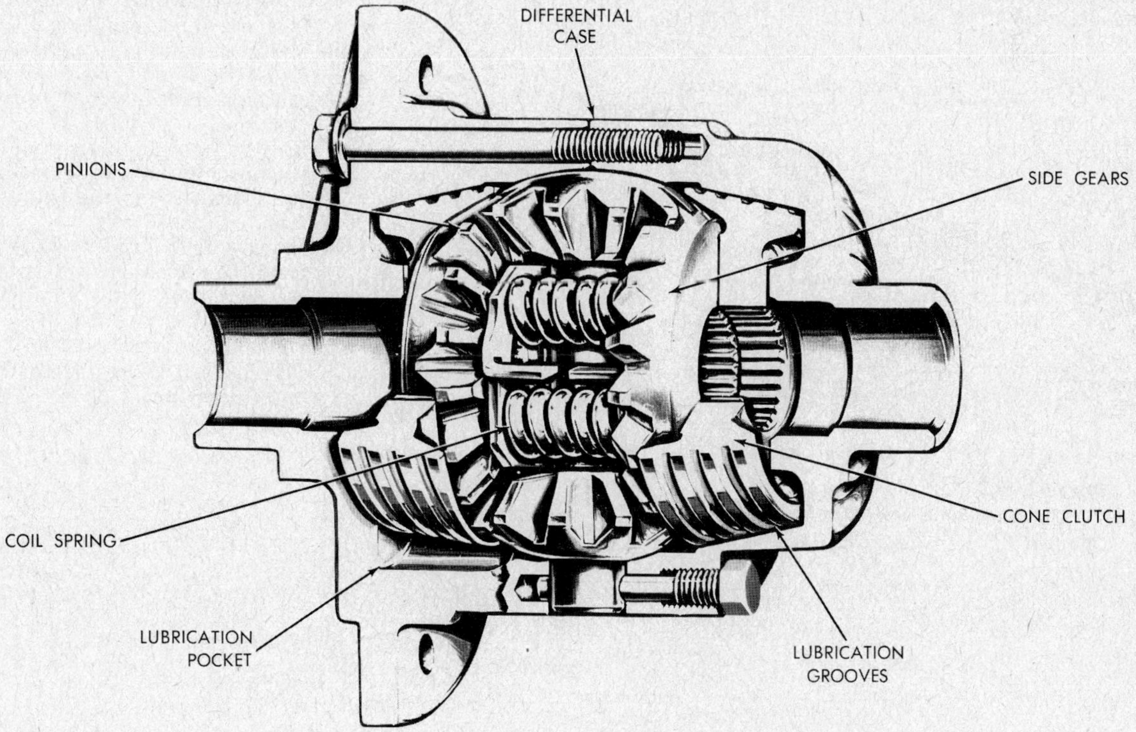

Differential case cutaway view (© Chrysler Corp.)

Ford Semi-Floating Single Speed Axle, Removable Carrier Type

This is a conventional type axle used on light duty Ford trucks. The axle design uses a removable carrier with the assembly bolted to the axle housing. The axle uses hypoid type gears and has the pinion gear mounted below the center line on the ring gear. The pinion gear is supported by two bearings in front of the gear and one behind. It is important to refer to the tag showing the axle and model number which is secured to the housing to obtain proper replacement parts.

Carrier Assembly

Removal

1. With the vehicle raised on a lift, remove the axle shafts from the housing.
2. Remove the drive shaft from the carrier assembly.
3. With a drain pan under the axle, remove the retaining bolts from the carrier and drain the gear lube.
4. Remove the carrier assembly from the axle.

Installation

1. Clean the surfaces of the carrier and the axle housing. Install a new gasket.
2. Position the carrier assembly on the studs in the housing and install the retaining nuts. Torque the nuts to 30-40 ft. lbs.
3. Install the drive shaft and torque the bolts to 13-17 ft. lbs.
4. Install the axles in the housing and secure.
5. Fill the axle housing to the proper level with gear lube and road test for proper operation.

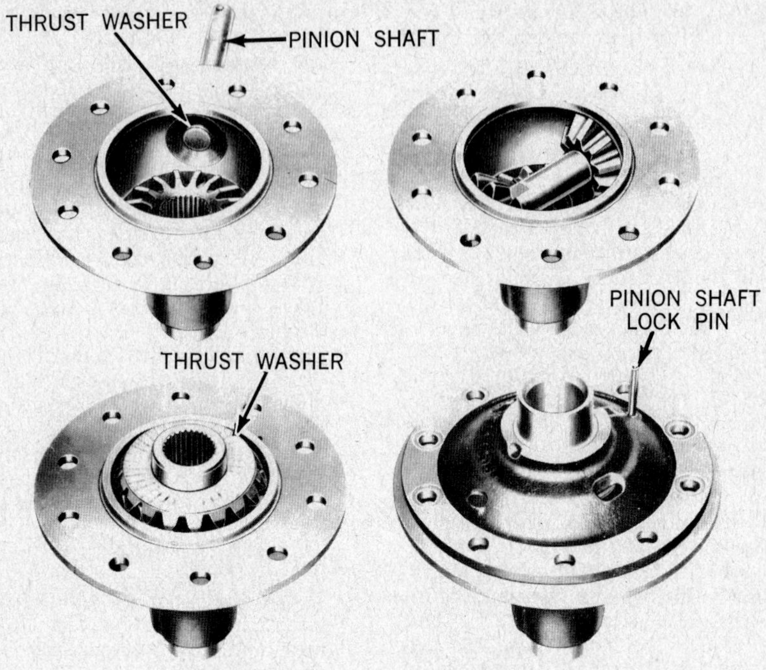

Differential case assembly

Differential Case

Removal and Disassembly

1. Remove the carrier assembly from the axle housing and mount the carrier in a holding fixture.
2. Mark the bearing caps and adjusting nuts so they may be installed in their original positions when assembling.
3. Remove the adjusting nut locks, bearing caps and adjusting nuts.
4. Lift the differential assembly out of the carrier. Using a bearing puller, remove the side bearings from the differential case.
5. Mark the side of the case, the ring gear and the cover so they can be installed in their original positions.
6. Remove the bolts that retain the ring gear to the case and using a soft hammer, tap the ring gear from the case.
7. Using a drift, drive the lock pin from the pinion shaft and seperate the halves of the differential case.
8. Drive the pinion shaft out of the case using a brass drift and remove the thrust washers and gears.

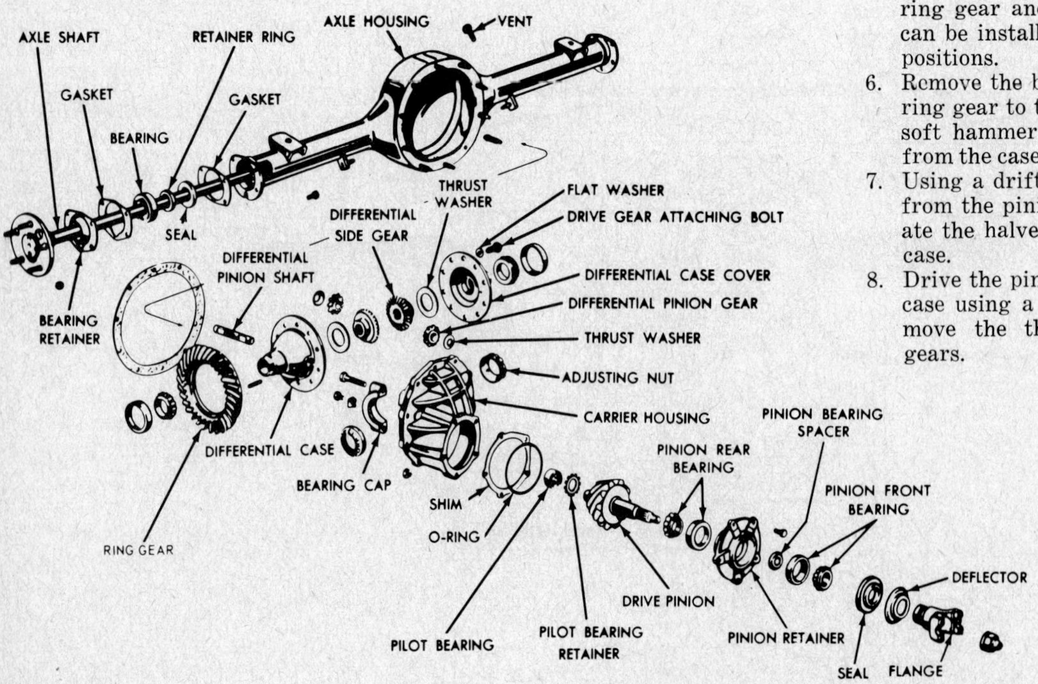

Removable carrier axle—disassembled (© Ford Motor Co.)

Drive Pinion and Bearing Retainer

Removal and Disassembly

1. With a holding fixture installed on the flange, remove the pinion nut and washer. Leave the holding fixture on the flange and using a puller, remove the flange from the pinion shaft.
2. Using a seal puller, remove the pinion seal from the retainer assembly.
3. Remove the bolts from the retainer assembly and lift the retainer from the carrier. Measure the thickness of the shim that was between the retainer and the carrier assembly. Record the result.
4. Install a piece of hose on the pinion pilot bearing surface in front of the pinion gear. Mount the retainer assembly in a press and press the pinion gear out of the retainer.
5. Mount the pinion shaft in a press and press the rear bearing from the pinion shaft.

Pinion Bearing Cup

Replacement

1. With the retainer assembly mounted in a press, using the proper tool, press the front and rear bearing cups from the assembly.
2. Check the inside surfaces of the retainer for any nicks, dirt or distortion.
3. Install the new cups by pressing them into place with the proper tool. When the cups are installed, make sure they are seated in the retainer by trying to fit a .0015 in. feeler gauge, between the cup and the bottom of the bore.

Pilot Bearing

Replacement

1. Using a bearing driver, drive the bearing and retainer out of the carrier assembly.
2. Using the same tool, drive the new bearing into place until the driver bottoms against the case.
3. Drive a new retainer into place with the concave side up.

Drive Pinion and Bearing Retainer

Assembly and Installation

1. Mount the pinion gear in a press and press the rear bearing into place.
2. Install the bearing spacer, bearing retainer and front bearing on the pinion shaft and press them into place. Be careful not to crush the bearing spacer.
3. Install a new O-ring in the groove in the retainer assembly. Do not twist the O-ring when fitting it into place.
4. Lubricate both pinion bearings.
5. Check the thickness of the original shim that was recorded earlier. Located on the head of the pinion gear is the shim adjustment number. Compare the number on the old pinion with the one on the new pinion. Refer to the table which indicates the amount of change to the original shim thickness for proper operation.
6. Install the new shim on the housing and install the pinion and retainer assembly, being careful not to damage the O-ring.
7. Install the bearing retainer bolts and torque them to 30-40 ft.lbs.
8. Using a seal driver, install a new pinion seal in the retainer assembly.
9. Position a holding tool on the flange and install the flange on the pinion shaft. With the holding tool still in place, install the washer and nut on the pinion shaft and torque the nut to 175 ft.lbs. Check the pinion bearing preload. The preload should be 8-14 in.lbs. for used bearings and 22-32 in.lbs. for new bearings. *Do Not* overtighten the nut. *Do Not* back off the nut to obtain the proper preload. If the 175 ft.lbs. initial torque was too much, the collapsible spacer must be replaced. Tighten the pinion only enough to obtain the right preload torque.

Differential Case

Assembly and Installation

1. Lubricate all of the differential parts with gear lube before assembling.
2. Install a side gear and thrust washer in the case bore. Using a soft hammer, drive the pinion shaft into the case far enough to hold a pinion thrust washer and gear. Place the second pinion thrust washer and gear in position and carefully tap the pinion shaft into place. Be sure to line up the holes for the lock pin in the pinion shaft.
3. With the second side gear and thrust washer in place, install the cover on the differential case. Drive the pinion lock pin into place. Insert an axle shaft spline into the side gear and check for free rotation of the gears.
4. Install two, two inch long 7/16 (N.F.) bolts through the differential case and thread them a little way into the ring gear. These will act as a guide when installing the ring gear on the case. Tap the ring gear into place.
5. Remove the guide pins and install the ring gear bolts. Tighten the bolts evenly to 65-85 ft.lbs.
6. If the differential bearings were removed, install the assembly in a press and press the new bearings into place.
7. Coat the bearing bores in the carrier with gear lube and install the bearing cups on the bearings. Place the differential assembly in the carrier.
8. Slide the differential case in the carrier bore until there is a slight amount of backlash between the gears.
9. Install the adjusting nuts in the carrier so that they just contact the bearing cups. The nuts should be engaged about the same number of threads on each side.
10. Position the bearing caps in the carrier. Be careful to line up the marks. Install the cap bolts and torque them to 70-80 ft.lbs. Make sure the adjusting nuts turn freely as the bolts are being tightened.
11. Adjust the backlash and bearing preload as follows;
    a. Loosen the bearing cap bolts then retighten them to 35 ft.-lbs.
    b. Loosen the adjusting nut on the pinion side so that it is away from the bearing cup. Tighten the nut on the opposite side so that the ring gear is forced into the pinion with no backlash.
    c. Recheck the nut on the pinion side to make sure it is still loose. Now tighten this nut until it contacts the bearing cup. After is contacts the cup, turn it two more notches.
    d. Rotate the ring gear several times in each direction. This helps to seat the bearings in the cups.
    e. Again loosen the nut on the pinion side. If there is any backlash between the gears, tighten the nut on the ring gear side until the backlash is removed.
    f. Install a dial indicator on the carrier assembly. Tighten the nut on the pinion side until it just contacts the cup. With the dial indicator set at zero, tighten the pinion side nut until the case is spread .008-.012 in. with new bearings and .005-.008 in. with old bearings. As this preload is applied the ring gear is forced away from the pinion and usually results in the correct backlash.
    g. Mount the dial indicator on the ring gear and check the gear for backlash. Make sure the bearing caps are torqued to 75-85 ft.lbs.

h. The backlash should be between .008-.012 in. If the backlash is not correct, loosen one nut and tighten the other an equal amount to move the ring gear in or out to correct the measurement. When making final adjustments, always move the adjusting nuts in a tightening direction. To do this, if a nut had to be loosened one notch, loosen it two notches and tighten it one. This makes certain the nut is in contact with the cup and will not shift when the vehicle is in operation.

i. Coat the ring gear teeth with a marking compound and check the tooth pattern. If the pattern is not correct make the necessary changes to bring it into adjustment.

12. Install the carrier assembly in the vehicle and road test for proper operation.

GMC Single Speed Axle Service

H052, H072, H110, H130, H135, H150, H170

Disassembly of Subassemblies

Differential Disassembly

1. Remove lock nut, adjusting screw, and thrust block.
2. Remove two adjuster lock cap screws and locks.
3. Punch-mark bearing caps and carrier to help in locating caps for assembly. Remove bearing adjusters and bearing caps. *NOTE: Do not pry caps free with a screwdriver or distort locating dowels.*
4. Carefully remove differential assembly from carrier.
5. Use differential side bearing remover to pull bearing cones off each side of case.
6. Make sure that differential case halves are punch-marked so that they can be reassembled in same position.
7. Remove drive gear, and separate case halves.
8. Remove two side gears; differential spider, and four differential pinions.
9. On H110, H135, and H150 models remove pinion and side gear thrust washers to complete differential disassembly.

Drive Pinion Disassembly

1. Remove seal retainer and gasket from carrier.
2. Use brass drift against inner end of pinion to drive out pinion and bearings assembly.
3. Remove shim pack from carrier from those models having tapered roller outer bearings.
4. According to the model, it may be necessary to use a drift to remove the pinion rear bearing.
5. Clamp yoke in soft-jawed vise. Remove yoke nut and washer and separate drive pinion from yoke.
6. Separate yoke from oil seal retainer.
7. Place retainer in a soft-jawed vise and, using a hammer and chisel, remove oil seal and then the felt oil seal.
8. On models with tapered roller outer bearing, remove bearing cup, outer tapered bearing cone, and bearing spacer from drive pinion.
9. Using bearing remover press plate with press, separate bearing cone (some models) or roller bearing (on all other models) from drive pinion.
10. On H110 and H135 models remove bearing lock ring, and use press plates with arbor press to remove roller bearing from inner end of drive pinion. This completes drive pinion disassembly.

Assembly of Subassemblies

NOTE: Thoroughly clean and lubricate all components with axle lubricant before reassembling.

Drive Pinion Assembly

1. Clean counterbore of oil seal retainer. Saturate felt seal in oil and install evenly in retainer. Soak oil seal in light engine oil for about one hour before installing. Coat outer surface of seal lightly with sealing compound to prevent oil leaks between seal and retainer.
2. Install oil seal into retainer with lip of seal toward inner side of retainer. Using a seal installer, press oil seal into retainer with face of seal flush with retainer face.
3. Retainer surface must be clean and smooth to prevent oil leaks between retainer and carrier.
4. On H052, H072, and H150 models, press bearing into place into carrier bore.
5. On H110 and H135 models, press roller bearing into position on drive pinion with chamfered side of inner race facing toward pinion shoulder. Position bearing lock ring to secure bearing on drive pinion. *NOTE: Opposed tapered roller bearing cones, two bearing cups, and spacer used on some models are serviced and replaced as a unit. The spacer is a preselected one to provide proper bearing adjustment.*
6. Models with tapered roller bearings:
   a. Press inner bearing cone into place with largest side of cone facing pinion gear end.
   b. Install original shim pack in carrier. If original ring gear and pinion are reinstalled, use shims that were removed. Shims are available in five thicknesses -0.012, 0.015, 0.018, 0.021, and 0.024 inch. When using new gears, start with one 0.021 inch shim and refer to "General Axle Service" section for details on checking pinion depth.
   c. Insert pinion assembly into carrier (on H150 model), align roller bearing with carrier boss. Install bearing spacer, bearing cup and bearing cone with wide side facing pinion splines.
7. Models with double-row ball bearing: Using a 2-inch pipe or tubing, drive bearing unit into proper seating position.
8. With pinion assembly properly positioned in carrier, install new gasket. Install seal retainer onto yoke, and assemble yoke and retainer assembly onto splined end of drive pinion.
9. Secure retainer to carrier with lock washers and cap screws and torque to specifications.
10. Secure pinion assembly with yoke washer and nut and torque to 220 ft. lbs. This completes drive pinion assembly.

Differential Assembly

1. To facilitate installation of drive gear, install two guide pins (cut ½"-20x2" bolts) in gear. Start guide pins through case flange holes and tap drive gear onto case. If one differential gear is bad, the complete set should be replaced.
2. Lubricate differential case inner walls and all component parts with axle lubricant. Place differential pinions and thrust wash-

ers (thrust washers are used only on H110, H135, and H150 axles) on spider.

3. Assemble side gears, pinions and side gear and pinion thrust washers to left half of differential.
4. Assemble drive gear half (right half of differential, being sure to line up marks on the two halves.
5. Install differential-to-drive gear cap screw and lock washers and tighten evenly until drive gear is flush with case flange. Remove guide pins and install cap screws and torque to specifications.
6. Differential side bearing cones can be installed with special installer tool.

Installation of Subassemblies

Differential Installation

1. Install bearing cap locating dowels in caps. Lubricate side bearings and place bearing cups on bearings.
2. Install differential assembly into carrier. Carefully install bearing adjusters into carrier.
3. Install bearing caps, aligning punch marks previously made. Be sure that bearing adjuster threads are engaged with carrier and caps. Tighten adjusters alternately and evenly. Tighten bearing cap screws until lock washers are flat.

Drive Gear and Pinion Adjustment

1. Loosen bearing cap screws just enough to loosen right-hand bearing adjuster (pinion side) and tighten left-hand bearing adjuster (opposite pinion side.) Using adjuster, remove all backlash between drive gear and pinion.
2. Back off left-hand bearing adjuster about two notches to point where notch in adjuster is aligned with lock. Tighten right-hand bearing adjuster solidly to seat bearing. Again loosen right-hand adjuster enough to free bearing; then retighten snugly against bearing. Draw up right-hand adjuster one or two more notches until adjuster notch aligns with lock.
3. With dial indicator on carrier adjuster, slowly oscillate drive gear and take backlash reading. Backlash should be 0.005 to 0.008-inch.
4. If backlash exceeds 0.008-inch, loosen right-hand adjuster one notch; then tighten left-hand adjuster one notch. If less than 0.005 inch, loosen left-hand adjuster one notch and tighten right-hand adjuster one notch.
5. After backlash has been adjusted, again tighten bearing cap screws until their respective lock washers flatten out.
6. Check drive gear run-out.
7. Install side bearing adjusting nut lock and secure with cap screws and lock washers.

Checking Pinion Depth (Models with Tapered Roller Bearings Only)

NOTE: Refer to tooth contact chart in the "General Axle Service" section.

1. Coat drive gear with red lead. Turn pinion shaft several revolutions in both directions while applying considerable drag on drive gear.
2. Pinion depth is determined by shim pack selection. Shim packs are available in thicknesses of: 0.012, 0.015, 0.018, 0.021, and 0.024- inch.
3. Changing pinion depth will again require adjusting backlash. After pinion depth and

SPECIFICATIONS

GMC H-052, H-072, H-110, H-135, H-150, H-170

Make	GMC
Type	Hypoid
Adjustment and Clearances	
Backlash—gear to pinion	0.005"-0.008"
Adjustment method	See text
Pinion backlash adjustment	
Models with tapered bearings	Shims
Models with ball bearing	None
Shim pack thickness	0.021" Initial
Shims available	0.012"-0.015"-0.018"-0.021"-0.024"
Differential bearing adjustment method	Threaded rings
Drive Gear	
Backlast—gear to pinion	0.005"-0.008"
Adjustment method	See text
Runout (mounted to case)	0.006"
Drive Pinion	
Backlash—pinion to drive gear	0.005"-0.008"
Adjustment method	See text
Differential Case	
Runout at flange (max.)	0.002"
Diameter at side gear	
H-052, H-072	1.927"-1.929"
H-110, H-135	2.193"-2.195"
H-150	2.409"-2.411"
Side Gear	
Backlash—side gear to pinion gear	0.004"-0.007"
Hub diameter—H-052, H-072	1.923"-1.925"
Hub diameter—H-110, H-135	2.189"-2.191"
Hub diameter—H-150	2.405"-2.407"
Pinion Gear	
Inside diameter—H-052 H-072	0.814"-0.815"
Inside diameter—H-110, H-135	0.880"-0.881"
Inside diameter—H-150	0.9435"-0.9445"
Thrust Washer Thickness (H-110, H-135, H-150)	
Side gear	0.058"-0.062"
Pinion gear	0.058"-0.062"
Spider	
Diameter of arms—H-052, H-072	0.808".0.809"
Diameter of arms—H-110, H-135	0.874"-0.875"
Diameter of arms—H-150	0.9365"-0.9375"
Thrust Block	
Thickness	0.1845"-0.1885"
Clearance—block to gear	0.005"-0.007"
Axle Shafts	
Diameter of splines—H-052, H-072	1.5275"-1.5325"
Number of splines—H-052, H-072	17
Diameter of splines—H-110, H-135	1.724"-1.732"
Number of splines—H-110, H-135	27
Diameter of Splines—H-150	1.848"-1.856"
Number of Splines—H-150	29
Torque Specifications (Ft. Lbs.)	
Drive gear bolts	
H-052, H-072	85-95
H-110, H-135	100-110
H-150	150-170
Differential side bearing cap bolts	
H-052, H-072	95-105
H-110, H-135, H-150	190-220
Pinion bearing retainer bolts	
H-052, H-072	90-100
H-110, H-135, H-150	160-170
Pinion flange nut	160-280
Diff. bearing adj. nut lock	10-20
Axle shaft flange to hub	
H-052, H-072	85-95
H-110, H-135, H-150	10-20
Carrier to housing	
H-052, H-072	40-50
H-110, H-1.5, H-150	75-90
Axle shaft nuts	
All models	80-100

backlash have been adjusted, torque bearing caps to specifications.

Thrust Block Installation

1. Install thrust block and lock nut to adjusting screw. Thread screw and block into carrier until block contacts drive gear. Rotate gear and note change of drag. Adjust these parts until point of greatest drag is reached. Back screw off about a 30 degree turn to provide 0.005 to 0.007-inch clearance between block and gear. Make certain screw does not turn at all when tightening lock nut to 135 foot-pounds torque.

Dana-Spicer Single Reduction Models 30, 44, 44-1, 60, 60-35, 70

Differential

Removal

1. Drain lubricant.
2. Remove cover and gasket.

NOTE: Attached to a cover bolt is a metal tag which shows the number of teeth on pinion and ring (drive) gear.

3. Remove bearing cap screws. Note the matching marks on cap and carrier and make sure caps are reassembled to correct markings.
4. Using a spreader tool, spread carrier a maximum of 0.020 inch and measure amount of spread with a dial indicator. *IMPORTANT: Carrier may be permanently damaged if spread more than 0.020 inch. Do not attempt differential removal without using a spreader.*
5. Carefully lift differential assembly out of carrier.
6. Remove the spreader assembly after removing the differential assembly from the housing.

Drive Pinion

Disassembly

1. Pull flange (yoke) from shaft splines of drive pinion.
2. Using a press or soft hammer, drive pinion and inner bearing cone assembly out of carrier.
3. Remove and tag shim pack from splined end of pinion. *NOTE: If either ring (drive) gear or pinion are to be replaced, write down markings (+), (—), or (0) located at face end of pinion for reassembly reference.*
4. Remove oil seal assembly from carrier bore. This frees oil seal gasket, oil slinger, and bearing cone.
5. If replacement of the pinion tapered bearings is necessary, the bearing cups should be removed from carrier as follows:
   a. Use remover with a driver or slide hammer to remove inner bearing cup from carrier. This frees shim pack. Remove and tag shims for reassembly.
   b. Remove outer bearing cup.
6. Use remover set to separate bearing cone from drive pinion.
7. Separate oil slinger from pinion.

NOTE: This oil slinger is only found on some axle models.

Differential

Disassembly

1. Remove and label the two bearing cups.
2. Use a suitable type puller to remove the bearing cones. Remove and label adjusting shims.
3. Drive out pinion shaft lock pin.

NOTE: On the Spicer Model 70 rear axle, punch-mark the differential case halves (for reassembly reference) and separate. Remove the differential spider, pinion gears, side gears and thrust washers.

4. Separate ring gear from case.
5. Remove pinion shaft, two pinions, two side gears, and four thrust washers from case.

Assembly

1. Place side gears with new thrust washers in position inside case.
2. Place pinions and thrust washers in position in case.
3. Install the differential pinion shaft in position in case between two pinions. Align shaft lock pin hole with lock pin hole in case and install pinion shaft lock pin. Peen hole to prevent pin from falling out. *NOTE: On the Spicer Model 70 rear axle, install the differential spider along with its pinion gears, side gears and thrust washers into the differential case halves. Bolt the two halves together making sure the punch-marks line up.*
4. Place ring (drive) gear in proper position against flange of case and bolt ring gear to case. Alternately tighten these bolts until all bolts are tightened to proper torque.

NOTE: Do not install differential cones or shim packs until pinion depth and bearing preload have been checked out. Differential bearing adjustment is a part of axle assembly procedure.

Mark locations on carrier and caps (© Dana Corp., Spicer Div.)

Installation of spreader and dial indicator (© Dana Corp., Spicer Div.)

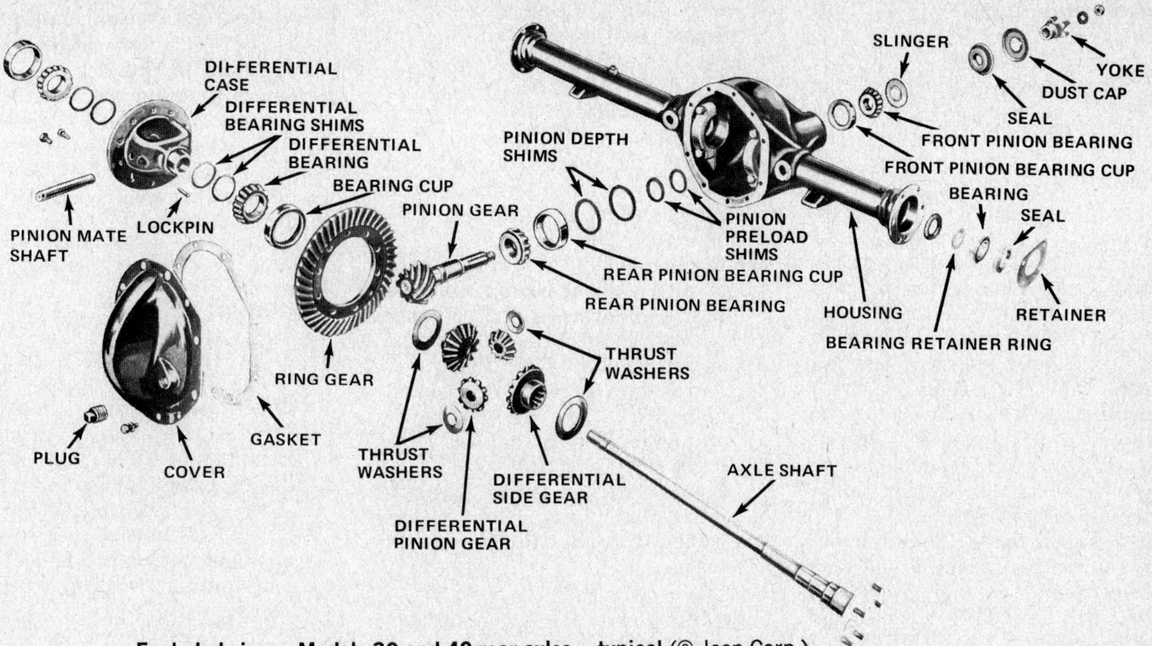

Exploded view—Models 30 and 40 rear axles—typical (© Jeep Corp.)

Differential Bearing

Adjustment

1. Press fit bearing cones tightly against shoulders on case.

IMPORTANT: Do not install shims at this time.

2. Install bearing cups.
3. Install spreader tool and dial indicator, and spread carrier as described in "Differential Removal."
4. Place differential assembly into carrier.
5. Install bearing caps using their respective cap screws. Make sure caps are assembled to their correct markings. Hand tighten bearing cap screws.
6. Install dial indicator at carrier with indicator button contacting back of ring (drive) gear. Rotate ring gear and check run-out.
7. If run-out exceeds 0.002-inch, remove the differential assembly and remove ring gear from the case.
8. Reinstall differential assembly without ring gear and check run-out of differential case flange. If run-out still exceeds 0.002-inch, the defect is probably due to bearings or case, and should be corrected before proceeding.
9. Remove differential from carrier.

NOTE: Do not install shims behind the bearings until final installation.

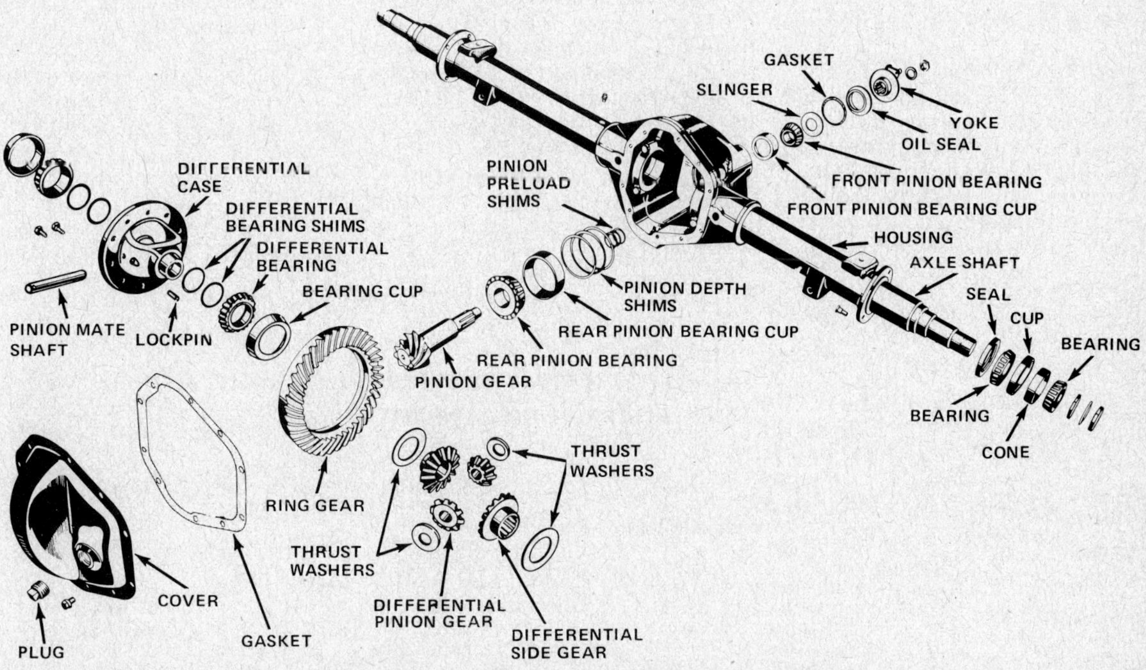

Exploded view—Model 60 rear axle—typical (© Jeep Corp.)

Drive Pinion

Installation

1. If either drive pinion or ring (drive) gear must be replaced, they must be installed as a set. (These parts are matched and lapped at time of manufacture to obtain the correct gear tooth contact.)
2. Whenever it is necessary to install a new drive pinion, the plus (+) or minus (−) marking on face of rear end of pinion must be considered. Select a new pinion and ring gear set with markings as near as possible to those on old pinion. If marking on both old and new pinion is the same, do not change thickness of shim pack.
3. The approximate difference between markings on old and new drive pinion is the adjustment that will have to be made in the shim packs.
4. In the first listing below note that the new pinion is a plus eight (+8) while the old pinion is a plus five (+5). Making a difference of plus three (+3). This means that the thickness of each shim pack must be decreased by 0.003-inch. Other examples are:

Pinions		*Difference*	*Amount*
New Pinion	*Old Pinion*	*Between Markings*	*To Change Each Shim Pack (in.)*
+8	+5	+3	Dec. 0.003
+5	+8	−3	Inc. 0.003
−5	−3	−2	Inc. 0.002
−3	−5	+2	Dec. 0.002
+5	−3	+8	Dec. 0.008
−4	+2	−6	Inc. 0.006

5. Once proper adjustment in shim packs has been made, place oil slinger, if so equipped, over pinion shaft. Install pinion inner bearing cone over shaft, and use bearing installer and an arbor press to press bearing onto pinion shaft. Bearing must be seated tightly against shoulder or oil slinger.
6. Use pinion front bearing cup installer to install outer bearing cup into carrier bore.
7. Install the selected inner shim pack in carrier. Then use pinion rear bearing cup installer to install inner bearing cup.
8. Insert pinion, oil slinger (when used) and inner bearing cone assembly into carrier and place the selected shim pack into position on outer end of pinion shaft.
9. Place outer bearing cone over pinion shaft, then use installer to seat bearing tight against shim pack.
10. Install pinion flange (yoke), washer and nut. Hold flange while tightening nut to proper torque.

NOTE: Install oil slinger and oil seal only after pinion depth and pinion bearing preload have been checked out.

Checking Pinion Depth Adjustment

1. A pinion depth gauge and correct adapter, which gives a micrometer reading, should be used to determine pinion depth. The actual pinion depth setting can be determined by adding gauge reading to thickness of step plate and comparing result with the nominal dimension of 2.625-inch (models 44/60-35) or 3.125-inch (model 60).
2. If the pinion setting is within minus (−) 0.001-inch to plus (+) 0.003-inch of this nominal dimension, the pinion position can be considered satisfactory.
3. If pinion setting exceeds these limits, it must be corrected by adjusting thickness of shim pack behind the pinion inner bearing cup.

Pinion Bearing Preload Adjustment

1. Use a torque wrench to check pinion bearing preload.
2. Rotating torque of pinion should be from 15 to 30 inch-pounds.
3. Add or remove shims from pack just behind outer bearing cone to bring preload within these torque limits.

Differential

Installation

1. Use dial indicator and spreader tool as described in "Differential Removal," to spread carrier a maximum of 0.020-inch.
2. Install bearing cups and place differential assembly in carrier. Rotate differential and, with a soft hammer, tap ring (drive) gear to assure a proper bearing seating.
3. Reinstall bearing caps in their proper locations as indicated by marks made during the removal procedure. Finger tighten cap screws. Relieve the spreader tool pressure, and tighten cap screws to 70-90 foot-pounds.
4. Move differential assembly tightly against drive pinion.
5. Install dial indicator securely to carrier, then set button at zero and against back of drive gear.
6. Move the differential toward the dial indicator and note the reading. For accuracy, repeat this operation several times.
7. Remove the differential assembly from carrier. Install a shim pack behind differential bearing cone at drive gear side, equal to the dimension indicated by dial indicator.
8. Subtract the indicator reading from the reading previously obtained in paragraph "Differential Bearing Adjustment."
9. To the above result should be added 0.015 to 0.020-inch in shims to provide bearing preload.

NOMINAL ASSEMBLY DIMENSION AND ADAPTER DISC CHART

Axle Model	*Nominal Assembly Dimension*	*Adapter Disc Tool Number*						
			1618-9	4.125″	SE-1065-9-G			SE-1065-9-I
					SE-1065-9-I	17800-1	4.4062″	SE-1065-9-M
			1790A-1A	4.2190″	SE-1065-9-CC			SE-1065-9-G
					SE-1065-9-E	G361	2.625″	SE-1065-9-PP
			G161	3.551″	SE-1065-9-E			SE-1065-9-O
			H140	3.551″	SE-1065-9-E	H340	2.625″	SE-1065-9-PP
			H162	3.719″	SE-1065-9-F			SE-1065-9-O
44	2.625″	SE-1065-9-SS	13800	3.6244″	SE-1065-9-G	H362	2.937″	SE-1065-9-R
60	3.125″	SE-1065-9-Y			SE-1065-9-E			SE-1065-9-PP
70*	3.500″	SE-1065-9-Y	16802-3	4.125″	SE-1065-9-G	28M	3.4725″	SE-1065-9-D

* Model 70—Use a 0.375 shim under dial pointer

SPECIFICATIONS

DRIVE PINION ADJUSTING SHIM THICKNESS CHANGES DANA

OLD PINION MARKING	NEW PINION MARKING .4	.3	.2	.1	0	+1	+2	+3	+4
+4	+0.008	+0.007	+0.006	+0.005	+0.004	+0.003	+0.002	+0.001	0
+3	+0.007	+0.006	+0.005	+0.004	+0.003	+0.002	+0.001	0	−0.001
+2	+0.006	+0.005	+0.004	+0.003	+0.002	+0.001	0	−0.001	−0.002
+1	+0.005	+0.004	+0.003	+0.002	+0.001	0	−0.001	−0.002	−0.003
0	+0.004	+0.003	+0.002	+0.001	0	−0.001	−0.002	−0.003	−0.004
−1	+0.003	+0.002	+0.001	0	−0.001	−0.002	−0.003	−0.004	−0.005
−2	+0.002	+0.001	0	−0.001	−0.002	−0.003	−0.004	−0.005	−0.006
−3	+0.001	0	−0.001	−0.002	−0.003	−0.004	−0.005	−0.006	−0.007
−4	0	−0.001	−0.002	−0.003	−0.004	−0.005	−0.006	−0.007	−0.008

MODEL 44-1F AND 44-7F—DANA

DANA AXLE ADJUSTMENTS

Description	Inch	Description	Scale Pull Lb
Backlash Between Ring Gear and Pinion	.004-.009	Steering Knuckle Turning Effort—Tie Rod Disconnected (1 Knuckle)	26
Backlash Maximum Variation Between Teeth	0.002		
Pinion Bearing Preload	15-35 in-lbs		

DANA AXLE TCRQUE LIMITS—(FT-LB)

Description	Ft-Lb	Description	Ft-Lb
Pinion Shaft Nut	200-220	Ball Joint Nut — Top	100
Differential Bearing Cap Bolts	70-90	— Bottom	80 ②
Ring Gear Attaching Bolts	45-65	Oil Filter Plug	40
Cover to Housing Bolts	30-40	U-Joint Bolts	15-20
Spindle Nut to Wheel Hub — Inner	50 ①	Backing Plate and Spindle to Steering Knuckle Retaining Bolts	30-40
— Outer	80-100		

① Torque to 50 ft-lb, then back off 90 degrees and rotate to closest pin hole.
② A torque prevailing nut. Do not reuse.

44-6CF AND 44-6CF-HD—DANA

DANA AXLE ADJUSTMENTS

Description	Inch	Description	Ft-Lb
Backlash Between Ring Gear and Pinion	.004-.009	Steering Knuckle Turning Torque (Starting)	
Backlash Maximum Variation Between Teeth	0.002	446CF	5-10
Pinion Bearing Preload	20-40 in-lbs	446CF-HD	10-15

DANA AXLE TORQUE LIMITS — (FT-LB)

Description	Ft-Lb	Description	446CF Ft-Lb	446CF-HD Ft-Lb
Pinion Shaft Nut	200-220	Ball Yoke Oil Seal Bolts	10-15	10-15
Differential Bearing Cap Bolts	70-90	Spindle Bearing Cap Bolts	30-40	80-90
Ring Gear Attaching Bolts	45-65	Spindle to Spindle Arm Bolts	30-40	80-90
Cover to Housing Bolts	30-40	Oil Filler Plug	40	40
Spindle Nut to Wheel Hub — Inner	50 ①	U-Joint Bolts	15-20	15-20
— Outer	80-90	Backing Plate and Spindle to Steering Knuckle Retaining Bolts	30-40	30-40

① Torque to 50 ft-lb, then back off 90 degrees and rotate to closest pin hole.

MODEL 44 AXLE

(Full-Floating and Semi-Floating Types)

Differential Bearing Preload	.015 in
Differential Side Gear-to-Case Clearance	.000-.006 in
Drive Gear-to-Pinion Backlash	.005-.010 in
Drive Pinion Bearing Break-Away Preload	
Original Bearings	10-20 in-lbs
New Bearings	20-40 in-lbs
Pinion depth dimension	2.625

SPECIFICATIONS
MODEL 30 FRONT AXLE

Differential Bearing Preload	.015 in
Differential Side Gear-to-Case Clearance	.000-.006 in
Drive Gear-to-Pinion Backlash	.005-.009 in
Drive Pinion Bearing Break-Away Preload	
Original Bearings	15-25 in-lbs
New Bearings	20-40 in-lbs
Pinion depth dimension	2.250

MODEL 44 AXLE

(Full-Floating and Semi-Floating Types)

Axle Housing Cover	20	15-25
Backing Plate Mounting Bolts/Nuts		
Front Brakes	28	25-30
Rear Brakes	30	25-35
Differential Bearing Bolts	80	70-90
Disc Brake Shield Bolt	8	5-10
Disc Brake Shield Nuts	35	30-40
Drive Gear-to-Case Bolts	55	45-65
Lower Ball Joint Nut	80	—
Pinion Yoke Nut	210	200-220
Upper Ball Joint Nut	100	—
Upper Ball Stud Seat	50	—
Universal Joint Flange Bolts	35	25-45
Universal Joint U-Bolts	15	13-18
Wheel-to-Hub Nuts	80	65-90

All torque values given in foot-pounds with dry fits unless otherwise specified.
Service Set-To Torques should be used when assembling components.
Service In-Use. Recheck Torques should be used for checking a pre-torqued item.

TORQUE SPECIFICATIONS
MODEL 30 FRONT AXLE

	Service Set-To Torques	Service In-Use Recheck Torques
Axle Housing Cover	20	15-25
Differential Bearing Bolts	45	35-50
Drive Gear-to-Case Bolts	55	45-65
Lower Ball Joint Nut	80	—
Pinion Yoke Nut	210	200-220
Universal Joint U-Bolts	15	13-18
Upper Ball Joint Nut	100	—
Upper Ball Stud Seat	50	—
Wheel-to-Hub Nuts	80	65-90

TORQUE SPECIFICATIONS
MODEL 44FBJ SPICER

Pinion and ring gear backlash—.005-.009 in.
Pinion depth setting—2.625 in.
Pinion depth adustment—Select shim
Pinion bearing preload—20-40 in. lbs. (New bearings)
—10-20 in. lbs. (Old bearings)
Differential bearing preload—.015 in. added to Zero Reading on drive tooth side

TORQUE SPECIFICATIONS

Companion flange nut—200-220 ft. lbs.
Differential bearing cap capscrew—70-90 ft. lbs.
Ring gear to differential case sapscrew—45-60 ft. lbs.
Cover to housing bolts—20 ft. lbs.

10. Install the above shim pack behind differential bearing cone at side opposite to drive gear.
11. Spread differential carrier, using spreader tool.
12. Install differential bearing cups then locate differential assembly in carrier.
13. Rotate differential assembly, tapping gear to seat bearings.
14. Install differential bearing caps in their correct location as indicated by marks made upon disassembly. Finger tighten cap screws.
15. Remove differential carrier spreader tool. Tighten differential bearing cap screws to proper torque.
16. Install dial indicator and check drive gear to drive pinion backlash at four equally spaced points around the drive gear. Backlash must be held to 0.003 to 0.006-inch and must not vary more than 0.002-inch between positions checked.
17. Whenever backlash is not within limits, differential bearing shim pack should be corrected.

International Harvester Co. Single Speed, Single Reduction Rear Axles

The rear axles may vary as to the design and the construction, but the components of the axles perform similarly regardless of the type. The components of the rear axle that the serviceman will be concerned with are the drive gears, the differential assembly and the axle housing. The removal and installation of the carrier assembly is accomplished in the conventional manner, regardless of a single or tandem axle.

Carrier Assembly

Disassembly

1. Mount the carrier assembly in a suitable fixture.
2. Remove the cotter pins from the bearing adjuster locks and remove the locks from the bearing caps.
3. Match mark the carrier legs to the bearing caps to identify properly upon reassembly.
4. Remove the ring gear thrust block and adjusting screw from the carrier housing.
5. Cut and remove the lock wire. Remove the bearing cap stud nuts or cap screws. Remove the bearing cap stud nots or cap screws. Remove the bearing caps and adjusting nuts. *NOTE: Bearing cap pilot rings may be used on some axle models. Do not lose or damage.*
6. Tip the differential assembly away from the pinion and lift the assembly from the housing.

NOTE: Due to the weight of the differential assembly, a lifting device may be used to assist in the removal.

Differential Case and Gear Aseembly

Disassembly

1. Match mark the differential case halves for the proper reassembly.
2. Cut the lock wire and remove the cap screws or stud nuts and separate the case halves.
3. Remove the spider, pinions, side gears and thrust washers from the case halves.
4. Remove the ring gear rivets by center punching each rivet head and using a drill, 1/32 inch smaller than the rivet body, drill through the rivet head. Use a punch to press out the remaining part of the rivet.

CAUTION: Never use a chisel to cut off the head of the rivets or damage to the differential case can result.

Pinion and Cage Assembly

Removal

1. Remove the pinion cage cap screws and remove the pinion cage assembly from the differential carrier. *NOTE: Puller screw holes are provided on some pinion cages, to assist in the removal of the cage from the housing. If no puller screw holes are present, a brass drift can be used on the inner end of the pinion to force the pinion and cage assembly from the carrier housing.*
   CAUTION: Do not use a drift on pinion shafts that have the straddle bearing retained by a snap ring. The snap ring groove may collapse.
2. Retain the shim pack for use during the reassembly.
3. Remove the companion flange from the pinion shaft, after the removal of the cotter pin and nut. *NOTE: The companion flange may have to be tapped of the pinion shaft with a soft hammer.*
4. Remove the outer bearing from the cage by holding the cage in a vise and tapping on the pinion shaft end, and forcing the shaft through the cage. **CAUTION: Do not allow the component parts to fall.**
5. Remove the spacer or spacer combination from the pinion shaft.
6. Remove the rear tapered thrust bearing from the pinion with the aid of a suitable puller.
7. Remove the straddle bearing retainer, if equipped, and remove the bearing with the aid of a suitable puller. *NOTE: The straddle bearing may be retained by staking of the pinion shaft end, by a snap ring, or by a cap screw and washer.*

Exploded view—differential assembly—typical
(© International Harvester Co.)

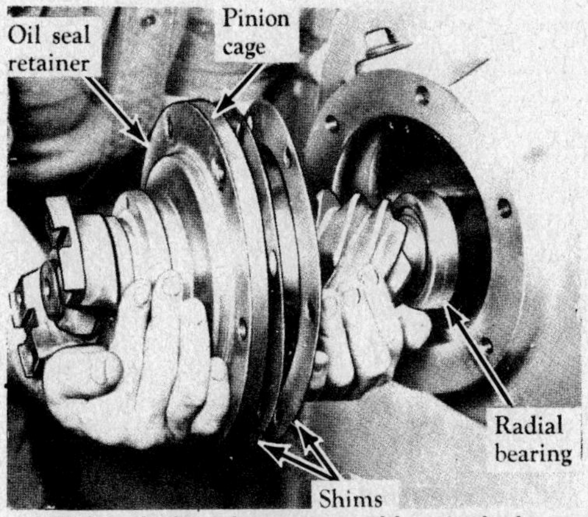

Pinion shaft and cage assembly—typical
(© International Harvester Co.)

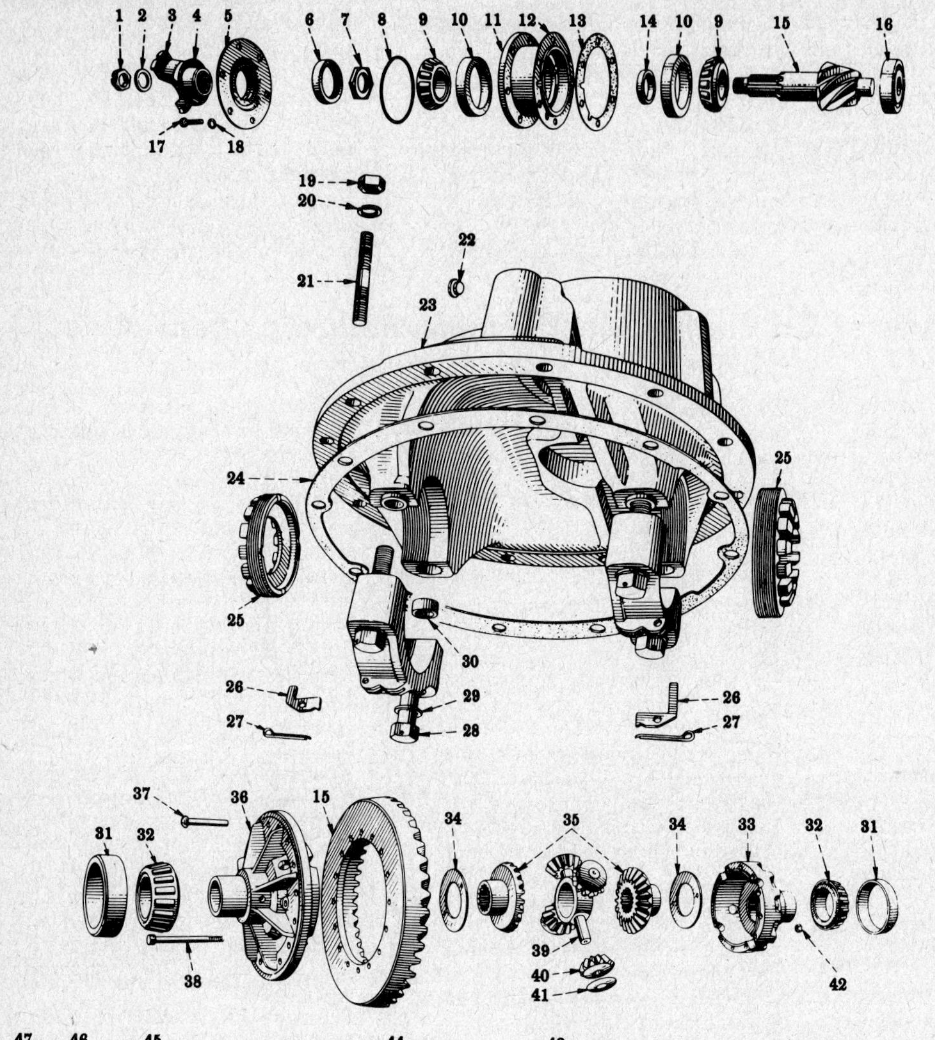

1 Nut, pinion end
2 Washer
3 Flange
4 Slinger
5 Retainer, pinion oil seal
6 Seal
7 No longer used
8 Seal, O-ring type
9 Bearing, pinion thrust
10 Cup, bearing
11 Cage, pinion bearing
12 Not used.
13 Shim pack
14 Spacer, pinion bearing
15 Gear set, drive and pinion
16 Bearing, radial
17 Bolt, hex head
18 Washer, lock
19 Nut, stud
20 Washer, lock
21 Stud
22 Plug, pipe
23 Carrier, with caps, assembly
24 Gasket, carrier to axle housing
25 Adjuster, bearing
26 Lock, adjuster
27 Pin, cotter.
28 Bolt, bearing cap
29 Washer
30 Bushing, pilot ring
31 Cup, bearing
32 Bearing, differential
33 Case, differential, plain half
34 Washer, thrust
35 Gear, differential side
36 Case, differential, flanged half
37 Rivet, drive gear to case
38 Bolt, differential case
39 Spider, differential
40 Gear, spider
41 Washer, thrust
42 Nut, hex
43 Breather, axle housing vent
44 Housing, axle assembly
45 Shaft, axle
46 Stud, wheel flange
47 Nut, hex
48 Plug, pipe

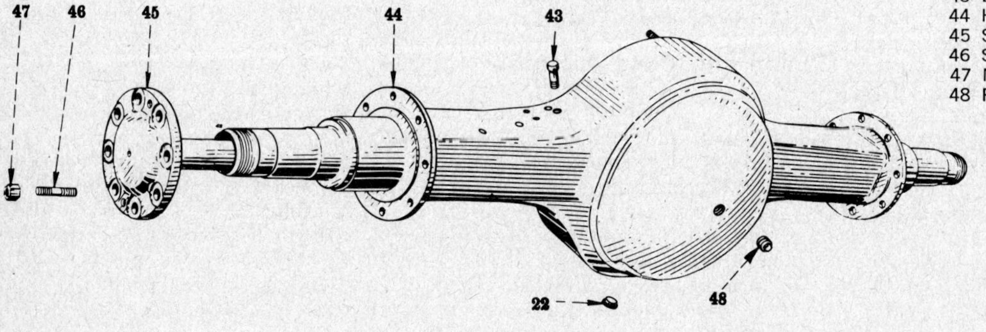

Exploded view—heavy duty single reduction rear axle (© International Harvester Co.)

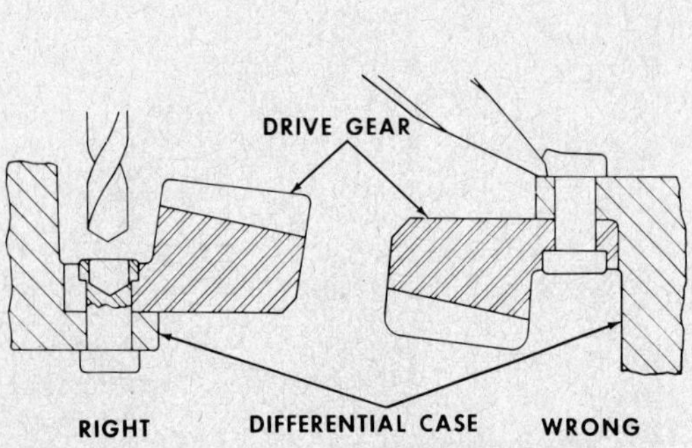

Right and wrong way to remove ring gear rivets
(© International Harvester Co.)

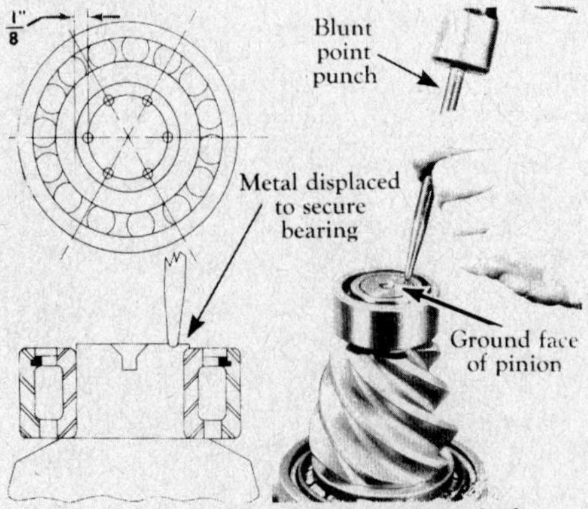

Staking straddle bearing to pinion shaft
(© International Harvester Co.)

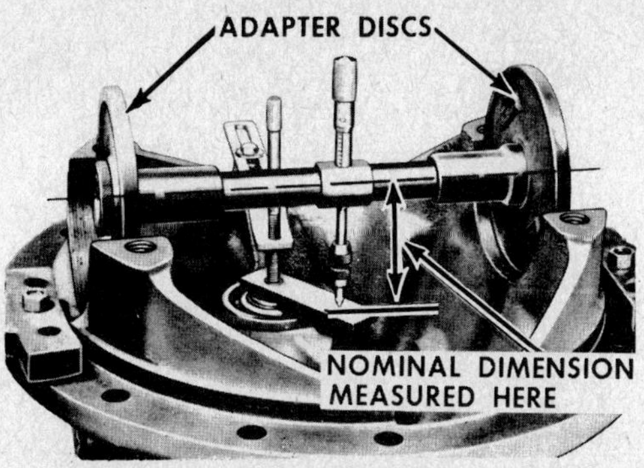

Use of the pinion setting gauge—typical
(© International Harvester Co.)

Location of pinion setting markings—typical
(© International Harvester Co.)

8. Remove the cork seal, and oil seal from the pinion cage.

Differential Carrier Assembly

Precautions to be Observed During the Reassembly

1. Before assembly, lubricate the bearings and cups and rewrap to maintain cleanliness.
2. Use correct rivet pressure when installing the ring gear to the differential case, or if bolts are available, be assured that the proper torque is applied in tightening.
3. Be sure that the bearing caps and adjusting nuts are correctly aligned and that the bearing cups fit properly. Irreparable damage can result to the differential carrier or bearing caps if the alignment is off.
4. Observe the proper torque settings when tightening any nuts or bolts.

Five Steps in the Reassembly of the Differential Assembly

1. *Pinion bearing preload*—This is determined by the thickness of the spacer between the two pinion thrust bearings, when tightened in the pinion cage.
2. *Establish pinion nominal dimension*—Use the manufacturers pinion setting gauge (SE-1065), or use an equivalent tool. Changes to this dimension can be made by adding or removing shims to move the pinion in or out of the carrier housing.
3. *Set the ring gear lash*—Move the ring gear to or from the pinion by means of the differential bearing adjusters.
4. *Preload the differential bearings*—This is accomplished by tightening the bearing adjusting nuts after zero end play has been obtained on the bearings.
5. *Check the gear tooth contact*—Use the paint impression method for this operation.

Differential Carrier

Assembly

1. Install the ring gear on the differential case with either the rivet method or by bolts.
2. When installing rivets, observe the pressures needed to upset the rivets.

RIVET SIZE	PRESSURE U.S. TONS
7/16	18-20
½	20-25
9/16	36
⅝	45-50
¾	50

NOTE: Hold the pressure force for one minute to assure that the rivet will fill the hole.

3. Install the side gear and thrust washer in the ring gear half of the differential case.
4. Place the spider, the pinion gears and thrust washers in position and install the component side gear and thrust washer.
5. Align the previously made match marks and position the component case half to the ring gear case half.
6. Install the cap screws or stud nuts and torque to specifications.
7. Check the gears for freedom of movement and install the lock wire.
8. Install the differential bearings on the differential case.

Pinion and Cage Assembly

Installation

1. Install the rear thrust tapered bearing and the straddle bearing on the pinion shaft.
2. Install the straddle bearing retainer. *NOTE: If the straddle bearing is of the type to be staked, use a blunt pin punch and stake in at least four to six equidistant places, approximately 1/8 inch in from the pinion circumference. The size of the pinion will dictate the number of staked points on the pinion end.*
3. Renew the bearing cups in the pinion cage, as necessary.
4. Lubricate the bearings and cups and install the pinion shaft through the pinion cage.
5. Install the spacer or spacer combination on the pinion shaft, followed by the outer pinion tapered bearing.
6. Temporarily assemble the companion flange and the washer and nut onto the pinion shaft, tightening the nut to specifications while holding the flange in a vise.
7. To measure the pinion bearing preload, wrap a strong cord or soft wire around the pinion cage and attach the other end to a inch-pound scale. Rotate the pinion cage by pulling on the spring scale and reading the scale while the cage is rotating. Refer to the specifications listed within this chapter.
8. If the preload does not agree with the specifications, a thicker or thinner spacer or spacer combination must be used.
9. When the proper preload is obtained, assemble the pinion bearing cage by removing the companion flange, install the oil seal, cork gasket, reinstall the campanion flange, washer and nut. Torque the nut to specifications and install the cotter pin.

Pinion Nominal Dimension

To locate the pinion nominal dimension, refer to the specifications listed within this chapter. Some pinions will have the dimension stamped or etched on the gear end of the shaft. Refer and compare to the specifications. The pinion variation, noted in thousands of an inch, will be etched on the gear end of the pinion shaft. This figure will be used in determining the amount of shims needed to locate the pinion gear in the proper relationship to the ring gear centerline. *NOTE: Refer to the beginning of the Rear Axe Drive Section for the procedure to follow in the use of the pinion setting gauge tool.*

If the pinion setting gauge tools are not available, the pinion depth will have to be adjusted by assembling the carrier assembly, installing the pinion cage assembly and the differential assembly into the carrier housing, and observing the tooth contact pattern on the ring gear. This is a trial and error method and very time consuming.

Differential Assembly

Installation, Preload, Backlash

1. Install the differential assembly with the bearing cups on the differential bearings into the legs of the carrier housing.
2. Install the bearing adjusting nuts and the bearing caps. Install the cap screws or stud nuts and turn the adjusting nuts while tightening the bearing caps to assure freedom of movement of the adjusting nuts. **CAUTION: If the bearing caps are not positioned properly, the adjusting nuts may be cross-threaded, and irreparable damage to the carrier housing or to the bearing cups may result.**
3. With the side bearing caps loosened to permit the bearing cup movement, loosen the adjusting nuts only enough to notice end play on a dial indicator, mounted on the carrier assembly with the button contacting the back side of the ring gear.
4. Tighten the adjusting nuts to obtain zero end play on the indicator.
5. Move the dial indicator to the coast side of the ring gear teeth, and determine the amount of back lash present between the pinion and the ring gear.
6. To adjust the back lash, move the ring gear towards or away from the pinion by means of the differential bearing adjusting nuts. Move the adjusting nuts the same distance, either in or out to maintain the differential bearing zero end play.
7. When the correct backlash clearance is established, tighten each adjusting nut one or two notches (depending upon the axle model), to preload the differential bearings. Tighten the bearing cap screws or stud nuts to the proper torque and recheck the gear backlash. Install the adjusting nut locks and cotter pins.
8. Coat approximately twelve teeth of the ring gear with oiled red lead paint and rotate the pinion in its normal rotation and check the drive side of the ring gear teeth for the tooth contact impression. *NOTE: A sharper tooth contact impression may be obtained by applying a small amount of resistance to the gear with a flat steel bar and using a wrench to turn the pinion.*
9. If the area of contact starts near the toe end of the ring gear and extends about ⅔ of the tooth length, the tooth contact is satisfactory.
10. Install the ring gear thrust block, if equipped. Adjust the block firmly a gainst the back face of the ring gear and back off the screw ¼ turn and lock the jam nut.
11. Install the carrier assembly into the housing, following the reverse procedure of the removal operation.

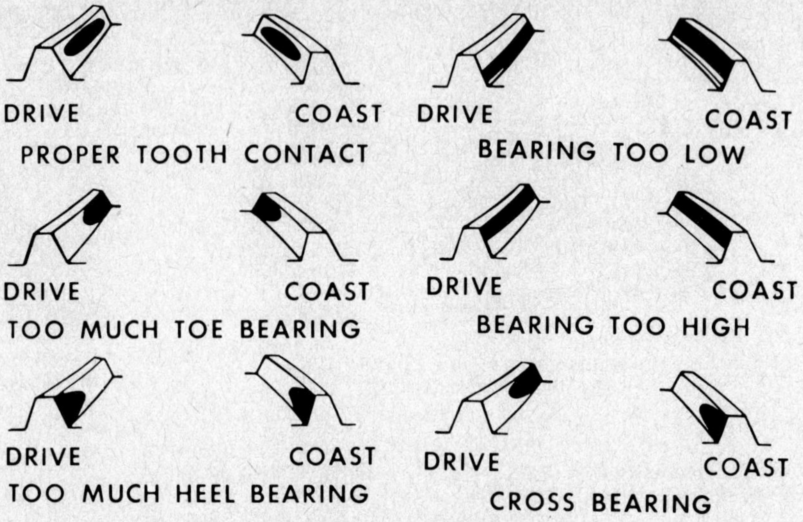

Typical gear tooth contact patterns

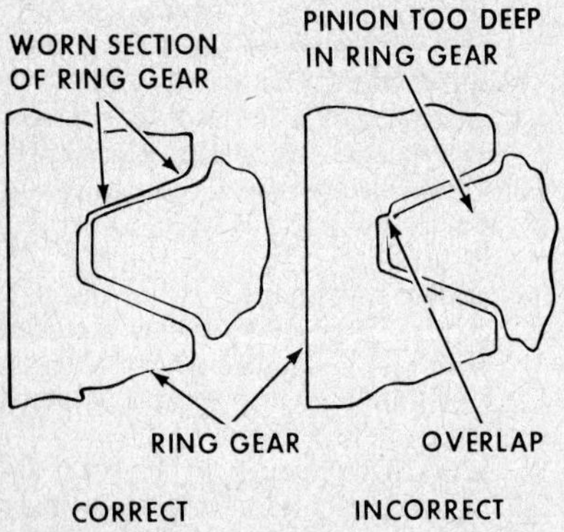

Correct and incorrect gear lash—using worn gears
(© International Harvester Co.)

INDEX

HYDRAULIC BRAKE SYSTEM TROUBLE DIAGNOSIS

Condition	*Possible Cause*	*Correction*
Insufficient brakes	1. Improper brake adjustment.	1. Adjust brakes.
	2. Worn lining.	2. Replace brake lining and adjust brakes.
	3. Sticking brakes.	3. Lubricate brake pivots and support platforms.
	4. Brake valve pressure low.	4. Inspect for leaks and obstructed brake lines.
	5. Slack adjuster to diaphragm rod not adjusted properly.	5. Adjust slack adjuster.
	6. Master cylinder low on brake fluid.	6. Fill master cylinder and inspect for leaks.
Brakes apply slowly	1. Improper brake adjustment or lack of lubrication.	1. Adjust brakes and lubricate linkage.
	2. Low air pressure.	2. Check belt tension and compressor for output. Adjust as necessary.
	3. Brake valve delivery pressure low.	3. Check valve pressure and clean or replace as necessary.
	4. Excessive leakage with brakes applied.	4. Inspect all fittings and lines for leaks and repair as necessary.
	5. Restriction in brake line or hose.	5. Clean or replace brake line or hose.
Spongy pedal	1. Air in hydraulic system.	1. Fill and bleed hydraulic system.
	2. Swollen rubber parts due to contaminated brake fluid.	2. Clean hydraulic system and recondition wheel cylinders and master cylinder.
	3. Improper brake shoe adjustment.	3. Adjust brakes.
	4. Brake fluid with low boiling point.	4. Flush hydraulic system and refill with proper brake fluid.
	5. Brake drums ground excessively.	5. Replace brake drums.
Erratic brakes	1. Linings soaked with grease or brake fluid.	1. Correct the leak and replace brake lining.
	2. Primary and secondary shoes mounted in wrong position.	2. Match the primary and secondary shoes and mount in proper position.
Chattering brakes	1. Improper adjustment of brake shoes.	1. Adjust brakes.
	2. Loose front wheel bearings.	2. Clean, pack and adjust wheel bearings.
	3. Hard spots in brake drum.	3. Grind or replace brake drums.
	4. Out-of-round brake drums.	4. Grind or replace brake drums.
	5. Grease or brake fluid on lining.	5. Correct leak and replace brake lining.
Squealing brakes	1. Incorrect lining.	1. Install correct lining.
	2. Distorted brakedrum.	2. Grind or replace brake drum.
	3. Bent brake support plate.	3. Replace brake support plate.
	4. Bent brake shoes.	4. Replace brake shoes.
	5. Foreign material embedded in brake lining.	5. Replace brake shoes.
	6. Dust or dirt in brake drum.	6. Use compressed air and blow out drums and support plate and shoes.
	7. Shoes dragging on support plate.	7. Sand support plate platforms and lubricate.
	8. Loose support plate.	8. Tighten support plate attaching nuts.
	9. Loose anchor bolts.	9. Tighten anchor bolts.
	10. Loose lining on brake shoes or improperly ground lining.	10. Replace brake shoes and cam-grind lining.
Brakes fading	1. Improper brake adjustment.	1. Adjust brakes correctly.
	2. Improper brake lining.	2. Replace brake lining.
	3. Improper type of brake fluid.	3. Drain, flush and refill hydraulic system.
	4. Brake drums ground excessively.	4. Replace brake drums.
Dragging brakes	1. Improper brake adjustment.	1. Correct adjust brakes.
	2. Distorted cylinder cups.	2. Recondition or replace cylinder.
	3. Brake shoe seized on anchor bolt.	3. Clean and lubricate anchor bolt.
	4. Broken brake shoe return spring.	4. Replace brake shoe return spring.
	5. Loose anchor bolt.	5. Adjust and tighten anchor bolt.
	6. Distorted brake shoe.	6. Replace defective brake shoes.
	7. Loose wheel bearings.	7. Lubricate and adjust wheel bearings.
	8. Obstruction in brake line.	8. Clean or replace brake line.
	9. Swollen cups in wheel cylinder or master cylinder.	9. Recondition wheel or master cylinder.
	10. Master cylinder linkage improperly adjusted.	10. Correctly adjust master cylinder linkage.
Hard pedal	1. Incorrect brake lining.	1. Install matched brake lining.
	2. Incorrect brake adjustment.	2. Adjust brakes and check fluid.
	3. Frozen brake pedal linkage.	3. Free up and lubricate brake linkage.
	4. Restricted brake line or hose.	4. Clean out or replace brake line hose.
Wheel locks	1. Loose or torn brake lining.	1. Replace brake lining.
	2. Incorrect wheel bearing adjustment.	2. Clean, pack and adjust wheel bearings.
	3. Wheel cylinder cups sticking.	3. Recondition or replace the wheel cylinder.
	4. Saturated brake lining.	4. Reline front, rear or all four brakes.

HYDRAULIC BRAKE SYSTEM TROUBLE DIAGNOSIS

Condition	*Possible Cause*	*Correction*
Brakes fade (high speed)	1. Improper brake adjustment. 2. Distorted or out of round brake drums. 3. Overheated brake drums. 4. Incorrect brake fluid (low boiling temperature). 5. Saturated brake lining.	1. Adjust brakes and check fluid. 2. Grind or replace the drums. 3. Inspect for dragging brakes. 4. Drain flush and refill and bleed the hydraulic brake system. 5. Reline brakes as necessary.

Hydraulic Brakes

General Information

Servicing the hydraulic system is chiefly a matter of adjustments, replacement of worn or damaged parts and correcting the damage caused by grit, dirt or contaminated brake fluid. It is highly important to make sure the brake system is clean and tightly sealed when a brake job is completed and that only approved heavy duty brake fluid is used.

The approved heavy duty type brake fluid retains the correct consistency throughout the widest range of temperature variation, will not affect rubber cups, helps protect the metal parts of the brake system against failure and assures long trouble-free brake operation.

Never use brake fluid from a container that has been used for any other liquid. Mineral oil, alcohol, anti-freeze, or cleaning solvents, even in very small quantities, will contaminate brake fluid. Contaminated brake fluid will cause piston cups and the valve in the master cylinder to swell or deteriorate.

Brake adjustment is required after installation of new or relined brake shoes. Adjustment is also necessary whenever excessive travel of pedal is needed to start braking action.

Low Pedal

Normal brake lining wear reduces pedal reserve. Low pedal reserve may also be caused by the lack of brake fluid in the master cylinder. The wear condition may be compensated for by a minor brake adjustment. Check fluid level in master cylinder and add as required.

Fluid Loss

If the master cylinder requires constant addition of hydraulic fluid, fluid may be leaking past the piston cups in the master cylinder or brake cylinders, the hydraulic lines; hoses or connections may be loose or broken. Loose connections should be tightened, or other necessary repairs or parts replacement made and the hydraulic brake system bled.

Fluid Contamination

To determine if contamination exists in the brake fluid, as indicated by swollen, deteriorated rubber cups, the following tests can be made.

Place a small amount of the drained brake fluid into a small clear glass bottle. Separation of the fluid into distinct layers will indicate mineral oil content. Be safe and discard old brake fluid that has been bled from the system. Fluid drained from the bleeding operation may contain dirt particles or other contamination and should not be reused.

Brake Adjustment

Normally self adjusting brakes will not require manual adjustment but in the event of a brake reline it may be advisable to make the initial adjustment manually to speed up adjusting time.

Automatic Adjuster Check

Place vehicle on a hoist, with a helper in the driver's seat to apply brakes. Remove plug from rear adjustment slot in each brake support plate to observe adjuster star wheel. Then, to exclude possibility of maximum adjustment; that is, the adjuster refuses to operate because the closest possible adjustment has been reached; the star wheel should be backed off approximately 30 notches. It will be necessary to hold adjuster lever away from star wheel to allow backing off of the adjustment.

Spin the wheel and brake drum in reverse direction and apply brakes vigorously. This will provide the necessary inertia to cause the secondary brake shoe to leave the anchor. The wrap up effect will move the secondary shoe, and cable will pull the

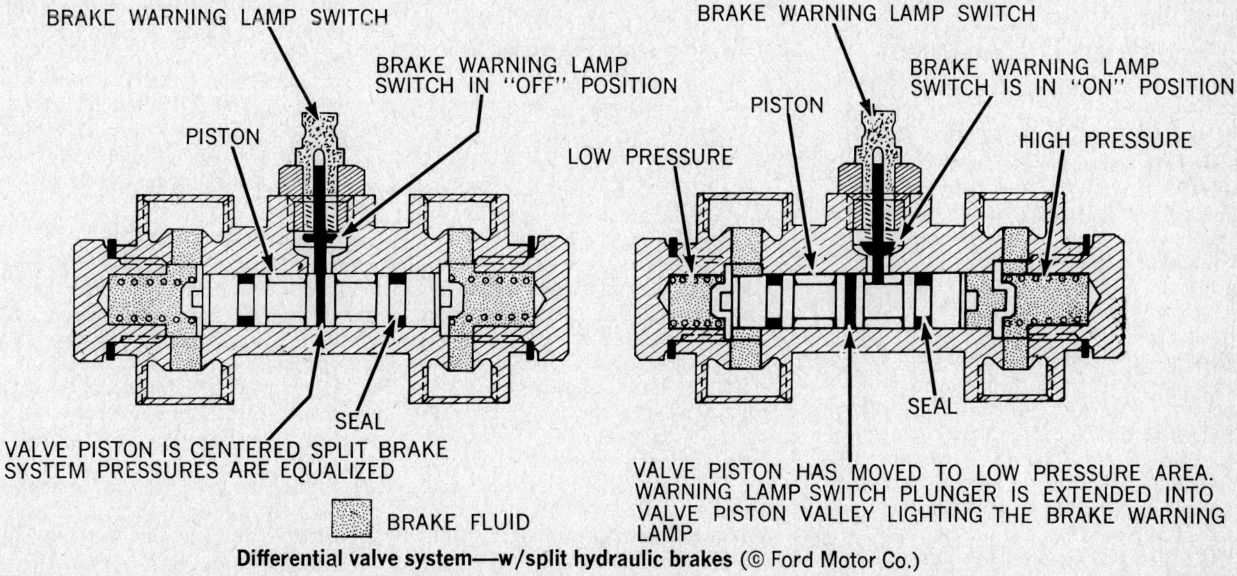

Differential valve system—w/split hydraulic brakes (© Ford Motor Co.)

adjuster lever up. Upon release of brake pedal, the lever should snap downward, turning star wheel. Thus, a definite rotation of adjuster star wheel can be observed if automatic adjuster is working properly. If by the described procedure one or more automatic adjusters do not function properly, the respective drum must be removed for adjuster servicing.

Hydraulic Line Repair

Steel tubing is used in the hydraulic lines between the master cylinder and the front brake tube connector, and between the rear brake tube connector and the rear brake cylinders. Flexible hoses connect the brake tube to the front brake cylinders and to the rear brake tube connector.

When replacing hydraulic brake tubing, hoses, or connectors, tighten all connections securely. After replacement, bleed the brake system at the wheel cylinders and at the booster, if so equipped.

Brake Tube

If a section of the brake tube becomes damaged,the entire section should be replaced with tubing of the same type, size, shape, and length. *Copper tubing should not be used in the hydraulic system.* When bending brake tubing to fit the frame or rear-axle contours, be careful not to kink or crack the tube.

All brake tubing should be double flared to provide good leak-proof connections. Always clean the inside of a new brake tube with clean isopropyl alcohol.

Brake Hose

A flexible brake hose should be replaced if it shows signs of softening, cracking, or other damage.

When installing a new brake hose, position the hose to avoid contact with other truck parts.

Pressure Differential Switch

The hydraulic system safety switch is used to warn vehicle operator that one of the hydraulic systems has failed. A failure in one part of the brake system does not result in failure of the entire hydraulic brake system.

As an example, failure of rear brake system will leave front brake system still operative.

As pressure falls in one system the other system's normal pressure forces piston to inoperative side contacting switch terminal, causing a red warning light to come on in instrument panel, thus, warning operator of vehicle that one of the systems has failed and should be repaired.

The safety switch body is mounted in a vertical position, with the brake tubes connected to opposite sides.

The component parts of the switch body are not serviced. However, terminal unit can be removed if a malfunction occurs and a new terminal unit installed.

Centralizing the Pressure Differential Valve

1. Turn the ignition switch to the ACC or ON position. Loosen the pressure differential valve inlet tube nut of the system that remained operative, or the side opposite the system that was bled last. Operate the brake pedal carefully and gradually until the pressure differential valve is returned to a centralized position and the brake warning light goes out. Tighten the tube nut.
2. Check the fluid level in the master cylinder reservoirs and fill them to within 1/4" of the top with the specified brake fluid.
3. Turn the ignition switch to the OFF position.

With Split Hydraulic Brakes

The pressure differential valve used with the split hydraulic brake system has a self-centering spring. Use the following procedure to reset the valve:

1. Remove the switch connector wire.
2. Remove the threaded hex-shaped electrical switch body from the center of the valve. This allows the valve centering springs to re-position the valve.
3. Install the electrical switch and connect the wire.
4. Apply the brakes a few times and check the operation of the warning light. The light should go on with the ignition switch in the START position only.

Bleeding Brakes

Manual Bleeding

1. Attach a rubber drain tube to the bleeder screw of the brake wheel cylinder. The end of the tube should fit snugly around the bleeder screw.
2. Submerge the free end of the tube in a container partially filled with clean brake fluid. Loosen the bleeder screw.
3. Push the brake pedal down slowly by hand, allowing it to return slowly to the fully-released position. Repeat this operation until air bubbles cease to appear at the submerged end of the tube.
4. When the fluid is completely free of air bubbles, close the bleeder screw and remove the drain tube.
5. Repeat this procedure at each brake cylinder. Refill the master cylinder reservoir after each brake cylinder is bled and when the bleeding operation is completed.

Master Cylinder Service

Bendix Tandem

Disassembly

1. Clean the outside of the master cylinder assembly. Remove the residual pressure valves.
2. Remove the tube seats by installing "easy outs" firmly into the seats. Tap lightly with a hammer to loosen, remove seats.
3. Slide clamp off master cylinder cover and remove the cover and its gasket. Drain the brake fluid from the master cylinder.
4. Remove the snap ring from the open end of the cylinder with snap ring pliers. Remove the washer from cylinder bore.
5. Remove the front piston retaining screw. Carefully remove the rear piston assembly.
6. Remove the front piston assembly.

Cleaning and Inspection

1. Clean all parts with a suitable solvent and dry with filtered compressed air. Wash cylinder bore with clean brake fluid and check for damage or wear.
2. If cylinder bore is lightly scratched or shows slight corrosion it can be cleaned with crocus cloth. Heavier scratches or corrosion can be removed by honing, providing that diameter of cylinder bore is not increased by more than .002 inch. If master cylinder bore does not clean up at .002 inch when honed, the master cylinder should be replaced.
3. If master cylinder pistons are badly scored or corroded, replace them with new ones. All caps and seals should be replaced when rebuilding a master cylinder.

Assembly

NOTE: Before assembly of master cylinder, dip all parts in clean brake fluid and place on clean paper. Assembling master cylinder dry can damage rubber seals.

1. Coat master cylinder bore with brake fluid and carefully slide the front piston into cylinder body.
2. Slide the rear piston assembly into the cylinder bore. Compress pistons and install the front piston retaining screw.

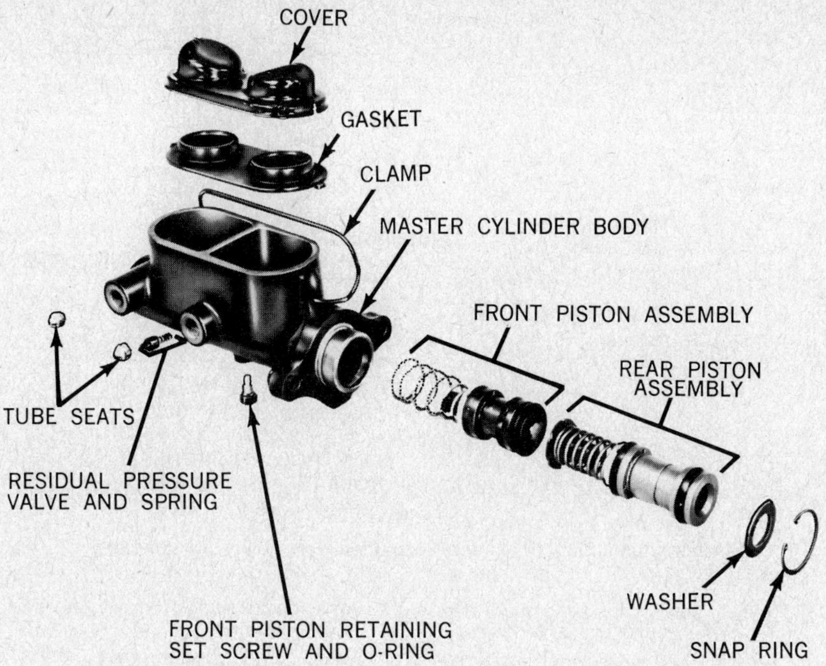

Bendix tandem master cylinder—exploded view (© Chrysler Corp.)

3. Position washer in cylinder bore and secure with snap ring.
4. Install the residual pressure valve and spring in the outlet port and install tube seats firmly.

Chrysler Tandem

Disassembly

1. Clean the outside of the master cylinder assembly. Remove the master cylinder cover and drain the brake fluid.
2. Remove the front piston retainer screw from inside reservoir and the snap ring from the outer end of cylinder bore. Slide the rear piston assembly out of cylinder bore.
3. Tamp the master cylinder assembly lightly on bench, open end down, to remove the front piston and spring. If the front piston sticks in cylinder bore, use air pressure to force it out.
4. Remove the front piston compression spring from the cylinder bore.
5. Remove the tube seats by installing "easy outs" firmly into the seats. Tap lightly with a hammer to loosen, remove the seats.
6. Take note of the position of cup lips and remove them from pistons. DO NOT remove the center cup of the rear piston. If this cup is damaged or worn, install a new rear piston assembly.

Cleaning and Inspection

1. Clean all parts with a suitable solvent and dry with filtered compressed air. Wash cylinder bore with clean brake fluid and check for damage or wear.
2. If cylinder bore is slightly scrached or shows slight corrosion it can be cleaned with crocus cloth. Heavier scratches or corrosion can be removed by honing, providing that the diameter of the cylinder bore is not increased by more than .002 inch. If master cylinder bore does not clean up at .002 inch when honed, the master cylinder should be replaced.
3. If master cylinder pistons are bady scored or corroded, replace them with new ones. All caps and seals should be replaced when rebuilding a master cylinder.

Assembly

NOTE: Before assembly of master cylinder, dip all parts in clean brake fluid and place on clean paper. Assembling a master cylinder dry can damage the new seals.

1. Carefully work the primary cup on the end of the front piston with the lip facing away from the piston.
2. Carefully, work the second seal cup over the rear end of the piston and into the second land. Be sure that the lip of the cup is facing the front of piston.
3. Carefully work the rear secondary cup over the piston and into the rear land. The lip must face the rear of the piston.
4. Slide the cup retainer over the stem of the front piston with the beveled side away from the piston cup.
5. Position the small end of the

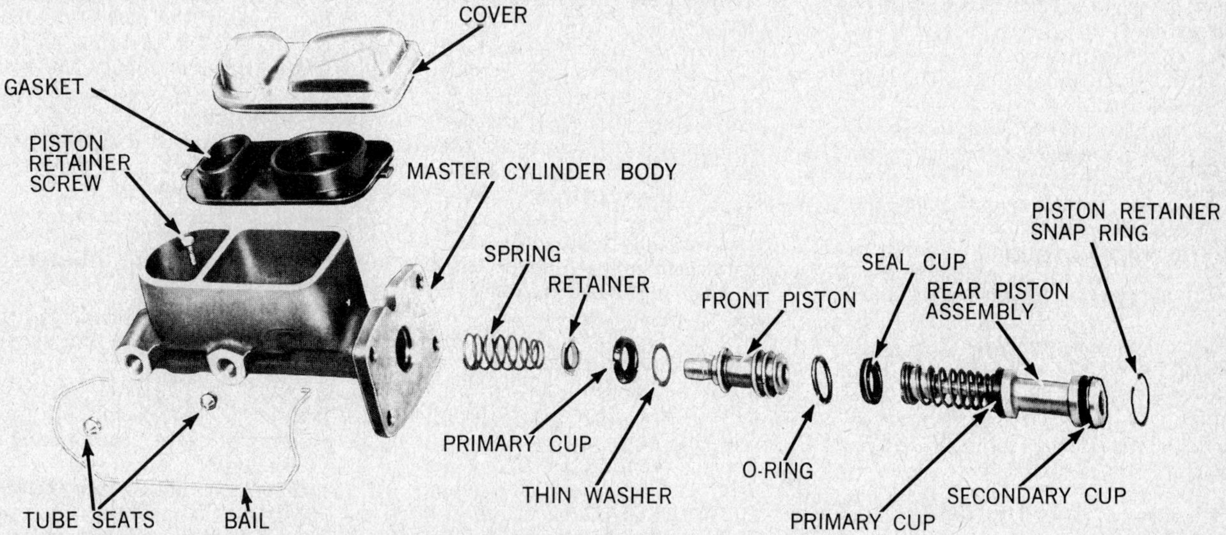

Chrysler tandem master cylinder—exploded view (© Chrysler Corp.)

pressure spring into the retainer, then slide the assembly into the master cylinder bore.

CAUTION: **Be sure that the cups enter the cylinder bore evenly in order that the sealing quality of the cups is not damaged, keep the seals and cylinder bore well lubricated with brake fluid.**

6. Carefully work the secondary cup over the rear end of the rear piston with the lip facing towards the front.
7. Center the spring retainer of the rear piston assembly over the shoulder of the front piston. Push the piston assemblies into the cylinder bore. Carefully work the cup lips into bore, then seat piston assemblies.
8. Holding the pistons in their seated position, install the piston retaining screw and tighten securely.
9. Install new tube seats. (When bench bleeding is performed, the tube seats will be correctly positioned.)

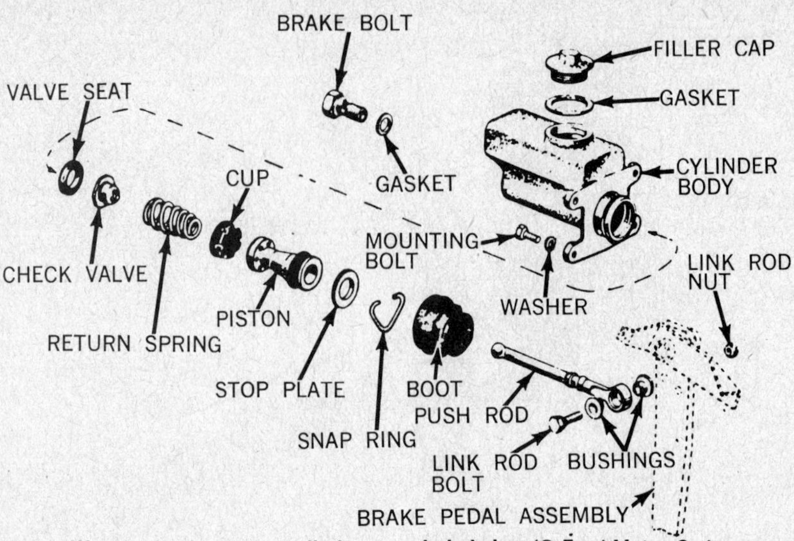

Wagner single master cylinder—exploded view (© Ford Motor Co.)

Wagner Single

Disassembly

1. Clean the outside of the master cylinder assembly. Remove the master cylinder cover and drain the fluid.
2. Remove the boot, stop retainer, piston stop and the end plug.
3. Remove the piston, cups, return spring and the valve assembly.

Cleaning and Inspection

1. Clean all parts with a suitable solvent and dry with filtered compressed air. Wash cylinder bore with clean brake fluid and check for damage and wear.
2. If cylinder bore is slightly scratched or shows slight corrosion it can be cleaned with crocus cloth. Heavier scratches or corrosion can be removed by honing, providing that the diameter of the cylinder bore is not increased by more than .002 inch. If the master cylinder bore does not clean up at .002 inch when honed, the master cylinder should be replaced.
3. If the master cylinder piston is badly scored or corroded, replace it with a new one. All caps and seals should be replaced when rebuilding a master cylinder.

Assembly

NOTE: Before assembly of master cylinder, dip all parts in clean brake fluid and place on clean paper. Assembling a master cylinder dry can damage the new seals.

1. Install the check valve and spring in the cylinder, with the valve facing toward the outlet of the master cylinder.
2. Install the cylinder cup in the cylinder with the open end of the cup over the closed end of the return spring.
3. Install the secondary cup on the piston and install the piston, piston stop and stop retainer.
4. Install the boot and push rod.

Wagner Tandem

Disassembly

1. Clean the outside of the master cylinder. Remove the cylinder cover screw or spring retaining clip. Lift off the cover and the diaphragm gasket and pour off excess brake fluid. Use the push rod to stroke the cylinder forcing fluid from the cylinder through the outlet ports.
2. Loosen and remove the piston stop screw and gasket from the right hand side of the cylinder.
3. Pull back the push rod boot and remove the snap ring from the groove in the end of the cylinder bore.
4. Remove the push rod and stop plate from the master cylinder.
5. Remove the internal parts from the master cylinder. If the parts will not slide out apply air pressure at the secondary outlet port. If after applying air, parts still do not move easily, check bore carefully for extensive damage which may eliminate possibility of rebuilding master cylinder.

Inspection and Repair

1. Clean all parts in clean brake fluid. Inspect the parts for chipping, excessive wear or damage. Replace them as required. When using a master cylinder repair kit, install all the parts supplied.
2. Check all recesses, openings and internal passages to be sure they are open and free of foreign matter. Passages may be probed with soft copper wire, 0.020" OD, or smaller.
3. Minor scratches or blemishes in the cylinder bore can be removed with crocus cloth or a clean up hone. Do not oversize the bore more than 0.007".

Assembly

1. Dip all parts except the master cylinder in clean hydraulic brake fluid of the specified type.
2. Install the rear rubber cup on the secondary piston with the cup lip facing the rear. All other cups face the front or closed end of the cylinder.
3. Assemble and install the secondary piston spring, front cup, and the secondary piston.
4. Install the piston stop screw and gasket, making sure the screw enters the cylinder behind the rear of the secondary piston.
5. Assemble and install the primary piston and push rod parts.
6. Locate the stop plate in the seat in the bore and engage the snap ring into the groove at the rear of the cylinder.
7. Install the push rod boot onto the push rod and the groove of the cylinder housing.
8. Bleed the master cylinder.

Bench Bleeding the Master Cylinder

Before the master cylinder is installed on the vehicle, the unit should be bled.

1. Support the master cylinder body in a vise, and fill both fluid reservoirs with the specified brake fluid.

CAUTION: **Do not tighten the vise too tightly on the master cylinder as this can cause damage to the cylinder which can not be repaired.**

2. Loosely intall plugs in the front and rear brake outlet bores. Depress the primary piston several times until air bubbles cease to appear in the brake fluid.
3. Tighten the plugs and attempt to depress the piston. The piston travel should be restricted after all air is expelled.
4. Remove the plugs. Install the cover and diaphragm gasket assembly, and make sure the cover screw is tightened securely.

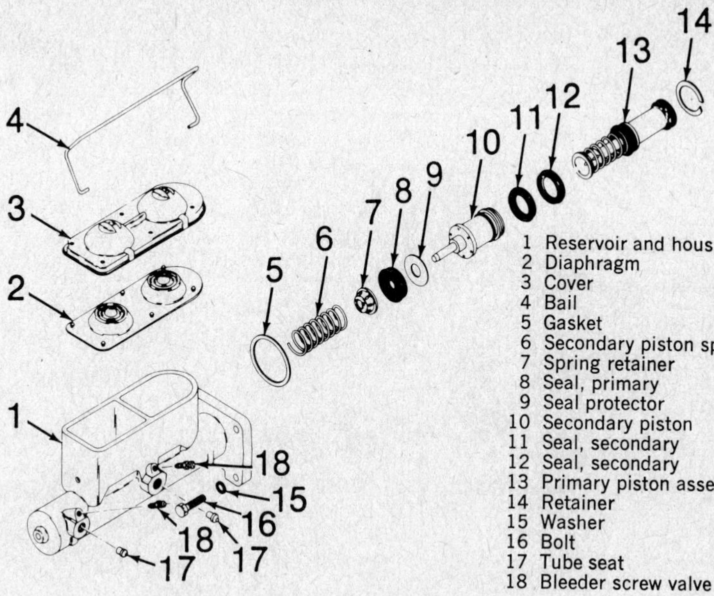

Split system master cylinder (© G.M. Corp.)

Single and Double Barrel-G.M.C.

Disassembly

1. Clean the outside of the master cylinder.
2. Remove the snap ring from the groove in the cylinder bore.
3. Remove the washer (stop plate) from the clutch bore.
4. Remove the piston assembly, primary cup, return spring and retainer assembly, check valve, and the check valve seat from the brake cylinder bore.
5. Remove the piston assembly, primary cup, and return spring and retainer assembly from the clutch cylinder bore.
6. Remove the cover and the bleeder screw valve from the housing.
7. Thoroughly clean all parts with brake fluid.
8. Check the clearance between the piston and the cylinder wall. It should be within 0.001" to 0.005"

Assembly

1. Coat all internal parts with brake fluid.
2. Install the parts in the brake cylinder bore.
   a. Install the check valve seat and then the check valve in the cylinder bore.
   b. Install the short return spring in the bore with the large diameter end of the spring over the check valve.
   c. Install the primary cup in the cylinder bore with the lip of the cup toward the outlet end. Make sure the end of the return spring seats inside the cup.
   d. Insert the piston and secondary cup assembly into the cylinder bore with the open end of the piston toward the open end of the cylinder bore.
   e. Press all parts into the cylinder bore and install the washer (stop plate) if used and the snap ring.
3. Install the parts in the clutch cylinder bore.
   a. Install the long return spring with the large diameter end first in the cylinder bore.
   b. Install the primary cup with the lip of the cup toward the outlet end.
   c. Insert the piston and secondary cup into the cylinder bore, with the open end of the piston toward the open end of the cylinder.
   d. Press all parts into the cylinder bore and install the washer (stop plate) if used and the snap ring.
4. Install the cover and the bleeder screw.

Split System—G.M.C. (Tandem)

Disassembly

1. Remove the cover and reservoir seal.
2. Remove the retaining ring from the groove in the end of the cylinder of the cylinder bore.
3. Remove all parts from the cylinder bore.
4. Remove the bleeder screw valves.

Assembly

1. Clean all parts in clean brake fluid.
2. Leave a coating of brake fluid on all internal parts and install parts in the cylinder bore using new rubber seals.
3. Install retainer ring and bleeder screws.

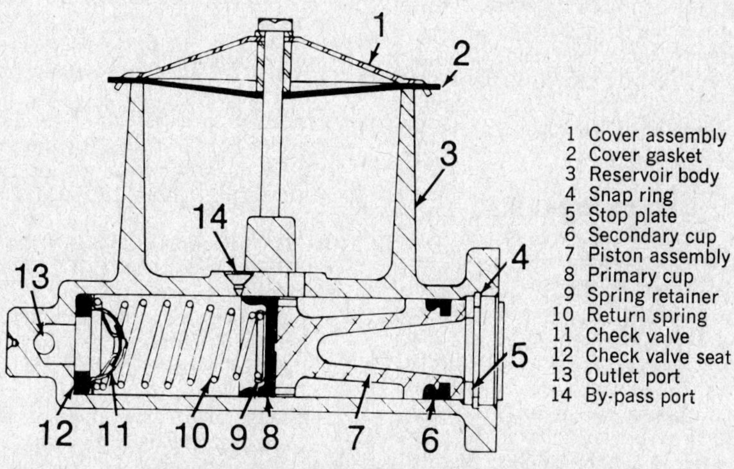

Single reservoir master cylinder (© G.M. Corp.)

Wheel Cylinders

Disassembly

1. In case of a leak, remove brake shoes (replace if soaked with grease or brake fluid), boots, piston wheel cylinder cups and wheel cylinder cup expansion spring.

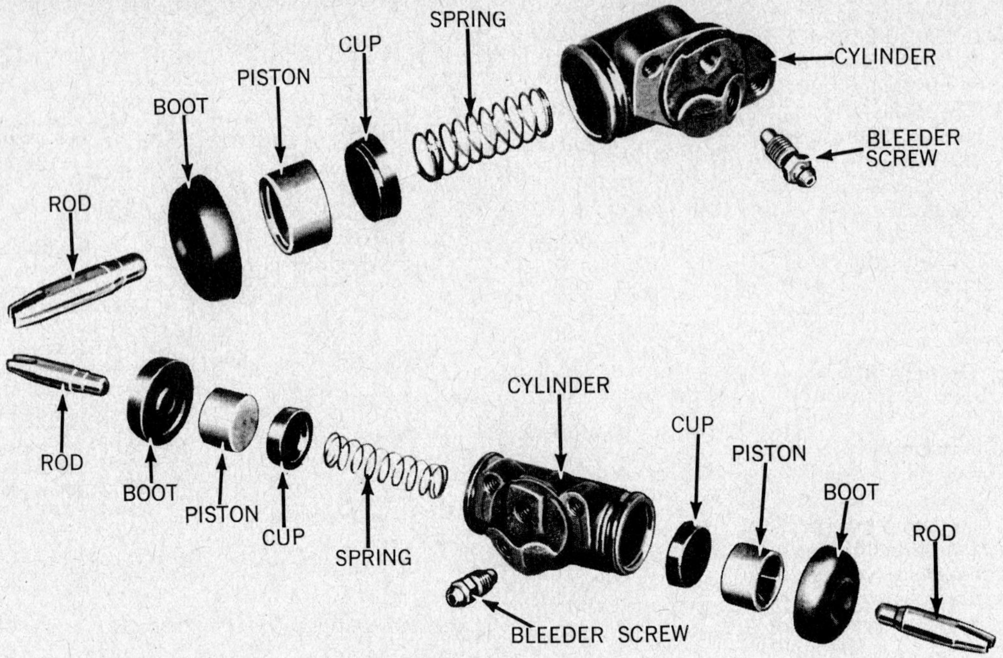

Wheel cylinder—typical (© Chrysler Corp.)

NOTE: A slight amount of fluid on boot may not be a leak, but may be preservative oil used on assembly.

2. Wash wheel cylinder bore with clean brake fluid and inspect for scoring or pitting.

Use extreme care in cleaning the wheel cylinder after reconditioning. Remove all dust or grit by flushing the cylinder with clean brake fluid; wipe dry with a clean lintless cloth and clean a second time with brake fluid. Dry the wheel cylinder with air pressure, then flush with clean brake fluid. (Be sure the bleeder screw port and the bleeder screw are clean and open.)

Wheel cylinder bores or pistons that are badly scored or coroded should be replaced. The old piston cups should be discarded when reconditioning wheel cylinders.

Cylinder walls that have light scratches, or show signs of corrosion, can usually be cleaned with crocus cloth, using a circular motion. However, cylinders that have deep scratches or scoring may be honed, providing the diameter of the cylinder bore is not increased more than .002″. *A cylinder that does not clean up at .002″ should be discarded and a new cylinder installed. (Black stains on the cylinder walls are caused by the piston cups and will do no harm.)*

Should inspection reveal the necessity of installing a new wheel cylinder proceed as follows:

1. Disconnect brake hose from brake tube at frame bracket (front wheels) or disconnect the brake tube from wheel cylinder (rear wheels).
2. Disconnect brake hose from wheel cylinder (front wheels only) and remove wheel cylinder attaching bolts, then slide wheel cylinder out of backing plate.

Assembly (Front or Rear)

Before assembling pistons and new cups in wheel cylinder, dip them in brake fluid. If boots are deteriorated, cracked or do not fit tightly on brake shoe push rod, as well as wheel cylinder casting, new boots should be installed.

1. Wash wheel cylinder with clean brake fluid and wipe dry.
2. Install expansion spring in cylinder. Install wheel cylinder cups in each end of cylinder with open end of cups facing each other.
3. Install wheel cylinder pistons in each end of cylinder with recessed end of pistons facing open ends of cylinder.
4. Install boots over ends of cylinder. Keep assembly compressed with aid of a brake cylinder clamp until brake shoes are assembled.

Brake Service

Non-Servo Type

This brake is a non-servo, floating shoe type brake. Upper ends of shoes extend through wheel cylinder boots and contact inserts in wheel cylinder pistons. Shoe ends are held firmly against pistons by the brake shoe return spring. Lower ends of shoes are held against a fixed anchor plate by the anchor spring. Hold-down spring at center of each shoe holds shoes in alignment. Lining-to-drum clearance adjustment is made through eccentric cam type adjusting studs.

Brake Shoe Removal

1. Back off brake adjustment, then remove brake drum.
2. Remove brake shoe return spring. Spread upper end of shoes until they are clear of wheel cylinders and hold-down springs, then disengage shoes from anchor plate at bottom. Remove anchor spring from shoes.
3. Do not depress brake pedal while shoes are removed.

Cleaning and Inspection

1. Clean all dirt out of brake drum. Inspect drum for roughness, scoring, or out-of-round. Replace or recondition drum as necessary.
2. Carefully pull lower edge of each wheel cylinder boot away from cylinder and note whether interior is excessively wet with brake fluid. Excessive fluid indicates leakage past piston cups, requiring overhaul of wheel cylinder.

NOTE: A slight amount of fluid is nearly always present and acts as a lubricant for pistons.

3. Check backing plate attaching bolts to make sure they are tight. Clean all rust and dirt from ledges on backing plate where shoe rims make contact using fine emery cloth.
4. Inspect the shoe return and anchor springs and hold-down

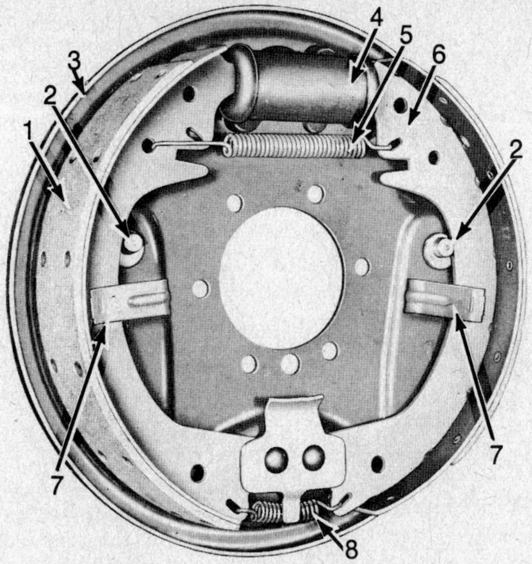

Non servo type brake installed (© G.M. Corp.)

1 Secondary shoe
2 Adjusting cam
3 Backing plate
4 Wheel cylinder
5 Shoe return spring
6 Primary shoe
7 Shoe hold-down spring
8 Shoe anchor spring

springs. If broken, cracked, or weakened by rust or corrosion, replace springs.

5. If brake linings are worn to the extent that replacement is necessary, replace linings.

Brake Shoe Installation

1. Inspect brake shoe lining assemblies and make sure there are no nicks or burrs on edges of shoes which contact backing plate.
2. Apply a light film of grease at the following points: where shoe webs contact hold-down springs: where anchor ends of shoe webs contact anchor plate; and at six places where shoe rims contact ledges on backing plate.
3. Install hold-down springs on backing plate. Hook anchor spring into slot at bottom of each shoe. Swing upper ends of shoes apart and position at backing plate, with lower ends of shoe webs engaging anchor plate and with anchor spring behind extension on anchor plate. *NOTE: The shoe with the shorter lining must be to the rear of the vehicle.*
4. Swing shoes up into position with center of shoe webs engaging hold-down springs, and with upper ends inserted through wheel cylinder boots.
5. Install brake shoe return spring, being sure short end is hooked into slotted hole in rear shoe and long end in round hole in front shoe.
6. Install brake drum and wheel. Adjust brakes.

Wagner

Twin Action Type

Twin-action brake is a four-anchor type. Brake shoes are self-centering in operation, and both shoes are self-energizing in both forward and reverse.

Two wheel cylinders are mounted on opposite sides of the backing plate. One brake shoe is mounted above wheel cylinders and one below. Sliding pivot type anchor is used at front end of upper shoe and at rear end of lower shoe. Adjustable anchor is used at front end of lower shoe and at rear end of upper shoe. Four shoe return springs hold shoe ends firmly against anchors when brakes are released.

Anchor brackets are steel forgings, attached to flange on axle housing in conjunction with the backing plate. At adjustable anchor end of each shoe, shoe web bears against flat head of adjusting screw which threads into anchor bracket. The adjusting screw heads are notched and are rotated for brake adjustment through access holes in backing plate. A lock spring which fits over anchor bracket holds adjusting screw in position.

The brake backing plate has six machined bearing surfaces, three for each shoe, against which the inner edge of each shoe bears. Two brake shoe guide bolts are riveted to backing plate and extend through holes in center of brake shoe web. Shoes are retained on guide bolts by flat washers, nuts, and cotter pins.

Wheel cylinder push rods make contact between wheel cylinder pistons and brake shoes.

Inner edge of brake drum has a

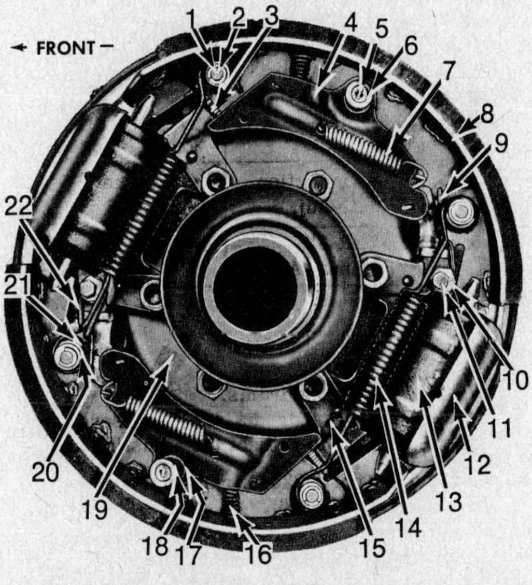

Twin action self adjusting brakes (© G.M. Corp.)

1 Hold-down pin spring lock
2 Hold-down pin
3 Adjusting screw
4 Adjusting lever
5 Adjusting lever pin spring
6 Hold-down spring cup
7 Lever override spring
8 Brake shoe and lining
9 Adjusting lever pivot
10 Adjusting lever cam
11 Adjusting lever bolt
12 Wheel cylinder shield
13 Wheel cylinder
14 Brake shoe return spring
15 Brake shoe anchor
16 Lever return spring
17 Adjusting lever pin sleeve
18 Hold-down spring
19 Brake backing plate
20 Hold-down pin retainer
21 Hold-down pin spring
22 Adjusting lever link

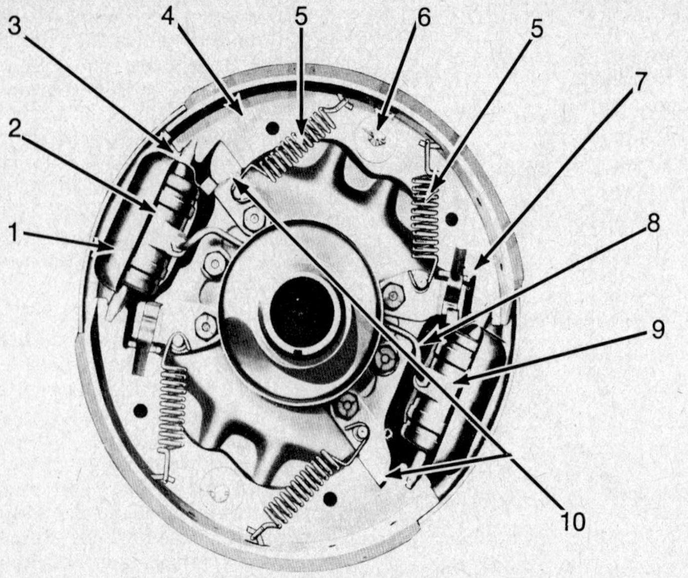

Twin action type brake installed (© G.M. Corp.)

1 Heat shield
2 Front wheel cylinder
3 Dust shield
4 Brake shoe
5 Brake shoe return spring
6 Brake shoe guide bolt
7 Adjusting screw
8 Hydraulic line
9 Rear wheel cylinder
10 Brake shoe anchor

groove which fits over a flange on the edge of backing plate, forming a seal against the entrance of dirt and mud.

Twin-Action Type Rear Brake

Brake Shoe Removal

1. Remove brake drums. *NOTE: If brake drums are worn severely, it may be necessary to retract the adjusting screws.*
2. Remove the brake shoe pull back springs. *NOTE: Since wheel cylinder piston stops are incorporated in the anchor brackets, it is not necessary to install wheel cylinder clamps when the brake shoes are removed.*
3. Loosen the adjusting lever cam cap screw, and while holding the star wheel end of the adjusting lever past the star wheel, remove the cap screw and cam.
4. Remove the brake shoe hold down springs and pins by compressing the spring and, at the same time, pushing the pin back through the flange plate toward the tool. Then, keeping the spring compressed, remove the lock ("C"-washer) from the pin with a magnet.
5. Lift off the brake shoe and self-adjuster lever as an assembly.
6. The self-adjuster lever can now be removed from the brake shoe by removing the hold-down spring and pin. Remove lever return spring also. *NOTE: The adjusting lever, override spring and pivot are an assembly. It is not recommended that they be disassembled for service purposes unless they are broken. It is much easier to assemble and disassemble the brake leaving them intact.*
7. Thread the adjusting screw out of the brake shoe anchor and remove and discard the friction spring.
8. Clean all dirt out of brake drum. Inspect drums for roughness, scoring or out-of-round. Replace or recondition drums as necessary.
9. Carefully pull lower edges of wheel cylinder boots away from cylinders. If brake fluid flows out, overhaul of the wheel cylinders is necessary. *NOTE: A slight amount of fluid is nearly always present and acts as a lubricant for the piston.*
10. Inspect flange plate for oil leakage past axle shaft oil seals. Install seals if necessary.

Brake Shoe Installation

1. Put a light film of lubricant on shoe bearing surfaces of brake flange plate and on threads of adjusting screw.
2. Thread adjusting screw completely into anchor without friction spring to be sure threads are clean and screw turns easily. Then remove screws, position a new friction spring on screw and reinstall in anchor.
3. Assemble self-adjuster assembly and lever return spring to brake shoe and position adjusting lever link on adjusting lever pivot.
4. Position hold-down pins in flange plate.
5. Install brake shoe and self-adjuster assemblies onto hold down pins. Insert ends of shoes in wheel cylinder push rods and legs of friction springs. *NOTE: Make sure the toe of the shoe is against the adjusting screw.*
6. Install cup, spring and retainer on end of hold-down pin. With spring compressed, push the hold-down pin back through the flange plate toward the tool and install the lock on the pin.
7. Install brake shoe return springs.
8. Holding the star wheel end of the adjusting lever as far as possible past the star wheel, position the adjusting lever cam into the adjusting lever link and assemble with cap screw.
9. Check the brake shoes for being centered by measuring the distance from the lining surface to the edge of the flange plate. To center the shoes, tap the upper or lower end of the shoes with a plastic mallet until the distances at each end become equal.
10. Locate the adjusting lever .020″ to .039″ above the outside diameter of the adjusting screw thread by loosening the cap screw and turning the adjusting cam. *NOTE: To determine .020″ to .039″, turn the adjusting screw 2 full turns out from the fully retracted position. Hold a .060″ wire gauge at a 90° angle with the star wheel edge of the adjusting lever. Turn the adjusting cam until the adjusting lever and threaded area on the adjusting screw just touch the wire.*
11. Secure the adjusting cam cap screw and retract the adjusting screw.
12. Install brake drums and wheels.
13. Adjust the brakes by making several forward and reverse stops until a satisfactory brake pedal height results.

Bendix

Duo Servo Type

Removing Front Brake Shoes

With the vehicle elevated on a hoist, jack or suitable stands remove front wheel and drums.

1. Remove brake shoe return springs.
   (*Note how secondary spring overlaps primary spring.*)
2. Remove brake shoe retainer, spring and nails.
3. Slide eye of automatic adjuster cable off anchor and unhook from lever. Remove cable, cable guide and anchor plate.
4. Disconnect lever spring from

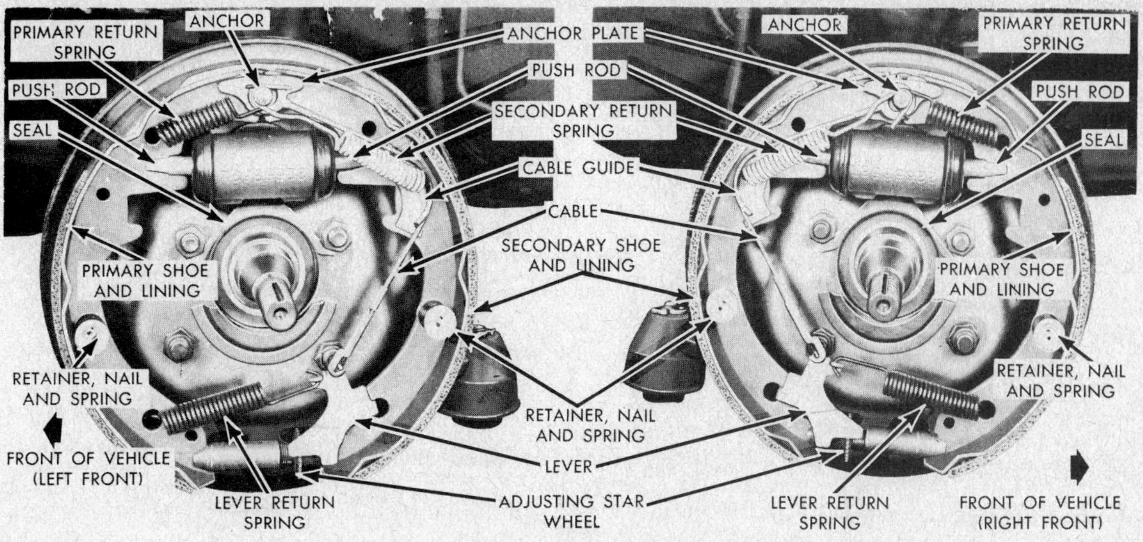

Brake assemblies front (© Chrysler Corp.)

lever and disengage from shoe web. Remove spring and lever.

5. Remove the primary and secondary brake shoe assemblies and adjusting star wheel from support. Install wheel cylinder clamps to hold pistons in cylinders.

Installing Front Brake Shoes

1. Match a primary with a secondary brake shoe and place them in their relative position on a work bench.
2. Lubricate threads of adjusting screw and install it between the primary and secondary shoes with star wheel next to secondary shoe. The star adjusting wheels are stamped "R" (right side) and "L" (left side), and indicate their location on vehicle.
3. Overlap anchor ends of primary and secondary brake shoes and install adjusting spring lever.
4. Spread anchor ends of brake shoes to maintain adjusting lever and spring in position.
5. Holding brake shoes in their relative position, place brake shoe assembly on support and over the anchor pin.
6. Install nails, cups, springs and retainers.
7. Install anchor pin plate.
8. Install cable guide in the secondary shoe and place the "eye" of adjusting cable over anchor pin.
9. Install return spring in primary shoe. Slide spring over anchor.
10. Install return spring in secondary shoe and slide over anchor. (Be sure the secondary spring overlaps primary).
11. Place adjusting cable cover guide and engage hook of cable into adjusting lever.
12. Install brake drum.
13. Adjust brakes.
14. After checking brake pedal operation, road test vehicle.

Removing Rear Brake Shoes

1. With the vehicle elevated on a hoist, jack or suitable stand, loosen parking brake equalizer nut, remove rear wheel, and drum retaining clips. Remove drum.
2. Remove brake shoe return springs. (Note how secondary spring overlaps primary spring.)
3. Remove brake shoe retainers, springs and nails.
4. Slide eye of automatic adjuster cable off anchor and then unhook from lever. Remove cable, cable guide and anchor plate.
5. Disconnect lever spring from lever and disengage from shoe web. Remove spring and lever.
6. Spread anchor ends of the primary and secondary shoes and remove parking brake strut and spring.
7. Disengage parking brake cable from parking brake lever and remove brake assembly.
8. Remove the primary and secondary brake shoe assemblies and adjusting star wheel from support. Install wheel cylinder to hold pistons in cylinders.

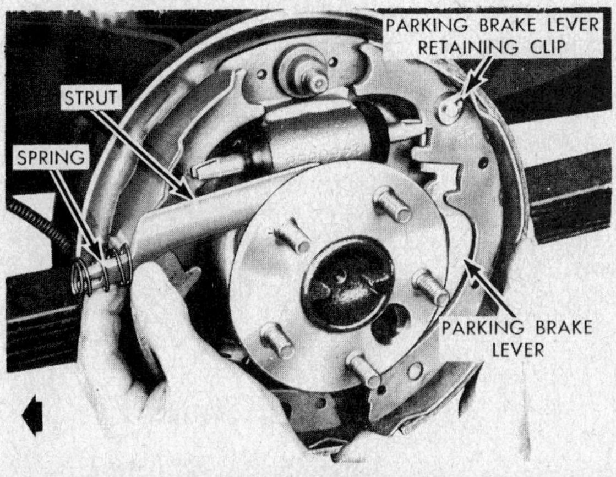

Removing or installing parking brake strut and spring—rear (© Chrysler Corp.)

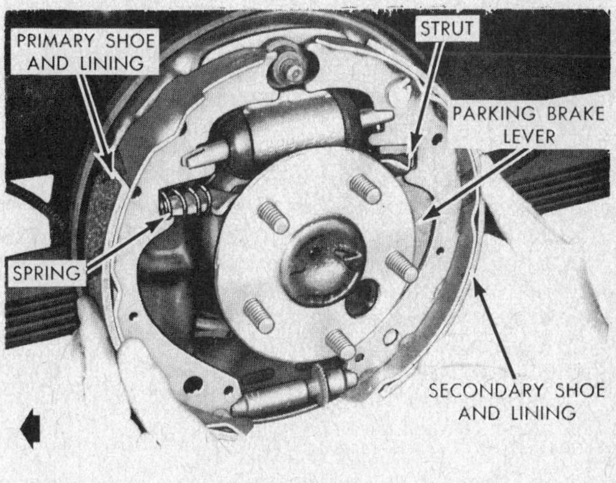

Installing brake shoes (© Chrysler Corp.)

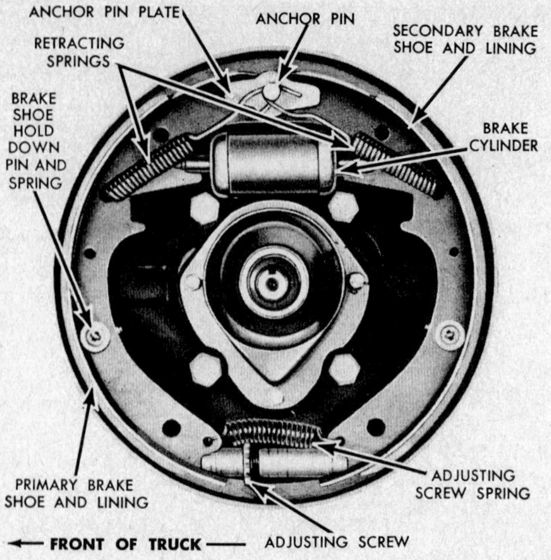

Duo-servo single anchor assembly (© Ford Motor Co.)

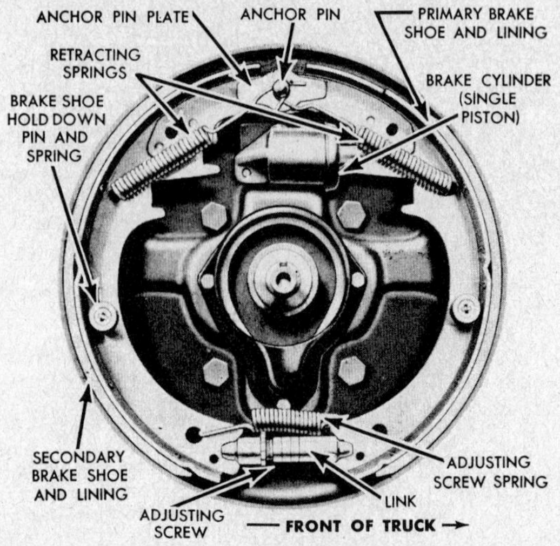

Uni-servo single anchor brake assembly (© Ford Motor Co.)

Installing Rear Brake Shoes

1. Inspect the platforms of support for nicks or burrs. Apply a thin coat of lubricant to support platforms.
2. Attach parking brake lever to the back side of the secondary shoe.
3. Place the secondary and primary shoe in their relative position on a work bench.
4. Lubricate threads of adjusting screw and install it between the primary and secondary shoes with star wheel next to secondary shoe. The star adjusting wheels are stamped "R" (right side) and "L" (left side), and indicate their location on vehicle.
5. Overlap anchor ends of the primary and secondary brake shoes and install adjusting spring and lever.
6. Hold the brake shoes in their relative position and engage parking brake cable into parking brake lever.
7. Install parking brake strut and spring between the parking brake lever and primary shoe.
8. Place brake shoes on the support and install retainer nails, springs and retainers.
9. Install anchor pin plate.
10. Install "eye" of adjusting cable over anchor pin and install return spring between primary shoe and anchor pin.
11. Install cable guide in secondary shoe then install secondary return spring. (Be sure secondary spring overlaps primary.)
12. Place adjusting cable in groove of cable guide and engage hook of cable into adjusting lever.
13. Install brake drum and retaining clips.
14. Adjust brakes.

Bendix

Two-Piston Single Cylinder Hydraulically Actuated Type

Description

Both shoes pivot on anchor pins at the bottom of the support plate. The shoes are actuated by one wheel cylinder which is of the double piston type. Specification for heel and toe clearance of shoes should be strictly followed to obtain efficient brake operation.

Brake Shoe Removal

1. Back off the adjusting cam and remove wheel and drum assembly.
2. Remove brake shoe return spring.
3. Install wheel cylinder brake clamp to prevent pistons from being forced out of cylinder.
4. Remove "C" washer, oil washer and retainer, guide spring retainer and guide spring from anchor bolts to remove brake shoes.

Brake Shoe Installation

1. Install brake shoes, oil washers and retainers on anchor bolts and secure with "C" washers.
2. Install brake return spring.
3. Install wheel and drum assembly.

Adjustments

Since tapered brake lining is thicker at the center than at the ends, the adjustment procedures outlined in the paragraphs that follow must be performed in order to assure maximum braking efficiency.

Minor Adjustment

1. Jack up truck so that one wheel can be rotated freely.
2. Then, while rotating that wheel forward and backward, bring the shoe out to the drum with the adjusting cam until a light drag is obtained.
3. Back off the adjustment until the wheel is free to turn.
4. Repeat this procedure on the other shoe.

Major Adjustment

1. Inspect the fluid level in the master cylinder and add fluid if the level is 3/8" to 1/2" from the top of the reservoir or lower.
2. Loosen lock nuts and turn brake shoe anchor bolts to the fully released position.
3. Adjust the anchor bolt and cam and the minor adjustment cam at the top of the shoe to give equal clearance at the toe and heel. Make sure that sufficient center contact is maintained to produce a slight drag.
4. Lock anchor adjusting nut. After adjusting the clearance on one shoe, repeat the procedure on the other shoe. Then apply the brakes a couple of times to make sure adjustment is up to specifications.

NOTE: Whenever cams are adjusted, check brakes by applying pressure on the brake pedal a couple of times so as to make sure wheel drag has not increased, since the spring loaded cams may cause shoe adjustment to change by shifting position. Wheel should only have a slight drag at room temperature.

Bendix

Brake Shoe Adjustment

The brake drums should be at normal room temperature, when the brake shoes are adjusted. If the shoes are adjusted when the shoes are hot and expanded, the shoes may drag as the drums cool and contract.

A minor brake adjustment re-establishes the brake lining-to-drum clearance and compensates for normal lining wear.

A major brake adjustment includes the adjustment of the brake shoe anchor pins as well as the brake shoes. Adjustment of the anchor pin permits the centering of the brake shoes in the drum.

Adjustment procedures for each type of brake assembly are given under the applicable heading.

Minor Adjustment

The brake shoe adjustment procedures for the uniservo single anchor brake assmebly are the same as those for the duo-servo single anchor type.

A major brake adjustment should be performed when dragging brakes are not corrected by a minor adjustment, when brake shoes are relined or replaced, or when brake drums are machined.

Duo-Servo Single Anchor Brake

The duo-servo single-anchor brake is adjusted by turning an adjusting screw located between the lower ends of the shoes.

1. Raise the truck until the wheels clear the floor.

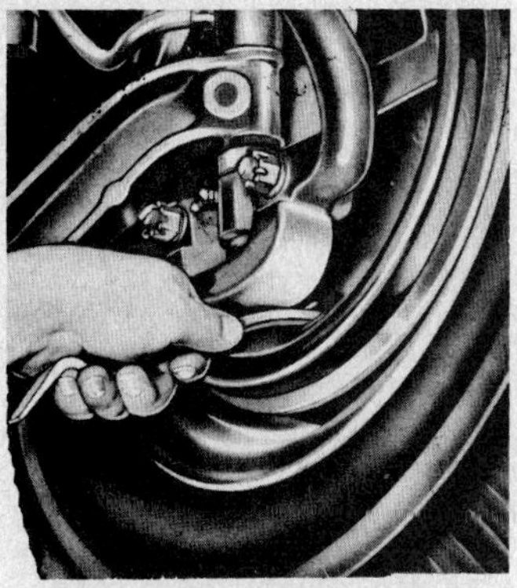

Duo-servo brake adjustment
(© Ford Motor Co.)

2. Remove the cover from the adjusting hole at the bottom of the brake carrier plate, and turn the adjusting screw inside the hole to expand the brake shoes until they drag against the brake drum.
3. When the shoes are against the drum, back off the adjusting screw 10 or 12 notches so that the drum rotates freely without drag.
4. Install the adjusting hole cover on the brake carrier plate.
5. Check and adjust the other three brake assemblies. When adjusting the rear brake shoes, check

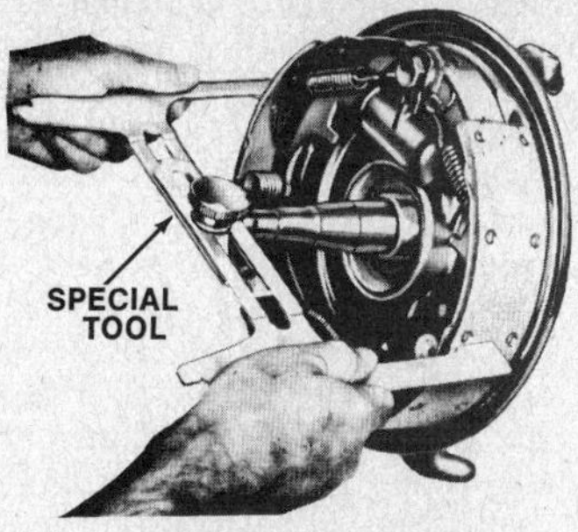

Measuring brake shoes
(© Ford Motor Co.)

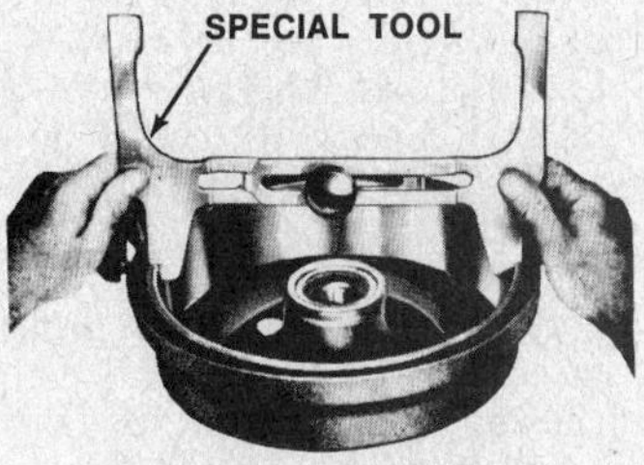

Measuring brake drum
(© Ford Motor Co.)

the parking brake cables for proper adjustment. Make sure that there is clearance between the ends of the parking brake link and the shoes.

6. Apply the brakes. If the pedal travels more than halfway down between the released position and the floor, too much clearance exists between the brake shoes and the drums. Repeat steps 2 and 3 above. Internal inspection and/or bleeding may be necessary.
7. When all brake shoes have been properly adjusted, road test the truck and check the operation of the brakes. *Perform the road test only when the brakes will apply and the truck can be safely stopped.*

Kelsey Hayes

Front Brake Shoes

Removal

1. Raise the vehicle until the wheel clears the floor. Remove the wheel, drum and hub assembly.
2. Clamp the wheel cylinder boots against the ends of the cylinder.
3. Remove the brake shoe retracting springs from both shoes.
4. Remove the adjusting lever link, anchor plate and the adjusting lever spring.
5. Remove the hold down spring cups, springs and the adjusting lever.
6. Remove the brake shoes and adjuster screw assembly from the backing plate.

Installation

1. Clean all brake dust from the brake assembly parts with a *clean dry* rag.
2. Coat all points of contact between the shoes and other brake parts with high temperature grease.
3. Coat the adjuster screw with high temperature grease before assembly. Thread the adjuster screw into the adjuster screw sleeve.
4. Position the brake shoes on the backing plate and install the adjusting lever, hold down pins, springs and cups.
5. Position the adjuster screw assembly on the brake shoes so that the star wheel is opposite the adjusting slot in the backing

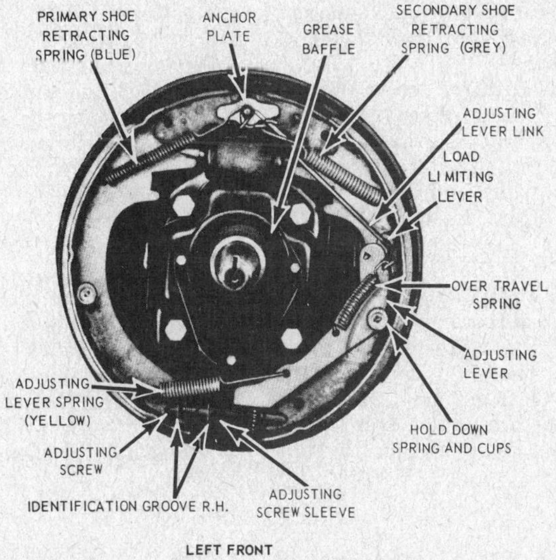

Kelsey-Hayes hydraulic brake assembly (© Ford Motor Co.)

plate. Install the adjusting lever spring.

6. Install the anchor plate and adjusting lever link.
7. Install the secondary brake shoe retracting spring.
8. Install the primary brake shoe retracting spring.
9. Remove the clamp from the wheel cylinder boots.
10. Install the wheel, drum and hub assembly.
11. Adjust the brakes. Subsequent adjustment will be automatic.

Rear Brake Shoes

Removal

1. Raise the truck until the wheel clears the floor.
2. Remove the wheel, hub and drum assembly.
3. Clamp the brake cylinder boots against the ends of the cylinder with brake piston clamps.
4. *Note the two different types of brake shoe retracting springs and remove the springs.*
5. Remove the brake shoe hold down post cotter key, nut, and shoe hold down washer.
6. Loosen and remove the eccentric adjuster bolt, lock washer, eccentric and adjusting link.
7. Remove the shoe and lining assembly from the backing plate.
8. Remove the anchor block spring and slide the adjuster assembly from the shoe web.
9. Remove the adjuster star wheel and screw from the adjuster block. Unthread the star wheel from the adjuster screw.

Installation

1. Wipe all brake dust from the brake assembly parts with a *clean dry* rag. Coat all points of contact between brake shoes and other parts with high temperature grease.
2. Coat the adjuster screw and the inside of the adjuster block with high temperature grease.
3. Thread the adjuster screw onto the star wheel and insert the adjuster screw assembly into the adjuster block. Maintain a 2.12-2.18 inch dimension from the end of the adjuster block to the adjuster screw web slot.
4. Install the adjuster assembly onto the shoe web and attach the anchor block spring.
5. Place the brake shoe over the retracting spring toggle pin and insert the ends of the shoe in the wheel cylinder links.
6. Install the shoe hold down washer and nut. Do not install the cotter pin.
7. Install the four brake shoe retracting springs. Make sure the retracting springs are installed. On 15 x 5″ brakes the inner hook ends face the wheel cylinders. On 15 x 4″ brakes the inner hook ends face the center of the axle.
8. Install the adjusting link, eccentric, lockwasher and adjuster bolt. Do not tighten.
9. Remove the brake piston clamps.
10. Tighten the shoe hold down nut until there is 0.015-0.025″ clearance between the shoe and hold down washer with the shoe held against the backing plate. Install the cotter pin.
11. Center the shoes on the backing plate. Using a ½″ wrench, rotate the adjuster eccentric until the adjusting lever is at the index mark. Tighten the eccentric adjuster bolt to specification.
12. Install the wheel, hub and drum assembly.
13. Adjust the brake to obtain a slight drag. Subsequent adjustments will be automatic.

Brake Shoe Adjustment

The brake drums should be at normal room temperature, when the brake shoes are adjusted. If the shoes are adjusted when the shoes are hot and expanded, the shoes may drag as the drums cool and contract.

The brake shoes are automatically adjusted when the vehicle is driven in reverse and the brakes applied. A manual adjustment is required only after the brake shoes have been relined or replaced. *The manual adjustment is performed while the drums are removed, using the tool and the procedure detailed below.*

When adjusting the rear brake shoes, check the parking brake cables for proper adjustment. Make sure that the equalizer operates freely.

To adjust the brake shoes:

1. Use special tool (see illustration) and adjust to the inside diameter of the drum braking surface.
2. Reverse the tool as shown in illustration and adjust the brake shoes to touch the gauge. The gauge contact points on the shoes must be parallel to the vehicle with the center line through the center of the axle. Hold the automatic adjusting lever out of engagement while rotating the adjusting screw, to prevent burring the screw slots. Make sure the adjusting screw rotates freely.
3. Apply a small quantity of high temperature grease to the points where the shoes contact the carrier plate, being careful not to get the lubricant on the linings.
4. Install the drums. Install the retaining nuts and tighten securely.
5. Install the wheels on the drums and tighten the mounting nuts to specification.
6. Complete the adjustment by applying the brakes several times while backing the vehicle.
7. After the brake shoes have been properly adjusted, check the operation of the brakes by making several stops while operating in a forward direction.

Parking Brakes

Internal Shoe Type

Adjustment

Nine-Inch Diameter Drum

1. Release the parking brake lever in the cab.
2. From under the truck, remove the cotter pin from the parking brake linkage adjusting clevis pin. Remove the clevis pin.
3. Lengthen the parking brake adjusting link by turning the clevis. Continue to lengthen the adjusting link until the shoes seat against the drum when the clevis pin is installed.
4. Remove the clevis pin and shorten the linkage adjustment until there is 0.010″ clearance between the shoes and the drum. The measurement should be taken at all points around the drum with the clevis pin installed.
5. Install a new cotter pin in the clevis retaining pin and check the brake operation.

Twelve-Inch Diameter Drum

There is no internal adjustment on this brake. Adjustment is made on the linkage. Remove the clevis pin, loosen the nuts on the adjusting rod, and turn the clevis on the rod until a ¼-⅜″ free play is obtained at the brake lever. Tighten the nuts, and connect the clevis to the bellcrank with the clevis pin.

DISC BRAKES—TROUBLE DIAGNOSIS

CAUSE	CORRECTION
1. Master cylinder fluid level low.	1. Fill to proper level with approved fluid. Note, fluid level drops as disc brake linings wear.
2. Poor quality brake fluid (low boiling point) in system.	2. Drain hydraulic system and fill with approved
3. Air in hydraulic system.	3. Bleed hydraulic system and refill with approved fluid.
4. Hoses soft or weak (expanding under pressure).	4. Replace defective hoses. combination valve and all cups and seals in complete brake s

1. Power brake malfunctioning.	1. Check and repair power unit.
2. Linings soiled with brake fluid, oil or grease.	2. Replace shoes and linings.
3. Lines, hoses or connections dented, kinked, collapsed, clogged or disconnected.	3. Repair or replace defective parts.
4. Master cylinder cups swollen.	4. Drain hydraulic system, flush system with brake fluid and replace combination valve and all cups and seals in complete brake system.
5. Master cylinder bore corroded or rough.	5. Repair or replace master cylinder.
6. Caliper pistons frozen or seized.	6. Disassemble caliper and free pistons (replace if necessary).
7. Caliper cylinder bores corroded or rough.	7. Disassemble caliper and remove corrosion or roughness, or replace caliper.
8. Pedal push rod and linkage binding.	8. Free and lubricate.
9. Metering valve not working.	9. Replace combination valve.

GRABBING OR PULLING (Severe Reaction To Pedal Pressure and Out of Line Stops)

CAUSE	CORRECTION
1. Linings soiled with brake fluid, oil or grease.	1. Replace shoes and linings.
2. Caliper loose.	2. Tighten caliper mounting bolts to specified torque.
3. Lines, hoses or connection dented, kinked, collapsed or clogged.	3. Repair or replace defective parts.
4. Master cylinder bore corroded or rough.	4. Repair or replace master cylinder.
5. Caliper pistons frozen or seized.	5. Disassemble caliper and free pistons (replace if necessary).
6. Caliper cylinder seals soft or swollen.	6. Drain hydraulic system, flush system with brake fluid and replace all cups and seals in complete brake system.
7. Caliper cylinder bores corroded or rough.	7. Disassemble caliper and remove corrosion or roughness, or replace caliper.
8. Pedal linkage binding (and suddenly releasing).	8. Free and lubricate linkage.
9. Metering valve not functioning properly.	9. Replace combination valve.

DISC BRAKES—TROUBLE DIAGNOSIS—Cont'd

FADING PEDAL (Pedal Falling Away Under Steady Pressure)

CAUSE	CORRECTION
1. Poor quality brake fluid (low boiling point) in system.	1. Drain hydraulic system and fill with approved fluid.
2. Hydraulic connections loose; lines or hoses ruptured (causing leakage).	2. Tighten or replace defective parts.
3. Master cylinder cup worn or damaged. (primary, secondary or both).	3. Repair master cylinder.
4. Master cylinder bore corroded, worn or scored.	4. Repair or replace master cylinder.
5. Caliper cylinder seals worn or damaged.	5. Replace seals.
6. Caliper cylinder bores corroded, worn or scored.	6. Disassemble caliper and remove corrosion or scoring, or replace caliper.
7. Bleed screw open.	7. Close bleed screw and bleed hydraulic system.

NOISE AND CHATTER (May Be Accompanied By Brake Roughness and Pedal Pumping)

CAUSE	CORRECTION
1. Disc has excessive lateral runout.	1. Replace or machine disc.
2. Disc has excessive thickness variations (out of parallel).	2. Replace or machine disc.
3. Disc has casting imperfections.	3. Replace disc.
4. Car creeping or moving slowly with brakes applied (may produce groan or crunching noise).	4. Increase or decrease pedal effort slightly.
5. Squeal, during application.	5. A small amount of high-pitched squeal is inherent in disc brake design and must be considered normal. Some relief may be obtained with service package backing.

DRAGGING BRAKES (Slow or Incomplete Release of Brakes)

CAUSE	CORRECTION
1. Lines, hoses or connections dented, kinked, collapsed or clogged.	1. Repair or replace defective parts.
2. Master cylinder compensating port restricted by swollen primary cup.	2. Drain hydraulic system, flush system with brake fluid and replace combination valve and all cups and seals in complete brake system.
3. Residual pressure check valve in lines to front wheels.	3. Remove check valve.
4. Caliper pistons frozen or seized.	4. Disassemble caliper and free pistons (replace if necessary).
5. Caliper cylinder seals swollen.	5. Drain hydraulic system, flush system with clean brake fluid and replace combination valve and all cups and seals in complete brake system.
6. Caliper cylinder bores corroded or rough.	6. Disassemble caliper and remove corrosion or roughness, or replace caliper.
7. Hydraulic push rod on power brake out of adjustment or binding (causing primary cup to restrict master cylinder compensating port).	7. Adjust or free and lubricate.

Floating Caliper Disc Brakes—Dual Piston

This disc brake is a floating caliper design with two pistons on one side of the rotor. It is a two piece unit consisting of the caliper and cylinder housing. The caliper is mounted to the anchor plate on two mounting pins which travel in bushings in the anchor plate. The bushings and pins are protected by boot type seals.

Two brake shoe and lining assemblies are used in each caliper, one on each side of the rotor. The shoes are identical and are attached to the caliper with two mounting pins.

The cylinder housing contains the two pistons. The pistons are fitted with an insulator on the front and a seal on the back lip. A friction ring is attached to the back of the piston with a shouldered cap screw. The pistons and cylinder bores are protected by boot seals which are fitted to a groove in the piston and attached to the cylinder housing with retainers. The cylinder assembly is attached to the caliper with two cap screws and washers.

The anchor plate is bolted directly to the spindle. It positions the caliper assembly over the rotor forward of the spindle.

Disc Brake Shoe Adjustment

The front disc brake assembly is designed so that it is inherently self-adjusting and requires no manual adjustment.

Automatic adjustment for lining wear is achieved by the piston and friction ring sliding outward in the cylinder bore. The piston assumes a new position in the cylinder and maintains the correct adjustment.

Front Disc Brake Shoe and Lining

Replace shoe and lining assemblies when lining is worn to a minimum of 1/16″ in thickness (combined thickness of shoe and lining ¼″ minimum).

Removal

1. Remove the shoe and lining mounting pins, anti-rattle springs and old shoe and lining assemblies.

Installation

1. Remove the master cylinder cover.
2. Loosen the piston housing-to-caliper mounting bolts sufficiently to permit the installation of new shoe and lining assemblies. *Do not move pistons.*
3. Install new shoe and lining assemblies. Install the brake shoe mounting pins and anti-rattle springs. *Be sure that the spring tangs are located in the holes provided in the shoe plates.*
4. Torque the brake shoe mounting pins to 17-23 ft lbs.
5. Reset the pistons to the correct location in the cylinders by placing shims or feeler gauges of .023 to .035″ thickness between the shoe plate of the outboard shoe and lining assembly and the caliper; then, retighten the piston housing-to-caliper mounting bolts. *Keep the cylinder housing square with the caliper.*
6. Loosen the piston housing-to-caliper mounting bolts and remove the shims.
7. Torque the piston housing-to-caliper mounting bolts to 155 to 185 ft lbs.
8. Check the master cylinder reservoirs.
9. Install the master cylinder cover.

Disc Brake Caliper

Removal

1. Remove the wheel and tire assembly.
2. Remove the pins and nuts retaining the caliper assembly to the anchor plate.
3. Disconnect the brake hose from the caliper and remove the caliper.

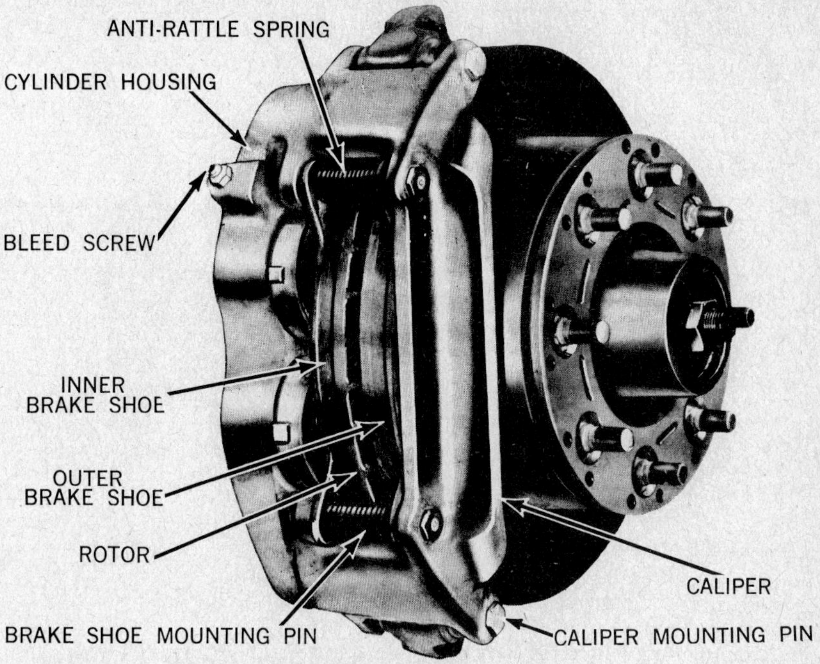

Floating caliper disc brake (© Ford Motor Co.)

Installation

1. Connect the brake hose to the caliper.
2. Position the caliper assembly to the anchor plate and install the retaining pins and nuts. Torque the nuts to specifications.
3. Install drum and wheel and bleed brake system.

If the caliper assembly is leaking, the piston assemblies must be removed from the piston housing and replaced. If the cylinder bores are scored, corroded or excessive wear is evident, the piston housing must be replaced. *Do not hone the cylinder bores.* Piston assemblies are not available for oversize bores. The piston housing must be removed from the caliper for replacement.

Disassembly

1. Remove the two pins and nuts retaining the caliper to the support. Disconnect the flexible brake hose and plug the end to prevent brake fluid leakage.
2. Remove the boot retainers and remove the dust boots from the pistons and cylinder housing.
3. Position the caliper assembly in a vise.
4. Place a block of wood between the caliper and the cylinders, and apply low pressure air to the brake hose inlet. One piston will be forced out.
5. Reverse the piston and install it by hand pressure back into the cylinder bore far enough to form a seal. Block the reversed piston

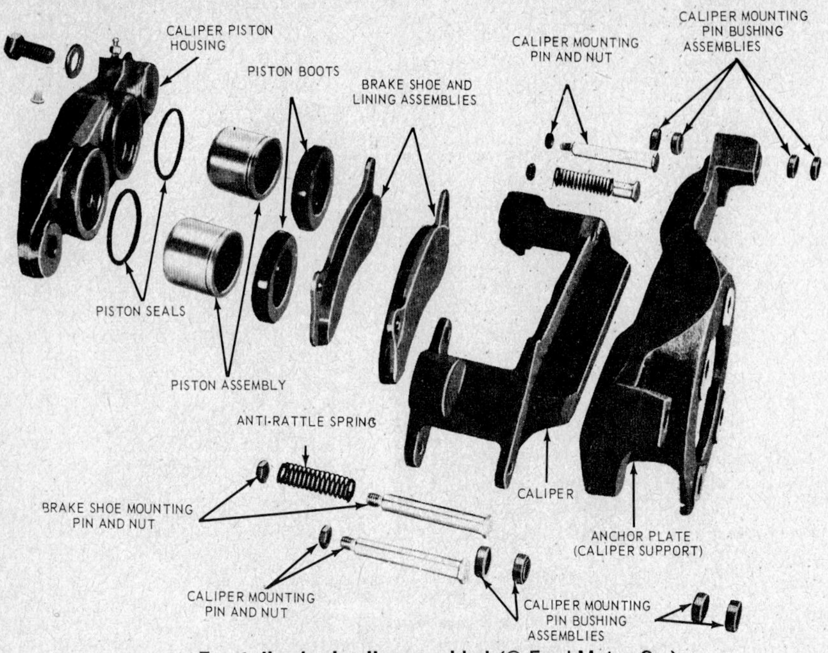

Front disc brake disassembled (© Ford Motor Co.)

from moving out of the bore and place the wooden block between the remaining piston and the caliper.

6. Force out the second piston with low pressure air. *Care should be taken as the piston is forced out of the bore.*
7. Remove the two bolts and separate the caliper from the cylinder housing.

Assembly

The piston assembly and dust boots are not to be reused. A new set is to be used each time the caliper is assembled.

1. Apply a film of clean brake fluid in the cylinder bores and on the piston assemblies. *Do not apply brake fluid on the insulators.*
2. Start the piston assemblies into the cylinder bores using firm hand pressure. *Exercise care to avoid cocking the piston in the bore.*
3. Lightly tapping with a rawhide mallet, seat each piston assembly until the friction ring bottoms out in the cylinder bore.
4. Install the piston dust boots and retainers.
5. Position the piston housing on the caliper and install the piston housing-to-caliper mounting bolts and washers. Torque the piston housing-to-caliper mounting bolts to 155 to 185 ft lbs.
6. Install the flexible brake hose.
7. Bleed the brake system and centralize the pressure differential valve.

Do not move the vehicle after working on the disc brakes until a firm brake pedal is obtained.

Sliding Caliper Disc Brakes—Single Piston

This caliper is a one piece type with a single piston on the inboard side. The piston is made of steel and is plated to resist wear and corrosion.

The piston has a square cut seal which provides for a seal between the piston and the caliper cylinder wall. A rubber dust boot located in a groove in the cylinder helps keep contamination from the piston and cylinder wall.

The caliper is mounted on an adapter which is mounted on the steering knuckle.

Disc Brake Adjustment

No adjustment is required on this unit other than applying the pedal several times after the unit has been worked on. This is to seat the shoes and after this is done the hydraulic pressure maintains the proper clearance between the brake shoes and the rotor.

Brake Shoe Removal

Replace the brake shoes when the linings are worn within 1/32" of the shoe or the rivets.

Removal

1. Remove the master cylinder cover and if the cylinder is more than ⅓ full remove the fluid necessary to make the cylinder only ⅓ full. This is done to prevent any overflow from the cylinder when the piston is pushed into the bore of the caliper.
2. Raise vehicle on hoise and remove the front wheels.
3. Compress the piston back into the bore by using a large C-clamp and compressing the unit until the piston bottoms in the bore.
4. Remove the two retaining bolts that hold the caliper into the support. If the caliper has retaining clips remove the retaining clips and anti-rattle springs. If the caliper has key type retainers, remove the key retaining screws, and using a hammer and drift, punch drive the key out of the caliper.
5. Slide the caliper off the rotor disc. Be careful not to damage the dust boot on the piston when removing the caliper.

NOTE: Do not let the caliper hang with the brake hose supporting the

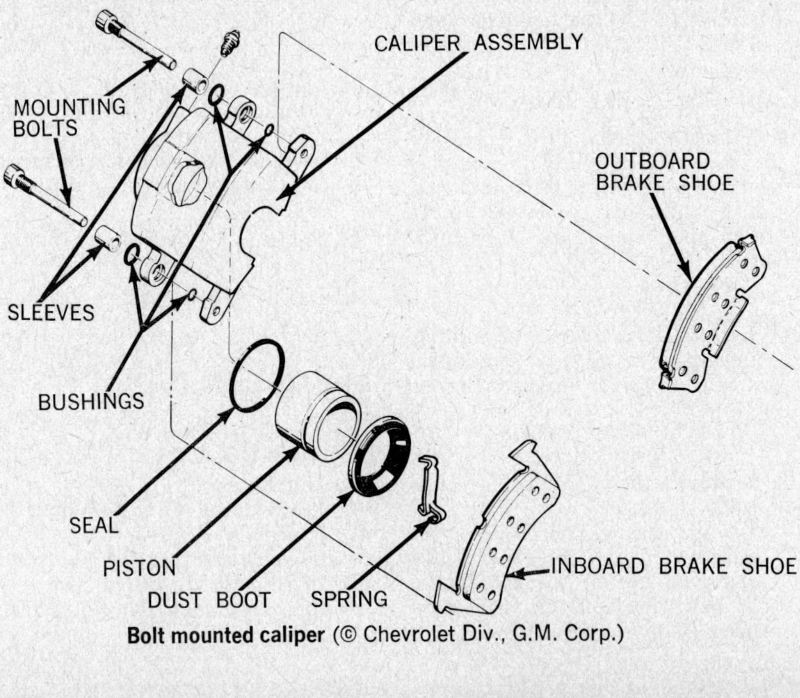

Bolt mounted caliper (© Chevrolet Div., G.M. Corp.)

weight. This can cause damage to the hose which could result in a loss of brakes. Set the caliper on the front suspension arm or tie rod.

6. Remove the outer shoe from the caliper. It may be necessary to tap the shoe to loosen it from the caliper. Remove the inner shoe from the caliper or spindle assembly depending on where the shoe stays.
7. Remove the shoe support spring from the piston.

Cleaning and Inspection

Clean the sliding surfaces of the caliper and clean any dirt from the mounting bolts, clips or keys.

Inspect the boot on the piston for signs of cracks, cuts or other damage. Check to see if there is signs of fluid leaking around the seal on the piston. This will show up in the boot. If there is an indication of a fluid leak, the entire caliper has to be disassembled and the seal replaced.

Installation

1. Make sure that the piston is fully bottomed in the cylinder bore and install the outboard shoe in the recess of the caliper. NOTE: On shoes with anti-rattle springs be sure to install the spring before installing the shoe in the caliper.
2. Place the outer shoe on the caliper and press it into place with finger pressure.
3. Position the caliper on the rotor and carefully slide it down into position over the rotor.
4. Install the caliper mounting bolts and torque them to 35 ft lbs. On models with retaining clips install the anti-rattle springs and the retaining clips and torque the retaining screws to 200 in lbs. On models with key type retainers press down the caliper and install the key in its slot and drive it in place with a hammer and drift. Install the retaining screw and torque to 12-18 ft lbs.
5. Install the wheels and lower the vehicle. Check the master cylinder fluid level and add any fluid necessary to bring it up to the proper level.
6. Pump the brake pedal several times until a firm brake pedal is established. Road test the vehicle to check for proper operation.

Disc Caliper

Removal

1. Remove the cover on the master cylinder and check if the fluid level is 1/3 full. If it is more than 1/3 full remove the necessary amount to bring the level down. This step is necessary to avoid overflow from the master cylinder when the piston is compressed into the cylinder bore.
2. Raise the vehicle and remove the wheel.
3. Compress the piston into the caliper bore and remove the brake hose from the caliper. Tape the end of the hose to prevent dirt from entering the line.
4. Remove the caliper retaining bolts, clips or wedges and remove the caliper from the vehicle.

Disassembly

1. Clean the outside of the caliper with clean brake fluid and drain any fluid from the caliper.
2. Remove the piston from the caliper by connecting the hydraulic line to the caliper and gently stroking the brake pedal. This will push the piston from the caliper bore.
3. With care remove the boot from the caliper piston bore.
4. Remove the piston seal from the caliper bore using a piece of wood or plastic.

NOTE: DO NOT use a metal tool to remove the seal. This can damage the bore or burr the edges of the seal groove.

5. Remove the bleeder valve.

Cleaning and Inspection

1. Clean all the parts with clean brake fluid and blow out all the passages in the caliper.

NOTE: When ever the caliper is disassembled discard the boot and piston seal. These parts must not be reused.

2. Inspect the outside of the piston for signs of wear, corrosion, scores or any other defects. If any defects are detected replace the piston.
3. Check the caliper bore for the same defects as the piston. However, the bore can be cleaned up to a point with crocus cloth. If there are any marks that will not clean up with the cloth the caliper must be replaced.

Assembly and Installation

1. Lube the caliper bore and the piston with clean brake fluid and position the seal for the piston in the cylinder bore groove.
2. Install the dust boot into the groove in the piston with the fold faces toward the open end of the piston.
3. Install the piston in the bore being careful not to unseat the piston seal in the bore.
4. With the piston bottomed in the cylinder position the boot in the groove in the caliper. Make sure that the retaining ring in the seal is pressed down evenly around the cylinder.
5. Install the bleeder screw in the caliper and install the caliper back on the vehicle.

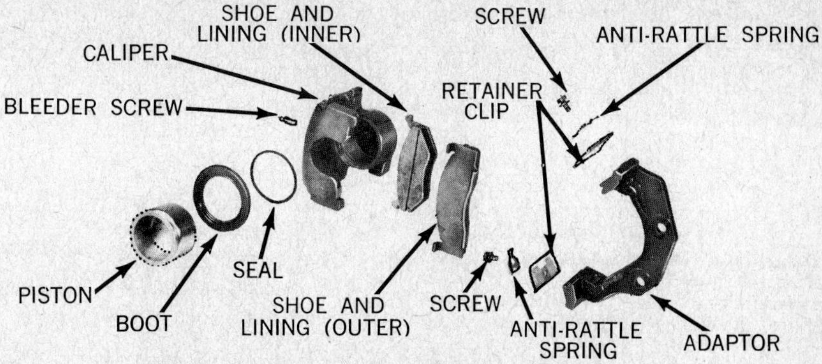

Caliper assembly retaining clip type (© Chrysler Corp.)

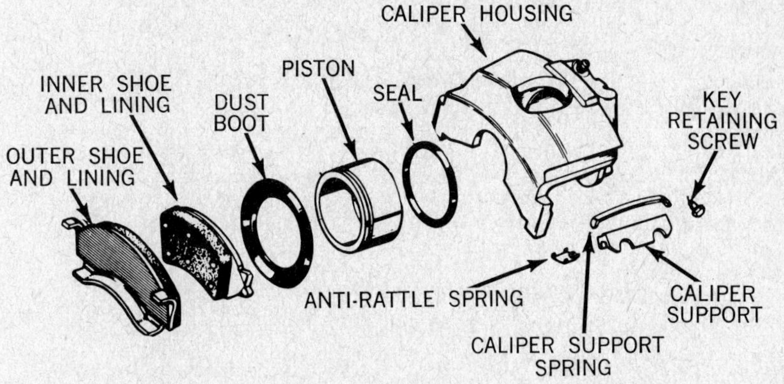

Disc brake caliper retainer key type (© Ford Motor Co.)

6. Connect the brake hoses and bleed the calipers of air. When bleeding is done pump the pedal several times to develop a firm brake pedal.

Sliding Caliper Disc Brakes (Double Piston)

Brake Shoe and Caliper

Removal

1. Drain about 2/3 of the total brake fluid from the reservoir.
2. Jack up the vehicle and remove the front wheels.
3. Remove the four screws and remove the caliper hold-down assembly.
4. Lift the caliper off the hub and rotor. If the caliper is to be removed, disconnect the hydraulic line; if not, lay the caliper on the suspension or support with a length of wire.
5. Remove the inner and outer shoe and lining.

Disassembly

1. Drain the brake fluid from the caliper and clean the exterior with clean brake fluid.
2. Place a small block of wood under the caliper pistons and place a protective pad over the exterior. Remove the pistons by directing compressed air into the caliper fluid outlet.
3. Remove and discard piston boots.

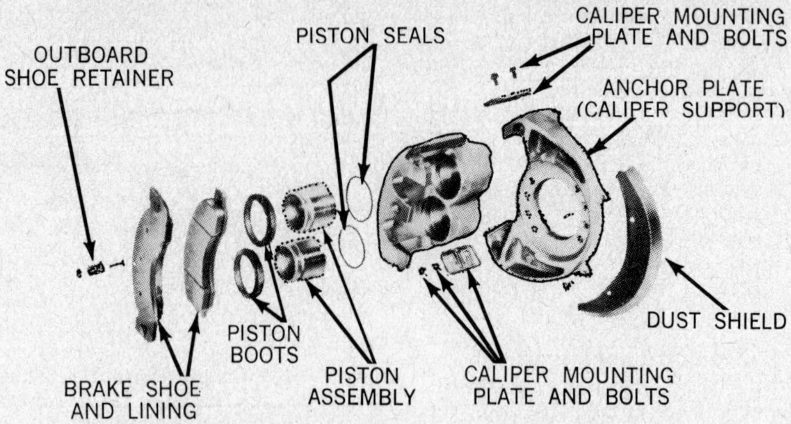

Sliding caliper disc brakes—double piston (© Ford Motor Co.)

4. Remove the piston seals from the groove in the caliper bore.

Assembly

1. Clean all parts in clean brake fluid and blow dry.
2. Dip the new piston seal in clean brake fluid and install it into the cylinder groove.

NOTE: Be sure that the seal is not rolled or twisted in the groove.

3. Install the dust boot in the cylinder groove.
4. Coat the outside diameter of the piston with clean brake fluid. Use something plastic or wood and gradually work the dust boot around the piston.
5. Press the piston straight into the caliper bore until it bottoms. Position the boot in the piston groove.

Installation

1. Install a new shoe and lining assembly into the anchor plate.
2. Push the pistons to the bottom of the piston bore. Place a small block of wood over both pistons and boots. Push the pistons to the bottom of the bores with a C-clamp.
3. Install the outer shoe and lining onto the caliper and install the shoe hold-down spring and pin.
4. Install the caliper assembly over the hub, rotor and inner shoe, and position into the inner grooves in the anchor plate.
5. Install the caliper hold-down parts and tighten to 40 ft. lbs.
6. Add extra heavy duty brake fluid to bring the level to ¼″ from the top of the reservoir.
7. Bleed the system and add fluid as necessary.

POWER BOOSTER TROUBLE DIAGNOSIS

Condition	*Possible Cause*	*Correction*
Vacuum leak (booster in released position)	1. End plate, center plate or control valve body gaskets leak. 2. Distortion of end plate. 3. Misalignment of control valve poppet. 4. Loose vacuum cylinder bolts. 5. Loose control valve body screws. 6. Large control valve poppet spring not centered in spring retainer.	1. Recondition booster unit. 2. Replace end plate. 3. Disassemble, clean and correctly reassemble. 4. Coat vacuum cylinder bolts lightly with a suitable sealing compound and tighten to specified torque. 5. Tighten control valve body screws to specified torque. 6. Disassemble unit and correctly reassemble.
Vacuum leak (booster in applied position)	1. Leak at control valve poppet and seat. 2. Dry or faulty piston leather packing. 3. Faulty control valve diaphragm assembly.	1. Clean and inspect poppet and seat for damage and repair as necessary. 2. Clean and lubricate piston leather or replace. 3. Replace faulty parts.
External hydraulic leaks	1. Gasket ("O" ring) leaking at hydraulic end plate joint. 2. Fluid leaking at copper gasket under hydraulic cylinder end cap.	1. Disassemble clean and replace ("O" ring) gasket and reassemble. 2. Remove end cap and inspect copper gasket and seat install new copper gasket.
Internal hydraulic leak at low pressures	1. Control valve hydraulic piston cup failure. 2. Faulty push rod seal.	1. Recondition control valve unit. 2. Replace push rod seal.
Internal leaks at high pressure	1. Fluid passing copper gasket under hydraulic fitting in control valve. 2. Inspect cups and seals of master cylinder for cuts and scores. 3. Inspect cups of the control valve hydraulic piston.	1. Clean and inspect gasket and fitting, replace if faulty. 2. Hone master cylinder and replace cups and seals. 3. Replace faulty cups.
Hydraulic pressure buildup (without added input)	1. Check hydraulic piston check valve and slot for foreign material under valve.	1. Clean or replace valve and seats as condition indicates.
Failure to release	1. Weak vacuum cylinder piston return spring. 2. Dry vacuum piston leather packing. 3. Swollen rubber cups due to inferior or contaminated brake fluid. 4. Damaged or dented vacuum cylinder shell. 5. Dirty or sticky control valve piston.	1. Replace vacuum cylinder piston return spring. 2. Lubricate vacuum piston leather packing. 3. Flush hydraulic system and recondition or replace all cylinders. 4. Replace vacuum cylinder shell. 5. Recondition control valve assembly.
Failure of booster to operate within specified pressures	1. Rusty, dirty or distorted vacuum cylinder shell. 2. Dry or worn vacuum cylinder leather packing. 3. Swollen rubber cups due to inferior brake fluid. 4. Worn or scored hydraulic cups. 5. Dirt, rust or foreign matter in any component of the system.	1. Clean or replace vacuum cylinder shell. 2. Recondition and lubricate the vacuum booster. 3. Recondition the master cylinder. Replace brake fluid. 4. Recondition the master cylinder. 5. Recondition and lubricate the brake booster assembly.
Loss of fluid	1. Fluid leaking past cup in master cylinder. 2. Brake wheel cylinders leaking. 3. Loose hydraulic hose connectors. 4. Leaking stop light switch.	1. Recondition master cylinder or replace. 2. Recondition or replace wheel cylinders. 3. Inspect and tighten all hydraulic connections. 4. Replace stop light switch.
Presence of brake fluid on hy-power vacuum cylinder	1. Piston cup or push rod seal leaking.	1. Recondition master cylinder.
Pedal kicks back against foot when brakes are applied	1. Vacuum leakage. 2. Dirt under control valve or damaged seat. 3. Weak or broken spring.	1. Inspect and correct vacuum leak. 2. Clean and recondition booster assembly. 3. Replace spring.
Engine runs unevenly at idle with brakes released	1. Vacuum leakage. 2. Dirt under control valve disc or damaged seat. 3. Defective spring.	1. Inspect and tighten all vacuum fittings. 2. Clean control valve or replace. 3. Replace defective spring.
Engine runs evenly and pedal is hard with brakes applied	1. Control valve piston assembly not seating on vacuum disc. 2. Defective control valve plate and diaphragm. 3. Defective pressure plate and diaphragm.	1. Clean or replace control valve piston assembly. 2. Replace control valve plate and diaphragm. 3. Replace pressure plate and diaphragm.

POWER BOOSTER TROUBLE DIAGNOSIS

Condition	Possible Cause	Correction
Brakes are slow to release Note: First, jack up truck and determine whether or not the wheels are dragging.	1. Incorrect pedal linkage adjustment. 2. Compensating port of master cylinder plugged. 3. Brake shoes sticking. 4. Weak brake shoe return spring. 5. Booster control valve piston sticking. 6. Booster air filter clogged. 7. Control valve diaphragm return spring missing. 8. Defective check valve in slave cylinder piston. 9. Dirt under atmospheric valve disc.	1. Adjust and lubricate pedal linkage. 2. Clean master cylinder with compressed air. 3. Free up and lubricate brake shoes. 4. Replace brake shoe return spring. 5. Clean booster control valve piston and lubricate. 6. Clean air filter in mineral spirits. 7. Install new control valve return spring. 8. Recondition slave cylinder pistons. 9. Clean atmospheric valve.
Brake pedal is hard at different intervals	1. Defective manifold check valve. 2. Slave cylinder piston sticking due to dirt or inferior brake fluid. 3. Brake booster air cleaner clogged.	1. Clean or replace manifold check valve. 2. Clean and recondition slave cylinder. 3. Clean air cleaner in mineral spirits and blow dry with compressed air.

Power Brake Boosters

Brake System Preliminary Checks

Always check the fluid level in the brake master cylinder reservoir(s) before performing the test procedures. If the fluid level is not within ¼" of the top of the master cylinder reservoirs, add the specified brake fluid.

Push the brake pedal down as far as it will go. If the pedal travels more than halfway between the released position and the floor, adjust the brakes. If the vehicle is equipped with automatic brake adjusters, several sharp brake applications while backing up may be necessary to adjust the brakes.

Road test the vehicle and apply the brakes at a speed of about 20 mph to see if the vehicle stops evenly. If not, the brakes should be adjusted. *Perform the road test only when the brakes will apply and the vehicle can be safely stopped.*

Dual Brake Warning Light System Tests

1. Turn the ignition switch to the ACC or ON position. If the light on the brake warning lamp remains on, the condition may be caused by a shorted or broken switch, grounded switch wires or the differential pressure valve is not centered. Centralize the differential pressure valve. If the warning light remains on, check the switch connector and wire for a grounded condition and repair or replace the wire assembly. If the condition of the wire is good, replace the brake warning lamp switch.
2. Turn the ignition switch to the start position. If the brake warning lamp does not light, check the light and wiring and replace or repair wiring as necessary. When both brake systems are functioning normally, the equal pressure at the pressure differential valve during brake pedal application keeps the valve centered. The brake warning light will be on only when the ignition key is in the start position.
3. If the brake warning lamp does not light when a pressure differential condition exists in the brake system, the warning lamp may be burned out, the warning lamp switch is inoperative or the switch to lamp wiring has an open circuit. Check the bulb and replace it, if required. Check the switch to lamp wires for an open circuit and repair or replace them, if required. If the warning lamp still does not light, replace the switch.

Power Brake Function Test

With the engine stopped, eliminate all vacuum from the system by pumping the brake pedal several times. Then push the pedal down as far as it will go, and note the effort required to hold it in this position. If the pedal gradually moves downward under this pressure, the hydraulic system is leaking and should be checked by a hydraulic pressure test.

With the brake pedal still pushed down, start the engine. If the vacuum system is operating properly, the pedal will move downward. If the pedal position does not change, the vacuum system is not operating properly and should be checked by a vacuum test.

Vacuum Booster Check Valve Test

Disconnect the line from the bottom of the vacuum check valve, and connect a vacuum gauge to the valve. Start the engine, run it at idle speed, and check the reading on the vacuum gauge.

The gauge should register 17-19" with standard transmission and 14-15" in Drive range if equipped with an automatic transmission. Stop the engine and note the rate of vacuum drop. If the vacuum drops more than one inch in 15 seconds, the check valve is leaking. If the vacuum reading does not reach 18" or is unsteady, an engine tuneup is needed.

Remove the gauge and reconnect the vacuum line to the check valve.

Vacuum Booster Test—Bendix Piston Type

Disconnect the vacuum line from the booster end plate. Install a tee fitting in the end plate, and connect a vacuum gauge (No. 1) and vacuum line to the fitting. Install a second vacuum gauge (No. 2) in place of the pipe plug in the booster control valve body.

Start the engine, and note the vacuum reading on both gauges. If both gauges do not register manifold vacuum, air is leaking into the vacuum system. If both gauges register manifold vacuum, stop the engine and note the rate of vacuum drop on both gauges. If the drop exceeds one inch in 15 seconds on either gauge, air is leaking into the vacuum system. Tighten all vacuum connections and repeat the test. If leakage still exists, the leak may be localized as follows:

1. Disconnect the vacuum line and gauge No. 1 from the booster.
2. Connect vacuum gauge No. 1 directly to the vacuum line. Start the engine and note the gauge reading. Stop the engine and check the rate of vacuum drop. If gauge No. 1 does not register manifold vacuum, or if the vacuum drop exceeds 1" in 15 seconds, the leak is in the vacuum

line or check valve connections.

3. Reconnect vacuum gauge No. 1 and the vacuum line to the tee fitting. Start the engine, and run it at idle speed for one minute. Depress the brake pedal sufficiently to cause vacuum gauge No. 2 to read from zero to 1 inch of vac uum. Gauge No. 1 should register manifold vacuum of 17-19″ with standard transmission and 14-16″ in Drive range if equipped with an automatic transmission. If the drop of vacuum on gauge No. 2 is slow, the air cleaner, or air cleaner line, may be plugged. Inspect and if necessary, clean the air cleaner.
4. Release the brake pedal and observe the action of gauge No. 2. Upon releasing the pedal, the vacuum gauge must register increasing vacuum until manifold vacuum is reached. The rate of increase must be smooth, with no lag or slowness in the return to manifold vacuum. If the gauge readings are not as outlined, the booster is not operating properly and should be removed and overhauled.

Vacuum Booster Test—Diaphragm Type

This procedure can be used to test all diaphragm boosters which are equipped with a pipe thread outlet on the atmosphere portion of the diaphragm chamber.

Remove the pipe plug from the rear half of the booster chamber, and install a vacuum gauge. Start the engine and run it at idle speed. The gauge should register 18-21″ of vacuum.

1. With the engine running, depress the brake pedal with enough pressure to show a zero reading on the vacuum gauge. Hold the pedal in the applied position for one minute. Any downward movement of the pedal during this time indicates a brake fluid leak. Any kickback (upward movement) of the pedal indicates brake fluid is leaking past the hydraulic piston check valve.
2. With the engine running, push down on the brake pedal with sufficient pressure to show a zero reading on the vacuum gauge. Hold the pedal down, and shut the engine off. Maintain pedal position for one minute. A kickback of the pedal indicates a vacuum leak in the vacuum check valve, in the vacuum line connections, or in the booster.

Bleeding Vacuum-Hydraulic Booster Systems

1. Eliminate vacuum in the booster by depressing the brake pedal several times while the engine is not running.
2. On trucks not equipped with reservoir tanks, disconnect the manifold tube at the booster side of the manifold check valve (engine not running).
3. Alternately loosen the brake tube at each unit until all air is expelled. Booster slave-cylinder is bled first.

CAUTION: **Where air pressure brake bleeding equipment is used to bleed brakes, do not use more than 25-30 psi.**

NOTE: A piston stop is provided in the slave cylinder to eliminate the possibility of damaging the return spring while bleeding the system. This damage occurs only when bleeding the brakes with a vacuum present in the booster system.

Hydraulic Tandem Brake Unit

Disassembly

1. Disconnect hydraulic and vacuum by-pass tube from valve body.
2. Remove control valve air inlet fitting from control valve body.
3. Remove control valve body and valve parts from end plate.
4. Make a special tool. *NOTE: If this to be a regular service this tool is recommended. For one time or emergency, a vise, "C" clamps, and a guide tube 10″ long may be used.*
5. Insert tool through end plate opening, and force vacuum cylinder piston forward.
6. Attach flange of tool to end plate with three valve body cover screws.
7. Loosen slave cylinder check nut, and remove slave cylinder.
8. Compress push rod pin retaining spring, remove retainer pin, then remove hydraulic piston from push rod.
9. Hold end cap in a vise, and remove hydraulic cylinder from cap.
10. Loosen vacuum hose clamps, then slide both hoses on the vacuum tube toward center plate.
11. Remove hydraulic by-pass tube from rear end plate, then remove return spring compression tool from end plate.
12. Remove the nuts and studs from power cylinder, then disassemble end plates, cylinder shells and center plate assembly.
13. Force center plate and vacuum piston together, and insert a rod through hole in piston rod to hold piston return spring in the compressed position.
14. Place assembly ring over piston, then remove piston assembly, but keep piston parts assembled in assembly ring. After vacuum tubes and tee fittings have been removed from center plate, position plate on a flat surface.
15. Remove fast application valve cover.
16. To disassemble the diaphragm assembly, hold valve shaft with a screw driver, and remove nut.
17. Lift retainer and diaphragm off valve shaft.
18. Turn center plate upside down, then remove valve seat plate screws and plate, gasket, valve, and spring from center plate.
19. Position front end plate assem bly on a flat surface with flat side down.
20. Remove the "O" ring seal, snap ring and retainer washer, push rod seal spring and flange washer, push rod rubber cup seal, and guide washer from end plate.
21. Drive push rod leather seal out of end plate.
22. Position end plate in a holding fixture, then remove hydraulic valve fitting with a 1-7/8″ socket wrench.
23. Push hydraulic piston out of valve fitting, and remove gasket from fittings.

Clean all metal parts in a suitable cleaning fluid. After cleaning, wash all the hydraulic system parts in alcohol.

Examine the bore of the cylinder shells for rust and corrosion, and polish with fine steel wool or crocus cloth if necessary.

If the cylinders are badly pitted or scored, install new cylinders.

If felt type wicks are worn, replace them with cotton type wicks.

Use overhaul kit and install ALL parts contained. Do not gamble on ANY old parts that the kit replaces.

Assembly

1. Install nut on piston rod with flat side of nut upward.
2. Position larger diameter piston plate on piston rod with chamfered side of hole at top. Guide rubber seal ring over threads of piston rod.
3. Place assembly ring on a flat surface, then install leather packing, with lip side upward; and smaller diameter piston plate with chamfered side of hole downward in the ring.
4. Cut a new piece of wick to the required length, then place it against inner face of leather packing lip.
5. Assemble expander ring against wick with gripper points upward, and hook notched end of

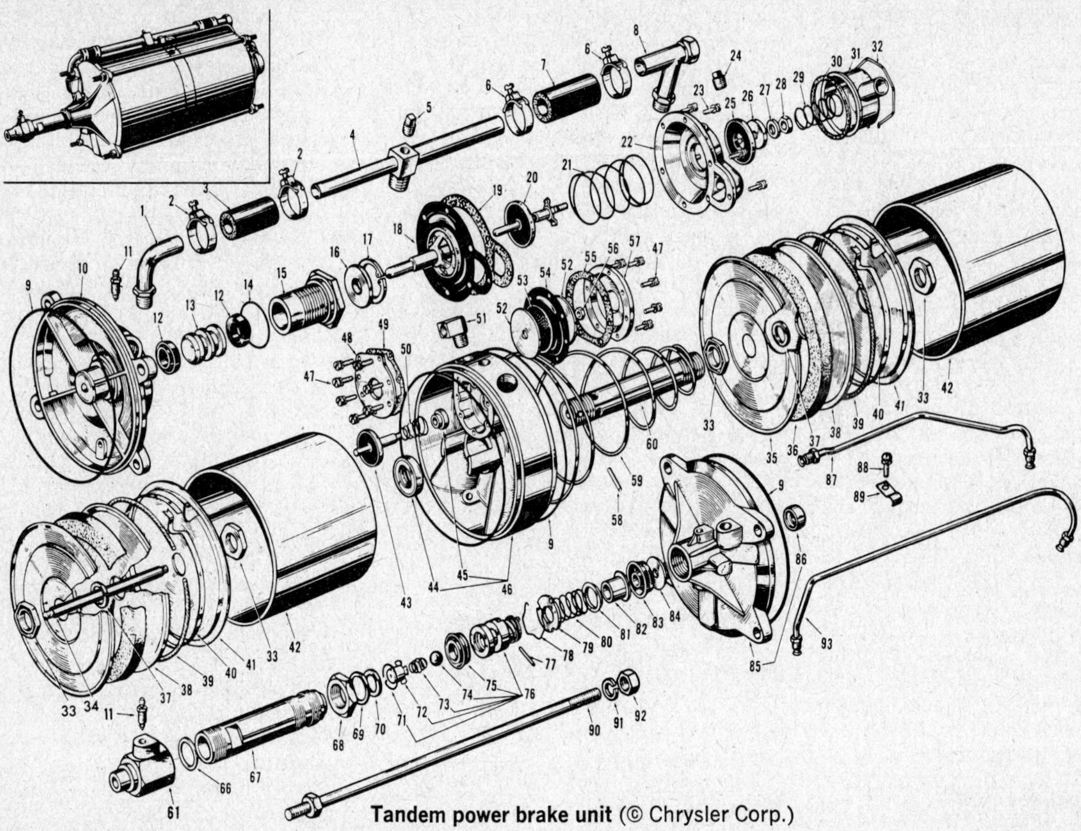

Tandem power brake unit (© Chrysler Corp.)

1 Tube & bushing
2 Clamp—hose
3 Hose—vacuum ¾x2½"
4 Tube # fitting—vacuum
5 Plug—pipe (⅛")
6 Clamp—hose (1")
7 Hose—vacuum 1"x3"
8 Tee—1" hose ¾" pipe, male & female
9 Gasket—center plate & end plate
10 Plate—cylinder end
11 Valve—bleeder
12 Cup—hydraulic valve piston
13 Piston—hydraulic valve
14 Seal—hyd. valve fitting
15 Fitting—hyd. valve piston
16 Washer—stop
17 Ring—retainer
18 Diaphragm & plates—control valve
19 Gasket—poppet (valve body)
20 Shaft & vac. poppet—control valve
21 Spring—poppet valve
22 Body—control valve
23 Screw & lockwasher
24 Plug—(⅜")
25 Seal—poppet valve
26 Valve—poppet
27 Washer—poppet valve
28 Nut—Hex (#6-32)
29 Spring—poppet valve (small)
30 Gasket—A. C. tube & cover
31 Tube & cover—air inlet
32 Snap ring—air inlet tube & cover
33 Nut—piston rod
34 Push rod—piston
35 Plate—piston (outer)
36 Packing—piston
37 Seal—vacuum piston
38 Plate—piston (inner)
39 Wick—piston
40 Ring—piston expander
41 Plate—retainer (piston felt & exp. ring)
42 Shell—vac. cyl.
43 Shaft & seal (fast application valve)
44 Seal—center plate piston rod
45 Seal—Center plate poppet valve
46 Center plate & seals
47 Screw & lockwasher fast application valve
48 Seat—poppet (fast application valve)
49 Gasket—poppet seat
50 Spring—return—valve poppet
51 Elbow—inverted flared tube
52 Plate—diaphragm
53 Gasket—diaphragm plate
54 Diaphragm—F. A. valve
55 Gasket—cover (F. A. valve)
56 Nut—thin hex. check (¼"-28)
57 Cover—fast application valve
58 Pin—retainer (push rod)
59 Spring return (vac. piston)
60 Piston rod & thrust cup
61 Cap—end—hydraulic cylinder
66 Gasket—end cap
67 Tube—hydraulic cylinder
68 Nut—hyd. cyl. tube
69 Seal—hyd. cyl. tube nut
70 Seal—hyd. cyl.
71 Snap ring—ball retainer
72 Retainer—ball
73 Spring—ball return
74 Ball (hyd. piston check valve)
75 Cup—hyd. piston
76 Piston—hydraulic
77 Pin—retainer, hydraulic piston
78 Snap ring
79 Washer—stop
80 Spring—retainer
81 Sleeve—retainer
82 Retainer—seal
83 Hyd. seal
84 Washer—guide
85 End plate & seal
86 Seal—oil (end plate)
87 Tube—vacuum by-pass
88 Screw & lockwasher—clip attached
89 Clip—tube (¼")
90 Stud—cylinder attaching
91 Lockwasher—cylinder attaching
92 Nut—hex. (½"-20) cylinder attaching
93 Tube—hyd. by-pass

spring under the clip near opposite end of spring. Position cut of retainer plate over loop of the spring.

6. Hold piston parts in the assembly ring, assemble them on end of piston rod, then install nut on tip of piston assembly. Tighten nut until it is flush with end of rod. Stake nuts securely at two places.
7. Clamp staked nut firmly in a vise, and tighten nut on opposite side of piston plate solidly against piston plate.
8. Press the fast application valve stem and push rod seals into center plate. The application valve seal must be flush with bottom of hole. The push rod seal should rest against the shoulder of center plate. Position center plate. Then place valve spring on top of seal with the small end at top.
9. Install the bullet-nosed tool at threaded end of valve shaft, and insert valve shaft through seal. Position gasket on center plate.
10. Place valve seat plate, with seat side downward, on gasket, and install screws and lockwashers.
11. Turn center plate over. Place lower diaphragm plate on valve shaft with rounded edge at top, then place diaphragm gasket at top of plate. Position diaphragm on top of gasket so screw holes and the bypass hole index with the identical holes in center plate.
12. Install the other diaphragm plate with rounded edge facing diaphragm.
13. Install valve shaft nut on valve shaft. Use a screw driver to prevent shaft from turning, and tighten nut. Stake nut securely at opposite points.
14. Position cover gasket and cover plate, then install screw and lockwashers.

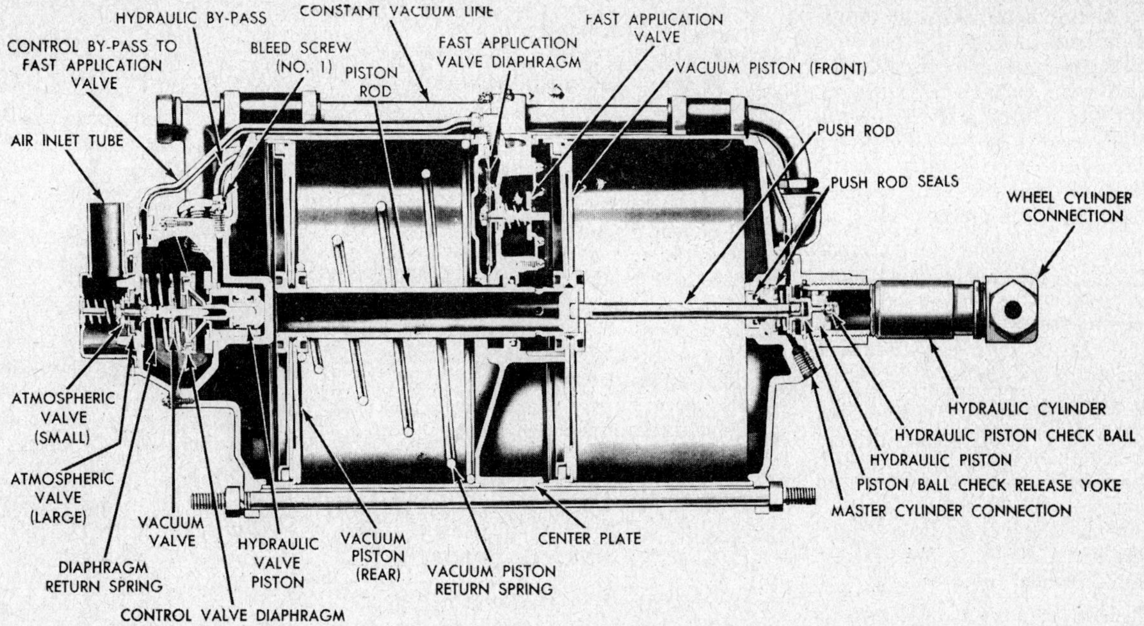

Tandem power brake—sectional view (© Chrysler Corp.)

15. Place piston return spring over piston rod with small end of spring at bottom.
16. Carefully guide piston rod through leather seal in center plate, with piston stop flanges of center plate facing upward. Press center plate down against spring, and insert a rod in piston rod. Thread piston rod nut on piston rod, with flat side of nut upward to limit of threads.
17. If forward piston was disassembled to replace leather piston packing, cotton wicking, or other parts, assemble the piston parts in the ring and turn assembly ring over.
18. Remove larger piston plate and "O" ring seal.
19. With assembly ring still in place, guide the remaining piston parts over end of push rod and against piston nut. Carefully install "O" ring seal over threads of piston rod.
20. Place the larger diameter piston plate on piston rod with chamfered side of hole toward "O" ring seal.
21. Assemble large end of push rod in end of piston rod and install retainer pin. Install piston rod nut on end of piston rod with flat side downward. Tighten nut until it is flush with face of piston rod, then stake nut securely at opposite points.
22. Hold piston rod nut in a vise or with a wrench, and tighten inner nut securely against piston. Care must be exercised when tightening inner nut to prevent expander spring retainer plate from shifting.
23. Remove assembly ring, then remove rod holding return spring compressed. Install a new copper gasket in end cap.
24. The hydraulic cylinder must be assembled with milled flats next to end cap. Tighten hydraulic cylinder solidly in end cap, then thread check nut on hydraulic cylinder up to the limit of the threads.
25. Install check nut seal (if used) in groove of cylinder tube. Install bleeder screw in cap.
26. Press push rod leather seal into hydraulic cylinder bore of front end plate from inner side of plate with lip of seal toward outer end of the plate. Install push rod seal parts.
27. The chamfered side of stop washer is down, lip of cup is up, flat side of washer is next to cup, and small end of spring is down. Place washer against spring. Install snap ring in inner groove of end plate.

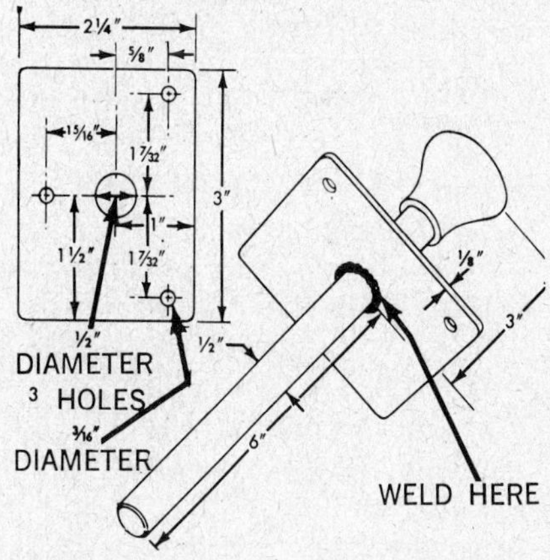

Compressor tool for vacuum piston return spring (© Chrysler Corp.)

28. Install stop washer with flat side in control valve hydraulic fitting. Install stop washer retaining ring.
29. Dip hydraulic piston cups in brake fluid, and assemble them on the hydraulic piston with lips of cups positioned away from each other. Insert piston into the fitting with open end of piston toward stop washer.
30. Install a new gasket on the hydraulic fitting (copper gasket on fitting without the groove, and a rubber seal gasket on fitting with the groove). Install the hydraulic fitting in end plate with a 1-7/8" socket wrench. Tighten fitting equipped with a rubber gasket firmly, and fitting equipped with a copper gasket to 324-330 foot-pounds.
31. Assemble vacuum control parts in control body. Install a new lead washer.
32. Hold slave cylinder end cap in a vise, and thread cylinder into end plate. Install T-fitting and tubes on center plate.
33. Position an end plate gasket on the plate, place cylinder shell on end plate, and coat interior of cylinder with vacuum cylinder oil.
34. Dip cylinder piston on packing in vacuum cylinder oil and allow the excess oil to drain off the wickings.
35. Position a gasket on ledge of center plate, then carefully guide push rod through seal in front end plate. At the same time, align the vacuum tube in end plate with vacuum tube on center plate. Slide hose in place to contact the two vacuum tubes.

36. Position a new gasket at center plate ledge.
37. Coat the interior of cylinder shell with vacuum cylinder oil, then tip cylinder at a 45 degree angle to prevent damage to the piston leather packing.
38. Carefully push the cylinder over piston and onto center plate.
39. Place a new gasket on ledge of end plate, then install end plate on cylinder, aligning end plate vacuum tube and center plate tube. Install cylinder studs and tighten nuts evenly.
40. To assemble the hydraulic piston parts, place large end of spring in retainer cup, then install check ball in piston body behind spring.
41. Dip piston cup in brake fluid, then install it on piston with lip of cup toward check ball.
42. Position the vacuum hoses on tubes, and tighten hose clamps firmly.
43. Connect hydraulic by-pass tube to front and rear end plate.
44. Remove slave cylinder from end plates, then insert and attach return spring compressing tool.
45. Assemble hydraulic piston on push rod.
46. Make certain lock ring is positioned over the retainer pin. Install hydraulic gasket in the plate. Carefully guide the hydraulic cylinder over piston cup, and thread cylinder into end plate.
47. Adjust cylinder $7\frac{3}{4}''$, measuring between points shown in illustration.
48. Align bleeder screw in end cap with bleeder screw in control valve.
49. Remove spring compressing tool. After cylinder length adjustment is completed, tighten cylinder check nut solidly.
50. Install guide pins, made from 8-32 x $2\frac{1}{2}''$ machine screws with the heads cut off, in end plate.
51. Install diaphragm with diaphragm stem inserted into hydraulic control piston hole. Place diaphragm return spring and control valve body on top of diaphragm.
52. Remove guide pins, one at a time, and replace each guide pin with an attaching screw and a new lock washer. Tighten screws progressively and firmly.
53. Install air inlet fitting in control body, then install retainer.
54. Install vacuum by-pass tube.
55. Inspect assembly to see that all bolts, nuts, screws, washers, and plugs are in place, and that all tubes, clamps, and fittings are firmly tightened.

Installation

1. Position assembly on mounting brackets, and install attaching bolts.
2. Tighten bolts firmly.
3. Connect stop light wires and hydraulic lines to stop light switch.
4. Attach vacuum hose to booster.
5. Connect master cylinder hydraulic line to booster control valve.
6. Connect wheel cylinder hydraulic line to booster end cap.
7. Attach air inlet hose to control valve air inlet fitting, then check and tighten connections.
8. Remove lubricating plugs from end and center plates.
9. Add vacuum cylinder oil to level of filler holes, install plugs, then bleed hydraulic system.

Bendix Hydro-Boost

The Bendix Hydro-Boost uses the hydraulic pressure supplied by the power steering pump to provide a power assist to brake application.

Disassembly

1. Place the booster in a vise with the bracket end up. Using a hammer and chisel, cut the bracket nut that holds the linkage bracket to the booster assembly. The nut should be cut at the open slot in the booster cover threads. Care must be exercised to avoid damage to the threads. Spread the nut and remove the bracket.
2. Remove the pedal boot by pulling it off over the pedal rod eyelet.
3. Position pedal rod removing tool around the pedal rod. The tool should be resting on the booster cover. Insert a punch through the pedal rod from the lower side of the special tool. Push the punch through until it rests on the higher side of the tool. Push up on the punch to shear the pedal rod retainer; remove the pedal rod
4. Remove the grommet from the groove near the end of the pedal rod and from the groove in the input rod.
5. Disengage the tabs of the spring retainer from the ledge inside the opening near the master cylinder mounting flange of the booster. Remove the retainer and piston return spring from the opening.
6. Pull straight out on the output push rod to remove the push rod and push rod retainer from inside the booster piston.
7. Press in on the spool plug, and insert a small punch into the hole on top of the housing. This unseats one side of the spool plug snap ring from the groove in the bore. Remove the snap ring.

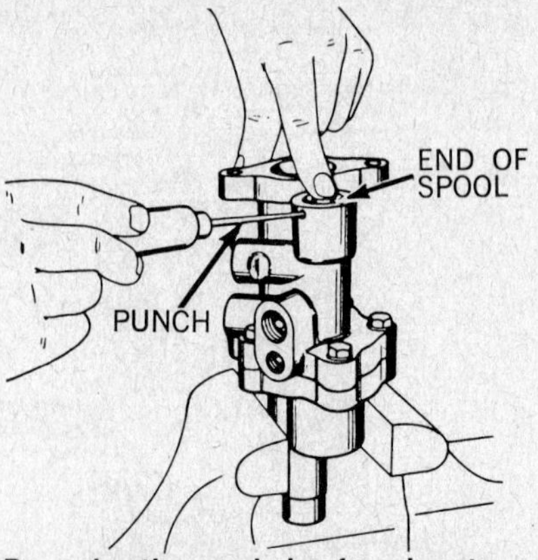

Removing the spool plug from booster—Bendix Hydro-Boost (© G.M. Corp.)

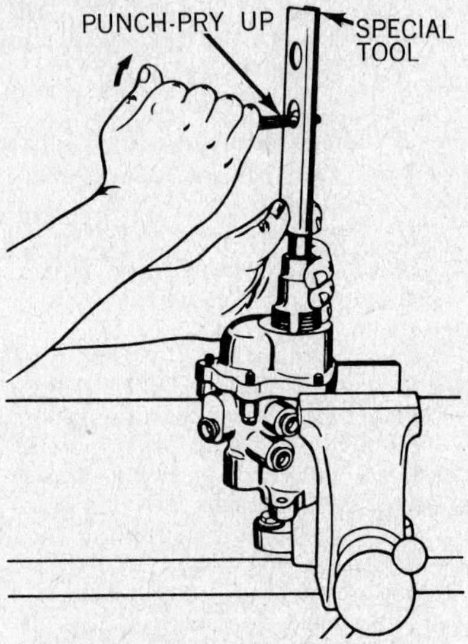

Removing the booster pedal rod—Bendix Hydro-Boost (© G.M. Corp.)

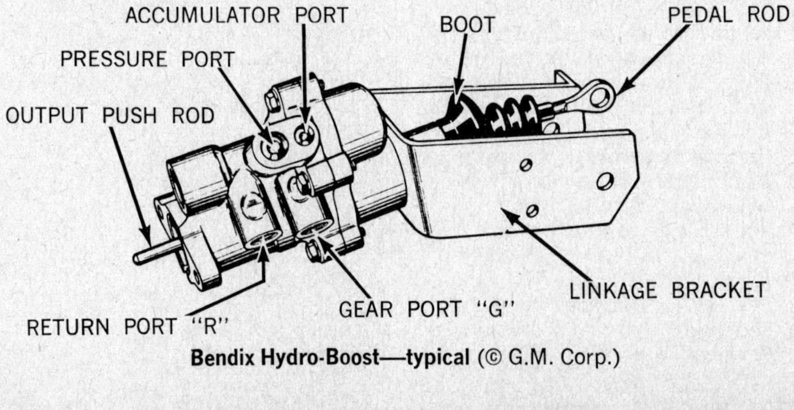

Bendix Hydro-Boost—typical (© G.M. Corp.)

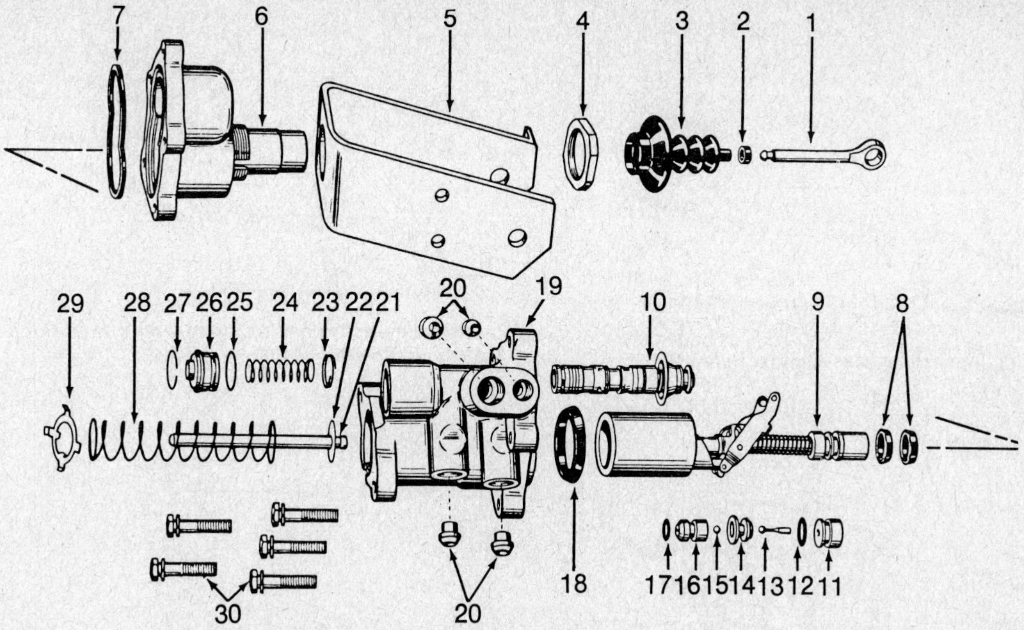

Bendix Hydro-Boost—exploded view (© G.M. Corp.)

1 Pedal push rod
2 Pedal push rod grommet
3 Pedal push rod boot
4 Bracket nut
5 Linkage bracket
6 Booster cover
7 Cover to housing seal
8 Input rod seals
9 Input rod and piston assy.
10 Spool assembly
11 Plunger seat
12 'O' ring
13 Spacer
14 Spacer
15 Check valve ball
16 Accumulator check valve
17 'O' ring
18 Piston seal
19 Booster housing
20 Tube seat inserts
21 Output push rod
22 Push rod retainer
23 Spiral snap ring
24 Spool spring
25 Plug 'O' ring
26 Spool plug
27 Snap ring
28 Piston return spring
29 Spring retainer
30 Housing to cover bolts

8. Remove the spool plug from the bore with a pair of pliers. Remove the 'O' ring from the plug and discard. Remove the spool spring from the bore.
9. Place the booster cover in a soft-faced vise and remove the cover retaining bolts. Remove the booster assembly from the vise and separate the booster cover from the housing. Remove the large seal ring and discard.
10. Press in on the end of the spool assembly, and use a spiral snap ring removing tool to remove the snap ring from the forward groove in the spool. Discard the snap ring.
11. Remove the input rod and piston assembly, and the spool assembly from the booster housing.
12. Remove the input rod seals from the input rod end, and the piston seal from the piston bore in the housing. Discard the seals.
13. Remove the plunger, seat, spacer and ball from the accumulator valve bore in the flange of the booster housing. Remove the 'O' ring from the seat and discard.
14. Thread a screw extractor into the opening in the check valve in the bottom of the accumulator valve bore, and remove the check valve from the bottom of the bore. Discard the check valve and 'O' ring.

NOTE: Using a screw extractor damages the seat in the check valve. A new check valve, 'O' ring and valve must be installed whenever the check valve is removed from the accumulator valve bore.

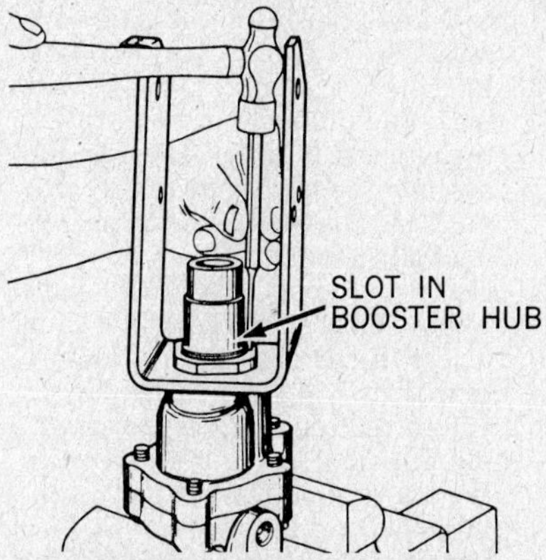

Staking linkage bracket nut—Bendix Hydro-Boost (© G.M. Corp.)

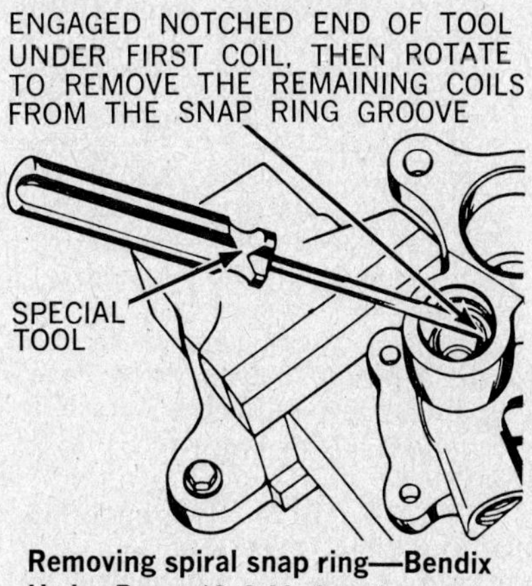

Removing spiral snap ring—Bendix Hydro-Boost (© G.M. Corp.)

15. Using a ¼″ or a 5/16″ spiral flute type screw extractor, remove the tube seats from the booster ports.

Cleaning & Inspection

1. Clean all parts in a suitable solvent.
2. Inspect the valve spool and the valve spool bore for any damage or ware. Discoloration of the spool or bore is normal, particulary in the grooves. If any damage is noted, replace the valve spool and housing.

NOTE: The clearance between the valve spool and the bore is very important. Because of this, the valve spool and housing are to be replaced only as an assembly.

3. Inspect the input rod and piston assembly for any damage or ware. Replace any defective components.
4. Inspect the piston bore in the housing for any damage or ware. If defective, replace the booster housing and spool valve assembly.

Assembly

CAUTION: Parts must be kept VERY clean. If there is any reason to doubt the cleanliness of the components, re-wash before assembly.

Lubricate all seals and metal friction points with power steering fluid before assembly. Whenever the booster is disassembled, be sure that seals, tube inserts, spiral snap ring, check valve and ball are replaced.

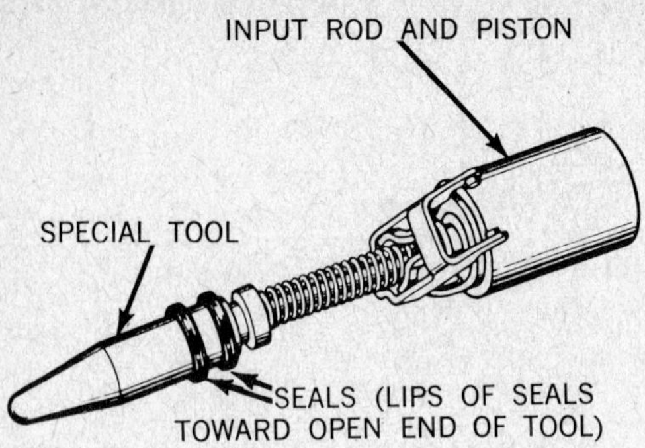

Installing input rod seals—Bendix Hydro-Boost (© G.M. Corp.)

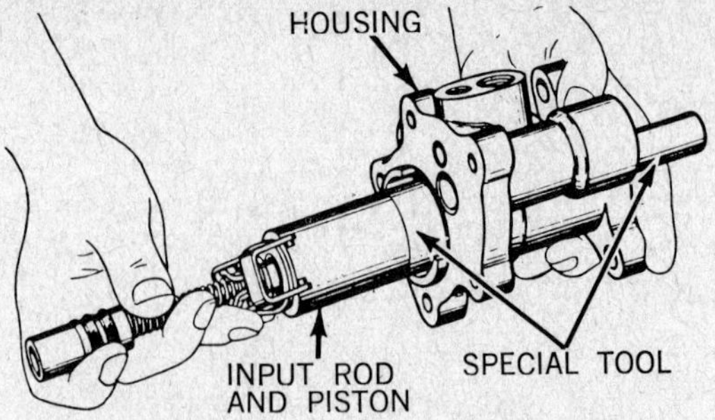

Installing input rod and piston assembly in booster—Bendix Hydro-Boost (© G.M. Corp.)

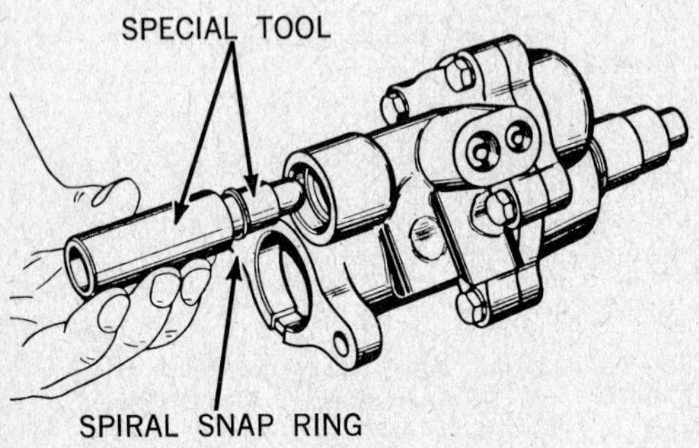

Installing spiral snap ring—Bendix Hydro-Boost (© G.M. Corp.)

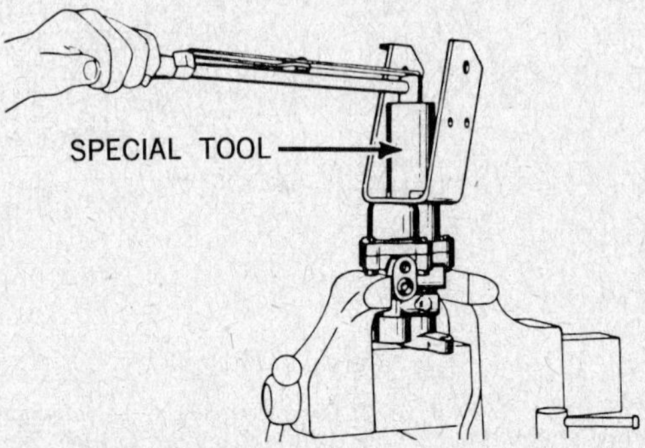

Installing linkage bracket nut—typical—Bendix Hydro-Boost (© G.M. Corp.)

1. Position a tube seat in each booster port and screw a spare tube nut in each port to press the seat down into the port. Do not tighten the tube nuts in the port as this may deface the seats. Remove the spare tube nuts and check for aluminium chips in the ports. Be sure that there is no foreign matter in the ports.
2. Coat the piston bore and piston seal with clean power steering fluid. Assemble the seal in the piston bore. The lip of the seal must be towards the rear (away from the master cylinder mounting flange). Be sure that the seal is fully seated in the housing.
3. Lubricate the input rod end, input rod seals and the seal installer tool with clean power steering fluid. Slide the seals on the tool with the lip of the cups towards the open end of the tool. Slide the tool over the input rod end end down to the second groove; then slide the forward seal off the tool and into the groove. Assemble the other seal in the first groove. Be sure that both seals are fully seated.
4. Lubricate the piston and piston installing tool with clean power steering fluid. Insert the large end of the tool into the piston and the tool and piston into the piston bore, through the seal.
5. Position the 'O' ring on the accumulator check valve and coat the assembly with clean power steering fluid. Insert the check valve in the accumulator valve recess in the housing flange. Place the ball and spacer in the same recess.
6. Place the 'O' ring on the changing valve plunger seat and insert the plunger into the seat. Dip the assembly in clean power steering fluid and insert it into the changing valve recess.
7. Coat the spool assembly with clean power steering fluid and insert in the spool bore. Be sure that the pivot pins on the upper end of the input rod lever assembly are engaged in the groove in the sleeve. Remove piston installing tool.
8. Separate the two components of the snap ring installation tool and place the spiral snap ring on the tool. Insert the rounded end of the installer into the spool bore. While pressing on the rear of the spool, slide the snap ring off the tool and into the groove near the forward end of the spool by pressing in on the tool sleeve. Check to be sure that the retaining ring is fully seated.
9. Place the housing seal in the groove in the housing cover. Join the booster housing and cover and secure with five attaching bolts. Tighten the bolts to 18-26 ft. lbs.

CAUTION: It is very important that the same cover attaching bolts are used as they are designed for the booster only. If they are damaged, replace with the same part numbers.

10. Place an 'O' ring on the spool plug. Insert the spool spring and the spool plug in the forward end of the spool bore. Press in on the plug and position the snap ring in its groove in the spool valve bore.
11. Place the linkage bracket on the booster assembly. The tab on the inside of the large hole in the bracket should fit into the slot in the threaded portion of the booster cover.
12. Install the bracket nut with a staking groove outward on the threaded portion to the booster cover. Use special tool and tighten to 95-120 ft. lbs.
13. Insert a small punch into the staking groove of the nut, at the slot in the booster cover, and with a hammer stake the nut in place. Be sure that the threads on the nut are deformed so the nut will not loosen.
14. Position a new boot and grommet on the pedal rod. Moisten the grommet and insert the grommet end of the pedal rod into the input rod of the booster. When the grommet is fully seated, the pedal rod will rotate freely.
15. Install the boot on the booster cover.

Bendix Master Vac

Removal

1. Disconnect clevis at brake pedal to push rod.
2. Remove vacuum hoses from power cylinder.

3. Disconnect hydraulic line from master cylinder.
4. Remove the four attaching nuts and lock washers that hold the unit to the firewall. Remove the power brake unit.

Disassembly

2. Remove four master cylinder to vacuum cylinder attaching nuts and washers.
2. Separate master cylinder from vacuum cylinder, then remove the rubber seal from the outer groove at end of master cylinder.
3. Remove the push rod from the power section. (Do not disturb adjusting screw.)
4. Remove push rod boot and valve operating rod.
5. Scribe alignment marks across the rear shell and vacuum cylinder. Remove all but two of the end plate attaching screws (opposite each other). Hold down on the rear shell while removing the two remaining screws to prevent the piston return spring from expanding.
6. Scribe a mark across the face of the piston, to index the mark on the rear shell, and remove rear shell with vacuum piston and piston return spring.
7. Remove vacuum hose from vacuum piston and from vacuum tube on inside of rear shell. Separate rear shell from vacuum piston.
8. Remove air cleaner and vacuum tube assembly, and air filter from the rear shell.
9. Spring the felt retaining ring enough to disengage ring from grooves in bosses on rear piston plate.
10. Remove piston felt and expander ring from piston assembly.
11. Remove six piston plate attaching screws and separate front piston plate and piston packing from piston plate.
12. Remove valve return spring, floating control valve and diaphragm assembly, valve spring and diaphragm plate. Separate floating control valve spring-retainer and control valve diaphragm from control valve.
13. Remove rubber reaction disc and shim (if present) from front piston plate. *NOTE: Do not remove the valve operating rod and valve plunger from the rear piston plate unless it is necessary to replace defective parts. Normally, the next two steps can be omitted.*
14. When it is necessary to replace the valve operating rod or valve plunger, remove valve rod seal from groove in piston plate and pull seal over end of rod.

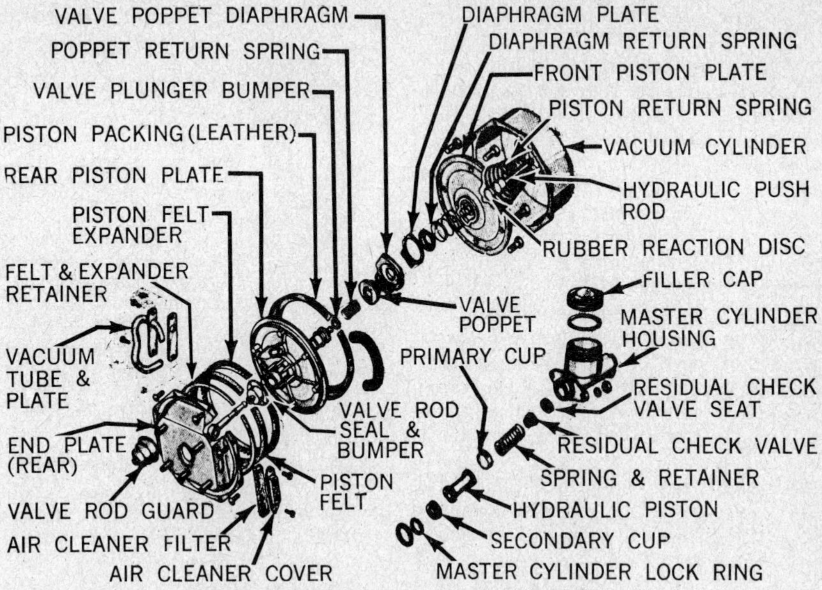

Bendix master vac unit (© Ford Motor Co.)

15. Hold piston with valve plunger side down and inject alcohol into valve plunger through opening around valve rod. This will wet the rubber lock in the plunger. Then drive or pry valve plunger off the valve rod. *NOTE: If master cylinder is not to be rebuilt, omit Steps 16-19*
16. Remove snap-ring from groove in base at end of master cylinder.
17. Remove piston assembly, primary cup, retainer spring, and check-valve from master cylinder.
18. Remove filler cap and gasket from master cylinder body.
19. Remove secondary cup from master cylinder piston.

Cleaning Note

After disassembly, cleaning of all metal parts in satisfactory commercial cleaner solvent is recommended. Use only alcohol or Declene on rubber parts or parts containing rubber. After cleaning and drying, metal parts should be rewashed in clean alcohol or Declene before assembly.

Assembly

Steps 1-5 apply to a completely disassembled master cylinder. Otherwise, omit these steps (1-5).

1. Coat bore of master cylinder with brake fluid.
2. Dip secondary cup in brake fluid and install on master cylinder piston.
3. Dip other piston parts in brake fluid and assemble the piston. Install piston.
4. Install snap-ring into groove of cylinder.
5. Use new gasket and install filler cap.
6. Assemble valve rod seal on rod and insert valve rod through the piston. Dip valve plunger in alcohol and assemble to ball end of valve rod. Be sure ball end of rod is locked in place in plunger.
7. Assemble floating control valve diaphragm over end of floating control valve. Be sure diaphragm is in recess of floating control valve. Press control valve spring retainer over end of control valve and diaphragm.
8. Clamp valve operating rod in a vise with rear piston plate up. Lay leather piston packing on rear piston plate with lip of leather over edge of piston plate.
9. Install floating control valve return spring over end of valve plunger.
10. Assemble diaphragm plate to diaphragm and assemble floating control valve with diaphragm in recess of rear piston plate.
11. Install floating control valve spring over retainer. Align and assemble front piston plate with rear piston plate. Center the floating control valve spring on front piston plate and center valve plunger stem in hole of piston.
12. Holding front and rear piston plates together, loosely install six piston plate cap screws.
13. Install shim and rubber reaction disc in recess at center of front piston plate. *NOTE: A piston assembling ring is handy in assembling the piston.*
14. Place the assembling tool over piston packing, turn piston assembly upside down and assemble the expander ring against inside lip of leather packing. Saturate felt with Vacuum Cylinder

Oil or shock absorber fluid—type A, then assemble in expander ring. Assemble retainer ring over bosses on rear piston plate. Be sure retainer is anchored in grooves of piston plate.

15. Assemble air cleaner filter over vacuum tube of air cleaner and attach air cleaner shell in position with screws.
16. Slide vacuum hose onto vacuum inlet tube of piston and align hose to lay flat against piston.
17. Wipe a coat of vacuum cylinder oil on bore of cylinder. Remove assembling ring from vacuum piston and coat leather piston packing with vacuum cylinder oil.
18. Install rear shell over end of valve operating rod and attach vacuum hose to tube end on each side of end plate.
19. Center small diameter end of piston return spring in vacuum cylinder. Center large diameter of spring on piston. Check alignment mark on piston with marks on vacuum cylinder and rear shell, compress spring and install two attaching screws at opposite sides to hold rear shell and cylinder together. Now, install balance of screws and tighten evenly.
20. Dip small end of pushrod boot in alcohol and assemble guard over end of valve operating rod and over flange of shell.
21. Insert large end of pushrod through hole in end of vacuum cylinder and guide into hole of front piston plate. *NOTE: Before going on with assembly, check the distance from the outer end of the pushrod to the master cylinder mounting surface on the vacuum cylinder. This measurement should be 1.195-1.200″.*
22. After pushrod adjustment is correct, replace rubber seal in groove on master cylinder body.
23. Assemble master cylinder to the vacuum cylinder at four studs. Replace lock washers and nut and securely tighten.

Kelsey-Hayes Diaphragm Type

Identification

The Kelsey-Hayes power brake unit can be identified by the twistlock method of locking the housing and cover together, plus the white-colored vacuum check valve assembly.

Removal

1. With engine off, apply brakes several times to equalize internal brake pressure.

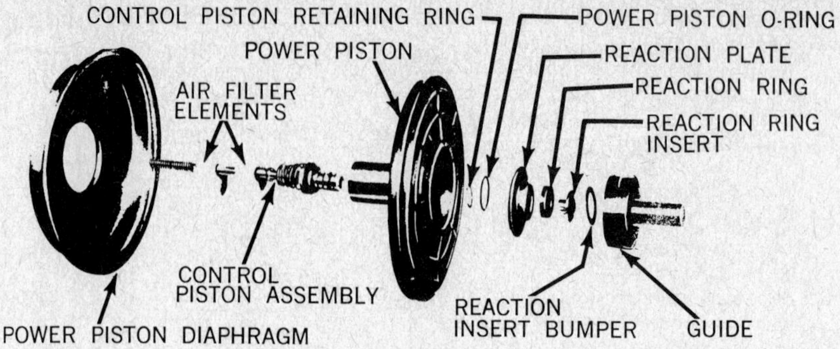

Power piston assembly (© G.M. Corp.)

2. Disconnect hydraulic line from master cylinder.
3. Disconnect vacuum hose from power brake check valve.
4. Disconnect power brake from brake pedal (under instrument panel).
5. Disconnect power brake unit from dash panel.
6. Remove power brake and master cylinder assembly from the vehicle.

Disassembly

1. Separate master cylinder from power brake unit.
2. Remove master cylinder pushrod and air cleaner plate.
3. Mount the power unit in a vise with the master cylinder attaching-studs up.
4. Scribe an index line across the housing and cover for reassembly reference.
5. Pry out the housing lock. Do not damage the lock, as it must be used at assembly.
6. Remove check valve from cover by prying out of rubber grommet.
7. Place parking brake flange holding tool over the master cylinder mounting studs.
8. Rotate the tool and cover in a counterclockwise direction. Then, separate the cover from the housing. This will expose the power piston return spring and diaphragm.
9. Lift out the power piston return spring. Remove the brake unit from the vise.
10. Remove power piston by slowly lifting the piston straight up.
11. Remove air cleaner, guide seal and seal retainer from the cover.
12. Remove the block seal from the center hole of the housing, using a blunt drift. (Don't scratch the bore of the housing, it could cause a vacuum leak.)

Power Piston Disassembly

1. Remove power piston diaphragm from the power piston. Keep it clean.
2. Remove screws that attach the plastic guide to the power piston. Remove guide and place to one side.
3. Remove the power piston square seal ring, reaction ring insert, reaction ring and reaction plate.
4. Depress operating rod slightly, then remove the Truarc snap-ring.
5. Remove control piston by pulling the operating rod.
6. Remove the O-ring seal from the end of the control piston.
7. Remove the filter elements and dust felt from the control piston rod.

Cleaning and Inspection

Thoroughly wash all metal parts in a suitable solvent and dry with compressed air. The power diaphragm, plastic power piston and guide should be washed in a mild soap and water solution. Blow dust and all cleaning material out of internal passages. All rubber parts should be replaced, regardless of condition. Install new air filters at assembly. Inspect all parts for scoring, pits, dents or nicks. Small imperfections can be smoothed out with crocus cloth. Replace all badly damaged parts.

Assembly

When assembling, be sure that all rubber parts, except the diaphragm and the reaction ring are lubricated with silicone grease.

1. Install control piston O-ring onto the piston.
2. Lubricate and install the control piston into the power piston. Install the Truarc snap-ring into its groove. Wipe all lubricant off the end of the control piston.
3. Install air filter elements and felt seal over the pushrod and down past the retaining shoulder on the rod. Install the power piston square seal ring into its groove.
4. Install the reaction plate in the power piston. Align the three holes with those in the power piston.
5. Install the rubber reaction ring in the reaction plate. Do not lubricate this ring.
6. Lubricate outer diameter of the

reacton insert and install in the reaction ring.
7. Install reaction insert bumper into the guide.
8. Place guide on the power piston, align the holes with the aligning points on the power piston. Install retaining screws and torque to 80-100 in. lbs.
9. Install diaphragm on power piston; be sure that the diaphragm is correctly seated in the power piston groove.
10. With the housing blocked to prevent damage, install the block seal in the housing.
11. Install a new cover seal on the retainer and lubricate thoroughly, inside and out, with silicone grease, then install in the cover bore. Install new air filter.
12. Lubricate check valve grommet and install the vacuum check valve.
13. Mount the power unit in a vise, with master cylinder attaching studs up.
14. Apply a light coating of silicone grease to the bead, *outer edge only*, of the power piston diaphragm.
15. Install the power piston assembly in the housing with the operating rod down.
16. Install the power piston return spring into the flange of the guide.
17. Place the cover over the return spring and press down on the cover. At the same time, pilot the guide through the seal.
18. Rotate the cover to lock it to the housing. Be sure the scribe lines are in correct index and that the diaphragm is not pinched during assembly.
19. Install the housing lock on one of the long tangs of the housing.
20. Remove the power unit from the vise.
21. Install the master cylinder push-rod and air cleaner plate, then install the master cylinder on the studs. Install attaching nuts and washers. Torque to 200 in. lbs.

Installation

1. Install the power brake seal to the firewall.
2. Install power brake unit onto firewall and torque the attaching nuts to 200 in. lbs.
3. Install pushrod to brake pedal attaching bolt. Torque to 30 ft. lbs.
4. Install vacuum hose onto the power brake unit.
5. Attach the hydraulic tube and fill the master cylinder. Bleed hydraulic system.
6. Adjust stop-light switch if necessary.

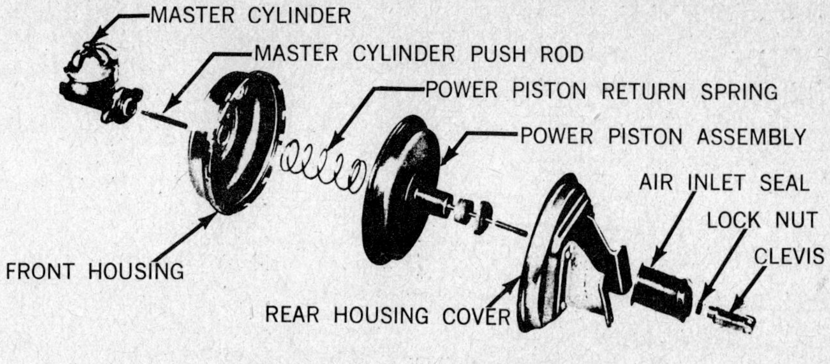

Power brake unit (© G.M. Corp.)

Delco Single Diaphragm Booster

Disassembly

1. Scribe a mark on the bottom center of front and rear housings for reassembly.
2. Attach a base tool to the front housing and clamp the base in a vise with the power section up.
3. Separate the front and rear housings by securing a spanner wrench to the bracket. Press down on the wrench and rotate rear housing counterclockwise to the unlocked position. Loosen the housing carefully as it is spring loaded.
4. Remove the spanner wrench, then lift the rear housing and power piston assembly from the unit. Remove the return spring.
5. Remove the silencer by removing the retaining ring on the push rod.
6. Remove the seal, vacuum check valve and grommet from the front housing.
7. Remove the power piston assembly from the rear housing.
8. Remove the silencer from the neck of the power piston tube.
9. Remove the lock ring from the power piston.
10. Remove the reaction retainer, piston, plate, levers, bumper and spring.
11. Place a power piston wrench in a vise and position the assembly so that the three lugs on the tool fit into the three notches in the piston.
12. Press down on the support plate and rotate it counterclockwise until it separates from the power piston.
13. Remove the diaphragm from the support plate.
14. Position the power piston, tube down, in a tool fabricated from a piece of wood 2″ x 4″ x 8″ long with a 1$^3/_8$″ hole in the center clamped in a vise.
15. Remove the snap ring on the air valve.
16. Using the power pump and press plate insert the power piston, tube down, in a press plate and remove the air valve assembly using a $^3/_8$″ drive extension as a remover.
17. Remove the floating control valve assembly from the push rod. Use a new one when rebuilding.

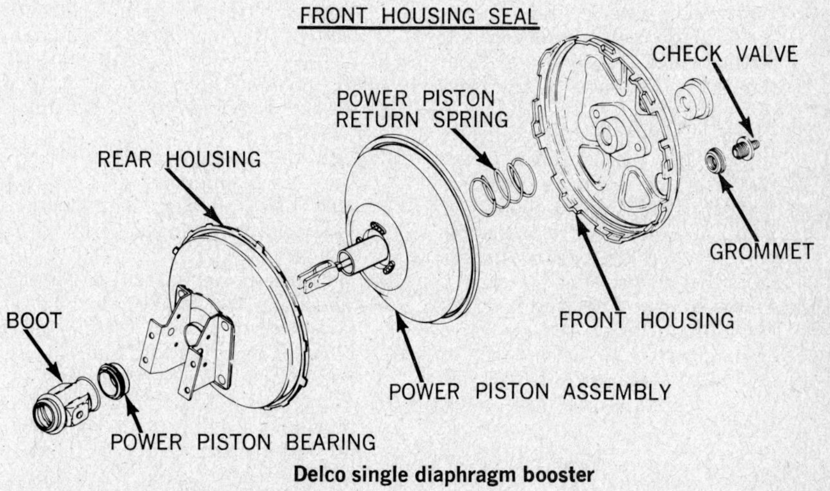

Delco single diaphragm booster

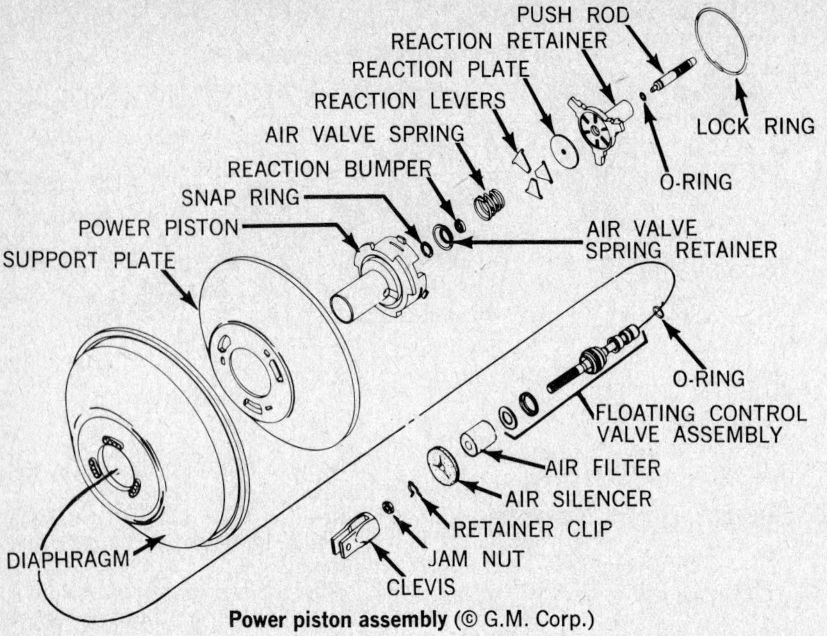

Power piston assembly (© G.M. Corp.)

18. Push the master cylinder push rod from the center of the reaction retainer.
19. Remove the O-ring from the groove in the master cylinder piston rod.

Assembly

1. Use clean brake fluid and thoroughly clean all resuable brake parts.
2. Inspect all rubber parts and replace if nicked, cut or damaged.
3. When rebuilding make sure that no grease or mineral oil comes in contact with any of the rubber parts.
4. Install a new vacuum check valve using a new grommet.
5. Position a new front housing seal so that the flat surface of the cup lies against the bottom depression in the housing.
6. Place a new O-ring in the groove on the master cylinder piston rod, wipe a thin film of silicone lubricant on the "O" ring.
7. Insert the master cylinder piston rod through the reaction retainer so the round end protrudes from the end of the tube on the reaction retainer.
8. Place the power piston wrench in a vise and position the power piston on the wrench so that the three lugs fit into the notches.
9. Position a new "O" ring on the air valve on the second groove from the push rod end.
10. Place a new floating control valve on the push rod-air valve assembly so that the flat face of the valve will seat against the valve seat on the air valve. *NOTE: The old floating control valve assembly must be replaced with a new one since the force required to remove it distorts component parts.*
11. Wipe a thin film of silicone lubricant on the control valve and the "O" ring on the air valve.
12. Press the air valve push rod assembly, air valve first, onto its seat in the tube of the power piston.
13. Place the control valve retainer over the push rod so that the flat side seats on the floating control valve.
14. Press the floating control valve and its retainer onto the power piston tube by use of an installer tool and pushing down by hand.
15. After the floating control valve is seated, position the push rod limiter washer over the push rod and down onto the valve.
16. Stretch the air filter element over the end of the push rod and press it into the the power piston tube.
17. Assemble the power piston diaphragm to the support plate. The raised flange of the diaphragm is pressed through the hole in the center of the support plate. *NOTE: Be sure that the edge of the center hole fits into the groove in the flange of the diaphragm.*
18. Pull the diaphragm away from the outside diameter of the support plate so that the support plate can be gripped with both hands.
19. With the power piston still positioned on the holding tool in a vise, coat the bead of the diaphragm that contacts the power piston with silicone lubricant.
20. Place the support plate and diaphragm assembly over the tube of the power piston with the locking tangs facing downward. *NOTE: The flange of the power piston will fit into the groove on the power piston.*
21. Press down and rotate the support plate clockwise, until the lugs on the power piston come against the stops on the support plate.
22. Turn the assembly over and place tube down in a tool, fabricated from a piece of wood 2" x 4" x 8" long with a 1⅜" hole in the center, clamped into a vise.
23. Replace the snap ring into the groove of the air valve.
24. Place the air valve spring retainer on the snap ring and assemble the reaction bumper into the groove in the end of the air valve.
25. Position the air valve return spring, large end down, on the spring retainer.
26. Place the three reaction levers into position with the wide ends in the slots of the power piston and the narrow ends resting on top of the air valve return springs.
27. Position the reaction plate (with the numbered side up) on top of the reaction levers. Press down on the plate until the large ends of the reaction levers pop up so the plate rests flat on the levers and is centered.
28. With the round end of the master cylinder piston rod up, and with the reaction retainer held toward the top of the piston rod, place the small end of the piston rod in the hole in the center of the reaction plate. Line up the ears on the reaction retainer with the notches in the power piston and push the reaction retainer down until the ears seat in the notches.
29. With pressure on the reaction retainer, position the large lock ring down over the master cylinder push rod.
30. There is a lug on the power piston which has a raised divider in the center. One end of the lock ring goes under the lug and on one side of the divider.
31. As you work your way around the power piston, the lockring goes over the ear of the reaction retainer and under a lug on the power piston until the other end of the lock ring is seated under the lug with the raised divider. *NOTE: Make certain both ends of the lock ring are securely under the large lug.*
32. Place a new power piston bearing in the center of the rear housing so the flange on the center hole of the housing fits into the groove of the power piston bearing. The large flange on the power piston bearing will be on

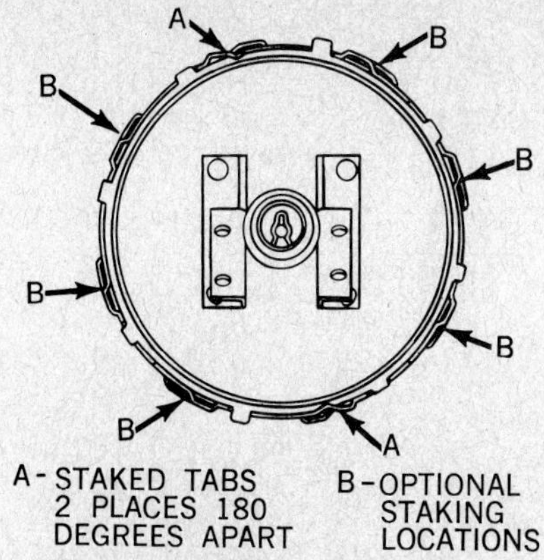

Housing locking tabs (© G.M. Corp.)

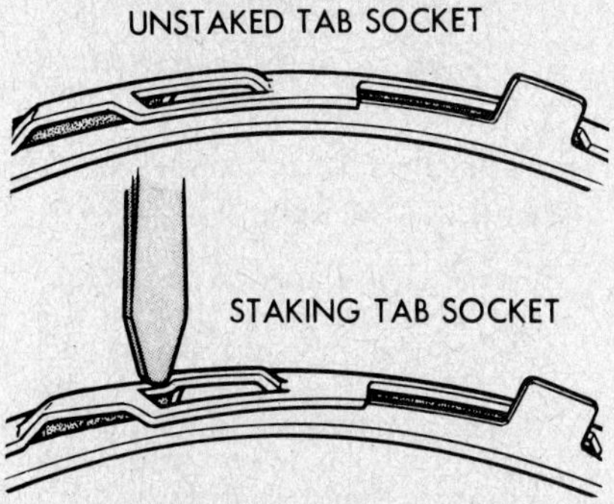

Staking housing tabs (© G.M. Corp.)

the stud side of the housing. Coat the inside of the bearing with silicone lubricant.

33. Place the air silencer over the holes on the tube of the power piston. Wipe the tube with silicone lubricant.
34. Attach the holding fixture to the front housing and clamp the base in a vise.
35. Place the power piston return spring over the insert in the front housing.
36. Lubricate the inside diameter of the support plate seal, the reaction retainer tube, and the beaded edge of the diaphragm with silicone lubricant.
37. Place the rear housing assembly over the front housing assembly and align the scribe marks of the two housings so they will match when in the locked position.
38. Place a spanner wrench on the rear housing and tighten the nuts and washers to the bolts.
39. Press down on the spanner wrench and twist the rear housing clockwise until fully locked.

NOTE: Do not break the studs loose in the rear housing or put pressure on the power piston tube when locking the housings.

40. Remove the spanner wrench and the holding fixture from the front housing.
41. Push the felt silencer over the pushrod and seat it against the end of the power piston tube.
42. Push the plastic boot and seat it against the rear housing. The raised tabs on the side of the boot will locate in the holes in the center of the brackets.
43. Stake the front and rear housing in two places: 180° apart.

NOTE: The interlock tabs should not be used for staking a second time. When all tabs have been staked once, the housing must be replaced.

Delco Tandem Dual Diaphragm Type

Disassembly

1. Scribe a line across the front and rear housing for reassembly.
2. Attach the base of a special holding fixture or equivalent to the front housing with nuts and washers and draw down tight to eliminate damage to the studs. Clamp the base in a vise with the power section up.
3. On vehicles with a straight mounting bracket place a spanner wrench over the studs on the rear housing and attach with nuts and washers.
4. On vehicles with a tilted mounting bracket there is a special tool placed inside the mounting bracket with the spanner wrench placed on top.
5. Press down on the spanner wrench and rotate the rear housing counterclockwise to separate the two housings. Remove the special tools.
6. Remove the power piston return spring, and remove and discard the vacuum check valve and grommet from the front housing.
7. Remove the front housing seal.
8. Remove the boot retainer and boot from the rear housing and remove the felt silencer from inside the boot.
9. Remove the power piston group from the rear housing and remove the primary power piston bearing from the center opening of the rear housing.

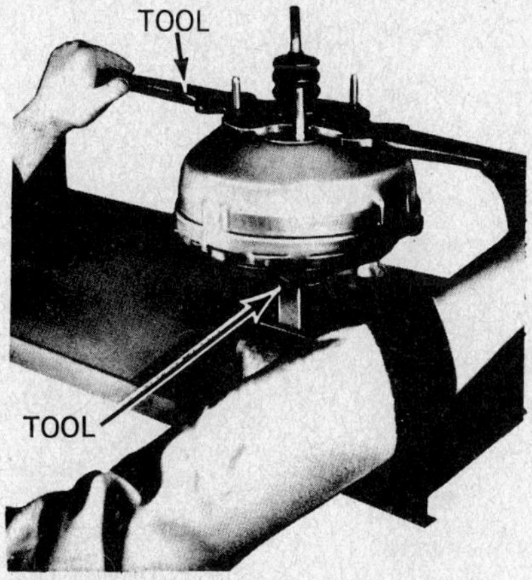

Unlocking front and rear housings (© G.M. Corp.)

10. Remove piston rod retainer and piston rod from the secondary piston.
11. Mount a special double ended tool with the large diameter end up in a vise. Position the secondary power piston so that the two radial slots in the piston fit over the ears of the tool.

NOTE: Due to an optional construction design on the primary and secondary power pistons the special tool used in step 11 will have to be reworked.

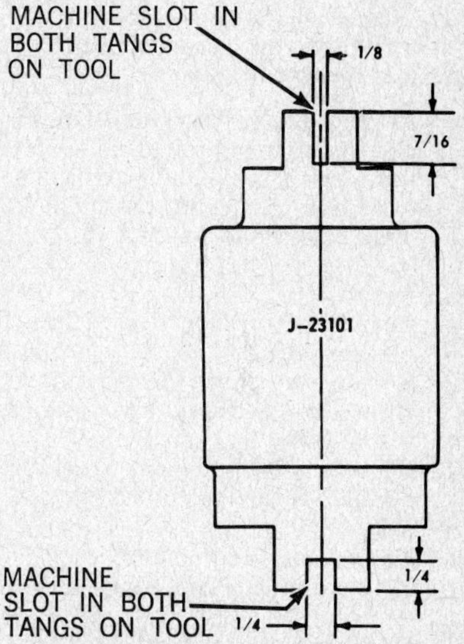

Reworking of tool for optional power piston design (© G.M. Corp.)

12. Fold back the primary diaphragm from the outside diameter of the primary support plate. Grip the edge of the support plate and rotate it counterclockwise to unscrew the primary power piston from the secondary power piston.
13. Remove the housing divider from the secondary power piston bearing from the housing divider.
14. The secondary power piston should still be positioned on the special double ended tool. Fold back the secondary diaphragm from the outside diameter of the secondary support plate. Rotate the support plate clockwise to unlock the secondary power piston.
15. Remove the secondary diaphragm from the secondary support plate.
16. Remove the reaction piston and disc from the center of the secondary power piston by pushing down on the end of the piston.
17. Remove the air valve spring from the end of the valve, if not removed earlier.

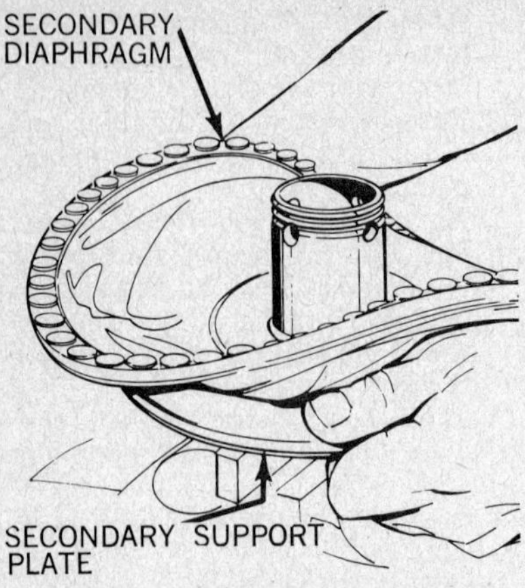

Locking or unlocking the secondary support plate and secondary power piston (© G.M. Corp.)

18. Remove the primary diaphragm and piston using the same procedure as the secondary with the exception of turning the support plate counterclockwise to unlock it.
19. Remove the air filter from the tubular section of the primary power piston.
20. Remove the power head silencer from the neck of the power piston tube.
21. Remove the rubber reaction bumper from the end of the air valve.
22. Using snap ring pliers, remove the retaining ring from the air valve.
23. Remove the air valve push rod assembly.
    a. The recommended method would be to place the primary power piston in an arbor press and press the air valve push rod assembly out the bottom of the power piston tube using a rod not larger than ½″ in diameter.
    b. An alternate method would be to insert a heavy, round shanked screwdriver on both sides of the pushrod and pull the air valve-push rod assembly straight out.
24. Remove the "O" ring seal from the air valve.

Assembly

1. Use clean brake fluid and thoroughly clean all reusable brake parts.
2. Inspect all rubber parts and replace if nicked, cut or damaged.
3. When rebuilding, make sure that no grease or mineral oil comes in contact with any of the rubber parts.
4. Install a new vacuum check valve and a new grommet in the front housing.
5. Place a new seal in the front housing so that the flat surface lies against the bottom of the depression in the housing.
6. Reassemble the power piston group.
7. Lubricate the inside and outside diameter of the "O" ring seal with silicone lubricant and place on the air valve.
8. Wipe a thin film of silicone lubricant on the large and small outside diameter of the floating control valve. If the floating control valve needs replacement, it will be necessary to replace the complete air valve-push rod assembly.
9. Place the air valve end of the air valve push rod assembly into the tube of the primary power piston. Manually press the air valve push rod assembly so that the floating control valve bottoms on the tube section of the primary power piston.
10. Place the inside diameter of the floating control valve retainer on the outside diameter of the special installer. Place it over the pushrol so that the closed side of the retainer seats on the floating control valve. Using the installer manually press the retainer and floating control valve to seat in the tube.
11. Stretch the filter element over the pushrod and press it into the piston tube.
12. Place the retaining ring into the groove in the air valve using snap ring pliers.
13. Position the rubber reaction bumper on the end of the air valve.
14. Determine the correct reaction piston and apply a light coat of silicone lubricant to the outside diameter of the rubber reaction disc.
15. Place the rubber reaction disc in the large cavity of the secondary

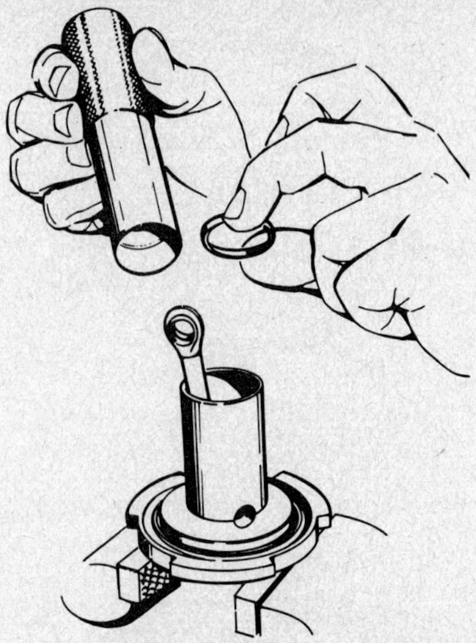

Installing the floating control valve retainer (© G.M. Corp.)

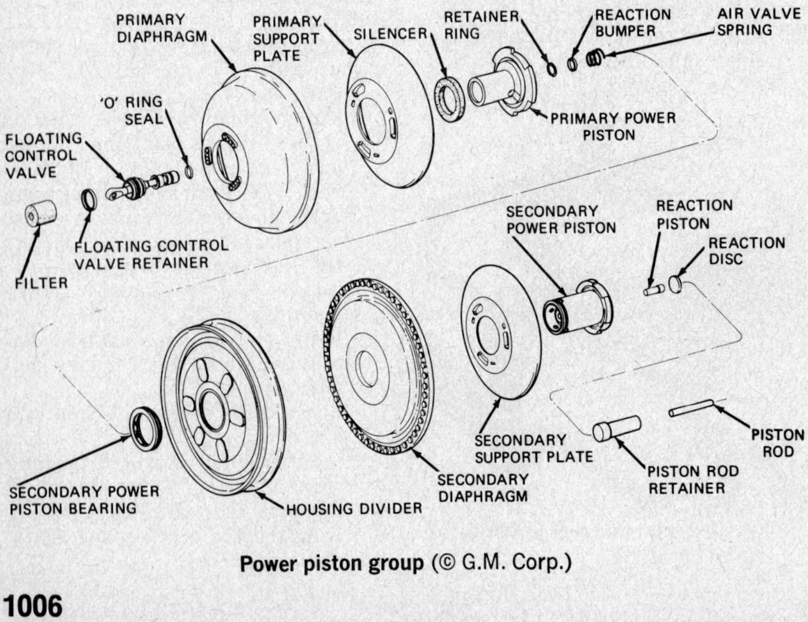

Power piston group (© G.M. Corp.)

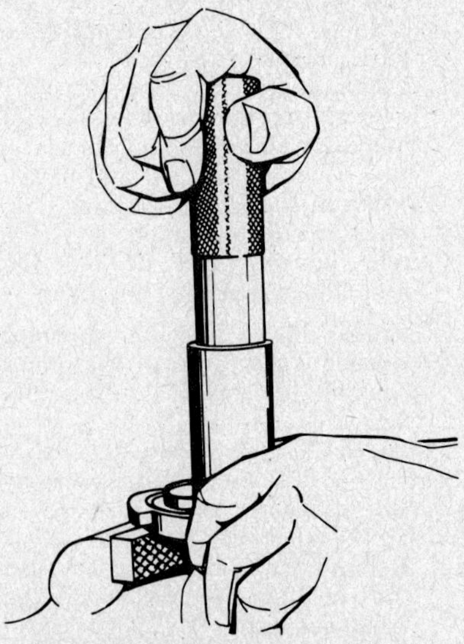

Seating the floating control valve assembly (© G.M. Corp.)

power piston and push the disc down to seat on the reaction piston.

16. Unlock the secondary power piston from the primary power piston.
17. Assemble the primary diaphragm to the primary support plate opposite the locking tangs. Press the raised flange on the inside diameter of the diaphragm through the center hole of the support plate. Be sure that the edge of the support plate center hole fits into the groove of the flange. *NOTE: Lubricate the inside diameter of the diaphragm and the raised surface of the flange with a light coat of silicone lubricant.*
18. Mount the special tool used in step 11 of the disassembly procedures in a vise with the small end up. Position the primary power piston so that the two radial slots in the piston fit over the ears (tangs) of the tool.
19. Fold the primary diaphragm away from the outside diameter of the primary support plate.
20. Place the primary support plate and diaphragm assembly over the tube of the primary piston. Make sure the locking tangs are facing down.
21. Press down and rotate the support plate clockwise until the tabs on the piston contact the stops.
22. Place the power head silencer on the tube of the piston so that the holes at the base of the tube are covered.
23. Coat the outside of the tube with silicone lubricant.
24. Remove the primary piston assembly from the special tool and lay it aside.
25. Assemble the secondary diaphragm to the secondary support plate following the same steps for assembling the primary support plate except mount the special tool with the large diameter up, and press down and turn the plate counterclockwise until the piston contacts the stops.
26. Leave the secondary power piston on the tool and in the vise.
27. Apply a light coat of talcum powder or silicone lubricant to the bead on the outside diameter of the secondary diaphragm. This will make it easier for reassembly of the front and rear housing.
28. Place the secondary bearing in the inside diameter of the housing divider so that the extended lip of the bearing faces up.
29. Lubricate the inside diameter of the bearing with silicone lubricant.
30. Using a special protector tool or equivalent, position the secondary bearing on the threaded end of the secondary power piston.
31. Hold the housing divider so that the six oblong protrusions on the middle of the divider are facing up. Press the divider down over the tool and onto the piston tube so it rests against the support ring. Remove the bearing protector tool.
32. Pick up the primary power piston assembly and fold the primary diaphragm away from the outside diameter of the support plate.
33. Place the small end of the air valve return spring on the air valve so that it contacts the air valve retaining ring.
34. Position the primary power piston. Make sure that the air valve return spring seats down over the raised center section of the secondary piston.
35. Rotate the secondary power piston clockwise into the threaded portion of the primary piston. Tighten to 5-15 ft. lbs.
36. Fold the primary diaphragm back into position.
37. Cover the outside diameter of the piston rod retainer with a light coat of silicone lubricant.
38. Insert the master cylinder piston rod retainer into the secondary power piston so that the flat end bottoms against the rubber reaction disc.
39. Place the new primary piston bearing in the rear housing center hole. The thin lip of the bearing will protrude to the outside of the housing. Coat the inside diameter of the bearing with silicone lubricant.
40. Mount the holding fixture in a vise and position the front housing so that the housing studs fit in the holes provided in the tool.
41. Place the power piston return spring over the inset in the front housing.
42. Assemble the power piston assembly to the rear housing by pressing the tube of the primary piston through the rear housing bearing until the housing divider seats in the rear housing and the primary piston bottoms against the housing.
43. Hold the rear housing with the mounting studs up and position it so that the tangs on the edge of the front housing are locked in the slots on the edge of the rear housing. The scribe marks on the top of the housings will be in line.
44. Lower the rear housing assembly onto the front housing.

NOTE: The power piston spring must seat in the despression in the face of the secondary power piston. Check that the bead on the outside diameter of the secondary diaphragm is positioned between the edges of the housing.

45. Assembly the front and rear housings with the spanner wrench.
46. Replace the silencer and boot.

Transfer Cases

INDEX

TRANSFER CASE APPLICATION CHART

	Chev./GMC	Dodge/Plymouth	Ford	International	Jeep
Dana 20	X		X	X	X
Dana 21			X		
Dana 24			X		
Dana 300				X	X
International TC-143				X	
New Process 201		X			
New Process 202				X	
New Process 203	X	X	X		
New Process 205	X		X	X	
New Process 208		X	X		X
New Process 219					X
Warner Quadra-Trac					X
Warner 1345			X		

Transfer Case Trouble Analysis

Slips Out of Gear (High-Low)

1. Shifting poppet spring weak.
2. Bearing broken or worn.
3. Shifting fork bent.
4. Improper control rod adjustment.

Slips Out of Front Wheel Drive

1. Shifting poppet spring weak or broken.
2. Bearing worn or broken.
3. Excessive shaft end-play.
4. Shifting fork bent.

Hard Shifting

1. Lack of lubricant.
2. Shift lever binding on shaft.
3. Shifting poppet ball scored.
4. Shifting fork bent.
5. Low tire pressure.

Backlash

1. Companion yoke loose.
2. Transfer case loose on mounts.
3. Internal parts excessively worn.

Noisy

1. Low lubricant level.
2. Bearings improperly adjusted or excessively worn.
3. Gears worn or damaged.
4. Improper alignment of driveshafts or U-joints.

Oil Leakage

1. Excessive amount of lubricant in case.
2. Vent clogged.
3. Gaskets or seals leaking.
4. Bearings loose or damaged.
5. Driveshaft yoke mating surfaces scored.

Overheating

1. Excessive or insufficient amount of lubricant.
2. Bearing adjustment too tight.

Cleaning and Inspection

Cleaning

During overhaul, all components of the transfer case (except bearing assemblies) should be thoroughly cleaned with solvent and dried with air pressure prior to inspection and reassembly.

1. Clean the bearing assemblies as follows.

   NOTE: Proper cleaning of bearings is of utmost importance. Bearings should always be cleaned separately from other parts.

   a. Soak all bearing assemblies in CLEAN solvent or fuel oil. Bearings should never be cleaned in a hot solution tank.

   b. Slush bearings in solvent until all old lubricant is loosened. Hold races so that bearings will not rotate; then clean bearings with a soft bristled brush until all dirt has been removed. Remove loose particles of dirt by tapping bearing flat against a block of wood.

   c. Rinse bearings in clean solvent; then blow bearings dry with air pressure.

   CAUTION: Do not spin bearings while drying.

   d. After drying, rotate each bearing slowly while examining balls or rollers for roughness, damage, or excessive wear. Replace all bearings that are not in first class condition.

   NOTE: After cleaning and inspecting bearings lubricate generously with recommended lubricant, then wrap each bearing in clean paper until ready for reassembly.

2. Remove all portions of old gaskets from parts, using a stiff brush or scraper.

Inspection

1. Inspect all parts for discoloration or warpage.
2. Examine all gears and splines for chipped, worn, broken or nicked teeth. Small nicks or burrs may be removed with a fine abrasive stone.
3. Inspect the breather assembly to make sure that it is open and not damaged.
4. Check all threaded parts for damaged, stripped, or crossed threads.
5. Replace all gaskets, oil seals and snap-rings.
6. Inspect housings, retainers and covers for cracks or other damage. Replace the damaged parts.

7. Inspect keys and keyways for condition and fit.
8. Inspect shift forks for wear, distortion or any other damage.
9. Check detent ball springs for free length, compressed length, distortion or collapsed coils.
10. Check bearing fit on their respective shafts and in their bores or cups. Inspect bearings, shafts and cups for wear.

    NOTE: If either bearings or cups are worn or damaged, it is advisable to replace both parts.
11. Inspect all bearing rollers or balls for pitting or galling.
12. Examine detent balls for corrosion or brinneling. If shift bar detents show wear, replace them.
13. Replace all worn or damaged parts. When assembling the transfer case, coat all moving parts with recommended lubricant.

Dana Model 20

Description

The Dana Model 20 is a two-speed gearbox that controls the power from the transmission to the front and rear driving axles. Positions of the transfer case are: four-wheel-drive low (4L), neutral (N), two-wheel-drive high (2H) and four-wheel-drive high (4H).

Disassembly

Transfer Case

1. Clean any dirt from the transfer case and remove the bottom cover plate.
2. Remove the retaining plug, flat washer, detent spring and ball which engages the front drive shift rail detent rod. Then, remove plug from front drive detent rod access hole.
3. Remove the retaining plug, detent spring and ball which engages the rear drive shift rail detent rod.
4. Remove the idler shaft lockplate.
5. Using a hammer and soft drift, drive the idler shaft rearward

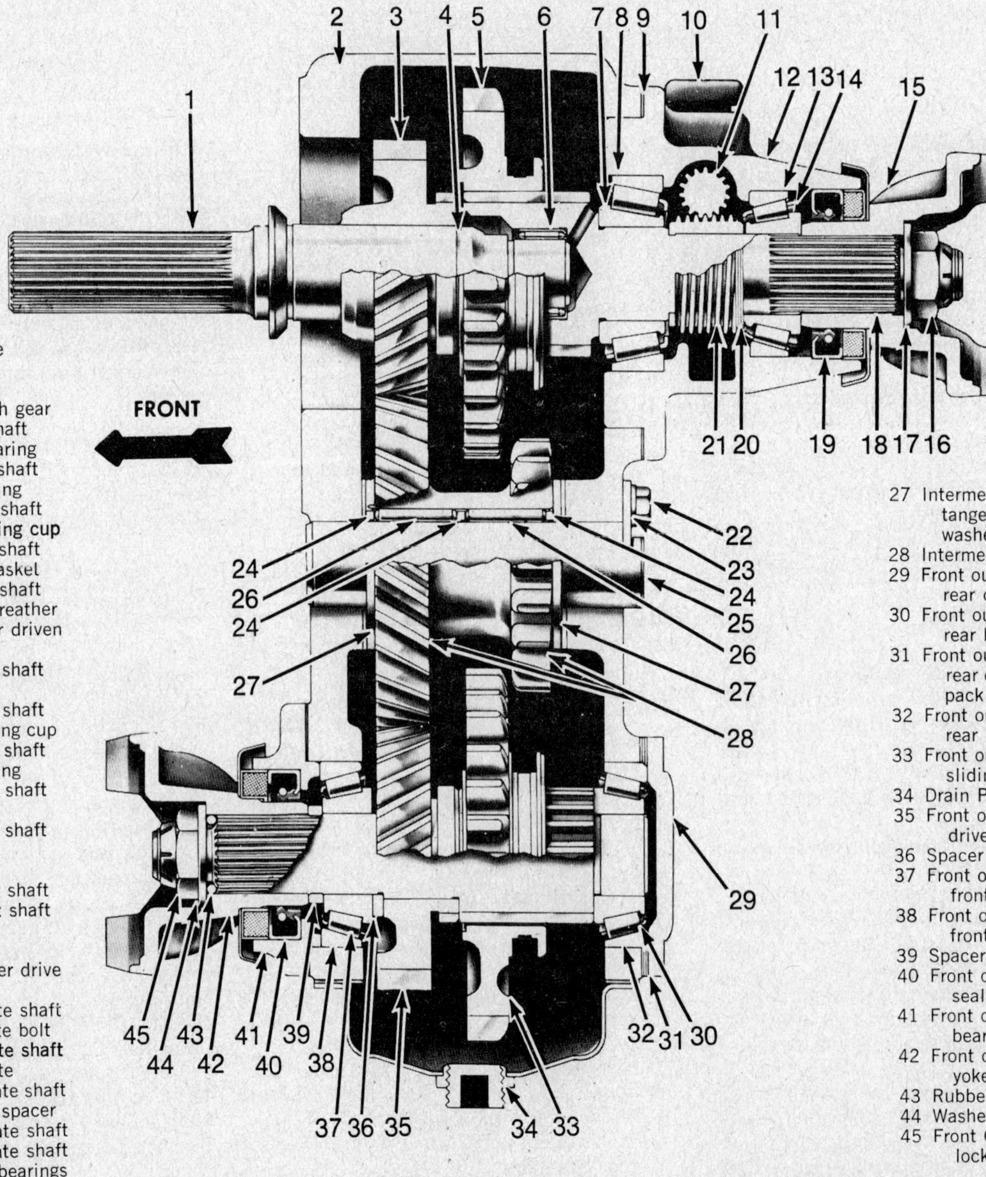

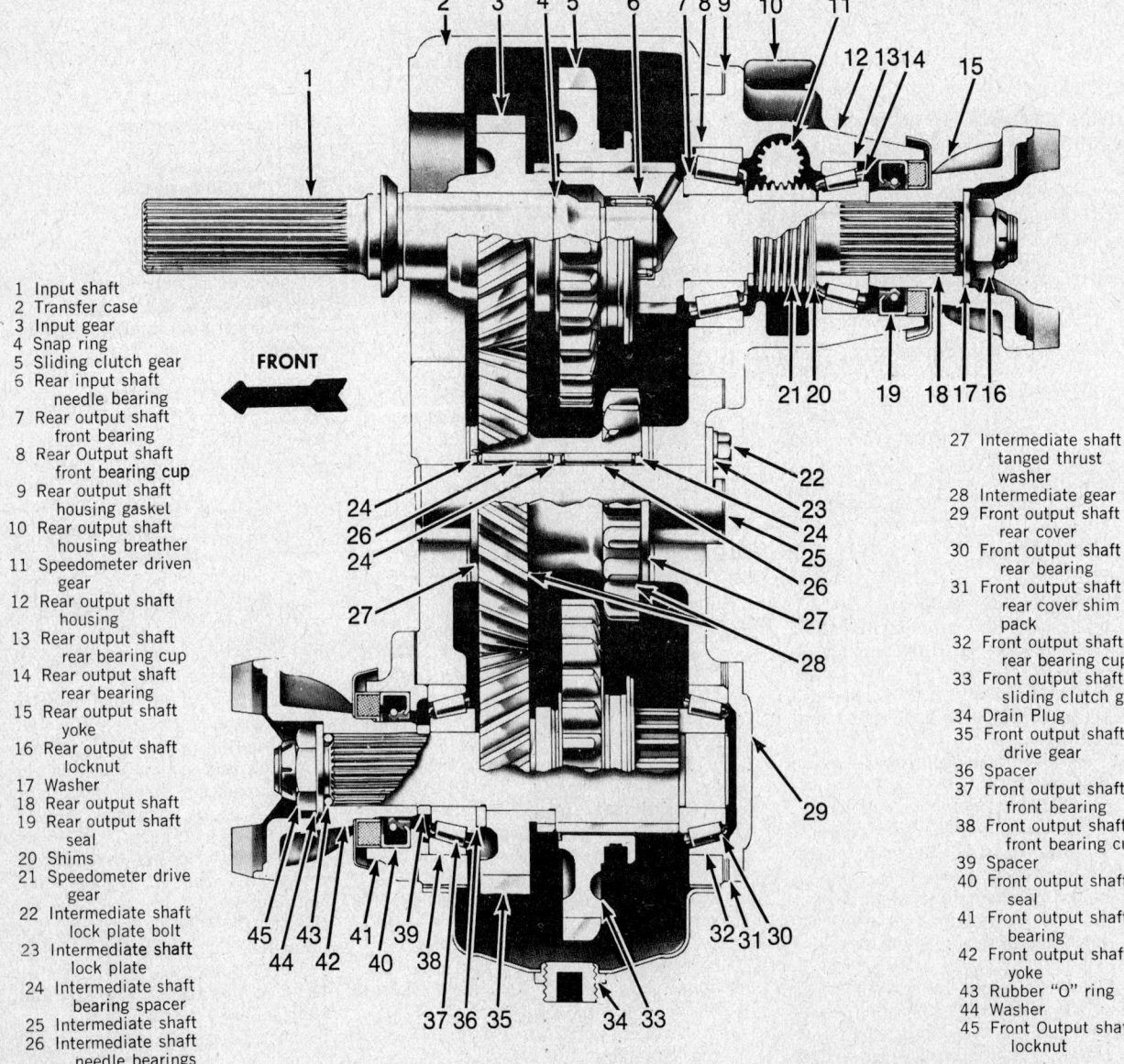

1 Input shaft
2 Transfer case
3 Input gear
4 Snap ring
5 Sliding clutch gear
6 Rear input shaft needle bearing
7 Rear output shaft front bearing
8 Rear Output shaft front bearing cup
9 Rear output shaft housing gasket
10 Rear output shaft housing breather
11 Speedometer driven gear
12 Rear output shaft housing
13 Rear output shaft rear bearing cup
14 Rear output shaft rear bearing
15 Rear output shaft yoke
16 Rear output shaft locknut
17 Washer
18 Rear output shaft
19 Rear output shaft seal
20 Shims
21 Speedometer drive gear
22 Intermediate shaft lock plate bolt
23 Intermediate shaft lock plate
24 Intermediate shaft bearing spacer
25 Intermediate shaft
26 Intermediate shaft needle bearings
27 Intermediate shaft tanged thrust washer
28 Intermediate gear
29 Front output shaft rear cover
30 Front output shaft rear bearing
31 Front output shaft rear cover shim pack
32 Front output shaft rear bearing cup
33 Front output shaft sliding clutch gear
34 Drain Plug
35 Front output shaft drive gear
36 Spacer
37 Front output shaft front bearing
38 Front output shaft front bearing cup
39 Spacer
40 Front output shaft seal
41 Front output shaft bearing
42 Front output shaft yoke
43 Rubber "O" ring
44 Washer
45 Front Output shaft locknut

Cross-section of Dana model 20 transfer case (© G.M.C.)

and out of the case; then lift out the thrust washers and idler gear.

NOTE: When removing the idler gear, do not lose any of the rollers.

6. Remove the flange retaining nuts from the front and rear output shafts.
7. Remove the flange from the front and rear output shafts. Discard the O-ring.
8. Remove the bolts securing the adapter housing to the case; then remove the adapter as an assembly.
9. Remove the bolts which attach the rear output shaft bearing retainer to the case; then remove the retainer and output shaft as an assembly.

NOTE: Be sure not to lose any of the rollers.

10. Disconnect the shift rail link from the two shift rails.
11. Lift out the rear output shaft sliding gear.
12. Remove the setscrew securing the rear fork to the shift rail; then remove the rear drive shift rail and fork.
13. Remove the front output shaft rear cover and shims. Fasten the shims together.
14. Remove the front output shaft bearing retainer and gasket.
15. Tap the threaded end of the front output shaft; then remove the rear cup.
16. Angle the front output shaft front bearing away from the main drive gear to allow removal of the snap-ring; then tap the shaft and rear bearing out of the case.
17. Lift out the sliding gear, main drive gear, front bearing, spacer and snap-ring.
18. Remove the front cup.
19. Remove the setscrew securing the front shift fork to the shift rail; then remove the rail and fork.
20. Remove the detent rods.
21. Remove shift rail oil seal.

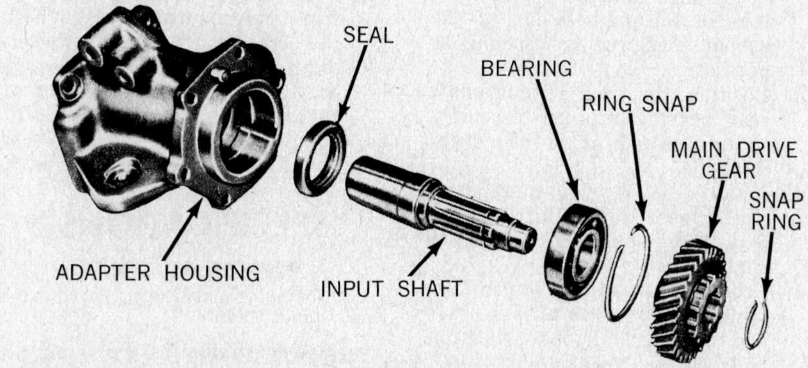

Exploded view of the input shaft of a Dana 20 transfer case (© Ford Motor Co.)

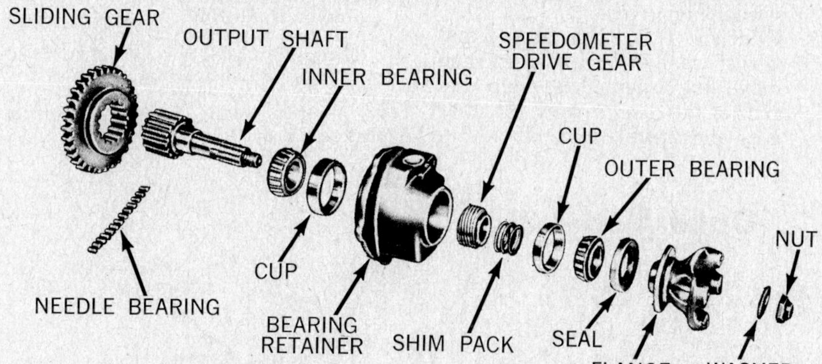

Exploded view of the rear output shaft of a Dana 20 transfer case (© Ford Motor Co.)

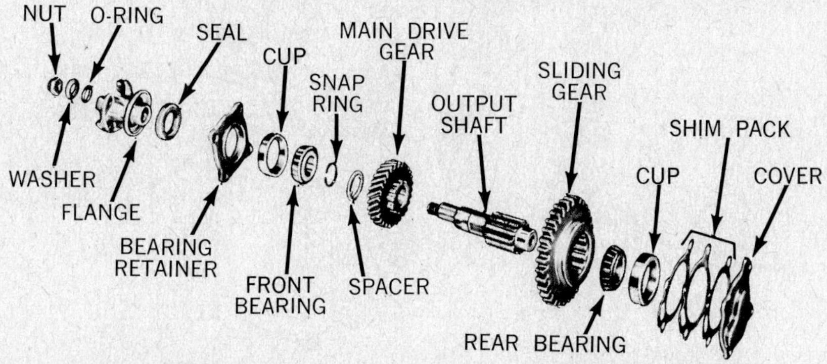

Exploded view of the front output shaft of a Dana 20 transfer case (© Ford Motor Co.)

Input Shaft

1. Remove the snap-ring from the front of the shaft.
2. Place the adapter housing and input shaft on a press and force the shaft out of the main drive gear and housing.
3. Remove the bearing retaining snap-ring; then remove bearing.
4. Remove the seal in the adapter housing.

Rear Output Shaft

1. Remove needle bearings from bore of shaft.
2. Remove speedometer driven gear.
3. Place bearing retainer and shaft assembly in a press; then force shaft out of retainer.
4. Lift off speedometer drive gear and shims. Tag shims for reassembly.
5. Press out the outer cup, bearing and seal.
6. Remove the inner cup.
7. Remove the inner bearing.

Front Output Shaft

Using the sliding gear as a base, press rear bearing off shaft.

Assembly

Input Shaft

1. Install a new seal in the adapter housing.
2. Install bearing in the housing and secure with snap-ring.
3. Using the main drive gear as a base, force the input shaft through the housing, seal, bearings and main drive gear. Secure with snap-ring on front of shaft.

Rear Output Shaft

1. Press the shaft into the inner bearing.
2. Install outer cup in the bearing retainer.
3. Install the inner cup.
4. Position the outer bearing in the retainer; then place the shims and speedometer drive gear on the shaft. Install shaft in the bearing retainer housing.
5. Place the bearing retainer and shaft in a vise. Install the output shaft flange and torque the retaining nut to specifications.

6. With a dial indicator on the flange end of the shaft, measure end-play. Adjust shim pack between the speedometer drive gear and outer bearing to achieve correct clearance.
7. After setting correct end-play, remove flange and press bearing retainer seal into housing.
8. Install the flange, washer and nut. Tighten the nut to specifications.

Front Output Shaft

Using a press, force front output rear bearing on shaft.

Shift Rail Oil Seals

Install the two shift rail oil seals with appropriate tools.

Transfer Case

1. Install the front detent rod in the case.
2. Slide the front drive shift rail all the way into the case and place the shift fork on the rail as it enters the case. Secure the fork to the rail with the setscrew.
3. Position the front output shaft sliding gear in the shift fork.
4. Install the rear detent rod.
5. Slide the rear drive shift rail into the case and position the shift fork on the rail as the rail enters the case. Secure the fork to the rail with the setscrew.

   NOTE: The shift rails should be inserted so that the detents are positioned as shown in illustration.
6. While holding the sliding gear and main drive gear in position, install the front output shaft and rear bearing assembly through the two gears.
7. Install the main drive gear spacer and secure with the snap-ring.
8. Install the front output shaft rear bearing cup.
9. Place the front output shaft rear cover and shims on the case and install the attaching bolts.
10. Install the front output shaft front bearing on the shaft. Install the front bearing cup.
11. If the front bearing retainer oil seal was removed, install a new seal. Position the bearing retainer and gasket to the case and install the attaching bolts.
12. Place the rear output shaft rear bearing retainer on a work bench and install 13 needle bearings in the splined hub of the output shaft, using vaseline or grease.
13. Position the rear output shaft rear bearing retainer assembly to the case and install the attaching bolts.
14. Install the rear output shaft sliding gear in the shifting fork and on the splines of the output shaft.
15. Position the adapter housing assembly on the rear output shaft and case. Install the attaching bolts.
16. Install the roller bearings in the bore of the idler shaft gear with vaseline or grease.
17. Position the idler gear and thrust washers in the case; then drive the idler shaft into the rear of the case through the idler gear and thrust washers.

    NOTE: After installing the idler shaft, tap the sides of the case to relieve any possible binding.
18. Install the idler shaft lock plate.
19. Secure the shift rail link to the two shift rails.
20. Install the front and rear drive shift rail detent balls, springs and retaining plugs.

    NOTE: Be sure that the heavier loaded spring and flat washer are installed in the front drive shift rail.
21. Install the rod access hole plug.
22. Install the flange, washer and retaining nut on each of the output shafts. Be sure to install a new O-ring in the front output shaft flange. Torque the attaching nuts to specifications.
23. With a dial indicator on the front drive output shaft, check the end-play. If not within specifications, adjust the shim pack at the front output shaft rear cover.
24. Place the cover plate on the case and install the attaching bolts.

SPECIFICATIONS

END PLAY (IN.)

Front Output Shaft	0.001-0.005
Rear Output Shaft	0.001-0.005

TORQUE LIMITS (FT. LBS.)

Transfer Case to Transmission Extension Bolts	20-30
Transfer Case to Transmission Output Shaft Nut	60-80
Front Output Shaft Rear Cover Bolts	25-32
Front Output Shaft Bearing Retainer Bolts	25-32
Idler Shaft Cover Bolts	25-32
Front and Rear Output Flanges	80-85

Dana Model 21

Description

The Dana Model 21 is a single-speed gearbox that transmits power to the front driving axle. There are two positions of the transfer case; front drive axle engaged and front drive axle disengaged.

Disassembly

Transfer Case

1. Clean all dirt from transfer case and drain lubricant.
2. Remove bolts that attach the cover to the top of the case; then remove the cover.
3. Remove the setscrew securing the shift fork to the rail. Tap the shift rail rearward; then remove the rail cap from the rear of the case.
4. Remove the shift rail and fork.
5. Remove the detent spring and ball which engages the front drive shift rail.

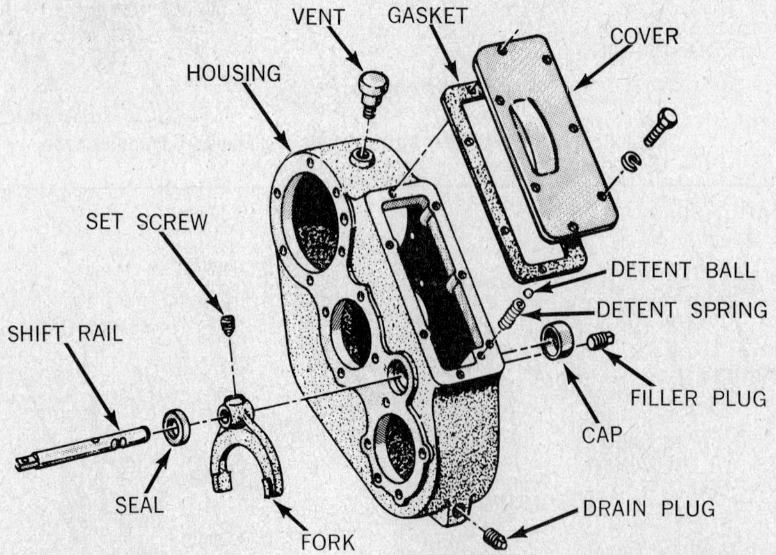

Exploded view of the case housing and shift mechanism of a Dana model 21 transfer case (© Ford Motor Co.)

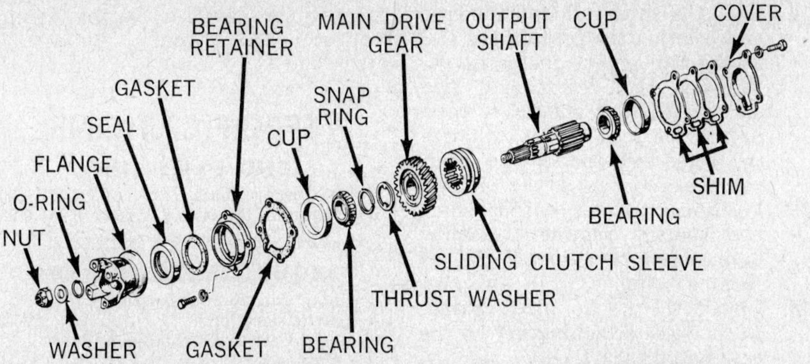

Exploded view of the front output shaft of a Dana 21 transfer case (© Ford Motor Co.)

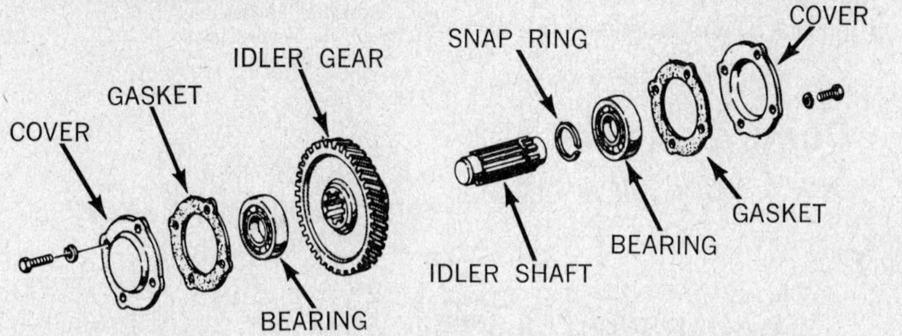

Exploded view of the idler shaft of a Dana 21 transfer case (© Ford Motor Co.)

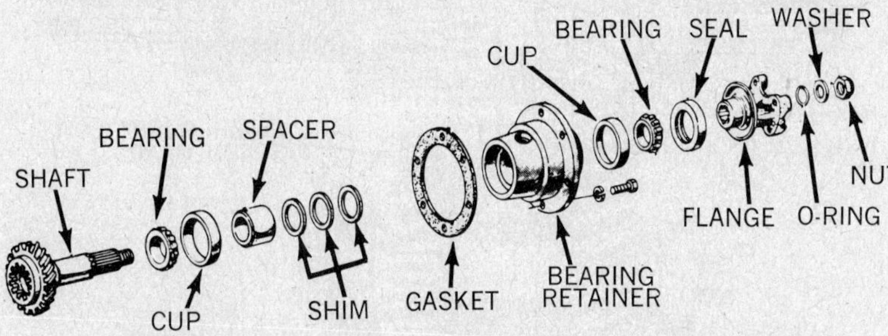

Exploded view of the rear output shaft of a Dana 21 transfer case (© Ford Motor Co.)

6. Remove the flange attaching nuts, flat washer and O-ring from the front and rear output shafts. Discard the O-rings.
7. Remove the flange from the front and rear output shafts.
8. Remove the bolts that attach the rear output shaft bearing retainer to the case; then remove the retainer and output shaft as an assembly.
9. Remove the front and rear idler shaft covers.
10. Using a hammer and soft drift, drive the idler shaft and rear idler bearing rearward out of the case; then lift out the front bearing and idler gear.
11. Remove the front output shaft bearing retainer and gasket. Remove the retainer seal if it is worn or damaged.
12. Remove the front output shaft rear cover and shims. Tie the shims together for reassembly.
13. Tap the end of the front output shaft toward the front of the case; then remove the front bearing cup. Remove the rear bearing cup by tapping the shaft rearward.
14. Angle the front output shaft front bearing away from the main drive gear to remove the snap-ring from its groove in the shaft. Drive the output shaft and rear bearing out of the case.
15. Remove the sliding gear, main drive gear, front bearing, thrust washer and snap-ring from the case.
16. Remove the shift rail seal.

Front Output Shaft Bearing

To remove the front output shaft rear bearing, use the sliding gear as a base and press off the bearing.

Idler Shaft

1. Remove the snap-ring from the idler shaft.
2. Using the idler gear as a base, press the idler shaft out of the rear bearing.

Rear Output Shaft

1. To remove the output shaft from the bearing retainer tap shaft rearward. Remove the shims and spacer.
2. Remove the inner bearing from the output shaft.
3. Place the bearing retainer on a press and force out the outer cup, outer bearing and oil seal.
4. Using a soft drift, drive out the inner bearing cup.

Assembly

Front Output Shaft

Using an arbor press, force rear bearing on front output shaft.

Idler Shaft

1. Using a press, install rear idler bearing on the shaft.
2. Install snap-ring.

Rear Output Shaft

1. Press the inner bearing on the output shaft.
2. Using a soft-faced hammer, tap the inner bearing cup into the retainer.
3. Install the outer cup.
4. Place spacer and shims on the output shaft; then install the shaft in the bearing retainer housing.
5. Install the outer bearing on the shaft.
6. Place the bearing retainer and output shaft in a vise. Measure end-play with a dial indicator on end of the shaft. If not within specifications, adjust shim pack between the spacer and the front and rear bearing cones.
7. After setting correct end-play, install the bearing retainer seal.

Transfer Case

1. While holding the drive gear, sliding gear and thrust washer in the case, install the front output shaft, from the rear, through the gears and washer. Install the snap-ring.
2. Install the front output shaft rear bearing cup.
3. Place the front output shaft rear cover and shims on the case. After removing old sealant from all mating surfaces with thinner, apply gasket sealer to the attaching bolts and torque to specifications. With the cover installed, apply sealer to the outside edge of the adjusting shims, case and cover joints.
4. Install the front output shaft rear bearing on the shaft. Install the front bearing.
5. If the front bearing retainer oil seal was removed, install a new seal. Position the bearing retainer and gasket to the case and install attaching bolts.

6. Install the flange, new O-ring, washer and attaching nut on the front output shaft.
7. With a dial indicator on the front drive output shaft, check the end-play. If not within specified limits, increase or decrease the shim pack thickness at the front output shaft rear cover.
8. Place the idler gear in the case; then install the idler shaft through the gear. Install the front bearing.
9. Place the front and rear idler covers and gaskets on the case; then install attaching bolts.
10. Install a new shift rail seal.
11. Install the shift rail detent ball and spring in the top of the case.
12. Slide the shift rail into the case and position the fork on the rail as the rail enters the case. Depressing the detent ball and spring will allow the rail to pass. Secure the fork to the rail with the setscrew. Install the shift rail cap.
13. Position the rear output shaft and bearing retainer assembly to the case, then install the attaching bolts.
14. Install the flange, new O-ring, washer and attaching nut on the rear output shaft.
15. Place the top cover and gasket on the case, then install attaching bolts.
16. Fill the transfer case to the proper level with the recommended lubricant.

SPECIFICATIONS

END PLAY (IN.)

Front Output Shaft	0.001-0.005
Rear Output Shaft	0.001-0.005

TORQUE LIMITS (FT. LBS.)

Transfer Case to Transmission Extension Bolts	20-30
Transfer Case to Transmission Output Shaft Nut	125-150
Front Output Shaft Rear Cover Bolts	25-32
Front Output Shaft Bearing Retainer Bolts	25-32
Idler Shaft Cover Bolts	25-32

Dana Model 24

Description

The Dana Model 24 is a two-speed gearbox that is manually controlled by a shift lever in the cab. The transfer case positions are: four-wheel-drive low (4L), neutral (N), two-wheel-drive high (2H) and four-wheel-drive high (4H).

Disassembly

1. Clean any dirt from the transfer case and remove the power take-off cover plate.
2. Remove both idler shaft bearing retainers.
3. Using a soft-faced hammer, tap the idler shaft and bearing to the rear until the bearing is free of the case.
4. Remove the idler shaft, two gears and spacer.
5. Remove the idler shaft front bearing.
6. Remove the flange retaining nuts from the front output shaft, the input shaft and the rear output shaft.
7. Remove the flanges and washers.
8. Remove the front output shaft front and rear bearing retainers.

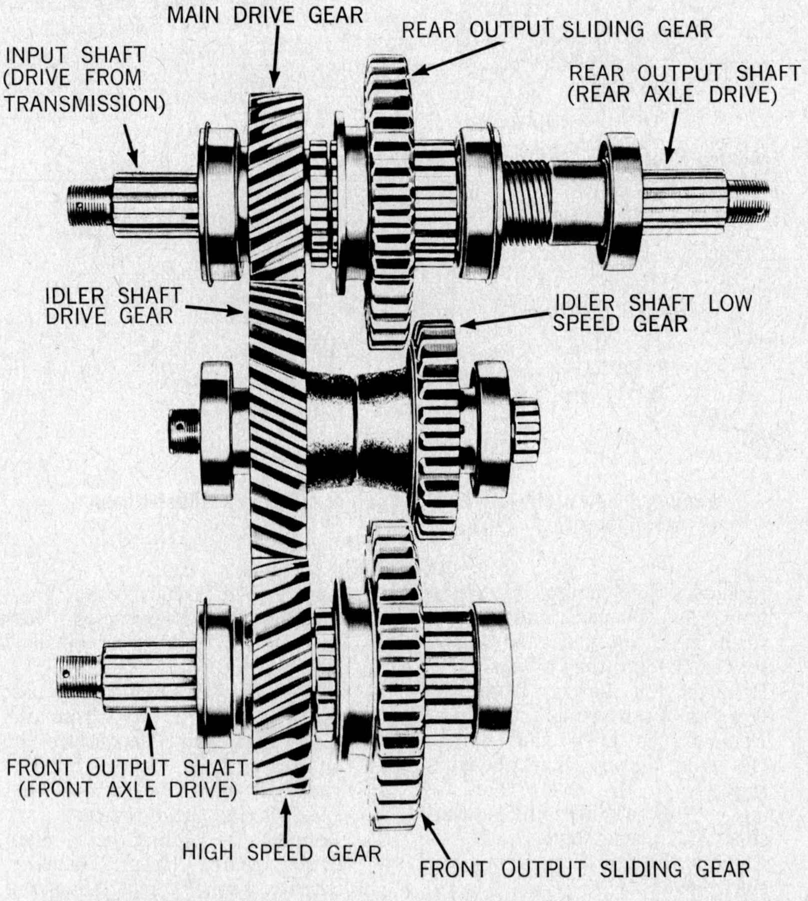

Dana Model 24 gear train—neutral position illustrated (© Ford Motor Co.)

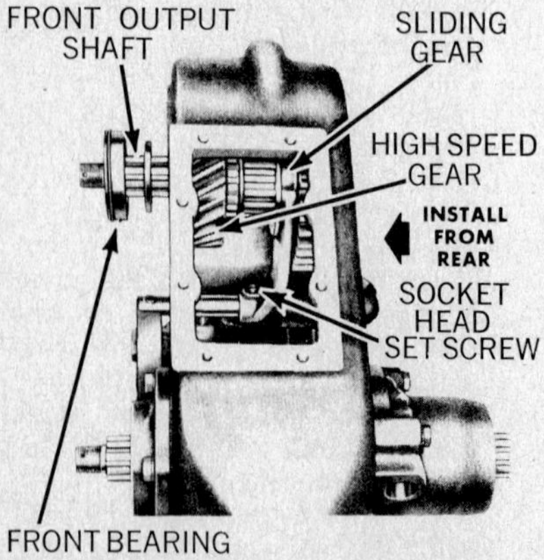

Removing/installing the front output shaft of a Dana 24 transfer case (© Ford Motor Co.)

9. Tap the front output shaft and rear bearing through the gears and case. Remove the high speed gear.
10. Remove the front output shaft front bearing and washer.
11. Remove the setscrew that retains the front drive shaft fork to the shift rail.
12. Remove the front output shaft sliding gear.
13. If the input shaft oil seal is to be replaced, remove it with a four-jaw puller and slide hammer.
14. Remove the input shaft bearing retainer.
15. If the output shaft bearing retainer oil seal is to be replaced, remove it with a puller and slide hammer.
16. Remove the rear output shaft bearing retainer; then remove the speedometer drive assembly.

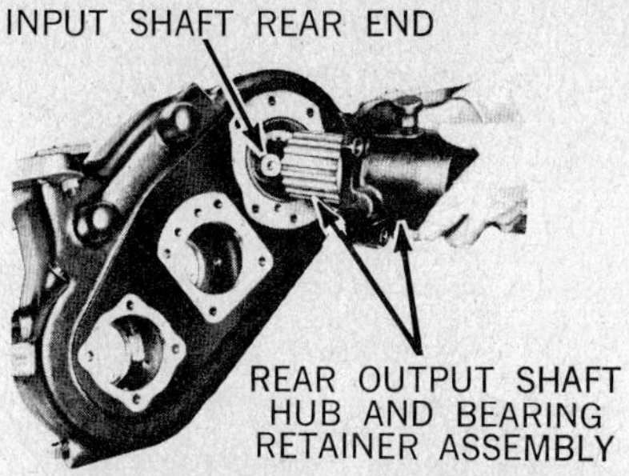

Removing/installing the rear output shaft of a Dana 24 transfer case
(© Ford Motor Co.)

17. Loosen the rear output shaft assembly from the case by driving on the front end of the input shaft with a soft-faced hammer.
18. Remove the rear output shaft and bearing retainer as an assembly.
19. Tap the input shaft through the front bearing, through the main drive gear, through the sliding gear and out of the case.

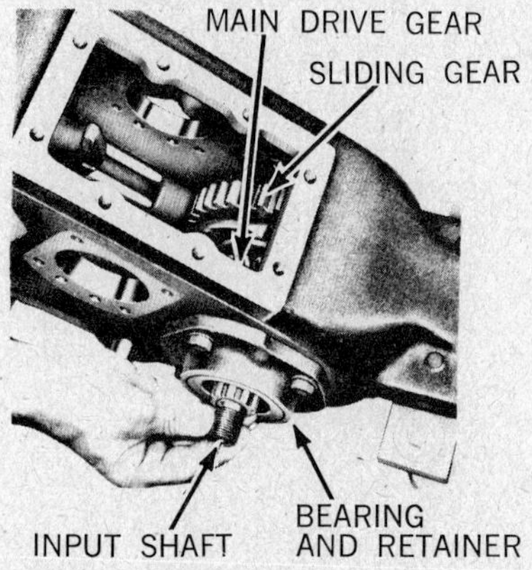

Removing/installing the input shaft of a Dana 24 transfer case
(© Ford Motor Co.)

20. Lift the main drive gear out of the case and then drive out the input shaft front bearing.
21. Remove the setscrew that retains the rear drive shift fork to the shift rail.
22. Remove the rear output shaft sliding gear.
23. Remove the shift rail link from the two shift rails.
24. Remove the retaining plug, detent spring and ball which engage the front drive shift rail detent rod.

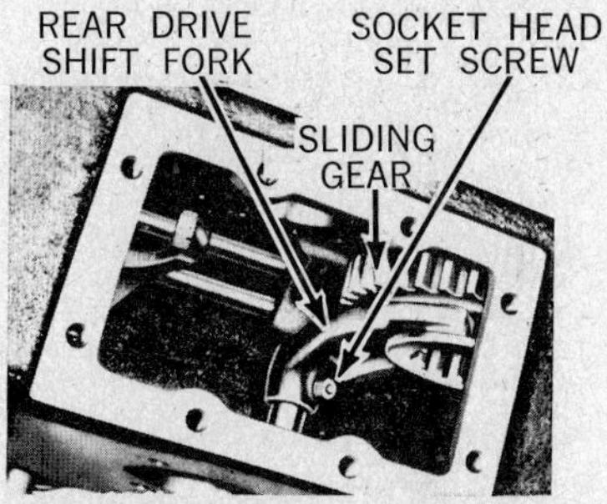

The rear drive shift fork and sliding gear of the Dana 24 transfer case
(© Ford Motor Co.)

25. Remove the retaining plug detent spring and ball which engages the rear drive shift rail detent rod. Remove the front drive detent rod access hole plug.
26. Pull the front drive shift rail to the furthest outward position.
27. Pull the rear drive shift rail far enough to allow the two detent rods to slide out.
28. Remove the rear drive shift rail and fork.
29. Remove the shift rail seals.

Assembly

1. Slide the front drive shift rail all the way into the case and position the shift fork on the rail as the rail enters the case.
2. Install the two detent rods in the case.
3. Install the rear drive shift fork and hold the detent rods and the fork in place as the rear drive shift rail is pushed in as far as possible.

   NOTE: In steps 2 and 3, the shift rails should be inserted so that the detents are positioned as shown in illustration.
4. Pull the front drive shift rail out to its next detent. This will permit the rear drive shift rail to be pushed in to the full extent of its travel. After pushing the rear drive shift rail all the way in, push the front drive shift rail back to its extreme inward position.

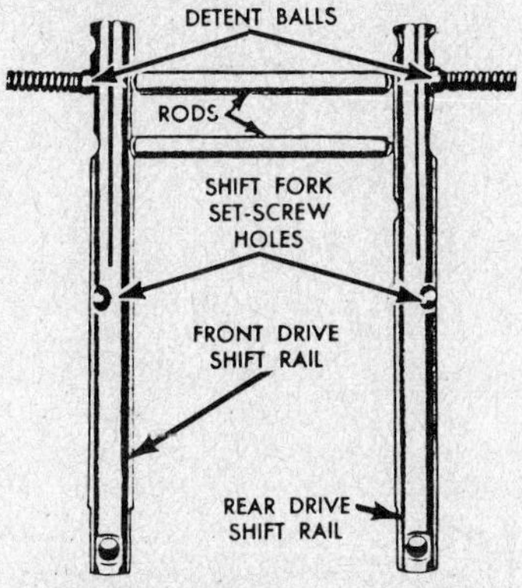

The shift mechanism of a Dana 24 transfer case (© Ford Motor Co.)

5. Install the rear drive shift detent ball, spring and retaining plug; then install the access hole plug.
6. Install the front drive shift rail detent ball, spring and retaining plug.
7. Secure the shift rail link in the two shift rails.
8. Place the rear output sliding gear in the shift fork and secure the fork to the rear drive shift rail with the setscrew.
9. Install the input shaft front bearing and retainer assembly. Coat retainer and bolts with sealer.
10. Place the main drive gear in the case; then slide the input shaft into the rear of the case through the main drive gear and through the front bearing and retainer.
11. Install the roller bearings in the splined hub of the rear output shaft assembly with petrolatum jelly or grease. Then install the shaft and bearing retainer assembly, making sure that the output shaft is aligned correctly with the input shaft. Coat the case, bearing retainer and bolts with sealer.
12. Position the front output sliding gear in the shift fork and secure the folk to the front drive shift rail with the setscrew.
13. While holding the sliding gear and high speed gear in position, install the front output shaft and rear bearing assembly through the two gears from the rear of the case.
14. After coating with sealer, install the front output shaft rear bearing retainer and gasket.
15. Install the washer and bearing over the front output shaft at the front of the case and then install the front bearing retainer and gasket. Coat retainer with sealer.
16. Install the flange, washer, flange retaining nut and cotter key on each of the three shafts. Torque to specifications.
17. Place the idler shaft gears in the case and install the shaft and rear bearing assembly from the rear. After applying sealer to the plate and bolts, install the rear bearing retainer.
18. Position the spacer on the front end of the idler shaft and install the front bearing. Tap the bearing lightly with a mallet or soft-faced hammer.
19. Install the washer, retaining nut and cotter pin on the front end of the idler shaft.
20. After applying sealer to the plates and bolts, install the idler shaft front bearing retainer and the power take-off cover plate.

SPECIFICATIONS

END PLAY (IN.)

Front Output Shaft	0.003-0.007
Rear Output Shaft	0.003-0.007

TORQUE LIMITS (FT. LBS.)

Transfer Case to Transmission Extension Bolts	20-30
Transfer Case to Transmission Output Shaft Nut	60-80
Front Output Shaft Rear Cover Bolts	25-32
Front Output Shaft Bearing Retainer Bolts	25-32
Idler Shaft Cover Bolts	25-32

Dana 300

The 300 is used in Jeep® CJ models only. It has a cast iron case, four gear positions and employs an external floor mounted gearshift linkage for range control. It is a part time, 2 speed unit with undifferentiated high and low ranges. It is used with both manual and automatic transmission. Low range reduction is 2.6:1.

Disassembly

1. Drain the unit and remove the shift lever assembly.
2. Remove the bottom cover.

   NOTE: The bottom cover has been coated with a sealant. Use a putty knife to break the seal and work the knife around the bottom of the cover to break it loose. Don't try to wedge the cover off.
3. With a puller, remove the front and rear yokes.
4. Unbolt and remove the input shaft support from the case. The rear output shaft gear and input shaft will come with it as an assembly.

   NOTE: The support has been coated with sealant, remove it as you did the bottom cover.
5. Remove the rear output shaft clutch sleeve from the case.
6. Remove and discard the snap ring retaining the rear output shaft gear on the input shaft and remove the gear.
7. Remove and discard the input bearing snap ring.

Shift rod oil seal removal

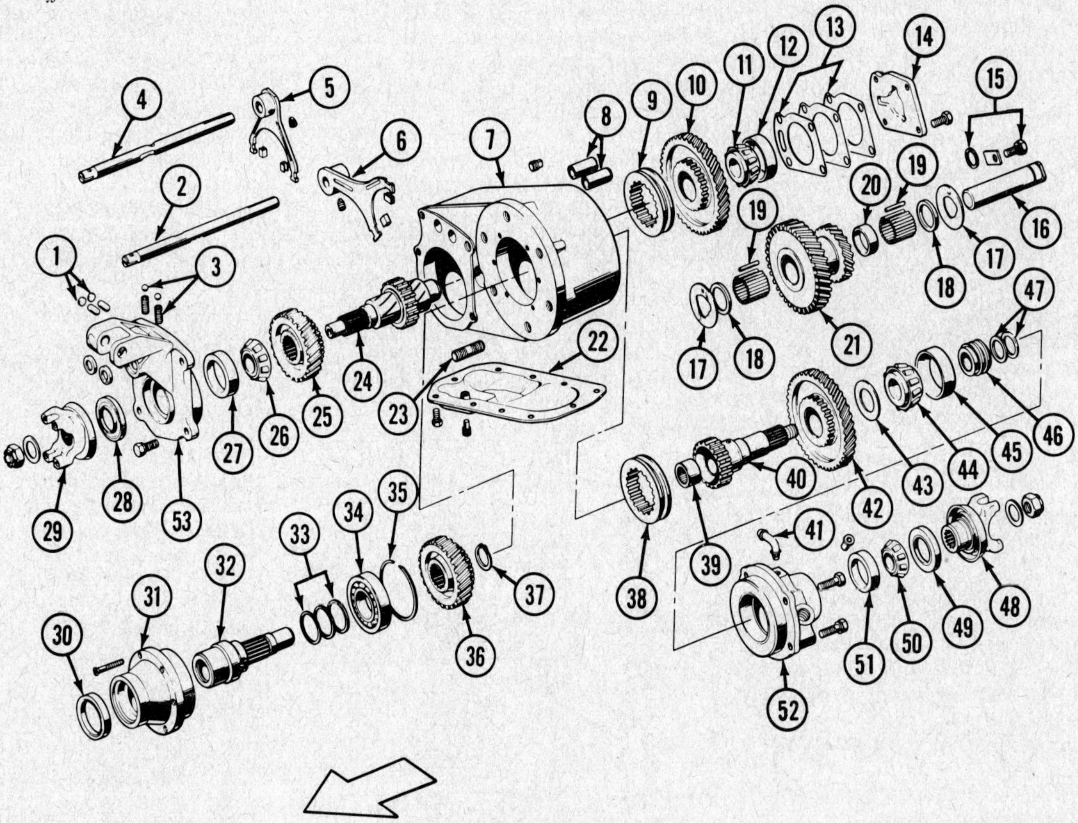

Dana 300 exploded view

1 Interlock plugs and interlocks
2 Shift rod—rear output shaft fork
3 Poppet balls and springs
4 Shift rod—front output shaft fork
5 Front output shaft shift fork
6 Rear output shaft shift fork
7 Transfer case
8 Thimble covers
9 Clutch sleeve—front output shaft
10 Clutch gear—front output shaft
11 Bearing—front output shaft rear
12 Race—front output shaft bearing
13 End play shims—front output shaft
14 Cover plate
15 Lock plate, bolt and washer
16 Intermediate gear shaft
17 Thrust washer
18 Bearing spacer (thin)
19 Intermediate gear shaft needle bearings
20 Bearing spacer (thick)
21 Intermediate gear
22 Bottom cover
23 Stud (case-to-trans.)
24 Front output shaft
25 Front ouptut shaft gear
26 Front output shaft bearing (front)
27 Front output shaft bearing race
28 Oil seal
29 Front yoke
30 Seal
31 Support—input shaft
32 Input shaft
33 Shims
34 Input shaft bearing
35 Input shaft bearing snap ring
36 Rear output shaft gear
37 Snap ring
38 Clutch sleeve—rear output shaft
39 Input shaft rear bearing (needle) (or pilot bearing)
40 Rear output shaft
41 Vent
42 Clutch gear—rear output shaft
43 Thrustwasher
44 Bearing—rear output shaft front
45 Race—rear output shaft bearing
46 Speedometer drive gear
47 End play shims
48 Rear yoke
49 Rear output shaft oil seal
50 Bearing—rear output shaft rear
51 Bearing race
52 Rear bearing cap
53 Front bearing cap

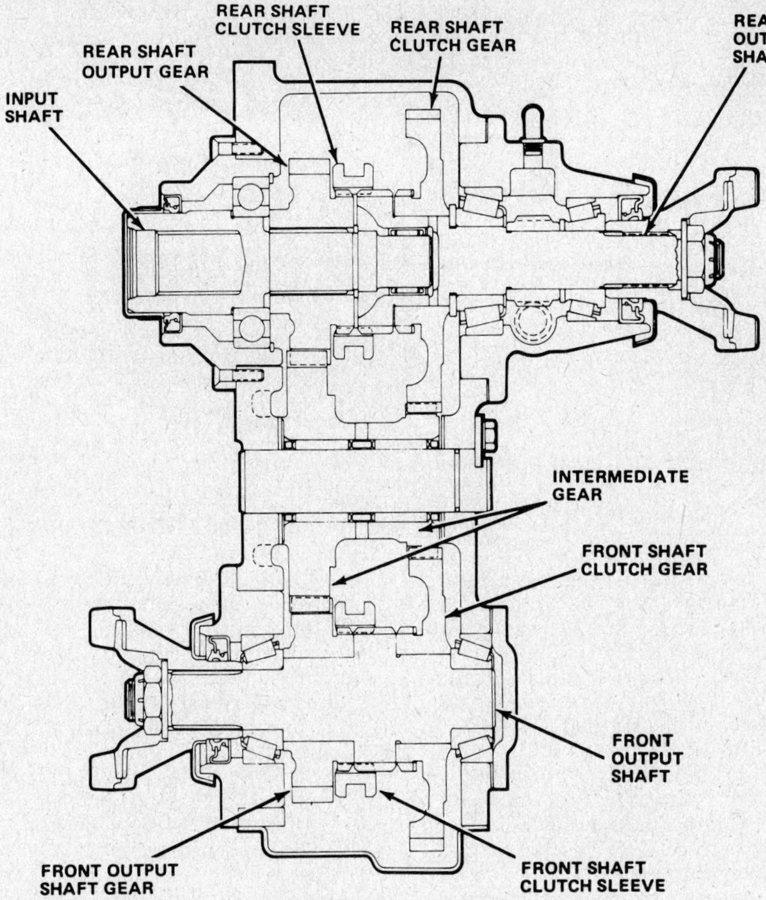

Dana 300 power flow

Yoke oil seal removal

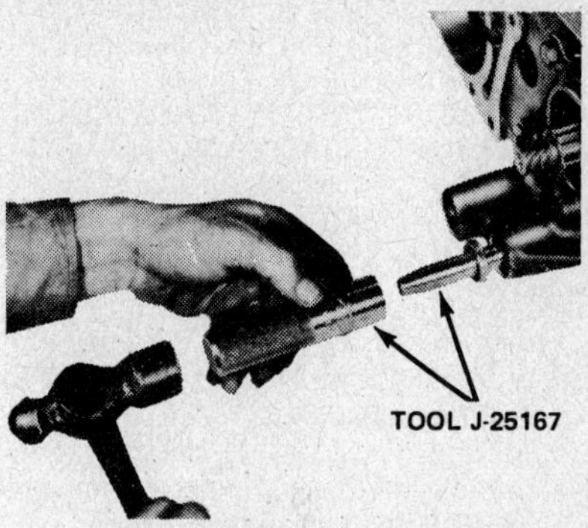

Shift rod oil seal positioning

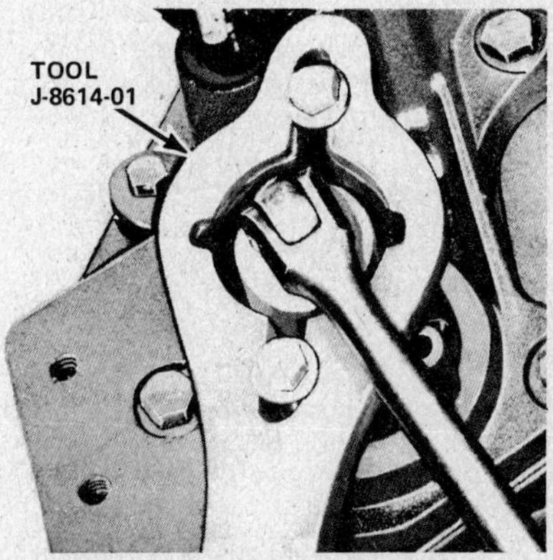

Output shaft yoke nut removal

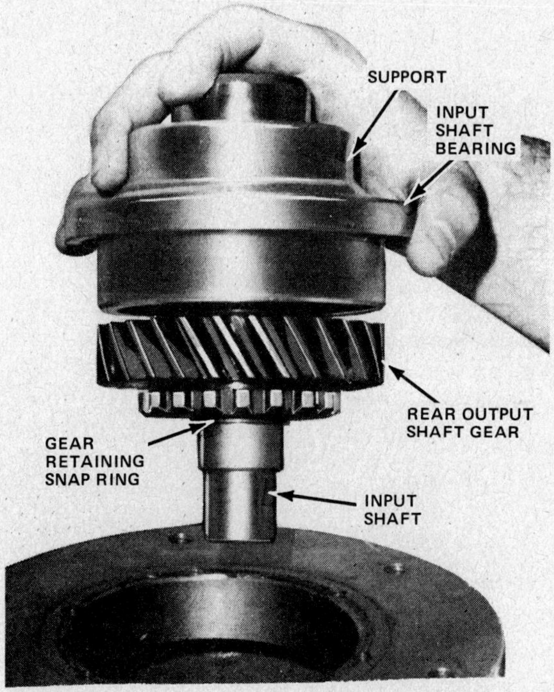

Front support, input shaft and rear output shaft gear removal

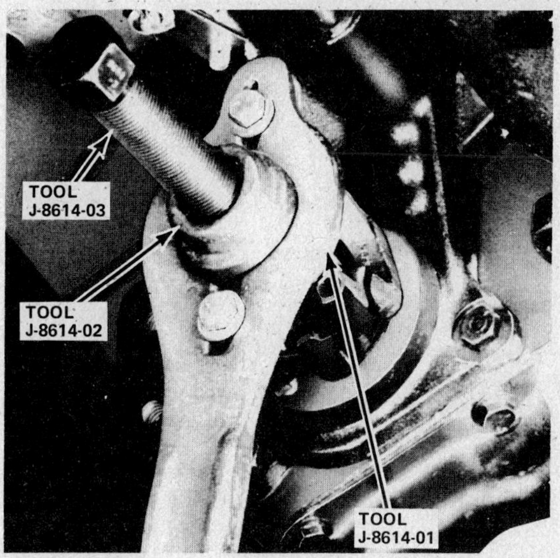

Yoke removal

Shift fork set screw removal

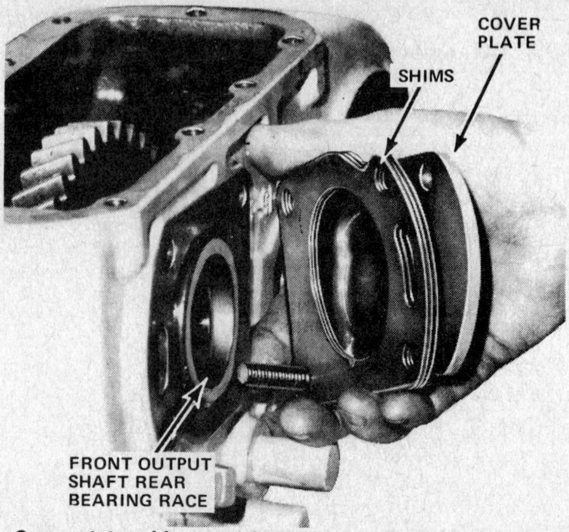

Cover plate, shims and front output shaft rear bearing race

8. Remove the input shaft bearing from the support. Tap the end of the shaft with a soft mallet to aid removal.
9. Remove the input shaft bearing and end play shims from the shaft with an arbor press.
10. Remove the input shaft oil seal from the support.
11. Unbolt and remove the intermediate shaft lockplate.
12. Remove the intermediate shaft. Tap the shaft out of the case using a brass punch and plastic mallet.
13. Remove and discard the intermediate shaft O-ring seal.
14. Remove the intermediate gear assembly and thrust washers.

    NOTE: The thrust washers have locating tabs which must fit into notches in the case at assembly.

15. Remove the needle bearings and spacers from the intermediate gear. There are 48 needle bearings and three spacers.
16. Remove the rear bearing cap attaching bolts and remove the cap. A plastic mallet will aid in removal.

    NOTE: The rear bearing cap has been coated with sealant.

17. Remove the end play shims and speedometer drive gear from the rear output shaft.
18. Remove and discard the rear output shaft oil seal. Remove the bearings and races from the rear cap.
19. Unbolt and remove the front and rear output shaft shift forks from the shift rods.
20. Remove the shift rods. Insert a punch through the clevis pin holes in the rods and rotate the rods while pulling them out of the case.

    NOTE: When the shift rods are free of the case, take care to avoid losing the shift rod poppet balls and springs.

21. Remove the shift forks from the case.
22. Remove the bolts attaching the front cap to the case and remove the cap.

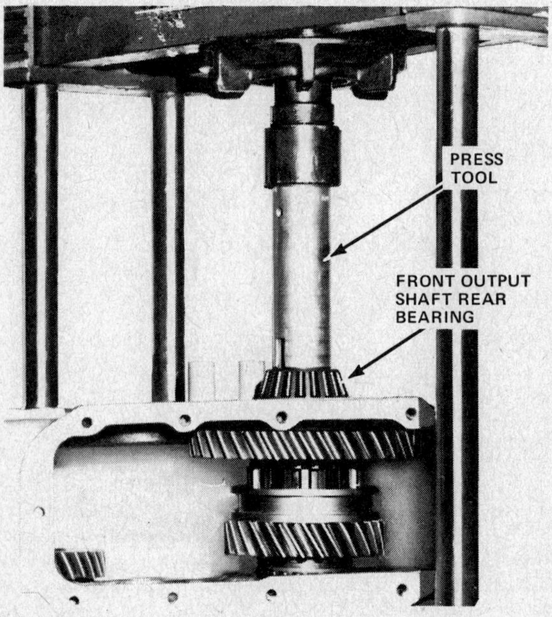

Front output shaft rear bearing positioning

Front output shaft rear bearing removal

NOTE: The front cap has been coated with sealant.

23. Remove the front output shaft and shift rod oil seals from the front cap.
24. Remove the bearing race from the front cap.
25. Remove the cover plate bolts and remove the plate and end play shims from the case. Keep the shims together for assembly.
26. Move the front output shaft toward the front of the case.
27. Remove the front output shaft rear bearing race.
28. Remove the rear output shaft front bearing. Position the case on wood blocks. Seat the clutch gear on the case interior surface and tap the shaft out of the bearing with a soft mallet.

NOTE: If the bearing is difficult to remove, an arbor press may have to be used.

29. Remove the rear output shaft front bearing, thrust washer, clutch gear and output shaft from the case.
30. Remove the front output shaft rear bearing with an arbor press.

CAUTION: Be sure to support the case with wood blocks positioned on either side of the case bore.

31. Remove the case from the press and remove the output shaft, clutch gear and sleeve and the shaft rear bearing.
32. Remove the front output shaft front bearing with an arbor press and tool J-22912-01 or its equivalent.
33. Remove the front output shaft from the gear.
34. Remove the input shaft rear needle bearing from the rear output shaft using tool J-29369-1 or its equivalent. Support the shaft in a vise during removal.
35. Using a ⅜" drive, 7/16" socket, remove the shift rod thimbles from the case.

Assembly

Coat all parts with SAE 85W-90 oil before assembly.

1. Apply Loctite® 220 or its equivalent to the thimbles and install them in the case.
2. Install the front output shaft gear on the front output shaft. Be sure that the clutch teeth on the gear face the shaft gear teeth.
3. Install the front bearing on the front output shaft using an arbor press. Be sure that the bearing is seated against the gear.
4. Install the front output shaft in the case and install the clutch sleeve and gear on the shaft.
5. Install the front output shaft rear bearing using an arbor press.

NOTE: Install an old yoke nut on the shaft to avoid damage to the threads.

6. Install the input shaft needle bearings in the rear output shaft with tool J-29179 or its equivalent.
7. Position the rear output shaft clutch gear in the case and insert the rear output shaft into the gear.
8. Install the thrust washer and front bearing on the rear output shaft using an arbor press.
9. Install the shims and bearing on the input shaft using an arbor press.
10. Install a new input shaft seal.
11. Using a new snap ring, install the input shaft and bearing in the support.
12. Install the rear output shaft gear on the input gear and install a new gear retaining ring.
13. Measure the clearance between the input gear and the gear retaining snap ring using a feeler gauge. Clearance should not exceed .003 in. If clearance is beyond tolerance, add shims between the input shaft and bearing.
14. Install the clutch sleeve on the rear output shaft.
15. Apply Loctite® 515 or equivalent to the mating surfaces of the input shaft support and install the support assembly, shaft and gear in the case. Use two support bolts to align the support on the case and tap the support into position with a soft mallet. Torque the support bolts to 10 ft-lb.
16. Install the rear bearing cap front bearing race.
17. Install the rear bearing cap rear bearing race.
18. Position the rear output shaft rear bearing in the rear bearing cap.
19. Install the rear output shaft yoke oil seal.
20. Install the speedometer gear and endplay shims on the rear output shaft.
21. Apply Loctite® 515 or equivalent to the mating surfaces of the cap and install the rear bearing cap. Use two cap bolts to align the cap and tap it into place with a soft mallet.
22. Tighten the cap bolts to 35 ft-lb.
23. Install the rear output shaft yoke. Torque a new locknut to 120 ft-lb.
24. Clamp a dial indicator on the rear output shaft bearing cap. Position the indicator stylus so that it contacts the end of the shaft.
25. Pry the shaft back and forth to check end play. End play should be .001-.005 in. If play is not correct, remove or add shims between the speedometer drive gear and the output shaft rear bearing.
26. Install the front output shaft rear bearing race.
27. Install the front output shaft end play shims and cover plate. Tighten the cover plate bolts to 35 ft-lb.

NOTE: Apply Loctite® 220 to the bolts before installation.

28. Install the front output shaft front bearing race.
29. Install the front output shaft yoke oil seal.
30. Install the shift rod oil seals.
31. Install the front bearing cap, using Loctite® 515 on the mating surfaces. Use two bolts to align the cap and tap it into position with a soft mallet.
32. Install and tighten the bearings cap bolts to 35 ft-lb.
33. Seat the rear bearing cup against the cover plate by tapping the

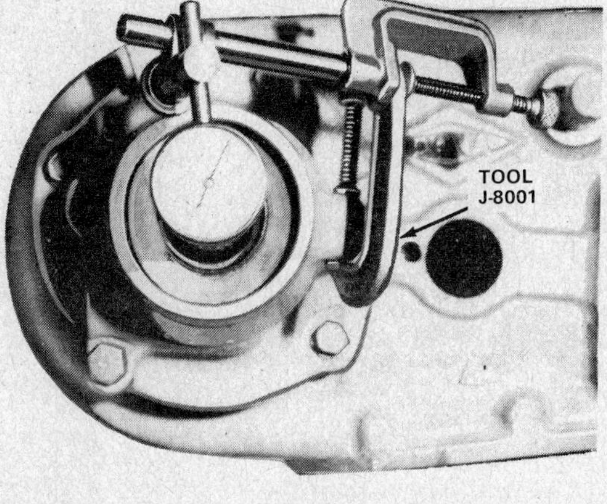

Checking rear output shaft end play

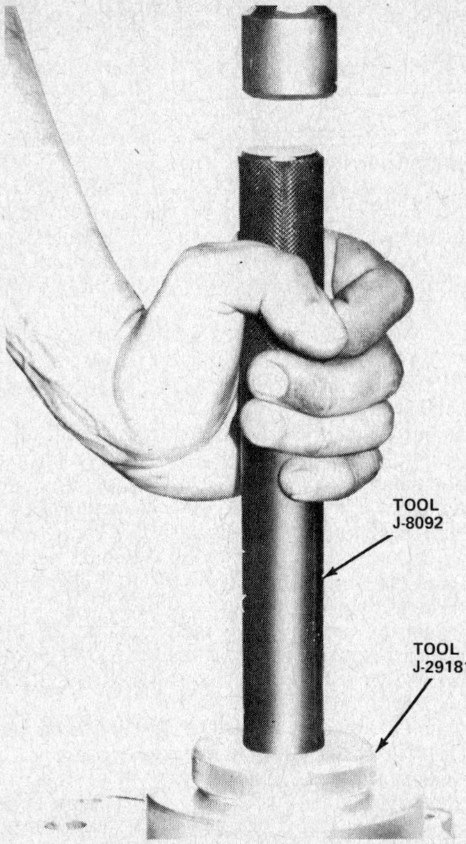

Front output shaft front bearing race installation

end of the front output shaft with a plastic mallet. Mount a dial indicator on the front bearing cap and position the stylus against the end of the output shaft. Pry the shaft back and forth to check end play. End play should be .001-.005 in. If the play is not correct, add or remove shims between the cover plate and case. If shims are added seat the rear bearing cup again before checking.

34. Install the front output shaft yoke. Tighten the new locknut to 120 ft-lb.
35. Install the front and rear output shaft shift forks.
36. Install the front output shaft shift rod poppet ball and spring in the front bearing cap.
37. Compress the poppet ball and spring and install the front output shaft shift rod part way in the case.
38. Insert the front output shaft shift rod through the shift fork.
39. Align the setscrew hole in the shift fork and rod. Install and tighten the setscrew to 14 ft-lb.
40. Install the rear output shaft shift rod poppet ball and spring in the front bearing cap.
41. Compress the ball and spring and install the rear output shaft shift rail part way. The front output shaft shift rod should be in neutral and the interlocks seated in the front bearing cap bore.
42. Insert the rear output shaft shift rod through the shift fork.
43. Align the setscrew holes in the fork and rod. Torque the setscrew to 14 ft-lb.
44. Insert tool J-25142 in the intermediate gear and install the needle bearings and spacer.
45. Install the intermediate gear thrust washers in the case. Make sure that the tangs are aligned with the grooves in the case. The thrust washers may be held in place with petroleum jelly.
46. Install a new O-ring seal on the intermediate shaft.
47. Position the intermediate gear in the case.
48. Install the intermediate shaft in the case bore. Tap the shaft into the gear until the shaft forces the tool out of the case.
49. Install the intermediate shaft lock plate and bolt. Torque the bolt to 23 ft-lb.
50. Install the bottom cover, applying Loctite® 515 or equivalent to the mating surfaces. Install and torque the bolts to 15 ft-lb.
51. Fill the case with 4 pints of SAE 85W-90 gear oil.

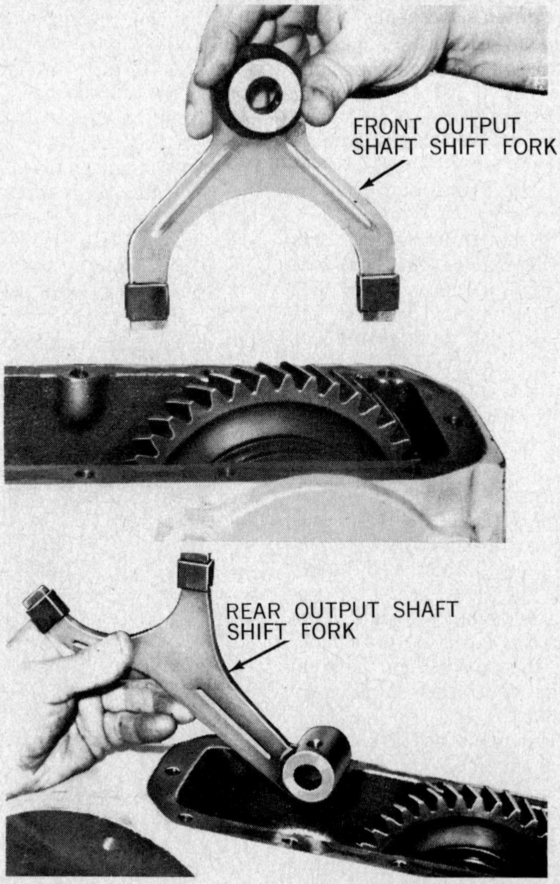

Shift fork installation

International Harvester Model TC-143

The IH Model TC-143 "Silent Drive" transfer case is a chain driven single speed unit. Unlike conventional gear driven transfer cases, this unit has a high-strength link-belt type loop of chain driving two broad-faced sprockets. There is no neutral position. There are two variations of this transfer case; one is frame mounted with a short intermediate drive shaft between the input shaft of the transfer case and the transmission output shaft and the other type is mounted directly to the rear of the transmission.

Disassembly

1. After removing the transfer case from the vehicle and draining all of the lubricant out, clean the outside of the case.
2. Remove the shift cover.
3. Unscrew and remove the indicator light switch from the case.
4. With the rear output shaft flange clamped in a soft jawed vise, remove the flange retaining nut. Remove the flange from the vise and remove the flange from the rear output shaft. Use a puller, if necessary.
5. Turn the case so it rests on the flanges and remove the bolts securing the two halves of the case. Lift the top (rear) half of the case from the assembly and discard the gasket.
6. If present, remove the short spacer from the rear side of the input shaft. Also, if the thrust washer did not stay with the cover when removed, remove it now from the front output shaft.
7. With the case again secured in a soft jawed vise, place your thumbs on the ends of the shafts with your fingers under the sprockets. Pull the sprockets together with the chain off the shafts and out of the case as an assembly.
8. Unhook and remove the shift spring.
9. Remove the shift assembly mounting bolt and spring stud from the case.
10. Pull the shift cranks from the bosses inside the case.
11. If present, remove the long spacer from the input shaft and the washer from the front output shaft.
12. Lift the sliding clutch and its shift shoe from the front output shaft.
13. The two shafts are removed from the case with a press or by tapping them out with a soft hammer.

NOTE: If the transfer case is a transmission mounted unit, a snap ring on the input shaft must be removed before the shaft can be removed from the case.

14. After the shafts are removed, remove the oil seals and the bearing snap rings, and press or tap out the two ball bearings.
15. Pry and remove the thrust washer from the boss for the front output shaft roller bearing in the other half of the case.
16. Press the roller bearing cage

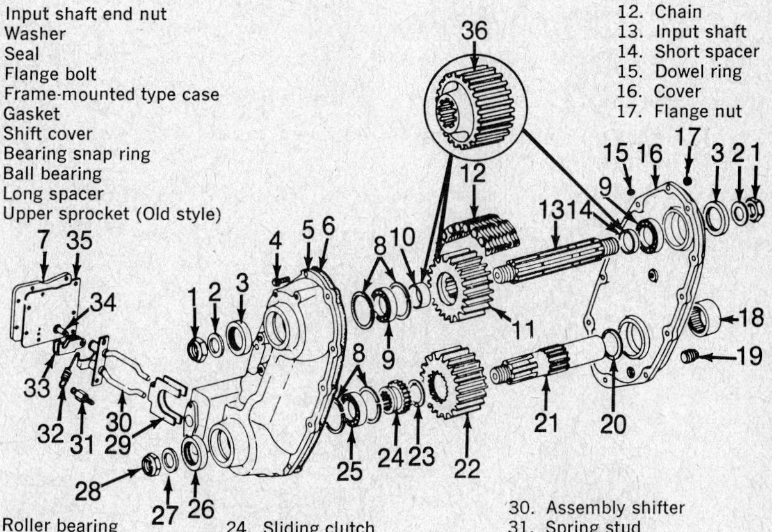

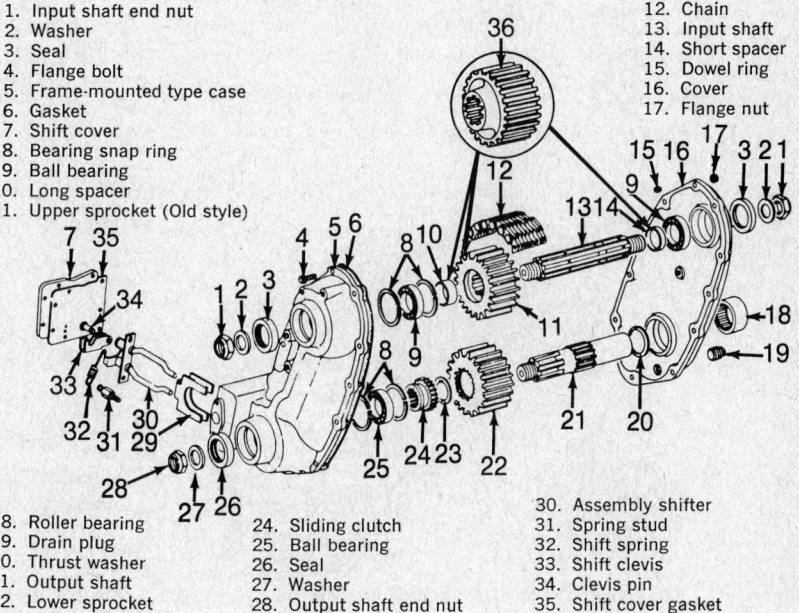

1. Input shaft end nut
2. Washer
3. Seal
4. Flange bolt
5. Frame-mounted type case
6. Gasket
7. Shift cover
8. Bearing snap ring
9. Ball bearing
10. Long spacer
11. Upper sprocket (Old style)
12. Chain
13. Input shaft
14. Short spacer
15. Dowel ring
16. Cover
17. Flange nut
18. Roller bearing
19. Drain plug
20. Thrust washer
21. Output shaft
22. Lower sprocket
23. Thrust washer
24. Sliding clutch
25. Ball bearing
26. Seal
27. Washer
28. Output shaft end nut
29. Shift shoe
30. Assembly shifter
31. Spring stud
32. Shift spring
33. Shift clevis
34. Clevis pin
35. Shift cover gasket
36. Upper sprocket (new style)

Exploded view of a frame mounted type International Harvester TC-143 transfer case (© International Harvester Co.)

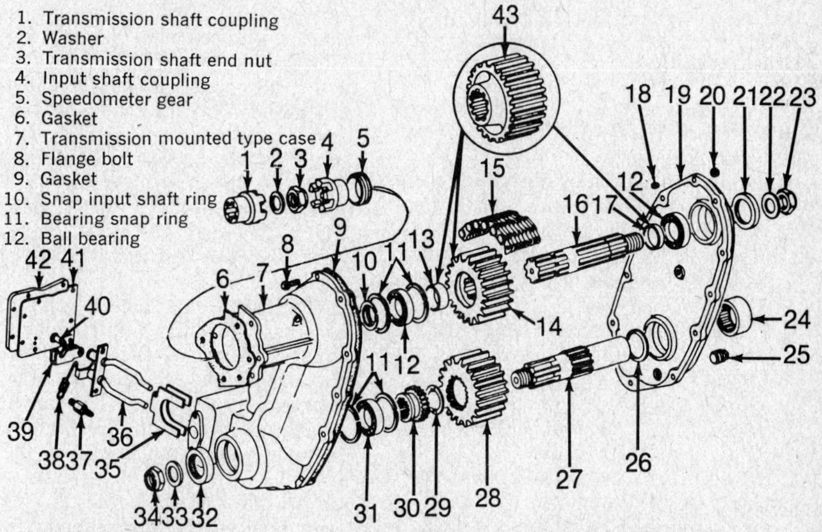

Exploded view of a transmission mounted type International Harvester TC-143 transfer case (© International Harvester Co.)

1. Transmission shaft coupling
2. Washer
3. Transmission shaft end nut
4. Input shaft coupling
5. Speedometer gear
6. Gasket
7. Transmission mounted type case
8. Flange bolt
9. Gasket
10. Snap input shaft ring
11. Bearing snap ring
12. Ball bearing
13. Long spacer
14. Upper sprocket (Old style)
15. Chain
16. Input shaft
17. Short spacer
18. Dowel ring
19. Cover
20. Flange nut
21. Seal
22. Washer
23. End nut
24. Roller bearing
25. Drain plug
26. Thrust washer
27. Output shaft
28. Lower sprocket
29. Thrust washer
30. Sliding clutch
31. Ball bearing
32. Seal
33. Washer
34. Output shaft end nut
35. Shift shoe
36. Assembly shifter
37. Spring stud
38. Shift spring
39. Shift clevis
40. Clevis pin
41. Shift cover gasket
42. Shift cover
43. Upper sprocket (new style)

Removing the shifter cover on a TC-143 transfer case
(© International Harvester Co.)

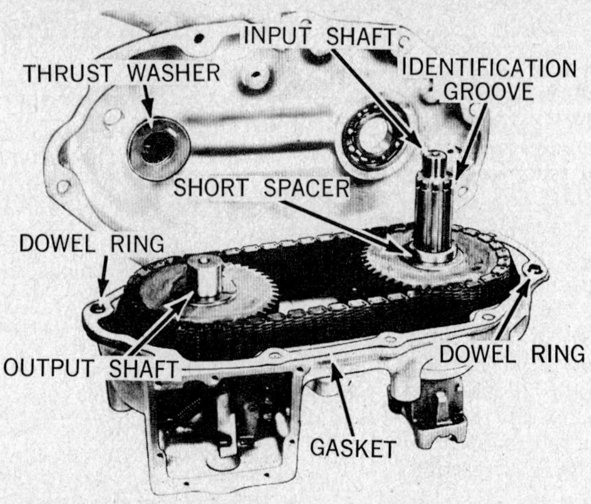

Removing the rear half of the case (cover) from the TC-143 transfer case (© International Harvester Co.)

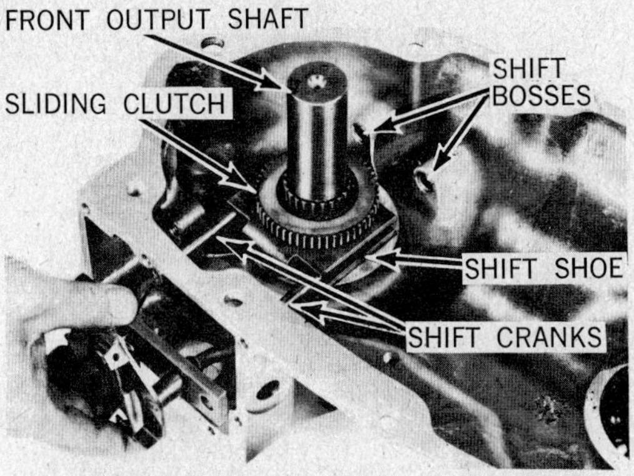

Removing the shifter mechanism from the TC-143 transfer case
(© International Harvester Co.)

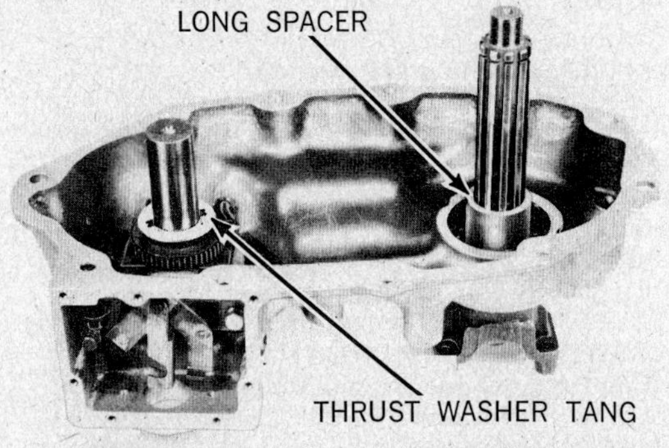

Installation of the thrust washer and long spacer, is so equipped, on the TC-143 transfer case
(© International Harvester Co.)

from the inside and out of the cover.

17. Press the ball bearing on the outer race from the outside and out of the cover.

Cleaning and Inspection

1. Clean all parts in solvent, removing all traces of old gaskets, sealants and lubricants, and dry the parts with compressed air.
2. Examine all the ball and roller bearings for wear or damage and replace as necessary.
3. Inspect the sprocket teeth and bores for damage and wear. Check the internal splines and clutch teeth for chipped surfaces. Small nicks or burrs can be removed with a file.
4. Check the smooth and splined surfaces of the shafts for wear or damage. The sliding clutch must move freely on the output shaft, but excessive clearance is remedied by replacement of parts.
5. Examine the chain for bent or broken links. If either condition exists, replace the chain.

Assembly

1. Install the two snap rings in the outer grooves of both bearing bores in the front half of the case.
2. Coat both bearing bores with lubricant and press or tap with a soft hammer both ball bearing assemblies into the case.
3. Install the two snap rings in the inner grooves of the two bearing bores in the front case half.
4. Install the shaft oil seals from the outside of the front case half. They are best installed with a press.
5. On a frame mounted transfer case, position the lightly lubricated shafts in the bearings, then, pull the shafts into the bearings by tightening the flange attaching nuts with the flanges installed. The input shaft is installed with the identification groove toward the rear of the transfer case. Tighten the flange attaching nut on the front output shaft to 200-250 ft. lbs., and the flange attaching nut on the input shaft until it bottoms, then back off two turns and retighten to 140-150 ft. lbs.
6. The output shaft in transmission mounted transfer cases is installed in the same manner as outlined for frame mounted units in step 5.
7. The input shaft in transmission mounted transfer cases has a snap ring to be installed on the front end of the shaft prior to installation in the bearing. The shaft is then pressed or tapped into the bearing with a soft hammer until the snap ring is bottomed against the bearing.
8. Assemble the shift shoe to the sliding clutch and install the sliding clutch to the front output shaft.
9. Insert the shifter assembly into the transfer case so the shift cranks of the shifter pass through the shift shoe before being guided into the shift bosses. Make sure the shifter operates the sliding clutch and then secure the assembly with the bolt and spring stud.

   NOTE: The flange bolt must be installed before the spring stud because the position of the spring stud when installed prevents the installation of the flange bolts.
10. Install the thrust washer to the front output shaft and the long spacer to the input shaft, if so equipped with a long spacer.

    NOTE: Be sure the thrust washer tangs fit down into the splines on the shaft.

11. Lightly lubricate the bores of both sprockets and secure the case in a soft jawed vise by the end of the input shaft.
12. Install the upper sprocket to the outer end of the input shaft. Do not slide the sprocket completely into the case.
13. Position the chain over the sprocket and place the lower sprocket inside the chain.
14. Pull down on the lower sprocket enough to slide the lower sprocket onto the output shaft.
15. Slide both sprockets and chain onto the sprockets as far as they will go.
16. Install the short spacer on the input shaft (not required on later models).
17. Install the shift spring between the spring post and the shifter assembly.
18. Press the ball bearing into the input shaft bore of the rear cover from the inside surface.
19. Press the roller bearing into the output shaft bore of the rear cover from the outside surface until it is flush with the bearing bore.
20. Press the seal for the rear of the input shaft (rear output) into the cover until it is flush.
21. Place the cover on a bench, inside facing up. Coat the back side of the thrust washer with a thin coat of sealant and position it on the roller bearing boss with the tang on the washer mated with the oil passage in the boss.

NOTE: Use the sealant sparingly and make sure none of it enters the bearing or blocks the two oil passages.

22. Position a new gasket and two dowel rings on the mating surface of the case.
23. Position the cover onto the case, guiding the two shafts into their respective bearings. Secure the cover to the case with the attaching nuts and bolts, tightening them to 29-38 ft. lbs.
24. Install the indicator light switch to the case and check its operation with a test light.
25. Install the shift cover gasket and cover on the case and secure it with bolts and lockwashers tightened to 4-6 ft. lbs. *Do not overtighten.*
26. Install the rear output flange on the rear of the input shaft so both the input flange and the output flange are on the same plane. The flanges must be assembled in this manner to prevent vibration.
27. Install the washer and a nylon insert locknut on the shaft tightened to 140-150 ft. lbs. to secure the flange.

New Process Model T201

Description

The New Process Model 201 transfer case (Dodge 91000) is a 2-speed gearbox which provides speed reduction and couples power to the front and rear driving axles.

CAUTION: Do not engage front driving axle when operating truck on hard surfaced roads at high speeds.

De-Clutch and Shift Rod Adjustment

NOTE: All adjustments must be made with the front axle engaged and the transfer case in low range.

1. Disconnect de-clutch and shift rods at shift levers.
2. Adjust de-clutch rod length until lever clears rear end of slot in cab underbody by 5/8 in. Secure adjusting yoke with locknut.
3. Adjust shift rod length until distance between protusions on shift and de-clutch levers is 1/4 in. Secure adjusting yoke with locknut.
4. Connect de-clutch and shift rods at shift levers and then road test vehicle.

Disassembly

Rear Output Shaft

1. Remove cotter pin and flange nut at rear output shaft.
2. Remove attaching bolts and nuts, then remove bearing retainer and gasket. Discard gasket.
3. Remove output shaft assembly from case.
4. Remove nut and washer at rear of shaft.
5. Remove brake drum by tapping on it lightly (if necessary).
6. Remove shaft and gear from bearing retainer.
7. Remove shims, spacer and speedometer drive gear. Tie shims together for reassembly.
8. Remove inner bearing cone, using a suitable puller.
9. Remove snap-ring and roller bearings from shaft gear bore.

NOTE: The rear output shaft and gear is serviced as an assembly. Do not remove gear from shaft.

10. Remove attaching nuts, brake support, bearing and oil seal. Discard seal.

Front Output Shaft

1. Remove attaching bolts and nuts, then remove rear bearing retainer and gasket. Discard gasket.
2. Remove cotter pin and nut at front output shaft.
3. Remove attaching nut, washer and companion flange.
4. Remove the front output shaft assembly through the rear of the case.
5. Remove sliding clutch gear.
6. Position front output shaft assembly in a soft-jawed vise.
7. Remove lock retainer and bearing nut.

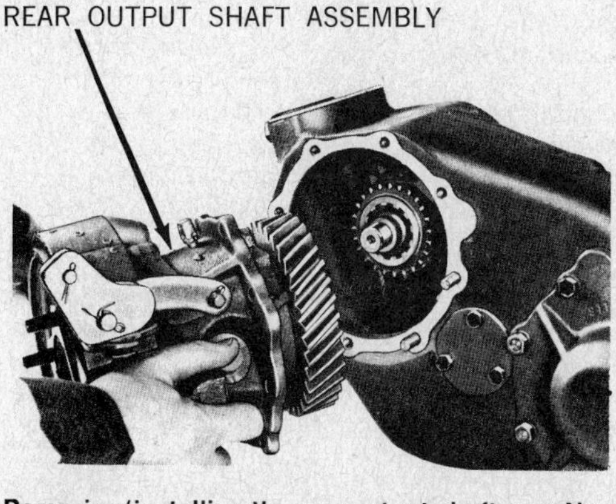

Removing/installing the rear output shaft on a New Process T-201 transfer case (© Chrysler Corp.)

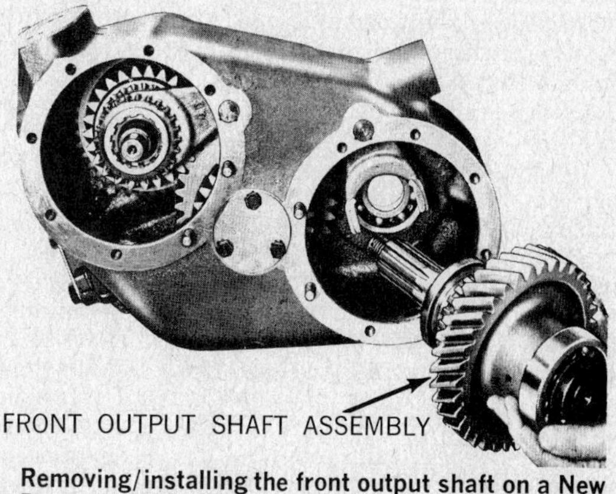

Removing/installing the front output shaft on a New Process T-201 transfer case (© Chrysler Corp.)

1 Ball, shift bar poppet
2 Spring, shift bar poppet ball
3 Bar, front output shaft
4 Fork, shift
5 Screw, set
6 Clutch, front output sliding
7 Fork, shift
8 Gear, front output drive
9 Bearing, roller (70 req'd)
10 Spacer, bearing
11 Shaft, front output front gear
12 Washer, thrust
13 Bearing, ball
14 Retainer, lock
15 Nut, bearing retaining
16 Shaft, idler gear
17 Cone, idler gear bearing
18 Cup, idler gear bearing
19 Shim, set
20 Spacer, bearing
21 Shaft input
22 Ring, snap
23 Bearing, roller (15 req'd)
24 Gear, rear output drive w/shaft
25 Gear, speedometer drive
26 Spacer, speedometer drive gear
27 Clutch, two-speed sliding
28 Plug, pipe
29 Gasket, set
30 Bolt, hex head, w/lock washer
31 Retainer, front output shaft rear bearing
32 Bolt, hex head, w/lock washer
33 Washer, lock
34 Nut, hex
35 Breather
36 Cup, rear output shaft outer bearing
37 Cone, rear output shaft outer bearing
38 Support, hand brake
39 Seal, rear output shaft outer bearing oil
40 Stud
41 Retainer, rear output drive gear bearing
42 Plate, idler shaft cover
43 Cup, rear output shaft inner bearing
44 Cone, rear output shaft inner bearing
45 Case, transfer
46 Bolt w/washer
47 Bolt, hex head
48 Washer, lock
49 Cover, power take-off opening

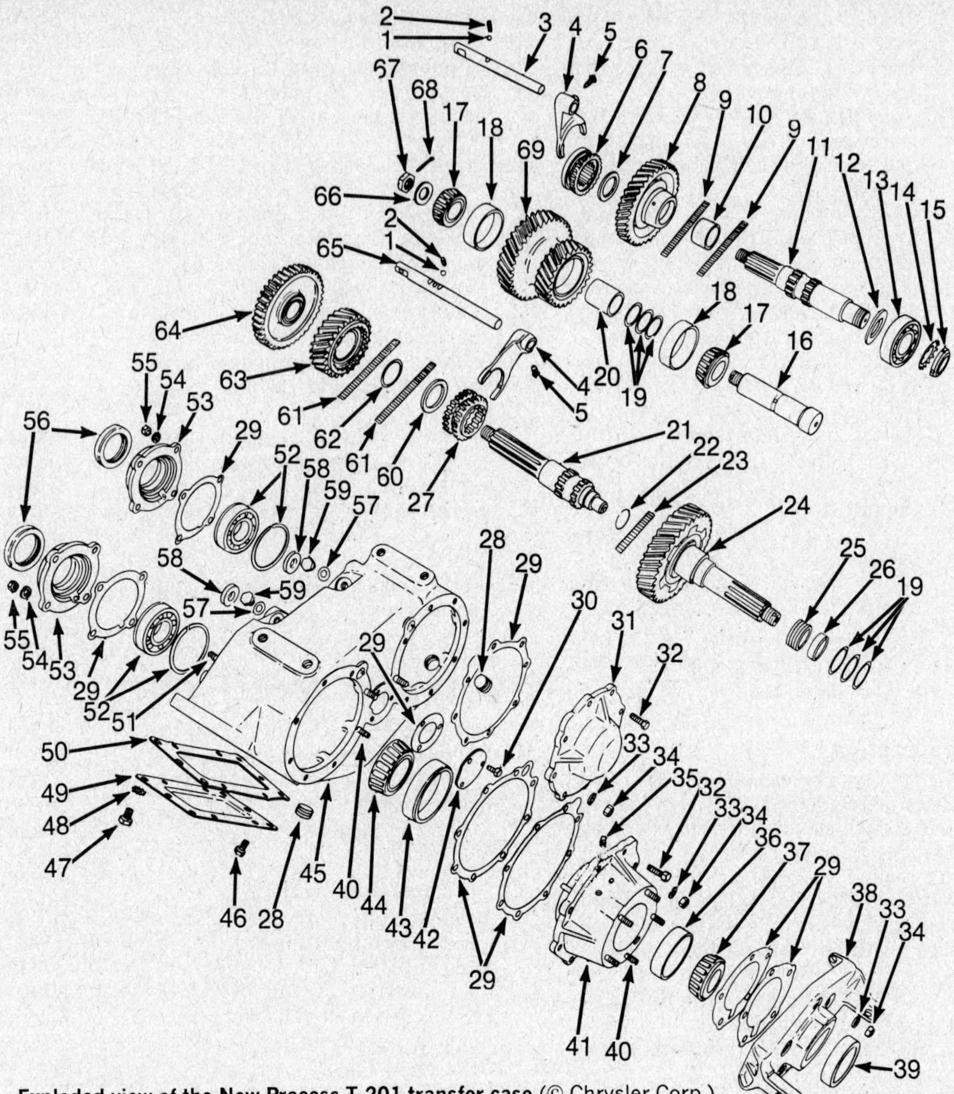

Exploded view of the New Process T-201 transfer case (© Chrysler Corp.)

50 Gasket, power take-off cover
51 Stud
52 Bearing, input and front output ball
53 retainer, input and front output bearing
54 Washer, lock
55. Nut, hex
56 Seal, input and front output bearing retainer oil
57 Gasket
58 Seal, front and rear output shift bar oil
59 Screw, poppet ball retainer
60 Washer, thrust
61 Bearing, roller (70 req'd)
62 Spacer, bearing
63 Gear, input drive
64 Gear, power take-off
65 Bar, two-speed shift
66 Washer
67 Nut, hex
68 Pin, cotter
69 Gear, idler

8. Using a suitable puller, remove bearing.
9. Remove front output shaft drive gear by lifting upward and holding the thrust washers against the hub to retain bearing rollers.
10. Carefully set aside thrust washers, then remove the two rows of bearing rollers (70 rollers) and the spacer separating them.
11. Remove attaching nuts and bearing retainer with gaskets. Note number of gaskets used.

Idler Gear, Shift Bar and Fork

1. Remove safety wire and setscrews securing shift forks to shift bars.
2. Remove poppet ball retaining plugs, gaskets and poppet ball springs.
3. Pull shift bars out of the case, then remove shift forks and poppet balls.
4. Remove cotter pin, nut and washer from front end of idler shaft.
5. Remove attaching bolts, gasket and idler gear shaft cover plate.
6. Remove idler gear assembly.

NOTE: When removing the idler gear assembly, use an arbor as shown in illustration and perform the following:

a. Install arbor on threaded end of shaft so that it seats against the shaft shoulder.
b. Drive arbor until shaft is free at rear of case.
c. Separate shaft and arbor.
d. Remove gear with arbor through front output shaft opening.
e. Remove arbor, shims, spacer and bearing cones. Tie shims together for reassembly.

Input Shaft

1. Remove cotter pin and input shaft flange nut.
2. Remove nut, flat washer and companion flange.
3. Remove input shaft assembly through rear output shaft opening in case.

NOTE: Make certain to retain power take-off and drive gear on the shaft.

4. Mount input shaft in a soft-jawed vise.
5. Remove power take-off gear.
6. Remove input drive gear while holding thrust washers tightly against hub.

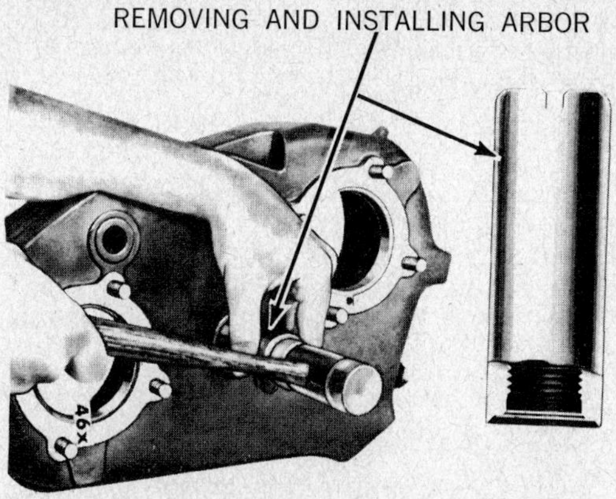

Removing/installing the idler gear shaft on a New Process T-201 transfer case (© Chrysler Corp.)

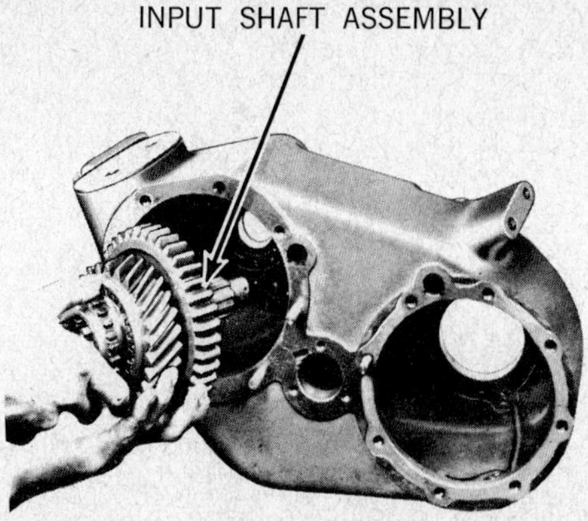

Removing/installing the input shaft assembly on a New Process T-201 transfer case (© Chrysler Corp.)

7. Carefully remove the two rows of bearing rollers (70 rollers) and the separating spacer.
8. Remove attaching nuts, bearing retainer, gaskets and oil seal. Note the number of gaskets used and discard the oil seal.

Assembly

The transfer case is assembled in the reverse order of disassembly. The following procedures concerning preloading bearings and bearing adjustment however, must all be completed before (or in some cases, during) installation of shaft and gear assemblies.

Input Shaft

1. The input shaft drive gear bearing consists of 70 rollers divided into two rows by a spacer.
2. Coat gear bore with grease, then position rollers and spacer.
3. Hold thrust washers against hub to retain rollers, then install gear on shaft.
4. Input shaft end-play is controlled by gasket thickness between case and bearing retainer.
5. Position retainer on case, then measure clearance with a feeler gauge.
6. Select gasket(s) with a thickness .005 in. more than measured clearance.
7. Remove retainer and install selected gasket(s), then reinstall retainer.

Rear Output Shaft

1. Rear output shaft bearing preload is set by shim set size selection.
2. Using an arbor press and suitable sleeve, install inner bearing cone on shaft. The cone should be firmly seated against gear.
3. Install speedometer drive gear, spacer and original bearing shim set.
4. Install rear output shaft in bearing retainer, then position outer bearing cone on shaft.
5. Install parking brake drum, flat washer and slotted nut. Torque nut to 125 ft. lbs.
6. Mount shaft and retainer assembly in a vise so that shaft is free to rotate.
7. Turn shaft until bearing rolls smoothly. Then, using an inch-pound torque wrench, measure bearing preload with the wrench in motion. Subtract or add shims as necessary to meet specifications.

   NOTE: Shims for adjusting bearing preload are available in four thicknesses.
8. After the final adjustment, remove slotted nut, washer and brake drum.
9. Install parking brake support and new support oil seal.
10. Reinstall brake drum, washer and slotted nut. Torque nut to specfications.

Idler Gear

1. Idler gear bearing end-play is controlled by shim set size selection.
2. Clamp the idler gear shaft (large end) in a soft-jawed vise.
3. Install bearing cone against shoulder on shaft.
4. Install bearing spacer and original shim set.
5. Install idler gear (small end down) on shaft, then install other bearing cone.

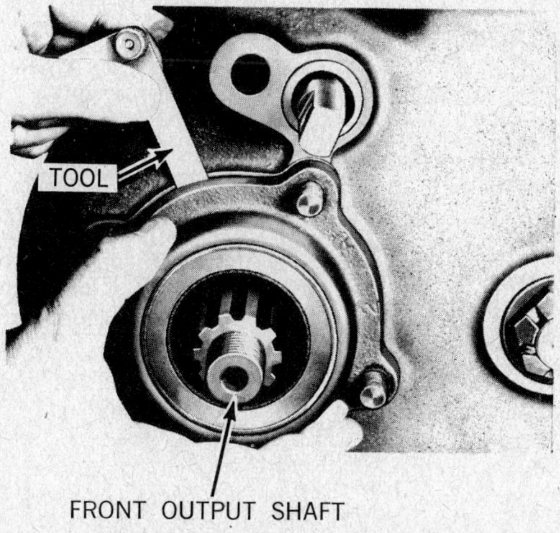

Checking clearance between case and bearing retainer

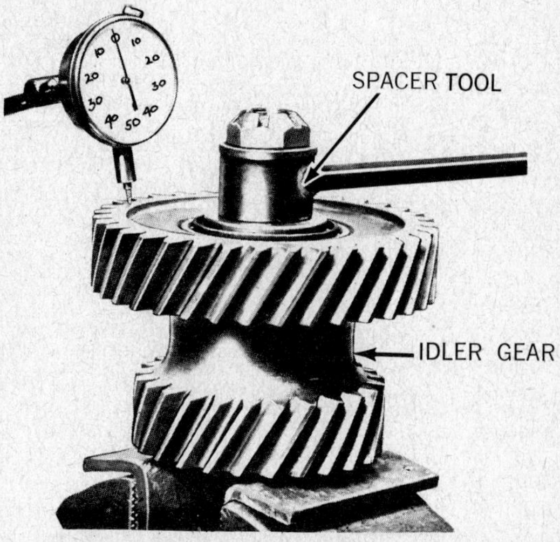

Checking idler gear bearing adjustment

6. Position spacer tool as shown in illustration, then install flat washer and nut. Torque nut to specifications.
7. Rotate gear until bearing rolls smoothly. Then using a dial indicator, measure idler gear bearing end-play. Add or subtract shims as necessary to meet specifications.
8. Disassemble idler gear shaft assembly. Tie newly selected shims together.
9. To install gear assembly in the case, position bearing cone in in the large end of the gear, then place gear (small end up) on a bench.
10. Install the same arbor used to remove idler gear shaft, a spacer, new shims and other bearing cone in the idler gear.
11. Hold the idler gear assembly in the case with the small diameter gear facing rearward, then insert the shaft through the case (from rear) and thread it into the previously installed arbor.
12. Tap on the shaft until arbor extends through opposite side of case.
13. Remove arbor.

Two-Speed Clutch

When installing the two-speed clutch on the input shaft, make certain that the recessed side of the gear is toward the front of the case.

Front Output Shaft

1. The front output shaft drive gear bearing consists of 70 bearing rollers divided into two rows by a spacer.
2. Coat gear bore with grease, then position rollers and spacer.
3. Hold thrust washers against each hub to retain rollers, then install gear on shaft.
4. Shaft end-play is controlled by gasket thickness between case and bearing retainer.
5. Position retainer on case, then measure clearance with a feeler gauge.
6. Select gasket(s) with a thickness .005 in. more than measured clearance.
7. Remove retainer and install selected gasket(s), then reinstall retainer.
8. When installing the front output shaft assembly in the case, locate front output shift bar as far toward rear of case as possible. This will make it possible to position shift fork in clutch gear collar and to align clutch gear splines on front output shaft.

SPECIFICATIONS

END PLAY (IN.)

Input Shaft	0.005
Front Output Shaft	0.005
Idler Gear	0.000-0.002

BEARING PRELOAD (IN. LBS.)

Rear Output Shaft Bearings	15-30

TORQUE LIMITS (FT. LBS.)

Front Retainer Nut	35-55
Poppet Screw	15-25
Idler Cover Screw	15-25
Drain and Filler Plugs	25-45
Top Cover	38-42
All Bearing Caps	38-42
Flange and Idler Shaft Nut	125
Input Shaft	300-400
Front Output Shaft	300-400
Rear Output Shaft	300-400
Idler Shaft Nut	140-160
Front Output Shaft Flange Nut	140-160
Input Shaft Flange Nut	140-160
Driveshaft Mating Flange Nuts	35
Breather	8-12
Brake Support Nut	25-45
Brake Retaining Screw	20-40
Brake Retainer Nut	25-45
Brake Drum	60-66
Brake Mounting	60-66
Brake Drum Nut	140-160
P.T.O. Screw	8-12
P.T.O. to Case	38-42
P.T.O. Bearing Cap	38-42
P.T.O. Top Cover	38-42
P.T.O. Shaft	300-400

New Process Model 202

Description

The New Process Model 202 transfer case is a two-speed gear box which is used to transmit power from the main transmission to a front driving axle, as well as to a conventional rear axle. Sliding clutch gears in the transfer case are controlled by a single lever to select various driving ranges. A separate control lever is provided for operating the power take-off assembly on units so equipped.

The transfer case should not be operated in four-wheel high range on dry, hard surface roads, as rapid tire wear will result.

CAUTION: **Do not operate transfer case in neutral range for extended periods of time when power take-off assembly is disengaged.**

Disassembly

NOTE: The following procedure covers a disassembly of the transfer case removed from the chassis and mounted in a suitable stand.

Rear (Upper) Output Shaft

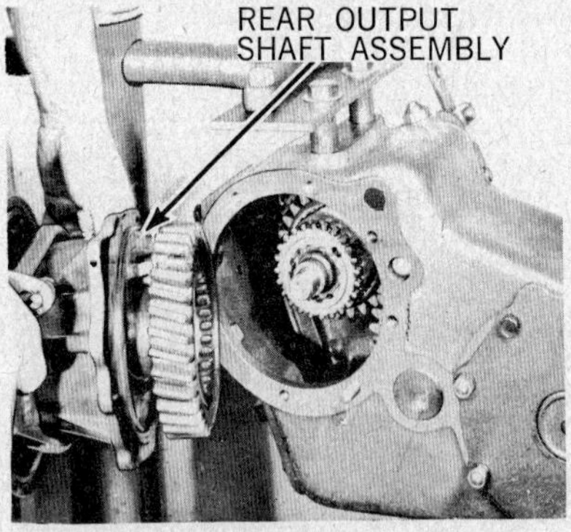

Removing/installing the rear output shaft from a New Process T-202 transfer case (© International Harvester Co.)

1. Remove cotter pin from flange nut located at end of rear output shaft. Apply hand brake to prevent shaft from rotating; then break the torque on nut.
2. Remove hex head bolts and two nuts securing bearing retainer to case. Remove the rear output shaft assembly. Remove and discard gasket.
3. Place the output shaft assembly on a bench.
4. Remove the nut and flat washer at rear of shaft. Tap brake drum lightly and remove drum from shaft. Slide off brake drum flange spacer.
5. Remove output shaft with drive gear from upper rear bearing retainer. Slide off speedometer drive gear, spacer and drive gear inner bearing. Remove snap-ring and fifteen roller bearings.
6. Remove hex nuts and lock washers securing hand brake support to upper rear bearing retainer. Remove brake support and drive gear outer bearing. Remove oil seal and discard.

Input Shaft

1. Remove ten capscrews and lock washers attaching power take-off cover or assembly (if so equipped). Remove and discard gasket.
2. Remove shift bar poppet screw, spring and ball. Through the rear output shaft opening in case, remove roll pin securing two-speed shift fork on bar. Use a 5/32 in. diameter steel rod to drive out roll pin.

NOTE: Where case interference prevents complete removal of roll pin, drive the pin until shift bar can be removed. Shift fork can then be moved toward input shaft clutch gear to provide clearance for removal of roll pin.

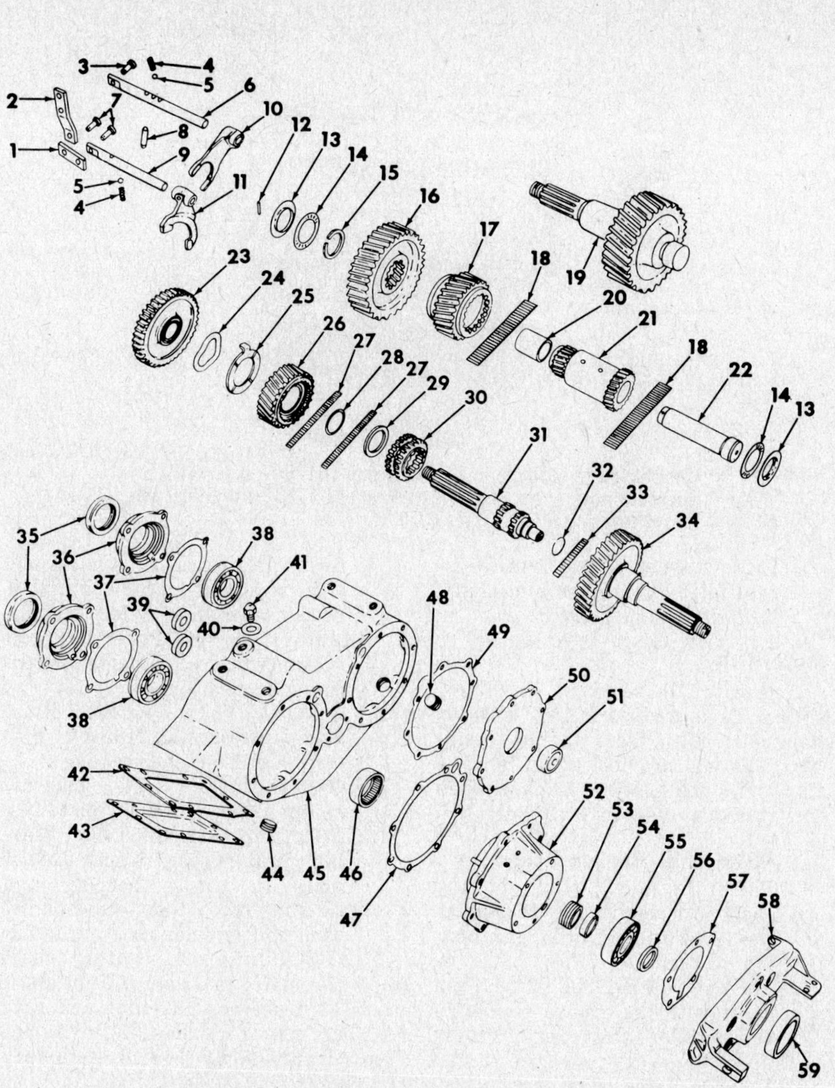

1 Link, shift lever
2 Lever, shift
3 Pin, rod
4 Spring, shift bar poppet
5 Ball, shift bar poppet
6 Bar, shift, two-speed
7 Pin, rod
8 Plunger, shift bar interlock
9 Bar, shift idler
10 Fork, shift, two-speed
11 Fork, shift, idler
12 Pin, idler shaft
13 Bearing, thrust, race
14 Bearing, thrust, needle
15 Ring, snap, idler
16 Gear, idler drive
17 Gear, sliding, idler
18 Bearing, roller, idler, shaft
19 Gear, lower shaft (front output)
20 Spacer, rotating shaft
21 Shaft, idler gear, rotating
22 Shaft, idler gear, stationary
23 Gear, PTO, input shaft, upper
24 Spring, friction washer, input shaft
25 Washer, friction, input shaft
26 Gear, drive, input shaft, upper
27 Bearing, roller, input shaft, front
28 Spacer, input shaft drive gear bearing
29 Washer, input shaft sliding clutch
30 Gear, clutch, input shaft, upper
31 Shaft, input
32 Ring, snap
33 Bearing, roller, drive gear
34 Gear, shaft, output drive
35 Seal, oil, input and output shaft, front
36 Retainer, bearing, input and output shaft, front
37 Gasket, bearing retainer
38 Bearing, input and output shaft, front
39 Seal, oil, shift bar
40 Gasket, shift bar poppet screw
41 Screw, shift bar poppet
42 Gasket, PTO cover
43 Cover, PTO opening
44 Plug, pipe
45 Case, transfer
46 Bearing, gear, output shaft, inner
47 Gasket, rear bearing retainer, upper
48 Plug, pipe
49 Gasket, rear bearing retainer, lower
50 Retainer, lower rear bearing (front output shaft)
51 Bearing, lower shaft, rear
52 Retainer, upper rear (output shaft) bearing
53 Gear, speedometer drive gear
54 Spacer, speedometer drive gear
55 Bearing, output shaft drive gear, outer
56 Spacer, brake drum flange
57 Gasket, brake drum support
58 Support, hand brake
59 Seal, oil, output shaft bearing, rear

Exploded view of the New Process T-202 Transfer case
(© International Harvester Co.)

3. Position idler shift bar in four-wheel high drive position (shift bar to extreme rear in case). Simultaneously remove input shaft clutch gear and two-speed shift fork.
4. Remove cotter pin from nut at outer end of input shaft. Use a suitable flange holder to prevent shaft from turning; then break torque on nut. Remove the nut, flat washer and companion flange.
5. Move the input shaft and gear assembly toward rear of case by lightly tapping on the outer end of shaft. This will free shaft from bearing and permit shaft and power take-off gear to be removed.

   CAUTION: Hold input drive gear firmly against shoulder on shaft to retain roller bearings in bore of gear.

6. Place input shaft on a bench and remove drive gear, roller bearings, spacer and sliding clutch gear washer. Remove friction washer and washer spring from hub of power take-off gear.

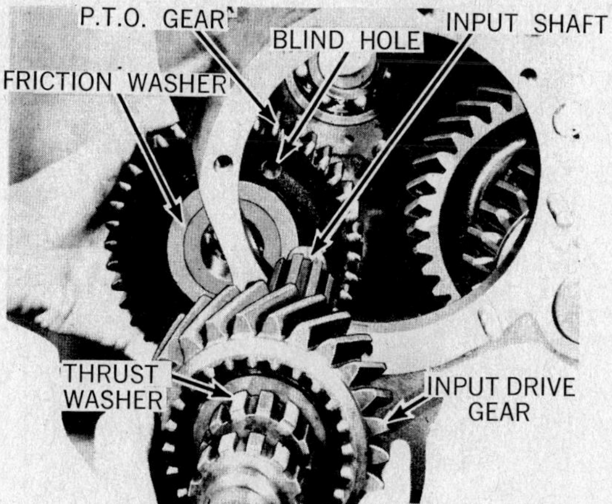

Removing the input shaft and P.T.O. gear from a New Process T-202 transfer case
(© International Harvester Co.)

7. Remove input shaft bearing retainer, gasket and bearing. If necessary, remove and discard oil seal from bearing retainer.

Front (Lower) Output Shaft

1. Remove cotter pin from nut at outer end of front output shaft. Use a suitable flange holder to prevent shaft from turning; then break torque on nut. Remove nut, flat washer and flange.
2. Remove hex head bolts and nuts attaching input shaft rear bearing retainer to case. Lightly tap on end of shaft, moving it toward rear of case to displace shoulder on rear bearing retainer. Remove drive gear and shaft.
3. Press drive gear rear bearing from retainer. Remove front bearing retainer and bearing. If lubricant leakage is evident at the retainer, remove oil seal and discard.

Idler Shift Bar and Gear

1. Remove roll pin securing fork to idler shift bar. Use a 5/32″ diameter steel rod to drive out pin. Withdraw shift bar and fork.

   NOTE: Spring tension on poppet ball will displace ball from case upon removing shift bar.
2. Remove shift bar interlock plunger and spring.
3. Remove roll pin from outer end of idler gear stationary shaft. Using a brass drift, drive the idler shaft toward rear of case. Remove shaft.
4. Remove idler gear rotating shaft assembly through the opening from which the rear output shaft assembly was removed. Place the gear assembly on a bench.
5. Remove thrust bearing and thrust bearing race at each end of rotating shaft. Remove individual roller bearing and spacer.

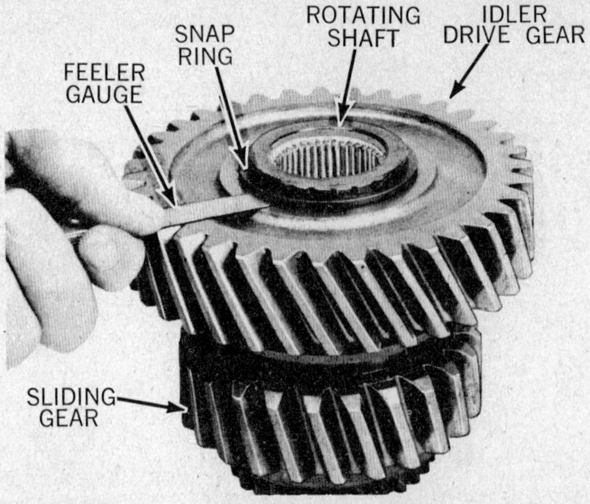

Checking the side clearance between the idler drive gear and retaining snap ring—New Process T-202 transfer case
(© International Harvester Co.)

6. Remove snap-ring; then separate idler drive gear and shaft. Remove sliding clutch gear.

Assembly

Lubricate all bearings, bushings, spline shafts and shift bar forks at their contact surfaces during assembly. This will provide initial lubrication and avoid possible damage when the transfer case is first operated.

Idler Shift Bar and Gear

1. Place the idler gear rotating shaft in a vertical position with the large splined gear end resting on bench.
2. Position sliding clutch gear on shaft with the groove which receives idler shift fork, facing upward.
3. Position drive gear on shaft so that gear internal splines engage splines on shaft.

   CAUTION: The long shoulder side of drive gear must face slid-clutch gear to provide clearance with the inside face of case.
4. Install snap-ring and check for proper side clearance with drive gear. This is accomplished by inserting a feeler gauge between the ring and gear. Three different thicknesses of snap-rings are available for obtaining proper clearance. Select and install proper size. Refer to Specifications for recommended snap-ring side clearance.

   NOTE: Snap-ring side clearance must be maintained to prevent possible ring breakage.
5. Coat the bore of idler gear rotating shaft with Lubriplate No. 110; then assemble roller bearings and spacer. Apply Lubriplate to thrust bearing and bearing race; then assemble at each end of idler rotating shaft. Carefully place rotating shaft assembly in case. Align shaft with opening in front and rear of case for installing the stationary shaft. Install stationary shaft, making certain not to disturb roller bearing arrangement in bore of rotating shaft. Tap the shaft lightly until seated. Install roll pin in shaft at front of case.
6. Position poppet spring and ball in case. Hold the spring and ball in a compressed position and insert idler shift bar at front side of case. Place idler shift fork in position on sliding gear (shoulder on fork toward front of case) and install on shift bar. Secure fork to shift bar with roll pin.

   NOTE: Side of shift bar employing only one detent must be facing upwards.

Input Shaft

1. Place the input drive gear on a bench and assemble roller bearings and spacer. Coat the gear bore with Lubriplate No. 110 to retain bearing rollers.
2. Install sliding clutch washer; then carefully position drive gear with bearings on shaft. Place friction washer on shaft

Removing the front output shaft assembly from a New Process T-202 transfer case (© International Harvester Co.)

next to drive gear, with the tang opposite gear.

3. Assemble friction washer spring on hub of power take-off gear.

   NOTE: Install spring on recess side of gear.

4. Assemble input shaft with drive gear and power take-off gear in case. Hold the drive gear firmly to clutch gear washer to keep roller bearings in place.

   NOTE: Rotate friction washer until tang engages blind hole in power take-off gear.

5. With the idler shift bar in four-wheel high drive position (shift bar to extreme rear of case), insert interlock plunger in case.
6. Install two-speed shift bar in case so that side of bar with the single detent is facing the idler shift bar. Install sliding clutch gear and two-speed shift bar fork. Install roll pin to secure fork to shift bar.
7. Install input shaft bearing.

   CAUTION: Movement of input shaft toward rear of case while installing bearing will permit rollers to become displaced from bore of drive gear.

8. Position bearing retainer to case and install hex head bolts finger tight. Do not torque bolts at this time since gasket thickness must be determined following installation of rear output shaft assembly.

Front (Lower) Output Shaft

1. Install front output shaft bearing in face of case.
2. Install front output shaft and drive gear.
3. Press drive gear rear bearing in retainer. Install bearing with stamped end of bearing resting on press. Position gasket and retainer at rear face of case. Install hex head bolts with lock washers and tighten securely.
4. Install new oil seal in bearing retainer. Assemble retainer to front face of case and install hex head bolts finger tight. Do not torque bolts at this time.

Rear (Upper) Output Shaft

1. Support rear output shaft bearing retainer in a press; then install shaft inner bearing flush with outer surface of retainer.
2. Place bearing retainer on a bench and assemble drive gear and shaft. Position speedometer drive gear and spacer on shaft. Assemble outer bearing on shaft and install in upper rear bearing retainer. Install hand brake drum spacer.
3. Install new oil seal in hand brake support. Install gasket and brake support to upper rear bearing retainer.
4. Position gasket to bearing retainer and install the rear output assembly on case.

Input and Front Output Shaft Bearing Adjustment

The fit of the input and front output shaft bearing retainer to their respective bearings is controlled by gasket thickness. To determine the correct thickness or number of gaskets required, measure the clearance between retainer and case with a feeler gauge. Select gasket(s) which will give a bearing retainer fit within specified limits. See Specifications. Remove the retainer; then install selected gasket(s) and retainer.

SPECIFICATIONS

BEARING CLEARANCE

Input and Front Output Shaft Bearings	0.003-0.006 in.
Gasket Thickness Available	0.009-0.011 in.
	0.0135-0.0165 in.

SNAP RING

Side Clearance	0.007-0.013 in.
Thickness Available	0.092-0.094 in.
	0.095-0.097 in.
	0.098-0.100 in.

POPPET BALL SPRING

Free Length	1.0 in.
Pressure @ 21/32"	30 Lbs.

TORQUE LIMITS

Flange Nut	Minimum 125 ft lbs.

New Process Model 205

Description

The New Process Model 205 transfer case is a two-speed gearbox mounted between the main transmission and the rear axle. The gearbox transmits power from the transmission and engine to the front and rear driving axles.

Disassembly

Transfer Case

1. Clean the exterior of the case.
2. Remove the nuts from the universal joint flanges.
3. Remove the front output shaft rear bearing retainer, front bearing retainer and drive flange.
4. Tap the front output shaft assembly from the case with a soft hammer. Remove the sliding clutch, front output high gear, washer and bearing from the case.
5. Remove the rear output shaft

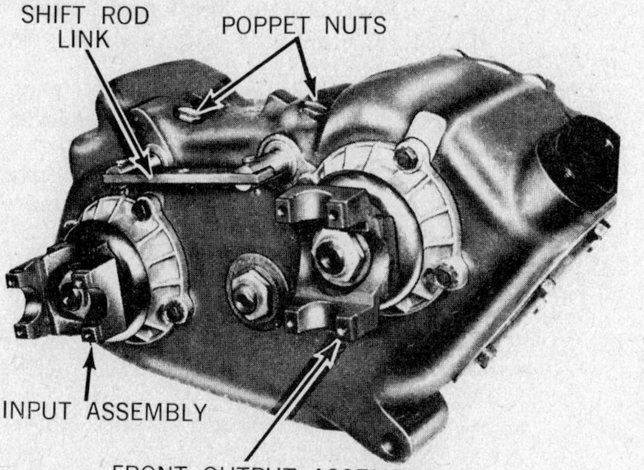

Front view of a New Process 205 transfer case. This unit would have a short driveshaft connected to the input shaft. Others are bolted directly to the transmission.
(© International Harvester Co.)

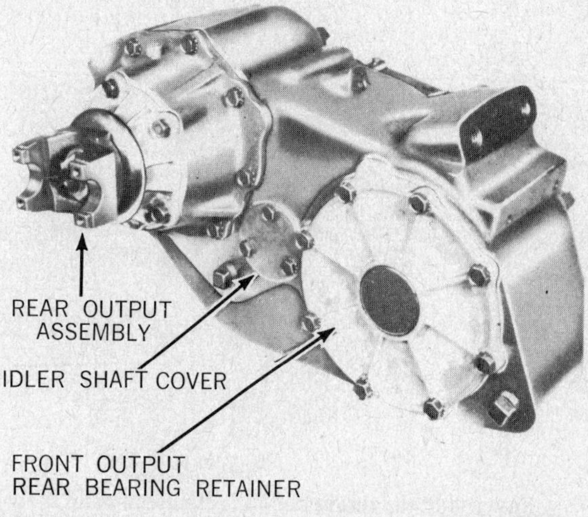

Rear view of a New Process 205 transfer case (© G.M.C.)

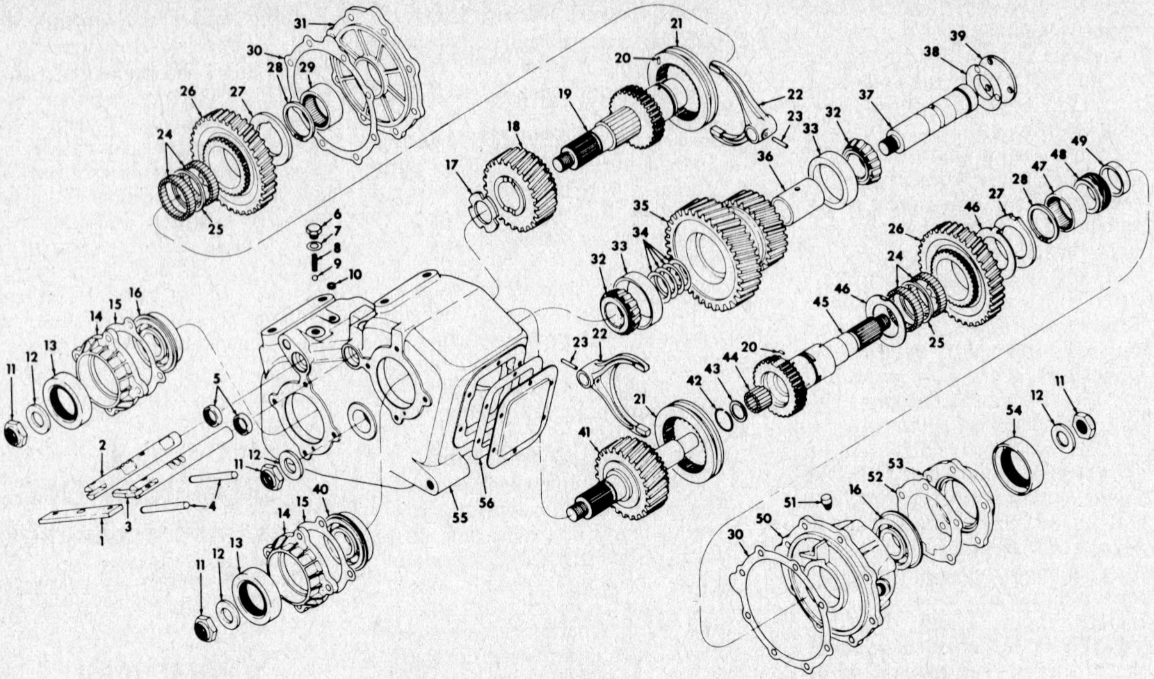

Exploded view of a New Process 205 transfer case (© International Harvester Co.)

1. Shift lever link
2. Bar
3. Bar
4. Plunger
5. Seal
6. Screw
7. Gasket
8. Spring
9. Ball
10. Plug
11. Nut
12. Washer
13. Seal
14. Retainer
15. Gasket
16. Bearing
17. Washer
18. Gear
19. Shaft
20. Pin
21. Clutch
22. Fork
23. Pin
24. Bearing
25. Spacer
26. Gear
27. Washer
28. Ring
29. Bearing
30. Gasket
31. Retainer
32. Cone
33. Cup
34. Shim set
35. Gear
36. Spacer
37. Shaft
38. Gasket
39. Cover
40. Bearing
41. Shaft
42. Ring
43. Washer
44. Bearing
45. Gear
46. Washer
47. Bearing
48. Gear
49. Spacer
50. Retainer
51. Breather
52. Gasket
53. Retainer
54. Seal
55. Case
56. Gasket

housing attaching bolts and remove the housing, output shaft, bearing retainer and speedometer gear.

6. Slide the rear output shaft from the housing.

   NOTE: Be careful not to lose the 15 needle bearings that will be loose when the rear output shaft is removed.

7. Drive the two 1/4 in. shift rail pin access hole plugs into the transfer case with a punch and hammer.
8. Remove the two shift rail detent nuts and springs from the case. Use a magnet to remove the two detent balls.
9. Position both shift rails in neutral and remove the shift fork retaining roll pins with a long punch.
10. Remove the clevis pin from one shift rail and rail link.
11. Remove the range shift rail first, then the 4WD shift rail.
12. Remove the shift forks and and sliding clutch from the case. Remove the input shaft bearing retainer, bearing and shaft.
13. Remove the cup plugs and rail pins, if they were driven out, from the case.
14. Remove the locknut from the idler gear shaft.
15. Remove the idler gear shaft rear cover.
16. Remove the idler gear shaft, using a soft hammer and a drift.
17. Roll the idler gear assembly to the front output shaft hole and remove the assembly from the case.

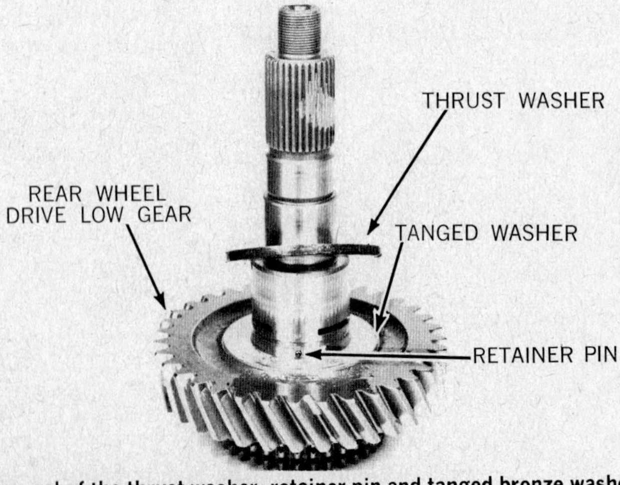

Removal of the thrust washer, retainer pin and tanged bronze washer from the rear output shaft assembly on a New Process 205 transfer case
(© International Harvester Co.)

Rear Output Shaft and Yoke

1. Loosen rear output shaft yoke nut.
2. Remove shaft housing bolts, then remove the housing and retainer assembly.
3. Remove retaining nut and yoke from the shaft, then remove the shaft assembly.
4. Remove and discard snap ring.
5. Remove thrust washer and pin.
6. Remove tanged bronze washer. Remove gear needle bearings, spacer and second row of needle bearings.
7. Remove tanged bronze thrust washer.
8. Remove pilot rollers, retainer ring and washer.
9. Remove oil seal retainer, ball bearing, speedometer gear and spacer. Discard gaskets.

Rear output shaft assembly removed; Removal of the bearing, spacer, and speedometer gear—New Process 205 transfer case
(© International Harvester Co.)

10. Press out bearing.
11. Remove oil seal from the retainer.

Front Output Shaft

1. Remove lock nut, washer and yoke.
2. Remove attaching bolts and front bearing retainer.
3. Remove rear bearing retainer attaching bolts.
4. Tap output shaft with a soft-faced hammer and remove shaft, gear assembly and rear bearing retainer.
5. Remove sliding clutch, gear, washer and bearing from output high gear.
6. Remove sliding clutch from the high output gear; then remove gear, washer and bearing.
7. Remove gear retaining snap-ring from the shaft, using large snap-ring picks. Discard ring.
8. Remove thrust washer and pin.
9. Remove gear, needle bearings and spacer.
10. Replace rear bearing, if necessary.

CAUTION: Always replace the bearing and retainer as an assembly. Do not try to press a new bearing into an old retainer.

Shift Rails and Forks

1. Remove the two poppet nuts, springs, and using a magnet, the poppet balls.
2. Remove cup plugs on top of case, using a ¼″ punch.
3. Position both shift rails in neutral, then remove fork pins with a long handled screw extractor.
4. Remove clevis pins and shift rail link.
5. Lower shift rails; upper rail first and then lower.
6. Remove shift forks and sliding clutch.
7. Remove the front output high gear, washer and bearing. Remove the shift rail cup plugs.

Input Shaft

1. Remove snap-ring in front of bearing. Tap shaft out rear of case and bearing out front of case, using a soft-faced hammer or mallet.
2. Tilt case up on power take-off and remove the two interlock pins from inside.

Idler Gear

1. Remove idler gear shaft nut.
2. Remove rear cover.
3. Tap out idler gear shaft, using a soft-faced hammer and a drift approximately the same diameter as the shaft.
4. Remove idler gear through the front output shaft hole.
5. Remove two bearing cups from the idler gear.

Assembly

Transfer Case

1. Assemble the idler shaft gears, bearings, spacer and shims, and bearings on a dummy shaft tool and install the assembly into the case through the front output shaft bore, large end first.
2. Install the idler shaft from the large bore side, using a soft hammer to drive it through the bearings, spacer, gears, and shims.
3. Install a washer and new locknut on the end of the idler shaft. Check to make sure the idler gear rotates freely. Tighten the locknut to specification.
4. Install the idler shaft cover with a new gasket so the flat side faces the rear bearing retainer of the front output shaft. Install and tighten the two retaining screws to the proper torque.
5. Install the interlock pins into the interlock bore through the front of the output shaft opening.
6. Start the 4WD shift rail into the front of the case, solid end of the rail first, with the detent notches facing up.
7. Position the shift fork onto the shift rail with the long end facing inward. Push the rail through the fork and into the Neutral position.
8. Position the input shaft and bearing in the case.
9. Start the range shift rail into the case from the front, with the detent notches facing up.
10. Position the sliding clutch to the shift fork. Place the sliding clutch on the input shaft and align the fork with the shift rail. Push the rail through the fork into the Neutral position.
11. Install the roll pins that lock the shift forks to the shift rails with a long punch.
12. Position the front wheel drive high gear and its thrust washer in the case. Position the sliding clutch in the shift fork. Shift the rail and fork into the front wheel drive (4WD-Hi) position ,while at the same time, meshing the clutch with the mating teeth on the front wheel drive high gear.
13. Align the thrust washer, high gear and sliding clutch with the bearing bore in the case and insert the front output shaft and low gear into the high gear assembly.
14. Install a new seal in the front bearing retainer of the front output shaft, and install the bearing and retainer and new gasket in the case. Tighten the bearing retainer cap screws to the proper torque.
15. Lubricate the roller bearing in the front output shaft rear bearing retainer, which is the aluminum cover, and install it over the front output shaft and to the case. Install and tighten the retaining screws to the proper torque.
16. Move the range shift rail to the High position and install the rear output shaft and retainer assembly to the housing and input shaft. Use one or two new gaskets, as required, to adjust the clearance on the input shaft pilot. Install the rear output shaft housing retaining bolts and tighten them to specification.
17. Using a punch and sealing compound, install the shift rail pin access plugs.
18. Install the fill and drain plugs and the cross-link clevis pin.

Idler Gear

1. Press the two bearing cups in the idler gear.
2. Assemble the two bearing cones, spacer, shims and idler gear on a dummy shaft, with bore facing up. Check end-play.
3. Install idler gear assembly (with dummy shaft) into the case, large end first, through the front output shaft bore.
4. Install idler shaft from large bore side, driving it through with a soft-faced hammer or mallet.
5. Install washer and new locknut. Check for free rotation and measure end-play. Torque locknut to specifications.
6. Install idler shaft cover and new gasket. Torque cover bolts to specifications.

NOTE: Flat side of cover must be positioned towards front output shaft rear cover.

Shift Rails and Forks

1. Press the two rail seals into the case.

NOTE: Install seals with metal lip outward.

2. Install interlock pins from inside case.
3. Insert slotted end of front output drive shift rail (with poppet notches up) into back of case.
4. While pushing rail through to neutral position, install shift fork (long end inward).
5. Install input shaft and bearing into case.
6. Install end of range rail (with poppet notches up) into front of case.
7. Install sliding clutch on fork, then place over input shaft in case.
8. Push range rail, while engaging sliding clutch and fork, through to neutral position.
9. Drive new lockpins into forks through holes at top of case.

NOTE: Tilt case on power take-off opening to install range rail lockpin.

Front Output Shaft and Gear

1. Install two rows of needle bearings in the front low output gear and retain with grease.

   NOTE: Each row consists of 32 needle bearings and the two rows are separated by a spacer.
2. Position front output shaft in a soft-jaw vise, with spline end down. Place front low gear over shaft with clutch gear facing down; then install thrust washer pin, thrust washer and new snap-ring.

   NOTE: Position snap ring gap opposite the thrust washer pin.
3. Place front drive high gear and washer in case. Install sliding clutch in the shift fork, then put fork and rail into 4-High position, meshing front drive high gear and clutch teeth.
4. Align washer, high gear and sliding clutch and bearing bore. Insert front output shaft and low gear assembly through the high gear assembly.
5. Install front output bearing and retainer with a new seal in the case.
6. Clean and grease rollers in front output rear bearing retainer. Install on case with one gasket and bolts coated with sealant. Torque bolts to specifications.
7. Install front output yoke, washer and locknut. Torque locknut to specifications.

Rear Output Shaft

1. Install two rows of needle bearings into the output low gear, retaining them with grease.

   NOTE: Each row consists of 32 needle bearings and the two rows are separated by a spacer.
2. Install thrust washer (with tang down in clutch gear groove) onto the rear output shaft.
3. Install output low gear onto shaft with clutch teeth facing downward.
4. Install thrust washer over gear with tab pointing up and away. Install washer pin.
5. Install large thrust washer over shaft and pin. Turn washer until tab fits into slot located approximately 90° away from pin.
6. Install snap-ring and measure shaft end-play.
7. Grease pilot bore and install needle bearings.

   NOTE: There are 15 pilot needle bearings.
8. Install thrust washer and new snap-ring in pilot bore.
9. Press new bearing into retainer housing.
10. Install housing on output shaft assembly.
11. Install spacer and speedometer gear. Install rear bearing.
12. Install rear bearing retainer seal.
13. Install bearing retainer assembly on housing, using one or two gaskets to achieve specified clearance. Torque attaching bolts to specifications.
14. Install yoke, washer and locknut on output shaft.
15. Position range rail in high, then install output shaft and retainer assembly on case. Torque housing bolts to specifications.

Case

1. Install power take-off cover and gasket. Torque attaching bolts to specifications.
2. Install cup plugs at rail pin holes.

   NOTE: After installing, seal the cup plugs.
3. Install drain and filler plugs. Torque to specifications.
4. Install shift rail cross link, clevis pins and lock pins.

SPECIFICATIONS

END PLAY (IN.)

Idler Gear	0.000-0.002 in.
Rear Output Shaft	0.002-0.027 in.

TORQUE LIMITS (FT. LBS.)

Idler Shaft Locknut	150
Idler Shaft Cover	20
Front Output Shaft Front Bearing Retainer	30-35
Front Output Shaft Yoke Locknut	130-150
Rear Output Shaft Bearing Retainer and Housing	30-35
Rear Output Shaft Yoke Locknut	130-150
P.T.O. Cover	15
Front Output Shaft Rear Bearing Retainer	30-35
Filler and Drain Plugs	30
Case to Frame	130
Case to Adapter	25
Adapter Mount	75
Case Bracket to Frame	
Upper	30
Lower	65
Adapter to Transmission	
Manual Transmission	30-35
Automatic Transmission	30-35

New Process 208

The 208 is a part-time unit with a two piece aluminum housing. On the front case half, the front output shaft, front input shaft, four wheel drive indicator switch and shift lever assembly are located. On the rear case half, the rear output shaft, bearing retainer and drain and fill plugs are located.

Disassembly

1. Drain the fluid from the case.
2. Remove the attaching nuts from the front and rear output yokes. Remove the yokes and sealing washers.
3. Remove the four bolts and separate the rear bearing retainer from the rear case half.

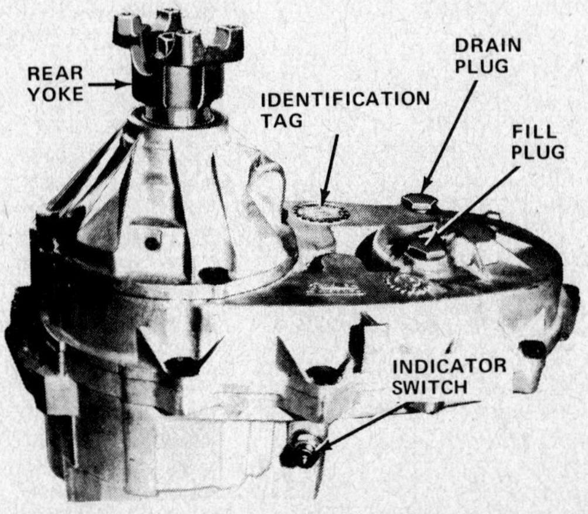

208 Indicator switch identification tag and drain and fill plug locations

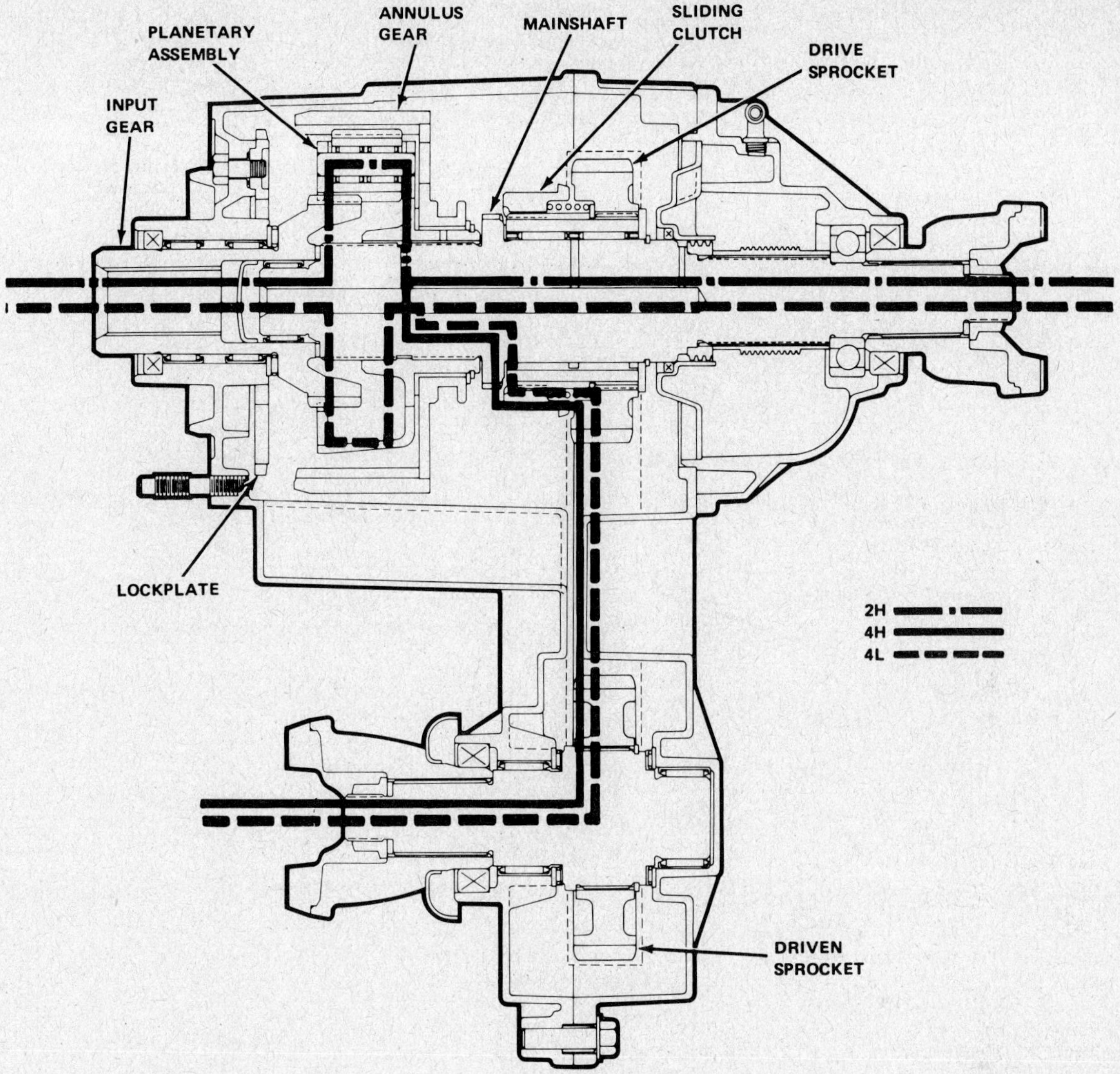

208 power flow

4. Remove the retaining ring, speedometer drive gear nylon oil pump housing, and oil pump gear from the rear output shaft.
5. Remove the eleven bolts and separate the case halves by inserting a screw driver in the pry slots on the case.
6. Remove the magnetic chip collector from the bottom of the rear case half.
7. Remove the thick thrust washer, thrust bearing and thin thrust washer from the front output shaft assembly.
8. Remove the drive chain by pushing the front input shaft inward and by angling the gear slightly to obtain adequate clearance to remove the chain.
9. Remove the output shaft from the front case half and slide the thick thrust washer, thrust bearing and thin thrust washer off the output side of the front output shaft.
10. Remove the screw, poppet spring and check ball from the front case half.
11. Remove the four wheel drive indicator switch and washer from the front case half.
12. Position the front case half on its face and lift out the rear output shaft, sliding clutch and clutch shift fork and spring.
13. Place a shop towel on the shift rail. Clamp the rail with a vise grip pliers so that they lay between the rail and the case edge. Position a pry bar under the pliers and pry out the shift rail.
14. Remove the snap ring and thrust washer from the planetary gear set assembly in the front case half.

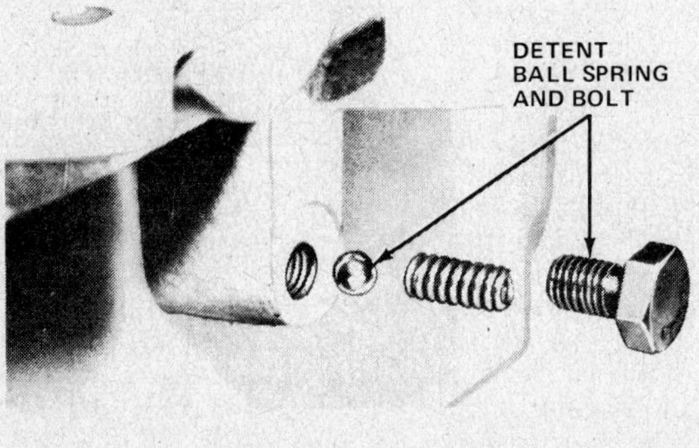

Detent ball, spring and bolt removal

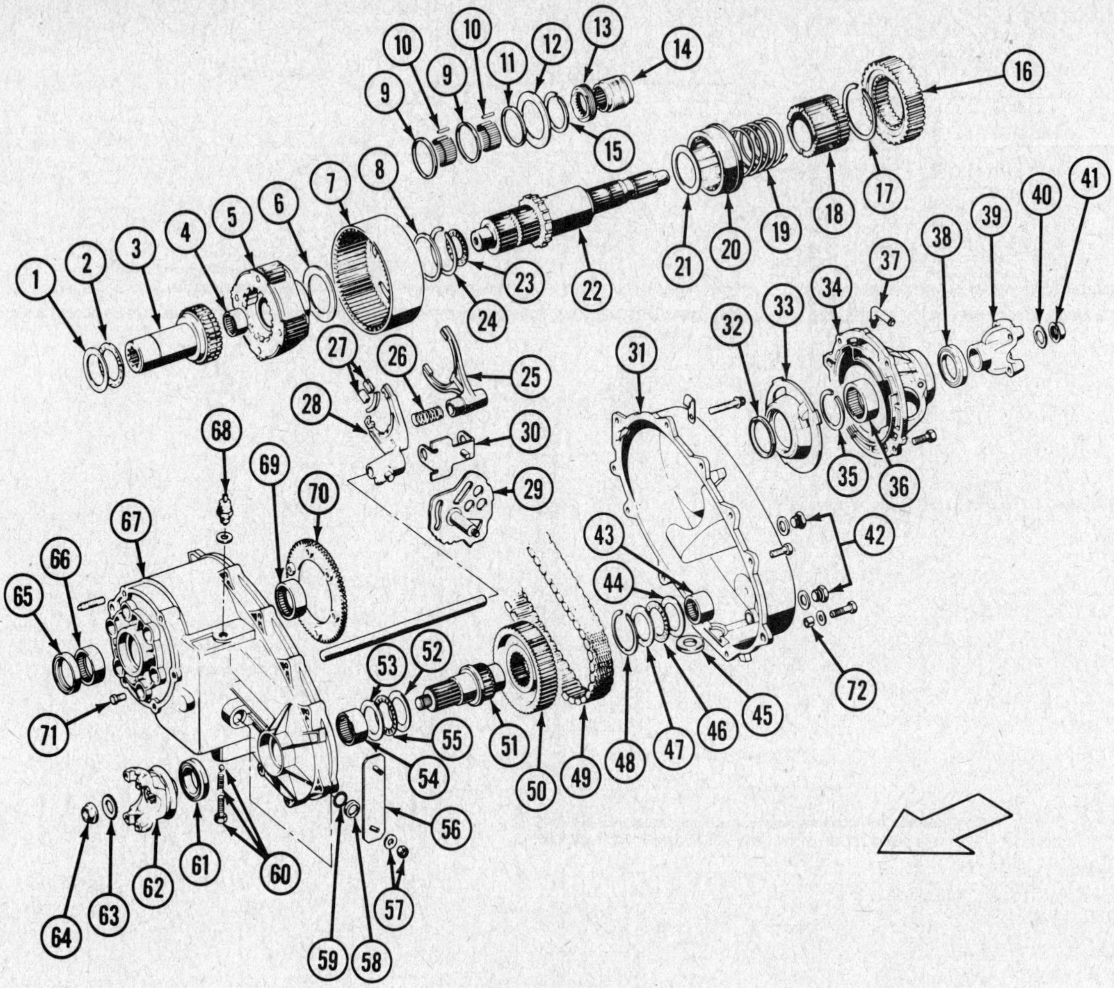

208 exploded view

1 Input gear thrust washer
2 Input gear thrust bearing
3 Input gear
4 Mainshaft pilot bearing
5 Planetary assembly
6 Planetary thrust washer
7 Annulus gear
8 Annulus gear thrust washer
9 Needle bearing spacers
10 Mainshaft needle bearings (120)
11 Needle bearing spacer
12 Thrust washer
13 Oil pump
14 Speedometer gear
15 Drive sprocket retaining ring
16 Drive sprocket
17 Sprocket carrier stop ring
18 Sprocket carrier
19 Clutch spring
20 Sliding clutch
21 Thrust washer
22 Mainshaft
23 Mainshaft thrust bearing
24 Annulus gear retaining ring
25 Mode fork
26 Mode fork spring
27 Range fork inserts
28 Range fork
29 Range sector
30 Mode fork bracket
31 Rear case
32 Seal
33 Pump housing
34 Rear retainer
35 Rear output bearing
36 Bearing snap ring
37 Vent tube
38 Rear seal
39 Rear yoke
40 Yoke seal washer
41 Yoke nut
42 Drain and fill plugs
43 Front output shaft rear bearing
44 Front output shaft rear thrust bearing race (thick)
45 Case magnet
46 Front output shaft rear thrust bearing
47 Front output shaft rear thrust bearing race (thin)
48 Driven sprocket retaining ring
49 Drive chain
50 Driven sprocket
51 Front output shaft
52 Front output shaft front thrust bearing race (thin)
53 Front output shaft front thrust bearing race (thick)
54 Front output shaft front bearing
55 Front output shaft front thrust bearing
56 Operating lever
57 Washer and locknut
58 Range sector shaft seal retainer
59 Range sector shaft seal
60 Detent ball, spring and retainer bolt
61 Front seal
62 Front yoke
63 Yoke seal washer
64 Yoke nut
65 Input gear oil seal
66 Input gear front bearing
67 Front case
68 Lock mode indicator switch and washer
69 Input gear rear bearing
70 Lockplate
71 Lockplate bolts
72 Case alignment dowels

15. Remove the annulus gear assembly and thrust washer from the front case half.
16. Lift the planetary gear assembly from the front case half.
17. Lift out the thrust bearing, sun gear, thrust bearing and thrust washer.
18. Remove the six bolts and lift the gear locking plate from the front case half.
19. Remove the nut retaining the external shift lever and washer. Press the shift control shaft inward and remove the shift selector plate and washer from the case.
20. From the rear output shaft, remove the snap ring and thrust washer retaining the chain drive sprocket and slide the sprocket from the drive gear.
21. Remove the retaining ring from the sprocket carrier gear.
22. Carefully slide the sprocket carrier gear from the rear output shaft. Remove the two rows of

Driven sprocket retaining snap ring removal

Front output shaft rear thrust bearing removal

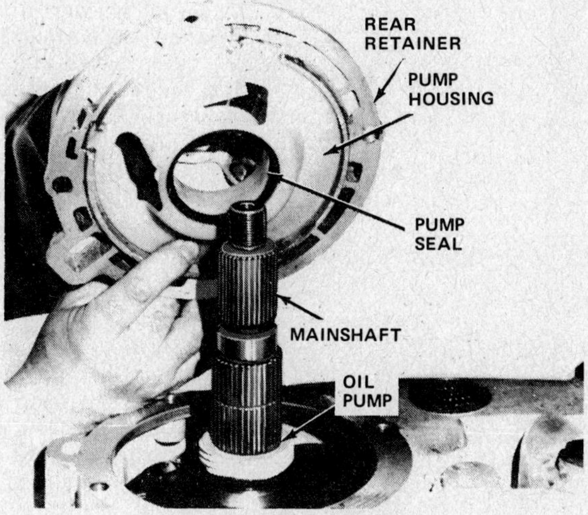

Rear retainer removal

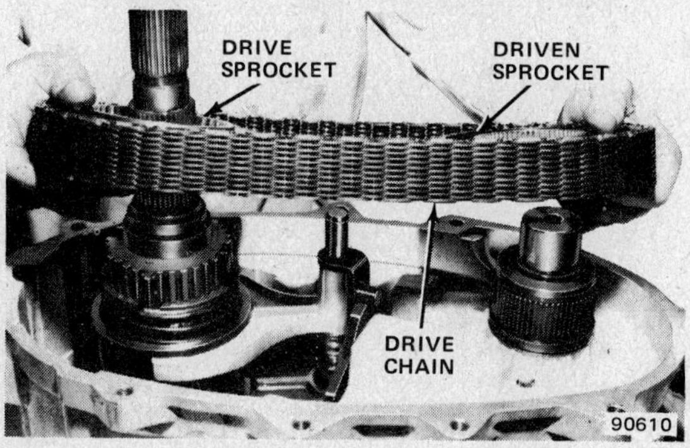

Sprocket and chain removal

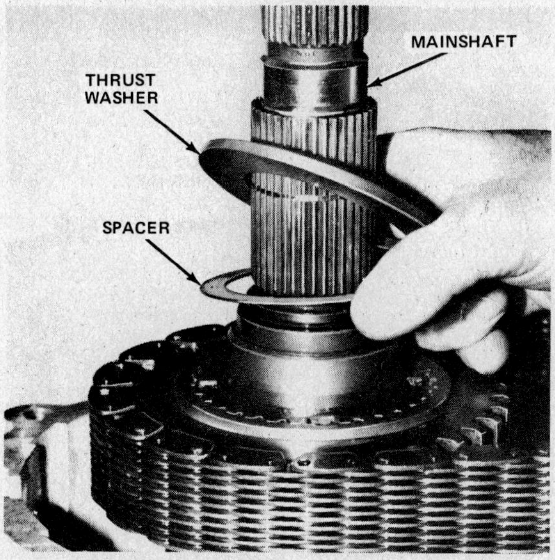

Drive sprocket thrust washer and spacer removal

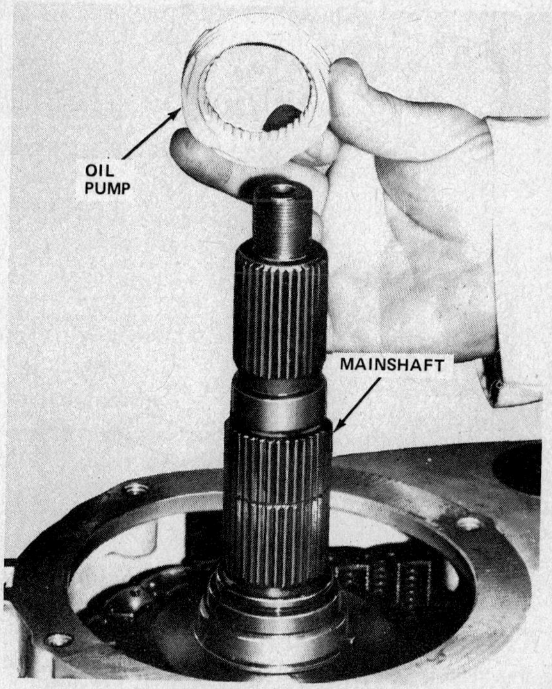

Oil pump removal

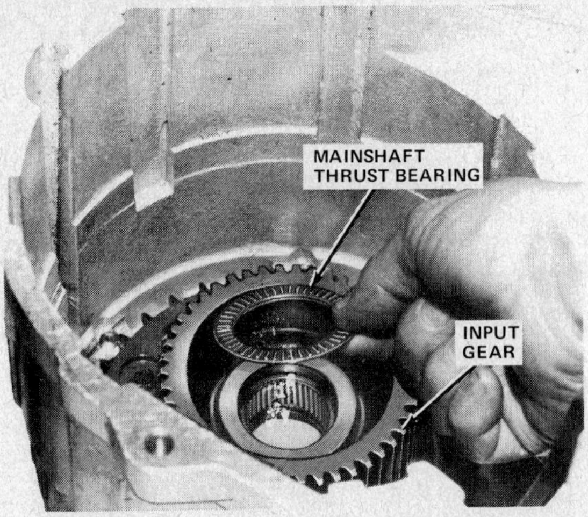

Mainshaft thrust bearing and input gear

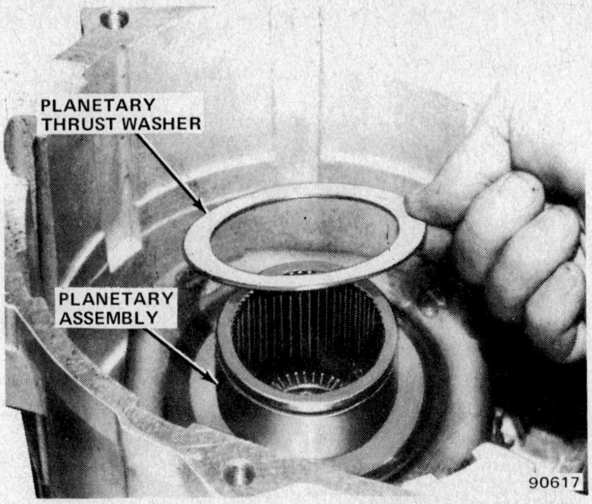

Planetary thrust washer and planetary assembly

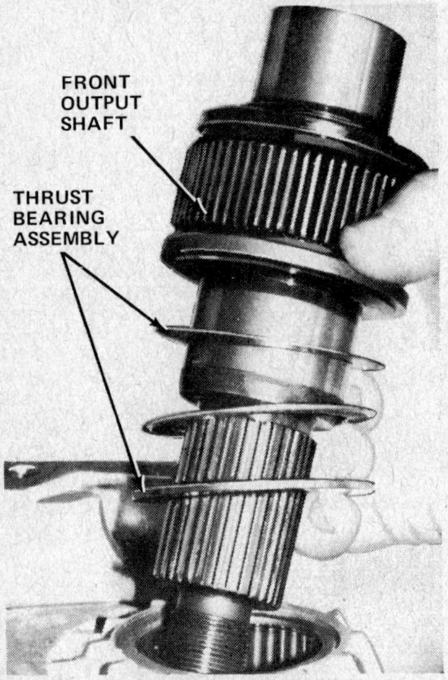

Front output shaft and front thrust bearing assembly removal

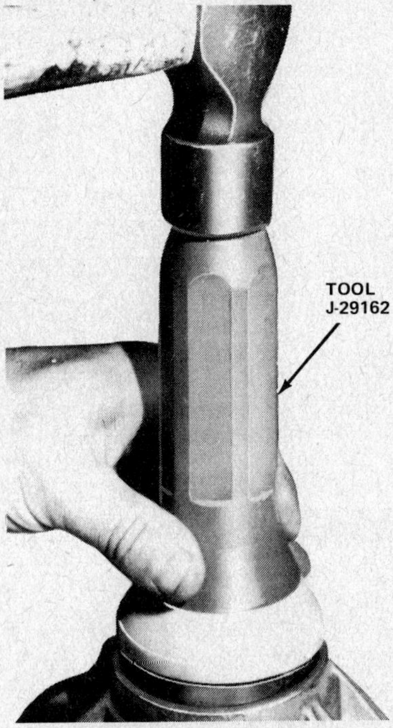

Rear seal installation

60 loose needle bearings. Remove the three separator rings from the output shaft.

Assembly

1. Slide the thrust washer against the gear on the rear output shaft.
2. Place the three space rings in position on the rear output shaft. Liberally coat the shaft with petroleum jelly and install the two rows (60 each) of needle bearings in position on the rear output shaft.
3. Carefully slide the sprocket gear carrier over the needle bearings. Be careful not to dislodge any of the needles.
4. Install the retaining ring on the sprocket gear.
5. Slide the chain drive sprocket onto the sprocket carrier gear.
6. Install the thrust washer and snap ring on the rear output shaft.
7. Install the shift selector plate and washer through the front of the case.
8. Place the shift lever assembly on the shift control shaft and torque the nut to 14-20 ft-lb.

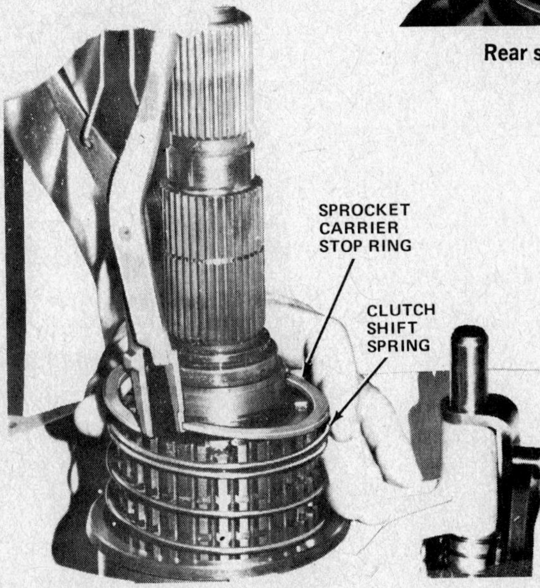

Sprocket carrier clutch ring and spring removal

Input gear thrust bearing and race removal

9. Place the locking plate in the front case half and torque the bolts to 25-35 ft-lb.
10. Place the thrust bearing and washer over the input shaft of the sun gear. Insert the input shaft through the front case half from the inside and insert the thrust bearing.
11. Install the planetary gear assembly so the fixed plate and planetary gears engage the sun gear.
12. Slide the annulus gear and clutch assembly with the shift fork assembly engaged, over the hub of the planetary gear assembly. The shift fork pin must engage the slot in the shift selector plate. Install the thrust washer and snap ring.
13. Position the shift rail through the shift fork hub in the front case. Tap lightly with a soft hammer to seat the rail in the hole.
14. Position the sliding clutch shift fork on the shift rail and place the sliding clutch and clutch shift spring into the front case half. Slide the rear output shaft into the case.
15. On the output side of the front output shaft, assemble the thin thrust washer, thrust bearing, and thick thrust washer and partially insert the front output shaft into the case.
16. Place the drive chain on the rear output shaft drive gear. Insert the rear output shaft into the front case half and engage the drive chain on the front output shaft drive gear. Push the front output shaft into position in the case.

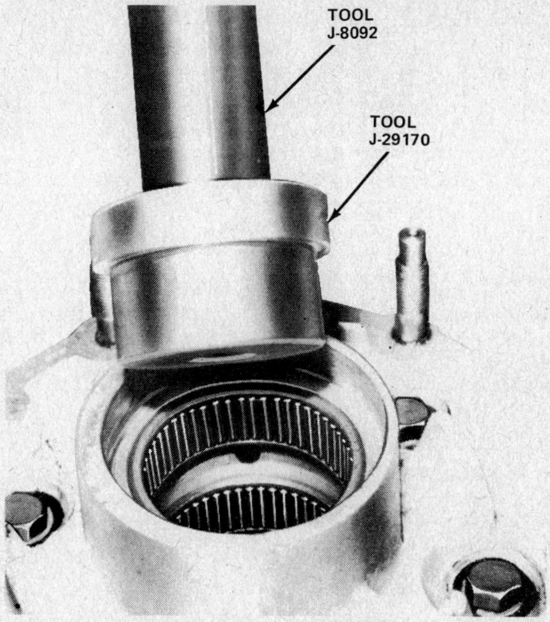

Input gear bearing removal

17. Assemble the thin thrust washer, thrust bearing and thick thrust washer on the inside of the front output shaft drive gear.
18. Position the magnetic chip collector into position in the front case half.
19. Place a bead of RTV sealant completely around the face of the front case half and assemble the case halves being careful that the shift rail and forward output shafts are properly retained.
20. Alternately tighten the bolts to 20-25 ft-lb.
21. Slide the oil pump gear over the input shaft and slide the spacer collar into position.
22. Engage the speedometer drive gear onto the rear output shaft and slide the retaining ring into position.
23. Use petroleum jelly to hold the nylon oil pump housing in position at the rear bearing retainer. Apply a bead of RTV sealant around the mounting surface of the retainer and carefully position the retainer assembly over the output shaft and onto the rear case half. The retainer must be installed so that the vent hole

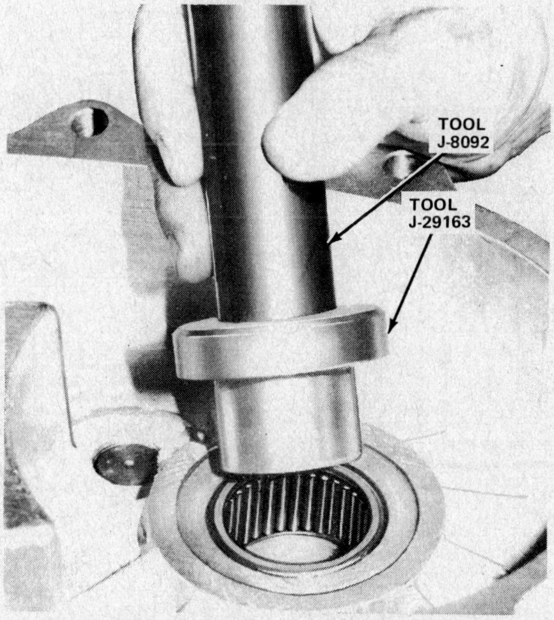

Front output shaft rear bearing installation

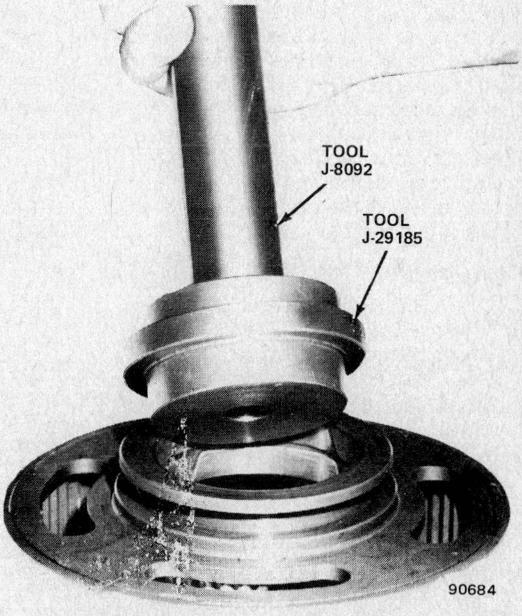

Annulus gear bushing installation

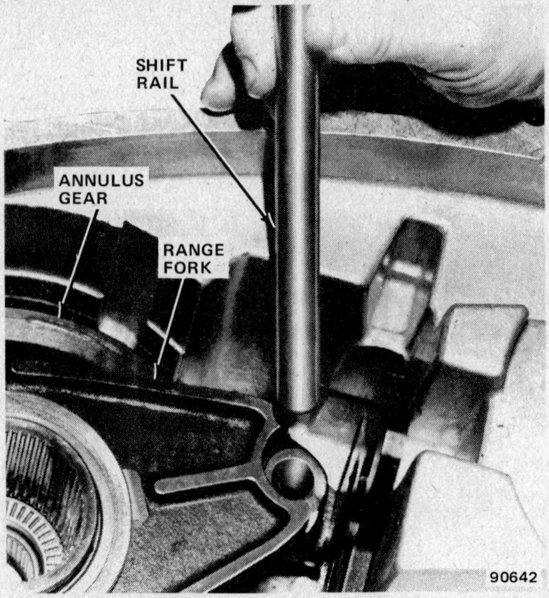

Annulus gear and shift rail installation

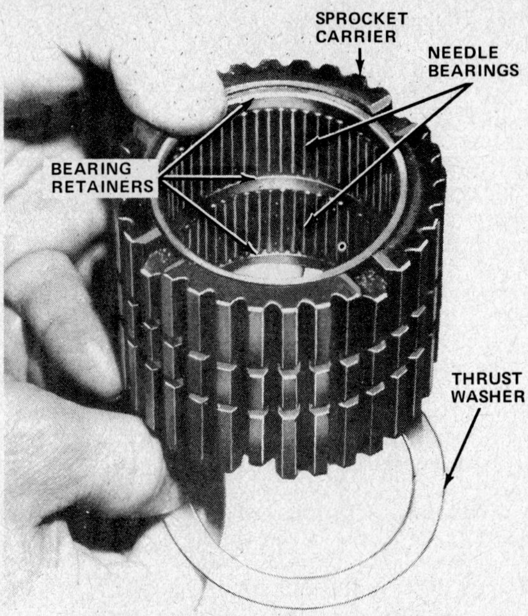

Assembling sprocket carrier components

is vertical when the case is installed.

24. Torque the retainer bolts alternately to 20-25 ft-lb.
25. Place a new thrust washer under each yoke and install the yokes on their respective shafts. Place the oil slinger under the front yoke. Torque the nuts to 90-130 ft-lb.
26. Install the poppet ball, spring and screw in the front case half. Torque the screw to 20-25 ft-lb.
27. Install the 4wd indicator switch and washer and tighten to 15-20 ft-lb.
28. Fill the unit with 6 pints of Ford CJ fluid or Dexron II.

New Process 219

Introduced in the 1980 model year of Jeep® vehicles as the Quadra-Trac®, this is a full-time unit. The 4wd mode is fully differentiated in 4H only. The 4L and Lock ranges are undifferentiated. The 4H differentiation is accomplished by a torque biasing viscous coupling and an open differential connected to the coupling. Two drive sprockets and an interconnecting drive chain are used to distribute input torque.

Disassembly

1. Drain the lubricant from the case.
2. Remove the front and rear output shaft yokes and discard the yoke seal washers and yoke nuts.
3. Mark the rear retainer and rear case for an alignment reference.
4. Unbolt and remove the rear retainer. If necessary, use a soft mallet to loosen the retainer. Under no circumstances should the retainer be pried off.
5. Remove the differential shims and speedometer drive gear from the rear output shaft. Mark the shims for reference.

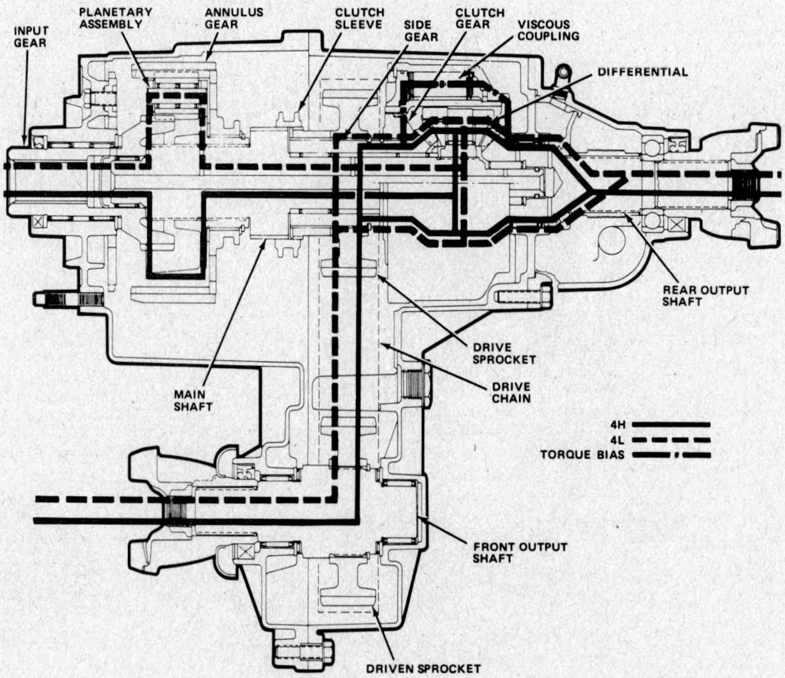

219 Quadra-Trac power flow

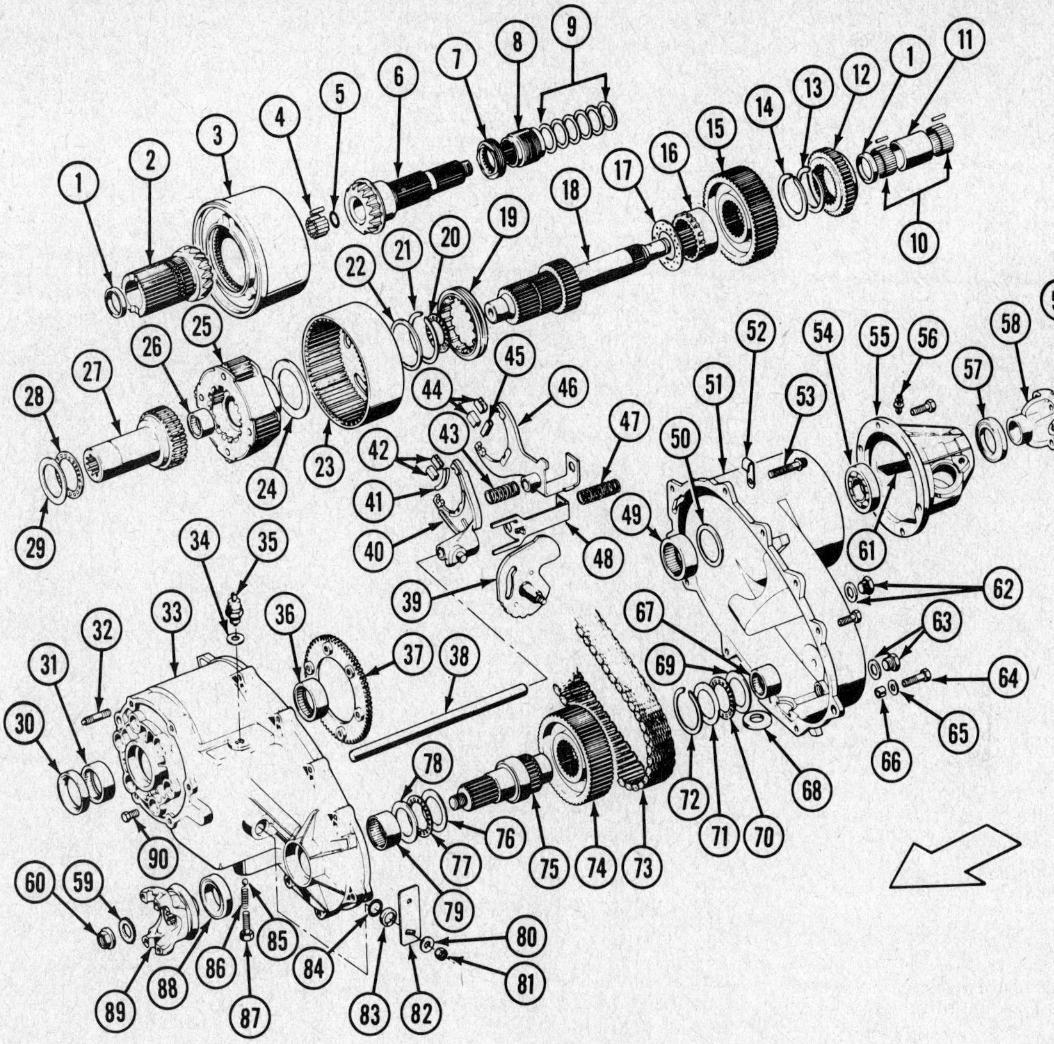

219 exploded view

1 Mainshaft rear bearing spacer—short (2)
2 Side gear
3 Viscous coupling and differential assembly
4 Mainshaft rear pilot roller bearings (15)
5 Mainshaft O-ring
6 Rear output shaft
7 Oil pump
8 Speedometer gear
9 Differential end play shims (selective)
10 Mainshaft needle bearings (82)
11 Mainshaft rear bearing spacer
12 Clutch gear
13 Clutch gear locating ring
14 Drive sprocket locating ring
15 Drive sprocket
16 Side gear clutch
17 Mainshaft thrust washer
18 Mainshaft
19 Clutch sleeve
20 Mainshaft thrust bearing
21 Annulus gear retaining ring
22 Annulus gear thrust washer
23 Annulus gear
24 Planetary thrust washer
25 Planetary assembly
26 Mainshaft front pilot bearing
27 Input gear
28 Input gear thrust bearing
29 Input gear thrust bearing race
30 Input gear oil seal
31 Input gear front bearing
32 Front case mounting stud (6)
33 Front case
34 Lock mode indicator switch gasket
35 Lock mode indicator switch
36 Input gear rear bearing
37 Low range lockplate
38 Shift rail
39 Range sector
40 Range fork
41 Range fork insert
42 Range fork pads
43 Mode fork spring
44 Mode fork pads
45 Mode fork insert
46 Mode fork
47 Shift rail spring
48 Mode fork bracket
49 Rear output shaft bearing
50 Rear output shaft bearing seal
51 Rear case
52 Wiring clip
53 Spline bolt
54 Rear output bearing
55 Rear retainer
56 Vent
57 Output shaft oil seal
58 Rear Yoke
59 Yoke seal washer
60 Yoke locknut
61 Vent chamber seal
62 Fill plug and gasket
63 Drain plug and gasket
64 Rear case bolt
65 Washer (2)
66 Case alignment dowel
67 Front output shaft rear bearing
68 Magnet
69 Front output shaft rear thrust bearing race (thick)
70 Front output shaft rear thrust bearing
71 Front output shaft rear thrust bearing race (thin)
72 Driven sprocket retaining snap ring
73 Drive chain
74 Driven sprocket
75 Front output shaft
76 Front output shaft front thrust bearing race (thin)
77 Front output shaft front thrust bearing
78 Front output shaft front thrust bearing race (thick)
79 Front output shaft front bearing
80 Washer
81 Locknut
82 Operating lever
83 Range sector shaft seal retainer
84 Range sector shaft seal
85 Detent ball
86 Detent spring
87 Detent retaining bolt
88 Front output shaft seal
89 Front yoke
90 Lockplate bolts

Differential shim, speedometer gear and oil pump

6. Remove the rear output bearing snap ring and remove the bearing from the retainer using a soft mallet.

   NOTE: The rear output bearing has one side shielded. Note this for reassembly.

7. Remove the rear output shaft seal from the retainer using a screwdriver or punch.
8. Position the front case assembly on wood blocks. The blocks should have V cuts made in them for more positive support of the case.
9. Remove the case halve bolts. The case halves may be pried apart using a screwdriver in the notches provided at the case ends.

   NOTE: The two case end bolts have flat washers and alignment dowels. Note their location for assembly.

10. Remove the rear output shaft and viscous coupling as an assembly. Tap the shaft with a plastic mallet if necessary.
11. Remove the O-ring seal and pilot roller bearings from the mainshaft.
12. Remove the rear output shaft from the viscous coupling.
13. Remove the shift rail spring from the rail.
14. Remove the plastic oil pump from the shaft bore in the rear case. Note the pump position for assembly reference. The end with the recess must face the shaft bore when installed.
15. Remove the rear output shaft bearing seal from the case. A screwdriver may be used to pry it out.
16. Remove the front output shaft thrust bearing assembly. Remove the thick washer, bearing and thin washer.
17. Remove the driven sprocket retaining snap ring.
18. Remove the drive sprocket, drive chain, driven sprocket, side gear clutch and clutch gear as an assembly. Place the assembly on a workbench and mark the components for assembly.
19. Remove the needle bearings and spacers from the mainshaft and side gear bore. A total of 82 bearings and three spacers is used.
20. Remove the side gear/clutch gear assembly from the drive sprocket. Remove two snap rings and remove the clutch gear from the side gear.
21. Remove the side gear clutch, mainshaft thrust washer and remaining mainshaft needle bearing spacer.
22. Remove the front output shaft and shaft thrust bearing assembly. Note the installation sequence of the bearing assembly.
23. Remove the front output shaft

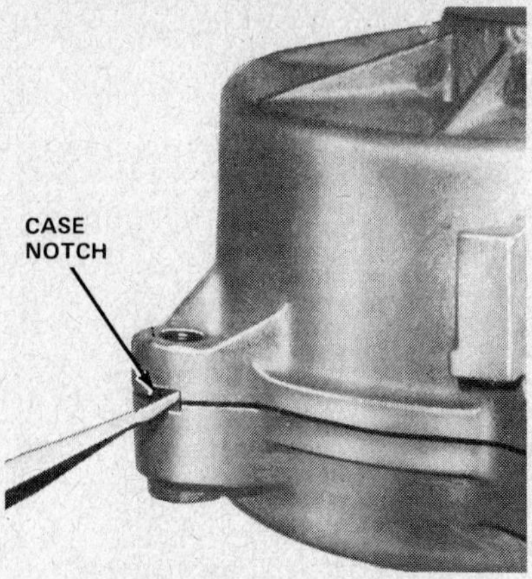

Rear case half removal

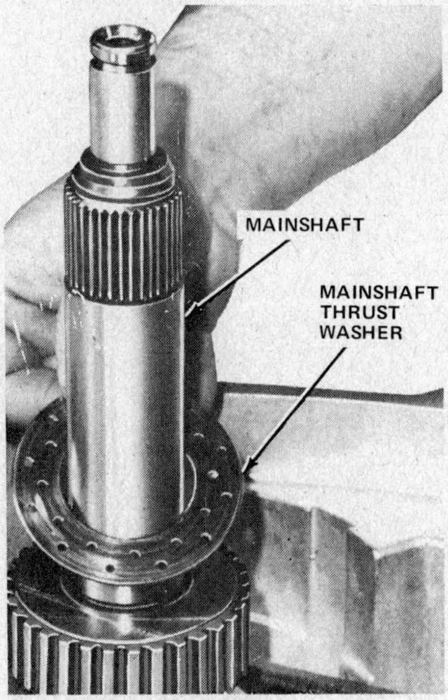

Mainshaft and thrust washer

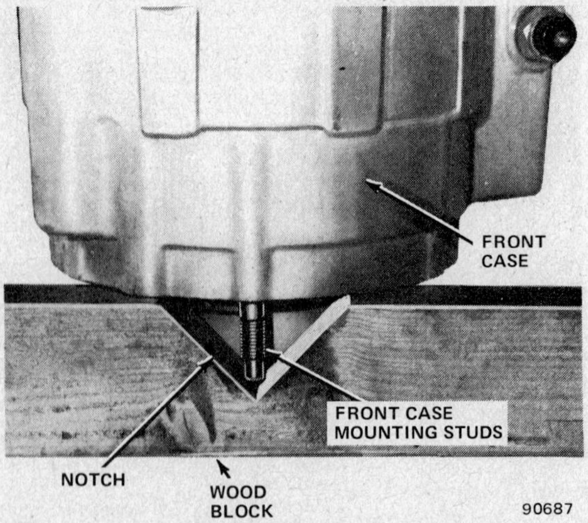

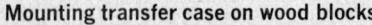

Mounting transfer case on wood blocks

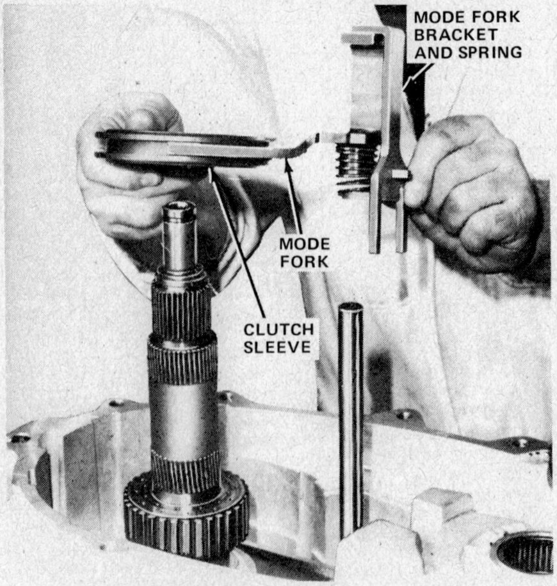

Clutch sleeve and mode fork removal

seal from the front case using a screwdriver or punch.
24. Remove the shift rail spring from the shift rail.
25. Remove the clutch sleeve, mode fork and spring as an assembly.
26. Remove the mainshaft thrust washer and mainshaft. Grasp the shaft and pull it straight up and out.
27. Move the range operating lever downward to the last detent position.
28. Disengage the range fork lug from the range sector slot.
29. Remove the annulus gear retaining snap ring and thrust washer.
30. Remove the annulus gear and range fork.
31. Remove the planetary thrust washer from the hub.
32. Remove the planetary assembly.

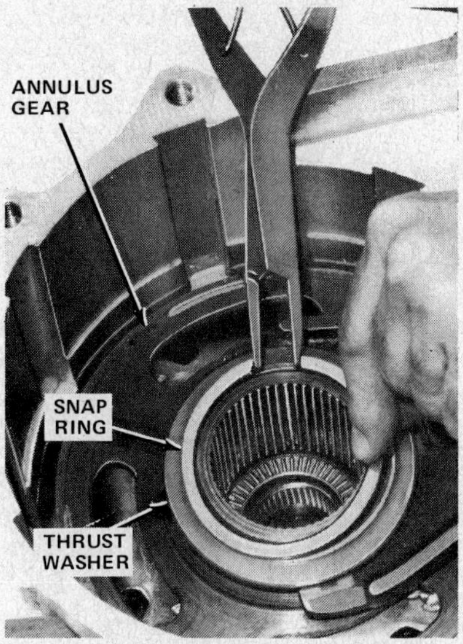

Annulus gear snap ring and thrust washer

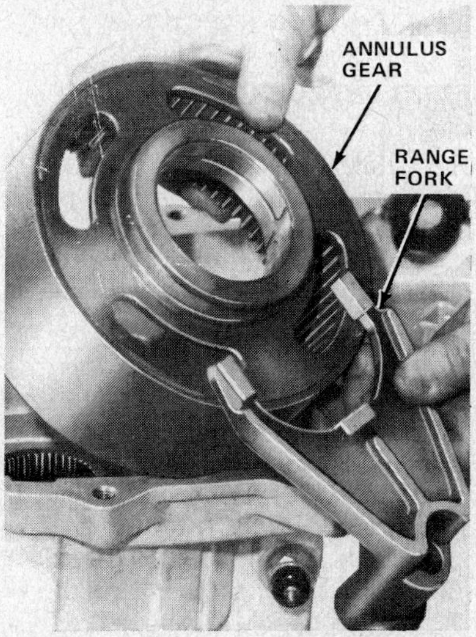

Annulus gear and range fork removal

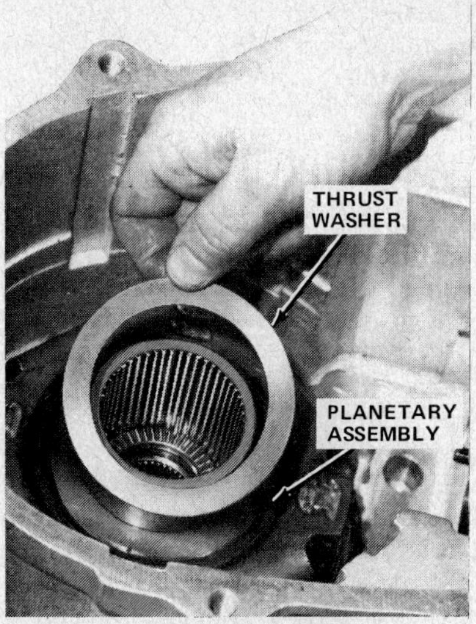

Planetary thrust washer removal

33. Remove the mainshaft thrust bearing from the input gear.
34. Remove the input gear and remove the input gear thrust bearing and race.

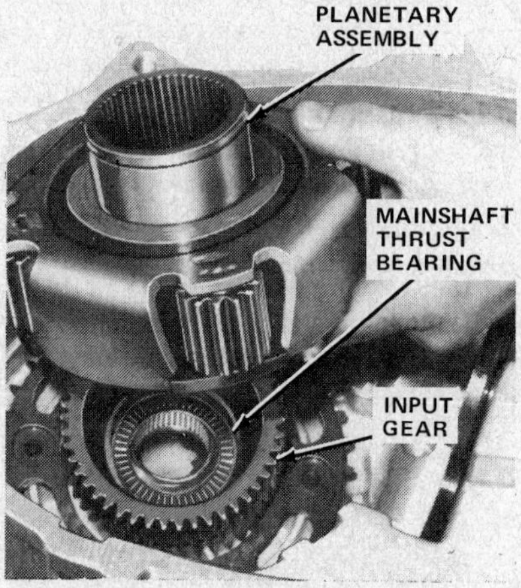

Planetary assembly removal

35. Remove the range selector detent ball and spring retaining bolt and remove the detent ball and spring.
36. Remove the range selector and operating lever attaching nut and lockwasher, and remove the lever.
37. Remove the range selector.
38. Remove the range selector O-ring and retainer.
39. Remove the input gear oil seal from the front case with a screwdriver.

Assembly

Lubricate all parts before assembly with 10W-30 motor oil. Petroleum jelly will be indicated for some assemblies. Do not use chassis lube or other heavy lubricants.

1. Install new input gear and rear output shaft bearing oil seals. Seat the seals flush with the edge of the seal bore or with the seal groove in the case. Coat the seal lips with petroleum jelly after installation.
2. Install the input gear thrust bearing race in the case counterbore.
3. Install the input gear thrust bearing on the input gear and install the gear and bearing in the case.
4. Install the mainshaft thrust bearing in the bearing recess in the input gear.
5. Install the planetary assembly on the input gear. Make sure that the planetary pinion teeth mesh fully with the input gear.
6. Install the planetary thrust washer on the planetary hub.
7. Install a new sector shaft O-ring and retainer in the shaft bore in the case.
8. Install the range selector in the front case. Install the operating lever on the sector shaft and install the lever attaching washer and locknut on the shaft. Tighten the locknut to 17 ft-lb.
9. Install the detent spring, ball and retaining bolt in the front case detent bore. Tighten the bolt to 22 ft-lb.

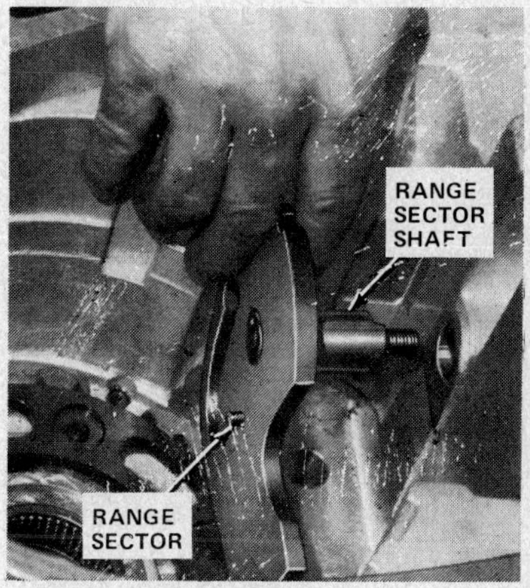

Range sector installation

10. Move the range selector to the last detent position.
11. Assemble the annulus gear and range fork. Install the assembled fork and gear over the planetary assembly. Be sure that the annulus gear is fully meshed with the planetary pinions.
12. Insert the range fork lug in the range detent slot.
13. Install the annulus thrust washer and retaining ring on the annulus gear hub.
14. Align the mainshaft thrust washer in the input gear, if necessary.
15. Install the mainshaft. Be sure

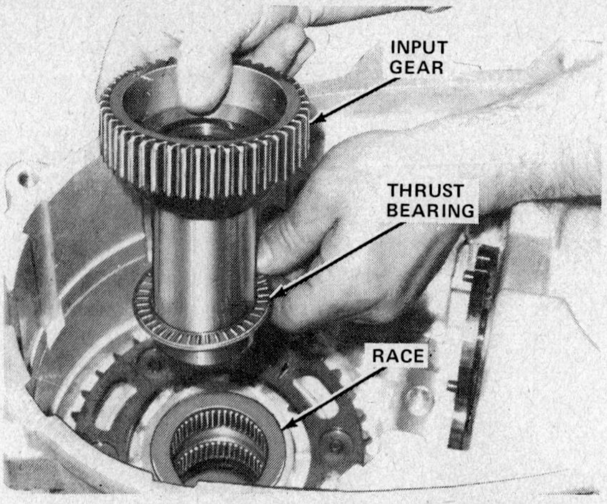

Input gear and thrust bearing removal and installation

the shaft is fully seated in the input gear.

16. Install the mainshaft thrust washer on the mainshaft.
17. Install the short mainshaft needle bearing spacer on the shaft.
18. Apply a liberal coating of petroleum jelly to the mainshaft needle bearing surface and install 41 of the 82 needle bearings on the shaft. Be sure the bearings seat on the short spacer.
19. Install the long needle bearing spacer on the shaft. Lower the spacer onto the previously installed needle bearings carefully to avoid displacing them.
20. Align the shift rail bore in the case with the bore in the range fork and install the shift rail.

    NOTE: Remove all traces of oil from the case shift rail bore before installing the rail. Oil in the case bore may prevent the rail from seating completely and prevent rear case installation.
21. Assemble the mode fork, mode fork spring and mode fork bracket.
22. Install the clutch sleeve in the mode fork. Be sure the sleeve is positioned so that the ID numbers on the sleeve face upward when the sleeve is installed.
23. Align the clutch sleeve and mode fork assembly with the shift rail and install the assembly on the shift rail and mainshaft. Be sure that the clutch sleeve is meshed with the mainshaft gear.
24. Lubricate the remaining 41 needle bearings and place them on the mainshaft.
25. Install the side gear clutch on the mainshaft with the teeth facing downward. Be sure the gear teeth mesh with the clutch sleeve.
26. Install the remaining short mainshaft needle bearing spacer. Install the spacer carefully to avoid displacing previously installed bearings.
27. Install the front output shaft front thrust bearing in the front case. Correct sequence is thick race, bearing, thin race.
28. Install the front output shaft in the front case.
29. Install the clutch gear on the side gear. The tapered side of the clutch gear teeth must face the side gear teeth.
30. Install the clutch gear and drive sprocket locating snap rings on the side gear. Install the snap rings so that they face each other.
31. Position the drive and driven sprockets in the drive chain and install the assembled side and clutch gears in the drive sprocket.
32. Install the assembled drive chain, sprockets and side gear on the mainshaft and front output shaft. Align the sprockets with the shaft, keeping the assembly level and carefully lower the assembly onto both shafts simultanteously. Do not displace any of the needle bearings.
33. Install the driven sprocket retaining snap ring.
34. Install the front output shaft rear thrust bearing assembly on the front output shaft. Correct installation sequence is thin race, thrust bearing, thick race.
35. Install the shift rail spring on the shift rail.
36. Install a new O-ring on the mainshaft pilot bearing hub.
37. Coat the mainshaft pilot roller bearing hub and bearings with a liberal amount of petroleum jelly and install the rollers on the shaft.
38. Install the rear output shaft in the viscous coupling. Be sure it is fully seated.
39. Install the assembled viscous coupling and rear output shaft on the mainshaft. Align the mainshaft pilot hub with the pilot bearing bore in the rear output shaft and carefully lower the assembly onto the mainshaft. Take care to avoid displacing the roller bearings.
40. Align the clutch gear teeth with the viscous coupling teeth and seat the coupling fully onto the clutch gear.

    NOTE: When correctly installed, the clutch gear teeth will not be visible or extend out of the coupling.
41. Install the magnet in the front case, if removed.
42. Clean the mating surfaces of the case halves thoroughly.
43. Apply Loctite® 515 or equivalent to the mating surfaces and all attaching bolts.
44. Join the case halves, aligning the dowels and install the bolts. Torque the bolts to 22 ft-lb.

    NOTE: The two end bolts require flat washers.
45. Install the oil pump on the rear output shaft and seat it in the case. The side with the recess should face the inside of the case.
46. Install the speedometer drive

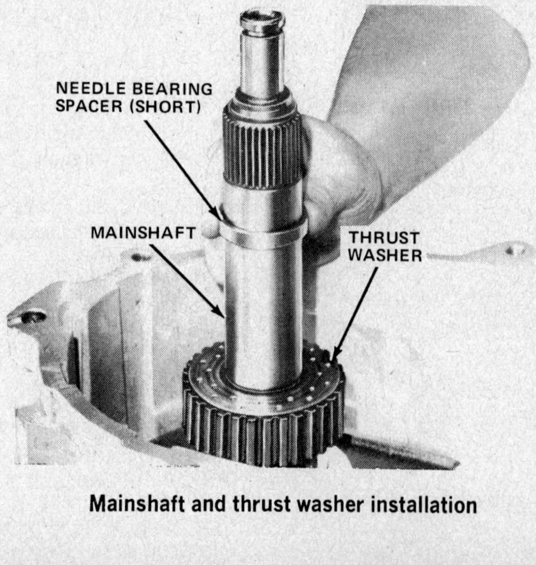

Mainshaft and thrust washer installation

gear and differential shift, on the output shaft.
47. Install the vent chamber seal in the rear retainer.
48. Align and install the rear retainer on the case. Make the retainer finger tight only.
49. Install the yoke on the rear output shaft. Make the yoke finger tight only.
50. Mount a dial indicator on the rear retainer. Position the indicator stylus so that it contacts the top of the yoke nut.
51. Install the yoke on the front output shaft and rotate the shaft ten complete revolutions.
52. Rotate the front output shaft again and note the play indicated on the dial. End play should be .002-.010 inch. If the end play must be adjusted, remove the rear retainer and add or subtract shims as required.
53. Remove both output shaft yokes and discard the nuts.
54. Install the front and rear yoke seals.
55. Remove the rear retainer bolts, apply Loctite® 515 or equivalent to the mating surface of the retainer and to the bolts and install the bolts. Torque them to 22 ft-lb.
56. Install new yoke seal washers on the output shafts, install yokes on the shafts and install new yoke nuts. Tighten the nuts to 110 ft-lb.
57. Install the drain plug and tighten to 18 ft-lb.
58. Pour 4 pints of 10W-30 motor oil into the case and install the fill plug. Tighten it to 18 ft-lb.

New Process Model 203 (Full Time Four Wheel Drive)

Description

The New Process Model 203 transfer case is a full-time 4WD unit that operates in 4WD at all times. The unit incorporates a differential similar to axle differentials; compensating for different speeds of the front and rear axles resulting from varying speeds while turning and operating over different surfaces.

There are five shift positions with this transfer case; Neutral, High and High Lock, and Low and Low Lock. The Lock positions are used under low traction conditions. In the Lock position, the differential action of the transfer case is eliminated, by locking the front and rear output shafts together. In this mode, neither the front or rear axle can rotate independently of the other.

Disassembly

1. Loosen rear output shaft flange retaining nut and remove front output shaft flange and washer.
2. Tap the front output shaft dust seal away from case assembly.

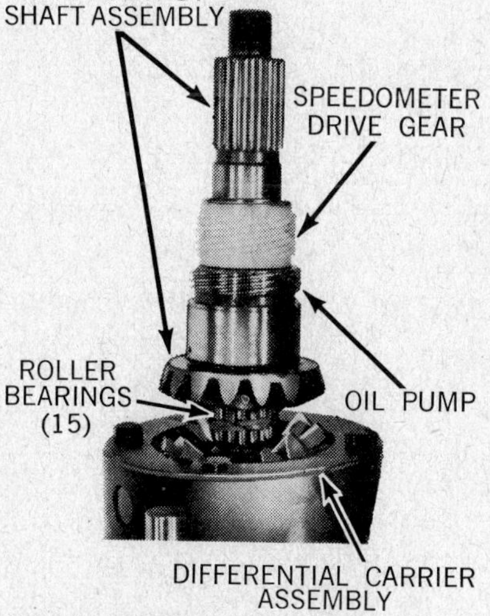

Removing the rear output shaft. The differential carrier assembly is removed next—New Process 203 transfer case (© Ford Motor Co.)

Remove front output shaft bearing retainer and gasket.
3. Position transfer case assembly on blocks with input shaft facing downward.
4. Remove rear output shaft assembly from transfer case. Slide the differential carrier off the shaft.
5. Place a 1½ in. to 2 in. band type hose clamp on input shaft to retain bearings.
6. Lift shift rail and driveout pin retaining shift fork.
7. Remove shift rail poppet ball plug, gasket and ball from case. Use a magnet to remove poppet ball.
8. Push shift rail down, lift up on lockout clutch and remove shift fork from clutch assembly.

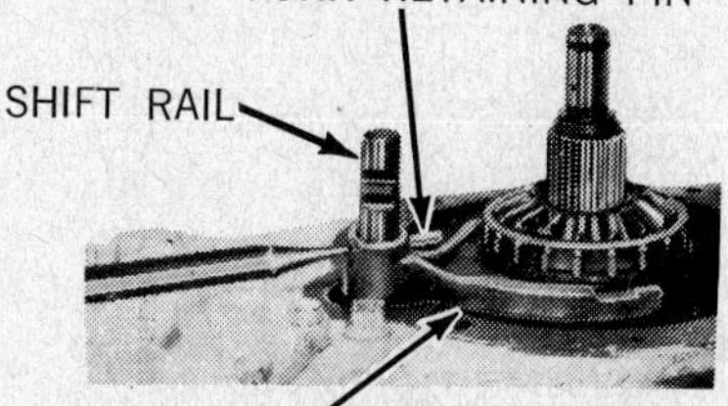

Removing the pin retaining the shift fork to the shift rail in a New Process 203 transfer case (© Ford Motor Co.)

9. Remove front output shaft rear bearing retainer. It may be necessary to gently tap front of shaft or cautiously pry retainer from case. Make certain that no roller bearings are lost from rear cover.
10. When necessary, remove rear bearing by pressing.
11. Pry front output shaft front bearing from lower side of case.
12. Remove front otuput shaft assembly from case.
13. Lift intermediate housing from range box, after removing bolts.
14. Remove chain from intermediate housing.
15. Remove lockout clutch, drive gear and input shaft from range box.

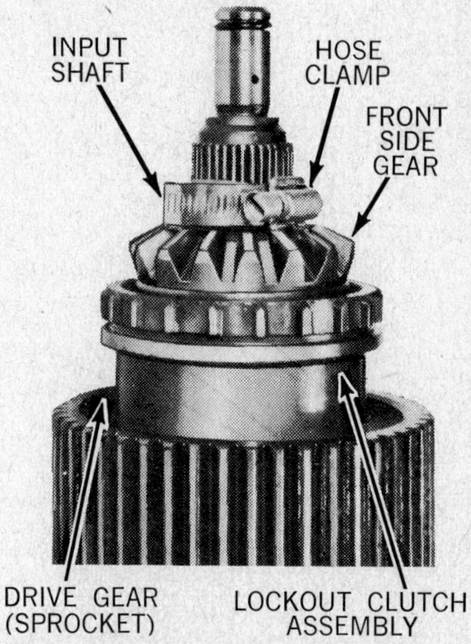

Place a hose clamp around the end of the input shaft to prevent losing the 123 roller bearings out of the clutch assembly—New Process 203 transfer case (© Ford Motor Co.)

16. Install a 1½″ to 2″ band type hose clamp on end of input shaft to retain roller bearings.
17. Pull up on shift rail and remove rail from link.
18. Lift input shaft assembly from range box.

Assembly

1. Position range box with input gear side down, on wood blocks.
2. Place gasket on input housing.
3. Install lockout clutch and drive sprocket on input shaft assembly. Install a 2″ band type hose clamp on end of input shaft to prevent loss of bearings during installation.
4. Place input shaft, lockout clutch and drive sprocket in range box. Align tab on bearing retainer with notch in gasket.
5. Engage lockout clutch shift rail to the connector link. Position rail in housing bore and turn shifter shaft lowering rail into the housing. This will prevent

1 Adapter
2 Input Gear Bearing Retainer
3 Input Gear Bearing Retainer Gasket
4 Input Gear Bearing Retainer Seals
5 Bearing Outer Ring
6 Bearing to Shaft Retaining Ring
7 Input Gear Bearing
8 Adapter to Selector Housing Gasket
9 Range Selector Housing (Range Box)
10 P.T.O. Cover Gasket
11 P.T.O. Cover
12 Selector Housing to Chain Housing Gasket
13 Main Drive Input Gear
14 Range Selector Sliding Clutch
15 Shift Lever Lock Nut
16 Range Selector Shift Lever
17 Shift Lever Retaining Ring
18 Lockout Shift Lever
19 Detent Plate Spring Plug
20 Detent Plate Spring Plug Gasket
21 Detent Plate Spring
22 Detent Plate
23 Lockout Shifter Shaft
24 "O" Ring Seal
25 Lockout Shaft Connector Link
26 "O" Ring Seal
27 Range Selector Shifter Shaft
28 Range Selector Shift Fork
29 Detent Plate Pivot Pin
30 Thrust Washer
31 Spacer (short)
32 Range Selector Counter Gear
33 Counter Roller Bearings and Spacers (72 Bearings Req'd.)
34 Countergear Shaft
35 Thrust Washer
36 Input Shaft Roller Bearings (15 Req'd.)
37 Thrust Washer Pins (2 Req'd.)
38 Input Shaft
39 "O" Ring Seal
40 Low Speed and Bushing
41 Thrust Washer
42 Input Shaft Bearing Retainer
43 Input Shaft Bearing
44 Input Shaft Bearing Retaining Ring (Large)
45 Input Shaft Bearing Retaining Ring
46 Chain Drive Housing
47 Lockout Shift Rail Poppet Plug, Gasket, Spring and Ball
48 Thrust Washer
49 Lubricating Thrust Washer
50 Retaining Ring
51 Flange Lock Nut
52 Washer
53 Seal
54 Front Output Yoke
55 Dust Shield
56 Front Output Shaft Bearing Retainer Seal
57 Front Output Shaft Bearing Retainer
58 Front Output Shaft Bearing
59 Bearing Outer Ring
60 Bearing Retainer Gasket
61 Front Output Shaft
62 Front Output Shaft Rear Bearing
63 Front Output Rear Bearing Retainer Cover Gasket
64 Front Output Rear Bearing Retainer
65 Drive Shaft Sprocket
66 Drive Chain
67 Retaining Ring
68 Sliding Lock Clutch
69 Lockout Shift Rail
70 Shift Fork Retaining Pin
71 Lockout Shift Fork
72 Lockout Clutch Spring
73 Spring Washer Cup
74 Front Side Gear
75 Front Side Gear Bearing and Spaces (123 Bearings Req'd.)
76 Differential Carrier Assembly (132 Bearings Req'd.)
77 Rear Output Shaft Roller Bearings (15 Req'd.)

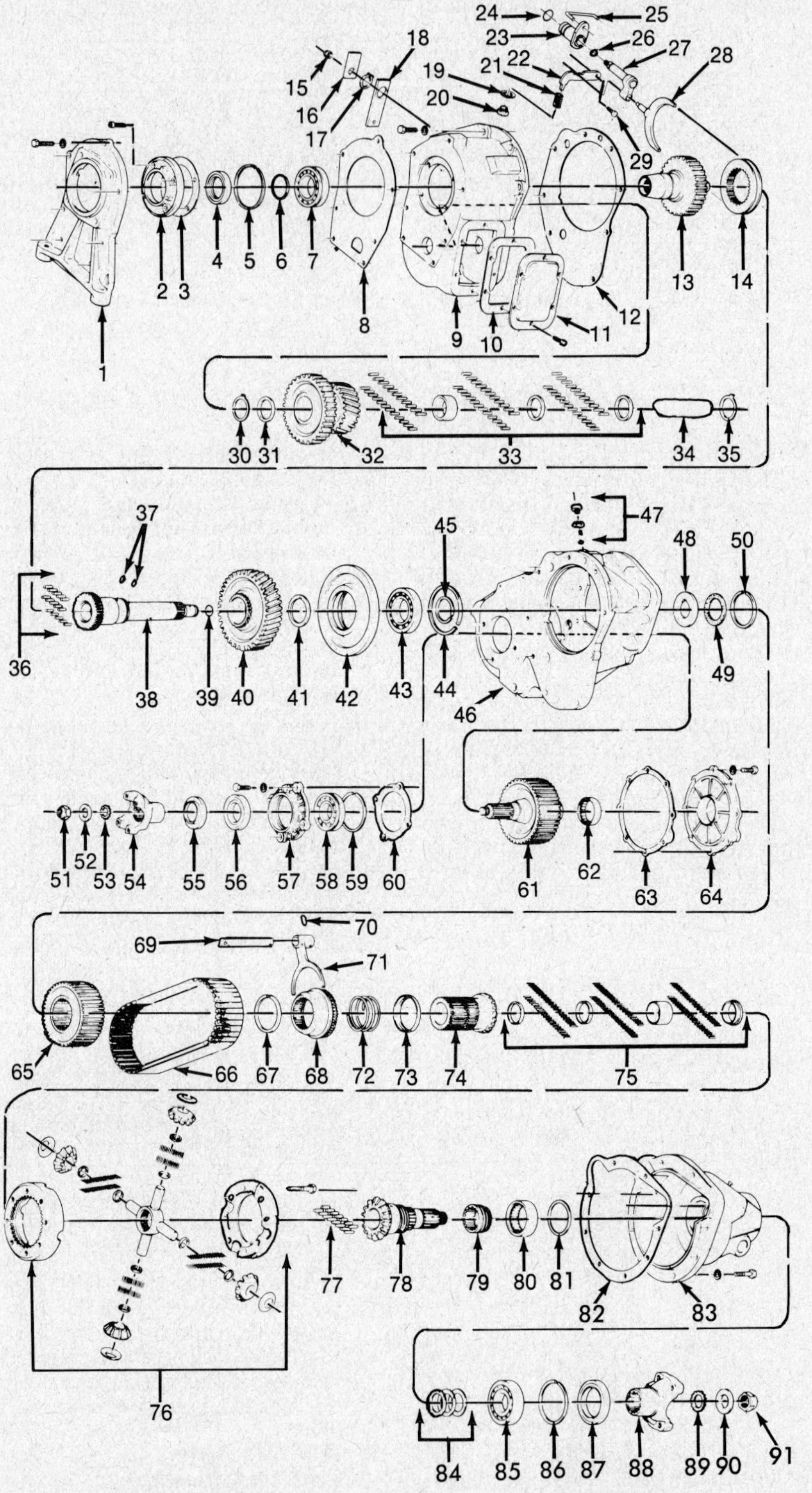

Exploded view of New Process model 203 full time transfer case
(© General Motors Corp.)

78 Rear Output Shaft
79 Speedometer Drive Gear
80 Rear Output Shaft Front Roller Bearing
81 Oil Pump "O" Ring Seal
82 Rear Output Housing Gasket
83 Rear Output Housing
84 Shim Pack
85 Rear Output Rear Bearing
86 Bearing Retainer
87 Rear Output Shaft Seal
88 Rear Output Flange
89 Rear Output Shaft Rubber Seal
90 Washer
91 Flange Nut

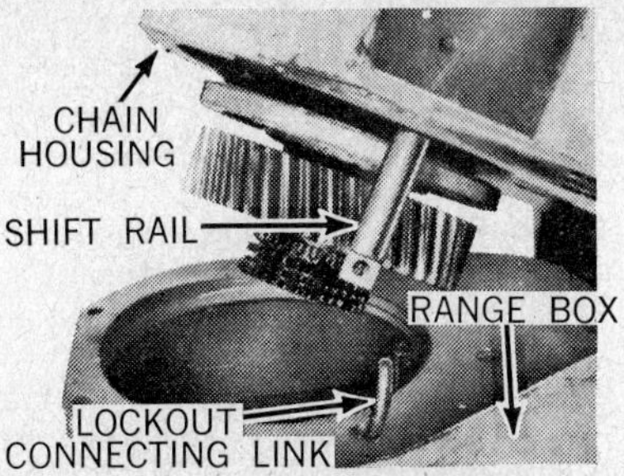

Disengaging the shift rail from the locknut connecting link in a New Process 203 transfer case (© Ford Motor Co.)

the link and rail from becoming disconnected.

6. Place the drive chain in housing with the chain around the outer wall.
7. Secure the chain housing to the range box. Be sure that the shift rail engages the channel of the housing. Place the chain on the input drive sprocket.
8. Place the front output sprocket in transfer case. Turn the clutch drive gear to assist in positioning chain on sprocket.
9. Position the shift fork and rail on the clutch assembly. Install the clutch assembly completely into the drive sprocket. Insert retaining pin in shift fork and rail.
10. Install front output bearing, gasket, retainer, bolts, flange, gasket, seal, washer and retaining nut.
11. If rear bearing was removed from front output shaft, press a new bearing into the outside face of cover until bearing is flush with opening.
12. Install front output shaft, rear bearing retainer, gasket and bolts.
13. Slip differential carrier assembly on the input shaft. Bolts on carrier must face rear of shaft.
14. Load bearings in pinion shaft, install rear output housing assembly, gasket and bolts.
15. Install a dial indicator on the rear housing. The indicator must contact the end of the output shaft. While holding the rear flange, rotate the front output shaft and find the highest point of gear hop. Reset indicator and with rear output shaft at high point, pull up on the end of the shaft to determine end play. Remove indicator and install shim pack to control end play to between 0 and .005″. The shim pack is positioned on the shaft in front of the rear bearing. Check for binding of rear output shaft.
16. Insert lockout clutch shift rail poppet ball, spring and screw plug in transfer case.
17. Install poppet plate spring, gasket and plug, if they were not previously installed.
18. Install shift levers on the range box, if these were not left on vehicle.
19. Torque all bolts, locknuts and plugs to specifications.
20. Fill transfer case with specified lubricant until the proper level is reached. Secure filler plug.

Transfer Case Subassemblies Overhaul

Lockout Clutch Assembly

Disassembly

1. Remove front side gear from input shaft assembly.
2. Remove thrust washer, roller bearings and spacers from front side gear bore. The position of the spacers must be noted.
3. Remove the snap ring which holds the drive sprocket to clutch assembly. Slip the drive sprocket from the front side gear.
4. Remove the lower snap ring.
5. Remove sliding gear, spring and spring cup washer from the front side gear.
6. Throughly clean and inspect all component parts. Replace any component that is worn or defective.

Assembly

1. Place spring cup washer, spring and sliding clutch gear on front side gear.
2. Secure sliding clutch to front side gear with a snap ring.
3. Spread petroleum jelly on front side gear and install roller bearings and spacers.
4. Place thrust washer in gear end of front side gear.
5. Slide drive sprocket on clutch splines and secure with snap ring.

Differential Carrier Assembly

Disassembly

1. Separate differential carrier sections and lift out pinion gear and spider assembly.
2. Note that undercut side of pinion gear spider faces toward front of side gear.
3. Remove pinion thrust washers, pinion roller washer gears and roller bearings from spider unit.
4. Throughly clean and inspect all component parts. Replace any component that is worn or damaged.

Assembly

1. Spread petroleum jelly on pinion gears and install roller bearings.
2. Position on the leg of each spider, pinion roller washer, pinion gear and thrust washer.
3. Position the spider assembly in front half of the carrier. The undercut surface of the spider thrust surface face downward or toward teeth.
4. Secure carrier halfs together. Make certain the marks are aligned. Torque all bolts to specifications.

Input Shaft Assembly

Disassembly

1. Remove thrust washer and spacer from shaft.
2. Remove bearing retainer assembly from input shaft.
3. Hold low speed gear and lightly tap shaft from gear. Note the position of the thrust washer pins in input shaft.
4. Remove snap ring holding input bearing in retainer using a screw driver. Lightly tap rear bearing out of retainer.
5. Remove pilot roller bearing and 'O' ring from end of input shaft.
6. Throughly clean and inspect all component parts. Replace any component that is worn or damaged.

Assembly

1. Tap or press input bearing into retainer. Be sure that ball loading slots are toward concave side of retainer. Install securing snap ring. Make certain that selective snap ring of proper thickness is used to provide tightest fit.
2. Position low speed gear on shaft, clutch end facing gear end of input shaft.
3. Place thrust washers on input shaft, align slot in washer with pin in shaft. Slide or tap washers into position.
4. Place input bearing retainer on shaft and secure with snap ring. Snap rings are selective. Use snap ring that provides tightest fit.
5. Slip spacer and thrust washer on shaft and align with locating pin.
6. Spread heavy grease on end of shaft and install roller bearings.
7. Install rubber 'O' ring at end of shaft.

Range Box

Disassembly

1. Remove poppet plate spring, plug and gasket.
2. Remove clutch fork and sliding gear by disengaging sliding clutch gear from input gear.
3. Remove upper shift lever from shifter shaft.
4. Remove snap ring and lower shift lever.
5. Push shifter shaft assembly down and remove lockout clutch

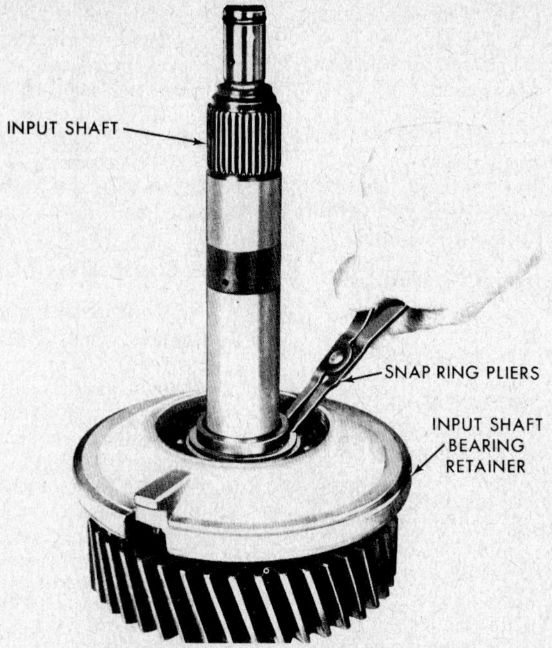

Removing input shaft bearing retainer

connector link. The long end of connector link engages poppet plate.

6. Remove shifter shaft assembly and separate shafts. Remove 'O' rings.
7. When necessary to remove poppet plate, drive pivot shaft out and remove plate and spring from bottom of case.
8. Remove input gear bearing retainer and seal assembly. Release snap ring from retainer and tap bearing out of assembly.
9. Release snap ring holding input shaft bearing to shaft and remove bearing.
10. Remove countershaft from cluster gear and case assembly from intermediate case side. Remove cluster gear assembly from range box.
11. Remove cluster gear thrust washers from case.
12. Thoroughly clean and inspect all component parts. Replace any component that is worn or damaged.

Assembly

1. Spread heavy grease in cluster bore and using proper tool install roller bearings and spacers.
2. Spread heavy grease on case and install thrust washers. Engage tab on thrust washers with slot in case.
3. Place cluster gear assembly in case and install countershaft through front of range box and into gear assembly. Flat face of countershaft must be aligned with case gasket.
4. Place bearing on input gear shaft with snap ring groove facing out, install a new retaining ring. Insert input gear and bearing in housing. The retaining ring used in this operation is a select fit. Use ring that provides the tightest fit.
5. Secure input gear and bearing with a snap ring.
6. Match up oil slot in retainer with drain hole in case and insert input gear bearing retainer and gaskets. Install bolts and torque to specifications.
7. Spread sealant on pin and install poppet pin and pivot pin in housing.
8. Lubricate and install new 'O' rings on inner and outer shifter shafts.
9. Insert shifter shafts in housing and engage long end of lockout clutch connector link with outer shifter shaft. Complete this operation before assembly bottoms out.
10. Install lower shift lever and retaining ring.
11. Install upper shift lever and shaft retaining nut.
12. Install shift fork and sliding clutch gear. Push fork up into shifter shaft and engage poppet plate. Move sliding clutch gear onto input shaft gear.
13. Insert poppet plate spring, gasket and plug in housing top. Make certain that spring engages poppet plate.

Input Gear Bearing

Replacement

1. Remove bearing retainer and gasket from housing.
2. Remove and discard snap ring holding bearing in retainer.
3. Pry bearing from case and remove from shaft.
4. Inspect input gear and bearing retainer for damage or wear. Replace if necessary.
5. Place new bearing and snap ring on input gear. Using a soft hammer, tap bearing into position. Secure snap ring.
6. Insert bearing retainer into housing and secure with attaching bolts. Tighten bolts to specifications.

Input Gear Retainer Seal

Replacement

1. Remove bearing retainer from housing.
2. Remove seal from retainer by prying.
3. Place new seal on retainer and install with proper seal driver.
4. Install bearing retainer in housing and secure with attaching bolts. Tighten bolts to specifications.

Rear Output Shaft Housing Assembly

Disassembly

1. Remove speedometer driven gear from housing.
2. Remove rear output flange and washer, if they have not been removed previously.
3. Using a soft hammer tap on flange end of pinion and remove the pinion. If speedometer drive gear does not come off with pinion reach into case and remove.
4. Remove old seal from bore with suitable prying tool.
5. Remove snap ring retaining rear output rear bearing.
6. Tap bearing out of housing.
7. Install a long drift into rear opening of housing and drive out front output bearing. Remove seal and discard.

Assembly

1. Spread grease on front bearing seal and place in bore. Place bearing in bore and press until it bottoms in housing.
2. Using a soft hammer tap rear bearing into place. Secure with proper snap ring. Snap rings are selective, use the one that provides the tightest fit.
3. Place rear seal in bore and drive into position with suitable tool.

When seal is in position it should be approximately 1/8″ to 3/16″ below housing face.

4. Place speedometer drive gear on output shaft with shims of approximately .050″ thickness. Insert output shaft into carrier through housing front opening.
5. Install flange and washer on output shaft. Leave retaining nut loose until shim requirements are known.
6. Install speedometer driven gear.

Front Output Shaft Bearing Retainer Seal

Replacement

1. Remove old seal from retainer bore.
2. Inspect and clean retainer.
3. Spread sealer on outer edge of new seal.
4. Place new seal in retainer bore and drive into position with proper tool.

Front Output Bearing

Replacement

1. Remove rear cover from case assembly and discard gasket.
2. Press old bearing from cover.
3. Place new bearing on outside face of cover. Cover bearing with a wood block and press into cover until bearing is flush with opening.
4. Place gasket on transfer case and tap cover into position using a soft hammer. Secure cover with attaching bolts and tighten to specifications.

SPECIFICATIONS

TORQUE (FT. LBS.)

Adapter to Transfer Case Bolts	38
Adapter to Transmission Bolts	40
Transfer Case to Frame Nuts (Upper)	50
Transfer Case to Frame Nuts (Lower)	65
Shift Lever Attaching Nuts	25
Shift Lever Rod Swivel Locknuts	50
Shift Lever Locking Arm Nut	150 in. lbs.
Skid Plate Bolt Retaining Nuts	45
Crossmember Bolt Retaining Nuts	45
Adapter Mount Bolts	25
Intermediate Case to Range Box Bolts	30
Front Output Bearing Retainer Bolts	30
Output Shaft Yoke Nuts	150
Front Output Rear Bearing Retainer Bolts	30
Differential Assembly Screws	45
Rear Output Shaft Housing	30
Poppet Ball Retainer Nut	15
PTO Cover Bolts	15
Front Input Bearing Retainer Bolts	20
Filler Plug	25

Warner Quadra-Trac®

Description

The Quadra-Trac transfer case provides full-time, four-wheel drive under all driving conditions. The front and rear driveshafts are driven by a limited slip differential in the transfer case. The limited slip differential is connected to the input shaft by a link-belt type chain. In operation, if the rear axle loses traction, then the engine torque will be transfered through the transfer case differential to the front axle.

The transfer case contains a manually actuated lockout system that locks the front and rear driveshafts together, cancelling the differential action. This feature is used under extreme marginal traction situations.

NOTE: In order to spare the transfer case differential side gears and brake cones from excessive, and possibly, damaging wear, do not spin the wheels excessively when the vehicile is stuck or bogged down.

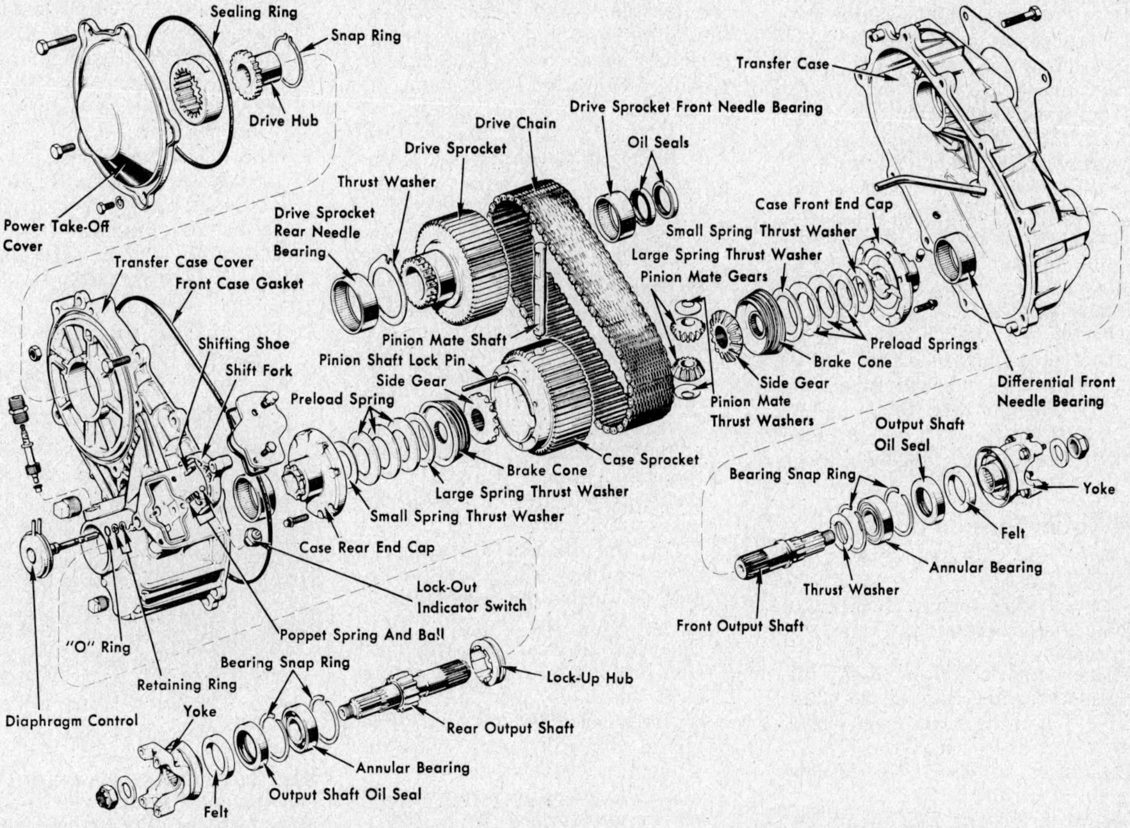

Exploded view of the Warner Quadra-Trac without the optional reduction unit (© Jeep Corp.)

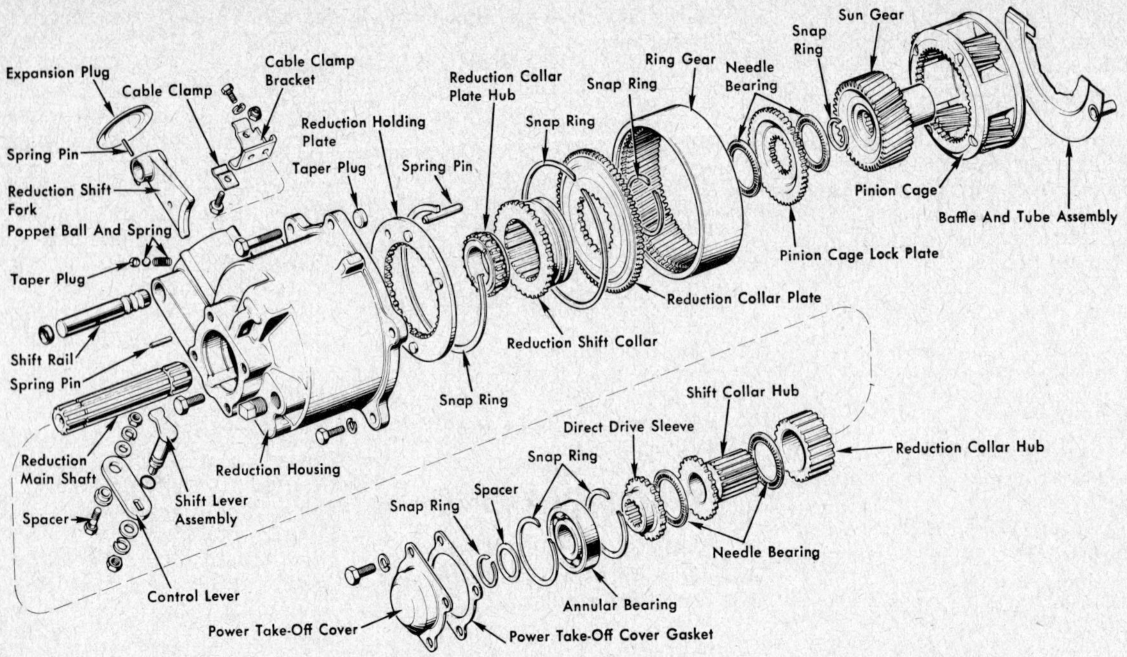

Exploded view of the Warner Quadra-Trac without the optional reduction unit (© Jeep Corp.)

An optional gear reduction unit mounted at the rear of the input shaft is available for the Quadra-Trac unit, making it a two-speed transfer case.

Performance Checks

Transfer Case Differential Torque Bias Check

1. With the lock-out feature *not* engaged and the transmission in Park, raise the vehicle until the front wheels are free of the ground.
2. Disconnect the rear driveshaft from the transfer case.
3. Turn the rear yoke retaining nut with a torque wrench and socket, taking note of how much torque is required to force the cone clutches to slip. They should slip when 110 to 270 ft. lbs. are applied.

Slippage below 110 ft. lbs. indicates replacement of the differential is needed. If no slippage occurs at 270 ft. lbs., improper lubrication is indicated. Drain and refill the transfer case and reduction unit, if so equipped, with the proper lubricant mixture.

Drive Chain Tension Check

1. Drain the lubricant from the transfer case.
2. Remove the chain inspection plug and insert a steel rule into the hole.
3. A new chain will be 1.575 in. from the outer edge of the plug hole. When the slack in the chain reaches ½-¾ in., the chain should be replaced. No adjustment is possible.
4. Reinstall the drain and chain inspection plugs, and refill the unit with the proper lubricant mixture.

Rear Case Cover

Removal

Most Quadra-Trac components can be serviced without removing the complete unit from the vehicle. To gain access to the rear output shaft, drive sprocket and thrust washer, chain, differential and needle bearing, or the diaphragm control system, just the rear cover has to be removed.

1. Lift and support the vehicle.
2. If the vehicle is equipped with a reduction unit, continue on to the next step for the reduction unit removal procedure. If the vehicle is not equipped with a reduction unit, proceed to Step 7.
3. Loosen all the bolts that attach the reduction unit to the transfer case cover.
4. Move the reduction unit backward just enough to allow the oil to drain from the unit.
5. Loosen the cable retaining bolt at the shift control lever. Loosen the cable clamp bolt and remove the control cable from the clamp bracket and control lever.
6. When the oil has drained, remove the bolts which hold the reduction unit to the transfer case cover. Move the reduction unit rearward to clear the transmission output shaft and pinion cage which is attached to the transfer case drive sprocket. The pinion cage will remain with the transfer case assembly.

   NOTE: The pinion cage should not be removed if the transfer case cover assembly is to be removed, but may be removed for inspection or replacement if the transfer case cover assembly is to remain in the vehicle. Removal of the pinion cage involves only removing the snap-ring which holds the cage to the sprocket and sliding the cage backward.
7. Remove the transfer case drain plug and allow the unit to drain.
8. Mark the rear output shaft yoke and universal joint to provide an alignment reference during reassembly. Disconnect the rear drive shaft front universal joint from the transfer case rear yoke.
9. Mark the diaphragm control vacuum hoses for identification during reassembly, then disconnect them. Also remove the lock-up indicator switch wire and the

Mark the end caps and case sprocket of the differential assembly before disassembling the differential—Warner Quadra-Trac (© Jeep Corp.)

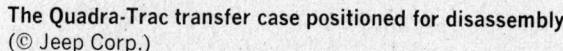

The Quadra-Trac transfer case positioned for disassembly
(© Jeep Corp.)

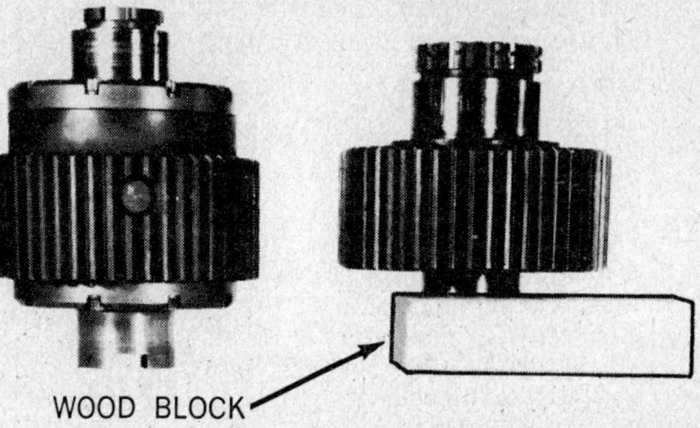

The differential and drive sprocket positioned for installation of the drive chain Warner Quadra-Trac
(© Jeep Corp.)

speedometer cable. Remove the indicator switch.

10. Disconnect the parking brake cable guide from the pivot on the right frame side.
11. Remove the bolts which attach the case cover assembly to the case (front housing). Carefully slide the cover assembly backward off the front output shaft and the transmission output shaft.

Disassembly

1. To disassemble the unit, remove the rear output shaft yoke.
2. If the unit is *not* equipped with a reduction unit, remove the power take-off cover from the rear of the transfer case cover. Remove the sealing ring from the transfer case cover.
3. Using a piece of wood 2 in. × 4 in. and 6 in. long, support the cover and drive sprocket.
4. If *not* equipped with a reduction unit, remove the drive hub and sleeve from the drive sprocket rear splines by expanding the internal snap-ring. The ring expanding tabs are accessible through a slot in the outside edge of the drive sleeve.
5. If equipped with a reduction unit, remove the pinion cage snap ring and carrier.
6. Lift the case cover from the drive sprocket and differential. The cover, rear output shaft, bearings and seal, drive sprocket rear needle bearing, and lock-up hub can now be serviced without any further disassembly of other components.
7. Slide the drive sprocket toward the differential unit and remove the chain. The differential unit may now be serviced without any further disassembly of other components.

Assembly

1. Position the drive sprocket on a block of wood 2 in. × 4 in. and 6 in. long.
2. Place the differential assembly about 2 in. from the drive sprocket and with the front end of the differential on the bench.
3. Position the drive chain around the drive sprocket and the differential assembly. Be sure that the chain is properly engaged with the sprocket and differential teeth and that the slack is removed from the chain.
4. Insert the rear output shaft into the differential.
5. Shift the lock-up hub rearward in the case cover. Lubricate the drive sprocket thrust washer and insert it in position on the case cover.
6. Carefully align the case cover and position it onto the drive sprocket and differential. The output shaft may have to be slightly rotated to align it with the lock-up hub. Be sure that the drive sprocket thrust washer stays positioned correctly.
7. If equipped with a reduction unit, install the pinion cage onto the drive sprocket rear splines. Install the snap-ring. Be sure that the snap-ring seats properly in the groove.
8. If the vehicle is *not* equipped with a reduction unit, assemble the drive hub, drive sleeve, and snap-ring, then install them onto the drive sprocket rear splines. Be sure the snap-ring seats properly.
9. Turn the drive sleeve or pinion cage to make sure the drive sprocket thrust washer did not come out of position. No binding should be present.
10. If *not* equipped with a reduction unit, install the power take-off sealing ring and cover and tighten the attaching screws.
11. Install the speedometer gear on the rear output shaft.
12. Install the rear output shaft oil

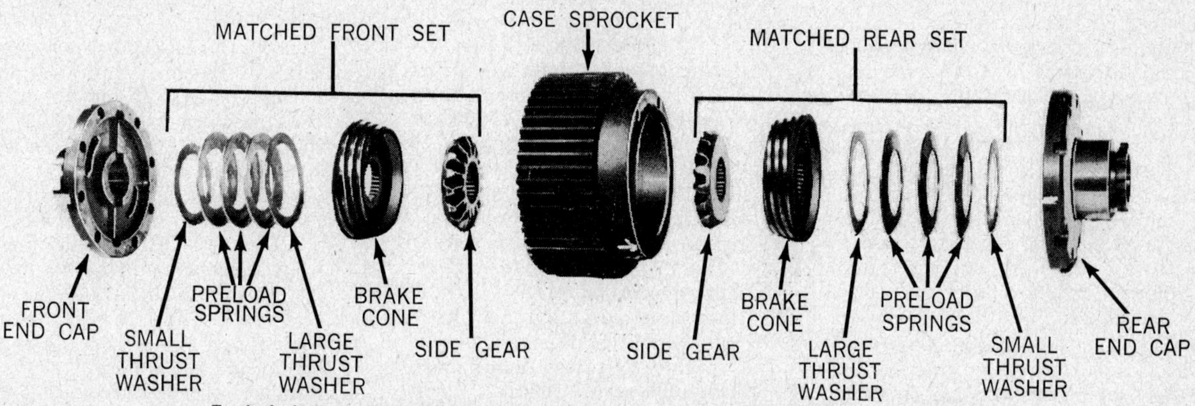

Exploded view of the differential assembly—Warner Quadra-Trac (© Jeep Corp.)

seal and the rear yoke and nut. Tighten the nut to specification.

Installation

13. Clean the groove which the front oil seal gasket fits into and install the seal.
14. Install two 3/8 in. 16 × 2 in. long pilot studs into the transfer case front cover housing.
15. On 1973-74 models only, insert the oil tube into the case bore at the front output shaft bearing boss. Insert a 6 in. length of 5/16 in. rod into the tube. The rod will be used as a pilot to align the tube with the case cover. Lift the cover assembly and align the tube pilot with the hole in the cover. Move the assembly forward over the pilot studs.
16. Move the cover assembly forward to mesh with the front output shaft and transmission output shaft. It may be necessary to rotate the rear output shaft slightly to allow the two sets of splines to engage.
17. After the cover assembly has been moved forward and is evenly touching the front half of the case, remove the pilot studs and install the rear cover attaching bolts. Tighten the bolts alternately and evenly to specifications.
18. Install the lock out indicator switch and connect the lock out switch wire, diaphragm control vacuum hoses, and the speedometer cable.
19. Install the rear drive shaft.
20. Install the parking brake cable guide to the pivot on the right frame side.
21. Install the reduction unit, if so equipped as follows:
22. Position the reduction unit to the transfer case and mesh the caged pinions with the sun gear and ring gear, and align the sun gear inner splines with the transmission output shaft splines.
23. Move the reduction unit forward until it touches the sealing ring.
24. Install the attaching screws loosely, then tighten them alternately to specification.
25. Connect the shift control cable and adjust it by first removing the swivel block from the control lever. Move the control lever to the most forward position. Thread the swivel block in or out on the cable end to obtain the correct length to fit the swivel block in the control lever.
26. Install the proper type and amount of lubricant and lower the vehicle.

NOTE: Use 8 oz. of Jeep Lubricant Concentrate Part No. 8123004 or 5356068 mixed with SAE 30 non-detergent motor oil or pre-mixed Jeep Quadra-Trac® Lubricant. 3.5 pints of the mixture is required to fill the transfer.

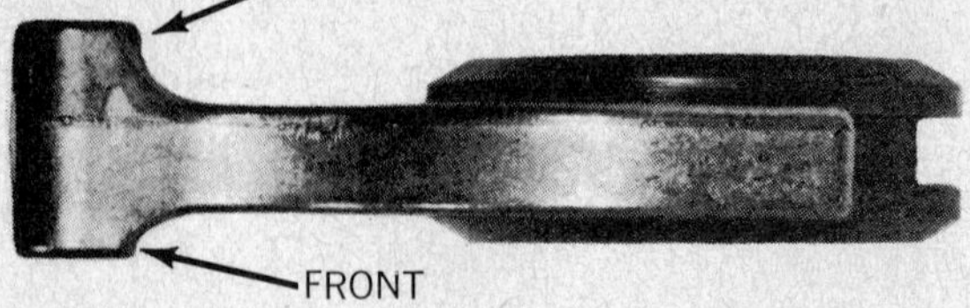

Install the lock-up hub assembly shift fork with the long side of the fork facing toward the rear—Warner Quadra-Trac (© Jeep Corp.)

Differential Assembly

Disassembly

1. Mark end caps and case sprocket with paint. Marks must be used to identify front end cap, rear end cap and proper orientation of caps to case sprocket.
2. Remove front end cap. If necessary, tap gently with a soft hammer.
3. Remove thrust washer, preload springs, brake cone and side gears from case sprocket. Care must be taken to keep the various pieces together as they must be installed as a unit.
4. Invert the case sprocket and remove rear cap. If necessary, tap gently with a soft hammer.
5. Remove the thrust washers, preload springs, brake cone and side gears. Care must be taken to keep the various pieces together as they must be installed as a unit.
6. Raise the case sprocket. The pinion shaft lock pin should fall out. If the pin does not fall, drive the pin out with a 1/4 in. pin punch.
7. Drive the pinion mate shaft out of case sprocket, using a brass drift and hammer. Care must be taken to avoid damaging the pinion mate thrust washers.
8. Thoroughly clean and inspect all component parts. Replace any damaged or worn parts with a complete matched set.

Assembly

Prelubricate all bearings and thrust surfaces with Jeep Lubricant Concentrate Part No. 8123004 or 5356068 or Jeep Quadra-Trac Lubricant prior to installation.

1. Slide the pinion mate shaft in the case sprocket three inches.
2. Install the pinion mate thrust washers and gears on shaft in the proper order.
3. Align the pinion mate shaft lockpin hole with hole in case sprocket. Lightly drive the pinion mate shaft into case sprocket until lockpin holes are exactly aligned.
4. Move the pinion mate gears apart until the gears are pressing the washers against the case sprocket.
5. Engage the pinion mate gear with the front side gears. Insert the brake cone over the gear and in case sprocket. Install the large thrust washer and preload springs, concave side of springs facing toward brake cone.
6. Lubricate the small thrust washer and place it on the front end cap. Install the front end cap, secure with attaching screws and alternately tighten to proper torque. Make certain that alignment marks are in order.
7. Invert the case sprocket and end cap and install the pinion shaft lock pin.
8. Mesh remaining side gear with pinion mate gears.
9. Insert the remaining brake cone over the side gear. Install the large thrust washer and preload spring, concave side of springs facing toward brake cone.
10. Lubricate the small thrust washer and place it on the rear end cap. Install the rear cap, tighten attaching screws finger tight.
11. Insert the front and rear output shafts in the differential and rotate until both shafts have aligned with the splines on the brake cones and side gears. Alternately tighten the retaining screws to proper torque.

Diaphragm Control, Shift Fork and Lock-Up Hub

Disassembly

1. Remove the vent cover and seal ring.
2. Remove the retaining rings positioning the shift fork on diaphragm. Carefully pry the shift fork forward to gain access to the retaining rings. Remove the spring with a magnet.
3. Caution must be exercised in removal of the diaphragm control rod as it is retained by a spring loaded detent ball. Insert a magnet into the hole to hold the detent ball. Slip the diaphragm control rod out of case. Remove detent ball and spring.
4. Remove shifting fork, plastic shifting shoes and lock-up hub.

Assembly

1. Lubricate the shifting shoes and place them in the shift fork.
2. Install the shift fork and lock-up hub assembly in the case cover, long end of shift fork first (toward rear). Make certain that the shift fork does not separate from the lock-up hub by reaching through the needle bearings.
3. Insert the diaphragm control rod in the case and shifting fork, stopping before the detent ball hole is reached.
4. Install the detent ball and spring. Depress the detent ball with a ¼ in. pin punch and slide the diaphragm control rod into place.
5. Install the shift fork retaining pin, (clips) and the diaphragm retaining spring, the spring should be below the surface of the bore.
6. Install the vent cover and seal ring.

Reduction Unit

Disassembly

1. Remove PTO cover and gasket.
2. Remove snap ring from reduction main shaft rear end, slide the reduction main shaft and sun gear assembly forward and out. Remove needle bearings.
3. Remove as an assembly, the ring gear, reduction collar plate, pinion cage lock plate, shift collar hub and reduction collar hub. Using a soft hammer, remove the shift collar hub from the pinion cage lock plate.
4. Remove the pinion cage lock plate, needle bearing, ring gear, reduction collar plate and shift collar hub. Separate the reduction collar hub and needle bearing from shift collar hub.
5. When necessary, separate the reduction collar plate and ring gear by removing retaining snap ring.
6. Remove needle bearing and direct drive sleeve from the reduction shift collar.
7. Shift the reduction shift collar to the neutral (center) detent with the control lever. Disengage the shift fork. Place the shift in the direct drive detent position (rear), align the collar outer teeth with the inner teeth in the reduction holding plate. Place the fork and collar in the reduction position (front) detent, and remove the reduction shift collar.
8. Remove the annular bearing rear snap ring and bearing.
9. Remove the shift fork locating spring pin, large expansion plug, shift rail taper plug, and control lever.
10. Drive the spring pin out of the shift fork and rail with a 3/16 in. pin punch. Slide the shift rail forward out of the shift fork, and remove the shift fork. Remove the spring shift fork poppet ball. Drive the poppet taper plug into the shift rail bore and remove the plug and spring.
11. Remove the shift lever retaining pin and the shift lever assembly.
12. Remove the reduction holding plate snap ring and reduction holding plate.

Assembly

1. Align the shift fork locating spring holes in the reduction holding plate and housing. Install the reduction holding plate. Locating pins should index the plate in the case. Secure the plate with a snap ring, tabs facing forward.
2. Install the shift lever assembly into the housing, lever towards the rear. Position seal ring on groove in shift lever shaft.
3. Move the shift lever assembly inward and install taper pin.
4. Install the shift rail in the shift rail rear bore, grooved end first. Position the shift rail with flat side towards the poppet spring. Engage the shift rail with the shift lever assembly and position the rail so it is flush with the edge of the poppet bore. Place the poppet ball on the end of spring and insert the assembly in the poppet bore, using a spring pin as an installation tool. Depress the poppet ball and slide the shift rail over the poppet ball as far as the spring pin will allow. Remove the spring pin and place the shift rail in the first detent position.
5. Position the shift rail so the flat side is facing the shift lever assembly and the spring pin bore is aligned with the spring pin bore in the shift fork. Once the spring pin holes are aligned, install the spring pin so that it is flush with the outside surface of the shift fork.
6. Install the shift rail taper plug, poppet bore taper plug, shift rail cover expansion plug, shift fork spring locating pin and the control lever.
7. Place the shift fork in the neutral position (center) detent. Install the reduction shift collar so that the outer teeth engage with the reduction holding plate inner teeth, and the shift collar fork groove forward of the shift fork. Place the shift fork in the direct drive (rear) detent. Move the shift collar away and to the rear of the shift fork until the groove aligns with the shift fork. Engage the collar groove with the shift fork.
8. Place the direct drive sleeve in the reduction shift collar, needle bearing surface facing toward the front. Lubricate and install the needle bearing, against the direct drive sleeve.
9. Assemble the reduction collar plate hub and ring gear. Make certain that snap rings are seated in their grooves.
10. Install the needle bearing and reduction collar hub on the shift collar hub.
11. Install the ring gear, reduction collar plate and hub on the shift collar hub.
12. Place a needle bearing on the shift collar hub and the reduction collar hub.
13. Tap the pinion cage lock into place on the shift collar hub with a soft hammer and install assembly in housing. Place needle bearings on the shift collar hub and the pinion cage lock plate.
14. Install the reduction main shaft and sun gear into shift collar hub and through the direct drive sleeve and annular bearing. With a brass drift gently tap the assembly as far to the rear as possible. Place the rear spacer on the main shaft and secure with the selective snap ring which gives the tightest fit, between .004 in. and .009 in. clearance. Snap rings are available in thicknesses ranging from 0.089 in. to 0.105 in.
15. Install PTO cover and gasket, tighten attaching bolts to proper torque.

SPECIFICATIONS

TORQUE (FT. LBS.)

Transfer Case	
Breather	6-10
Chain Measuring Access Hole Plug	6-14
Drain Plug	15-25
Fill Plug	15-25
Lock-Up Cover to Transfer Case	8-10
Lock-Out Indicator Switch	10-15
Output Shaft Nut	90-150
PTO Cover to Transfer Case bolts: ⅜ in.-16	15-25
5/16 in.-18	10-20
Speedometer Adapter	20-30
Transfer Case Cover to Transfer Case	15-25
Transfer Case to Transmission Extension Bolt	30-50
Reduction Unit	
Cable Housing Clamp Nut	7-12
Fill Plug	15-25
Shift Lever Cable Clamp Nut	10-20
Shift Lever to Shift Nut	15-25
Reduction PTO Cover to Case	15-25
Reduction Unit to Transfer Case Bolts: 3/8 in.-16	15-25
5/16 in.-18	8-10

Warner 1345

The 1345 is a two piece all aluminum part time unit, lubricated by a positive displacement oil pump that channels oil through drilled holes in the rear output shaft. The pump turns with the output shaft and allows towing of the vehicle for extended distances.

Disassembly

1. Drain the fluid from the case.
2. Remove both output shaft yokes.
3. Remove the 4wd indicator switch.
4. Unbolt and remove the case cover. The cover may be pried off using a screwdriver in the pry bosses.
5. Remove the magnetic chip collector from the bottom of the case.
6. Slide the shift collar hub off the rear output shaft.
7. Compress the shift fork spring and remove the upper and lower spring retainers from the shaft.
8. Lift the four wheel drive lockup fork and lockup shift collar assembly from the case.
9. Remove the thrust washer being careful not to lose the nylon wear pads on the lockup fork.
10. Remove the snap ring and thrust washer from the front output shaft.
11. Grip the chain and both sprockets and lift them straight up to remove the drive sprocket, driven sprocket and chain from the output shafts.
12. Lift the front output shaft from the case.

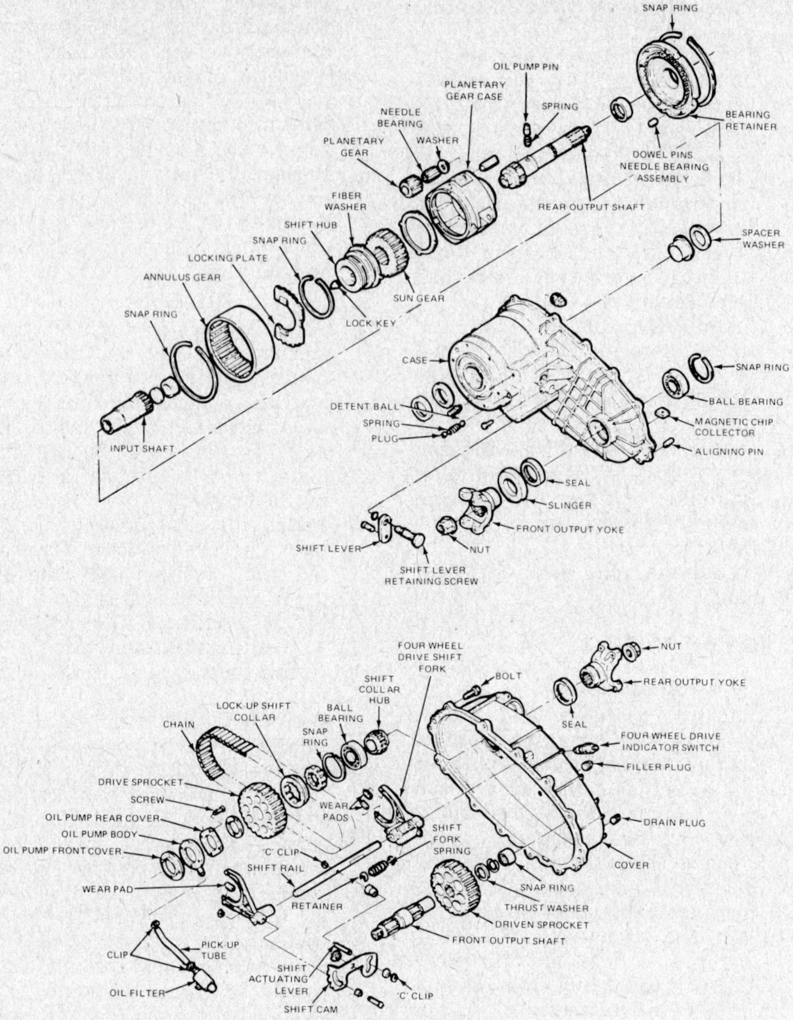

1345 exploded view

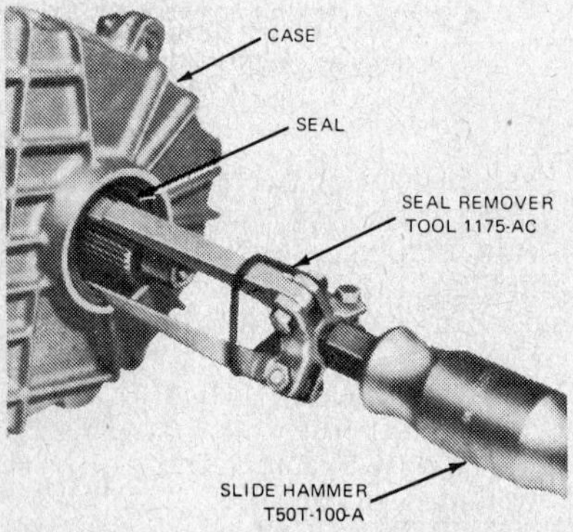

Removing the front output shaft seal

13. Remove the four oil pump attaching screws and remove the oil pump rear cover, pickup tube, filter and pump body, two pump pins, pump spring and oil pump front cover from the rear output shaft.
14. Remove the snap ring that holds the bearing retainer inside the case. Lift the rear output shaft while tapping on the bearing retainer with a plastic hammer.

    NOTE: Two dowel pins will fall into the case when the retainer is removed.

    Lift the rear output shaft and bearing retainer from the case.
15. Remove the rear output shaft from the bearing retainer. If necessary, press the needle bearing assembly out of the retainer.
16. Remove the C-clip that holds the shift cam to the actuating lever inside the case.

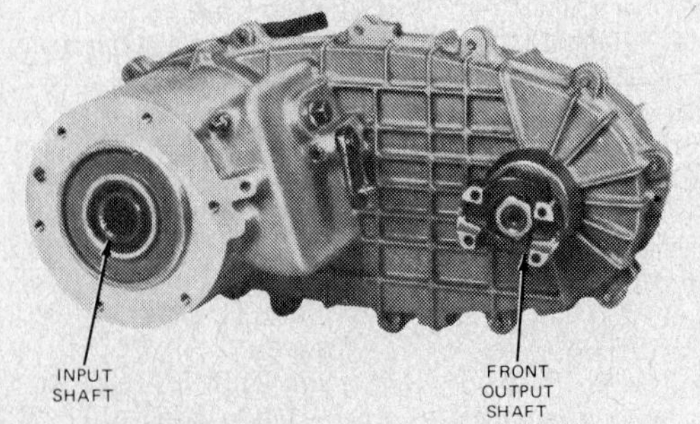

1345 transfer case front view

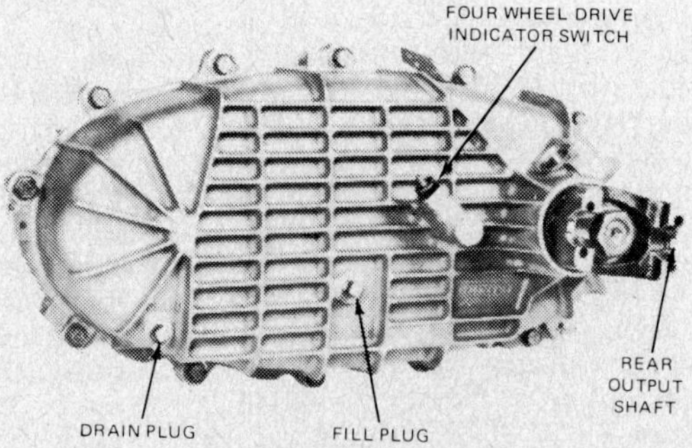

1345 transfer case rear view

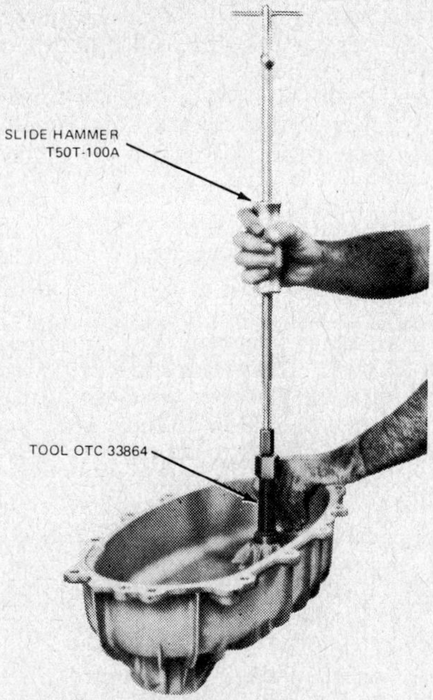

Removing the needle bearing

17. Remove the retaining screw and lift the shift lever from the case.

    NOTE: When removing the lever the shift cam will disengage from the shift lever shaft and may release the detent ball and spring from the case.
18. Remove the planetary gear set, shift rail, shift cam, input shaft and shift forks, as an assembly, from the case. Be careful not to lose the two nylon wear pads on the shift fork.

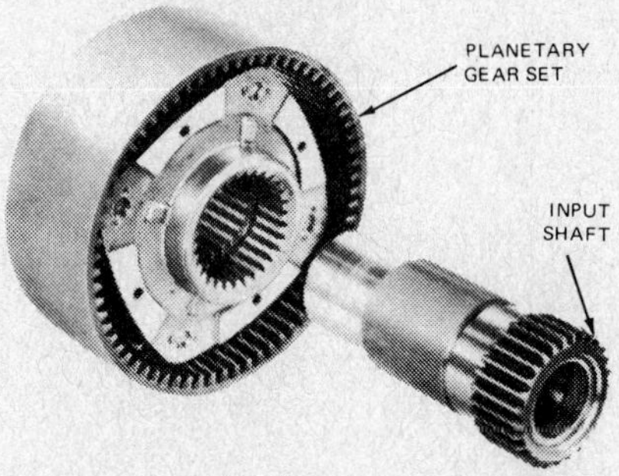

Removing the input shaft from the planetary gear set

19. Remove the spacer washer from the bottom of the case.
20. Drive the plug from the detent spring bore.

Assembly

Before assembly, lubricate all parts with clean automatic transmission fluid; either Ford CJ or Dexron II.

1. Assemble the planetary gear set, shift rail, shift cam, input shaft and shift fork together as a unit. Make sure that the boss on the shift cam is installed toward the case. Install the spacer washer on the input shaft.

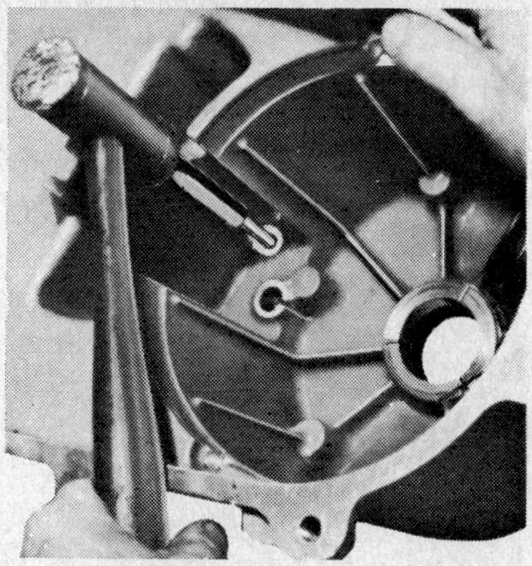
Removing the detent ball plug

2. Place the rear output shaft in the planetary gear set, making sure that the shift cam engages the shift fork actuating pin.
3. Lay the case on its side. Insert the rear output shaft and planetary gear set into the case. Make sure the spacer washer remains on the input shaft.
4. Install the shift rail into the hole in the case. Install the outer roller bushing into the guide in the case.
5. Remove the rear output shaft and position the shift fork in neutral.
6. Place the shift control lever shaft through the cam, and install the clip ring. Make sure that the shift control lever is pointed downward and is parallel to the front face of the case.
7. Check the shift fork and planetary gear engagement.
8. If removed, press a new needle bearing assembly into the bearing retainer.
9. Insert the output shaft through the bearing retainer from the bottom outward.

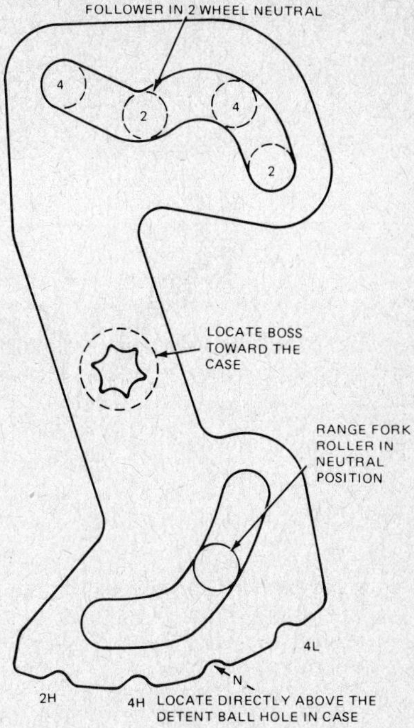

Connect shift cam engagement

10. Insert the rear output shaft pilot into the input shaft bushing. Align the dowel holes and the lower bearing.
11. Install the dowel pins. Install the snap ring that retains the bearing retainer in the case.
12. Insert the detent ball and spring in the detent bore in the case. Coat the seal plug with RTV sealant or its equivalent. Drive the plug into the case until the lip of the plug is 1/32 in. below the surface of the case. Peen the case over the plug in two places.
13. Install the pump front cover over the output shaft with the flanged side down. The word "TOP" must be facing the top of the transfer case.
14. Install the oil pump spring and two pump pins with the flat side

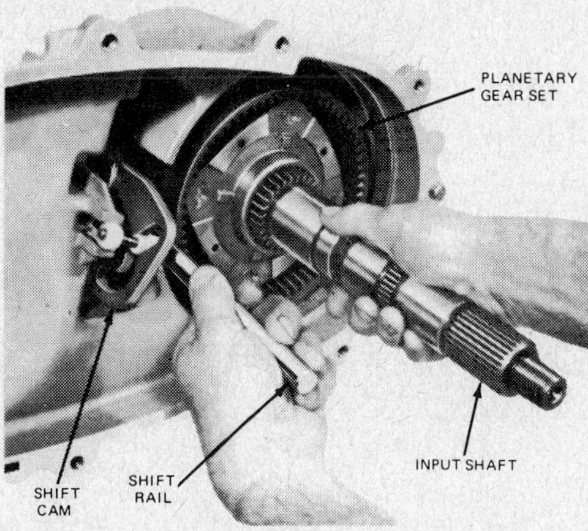

Installing the planetary gear set and shifter mechanism

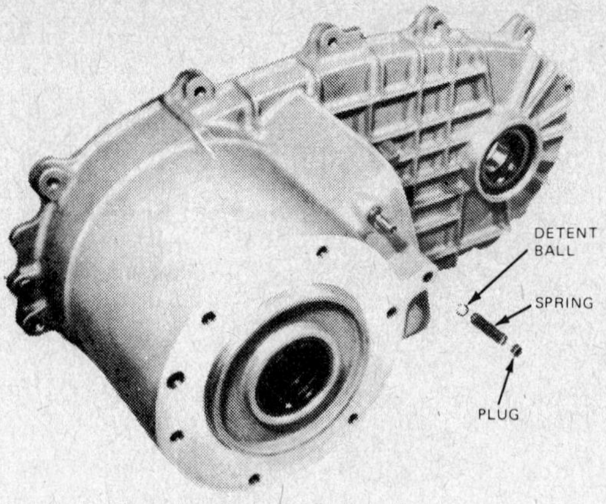

Installing the detent ball

outward in the hole in the output shaft. Push both pins in to install the oil pump body, pickup tube and filter.

15. Place the oil pump rear cover on the output shaft with the flanged side outward. The word "TOP" must be positioned toward the top of the case. Apply Loctite® or its equivalent to the oil pump bolts and torque them to 36-40 in-lb.
16. Install the thrust washer on the rear output shaft nest to the oil pump.
17. Place the drive sprocket on the front output shaft. Install the snap ring and thrust washer.
18. Install the chain on the drive sprocket and driven sprocket. Lower the chain into position in the case. The driven sprocket is installed through the front output shaft bearing and the drive sprocket is installed in the rear output shaft.
19. Engage the 4wd shift fork on the shift collar. Slide the shift fork over the shift shaft and the shift collar over the rear output shaft. Make sure the nylon wear pads are installed on the shift fork tips and the necked-down part of the shift collar is facing downward.
20. Push the 4wd shift spring downward and install the upper spring retainer. Push the spring upward and install the lower retainer.
21. Install the shift collar hub on the rear output shaft.
22. Apply a bead of RTV sealant on the case mounting surface. Lower the cover over the rear output shaft. Align the shift rail with its blind hole in the cover. Make sure the front output shaft is fully seated in its support bearing. Install the tighten the bolts to 40-45 ft-lb. Allow one hour curing time for the RTV sealant prior to using the case.
23. Install the 4wd indicator switch. Torque to 8-12 ft-lb.
24. Press the oil slinger on the front yoke. Install the front and rear output shaft yokes. Coat the nuts with Loctite® or equivalent and torque to 100-130 ft-lb.
25. Fill the unit with 6 pints of Ford CJ or Dexron II ATF. Tighten the fill plug to 18 ft-lb.
26. Install the unit in the vehicle and start the engine. Remove the level plug. If the fluid is flowing from the hole in a stream, the pump is not operating properly. The fluid should drip slowly from the hole.

IMPORT TRUCK SECTION

INDEX

INTRODUCTION

The Chevrolet Light Utility Vehicle (LUV) is exactly what the name implies. The LUV is a 1/2 ton mini-pickup truck, powered by a 4 cylinder engine with a manual 4-speed or automatic transmission.

The LUV was introduced in 1972 (model year). Designed to compete with the Japanese imports, the LUV is made by a Japanese automobile manufacturer, Isuzu Motors of Tokyo, Japan.

MODEL IDENTIFICATION

The LUV is available in conventional pick-up design with a 1/2 ton rating. A 4-wheel drive option is available beginning with the series 9.

Chevrolet LUV pickup

SERIAL NUMBER IDENTIFICATION

Vehicle

The chassis number plate is attached to the left-side rear door pillar within the cab. It has the date of manufacture and chassis number stamped on its face.

Engine

The engine number is stamped on the right upper center part of the cylinder block, adjacent to the distributor.

Location of the chassis number plate on the left side rear door panel

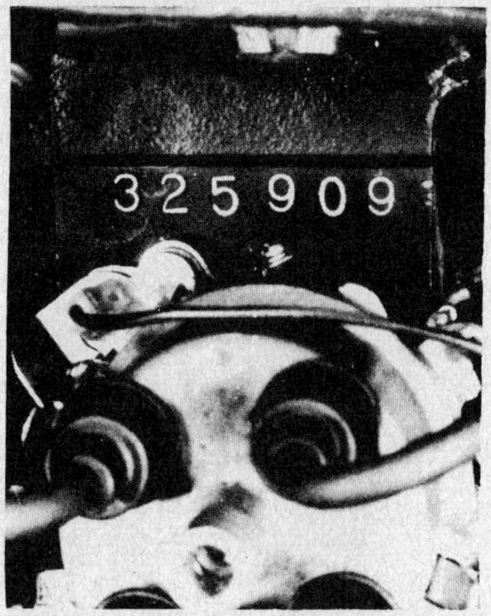

Location of the engine identification number on the center of the right side of the cylinder block

GENERAL ENGINE SPECIFICATIONS

Year	Engine Displacement cu in. (cc)	Carb Type	Advertised Horsepower (@ rpm)	Advertised Torque @ rpm (ft lbs)	Bore and Stroke (in.)	Advertised Compression Ratio	Oil Pressure (psi)
1973-75	110.8 (1817)	2-bbl	75 @ 5000	88 @ 3000	3.31 x 3.23	8.2:1	57
1976-80	110.8 (1817)	2-bbl	80 @ 4800	95 @ 3000	3.31 x 3.23	8.5:1	64

TUNE-UP SPECIFICATIONS

(When analyzing compression results, look for uniformity among cylinders, rather than specific pressures)

Year	Engine No. Cyl. Displacement cu in. (cc)	Spark Plugs Type	Spark Plugs Gap (in.)	Distributor Point Dwell (deg)	Distributor Point Gap (in.)	Ignition Timing (deg) MT	Ignition Timing (deg) AT	Intake Valve Opens (deg)	Fuel Pump Pressure (psi)	Idle Speed (rpm) MT	Idle Speed (rpm) AT	Valve Clearance (in.)⑦ In	Valve Clearance (in.)⑦ Ex
1973-74	4-110.8 (1817)	BP-6ES④	0.030 ④	49-55	②	③	—	31	3-4.5	⑤	—	0.004	0.006
1975	4-110.8 (1817)	BP-6ES	0.030	49-55	0.018-0.022	12B	—	31	3-4.5	900	—	0.004	0.006
1976	4-110.8 (1817)	BPR-6ES	0.030	47-57	0.016-0.020	6B	6B	21	3-4.5	900	900	0.006	0.010
1977-80	4-110.8 (1817)	BPR-6ES⑥	0.030	47-57	0.016-0.020	6B	6B	21B	2.6-3.3	900	900	0.006	0.010

① See tune-up sticker in the engine compartment
② On 1973 dual point distributor: Retarded points—0.016-0.024 in; Advanced points—0.018-0.022 in. On 1974 single point distributor: 0.016-0.024 in.
③ 8°B @ 700 rpm—1973; 12°B @ 700 rpm—1974
④ AC-44XLS with 0.035 in. gap—1974
⑤ 700 rpm—1973; 700 rpm w/o AC and 900 rpm w/AC—1974
⑥ AC-R44XLS
⑦ Cold
— Not applicable

NOTE: The underhood specifications sticker often reflects tune-up specification changes made in production. Sticker figures must be used if they disagree with those in this chart.

FIRING ORDER

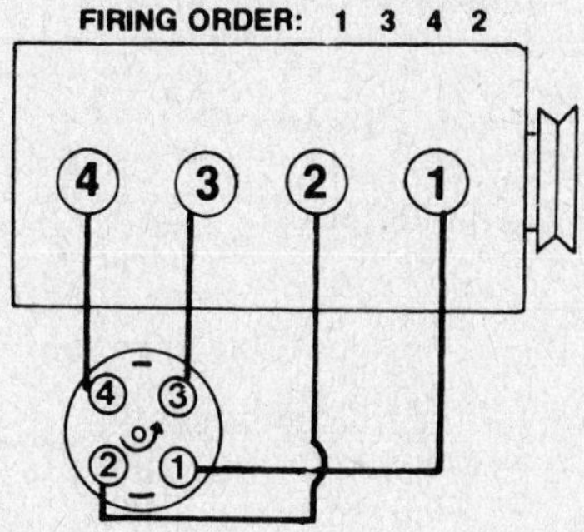

CRANKSHAFT AND CONNECTING ROD SPECIFICATIONS

(All measurements given in in.)

Year	Engine Displacement cu in. (cc)	Crankshaft Main Brg Journal Dia	Crankshaft Main Brg Oil Clearance	Crankshaft Shaft End-Play	Thrust on No.	Connecting Rod Journal Dia	Connecting Rod Oil Clearance	Connecting Rod Side Clearance
1973-75	110.8 (1817)	2.2016-2.2022	0.0015-0.0047	0.0059-0.0120	3	1.9262-1.9268	0.0020-0.0047	0.0079-0.0130
1976-80	110.8 (1817)	2.2016-2.2022	0.0008-0.0025	0.0024-0.0094	3	1.9262-1.9268	0.0007-0.0030	0.0137-Max.

CAPACITIES

Year	Engine No. Cyl. Displacement cu in. (cc)	Engine Crankcase (qts) With Filter	Engine Crankcase (qts) Without Filter	Transmission Pts to Refill After Draining 4-Speed	Transmission Pts to Refill After Draining Auto	Drive Axle (pts)	Gas Tank (gals)	Cooling System (qts) With Heater	Cooling System (qts) Without Heater
1973-1980	4-110.8 (1817 cc)	5.3	4.8	2.6②	6	2.7③	10①	6.4	5.3

① 13.2 gals. in 1974-80 ② W/transfer case—5.3 pts. ③ Front and rear

VALVE SPECIFICATIONS

Year	Engine Displacement cu. in. (cc)	Seat Angle (deg)	Face Angle (deg)	Spring Test Pressure (lbs @ in.) Outer	Spring Test Pressure (lbs @ in.) Inner	Free Length (in.) Outer	Free Length (in.) Inner	Stem-to-Guide Clearance (in.) Intake	Stem-to-Guide Clearance (in.) Exhaust	Stem Diameter (in.) Intake	Stem Diameter (in.) Exhaust
1973-1975	110.8 (1817)	45	45	41.8-50.1 @ 1.58	15.4-19.0 @ 1.50	2.05-1.99	1.78-1.73	.0016-.0079	.0020-.0098	.3150-.3102	.3150-.3091
1976-1980	110.8 (1817)	45	45	32.2-37.0 @ 1.614	18.7-21.5 @ 1.516	1.7874-1.8465	1.7244-1.7835	0.0009-0.0022	0.0015-0.0031	0.3102	0.3091

PISTON AND RING SPECIFICATIONS

(All measurements in inches)

Year	Engine Displacement cu in. (cc)	Piston Clearance	Ring Gap Top Compression	Ring Gap Bottom Compression	Ring Gap Oil Control	Ring Side Clearance Top Compression	Ring Side Clearance Bottom Compression	Ring Side Clearance Oil Control
1973-75	110.8 (1817)	0.0018-0.0026	0.008-0.016	0.008-0.016	0.012-① 0.039	0.0012-0.0028	0.0012-0.0028	0.0008-0.0024
1976-80	110.8 (1817)	0.0018-0.0026	0.008-0.016	0.008-0.016	0.008-0.035	0.0059	0.0058	0.0059

① 1977: .008-.035

TORQUE SPECIFICATIONS

(All readings in ft lbs unless noted)

Year	Engine Displacement cu in. (cc)	Cylinder Head Bolts	Rod Bearing Bolts	Main Bearing Bolts	Crankshaft Pulley Bolt	Flywheel-to-Crankshaft Bolts
1973-80	110.8 (1817)	①	43	72	50③	36②

① On 1973 models, tighten, in sequence to 60 ft lbs; on 1974-75 models, tighten to 43 ft lbs first, then loosen completely and retighten 1, 2, 3, and 6 to 70 ft lbs, and the remaining bolts to 60 ft lbs.
On 1976 and later models, tighten to 61 ft lbs first, then retighten to 72 ft lbs.
② 69 ft lbs in 1974-79.
③ 1976-79—87 ft lbs.

TORQUE SEQUENCES

Cylinder Head

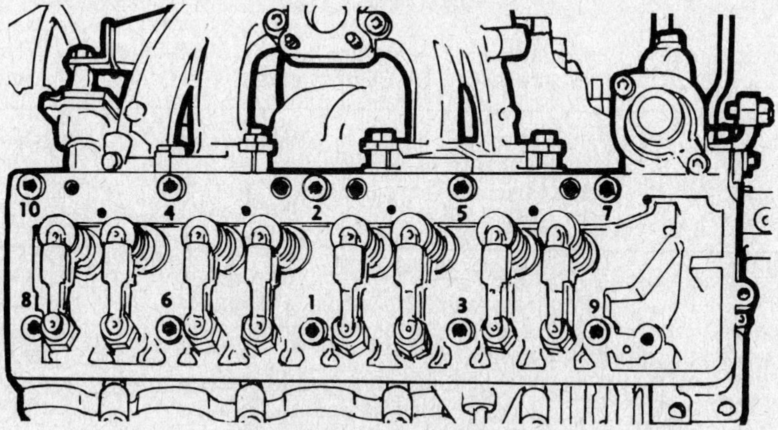

1973-75 torque sequence

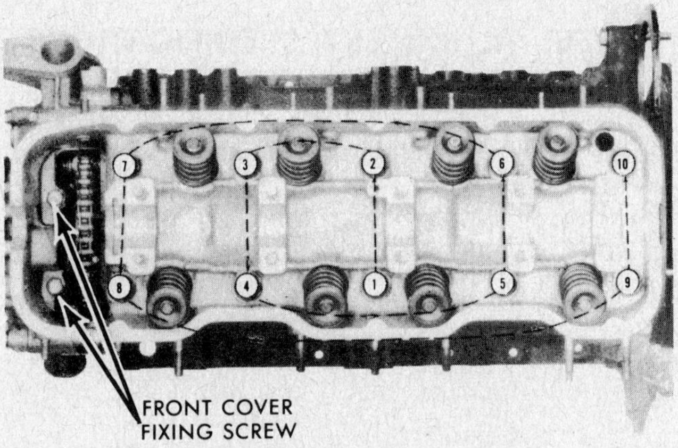

1976 and later torque sequence

ALTERNATOR AND REGULATOR SPECIFICATIONS

	ALTERNATOR				REGULATOR				
					Field Relay		Regulator		
Year	Part No.	Field Current @ 12V (amps)	Output (amps)	Part No.	Core Cap (in.)	Point Gap (in.)	Core Gap (in.)	Point Gap (in.)	Volts @ 75F°
1973-76	LT 130 83	1.2-1.7	30	TL 12 66	.032-.039	.016-.024	.024-.039	.012-.016	13.5-14.5
1977-80	LT 135-30	—	35	TL 12 87	.032-.039	.016-.024	.024-.039	.012-.016	13.8-14.8

BATTERY AND STARTER SPECIFICATIONS

(All trucks use 12 volt, negative ground electrical systems)

			STARTER							
			Lock Test			No Load Test				
Year	Model	Battery Amp Hour Capacity	Amps	Volts	Torque (ft/lb)	Amps	Volts	RPM	Brush Spring Tension (oz)	Min. Brush Length (in.)
1973-80	All	50	330 or less	5.1	5:8	60 or less	12	6000 or more	56	0.49①

① 1977: 0.47

BRAKE SPECIFICATIONS

(All measurements given are (inches) unless noted)

				Brake Disc			Brake Drum		Minimum Lining Thickness	
Year	Model	Lug Nut Torque (ft/lb)	Master Cylinder Bore	Minimum Thickness	Maximum Run-Out	Diameter	Max. Machine O/S	Max. Wear Limti	Front	Rear
1973-80	All	65	0.875	0.668 (after refinishing) 0.653 (discard) ①	②	10.00	10.059	10.079	0.059 ③	0.059

① Discard dimension stamped into disc.

② Maximum run-out—0.005 in. Rate of change must not exceed 0.001 in. in 30°.

③ 1976-79—0.264 in. measured from backside of shoe table. Is point of contact of warning sensor.

NOTE: Minimum lining thickness is as recommended by the manufacturer. Due to variations in state inspection regulations, the minimum allowable thickness may be different than recommended by the manufacturer.

WHEEL ALIGNMENT SPECIFICATIONS

		Caster		Camber			
Year	Model	Range (deg)	Preferred Setting (deg)	Range (deg)	Preferred Setting (deg)	Toe-in (in)	Steering Axis Inclination (deg)
1973-75	All	0 to 1P	½P①	½P to 1½P	1P②	+ ⅛ ± $^{1}/_{16}$③	7
1976	All	1$^{1}/_{16}$N to $^{15}/_{16}$P	$^{1}/_{16}$N	¼N to 1¼P	½P	0	7
1977-80	All	1$^{1}/_{16}$N to $^{15}/_{16}$P	$^{1}/_{16}$N	¼N to 1¼P	½P	0	7½

① Caster should not vary more than ½° from side-to-side

② Camber should not vary more than ½° from side-to-side

③ Always adjust the toe-in after adjusting caster and camber

TUNE-UP PROCEDURES

Spark Plugs

REMOVAL

1. Remove the wire from the end of the spark plug by grasping the wire by the rubber boot. If the boot sticks to the plug, remove it by twisting and pulling at the same time. Do not pull the wire itself or you will most certainly damage the delicate carbon core.

2. Use a $^{13}/_{16}$ in spark plug socket to loosen all of the plugs about two turns.

3. If compressed air is available, blow off the area around the spark plug holes. Otherwise, use a rag or a brush to clean the area. Be careful not to allow any foreign material to drop into the spark plug holes.

4. Remove the plugs by unscrewing them the rest of the way from the engine.

INSPECTION

Check the plugs for deposits and wear. If they are not going to be replaced, clean the plugs thoroughly. Remember that any kind of deposit will decrease the efficiency of the plug. Plugs can be cleaned on a spark plug cleaning machine, or you can do an acceptable job of cleaning with a stiff brush.

Check the spark plug gap before installation. The ground electrode must be parallel to the center electrode and the specified size wire gauge should pass through the gap with a slight drag. If the electrodes are worn, it is possible to file them level.

INSTALLATION

1. Insert the plugs in the spark plug hole and tighten them hand-tight. Take care not to cross-thread them.

2. Tighten the plugs to 18–25 ft lbs.

3. Install the spark plug wires on their plugs. Make sure that each wire is firmly connected to each plug.

Breaker Points and Condenser

Never replace the points without replacing the condenser and vice versa.

Remember that a change in the point gap or dwell also changes the ignition timing. Therefore, if the points are adjusted, you must also correct the ignition timing.

***NOTE:** See "Emission Controls" for an explanation of the dual point distributor and how it works.*

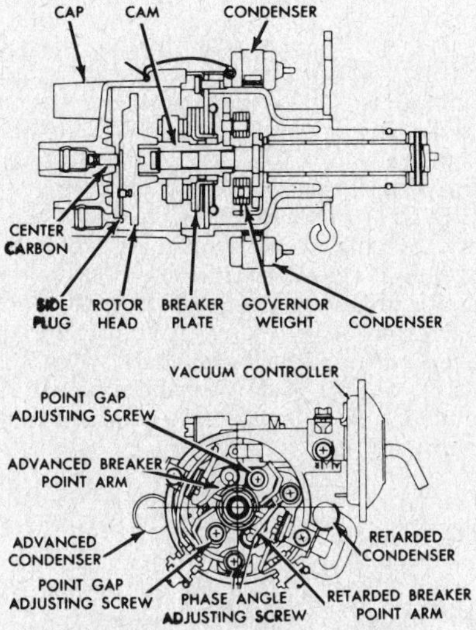

Dual point distributor

INSPECTION OF POINTS

1. Disconnect the high-tension wire from the top of the distributor.
2. Remove the distributor cap by prying off the spring clips on the sides of the cap.
3. Remove the rotor from the distributor shaft by pulling it straight up. Examine the condition of the rotor. If it is cracked or the metal tip is excessively worn or burned, it should be replaced. Clean the metal tip with fine emery paper.
4. Pry open the contacts of the points with a screwdriver and check the condition of the contacts. If they are excessively worn, burned or pitted, they should be replaced.
5. If the points are in good condition, adjust them and replace the rotor and the distributor cap. If the points need to be replaced, follow the replacement procedure given below.

REMOVAL AND INSTALLATION

***NOTE:** Dual point distributors are serviced in a similar manner as single point units as far as replacement of the breaker points is concerned.*

1. Remove the coil high-tension wire from top of the distributor cap. Remove the distributor cap from the distributor and place it out of the way. Remove the rotor from the distributor shaft.
2. Loosen the screw that holds the condenser lead to the body of the breaker points and remove the condenser lead from the points.
3. Remove the screw that holds and grounds the condenser to the distributor body. Remove the condenser from the distributor and discard it.
4. Remove the points assembly attaching screws and adjustment lockscrews. A screwdriver with a holding mechanism will come in handy here, so that you don't drop a screw into the distributor and have to remove the entire distributor to retrieve it.
5. Remove the points by lifting them straight up and off the locating dowel on the plate. Wipe off the cam and and apply new cam lubricant. Discard the old set of points.
6. Slip the new set of points onto the locating dowel and install the screws that hold the assembly onto the plate. Do not tighten them all the way.
7. Attach the new condenser to the plate with the ground screw.
8. Attach the condenser lead to the points at the proper place.
9. Apply a small amount of cam lubricant to the shaft where the rubbing block of the points touches.

ADJUSTMENT OF THE BREAKER POINTS WITH A FEELER GAUGE

Single Point Distributor

1. If the contact points of the assembly are not parallel, bend the stationary contact so that they make contact across the entire surface of the contacts. Bend only the stationary bracket part of the point assembly; not the moveable contact.
2. Turn the engine until the rubbing block of the points is on one of the high points of the distributor cam. You can do this by either turning the ignition switch to the start position and releasing it quickly ("bumping" the engine) or by using a wrench on the bolt that holds the crankshaft pulley to the crankshaft.
3. Place the correct size feeler gauge between the contacts. Make sure it is parallel with the contact surfaces.
4. With your free hand, insert a screwdriver into the notch provided for adjustment or into the eccentric adjusting screw, then twist the screwdriver to either increase or decrease the gap to the proper setting.
5. Tighten the adjustment lockscrew and recheck the contact gap to make sure that it didn't change when the lockscrew was tightened.
6. Replace the rotor and distributor cap, and the high-tension wire that connects the top of the distributor and the coil. Make sure that the rotor is firmly seated all the way onto the distributor shaft and that the tab of the rotor is aligned with notch in the shaft. Align the tab in the base of the distributor cap with the notch in the distributor body. Make sure that the cap is firmly seated on the distributor and that the retainer springs are in place. Make sure that the end of the high-tension wire is firmly placed in the top of the distributor and the coil.

Dual Point Distributor

The two sets of breaker points are adjusted with a feeler gauge in the same manner as those in a single point distributor. Check the "Tune-Up Specifications" chart for the correct setting for either set of points; they are not the same.

ADJUSTMENT OF THE BREAKER POINTS WITH A DWELL METER

Single Point Distributor

1. Adjust the points with a feeler gauge as previously described.
2. Connect the dwell meter to the ignition circuit according to the manufacturer's instructions. One lead of the meter is connected to a ground and the other lead is connected to the distributor post on the coil. An adapter is usually provided for this purpose.
3. If the dwell meter has a set line on

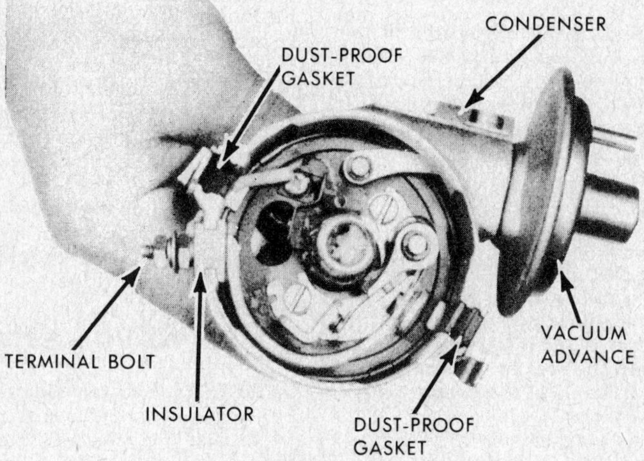

Single point distributor

it, adjust the meter to zero the indicator.

4. Start the engine.

***NOTE:** Be careful when working on any vehicle while the engine is running. Make sure that the transmission is in Neutral and that the parking brake is applied. Keep hands, clothing, tools and the wires of the test instruments clear of the rotating fan blades.*

5. Observe the reading on the dwell meter. If the reading is within the specified range, turn off the engine and remove the dwell meter.

***NOTE:** If the meter does not have a scale for 4 cylinder engines, multiply the 8 cylinder reading by two.*

6. If the reading is above the specified range, the breaker point gap is too small. If the reading is below the specified range, the gap is too large. In either case, the engine must be stopped and the gap adjusted in the manner previously covered.

After making the adjustment, start the engine and check the reading on the dwell meter. When the correct reading is obtained, disconnect the dwell meter.

7. Check the adjustment of the ignition timing.

Dual Point Distributor

The breaker point dwell is set with a dwell meter in the same manner as for a single point distributor. However, the retard set of points is deenergized at curb idle and it will be necessary to energize the retard set of points in order to get a reading on a dwell meter. After adjusting the dwell of the advance set of points at curb idle speed, have an assistant depress the accelerator pedal at least 7° or move the throttle linkage enough to energize the accelerator switch, opening the accelerator relay-to-distributor relay circuit, thus energizing the retard set of breaker points, and getting retard breaker point dwell reading.

Ignition Timing

The timing marks are located at the front crankshaft pulley and consist of a pointer attached to the engine block and graduations on the crankshaft pulley.

1. Set the dwell angle to the proper specification.

2. Locate the timing marks on the crankshaft pulley and the front of the engine.

3. Clean off the timing marks, so that you can see them.

4. Use chalk or white paint to color the mark on the crankshaft pulley that will indicate the correct timing, when aligned with the pointer. It is also helpful to mark the tip of the pointer with a small dab of color.

5. Attach a tachometer to the engine.

6. Attach a timing light to the engine according to the manufacturer's instructions. If the timing light has three wires, one, usually green or blue, is attached to the No. 1 spark plug with an adapter. The other wires are connected to the battery. The red wire goes to the positive side of the battery and the black wire is connected to the negative terminal of the battery.

7. Disconnect the vacuum line to the distributor at the distributor and plug the vacuum line. A golf tee does a good job.

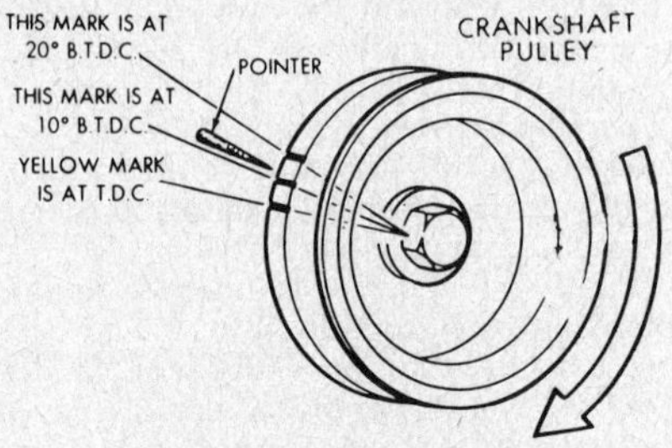

1973-75 timing marks

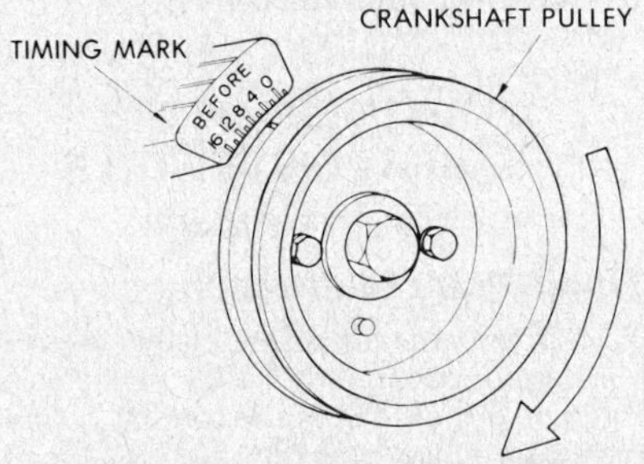

1976 and later timing marks

8. Check to make sure that all of the wires clear the fan and then start the engine.

9. Adjust the idle to the correct setting.

10. Aim the timing light at the timing marks. If the marks that you put on the pulley and the engine are aligned when the light flashes, the timing is correct. Turn off the engine and remove the tachometer and the timing light. If the marks are not in alignment, proceed with the following steps.

11. Turn off the engine.

12. Loosen the distributor lockbolt just enough so that the distributor can be turned with a little effort.

13. Start the engine. Keep the wires of the timing light clear of the fan.

14. With the timing light aimed at the pulley and the marks on the engine, turn the distributor in the direction of rotor rotation to retard the spark, and in the opposite direction of the rotor rotation to advance the spark. Align the marks on the pulley and the engine with the flashes of the timing light.

Valve Lash

***NOTE:** While all valve adjustments must be made as accurately as possible, it is better to have the valve adjustment slightly loose than slightly tight, as a burned valve may result from overly tight adjustments.*

ADJUSTMENT

***NOTE:** The valves are adjusted with the engine cold.*

1. Make sure that the cylinder head and camshaft retaining bolts are tightened to the proper torque.

2. Remove the camshaft carrier sidecover.

3. Turn the crankshaft with a wrench on the front pulley attaching bolt or by "bumping" the engine with the starter until the No. 1 piston is at TDC of the compression stroke. You can tell when the piston is coming up on the compression stroke by removing the spark plug and placing your thumb over the hole; you will feel air being forced out of the spark plug hole past your thumb. Both valves on No. 1 cylinder will be closed. Stop turning the crankshaft when the TDC timing mark on the crankshaft pulley is directly aligned with the timing mark pointer.

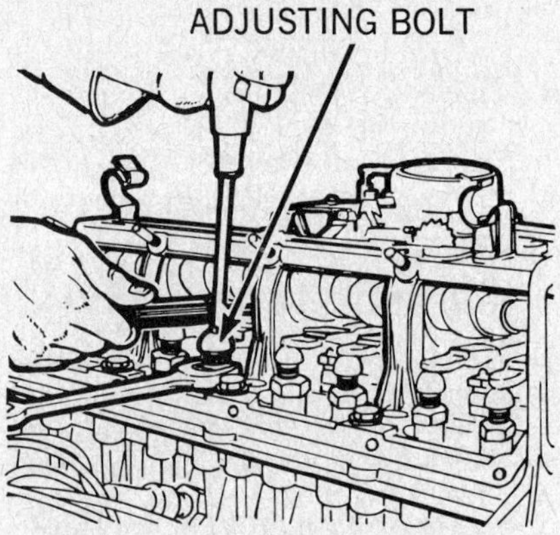

Adjusting the valves. The feeler gauge is placed between the rocker arm and camshaft lobe

Number of Cylinders	1		2		3		4	
Valve Arrangement	Exh.	In.	In.	Exh.	Exh.	In.	In.	Exh.
When piston in No. 1 cylinder is held at T.D.C.	0	0	0		0			
When piston in No. 4 cylinder is held at T.D.C.				0		0	0	0

Valve adjusting sequence

4. With the No. 1 piston at TDC of the compression stroke, check the clearance between the rocker arm and the camshaft on 1973–76 models, and between the rocker arm and valve stem on 1977–79 models with the proper thickness feeler gauge on Nos. 1 and 2, intake valves and Nos. 1 and 3 exhaust valves.

5. Adjust the clearance by loosening the locknut with an open-end wrench, turning the adjusting screw with a phillips head screwdriver and retightening the locknut. The proper thickness feeler gauge should pass between the camshaft or valve stem and the rocker with a slight drag when the clearance is corrected.

6. Turn the crankshaft one full turn to position the No. 4 piston at TDC of its compression stroke. Adjust the remaining valves: Nos. 2 and 4 exhaust and Nos. 3 and 4 intake in the same manner as outlined in Step 5.

7. Install the camshaft carrier side-cover.

Carburetor

This section contains only tune-up adjustment procedures for carburetors. Descriptions, adjustments, and overhaul procedures for carburetors can be found in the "Fuel System" section.

IDLE SPEED AND MIXTURE ADJUSTMENT

1. Start the engine and run it until it reaches operating temperature.
2. If it hasn't already been done, check and adjust the ignition timing. After you have set the timing, turn off the engine.
3. Attach tachometer to the engine.
4. Remove the air cleaner.
5. Start the engine and, with the transmission in Neutral, check the idle speed on the tachometer. If the reading on the tachometer is correct, turn off the engine and remove the tachometer. If it is not correct, proceed to the following steps.
6. Turn the idle adjusting screw with a screwdriver—clockwise to increase idle speed and counterclockwise to decrease it.
7. If the vehicle is equipped with air conditioning:
   a. Turn on the AC to maximum cold and high blower. Disconnect the vacuum line to the air cleaner housing air compensator and plug the inlet manifold;
   b. Open the throttle approximately $^1/_3$ and allow the throttle to close. This will allow the speed-up solenoid to reach full travel;
   c. Adjust the speed-up controller adjusting screw to set the idle speed to 900 rpm;
   d. Open the throttle about $^1/_3$ and allow it to close. Read the idle rpm. If it is not at 900 rpm, repeat step c until the correct reading is obtained. Shut off the engine.
8. Turn the mixture adjusting screw all the way. Seat the needle tip *lightly* to avoid damaging the tip. Back the screw out $3^1/_2$ turns.
9. Start the engine. Turn the mixture screw until the maximum engine rpm is achieved.
10. Reset the engine idle speed to 900 rpm.
11. Turn the idle mixture screw clockwise (lean) until the engine speed drops to 850 rpm.
12. Reset the idle mixture screw $^1/_2$ turn counter-clockwise (rich) from step 11 position.
13. Rest the throttle adjusting screw to 900 rpm.
14. Reconnect any plugged vacuum lines that may have been disconnected.

ENGINE ELECTRICAL

Distributor

REMOVAL AND INSTALLATION

1. Remove the high-tension wires from the distributor cap terminal towers, noting their positions to assure correct reassembly.
2. Remove the primary lead from the coil terminal.
3. Disconnect the vacuum line.
4. Unlatch the two distributor cap retaining clips and remove the distributor cap.
5. Note the position of the rotor in relation to the base. Scribe a mark on the base of the distributor and on the engine block to facilitate reinstallation. Align the marks with the direction the metal tip of the rotor is pointing.
6. Remove the bolt which holds the distributor to the engine.
7. Lift the distributor assembly from the engine.

To install:

8. Insert the distributor into the engine. Line up the mark on the engine with the metal tip of the rotor. Make sure that the vacuum advance diaphragm is pointed in the same direction as it was pointed originally. This will be done automatically if the marks on the engine and the distributor are lined up with the rotor.
9. Install the distributor hold-down bolt and clamp. Leave the screw loose enough so that you can move the distributor with heavy hand pressure.
10. Connect the primary wire to the coil. Install the distributor cap on the distributor housing. Secure the distributor cap with the spring clips.
11. Install the spark plug wires. Make sure that the wires are pressed all the way into the top of the distributor cap and firmly onto the spark plug.
12. Adjust the point dwell and set the ignition timing.

NOTE: If the crankshaft has been tuned or the engine disturbed in any manner while the distributor was removed, or if the marks were not drawn, it will be necessary to initially time the engine. Follow the procedure given below.

1. It is necessary to place the No. 1 cylinder in the firing position to correctly install the distributor. To locate

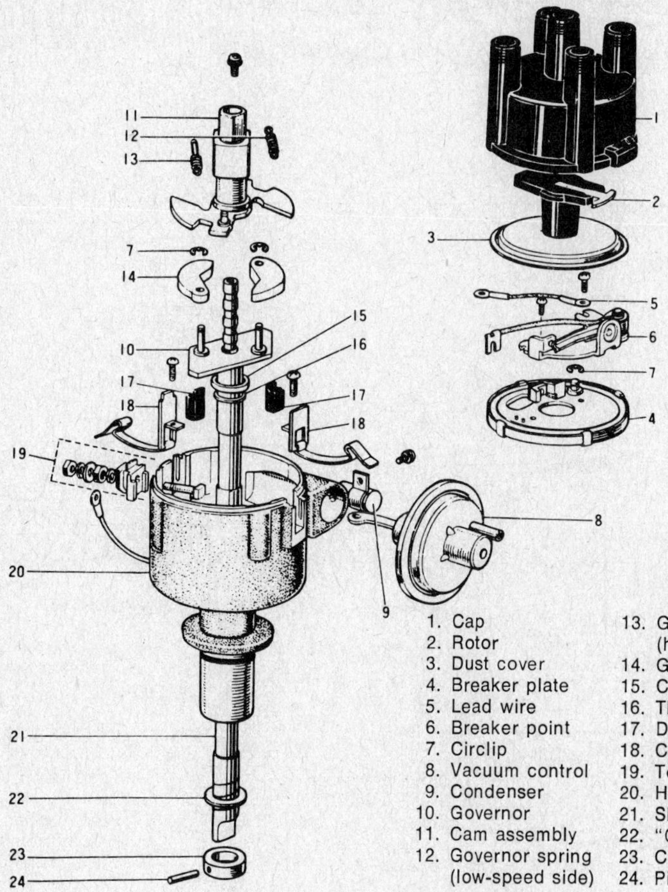

1. Cap
2. Rotor
3. Dust cover
4. Breaker plate
5. Lead wire
6. Breaker point
7. Circlip
8. Vacuum control
9. Condenser
10. Governor
11. Cam assembly
12. Governor spring (low-speed side)
13. Governor spring (high-speed side)
14. Governor weight
15. Cap washer
16. Thrust washer
17. Dust gasket
18. Cap clamp
19. Terminal
20. Housing
21. Shaft
22. "O" ring
23. Collar
24. Pin

Exploded view of the distributor

this position, the ignition timing marks on the crankshaft front pulley are used.

2. Remove the No. 1 cylinder spark plug. Turn the crankshaft until the piston in the No. 1 cylinder is moving up on the compression stroke. This can be determined by placing your thumb over the spark plug hole and feeling the air being forced out of the cylinder. Stop turning the crankshaft when the timing marks that are used to time the engine are aligned.

3. Oil the distributor housing lightly where the distributor bears on the cylinder block.

4. Install the distributor so that the rotor, which is mounted on the shaft, points toward the No. 1 spark plug terminal tower position when the cap is installed. Of course you won't be able to see the direction in which the rotor is pointing if the cap is on the distributor. Lay the cap on the top of the distributor and make a mark on the side of the distributor housing just below the No. 1 spark plug terminal. Make sure that the rotor points toward that mark when you install the distributor.

5. When the distributor shaft has reached the bottom of the hole, move the rotor back and forth slightly until the driving lug on the end of the shaft enters the slots cut in the end of the oil pump shaft and the distributor assembly slides down into place.

6. When the distributor is correctly installed, the breaker points should be in such a position that they are just ready to break contact with each other. This is accomplished by rotating the distributor body after it has been installed in the engine. Once again, line up the marks that you made before the distributor was removed from the engine.

7. Install the distributor hold-down bolt.

8. Install the spark plug into the No. 1 spark plug hole and continue from Step 3 of the distributor installation procedure.

Alternator

1973–76 Chevrolet LUV vehicles are equipped with a 30 amp alternator with an electro-mechanical, adjustable voltage regulator. 1977 and later models use a similar 35 amp unit.

ALTERNATOR PRECAUTIONS

To prevent damage to the alternator and regulator, the following precautionary measures must be taken when working with the electrical system.

1. Never reverse battery connections. Always check the battery polarity visually. This is to be done before any connections are made to be sure that all of the connections correspond to the battery ground polarity of the LUV.

2. Booster batteries for starting must be connected properly. Make sure that the positive cable of the booster battery is connected to the positive terminal of the battery that is getting the boost.

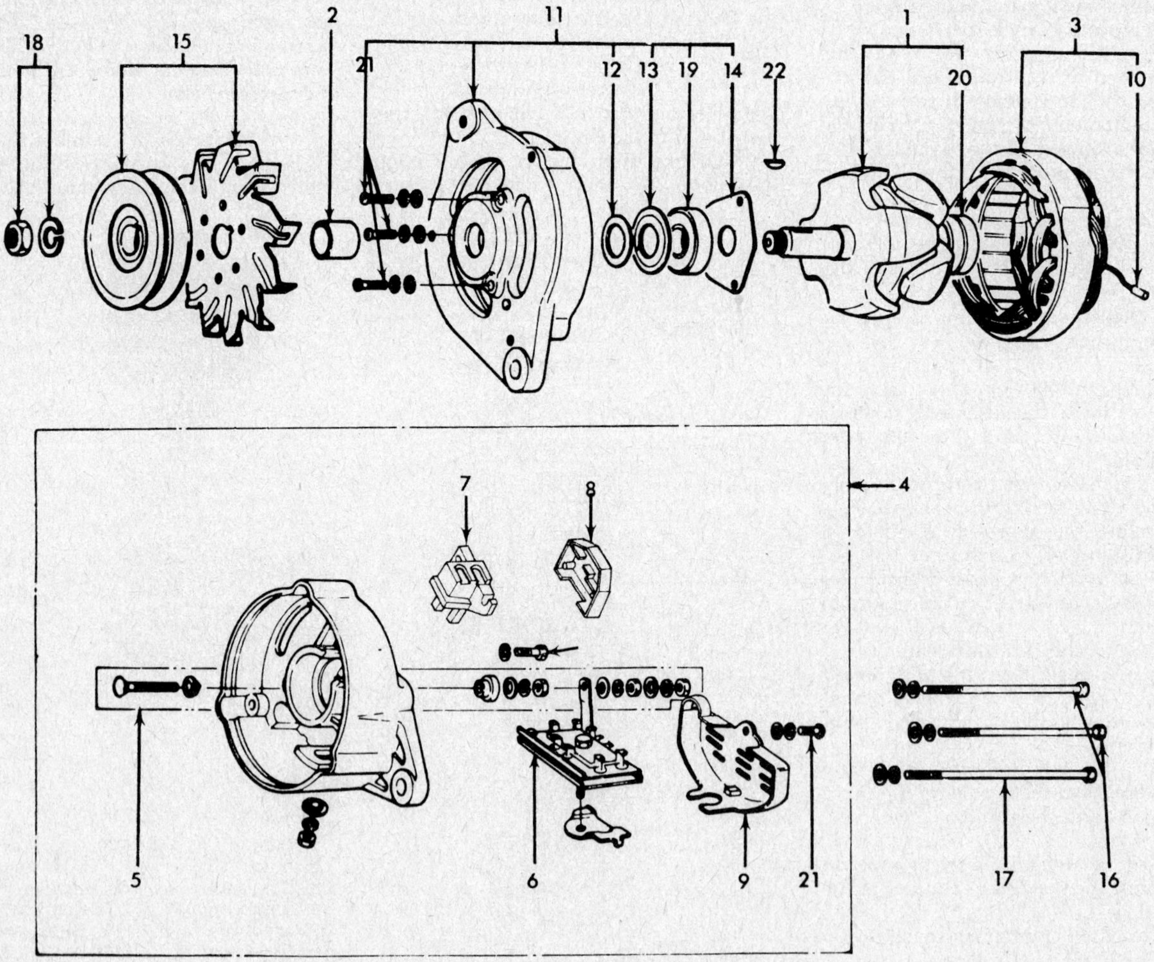

1. Rotor assembly
2. Spacer
3. Stator assembly
4. Rear cover assembly
5. Terminal bolt assembly
6. Diode assembly
7. Brush holder assembly
8. Cover
9. Diode cover
10. Terminal
11. Front cover assembly
12. Seal
13. Seal retainer
14. Bearing retainer
15. Pulley assembly w/fan
16. Through-bolt
17. Through-bolt
18. Nut and lockwasher assembly
19. Front ball bearing
20. Rear ball bearing
21. Screw
22. Key

Exploded view of the alternator—typical

This applies to both negative and ground cables.

3. Disconnect the battery cables before using a fast charger; the charger has a tendency to force current through the diodes in the opposite direction for which they were designed. This burns out the diodes.

4. Never use a fast charger as a booster for starting the vehicle.

5. Never disconnect the voltage regulator while the engine is running.

6. Do not ground the alternator output terminal.

7. Do not operate the alternator on an open circuit with the field energized.

8. Do not attempt to polarize an alternator.

REMOVAL AND INSTALLATION

1. Remove the air pump.
2. Disconnect the battery ground cable before disconnecting the cable from the alternator "A" terminal. This is a hot cable connected directly to the battery.
3. Disconnect the alternator circuit at the connector and disconnect the cable from the "A" terminal.
4. Remove the mounting bolts on the lower part of the alternator and the fan belt adjusting bolt and remove the alternator.
5. Install the alternator in the reverse order of removal and tighten the fan belt and air pump belt tension.

BELT TENSION ADJUSTMENT

Any engine V-belt is correctly tensioned when the longest span of belt between pulleys can be depressed about 1/4 in. in the middle by moderate thumb pressure. To adjust, loosen the accessory's slotted adjusting bracket bolt. If the hinge bolt is very tight, it may be necessary to loosen it slightly to move the item.

CAUTION: ***Be careful not to overtighten belts, as this will damage the bearings, particularly in air or water pumps and alternators.***

Regulator

REMOVAL AND INSTALLATION

1. Remove the negative battery cable from the battery.
2. Disconnect the electrical leads at the regulator, taking note to the positions in order to facilitate correct reconnection.
3. Remove the two mounting screws and remove the regulator.
4. Install the regulator in the reverse order of removal.

ADJUSTMENT

1. Remove the regulator from the vehicle and remove the regulator cover.
2. If the contact points are rough, dress them with fine sandpaper.
3. Check and adjust core gap first, and then the point gap. Adjustment of the yoke gap is unnecessary.
4. Adjust the core gap by loosening the screws attaching the contact set to the yoke. Move the contact set up or down as required. The standard core gap is 0.024–0.039 in. Tighten the attaching screw.
5. Adjust the point gap by loosening the screw attaching the upper contact. Move the upper contact up or down as required. The standard point gap is 0.012–0.016 in.
6. Adjust the regulated voltage by means of the adjusting screw. Turn the adjusting screw in to increase voltage and out to reduce voltage. When the correct adjustment is obtained, secure the adjusting screw by tightening the locknut. The regulated voltage is 13.5–14.5 volts for 1973–76 models and 13.8–14.8 for 1977 and later.
7. Install the regulator cover, reconnect the electrical leads and install the regulator.

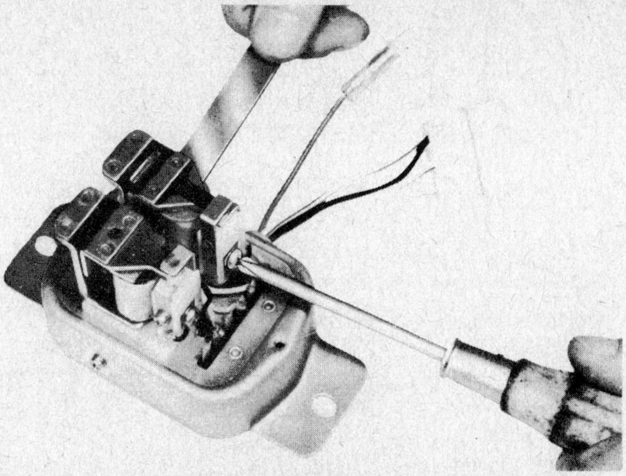

Adjusting the regulator core gap

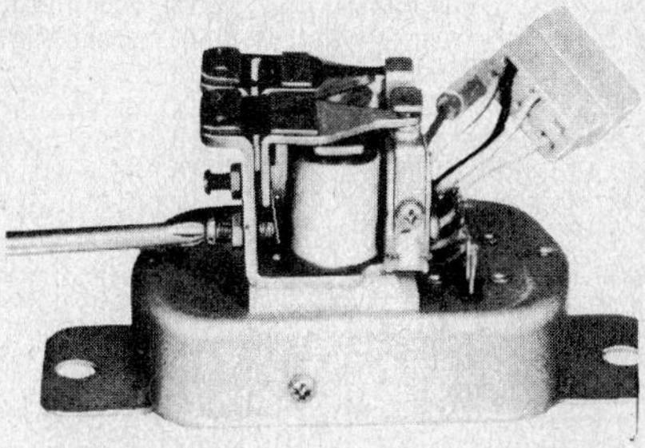

Adjusting the voltage regulator

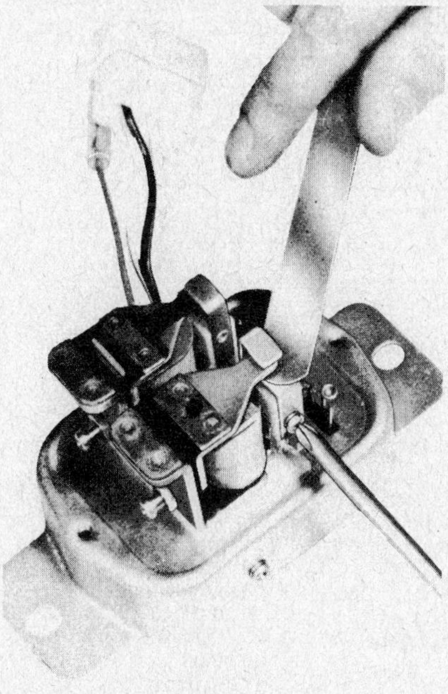

Adjusting the regulator point gap

Starter

REMOVAL AND INSTALLATION

1. Disconnect the negative battery cable from the battery.
2. Disconnect the starter wiring at the starter, taking note of the positions for correct reinstallation.
3. Remove the bolts attaching the starter to the engine and remove the starter from the vehicle.
4. Install the starter in the reverse order of removal.

BRUSH REPLACEMENT

1. With the starter out of the vehicle, remove the bolts holding the solenoid to the top of the starter and remove the solenoid.
2. To remove the brushes, remove the two thru-bolts and the two rear cover attaching screws and remove the rear cover.
3. Disconnect the brushes electrical leads and remove the brushes.
4. Install the brushes in the reverse order of removal.

STARTER DRIVE REPLACEMENT

1. With the starter motor removed from the vehicle, remove the solenoid from the starter.
2. Remove the two thru-bolts and separate the gear case from the yoke housing.

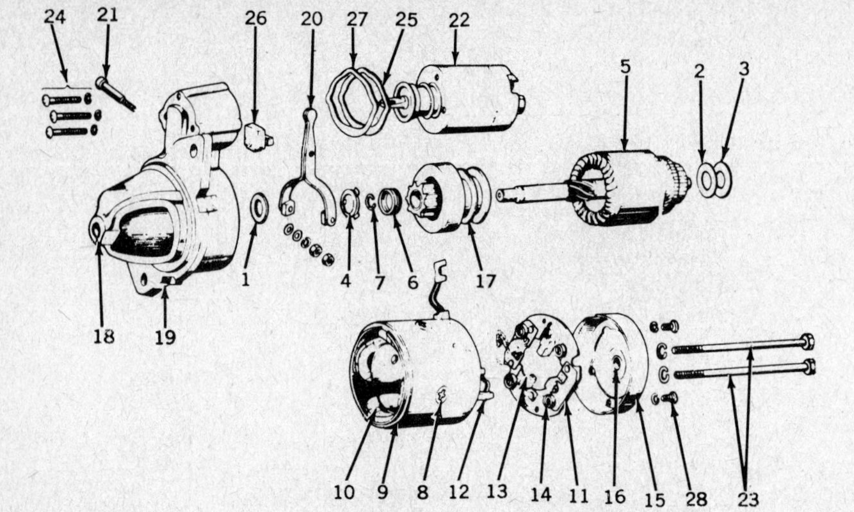

1. Thrust washer
2. Spacer
3. Washer
4. Stopper washer
5. Armature
6. Pinion stopper
7. Snap-ring
8. Field coil retaining screw
9. Yoke housing
10. Field coils
11. Brush holder
12. Brush (field coil)
13. Brush (ground)
14. Brush tension spring
15. Rear cover
16. Rear armature bearing
17. Clutch drive
18. Front armature bearing
19. Gear case
20. Shift lever
21. Shift lever pivot bolt
22. Solenoid switch
23. Through-bolts
24. Solenoid-to-gear case attaching bolts
25. Washer
26. Dust cover
27. Insulator
28. Brush holder-to-rear cover attaching screw

Exploded view of the starter—1973-75

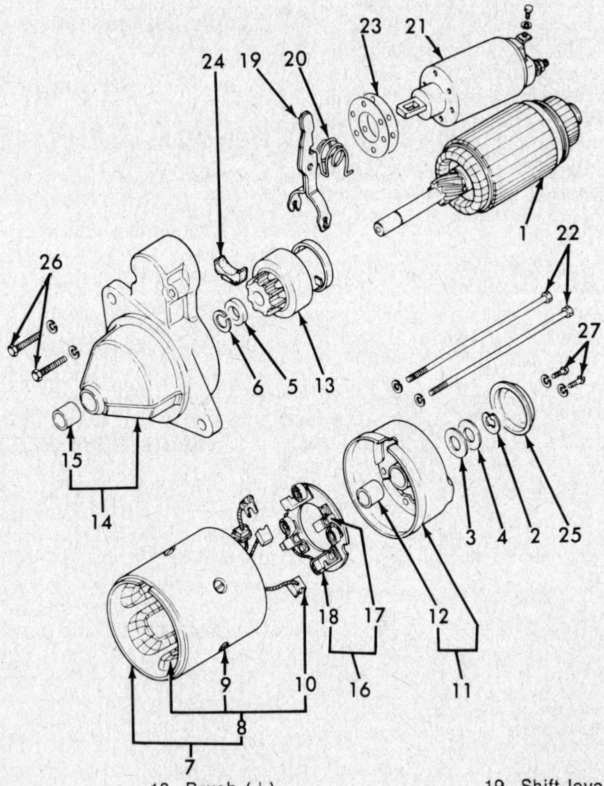

1. Armature
2. Snap ring
3. Thrust washer
4. Thrust washer
5. Pinion stop
6. Pinion stop clip
7. Yoke
8. Field coil
9. Screw
10. Brush (+)
11. Rear cover assembly
12. Rear cover bushing
13. Pinion
14. Gear case assembly
15. Gear case bushing
16. Brush holder assembly
17. Brush (—)
18. Brush spring
19. Shift lever
20. Torsion spring
21. Magnetic Switch
22. Bolt
23. Adjusting plates
24. Dust cover, gear case
25. Dust cover, rear cover
26. Bolt
27. Screw

Exploded view of the starter—1976 and later

3. Remove the pinion stopper clip and the pinion stopper.

4. Slide the starter drive off the armature shaft.

5. Install the starter drive and reassemble the starter in the reverse order of removal.

ENGINE MECHANICAL

Engine Removal and Installation

1973–75

1. Disconnect the battery ground cable.

2. Prior to removing the hood, scribe a mark in the area of the hinges to ensure that the hood is reinstalled in its original position. Remove the hood.

3. Drain the cooling system through the drain cock on the radiator and on the cylinder block.

4. Drain the engine oil.

5. Disconnect the upper and lower hoses from the radiator and remove the radiator.

6. Disconnect the hoses from the air cleaner and remove the air cleaner assembly.

7. Remove the carburetor control cable.

8. Remove the choke control cable.

9. Disconnect the carburetor wiring.

10. Disconnect the exhaust pipe from the exhaust manifold at the flange.

11. Disconnect the alternator and starter wiring.

12. Disconnect the heater hose at the fender side.

13. Disconnect the vacuum hose.

14. Disconnect the spark plug wires from the distributor.

15. Disconnect the grounding cable between the cylinder head cover and the dashboard at the cylinder head cover side.

16. Disconnect the engine wiring at the two connectors.

17. Disconnect the oil pressure unit cord and temperature sending unit lead and the distributor ground wire; remove the wire from the three clips on the engine.

18. Disconnect the fuel line from the fuel pump.

19. Disconnect the ground cable on the timing gear case at the engine side.

20. Disconnect the two hoses from the fuel tank evaporative emission control check and relief valve.

21. Disconnect the driveshaft at the rear axle.

22. Remove the driveshaft from the transmission and install a plug in the end of the transmission to prevent loss of lubricant.

23. Disconnect the clutch slave cylinder.

24. Remove the exhaust pipe bracket from the clutch housing.
25. Disconnect the speedometer drive cable at the transmission.
26. Disconnect the body grounding cable between the transmission and the body at the floor side.
27. Remove the gearshift lever assembly.
28. Insert a lifting device into the engine hangers and lift the engine slightly.
29. Remove the engine rear mounts.
30. Check that the engine and auxiliary parts are separated completely from the chassis frame, then lift the engine out of position. When hoisting the engine, adjust the tension so that the front end of the engine is elevated slightly above the rear of the engine.
31. When the front of the engine clears the deflector, continue raising and move the engine toward the front of the truck.
32. Install the engine in the reverse order of removal. After the installation is complete, fill the crankcase with oil, the cooling system with coolant, adjust the clutch pedal free-play, and start the engine and check for leaks.

1976–80

1. Raise hood and disconnect the battery cables.
2. Remove the skid plate and drain both the cooling system and the oil pan.
3. Remove the air cleaner assembly and vacuum hoses. Mark the vacuum hoses for reinstallation.
4. Disconnect all hoses, tubing and electrical leads from the engine and mark them for reinstallation.
5. Remove the radiator and fan blade assembly.
6. Disconnect the exhaust pipe from the exhaust manifold.
7. Raise the vehicle and, if equipped with a manual transmission, remove the clutch return spring and slave cylinder. Fasten the cylinder to the frame rail with a piece of wire.
8. Remove the starter motor and fasten it to the frame rail with a piece of wire.
9. Remove the flywheel cover pan.
10. Remove the bell housing bolts and support the transmission.
11. Lift the engine slightly and remove the engine mount nuts.
12. Make certain that all lines, hoses, wires and cables have been disconnected from the engine and the frame.
13. Remove the engine from the vehicle with the front of the engine raised slightly.
14. Installation is the reverse of removal.

Cylinder Head

REMOVAL AND INSTALLATION

1973–75

1. Disconnect the negative battery cable, drain the cooling system and remove the air cleaner and attendant hoses.
2. Remove the air pump.
3. Remove the alternator.
4. Disconnect the carburetor throttle linkage and fuel line together with the solenoid electrical lead.
5. Disconnect the exhaust pipe from the exhaust manifold.
6. Remove the six bolts retaining the camshaft carrier front cover and remove the front cover.
7. Remove the oil line from the secondary chain tensioner plug.
8. Remove the chain tensioner plug along with the tensioner spring.
9. Remove the bolt and plate washer retaining the timing (camshaft) sprocket.
10. Remove both upper secondary timing chain damper bolts, located in the front of the cylinder head.
11. Loosen both lower timing chain damper bolts.
12. Separate the timing (camshaft) sprocket from the camshaft, together with the chain.
13. Carefully separate the sprocket from the chain to prevent the timing sprocket pin from falling out.

NOTE: When removing the camshaft from the timing sprocket, the pin should be positioned in the top. Mark the position of the pin on the timing sprocket prior to disassembling the parts.

14. Hold the chain in position with a wire or cord.
15. Remove the 10 bolts retaining the camshaft cover and remove the cover.
16. Loosen the 12 camshaft carrier bolts evenly in progression and remove them. The camshaft carrier is under tension from the valve springs. Loosen all the bolts alternately in progression, so that a single bolt will not receive the tension of the valve springs. Care must be taken not to loosen the camshaft carrier locating dowel.
17. Loosen the sleeve nut on the air injection nozzle and remove the nozzle by turning it about 180°.
18. Remove the three bolts retaining the timing gear case to the cylinder head.
19. Loosen the cylinder head bolts in a progressional sequence.
20. Remove the cylinder head, gasket and O-rings.

Install the cylinder head in the reverse order of removal, as follows:

21. Position the cylinder head gasket on the block with the "Top" side up. Insert the O-rings into the oil ports.
22. Position a gear case-to-cylinder head gasket on the gear case, if necessary.

Removing the camshaft carrier front cover through 1975

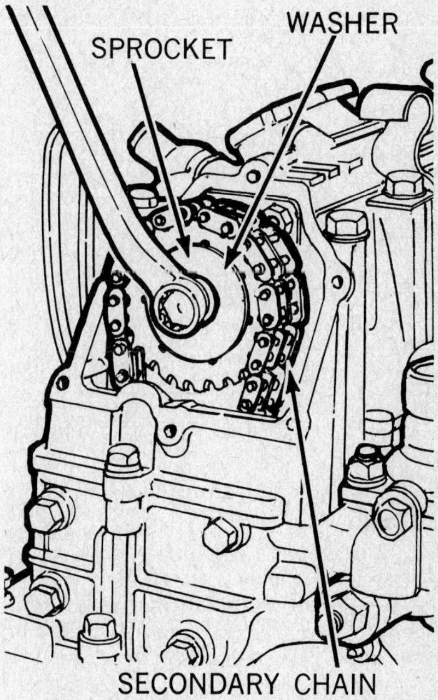

Removing the camshaft timing sprocket retaining bolt through 1975

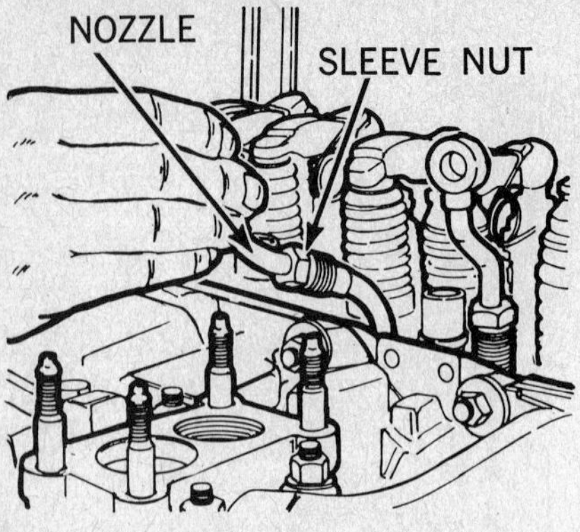

Removal of the air injection nozzle

23. Install the cylinder head on the block and tighten the cylinder head bolts to specifications.

24. Tighten the three bolts attaching the timing gear case to the cylinder head.

25. Install the air injection nozzles. Do not tighten them securely at this time.

26. Align the setting mark on the camshaft thrust plate with the corresponding mark on the camshaft.

27. Position the O-rings to the camshaft carrier. Install these parts in position and lightly tighten the bolts retaining the dowels. Install the longest bolts in the position of the dowel.

28. Install the camshaft carrier bolts. Tighten the bolts alternately, in progression to 15 ft lbs to compress the valve springs evenly. Note that the camshaft carrier is also used to retain two portions of the air manifold bracket and PCV hose clips.

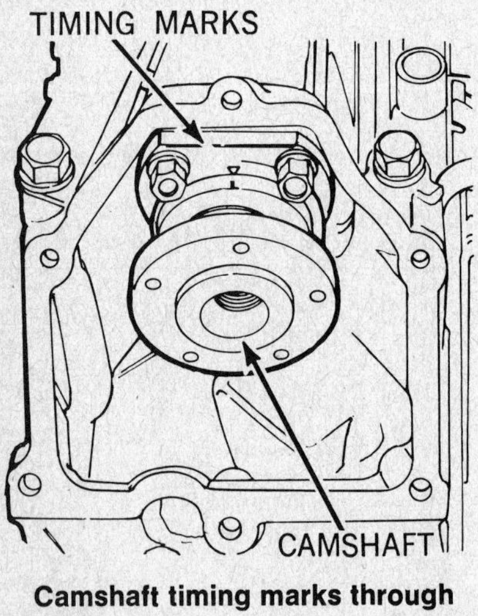

Camshaft timing marks through 1975

29. With the No. 4 cylinder at TDC of the compression stroke, check that the setting mark on the camshaft and on the thrust plate are correctly aligned. If the setting marks are not in good alignment, make the necessary adjustment as follows:

a. If the setting mark on the camshaft and the thrust plate are not in alignment, attach the camshaft sprocket to the camshaft, insert the pin into a hole in the camshaft timing sprocket and turn the crankshaft until the marks line up. Then, bring the camshaft into a free state by removing the camshaft timing sprocket from the camshaft and, set the piston in the No. 4 cylinder to TDC of the compression stroke. If the engine has been turned in reverse in the course of this adjustment, make a final adjustment by turning the engine in the normal direction of rotation so that the marks are lined up, with the chain properly tensioned on the correct side.

b. When installing the camshaft timing sprocket on the camshaft, keep their mating faces free of foreign matter because the drive torque is relayed to the timing sprocket from the camshaft by means of frictional contact.

30. Bring the camshaft timing sprocket together with the timing chain, so that the punched mark on the sprocket is located at the 12 o'clock position. Assemble the sprocket to the camshaft.

31. Adjust the position of the camshaft timing sprocket, relative to the camshaft, so that the punched mark on the camshaft timing sprocket is turned up when the drive side of the timing chain is tensioned by pushing the chain tensioner shoe from the plug hole in the secondary chain tensioner. When the camshaft timing sprocket is correctly installed, the punched mark on the sprocket is brought to a position 6° 20′ from the top in the direction of rotation.

32. Hold the parts in their relative position. Look through each of the five holes in the camshaft timing sprocket to find a hole in alignment with the hole in the camshaft flange and insert the pin into that hole.

33. Tighten the camshaft timing sprocket attaching bolt, with the plate washer installed, to 33 ft lbs.

34. Install the camshaft carrier front cover.

35. Install the secondary chain tensioner.

36. Assemble the remaining components to the engine in the reverse order of removal, working backwards from Step 5.

37. Adjust the valves.

1976–80

1. Remove the cam cover.
2. Remove the EGR pipe clamp bolt at the rear of the cylinder head.
3. Raise the vehicle on a hoist and disconnect the exhaust pipe at the exhaust manifold.
4. Lower the vehicle from the hoist and drain the cooling system.
5. Disconnect the heater hoses at the inlet manifold and at the rear of the cylinder head.
6. Disconnect the accelerator linkage and fuel line at the carburetor, all necessary electrical connections, spark plug wires and vacuum lines.
7. Rotate the camshaft until the No. 4 cylinder is in the firing position. Remove the distributor cap and mark the rotor to housing relationship.
8. Lock the timing chain adjuster by depressing and turning the automatic adjuster side pin 90° clockwise.
9. Remove the timing sprocket to camshaft bolt and remove the sprocket from the camshaft.

NOTE: Keep the sprocket on the chain damper and chain.

10. Disconnect the AIR hose and the check valve at the exhaust manifold.
11. Remove the cylinder head to timing cover bolts.
12. Remove the cylinder head bolts in a progressional sequence, starting with the outer bolts.
13. Remove the cylinder head, intake and exhaust manifold as a unit.
14. To install, reverse the removal procedure and tighten the bolts in the sequence and torque shown in the specifications table in the front of the section.

VALVE GUIDE REPLACEMENT

1. With the cylinder head removed from the vehicle and the valves removed from the head, drive the guides out toward the upper face of the cylinder head with a suitable driver. The valve guides cannot be driven out downward because they are secured in place with a snap-ring.
2. Lubricate the outside of the new valve guide with oil. Press it all the way into position, from the upper face of the cylinder head, until it is brought in contact with the snap-ring. Allowable interference between the cylinder head and the valve guide is 0.0016 in.

Valve Rockers

REMOVAL AND INSTALLATION

1973–75

1. Remove the camshaft cover as outlined under "Cylinder Head Removal."

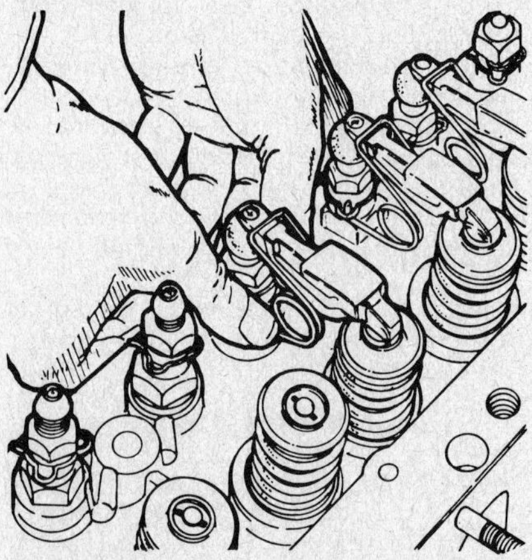

Removing or installing the rocker retaining spring

2. Remove the rocker spring from the pivot and lift the rocker from the cylinder head. Be careful not to lose the rocker guide resting on the top of each of the valves.

3. Install in the reverse order of removal.

1976–80

1. Remove the cam cover.

2. Loosen the rocker arm shaft bracket nuts a little at a time, in sequence, starting with the outer brackets.

3. Remove the nuts from the rocker arm shaft brackets.

4. Remove the spring from the rocker arm shaft and remove the rocker brackets and arms.

5. Before installing apply a generous amount of clean engine oil to the rocker arm shaft, rocker arms and valve stems.

6. Install the longer shaft on the exhaust valve side and the shorter shaft on the intake side, so that the aligning marks on the shafts are turned on the front side.

7. Assemble the rocker arm shaft brackets and rocker arms to the shafts so that the cylinder number that is on the upper face of the brackets is pointed toward the front of the engine.

8. Align the mark on the No. 1 rocker arm shaft bracket with the mark on the intake and exhaust valve side rocker arm shafts.

9. Make certain the amount of projection of the rocker arm shaft beyond the face of the No. 1 rocker arm shaft bracket is longer on the exhaust side shaft than on the intake shaft when the rocker arm shaft stud holes are aligned with the rocker arm shaft bracket stud holes.

10. Place the rocker arm shaft springs in position between the shaft bracket and rocker arm.

11. Check that the punch mark on the rocker arm shaft is turned upward, then install the rocker arm shaft bracket assembly onto the cylinder head studs. Align the mark on the camshaft with the mark on the No. 1 rocker arm shaft bracket.

12. Tighten the rocker arm shaft brackets stud nuts to 16 ft lbs.

***NOTE:** Hold the rocker arm springs with an adjustable wrench while torquing nuts to prevent damage to the spring. Start with the center nut and work outward.*

13. Adjust the valves and install the cam cover.

Combination Manifold

REMOVAL AND INSTALLATION

Although the intake and exhaust manifolds are separate pieces, they are removed and installed as a unit.

1. Remove the air cleaner with all of the hoses.

2. Disconnect all of the electrical leads, throttle linkage, fuel and vacuum lines from the carburetor.

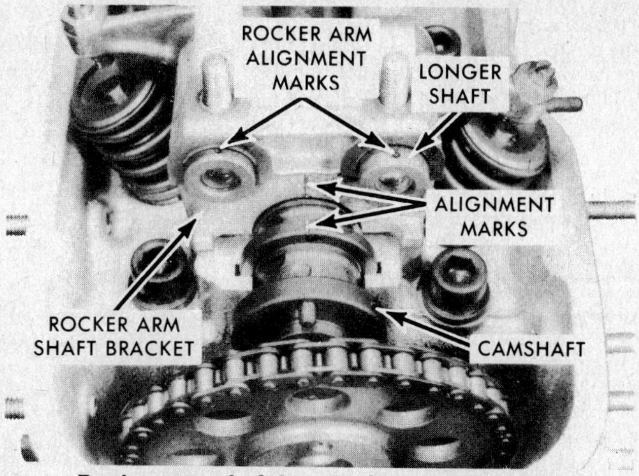

Rocker arm shaft installation—1976 and later

3. The carburetor can be removed from the manifold at this point or can be removed as an assembly with the intake manifold.

4. Disconnect the exhaust pipe from the exhaust manifold.

5. Slightly loosen all of the manifold attaching nuts, and then remove them, working from the outside toward the center. Remove the two manifolds.

6. Install the manifolds in the reverse order of removal, making sure that the mating surfaces are clean before installation.

Intake Manifold

REMOVAL AND INSTALLATION

1976–80

1. Disconnect the battery ground cable and remove the air cleaner assembly.

2. Remove the EGR pipe clamp bolt at the rear of the cylinder head.

3. Raise the vehicle and remove the EGR pipe from the intake and exhaust manifolds.

4. Remove the EGR valve and bracket assembly from the intake manifold.

5. Lower the vehicle and drain the cooling system.

6. Remove the upper coolant hoses from the manifold.

7. Disconnect the accelerator linkage, vacuum lines, electrical wiring and fuel line from the intake manifold.

8. Remove the retaining nuts and remove the manifold from the cylinder head.

9. Remove the lower heater hose while holding the manifold away from the engine. Remove the manifold from the vehicle.

10. Installation is reverse of removal.

Exhaust Manifold

REMOVAL AND INSTALLATION

1976–80

1. Disconnect the battery ground cable and remove the air cleaner assembly.

2. Remove the EGR pipe clamp bolt at the rear of the cylinder head.

3. Raise the vehicle and remove the EGR pipe from the intake and exhaust manifolds.

4. Separate the exhaust pipe from the manifold.

5. Remove the manifold shield and remove the heat stove.

6. Remove the manifold retaining nuts and remove the manifold from the engine.

7. Installation is the reverse of removal.

Timing Gear Cover

REMOVAL AND INSTALLATION

1973–75

1. Disconnect the negative battery cable, drain the cooling system, and remove the alternator and air pump with their respective mounting brackets and drive belts.

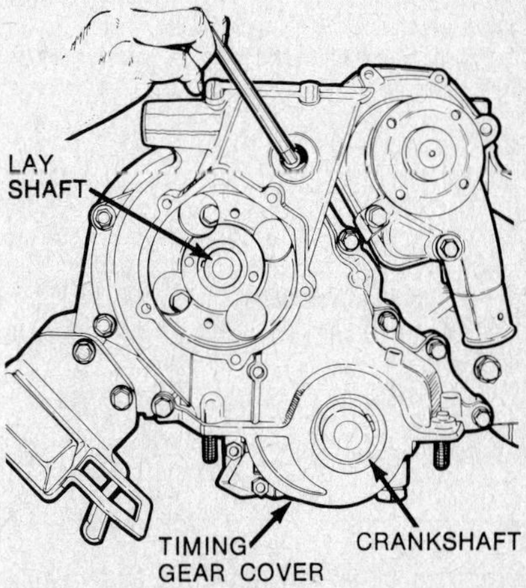

With the access plug removed, remove the bolt on the inner face of the gear cover. The layshaft in the illustration is the jackshaft referred to in the text through 1975

2. Remove the crankshaft pulley bolt and remove the pulley.
3. Remove the six bolts retaining the front cover and remove the front camshaft carrier cover.
4. Remove the 17 bolts retaining the timing gear case.
5. Remove the access plug and take out the bolt on the inner face of the gear case.
6. Insert the edge of a screwdriver into the cutaway portions on the outer rim of the timing gear case and pry it off the engine.
7. Install the timing gear case and the camshaft carrier front cover in the reverse order of removal and assemble the engine in the reverse order of disassembly.

1976–80

1. Remove the cylinder head.
2. Remove the oil pan.
3. Remove the oil pickup tube from the oil pump.
4. Remove the harmonic balancer. (See Timing Cover Seal—Removal and Installation)
5. Remove the air pump drive belt.
6. If equipped with air conditioning, remove the compressor and lay it to one side. Then remove the mounting brackets.
7. Remove the distributor cap and the distributor.
8. Remove the front cover attaching bolts, then the cover.
9. Install a new gasket onto the cylinder block.
10. Align the oil pump drive gear punch mark with the oil filter side of the cover; then align the center of the dowel pin with the alignment mark on the oil pump case.
11. Rotate the crankshaft until the no. 1 and the no. 4 cylinders are at top dead center.
12. Install the front cover by engaging the pinion gear with the oil pump drive gear on the crankshaft.
13. Check that the punch mark on the oil pump drive gear is turned to the rear side as viewed through the clearance between the front cover and the cylinder block.
14. Check that the slit at the end of the oil pump shaft is parallel with the front face of the cylinder block and is offset forward.
15. Reverse steps 1 thru 7.

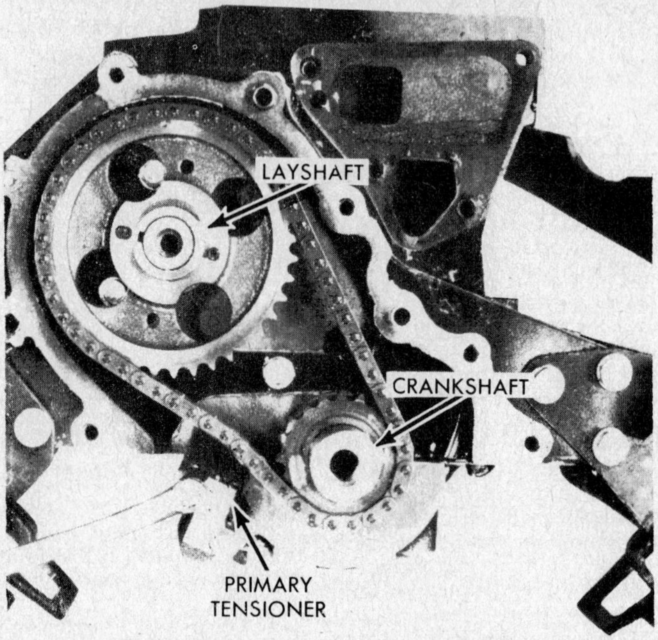

Removing the primary chain tensioner

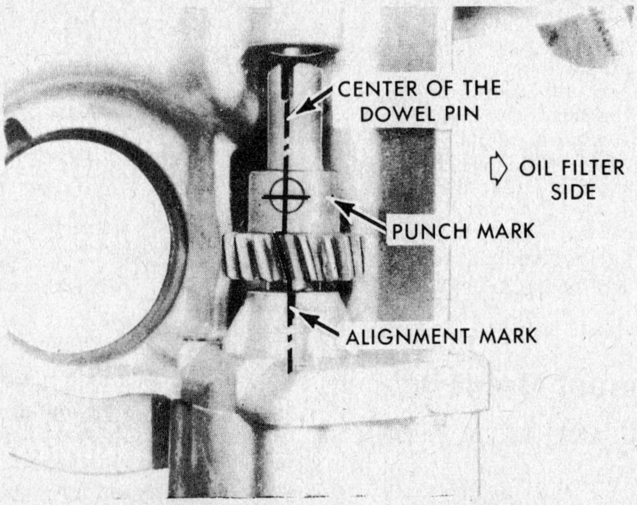

Oil pump alignment—1976 and later

Timing Cover Seal

REMOVAL AND INSTALLATION

1. Disconnect the negative battery cable.
2. Drain the cooling system.
3. Disconnect the radiator inlet and outlet hoses.
4. Remove the radiator assembly.
5. Remove the generator and compressor drive belts.
6. Remove the engine fan.
7. Remove the crankshaft pulley center bolt and remove the pulley and balancer assembly.
8. Pry out the timing cover seal using a suitable size screwdriver.
9. Using the appropriate tool install the new seal in the timing cover.
10. Reverse steps 1 thru 7.

Timing Chains, Sprockets, and Tensioner

REMOVAL AND INSTALLATION

1973–75

1. Disconnect the battery ground cable, drain the cooling system, and remove the alternator and air pump with their respective mounting brackets and drive belts. Remove the fan.
2. Remove the timing gear cover.
3. Remove the oil line from the secondary chain tensioner plug.
4. Remove the chain tensioner plug with the tensioner spring.
5. Remove the bolt and plate washer retaining the camshaft timing sprocket.
6. Remove both of the upper secondary timing chain damper bolts, located in front of the cylinder head.
7. Loosen both of the lower timing chain damper bolts.
8. Separate the timing sprocket from the camshaft, together with the chain. Then, carefully remove the timing sprocket from the chain to prevent the timing sprocket pin from falling out. When removing the timing sprocket from the camshaft, the pin should be positioned at the top. Mark the position of the pin on the timing sprocket before disassembling the parts.
9. Remove the bolt retaining the secondary timing sprocket to the jackshaft.

Remove the secondary sprocket by alternately screwing two bolts into the threaded holes in the timing sprocket one turn at a time.

10. Remove the secondary sprocket from the chain.

11. Remove the chain from the top, through the camshaft carrier front cover hole.

12. Remove the secondary chain tensioners from the cylinder head.

13. Remove the two nuts retaining the primary chain tensioner. Be careful to prevent the tensioner shoe from jumping out of position by the action of the spring. Remove the chain tensioner.

14. Remove the timing sprockets together with the chain, by inserting screws into the threaded holes in the jackshaft sprocket and turning them alternatively and evenly until the sprockets are free.

To install the timing chain, tensioners and sprockets:

15. If the engine was not disturbed while the components were removed, then install everything in the reverse order of removal, using the procedure below as a guide. If, however, the crankshaft or camshaft was turned or the engine disassembled further, start the assembly procedure by bringing the No. 1 and No. 4 pistons to top dead center (TDC).

16. Check that the pistons are at TDC by positioning the timing gear cover on the locating dowels and place the crankshaft pulley in position. The TDC timing mark should be in direct line with the timing mark pointer.

17. Position the crankshaft and jackshaft timing sprocket into position with the primary chain attached to them. When installing the primary timing sprockets, the timing mark on the jackshaft sprocket must align with the timing mark on the crankshaft sprocket.

18. Align the keyway of the jackshaft with the key in the sprocket by turning the jackshaft, then set both sprockets in position by lightly tapping each sprocket alternately.

***NOTE:** The jackshaft can be prevented from turning while driving the sprockets into position by holding it through the fuel pump opening.*

19. Install the primary chain tensioner.

20. Install a new oil seal in the timing gear case and fill the space between the lips of the oil seal with grease. Position a new gasket to the mating face of the gear case with adhesive. Align the locating dowels with the proper holes and mount the gear case onto the engine. Install and tighten the retaining screws.

21. With the No. 4 piston at TDC on the compression stroke, check to make sure that the setting mark on the camshaft and on the camshaft thrust plate are aligned. If they are not aligned, go on to the next numbered step.

a. Attach the camshaft sprocket to the camshaft, insert the pin into a hole in the camshaft sprocket and turn the crankshaft until the marks on the camshaft and the thrust plate align.

b. Remove the camshaft sprocket from the camshaft and bring the No. 4 piston to TDC of the compression stroke.

***NOTE:** If the engine has been turned in the opposite direction of normal rotation to align the marks on the thrust plate and the camshaft, make the final adjustment by turning the engine in the direction of normal rotation so that the marks are lined up and the chain is tensioned on the normal side.*

22. Insert the timing chain into the gear case from the upper opening and hold it in position.

23. Bring the jackshaft timing sprocket together with the chain, and install it in position so that the punched mark on the sprocket is pointed to the key on the jackshaft. When the sprocket is correctly installed, the punched mark is located approximately at the 2 o'clock position.

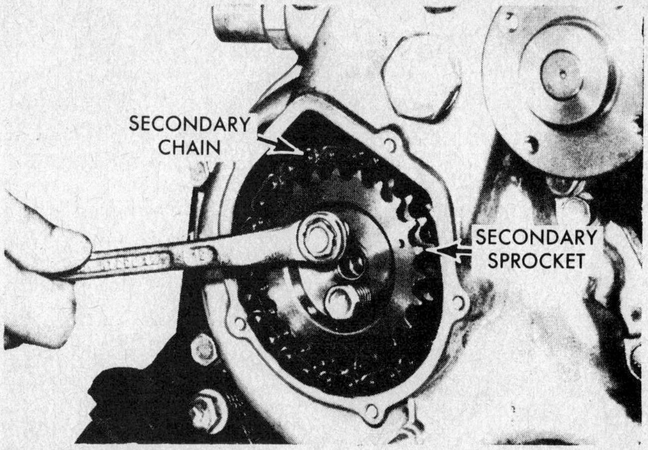

Removing the secondary timing sprocket from the jackshaft by installing two screws in the holes provided and turning them alternately—through 1975

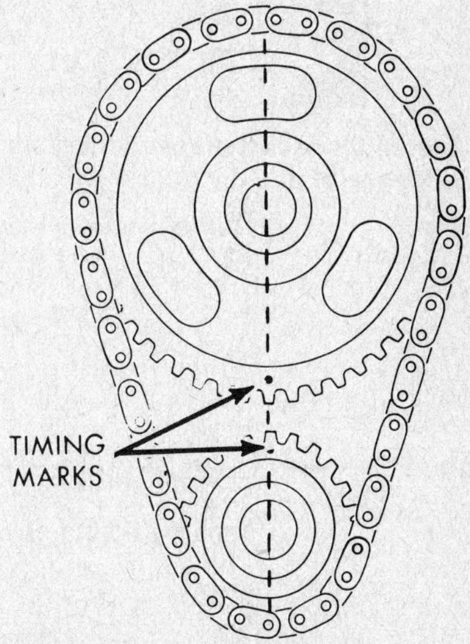

With the No. 1 and 4 pistons at TDC, install the crankshaft and jackshaft sprockets with the chain so the timing marks on the sprockets are aligned—through 1975

Locking the timing chain adjuster—1976 and later

Install the jackshaft secondary timing sprocket so that the punched mark aligns with the key on the jackshaft—through 1975

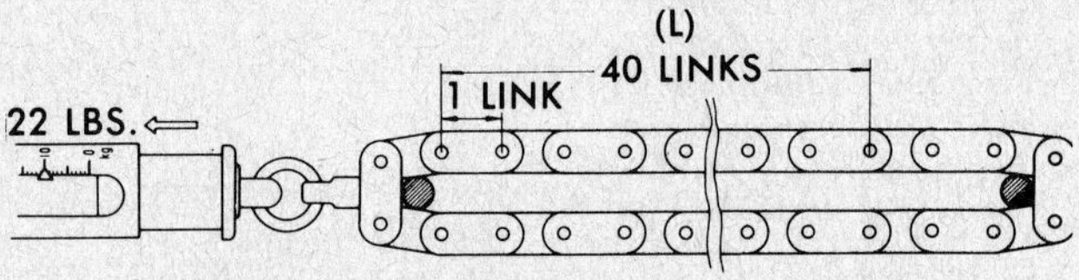

Checking timing chain wear—1976 and later

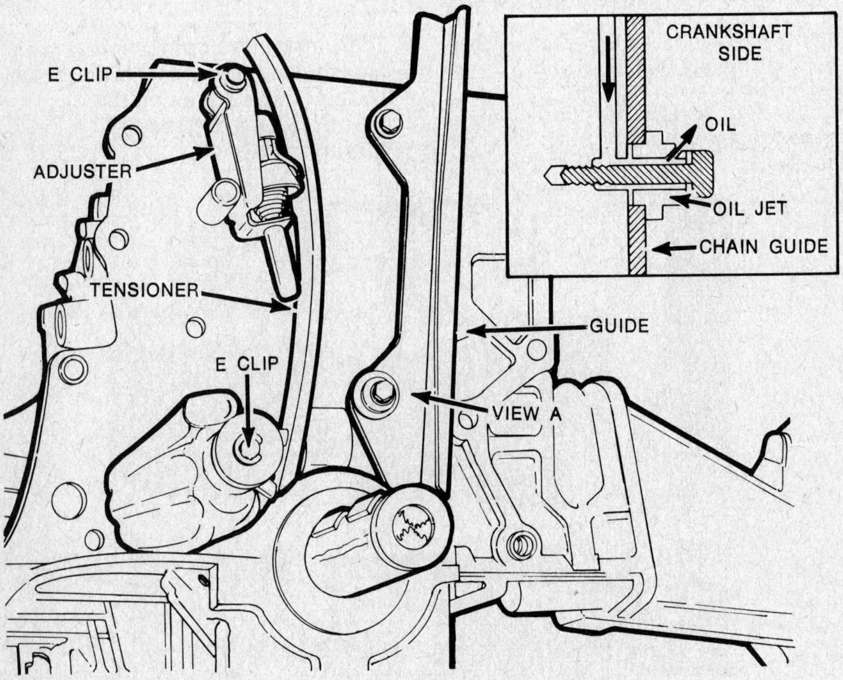

Timing chain adjuster—1976 and later

24. Bring the camshaft timing sprocket together with the timing chain, so that the punched mark on the sprocket is located at the 12 o'clock position and assemble the sprocket to the camshaft.

25. Adjust the position of the camshaft timing sprocket, relative to the camshaft, so that the punched mark on the camshaft timing sprocket is turned up when the drive side of the timing chain is tensioned by pushing the chain tensioner shoe from the plug hole in the secondary chain tensioner.

NOTE: When the camshaft timing sprocket is correctly installed, the punched mark on the sprocket is brought to a position 6° 20′ from the top in the direction of normal rotation.

26. Hold all of the parts in position and look through each of the five holes in the camshaft timing sprocket to find a hole in alignment with the hole in the camshaft flange. Insert the pin into that hole.

27. Tighten the jackshaft timing sprocket attaching bolt to 33 ft lbs. Install the plate washer and tighten the camshaft timing sprocket attaching bolt to 33 ft lbs.

28. Install the gear case front cover and the camshaft carrier front cover.

29. Install the secondary chain tensioner.

30. Assemble the remaining components in the reverse order of removal.

1976–80

1. Remove the front cover assembly as previously described.
2. Remove the timing chain from the crankshaft sprocket.
3. Remove the sprocket and the pinion gear from the crankshaft using a puller.
4. Remove the E-clip and remove the automatic chain adjuster.
5. Remove the E-clip and remove the chain tensioner.
6. Check thetiming chain for wear. With a pull of approximately 22 lbs. as shown in the illustration the standard length is 15.00″; replace the chain if it is greater than 15.16″.
7. Check tensioner pins for wear or damage, and replace if necessary.
8. Replace the chain tensioner and adjuster using the "E" clips.
9. Install the timing sprocket and pinion gear with the groove side toward the front cover. Align the key grooves with the key on the crankshaft, then drive into position using the appropriate tool.
10. Turn the crankshaft so that the key is turned toward the cylinder head side (No.1 and No.4 pistons at top dead center).
11. Install the timing chain by aligning the mark plate on the chain with the mark on the crankshaft timing sprocket. The side of the chain with the mark plate

is on the front side and the side of the chain with the most links between the mark plates is on the chain guide side.

12. Install the camshaft timing sprocket so that the mark side of the sprocket faces forward and so that the triangular mark aligns with the chain mark plate.

NOTE: Keep the timing chain engaged with the camshaft timing sprocket until the sprocket is installed on the camshaft.

13. Install the front cover assembly.

Camshaft

REMOVAL AND INSTALLATION

1973–75

1. Remove the camshaft carrier as outlined under "Cylinder Head Removal and Installation".
2. Remove the two bolts retaining the thrust plate in position on the front of the camshaft carrier.
3. Remove the thrust plate and slide the camshaft out through the front of the carrier.

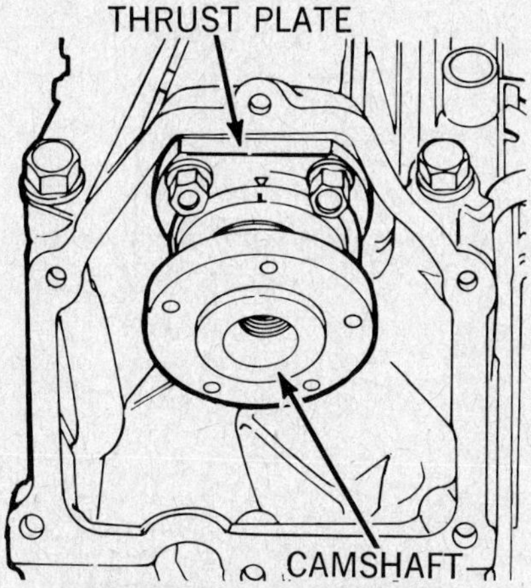

Removing the camshaft thrust plate through 1975

4. Install the camshaft in the carrier in the reverse order of removal, coating it liberally with engine oil before sliding it into position. Exercise care not to damage the camshaft bearing journals during the installation.

1976–80

1. Remove the cam cover.
2. Rotate the camshaft until the No. 4 cylinder is in firing position. Remove the distributor cap and mark the rotor to housing position.
3. Lock the timing chain adjuster by depressing and turning the automatic adjuster slide pin 90° in a clockwise position.

NOTE: Make sure that the chain is in a free state, after locking the chain adjuster.

4. Remove the bolt retaining the sprocket to the camshaft and remove the sprocket.

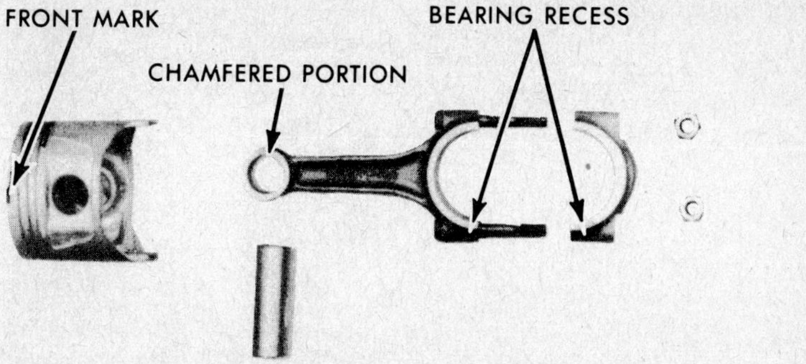

Piston and connecting rod assembly

NOTE: Keep the timing sprocket on the chain damper and tensioner without removing the chain from the sprocket.

5. Remove the rocker arm, shaft and bracket assembly.
6. Remove the camshaft assembly.
7. To install reverse the removal procedure.

Pistons and Connecting Rods

PISTON AND CONNECTING ROD IDENTIFICATION AND POSITIONING

The pistons are marked with the word "Front" and a notch in the piston head. When installed in the engine the "Front" and notch markings are to be facing the front of the engine. The connecting rods are numbered corresponding to the cylinders in which they are to be installed. Install the connecting rods in their correct cylinders with the marking to the right of the notch in the piston (looking from the rear of the engine), on the same side as the jackshaft.

ENGINE LUBRICATION

Oil Pan

REMOVAL AND INSTALLATION

1973–75

All models have a one-piece stamped steel oil pan. To remove the oil pan it may be necessary to unbolt the motor mounts and jack the engine to gain clearance. Remove the attaching screws and remove the oil pan. Install in the reverse order of removal, using new gaskets. Tighten the retaining bolts to 50 in. lbs.

1976–80

1. Raise the hood and disconnect the battery ground cable.

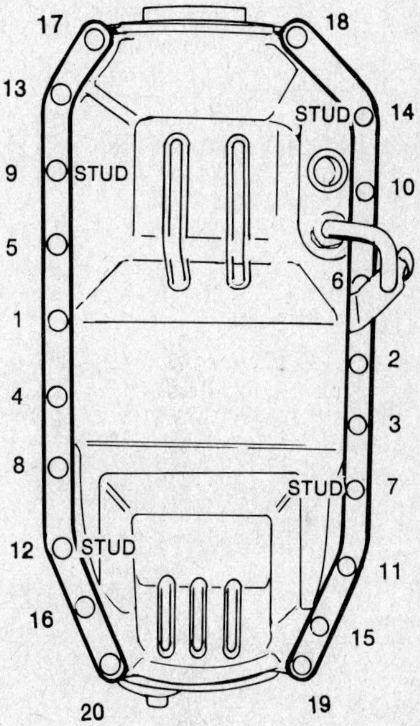

1973-75 oil pan tightening sequence

2. Raise the vehicle on a lift.
3. Drain the crankcase.
4. Remove the front splash shield.
5. Remove the front crossmember.
6. Disconnect the relay rod at the idler arm and lower the relay rod.
7. Remove the left hand bell housing brace.
8. Disconnect the vacuum line at the oil pan.
9. Remove the oil pan bolts and remove the oil pan.
10. To install reverse the removal procedure. Tighten the bolts evenly to 43 in. lbs.

Rear Main Oil Seal

REPLACEMENT

1. Remove the transmission.
2. Remove the oil pan and remove the rear main oil seal retainer from the cylinder block.
3. Fill the space between the lips of the oil seal with grease.
4. Position a new gasket on the mating surface of the cylinder block with adhesive.

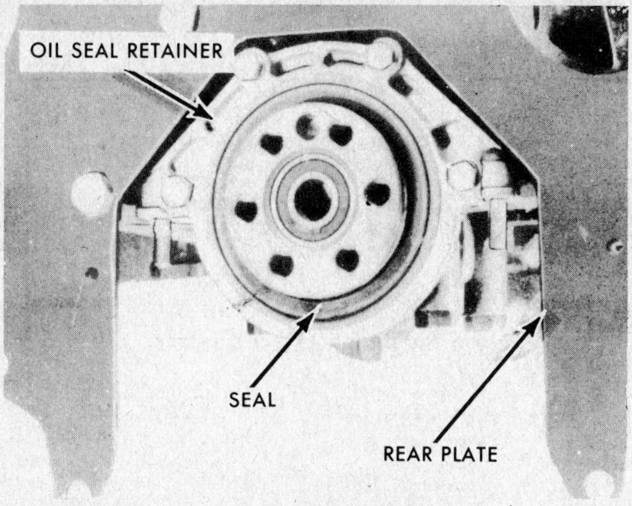

Rear main bearing oil seal

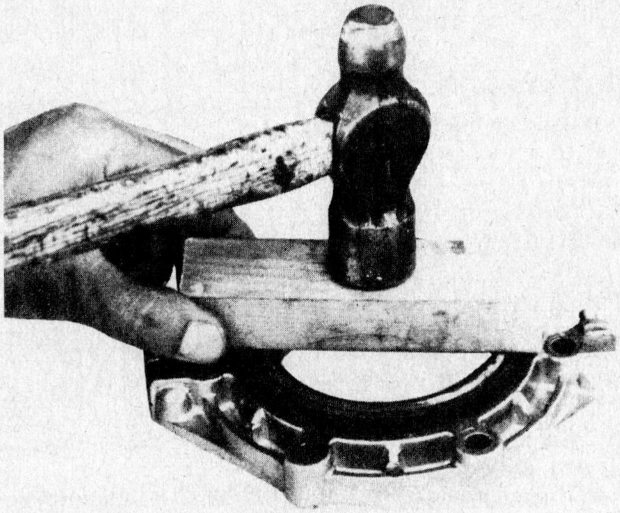

Installing rear main seal retainer

5. Align the dowel holes with the locating dowels and mount the oil seal retainer to the cylinder block.
6. Install the oil pan.

Oil Pump

REMOVAL AND INSTALLATION

1973–75

1. Drain and remove the oil pan or crankcase.

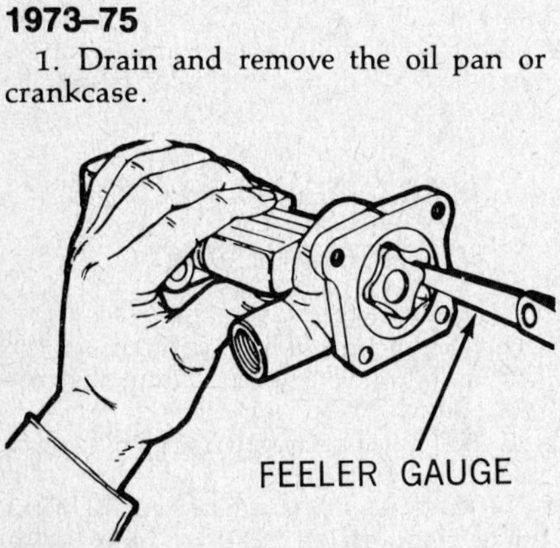

Measuring tip clearance—1973-75

2. Disconnect the oil feed pipe.
3. Remove the two bolts securing the oil pump to the cylinder block and remove the oil pump.
4. Install in the reverse order of removal.

1976–80

1. Remove the cam cover.
2. Remove the distributor cap, then the distributor.
3. Remove the engine oil pan.
4. Remove the bolt attaching the oil pickup tube to the block and remove the tube from the oil pump.
5. Remove the oil pump mounting bolts and remove the pump assembly.
6. To install align the mark on the camshaft with the mark on the no. 1 rocker arm shaft bracket. Align the notch on the crankshaft pulley with the "O" mark on the front cover. When the two sets of marks are aligned the no. 4 cylinder is at top dead center on the compression stroke.
7. Install the oil pump assembly by engaging the oil pump drive gear with the pinion gear on the crankshaft, so that the alignment mark on the drive gear is turned rearward and is away

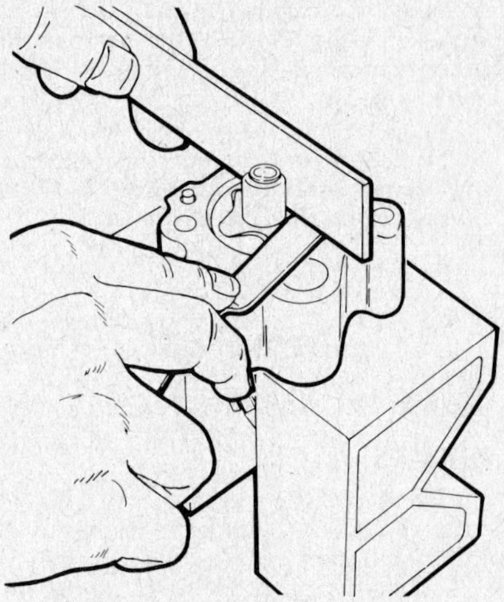

Measuring pump cover to rotor clearance—1976 and later

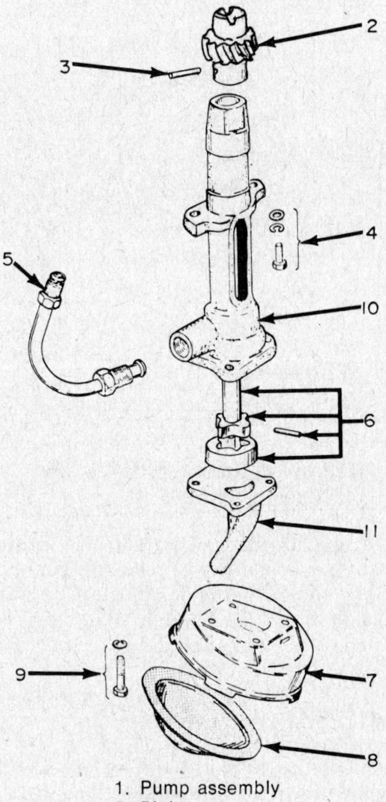

1. Pump assembly
2. Pinion
3. Pin
4. Bolt, lockwasher, plain washer
5. Pipe assembly
6. Rotor set
7. Case
8. Screen
9. Bolt, lockwasher
10. Body
11. Cover

Exploded view of the oil pump—through 1975

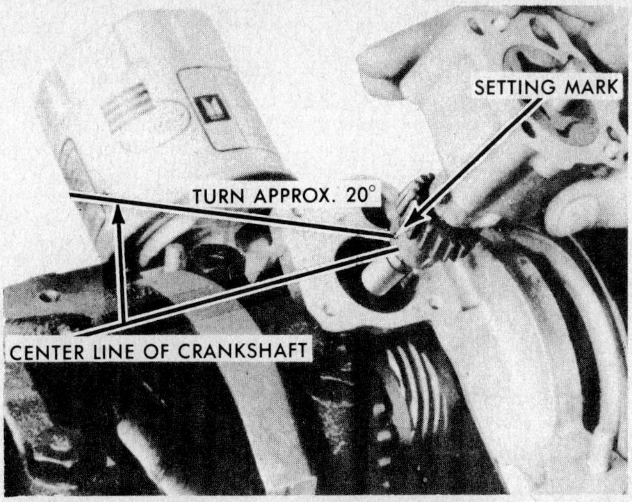

Installing oil pump—1976 and later

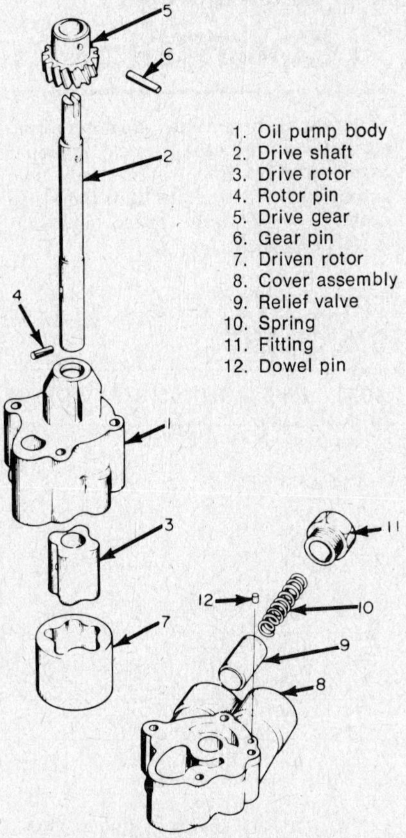

1. Oil pump body
2. Drive shaft
3. Drive rotor
4. Rotor pin
5. Drive gear
6. Gear pin
7. Driven rotor
8. Cover assembly
9. Relief valve
10. Spring
11. Fitting
12. Dowel pin

Exploded view of the oil pump—1976 and later

from the crankshaft by approximately 20° in a clockwise direction.

8. Install the oil pump mounting bolts.
9. Connect the oil pipe to the rubber hose and attach the oil pipe to the cylinder block.
10. Install the oil pan and cam cover.
11. Install the distributor by turning the distributor shaft, so that the boss on the shaft is fitted into the slit at the end of the oil pump drive shaft.
12. Install the distributor cap.

CHECKING CLEARANCES

1973–75

1. To disassemble the oil pump, first flatten out the tab bent to the case.
2. Remove the four bolts and remove the strainer case and pump body cover.
3. Measure the clearance between the tips of the rotor (center piece) and the high sections of the vane with a feeler gauge. The clearance should be between 0.0012–0.0059 in.
4. Measure the clearance between the vane and wall of the pump body with a feeler gauge. Replacement of either the vane or the pump body is necessary if the clearance is not within the limits of 0.008–0.011 in.
5. Place a straight edge over the rotor and vane, resting the straight edge on the pump cover mating surface of the pump body. Measure the clearance between the straight edge and the rotor and vane. The standard clearance should be between 0.0016–0.0035 in. Replace either the rotor, vane, or the pump body cover if the clearance is more than 0.0060 in.
6. Assemble the oil pump in the reverse order of disassembly.

1976–80

1. Measure tip clearance between the drive roter and the driven rotor with a feeler gauge. The clearance should be 0.005–0.0059 inch.
2. Measure the clearance between the driven rotor and the inner wall of the pump body. The clearance should be 0.0063–0.0087 inch.
3. Measure the clearance between the rotors and oil pump cover with a square and feeler gauge. The clearance should be 0.0012–0.0035 inch.
4. Measure the outside diameter of the drive shaft and the inside diameter of

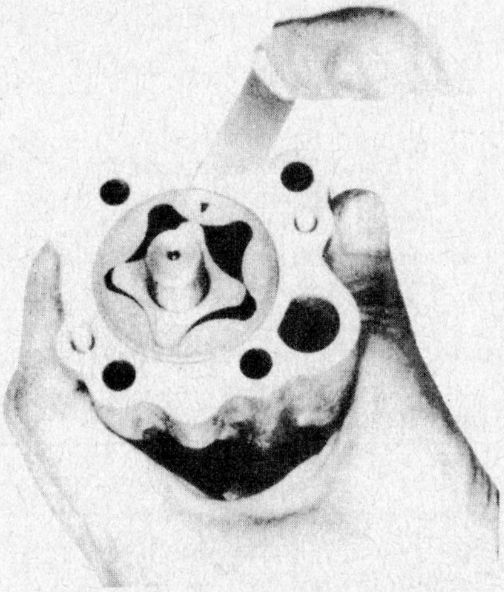

Measuring driven rotor to body clearance—1976 and later

Measuring body cover clearance—1973-75

the shaft hole in the pump cover. The clearance should be 0.0028–0.0043.

ENGINE COOLING

Radiator

REMOVAL AND INSTALLATION

1. Drain the radiator by opening the drain cock on the lower part of the radiator.
2. Disconnect the radiator upper and lower hoses.
3. Remove the four bolts retaining the radiator and remove the radiator assembly.
4. Install the radiator in the reverse order of removal.

Water Pump

REMOVAL AND INSTALLATION

1973–75

1. Disconnect the battery ground cable.
2. Drain the cooling system and disconnect the upper and lower radiator hoses. Disconnect and move heater hose out of work area.
3. Remove the radiator and shroud assembly.
4. Remove the alternator and air pump belts, fan pulley, spacer and fan blades.
5. Remove the water pump assembly.

NOTE: Loosen, but do not remove the bolt from behind the timing gear cover.

6. Installation is the reverse of removal.

Loosen, but do not remove, the bolt behind the timing gear cover when removing the 1973-75 oil pump

1976–80

1. Disconnect the battery ground cable.
2. Remove the lower cover and drain the cooling system. Remove the coolant hoses from the pump body.
3. On non air conditioned models, remove the fan blades and pulleys from the hub.
4. On air conditioned models, remove the air pump and alternator belts, fan blades and pulleys.
5. Remove the water pump assembly.
6. Installation is the reverse of removal.

Thermostat

REMOVAL AND INSTALLATION

1973–75

1. Drain the radiator by opening the drain petcock on the bottom of the radiator.
2. Disconnect the upper and lower radiator hoses.
3. Disconnect the water outlet from the engine.
4. Remove the thermostat.
5. Replace the thermostat in the reverse order of removal, using a new gasket under the outlet housing and making sure that the thermostat is placed so that the spring end is inside the engine.

1976–80

1. Remove the drain plug and drain the cooling system.
2. Disconnect the PCV, ECS, AIR, CCS hoses and remove the two bolts attaching the air cleaner, then loosen the clamp bolt.
3. Lift the air cleaner from the carburetor and disconnect the CCS hose from the air cleaner, then remove the air cleaner assembly.
4. Remove the two bolts attaching the outlet pipe and remove the outlet pipe and water hose.
5. Remove the thermostat from the intake manifold.
6. To install reverse the removal procedure.

EMISSION CONTROLS

There are three types of automotive pollutants; crankcase fumes, exhaust gases, and gasoline evaporation. The equipment that is used to limit these polutants is commonly called emission control equipment.

EMISSION CONTROL SYSTEMS APPLICATION CHART

Year	1973	1974	1975	1976	1977	1978-80
Positive Crankcase Ventilation System (PCV)	X	X	X	X	X	X
Controlled Combustion System (CCS)	X①	X	X	X	X	X
Evaporation Control System (ECS)	X	X	X	X	X	X
Exaust Gas Recirculation System (EGR)		X	X	X	X	X
Air Injector Reactor System (AIR)	X	X	X	X②	X②	X②
Coasting Richer System	X	X	X	X③	X③	X③
Oxidizing Catalytic Converter System (OCS)				X④	X④	X④
Over Temperature Control System (OTC)				X④	X④	X④
Dashpot			X		X	X⑤
Transmission Control Spark System (TCS)			X			
Dual Contact Point Distributor	X					

① Called Thermostatically Controlled Air Cleaner System in 1973
② Federal uses Air By-pass Valve; California uses Mixture Control Valve
③ Federal with manual transmission; California with automatic and manual transmission
④ California only
⑤ Federal cab and chassis only with manual transmission

Crankcase Emission Controls

1973–75

The crankcase emission control equipment consists of a positive crankcase ventilation valve (PCV), a closed or open oil filler cap and hoses to connect this equipment.

Crankcase gases are recycled in the following manner: while the engine is running, clean filtered air is drawn into the crankcase through the carburetor air filter and then through a hose leading to the rocker cover. As the air passes through the crankcase it picks up the combustion gases and carries them out of the crankcase, up through the PCV valve and into the intake manifold they are drawn into the combustion chamber and burned.

The most critical component in the system is the PCV valve. This vacuum controlled valve regulates the amount of gases which are recycled into the combustion chamber. At low engine speeds the valve is partially closed, limiting the flow of gases into the intake manifold. As engine speed increases, the valve opens to admit greater quantities of the gases into the intake manifold. If the valve should become blocked or plugged, the gases will be prevented from escaping from the crankcases by the normal route. Since these gases are under pressure, they will find their own way out of the crankcase. This alternate route is usually a weak oil seal or gasket in the engine. As the gas escapes by the gasket, it also creates an oil leak. Besides causing oil leaks, a clogged PCV valve also allows these gases to remain in the crankcase for an extended period of time, promoting the formation of sludge in the engine.

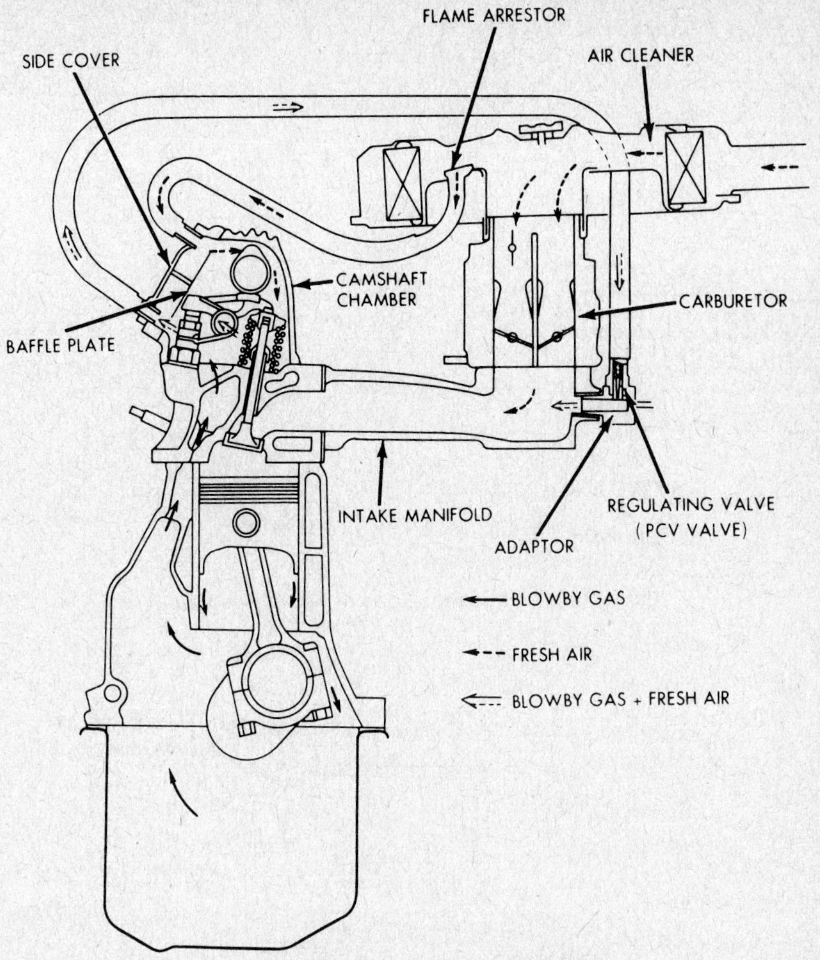

PCV system—through 1975

TESTING

Check the PCV system hoses and connections, to see that there are no leaks; then replace or tighten, as necessary.

To check the valve, remove it and blow through both of its ends. When blowing from the side which goes toward the intake manifold, very little air should pass through it. When blowing from the crankcase (valve cover) side, air should pass through freely.

Replace the valve with a new one, if the valve fails to function as outlined.

*NOTE: **Do not attempt to clean or adjust the valve; replace it with a new one.***

REMOVAL AND INSTALLATION

To remove the PCV valve, simply loosen the hose clamp and remove the valve from the manifold-to-crankcase hose and intake manifold. Install the PCV valve in the reverse order of removal.

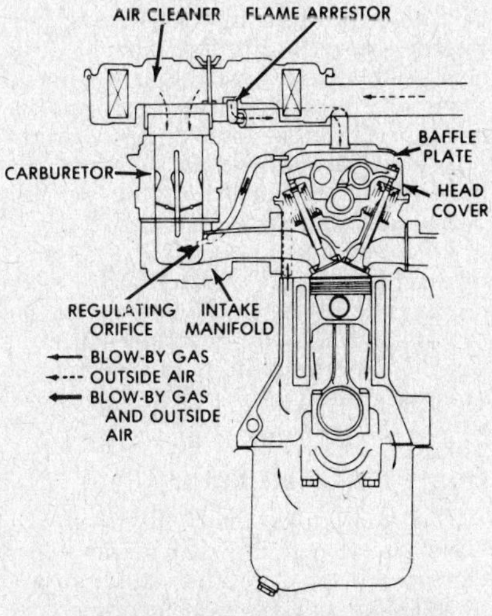

PCV system—1976 and later

1976–80

A regulated orifice, located in the intake manifold and connected to the cylinder head cover by a hose, replaces the PCV valve.

During wide open throttle operation, low vacuum exists in the intake manifold and the regulating orifice cannot admit the entire amount of engine blow-by gases. Since the air movement is greater through the air cleaner assembly, part of the blow–by gases are drawn into the air cleaner from the rear end of the cylinder head cover.

Service

1. Clean the internal parts of the hoses and regulating orifice.
2. Check the hoses for cracks, fatigue and swelling.

Evaporative Emission Control System

When raw fuel evaporates, the vapors contain hydrocarbons. To prevent these nasties from escaping into the atmosphere, the fuel evaporative emission control system was developed.

The system consists of a sealed fuel tank, a vapor separator tank, check and relief valve and the hoses connecting these components, leading from the fuel tank, to the crankcase of the engine.

In operation, the vapor formed in the fuel tank passes through the vapor separator, which allows liquid fuel to flow back into the fuel tank while allowing fuel vapor to pass into the check and relief valve and the crankcase. When the

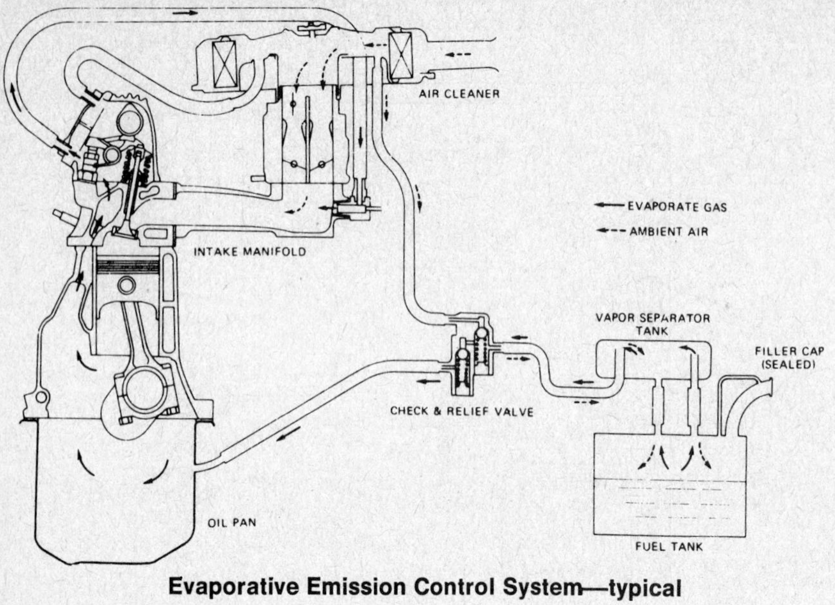

Evaporative Emission Control System—typical

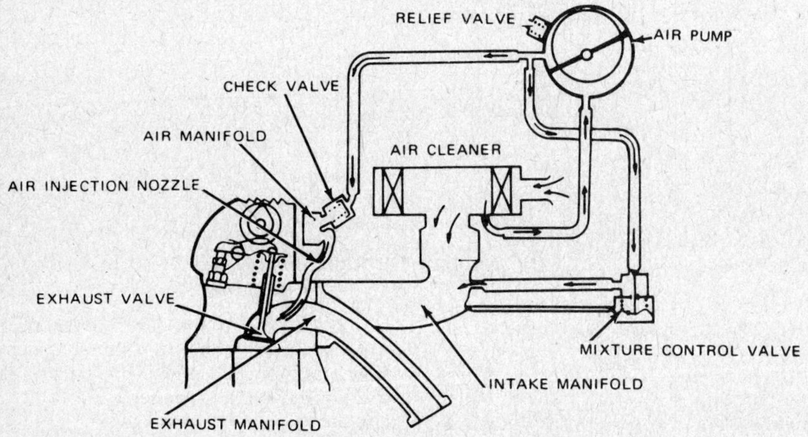

Diagram of the AIR system

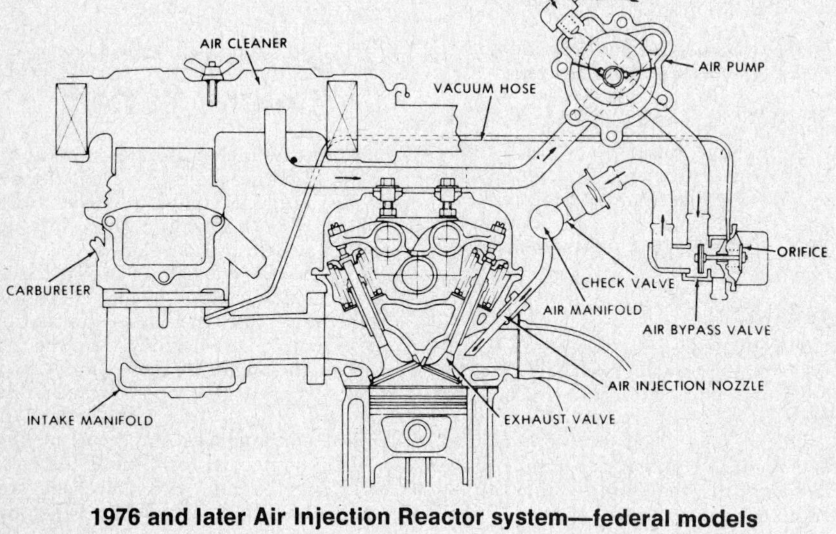

1976 and later Air Injection Reactor system—federal models

engine is not running, if the fuel vapor pressure in the vapor separator becomes as high as 1 to 1.4 in. Hg, the check valve opens and allows the vapor to enter the engine crankcase.

INSPECTION AND SERVICE

Check the hoses for proper connections and damage. Replace as necessary. Check the vapor separator tank for fuel leaks, distortion and dents, and replace as necessary.

Remove the check valve and inspect it for leakage by blowing air into the ports in the check valve. When air is applied from the fuel tank side, the check valve is normal if air passes into the check side (crankcase side), but not leaking into the relief side (air cleaner side). When air is applied from the check side, the valve is normal if the passage of air is restricted. When air is applied from the relief side (air cleaner side), the valve is normal if air passes into the fuel tank side but not into the check side.

REMOVAL AND INSTALLATION

Removal and installation of the various evaporative emission control system components consists of disconnecting the hoses, loosening retaining screws, and removing the part which is to be replaced or checked. Install in the reverse order. When replacing hose, make sure that it is fuel and vapor resistant.

Exhaust Emission Control Systems

Air Injection Reactor System

In gasoline engines, it is difficult to burn the air/fuel mixture completely through normal combustion in the combustion chambers. Under certain operating conditions, unburned fuel is exhausted into the atmosphere.

The air injection reactor system is designed so that ambient air, pressurized by the air pump, is injected through the injection nozzles into the exhaust ports near each exhaust valve. The exhaust gases are at high temperatures and ignite when brought into contact with the oxygen of the ambient air. Thus, the unburned fuel is burned in the exhaust ports and manifold.

To act against over-rich air/fuel mixture which occurs momentarily when the throttle plates in the carburetor are rapidly closed, additional ambient air is supplied intermittently into the intake manifold through the mixture control valve.

Dual Point Distributor

The dual point distributor has two sets of breaker points which operate independently of each other and are positioned with a relative phase angle of 1° apart. This makes one set the advanced

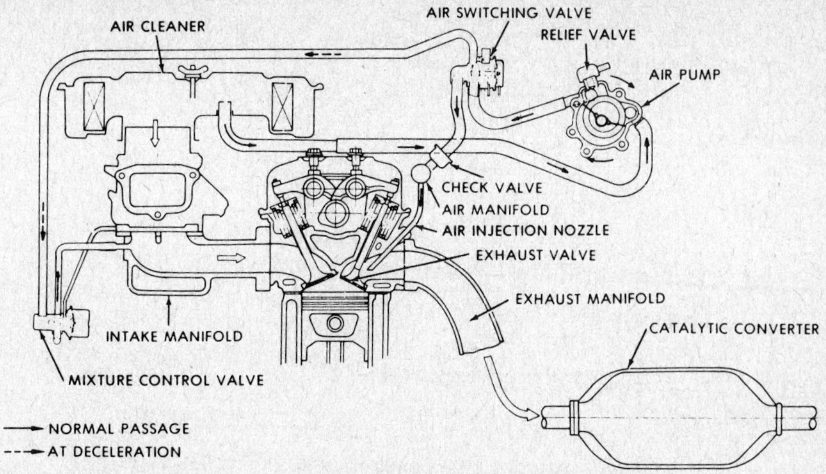

1976 and later Air Injection Reactor system—California models

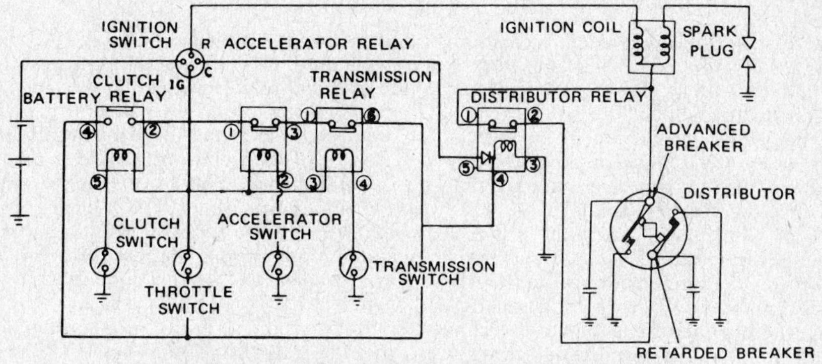

Electrical diagram of the dual point distributor system

points and the other set the retarded points.

The two sets of points, which mechanically operate continuously, are connected in parallel to the primary side of the ignition circuit. One set of points controls the firing of the spark plugs and hence, the ignition timing, depending on whether or not the retarded set of points is energized.

When both sets of points are electrically energized, the first set to open (the advanced set) has no control over breaking the ignition coil primary circuit because the retarded set is still closed and maintaining a complete circuit to ground. When the retarded set of points opens, the advanced set is still open, and the primary circuit is broken causing the electromagnetic field in the coil to collapse and the ignition spark is produced.

When the retarded set of points is removed from the primary ignition circuit through the operation of a distributor relay inserted into the retarded points circuit, the advanced set of points controls the primary circuit.

The retarded set of points is energized under the following conditions:

1. Light throttle application in Low gears: the accelerator pedal is depressed to between 7° and 35° of throttle valve opening, the clutch is engaged, and the transmission is in either 1st or 2nd gear.

2. Light throttle application or coasting in High gears: the accelerator pedal is depressed up to 35° of throttle valve opening, the clutch is engaged, and the transmission is in either 3rd or 4th gear.

In any other mode of operation, for example, with the accelerator pedal depressed less than 7° in condition No. 1, or more than 35° in condition No. 1 or No. 2, or at any time the clutch is disengaged, the circuit from any of the controlling switches is incomplete. This results in the distributor relay being energized which breaks the flow of current to the retarded set of points, and leaves the advance points in control of engine ignition timing.

There are four switches and relays which control the operation of the distributor relay. When the switches are On, their respective relays are energized and break an electrical circuit to the distributor relay, which in turn closes the electrical circuit to the retarded set of points, energizing them.

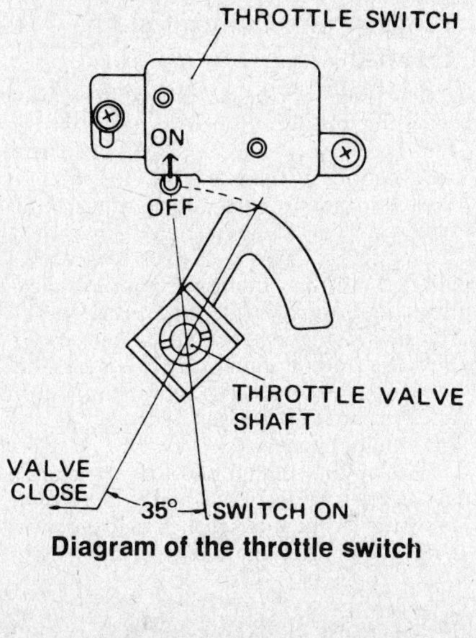

Diagram of the throttle switch

The switches are as follows:

1. The throttle switch: located on the carburetor primary throttle valve linkage and is turned On when the throttle valve is opened beyond 35°.

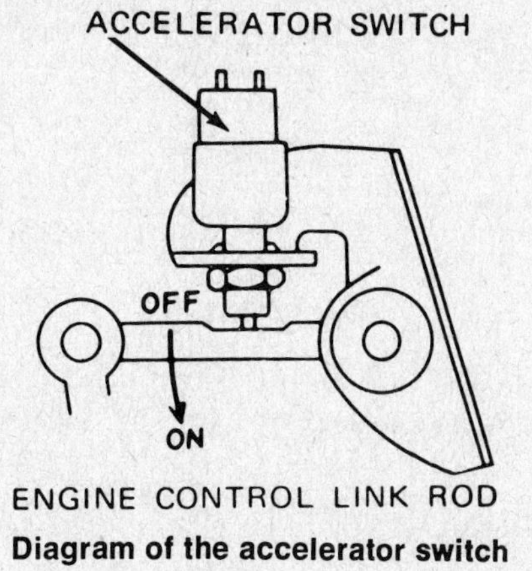

Diagram of the accelerator switch

2. The transmission switch: located on the upper part of the transmission gearbox and is turned On when the transmission is shifted into 3rd or 4th gear.

3. The clutch switch: located on the clutch pedal arm and is turned on when the clutch pedal is depressed.

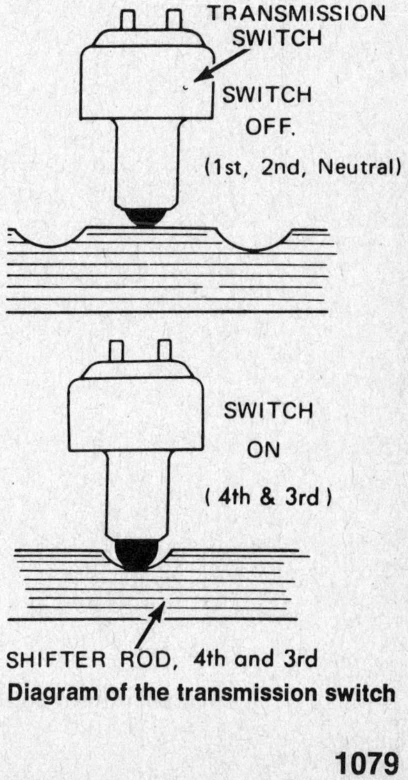

Diagram of the transmission switch

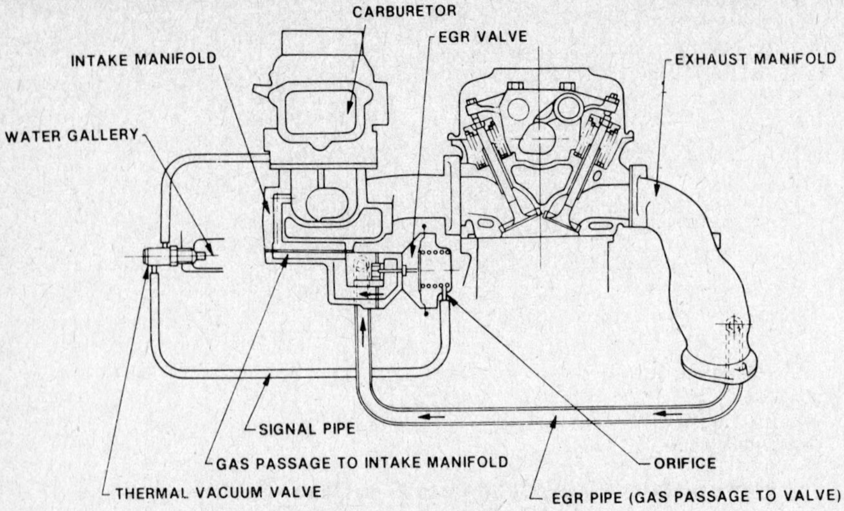

1976 and later EGR system

4. The accelerator switch: located on the accelerator pedal linkage and is turned On when the throttle valve is opened to an angle of 7°.

The purpose of the dual point distributor is to allow ignition advance only when the vehicle is accelerating heavily, or when the engine is at idle.

The distributor vacuum advance mechanism produces a spark advance based on the amount of vacuum in the intake manifold. With a high vacuum, less air/fuel mixture enters the engine cylinders and the mixture is therefore less highly compressed. Consequently, this mixture burns more slowly and the advance mechanism gives it more time to burn. This longer burning time results in higher combustion temperatures at peak pressure and hence, more time for nitrogen to react with oxygen and form oxides of nitrogen. NO_X. At the same time, this advanced timing results in less complete combustion due to the greater area of cylinder wall (quench area) exposed at the instant of ignition. This "cooled" fuel will not burn as readily and hence, results in higher unburned hydrocarbons (HC). The production of NO_X and HC resulting from vacuum advance is highest during idle and moderate acceleration in lower gears.

Retardation of the ignition timing is necessary to reduce emissions. Various ways of retarding the ignition spark have been used in domestic automobiles, all of which remove vacuum to the distributor vacuum advance mechanism at different times under certain conditions. Another way of accomplishing the same goal is the dual point distributor system.

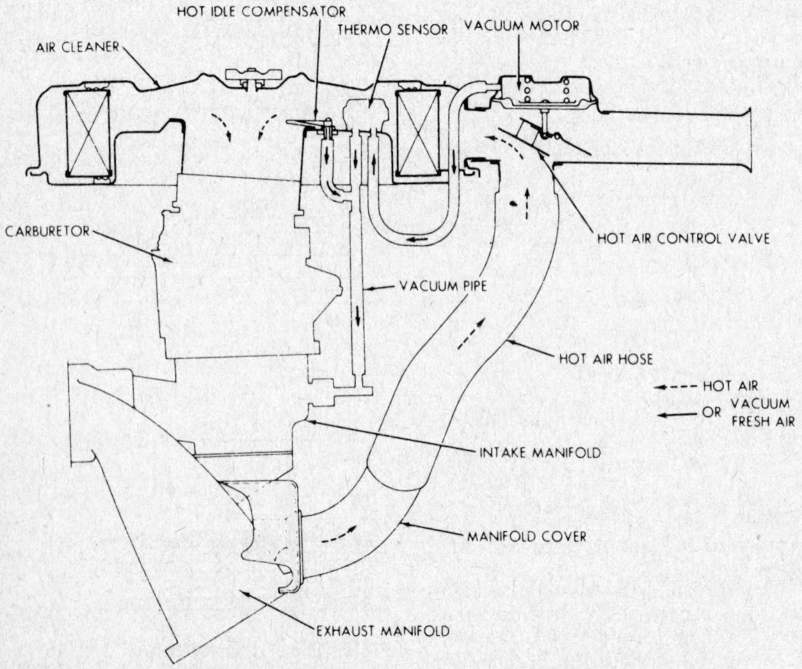

Diagram of the temperature controlled air cleaner

NOTE: The transmission, clutch, and accelerator switches and relays also control the operation of the Coasting Richer System.

Exhaust Gas Recirculation System (EGR)

Exhaust gas recirculation is used to reduce combustion temperatures in the engine, thereby reducing the oxides of nitrogen emissions.

An EGR valve is mounted on the center of the intake manifold. The recycled exhaust gas is drawn into the bottom of the intake manifold riser portion through the exhaust manifold heat stove and EGR valve. A vacuum diaphragm is connected to a timed signal port at the carburetor flange.

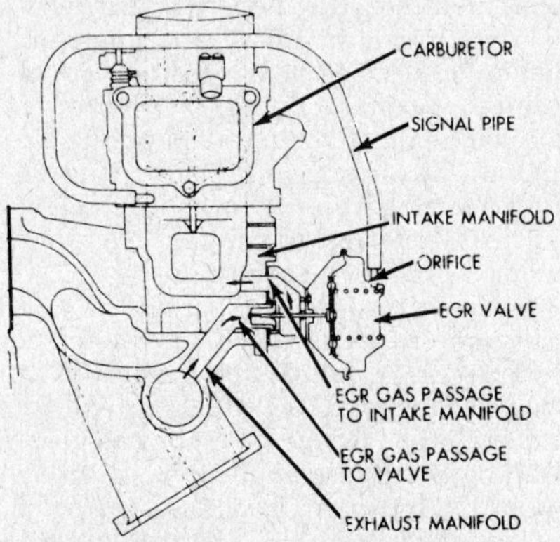

Diagram of the EGR system—through 1975

As the throttle valve is opened, vacuum is applied to the EGR valve vacuum diaphragm. When the vacuum reaches about 3.5 in. Hg, the diaphragm moves against spring pressure and is in a fully up position at 8 in. Hg of vacuum. As the diaphragm moves up, it opens the exhaust gas metering valve which allows exhaust gas to be pulled into the engine intake manifold. The system does not operate when the engine is idling because the exhaust gas recirculation would cause a rough idle.

Temperature Controlled Air Cleaner

The rate of fuel atomization varies with the temperature of the air that the fuel is being mixed with. The air/fuel ratio cannot be held constant for efficient fuel combustion with a wide range of air temperatures. Cold air being drawn into the engine causes a denser and richer air/fuel mixture, inefficient fuel atomization, and thus, more hydrocarbons in the exhaust gas. Hot air being drawn into the engine causes a leaner air/fuel mixture and more efficient atomization and combustion for less hydrocarbons in the exhaust gases.

The automatic temperature controlled air cleaner is designed so that the temperature of the ambient air being drawn into the engine is automatically con-

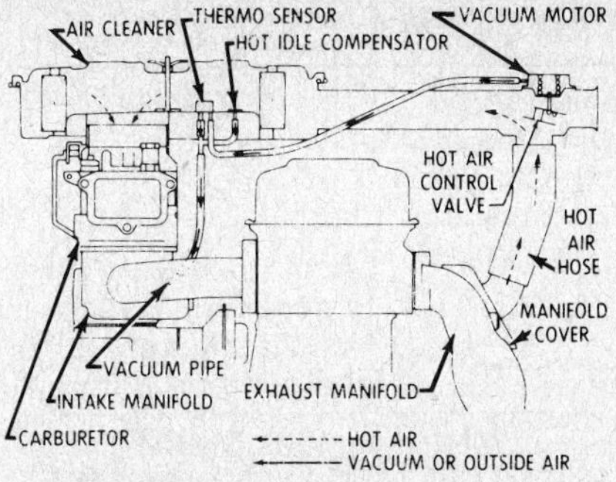

1976 and later Controlled Combustion system

trolled, to hold the temperature of the air and, consequently, the fuel/air ratio at a constant rate for efficient fuel combustion.

A temperature sensing vacuum switch controls vacuum applied to a vacuum motor operating a valve in the intake snorkel of the air cleaner. When the engine is cold or the air being drawn into the engine is cold, the vacuum motor opens the valve, allowing air heated by the exhaust manifold to be drawn into the engine. As the engine warms up, the temperature sensing unit shuts off the vacuum applied to the vacuum motor which allows the valve to close, shutting off the heated air and allowing cooler, outside (under hood) air to be drawn into the engine.

INSPECTION AND ADJUSTMENTS

Air Pump

If the air pump makes an abnormal noise and cannot be corrected without removing the pump from the vehicle, check the following in sequence:

1. Turn the pulley ³/₄ of a turn in the clockwise direction and ¹/₄ turn in the counterclockwise direction. If the pulley is binding and if rotation is not smooth, a defective bearing is indicated.
2. Check the inner wall of the pump body, vanes and rotor for wear. If the rotor has abnormal wear, replace the air pump.
3. Check the needle roller bearing for wear and damage. If the bearings are defective, the air pump should be replaced.
4. Check and replace the rear side seal if abnormal wear of damage is noticed.
5. Check and replace the carbon shoes holding the vanes if they are found to be worn or damaged.
6. A deposit of carbon particles on the inner wall of the pump body and vanes is normal, but should be removed with compressed air before reassembling the air pump.

Check Valve

Remove the check valve from the air manifold. Test it for leakage by blowing air into the valve from the air pump side and from the air manifold side. Air should only pass through the valve from the air pump side if the valve is functioning normally. A small amount of air leakage from the manifold side can be overlooked. Replace the check valve if it is found to be defective.

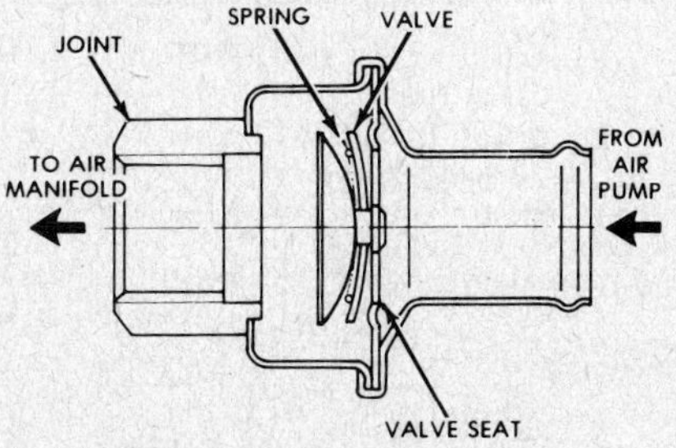

Check valve cross section

Mixture Control Valve

1976–80 CALIFORNIA AND HIGH ALTITUDE MODELS

Disconnect the rubber hose connecting the mixture control valve with the intake manifold and plug the intake manifold side of the valve. If the mixture control valve is operating correctly, air will continue to blow out the mixture control valve for a few seconds after the accelerator pedal is fully depressed (engine running) and released quickly. If air continues to blow out for more than five seconds, replace the mixture control valve.

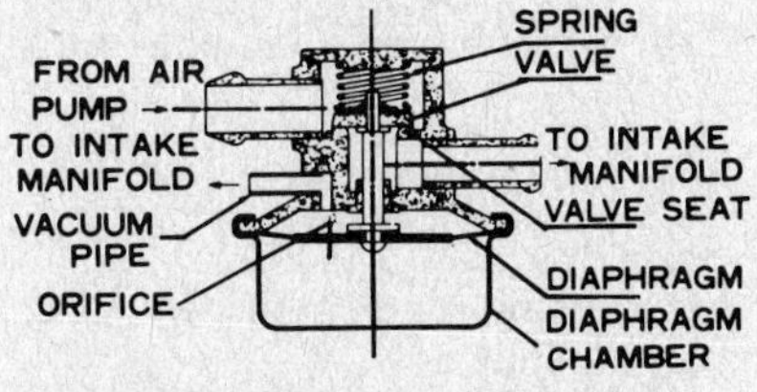

Cut away diagram of the mixture control valve

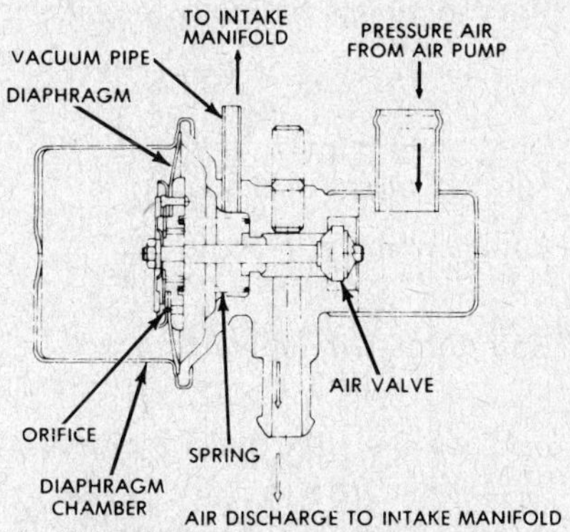

Mixture control valve—cross section

Air Manifold and Air Injection Nozzles

Check around the air manifold for air leakage with the engine running at 2,000 rpm. If air is leaking from the eye joint bolt, retighten or replace the gasket. Check the air nozzles for restrictions by blowing air into the nozzles.

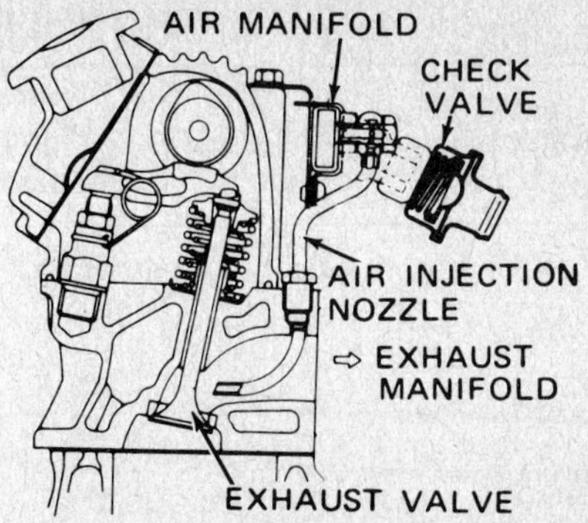

The air injection manifold and nozzles—through 1975

Air By-pass valve

1976–80 FEDERAL MODELS

The purpose of the air by-pass valve is to prevent the afterburning of the exhaust gases in the manifold when the throttle is closed for deceleration. High intake vacuum at the moment of deceleration causes the air by-pass valve to cut off the secondary air to the exhaust manifold and diverts the air to the atmosphere, thus preventing the afterburning.

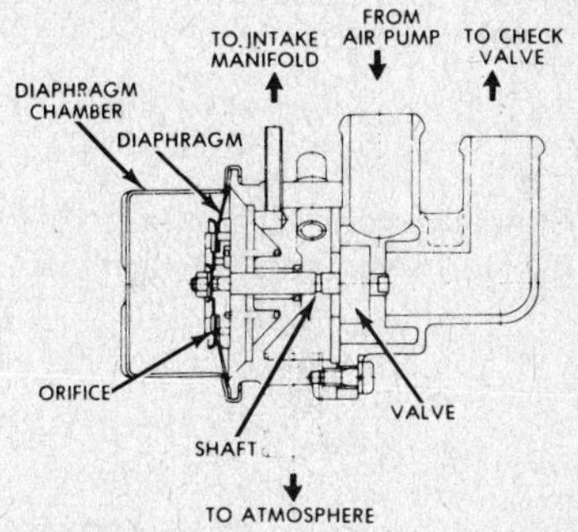

Air bypass valve—cross section

To test the air by-pass valve, remove the outlet hose and with the engine running, open the throttle completely and close it quickly. Air should flow out for a few seconds. If the air continues to flow out for more than five seconds, replace the air by-pass valve.

Hoses

Check and replace hoses if they are found to be weakened or cracked. Check all hose connections and clips. Be sure that the hoses are not in contact with other parts of the engine.

Coasting Richer System

This system functions when the engine is coasting, to enrich the air/fuel mixture, which minimizes hydrocarbon

TROUBLESHOOTING COASTING RICHER SYSTEM

Checking Order	Ignition Switch	Trans-mission	Throttle	Clutch	Solenoid Valve Normal Condition	Solenoid Valve Abnormal Condition	Defective Part or Check Point
1	ON	4th or 3rd gear	When opening angle is 7° or less	Engage	ON	OFF	Check fuse then refer to checking order No. 6 if still not operating properly
2	OFF	*	*	*	OFF	ON	Ignition Switch
3	ON	1st, 2nd, Neutral, Reverse	*	*	OFF	ON	Transmission Switch
4	ON	*	When opening angle is 7° or more	*	OFF	ON	Accelerator Switch
5	ON	*		Disengage	OFF	ON	Clutch Switch

* Operating condition is unimportant.

SOLENOID VALVE CIRCUIT TEST

If the solenoid valve does not function properly when the ignition switch, transmission switch, clutch switch, and accelerator switch are turned ON, perform the following checks to determine the cause of trouble.

Test	Result	Cause
A. Check the solenoid valve terminal voltage.	One terminal indicates 12V.	Solenoid valve defective or grounding cable poorly connected
	Both terminals also indicate zero V.	Check parts mentioned under paragraph (b).
B. Check voltage at ignition switch AM terminal and IG terminal.	Both terminals indicate zero V.	Cable between solenoid valve and ignition switch poorly connected.
	AM terminal indicates 12V and 1G terminal zero V.	Ignition switch defective.
	Both terminals indicate 12V.	Check parts mentioned under paragraph (c) below.
C. Check voltage at transmission switch terminals.	Both terminals indicate zero V.	Cable between ignition switch and transmission switch poorly connected.
	One of terminals indicates 12V and the other zero V.	Transmission switch defective or incorrectly installed
	Both terminals indicate 12V.	Check parts mentioned under paragraph (d) below.
D. Check voltage at clutch switch terminals.	Both terminals indicate zero V.	Cables between transmission switch and clutch switch poorly connected.
	One of the terminals indicates 12V, other zero V.	Clutch switch defective or incorrectly installed.
	Both terminals indicate 12V.	Check parts mentioned under paragraph (e) beow.
E. Check voltage at accelerator switch terminals.	Both terminals indicate zero V.	Cable between clutch switch and accelerator switch poorly connected.
	One of the terminals indicates 12V and another zero V.	Accelerator switch defective or incorrectly installed.

TCS SYSTEM TROUBLESHOOTING

Test	Result	Cause
1. Check the vacuum switching valve terminal voltage.	One terminal indicates 12V.	Vacuum switching valve defective or grounding cable poorly connected.
	Both terminals also indicate zero V.	Check parts mentioned under Test 2.
2. Check voltage at ignition switch AM terminal and IG terminal.	Both terminals indicate zero V.	Cable between vacuum switching and ignition switch poorly connected.
	AM terminal indicates 12V and IG terminal zero V.	Ignition switch defective.
	Both terminals indicate 12V.	Check parts mentioned under Test 3.
3. Check voltage at transmission switch terminals.	Both terminals indicate zero V.	Cable between ignition switch and transmission switch poorly connected.

content of the exhaust gases through efficient combustion.

A solenoid operated valve in the carburetor allows extra fuel to be drawn into the intake manifold during coasting.

The solenoid is energized by the following switches:

1973–75

a—Accelerator switch
b—Clutch switch (two types)
c—3rd—4th transmission switch

1976–80 Federal with manual transmission

a—Accelerator switch
b—Clutch switch
c—3rd —4th gear switch

1976–80 California with manual transmission

a—Accelerator switch
b—Clutch switch
c—Transmission neutral switch
d—Engine speed sensor

1976–80 California with automatic transmission

a—accelerator switch
b—inhibitor switch
c—Engine speed sensor

When all of these switches turn on and the engine is coasting, the solenoid valve on the secondary side of the carburetor engerizes and causes the valve to open. When the valve opens, fuel is drawn out of the float chamber by engine vacuum and metered by the coasting jet below the secondary throttle valve. On acceleration the coasting richer circuit is opened causing the coasting richer valve to close, shutting off the supply of extra fuel.

TESTING

Solenoid Valve

The valve should open when the circuit is energized. A clicking noise should be heard when the valve operates.

Accelerator switch

The accelerator switch should be closed when the pedal is not depressed and open when the pedal is depressed. Check with a test lamp.

Clutch Switch

1973

When the clutch pedal is depressed, the clutch switch contacts are closed and current flows to a clutch relay switch which energizes the advance point set in the distributor and the coasting richer system is de-energized.

1974–80

When the clutch pedal is depressed, the switch contacts are opened and the coasting richer system is de-energized.

Test all years' clutch switches with a test lamp.

Transmission Switch

FEDERAL MANUAL TRANSMISSION MODELS

The transmission switch turns on when the transmission is shifted into 3rd or 4th gear and energizes the coasting richer system. It de-energizes the system when the transmission is shifted into any other position.

CALIFORNIA MANUAL TRANSMISSION MODELS

The transmission switch turns on when the transmission is shifted into any gear and turns off when it is shifted into neutral position. The solenoid is energized when the switch is in the On position. Test with a test lamp.

Inhibitor Switch

CALIFORNIA AUTOMATIC TRANSMISSION MODELS

The inhibitor switch is installed on the shift linkage lever and energizes the

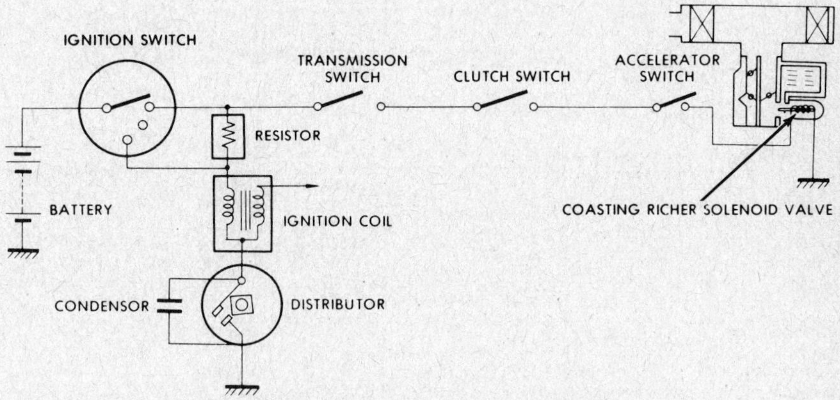

Coasting Richer system—Federal models

coasting richer system in drive, low or second gear positions. Test with a test lamp.

EGR Valve

NOTE: The EGR valve cannot be disassembled. No actual service is required except to determine proper operation of the valve

Check the valve shaft for proper movement by opening the throttle to give 2,000–2,500 rpm. The shaft should move upward at these speeds and return to the downward position when the engine speed is reduced to normal idle speed.

Check the vacuum diaphragm function by applying an outside vacuum source to the vacuum supply tube at the top of the vacuum diaphragm. The diaphragm should not leak down and should move to the fully up position at about 8–10 in. Hg of vacuum.

Transmission Controlled Spark Advance System

CALIFORNIA ONLY

This system was used on the 1975 models and was designed to control the ignition timing while in third gear by eliminating the vacuum advance.

An electrically operated switch, controlled by the transmission shift rail, controls distributor vacuum advance by the use of a vacuum switching valve, located on the firewall.

TESTING

Test the circuit with a test lamp. No current will flow through the transmission switch when in third gear.

When energized, the switching valve should allow vacuum to the distributor.

Engine Speed SensorCalifornia Only

Disconnect the engine speed sensor wiring connector and connect "B", "BR" and "BY" color-coded wiring terminals to each other with suitable cables. Then start the engine and check for the continuity between "LgB" color coded wiring terminals. When the engine runs over 1500–1700 rpm, the engine speed sensor is normal, if the continuity exists.

Catalytic Converter System—California Only

1976–80 California Models

A 2.6 liter converter is used to control hydrocarbon and carbon monoxide emissions. The converter oxidizes hydrocarbons and carbon monoxide into water and carbon dioxide.

Over-Temperature Control System

While the engine is coasting, the coasting richer system is operated to prevent catalyst overheating caused by poor combustion. The secondary air injection is operated simultaneously with the coasting richer system. When the catalyst temperature reaches 1350°F, due to high speed and/or high load driving, the secondary air is diverted to the atmosphere to reduce chemical reaction in the catalyst. When the catalyst temperature reaches 1830°F, due to engine malfunction or ignition system failure, the warning lamp and buzzer are turned on.

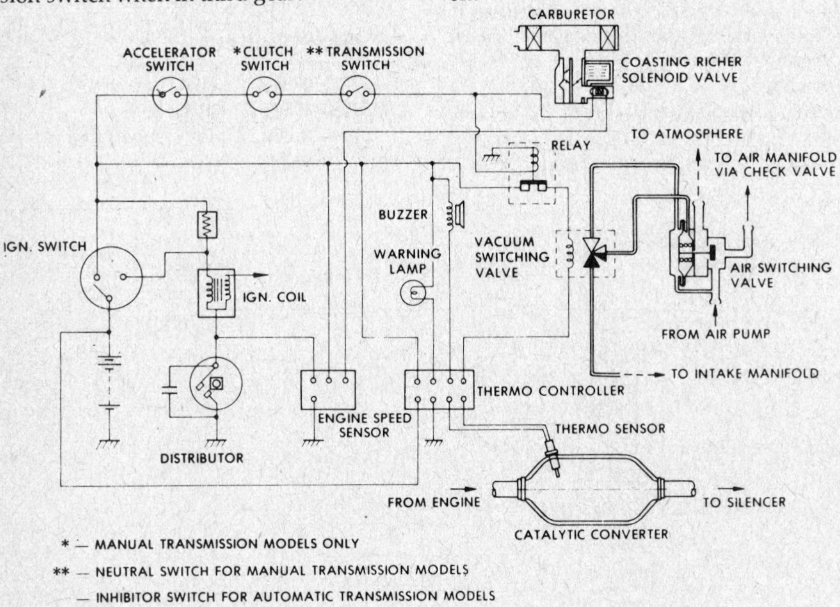

Overtemperature Control system—California models

Vacuum Switching Valve

The Vacuum switching valve has three ports, two of which are activated electrically by the solenoid plunger. The plunger is energized when the catalyst temperature exceeds 1350°F. It connects the diaphragm chamber of the air switching valve with the intake manifold permitting manifold vacuum to be applied to the diaphragm chamber.

Air Switching Valve

This valve diverts air flow from the pump and is operated by manifold vacuum and air pump pressure which are operated by the vacuum switching valve.

FUEL SYSTEM

Fuel Filter

A fuel filter is located in the fuel line leading from the fuel tank to the fuel pump. It is of the cartridge type with a paper filter element. If the fuel line is suspected of being clogged, check the fuel filter. Otherwise, the filter never has to be serviced.

MECHANICAL FUEL PUMP

The fuel pump is a mechanically operated, diaphragm-type driven by the fuel pump eccentric cam on the jackshaft.

Design of the fuel pump permits disassembly, cleaning and repair or replacement of defective parts.

REMOVAL AND INSTALLATION

1. Disconnect the rubber hose at the side of the fuel pump.
2. Remove the joint bolt and disconnect the fuel line at the side of the fuel pump. Be careful not to lose the joint bolt gaskets when removing the joint bolt.
3. Remove the two fuel pump mounting nuts and remove the fuel pump assembly from the side of the engine.
4. Install the fuel pump in the reverse order of removal, using a new gasket and sealer on the mating surface.

Electric Fuel Pump

The fuel pump is of the electro-magnetic type and is installed on the inner face of the third crossmember at the left hand side. This fuel pump is a totally enclosed type and cannot be disassembled.

REMOVAL AND INSTALLATION

1. Disconnect the hoses at the fuel pump.
2. Remove the two bolts and one nut mounting the fuel pump and remove the fuel pump assembly.

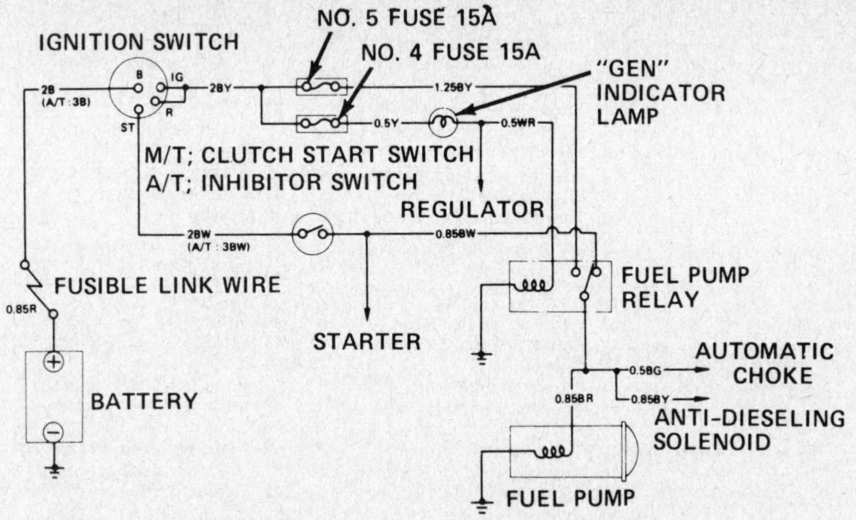

Schematic of the electric fuel pump circuit

Carburetor

The carburetor, used on the Chevy LUV is a two-barrel downdraft type with a low-speed (primary) side and a high-speed (secondary) side.

REMOVAL AND INSTALLATION

1. Remove the air cleaner wing nut and disconnect the rubber hoses from the clips on the air cleaner cover and the vacuum hose from the vacuum motor.
2. Remove the bracket bolts at the air cleaner and remove the air cleaner cover and filter element.
3. Disconnect the hot air hose (to the hot air duct), the air hose to the air pump at the air cleaner, and the vacuum hose at the joint nipple side of the intake manifold.
4. Loosen the bolt clamping the air cleaner to the carburetor. Separate the air cleaner body from the carburetor but do not remove it completely as the hoses remain connected.
5. Disconnect the PCV hose (to the camshaft cover), the rubber hoses to the check and relief valve and remove the air cleaner body.
6. On the 1974 and later models, disconnect the vacuum hoses from the EGR valve.
7. Disconnect the choke control wire.
8. Disconnect the lead from the throttle solenoid.
9. Disconnect the throttle linkage return spring.
10. Disconnect the accelerator linkage wire.
11. Disconnect the fuel line at the carburetor.
12. On 1974–75, remove the check valve from the air manifold.
13. Remove the four retaining nuts and lockwashers securing the carburetor

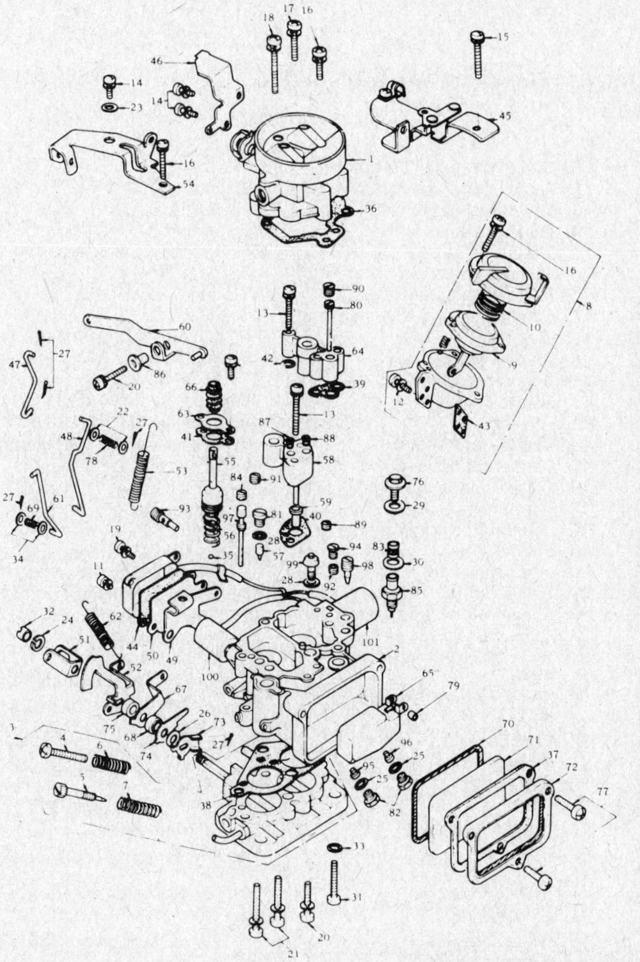

1. Choke chamber assembly
2. Float chamber assembly
3. Throttle chamber assembly
4. Throttle adjusting screw
5. Idle adjusting screw
6. Adjusting spring screw
7. Adjusting screw spring
8. Diaphragm chamber assembly
9. Diaphragm assembly
10. Diaphragm spring
11-21. Screw
22-24. Washer
25. Gasket
26. Washer
27. Pin
28. Gasket
29. Washer
30. Gasket
31. Screw
32. Nut
33-34. Washer
35. Inlet valve
36-44. Gasket
45. Choke wire bracket
46. Spring hanger
47. Choke connecting rod
48. Choke connecting rod
49. Accelerator switch holder
50. Plate
51. Throttle lever
52. Accelerator switch lever
53. Return spring
54. Accelerator switch bracket
55. Accelerator pump piston
56. Pump return spring
57. Injector weight
58. Pri. small venturi
59. Outer emulsion tube
60. Pump lever
61. Pump connecting lever
62. Return spring
63. Piston plate
64. Sec. small venturi
65. Float
66. Dust cover
67. Choke connecting lever
68. Sleeve (B)
69. Spring
70. Rubber seal
71. Level gauge
72. Level gauge cover
73. Adjust lever
74. Return plate
75. Sleeve (A)
76. Set screw
77. Screw
78. Spring
79. Float collar
80. Sec. emulsion tube
81. Injector weight plug
82. Main jet plug
83. Strainer
84. Pri. slow jet plug
85. Float needle valve assembly
86. Collar
87. Pri. main air bleed
88. Accelerator air bleed
89. Sec. slow air bleed
90. Sec. main air bleed
91. Pri. slow air bleed
92. Coasting jet
93. Vacuum jet
94. Coasting air bleed
95. Pri. main jet
96. Sec. main jet
97. Pri. slow jet
98. Sec. slow jet
99. Power valve
100. Anti dieseling solenoid
101. Coasting valve solenoid

Exploded view of the 1973 carburetor

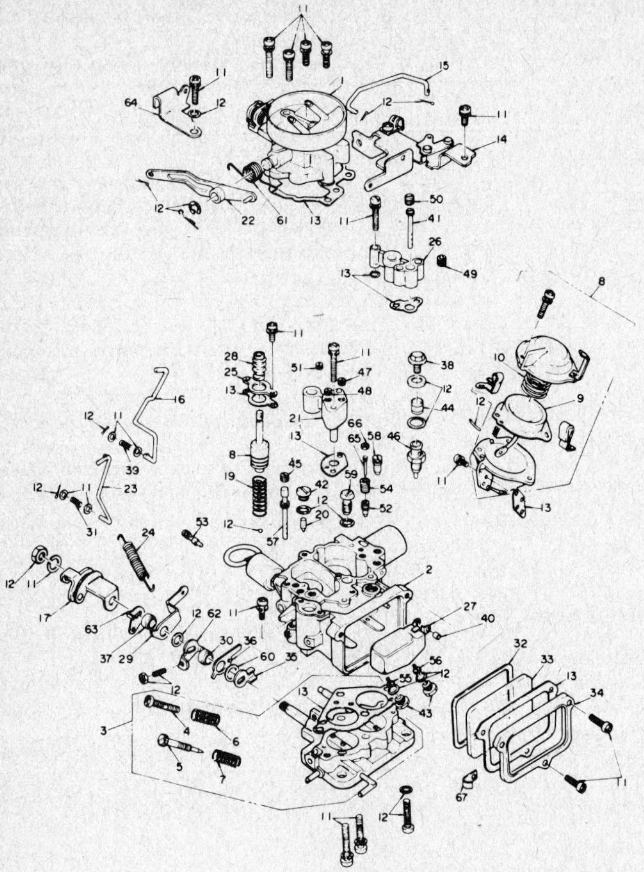

1. Choke chamber assembly
2. Float chamber assembly
3. Throttle chamber assembly
4. Throttle adjust screw
5. Idle adjust screw
6. Throttle adjust screw spring
7. Idle adjust screw spring
8. Diaphragm chamber assembly
9. Diaphragm
10. Diaphragm spring
11. Screw & washer kit, A
12. Screw & washer kit, B
13. Gasket
14. Choke control arm
15. Choke connecting rod
16. Choke connecting rod
17. Throttle lever (primary)
18. Accelerator pump piston
19. Piston spring
20. Injector weight
21. Small venturi (primary)
22. Accelerator pump lever
23. Connecting rod
24. Throttle return spring
25. Plate
26. Small venturi (secondary)
27. Float
28. Dust cover
29. Starting lever
30. Sleeve
31. Spring
32. Rubber seal
33. Fuel level gage
34. Cover
35. Adjust lever, B
36. Return plate
37. Sleeve
38. Filter set screw
39. Spring
40. Collar
41. Secondary emulsion tube
42. Plug
43. Drain plug
44. Filter
45. Slow jet plug (primary)
46. Needle valve
47. Accel air bleed
48. Main air bleed (primary)
49. Slow air bleed (secondary)
50. Main air bleed (secondary)
51. Slow air bleed (primary)
52. Coasting jet
53. Vacuum jet
54. Coasting air bleed
55. Main jet (primary)
56. Slow jet (secondary)
57. Slow jet (primary)
58. Slow jet (secondary)
59. Power valve
60. Thrust washer
61. Pump lever return spring
62. Kick lever
63. Crank
64. Choke control cable hanger
65. Coasting adjust screw
66. Coasting adjust screw

Exploded view of the carburetor on 1974-75 models without A/C

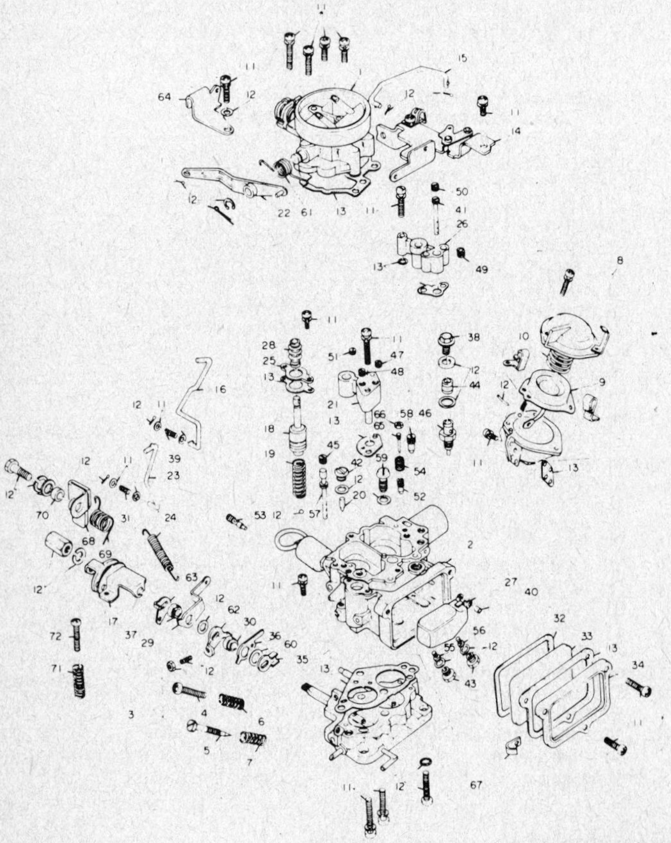

1. Choke chamber assembly
2. Float chamber assembly
3. Throttle chamber assembly
4. Throttle adjust screw
5. Idle adjust screw
6. Throttle adjust screw spring
7. Idle adjust screw spring
8. Diaphragm chamber assembly
9. Diaphragm
10. Diaphragm spring
11. Screw & washer kit, A
12. Screw & washer kit, B
13. Gasket
14. Choke control arm
15. Choke connecting rod
16. Choke connecting rod
17. Throttle lever (Primary)
18. Accelerator pump piston
19. Piston spring
20. Injector weight
21. Small venturi (Primary)
22. Accelerator pump lever
23. Connecting rod
24. Throttle return spring
25. Plate
26. Small venturi (Secondary)
27. Float
28. Dust cover
29. Starting lever
30. Sleeve
31. Spring
32. Rubber seal
33. Fuel level gage
34. Cover
35. Adjust lever, B
36. Return plate
37. Sleeve
38. Filter set screw
39. Spring
40. Collar
41. Secondary emulsion tube
42. Plug
43. Drain plug
44. Filter
45. Slow jet plug (Primary)
46. Needle valve
47. Accel air bleed
48. Main air bleed (Primary)
49. Slow air bleed (Secondary)
50. Main air bleed (Secondary)
51. Slow air bleed (Primary)
52. Coasting jet
53. Vacuum jet
54. Coating air bleed
55. Main jet (Primary)
56. Main jet (Secondary)
57. Slow jet (Primary)
58. Slow jet (Secondary)
59. Power valve
60. Thrust washer
61. Pump lever return spring
62. Kick lever
63. Crank
64. Choke control cable hanger
65. Coasting adjust screw
66. Lock nut
67. EGR vacuum pipe clip
68. Fast idle lever
69. Spring
70. Collar
71. Fast idle adjust spring
72. Fast idle adjust screw

Exploded view of the carburetor on 1974-75 models with A/C

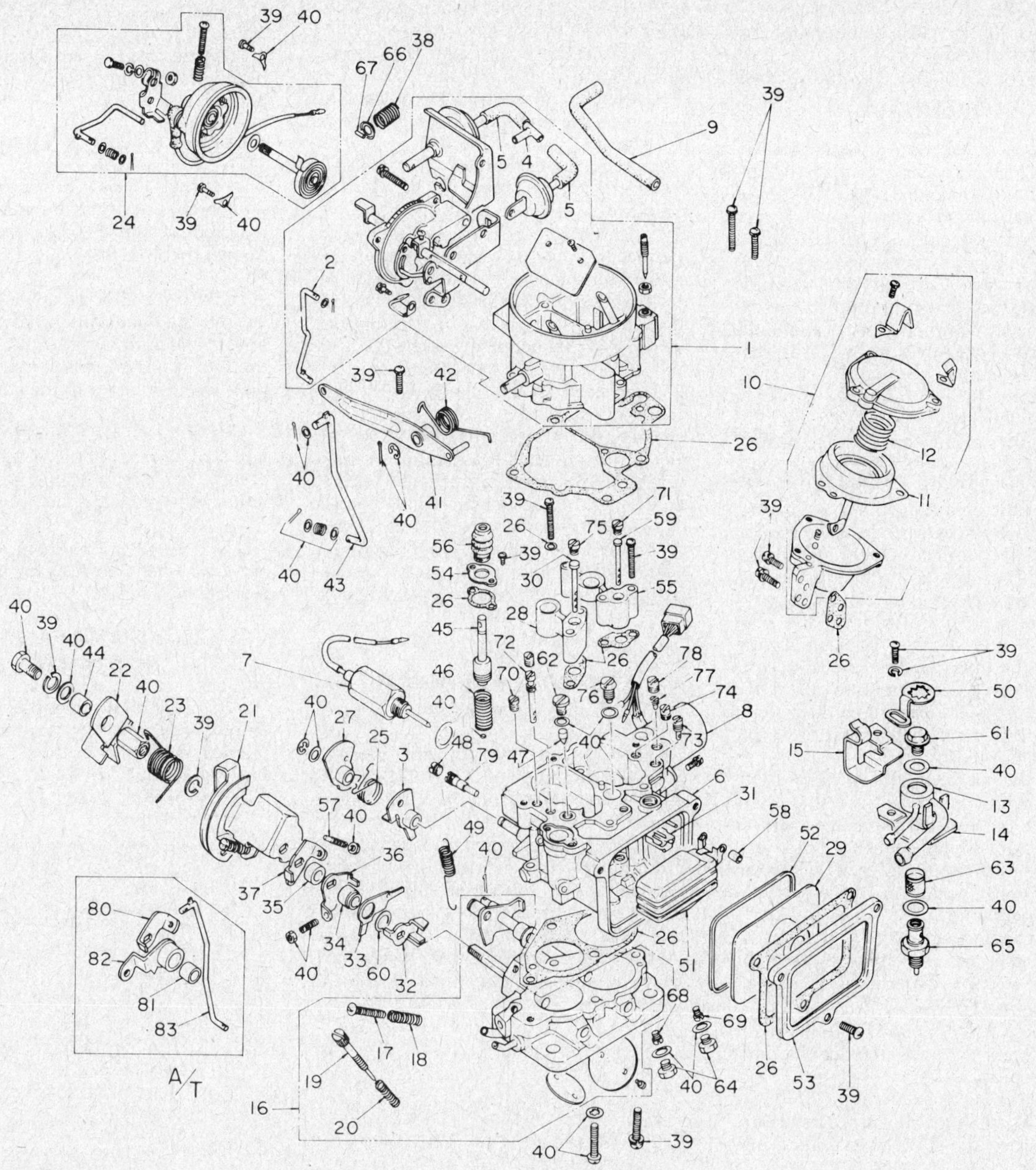

1. Choke chamber assembly
2. Choke connecting rod
3. Counter lever
4. Nipple
5. Hose
6. Float chamber assembly
7. Anti-dieseling solenoid
8. Coasting richer solenoid
9. Hose
10. Diaphragm chamber assembly
11. Diaphragm
12. Diaphragm spring
13. Nipple
14. Nipple stop late
15. EGR vacuum hose clip
16. Throttle chamber assembly
17. Throttle adjusting screw
18. Adjusting screw spring
19. Idle adjusting screw
20. Adjusting screw spring
21. Throttle lever (Primary)
22. Fast idle lever
23. Fast idle lever spring
24. Thermostat cover assembly
25. Fast idle cam spring
26. Gasket kit
27. Fast idle cam
28. Small venture (Primary)
29. Fuel level gauge
30. Primary emulsion tube
31. Baffle plate
32. Throttle adjusting lever
33. Throttle return plate
34. Kick lever sleeve
35. Throttle lever sleeve
36. Kick lever
37. Fast idle lever
38. Auto choke piston spring
39. Screw & Washer kit, A
40. Screw & Washer kit, B
41. Accelerator pump lever
42. Pump lever return spring
43. Accelerator pump rod
44. Fast idle lever collar
45. Accelerator pump piston
46. Piston return spring
47. Injector weight
48. Vacuum jet plug
49. Throttle return spring
50. Lock lever
51. Float
52. Rubber seal
53. Cover
54. Plate
55. Small venturi (Secondary)
56. Dust cover
57. Fast idle adjusting screw
58. Collar
59. Secondary emulsion tube
60. Thrust washer
61. Filter set screw
62. Injector weight plug
63. Filter
64. Drain plug
65. Needle valve
66. Piston spring carrier
67. Piston spring stop pin
68. Main jet (Primary)
69. Main jet (Secondary)
70. Slow air bleed (Primary)
71. Main air bleed (Secondary)
72. Slow jet (Primary)
73. Slow jet (Secondary)
74. Slow air bleed (Secondary)
75. Main air bleed (Primary)
76. Power valve
77. Coasting jet
78. Coasting air bleed
79. Vacuum jet
80. Connecting lever
81. Collar A
82. Down shift lever
83. Pump rod

Exploded view of the carburetor—1976-78

to the manifold and remove the carburetor.

14. Install the carburetor in the reverse order of removal.

OVERHAUL

Efficient carburetion depends greatly on careful cleaning and inspection during overhaul, since dirt, gum, water, or varnish in or on the carburetor parts are often responsible for poor performance.

Ovcerhaul your carburetor in a clean, dust-free area. Carefully disassemble the carburetor, referring often to the exploded views. Keep all similar and look-alike parts segregated during disassembly and cleaning to avoid accidental interchange during assembly. Make a note of all jet sizes.

When the carburetor is disassembled, wash all parts (except diaphragms, electric choke units, pump plunger, and any other plastic, leather, fiber, or rubber parts) in clean carburetor solvent. Do not leave parts in the solvent any longer than is necessary to sufficiently loosen the deposits. Excessive cleaning may remove the special finish from the float bowl and choke valve bodies, leaving these parts unfit for service. Rinse all parts in clean solvent and blow them dry with compressed air or allow them to air dry. Wipe clean all cork, plastic, leather with lint-free cloth.

Blow out all passages and jets with compressed air and be sure that there are no restrictions or blockages. Never use wire or similar tools to clean jets, fuel passages, or air bleeds. Clean all jets and valves separately to avoid accidental interchange.

Check all parts for wear or damage. If wear or damage is found, replace the defective parts. Especially check the following:

1. Check the float needle and seat for wear. If wear is found, replace the complete assembly.
2. Check the float hinge pin for wear and the float(s) for dents or distortion. Replace the float if fuel has leaked into it.
3. Check the throttle and choke shaft bores for wear or an out-of-round condition. Damage or wear to the throttle arm, shaft, or shaft bore will often require replacement of the throttle body. These parts require a close tolerance of fit; wear may allow air leakage, which would affect starting and idling.

***NOTE:** Throttle shafts and bushings are not included in overhaul kits. They can be purchased separately.*

4. Inspect the idle mixture adjusting needles for burrs or grooves. Any such condition requires replacement of the needle, since you will not be able to obtain a satisfactory idle.
5. Test the accelerator pump check valves. They should pass air one way but not the other. Test for proper setting by blowing and sucking on the valve. Replace the valve if necessary. If the valve is satisfactory, wash the valve again to remove breath moisture.
6. Check the bowl cover for warped surfaces with a straightedge.
7. Closely inspect the valves and seats for wear and damage, replacing as necessary.
8. After the carburetor is assembled, check the choke valve for freedom of operation.

Carburetor overhaul kits are recommended for each overhaul. These kits contain all gaskets and new parts to replace those that deteriorate most rapidly. Failure to replace all parts supplied with the kit (especially gaskets) can result in poor performance later.

After cleaning and checking all components, reassemble the carburetor, using new parts and referring to the exploded view. When reassembling, make sure that all screws and jets are tight in their seats, but do not overtighten as the tips will be distorted. Tighten all screws gradually, in rotation. Do not tighten needle valves into their seats; uneven jetting will result. Always use new gaskets. Be sure to adjust the float lever when reassembling.

THROTTLE LINKAGE ADJUSTMENT

When the primary throttle valve is opened to an angle of 50°—1973–75, 47°—1976 and later from its closed position, the adjust plate which is interlocked with the primary throttle valve, is brought into contact with portion A (see illustration) of the return plate. When the primary throttle valve is opened farther, the return plate is pulled apart from the stopper (B in the illustration), allowing the secondary throttle valve to open.

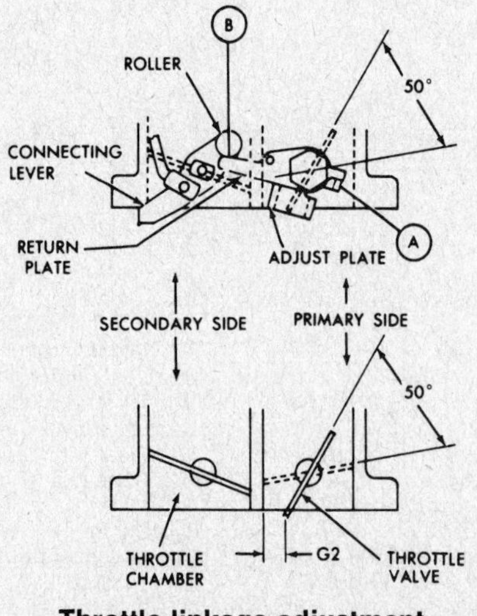

Throttle linkage adjustment

To adjust linkage:

1. Measure the clearance between the primary throttle valve and the wall of the throttle chamber at the center of the throttle valve when the adjust plate is brought into contact with portion A of the return plate. Standard clearance is 0.26–0.32 in.—1973–75, 0.24–0.30 in.—1976 and later.
2. If necessary, make the adjustment by bending the portion A of the return plate.

FLOAT LEVEL ADJUSTMENT

The fuel level is normal if it is is within the lines on the window glass of the float chamber when the vehicle is resting on level ground and the engine is off.

If the fuel level is outside the lines, remove the float housing cover. Have an absorbent cloth under the cover to catch the fuel from the fuel bowl. Adjust the float level by bending the needle seat on the float.

The needle valve should have an effective stroke of about 0.059 in. When necessary, the needle valve stroke can be adjusted by bending the float stopper.

***NOTE:** Be careful not to bend the needle valve rod when installing the float and baffle plate, if removed.*

CHOKE AND FAST IDLE ADJUSTMENT

When the choke is pulled completely closed, the primary throttle valve is opened, by means of the choke connecting rod to an angle of 17.5°—1973–74, 17°—1975–79.

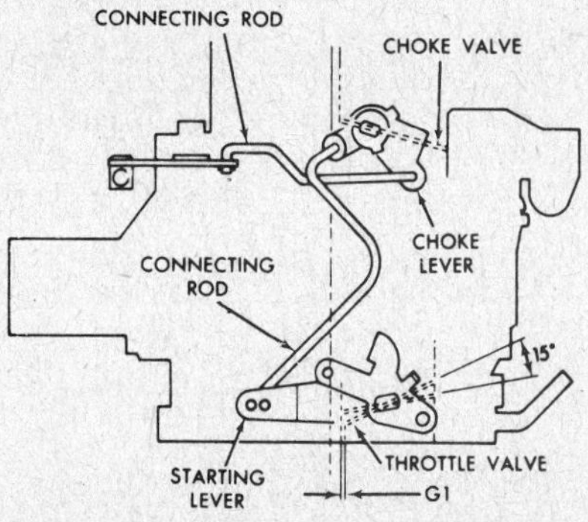

Choke and fast idle adjustment—1973-74

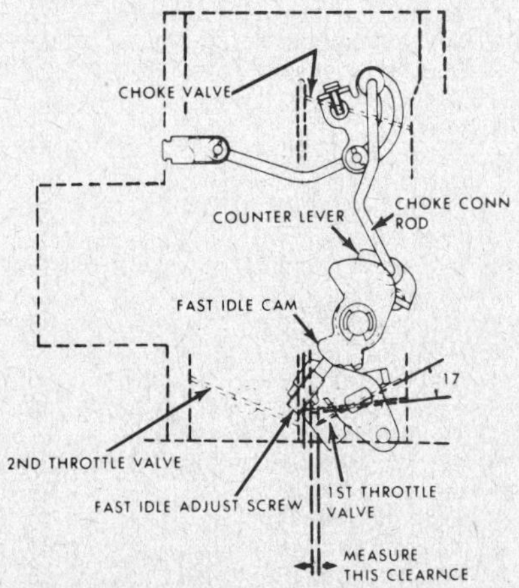

Choke and fast idle adjustment—1975 and later

To check the opening angle of the primary throttle valve, close the choke valve completely and measure the clearance between the throttle valve and the wall of the throttle valve chamber at the center part of the throttle valve. The clearance should be 0.057–0.065 in.—1973–74, 0.047–0.051 in.—1975 and later. If necessary, adjust the throttle valve opening angle by bending the connecting rod. Make sure to turn the throttle stop screw all the way in before measuring the clearance.

ELECTRIC CHOKE ADJUSTMENT

Align the thickest line on the thermostat housing with the line on the thermostat cover. Measure clearance (I) between the cover side stopper and the bimetal lever side stopper when the diaphragm (B) is fully stroked with negative pressure or finger pressure. If the measured valve deviates from the standard clearance of 0.28–0.29 in. or the equivalent bimetal lever angle of 20 degrees adjust with the adjusting screw.

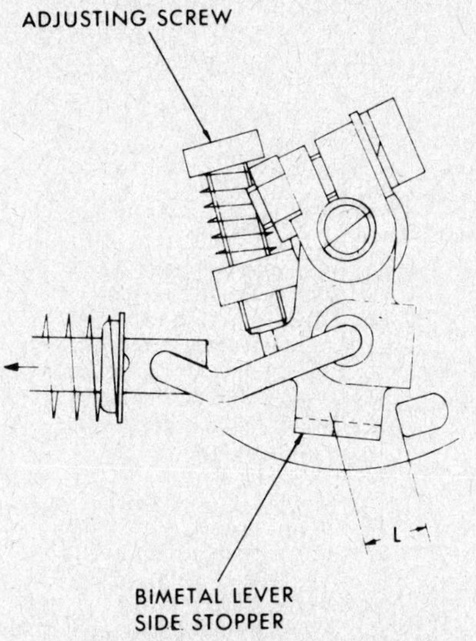

Electric choke stopper clearance

MANUAL TRANSMISSION

2-Wheel Drive Models

REMOVAL AND INSTALLATION

1. Disconnect the negative battery cable.
2. Remove the air cleaner assembly, and on 1974 and later models, disconnect the accelerator linkage at the carburetor throttle lever.
3. Slide the gearshift lever boot upward on the lever, remove the two gearshift lever attaching bolts and remove the lever.

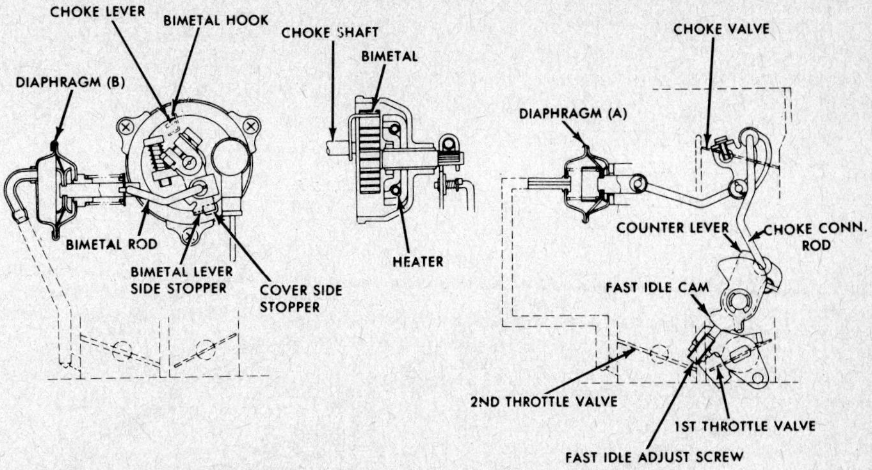

Exploded view of the automatic choke mechanism

4. Remove the starter attaching bolts and lay the starter assembly aside.
5. Raise the vehicle on a hoist and disconnect the exhaust pipe at the flange and disconnect the exhaust pipe hanger at the transmission.
6. Disconnect the speedometer cable at the transmission and disconnect the driveshaft at the differential. Remove the driveshaft. At this point you will have to either drain the transmission lubricant or plug the output shaft opening to prevent spillage.
7. On 1973–77 models, disconnect the clutch slave cylinder and pushrod from the transmission case and wire the slave cylinder to the frame. On 1978–80 models, disconnect the clutch cable from the bell housing and clutch fork.
8. Remove the bolts attaching the stiffeners, then remove the stone shield (all models).
9. Remove the frame bracket-to-rear transmission mounting attaching bolts.

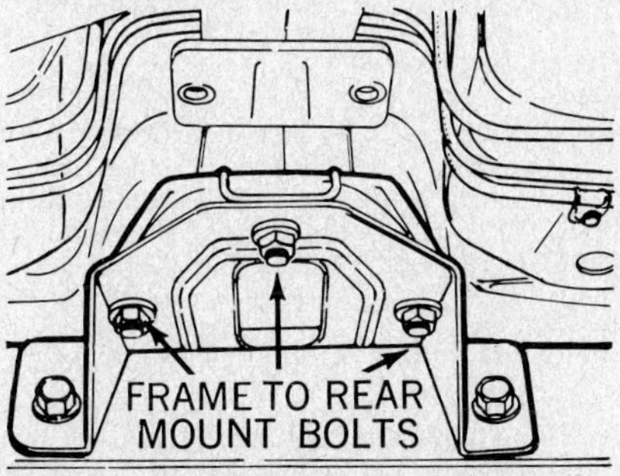

Remove the three frame bracket-to-transmission rear mounting bolts

10. Raise the engine and transmission as required and remove the four crossmember-to-frame bracket bolts.
11. On 1973–75 models, remove the mounting from the transmission rear cover.
12. Lower the engine and transmission assembly and support the rear of the engine.
13. Disconnect the electrical connectors at the TCS or CRS switch and the back-up light switch.
14. Remove the transmission-to-engine attaching bolts and slide the transmission straight back until the input shaft is clear of the clutch. Tip the front of the transmission downward and remove the transmission from the vehicle.
15. Install the transmission in the reverse order of removal, using a clutch aligning arbor or discarded transmission input shaft to align the clutch disc and the pilot bearing, if necessary (if the clutch was removed).

OVERHAUL

1973–75

1. Drain the transmission oil.
2. Remove the clutch fork, cover and release bearing.
3. Remove the five bolts from the front bearing retainer and the Belleville spring.
4. Remove the eight transmission top cover retaining bolts and remove the cover. Take care not to lose the three detent springs and balls.
5. Remove the four shift quadrant cover retaining bolts and remove the cover.
6. Remove the TCS or CRS switch and back-up lamp switch. Take care not to lose the back-up switch actuating pin and detent ball when removing the switch.
7. Remove the fulcrum bracket and the reverse idler gear control lever and the shift block.
8. Remove the three rollpins from the shift forks.
9. Remove the reverse shifter shaft through the front of the case and remove the shift fork. Be careful not to lose the three detent balls at the front of the case.
10. Remove the speedometer adapter from the transmission extension housing.
11. Remove the rear extension housing.
12. Remove the third and fourth gear shifter shaft through the rear of the case. Take care not to lose the two interlock balls at the front of the case.

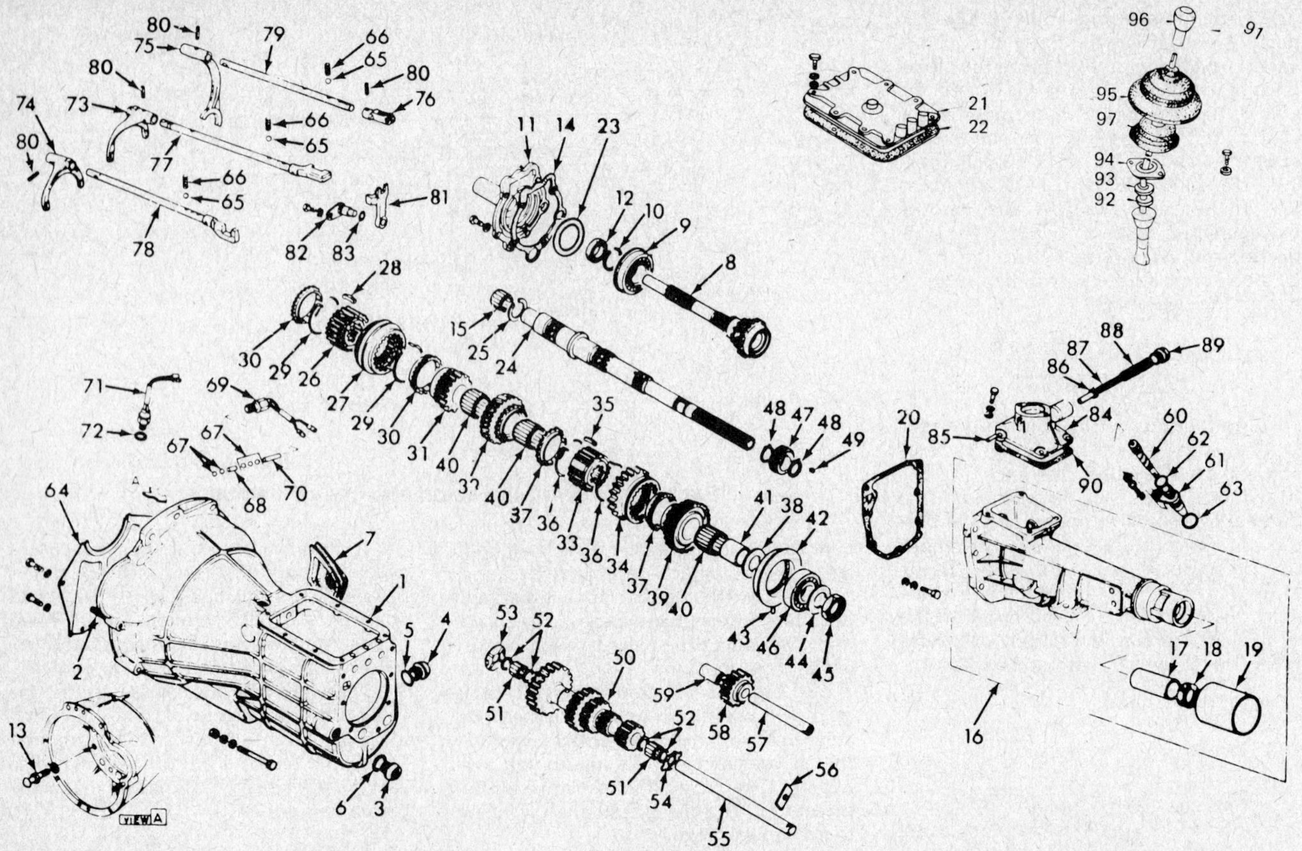

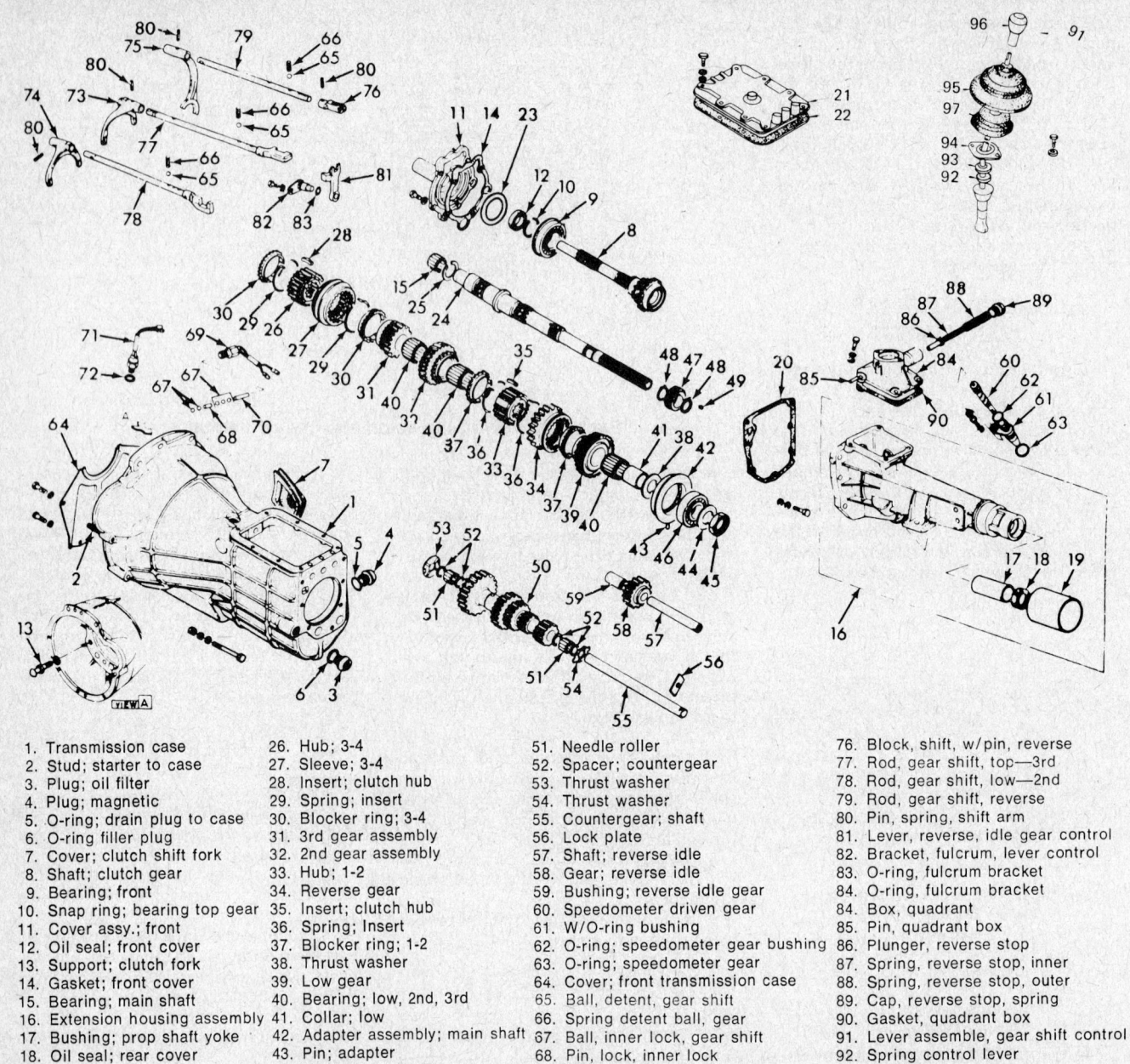

1. Transmission case
2. Stud; starter to case
3. Plug; oil filter
4. Plug; magnetic
5. O-ring; drain plug to case
6. O-ring filler plug
7. Cover; clutch shift fork
8. Shaft; clutch gear
9. Bearing; front
10. Snap ring; bearing top gear
11. Cover assy.; front
12. Oil seal; front cover
13. Support; clutch fork
14. Gasket; front cover
15. Bearing; main shaft
16. Extension housing assembly
17. Bushing; prop shaft yoke
18. Oil seal; rear cover
19. Cover: dust rear cover
20. Gasket; rear cover
21. Cover assembly
22. Gasket; top cover
23. Belleville spring
24. Main shaft
25. Snap ring; main shaft
26. Hub; 3-4
27. Sleeve; 3-4
28. Insert; clutch hub
29. Spring; insert
30. Blocker ring; 3-4
31. 3rd gear assembly
32. 2nd gear assembly
33. Hub; 1-2
34. Reverse gear
35. Insert; clutch hub
36. Spring; Insert
37. Blocker ring; 1-2
38. Thrust washer
39. Low gear
40. Bearing; low, 2nd, 3rd
41. Collar; low
42. Adapter assembly; main shaft
43. Pin; adapter
44. Spacer
45. Nut; main shaft
46. Bearing; main shaft
47. Speedometer drive gear
48. Snap ring; speedometer gear
49. Key; speedometer gear
50. Counter gear
51. Needle roller
52. Spacer; countergear
53. Thrust washer
54. Thrust washer
55. Countergear; shaft
56. Lock plate
57. Shaft; reverse idle
58. Gear; reverse idle
59. Bushing; reverse idle gear
60. Speedometer driven gear
61. W/O-ring bushing
62. O-ring; speedometer gear bushing
63. O-ring; speedometer gear
64. Cover; front transmission case
65. Ball, detent, gear shift
66. Spring detent ball, gear
67. Ball, inner lock, gear shift
68. Pin, lock, inner lock
69. Switch assembly, reverse lamp
70. Plunger, reverse lamp switch
71. Switch assembly, top—3rd
72. Gasket, switch
73. Arm, shift, top—3rd
74. Arm, shift low—2nd
75. Arm, shift, reverse
76. Block, shift, w/pin, reverse
77. Rod, gear shift, top—3rd
78. Rod, gear shift, low—2nd
79. Rod, gear shift, reverse
80. Pin, spring, shift arm
81. Lever, reverse, idle gear control
82. Bracket, fulcrum, lever control
83. O-ring, fulcrum bracket
84. O-ring, fulcrum bracket
84. Box, quadrant
85. Pin, quadrant box
86. Plunger, reverse stop
87. Spring, reverse stop, inner
88. Spring, reverse stop, outer
89. Cap, reverse stop, spring
90. Gasket, quadrant box
91. Lever assemble, gear shift control
92. Spring control lever
93. Cage, control lever
94. Cover, control lever
95. Grommet, lever, gear shift
96. Knob, lever, gear shift control
97. Cover, dust, control lever

1973-75 transmission

13. Remove the first and second shifter shaft through the rear of the case. Avoid losing the interlock pin through the front of the shaft.

14. Remove the first and second, and the third and fourth gear shift forks through the top of the case.

15. Remove the lock plate at the rear of the case and remove the reverse idler gear shaft through the rear of the case.

16. Drive the countergear shaft through the rear of the case with a drift.

17. Remove the mainshaft from the rear of the transmission case. Remove the clutch gear pilot roller from the clutch gear. Remove the clutch gear and the bearing assembly from the front of the case. Press the front bearing from the clutch gear.

18. Remove the countergear and reverse idler gear from the transmission case.

19. Remove the snap-ring and remove the front bearing from the clutch gear shaft.

20. Remove the rear speedometer drive gear snap-ring, speedometer gear and drive key, and remove the front snap-ring.

21. Remove the rear bearing retainer nut and lockwasher and remove the rear bearing retainer.

22. Press the rear bearing from the retainer.

23. Remove the first gear rear thrust washer, gear, caged roller bearing, sleeve and blocker ring.

24. Remove the first and second gear synchronizer hub and gear assembly.

25. Remove the second speed gear, caged roller bearing and blocker ring.

26. Remove the third and fourth gear synchronizer hub snap ring and remove the synchronizer assembly, blocker ring, third speed gear and caged roller bearing.

To assemble the transmission:

27. Lightly oil the third gear bearing journal on the mainshaft. Install the caged roller bearing, the third gear blocker ring, and the third and fourth gear synchronizer hub assembly with the chamfer on the synchronizer hub toward the front of the transmission. Install the snap-ring.

28. Hold the shaft in a vertical position so that the rearward end is up. Lightly oil the second speed journal on the main shaft. Install the clutch pilot roller bearing, second speed gear and blocker ring.

29. Install the first and second gear synchronizer hub and gear assembly. The toothed portion of the reverse sliding gear on the synchronizer assembly should be located toward the front of the transmission.

30. Install the first gear sleeve and lightly oil the sleeve. Install the caged roller bearing over the sleeve and install the blocker ring, first gear and the rear thrust washer. The thrust washer oil groove side faces first gear.

31. Press the rear bearing into the rear bearing retainer. The sealed portion of the bearing should be positioned toward the front of the retainer.

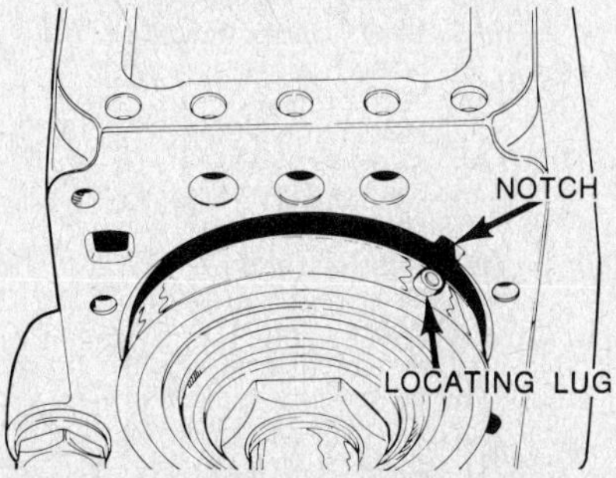

Install the main drive assembly into the rear case insuring that the lug on the rear of the bearing retainer assembly is located in the notch in the rear of the case

32. Install the rear bearing and retainer assembly on the rear of the main shaft and install the lockwasher and nut. Tighten the nut to 80 ft lbs and bend the tab on the lockwasher over one flat portion of the nut. Be sure the notches of the blocker rings align with the keys on the synchronizer assemblies.

33. Insert the reverse idler gear into the case. The shift fork groove should be toward the rear of the transmission.

34. Install the inner thrust washers, of which there are 46 (23 on each side), the needle bearings and the outer thrust washers into the front and rear of the counter gear using chassis lube to retain the bearings. Install the dummy shaft.

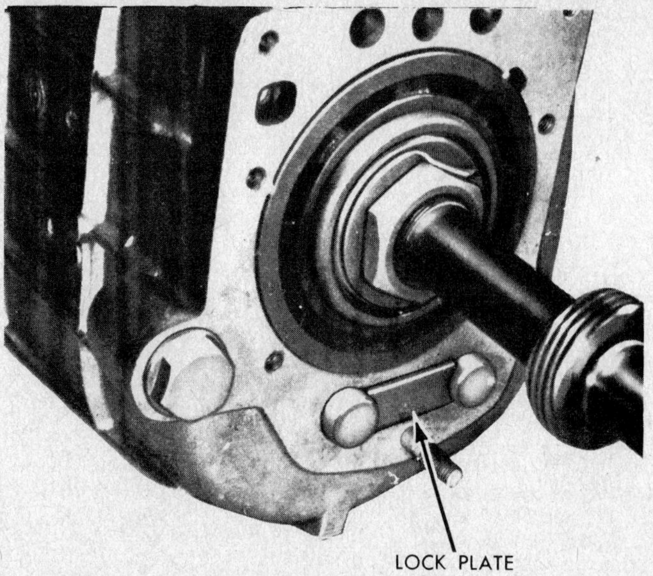

Remove the lockplate at the rear of the transmission housing before removing the reverse idler gear shaft through the rear of the housing

35. Install the front and rear countergear thrust washers and install the countergear into the case locating the large diameter gear toward the front of the case.

36. Install the front bearing onto the clutch gear and install the snap-ring.

37. Install the clutch gear into the transmission case. Make sure the clutch gear is properly positioned when driving it into the case so as not to gall the bearing race.

38. Install the clutch gear pilot roller into the clutch gear, pack the bearing with chassis lube and install the blocker ring on the clutch gear cone.

39. Install the main drive assembly into the case insuring that the lug on the rear bearing retainer assembly is located into the notch in the rear of the case.

40. With the main drive assembly installed, invert the case and drive the reverse idle shaft into the rear of the case. Rotate the mainshaft slightly to lcoate the counter gear for installation of the counter gear shaft.

To insure that the thrust washers are properly positioned, lightly oil the counter-gear shaft and install it through the rear of the case. Tap the countergear shaft lightly with a soft faced hammer, driving the dummy shaft out through the front of the case. Install the lock plate into the key slots of the reverse idler gear shaft and counter gear shaft and drive the lock-plate against the rear of the case.

41. Install the shift forks into the case, positioning the shift forks into the grooves of the synchronizer sleeves on the first and second, and the third and fourth gear synchronizer assemblies. Install the reverse gear shift fork into the groove on the reverse idler gear.

42. Install the interlock pin into the first and second shifter shaft and install the shaft through the rear of the case, picking up the first and second gear shift fork.

43. Rotate the transmission case and install the two interlock balls into the front shifter shaft bosses. Install the third and fourth shifter shaft through the rear of the case, picking up the third and fourth shift fork and locate the shaft to the front of the case to retain the interlock balls.

44. Install the speedometer drive gear and snap rings.

45. Install the rear extension housing and tighten the attaching bolts and nut to 10 ft. lbs. Install the extension housing seal.

46. Install the speedometer driven gear assembly.

47. Install the two interlock balls and insert the reverse shifter shaft through the front of the case, picking up the reverse shift fork.

48. Install the roll pins through the first and second, third and fourth, and the reverse shift forks into the shafts.

49. Install the reverse shift block, fulcrum bracket and reverse idler gear control lever and roll pin.

50. Install the interlock ball and actualing pin in the back-up light switch orifice and install the back-up light switch and TCS switch.

51. Install the shift quadrant top and tighten the attaching bolts to 10 ft lbs.

52. Put the transmission in Neutral and install the three detent balls, springs, gasket and top cover and tighten the cover attaching bolts to 10 ft lbs.

53. Install the front cover attaching bolts to 10 ft lbs.

54. Install the speedometer driven gear.

55. Install the shift fork ball stud and tighten to 65–70 ft lbs.

56. Install the clutch shift fork and release the bearing assembly.

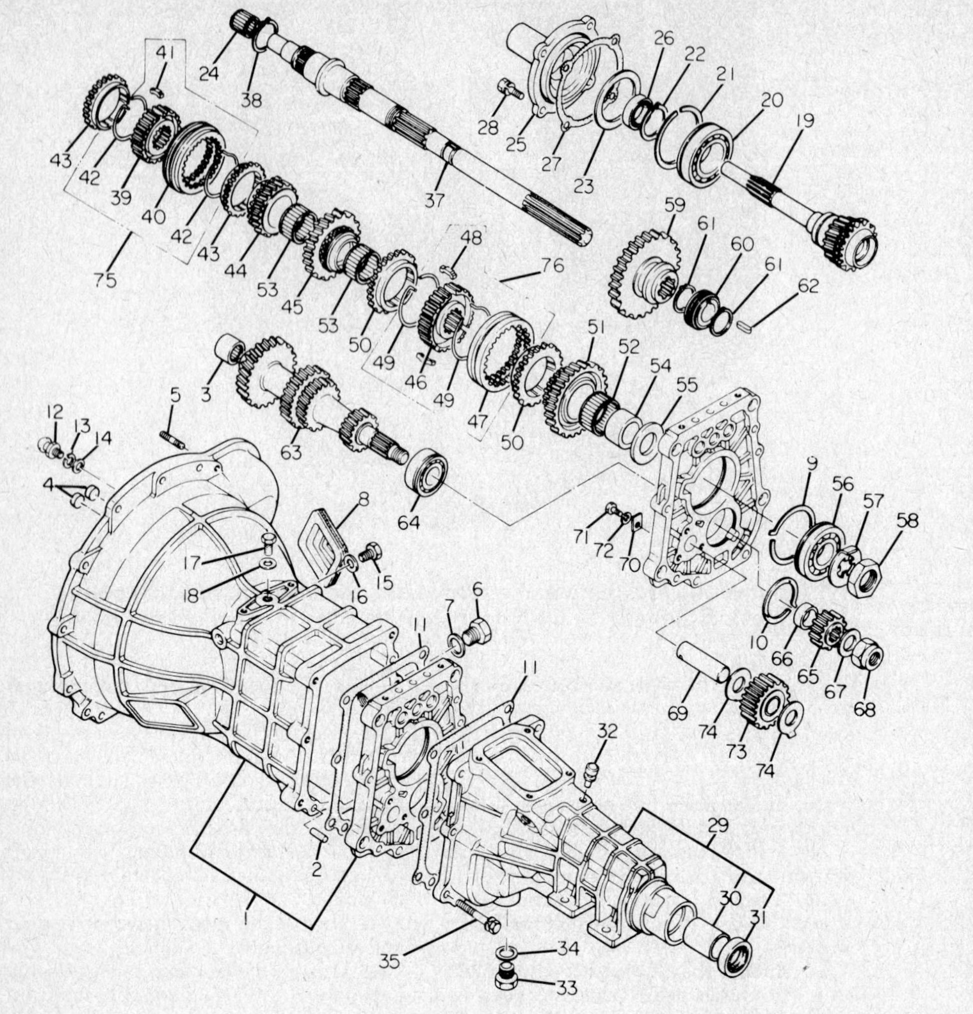

1. Case, w/center support
2. Pin, guide
3. Bearing, needle
4. Plug, shift rod
5. Stud
6. Plug, oil filler
7. O-ring, oil filler
8. Dust cover, shift fork
9. Ring, snap, mainshaft
10. Ring, snap counter gear
11. Gasket, case and rear cover
12. Ball stud
13. Washer, lock
14. Washer, plain
15. Plug, screw
16. Gasket, plug (Calif. spec.)
17. Plug, screw (Calif. spec.)
18. Gasket, plug (Calif. spec.)
19. Shaft, clutch gear
20. Bearing, ball
21. Ring, snap
22. Ring, snap
23. Spring, Belleville
24. Bearing, needle
25. Bearing retainer
26. Seal, oil, bearing retainer
27. Gasket, bearing retainer
28. Bolt
29. Extension assembly, rear, w/bushing and seal
30. Bushing
31. Seal, oil, rear extension
32. Breather assembly
33. Plug, oil drain
34. O-ring, oil drain
35. Bolt
37. Shaft main
38. Ring, snap
39. Hub, synchronizer, 3rd-4th
40. Sleeve, synchronizer
41. Key, synchronizer
42. Spring, synchronizer
43. Ring, blocker
44. Gear assembly, 3rd
45. Gear assembly, 2nd
46. Hub, synchronizer, 1st-2nd
47. Sleeve, synchronizer
48. Key, synchronizer
49. Spring, synchronizer
50. Ring blocker
51. Gear assembly, 1st
52. Bearing needle, 1st
53. Bearing, needle, 2nd
54. Collar, needle bearing
55. Washer, thrust, 1st
56. Bearing, mainshaft
57. Washer, lock, mainshaft
58. Nut, mainshaft
59. Gear, reverse
60. Gear, speed drive
61. Ring, snap, drive gear
62. Key
63. Gear, counter
64. Bearing, angular ball
65. Gear, counter reverse
66. Spacer
67. Washer, plain
68. Nut, self lock
69. Shaft, reverse idle
70. Plate lock
71. Bolt, lock
72. Washer, spring
73. Gear, reverse idle
74. Washer, thrust
75. Synchronizer assembly, 3rd-4th
76. Synchronizer assembly, 1st-2nd

1975 and later transmission

57. Fill the transmission with SAE 30 oil.

1976–80

1. Remove the drain plug and drain the transmission pan.
2. Remove the boot, clutch fork and throwout bearing.
3. Remove the four bearing retainer bolts and remove the retainer, gasket and spring washer.
4. Remove the bolt holding the speedometer gear bushing and remove the speedometer driven gear assembly.
5. Remove the four bolts holding the shifter cover and remove the shifter cover and gasket.
6. Remove the back-up switch on California vehicles and both back-up and CRS switches on all others.
7. Remove the eight bolts holding the rear extension, then remove the rear extension and gasket.
8. Remove the thrust washers and reverse idler gear from the reverse idler gear shaft.
9. Remove the snap rings, speedometer drive gear and key from the mainshaft.
10. Remove the spring pin from the reverse shifter fork and reverse gear.
11. Remove the snap ring from the outer circumference of the clutch gear shaft ball bearing.
12. Remove the center support assembly from the transmission case.
13. Drive out the spring pins from the third and fourth and first and second shift forks.

*NOTE: **When removing the spring pin, hold a round bar against the end of the shifter rods to prevent damage.***

14. Remove the detent spring plate from the center support, then remove the detent springs and balls.
15. Remove the first and second and third and fourth shifter rods from the center support, then remove the shifter forks.
16. Remove the reverse shifter rod forward as it is fitted with a stopper pin.

*NOTE: **Be careful not to loose the detent interlock plugs located between the shifter rods in the center support.***

17. Move both synchronizers rearward to prevent turning of the mainshaft.

*NOTE: **It may be necessary to tap the synchronizers with a hammer handle to get them engaged.***

18. Flatten out the lock washer and remove the lock nut and washer from the mainshaft.
19. Remove the self locking nut, washer, countershaft reverse gear and collar from the rear of the countergear.

20. Insert the nose of snap ring pliers into the countergear bearing snap ring hole in the center support and disengage the snap ring from the ring groove by tapping on the front face of the center support while expanding the countergear bearing snap ring.

21. Remove the center support by expanding the mainshaft rear bearing snap ring with the snap ring pliers.

22. Separate the clutch gear, needle bearings and blocker ring from the mainshaft assembly.

23. Press the rear bearing from the mainshaft.

24. Remove the thrust washer, 1st speed gear, needle roller bearing, a collar and blocker ring.

25. Remove the 1st and 2nd gear synchronizer assembly.

26. Remove the 2nd gear, blocker ring and needle roller bearing frm the mainshaft.

27. Remove the snap ring, 3rd and 4th sychronizer assembly, and blocker ring from the mainshaft.

28. Remove 3rd gear and needle bearings.

29. Remove the snap ring and press off the clutch bearing and countergear bearing from the shaft.

To assemble the transmission:

30. Stand the front of the mainshaft upward and install the 3rd speed gear and needle roller bearing with the tapered side of the gear facing the front of the mainshaft.

31. Install a blocker ring with the clutching teeth upward over the synchronizing surface of the 3rd speed gear.

32. If it is necessary to reassemble the synchronizer assembly turn the face of the synchronizer hub with the heavy boss to the face of the sleeve with the light chamfering on the outer rim.

33. Fit the keys into the key groove and position the synchronizer springs into the hole in the side face of the hub.

34. Install the 3rd and 4th synchronizer assembly on the mainshaft with the face of the sleeve with the light chamfer rearward.

35. Install the snap ring.

36. Now turn the rear of the mainshaft upward and install the 2nd speed gear and needle roller bearing on the mainshaft with the tapered surface of the gear facing the rear of the mainshaft.

37. Install a blocker ring with the clutching teeth downward over the synchronizing surface of the 2nd speed gear.

38. Install the 1st and 2nd synchronizer assembly with the chamfer on the sleeve facing the front of the mainshaft.

39. Install a blocker ring with the clutching teeth rearward.

40. Install the collar, needle roller bearing and 1st speed gear on the mainshaft.

***NOTE:** The tapered side of the gear should be facing the front of the mainshaft.*

40. Install the 1st speed gear thrust washer on the mainshaft with the grooved side facing 1st gear.

41. Press the rear bearing on the mainshaft with the snap ring groove facing the front of the mainshaft.

42. If removed, press the ball bearing on the clutch gear shaft with the snap ring groove on the bearing facing the front of the transmission. Install the snap ring on the clutch gear shaft.

43. Assemble the needle roller bearing, blocker ring and clutch gear to the front of the mainshaft.

44. If removed, press on the counter gear ball bearing with the snap ring groove facing the rear of the transmission.

45. If removed, install the snap rings in the snap ring groove in the inner circumference of the mainshaft and countergear holes of the center support.

46. If removed, insert the idler gear shaft with the lock plate groove side into the center support from the rear, then install the lock plate into the groove and tighten the bolt to 14 ft. lbs.

47. Mesh the countergear with the mainshaft assembly and install a holding tool on the mainshaft and countergear.

48. Place the tool with mainshaft and countergear assembled into a vise, then install the center support.

49. Expand the mainshaft bearing snap ring in the center support and press the center support onto the shaft until the countergear bearing is brought into contact with its snap ring.

50. Expand the countergear bearing snap ring and press the center support further until the mainshaft and countergear snap rings are fitted into their grooves.

51. Remove the holding tool from the mainshaft and countergear and remove the assembly from the vise.

52. Move both synchronizers rearward to prevent turning of the mainshaft.

53. Install the collar, countershaft reverse gear, washer and self locking nut on the rear of the countergear; torque the nut to 100 ft. lbs.

***NOTE:** New self-locking nuts should be used.*

54. Install the lock nut and lock washer on the mainshaft and torque the nut to 94 ft. lbs., then bend down the lock washer.

***NOTE:** Install the lock nut so that the chamfered side is facing the lock washer.*

55. Apply grease to the two detent holes from the middle hole of the center support.

56. Install the 1st and 2nd and the 3rd and 4th shifter forks into their grooves in the synchronizer assembly.

57. Install the 3rd and 4th shifter rod from the rear of the center support through the middle hole and into the 1st and 2nd, 3rd and 4th shifter forks. Align the spring pin hole in the shifter fork with the hole in the shifter rod.

***NOTE:** Identify the 3rd and 4th shifter rod by the two detent grooves on the side of the rod.*

58. Install the 1st and 2nd shifter rod from the rear of the center support through the 1st and 2nd shifter fork and align the hole in the rod to the hole in the shifter fork.

59. If removed, install the stopper pin in the reverse shifter rod and the front of the center support.

60. Install the two spring pins in the 1st/2nd and 3rd/4th shifter forks.

***NOTE:** When installing the spring pins place a round bar against the end of the shifter rod to prevent damage.*

61. Install the detent balls, spring, gasket and retainer on the center support and torque the bolts to 14 ft. lbs.

62. Place the transmission case upright on wooden blocks and install the center support assembly and gasket into the transmission case aligning the dowel pin holes with the dowel pins.

63. Assemble the reverse shifter fork to the reverse gear and install these parts into position from the rear side of the mainshaft, then connect them to the reverse shifter rod.

64. Install the spring pin in the reverse shifter fork.

65. Install the thrust washer and reverse idler gear on the idler shaft.

***NOTE:** The reverse idler gear should be installed with undercut teeth forward.*

66. Install the speedometer drive gear snap ring and key on the mainshaft.

67. If removed install a new oil seal to the rear extension.

68. Apply grease to the outer thrust washer of the reverse idler shaft and insert it in the rear extension.

69. Install the rear extension and gasket to the transmission case aligning the dowel pin hole with the dowel pin. Torque the eight bolts to 27 ft. lbs.

70. Install the back-up lamp switch and CRS switch if removed.

71. Install the shifter cover and gasket and torque the bolts to 10 ft. lbs.

72. Install the oil "O" ring to the speedometer driven gear and install the gear to the rear extension.

73. Install the front bearing retainer seal.

74. Install a snap ring to the outer circumference of the clutch gear bearing.

75. Apply grease to the bearing retainer spring washer and place it in the bearing retainer with the dished face turned to the being outer space.

76. Install the bearing retainer to the front of the transmission case and torque the four bolts to 14 ft. lbs.

***NOTE:** The shorter bolts are used on countergear front bearing side of the bearing retainer.*

77. Install the ball stud to the bearing retainer and torque to 30 ft. lbs.

78. Install the boot clutch fork and throwout bearing, then install the retaining spring.

79. Install the drain plug on the transmission case, then install the rear cover plug. Fill the transmission case to the specified level of 1.35 qt.

MANUAL TRANSMISSION AND TRANSFER CASE

4 Wheel Drive Models

REMOVAL AND INSTALLATION

1. Disconnect the battery ground.
2. Drain the transmission oil.
3. Slide the shift lever boots upward and unbolt each lever.
4. Remove the return spring from the transfer case shift lever and remove both levers.
5. Remove the starter attaching bolts and remove the starter assembly.
6. Raise the support the vehicle. Disconnect the exhaust pipe from the manifold and disconnect the pipe support from the transmission.
7. Disconnect the speedometer cable at the transmission. Disconnect the rear driveshaft at the differential. Disconnect the ground strap.
8. Remove the rear driveshaft from the transfer case. Remove the front driveshaft.
9. Disconnect the clutch return spring.
10. Disconnect the clutch cable at the fork.
11. Remove the flywheel stoneguard.
12. Remove the transmission rear crossmember bolts.
13. Raise the engine and transmission, and remove the rear crossmember-to-frame bolts.
14. Remove the rear mounting bolts from the transfer case.
15. Unbolt and remove the side case from the transmission.
16. Remove the stud bolt from the transfer case.
17. Lower the engine and transmission assembly and support the rear of the engine.
18. Disconnect the CRS switch and backup light switch.
19. Remove the shifter cover and gasket from the transfer case.
20. Remove the transmission-to-engine bolts. When removing the transmission, turn the side case fitting face of the case downward and pull the case straight back until free from the clutch. Tip the front of the transmission downward and remove it.
21. Installation is the reverse of removal. Torque shifter cover bolts to 14 ft lb.

CLUTCH

The clutch is a hydraulically operated single-plate, dry friction disc, diaphragm spring type.

1973–77

The clutch is operated by a clutch pedal which is mechanically connected to a clutch master cylinder. When the pedal is depressed, the piston in the master cylinder is moved in the master cylinder bore. This movement compresses the fluid in the master cylinder causing hydraulic pressure which is transferred through a tube to the slave cylinder. The slave cylinder is mounted to the clutch housing with its piston connected to the clutch release lever. The hydraulic pressure in the slave cylinder forces the slave cylinder piston to travel out the cylinder bore and move the clutch release lever, disengaging the clutch.

1978–80

The clutch is operated by a steel cable connecting the pedal with the throw-out arm.

REMOVAL AND INSTALLATION

1. Raise the vehicle on a hoist.
2. Remove the transmission.
3. Mark the clutch assembly-to-flywheel relationship with paint or a center punch so that the clutch assembly can be reassembled in the same position from which it is removed.
4. Loosen the six clutch cover-to-flywheel attaching bolts, one turn at a time in an alternating sequence, until the spring tension is relieved to avoid distorting or bending the clutch cover.
5. Support the clutch pressure plate and cover assembly with a clutch aligning arbor, then remove the bolts and the clutch assembly.
6. Apply a thin coat of grease to the pressure plate wire ring, diaphragm spring, clutch cover grooves and the drive bosses on the pressure plate.
7. Apply a thin coat of Lubriplate to the splines in the driven plate.
8. Assemble the clutch cover and pressure plate and the driven plate on a clutch alignment arbor.
9. Align the marks made on the clutch cover and the flywheel and install the six clutch cover-to-flywheel attaching bolts. Tighten the bolts to 50 in. lbs. Remove the aligning arbor.

PEDAL HEIGHT ADJUSTMENT

1973–77

1. Disconnect the battery ground cable.
2. Measure the clutch pedal height after making sure that the pedal is fully returned by the pedal return spring. The pedal height should be between 5.9 and 6.3 in.
3. To adjust the height, disconnect the clutch switch and remove it from its mounting bracket.
4. Loosen the locknut on the master cylinder pushrod.
5. Adjust the clutch pedal to the specified height by rotating the pushrod in the appropriate direction. Tighten the locknut when finished with the adjustment.
6. Install the clutch switch. Adjust the clearance between the switch hous-

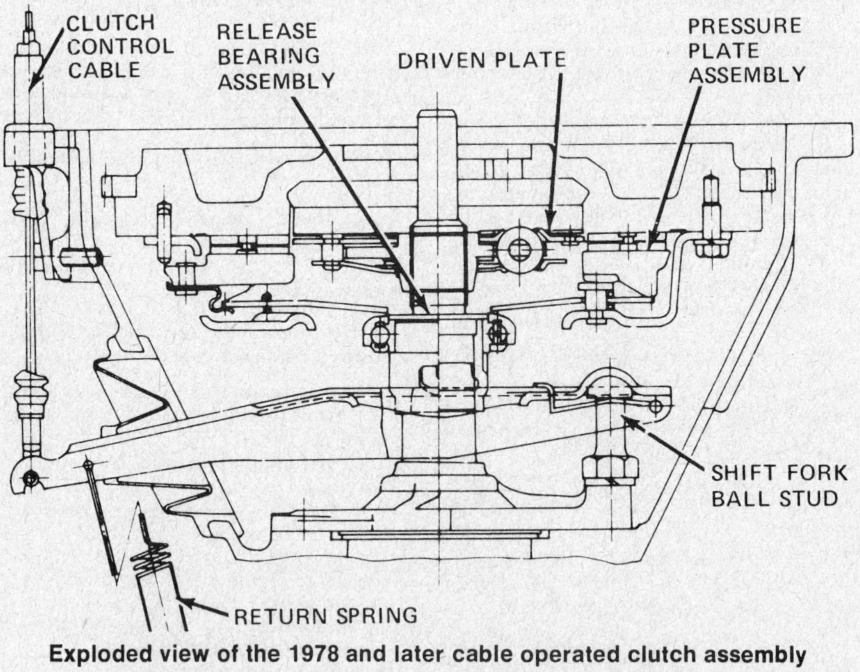

Exploded view of the 1978 and later cable operated clutch assembly

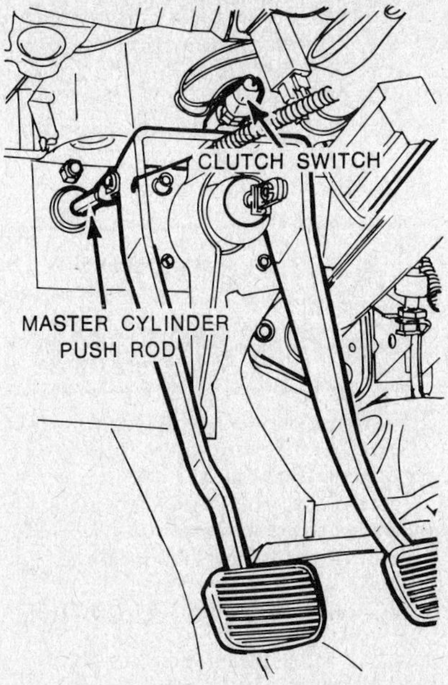

Clutch pedal height adjustment

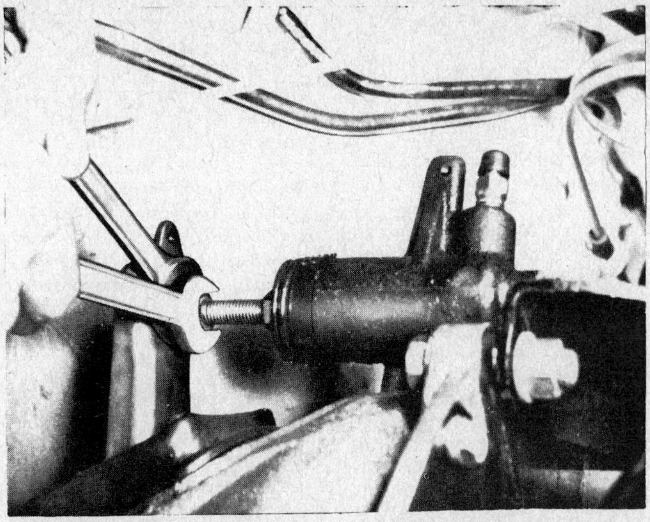

Clutch release fork adjustment

ing (not the switch actuating pin) and the clutch pedal tab to 0.02–0.04 in. Tighten the switch locknut.

7. Connect the electrical leads to the clutch switch and connect the negative battery cable.

1978–80

Adjust the pedal stop so that the clutch and brake pedals are the same height. Make sure that the clutch switch is in contact with the clutch pedal bracket.

CLUTCH RELEASE FORK ADJUSTMENT

1973–77

1. Remove the clutch release fork return spring and move the release fork slightly rearward.
2. Loosen the adjusting nut and adjust the pushrod until it contacts the release fork.
3. Back off the pushrod about 1$^{3}/_{4}$ turns and tighten the locknut.

NOTE: Excess clearance between the release (throwout) bearing and the diaphragm spring fingers will cause the clutch to drag while too little clearance can cause the clutch to slip.

Clutch Master Cylinder

REMOVAL AND INSTALLATION

1. Disconnect the clutch pedal arm from the pushrod.
2. Disconnect the clutch hydraulic line from the master cylinder.

NOTE: Take precautions to keep brake fluid from coming in contact with any painted surfaces.

3. Remove the nuts attaching the master cylinder and remove the master cylinder and pushrod toward the engine compartment side.
4. Install the master cylinder in the reverse order of removal and bleed the clutch hydraulic system.

OVERHAUL

1. Remove the master cylinder from the vehicle.
2. Drain the clutch fluid from the master cylinder reservoir.
3. Remove the boot and circlip and remove the pushrod.
4. Remove the stopper, piston, cup and return spring.
5. Clean all of the parts in clean brake fluid.
6. Check the master cylinder and piston for wear, corrosion and scores and replace the parts as necessary. Light scoring and glaze can be removed with crocus cloth soaked in brake fluid.
7. Generally, the cup seal should be replaced each time the master cylinder is disassembled. Check the cup and replace it if it is worn, fatigued, or damaged.
8. Check the clutch fluid reservoir, filler cap, dust cover and the pipe for distortion and damage and replace the parts as necessary.
9. Lubricate all new parts with clean brake fluid.
10. Reassemble the master cylinder parts in the reverse order of disassembly, taking note of the following:
    a. Reinstall the cup seal carefully to prevent damaging the lipped portions;
    b. Adjust the height of the clutch pedal after installing the master cylinder in position on the vehicle;
    c. Fill the master cylinder and clutch fluid reservoir and then bleed the clutch hydraulic system.

Hydraulic System Bleeding

1. Bleed the clutch master cylinder by pumping the clutch pedal several times

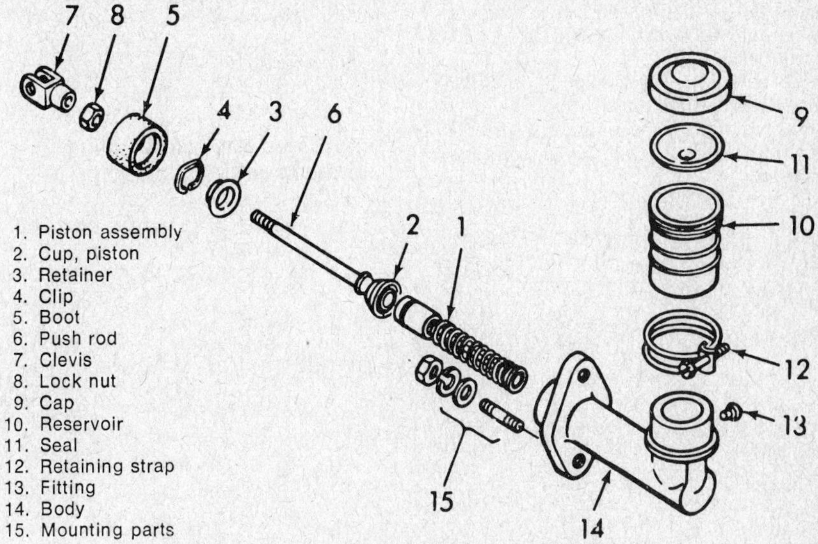

Exploded view of the clutch master cylinder

and while holding the pedal down, slowly open the bleeder screw.

2. Repeat step one until all signs of air bubbles disappear in the released fluid.

CAUTION: Don't let the master cylinder fluid level get too low.

3. Connect a tube to the clutch slave cylinder bleeder screw and insert the other end into a clean glass container, $^1/_4$ to $^1/_2$ filled with brake fluid.

4. Bleed the slave cylinder in the same manner as the master cylinder until the air bubbles disappear.

5. Refill the system reservoir and depress the clutch pedal several times.

6. Check for leaks and smooth operation.

Clutch Slave Cylinder

REMOVAL AND INSTALLATION

1. Remove the slave cylinder attaching bolts and the pushrod from the shift fork.

2. Disconnect the flexible fluid hose from the slave cylinder and remove the unit from the vehicle.

3. Install the slave cylinder in the reverse order of removal and bleed the clutch hydraulic system.

OVERHAUL

1. Remove the slave cylinder from the vehicle.

2. Remove the pushrod and boot.

3. Force out the piston by blowing compressed air into the slave cylinder at the hose connection.

NOTE: Be careful not to apply excess air pressure to avoid possible injury.

4. Clean all of the parts in brake fluid.

5. Check and replace the slave cylinder bore and piston if wear or severe scoring exists. Light scoring and glaze can be removed with crocus cloth soaked in brake fluid.

6. Normally the piston cup should be replaced when the slave cylinder is disassembled. Check the piston cup and replace it if it is found to be worn, fatigued or scored.

7. Replate the rubber boot if it is cracked or broken.

8. Lubricate all of the new parts in clean brake fluid and reassemble in the reverse order of disassembly, taking note of the following:

a. Use care when reassembling the piston cup to prevent damaging the lipped portion of the piston cup:

b. Fill the master cylinder with brake fluid and bleed the clutch hydraulic system;

c. Adjust the clearance between the pushrod and the shift fork to 5/64 in.

Clutch Cable

REMOVAL AND INSTALLATION

1978–80

1. Loosen the clutch cable lock and adjusting nuts. Remove the clutch cable clip at the engine compartment location.

2. Raise the vehicle and remove the spring from the shift fork end.

3. Disconnect the cable end from the shift fork and pull the cable assembly through the bracket.

4. Lower the vehicle enough to disengage the hooked part of the clutch pedal from the cable eye. Pull the cable assembly towards the engine compartment and remove the cable from the vehicle.

5. Installation is the reverse of removal.

ADJUSTMENT

1. Pull the outer cable forward and turn the adjusting nut inward until the rubber lip on the washer damper touches the firewall.

2. Depress and release the clutch pedal a few times.

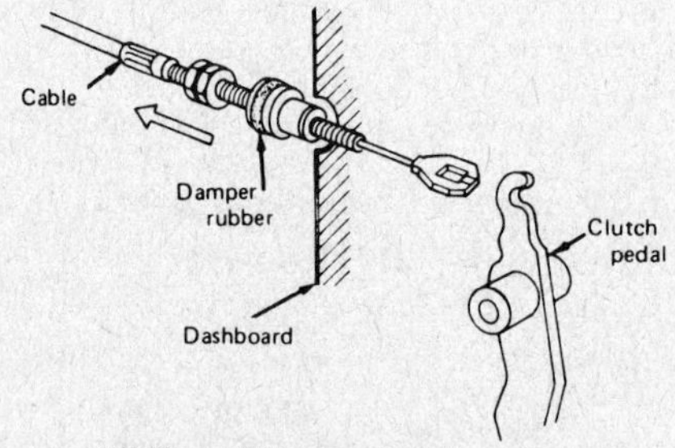

1978 and later clutch cable adjustment locations

3. Pull the outer cable forward again and fully tighten the adjusting nut. Back the adjusting nut off to provide a clearance of 0.20 in.

4. Release the outer cable and tighten the nut.

AUTOMATIC TRANSMISSION

The Turbo Hydra-Matic 200 transmission is a fully automatic unit having three speeds forward and one in reverse. It is coupled to the engine by a torque converter which supplies hydraulic torque multiplication when required.

REMOVAL AND INSTALLATION

1. Disconnect the negative battery cable and remove the throttle valve cable from the carburetor.

2. Remove the transmission dipstick assembly.

3. Raise the vehicle and remove the pan from the converter housing.

4. Remove the starter assembly.

5. Disconnect the driveshaft and remove it from the vehicle.

NOTE: Plug the rear of the transmission to avoid fluid leakage.

6. Disconnect the shift lever control rod from the transmission shift lever.

7. Remove the exhaust pipe bracket. Remove the speedometer cable from the transmission.

8. Remove the oil cooler lines and position them along the vehicle frame to prevent damage.

9. Remove the bolts and nuts coupling the drive plate to the converter.

10. Remove the bolts holding the frame bracket to the transmission rear mount.

11. Raise the engine and transmission assembly and remove the frame bracket from the cross member. Remove the rear mount from the transmission.

12. Remove the bell housing bolts and move the transmission rearward together with the throttle cable and the oil filler tube.

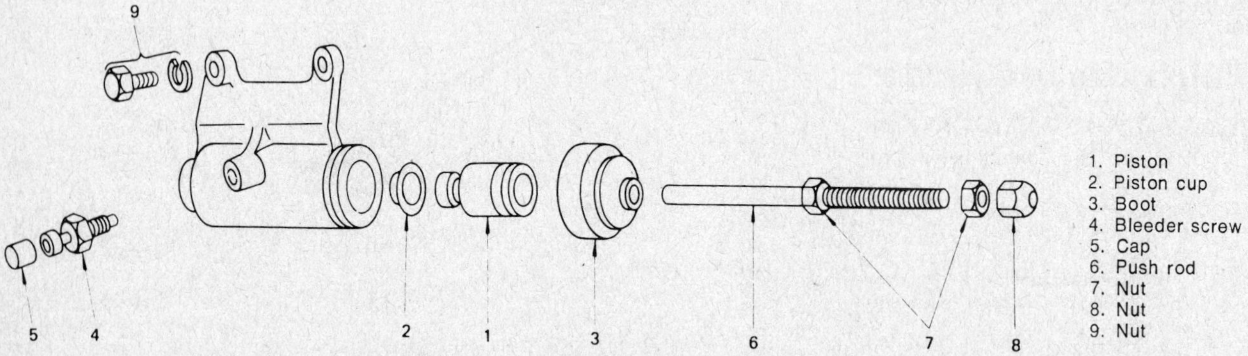

Exploded view of the clutch slave cylinder

CAUTION: Do not allow the torque converter to drop from the transmission.

Shift Linkage Adjustment

1. Loosen the control rod lock nuts so that trunnion will slide on the control rod.
2. Turn the manual shaft of the transmission counterclockwise, viewed from the left side of the transmission, as far as it will go.
3. Back off the manual shaft three stops to the neutral position.
4. Holding the shaft in this position, move the shift lever to the neutral position and push the shift control lower lever rearward to remove play. Tighten the lock nuts.
5. Check for proper operation of the transmission in all transmission ranges.

Throttle Valve Control Cable

REMOVAL AND INSTALLATION

1. Loosen the throttle valve control cable adjusting nuts and disconnect the cable from the carburetor throttle lever by removing the pin.
2. Remove the throttle valve cable clip from the right side of the cylinder body.
3. Remove the bolt holding the throttle cable to the transmission and pull the cable upward. Disconnect the end of the inner cable from the throttle lever link on the transmission side.
4. Remove the cable assembly from the vehicle.
5. Installation is the reverse of removal.

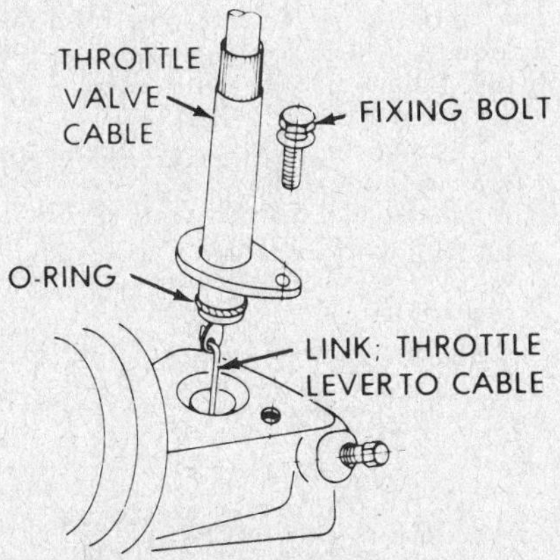

Throttle cable attachment to transmission

ADJUSTMENT

1. Loosen the throttle valve control cable adjusting nuts.
2. Open the carburetor throttle lever to the wide open position and adjust the inner cable by turning the adjustment

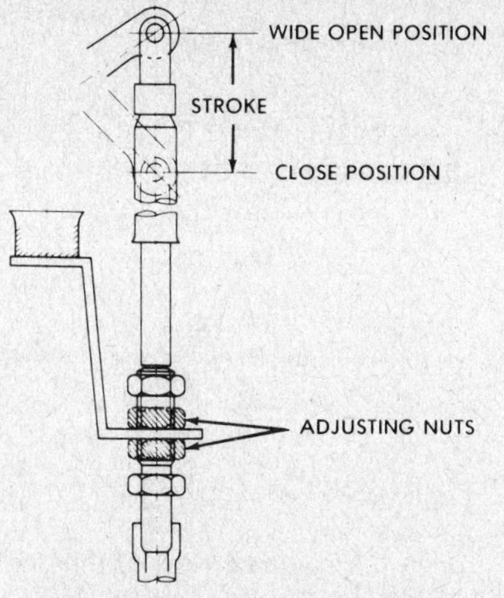

Checking throttle valve cable adjustment—Turbo Hydra-Matic 200 transmission

nut (lower) on the outer cable by hand so that the inner cable has a free play of approximately 0.040 in.

3. Tighten the lock nut (upper) securely.
4. Make sure that the stroke of the inner cable from the wide open position to the closed position is within the range of 1.37 to 1.41 inches.

Detent Downshift

Forced downshifting of the automatic transmission is accomplished by depressing the accelerator pedal to the floor.

The throttle valve control cable must be properly adjusted for the downshifting to occur.

Inhibitor Switch

ADJUSTMENT

1. Loosen the screws holding the switch. Move the switch body so that the center of the moveable part of the switch, aligns with the neutral position indicator line on the steel case when the shift lever is in the neutral position.
2. Tighten the holding screws, make sure that the engine does not start in gear.

Intermediate Band

The bands are not adjustable. A selective band apply pin is installed at time of assembly or overhaul that compensates for normal band wear.

Transmission Fluid Drain and Refilling

1. Raise the vehicle, support the transmission at the vibration damper, and remove the fluid pan retaining bolts from the front and sides of the fluid pan.
2. Loosen the rear fluid pan bolts approximately four (4) turns.
3. Carefully pry the front of the fluid pan loose from the transmission case and allow the fluid to drain into a waste container.

CAUTION: The operating temperature of the fluid can exceed 350°F.

4. Remove-and clean the pan.
5. Remove the two (2) retaining screen-to-valve body bolts, screen and gasket and clean the screen thoroughly.
6. Install screen and new gasket in place on valve body. Tighten retaining bolts to 6–10 ft. lbs.
7. Install the fluid pan with a new gasket and torque the pan retaining bolts to 10–13 ft. lbs.
8. Lower the vehicle and install six (6) pints of Dexron II® in the transmission. Start the engine and move the selector lever through each gear position.
9. Recheck the fluid level and fill to the following levels.
   a. **Fluid at room temperature:** Level should be 1/8 to 3/8 in. below the add mark on the dip stick.
   b. **Fluid at normal operating temperature:** Fluid level should be at the full mark on the dip stick.

NOTE: Normal operating temperature is reached after approximately 15 miles of highway type driving or equivalent.

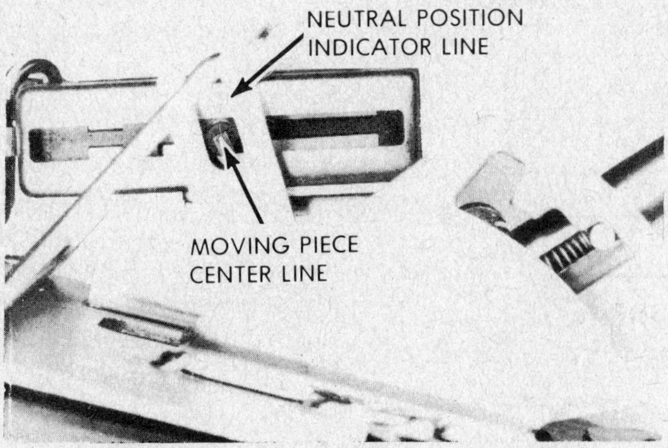

Adjusting the inhibitor (neutral start) switch

DRIVE AXLES

Driveshaft and U-Joints

Standard Wheel Base Models

NOTE: Match-mark all parts for installation.

1. Disconnect the driveshaft rear flange from the differential pinion flange.
2. Pull the one piece driveshaft from the end of the transmission housing cover.
3. Plug or cover the transmission housing cover end to prevent lubricant leakage.
4. Installation is the reverse of removal.

Long Wheel Base Models

NOTE: Match-mark all parts for installation.

1. Disconnect the flanged yokes between the front and the rear driveshafts.
2. Disconnect the rear driveshaft flange from the differential pinion flange and remove the rear shaft.
3. Remove the center bearing support bracket from the fourth crossmember and pull the front driveshaft from the rear of the transmission housing cover.
4. Install a plug or cover the transmission housing cover end to prevent lubricant loss.
5. Installation is the reverse of removal.

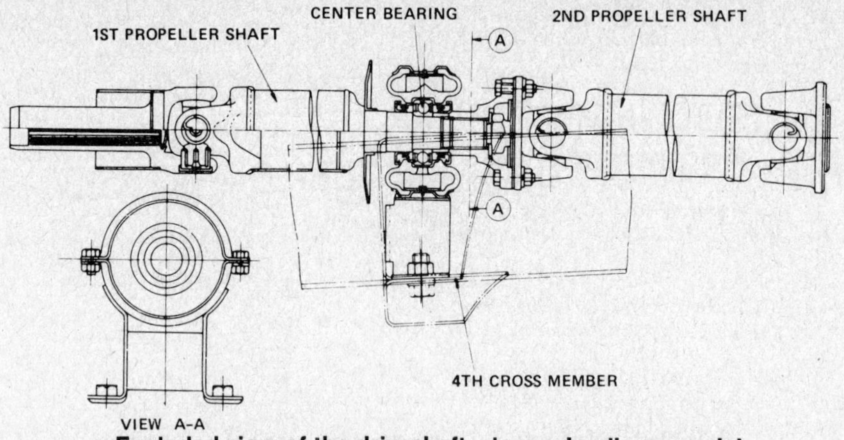

Exploded view of the driveshaft—long wheelbase model

U-Joint

OVERHAUL

1. Remove the driveshaft from the vehicle.
2. Punch mating marks on both the yokes at either end of the driveshaft and the driveshaft itself so that the driveshaft assembly can be reassembled in the same position.
3. Remove the snap-rings from the bearing hole of the yokes.
4. Place the yoke in a vise with a small socket positioned against one of the bearing cups and a larger socket placed against the yoke on the opposite side. The larger socket must be able to receive the bearing cap when it is pressed out of the yoke.
5. Tighten the vise until the bearing caps are free of the yoke.
6. Remove the two remaining bearings from the opposite yoke in the same manner and remove the spider bearing journal.
7. Make sure that the new spiders and needle bearings in the bearing caps are well lubricated.
8. Assemble the universal joint spider and bearing caps to the yoke in the reverse manner of removal, using the smaller socket to press the bearing caps into the yoke and the larger socket to bear against the yoke bearing cap hole at the opposite end. Use a vise to press the bearing caps in place.
9. Install the hole snap-ring to secure the bearing caps.
10. Assemble the slide yoke to the driveshaft, aligning the marks made prior to disassembly.
11. Install the driveshaft assembly on the vehicle.

Axle Shaft, Bearing and Seal—2 Wheel Drive

AXLE SHAFT REMOVAL AND INSTALLATION

1. Raise the vehicle on a hoist.
2. Remove the rear wheel cover and the wheel and tire.
3. Remove the brake drum, brake shoes, and disconnect the parking brake inner cable.
4. Disconnect the brake line at the wheel cylinder and plug the end of the line.
5. Remove the four nuts from the bearing holder through-bolts from the inside of the brake backing plate.
6. Using an axle puller, pull out the axle shaft assembly. Never strike the brake backing plate with a hammer in an attempt to remove the axle shaft.
7. Install the axle shaft in the reverse order of removal, tighten the bearing holding plate attaching nuts to 55 ft lbs, bleeding the brake hydraulic system after installing the brakes and adjusting the parking brake cable as necessary.

BEARING AND/OR SEAL REMOVAL AND INSTALLATION

Axle Shaft End-Play Adjustment

Tool J-24246 (or substitute) is necessary to break the locknut loose from the axle shaft. The locknut is torqued to 190 ft/lbs. Adjust the axle shaft end-play.

1. Remove the axle shaft.
2. Flatten the locktab and clamp the axle shaft nut in a vise.
3. Install tool J-24246 and clamp in place with two wheel nuts.
4. Turn the axle shaft nut loose from the locknut.

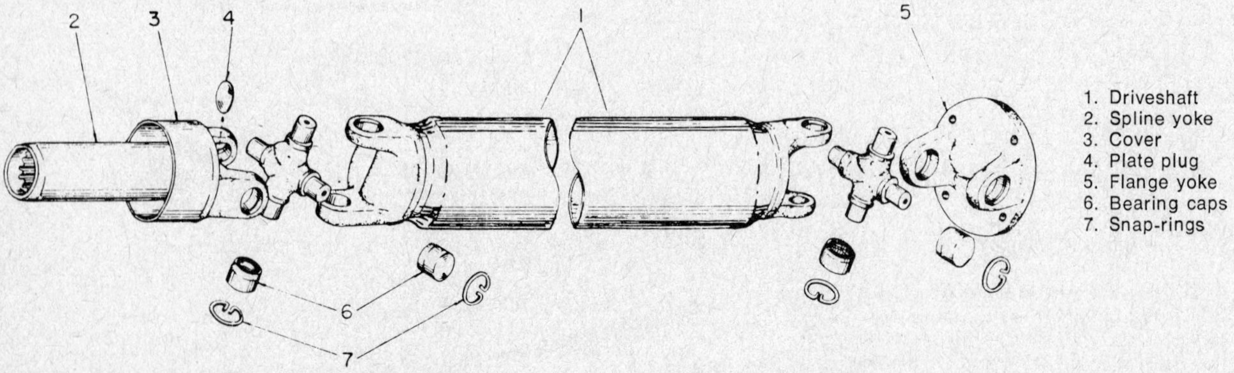

Exploded view of the driveshaft and U-joints

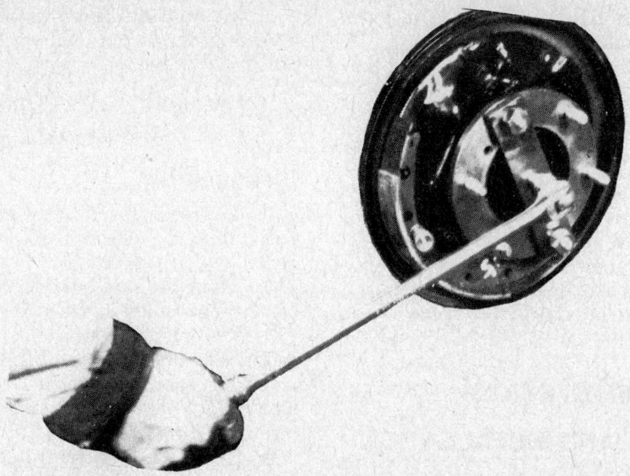

Removing the axle shaft from the brake backing plate

5. Press the backing plate, bearing and holder, locknut and washer from the axle shaft.
6. Remove the oil seal.
7. Install the bearing outer race and seal in the holder.
8. Install the bearing outer race and seal in the holder.
8. Install the bearing holder on the backing plate with the four through bolts. The oil seal side of the bearing holder goes against the backing plate.
9. Install the axle shaft through the backing plate and bearing holder.
10. Install a new lockwasher with dished side away from the bearing.
11. Clamp the locknut in a vise and using tool J-24246 tighten the axle shaft into the locknut to 190 ft/lbs. Bend the locktab.
12. Install the axle shaft.
13. To adjust the end-play:

If one shaft has been serviced, start with step B.

A. Insert a .079 in. shim between bearing holder and axle tube flange. Install the axle shaft.

B. Install the opposite axle shaft without shims until it contacts the differential thrust block. Measure the clearance between the bearing holder and flange.

C. The proper shim size is this measurement (Step B) plus 0.004 in.

D. Remove the axle shaft, install shim pack and reinstall the axle shaft.

FRONT AXLE AND AXLE SHAFT —4-WHEEL DRIVE

Removal and Installation

1. Raise and support the vehicle.
2. Disconnect the front driveshaft at the differential.
3. Remove the wheels and skid plate.
4. Loosen the torsion bar completely with the height control adjusting bolts.
5. Remove the strut bars.
6. Disconnect the stabilizer bars at the lower control arms.
7. Remove the caliper assemblies and wire them to the frame. It is not necessary to disconnect the brake lines.
8. Remove the ball joints from the tie rods.
9. Disconnect the upper control arms at the frame. Make sure to note the number and positions of the shims.
10. Remove the steering link ends from the lower control arms.
11. Disconnect the shock absorbers from the lower control arms.
12. Disconnect the lower control arms from the frame.
13. Remove the free wheeling hub. See Front Bearing Removal.
14. Remove the rotors and upper links.
15. Remove the pitman arm and idler

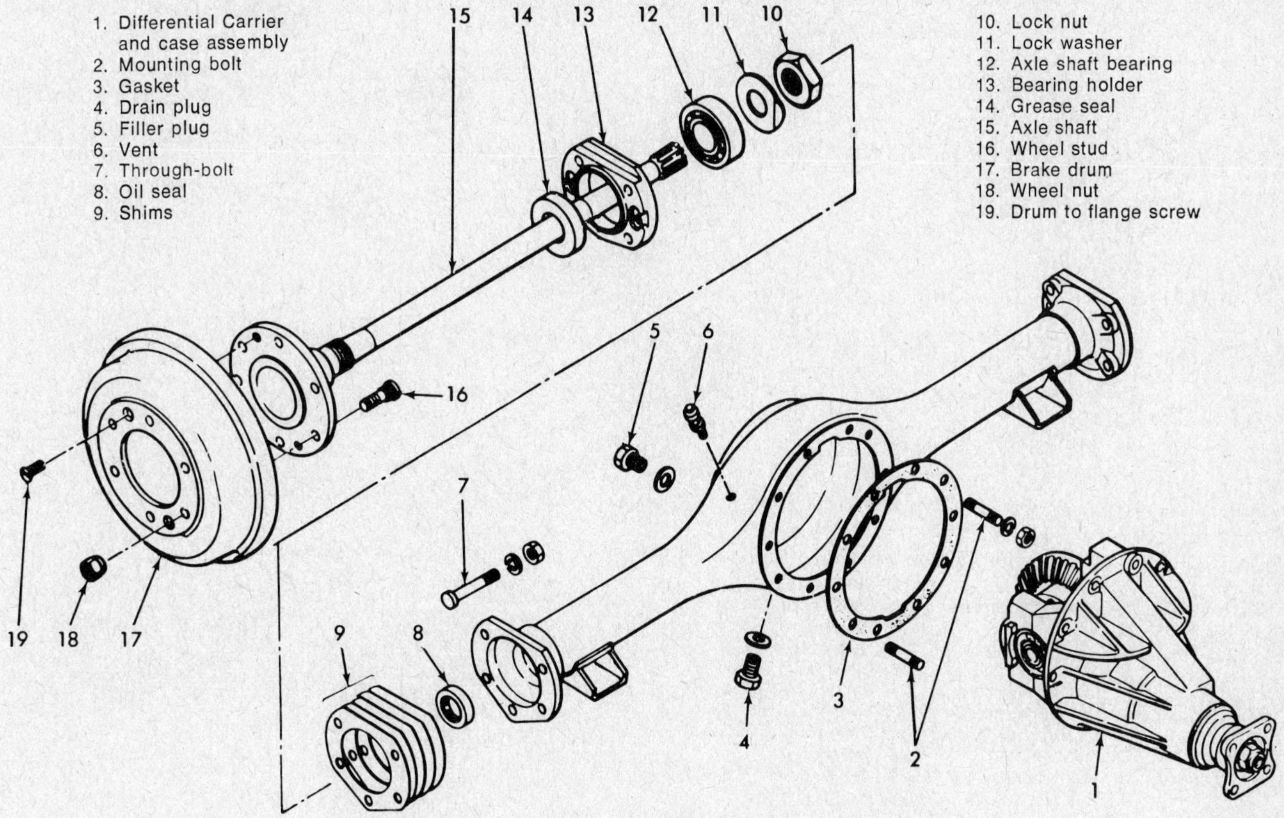

Exploded view of the axle shaft and housing assembly

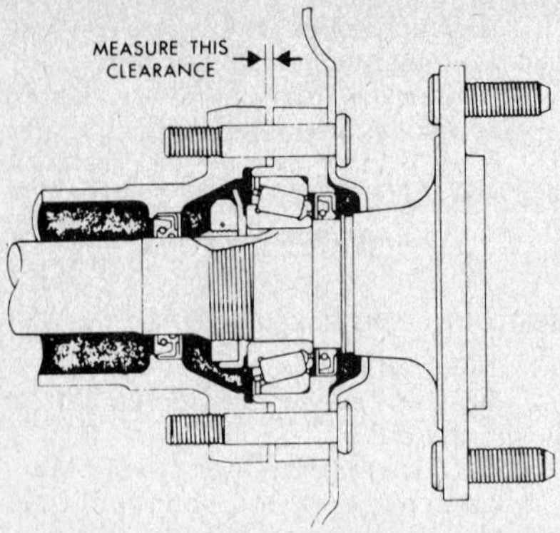

Axle shaft bearing holder-to-flange clearance. This dimension plus 0.0004 in. equals the thickness of the shim pack

arm along with the steering linkage assembly.

16. Support the differential housing with a jack, lower it clear of the vehicle and roll it out. Take care to avoid damaging the birfield joints.

17. Drain the differential case and remove the four bolts attaching the axle mounting bracket to the case.

18. Pull the shaft assemblies from the case on both sides.

19. Installation is the reverse of removal. Observe the following torque valves:

Axle shaft-to-case: 43 ft. lb.
Differential case-to-frame: 15 ft.lb
Pitman arm-to-sector shaft: 160 ft.lb.
Idler arm-to-pivot shaft: 87 ft.lb.
Lower control arm-to-frame: 94 ft.lb.
Ball joint castellated nut: 100 ft.lb.

Differential

REMOVAL AND INSTALLATION

1. Raise the vehicle on a hoist.
2. Remove the wheels and brake drums.
3. Remove the axle shafts.
4. Remove the driveshaft.
5. Remove the ten attaching nuts retaining the differential carrier and case assembly to the axle housing and remove the carrier from the vehicle.
6. Install the differential carrier in the reverse order of removal, tightening the nuts to 18 ft lbs.

OVERHAUL

Disassembly

1. Before disassembling the differential, make a pattern check of the ring gear.
2. Mark the side bearing caps so they can be reinstalled in the same positions.
3. Remove the nuts and the bearing caps, then remove the differential case and ring gear assembly. Keep left and right side bearings separate to avoid interchanging.
4. Remove the differential side bearings from the case. Carefully record the thickness of each side bearing and each shim pack removed and keep them separated.
5. Remove the ring gear bolts and separate the ring gear from the differential case.
6. Drive out the pinion shaft lock-pin with a long drift. It may be necessary to

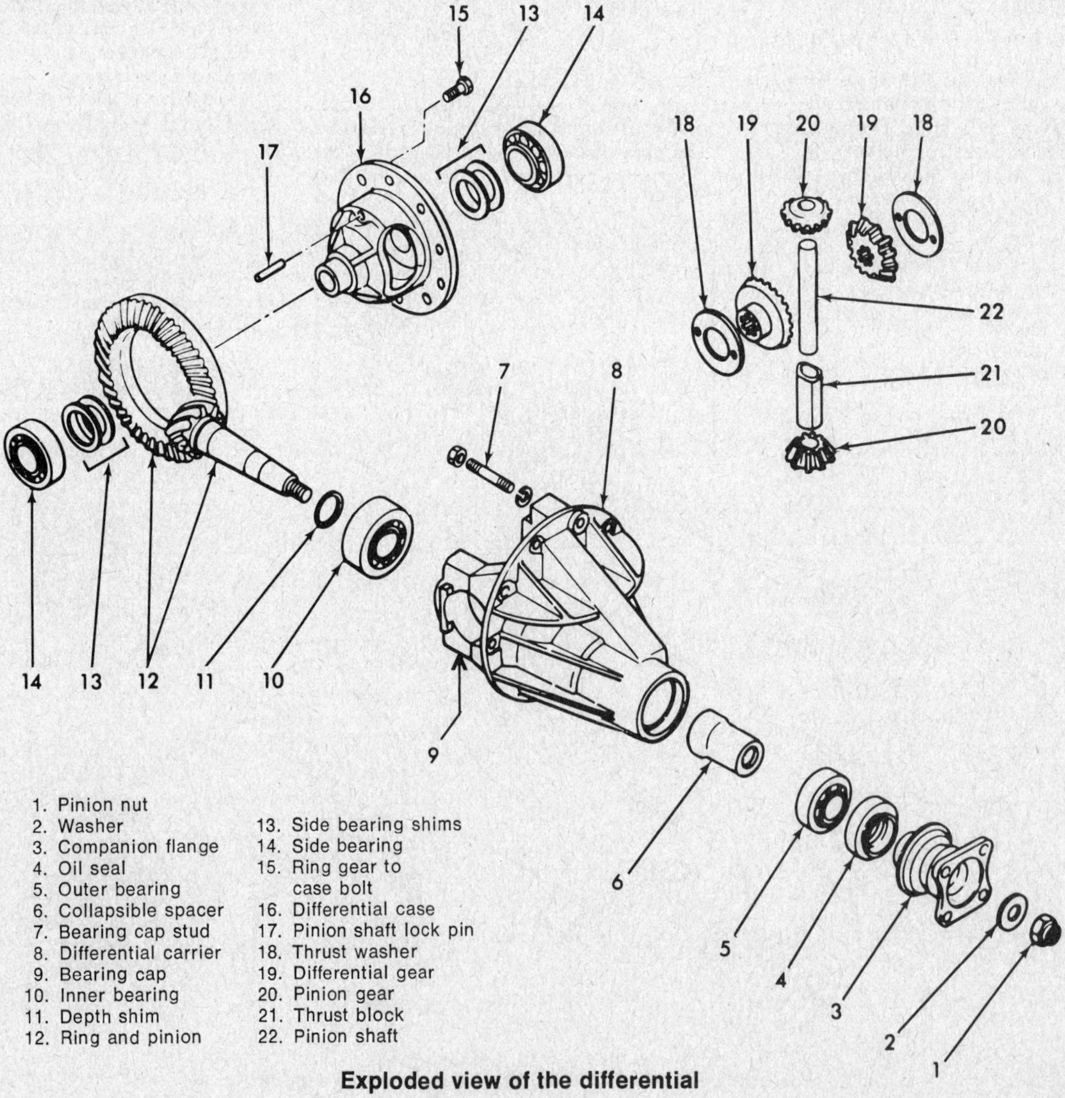

1. Pinion nut
2. Washer
3. Companion flange
4. Oil seal
5. Outer bearing
6. Collapsible spacer
7. Bearing cap stud
8. Differential carrier
9. Bearing cap
10. Inner bearing
11. Depth shim
12. Ring and pinion
13. Side bearing shims
14. Side bearing
15. Ring gear to case bolt
16. Differential case
17. Pinion shaft lock pin
18. Thrust washer
19. Differential gear
20. Pinion gear
21. Thrust block
22. Pinion shaft

Exploded view of the differential

first remove the caulking in the lock-pin with a 5 mm drill.

7. Remove the pinion shaft with a drift and take out the thrust block, pinion gears, side gears and thrust washers from the differential case.

8. Remove the pinion nut.

9. Remove the companion flange.

10. Drive the pinion from the carrier by hitting a soft metal drift held against the splined end of the drive pinion. The outer (front) bearing will fall loose in the carrier, while the inner (rear) bearing will remain pressed on the drive pinion. Both bearing races will remain in the carrier bores.

11. Remove the rear bearing from the drive pinion by use of a press.

Wash all of the parts, being careful not to interchange any. Look for damaged excessively worn, or bent parts. Replace any defective parts.

*NOTE: **Ring gears and drive pinions come only in matched sets. If either part is defective, both must be replaced together.***

It is very important to clean and assemble the differential parts with care, and to follow adjustment procedures. Units that are contaminated with dirt or other foreign material, or which are incorrectly adjusted may be noisy and have a short service life. Be sure to use all new seals, gaskets and flange nuts when reassembling the axle.

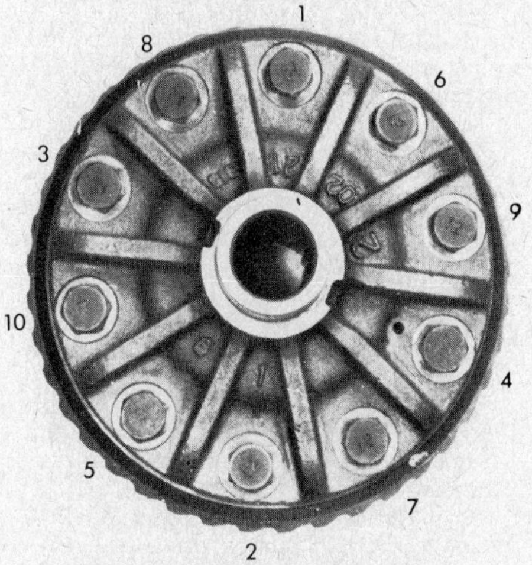

Ring gear tightening sequence

Pinion Depth Adjustment

If the old ring and pinion are going to be reinstalled and the contact pattern was found to be satisfactory before disassembly, install the pinion in the housing in the reverse order of removal, using the old shims installed in the original locations with a new collapsible spacer.

However, if the contact pattern was found to be unsatisfactory due to assumed wear of a depth adjusting shim, measure the thickness of the shim(s) and install or subtract shims accordingly to gain a satisfactory contact pattern between the ring and pinion gear in regard to pinion depth.

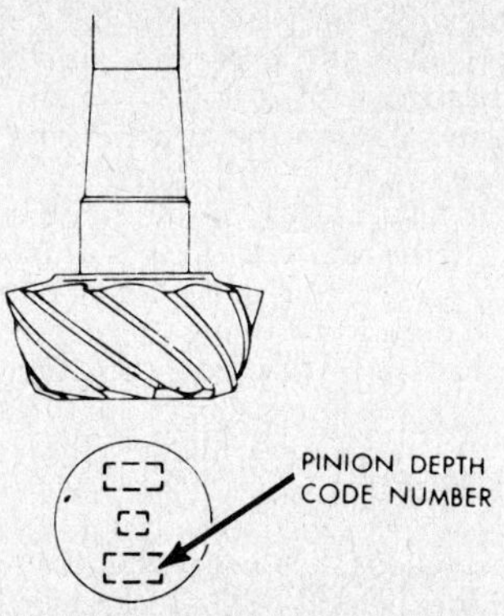

Pinion depth code number location

*NOTE: **Shims are available in sizes ranging from 0.086 in. to 0.101 in.***

If a new ring and pinion are being installed, compute the difference between the old and new pinions' depth code numbers then add or subtract shims accordingly as follows:

After installing a new ring and pinion together with the correct size shims, conduct another gear tooth contact pattern check. If the pattern is satisfactory, install the differential in the housing. If the pattern must be changed, disassemble the differential, install different shims accordingly, and reassemble the differential with a new crush collar (collapsible spacer). Make another gear tooth contact pattern check.

PINION SHIM ADJUSTMENT CHART

Pinion Depth Code Number	Thickness Shim Required
+10	Subtract 0.005 in.
+8	Subtract 0.004 in.
+6	Subtract 0.003 in.
+4	Subtract 0.002 in.
+2	Subtract 0.001 in.
0	No shim required
−2	Add 0.001 in.
−4	Add 0.002 in.
−6	Add 0.003 in.
−8	Add 0.004 in.
−10	Add 0.005 in.

Pinion Bearing Preload Adjustment

Upon installation of the drive pinion, it is necessary to tighten the companion flange-to-pinion attaching nut to the proper specification in order to place the right amount of preload on the drive pinion bearings.

1. Place the drive pinion and the crush collar into the carrier.

2. Lubricate, then position the front bearing into the carrier. Install a new oil seal.

3. Mount the companion flange to the drive pinion. Apply hypoid lubricant to the pinion threads. Install a new pinion nut and tighten it to 85 ft lbs.

4. Rotate the drive pinion to insure that the bearings are seated.

5. Wind a length of string around the pinion flange. Attach a pull scale to the loose end of the string. Note the scale reading required to rotate the pinion by pulling the scale.

6. Continue to tighten the pinion nut in small amounts until the pull required to rotate the drive pinion becomes 17 lbs for new bearings and 7–9 lbs for used bearings.

*NOTE: **Tighten the drive pinion nut in small increments only, so as to be sure of not exceeding the preload specifications. If the preload specifications are exceeded, the crush collar will be compressed too far and will require replacement.***

Differential Case Reassembly

1. Install the side gears and thrust washers in the differential case.

2. Position the pinion gears 180° apart. Roll the gears into position, making sure they are in alignment, to allow installation of the pinion shaft.

3. Place the thrust block between the pinion gears, and drive the pinion shaft into position. Make sure that the lockpin hole in the cross shaft aligns with the hole in the case.

4. Measure the amount of backlash between the differential gears and the pinion gears. If the backlash is greater than 0.003 in., make the necessary adjustment with the thrust washers, available in thicknesses of 0.037 in., 0.041 in., and 0.045 in. Remember that increasing the thickness of the washers will decrease backlash and vice versa.

5. Install the lockpin into the cross-shaft and caulk its end to prevent loosening.

6. Clean the bolts. Apply thread locking compound to the threaded portion of the bolts. Install the ring gear in position on the differential case. Tighten the bolts in a diagonal sequence to 80–87 ft. lbs.

Side Bearing Preload and Initial Backlash Adjustment

If the original side bearings, differential case, ring and pinion, and differential carrier are being reused, and if the pattern check taken before disassembly showed a satisfactory contact pattern, the original shims (or new shims of the same dimension) can be reinstalled in the same positions from which they were removed.

If you are going to install *new side bearings only,* and if the contact pattern was satisfactory, select the shims in the following manner:

1. Measure the new bearing with a micrometer, and compare its thickness with the original bearing.

2. If the new bearing is thicker, subtract the numerical difference between

the new and old bearing from the original shim pack.

3. If the new bearing is thinner, add the numerical difference between the old and new bearing to the original shim pack.

If new bearings *and/or* differential case, ring and pinion, or differential carrier are being installed, new shims will have to be selected for installation behind the side bearings for proper ring and pinion gear tooth contact.

1. Install the side bearings to be used in the final assembly onto the differential case. Do not install shims at this time.
2. Mount the case into the carrier bores.
3. Move the ring gear tightly against the carrier on the ring gear side, away from the drive pinion, and hold in this position. Using a feeler gauge just thick enough to produce a slight drag, carefully measure the clearance between the bearing and the differential carrier on the side opposite the ring gear. Record this measurement.
4. To determine the proper shims for installation, carry out the following procedure:
   a. A predetermined dimension of 0.002 in. is always needed to establish proper preload. Therefore, add 0.002 in. to the clearance measured in Step 3. This will give the necessary combined total thickness of both shim packs.
   b. Divide the total dimension into two shim packs, so that the numerical difference between the packs equals the numerical difference between the original shim packs.
5. Remove the case from the carrier. Carefully remove both side bearings. Install the shims as determined in Step 4 behind each bearing.
6. Install the case onto the carrier, tapping carefully into place. Install the side bearing caps in their original positions and tighten the attaching bolts to 75 ft lbs.
7. Measure the run-out of the ring gear. If the run-out exceeds 0.002 in., correct by cleaning or replacing parts.
8. Mount a dial indicator against the ring gear teeth with the indicator pin inline with the direction of tooth travel. Measure the gear backlash in three locations. Backlash should be 0.005–0.007 in.
9. If backlash is not within the limits, the shims behind each side bearing will have to be adjusted.

***NOTE:** In order to maintain the proper preload on the side bearings, the total thickness of the shim packs must not be changed. Therefore, if the thickness of one shim pack must be increased, the thickness of the opposite shim pack must be decreased by an equal amount.*

10. To increase backlash, the right side bearing shim must be increased, and the left side decreased. To decrease backlash, the right side shim must be decreased, while the left side is increased.

***NOTE:** Backlash changes about 0.002 in. for each 0.003 in. shim change.*

Gear Tooth Contact Pattern Check

A gear tooth contact pattern check before final assembly is necessary to verify whether or not the drive pinion and the ring gear are meshed properly.

1. Wipe any oil out of the assembly and carefully clean each tooth of the ring gear.
2. Apply red lead gear marking compound sparingly to the ring gear teeth.
3. Rotate the drive pinion by hand 1/4 of a turn in both directions so as to mark both the drive (convex) side and coast (concave) side of the ring gear teeth. Excessive turning of the ring gear is not recommended.
4. Observe the pattern made on the ring gear teeth and compare it with the illustration. Make the necessary adjustments recommended.

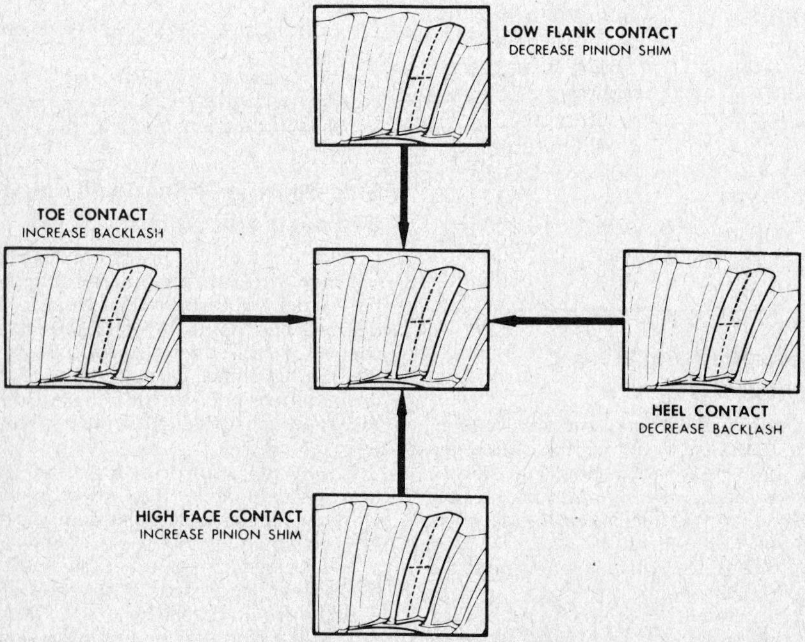

Gear tooth contact patterns

REAR SUSPENSION

The rear suspension consists of semi-elliptical leaf springs with hydraulic double-acting shock absorbers. There is a straight "helper" spring added to the bottom of the spring pack. When the semi-elliptical springs straighten out due to the vehicle being loaded, they come in contact with the helper spring which helps to support any additional weight.

Springs

REMOVAL

1. Jack up the rear of the vehicle and place jackstands under the frame near the rear end of the rear spring brackets.
2. Remove the rear shock absorbers.
3. Remove the parking brake cable clips.
4. Remove the nuts form the U-bolts holding the springs to the axle housing.
5. Jack the rear axle up to remove the weight of the axle housing from the springs.
6. Remove the front and rear shackle pin nuts.
7. Drive out the rear shackle pin by using a hammer and drift and lower the rear end of the leaf spring assembly to the floor.
8. Drive out the front shackle pin and remove the leaf spring assembly rearward.
9. Remove the shackle pin from the rear spring bracket and remove the shackle.

INSPECTION

1. Check the leaf springs for cracks, wear and broken leaves. Replace any leaves found to be cracked, broken, fatigued or seriously worn.
2. Check the shackles for bending and the pins for wear.
3. Check the U-bolts for distortion or other damage.

INSTALLATION

1. Mount the shackle to the bracket.
2. Align the front end of the leaf

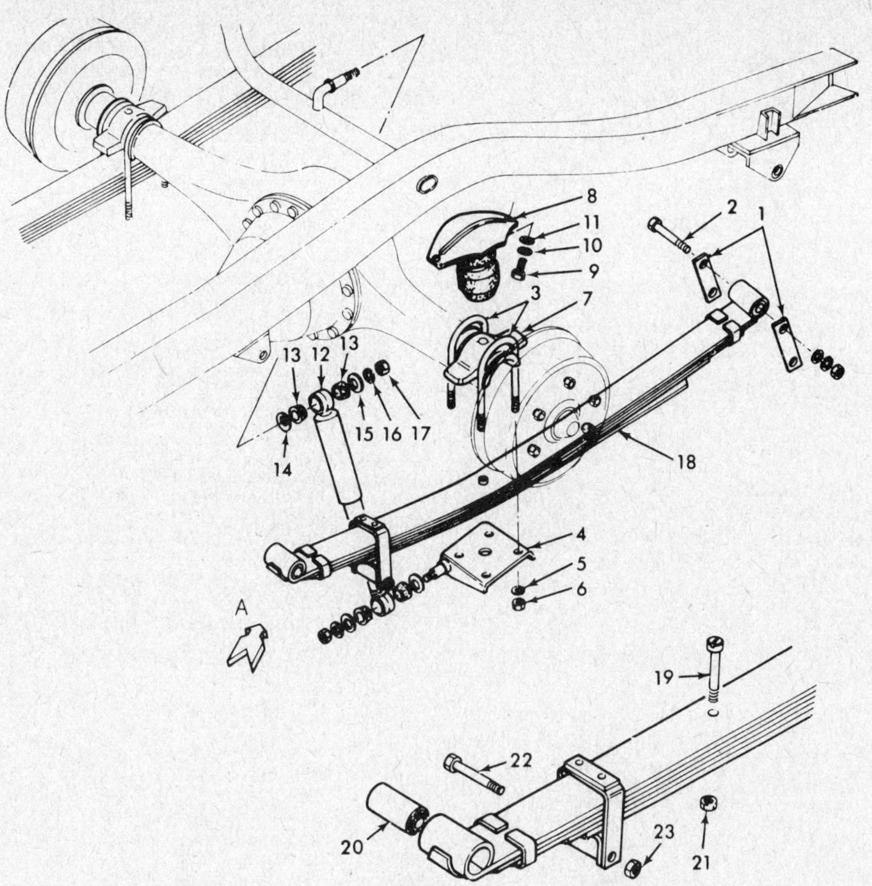

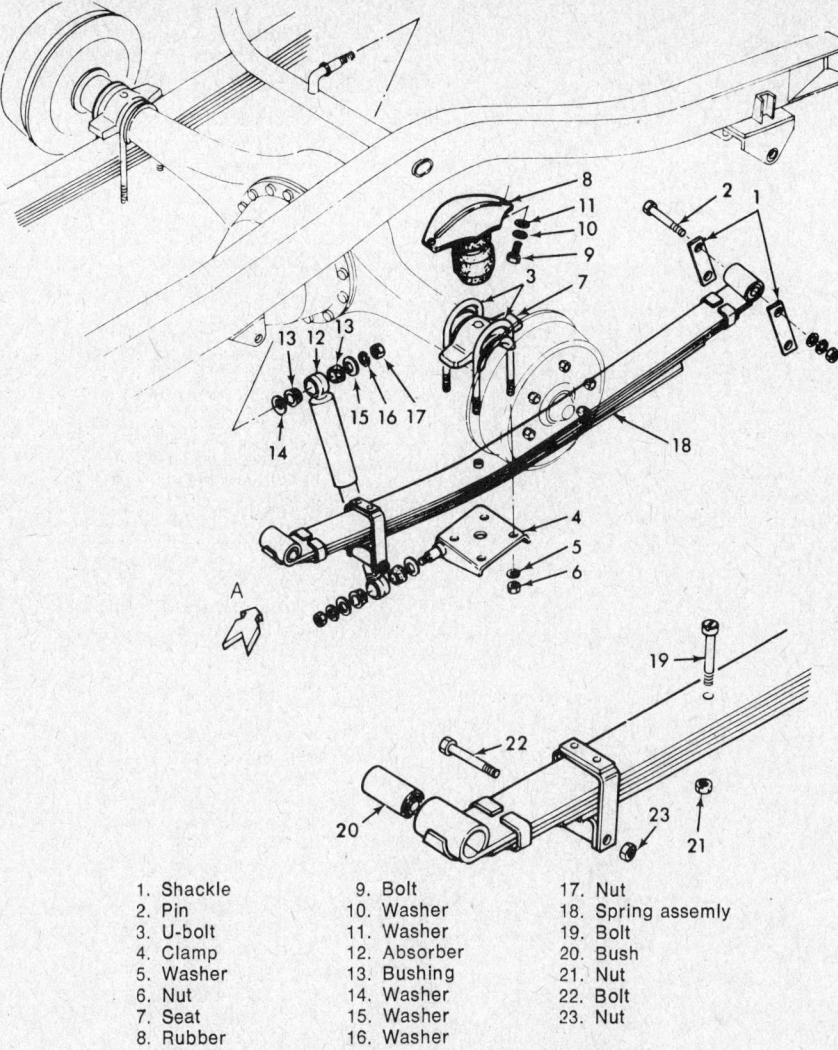

1. Shackle
2. Pin
3. U-bolt
4. Clamp
5. Washer
6. Nut
7. Seat
8. Rubber
9. Bolt
10. Washer
11. Washer
12. Absorber
13. Bushing
14. Washer
15. Washer
16. Washer
17. Nut
18. Spring assemly
19. Bolt
20. Bush
21. Nut
22. Bolt
23. Nut

Exploded view of the rear suspension

spring assembly with the front bracket and install the shackle pin.

3. Align the rear end of the leaf spring assembly with the shackle and install the shackle pin.
4. Loosely install the shackle pin nuts and install the U-bolts. Tighten the U-bolt nuts to 40 ft lbs.
5. Install the shock absorbers.
6. Clip the parking brake cable to the bracket.
7. Remove the jackstands and lower the vehicle so that the vehicle weight is on the left springs.
8. Tighten the shackle pin nuts to 130 ft lbs.

Shock Absorbers

REMOVAL AND INSTALLATION

Remove the rear shock absorbers by loosening and removing the upper and lower attaching nuts and pulling the shock absorber ends off the mounting studs, together with the washers and rubber brushings. Install the shock absorbers in the reverse order of removal, making sure that you use new rubber bushings and that they are installed correctly in the bevel shaped mounting holes in the end of the shock absorbers.

FRONT SUSPENSION

LUV trucks are equipped with the short and long arm type front suspension. The control arms are attached to the vehicle with bolts and bushings at their inner pivot points and to the steering knuckle, which is part of the front wheel spindle, at their outer points.

The front suspension is an independent type utilizing torsion bar springs. The torsion bar has splines on each end. Height control is provided on the third crossmember of the frame. Both upper and lower control arms are pressed steel and the torsion bar is supported at the ends by forged links. The links are bolted to the third frame crossmember in the rear and the lower control arms in front.

Fore and aft movement of the front suspension is controlled by strut bars bolted to the lower control arms at one end and mounted to the chassis frame using a rubber bumper at the other end. A torsion bar type stabilizer is connected to the lower control arm by shackle rods.

Torsion Bars

REMOVAL AND INSTALLATION

1. Jack up the front of the vehicle and support it with jackstands.
2. Remove the adjusting bolt from the height control arm.
3. Mark the location and remove the height control arm from the torsion bar and the third crossmember.
4. Mark the location and withdraw the torsion bar from the lower control arm.
5. For installation, apply a generous amount of grease to the serrated ends of the torsion bars.
6. Hold the rubber bumpers in contact with the lower control arm. Jack the vehicle up under the lower control arm to accomplish this.
7. Insert the front end of the torsion bar into the control arm.
8. Install the height control arm in position so that its end is reaching the adjusting bolt. Be sure to lubricate the part of the height control arm that fits into the chassis with grease.
9. Install a new cotter pin in the height control arm.
10. Turn the adjusting bolt to the location marked before removal.
11. Lower the vehicle and check the vehicle height and trim attitude.

Shock Absorbers

REMOVAL AND INSTALLATION

1. Raise the vehicle and support it with jackstands.
2. Hold the upper stem of the shock absorber from turning with an open-end wrench, and then, remove the upper stem retaining nut, retainer and rubber grommet.
3. Remove the bolt retaining the lower shock absorber pivot to the lower control arm and remove the shock absorber from the vehicle.
4. Install the shock absorber by first installing the lower retainer and rubber grommet over the upper stem and then, installing the shock fully extended up through the upper control arm so that the upper stem passes through the mounting hole in the frame bracket.
5. Install the upper rubber grommet, retainer and attaching nut over the shock absorber upper stem.
6. Hold the upper stem of the shock absorber from turning with an open-end wrench and tighten the retaining nut.

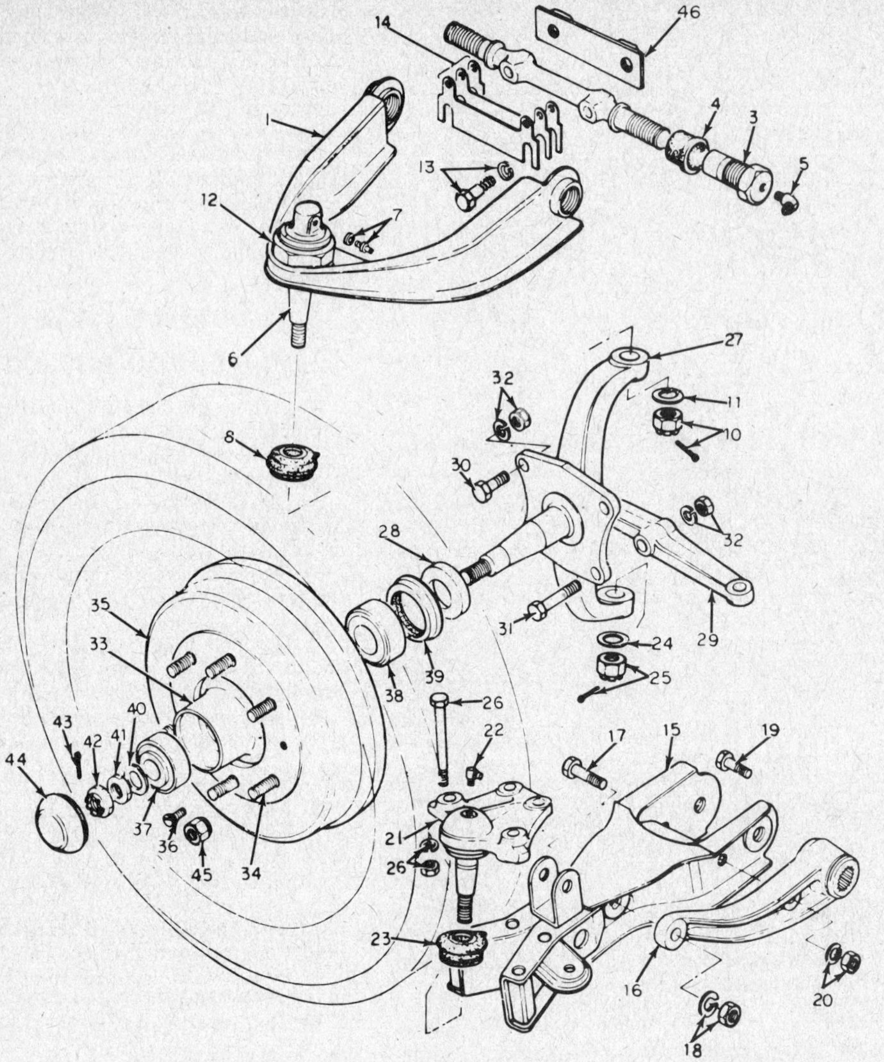

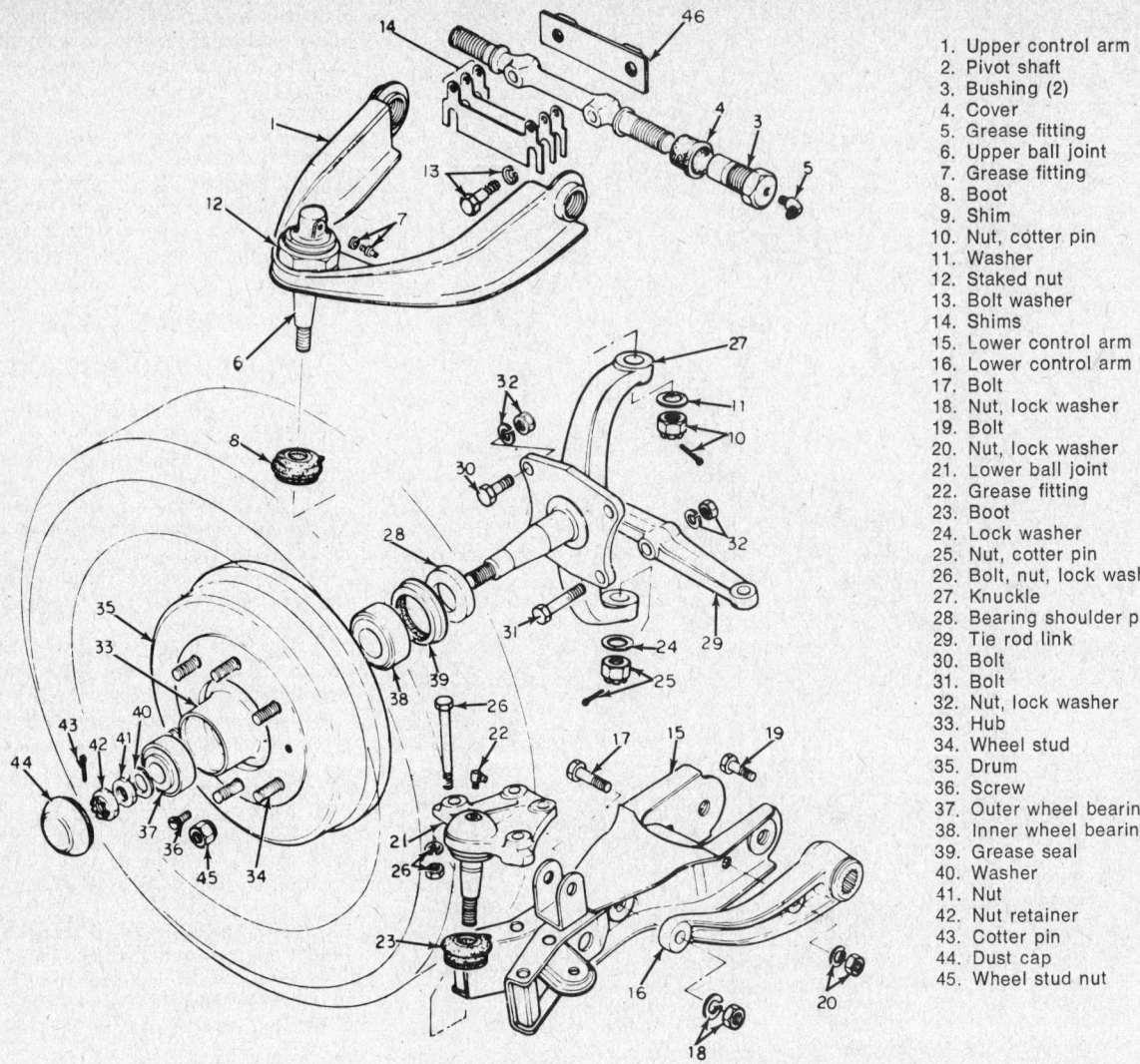

1. Upper control arm
2. Pivot shaft
3. Bushing (2)
4. Cover
5. Grease fitting
6. Upper ball joint
7. Grease fitting
8. Boot
9. Shim
10. Nut, cotter pin
11. Washer
12. Staked nut
13. Bolt washer
14. Shims
15. Lower control arm
16. Lower control arm link
17. Bolt
18. Nut, lock washer
19. Bolt
20. Nut, lock washer
21. Lower ball joint
22. Grease fitting
23. Boot
24. Lock washer
25. Nut, cotter pin
26. Bolt, nut, lock washer
27. Knuckle
28. Bearing shoulder piece
29. Tie rod link
30. Bolt
31. Bolt
32. Nut, lock washer
33. Hub
34. Wheel stud
35. Drum
36. Screw
37. Outer wheel bearing
38. Inner wheel bearing
39. Grease seal
40. Washer
41. Nut
42. Nut retainer
43. Cotter pin
44. Dust cap
45. Wheel stud nut

Exploded view of the upper and lower control arms, ball joints, spindle and hub assemblies

7. Install the retainers attaching the shock absorber lower pivot to the lower control arm and tighten them.

Upper Control Arm and Ball Joint

REMOVAL AND INSTALLATION

NOTE: The upper control arm and ball joint are replaced as an assembly.

1. Raise the vehicle and support it on jackstands placed under the lower control arms.
2. Remove the wheel and tire assembly.
3. Remove the cotter pin nut fastening the upper control arm and upper ball joint assembly and disconnect the upper control arm from the steering knuckle.

NOTE: Do not allow the steering knuckle to hang by the flexible brake line. Wire the steering knuckle up to the frame temporarily.

4. Remove the two bolts from the upper pivot shaft and remove the upper control arm from the bracket. Be sure to note the position and number of shims used for adjusting the camber and caster angles when removing the upper control arm. This is to ensure that the shims are reinstalled in their original positions.
5. To remove the pivot shaft and bushings from the upper control arm assembly, remove the bushing nuts from the pivot shaft by loosening them alternately, then remove the pivot shaft.
6. To install the upper control arm and ball joint assembly, first install the pivot shaft boots to the pivot shaft.
7. Fill the internal part of the bushings with grease (molybdenum disulfide) and screw the bushings into the pivot shaft. Be sure to screw the right-side and the left-side bushings alternately into the pivot shafts carefully avoiding getting grease on the outer face of the bushings. Tighten the nuts to 250 ft lbs.

NOTE: Be sure that the control arm and bushings are centered properly and that the control arm rotates with resistance but is not binding on the pivot shaft when tightened to the proper torque.

8. Install the grease fittings and lubricate the parts with grease through the grease fittings.
9. Install the ball joint stub through the steering knuckle. Install the castellated nut and tighten it to 75 ft lbs and just enough additional torque to install the cotter pin. Use a new cotter pin.
10. Mount the upper control arm to the chassis frame and install the shims in their original positions between the pivot shaft and bracket. Tighten the pivot shaft attaching nuts to 55 ft lbs.

NOTE: Tighten the thinner shim pack's nut first for improved shaft-to-frame clamping force and torque retention.

11. Install the dust cover.
12. Install the wheel and tire assembly and lower the vehicle to the floor.

Lower Ball Joint

REMOVAL AND INSTALLATION

1. Raise the front of the vehicle and support it with jackstands.
2. Remove the wheel and tire assembly.
3. Remove the cotter pin and castellated nut which retains the ball joint to the steering knuckle.
4. Remove the two bolts retaining the lower ball joint and strut rod.
5. Remove the two bolts retaining the strut rod and ball joint to the lower arm. Remove the remaining bolts from the ball joint.
6. Remove the ball joint.
7. Install the lower ball joint by mounting the joint to the lower control arm and tightening the four bolts to 45 ft lbs.
8. Install the ball joint stud into the steering knuckle and install the castellated nut and torque it to 75 ft lbs and just enough additional torque to align the cotter pin hole with one of the castellations on the nut. Install a new cotter pin.
9. Lubricate the lower ball joint through the grease fitting.
10. Install the wheel and tire assembly and lower the vehicle to the ground.

Lower Control Arm

REMOVAL AND INSTALLATION

1. Jack up the vehicle and support it with jackstands.
2. Remove the wheel and tire.
3. Remove the strut bar by removing the frame side bracket and the double nuts, washer and the rubber bushing from the front side of the strut bar. Next, remove the two bolts fastening the strut bar to the lower control arm and remove the bar.
4. Disconnect the stabilizer bar from the lower control arm.
5. Remove the torsion bar.
6. Disconnect the shock absorber from the lower control arm.
7. If you so desire, remove the lower ball joint from the lower control arm joint at this time.
8. Remove the retaining nut and drive out the bolt holding the lower control arm to the chassis with a soft metal drift. Remove the lower control arm from the vehicle.
9. To install the lower control arm, first, install the lower ball joint to the lower control arm. Tighten the retaining nuts to 45 ft lbs.
10. Mount the lower control arm to the frame. Drive the bolt into position carefully with a soft metal drift. Use care not to damage the serrated portions. Tighten the nut on the end of the pivot bolt to 135 ft lbs.
11. Install the stabilizer bar to the lower control arm.
12. Place the washers and bushings on the strut rod and install it through the frame bracket. Install the second set of washers and bushings on the strut rod together with the lockwashers and nut. Leave the nut loose temporarily.
13. Install the strut rod to the lower control arm and tighten the bolts to 45 ft lbs.
14. Assemble the lower ball joint to the steering knuckle.
15. Install the wheel and tire and lower the vehicle.
16. Tighten the first strut bar-to-chassis frame attaching nut to 175 ft lbs, and the second locknut to 55 ft lbs.

Front End Alignment

Proper alignment of the front wheels must be maintained in order to ensure ease of steering and satisfactory tire life.

The most important factors of front wheel alignment are wheel camber, axle caster, and wheel toe-in.

Wheel toe-in is the distance by which the wheels are closer together at the front than at the rear.

Wheel camber is the amount in which the top of the wheels incline outward from the vertical.

Front axle caster is the amount in degrees which the steering knuckle pivot axis is tilted toward the rear of the vehicle. Positive caster is the inclination of the top of the steering knuckle toward the rear of the vehicle.

When checking alignment, it is important that the wheel bearings be properly adjusted and the ball joints have no freeplay.

CASTER ADJUSTMENT

The purpose of caster is to provide steering stability which will keep the front wheels in the straight-ahead position and also assist in straightening up the wheels when coming out of a turn.

The caster is adjusted by adding or subtracting spacer shims from either the front or rear upper control arm pivot shaft attaching bolts.

CAMBER ADJUSTMENT

The purpose of camber is to more nearly place the weight of the vehicle over the tire contact patch on the road to facilitate ease of steering. The result of excessive camber is irregular wear of the tires on the outside shoulder and is usually caused by bent parts. Excessive negative camber will also cause hard steering and possibly wandering. The tires will wear on the inside shoulders.

The camber angle is adjusted by adding or subtracting spacer shims from both the front and rear upper control arm pivot shaft attaching bolts. The same amount of shims is added or subtracted to both of the bolts at the same time.

TOE-IN

The toe-in measurement is the difference between the distances between the front and rear center of the tread of the two front tires.

The toe-in can be adjusted by turning the intermediate rod after loosening the locknuts on the intermediate rod ends. The locknuts have left-hand and right-hand threads to allow for equal adjustment of both wheels at the same time. Turn the intermediate rod toward the front of the vehicle to reduce the toe-in angle and toward the rear of the vehicle to increase the toe-in angle.

RIDE HEIGHT ADJUSTMENT

NOTE: ***The ride height should be measured with a full tank of gas, spare tire, jack, no passengers, and with the tires inflated to the correct pressure.***

The vehicle ride height adjustment end of the torsion bar

1. Place the vehicle on a smooth level floor and bounce the front end several times. Raise the vehicle and then allow it to settle to a normal height.

2. Measure the distance between the bottom of the lower ball joint stud which fits through the steering knuckle and the ground and the distance between the frame crossmember that the lower control arm attaches to and the ground.

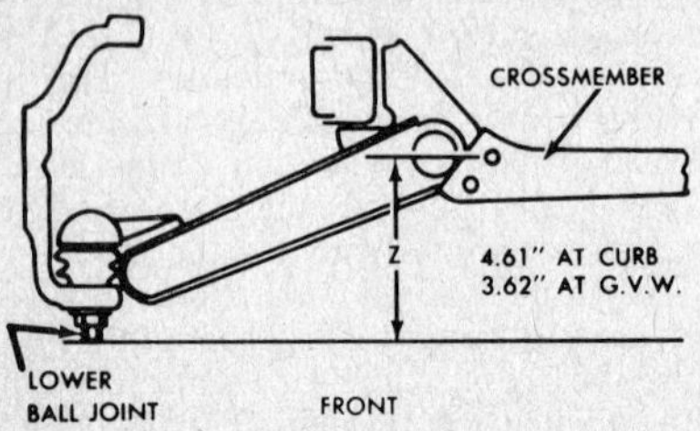

Ride height measurement at the front of the vehicle

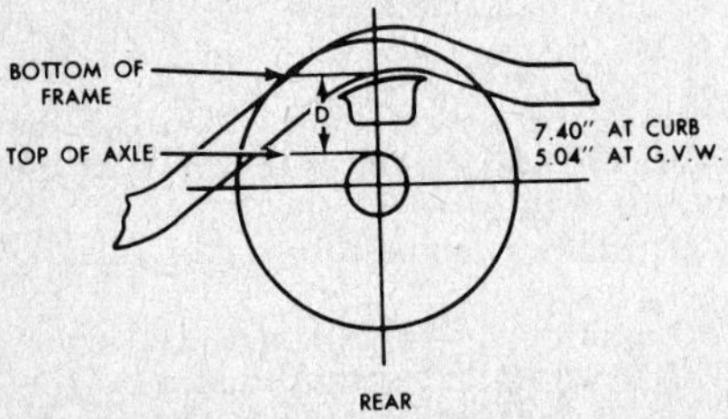

Ride height measurement at the rear of the vehicle

The difference between these two measurements should be 2.52 in. (1.54 in. with the vehicle loaded to GVW).

3. Adjust the vehicle height by first loosening the nuts on the front end of the strut bar and then turning the vehicle height adjusting bolt. Turn the bolt clockwise to raise the vehicle. As an additional check, measure the clearance between the rubber bumper and the lower control arm. The clearance should be 7/8 in.

4. Check the ride height at the front of the vehicle as outlined in Step 2 and the ride height at the rear axle by measuring the clearance between the top of the axle and the bottom of the frame where the frame rises to clear the axle. The clearance between the frame and axle at this point should be 7.90 in. (6.26 in. with the vehicle loaded to GVW).

5. After obtaining the correct clearances, securely tighten the strut bar attaching nuts to the proper torque.

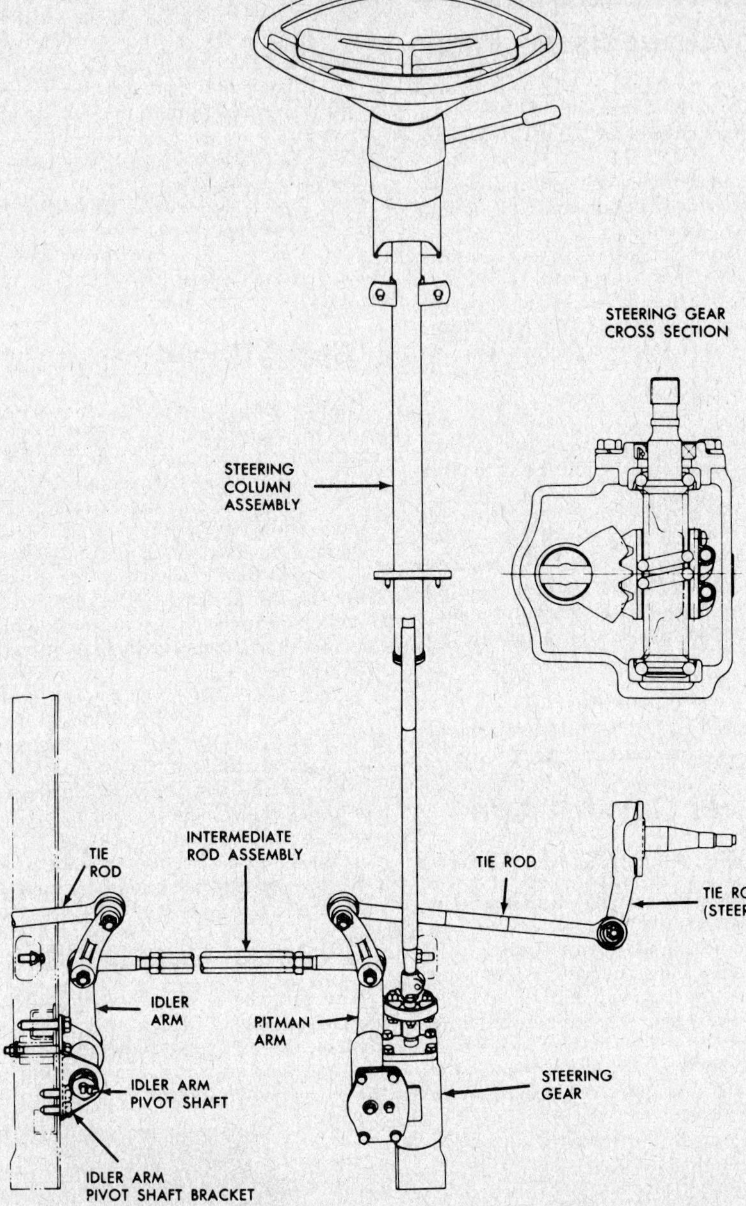

Steering linkage and cross-sectional view of the steering gear

STEERING

Steering Wheel

REMOVAL AND INSTALLATION

1. Disconnect the battery ground cable.

2. Remove the horn shroud and spring by pushing and turning it counterclockwise. Remove the horn contact ring and wire.

3. Remove the steering wheel-to-steering shaft retaining nut, washer and lockwasher.

4. Mark the relative position of the steering wheel and shaft to each other.

5. Remove the steering column cowling by removing the four attaching screws and washers.

6. Remove the steering wheel from the shaft with a puller.

***NOTE:** Under no circumstances is the steering shaft to be hammered jarred, or leaned upon. The steering column is a collapsible, energy-absorbing type and can be easily damaged through mistreatment.*

7. Install the steering wheel in the reverse order of removal, aligning the marks made on the steering wheel and the shaft. Draw the steering wheel onto the shaft with the attaching nut.

Turn Signal and Dimmer Switch

REMOVAL AND INSTALLATION

1. Disconnect the battery ground cable.

2. Remove the four screws retaining the steering column cowling and remove the cowling.

3. Remove the wire connectors from the switch.

4. Remove the switch by removing

1. Coupling
2. Flange, upper coupling
3. Flange, lower coupling
4. Cross-strap
5. Cross-strap
6. Thrust washer
7. Spring
8. Thru-bolt
9. Lock nut
10. Pinch bolt, lock washer
11. Mast jacket
12. Shaft assembly
13. Bushing
14. Grommet
15. Gasket
16. Bolt and washers
17. Screw and washers
18. Wheel assembly
19. Horn shroud seat
20. Screw
21. Horn shroud
22. Spring
23. Nut
24. Shaft nut and washers
25. Column cowling
26. Cowling screws and washers
27. Bolt, washer
28. Steering gear housing
29. Sector shaft bushings
30. Wormshaft seal
31. Sector (Pitman) shaft seal
32. Filler plug
33. Worm & ball nut assembly
34. Wormshaft bearing
35. End cover
36. Top cover
37. Worm preload shims
38. Gasket
39. Bolt, lock washer
40. Sector adjuster screw
41. Lock nut
42. Sector shaft
43. Adjusting shim
44. Pitman shaft nut
45. Lock washer
46. Bolt, nut (stopper)
47. Hazard warning switch assembly

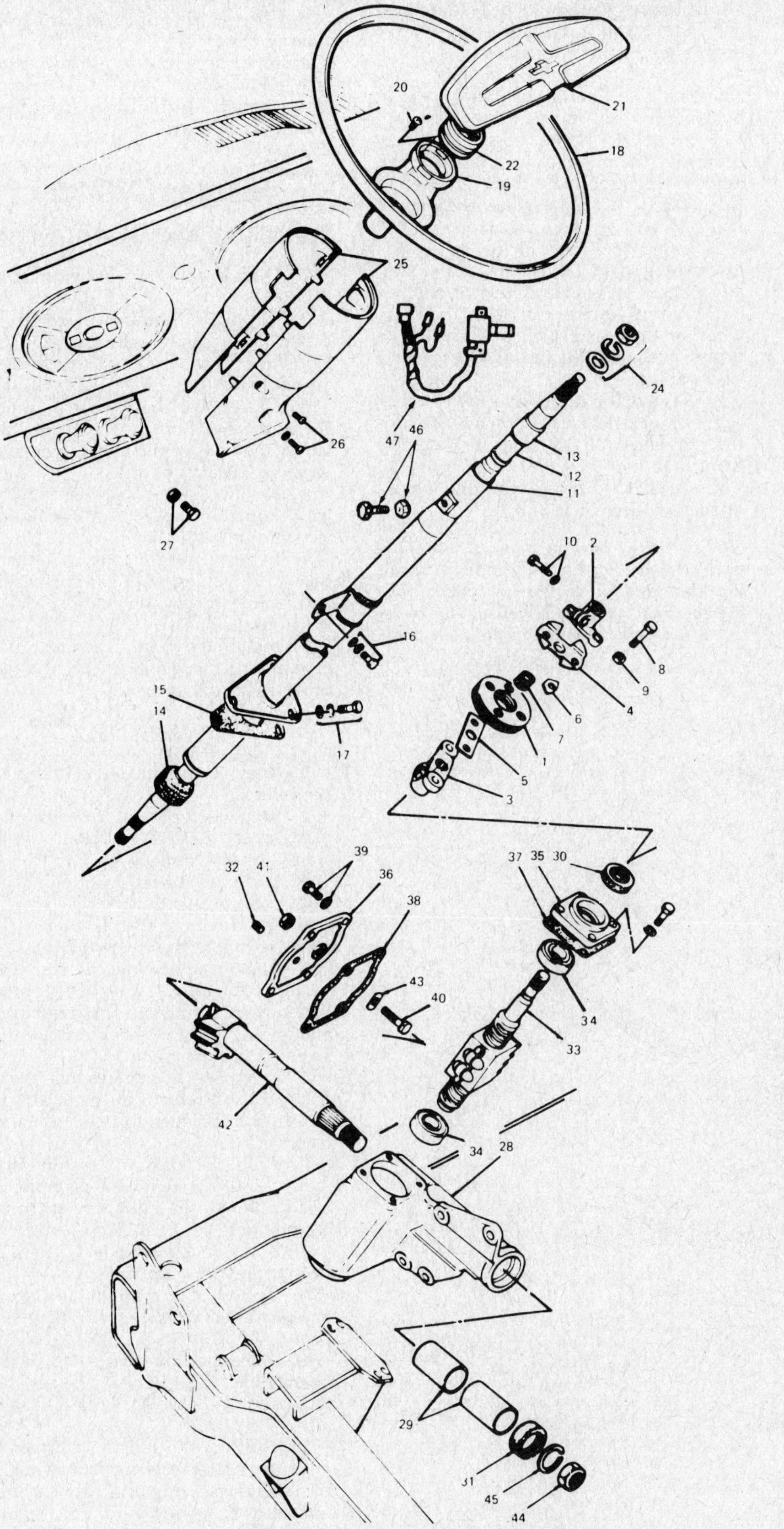

Exploded view of the steering system components

the two screws which retain the switch clamp to the steering column mast jacket.

5. Replace the switch in the reverse order of removal.

Manual Steering Gear

REMOVAL AND INSTALLATION

1. Raise the vehicle on a hoist.
2. Remove the pitman arm nut and washer and mark the relationship of the shaft to the arm. Using a puller, remove the pitman arm from the pitman shaft.
3. Remove the engine stone shield.
4. Remove the two lower flexible coupling clamp bolts.
5. Remove the steering gear-to-frame bolts and remove the steering gear from the vehicle.
6. Install the steering gear in the reverse order of removal, installing the mounting bolts loosely at first and tightening the large bolts to 55 ft lbs and the small ones to 20 ft lbs only after the flexible coupling bolts have been tightened to 20 ft lbs.

BRAKE SYSTEMS

The Chevy LUV is equipped with vacuum assisted hydraulic self-adjusting type brakes.

On 1973–75 models the front brakes are of the two leading shoe type which incorporate two wheel cylinders at each wheel. The front wheel cylinder actuates the lower brake shoe and the rear cylinder the upper brake shoe. On 1976–80 models the front brakes are the floating disc brake type which incorporates a single piston actuating both inner and outer shoe and lining assemblies. The brake linings are molded and bonded to the brake shoes.

The rear brakes are the duo-servo type with a single wheel cylinder on each wheel. The wheel cylinder has two pistons, actuating both the secondary and primary brake shoes. The brake lining is also molded and bonded to the brake shoes. The primary lining is smaller than the secondary lining.

The self-adjusters on the front brakes operate during forward stops and the self-adjusters on the rear brakes adjust on reverse stops.

The parking brake is actuated by a rachet type L-handle mounted to the dash at the right of the steering column. A cable connects the handle to the intermediate cable by means of a lever. The intermediate cable attaches to the two rear cables which operate the rear service brakes. Adjustment of the parking brake is provided at the equalizer.

Adjustment

Disc brakes require no adjustments. Drum brakes, although self-adjusting, may require an initial adjustment after the brakes have been replaced, or whenever the adjuster position has been changed. The final adjustment is made by using the self-adjusting mechanism.

1. With the brake drum removed, disengage the pullback springs from the adjuster plates on the front brakes, or the actuator from the starwheel on the rear brakes.
2. Using the brake drum as an adjustment gauge, adjust the upper and lower shoes an equal number of notches on the front brakes, or turn the starwheel on the rear brakes until the brake drum slides over the brake shoes with a slight drag.
3. Retract the upper and lower shoes of the front brakes two notches, or turn the starwheel on the rear brakes 1¼ turns to retract the shoes.
4. Install the brake drums and wheels and lower the vehicle.

NOTE: If the backing place access plugs were removed on the front brakes, make sure that they are reinstalled before making the final adjustment. Also, the brake drums are to be installed in the same position from which they were removed. Make sure that you install the drum-to-flange locating screw.

5. Perform the final adjustment by making a number of forward and reverse stops, applying the brakes with a firm pedal effort until a satisfactory brake pedal height, and straight-line braking is achieved.

Master Cylinder

REMOVAL AND INSTALLATION

1. Disconnect the battery ground cable.
2. Wipe the master cylinder and brake lines clean. Place absorbent cloths below the master cylinder area to absorb any fluid leakage.
3. Disconnect the hydraulic lines at the connections on the master cylinder. Cover the ends of the brake lines to prevent the entrance of dirt.
4. Remove the master cylinder bracket bolt at the front end of the master cylinder.
5. Remove the master cylinder-to-booster attaching nuts and lockwashers and remove the master cylinder and gasket from the booster.
6. Install the master cylinder in the reverse order of removal, and bleed the brake hydraulic system.

OVERHAUL

1. Remove the master cylinder from the vehicle.
2. Remove the fluid reservoir caps, plates and strainers and drain the fluid from the reservoirs.
3. Place the master cylinder in a vise.
4. Loosen the fluid reservoir clamp screws and remove the plastic reservoirs from the master cylinder body.
5. Remove the connector bolt, connector and gaskest from the front system side (rear outlet). Then, remove the end plug, gasket, check valve, return spring and spring seat.
6. Remove the connector, gasket, check valve, return spring and spring seat from the rear system side (front outlet).
7. Push the primary piston all the way in and then remove the stopper bolt and gasket on the right-side of the master cylinder.
8. Using snap-ring pliers, remove the primary piston snap-ring.
9. Remove the primary and secondary piston assemblies from the cylinder bore.
10. Clean all of the parts in clean brake fluid. Blow out all passages, orifices, and valve holes with compressed air.
11. Inspect the master cylinder bore and pistons for scoring, corrosion, and rust. Slight scoring and rust can be removed by polishing with crocus cloth or fine emery paper soaked with brake fluid.

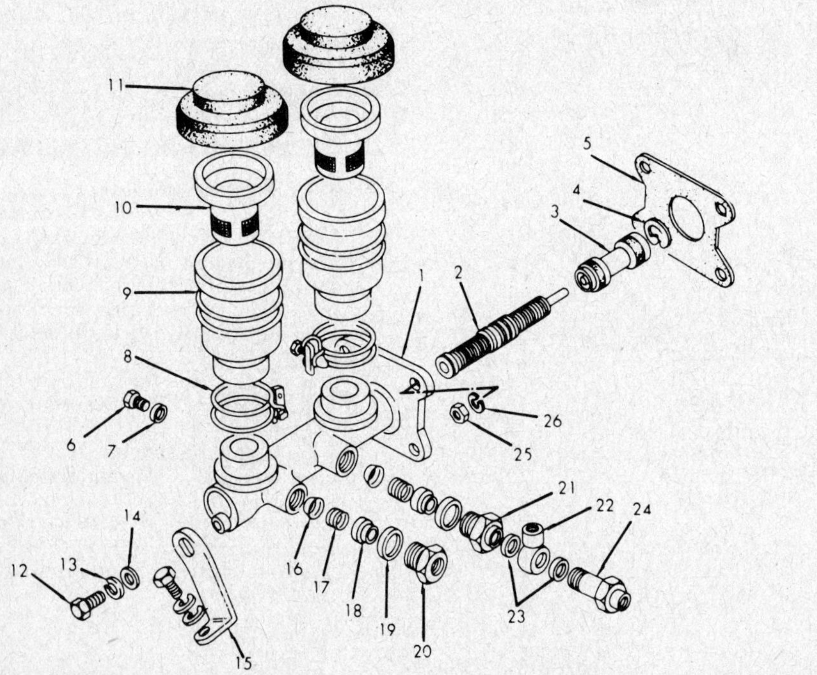

1. Master cylinder
2. Secondary piston
3. Primary piston
4. Snap ring
5. Gasket*
6. Stopper bolt
7. Gasket*
8. Clamp
9. Reservoir
10. Filter
11. Cover
12. Bolt
13. Lock washer
14. Washer
15. Bracket
16. Spring seat
17. Return spring
18. Check valve
19. Gasket*
20. Connector
21. End pulg
22. Connector
23. Gasket*
24. Connector bolt*
25. Nut
26. Washer

NOTE (*) Included in REPAIR KIT

Exploded view of the brake master cylinder

12. Soak all new and old parts in clean brake fluid before reassembling.

13. Insert the secondary piston assembly into the master cylinder bore, so that the primary stem guide is projected slightly beyond the cylinder bore end.

14. Insert the primary piston into the master cylinder bore so that the secondary piston stem guide enters the hole in the primary piston.

15. Install the snap-ring into the groove in the master cylinder housing.

16. Depress the primary piston and install the piston stopper bolt and new gasket.

17. Install the spring seat, return spring, check valve, new gasket and end plug in the front system side of the master cylinder (rear outlet).

18. Install a new gasket on either side of the connector and secure ti into position with the connector bolt.

19. Install the spring seat, return spring, check valve, new gasket and connector in the rear system side of the master cylinder (front outlet).

20. Install the clamps over the lower ends of the fluid reservoirs, place the reservoirs in position on the master cylinder body and then tighten the clamp bolts.

21. Install the reservoir filters, and fill the reservoirs with clean brake fluid. Push in on the primary piston to determine that it returns smoothly. Test the piston assembly two or three times to make sure that fluid comes out of the front and rear outlets.

22. Install the plates and covers.

23. Install plugs in all of the connector outlet ports.

24. Fill the reservoirs to the proper level with clean brake fluid.

25. Insert a rod with a smooth round end to the piston end and press it in to compress the piston return spring.

26. Release the pressure on the rod. Watch for air bubbles in the reservoir fluid.

27. Repeat Steps 25 and 26 as long as bubbles appear in the fluid.

28. Install the master cylinder on the vehicle and bleed the brake hydraulic system.

Power Cylinder

REMOVAL AND INSTALLATION

1. Disconnect the battery ground cable.

2. Disconnect the hydraulic lines at the master cylinder. Cap them immediately.

3. Remove the bracket connecting the power unit to fender skirt.

4. Remove the vacuum line from the vacuum check valve and move line out of the way.

5. Disconnect the brake pedal return spring, and brake pedal pin from the push rod clevis.

6. Remove the power cylinder-to-firewall nuts and carefully remove the master cylinder and power cylinder as a unit.

7. Installation is the reverse of removal.

NOTE: The piston rod height should be checked before the power unit is installed. The height is 0.729 to 0.736 inches, measured from the master cylinder mounting face of the power unit to the top of the push rod, when the rod is bottomed in the power cylidner.

Bleeding

The brake hydraulic system must be bled after any line has been disconnected or air has somehow found its way into the system.

The bleeding operation should start with the wheel cylinder nearest the master cylinder and end with the one farthest away.

NOTE: Do not bleed the brakes with the brake drums or calipers removed.

1. Make sure that the master cylinder is full and kept at least $^3/_4$ full throughout the entire bleeding process. Check the fluid level in the master cylinder reservoirs frequently during the bleeding operation.

2. Remove the cap from the wheel cylinder or caliper bleeder valve. Position a wrench on the bleeder valve and place a rubber hose over the bleeder valve nipple.

3. Place the other end of the bleeder hose into a a clear container containing enough brake fluid to ensure that the end of the bleeder hose will remain submerged.

4. Start the engine and allow it to run during the actual bleeding of each wheel cylinder. This is so to have vacuum applied to the brake booster during the bleeding process.

5. Open the wheel cylinder bleeder valve by turning the wrench counterclockwise about $^3/_4$ of a turn. Have an assistant depress the brake pedal. Just before the brake pedal reaches the end of its travel, close the bleeder valve and allow the brake pedal to return slowly to the released position. Repeat this operation until the brake fluid being expelled is free from air bubbles, then close the bleeder valve tightly.

6. Remove the bleeder hose and the wrench from the bleeder valve and install them onto the next wheel cylinder or caliper to be bled. Repeat Step 5 on all of the remaining wheel cylinders. Don't forget to check and replenish the brake fluid in the master cylinder reservoirs.

7. After bleeding the brake hydraulic system, check the operation of the brakes. Depress the brake pedal several times then hold it depressed. Notice how far the pedal can be depressed. Release the pedal for about 10 seconds, then depress it again and hold it, taking notice of the distance which it can be depressed before it stops with the same amount of pedal pressure applied as before. If the pedal depresses further or can be "pumped up", then it can be assumed that there is still air in the hydraulic system and further bleeding is required.

Front Disc Brakes

DISC BRAKE PADS

Inspection

Replace the front disc brake linings whenever the lining wear indicator makes a squeaking noise or when the

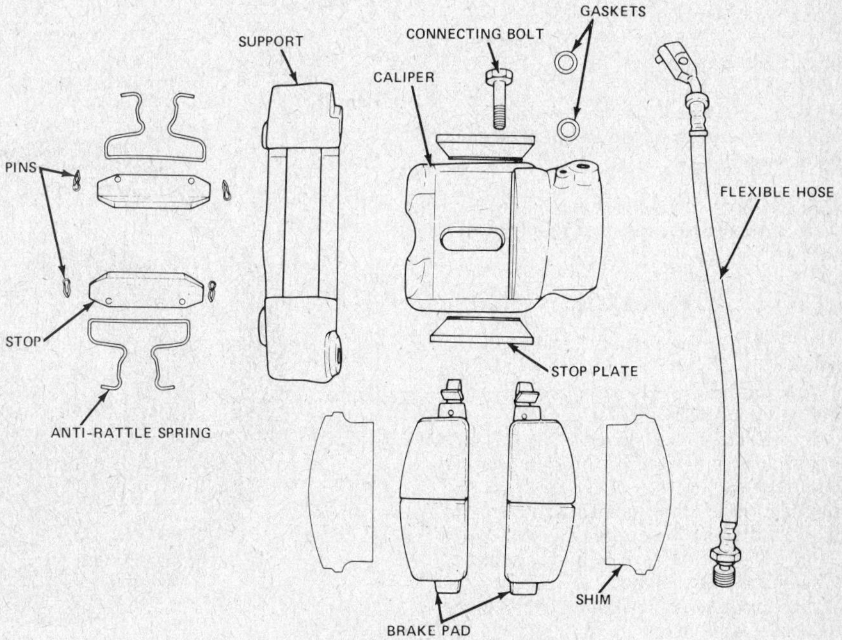

Disc brake components

lining is worn to within .039" of the shoe surface. All four brake linings should always be replaced at the same time.

REMOVAL AND INSTALLATION

1. Raise the vehicle on a lift.
2. Remove the wheel and tire assembly.
3. Remove the pins from the caliper stops and then remove the stops.
4. Remove the caliper from the support, remove the stop plates from the caliper then suspend the caliper assembly from the upper link or frame using a piece of heavy wire.
5. Remove the shoe and lining assemblies and shims and mark the locations if to be reinstalled.
6. Remove the anti-rattle springs from the support.
7. Wipe the inside of the caliper clean, including the exterior of the dust seal. Check to see that the dust seal is in good condition.
8. Install the anti-rattle springs, shims and the shoe and lining assemblies to the support.

NOTE: If original linings are being reinstalled, they must be installed in the original position. Also position the wear indicators to the lower side of the support.

9. Install new stop plates to the caliper, then install the caliper, stops and stop pins.
10. Install the wheel and tire assembly.

Disc Brake Calipers

REMOVAL AND INSTALLATION

1. Raise the vehicle on a lift.
2. Remove the wheel and tire assembly.
3. Remove the pins from the caliper stops and then remove the stops.
4. Disconnect the front flexible hose from the brake line.

NOTE: To keep dirt from entering, cap or tape the openings of the flexible hose and brake line.

5. Remove the caliper from the support and remove the stop plates from the caliper.

OVERHAUL

1. Remove the flexible hose from the caliper.
2. Remove the dust seal from the caliper using a small screwdriver.
3. Insert a block of wood into the caliper and force out the piston by applying compressed air into the caliper at the flexible hose attachment. Remove and discard the piston square ring seal.
4. Clean all parts in clean brake fluid. Check the cylinder bore and pistons for wear, scuffing or corrosion and replace as necessary.
5. Apply a silicone lube to the caliper bore and the piston square ring seal and insert the piston seal into the caliper bore using finger pressure only.
6. Apply a silicone lubricant to the piston and assemble the dust seal to the piston and caliper. Install the seal ring into the dust seal.
7. Install the flexible hose to the caliper using new gaskets.
8. Lubricate the stop plates and the sliding surfaces of the caliper than install the new stop plates to the caliper, the caliper and the new stop pins.
9. Connect the flexible brake hose to the brake line.
10. Install the wheel and tire assembly.

Brake Disc

REMOVAL AND INSTALLATION

1. Raise the vehicle on a lift.
2. Remove the front tire and wheel assembly.
3. Remove the bolts attaching the caliper support to the adapter and then suspend the caliper and support from the upper link or frame using a piece of heavy wire.
4. Remove the hub grease cap, cotter pin, spindle nut retainer and nut and remove the hub and rotor assembly.
5. Replace the hub and disc as an assembly if either needs replacement.

NOTE: All brake disc have a minimum thickness dimension cast into them. This dimension is the minimum wear dimension and not a refinish dimension.

6. Install the dust shield and adapter to the steering knuckle and torque to the long bolts to 55 ft lbs. and the small bolts to 35 ft. lbs.
7. Install the front hub and disc assembly and adjust the wheel bearings.
8. Assemble the caliper and support assembly to the adapter and torque the bolts to 64 ft. lbs.
9. Install the front wheel and tire assembly.

Front Drum Brakes

BRAKE DRUMS

Removal and Installation

1. Jack up the vehicle and support it on jackstands.
2. Remove the wheel cover and remove the wheel and tire assembly.
3. Remove the brake drum and hub retaining screws and remove the drum. Identify the drum so that it can be reinstalled in the same position.

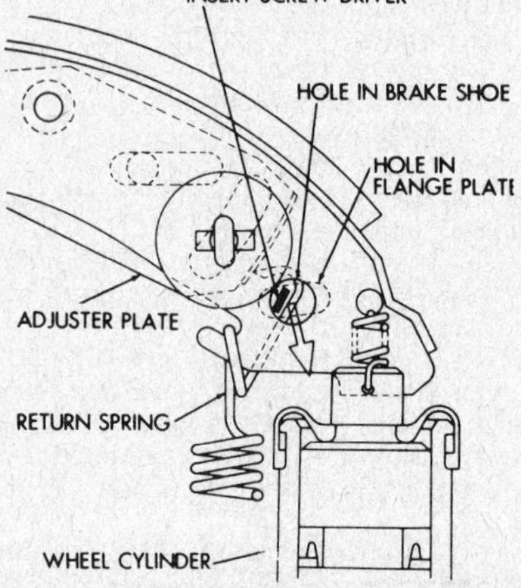

Insert a brake adjusting tool through the hole in the backing plate and the brake shoe. Raise and release the end of the return spring and move the brake in towards the wheel cylinder

If the brake drums are worn considerably, it may be necessary to retract the brake shoes before the drum can be removed. Remove the rubber hole plugs in the backing plate and insert a screwdriver through the hole and into the hole in the brake shoe. Raise the end of the brake shoe return spring to release it from the serration and contact the brake shoe by moving it in toward the wheel cylinder.

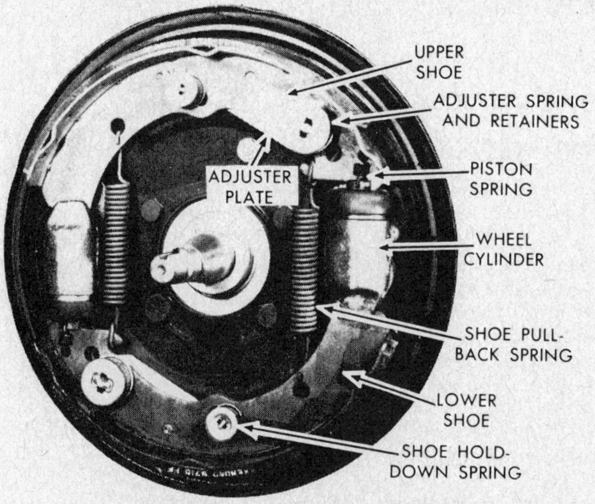

Front drum brake components

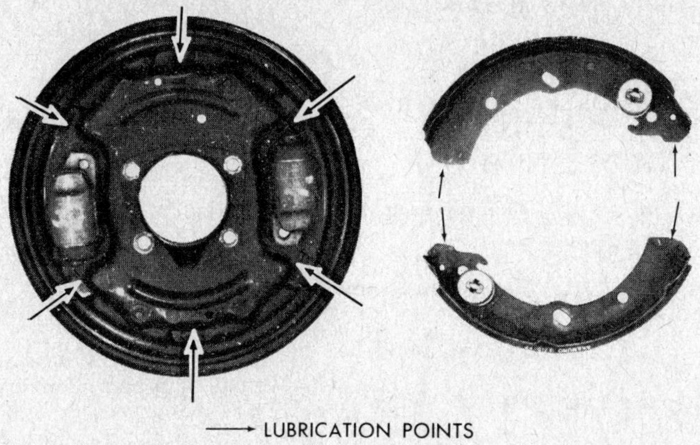

Lubrication point for front drum brakes

NOTE: Never depress the brake pedal while the brake drums are removed.

4. Install the brake drums in the reverse order of removal.

Inspection

After removing the brake drum, remove any dirt and inspect the drum for cracks, deep grooves, roughness, scoring, or out-of-roundness. Replace any brake drum which is cracked completely through.

Smooth any slight scores by polishing the friction surface with fine emery cloth. Heavy or extensive scoring will cause excessive brake lining wear and should be removed from the brake drum through resurfacing of the brake drum friction surface. The maximum finished diameter of the brake drums must not exceed 10.059 in. The brake drum must be replaced if the diameter is 10.079 in. or greater.

BRAKE SHOES

Removal and Installation

The brake linings must be replaced when the lining thickness is 0.059 in. or less.

1. Remove the brake drum.
2. Disconnect the wheel cylinder piston springs from the pistons and shoes with a pair of pliers.
3. Depress and rotate the hold-down spring retainers 90° with a pair of pliers and then remove the springs and retainers.
4. Remove the upper and lower brake shoes.
5. Depress the self-adjusting spring retainers, rotate the shoe 90° while holding the retainer and then separate the self-adjuster retainer, washer, spring, pin, adjuster lever and the brake shoe from each other.

NOTE: If the shoes, adjuster levers and return springs are to be reinstalled, be sure to mark their location so that they will be reinstalled in their original positions.

6. Before you install the brake shoes, make sure that your hands and tools are free from grease and oil that could possibly contaminate the brake linings.
7. Place the brake shoe in an arbor press or similar tool and install the adjuster pivot pin, adjuster lever, washer, spring and retainers to each brake shoe. Compress the spring and rotate the retainer 90° while compressing the spring, making sure that the pin end is seated in the retainer groove.

NOTE: Install the washer so that its lining side is facing the lever. Also, the left and right-side adjuster levers are not interchangeable and must be reinstalled in their original positions.

8. Lubricate the brake shoe contact points on the backing plate and the wheel cylinder contact points on the brake shoes with Lubriplate.
9. Hook the return springs to the brake shoes. Be sure to install the left and right springs in their original positions as they are not interchangeable. The left springs are light blue; right springs are black.
10. Fit the grooved portion of the adjuster lever to the guide pin and install the brake shoes in position. Make sure that the shoes are fitted properly to the guide pin. If the end of the brake shoe is not inserted in the groove, it is an indication that the brake shoes are lifted off the ridged portion. Make sure that the return spring end is fitted properly to the adjuster lever.
11. Install the piston springs on the wheel cylidner piston ends.
12. Install the brake shoe hold-down springs and retainers. With a pair of pliers, compress the spring and rotate the retainer 90°, making sure that the pin end is seated in the retainer groove.
13. Reinstall the brake drum and adjust the brakes.

WHEEL CYLINDERS

Removal and Installation

It is not necessary to remove the wheel cylinders from the backing plates to disassemble, inspect, and overhaul the cylinder. Removal is necessary only when the wheel cylinder is damaged beyond repair and must be replaced.

It is a good practice to inspect the wheel cylinders for leakage whenever the brake drums are removed. Simply pull the edge of the wheel cylidner boot carefully away from the cylinder and note whether or not the interior is wet with brake fluid. Excessive fluid at this point indicates leakage past the piston cup, requiring overhaul or replacement. A slight amount of fluid on the inside of the wheel cylinder is almost always present and acts as a lubricant for the piston.

1. Remove the wheel and tire assembly, the brake drum and the brake shoes.
2. Disconnect the brake system hydraulic line from the wheel cylidner at the rear of the backing plate.
3. Remove the screws securing the wheel cylinder to the backing plate and remove the wheel cylinder from the backing plate.
4. Install the wheel cylinder in the reverse order of removal and bleed the brake hydraulic system.

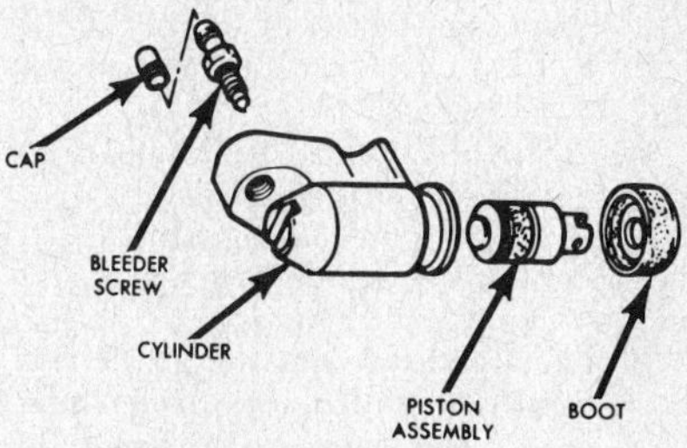

Exploded view of the front wheel cylinder

Overhaul

1. Either with the wheel cylinder removed or still on the brake backing plate remove the boot(s) from the cylinder end(s).
2. Remove the piston(s) and cup(s).

NOTE: The front wheel cylinder pistons and cups are serviced as an assembly.

3. Inspect the cylinder bore. Check for staining and corrosion. Discard any wheel cylinder which is excessively corroded. Inspect the piston and discard it if it is excessively pitted, scored or damaged.
4. Polish any stained or slightly scored areas in the cylinder bore with crocus cloth. Move the crocus cloth in a circular motion around the circumference of the cylinder bore, not in a lengthwise manner.
5. Wash the master cylinder body thoroughly in clean brake fluid, allowing it to remain lubricated for assembly. Do not lubricate the pistons or cups prior to their installation in the cylinder.
6. On front wheel cylinders, install the piston assembly into the cylinder, being careful not to damage the boot.
7. On rear wheel cylinders, insert the spring-expander into the cylinder bore. Install the new cups with the flat surface

toward the outer ends of the cylinder. Be sure that the cups are lint-free. Do not lubricate the cups prior to installation. Install the new pistons into the cylinder with the flat surfaces toward the center of the cylinder. Do not lubricate prior to installation.

8. Press the new boot(s) onto the wheel cylinder.

9. Install the wheel cylinder onto the brake backing plate, if it was removed, assemble the brake shoes to the backing plate, install the brake drum and bleed the brake hydraulic system.

Front Wheel Bearings —2 Wheel Drive

REMOVAL AND INSTALLATION

1. Remove the hub assembly.
2. Remove the outer roller bearing assembly from the hub. Pry out the inner bearing lip seal and remove the inner bearing assembly.
3. Wash all parts in a cleaning solvent and blow dry.
4. Check the bearings for pitting or scoring. Also check for smooth rotation and lack of noise.
5. Thoroughly lubricate the bearings with new wheel bearing lubricant.
6. Apply a light coat of lubricant to the spindle and inside surface of the hub.
7. Place the inner bearing in the race of the hub and install a new grease seal.
8. Install the hub assembly on the spindle.
9. Install the outer wheel bearing, washer and adjust nut.
10. Adjust the wheel bearings as outlined below.
11. Install the dust cap on the hub.
12. Install the brake caliper and support assembly.
13. Install the wheel and tighten the nuts.

WHEEL BEARING ADJUSTMENT

1. With the wheel raised, remove the hub cap and dust cap and then remove the cotter pin and nut retainer from the end of the spindle.
2. While rotating the wheel, tighten the spindle nut to 22 ft. lbs.
3. Turn the hub 2–3 turns and loosen the nut just enough so that it can be turned with your fingers.
4. Turn the nut all the way in with your fingers and check to be sure the hub has no free play.
5. Measure the starting torque by pulling one of the wheel hub studs with a pull scale. Tighten the spindle nut so that the pull scale reads 1.1–2.6 lbs. when the hub begins to rotate.

*NOTE: **Make sure that the brake pads are not in contact with the drum when measuring rotating torque.***

6. Install the nut retainer, cotter pin, dust cap and hub cap.

7. Perform the same procedure for each wheel.

Wheel Bearings—4 Wheel Drive

REMOVAL, INSTALLATION AND ADJUSTMENT

1. Raise and support the front end. Place the hub in 2H.
2. Remove the free wheeling hub cover assembly.
3. Remove the snap ring and shims from the spindle.
4. Remove the free wheeling hub body and lock washer.
5. Remove the outer roller bearing assembly from the hub with your fingers.
6. Using a brass or wood drift, drive out the inner bearing assembly along with the oil seal. Replace the seal.
7. Wash all parts in a non-flammable solvent.
8. Check all parts for cracks or wear. Thoroughly lubricate all bearings parts with a high temperature wheel bearing grease. Remove any excess. Apply about 2 ounces of the grease to the hub.
9. Lightly coat the spindle with the same grease.
10. Place the inner bearing into the hub race and install a new seal and retaining ring.
11. Carefully install the hub on the spindle and install the outer bearing.
12. Install the spindle nut.
13. While rotating the hub, tighten the hub not so that the wheel cannot be turned by hand.
14. Turn the hub 2–3 turns and back off the nut just enough so that it can be loosened with the fingers.
15. Finger-tighten the nut so that all play is taken up at the bearing.
16. Attach a pull scale to one of the lugs and check the amount of pull needed to start the wheel turning. Initial pull should be 2.6–4.0 lbs. When performing this test, make sure the brake pads are not touching the rotor. If the rotating torque is not correct, tighten the spindle nut until it is.
17. Install the snap ring and shims, gasket and cover. Torque the cover bolts to 14 ft lb.

Rear Drum Brakes

BRAKE DRUMS

Removal and Installation

1. Raise the vehicle and support it on jackstands.
2. Remove the hub caps and remove the rear tire and wheel.
3. Loosen the check nuts at the parking brake equalizer sufficiently to remove all tension from the brake cable.
4. Remove the drum-to-hub retaining screws and remove the drum from the vehicle. Identify each brake drum so that it can be reinstalled in its original position. Never depress the brake pedal while any of the brake drums are removed.
5. Install the brake drums in the reverse order of removal.

Inspection

Inspect the rear brake drums in the same manner as is outlined for the front brake drums.

BRAKE SHOES

Removal and Installation

1. Remove the brake drums.
2. Unhook the brake return springs from the anchor pin using a brake tool and remove the springs.
3. Remove the brake shoe hold-down springs using pliers. Depress the spring retainer while rotating it 90° to align the slot in the retainer with the flanged end of the pin.
4. Remove the self-adjuster cable assembly by disconnecting the spring at the adjuster lever and removing the cable end from the anchor pin. Remove the guide plate from the anchor pin.
5. Remove the adjuster lever and the lever hold-down wire from the shoe pivot.
6. Separate the shoes from the wheel cylinder pushrods.
7. Separate the primary and second-

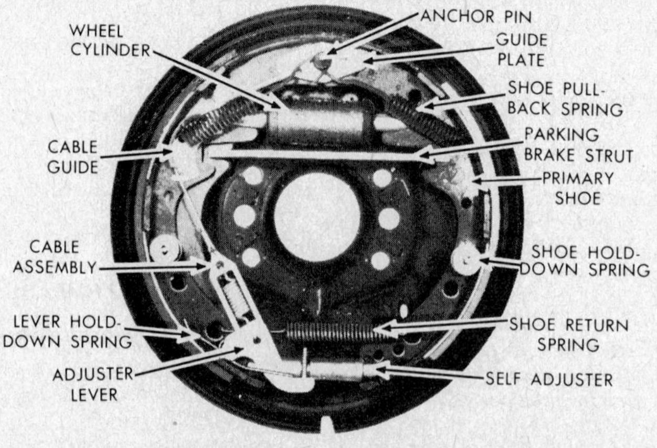

Rear drum brake components

ary brake shoes, adjuster, return spring, and parking brake strut assemblies.

*NOTE: **If the brake shoes are to be reinstalled, be sure to identify them so that they can be reinstalled in their original positions.***

8. Separate the parking brake lever and the rear cable. Remove the clip and washer and remove the parking brake lever from the secondary shoe.
9. Lubricate the parking brake cable with Lubriplate.
10. Assemble the parking brake lever to the secondary shoe and then assemble the parking brake cable to the lever.
11. Before installation, make sure that the adjusting screw is clean, lubricated and operable.
12. Connect the brake shoes together with bottom return spring and then place the adjuster screw into position. The adjuster screw is installed with the starwheel nearest to the secondary shoe.
13. Assemble the parking brake strut with the spring on the primary shoe end, and assemble the shoes to the wheel cylinder pushrods.
14. Install the shoe hold-down springs using a pair of pliers. Compress the springs and rotate the retainers 90°.
15. Install the guide plate on the anchor pin. Assemble the self-adjuster lever and the lever hold-down wire to the secondary shoe pivot pin. Place the adjuster cable over the anchor pin, route the cable around the shoe shield and then attach the spring at the opposite end to the adjuster lever.
16. Install the return springs using a brake tool.
17. Pry the shoes away from the backing plate and lubricate the shoe contact areas with a thin coat of Lubriplate.
18. Check the operation of the parking brake. *Do not step on the brake pedal.*
19. Install the brake drum and adjust the brake shoes.

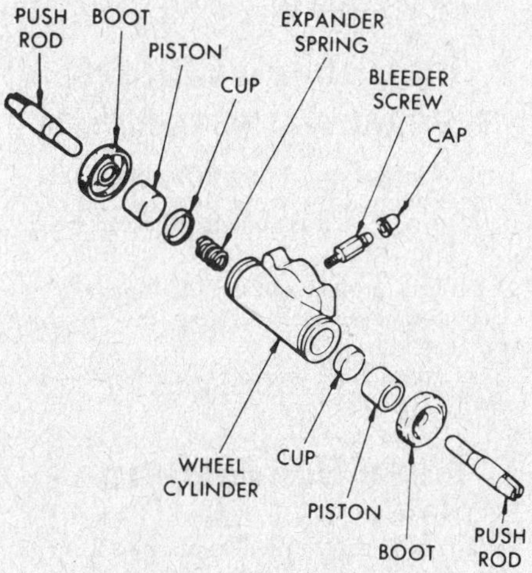

Exploded view of the rear wheel cylinder

WHEEL CYLINDERS

Removal and Installation

Remove and install the rear wheel cylinders in the same manner as outlined for the front wheel cylinders.

Overhaul

Follow the procedure given for overhauling the front wheel cylinders to overhaul the rear wheel cylinders.

Parking Brake

Adjustment

Since the rear brakes are utilized as service brakes and parking brakes, the service brake must be properly adjusted as a base for parking brake adjustment.

1. Raise the vehicle on a hoist.

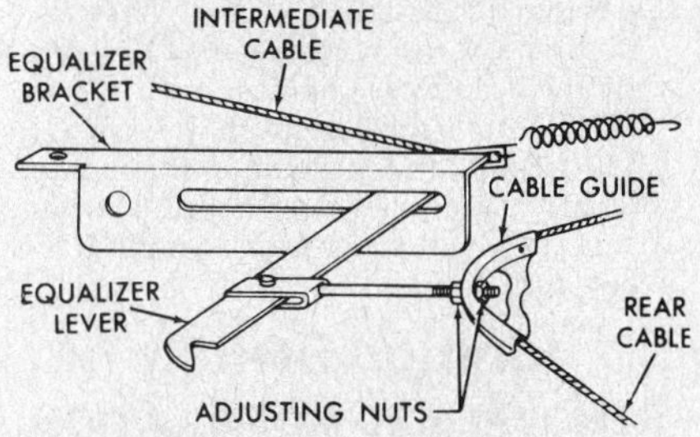

Parking brake adjustment

2. Apply the parking brake two notches from the fully released position.
3. Loosen the equalizer check nut, and tighten or loosen the front jam nut until a light to moderate drag is felt when the rear wheels are rotated frontward.
4. Tighten the nuts securely. Hold the front nut while tightening the jam nut.
5. Fully release the parking brake and rotate the rear wheels. No drag should be present.
6. Lower the vehicle.

FRONT CABLE

Removal and Installation

1. Disconnect the battery ground cable.
2. Remove the carburetor air cleaner.
3. Drain the cooling system. Disconnect the heater hoses at the heater core outlet tubes at the dash panel and secure the hoses in an upright position to minimize coolant loss.
4. Disconnect the parking brake front cable at the control lever on the rightside of the engine compartment.
5. Remove the right-hand pulley center bolt and remove the pulley.
6. Remove the cable cover nuts at the dash panel and remove the cover.
7. Remove the windshield wiper switch on the instrument panel.
8. Remove the screws attaching the lever assemb!y to the instrument panel.
9. Pull the assembly rearward and lay it on the floor.
10. Loosen the parking brake light switch bracket screw and rotate the switch and bracket 90°.
11. Manually release the ratchet and then depress the handle all the way in.
12. Remove the cotter pin, washer, pivot pin and the pulley. Remove the cable assembly.
13. To install the cable, install the cable to handle lower end and then pull the handle rearward several notches.
14. Rotate the parking brake light switch and bracket into position and tighten the bracket screw.
15. Install the pulley, pivot pin, washer and cotter pin.
16. For the remainder of the installation procedure follow the removal procedure in reverse starting with Step 8.

INTERMEDIATE CABLE

Removal and Installation

1. Raise the vehicle on a hoist.
2. Disconnect the equalizer lever spring at the lever.
3. Loosen the cable guide nut and remove the cable assembly.
4. Install the intermediate cable in the reverse order of removal and adjust the parking brake.

REAR CABLE

Removal and Installation

1. Raise the vehicle on a hoist.
2. Remove the rear cable retaining clamps on the left and right-sides.
3. Disconnect the equalizer lever return spring at the lever.
4. Remove the cotter pin, washer and pin and remove the equalizer lever from the front cable and equalizer adjusting bolt clevis.
5. Remove the left and right rear wheel and tire assemblies.
6. Remove the brake drums and shoes, disconnecting the rear cable from the brake lever.
7. Remove the rear cable spring cup using a box wrench.
8. Withdraw the cable ends from the

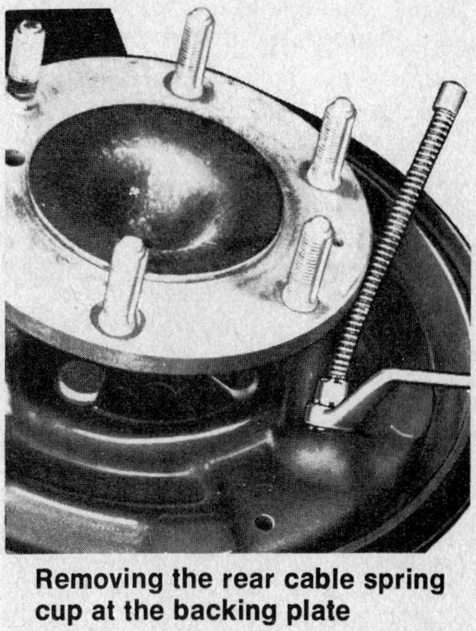

Removing the rear cable spring cup at the backing plate

backing plates on either side and remove the cable assembly.

9. Install the cable in the reverse order of removal and adjust the parking brake.

CHASSIS ELECTRICAL

Heater Blower

REMOVAL AND INSTALLATION

1. Disconnect the battery ground cable.
2. Disconnect the blower motor electrical leads.
3. Remove the blower-to-heater core screws and remove the blower motor assembly.
4. Install in the reverse order.

Heater Core

REMOVAL AND INSTALLATION

1. Disconnect the battery ground cable.
2. Place a drain pan under the heater hoses at the heater and remove the heater hoses from the core tubes, securing the heater hoses in a raised position to prevent further loss of coolant. Plug or tape the heater core tubes to prevent spillage of coolant in the passenger compartment when removing.
3. Remove the parcel shelf.
4. Loosen the air diverter and defroster door bowden cable clamps at the heater case and disconnect the cables from the doors.
5. Disconnect the blower resistor leads.
6. Remove the control assembly-to-instrument panel screws and swing the control to the left and lay it on the floor. Be careful not to kink the water valve bowden cable.
7. Remove the four heater-to-firewall screws. Pull the heater rearward until the core tubes clear the firewall opening, then remove the heater by moving it to the right and down.
8. Remove the core tube clamp screw and remove the clamp.
9. Remove the seven screws and separate the heater case halves.
10. Remove the core from the case.
11. Install and assemble the heater core and heater case in the reverse order of removal, using new seals around the heater core.

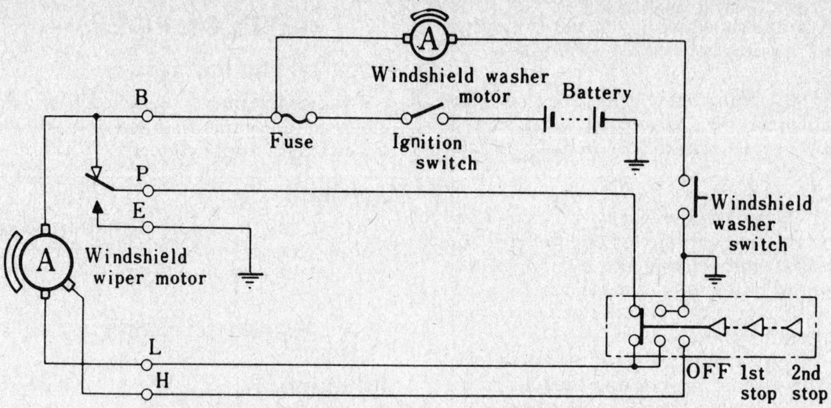

Windshield wiper and washer electrical circuit

Ignition Switch

REMOVAL AND INSTALLATION

1. Disconnect the battery ground strap.
2. Remove the multi-connector from the rear of the ignition switch.
3. Remove the lock nut from the front of the switch. Remove the switch from the rear of the instrument panel.
4. Installation is the reverse of removal.

***NOTE:** Align the locating lug on the switch body with the slot in the instrument panel mounting hole during installation.*

Radio

REMOVAL AND INSTALLATION

1. Disconnect the battery ground cable.
2. Remove the ash tray and ash tray plate.
3. Remove the tuner and volume control knobs, jam nuts, plain washers and face panel.
4. Remove the screws from the front and rear mounting brackets.
5. Disconnect the electrical connections, antenna lead and remove the radio. Remove the front mounting brackets from the radio.
6. Install the radio in the reverse order of removal.

Windshield Wiper Motor and Linkage

REMOVAL AND INSTALLATION

1. Remove the wiper blades and arms.
2. Remove the two bolts attaching the pivot.
3. Remove the four wiper motor mounting bolts and remove the wiper motor and linkage.
4. To remove the motor independently, take out the motor shaft nut and three bolts and then pull off the connector and disconnect the ground cable.
5. Install and assemble in the reverse order of removal. Make sure to install the wiper motor linkage so that it is not twisted or touching any adjacent parts; otherwise, the wiper motor will be loaded and cause poor wiper action.

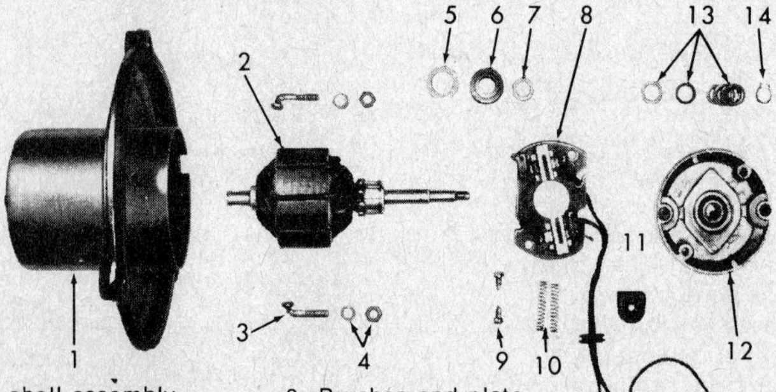

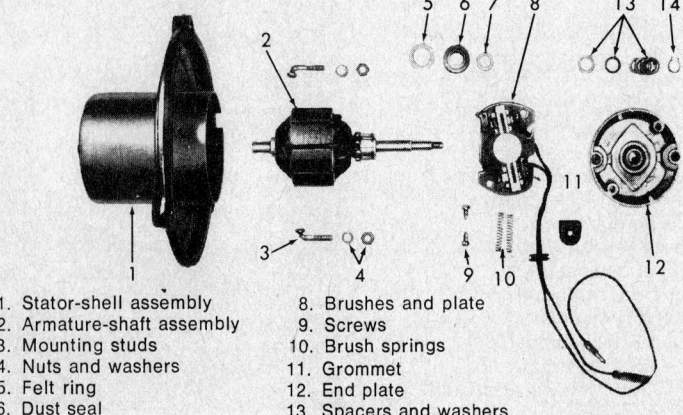

1. Stator-shell assembly
2. Armature-shaft assembly
3. Mounting studs
4. Nuts and washers
5. Felt ring
6. Dust seal
7. Spacer
8. Brushes and plate
9. Screws
10. Brush springs
11. Grommet
12. End plate
13. Spacers and washers
14. Snap ring

Blower motor

Instrument Cluster

REMOVAL AND INSTALLATION

1. Disconnect the speedometer cable.
2. Remove the wing nuts on the rear side of the instrument panel and pull the assembly part way out.
3. Disconnect the wiring harness at the connector and remove the instrument panel.
4. Install the panel in the reverse of removal.

Fuse Box Location

The fuse box is located under the hood, on the left inner fender panel, near the firewall, adjacent to the master cylinders. The fuse box contains ten fuses in use and four positions for spares.

INDEX

INTRODUCTION

Datsun, then known as D.A.T., began producing cars in 1913. The name D.A.T. was derived from the beginning letters of the founder's last names. The name Datson, for son of D.A.T., was used later and finally evolved into Datsun. The first Datsun was a two seater with motorcycle fenders and a four-speed transmission. In 1933, a reorganization led to the formation of Nissan Motor Company, Ltd., which is now the parent company of Datsun. Datsun cars made their first United States appearance at the 1958 Los Angeles Imported Car Show. Cars and pick-ups were first imported in 1960.

The first Datsun pick-up imported (until 1966) was the model L320 with a 1200 cc engine. Next came the L520 and L521 with 1300 cc engines. In 1970, the model PL521 pick-up with a 1600 cc engine was introduced. In midyear 1973, the 1800 cc engine was installed in the PL620 pick-up. The PL620 model was introduced in 1972 using the 1600 cc engine. The L20B engine was introduced in 1975. An optional automatic transmission was made available in 1972; a five speed overdrive manual transmission was introduced in 1977. Transistorized ignition was installed on trucks sold in California starting in 1976, and nationwide in 1978. Front disc brakes were also first installed in 1978.

SERIAL NUMBER IDENTIFICATION

Vehicle

The vehicle identification plate is located on the firewall in the engine compartment. The plate gives the vehicle type, engine capacity, maximum engine horsepower, wheelbase, engine number, and truck serial numbers.

The chassis serial number is stamped on the upper face of the right-side frame member.

The vehicle identification model codes may be interpreted as follows:

1973–74: The first letter, P, indicates the 1600 cc engine through mid-1973 and the 1800 cc engine thereafter. The second letter, L, means left hand drive. 620 is the model number. Four suffix letters are used. The first is either a K or blank; K indicates an automatic transmission. The second and third suffix letters are T and U; T indicates a floor shift, and U a U.S. and Canada specifications model. The fourth suffix letter is an H or blank; H indicates that no heater is installed.

1975–76: Three prefix letters and four suffix letters are used. The first letter is an H, for the L20B engine. The second letter is L, for left hand drive. The third letter is either a G or a blank; G is for long-wheelbase (long bed) trucks. The next three numbers, 620, are the model number. The four suffix letters remain the same as in 1973–74, with the exception of the last letter in 1976, which may be a V or a blank; V indicates a California model.

1977–80: Four prefix and four suffix letters are used. The first letter is a K or a blank; K indicates a king cab model. The second, third, and fourth letters are the same as those used in 1975–76. The next three numbers are the model number, 620. The first suffix letter is either a K, an F, or a blank; K indicates automatic transmission, F indicates a 5-speed, a blank indicates a 4-speed. The second and third suffix letters, T and U, have the same meaning as in earlier years. The last letter is either a V, an N, or a blank; V indicates a California model, N indicates a Canada model, a blank indicates a 49 States model.

Engine

The engine serial number is stamped on the right side of the cylinder block, just below the number four spark plug.

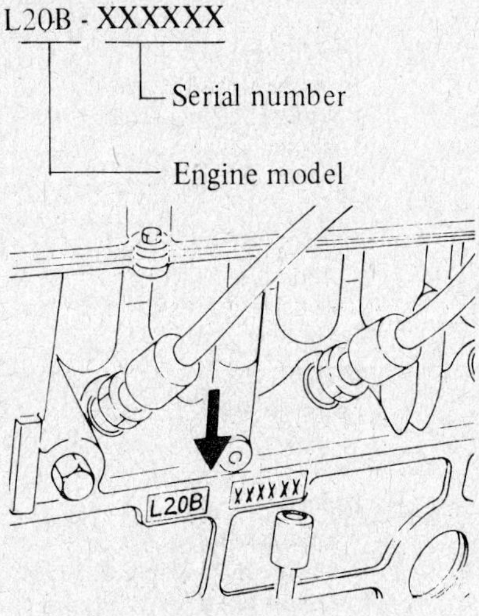

Engine serial number location

Transmission

The transmission serial number is stamped on the front upper face of the transmission case on manual transmissions, or on the right side of the transmission case on automatic transmissions.

GENERAL ENGINE SPECIFICATIONS

Year	Type (model)	Engine Displacement cu. in. (cc)	Carburetor Type	Horsepower (SAE) @ rpm	Torque @ rpm (ft lbs)	Bore x Stroke (in.)	Compression Ratio	Normal Oil Pressure (psi)
1973-74	OHC 4 (L18)	108.0 (1,770)	Dual throat downdraft	93 @ 6,000	99 @ 3,200	3.35 x 3.07	8.5:1	50-57
1975	OHC 4 (L20B)	119.1 (1,952)	Dual throat downdraft	100 @ 5,600	100 @ 3,600	3.35 x 3.39	8.5:1	50-57
1976-80	OHC 4 (L20B	119.1 (1,952)	Dual throat downdraft	100 @ 5,800	100 @ 3,600	3.35 x 3.39	8.5:1	50-57

TUNE-UP SPECIFICATIONS

(When analyzing compression test results, look for uniformity among cylinders, rather than specific pressures)

Year	Spark Plugs Type	Spark Plugs Gap (in.)	Distributor Point Dwell (deg)	Distributor Point Gap (in.)	Ignition Timing (deg) MT	Ignition Timing (deg) AT	Fuel Pump Pressure (psi)	Idle Speed (rpm) MT	Idle Speed (rpm) AT①	Valve Clearance (in.) (Hot) In	Valve Clearance (in.) (Hot) Ex	Percentage of CO at idle
1973-74	BP-6ES	0.028-0.031	49-55	0.018-0.022	5B @ 200	5B @ 650	2.6 3.4	800	650	0.008 cold/ 0.010	0.010 cold/ 0.012	1.5
1975	BP-6ES	0.031-0.035	49-55	0.017-0.022	12B ②	12B	3.8	750	650	0.010	0.012	2.0
1976 (Federal)	BP-6ES	0.031-0.035	49-55	0.018-0.022	12B	12B	3.8	750	650	0.010	0.012	2.0
1976 (California)	BP-6ES	0.039-0.043	Electronic	③	10B	12B	3.8	750	650	0.010	0.012	2.0
1977 (Federal)	BP 6ES	0.031-0.035	49-55	0.018-0.022	12B	12B	3.8	750	650	0.010	0.012	2.0
1977 (California)	BPR-6ES	0.031-0.035	Electronic	③	10B	12B	3.8	750	650	0.010	0.012	2.0
1978-80	BP-6ES-11	0.039-0.043	Electronic	③	12B	12B	3.0-3.9④	600	600	0.010	0.012	1.0

NOTE: The underhood specifications sticker sometimes reflects tune-up specification changes made in production Sticker figures must be used if they disagree with this chart.

① In Drive
② 10B—California
③ Reluctor Gap 0.008-0.16 in.
④ W/Electric Fuel Pump—4.6 lbs

FIRING ORDER

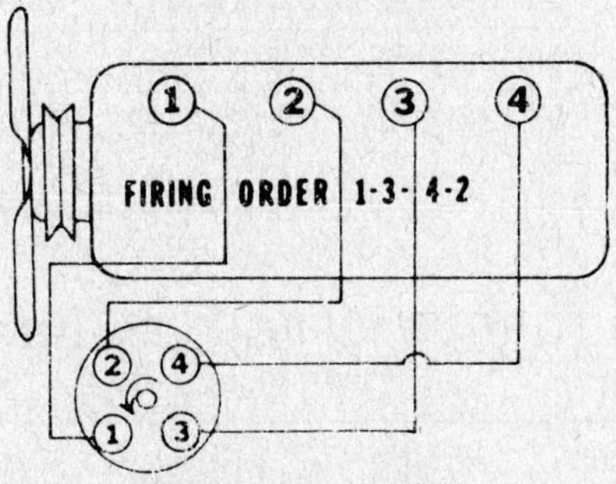

Firing order 1-3-4-2

CAPACITIES

Model	Engine Crankcase With Filter	Engine Crankcase Without Filter	Transmission (pts) Manual 4-sp	Transmission (pts) Automatic (total capacity)	Drive Axle (pts)	Gas Tank (gals)	Cooling System (qts)
1973-74	5.0	4.5	4.0	11.8	2.0	11.8	6.5
1975	5.0	4.5	3.5	11.8	2.0	11.8	10.5①
1976	4.5	4.0	2.5	11.8	2.12	11.8	8.5
1977	4.5	4.0	②	11.8	2.12	11.8	8.5
1978-80	4.5	4.0	②	11.8	2.12	11.8	9.4③

① With heater
② 4-spd—3.7 5-spd—4.25
③ W/Auto trans.

CRANKSHAFT AND CONNECTING ROD SPECIFICATIONS

(All measurements are given in inches)

Engine Model	Main Brg. Journal Dia.	Crankshaft Main Brg. Oil Clearance	Shaft End-Play	Thrust on No.	Connecting Rod Bearings Journal Dia.	Oil Clearance	Side Clearance
L16	2.1631-2.1636	0.001-0.003	0.002-0.006	3	1.9670-1.9675	0.001-0.003	0.008-0.012
L18	2.1631-2.1636	0.001-0.002	0.002-0.007	3	1.9670-1.9675	0.001-0.002	0.008-0.012
L20B	2.333-2.360	0.0008-0.002	0.002-0.007	3	1.9660-1.9670	0.001-0.002	0.008-0.012

VALVE SPECIFICATIONS

Engine Model	Seat Angle (deg)	Valve Spring Pressure (lb. @ in.) Outer	Inner	Valve Spring Free Length (in.) Outer	Inner	Stem To Guide Clearance (in.) Intake	Exhaust	Valve Guide Removable
L16	45	105 @ 1.21 64 @ 1.53	56 @ .96 27 @ 1.38	2.05	1.77	0.001-0.002	0.002-0.003	Yes
L18	45	108 @ 1.16	56 @ .97	1.97	1.77	0.001-0.002	0.002-0.003	Yes

PISTON AND RING SPECIFICATIONS

(All measurements in inches)

Engine Model	Piston Clearance	Ring Gap Top Compression	Bottom Compression	Oil Control	Ring Side Clearance Top Compression	Bottom Compression	Oil Control
L16	0.001-0.002	0.009-0.015	0.006-0.012	0.006-0.012	0.002-0.003	0.001-0.003	0.001-0.003
L18	0.001-0.002	0.014-0.022	0.012-0.020	0.012-0.035	0.002-0.003	0.002-0.003	0.002-0.003
L20B	0.001-0.002	0.010-0.020	0.010-0.020	0.010-0.020	0.002-0.003	0.002-0.003	N.A.
L20B (1975)	0.001-0.002	0.010-0.016	0.012-0.020	0.012-0.022	0.002-0.003	0.001-0.003	N.A.

N.A. Not Applicable

TORQUE SPECIFICATIONS

(All readings in ft lbs)

Engine Model	Cylinder Head Bolts	Main Bearing Bolts	Rod Bearing Bolts	Crankshaft Pulley Bolt	Flywheel to Crankshaft Bolts
L16	40	33-40	20-24	116-130	69-76
L18	47-62	33-40	33-40	87-116	101-116
L20B	47-61	33-40	33-40	87-116	101-116

TORQUE SEQUENCES

Cylinder Head

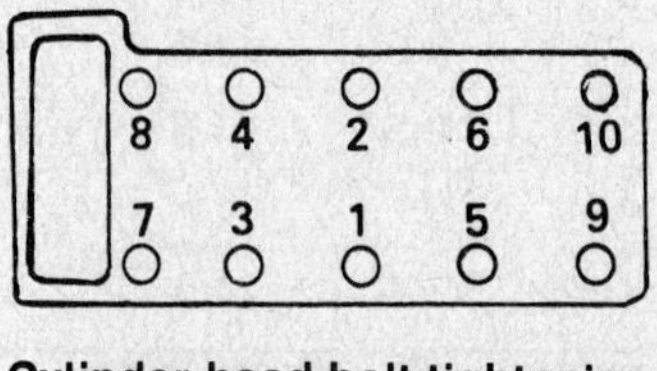

Cylinder head bolt tightening sequence

ALTERNATOR AND REGULATOR SPECIFICATIONS

Year	Alternator Identification Number	Rated Output @ 5000 RPM	Output @ 2500 RPM (not less than)	Brush Length	Brush Spring Tension	Regulated Voltage
1973-76	LT135-13B	35	28	0.571	8.99-12.17	14.3-15.3
	LT135-19B②	35	28	0.571	8.99-12.17	14.3-15.3
1977	LT135-36B	35	28	0.295	9.0-12.2	14.3-15.3
	LT138-01B②	38	30	0.295	9.0-12.2	14.3-15.3
1978-80	LR135-44①	35	27.5	0.295	8.99-12.17	14.4-15.0
	LR138-01①②	38	30	0.295	8.99-12.17	14.4-15.0

① Uses integral voltage regulator ② With air conditioning

BATTERY AND STARTER SPECIFICATIONS

(All trucks use 12 volt, negative ground electrical systems)

Year	Battery Amp Hour Capacity	STARTER Lock Test Amps	Lock Test Volts	Lock Test Torque (ft/lbs)	No Load Test Amps	No Load Test Volts	No Load Test RPM	Brush Spring Tension (oz)	Min. Brush Length (in.)
All	50,60	430 MT	6.0	6.3	60	12	7,000	49-64	0.7283
		340 AT	5.9	6.0	60	12	6,000	49-64	0.7283

MT Manual Transmission AT Automatic Transmission

BRAKE SPECIFICATIONS

(All measurements given are in inches unless noted)

Year	Lug Nut Torque (ft/lbs)	Master Cylinder Bore	Brake Disc Minimum Thickness	Brake Disc Maximum Run-out	Drum Diameter	Drum Max. Wear Limit	Minimum Lining Thickness Front	Minimum Lining Thickness Rear
1973-77	58-65	0.750	—	—	10.000①	10.060	0.039	0.039
1978-80	58-65	0.8125	0.413	0.0059	10.000	10.060	0.080	0.059

NOTE: Minimum lining thickness is as recommended by the manufacturer. Due to variation in state inspection regulations, the minimum allowable thickness may be different than recommended.

— Not Applicable ① Uses Front and Rear Brake Drums

WHEEL ALIGNMENT SPECIFICATIONS

Year	Caster Range (deg)	Caster Preferred Setting (deg)	Camber Range (deg)	Camber Preferred Setting (deg)	Toe-in (in.)	Steering Axis Inclination (deg)	Wheel Pivot Ratio (deg) Inner Wheel	Wheel Pivot Ratio (deg) Outer Wheel
1973-74	—	1°50′	—	1°15′	0.08-0.12	6°15′	36°	31°
1975-76	1°15′-2°15′	1°50′	0°15′-2°15′	1°15′	0.04-0.20	6°15′	35°-37°	30°32′
1977	—	1°50′	—	1°15′	0.079-0.118	6°15′	36°	31°
1978-80	35′-2°05′	—	15′-1°15′	—	0.20-0.28	—	34°-36°	29°30′-31°30′

— Not specified

TUNE-UP PROCEDURES

Spark Plugs

Number the spark plug wires and clean any foreign material from around the spark plugs prior to removing them. Use a spark plug socket with a rubber insert to remove the plugs. This will prevent cracking the procelain insulator. Each spark plug should be individually inspected and, if necessary, replaced. Refer to the Troubleshooting Section for an analysis of plug tip conditions. Clean reusable spark plugs and file the center electrode flat. Adjust the spark plug gap, according to the Tune-Up Specifications chart, with a wire type feeler gauge. Lightly oil the threads and torque the spark plugs to 11-15 ft lbs.

Breaker Points and Condenser

Either single points or dual points systems may be used. Dual points are serviced in the same manner as single points, with the exception of setting dwell, which is covered later.

1. Release the distributor cap clips and remove the cap.
2. Remove the distributor rotor by pulling straight up. Replace it if the contact tip is burned or corroded. Do not file the tip.
3. Inspect the points; if they are burned, worn, or corroded, replace them.
4. Use a magnetic screwdriver to remove the points hold-down screws. On distributors with the condenser mounted inside, the points screws also retain the condenser. Remove the points (and condenser, if inside). Loosen the screw in the side of the distributor to allow the points wire to slip out.
5. On dual points distributors and single points distributors with the condensers mounted outside the distributor, remove the condenser lead screw(s) and remove the condenser(s). On dual points models, note the locations of the condensers; they have different electrical capacities, and replacements must be installed in the same relationship.
6. Place a dap of grease on the distributor points cam and spread it around evenly. Do not use oil.
7. Install the new points and condenser(s). Tighten the condenser mounting screws, but leave the points screws slightly loose.
8. Check that the points meet squarely. The fixed point can be bent slightly if necessary.
9. Adjust the point gap. The rubbing block of the points must be on one of the high points of the distributor cam. The engine can be rotated with a wrench on the crankshaft pulley bolt (sparkplugs removed) or bumped around with the starter. Insert a flat feeler gauge of the correct thickness (see the specifications chart) between the points. Adjust the gap until the feeler gauge slides through with a slight drag.
10. Tighten the points hold down screws and recheck the adjustment. When the gap is correct, pull a matchbook cover or business card through (between) the points to clean them. Install the rotor and cap, and set the dwell and ignition timing.

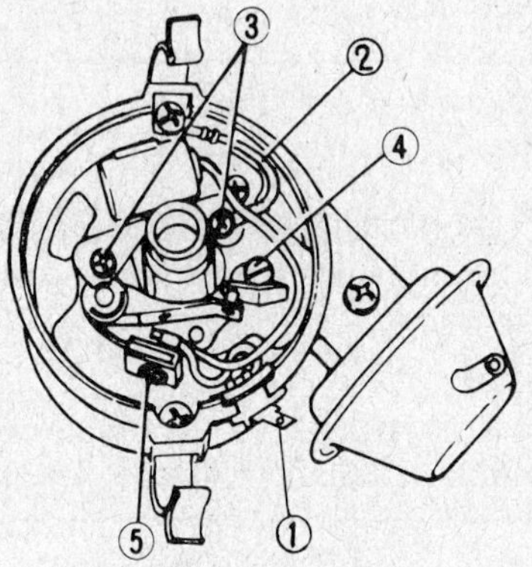

1. Primary lead terminal
2. Ground lead wire
3. Set screw
4. Adjuster
5. Screw

Point type ignition distributor component identification

Dwell Angle

1. Hook up a dwell meter according to the manufacturer's instructions. Zero the meter needle if necessary. Start the engine and read the dwell on the meter. If the dwell is correct, shut off the engine and remove the meter.
2. If the dwell requires adjustment, shut off the engine, remove the distributor cap, and adjust the point gap. Open the point gap to decrease dwell, close the gap to increase dwell.
3. Replace the cap and start the engine. Check the dwell, and repeat the process as necessary.

If the distributor has two sets of points, proceed as follows:

1. Unplug the distributor from the engine wiring harness.
2. Connect the two black wires with a jumper wire. This activates the advanced set of points.
3. Check and adjust the dwell of the advanced set of points.
4. Take one end of the jumper wire from the distributor side of the plug. Connect the black wire in the engine harness to the yellow wire from the distributor. This activates the retarded set of points.
5. Check and adjust the dwell of the retarded set of points.
6. Reconnect the plug.

Solid State Breakerless Ignition

AIR GAP

Through 1978

Reluctor air gap should be checked periodically. Standard air gap is 0.012-0.016 in. for both single and dual gap distributors. If the gap is incorrect, adjustment may be made by loosening the pick-up coil screws and inserting a feeler gauge.

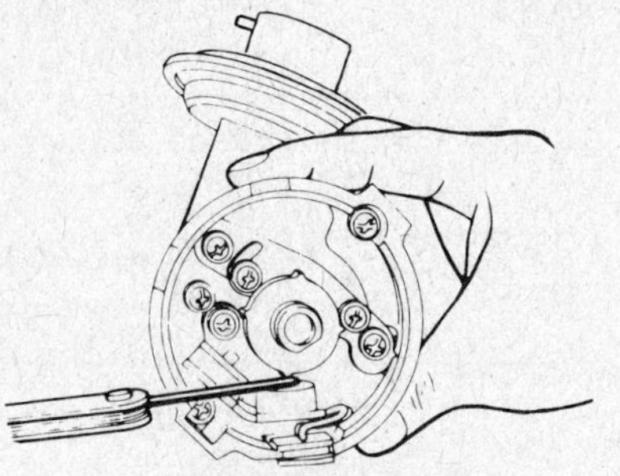

1. Reservoir cap
2. Strainer
3. Stopper ring
4. Stopper screw
5. Stopper
6. Primary piston
7. Spring
8. Secondary piston
9. Spring
10. Plug
11. Check valve

Measuring reluctor air gap in pointless ignition distributor

NOTE: The use of a non-magnetic feeler gauge such as plastic or brass, is recommended for accurate gapping.

Remove the rubber cap from the tip of the rotor shaft. Add grease if necessary. The reluctor cannot be removed. To remove the pick-up coil, take out the two pick-up coil assembly and core screws clamping the primary wire. Reverse the sequence to install.

1979–80

1979-80 models use a ring-type pick-up instead of the arm type used in earlier years. There is no provision for air gap adjustment.

Ignition Timing

Timing settings are given in the Tune-Up Specifications Chart.

1. Set the dwell to proper specification.
2. Locate the timing marks on the crankshaft pulley and the front of the engine.
3. Clean off the timing marks so that you can see them.
4. Use chalk or white paint to color the mark on the crankshaft pulley and the mark on the scale which will indicate the correct timing when aligned with the notch on the crankshaft pulley.

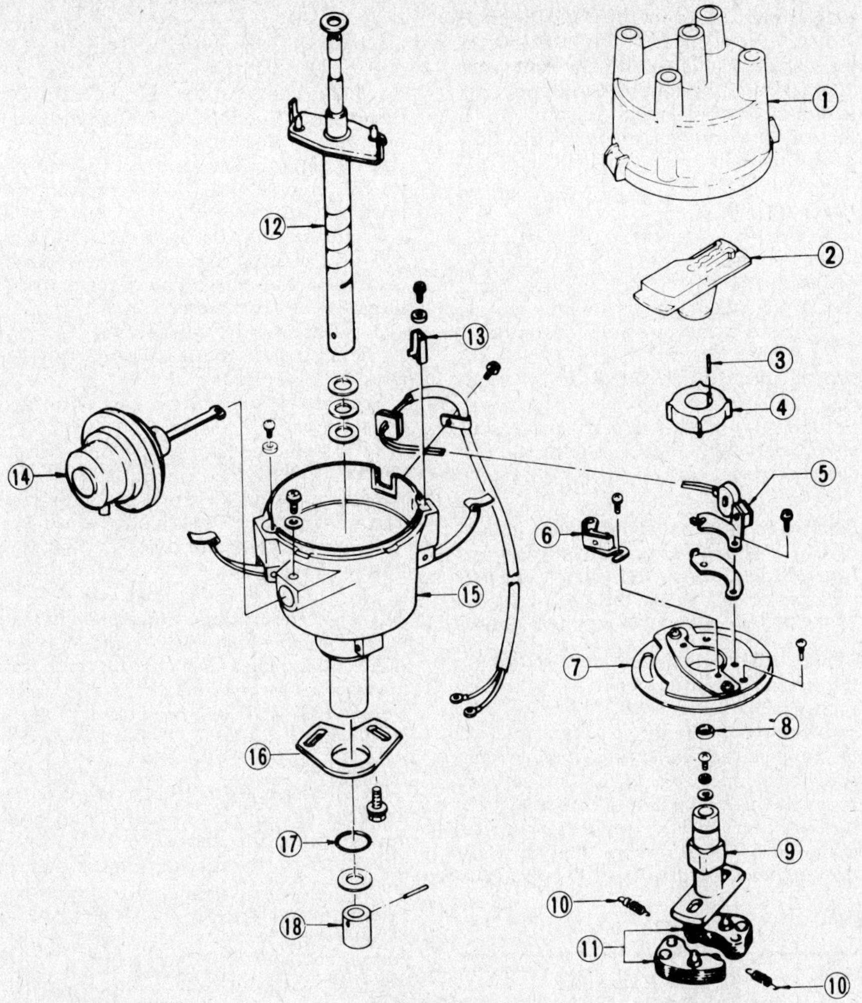

1. Cap assembly
2. Rotor head assembly
3. Roll pin
4. Reluctor
5. Pick-up coil
6. Contactor
7. Breaker plate assembly
8. Packing
9. Rotor shaft
10. Governor spring
11. Governor weight
12. Shaft assembly
13. Cap setter
14. Vacuum controller
15. Housing
16. Fixing plate
17. O-ring
18. Collar

Electronic ignition distributor

5. Attach a tachometer to the engine.
6. Attach a timing light to the engine, according to the manufacturer's instructions.
7. Leave the vacuum line connected to the distributor vacuum diaphragm.
8. Check to make sure that all of the wires clear the fan and then start the engine. Allow the engine to reach normal operating temperature.
9. Adjust the idle to the correct setting.
10. Aim the timing light at the timing marks. If the marks that you put on the pulley and the engine are aligned when the light flashes, the timing is correct. Turn off the engine and remove the tachometer and the timing light. If the marks are not in alignment, proceed with the following steps.
11. Turn off the engine.
12. Loosen the distributor lockbolt just enough so that the distributor can be turned with a little effort.
13. Start the engine. Keep the wires of the timing light clear of the fan.
14. With the timing light aimed at the pulley and the marks on the engine, turn the distributor in the direction of rotor rotation to retard the spark, and in the opposite direction of rotor rotation to advance the spark. Align the marks on the pulley and the engine with the flashes of the timing light. Tighten the hold-down bolt.

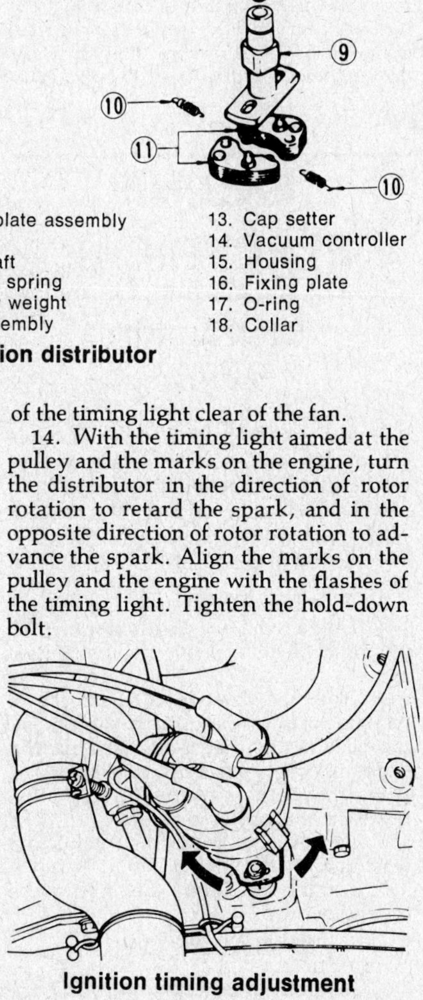

Ignition timing adjustment

***NOTE:** See the "Emission Controls" section for adjustment of phase difference on dual point models.*

Valve Lash

1. The valves are adjusted with the engine at normal operating temperature. Run the engine for at least fifteen minutes to ensure that all the parts have reached their full expansion. After the engine is warmed up, shut it off.
2. Remove the bolts which hold the cam cover in place and remove the cam cover.
3. Place a wrench on the crankshaft pulley bolt and turn the engine over until the valves for No. 1 cylinder are closed. When both cam lobes are pointing up, the valves are closed.
4. Check the clearance of the intake and exhaust valves. You can differentiate between them by lining them up with the tubes of the intake and exhaust manifolds. The correct size feeler gauge should pass between the base circle of the cam and the rocker arm with just a slight drag. Be sure the feeler gauge is inserted *straight* and not on an angle.
5. If the valves need adjustment, loosen the locking nut and then adjust the clearance with the adjusting screw. After you have the correct clearance, tighten the locking nut and recheck the clearance.
6. Repeat this procedure until you have checked and/or adjusted all the valves.
7. Install the cam cover gasket, the cam cover, and any wires and hoses which were removed.

Engine valve arrangement

Carburetor

This section contains only tune-up adjustment procedures for carburetors. Descriptions, adjustments, and overhaul procedures for carburetors can be found in the "Fuel System" section.

When the engine is running, the air-fuel mixture from the carburetor is being drawn into the engine by a partial vacuum which is created by the movement of the pistons downward on the intake stroke. The amount of air-fuel mixture that enters into the engine is controlled by the throttle plates in the bottom of the carburetor. When the engine is not running the throttle plates are closed, completely blocking off the bottom of the carburetor from the inside of the engine. The throttle plates are connected by the throttle linkage to the accelerator pedal in the passenger compartment. When you depress the pedal, you open the throttle plates in the carburetor to admit more air-fuel mixture to the engine.

When the engine is not running, the throttle plates are closed. When the engine is idling, it is necessary to have the throttle plates open slightly. To prevent having to hold your foot on the pedal when the engine is idling, an idle speed adjusting screw is added to the carburetor linkage.

The idle adjusting screw contacts a lever (throttle lever) on the outside of the carburetor. When the screw is turned, it either opens or closes the throttle plates of the carburetor, raising or lowering the idle speed of the engine. This screw is called the curb idle adjusting screw.

A special mixture circuit is incorporated into the carburetor to enable the engine to run smoothly at idle. This circuit is controlled by the mixture screw, which determines the amount of fuel admitted at idle.

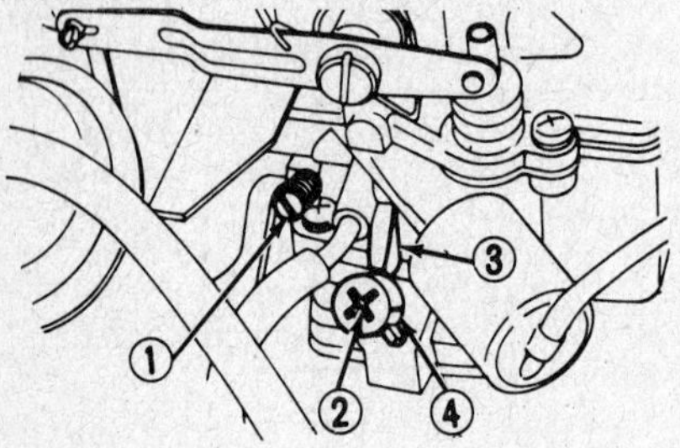

1. Throttle adjusting screw
2. Idle adjusting screw
3. Stopper
4. Idle limiter cap

Carburetor idle adjustment screw

IDLE SPEED AND MIXTURE ADJUSTMENT

1. Start the engine and run it until it reaches operating temperature.
2. Allow the engine idle speed to stabilize by running the engine at idle for at least one minute.
3. If it hasn't already been done, check and adjust the ignition timing to the proper setting.
4. Turn off the engine and connect a tachometer to the engine.
5. Disconnect and plug the air hose between the three way connector and the check valve, if equipped. Start the engine. With the transmission in Neutral, check the idle speed on the tachometer. If the reading on the tachometer is correct, continue on to Step 6. If it is not correct, turn the idle adjusting screw clockwise with a screwdriver to increase the idle speed and counterclockwise to decrease it.
6. With an automatic transmission in Drive (wheels chocked and parking brake applied) or a manual transmission in Neutral, turn the mixture screw out until the engine rpm starts to drop due to an overly rich mixture.
7. Turn the screw in past the starting point until the engine rpm start to drop because of a too lean mixture. On 1975–77 models, turn the mixture screw in until the idle speed drops 60–70 rpm with manual transmission, or 15–25 rpm with automatic transmission (in Drive). On 1978 models, the rpm drop should be 45–55 rpm for all trucks. For 1979–80 the rpm drop should be 45–55 rpm with manual transmission, or 25–35 rpm with automatic transmission (in Drive). If the mixture limiter cap will not allow this adjustment, remove it, make the adjustment, and reinstall it. Go on to Step 10 for 1975–80 trucks.
8. On 1973–74 models, turn the mixture screw back out to the point midway between the two extreme positions where the engine began losing rpm to achieve the fastest and smoothest idle.
9. Adjust the curb idle speed to the proper specification, on 1973–74 models.
10. Install the air hose. If the engine speed increases, reduce it with the idle speed screw.

NOTE: To be sure that the vehicle is complying with emission laws, have the exhaust checked with a "CO" meter. The percentages of CO should be 1.5% 1973–74, 2% 1975–77, and 1% 1978–80 at idle speed.

NOTE: Idle limiter caps are installed on the mixture adjusting screws so that an incorrect adjustments cannot be made. If a satisfactory idle cannot be obtained within the range of the limiter caps, remove them and make the adjustment as outlined above. Reinstall the limiter caps so that the cap can be turned only 1/8 of a turn counterclockwise before it reaches the stop. Have the engine checked with a CO meter after making the adjustment.

ENGINE ELECTRICAL

Distributor

REMOVAL

1. Remove the high-tension wires from the distributor cap terminal towers, noting their positions to assure correct reassembly. Number the wires with pieces of adhesive tape if they are not already numbered.
2. Disconnect the distributor wiring harness.
3. Disconnect the vacuum line(s).
4. Unlatch the two distributor cap retaining clips and remove the distributor cap.
5. Note the position of the rotor in relation to the base. Scribe a mark on the base of the distributor and on the engine block to facilitate reinstallation. Align the marks with the direction the metal tip of the rotor is pointing.
6. Remove the bolt which holds the distributor to the engine.
7. Lift the distributor assembly from the engine.

INSTALLATION

1. Insert the distributor shaft and assembly into the engine. Line up the mark on the distributor and the one on the engine with the metal tip of the rotor. Make sure that the vacuum advance diaphragm is pointed in the same direction as it was pointed originally. This will be done automatically if the marks on the engine and the distributor are lined up with the rotor.
2. Install the distributor hold-down bolt and clamp. Leave the screw loose enough so that you can move the distributor with heavy hand pressure.
3. Connect the distributor wiring harness. Install the distributor cap on the distributor housing.

   Secure the distributor cap with the spring clips.
4. Install the spark plug wires. Make sure that the wires are pressed all the way into the top of the distributor cap and firmly onto the spark plug.
5. Adjust the point dwell and set the ignition timing.

NOTE: If the crankshaft has been turned or the engine disturbed in any manner (i.e., disassembled and rebuilt) while the distributor was removed, or if the marks were not drawn, it will be necessary to initially time the engine. Follow the procedure given below.

1. It is necessary to place the No. 1 cylinder in the firing position to correctly install the distributor. To locate this position, the ignition timing marks on the crankshaft front pulley are used.
2. Remove the No. 1 cylinder spark plug. Turn the crankshaft until the piston in the No. 1 cylinder is moving up on the compression stroke. This can be determined by placing your thumb over the spark plug hole and feeling the air being forced out of the cylinder. Stop turning the crankshaft when the timing marks that are used to time the engine are aligned.
3. Oil the distributor housing lightly where the distributor bears on the cylinder block.
4. Install the distributor so that the rotor points toward the No. 1 spark plug terminal tower position.
5. When the distributor shaft has reached the bottom of the hole, move the rotor back and forth slightly until the driving lug on the end of the shaft enters the slots cut in the end of the oil pump shaft and the distributor assembly slides down into place.
6. When the distributor is correctly installed, the breaker points should be in such a position that they are just ready to break contact with each other. This is accomplished by rotating the distributor body after it has been installed in the engine. Once again, line up the marks that you made before the distributor was removed from the engine.
7. Install the distributor hold-down bolt.
8. Install the spark plug into the No. 1 spark plug hole and continue from Step 3 of the distributor installation procedure.

Alternator

Datsun pick-ups are equipped with 35 amp alternators with electromechanical, adjustable voltage regulators through 1976. 1977 models are the same, except that trucks with factory air conditioning have 38 amp alternators. 1978–80 models use 35 amp alternators (38 amp with A/C), but have a transistorized, non-adjustable regulator integral with the alternator.

ALTERNATOR PRECAUTIONS

To prevent damage to the alternator and regulator, the following precautionary measures must be taken when working with the electrical system.

1. Never reverse battery connections. Always check the battery polarity visually. This is to be done before any connections are made to be sure that all of the connections correspond to the battery ground polarity of the truck.
2. Booster batteries for starting must be connected properly. Make sure that the positive cable of the booster battery is connected to the positive terminal of the battery which is getting the boost.
3. Disconnect the battery cables before using a fast charger; the charger has a tendency to force current through the diodes in the opposite direction for which they were designed. This burns out the diodes.
4. Never use a fast charger as a booster for starting the vehicle.
5. Never disconnect the voltage regulator while the engine is running.
6. Do not ground the alternator output terminal.
7. Do not operate the alternator on an open circuit with the field energized.
8. Do not attempt to polarize an alternator.
9. Disconnect the battery cables before using an electric arc welder on the truck.

REMOVAL AND INSTALLATION

1. Disconnect the negative battery terminal.
2. Disconnect the two lead wires and connector from the alternator.
3. Loosen the drive belt adjusting bolt and remove the belt.
4. Unscrew the alternator attaching bolts and remove the alternator from the vehicle.
5. Install the alternator in the reverse order of removal.

Regulator

REMOVAL AND INSTALLATION

1973–77

1. Disconnect the negative battery terminal.
2. Disconnect the electrical lead connector of the regulator.
3. Remove the two mounting screws and remove the regulator from the vehicle.

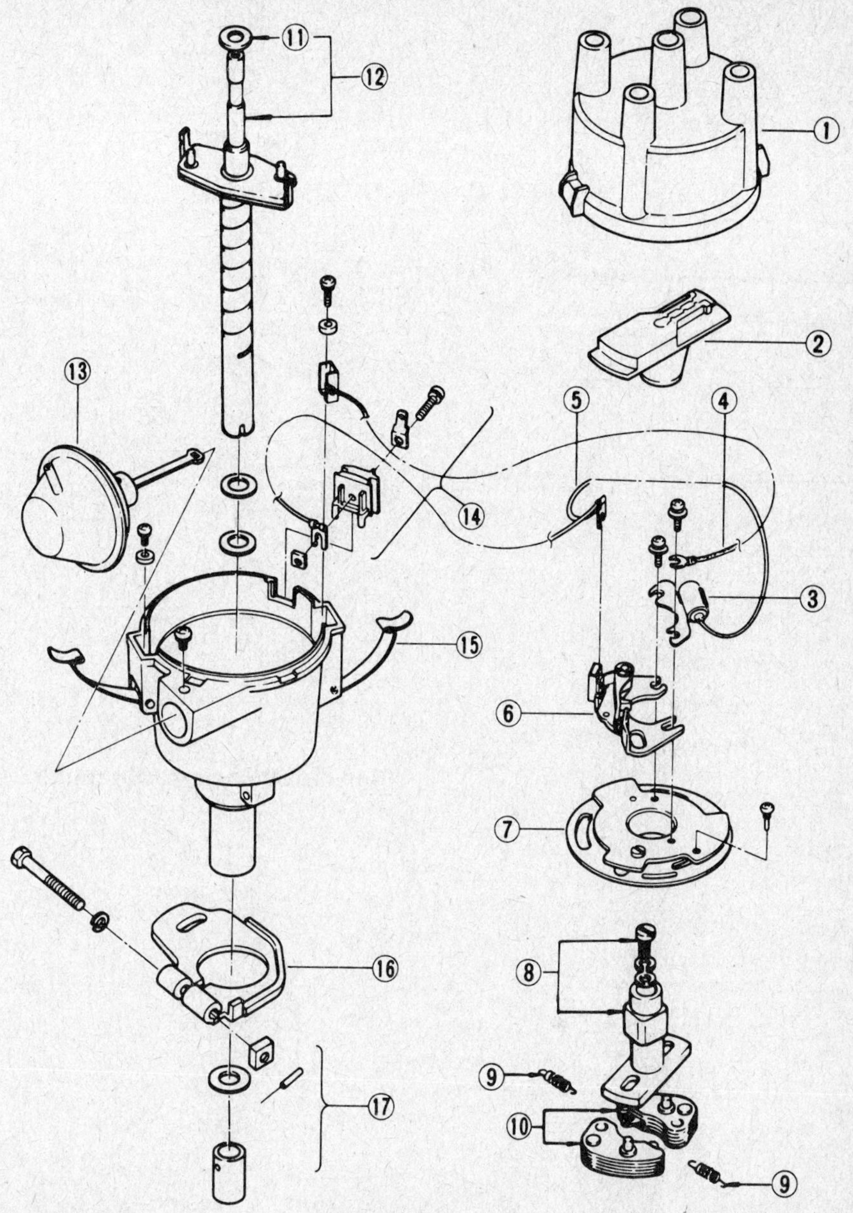

1. Cap assembly
2. Rotor head assembly
3. Condenser assembly
4. Ground wire assembly
5. Lead wire assembly
6. Contact set
7. Breaker plate assembly
8. Cam assembly
9. Governor spring
10. Governor weight
11. Thrust washer
12. Shaft assembly
13. Vacuum control assembly
14. Terminal assembly
15. Clamp
16. Fixing plate
17. Collar set

Point type ignition distributor

4. Install the regulator in the reverse order of removal.

1978–80

The transistorized regulator is soldered to the brush assembly inside the alternator. It is non-adjustable, and must be replaced together with the brush assembly if faulty.

1. Remove the alternator.
2. Remove the through bolts and separate the front cover from the stator housing.
3. Unsolder the wire connecting the diode plate to the brush at the brush terminal.
4. Remove the bolt retaining the diode plate to the rear cover.
5. Remove the nut securing the battery terminal bolt.
6. Lift the stator slightly, together with the diode plate, to gain access to the diode plate screw. Remove the screw.
7. Separate the stator and diode, and remove the brush and regulator assembly.
8. Assembly is the reverse. Apply soldering head sparingly, carrying out the operation as quickly as possible, to avoid head damage to the transistors and diodes. Before assembling the alter-

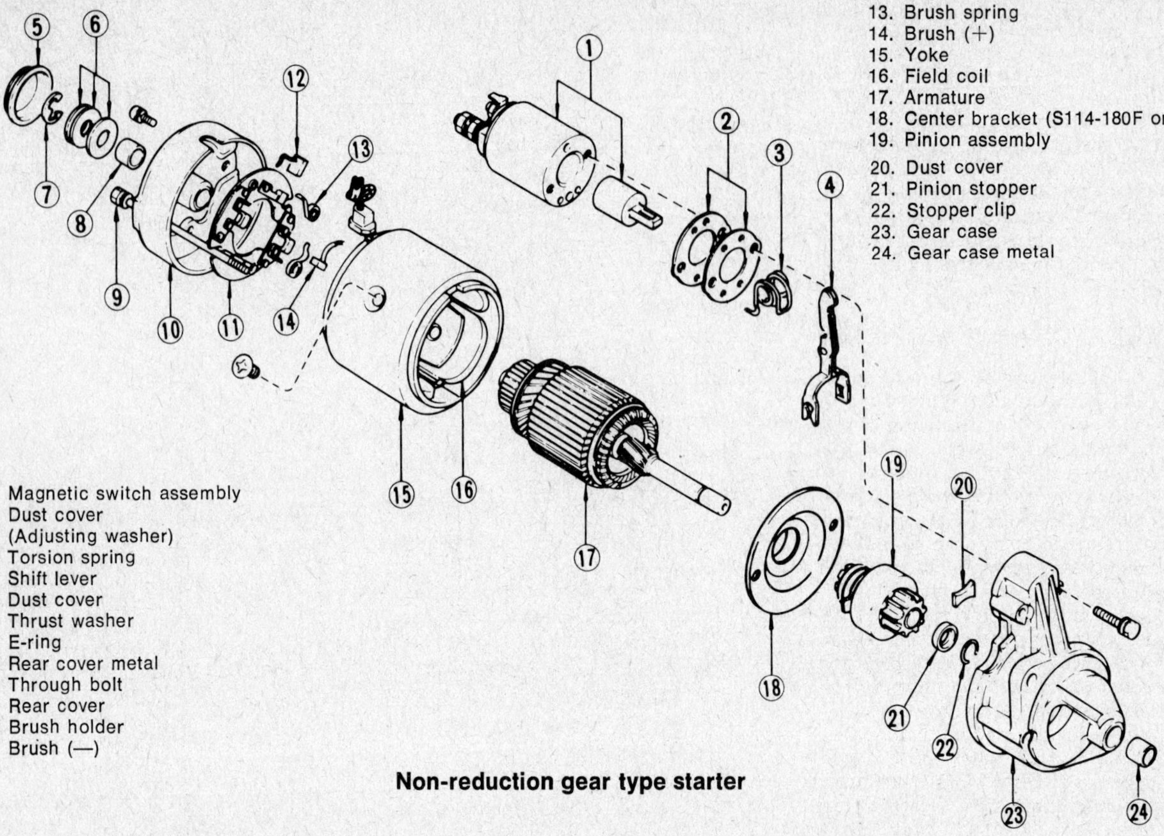

13. Brush spring
14. Brush (+)
15. Yoke
16. Field coil
17. Armature
18. Center bracket (S114-180F only)
19. Pinion assembly
20. Dust cover
21. Pinion stopper
22. Stopper clip
23. Gear case
24. Gear case metal

1. Magnetic switch assembly
2. Dust cover (Adjusting washer)
3. Torsion spring
4. Shift lever
5. Dust cover
6. Thrust washer
7. E-ring
8. Rear cover metal
9. Through bolt
10. Rear cover
11. Brush holder
12. Brush (—)

Non-reduction gear type starter

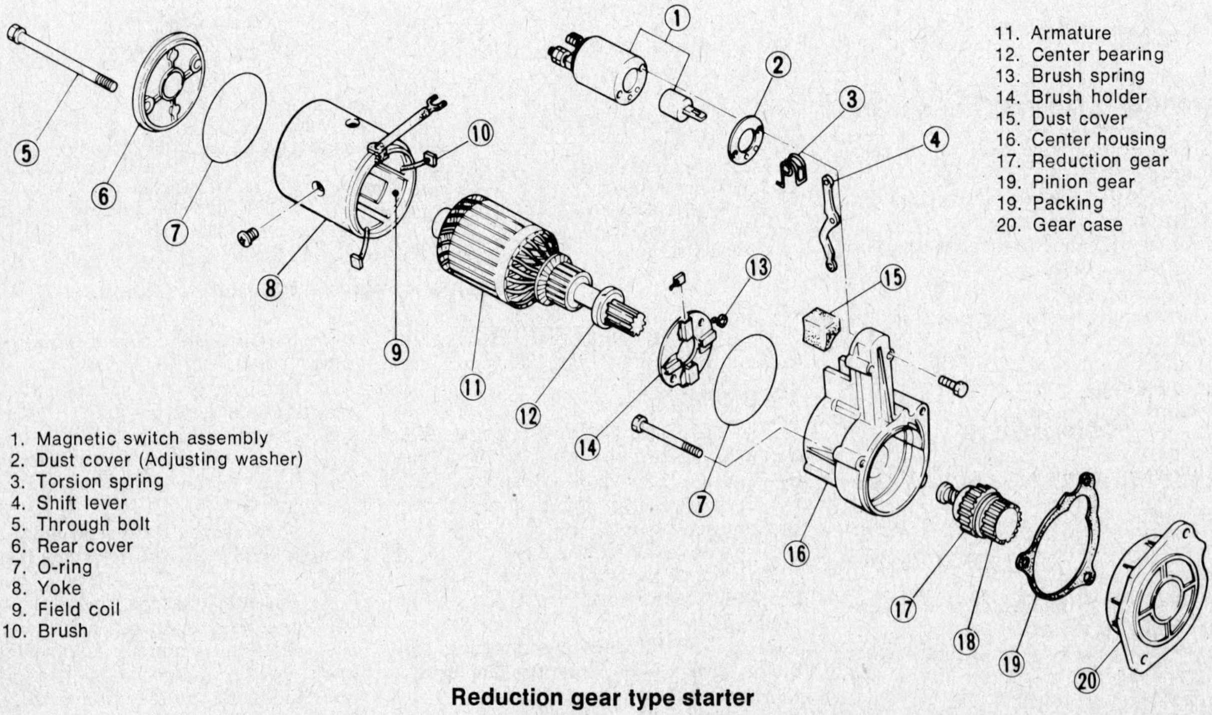

11. Armature
12. Center bearing
13. Brush spring
14. Brush holder
15. Dust cover
16. Center housing
17. Reduction gear
19. Pinion gear
19. Packing
20. Gear case

1. Magnetic switch assembly
2. Dust cover (Adjusting washer)
3. Torsion spring
4. Shift lever
5. Through bolt
6. Rear cover
7. O-ring
8. Yoke
9. Field coil
10. Brush

Reduction gear type starter

nator halves, bend a piece of wire in an "L" and slip it through the rear cover next to the brushes. Use the wire to hold the brushes in a retracted position until the case halves are assembled. Remove the wire carefully, to prevent damage to the slip rings.

ADJUSTMENT

1973–77

1. Adjust the voltage regulator core gap by loosening the screw which is used to secure the contact set on the yoke, and move the contact up or down as necessary. Retighten the screw. The gap should be 0.024–0.039 in.
2. Adjust the point gap of the voltage regulator coil by loosening the screw used to secure the upper contact and move the upper contact up or down. The gap should be 0.012–0.016 in. through 1975, 0.014–0.018 1976–77.
3. The core gap and point gap on the charge relay coil is or are adjusted in the same manner as previously outlined for the voltage regulator coil. The core gap is to be set as 0.032–0.039 in. and the point gap adjusted to 0.016–0.024 in.
4. The regulated voltage is adjusted by loosening the locknut and turning the adjusting screw clockwise to increase, or counterclockwise to decrease the regulated voltage. The voltage should be between 14.3–15.3 volts at 68° F.

Starter

A standard non-reduction gear starting motor is used on all models through 1977, and most 1978–80 models. This motor has its brushes located within the rear cover. A reduction gear starting motor is installed in all 1978–80 Canadian models, and is optional for U.S. trucks in 1979–80. The reduction gear motor brushes are on a plate located just behind the starter drive housing.

REMOVAL AND INSTALLATION

1. Disconnect the negative battery cable from the battery.
2. Disconnect the starter wiring at the starter, taking note of the positions for correct reinstallation.
3. Remove the bolts attaching the starter to the engine and remove the starter from the vehicle.
4. Install the starter in the reverse order of removal.

BRUSH REPLACEMENT

Non-Reduction Gear Type

1. With the starter out of the vehicle, remove the bolts holding the solenoid to the top of the starter and remove the solenoid.
2. To remove the brushes, remove the two thru-bolts, and the two rear cover attaching screws and remove the rear cover.
3. Disconnect the electrical leads and remove the brushes.
4. Install the brushes in the reverse order of removal.

Reduction Gear Type

1. Remove the starter. Remove the solenoid.
2. Remove the through bolts and the rear cover. The rear cover can be pried off with a screwdriver, but be careful not to damage the O-ring.
3. Remove the starter housing, armature, and brush holder from the center housing. They can be removed as an assembly.
4. Remove the positive side brush from its holder. The positive brush is insulated from the brush holder, and its lead wire is connected to the field coil.
5. Carefully lift the negative brush from the commutator and remove it from the holder.
6. Installation is the reverse.

STARTER DRIVE REPLACEMENT

Non-Reduction Gear Type

1. With the starter motor removed from the vehicle, remove the solenoid from the starter.
2. Remove the two thru-bolts and separate the gear case from the yoke housing.
3. Remove the pinion stopper clip and the pinion stopper.
4. Slide the starter drive off the armature shaft.
5. Install the starter drive and reassemble the starter in the reverse order of removal.

Reduction Gear Type

1. Remove the starter.
2. Remove the solenoid and the shift lever.
3. Remove the bolts securing the center housing to the front cover and separate the parts.
4. Remove the gears and starter drive.
5. Installation is the reverse.

Battery

REMOVAL AND INSTALLATION

1. Disconnect the negative (ground) cable from the terminal, and then the positive cable.

NOTE: To avoid sparks, always disconnect the ground cable first, and connect it last.

2. Remove the battery hold-down clamp.
3. Remove the battery, being careful not to spill the acid.

NOTE: Spilled acid can be neutralized with a baking soda/water solution. If you somehow get acid into your eyes, flush it out with lots of water and get to a doctor.

4. Clean the battery posts thoroughly before reinstalling, or when installing a new battery.
5. Clean the clamps, using a wire brush, both inside and out.
6. Install the battery and the hold-down clamp or strap. Connect the positive, and then the negative cable. Do not hammer them in place. The terminals should be coated lightly (externally) with grease to prevent corrosion. There are also felt washers impregnated with an anti-corrosion substance which are slipped over the battery posts before installing the cables; these are available in auto parts stores.

CAUTION: Make absolutely sure that the battery is connected properly before you turn on the ignition switch. Reversed polarity can burn out your alternator and regulator within a matter of seconds.

ENGINE MECHANICAL

Design

The engine used in the Datsun pickup is a water-cooled, 4 cycle, 4 cylinder, overhead camshaft gasoline engine.

The cylinder head is cast aluminum alloy with wedge-type combustion chambers.

The valve system consists of a chain-driven overhead camshaft working directly on the rocker arms which operate valves with dual valve springs.

The crankshaft is fully balanced and is supported by five main bearings.

The intake and exhaust manifolds are mounted on the same side of the engine. The intake manifold is of cast aluminum upon which is mounted a single, two barrel, downdraft carburetor.

Engine Removal and Installation

It is much easier to remove the engine and the transmission together as an assembly than to remove only the engine from the engine compartment. After the engine and transmission are removed from the vehicle, the two can be separated.

1. Disconnect the battery ground cable. Remove the battery.
2. Mark the location of the hood hinges on the body in order to facilitate installation, and remove the hood.
3. Remove the air cleaner after disconnecting the PCV hose from the rocker cover.
4. Drain the radiator of coolant and the engine crankcase of oil.
5. Disconnect the upper and lower radiator hoses from the engine. Disconnect and plug the automatic transmis-

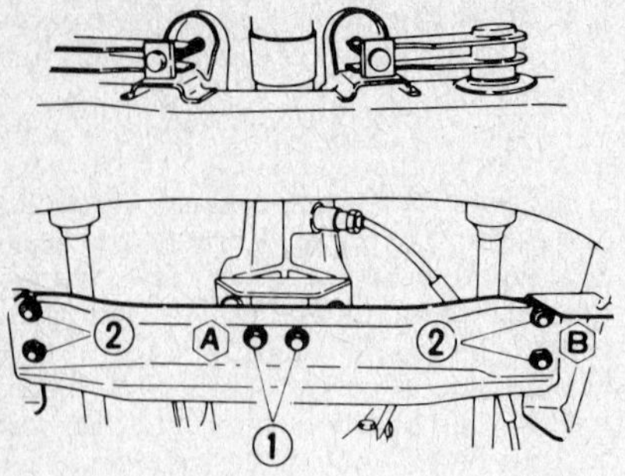

Tightening torque:
A. 1.6 to 2.2 kg-m (12 to 16 ft-lb)
B. 3.2 to 4.3 kg-m (23 to 31 ft-lb)

Engine rear mount

sion cooler lines at the radiator, if so equipped. Use a flare nut wrench if one is available.

6. Remove the four bolts securing the radiator and remove the radiator from the vehicle.

7. Disconnect the engine ground cable at the cylinder head.

8. Disconnect the electrical leads at the starter, alternator, distributor, the high-tension ignition coil cable, and the oil pressure and temperature sending units wires.

9. Disconnect the fuel line at the fuel pump (or filter on electric pump models), the heater hose at the engine side, and the choke wire and accelerator cable at the carburetor. Disconnect the emission hoses or wires to the carbon canister, air pump, B.C.D.D. solenoid, and fuel cut solenoid; the vacuum hose to the brake booster (on models so equipped), and any other wires or hoses running to the engine. Tag all wires as they are disconnected for assembly.

10. Remove the transmission control linkage from the transmission; in the case of an automatic transmission, remove the cross-shaft assembly from the transmission. Remove the selector rod from the selector lever on the automatic transmission. On manual transmissions, lift the rubber boot and remove the nut or c-clip from the shift lever and detach the shift lever from the transmission.

11. Remove the two bolts securing the clutch slave cylinder. Disconnect the clutch slave cylinder and the flexible tubing as an assembly.

12. Disconnect the speedometer cable and the back-up light wiring (and neutral switch, if equipped) from the rear section of the transmission.

13. Disconnect the exhaust pipe from the exhaust manifold.

14. Disconnect the driveshaft center bearing bracket from the third crossmember of the frame. Disconnect the driveshaft at the differential housing. Remove the driveshaft assembly from the vehicle and plug the rear end of the transmission extension housing to prevent loss of transmission lubricant.

15. Attach a suitable lifting device to the engine and lift the engine slightly.

16. Remove the front engine mount bolts on both sides of the engine.

17. Place a jack under the transmission and lift it slightly.

18. Loosen the two combination engine rear mounting/transmission mounting bolts. On models with a catalytic converter, loosen the two exhaust pipe hanger bolts.

19. Remove the four bolts (two on each side) securing the engine rear mounting/transmission support side member and detach the support from the frame.

20. On 1976 and later models, remove the bolts securing the idler arm to the frame, and push down the tie-rod.

21. Pull the engine toward the front as far as possible and carefully raise the engine with the transmission up and out of the vehicle.

22. Install the engine in the reverse order of removal, taking note of the following:

Do not connect any parts to the engine or transmission until the engine and transmission are in place on the engine/transmission mounts and secured by the mounting bolts. Secure the rear support first and then the front engine mounts, using the upper bolt hole as a guide.

Cylinder Head

REMOVAL AND INSTALLATION

1. Crank the engine until the No. 1 piston is at TDC of the compression stroke and disconnect the negative battery cable, drain the cooling system, and remove the air cleaner and attending hoses.

2. Remove the alternator.

3. If equipped with air conditioning, unbolt the compressor and move it aside onto the fender. Do not detach any of the compressor lines the escaping refrigerant will freeze any surface it contacts, including your skin.

4. Disconnect the carburetor throttle linkage, the fuel line and any other vacuum lines or electrical leads, and remove the carburetor.

5. Disconnect the exhaust pipe from the exhaust manifold.

6. Remove the fan and fan pulley.

7. Remove the spark plugs to protect them from damage. Lay the spark plugs aside and out of the way.

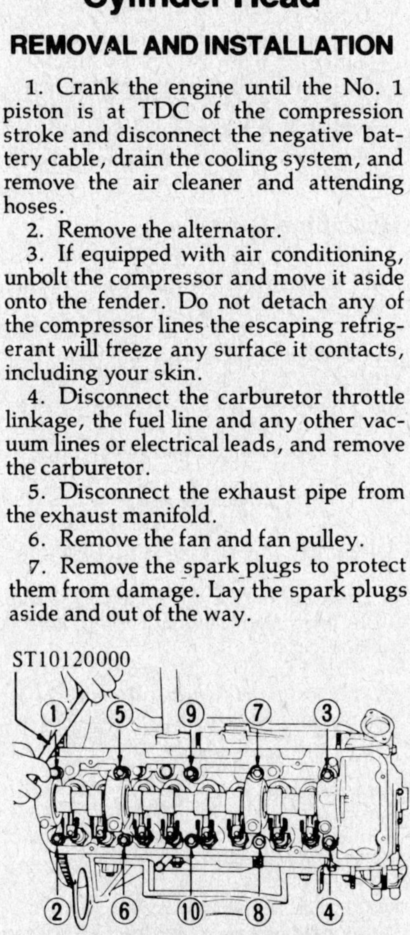

Cylinder head mount bolt loosening sequence

8. Remove the rocker cover.

9. Remove the water pump.

10. Remove the fuel pump from the head, on models without the electric pump.

11. Remove the fuel pump drive cam.

12. Mark the relationship of the camshaft sprocket to the timing chain with paint or chalk. If this is done, it will not be necessary to locate the factory timing marks. Before removing the camshaft sprocket, it will be necessary to wedge the chain in place so that it will not fall down into the front cover. The factory procedure is to wedge the timing chain in place with the wooden wedge shown here. The problem with this is that it may allow the chain tensioner to move out far enough to cock itself against the chain. If this happens, you'll find that the chain won't go back over the sprocket after you've put the sprocket back on. In this case, you'll have to remove the front cover and push the tensioner back.

After installing the wedge, unbolt and remove the camshaft sprocket.

13. Loosen and remove the cylinder head bolts. You will need a 10 mm Allen wrench to remove the head bolts. Keep the bolts in order, because they are different sizes. Lift the cylinder head assembly from the engine. Remove the intake and exhaust manifolds as necessary.

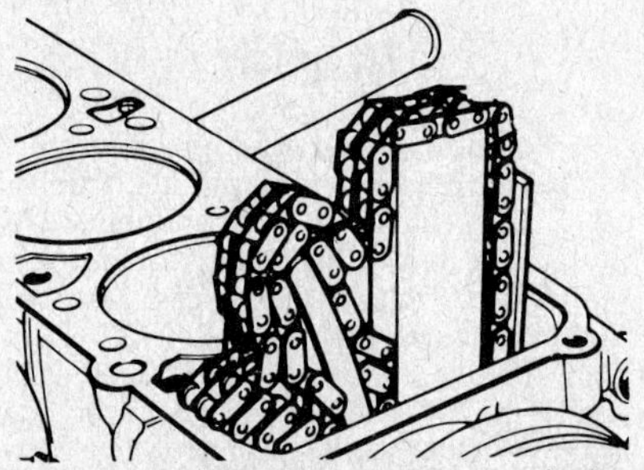

Use a wedge to prevent timing chain from slipping off crankshaft sprocket

14. Thoroughly clean the cylinder block and head mating surfaces. Check the block and head for flatness before installing the head. Install a new cylinder head gasket. Do not use sealer on the cylinder head gasket.

15. With the crankshaft turned so that the No. 1 piston is at TDC of the compression stroke (if not already done so as mentioned in Step 1), make sure that the camshaft sprocket timing mark and the oblong groove in the camshaft retaining plate are aligned.

16. Place the cylinder head in position on the cylinder block, being careful not to allow any of the valves to come in contact with any of the pistons. Do not rotate the crankshaft or camshaft separately because of possible damage which might occur to the valves.

17. Temporarily tighten the two center right and left cylinder head bolts to 14.5 ft lbs.

18. Install the camshaft sprocket to-

gether with the timing chain to the camshaft. Make sure that the marks you made earlier line up. If the chain will not stretch over the sprocket, the problem lies in the tensioner. See "Timing Chain Removal and Installation" for timing procedure, if necessary.

19. Install the cylinder head bolts. Note that there are two sizes of bolts used; the longer bolts are installed on the driver side of the engine with a smaller bolt in the center position. The remaining small bolts are installed on the opposite side of the cylinder head.

20. Tighten the cylinder head bolts in three stages: first to 29 ft lbs, second to 43 ft lbs, and lastly to 47–62 ft lbs.

Tighten the cylinder head bolts in the proper sequence.

21. Install and assemble the remaining components of the engine in the reverse order of removal.

Valve Guide

REMOVAL AND INSTALLATION

1. With the cylinder head removed from the engine, and the valves removed from the head, use a drift and a hammer or press. Drive the valve guides out from the combustion chamber side toward the rocker cover side. A heated cylinder head will facilitate the operation.

2. Ream the cylinder head side guide hole at room temperature. The guide hole should be 0.4719–0.4723 in. for standard valves and 0.4797–0.4802 in. for 0.0079 in. oversize valves which are available for service.

3. After heating the cylinder head to 302–392° F, press the new valve guide carefully into the cylinder head. The top of the valve guide should protrude out the top of the guide hole 0.4173 in.

4. Ream the bore of the valve guide with the valve guide pressed into the cylinder head. The standard valve guide bore size is 0.3150–0.3157 in.

5. Assemble the cylinder head and install it on the engine in the reverse order of removal.

Valve Seat

REMOVAL AND INSTALLATION

1. With the cylinder head removed from the engine and the valves removed from the cylinder head, old valve seat inserts can be removed by boring them out until they collapse. Be careful that the boring doesn't continue beyond the bottom face of the insert recess in the cylinder head.

2. Select the suitable valve seat insert and check its outside diameter.

3. Machine the cylinder head recess using the center of the valve guide as the center of the valve seat insert so that the insert will have the correct fit.

4. Ream the cylinder head recess at room temperature.

5. Heat the cylinder head to 302–392° F.

6. Fit the insert, making sure that it seats fully in the recess in the cylinder head. Peen the insert with a punch in at least four places equally spaced around its circumference.

7. Grind the valve seats to the proper angle.

8. Lap the valves with lapping compound to each seat to which they are to be mated. Thoroughly clean both the valve and the seat of all lapping compound before installing the valves.

Valve Rockers and Rocker Pivots

REMOVAL AND INSTALLATION

1. Loosen the rocker pivot locknut, lower the pivot by screwing it down into the cylinder head, and remove the rocker arm by pressing down on the valve spring.

2. To remove the rocker pivots, loosen the locknut, then unscrew the pivot from the cylinder head.

3. Install the pivots and rockers and assemble the engine in the reverse order of removal.

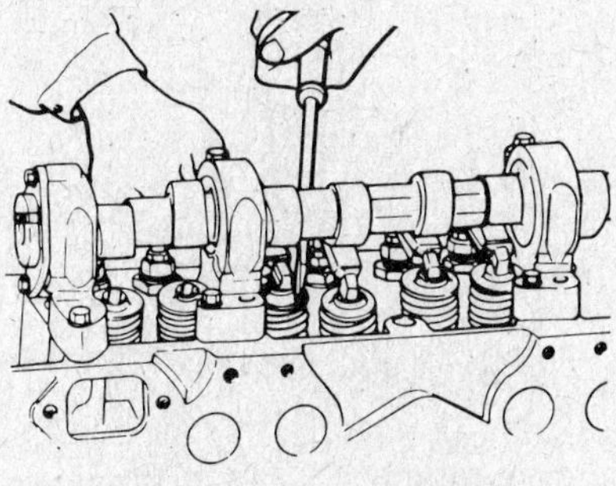

Rocker arm removal

Intake Manifold

REMOVAL AND INSTALLATION

NOTE: It is important to replace the gasket whenever the intake manifold is removed. Because the intake and exhaust manifolds share a common gasket, when ever the intake manifold is removed, the exhaust manifold must also be removed, so that the gasket can be replaced.

1. Remove the air cleaner assembly together with all of the attending hoses. Remove the EGR tube on 1974 and later models.

2. Disconnect the throttle linkage, fuel, and vacuum lines from the carburetor. Label all wires and hoses as they are removed to simplify installation.

3. The carburetor can be removed from the manifold at this point or can be removed as an assembly with the intake manifold.

4. Loosen the intake manifold attaching nuts, working from the two ends toward the center, and then remove them.

5. Remove the intake manifold from the engine.

6. Install the intake manifold in the reverse order of removal. Always use a new gasket when installing the manifold

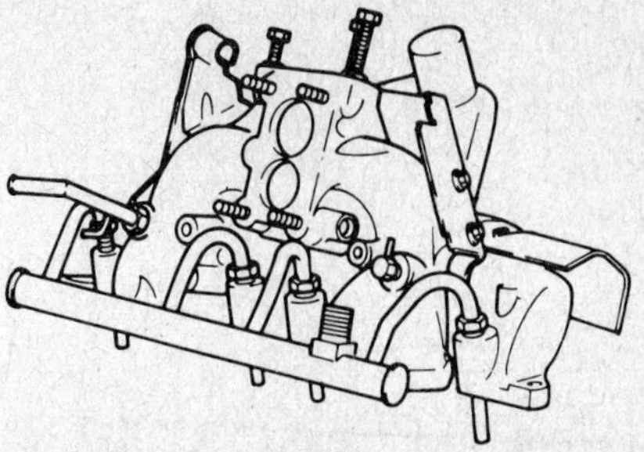

Intake and exhaust manifolds

air leaks will cause burnt valves. Tighten the manifold bolts from the center outwards, in two progressive steps, to 9–12 ft lbs.

Exhaust Manifold

REMOVAL AND INSTALLATION

NOTE: It is not absolutely necessary to replace the gasket when only the exhaust manifold is removed, unless the gasket is damaged, or leaks develop.

1. Remove the air cleaner assembly.

2. Disconnect the exhaust pipe from the exhaust manifold.

3. Loosen and remove the exhaust manifold attaching nuts and remove the manifold from the engine.

4. Install the exhaust manifold in the reverse order of removal. Use new gaskets at the cylinder head (if necessary) and exhaust pipe. Tighten the mounting bolts in a circular pattern, working from the center to the ends, in two progressive steps to 9–12 ft lbs.

NOTE: On 1978–80 models, install the stud bolt into the center of the outermost guide hold (no. 4 cylinder) of the manifold.

Timing Gear Cover

REMOVAL AND INSTALLATION

1. Disconnect the negative battery cable from the battery, drain the cooling system, and remove the radiator together with the upper and lower radiator hoses.

2. Loosen the alternator drive belt adjusting screw and remove the drive belt. Remove the bolts which attach the alternator bracket to the engine and set the alternator aside out of the way.

3. Remove the distributor.

4. Remove the oil pump attaching screws, and take out the pump and its drive spindle.

5. Remove the cooling fan and the fan pulley together with the drive belt.

6. Remove the water pump.

7. Remove the crankshaft pulley bolt and remove the crankshaft pulley.

8. Remove the bolts holding the front cover to the front of the cylinder block, the four bolts which retain the front of the oil pan to the bottom of the front cover and the two bolts which are

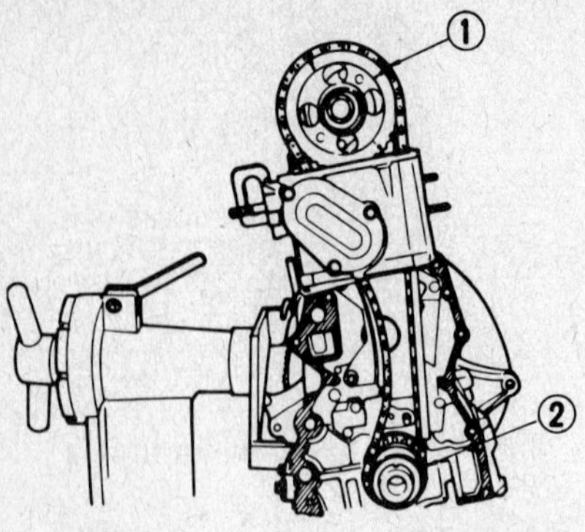

1. Timing mark 2. Timing mark

Engine front cover installation

screwed down through the front of the cylinder head and into the top of the front cover.

9. Carefully pry the front cover off the front of the engine.

10. Cut the exposed front section of the oil pan gasket away from the oil pan. Do the same to the gasket at the top of the front cover. Remove the two side gaskets and clean all of the mating surfaces.

11. Cut the portions needed from a new oil pan gasket and top front cover gasket.

12. Apply sealer to all of the gaskets and position them on the engine in their proper places.

13. Apply a light coating of oil to the crankshaft oil seal and carefully mount the front cover to the front of the engine and install all of the mounting bolts. Tighten the 8 mm bolts to 7–12 ft lbs and the 6 mm bolts to 3–6 ft lbs. Tighten the oil pan attaching bolts to 4–7 ft lbs.

14. Before installing the oil pump, place the gasket over the shaft and make sure that the mark on the drive spindle faces (aligned with) the oil pump hole. Install the oil pump so that the projection on the top of the shaft is located in the exact position as when it was removed or is in the 11:25 o'clock position with the piston in the No. 1 cylinder is placed at TDC on the compression stroke, if the engine was disturbed since disassembly. Tighten the oil pump attaching screws to 8–10 ft lbs.

Oil Seal

1. Remove the front cover.
2. Pry the old seal from the cover with a pointed piece of plastic or wood.
3. Oil the lip of the new seal. Do not use grease. Press it into place, making sure the flat side faces forward and the lip faces the engine.
4. Install the front cover.

Apply sealant at these points.

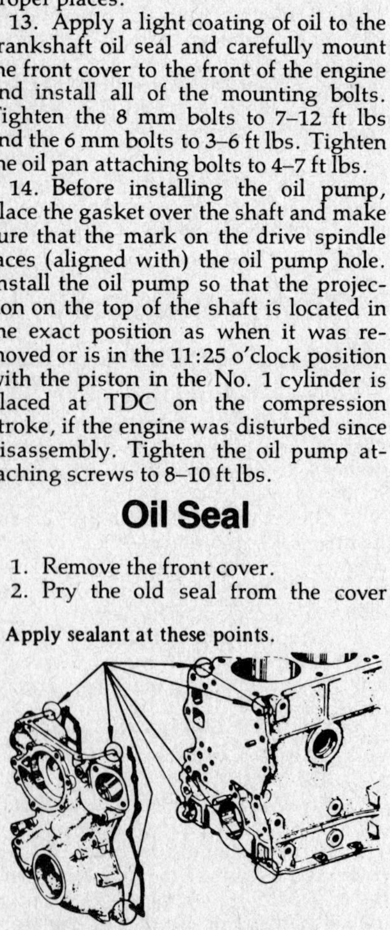

Sealing engine front cover

Timing Chain and Tensioner

REMOVAL AND INSTALLATION

1. Before beginning any disassembly procedures, position the no. 1 piston at TDC on the compression stroke.

2. Remove the front cover. Remove the camshaft cover.

3. With the no. 1 piston at TDC, the timing marks on the camshaft sprocket and the timing chain should be visible. Mark both of them with paint. Also mark the relationship of the camshaft sprocket to the camshaft. At this point

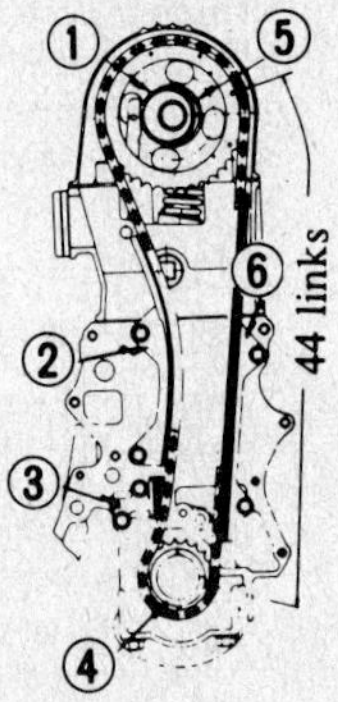

1. Fuel pump drive cam
2. Chain guide
3. Chain tensioner
4. Crank sprocket
5. Cam sprocket
6. Chain guide

Timing chain installation

you will see that there are three sets of timing marks and locating holes in the sprocket. They are for making adjustments to compensate for timing chain stretch. See the "Timing Chain Adjustment" section for details.

4. With the timing marks on the cam sprocket clearly marked, locate and mark the timing marks on the crankshaft sprocket. Also mark the chain timing mark if it is to be reused.

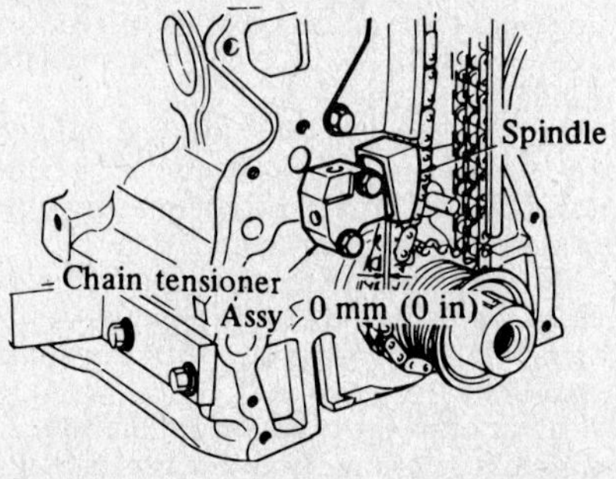

Timing chain tensioner installation

5. Unbolt the camshaft sprocket and remove the sprocket along with the chain. As you remove the chain, hold it where the chain tensioner contacts it.

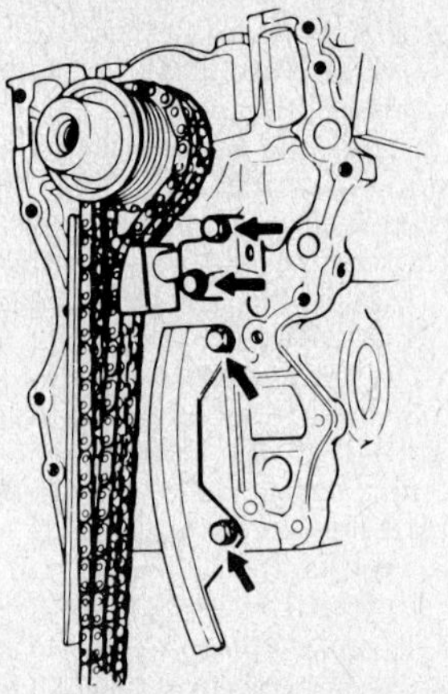

Timing chain and tensioner removal

When the chain is removed, the tensioner will come apart. Hold on to it and you won't lose any of the parts.

The crankshaft sprocket can be removed with a puller, if necessary. There is no need to remove the chain guide unless it is being replaced.

6. Install the timing chain and the camshaft sprocket together after first positioning the chain over the crankshaft sprocket. Position the sprocket so that the marks made earlier line up. This is assuming that the engine has not been

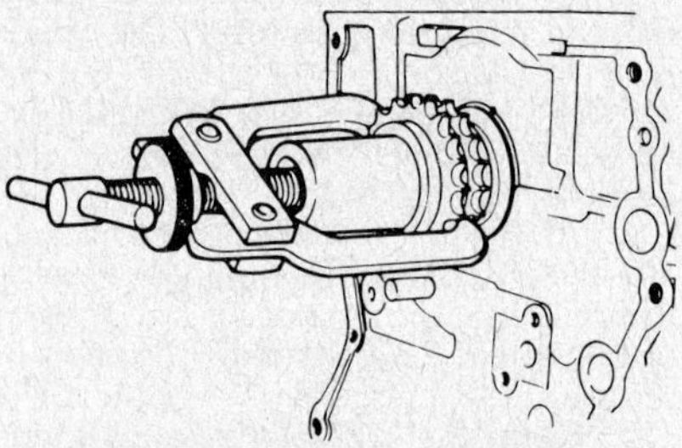

Removing timing chain drive sprocket

disturbed. The camshaft and the crankshaft keys should both be pointing upward. If a new chain and/or gear is being installed, position the sprocket so that the timing marks on the chain align with the marks on the sprocket (with both keys pointing up). The marks are on the right-hand side of the sprockets as you face the engine. 1973 Engines have 42 pins between the mating marks of the chain and sprockets when the chain is installed correctly. 1974 and later engines have 44 pins. The factory refers to the pins as links, but in American terminology this is incorrect. Count the pins. There are two pins per chain link. This is an important step. If you do not get the exact number of pins between the timing marks, valve timing will be incorrect, and the engine will either not run at all or run very badly.

7. Install the chain tensioner. Adjust the protrusion of the chain tensioner spindle to zero clearance.

8. With a new seal installed in the front cover and a light coat of oil applied to the seal, assemble the remaining com-

ponents of the engine in the reverse order of disassembly.

TIMING CHAIN ADJUSTMENT

When the timing chain stretches excessively, the valve timing will be adversely affected. There are two camshaft sprocket locating holes provided to correct the valve timing. Actually there are three sets of holes and timing marks on the camshaft sprocket, the third hole and timing mark are for 6 cylinder Datsun engines and in the case of the Datsun pick-up 4 cylinder engines are obviously ignored.

If the stretch of the chain roller links is excessive, adjust the camshaft sprocket location by transferring the camshaft set position of the camshaft sprocket from the factory position of No. 1 to No. 2 as follows:

1. Turn the crankshaft until the No. 1 piston is at TDC on its compression stroke. Examine whether the camshaft sprocket location notch is to the left of the oblong groove on the camshaft retaining plate. If the notch in the sprocket is to the left of the groove in the retaining plate, then the chain is stretched and needs adjusting.
2. Remove the camshaft sprocket together with the chain and reinstall the sprocket and chain with the locating dowel on the camshaft inserted into the No. 2 hole of the sprocket and the timing mark on the timing chain aligned with the No. 2 mark on the sprocket. The amount of modification is 4° of the crankshaft rotation.
3. Recheck the valve timing as outlined in Step 1. The notch in the sprocket should be to the right of the groove in the camshaft retaining plate.
4. If and when the notch cannot be brought to the right of the groove with the sprocket installed in the No. 2 hole, the timing chain must be replaced to gain the proper valve timing.

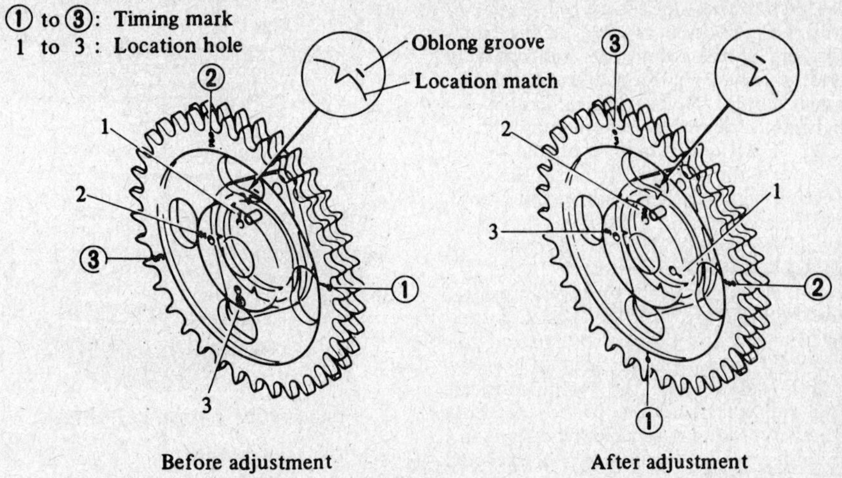

Camshaft sprocket adjusting locations

Camshaft

REMOVAL AND INSTALLATION

1. Removal of the cylinder head from the engine is optional. Remove the camshaft sprocket from the camshaft together with the timing chain.
2. Loosen the valve rocker pivot locknut and remove the rocker arm by pressing down on the valve spring. Remove all of the rocker arms in this manner.
3. Remove the two retaining nuts on the camshaft retainer plate at the front of the cylinder head and carefully slide the camshaft out of the camshaft carrier.
4. Lightly coat the camshaft bearings with clean motor oil and carefully slide the camshaft in place in the camshaft carrier.
5. Install the camshaft retainer plate with the oblong groove in the face of the plate facing toward the front of the engine.
6. Check the valve timing as outlined under "Timing Chain Removal and Installation" and install the timing sprocket on the camshaft, tightening the bolt together with the fuel pump cam to 86–116 ft lbs.
7. Install the rocker arms by pressing down the valve springs with a screwdriver and install the valve rocker springs.
8. Install the cylinder head, if it was removed, and assemble the rest of the engine in the reverse order of removal.

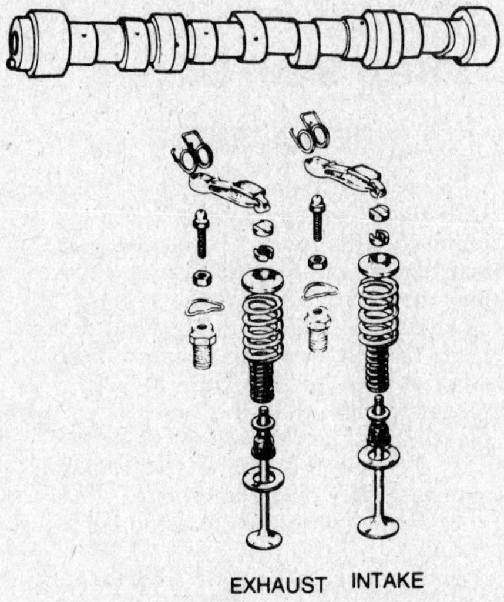

Camshaft and valve assemblies

Pistons and Connecting Rods

REMOVAL AND INSTALLATION

1. Remove the cylinder head.
2. Remove the oil pan.
3. Remove any carbon buildup from the cylinder wall at the top end of the piston travel with a ridge reamer tool.
4. Position the piston to be removed at the bottom of its stroke so that the connecting rod bearing cap can be reached easily from under the engine.
5. Unscrew the connecting rod bearing cap and remove the cap and lower half of the bearing.
6. Push the piston and connecting rod up and out of the cylinder block with a length of wood. Use care not to scratch the cylinder wall with the connecting rod or the wooden tool.
7. Keep all of the components from each cylinder together and install them in the cylinder from which they were removed.
8. Coat the bearing face of the connecting rod and the outer face of the pistons with engine oil.
9. Turn the top compression ring to bring its gap to about the 1:30 o'clock position. Set the remaining rings so that their gaps are position 180° apart around the piston. The oil ring gap will be directly under the top compression ring gap.
10. Turn the crankshaft until the rod journal of the particular cylinder you are working on is brought to the TDC position.
11. With the piston and rings clamped in a ring compressor, the notched mark on the head of the piston toward the front of the engine, and the oil hole side of the connecting rod toward the right side of the engine, push

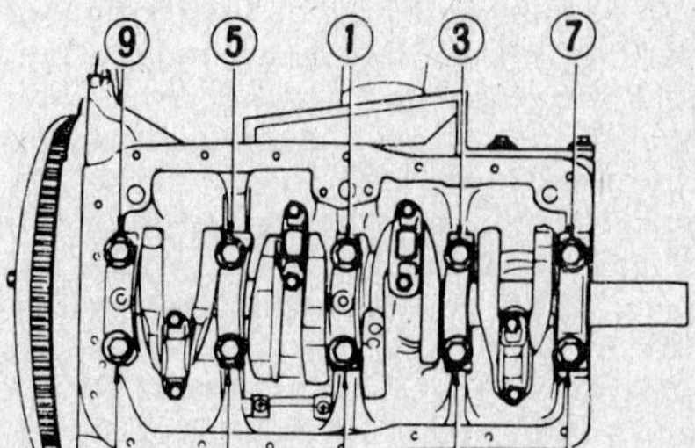

Engine bearing cap bolt tightening sequence

the piston and connecting rod assembly into the cylinder bore until the big bearing end of the connecting rod contacts and is seated on the rod journal of the crankshaft. Use care not to scratch the cylinder wall with the connecting rod.

12. Push down farther on the piston and turn the crankshaft while the connecting rod rides around on the crankshaft rod journal. Turn the crankshaft until the crankshaft rod journal is at BDC (bottom dead center).

13. Align the mark on the connecting rod bearing cap with that on the connecting rod and tighten the bearing cap bolts to the specified torque.

14. Install all of the piston/connecting rod assemblies in the manner outlined above and assemble the oil pan and cylinder head to the engine in the reverse order of removal.

Piston and Connecting Rod Identification and Positioning

The pistons are marked with a notch in the piston head. When installed in the engine, the notch markings are to be facing toward the front of the engine.

The connecting rods are installed in the engine with the oil hole facing toward the fuel pump side (right) of the engine.

NOTE: It is advisable to number the pistons, connecting rods, and bearing caps in some manner so that they can be reinstalled in the same cylinder, facing the same direction from which they are removed.

ENGINE LUBRICATION

Oil Pan

REMOVAL AND INSTALLATION

To remove the oil pan it will be necessary to unbolt the motor mounts and jack the engine to gain clearance. Drain the oil and remove the attaching screws and remove the oil pan and gasket. Install the oil pan in the reverse order with a new gasket. Apply a thin bead of silicone seal to the engine block at the junction of the block and front cover, and the junction of the block and main bearing cap. Then apply a thin coat of silicone seal to the new oil pan gasket, install the gasket to the block, and install the pan. Tighten the pan bolts in a circular pattern from the center to the ends, to 4–7 ft lbs. Overtightening will distort the pan lip, causing leakage.

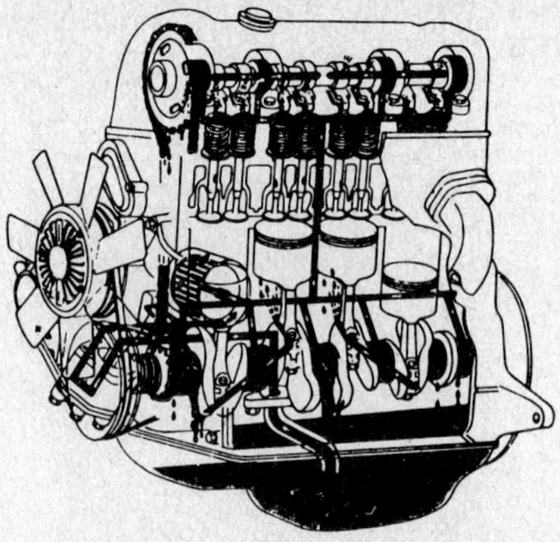

Engine lubrication schematic

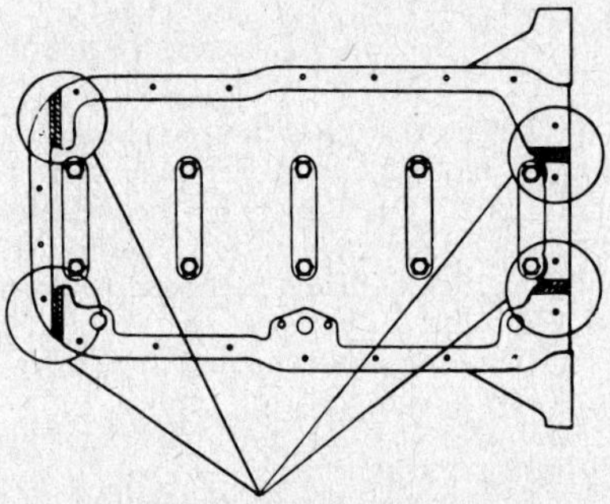

Apply sealant at these points

Oil pan sealing locations

Rear Main Oil Seal

REPLACEMENT

In order to replace the rear main oil seal, the rear main bearing cap must be removed. Removal of the rear main bearing cap requires the use of a special rear main bearing cap puller. Also, the oil seal is installed with a special crankshaft rear oil seal drift. Unless these or similar tools are available to you, it is recommended that the oil seal be replaced by a Datsun service center.

1. Remove the engine and transmission assembly from the vehicle.
2. Remove the transmission from the engine.
3. Remove the clutch from the flywheel.
4. Remove the flywheel from the crankshaft.

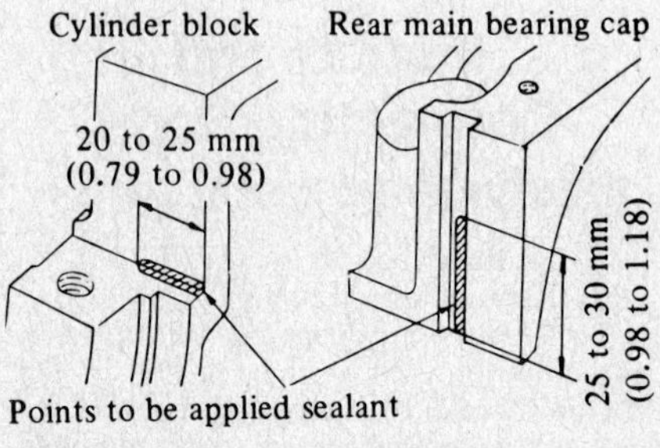

Main bearing cap sealing locations

5. Remove the rear main bearing cap together with the bearing cap side seals.
6. Remove the rear main oil seal from around the crankshaft.
7. Apply oil to the sealing lip of the oil seal and install the seal around the crankshaft using a suitable tool.
8. Apply sealer to the rear main bearing cap as indicated and install the rear main bearing cap and tighten the cap bolts to 33–40 ft lbs.
9. Apply sealant to the rear main bearing cap side seals and install the side seals, driving the seals into place with a suitable drift.
10. Assemble the engine and install it in the vehicle in the reverse order of removal.

Oil Pump

REMOVAL AND INSTALLATION

The oil pump is mounted externally on the engine, eliminating the need to remove the oil pan in order to remove the oil pump.

Oil strainer and oil pump removal

1. Remove the distributor.
2. Drain the engine oil.
3. Remove the front stabilizer.
4. Remove the splash shield board.

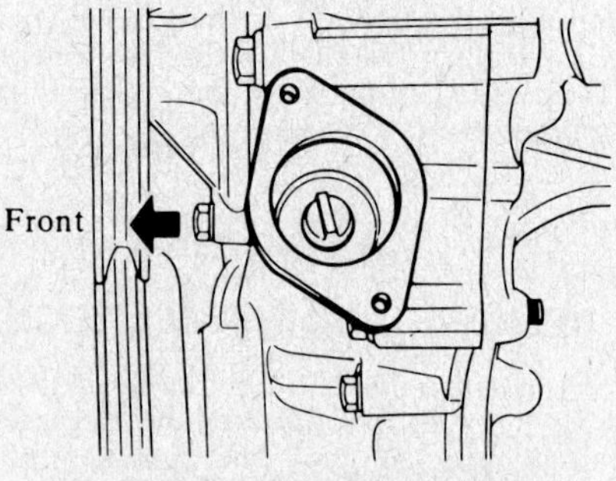

Setting oil pump drive spindle

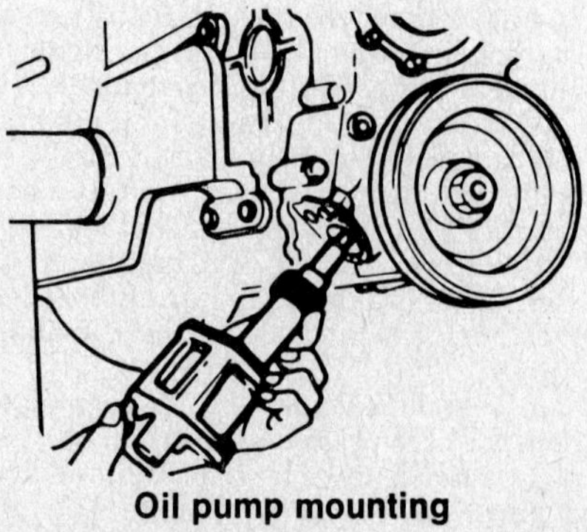

Oil pump mounting

OIL PUMP SPECIFICATIONS

Engine	Pump Type	Clearance Between Inner and Outer Rotor (in.)	Tip Clearance Gear or Rotor to Cover or Outer Rotor (in.) (max.)	Clearance Between Outer Rotor and Body (in.)	Maximum Oil Pressure (psi)	Minimum Oil Pressure (psi) at Idle	Relief Valve Spring Free Length (in.)	Relief Valve Opening Pressure (psi)
L16, L18	Rotor	0.002-0.005	0.005	0.006-0.008	54-60	14-17	2.24	54.0-59.7
L20B	Rotor	0.001-0.003	0.005	0.006-0.008	71	11	2.067	50

5. Remove the oil pump body with the drive spindle assembly.
6. Before installing the oil pump in the engine, turn the crankshaft so that the No. 1 piston is at TDC of the compression stroke.
7. Fill the pump housing with engine oil, then align the punch mark on the spindle with the hole in the oil pump.
8. With a new gasket placed over the drive spindle, install the oil pump and drive spindle assembly so that the projection on the top of the drive spindle is located in the 11:25 o'clock position.

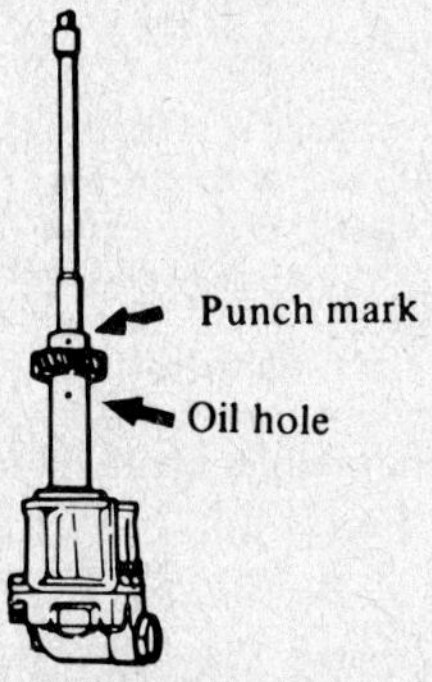

Aligning oil pump punch mark and oil hole

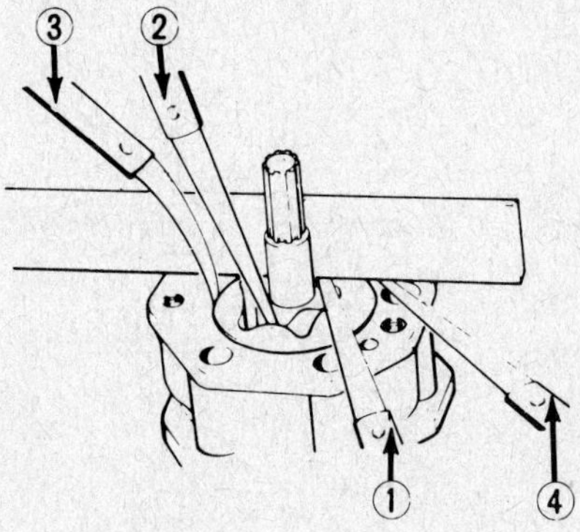

1. Side clearance
2. Tip clearance
3. Outer rotor to pump body clearance
4. Rotor to cover clearance

Oil pump clearance measurements

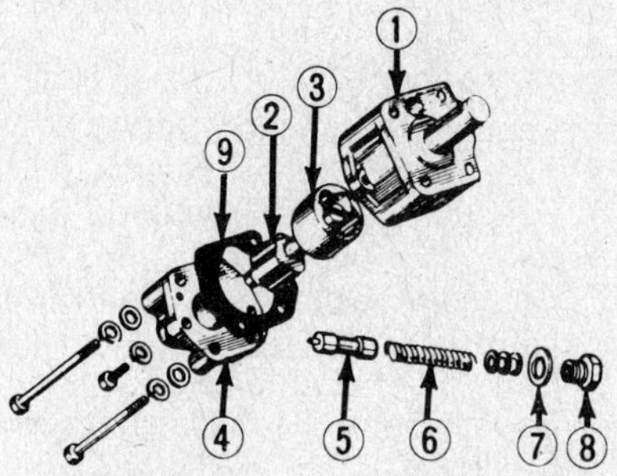

1. Pump body
2. Inner rotor and shaft
3. Outer rotor
4. Pump cover
5. Pressure regulator valve
6. Valve spring
7. Washer
8. Cap
9. Gasket

Oil pump components

9. Install the distributor with the metal tip of the rotor pointing toward the No. 1 spark plug tower of the distributor cap.
10. Assemble the remaining components in the reverse order of removal.

ENGINE COOLING

Coolant Changes

DRAINING, FLUSHING, AND REFILLING

Once every 24 months or 24,000 miles, the cooling system should be drained, thoroughly flushed, and refilled. This should be done with the engine cold.

1. Remove the radiator cap.
2. There are two drain plugs in the cooling system; one at the bottom of the radiator and one at the rear of the driver's side of the engine. Both should be loosened to allow the coolant to drain.
3. Turn on the heater inside the truck to its hottest position. This ensures that the heater core is flushed out completely. Flush out the system thoroughly by refilling it with clean water through the radiator opening as it escapes from the two drain cocks. Continue until the water running out is clear. Also clean out the coolant recovery tank.
4. If the system is badly contaminated with rust or scale, use a commercial flushing solution to clear it out. Follow the manufacturer's instructions. Some causes of rust are air in the system, caused by a leaky radiator cap or an insufficiently filled or leaking system, failure to change the coolant regularly, use of excessively hard or soft water, and failure to use a proper mix of antifreeze and water.
5. When the system is clear, allow all the water to drain, then close the drain plugs. Fill the system through the radiator with a 50/50 mix of ethylene glycol type antifreeze and water.
6. Start the engine and top off the radiator with water. If your truck has a coolant recovery tank, fill it half full with the coolant mix.
7. Replace the radiator and coolant tank caps, and check for leaks. When the engine has reached normal operating temperature, shut it off, allow it to cool, then top off the radiator or coolant tank as necessary.

Radiator

REMOVAL AND INSTALLATION

1. Drain the engine coolant into a clean container.
2. Remove the front grille.
3. Disconnect the upper and lower radiator hoses. On a truck with an automatic transmission, disconnect the fluid cooler inlet and outlet lines from the radiator. Plug the lines to prevent the loss of transmission fluid and the entrance of dirt. Remove the fan shroud, if equipped.
4. Remove the bolts retaining the radiator from the radiator side supports and remove the radiator upward.
5. Install the radiator in the reverse order of removal.

Water Pump

REMOVAL AND INSTALLATION

1. Drain the engine coolant into a clean container.
2. Loosen the four bolts retaining the fan shroud to the radiator and remove the shroud.
3. Loosen the belt, then remove the fan and pulley from the water pump hub.
4. Remove the five bolts retaining the pump and remove the pump together with the gasket from the front cover.
5. Remove all traces of gasket material and install the water pump in the reverse order with a new gasket and sealer. Tighten the bolts uniformly.

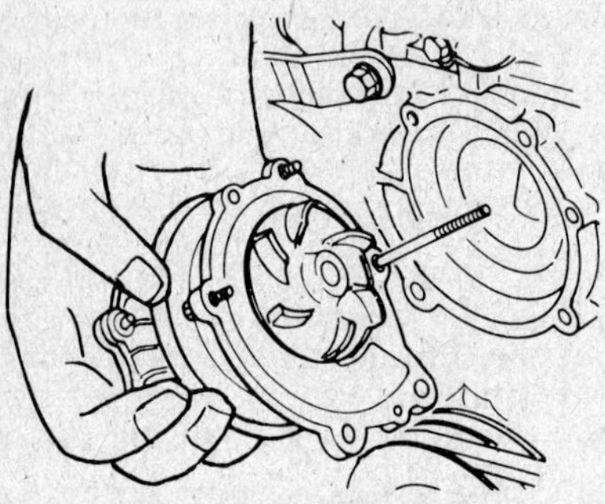

Water pump mounting

Thermostat

The factory-installed thermostat opening temperature is 180° F for trucks sold in the U.S., 190° F for trucks sold in Canada.

REMOVAL AND INSTALLATION

1. Drain the engine coolant into a clean container so that the level is below the thermostat housing.
2. Disconnect the upper radiator hose at the water outlet.
3. Loosen the two securing nuts and remove the water outlet, gasket, and the thermostat from the thermostat housing.
4. Install the thermostat in the revers order of removal, using a new gasket with sealer and with the thermostat spring toward the inside of the engine.

EMISSION CONTROLS

Emission Controls

Various systems are used to control crankcase vapors, exhaust emissions, and fuel vapors. The accompanying chart shows the systems used with various models and engines.

EMISSION CONTROL EQUIPMENT APPLICATIONS TABLE

Year	Model	Engine	Emission Control Systems
1973-1975	620	L18	1,4,5
1976-1980	620	L20B	1,3,4,6,7,8,9,10

1. Closed Crankcase Ventilation System
2. Not used
3. Air Pump System
4. Engine Modification System
5. Fuel Vapor Control System
6. Exhaust Gas Recirculation System
7. Catalytic Converter California Only
8. Early Fuel Evaporation System
9. Boost Controlled Deceleration Device
10. High Altitude Compensator—California Option
11. TCS—Manual Transmisson exc. California
12. Floor Temperature Sensing Device
13. Spark Timing Control

Crankcase Ventilation System

The closed crankcase ventilation system is used to route the crankcase vapors to the intake manifold to be mixed and burned with the air/fuel mixture.

An air intake hose is connected between the air cleaner assembly or the throttle chamber, and the valve cover. A return hose is connected between a steel net baffle on the side of the crankcase to the intake manifold or throttle chamber, with a metering positive crankcase ventilation (PCV) valve in the hose.

To test the system, allow the engine to idle. With the PCV valve removed from the hose, a hissing sound should be heard, and vacuum should be felt when you cover the engine side of the valve with your finger. The PCV valve should be replaced at regular intervals of 12,000 miles, through 1974, or 24,000 miles thereafter.

Air Injection System (AIS)

The air injection reactor system is designed so that ambient air, pressurized by an air pump, is injected through the injection nozzles into exhaust ports near each exhaust valve. The exhaust gases are at high temperatures and ignite when brought into contact with the oxygen of the ambient air. Thus, the un-

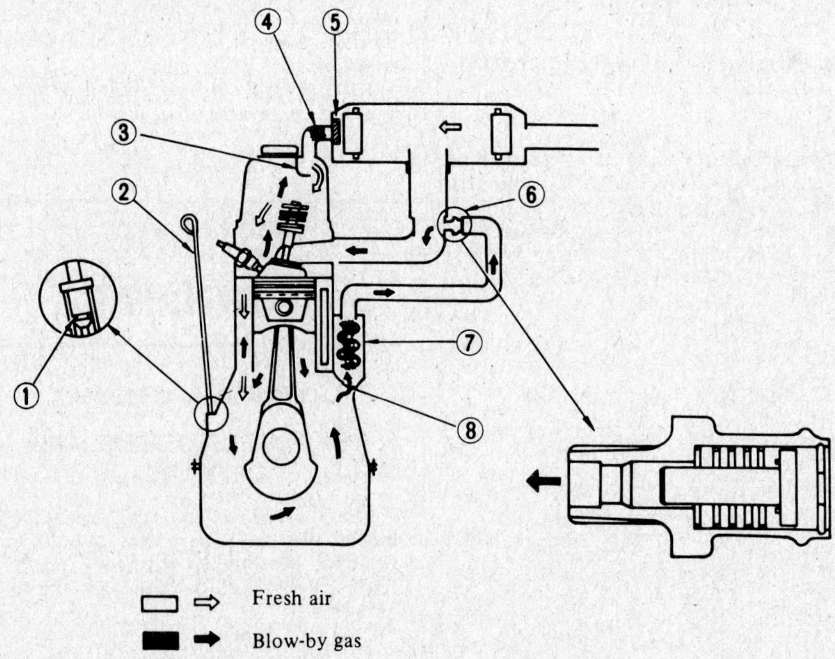

1 O-ring
2. Oil level gauge
3. Baffle plate
4. Flame arrester
5. Filter
6. P.C.V. valve
7. Steel net
8. Baffle plate

Crankcase emission control system

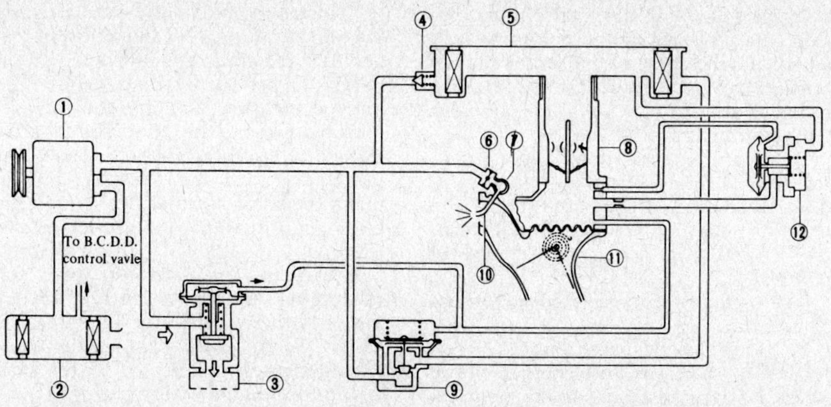

1. Air pump
2. Air pump air cleaner
3. Emergency air relief valve
4. Air relief valve
5. Air cleaner
6. Check valve
7. Air gallery pipe
8. Carburetor
9. Air control valve
10. Injection nozzle
11. Exhaust manifold
12. Anti-backfire valve

Air injection system schematic

burned fuel is burned in the exhaust ports and manifold.

A check valve is installed in the air pump discharge line to prevent the airflow from reversing due to a broken drive belt, relief valve spring failure, or backfire in the exhaust manifold. Reversed airflow could damage the air pump.

The air pump relief valve bleeds off excess air from the pump at high speeds. The valve is mounted on the carburetor air cleaner.

Trucks with a catalytic converter (1976 and later pick-ups sold in California) have protection devices to prevent converter overheating due to large quantities of injected air. 1976–77 models use an emergency air relief valve and an air control valve. The emergency valve has a diaphragm operated by engine vacuum. When intake manifold vacuum reaches a predetermined level, the valve opens, diverting air from the pump into the atmosphere. When vacuum drops, the valve closes allowing normal AIS operation.

The air control valve is also controlled by engine vacuum. High vacuum and high pressure from the air pump open the control valve, venting air from the pump into the air cleaner.

1978–80 models have a combined air control valve instead of the relief valve, emergency valve, and air control valve. The combined air control valve regulates the amount of injected air according to intake manifold and air pump discharge pressure, to prevent the converter from overheating.

An anti-backfire valve is installed in an air delivery hose. The purpose of the valve is to prevent backfiring in the exhaust manifold during deceleration. When the throttle closes suddenly, an overly rich air/fuel mixture exists in the intake manifold due to the lack of air getting past the throttle valves. This rich mixture will not completely burn in the combustion chamber. If the unburned gases were to come in contact with the oxygen pumped into the exhaust ports by the air pump, they would ignite and cause backfiring and possible damage.

The anti-backfire valve is connected to the intake manifold by a vacuum line and when the vacuum rises, the valve opens a port in the intake manifold, allowing extra filtered air from the air cleaner to be admitted into the combustion chambers, leaning out the overly rich mixture.

1979–80 cab and chassis models have a transistorized programmed control unit, a vacuum switching valve, and an air control switch which govern air flow through the AIS. The air control switch, located between the intake manifold and the control unit, turns off when manifold vacuum is high, and on when vacuum is low. This provides a signal to the control unit, which determines when to turn the vacuum switching valve on or off accordingly. The vacuum switching valve controls the upper chamber of the CAC valve diaphragm, opening or closing the CAC valve according to signals received from the control unit. Thus, the amount of air injected into the AIS is monitored and adjusted as conditions warrant.

TESTING

Air Pump

If the air pump makes an abnormal noise and cannot be corrected without removing the pump from the vehicle, check the following in sequence:

1. Turn the pulley 3/4 of a turn in the clockwise direction and 1/4 of a turn in the counterclockwise direction. If the pulley is binding and if rotation is not smooth, a defective bearing is indicated.
2. Check the inner wall of the pump body, vanes, and rotor for wear. If the rotor has abnormal wear, replace the air pump.
3. Check the needle roller bearing for wear and damage. If the bearings are defective, the air pump should be replaced.
4. Check and replace the rear side seal if abnormal wear or damage is noticed.
5. Check and replace the carbon shoes holding the vanes if they are found to be worn or damaged.
6. A deposit of carbon particles on the inner wall of the pump body and vanes is normal, but should be removed with compressed air before reassembling the air pump.

Check Valve

Remove the check valve from the air pump discharge line. Test it for leakage by blowing air into the valve from the air pump side and from the air manifold side. Air should only pass through the valve from the air pump side if the valve is functioning normally. A small amount of air leakage from the manifold side can be overlooked. Replace the check valve if it is found to be defective.

Anti-Backfire Valve

To check the valve, disconnect the hose from the air cleaner and place a finger on the end. Run the engine up to about 3,000 rpm, then quickly release the throttle. If the valve is performing correctly, suction should be felt at the end of the hose. If no suction is felt, replace the anti-backfire valve.

Air Pump Relief Valve

1. Disconnect the hoses leading to the check valve (on the air injection manifold) and the air control valve from the air hose connector. Plug the connector.
2. Start the engine and increase the engine speed to about 3000 rpm. Place your finger on the outlet of the relief valve (inside the air cleaner housing) and check for air discharge. If you do not feel any air coming out, the relief valve is faulty, and must be replaced.

Air Injection Nozzles

Check around the air manifold for air leakage with the engine running at 2,000 rpm. If air is leaking from the eye joint bolt, retighten or replace the gasket. Check the air nozzles for restrictions by blowing air into the nozzles.

Hose

Check and replace the hoses if they are found to be weakened or cracked. Check all hose connections and clips. Be sure that the hoses are not in contact with other parts of the engine.

Emergency Air Relief Valve

1. Warm up the engine.
2. Check all hoses for leaks, kinks, improper connections, etc.
3. Run the engine up to 2000 rpm under no load. No air should be discharged from the valve.
4. Disconnect the vacuum hose from the valve. This is the hose which runs to the intake manifold. Run the engine up to 2000 rpm. Air should be discharged from the valve. If not, replace it.

Combined Air Control Valve

1. Check all hoses for leaks, kinks, and improper connections.
2. Thoroughly warm up the engine.
3. With the engine idling, check for air discharge from the relief opening in the air cleaner case.
4. Disconnect and plug the vacuum hose from the valve. Air should be discharged from the valve with the engine idling. If the disconnected vacuum hose is not plugged, the engine will stumble.
5. Connect a hand-operated vacuum pump to the vacuum fitting on the valve and apply 7.8–9.8 in. Hg. of vacuum. Run the engine speed up to 3000 rpm. No air should be discharged from the valve.
6. Disconnect and plug the air hose at the check valve, with the conditions as in the preceding step. This should cause the valve to discharge air. If not, or if any of the conditions in this procedure are not met, replace the valve.

Spark Timing Control System Dual Point Distributor—1973

The dual point distributor has two sets of breaker points which operate independently of each other and are positioned with a relative phase angle of 7° apart. This makes one set the advanced points and the other set the ratarded points.

The two sets of points, which mechanically operate continuously, are connected in parallel to the primary side of the ignition circuit. One set of points controls the firing of the spark plugs and hence, the ignition timing, depending on whether or not the retarded set of points is energized.

When both sets of points are electrically energized, the first set to open (the advanced set, 4° or 1° sooner) has no control over breaking the ignition coil primary circuit because the retarded set is still closed and maintaining a complete circuit to ground. When the retarded set of points opens, the advanced set is still open, and the primary circuit is broken causing the electromagnetic field in the coil to collapse and the ignition spark is produced.

When the retarded set of points is removed from the primary ignition circuit through the operation of a distributor relay inserted into the retarded points circuit, the advanced set of points controls the primary circuit. The retarded set of points is activated as follows: The retarded set of points is activated only while the throttle is partially open, the temperature is above 50° F, and the transmission is in any gear but Fourth gear.

NOTE: When the ambient temperature is below 34° F, the retarded set of points is removed from the ignition circuit no matter what switch is on.

In the case of an automatic transmission, the retarded set of points is activated at all times except under heavy acceleration and high-speed cruising (wide open throttle) with the ambient temperature above 50° F.

There are three switches which control the operation of the distributor relay. All of the switches must be ON in order to energize the distributor relay thus energizing the retarded set of points.

The switches and their operation are as follows:

A transmission switch located in the transmission closes an electrical circuit when the transmission is in any gear except Fourth.

A throttle switch located on the throttle linkage at the carburetor is ON when the throttle valve is moved within a predetermined angle of 45°.

The temperature sensing switch is located near the hood release lever inside the passenger compartment. The temperature sensing switch comes ON between 41° F and 55° F when the temperature is rising and goes OFF at about 34° F when the temperature falls.

TESTING

Spark Timing Control System Dual Point Distributor Phase Difference

1. Disconnect the wiring harness of the distributor from the engine harness.
2. Connect the black wire of the engine harness with the black wire of the distributor harness with a jumper wire. This connects the advanced set of points.
3. With the engine idling, adjust the ignition timing by rotating the distributor.

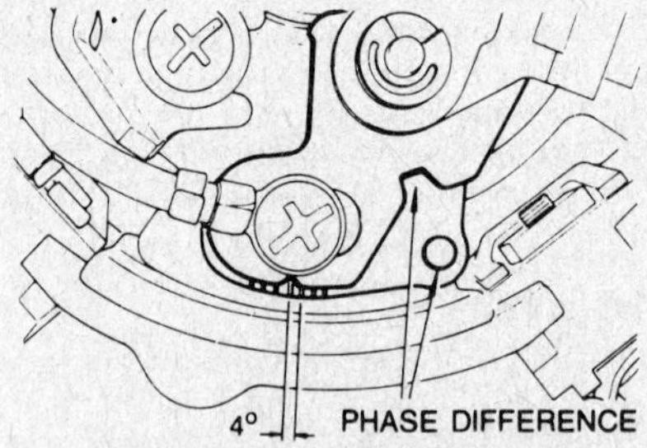

Dual point ignition distributor phase angle adjusting screw

4. Disconnect the jumper wire from the black wire of the distributor harness and connect it to the yellow wire of the distributor harness. The retarded set of points is now activated.
5. With the engine idling, check the ignition timing. The timing should be retarded from the advanced setting 7°.
6. To adjust the out-of-phase angle of the ignition timing, loosen the adjuster plate set screws on the same side as the retarded set of points.
7. Place the blade of a screwdriver in the adjusting notch of the adjuster plate and turn the adjuster plate as required to obtain the correct retarded ignition timing specification. The ignition timing is retarded when the adjuster plate is turned counterclockwise. There are graduations on the adjuster plate to make the adjustment easier; one graduation is equal to 4° of crankshaft rotation.
8. Replace the distributor cap, start the engine, and check the ignition timing with the retarded set of points activated (yellow wire of the distributor wiring harness connected to the black wire of the engine wiring harness).
9. Repeat the steps above as necessary to properly set the retarded ignition timing.

Transmission Switch

Disconnect the electrical leads at the switch and connect a self-powered test light to the electrical leads. The switch should conduct electricity only when the gearshift is moved to Fourth gear.

Throttle Switch

The throttle switch located on the throttle linkage at the carburetor is checked with a self-powered test light. Disconnect the electrical leads of the switch and connect the test light. The switch should not conduct current when the throttle valve is opened up to 45°. When the throttle is fully opened, the switch should conduct current.

Temperature Sensing Switch

The temperature sensing switch mounted in the passenger compartment (near the hood release lever) should not conduct current when the temperature is above 55° F.

Boost Control Deceleration Device (BCDD)

The BCDD reduces hydrocarbon emissions during coasting conditions.

The BCDD consists of an independently operated auxiliary fuel system. This system functions when the engine is coasting to enrich the air-fuel mixture which minimizes the hydrocarbon content of the exhaust gases through more efficient combustion. This is accomplished without adversly affecting engine idle and the carbon monoxide content of the exhaust gases.

When intake manifold vacuum exceeds a predetermined value, a vacuum-actuated diaphragm opens an air passage allowing additional air to enter the intake manifold. When the additional air passage is opened, vacuum is brought to bear on another diaphragm which opens a fuel passage allowing additional fuel to enter the intake manifold.

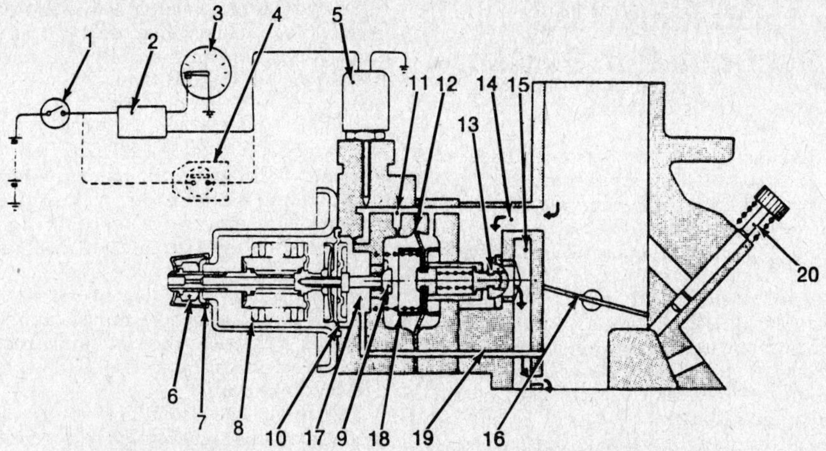

1. Ignition switch
2. Amplifier
3. Speed detecting switch
   Blow 10 M.P.H.: ON
   (for M/T)
4. Inhibitor switch
   "N" or "P" position: ON
   (For A/T)
5. Vacuum control
   solenoid valve
6. Adjusting nut
7. Lock spring
8. Altitude corrector
9. Vacuum control valve
10. Diaphragm I
11. Air passage
12. Diaphragm II
13. Air control valve
14. Air passage
15. Air passage
16. Throttle valve
17. Vacuum chamber I
18. Vacuum chamber II
19. Vacuum passage
20. Idle speed adjusting screw

BCDD components

When the engine changes from a coasting condition to that of idling, the transmission speed sensor closes an electrical circuit, energizing the vacuum control solenoid valve. When energized, the vacuum control solenoid valve vents the intake manifold vacuum to the atmoshpere, thus causing the two diaphragms to return to their normal positions, closing off the additional air and fuel mixture. The transmission switch is not used on 1978 and later models.

TESTING

Boost Controlled Deceleration Device (BCDD)

Normally, the BCDD never needs adjustment. However, if the need should arise because of suspected malfunction of the system, proceed as follows:

1. Connect a tachometer to the engine.
2. Connect a quick-response vacuum gauge to the intake manifold.
3. Disconnect the BCDD solenoid valve electrical leads.
4. Start and warm up the engine until it reaches normal operating temperature.
5. Adjust the idle speed to the proper specification.

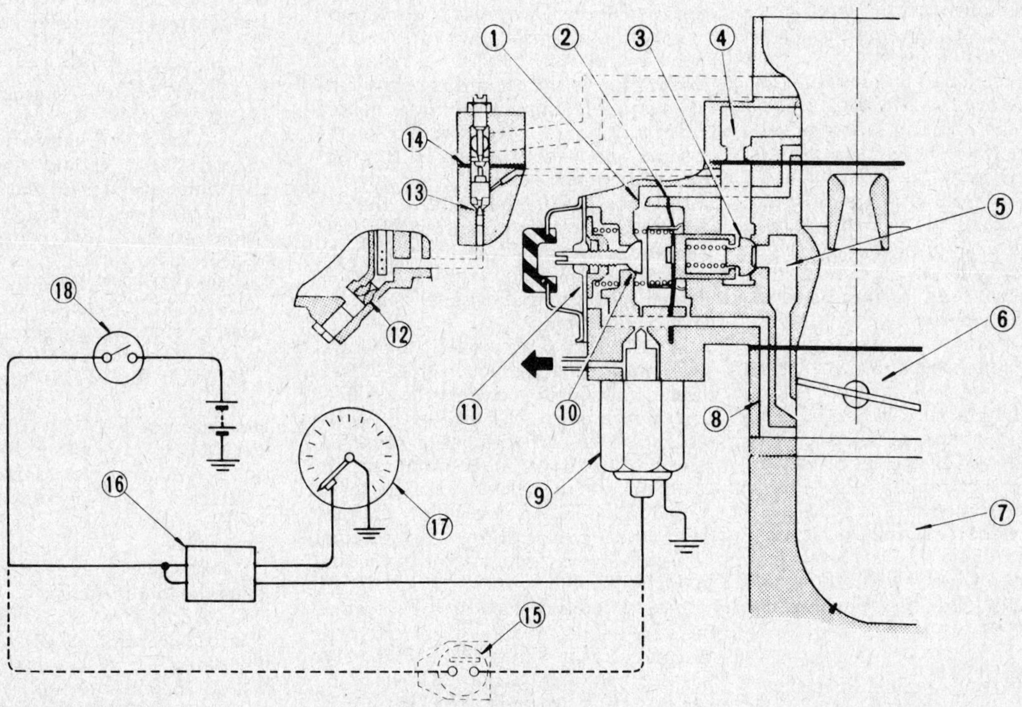

1. Air jet
2. Diaphragm II
3. Mixture control valve
4. Coasting air bleed II
5. Mixture air passage
6. Secondary barrel
7. Intake manifold
8. Boost passage
9. Vacuum control solenoid valve
10. Vacuum control valve
11. Diaphragm I
12. Secondary main jet
13. Coasting jet
14. Coating air bleed I
15. Inhibitor switch "N", "P": ON (for automatic transmission)
16. Amplifier
17. Speed detecting switch below 10 M.P.H.: ON (for manual transmission)
18. Ignition switch

BCDD system schematic

6. Raise the engine speed to 3,000–3,500 rpm under no-load (transmission in Neutral or Park), then allow the throttle to close quickly. Take notice as to whether or not the engine rpm returns to idle speed and if it does, how long the fall in rpm is interrupted before it reaches idle speed.

At the moment the throttle is snapped closed at high engine rpm, the vacuum in the intake manifold reaches −27.7 in. Hg on pre-1975 vehicles and −23.6 in. Hg on 1975 models, and then gradually falls to about −16.5 in. Hg at idle speed. The process of the fall of intake manifold vacuum and engine rpm will take one of the following three forms:

a. When the operating pressure of the BCDD is too high, the system remains inoperative, and the vacuum in the intake manifold decreases without interruption just like that of an engine without a BCDD;

b. When the operating pressure is lower than that of the case given, but still higher than the properly set pressure, the fall of vacuum in the intake manifold is interrupted and kept constant at a certain level (operating pressure) for about one second and then gradually falls down to the normal vacuum at idle speed;

c. When the set operating pressure of the BCDD is lower than the intake manifold vacuum when the throttle is suddenly released, the engine speed will not lower to idle speed.

To adjust the set operating pressure of the BCDD, remove the adjusting screw cover from the BCDD mechanism mounted on the side of the carburetor.

The adjusting screw is a left-handed threaded screw. Turning the screw 1/8 of a turn in either direction will change the operation pressure about 0.79 in. Hg. Turning the screw counterclockwise will increase the amount of vacuum needed to operate the mechanism and turning the screw clockwise will decrease the amount of vacuum needed to operate the mechanism.

The operating pressure for the BCDD on a vehicle with a manual transmission is −19.7 ±0.79 in. Hg and for a vehicle with an automatic transmission −18.9 ±0.79 in. Hg. through 1974. The decrease in intake manifold vacuum should be interrupted at these levels for about one second when the BCDD is operating correctly. The figures for later years are:

1975–76:
- −20.7 to −21.1, manual transmission;
- −19.9 to −20.3, automatic transmission;

1977:
- −20.1 to −21.7, manual transmission;
- −19.3 to −20.9, automatic transmission;

1978:
- −22.05±0.79, all models;

1979–80:
- −21.65±0.75, all models.

Exhaust Gas Recirculation System (EGR)

Exhaust gas recirculation is used to reduce combustion temperatures in the engine, thereby reducing the oxides of nitrogen emissions.

An EGR valve is mounted on the center of the intake manifold. The recycled exhaust gas is drawn into the bottom of the intake manifold riser portion through the exhaust manifold heat stove and EGR valve. A vacuum diaphragm is connected to a timed signal port at the carburetor flange.

As the throttle valve is opened, vacuum is applied to the EGR valve vacuum diaphragm. When the vacuum reaches about 2 in. Hg, the diaphragm moves against spring pressure and is in a fully up position at 8 in. Hg of vacuum. As the diaphragm moves up, it opens the exhaust gas metering valve which allows exhaust gas to be pulled into the engine intake manifold. The system does not operate when the engine is idling because the exhaust gas recirculation would cause a rough idle.

On pre-1975 models, an electrically-operated solenoid vacuum line between the EGR valve and the carburetor. The operation of the solenoid is controlled by a temperature sensing switch mounted in the coolant outlet housing. When the temperature of the coolant is below normal operating temperature, the solenoid is electrically activated and blocks the vacuum line leading to the EGR valve, thus preventing exhaust gas recirculation. When the temperature of the engine coolant reaches operating temperature, the solenoid is deactivated and the vacuum is allowed to act upon the EGR valve diaphragm and exhaust gas recirculation takes place.

On 1975 and later models, a thermal vacuum valve inserted in the engine thermostat housing controls the application of vacuum to the EGR valve. When the engine coolant reaches a predetermined temperature, the thermal vacuum valve opens and allows vacuum to be routed to the EGR valve. Below the predetermined temperature, the thermal vacuum valve closes and blocks vacuum to the EGR valve.

1978–80 models have a B.P.T. valve installed between the EGR valve and the thermal vacuum valve. The B.P.T. valve has a diaphragm raised or lowered by exhaust back pressure. The diaphragm opens or closes an air bleed, which is connected into the EGR vacuum line. High pressure results in higher levels of EGR, because the diaphragm is raised, closing off the air bleed, which allows more vacuum to reach and open the EGR valve. Thus, the amount of recirculated exhaust gas varies with exhaust pressure.

1978–80 California models have a vacuum delay valve installed in the line between the thermal vacuum valve and the EGR valve. This valve delays rapid drops in vacuum in the EGR line, thus effecting a longer EGR time.

On all 1975 model trucks (except Canadian models) and all 1976–77 49 States model trucks, the EGR system is equipped with a warning system which monitors the distance the pick-up has traveled and activates a warning light when the EGR system must be checked and possibly serviced. The EGR warning light, mounted on top of the dash, comes on when a predetermined number of miles has been traveled and every time the starter is engaged as a check for a burned-out bulb.

To reset the counter, which is mounted on the right fender apron under the hood, remove the grommet installed in the side of the counter and insert the tip of a small screwdriver into the hole. Press down on the knob inside the hole. Reinstall the grommet.

TESTING

Exhaust Gas Recirculation

PRE-1975

Check the operation of the EGR system as follows:

1. Visually inspect the entire EGR control system. Clean the mechanism free of oil and dirt. Replace any rubber hoses found to be cracked or broken.
2. Make sure that the EGR solenoid valve is properly wired.
3. Increase the engine speed from idling to 3,000–3,500 rpm. The plate of the EGR control valve diaphragm and the valve shaft should move upward as the engine speed is increased.
4. Disconnect the EGR solenoid valve electrical leads and connect them directly to the vehicle's 12 volt electrical supply (battery). Race the engine again with the EGR solenoid valve connected to a 12 volt power source. The EGR control valve should remain stationary.
5. With the engine running at idle, push up the EGR control valve diaphragm by pressing it up with your finger. When this is done, the engine idle should come rough and uneven.

Inspect the two components of the EGR system as necessary in the following manner:

1. Remove the EGR control valve from the intake manifold.
2. Apply 4.7–5.1 in. Hg of vacuum to the EGR control valve by sucking on a tube attached to the outlet on top of the valve. The valve should move to the full up position. The valve should remain open for more than 30 seconds after the application of vacuum is discontinued and the vacuum hose is blocked.
3. Inspect the EGR valve for any signs of warpage or damage.
4. Clean the EGR valve seat with a brush and compressed air to prevent clogging.
5. Connect the EGR solenoid valve to a 12 volt DC power source and notice if the valve clicks when intermittently

electrified. If the valve clicks, it is considered to be working properly.

6. Check the EGR temperature sensing switch by removing it from the engine and placing it in a container of water together with a thermometer. Connect a self-powered test light to the two electrical leads of the switch.

7. Heat the container of water.

8. The switch should conduct current when the water temperature is below 77° F and stop conducting current when the water reaches a temperature somewhere between 88–106° F. Replace the switch if it behaves otherwise.

1975 AND LATER

1. Remove the EGR valve and apply enough vacuum to the diaphragm to open the valve.

2. The valve should remain open for over 30 seconds after the vacuum is removed.

3. Check the valve for damage, such as warpage, cracks, and excessive wear around the valve and seat.

4. Clean the seat with a brush and compressed air and remove any deposits from around the valve and port (seat).

5. To check the operation of the thermal vacuum valve, remove the valve from the engine and apply vacuum to the ports of the valve. The valve should not allow vacuum to pass.

6. Place the valve in a container of water with a thermometer and heat the water. When the temperature of the water reaches 134°–145° F, remove the valve and apply vacuum to the ports; the valve should allow vacuum to pass through it.

7. To test the B.P.T. valve installed on 1978 and later models, disconnect the two vacuum hoses from the valve. Plug one of the ports. While applying pressure to the bottom of the valve, apply vacuum to the unplugged port and check for leakage. If any exists, replace the valve.

8. To test the check valve installed in some 1978 and later models, remove the valve and blow into the side which connects to the EGR valve. Air should flow. When air is applied to the other side, air flow resistance should be greater. If not, replace the valve.

Automatic Temperature Controlled (ATC) Air Cleaner

The rate of fuel atomization varies with the temperature of the air with which the fuel is being mixed. The air/fuel ratio cannot be held constant for efficient fuel combustion with a wide range of air temperatures. Cold air being drawn into the engine causes a denser and richer air/fuel mixture, inefficient fuel atomization, and thus, more hydrocarbons in the exhaust gas. Hot air being drawn into the engine causes a

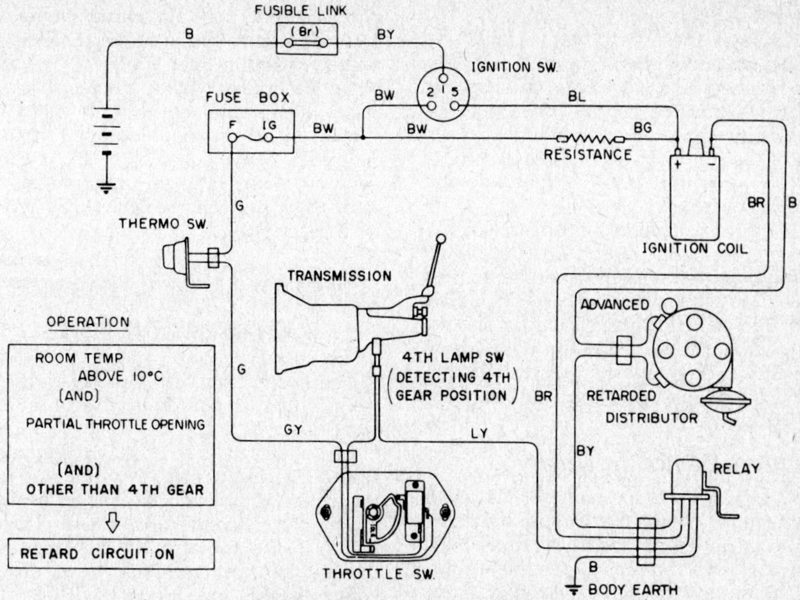

Dual ignition point system

leaner air/fuel mixture and more efficient atomization and combustion for less hydrocarbons in the exhaust gases. The automatic temperature controlled air cleaner is designed so that the temperature of the ambient air being drawn into the engine is automatically controlled, to hold the temperature of the air and, consequently, the fuel/air ratio at a constant rate for efficient fuel combustion.

A temperature sensing vacuum switch controls vacuum applied to a vacuum motor operating a valve in the intake snorkle of the air cleaner. When the engine is cold or the air being drawn into the engine is cold, the vacuum motor opens the valve, allowing air heated by the exhaust manifold to be drawn into the engine. As the engine warms up, the temperature sensing unit shuts off the vacuum applied to the vacuum motor which allows the valve to close, shutting off the heated air and allowing cooler, outside (underhood) air to drawn into the engine.

TESTING

When the air around the temperature sensor of the unit mounted inside the air cleaner housing reaches 100° F, the sensor should block the flow of vacuum to the air control valve vacuum motor. When the temperature around the temperature sensor is below 100° F, the sensor should allow vacuum to pass onto the air valve vacuum motor, thus blocking off the air cleaner snorkle to underhood (unheated) air.

When the temperature around the sensor is about 118° F, the air control valve should be completely open to underhood air.

When the engine is operating under a heavy load (wide open throttle acceleration), the air control valve fully opens to underhood air to obtain full power no matter what the temperature is around the temperature sensor.

Electric Choke

The purpose of the electric choke is to shorten the time that the choke is in operation after the engine is started, thus shortening the time of high HC output.

An electric heater warms the bimetal spring which controls the opening and closing of the choke valve. The heater starts to heat as soon as the engine starts.

Spark Timing Control System

A spark timing control system is added to manual transmission models sold in the U.S. in 1979–80. The system controls distributor vacuum advance, giving full vacuum advance when the transmission is in 4th or 5th, and partial advance in the first three gears. This provides better control of the combustion process, lowering emissions of HC and NOx.

The system components include a top detecting switch, installed into the transmission, and a vacuum switching valve spliced into the distributor vacuum advance hose by means of a three way connector. When the transmission is shifted into either of the two top gears, the transmission switch goes on, thus activating the vacuum switching valve which closes its air bleed, giving full advance. Shifting into any gear but 4th or 5th turns the transmission switch off, deactivating the vacuum switching valve. The valve opens a vacuum leak, providing only partial vacuum advance to the distributor.

TESTING

1. Check all hoses and electrical wires for proper connections, leaks or

corrosion, and so on.

2. Check the distributor vacuum advance unit for proper operation. This can be checked by hooking up a timing light, starting the engine, then increasing engine speed and observing whether or not the timing marks advance. If not, the advance unit must be checked for binding or leaks.

3. With the timing light installed, increase the engine speed to 2000 rpm. Disengage the clutch, then shift between 3rd, 4th, and 5th, then back down and into neutral. Spark timing should vary when the transmission is in 4th or 5th (advance should be greater). If this is not the case, check the vacuum switching valve.

Vacuum Switching Valve

1. Disconnect the valve's electrical connectors. With the timing light installed, run the engine up to about 2000 rpm and keep it there. Check the timing.

2. Connect the valve's electrical connectors directly to the battery with a pair of jumper wires. Be sure to observe correct polarity. If spark timing varies, the valve is ok. If not, replace it.

Transmission Switch

1. The switch can be checked easily with an ohmmeter. Connect the ohmmeter leads to the switch leads on the transmission. Shift back and forth between either 4th or 5th and one of the other gears. If the resistance does not change, replace the switch.

Catalytic Converter

1976 and later trucks sold in California have a catalytic converter, which is a muffler-shaped device installed into the exhaust system. The converter is filled with a monolithic substrate coated with small amounts of platinum and palladium. Through catalytic action, a chemical change converts carbon monoxide and hydrocarbons into carbon dioxide and water. The catalytic process is aided by the injection of air from the air pump system, which oxidizes the HC and CO before they reach the converter.

1976–78 catalyst-equipped trucks have a floor temperature warning system, consisting of a temperature sensor, installed onto the floor of the cab above the converter; a relay, located with the other relays on the right fender of the engine compartment; and a light, installed on the instrument panel. The lamp turns on when floor temperatures become abnormally high, due to converter or engine malfunction. The light also comes on when the ignition switch is turned to Start to check its operation. 1979 and later models do not have the warning system.

Trucks with the catalytic converter also have a combined air control valve in 1978 and 1979, which controls the amount of secondary air injected into the exhaust manifold. It is regulated by engine vacuum and air pump pressure, and works to keep the converter temperatures within proper limits. The combined air control valve replaces the air pump relief valve, found in the air pump system of trucks not equipped with a catalytic converter. 1976–77 models have an emergency air relief valve for catalyst protection. See the AIS section for a description.

Evaporative Emission Control System

There are two different evaporative emission control systems used on Datsun pick-ups.

The system, until 1974, consists of a sealed fuel tank, a vapor-liquid separator, a flow guide (check) valve, and all of the hoses connecting these components, in the above order, leading from the fuel tank to the PCV hose, which connects the crankcase to the PCV valve.

In operation, the vapor formed in the fuel tank passes through the vapor separator, into the flow guide valve and the crankcase. When the engine is not running, if the fuel vapor pressure in the vapor separator goes above 0.4 in. Hg, the flow guide valve opens and allows the vapor to enter the engine crankcase. Otherwise the flow guide valve is closed to the vapor separator while the engine is not running. When the engine is running, a vacuum is developed in the fuel tank or in the engine crankcase and the difference of pressure between the relief side and the fuel tank or crankcase becomes 2 in. Hg, the relief valve opens and allows ambient air from the air cleaner into the fuel tank or the engine crankcase. This ambient air replaces the vapor within the fuel tank or crankcase, bringing the fuel tank or crankcase back into a neutral or positive pressure range.

The system used on 1975 and later models consists of a sealed fuel tank, vapor-liquid separator, vapor vent line, carbon canister, vacuum signal line, and a canister purge line.

In operation, fuel vapors and/or liquid are routed to the liquid/vapor separator where liquid fuel is directed back into the fuel tank as fuel vapors flow into the charcoal-filled canister. The charcoal absorbs and stores the fuel vapors when the engine is not running or is at idle. When the throttle valves in the carburetor are opened, vacuum from above the throttle valves is routed through a vacuum signal line to the purge control valve on the canister. The control valve opens and allows the fuel vapors to be drawn from the canister through a purge line and into the intake manifold and combustion chambers.

INSPECTION AND SERVICE

Check the hoses for proper connections and damage. Replace as necessary. Check the vapor separator tank for fuel leaks, distortion and dents, and replace as necessary.

Flow Guide Valve—Pre-1975

Remove the flow guide valve and inspect it for leakage by blowing air into the ports in the valve. When air is applied from the fuel tank side, the flow guide valve is normal if air passes into the check side (crankcase side), but not leaking into the relief side (air cleaner side). When air is applied from the check side, the valve is normal if the passage of air is restricted. When air is applied from the relief side (air cleaner side), the valve is normal if air passes into the fuel tank side or into the check side.

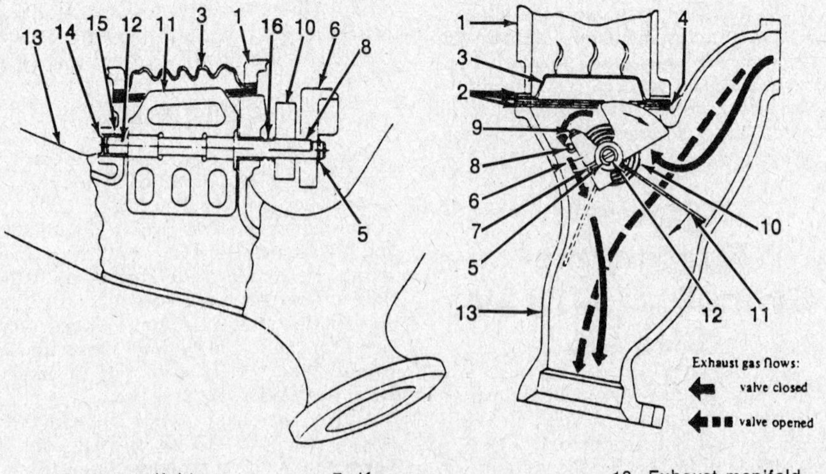

1. Intake manifold
2. Stove gasket
3. Manifold stove
4. Heat shield plate
5. Snap ring
6. Counterweight
7. Key
8. Stopper pin
9. Screw
10. Thermostat spring
11. Heat control valve
12. Control valve shaft
13. Exhaust manifold
14. Cap
15. Bushing
16. Coil spring

Early fuel evaporation system

Carbon Canister and Purge Control Valve—1975 and Later

To check the operation of the carbon canister purge control valve, disconnect the rubber hose between the canister control valve and the T-fitting, at the T-fitting. Apply vacuum to the hose leading to the control valve. The vacuum condition should be maintained indefinitely. If the control valve leaks, remove the top cover of the valve and check for a dislocated or cracked diaphragm. If the diaphragm is damaged, a repair kit containing a new diaphragm, retainer, and spring is available and should be installed.

The carbon canister has an air filter in the bottom of the canister. The filter element should be checked once a year or every 12,000 miles; more frequently if the truck is operated in dusty areas. Replace the filter by pulling it out of the bottom of the canister and installing a new one.

FUEL SYSTEM

Mechanical Fuel Pump

The fuel pump is a mechanically-operated, diaphragm-type driven by the fuel pump eccentric cam on the front of the camshaft. Design of the fuel pump permits disassembly, cleaning, and repair or replacement of defective parts.

TESTING

1. Disconnect the line between the carburetor and the pump at the carburetor.
2. Connect a fuel pump pressure gauge into the line.
3. Start the engine. The pressure should be between 3.0 and 3.9 psi. There is usually enough gas in the float bowl to perform this test.
4. If the pressure is ok, perform a capacity test. Remove the gauge from the line. Use a graduated container to catch the gas from the fuel line. Fill the carburetor float bowl with gas. Run the engine for one minute at about 1000 rpm. The pump should deliver 1000cc in one minute or less.

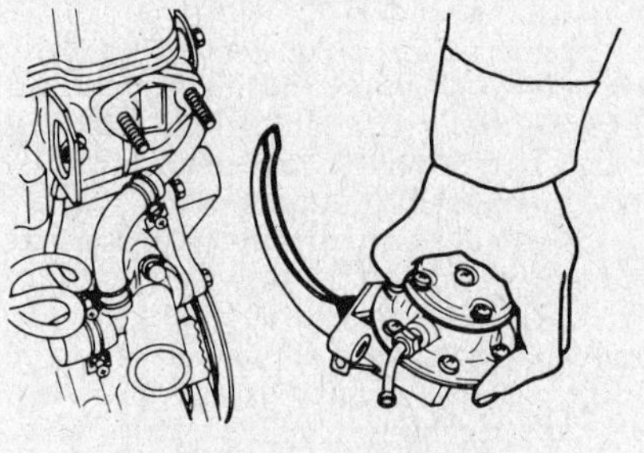

Fuel pump mounting

REMOVAL AND INSTALLATION

1. Disconnect the two fuel lines from the fuel pump. Be sure to keep the line leading from the fuel tank up high to prevent the excessive loss of fuel.
2. Remove the two fuel pump mounting nuts and remove the fuel pump assembly from the side of the engine.
3. Install the fuel pump in the reverse order of removal, using a new gasket and sealer on the mating survace.

Electric Fuel Pump

An electric fuel pump is used on 1977 and later models with factory-installed air conditioning, and also on 1979–80 cab and chassis models. The pump is mounted on a bracket located on the right frame rail next to the fuel tank. There is a filter mounted in the body of the pump, which does not normally require service. The pump can be disassembled, if necessary, but all electronic parts within the body (one transistor, two diodes, and three resistors) must be replaced as an assembly.

TESTING

1. Disconnect the hose from the pump outlet at the pump.
2. Connect a length of hose to the outlet. The hose should have an inside diameter of 1/4 in. (6mm). The diameter of the hose is important for accurate measurements.
3. Raise the end of the hose above the level of the pump. Turn the ignition switch on and catch the gasoline in a graduated container. Pump output should be 1400 cc in one minute or less.
4. Fuel pump pressure should be 4.6 psi through 1978, and between 3.1 and 3.8 psi in 1979–80.

REMOVAL AND INSTALLATION

1. Remove the inlet and outlet hoses, catching the fuel that drains in a metal container.
2. Disconnect the wiring at the connector.
3. Remove the two bolts securing the pump to the bracket and remove the pump.
4. Installation is the reverse. Replace the hose clamps if their condition warrants.

Carburetor

The carburetor used on the Datsun pick-up is a two-barrel, downdraft-type with a low-speed (primary) side and a high-speed (secondary) side. It has an electrically-operated anti-dieseling solenoid. As the ignition switch is turned off, the valve is energized and shuts off the supply of fuel to the idle circuit of the carburetor.

REMOVAL AND INSTALLATION

1. Remove the air cleaner.
2. Disconnect and label the fuel and vacuum lines from the carburetor.
3. Remove the throttle linkage.
4. Remove the four nuts and washers retaining the carburetor to the manifold.
5. Lift the carburetor from the manifold.
6. Remove and discard the gasket used between the carburetor and the manifold.
7. Install the carburetor in the reverse order of removal using a new carburetor base gasket.

AUTOMATIC CHOKE ADJUSTMENT

1. With the engine cold, make sure the choke is fully closed (press the gas pedal all the way to the floor and release, or pull the choke knob out on early models with that system).
2. Check the choke linkage for binding. The choke plate should be easily opened and closed with your finger. If the choke sticks or binds, it can usually be freed with a liberal application of a carburetor cleaner made for the purpose. A couple of quick shots from a spray can of this stuff normally does the trick. If not, the carburetor will have to be disassembled for repairs.
3. The choke is correctly adjusted when the index mark on the choke housing (notch) aligns with the center mark on the carburetor body. If the setting is correct, loosen the three screws clamping the choke body in place and rotate the choke cover left or right until the marks align. Tighten the screws carefully to avoid cracking the housing.

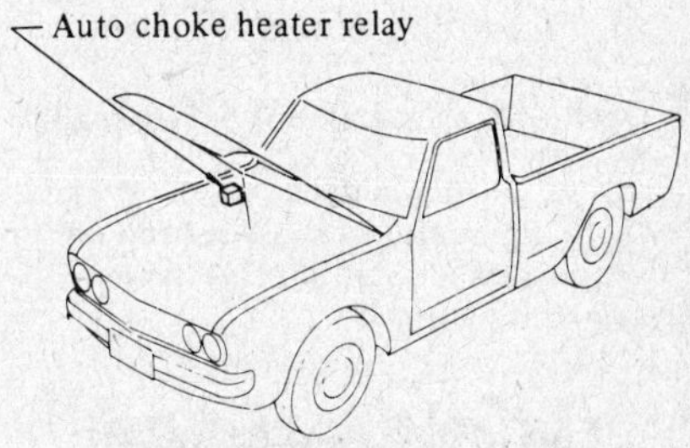

Automatic choke relay location

THROTTLE LINKAGE ADJUSTMENT

When the primary throttle valve is opened to an angle of 50° from its closed position, the adjust plate which is integral with the primary throttle valve, is brought into contact with portion A (see illustration) of the return plate. When the primary throttle valve is opened farther, the return plate is pulled apart from the stopper (B in the illustration), allowing the secondary throttle valve to open.

To adjust the linkage:

1. Measure the clearance between the primary throttle valve and the wall of the throttle chamber at the center of the throttle valve when the adjust plate is brought into contact with portion A of

the return plate. Standard clearance is 0.26–0.32 in.

2. If necessary, make the adjustment by bending the portion A of the return plate.

FLOAT LEVEL ADJUSTMENT

The fuel level is normal if it is within the lines on the window glass of the float chamber when the vehicle is resting on level ground and the engine is off.

If the fuel level is outside the lines, remove the float housing cover. Have an absorbent cloth under the cover to catch the fuel from the fuel bowl. Adjust the float level by bending the needle seat on the float.

The needle valve should have an effective stroke of about 0.0591 in. When necessary, the needle valve stroke can be adjusted by bending the float stopper.

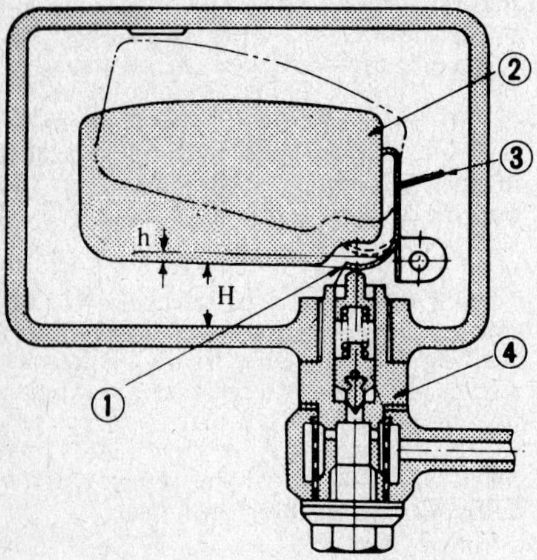

1. Float seat
2. Float
3. Float chamber
4. Needle valve

Carburetor float level adjustment

NOTE: Be careful not to bend the needle valve rod when installing the float and baffle plate, if removed.

FAST IDLE ADJUSTMENT

1. With the carburetor removed from the vehicle, place the upper side of the fast idle screw on the second step of the fast idle cam and measure the clearance between the throttle valve and the wall of the throttle valve chamber at the center of the throttle valve (A in the illustration). The clearance should be 0.035–0.039 in. with manual transmission, or 0.044–0.048 in. with automatic transmission through 1974. For 1975–76 the figures are 0.040–0.048 in., manual, 0.048–0.052 in. automatic.

For 1977–80 models, the fast idle screw should be placed on the first step of the fast idle cam. This is the highest of the four. Clearance A should be 0.052–0.058 in., manual transmission, or 0.062–0.068 in. automatic.

2. Install the carburetor on the engine. Place the fast idle screw on the second step of the cam.

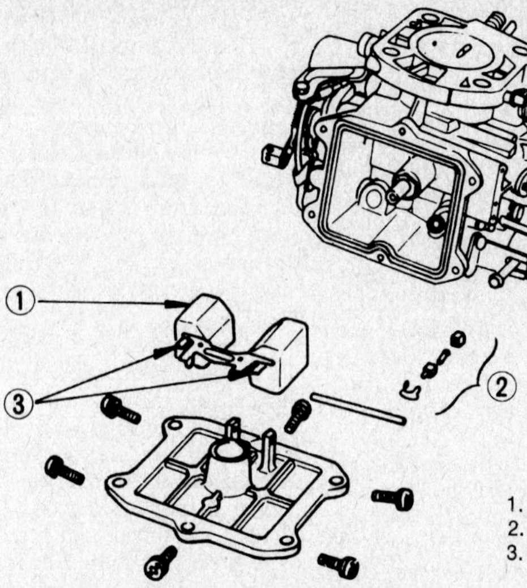

1. Float
2. Needle valve parts
3. Float stopper

Carburetor float chamber

3. Start the engine and measure the fast idle rpm with the engine at operating temperature. The rpm should be about 2,000 rpm with a manual transmission and 2,400 rpm with an automatic transmission through 1976. For 1977–80, the idle should be between 1900 and 2800 for manual transmission, 2200–3200 for automatic. For 1977–80, there is a "reference" value given for distance A, with the carburetor mounted on the engine and the fast idle screw on the *second* step of the cam: 0.037–0.046 in., manual transmission, 0.046–0.055 in., automatic transmission.

4. To adjust the fast idle speed, loosen the locknut and turn the fast idle adjusting screw.

NOTE: The first step of the fast idle adjustment procedure is not absolutely necessary; it should be used as a guide to correct adjustment at overhaul.

CHOKE UNLOADER ADJUSTMENT

1. Close the choke valve completely.
2. Hold the choke valve closed by stretching a rubber band between the choke piston lever and a stationary part of the carburetor.
3. Open the throttle lever fully.
4. With the throttle lever fully open, adjust the clearance between the choke valve and the carburetor body to 0.173 in. through 1974, or 0.096 in., 1975 and later by bending the unloader tongue.

NOTE: Make sure that the throttle valve opens completely when the carburetor is mounted on the engine.

DASHPOT ADJUSTMENT

Only trucks with an automatic transmission have a dashpot through 1974. All 1975 and later models have a dashpot. The purpose of this device is to prevent the throttle from suddenly snapping shut. The dashpot has a plunger which extends when the throttle is closed suddenly. The plunger contacts a tab on the throttle lever and holds the throttle open slightly for a second, then closes the throttle slowly over the period of another second or so.

1. Adjust the idle speed and mixture before making adjustments to the dashpot. Warm the engine to operating temperature, and connect a tachometer to the engine.
2. Move the throttle lever by hand, and note the engine speed when the dashpot plunger just touches the throttle lever.
3. The engine speed should be 1600–1800 rpm through 1974. For 1975 and later trucks, the speed should be 1650–1850 rpm with automatic transmission, or 1900–2100 rpm with manual transmission.
4. If not, loosen the locknut and turn the adjusting screw until the engine speed is in the proper range. Tighten the locknut. On 1978–80 models with air conditioning, a different dashpot is used. Adjustment is made by turning the screw on the throttle lever which contacts the plunger.
5. Open the throttle and allow it to close by itself. The dashpot should smoothly reduce the idling speed from 2000 to 1000 rpm in about three seconds.

OVERHAUL

Efficient carburetion depends greatly on careful cleaning and inspection during overhaul, since dirt, gum, water, or varnish in or on the carburetor parts are often responsible for poor performance.

Overhaul your carburetor in a clean, dust-free area. Carefully disassemble the carburetor, referring often to the exploded views. Keep all similar and look-alike parts segregated during disassembly and cleaning to avoid accidental interchange during assembly. Make a note of all jet sizes.

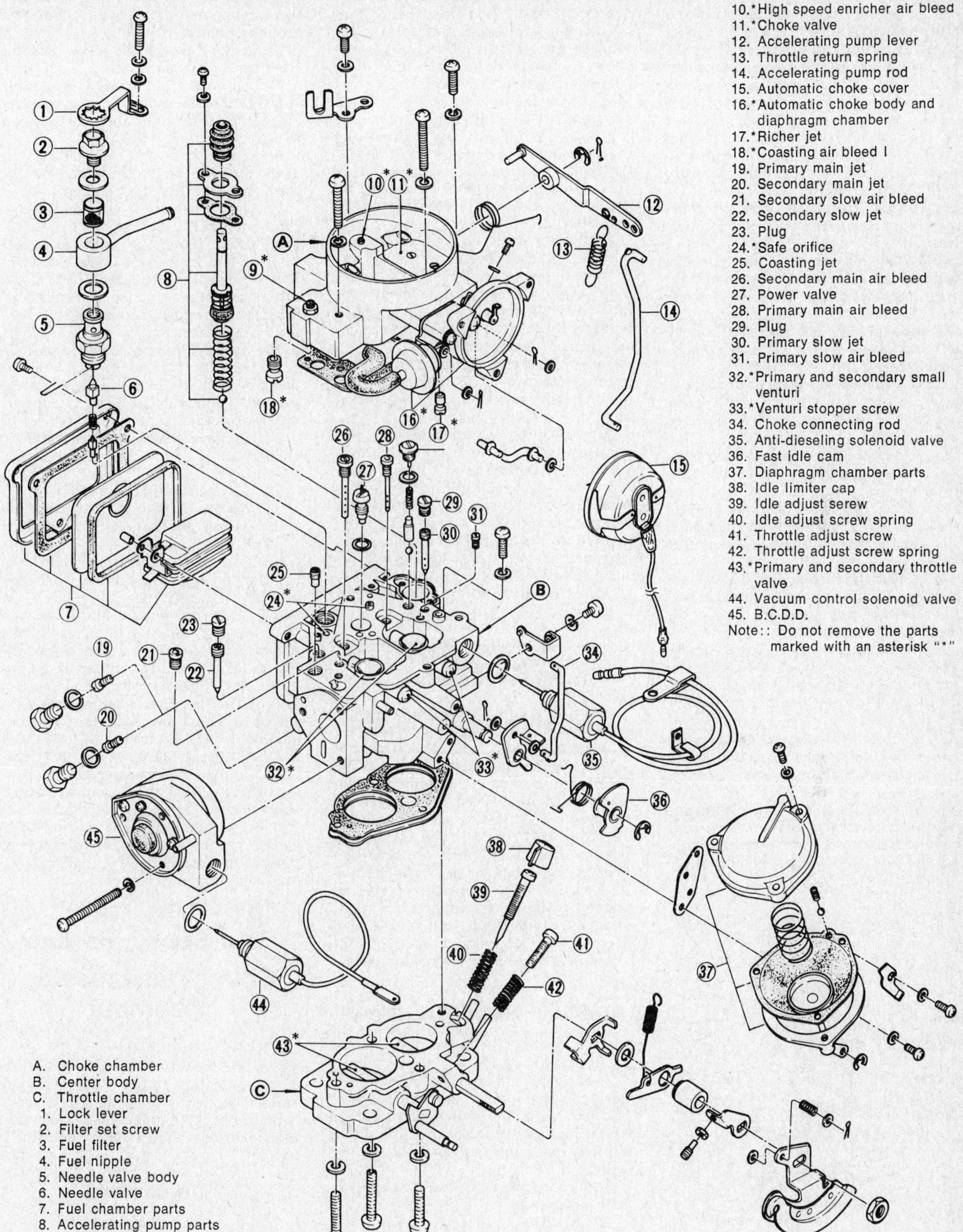

A. Choke chamber
B. Center body
C. Throttle chamber
1. Lock lever
2. Filter set screw
3. Fuel filter
4. Fuel nipple
5. Needle valve body
6. Needle valve
7. Fuel chamber parts
8. Accelerating pump parts
9. Coasting air bleed adjusting screw
10.*High speed enricher air bleed
11.*Choke valve
12. Accelerating pump lever
13. Throttle return spring
14. Accelerating pump rod
15. Automatic choke cover
16.*Automatic choke body and diaphragm chamber
17.*Richer jet
18.*Coasting air bleed I
19. Primary main jet
20. Secondary main jet
21. Secondary slow air bleed
22. Secondary slow jet
23. Plug
24.*Safe orifice
25. Coasting jet
26. Secondary main air bleed
27. Power valve
28. Primary main air bleed
29. Plug
30. Primary slow jet
31. Primary slow air bleed
32.*Primary and secondary small venturi
33.*Venturi stopper screw
34. Choke connecting rod
35. Anti-dieseling solenoid valve
36. Fast idle cam
37. Diaphragm chamber parts
38. Idle limiter cap
39. Idle adjust serew
40. Idle adjust screw spring
41. Throttle adjust screw
42. Throttle adjust screw spring
43.*Primary and secondary throttle valve
44. Vacuum control solenoid valve
45. B.C.D.D.

Note:: Do not remove the parts marked with an asterisk "*"

Carburetor components

When the carburetor is disassembled, wash all parts (except diaphragms, electric choke units, pump plunger, and any other plastic, leather, fiber, or rubber parts) in clean carburetor solvent. Do not leave parts int the solvent any longer than is necessary to sufficiently loosen the deposits. Excessive cleaning may remove the special finish from the float bowl and choke valve bodies, leaving these parts unfit for service. Rinse all parts in clean solvent and blow them dry with compressed air or allow them to air dry. Wipe clean all cork, plastic, leather, or fiber parts with a clean, lint-free cloth.

Blow out all passages and jets with compressed air and be sure that there are no restrictions or blockages. Never use wire or similar tools to clean jets, fuel passages, or air bleeds. Clean all jets and valves separately to avoid accidental interchange.

Check all parts for wear or damage. If wear or damage is found, replace the defective parts. Especially check the following:

1. Check the float needle and seat for wear. If wear is found, replace the complete assembly.
2. Check the float hinge pin for wear and the float(s) for dents or distortion. Replace the float if fuel has leaked into it.
3. Check the throttle and choke shaft bores for wear or an out-of-round condition. Damage or wear to the throttle arm, shaft, or shaft bore will often require replacements of the throttle body. These parts require a close tolerance of fit; wear may allow air leakage, which could affect satrting and idling.

NOTE: Throttle shafts and bushings are not included in overhaul kits. They can be purchased separately.

4. Inspect the idle mixture adjusting needles for burrs or grooves. Any such condition requires replacement of the needle, since you will not be able to obtain a satisfactory idle.

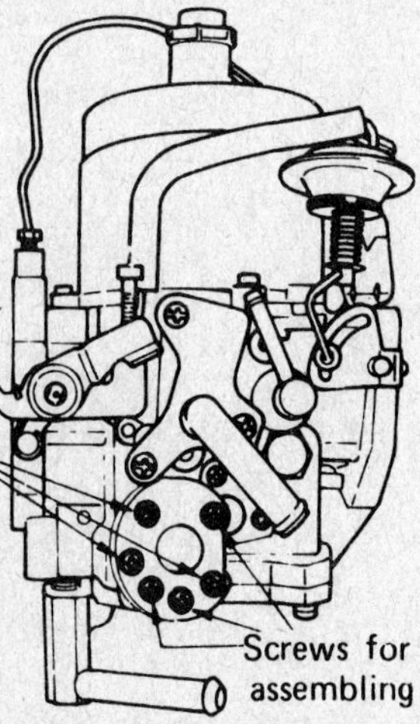

Carburetor power valve

5. Test the accelerator pump check valves. They should pass air one way but not the other. Test for proper seating by blowing and sucking on the valve. Replace the valve if necessary. If the valve is satisfactory, wash the valve again to remove breath moisture.
6. Check the bowl cover for warped surfaces with a straightedge.
7. Closely inspect the valves and seats for wear and damage, replacing as necessary.
8. After the carburetor is assembled, check the choke valve for freedom of operation.

Carburetor overhaul kits are recommended for each overhaul. These kits contain all gaskets and new parts to replace those that deteriorate most rapidly. Failure to replace all parts supplied with the kit (especially gaskets) can result in poor performance later.

Some carburetor manufacturers supply overhaul kits of three basic types; minor repair; major repair; and gasket kits.

After cleaning and checking all components, reassemble the carburetor. When reassembling, make sure that all screws and jets are tight in their seats, but do not overtighten as the tips will be distorted. Tighten all screws gradually, in rotation. Do not tighten needle valves into their seats; uneven jetting will result. Always use new gaskets. Be sure to adjust the float level when reassembling.

MANUAL TRANSMISSION

The Datsun pick-up uses an F4W63 four speed transmission through 1974, an F4W71B four speed 1975–80, or an optional FS5W71B five speed transmission from 1977 to 1980. The F4W63 is a bottom cover unit, with an extension housing for the shift rail, while the two later models have a one piece case, an adapter plate which supports the mainshaft and countershaft, and an extension housing. All units have internal shift rails; no linkage adjustments are necessary.

REMOVAL AND INSTALLATION

1. Disconnect the battery ground cable from the battery.
2. On 1975 and later models only, remove the shift lever from inside the cab. It is retained to the shift rail by a c-clip, accessible under the boot. Remove the c-clip and retaining pin, and remove the lever.
3. Jack up the vehicle and support it with jackstands.
4. On 1973–74 models, unscrew the nut securing the bottom of the shifter to the transmission shifting mechanism.
5. Disconnect the exhaust pipe from the exhaust manifold. On trucks with a catalytic converter, also remove the exhaust pipe bracket next to the speedometer cable by unscrewing the two mounting bolts.
6. Remove the clutch slave cylinder from the transmission case.
7. Disconnect the speedometer cable from the transmission extension housing and the back-up light and transmission switch wires at the switch(es).
8. Remove the bracket holding the center bearing of the driveshaft on the third crossmember of the frame.
9. Matchmark the u-joint and flange for installation. Disconnect the driveshaft from flange at the differential housing and remove the driveshaft from under the vehicle by sliding it out of the extension housing of the transmission. Plug the rear of the transmission to prevent loss of lubricant.
10. Support the engine with a jack located under the oil pan. Place a block of wood between the jack and the oil pan to prevent damage to the oil pan. Support the transmission with a jack.
11. Remove the rear engine mount securing bolts and the crossmember mounting bolts.
12. Remove the starter motor.
13. Remove the bolts securing the transmission to the engine, pull the transmission toward the rear until the transmission mainshaft is free of the back of the engine. Separate the transmission from the engine than lower the transmission out from under the truck.
14. Install the transmission in the reverse order of removal. Before installing, clean the mating surfaces of the engine and transmission thoroughly. Lightly coat the input shaft splines with grease. Tighten the engine-to-transmission bolts to 17–20 ft lbs, 1973, 29–36 ft lbs, 1974–76; or 32–43 ft lbs, 1977 and later. Tighten the crossmember to chassis bolts to 20–27 ft lbs, and the clutch slave cylinder mounting bolts to 18–22 ft lbs. Be sure to align the marks made earlier on the U-joint and differential flange when installing the driveshaft, to maintain driveline balance.

Four Speed, Bottom Cover Transmission Overhaul

The reverse and reverse idler drive gears are contained in the extension housing of this transmission. On late units, the cast, ribbed bottom cover is replaced by a stamped steel cover. The transmissions have a floorshift mechanism.

Disassembly

1. Drain the transmission.
2. Remove the clutch withdrawal lever and release bearing.
3. Remove the clevis pin which connects the striker rod to the shift lever.

4. Remove the speedometer drive pinion assembly.

5. Unbolt and remove the extension housing, disengaging the striker rod from the shift rod gates.

6. Remove the bottom and front covers.

7. Remove the three detent plugs, springs, and balls.

8. Drive out the shift fork retaining pins. Remove the rods and forks.

9. Move the first/second and third/fourth coupling sleeves into gear at the same time to lock the mainshaft.

10. Pull out the countershaft and countergear with the two needle roller bearings and spacers.

11. Remove the snap-ring, reverse idler gears, and shaft.

12. Unbolt the mainshaft rear bearing retainer.

13. Pull out the mainshaft assembly to the rear. Pull out the clutch shaft to the front.

14. To disassemble the mainshaft, remove the snap-ring, third/fourth synchronizer hub and coupling sleeve. Remove third gear, with the roller bearing. Remove the mainshaft nut, lockplate, speedometer drive gear, and steel ball. Take off reverse gear and the hub. Press off the bearing and retainer. Remove the thrust washer and first gear with the needle roller bearing and bushing. Be careful not to lose the steel ball which locates the thrust washer. Take off the first/second synchronizer and hub. Remove second gear with the needle roller bearing.

INSPECTION

1. Clean all parts with a safe solvent. Lubricate the bearings with gear oil.

2. Check the mainshaft for straightness. Runout at the rear of the shaft should not exceed 0.0059 in. (0.15 mm.). Make sure the synchronizer hubs slide freely without excessive clearance.

3. Place the synchronizer baulk ring in position on the cone of its gear. Check the gap between the baulk ring end face and the front face of the clutch teeth. The gap should be 0.0472–0.0360 in. (1.2–1.6 mm.). If it is less than 0.0315 in. (0.8 mm.) replace the ring.

4. The clearance between the shift forks and their grooves should be 0.0059–0.0118 in. (0.15–0.30 mm.).

5. Replace all O-rings and oil seals.

ASSEMBLY

Assembly procedures are generally the reverse of disassembly, however the following special instructions are required.

1. On the clutch shaft, there should be no end-play between the bearing and the snap-ring. Snap-rings are available in sizes from 0.0598 in. (1.52 mm.) to 0.0697 in. (1.77 mm.).

2. Some of these transmissions use a servo type synchronizer which utilizes brake bands. To assemble these synchronizers, place each gear on a flat sur-

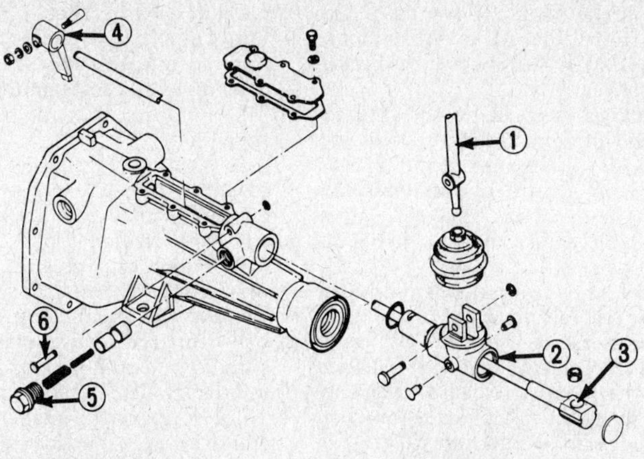

1. Control lever
2. Striking rod guide
3. Striking rod
4. Striking lever
5. Return spring plug
6. Selector rod

Four speed transmission shifting mechanism

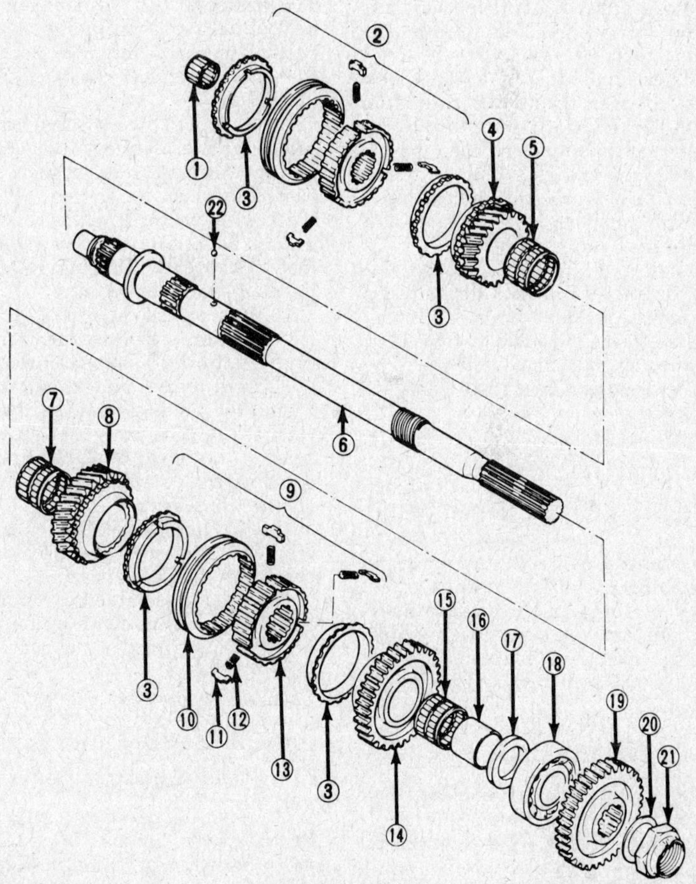

1. Pilot bearing
2. 3rd & 4th synchronizer assembly
3. Baulk ring
4. 3rd speed gear, mainshaft
5. Needle bearing
6. Mainshaft
7. Needle bearing
8. 2nd speed gear, mainshaft
9. 1st & 2nd synchronizer assembly
10. Coupling sleeve
11. Shifting insert
12. Shifting insert spring
13. Synchronizer hub
14. 1st speed gear, mainshaft
15. Needle bearing
16. Bush, 1st speed gear
17. Thrust washer, mainshaft
18. Mainshaft bearing
19. Reverse gear, mainshaft
20. Thrust washer
21. Nut
22. Steel ball

Four speed transmission main shaft assembly

face. Install the synchronizer ring into the clutch gear. Place the thrust block and anchor block and install the circlip into the groove.

3. Third gear should be adjusted to give an end-play of 0.0020–0.0059 in. (0.05–0.15 mm.). Snap-rings for adjustment are available in sizes from 0.551 in. (1.40 mm.) to 0.0630 in. (1.60 mm.).

4. Tighten the mainshaft nut to 65–80 ft lbs.

5. Install the reverse idler driving gear on the reverse shaft and fasten with a snap-ring. Install the shaft and gear into the case, placing a thrust washer between the gear and case. Place a thrust washer, idler gear, and snap-ring on the inside end of the shaft. Idler gear end-play should be 0.0039–0.0118 in. (0.1–0.3 mm.). Snap-rings are available in sizes from 0.0433 in. (1.1 mm.) to 0.0591 in. (1.5 mm.).

6. Countergear end-play should be 0.0020–0.0059 in. (0.05–0.15 mm.). Thrust washers for adjustment are available from 0.0945 in. (2.40 mm.) to 0.1024 in. (2.60 mm.).

7. To assemble the shift mechanism, place the first/second and third/fourth forks onto their sleeves. Insert the first/second shift rod. Install an interlock plunger and then the third/fourth shift rod with the interlock pin. Install the other interlock plunger and then the reverse shift fork and rod. Place a detent ball and spring into each detent hole. Use sealant on the plug threads and torque the plug to 12–15 ft lbs.

8. Install the extension housing, engaging the striker rod with the shift rod gates. Torque the bolts to 16–22 ft lbs. Torque the front cover bolts to 8–12 ft lbs. Torque the bottom cover bolts to 8–12 ft lbs. See the Capacities Chart for refill capacity.

Four Speed Transmission Overhaul

This transmission is constructed in three sections: clutch housing, transmission housing, and extension housing. There are no case cover plates. There is a cast iron adapter plate between the transmission and extension housings.

DISASSEMBLY

1. Remove the clutch housing dust cover. Remove the retaining spring, release bearing sleeve, and withdrawal lever.

2. Remove the backup light/neutral safety switch.

3. Unbolt and remove the clutch housing, rapping with a soft hammer if necessary. Remove the gasket, mainshaft bearing shim, and countershaft bearing shim.

4. Remove the speedometer pinion sleeve.

5. Remove the striker rod pin from the rod. Separate the striker rod from the shift lever bracket.

6. Unbolt and remove the rear extension. It may be necessary to rap the housing with a soft hammer.

7. Remove the mainshaft bearing snap-ring.

8. Remove the adapter plate and gear assembly from the transmission case by rapping with a soft hammer. Hold the adapter plate in a vise.

9. Punch out the shift fork retaining pins. Remove the shift rod snap-rings. Remove the detent plugs, springs, and balls from the adapter plate. Remove the shift rods, being careful not to lose the interlock balls.

10. Remove the snap-ring, speedometer drive gear, and locating ball.

11. Bend back the mainshaft lock tab. Remove the nut, lockwasher, thrust washer, reverse hub, and reverse gear.

12. Remove the snap-ring and countershaft reverse gear. Remove the snap-ring, reverse idler gear, thrust washer, and needle bearing.

13. Support the gear assembly while rapping the rear of the mainshaft with a soft hammer. An assistant would be helpful to avoid dropping any of the parts. The mainshaft will separate into the forward clutch shaft and the rear mainshaft.

14. Remove the setscrew from the adapter plate. Remove the shaft nut, spring washer, plain washer, and reverse idler shaft.

15. Remove the machine screws holding the bearing retainer with an impact tool. Remove the bearing retainer and the mainshaft rear bushing.

16. To disassemble the mainshaft (rear section), remove the front snap-ring, third/fourth synchronizer assembly, third gear, and needle bearing. From the rear, remove the thrust washer, locating ball, first gear, needle bearing, first gear bushing, first/second synchronizer assembly, second gear, and needle bearing.

17. To disassemble the clutch shaft, remove the snap-ring and bearing spacer and press off the bearing.

18. To disassemble the countershaft, press off the front bearing. Press off the rear bearing, press of the gears and remove the keys.

19. Remove the retaining pin, control arm pin, and shift control arm from the rear of the extension housing.

INSPECTION

1. Wash all parts in a safe solvent. Oil bearings immediately. Check all parts for wear or damage. Replace all seals, O-rings, and gaskets.

2. When reassembling, gear backlash between mating gears should be 0.0020–0.0059 in. (0.05–0.15 mm.). If excessive, replace both driving and driven gears.

3. Gear end-play should be 0.0047–0.0075 in. (0.12–0.19 mm.) for all gears except the reverse idler. Reverse idler gear end-play should be 0.0020–0.0138 in. (0.05–0.35 mm.). End-play is adjusted by installing snap-rings of different thicknesses.

4. Check the synchronizer baulk ring inside serration for wear. The slot should be 0.0472–0.0550 in. (1.2–1.4 mm.) wide.

ASSEMBLY

1. Place the O-ring in the front cover. Install the front cover to the clutch housing with a press. Put in the front cover oil seal.

2. Install the rear extension oil seal with a drift.

3. Assemble the first/second and third/fourth synchronizer assemblies. Make sure that the ring gaps are not both on the same side of the unit.

4. On the rear end of the mainshaft, install the needle bearing, second gear, baulk ring, first/second synchronizer assembly, baulk ring, first gear bushing, needle bearing, first gear, locating ball, and thrust washer.

5. Drive or press on the mainshaft rear bearing.

6. Install the countershaft rear bearing to the adapter plate. Drive or press the mainshaft rear bearing into the adapter plate until the bearing snap-ring groove comes through the rear side of the plate. Install the snap-ring. If it is not tight against the plate, press the bearing back in slightly.

7. Insert the countershaft bearing ring between the countershaft rear bearing and bearing retainer. Install the bearing retainer to the adapter plate, torquing the screws to 9–13 ft lbs. Stake both ends of the screws with a punch.

8. Insert the reverse idler shaft from the rear of the adapter plate. Torque the set-screw to 9–13 ft lbs. Install the spring washer and plain washer to the idler shaft. Torque the shaft nut to 43–58 ft lbs.

9. Place the two keys on the countershaft and oil the shaft lightly. Press on third gear and install a snap-ring.

10. Install the countershaft into its rear bearing.

11. From the front of the mainshaft, install the needle bearing, third gear, baulk ring, third/fourth synchronizer assembly, and snap-ring. Snap-rings are available in thicknesses from 0.0561 in. (1.425 mm.) to 0.0640 in. (1.625 mm.) to adjust gear end-play to the figure specified under "Inspection."

12. Press the main drive bearing onto the clutch shaft. Install the main drive gear spacer and a snap-ring. Snap-rings are available in thicknesses from 0.0710 in. (1.80 mm.) to 0.0820 in. (2.08 mm.) to adjust gear end-play to the figure specified under "Inspection."

13. Insert a key into the countershaft. Insert the pilot bearing in the clutch shaft assembly. Engage the countershaft drive gear with fourth gear and drive on the countershaft fourth gear with a drift. The rear end of the countershaft should be held steady while driving on the gear, to prevent rear bearing damage.

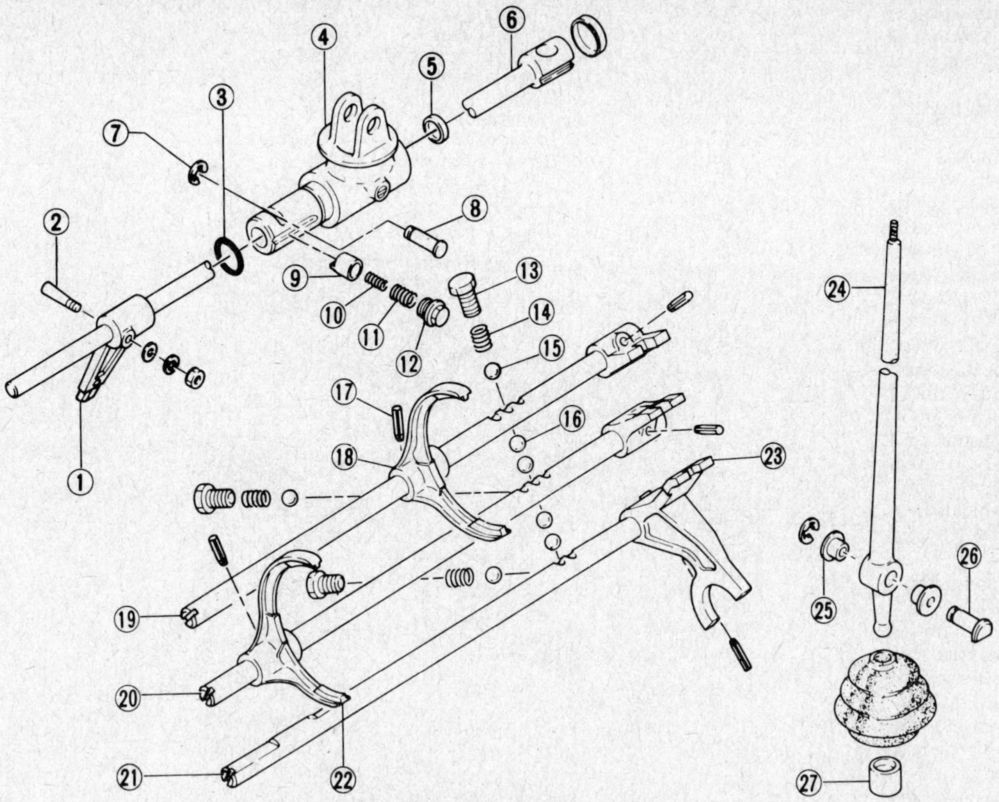

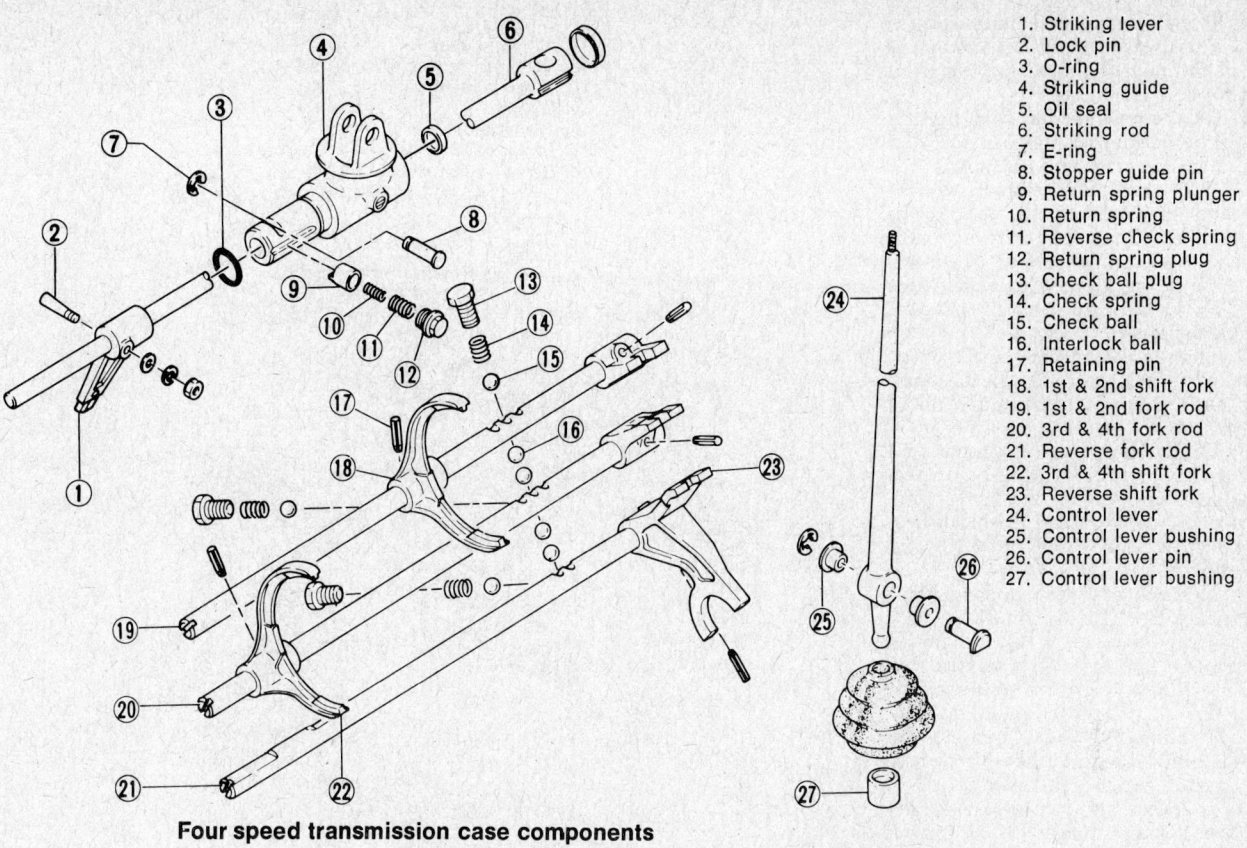

1. Striking lever
2. Lock pin
3. O-ring
4. Striking guide
5. Oil seal
6. Striking rod
7. E-ring
8. Stopper guide pin
9. Return spring plunger
10. Return spring
11. Reverse check spring
12. Return spring plug
13. Check ball plug
14. Check spring
15. Check ball
16. Interlock ball
17. Retaining pin
18. 1st & 2nd shift fork
19. 1st & 2nd fork rod
20. 3rd & 4th fork rod
21. Reverse fork rod
22. 3rd & 4th shift fork
23. Reverse shift fork
24. Control lever
25. Control lever bushing
26. Control lever pin
27. Control lever bushing

Four speed transmission case components

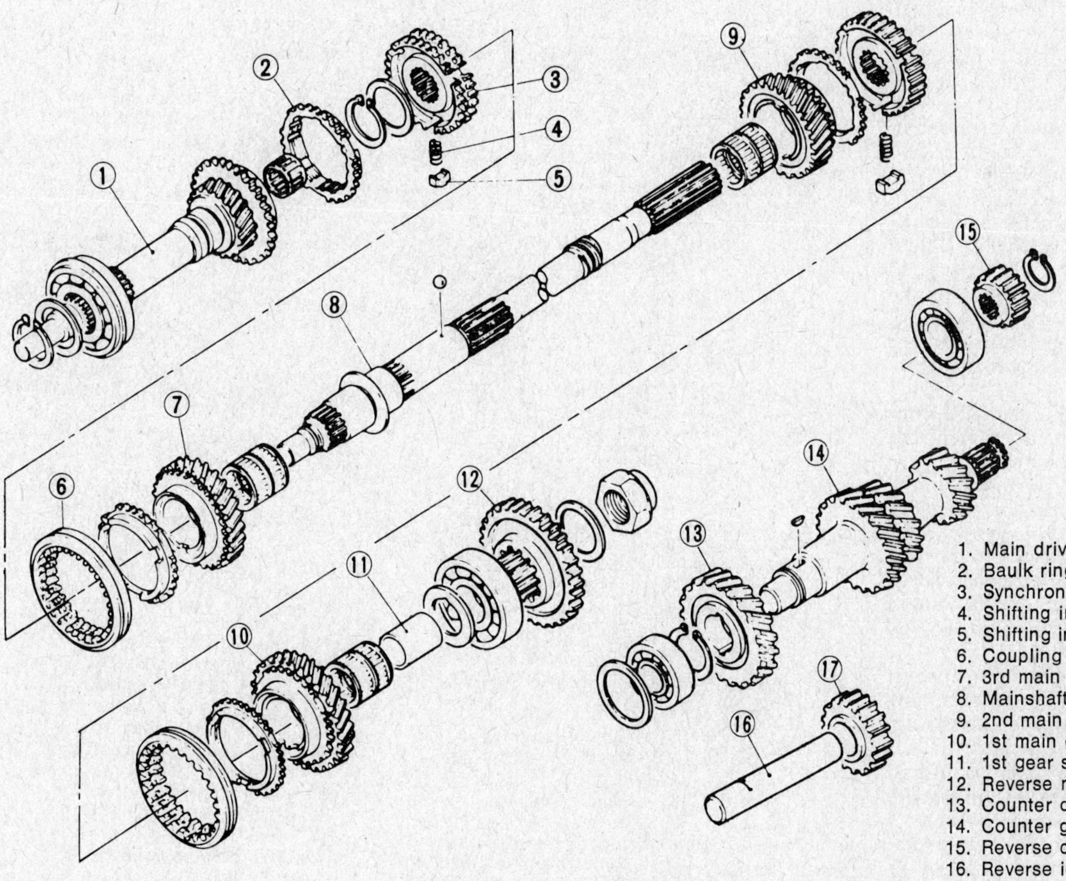

1. Main drive gear
2. Baulk ring
3. Synchronizer hub, 3rd & 4th
4. Shifting insert spring
5. Shifting insert
6. Coupling sleeve
7. 3rd main gear
8. Mainshaft
9. 2nd main gear
10. 1st main gear
11. 1st gear spacer
12. Reverse main gear
13. Counter drive gear
14. Counter gear
15. Reverse counter gear
16. Reverse idler shaft
17. Reverse idler gear

Four speed transmission gear components

14. Install the reverse hub, reverse gear, thrust washer, and lock tab on the rear of the mainshaft. Install the shaft nut temporarily.

15. Oil the reverse idler shaft lightly. Install the needle bearing, reverse idler gear, thrust washer, and snap-ring.

16. Place the countershaft reverse gear and snap-ring on the rear of the countershaft. Snap-rings are available in thicknesses from 0.0433 in. (1.1 mm.) to 0.0590 in. (1.5 mm.) to adjust gear end-play to the figure specified under "Inspection."

17. Engage both first and second gears to lock the shaft. Torque the mainshaft nut to 130–152 ft lbs. and bend up the lock tab.

18. On the rear of the mainshaft, install the snap-ring, locating ball, speedometer drive gear, and snap-ring. Snap-rings are available in thicknesses from 0.0433 in. (1.1 mm.) to 0.0590 in. (1.5 mm.).

19. Recheck end-play and backlash of all gears. See "Inspection."

20. Place the reverse shift fork on the reverse gear and install the reverse shift rod. Install the detent ball, spring, and plug. Install the fork retaining pin. Place two interlock balls between the reverse shift rod and the third/fourth shift rod location. Install the third/fourth shift fork and rod. Install the detent ball, spring, and plug. This plug is shorter than the other two. Install the fork retaining pin. Place two interlock balls between the first/second shift rod location and the third/fourth shift rod. Install the first/second shift fork and rod. Install the detent ball, spring, and plug. Apply locking agent to each detent plug and torque them to 16–22 ft lbs. Install the fork retaining pin.

21. Install the shift rod snap-rings.

22. Oil all moving parts and make sure that all gears can be shifted smoothly.

23. Apply sealant sparingly to the adapter plate and transmission housing. Install the transmission housing to the adapter plate and bolt it down temporarily.

24. Drive in the countershaft front bearing with a drift. Place the snap-ring in the mainshaft front bearing.

25. Apply sealant sparingly to the adapter plate and extension housing. Align the shift rods in the neutral positions. Position the striker rod to the shift rods and bolt down the extension housing. Torque to 11–16 ft lbs. Be careful not to damage the extension housing oil seal in installation.

26. Insert the striker rod pin, connect the rod to the shift lever bracket, and install the striker rod pin retaining ring. Replace the shift control arm.

27. To select the proper mainshaft bearing shim, first measure the amount the bearing protrudes from the front of the transmission case. This is measurement (B). Then measure the depth of the bearing recess in the rear of the clutch housing. This is measurement (A). Re-

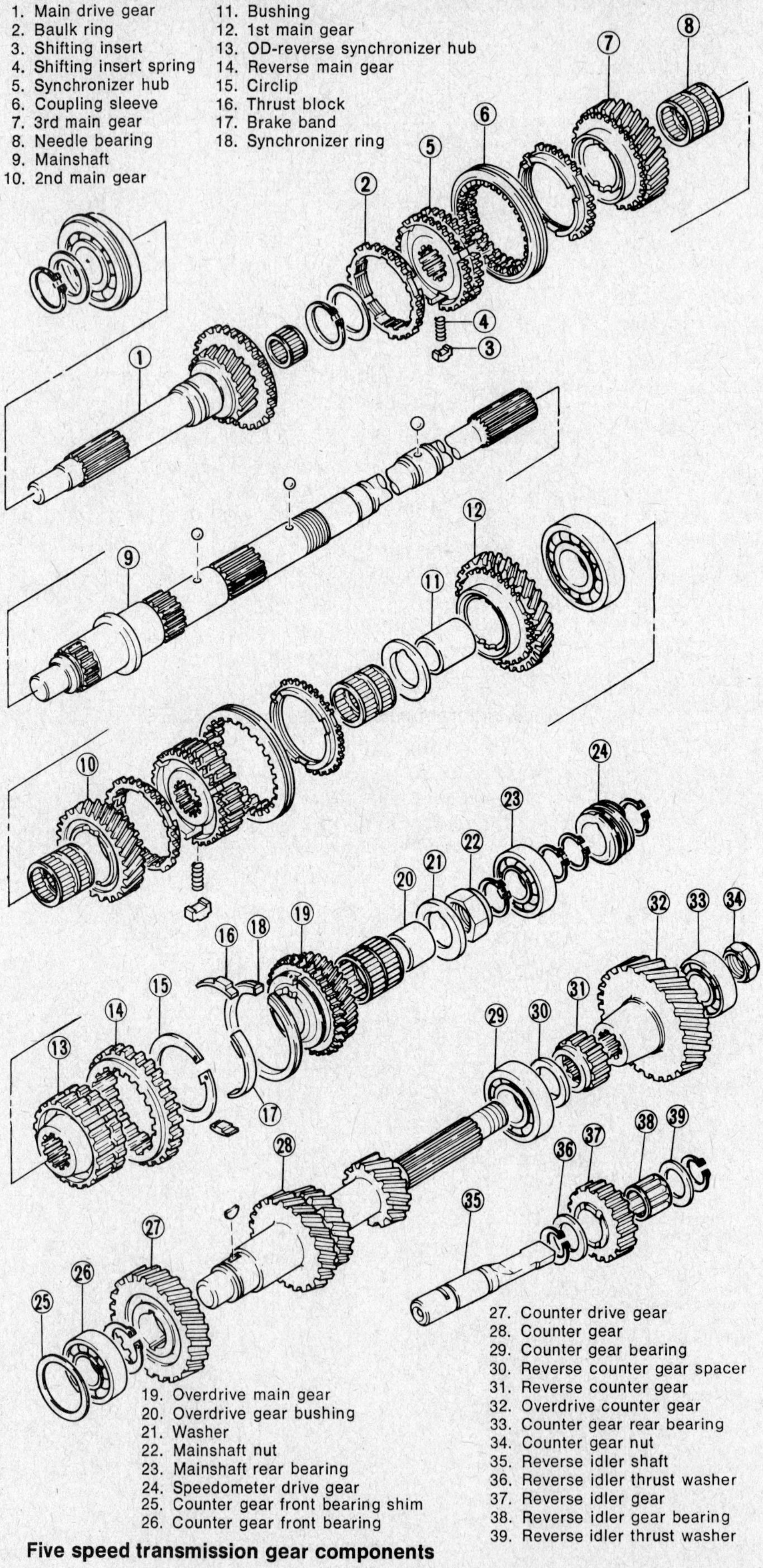

1. Main drive gear
2. Baulk ring
3. Shifting insert
4. Shifting insert spring
5. Synchronizer hub
6. Coupling sleeve
7. 3rd main gear
8. Needle bearing
9. Mainshaft
10. 2nd main gear
11. Bushing
12. 1st main gear
13. OD-reverse synchronizer hub
14. Reverse main gear
15. Circlip
16. Thrust block
17. Brake band
18. Synchronizer ring
19. Overdrive main gear
20. Overdrive gear bushing
21. Washer
22. Mainshaft nut
23. Mainshaft rear bearing
24. Speedometer drive gear
25. Counter gear front bearing shim
26. Counter gear front bearing
27. Counter drive gear
28. Counter gear
29. Counter gear bearing
30. Reverse counter gear spacer
31. Reverse counter gear
32. Overdrive counter gear
33. Counter gear rear bearing
34. Counter gear nut
35. Reverse idler shaft
36. Reverse idler thrust washer
37. Reverse idler gear
38. Reverse idler gear bearing
39. Reverse idler thrust washer

Five speed transmission gear components

quired shim thickness is found by subtracting (B) from (A). Shims are available in thicknesses of 0.0551 in. (1.4 mm.) and 0.0630 in. (1.6 mm.).

28. To select the proper countershaft front bearing shim, measure the amount that the bearing is recessed into the transmission case. Shim thickness should equal this measurement. Shims are available in thicknesses from 0.0157 in. (.4 mm.) to 0.0394 in. (1.0 mm.).

29. Apply sealant sparingly to the clutch and transmission housing mating surfaces and torque the bolts to 11–16 ft lbs.

30. Replace the clutch operating mechanism.

31. Install the shift lever temporarily and check shifting action.

32. Refill the transmission. See the Capacities Chart.

Five Speed Transmission Overhaul

This transmission is quite similar to the four speed unit. Servo type synchromesh is used, instead of the Borg Warner type in the four speed. Shift linkage and interlock arrangements are the same, except the reverse shift rod also operates fifth gear. Most service procedures are identical to those for the four speed unit. Those unique to the five-speed follow.

DISASSEMBLY

To disassemble the synchronizers, remove the circlip, synchronizer ring, thrust block, brake band, and anchor block. Be careful not to mix parts of the different synchronizer assemblies.

INSPECTION

1. Gear backlash should be 0.0016–0.0059 in. (0.04–0.15 mm.) for the main drive gear and reverse gear. For first, second, third, and fifth gears it should be 0.0016–0.0079 in. (0.04–0.20 mm.).

2. Gear end-play should be:

5-SPEED TRANSMISSION END-PLAY SPECIFICATIONS

Gear	End-Play In. (mm.)
First, Second, Fifth	0.0039-0.0075 (0.12-0.19)
Third	0.0039-0.0094 (0.12-0.24)
Reverse Idler	0.0019-0.0137 (0.05-0.35)

ASSEMBLY

1. The synchronizer assemblies for second, third, and fourth are identical. When assembling the first gear synchronizer, be sure to install the 0.0866 in (2.2 mm.) thick brake band at the bottom.

2. When assembling the mainshaft, select a third gear synchronizer hub snap-ring to minimize hub end-play. Snap-rings are available in thicknesses of 0.0610–0.0630 in. (1.55–1.60 mm.), 0.–0591–0.0610 in. (1.50–1.55 mm.), and 0.–0571–0.0591 in. (1.45–1.50 mm.). The synchronizer hub must be installed with the longer boss to the rear.

3. When reassembling the gear train, install the mainshaft, countershaft, and gears to the adapter plate. To tighten the mainshaft locknuts, tighten the front nut to 15–22 ft lbs. and the rear nut to 7–15 ft lbs. Hold the rear nut and force the front nut against it to a torque of 217 ft lbs. Select a snap-ring to minimize end-play of the fifth gear bearing at the rear of the mainshaft. Snap-rings are available in thicknesses from 0.0433 in. (1.1 mm.) to 0.0551 in. (1.4 mm.).

CLUTCH

The clutch is a hydraulically-operated single-plate, dry friction disc, diaphragm spring type.

The clutch is operated by a clutch pedal which is mechanically connected to a clutch master cylinder. When the pedal is depressed, the piston is the master cylinder is moved in the master cylinder bore. This movement compresses the fluid in the master cylinder causing hydraulic pressure which is transferred through a tube to the slave cylinder. The slave cylinder is mounted to the clutch housing with its piston connected to the clutch release lever. The hydraulic pressure in the slave cylinder forces the slave cylinder piston to travel out the cylinder bore and move the clutch release lever, disengaging the clutch.

Pedal Height and Free-Play Adjustment

1. Disconnect the pushrod clevis from the clutch pedal and adjust the clutch pedal height to 5.91 in., 1973; 6.02 in., 1974–77; 6.42 in., 1978–80, by loosening the locknut on the pedal stopper. Turn the pedal stopper in or out as necessary and retighten the locknut.

2. Loosen the locknut on the pushrod and adjust the position of the clevis so

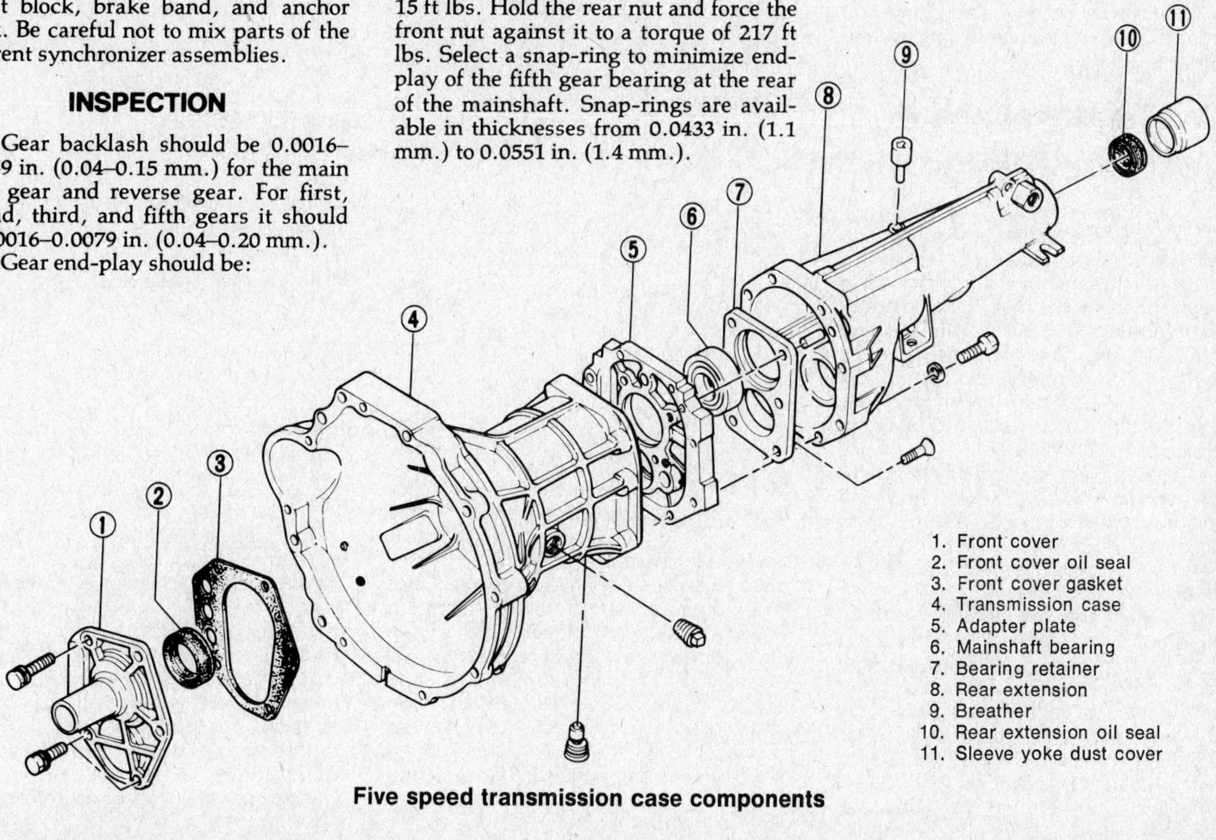

1. Front cover
2. Front cover oil seal
3. Front cover gasket
4. Transmission case
5. Adapter plate
6. Mainshaft bearing
7. Bearing retainer
8. Rear extension
9. Breather
10. Rear extension oil seal
11. Sleeve yoke dust cover

Five speed transmission case components

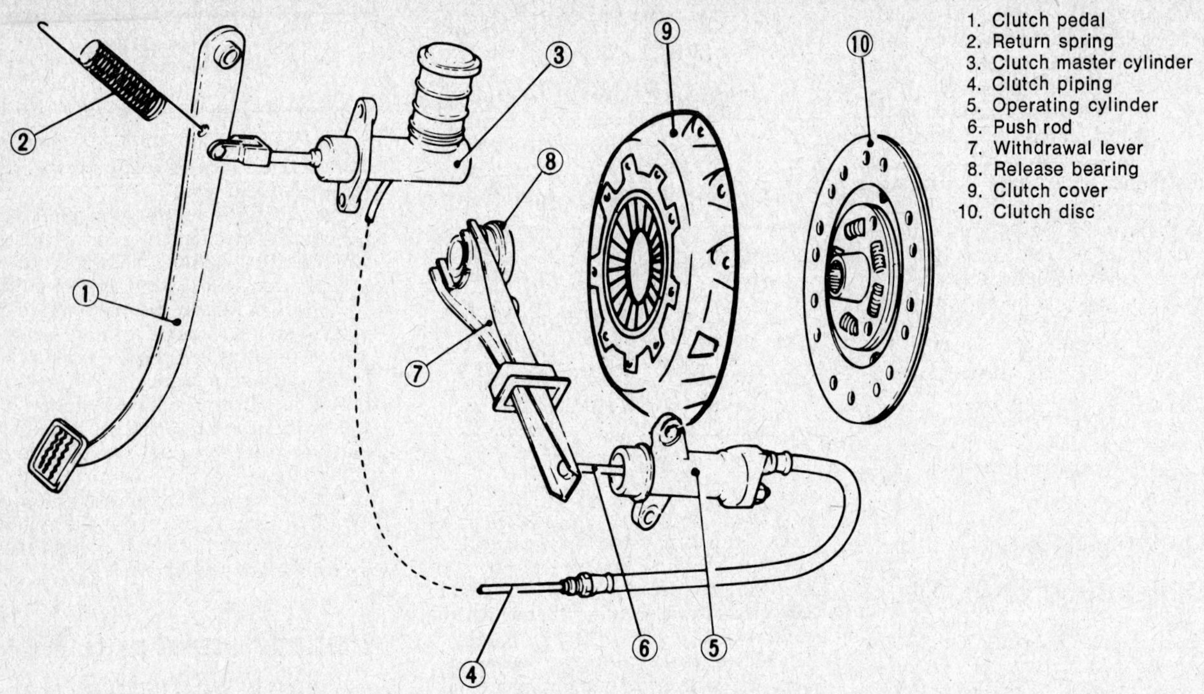

Clutch system components

that 0.039–0.118 in. (through 1977) or 0.04–0.20 in. (1978–80) of free-play exists between the clevis and the clutch pedal. Retighten the locknut and install the clevis pin and cotter pin.

3. After making the adjustments, make sure that the clutch pedal travels its full stroke of: 5.08 in., 1973; 4.61–4.84 in., 1974–77; 4.69–4.92 in., 1978–80. The clutch linkage should operate smoothly and completely disengage and engage the clutch.

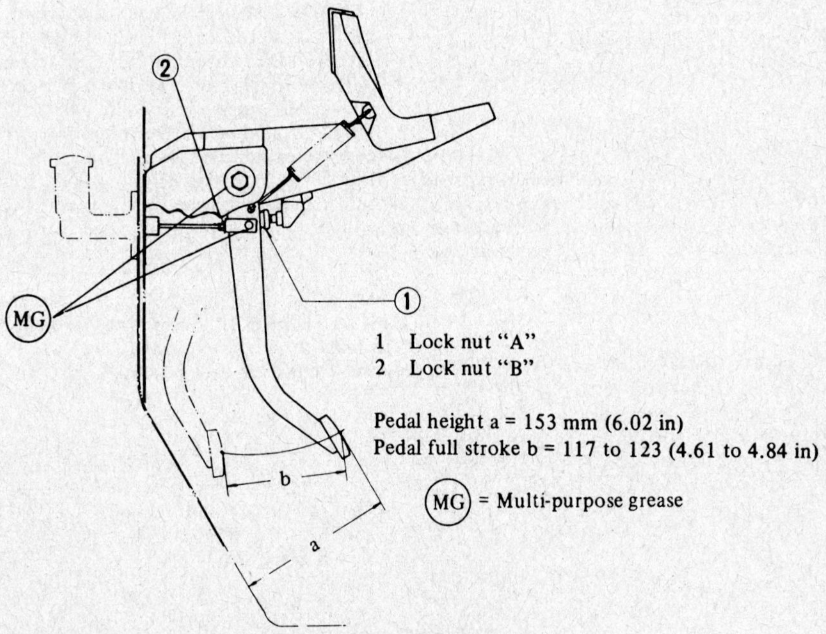

Clutch pedal adjustment

Removal and Installation

1. Raise the vehicle on a hoist.
2. Remove the transmission.
3. Mark the clutch assembly-to-flywheel relationship with paint or a center punch so that the clutch assembly can be reassembled in the same position from which it is removed. Insert a clutch aligning tool (dummy shaft) into the hub. It is important to support the weight of the clutch while the retaining bolts are being removed.
4. Loosen the six clutch cover-to-flywheel attaching bolts, one turn at a time in an alternating sequence, until the spring tension is relieved to avoid distorting or bending the clutch cover. Remove the clutch assembly.
5. Inspect the flywheel for scoring, roughness, or signs of overheating. Light scoring may be cleaned up with emery cloth, but any deep grooves or scoring warrant replacement or refacing (if possible) of the flywheel. If the clutch facings or flywheel are oily, inspect the transmission front cover oil seal, the pilot bushing, and engine rear seals, etc. for leakage, and correct before replacing the clutch. If the pilot bushing in the crankshaft is worn, replace it. Install it using a soft hammer. The factory-supplied part does not have to be oiled, but check the procedure if you are using an aftermarket part. Inspect the clutch cover for wear or scoring, and replace as necessary. The pressure plate and spring cannot be disassembled; you must replace the clutch cover as an assembly.
6. Inspect the clutch release bearing. If it is rough or noisy, it should be replaced. The bearing can be removed from the sleeve with a puller; this requires a press to install the new bearing. After installation, coat the groove in the sleeve, the contact surfaces of the release lever, pivot pin and sleeve, and the release bearing contact surfaces on the transmission front cover with a light coat of grease. Be careful not to use too much grease, which will run at high temperatures and get onto the clutch facings. Reinstall the release bearing on the lever.
7. Apply a thin coat of grease to the

1. Control lever knob
2. Pusher
3. Control lever assembly
4. Selector range lever
5. Control lever bracket
6. Selector rod

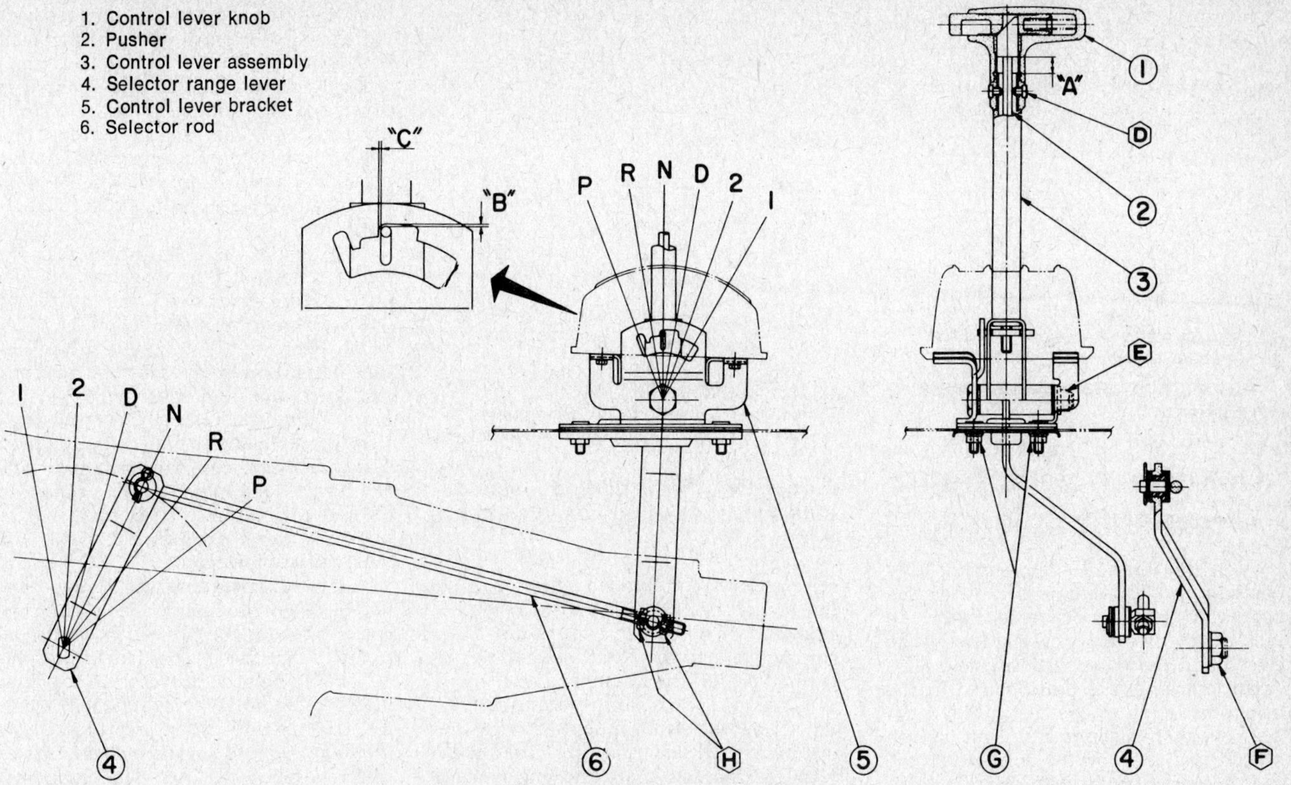

Automatic transmission control linkage

pressure plate wire ring, diaphragm spring, clutch cover grooves and the drive bosses on the pressure plate.

8. Slide the clutch disc onto the splines, and move it back and forth several times. Remove the disc and wipe off

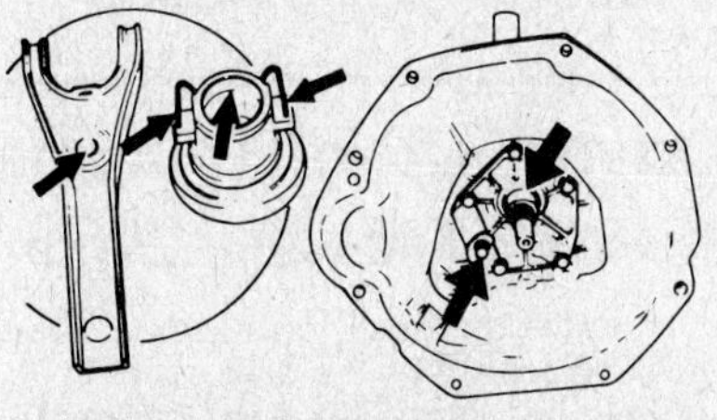

Lubricating points of clutch withdrawal lever and front cover

the excess lubricant. Be very careful not to get any grease on the clutch facings.

9. Assemble the clutch cover and the clutch plate on the clutch alignment arbor.

10. Align the marks made on the clutch cover and the flywheel (if the old cover is being used) and install the six clutch cover-to-flywheel attaching bolts. Three dowels are used to locate the clutch cover on the flywheel properly. Tighten the bolts in an alternating sequence one at a time to 12–15 ft lbs. Remove the aligning arbor.

11. Install the transmission.

Bleeding the Clutch Hydraulic System

1. Check and fill the clutch fluid reservoir to the full mark if necessary. During the bleeding process, continue to check and replenish the reservoir to prevent the fluid level from getting lower than 1/2 full.

2. Connect a clear vinyl hose to the bleeder screw on the slave cylinder. Immerse the other end of the hose in a clear jar half filled with brake fluid.

3. Have an assistant pump the clutch pedal several times and hold it down. Loosen the bleeder screw slowly.

4. Tighten the bleeder screw and release the clutch pedal gradually. Repeat this operation until air bubbles disappear from the brake fluid being expelled out through the bleeder screw.

5. When the air is completely removed, securely tighten the bleeder screw and replace the dust cap.

6. Check and refill the master cylinder reservoir as necessary.

7. Depress the clutch pedal several times to check the operation of the clutch and check for leaks.

AUTOMATIC TRANSMISSION

Only external transmission adjustments and repairs, and transmission removal and replacement, are covered in this book.

All models use a JATCO automatic transmission, model 3N71B. This transmission uses Dexron fluid.

Pan Removal

Loosen the automatic transmission pan attaching bolts more at one corner than the other three corners. Allow the fluid to drain out the one corner. Remove all of the pan attaching bolts and remove the pan. Install the pan in the reverse order of removal. Always use a new gasket.

Shift Linkage Adjustment

Adjustment of the shift linkage is a critical operation. If the adjustment is made sloppily, the result will be partial application of the band or clutches, and will eventually damage the transmission.

1. If the control knob is removed, prior to installation set dimension "A" in the illustration to 0.43–0.47 in. (11–12 mm).

2. Install the control knob, adjusting dimension "B" to 0.004–0.043 in. (0.1–1.1 mm) by turning the pushing rod (2).

3. Loosen the adjusting nuts ("H"). Set both the shift lever (3) and the transmission selector lever (4) into the neutral positions. Set clearance "C" to 0.04 in. (1 mm) by turning the adjusting nuts which connect to the selector rod (6).

After making the adjustments, check for proper engagement in each gear, and that the mechanism operates without binding. Readjust as necessary.

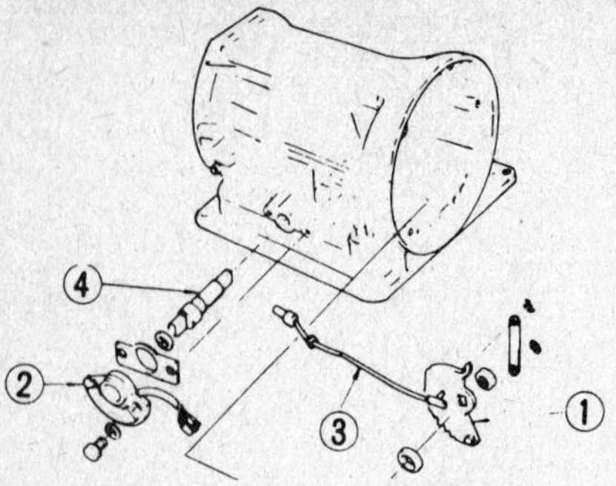

1. Manual plate
2. Inhibitor switch
3. Parking rod
4. Manual shaft

Automatic transmission manual linkage

Kick-Down Switch and Downshift Solenoid

With the ignition switch in the ON position and the engine off, when the accelerator pedal is depressed fully, the kick-down switch contacts should be closed and the downshift solenoid activated, emitting a clicking sound. If the components fail to operate in this manner, check for continuity first at the switch and then at the solenoid if the switch checks out as being satisfactory. Replace either of the components as necessary.

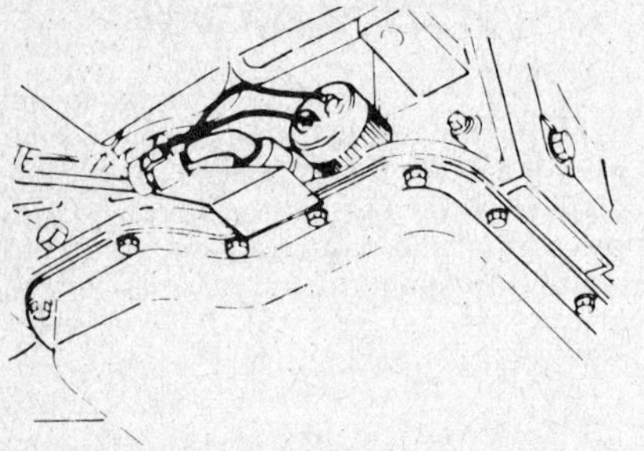

Automatic transmission downshift solenoid

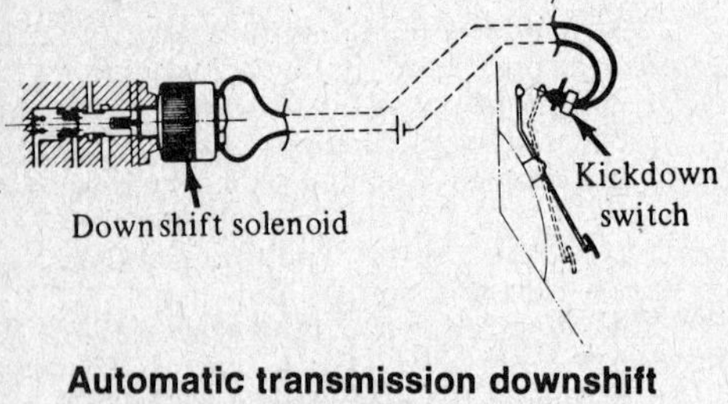

Automatic transmission downshift solenoid and switch

Neutral Safety Switch

The neutral safety switch is located on the transmission range selector lever. The switch operated the back-up lights and controls the operation of the starter. The starter should only operate when the transmission is in Park or Neutral.

To adjust the neutral safety switch, unscrew the securing nut of the range

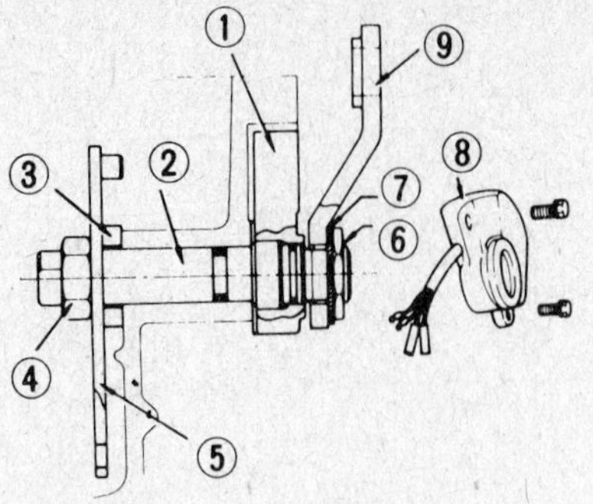

1. Inhibitor switch
2. Manual shaft
3. Washer
4. Nut
5. Manual plate
6. Washer
7. Nut
8. Inhibitor switch
9. Range select lever

Automatic transmission neutral start and back-up light switch components

selector lever and the two bolts securing the switch body. Remove the machine screw under the switch body. Adjust the shift selector to the Neutral position (in vertical position and detent clicks).

Move the switch slightly aside so that the screw hole will be aligned with the pin hole of the internal rotor combined with the manual shaft and check their alignment by inserting a 0.0591 in. (1.5 mm) diameter pin into the holes. A # 53 drill bit will work for this. Fasten the switch body with the bolts, pull out the pin, and tighten the screw into the hole. Connect the selector lever.

If the neutral safety switch does not perform satisfactorily after adjustment, replace it with a new one.

Removal and Installation

1. Disconnect the negative battery cable.
2. Disconnect the shaft from the accelerator linkage.
3. Raise and support the truck.
4. Matchmark the U-joint and differential flange and disconnect them. Remove the center bearing mounting bolts and remove the driveshaft. Plug the transmission extension housing.
5. Disconnect the exhaust pipe from the manifold and discard the gasket. Use a new gasket upon assembly. On trucks with a catalytic converter, disconnect the exhaust pipe bracket.
6. Disconnect the shift linkage at the transmission.
7. Disconnect the neutral switch wires. Disconnect the vacuum hose from the diaphragm, and the wire from the downshift solenoid. Disconnect the speedometer cable from the extension housing.
8. Remove the fluid filler tube.
9. Disconnect the fluid cooler lines at the transmission.
10. Support the engine with a jack under the oil pan, placing a wooden block between the pan and the jack as a buffer. Also support the transmission with a jack.
11. Remove the torque converter cover. Matchmark the converter and the drive plate for reassembly. Remove the bolts attaching the converter to the drive plate (flywheel). Rotate the engine to do this, using a wrench on the crankshaft pulley bolt.
12. Remove the bolts for the rear engine mount and the crossmember. Remove the crossmember.
13. Remove the starter.
14. Remove the transmission-to-engine bolts. Lower the transmission back and down, out from under the truck.
15. Before installing the transmission, check the drive plate runout with a dial indicator. Turn the crankshaft one full turn. Maximum allowable runout is 0.012 in. (0.3 mm). Replace the drive plate if runout exceeds 0.020 in. (0.5 mm); otherwise, reface it.
16. When installing the torque converter, be sure to line up the notch in the converter with the projection on the oil pump. Align the marks made during removal and bolt the converter to the drive plate, tightening the bolts to 29–36 ft lbs. Then rotate the engine a few turns to make sure the transmission rotates freely without binding. The engine-to-transmission bolt torque is 29–36 ft lbs. Adjust the shift linkage and neutral switch after installation.

DRIVE AXLES

Driveshaft and U-Joints

REMOVAL AND INSTALLATION

1. Raise the truck on a hoist. Mark the relationship of the driveshaft to the companion flange at the differential housing so that the driveshaft can be reinstalled in the same position. It is important to reassemble the parts in their correct relationship, because they were balanced as an assembly at the factory.
2. Remove the bolts retaining the center bearing bracket.
3. Remove the bolts connecting the driveshaft to the companion flange at the differential housing (and at the front flange on early models).
4. Move the driveshaft assembly toward the rear of the truck, passing it under the rear axle, removing the sleeve yoke from the transmission. Watch for oil leaking out the end of the transmission. Plug if necessary.
5. Install the driveshaft in the reverse order of removal. Be careful not to bang the sleeve yoke (620 models) into the seal inside the transmission extension housing, which will damage the seal, causing leakage. Align the driveshaft with the differential housing companion

flange in their original position. Tighten the U-joint nuts to 15–20 ft. lbs. (17–24 ft. lbs., 1974 and later) and the nuts retaining the center bearing bracket to 12–16 ft lbs.

U-JOINT OVERHAUL

1. Remove the driveshaft.
2. Punch mating marks on both the yokes at either end of the driveshaft and the driveshaft itself so that the driveshaft assembly can be reassembled in the same position.
3. Remove the snap-rings from the bearing hole of the yokes with a screwdriver.
4. Place the yoke in a vise with a small socket positioned against one of the bearing cups and a larger socket placed against the yoke on the opposite side. The larger socket must be able to receive the bearing cap when it is pressed out of the yoke.
5. Tighten the vise until the bearing caps are free of the yoke.
6. Remove the two remaining bearings from the opposite yoke in the same manner and remove the spider bearing journal.
7. Make sure that the new spiders and needle bearings in the bearing caps are well lubricated.
8. Assemble the universal joint spider and bearing caps to the yoke in the reverse manner of removal, using the smaller socket to press the bearing caps into the yoke and the larger socket to bear against the yoke.

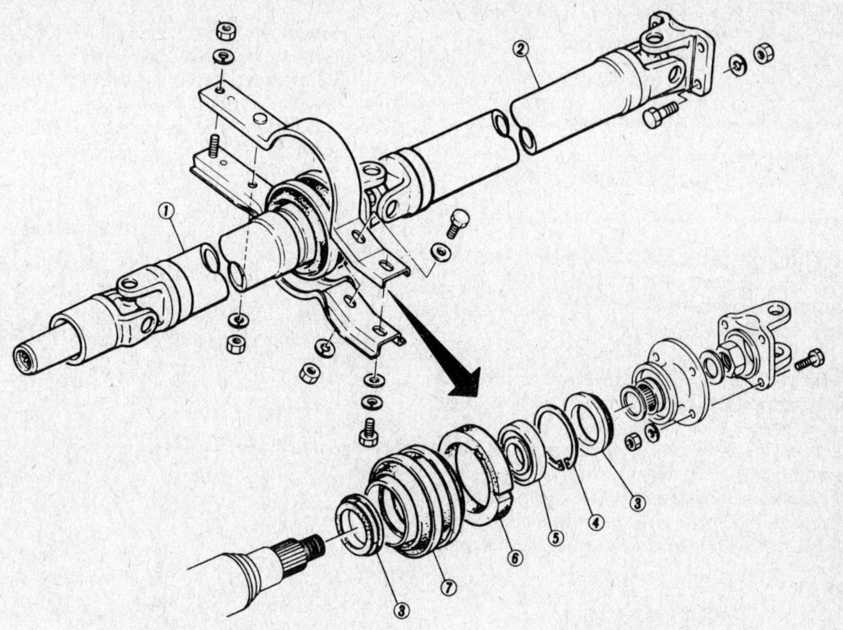

1. Front propeller shaft
2. Rear propeller shaft
3. Dust seal
4. Snap ring
5. Ball bearing
6. Cushion
7. Center bearing insulator

Two piece driveshaft with center bearing and three U-joints

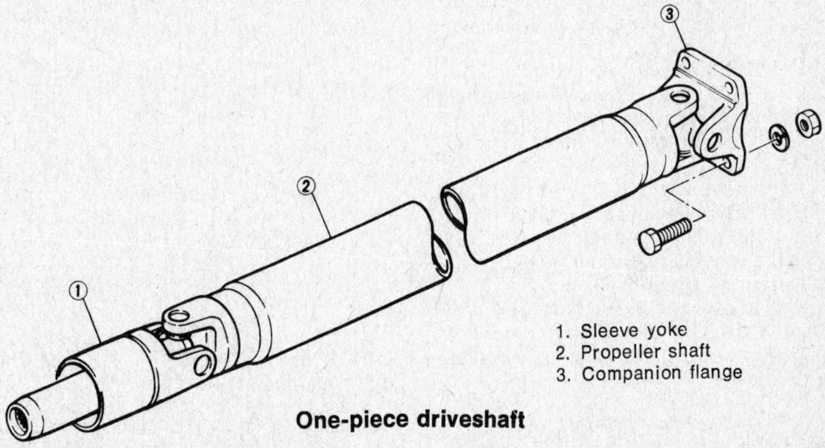

1. Sleeve yoke
2. Propeller shaft
3. Companion flange

One-piece driveshaft

Axle Shaft, Bearing and Seal

REMOVAL AND INSTALLATION

1. Raise the rear of the vehicle and support it. Remove the rear wheel and tire.
2. Disconnect the rear parking brake cable by removing the adjusting nut and clamps.
3. Disconnect the brake tube at the rear brake backing plate. Plug the end of the brake tube to prevent loss of brake fluid.
4. Remove the brake drum.
5. Remove the nuts securing the wheel bearing retainer to the brake backing plate.

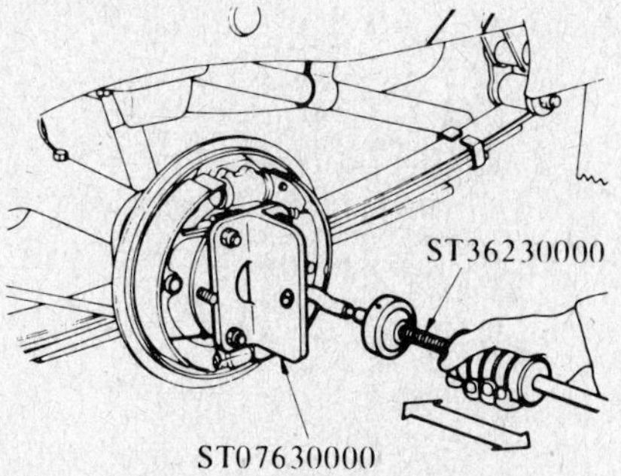

Rear axle shaft removal

6. Pull out the axle shaft assembly together with the brake backing plate using a slide hammer.
7. Remove the oil seal in the axle housing if necessary. It can be pried out with a screwdriver. Oil the lips of the new seal and install it carefully to avoid damage to the lip.
8. To replace the bearing, unbend and discard the lockwasher. Remove the locknut with a soft drift and a hammer.
9. Press the old bearing and cage off the shaft.
10. Remove the oil seal in the cage. Use a brass drift to remove the bearing cup after the seal has been removed.
11. Install the new cup with a brass drift. Install a new oil seal over the bearing cup. Lubricate the area between the seal lips with grease after installation.
12. Place the bearing cage and spacer on the axle shaft, then fit the bearing, tapping it into place with a soft drift and light hammer blows.
13. Place the flat bearing lockwasher over the bearing, then the new nut lockwasher. Install the locknut, tightening to 108 ft lbs. Continue to tighten after that until the grooves line up with the lockwasher tabs. The nut can be tightened up to 145 ft lbs. Bend the lockwasher tabs into place.
14. Lubricate the bearing and the recess in the axle housing with wheel bearing grease. Coat the axle splines with gear oil. Coat the seal surface of the shaft with grease.
15. Install the axle shaft in the reverse order of removal. The axle endplay should be 0.012–0.035 in. The endplay is adjusted by adding or removing shims behind the brake backing plate.

Tighten the backing plate attaching nuts to 27–35 ft lbs. through 1973, or 39–46 ft lbs, 1974 and later.

DIFFERENTIAL

The axle ratio for all trucks is 4.375 (35/8), except for 1973–74 pick-ups with automatic transmission, which have a ratio of 4.625 (37/8).

NOTE: Two types of differential pinion bearing preload adjustment are used on the solid axles. One type uses a collapsible sleeve; the other uses selective washers and a non-collapsible sleeve. In other aspects, including selection and placement of shims for pinion depth, ring gear backlash and side carrier preload, the procedures are the same.

DISASSEMBLY

1. Remove the side bearing caps, marking their locations for reassembly. Remove the differential assembly from the carrier.
2. Pull off the side bearings. Do not mix left and right side parts.
3. Flatten the lock tabs and unbolt the ring gear, loosening the bolts diagonally.
4. Drive out the pinion shaft lock pin from left to right. Remove the pinion shaft and pinions, side gears, and thrust washers. Separate these parts by original location.
5. Remove the drive pinion nut and pull off the flange. Tap the drive pinion back with a soft hammer and remove it with the rear bearing inner race, bearing spacer, and adjusting washer.
6. Remove and discard the oil seal. Remove the front bearing inner race.
7. Pull out the front and rear bearing outer races.

INSPECTION

1. Wash all parts in a safe solvent. Oil the bearings immediately.
2. Ring and pinion gears must be replaced only in pairs. If the ring gear is warped more than 0.002 in., replace it.
3. Check all parts for wear or distortion. Replace any suspected bearings.

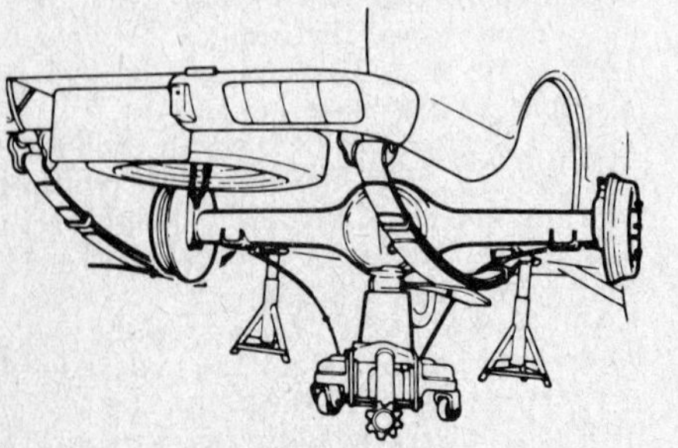

Rear axle removal

ASSEMBLY

1. Assemble the pinions, side gears, pinion shaft, and thrust washers in the case. Clearance between the side gears and thrust washers should be 0.004–0.008 in. Thrust washers are available in various thicknesses for adjustment.
2. Drive in and peen over the lock pin.
3. Bolt on the ring gear using new lock tabs. Tighten the bolts diagonally.
4. Press the side bearing inner races onto the differential case without shims.
5. The drive pinion height is adjusted with shims behind the rear bearing race.

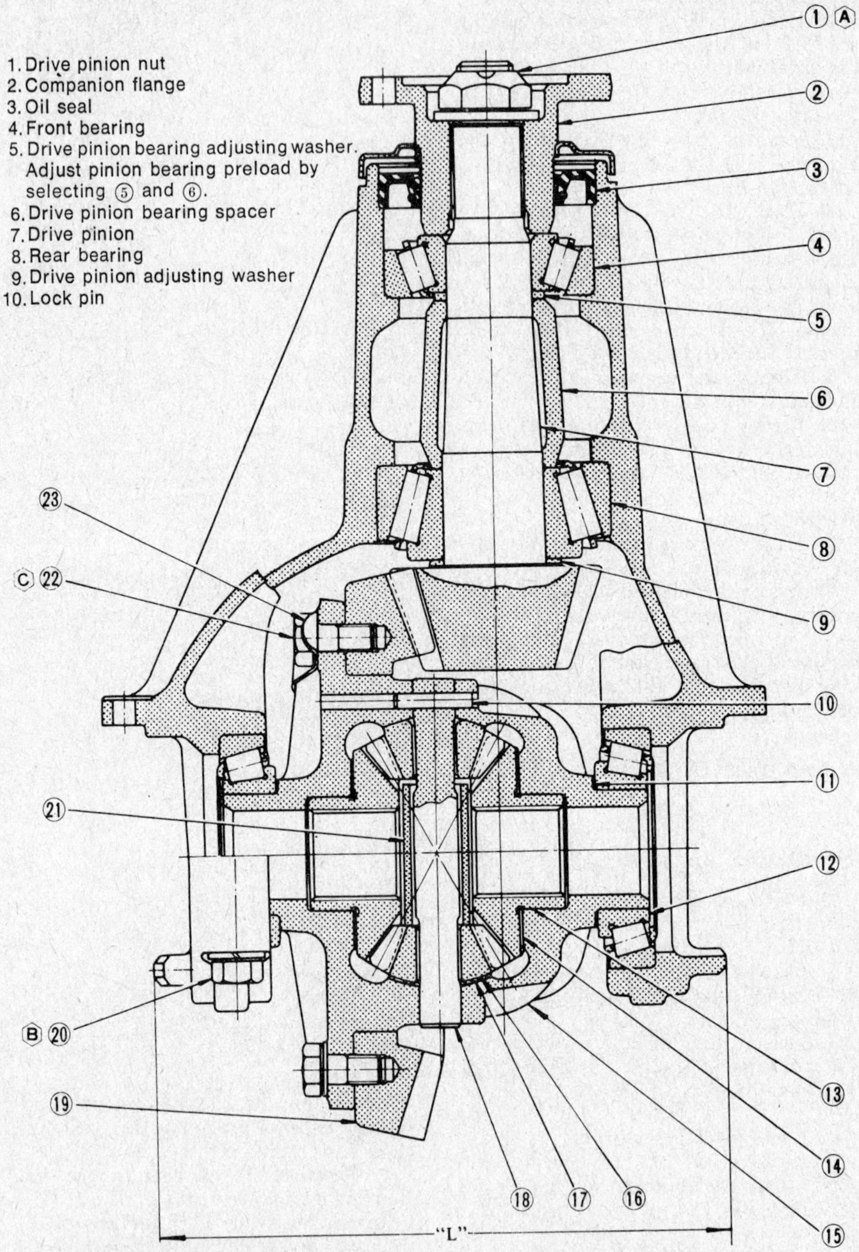

1. Drive pinion nut
2. Companion flange
3. Oil seal
4. Front bearing
5. Drive pinion bearing adjusting washer. Adjust pinion bearing preload by selecting ⑤ and ⑥.
6. Drive pinion bearing spacer
7. Drive pinion
8. Rear bearing
9. Drive pinion adjusting washer
10. Lock pin
11. Side bearing adjusting shim. Adjust side bearing preload and backlash between ring gear and drive pinion by selecting ⑪.
12. Side bearing
13. Side gear
14. Thrust washer. Adjust pinion mate-to-side gear backlash (or the clearance between the rear face of side gear and thrust washer) to 0.02 to 0.08 mm (0.0008 to 0.0031 in) by ⑭.
15. Differential case
16. Thrust washer
17. Pinion mate
18. Pinion shaft
19. Ring gear. Backlash between ring gear and drive pinion: 0.15 to 0.20 mm (0.0059 to 0.0079 in)
20. Bearing cap bolt
21. Thrust block
22. Ring gear bolt
23. Lock strap

Differential carrier

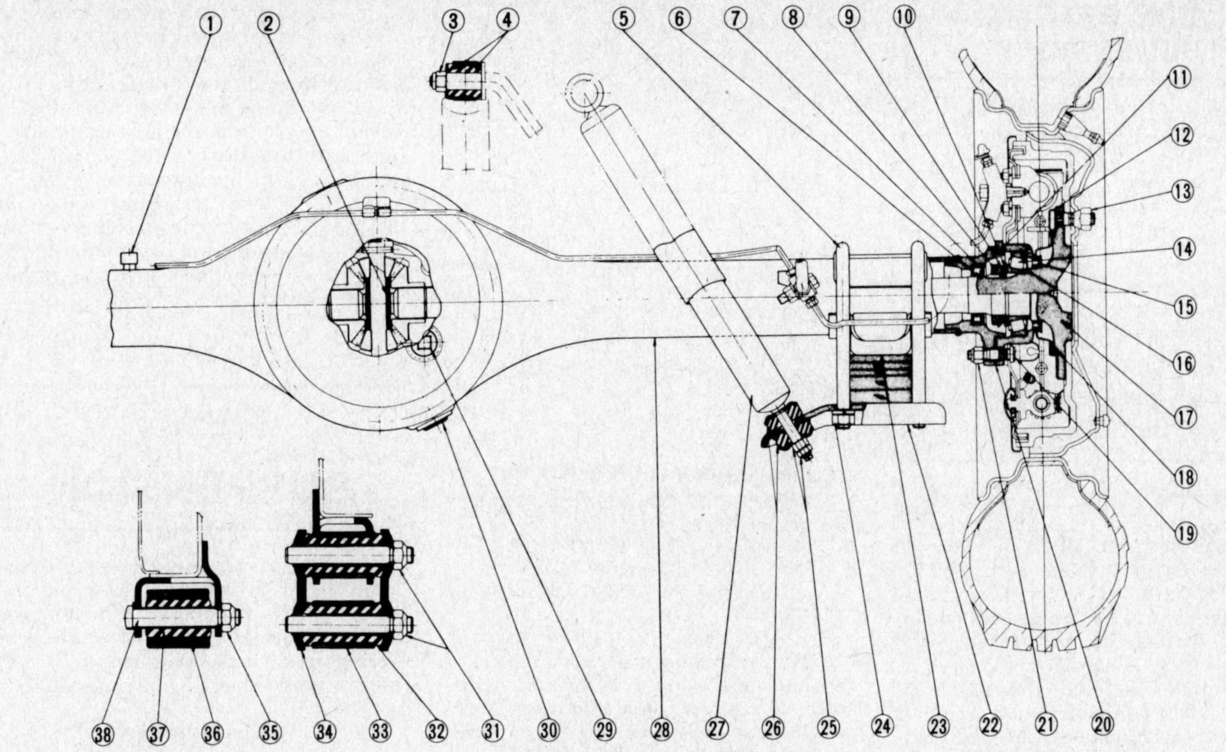

1. Air breather
2. Thrust block
3. Nut
   T = 3.1 to 4.1 kg-m
   (22 to 30 ft-lb)
4. Shock absorber mounting rubber bush
5. Rear spring clip (U-bolt)
6. Rear axle oil seal spacer
7. Rear axle shaft oil seal
   Apply wheel bearing grease to oil seal lip when assembling
8. Rear axle bearing lock nut
   T = 15 to 20 kg-m
   (108 to 145 ft-lb)
9. Rear axle bearing lock washer
10. Plain washer
11. Rear axle bearing cage
12. Road wheel bolt
13. Road wheel nut
    T = 8 to 9 kg-m
    (58 to 65 ft-lb)
14. Wheel bearing
15. Rear axle bearing grease seal.
    Apply wheel bearing grease to oil seal lip when assembling
16. Rear axle bearing spacer
17. Rear axle shaft
18. Grease catcher
19. Bearing cage bolt
20. Rear axle case end shim
21. Nut
    T = 5.4 to 6.4 kg-m
    (39 to 46 ft-lb)
22. Rear spring pad
23. Rear spring
24. Nut
    T = 7.3 to 9.9 kg-m
    (53 to 72 ft-lb)
25. Nut
    T = 1.6 to 2.2kg-m
    (12 to 16 ft-lb)
26. Shock absorber rubber bush
27. Shock absorber
28. Rear axle case
29. Filler plug
    T = 6 to 10 kg-m
    (43 to 72 ft-lb)
    Oil capacity (about) = 1.0 liter
    (1 US qt., 7/8 Imp. qt.)
30. Drain plug
    T = 6 to 10 kg-m
    (43 to 72 ft-lb)
31. Nut
    T = 11.5 to 13.0 kg-m
    (83 to 94 ft-lb)
32. Rear spring rear bush
33. Rear spring
34. Rear spring shackle
35. Nut
    T = 11.5 to 13.0 kg-m
    (83 to 94 ft-lb)
36. Rear spring
37. Rear spring front bush
38. Rear spring front pin

T: Tightening torque

Rear axle and suspension components

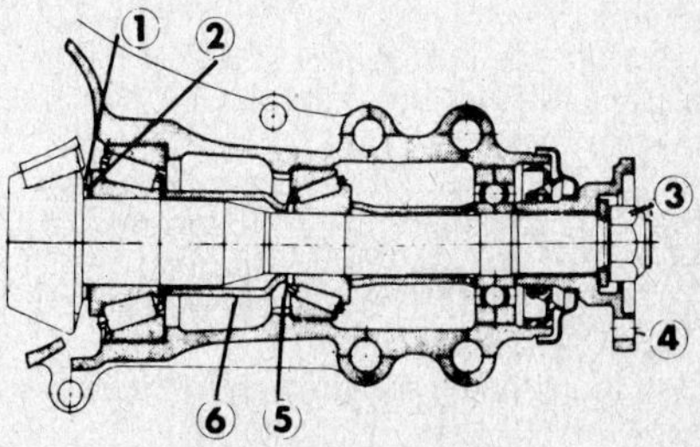

1. Pinion bearing adjusting washer
2. Pinion height adjusting shims
3. Pinion nut
4. Pinion flange
5. Pinion bearing adjusting washer
6. Pinion bearing adjusting spacer

Drive pinion components

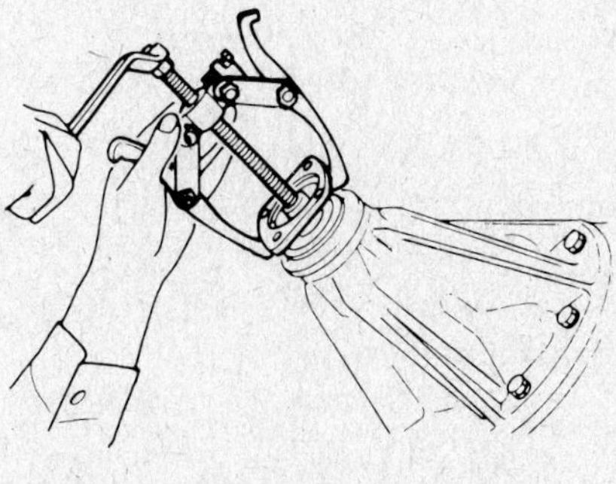

Removing differential companion flange

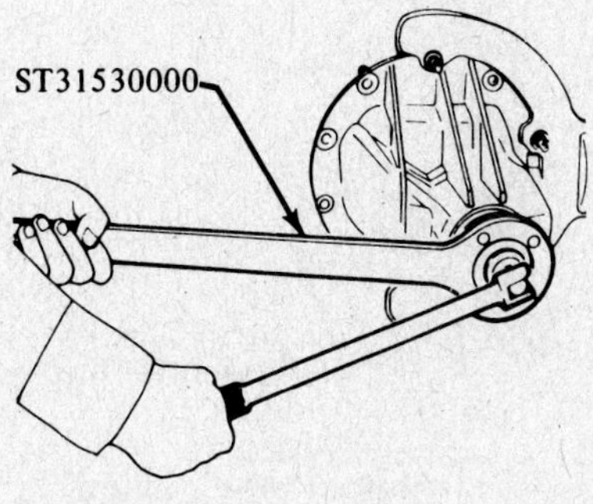

Removing differential drive pinion nut

SIDE BEARING DIMENSIONS

Figure	Location
A	left bearing housing of gear carrier
B	right bearing housing
C,D	differential case
E	difference from standard size (0.7874 in.) of left bearing
F	difference from standard size of right bearing

Dealers have special tools for making this measurement.

Standard pinion height is measured from the axle centerline to the pinion face. The deviation of the drive pinion from standard size is marked on the pinion face with + for larger and − for smaller. There is usually an M mark on pinions graded in hundredths of a millimeter. If no standard pinion height is specified, the adjustment must be made by use of special tools or by comparing the marks on the old and new drive pinion and adjusting the original shim pack to suit.

6. Press in the drive pinion rear bearing outer race and shims. Press in the front bearing outer race. Press the rear bearing inner race onto the drive pinion.
7. Install the drive pinion and collapsible spacer or the selected washer and spacer into the differential carrier. The front bearing inner race and the flange should be installed. Tighten the flange nut until the torque required to turn the shift (bearing preload) is:
8. Check the drive pinion height again.
9. Torque the flange nut to the specified torque.
10. Make sure that pinion bearing preload is as in Step 7. If it is excessive, a new spacer or washer must be installed.
11. If the cotter pin does not align, replace the nut and retorque. Do not overtorque.
12. The required side bearing adjusting shim thickness can be determined by the use of the following formulae:

$T_1 = (A - C + D - H') \times 0.01 + 0.20 + E$

$T_2 = (B - D + H') \times 0.01 + 0.09 + F$

a. T_1 is the required shim thickness on the left side.

b. T_2 is the required shim thickness on the right side.

c. A is the figure marked on the left side bearing housing of the gear carrier.

d. B is the figure marked on the right side bearing housing of the gear carrier.

e. C and D are figures marked on the differential case.

f. E and F are differences in the width of the left and right side bearings against the standard width.

g. H' is the figure marked on the ring gear.

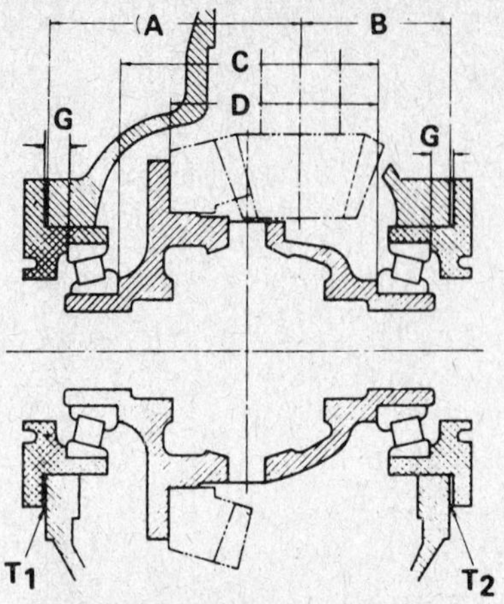

Measurements for selecting differential side bearing shims

NOTE: Because the markings on the parts are in metric figures, it is advisable to use them to compute shim thicknesses, converting to inches as necessary when completed.

13. Locate and substitute the figures in the formulae.

NOTE: If the valves for A, B, C, D, and H' are not given, regard them as zero.

14. Place the determined side bearing adjusting shims on the differential case and press the side bearings in place.
15. Install the differential case assembly into the gear carrier and install the caps and bolts.

NOTE: After the assembly, make sure the preload and back-lash are correct. It may be necessary to readjust.

16. If the back-lash is too small, decrease the thickness of the left shim and increase the thickness of the right shim by the same amount.
17. If the preload does not agree with the specifications, adjust it with the side bearing shims.
18. Check the tooth contact pattern of the ring gear and pinion gear by painting the rear gear teeth with a suitable mixture to produce a contact pattern.
19. Rotate the pinion through several revolutions in both the forward and the reverse directions so that a definite pattern is made on the ring gear teeth.
20. If the tooth contact is proper and no adjustment is needed, clean the paint mixture from the ring and pinion teeth. The installation of the carrier assembly is in the reverse of the removal.

REAR SUSPENSION

The rear suspension consists of semielliptic leaf springs and telescopic hydraulic shock absorbers. There are rubber bushings at either end of the leaf springs and shock absorbers to absorb vibration and noise.

Springs

REMOVAL AND INSTALLATION

CAUTION: The leaf springs are under a considerable amount of tension. Be very careful when removing or installing them; they can exert enough force to cause serious injuries.

1. Jack up the rear of the truck and support it with jackstands placed under the frame.
2. Disconnect the shock absorbers at their lower end.
3. Remove the nuts securing the U-bolts around the axle housing.
4. Place a jack under the rear axle housing and raise the housing to remove the weight off the springs.
5. Remove the nuts from the spring shackles, drive out the shackle pins and remove the spring from the vehicle.
6. Install the spring in the reverse order of removal. The weight of the truck

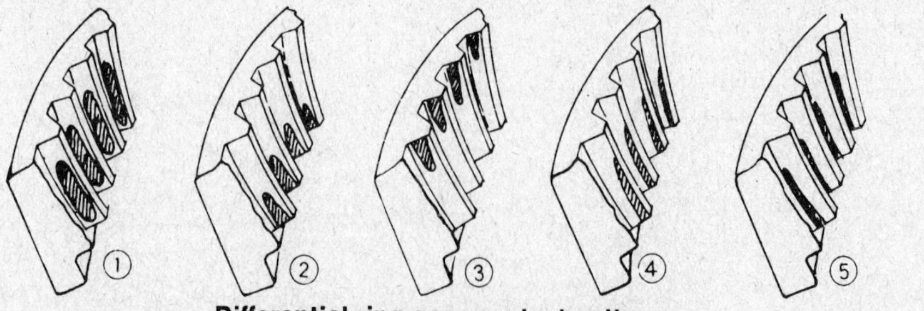

Differential ring gear contact patterns

1. Correct tooth contact
2. Short toe contact; move ring gear away from pinion
3. Short heel contact; move ring gear toward pinion
4. Contact too high and narrow; pinion should be moved toward center of axle
5. Contact too low and narrow; pinion should be moved away from center of axle.

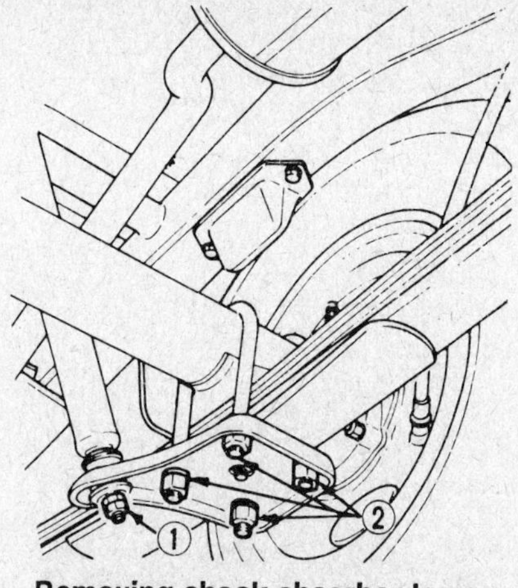

Removing shock absorber lower end and U-bolts

must be on the rear wheels before tightening the front pin, shackle, and shock absorber attaching nuts. Tighten the front pin and shackle nuts to 83–94 ft lbs (37–59 ft lbs for the spring shackle nuts, 1978–80), the U-bolt nuts to 53–72 ft lbs, and the shock absorber lower end nut to 12–16 ft lbs.

Shock Absorbers

REMOVAL AND INSTALLATION

The rear shock absorbers are removed by removing the upper and lower attaching nuts, and removing the component from the vehicle. They are installed in the reverse order. The weight of the vehicle must be on the rear wheels before tightening the shock absorber attaching nuts to 12–16 ft lbs.

FRONT SUSPENSION

This independent front suspension uses torsion bar springs, upper and lower links (control arms), tubular shock absorbers, and kingpins through 1977. Ball joints replace the kingpins in 1978–80. The lower suspension links are located fore and aft by tension rods from the front of the frame. The front end height can be adjusted to compensate for normal spring sagging.

Shock Absorbers

REMOVAL AND INSTALLATION

1. Raise and support the front of the truck.
2. Remove the wheel.
3. Hold the upper stem of the shock with a pair of pliers and remove the locknut and mounting nut at that end.
4. Remove the nut and bolt retaining

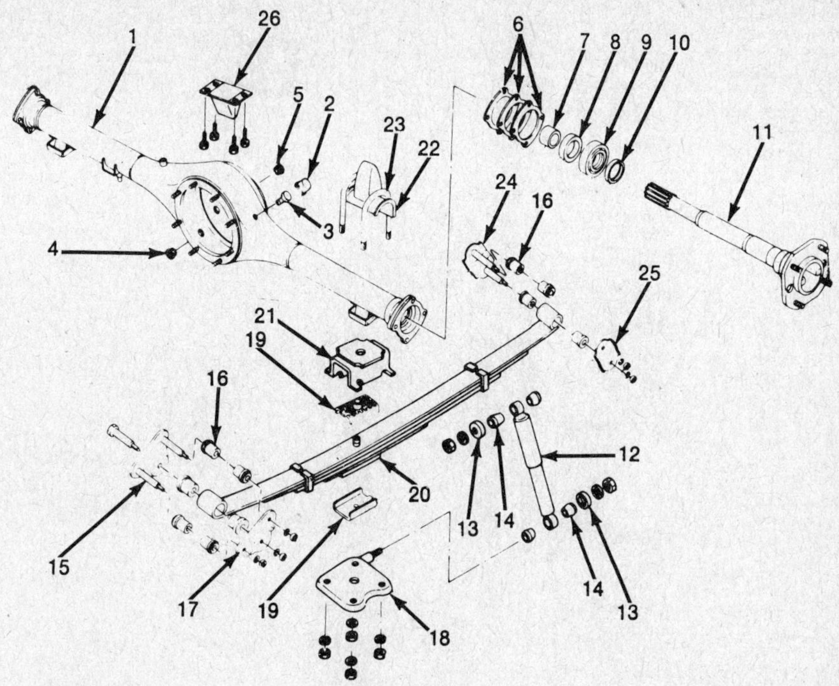

1. Rear axle case
2. Breather cap
3. Breather
4. Drain plug
5. Filler plug
6. Rear axle case end shim
7. Bearing collar
8. Oil seal
9. Rear axle bearing
10. Bearing spacer
11. Rear axle shaft
12. Shock absorber assembly
13. Special washer
14. Shock absorber bushing
15. Front pin assembly
16. Spring bushing
17. Front pin outer plate
18. Lower spring seat
19. Spring seating pad
20. Rear spring assembly
21. Location plate
22. Rear axle bumper
23. U-bolt (spring clip)
24. Shackle pin assembly
25. Shackle
26. Torque arrester

Rear suspension component parts

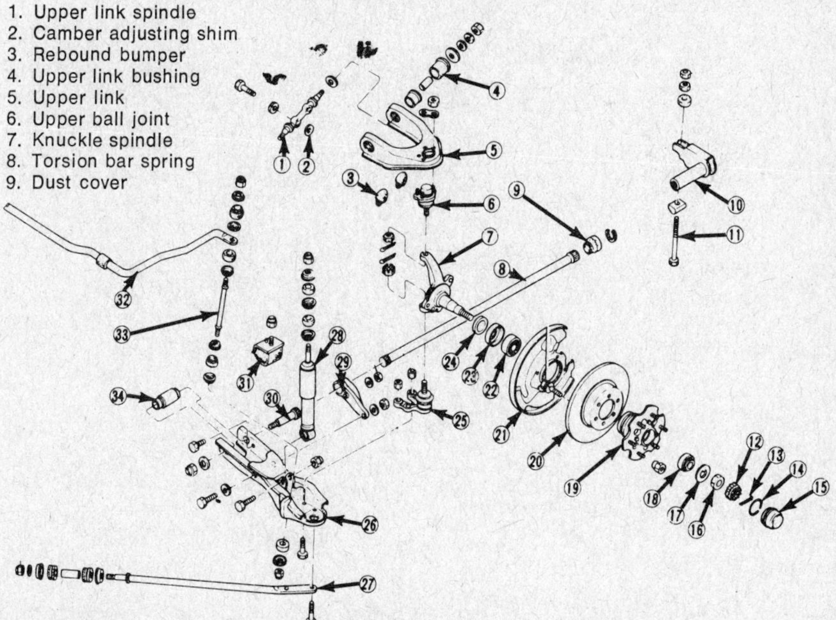

1. Upper link spindle
2. Camber adjusting shim
3. Rebound bumper
4. Upper link bushing
5. Upper link
6. Upper ball joint
7. Knuckle spindle
8. Torsion bar spring
9. Dust cover
10. Anchor arm
11. Anchor arm adjusting bolt
12. Adjusting cap
13. Cotter pin
14. "O" ring
15. Hub cap
16. Spindle nut
17. Washer
18. Outer wheel bearing
19. Wheel hub
20. Rotor
21. Baffle plate
22. Inner wheel bearing
23. Grease seal
24. Spacer
25. Lower ball joint
26. Lower link
27. Tension rod
28. Shock absorber
29. Torque arm
30. Lower link spindle
31. Rebound bumper
32. Stabilizer
33. Stabilizer connecting rod
34. Lower link bushing

1978 and later front suspension components

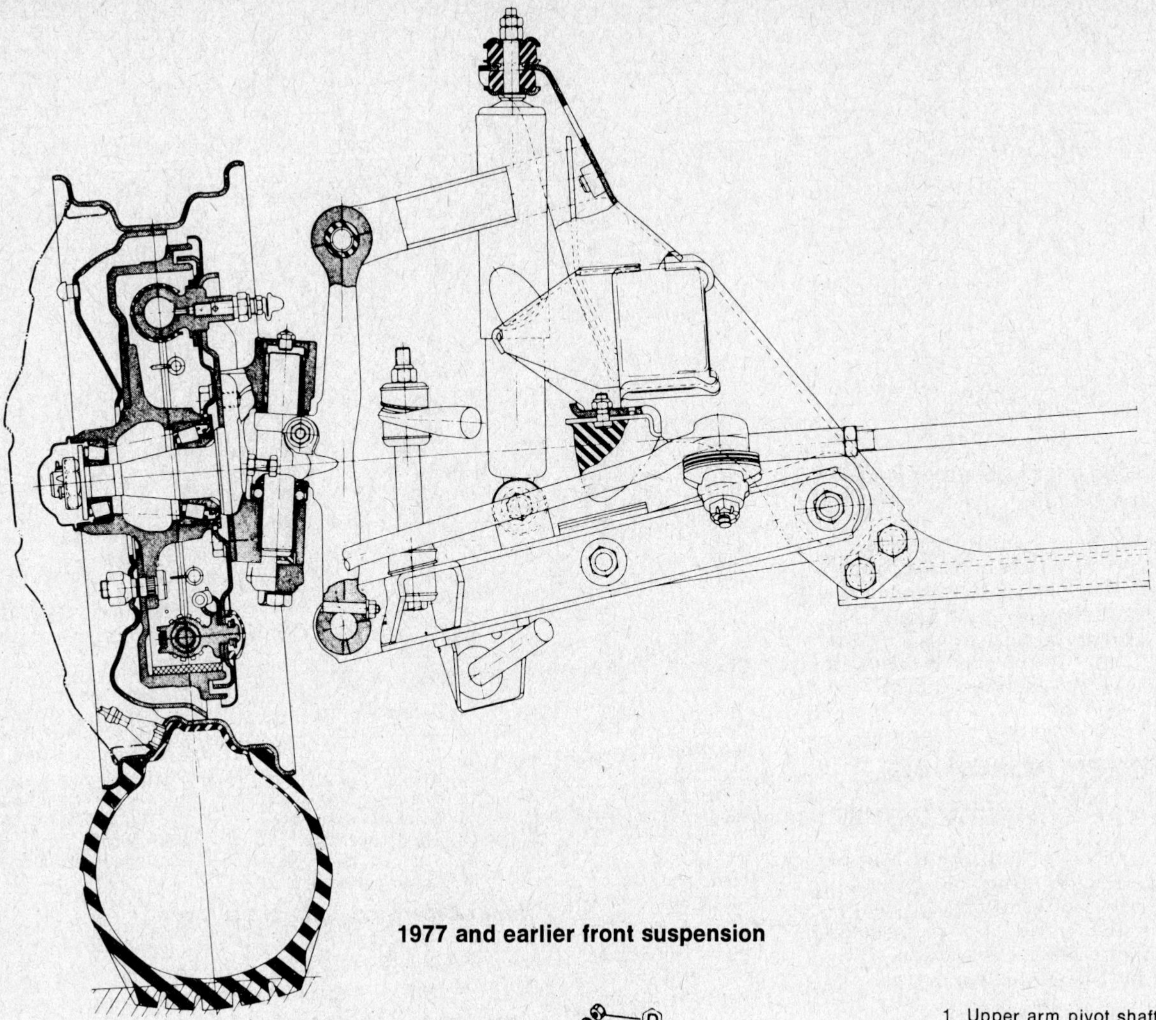

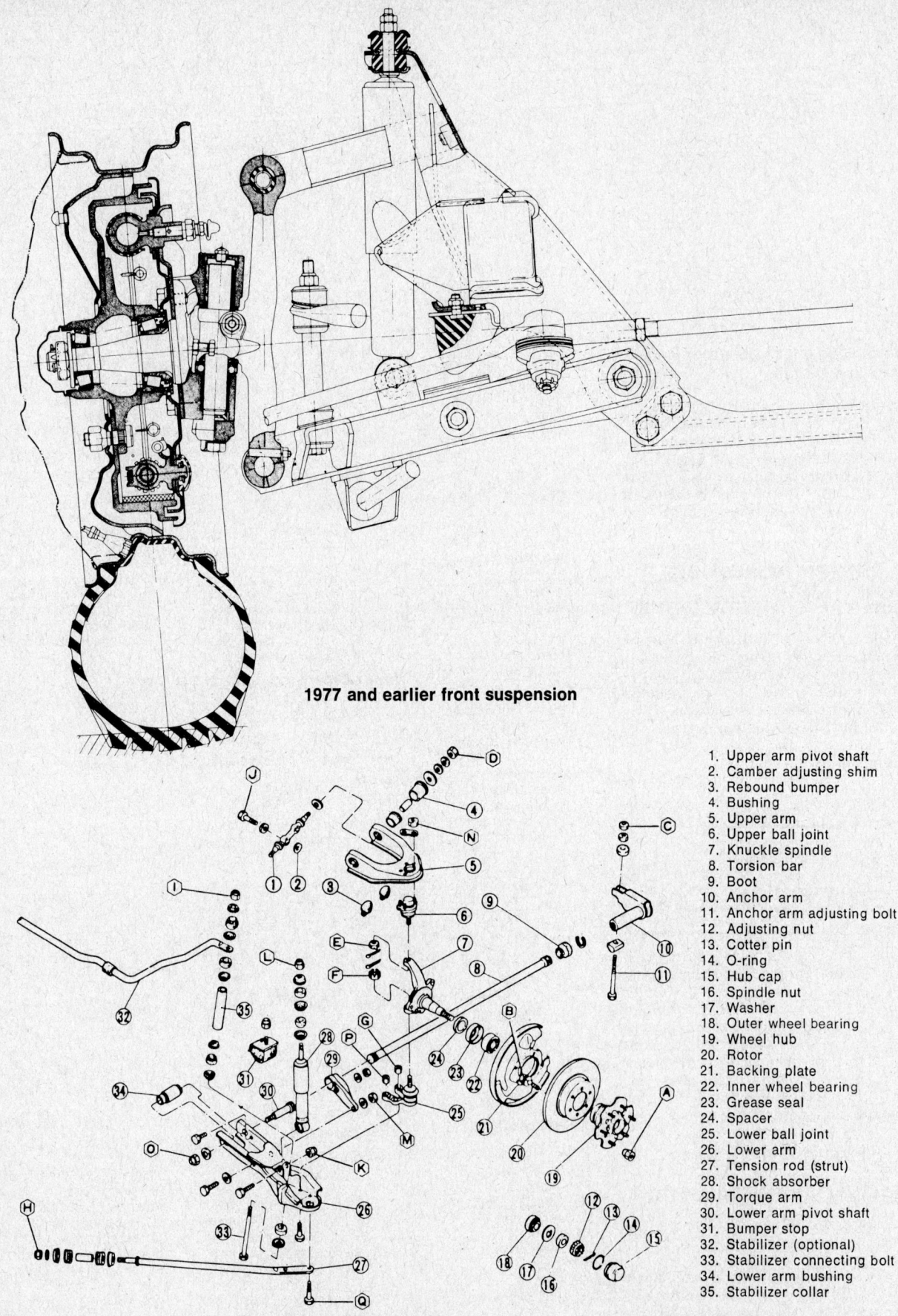

1977 and earlier front suspension

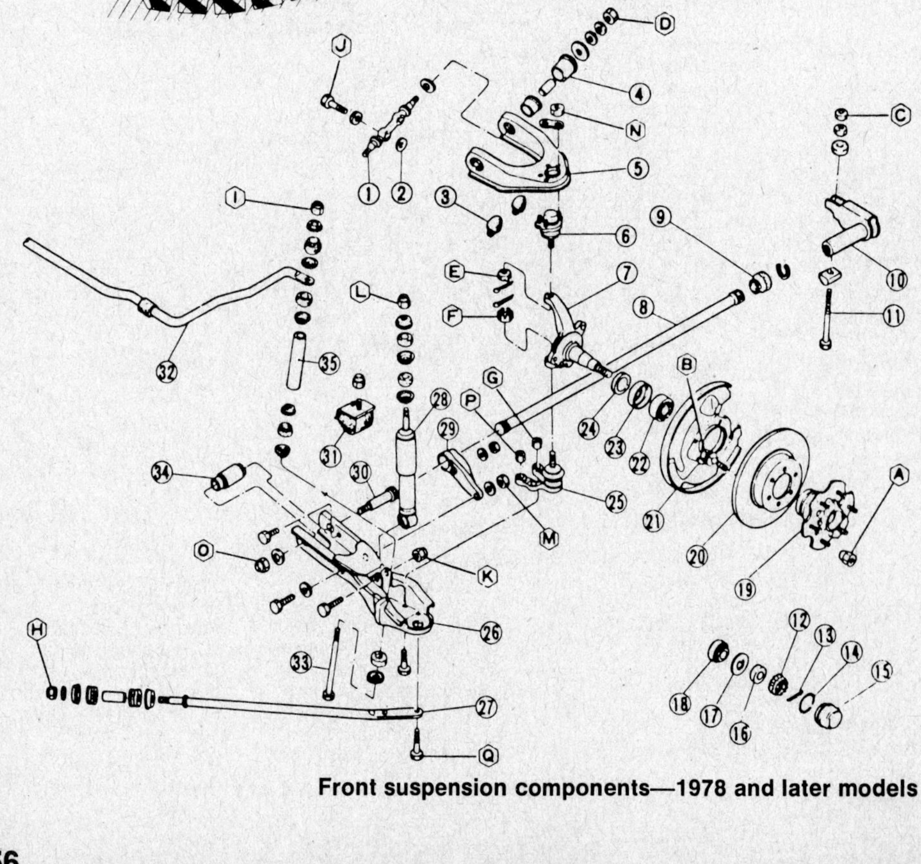

1. Upper arm pivot shaft
2. Camber adjusting shim
3. Rebound bumper
4. Bushing
5. Upper arm
6. Upper ball joint
7. Knuckle spindle
8. Torsion bar
9. Boot
10. Anchor arm
11. Anchor arm adjusting bolt
12. Adjusting nut
13. Cotter pin
14. O-ring
15. Hub cap
16. Spindle nut
17. Washer
18. Outer wheel bearing
19. Wheel hub
20. Rotor
21. Backing plate
22. Inner wheel bearing
23. Grease seal
24. Spacer
25. Lower ball joint
26. Lower arm
27. Tension rod (strut)
28. Shock absorber
29. Torque arm
30. Lower arm pivot shaft
31. Bumper stop
32. Stabilizer (optional)
33. Stabilizer connecting bolt
34. Lower arm bushing
35. Stabilizer collar

Front suspension components—1978 and later models

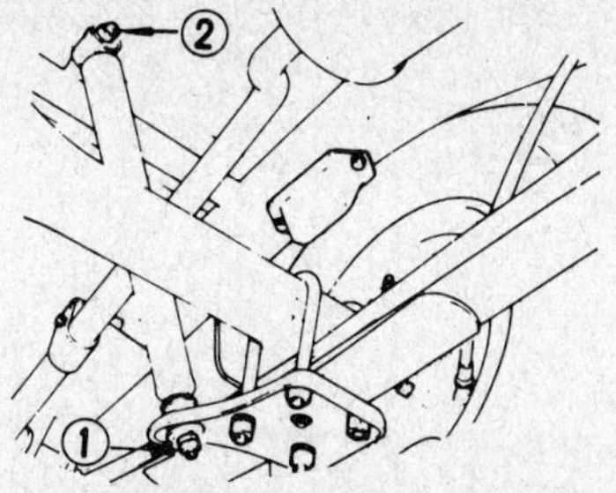

Rear shock absorber removal

the lower end of the shock. Remove the shock.

5. Installation is the reverse.

Kingpin and Bushing Replacement

1973–77

1. Block the front of the truck.
2. Remove the wheels.
3. Unscrew the front wheel brake hose connections.
4. Remove the hubcap and spindle nut. Remove the hub and drum with the wheel bearing.
5. Remove the brake backing plate from the spindle.
6. Disconnect the tie rod from each spindle.
7. Take out the kingpin lock bolt and remove the upper spindle plug. It may be necessary to drill and tap a hole to pull the plug out. Drive the kingpin down to remove the bottom plug. Tap out the kingpins.
8. Remove the spindle with the shims and thrust washer.
9. The old bushings should be driven out of the spindle and new ones driven in. It is advisable to replace the kingpin also. Ream the new bushings to fit the kingpin. The fit should be such that the kingpin, when oiled, can be turned or pushed in or out readily with thumb pressure. Make sure that the bushing holes for the grease fittings are open.
10. On reassembly, use a new spindle thrust washer. Install spindle shims so that the clearance between the upper end of the kingpin boss on the spindle support knuckle and the spindle is 0.003–0.005 in. Use new kingpin expansion plugs. Use a new front hub grease seal.

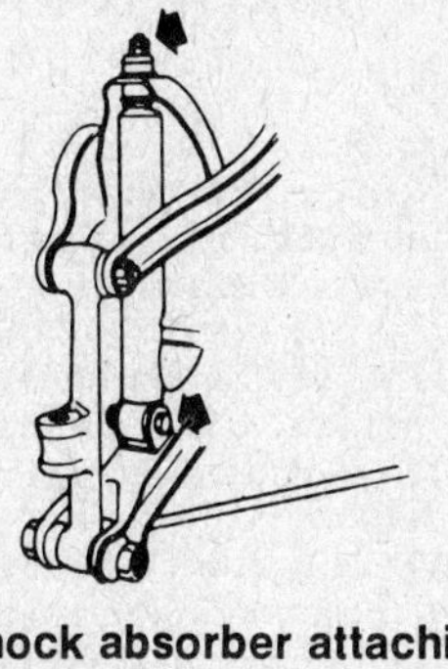

Front shock absorber attaching points

1. Upper ball joint
2. Baffle plate
3. Rotor
4. Grease seal
5. Wheel nut
6. Spacer
7. Outer bearing
8. Knuckle spindle
9. Hub cap
10. Cotter pin
11. Adjusting cap
12. Spindle nut
13. Inner bearing
14. Wheel hub
15. Knuckle arm
16. Lower ball joint

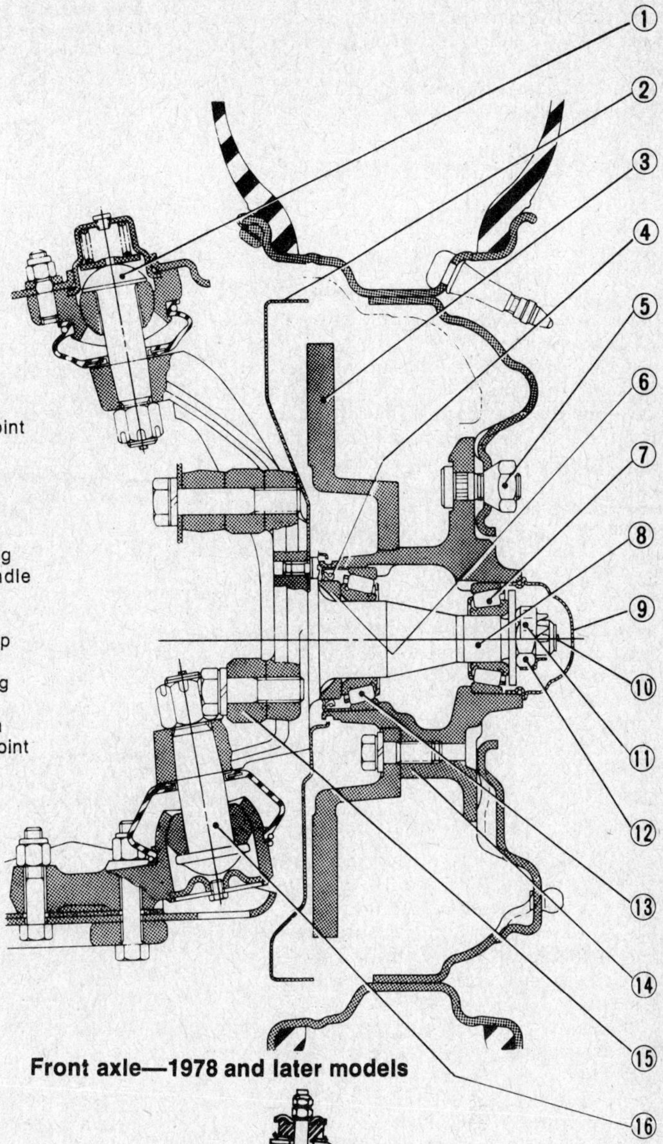

Front axle—1978 and later models

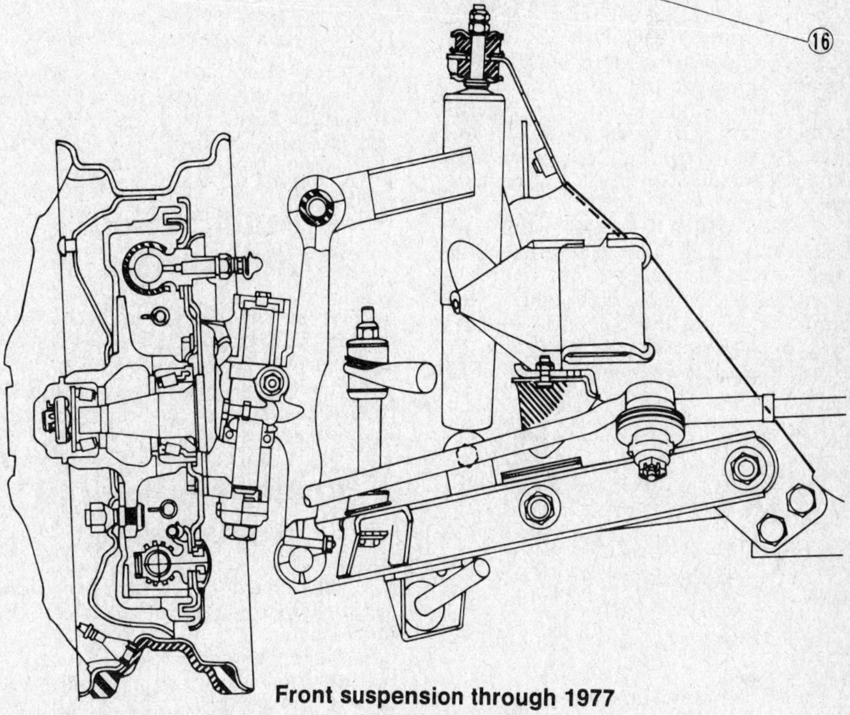

Front suspension through 1977

Adjust the front wheel bearing by torquing it to 22–25 ft lbs. and backing off 1/8 turn.

11. Grease the suspension and bleed the brake system.

Ball Joint Replacement

UPPER

1978–80

1. Raise and support the truck on stands placed on the frame rails.
2. Remove the wheels.
3. Loosen the torsion bar anchor lock and adjusting nuts.
4. Remove and discard the cotter pin from the ball joint stud and remove the nut. Separate the stud from the knuckle spindle with a ball joint removal tool.
5. Loosen the bolts retaining the ball joint to the control arm, and remove the joint.
6. Install the new ball joint into the control arm, tightening the bolts to 12–16 ft. lbs. Install the ball joint stud into the knuckle spindle and install the nut. Tighten the nut to 60 ft. lbs, then continue to tighten until the holes align (limit:72 ft. lbs.). Install a new cotter pin. Adjust the ride height after assembly.

LOWER

1. Perform Steps 1 and 2 of the upper ball joint removal procedure. Remove the lower shock absorber mounting bolt.
2. Loosen the torsion bar spring anchor lock and adjusting nuts, and remove the anchor arm bolt from the anchor arm.
3. Remove the snap ring, then move the anchor arm and torsion bar fully rearward.
4. Disconnect the stabilizer bar from the lower arm.
5. Disconnect the strut (tension rod) from the lower control arm.
6. Remove and discard the cotter pin from the ball joint stud, and remove the nut. Separate the ball joint from the knuckle spindle with a ball joint removal tool.
7. Remove the attaching bolts, and remove the ball joint from the lower arm.
8. Install the new ball joint to the arm, tightening the bolts to 28–38 ft. lbs. Install the ball joint stud into the knuckle spindle and tighten the nut to 127 ft lbs. Continue to tighten until the holes align, then install the new cotter pin (torque limit: 141 ft. lbs.). The torsion bar ride height must be adjusted after assembly.

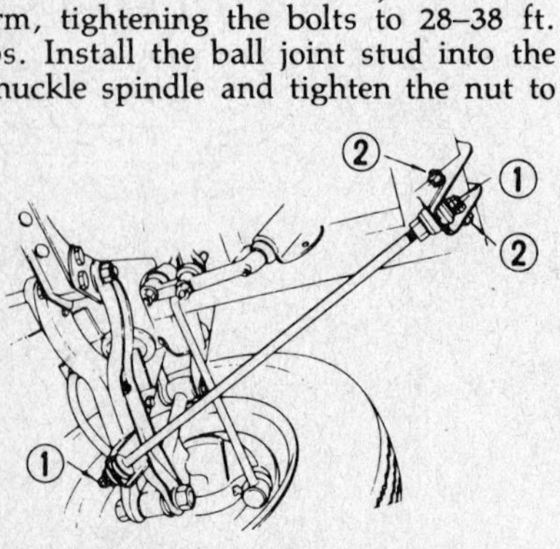

Tension rod mounting

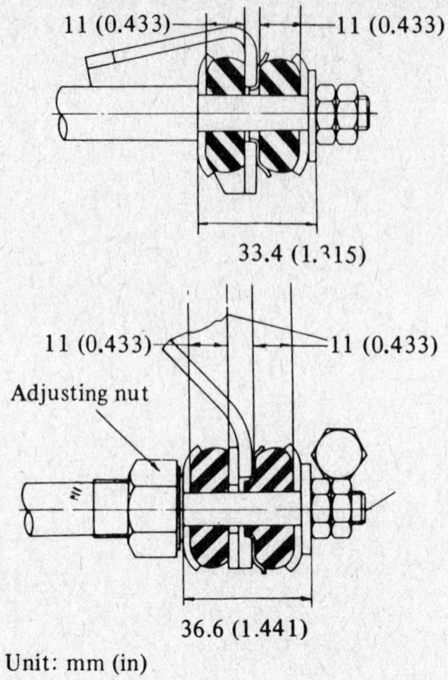

Tension rod installation

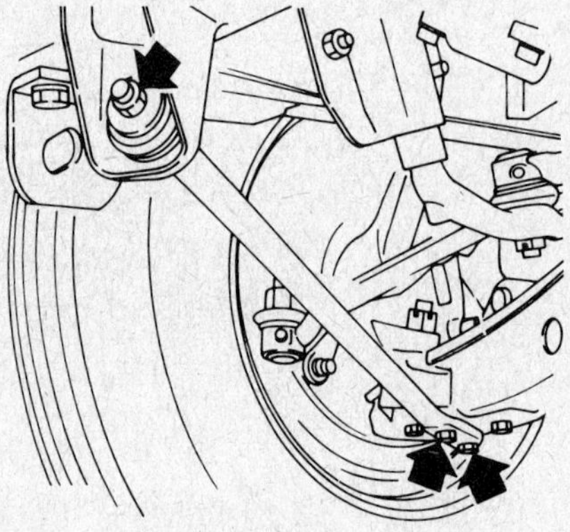
Tension rod mounting

Tension Rod Adjustment

There are three adjusting nuts on each tension rod (strut). There is one at the lower suspension link end and two at the frame end. Adjust these nuts until both rubber bushings at the frame end are compressed to 0.43 in.

Suspension Height Adjustment

1. Jack up the vehicle under the front suspension crossmember to unload the torsion bars.
2. Turn the rear torsion bar anchor bolt right to lower the vehicle and left to raise it.

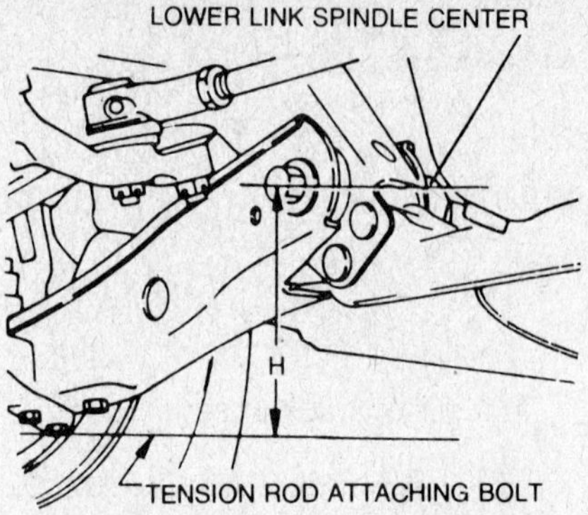

Suspension height measurement for 1978 and later models

3. For models through 1976, dimension B in the illustration should be 3.07–3.23 in. with the truck empty and resting on its wheels. For 1977 models, the distance should be 3.11–3.31 in.

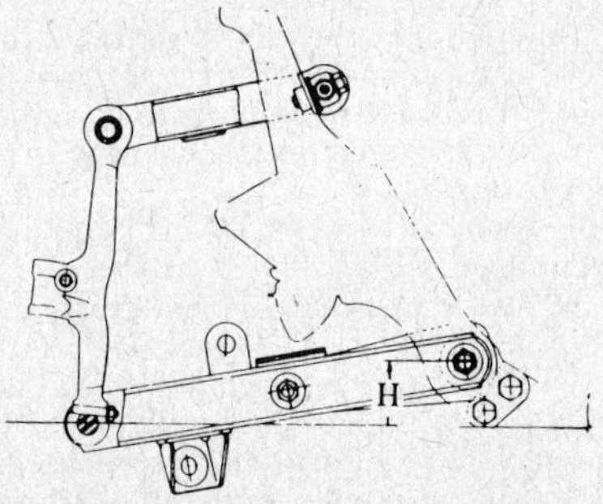

Suspension height measurement through 1977

4. For 1978–80 models, measure the distance H between the center of the lower control arm pivot bolt and the tension rod attaching bolt, as shown in the illustration; H should be 4.92 in.

Wheel Alignment

Caster and camber are adjusted by shims placed between the upper suspension link spindle and the crossmember. Toe-in is adjusted at the center tie-rod. See the Wheel Alignment Specifications Chart for alignment specifications.

Wheel Bearing Adjustment

1. Raise and support the front of the car or truck.
2. Remove the wheel and tire, hub cap, and cotter pin. Discard the cotter pin. Remove the adjusting cap over the wheel bearing nut.
3. Remove the brake pads on disc brake models. Check to make sure the shoes are not dragging on models with drum brakes.
4. While turning the hub forward, tighten the adjusting nut to 22–29 ft lbs.
5. Rotate the hub a few more times to snug down the bearings.

6. Retighten the nut to 22–29 ft lbs. Unscrew the adjusting nut 1/8 of a turn (45 degrees). Install the lock nut (castellated nut) and snug it down against the adjusting nut until one of its grooves lines up with the hole in the spindle. It is okay to tighten the adjusting nut up to 15 degrees to allow the lock nut holes to align. Install a new cotter pin, bending its ends around the lock nut.

7. Install the wheel and couple of lug nuts. Check the axial play of the wheel by shaking it back and forth. The bearing free play should feel close to zero, but the wheel should spin freely. Be sure the brake shoes are not dragging against the drum.

8. If the bearing play is correct, with drum brakes you can install the grease cap and the rest of the lug nuts. With disc brakes, remove the wheel, replace the caliper, then install the wheel and grease cap.

STEERING

Steering Wheel

REMOVAL AND INSTALLATION

1. Position the wheels in the straight-ahead position.

2. Disconnect the battery ground cable from the battery.

3. Remove the horn pad by unscrewing the two screws from the rear side of the steering wheel crossbar.

4. Punch mark the top of the steering column shaft and the steering wheel flange.

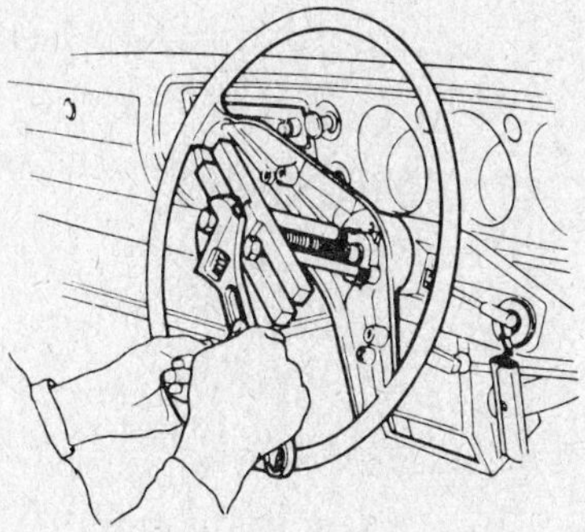

Steering wheel removal

5. Remove the attaching nut and remove the steering wheel with a puller.

CAUTION: Do not strike the shaft with a hammer, which may cause the column to collapse.

6. Install the steering wheel in the reverse order of removal aligning the punch marks. Tighten the steering wheel attaching nut to 51–54 ft lbs.

Turn Signal and Dimmer Switch

REMOVAL AND INSTALLATION

1. Disconnect the negative cable from the battery.

2. Remove the steering wheel.

3. Disconnect the wiring harness from the clip which retains it to the lower instrument panel.

4. Disconnect the multiple connector and lead wire from the instrument panel wiring harness.

5. Remove the steering column shell covers (upper and lower).

6. Loosen the two screws attaching the switch assembly to the steering column jacket and remove the switch assembly.

7. Install the turn signal and dimmer switch and the steering wheel in the reverse order of removal.

Ignition Switch

REMOVAL AND INSTALLATION

1. Disconnect the negative cable from the battery.

2. Unscrew and remove the escutcheon from the front of the ignition switch.

3. Remove the ignition switch and wiring harness with spacer from the steering shell cover.

4. Disconnect the wiring connector from the back of the ignition switch.

5. Install the ignition switch in the reverse order of removal.

NOTE: On models with the optional steering lock cylinder, remove the switch by removing the two retaining screws from the back of the steering lock cylinder.

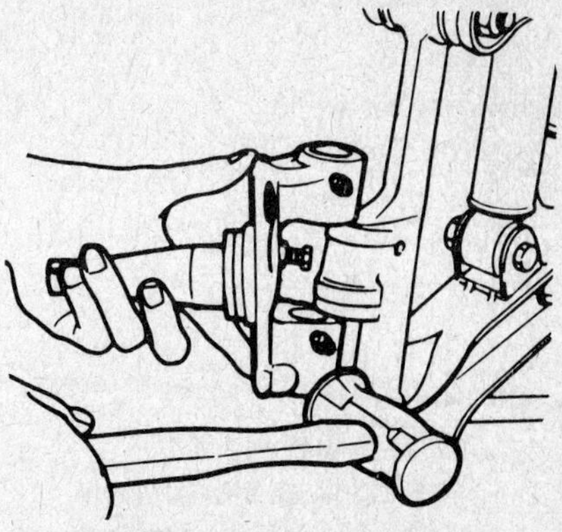

Knuckle spindle removal

Steering Lock

REMOVAL AND INSTALLATION

1. Remove the ignition switch.

2. Drill out the two shear screws.

3. Remove the two other normal type screws and dismount the steering lock from the steering jacket tube.

4. Install a new steering lock in the reverse order, being sure to tighten the two shear screws until they shear.

Steering Linkage

REMOVAL AND INSTALLATION

1. Jack up the front of the truck and support it with jackstands placed under the frame.

2. Remove the cotter pins and nuts securing the side rod ball studs to the steering knuckle/spindle arms.

3. Use a puller to disconnect the side rod ball studs from the steering knuckle arms. If a puller is not available, strike the side of the steering knuckle arm boss with a hammer, backing it up with a

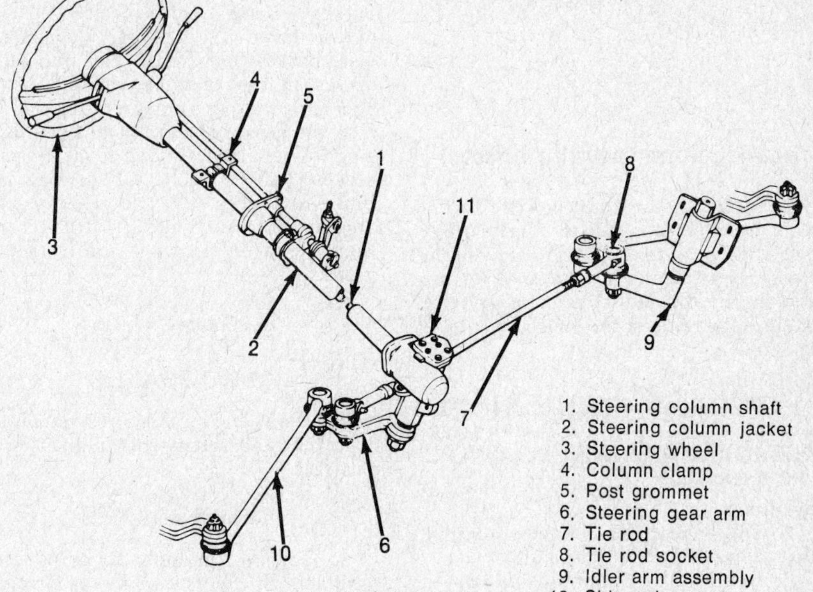

1. Steering column shaft
2. Steering column jacket
3. Steering wheel
4. Column clamp
5. Post grommet
6. Steering gear arm
7. Tie rod
8. Tie rod socket
9. Idler arm assembly
10. Side rod
11. Steering gear assembly

Steering system components

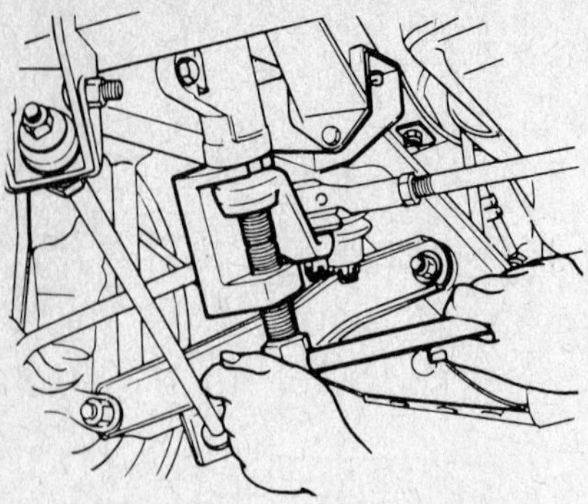

Steering gear arm removal

heavy hammer on the opposite side, and at the same time having an assistant pull the ball stud out of the steering knuckle arm.

NOTE: Do not strike the ball stud head, the ball socket on the side rod, or the side rod with the hammer.

4. Remove the nut securing the steering gear arm on the sector shaft and remove the gear arm with a puller. If a puller is not available, and the steering gear arm need not be removed, disconnect the side arm and tierod ball studs from the steering gear arm in the same manner as outlined in Step 3.

5. Remove the idler arm assembly from the frame by unscrewing the two attaching nuts.

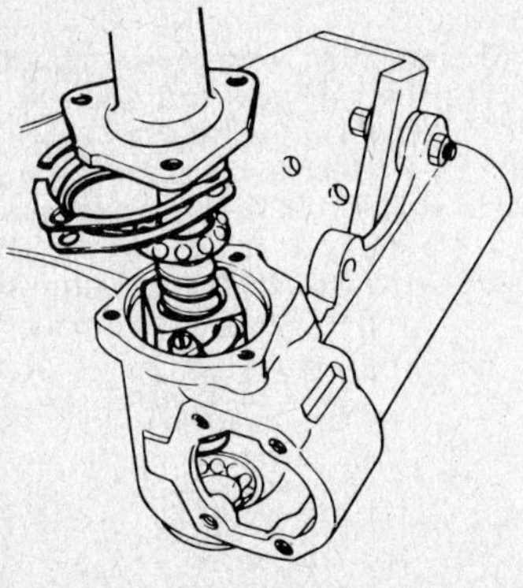

Steering worm assembly removal

6. Install the steering linkage in the reverse order of removel. Tighten the ball stud nuts to 40–55 lbs, idler arm assembly attaching nuts to 23–27 ft lbs, and the tie-rod adjustment locknuts to 58–72 ft lbs. Adjust the toe-in and steering angle.

Power Steering Pump

REMOVAL AND INSTALLATION

1. Disconnect and plug the hoses at the pump.

2. Disconnect the pump mounting bolts and remove the drive belt.

3. Remove the pump. Installation is the reverse. Adjust the belt tension after installation, and fill and bleed the system.

BELT TENSION ADJUSTMENT

1. Loosen the tension adjustment and mounting bolts.

2. Move the pump toward or away from the engine so that the belt deflects $^{1}/_{4}$-$^{1}/_{2}$ in. midway between the idler pulley and the pump pulley under moderate thumb pressure.

3. Tighten the bolts and recheck the tension adjustment.

SYSTEM BLEEDING

1. Fill the pump reservoir and allow to remain undisturbed for a few minutes.

2. Raise the car until the front wheels are clear of the ground.

3. With the engine off, quickly turn the wheels right and left several times, lightly contacting the stops.

4. Add fluid if necessary.

5. Start the engine and let it idle.

6. Repeat Steps 3 and 4 with the engine idling.

7. With the steering wheel all the way to the left, open the bleeder screw on the steering gear to allow the air to bleed. Close the screw when fluid is expelled.

8. Stop the engine, lower the car until the wheels just touch the ground. Start the engine, allow it to idle, and turn the wheel back and forth several times. Check the fluid level and refill if necessary.

BRAKE SYSTEMS

Datsun pick-ups are equipped with hydraulically-operated drum brakes through 1977, with single-servo brakes on the front wheels and duo-servo brakes on the rear wheels. 1978–80 models have single caliper, dual-piston disc brakes up front and duo-servo drums at the rear. A vacuum brake booster is standard equipment. 1976 and later models have the Nisan Load Sensing Valve, a proportioning valve which senses changes in the vehicle load and brake fluid pressure, and regulates the amount of rear braking force accordingly, to reduce the possibility of rear brake lock-up.

Adjustment

DISC BRAKES

The front disc brakes are self-adjusting. No adjustments are necessary or possible.

DRUM BRAKES

1. Jack up the wheel to be adjusted until it completely clears the ground.

2. Make sure that the parking brake is completely released if the rear brakes are being adjusted.

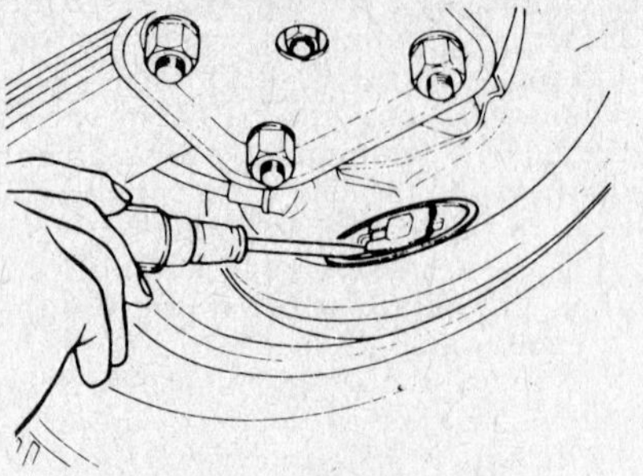

Drum brake adjustment

3. Remove the rubber boot from the rear of the brake backing plate.

4. Lightly tap the adjuster housing forward with a hammer and screwdriver.

5. Turn the adjuster wheel downward with a screwdriver to spread the brake shoes. Stop turning the adjuster wheel when the brake drum is locked and the wheel cannot be turned by hand.

6. Turn the adjuster wheel upward, backing off the shoes from the brake drum 12 notches, to obtain the correct clearance between the brake shoes and drum. Turn the wheel to make sure that the brake drum turns without dragging.

7. Install the rubber boot.

BRAKE PEDAL

These models have adjustable master cylinder pushrods for setting free-play.

1. Adjust the height of the stop light switch so that the top surface of the brake pedal is 5.5 in. off the surface of the floor board (without rugs) through 1975. The distance should be 5.8 in., 1976–77, or 6.06 in., 1978–80. Tighten the stop light switch locknut.

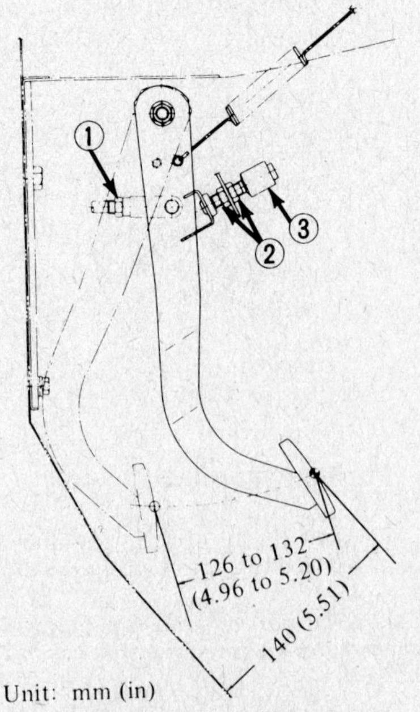

1. Push rod adjusting nut
2. Switch adjusting nuts
3. Brake lamp switch

Brake pedal adjustment

2. Adjust the length of the master cylinder pushrod (booster pushrod on vehicles so equipped) clevis so that 0.04–0.12 in. of free-play exists between the brake pedal and the pushrod through 1975. Free-play should be 0.024–0.047 in., 1976–77, or 0.04–0.20 in., 1978–80.

3. Operate the brake pedal to make sure that it operates freely with no noise or interference.

Overhaul

MASTER CYLINDER

Removal and Installation

1. On a truck not equipped with power brakes, remove the cotter pin, pull out the clevis pin, and separate the brake pedal from the master cylinder pushrod.

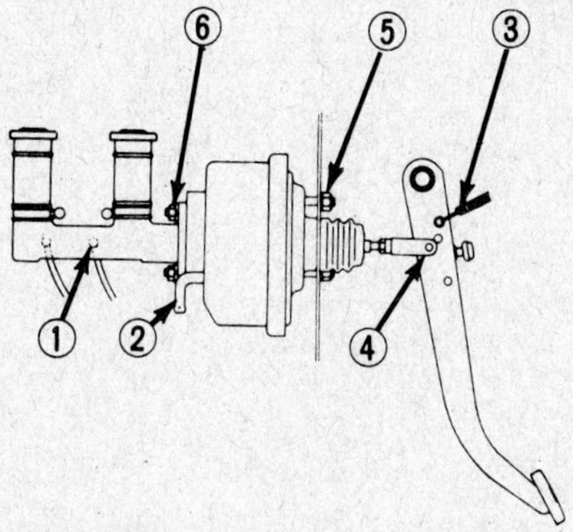

For removal of master-vac, remove the parts in the numerical order indicated

2. Place a number of cloths or a container under the master cylinder to catch the brake fluid. Disconnect the brake tubes from the master cylinder; use a flare nut wrench if one is available.

*NOTE: **Brake fluid eats paint; wipe up any spilled fluid immediately, then flush the area with clear water.***

3. Remove the master cylinder securing nuts and withdraw the master cylinder from the firewall or power brake booster.

4. Install the master cylinder in the reverse order of removal and bleed the brake hydraulic system.

Disassembly

The master cylinder can be disassembled using the illustrations as a guide. Clean all parts in clean brake fluid. Replace the cylinder or piston as necessary if clearance between the two exceeds 0.006 in. Lubricate all parts with clean brake fluid on assembly. Master cylinder rebuilding kits, containing all the wearing parts, are available to simplify overhaul. Master cylinders are supplied to Datsun by two manufacturers: Nabco and Tokico. Parts between these

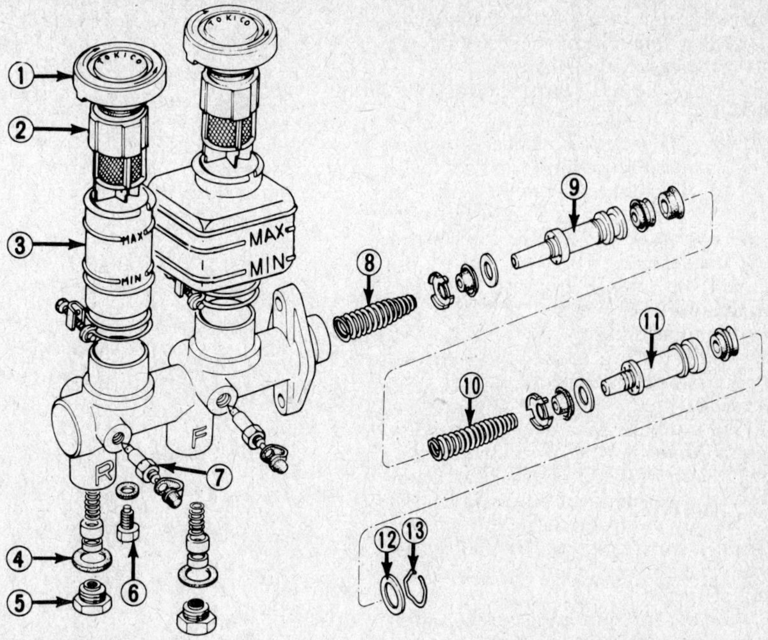

1. Reservoir cap
2. Oil filter
3. Oil reservoir
4. Packing
5. Valve cap
6. Secondary piston stopper
7. Bleeder screw
8. Secondary return spring
9. Secondary piston
10. Primary return spring
11. Primary piston
12. Piston stopper
13. Piston stopper ring

Disc brake master cylinder

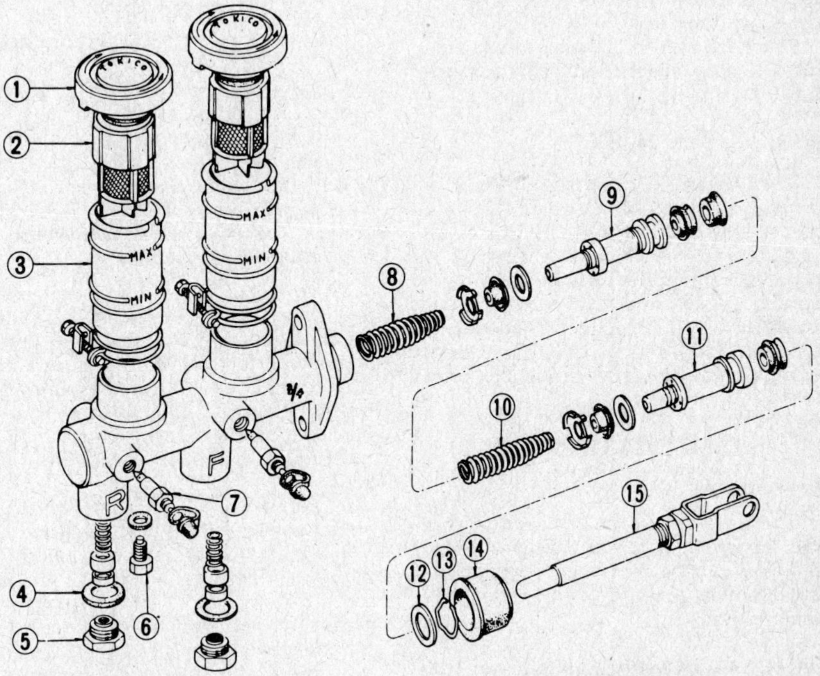

1. Reservoir cap
2. Oil filter
3. Oil reservoir
4. Packing
5. Valve cap
6. Secondary piston stopper
7. Bleeder screw
8. Secondary return spring
9. Secondary piston
10. Primary return spring
11. Primary piston
12. Piston stopper
13. Piston stopper ring
14. Dust cover
15. Push rod assembly

Drum brake master cylinder

manufacturers are not interchangeable. Be sure you obtain the correct rebuilding parts for your master cylinder.

Bleeding

Bleeding is required whenever air in the hydraulic fluid causes a spongy feeling pedal and sluggish response. This is almost always the case after some part of the hydraulic system has been repaired or replaced.

1. Fill the master cylinder reservoir with the proper fluid. Special fluid is required for disc brakes.
2. The usual procedure is to bleed at the points furthest from the master cylinder first.
3. Fit a rubber hose over the bleeder screw. Submerge the other end of the hose in clean brake fluid in a clear glass container. Loosen the bleeder screw.
4. Slowly pump the brake pedal several times until fluid free of bubbles is discharged. An assistant is required to pump the pedal.
5. On the last pumping stroke, hold the pedal down and tighten the bleeder screw. Check the fluid level periodically during the bleeding operation.
6. Bleed the front brakes in the same way as the rear brakes. Note that some front drum brakes have two hydraulic cylinders and two bleeder screws. Both cylinders must be bled.
7. Check the fluid level in the master cylinder periodically during the bleeding procedure, and refill as necessary. Do not allow it to run dry.
8. Check that the brake pedal is now firm. If not, repeat the bleeding operation.

NLSV

The Nissan Load Sensing Valve is a proportioning valve installed between the master cylinder and the brakes. It limits fluid pressure to the rear brakes to prevent rear wheel lock–up. The valve is not rebuildable, and must be replaced as an assembly if defective. It should be replaced if, in a stop on dry pavement from 30 mph, the rear wheels lock prior to the front wheels.

DISC BRAKE PADS

Inspection

The pads should be removed so that the thickness of the remaining friction material can be measured. If the pads are less than 2 mm (0.08 in.) thick, they must be replaced.

NOTE: Always replace all pads on both wheels at the same time. The factory kit includes four pads, clips, pins, and springs; all parts should be used.

Removal and Installation

1. Raise and support the front of the truck. Remove the wheels.
2. Remove the retaining clip from the outboard pad.

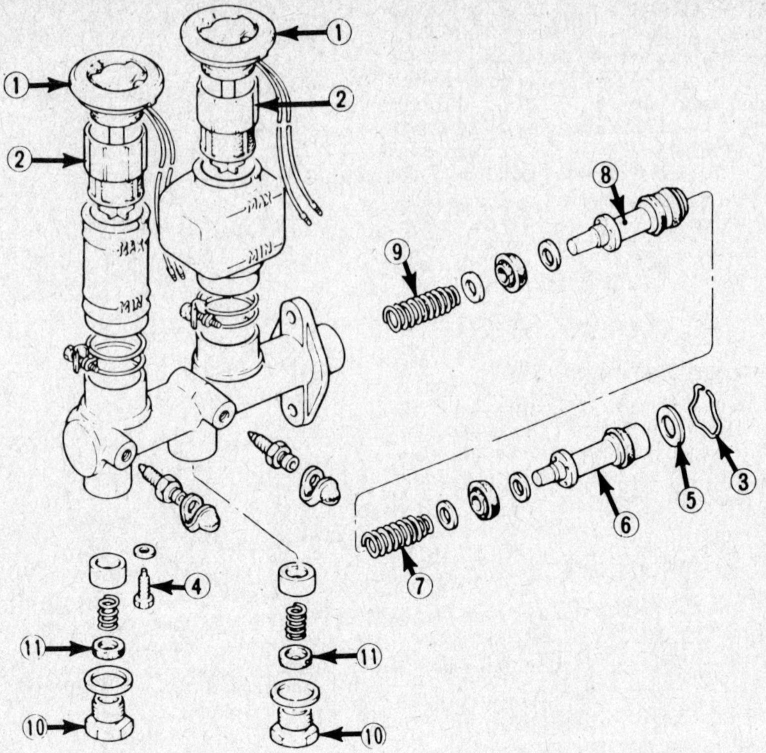

1. Reservoir cap
2. Strainer
3. Stopper ring
4. Stopper screw
5. Stopper
6. Primary piston
7. Spring
8. Secondary piston
9. Spring
10. Plug
11. Check valve

Brake master cylinder components

3. Remove the pad pins retaining the antisqueal springs.
4. Remove the pads.

NOTE: When replacing the pads, always check the surface of the rotors for scoring or wear. The rotors should be removed for resurfacing if badly worn.

5. To install, open the bleeder screw slightly and push the outer piston into the cylinder until the dust seal groove aligns with the end of the seal retaining ring, then close the bleeder screw. Be careful, because the piston can be pushed too far, requiring disassembly of the caliper to repair. Install the inner pad.
6. Pull the yoke to push the inner piston into place. Install the outer pad.
7. Lightly coat the areas where the pins touch the pads, and where the pads touch the caliper (at the top) with grease. Do not allow the grease to get on the pad friction surfaces.
8. Install the anti-squeal springs and pad pins. Install the clip.
9. Apply the brakes a few times to seat the pads. Check the master cylinder leve; add fluid if necessary. Bleed the brakes if necessary.

CALIPER

Removal and Installation

1. Remove and plug the brake tube.

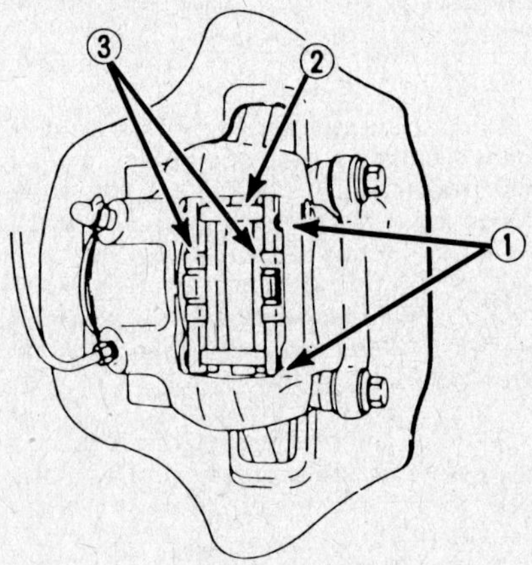

1. Clip
2. Pan pin
3. Anti-squeal spring

Disc brake pads

2. Unbolt and remove the caliper from the spindle.
3. Installation is the reverse. Tighten the mounting bolts to 53–72 ft. lbs.

Disassembly

1. Remove the caliper.
2. Remove the pads.
3. Remove the gripper pin attaching nuts and separate the yoke from the caliper body.

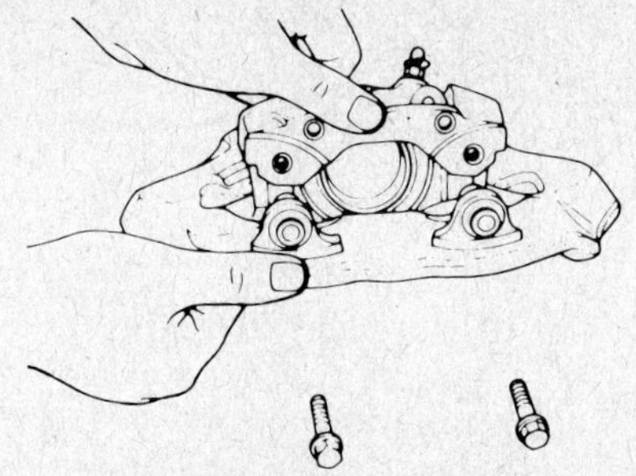

Disc brake yoke removal

4. Remove the yoke holder from the piston and remove the retaining rings and dust seals from the ends of both pistons.

5. Apply air pressure gradually into the fluid chamber of the caliper, to force the pistons from the cylinders.

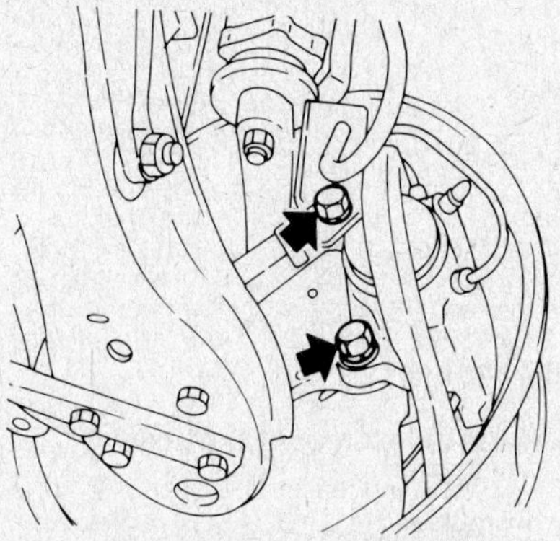

Disc brake caliper mount bolts

6. Remove the piston seals.

7. Inspect the parts for wear or damage. Check the inside surface of the cylinder for scoring or wear, and replace the caliper as necessary. Minor damage can be cleaned up with crocus cloth, but deep pitting or scoring warrants replacement of the caliper. The piston should be examined for wear, but do not polish it with crocus cloth; it has a plated surface which will be damaged by sanding. Replace the piston as necessary.

8. To assemble, coat the seals and pistons with clean brake fluid. Install the seals into the cylinder bore.

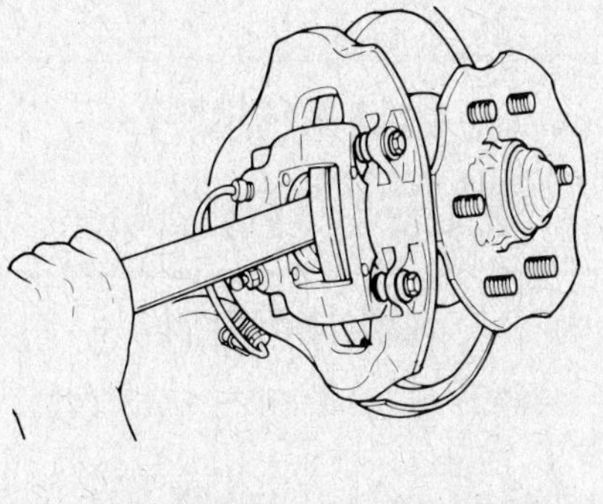

Push disc brake piston back into housing when replacing pads

9. Slide the "A" piston into the cylinder, followed by the "B" piston, so that its yoke groove coincides with the yoke groove of the cylinder.

10. Install the dust seal and secure tightly with the retaining ring.

11. Install the yoke holder onto the "A" piston and install the gripper to the yoke. If you lightly coat the gripper pins with soapy water, they will be easier to install.

12. Support the end of the "B" piston, and press the yoke into the yoke holder. This will require a good deal of force. Be careful to insert the yoke straight into the holder, to avoid cracking the yoke holder.

13. Install the pads, anti-squeal springs, and pad pins and retain with the clip.

14. Tighten the gripper pin attaching nuts to 12–15 ft lbs, and install the caliper on the spindle.

DISC (ROTOR)

Removal and Installation

1. Remove the caliper.
2. Remove the hub cap, cotter pin, and adjusting nut.
3. Remove the wheel bearing nut and remove the hub and rotor.
4. Hold the hub in a vise and loosen the bolts to remove the rotor from the hub.
5. Installation is the reverse. Tighten the rotor-to-hub bolts to 28–38 ft lbs. Adjust the wheel bearings after installation.

Inspection

1. Check the rotor for wear or scoring. Deep scoring, grooves, or rust pitting can be removed by refacing. Minimum disc thickness is 10.5 mm (0.413 in.). If the rotor will be thinner than this after refinishing, it must be replaced.

2. Check disc parallelism; it must be under 0.03 mm (0.0012 in.). If over this specification, the disc must be replaced.

3. With the disc and hub installed, and the wheel bearings adjusted to specification, measure the disc runout with a dial indicator. If runout exceeds 0.15 mm (0.0059 in.), the disc needs to be refinished or replaced.

BRAKE DRUM

Removal and Installation

1. Jack up the front of the vehicle so that the wheel which is to be serviced is off the ground.
2. Remove the wheel and tire assembly.
3. Pull the brake drum off of the hub. If the drum cannot be easily removed, back off on the brake adjustment.

NOTE: Never depress the brake pedal while the brake drum is removed.

4. Install the brake drum in the reverse order of removal and adjust the brakes.

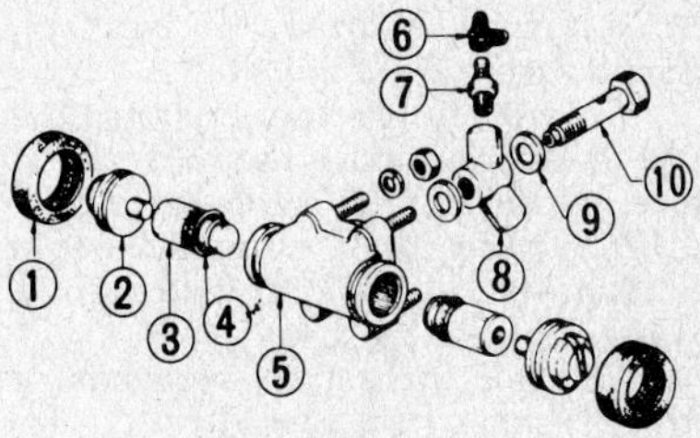

1. Dust cover
2. Piston head
3. Piston
4. Piston cup
5. Wheel cylinder housing
6. Bleeder cap
7. Bleeder screw
8. Connector
9. Washer
10. Connector bolt

Rear wheel cylinder

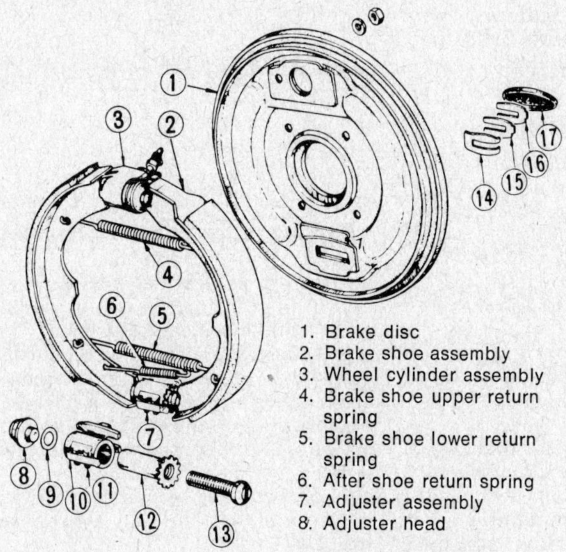

1. Brake disc
2. Brake shoe assembly
3. Wheel cylinder assembly
4. Brake shoe upper return spring
5. Brake shoe lower return spring
6. After shoe return spring
7. Adjuster assembly
8. Adjuster head
9. Adjuster head shim
10. Lock spring
11. Adjuster housing
12. Adjuster wheel
13. Adjuster screw
14. Retaining spring
15. Lock plate
16. Adjuster shim
17. Rubber boot

Drum front brake

Inspection

After removing the brake drum, wipe out the accumulated dust with a damp cloth.

CAUTION: Do not blow the brake dust out of the drums. Brake linings contain asbestos, a known cancer causing substance. Dispose of the cloth after use.

Inspect the drum for cracks, deep grooves, roughness, scoring, or out-of-roundness. Replace any brake drum which is cracked.

Smooth any slight scores by polishing the friction surface with fine emery cloth. Heavy or extensive scoring will cause excessive brake lining wear and should be removed from the brake drum through resurfacing. The maximum finished diameter of the brake drums must not exceed 10.059 in. The brake drum must be replaced if the diameter is 10.079 in. or greater.

Front Removal and Installation

1. Raise and support the front of the truck. Remove the wheels.
2. Remove the drum. If removal is difficult, back off the adjuster.
3. To provide working clearance, remove the hub: remove the hub cap, remove and discard the cotter pin, remove the adjusting cap and nut from the spindle, then remove the hub together with the bearings and washers.
4. Unhook the return springs. Remove the shoes.
5. Disconnect and plug the brake hose at the wheel cylinder. Remove the cylinder.
6. Remove the rubber boot, shim, lock plate and spring, and remove the adjuster.
7. Wear limit for the drum is 10.06 in.; maximum out of round is 0.0008 in. Minimum lining thickness is 0.039 in. Wheel cylinder piston clearance maximum is 0.006 in.
8. To install, apply grease sparingly to the adjuster bore, wheel and screw, the backing plate contact surfaces, and the adjuster sliding surfaces. Bleed the system after installation and adjust the wheel bearings.

Rear Removal and Installation

1. Raise and support the rear of the truck. Remove the wheels.
2. Loosen the parking brake cable and remove the drum.
3. Turn the shoe retainers 90° and remove together with hold down springs.
4. Spread the shoes apart and remove the link.
5. Remove the return springs.
6. Remove the shoes. The secondary shoe must be separated from the parking brake toggle lever.
7. Disconnect and plug the brake line at the cylinder and remove the cylinder.
8. Remove the boot, shim, lock plate and springs and remove the adjuster.
9. All wear specifications are the same as for the front, except the piston to wheel cylinder clearance, which is 0.06 in. maximum.
10. When installing, adjust the clearance between the parking brake toggle lever and the rear shoe to 0.0118 in. maximum. Toggle pin washers are available in different thicknesses.

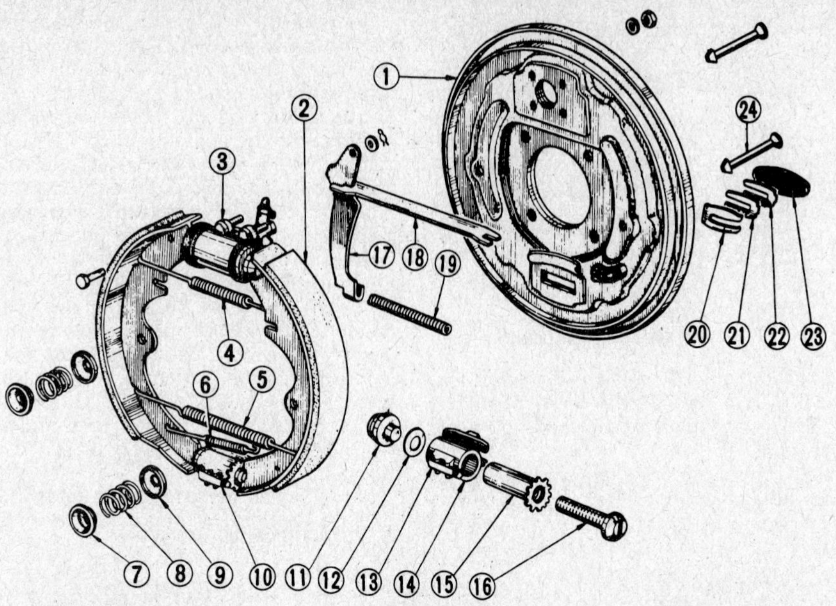

Rear brake components

PARKING BRAKE

Cable Adjustment

1. Jack up the rear of the vehicle until the rear wheels clear the ground.
2. Adjust the rear brakes as outlined under "Brake System Adjustment."
3. Loosen the locknut at the parking cable lever assembly mounted on the driveshaft center bearing crossmember.
4. Turn the adjusting nut until the parking brake control lever operating stroke is between 3 in. and 4 in.
5. Release the parking brake and make sure that the rear wheels turn freely with no drag.
6. Lower the vehicle.

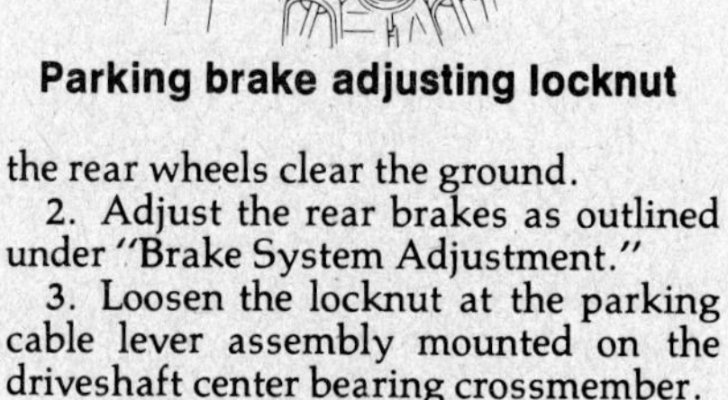

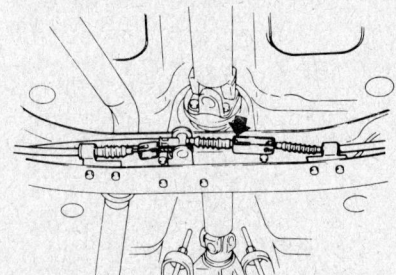

Parking brake adjusting locknut

Removal and Installation

1. Fully release the parking brake control lever.
2. Loosen the adjusting nut at the cable lever mounted to the frame crossmember.
3. Disconnect the cable from the control lever.
4. Remove the rear brake drums, and disconnect the parking brake cables from the parking brake toggle levers of the rear service brake assemblies.
5. Remove the lockplate, spring and clip, and pull the parking brake cable out toward the cable lever.
6. Remove the cotter pin at the cable lever and disconnect the cable.
7. Install the cables in the reverse order of removal. Apply a light coat of grease to the cables to make sure that they slide properly. Adjust the parking brake cables.

CHASSIS ELECTRICAL

Heater Unit

REMOVAL AND INSTALLATION

1. Disconnect the battery ground cable.
2. Drain the engine coolant.
3. Remove the defroster hoses.

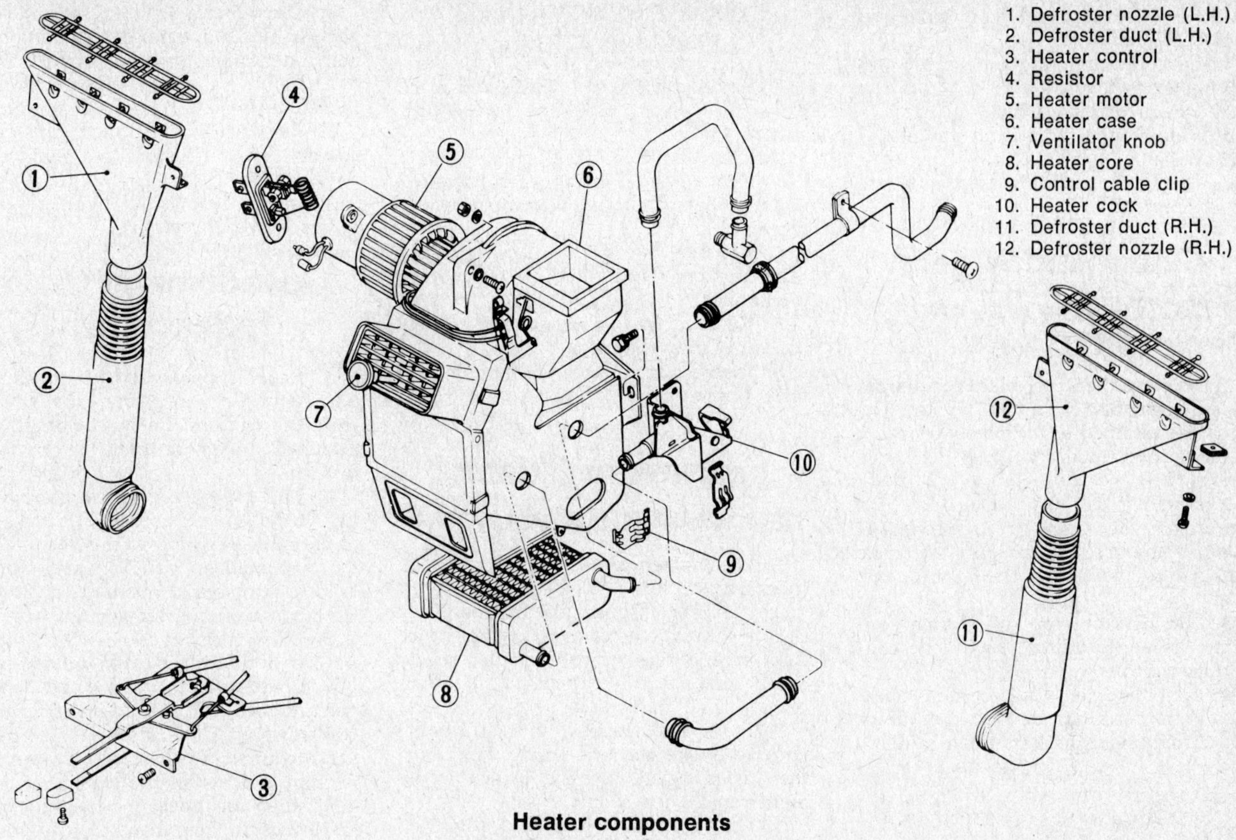

Heater components

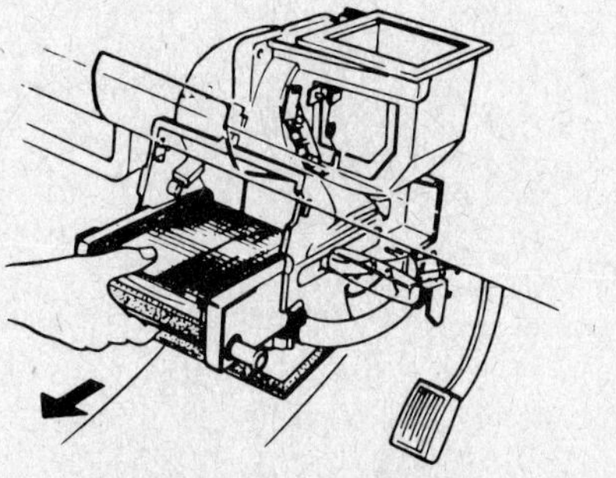

Heater core removal

4. Remove the three cable retaining clips and disconnect the control cables from the valves and water cock.
5. Disconnect the two fan motor leads from each connector.
6. Disconnect the two resistor lead wires from each connector.
7. Disconnect the water hoses from the heater core and water cock.
8. Remove the three heater housing mounting bolts and remove the heater assembly from the vehicle.
9. Install the heater assembly in the reverse order of removal.

Blower

REMOVAL AND INSTALLATION

1. Remove the heater assembly from the vehicle as previously outlined.
2. Remove the nine spring clips and disassemble the heater housing.
3. Remove the fan from the electric motor.
4. Remove the fan motor retaining screws and remove the motor.
5. Install the blower motor and heater assembly in the reverse order.

Heater Core

REMOVAL AND INSTALLATION

1. Drain the engine coolant.
2. Remove the defroster hoses.
3. Disconnect the water hoses from the inlet and outlet pipes of the heater core.
4. Remove the four clips and front cover.
5. Remove the heater core from the heater housing.
6. Install the heater core in the reverse order of removal.

Radio

REMOVAL AND INSTALLATION

1. Pull the knobs off the radio control shafts.
2. Remove the radio retaining nuts and washer from the radio control shafts.

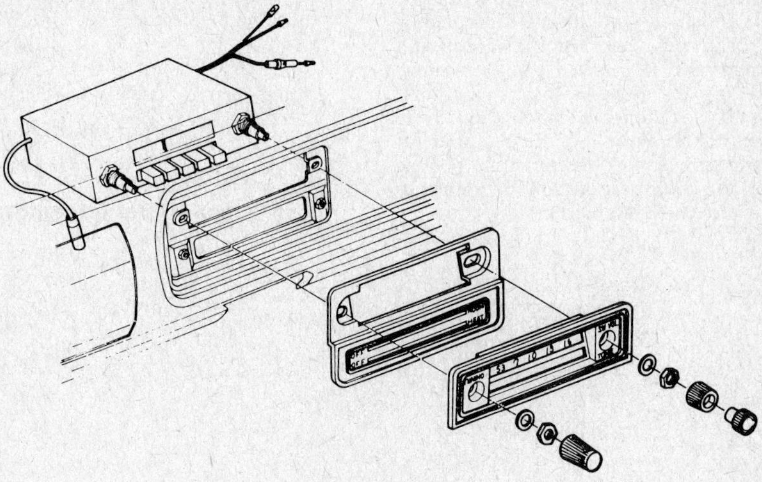

Radio mounting

3. Remove the bezel plate from the front of the radio.
4. Disconnect the antenna cable and the power and speaker wires from the under the instrument panel.
5. Remove the radio from the instrument panel.
6. Install the radio in the reverse order of removal.

Windshield Wipers

MOTOR REMOVAL AND INSTALLATION

1. Remove the wiper blades and arms as an assembly from the pivots. The arms are retained to the pivots by nuts. Remove the nuts and pull the arms straight off.
2. Remove the cowl top grille. It is retained by four screws at its front edge. Remove the screws and pull the grille forward to disengage the tabs at the rear.
3. Remove the stop ring which connects the wiper motor arm to the connecting rod.
4. Disconnect the wiper motor harness at the connector on the wiper motor body from under the instrument panel.

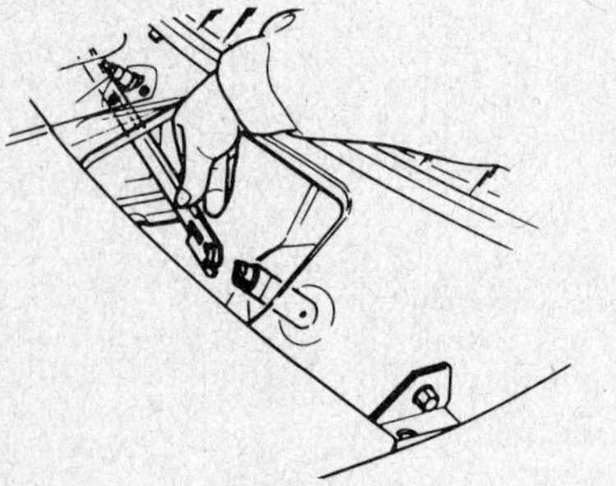

Windshield wiper linkage mounting

5. Remove the three retaining screws and pull the wiper motor outward and remove the motor from the vehicle.
6. Install the wiper motor in the reverse order of removal. The wiper arms should be installed so that the blades are .98 in. (25 mm) above, and parallel to, the windshield molding. If the motor has been run, be sure the motor and linkage is in its parked position before installing the wiper arms. To do this, turn the ignition switch on, and cycle the motor three or four times. Shut off the motor with the wiper switch (not the ignition switch), and allow the motor to return to the park position.

LINKAGE REMOVAL AND INSTALLATION

1. Remove the wiper blade and arm from the pivot. See the preceding section.
2. Remove the cowl top grille.
3. Remove the two flange nuts retaining the wiper linkage pivot to the cowl top.
4. Remove the stop ring which retains the connecting rod to the wiper motor arm.
5. Remove the wiper motor linkage assembly from the truck.
6. Install the linkage in the reverse order of removal.

Instrument Cluster

REMOVAL AND INSTALLATION

1. Disconnect the battery ground (negative) cable.
2. Working through the openings of the instrument cluster cover, remove the three screws retaining the cluster cover to the instrument panel and remove cover.
3. From underneath the instrument panel, remove the one screw retaining the cluster assembly to the lower instrument panel.
4. Withdraw the cluster lid slightly. Press the windshield wiper control knob in, turn it counterclockwise and pull it off the switch. Remove the headlight/parking light switch knob in the same manner.
5. From behind the instrument cluster, disconnect the speedometer cable at the speedometer head and the multiple connector from the printed circuit.

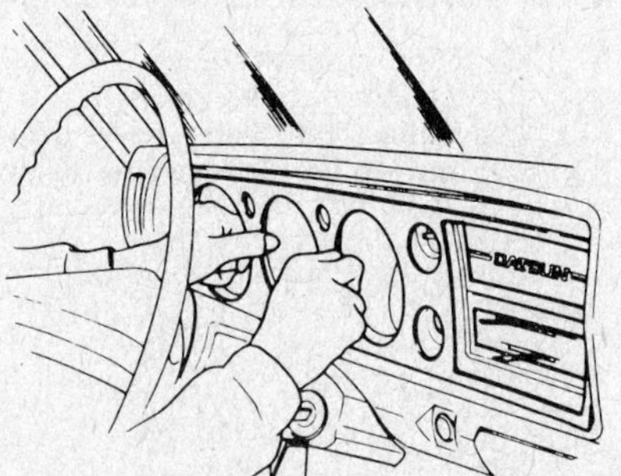

Instrument cluster lid removal

6. On vehicles with a clock, disconnect the wires at each connection on the instrument panel printed circuit.
7. Remove the four screws retaining the cluster assembly to the cluster lid.
8. Remove the instrument cluster assembly from under the instrument panel.
9. Install the instrument cluster in the reverse order of removal.

Speedometer Cable Replacement

1. Reach up under the instrument panel and disconnect the cable housing from the back of the speedometer. It is attached by a knurled knob which unscrews.
2. Pull the cable from the cable housing. If the cable is broken, the other half of the cable will have to be removed from the transmission end. Unscrew the retaining knob and remove the cable from the transmission extension housing.
3. Lubricate the cable with graphite powder and feed the cable into the housing. It is best to start at the speedometer end and feed the cable down towards the transmission. It is also usually necessary to unscrew the transmission connection and install the cable end to the gear, then reconnect the housing to the transmission. Slip the cable end into the speedometer, and reconnect the cable housing.

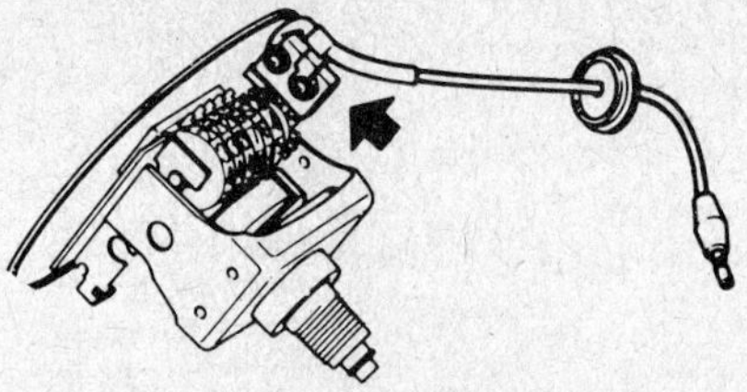

Speedometer

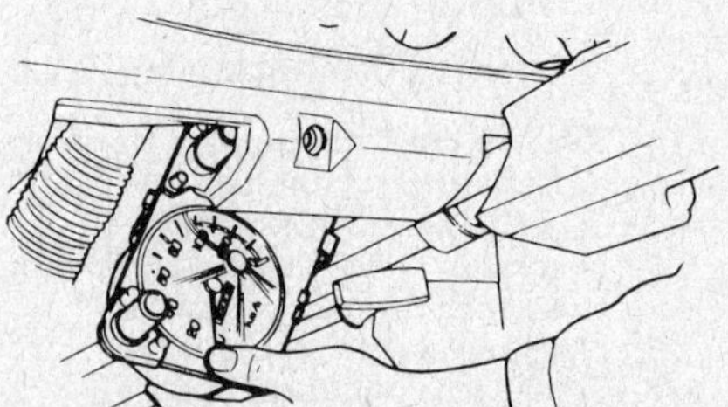

Combination meter removal

INDEX

VEHICLE IDENTIFICATION

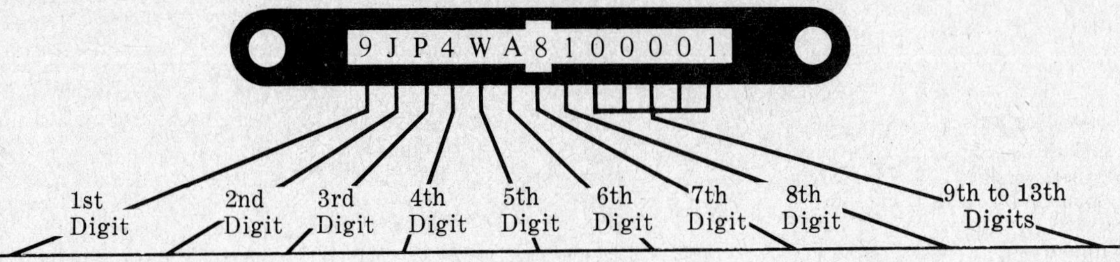

Truck Line	G.V.W. and Wheelbase	Price Class	Body Code	Engine Code	Model Year	Transmission① Code	Trim Code	Sequential Serial Number
9: Dodge 0: Plymouth	J: G.V.W.—Less than 6,000 lbs. W/B—Less than 110.2 in.	L: Low Price P: Premium Price	4: For conventional cab with swept-line box	L:2.0 liters (121.7 CID) W:2.6 liters (155.9 CID)	A: 1980	1: 4 speed M/T 49 states 2: 4 speed M/T Calif. 3: 4 speed M/T Canada 4: 5 speed M/T 49 states 5: 5 speed M/T Calif. 6: 5 speed M/T Canada 7: A/T 49 states 8: A/T Calif. 9: A/T Canada	1: Low 3: High 1 5: High 2	00001 ~

① M/T: Manual transmission, A/T: Automatic transmission

G.V.W. Gross Vehicle Weight

W/B: Wheel Base

ENGINE IDENTIFICATION

Model	Year	Cu. in. (cm³)	Number of Cylinders	Type	Engine Series Identification
D-50 Dodge	1979-80	121.7 (2000)	4	OHC	U
Plymouth Arrow	1979-80	121.7 (2000)	4	OHC	U
D-50 Dodge Sport	1979-80	155.92 (2555)	4	OHC	W
Plymouth Arrow Sport	1979-80	155.92 (2555)	4	OHC	W

OHC: Overhead Cam shaft

GENERAL ENGINE SPECIFICATIONS

Year	Engine Displacement cu in. (cc)	Carburetor Type	Horsepower @ rpm	Torque @ rpm (ft-lbs)	Bore X Stroke (in.)	Compression Ratio	Oil Pressure (psi)
1979-80	121.7 (1995)	1 x 2 bbl	93 @ 5200①	108 @ 3000②	3.31 x 3.54	8.5:1	50-64
	155.92 (2555)	1 x 2 bbl	105 @ 5000③	139 @ 2500④	3.59 x 3.86	8.2:1	50-64

① Canada: 96 @ 5500 HP
② Canada: 109 @ 3500 Torque
③ Canada: 108 @ 5000 HP
④ Canada: 140 @ 2500 Torque

ENGINE TUNE-UP SPECIFICATIONS

U.S.A. engines

Engine	Transmission	Curb Idle Speed	Curb Idle CO	Enriched Idle Speed	Enriched Idle CO	Ignition Timing
49-state						
U-engine	Manual	650 ± 50 rpm	Below 0.1%	730 ± 10	1.0 ± 0.1%	5° BTDC ± 1°
	Automatic	700 ± 50 rpm	Below 0.1%	780 ± 10	1.0 ± 0.1%	5° BTDC ± 1°
W-engine	Manual	750 ± 50 rpm	*1.0 ± 0.5%	—	—	7° BTDC ± 1°
	Automatic	750 ± 50 rpm	*1.0 ± 0.5%	—	—	7° BTDC ± 1°
California						
U-engine	Manual	650 ± 50 rpm	*1.0 ± 0.5%	—	—	5° BTDC ± 1°
	Automatic	700 ± 50 rpm	*1.0 ± 0.5%	—	—	5° BTDC ± 1°
W-engine	Manual	750 ± 50 rpm	*1.0 ± 0.5%	—	—	7° BTDC ± 1°
	Automatic	750 ± 50 rpm	*1.0 ± 0.5%	—	—	7° BTDC ± 1°

* With air injection system disconnected

TUNE-UP SPECIFICATIONS

(When analyzing compression test results, look for uniformity among cylinders, rather than specific pressures)

Year	Engine Displacement cu in. (cc)	Spark Plugs Type①	Spark Plugs Gap (in.)	Ignition Timing (deg) MT	Ignition Timing (deg) AT	Intake Valve Opens (deg) BTDC	Fuel Pump Pressure (psi)	Idle Speed (rpm)	Valve Clearance (in.) In	Valve Clearance (in.) Ex
1979-80	121.7 (2000)	BPR6ES-11	0.039-0.043②	5B	5B	25	4.6-6.0	650 ± 50④	0.066③ Hot	0.010 Hot
	155.92 (2555)	BPR5ES-11	0.039-0.043②	7B	7B	25	4.6-6.0	750 ± 50	0.066③ Hot	0.010 Hot

NOTE: The underhood specifications sticker sometimes reflects tune-up specification changes made in production. Sticker figures must be used if they disagree with this chart.

① NGK Spark Plugs. For Canada, 2000 cc—BRP6ES: 2555 cc—BPR5ES.

② Canada: 0.028-0.031 in.

③ Jet Valve clearance: 0.006 (Hot)

④ Automatic Transmission: 700 ± 50 rpm.

MT: Manual Transmission

AT: Automatic Transmission

FIRING ORDERS

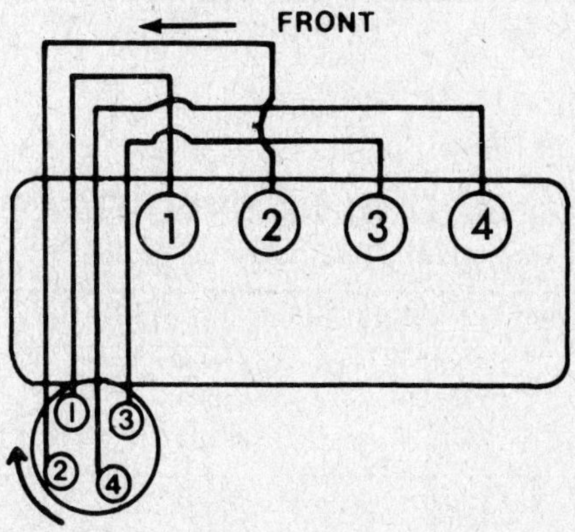

CAPACITIES

Year	Model	Engine Displacement (cc)	Crankcase (qts) With Filter	Crankcase (qts) Without Filter	Transmission (qts) Manual 4-spd	Transmission (qts) Manual 5-spd	Transmission (qts) Automatic	Drive Axle (pts)	Gasoline Tank (gals)	Cooling System (qts) With AC	Cooling System (qts) Without AC
1979-80	All	2000	4.5	4.0	2.2	—	6.8①	2.8	15.8	9.5	9.5
		2555	4.5	4.0	—	2.4	6.8①	2.8	15.8	9.7	9.7

① 1980: 7.2 U.S. quarts

CRANKSHAFT AND CONNECTING ROD SPECIFICATIONS

(All measurements given in inches)

Year	Engine cu in.	Crankshaft Main Brg. Journal Dia.	Crankshaft Main Brg. Oil Clearance	Crankshaft Shaft End Play	Crankshaft Thrust on No.	Connecting Rod Journal Diameter	Connecting Rod Oil Clearance	Connecting Rod Side Clearance
1979-80	121.7 155.9	2.3622	0.0008- 0.0028	0.002- 0.007	3	2.0866	0.0008- 0.0028	0.004- 0.010

VALVE SPECIFICATIONS

Year	Engine Displacement cu in. (cc)	Seat Angle (deg)	Face Angle (deg)	Spring Test Pressure (lbs @ in.)	Spring Installed Height (in.)	Stem to Guide Clearance (in.) Intake	Stem to Guide Clearance (in.) Exhaust	Stem Diameter (in.) Intake	Stem Diameter (in.) Exhaust
1979-80	121.7 (2000)	45	45	61 @ 1.59	1.590	0.0012- 0.0024	0.002- 0.0035	0.315	0.315
	155.92 (2555)	45	45	61 @ 1.59	1.590	0.0012- 0.0024	0.002- 0.0035	0.315	0.315
	Jet Valve	45	45	5.5 @ .846	—	—	—	0.1693	0.1693

PISTON AND RING SPECIFICATIONS

(All measurements given in inches)

Year	Engine cu in.	Piston to Bore Clearance	Ring Side Clearance Top Compression	Ring Side Clearance Bottom Compression	Ring Side Clearance Oil Control	Ring Gap Top Compression	Ring Gap Bottom Compression	Ring Gap Oil Control
1979-80	121.7 155.92	0.0008- 0.0016	0.0024- 0.0039	0.0008- 0.0024	—	0.010- 0.018	0.010- 0.018	0.0078- 0.035

TORQUE SPECIFICATIONS

(All readings in ft-lb)

Year	Engine Displacement cu in. (cc)	Cylinder Head Bolts	Rod Bearing Bolts	Main Bearing Bolts	Crankshaft Pulley Bolt	Flywheel to Crankshaft Bolts	Manifolds Intake	Manifolds Exhaust
1979-80	All	65-72	33-34	55-61	80-94	94-101	11-14	11-14

TORQUE SEQUENCES

Cylinder Head

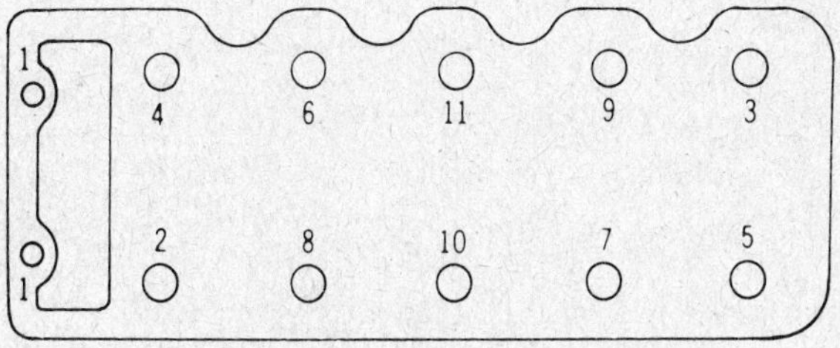

Head torque removal sequence
(© Chrysler Corp.)

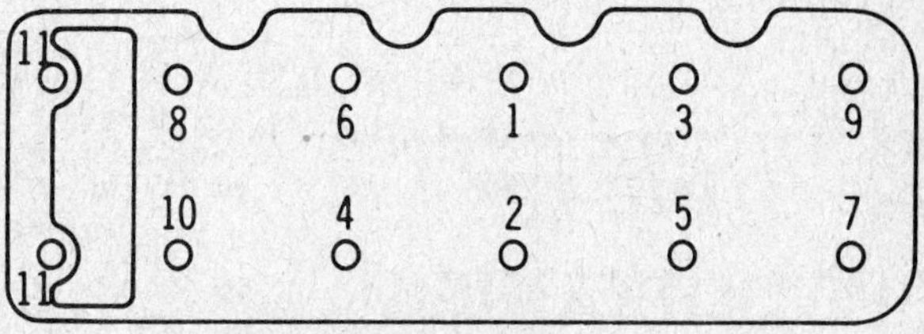

Head torque installation sequence
(© Chrysler Corp.)

ALTERNATOR AND REGULATOR SPECIFICATIONS

Model	Year	Alternator Identification Number	Rated Output @ 5000	Rated Output @ 2500	Brush Length (in.)	Brush Spring Tension (lbs.)	Regulated Voltage
All	1979	AQ2245G	41 amps	34 amps	0.669①	2.9-3.7②	14.1-14.7
	1980	A2T16471	44 amps	37 amps	0.709	0.7-1	14.1-14.7

① Built-in type brush: 0.709 in.
② Built-in type spring: 0.7-1 lbs.

BATTERY AND STARTER SPECIFICATIONS

Year	Engine Model	Battery Amp Hour Capacity	Starter Amps	Starter No Load Test Volts	Starter RPM	Starter Brush Spring Tension (lbs)	Starter Min. Brush Length (in.)	Type of Starter
1979-80	U, W w/MT	45, 60①	60	11.5	6,600	2.9-3.7	0.453	Direct Drive
	U, W w/AT	45, 60①	90④	11.5③	②3,300	2.9-3.7	0.453	Gear Reduction

MT: Manual Transmission
AT: Automatic Transmission
① 60 amp for Canada
② 1979: 4,500 rpm
③ 1979: 11 volts
④ 1979: 62 amps

WHEEL ALIGNMENT

Year	Model	Caster (degrees)	Camber (degrees)	Toe-in (in.)	Steering Angle Inner Wheel (degrees)	Steering Angle Outer Wheel (degrees)	King Pin Angle
1979	All	3° ± 1°	1° ± 30′	0.08-0.35	37°	30.5°	8°
1980	All	2°30′ ± 1°	1° ± 30′	0.08-0.35	37°	30.5°	8°

BRAKE SPECIFICATIONS

(All measurements are given in inches unless noted)

		Lug Nut Torque	Master Cyl-inder	Brake Disc Thickness			Brake Drum		Lining Thickness	
Model	Year	Ft-lb	Bore	Std.	Min.	Runout	Diameter	Maximum Wear	Front Min.	Rear Min.
All	1979	51-58	7/8	0.79	0.72	0.006	9.5	9.579	0.04①	0.04①
	1980	51-58	7/8	0.79	0.72	0.006	9.5	9.579	0.04①	0.04①

① Due to the variations in state inspection regulations, the minimum allowable lining thickness may be different from that recommendad by the manufacturer.

TUNE-UP PROCEDURES

NOTE: The procedures outlined below are the specific procedures for the D-50/Plymouth Arrow Pick-up truck; general tune-up procedures may be found in the section at the end of this book.

Spark Plugs

Check, clean and adjust the spark plugs every 6,000 miles. Replace them every 12,000 miles.

Clean any foreign material from around the spark plugs before removing them. When removing plug cables, grasp them at the cable caps.

Inspect the plugs for cracked or damaged threads or insulators, worn electrodes and damaged or worn plug gaskets. Use the diagnosis guide at the end of this book to check the burning patterns of the plugs. Always replace all four plugs as a set, it will be cheaper and more effective in the long run.

Set the plug gap to 0.039-0.043 in. (USA), 0.028-0.031 in. (Canada) using a wire feeler gauge.

NOTE: Do not use a flat gauge; an inaccurate reading will result. Hand start, then torque each plug into its hole at 18-21 ft-lb.

CAUTION: Don't over-torque plugs or thread stripping could result.

Electronic Ignition System (EIS)

All D-50/Plymouth Arrow pick-ups are equipped with electronic ignition systems which replace the contact points and condenser with a transistorized integrated circuit. There are no adjustments that can be done on this type of ignition system.

IGNITION SYSTEM TEST

If you suspect that the ignition system may be defective perform the following test:

1. Remove the distributor cap by inserting a screwdriver in the ends of the two retaining screws, pushing in and turning the screws clockwise.
2. Remove the mounting screws holding the rotor assembly and lift out the rotor assembly.
3. Set the ignition switch to ON.
4. Disconnect the high tension cable from the center terminal of the distributor cap and hold its end about a quarter of an inch away from ground (cylinder block, etc.). Insert a flatblade screwdriver between the reluctor and the stator of the distributor (see illustration). A spark should jump from the high tension wire to ground. If a spark is not produced, a defective control unit, pick-up coil, ignition coil or faulty wiring may be the problem. Further service should be left to a qualified service technician.

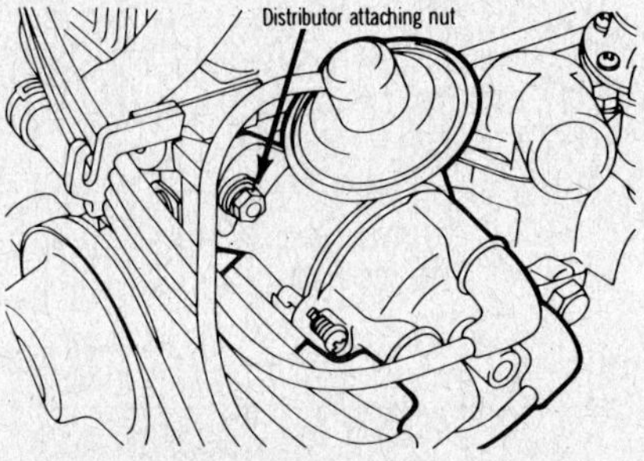

Ignition timing adjustment nut
(© Chrysler Corp.)

Ignition Timing

1. Warm up the engine. Connect a tachometer and check the engine idle speed. Adjust it as outlined below if it is not within specifications.

If the timing mark on the front pulley is difficult to see, use chalk or a dab of paint to make it more visible.

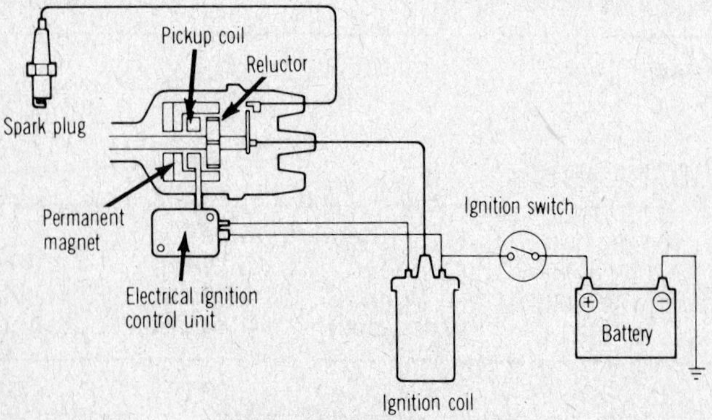

Electronic ignition system
(© Chrysler Corp.)

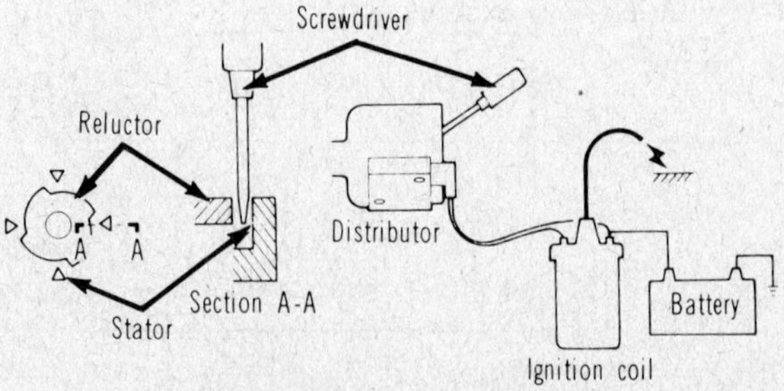

Electronic ignition system test
(© Chrysler Corp.)

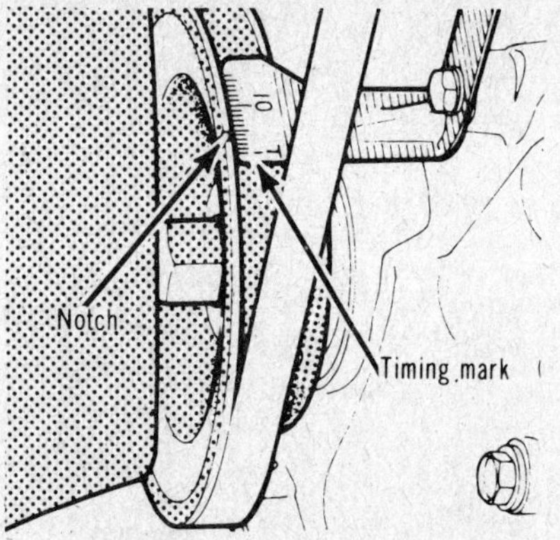

Crankshaft pulley timing mark
(© Chrysler Corp.)

2. Connect a timing light to the engine, as outlined in the instructions supplied by the manufacturer of the light.

3. Allow the engine to run at the specified idle speed with the gear shift in Neutral and the air conditioning compressor and lights off.

CAUTION: Be sure the parking brake is firmly set and that the wheels are chocked.

4. Point the timing light at the timing marks indicated on the front timing chain cover. With engine at idle, timing should be at the specifications given in the tune-up chart at the beginning of this section. If it is not, loosen the attaching nut at the base of the distributor and rotate the distributor until the correct timing is achieved.

5. Stop the engine and retighten the attaching nut. Start the engine and recheck the timing.

6. Stop the engine and disconnect the timing light and tachometer.

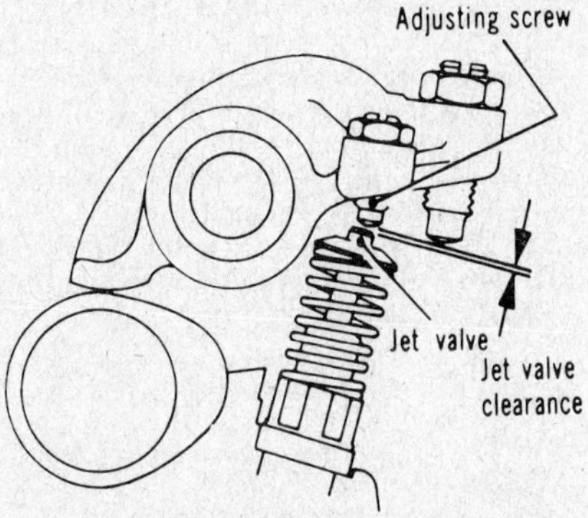

Adjusting the Jet Valve (U.S.A. only)
(© Chrysler Corp.)

Adjusting intake and exhaust valve lash
(© Chrysler Corp.)

Valve Lash

Both the U engine (1995 c.c.) and the W engine (2555 c.c.) which are sold in the United States have a jet valve located beside the intake valve of each cylinder. The jet valve works off the intake valve rocker arm and injects a swirl of air into the combustion chamber to promote more complete burning of fuel.

NOTE:** **When adjusting valve clearances, the jet valve must be adjusted before the intake valve.

1. Start the engine and allow it to reach normal operating temperature (170-190°F).

2. Stop the engine and remove the air cleaner and its hoses. Remove any other cables, hoses, wires, etc., which are attached to the valve cover, and remove the valve cover.

3. Disconnect the high tension coil-to-distributor wire at the coil.

4. Watch the rocker arms for No. 1 cylinder and rotate the crankshaft until the exhaust valve is closing and the intake valve has just started to open. At this point, no. 4 cylinder will be at Top Dead Center (TDC) commencing its firing stroke.

5. Loosen the lock nut on cylinder no. 4 intake valve and back off the intake valve adjusting screw 2 or more turns.

6. Loosen the lock nut on the jet valve adjusting screw.

7. Turn the jet valve adjusting screw counter-clockwise and insert a 0.006 in. feeler gauge between the jet valve stem and the adjusting screw.

8. Tighten the adjusting screw until it touches the feeler gauge.

Take care not to press in the valve while adjusting because the jet valve spring is very weak.

NOTE: If the adjusting screw is tight, special care must be taken to avoid pressing down on the jet valve when adjusting the clearance or a false reading will result.

9. Tighten the lock nut securely while holding the rocker arm adjusting screw with a screwdriver to prevent it from turning.

10. Make sure that a 0.006 in. feeler gauge can be easily inserted between the jet valve and the rocker arm.

11. Adjust no. 4 cylinder's intake valve to 0.006 in. and its exhaust valve to 0.010 in. Tighten the adjusting screw locknuts and re-check each clearance.

12. Perform step 4 in conjunction with the chart below to set up the remaining three cylinders for valve adjustments.

13. Replace the valve cover and all other components. Run the engine and check for oil leaks at the valve cover.

Carburetor

***NOTE:** See "Fuel System", below, for other carburetor adjustments.*

IDLE SPEED AND MIXTURE ADJUSTMENTS

U engine—U.S.A. except 1980 California, 1979 W engine

1. Place the transmission in "N" (Neutral) position and set the parking brake.

2. Make sure the air conditioner, lights and all accessories are off.

3. Run the engine at idle until the coolant temperature reaches 170-190°F.

4. Adjust the engine speed and idle CO concentration to the enriched idle speed and enriched idle CO as specified in the following chart. Adjust the CO-concentration using the idle speed adjusting screw (SAS) and the idle mixture adjusting screw (MAS).

5. Reset the engine speed to curb idle speed by adjusting the idle mixture adjusting screw (MAS—See illustration).

6. The engine should now run smoothly.

7. If the adjustment procedure does not bring the CO concentration and speed to specifications, reset the idle mixture adjusting screw or repeat steps 3 through 5.

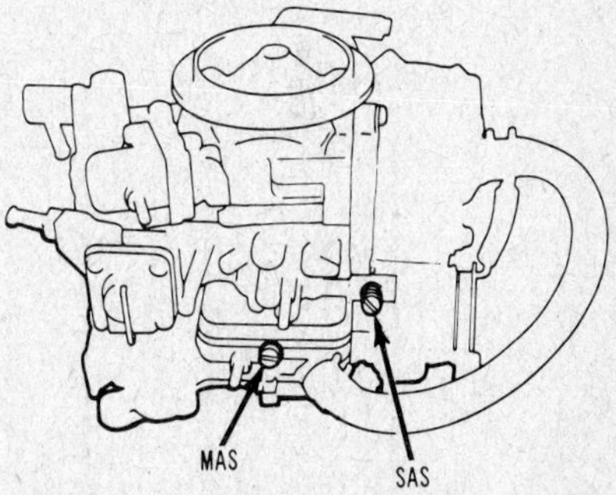

Idle mixture adjusting screw (MAS) and idle speed adjusting screw (SAS) (© Chrysler Corp.)

U engine—1980 California, 1980 W engine

1. Complete steps 1 through 3 under U engine, above.

2. Remove the air hose running from the reed valve to the air cleaner and plug the air inlet of the reed valve with your thumb.

3. Set the engine speed and the idle CO concentration to their respective values given in the chart by adjusting the idle speed adjusting screw (SAS) and

the idle mixture adjusting screw (MAS). See illustration.

4. Unplug the air inlet of the reed valve and reconnect the air hose to the reed valve.

5. Reset the engine speed to the chart specifications by adjusting the idle speed adjusting screw if the engine is not running within idling limits.

Canada

1. Place the transmission in "N" (Neutral) position and set the parking brake.

2. Make sure the air conditioner, lights and accessories are off.

3. Run the engine at idle until the coolant temperature reaches 170-190°F.

4. Set the engine speed and the idle CO to the value specified in the chart by adjusting the idle speed adjusting screw (SAS) and the idle mixture adjusting screw (MAS). Ideally, the idle CO should be as lean as possible without causing misfiring within the specified values.

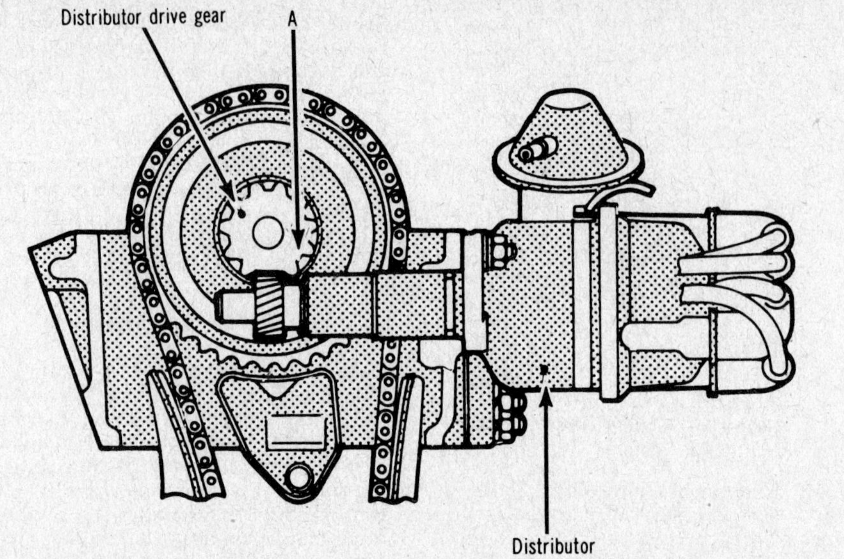

Distributor mounting in relation to cam shaft mounted drive gear
(© Chrysler Corp.)

ENGINE ELECTRICAL

Distributor

REMOVAL

1. Disconnect the battery ground cable.

2. Disconnect the wiring harness from the distributor control unit.

3. Mark the spark plug cables and pull them off the spark plugs.

NOTE: Always pull spark plug and coil cables at their caps to avoid breaking the wires inside the cables.

4. Remove the distributor cap by inserting a screwdriver into the two retaining screws, pushing in and turning clockwise.

5. Match-mark the distributor housing and the engine block; mark the rotor position in the distributor as well. This will aid in correct positioning of the distributor during installation.

6. Disconnect the vacuum hose from the vacuum control unit.

7. Remove the distributor mounting nut and lift off the distributor assembly.

INSTALLATION—ENGINE DISTURBED

1. Turn the engine crankshaft until the No. 1 cylinder is at top dead center on compression stroke. To find No. 1 cylinder, compression stroke, take off the distributor cap and turn over the engine until the rotor assembly is pointing toward the number 1 cylinder lead in the distributor cap. Verify Top Dead Center on the crankshaft pulley.

2. Align the mating mark (line) on the distributor housing with the mating

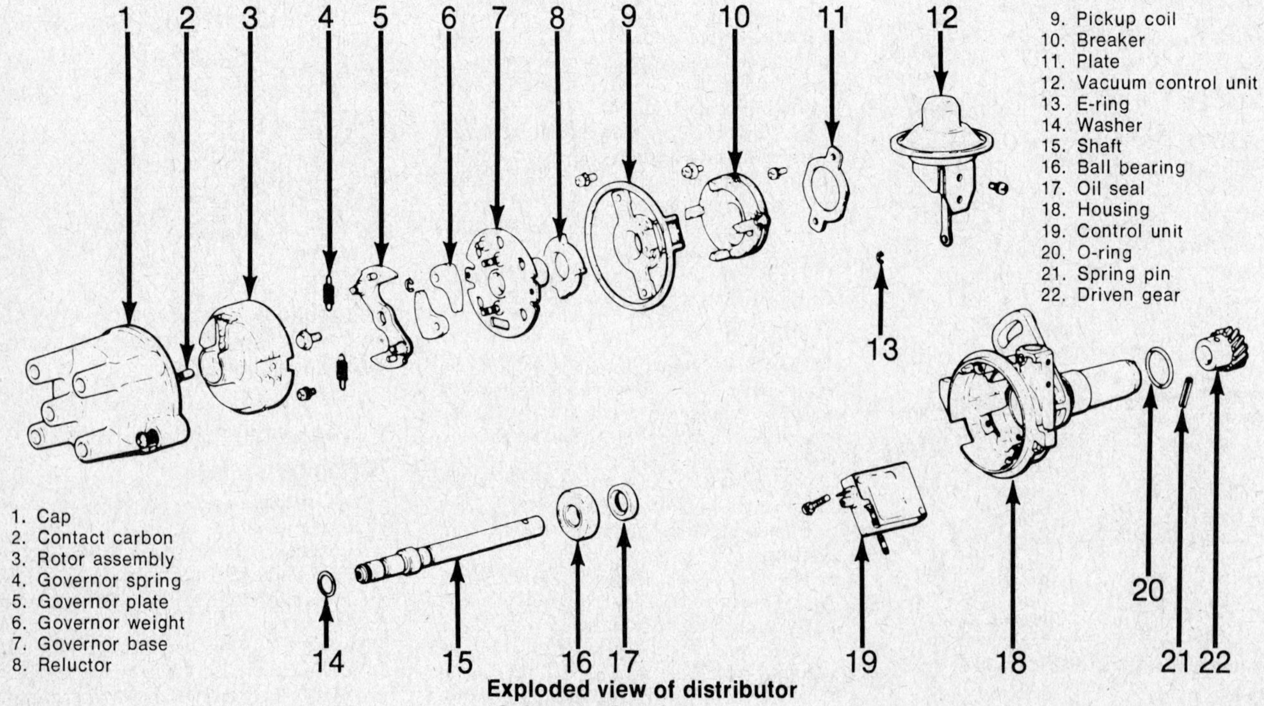

Exploded view of distributor
(© Chrysler Corp.)

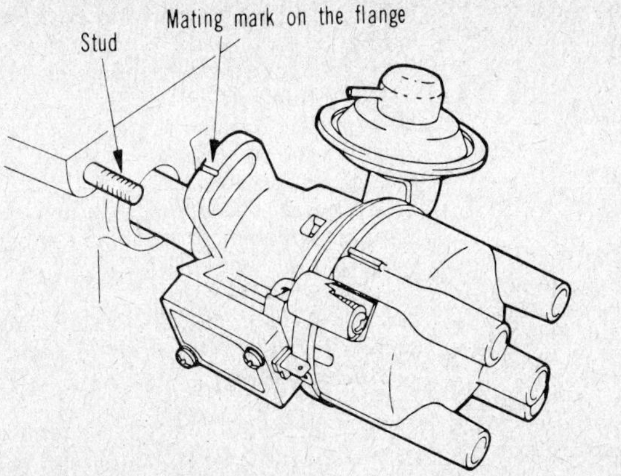

Distributor installation: align mark on flange with center of stud
(© Chrysler Corp.)

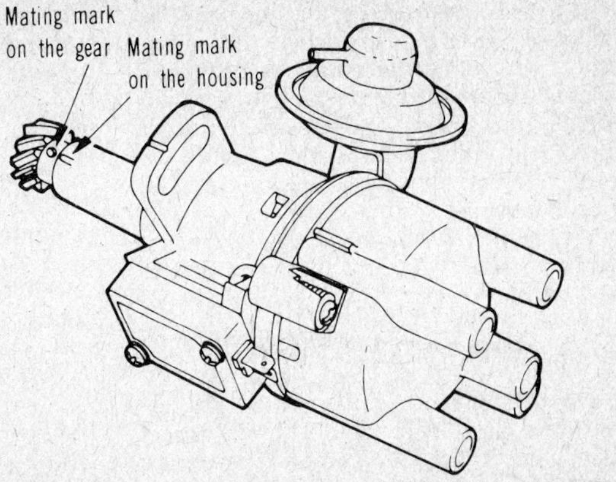

Align mating marks on distributor driven gear and housing
(© Chrysler Corp.)

mark (punch mark) on the distributor driven gear.

3. Install the distributor with the mating mark on the distributor attaching flange even with the center of the distributor retaining stud. Tighten the nut and replace the distributor cap, wires, and plug wires.

4. Set ignition timing as described above.

INSTALLATION—ENGINE NOT DISTURBED

1. Insert the distributor in the engine and align the marks made during removal.

2. Install the mounting nut, distributor cap, wires and plug wires, and vacuum line.

3. Start engine and check ignition timing as outlined above.

Alternator

ALTERNATOR PRECAUTIONS

1. Always observe proper polarity of the battery connections; be especially careful when jump-starting the car.

2. Never ground or short out any alternator or alternator regulator terminals.

3. Never operate the alternator with any of its or the battery's leads disconnected.

4. Always remove the battery or disconnect its output lead while charging it.

5. Always disconnect the ground cable when replacing any electrical components.

6. Never subject the alternator to excessive heat or dampness if the engine is being steam-cleaned.

7. Never use arc-welding equipment with the alternator connected.

REMOVAL AND INSTALLATION

1. Disconnect the battery ground cable.

2. Disconnect the cable from terminal "B" on the back of the alternator. Disconnect the other cables.

3. Remove the alternator brace bolt and the support bolt nut. Remove the drive belt.

4. Pull out the support bolt and remove the alternator assembly.

To install alternator:

1. Align the hole in the alternator leg with the hole in the front case and insert the alternator support bolt from the front bracket side.

2. Install the brace bolt.

3. Install drive belt.

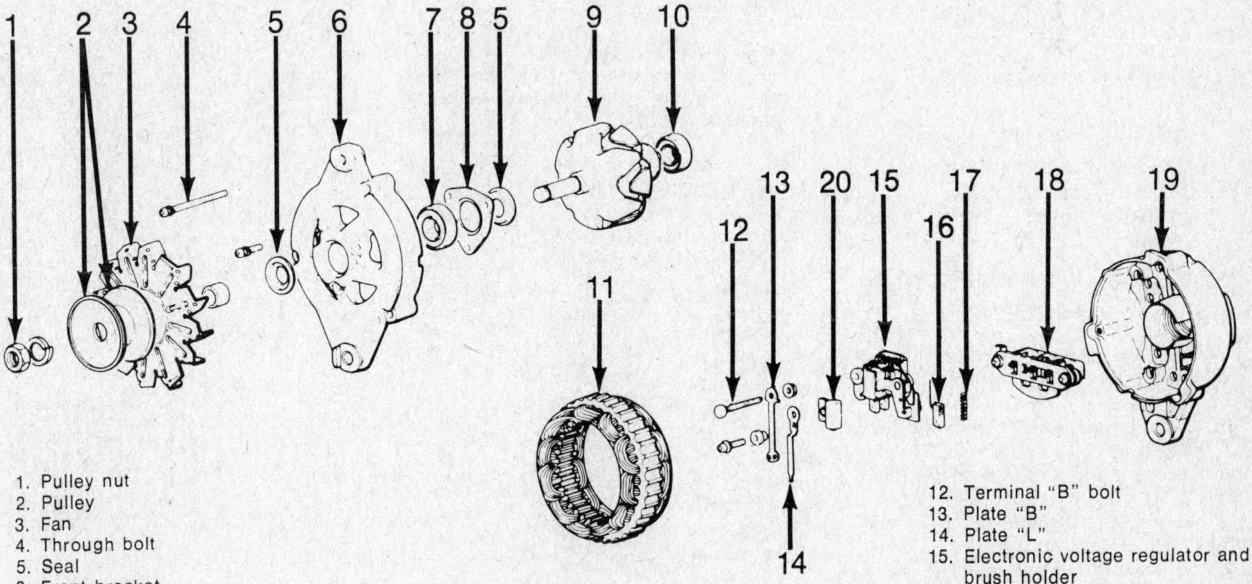

1. Pulley nut
2. Pulley
3. Fan
4. Through bolt
5. Seal
6. Front bracket
7. Ball bearing
8. Bearing retainer
9. Rotor assembly
10. Ball bearing
11. Stator assembly
12. Terminal "B" bolt
13. Plate "B"
14. Plate "L"
15. Electronic voltage regulator and brush holder
16. Brush
17. Brush spring
18. Rectifier assembly
19. Rear bracket
20. Condenser

Exploded view of alternator
(© Chrysler Corp.)

4. Push the alternator toward the front of the engine and check the clearance between the alternator leg and the front case. If the clearance is more than 0.008 in., insert spacers as required. 0.0078 in. thick spacers are available.

5. Adjust the belt tension as described below.

6. Tighten the alternator support bolt nut to 15-18 ft-lb, and the brace bolt to 9-11 ft-lb.

BELT ADJUSTMENT

Inspection and adjustment to the alternator drive belt should be performed every 15,000 miles. The belt should be replaced every 30,000 miles.

1. Inspect the drive belt to see that it is not cracked or worn. Be sure that its surfaces are free of grease or oil.

2. Pull the belt with a force of about 22 lbs. at a point halfway between the alternator pulley and the water pump pulley. The belt deflection should be $1/4$ to $3/8$ in.

3. If the belt requires adjustment, loosen the alternator support bolt and alternator brace bolt and move the alternator to obtain specified deflection at 22 lbs. pressure.

4. After adjustment, tighten the alternator support bolt to 14-18 ft-lb, and the alternator brace bolt to 9 to 11 ft-lb.

CAUTION: Do not overtighten the belt, or damage to the alternator bearings might result.

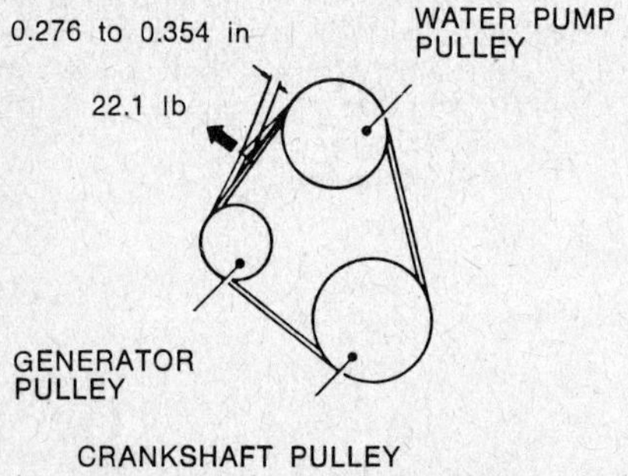

Adjusting the tension of the alternator drive belt
(© Chrysler Corp.)

CHARGING SYSTEM TEST (ON-VEHICLE)

1. Place the ignition switch at off.

2. Disconnect the battery ground cable.

3. Disconnect the cable from terminal "B" of the alternator and connect an ammeter between the terminal "B" and the cable.

4. Connect a voltmeter between terminal "B" (+) and ground (−).

5. Set the engine tachometer.

6. Connect the battery ground cable to the battery. The voltmeter should indicate the battery voltage.

7. Start the engine.

8. Turn on the lamps, accelerate the engine to the speed specified in the chart at the beginning of this section and measure the output current. Check it against the chart.

OVERHAUL

1. Remove alternator from vehicle.

2. Remove the three through bolts from the alternator body.

3. Insert a screwdriver between the front bracket and stator (see illustration). Pry the front bracket away from the stator. Remove the front bracket along with the rotor.

NOTE: If the screwdriver is inserted too deeply, the stator coil might be damaged.

4. Hold the rotor in a vise and remove the pulley nut. Then remove the pulley, fan, spacer and seal. Remove the rotor from the front bracket and remove the seal.

5. Unsolder the rectifier from the stator coil lead wires and remove the stator assembly.

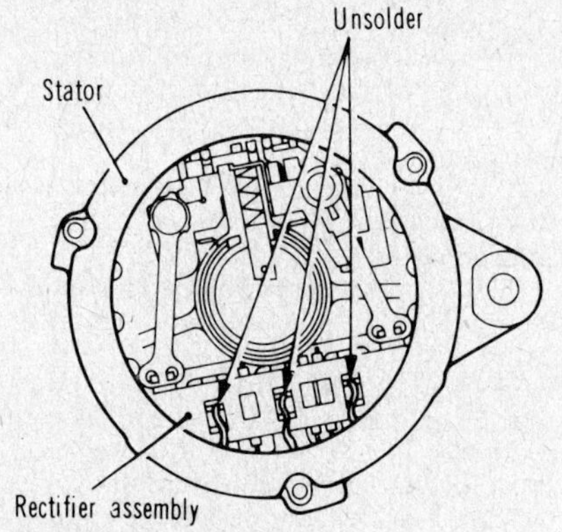

Unsolder the three wires to remove the stator assembly
(© Chrysler Corp.)

NOTE: Make sure the solder is removed quickly (in less than five seconds). If a diode is heated to more than 150°C, it might be damaged.

6. Remove the condenser from the terminal "B".

7. Unsolder the plates "B" and "L" from the rectifier assembly.

8. Remove the mounting screw and terminal "B" bolt and remove the electronic voltage regulator and brush holder. The regulator and brush holder cannot be separated.

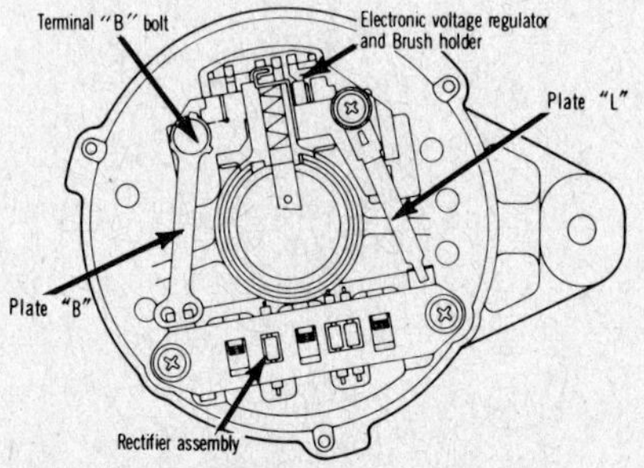

Rear view of alternator showing rectifier assembly and brush holder
(© Chrysler Corp.)

9. Remove the rectifier assembly.

10. Brush and brush spring replacement; When only a brush or brush spring is to be replaced, it is not necessary to remove the stator, etc. Raise the brush holder assembly and unsolder the wire pigtail of the brush and remove the brush.

NOTE: Be very careful when bending the plates "B" and "L" so as not to disturb the rectifier moulding.

11. Check the outside circumference of the slip ring for dirtiness and roughness. Clean or polish with fine sandpaper, if required. A badly damaged slip ring or a slip ring worn down beyond the service limit should also be replaced. The service limit for the slip ring outside diameter is 1.268 in.

12. Check for continuity between the field coil and slip ring. If there is no continuity, the field coil is defective and the rotor must be replaced.

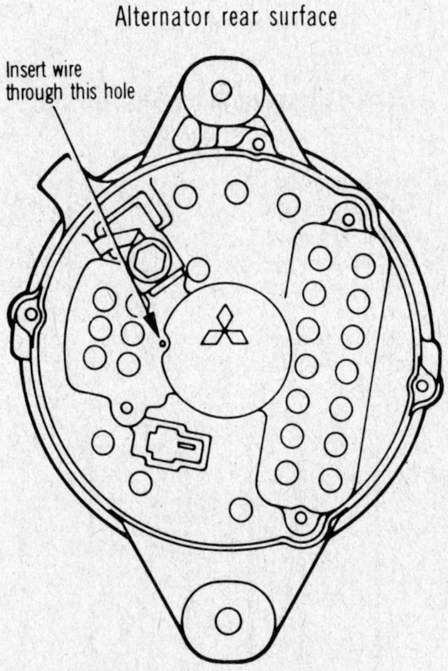

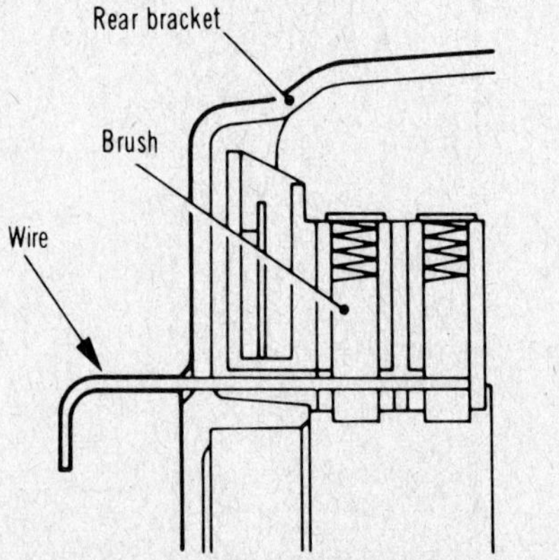

When replacing the end case, insert a wire to hold the brushes up
(© Chrysler Corp.)

13. Check for continuity between the slip ring and the shaft (or core). If there is continuity, the rotor assembly must be replaced.

14. Check for continuity between the leads of the stator coil. If there is no continuity, the stator coil is defective.

15. Check for an open circuit between the stator coil leads and the stator core. If there is continuity between the stator core and the coil leads, the stator assembly must be replaced.

16. Check for continuity between the (+) heat sink and the stator coil lead connection terminal with a circuit tester. If there is continuity in both directions, the diode is short-circuited and the rectifier assembly must be replaced.

17. Perform step 16 between the (−) heat sink and the stator coil lead connection.

18. Using a circuit tester, check the three diodes for continuity in both directions. If there is either continuity or an open circuit in both directions, the diode is defective and must be replaced.

19. Measure the length of the brush. If it is worn below 0.315 in., it must be replaced.

Assembly is the reverse of disassembly with the following notes:

20. Be sure to install both the front and rear seals on the front bearing.

21. To install the rotor assembly in the rear bracket, push the brushes into the brush holder, insert a wire to hold them in the raised position and install the rotor. Remove the wire.

Regulator

REMOVAL AND INSTALLATION

Both the 1979 and '80 D-50/Plymouth Arrow Pick-ups use an integrated circuit-type regulator which is contained in the alternator. See above for removal procedures. Adjustments of the regulator are confined to replacement.

Starter

REMOVAL AND INSTALLATION

1. Disconnect the battery ground cable.

2. Disconnect the starter motor wiring.

3. Loosen and remove the two starter motor mounting bolts and remove the starter motor.

4. Installation is the reverse of removal.

STARTER DRIVE, SOLENOID AND BRUSH REPLACEMENT

*NOTE: **Starter must be removed from vehicle for this operation.***

Direct Drive Type

1. Remove the wire connecting the starter solenoid to the starter.

2. Remove the two screws holding the starter solenoid on the starter-drive housing and remove the solenoid.

3. Remove the two long through bolts at the rear of the starter and separate the armature yoke from the armature.

4. Carefully remove the armature and the starter drive engagement lever from the front bracket, after making a mental note of the way they are positioned along with the attendant spring and spring retainer.

5. Loosen the two screws and remove the rear bracket.

6. Tap the stopper ring at the end of the drive gear engagement shaft in towards the drive gear to expose the snap ring. Remove the snap ring.

7. Pull the stopper, drive gear and overrunning clutch from the end of the shaft. For 1979 models with automatic transmissions, remove the center bracket, spring and spring retainer.

Inspect the pinion and spline teeth for wear or damage. If the engagement teeth are damaged, visually check the flywheel ring gear through the starter hole to insure that it is not damaged. It will be necessary to turn the engine over by hand to completely inspect the ring gear.

Check the brushes for wear. Their service limit length is 0.453 in. Replace if necessary.

Assembly is performed in the following manner. For 1979 models with automatic transmissions, fit the spring retainer, spring and center bracket on the shaft.

8. Install the spring retainer and spring on the armature shaft.

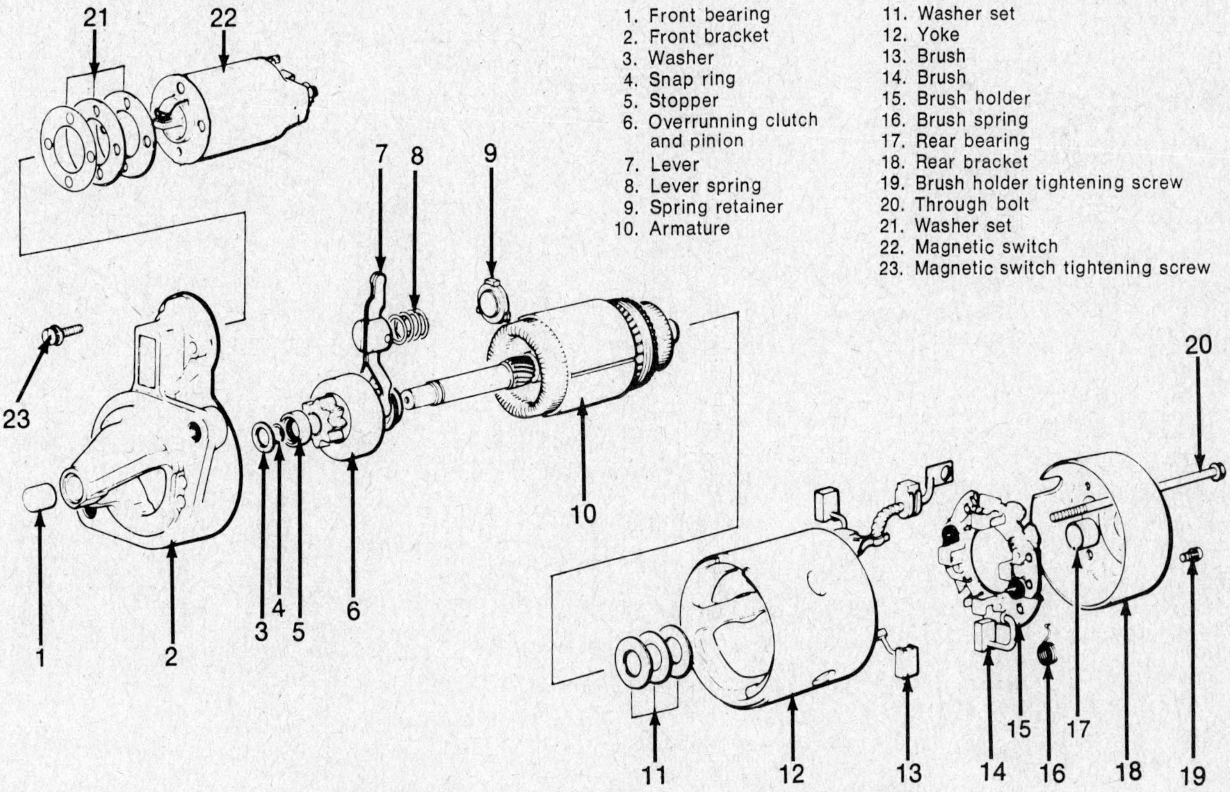

Exploded view of direct drive starter (manual transmission)
(© Chrysler Corp.)

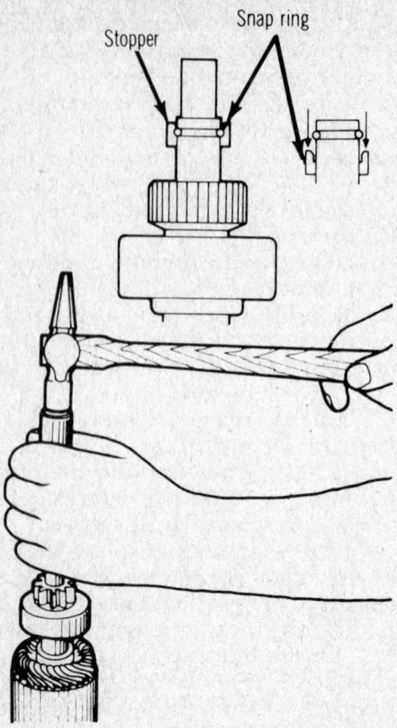

To remove the overrunning clutch, tap down the stopper and remove the snap ring
(© Chrysler Corp.)

9. Install the overrunning clutch assembly on the armature shaft.
10. Fit the stopper ring with its open side facing out on the shaft.
11. Install a new snap ring and, using a gear puller, pull the stopper ring into place over the snap ring.
12. Fit the small washer on the front end of the armature shaft.
13. Fit the engagement lever into the overrunning clutch and refit the armature into the front housing.
14. Fit the engagement lever spring and spring retainer into place and slide the armature yoke over the armature. Make sure you position the yoke with the spring retainer cut-out space in line with the spring retainer.

NOTE: Make sure the brushes are seated on the commutator.

15. Replace the rear bracket and two retainer screws.
16. Install the two through bolts in the end of the yoke.
17. Refit the starter solenoid, making sure you fit the plunger over the engagement lever. Install the screws and connect the wire running from the starter yoke to the starter solenoid.

Gear Reduction Type

1. Remove the wire connecting the starter solenoid to the starter.
2. Remove the two screws holding the solenoid and, pulling out, unhook it from the engagement lever.
3. Remove the two through bolts in the end of the starter and remove the two bracket screws. Pull off the rear bracket.

NOTE: Since the conical spring washer is contained in the rear bracket, be sure to take it out.

4. Remove the yoke and brush holder assembly while pulling the brush upward.
5. Pull the armature assembly out of the mounting bracket.
6. In the side of the mounting bracket that the armature fits into, there is a small dust cap held by two screws. Remove it and remove the snap ring and washer under it.
7. Remove the remaining bolts in the mounting bracket and split the reduction case.

NOTE: Several washers will come out when the case is split. These adjust the end play for the pinion shaft. Do not lose them.

8. Remove the reduction gear, lever and lever spring from the front bracket.
9. Using a brass drift or deep socket, knock the stopper ring on the end of the shaft in toward the pinion. Remove the snap ring. Remove the stopper, pinion and pinion shaft assembly.
10. Remove the ball bearings at both ends of the armature.

NOTE: The ball bearings are pressed in the front bracket and are not replaceable. Replace them together with the bracket.

Inspect the pinion and spline teeth for wear or damage. If the engagement teeth are damaged, visually check the flywheel ring gear through the starter hole to insure that it is not damaged also. It will be necessary to turn the engine over by hand to completely inspect the ring gear.

Check the brushes for wear. Their service limit length is 0.0453 in. Replace if necessary.

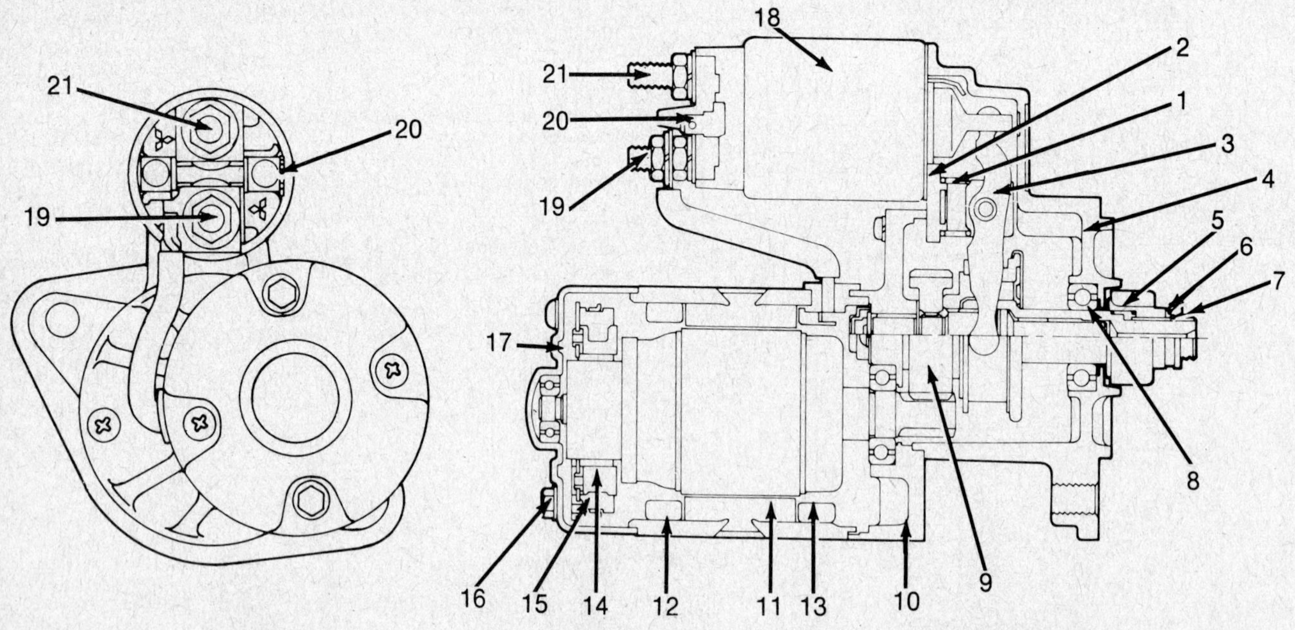

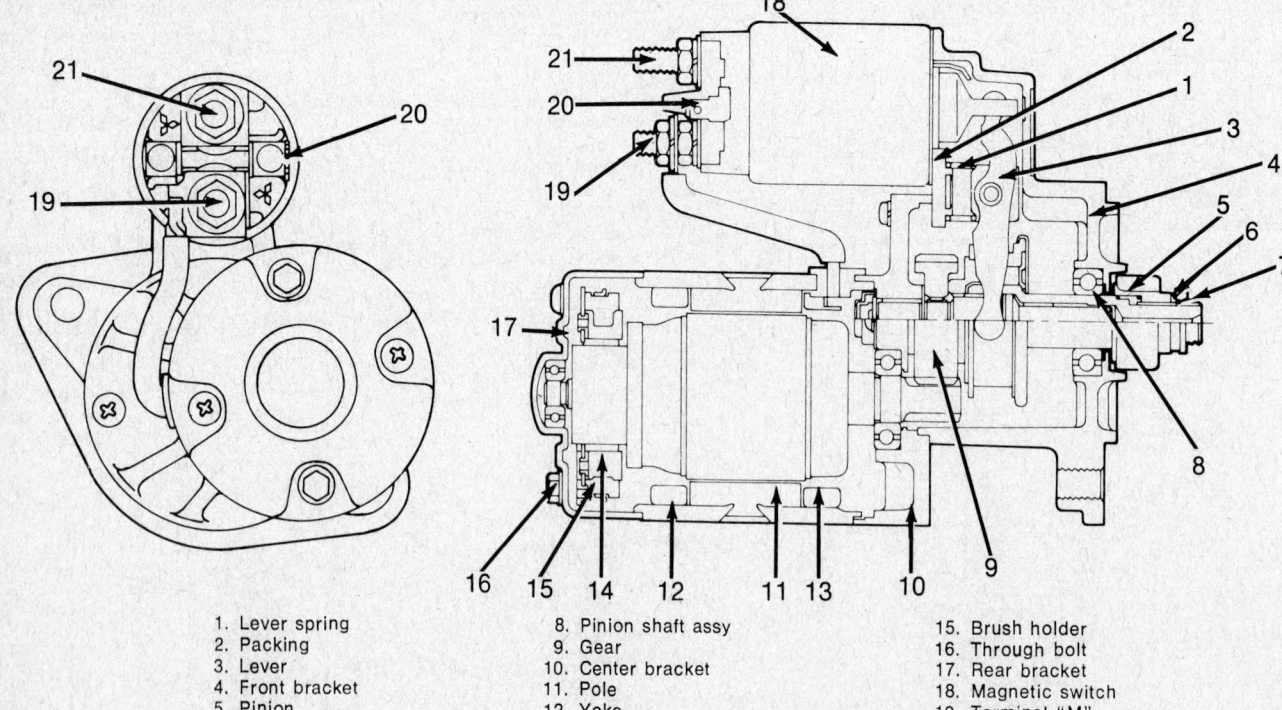

1. Lever spring
2. Packing
3. Lever
4. Front bracket
5. Pinion
6. Stopper
7. Ring
8. Pinion shaft assy
9. Gear
10. Center bracket
11. Pole
12. Yoke
13. Field coil
14. Brush
15. Brush holder
16. Through bolt
17. Rear bracket
18. Magnetic switch
19. Terminal "M"
20. Terminal "S"
21. Terminal "B"

Cross-section of reduction gear starter (automatic transmission)
(© Chrysler Corp.)

Assembly is the reverse of disassembly. Be sure to replace all adjusting and thrust washers. When replacing the rear bracket, fit the conical spring pinion washer with its convex side facing out. Make sure that the brushes seat themselves on the commutator.

ENGINE MECHANICAL

REMOVAL AND INSTALLATION

CAUTION: Be sure the car is supported securely during engine removal.

NOTE: The engine and transmission are removed as a unit. For transmission removal only, see section below.

1. Working inside the engine compartment, remove the splash shield below the engine. Drain the coolant from the radiator and the engine by opening the drain plug at the bottom of the radiator and the drain cock located at the right rear of the cylinder block. Use a suitable container to catch coolant.

NOTE: It would be wise to drain the radiator in an area other than the one in which the engine is to be removed so that you will not be in contact with coolant when working under the vehicle.

2. Disconnect and remove the battery.
3. Disconnect the ground strap and the wiring of the ignition coil, fuel cut-off solenoid valve, alternator, starter motor, water temperature gauge unit and oil pressure gauge unit.
4. Disconnect the air cleaner breather hose. Remove the air cleaner and disconnect the hot air duct and the vacuum hose.
5. Disconnect the accelerator control cable. For automatic transmissions, disconnect the transmission control rod.
6. Disconnect the radiator hoses by loosening their clips.
7. Disconnect the heater hose.
8. Disconnect the exhaust pipe from the exhaust manifold. The muffler pipe bracket should be detached at the transmission.
9. Disconnect the fuel hoses and vapor hose.
10. Remove the radiator and radiator cowl. Four bolts hold the radiator in place. On vehicles with automatic transmissions, remove and plug the two oil cooling pipes in the bottom of the radiator.
11. For trucks with four and five speed transmissions:
    a. Remove the lock screws and lift up the console box, inside the driver's compartment. In trucks without a console box, remove the carpet.
    b. Remove the attaching screws and lift out the dust cover retainer plate.
    c. Pull up the dust cover and remove the four attaching bolts holding the shift lever to the transmission extension housing. Remove the shift lever control assembly.

NOTE: On four speed transmissions, remove the gear shift lever with the lever in 2nd speed position. On five speed transmissions, place the lever in 1st speed position.

12. Mark the position of the hood retaining bolts in relation to the hood and remove the hood.
13. Jack up the vehicle and support it on stands.
14. Disconnect the speedometer cable and backup light switch wiring from the transmission.
15. For trucks with manual transmissions, disconnect the clutch cable from the transmission by removing the cotter key and sliding it off the arm. Disconnect the cable from the cable bracket. For automatic transmissions, remove shift linkage between transmission and shift lever.
16. Drain the transmission.
17. Remove the bolts holding the rear of the driveshaft to the rear axle. Remove the two nuts holding the center bearing assembly of the driveshaft to the frame and pull the driveshaft out of the rear of the transmission.
18. Support the transmission on a jack and remove the bolts holding the front motor mounts.
19. Unbolt the rear transmission mount crossmember and remove the two bolts holding it to the transmission. Remove the crossmember.
20. Attach steel lifting cables to the engine front and rear hangers and attach the cables to a suitable hoist.
21. Have an assistant slowly lower the jack under the transmission and pull the engine/transmission out of the vehicle by tilting it upwards and pulling forward.

NOTE: If the transmission will not clear the steering relay rod, raise it until the bell housing is above the rod, then remove the engine/transmission from the truck.

Installation is the reverse of removal. Adjust all transmission and carburetor linkages as detailed in the appropriate sections. Install and adjust the hood. Refill the engine, transmission and radiator to capacity.

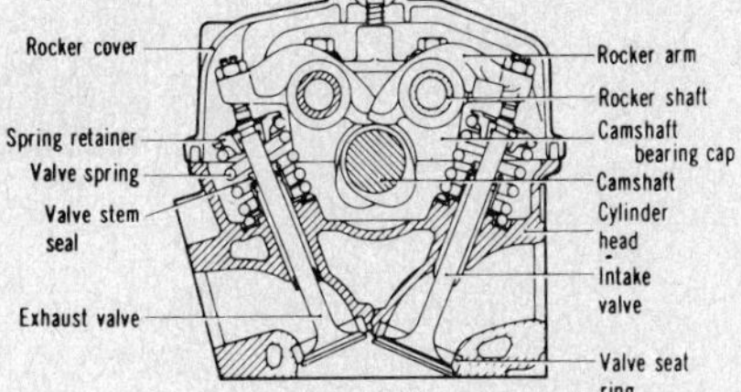

Cross-section of cylinder head
(© Chrysler Corp.)

NOTE: Refer to the engine rebuilding section at the end of this book for complete overhaul procedures not covered in this chapter.

Cylinder Head

REMOVAL AND INSTALLATION

CAUTION Do not perform this operation on a warm engine. Remove the head bolts in the sequence shown at the front of this section and in several steps. Loosen the head bolts evenly, not one at a time. Do not attempt to slide the cylinder head off the block, as it is located with dowel pins. Lift the head straight up and off the block.

1. Disconnect the battery and drain the cooling system. Disconnect the upper radiator hose.
2. Remove the breather hoses and purge hose.
3. Remove the air cleaner and fuel line.
4. Remove the vacuum hose at the distributor and purge control valve.
5. Disconnect the spark plug wires after marking them for reinstallation.
6. Remove the distributor cap, and distributor by removing the retainer nut and pulling the unit out.
7. Disconnect the heater hose at the intake manifold.
8. Disconnect the water temperature gauge unit wire.
9. Place no. 1 piston in the Top Dead Center position to take pressure off the fuel pump rocker arm. Disconnect the fuel hoses and plug the line leading to the gas tank to prevent fuel leakage.
10. Remove the fuel pump mounting nuts or bolts and remove the fuel assembly. Remove the insulator and gaskets.
11. Disconnect the exhaust pipe at the exhaust manifold flange.
12. Remove the rocker cover.
13. Remove its breather and semi-circular seal.
14. After slightly loosening the camshaft sprocket bolt, turn the crankshaft until no. 1 piston is at top dead center on compression stroke (both valves closed).

NOTE Never turn the engine over using the camshaft bolt: it puts undue strain on the chain and other components.

15. Remove the camshaft sprocket bolt and distributor drive gear. Remove the camshaft sprocket and allow it to rest in the chain on the holder below.
16. Remove the cylinder head bolts in the sequence shown in the illustration. Head bolts should be loosened in two or three stages to prevent head warpage.

NOTE: The cylinder head assembly is located with two dowl pins, front and rear, on the cylinder block. When removing, be careful not to slide it, or twist the camshaft sprocket and chain.

17. Remove the cylinder head assembly and cylinder head gasket.

Installation is performed in the following manner.

18. Clean all gasket surfaces of cylinder block and cylinder head.

19. Install a new cylinder head gasket. Install the cylinder head assembly.

NOTE: Do not apply sealant to the head gasket and do not reuse an old head gasket.

NOTE: The head gasket for the U engine has a number "52" stamped at the front of its upper surface, while the W engine has the number "54" in that position.

20. Install the ten cylinder head bolts. Starting at top center, tighten all cylinder head bolts to 35 ft-lb. in the sequence shown in the illustration. Repeat the tightening procedure, this time torque the bolts to 65-72 ft-lb. (cold engine), (72-80 ft-lb. hot engine).

21. Tighten the two front bolts (number 11 in illustration) to 11-15 ft-lb.

22. Verify that no. 1 cylinder is at top dead center. Align the dowel pin in the end of the camshaft sprocket with the groove in the top of the front camshaft bearing cap and install the camshaft sprocket and chain while pulling up on the sprocket.

23. Install the distributor drive gear and the sprocket bolt.

24. Turn the crankshaft about 90° back, and tighten the camshaft sprocket bolt to 37-43 ft-lb.

Very slowly turn the engine over two times to make sure the valve timing is correct. If the engine locks at a certain point in these two revolutions, the valve timing is not correct. Repeat steps 22-24.

CAUTION: At this point, do not turn the engine over using the starter. If the valve timing is off, several of the valves could be bent.

25. Install the breather and semicircular seal to the cylinder head after applying sealant to surface contact points. Install the rocker cover with a new gasket.

26. Connect the exhaust pipe to the exhaust manifold flange. Tighten the bolts to 11-18 ft-lb.

27. Put no. 1 cylinder at Top Dead Center and install the fuel pump with a new gasket and insulator. Connect all hoses.

28. Connect the water temperature gauge unit wire. Connect the heater hose to the intake manifold.

Install the distributor and spark plug cables. See distributor section, above, for procedure.

29. Connect the vacuum hose to the distributor and purge control valve. Connect the upper radiator hose and fill the cooling system with coolant.

Many mechanics recommend that the engine oil be replaced after the head is removed to avoid water contamination from the coolant.

Intake Manifold

REMOVAL AND INSTALLATION

1. Drain the cooling system.
2. Remove the air cleaner assembly with its hoses from the engine.
3. Disconnect the fuel line and EGR lines.
4. Disconnect the accelerator linkage and, if so equipped, the automatic transmission shift cables at the carburetor.
5. Remove the water hose at the intake manifold. Remove the water hose at the carburetor.
6. Disconnect the water temperature sending unit.
7. Remove the manifold with the carburetor as a unit.

Installation is the reverse of removal. Tighten manifold nuts to 11-14 ft-lbs.

Exhaust Manifold

REMOVAL AND INSTALLATION

1. Remove air cleaner.
2. Remove the heat shield from the exhaust manifold. Remove the EGR lines and reed valve, if equipped.
3. Unbolt the exhaust flange connection.
4. Remove nuts holding manifold to cylinder head.
5. Remove manifold.

Installation is the reverse of removal. Tighten flange connection bolts to 11-18 ft-lb. Tighten manifold bolts to 11-14 ft-lb.

Timing Chain, Cover, "Silent Shafts" and Tensioner

REMOVAL AND INSTALLATION

NOTE: All D-50/Plymouth Arrow Pickups are equipped with two "Silent Shafts" which cancel the vertical vibrating force of the engine and the secondary vibrating forces, which include the sideways rocking of the engine due to the turning direction of the crankshaft and other rolling parts. The secondary vibrating forces can be cancelled if forces equivalent in magnitude but opposite in direction are produced. In these engines, the opposite force is produced by silent shafts located in the upper left and lower right sides in the front of the cylinder block. The shafts are driven by a duplex chain and are turned by the crankshaft. The silent shaft chain assembly is mounted in front of the timing chain assembly and

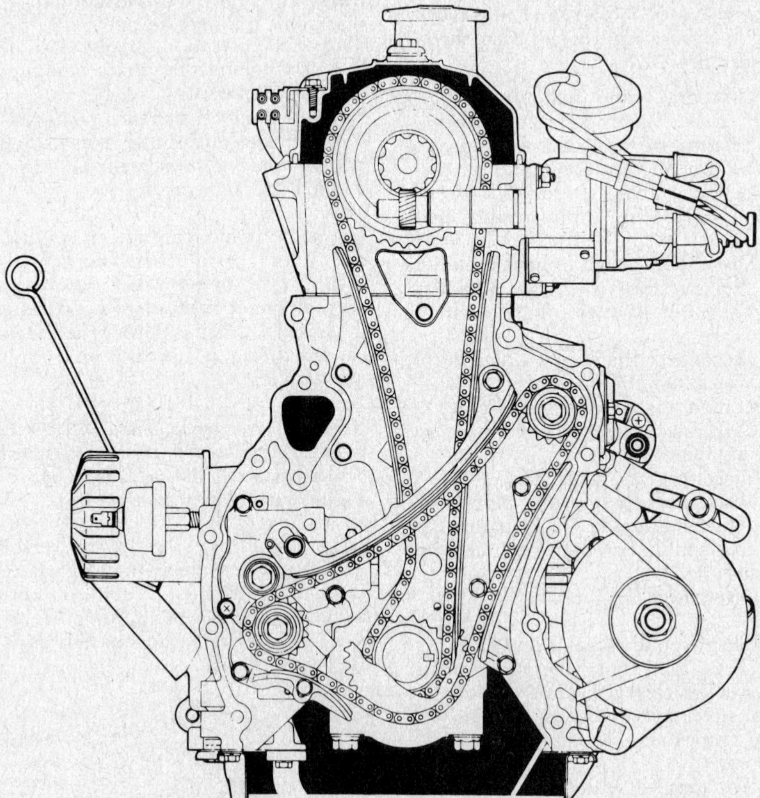

"Silent Shaft" chain mounting in relation to timing chain
(© Chrysler Corp.)

must be removed to service the timing chain.

1. Remove the battery cables.
2. Drain the radiator and remove it from the vehicle.
3. Remove the cylinder head (refer to cylinder head section, above, for procedures).
4. Remove the cooling fan, spacer, water pump pulley and belt.
5. Remove the alternator. Remove the water pump.
6. Raise the front of the vehicle and support it on jack stands.
7. Remove the oil pan and screen. Remove the crankshaft pulley.
8. Remove the timing case cover.
9. Remove the chain guides, side (A), top (B), bottom (C), from the "B" chain (outer).
10. Remove the locking bolts from the "B" chain sprockets.
11. Remove the crankshaft sprocket, silent shaft sprocket and the outer chain.
12. Remove the crankshaft and camshaft sprockets and the timing chain.
13. Remove the camshaft sprocket holder and the chain guides, both left and right.
14. Remove the tensioner.
15. Remove the sleeve from the oil pump. Remove the oil pump by first removing the bolt locking the oil pump driven gear and the right silent shaft, then remove the oil pump mounting bolts. Remove the silent shaft from the engine block.

NOTE: If the bolt locking the oil pump and the silent shaft is hard to loosen, remove the oil pump and the shaft as a unit.

16. Remove the left silent shaft thrust washer and take the shaft from the engine block.

Installation is performed in the following manner:

1. Install the right silent shaft into the engine block.
2. Install the oil pump assembly. Do not lose the woodruff key from the end of the silent shaft. Torque the oil pump mounting bolts to 6 to 7 ft. lbs.
3. Tighten the silent shaft and the oil pump driven gear mounting bolt.

NOTE: The silent shaft and the oil pump can be installed as a unit, if necessary.

4. Install the left silent shaft into the engine block.
5. Install a new "O" ring on the thrust plate and install the unit into the engine block, using a pair of bolts without heads, as alignment guides.

CAUTION: If the thrust plate is turned to align the bolt holes, the "O" ring may be damaged.

6. Remove the guide bolts and install the regular bolts into the thrust plate and tighten securely.
7. Rotate the crankshaft to bring no. 1 piston to TDC.
8. Install the cylinder head.
9. Install the sprocket holder and the right and left chain guides.
10. Install the tensioner spring and sleeve on the oil pump body.
11. Install the camshaft and crankshaft sprockets on the timing chain, aligning the sprocket punch marks to the plated chain links.
12. While holding the sprocket and chain as a unit, install the crankshaft sprocket over the crankshaft and align it with the keyway.
13. Keeping the dowel pin hole on the camshaft in a vertical position, install the camshaft sprocket and chain on the camshaft.

NOTE: The sprocket timing mark and the plated chain link should be at the 2 to 3 O'clock position when correctly installed.

CAUTION: The chain must be aligned in the right and left chain guides with the tensioner pushing against the chain. The tension for the inner chain is predetermined by spring tension.

14. Install the crankshaft sprocket for the outer or "B" chain.
15. Install the two silent shaft sprockets and align the punched mating marks with the plated links of the chain.
16. Holding the two shaft sprockets and chain, install the outer chain in alignment with the mark on the crankshaft sprocket. Install the shaft sprockets on the silent shaft and the oil pump driver gear. Install the lock bolts and recheck the alignment of the punch marks and the plated links.
17. Temporarily install the chain guides, *Side* (A), *Top* (B), and *Bottom* (C).

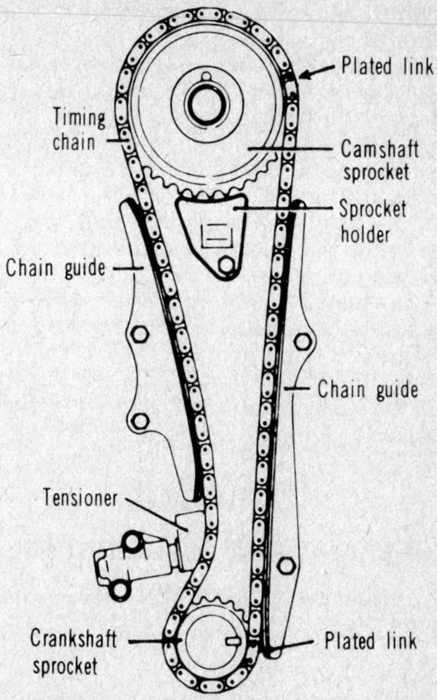

Timing chain installation: align the plated links with the punch-marks on the cam sprocket and the crankshaft sprocket
(© Chrysler Corp.)

18. Tighten *Side* (A) chain guide securely.
19. Tighten *Bottom* (B) chain guide securely.
20. Adjust the position of the *Top* (B) chain guide, after shaking the right and left sprockets to collect any chain slack, so that when the chain is moved toward the center, the clearance between the chain guide and the chain links will be

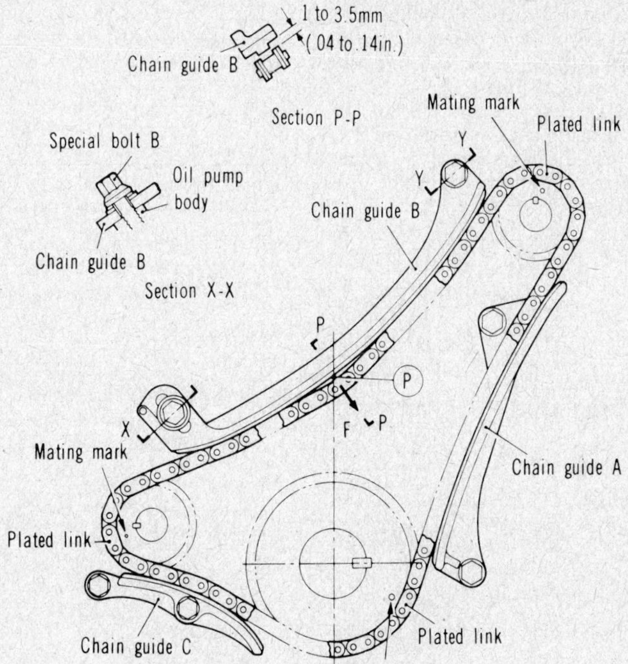

"Silent Shaft" balancing system
(© Chrysler Corp.)

approximately ⁹⁄₆₄ inch. Tighten the *Top* (B) chain guide bolts.

21. Install the timing chain cover using a new gasket, being careful not to damage the front seal.

22. Install the oil screen and the oil pan, using a new gasket. Torque the bolts to 4.5 to 5.5 ft. lbs.

23. Install the crankshaft pulley, alternator and accessory belts, and the distributor.

24. Install the oil pressure switch, if removed, and install the battery ground cable.

25. Install the fan blades, radiator, fill the system with coolant and start the engine.

Camshaft

REMOVAL AND INSTALLATION

1. Remove the breather hoses and purge hose.
2. Remove the air cleaner and fuel line.
3. Remove the fuel pump. Remove the distributor.
4. Disconnect the spark plug cables.
5. Remove the rocker cover.
6. Remove the breather and semi-circular seal.
7. After slightly loosening the camshaft sprocket bolt, turn the crankshaft until no. 1 piston is at Top Dead Center on compression stroke (both valves closed).
8. Remove the camshaft sprocket bolt and distributor drive gear.
9. Remove the camshaft sprocket with chain and allow it to rest on the camshaft sprocket holder.
10. Remove the camshaft bearing cap tightening bolts. Do not remove the front and rear bearing cap bolts altogether, but keep them inserted in the bearing caps so that the rocker assembly can be removed as a unit.
11. Remove the rocker arms, rocker shafts and bearing caps as an assembly.
12. Remove the camshaft.

Installation is performed in the following manner.

13. Lubricate the camshaft lobes and bearings and fit camshaft into head.
14. Install the assembled rocker arm shaft assembly. The camshaft should be positioned so that the dowel pin on the front end of the cam is in the 12 o'clock position and in line with the notch in the top of the front bearing cap.

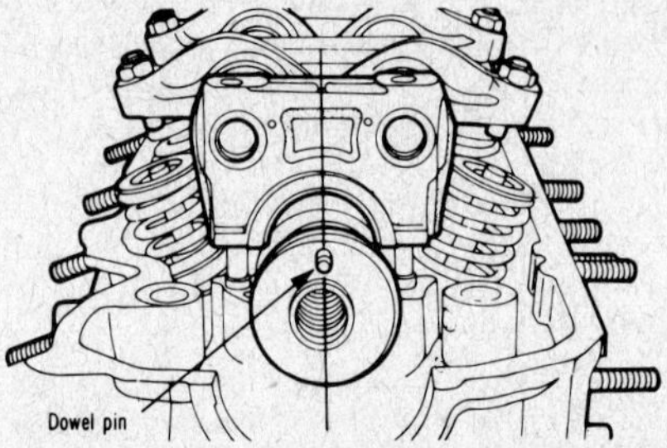

Installing the cam shaft: align the dowel pin with the notch in the top of the front bearing cap
(© Chrysler Corp.)

15. Install the bearing cap bolts. Starting at the center and working out, tighten the bolts to 7 ft-lb. Repeat the procedure, this time tightening them to 14-15 ft-lb.
16. Install the camshaft sprocket and distributor drive gear onto the camshaft while pulling it upward. Temporarily tighten the locking bolt.
17. Turn the crankshaft about 90° back and tighten the camshaft sprocket bolt to 37–43 ft-lb.
18. Temporarily set the valve clearance to cold engine specifications (see Valve Lash section, above).
19. Temporarily install the breather, semicircular seal and rocker cover and start the engine and run it at idle speed.
20. After the engine is at normal operational temperature, adjust the valves to hot engine specifications (see Valve Lash section, above).
21. Install breather and seal and apply sealant to the contact surfaces.
22. Install the rocker cover and tighten to 4–5 ft-lb.
23. Install distributor, fuel pump, air cleaner, fuel line, plug leads and other assemblies.

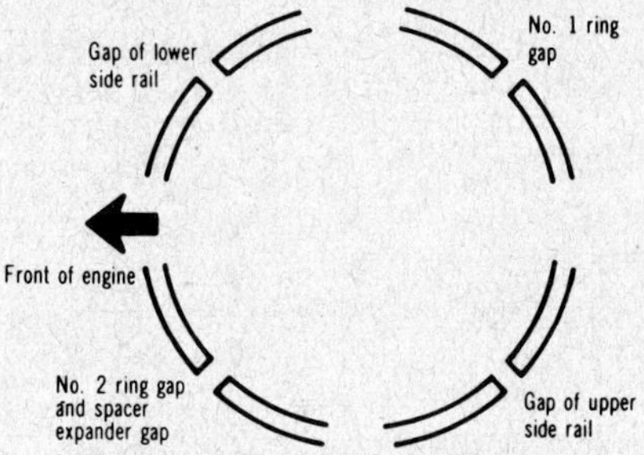

Ring end gap positioning
(© Chrysler Corp.)

PISTON AND PISTON RING APPLICATION

Description	Engine	Identification Mark	
Piston	U (for U.S.A.)	52J	Stamped on top of piston
	U (for Canada)	52	
	W (for U.S.A.)	54J	
	W (for Canada)	54	
Piston ring No. 1	U	N1	Stamped on ring end
	W	T	
No. 2	U	N	
	W	2T	
Oil ring		None	

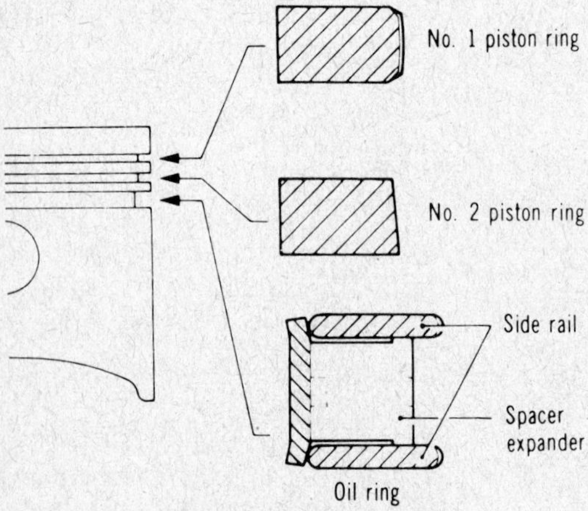

Piston ring installation
(© Chrysler Corp.)

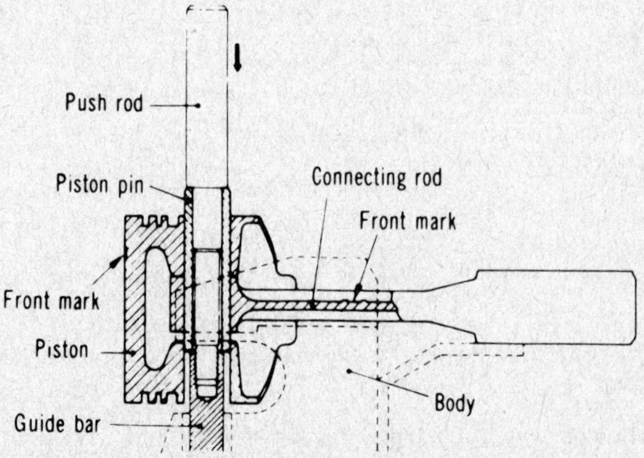

Installing the piston pin. Also shown: front marks on piston and connecting rod
(© Chrysler Corp.)

PISTON RING SERVICE SIZE

Size mm (in.)	Size Mark
STD	None
0.25 (.010) O.S.	25
0.50 (.020) O.S.	50
0.75 (.030) O.S.	75
1.00 (.039) O.S.	100

ENGINE LUBRICATION

Oil Pan

REMOVAL AND INSTALLATION

The engine must be raised off its mounts for the pan to clear the suspension crossmember.

1. Remove the underbody splash shield.
2. Unbolt the left and right engine mounts.
3. Jack up the engine under the bell housing.
4. Remove the oil pan.
5. Installation is the reverse of removal.

Rear Main Oil Seal

REPLACEMENT

The rear main oil seal is located in a housing on the rear of the block. To replace the seal, remove the transmission and do the work from underneath the vehicle or remove the engine and do the work on the bench.

1. Remove the housing from the block.

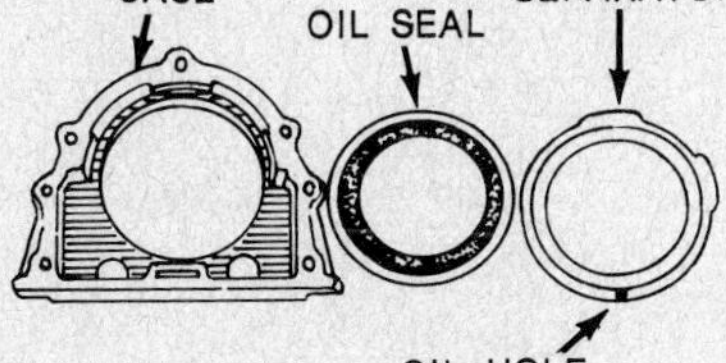

Rear main oil seal
(© Chrysler Corp.)

2. Remove the separator from the housing.
3. Pry out the old seal.
4. Lightly oil the replacement seal. The oil seal should be installed so that the seal plate fits into the inner contact surface of the seal case. Install the separator with the oil holes facing down.

Oil Pump

REMOVAL AND INSTALLATION

See Timing Chain, Cover, "Silent Shaft" and Tensioner removal and installation procedure, above.

OVERHAUL

1. Remove the two screws at the rear of the oil pump and remove the cover and gear.
2. Remove the relief valve plug and withdraw the relief spring and plunger.
3. Check the pump for cracks and wear. Check all oil holes for clogging.
4. Clearance between the gears and the pump assembly (tip clearance) should be 0.0043–0.0059 in.
5. Both gears front bearing clearance should be within 0.0008 and 0.0020 in.
6. The rear bearing clearance of the drive gear should be 0.0016–0.0028 in.

***NOTE:** When bearing replacement is necessary, replace the oil pump body assembly.*

7. Insert the relief plunger into the pump body and make sure it operates smoothly. Check the relief spring for breakage or sagging.

When reassembling, observe the following:

8. Coat all parts in oil before reassembling.
9. Match the two punch marks on the gears so that they mate where the gears meet.

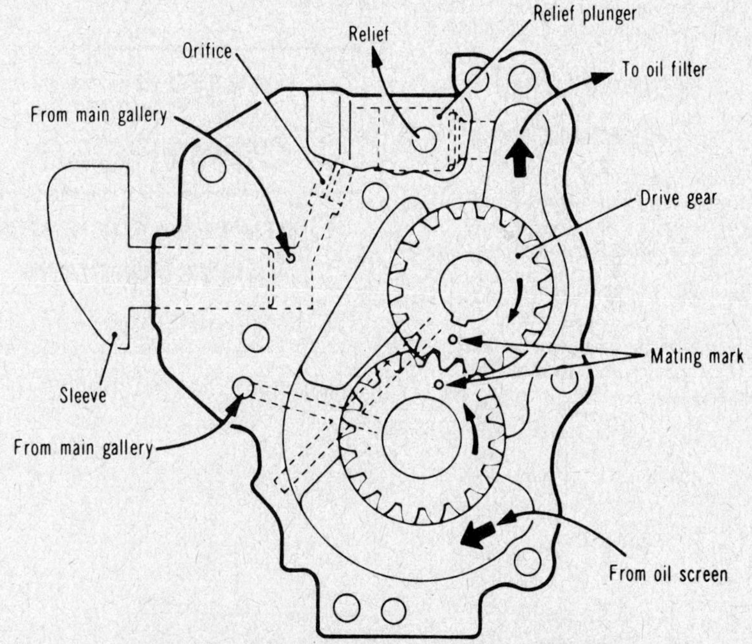

Oil pump layout. Notice mating marks on gears
(© Chrysler Corp.)

OIL PUMP SPECIFICATIONS

Engine	Type	Drive Gear Rear End Clearance With Bearing	Tip Clearance; Gear to Cover (in.)	Maximum Oil Pressure (psi)	Relief Valve Spring Free Length (in.)	Relief Valve Opening Pressure (psi)
U, W	Gear	0.0016-0.0028	0.0043-0.0059	64.0	1.850	49.8-64

10. Check for smooth rotation after assembly.

CAUTION: Make sure the mating marks meet, or the silent shaft will be out of time and cause vibration.

Before installing the pump, fill the delivery port with clean oil to prime it.

ENGINE COOLING

Radiator

REMOVAL AND INSTALLATION

1. Remove the splash panel from the bottom of the vehicle. Drain the radiator by opening the petcock. Remove the shroud on models so equipped.
2. Disconnect the radiator hoses at the engine. On automatic transmission vehicles, disconnect and plug the transmission lines to the bottom of the radiator.
3. Remove the two retaining bolts from either side of the radiator. Lift out the radiator.
4. Install the radiator in the reverse order of removal. Tighten the retaining bolts gradually in a criss-cross pattern.

Water Pump

REMOVAL

1. Drain the cooling system.
2. Remove the fan shroud and radiator if necessary for working room.
3. Remove the alternator and accessory belts.
4. Remove the fan blades and/or automatic hub, if equipped.
5. Remove the water pump assembly from the timing chain case or the cylinder block.

INSTALLATION

1. Install the water pump to the timing chain case or the engine block and tighten the bolts securely.
2. Install the fan blades and/or the automatic clutch fan hub.
3. Install the alternator and accessory belts and adjust as necessary.
4. Install the fan shroud and the radiator, if removed.
5. Fill the cooling system, start the engine, and check for coolant leakage.

Thermostat

REMOVAL AND INSTALLATION

The thermostat is located in the intake manifold under the upper radiator hose.

1. Drain the coolant below the level of the thermostat.
2. Remove the two retaining bolts and lift the thermostat housing off the intake manifold with the hose still attached.

NOTE: If you are careful, it is not necessary to remove the upper radiator hose.

3. Lift the thermostat out of the manifold.
4. Install the thermostat in the reverse order of removal. Use a new gasket and coat the mating surfaces with sealer.

EMISSION CONTROLS

Crankcase Emission Control System

A closed-type crankcase ventilation system is used to prevent engine blow-by gases from escaping into the atmosphere.

A small fixed orifice, located in the intake manifold, is connected to the rear section of the rocker arm cover by a hose.

A larger hose is connected from the front of the rocker arm cover to the air cleaner assembly. Under light to medium carburetor throttle opening, the blow-by gases are drawn through the fixed orifice. Under heavy acceleration, both the fixed orifice and the large hose route the gases into the engine.

The only maintenance required is to regularly check the breather hose condition, clean the orifice in the intake manifold, and clean the steel wool filter, in the air cleaner.

A PCV valve is not used in the system.

Fuel Evaporation Control System

This system is designed to prevent hydrocarbons from escaping into the atmosphere from the fuel tank, due to normal evaporation.

The parts of the system are as follow:

Separator tank Located near the gasoline tank, used to accommodate expansion, and to allow maximum condensation of the fuel vapors.

Canister Located in the engine compartment to trap and retain gasoline vapors while the engine is not operating. When the engine is started, fresh air is drawn into the canister, removing the stored vapors, and is directed to the air cleaner.

Two-way Valve Because of different methods of tank venting and the use of sealed gasoline tank cap, the two-way valve is used in the vapor lines. The valve relieves either pressure or vacuum in the tank.

Purge Control Valve The purge control valve replaces the check valve used in previous years. During idle, the valve closes off the vapor passage to the air cleaner.

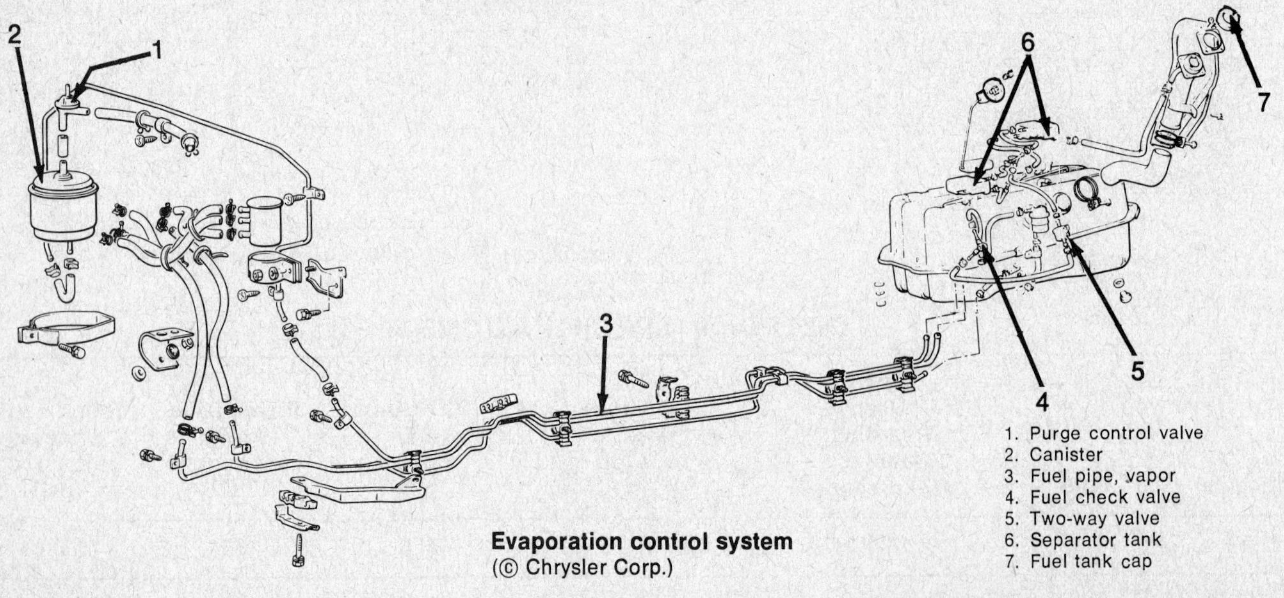

1. Purge control valve
2. Canister
3. Fuel pipe, vapor
4. Fuel check valve
5. Two-way valve
6. Separator tank
7. Fuel tank cap

Evaporation control system
(© Chrysler Corp.)

Fuel Check Valve This valve is used to prevent fuel leakage in case of roll over. It is installed in the vapor line between the separator and the two-way valve.

MAINTENANCE

Be sure that all hoses are clamped and not dry-rotted or broken. Check the valves for cracks, signs of gasoline leakage, and proper operating condition.
The canister air filter should be inspected and changed at least every 24,000 miles.

Heated Air Intake System

All models are equipped with a temperature regulated air control valve in the air cleaner snorkel.

When the underhood air temperature is 41 degrees or lower, the air control valve allows preheated air to flow through the heat cowl of the exhaust manifold, via a flexible hose, to the air cleaner and into the carburetor.

When the underhood temperature is 108 degrees or above, the air flow is directed through the air cleaner snorkel.

At intermediate temperatures, the carburetor intake air is a blend of the direct underhood and preheated air.

MAINTENANCE

Visually check the control valve assembly when the engine is cold, to be sure that the valve is closed.

Warm up the engine and check that the control valve opens to the outside air.

Secondary Air Supply System

This system supplies air for the further combustion of unburned gases in the thermal reactor (California only) or exhaust manifold and consists of a reed valve, air hoses, and air passages built into the cylinder head.

The reed valve is operated by exhaust pulsations in the exhaust manifold. It draws fresh air through the air cleaner and supplies it to the exhaust ports.

MAINTENANCE

Check for damage to the air hoses and air pipes. Make sure the air passages are open in the head.

Exhaust Gas Recirculation System

The EGR system recirculates part of the exhaust gases into the combustion chambers. This dilutes the air/fuel mixture, reducing formation of oxides of nitrogen in the exhaust gases by lowering the peak combustion temperatures.

The parts of the EGR system are:
EGR valve - Operated by vacuum drawn from a point above the carburetor throttle plate. The vacuum controls the raising and lowering of the valve pintle to allow exhaust gases to pass from the exhaust system to the intake manifold.
Thermo Valve - Used to stop EGR valve operation below approximately 131 degrees, in order to improve cold driveability and starting.

Dual EGR Control Valve

The EGR vacuum flow is suspended during idle and wide open throttle operation.

The primary valve controls EGR flow when the throttle valve opening is relatively narrow, while the secondary control valve operates at wider openings.
Sub EGR Control Valve - Linked to the throttle valve to closely modulate the EGR gas flow.

EGR Maintenance Warning Light

A light in the speedometer assembly to alert the driver to the need for EGR system maintenance.

This device has a mileage sensor to light the visual signal at 15,000 mile intervals.

Upon completion of the required EGR system maintenance, the warning light can be turned off by resetting the switch. It is in the speedometer cable, under the instrument panel.

MAINTENANCE

1. Check all vacuum hoses for cracks, breakage and correct installation.
2. Check EGR valve operation by applying vacuum to the EGR valve vacuum nipple with the engine idling. The idle should become rough.
3. Check the passages in the cylinder head and intake manifold for clogging. Clean as necessary.
4. Cold start the engine. The EGR port nipple should be open. When the coolant is warmed to over 131 degrees, the port should be closed.

Catalytic Converter

This unit replaces the thermal reactor. It is filled with catalyst to oxidize hydrocarbons and carbon monoxide in the exhaust gases.

MAINTENANCE

1. Check the core for cracks and damages.
2. If the idle carbon monoxide and hydrocarbon content exceeds specifications and the ignition timing and idle mixture are correct, the converter must be replaced.

Jet Air System

A jet air passage is provided in the carburetor, intake manifold, and cylinder head to direct air to a jet valve, operated simultaneously with the intake valve.

On the intake stroke, jet air is forced into the combustion chamber because of the pressure difference between the ends of the air jet passage.

This jet of air produces a strong swirl in the combustion chamber scavenging the residual gases around the spark plug.

The jet air volume lessens with increased throttle opening. It is at a maximum at idle.

MAINTENANCE

NOTE: Refer to Valve Lash Adjustment for adjusting jet valve clearance.

No maintenance is required other than clearance adjustment during valve

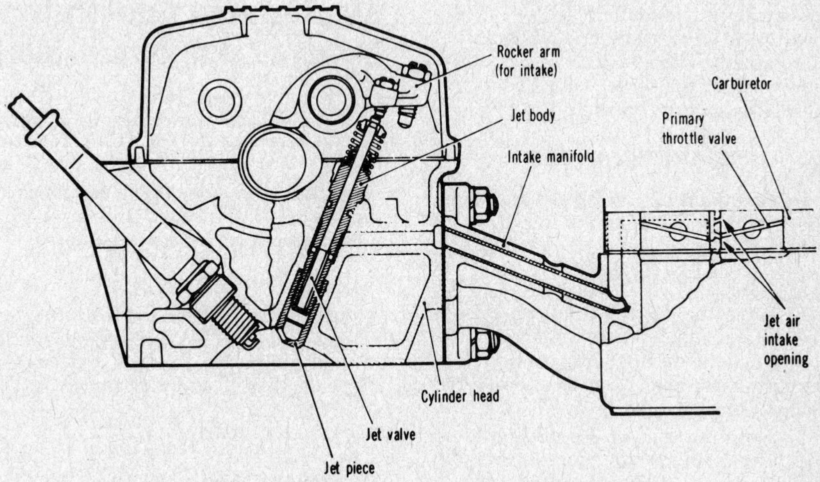

Cross-section of Jet Valve (U.S.A. only)
(© Chrysler Corp.)

adjustment. The valve can be removed from the cylinder head for service or replacement.

Ignition Timing Control System

When the engine is idling or operating at low speeds under light load or deceleration, the exhaust gas temperature is low, resulting in incomplete combustion of the air/fuel mixture. To prevent this, ignition timing is retarded under these conditions to maintain high exhaust gas temperature.

The units in the Ignition Timing Control system are as follow:

Thermo Valve - This valve is used to protect the engine from overheating. When coolant temperature reaches 203 degrees, the advance unit is allowed to operate, causing an increase in engine speed and a decrease in coolant temperature.

Single diaphragm distributor - This distributor has a single diaphragm vacuum advance unit, which advances the ignition timing as engine vacuum dictates. The single diaphragm distributor must not be interchanged with the dual diaphragm distributor. The distributor operating curves are different and would cause increased emissions. A thermo valve is *not* used with this type of distributor.

MAINTENANCE

Distributor maintenance is at tune-up intervals.

Deceleration Device

Closing of the throttle valve on deceleration is delayed in order to burn the air/fuel mixture more thoroughly. A vacuum controlled dashpot, attached to the carburetor linkage is used.

A servo valve detects intake manifold vacuum and closes if vacuum exceeds a preset value. Since the air in the dash pot diaphragm chamber can not escape, the throttle linkage opening is temporarily retained. If the vacuum is below the preset value, the servo valve opens and the dashpot works normally.

MAINTENANCE

Inspect the hoses for breaks and damage, and the valve body for cracks.

ADJUSTMENT

1. Have the engine running, brakes locked, and a tachometer attached.
2. Push the dashpot rod, connected to the carburetor arm, upward and into the dashpot until it stops.
3. Note the rpm at the dashpot stop and adjust to specifications. Note the time required between suddenly releasing the dashpot rod and the return to normal curb idle.

DASH POT ADJUSTMENTS

Description	Standard value U-engine	Standard value W-engine
Set speed (rpm)	2200 ± 100	1700 ± 100
Required time (sec.)	3 to 6	
Speed specified for measurement of required time (rpm)	900	

Mixture Control Valve

This control valve is used to supply additional air into the intake manifold to decrease manifold vacuum during deceleration, and is activated by the intake manifold vacuum level.

Manual Altitude Compensation System

An off-on valve is used to increase the air supply to the carburetor to lean the mixture and decrease the EGR flow for high altitude operation.

MAINTENANCE

The required maintenance is to inspect any vacuum hoses and routing for kinks, breakage and cracks. The off-on valve should be on for high altitude and off for driving under 4000 ft.

FUEL SYSTEM

Fuel Filter

REPLACEMENT

All models use an in-line filter which should be replaced every 12,000 miles.

Mechanical Fuel Pump

REMOVAL AND INSTALLATION

1. Remove the fuel lines.
2. Unbolt the pump mounting bolts, and remove the pump, insulator, and gasket.
3. Coat both sides of a new insulator and gasket with sealer, and install the pump in the reverse order of removal.

TESTING

Disconnect the fuel line from the carburetor and attach a pressure tester to the end of the line. Crank the engine. The tester should show 4.6-6 psi.

Carburetors

REMOVAL AND INSTALLATION

1. Remove the solenoid valve wiring.
2. Disconnect the air cleaner breather hose, air duct and vacuum tube.
3. Remove the air cleaner.
4. Remove the air cleaner case.
5. Disconnect the accelerator and shift cables (automatic transmission) at the carburetor.
6. Disconnect the purge valve hose; remove the vacuum compensator, and fuel lines.
7. Drain the coolant.
8. Remove the water hose between the carburetor and the cylinder head.
9. Remove the carburetor.
10. Installation is the reverse of removal.

OVERHAUL

1. Disconnect the water hose.
2. Remove the throttle return spring and damper spring.

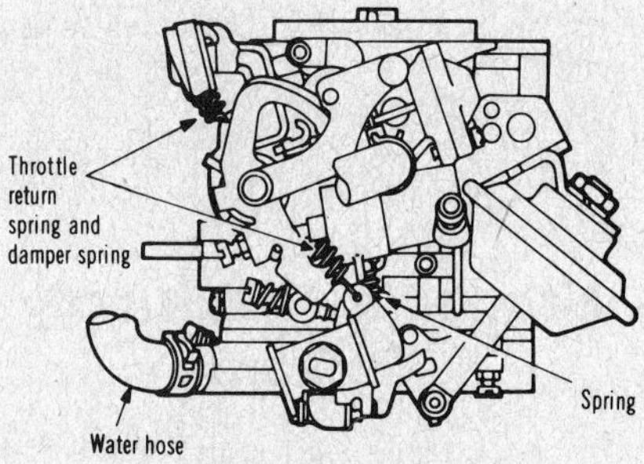

Removing springs
(© Chrysler Corp.)

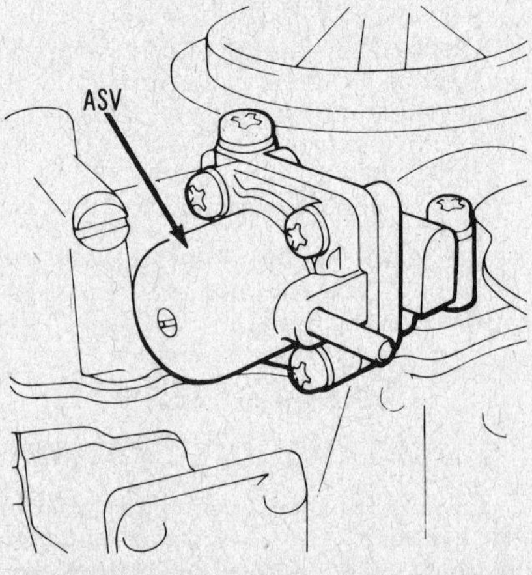

Removing the Air Switching Valve (ASV)
(© Chrysler Corp.)

3. Remove the throttle adjuster lever spring and the secondary return spring.
4. Remove the choke unloader link retaining clip and disconnect the choke unloader link.
5. Disconnect the vacuum hose.
6. Disconnect the lower end of the diaphragm chamber link and remove the diaphragm chamber. *Do not immerse the diaphragm chamber assembly in cleaner.*
7. Remove the two screws and remove the air switching valve (ASV).
8. Remove the six float chamber cover screws. Separate the float chamber cover from the carburetor main body by tapping with a plastic hammer. Do not pry it off.
9. Remove the float chamber cover gasket.
10. Remove the float lever pin and the float.
11. Remove the needle valve assembly, gasket and filter.
12. Do not remove the automatic choke system because the factory setting will be disturbed.
13. Turn the main body upside down and remove the pump discharge check ball and weight.
14. Remove the fuel cut-off solenoid.
15. Remove the main jets and pilot jets. Do not tamper with the screws with white paint on heads.

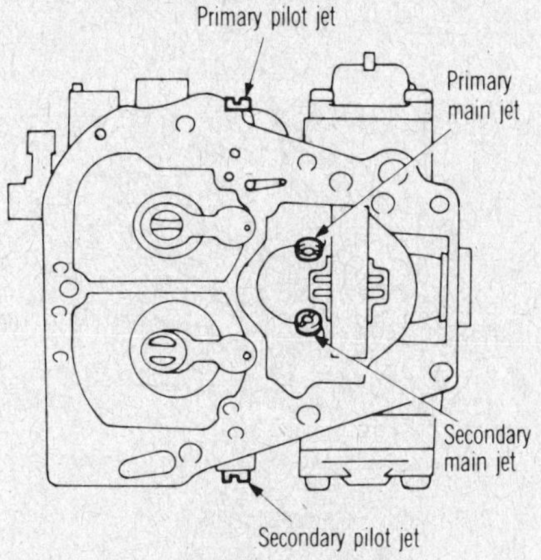

Location of jets
(© Chrysler Corp.)

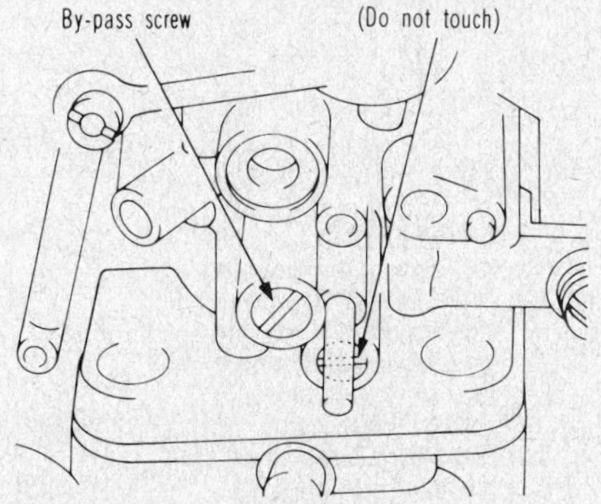

Do not touch these screws (painted white) when disassembling carburetor
(© Chrysler Corp.)

16. Remove the enrichment assembly.
17. Disconnect the pump rod from the throttle shaft lever and remove the accelerator pump assembly.
18. Remove the sub-EGR valve link retaining clip and remove the washer and spring, then disconnect the link. Do not touch the EGR adjusting screw because it was preset at the factory. Do not distort the sub-EGR valve link.
19. Remove the two main body-to-throttle body screws. Separate the throttle body from the main body and remove the gasket.
20. Remove the idle speed adjusting screw, spring washer and packing from the throttle body.

Assembly is the reverse of disassembly.

When the carburetor is disassembled, wash all parts (except diaphragms, electric choke units, pump plunger, and any other plastic, leather, fiber, or rubber parts) in clean carburetor solvent. Do not leave parts in the solvent any longer than is necessary to sufficiently loosen the deposits. Excessive cleaning may remove the special finish from the float bowl and choke valve bodies, leaving these parts unfit for service. Rinse all parts in clean solvent and blow them dry with compressed air or allow them to air dry. Wipe clean all cork, plastic, leather, and fiber parts with a clean, lint-free cloth.

Blow out all passages and jets with compressed air and be sure that there are no restrictions or blockages. Never use wire or similar tools to clean jets, fuel passages, or air bleeds. Clean all jets and valves separately to avoid accidental interchange.

Check all parts for wear or damage. If wear or damage is found, replace the defective parts. Especially check the following:

1. Check the float needle and seat for wear. If wear is found; replace the complete assembly.
2. Check the float hinge pin for wear and the float(s) for dents or distortion. Replace the float if fuel has leaked into it.
3. Check the throttle and choke shaft bores for wear or an out-of-round condition. Damage or wear to the throttle arm, shaft, or shaft bore will often require replacement of the throttle body. These parts require a close tolerance of fit; wear may allow air leakage, which could affect starting and idling.

***NOTE:** Throttle shafts and bushings are not included in overhaul kits. They can be purchased separately.*

4. Inspect the idle mixture adjusting needles for burrs or grooves. Any such condition requires replacement of the needle, since you will not be able to obtain a satisfactory idle.
5. Test the accelerator pump check valves. They should pass air one way but not the other. Test for proper seating by blowing and sucking on the valve. Replace the valve if necessary. If the valve is satisfactory, wash the valve again to remove breath moisture.
6. Check the bowl cover for warped surfaces with a straight edge.
7. Closely inspect the valves and seats for wear and damage, replacing as necessary.
8. After the carburetor is assembled, check the choke valve for freedom of operation.

Carburetor overhaul kits are recommended for each overhaul. These kits contain all gaskets and new parts to replace those that deteriorate most rapidly. Failure to replace all parts supplied with the kit (especially gaskets) can result in poor performance later.

After cleaning and checking all components, reassemble the carburetor, using new parts and referring to the exploded view. When reassembling, make sure that all screws and jets are tight in their seats, but do not overtighten as the tips will be distorted. Tighten all screws gradually, in rotation. Do not tighten needle valves into their seats; uneven jetting will result. Always use new gaskets. Be sure to adjust the float level when reassembling.

FLOAT AND FUEL LEVEL ADJUSTMENT

A sight glass is fitted at the float chamber and the fuel level can be checked without disassembling the carburetor. Normal fuel level is within the level mark on the sight glass.

The fuel level adjustment is corrected by increasing or decreasing the number of needle valve packings. The float level may be off 0.160 inch, above or below the level mark and the operation of the engine would not be affected.

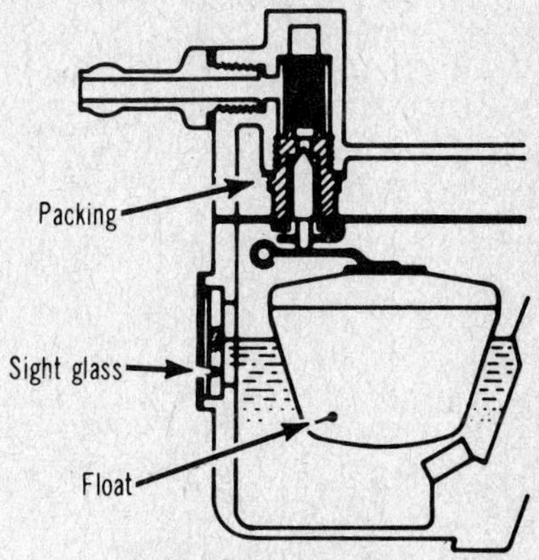

Float adjustment
(© Chrysler Corp.)

FAST IDLE ADJUSTMENT

1. Start the engine and open the throttle valve about 45 degrees. Manually close the choke valve and slowly return the throttle valve to the stop position.
2. With a tachometer, check that the fast idle speed is 2,000 rpm or lower.

(Not less than 1700 rpm). Adjust the speed as necessary with the fast idle speed screw.

3. Cold start the engine and check the automatic choke and fast idle operation.

AUTOMATIC CHOKE ADJUSTMENT

The choke case has five small projections. Align the center projection with the yellow punch mark of the bimetal case.

MANUAL TRANSMISSION

Four and Five Speed

REMOVAL AND INSTALLATION

1. Disconnect the battery ground cable, remove the air cleaner and the starter.
2. Remove the top transmission mounting bolts from the bell housing.
3. From inside the vehicle, raise the console assembly, if equipped, or the carpet and remove the dust cover retaining plate at the shift lever.
4. Place the four speed transmission in second gear and the five speed transmission in first gear. Remove the control lever assembly.
5. Raise the vehicle and support it safely. Drain the transmission. Disconnect the speedometer and the back up light switch.
6. Remove the drive shaft, exhaust pipe, and the clutch cable.
7. Support the transmission and remove the engine rear support bracket.
8. Remove the bell housing cover and bolts, move the transmission rearward, and lower it carefully to the floor. Remove the transmission from under the vehicle.
9. To install the transmission, reverse the removal procedure. Make sure the transmission is in the proper gear before installing the gear shift lever.

OVERHAUL

NOTE: Proper transmission overhaul requires the use of certain special tools. If these are not available, the job should not be undertaken.

4-Speed

1. Remove the undercover.
2. Remove the backup light switch. Be careful not to lose the steel ball.
3. Remove the speedometer gear sleeve clamp and remove the speedometer driven gear and sleeve assembly from the extension housing assembly.
4. Remove the extension housing bolts. Turn the shift lever to the left and pull off the extension housing.
5. Loosen the three poppet plugs, then remove the three poppet springs and the three steel balls.
6. Place the 1st-2nd speed shift rod in Neutral position.
7. Remove the reverse shift rail and fork assembly together with the reverse idler gear.
8. Using a $^{3}/_{16}$ in. punch, drive off the 3rd-4th and 1st-2nd speed shift fork spring pins. Push each shift rod toward the rear of the transmission case and remove the shift forks. Remember to remove the interlock plunger.
9. Remove the snap ring from the rear end of the counter gear and then remove the reverse counter gear.
10. Unlock the main shaft lock nut and remove the lock nut. The lock nut can be loosened by double-engaging the 3rd speed gear and the 1st speed gear.
11. Remove the reverse gear from the main shaft.
12. Remove the five attaching screws and then remove the rear bearing retainer.
13. Remove the front bearing retainer.
14. With the counter gear pressed to the rear, remove the rear bearing snap

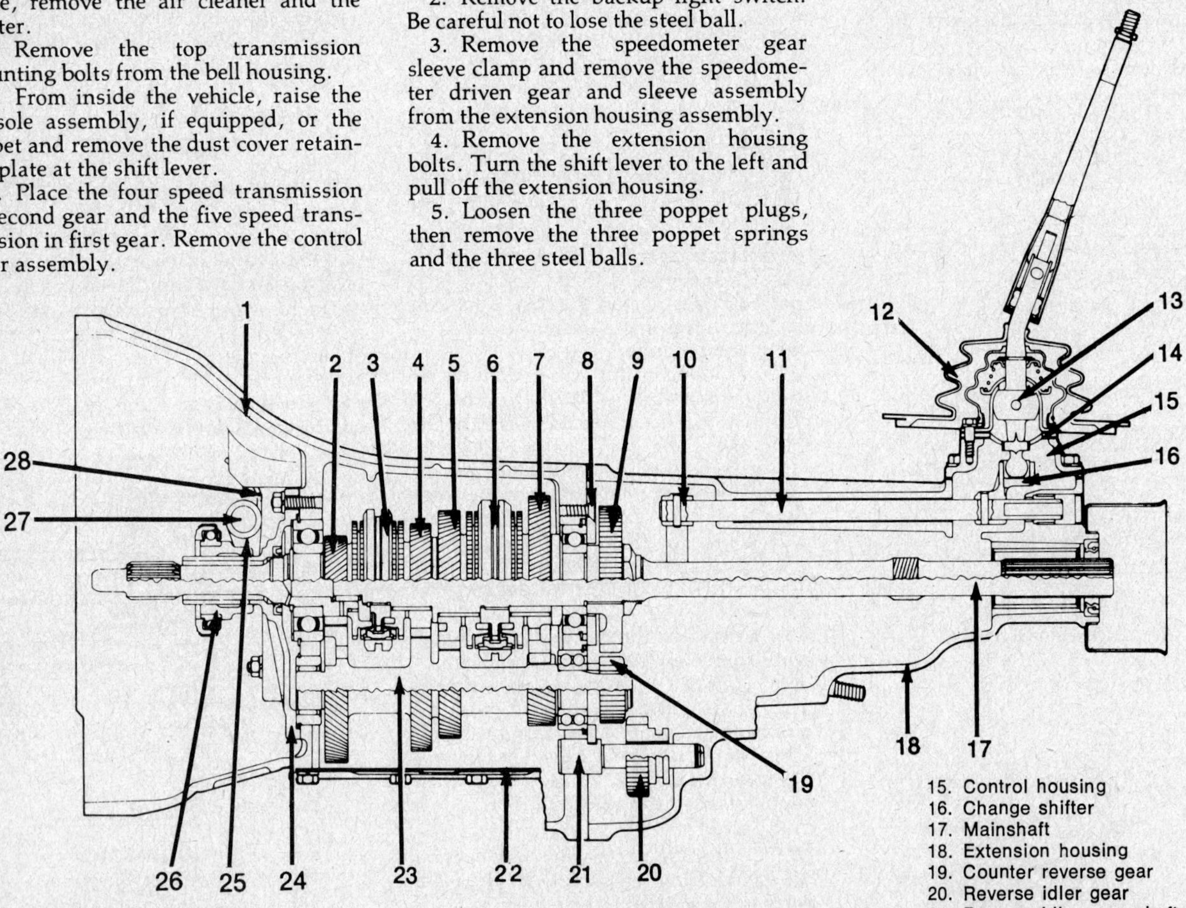

1. Transmission case
2. Main drive pinion
3. Synchronizer assy (3-4 speed)
4. 3rd speed gear
5. 2nd speed gear
6. Synchronizer assy (1-2 speed)
7. 1st speed gear
8. Rear bearing retainer
9. Reverse gear
10. Control finger
11. Control shaft
12. Control lever cover
13. Control level assy
14. Stopper plate
15. Control housing
16. Change shifter
17. Mainshaft
18. Extension housing
19. Counter reverse gear
20. Reverse idler gear
21. Reverse idler gear shaft
22. Under cover
23. Counter gear
24. Front bearing retainer
25. Clutch shift arm
26. Release bearing carrier
27. Clutch control shaft
28. Return spring

Cross section of four speed transmission
(© Chrysler Corp.)

ring. Then using a bearing puller remove the rear counter bearing.

15. Remove the snap ring from the front counter bearing. Pull off the bearing with a bearing puller.

16. Pull the counter gear out of the case.

17. Remove the main drive pinion from the front of the case. To remove the bearing from the main drive pinion, remove the two snap rings and then remove the bearing with a bearing puller.

18. Remove the mainshaft bearing snap ring and remove the bearing using a dual post bearing puller (D-50/Plymouth Arrow special tool MD998056-10 and MD998056).

19. Remove the main shaft assembly by lifting it up through the case.

20. Disassemble the mainshaft assembly in the following order.

a. Pull off the 1st speed gear, the 1st-2nd speed synchronizer and the 2nd speed gear toward the rear of the mainshaft.

b. Remove the snap ring from the forward end of the mainshaft, then remove the 3rd-4th speed synchronizer and the 3rd speed gear.

21. If removing the shift control shaft assembly, remove the pin locking the gear shifter using a $^{3}/_{16}$ in. punch. To remove the lock pin, press the gear shifter forward and drive the lock pin off, being careful not to bend the control shaft.

Inspect the parts after cleaning. Replace any worn, damaged or defective.

Assembly is as follows.

22. If the main drive pinion bearing has been removed, replace it using a pipe fit over the end of the pinion shaft.

CAUTION: Make sure the pipe does not apply pressure on the ball bearings but only on the bearing race, or bearing damage could result.

23. Fit a snap ring which gives a clearance of no more than 0-0.002 in. and install it on the drive pinion.

24. Assemble the main shaft in the following order.

a. Assemble the 3rd-4th speed and the 1st-2nd speed synchronizers. The front and rear ends of the synchronizer sleeve and hub can be identified as shown in the illustration. The synchronizer spring is installed as shown.

b. Install the needle bearing, 3rd speed gear, synchronizer ring and the 3rd-4th speed synchronizer assembly onto the mainshaft from the front end. Be careful not to confuse the front and the rear of the synchronizer assembly.

25. Select and install a snap ring that will give the 3rd-4th speed synchronizer hub an end-play from 0.0 to 0.003 in.

26. Third speed gear end-play should be from 0.002 to 0.008 in.

27. Install the needle bearing, the 2nd speed gear, the synchronizer assembly, the bearing sleeve, the needle bearing, the 1st speed gear, and the bearing spacer onto the mainshaft from the rear end.

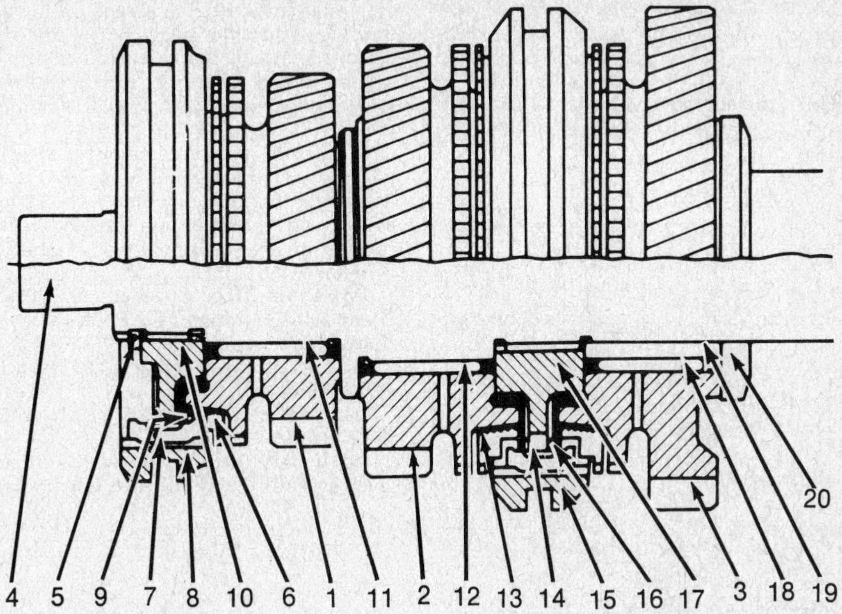

1. 3rd speed gear
2. 2nd speed gear
3. 1st speed gear
4. Mainshaft
5. Snap ring
6. Synchronizer ring (3-4 speed)
7. Synchronizer piece
8. Synchronizer sleeve (3-4 speed)
9. Synchronizer spring (3-4 speed)
10. Synchronizer hub (3-4 speed)
11. Needle bearing (3rd speed gear)
12. Needle bearing (2nd speed gear)
13. Synchronizer ring (1-2 speed)
14. Synchronizer piece
15. Synchronizer sleeve (1-2 speed)
16. Synchronizer spring (1-2 speed)
17. Synchronizer hub (1-2 speed)
18. Needle bearing (1st speed gear)
19. 1st gear bearing sleeve
20. Bearing spacer

Mainshaft assembly—four and five speed transmissions
(© Chrysler Corp.)

28. Push the bearing spacer forward and check the 1st and 2nd speed gear end play. Clearance should be within 0.002-0.008 in.

29. Insert the mainshaft assembly into the transmission case and fit the mainshaft center bearing using a bearing driver. Hold the forward end of the mainshaft by hand at the front of the case.

30. Install the needle bearing and the synchronizer ring, then insert the main drive pinion assembly into the case from the front.

31. Insert the countershaft gear into the case. With a snap ring fitted to the countershaft front needle bearing, drive the bearing into the case by hammering on the outer race of the bearing.

32. Fit a snap ring to the countershaft rear ball bearing and then install the bearing with a bearing installer.

33. Install the front bearing retainer. When installing the retainer, install a spacer that will give a clearance (C) of 0.0-0.004 in. (see illustration). Apply sealant to both sides of the front bearing retainer packing and apply gear oil to the oil seal lip. Install packing and oil seal.

34. Install the rear bearing retainer and its five screws. It is suggested that each screw head be staked with a pointed punch to prevent them from coming loose.

35. Install the reverse gear on the mainshaft and tighten the lock nut to 73-94 ft-lb. Lock the nut at the notch of the mainshaft.

36. Install the spacer and counter reverse gear to the counter gear rear end.

37. Install a snap ring of the proper size so that the reverse counter gear and play will be from 0.0 to 0.003 in.

38. Install the 3rd-4th and 1st-2nd speed shift forks into their respective synchronizer sleeves. Insert each shift rod from the rear of the case. Lock the shift forks and rod with spring pins, install the interlock plunger between the shift rods.

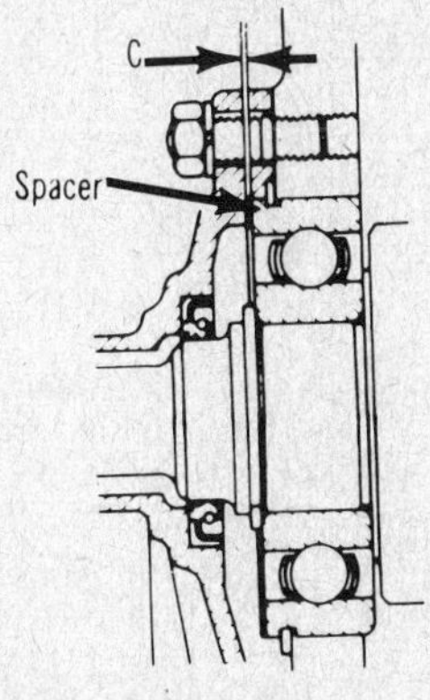

Retainer-to-bearing clearance adjustment
(© Chrysler Corp.)

NOTE: The spring pins should be installed with the slits parallel to the shift rod.

39. Install the reverse shift rod and fork assembly together with the reverse idler gear.

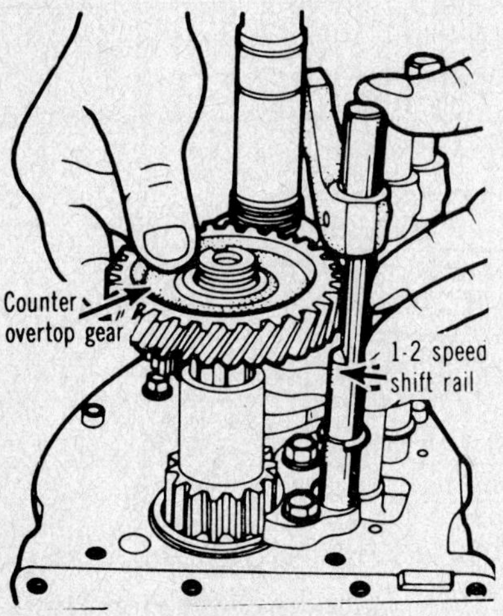

Installing reverse idler gear—four speed transmission
(© Chrysler Corp.)

40. Insert the ball and poppet spring with the small end on the ball side into each shift rod. Tighten the plugs to the specified positions. After installation, seal each plug head with sealant.
41. Apply sealant to both sides of the extension housing packing and fit the packing into the housing.
42. Turn the gear shift control down to the left and install the extension to the transmission case.
43. Make sure the forward end of the control finger is snug in the slot of the shift lug and fit the extension housing bolts after coating their threads with sealant.
44. Apply gear oil to the speedometer driven gear and install the gear and sleeve assembly in the extension housing. Make sure the sleeve flange and its mating areas on the extension housing are free of dirt, or it will cause the gears to be misaligned and could damage them.
45. Rotate the speedometer driven gear and sleeve assembly so that the number on the sleeve, which is the same as the number of teeth on the gear, is in the "U" mark position as the assembly is installed.
46. Install the speedometer gear clamp with its tongs in the sleeve positioning slots.
47. Install the backup light switch with its steel ball.
48. Refit the under cover and torque the bolts to 6–7 ft-lb.
49. Install the transmission control lever assembly and fill the gear shifter area with grease. Fill the transmission with lubricant.

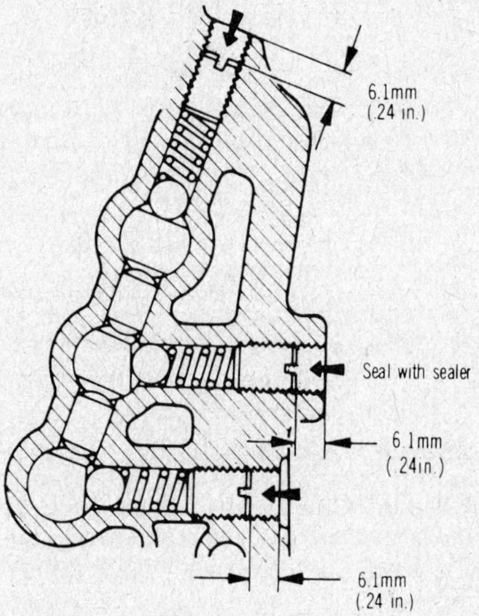

Installing poppet spring and plug assembly; four and five speed transmissions
(© Chrysler Corp.)

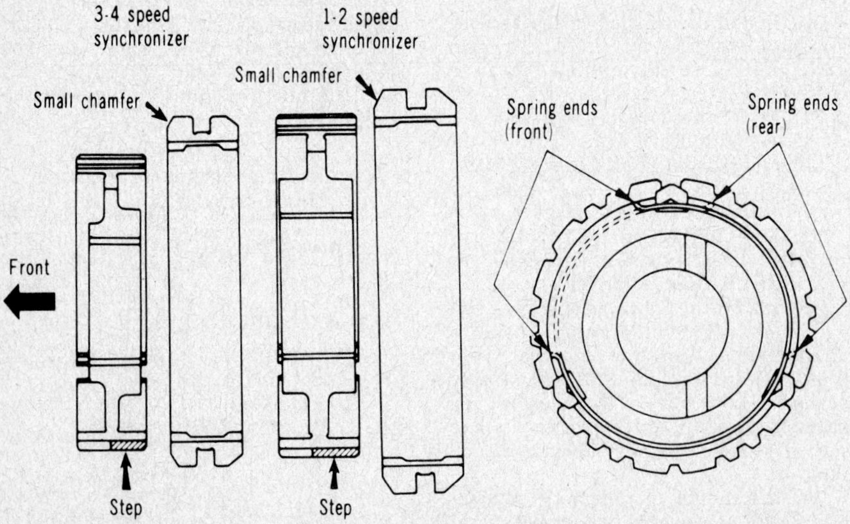

Synchronizer hub assemblies and spring installation. Note direction of hubs in relation to arrow
(© Chrysler Corp.)

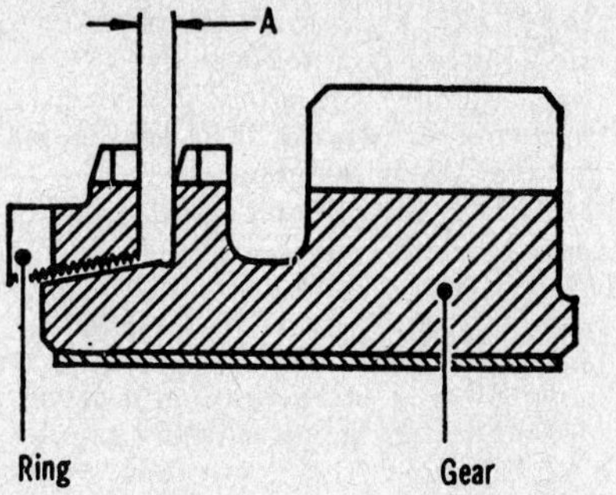

Synchronizer ring to gear clearance: "A" equals 0.032 in. on both four and five speed transmissions
(© Chrysler Corp.)

5 Speed

1. Drain the oil and remove the case cover.
2. Remove the backup light switch and ball.
3. Remove the extension housing attaching bolts, back off the plug of the neutral return plunger, turn the shift lever down to the left and pull off the extension housing.
4. Remove the snap ring and speedometer drive gear.
5. Remove the snap ring and mainshaft rear bearing.
6. Remove the three plugs and remove the poppet springs and balls.
7. Remove the 1–2 and 3–4 shift fork pins with a $^3/_{16}$" punch. Pull each rail toward the rear of the case and remove the forks and interlock plunger.
8. In the same manner, remove the 5th-reverse forks.
9. Engage the reverse and 2nd gears and remove the mainshaft and countershaft rear locknuts.
10. Remove the 5th counter gear and bearing with a puller. Remove the spacer and reverse counter gear.
11. Remove the 5th gear and sleeve from the mainshaft. Remove the 5th synchronizer and spacer.
12. Remove the cotter pin, nut and reverse idler gear.
13. Remove the rear bearing retainer.
14. Drive the reverse idler gear shaft from the case.
15. Remove the front bearing retainer.
16. Press the countergear to the rear and remove the rear bearing snap ring.
17. Using a puller, remove the counter rear bearing.
18. Remove the snap ring and pull the counter front bearing. Remove the countergear from the case.
19. Remove the main drive pinion from the case.
20. Remove the two snap rings and pull the bearing.
21. Remove the snap ring and pull the mainshaft bearing.
22. Remove the mainshaft from the case.

23. Disassemble the mainshaft.
24. Disassemble the extension housing.

To assemble:

25. Install the bearing on the main drive pinion and select a snap ring which will give a clearance of 0–0.0024" between the snap ring and the bearing.
26. Assemble the mainshaft. Use a spacer which will give a 3–4 synchronizer end play of 0–0.003". Use a snap ring which will give a 1–2 gear end play of 0.002–0.008".
27. Insert the mainshaft into the case and drive in the center bearing.
28. Install the needle bearing and synchronizer ring, then insert the main drive pinion into the case from the front.
29. Insert the countershaft gear into the case.
30. Install the snap ring on the countershaft front needle bearing and drive the bearing into the case by hammering the outer race.
31. Install the snap ring on the countershaft rear bearing and install it in place.
32. Install the front bearing retainer using a spacer which will give clearance of 0–0.004" between the bearing and retainer.
33. Install the front retainer oil seal.
34. Install the rear retainer.
35. Install the reverse idler gear shaft.
36. Install the needle bearing, reverse idler gear and thrust washer. Tighten the locknut and install the cotter pin. Idler gear end play should be 0.0047–0.0110". If not, replace the thrust washer.

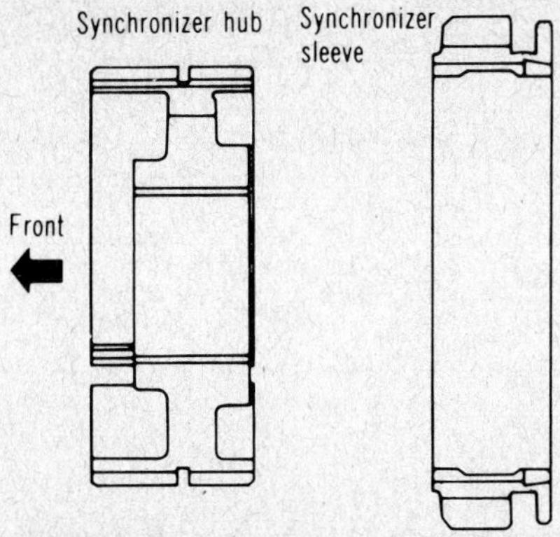

Fifth speed (overdrive) synchronizer hub installation direction
(© Chrysler Corp.)

37. Assemble the 5th synchronizer.
38. Install the spacer, stop plate and 5th synchronizer assembly, the 5th gear bearing sleeve and needle bearing, the synchronizer ring and 5th gear, in that order, to the mainshaft from the rear. 5th gear end play should be 0.004–0.010".
39. Install the spacer, counter reverse gear spacer, counter 5th gear and the ball bearing onto the countershaft gear from the rear. Tighten and lock the nut.
40. Insert the 3–4 and 1–2 forks into their synchronizer sleeves. Insert each shift rail from the rear of the case. Install the spring pins and interlock plunger.

NOTE: ***The slit in the pins should be parallel with the rail.***

41. Insert the ball and poppet spring into each shift rail. Tighten the plugs flush with the case.
42. Install the ball bearing on the rear of the mainshaft.
43. Install the speedometer drive gear.
44. Turn the shifter down and to the left and install the extension housing.
45. Install the neutral return plungers, spring, and resistance spring and ball. Tighten the plugs flush with the case.
46. Install the speedometer driven gear sleeve and lock plate.

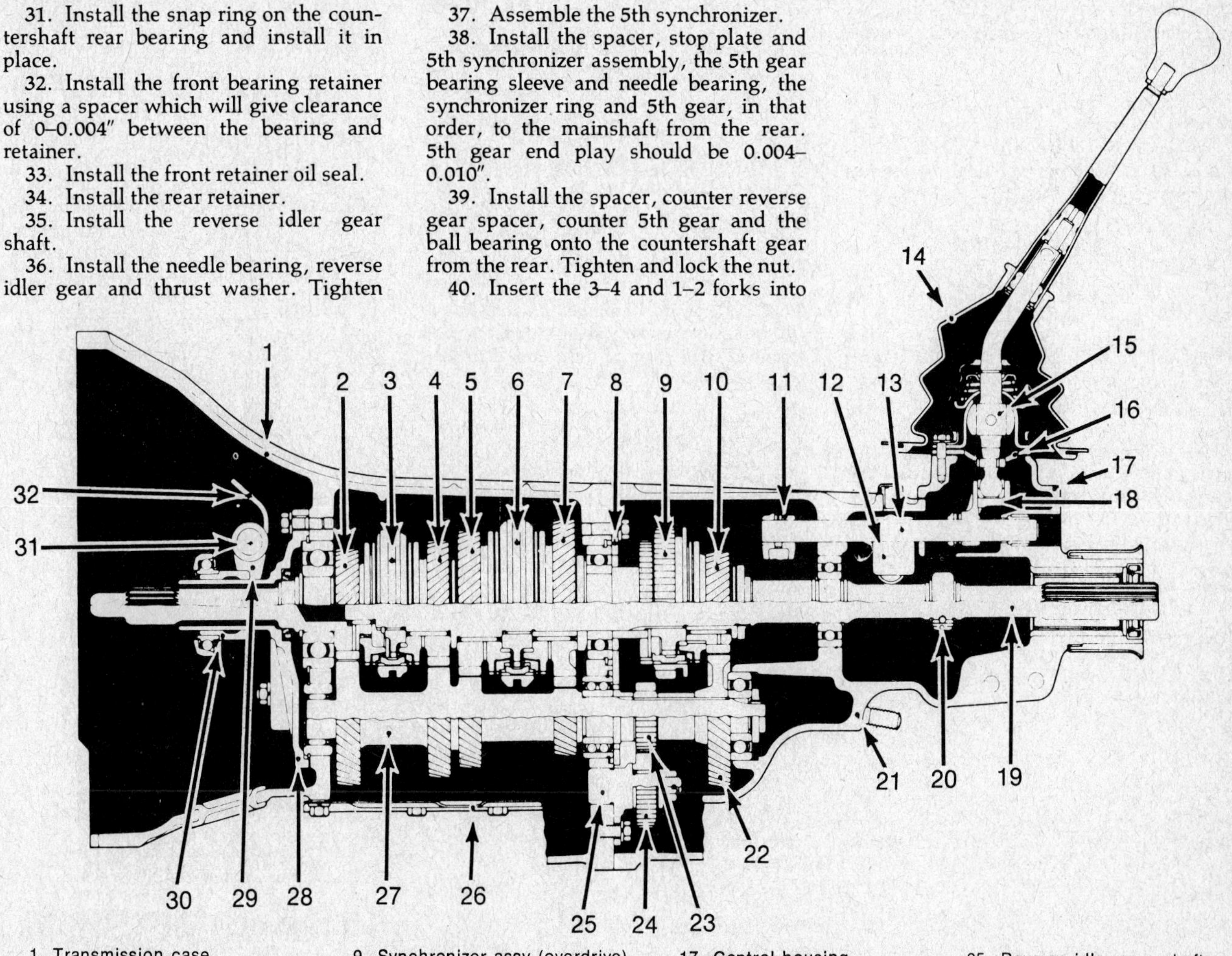

1. Transmission case
2. Main drive pinion
3. Synchronizer assy (3-4 speed)
4. 3rd speed gear
5. 2nd speed gear
6. Synchronizer assy (1-2 speed)
7. 1st speed gear
8. Rear bearing retainer
9. Synchronizer assy (overdrive)
10. Overdrive gear
11. Control finger
12. Neutral return finger
13. Control shaft
14. Control lever cover
15. Control lever assy
16. Stopper plate
17. Control housing
18. Change shifter
19. Mainshaft
20. Speedometer drive gear
21. Extension housing
22. Counter overdrive gear
23. Counter reverse gear
24. Reverse idler gear
25. Reverse idler gear shaft
26. Under cover
27. Counter gear
28. Front bearing retainer
29. Clutch shift arm
30. Release bearing carrier
31. Clutch control shaft
32. Return spring

Cross-section of five speed transmission
(© Chrysler Corp.)

47. Install the backup light switch and ball.
48. Install the bottom cover and torque the bolts to 6–7 ft lb.
49. Install the control lever assembly.

CLUTCH

Clutch Cable

REMOVAL AND INSTALLATION

1. Loosen the cable adjusting wheel inside the engine compartment.
2. Loosen the clutch pedal adjusting bolt locknut and loosen the adjusting bolt.
3. Remove the cable end from the clutch throwout lever.
4. Remove the cable end from the clutch pedal.
5. Installation is the reverse of removal.

NOTE: Apply engine oil to the cable before replacing. Make sure the isolating pad is fitted on the cable after installation to keep the cable from rubbing the motor mount during operation.

Adjustment

PEDAL HEIGHT

1. Adjust the pedal height to the standard value with the adjusting bolt (see illustration), and check the pedal stroke and distance "A".

CAUTION: Insufficient pedal stroke results in only partial clutch release, causing hard gear shifting and gear grinding when shifting.

2. In the engine compartment, at the fire wall, pull out the clutch cable a little and adjust the cable by turning the adjusting wheel until it is 0.12–0.16 in from the insulator.
3. Clutch pedal free play should be within 0.8–1.4 in.

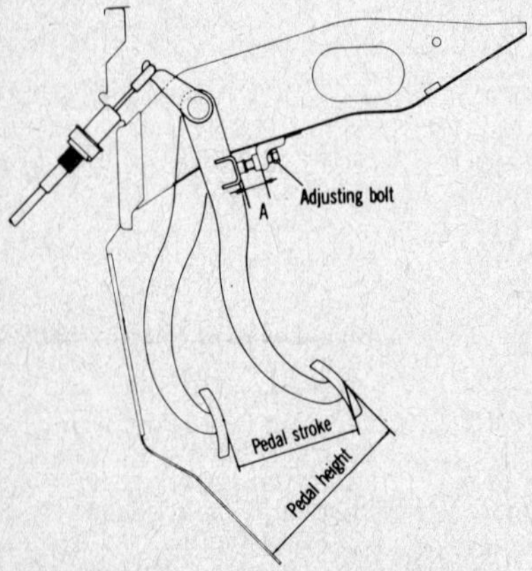

Adjusting clutch pedal height
(© Chrysler Corp.)

PEDAL HEIGHT ADJUSTMENT

Description	Standard value mm (in.) U-engine	W-engine
Distance A	22 (.9)	20 (.8)
Pedal height	166 (6.5)	176 (6.9)
Pedal stroke	140 (5.5)	150 (5.9)

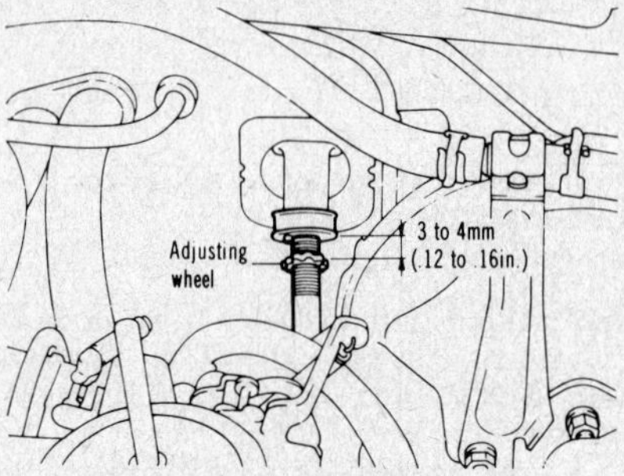

Adjusting the clutch cable
(© Chrysler Corp.)

Clutch Disc Replacement

1. Remove the transmission as outlined in the Manual Transmission Removal and Installation section.

NOTE: It is recommended that a clutch aligning tool be inserted in the clutch hub to prevent dropping of the clutch disc during disassembly.

2. Remove pressure plate bolts, pressure plate and clutch disc.
3. From inside the transmission bell housing, remove the return spring clip and remove the release bearing assembly.
4. If necessary, remove the release control lever and spring pin with a ³/₁₆ inch punch. Remove the control lever shaft assembly and clutch shift arm, two felt packings and two return springs.
5. Installation is the reverse of removal.

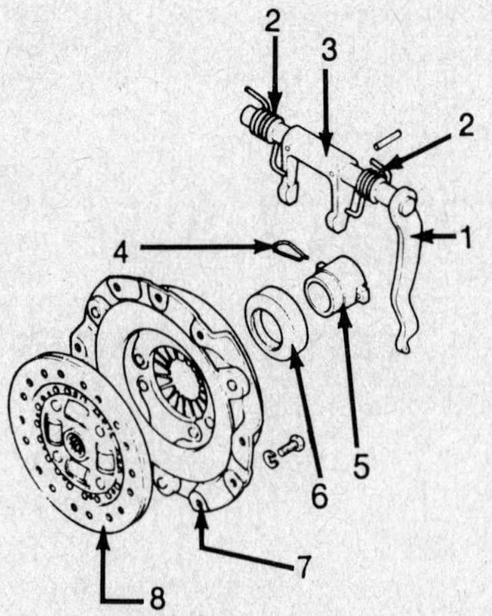

1. Clutch control shaft
2. Return spring
3. Clutch shift arm
4. Return clip
5. Release bearing carrier
6. Release bearing
7. Pressure plate assembly
8. Clutch disc

Exploded view of clutch assembly
(© Chrysler Corp.)

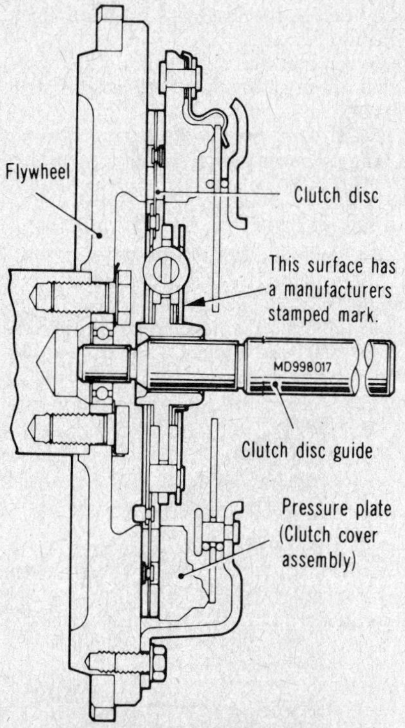

Installing the clutch disc—use clutch disc guide as shown
(© Chrysler Corp.)

TORQUEFLITE AUTOMATIC TRANSMISSION

Removal and Installation

The transmission and converter must be removed as an assembly; otherwise, the converter drive plate, pump bushing, or oil seal may be damaged. The drive plate will not support a load; therefore, none of the weight of the transmission should be allowed to rest on the plate during removal.

1. Disconnect battery ground cable, drain the transmission, and remove cooler lines at transmission.
2. Remove starter and cooler line bracket.
3. Rotate crankshaft clockwise and remove bolts attaching torque converter to drive plate.
4. Remove the driveshaft.
5. Disconnect gearshift rod and torque shaft.
6. Disconnect throttle rod from lever at the left side of transmission. Remove linkage bellcrank from transmission if so equipped.
7. Remove the oil filler tube and speedometer cable.
8. Support the rear of the engine with jack.
9. Raise transmission slightly.
10. Remove crossmember.
11. Remove all bell housing bolts.
12. Carefully work transmission converter assembly rearward off engine block dowels and disengage converter hub from end of crankshaft. Attach a small C-clamp to edge of bell housing to hold converter in place during transmission removal.
13. Remove transmission.
14. Installation is the reverse of removal.

Pan and Filter Removal and Installation

1. Raise and support vehicle.
2. Loosen the pan bolts from one end to the other allowing the fluid to drain out.
3. Unbolt the old filter from the pan.
4. Clean the pan and install a new filter. Tighten filter bolts to 35 in lb.
5. Install the pan and new gasket. Torque pan bolts to 6–9 ft lb.
6. Add four quarts of Dexron fluid, start the engine and move the lever through all positions, pausing momentarily in each. Add enough fluid to bring the level to the full mark on the dipstick.

Adjustments

THROTTLE LINKAGE

The throttle rod adjustment is very important to proper transmission operation. This adjustment positions a valve which controls shift speed, shift quality and part throttle-down shift sensitivity. If the setting is too short, early shifts and slippage between shifts may occur. If the setting is too long, shifts may be delayed and part throttle-down shifts may be very sensitive.

To adjust the throttle rod:

1. Warm up the engine until it reaches the normal operating temperature. With the carburetor automatic choke disengaged from the fast idle cam, adjust the engine idle speed by rotating speed adjusting screw (SAS). See "Tune-up Procedures" at the beginning of this section.
2. Loosen the bolts on the linkage so that both rod "B" and "C" can slide properly.
3. Lightly push rod "A" or the transmission throttle lever and rod "C" toward the idle stopper, and set the rods to the idle position. Tighten the bolt securely that connects rods "B" and "C".
4. Make sure that when the carburetor throttle valve is wide-open, the transmission throttle lever smoothly moves from the IDLE to the WIDE OPEN position (from 47.5° to 54°), and that there is some range in the lever stroke.
5. Also make sure that when the throttle linkage alone is slowly returned from the fully closed position, the transmission throttle lever completely returns to *idle* by return spring force.

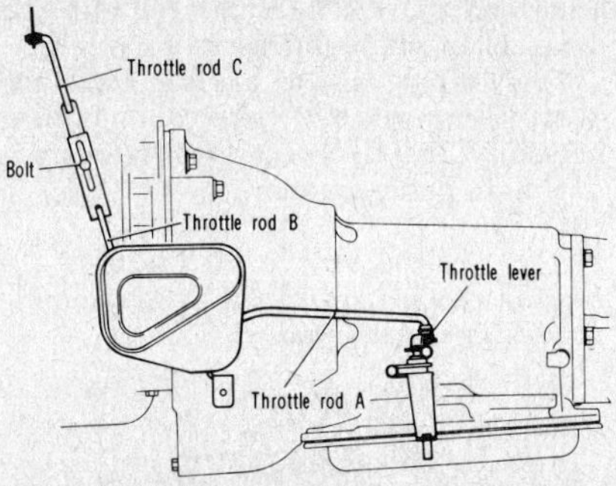

Throttle rod adjustment—automatic transmission
(© Chrysler Corp.)

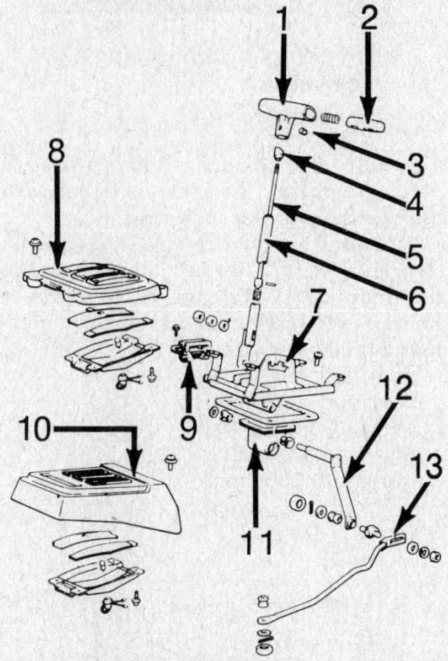

1. Selector handle
2. Push button
3. Set screw
4. Rod adjusting cam
5. Selector lever rod
6. Selector lever
7. Detent plate
8. Position indicator cover (for sports)
9. Inhibitor switch
10. Position indicator cover
11. Lever bracket cover
12. Control cover
13. Control rod

Exploded view of automatic transmission shift control
(© Chrysler Corp.)

KICKDOWN BAND

The kickdown band adjusting screw is located on the left side of the transmission case.

1. Loosen locknut and back off approximately 5 turns. Test adjusting screw for free turning in the transmission case.
2. Tighten the adjusting screw to 72 in. lbs.
3. Back off adjusting screw 3 turns from Step 2. Tighten the locknut to 35 ft lbs.

LOW & REVERSE BAND

1. Raise vehicle, drain transmission fluid and remove the pan.
2. This transmission has an allen socket adjustment screw at the servo end of lever. After removing the locknut this screw is tightened to 41 in. lbs. torque then backed off $7^1/_2$ turns. Tighten locknut to 30 ft lbs.
3. Reinstall the pan.

NEUTRAL SAFETY SWITCH

1. When testing the safety switch, check to see if the switch has been properly installed. Move the selector lever into N position and adjust the switch by moving it so that the pin on the forward end of the rod assembly will be in the position near the lobe of detent plate and that this position will be at the front end of the range of N connection of the switch. Temporarily tighten the attaching screws. After adjusting the selection lever clearance to 0.059 in. securely tighten the screws.
2. Test the continuity of the switch circuit by using a test light with switch connector disconnected.

SHIFT LINKAGE ADJUSTMENT

To adjust the shift linkage, the control cover must be removed.

Removal and Installation

1. Remove the shift handle assembly from the lever.
2. Take the position indicator assembly out upward.
   Remove the position indicator lamp.
3. Disconnect the control rod from the arm.
   Remove the lever bracket assembly.
4. Installation is the reverse of removal.
   If the proper turning effort (13–29 in. lbs) is not obtained, adjust it by using a selective wave-washer of proper size.

CAUTION: When the turning effort at the pivot A is checked, the pin at the forward end of the rod assembly must not slide with the detent plate. If the arm is loose, the bushing should be replaced.

DRIVELINE

Driveshaft

REMOVAL AND INSTALLATION

1. Make mating marks on the flange yoke and the differential companion flange.
2. Remove the bolts connecting the flange yoke to the differential companion flange, and remove the nuts attaching the center bearing assembly.
3. Remove the propeller shaft by drawing it out. Installation is reverse of removal.

NOTE: When the sleeve yoke end of the propeller shaft is pulled out from the transmission extension housing, transmission oil will flow out it if the front of the truck is raised higher, than the rear.

CAUTION: When removing the propeller shaft, be careful not to damage the oil seal lip and see that no foreign substance is present in the lip area.

U-Joint Overhaul

1. Remove the bearing retainer snap rings from the flange yoke.
2. With a vise and suitable sockets, force one needle bearing cup outward from the yoke, using the cross as a ram.
3. Grasp the protruding bearing with pliers or vise grips and remove it from the yoke.
4. Reverse the sockets and again using the cross as a ram, force the opposite bearing outward from the yoke and remove it with pliers or vise grips.
5. Follow the same procedure to remove the remaining bearing in the yoke.
6. To install, place the cross in the yoke and start a bearing cup into the yoke collar, engaging the cross arm.
7. With the aid of a vise, force the bearing cup into the yoke collar until it bottoms. Install the opposite bearing cup in the same manner.

NOTE: Sockets may be used to force the bearing cup inward so that the retaining snap rings can be installed.

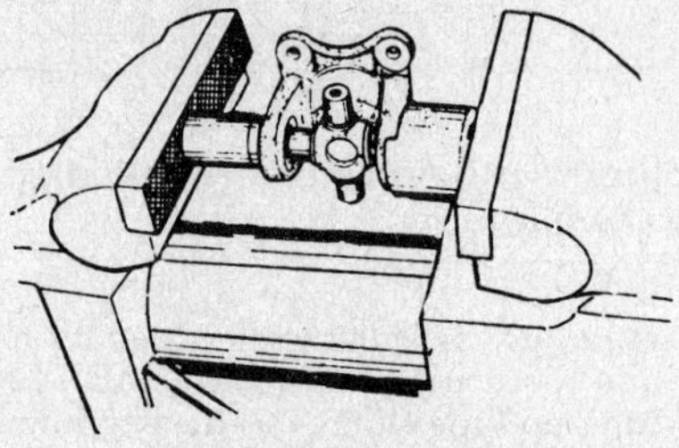

U-joint overhaul
(© Chrysler Corp.)

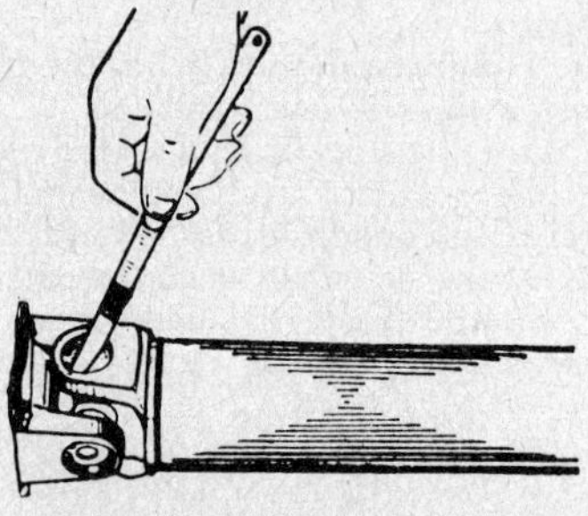

Checking U-joint snap ring clearance
(© Chrysler Corp.)

8. Different thickness snap rings are used to control the clearance between the bearing and the snap ring.
9. Install a snap ring and measure the clearance with a feeler gauge. Replace the snap ring with one of the proper thickness to have a total clearance tolerance of .000 to .001 inch.

Snap ring selection range
No color - 0.0504 inch
Yellow - 0.0561 inch
Blue - 0.0528 inch
Purple - 0.0539 inch

NOTE: When snap rings are installed, press each bearing towards the opposite side to measure the maximum clearance.

Center Bearing

REMOVAL AND INSTALLATION

1. Remove driveshaft.
2. Disconnect the center universal joint.
3. Remove the nut holding the center yoke and remove the yoke. Remove the center bearing bracket from the bearing by prying on it.
4. Remove the center bearing using a gear puller.

NOTE: The center bracket and the mounting rubber are welded together and must be replaced as a unit.

To assemble:

5. Fill the bearing grease cavity with multipurpose grease.
6. Partially insert the center bearing into the shaft and install the bracket to the bearing.
7. Verify that the bracket mounting rubber is properly fitted in the bearing groove.

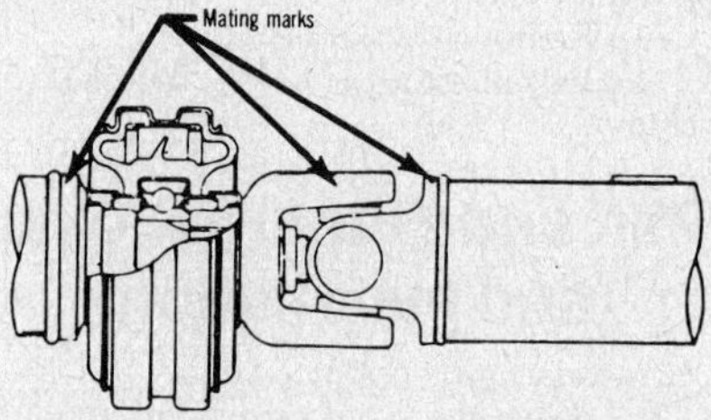

When installing center bearing align three mating marks
(© Chrysler Corp.)

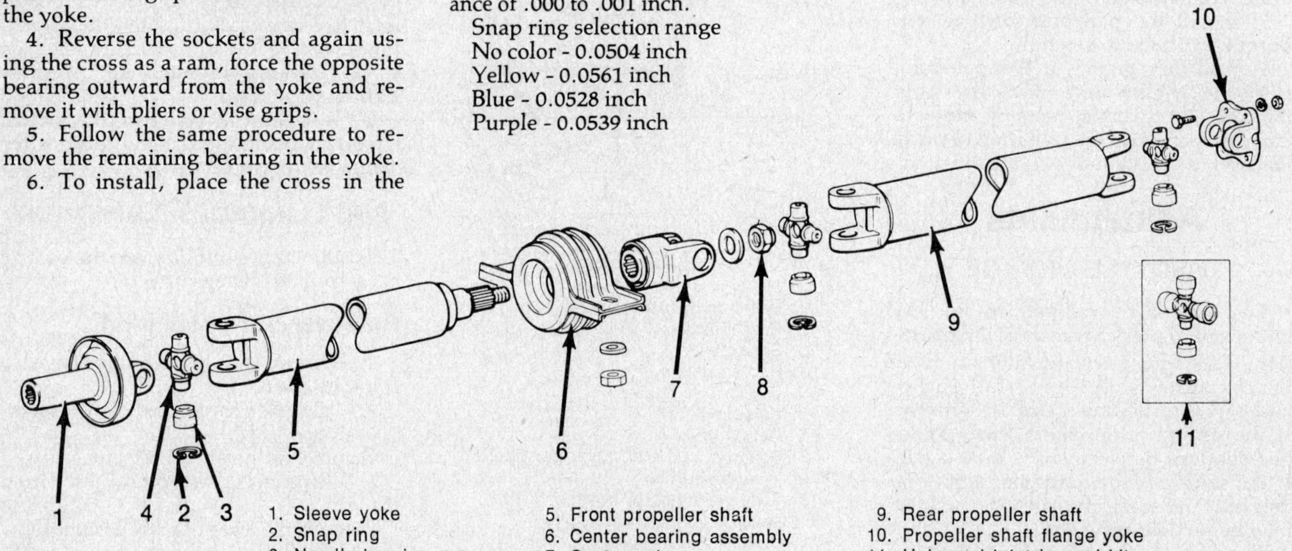

1. Sleeve yoke
2. Snap ring
3. Needle bearing
4. Universal joint journal
5. Front propeller shaft
6. Center bearing assembly
7. Center yoke
8. Center yoke attaching nut
9. Rear propeller shaft
10. Propeller shaft flange yoke
11. Universal joint journal kit

Exploded view of driveshaft
(© Chrysler Corp.)

8. Refit the center yoke, making sure you align the notch on the yoke with the notch on the front propeller shaft. Replace the attaching nut and tighten to 116-159 ft-lb.

9. Replace the center universal joint, making sure you align the notch on the rear propeller shaft with the notch on the yoke.

10. Install the driveshaft.

***NOTE:** The manufacturer suggests that a new center yoke locking nut be used when the center bearing is removed.*

DRIVE AXLE

Axle Shaft, Bearing and Seal

REMOVAL AND INSTALLATION

1. Jack up the vehicle and support it on stands.

2. Remove the rear wheels and brake drums.

3. Disconnect the brake line from the wheel cylinder and plug it to prevent fluid loss.

4. Remove the four nuts behind the brake backing plate holding the bearing case to the axle housing assembly.

5. Remove the braking plate, bearing case and the axle shaft as an assembly.

***NOTE:** It may be necessary to use a slide hammer to remove the assembly.*

6. Remove the "O" ring and the bearing preload shims. Save the preload shims, as you will need them for reasembly.

7. Remove the oil seal with a hooked slide hammer.

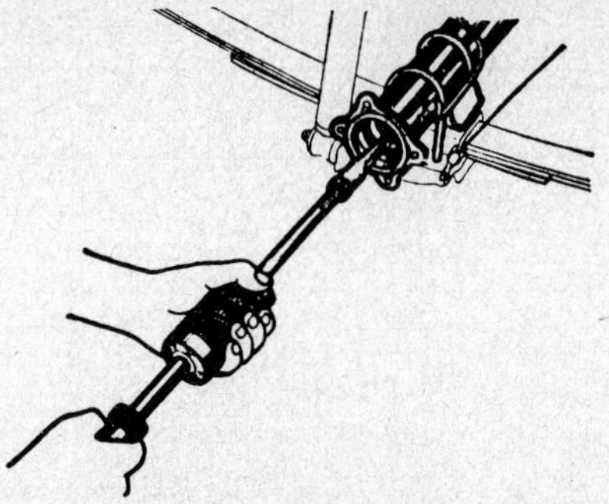

Removing the oil seal
(© Chrysler Corp.)

8. To remove the axle shaft bearing, remove the notched locknut. This calls for a special tool, but you should be able to use a brass drift to knock it loose.

9. Remove the lock washer and plain washer.

10. Screw the lock nut back on to the axle shaft about three turns.

11. It will be necessary to fabricate a metal plate that fits over the axle shaft and butts the lock nut. Drill four holes in the plate that align with the four bearing case studs and fit the plate. Refit two nuts and washers to the bearing case studs diagonally across from each other and tighten them evenly to free the bearing case and the bearing.

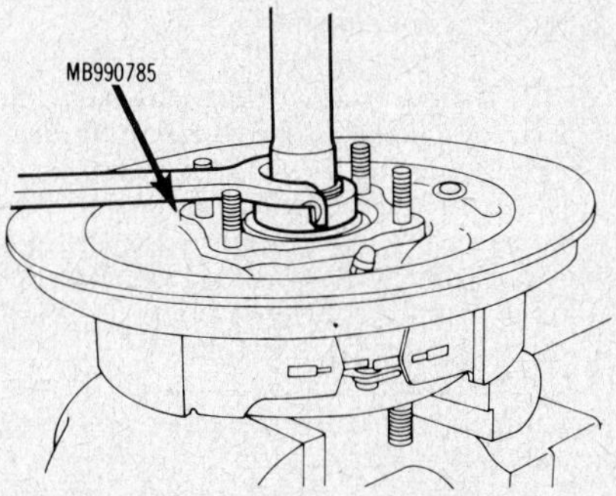

Removing the axle shaft lock nut
(© Chrysler Corp.)

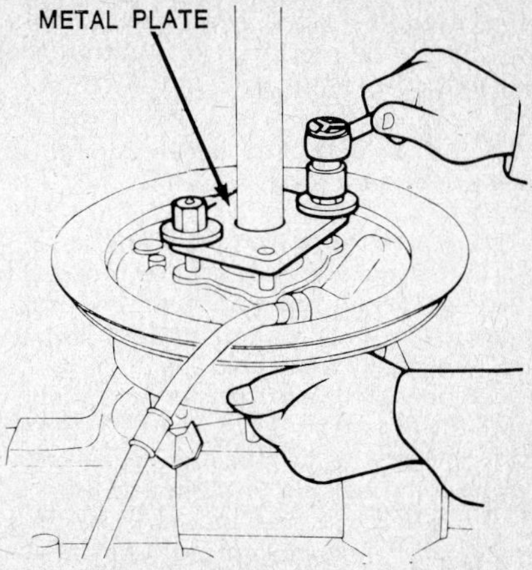

Removing axle bearing—fabricate metal plate indicated in picture
(© Chrysler Corp.)

12. Use a hammer and drift to remove the bearing outer race from the bearing case.

13. Remove the outer oil seal from the bearing case.

To assemble:

***NOTE:** Always use new "O" rings and check the condition of all oil seals and dust covers.*

14. Apply grease to the outer surface on the bearing outer race and to the lip of the outer oil seal, and drive them into the bearing case from each side.

15. Slide the bearing case and bear-

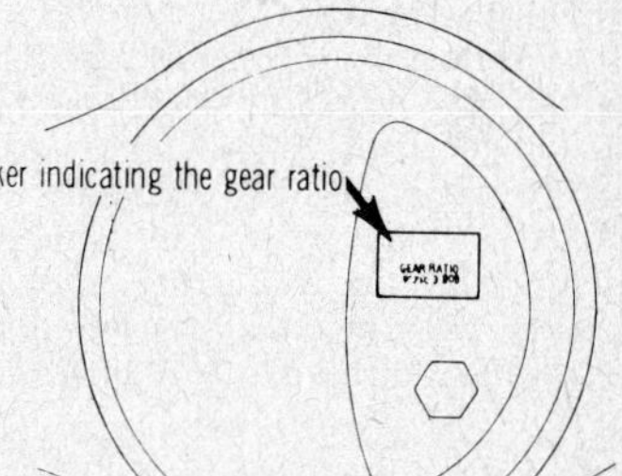

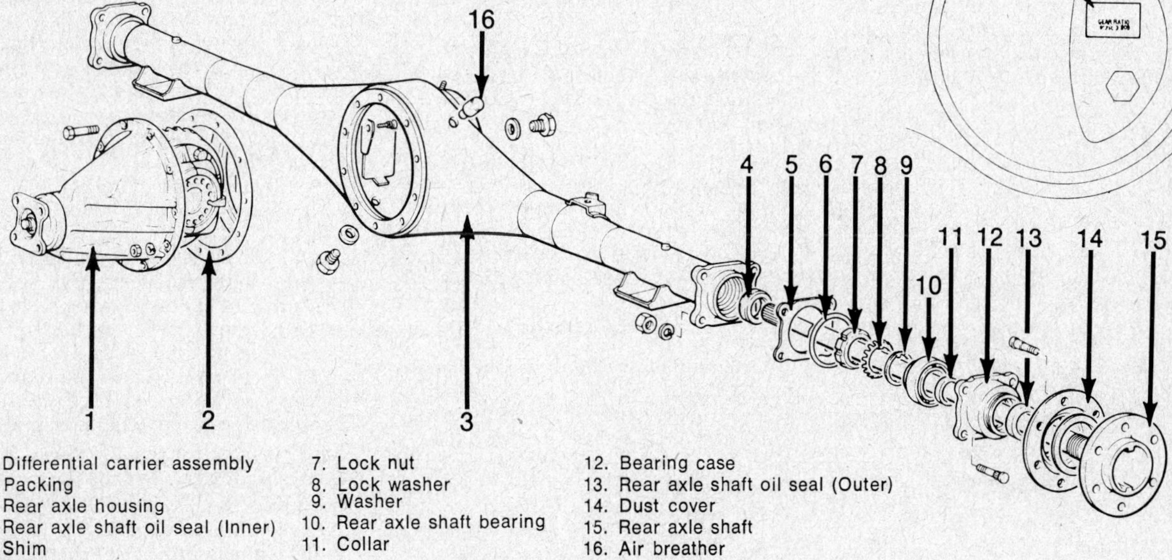

1. Differential carrier assembly
2. Packing
3. Rear axle housing
4. Rear axle shaft oil seal (Inner)
5. Shim
6. O-ring
7. Lock nut
8. Lock washer
9. Washer
10. Rear axle shaft bearing
11. Collar
12. Bearing case
13. Rear axle shaft oil seal (Outer)
14. Dust cover
15. Rear axle shaft
16. Air breather

Exploded view of drive axle assembly
(© Chrysler Corp.)

ing over the rear axle shaft. Apply grease on the bearing rollers and fit the inner race by pressing it into place.

CAUTION: Be careful not to damage or deform the dust cover.

16. Pack the bearing with grease.
17. Install the washer, the crowned lock washer and the lock nut in the order just given and tighten the lock nut to 130-159 ft-lb. if possible.
18. Bend the tab on the lock washer into the groove on the lock nut. If the tab and the groove do not line up, slightly tighten the lock nut until they do.
19. Drive the new inner oil seal into place after greasing it and refit the assembly. Be sure to fit the "O" ring and shim and apply silicone rubber sealant to the bearing case face.

NOTE: Be sure to bleed the brakes before road testing!

To adjust preload:

1. Begin with the left side rear axle assembly and insert a 0.04 in. shim between the bearing case and the axle shaft housing. Tighten the four nuts to 36-43 ft-lb.

NOTE: Be sure to fit the "O" ring and apply sealant.

2. Install the right side axle assembly into the right side housing without its shim and "O" ring. Tighten the four nuts to 0.4 ft-lb.
3. Using a flat blade feeler gauge, measure the gap between the bearing case and the axle housing face. It should range between 0.002-0.008 in. Record the measurement.
4. Remove the axle shaft and select a shim that is the same thickness as the gap between the faces just measured, plus a shim with a thickness from 0.002-0.0079 in. and install them on the housing. Fit the "O" ring and apply sealant. Fit the axle assembly and tighten the four nuts to 36-43 ft-lb.

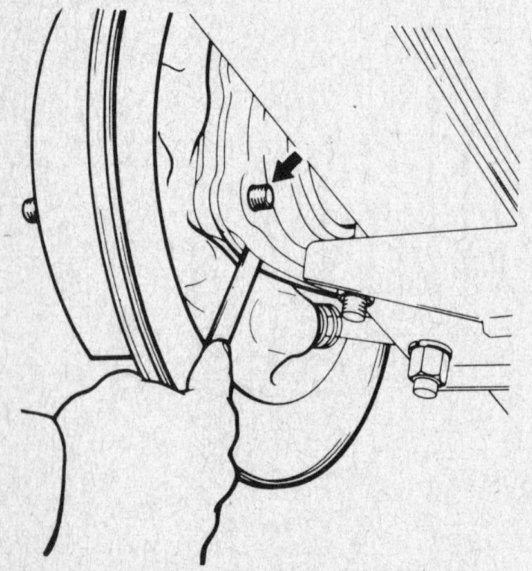

Measuring clearance between bearing case and axle housing face
(© Chrysler Corp.)

AXLE SHAFT ASSEMBLY PRELOAD SHIMS

Part No.	Thickness of shim mm (in).
MB092491	0.05 ± 0.005 (.0020 ± .0002)
MB092492	0.10 ± 0.010 (.0040 ± .0004)
MB092493	0.20 ± 0.015 (.0079 ± .0006)
MB092494	0.30 ± 0.020 (.0118 ± .0008)
MB092495	0.50 ± 0.025 (.0197 ± .0010)
MB092496	1.00 ± 0.040 (.0394 ± .0016)
MB092497	1.50 ± 0.050 (.0591 ± .0020)
MB092498	2.00 ± 0.055 (.0787 ± .0022)

5. Assemble remaining components. Be sure to bleed the brakes!

Rear Axle Assembly

REMOVAL AND INSTALLATION

1. Loosen the rear wheel hub nuts and jack up the truck. Support the truck on jack stands placed forward of the rear spring front brackets.
2. Remove the rear wheels and remove the propeller shaft.

NOTE: Support the differential housing with a jack to keep a slight amount of pressure on the springs.

3. Loosen the joint between the brake hose and the brake line and remove the stops to disconnect the brake hose. Plug the lines to prevent fluid loss.
4. Disconnect the rear cable of the parking brake at the balancer (refer to brake section for procedure.
5. Remove the shock absorbers, and the spring seats after removing the spring U-bolts.
6. Remove the spring shackle pin nuts and the shackle plate.

CAUTION: The axle assembly will be supported solely by the jack under the differential case. Be careful not to allow it to drop.

7. With an assistant holding the axle assembly, slowly lower it to the ground.

Installation is the reverse of removal. Bleed the brakes after assembly.

For installation of the rear suspension, see Rear Suspension section.

OVERHAUL

Differential overhaul requires many special tools and access to a range of preload shims and other dealer equipment. If you have never overhauled a rear axle assembly before, it would be wise to let your dealer perform this operation for you.

1. Remove the lock bolts and plates holding the side bearing nut in place.
2. Remove the side bearing nuts with the special adjusting spanner no. MB990201.
3. Remove the carrier caps and pry out the differential.
4. Pull off the differential side bearings.

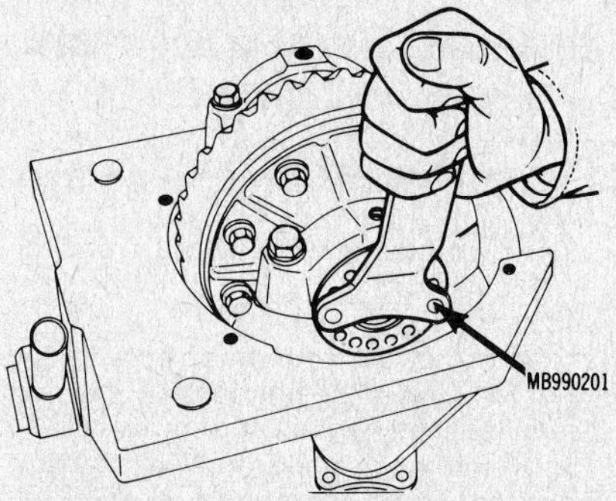

Removing side bearing nuts with special spanner
(© Chrysler Corp.)

NOTE: Be sure to keep the right and left bearings and shims separated.

5. Loosen the ring gear mounting bolts in diagonal sequence. Remove the ring gear.
6. Drive the pinion shaft lock pin out from the rear of the ring gear using a punch, and remove the pinion shaft.
7. Remove the side gears with their spacers. Keep left and right side gears and spacers separate.
8. Hold the end yoke and remove the pinion lock nut.
9. Remove the end yoke.
10. Tap the end of the drive pinion shaft with a plastic hammer and force out the drive pinion along with its adjusting shim, the rear inner race, the drive pinion spacer and the preload adjusting shim. The rear bearing inner race can be pressed off the pinion shaft.
11. Remove the front and rear pinion bearing outer races. The front race should be removed with its oil seal.

NOTE: Do not reuse the old oil seal. If the unit is to be assembled using no replacement parts except oil seals, the same spacers and shims can generally be used. If either pinion bearing or ring gear and drive pinion are being replaced, new shims should be used. Only replace the drive pinion and ring gear in matched sets.

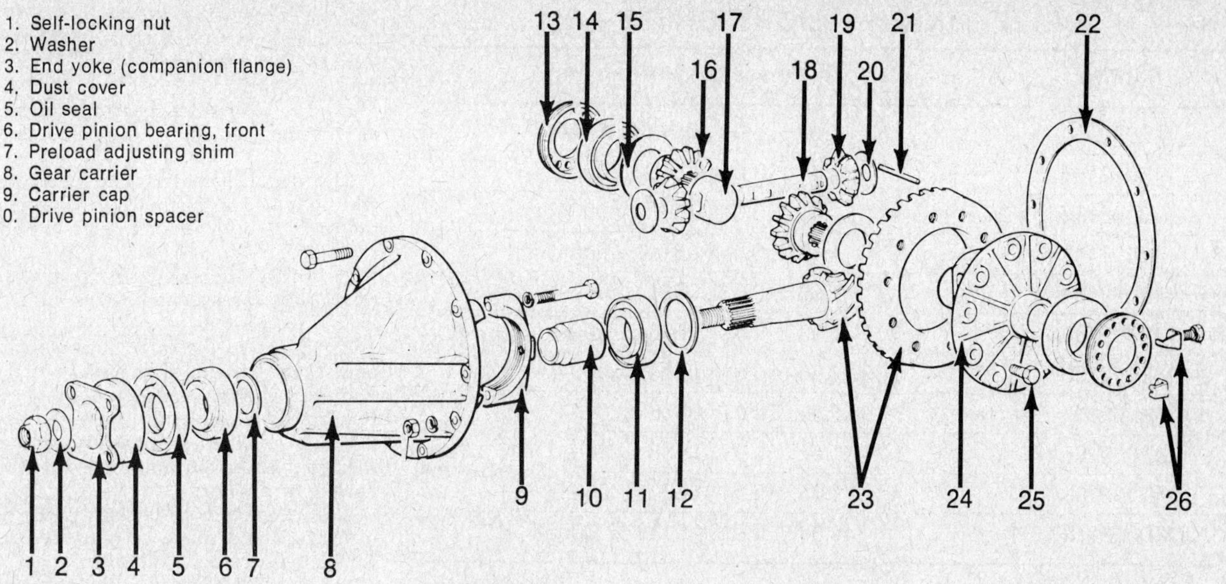

1. Self-locking nut
2. Washer
3. End yoke (companion flange)
4. Dust cover
5. Oil seal
6. Drive pinion bearing, front
7. Preload adjusting shim
8. Gear carrier
9. Carrier cap
10. Drive pinion spacer
11. Drive pinion bearing, rear
12. Drive pinion height adjusting shim
13. Side bearing nut
14. Side bearing
15. Side gear thrust spacer
16. Side gear
17. Center block
18. Pinion shaft
19. Pinion gear
20. Pinion washer
21. Lock pin
22. Packing
23. Final gear set
24. Differential case
25. Lock bolt
26. Lock plate

Exploded view of rear end drive gears
(© Chrysler Corp.)

Assemble the side gears in the differential case. Install the spacers in the same positions they were in when removed.

12. With the washers, insert both differential gears at the same time to mesh with the side gears. Insert the pinion shaft.

13. Measure the backlash of the differential pinion gears and the side gears. Backlash should be within 0.002-0.005 in. If not, replace the side gear spacers with the appropriate ones listed below.

14. Align the differential drive pinion shaft with the lock pin hole in the differential case and drive the pin in from the rear of the case. Stake the pin with a small pointed punch to secure it.

15. Remove the old adhesive from the ring gear mounting bolts and apply new adhesive. Snug up all bolts then tighten them on a criss-cross pattern of 58-65 ft-lb.

***NOTE:** To allow the adhesive to set on the bolt threads, keep the unit stationary for about an hour.*

16. Press the front and rear bearing outer races into the gear carrier.

***CAUTION:** Make sure that the races do not tilt and that they sit fully in the case.*

Look at the top face of the drive pinion (gear side). If there is an etched number, such as −0,−1,−2,+1,+2, etc., Complete step 17. If not, skip step 17 and go on to step 18.

17. Insert a shim between the drive pinion and rear bearing. If the original gear set is being replaced, the original shims may be used. If a new gear set is being installed, calculate the shim dimension in the following manner. Assuming the pinion height before disassembly is correct, subtract the new pinion variation marking (on the pinion head) from the old pinion variation marking. If the answer is positive, add shims in the corresponding amount. If the answer is negative, subtract shims in the corresponding amount. This will produce a reasonable starting point for assembly. If the shim choice is proved incorrect, the entire pinion must be disassembled, and the shim changed accordingly. The etched marking on the face of the pinion represents a positive or negative variation from the standard in millimeters.

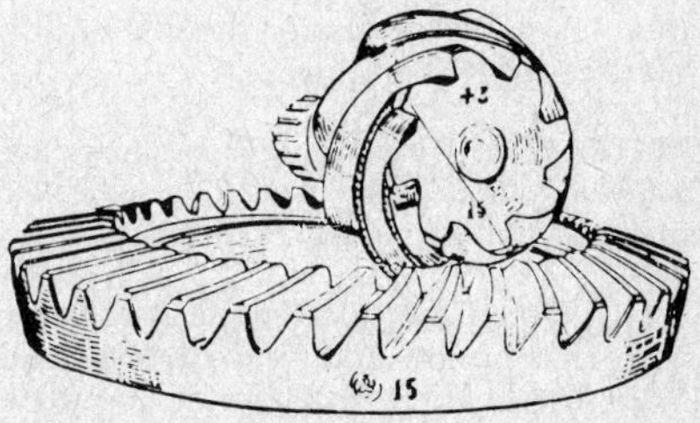

Pinion and ring gear markings
(© Chrysler Corp.)

***NOTE:** If the original gear set is being reused in the differential case, the original shims may be used.*

18. If the drive pinion has no marking on its gear-side face, it will be necessary to obtain two D-50/Plymouth Arrow dealer special tools; MB990819 and MB990552. Install parts marked 1,-6,2,7,3,4, and 5 in the illustration labeled "Measuring Pinion Height (Clearance)" with special tool MB990819 into the carrier case. Grad-

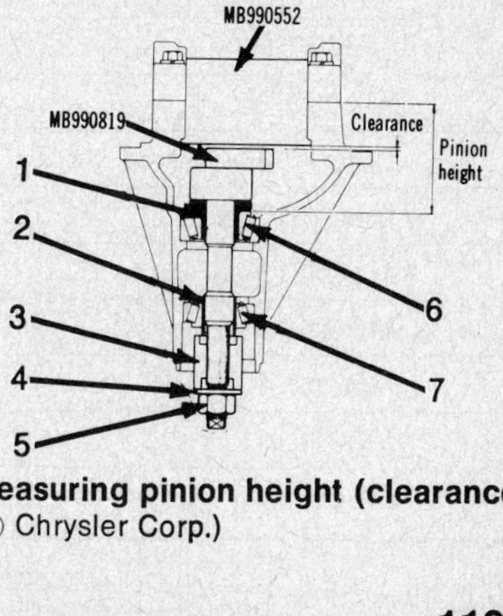

Measuring pinion height (clearance)
(© Chrysler Corp.)

SIDE GEAR SPACERS

Part No.	Thickness of spacer mm (in.)
MB092034	$0.8^{-0.08}_{-0.17}$ ($.0315^{-.0031}_{-.0067}$)
MB092035	$0.8^{-0.18}_{-0.27}$ ($.0315^{-.0071}_{-.0106}$)
MB092036	$0.8^{0}_{-0.07}$ ($.0315^{0}_{-.0028}$)

DRIVE PINION HEIGHT SHIMS

Part No.	Thickness of shim mm (in.)
MB092160	1.38 ± 0.01 (.0543 ± .0004)
MB092161	1.41 ± 0.01 (.0555 ± .0004)
MB092162	1.44 ± 0.01 (.0567 ± .0004)
MB092163	1.47 ± 0.01 (.0579 ± .0004)
MB092164	1.50 ± 0.01 (.0591 ± .0004)
MB092165	1.53 ± 0.01 (.0603 ± .0004)
MB092166	1.56 ± 0.01 (.0614 ± .0004)
MB092167	1.59 ± 0.01 (.0626 ± .0004)
MB092168	1.62 ± 0.01 (.0638 ± .0004)
MB092169	1.65 ± 0.01 (.0650 ± .0004)
MB092170	0.30 ± 0.013 (.0118 ± .0005)

ually tighten the nut to produce 6-9 in-lb. without the oil seal. Fit special tool MB990552 in the differential caps and replace the caps on the case. Measure the clearance between the two special tools (see illustration) and select a shim of an equivalent thickness to the clearance to make the pinion height within tolerance of ± 0.0012 in.

NOTE: If the pinion height has to be adjusted by more than 0.0650 in. use two shims including one 0.0118 in. thick.

19. Install the selected shim between the drive pinion and the rear bearing. Press the bearing onto the drive pinion shaft.

20. Assemble the drive pinion in the case and torque the pinion nut gradually to 137-180 ft-lb. Check the pinion preload. With oil seal, it should be between 9-11 in.-lb. Without the oil seal, it should be 6-9 in.-lb. The preload shim selection ranges from 0.0118 to 0.0917 in.

21. If you have not already done so, apply a thin coat of grease to the drive pinion oil seal and insert it in the case. Refit the yoke and tighten to 137-180 ft-lb.

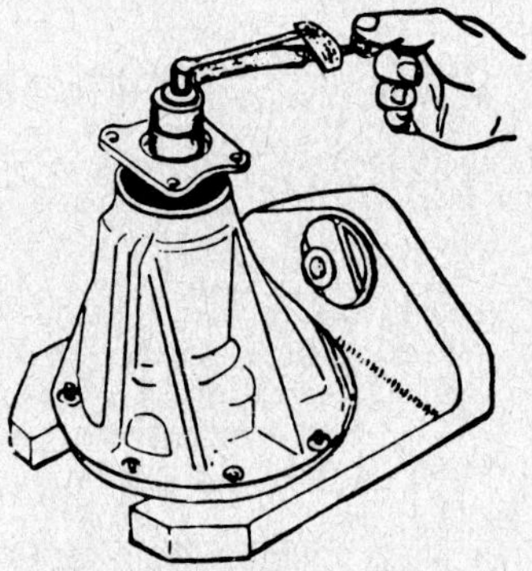

Measuring pinion preload
(© Chrysler Corp.)

22. Press the side bearings into the differential case and fit the case into the carrier.

23. Install the carrier caps with their mating marks in line with the marks on the carriers and finger tighten the four set bolts.

24. Install the side bearing nuts, and tighten the carrier cap bolts to 40-47 ft-lb.

25. Screw in the side bearing nuts to adjust the standard backlash value. Each nut should be tightened to 11 lb. Repeatedly loosen and tighten the bearing nuts to insure smooth operation, then tighten them until they become hard to turn.

26. Attach a dial indicator to the ring gear teeth and make certain the backlash is between 0.005-0.007 in.

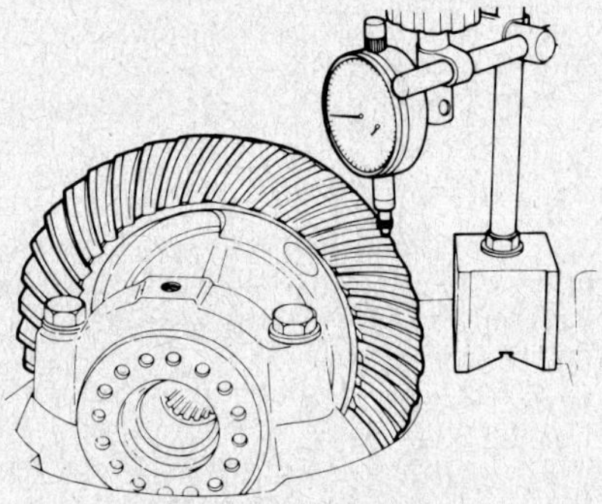

Backlash adjustment
(© Chrysler Corp.)

NOTE: If the backlash is less than the limit, loosen the bearing nut on the back side of the ring gear and tighten the bearing nut on the teeth side by the same amount.

27. After adjusting backlash, tighten the bearing nuts 1/2 pitch.

NOTE: One pitch is the space between two adjacent holes on the side of the bearing nut.

28. Again measure the backlash and install a one or two pronged lock plate, whichever lines up with the bearing nut holes. Tighten the lock plate bolts to 11-16 ft-lb.

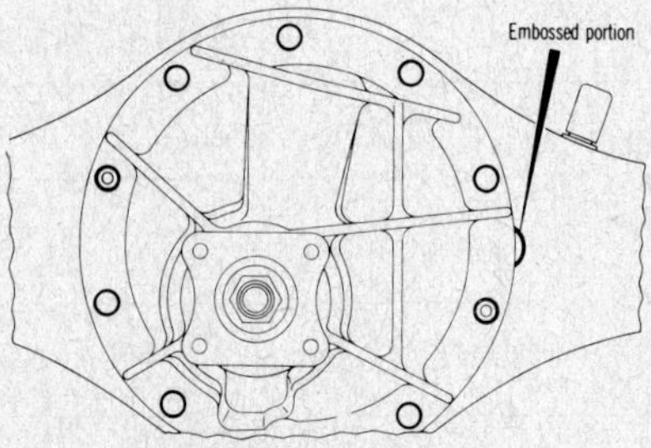

Installing the packing
(© Chrysler Corp.)

PINION BEARING PRELOAD SHIMS

Part No.	Thickness of shim mm (in.)
MB092130	0.30 ± 0.01 (.0118 ± .0004)
MB092131	2.00 ± 0.01 (.0787 ± .0004)
MB092132	2.03 ± 0.01 (.0799 ± .0004)
MB092133	2.06 ± 0.01 (.0811 ± .0004)
MB092134	2.09 ± 0.01 (.0823 ± .0004)
MB092135	2.12 ± 0.01 (.0835 ± .0004)
MB092136	2.15 ± 0.01 (.0846 ± .0004)
MB092137	2.18 ± 0.01 (.0858 ± .0004)
MB092138	2.21 ± 0.01 (.0870 ± .0004)
MB092139	2.24 ± 0.01 (.0882 ± .0004)
MB092140	2.27 ± 0.01 (.0894 ± .0004)
MB092141	2.30 ± 0.01 (.0906 ± .0004)
MB092142	2.33 ± 0.01 (.0917 ± .0004)

Proper tooth contact
(© Chrysler Corp.)

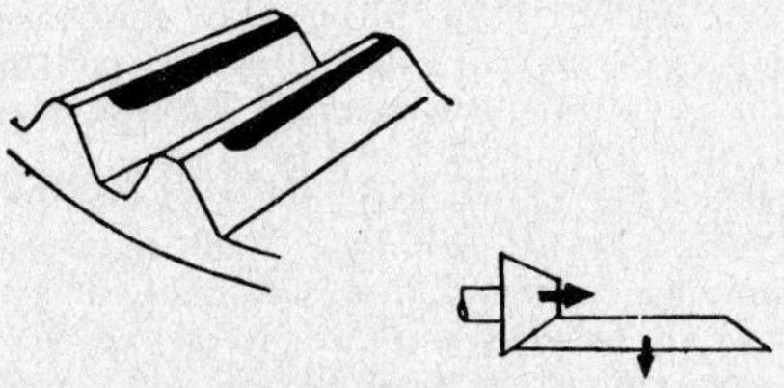

Face contact
(© Chrysler Corp.)

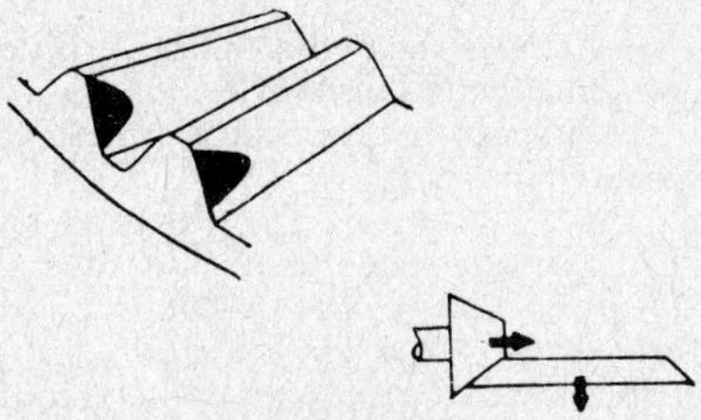

Heel contact
(© Chrysler Corp.)

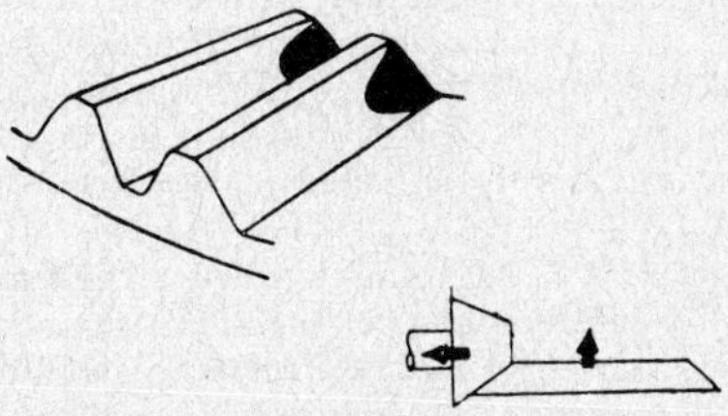

Toe contact
(© Chrysler Corp.)

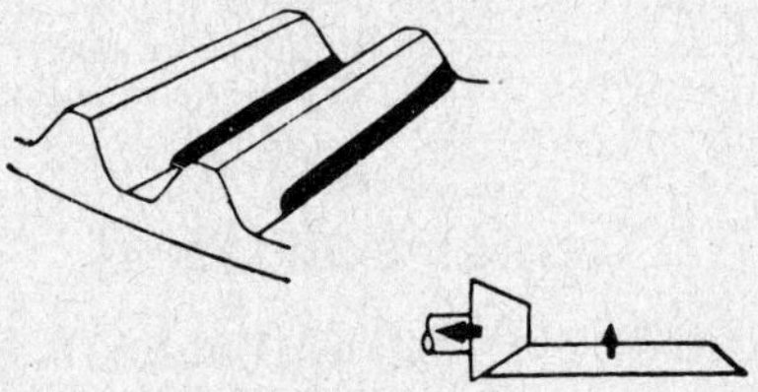

Flank contact
(© Chrysler Corp.)

29. Measure the ring gear runout in four or more spots. Runout should be 0.002 in. or less.
30. Make a ring gear tooth pattern check.
31. Apply gear oil to all moving parts and use sealant when assembling. Install the packing with the embossed portion at about 3 o'clock position on the axle housing.
32. Fit the differential and tighten the mounting nuts to 18-22 ft-lb.
33. Be sure to fill the rear axle with about 3 pints of gear oil before testing.

FRONT SUSPENSION

Coil Spring

REMOVAL AND INSTALLATION

1. Raise the front of the vehicle and support it on jack stands.
2. Remove the wheel.
3. Remove the shock absorber (see below for procedures).
4. Remove stabilizer and strut bar (see below for procedures).
5. Compress the coil spring with a spring compressor.
6. Remove the relay rod from the steering arm.
7. Remove the upper and lower ball joints using a ball joint remover.
8. Remove the coil spring.

Installation is the reverse of removal.

NOTE: The coil springs are color coded. The left side spring has a green band on it and the right side spring has a pink band on it. Do not mix the left and right springs.

9. Tighten the ball joint castle nuts to: upper, 43–65 ft-lb.; lower, 87–130 ft-lb.

Shock Absorbers

REMOVAL AND INSTALLATION

1. Raise the vehicle and support it on jack stands.
2. Remove the wheel.
3. Remove the double lock nuts at the top of the shock absorber along with the rubber washer and its metal caps.
4. Remove the two bolts at the bottom of the shock absorber and withdraw

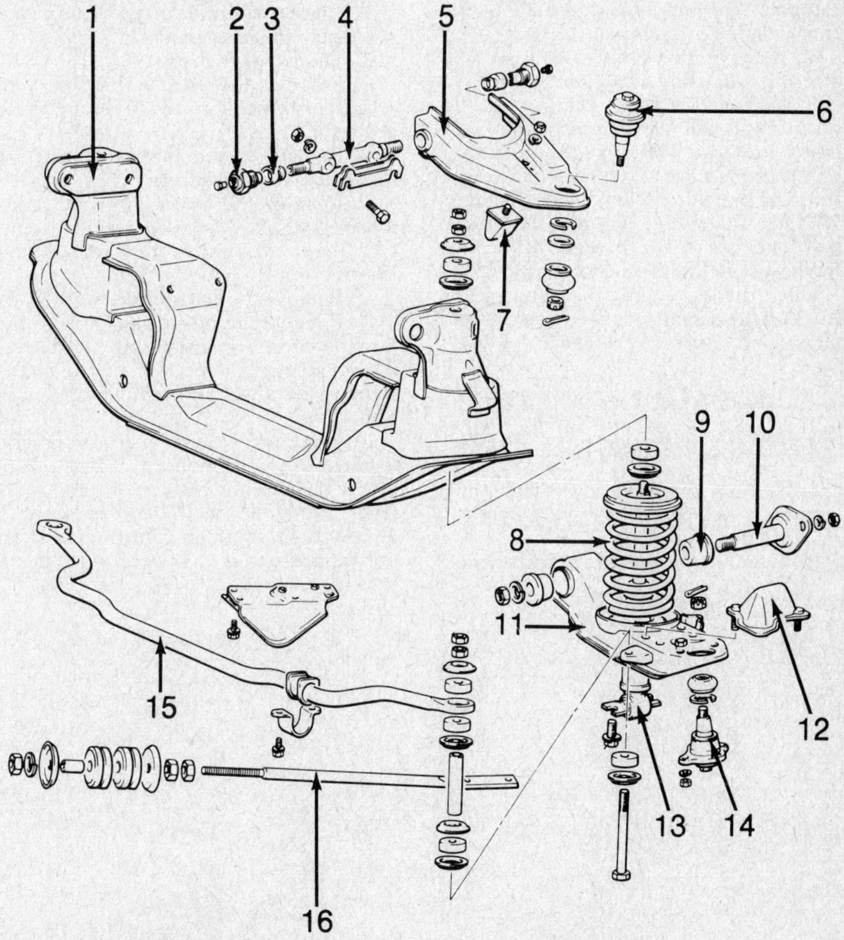

1. Crossmember
2. Pivot bushing
3. Dust seal
4. Upper arm shaft
5. Upper arm
6. Upper ball joint
7. Rebound stop
8. Front coil spring
9. Lower arm bushing
10. Lower arm shaft
11. Lower arm
12. Bump stop
13. Shock absorber
14. Lower ball joint
15. Stabilizer
16. Strut bar

Exploded view of front suspension
(© Chrysler Corp.)

the shock absorber through the bottom arm.

Installation is the reverse of removal.

5. Be sure to refit all of the rubber cushion washers and their metal caps in the correct order. Tighten the upper shock absorber nut to 9–13 ft-lb. and install the lock nut. Tighten the two lower shock absorber bolts to 6–9 ft-lb.

Steering Knuckle

REMOVAL AND INSTALLATION

1. Raise the vehicle and support it on jack stands.
2. Remove the wheel.
3. Remove the brake caliper assembly and the front hub assembly (see brake caliper and hub removal section, below).
4. Disconnect the stabilizer and strut bar from the lower arm (see stabilizer and strut bar removal section, below).
5. Remove the shock absorber and compress the coil spring (see above for shock absorber removal).
6. Remove the relay rod from the steering arm using a ball joint remover.
7. Remove the cotter pins and castle nuts from the steering knuckle ball joints, and using either a gear puller or a ball joint remover, free the ball joints from the knuckle. Remove the knuckle.

When installing, tighten the upper ball joint castle nut to 43–65 ft-lb. and the lower ball joint nut to 87–130 ft-lb. Tighten the tie rod end ball joint nut to 25–33 ft-lb. Fit new cotter keys. Installation is the reverse of removal.

Upper Control Arm

REMOVAL AND INSTALLATION

1. Jack up the front of the truck and support it on stands.
2. Remove the wheel.
3. Remove the shock absorber and compress the coil spring (see illustration).
4. Remove the cotter pin and castle nut from the upper ball joint.
5. Using a gear puller or ball joint remover, free the ball joint from the steering knuckle.
6. Remove the bolts holding the upper control arm to the crossmember and remove the control arm as an assembly.

NOTE: Save all of the adjustment shims from the upper control arm for reassembly.

Installation is the reverse of removal. Replace all camber adjustment shims behind the upper control arm. Observe the following torques: upper control arm to crossmember bolts, 40–54 ft-lb.; ball joint to knuckle, 43–65 ft-lb.

Lower Control Arm

REMOVAL AND INSTALLATION

1. Raise the front of the truck and support it on jackstands.
2. Remove the wheel.
3. Remove the shock absorber and compress the coil spring (see above for procedure).
4. Remove the stabilizer and strut bar (see below for procedures).
5. Remove the cotter pin and castle nut from the lower ball joint and separate the ball joint from the steering knuckle using a ball joint remover.
6. Remove the coil spring.
7. Remove the nut in the front of the lower control arm mounting shaft. Remove the nuts at the rear of the shaft. Remove the shaft and remove the lower arm.

Installation is the reverse of removal. Tighten the front mounting shaft nut to 40–54 ft-lb. Tighten the rear nut to 6–9 ft-lb. Tighten the ball joint castle nut to 87–130 ft-lb. Tighten control arm shaft only after truck is on the ground.

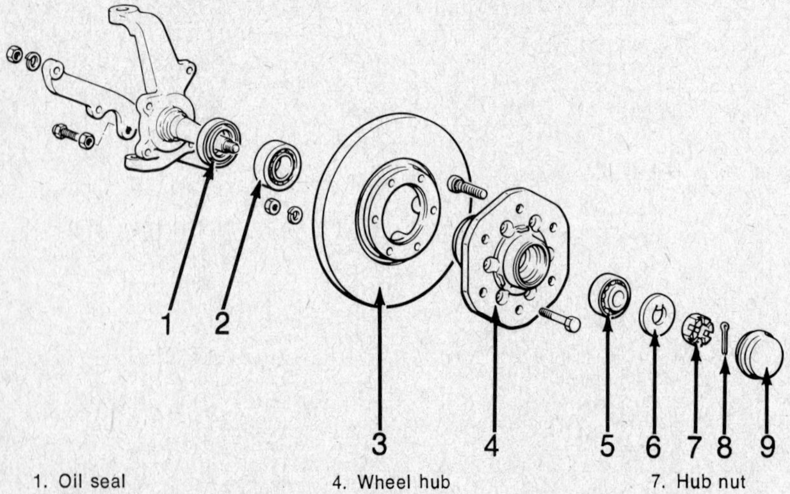

1. Oil seal
2. Wheel bearing (inner)
3. Brake disc
4. Wheel hub
5. Wheel bearing (outer)
6. Washer
7. Hub nut
8. Cotter pin
9. Hub cap

Steering knuckle and hub assembly
(© Chrysler Corp.)

Stabilizer and Strut Bar

REMOVAL AND INSTALLATION

1. Raise the vehicle and support it on jack stands.
2. Remove the wheels.
3. Disconnect the stabilizer and the strut bars from the lower control arms.

CAUTION: When removing the strut bar, loosen the adjusting nut at the other end of the bar before loosening the bolts at the control arm.

NOTE: Before removing stabilizer bar, note the order and direction of the rubber cushion washers and their metal caps for reassembly.

4. Remove the nut and spacers at the threaded end of the strut bar and remove the bar.
5. Remove the two stabilizer brackets and remove the stabilizer.

Installation is the reverse of removal. Observe the following.

There is a letter "L" on the left side strut bar, do not confuse it with the right side bar. The rubber cushions on the front of the strut bar are different; the cushion with a protruded lip is mounted at the front and the regular cushion is mounted at the back.

When installing the strut bar, set the standard distance (A) in illustration to 3.8 in. from the tip of the threaded end of the bar to the rear face of the rear double nut. Lower the vehicle to the ground and tighten all nuts and bolts.

CAUTION: Make sure you check the front wheel alignment after installing the strut bar in order to obtain the correct caster, and then re-adjust the distance (A) (see illustration) as required.

When installing both ends of the stabilizer, tighten the first nut (adjustment nut) to obtain length (B) (see illustration) 0.87–0.94 in., then tighten the lock nut to 18–25 ft-lb.

Upper Ball Joint

REMOVAL AND INSTALLATION

1. Remove the upper control arm from the vehicle (see above for procedure).
2. Remove the ball joint dust seal by prying up the dust seal ring evenly with a screwdriver.
3. Remove the snap ring using snap ring pliers.
4. Using a ball joint remover and installer tool, press off the ball joint.

NOTE: A minimum of 2200 lb. pressure will be required to remove the upper ball joint from the control arm.

5. To install the ball joint, press it into the burred hole, with the ball joint and upper arm mating marks aligned.

6. Make sure the ball joint snap ring is a tight fit and install the dust cover.

Lower Ball Joint

REMOVAL AND INSTALLATION

1. Jack up the vehicle and remove the wheel.
2. Remove the coil spring (see above for procedures).
3. If you have not already done so, free the lower ball joint from the steering knuckle using a ball joint remover. Remove the dust cover from the ball joint.
4. Unbolt and remove the ball joint.
5. Installation is the reverse of removal. Install the ball joint with its tab side pointing to the rear of the vehicle. Tighten the ball joint to lower control arm bolts to 22–30 ft-lb.

REAR SUSPENSION

Leaf Springs

REMOVAL AND INSTALLATION

1. Loosen the wheel nuts and jack up the vehicle. Support the frame on jack stands and lower the jack under the rear axle housing.

CAUTION: Do not put jack stands under axle housing shafts.

2. Remove the parking break cable clamp from the leaf spring.
3. Disconnect the upper end of the shock absorber and the lower end at the spring U-bolt seat.

NOTE: If the shock absorber is not going to be replaced or serviced, leave the lower end on the spring U-bolt seat.

4. Loosen the U-bolt nuts and jack up the rear axle housing until it clears the spring seat. Remove the spring seat.
5. Remove the front spring pin and the rear shackle pin and remove the spring.

Installation is the reverse of removal. Observe the following:

6. Install the spring front eye bushings from both sides of the eye with the bushing flanges facing out. Insert the spring pin assembly from the wheel side and secure it to the hanger bracket with its bolt. Temporarily tighten the spring pin nut.
7. Repeat step 6 on the rear spring mount.
8. Align the center of the U-bolt seat with the center bolt hole in the spring. Tighten the U-bolts to 47–54 ft-lb.

NOTE: Tighten the nuts on the U-bolts until all of the U-bolt threads protrude evenly.

Tighten the spring pins and shackle pins to 22–33 ft-lb.

Shock Absorbers

REMOVAL AND INSTALLATION

1. Jack up the vehicle and remove the wheel.
2. Unbolt the top and bottom of the shock absorber and remove.

Installation is the reverse of removal. Tighten the shock absorber upper and lower mounting nuts to 13–18 ft-lb.

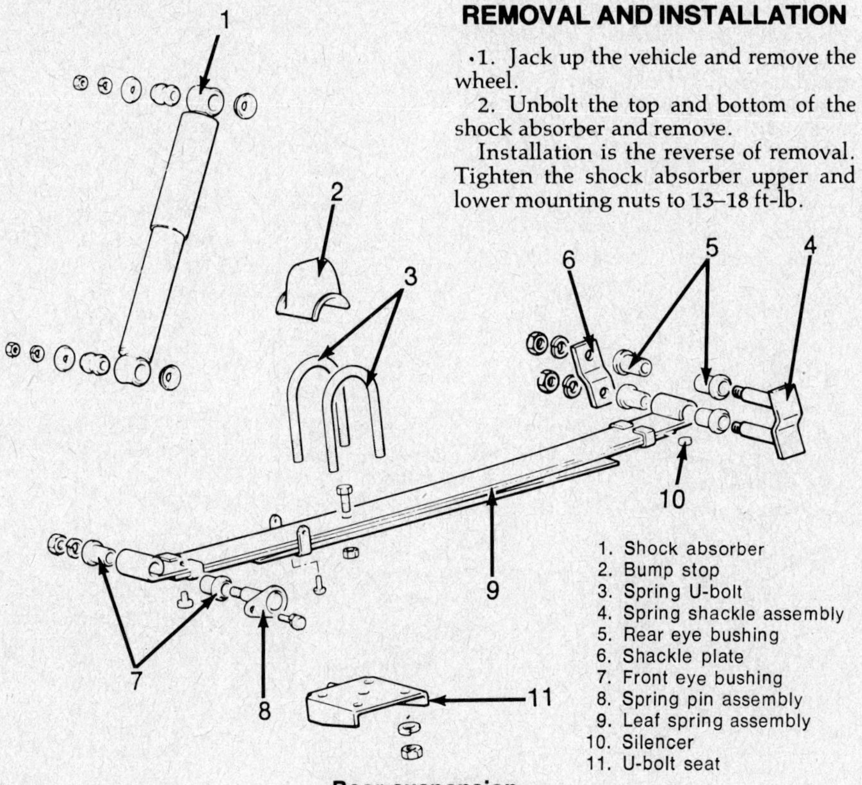

Rear suspension
(© Chrysler Corp.)

STEERING

Steering Wheel

REMOVAL AND INSTALLATION

1. Pry off the steering wheel center foam pad.
2. Remove the steering wheel retaining nut.
3. Using a steering wheel puller, remove the wheel.
4. Be sure the front wheels are in a straight ahead position. Reverse the removal procedure for installation.

Steering Column

REMOVAL AND INSTALLATION

1. Remove the air cleaner. Match mark the column shaft on the steering gear shaft.
2. Remove the clamp bolt which holds the steering column shaft on the steering gear shaft.

NOTE: On vehicles with air conditioning, step 2 must be done from under the truck.

3. Remove the horn pad and steering wheel retaining nut, then remove the steering wheel using a puller.
4. Loosen the tilt lock knob and lower the steering column fully.
5. Remove the steering column cover and disconnect the column wiring under the dashboard.
6. Remove the five bolts holding the base of the column at the fire wall.
7. Remove the four bolts holding the tilt column and remove the steering column from the vehicle.

Installation is the reverse of removal. Align the match marks on the steering column shaft and the steering gear shaft and couple the shafts before installing any bolts. Tighten the clamp bolt to 15–18 ft-lb.

Ignition Switch/Lock

REMOVAL AND INSTALLATION

1. Remove the column cover.
2. Cut a notch in the lock bracket bolt head with a hack saw.
3. Remove the lock bolts.
4. Disconnect the ignition harness and remove the switch/lock as a unit.
5. To remove the ignition switch, remove the screw holding it on the harness side and pull out the switch.

Installation is the reverse of removal.

NOTE: The steering wheel upper lock bracket and bolts should be replaced with new parts when the unit is installed.

Before fully tightening the screw in the back of the ignition switch, insert the key and make sure the switch works smoothly.

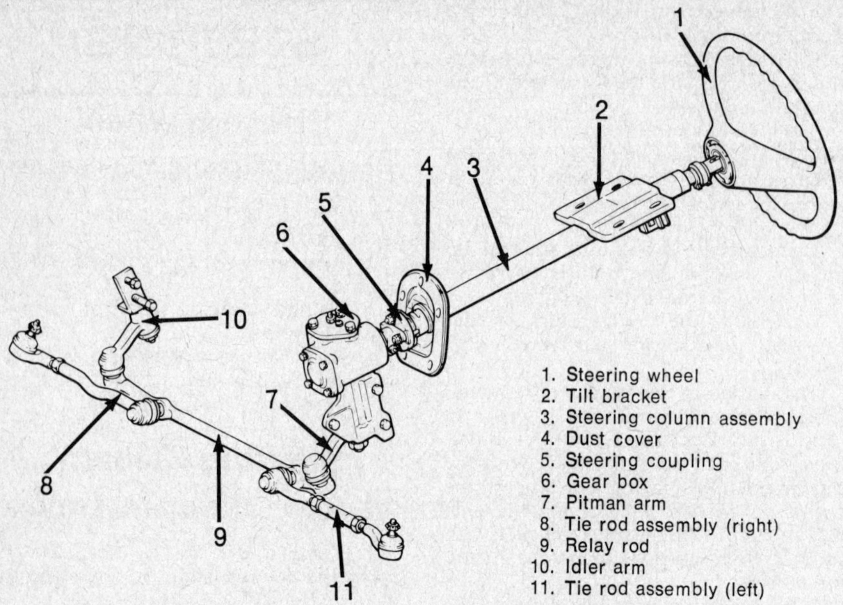

1. Steering wheel
2. Tilt bracket
3. Steering column assembly
4. Dust cover
5. Steering coupling
6. Gear box
7. Pitman arm
8. Tie rod assembly (right)
9. Relay rod
10. Idler arm
11. Tie rod assembly (left)

Manual steering column and gear assembly
(© Chrysler Corp.)

Turn Signal Switch

REMOVAL AND INSTALLATION

1. Remove the steering wheel (see above for procedure).
2. Put the tilt handle in its lowest position.
3. Remove the upper and lower column covers.
4. Remove the wiring harness band clip and disconnect the harness.
5. Remove the switch.

Installation is the reverse of removal with the following notes.

6. Make sure the column switch aligns with the steering shaft center.
7. Place the wiring harness along the column tube as close as possible to the center line. Be sure to replace the adjustable wiring harness bands.

Steering Linkage

REMOVAL AND INSTALLATION

1. Jack up the vehicle and support it on stands.
2. Remove the cotter pins and castle nuts holding the tie rod ends to the steering arms and the relay rod, and free the tie rods using either a suitable gear puller or a ball joint remover.
3. Unbolt and remove the relay rod in the same manner.
4. To remove the idler arm, remove the two bolts holding it to the frame and pull it out.

NOTE: The outer tie rod end has a left hand thread and the inner tie rod has a right handed thread on the driver's side.

Installation is the reverse of removal. Tighten all tie rod end nuts and relay rod nuts to 25-33 ft-lbs.

Manual Steering

GEAR BOX

Removal and Installation

1. Remove the clamp bolt connecting the sterring shaft with the sterring gear housing mainshaft.
2. Disconnect the tie rod and pitman arm from the relay rod using a ball joint remover or gear puller.
3. Remove the three bolts holding the gear box to the frame and remove the gear box from under the vehicle.

Installation is the reverse of removal. Tighten the pitman arm to relay rod nut to 94-109 ft-lb., and the tie rod socket to relay rod to 29-33 ft-lb.

Overhaul and Adjustments

1. Remove the gear box from the vehicle.
2. Remove the nut holding the pitman arm on the cross shaft and using a gear puller, pull the arm from the shaft.
3. Before disassembling any further, record the starting preload of the mainshaft as a guide for reassembly.
4. Loosen the lock nut on the cross shaft adjusting bolt and turn the bolt slightly counterclockwise. Remove the cover bolts.
5. Lift the cover up slightly and turn the adjusting bolt in until it unfastens from the cover and remove the cover.
6. Turn the cross shaft until its teeth will fit through the cover hole and pull it out of the gear housing.

NOTE: Use care not to damage the cross shaft splines and the oil seal when removing the cross shaft.

7. Measure the main shaft starting preload with the cross shaft removed.
8. Loosen the end cover attaching bolts and remove the end cover and shim.

NOTE: Keep the shim for reassembly.

9. Gently pull out the main shaft, ball nut assembly and the bearings.

CAUTION: Never attempt to disassemble the main shaft and ball nut assembly.

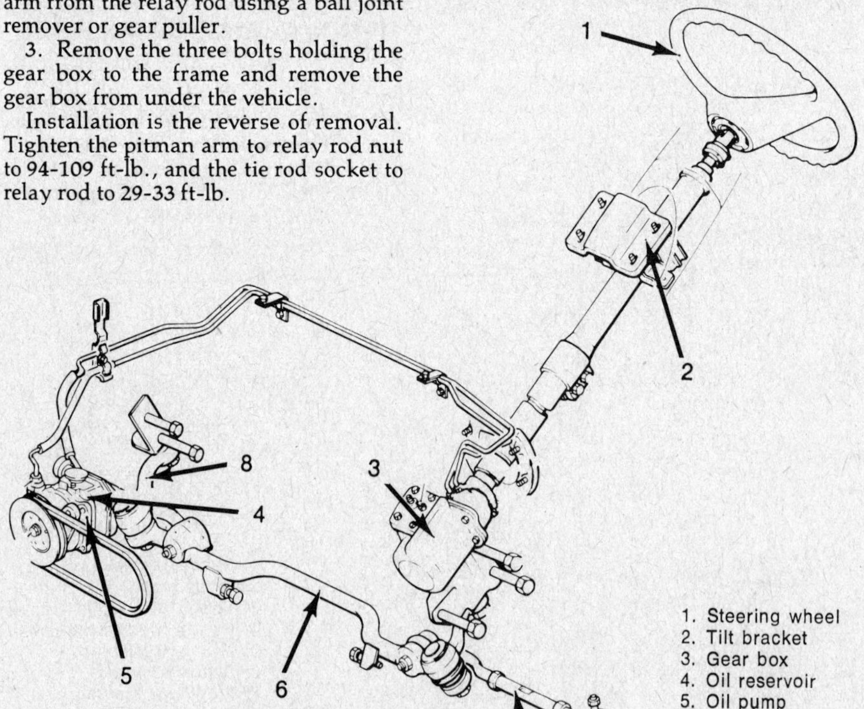

1. Steering wheel
2. Tilt bracket
3. Gear box
4. Oil reservoir
5. Oil pump
6. Relay rod
7. Tie rod
8. Idler arm

Power steering column and assembly
(© Chrysler Corp.)

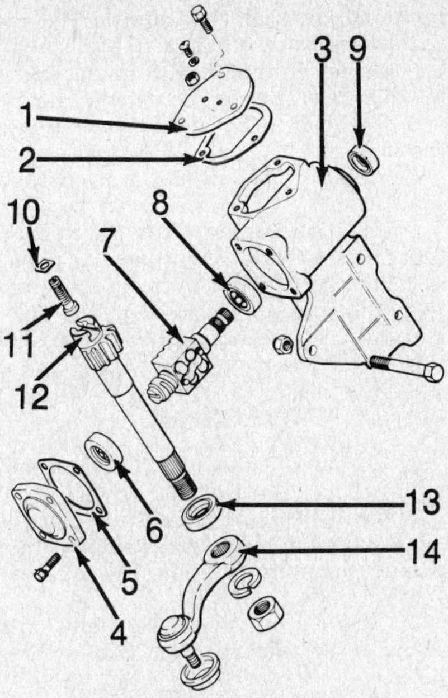

1. Gear housing upper cover
2. Packing
3. Gear housing
4. Gear housing end cover
5. Mainshaft adjusting shim
6. Mainshaft bearing
7. Mainshaft assembly
8. Mainshaft bearing
9. Mainshaft oil seal
10. Gear adjusting spacer
11. Gear adjusting bolt
12. Cross shaft
13. Cross shaft oil seal
14. Pitman arm

Exploded view of manual steering gear
(© Chrysler Corp.)

Check the component parts for wear or damage. Make sure the ball nut slides easily on the mainshaft. There should not be excessive free play.

CAUTION: Never allow the ball not to run entirely to the end of its travel, or it could be damaged.

To assemble:

10. Insert the main shaft assembly into the gear housing. Hold the main shaft horizontally.

11. Install the oil seal after applying a small amount of grease to its lip.

12. Install the gasket, shim and gasket end cover to the housing. Tighten the four end cover bolts to 11-45 ft-lb. Use sealant on both the cover gasket and the bolt threads.

13. Measure the main shaft preload. It should be between 3-4.8 ft-lb. If not, adjust it replacing the shim with a thicker or thinner shim. Shims come in thicknesses from 0.0020 to 0.0200 in.

14. Fit the adjusting bolt and shim in the top of the cross shaft and, using a feeler gauge, check the clearance between the adjusting bolt head and the cross shaft. Clearance should be 0-0.002. If not, replace the shim.

MANUAL STEERING MAINSHAFT SHIMS

Part No.	Thickness mm (in.)
MB005890	0.05 (.0020)
MB005891	0.06 (.0024)
MB005892	0.07 (.0030)
MB005893	0.10 (.0040)
MB005894	0.20 (.0080)
MB005895	0.30 (.0120)
MB005896	0.50 (.0200)

15. Insert the cross shaft into the gear housing. Be sure to align the teeth on both shafts in the center of their travel.

16. Install the cover and torque the bolts to 11-14 ft-lbs. Apply sealant to the cover gasket and the threads of the bolts.

17. Verify that the unit works smoothly, then screw the adjusting bolt in and out of the cover two or three times to adjust the cross shaft into proper mesh with the main shaft.

18. Then loosen the adjusting bolt, making sure there is no free play at the mainshaft center position. Back lash should be 0-0.002 in.

19. Test the main shaft preload. Starting torque should be 5.7-7.4 ft-lb.

20. Fill the unit with multipurpose gear oil and install the pitman arm. Its two match marks should aign with the match mark on the cross shaft. Tighten the nut to 94-109 ft-lb.

Power Steering

POWER STEERING PUMP

Removal

1. Remove the drive belt. If the pulley is to be removed, do so now.
2. Disconnect the pressure and return lines. Catch any leaking fluid.
3. Remove the pump attaching bolts and lift the pump from the brackets.

Installation

1. Make sure the bracket bolts are tight and install the pump to the brackets.
2. If pulley had been removed, install it and tighten the nut securely. Bend the lock tab over the nut.
3. Install the drive belt and adjust to a tension of 22 lbs. at a deflection of .28 to .39 inches at the top center of the belt.

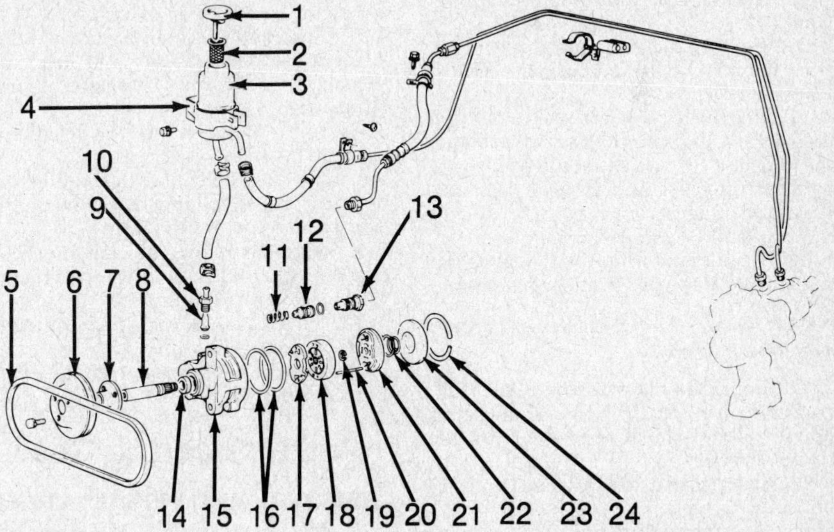

1. Oil reservoir cap
2. Oil filter
3. Oil reservoir
4. Oil reservoir bracket
5. Drive belt
6. Oil pump pulley
7. Pulley bracket
8. Drive shaft
9. Fitting pipe
10. Fitting connector
11. Flow control spring
12. Flow control plunger
13. Connector & fitting assembly
14. Drive shaft seal
15. Oil pump body
16. O-ring
17. Thrust plate
18. Pump ring & rotor
19. Drive shaft retaining ring
20. Dowel
21. Pressure plate
22. End plate spring
23. End plate
24. Retaining ring

Separate reservoir power steering pump assembly—others similar
(© Chrysler Corp.)

Tighten the pump bolts securely to hold the tension.

4. Connect the pressure and return lines and fill the reservoir with approved fluid. (Dexron II®).

5. Bleed the system. (Refer to the bleeding procedure).

OVERHAUL

Separate Reservoir Type

1. Remove the pulley bracket with a gear puller.

2. Loosen and remove the suction port assembly.

3. Remove the pressure hose fitting assembly.

4. Remove the end plate retaining ring by inserting a small punch in the 0.13 in. diameter hole in the housing opposite the flow control valve hole. Compress the retaining ring with the punch and remove it by inserting a screwdriver under the ring and twisting.

5. Remove the end plate and the end plate "O" ring. The end plate is spring loaded and should pop out. If it sticks, rocking it from side to side should free it.

6. Turn the pump over and allow the flow control valve and the valve spring to fall out.

7. With the end cover "O" ring removed, tap lightly on the end of the drive shaft to free the pressure plate.

8. Remove the pressure plate, drive shaft, pump ring, vanes and rotor.

CAUTION: Do not remove the welch plug. If it is cracked or otherwise damaged, replace the whole housing body.

9. Remove the drive shaft retaining ring.

10. Remove the rotor and thrust plate from the drive shaft and both dowel pins from the housing.

11. Pry the drive shaft seal out of the housing, being careful not to damage the housing, discard the shaft seal.

Clean all parts and inspect them for wear or damage.

To assemble, proceed as follows.

12. Install new drive shaft seal using a seal installer with a press or hammer.

NOTE: Only use as much force as necessary to seat the seal.

13. Lubricate the pressure plate "O" ring with Dexron II® or its equivalent, and install it in the third groove from the rear of the housing.

14. Insert both dowel pins in the housing.

15. Assemble the drive shaft, thrust plate and rotor, then fit a new snap ring on the drive shaft. The rotor must have its countersunk side toward the thrust plate.

16. Lubricate the oil seal and drive shaft with ATF Dexron II® or its equivalent and insert the drive shaft in the housing. Be sure to align the dowel pins with the thrust plate so as not to damage the oil seal lip.

17. Install the pump ring on the dowel pins with the arrow in the pump ring facing the rear of the housing.

18. Insert all ten vanes in the rotor slots with their rounded edges outward. They should slide freely in the rotor.

19. Lubricate the pressure plate and install with "O" ring on the dowel pins with the circular depression which holds the spring toward the rear of the housing. The pressure plate must be pressed about 0.06 in. over the "O" ring to seat properly.

20. Fit the end plate "O" ring in the second groove from the rear of the housing.

21. Install the end plate spring in the groove provided in the pressure plate.

22. Lubricate the end plate to avoid damage to the "O" ring and press it into the housing. Fit the end plate retaining ring.

23. Be sure to bleed the system (refer to bleeding procedure).

Reservoir in Unit Type

1. Remove the oil reservoir.

2. Hold the pump in a vise, loosen the pump cover bolts and remove the cover.

3. Remove the following parts from the pump body: cam ring, vanes, "O" ring, side plate assembly, and the shaft assembly which includes the shaft, rotor, side plate, collar and snap ring.

4. Remove the shaft assembly snap ring and remove the collar, rotor side plate.

5. Remove the oil seal with a screw driver. Remove the suction connector.

6. Remove the connector at the top of the pump body and remove the flow control valve assembly and flow control spring.

7. Clean and check all parts for wear. Always use new gaskets and lubricate all parts with Dexon II® before assembling.

Assembly is the reverse of disassembly with the following notes.

8. Pay close attention to the illustrations for the installing direction of the side plate, rotor and collar.

9. When installing the cam ring, the counter-sunk holes at the end of the vanes face toward the cover.

10. Fit the vanes with their rounded sides pointed out.

11. Bleed the system (see bleeding procedures).

Power Steering Gear

REMOVAL AND INSTALLATION

1. Disconnect the steering shaft from the gear box mainshaft.

2. Disconnect the tie rod from the relay rod, and the pitman arm from the relay rod using a gear puller.

3. Remove the air cleaner and disconnect the pressure hose and the return hose from the gear box using a pipe wrench, then remove the undercover.

4. Loosen the gear box mounting bolts. On vehicles with automatic transmissions, remove the throttle linkage with the throttle linkage splash shield. On vehicles with manual transmissions, remove the starter on the transmission.

5. Remove the gear box from under the vehicle.

6. Remove the pitman arm with a gear puller.

Installation is the reverse of removal. Observe the following torques: gear box to frame, 40-47 ft-lb.; tie rod socket and relay rod connection, 25-33 ft-lb.; pressure hose connection, 22-29 ft-lb.; return hose connection 29-36 ft-lb.

OVERHAUL

1. Loosen the adjusting lock nut and remove it.

2. With the gear in neutral position, tap the bottom of the cross shaft with a plastic hammer to remove the cross shaft.

3. Remove the side cover bolts, and screw in the adjusting bolt two or three turns.

4. Remove the valve housing nut.

5. Remove the valve housing bolts and take out the valve housing and rack piston, holding the rack piston to avoid turning it.

NOTE: Be careful not to let the rack piston fall off of the shaft.

6. Hold the valve housing in a vise and move the rack piston up and down to check the backlash between the groove of the rack piston and the balls. Measure the backlash after fully tightening the rack piston on the shaft and then lossening it two turns. Service limit is 0.008 in. If backlash exceeds the service limit, replace the ball screw unit and the rack piston as an assembly.

7. To remove the rack piston, turn it counter-clockwise.

CAUTION: There are twenty-six steel balls in the rack piston which will probably fall out when you remove it from the shaft. Do not lose them.

8. To disassemble the rack piston, remove the circulator holder, the circulator, the steel balls, the seal ring and the "O" ring. Do not disassemble the rack piston end cap.

9. Loosen the top cover and remove it and the input worm shaft from the valve housing.

10. Remove worm shaft thrust plate, thrust needle roller bearing, two seal rings and two "O" rings.

11. Screw in the adjusting bolt at the tip of the cross shaft and remove the side cover.

CAUTION: There are thirty-three needle bearing rollers which may fall out when you remove the cross shaft. Do not lose them.

12. Remove the following parts from the side cover: "O" ring, needle bearings, adjusting bolt and adjusting plate.

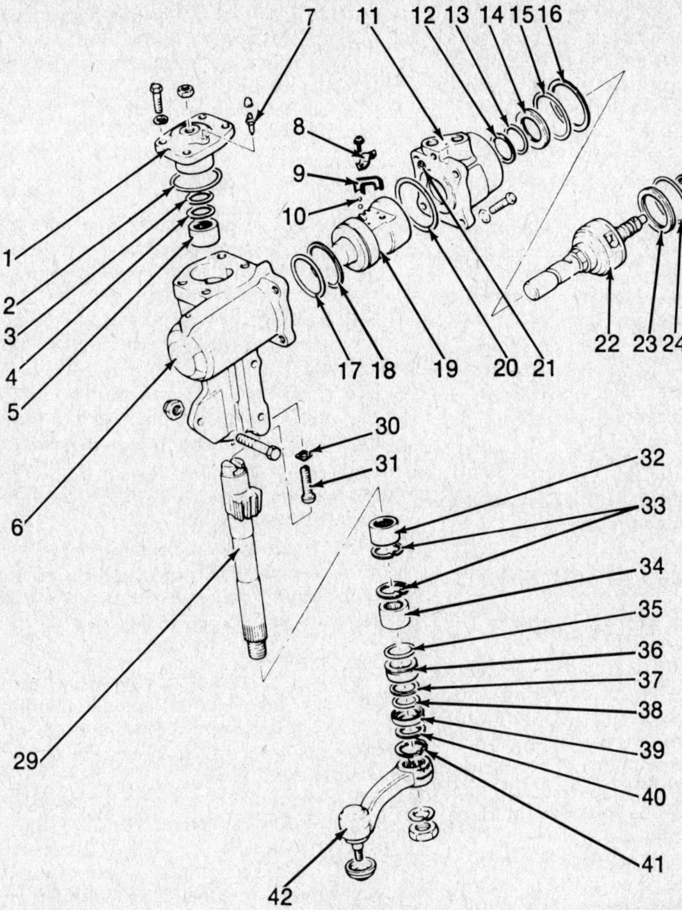

1. Side cover
2. O-ring
3. O-ring
4. Seal ring
5. Needle bearing
6. Gear box
7. Bleeder plug
8. Circulator holder
8. Circulator
10. Ball
11. Valve housing
12. Seal ring
13. O-ring
14. Thrust needle bearing
15. O-ring
16. Seal ring
17. O-ring
18. Seal ring
19. Rack piston
20. O-ring
21. O-ring
22. Input worm shaft
23. Thrust needle bearing
24. O-ring
25. Ball bearing
26. Oil seal
27. Top cover
28. Nut
29. Cross shaft
30. Adjusting plate
31. Adjusting bolt
32. Needle bearing, upper
33. Snap ring
34. Needle bearing, lower
35. O-ring
36. Seal housing
37. Seal ring
38. O-ring
39. Oil seal
40. Backup ring
41. Snap ring
42. Pitman arm

Exploded view of power steering gear assembly
(© Chrysler Corp.)

NOTE: If no oil leaks through the threads of the adjusting bolt, do not remove the sealing at the rear of the needle bearing seat.

13. Remove the seal ring and "O" ring from the valve housing.
14. To remove the ball bearing and oil seal in the top cover, use a brass drift.
15. Remove the oil seal and seal ring from the gear box using a screw driver.

Clean and inspect all parts for wear or damage. Always use new gaskets and oil seals and coat indicated parts with Dexron II® before installing.

To assemble, proceed as follows.

16. Apply a thin coat of multipurpose grease to the bearing race in the side cover and insert the thirty-three roller bearings. Apply a dab of grease to bottom of the side cover. Be careful not to disturb the needle bearings.
17. Install the side cover "O" ring.
18. With the adjusting bolt and adjusting plate inserted in the top of the cross shaft, measure the clearance between the bolt head and the cross shaft. It should be from 0 to 0.002 in. Adjust clearance by replacing shim plate.

NOTE: Install the adjusting plate with its chamfered side in contact with the surface of the cross shaft.

19. Align the cross shaft with the side cover and install. Attach them by tightening the adjusting bolt. Take care not to disturb the needle bearings while installing the cross shaft. Make sure you don't damage the oil seal. Tighten the adjusting bolt lock nut temporarily.
20. To assemble the top cover, apply a thin coat of multipurpose grease to the lip of the oil seal and press fit it in the cover.
21. Press fit the ball bearing.
22. Apply a thin coat of multipurpose grease on the gear box oil seal and install it.
23. Install the "O" ring first and then the seal ring on the input worm shaft. Lubricate with ATF.
24. Install the thrust plate, thrust needle bearing and the thrust plate in the order given on the input worm shaft.
25. Install the "O" rings and the seal ring into their seats in the valve housing without using undue force. The seal ring should be compressed into a heart shape when fit.
26. Install the input worm shaft in the valve housing.
27. Install the thrust plate, needle roller bearing and the thrust plate in the given order in the top cover.

NOTE: Install the thinner thrust plate on the top cover side.

28. Temporarily tighten the top cover to the valve housing.

NOTE: Take care not to disturb the thrust plate and needle roller bearing in the top cover.

29. Tighten the top cover bolts to 12–16 in. lb.

NOTE: Turn the input worm shaft and check for smooth rotation and noise.

30. Tighten the valve housing nut to 130–166 ft-lb.

NOTE: Do not allow the top cover to rotate while tightening the nut.

31. Measure the starting preload of the input worm shaft. It should be from 3–5 in. lb. If not, adjust by tightening or

POWER STEERING CROSS SHAFT SHIM PLATES

Part No.	Thickness mm (in.)
MB076596	1.95 (.077)
MB076196	2.00 (.079)
MB076597	2.05 (.081)
MB076598	2.10 (.083)
MB076599	2.15 (.085)

loosening the valve housing nut in accordance with steps 30 and 31.

32. Install the "O" ring and seal ring on the rack piston in the given order.

33. Insert the rack piston in the input worm shaft until the piston reaches the end of its travel. Rotate the input shaft and align the ball running surface on the worm with the ball insertion holes. Insert nineteen balls into the hole, pushing them lightly with a brass rod.

CAUTION: Do not rotate the worm shaft or rack piston at this point or the balls might enter other grooves.

After installing all nineteen of the balls, make sure the last ball is about half an inch below the end of the rack piston. If there is more than a half inch clearance, it probably means one or more of the balls has fallen into a different worm groove. Remove the assembly and begin again.

34. Insert the remaining seven balls in the circulator, holding them in place with grease. Fit the circulator in place and tighten the screws.

35. Hold the gear box in a vise and install the ball screw unit. Tighten the valve housing to 33–40 ft-lb. After installation, rotate the input worm shaft to move the rack piston to the neutral (center) position.

NOTE: Be careful not to damage the seal ring when installing the rack piston.

36. Install the cross shaft assembly (with side cover) in to the gear box and tighten the side cover to 33–40 ft-lb. When installing the cross shaft, apply a thin coat of ATF to the teeth and shaft of the rack piston and multipurpose grease to the oil seal lip. Do not rotate the side cover during installation or risk damage to the "O" ring. It might be a good idea to wrap tape around the splined end of the cross shaft to prevent damage to the seals.

37. Measure the total starting torque of the input worm shaft to neutral position (center). Make sure the ball screw operates smoothly through its entire travel. Starting torque should be between 4–6 in.-lb. Tighten the valve housing nut to 130–166 ft.-lb. Measure the preload after tightening.

38. Install the pitman arm on the cross shaft aligning the slit in the end of the shaft with the two slits on the pitman arm. Tighten the pitman nut to 94–109 ft-lb.

39. After tightening the pitman arm, measure the distance between the center of the frame mounting bolt hole closest to the pitman arm and the inner surface of the pitman arm. This length should be about 0.77 in.

BLEEDING THE SYSTEM

1. The reservoir should be full of Dexron II®

2. Jack up the front wheels and support the vehicle safely.

3. Turn the steering wheel fully to the right and left until no air bubbles appear in the fluid. Maintain the reservoir level.

4. Lower the vehicle and with the engine idling, turn the wheels fully to the right and left. Stop the engine.

5. Install a tube from the bleeder screw on the steering gear box to the reservoir.

6. Start the engine, turn the steering wheel fully to the left and loosen the bleeder screw.

7. Repeat the procedure until no air bubbles pass through the tube.

8. Tighten the bleeder screw and remove the tube. Refill the reservoir as needed, and check that no further bubbles are present in the fluid.

CAUTION: An abrupt rise in the fluid level after stopping the engine is a sign of incomplete bleeding. This will cause noise from the pump or control valve.

Front End Alignment

CASTER AND CAMBER

To adjust caster, adjust the tightening of the upper arm shaft. A half turn of the upper arm shaft will cause 0.049 in. play in the upper arm shaft resulting in a $^1/_4$ degree caster adjustment. The standard caster value and other wheel alignment specifications can be found at the beginning of this chapter.

To adjust the camber, it is necessary to adjust the number and thickness of the shims under the upper arm shaft. A total of 0.16 in. shim thickness between the upper arm shaft and the crossmember is normally required for standard camber. A 0.024 in. adjustment in thickness of shims will provide about 8 minutes adjustment of camber.

TOE-IN

Toe-in can be adjusted by screwing the left tie rod turnbuckle in or out. One revolution of the turnbuckle will vary in about 0.3 in. of toe-in adjustment. The toe-in may be increased or decreased by turning the tie rod turnbuckle toward the front or the rear of the vehicle respectively. After completion of the toe-in adjustment, check the difference in the length of the left and the right tie rods. If the difference exceeds 0.2 in., remove the right tie rod and adjust the length until the difference is reduced to 0.2 in. or less. An "L" stamped on the outer surface of the tie rod stands for left-hand thread end.

BRAKES

Master Cylinder

REMOVAL AND INSTALLATION

1. Remove all lines connected to the master cylinder. Slowly depress the brake pedal to remove the fluid.

2. Remove the master cylinder from the booster assembly.

3. Installation is the reverse of removal. Bleed the brakes.

OVERHAUL

1. Remove the stop ring, piston stop, primary piston assembly, secondary piston assembly and the secondary return spring in the given order.

2. Loosen the valve case and remove the check valve and the check valve spring.

3. Wash the master cylinder, pistons and cups in brake fluid. Use care not to damage the cylinder, piston or cups.

CAUTION: Do not attempt to disassemble the primary piston assembly; its length is factory adjusted.

NOTE: When any related parts such as the return spring, piston cup and piston require replacement, you must replace the entire piston assembly.

To assemble:

4. Hone the master cylinder slightly. The cylinder bore inside diameter should be between 0.8748–0.8768 in. If not, replace cylinder. Coat the cylinder with brake fluid.

5. Measure the piston outside diameter. It should be between 0.8719–0.8732. If not replace.

6. Assemble the master cylinder components in the master cylinder after coating the rubber seals with brake fluid. Bleed the brakes after installation.

NOTE: Prime the cylinder by pouring a little fluid in the reservoirs and working the piston until fluid squirts out of the two brake line ports.

SYSTEM BLEEDING

1. Check the master cylinder fluid level.

2. Remove the cap from the bleeder screw of the wheel farthest from the master cylinder.

3. Connect a length of rubber tubing to the screw and place the other end in a jar half full of clean brake fluid.

4. Pump the brake pedal until no bubbles are visible in the container.

5. Hold the pedal in the depressed position and tighten the screw. Replace the cap and proceed to each wheel in turn.

NOTE: Periodically check the master cylinder during the bleeding operation to check the fluid level does not go too low. If it does, air will enter the master cylinder and it will have to be bled as well.

Front Disc Brakes

PAD REMOVAL AND INSTALLATION

1. Remove the wheel and expose the caliper.

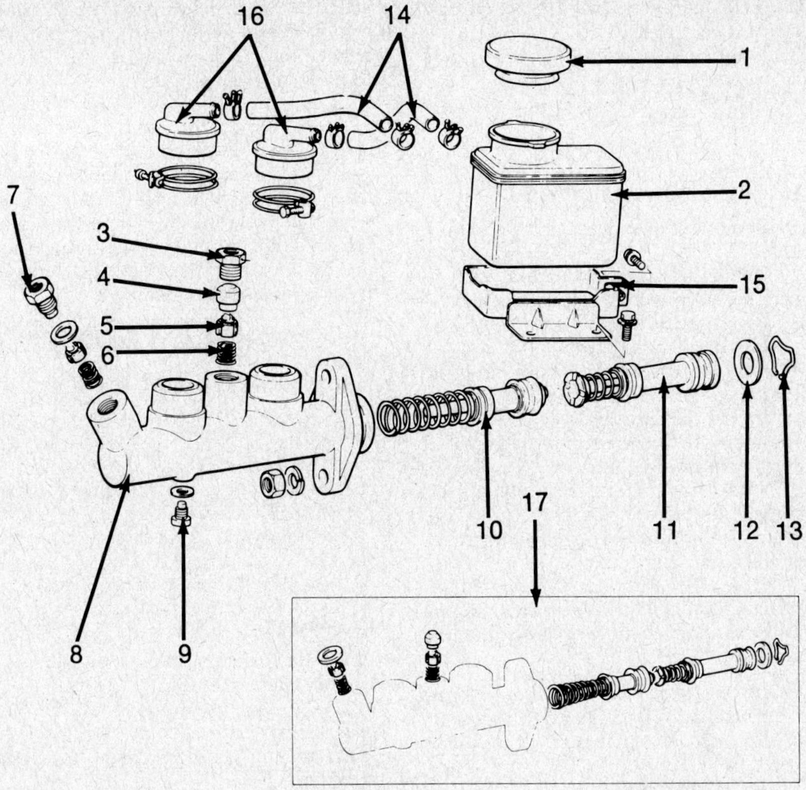

1. Reservoir cap
2. Fluid reservoir
3. Check valve cap
4. Outer pipe seat
5. Check valve
6. Check valve spring
7. Valve case
8. Master cylinder
9. Secondary piston stop
10. Secondary piston assembly
11. Primary piston assembly
12. Piston stop
13. Stop ring
14. Reservoir hose
15. Bracket
16. Nipple
17. Master cylinder kit

Master cylinder
(© Chrysler Corp.)

2. Remove approximately 1/2 the fluid from the master cylinder reservoir.

3. Remove the spring (spigot) pin and pull the stopper plug from the upper end of the caliper.

4. Move the caliper back and forth to loosen and remove it from the caliper support.

NOTE: The hydraulic brake hose need not be removed from the caliper, but do not allow the caliper weight to hang from the hose.

5. To install, push the piston into its original position in the caliper, using a piston expander tool or a hammer handle.

NOTE: The bleeder may have to be opened to allow the piston to bottom.

6. Install the pads, pad clip B, and pad clips inner and outer.

7. Slip the caliper over the pads and install the pad support plate, stopper plug, and the spring pin.

8. Check the brake drag torque after the brakes have been applied several times on a test drive. The torque should be 29 in. lbs., measured at a wheel mounting bolt.

CALIPER OVERHAUL

1. Remove the wheel and caliper. Disconnect the hydraulic brake line.
2. Remove the dust boot. Cover the outer side of the caliper with a cloth, inject air pressure into the brake hose fitting and push the piston out of the caliper.
3. Remove the piston seal from the piston and clean all parts.
4. Hone the caliper piston bore, if necessary.
5. Install a new seal on the piston, lubricate and install the piston into the caliper bore. Seat the piston at the bottom of its travel and install the dust shield.
6. Install the brake hose to the caliper and place the caliper on the support. Lock the caliper into place.
7. Fill the reservoir and bleed the brakes throughly.

BRAKE DISC AND WHEEL BEARING

Removal and Installation

1. Remove the caliper.
2. Pry off the dust cap. Tap out and discard the cotter pin. Remove the locknut.
3. Remove the brake disc and wheel hub.
4. Using a brass drift, carefully drive the outer bearing race out of the hub.

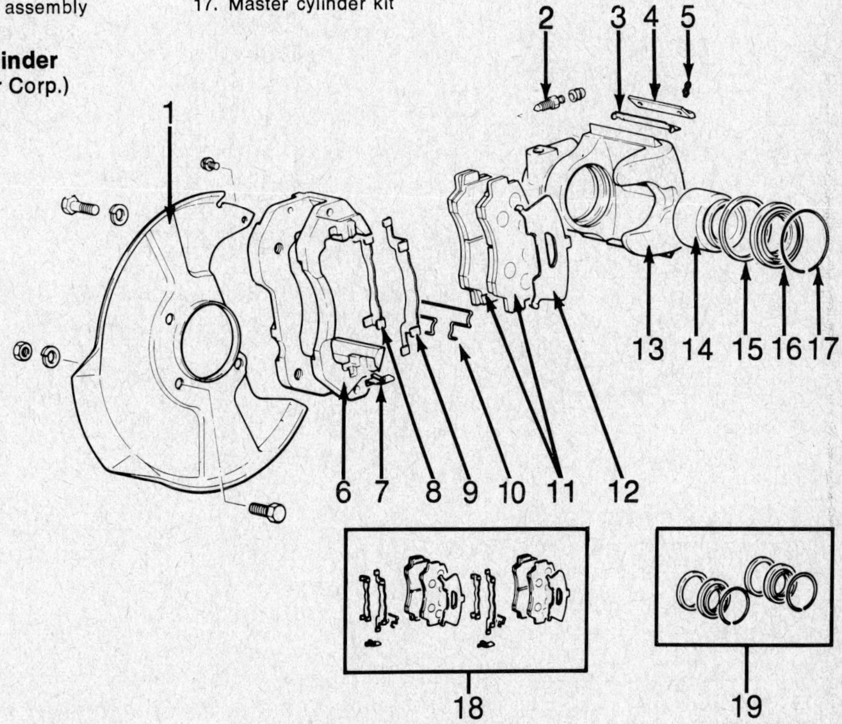

1. Dust cover
2. Bleeder screw
3. Pad support plate
4. Stopper plug
5. Spigot pin
6. Caliper support
7. Pad clip (inner)
8. Pad clip B
9. Pad clip (outer)
10. Anti-rattle spring
11. Brake pad
12. Anti-squeak shim
13. Caliper body
14. Piston
15. Piston seal
16. Dust boot
17. Boot ring
18. Pad repair kit
19. Seal and boot repair kit

Front disc brake caliper assembly
(© Chrysler Corp.)

5. Remove the inner bearing seal and bearing.
6. Check the bearings for wear or damage and replace them if necessary. Drift the bearing race into place in the hub.
7. Pack the inner and outer wheel bearings with grease.
8. Install the inner bearing in the hub. Drive the seal on until its outer edge is even with the edge of the hub.
9. Install the hub/disc assembly on the spindle, being careful not to damage the oil seal.
10. Install the outer bearing, washer, and spindle nut. Adjust the bearing.

Adjustment

1. Tighten the spindle nut to 22 ft-lbs. and then loosen it.
2. Tighten the nut to 6 ft-lbs.
3. Install the cap on the nut. Do not back off the nut more than 30° for cotter pin hole-to-slot alignment.

Drum Brakes

BRAKE DRUM REMOVAL AND INSTALLATION

1. Release the parking brake. Block the front wheels.
2. Jack up the rear of the truck and support it on stands.
3. Remove the wheel.
4. Remove the brake drum.

Installation is the reverse of removal.

BRAKE SHOES

Removal and Installation

1. Remove the wheel and the brake drum.
2. Using a standard brake return spring tool, remove the return spring.
3. Remove the adjusting spring and the adjusting lever.
4. Remove the brake shoes and the adjusting assembly then remove the cable from the parking brake lever.

Installation is the reverse of removal with the following notes.

5. After the primary shoes have been installed, install the parking brake cable. Set the adjuster assembly, then secure the secondary shoes.

NOTE: Grease the threaded area on the adjuster assembly and make sure it turns smoothly.

6. Install the primary shoe return springs, adjusting cable and the secondary shoe return springs in the given order.

NOTE: The spring for the primary shoe is colored green, while the spring for the secondary shoe is gray. Do not mix them, as they are different lengths.

7. To check the adjuster assembly operation: pull the adjuster cable toward you to see if the adjuster lever goes into mesh with the next tooth on the adjuster wheel. Make sure that when the cable is released, the adjuster lever returns to its original position after the adjuster wheel has moved a tooth ahead.

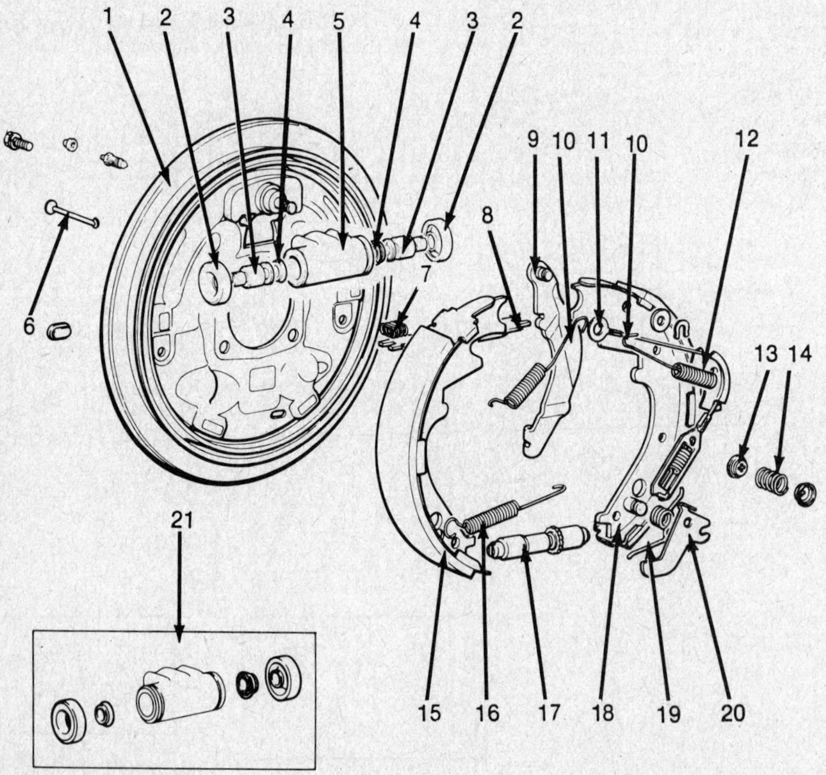

1. Backing plate
2. Wheel cylinder boot
3. Wheel cylinder piston
4. Wheel cylinder piston cup
5. Wheel cylinder body
6. Shoe hold-down pin
7. Anti-rattle spring
8. Parking brake strut
9. Parking brake lever
10. Shoe return spring
11. Adjusting cable
12. Cable guide
13. Shoe hold-down cup
14. Shoe hold-down spring
15. Primary shoe assembly
16. Adjusting spring
17. Adjuster assembly
18. Secondary shoe assembly
19. Adjuster spring
20. Autoadjuster lever
21. Wheel cylinder repair kit

Rear drum brake components

WHEEL CYLINDER

Removal and Installation

1. Remove brake shoes (see above for procedures).
2. Disconnect the brake pipe from the rear of the wheel cylinder and plug it to prevent it from leaking fluid.
3. Remove the wheel cylinder from the brake backing plate.

Installation is the reverse of removal.

Overhaul

1. Remove dust caps from both ends of the wheel cylinder.
2. Pull out the plungers, rubber seals and piston cups.

Clean and lightly hone the wheel cylinder.

Assembly is the reverse of disassembly. Lubricate all parts with brake fluid before assembly.

Power Brake Unit

REMOVAL AND INSTALLATION

1. Remove the master cylinder.
2. Disconnect the vacuum hose from the power brake.
3. Remove the pin connecting the power brake operating rod to the pedal.
4. Loosen the nuts attaching the power brake to the fire wall and remove the power brake.

Installation is the reverse of removal. Apply sealer to all mounting surfaces before assembling.

Parking Brake

ADJUSTMENT

1. Release the parking brake.
2. Jack up the vehicle and support it on jack stands.
3. Make sure the balancer that the front of the cable rides in is parallel with the center line of the truck. The clearance between the balancer and the crossmember should be about 8 in.
4. Adjust the parking brake by turning the turnbuckle on the cable. The brake is properly adjusted when the parking brake handle can be pulled 16 to 17 notches (approx. 4.3 in.)
5. After adjusting the parking brake, make sure there is slack in the cable when the brake is in the off position.

If the brake will not adjust correctly or fails on a hill, the rear brake shoes should be inspected for wear, oil or grease covered surfaces or malfunction.

CHASSIS ELECTRICAL

Blower Motor Without Air Conditioning

REMOVAL AND INSTALLATION

1. Remove the cluster panel.
2. Disconnect the cable between the motor and the heater unit.
3. Remove the three bolts holding the motor in the heater unit and pull out the fan.

NOTE: It may be necessary to unfasten the fan from the motor to remove them from under the dashboard.

Installation is the reverse of removal.

Blower Motor With Air Conditioning

REMOVAL AND INSTALLATION

The air conditioning system used on D-50/Plymouth Arrow pick-up trucks utilizes the blower motor assembly of the heater unit. See above for removal and installation procedures. However, it may be necessary to remove some of the air conditioning components to gain access to the motor. If this is the case, never attempt to loosen any of the air conditioning hoses during your work. They contain refrigerant under pressure, which could severely damage your eyes or skin on contact.

Heater Unit Without Air Conditioning

REMOVAL AND INSTALLATION

1. Drain the cooling system.
2. Place the hot water flow control lever in the off position.
3. Remove the glove box, the center ventilation grille and duct, and the defroster duct.
4. Disconnect all control cables at the heater side.
5. Disconnect the water hoses.
6. Disconnect the harness from the heater fan motor.
7. Remove the top mounting bolts and the center mounting nuts, and remove the heater assembly.

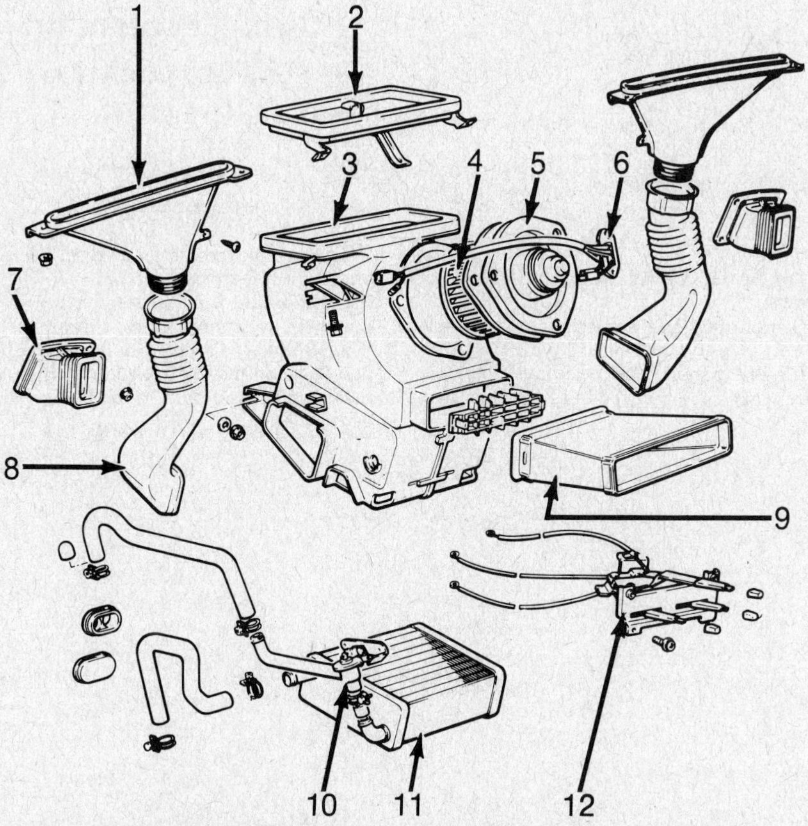

1. Defroster nozzle
2. Ventilator assembly
3. Heater assembly
4. Turbo fan
5. Motor
6. Heater resistor
7. Side ventilation duct
8. Defroster duct
9. Center ventilation duct
10. Water valve
11. Heater core
12. Heater control panel assembly

Heater assembly
(© Chrysler Corp.)

Heater Unit With Air Conditioning

REMOVAL AND INSTALLATION

Removing the heater unit with air conditioning attached is similar to procedures used on units without air conditioning. It may be necessary to loosen or remove certain components of the air conditioning system to facilitate heater unit removel, however, *never* loosen the refrigerant pipes that lead into the air conditioning evaporator assembly. They are filled with a noxious fluid which, under certain conditions, could cause severe damage to your face or skin. Always leave all air conditioning work to skilled professionals.

Radio

REMOVAL AND INSTALLATION

1. Remove the instrument cluster bezel.
2. Remove the radio bracket attaching screws from the instrument panel, and remove the radio bracket.
3. Pull the radio out slightly, disconnect the antenna lead-in, speaker connector and the power supply connector.
4. Take out the radio.

Installation is the reverse of removal.

Windshield Wipers Motor and Linkage

REMOVAL AND INSTALLATION

1. Remove the wiper arms. Remove the arm shaft lock nuts and push in the shafts. Disconnect the electrical wiring.
2. Remove the bolts holding the motor bracket to the body and pull the wiper assembly outward and away from the body.
3. Hold the motor shaft and the linkage at right angles to each other and disconnect them. Remove the motor.
4. The linkages can be pulled from the opening in the front deck.
5. The installation is in the reverse of the removal, being sure to insert the linkage shaft bracket positioning boss positively in the hole provided in the body before tightening the wiper shaft nut.
6. Locate the wiper blades in the stopped position approximately 1/2 to 3/4 inch above the bottom moulding or sealer of the windshield.

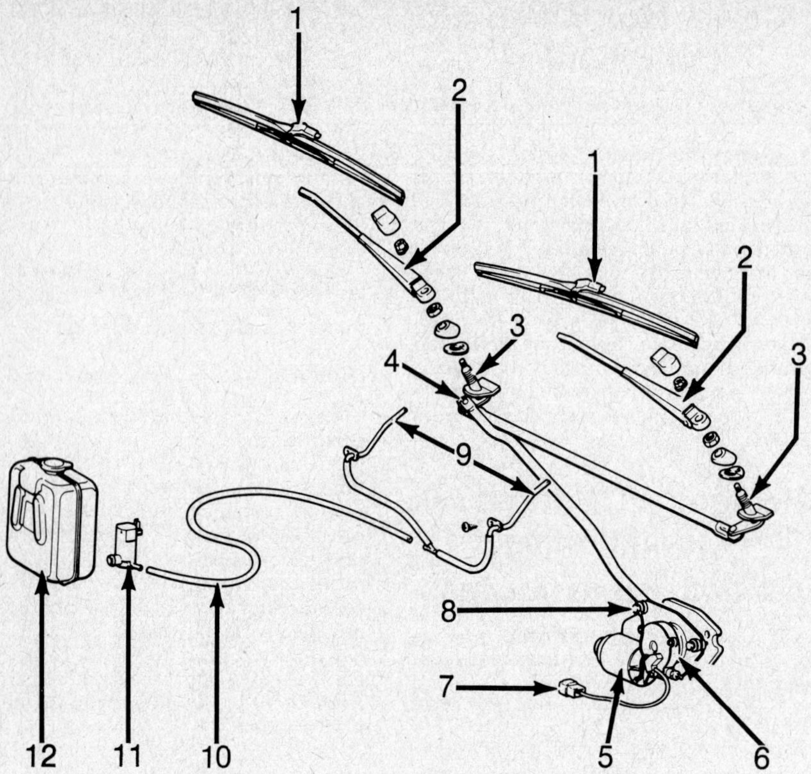

1. Wiper blade
2. Wiper arm
3. Pivot shaft
4. Wiper linkage
5. Wiper motor
6. Motor gear box
7. Motor wire connector
8. Wiper motor assembly grounding point
9. Washer nozzle
10. Washer tube
11. Washer motor assembly
12. Washer liquid tank

Windshield wipers, linkage and washer assembly
(© Chrysler Corp.)

Instrument Panel

REMOVAL AND INSTALLATION

1. Disconnect the negative battery cable.
2. Remove the heater fan control knob, heater control knobs and the radio knobs.
3. Remove the ash tray and remove the two screws behind it holding the instrument panel bezel. Remove the two screws at the top of the bezel and remove the bezel.
4. Remove the four screws in the corners of the meter case.
5. Disconnect the speedometer cable and connectors from the back of the meter, and remove the meter assembly.

Installation is the reverse of removal.

Speedometer Cable

REMOVAL AND INSTALLATION

1. Unfasten the speedometer cable from the rear of the speedometer. The instrument panel may have to be removed.

NOTE: ***The cable is fastened to the speedometer via a snap clip, which must be pressed down while the cable is being unfastened.***

2. Unfasten the speedometer cable from the transmission.
3. Remove the bands holding the cable with the wiring harness and withdraw the cable through the engine compartment.

Installation is the reverse of removal.

CAUTION: ***Always install the speedometer cable with the largest radius possible to prevent cable binding and noise.***

Circuit Protection

FUSE BOX LOCATION

The fuse box is located below the hood release handle on the driver's side of the vehicle.

FUSIBLE LINK

The fusible link is located on the battery running from the positive (+) battery terminal. It is necessary to test the link for continuity with a circuit tester, since visual inspection is not enough to detect a melted fusible link. When the fusible link is melted, a dead short may be the cause.

INDEX

INTRODUCTION

The Courier was introduced by Ford in 1972 to compete with the already well established Toyotas and Datsuns. The Courier fills the need for a vehicle between the family car and an all-out truck. The small wheel-base and stiff suspension to accommodate the substantial payload capacity all blend together to form a pleasant compromise.

The courier is made for Ford Motor Co. by Toyo Kogyo, in Japan. Very similar, both in appearance and performance to its counterparts, the Courier was one of the first to offer an automatic transmission in trucks of this type and also has one of the higher GVWs. It also comes equipped with a skid plate under the oil pan on earlier models, a worthwhile feature for off-roaders.

Power for the Courier is supplied by a SOHC engine of 1796 cc, enlarged to 2000 cc in 1979, and a SOHC engine of 2300 cc providing sufficient on or off-road performance with excellent gas mileage. A 4-speed manual, fully synchronized transmission is standard with the 3-speed automatic and 5-speed manual optional. Drum brakes front and rear through 1976, and disc and drum brakes 1977 and later provide stopping power.

SERIAL NUMBER IDENTIFICATION

Vehicle

The vehicle identification information is stamped on the model plate reveted to the body at the right rear corner of the engine compartment. This plate contains the truck model code and year, the engine model codes, the cylinder displacement of the engine, the chassis number (which is the same as the vehicle and warranty identification number) and the name of the manufacturer.

Vehicle Safety Certification Label

The Vehicle Safety Certification Label is attached to the left door lock pillar and contains the following information:

GVWR—Gross Vehicle Weight Rating, which is the maximum loaded weight at which the vehicle can be operated;

GAWR—Gross Axle Weight Rating, which is the maximum loaded weight of each axle measured at the ground. However, if one axle is loaded to its maximum, the weight of both axles cannot exceed the vehicle's weight at the ground;

This label also contains the name of the manufacturer, the month and year of manufacture and the statement of certification;

The VIN (Vehicle Identification Number) is also located on the certification label and is used for warranty identification.

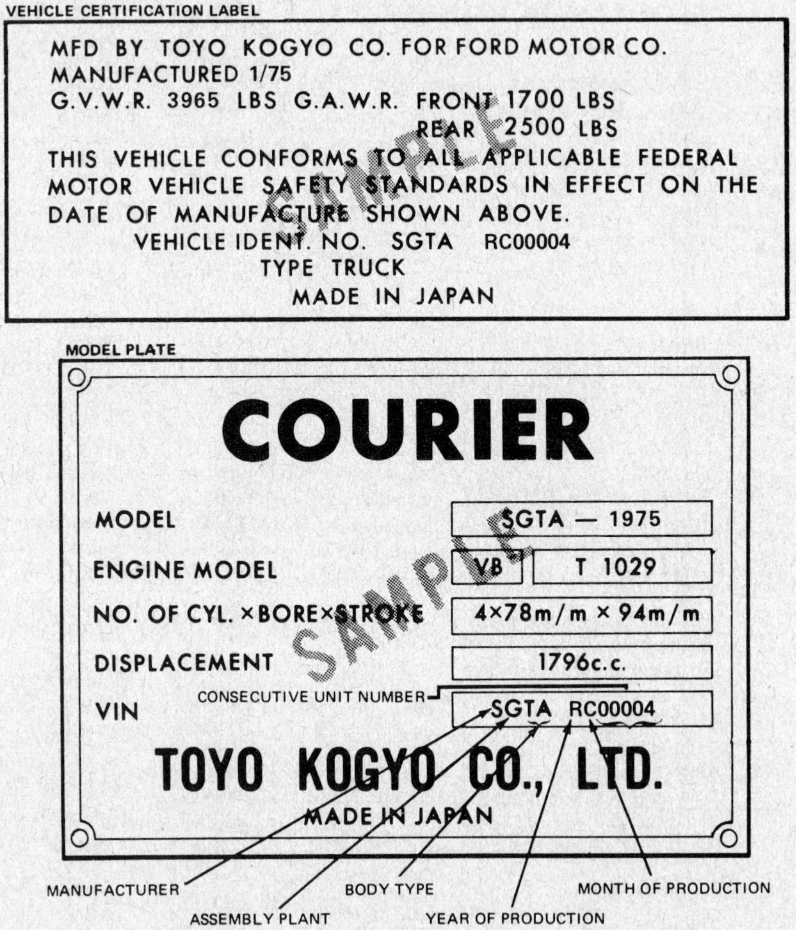

Vehicle certification label and model plate

GENERAL ENGINE SPECIFICATIONS

Year	Engine Displacement cu. in. (cc)	Carb Type	Advertised Horsepower (@ rpm)	Advertised Torque @ rpm (ft lbs)	Bore and Stroke (in.)	Advertised Compression Ratio	Oil Pressure (@ rpm)
1973-75	109.6 (1796)	2V	74 @ 5000	92 @ 3500	3.07 x 3.70	8.6:1	50-64 @ 3000
1976-78	109.6 (1796)	2V	67 @ 5000	88 @ 3000	3.07 x 3.70	8.6:1	50-64 @ 3000

GENERAL ENGINE SPECIFICATIONS

Year	Engine Displacement cu. in. (cc)	Carb Type	Advertised Horsepower (@ rpm)	Advertised Torque @ rpm (ft lbs)	Bore and Stroke (in.)	Advertised Compression Ratio	Oil Pressure (@ rpm)
1977-80	140 (2300)	2V	92 @ 5000	121 @ 3000	3.78 x 3.126	9.0:1	40-60 @ 2000
1979-80	120.2 (2000)	2V	NA	NA	3.15 x 3.86	8.6:1	50-64 @ 3000

N.A. Not available

TUNE-UP SPECIFICATIONS

When analyzing compression results, look for uniformity among cylinders, rather than specific pressures.

Year	Engine cu. in. Displacement (cc)	Spark Plugs Type	Spark Plugs Gap (in.)	Distributor Point Dwell (deg)	Distributor Point Gap (in)	Ignition Timing (deg) MT	Ignition Timing (deg) AT	Intake Valve Opens (deg)	Fuel Pump Pressure (psi)	Compression Pressure (psi)	Idle Speed (rpm) MT	Idle Speed (rpm) AT	Valve Clearance (in.) In ②	Valve Clearance (in.) Ex ②
1973	109.6 (1796)	AG32A	0.032	49-55	0.020	3B	—	26B	2.8-3.6	①	750	—	0.012	0.013
1974	109.6 (1796)	AG32A	0.032	49-55	0.020	3B	3B	13B	2.8-3.6	①	750	750	0.012	0.012
1975	109.6 (1796)	AG32A	0.032	49-55	0.020	5B	5B	13B	2.8-3.6	①	750	750	0.012	0.012
1976	109.6 (1796)	AG32	0.032	49-55	0.020	5B	5B	13B	2.8-3.6	①	750	750	0.012	0.012
1977	109.6 (1796)	AG32	0.032	49-55	0.020	5B	5B	13B	2.8-3.6	①	700	700	0.012	0.012
	140.0 (2300)	AGRF52	0.034	Electronic		6B	6B	NA	2.8-3.6	①	825	700	Hyd.	Hyd.
1978	109.6 (1796)	AG32	0.032	49-55	0.020	8B	8B	18B	2.8-3.6	①	700	700	0.012	0.012
	140.0 (2300)	AGRF52	0.034	Electronic		6B	6B	NA	2.8-3.6	①	825	700	Hyd.	Hyd.
1979	120.2 (2000)	AGR32	0.031	Electronic		8B	8B	14B	2.8-3.6	①	650	650	0.012	0.012
	140.0 (2300)	AGRF52	0.043	Electronic		6B	6B	NA	2.8-3.6	①	800	700	Hyd.	Hyd.
1980	120.2 (2300)	AGR32	0.031	Electronic		8B	8B	14B	2.8-3.6	①	650	650	0.012	0.012
	140.0 (2300)	AGRF52	0.043	Electronic		6B	6B	NA	2.8-3.6	①	800	700	Hyd.	Hyd.

NOTE: If the specifications on the engine decal differs from the above information, use the specifications as listed on the engine decal.

① The lowest reading cylinder should be within 75% of the highest.

② Measured at the valve (Engine hot).

N.A. Not Available

FIRING ORDERS

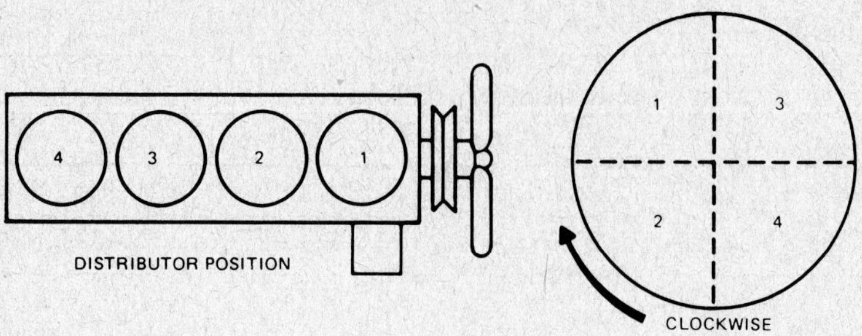

FIRING—1-3-4-2

TIMING MARK SKETCH

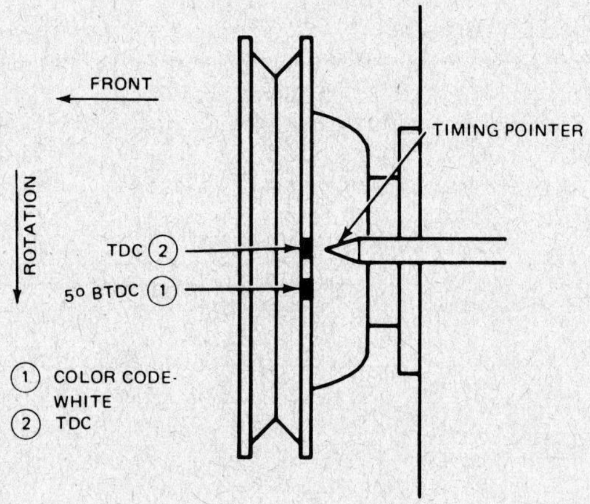

VIEWED FROM RIGHT SIDE OF ENGINE

1800 and 2000cc engines

TIMING MARK SKETCH CALIFORNIA

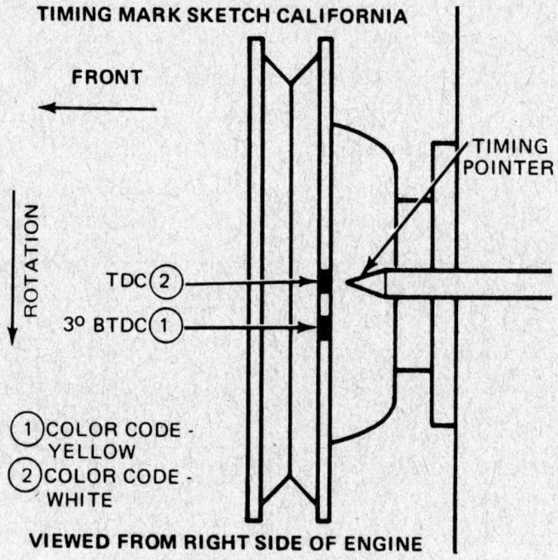

VIEWED FROM RIGHT SIDE OF ENGINE

1973-76 timing marks

CYLINDER NUMBERING AND DISTRIBUTOR LOCATION

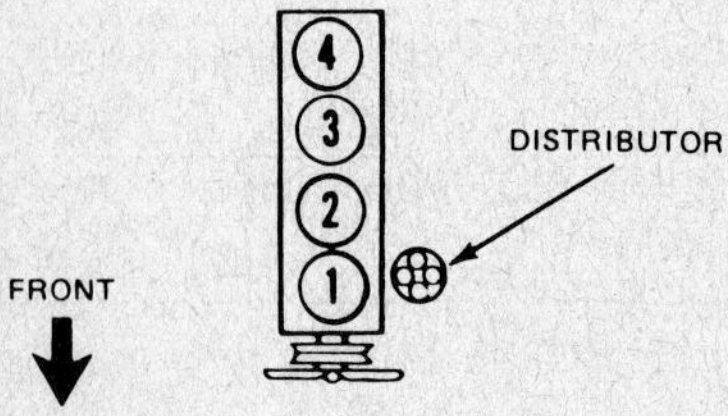

FIRING ORDER AND POSITION

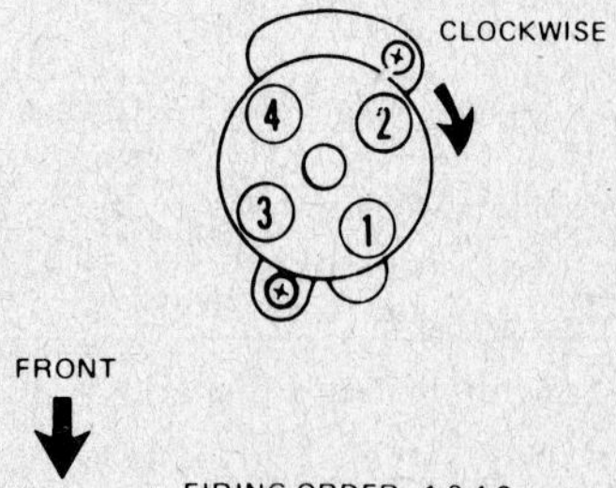

FIRING ORDER—1-3-4-2

TIMING MARKER

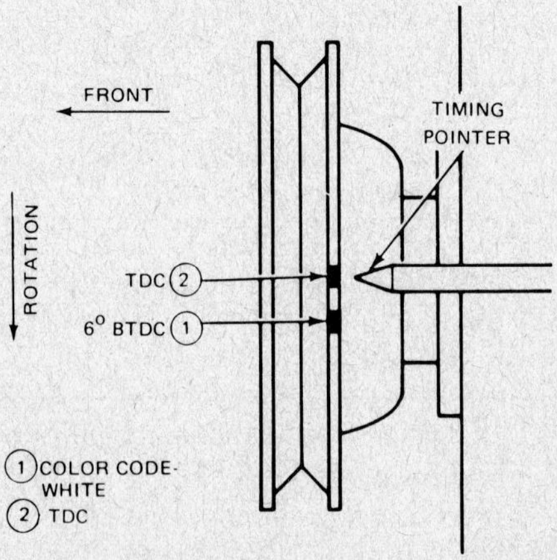

2300cc engine

CAPACITIES

Year	Engine Displacement cu. in. (cc)	Crankcase Qts. (L) With Filter	Crankcase Qts. (L) Without Filter	Transmission 4-speed Pts. (L)	Transmission 5-speed Pts. (L)	Auto Qts. (L)	Axle Pts. (L)	Gas Tank Gals. (L)	Cooling System with Heater Qts. (L)
1973	109.6 (1796)	5 (4.7)	4 (3.8)	3 (1.4)	—	—	2.7 (1.3)	11.7 (44)	7.5 (7.2)
1974-76	109.6 (1796)	5 (4.7)	4 (3.8)	3 (1.4)	3.6 (1.7)	6.6 (6.3)	3.2 (1.5)	11.7 (44)	7.5 (7.2)
1977-80	109.6 (1796) 120.2 (2000)	5 (4.7)	4 (3.8)	3 (1.4)	3.6 (1.7)	6.6 (6.3)	2.8 (1.3)	Short Bed 15 (57)	7.5 (7.2)
1977-80	140 (2300)	4.5 (4.3)	4 (3.8)	3 (1.4)	3.6 (1.7)	6.6 (6.3)	2.8 (1.3)	Long Bed 17.5 (66)	8.8 (8.3)

CRANKSHAFT AND CONNECTING ROD SPECIFICATIONS

(All measurements given in in.)

Year	Engine Displacement cu. in. (cc)	Crankshaft: Main Brg Journal Dia	Crankshaft: Main Brg Oil Clearance	Crankshaft: Shaft End Play	Crankshaft: Thrust on No.	Connecting Rod: Journal Dia	Connecting Rod: Oil Clearance	Connecting Rod: Side Clearance
1973	109.6 (1796)	2.4746-2.4780	0.0005-0.0015①	0.003-0.012	4	2.0842-2.0866	0.001-0.0011②	0.004-0.008 ③
1974	109.6 (1796)	2.4779-2.4785	0.0005-0.0015①	0.003-0.012	4	2.0842-2.0848	0.001-0.011②	0.004-0.008 ③
1975-78	109.6 (1796)	2.4779-2.4785	0.0005-0.0015①	0.003-0.012	4	2.0842-2.0848	0.001-0.011②	0.004-0.008 ③
1977-80	140.3 (2300)	2.3990-2.3982	0.0008-0.0015⑤	0.004-0.008	4	2.0464-2.0472	0.0008-0.0015⑤	0.0035-0.0105 ⑥
1979-80	120.2 (2000)	2.4780-2.4786	0.0005-0.0015①	0.003-0.009	4	2.0842-2.0848	0.0010-0.0026②	0.004-0.008 ③

① Wear limit: 0.0012-0.0024 in.
② Wear limit: 0.0008-0.003 in.
③ Wear limit: 0.014 in.
④ Wear limit: 0.001 to 0.003 in.
⑤ Wear limit: 0.0008 to 0.0026 in.
⑥ Wear limit: 0.0150 in.

VALVE SPECIFICATIONS

Year	Engine Displacement cu. in. (cc)	Seat Angle (deg)	Face Angle (deg)	Spring Test Pressure (lbs. @ in.)	Free Length (in.)	Stem to Guide Clearance (in.) Intake	Stem to Guide Clearance (in.) Exhaust	Stem Diameter (in.) Intake	Stem Diameter (in.) Exhaust
1973	109.6 (1796)	45	45	20.9 @ 1.25① 31.5 @ 1.34②	1.438① 1.469②	.0007-.0021③	.0007-.0023③	.3161-.3167	.3159-.3161
1974-78	109.6 (1796)	45	45	16.3 @ 1.30① 26.8 @ 1.36②	1.438① 1.469②	.0007-.0021③	.0007-.0023③	.3161-.3167	.3159-.3167
1977-80	140.3 (2300)	45	44	71-79 @ 1.56	1.82	.0010-.0027④	.0015-.0032④	.3416-.3423	.3411-.3418
1979-80	120.2 (2000)	45	45	20.9 @ 1.26① 31.4 @ 1.34②	1.438① 1.469②	.0007-.0021③	.0007-.0023③	.3162-.3168	.3160-.3168

① Inner
② Outer
③ Wear limit: 0.008 in.
④ Service clearance 0.0055 in.

PISTON AND RING SPECIFICATIONS

(All measurements in in.)

			RING GAP			RING SIDE CLEARANCE		
Year	Engine Displacement cu. in. (cc)	Piston Clearance	Top Compression	Bottom Compression	Oil Control	Top Compression	Bottom Compression	Oil Control
1973-78	109.6 (1796)	0.0022-0.0028	0.008-0.016	0.008-0.016	0.008-0.016	0.0014-0.0028	0.0012-0.0026	0.0012-0.0025
1977-80	140 (2300)	0.0014-0.0022	0.010-0.020	0.010-0.020	0.015-0.055	0.002-0.004①	0.002 0.004①	Snug
1979-80	120.2 (2000)	0.0014-0.0030	0.008-0.016	0.008-0.016	0.012-0.035	0.001-0.003	0.001-0.003	Snug

① Service Limit—0.006 in.

TORQUE SPECIFICATIONS

(All readings in ft lbs unless noted)

Year	Engine Displacement cu. in. (cc)	Cylinder Head Bolts	Rod Bearing Bolts	Main Bearing Bolts	Camshaft Sprocket-to-Cam	Flywheel-to-Crankshaft Bolts	Manifolds Intake	Manifolds Exhaust
1973	109.6 (1796)	①	30	60-65	50-58	115	20	20
1974	109.6 (1796)	①	29-33	60-65	50-64	115	20	20
1975	109.6 (1796)	①	29-33	60-65	50-64	115	20	20
1976-78	109.6 (1796)	②	29-33	60-65	50-64	112-118	14-19	16-21
1977-80	140.3 (2300)	80-90③	30-36	80-90	80-90	54-64	14-21④	16-23⑥
1979-80	120.2 (2000)	⑤	36-40	61-65	51-58	112-118	14-20	16-21

NOTE: The following chart gives torque limits for various size bolts; if the torques listed above conflict with those listed below, use the torques above.

① 60-65 ft lbs (cold); 70 ft lbs (normal operating temperature)
② 63-68 ft lbs (cold); 69-73 ft lbs (normal operating temperature)
③ Torque in two steps: (1) 50-60 ft lbs, (2) 80-90 ft lbs
④ Torque in two steps: (1) 5-7 ft lbs, (2) 14-21 ft lbs
⑤ 59-64 cold, 69-72 hot
⑥ 27-38, 1979-80

6 mm— 6 ft lbs
8 mm—15 ft lbs
10 mm—30 ft lbs
12 mm—50 ft lbs
14 mm—65 ft lbs

TORQUE SEQUENCES

Cylinder Head

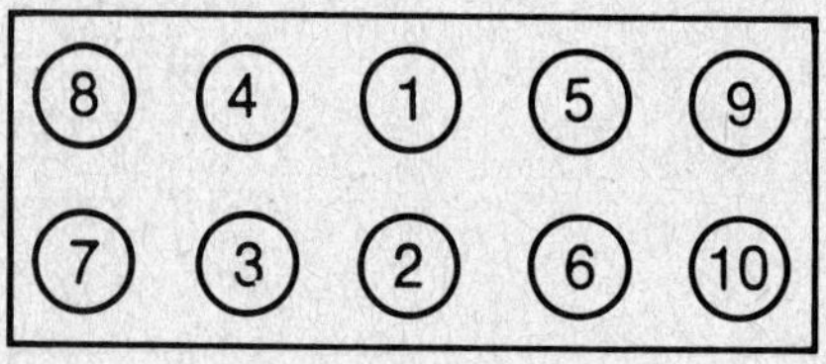

1800cc and 2000cc

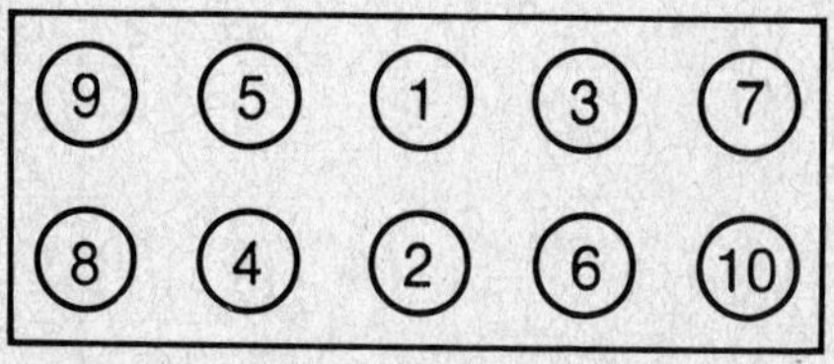

2300cc engine cylinder head torque (two progressive steps)

BATTERY AND STARTER SPECIFICATIONS

(All trucks use 12 volt, negative ground electrical systems)

Year	Model	Battery Amp Hour Capacity	STARTER Lock Test Amps	Lock Test Volts	Lock Test Torque (ft/lbs)	No Load Test Amps	No Load Test Volts	No Load Test RPM	Brush Spring Tension (oz.)	Min. Brush Length (in.)
1973-80	All	60①	—Not Recommended—			50 (or less)	11	5000 (or more)	38	0.16②

① 70 amp/hr battery optional
② New length—0.55 in.

BRAKE SPECIFICATIONS

(All measurements given are (in.) unless noted)

Year	Model	Lug Nut Torque (ft/lb)	Master Cylinder Bore	Brake Disc Minimum Thickness	Brake Disc Maximum Run-Out	Brake Drum Diameter	Brake Drum Max. Machine O/S	Brake Drum Max. Wear Limit	Minimum Lining Thickness Front	Minimum Lining Thickness Rear
1973-76	All	55-65	0.750	—	—	10.236	10.296	10.30	0.039①	0.039①
1977-78	All	55-65	0.875	0.4331	0.0039	10.236	10.245	10.275	0.315	1/32 Above Shoe
1979-80	All	58-65	0.875	0.4331	0.0039	10.236	10.245	10.275	0.276	0.039

NOTE: Minimum lining thickness is as recommended by the manufacturer. Due to variations in state inspection regulations, the minimum allowable thickness may be different than recommended by the manufacturer.

① or within 1/32 in. of the shoe. New lining thickness is 0.217 in.
— Not Applicable

WHEEL ALIGNMENT SPECIFICATIONS

Year	Model	Caster Range (deg)	Caster Pref. Setting (deg)	Camber Range (deg)	Camber Pref. Setting (deg)	Toe-in (in.)	Front Wheel Turning Angle (deg) Inward	Front Wheel Turning Angle (deg) Outward
1973-76	All	¾P-1¼P	1P	1P-1¾P	⅜P	0-¼	34-38	32-33
1977-80	All	¾P-1¼P	1P	½P-1¼P②	⅞P②	0-¼	32°30′①	30°40′①

P Positive
① Maximum
② 1980: ¾P Preferred
Range 1⅛P-½P

TUNE-UP PROCEDURES

Breaker Points and Condenser

REMOVAL AND INSTALLATION

1. Remove the distributor cap and rotor.
2. Disconnect the primary and condenser wires.
3. Remove the breaker points from the base plate.
4. Place the breaker points assemblies on the base plate. Install the attaching screws, using a magnetic screwdriver.

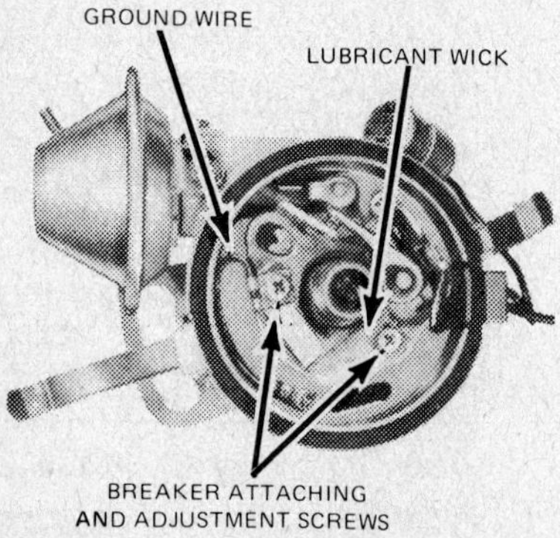

Distributor components

5. Install the condenser. It is always best to install a new condenser each time you replace the points.
6. Connect the primary and condenser wires to the points terminal and tighten the connection.
7. Be sure that the points are aligned.
8. Set the point gap or dwell angle and install the rotor and distributor cap.

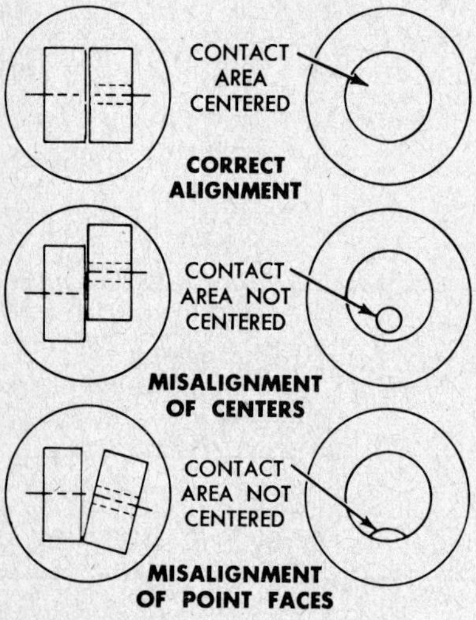

Alignment of breaker points

Dwell Angle

When setting ignition contact points, it is advisable to observe the following general rules:

1. If the points are used, they should not be adjusted using a feeler gauge. The gauge will not give an accurate reading on a pitted surface.
2. Never file the points—this removes their protective coating and results in rapid pitting.
3. When using a feeler gauge to set new points, be certain that the points are fully open. The fiber rubbing block must rest on the highest point of the cam lobe.
4. Always make sure that a feeler gauge is free of oil or grease before setting the points.
5. Make sure that the points are properly aligned and that the feeler gauge is not tilted. If points are misaligned, bend the fixed contact support only, never the movable breaker arm.

A dwell meter virtually eliminates errors in point gap caused by the distributor cam lobes being unequally worn, or human error. In any case, point dwell should be checked as soon as possible after setting with a feeler gauge because it is a far more accurate check of point operation under normal operating conditions. The dwell meter is also capable of detecting high point resistance (oxidation) or poor connections within the distributor.

To connect the dwell meter, switch the meter to the four cylinder range, and connect one lead to ground. The other lead should be connected to the coil distributor terminal (the one having the wire going to contact points) Follow the manufacturer's instructions if they differ from those listed. Zero the meter, start the engine and gradually allow it to assume normal idle speed. (See "Tune-Up Specifications.") The meter should agree with the specifications. Any excessive variation in dwell (more than 3 degrees at 1500 rpm) indicates a worn distributor shaft or bushings, or perhaps a worn distributor cam or breaker plate.

ADJUSTMENT

There are two methods to adjust the breaker point gap. By far the more accurate is the method of measuring dwell angle electronically.

Feeler Blade Method

1. Check and adjust the breaker point alignment. Bend the fixed contact support only.
2. Crank the engine in short bursts until the rubbing block rests on a peak of a cam lobe.
3. Insert a feeler blade of the specified thickness between the breaker points. Adjust the gap until the feeler blade will slide through the gap with a slight drag, by loosening the adjustment screw and moving the point base. When the correct

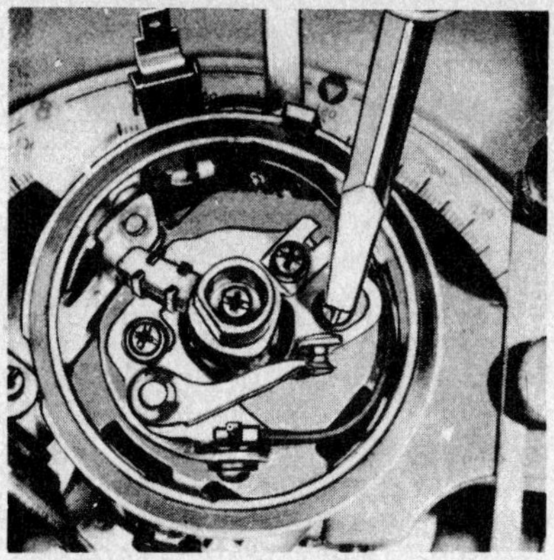

Point gap adjustment

gap is obtained, tighten the adjustment screw.

4. Clean the breaker cam and apply a thin coat of distributor cam lubricant to the cam. Do not use engine oil.
5. After setting the breaker point gap, set the ignition timing.
6. Install the distributor rotor and cap.

Dwell Meter Method

1. Connect a dwell/tach to the engine.
2. Remove the distributor cap and rotor.
3. If the dwell angle is not as specified, adjust the point gap. Crank the engine again and note the dwell reading. Repeat this process until the dwell is within specifications.

Electronic Ignition

2000 cc and 2300 cc Engine

An electronic ignition system is used on these engines, which eliminates the points and condenser. The system includes an ignition module, a high tension ignition coil, a magnetic pick-up coil in the distributor triggered by a timing rotor, and special secondary wiring.

Dwell is determined by the position of one of the four timing rotor spokes in relation to the magnetic pick-up coil, located on a predetermined spot of the distributor plate. No adjustment is needed. The timing is checked and adjusted in the conventional manner.

Ignition Timing

1. Clean and mark the timing marks.
2. Disconnect and plug the vacuum line to the distributor.
3. Connect a timing light and tachometer.
4. Start the engine and reduce the idle to 700–750 rpm to be sure that the centrifugal advance mechanism is not working.
5. With the engine running, shine the timing light at the timing pointer and observe the position of the pointer in relation to the timing mark on the crankshaft pulley.

6. If the timing is not as specified, adjust the timing by loosening the distributor hold down bolt and rotating the distributor in the proper direction. When the proper ignition timing is obtained, tighten the hold down bolt on the distributor.

7. Check the centrifugal advance mechanism by accelerating the engine to about 2,000 rpm. If the ignition timing advances, the mechanism is working properly.

8. Stop the engine and remove the timing light.

9. Reset the idle to specifications.

10. Remove the tachometer.

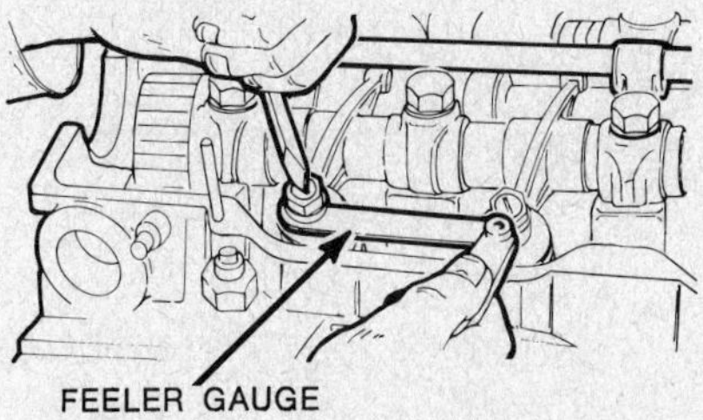

Checking valve clearance at the valve

Valve Lash

1800 and 2000 cc Engines

1. Run the engine until normal operating temperature is reached.
2. Remove the rocker cover.
3. Torque the cylinder head bolts to specifications.
4. Rotate the crankshaft so that No. 1 cylinder (front) is in the firing position. This can be determined by removing the spark plug from No. 1 cylinder and putting your thumb over the spark plug port. When compression is felt, No. 1 cylinder is on the compression stroke. Rotate the engine with a wrench on the crankshaft pulley and stop it at TDC of the compression stroke on No. 1 cylinder.
5. Check the valve clearance. The clearance can be checked at the camshaft or at the valve.
6. Loosen the adjusting screw locknut and adjust the clearance by turning the adjusting screw with the feeler blade inserted. Tighten the locknut.
7. Rotate the crankshaft, adjusting the valves for each cylinder at TDC of the compression stroke for each cylinder in the firing order—1-3-4-2.

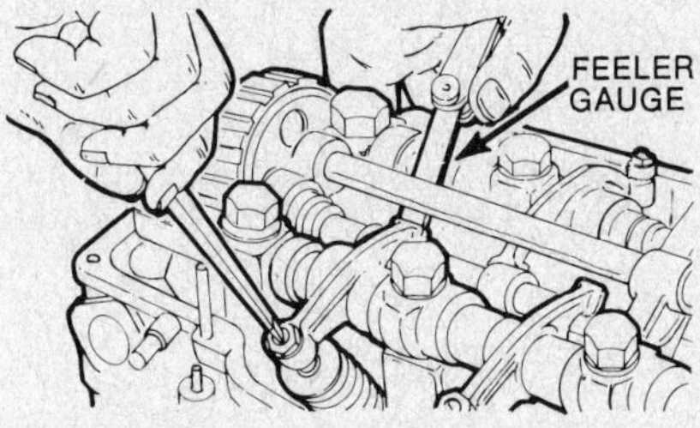

Checking valve clearance at the camshaft

8. Install the rocker arm cover with a new gasket.

2300 cc Engine

The lash adjusters are a zero lash, hydraulic device, similar in both construction and operation to conventional type hydraulic lifters.

A collapsed tappet gap is the only check that can be made to determine if abnormal wear exists.

The allowable tappet gap when collapsed is 0.035 to 0.055 in. (0.040–0.050 in. preferred), measured at the cam.

Carburetor

IDLE SPEED AND MIXTURE

1. Put the transmission in Neutral.
2. Connect a tachometer.
3. Set the curb idle speed to specifications, using the curb idle speed adjusting screw.
4. Check the idle mixture with a HC/CO analyzer, to prevent disturbing the emission level by over-richening it.

***NOTE:** The only recommended procedure for air/fuel mixture adjustment is with the use of an exhaust gas analyzer. The specifications listed on the Vehicle Emission Control label, located in the engine compartment, must be followed.*

ENGINE ELECTRICAL

Distributor

REMOVAL AND INSTALLATION

1. Remove the distributor cap.
2. Disconnect the vacuum hose.

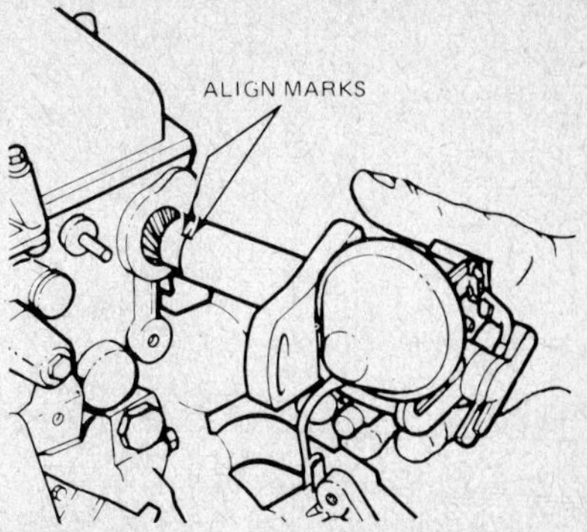

Distributor removal or installation

3. Scribe matchmarks on the distributor body and the cylinder block to indicate the relative positions.
4. Scribe another mark on the distributor body indicating the position of the rotor.
5. Disconnect the primary wires.
6. Remove the distributor hold down bolt and remove the distributor from the engine.

***NOTE:** Do not crank the engine while the distributor is removed.*

To install the distributor:

7. If the engine was cranked while the distributor was removed, turn the crankshaft until No. 1 cylinder is at the top of the compression stroke. This can be determined by feeling compression with your thumb through the spark plug port. The TDC mark on the crankshaft pulley should also be aligned with the timing pointer. Slide the distributor into the engine with the rotor pointing to No. 1 firing position (see "Firing Order").
8. If the engine has not been cranked while the distributor was removed, slide the distributor (with the O-ring if equipped) into the engine, aligning the matchmarks made during removal.

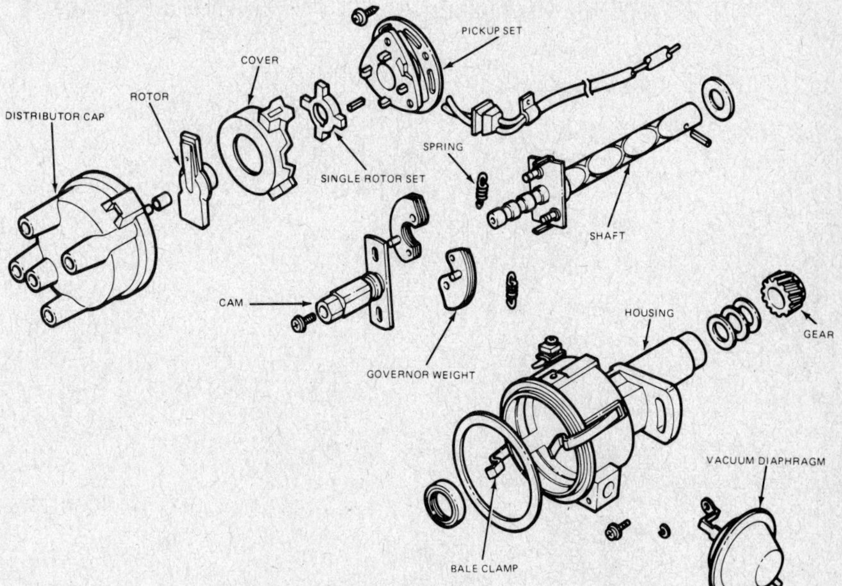

Electronic ignition distributor components

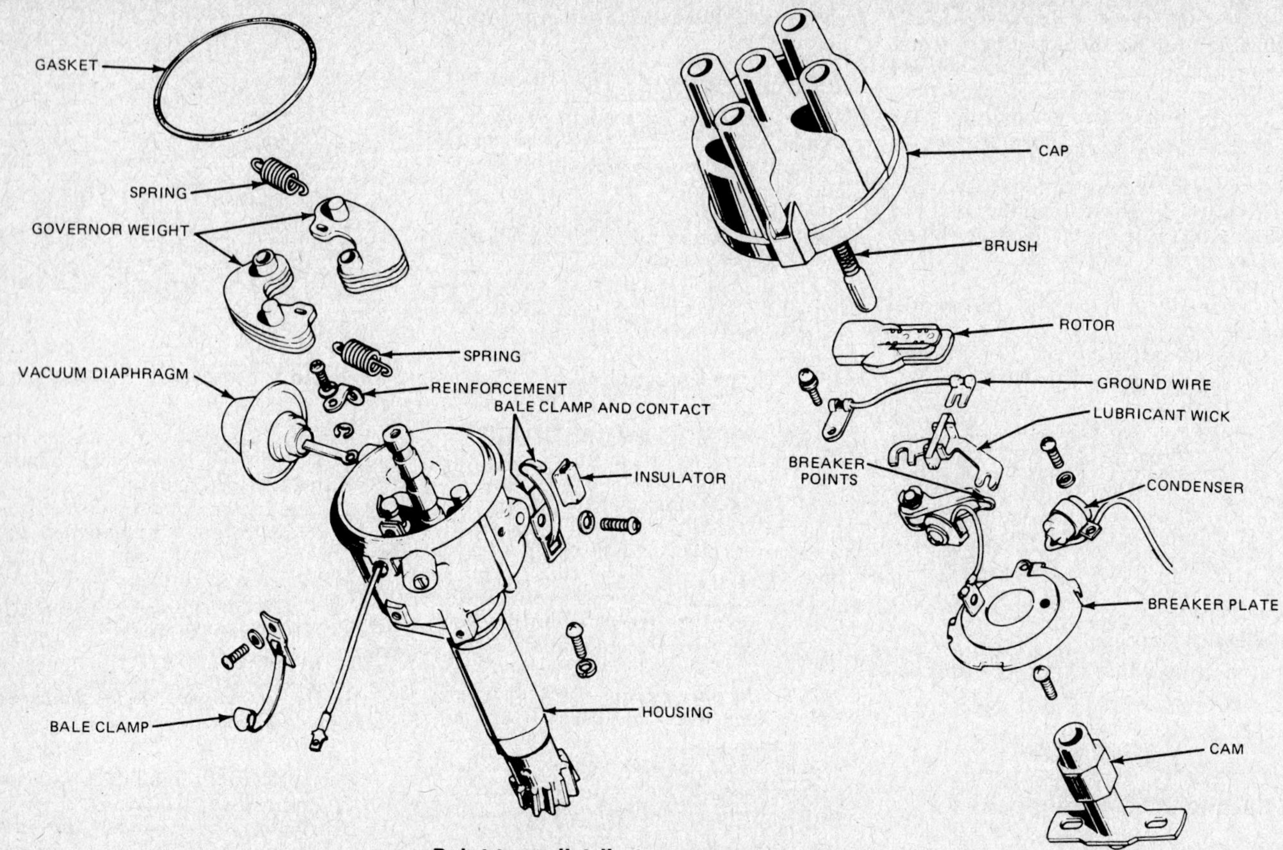

Point type distributor component parts

9. Install the flat washer, lockwasher and hold-down nut, but do not tighten the nut.
10. Install the distributor cap and connect the primary wires.
11. Set the ignition timing, and tighten the hold-down nut.
12. Connect the vacuum line.

Alternator

A 40 amp fuse protects the charging circuit on Couriers through 1975; a fusible link is used on 1976 and later models. Either can be found on the right fender splash shield in the engine compartment.

ALTERNATOR PRECAUTIONS

Some precautions should be taken when working on this, or any other, AC charging system.

1. Never switch battery polarity.
2. When installing a battery, always connect the grounded terminal first.
3. Never disconnect the battery while the engine is running.
4. If the molded connector is disconnected from the alternator, never ground the hot wire.
5. Never run the alternator with the main output cable disconnected.
6. Never electrically weld around the truck without disconnecting the alternator.
7. Never apply any voltage in excess of battery voltage while testing.
8. Never "jump" a battery for starting purposes with more than 12 volts.

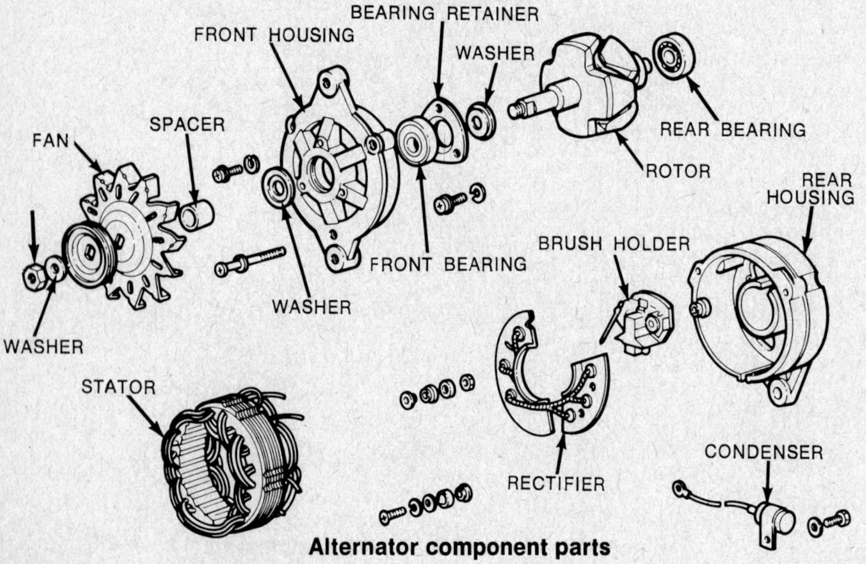

Alternator component parts

Removal and Installation

1. Disconnect the wire at the terminal at the rear of the alternator.
2. Pull the multiple connector from the rear of the alternator.
3. Remove the fan belt.
4. Remove the distributor cap and rotor from the distributor to provide clearance, if necessary.
5. Remove the alternator.
6. Installation is the reverse of removal. Be sure to adjust the drive belt tension and to connect the battery properly.

Regulator

An external regulator is located on the fender splash shield.

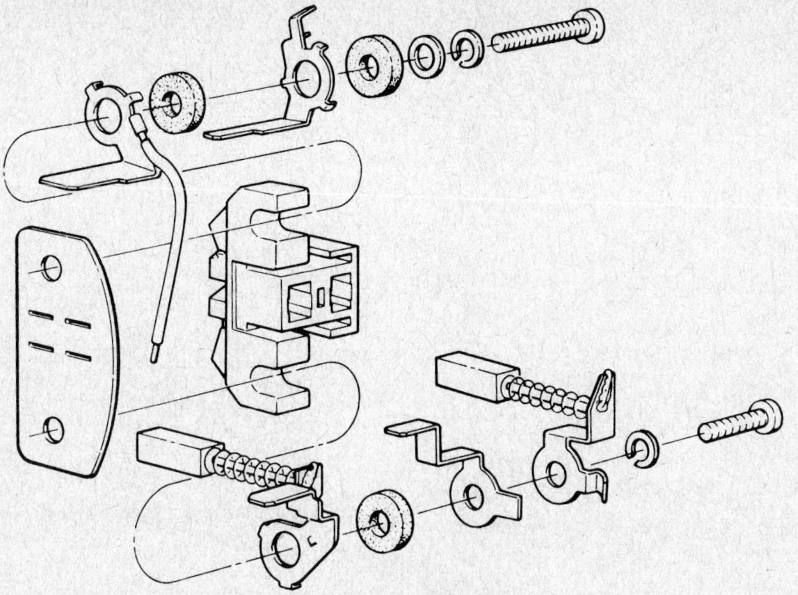

Alternator brush holder

REMOVAL AND INSTALLATION

1. Disconnect the regulator wires at the multiple connector.
2. Remove the regulator from the splash shield.
3. Installation is the reverse of removal.

REGULATOR TEST

The alternator regulator is not adjustable, but if it is suspected to be malfunctioning, the following test can be performed.

1. Connect a tachometer.
2. Connect the positive lead of a voltmeter to the alternator B terminal, and the negative lead to ground.
3. Set a voltmeter to the 20 volt scale.
4. Put the transmission in Neutral and set the parking brake.
5. Start the engine and run it at 1,800 rpm. The voltmeter should read 14–15 volts. If not replace the regulator.

Starter

REMOVAL AND INSTALLATION

1. Raise the hood and disconnect the battery ground cable.
2. Remove the carburetor air cleaner and air intake tube.
3. Disconnect the battery cable from the starter solenoid battery terminal.
4. Pull the ignition switch wire from the solenoid 50 terminal.
5. Raise and support the truck on jackstands.
6. Working under the truck, remove the two starter attaching bolts, washers and nuts.
7. Tilt the drive end of the starter and remove the starter by working it out below the emission system hoses.

To install the starter:

8. Install the starter and 2 bolts, washers and nuts.
9. Connect the ignition switch wire to the solenoid 50 terminal.
10. Connect the battery cable to the solenoid battery terminal.
11. Install the carburetor air cleaner and air intake tube.
12. Connect the ground cable to the battery.
13. Lower the truck and check the operation of the starter.

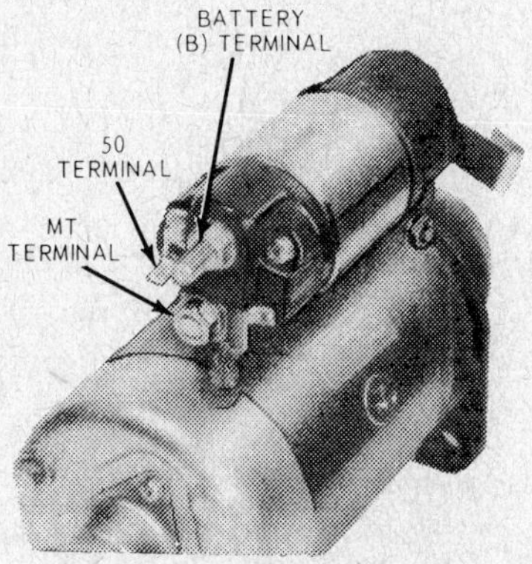

Starter solenoid terminals

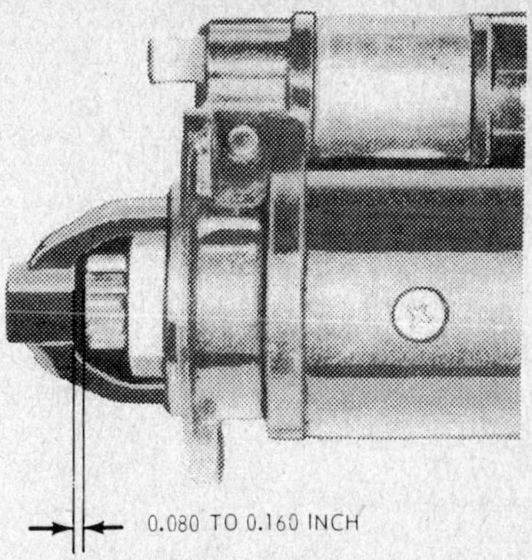

Starter drive end clearance

STARTER DRIVE REPLACEMENT

1. Remove the field strap.
2. Disengage the solenoid plunger hook from the shift fork and remove the solenoid.
3. Remove the shift fork pivot bolt, nut and lock washer.
4. Remove the drive end housing while disengaging the shift fork.
5. Slide the drive stop-ring retainer toward the armature and remove the stop-ring.
6. Slide the retainer and drive assembly from the shaft.
7. Installation is the reverse of removal.

ENGINE MECHANICAL

REMOVAL AND INSTALLATION

1. Remove the hood.
2. Drain the coolant and oil.
3. Remove all coolant lines, electrical wires, control cables and vacuum lines from the engine.
4. Remove the following:
   a. radiator
   b. fuel line
   c. fan
   d. drive belts
   e. alternator
   f. thermactor pump and filter hose
   g. front lower skid plate (1800 cc)

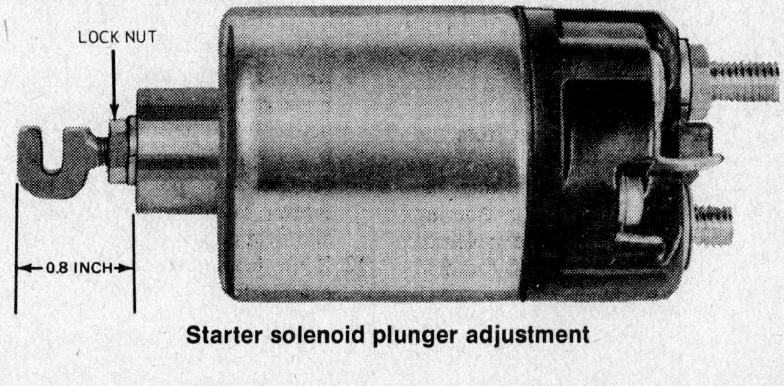

Starter solenoid plunger adjustment

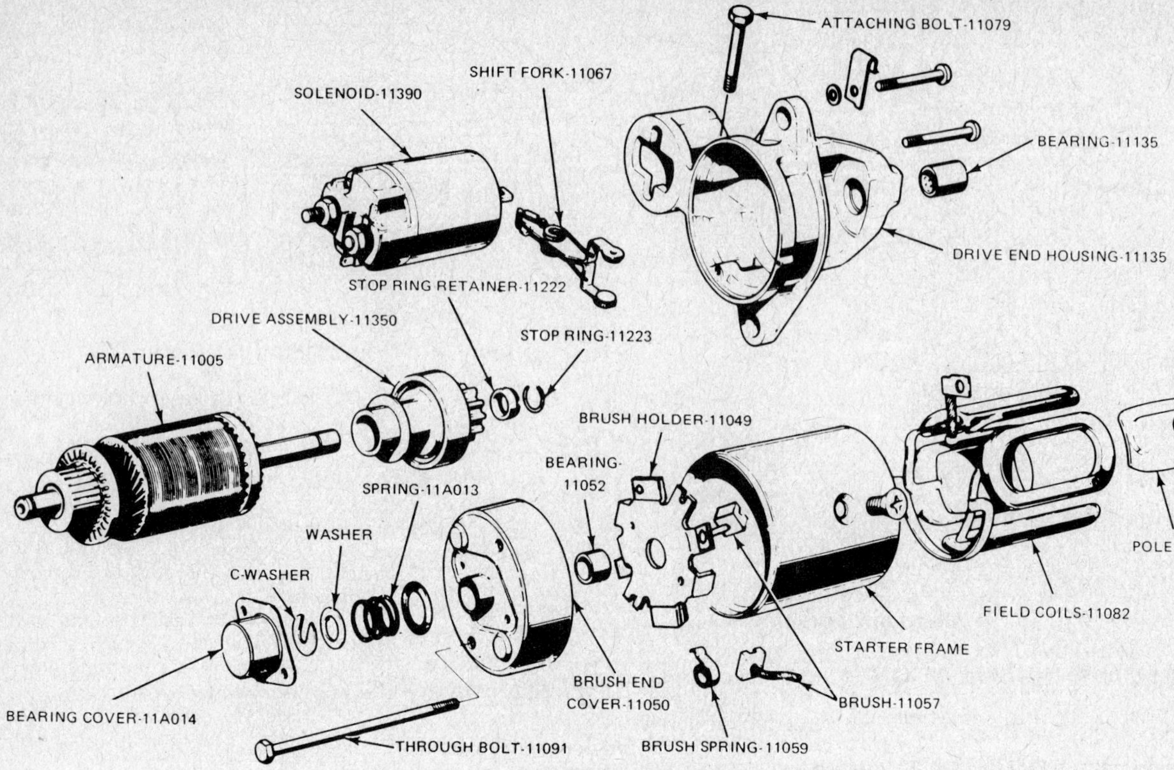

Starter component parts

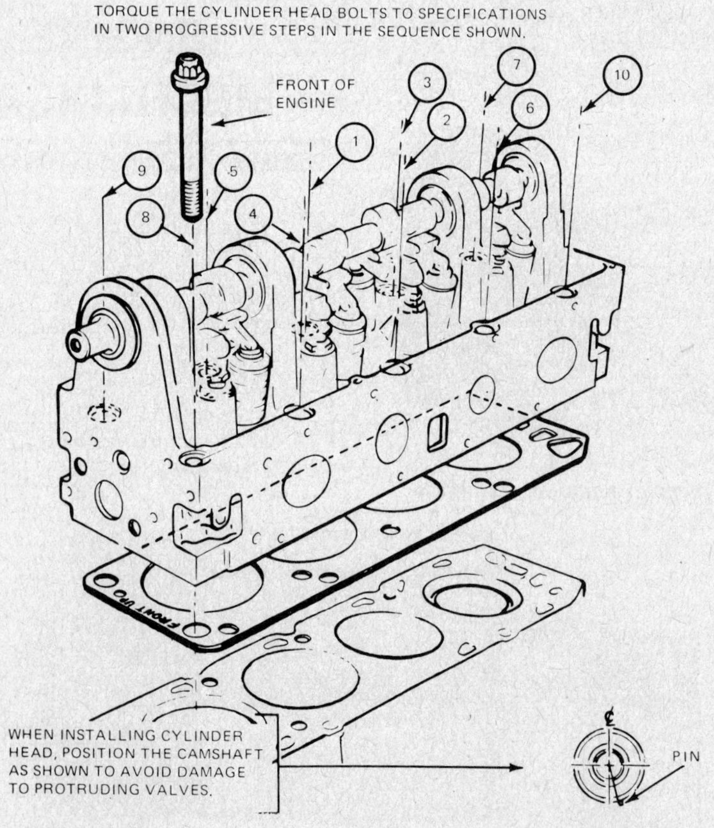

Cylinder head removal and installation—2300cc engine

h. exhaust pipe
i. flywheel housing bolts
j. lower starter nuts and one lower bolt, and
k. starter.

5. Support the transmission and attach an engine hoist. Remove the engine mount bolts and nuts.
6. Slide the engine forward, clear of the transmission, and out of the truck.
7. Installation is the reverse of removal.

Cylinder Head

REMOVAL AND INSTALLATION

1800 and 2000 cc Engines

1. Drain the cooling system and remove the hood.
2. Rotate No. 1 cylinder to TDC of compression stroke and remove the distributor.
3. Remove the following:
   a. air cleaner
   b. rocker arm cover
   c. exhaust pipe
   d. accelerator linkage
   e. exhaust pipe
   f. distributor gear from camshaft
   g. camshaft gear
   h. Rocker arm assembly
   i. head bolts, and
   j. camshaft.
4. Lift off the cylinder head and remove all tension from the timing chain.
5. Installation is the reverse of removal. Follow procedures under "Timing Chain Installation" and "Tensioner Adjustment". Adjust valve clearance hot.

2300 cc Engine

1. Remove the air cleaner, disconnect the hoses running across the valve cover, and remove the valve cover.
2. Remove the exhaust manifold.
3. Remove the intake manifold, complete with carburetor and decal valve.
4. Remove the camshaft drive belt cover. Note the positions of the rubber grommets underneath.
5. Remove the camshaft belt.
6. Remove the coolant outlet elbow from the cylinder head, with the hose attached.
7. Using special socket, remove the cylinder head bolts.
8. Lift the cylinder head and camshaft assembly from the engine. Do not pry under the head to remove.
9. To install, clean all the gasket surfaces, install a new head gasket, and install the head on the block. Torque the cylinder head bolts to specifications in three progressive steps. Install the cam belt, using the procedure outlined later in this section. The rest of installation is the reverse of removal.

OVERHAUL

See the "Engine Rebuilding Section".

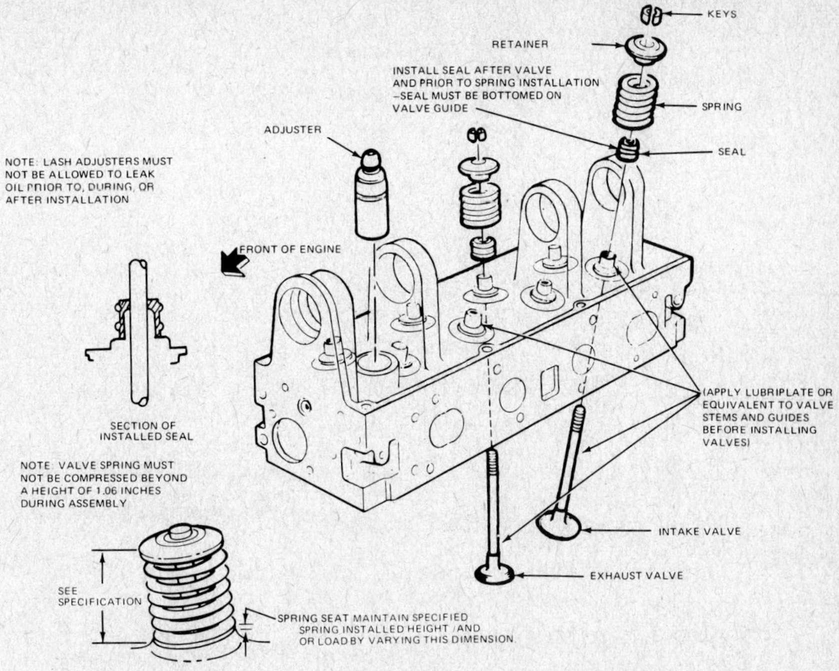

Cylinder head valves, springs, seals, retainers and lash adjusters —2300cc engine

Rocker Shafts

REMOVAL AND INSTALLATION

1800 and 2000 cc Engines

This operation should only be performed on a cold engine; the bolts which hold the rocker shafts in place also hold the cylinder head to the block.

1. Disconnect the choke cable.
2. If equipped, disconnect the air bypass valve cable.
3. Disconnect the spark plug wires.
4. Remove the rocker cover.
5. Remove the rocker arm shaft attaching bolts evenly and remove the rocker arm shafts.
6. Installation is the reverse of removal. Torque the rocker arm bolts in the three progressive steps and adjust the valves cold. Later perform a hot adjustment.

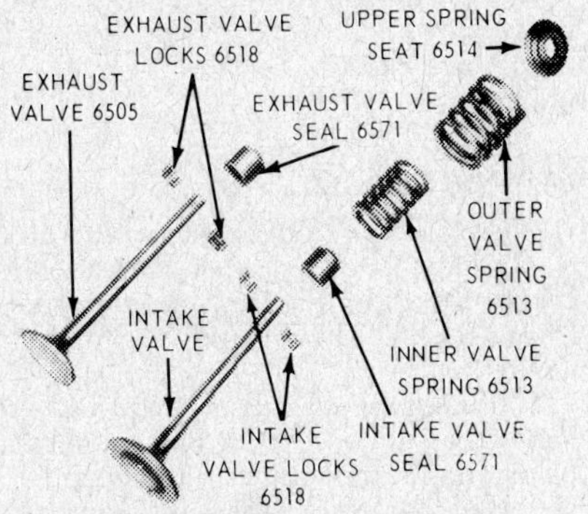

Valve assemblies—1800 and 2000cc engines

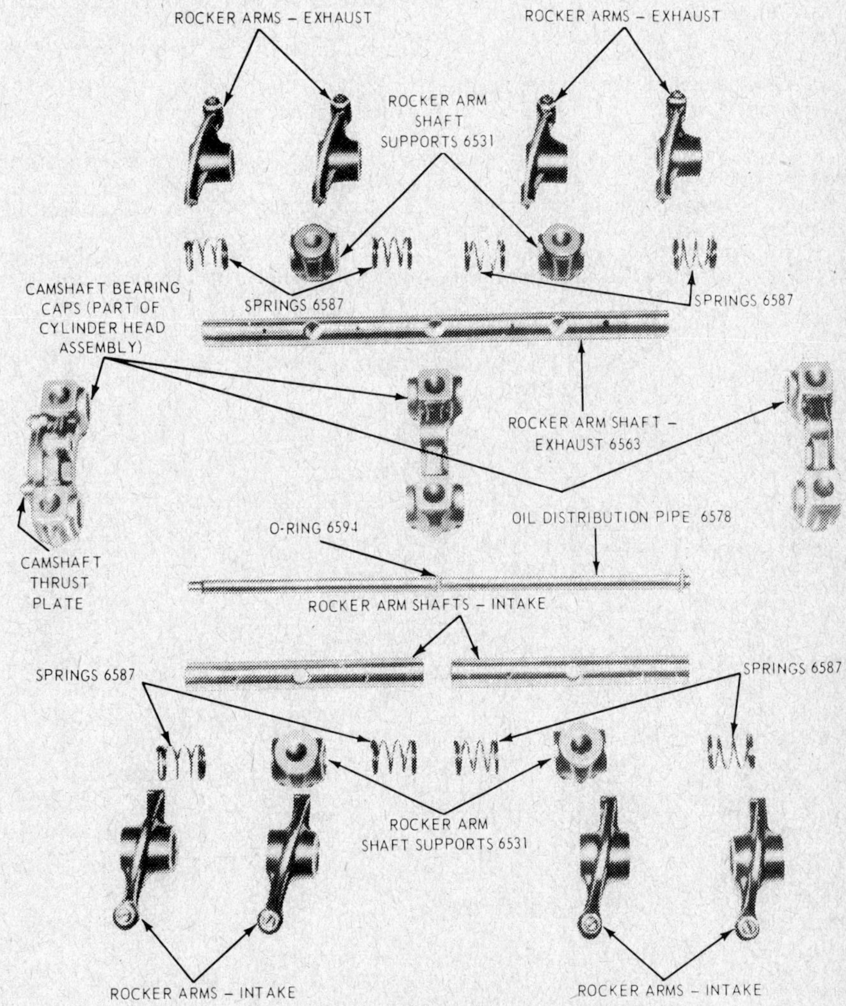

Rocker arms and shafts—1800 and 2000cc engines

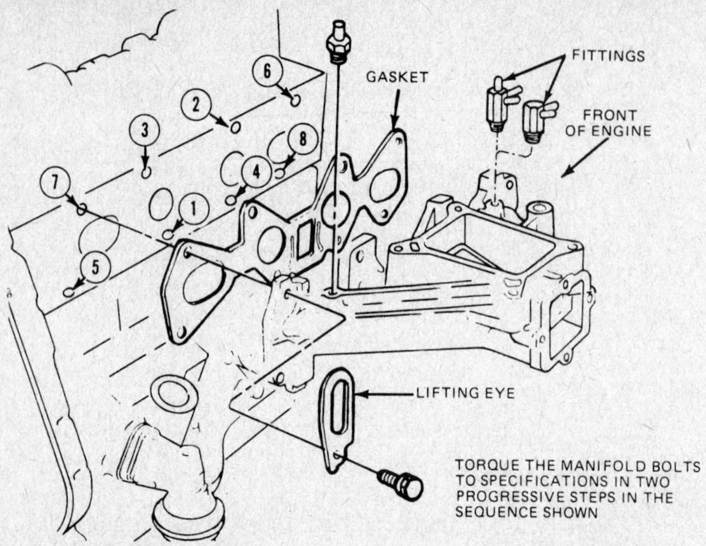

Intake manifold torque sequence— 2300cc engine

Intake Manifold

REMOVAL AND INSTALLATION

1. Drain the cooling system.
2. Remove the air cleaner.
3. Remove the accelerator linkage.
4. Disconnect the choke cable and fuel line. Plug the fuel line.
5. Disconnect the Thermactor hoses, if equipped.
6. Disconnect the PCV valve hose.
7. Disconnect the heater return hose and by pass hose.
8. Remove the manifold and carburetor as an assembly.
9. Installation is the reverse of removal. Use a new gasket. Tighten the manifolds bolts in a pattern from the center outwards in three progressive steps.

Exhaust Manifold

REMOVAL AND INSTALLATION

1. Remove the hot air duct and spark plug wires.
2. Remove the air injection nozzles or fitting, if equipped, and the upper and lower heat insulator.
3. Disconnect the EGR pipe, if present.
4. Raise the truck and disconnect the exhaust pipe at the flange.
5. Remove the manifold attaching bolts and remove the exhaust manifold.
6. Installation is the reverse of removal. Apply a light film of graphite grease to the manifold mounting surfaces, since no gasket is used. Use a new ring gasket at the exhaust pipe flange. Torque the manifold bolts in a circular pattern, working from the center outwards, in two progressive steps.

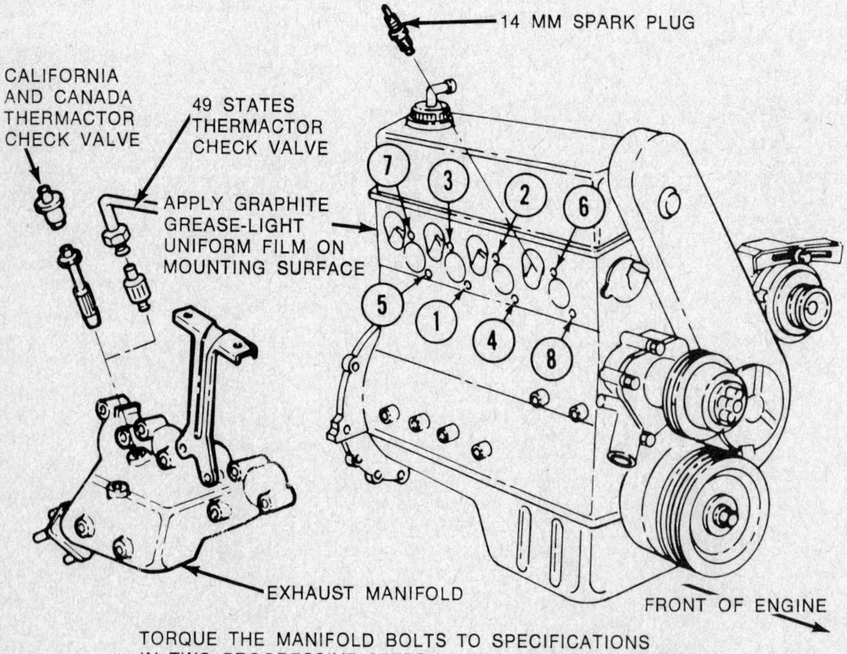

Exhaust manifold torque sequence—2300cc engine

Cylinder Front Cover

REMOVAL AND INSTALLATION

1800 and 2000 cc Engines

1. Scribe alignment marks on the hood hinges and remove the hood.
2. Drain the cooling system.
3. Remove the radiator.
4. Remove the accessory drive belts.
5. Remove the crankshaft pulley and the water pump.
6. Remove the cylinder head-to-front cover bolt.
7. Raise and support the truck.
8. Remove the engine skid plate.
9. Disconnect the emission line from the oil pan. Drain the oil.

Cylinder head-to-front cover bolt—1800 and 2000cc engines

10. Remove the oil pan.
11. Remove the alternator and bracket and lay the alternator aside.
12. Remove the Thermactor pump (if equipped) and lay the pump aside.
13. Remove the steel tube from the front of the engine.
14. Unbolt and remove the front cover.
15. Installation is the reverse of removal.

2300 cc Engine

There are two front covers on the 2300 cc engine; one is the cylinder front cover, the other is the auxiliary shaft front cover. They share a common gasket.

1. Drain the cooling system and remove the radiator. Plug the automatic transmission cooler lines, if equipped.
2. Remove the fan and accessory drive belts. Remove the fan and pulley.
3. Remove the camshaft belt outer

cover, crankshaft pulley, camshaft belt, and belt inner cover. See the timing belt section following for details.

4. Remove the crankshaft cam belt sprocket with a puller.

5. Drain the engine oil and remove the oil pan.

6. Unbolt and remove the cylinder front cover and the auxiliary shaft front cover.

If only one cover is to be removed, cut the gasket around the remaining cover, then use the necessary half of a new gasket when the cover is replaced.

Pry the old seals from the covers but do not install new shaft seals until the covers are in place.

Use a stepped tool to align the cylinder front cover and the crankshaft upon installation to prevent the timing belt from interfering with the front cover. Torque the cover bolts to 6–9 ft. lbs.

Install new shaft seals after cover installation. Oil the lips of the seals and install them with a seal driver of the proper size.

Front Cover Oil Seal

REMOVAL AND INSTALLATION

1800 and 2000 cc Engines

The front cover oil seal can be removed and a new one installed without removing the front cover.

1. Drain the cooling system.
2. Remove the radiator.

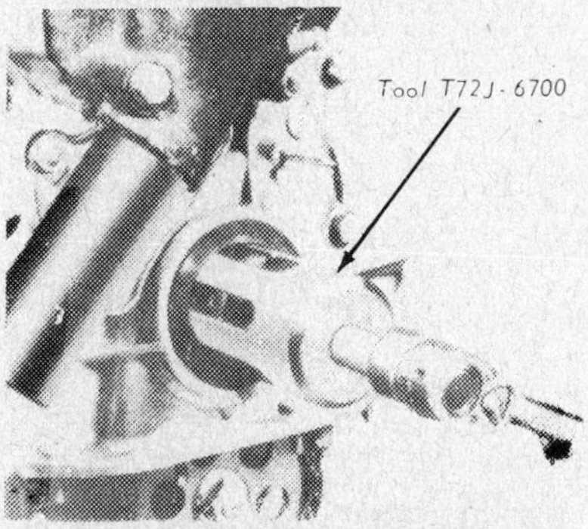

Removing front cover oil seal—1800 and 2000cc engines

Installing front cover oil seal—1800 and 2000cc engines

3. Remove the drive belt(s).
4. Remove the crankshaft pulley.
5. Pry the front oil seal from the front cover.
6. Press a new front seal into position (flush).
7. Install the crankshaft pulley.
8. Install the drive belt(s) and adjust the tension.
9. Install the radiator. Fill the cooling system.

2300 cc Engine

The cylinder and auxiliary shaft front cover seals can be replaced without removing the covers. Follow Steps 1, 2, 3, and 4 of the cylinder Front Cover procedure; it is not necessary to remove the belt inner cover. Remove the old seal with a puller. Coat the lips of a new seal with engine oil and install with a seal driver of the proper size.

Timing Chain and Tensioner

REMOVAL AND INSTALLATION

1800 and 2000 cc Engines

1. Remove the cylinder head and front cover. It is not necessary that the intake and exhaust manifolds be removed.
2. Remove the oil pump and chain.
3. Remove the timing chain tensioner.
4. Loosen the timing chain guide strip screws.
5. Remove the oil slinger.
6. Remove the oil pump sprocket and chain as an assembly.
7. Remove the timing chain, crankshaft and camshaft sprockets from the engine.

To install the timing chain, timing sprockets and tensioner:

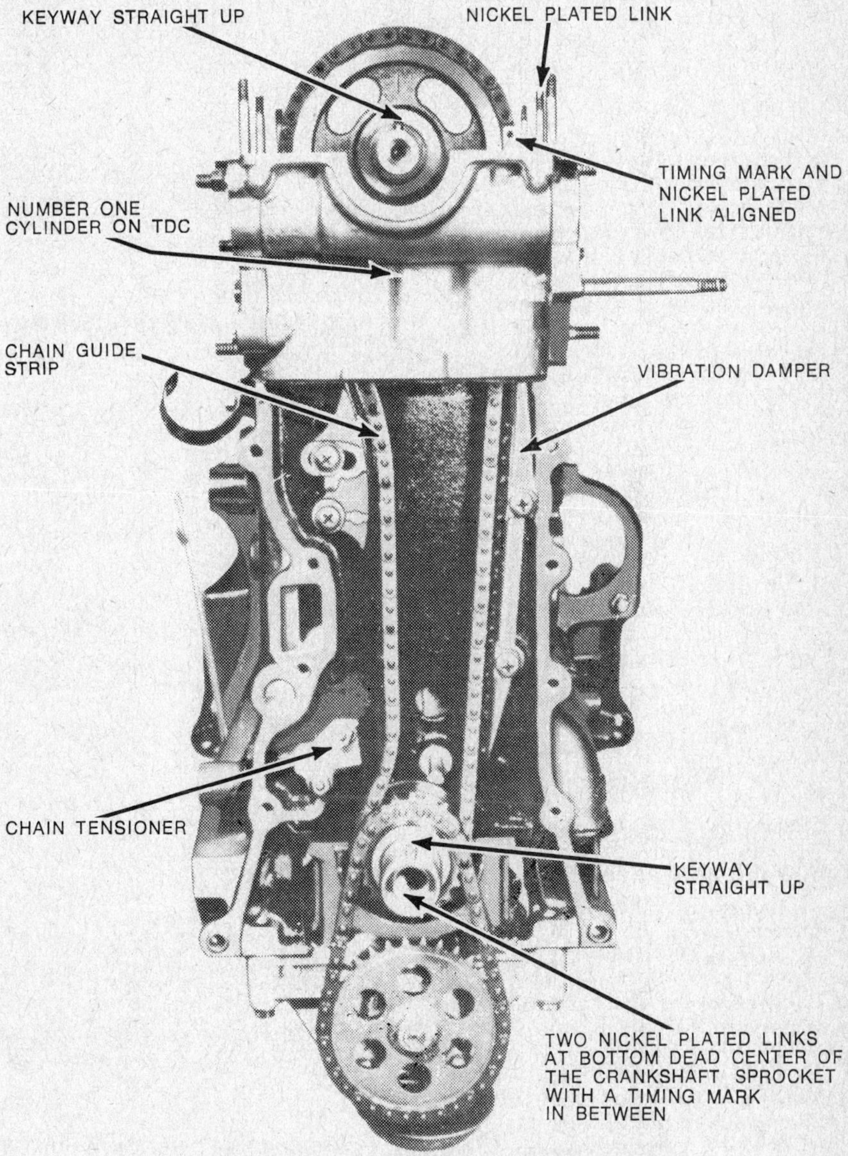

Correct valve timing—1800 and 2000cc engines

Installing the 1800 and 2000cc engine oil pump drive gear and chain

8. Position the crankshaft sprocket in the timing chain.
9. Position the oil pump chain and sprocket on the crankshaft and oil pump.
10. Install the oil slinger.
11. Install the oil pump washer and nut. Bend the washer over the nut.
12. Install the timing chain tensioner. Fully compress the snubber spring and wedge a screwdriver into the tensioner release mechanism. Without removing the screwdriver, install the tensioner.
13. Install the cylinder head and camshaft. Be sure that the valve timing is as illustrated.
14. Install the rocker arm shafts and cam bearing caps.
15. Install and torque the cylinder head bolts.
16. Adjust the timing chain tension. Press in on the chain guide strip. Tighten the guide strip attaching screws. Remove the screwdriver from the tensioner, allowing the snubber to take up the chain slack.
17. Replace the front cover.
18. Adjust the valve clearance cold. Torque the cylinder head bolts and adjust the valve clearance hot.

Timing Chain Tensioner

REMOVAL AND INSTALLATION

1800 and 2000 cc Engines

This operation can be performed with front cover installed.
1. Remove the water pump.
2. Remove the tensioner cover.
3. Remove the attaching bolts from the tensioner. Remove the tensioner.
To install the tensioner:
4. Fully compress the snubber spring. Insert a screw driver into the tensioner release mechanism.
5. Without removing the screwdriver, insert the tensioner and align the bolt holes. Install and torque the bolts.
6. Adjust the chain tension as follows:

ADJUSTMENT

1. Remove the two blind plugs and aluminum washers from the front cover.
2. Loosen the guide strip attaching screws.
3. Press the top of the chain guide strip through the adjusting hole in the cylinderhead.
4. Tighten the guide strip attaching screws.
5. Remove the screwdriver from the tensioner and let the snubber take up the slack in the chain.

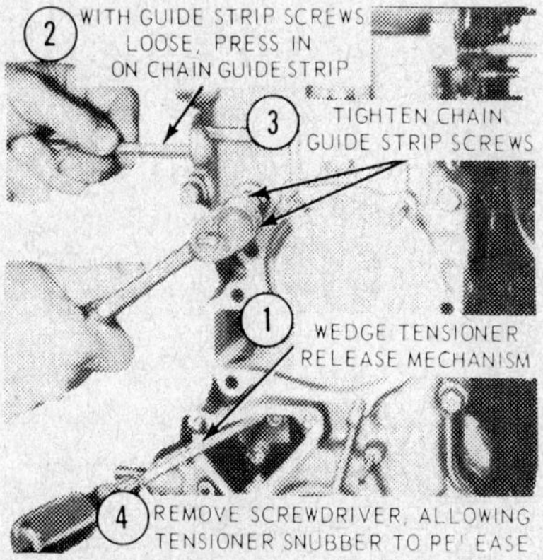

Adjusting timing chain tensioner (front cover installed)—1800 and 2000cc engines

6. Install the blind plugs and aluminum washers.
7. Install the tensioner cover and gasket.
8. Install a new gasket and water pump. Install the crankshaft pulley and drive belt and adjust the tension. Check the coolant level.

Timing Belt Cover, Belt, and Tensioner

CHECKING TIMING

2300 cc Engine Only

1. Remove the access plug from the belt cover.
2. Turn the crankshaft with a wrench on the pulley bolt (spark plugs removed) until the engine is at TDC. The timing pointer will be aligned with the notch on the crankshaft pulley.

CAUTION: Always turn the engine in a clockwise direction (facing the engine).

3. Remove the distributor cap. The rotor should point to the No. 1 plug tower.
4. Look through the access hole in the belt cover. The cam sprocket timing mark should be aligned with the timing pointer attached to the inner belt cover.

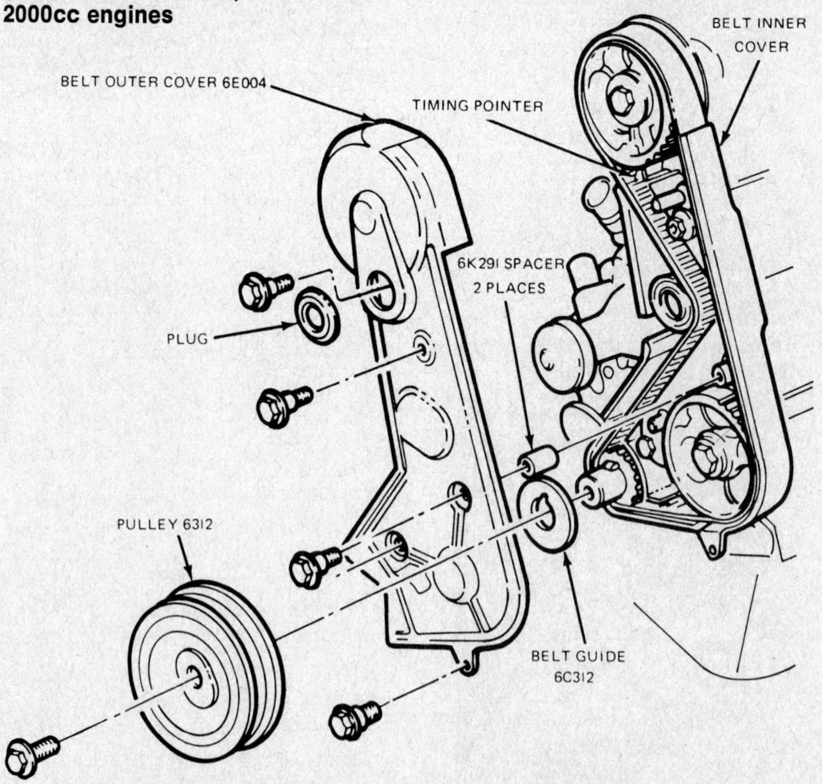

Timing belt outer cover, belt guide and inner cover and crankshaft pulley—2300cc engine

TIMING ADJUSTMENT; BELT REPLACEMENT

2300 cc Engine Only

1. If the engine is in time, and the belt is to be replaced, set the engine to TDC. Use the Checking Timing procedure.
2. Remove the fan and accessory drive belts. Remove the fan and pulley from the water pump shaft.
3. Remove the belt outer cover. There are tubular spacers underneath the two lower bolts.
4. Loosen the belt tensioner adjustment and pivot bolts. Lever the tensioner away from the belt and retighten the adjustment bolt to hold the tensioner.
5. Remove the crankshaft pulley and the belt guide behind it.
6. Remove the camshaft drive belt.
7. To time the engine, turn the crankshaft until the key is vertical. Remove the distributor cap and set the rotor to the No. 1 firing position by turning the auxiliary shaft sprocket. Turn the camshaft until the sprocket timing mark is aligned with the inner belt cover pointer.
8. Install the timing belt, crankshaft sprockets first, then auxiliary and cam sprockets. Center the belt fore and aft.
9. Loosen the tensioner adjustment bolt.
10. Rotate the crankshaft two complete turns in the direction of normal rotation, to remove belt slack. Tighten the tensioner adjustment bolt to 14–21 ft. lbs., the pivot bolt to 28–40 ft. lbs.
11. Check the belt timing.
12. Replace the belt guide, crankshaft pulley, spark plugs, distributor cap, outer cover, fan and pulley, and drive belts. Start the engine and adjust the ignition timing.

Camshaft

REMOVAL AND INSTALLATION

1800 and 2000 cc Engines

Perform this operation on a cold engine.

1. Scribe alignment marks on the hood hinges and remove the hood.
2. Remove the water pump.
3. Disconnect the coil wire and vacuum line from the distributor.
4 Rotate the crankshaft to place No. 1 cylinder on TDC of the compression stroke. This can be determined by removing the spark plug and feeling compression with your thumb. When compression is felt, rotate the crankshaft until the pointer aligns with he TDC mark on th pulley.
5. Remove the plug wires and distributor cap. Remove the distributor.
6. Remove the valve cover.
7. Release the tension on the timing chain.
8. Remove the cylinder head bolts.
9. Remove the rocker arm assembly.
10. Remove the nut, washer and distributor gear from the camshaft.

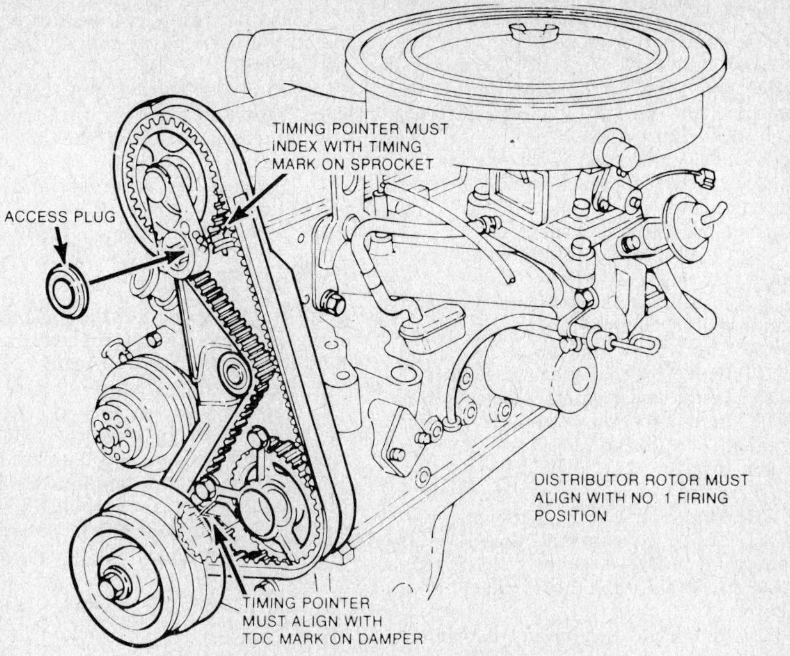

Timing belt installation—2300cc engine

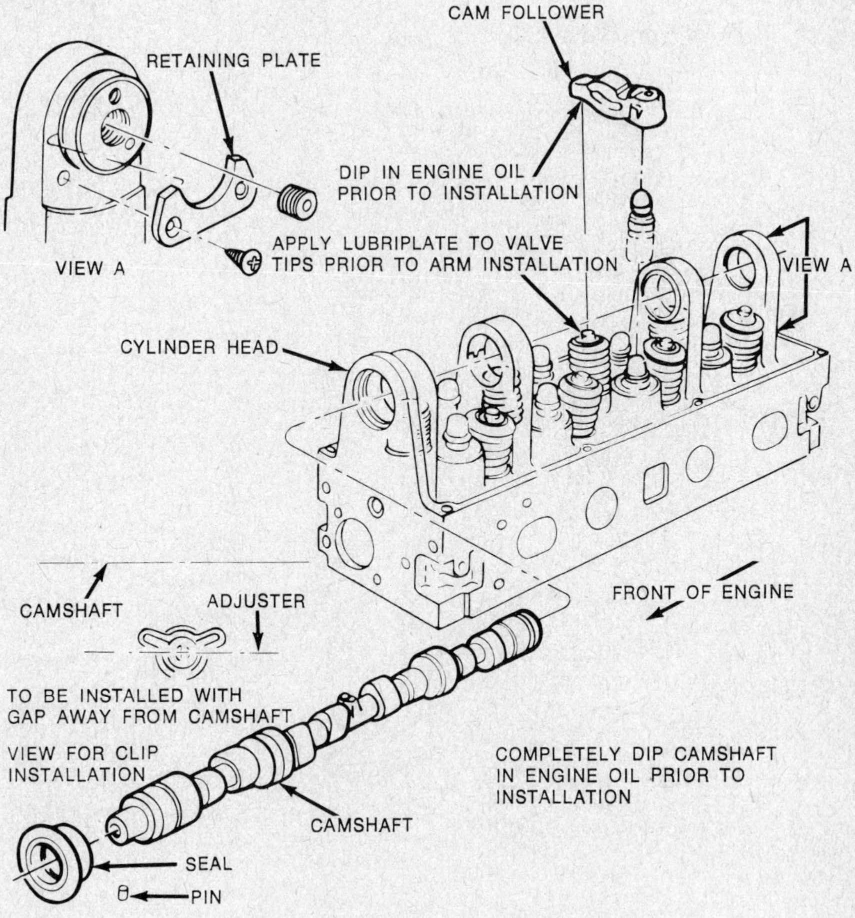

Camshaft installation—2300cc engine

11. Remove the nut and washer holding the camshaft sprocket.

12. Remove the camshaft. Do not remove the camshaft sprocket from the timing chain. Be sure that the sprocket teeth and chain relationship is not disturbed. Wire the chain and cam sprocket in place so that they will not fall behind the front cover.

To install the gasket surfaces.

14. Clean the cylinder head bolt holes.

15. Install the camshaft on the head and install the camshaft gear.

16. Check the valve timing.

17. Install the rocker arm assembly.

18. Install and torque the head bolts.

19. Install the cam sprocket washer and nut.

20. Install the distributor gear, washer, and nut.

21. Adjust the timing chain tension.

22. Check the camshaft end-play. It should be 0.001–0.007 in. If it exceeds 0.008 in., replace the thrust plate with a new one.

23. Install the distributor, distributor cap and plug wires.

24. Connect the vacuum line and coil wire.

25. Adjust the valve clearance cold. Install the valve cover and fill the cooling system.

26. Run the engine and check for leaks. When normal operating temperature is reached, adjust the hot valve clearance.

27. Adjust the carburetor and ignition timing.

28. Install the air cleaner and hood.

2300 cc Engine

1. Set the engine to TDC, as outlined in the Checking Timing procedure.
2. Remove the valve cover.
3. Remove the cam belt outer cover.
4. Loosen the tensioner bolts, lever the tensioner away from the belt, and retighten the tensioner adjustment bolt.
5. Slip the belt off the cam sprocket.
6. Remove the cam sprocket bolt and remove the sprocket with a puller. Remove the belt guide.

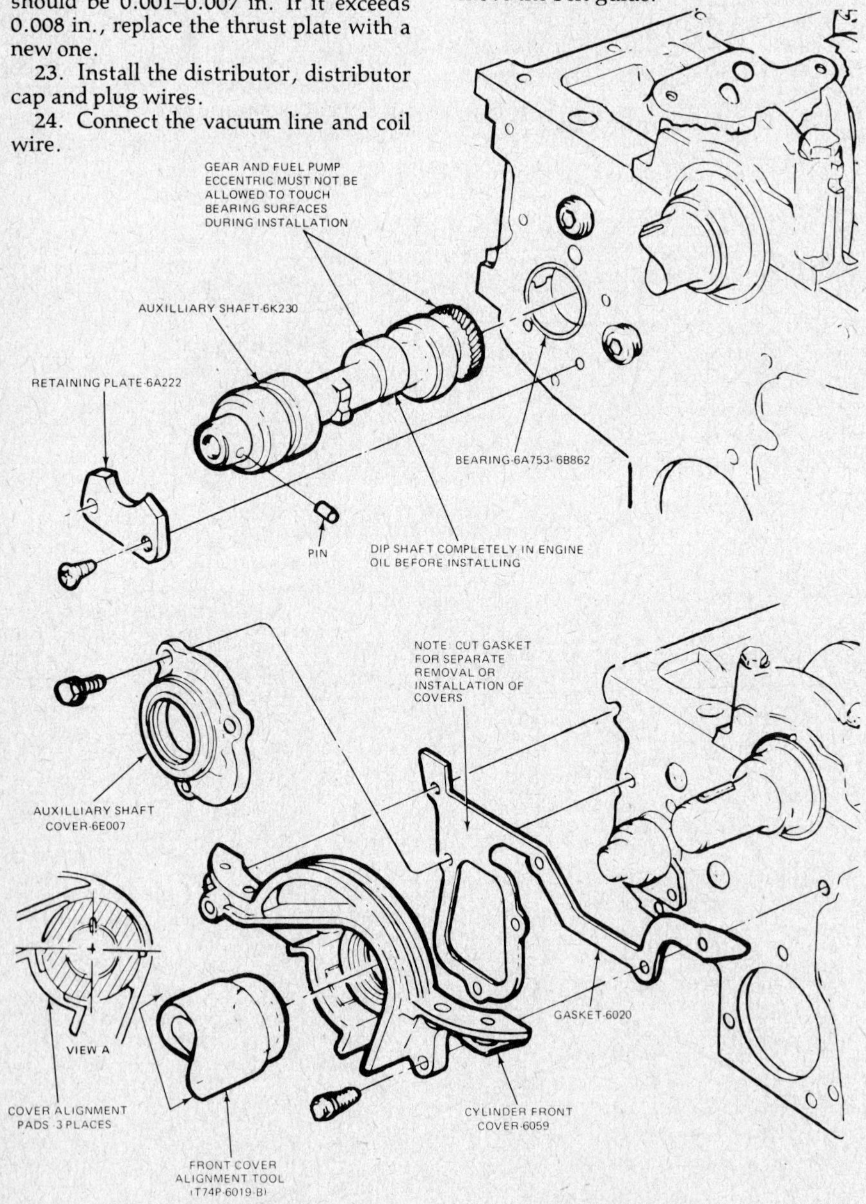

Auxiliary shaft installation—2300cc engine

7. Rotate the cam so that the base circle (low point) of the cam lobe is on the cam follower of the rearmost valve. Use a forked compressing tool to collapse the lash adjuster. Slide the cam follower over the lash adjuster and out.

8. Repeat this procedure with all seven remaining followers, working from the rear of the engine to the front. Keep all the parts in order; they must be returned to their original positions.

9. Remove the retaining plate from the rear cam bearing tower.

10. Remove the front cam seal. Slide the camshaft out through the front of the head.

11. Coat the cam and bearings with engine oil. If new bearings are installed, align their oil holes with those in the cam bearing towers. Slide the camshaft into the head.

12. Replace the retaining plate. Install a new front cam seal; oil the lips of the seal before installation.

13. Lubricate the valve tips and cam followers. Working from the front to the rear, replace the cam followers. Rotate the cam so that the base circle faces the head in each case. Compress the lash adjuster, install the follower, then fully collapse and release the lash adjuster again before rotating the camshaft for the next valve. This is important to prevent incorrect lash adjustment.

14. Install the belt guide. Install the cam sprocket. Wrap the sprocket bolt threads with Teflon tape and install the bolt and washer.

15. Measure the cam end play. If it exceeds 0.009 in., replace the retaining plate.

16. Align the cam sprocket mark with the inner belt cover pointer. Install the belt. Release the tensioner. Rotate the engine two complete turns in the direction of normal rotation to remove belt slack. Tighten the tensioner adjuster bolt to 14–21 ft. lbs., the pivot bolt to 28–40 ft. lbs. Check the belt timing.

17. Replace the outer cover. Replace the valve cover, using a new gasket.

Auxiliary Shaft

REMOVAL AND INSTALLATION

2300 cc Engine Only

1. Set the engine to TDC according to the Checking Timing procedure.
2. Remove the cam drive belt.
3. Remove the auxiliary shaft sprocket with a puller.
4. Remove the distributor.
5. Remove the auxiliary shaft cover and retaining plate.
6. Remove the shaft.

CAUTION: Do not allow the distributor drive gear teeth to touch the bearings.

7. Clean the shaft cover and front of the block. Coat the auxiliary shaft with oil and install into the block.
8. Replace the retaining plate. Coat

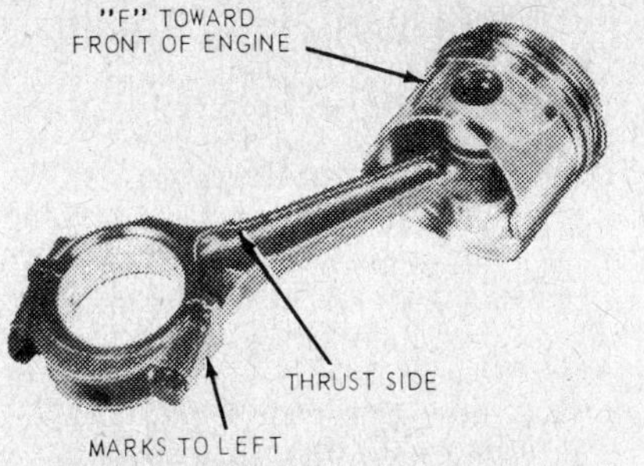
"F" TOWARD
FRONT OF ENGINE
THRUST SIDE
MARKS TO LEFT

Correct installation of piston and rod—1800 and 2000cc engines

the appropriate half of a new gasket with sealer and install the auxiliary shaft cover.

9. Install the distributor and the auxiliary shaft sprocket. Rotate the auxiliary shaft until the distributor rotor points to the No. 1 plug tower. Install the camshaft drive belt. Check the ignition timing.

Pistons and Connecting Rods

REMOVAL AND INSTALLATION

Refer to the "Engine Rebuilding" section for general engine service.

ENGINE LUBRICATION

Oil Pan

REMOVAL AND INSTALLATION

1800 and 2000 cc Engines

1. Raise and support the truck.
2. Remove the engine skid plate.
3. Drain the engine oil.
4. Remove and support the clutch release cylinder.
5. Remove the engine rear brace and loosen the bolts on the left-side.
6. Disconnect the emission line from the oil pan if equipped.
7. Remove the oil pan and rest it on the crossmember.
8. Remove the oil pump pickup tube from the pump.
9. Remove the oil pan.

To install the oil pan:

10. Clean all the gasket surfaces.
11. Clean the oil pan, oil pump pickup tube and oil pump screen.
12. Install a new oil pan gasket with oil-resistant sealer.
13. Install the oil pump pickup tube and screen.
14. Install the oil pan on the block. Torque the nuts and bolts to 5–8 ft. lbs.
15. Connect the emission line to the oil pan.

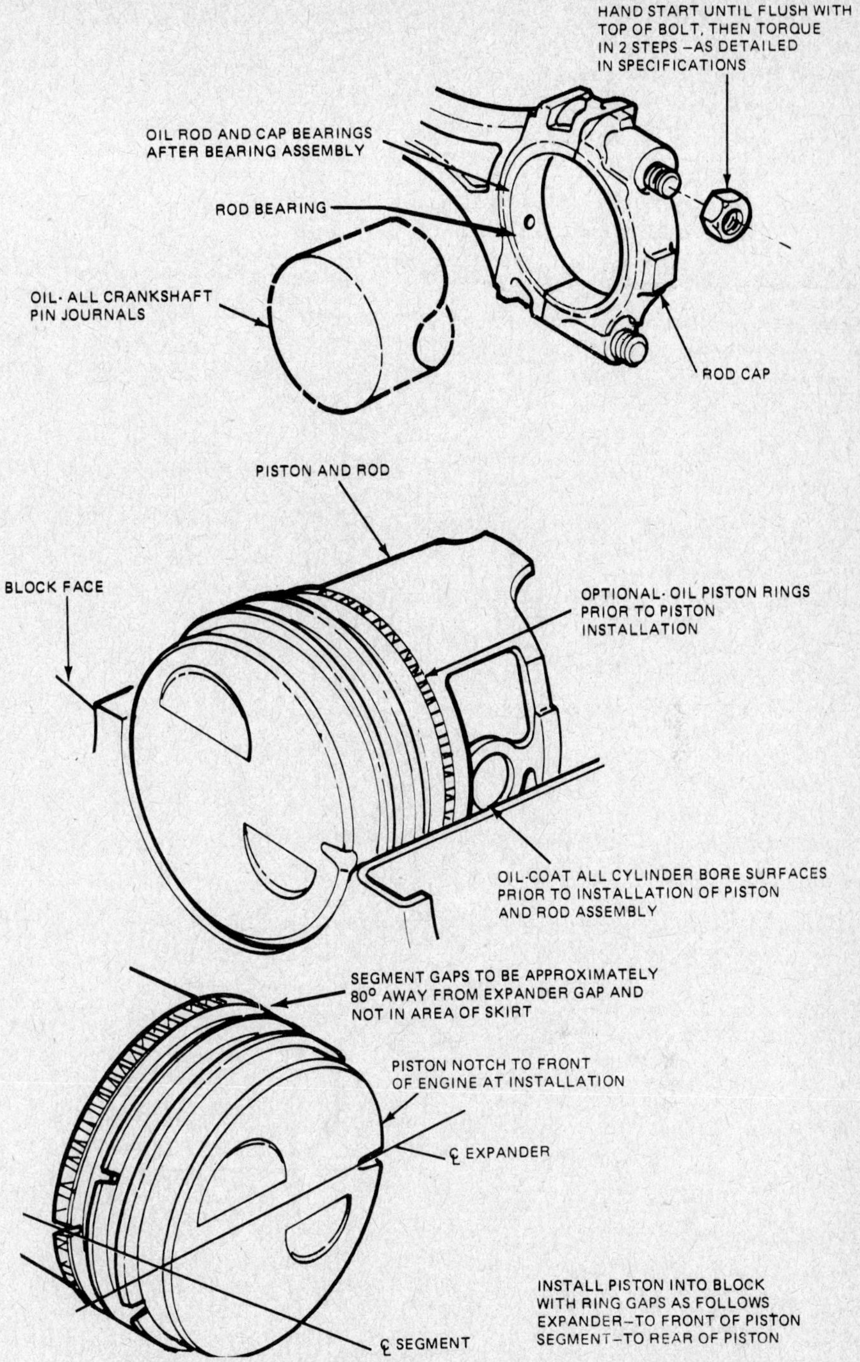
HAND START UNTIL FLUSH WITH
TOP OF BOLT, THEN TORQUE
IN 2 STEPS –AS DETAILED
IN SPECIFICATIONS
OIL ROD AND CAP BEARINGS
AFTER BEARING ASSEMBLY
ROD BEARING
OIL- ALL CRANKSHAFT
PIN JOURNALS
ROD CAP
PISTON AND ROD
BLOCK FACE
OPTIONAL- OIL PISTON RINGS
PRIOR TO PISTON
INSTALLATION
OIL-COAT ALL CYLINDER BORE SURFACES
PRIOR TO INSTALLATION OF PISTON
AND ROD ASSEMBLY
SEGMENT GAPS TO BE APPROXIMATELY
80° AWAY FROM EXPANDER GAP AND
NOT IN AREA OF SKIRT
PISTON NOTCH TO FRONT
OF ENGINE AT INSTALLATION
℄ EXPANDER
INSTALL PISTON INTO BLOCK
WITH RING GAPS AS FOLLOWS
EXPANDER–TO FRONT OF PISTON
SEGMENT–TO REAR OF PISTON
℄ SEGMENT

Installing pistons, rings and connecting rods—2300cc engine

16. Attach the rear engine bracket. Torque the bolts to specification.
17. Reinstall the clutch release cylinder. Torque the nuts to specification.
18. Replace the engine skid plate.
19. Lower the truck. Fill the crankcase, and run the engine. Check for leaks and oil pressure.

2300 cc Engine

1. Raise and support the truck.
2. Drain the engine oil. Remove the flywheel cover and dipstick.
3. Loosen and move the steering rack forward to gain clearance.
4. Remove the bolts and oil pan.
5. Clean the gasket mounting surfaces. Use new pan side gaskets, and new front and rear seals. Apply oil resistant sealer to the pan flange and the pan side gaskets. Install the gaskets on the pan.
6. Apply sealer to the joint of the block and front cover, then install the front and rear seals to the block. Press the seal tabs firmly into the block.
7. Install the oil pan and bolts. Torque to bolts to 5–8 ft. lbs. in a clockwise pattern, beginning at the left rear of the pan. The remainder of installation is the reverse of removal.

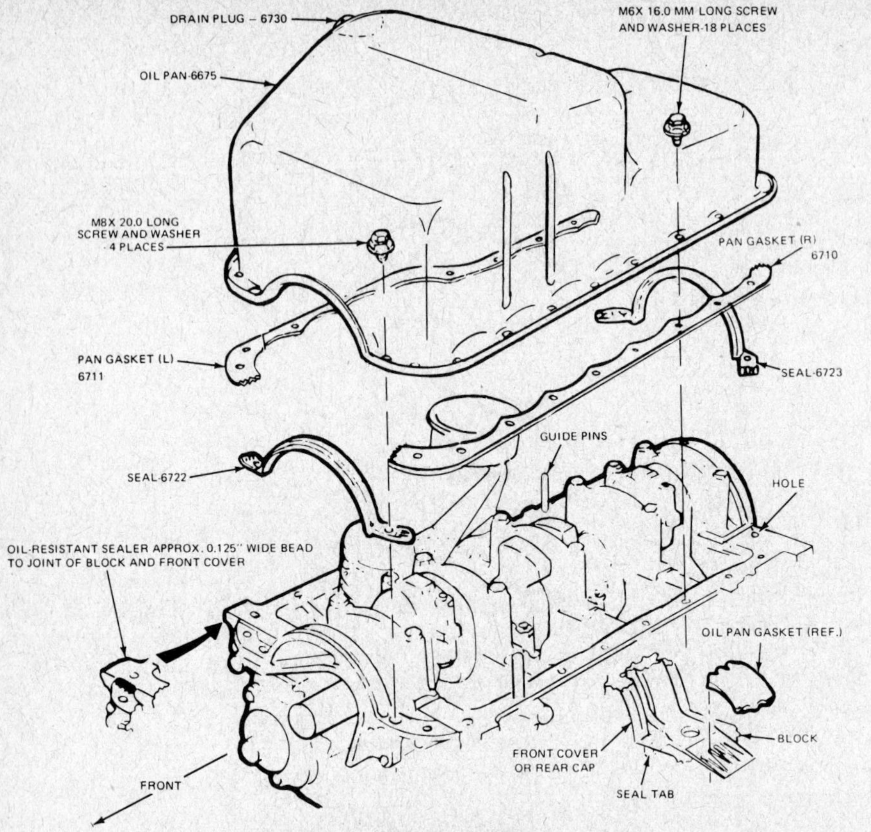

Oil pan installation—2300cc engine

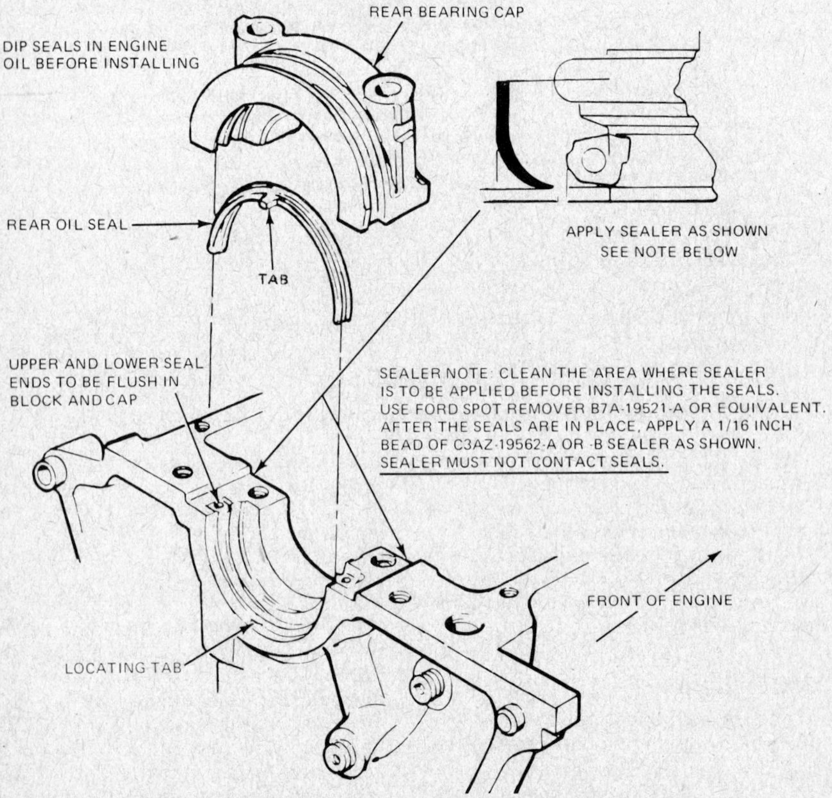

Rear main bearing seal installation—2300cc engine

Rear Main Oil Seal

REPLACEMENT

1800 and 2000 cc Engines

If the rear main oil seal in being replaced independently of any other parts, it can be done with the engine in place. If the rear main oil seal and the rear main bearing are being replaced together, the engine must be removed.

1. Remove the transmission.
2. Remove the clutch disc, pressure plate and flywheel.
3. Using an awl, punch two holes in the crankshaft rear oil seal. They should be punched on opposite sides of the crankshaft, just above the bearing cap-to-cylinder block split line.
4. Install a sheet metal screw in each hole. Pry against both screws at the same time to remove the oil seal. Do not scratch the oil seal surface on the crankshaft.
5. Clean the oil recess in the cylinder block and bearing cap. Clean the oil seal surface on the crankshaft.
6. Coat the oil seal surfaces with oil. Coat the oil seal surface and the seal surface on the crankshaft with Lubriplate. Install the oil seal and be sure that it is not cocked. Be sure that the seal surface was not damaged.
7. Install the flywheel. Coat the threads of the flywheel attaching bolts with oil-resistant sealer.
8. Install the clutch, pressure plate, and transmission.

2300 cc Engine

1. Remove the oil pan.
2. Loosen all the main bearing cap bolts enough to allow the crankshaft to lower slightly.

NOTE: It may be necessary to remove the oil pump for access to the cap bolts.

3. Remove the rear main bearing cap, and remove the oil seal from the cap.
4. Install a sheet metal screw into one end of the cylinder block half of the seal and remove the seal from the block.
5. Clean the cap and block seal grooves with solvent. Lubricate the seal halves in engine oil.
6. Install the upper half of the seal into the block groove with the undercut side of the seal towards the front of the engine.
7. Pull the seal until both ends are flush with the engine block.
8. Install the lower seal in the rear main bearing cap so that the tab faces to the rear and the undercut side faces to the front of the engine.
9. Apply a small amount of sealer to the mating surface of the rear main bearing cap and the engine block. Do not allow the sealer to contact the seal.
10. Install the rear main bearing cap and torque all the main caps to specifications.
11. Install the oil pan.

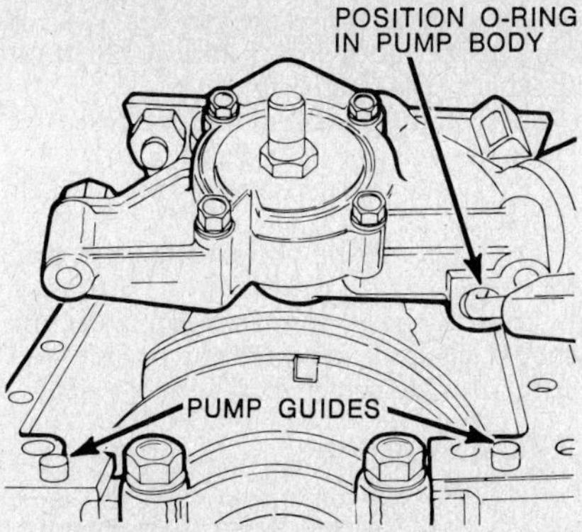

1800 and 2000cc engine oil pump installation

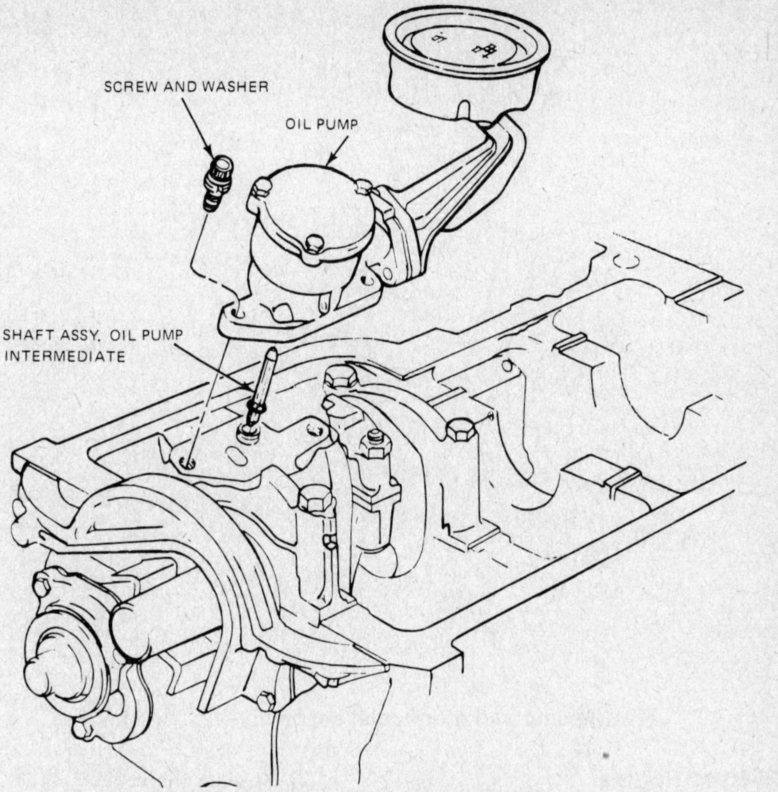

Oil pump installation—2300cc engine

Oil Pump

REMOVAL AND INSTALLATION

1800 and 2000 cc Engines

1. Remove the oil pan.
2. Remove the oil pump gear attaching nut.
3. Remove the bolts attaching the oil pump to the block. Loosen the sprocket on the pump.
4. Remove the oil pump and sprocket.

To install the oil pump:

5. Install the oil pump sprocket in the chain.
6. Prime the oil pump and install it on the sprocket and cylinder block. Install the bolts and torque them to specification.
7. Install the washer, gear and nut. Bend the locktab on the washer.
8. Install the oil pan. Fill the engine with oil. Start the engine and check for oil pressure. Check for leaks.

2300 cc Engine

The oil pump is mounted on the bottom of the engine block, enclosed by the oil pan. To remove the pump, remove the oil pan, the pump attaching bolts, and the pump. The pump is not rebuildable; if defective, it should be replaced. When installing, use a new gasket, and fill the pump with oil to prime it.

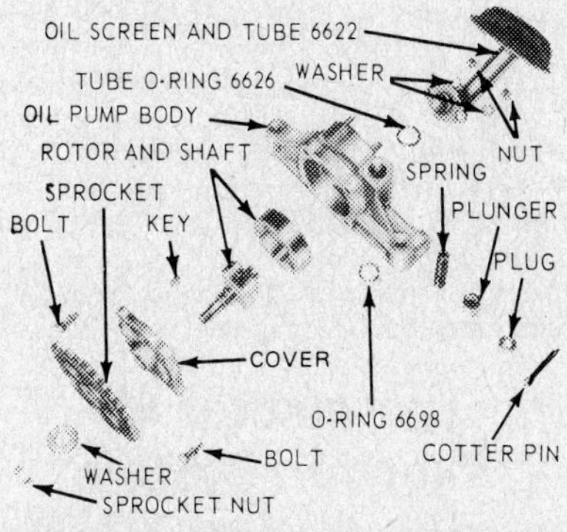

1800 and 2000cc engine oil pump components and related parts

ENGINE COOLING

Radiator

REMOVAL AND INSTALLATION

1. Drain the cooling system.
2. If equipped, remove the fan shroud.
3. Remove the fan on the 1800 and 2000 cc engines only. On California models remove the fan clutch.
4. Disconnect the upper and lower radiator hoses.
5. If equipped with automatic transmission, disconnect and plug the fluid cooler lines.
6. Unbolt and remove the radiator.
7. Installation is the reverse of removal.

Water Pump

REMOVAL AND INSTALLATION

1800 and 2000 cc Engines

1. Drain the cooling system.
2. Remove the lower hose from the water pump.
3. Disconnect the upper radiator hose from the engine and the lower radiator hose at the radiator.
4. Remove the radiator.
5. Remove the drive belts.
6. Remove the fan and pulley. Remove the crankshaft pulley.
7. Unbolt and remove the water pump.

To install the water pump:

8. Clean the gasket surfaces of the water pump and cylinder block.
9. Install the water pump and new gasket on the block. Torque the bolts to specification.
10. Install the lower hose on the water pump.
11. Install the fan and pulley. Install the crankshaft pulley.
12. Install the drive belts and adjust the tension.
13. Install the radiator.
14. Refill the cooling system with the specified amount and type of coolant. Install the radiator cap and start the engine. Check for leaks.

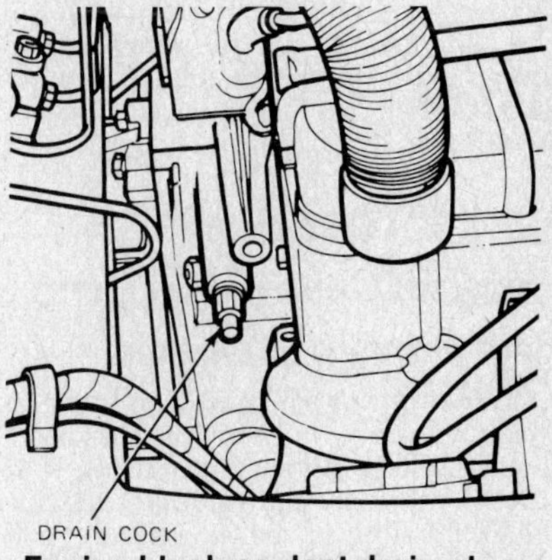

Engine block coolant drain plug

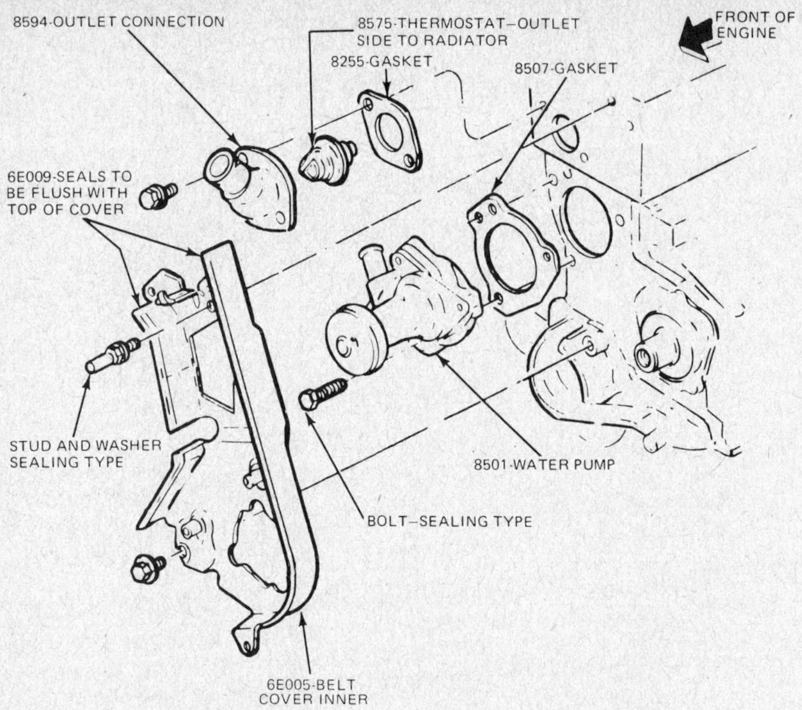

Water pump and thermostat assembly—2300cc engine

2300 cc Engine

1. Drain the cooling system. Disconnect the lower radiator hose and the heater hose from the water pump.
2. Remove the fan and accessory drive belts. Remove the fan shroud, if equipped.
3. Remove the fan and pulley.
4. Remove the camshaft drive belt outer cover.
5. Remove the water pump attaching bolts and the water pump. Wrench clearance has been provided in the inner belt cover; removal is not necessary.
6. To install, clean all gasket material from the mounting surfaces.
7. Transfer the heater hose fitting to the new pump.
8. Coat the new gasket with sealer and install the pump and gasket on the engine.
9. Install the belt outer cover, fan and pulley, and accessory drive belts. Install the fan shroud, if equipped. Connect the radiator and heater hoses. Fill the cooling system, turn the heater on, install the radiator and coolant recovery tank caps, and run the engine. Check for leaks. When cool, check the coolant level and add as necessary.

Thermostat

REMOVAL AND INSTALLATION

1800 and 2000 cc Engines

1. Drain enough coolant to bring the coolant level down below the thermostat housing. The thermostat housing is located on the left front side of the cylinder block. Disconnect the temperature sending unit wire.
2. Remove the coolant outlet elbow. If so equipped, position the vacuum control valve out of the way. The vacuum control valve is not used on California models.
3. Disconnect the coolant by-pass hose from the thermostat housing.
4. Remove the thermostat and housing from the engine.
5. Remove the thermostat from the housing and note the position of the jiggle pin.

To install the thermostat:

6. Remove all gasket material from the parts.
7. Install the thermostat housing using a new gasket with water-resistant sealer.
8. Position the thermostat in the housing with the jiggle pin up. Coat a new gasket with sealer and install it on the thermostat housing.
9. Install the coolant outlet elbow and vacuum control valve (if equipped).
10. Connect the by-pass and radiator hoses.
11. Connect the temperature sending unit wire.
12. Fill the cooling system with the proper coolant. Operate the engine and check the coolant level. Check for leaks.

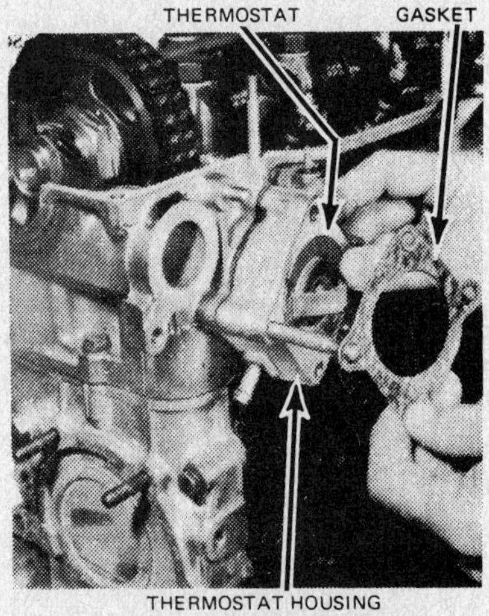

1800 and 2000cc engine thermostat installation

2300 cc Engine

1. Drain the coolant so that the level is below the thermostat.
2. It is not necessary to remove the hose from the outlet connection, if you're careful. Remove the two bolts holding the outlet to the block and pull it away enough to provide access to the thermostat.
3. Remove the thermostat and gasket.
4. Clean the mounting surface and outlet housing of all old gasket material.
5. Coat a new gasket with silicone sealer. The gasket must go on before the thermostat.
6. Position the gasket against the engine, then place the thermostat on top of it with the outlet side towards the radiator.
7. Install the coolant outlet and the two retaining bolts. Torque the bolts to 14–21 ft lbs. Refill the cooling system, start the engine, and check for leaks and proper thermostat operation.

EMISSION CONTROLS

Hydrocarbons, carbon monoxide (CO), oxides of nitrogen (NO) and fuel vapors are controlled by four basic systems. A Thermactor air injection system is used on California trucks only in 1973, and all trucks thereafter. A positive crankcase ventilation (PCV) system is used on all trucks. All Couriers use an evaporative emission control system to absorb fuel vapors and a deceleration control system to augment the Thermactor air pump.

Three additional systems were introduced in 1976 and 1977. An Exhaust Gas Recirculation (EGR) system was introduced on the 1976 California models with manual transmission, and expanded to all models in 1977. 1976 and later Couriers sold in California have a catalytic converter. 1977 and later 1800 cc engines have a spark delay system.

Thermactor Air Injection System

The Thermactor system consists of an air pump, check valve, one air injection nozzle for each cylinder, an air injection manifold, air by-pass valve and the associated hoses and connection.

TESTING THE SYSTEM

Air Pump Drive Belt

Be sure that the air pump drive belt is adjusted to the proper tension.

Air Pump

1. Disconnect the air pump outlet hose from the air by-pass valve.
2. Connect a "T" fitting and pressure gauge into the outlet line. The other end of the fitting should have a plug with an 11/32 in. hole drilled through it.
3. Start the engine and run it briefly at 1,500 rpm, choke fully open.
4. If the pressure reading is below 1 psi, replace the pump.

Air Pump Relief Valve

1. Operate the engine at idle.
2. Check the relief valve for airflow. No flow should be evident. If airflow out is noted, replace the relief valve and air pump.
3. Increase the engine speed to 3,000 rpm. If air flows out of the relief valve, the valve is in good condition. If air does not flow from the releif valve, or if the valve is excessively noisy, the relief valve and air pump assembly should be replaced.

Air Manifold Check Valve

1. Remove the check valve from the air injection manifold. Blow through the valve from the intake side and the outlet side. Air should pass through the valve from the intake side only. If air passes through the valve from the outlet side, replace the valve.

Air By-pass Valve

This valve is used through 1974.

1. Disconnect the air line at the check valve.
2. Push the choke knob all the way in.
3. Run the engine at 1,500 rpm.
4. Hold your hand over the end of the air pump air line. Air should flow from the hose.
5. Pull the choke knob all the way out. No air should flow from the air line.
6. If the valve is not operating properly, replace the valve.

Air Control Valve

This valve is used 1975–76.

1. Disconnect the outlet hose from the bottom of the air control valve at the air cleaner. With the engine idling, air should not flow from the outlet.
2. Unplug the air control valve solenoid electrical connector. Air should flow from the outlet.
3. Reconnect the plug. Increase the engine speed above 4,300 rpm and check for air discharge. Allow the engine to return to idle; air discharge should stop.
4. If the valve is not operating cor-

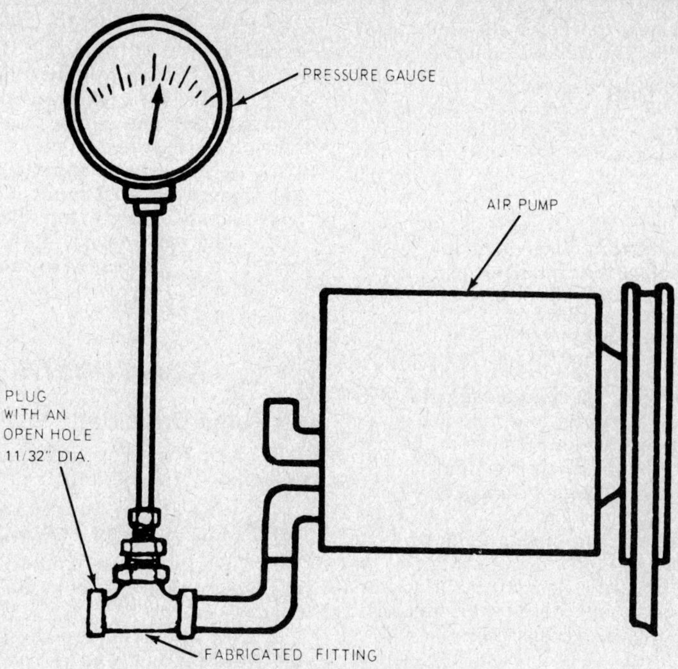

Checking air pump pressure

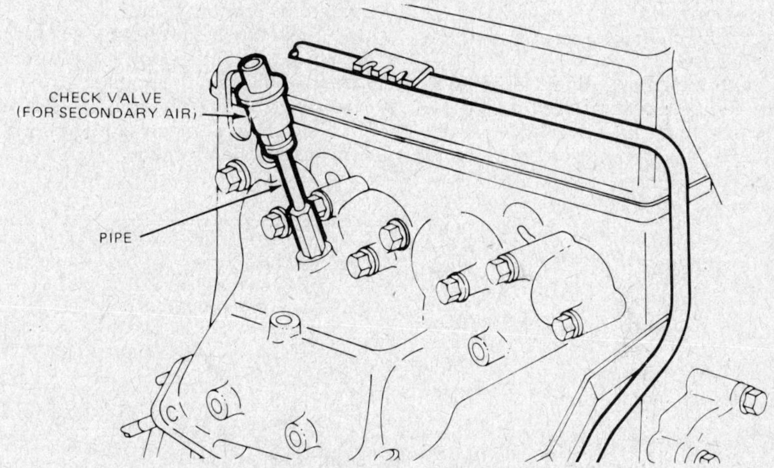

Air injection nozzle—2300cc engine

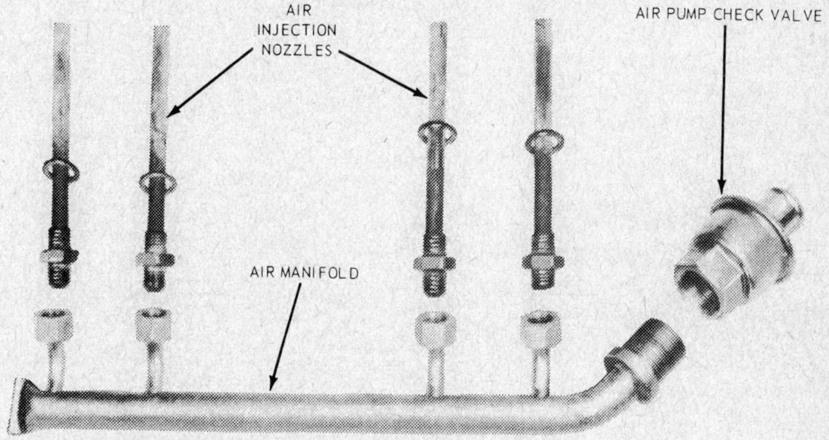

Air manifold assembly—1800 and 2000cc engines

rectly, check the hoses for soundness. Replace the valve as necessary.

Control Unit

The unit is only used 1975–76.

1. Attach a test light to the unit connector. The light should be on with the engine idling.
2. When engine speed is increased above 4,300 rpm, the light should go off.
3. Replace the unit if defective.

Air Control Valve

Only 1977–80 trucks sold in California with either the 1800 or 2000 cc engine, or the 2300 engine equipped with automatic transmission, have this valve.

1. Unplug the outlet hose at the bottom of the valve. Start the engine.
2. With the engine idling, air should not flow from the outlet.
3. Unplug the small diameter hose from the valve top. Air should flow.
4. If the valve is not operating correctly, check the hoses for soundness. Replace the valve as necessary.

Air Control Valve

This valve is used only on 1977 and later 2300 cc engines with manual transmission.

1. Unplug the outlet hose at the bottom of the valve.
2. With the engine idling, disconnect the small diameter hose from the air by-pass valve (not the air control valve). Air should flow from the outlet.
3. Plug the small hose. Air flow should stop.
4. Remove the vacuum hose connected to the No. 2 relief valve on the air control valve. This is the small hose at the side of the valve. Remove the plug from the hose disconnected in Step 2, and connect this hose to the No. 2 relief valve. Air should flow from the outlet.
5. If the valve is not operating correctly, check the hoses, and replace the valve as necessary.

ADJUSTMENTS

Air Pump Drive Belt

Be sure the drive belt is adjusted properly.

Air By-pass Valve Through 1974

1. Push the choke handle all the way in. Be sure that the choke plate is fully open.
2. Loosen the cable retaining screw in the valve plunger and the screw in the cable retaining bracket.
3. Be sure that the plunger is fully bottomed.
4. Insert the cable in the plunger and tighten the retaining screw.
5. Push down on the cable as much as possible without bending the control wire, then tighten the bracket screw.
6. Pull the choke knob all the way out. The valve plunger should be pulled to the top of the bracket.

Deceleration Control System

1973–74 Couriers use an anti-afterburn valve and a coasting to prevent detonation in the exhaust system. The coasting richer valve also prevents an overly lean mixture. The coasting richer valve is controlled by three switches; the speedometer switch, the accelerator switch and the clutch switch. In order for the coasting richer valve to operate, all three switches must be closed. The accelerators switch closes when the accelerator pedal is in the released position. The speedometer switch closes at speeds above approximately 17–23 mph. The clutch switch is closed when the clutch pedal is released.

1975–76 Couriers use the same system, but the clutch switch is not used. 1977–78 1800 and 2000 cc engine 49 State trucks use an air by-pass valve, a carburetor dashpot, and a throttle opener system. 1977–80 1800 and 2000 cc engine trucks sold in California and 1979–80 2000 cc, 49 State trucks use an anti-afterburn valve and a throttle opener system. 1977 and later 2300 cc 49 State engines use an air by-pass valve, a coasting richer valve controlled by speed and accelerator switches, and on trucks with manual transmission, a dashpot. 2300 cc engines sold in California use the air by-pass valve, and the dashpot with manual transmission.

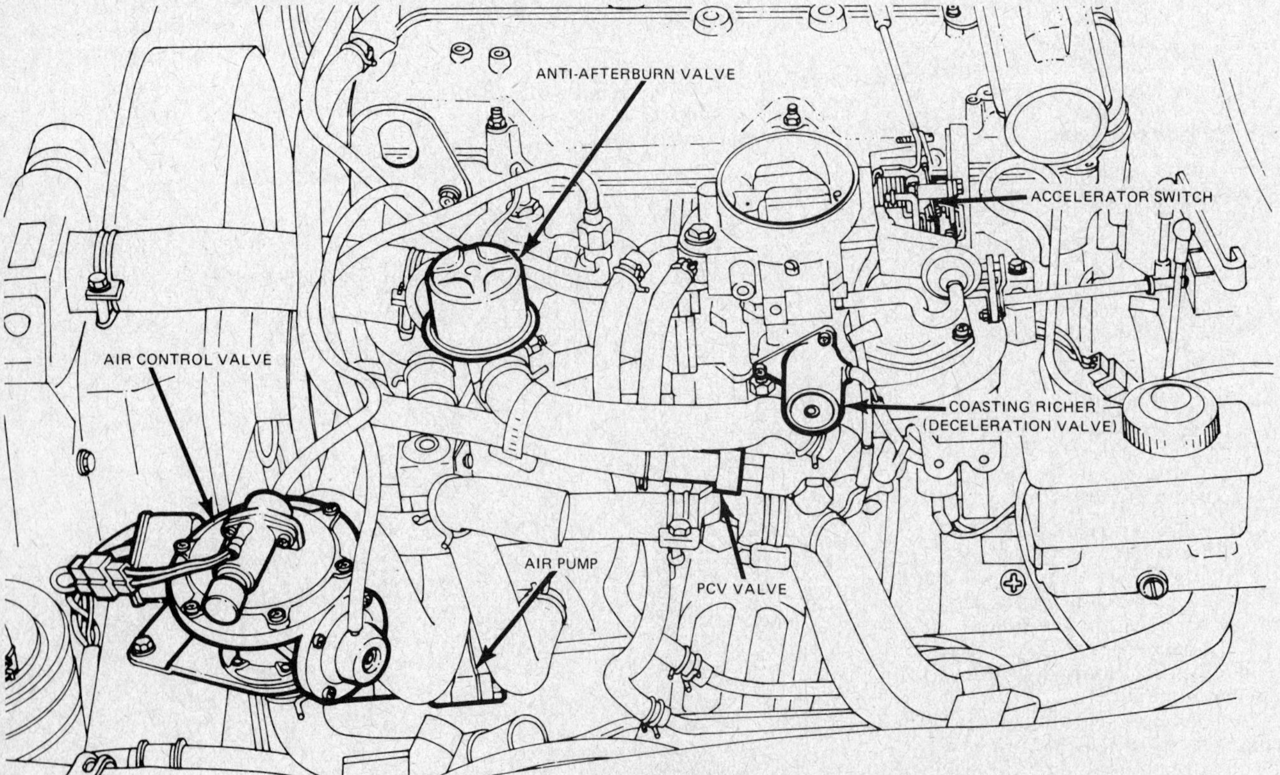

Deceleration Control System

TESTING THE SYSTEM

Anti-Afterburn Valve

1. Remove the outlet hose from the anti-afterburn valve.
2. Hold a hand over the outlet fitting and raise the engine rpm. Quickly release the accelerator. Air should flow for approximately three seconds. If the valve passes air for more than three seconds, or does not pass air at all, it should be replaced.

Coasting Richer Valve (Deceleration Valve)

1. Remove the coasting richer valve from the carburetor.
2. Connect the coasting richer valve to the battery.
3. As power is applied to the valve, the solenoid plunger should be pulled into the valve body.
4. Reinstall the coasting richer valve. Connect a test light.
5. Raise the rear wheels and support the truck on stands.
6. Start the engine and raise the engine speed above 30 mph. Release the accelerator pedal. The test light should come ON and remain ON until the speed falls below 17–23 mph.
7. If the system is operating properly no further tests are required. If not, proceed with the other tests.

Clutch Switch

When checking the circuit the test light should be on when the clutch pedal is fully released, and should be OFF when the clutch pedal is fully depressed.

Accelerator Switch

The accelerator switch is actuated by a throttle lever link on the carburetor. When checking the switch with a circuit tester, the test light should be ON when the accelerator pedal is fully released and should be OFF when the pedal is depressed.

Speed Switch

1. Remove the instrument cluster and attach a test light to the speedometer switch.
2. Reconnect the speedometer cable and ground wire.
3. Raise both wheels off the ground and support the truck on stands.
4. Start the engine.
5. Depress the accelerator pedal to accelerate the engine and confirm that the speed switch is ON at speeds of 17–23 mph and OFF at speeds below 17-23 mph.
6. If not replace the switch.

Speed Switch Relay

Check the speed switch relay with a test light to be sure that it is operating at 17–23 mph.

Servo Diaphragm

1. Disconnect the vacuum line between the vacuum control valve and the diaphragm at the diaphragm.
2. Disconnect the vacuum line between the intake manifold and the vacuum control valve at the manifold.
3. Disconnect the vacuum line between the carburetor and the distributor.
4. Connect a length of vacuum hose between the intake manifold and the servo diaphragm.
5. Connect a tachometer and start the engine. It should idle at 1300–1500 rpm. If the speed is within the 750–1700 rpm range, adjust the speed using the servo diaphragm adjusting screw. If adjustment is impossible, replace the servo diaphragm.

Vacuum Control Valve

1. Disconnect the hose between the valve and the intake manifold, at the manifold.
2. Attach a vacuum gauge in the line using a T-fitting.
3. Connect a tachometer. Raise the engine speed to 3000 rpm, then suddenly release the throttle. The vacuum reading should rise above 21.3 in. Hg., drop to that figure, then drop to 16–18 in. Hg. a few seconds later. Adjust these figures at altitudes other than sea level.
4. Adjust the valve with the screw in the top of the valve. Replace the valve if necessary.

Vacuum Switch

1. Disconnect the hose between the switch and the vacuum control valve.
2. Connect a vacuum gauge between the switch and an external vacuum source.
3. Raise the vacuum above 8 in. Hg., then allow the vacuum to drop. The switch should click at 6 in. Hg. If not, replace.

Air By-Pass Valve

1. Disconnect the hose from the side of the valve.
2. Start the engine and run above 2000 rpm.
3. Release the throttle and check for air flow from the side port of the valve. If there is no airflow, replace the valve.

Dashpot

1. With the engine idle speed and mixture properly adjusted, remove the air cleaner.
2. Loosen the dashpot locknut. Raise the engine speed to 2400–2600 rpm (2100–2300 rpm for California trucks).
3. Turn the dashpot until its rod contacts the throttle lever. Release the throttle and tighten the locknut.
4. Move the throttle lever until it contacts the dashpot rod, and recheck the engine speed. Repeat the adjustment if necessary.

Accelerator Switch Adjustment

1. Be sure that the throttle valve is fully closed.
2. Loosen the switch adjusting screw and turn the switch off.
3. Gradually tighten the adjusting screw until the switch produces a clicking sound and is turned on.
4. Tighten the adjusting screw another $1^1/_2$ turns.

Positive Crankcase Ventilation (PCV) System

The function of the PCV valve is to divert blow-by gases from the crankcase to the intake manifold to be burned in the cylinders. The system consists of a PCV valve and the hoses necessary to connect the components.

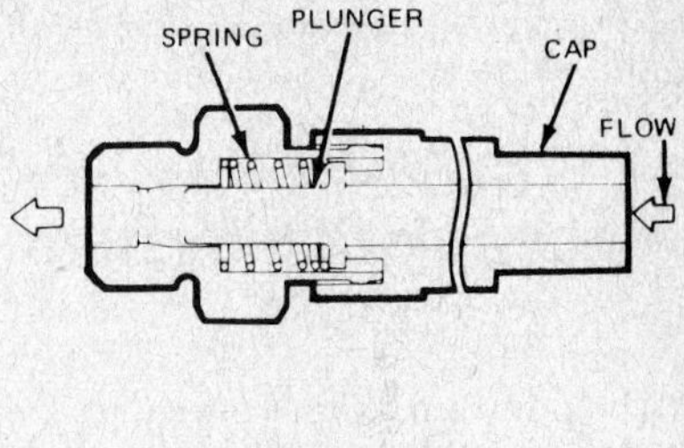

2.0L ENGINE

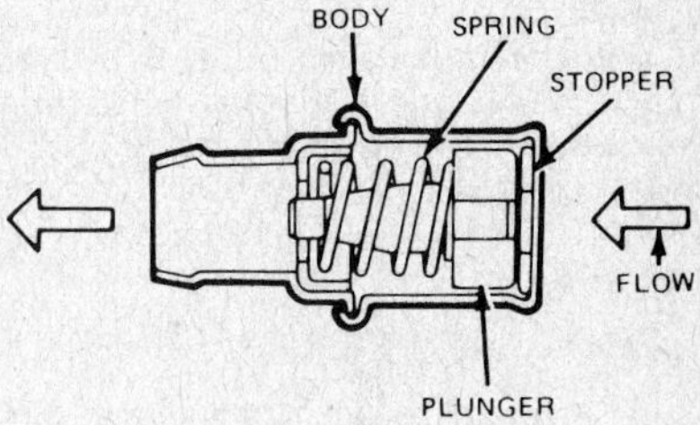

2.3L ENGINE

PCV valve operation

TESTING THE SYSTEM

PCV Valve

1. Remove the hose from the PCV valve.
2. Start the engine and run it at approximately 700–1,000 rpm.
3. Cover the end of the PCV valve with a finger. A distinct vacuum should be felt. If no vacuum is felt, replace the valve.

Evaporative Emission Control System

The system consists of a fuel tank, a condenser tank, a check valve, and a charcoal canister through 1976. 1977 and later models have a sealed fuel tank, a vapor controlling orifice in the line between the tank and the charcoal canister, and the canister. The check valve is eliminated through the use of a fuel filler

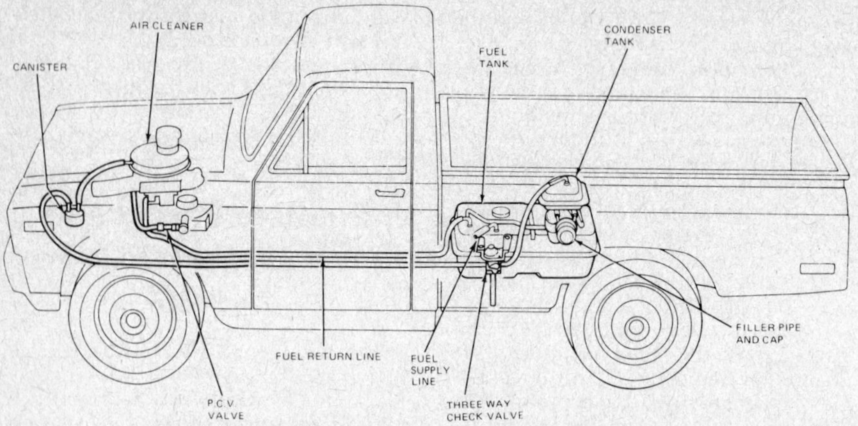

Evaporative Emission Control System 1971-77

cap with vacuum and pressure relief valves, and a fuel vapor valve on the tank.

Exhaust Gas Recirculation System (EGR)

The purpose of this system is to reduce peak combustion temperature by rerouting a small part of the exhaust gases back into the intake charge. This reduces the formation of oxides of nitrogen.

The system consists of an EGR control valve, an electrically controlled three way solenoid valve, a vacuum amplifier, and a coolant temperature operated switch.

EGR CONTROL VALVE TEST

1. With the engine idling, on 1976 trucks, disconnect the vacuum hose from the EGR valve, disonnect the intake manifold vacuum hose from the amplifier, and connect it to the EGR valve. On 1977 and later trucks, disconnect the vacuum hose from the EGR valve to the solenoid valve at the solenoid, disconnect the intake manifold vacuum hose at the manifold, and connect the EGR valve vacuum hose to the manifold fitting.
2. The engine should stall or idle roughly. If not, remove the EGR valve and pipe and clean them with a brush and wire. Replace and repeat the test. If unsuccessful, replace the EGR valve.

THREE-WAY SOLENOID VALVE TEST

1. Disconnect the electrical connectors from the thermo switch. Connect a jumper wire between the connectors to simulate a complete circuit.
2. Turn the ignition switch to ON.
3. Disconnect the vacuum hose from the EGR valve and blow into the hose. Air should be discharged from the three-way solenoid valve relief port. If it is not, replace the three-way valve.
4. Turn the ignition switch off, and remove the jumper wire from the thermo switch connectors. Disconnect the vacuum amplifier vacuum line from the three-way solenoid. Turn the ignition switch back to ON.
5. Blow into the vacuum line disconnected from the EGR valve, and check for air discharge from the vacuum amplifier port on the three-way solenoid valve. If there is no discharge, replace the solenoid valve.
6. After completion of all tests, reconnect the hoses to their original locations.

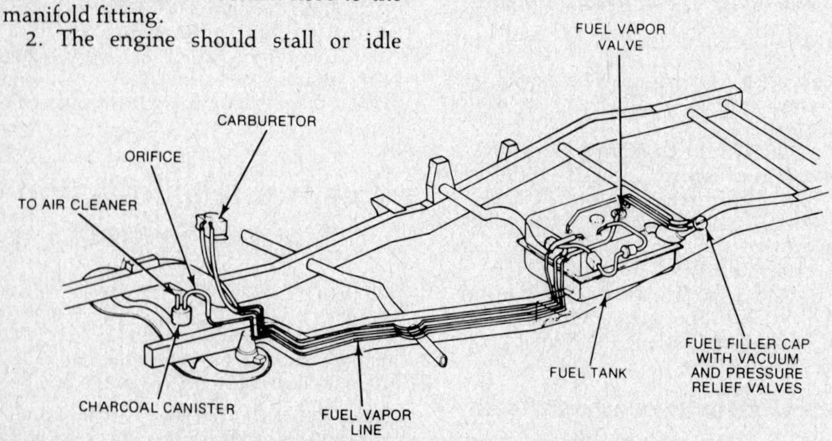

Evaporative Emission Control System 1978-80

VACUUM AMPLIFIER TEST

1. Start the engine and warm it to normal operating temperature.
2. Disconnect the vacuum amplifier vacuum hose from the solenoid valve. Connect a vacuum gauge to this hose.
3. Disconnect the vacuum amplifier vacuum hose from the carburetor. The vacuum hose to the intake manifold should remain connected.
4. Depress and release the accelerator several times, then allow the engine to idle. The vacuum gauge reading should be 2.0±.04 in. Hg.
5. Reconnect the vacuum amplifier vacuum hose to the carburetor.
6. Increase engine speed to 3500 rpm. The vacuum gauge reading should be 3.54 in. Hg. If the vacuum amplifier does not test properly, replace it.
7. After all tests are completed, return the hoses to their original positions.

EGR WARNING LIGHT - 1976 ONLY

1976 Couriers with EGR are equipped with a maintenance warning light on the instrument panel, which lights every 12,500 miles. The light indicates that the EGR system should be checked for proper operation, using the procedures outlined. The EGR valve should be removed and cleaned every 25,000 miles.

The switch controlling the light is installed behind the speedometer. To reset the switch after the maintenance has been performed, remove the cover from the switch, and move the switch knob to the opposite position.

Catalytic Converter

1976 and later trucks sold in California have a catalytic converter installed in the exhaust system to aid in the reduction of HC and CO emissions. The catalytic converter is a muffler-shaped device located between the exhaust manifold and the muffler. It is filled with beads containing platinum and palladium which, through catalytic action, enable the HC and CO gases to be converted into water vapor (H_2O) and carbon dioxide (CO_2). The converter also has a warning system, consisting of a thermo sensor inserted into the side of the converter, which monitors temperatures, and a warning light on the instrument panel which lights when the sensor detects converter temperatures exceeding 1742°F. The converter should be inspected periodically for cracks, corrosion, and any sign of external burning, and replaced as required.

WARNING SYSTEM TEST

1. Turn the ignition switch ON. The warning light on the instrument panel should light. Start the engine. The warning light should go off.
2. If the light does not light, check the bulb. If burned out, replace and retest the system.

3. If the light does not go out after the engine has started, shut off the engine and tilt the seatback forward.

4. Disconnect the thermo sensor wire electrical connectors.

5. Using an ohmmeter, check the thermo sensor circuit for continuity, on the sensor side of the wiring. If there is no continuity, replace the sensor. Reconnect the wires and repeat the test.

REMOVAL AND INSTALLATION

Catalytic Converter

CAUTION: Be very careful when working on or near the converter. External temperatures can reach 1500°F and more, causing severe burns. Removal or installation should only be performed on a cold exhaust system.

1. Raise the truck and support it on safety stands.
2. Loosen the nut and remove the thermo sensor from the side of the converter.
3. Remove the front and rear flange attaching nuts.
4. Remove the nut and rubber support which secures the converter bracket, and remove the converter.
5. Installation is the reverse of removal.

Spark Timing Control System

A spark delay system is used on 1977 and later 1800 and 2000 cc engines. Its purpose is to reduce the formation of CO and NOx emissions by delaying the vacuum advance to the distributor during normal acceleration. The system consists of a spark delay valve installed in the vacuum hose between the carburetor and the distributor advance diaphragm. The valve has an internal restrictor to slow the air flow in one direction, and a check valve which allows air to flow freely in the opposite direction.

To test the system:

1. Remove the air cleaner. Disconnect the vacuum hose from the distributor.
2. Disconnect the vacuum control valve hose at the intake manifold fitting, and install the distributor hose on that fitting.
3. Remove the vacuum hose from the carburetor side of the spark delay valve. Plug this hose, and attach a vacuum gauge to the delay valve.
4. Start the engine and allow it to idle.
5. Disconnect the vacuum hose from the intake manifold fitting (the hose from the spark delay valve to the distributor which has been connected to the intake manifold in Step 2) and note the time for the vacuum gauge reading to drop to 11.8 in. Hg. It should drop to this figure within 2–7 seconds (2–10 seconds on California trucks). If the reading is not correct, replace the spark delay valve.
6. After all tests have been completed, return the hoses to their original positions.

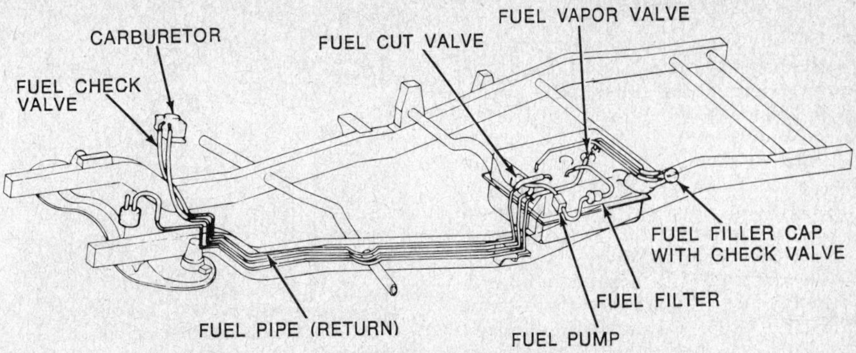

Fuel pump location and fuel system schematic

FUEL SYSTEM

Couriers use an electric fuel pump and a 2–barrel downdraft carburetor with a manual choke.

Fuel Filter

REPLACEMENT

A disposable fuel filter is used, located in the outlet line next to the fuel pump, under the left frame rail. To replace, loosen the hose clamps on each side of the filter and slide the clamps down the hoses. Pull the hoses from the old filter, install the new filter, and replace the clamps.

Electric Fuel Pump

An external electric fuel pump is mounted on the left frame rail adjacent to the fuel tank.

TESTING THE FUEL PUMP

To determine that the fuel pump is in good operating condition, tests for both volume and pressure should be performed. The tests are performed with the fuel pump installed, and the engine at normal operating temperature and idle speed.

Be sure that the fuel filter is in good condition.

Pressure Test

1. Remove the air cleaner.
2. Disconnect the fuel inlet line at the carburetor.
3. Connect a pressure gauge, a restrictor and a flexible hose between the fuel filter and the carburetor. Position the flexible hose and restrictor so that the fuel can be discharged into a suitable graduated container.
4. Operate the engine at idle speed and vent the system into the container by momentarily opening the hose restrictor.
5. Close the hose restrictor and allow the pressure to stablize and note the reading. It should be 2.8–3.6 psi.
6. If the pump pressure is not within specifications, and the fuel filter and fuel lines are not blocked, the pump is malfunctioning and should be replaced.
7. If the pressure is within specifications, perform the volume test.

Volume Test

1. Open the hose restrictor and expel the fuel into the container, while observing the time required to discharge 1 pint. Close the restrictor. Fuel pump volume should be approximately 2 pints/minute.
2. If the pump volume is below specifications, repeat the test using an auxiliary fuel supply and a new filter. If the pump volume meets specifications while using the auxiliary fuel supply, check for a restriction in the fuel lines or vent.

REMOVAL AND INSTALLATION

1. Remove the fuel pump shield from the frame. Disconnect the electrical leads from the pump.
2. Disconnect the inlet and outlet lines from the pump. Plug the lines.
3. Unbolt and remove the pump from its mounting bracket.
4. Installation is the reverse of removal.

Carburetor

REMOVAL AND INSTALLATION

1. Remove the air cleaner and duct.
2. Disconnect the accelerator shaft from the throttle lever.
3. Disconnect and plug the fuel supply and return lines.
4. Disconnect the throttle solenoid and deceleration valve at the quick-disconnects.
5. Disconnect the carburetor-to-distributor vacuum line.
6. Disconnect the throttle return and choke cable.
7. Remove the carburetor.
8. Installation is the reverse of removal.

OVERHAUL

The following instructions are general overhaul procedures. Most good carburetor rebuilding kits come replete with exploded views and specific instructions.

Efficient carburetion depends greatly on careful cleaning and inspection during overhaul, since dirt, gum, water, or varnish in or on the carburetor parts are often responsible for poor performance.

Overhaul your carburetor in a clean, dust-free area. Carefully disassemble the carburetor, referring often to the exploded views. Keep all similar and look-alike parts segregated during disassembly and cleaning to avoid accidental interchange during assembly. Make a note of all jet sizes.

When the carburetor is disassembled, wash all parts (except diaphragms, electric choke units, pump plunger, and any other plastic, leather, fiber, or rubber parts) in clean carburetor solvent. Do not leave parts in the solvent any longer than is necessary to sufficiently loosen the deposits. Excessive cleaning may remove the special finish from the float bowl and choke valve bodies, leaving these parts unfit for service. Rinse all parts in clean solvent and blow them dry with compressed air or allow them to air dry. Wipe-clean all cork, plastic, leather, and fiber parts with a clean, lint-free cloth.

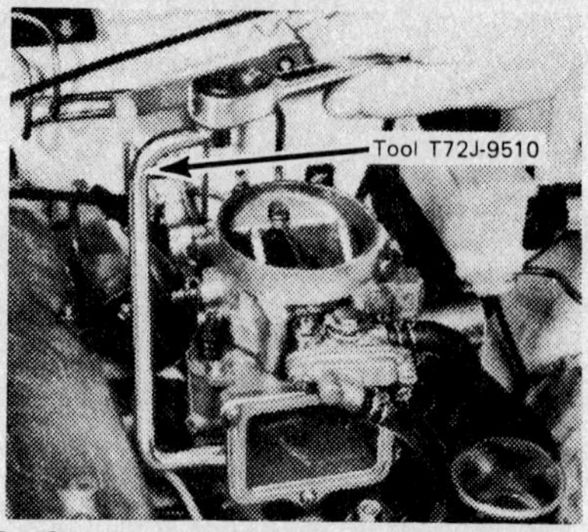

Carburetor removal or installation; a normal wrench can be bent to the same angle as the special tool shown

Blow out all passages and jets with compressed air and be sure that there are no restrictions or blockages. Never use wire or similar tools to clean jets, fuel passages, or air bleeds. Clean all jets and valves separately to avoid accidental interchange.

Check all parts for wear or damage. If wear or damage is found, replace the defective parts. Especially check the following:

1. Check the float needle and seat for wear. If wear is found, replace the complete assembly.
2. Check the float hinge pin for wear and the float(s) for dents or distortion. Replace the float if fuel has leaked into it.
3. Check the throttle and choke shaft bores for wear or an out-of-round condition. Damage or wear to the throttle arm, shaft, or shaft bore will often require replacement of the throttle body. These parts require a close tolerance of fit; wear may allow air leakage, which could affect starting and idling.

NOTE: Throttle shafts and bushings are not included in overhaul kits. They can be purchased separately.

4. Inspect the idle mixture adjusting needles for burrs or grooves. Any such condition requires replacement of the needle, since you will not be able to obtain a satisfactory idle.
5. Test the accelerator pump check valves. They should pass air one way but not the other. Test for proper seating by blowing and sucking on the valve. Replace the valve if necessary. If the valve is satisfactory, wash the valve again to remove breath moisture.
6. Check the bowl cover for warped surfaces with a straightedge.
7. Closely inspect the valves and seats for wear and damage, replacing as necessary.
8. After the carburetor is assembled, check the choke valve for freedom of operation.

Carburetor overhaul kits are recommended for each overhaul. These kits contain all gaskets and new parts to replace those which deteriorate most rapidly. Failure to replace all parts supplied with the kit (especially gaskets) can result in poor performance later.

After cleaning and checking all components, reassemble the carburetor, using new parts and referring to the exploded view. When reassembling, make sure that all screws and jets are tight in

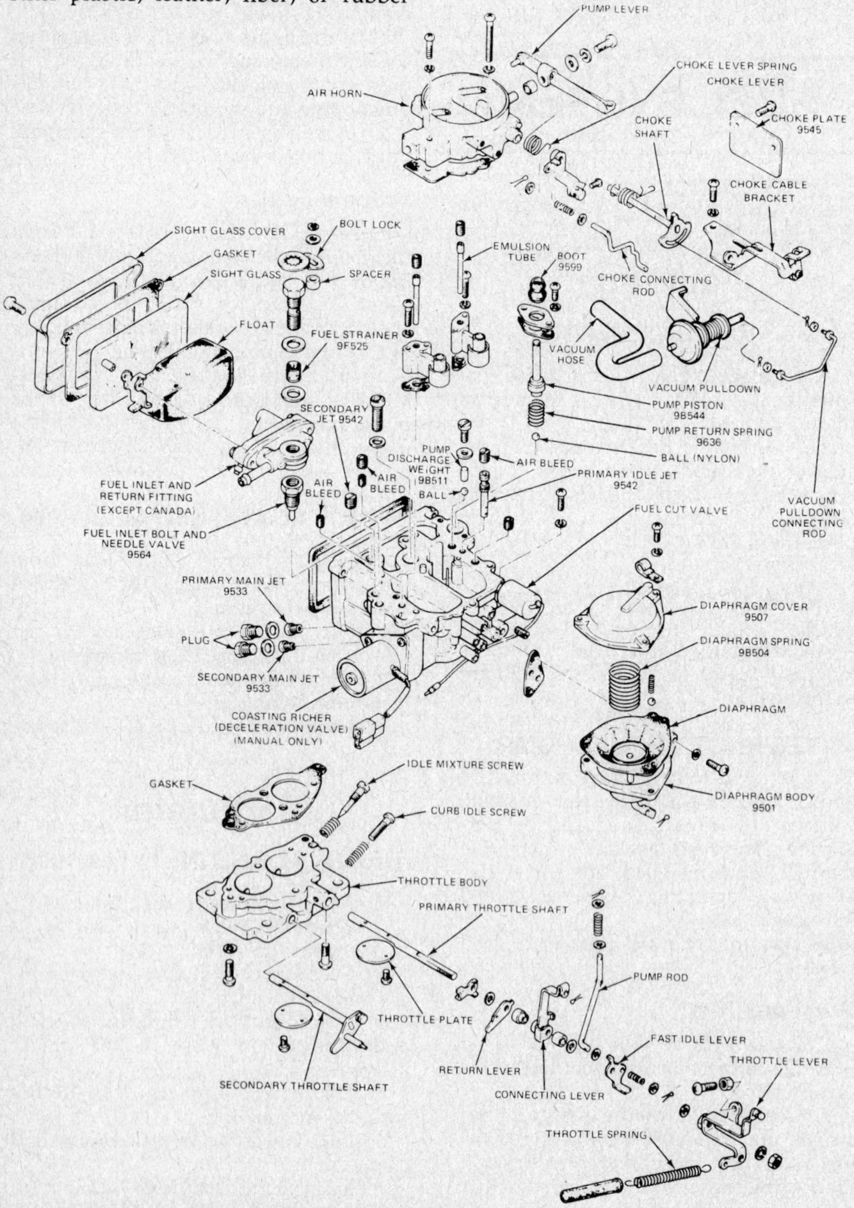

Exploded view of Zenith-Stromberg 2 barrel—1800cc engine

their seats, but do not overtighten as the tips will be distorted. Tighten all screws gradually, in rotation. Do not tighten needle valves into their seats; uneven jetting will result. Always use new gaskets. Be sure to adjust the float level when reassembling.

FAST IDLE ADJUSTMENT

1. Remove the air cleaner.
2. With the choke plate fully closed, measure the clearance between the primary throttle plate and the wall of the throttle bore. The clearance should measure 0.063–0.067 in. through 1976, and 0.071 in. 1977–78, or 0.067 in. for 1977-78 California models, and 0.051–0.059 in. for 1979–80 2000 cc engines or 0.058–0.066 for 1979–80 2300 cc engines.
3. If the clearance is not as specified, on 1972–78 bend the fast idle lever where it contacts the throttle lever tang until the proper clearance is obtained. On 1979–80, turn the adjusting screw on the fast idle lever to obtain the proper clearance.

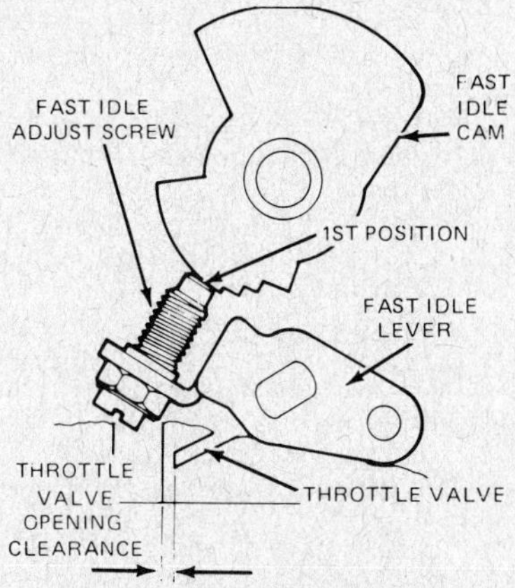

Fast idle cam adjustment

FLOAT AND FUEL LEVEL ADJUSTMENT

1. With the engine running, check the fuel level in the sight glass.
2. If the fuel level is not at the mark on the sight glass, remove the carburetor.
3. Remove the fuel bowl cover.
4. Invert the carburetor and lower the float until the tang on the float just contacts the needle valve.
5. Measure the clearance between the float and the edge of the bowl.

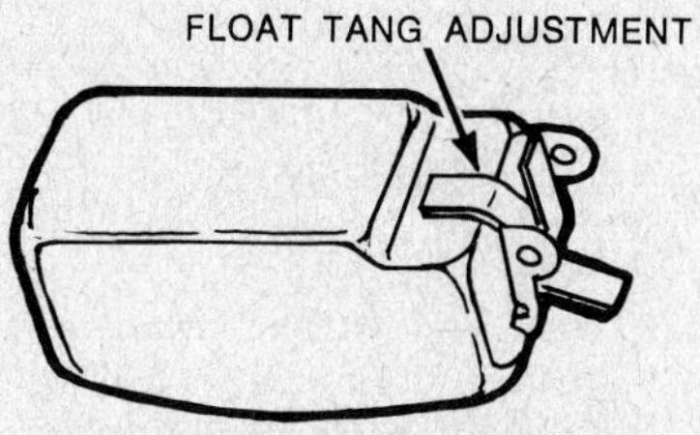

Bend tang to adjust float level

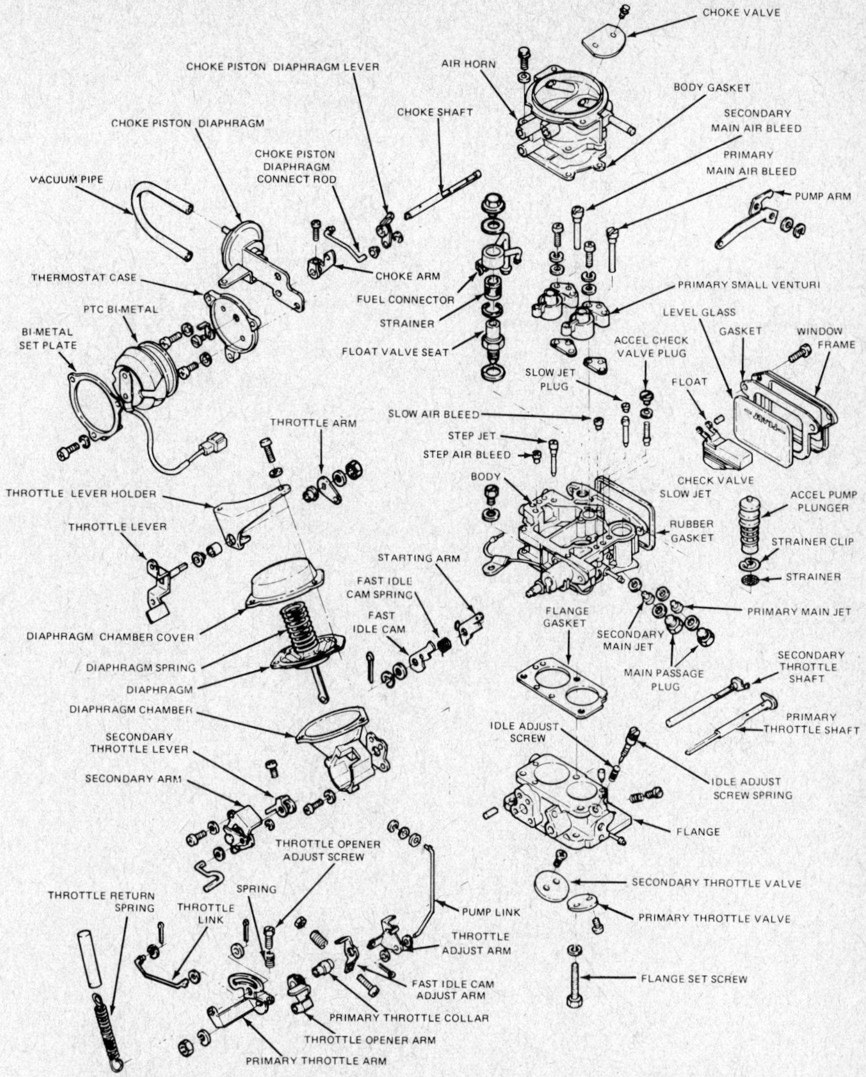

Exploded view of Zenith-Stromberg 2 barrel—2000cc engine

6. If the clearance is not 0.256 in. through 1976, 0.247 in. for 1977, or 0.236 1978 and later 2300 cc and 0.335 for 1979–80 2000 cc, bend the float tang until the proper clearance is obtained.
7. Install the fuel bowl cover.

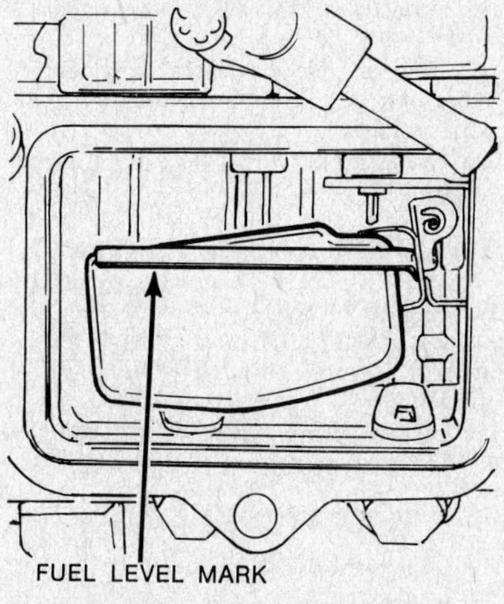

Fuel level mark on sight glass

8. Reinstall the carburetor.
9. Recheck the fuel level at the sight glass.

VACUUM PULLDOWN ADJUSTMENT

1975 and Later Only

1. On California models, unplug the electrical connectors from the water

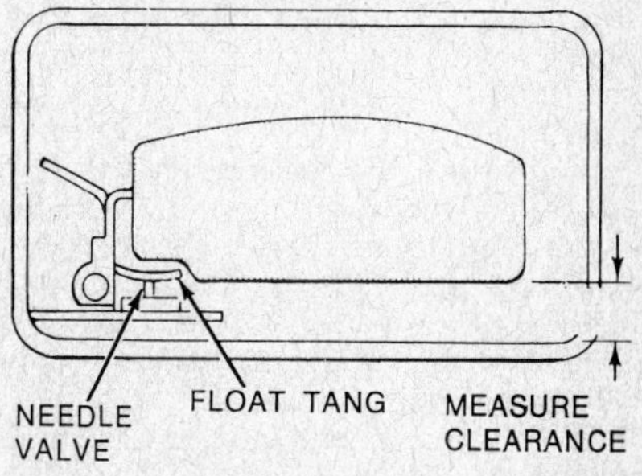

Float level adjustment—measure the clearance between the float and the edge of the bowl

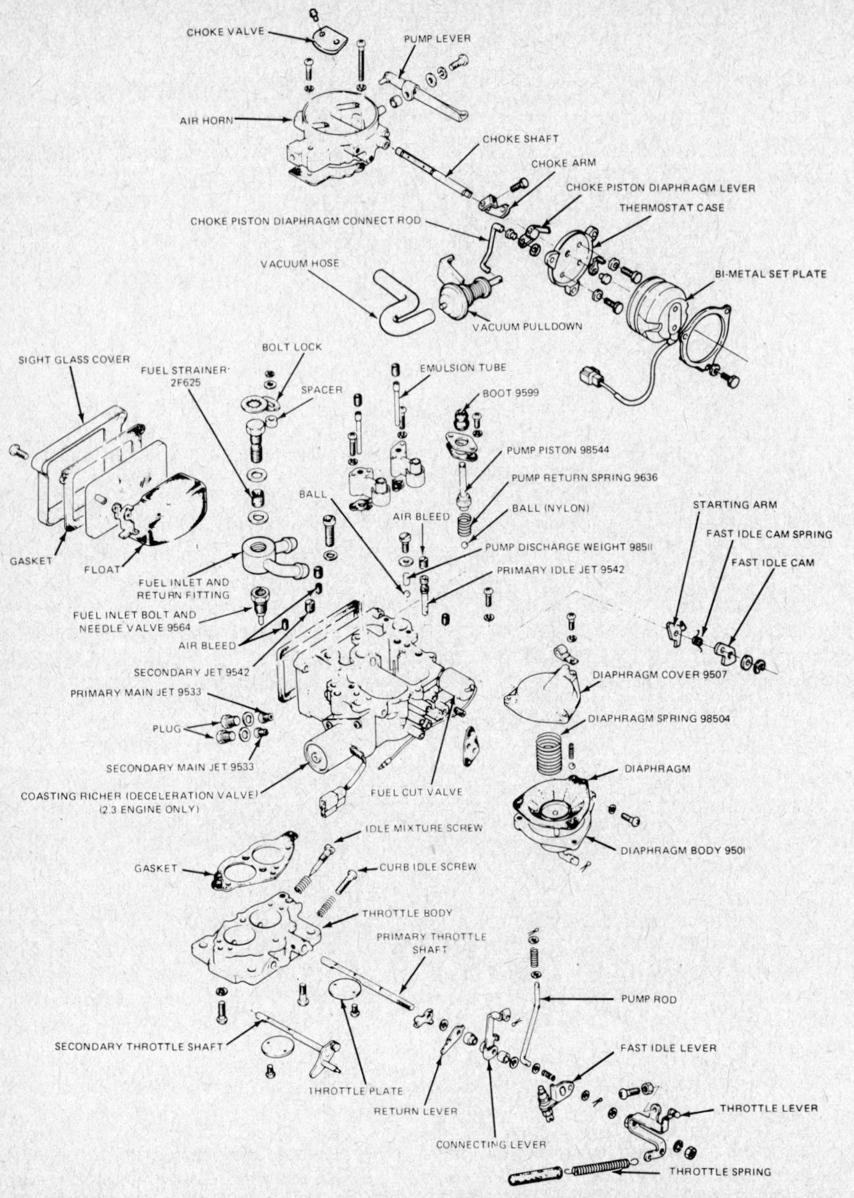

Exploded view of carburetor—2300cc engine carburetor; used through 1980

thermo switch and connect a jumper wire between the connectors. Turn the ignition switch on.

2. Pull the choke knob fully out.
3. Disconnect the vacuum hose from the pulldown diaphragm.
4. Connect an external vacuum source to the pulldown diaphragm. Applying vacuum gradually, the pulldown should start to open the choke at 5.9–7.5 in. Hg.
5. Increase the vacuum to 9.8–12.0 in. Hg. Use a wire gauge to check the choke plate-to-air horn wall clearance. It should be 0.06–0.08 in. 1975–76. 0.066–0.075 in. all 1977–80 1800 and 2000 cc models and 1977–80 2300 cc 49 States and Canada models, or 0.076–0.084 in. for 1977–80 2300 cc California models.
6. Adjust the clearance if necessary by bending the pulldown connecting rod.

CHOKE ADJUSTMENT

1. Push the choke knob all the way in.
2. Loosen the choke cable attaching screws at the choke lever and the choke cable bracket.
3. Be sure that the choke plate is fully open.
4. Insert the choke cable into the choke lever. Tighten the screw.
5. Pull the cable outward to remove all slack between the choke lever and choke cable bracket and tighten the attaching screw at the choke cable bracket.
6. Operate the choke to be sure that there is no binding.

THROTTLE LINKAGE ADJUSTMENT

1. Loosen the locknut on the longer linkage rod and rotate both ends in the sockets until the proper accelerator travel from idle to wide-open throttle is obtained.
2. Tighten the locknuts to set the adjustment.

MANUAL TRANSMISSION

Couriers are equipped with a fully synchronized manual transmission. There are no linkage or shifter adjustments.

REMOVAL AND INSTALLATION

4 Speed

1. Remove the following:
   a. gearshift boot
   b. shift lever, tower and gasket assembly
   c. driveshaft
   d. exhaust pipe brackets
   e. exhaust pipe
   f. clutch return spring and slave cylinder
   g. speedometer cable from case
   h. starter cables and backup light wires, and
   i. starter.
2. Support the transmission and engine with separate jacks.
3. Unbolt the transmission from the engine.
4. Remove the transmission crossmember.
5. Remove the transmission.
6. Installation is the reverse of removal.

5 Speed

1. Remove the gearshift boot and retainer cover from the lever.
2. Pull the lever, shim and bushing straight up and away from the retainer.
3. Disconnect the driveshaft.
4. Remove the following:
   a. exhaust pipe brackets
   b. exhaust pipe and resonator
   c. slave cylinder
   d. speedometer cable
   e. starter and backup light wires
   f. starter, and
   g. transmission-to-engine rear plate bolts.
5. Support the transmission and unbolt it from the crossmember; remove the crossmember and lower the transmission.
6. Installation is the reverse of removal.

OVERHAUL

4 Speed Disassembly

1. Drain and remove the transmission.
2. Disconnect the throwout bearing return spring and remove the bearing.

3. Remove the clutch housing, gasket and input shaft bearing thrust washers.
4. Unbolt the extension housing. With the control lever in Neutral, press the lever as far downward as possible and slide the extension housing off.
5. Unbolt the case halves and remove the right half from the left half.
6. Lift out the countershaft and gear assembly.
7. Roll the input and output shaft from under the shift forks and remove them as an assembly.
8. Separate the input shaft from the output shaft.
9. To remove the reverse idler gear, push the center (3rd and 4th) shift rail as far forward as possible. This will provide working clearance. Remove the gear.
10. Remove the setscrew on the outside of the case to remove the reverse idler shaft.
11. Remove the bearing from the bearing pocket in the shaft.
12. Remove the snap-ring that holds the input bearing on the shaft.
13. Press the input bearing off the shaft.
14. Position the input shaft bearing on the input shaft and press it into position.
15. Install the snap-ring.
16. Install the bearing in the bearing pocket.
17. Remove the snap-ring at the front end of the output shaft and remove the 3rd and 4th gear synchronizer, synchronizer ring and 3rd gear. The part number on the 3rd gear should face rearward; if not, mark the gear for reassembly.
18. Remove the rearmost snap-ring and slide the speedometer gear and drive ball off the shaft. Remove the other speedometer gear snap-ring.
19. Remove the selective fit snap-ring and washer holding reverse gear, output shaft bearing, low gear, low gear bushing, 1st and 2nd gear synchronizer and 2nd gear on the shaft. Slide the parts off the shaft. Note that the oil groove on the synchronizer hub should face forward.
20. Assemble 3rd gear and the synchronizer ring on the front end of the output shaft, along with the 3rd and 4th gear synchronizer.
21. Be sure the part number on the synchronizer hub faces rearward.
22. Install the front snap-ring.
23. Slide the 2nd gear and synchronizer ring on the rear end of the shaft.
24. Install the 1st and 2nd gear synchronizer and ring on the shaft with the oil groove in the synchronizer forward.
25. Install the 1st gear synchronizer ring, 1st gear and sleeve, thrust washer, bearing and reverse gear on the shaft.
26. Slide the selective fit thrust washer on the shaft and install the selective fit snap-ring. Check the clearance between the rear face of reverse gear and the selective thrust washer. The clearance should be 0–0.004 in. Adjust the end-play using combinations of thrust washers and snap rings.

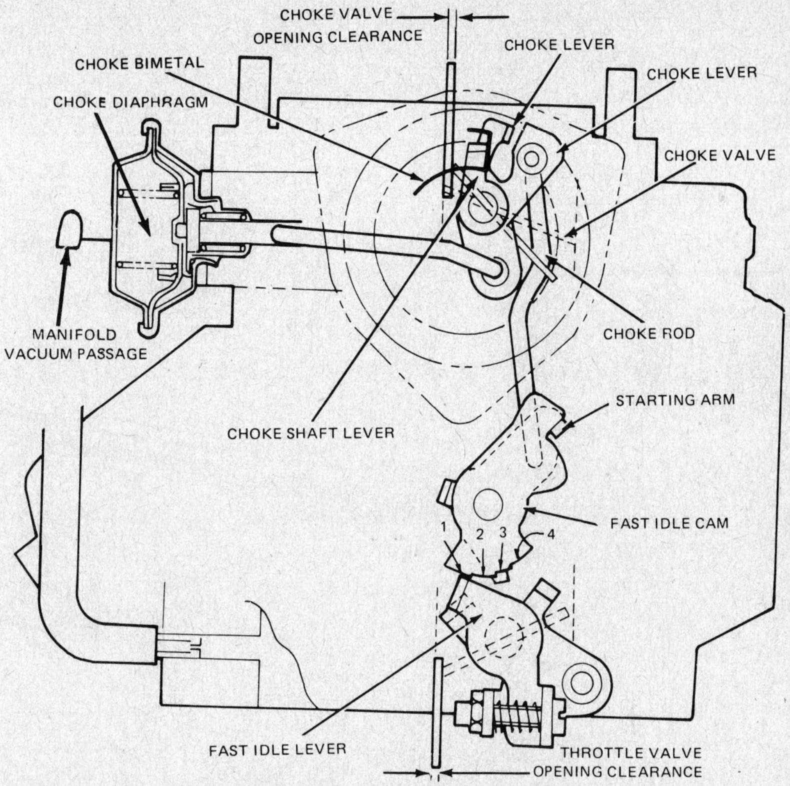

Choke linkage—2000cc engine

27. Remove the snap-ring from the rear end of the shaft and slide off reverse gear and the bearing.

28. If it is necessary to replace the bearing sleeve, it can be pressed off using sharp edged press plates.

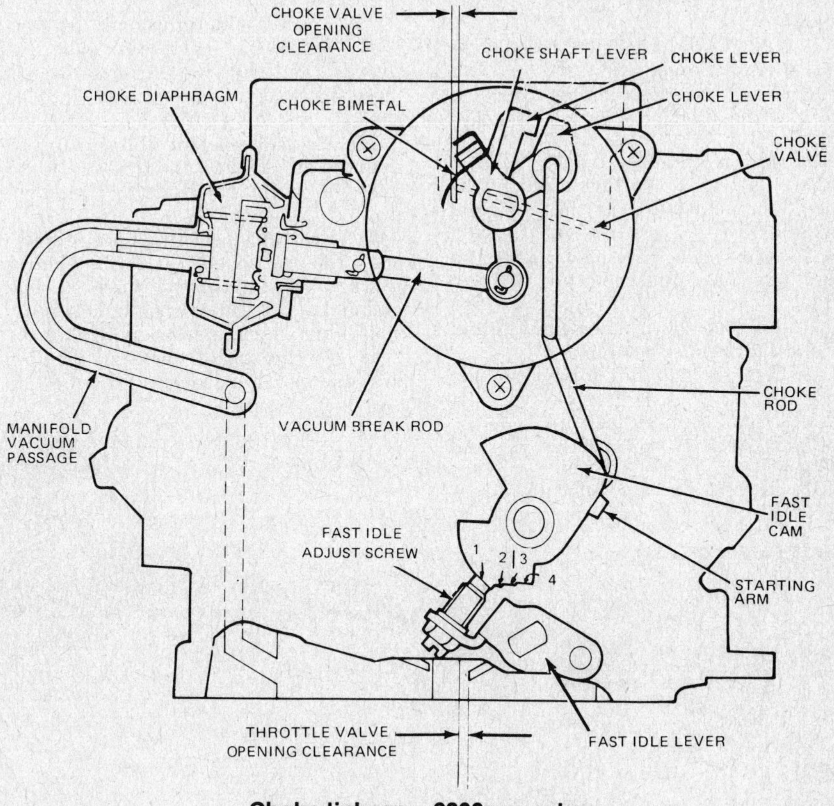

Choke linkage—2300cc engine

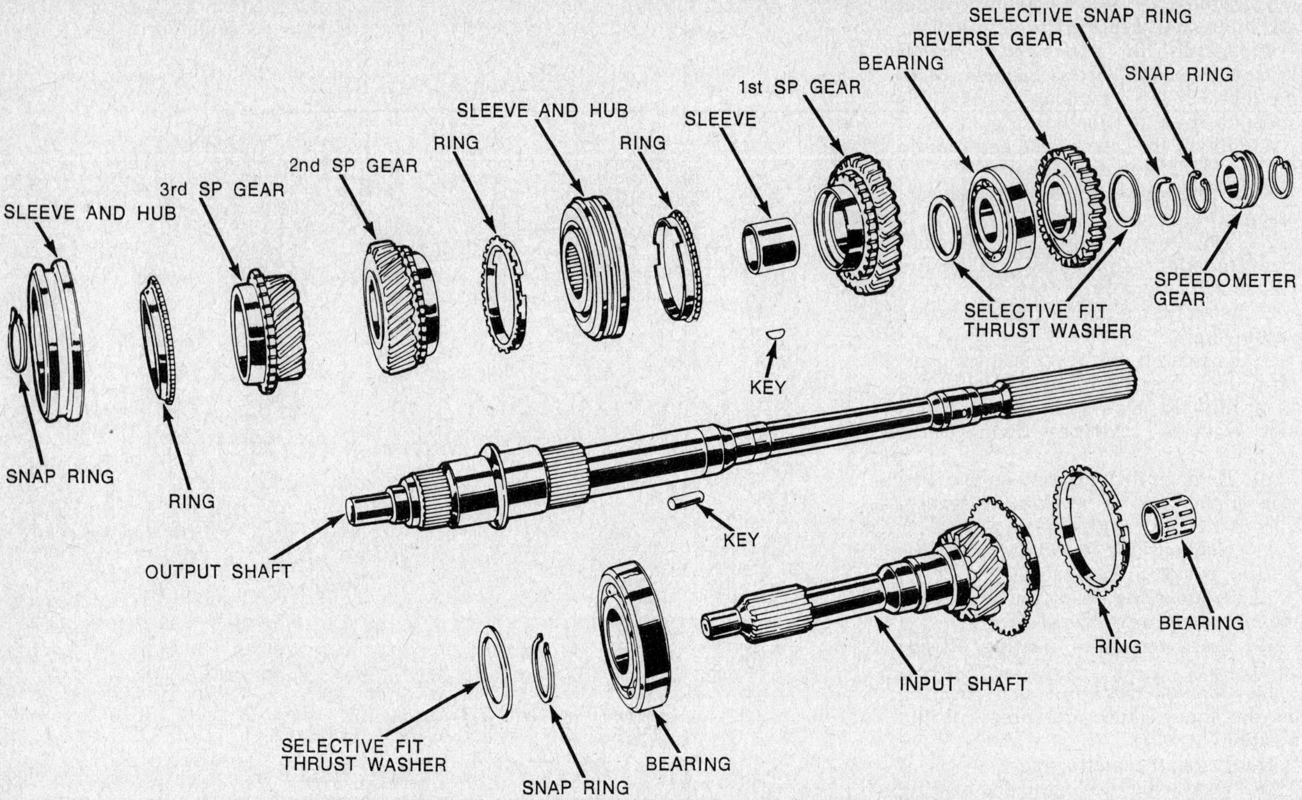

Four speed input and output shafts and component parts

29. Remove the snap-ring on the front end of the shaft and press the bearing off.

30. If the sleeve on the rear end of the shaft was removed, press it into position.

31. Install the bearing and reverse gear. Install the snap-ring.

32. Press the ball bearing onto the front of the shaft and install the snap-ring.

Detent assemblies, caps, plaltes, shims, gaskets, springs and balls should be reinstalled in their original locations.

33. Remove each spring cap, one at a time, and shake out the spring, ball and shim.

34. Remove the interlock bore plug. Shake out the interlock pins.

35. Remove the shift forks from the case.

36. Install the shift fork and slide the 1st and 2nd shift rail into the case and fork.

37. Install 2 dummy shift rails.

38. Align the holes in the dummy shift rails with the holes in the 1st and 2nd gear shift rail.

39. Holding the case on edge, drop a detent pin into position.

40. Remove a dummy shaft.

41. Install the 3rd and 4th gear shift fork rail and slide the 3rd and 4th gear shift rail (and washer, if used) into the case.

42. Align the detent holes in the remaining dummy rail and the 3rd and 4th gear shift rail. Install another interlock pin.

43. Remove the remaining dummy shaft rail and install the reverse shifter rail and fork. Align the interlock hole and install the remaining interlock pin.

44. Install the interlock bore plug.

45. Align the shift forks on the shift rails and install the lockbolts.

46. Position the case open side down and install each detent into the bore from which it was removed. Lubricate the moving parts.

47. Place the housing on its right side and remove the speedometer gear, back-up light switch and spring loaded friction piece.

48. Disconnect the control lever from the control rod and slide the rod from the housing. Remove the key.

49. Assembly is the reverse of disassembly. Lubricate the speedometer gear housing seal before installation.

4 Speed Assembly

1. Install the reverse idler gear. Install the idler gear and setscrew.

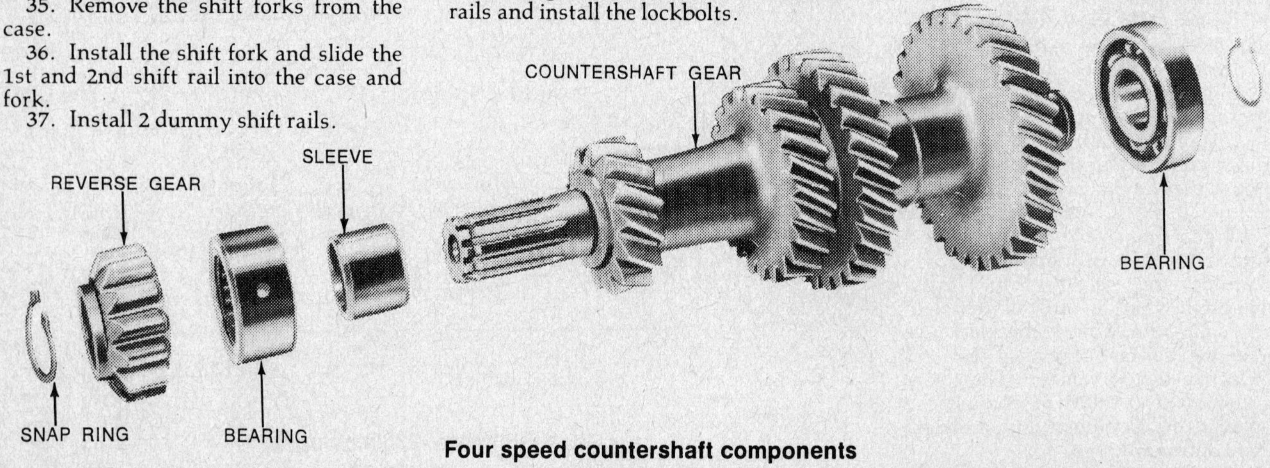

Four speed countershaft components

2. Lubricate the input shaft roller bearing with transmission fluid and install it in the bearing pocket.

3. Set the shift forks in Neutral. Assemble the output shaft to the input shaft and install the assembly in the case.

4. Install the countershaft assembly. Be sure the dowel hole in the bearing is aligned with the hole in the case. The main gear train will rotate freely if the holes are aligned.

5. Install the input bearing thrust washer in the clutch housing.

6. Assemble the clutch housing to the left half of the case.

7. Check the end-play between the rear face of the input shaft bearing and the shoulder in the case by moving the input shaft as far forward as possible. It should be 0–0.004 in. If it is incorrect, remove the clutch housing and install another selective fit input shaft thrust washer and check the end-play again.

8. Shift the transmission into 3rd gear. Check the clearance between the synchronizer key and the exposed edge of the synchronizer ring. It should be 0.030–0.080 in. If not, remove the clutch housing, countershaft, and the input shaft and output shaft as an assembly. Disassemble the output shaft and substitute a thicker selective fit washer for the key slotted thrust washer. Assemble complete output shaft and adjust the overall end-play at the reverse gear using the selective fit thrust washer described under "Output Shaft Disassembly and Assembly."

9. Install the input and output shaft assembly into the case. Install the countershaft. Install the clutch housing.

10. Recheck the synchronizer key clearance as described in Step 8.

11. Recheck the input shaft end-play as described in Step 7.

12. Shift the transmission into 4th gear. Measure the distance between the shift gate end of the shift rail and transmission case boss. The clearance should be 0–0.028 in. If the clearance is excessive, install a selective fit thrust washer (or washers) on the 3rd and 4th gear shift rail between the shift gate fitting and the transmission case boss.

13. Remove the clutch housing.

14. Lubricate all moving parts with transmission fluid. Lubricate the input shaft and output shaft seals in the clutch and extension housings.

15. Coat the mating surfaces of the case halves with a thin coat of sealer and allow them to dry.

16. Shift the transmission into Neutral.

17. Assemble the case halves.

18. Install a new extension housing gasket and install the extension housing.

19. Install the clutch housing using a new gasket.

20. Install the clutch release lever, bearing and related parts.

21. Install the transmission.

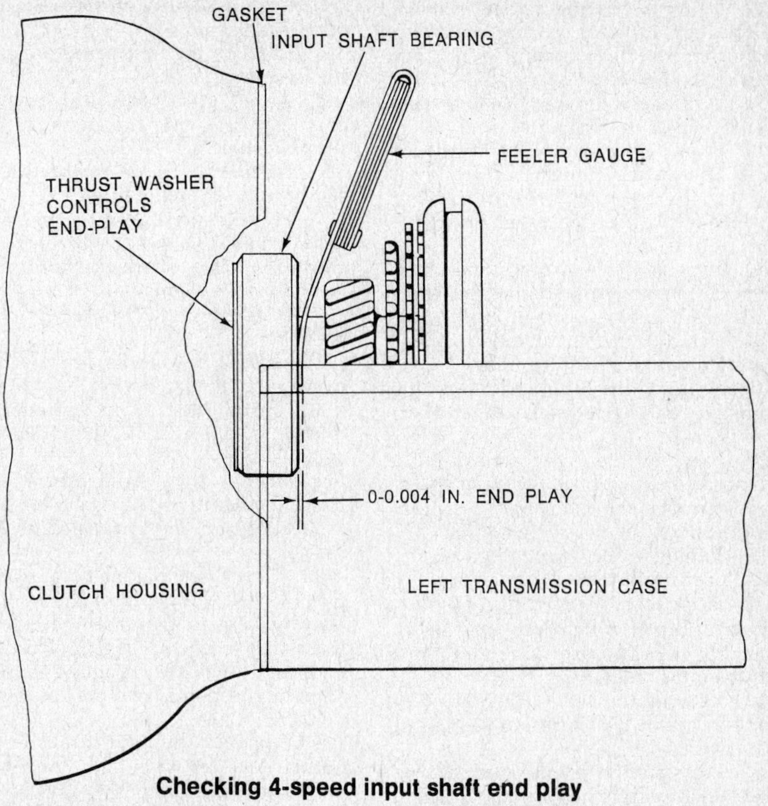

Checking 4-speed input shaft end play

5 Speed Disassembly

NOTE: The use of special tools is required for the following procedure.

1. Pull the release fork outward until the spring clip of the fork releases from the ball pivot.

2. Remove the fork and release bearing from the clutch housing.

3. Remove the nuts attaching the clutch housing and remove the housing, shim and gasket.

4. Remove the bolts attaching the gearshift lever retainer to the extension housing and remove the retainer and gasket.

5. Remove the spring and steel ball, select lock spindle and spring from the gearshift lever retainer.

6. Unbolt and remove the estension housing with the control lever end down to the left as far as it will go.

7. Unbolt and remove the control lever end, key and control rod.

8. Remove the lock plate and speedometer gear assembly from the extension housing.

9. Remove the back-up light switch from the extension housing.

10. Remove the snap ring and slide the speedometer drive gear from the mainshaft.

11. Remove the bottom cover and gasket.

12. Unbolt and remove the shift rod ends.

13. Remove the rear bearing housing from the intermediate housing.

14. Remove the snap ring and remove the main shaft rear bearing, thrust washer and race. A puller may be necessary.

15. Using the puller, remove the washer and countershaft rear bearing.

16. Remove the counter fifth gear.

17. Remove the intermediate housing from the case.

18. Unbolt and remove the springs and shift locking balls.

19. Remove the two blind covers and gaskets from the case.

20. Unbolt and remove the reverse/fifth shift rod, fork and interlock pin.

21. Unbolt and remove the first/second and third/fourth shift forks, rods and interlock pins.

22. Remove the snap ring and slide the washer, fifth gear and synchronizer ring from the main shaft. Also, remove the steel ball and needle bearing.

23. Lock the rotation of the mainshaft with second and reverse.

24. Remove the locknut and slide the reverse/fifth clutch hub and sleeve assembly, synchronizer ring, reverse gear and needle bearing from the mainshaft.

25. Remove the spacer and counter reverse gear from the countershaft.

26. Remove the reverse idler gear, thrust washers and shaft from the transmission case.

27. Remove the bearing rear cover plate.

28. Remove the snap ring from the front end of the countershaft and install Mazda tool number 49 0839 445 synchronizer ring holder or its equivalent between the fourth synchronizer ring and the synchromesh gear on the main driveshaft.

29. Using a bearing puller, remove the countershaft front bearing.

30. Remove the adjusting shim from the countershaft front bearing bore.

31. With the puller, remove the countershaft center bearing outer race.

32. With a special puller and attachment, remove the mainshaft front bearing, thrust washer and inner race along with the adjusting shim front the mainshaft front bearing bore.

33. Remove the snap ring, and using the puller, remove the main drive shaft bearing.

34. Remove the countershaft center bearing inner race with the puller.

35. Separate the input shaft from the mainshaft and remove the input shaft from the case.

36. Remove the synchronizer ring and needle bearing from the input shaft.

37. Remove the mainshaft assembly from the case.

38. Remove the first/second and third/fourth shift forks from the case.

39. Remove the snap ring and slide the third/fourth clutch hub and sleeve assembly, synchronizer ring and third gear from the mainshaft.

40. Remove the thrust washer, first gear and needle bearing from the rear of the mainshaft.

41. Press out the needle bearing inner race, synchronizer ring, first and second clutch hub, sleeve assembly, synchronizer ring and second gear from the mainshaft.

5 Speed Assembly

1. Install the third/fourth clutch hub into the sleeve, place the three keys into the clutch hub slots and install the springs onto the hub.

2. Assembly the first/second and reverse/fifth clutch hub and sleeve as described in step 1.

3. Install the needle bearing, second gear, synchronizer ring, and first/second clutch assembly on the rear section of the mainshaft.

4. Press on the first gear needle bearing inner race.

5. Install the third gear and synchronizer ring onto the front section of the mainshaft.

6. Install the third/fourth clutch assembly onto the mainshaft.

7. Fit the snap ring on the mainshaft.

8. Install the needle bearing, synchronizer ring, first gear and thrust washer on the mainshaft.

9. Install the mainshaft assembly in the case.

10. Install the needle bearing on the front end of the mainshaft.

11. Install the first/second and third/fourth shift forks in their respective clutch sleeves.

12. Press the countershaft center bearing inner race on the countershaft.

13. Position the countershaft in the case.

14. Check the mainshaft bearing end play. Check the depth of the mainshaft bearing bore in the case. Measure the mainshaft bearing height. The difference indicates the required adjusting shim to give a total end play of less than 0.0039".

15. Install the synchronizer ring holder tool between the fourth synchronizer ring and the synchromesh gear on the input shaft.

16. Position the shims and mainshaft bearing in the bore and install with a press.

17. Install the input shaft bearing in the same way.

18. Check the countershaft front bearing end play in the same way as the mainshaft bearing end play.

19. Install the front bearing snap ring.

20. Press the countershaft center bearing into position.

21. Install the bearing cover plate.

22. Install the reverse idler gear shaft, thrust washers and reverse idler gear in the case.

23. Install the counter reverse gear and spacer on the rear end of the countershaft.

24. Install the thrust washer and press the needle bearing inner race of the reverse gear on the mainshaft.

25. Install the needle bearing, reverse gear, synchronizer ring, reverse/fifth clutch assembly and new mainshaft lock nut on the mainshaft.

26. Lock the mainshaft with the second and reverse gears. Tighten the locknut to 115–173 ft lb. Bend the tabs of the locknut.

27. Install the needle bearing, synchronizer ring and fifth gear on the mainshaft.

28. Install the thrust washer, steel ball and snap ring on the mainshaft.

29. Check the thrust washer-to-snap ring clearance. Clearance should be 0.0039–0.0118".

30. Install the first/second shift rod through the holes in the case and fork.

31. Install the interlock pin with a special installer and guide.

32. Install the third/fourth shift rod through the holes in the case and fork.

33. Align the holes and install the lock bolts of each shift fork and rod.

34. Install the interlock pin as above.

35. Position the reverse/fifth shift fork on the clutch sleeve and install the shift rod.

36. Tighten the lock bolt.

37. Install the three shift locking balls, springs and cap bolts.

38. Place the third/fourth clutch sleeve in third gear.

39. Check the clearance between the synchronizer key and the exposed edge of the synchronizer ring with a feeler gauge. The gap should be 0.026–0.079". Adjust by varying thrust washers.

40. Install the two blind covers and gaskets.

41. Install the undercover and gasket. Torque to 4–7 ft lb.

42. Apply a thin coat of sealer to the mating edges and install the intermediate housing on the transmission case. Align the lock bolt holes of the housing and reverse idler gear shaft, install and tighten the lock bolt.

43. Position the counter fifth gear and bearing to the rear end of the countershaft and install with a press.

44. Install the thrust washer and snap ring.

45. Check the clearance between the washer and snap ring. Clearance should be less than 0.0039".

46. Install the mainshaft rear bearing with a press.

47. Install the thrust washer and snap ring.

48. Check the thrust washer-to-snap

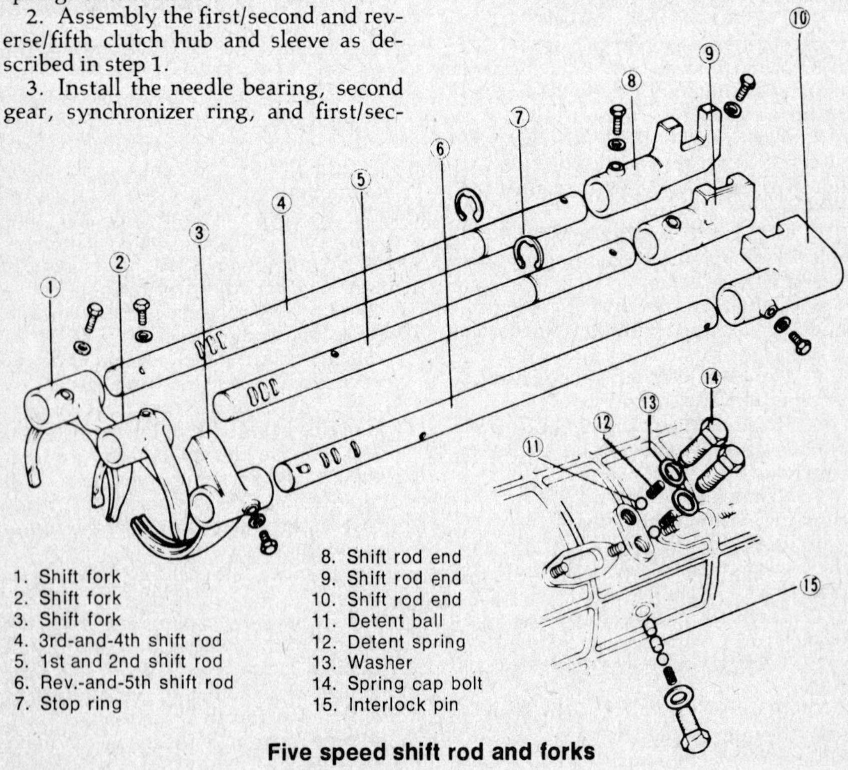

1. Shift fork
2. Shift fork
3. Shift fork
4. 3rd-and-4th shift rod
5. 1st and 2nd shift rod
6. Rev.-and-5th shift rod
7. Stop ring
8. Shift rod end
9. Shift rod end
10. Shift rod end
11. Detent ball
12. Detent spring
13. Washer
14. Spring cap bolt
15. Interlock pin

Five speed shift rod and forks

1. Shim
2. Snap ring
3. Main drive shaft bearing
4. Main drive shaft gear
5. Synchronizer ring
6. Synchronizer key
7. Synchronizer key spring
8. 3rd-and-4th clutch hub
9. Clutch sleeve
10. 3rd gear
11. Needle bearing
12. Needle bearing
13. Main shaft
14. Needle bearing
15. 2nd gear
16. 1st-and-2nd clutch hub
17. Clutch sleeve
18. Bearing inner race
19. Needle bearing
20. 1st gear
21. Thrust washer
22. Shim
23. Main shaft front bearing
24. Bearing cover
25. Thrust washer
26. Bearing inner race
27. Needle bearing
28. Reverse gear
29. Stop ring
30. Rev.-and-5th clutch hub
31. Clutch sleeve
32. Main shaft lock nut
33. Needle bearing
34. 5th gear
35. Thrust washer
36. Lock ball
37. Main shaft rear bearing
38. Thrust washer
39. Lock ball
40. Speedometer drive gear
41. Counter shaft front bearing
42. Shim
43. Counter shaft
44. Counter shaft center bearing
45. Counter reverse gear
46. Spacer
47. Reverse gear
48. Counter shaft rear bearing
49. Thrust washer
50. Thrust washer
51. Reverse idler gear
52. Idler gear shaft
53. Thrust washer

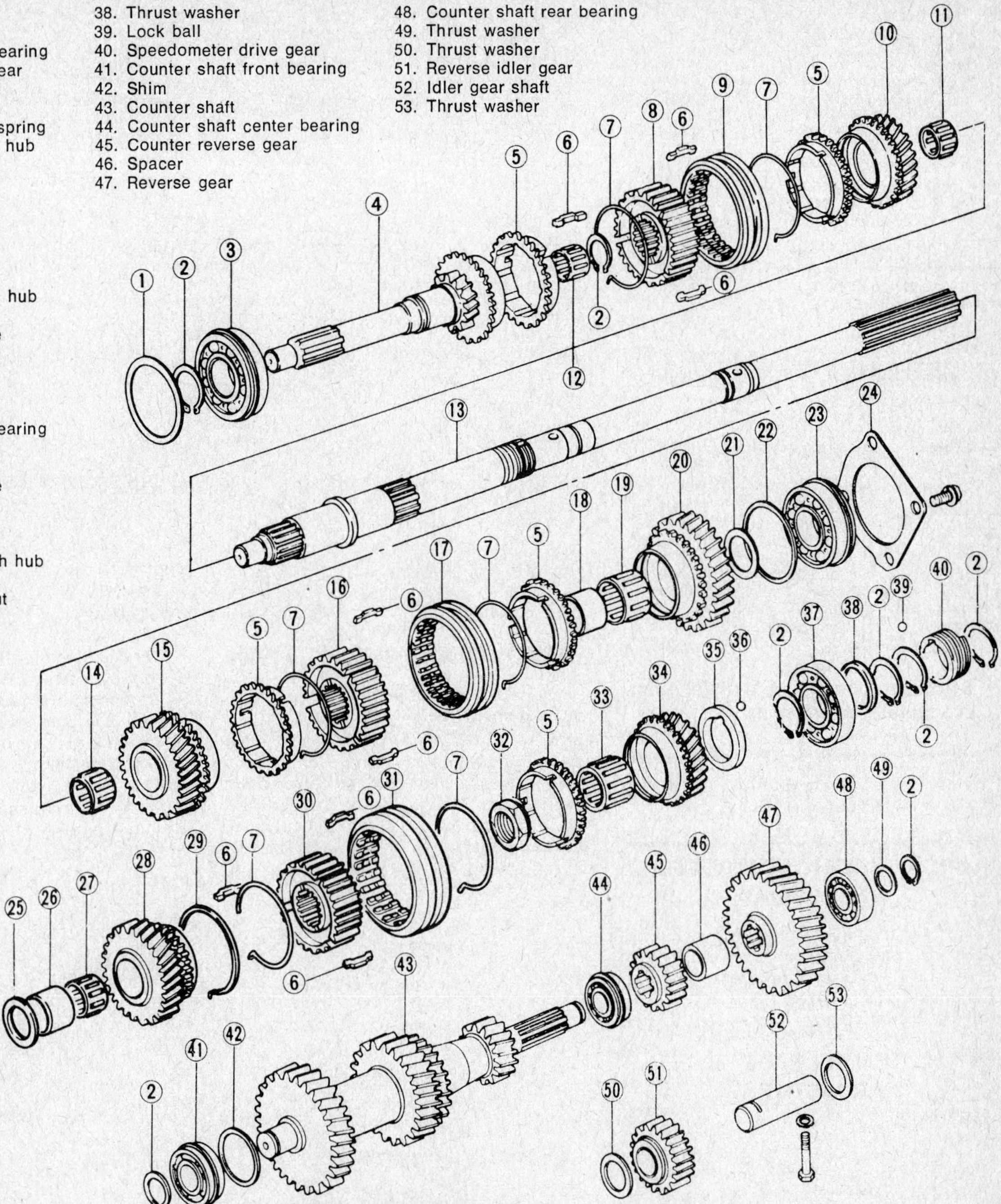

Five speed gear train

ring clearance. Clearance should be less than 0.0059″.

49. Apply a thin coat of sealing agent to the mating surfaces and install the bearing housing on the intermediate housing.

50. Install the shift rod ends of their respective rods.

51. Install the speedometer drive gear and steel ball on the mainshaft. Secure it with a snap ring.

52. Install a speedometer driven gear assembly on the extension housing and secure it with the bolt and lock plate.

53. Insert the control rod through the holes from the front side of the extension housing.

54. Align the key and insert the control lever end in the control rod.

55. Install the bolt and tighten it to 20–30 ft lb.

56. Install the back-up light switch and tighten to 20–30 ft lb.

57. Place the gasket on the case and install the extension housing with the control lever end down and as far to the left as it will go.

58. Tighten the bolts.

59. Check for proper operation of the gear shift lever.

60. Insert the select lock spindle and spring from the underside of the shift lever retainer.

61. Install the steel ball and spring in alignment with the spindle groove and install the spring cap bolt.

62. Install the gearshift lever retainer and gasket on the extension housing.

63. Check the bearing end play. Measure the depth of the bearing bore in the housing. Measure the height of the bearing protrusion. The difference indicates the thickness of the shim needed. The end play should be less than 0.0039″.

64. Place the gasket on the front side of the case. Apply lubricant to the lip of the oil seal and install the clutch housing on the case.

65. Install the release bearing and fork on the clutch housing.

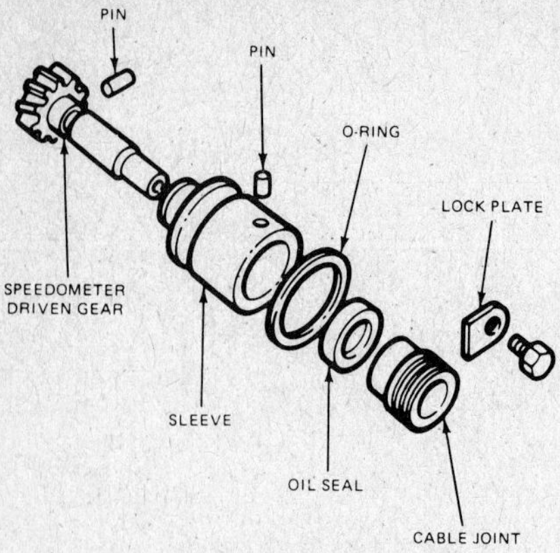

Speedometer gear and adapter

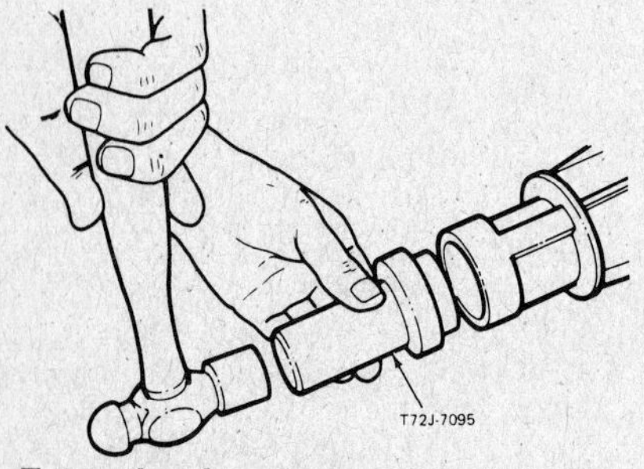

Extension housing seal installation five speed transmission

CLUTCH

PEDAL HEIGHT ADJUSTMENT (FREE-PLAY)

Adjust the pushrod length by rotating the rod. The clutch pedal should have a free travel of $^{13}/_{16}$–$1^{3}/_{16}$ in. measured at the pedal pad through 1975, and $^{1}/_{64}$–$^{1}/_{8}$ in. 1976 and later.

CLUTCH RELEASE LEVER ADJUSTMENT

1973–75

***NOTE:** This adjustment must be maintained to prevent release bearing and clutch damage.*

1. Raise and support the truck.
2. Disconnect the release lever return spring at the lever.
3. Loosen the locknut and rotate the adjusting nut until a clearance of 1/8–9/64 in. (0.12–0.14 in.) is obtained between the bullet nosed end of the adjusting nut and the release lever.
4. Tighten the locknut.

1976 and Later

No adjustment is possible on these trucks. Instead, the stroke can be checked by raising the truck and moving the release rod. If the stroke measures less than 0.196 in., the clutch should be replaced.

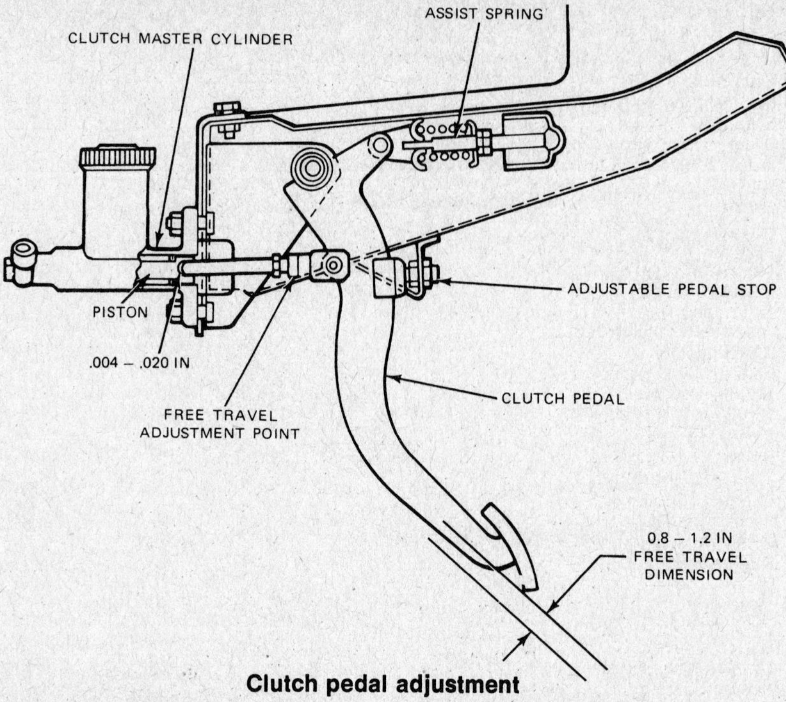

Clutch pedal adjustment

REMOVAL AND INSTALLATION

1. Remove the transmission.
2. Remove the four attaching and two pilot bolts holding the clutch cover to the flywheel. Loosen the bolts evenly and a turn or two at a time. If the clutch cover is to be reinstalled, mark the flywheel and clutch cover to show the location of the two pilot holes.
3. Remove the clutch disc.

To install the clutch:

4. Install the clutch disc on the flywheel. Do not touch the facing or allow the facing to come in contact with grease or oil. The clutch disc can be aligned using a tool made for that purpose, or with an old mainshaft.

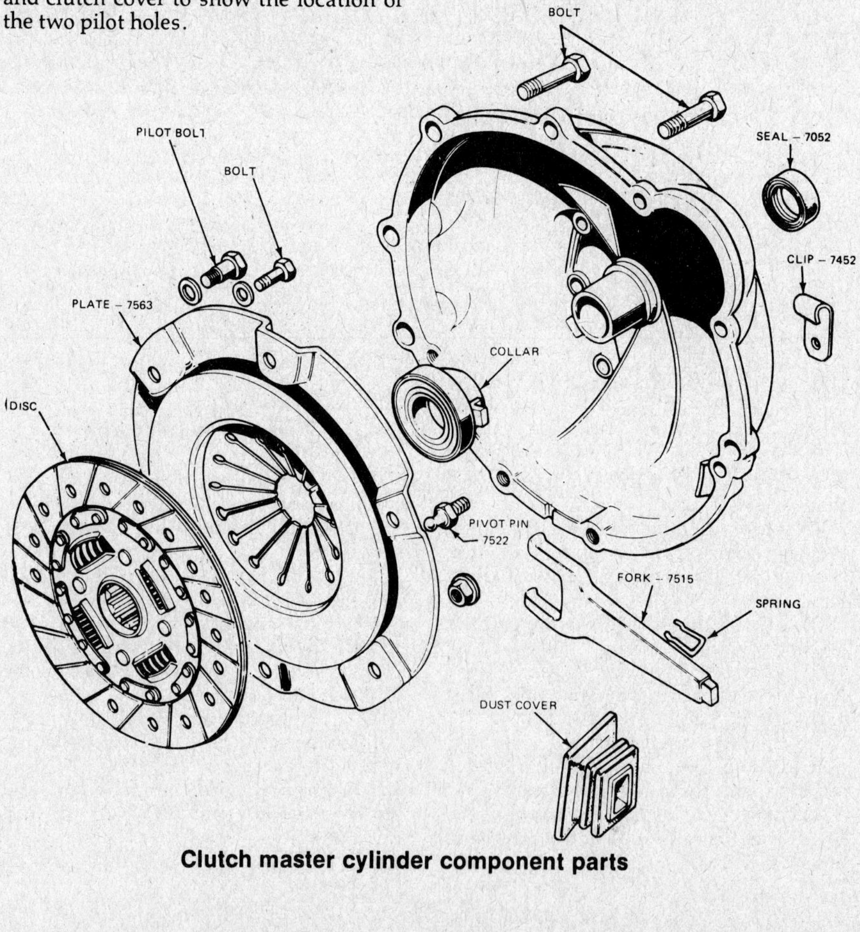

Clutch master cylinder component parts

5. Install the clutch cover on the flywheel aligning the marks made during removal, and install the four standard bolts and the two pilot bolts.
6. To avoid distorting the pressure plate, tighten the bolts evenly a few turns at a time until they are all tight.
7. Torque the bolts to 13–20 ft lbs using a crossing pattern.
8. Remove the aligning tool.
9. Apply a light film of lubricant to the release bearing, release lever contact area on the release bearing hub and to the input shaft bearing retainer.
10. Install the transmission.
11. Check the operation of the clutch and if necessary, adjust the pedal freeplay and the release lever.

Clutch Master Cylinder

REMOVAL AND INSTALLATION

1. Disconnect and plug the hydraulic line.
2. Unbolt and remove the master cylinder.

OVERHAUL

1. Remove the master cylinder.
2. Clean the outside of the cylinder thoroughly and drain the fluid.
3. Remove the boot (through 1975).
4. Use a screwdriver to remove the piston stop-ring. Remove the stop washer.
5. Remove the piston, piston cup and piston return spring from the cylinder.
6. Carefully remove and disassemble the one-way valve. 1976–78 1800 cc models do not have one. All 2000 and 2300 cc models have the valve.
7. Wash all parts (except rubber parts) in clean alcohol or brake fluid. Never use mineral spirits of any kind to clean a master cylinder.
8. Check the rubber cups. If they have become worn, softened or swelled, replace them.
9. Check the clearance between the cylinder bore and piston. If it exceeds 0.004 in., replace the cylinder or piston.
10. Be sure that the one-way valve is free to operate. 1976–78 1800 cc models have a compensating port which must be open.

To assemble the master cylinder:

11. Dip the piston and cups in clean brake fluid.
12. Install the return spring in the cylinder bore.
13. Install the primary cup so that the flat side of the cup is toward the piston.
14. Install the secondary cup on the piston and insert the cup and piston into the cylinder.
15. Install the stop washer and stopring.
16. Assemble and install the one-way valve, if equipped.
17. Fill the reservoir with clean brake fluid and operate the piston with a screwdriver until fluid is ejected through the outlet fitting.

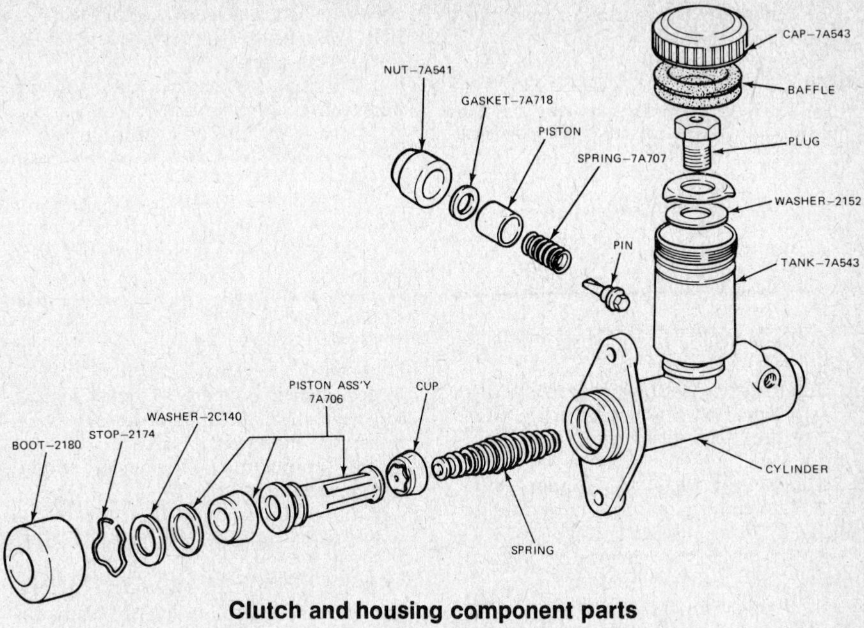

Clutch and housing component parts

18. Install the master cylinder.
19. Bleed the hydraulic system.

BLEEDING THE HYDRAULIC SYSTEM

The clutch hydraulic system must be bled whenever the line has been disconnected.

To bleed the system, remove the rubber cap from the bleeder valve and attach a rubber hose to the valve. Submerge the other end of the hose in a large jar of clean brake fluid. Open the bleeder valve. Depress the clutch pedal and allow it to return slowly. Continue this pumping action and watch the jar of brake fluid. When air bubbles stop appearing, close the bleeder valve and remove the tube.

During the bleeding process, the master cylinder must be kept at least $^3/_4$ full. After the bleeding operation is finished, install the cap on the bleeder valve and fill the master cylinder to the proper level. Always use fresh brake fluid, and above all, do not use the fluid that was in the jar for bleeding, since it contains air. Install the master cylinder reservoir cap.

Clutch Slave Cylinder

REMOVAL AND INSTALLATION

1. Disconnect and plug the slave cylinder hydraulic line.
2. Unhook the release lever return spring, through 1975. Unhook the lever from the pushrod, 1976 and later.
3. Remove the nuts and washers attaching the slave cylinder to the clutch housing.

To install the slave cylinder:

4. Install the slave cylinder on the clutch housing, torquing the nuts to 12–17 ft lbs.
5. Connect the slave cylinder inlet line to the slave cylinder.

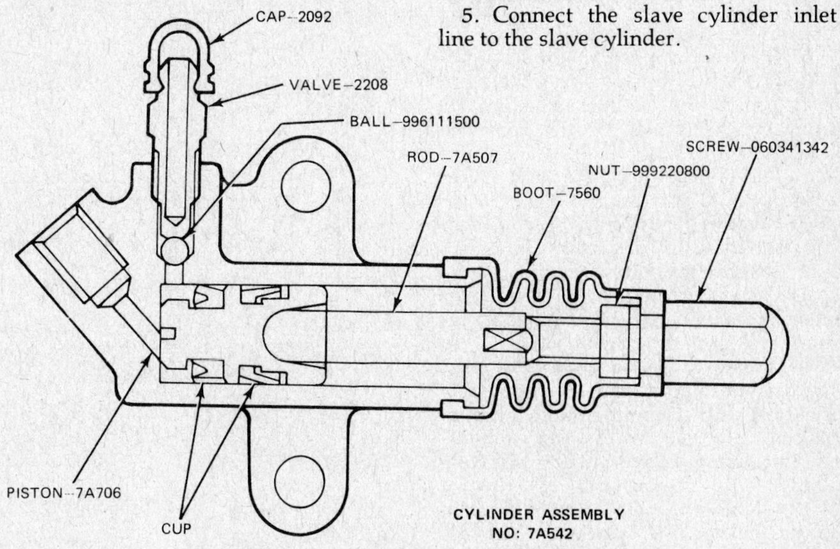

Clutch slave cylinder cross sectional view

6. Fill the master cylinder and bleed the hydraulic system.
7. Check and adjust the release lever, through 1975.
8. Connect the return spring on earlier models, or hook the release lever onto the pushrod, 1976 and later.

OVERHAUL

1. Remove the slave cylinder.
2. Clean the outside thoroughly.
3. Remove the dust cover and release rod.
4. Remove the piston from the cylinder.
5. Disassemble the bleeder valve.
6. Inspect the cylinder, using Steps 7–9 of the "Master Cylinder Overhaul" procedure.

To assemble the slave cylinder:

7. Dip the pistons and cups in clean brake fluid.
8. Assemble the cups to the piston as shown and install the piston.
9. Install the release rod and release rod boot.
10. Install the steel ball and bleeder into the bleeder orifice. Install the bleeder cap.
11. Install the slave cylinder.

AUTOMATIC TRANSMISSION

Couriers use a JATCO automatic transmission as optional equipment beginning in 1974. It is a 3-speed unit with manual selection of 1st and 2nd gears possible.

NOTE: The adjustments should be performed in the order given. Be sure the idle speed is set before performing any adjustments.

REMOVAL AND INSTALLATION

1. Disconnect the battery.
2. Raise and support the truck.
3. Drain the transmission fluid.
4. Unbolt the exhaust pipe bracket from the right side of the converter housing.
5. Disconnect the driveshaft at the rear axle.
6. Remove the driveshaft center bearing support.
7. Remove the driveshaft.
8. Disconnect the speedometer cable.
9. Disconnect the shift rod from the manual lever at the transmission.
10. Remove the vacuum hose from the vacuum diaphragm, the wires from the downshift solenoid and the inhibitor switch.
11. Disconnect and plug the oil cooler lines.
12. Remove the access cover from the lower end of the converter housing. Matchmark the drive plate and torque converter for reassembly. Remove the 4 bolts attaching the drive plate to the torque converter.
13. Unbolt the rear transmission support from the crossmember.
14. Support the transmission with a jack and unbolt and remove the crossmember.
15. Lower the transmission enough to remove the starter.
16. Remove the converter housing-to-engine bolts.
17. Remove the transmission fluid filler tube.
18. Using a pry bar, exert pressure between the flex plate and the converter to prevent the converter from disengaging from the transmission as the transmission is moved rearward.
19. Remove the transmission and onverter as an assembly.
20. Installation is the reverse of removal.

SHIFT LINKAGE ADJUSTMENT

1. Put the gearshift lever in Neutral.
2. Raise and support the truck.
3. Disconnect the clevis from the lower end of the selector lever operating arm.
4. Move the transmission manual lever to Neutral, the 3rd detent position from the rear of the transmission.
5. Loosen the two clevis retaining nuts and adjust the clevis so that it freely enters the hole of the lever. Tighten the retaining nuts to secure the adjustment.
6. Connect the clevis to the lever and attach it with the spring washer, flat washer and retaining clip.

THROTTLE LINKAGE ADJUSTMENT

See "Fuel System".

KICK-DOWN SWITCH ADJUSTMENT

1. Turn the ignition switch to the ON position.

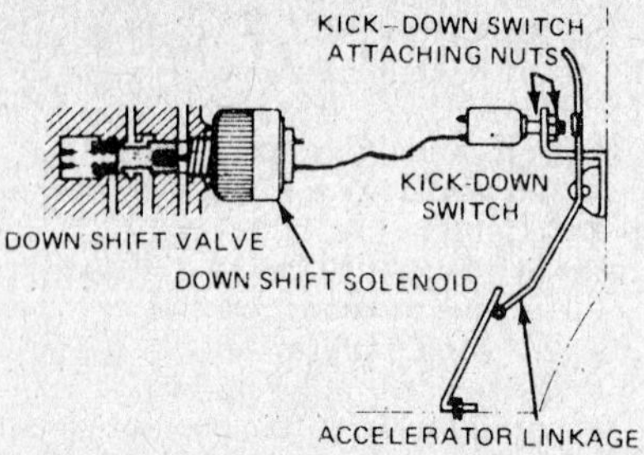

Automatic transmission kick-down switch adjustment

2. Loosen the kick-down switch attaching nut and adjust the switch to engage when the accelerator pedal is depressed about 7/8 of the way. The downshift solenoid will click when the switch engages.

NEUTRAL START SWITCH ADJUSTMENT

1. Adjust the shift linkage.
2. Place the transmission manual lever in Neutral (3rd detent from the rear of the transmission).
3. Remove the transmission manual lever retaining nut and lever.
4. Loosen the switch attaching bolts. Remove the screw from the alignment pin hole at the bottom of the switch.
5. Rotate the switch and insert an alignment pin, 0.059 in. diameter for 1974, or 0.079 in. 1975 and later into the alignment pin hole and internal rotor.
6. Tighten the two switch attaching bolts and remove the alignment pin.
7. Reinstall the alignment pin hole screw in the switch body.
8. Install the manual lever. The engine should only start with the transmission selector lever in Neutral or Park.

BAND ADJUSTMENT

1. Raise and support the truck.
2. Place a drainpan under the transmission and loosen the pan attaching bolts to drain the fluid. Finally remove all the bolts except the two at the front.

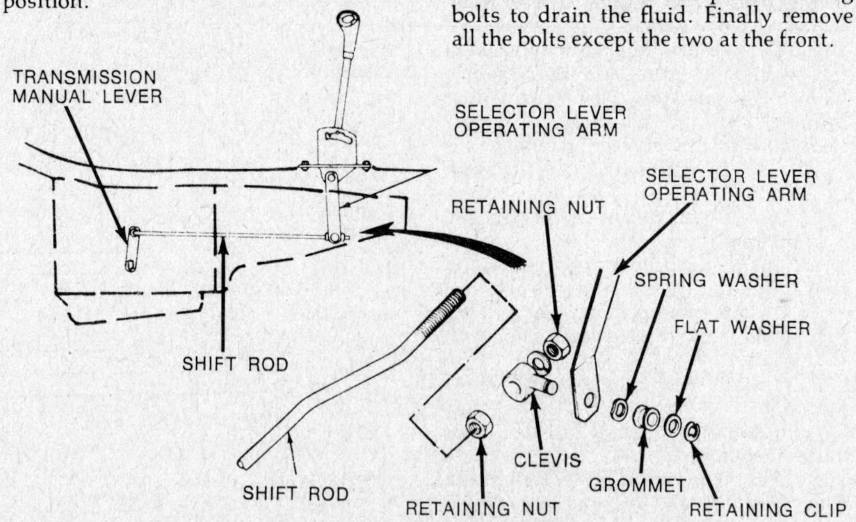

Automatic transmission manual linkage adjustment

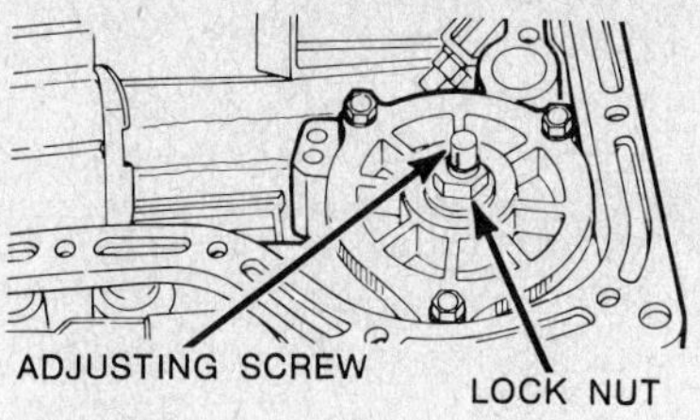

Automatic transmission band adjustment

3. When the fluid has drained, remove and thoroughly clean the pan.
4. Discard the pan gasket.
5. Loosen the band adjusting screw locknut and tighten the adjusting screw to 9–11 ft lbs.
6. Back the adjusting screw off two turns.
7. Hold the adjusting screw stationary and tighten the adjusting screw locknut to 22–29 ft lbs.
8. Install a new pan gasket and install the pan on the transmission. Fill the transmission.

PAN REMOVAL AND INSTALLATION

See Steps 1, 2, 3, 4, and 8 of the preceding procedure.

DRIVE AXLES

Driveshaft and U-Joints

REMOVAL AND INSTALLATION

1. Mark the driveshaft and companion flange for correct alignment when it is installed.
2. Remove the center support bearing bracket on two piece driveshafts.
3. Pull the driveshaft rearward and remove it from the transmission.

To install the transmission:

4 Position the driveshaft and slide the front yoke into the extension housing of the transmission.
5. Attach the center support bearing bracket if equipped.
6. Install the rear shaft to the companion flange and torque the bolts to 39–47 ft lbs. Be sure that the alignment marks made during removal are aligned.

U-Joint Overhaul

1. Remove the driveshaft from the vehicle and place it in a vise, being careful not to damage it.
2. Remove the snap-rings which retain the bearings in the flange and in the driveshaft.
3. Remove the driveshaft tube from the vise and position the U-joint in the vise with a socket smaller than the bearing cap on one side and a socket larger than the bearing cap on the other side.
4. Slowly tighten the jaws of the vise so that the small socket forces the U-joint spider and the opposite bearing into the larger socket.

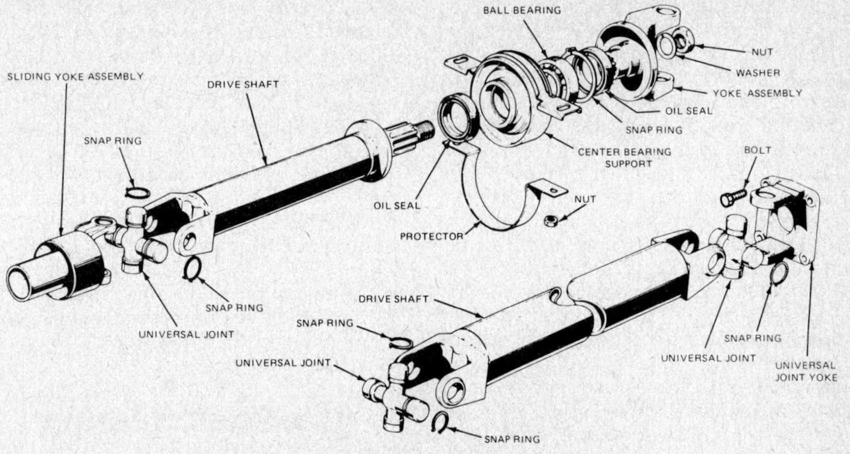

Two piece drive shaft disassembled

5. Remove the other side of the spider in the same manner (if applicable) and remove the spider assembly from the driveshaft. Discard the spider assemblies.
6. Clean all foreign matter from the yoke areas at the end of the driveshaft(s).
7. Start the new spider and one of the bearing cap assemblies into a yoke by positioning the yoke in a vise with the spider positioned in place with one of the bearing cap assemblies positioned over one of the holes in the yoke. Slowly close the vise, pressing the bearing cap assembly in the yoke. Press the cap in far enough so that the retaining snap-ring can be installed. Use the smaller socket to recess the bearing cap.

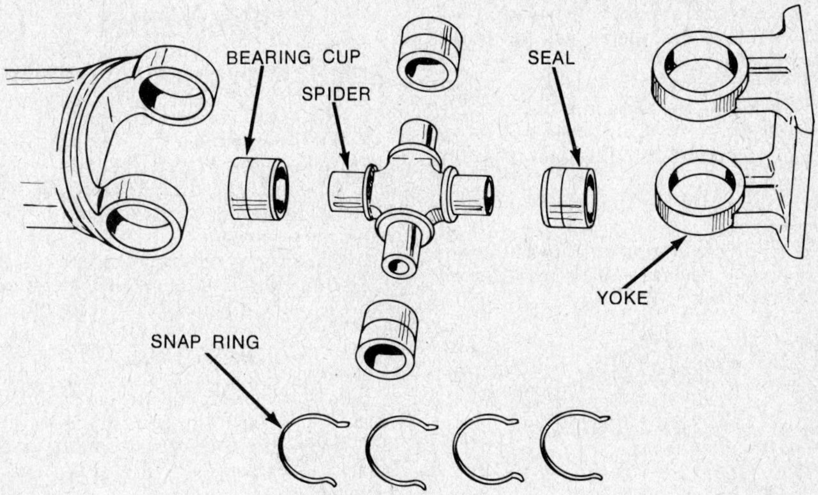

U-joint component parts

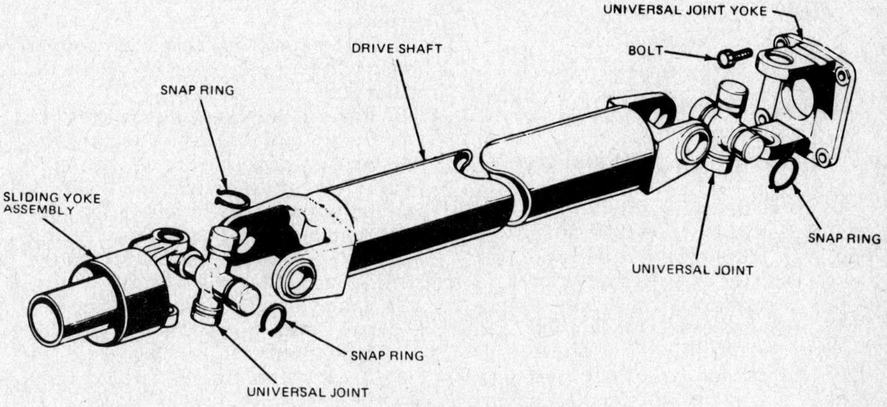

One piece drive shaft

8. Open the vise and position the opposite bearing cap assembly over the proper hole in the yoke with the socket that is smaller than the diameter of the bearing cap located on the cap. Slowly close the vise, pressing the bearing cap into the hole in the yoke with the socket. Make sure that the spider assembly is in line with the bearing cap as it is pressed in. Press the bearing cap in far enough so that the retaining snap-ring can be installed. Snap-rings are available in 0.057–0.064 in. thicknesses to assure good centering of the yokes and spiders, preventing out-of-balance. When selecting snap-rings, to give a suitable slight drag fit (not binding), use similar snap-rings in any given yoke. For example, do not use a 0.059 in. snap-ring opposite a 0.063 in. snap-ring, as this would create an out-of-balance condition.

9. Install all remaining U-joints in the same manner. The nut attaching the yoke and bearing to the front coupling shaft should be torqued to 115–130 ft lbs.

10. Install the driveshaft and grease the new U-joints.

Axle Shaft

REMOVAL AND INSTALLATION

1. Raise and support the truck.
2. Remove the rear wheel and brake drum.
3. Remove the brake shoes.
4. Remove the parking brake cable retainer.
5. Disconnect and plug the hydraulic brake lines.
6. Unbolt the backing plate and bearing housing.
7. Slide the complete axle shaft from the housing. If necessary, remove the oil seal from the housing.

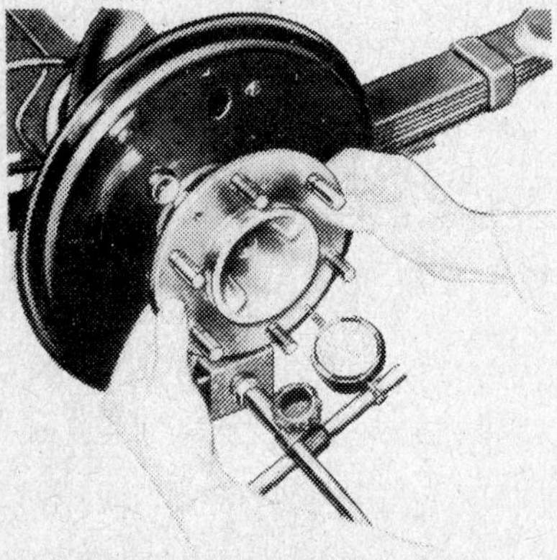

Checking axle shaft end play

To install the axle shaft:

8. Install a new axle oil seal in the housing if the old one was removed.
9. Install the axle shaft assembly.
10. Using two bolts and nuts, temporarily install the bearing housing and backing plate to the housing flange.
11. Check the axle shaft end-play with a dial indicator mounted on the backing plate.
12. If only one axle shaft has been removed, the end-play should be 0.002–0.006 in. If both axle shafts have been removed, check the end-play after the first shaft is installed. It should be 0.026–0.033 in. The end-play of the second shaft should then be 0.002–0.006 in. Shims are available to adjust the end-play.
13. After adjusting the end play, install bolts and torque them to 12–16 ft lbs.
14. Install the brake shoes.
15. Install the brake drum and wheel.
16. Connect the brake lines.
17. Bleed the brakes.

Axle Shaft Bearing

REMOVAL AND INSTALLATION

1. Remove the axle shaft. Straighten the tabs of the lock washer.
2. Using a spanner wrench, loosen and remove the lock nut from the axle.
3. Remove the bearing from the axle with the use of a puller.
4. Installation is the reverse of removal. Be sure the bearing taper points in the right direction. Tighten the lock nut to 130–190 ft. lbs., and bend the lock washer tabs over the nut.

Differential

REMOVAL AND INSTALLATION

1. Raise and support the truck.
2. Drain the fluid.
3. Remove the axle shafts.
4. Matchmark the driveshaft and companion flange for reassembly. Remove the driveshaft.
5. Unbolt and remove the carrier.
6. Installation is the reverse of removal. Clean the magnetic drain plug.

OVERHAUL

Before disassembling the carrier, perform a few tests for future reference.

1. Wipe the lubricant from the gear teeth and perform a tooth contact pattern test.
2. Measure and record the ring gear backlash. The limits are 0.007–0.008 in.
3. Measure and record the ring gear runout.
4. Matchmark the carrier, differential bearing caps and the adjusters for reassembly.
5. Remove the adjuster lockplates.
6. Set up a dial indicator to read the side bearing preload. Loosen the nuts securing the bearing cap and slowly back off the adjuster to relieve the preload. As this is being done, observe and record the preload. The adjuster on the left side has a left-hand thread.
7. Remove the nuts, bearing caps and adjusters. Keep each bearing cap with its own adjuster.
8. Remove the differential and keep each bearing outer race with its own bearing.

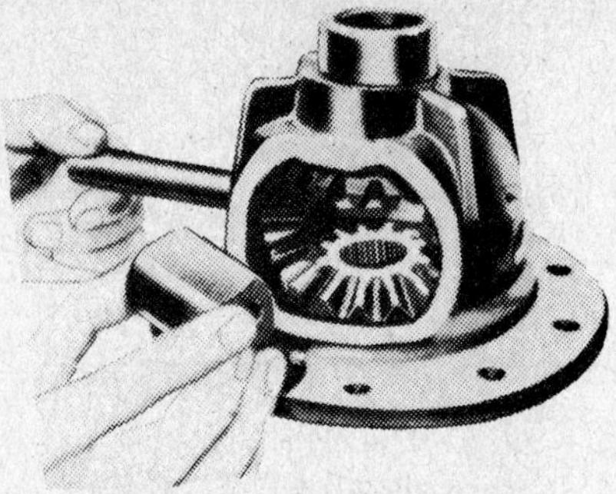

Pinion shaft and thrust block removal

9. If the differential bearings are to be replaced, remove them.
10. Unbolt and remove the ring gear.
11. Drive the lockpin from the ring gear.
12. Remove the pinion shaft and thrust block.
13. Rotate the differential pinion gears 90° and remove them and the thrust washers.
14. Remove the side gears and thrust washers.
15. Remove the pinion nut.
16. Remove the companion flange.
17. Remove the pinion and rear bearing from the carrier with a plastic or rubber mallet. Do not damage the gear teeth.
18. Remove the pinion oil seal and front bearing.
19. The pinion bearing outer races can be remove with a drift.
20. Remove and save the shims from underneath the outer race.
21. Remove the bearing from the pinion.

With the carrier disassembled, check all parts for wear or damage, replacing parts as necessary. Do not use old bearings with new races or vice versa. Replace ring and pinion gears in matched sets only. Always use a new oil seal.

22. Find the pinion depth. If the same ring and pinion are used, the shim combination under the outer race may prove satisfactory. If replacing a ring and pinion with a new set, examine the new pinion gear. There may be a mark on the face end from −1 to +1. This indicates an oversize or undersize pinion.

PINION GEAR MARKING CHART

Gear Mark	Inches O/S or U/S
±1	±0.0004
±2	±0.0008
±3	±0.0012

If there is no mark, the shim pack already with the carrier should be satisfactory. For example, if the new pinion is marked +3 and the old pinion is marked +2, the shim pack must be in-

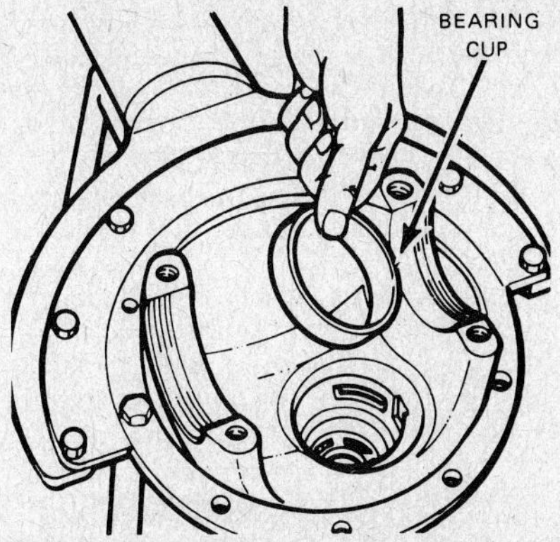

Positioning differential bearing cup

creased by 0.0004 in. In any case, no more than 4 shims should be used.

23. Position the determined shim pack and bearing races.

24. Find the pinion bearing preload. If the bearing was removed from the pinion gear or a new gear is being used, press the bearing on the pinion.

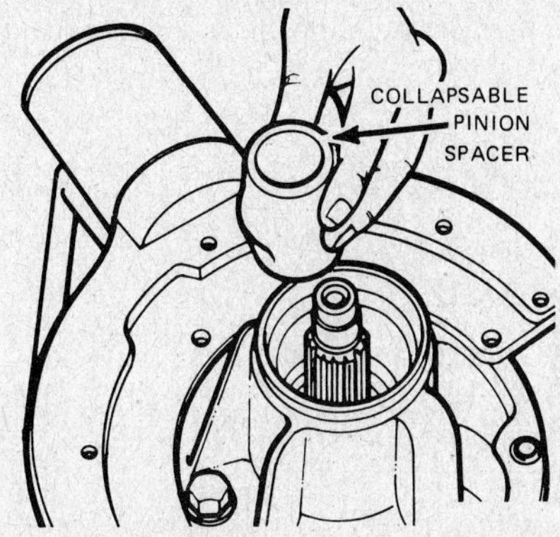

Installing differential pinion spacer

25. Install the pinion and bearing in the carrier.

26. Install the spacer and shims.

27. Install the front bearing and companion flange without the oil seal.

28. Tighten the pinion nut to 145–250 ft lbs, while checking the pinion preload

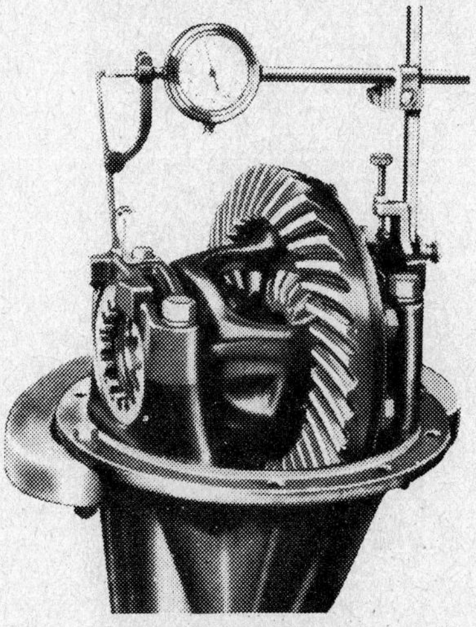

Checking side bearing preload

with an in. lb torque wrench. The rotating torque, through one complete revolution should be 1.3–2.5 ft lbs, within the 145–250 ft lbs of nut torque. Tighten the pinion nut slowly in small increments as the rotating torque builds up in a hurry. If the rotating torque is not within limits, it must be adjusted with shims and spacers selected from the following tables.

SHIM THICKNESS CHART

Identification Mark	Thickness (in.)
4	0.013
6	0.014
8	0.015

SPACER THICKNESS CHART

Identification Mark	Thickness (in.)
20	2.291
28	2.294
36	2.298
48	2.300

29. Following the adjustment, install a new oil seal and tighten the pinion nut to 200 ft lbs.

To assemble the differential:

30. Install the thrust washer on each differential side gear and install the side gears.

31. Insert the pinion gears and thrust washers in the case 180° apart.

32. Align the holes in the case and gears and install the pinion shaft.

33. Check the backlash of the side gears which should not exceed 0.008 in. If it does, adjust the backlash with the side gear thrust washers.

SIDE GEAR THRUST WASHER CHART

Identification Mark	Thickness (in.)
6	0.063
7	0.067
8	0.071

34. After adjustment, remove the pinion shaft and install the thrust block. The hole should be centered between the side gears. Reinstall the pinion shaft until the lockpin hole in the pinion shaft is aligned with the hole in the case.

35. Install the lockpin in the pinion shaft and stake it in place.

36. Install the ring gear and torque the bolts to 40–45 ft lbs. Bend the lock-tabs over the bolts.

37. Install each differential bearing in the case. Install the outer races on their respective bearings.

38. Install the differential gear assembly in the carrier so that the marks on the face of the pinion and ring gear are in alignment.

39. Note the identification marks on the adjusters (right and left-hand) and install these.

40. Install the bearing caps and align the matchmarks previously made.

41. Turn the adjusters until the bearings are properly positioned and some amount of backlash exists in the ring gear teeth. End-play in the bearings should be eliminated.

42. Slightly tighten one of the bearing cap nuts on each side and adjust the backlash.

43. Install a dial indicator on the carrier flange and index it at right angles to one of the ring gear teeth. Check the backlash at 4 or 5 different teeth. Turn both adjusters equally, until the backlash is 0.007–0.008 in.

44. Torque the bearing cap nuts to 45 ft lbs.

45. Install the adjuster lockplates.

REAR SUSPENSION

Springs

REMOVAL AND INSTALLATION

1. Raise and support the truck.
2. Support the rear axle.
3. Disconnect the shock absorber at the lower mount.
4. Remove the spring clip nuts and the spring plate.
5. Remove the spring pin nut and remove the two bolts and nuts attaching the spring pin to the frame bracket.
6. Remove the spring pin and remove the front end of the spring from the truck.
7. Remove the shackle plate nuts and the shackle plate.
8. Remove the spring from the truck.

To install the spring:

9. Install the rubber bushings in the front eye of the spring and position it in the frame bracket. Align the holes of the bushings with the hole of the frame bracket.
10. Insert the spring pin from the outside through the rubber bushing.
11. Install the spring pin plate to the frame bracket and torque the nuts to 15–18 ft lbs.
12. Install the rubber bushings in the rear spring eye and shackle plate. Install the spring and shackle plate to the frame bracket. Do not tighten the nuts.
13. Lower the rear axle and place the

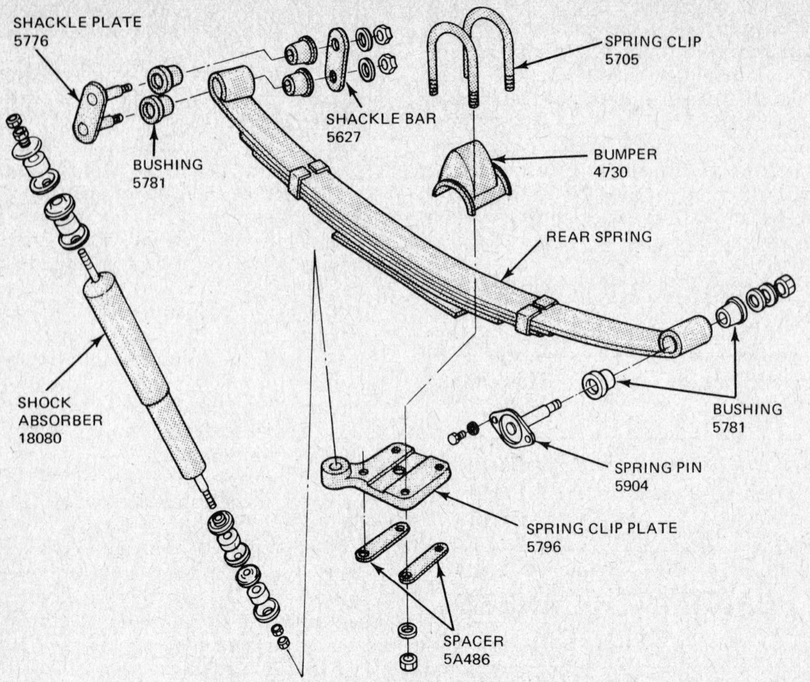

Rear suspension component parts

center hole of the axle spring clip plate over the head of the spring center bolt.

14. Install the spring plate under the spring and install the spring clips. Torque the nuts to 46–58 ft lbs.

15. Connect the shock absorber at the lower mount and torque the mount to 18–26 ft lbs.

16. Lower the vehicle and bounce it several times to seat the springs.

17. Tighten the spring pin nuts to 62–76 ft lbs. and the shackle plate nuts to 44–58 ft lbs.

Shock Absorber

REMOVAL AND INSTALLATION

1. Raise and support the truck.
2. Remove the nuts washers and bushings from the upper and lower shock mounts.
3. Compress the shock absorber and remove it.

To install the shock absorber:

4. If the rubber bushings are worn or damaged, use new ones.
5. Compress the shock absorber and install it in the truck.

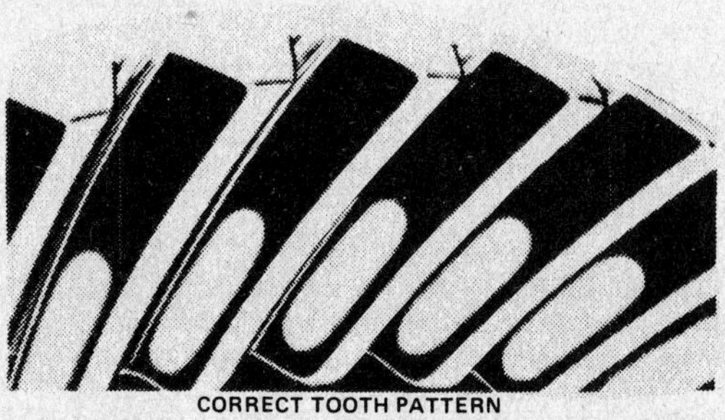

CORRECT TOOTH PATTERN
THIS PATTERN PROVIDES PROPER GEAR MESH AND AXLE PERFORMANCE.
ALL ADJUSTMENTS MUST BE MADE TO SECURE THIS TYPE OF PATTERN.

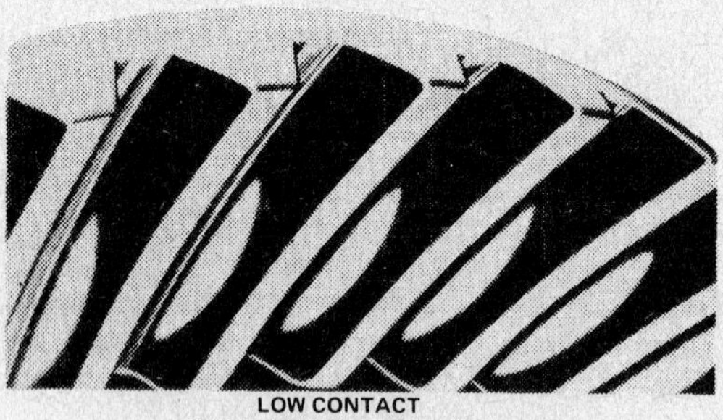

LOW CONTACT
THE PINION IS IN TOO FAR.
REMOVE SHIMS, AND READJUST BACKLASH.

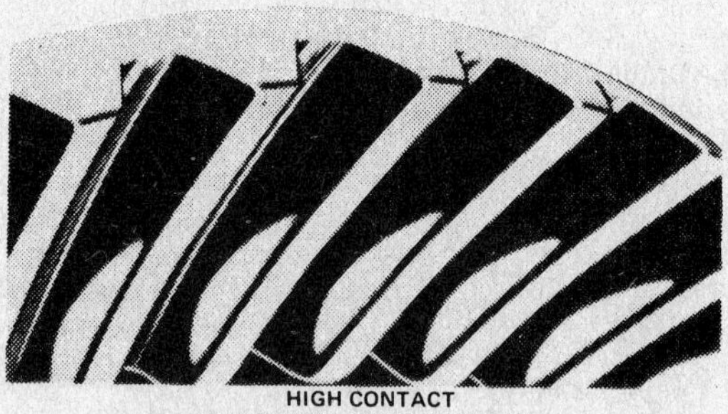

HIGH CONTACT
THE PINION IS OUT TOO FAR.
ADD SHIMS, AND READJUST BACKLASH.

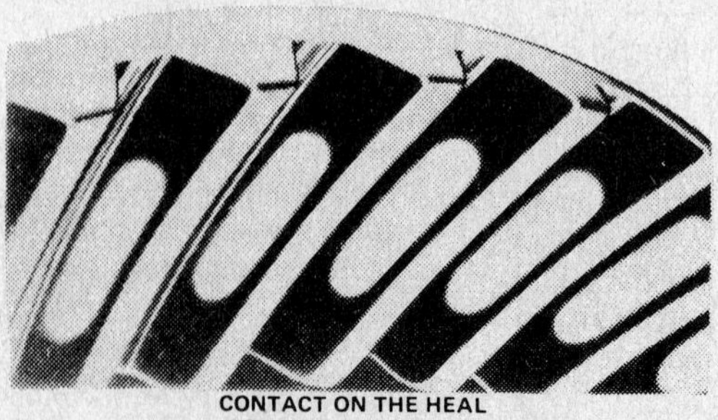

CONTACT ON THE HEAL
TOO MUCH BACKLASH.
MOVE RING GEAR TOWARD PINION.

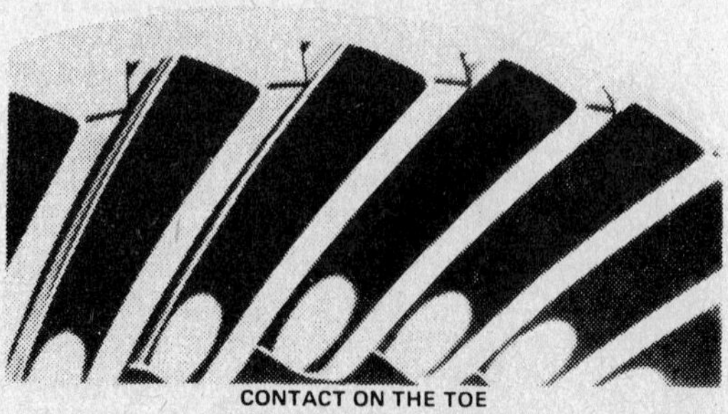

CONTACT ON THE TOE
NOT ENOUGH BACKLASH.
MOVE RING GEAR AWAY FROM PINION.

Gear tooth patterns

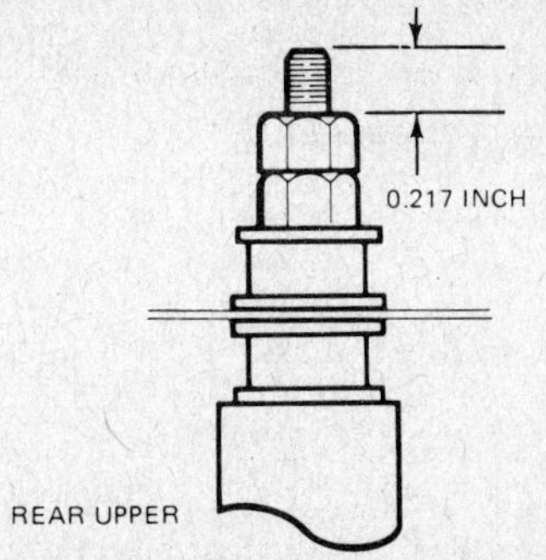

Rear shock absorber is correctly installed when this measurement is obtained

6. Install the rubber bushings, washers and nuts on both the upper and lower mounts. Torque all mounts to 18–26 ft lbs through 1974. Both the lower and upper mounts must be tightened to provide 0.138 in. between the outside nut and the end of the shock rod in 1975, and 0.217 in. for 1976–80.
7. Lower the truck.

FRONT SUSPENSION

Shock Absorber

REMOVAL AND INSTALLATION

1. Raise and support the truck.
2. Unbolt the upper mount from the crossmember.
3. Remove the rubber bushings and washers.
4. Unbolt the lower end from the control arm.
5. Remove the shock from under the lower control arm.

To install the shock absorber:

6. Replace any worn or damaged bushings.
7. From under the lower control arm, install the shock with bushings and attach the shock to the lower control arm. Torque the lower mount to 12–17 ft lbs.
8. Attach the upper end of the shock to the crossmember and torque the upper mount bolt to 18–26 ft lbs. through 1974. For 1975 and later models, tighten the nuts so that there is 0.256 in. between the top of the shock absorber rod and the top of the upper nut.
9. Lower the truck.

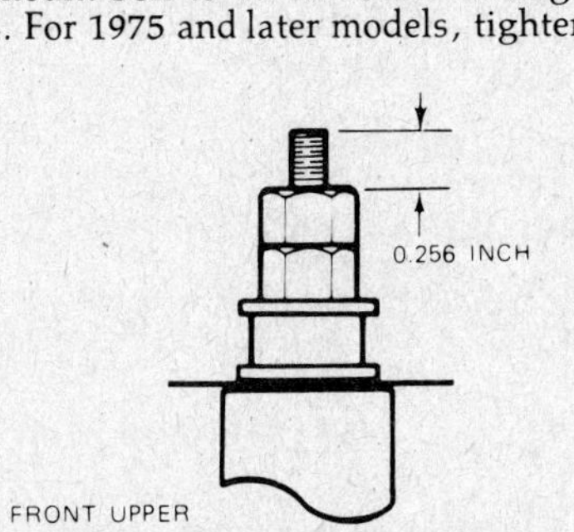

Front shock absorber is correctly installed when this measurement is obtained

Spring

REMOVAL AND INSTALLATION

Follow procedures under "Upper Control Arm".

Upper Control Arm

REMOVAL AND INSTALLATION

1. Raise and support the truck.
2. Support the lower control arm.
3. Lower the truck until the upper control arm is off the bumper stop.
4. Remove the wheel. Install a spring compressor.
5. Remove the cotter pin and nut retaining the upper ball joint.
6. Separate the ball joint from the spindle.
7. From under the hood, remove the two upper arm retaining bolts and remove the arm from the vehicle. Keep track of the alignment shims under the bolts.
8. Remove the ball joint from the upper arm.
9. Install the ball joint in the upper control arm. Torque the nut to 15–20 ft. lb.
10. Position the upper control arm in the truck and install the alignment shims from where they were removed. Torque the shaft nuts to 62–76 ft. lb.
11. Install the spindle on the ball joint. Torque to 40–55 ft. lb.
12. Remove the spring compressor.

Lower Control Arm

REMOVAL AND INSTALLATION

1. Raise and support the front of the truck.
2. Remove the wheel.
3. Disconnect the shock absorber and push the shock up into the spring.
4. Remove the front stabilizer bar.
5. Position a floor jack under the lower control arm and raise the arm to take the spring pressure off. Install a spring compressor.
6. Unbolt the ball joint from the lower control arm.
7. Pull the spindle and ball joint away from the lower arm.
8. If necessary, the lower ball joint can be removed by removing the cotter pin and nut and loosening the ball joint with a hammer.
9. Lower the arm on the jack. Remove the lower arm shaft-to-frame bolts and remove the lower arm.
10. Install the lower control arm. Do not tighten. If removed, install the ball joint. Torque the ball joint nuts to 60–70 ft. lb.
11. Install the spring.
12. Use a C-clamp to clamp the spring to the lower control arm.
13. Raise the lower control arm with a floor jack and position the ball joint and spindle in the lower arm.
14. Loosely install the three lower arm-to-ball joint bolts. Remove the spring compressor, and remove the floor jack and C-clamp.
15. Torque the shaft to frame nuts to 54–69 ft. lb.

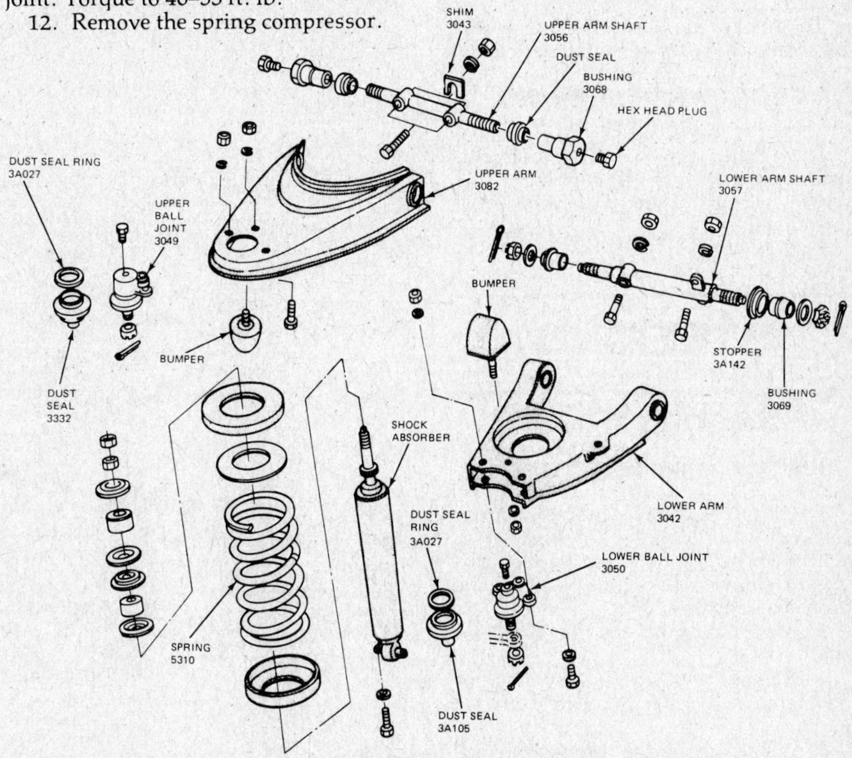

Front suspension component parts

16. Pull the shock absorber down and install the bolts and nuts.
17. Install the stabilizer bar on the lower control arm.
18. Check front wheel alignment.

Ball Joints

CHECKING

1. Check the ball joint dust seals and replace them if they are defective.
2. Check the end-play of the upper and lower ball joints. If the end-play exceeds 0.031 in., replace the ball joint.

REPLACEMENT

Use the applicable procedure under "Upper Control Arm Removal and Installation," or "Lower Control Arm Removal and Installation".

Front End Alignment

CASTER

Caster is adjusted by changing the shim(s) between the upper arm shaft and the frame, or, by turning the eccentric shaft until the correct angle is obtained.

CAMBER

Camber is adjusted by adding or subtracting the shim(s) between the upper arm shaft and the frame. The shims are available in thicknesses of 0.040 in., 0.064 in., 0.080 in., and 0.128 in.

TOE-IN

Toe-in can be increased or decreased by changing the length of the tie-rods.

FRONT WHEEL TURNING ANGLE

The turning stop screws are located at the steering knuckle. If necessary, the screws can be adjusted to adjust the turning angle.

STEERING

Steering Wheel

REMOVAL AND INSTALLATION

1. Disconnect the negative battery cable.
2. Remove the horn button by turning it counterclockwise. Remove the horn contact spring.
3. Matchmark the steering wheel and shaft.
4. Remove the wheel attaching nut and remove the steering wheel with a puller.
5. Installation is the reverse of removal.

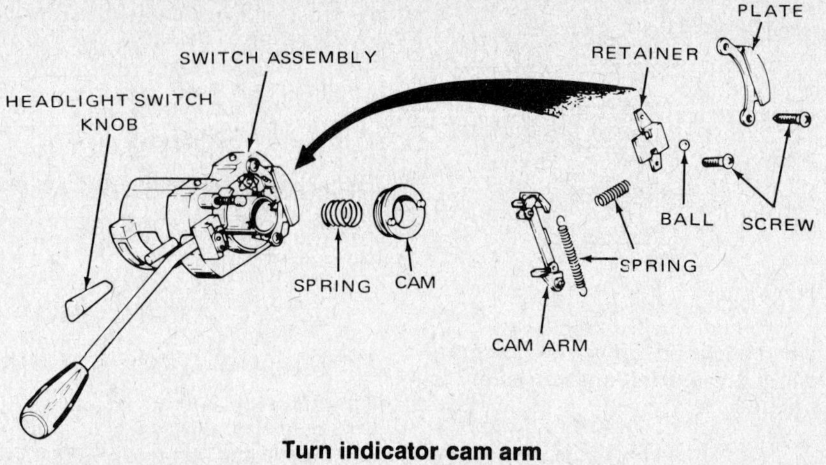

Turn indicator cam arm

Combination Switch

REMOVAL AND INSTALLATION

1. Disconnect the battery ground and remove the steering wheel.
2. Remove the plastic lights, hazard indicator and shroud.
3. Disconnect the multiple connector at the base of the column and pull off the headlight switch knob.
4. Remove the snap-ring and pull the indicator cancelling cam off the shaft.
5. Unbolt and remove the switch from the column.
6. Installation is the reverse of removal.

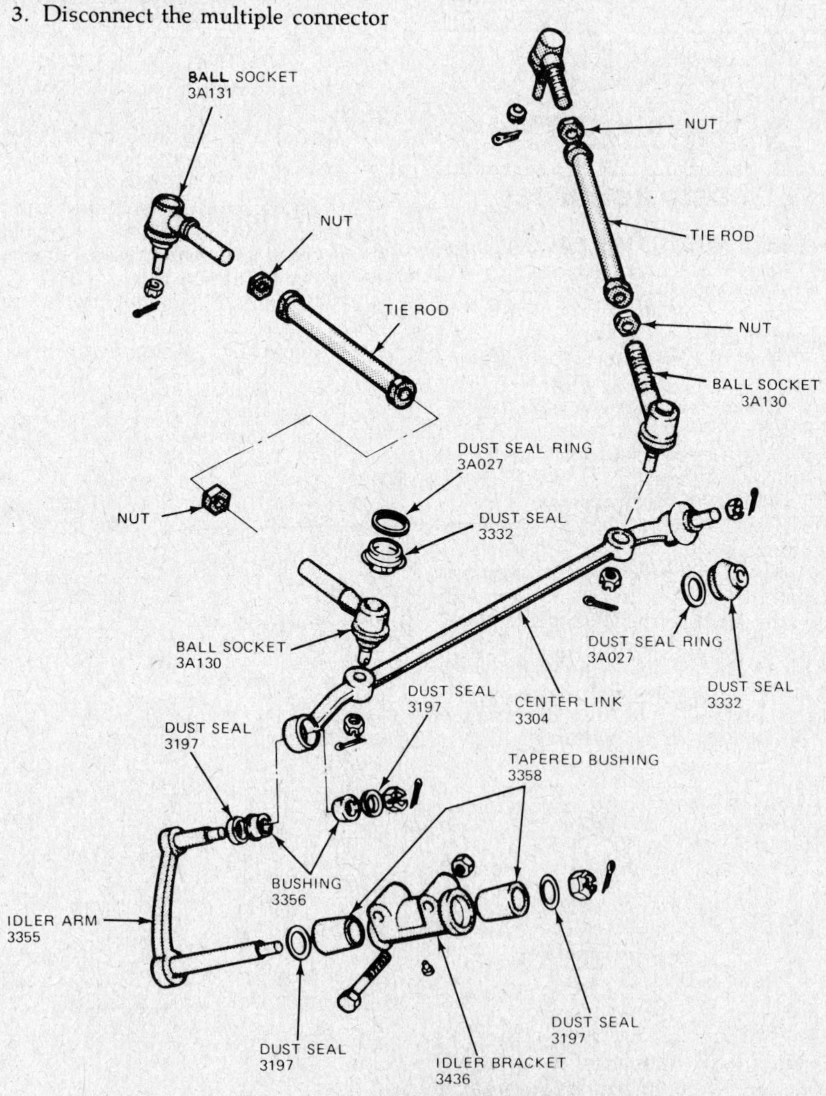

Steering linkage components

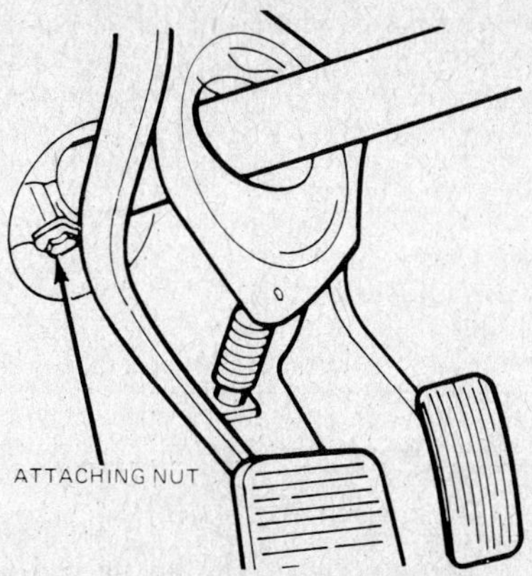

Steering column jacket attaching nut

Ignition Switch

REMOVAL AND INSTALLATION

1. Disconnect the battery ground cable.
2. Reach under the instrument panel and pull the wire connector from the rear of the switch.
3. Hold the switch body from behind the instrument panel and remove the black retaining nut by turning it counterclockwise.
4. Remove the switch from the rear of the instrument panel.
5. Installation is the reverse of removal.

Steering Column and Gear

REMOVAL AND INSTALLATION

1. Disconnect the negative battery cable.
2. Remove the steering wheel.
3. Remove the canceling cam snap-ring and cam from the top of the steering shaft.
4. Remove the dimmer and turn signal wires from the switch.
5. Remove the steering column support bracket.
6. Remove the floor covering and insulator pad from the bottom end of the steering column.
7. Unbolt the toe plate and boot from the dash.
8. Remove the column jacket from the shaft.
9. Remove the air cleaner.
10. Disconnect the heater hoses and brackets and position them aside.
11. Remove and plug the hydraulic lines from the clutch and master cylinders.
12. Remove the brake and clutch master cylinders.
13. Raise and support the truck. Disconnect the pitman arm.
14. Unbolt the steering gear from the frame. Check for the presence of an aligning shim between the gear and the frame.

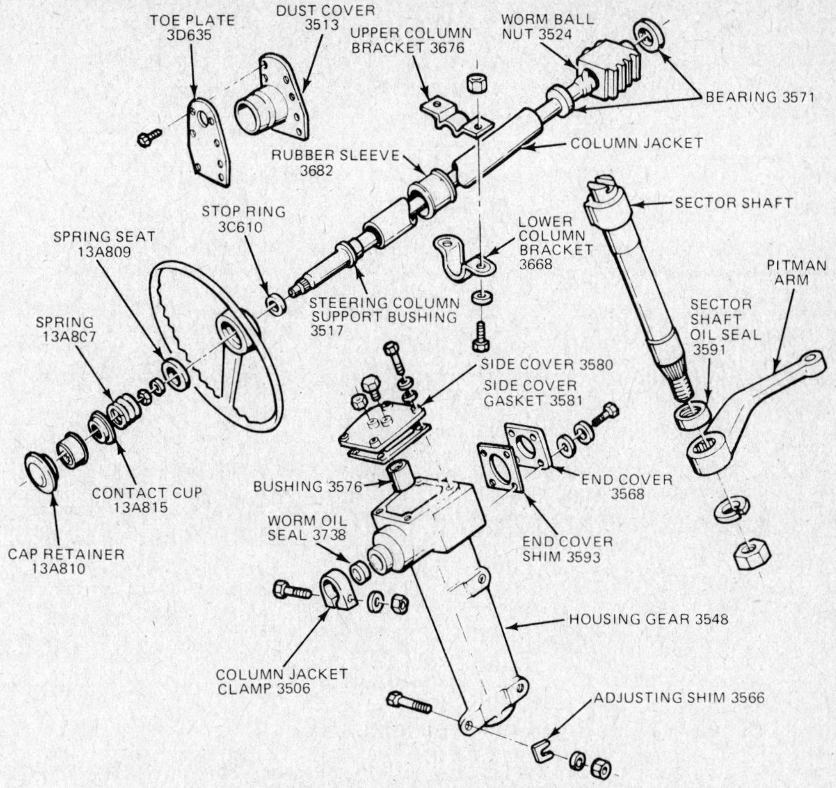

Steering wheel, steering column and gear

15. Lower the truck and remove the gear and shaft.
16. Installation is the reverse of removal. Reinstall the aligning shim in its original location, if equipped. Bleed the clutch and master cylinders. Bleed the brakes.

WORM BEARING PRELOAD ADJUSTMENT

1. It is necessary to drain the steering gear to make this adjustment. Refill the steering gear after adjustment.
2. Disconnect the pitman arm from the gear.
3. Loosen the sector adjusting screw locknut and turn the adjusting screw counterclockwise.
4. Rotate the worm shaft with a torque wrench. The preload should be 1–3.5 in. lb. If it is not, unscrew the end cover bolts and remove the end cover with the shim pack. If the preload is less than specified, reduce the shim size. If it is more than specified, increase the shim size. Shims are available in 0.002, 0.003, 0.004 and 0.008 in.
5. Reconnect the pitman arm.

SECTOR GEAR AND BALL NUT MESH LOAD

The adjustment must be done after the worm bearing preload is adjusted.

1. Disconnect the pitman arm from the center link.
2. Loosen the locknut on the sector adjusting screw.
3. Turn the steering wheel slowly to either stop. Turn it to the other stop, counting the number of turns. Position the steering wheel in the center, by dividing the number of turns in half.
4. Turn the sector adjusting screw clockwise until a torque of 5–7 in. lbs is obtained while rotating the worm past the center (high spot).
5. Tighten the locknut while holding the adjusting screw. Recheck the mesh load.
6. Reconnect the pitman arm to the center link.

BRAKE SYSTEMS

ADJUSTMENT

Front disk brakes introduced in 1977 are self-adjusting.

Front Drum Brakes

ADJUSTMENT

1. Raise and support the truck.
2. Remove the adjusting slot covers from the brake backing plate.
3. Insert a brake adjusting spoon and rotate the starwheel of one wheel cylinder toward the inside of the brake drum until the wheel is locked. Then back off the starwheel 6–8 notches through 1974, 5 notches 1975–76.

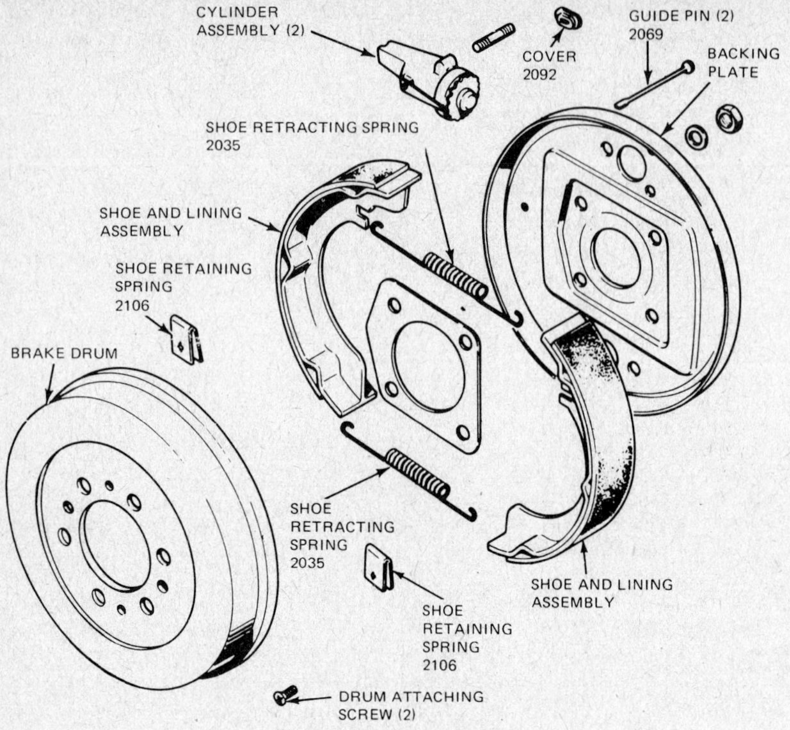

Drum type front brake

4. Repeat Step 3 for each wheel cylinder of each wheel.
5. Install the adjusting slot covers.
6. Check the brake adjustment by spinning the wheel by hand. There should be no drag.

Rear Brakes

ADJUSTMENT

1. Be sure that the parking brake is fully released. Disconnect the equilizer clevis pin.
2. Raise and support the truck.
3. Remove the adjusting slot covers from the brake backing plate.
4. Insert a brake spoon into the lower adjusting slot to contact the starwheel of the lower wheel cylinder.
5. Turn the lower wheel cylinder starwheel to expand the brake shoe until it locks against the drum. Back the starwheel off 6–8 notches through 1974, 5 notches 1975 and later. Check the wheel, by rotating, to be sure that there is no drag.
6. Repeat Step 5 for each wheel cylinder of each wheel.
7. Connect the parking brake equalizer clevis pin and check the parking brake adjustment.
8. Install the adjusting hole covers.
9. Lower the truck and road-test the brakes. Readjust if necessary.

BRAKE PEDAL FREE-TRAVEL ADJUSTMENT

1. Loosen the locknut on the master cylinder pushrod at the clevis, which attaches the pushrod to the pedal.
2. Turn the master cylinder pushrod either in or out to obtain $^5/_8$–1 in. free travel through 1974, $^1/_8$–$^{11}/_{32}$ 1975–76, or $^{11}/_{32}$–$^7/_{16}$ 1977 and later.
3. Tighten the locknut.

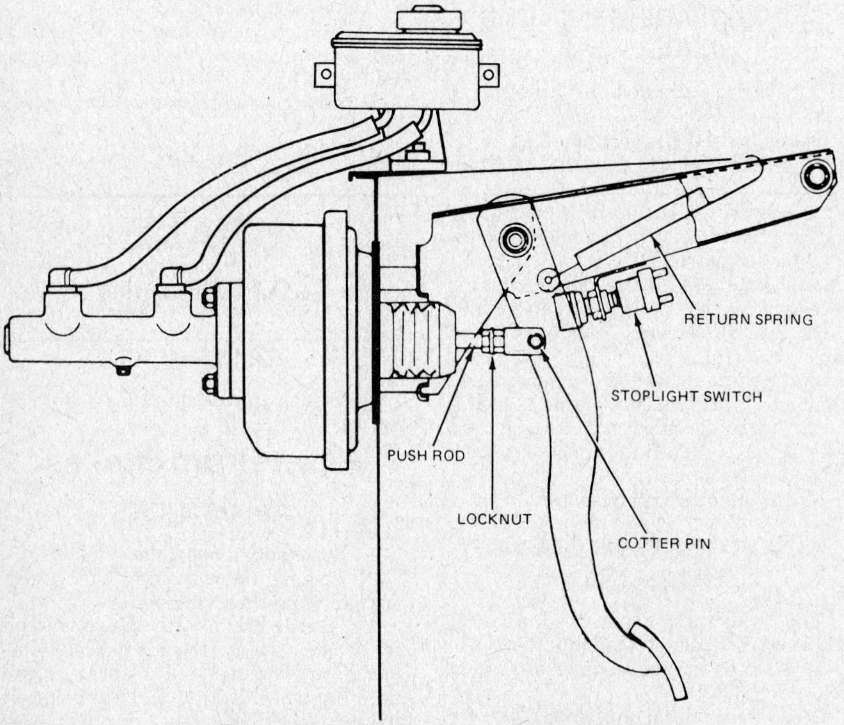

Brake pedal free-travel adjustment

Master Cylinder

REMOVAL AND INSTALLATION

1. Disconnect and plug the brake lines from the master cylinder outlets. 1977 and later models have a remote reservoir, so the two inlet hoses also should be disconnected at the master cylinder and plugged.
2. Unbolt the master cylinder and lift it and the boot outward and upward away from the firewall and brake rod.

To install the master cylinder:

3. Install the master cylinder (and boot through 1976) on the firewall or vacuum booster, while carefully guiding the brake pushrod into contact with the master cylinder piston.
4. Install the two nuts and lockwashers and tighten the nuts to 11–17 ft lbs.
5. Connect the brake lines to the master cylinder outlet ports. Reconnect the reservoir inlet hoses on the 1977 and later models.
6. Bleed the brake system.
7. Check the brake pedal free-travel adjustment.

OVERHAUL

1. Remove the master cylinder.
2. Remove the master cylinder reservoir (through 1976) and drain the master cylinder.
3. Remove the two grommets from the master cylinder body through 1976. Remove the elbow connectors 1977 and later.
4. Remove the dust boot through 1976.
5. Use a small screwdriver to remove the piston stopring.
6. Remove the piston stopwasher, primary piston and primary piston return spring.
7. Remove the secondary piston stopscrew and O-ring through 1976. On 1977 and later models, first fabricate a guide pin 0.193 in. in diameter by 0.315

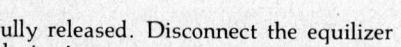

in. long. Push the secondary piston toward the front of the cylinder with a screwdriver, then remove the stop screw and its O-ring. Insert the guide pin into the stop screw hole, slowly release pressure on the secondary piston, and allow it to pass over the guide pin and out.

8. Remove the secondary piston and secondary return spring.

9. Remove the outlet port fittings, gaskets, check valves and check valve springs.

10. Clean all the parts (except rubber) in isopropyl alcohol. Do not use mineral base fluids. Allow all parts to air dry.

To assemble the master cylinder:

11. Dip all parts in clean brake fluid before assembly.

12. Install the check valve spring and check valves into the cylinder outlets and install the outlet port fittings and gaskets.

13. For models through 1976: Position the secondary piston return spring on the secondary piston and install the assembly spring first.

Position the primary piston spring on the primary piston and install the assembly, spring first into the cylinder.

Install the piston stopwasher and piston stopring.

Install the secondary piston stopbolt.

Install the two grommets in the cylinder body.

Install the reservoir so that the outlet tubes are seated in the grommets.

14. For 1977 and later: Install the secondary and primary cups on the secondary piston. Install the guide pin used during disassembly into the stop screw hole.

Install the secondary piston assembly and spring into the cylinder, pushing them in as far as they will go with a screwdriver. Holding them there, remove the guide pin and install the stop screw and O-ring.

Install the cups on the primary piston, and install the piston assembly and its spring into the cylinder. Install the washer and snap ring into the end of the cylinder.

15. Fill the master cylinder and pump the piston with a screwdriver until fluid flows from the outlet ports.

16. Install the master cylinder and bleed the brakes.

Vacuum Booster

REMOVAL AND INSTALLATION

1. Remove the master cylinder.
2. Remove the vacuum hose from the check valve.
3. Working under the instrument panel, disconnect the booster pushrod from the brake pedal by removing the cotter pin at the fork.
4. Remove the four booster mounting nuts from under the instrument panel.
5. Remove the vacuum booster.
6. To install, reverse the removal procedure. Bleed the brakes after installation.

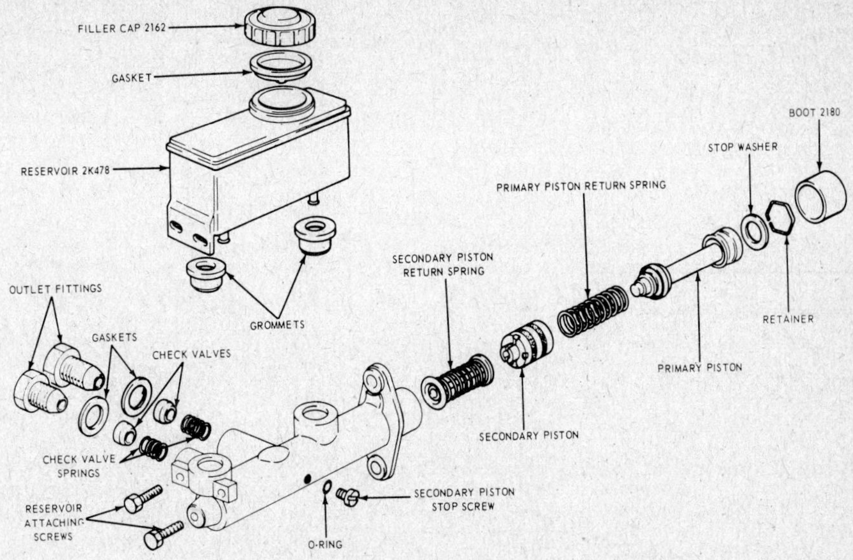

Master cylinder component parts—1971-75

Pressure Differential Valve

REMOVAL AND INSTALLATION

1. Disconnect the warning light switch connector from the warning light switch.
2. Disconnect the brake inlet and outlet lines. Plug the lines.
3. Remove the valve and switch assembly.
4. Position the valve and switch on the cowl. Install the retaining bolt.
5. Connect the brake lines to the valve.
6. Connect the warning light to the switch wiring connector.
7. Depress the brake pedal several times, then bleed the brake system.
8. Fill the master cylinder and check for proper operation.

CENTRALIZING THE PRESSURE DIFFERENTIAL VALVE

Normally, the brake warning light will remain ON after any repairs to the brake system, or after bleeding the brakes. This is caused by the pressure differential valve remaining in the off center position.

1. Turn the ignition switch ON.
2. Check the fluid levels in the master cylinder reservoir and fill them to within $1/4$ in. of the top, if necessary.
3. Depress the brake pedal and the piston will center itself, causing the warning light to go out.
4. Turn the ignition switch OFF. The light should go out.

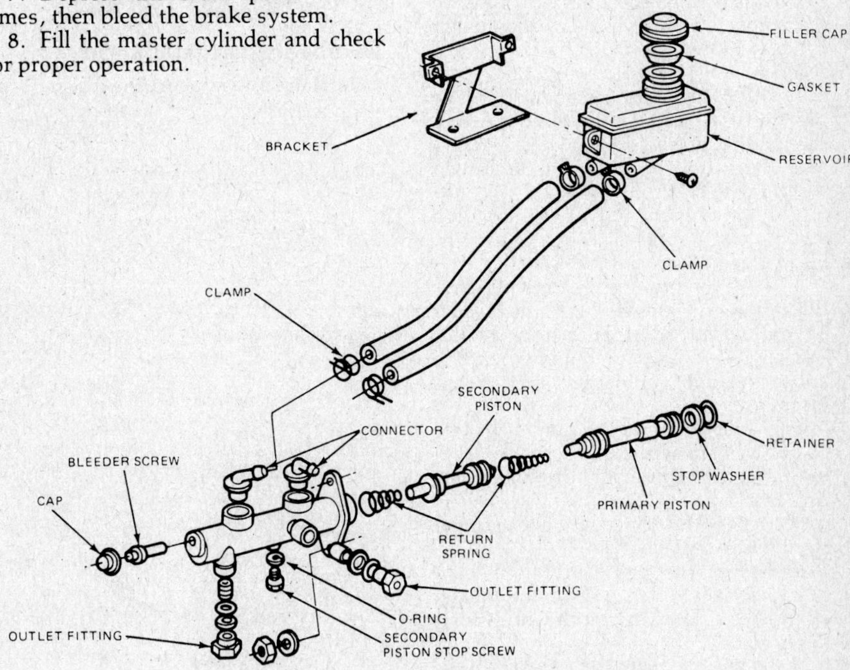

Master cylinder component parts—1976-80

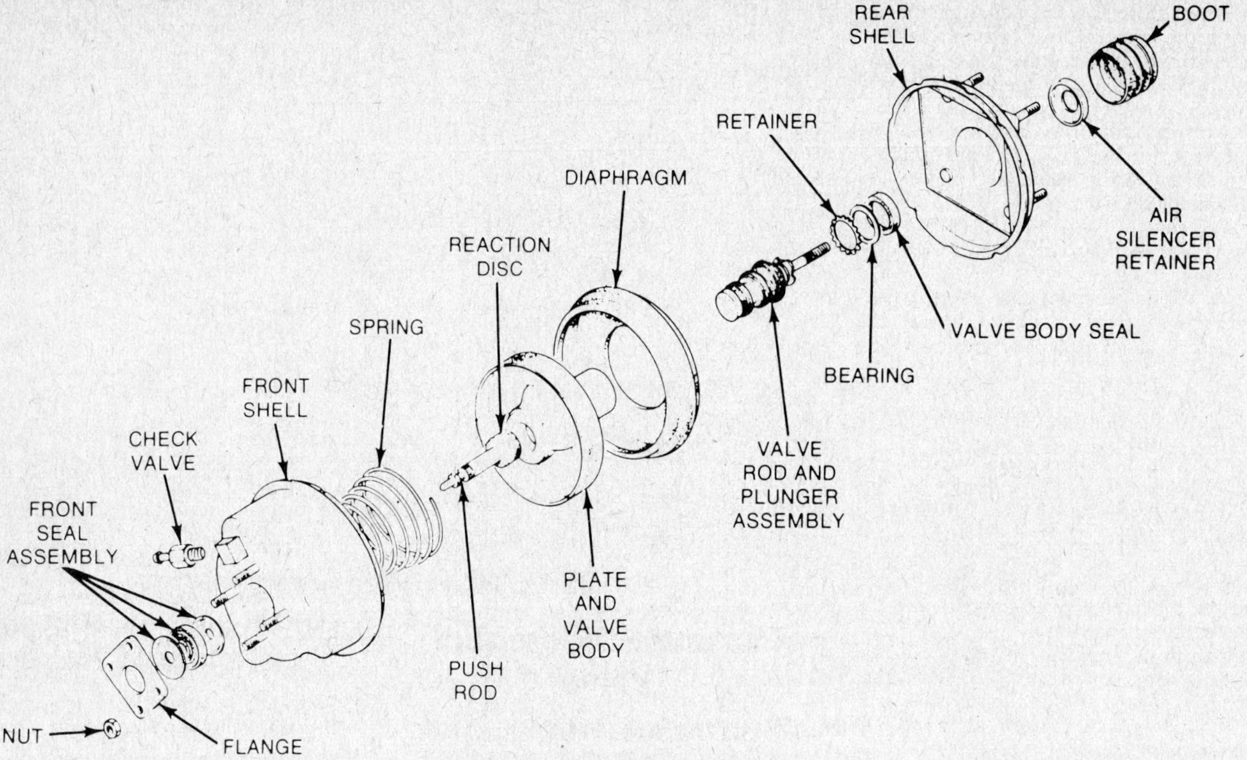

Power brake booster components

Bleeding

The primary and secondary (front and rear) systems are independent systems and are bled separately. Bleed the longest line first on an individual system. In the case of the rear brakes, bleed at the lower right rear wheel cylinder then at the upper right rear wheel cylinder. Keep the master cylinder reservoirs full of extra heavy duty brake fluid.

Do not use the secondary piston stop screw located on the side of the master cylinder to bleed with, as damage to the secondary piston could result.

1. Bleed the rear (secondary) brake system first. Remove the bleeder fitting cap and attach a rubber hose snugly over the fitting at the right rear lower wheel cylinder.
2. Submerge the end of the hose in a jar of clean brake fluid. Open the bleeder valve $^3/_4$ turn.
3. Push the brake pedal down slowly through its full travel. Close the bleeder fitting and let the pedal return. Repeat this operation until air bubbles cease to appear at the submerged end of the bleeder tube.
4. When the fluid is completely free of bubbles, close the bleeder fitting, remove the tube and install the bleeder fitting cap.
5. Repeat this procedure at the upper right wheel cylinder.
6. Repeat the procedure at the left rear wheel cylinders. Refill the master cylinder reservoir after each wheel cylinder is bled.
7. Bleed the primary (front) brake system in the same manner, ending by bleeding each left front wheel cylinder or the left front caliper.
8. When the bleeding operation is complete, the master cylinder should be filled to within $^1/_4$ in. of the top. Install the master cylinder cover.
9. Centralize the pressure differential valve.

Drum Brakes

BRAKE DRUM

Removal and Installation

1. Raise and support the truck.
2. Remove the wheel.
3. Remove the brake drum attaching screws and install them in the tapped holes in the brake drum.
4. Turn these screws in evenly to force the brake drum away from the wheel hub.
5. Remove and inspect the brake drum.

To install the brake drum:

6. Install the brake drum with the attaching screw holes aligned with the holes in the hub.

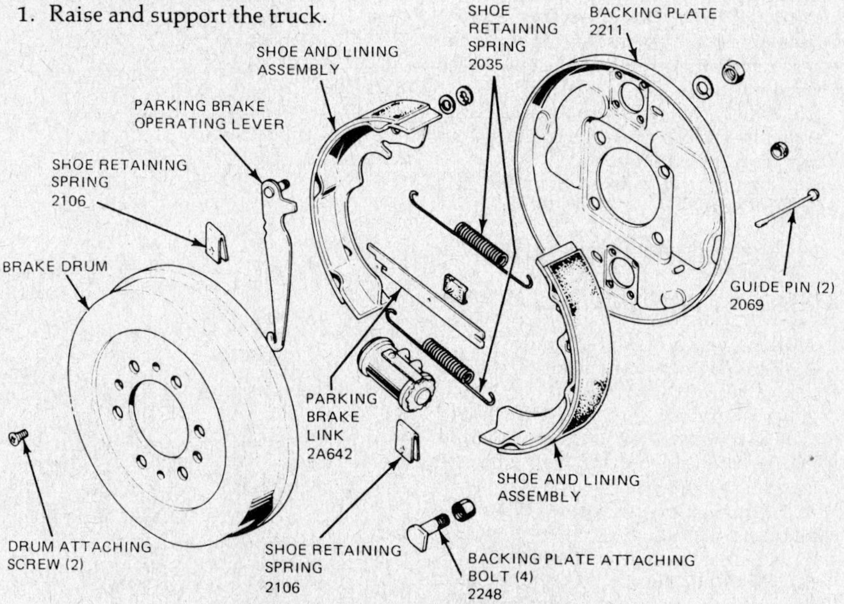

Rear brake assembly 1971-77

7. Transfer the attaching screws from the tapped holes in the brake drum to the attaching holes in the hub.
8. Tighten the screws evenly to secure the hub.
9. Install the wheel.
10. Lower the truck check the brake adjustment.

Inspection

1. Check the brake drum diameter with a brake drum gauge. Replace any drums which have a diameter greater than 10.2962 in. through 1974, 10.2756 1975 and later.
2. Inspect the brake drums for cracks.

BRAKE SHOES

Inspection

1. Wipe out the accumulated dust and grit with a damp cloth.
2. If the lining is worn to within $^1/_{32}$ in. of the shoe or if the shoes are damaged, they must be replaced.
3. Replace any linings (in axle sets only) that are contaminated with grease or brake fluid from leaking wheel cylinders.
4. Check the condition of the shoes, retracting springs and hold-down springs for signs of overheating. If the shoes have a slight blue color, this indicates over heating and replacement of the springs as well as the linings is recommended.
5. If signs of overheating are present, the wheel cylinders should be rebuilt as a precaution against future problems.

Removal and Installation

1. Raise and support the truck.
2. Remove the wheel.
3. Remove the brake drum.
4. Remove the brake shoe retracting springs.
5. Remove the shoe retaining spring guide pin and the retaining spring.
6. On rear brakes only, remove the parking brake link, and disconnect the parking brake cable from the parking brake lever.
7. Remove the brake shoes.

To install new brake shoes:

8. Lubricate the threads of the adjusting screw with brake paste and one or two spots on the adjuster wheel inside threads. Lubricate the backing plate shoe pads.
9. On front wheel brakes, position each brake shoe on the brake backing plate so that the slot in the shoe web is toward the starwheel in the wheel cylinder.
10. On rear brakes, install the parking brake lever on the rear shoe and install the retaining clip. Hold the rear brake shoe near the brake backing plate and connect the eye of the parking brake cable to the parking brake operating lever. Position both shoes on the backing plate and connect the parking brake link between both shoes. Engage the brake

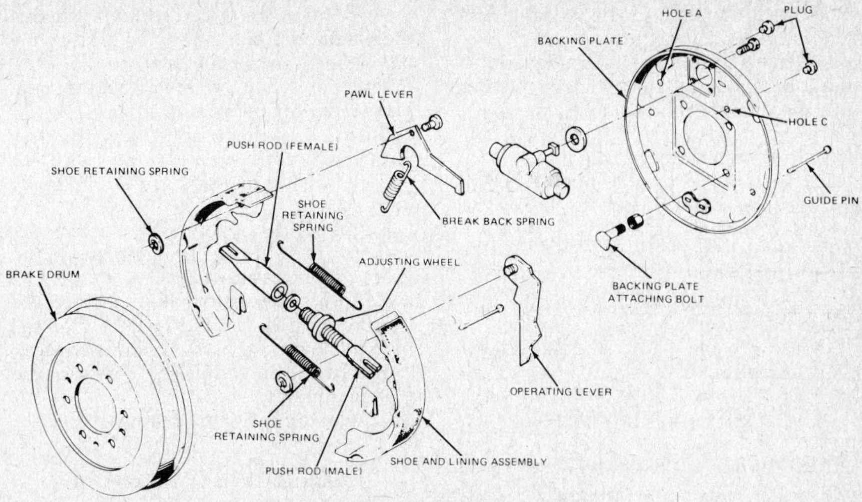

Rear brake assembly 1978-80

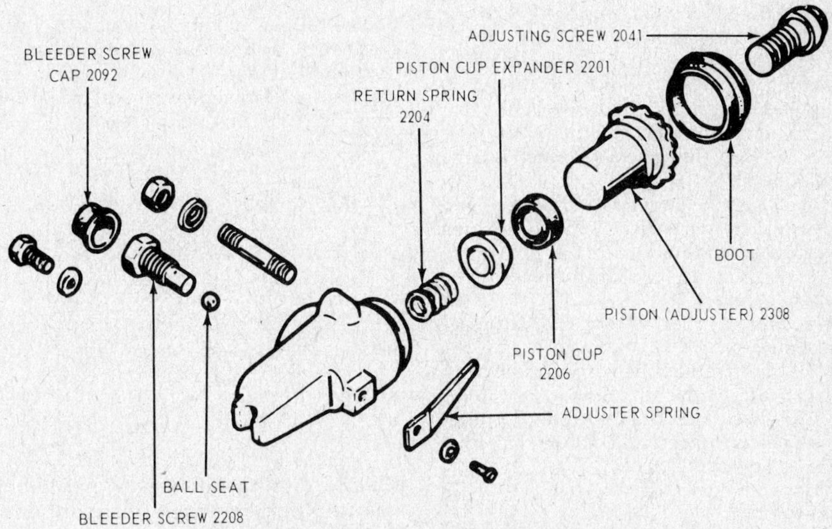

Front wheel cylinder component parts

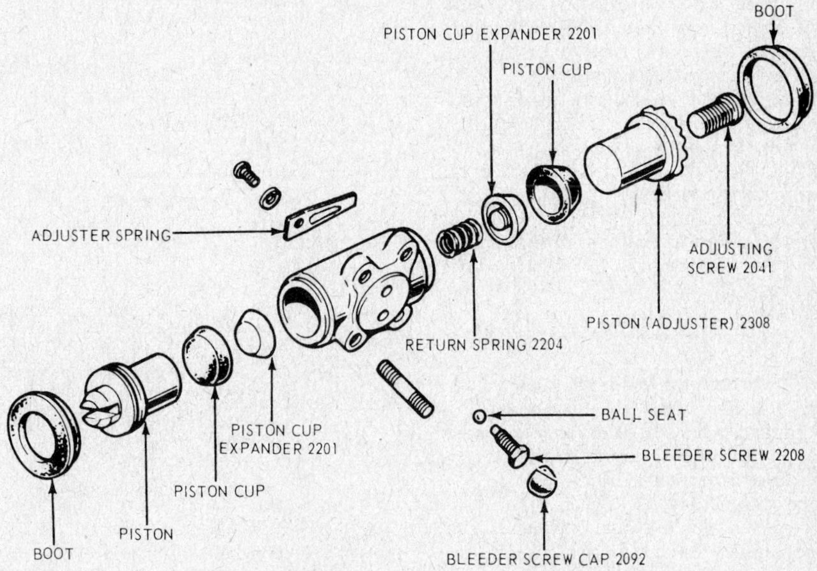

Rear wheel cylinder component parts

shoes with the slots in the wheel cylinder pistons and adjusting screws.

11. Install the shoe retaining spring guide pins. Install the retaining spring over the guide pin, hold the guide pin in place and depress the retaining spring. Turn it 90° to lock the spring in place.

12. Install the brake shoe retracing springs. Be careful not to bend the springs or stretch the hooks.

13. Install the brake drum.

14. Install the wheel.

15. Adjust the brakes.

16. Bleed the brakes.

17. Lower the truck and check for proper operation.

WHEEL CYLINDER

Removal and Installation

1. Raise and support the truck.
2. Remove the wheel.
3. Remove the brake drum and brake shoes.
4. Disconnect and plug the brake line at the wheel cylinder.
5. Remove the stud nuts and bolt attaching the wheel cylinder to the backing plate and remove the wheel cylinder.

To install the wheel cylinder:

6. Install the wheel cylinder on the backing plate.
7. Clean the end of the brake line and attach it to the wheel cylinder. Tighten the tube fitting nut.
8. Install the links in the end of the wheel cylinder.
9. Install the shoes and adjuster assemblies.
10. Install the brake drum and wheel.
11. Adjust the brakes.
12. Bleed the brakes and centralize the pressure differential valve.
13. Lower the truck.

Overhaul

1. Remove the wheel cylinder.
2. Remove the piston and adjusting screw with the boot attached to the adjuster. Separate the adjuster screw and boot from the adjuster. On rear wheel cylinders, remove the other piston and boot and separate the parts.
3. On front cylinders, using compressed air, if possible, remove the piston cup, expander and spring. Lay the cylinder face down and apply air pressure to the brake line port.

On rear cylinders, press in on either piston cup and force the piston cups, expanders, and return spring from the cylinder.

4. Wash all parts in isopropyl alcohol, except the rubber boots. Discard the piston cups.
5. Examine the cylinder bore, piston and adjuster for wear, roughness or damage. Check the clearance between the piston and cylinder bore. If the clearance is greater than 0.006 in., replace with new parts.

To assemble the wheel cylinder:

6. Lubricate the cylinder bore, adjuster and new piston cups with clean brake fluid.
7. Position the piston return spring in the piston cup expander. On rear cylinders, use either expander, then place the other piston cup expander and a new piston cup on the return spring. On all cylinders, install the return spring, piston cup expander(s) and cup(s) into the cylinders. The flat side of the cup faces out.
8. Install the piston boot to the piston adjuster (smaller lip of the boot in the groove of the piston adjuster.)
9. Insert the piston adjuster into the cylinder and install the larger lip of the boot in the groove on the cylinder body.
10. Install the adjusting screw in the piston adjuster.
11. Install the wheel cylinder.

Front Disc Brakes

PADS

Inspection

The caliper must be removed to check pad wear. Follow the procedure under Pad Replacement. Measure the lining thickness. Pads should be replaced if the lining is 0.315 in. thick or less.

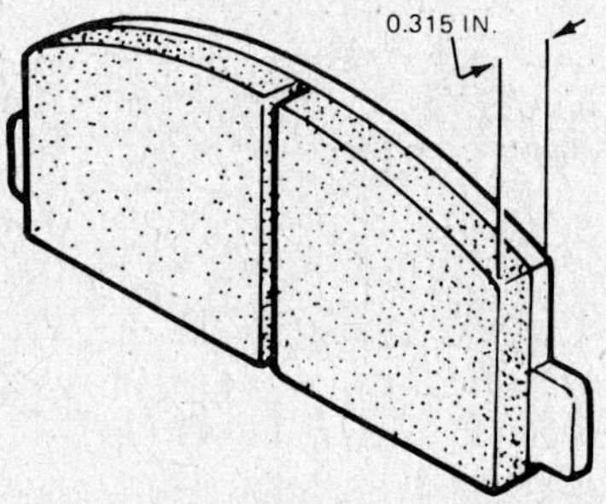

Caliper lining thickness measurement. Replace when measurement is 0.315 inch or less

Replacement

1. Raise the truck and remove the wheel.
2. Remove the four locking clips.
3. Remove the two stopper plates (wedges) with a hammer and drift.
4. Remove the caliper body and anti-rattle spring. Support the caliper; do not allow it to hang by the brake hose.
5. Pull out the brake pads.
6. To install: Press the piston back into the caliper body. Use a C-clamp, and, while tightening, open the bleeder screw slightly. Close the bleeder screw when the piston is in place.
7. Install new pads (and shims, if necessary). Replace all pads at the same time. Do not mix different lining types.
8. Replace the anti-rattle spring and the caliper body.
9. Apply a thin coat of grease to the stopper plates, and push them into place. Install the locking clips.
10. Install the wheel and lower the truck. Check the fluid level and add, if necessary. Check for a hard brake pedal.

CALIPER

Removal and Installation

1. Follow Steps 1–5 of the Pad Replacement procedure.
2. Disconnect and plug the brake hose.
3. Remove the caliper body.
4. If necessary, remove the caliper bracket by removing the two retaining bolts.
5. Installation is the reverse. Bleed the system after installation.

OVERHAUL

1. Clean off the caliper body. Remove the boot retainer and dust boot.

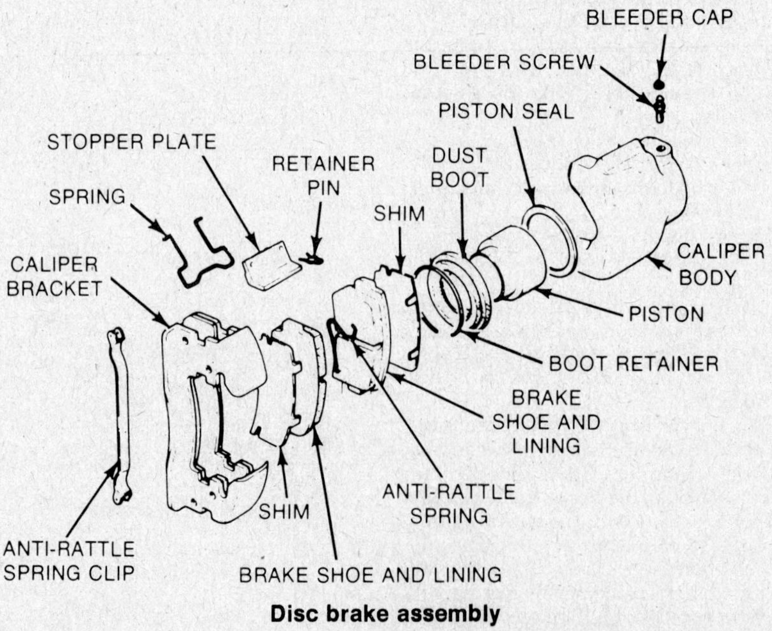

Disc brake assembly

2. Place some cloths in front of the piston to prevent damage. Apply compressed air to the brake line hole and remove the piston. Seized pistons can be removed by tapping around the piston with a plastic mallet while applying air pressure.
3. Remove the piston seal from the caliper bore. Discard the seal and boot.
4. Remove the bleeder valve only if necessary.
5. Clean all parts in clean brake fluid or denatured alcohol only.
6. Inspect the caliper bore and piston for scratches, corrosion, or scoring. Damaged parts should be replaced.
7. Coat the new seal with brake fluid, and install it into the groove in the bore.
8. Coat the piston and bore with clean brake fluid, and install the piston.
9. Install the dust boot by pressing its flange squarely into the inner groove of the caliper bore. Install the boot retainer.
10. Install the caliper. Bleed the system after installation.

ROTOR INSPECTION

1. Inspect the surface for scratches, scoring, or deep rust pitting. Reface the disc if these conditions exist. If the disc is less than 0.433 in. thick after refinishing, replace it.
2. Inspect the lateral runout of the disc with a dial indicator. If it exceeds 0.0039 in., the disc should be refinished or replaced. The wheel bearings must be properly adjusted before making this measurement.

FRONT WHEEL BEARINGS

Adjustment

The front wheel bearings should be adjusted if the wheel is loose on the spindle or if the wheel does not rotate freely.
1. Raise and support the truck.
2. Remove the wheel cover and pry the grease cap from the hub.
3. Remove the cotter pin and locknut.
4. While rotating the wheel, drum and hub, tighten the adjusting nut to 17–25 ft lbs.
5. Back off the adjusting nut 1/2 turn, then retighten the nut to 10–15 in. lbs. for trucks through 1973, or 6–8 ft. lbs. 1974–76. For 1977 and later trucks, simply back off the adjusting nut 1/4 turn.
6. Install the nut lock on the adjusting nut so that the castellations are aligned with the cotter pin hole in the spindle.
7. Install a new cotter pin.

Removal, Installation and Packing

1. Raise and support the truck.
2. Remove the wheel cover.
3. Remove the wheel and tire.
4. Remove the grease cap from the hub. Remove the cotter pin, nut lock, adjusting nut and flat washer from the spindle.

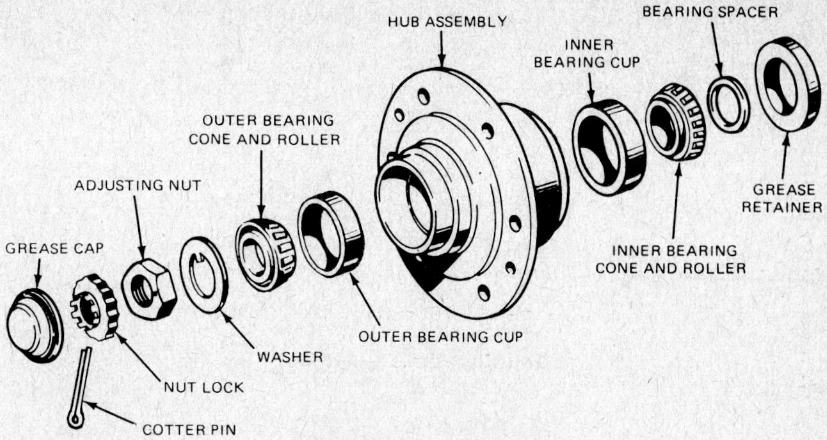

Front hub, typical

Front wheel bearing adjustment 1971-77

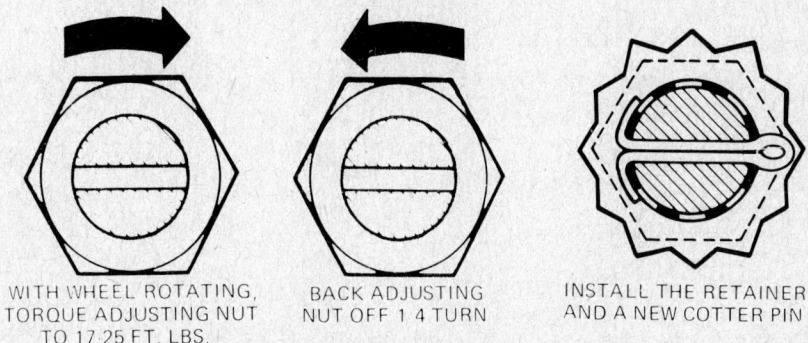

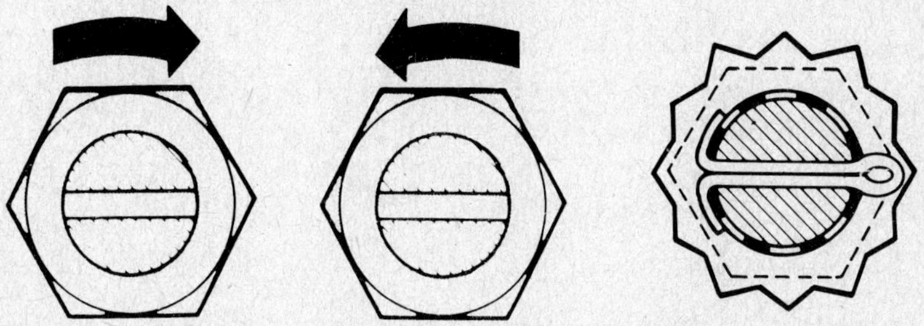

Front wheel bearing adjustment 1978-80

5. Remove the hub and drum.
6. Remove and discard the old grease retainer. Remove the inner bearing cone and roller from the hub.
7. Clean the grease from the inner and outer bearing cups with solvent and inspect the cups for scratches, pits, or wear.
8. If the cups are worn or damaged, remove them with a drift.
9. Thoroughly clean the inner and outer bearing cones and rollers. DO NOT SPIN THE BEARINGS TO DRY THEM.
10. Inspect the cones and roller for wear and replace as necessary. The cone and roller assemblies should be replaced as a set. Do not use new bearings or cups with old bearings or cups.
11. Clean the spindle and the inside of the hub with solvent to remove all of the old grease.
12. Cover the spindle with a cloth and clean the dirt from the dustshield. Remove the cloth carefully. Do not get dirt on the spindle.
13. If the inner or outer bearing cups were removed, install the new replacement cups in the hub. Be sure that they are seated squarely and properly.
14. Pack the inside of the hub with wheel bearing grease.

NOTE: It is important that all the old grease is removed, because lithium base grease is not compatible with the sodium base grease that was originally installed.

15. Pack the bearing cone and roller with wheel bearing grease. Work as much grease as possible between the cone and rollers. Lubricate the outside cone surfaces with grease.
16. Installing the inner bearing cone

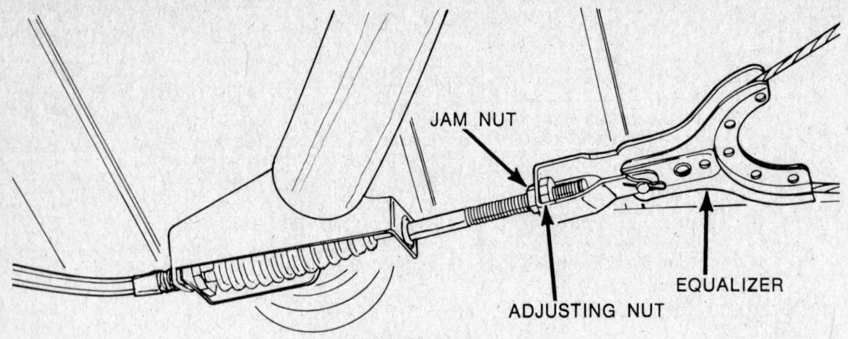

Parking brake adjustment

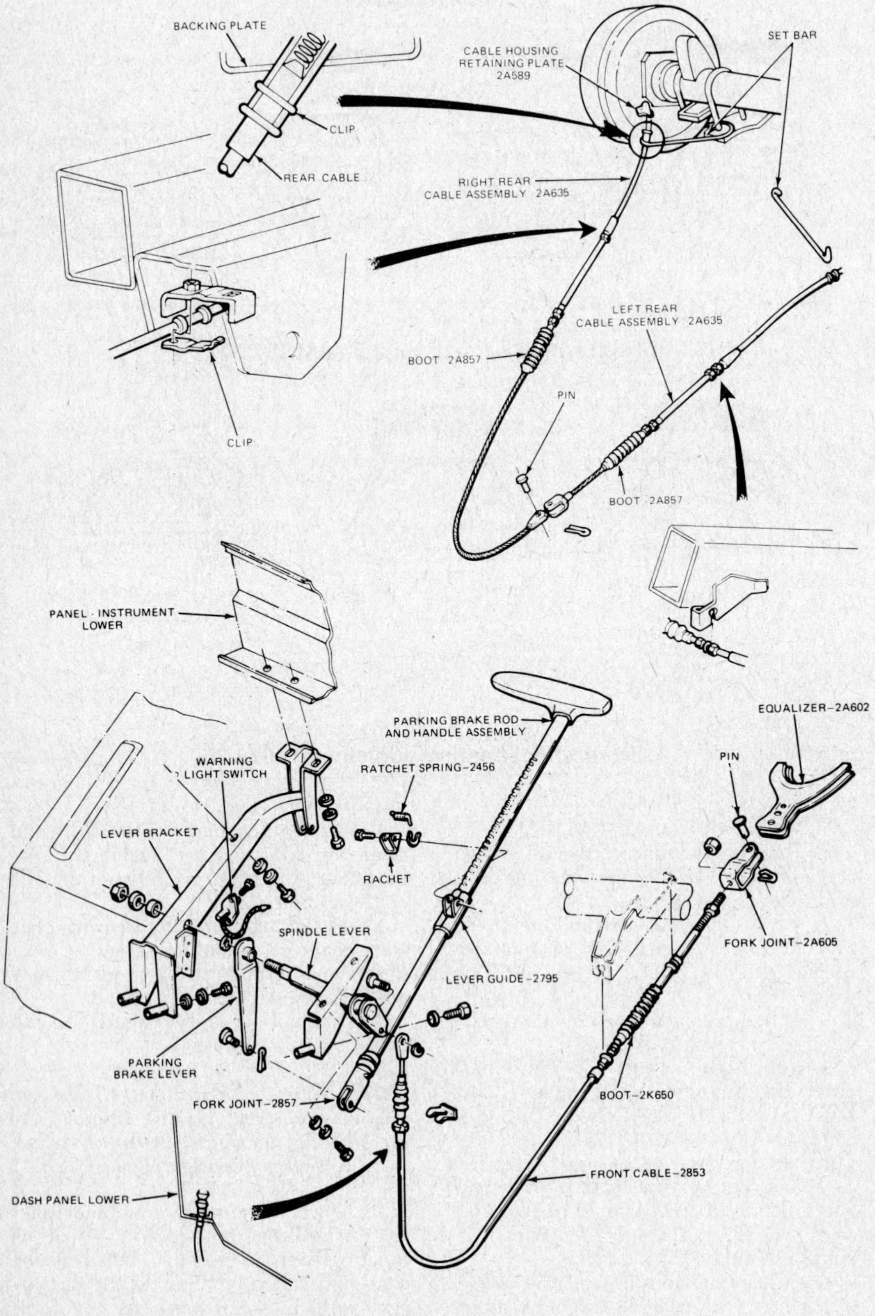

Parking brake linkage

and roller in the inner cup. Apply a light film of grease to the grease seal and install the seal. Be sure that the seal is properly seated.

17. Install the hub and drum on the spindle. Keep the hub centered on the spindle to prevent damaging the grease seal.
18. Install the outer bearing cone and roller and the flat washer on the spindle. Install the adjusting nut.
19. Install the wheel and tire.
20. Adjust the wheel bearings.
21. Install the hub cap.
22. Pump the brake pedal several times to restore normal brake lining-to-drum clearance and normal brake pedal pressure.

Parking Brake

ADJUSTMENT

1. Adjust the service brakes before attempting to adjust the parking brake.
2. Use the adjusting nut to adjust the length of the front cable so that the rear brakes are locked when the parking brake lever is pulled out 5–10 notches.
3. After adjustment, apply the parking brake several times. Release the parking brake and make sure that the rear wheels rotate without dragging. If they drag, repeat the adjustment.

FRONT PARKING BRAKE CABLE

Removal and Installation

1. Raise and support the truck.
2. Remove the serrated adjusting nut.
3. Separate the front brake cable from the equalizer and remove the jam nut.
4. Remove the cable return spring and pull the protective boot from the lower end of the front cable housing.
5. Pull the lower cable housing forward out of the slotted frame bracket and slip the cable shaft sideways through the slot until the cable and housing is free fo the bracket.
6. Disengage the upper cable connector from the brake lever by removing the clevis pin and retainer.
7. Remove the upper cable housing retaining clip and pull the upper cable and housing from out of the slotted bracket on the firewall.
8. Push the upper cable, cable housing, and dust shield grommet through the firewall opening and into the engine compartment.
9. Remove the cable and housing.
10. Installation is the reverse of removal.

REAR PARKING BRAKE CABLE

Removal and Installation

1. Raise and support the truck.
2. Remove the equalizer clevis pin and disconnect the equalizer from the front brake clevis.

3. Disconnect the right-hand cable from the left-hand cable at the cable connector.
4. Remove the rear brake shoes.
5. Disengage the parking brake levers from the cable connectors by rotating the hooked ends of the levers out of the cable connector.
6. Remove the cable housing retainer from the brake backing plate.
7. Pull the return spring to release the retainer plate from the end of the cable housing.
8. Pull the boot from the forward end of the housing.
9. Loosen the cable housing-to-frame bracket locknut and remove the forward end of the cable housing from the frame bracket.
10. Remove the cable housing retaining clip bolts.
11. Disengage the cable housing-to-frame tension springs and pull the cable housing and cable out of the brake backing plate.
12. Installation is the reverse of removal.

CHASSIS ELECTRICAL

Heater Assembly

REMOVAL AND INSTALLATION

1. Disconnect the battery.
2. Drain the cooling system.
3. Remove the water valve shield at the left-side of the heater.
4. Disconnect the two hoses from the left-side of the heater.
5. At the heat-defrost door, at the water valve and at the outside recirculation door, disengage the control cable housing from the mounting clip on the heater. Disconnect each of the three cable wires from the crank arms.
6. Disconnect the fan motor electrical lead.
7. Remove the glove compartment for clearance.
8. At the engine side of the firewall, remove the retaining nut and bolt.
9. Disconnect the two defroster ducts from the heater and remove the heater.
10. Installation is the reverse of removal. Note the following:
   a. Connect the heat-defrost door control cable to the door crank arm. Set the control lever (upper) in the HEAT position and turn the crank arm toward the mounting clip as far as it will go. Engage the cable housing in the clip and install the screw in the clip.
   b. Connect the water valve control cable wire to the crank arm on the water valve lever. Locate the cable housing in the mounting clip. Set the control lever in the HOT position and pull the valve plunger and lever to the full outward position. This will move the lever crank arm toward the cable mounting clip as far as it will go. Tighten the clip and screw.
   c. Insert the outside-recirculation door control cable into the hole in the door crank arm. Bend the wire over and tighten the screw. Set the center control lever in the REC position and turn the door crank arm toward the mounting clip as far as it will go. Engage the cable housing in the clip and install the screw in the clip.

Heater Motor and Fan

REMOVAL AND INSTALLATION

1. Remove the heater.
2. Remove the five screws and separate the halves of the heater assembly.
3. Loosen the fan retaining nut. Lightly tap on the nut to loosen the fan. Remove the fan and nut from the motor shaft.
4. Remove the three motor-to-case retaining screws and disconnect the bullet connector to the resistor and ground screw.
5. Rotate the motor and remove it from the case.

Heater Core

REMOVAL AND INSTALLATION

1. Remove the heater.
2. Separate the halves of the case.
3. Loosen the hose clamps and slide the heater core from the case.
4. Slide the replacement core into the case. At the same time, connect the core tube to the water valve tube with the short hose and clamps.
5. Assemble the halves of the heater and install the five screws.
6. Install the heater.

Radio

REMOVAL AND INSTALLATION

1. Remove the ash tray, ash tray re-

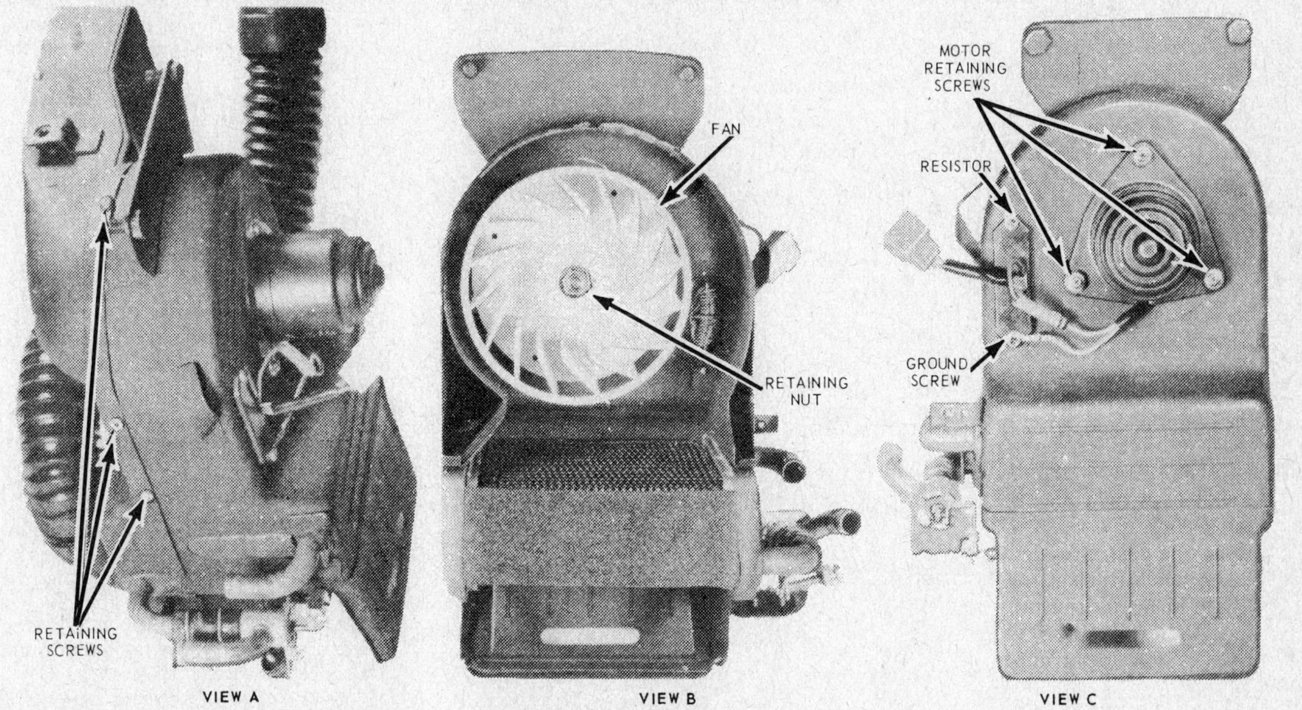

Heater system components

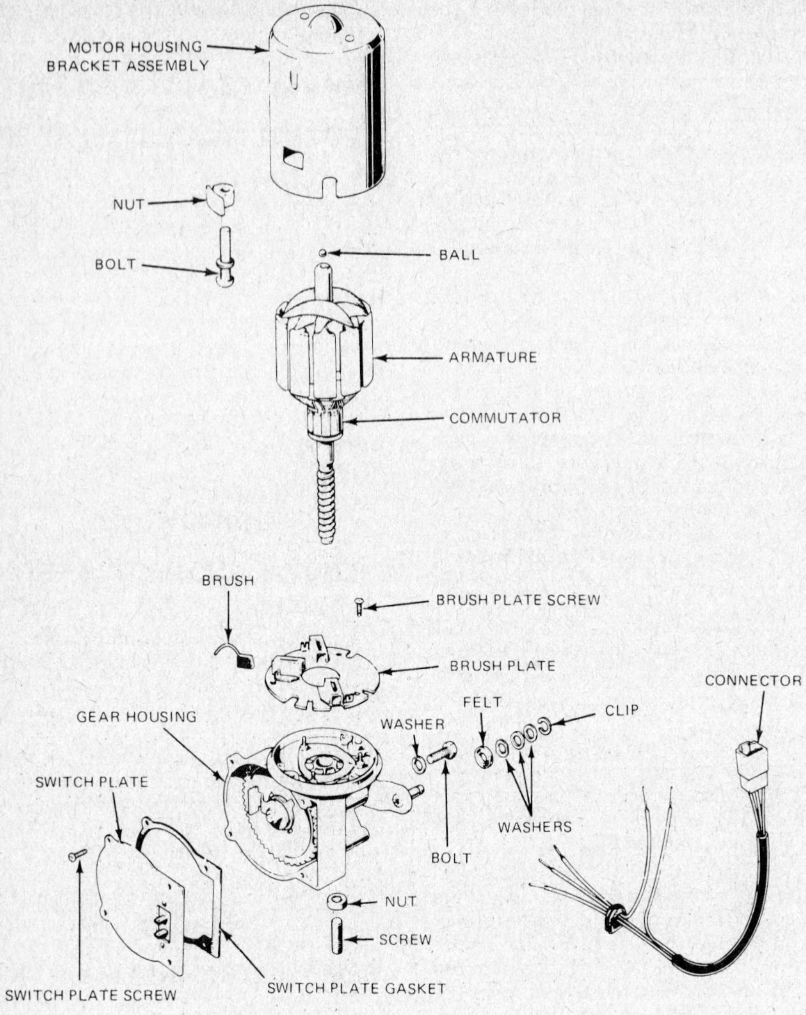

Windshield wiper motor components

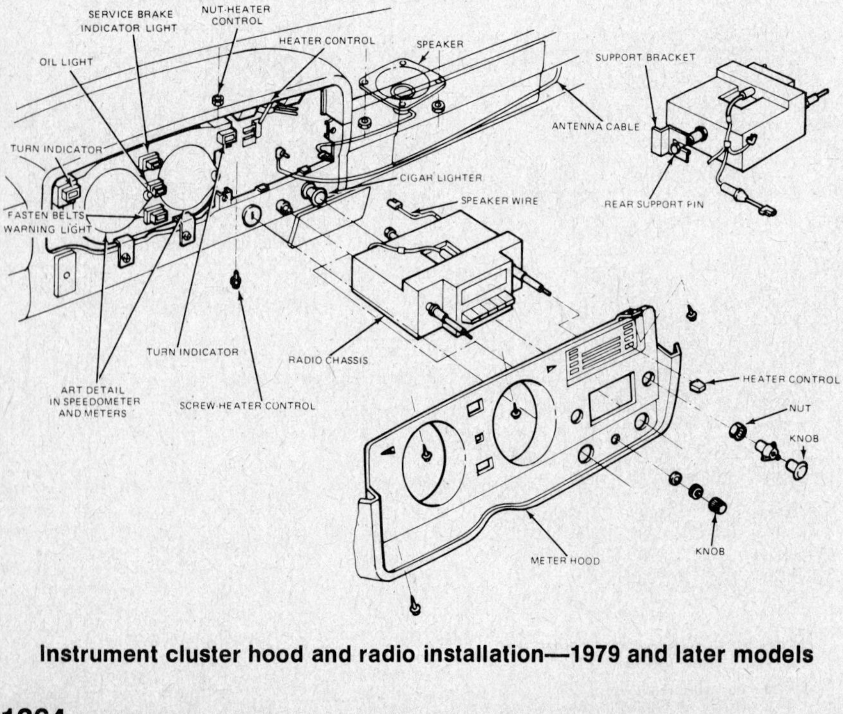

Instrument cluster hood and radio installation—1979 and later models

tainer and rear retainer support. Remove the heater control knobs, heater control bezel and right-hand defroster hose.

2. Remove the heater control and position it to the left.
3. Remove the radio chassis rear support bracket.
4. Bend the bracket down 90°.
5. Remove the radio knobs, attaching nuts and bezel.
6. Pull the chassis forward until the control shafts clear the holes in the instrument panel. Disconnect the speaker wires, power lead and antenna lead. Rotate the chassis so that the control shafts point upward and lower the radio.
7. Installation is the reverse of removal.

Wiper Motor, Linkage and Bracket

REMOVAL AND INSTALLATION

1. Disconnect the battery.
2. Remove the wiper arms and blades by removing the retaining nuts.
3. Remove the rubber cap, nut, tapered spacer and rubber grommet from each pivot shaft.
4. Remove the two motor and bracket retaining bolts and washers.
5. Disconnect the wiper motor leads at the multiple connector.
6. Remove the motor and bracket assembly. Note the position of the ground washer and the rubber washer at the bracket mounting holes. Remove the plastic water shield.
7. To disconnect the motor from the bracket, remove the retaining clip that holds the linkage to the motor output arm. Note the position of the washers before removing the motor from the bracket.
8. Remove the four motor-to-bracket retaining bolts and remove the motor.
9. Installation is the reverse of removal.

Instrument Cluster

REMOVAL AND INSTALLATION

1. Disconnect the battery.
2. Remove the screws holding the cluster to the instrument panel.
3. Pull the cluster rearward enough to gain access to the cluster assembly.
4. Reach behind the cluster and disconnect the speedometer cable.
5. Pull the multiple connector from the printed circuit.
6. Note the position of the two ammeter leads and disconnect them.
7. Remove the screw attaching the ground wire to the rear of the cluster. On trucks equipped with a coasting richer valve, remove the two connectors at the speedometer sensor switch.
8. Remove the instrument cluster.
9. Installation is the reverse of removal.

INDEX

MODEL IDENTIFICATION

1977-78 B-1800 Pick-Up
(© Toyo Kogyo Co. Ltd.)

1979-80 B-2000 Pick-Up
(© Toyo Kogyo Co. Ltd.)

1974-77 rotary Pick-Up
(© Toyo Kogyo Co. Ltd.)

GENERAL ENGINE SPECIFICATIONS—PISTON ENGINE

Year	Engine Displacement Cu in. (cc)	Carb Type	Net Horsepower (@ rpm)	Net Torque @ rpm (ft lbs)	Bore and Stroke (in.)	Compression Ratio	Oil Pressure (@ rpm)
1974-76	96.8 (1586)	2-bbl	70 @ 5000	82 @ 3400	3.07 x 3.27	8.6:1	50-64 @ 3000
1977-78	109.6 (1796)	2-bbl	66 @ 4500	92 @ 3000	3.07 x 3.07	8.6:1	48-64 @ 3000
1979-80	120.2 (2000)	2-bbl	NA	NA	3.15 x 3.86	8.6:1	50-64 @ 3000

NA—Not available

GENERAL ENGINE SPECIFICATIONS—ROTARY

Model	Engine Displacement Cu in. (cc)	Carburetor Type	Net Horsepower	Net Torque	Rotor Displacement (cu in.)	Compression Ratio	Oil Pressure @ prm (psi)
Pick-up	80 (1,308)	4-bbl	110	117	40	9.2:1	71.1 @ 3,000

TUNE-UP SPECIFICATIONS—PISTON ENGINE

Year	Engine Displacement Cu in.	(cc)	Spark Plugs Type	Spark Plugs Gap (in.)	Distributor Point Dwell (deg)	Distributor Point Gap (in.)	Ignition Timing (deg) MT	Ignition Timing (deg) AT	Intake Valve Opens (deg)	Fuel Pump Pressure (psi)	Idle Speed (rpm) MT	Idle Speed (rpm) AT	Valve Clearance (in.)▲ In	Valve Clearance (in.)▲ Ex
1974-76	96.8	(1586)	BP-6ES	.031	49-55	0.020	5B②	5B②	13B	2.8-3.6	800-850	650-① 700	.012-	.012
1977-78	109.6	(1796)	BP-6ES	.031	49-55	0.020	8B	8B	18B	2.8-3.6	700-750	—	.012-	.012
1979-80	120.2	(2000)	BPR-6ES	.031	Elec.	Elec.	8B	—	14B	2.8-3.6	600-700	—	.012-③	.012③

▲ At the valve (warm engine)
— Not Applicable
① Transmission in Drive
② 1976 Calif.: 8B
③ 0.009 on the cam side
CO—% at idle: 1973-75—1.5-2.5%
B—BTDC (Before Top Dead Center)

FIRING ORDERS

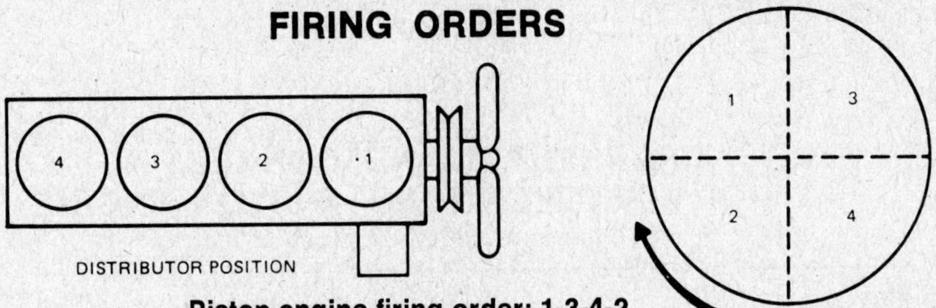

Piston engine firing order: 1-3-4-2
(© Toyo Kogyo Co. Ltd.)

TUNE-UP SPECIFICATIONS—ROTARY

Year	Engine Cu in.	Spark Plugs Type	Spark Plugs Gap	Distributors (both)▲ Point Gap (in.)	Distributors (both)▲ Point Dwell (deg)	Ignition Timing (deg) Leading Normal	Ignition Timing (deg) Leading Retarded	Ignition Timing (deg) Trailing Normal	Idle Speed (rpm) MT	Idle Speed (rpm) AT
1974	80	N-80B	0.024-0.028	0.018	58 ± 3	5A	—	15A	900	750①
1975	80	N-80B	0.024-0.028	0.018	58 ± 3	TDC	20A	15A	800-850	750-800①
1976	80	RN 278B	0.039-0.043	0.018	58 ± 3	5A	20A	20A	725-775	725-① 775
1977	80	RN-278B	0.039-0.043	0.018	58 ± 3	5A	—	25A	725-775	725-775

▲ 1974-75 models have only one distributor
① Transmission in drive (D)
TDC Top dead center
A After top dead center
deg degrees

FIRING ORDERS

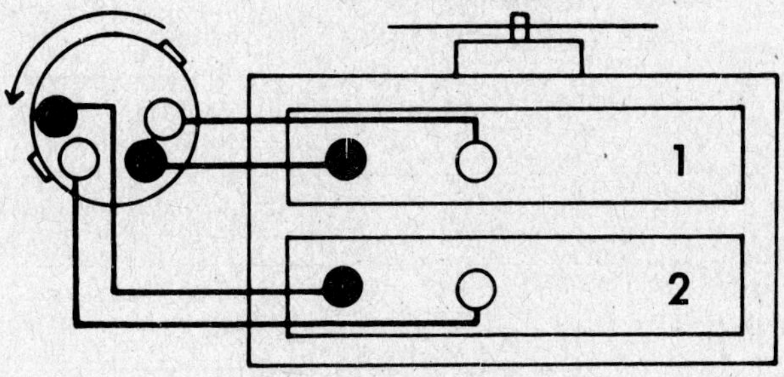

Rotary engine firing order
(© Toyo Kogyo Co. Ltd.)

CAPACITIES

Year	Model	Engine Displacement Cu in. (cc)	Engine Crankcase (qts) With Filter	Engine Crankcase (qts) Without Filter	Transmission (pts) Manual 4-spd	Transmission (pts) Manual 5-spd	Transmission (pts) Automatic	Drive Axle (pts)	Gasoline Tank (gals)	Cooling System (qts) W/ AC	Cooling System (qts) W/O AC
1974-76	B-1600	96.8 (1586)	4.00	3.00	3.00①	—	—	2.80	11.7	—	6.80
1974-75	Rotary Pick-up	80 (1308)	5.50	4.50	3.60	—	13.20	2.80	20.4	—	10.80
1976-77	Rotary Pick-up	80 (1308)	6.80	5.30	3.60	4.60	13.20	2.80	20.8	—	10.30
1977-78	B-1800	109.6 (1796)	3.8	—	3.00	3.8	—	3.0	14.8②	—	7.6
1979-80	B-2000	120.2 (2000)	4.1	—	3.2	3.6	—	2.8	14.8②	—	7.6③

① After #49825—3.20
② Long body—17.4 gal.
③ 7.0 without heater

CRANKSHAFT AND CONNECTING ROD SPECIFICATIONS—PISTON ENGINE

(All measurements are given in inches)

Year	Engine Displacement Cu in. (cc)	Crankshaft Main Brg Journal Dia	Crankshaft Main Brg Oil Clearance	Crankshaft Shaft End-Play	Crankshaft Thrust on No.	Connecting Rod Journal Dia	Connecting Rod Oil Clearance	Connecting Rod Side Clearance
1974-76	96.8 (1586)	2.4804	.001-..002	.003-.009	4	2.0866	.001-.003	.004-.008
1977-78	109.6 (1796)	2.4804	.0012-.0019	.003-.009	5	2.0866	.0011-.0030	.004-.008
1979-80	120.2 (2000)	2.4804	.0012-.0020	.003-.009	5	.7874①	.0011-:0030	.004-.008

① Small end, inner diameter

VALVE SPECIFICATIONS—PISTON ENGINE

Year	Engine Displacement Cu in. (cc)	Seat Angle (deg)	Face Angle (deg)	Spring Test Pressure (lbs @ in.)	Spring Installed Height (in.)	Stem-to-Guide Clearance (in.) Intake	Stem-to-Guide Clearance (in.) Exhaust	Stem Diameter (in.) Intake	Stem Diameter (in.) Exhaust
1974-76	96.8 (1586)	45	45	①	②	.0007-.0021	.0007-.0023	.3150	.3150
1977-78	109.6 (1796)	45	45	③	②	.0007-.0021	.0007-.0023	.3150	.3150
1979-80	120.2 (2000)	45	45	①	②	.0007-.0021	.0007-.0023	.3150	.3150

① Outer: 31.4 @ 1.339
Inner: 20.9 @ 1.260

② Outer: 1.339
Inner: 1.260

③ Outer: 31.4 @ 1.339
Inner: 20.9 @ 1.260

PISTON AND RING SPECIFICATIONS

(All measurements are given in inches)

Year	Engine Displacement Cu in. (cc)	Piston Clearance	Ring Gap			Ring Side Clearance		
			Top Compression	Bottom Compression	Oil Control	Top Compression	Bottom Compression	Oil Control
1974-76	96.8 (1586)	.0022-.0028	.008-.016	.008-.016	.008-.016	.0014-.0028	.0012-.0025	.008-.016
1977-78	109.6 (1796)	.0022-.0028	.008-.016	.008-.016	.012-.035	.0014-.0028	.0012-.0025	—
1979-80	120.2 (2000)	.0014-.0030	.008-.016	.008-.016	.012-.035	.0012-.0028	.0012 .0025	—

TORQUE SPECIFICATIONS—PISTON ENGINE

(All figures given in ft-lb)

Year	Cylinder Head Bolts	Rod Bearing Bolts	Main Bearing Bolts	Crankshaft Pulley Bolt	Flywheel-to-Crankshaft Bolts	Manifold	
						Intake	Exhaust
1974-78	②	36-40	61-65	101-108	112-118	14-19	12-17①
1979-80	③	30-33	61-65	101-108	112-118	14-19	16-21

① B1800—16-21
② Cold—56-60
Hot—69-72
③ Cold—59-64
Hot—69-72

TORQUE SEQUENCES

Cylinder Head

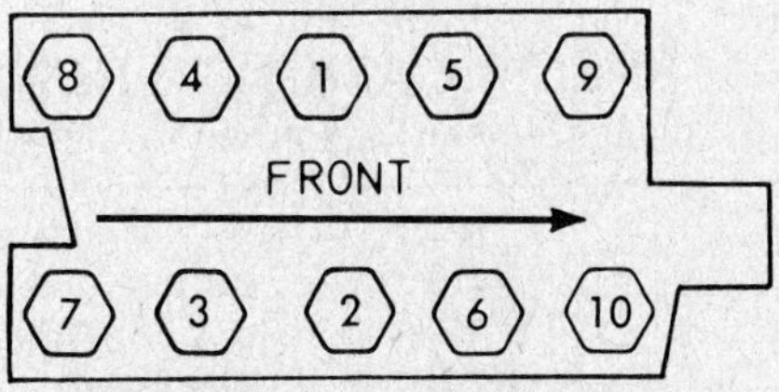

Piston engine cylinder head bolt tightening sequence

TORQUE SPECIFICATIONS—ROTARY

(All figures in ft-lb)

Engine Displacement Cu In. (cc)	Front Cover	Bearing Housing	Rear Stationary Gear	Eccentric Shaft Pulley Bolt	Flywheel to Eccentric Shaft Nut	Manifolds		Oil Pan	Tension Bolts
						Intake	Exhaust		
80 (1,308)	—	—	—	54-69	289-362	15	32-43	5-7	23-27

TORQUE SEQUENCES

Cylinder Head

Tension bolt loosening sequence
(© Toyo Kogyo Co. Ltd.)

Tension bolt tightening sequence
(© Toyo Kogyo Co. Ltd.)

ECCENTRIC SHAFT SPECIFICATIONS—ROTARY

(All measurements are given in inches)

Model	Journal Diameter Main Bearing	Journal Diameter Rotor Bearing	Oil Clearance Main Bearing	Oil Clearance Rotor Bearing	Eccentric Shaft End-Play Normal	Eccentric Shaft End-Play Limit	Min. Shaft Runout
Pick-up	1.6929	2.9134	.0016-.0028	.0016-.0031	.0016-.0028	.0035	.0024

SEAL SPECIFICATIONS—ROTARY

(All measurements are given in inches)

Model	Apex Seal Normal Height	Apex Seal Height Limit	Corner Seal Width (OD)	Side Seal Thickness	Side Seal Width	Oil Seal Contact Width of Lip Normal	Oil Seal Contact Width of Lip Limit
Pick-up	.33500	.27600	.4331	.0394	.1378	.008	.031

SEAL CLEARANCES—ROTARY

(All measurements are given in inches)

Model	Apex Seals To Side Housing Normal	Apex Seals To Side Housing Limit	Apex Seals To Rotor Groove Normal	Apex Seals To Rotor Groove Limit	Corner Seal to Rotor Groove Normal	Corner Seal to Rotor Groove Limit	Side Seal To Rotor Groove Normal	Side Seal To Rotor Groove Limit	Side Seal To Corner Seal Normal	Side Seal To Corner Seal Limit
Pick-up	.0051-.0067	.012	.0020-.0035	.006	.0008-.0019	.0031	.0016-.0028	.0040	.0020-.0059	.016

ROTOR AND HOUSING SPECIFICATIONS—ROTARY

(All measurements are given in inches)

Model	Rotor: Side Clearance	Rotor: Standard Protrusion of Land	Rotor: Limit of Protrusion of Land	Rotor: Front and Rear Distortion Limit	Rotor: Front and Rear Wear Limit	Housing: Rotor Width	Housing: Rotor Distortion Limit	Housing: Intermediate Distortion Limit	Housing: Intermediate Wear Limit
Pick-up	.0047-.0083	.004-.006	.003	.002	.004	3.1438	.002	.002	.004

ALTERNATOR AND REGULATOR SPECIFICATIONS

Year	Model	Alternator: Field Current @ 14V	Alternator: Output (amps)	Regulator: Air Gap (in.)	Regulator: Point Gap (in.)	Regulator: Back Gap (in.)	Regulator: Volts @ 75°
1974-75	Rotary Pickup	40	50	0.028-0.051	0.012-0.018	0.028-0.059	14.5
1973-76	B1600	28	35	0.028-0.043	0.012-0.016	0.028-0.043	14.5
1976-77	Rotary Pickup	56	63	0.028-0.051	0.012-0.018	0.028-0.059	14.0
1977-78	B1800	—	—	0.028-0.051	0.012-0.018	0.028-0.059	14-15①
1979-80	B2000	—	—	0.028-0.051	0.012-0.018	0.028-0.059	14-15①

① Alternator @ 4,000 RPM and battery fully charged

BATTERY AND STARTER SPECIFICATIONS

(All trucks use 12 volt, negative ground electrical systems)

Year	Model	Battery Amp Hour Capacity	Starter: Lock Test Amps	Starter: Lock Test Volts	Starter: Lock Test Torque (ft/lbs)	Starter: No Load Test Amps	Starter: No Load Test Volts	Starter: No Load Test RPM	Starter: Brush Spring Tension (oz)	Starter: Min. Brush Length (in.)
1974-75	Rotary Pickup	70	1100	5.0	17.0	100	11.5	7800	49-63	0.45
1976-77	Rotary Pickup	60MT 70AT	780MT 1100AT	5.0	8.0MT 17.4AT	75MT 100AT	11.5	4900MT 7800AT	49-63	0.45
1973-76	B1600	60	560	7.5	9.4	60	11.5	6000	35-46	0.45
1977-78	B1800	45	310	5.0	5.4	53	11.5	6800	49-63	0.45
1979-80	B2000	45①	310	5.0	5.4	53	11.5	6800	49-63	0.45

① Heavy duty—70

BRAKE SPECIFICATIONS

(All measurements are (in.) unless noted)

Model	Lug Nut Torque (ft/lb)	Master Cylinder Bore	Brake Disc Minimum Thickness	Brake Disc Maximum Run-Out	Brake Drum Diameter	Brake Drum Max. Machine O/S	Brake Drum Max. Wear Limit	Minimum Lining Thickness Front	Minimum Lining Thickness Rear
B1600	65-72	0.750	—	—	10.236	10.276	—	0.039	0.039
Rotary Pickup	65-72	0.875	0.433	0.004	10.236	10.275	—	0.276	0.039
B1800	58-65	0.750	0.433	0.004	10.236	—	10.276	0.276	0.039
B2000	58-65	0.875	0.433	0.0039	10,236	—	10.276	—	0.039

NOTE: Minimum lining thickness is as recommended by the manufacturer. Due to variations in state inspection regulations, the minimum allowable thickness may be different than recommended by the manufacturer.

WHEEL ALIGNMENT SPECIFICATIONS

Year	Model	Camber Range (deg)	Camber Preferred Setting (deg)	Caster Range (deg)	Caster Preferred Setting (deg)	Toe-in (in.)	Steering Axis Inclination (deg)
1975	Rotary pickup	⅔P-1½P	1⅙P	0-½P	¼P	0-0.24	8¾P
1976-77	Rotary pickup	1⅓P-2⅓P	1⅚P	0-½P	¼P	0-0.12	8¾P
1973-76	B1600	½P-1½P	1P	1P-2P	1½P	0-0.24	7⅓P
1977-78	B1800	⅜P-1¼P	¾P	⅔P-1⅓P	1P	0-0.24	8°15′
1979-80	B2000	⅜P-1⅓P	¾P	⅔P-1⅓P	1P	0-0.24	8°15′

TUNE-UP PROCEDURES

Spark Plugs

The spark plugs should be checked and adjusted every 4,000 miles or 4 months for rotary engine-models or every 6,000 miles for piston engine-models. New plugs should be installed every 12,000 miles or 12 months.

The Mazda rotary engine has four spark plugs. Each of the two combustion chambers uses two plugs. The leading bottom spark plug fires first, igniting the fuel/air mixture, as in conventional engines; the trailing top plug fires a short time afterward (10° later), igniting any unburned mixture. This aids in more complete combustion in the long narrow chamber, which helps to reduce exhaust emissions of unburned fuel.

The spark plugs are specially constructed and designed for use only in the Mazda rotary engine.

1. Remove the wire from one of the plugs. Use a spark plug wrench with a rubber insulator to remove the plug.

***NOTE:** Both the distributor and the engine housing are marked to aid in identification of the spark plug and distributor connections. However, to avoid confusion, it is easier to remove one plug at a time.*

2. Check each plug for badly worn electrodes, black deposits, fouling, or cracked porcelain.
3. Clean the plug with a wire brush, if it is dirty.
4. Replace any plug which has a badly worn or burned electrode.
5. Measure the electrode gap with a *wire* gauge.
6. Adjust the gap to the specifications given in the "Tune-Up" Specifications Chart.
7. If the electrodes show signs of burning white or if the electrodes are burning rapidly, replace the plugs with cold range plugs.

***NOTE:** When replacing spark plugs be sure all plugs are of the same manufacture and heat range. It is a good idea to replace plugs in sets of four, if possible.*

8. Replace the spark plug and torque it to 10 ft lbs.

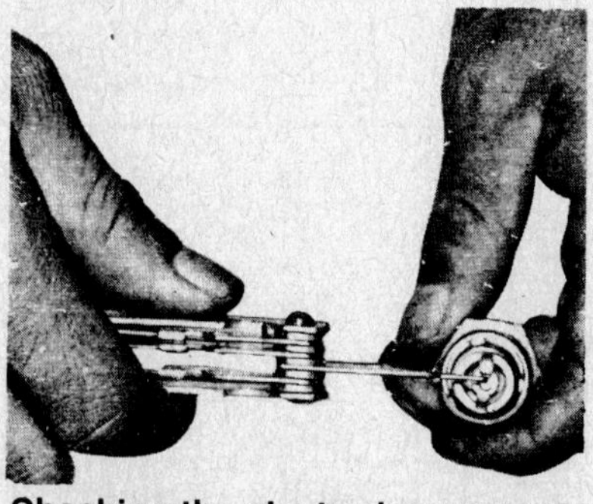

Checking the electrode gap; note the dual electrodes
(© Toyo Kogyo Co. Ltd.)

Breaker Points

NOTE: 1976 and later 1300 models, 1977 1600 models, and 1979–80 B2000 models have electronic ignition, eliminating the points and condenser. California and Canada models through 1978 have conventional ignition.

1. Release the clips on the distributor cap with a screwdriver. Lift off the cap and move it aside, leaving the wires attached. Pull the rotor from the shaft.
2. Inspect the points. If they are badly pitted or burned, they must be replaced. If they are only slightly burned, they may be filed flat and reused. In either case, they must be removed from the distributor. If the points are in good shape and only require adjustment, proceed to Step 8.
3. Remove the screws securing the points to the distributor breaker plate. Use a magnetic screwdriver to avoid dropping the screws. Remove the points.
4. If the points are slightly burned and are to be reused, clean them with a few strokes of a flat points file. Do this with the points removed from the distributor to avoid getting filings and grit in the works. Do not use an emery board, sandpaper, or the like for this job.
5. Install the new or cleaned points onto the breaker plate, but leave the mounting screws slightly loose. Apply a small dab of grease onto the distributor cam. Do not use oil, which will get onto the points, causing them to burn.
6. The condenser should be replaced whenever the points are replaced. Disconnect the condenser leads and remove the condenser mounting screws. Dual points models have a condenser for each set of points. A smaller condenser, used for radio noise suppression, is mounted next to the other condenser; it need only be replaced if ignition noise (clicking or popping) is heard over the radio. Install and connect the new condenser.
7. Check the breaker point alignment. If the points do not meet squarely, gently bend the fixed point slightly. Do not bend the movable point arm to adjust.

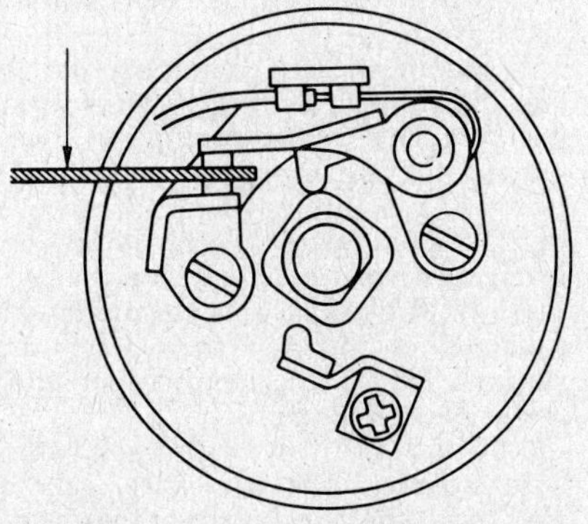

Adjusting the points with the rubbing block on the high point of the cam lobe

8. Rotate the engine until the rubbing block of the points arm is on one of the four high spots (lobes) of the distributor cam. The cam must open the points fully before the gap can be adjusted. The engine can be rotated by cranking it around in short bursts with the starter. You can also rotate the engine by hand with a wrench on the crankshaft (or eccentric shaft) pulley bolt; this is easier with the spark plugs removed. Move the engine only in the direction of normal rotation, to avoid damage to the apex seals (rotary engines).
9. Check the point gap with a flat feeler gauge of the proper thickness (see the Tune-Up Specifications). The feeler gauge should move through the points with only a light drag. If there is no drag, or if the gauge cannot be inserted at all, the gap is incorrect.
10. If the gap is incorrect, loosen the point set mounting screws slightly, if they are not already loose. Insert a screwdriver into the adjusting slot and lever the points open or closed until the gap is correct. Tighten the mounting screws and recheck the adjustment.
11. Install the rotor onto the distributor shaft (if the tip is burned or pitted, a new rotor should be used; similarly, if the distributor cap contacts are burned, a new cap should be installed). Install the distributor cap. If a new cap is being installed, hold the new cap next to the old and transfer the wires one at a time to avoid cross-wiring.

After adjusting the point gap, the timing must be checked; any change the gap (dwell) automatically changes ignition timing.

Dwell Angle

Dwell angle is the number of degrees of crankshaft rotation throuch which the points remain closed, conducting electricity. It is nothing more than an electric method of measuring point gap. All models are measured and adjusted in the same way.

1. Disconnect and plug the vacuum line(s) at the distributor.
2. Connect the dwell meter in accordance with its manufacturer's instructions.
3. Run the engine at idle, after it has been allowed to warm up.
4. Observe the dwell meter reading. It should be within the specifications in the "Tune-Up Specifications" chart.
5. If dwell is not within specifications, shut off the engine, remove the distributor cap and rotor and adjust the point gap. Increasing the gap decreases dwell, and vice-versa.
6. If the dwell angle cannot be brought to within specifications, check for one or more of the following:
   a. Worn distributor cam
   b. Worn rubbing block
   c. Bent movable contact arm

Replace any of the parts, if necessary.

7. When the dwell angle check is completed, disconnect the meter and reconnect the vacuum line(s).

Ignition Timing

1974–75 ROTARY

1. Connect a tachometer to the engine.
2. Disconnect and plug the vacuum tube on the distributor.
3. Connect a timing light to the wire from the leading (lower) plug of the front rotor housing.
4. Start the engine and run it at idle speed.
5. Shine the timing light on the indicator pin located on the front cover.
6. If the leading timing mark is not correctly aligned with the pointer, stop the engine.
7. Loosen the distributor locknut and rotate the distributor housing (with the engine running) until the timing marks align. Stop the engine and tighten the distributor locknut.
8. Recheck the timing.

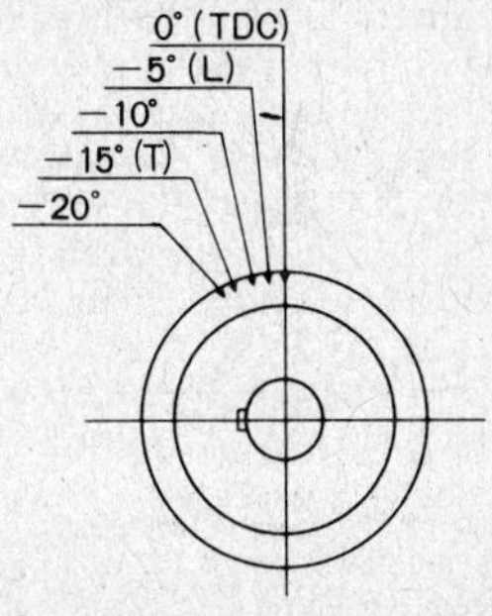

Ignition timing marks—1974-75 rotary
(© Toyo Kogyo Co. Ltd.)

9. Change the connection of the timing light to the wire from the trailing (top) plug in the front rotor housing.
10. Start the engine and shine the timing light at the indicator pin. If the trailing timing falls within the specifications, no further adjustments are necessary.
11. Adjust the trailing timing to specification by rotating the distributor body, as in Step 7.
12. Check the leading timing and record how much it differs from specification.
13. Remove the distributor cap and rotor.
14. Loosen the breaker base setscrews (the ones directly opposite each other near the outside of the distributor body) and turn the distributor base plate until the correct leading plug timing is obtained again.
15. Recheck the timing. The leading and trailing plug timing marks should both be aligned (or within specifications). If not, repeat the procedure until they are.

1976 ROTARY

1. Run the engine at normal operating temperature.

2. Connect a tachometer to the engine.
3. Connect a timing light to the leading spark plug of the front rotor.
4. Run engine at specified idle speed.
5. Aim the timing light at the timing indicator pin on the front cover.
6. If the timing is not correct, loosen the distributor locknut and rotate the distributor housing until the timing mark on the pulley aligns with the indicator pin.
7. Tighten the distributor locknut and recheck the lead timing.
8. Connect the timing light to the trailing spark plug.
9. Check the trailing timing with the timing light.
10. If the trailing timing is not correct, note the amount of error and stop the engine.
11. Remove the distributor cap and rotor.
12. Disconnect the primary wire from the leading point set.
13. Remove the breaker base plate and external lever for leading set.
14. Slightly loosen the breaker base set screws of the trailing side and turn the base plate as required. Install the leading breaker base assembly, rotor and cap.
15. Check the trailing and leading timing. If they are not correct, repeat the above steps.
16. Leave timing light connected to trailing plug of the front rotor housing.

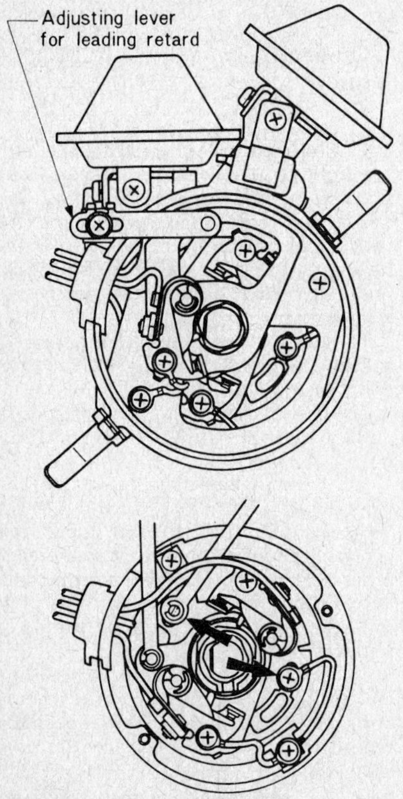

Adjusting the rotary engine ignition timing
(© Toyo Kogyo Co. Ltd.)

17. Connect a jumper between both terminals in the coupler of the primary lead wire.
18. Check the leading retard timing. Adjust by moving the external adjusting lever.

1977 ROTARY

1. Check the point gap for both leading and trailing sets. Adjust if necessary.
2. Warm-up engine and run it at specified idle speed.
3. Connect a timing light to the leading spark plug and aim it at the pointer on the front cover. If timing mark and pointer do not align as specified, adjust by loosening and rotating distributor body.
4. Tighten distributor body and switch timing light to trailing plug.
5. Check trailing timing by pointing timing light at pointer on front cover. If not within specifications, adjust by loosening and rotating distributor body.
6. Adjust leading timing by loosening the breaker base set screws in the distributor body and rotating the breaker base. Then, tighten the base, replace the cap and rotor. Start the engine and check the timing. Adjust the timing to specifications by loosening and rotating the distributor body.
7. Recheck the trailing timing and adjust as above, if necessary.

PISTON ENGINE

1. Raise the hood and clean and mark the timing marks. Chalk or fluorescent paint makes a good, visible mark.
2. Disconnect the vacuum line at the distributor and plug the disconnected line.
3. Connect a timing light to the front (No. 1) cylinder, a power source and ground. Follow the manufacturer's instructions.
4. Connect a tachometer to the engine.
5. Start the engine and reduce the idle to 700–750 rpm to be sure that the centrifugal advance mechanism is not working.
6. With the engine running, shine the timing light at the timing pointer and observe the position of the pointer in relation to the timing mark on the crankshaft pulley.
7. If the timing is not as specified, adjust the timing by loosening the distributor hold-down bolt and rotating the distributor in the proper direction. When the proper ignition timing is obtained, tighten the hold-down bolt on the distributor.
8. Check the centrifugal advance mechanism by accelerating the engine to about 2,000 rpm. If the ignition timing advances, the mechanism is working properly.
9. Stop the engine and remove the timing light.
10. Reset the idle to specifications.
11. Remove the tachometer.

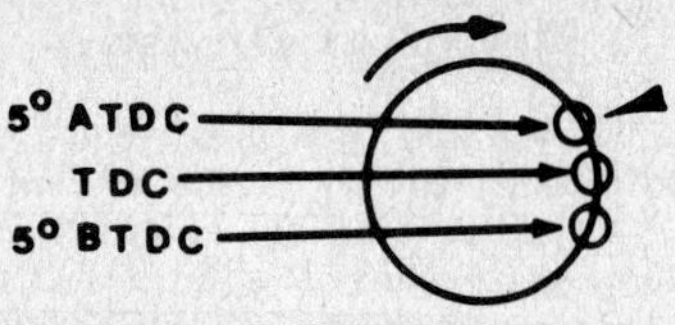

1600 engine timing marks—except California
(© Toyo Kogyo Co. Ltd.)

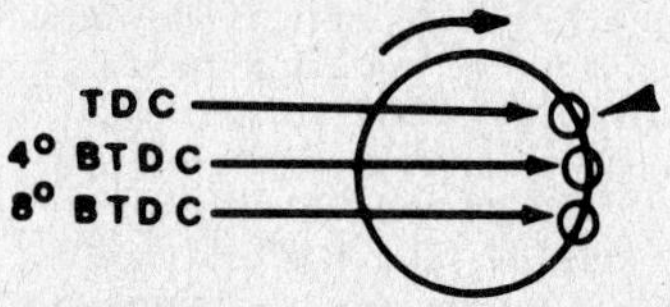

1600 engine timing marks—California
(© Toyo Kogyo Co. Ltd.)

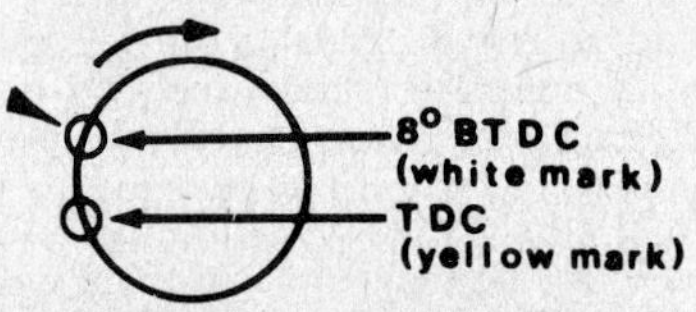

1800 engine timing marks
(© Toyo Kogyo Co. Ltd.)

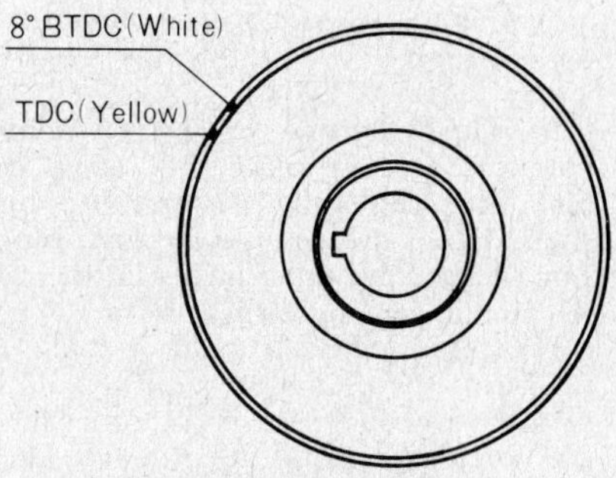

2000 engine timing marks
(© Toyo Kogyo Co. Ltd.)

Valve Lash

PISTON ENGINE

1. Run the engine until normal operating temperature is reached.
2. Shut off the engine and remove the rocker cover.
3. Torque the cylinder head bolts to 70 ft lbs.
4. Rotate the crankshaft so that the No. 1 cylinder (front) is in the firing position. This can be determined by removing the spark plug from the No. 1 cylinder and putting your thumb over the spark plug port. When compression is felt, the No. 1 cylinder is on the compression stroke. Rotate the engine with a wrench on the crankshaft pulley and stop it a TDC of the compression stroke on the No. 1 cylinder.
5. Check the valve clearance with a feeler blade. The clearance can be checked at the camshaft or at the valve.
6. If the valve clearance is incorrect, loosen the adjusting screw locknut and adjust the clearance by turning the ad-

justing screw with the feeler blade inserted. Hold the adjusting screw in the correct position and tighten the locknut.

7. Rotate the crankshaft (in the normal direction of rotation), adjusting the valves for each cylinder at TDC of the compression stroke. Adjust the valves for each cylinder, in the firing order, 1–3–4–2.

8. Install the rocker arm cover and torque the nuts to 18 in. lbs.

Compression

ROTARY ENGINE

Because of the unusual shape of the combustion chamber, the lack of valves, and because there are three chambers for each rotor, a normal gauge is useless for the measurement of rotary engine compression.

Mazda makes a special recording compression tester which produces a separate graph for each of the three chambers.

This is an expensive piece of equipment and not one that most mechanics are likely to have. If low compression is suspected, check with your local Mazda dealer.

Carburetor

***NOTE:** For further carburetor adjustments, see the "Fuel System" section below.*

IDLE SPEED AND MIXTURE

1974 Rotary

1. Warm the engine to normal operating temperature.
2. Be sure that the secondary throttle valve is fully returned.
3. Set the parking brake and block the front wheels.
4. Connect a tachometer according to the manufacturer's instructions.
5. Adjust the idle speed to specifications. The idle speed should ONLY be adjusted with the idle air screw. Never use the idle fuel jet screw to adjust the idle. This screw is preset at the factory and should not be moved.

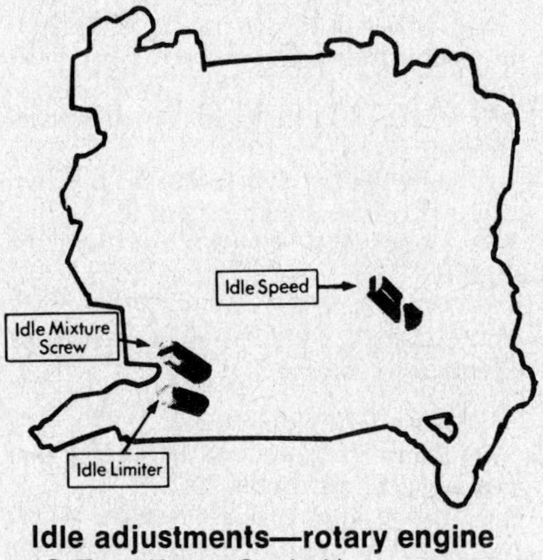

Idle adjustments—rotary engine
(© Toyo Kogyo Co. Ltd.)

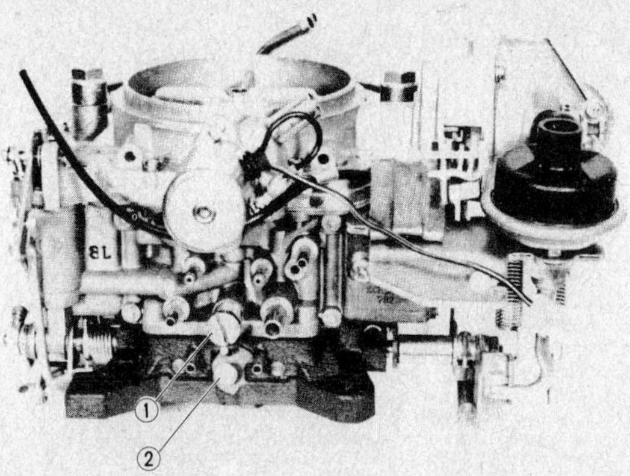

Adjusting the idle speed—1976-77 rotary; (1) air adjustment screw, (2) mixture screw
(© Toyo Kogyo Co. Ltd.)

6. After idle speed adjustment, you should also have the mixture checked with a CO analyzer.

IDLE AND THROTTLE SCREW ADJUSTMENT

If for some reason (tampering or carburetor overhaul) the idle and throttle screws need adjustment, use the following procedures. Two procedures are given; one for HC/CO analyzer and one for a fuel flow meter.

FUEL FLOW METER

It is best to use this procedure to set the idle and throttle screws after they have been disturbed. After you are finished, check the adjustment with a HC/CO analyzer.

1. Adjust the throttle angle opening to specifications with the throttle adjustment screw. The adjustment should be made from the fully closed position. Tighten the locknut after the adjustment is complete.
2. Connect a fuel flow meter.
3. Start the engine and set the approximate idle speed with the idle air screw.
4. Adjust the idle fuel flow to specifications with the idle fuel screw.
5. Use the idle air screw to set the idle speed again.
6. Repeat this procedure (Steps 4 & 5) until both the idle fuel flow and the idle speed are within specifications.
7. Disconnect the fuel flow meter.

HC/CO ANALYZER

1. If you have not already done so, adjust the throttle angle opening to specifications. Make the adjustment from the fully closed position.
2. Lock the nut after adjustment.
3. Start the engine and adjust the idle speed with the idle air screw.
4. Using the gas analyzer, check the HC (hydrocarbon) and CO (carbon monoxide) readings. If the HC is less than 200 ppm (parts per million) and the CO is between 0.1–2.0%, no further adjustment is needed.
5. If the HC and CO are not within specifications, adjust the CO reading to as close to 0.1% as possible, keeping the HC reading below 200 ppm. Use the idle fuel screw to make this adjustment.
6. Recheck the idle speed and adjust, if necessary, using the idle air screw.
7. Recheck the HC and CO readings to be sure that they are within limits. Repeat Steps 5 and 6 until the HC, CO and idle speed are all within specifications.

1975 Rotary

Idle speed changes with air temperature. It is suggested by Mazda that the idle adjustment be made indoors with a floor fan blowing through the radiator to assist in cooling. Whenever operating an engine indoors, make certain that provision is made for removal of exhaust gases. Idle speed should be adjusted with the engine at normal operating temperature, all accessories off and fuel tank cap removed.

1. Connect a tachometer to the engine.
2. Set idle speed to specification by turning the adjusting screw.

Mixture can be adjusted by:

3. Check the float level as described in the Fuel System Section.
4. Using a reliable CO meter, check the CO density at idle.
5. If density is not within 0.1%, adjust the idle mixture by turning the mixture screw.
6. Adjust the CO density to 0%, then turn the adjusting screw counterclockwise until the density is 0.5%.
7. Turn the screw clockwise until the density reaches 0.1%. Then turn the screw an additional on quarter turn.
8. Check the idle speed and reset if necessary.

1976–77 Rotary

As with 1975 models, the idle speed should be set indoors. See the starting paragraph and Steps 1 and 2 under 1975 Rotary.

1. Disconnect the idle compensator tube at the air cleaner.
2. Run the engine at normal operating temperature and make sure that the choke is wide open.

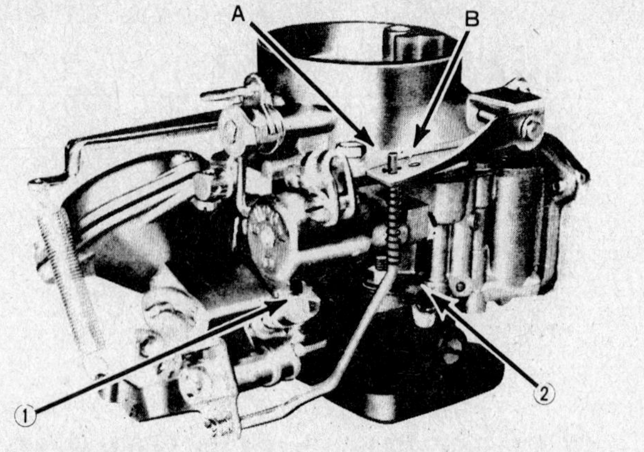

Idle speed (1) and mixture (2) screws—piston engine
(© Toyo Kogyo Co. Ltd.)

3. Check the float level as described in the Fuel System Section.
4. Connect an exhaust gas analyzer and tachometer to the engine.
5. With engine at idle, check the CO density.
6. Adjust the idle speed to specification by turning the idle adjusting screw.
7. Turn the mixture adjusting screw clockwise until the engine lopes severely.
8. Turn the screw slowly counterclockwise until the CO density reaches 0.1%, then turn it an additional one quarter turn in the same direction.

Piston Engines

1. Connect a tachometer to the engine. Warm the engine to normal operating temperature.
2. Run the engine (in neutral) to 2,000 rpm for a minute or two.
3. Allow the engine to return to idle. Adjust the idle to specifications by means of the idle speed screw.
4. The mixture can only be adjusted with the aid of an exhaust gas analyzer. Connect the CO meter to the exhaust and note the reading.
5. On models sold in California, disconnect the air hose between the air pump and the check valve, and plug the port of the check valve.
6. Adjust the mixture by means of the mixture screw until the CO concentration meets specifications.
7. If the limiter cap was removed from the mixture screw, reinstall it.

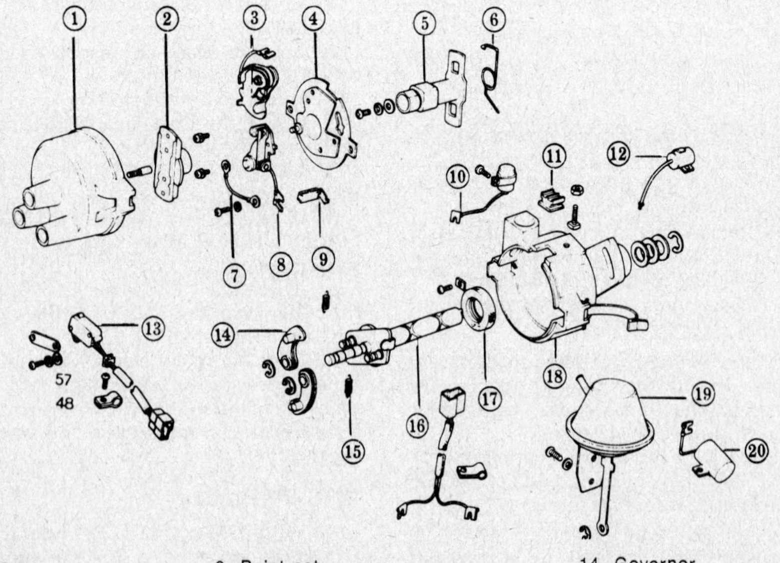

1. Cap
2. Rotor
3. Point set
4. Breaker plate
5. Cam
6. Spring
7. Ground wire
8. Point set
9. Felt
10. Ignition condenser
11. Terminal
12. Radio supression condenser
13. Vacuum switch—trailing distributor only
14. Governor
15. Governor spring
16. Shaft
17. Oil seal
18. Distributor housing
19. Vacuum advance unit
20. Ignition condenser

Rotary engine distributor components

ENGINE ELECTRICAL

Distributor

REMOVAL AND INSTALLATION

Rotary Engine—1974–78

The distributor is located on the right front side of the engine.

1. Open the hood and locate the distributor.
2. Remove the distributor cap.
3. Disconnect the vacuum tube from the advance unit.
4. Disconnect the primary wires from the distributor.
5. Matchmark the distributor body in relation to the engine front housing.
6. Remove the distributor hold-down bolt.
7. Pull the distributor from the front cover.

To install the distributor:

8. Turn the eccentric shaft until the TDC mark on the drive pulley aligns with the indicator pin on the front cover.
9. Align the matchmarks on the distributor housing and drive gear.
10. Install the distributor so that the distributor lockbolt is located in the center of the slot. Engage the gears.
11. Rotate the distributor clockwise until the leading contact point set starts to separate, and tighten the distributor lockbolt.
12. Install the distributor cap and connect the primary wires.
13. Set the ignition timing.
14. Connect the vacuum tube to the vacuum unit on the distributor.

Piston Engine

1. Matchmark the distributor cap and the body of the distributor. Remove the distributor cap.
2. Disconnect the vacuum hose from the diaphragm. Disconnect the electrical wire at the distributor, if so equipped.
3. Scribe matchmarks on the distributor body and the cylinder block to indicate the relative positions.
4. Scribe another mark on the distributor body indicating the position of the rotor.
5. Disconnect the primary wires from the distributor.
6. Remove the distributor hold-down nut, lockwasher and flat washer.
7. Remove the distributor from the engine.

***NOTE:** Do not crank the engine while the distributor is removed.*

To install the distributor:

8. Align the matchmarks on the distributor gear and body.
9. If the engine was cranked while the distributor was removed, turn the crankshaft until the No. 1 cylinder is at

the top of the compression stroke. This can be determined by feeling compression with your thumb over the spark plug port. The timing mark on the crankshaft pulley should also be aligned with the timing pointer. Slide the distributor into the engine with the rotor pointing to the No. 1 cylinder firing position (see "Firing Order").

10. If the engine has not been cranked while the distributor was removed, slide the distributor (with the O-ring) into the engine, aligning the matchmarks made during removal.

11. Install the flat washer, lockwasher and hold-down nut, but do not tighten the nut.

12. Install the distributor cap and connect the primary wires.

13. Set the ignition timing, and tighten the hold-down nut.

14. Connect the vacuum line wire, it so equipped.

FIRING ORDER

The firing order for the Mazda rotary engine is 1–2, with the trailing spark plugs firing ten degrees after the leading.

The firing order for the piston engine is 1–3–4–2.

Alternator

ALTERNATOR SERVICE PRECAUTIONS

Because of the nature of alternator design, special care must be taken when servicing the charging system.

1. Battery polarity should be checked before making any connections such as jumper cables or battery charger leads. Reversed battery connections will damage the diode rectifiers.
2. The battery must never be disconnected while the alternator is running because the regulator will be ruined.
3. Always disconnect the battery ground cable before replacing the alternator.
4. Do not attempt to polarize an alternator.
5. Do not short across or ground any alternator terminals.
6. Always disconnect the battery ground cable before removing the alternator output cable whether the engine is running or not.
7. If electric arc welding equipment is to be used on the car, first disconnect the battery and alternator cables. Never operate the car with the electric arc welding equipment attached.
8. If the battery is to be "quick charged", disconnect the positive cable from the battery.

REMOVAL AND INSTALLATION

1. Disconnect the battery ground cable at the negative (–) terminal.
2. Disconnect and tag all of the leads from the alternator.

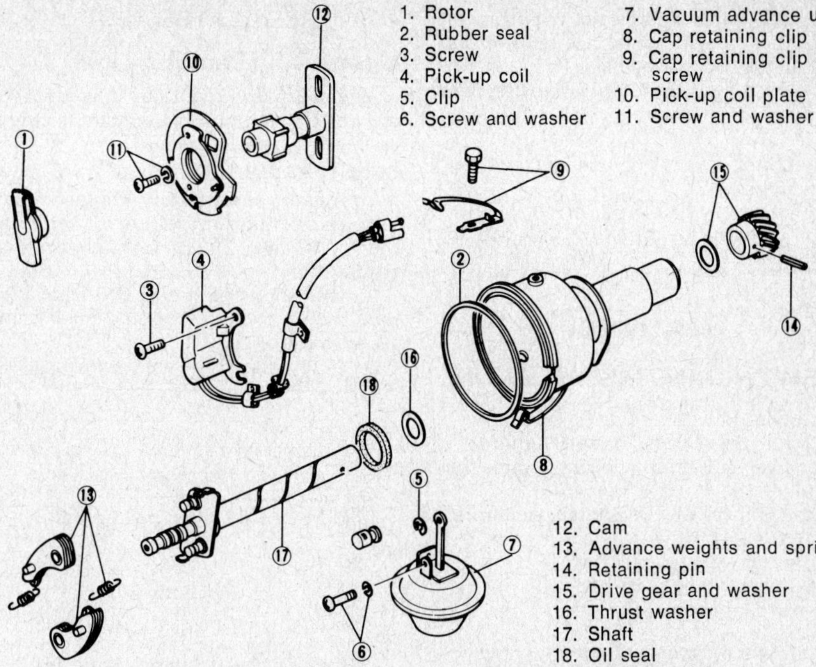

1. Rotor
2. Rubber seal
3. Screw
4. Pick-up coil
5. Clip
6. Screw and washer
7. Vacuum advance unit
8. Cap retaining clip
9. Cap retaining clip and screw
10. Pick-up coil plate
11. Screw and washer
12. Cam
13. Advance weights and springs
14. Retaining pin
15. Drive gear and washer
16. Thrust washer
17. Shaft
18. Oil seal

Exploded view of the electronic ignition distributor

3. Remove the alternator adjusting link bolt. Do not remove the adjusting link.
4. Remove the alternator securing nuts and bolts. Withdraw the drivebelt and remove the alternator.

Installation is performed in the reverse order of removal. Adjust the drivebelt tension as detailed below.

BELT TENSION ADJUSTMENT

1. Check the drivebelt tension by applying about 22 lbs of thumb pressure to the belt, at the midpoint of the longest span between pulleys. The belt should deflect to the following specifications:

Old belt—0.59–0.67 in.
New belt—0.47–0.55 in.

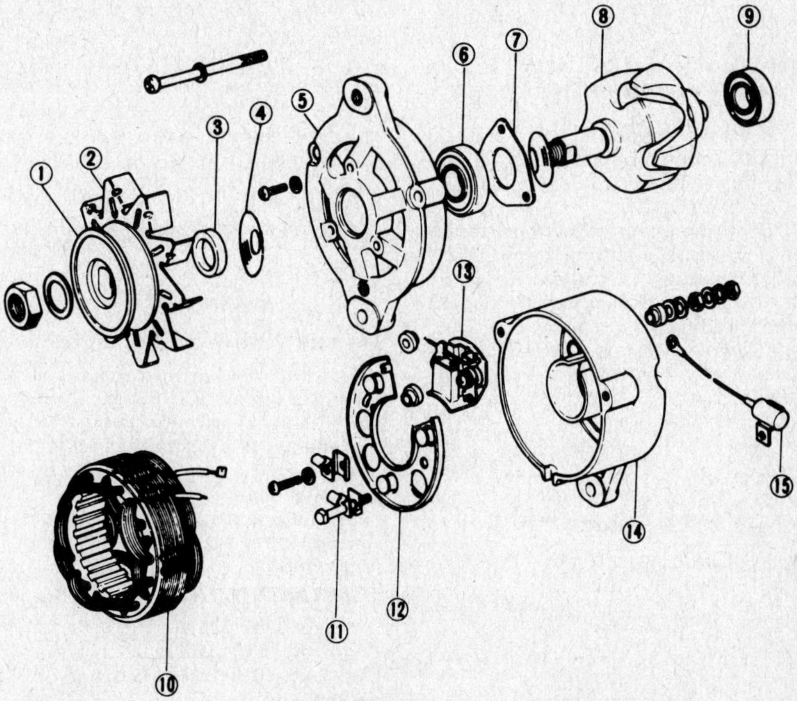

1. Pulley
2. Fan
3. Spacer
4. Slinger
5. Front housing
6. Front bearing
7. Bearing retainer
8. Rotor
9. Rear bearing
10. Stator
11. Terminal bolt
12. Diode plate (rectifiers)
13. Brush holder
14. Rear housing
15. Condenser

Exploded view of the alternator

2. If belt deflection is not within specifications loosen but do not remove the bolt on the adjusting link.
3. Push the alternator in the direction required to obtain proper belt deflection.

CAUTION: Do not pry or pound the alternator housing.

4. Tighten the adjusting link bolt to 20 ft lbs.

Regulator

REMOVAL AND INSTALLATION

1. Disconnect the battery ground cable at the negative (–) battery terminal.
2. Disconnect the wiring from the regulator.
3. Remove the regulator mounting screws.
4. Remove the regulator.

Installation is performed in the reverse order of removal.

VOLTAGE ADJUSTMENTS

Models With Ammeters Only

1. Remove the cover from the regulator.
2. Check the air gap, the point gap, and the back gap with a feeler gauge (see illustration).
3. If they do not fall within the specifications given in the "Alternator and Regulator" chart, adjust the gaps by bending the stationary contact bracket.
4. Connect a voltmeter between the "A" and "E" terminal of the regulator.

NOTE: Be sure that the battery is fully charged before proceeding with this test.

5. Start the engine and run it at 2,000 rpm (4,000 alternator rpm). The voltmeter reading should be 13.5–14.5 V.
6. Stop the engine.
7. Bend the upper plate *down* to decrease the voltage setting or *up* to increase the setting, as required.
8. If the regulator cannot be brought within specifications, replace it.
9. When the test is completed, disconnect the voltmeter and replace the regulator cover.

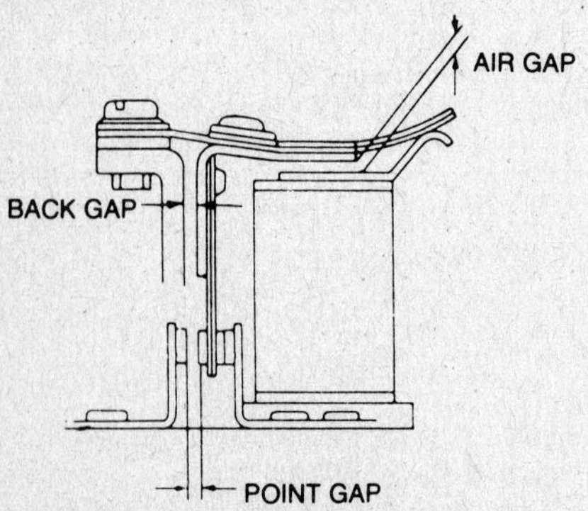

Regulator mechanical adjustments
(© Toyo Kogyo Co. Ltd.)

REGULATOR TEST

Models With Warning Light

The alternator regulator is composed of two control units: a constant voltage relay and a pilot lamp relay.

CONSTANT VOLTAGE RELAY

1. Use an almost fully charged battery and connect a voltmeter between the "A" and "E" terminals of the regulator.
2. Run the engine at 2,000 rpm and read the voltmeter. It should read from 14–15 volts.
3. If not, adjust the voltage relay.

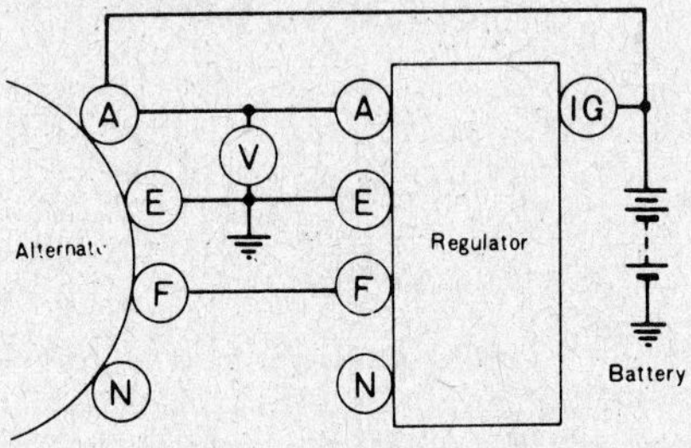

Testing the voltage regulator
(© Toyo Kogyo Co. Ltd.)

PILOT LAMP RELAY

1. Using a voltmeter and variable resistor, construct a circuit as shown.
2. Light the pilot lamp.
3. Slide the knob of the variable resistor so that the voltage gradually increases.
4. Read the voltage between the "N" and "E" terminals of the regulator. If the voltage is 3.7–5.7 (4.2–5.2 for 1977 and later) volts, it is operating properly.
5. Slide the knob of the variable resistor to decrease the voltage. Note the point on the voltmeter where the light will light again. If the reading is less than 3.5 volts through 1976 or 3.0 volts for 1977–80, the unit is working properly.
6. Disconnect the test instruments.

REGULATOR

Models With Warning Light

1. Check the air gap, back gap and point gap with a wire gauge. If they are not within specification, adjust the gap by bending the stationary bracket.
2. After the gaps are correctly set, adjust the voltage setting. Bend the upper plate down to decrease the voltage setting, or bend it up to increase the voltage setting.

CONSTANT VOLTAGE RELAY

Air Gap .028–.051 in.
Point Gap .012–.018 in.
Back Gap .028–.059 in.

PILOT LAMP RELAY

Air Gap .035–.055 in. through 1976, .039–.059 for 1977–80
Point Gap .028–.043 in. through 1976, .020–.035 in. for 1977–80
Back Gap 0.28–.059 in.

Starter

REMOVAL AND INSTALLATION

Rotary Engine

NOTE: There are two possible locations for the starter motor; one is on the lower right-hand side of the engine and the other is on the upper right-hand side.

1. Remove the ground cable from the negative (–) battery terminal.
2. If the car is equipped with the lower mounted starter, remove the gravel shield from underneath the engine.

CAUTION: Be extremely careful not to contact the hot exhaust pipe while working underneath the car.

3. Remove the battery cable from the starter terminal.
4. Disconnect the solenoid leads from the solenoid terminals.
5. Remove the starter securing bolts and withdraw the starter assembly.

Installation is the reverse.

Piston Engine

1. Raise the hood and disconnect the battery ground cable.
2. Remove the carburetor air cleaner and intake tube for clearance, if necessary.
3. Disconnect the battery cable from the starter solenoid battery terminal.
4. Pull the ignition switch wire from the solenoid terminal.
5. Raise and support the vehicle on jackstands.
6. Working under the vehicle, remove the starter attaching bolts, washers and nuts.
7. Tilt the drive end of the starter and remove the starter.
8. Installation is the reverse of removal.

SOLENOID REPLACEMENT

Perform solenoid replacement with the starter motor removed from the car.

1. Detach the field strap from the solenoid terminals.
2. Remove the solenoid securing screws.
3. Withdraw the solenoid spring and washers from the starter drive housing.

Solenoid installation is performed in the reverse order of removal.

STARTER DRIVE REPLACEMENT

1. Perform the solenoid removal procedure as above.
2. Remove the plunger from the drive engagement fork.
3. Unfasten the nuts from the thru-bolts.

NOTE: Unless further disassembly of the starter is desired, do not remove the thru bolts.

4. Remove the drive housing from the front of the starter.
5. Remove the engagement fork, spring, and spring seat.
6. Withdraw the over-running clutch from the armature shaft.

Assembly is performed in the reverse order of disassembly. Check the clearance between the pinion and the stop collar with the solenoid engaged. It should be 0.02–0.08 in.

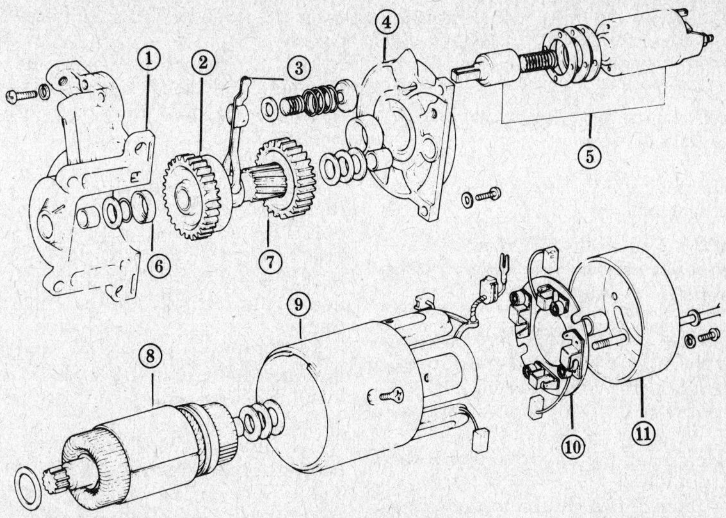

1. Front housing
2. Overrunning clutch
3. Engagement fork
4. Center frame
5. Solenoid
6. Stop
7. Idler gear
8. Armature
9. Field coil
10. Brush holder
11. End frame

Starter motor components

ENGINE MECHANICAL

Rotary

NOTE: Because of the unique design of the Mazda rotary engine, some procedures require the use of special factory tools. The text notes where these tools are necessary. If the tools are not available, the job should not be undertaken.

Design

The Mazda rotary engine replaces conventional pistons with three-cornered rotors which have rounded sides. The rotors are mounted on a shaft which has eccentrics rather than crank throws.

The chamber which the rotor travels in is roughly oval-shaped, but with the sides of the oval bowed in slightly. The technical name for this shape is a two-lobe epitrochoid.

As the rotor travels its path in the chamber, it performs the same four functions as the piston in a traditional piston engine: intake, compression, ignition, and exhaust.

But all four functions in a rotary engine are happening concurrently, rather than in four separate stages.

Ignition of the compressed fuel/air mixture occurs each time a side of the rotor passes the spark plugs. Since the rotor has three sides, there are three complete power impulses for each complete revolution of the rotor.

As it moves, the rotor exerts pressure on the cam of the eccentric shaft, causing the shaft to turn.

Because there are three power pulses for every revolution of the rotor, the eccentric shaft must make three complete revolutions for every one of the rotor. To maintain this ratio, the rotor has an internal gear that meshes with a fixed gear in a three-to-one ratio. If it were not for this gear arrangement, the rotor would spin freely and timing would be lost.

The Mazda rotary engine has two rotors mounted 60 degrees out of phase. This produces six power impulses for each complete revolution of both rotors and two power impulses for each revolution of the eccentric shaft.

Because of the number of power impulses for each revolution of the rotor, and because all four functions are concurrent, the rotary engine is able to produce a much greater amount of power for its size and weight than a comparable reciprocating piston engine.

Instead of using valves to control the intake and exhaust operations, the rotor uncovers and covers ports on the wall of the chamber as it turns. Thus, a complex valve train is unnecessary. The resulting elimination of parts further reduces the size and weight of the engine, as well as eliminating a major source of mechanical problems.

Spring-loaded carbon seals are used to prevent loss of compression around the rotor apexes and cast iron seals are used to prevent loss of compression around the side faces of the rotor. These seals are equivalent to compression rings on a conventional piston but must be more durable because of the high rotor rpm to which they are exposed.

Oil is controlled by means of circular seals mounted in two grooves on the side face of the rotor. These oil seals function to keep oil out of the combustion chamber and gasoline out of the crankcase, in a similar manner to the oil control ring on a piston.

The rotor housing is made of aluminum and the surfaces of the chamber are chrome plated for durability and the prevention of wear damage.

Engine Removal and Installation

CAUTION: Be sure that the engine has completely cooled before attempting to remove it.

1. Scribe matchmarks on the hood and hinges. Remove the hood from the hinges.
2. Working from underneath the car, remove the gravel shield; then drain the cooling system and the engine oil.
3. Disconnect the cable from the negative (−) battery terminal.
4. Remove the air cleaner, its bracket, and its attendant hoses.
5. Detach the accelerator cable, choke cable, and fuel lines from the carburetor.
6. Remove the nuts which secure the thermostat housing. Disconnect the ground cable from the housing and install the housing again after the cable is removed.
7. Disconnect the power brake vacuum line from the intake manifold.
8. Remove the fan shroud securing bolts and then the shroud itself.
9. Remove the bolts which secure the fan clutch to the eccentric shaft pulley. Withdraw the fan and clutch as a single unit.

NOTE: Keep the fan clutch in an upright position, so that its fluid does not leak out.

10. Unfasten the clamps and remove both of the radiator hoses.
11. Note their respective positions and remove the spark plug cables. Disconnect the primary leads from the distributors and remove both of the distributor caps.
12. Detach all of the leads from the alternator, the water temperature sender, the oil pressure sender, and the starter motor.
13. Disconnect all of the wiring from the emission control system components.
14. Detach the heater hoses at the engine.
15. Detach the oil lines from the front and the rear of the engine.
16. Disconnect the battery cable from the (+) battery terminal and from the engine.

17. Unfasten the nuts which secure the clutch slave cylinder and tie the cylinder up out of the way.

NOTE: Do not remove the hydraulic line from the slave cylinder.

18. Remove the exhaust pipe and the thermal reactor.

CAUTION: Be sure that the thermal reactor has completely cooled; severe burns could result if it has not.

19. Evenly and in two or three stages, remove the nuts and bolts which secure the clutch housing to the engine.
20. Support the transmission with a jack.
21. Remove the nuts from each of the engine mounts.
22. Attach a lifting sling to the lifting bracket on the rear of the engine housing.
23. Use a hoist to take up the slack on the sling.

CAUTION: Be sure that the hoist is secure to prevent possible personal injury or damage to the engine.

24. Pull the engine forward until it clears the transmission input shaft. Lift the engine straight up and out of the car.

NOTE: Be careful not to damage any of the components which remain in the car.

25. Remove the heat stove from exhaust manifold.
26. Remove the thermal reactor.

Engine installation is performed in the reverse order of removal.

Rotary Engine Overhaul

ENGINE DISASSEMBLY

1. Mount the engine on a stand.
2. Remove the oil hose support bracket from the front housing.
3. Disconnect the vacuum hoses, air hoses and remove the decel valve.
4. Remove the air pump and drive belt. Remove the air pump adjusting bar.
5. Remove the alternator and drive belt.
6. Disconnect the metering oil pump connecting rod, oil tubes and vacuum sensing tube from the carburetor.
7. Remove the carburetor and intake manifold as an assembly.
8. Remove the gasket and two rubber rings.
9. Remove the thermal reactor and gaskets.
10. Remove the distributor from the front cover.
11. Remove the water pump and gasket.
12. Invert the engine on the stand.
13. Remove the oil pan and gasket.
14. Remove the oil pump screen and gasket.
15. Identify the front and rear rotor housings with a felt tip pen. These are common parts and must be identified to be reassembled in their respective locations.
16. Turn the engine on the stand so that the top of the engine is up.
17. Remove the engine mounting bracket from the front cover.
18. Hold the flywheel with a flywheel holder and remove the eccentric shaft pulley.
19. Turn the engine on a stand so that the front end of the engine is up.
20. Remove the front cover and gasket.
21. Remove the O-ring from the oil passage on the front housing.
22. Remove the oil slinger and distributor drive gear from the shaft.
23. Unbolt and remove the chain adjuster.
24. Remove the locknut and washer from the oil pump driven sprocket.
25. Slide the oil pump drive sprocket and driven sprocket together with the drive chain off the eccentric shaft and oil pump simultaneously.
26. Remove the keys from the eccentric and oil pump shafts.
27. Slide the balance weight, thrust washer and needle bearing from the shaft.
28. Unbolt the bearing housing and slide the bearing housing, needle bearing, spacer and thrust plate off the shaft.
29. Turn the engine on the stand so that the top of the engine is up.
30. If equipped with a manual transmission, remove the clutch pressure plate and clutch disc. Loosen the pressure plate bolts evenly in small stages to prevent distortion and possible injury from the pressure plate flying off. Straighten the tab of the lockwasher and remove the flywheel nut. Remove the flywheel with a puller.
31. If equipped with an automatic transmission, remove the drive plate. Straighten the tab on the lockwasher and remove the counterweight nut, while holding the flywheel with a flywheel holder. Remove the counterweight using a puller.
32. Working at the rear of the engine, loosen the tension bolts in the sequence shown, and remove the tension bolts.

NOTE: Do not loosen the tension bolts one at a time. Loosen the bolts evenly in small stages to prevent distortion.

33. Lift the rear housing off the shaft.
34. Remove any seals that are stuck to the rotor sliding surface of the rear housing and reinstall them in their original locations.
35. Remove all the corner seals, corner seal springs, side seal and side seal springs from the rear side of the rotor. Mazda has a special tray which holds all the seals and keeps them segregated to prevent mistakes during reassembly. Each seal groove is marked to prevent confusion.
36. Remove the two rubber seals and two O-rings from the rear rotor housing.
37. Remove the dowels from the rear rotor housing.
38. Life the rear rotor housing away from the rear rotor, being very careful not to drop the apex seals on the rear rotor.
39. Remove each apex seal, side piece and spring from the rear rotor and segregate them.
40. Remove the rear rotor from the eccentric shaft and place it upside down on a clean rag.
41. Remove each seal and spring from the other side of the rotor and segregate these.
42. If some of the seals fall off the rotor, be careful not to change the original position of each seal.
43. Identify the rear rotor with a felt tip pen.
44. Remove the oil seals and the springs. Do not exert heavy pressure at only one place on the seal, since it could be deformed. Replace the O-rings in the oil seal when the engine is overhauled.
45. Hold the intermedidate housing down and remove the dowels from it.
46. Lift off the intermediate housing being careful not to damage the eccentric shaft. It should be removed by sliding it beyond the rear rotor journal on the eccentric shaft while holding the intermediate housing up and, at the same time, pushing the eccentric shaft up.
47. Lift out the eccentric shaft.
48. Repeat the above procedures to remove the front rotor housing and front rotor.

ENGINE ASSEMBLY

1. Place the rotor on a rubber pad or cloth.
2. Install the oil seal rings in their respective grooves in the rotors with the edge of the spring in the stopper hole. The oil seal springs are painted cream or blue in color. The cream colored springs must be installed on the front faces of both rotors. The blue colored springs must be installed on the rear faces of both rotors. When installing each oil seal spring, the painted side (square side) of the spring must face upward (toward the oil seal).
3. Install a new O-ring in each groove. Place each oil seal in the groove so that the square edge of the spring fits in the stopper hole of the oil seal. Push the head of the oil seal slowly with the fingers, being careful that the seal is not deformed. Be sure that the oil seal moves smoothly in the groove before installing the O-ring.
4. Lubricate each oil seal and groove with engine oil and check the movement of the seal. It should move freely when the head of the seal is pressed.
5. Check the oil seal protrusion and

install the seals on the other side of each rotor.

6. Install the apex seals without springs and side pieces into their respective grooves so that each side piece positions on the side of each rotor.

7. Install the corner seal springs and corner seals into their respective grooves.

8. Install the side seal springs and side seals into their respective grooves.

9. Apply engine oil to each spring and check each spring for smooth movement.

10. Check each seal protrusion.

11. Invert the rotor being careful that the seals do not fall out, and install the oil seals on the other side in the same manner.

12. Mount the front housing on a workstand so that the top of the housing is up.

13. Lubricate the internal gear of the rotor with engine oil.

14. Hold the apex seals with used O-rings to keep the apex seals installed and place the rotor on the front housing. Be careful not to drop the seals. Turn the front housing so that the sliding surface faces upward.

15. Mesh the internal and stationary gears and remove the old O-ring which is holding the apex seals in position.

16. Lubricate the front rotor journal of the eccentric shaft with engine oil and lubricate the eccentric shaft main journal.

17. Insert the eccentric shaft. Be careful that you do not damage the rotor bearing and main bearing.

18. Apply sealing agent to the front side of the front rotor housing.

19. Apply a light coat of petroleum jelly onto new O-rings and rubber seals (to prevent them from coming off) and install the O-rings and rubber seals on the front side of the rotor housing.

NOTE: The inner rubber seal is of the square type. The wider white line of the rubber seal should face the combustion chamber and the rubber seal should be positioned as shown. Do not stretch the rubber seal.

20. If the engine is being overhauled, install the seal protector to only the inner rubber seal to improve durability.

21. Invert the front rotor housing, being careful not to let the rubber seals and O-rings fall from their grooves, and mount it on the front housing.

22. Lubricate the dowels with engine oil and insert them through the front rotor housing holes and into the front housing.

23. Apply sealer to the front side of the rotor housing.

24. Install new O-rings and rubber seals on the front rotor housing in the same manner as for the other side.

25. Insert each apex spring seal, making sure that the seal is installed in the proper direction.

26. Install each side piece in its original position and be sure that the springs seat on the side piece.

27. Lubricate the side pieces with engine oil. Make sure that the front rotor housing is free of foreign matter and lubricate the sliding surface of the front housing with engine oil.

28. Turn the front housing assembly with the rotor, so that the top of the housing is up. Pull the eccentric shaft about 1 in.

29. Position the eccentric portion of the eccentric shaft diagonally, to the upper right.

30. Install the intermediate housing over the eccentric shaft onto the front rotor housing. Turn the engine so that the rear of the engine is up.

31. Install the rear rotor and rear rotor housing following the same steps as for the front rotor and the front housing.

32. Turn the engine so that the rear of the engine is up.

33. Lubricate the stationary gear and main bearing.

34. Install the rear housing onto the rear rotor housing. If necessary, turn the rear rotor slightly to mesh the rear housing stationary gear with the rear rotor internal gear.

35. Install a new washer on each tension bolt, and lubricate each bolt with engine oil.

36. Install the tension bolts and tighten them evenly, in several stages in sequence. The specified torque is 23-27 ft lbs.

37. After tightening the bolts, turn the eccentric shaft to be sure that the shaft and rotors turn smoothly and easily.

38. Lubricate the oil seal in the rear housing.

39. On vehicles with manual transmission, install the flywheel on the rear of the eccentric shaft so that the keyway of the flywheel fits the key on the shaft.

40. Apply sealer to both sides of the flywheel lockwasher and install the lockwasher.

41. Install the flywheel locknut. Hold the flywheel *securely* and tighten the nut to *three hundred and fifty ft lbs* (350 ft lbs) of torque.

NOTE: 350 ft lbs is a great deal of torque. In actual practice, it is practically impossible to accurately measure that much torque on the nut. At least a 3 ft bar will be required to generate sufficient torque. Tighten it as tight as possible, with no longer than 3 ft of leverage. Be sure the engine is held SECURELY.

42. On vehicles with automatic transmission, install the key, counterweight, lockwasher and nut. Tighten the nut to 350 ft lbs. *See step 41 and the note following step 41.* Install the drive plate on the counterweight and tighten the attaching nuts.

43. Turn the engine so that the front faces up.

44. Install the thrust plate with the tapered face down, and install the needle bearing on the eccentric shaft. Lubricate with engine oil.

45. Install the bearing housing on the front housing. Tighten the bolts and bend up the lockwasher tabs.

The spacer should be installed so that the center of the needle bearing comes to the center of the eccentric shaft and the spacer should be seated on the thrust plate.

46. Install the needle bearing on the shaft and lubricate it with engine oil.

47. Install the balancer and thrust washer on the eccentric shaft.

48. Install the oil pump drive chain over both of the sprockets. Install the sprocket and chain assembly over the eccentric shaft and oil pump shafts simultaneously. Install the key on the eccentric shaft.

NOTE:Be sure that both of the sprockets are engaged with the chain before installing them over the shafts.

49. Install the distributor drive gear onto the eccentric shaft with the "F" mark on the gear facing the front of the engine. Slide the spacer and oil slinger onto the eccentric shaft.

50. Align the keyway and install the eccentric shaft pulley. Tighten the pulley bolt to 60 ft lbs.

51. Turn the engine top so the engine faces up.

52. Check eccentric shaft end-play in the following manner:

a. Attach a dial indicator to the flywheel. Move the flywheel forward and backward.

b. Note the reading on the dial indicator; it should be 0.0016–0.0028 in.

c. If the end-play is not within specifications, adjust it by replacing the front spacer. Spacers come in four sizes, ranging from 0.3150–0.3181 in. If necessary, a spacer can be ground on a surface plate with emery paper.

d. Check the end-play again and, if it is now within specifications, proceed with the next step.

ECCENTRIC SHAFT SPACER THICKNESS CHART

Marking	Thickness
X	8.08 ± 0.01 mm (0.3181 ± 0.0004 in)
Y	8.04 ± 0.01 mm (0.3165 ± 0.0004 in)
V	8.02 ± 0.01 mm (0.3158 ± 0.0004 in)
Z	.800 ± 0.01 mm (0.3150 ± 0.0004 in)

53. Remove the pulley from the front of the eccentric shaft. Tighten the oil pump drive sprocket nut and bend the locktabs on the lockwasher.

54. Fit a new O-ring over the front cover oil passage.
55. Install the chain tensioner and tighten its securing bolts.
56. Position the front cover gasket and the front cover on the front housing, then secure the front cover with its attachment bolts.
57. Install the eccentric shaft pulley again. Tighten its bolt to 60 ft lbs.
58. Turn the engine so that the bottom faces up.
59. Cut off the excess gasket on the front cover along the mounting surface of the oil pan.
60. Install the oil strainer gasket and strainer on the front housing and tighten the attaching bolts.
61. Apply sealer to the joint surfaces of each housing.
62. Install the gasket and oil pan. Tighten the bolts evenly in two stages to 3.5 ft lbs.
63. Turn the engine so that the top is up.
64. Install the water pump and gasket on the front housing. Tighten the attaching bolts.
65. Rotate the eccentric shaft until the yellow mark (leading side mark) aligns with the pointer on the front cover.
66. Align the marks on the distributor gear and housing and install the distributor so that the lockbolt is in the center of the slot.
67. Rotate the distributor until the leading points start to separate and tighten the distributor locknut.
68. Install the gaskets and thermal reactor and tighten the attaching nuts.
69. Install the hot air duct.
70. Install the carburetor and intake manifold assembly with a new gasket. Tighten the attaching nuts.
71. Connect the oil tubes, vacuum tube and metering oil pump connecting rod to the carburetor.
72. Install the decel valve and connect the vacuum lines, air hoses and wires.
73. Install the alternator bracket, alternator and bolt and check the clearance. If the clearance is more than 0.006 in., adjust the clearance using a shim. Shims are available in three sizes: 0.0059 in., 0.0118 in., and 0.0197 in.
74. Install the alternator drive belt. Attach the alternator to the adjusting brace and adjust the belt tension to specification.
75. Install the air pump with the adjusting brace and install the air pump drive belt. Adjust the air pump drive belt to specifications.
76. Install the engine hanger bracket to the front cover.
77. Remove the engine from the stand.
78. Install the engine in the vehicle.
79. Fill the engine with fresh engine oil and install a new filter. Fill the engine with coolant. Start the engine, check the oil pressure, and warm it to normal operating temperature. Adjust the idle speed, timing and dwell. Recheck all capacities and refill if necessary. Check for leaks.

Intake Manifold

REMOVAL AND INSTALLATION

To remove the intake manifold and carburetor assembly with the engine remaining in the automobile, proceed in the following manner:

1. Perform steps 2, 3, 4, 5, 7, and 13 of "Engine Removal and Installation", above. Do no remove the engine. Do not drain the engine oil; merely remove the metering oil pump hose from the carburetor.
2. Perform steps 6 and 7 of the "Engine Disassembly" procedure.

Install the intake manifold and carburetor assembly in the reverse order of removal. Tighten the manifold securing nuts, working from the inside out, and in two or three stages, to the torque specifications found in the "Torque Specifications" chart. Refill the cooling system.

Thermal Reactor

REMOVAL AND INSTALLATION

CAUTION: The thermal reactor operates at extremely high temperatures. Allow the engine to cool completely before attempting to remove it.

To remove the thermal reactor, which replaces the exhaust manifold, proceed in the following manner:

1. Remove the air cleaner assembly from the carburetor.
2. Unbolt and remove the air injection pump as outlined in "Emission Controls."
3. Remove the intake manifold assembly, complete with carburetor.
4. Remove the heat stove from the thermal reactor.
5. Unfasten the thermal reactor securing nuts, including those on the exhaust pipe flange.

Measure the clearance between the rotors with a feeler gauge
(© Toyo Kogyo Co. Ltd.)

NOTE: The bottom nut is difficult to reach. Mazda makes a special wrench (part number 49 213 001) to remove it. If the wrench is unavailable, a flexible drive metric socket wrench may be substituted.

6. Lift the thermal reactor away from the engine.

Installation of the thermal reactor is performed in the reverse order of removal.

ENGINE LUBRICATION

Rotary

A conventional pump, which is chain driven, circulates oil through the rotary engine. A full-flow filter is mounted on the top of the rear housing and an oil cooler is used to reduce the temperature of the engine oil.

An unusual feature of the rotary engine lubrication system is a metering oil pump which injects oil into the float chamber of the carburetor. Once there, it is mixed with the fuel which is to be burned, thus providing extra lubrication for the seals. The metering oil pump is designed to work only when the engine is working under a load.

Oil Pan

REMOVAL AND INSTALLATION

1. Raise the front of the car and support it with jackstands.

CAUTION: Be sure that the car is supported securely.

2. Remove the drain plug and drain the engine oil.
3. Remove the nuts and bolts which secure the gravel shield and withdraw it from underneath the car.
4. Unfasten the retaining bolts and remove the oil pan with its gasket.

Oil pan installation is performed in the reverse order of removal. Coat both the oil pan flange and its mounting flange with sealer, prior to assembly.

Oil Pump

REMOVAL AND INSTALLATION

Oil pump removal and installation is contained in the engine overhaul section above. Perform only those steps needed to remove the oil pump.

CHECKING CLEARANCES

1. Separate the halves of the oil pump housing.
2. Measure the clearance between the lobes of the rotors with a feeler gauge.

Measure the gap between the straight edge and the housing
(© Toyo Kogyo Co. Ltd.)

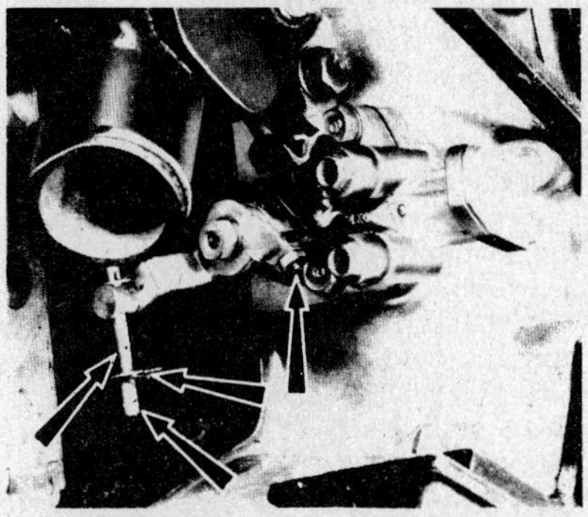

Arrow (right) indicates the metering oil pump adjusting screw. The three arrows (left) indicate the connecting rod adjusting holes
(© Toyo Kogyo Co. Ltd.)

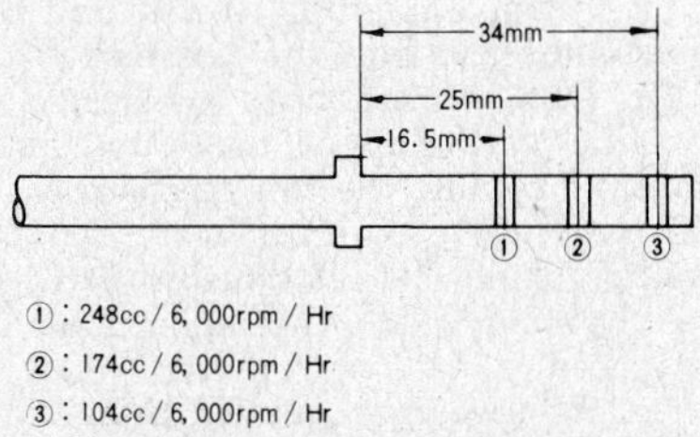

Connecting rod adjusting holes
(© Toyo Kogyo Co. Ltd.)

The clearance should be 0.0004–0.0035 in. Replace both of the rotors if the clearance exceeds 0.006 in.

3. Check the clearance between the outer rotor and the housing with a feeler gauge. The clearance should be 0.008–0.010 in. If the clearance is greater than 0.012 in., replace both of the rotors.

4. Place a straightedge across the pump housing. Measure the gap between the straightedge and the housing with a feeler gauge. The gap should be 0.001–0.005 in. If the gap exceeds 0.012 in., replace the rotors or the pump housing.

Metering Oil Pump

OPERATION

A metering oil pump, mounted on the top of the engine, is used to provide additional lubrication to the engine when it is operating under a load. The pump provides oil to the carburetor, where it is mixed in the float chamber with the fuel to be burned.

The metering pump is a plunger type and is controlled by throttle opening. A cam arrangement, connected to the carburetor throttle lever, operates a plunger. The plunger, in turn, acts on a differential plunger, the stroke of which determines the amount of oil flow.

When the throttle opening is small, the amount of the plunger stroke is small; as the throttle opening increases, so does the amount of the plunger stroke.

TESTING

1. At the carburetor, disconnect the oil lines which run from the metering oil pump to the carburetor.
2. Use a container which has a scale calibrated in cubic centimeters (cc) on its side to catch the pump discharge from the oil lines.
3. Run the engine at 2,000 rpm for six minutes.
4. At the end of this time, 2.0–2.5 should be collected in the container. If not, adjust the pump as explained below.

ADJUSTMENTS

Rotate the adjusting screw on the metering oil pump to obtain the proper oil flow. Clockwise rotation of the screw *increases* the flow; counterclockwise rotation *decreases* the flow.

If necessary, the oil discharge rate may be further adjusted by changing the position of the cam in the pump connecting rod. The shorter the rod throw, the more oil will be pumped. Adjust the throw by means of the three holes provided.

Oil Cooler

REMOVAL AND INSTALLATION

1. Raise the car and support it with jackstands.

*CAUTION: **Be sure that the car is securely supported.***

2. Drain the engine oil.
3. Unfasten the screws which retain the gravel shield and remove the shield.
4. Unfasten the oil lines from the oil cooler.
5. Unfasten the nuts which secure the oil cooler to the radiator.
6. Remove the oil cooler.

Examine the oil cooler for signs of leakage. Blow the cooler fins clean with compressed air. Later models coolers are made from aluminum; they must be repaired by aluminum welding.

Installation is performed in the reverse order of removal.

ENGINE COOLING

Rotary

RADIATOR REMOVAL AND INSTALLATION

*CAUTION: **Perform this operation when the engine has cooled completely.***

1. Drain the engine coolant into a large, clean container so that it may be reused.
2. Remove the nuts and bolts which attach the shroud to the radiator. Withdraw the shroud.
3. Remove the upper, lower, and expansion tank hoses from the radiator.
4. Unfasten the bolts which attach the radiator to its mounting bracket. Remove the oil cooler nuts and bolts.
5. Withdraw the radiator from the car.

Install the radiator in the reverse order of removal.

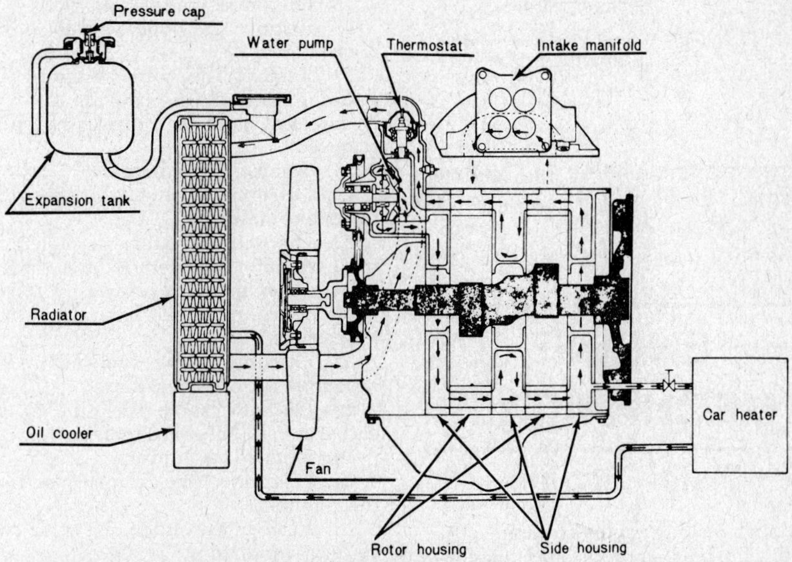

Rotary engine cooling system (© Toyo Kogyo Co. Ltd.)

Water Pump

REMOVAL AND INSTALLATION

1. Drain the cooling system.
2. Remove the air cleaner.
3. Remove the bolts attaching the rear of the fan drive and remove the fan drive.
4. If necessary to disassemble the water pump, loosen the bolts attaching the water pump pulley to the water pump boss.
5. Remove the air pump and drive belt.
6. Remove the alternator and disconnect the drive belt.
7. If necessary, remove the water pump pulley and bolts.
8. Unbolt and remove the water pump.
9. Installation is the reverse of removal.

Thermostat

REMOVAL AND INSTALLATION

1. Drain the engine coolant into a large, clean container for reuse.
2. Remove the nuts which secure the thermostat housing to the water pump.
3. Lift out the thermostat.

Thermostat installation is performed in the reverse order of removal.

CAUTION: The thermostat is equipped with a plunger which covers and uncovers a by-pass hole at its bottom. Because of this unusual construction, only the specified Mazda thermostat should be used for replacement. A standard thermostat will cause the engine to overheat.

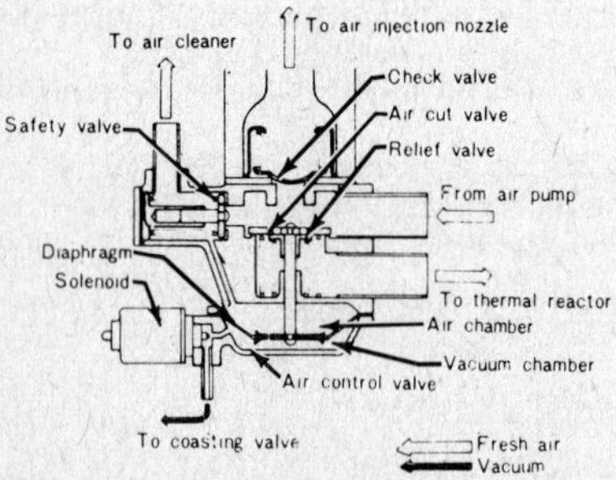

Thermostat installation and by-pass circuit
(© Toyo Kogyo Co. Ltd.)

ENGINE MECHANICAL

Piston Engine

Mazda piston engines are single overhead camshaft, four-cylinder engines. Water cools the thin cast iron block and cast aluminum alloy cylinder head with multi-spherical type combustion chambers.

The camshaft bearing caps are machined with the cylinder head and are not interchangeable. The cylinder head bolts also retain the camshaft bearing caps and the rocker arm shaft supports.

Exhaust valves are free rotating to prevent uneven valve wear. Intake rocker arm shafts are a two-piece unit, while the exhaust rocker arm shafts are single piece units.

The timing chain is a dual cog type encircling the crankshaft and camshaft sprockets. The crankshaft sprocket also holds the rotor type oil pump drive chain.

REMOVAL AND INSTALLATION

The engine is removed through the engine compartment, leaving the transmission in place.

1. Scribe the locations of the hood hinges and remove the hood.
2. Remove the engine splash shield.
3. Drain the coolant.
4. Drain the engine oil.
5. Disconnect and remove the battery.
6. Disconnect the primary wire and coil wire from the distributor.
7. Disconnect the wire at the "B" terminal of the alternator and disconnect the plug from the rear of the alternator.
8. Disconnect the wire from the oil pressure switch.
9. Disconnect the engine ground wire.
10. Remove the air cleaner and heat insulator.
11. Disconnect the breather hose from the rocker cover.
12. Disconnect the water temperature gauge wire and solenoid valve wire.
13. Disconnect the coupler for the back-up light switch.
14. Disconnect the vacuum tubes at the intake manifold and the carburetor.
15. Disconnect the starter wires.
16. Remove the upper and lower radiator hoses.
17. Remove the bolts attaching the radiator cowling. The cowling can only be removed after the radiator has been removed.
18. Remove the radiator.
19. Disconnect the heater hoses from the intake manifold.
20. Disconnect the throttle cable from the carburetor and remove the throttle linkage from the rocker cover.
21. Disconnect the choke cable from the carburetor.
22. Disconnect the fuel ventilation hose from the oil separator.
23. Disconnect the fuel line at the carburetor and plug the fuel line.
24. Remove the starter.
25. Disconnect the exhaust pipe from the manifold.
26. Remove the clutch or torque converter cover plate.
27. Support the transmission with a jack and remove the bolts attaching the engine to the transmission.
28. Unbolt the engine mounts.
29. Attach a lifting sling to the engine and pull the engine forward until it clears the transmission shaft.
30. Lift the engine from the vehicle.
31. Installation is the reverse of removal. Be sure to check all fluid levels.

Cylinder Head

REMOVAL AND INSTALLATION

Be sure that the cylinder head is cold before removal. This will prevent warpage.

1. Drain the cooling system. Disconnect the negative battery cable.
2. Scribe alignment marks around the hood hinges and remove the hood.
3. Remove the air cleaner.
4. Disconnect the coil wire and vacuum line from the distributor.
5. Rotate the crankshaft to put the No. 1 cylinder at TDC on the compression stroke.
6. Remove the plug wires and distributor cap as a unit.
7. Remove the distributor.
8. Remove the rocker arm cover.
9. Disconnect the exhaust pipe from the manifold.
10. Remove the accelerator linkage.
11. Remove the nut, washer and the distributor gear from the camshaft.
12. Remove the nut, washer, and camshaft gear. Support the timing chain from falling into the timing chain case. Do not remove the cam gear from the timing chain. The relationship between the chain and gear teeth should not be disturbed.
13. Remove the cylinder head bolts and cylinder head-to-front cover bolt.
14. Remove the rocker arm assembly.
15. Remove the camshaft from the camshaft gear.
16. Lift off the cylinder head.
17. Remove all tension from the timing chain.

To install the cylinder head:

18. Clean the rocker cover gasket surface at the head and the cover. Clean the head gasket surface at the head and the block. Clean the water pump gasket surface at the head gasket surface and the front cover.
19. Check the cylinder head flatness with a straightedge and feeler blades. It should not exceed 0.003 in. in any six in. span or 0.006 in. overall. If necessary, the cylinder head can be resurfaced, not to exceed 0.008 in.
20. Clean the cylinder head bolt holes of oil and dirt.
21. Position a new head gasket on the cylinder block.
22. Install the cylinder head on the block using the guides at either end of the block.
23. Install the camshaft on the head and camshaft gear.

24. Install the rocker arm assembly.
25. Install the head bolts. Torque the bolts to specifications in three progressive stages, in the sequence illustrated at the front of this section.
26. Install the camshaft gear washer and nut.
27. Install the distributor gear, washer and nut.
28. Time the engine. Follow the instructions under "Timing Chain and Sprocket Installation."
29. Adjust the timing chain tension. See "Timing Chain Tensioner Adjustment".
30. Connect the exhaust pipe to the exhaust manifold.
31. Install the distributor, distributor cap and plug wires.
32. Install the lower intake bracket bolt.
33. Install the accelerator linkage.
34. Connect the vacuum line and coil wire.
35. Adjust the valve clearance cold.
36. Install the rocker arm cover. Fill the cooling system.
37. Run the engine until normal operating temperature is reached, and check for leaks. Adjust the valve clearance hot.
38. Adjust the carburetor and ignition timing. Install the air cleaner and install the hood.

VALVE GUIDE REMOVAL AND INSTALLATION

Before attempting this, consult the "Engine Rebuilding" section for general procedures that will apply.

1. Remove the cylinder head.
2. Remove the deposits from the combustion chambers with a stiff wire brush and scraper before removing the valves. Do not scratch the cylinder head surface.

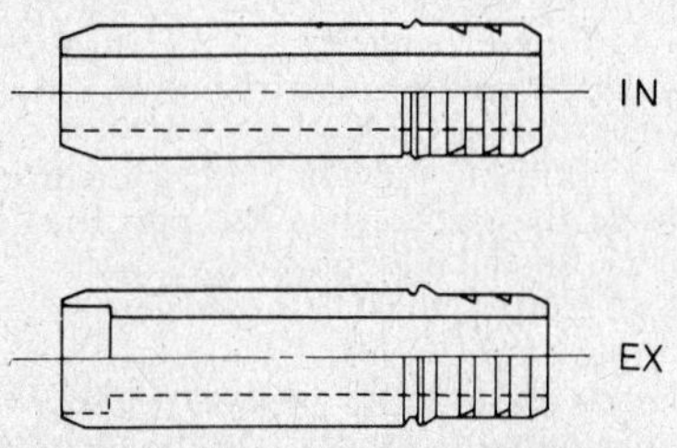

Intake (IN) and exhaust (EX) valve guides (© Toyo Kogyo Co. Ltd.)

3. Compress the valve springs with a valve spring compressor. Remove the valve spring retainer locks and release the springs.
4. Keep the exhaust and intake valve retainers separate. They should be reassembled to the valve from which they were removed.
5. Remove the spring retainer, springs and valve.
6. Remove the valve stem seals. Identify all parts so that they can be reinstalled in their original locations.
7. Drive out the valve guides.
8. Check the cylinder head flatness as described under "Cylinder Head Removal and Installation."

Assemble the cylinder head using new parts where applicable:

a. Lubricate all valves, valve stems, and valve guides with heavy-duty oil (SE). The valve tips should be lubricated with Lubriplate or the equivalent. Apply this before installation.
b. Press new valve guides into each bore until the ring on the guide touches the cylinder head. Note that the intake and exhaust valve guides are different.
c. Install new valve seals on the valve guides.
d. Install each valve into the valve from which it was removed or fitted.
e. Install the valve springs over the valve. Install the spring retainer.
f. Compress the springs and install the retainer locks. Be sure that the exhaust and intake locks are assembled to the correct valves.

9. Install the cylinder head. See "Cylinder Head Installation." Adjust the valves (hot) and set the timing and carburetor.

Rocker Shafts

REMOVAL AND INSTALLATION

This operation should only be performed on a cold engine; the bolts which hold the rocker shafts in place also hold the cylinder head to the block.

1. Raise the hood and cover the fenders.
2. Disconnect the choke cable.
3. If equipped, disconnect the air by-pass valve cable.
4. Disconnect the spark plug wires. Remove the wires from the spark wire guides on the rocker covers and position them out of the way.
5. Remove the rocker cover and discard the gasket.
6. Remove the rocker arm shaft attaching bolts evenly and remove the rocker arm shafts.

To install the rocker shafts: Install the rocker arm assemblies on the cylinder head. Temporarily tighten the cylinder head bolts to specifications and offset each rocker arm support 0.04 in. from the valve stem center. Torque the bolts to specifications.

7. Adjust the valves cold.
8. Clean the mating surfaces of the cylinder head and rocker cover.
9. Install the rocker cover with a new gasket.
10. Install the spark plug wires on the plugs. Place the wires in the clips on the rocker cover. Connect the choke and air by-pass valve cable.
11. Start the engine and check for leaks.
12. Allow the engine to reach operating temperature, torque the head bolts to specifications and adjust the valves hot.

Intake Manifold

REMOVAL AND INSTALLATION

1. Drain the cooling system.
2. Remove the air cleaner.
3. Remove the accelerator linkage.
4. Disconnect the choke cable and fuel line. Plug the fuel line.
5. Disconnect the PCV valve hose.
6. Disconnect the heater return hose and by-pass hose.
7. Disconnect and label any attaching vacuum lines.
8. Remove the intake manifold-to-cylinder head attaching nuts.
9. Remove the manifold and carburetor as an assembly.
10. Installation is the reverse of removal.

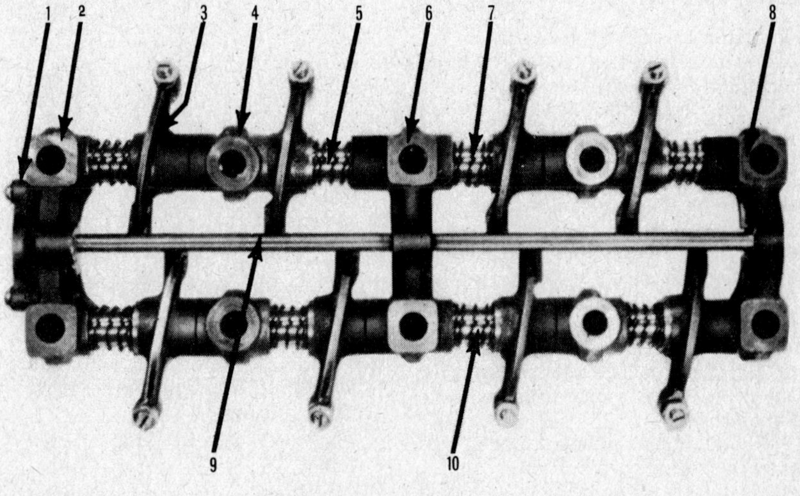

1. Thrust plate
2. Front bearing cap
3. Rocker arm (exhaust)
4. Support
5. Rocker arm shaft (exhaust)
6. Center bearing cap
7. Spring
8. Rear bearing cap
9. Oil pipe
10. Rocker arm shaft (intake)

Rocker arm assembly—piston engine

Exhaust Manifold

REMOVAL AND INSTALLATION

1. Raise and support the vehicle.
2. Remove the two attaching nuts from the exhaust pipe at the manifold.
3. Remove the air pump air injection hose from the check valve or air injection manifold, if equipped. Remove the heat stove and hot air tube to the air cleaner, if equipped.
4. Disconnect the EGR pipe, if so equipped.
5. Remove the exhaust pipe hanger from the bracket on the transmission, if so equipped.
6. Remove the manifold attaching nuts.
7. Remove the manifold.
8. Installation is the reverse of removal.

Front Cover

REMOVAL AND INSTALLATION

1. Drain the cooling system.
2. Disconnect the upper and lower radiator hoses. Remove the radiator.
3. Remove the accessory drive belts.
4. Remove the crankshaft pulley and the water pump.
5. Remove the cylinder head-to-front cover bolt.
6. Drain the oil from the engine.
7. Remove the oil pan-to-front cover bolts.
8. Remove the alternator and bracket and lay the alternator aside.
9. Remove the front cover.
10. Installation is the reverse.

Front Cover Oil Seal

REMOVAL AND INSTALLATION

The front cover oil seal can be removed and a new one installed without removing the front cover.

1. Drain the cooling system.
2. Disconnect the upper and lower radiator hoses and remove the radiator.
3. Remove the drive belt(s).
4. Remove the crankshaft pulley.
5. Pry the front oil seal from the front cover using a wooden or plastic tool to avoid damage to the seal mating surfaces.

To install a new oil seal:

6. Clean the pulley and seal area.
7. Oil the lip of the new seal and the front cover. Press a new front seal into position (flush).
8. Install the crankshaft pulley and torque the bolt to specifications.
9. Install the drive belt(s) and adjust the tension.
10. Install the radiator and connect the upper and lower hoses. Fill the cooling system. Start the engine and check for leaks.

Timing Chain and Tensioner

REMOVAL AND INSTALLATION

1. Remove the cylinder head and front cover. It is not necessary that the intake and exhaust manifolds be removed from the head.
2. Remove the oil pump and chain.
3. Remove the timing chain tensioner.
4. Loosen the timing chain guide strip screws.
5. Remove the oil slinger.
6. Remove the oil pump gear and chain as an assembly.
7. Remove the timing chain, crankshaft gear and camshaft gears from the engine.

To install the timing chain, timing gears and tensioner:

8. Position the crankshaft gear in the timing chain.
9. Position the oil pump chain and gear on the crankshaft and oil pump. Check the oil pump drive chain slack. It should be 0.15 in. Adjusting shims (between the oil pump body and cylinder block) are available in thickness of 0.006 in.
10. Install the oil slinger.
11. Install the oil pump washer and nut. Bend the washer over the nut.
12. Install the timing chain tensioner. Fully compress the snubber spring and wedge a screwdriver into the tensioner release mechanism. Without removing the screwdriver, install the tensioner.

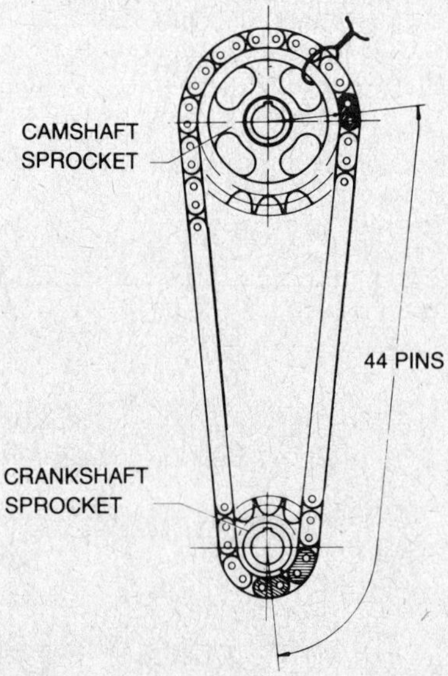

Installing timing chain—1800 and 2000 engines
(© Toyo Kogyo Co. Ltd.)

13. Install the cylinder head and camshaft. Be sure that the valve timing is as illustrated. It must be exact. You may have to move the cam gear one or two teeth to obtain the correct alignment.

Align the bright links and the marks on the 1600 engine
(© Toyo Kogyo Co. Ltd.)

14. Install the rocker arm shafts and cam bearing caps.
15. Install and torque the cylinder head bolts.
16. Adjust the timing chain tension. Press in on the chain guide strip. Tighten the guide strip attaching screws. Remove the screwdriver from the tensioner, allowing the snubber to take up the chain slack.
17. Replace the front cover.
18. Adjust the valve clearance cold. Run the engine. Torque the cylinder head bolts and adjust the valve clearance hot.

Timing Chain Tensioner

REMOVAL AND INSTALLATION

1. Remove the water pump.
2. Remove the tensioner cover.
3. Remove the attaching bolts from the tensioner. Remove the tensioner.

To install the tensioner:

4. Fully compress the snubber spring. Insert a screwdriver into the tensioner release mechanism.
5. Without removing the screwdriver, insert the tensioner and align the bolt holes. Install and torque the bolts.
6. Adjust the chain tension as follows:
   a. Remove the two blind plugs and aluminum washers from the front cover.
   b. Loosen the guide strip attaching screws.
   c. Press the top of the chain guide strip through the adjusting hole in the cylinder head.
   d. Torque the guide strip screws.
   e. Remove the screwdriver from the tensioner and let the snubber take up the slack in the chain.
   f. Install the blind plugs and aluminum washers.
   g. Install the tensioner cover and gasket.
   h. Install a new gasket and water pump. Install the crankshaft pulley and drive belt and adjust the tension. Check the cooling system level.

TIMING CHAIN TENSIONER ADJUSTMENT

To adjust the tensioner, repeat the above procedure omitting Steps 2 and 3.

Camshaft

REMOVAL AND INSTALLATION

Perform this operation on a cold engine only.

1. Disconnect the coil wire and vacuum line from the distributor.
2. Rotate the crankshaft to place the No. 1 cylinder on TDC of the compression stroke. This can be determined by removing the spark plug and feeling compression with your thumb. When compression is felt, rotate the crankshaft until the pointer aligns with the TDC mark on the pulley.
3. Remove the plug wires and distributor cap. Remove the distributor.
4. Remove the valve cover.
5. Release the tension on the timing chain.
6. Remove the cylinder head bolts. Only do this on a *cold* engine.
7. Remove the rocker arm assembly.
8. Remove the nut, washer and distributor gear from the camshaft.
9. Remove the nut and washer holding the camshaft gear.
10. Remove the camshaft. Do not remove the camshaft gear from the timing chain. Be sure that the gear teeth and chain relationship is not disturbed. Wire the chain and cam gear to a place so that they will not fall into the front cover.

To install the camshaft:

11. Clean all the gasket surfaces.
12. Clean the cylinder head bolt holes.
13. Install the camshaft on the head and install the camshaft gear.
14. Check the valve timing.
15. Install the rocker arm assembly.
16. Install and torque the head bolts.
17. Install the cam gear washer and nut.
18. Install the distributor gear, washer and nut.
19. Adjust the timing chain tension.
20. Check the camshaft end-play. It should be 0.001–0.007 in. If it exceeds 0.008 in., replace the thrust plate with a new one.
21. Install the distributor, distributor cap and plug wires.
22. Connect the vacuum line and coil wire.
23. Adjust the valve clearance cold. Install the valve cover and fill the cooling system.
24. Run the engine and check for leaks. When normal operating temperature is reached, adjust the valve clearance hot.
25. Adjust the carburetor and ignition timing.

The "F" marks (arrow) face the front of the engine
(© Toyo Kogyo Co. Ltd.)

Piston and Connecting Rod Positioning

REMOVAL AND INSTALLATION

Refer to the "Engine Rebuilding" section for general engine service.

ENGINE LUBRICATION

Piston Engine Oil Pan

REMOVAL AND INSTALLATION

1. Raise and support the vehicle.
2. Remove the engine skid plate.
3. Drain the engine oil.
4. Remove the clutch release cylinder attaching nuts. Let the cylinder hang.
5. Remove the engine rear brace attaching bolts and loosen the bolts on the left side.
6. Disconnect the emission line from the oil pan.
7. Remove the oil pan nuts and bolts and let the oil pan rest on the crossmember.
8. Remove the oil pump pickup tube from the pump.
9. Remove the oil pan.
10. Installation is the reverse of removal.

Rear Main Oil Seal

REPLACEMENT

If the rear main oil seal is being replaced independently of any other parts, it can be done with the engine in place. If the rear main oil seal and the rear main bearing are being replaced, together, the engine must be removed from the vehicle.

1. Remove the transmission.
2. Remove the clutch disc, pressure plate and flywheel.
3. Using an awl, punch two holes in the crankshaft rear oil seal. They should be punched on opposite sides of the crankshaft, just above the bearing cap-to-cylinder block split line.
4. Install a sheet metal screw in each hole. Pry against both screws at the same time to remove the oil seal. Do not scratch the oil seal surface on the crankshaft.
5. Clean the oil recess in the cylinder block and bearing cap. Clean the oil seal surface on the crankshaft.
6. Coat the oil seal surfaces with oil. Coat the oil surface and the seal surface on the crankshaft with Lubriplate. Install the new oil seal and make sure that it is not cocked. Be sure that the seal surface was not damaged.
7. Install the flywheel. Coat the threads of the flywheel attaching bolts to specifications in sequence across from each other.

1. Oil strainer
2. O-ring
3. Adjusting shim
4. Body
5. Adjusting shim
6. O-ring
7. Outer rotor
8. Inner rotor

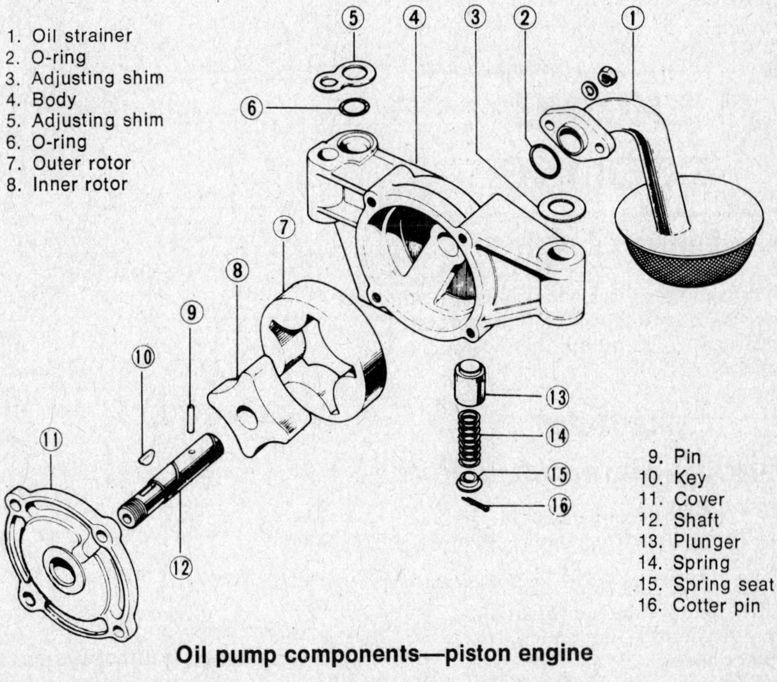

9. Pin
10. Key
11. Cover
12. Shaft
13. Plunger
14. Spring
15. Spring seat
16. Cotter pin

Oil pump components—piston engine

8. Install the clutch, pressure plate and transmission.

Oil Pump

CHECKING OIL PUMP

1. Measure the clearance between the lobes of the rotors with a feeler gauge. If the clearance exceeds 0.010 in., replace both rotors.
2. Check the clearance between the outer rotor and the pump body with a feeler gauge. Clearance should be 0.006–0.010 in. If it exceeds 0.012 in., replace the pump.
3. Place a straight-edge across the pump body and measure the clearance between the rotor and the straight-edge with a feeler gauge. Then, place a straight-edge across the pump cover and measure the clearance between the straight-edge and the cover. The combined clearances is the rotor end float. If it is 0.006 in. or more, correct it by grinding the cover. End float should be 0.002–0.004 in.

REMOVAL AND INSTALLATION

1. Remove the oil pan.
2. Remove the oil pump gear attaching nut.
3. Remove the bolts attaching the oil pump to the block. Loosen the gear on the pump.
4. Remove the oil pump gear.

To install the oil pump:

5. Install the oil pump gear in the chain.
6. Prime the oil pump and install it on the gear and cylinder block. Install the bolts and torque them to specifications.
7. Install the washer, gear and nut. Bend the locktab on the washer.
8. Install the oil pan. Fill the engine with oil. Start the engine and check for oil pressure. Check for leaks.

ENGINE COOLING

Piston Engine

The completely sealed cooling system consists of a radiator with pressure cap, centrifugal water pump, thermostat and a fan.

Radiator

REMOVAL AND INSTALLATION

1. Drain the cooling system.
2. If equipped, remove the fan shroud.
3. Remove the fan. On California models, remove the fan clutch.
4. Disconnect the upper and lower radiator hoses.
5. Disconnect and plug the automatic transmission cooler lines at the base of the radiator, if equipped.
6. Unbolt and remove the radiator.
7. Installation is the reverse of removal.

Water Pump

REMOVAL AND INSTALLATION

1. Drain the cooling system. Remove the fan shroud, if so equipped.
2. Remove the hoses from the water pump.
3. Remove the drive belts.
4. Remove the fan and pulley.
5. Unbolt and remove the water pump.
6. Installation is the reverse of removal. Use sealer or a new gasket upon assembly.

Thermostat

REMOVAL AND INSTALLATION

1. Drain enough coolant to bring the coolant level down below the thermostat housing. The thermostat housing is located on the left front side of the cylinder block. Disconnect the temperature sending unit wire.
2. Remove the coolant outlet elbow.
3. Remove the thermostat from the housing and note the position of the jiggle pin.
4. Install the thermostat with the jiggle pin up.
5. Installation is the reverse of removal. Use sealer or a new gasket upon assembly.

EMISSION CONTROLS

Rotary Engine

Positive Crankcase Ventilation (PCV) System

The positive crankcase ventilation valve (PCV) is located on the intake manifold below the carburetor. The PCV valve, which is operated by intake manifold vacuum, is used to meter the flow of air and fuel vapors through the rotor housing.

TESTING

1. Make sure that the air cleaner element is not clogged.
2. Connect a vacuum gauge into the line which runs between the PCV valve

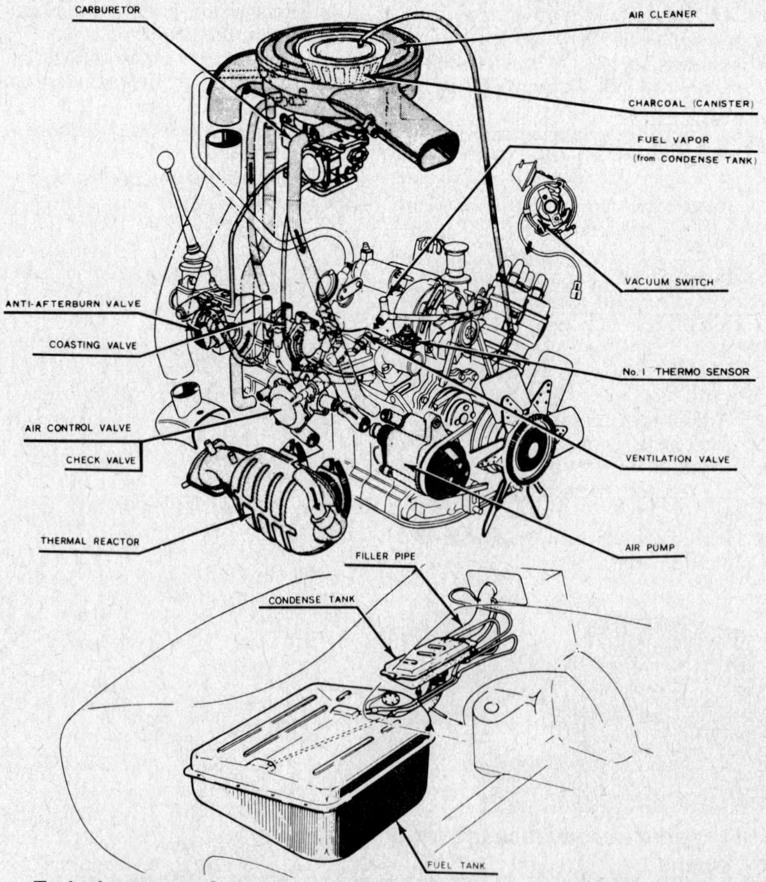

Emission control system components (© Toyo Kogyo Co. Ltd.)

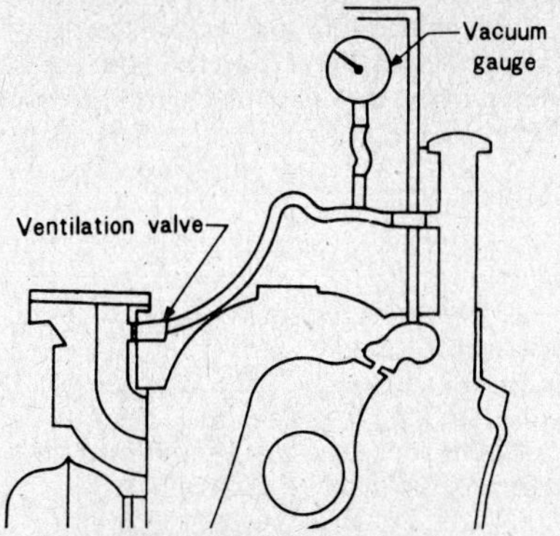

Testing the PCV valve
(© Toyo Kogyo Co. Ltd.)

and the oil filler tube, by means of a T-connector.

3. Increase the engine speed to 2,500–3,000 rpm. The vacuum reading should be below 2.4 in. Hg. If it is not, replace the PCV valve.

PCV VALVE REMOVAL AND INSTALLATION

1974

1. Remove the air cleaner assembly.
2. Remove the fuel return valve or the deceleration valve from the carburetor.

NOTE: It may be necessary to remove the starter motor.

3. Unfasten the distributor vacuum lines at the carburetor.
4. Disconnect the house from the PCV valve.
5. Use a flexible drive metric socket wrench to remove the valve from the intake manifold.

NOTE: If a flexible drive metric socket wrench is not available, the intake manifold must be removed in order to gain access to the PCV valve.

Installation of a new PCV valve is performed in the reverse order of removal.

1975 and Later

1. Remove the air cleaner.
2. Disconnect the hose at the PCV valve.
3. Unscrew the valve from the manifold.
4. Installation is reverse of removal.

Air Injection System

The air injection system used on the Mazda rotary engine differs from one used on a conventional piston engine in two respects:

1. Air is supplied not only to burn the gases in the exhaust ports, it is also used to cool the thermal reactor.

2. A three-way "air control valve" is used in place of the conventional anti-backfire and diverter valves. It contains an air cut-out valve, a relief valve, and a safety valve.

Air is supplied to the system by a normal vane-type air pump. The air flows from the pump to the air control valve where it is routed to the air injection nozzles, to cool the thermal reactor or, in case of a system malfunction, to the air cleaner. A check valve, located beneath the air control valve seat, prevents the back-flow of hot exhaust gases into the air injection system, in case of loss of air pressure.

Air injection nozzles are used to feed air into the exhaust ports, just as in a conventional piston engine.

COMPONENT TESTING

Air Pump

1. Check the air pump drive belt tension by applying 22 lbs of pressure halfway between the water pump and air pump pulleys. The belt should deflect 0.28–0.35 in. Adjust the belt, if necessary, or replace it if it is cracked or worn.

2. Turn the pump by hand. If it has seized, the drive belt will slip producing noise.

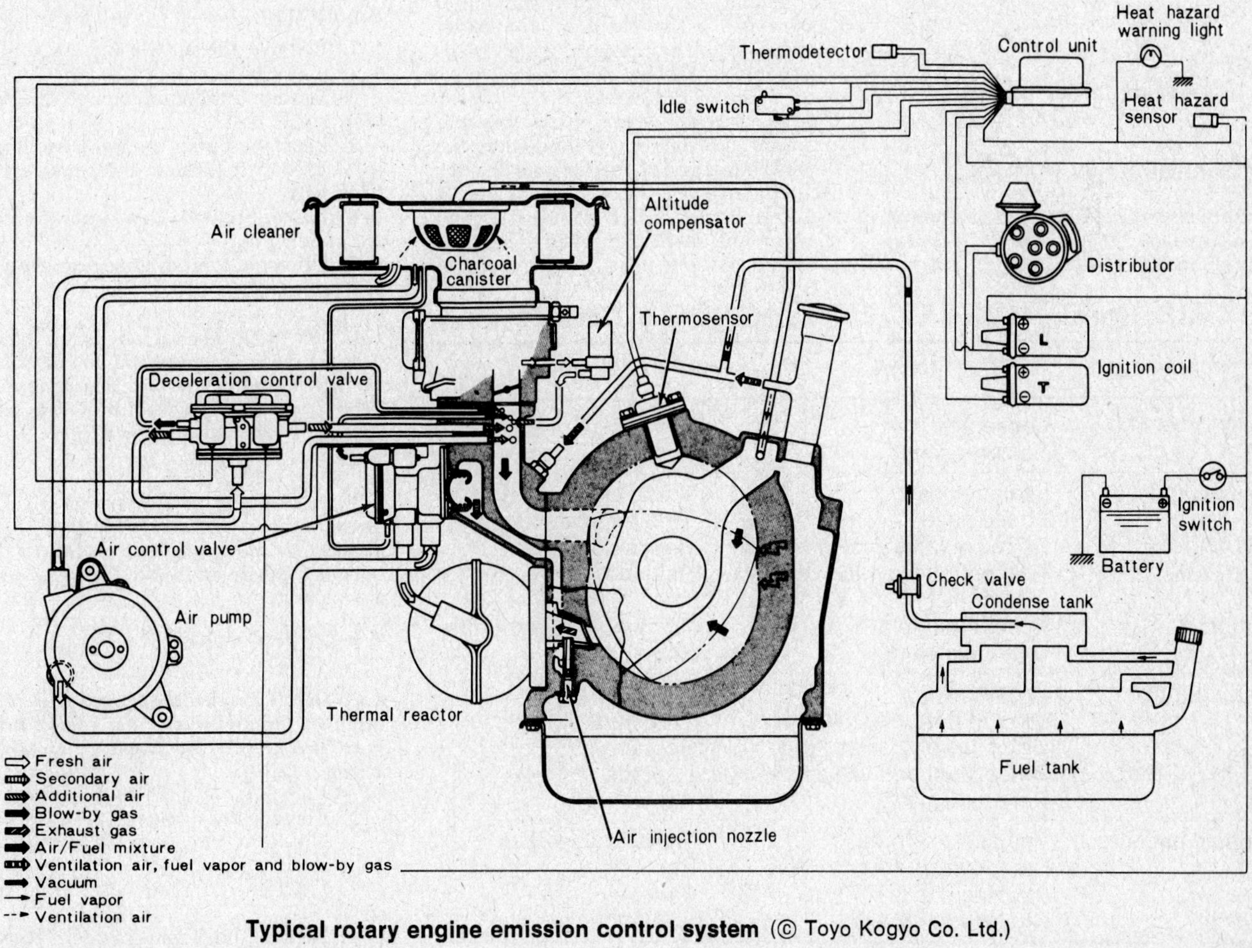

Typical rotary engine emission control system (© Toyo Kogyo Co. Ltd.)

NOTE: Disregard any chirping, squealing, or rolling sounds coming from inside of the pump; these are normal when it is being turned by hand.

3. Check the hoses and connections for leaks. Hissing or a blast of air is indicative of a leak. Soapy water, applied around the area in question, is a good method for detecting leaks.
4. Connect a pressure gauge between the air pump and the air control valve with a T-fitting.
5. Plug the other hose connections (outlets) on the air control valve.

CAUTION: Be careful not to touch the thermal reactor; severe burns will result.

6. With the engine at normal idle speed, the pressure gauge should read 0.48-0.68 psi for 1974-75 and more than 1.64 psi for 1976 and later. Replace the air pump if it is less than this.
7. If the air pump is not defective, leave the pressure gauge connected but unplug the two connections at the air control valve and proceed with the next test.

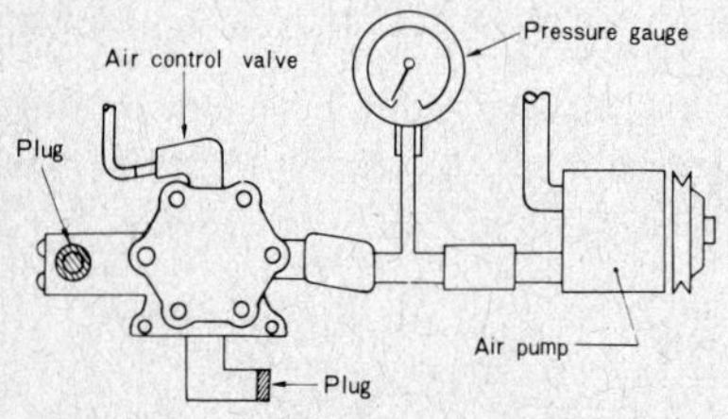

Testing the air pump
(© Toyo Kogyo Co. Ltd.)

Air Control Valve

CAUTION: When testing the air control valve, avoid touching the thermal reactor as severe burns will result.

1. Test the air control valve solenoid as follows:
   a. Turn the ignition switch off and on. A click should be heard coming from the solenoid. If no sound is audible, check the solenoid wiring.
   b. If no defect is found in the solenoid wiring, connect the solenoid directly to the truck's battery. If the solenoid still does not click, it is defective and must be replaced. If the solenoid is functioning, then check the components of the air flow control system, below.

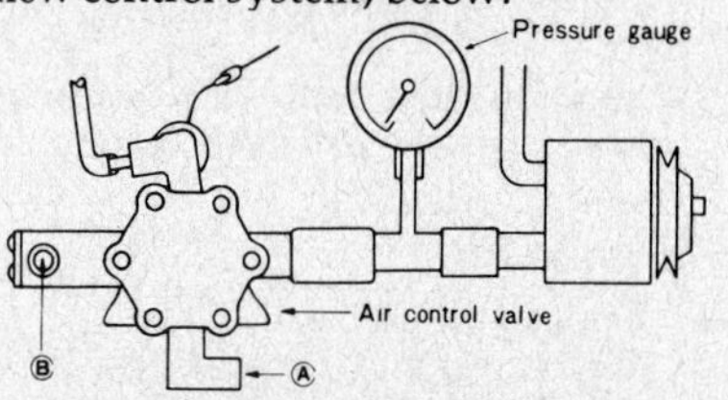

Testing the air control valve
(© Toyo Kogyo Co. Ltd.)

2. Start the engine and run it at idle speed. The pressure gauge should read 0.37-0.75 psi. No air should leak from the two outlets which were unplugged.
3. Increase the engine speed to 3,500 rpm (3,000—automatic transmission). The pressure gauge should now read 1,2-2.8 psi and the two outlets still should not be leaking air.
4. Return the engine to idle.
5. Disconnect the solenoid wiring. Air should not flow from the outlet marked "A", but not from the outlet marked "B". The pressure gauge reading should remain the same as in step 2.
6. Reconnect the solenoid.
7. If the relief valve is faulty, air sent from the air pump will flow into the cooling passages of the thermal reactor when the engine is at idle speed.
8. If the safety valve is faulty, air will flow into the air cleaner when the engine is idling.
9. Replace the air control valve if it fails to pass any one of the above tests. Remember to disconnect the pressure gauge.

Check Valve 1974

1. Remove the check valve as detailed below.
2. Depress the valve plate to see if it will seat properly.
3. Measure the free length of the valve spring; it should be 1.22 in.
4. Measure the installed length of the spring; it should be 0.68 in.

NOTE: The free length of the check valve spring should be 0.75 in. on models with automatic transmissions.

Replace the check valve if it is not up to specifications.

Check Valve 1975 and Later

1. Run engine at operating temperature.
2. Disconnect air house at air control valve.
3. Run engine at 1500 rpm. No exhaust leakage should be felt at the air inlet fitting of the air control valve.

COMPONENT REMOVAL AND INSTALLATION

Air Pump

1. Remove the air cleaner assembly from the carburetor.
2. Loosen, but do not remove, the adjusting link bolt.
3. Push the pump toward the engine to slacken belt tension and remove the drive belt.
4. Disconnect the air supply hoses from the pump.
5. Unfasten the pump securing bolts and remove the pump.

CAUTION: Do not pry on the air pump housing during removal and do not clamp the housing in a vise once the pump has been removed. Any type of heavy pressure applied to the housing will cause it to distort.

Installation is performed in the reverse order of removal. Adjust the belt tension by moving the air pump to the specification given in the "Testing" section, above.

Air Control Valve

CAUTION: Remove the control valve only after the thermal reactor has cooled sufficiently to prevent the danger of a serious burn.

1. Remove the air cleaner assembly.
2. Unfasten the leads from the air control valve solenoid.
3. Disconnect the air hoses from the valve.
4. Loosen the screws which secure

AIR INJECTION SYSTEM DIAGNOSIS CHART

Problem	Cause	Solution
Noisy drive belt	Loose belt	Tighten belt
	Seized pump	Replace
Noisy pump	Leaking hose	Trace and fix leak
	Loose hose	Tighten hose clamp
	Hose contacting other parts	Reposition hose
	Air control or check valve failure	Replace
	Pump mounting loose	Tighten securing bolts
	Defective pump	Replace
No air supply	Loose belt	Tighten belt
	Leak in hose or at fitting	Trace and fix leak
	Defective air control vave	Replace
	Defectve check valve	Replace
	Defective pump	Replace
Exhaust backfire	Vacuum or air leaks	Trace and fix leak
	Defective air control valve	Replace
	Sticking choke	Service choke
	Choke setting rich	Adjust choke

the air control valve and remove the valve.

Valve installation is performed in the reverse order of removal.

Check Valve

1. Perform the air control valve removal procedure, detailed above. Be sure to pay attention to the **CAUTION.**
2. Remove the check valve seat.
3. Withdraw the valve plate and spring. Install the check valve in the reverse order of removal.

Air Injection Nozzle

1. Remove the gravel shield from underneath the car.
2. Perform the oil pan removal procedure, as detailed in "Engine Lubrication", above.
3. Unbolt the air injection nozzles from both of the rotor housings.

Nozzle installation is performed in the reverse order of removal.

Thermal Reactor

A thermal reactor is used in place of a conventional exhaust manifold. It is used to oxidize unburned hydrocarbons and carbon monoxide before they can be released into the atmosphere.

If the engine speed exceeds 4,000 rpm, or if the car is decelerating, the air control valve diverts air into passages in the thermal reactor housing in order to cool the reactor.

A one-way valve prevents hot exhaust gases from flowing back into the air injection system. The valve is located at the reactor air intake.

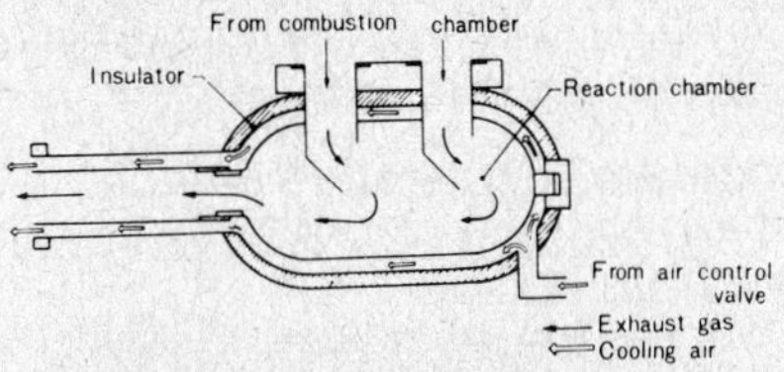

Thermal reactor cooling circuit
(© Toyo Kogyo Co. Ltd.)

INSPECTION

CAUTION: Perform thermal reactor inspection only after the reactor has cooled sufficiently to prevent severe burns.

1. Examine the reactor housing for cracks or other signs of damage.
2. Remove the air supply hose from the one-way valve. Insert a screwdriver into the valve and test the butterfly for smooth operation. Replace the valve if necessary.
3. If the valve is functioning properly, connect the hose to it again.

NOTE: Remember to check the components of the air injection system which are related to the thermal reactor.

REMOVAL AND INSTALLATION

Thermal reactor removal and installation procedures are given in the "Engine Mechanical" section.

Air Flow Control System

The control box is located beneath the dash, next to the fuse box and the thermodetector is behind the radiator grille.

COMPONENT TESTING

No. 1 Thermosensor

NOTE: Begin this test procedure with the engine cold.

1. Remove the air cleaner.
2. Examine the No. 1 thermosensor, which is located next to the thermostat housing, for leakage around the boot and for signs of wax leakage.
3. Disconnect the multiconnector from the thermosensor and place the prods of an ohmmeter on the thermosensor terminals.

The ohmmeter should read over 7 k-ohms with the engine cold and less than 2.3 k-ohms after the engine has been warmed up.

4. Replace the thermosensor with a new one, if the reading on the ohmmeter is not within specifications.
5. If the No. 1 thermosensor is functioning properly, proceed with the appropriate test for the thermodetector below.

Thermodetector

1. Unfasten the thermodetector connections.
2. Connect the test prods of an ohmmeter to the leads coming out of the thermodetector.
3. If the ohmmeter reading is below 200 k-ohms, the thermodetector is functioning satisfactorily.
4. Replace the thermodetector if it is defective and proceed with the vacuum switch if it is not.

Use the following chart to determine the correct ohmmeter reading for the ambient temperature at the time of the test.

THERMODETECTOR RESISTANCE SPECIFICATIONS

Ambient Temperature (°F)	Resistance (k-ohms ± 5%)
−4	10.0
+32	3.0
+68	1.2
+105	0.5

COMPONENT REMOVAL AND INSTALLATION

No. 1 Thermosensor

1. Remove the air cleaner assembly.

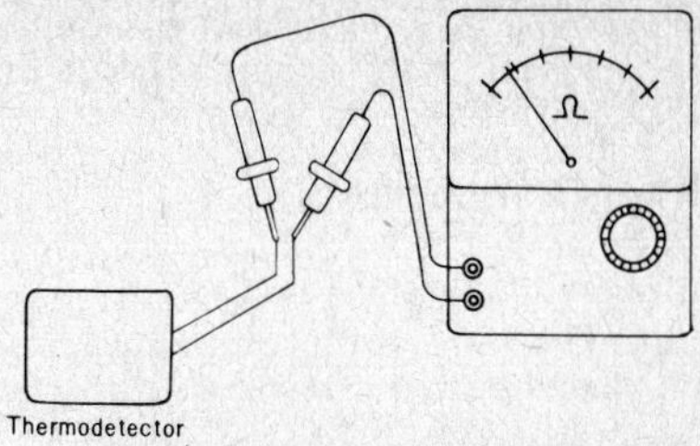

Testing the thermodetector
(© Toyo Kogyo Co. Ltd.)

2. If necessary, remove the starter motor as detailed under "Engine Electrical" or the deceleration control valve (see below).
3. Unplug the thermosensor multiconnector.
4. Withdraw the boot from the thermosensor.

Arrow indicates position of no. 1 thermosensor
(© Toyo Kogyo Co. Ltd.)

5. Unfasten its securing nuts and remove the thermosensor.

Installation is performed in the reverse order of removal.

Control Box

CAUTION: Be sure that the ignition switch is turned off to prevent damage to the control box.

1. Working from underneath the instrument panel, locate and disconnect the control box multiconnector.
2. Remove the screws which secure the control box.
3. Remove the control box.

Installation is performed in the reverse order of removal.

No. 2 Thermosensor

1. Drain the engine oil into a large, clean container for reuse.
2. Unfasten the connector from the No. 2 thermosensor.
3. Unscrew the thermosensor from the oil pan.

Installation is performed in the reverse order of removal.

No. 2 Control Box

The No. 2 control box is located in the luggage compartment next to the No. 1

control box. Its removal and installation are performed in the same manner as the No. 1 control box (see above).

Other Components

Any of the other components used in the air flow control system are removed by unfastening their multiconnectors and removing the screws which secure them.

Deceleration Control System

The deceleration control system uses an anti-afterburn valve, a coasting valve, and an air supply valve. In addition, an idle sensing switch is fitted to the carburetor. The No. 1 control box is shared with the air flow control system.

The anti-afterburn valve, which is located on the intake manifold, is used to supply frash air to the manifold during deceleration or when the engine is shut off, in order to prevent afterburning.

A coasting valve, which functions in a similar manner, is used to prevent an overly rich mixture during deceleration. The coasting valve also vents the vacuum chamber of the air control valve during deceleration. The valve is operated by a solenoid which is controlled by the No. 1 control box and the idle sensing switch.

An idle sensing switch is attached to the carburetor. When the throttle closes, its linkage contacts a plunger on the switch which completes the circuit from the No. 1 control box to the coasting valve thus causing the coasting valve to operate. On automatic transmission equipped models, it also determines trailing distributor operation.

A solenoid-operated air supply valve opens when the ignition is shut off to prevent the engine from dieseling (running on).

In addition to the above components, the truck is equipped with an altitude compensator which provides air to lean out the overly rich mixture that accrues at high altitudes.

On models with an automatic transmission, a kick-down control system is used. Regardless of the gear selected, the transmission will not go above second gear when the choke knob is pulled out.

COMPONENT TESTING

Anti-Afterburn Valve

1. Remove the air cleaner assembly.
2. Remove the hose from the air intake on the anti-afterburn valve.
3. With the engine idling, place your hand over the air intake. If a strong suction is felt, the valve is defective and should be replaced.
4. Increase the engine speed to 3,500–3,800 rpm. Release the throttle and allow it to snap shut. Air should be drawn in through the valve air intake for no longer than one second.
5. Keep the engine idling and disconnect the anti-afterburn valve solenoid wiring. Air should flow into the air intake while the solenoid is disconnected.

If the anti-afterburn valve fails to function properly, replace it with a new one. Remember to connect the air supply hose and the solenoid wiring after completing the test.

Combination Anti-Afterburn and Coasting Valve

1. Disconnect the hose which runs from the air cleaner to the combination valve at the air cleaner end.
2. Start the engine and run it at curb idle.
3. There should be no vacuum present at the end of the hose which you disconnected in step 1.
4. Turn the engine off.
5. Disconnect the hose which runs from the coasting valve portion of the combination valve to the intake manifold from the coasting valve end and plug up the port.
6. Operate the engine at idle.
7. Disconnect the anti-afterburn valve solenoid connector.
8. Check for vacuum at the end of the hose which you disconnected in step 1; there should be vacuum present. If not, the anti-afterburn valve is defective.
9. Turn the engine off. Reconnect the anti-afterburn valve electrical leads and the hose to the coasting valve.
10. Disconnect the intake manifold-to-anti-afterburn valve vacuum line at the valve end, and plug the vacuum fitting on the valve.
11. Start the engine and allow it to idle.
12. Disconnect the coasting valve solenoid at the multiconnector.
13. Hold your hand over the end of the vacuum line which you disconnected in step 10. Vacuum should be felt; if not, replace the defective coasting valve.
14. Turn the engine off and reconnect the leads and hoses that were disconnected above.

Altitude Compensator—1975

1. Detach the air intake hose from the altitude compensator.
2. Start the engine and run it at idle.
3. Hold your finger over the altitude compensator air intake; the engine speed should decrease. If it doesn't, replace the compensator.
4. Reconnect the air intake hose, if the compensator is in good working order.

Idle Switch

1. Unfasten the idle switch leads.
2. Connect a test meter to the switch terminals.
3. With the engine at idle, the meter should indicate a completed circuit.
4. Depress the plunger on the idle switch; the circuit should be broken (no meter reading).

If the idle switch is not functioning properly, replace it with a new one.

Coolant Temperature Switch

Start this test with the coolant temperature below 68°F.

1. Disconnect the electrical lead from the temperature switch.
2. Connect a test electrical lead from the temperature switch.
2. Connect a test light between one

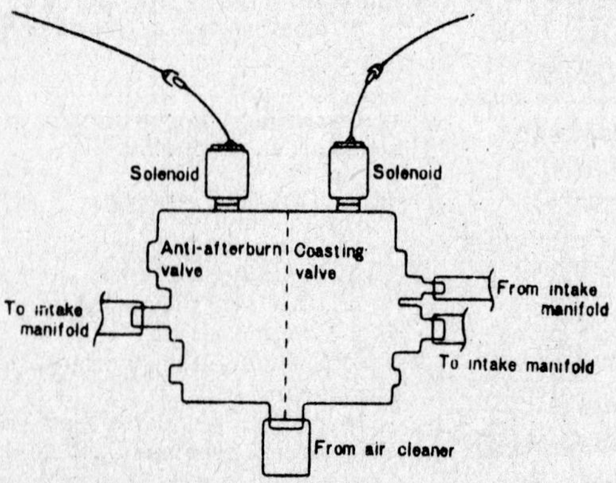

Combination anti-afterburn and coasting valve connections
(© Toyo Kogyo Co. Ltd.)

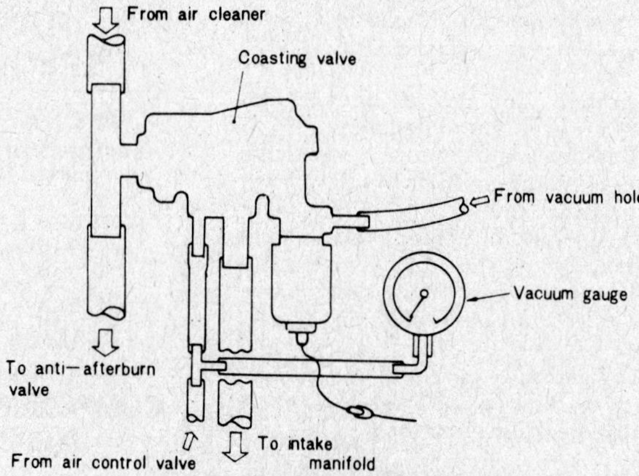

Testing the coasting valve
(© Toyo Kogyo Co. Ltd.)

terminal of the switch and a 12 volt battery. Ground the other terminal.
3. The test light should light.
4. Start the engine and allow it to warm up. Once the engine reaches normal operating temperature, the test light should go out.
5. Replace the switch if it doesn't work as outlined.

Choke Switch (Semi-Automatic Choke)

1. Working underneath the instrument panel, disconnect the lead at the back of the choke switch.
2. Connect a ohmmeter to the terminals on the choke switch side of the connector.
3. With the choke knob in (off), the meter should show continuity (resistance reading).
4. Pull the choke knob out, about 1/2 in. for manual transmission cars or 1 in. for automatics. The meter should show no continuity (read zero).
5. Replace the switch if defective.

COMPONENT REMOVAL AND INSTALLATION

Anti-Afterburn Valve

1. Remove the air cleaner assembly.
2. Disconnect the air hoses and vacuum lines from the valve.
3. Unfasten the solenoid wiring.

Arrow indicates the position of the anti-afterburn valve
(© Toyo Kogyo Co. Ltd.)

4. Remove the securing nuts and withdraw the valve.

Installation is performed in the reverse order of removal.

Arrow indicates the position of the coasting valve
(© Toyo Kogyo Co. Ltd.)

Coasting Valve

The coasting valve is removed and installed in the same manner as the anti-afterburn valve.

Idle Switch

1. Remove the coasting valve.
2. Remove the carburetor as detailed elsewhere, in this section.
3. Disconnect the wiring from the switch.
4. Unfasten the securing screws and remove the switch.

Installation is performed in the reverse order of removal. After installing the switch, adjust it as outlined under "Adjustments", below.

Idle switch position
(© Toyo Kogyo Co. Ltd.)

Air Supply Valve

1. Remove the air cleaner and the hot air duct.
2. Disconnect the air hose, the vacuum lines, and the solenoid wiring from the valve.
3. Unfasten the screws which secure the valve and remove it.

Air supply valve installation is performed in the reverse order of removal.

Altitude Compensator

1. Disconnect both hoses from the altitude compensator. Be sure to note their positions for correct hook-up.
2. Unfasten the altitude compensator securing bolts.
3. Remove the compensator from its bracket.

Installation is the reverse of removal.

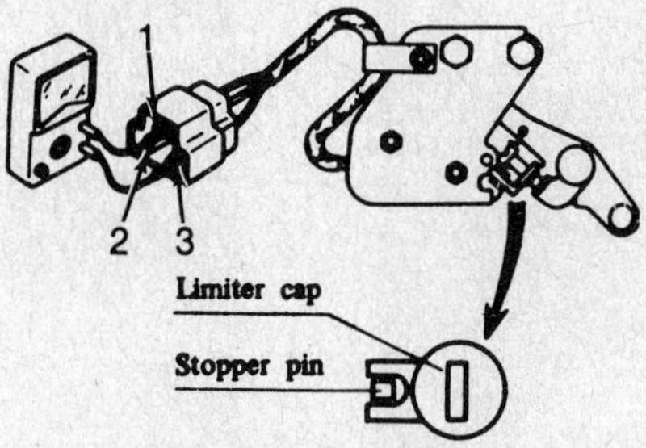

Adjusting the idle switch
(© Toyo Kogyo Co. Ltd.)

Coolant Temperature Switch

1. Drain the coolant from the radiator enough to bring the coolant level below the temperature switch.
2. Remove the alternator and drive belt if they are in the way.
3. Disconnect the switch multiconnector.
4. Use an open-end wrench to remove the switch.
5. Installation is the reverse of removal.

ADJUSTMENTS

Idle Switch

1. Warm up the engine until the water temperature is at least 159°F.
2. Make sure that the mixture and idle speed are properly adjusted.
3. Adjust the idle speed to 975–1,100 rpm (1,200–1,300 rpm-automatic transimssion) by rotating the throttle adjusting screw.
4. Rotate the idle switch adjusting screw until the switch changes from OFF to ON position.
5. Slowly turn the idle switch adjusting screw back to the point where the switch just changes from ON to OFF.
6. Turn the throttle screw back so that the engine returns to idle.

NOTE: Be sure that the idle switch goes on when the idle speed is still above 1,000 rpm.

Evaporative Emission Control System

The vapors rising from the gasoline in the fuel tank are vented into a separate condensing tank which is located in the luggage compartment. There they condense and return to the fuel tank in liquid form when the engine is not running.

When the engine is running, the fuel vapors are sucked directly into the engine through the PCV valve and are burned along with the air/fuel mixture.

Any additional fuel vapors which are not handled by the condensing tank are stored in a filter which is incorporated into the air cleaner. When the engine is running, the charcoal is purged of its stored fuel vapor.

A check valve vents the fuel vapor into the atmosphere if pressure in the fuel tank becomes excessive.

When the vehicle is parked for a short time following a long run, there is a tendency for the fuel in the float chamber to evaporate and enter the intake manifold through the air vent. To prevent this overrich condition, an air vent solenoid valve is installed on 1977 models to divert the fumes to the canister filter.

SYSTEM TESTING

There are several things to check for if

a malfunction of the evaporative emission control system is suspected.

1. Leaks may be traced by using an infrared hydrocarbon tester. Run the test probe along the lines and connections. The meter will indicate the presence of a leak by a high hydrocarbon (HC) reading. This method is much more accurate than a visual inspection which would indicate only the presence of a leak large enough to pass liquid.

2. Leaks may be caused by any of the following, so always check these areas when looking for them:

   a. Defective or worn lines;
   b. Disconnected or pinched lines;
   c. Improperly routed lines;
   d. A defective check valve.

NOTE: If it becomes necessary to replace any of the lines used in the evaporative emission control system, use only those hoses which are fuel resistant or are marked "EVAP."

3. If the fuel tank has collapsed, it may be the fault of clogged or pinched vent lines, a defective vapor separator, or a plugged or incorrect fuel filler cap.

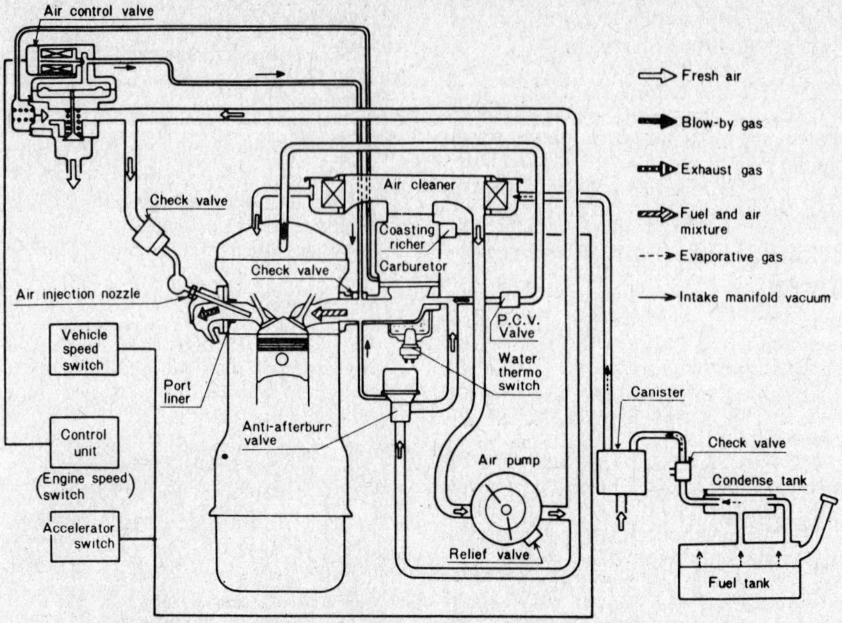

Typical piston engine emission system (© Toyo Kogyo Co. Ltd.)

EMISSION CONTROLS

Piston Engine Throttle Opener

The throttle opener system consists of a servo-diaphragm connected to the throttle lever and a vacuum control valve which controls intake manifold vacuum through the servo-diaphragm.

TESTING THE SYSTEM

Servo-Diaphragm

1. Start the engine and set the idle speed to 800 rpm. Stop the engine.

2. Disconnect the vacuum sensing tube between the servo-diaphragm and the vacuum control valve at the diaphragm.

3. Remove the intake manifold suction hole plug.

4. Connect the intake manifold and the servo-diaphragm with a tube so that the intake manifold vacuum goes directly to the servo-diaphragm.

5. Connect a tachometer and remove the vacuum sensing tube between the carburetor and distributor.

6. Start the engine and read the speed. If the engine is running 1300–1500 rpm, the servo-diaphragm is operating normally. If the engine speed is 800–1300, adjust the speed with the throttle opening screw. If the engine speed remains normal, about 800 rpm, the servo-diaphragm is defective and should be replaced.

7. Remove the test equipment and reconnect all the lines.

SERVICE

Servo-Diaphragm

REMOVAL AND INSTALLATION

1. Remove the air cleaner.

2. Disconnect the vacuum sensing tube from the diaphragm.

3. Remove the cotter pin and link.

4. Loosen the locknut and remove the servo-diaphragm.

5. Installation is the reverse of removal. Adjust the servo-diaphragm.

Vacuum Control Valve

REMOVAL AND INSTALLATION

1. Remove the air cleaner.

2. Disconnect the vacuum sensing tubes from the vacuum control valve.

3. Unbolt and remove the vacuum control valve.

4. Installation is the reverse of removal.

Positive Crankcase Ventilation (PCV) System

The function of the PCV valve is to divert blow-by gases from the crankcase

Servo diaphragm (© Toyo Kogyo Co. Ltd.)

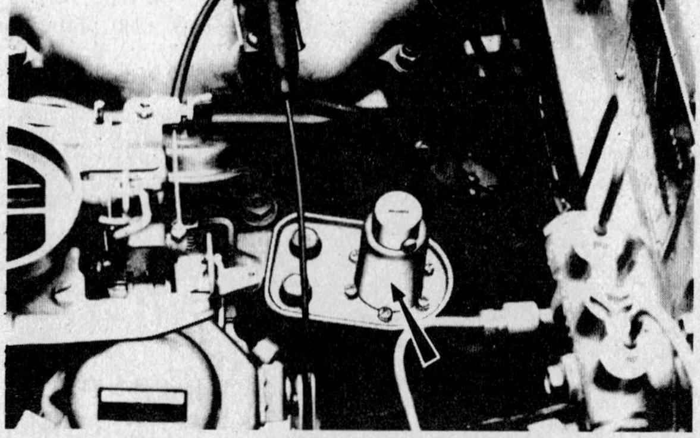

Vacuum control valve—B-1600 (© Toyo Kogyo Co. Ltd.)

to the intake manifold to be burned in the cylinders. The system consists of a PCV valve, an oil separator and the hoses necessary to connect the components.

Ventilating air is routed into the rocker cover from the air cleaner. The air is then moved to the oil separator and from the separator to the PCV valve. The PCV valve is operated by differences in air pressure between the intake manifold and the rocker cover.

TESTING THE SYSTEM

PCV Valve

STANDARD TEST

1. Remove the hose from the PCV valve.
2. Start the engine and run it at approximately 700–1000 rpm.
3. Cover the end of the PCV valve with your finger. A distinct vacuum should be felt. If no vacuum is felt, replace the valve.

ALTERNATE TEST

Remove the valve from its fitting. Shake the valve. If a rattle is heard, the valve is probably functioning normally. If no rattle is heard, the valve is probably stuck (open or shut) and should be replaced.

SERVICE

Removal and Installation

1. Remove the air cleaner.
2. Disconnect the hose from the PCV valve.
3. Remove the valve from the intake manifold fitting.

To install the valve, reverse the removal procedure.

Evaporative Emission Control System

The evaporative emission control system is designed to control the emission of gasoline vapors into the atmosphere. The system consists of a fuel tank, charcoal canister and a check valve.

When the engine is not running, fuel vapors are channeled to the canister. The fuel returns to the fuel tank as the vapors condense. During periods of engine operation, fuel vapors are removed from the charcoal by fresh air moving through the inlet hole in the bottom of the canister.

SERVICE

Check Valve Removal and Installation

The check valve is used only through 1976.

1. Disconnect the hoses from the check valve.
2. Unscrew and remove the valve from the crossmember.

Installation is the reverse of removal.

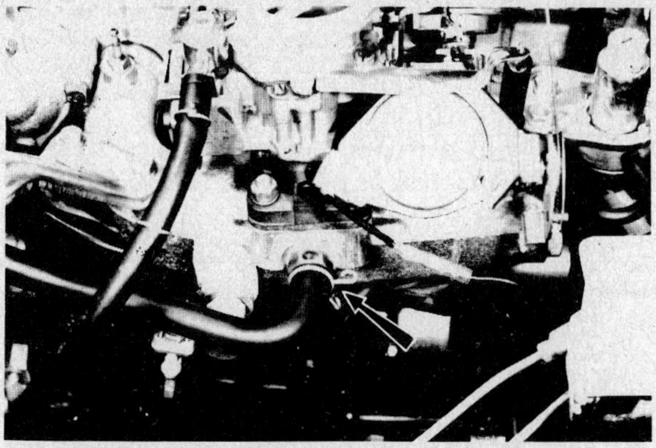

PCV valve—B-1600 (© Toyo Kogyo Co. Ltd.)

Air Injection System

CHECKING THE AIR PUMP

1. Disconnect the hose from the air pump outlet.
2. Connect a pressure gauge to the outlet.
3. Check the drive belt for proper tension and run engine at 1500 rpm. Gauge reading should be at least 1 psi. If not, replace the pump.

TESTING THE RELIEF VALVE

1. Run the engine at idle.
2. At idle, no air should be felt at the relief valve. If air flow is felt, replace the valve.
3. Increase the engine speed to 4500 rpm. If air flow is felt, valve is working properly.

PUMP REPLACEMENT

1. Disconnect the inlet and outlet hoses at the pump.
2. Remove the adjusting bolt and lift off the drive belt.
3. Support the pump and remove the mounting bolts. Lift out the pump.
4. Installation is the reverse of removal. Adjust drive belt to specification. Correct belt adjustment will give a 0.5 in. flex at the mid-point with a 22 lb push.

CHECK VALVE REPLACEMENT

Check valve is replaced by disconnecting the hose and unscrewing the valve from the manifold.

AIR CONTROL VALVE TEST

1. Start the engine and run it at idle.
2. Hold a finger over the relief valve port of the air control valve. Discharge air should be felt.
3. Disconnect the vacuum sensing tube from the air control valve and plug the tube. No air should be felt at the relief port.

REPLACING AIR CONTROL VALVE

1. Disconnect the vacuum lines from the valve.
2. Disconnect the wiring from the valve.
3. Disconnect the air hoses from the valve.
4. Unbolt and remove the valve.
5. Install in reverse of removal.

AIR CONTROL VALVE CHECK VALVE TEST

1. Disconnect the vacuum sensing tube from the air control valve solenoid.
2. Blow through the vacuum tube. Air should pass through the valve. Suck on the tube. No air should pass through the valve.

Exhaust Gas Recirculation System

EGR CONTROL VALVE TEST

1. Remove the air cleaner.
2. Run the engine at idle.
3. Disconnect the vacuum sensing tube from the EGR control valve.
4. Disconnect the vacuum sensing tube from the intake manifold vacuum control valve.
5. Connect this vacuum tube to the EGR control valve. The engine should stop. If not, clean or replace the EGR control valve.

REPLACING EGR CONTROL VALVE

1. Remove air cleaner.
2. Disconnect the vacuum sensing tube from the EGR control valve.
3. Disconnect the EGR control valve to exhaust manifold pipe.
4. Disconnect the pipe between the EGR control valve and the intake manifold.
5. Unbolt and remove the EGR control valve.
6. If old valve is to be reused, it

should be cleaned with a wire brush before installation.

7. To install, reverse the above procedure.

REPLACING AND/OR TESTING THE WATER TEMPERATURE SWITCH

1. Drain the radiator until the coolant level is below the intake manifold.
2. Disconnect the wires from the switch.
3. Unscrew the switch from the manifold.
4. Suspend the switch in a container of water so that it does not touch the sides or bottom.
5. Heat the water to no more than 113°F. and check the switch with an ohmmeter. Continuity should exist between the terminals.
6. Heat the water until the temperature becomes 149°F or more.
7. No continuity should exist. If the switch fails either test, replace it.
8. To replace the switch, reverse the removal procedure.

TESTING THE THREE-WAY SOLENOID VALVE

The valve is located at the top center of the firewall in the engine compartment.

1. Disconnect the wiring to the water thermo switch and connect a jumper wire to the two connectors of the switch.
2. Disconnect the vacuum sensing tube from the EGR valve.
3. Disconnect the vacuum sensing tube which runs to the vacuum amplifier from the three way solenoid valve.
4. Turn the ignition switch on.
5. Blow through the solenoid valve from the tube disconnected from the EGR valve. Air should pass through the valve to the valve air filter.
6. Disconnect the jumper wire from the thermo switch.
7. Blow through the tube disconnected from the EGR valve and make sure that the air passes through the opening to the vacuum amplifier tube.
8. If the solenoid valve does not operate properly, replace.

REPLACING THE THREE-WAY SOLENOID VALVE

1. Disconnect the wiring from the valve.
2. Disconnect the hoses from the valve.
3. Remove the screws and replace the valve.

EGR MAINTENANCE WARNING SYSTEM

1976 Only

Every 12,500 miles, the EGR warning light will come on when the ignition switch is turned on. When this occurs the valve should be removed and cleaned and checked for proper operation. When this is done reset the switch by taking off the cover from the switch and sliding the knob in the opposite direction. The switch is located behind the instrument panel, next to the speedometer.

Catalytic Converter

Periodically, the converter should be checked for excessive rust, cracks or corrosion. To replace the converter, raise and support the car and unbolt the converter from the flanges and body. A temperature sensor is located in the right side of the converter. To test its operation, remove a small plate under the floor mat on the passengers side. Remove the coupling and check across the terminals of the coupling with a circuit tester. If there is no current flow, replace the sensor.

Deceleration Control System

CHECKING ANTI-AFTERBURN VALVE

1. Disconnect the outlet hose from the valve.
2. Raise the engine speed and hold your finger over the outlet. Quickly release the accelerator linkage. Air should flow for a few seconds. If air is discharged for longer than three seconds or not at all, replace the valve.

REPLACING THE ANTI-AFTERBURN VALVE

1. Remove the air cleaner.
2. Disconnect all hoses from the valve and unbolt and remove the valve.

FUEL SYSTEM

Electric Fuel Pump

REMOVAL AND INSTALLATION

An external electric fuel pump is mounted on the left frame rail adjacent to the fuel tank. Current is supplied to the pump through the ignition circuit and the pump will operate with the key in the RUN position.

1. Remove the fuel pump shield from the frame. Disconnect the electrical leads from the pump.
2. Disconnect the inlet and outlet lines from the pump. Plug the lines.
3. Unbolt and remove the pump from its mounting bracket.

To install the fuel pump:

4. Position the fuel pump on the mounting bracket and install the bolts. Be sure that both mounting surfaces are clean.
5. Connect the inlet and outlet hoses.
6. Connect the electrical leads to the pump.
7. Install the fuel pump shield.

Carburetor

REMOVAL AND INSTALLATION

Rotary Engine

1. Remove the air cleaner assembly complete with its hoses and mounting bracket.
2. Detach the choke and accelerator cables from the carburetor.
3. Disconnect the fuel and vacuum lines from the carburetor.
4. Remove the oil line which runs to the metering oil pump, at the carburetor.
5. Remove all electrical wiring from carburetor.
6. Remove the carburetor attaching nuts and/or bolts, gasket or head insulator, and remove the carburetor.

Installation is performed in the reverse order of removal. Use a new gasket. Fill the float bowl with gasoline to aid in engine starting.

Piston Engine

1. Remove the air cleaner and duct.
2. Disconnect the accelerator shaft from the throttle lever.
3. Disconnect and plug the fuel supply and fuel return lines and plug these.
4. Disconnect the leads from the throttle solenoid and deceleration valve at the quick-disconnects.
5. Disconnect the carburetor-to-distributor vacuum line.
6. Disconnect the throttle return spring.
7. Disconnect the choke cable.
8. Remove the carburetor attaching nuts from the intake manifold studs and remove the carburetor. The attaching nuts are tucked underneath the carburetor body and are difficult to reach; a small socket with an "L" shaped hex drive, or a short, thin wrench sold for work on ignition systems will make removal easier.

To install the carburetor:

9. Install a new carburetor gasket on the manifold.
10. Install the carburetor and tighten the carburetor attaching nuts.
11. Connect the various wires and hoses to the carburetor, adjust the choke and accelerator linkage, start the engine, and check for fuel or vacuum leaks.

OVERHAUL

Efficient carburetion depends greatly on careful cleaning and inspection during overhaul since dirt, gum, water, or varnish in or on the carburetor parts are often responsible for poor performance.

Overhaul your carburetor in a clean,

1. Air horn
2. Choke valve lever
3. Clip
4. Choke lever shaft
5. Screw
6. Setscrew
7. Spring
8. Choke valve
9. Connector
10. Connecting rod
11. Spring
12. Fuel return valve
13. Hanger
14. Screw
15. Ring
16. Bolt
17. Carburetor body
18. Bolt
19. Diaphragm cover
20. Screw
21. Diaphragm
22. Accelerator pump arm
23. Float
24. Gasket
25. Connecting rod
26. Spring
27. Spring
28. Small venturi
29. Small venturi
30. Bolt
31. Check ball plug
32. Steel ball
33. Flange
34. Throttle shaft
35. Throttle shaft
36. Throttle lever
37. Spring washer
38. Nut
39. Lock
40. Adjusting arm
41. Starting lever
42. Arm
43. Screw
44. Gasket
45. Valve
46. Screw
47. Throttle valve
48. Throttle lever link
49. Ring
50. Throttle return spring
51. Arm
52. Retainer
53. Metering pump lever
54. Metering pump arm
55. Screw
56. Pin
57. Union bolt
58. Cover
59. Diaphragm spring
60. Diaphragm lever
61. Diaphragm pin
62. Diaphragm chamber
63. Screw
64. Diaphragm
65. Gasket
66. Connecting rod
67. Pin
68. Ring
69. Washer
70. Diaphragm stop ring
71. Diaphragm stop ring
72. Screw
73. Level gauge screw
74. Gasket
75. Gasket
76. Stop ring
77. Float pin
78. Needle valve seat
79. Gasket
80. Collar
81. Throttle adjusting screw
82. Idle adjusting screw
83. Spring
84. Main jet
85. Main jet
86. Gasket
87. Plug
88. Gasket
89. Air bleed
90. Air bleed
91. Slow jet
92. Step jet
93. Air bleed screw
94. Air bleed step
95. Cover
96. Diaphragm
97. Spring
98. Gasket
99. Washer
100. Shim
101. Jet
102. Bleed plug
103. Retainer
104. Pin
105. Screw
106. Gasket
107. Plug
108. Gasket
109. Gasket
110. Bolt
111. Nut
113. Cover
114. Gasket
115. Sight glass
116. Gasket
117. Filter
118. Accelerator
119. Gasket
120. Plug
121. Cover
122. Coasting valve bracket
123. Clip
124. Screw
125. Spring
126. Screw
127. Spring
128. Shim
129. Throttle positioner
130. Nut
131. Rod
132. Collar
133. Shim
134. Collar
135. Arm
136. Plate
137. Retaining spring
138. Lever
139. Setscrew
140. Ring

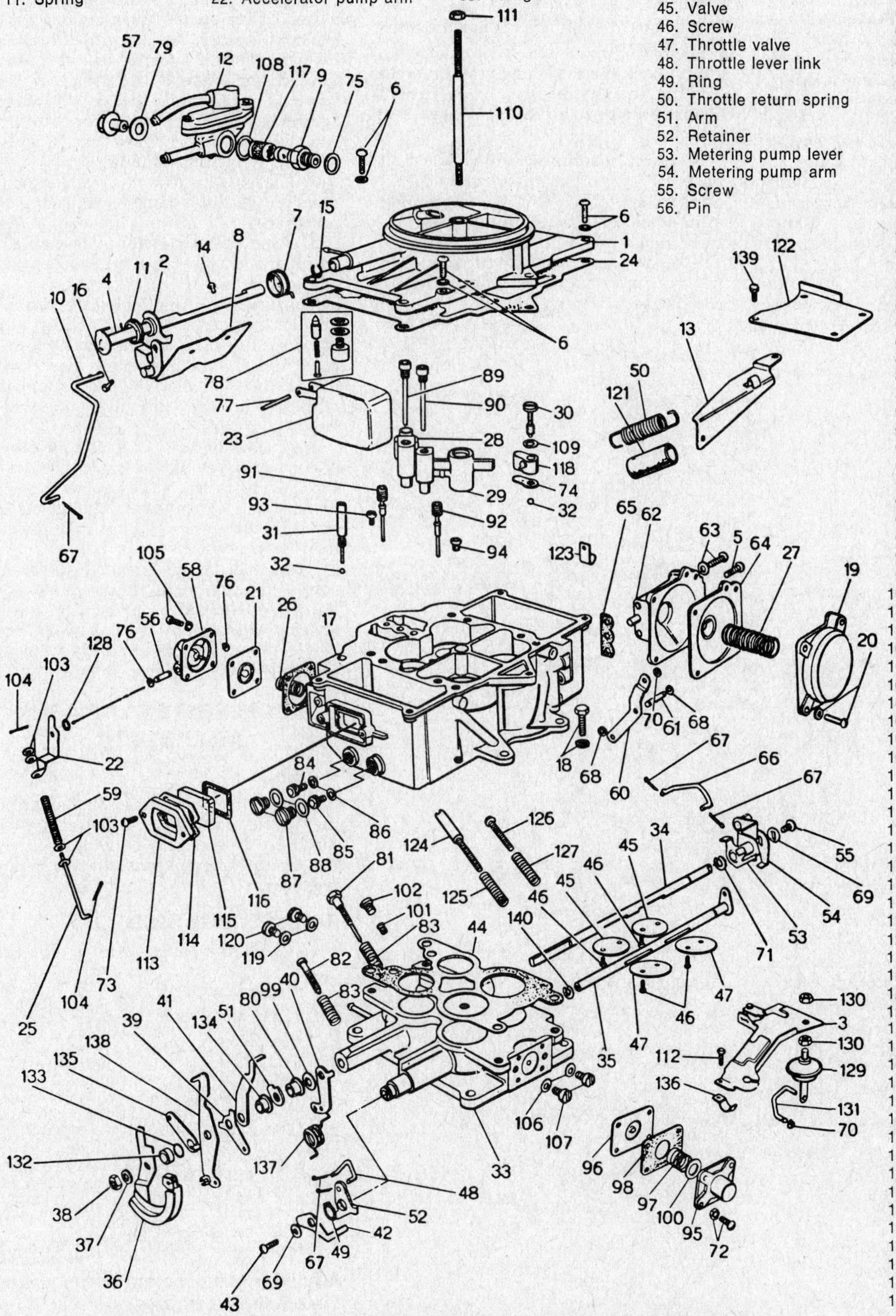

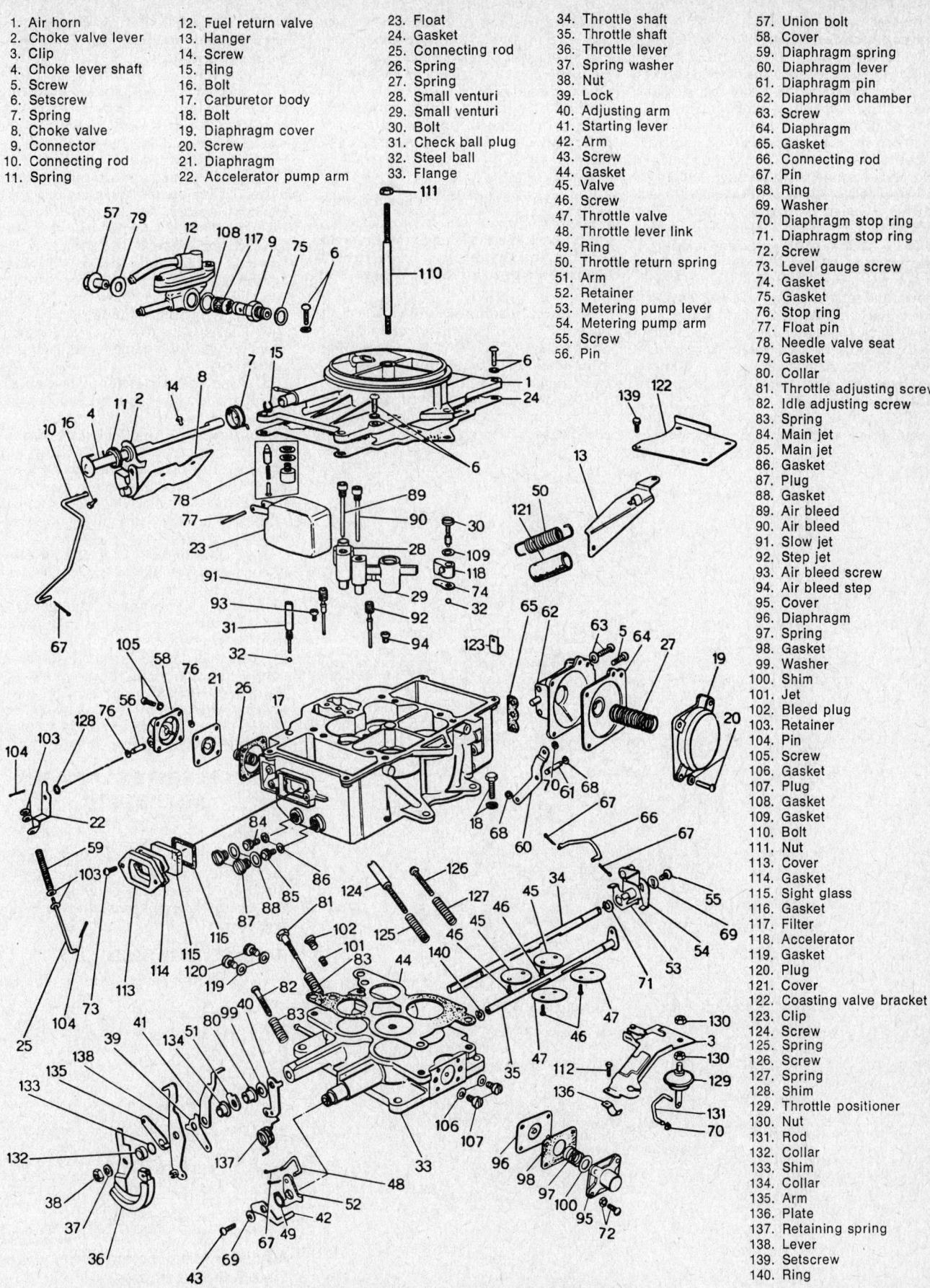

Rotary engine carburetor—exploded view

dust-free area. Carefully disassemble the carburetor, referring often to the exploded views. Keep all similar and look-alike parts segregated during disassembly and cleaning to avoid accidental interchange during assembly. Make a note of all jet sizes.

When the carburetor is disassembled, wash all parts (except diaphragms, electric choke units, pump plunger, and any other plastic, leather, fiber, or rubber parts) in clean carburetor solvent. Do not leave parts in the solvent any longer than is necessary to sufficiently loosen the deposits. Excessive cleaning may remove the special finish from the float bowl and choke valve bodies, leaving these parts unfit for service. Rinse all parts in clean solvent and blow them dry with compressed air or allow them to air dry. Wipe clean all cork, plastic, leather, and fiber parts with a clean, lint-free cloth.

Blow out all passages and jets with compressed air and be sure that there are no restrictions or blockages. Never use wire or similar tools to clean jets, fuel passages, or air bleeds. Clean all jets and valves separately to avoid accidental interchange.

Check all parts for wear or damage. If wear or damage is found, replace the defective parts. Especially check the following:

1. Check the float needle and seat for wear. If wear is found, replace the complete assembly.

2. Check the float hinge pin for wear and the float(s) for dents or distortion. Replace the float if fuel has leaked into it.

3. Check the throttle and choke shaft bores for wear or an out-of-round condition. Damage or wear to the throttle arm, shaft, or shaft bore will often require replacement of the throttle body. These parts require a close tolerance of fit; wear may allow air leakage, which could affect starting and idling.

NOTE: Throttle shafts and bushings are not included in overhaul kits. They can be purchased separately.

4. Inspect the idle mixture adjusting needles for burrs or grooves. Any such condition requires replacement of the needle, since you will not be able to obtain a satisfactory idle.

5. Test the accelerator pump check valves. They should pass air one way but not the other. Test for proper seating by blowing and sucking on the valve. Replace the valve if necessary. If the valve is satisfactory, wash the valve again to remove breath moisture.

6. Check the bowl cover for warped surfaces with a straightedge.

7. Closely inspect the valves and seats for wear and damage, replacing as necessary.

8. After the carburetor is assembled, check the choke valve for freedom of operation.

Carburetor overhaul kits are recommended for each overhaul. These kits contain all gaskets and new parts to replace those that deteriorate most rapidly. Failure to replace all parts supplied with the kit (especially gaskets) can result in poor performance later.

After cleaning and checking all components, reassemble the carburetor, using new parts and referring to the exploded view. When reassembling, make sure that all screws and jets are tight in their seats, but do not overtighten, as the tips will be distorted. Tighten all screws gradually, in rotation. Do not tighten needle valves into their seats; uneven jetting will result. Always use new gaskets. Be sure to adjust the float level when reassembling.

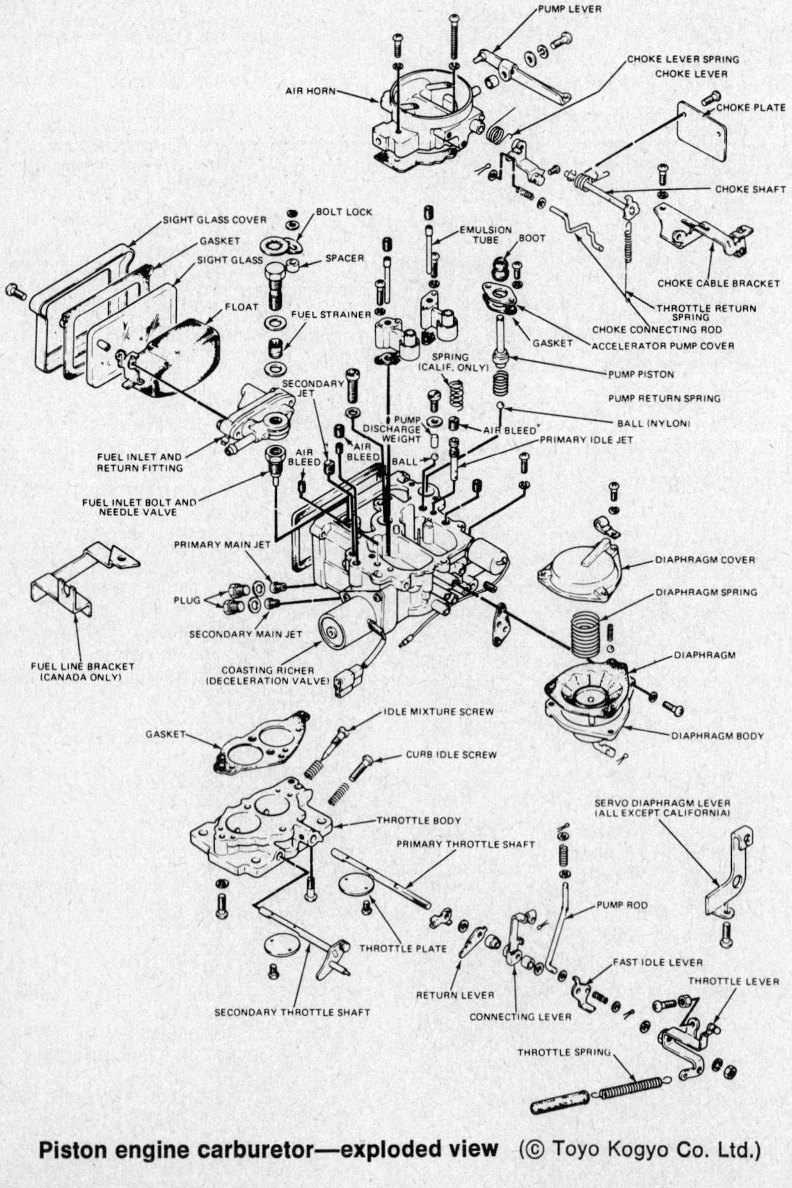

Piston engine carburetor—exploded view (© Toyo Kogyo Co. Ltd.)

ACCELERATOR LINKAGE ADJUSTMENT

B-1600

Remove the air cleaner and depress the accelerator fully. The carburetor throttle valves should be wide open. If not, check for proper installation, binding or wear.

Rotary, B1800, B2000

1. Check the pedal position. The ac-

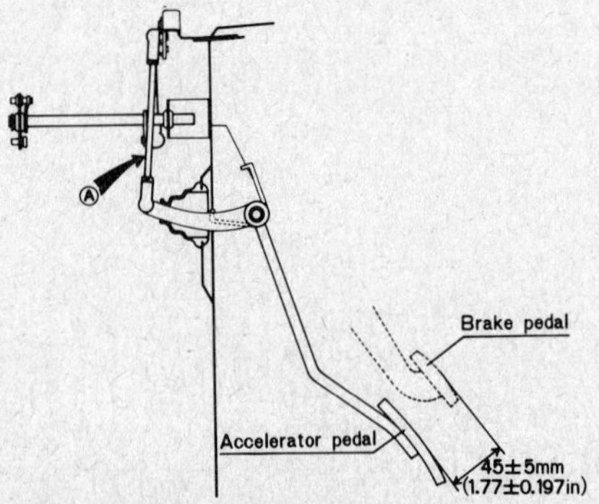

Adjusting the accelerator linkage on piston engine models
(© Toyo Kogyo Co. Ltd.)

celerator pedal should be lower than the brake pedal by 2.3" on the rotary pickup and 1.75 inches on the piston engine pick up.

2. If necessary, adjust the nut on the linkage above the pedal to obtain the proper height.

3. Check the free-play of the cable at the carburetor. It should be 0.04–0.12". If not, adjust by turning the clevis nut.

FLOAT AND FUEL LEVEL ADJUSTMENTS—ROTARY ENGINE

1. With the engine running, check the fuel level in the sight glass, using a mirror.

2. If the fuel levels are not within the specified marks on the sight glass, remove the air horn with the floats.

3. Invert the air horn and let the float hang so that it just contacts the needle valve.

4. Measure the clearance between the float and the air horn gasket, which should be 0.43 in. for 1974 models, and 0.10 in. for 1975–78 models. Bend the float seat lip to adjust the clearance if necessary.

5. Install the air horn and recheck the fuel levels in the sight glass.

FLOAT DROP

Rotary Pick-Up

1. Remove the air horn with the floats and allow the floats to hang free.

2. Measure the clearance between the bottom of the float and the air horn gasket. The clearance should be 2.03–2.07 in.

3. If not, adjust the distance by bending the float stop.

4. Install the air horn and recheck the fuel level in the sight glass.

B 1800, B2000

1. Check the fuel level within the float bowl through the sight glass, with the engine running. If the float is not aligned with the level mark, adjustment is necessary.

2. For adjustment, remove the carburetor. Remove the sight glass and invert the carburetor.

3. Measure the distance between the float and the top of the bowl. It should be 0.236 in. on the B1800, and 0.335 in. on the B2000

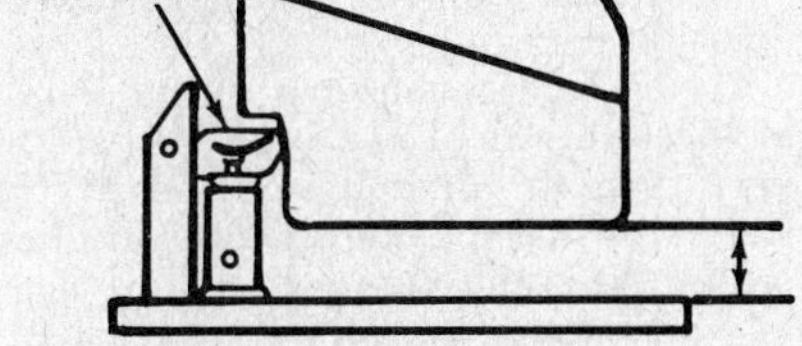

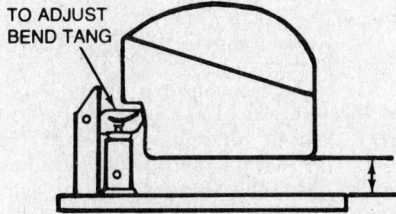

Float level adjustment—float bowl inverted and gasket installed
(© Toyo Kogyo Co. Ltd.)

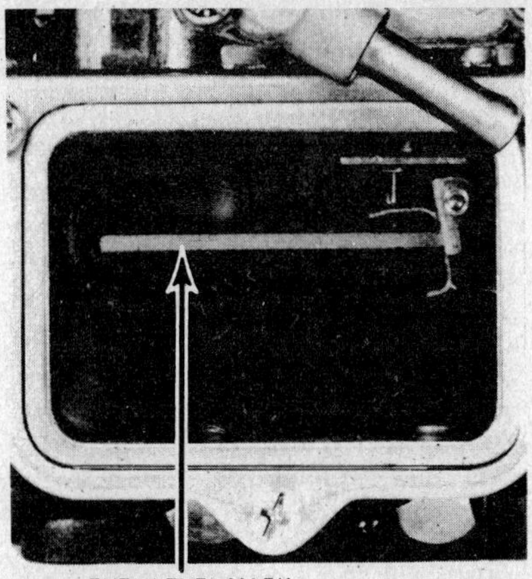

Fuel level mark on the sight glass—piston engine
(© Toyo Kogyo Co. Ltd.)

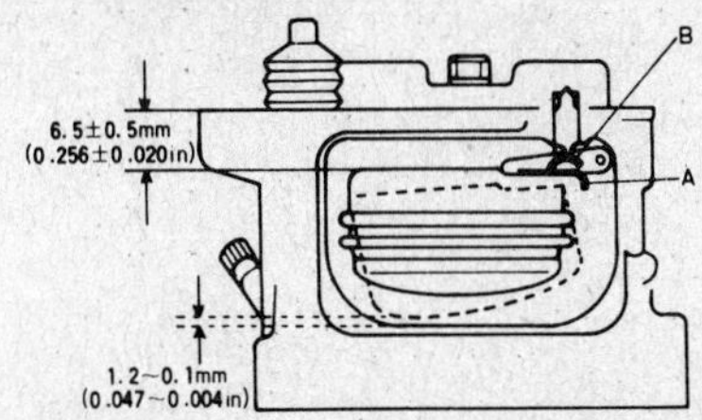

Piston engine float adjustment; bend tab "A" to adjust float drop and bend tab "B" to adjust float level
(© Toyo Kogyo Co. Ltd.)

4. Adjust by bending the float seat lip.

5. Turn the carburetor upright and allow the float to drip by its own weight.

6. Measure the clearance between the bottom of the float and the bowl. It should be 0.047 in. on the B1800 and 0.039 in. on the B2000. Bend the float stopper to adjust.

FAST IDLE ADJUSTMENT

1. Remove the carburetor.

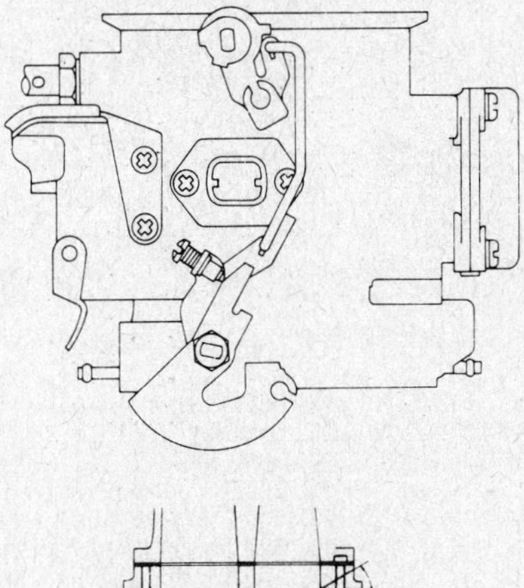

Fast idle adjustments; measure the angle "A" and clearance "B"
(© Toyo Kogyo Co. Ltd.)

2. With the choke plate fully closed, adjust the clearance between the primary throttle plate and the wall of the throat by bending the connecting rod between the choke plate linkage and the throttle plate. Clearances are as follows:
B1600—0.070 inch
B1800—0.071 ± 0.008 inch
Rotary Pick-up—0.060 ± 0.008 inch
(Calif. 0.080 ± 0.006 inch)

MANUAL TRANSMISSION

REMOVAL AND INSTALLATION

B-1600, B-1800, B-2000

1. Raise and support the truck. Drain the lubricant from the transmission.

2. Disconnect the ground wire from the battery.

3. Remove the gearshift lever boot.

4. Unbolt the cover plate from the gearshift lever retainer.

5. Pull the gearshift lever, shim and bushing straight up and away from the gearshift lever retainer.

6. Disconnect the wires from the starter motor and back-up light switch.

7. Disconnect the speedometer cable from the extension housing.

8. Remove the driveshaft.

9. Unbolt the exhaust pipe from the bracket on the transmission case.

10. Disconnect the exhaust pipe at the exhaust manifold.

11. Unhook the clutch release fork return spring and remove the clutch release cylinder from the clutch housing.

12. Remove the starter.

13. Support the transmission with a jack.

14. Unbolt the transmission from the rear of the engine.

15. Place a jack under the engine, protecting the oil pan with a block of wood.

16. Unbolt the transmission from the crossmember.

17. Unbolt and remove the crossmember.

18. Lower the jack and slide the transmission rearward until the mainshaft clears the clutch disc.

19. Remove the transmission from under the truck.

20. Installation is the reverse of removal.

Rotary Pick-Up 4 Speed or 5 Speed

1. Remove the knob from the gearshift lever.

2. Remove the gearshift lever boot.

3. Unbolt the retainer cover from the gearshift lever retainer.

4. Pull the gearshift lever, shim and bushing straight up and away from the gearshift lever retainer.

5. Disconnect the battery ground wire.
6. Remove the bolt attaching the power brake vacuum pipe to the clutch housing.
7. Disconnect the ground strap from the transmission case.
8. Remove the clutch release cylinder.
9. Remove the one upper bolt holding the starter and the three upper bolts and nuts securing the transmission to the engine.
10. Raise and support the truck.
11. Disconnect the wires from the starter motor and the back-up light switch wires.
12. Unbolt and remove the heat insulator from the front exhaust pipe.
13. Disconnect the exhaust pipe from the brackets.
14. Disconnect the exhaust pipe front flange from the exhaust manifold. Remove the front exhaust pipe.
15. Remove the driveshaft.
16. Insert a transmission oil plug into the extension housing.
17. Remove the starter.
18. Install a jack under the engine and support the engine.
19. Unbolt the transmission support from the body.
20. Remove the two lower bolts holding the transmission to the engine.
21. Slide the transmission rearward until the mainshaft clears the clutch disc and remove the transmission from under the truck.
22. Installation is the reverse of removal.

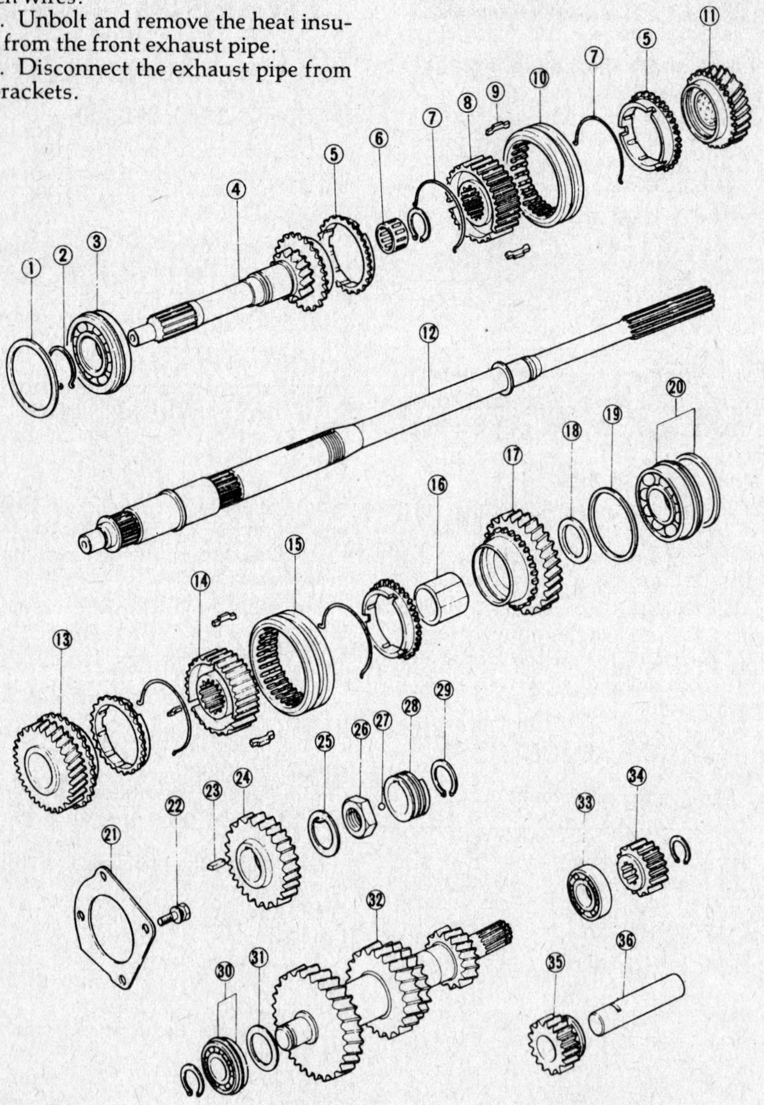

1. Adjusting shim
2. Snap-ring
3. Input shaft bearing
4. Input shaft
5. Synchronizer ring
6. Needle bearing
7. Synchronizer key spring
8. Third-and-Fourth clutch hub
9. Synchronizer key
10. Clutch hub sleeve
11. Third gear
12. Output shaft
13. Second gear
14. First-and-Second clutch hub
15. Clutch hub sleeve
16. Gear sleeve
17. First gear
18. Thrust washer
19. Adjust shim
20. Ball bearing and clip
21. Bearing stop
22. Bolt
23. Key
24. Reverse gear
25. Lockwasher
26. Locknut
27. Steel ball
28. Speedometer drive gear
29. Snap-ring
30. Ball bearing and clip
31. Adjusting shim
32. Countershaft
33. Needle bearing
34. Reverse countergear
35. Reverse idler gear
36. Reverse idler gear shaft

Mainshaft drive train—Rotary pick-up 4-speed

OVERHAUL

Disassembly Rotary Pick-up 4 Speed

1. Install the transmission in a workstand.
2. Drain the oil from the transmission, if you haven't already done so. Clean any metal chips off the drain plug and reinstall it.
3. Pull outward on the release fork, until it becomes disengaged from the ball stud. Slide the fork and throwout bearing out of the housing.
4. Remove the bellhousing nuts and remove the housing, complete with gasket.
5. Withdraw the adjusting shim from the bellhousing bearing bore.
6. Unfasten the nuts which secure the shift lever tower to the extension housing. Remove the tower and gasket.
7. Remove the extension housing securing nuts, set the control lever end in the neutral position, press the control lever end as far left as possible, and slide the extension housing off the transmission.
8. Remove the neutral switch from the transmission (models with seat belt interlock).
9. Unfasten the gearshift control lever yoke bolt and remove the yoke from the central lever.
10. Remove the speedometer sleeve lockplate. Withdraw the sleeve and driven gear from the extension housing. Remove the back-up light switch, also.
11. Unfasten the speedometer drive gear snap-ring, slide the drive gear off of the output shaft, and remove the lockball.
12. Loosen the bottom cover bolts evenly, and in several stages; then remove the bottom cover and gasket.
13. Remove the cap bolts, the detent springs, and detent balls from the transmission case.
14. Remove the blind covers and gaskets from the transmission case.
15. Remove the Reverse shift rod and idler gear from the rear of the transmission case. Unfasten the Reverse shift fork securing bolt and remove the fork.
16. Unfasten Third/Fourth shift fork securing bolt and remove the Third/Fourth shift rod from the rear of the case.
17. Repeat step 16 for the First/Second shift rod.
18. Straighten out the output shaft lockwasher. Hold the output shaft to keep it from turning, and loosen the locknut. Slide the reverse gear and key off the end of the output shaft.
19. Remove the countershaft snap-ring (rear) and remove the Reverse countergear.
20. Unfasten the bearing cover bolts and remove the cover.

21. Remove the reverse idler gear.
22. Hold the fourth synchronizer ring and gear on the output shaft.
23. Remove the countershaft front bearing snap-ring. Using a puller remove the front bearing. Withdraw the adjusting shim from the case bearing bore.
24. Remove the countershaft rear bearing with the puller. Remove the adjusting shim from the case bearing bore.
25. Remove the input shaft bearing snap-ring and remove the bearing with the puller.
26. Lift the countershaft out of the case.
27. Separate the input and output shafts. Remove the input shaft. Remove the fourth synchronizer ring and needle bearing from the input shaft.
28. Lift the output shaft gear assembly out of the case.
29. Remove First/Second and Third/Fourth shift forks from the case. Withdraw the shift interlock pins from the case.
30. Remove the Third/Fourth clutch hub snap-ring, then slide the clutch hub sleeve, third synchronizer ring and Third gear off the front of the output shaft. Be careful not to mix-up the synchronizer rings.
31. Slide the First gear and the synchronizer ring off the rear of the output shaft.
32. Slide the First gear sleeve, Second gear, second synchronizer ring and First/Second clutch hub/sleeve assembly off the output shaft.

Inspection

Clean the transmission case thoroughly with solvent and blow it dry with compressed air. Inspect the case for cracks or other signs of damage.

Inspect all of the bearings for wear or roughness.

Examine each of the gears. Replace any gears that have chipped or missing teeth, or gears that show signs of excessive wear.

Check the operation of the synchronizers. Replace any which are worn or damaged.

Place the mainshaft on V-blocks, and measure its runout with a dial indicator. If runout exceeds 0.0012 in., replace the mainshaft.

Assembly

1. Install the First/Second clutch hub on its sleeve, place the three shift keys in the clutch hub key slots, and install the key springs. Be sure to keep the open ends of the key springs 120° apart.
2. Perform step 1 for the Third/Fourth synchronizer assembly.
3. Place the synchronizer ring on Second gear and then slide Second gear on the output shaft, so that the synchronizer ring faces the rear of the shaft.
4. Slide the First/Second clutch hub and sleeve on the output shaft so that the clutch oil grooves face forward. Be sure that the three synchronizer keys engage the notches on the Second gear synchronizer ring.
5. Install the First gear sleeve in the output shaft.
6. Fit the synchronizer ring in the First gear and install the gear on the output shaft so that the ring faces the front of the shaft.
7. Install the same thrust washer on the output shaft that you removed during disassembly.
8. Perform step 6 for Third gear.
9. Install the Third/Fourth clutch hub and sleeve on the output shaft, being sure to engage the three synchronizer keys with the notches in the ring.

NOTE: The larger boss on the Third/Fourth clutch hub goes toward the front.

10. Install the snap-ring on the front of the output shaft. Install the output shaft/gear set assembly in the case. Fit the needle bearing on the front of the output shaft.
11. Place the synchronizer ring on the input shaft gear (Fourth) and install the gear on the front of the output shaft. Be sure that the synchronizer keys engage the notches in the synchronizer ring.
12. Position the First/Second and Third/Fourth shift forks in the groove on the clutch hub/sleeve assembly.
13. Install the countergear assembly in the case, being careful to engage each countergear with its respective output shaft gear.
14. Check the output shaft bearing end-play as follows:
    a. Measure the depth of the transmission case output shaft bearing bore.
    b. Measure the height of the bearing.
    c. The difference of these two measurements indicates the correct thickness of the adjusting shim to be used. The amount of end-play permitted is 0–0.0039 in.
    d. Shims are available in thicknesses of 0.0039 or 0.0118 in.
15. Hold the Fourth synchronizer ring off the input shaft synchronizer gear.
16. Install the input and output shaft bearings in their respective bores with a press.
17. Install the input shaft bearing snap-ring.
18. Check the countershaft bearing end-play, as outlined in step 14 for the input shaft. The amount of end-play allowed and available shim size are the same for both bearings.
19. Perform step 15 again.
20. Press the countershaft front and rear bearings into their respective bores. Install the snap-ring on the front bearing.
21. Install the Reverse countergear on the rear of the countershaft and secure with its snap-ring.
22. Fit the reverse gear idler shaft in the transmission case.
23. Install the bearing cover on the case.
24. Secure the reverse gear on the output shaft with its key.
25. Hold the output shaft to keep it from turning and tighten its locknut 150–180 ft lbs. Secure the locknut by bending the tabs on the lockwasher.
26. Fit the first/second shift rod into the case and secure it to the shift fork with the lockbolt. Place the shift rod in Neutral. Drift the interlock pin into its bore.
27. Perform step 26 for the Third/Fourth shift rod.
28. Slide the Reverse shift rod, complete with the Reverse idler gear, in from the rear of the case. Secure the shift rod to the Reverse fork with its lockbolt.
29. Install the detent balls and springs in their bores and secure them with their cap bolts.
30. Check the synchronizer key-to-exposed edge of the synchronizer ring clearance with a feeler gauge; it should be 0.026–0.079 in. If the clearance is greater, the synchronizer key could pop out. If the clearance is greater than specified, replace the selective-fit thrust washer with one of the three available sizes.
31. Install the blind covers over the gaskets.
32. Fit the lockball, speedometer drive gear, and snap-ring, in that order, on the rear of the output shaft.
33. Install the gearshift control lever through the holes in the front of the extension housing. Fit the Woodruff key on the control lever and install the yoke over it. Secure the yoke with its setbolt.
34. Thread the Neutral switch (for seat belt interlock) into the extension housing.
35. Fit the spring and plunger in the extension housing and secure them with the cap bolt.
36. Install the back-up light switch.
37. Secure the speedometer driven gear in its extension housing bore with the lockplate and bolt.
38. Push the gearshift control lever over to the left as far as possible. Place a gasket on the rear of the transmission case and install the extension housing over it. Secure the extension housing with its bolts. Check the operation of the gearshift control lever.
39. Install the bottom cover on the case. Secure it with its bolts.
40. Insert the select lockpin and spring in the shift tower. Align the slot in the pin with the lockball bore. Drop the lock ball and spring into the bore; secure with the cap bolt.
41. Install the shift tower on the extension housing and secure it with its bolts.
42. Perform step 14 for the input shaft bearing and clutch housing bore. The end-play and shim thickness are the same as in step 14.
43. Lubricate the lip of the bellhousing oil seal.
44. Put a gasket on the front of the

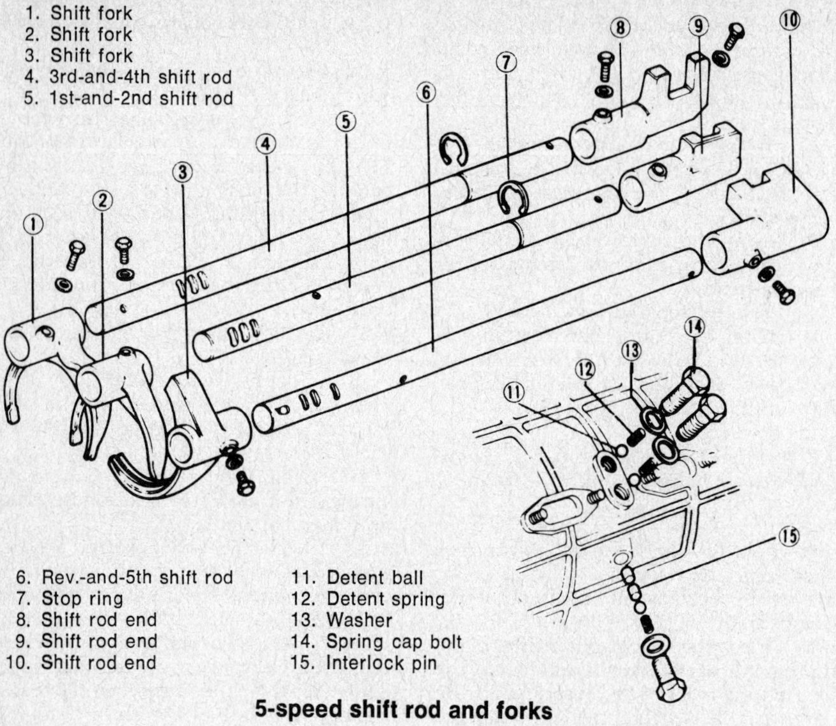

1. Shift fork
2. Shift fork
3. Shift fork
4. 3rd-and-4th shift rod
5. 1st-and-2nd shift rod
6. Rev.-and-5th shift rod
7. Stop ring
8. Shift rod end
9. Shift rod end
10. Shift rod end
11. Detent ball
12. Detent spring
13. Washer
14. Spring cap bolt
15. Interlock pin

5-speed shift rod and forks

transmission case, install the bellhousing on the case, and secure it with the nuts.

45. Install the throwout bearing, release fork and boot in the bellhousing.

Disassembly—B1800, B-2000, and Rotary Pick-up 5 Speed

NOTE: The use of special tools is required for the following procedure.

1. Pull the release fork outward until the spring clip of the fork releases from the ball pivot.
2. Remove the fork and release bearing from the clutch housing.
3. Remove the nuts attaching the clutch housing and remove the housing, shim and gasket.
4. Remove the bolts attaching the gearshift lever retainer to the extension housing and remove the retainer and gasket.
5. Remove the spring and steel ball, select lock spindle and spring from the gearshift lever retainer.
6. Unbolt and remove the extension housing with the control lever end down to the left as far as it will go.
7. Unbolt and remove the control lever end, key and control rod.
8. Remove the lock plate and speedometer gear assembly from the extension housing.
9. Remove the back-up light switch from the extension housing.
10. Remove the snap-ring and slide the speedometer drive gear from the mainshaft.
11. Remove the bottom cover and gasket.
12. Unbolt and remove the shift rod ends.
13. Remove the rear bearing housing from the intermediate housing.
14. Remove the snap-ring and remove the mainshaft rear bearing, thrust washer and race. A puller may be necessary.
15. Using the puller, remove the washer and countershaft rear bearing.
16. Remove the counter fifth gear.
17. Remove the intermediate housing from the case.
18. Unbolt and remove the springs and shift locking balls.
19. Remove the two blind covers and gaskets from the case.
20. Unbolt and remove the reverse/fifth shift rod, fork and interlock pin.
21. Unbolt and remove the first/second and third/fourth shift forks, rods and interlock pins.
22. Remove the snap ring and slide the washer, fifth gear and synchronizer ring from the main shaft. Also, remove the steel ball and needle bearing.
23. Lock the rotation of the mainshaft with second and reverse.
24. Remove the locknut and slide the reverse/fifth clutch hub and sleeve assembly, synchronizer ring, reverse gear and the needle bearing from the mainshaft.
25. Remove the spacer and counter reverse gear from the countershaft.
26. Remove the reverse idler gear, thrust washers and shaft from the transmission case.
27. Remove the bearing rear cover plate.
28. Remove the snap ring from the front end of the countershaft and install Mazda tool number 49 0839 445 synchronizer ring holder or its equivalent between the fourth synchronizer ring and the synchromesh gear on the main driveshaft.
29. Using a bearing puller, remove the countershaft front bearing.
30. Remove the adjusting shim from the countershaft front bearing bore.
31. With the puller, remove the countershaft center bearing outer race.
32. With a special puller and attachment, remove the mainshaft front bearing, thrust washer, and inner race along with the adjusting shim from the mainshaft front bearing bore.
33. Remove the snap-ring, and using the puller, remove the main drive shaft bearing.
34. Remove the countershaft center bearing inner race with the puller.
35. Separate the input shaft from the mainshaft and remove the input shaft from the case.
36. Remove the synchronizer ring and needle bearing from the input shaft.
37. Remove the mainshaft assembly from the case.
38. Remove the first/second and third/fourth shift forks from the case.
39. Remove the snap-ring and slide the third/fourth clutch hub and sleeve assembly, synchronizer ring and third gear from the mainshaft.
40. Remove the thrust washer, first gear and needle bearing from the rear of the mainshaft.
41. Press out the needle bearing inner race, synchronizer ring, first and second clutch hub, sleeve aasembly, synchronizer ring and second gear from the mainshaft.

Inspection

Inspection of components is carried out in the same manner as described in the Rotary Pick-up 4 Speed section.

Assembly

1. Install the third/fourth clutch hub into the sleeve, place the three keys into the clutch hub slots and install the springs onto the hub.
2. Assemble the first/second and reverse/fifth clutch hub and sleeve as described in step 1.
3. Install the needle bearing, second gear, synchronizer ring, and first/second clutch assembly on the rear section of the mainshaft.
4. Press on the first gear needle bearing inner race.
5. Install the third gear and synchronizer ring onto the front section of the mainshaft.
6. Install the third/fourth clutch assembly onto the mainshaft.
7. Fit the snap ring on the mainshaft.
8. Install the needle bearing, synchronizer ring, first gear and thrust washer on the mainshaft.
9. Install the mainshaft assembly in the case.
10. Install the needle bearing on the front end of the mainshaft.
11. Install the first/second and third/fourth shift forks in their respective clutch sleeves.

1. Shim
2. Snap ring
3. Main drive shaft bearing
4. Main drive shaft gear
5. Synchronizer ring
6. Sychronizer key
7. Synchronizer key spring
8. 3rd-and-4th clutch hub
9. Clutch sleeve
10. 3rd gear
11. Needle bearing
12. Needle bearing
13. Main shaft
14. Needle bearing
15. 2nd gear
16. 1st-and-2nd clutch hub
17. Clutch sleeve
18. Bearing inner race
19. Needle bearing
20. 1st gear
21. Thrust washer
22. Shim
23. Main shaft front bearing
24. Bearing cover
25. Thrust washer
26. Bearing inner race
27. Needle bearing
28. Reverse gear
29. Stop ring
30. Rev.-and-5th clutch hub
31. Clutch sleeve
32. Main shaft lock nut
33. Needle bearing
34. 5th gear
35. Thrust washer
36. Lock ball
37. Main shaft rear bearing
38. Thrust washer
39. Lock ball
40. Speedometer drive gear
41. Counter shaft front bearing
42. Shim
43. Counter shaft
44. Counter shaft center bearing
45. Counter reverse gear
46. Spacer
47. Reverse gear
48. Counter shaft rear bearing
49. Thrust washer
50. Thrust washer
51. Reverse idler gear
52. Idler gear shaft
53. Thrust washer

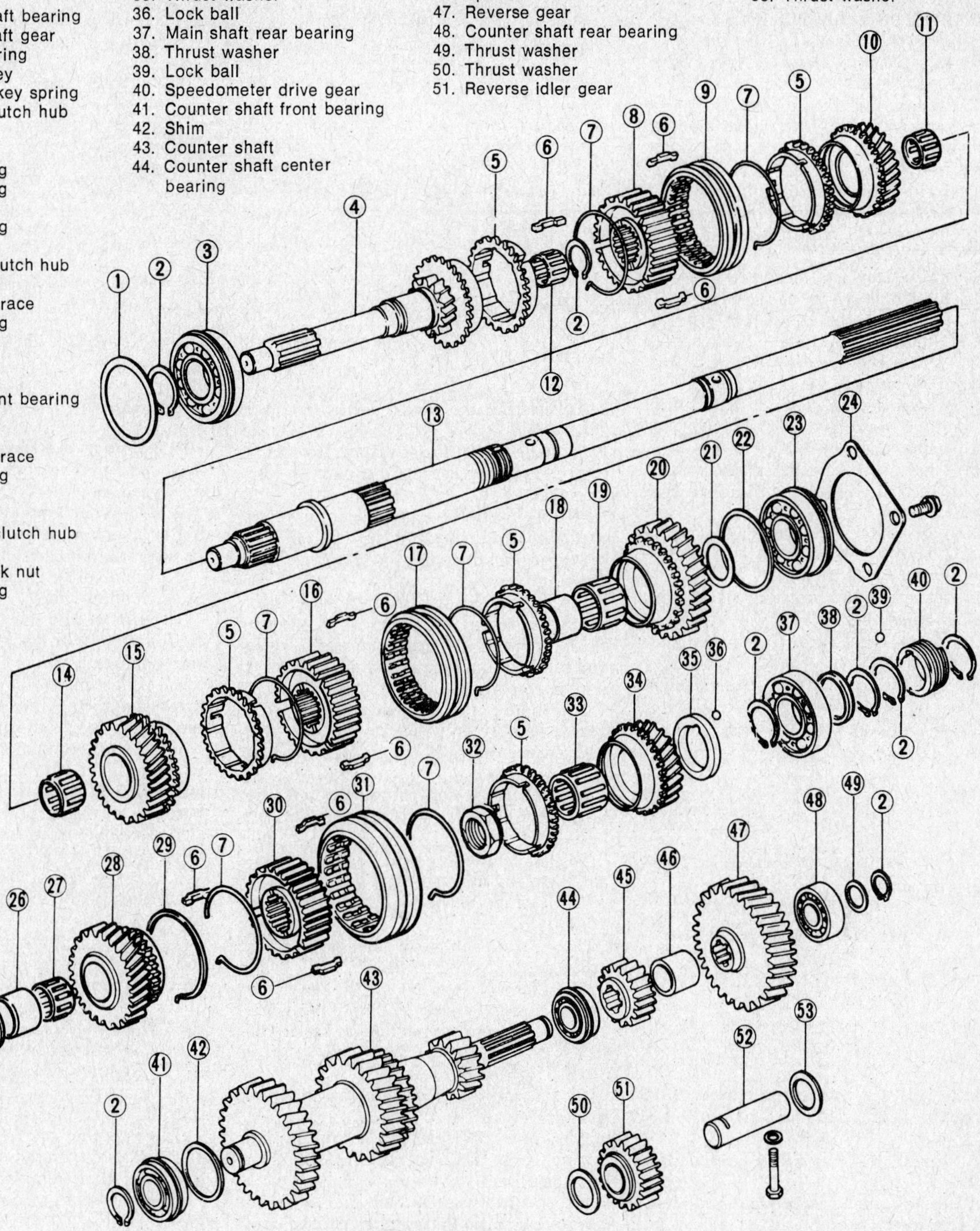

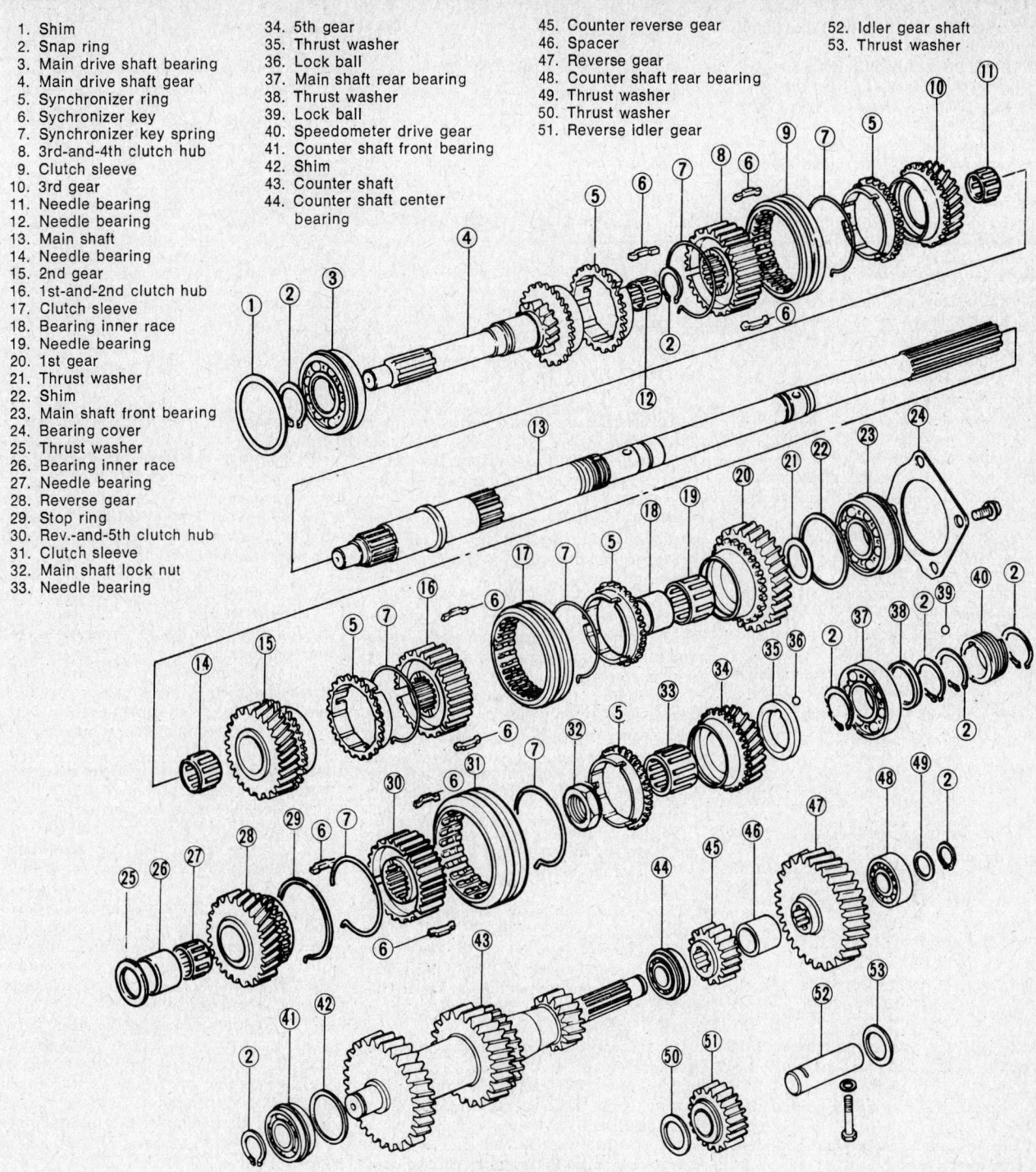

5-speed gear train

12. Press the countershaft center bearing inner race on the countershaft.

13. Position the countershaft in the case.

14. Check the mainshaft bearing end play. Check the depth of the mainshaft bearing bore in the case. Measure the mainshaft bearing height. The difference indicates the required adjusting shim to give a total end play of less than 0.0039″.

15. Install the synchronizer ring holder tool between the fourth synchronizer ring and the synchromesh gear on the input shaft.

16. Position the shims and mainshaft bearing in the bore and install with a press.

17. Install the input shaft bearing in the same way.

18. Check the countershaft front bearing end play in the same way as the mainshaft bearing end play.

19. Install the front bearing snap-ring.

20. Press the countershaft center bearing into position.

21. Install the bearing cover plate.

22. Install the reverse idler gear shaft, thrust washers and reverse idler gear in the case.

23. Install the counter reverse gear and spacer on the rear end of the countershaft.

24. Install the thrust washer and press the needle bearing inner race of the reverse gear on the mainshaft.

25. Install the needle bearing, reverse gear, synchronizer ring, reverse/fifth

clutch assembly and new mainshaft lock nut on the mainshaft.

26. Lock the mainshaft with the second and reverse gears. Tighten the locknut to 115–173 ft lb. Bend the tabs of the locknut.

27. Install the needle bearing, synchronizer ring and fifth gear on the mainshaft.

28. Install the thrust washer, steel ball and snap ring on the mainshaft.

29. Check the thrust washer-to-snap-ring clearance. Clearance should be 0.0039–0.0118″.

30. Install the first/second shift rod through the holes in the case and fork.

31. Install the interlock pin with a special installer and guide.

32. Install the third/fourth shift rod through the holes in the case and fork.

33. Align the holes and install the lock bolts of each shift fork and rod.

34. Install the interlock pin as above.

35. Position the reverse/fifth shift fork on the clutch sleeve and install the shift rod.

36. Tighten the lock bolt.

37. Install the three shift locking balls, springs and cap bolts.

38. Place the third/fourth clutch sleeve in third gear.

39. Check the clearance between the synchronizer key and the exposed edge of the synchronizer ring with a feeler gauge. The gap should be 0.026–0.079″. Adjust by varying thrust washers.

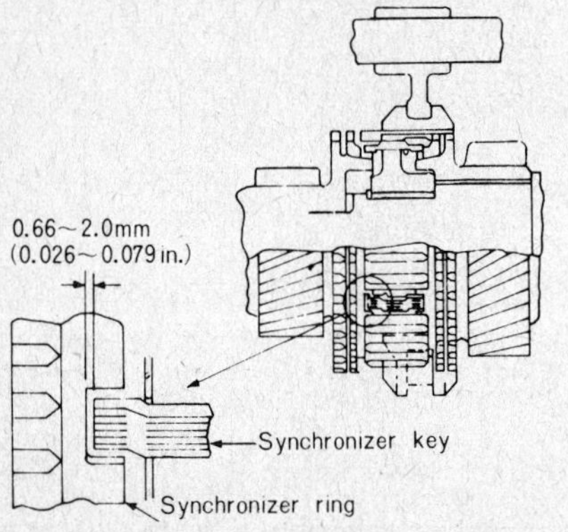

Checking the synchronizer clearance (© Toyo Kogyo Co. Ltd.)

40. Install the two blind covers and gaskets.

41. Install the undercover and gasket. Torque to 4-7 ft lb.

42. Apply a thin coat of sealer to the mating edges and install the intermediate housing on the transmission case. Align the lock bolt holes of the housing and reverse idler gear shaft, install and tighten the lock bolt.

43. Position the counter fifth gear and bearing to the rear end of the countershaft and install with a press.

44. Install the thrust washer and snap-ring.

45. Check the clearance between the washer and snap-ring. Clearance should be less than 0.0039″.

46. Install the mainshaft rear bearing with a press.

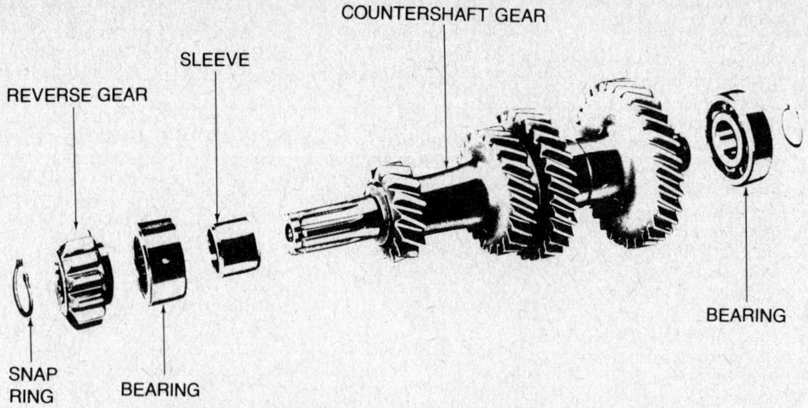

B-1600 countershaft (© Toyo Kogyo Co. Ltd.)

47. Install the thrust washer and snap-ring.

48. Check the thrust washer-to-snap-ring clearance. Clearance should be less than 0.0059″.

49. Apply a thin coat of sealing agent to the mating surfaces and install the bearing housing on the intermediate housing.

50. Install the shift rod ends on their respective rods.

51. Install the speedometer drive gear and steel ball on the mainshaft. Secure it with a snap-ring.

52. Install the speedometer driven gear assembly on the extension housing and secure it with the bolt and lock plate.

53. Insert the control rod through the holes from the front side of the extension housing.

54. Align the key and insert the control lever end in the control rod.

55. Install the bolt and tighten it to 20-30 ft lb.

56. Install the back-up light switch and tighten to 20–30 ft lb.

57. Place the gasket on the case and install the extension housing with the control lever end down and as far to the left as it will go.

58. Tighten the bolts.

59. Check the proper operation of the gear shift lever.

60. Insert the select lock spindle and spring from the underside of the shift lever retainer.

61. Install the steel ball and spring in alignment with the spindle groove and install the spring cap bolt.

62. Install the gearshift lever retainer and gasket on the extension housing.

63. Check the bearing end play. Measure the depth of the bearing bore in the housing. Measure the height of the bearing protrusion. The difference indicates the thickness of the shim needed. The end play should be less than 0.0039″.

64. Place the gasket on the front side of the case. Apply lubricant to the lip of the oil seal and install the clutch housing on the case.

65. Install the release bearing and fork on the clutch housing.

Disassembly—B-1600 4 Speed

1. Remove the throwout bearing return spring, throwout bearing, and the release fork.

2. Unfasten the bearing housing, bolts, then remove the housing and gasket.

3. Remove the input shaft and countershaft snap-rings.

4. Remove the floorshift lever retainer, complete with gasket from the extension housing.

5. Unfasten the cap bolt and withdraw the spring, steel ball, select lock pin and spring from the retainer.

6. Remove the extension housing securing nuts. Turn the control lever as far left as it will go and slide the extension housing off the output shaft.

7. Remove the spring seat and spring from the end of the shift control lever.

8. Loosen the spring cap and withdraw the spring and plunger from their bore.

9. Unfasten the bolt from the control rod yoke, then remove the control rod and boss from the extension housing.

10. Loosen the setscrew and remove the speedometer driven gear. Remove the back-up light switch.

11. Remove the speedometer drive gear snap-ring, slide the gear off the output shaft and take off the lockball.

12. Tap the front ends of the input shaft and countershaft with a plastic hammer; then remove the intermediate housing assembly from the transmission case.

13. Remove the three cap bolts; then withdraw the springs and lockballs.

14. Unfasten the shift lever securing nut. Remove the reverse shift rod. Reverse idler gear, and shift lever from the intermediate housing.

15. Remove the setscrews from all the shift forks and push the shift rods rearward to remove them. Remove the shift forks as well.

16. Withdraw the Reverse shift rod lockball, spring, and interlock pins from the intermediate housing.

17. Keep the output shaft from turning; straighten the tabs on its lockwasher, and remove its locknut. Remove

Reverse gear and key from the output shaft.

18. Remove the snap-ring from the rear of the countershaft and slide the reverse countergear off.

19. Using a plastic hammer, tap the rear of the output shaft and countershaft in turn, being careful not to damage them. Remove both shafts from the intermediate housing.

20. Remove the bearings from the intermediate housing and transmission case.

21. Remove the snap-ring from the output shaft.

22. Slide the Third/Fourth clutch hub, sleeve, synchronizer ring, and Third gear off the output shaft.

23. Remove the thrust washer, First gear, sleeve, synchronizer ring, and second gear from the rear of the output shaft.

Inspection

The inspection procedures for this transmission are identical to those outlined for the Rotary engine 4 speed.

Assembly

1. Install the Third/Fourth synchronizer clutch hub on the sleeve. Place the three synchronizer keys in the clutch hub key slots. Install the key springs with their open ends 120° apart.

2. Install Third gear and the synchronizer ring on the front of the output shaft. Install the Third/Fourth clutch hub assembly on the output shaft. Be sure that the larger boss faces the front of the shaft.

3. Secure the gear and synchronizer with the snap ring.

Remove the reverse shift lever from the intermediate housing on the B-1600
(© Toyo Kogyo Co. Ltd.)

4. Perform step 1 to the First/Second synchronizer assembly.

5. Position the synchronizer ring on second gear. Slide Second gear on the output shaft so that the synchronizer ring faces the rear of the shaft.

6. Install the First/Second clutch hub assembly on the output shaft so that its oil grooves face the front of the shaft. Engage the keys in the notches on the Second gear synchronizer ring.

7. Slide the First gear sleeve onto the output shaft. Position the synchonizer ring on First gear. Install the First gear on the output shaft so that the synchronizer ring faces frontward. Rotate the First gear as required to engage the notches in the synchronizer ring with the keys in the clutch hub.

8. Slip the thrust washer on the rear of the output shaft. Install the needle bearing on the front of the output shaft.

9. Install the synchronizer ring on Fourth gear and install the input shaft on the front of the output shaft.

10. Press the countershaft rear bearing and shim into the intermediate housing; then press the countershaft into the rear bearing.

11. Keep the thrust washer and First gear from falling off the output shaft by supporting the shaft. Install the output shaft on the intermediate housing. Be sure that each output shaft gear engages with its opposite number on the countershaft.

12. Tap the output shaft bearing and shim into the intermediate housing with a plastic hammer. Fit the cover on the housing.

13. Install Reverse gear on the output shaft and secure it with its key. Keep the

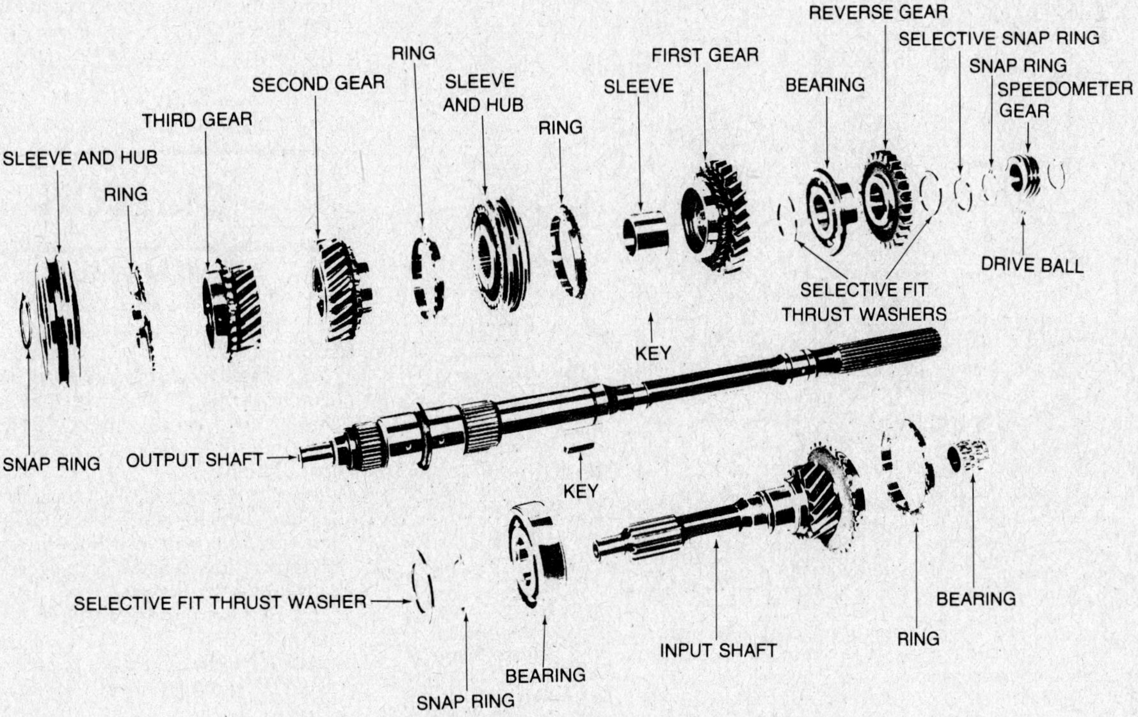

Input and output shafts—B-1600 (© Toyo Kogyo Co. Ltd.)

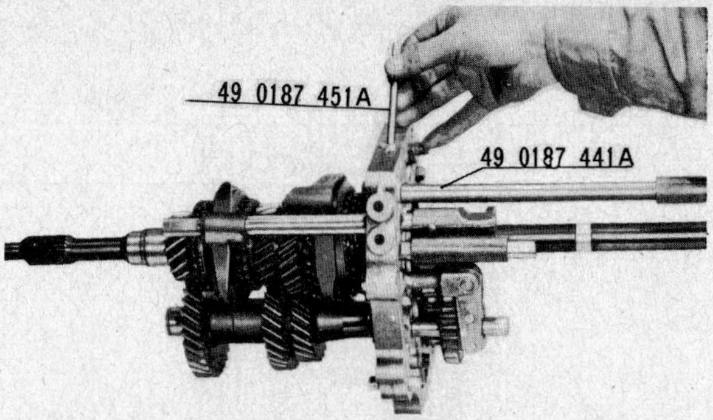

Input shaft, output shaft and countershaft assembled to the intermediate housing—B-1600
(© Toyo Kogyo Co. Ltd.)

output shaft from turning while tightening its locknut. Secure the nut by bending the tabs on the lockwasher.

NOTE: The chamfer on the teeth of both the Reverse gear and the Reverse countergear should face rearward.

14. Install the Reverse countergear and secure it with its snap-ring.
15. Install the lockball and spring into the bore in the intermediate housing. Depress the ball with a screwdriver.
16. Install the Reverse shift rod, lever, and idler gear at the same time. Tighten the nut which secures the shift lever to the intermediate housing. Place the Reverse shift rod in the neutral position.
17. Align the bores and insert the shift interlock pin.
18. Install the Third/Fourth shift rod into the intermediate housing end shift bores. Place the shift rod in Neutral.
19. Install the next interlock pin in the bore.
20. Install the First/Second shift rod.
21. Install the lockballs and springs in their bores. Install the cap bolt.
22. Fit the speedometer drive gear and lockball on the output shaft, and install its snap-ring.
23. Apply sealer to the mating surfaces of the intermediate housing. Install the intermediate housing in the transmission case.
24. Install the input shaft and countershaft front bearings in the transmission case. Fit the snap-ring on the input shaft bearing.
25. Secure the speedometer driven gear to the extension housing with its setscrew.
26. Install the control rod through the holes in the front of the extension housing.
27. Align the key with the keyway and install the yoke on the end of the control rod. Install the yoke lockbolt.
28. Fit the plunger and spring into the extension housing bore and secure with the spring cap.
29. Turn the control rod all the way to the left, install the extension housing on the intermediate housing, and tighten its securing nuts. Check control rod operation.
30. Insert the spring and select lockpin inside the gearshift retainer. Align the steel ball and spring with the lockpin slot, and secure it with the spring cap.
31. Install the spring and spring seat in the control rod yoke.
32. Install the gearshift lever retainer over its gasket on the extension housing.
33. Lubricate the lip of the front bearing cover oil seal and secure the cover on the transmission case.
34. Check the clearance between the front bearing cover and bearing. It should be less than 0.006 in. If it is not within specifications insert additional adjusting shims. The shims are available in 0.006 in. or 0.012 in. sizes.
35. Install the throwout bearing, return spring and release fork.

SHIFT LEVER ADJUSTMENT

The shift lever may be adjusted during transmission installation by means of the adjusting shims on the three bolts between the cover plate and the packing. The force required to move the shift knob should be 4.4–8.8 lbs.

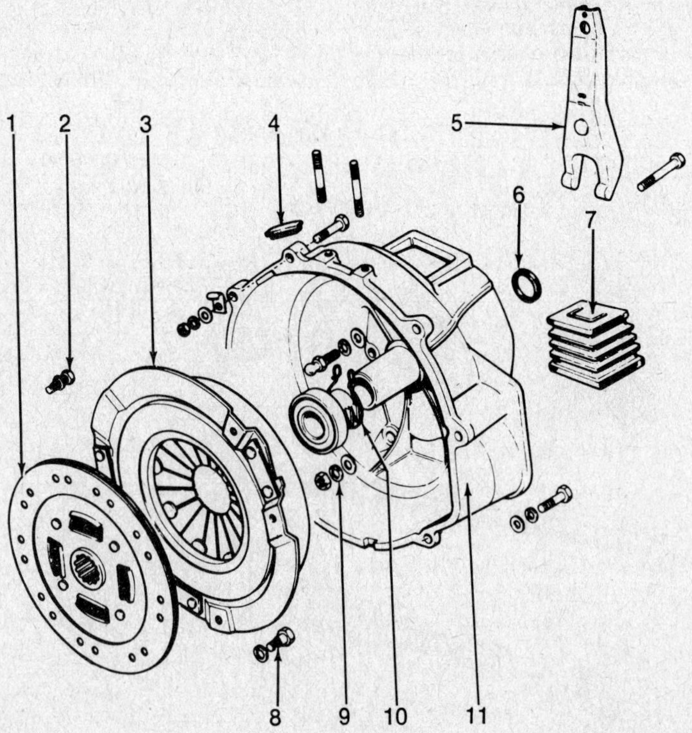

1. Clutch disc
2. Bolt
3. Clutch cover and pressure plate assembly
4. Service hole cover
5. Release fork
6. Oil seal
7. Dust boot
8. Reamer bolt
9. Release bearing
10. Spring
11. Clutch housing

Clutch components

CLUTCH

REMOVAL

1. Remove the transmission.
2. Attach a locking tool to the flywheel.
3. Install a clutch arbor to hold the clutch in place. An old input shaft makes an excellent arbor. Matchmark the pressure plate and flywheel for installation.
4. Unfasten the bolts (4 securing and 2 pilot) which secure the clutch cover, one turn at a time in sequence, until the clutch spring tension is released. Remove the bolts evenly.
5. Remove the clutch disc.

CAUTION: Be careful not to get grease or oil on the surface of the clutch disc.

6. Unfasten the nut which secures the

flywheel to the eccentric shaft, using a suitably large wrench.

7. Remove the flywheel with a puller.

8. Unhook the return spring from the throwout bearing and remove the bearing.

9. Pull out the release fork until the retaining spring frees itself from the ball stud. Withdraw the fork from the housing.

INSTALLATION

Clutch installation is performed in the following order:

1. Clean the flywheel and pressure plate surfaces with fine sandpaper. Check the flywheel and pressure plate for warpage, scoring, or signs of heat distortion. If scoring damage is minor, it can usually be cleaned up. Heavy wear or damage warrants replacement of the parts. Be sure that there is no oil or grease on them. Grease the eccentric shaft needle bearing.

2. Install the flywheel with its keyway over the key on the eccentric shaft.

3. Apply sealer to both sides of the flywheel lockwasher and position the lockwasher on the eccentric shaft.

4. Install the flywheel locknut(s) and tighten it to 350 ft. lbs. (rotary engines) or 112–118 ft. lbs. (piston engines); then bend the tabs of the lockwasher up around it.

5. Use an arbor to center the clutch disc during installation. Install the clutch disc with the long end of its hub facing the transmission.

NOTE: Use an old input shaft to center the clutch disc, if an arbor is not available.

6. Align the O-mark on the clutch cover with the reamed hole or the O-mark on the flywheel or align the matchmarks made during removal.

7. Tighten the clutch cover bolts evenly, and in two or three stages, to 13–20 ft lbs.

CAUTION: Do not tighten the bolts one at a time.

8. Grease the pivot pin. Insert the release fork through its boot so that its retaining spring contacts the pivot pin.

9. Lightly grease the face of the throwout bearing and its clutch housing retainer.

10. Install the throwout bearing and return spring. Check the operation of the release fork and throwout bearing for smoothness.

11. Install the transmission.

PEDAL HEIGHT ADJUSTMENT

Except B-1600

1. Loosen the locknut on the adjusting bolt.

2. Turn the adjusting bolt until the clearance between the pedal pad and the floormat is 8.46 in.

3. Carefully tighten the locknut.

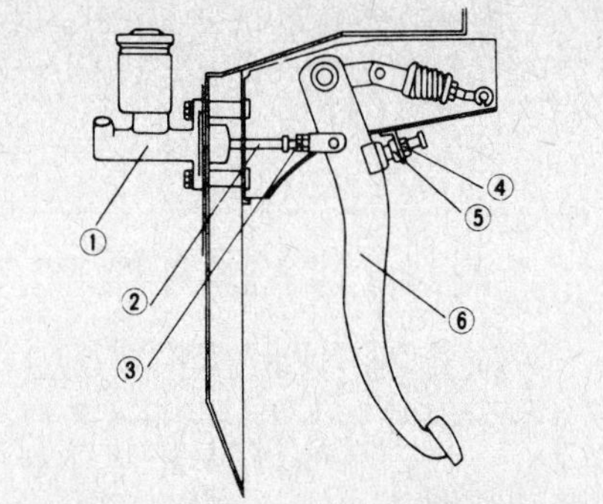

1. Master cylinder
2. Rod
3. Locknut
4. Adjusting bolt
5. Locknut
6. Clutch pedal

Clutch pedal height adjustment

PEDAL FREE-PLAY ADJUSTMENT

The free-play of the clutch pedal before the pushrod contacts the piston in the master cylinder should be 0.02–0.12 in.

To adjust the free-play, loosen the locknut and turn the pushrod until the proper adjustment is obtained. Tighten the locknut after the adjustment is complete.

RELEASE FORK FREE-PLAY ADJUSTMENT

Through 1975 Only

1. Unfasten the return spring from the release fork.

2. Loosen the locknut on the release rod.

3. Turn the adjusting nut on the release rod until the proper release fork free-play is obtained:

Rotary Pick-Ups—0.14–0.18 in.
B—1600—0.12–0.14

4. Carefully tighten the locknut and hook the return spring back on the release fork.

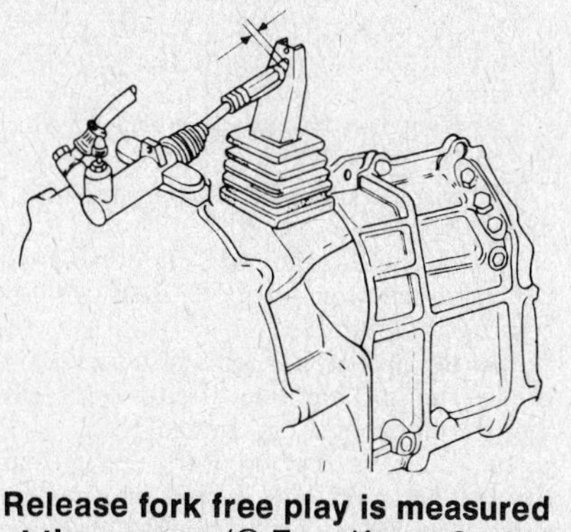

Release fork free play is measured at the arrows (© Toyo Kogyo Co. Ltd.)

Clutch Master Cylinder

REMOVAL AND INSTALLATION

1. Unfasten the hydraulic line from the master cylinder outlet and plug the outlet.

CAUTION: Use care not to drip any hydraulic fluid on painted surfaces, as it is an excellent paint remover.

2. Remove the nuts which secure the master cylinder assembly to the firewall.

3. Withdraw the master cylinder straight out and away from the firewall.

Installation is performed in the reverse order of removal. Bleed the hydraulic system as detailed below.

OVERHAUL

1. Thoroughly clean the outside of the master cylinder.

2. Drain the hydraulic fluid from the cylinder. Unbolt the reservoir from the cylinder body.

3. Remove the boot from the cylinder.

4. Release the wire piston stop ring with a screwdriver and withdraw the stop washer.

5. Withdraw the piston, piston cups, and return spring from the cylinder bore.

6. Wash all of the parts in clean hydraulic (brake) fluid. Do not use mineral spirits.

7. Examine the piston cups. If they are damaged, softened, or swollen, replace them with new ones.

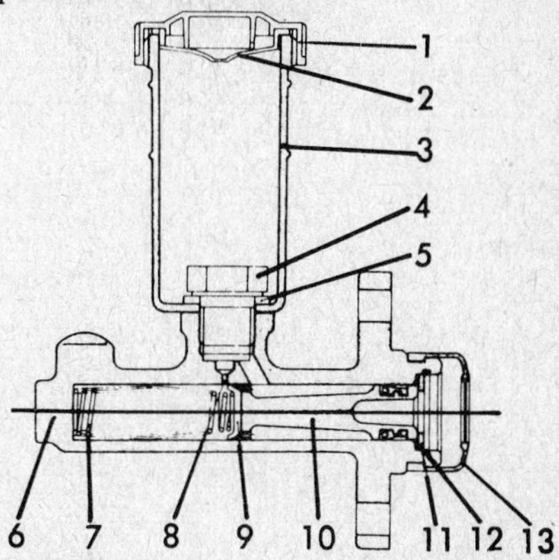

1. Cap
2. Baffle
3. Reservoir
4. Bolt
5. Washer
6. Cylinder
7. Return spring
8. Compensating port
9. Primary cup
10. Piston
11. Stop washer
12. Stop wire
13. Boot

Cutaway view of the master cylinder

8. Check the piston and bore for scoring or roughness.

9. Use a wire gauge to check the clearance between the piston and its bore. Replace either the piston or the cylinder if the clearance is greater than 0.006 in.

10. Be sure that the compensating port in the cylinder is not clogged.

ASSEMBLY

Assembly of the master cylinder is performed in the following order:

1. Dip the piston and cups in clean hydraulic (brake) fluid.

2. Bolt the reservoir up to the cylinder body.

3. Fit the return spring into the cylinder.
4. Insert the primary cup in the bore so that its flat side is facing the piston.
5. Place the secondary cup on the piston and insert them in the cylinder bore.
6. Install the stop washer and the wire piston stop.
7. Fill the reservoir half-full of hydraulic fluid. Operate the piston with a screwdriver until fluid spurts out of the cylinder outlet.
8. Fit the boot on the cylinder.

Clutch Release Cylinder

REMOVAL AND INSTALLATION

1. Unscrew the hydraulic line from the release cylinder and plug it.
2. Unhook the release fork return spring from the cylinder.
3. Unfasten the nuts which secure the release cylinder to the transmission.

Installation is performed in the reverse order of removal. Bleed the hydraulic system, as detailed below, and adjust the release fork free-play, as detailed above.

OVERHAUL

Consult the master cylinder overhaul section above for release cylinder overhaul procedures.

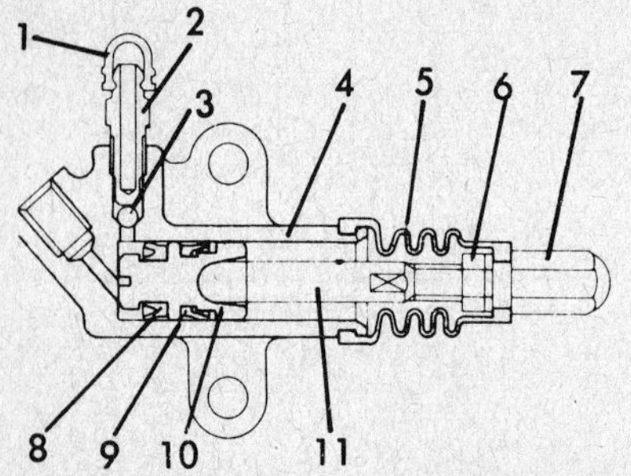

1. Cap
2. Bleeder screw
3. Valve
4. Cylinder
5. Boot
6. Lock nut
7. Adjusting nut
8. Primary cup
9. Secondary cup
10. Piston
11. Push rod

Cutaway view of the release cylinder

SYSTEM BLEEDING

1. Remove the rubber cap from the bleeder screw on the release cylinder.
2. Palce a bleeder tube over the end of the bleeder screw.
3. Submerge the other end of the tube in a jar half-filled with hydraulic (brake) fluid.
4. Depress the clutch pedal fully and allow it to return slowly.
5. Keep repeating step 4, while watching the hydraulic fluid in the jar. As soon as the air bubbles disappear, close the bleeder screw.

NOTE: During the bleeding procedure the reservoir must be kept at least 3/4 full.

6. Remove the tube and refit the rubber cap. Fill the reservoir with hydraulic fluid.

AUTOMATIC TRANSMISSION

REMOVAL

Rotary Pick-Up

1. Disconnect the cable from the negative (–) battery terminal.
2. Remove the power brake vacuum line bracket from the converter housing.
3. Remove the converter access hole cover. Lock the flex-plate by holding the drive pulley lockbolt with a wrench.
4. Matchmark the converter and flexplate. Unfasten the four converter-to-flexplate securing bolts.
5. Jack up the vehicle and securely support it with jackstands.

CAUTION: The exhaust system on rotary engine-equipped Mazdas gets considerably hotter than a conventional system; be sure to allow enough time for it to cool before performing steps 6 and 7.

6. Remove the heat shroud. Unfasten the exhaust pipe bracket on the right-hand side of the torque converter housing.
7. Unfasten the bolts which secure the exhaust pipe to the rear side of the front muffler. Detach the exhaust pipe.
8. Unfasten the bolts from the driveshaft flange and center bearing. Push the driveshaft out of the extension housing. Plug the hole in the extension housing, so that fluid doesn't leak out.
9. Detach the speedometer cable at the extension housing.
10. Remove the control rod.
11. Disconnect the starter wiring. Remove the starter from the converter housing.
12. Remove the bottom cover from the converter housing.
13. Support the transmission with a jack.
14. Unfasten the nuts which secure the transmission support member and remove the member.
15. Lower the transmission jack to increase the gap between the transmission and the underbody of the truck.
16. Remove the vacuum fitting from the intake manifold. Unfasten the vacuum line from the converter housing, transmission case, and extension housing. Disconnect the hose from the vacuum modulator and remove the vacuum line.
17. Disconnect the downshift solenoid wiring and separate the wires from the clip.
18. Disconnect the lines which run to the cooler at the left-hand side of the transmission. Remove the clips for these lines from the converter housing and transmission case.
19. Unfasten evenly, and in several stages, the bolts which secure the torque converter housing to the top of the engine.
20. Raise the transmission so that it is level again.
21. Use a screwdriver to carefully apply pressure between the torque converter and the flex-plate.
22. Slide the transmission rearward and lower it from the truck.

CAUTION: Do not rest the weight of the transmission on the torque converter splines.

INSTALLATION

Automatic transmission installation is performed in almost the reverse order of removal. There are several points which should be noted, however:

1. Before installing the transmission, use a dial indicator to measure flex-plate runout. Runout should be about 0.012 in. If runout exceeds 0.020 in., the flex-plate must be replaced.
2. Hand-tighten the four torque converter installation bolts and then lock the flex-plate with a locking tool. Next, tighten the four bolts evenly, and in several stages, to 27–40 ft lbs.
3. After completing transmission installation, rotate the eccentric shaft to be sure that there is no interference in the transmission.
4. Fill the transmission with type F transmission fluid. Converter capacity is 6.6 qts.
5. Check and adjust the following items, after completing installation:
   a. Shift linkage.
   b. Neutral safety switch.
   c. Engine idle speed.
   d. Kickdown switch and downshift solenoid.
6. Check the fluid level again and road test the car.

SHIFT LINKAGE ADJUSTMENT

1974-75

1. Unfasten the T-joint on the intermediate lever.
2. Place the range selector lever, which is mounted on the side of the transmission case, in Neutral (N); i.e., so that the slot in the selector shaft is pointing straight up and down.
3. Adjust the console-mounted gear selector lever by turning the T-joint until it indicates Neutral (N).
4. Reconnect the T-joint. Check the gear selector operation in all other ranges and to see that the linkage has no slack.

1976 and Later

1. Place the transmission selector lever in N.
2. Raise the vehicle and disconnect the clevis from the lower end of the selector arm.

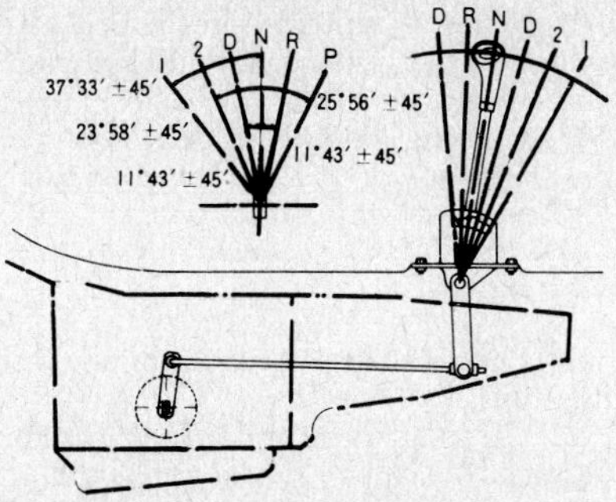

Transmission linkage adjustment
(© Toyo Kogyo Co. Ltd.)

3. Move the manual lever to the N position.

NOTE: The N position is the third detent from the back.

4. Loosen the two clevis retaining nuts and adjust the clevis so that it freely enters the lever hole.
5. Tighten the retaining nuts.
6. Connect the clevis to the lever and secure with the spring washer, flat washer and retaining clip.

NEUTRAL SAFETY SWITCH ADJUSTMENT

Rotary Pick-Up

1. Remove the housing from the shift lever.
2. Adjust the shift lever so that there is 0.–0.012 in. clearance between the pin and the guide plate, when the lever is in neutral.
3. Adjust the neutral safety switch so that the pin hole in the switch body is aligned with the pin hole of the sliding plate when the shift lever is in Neutral.
4. Check the adjustment by trying to start the engine in all gears. It should only start in Park or Neutral.
5. Reinstall the housing on the shift lever.

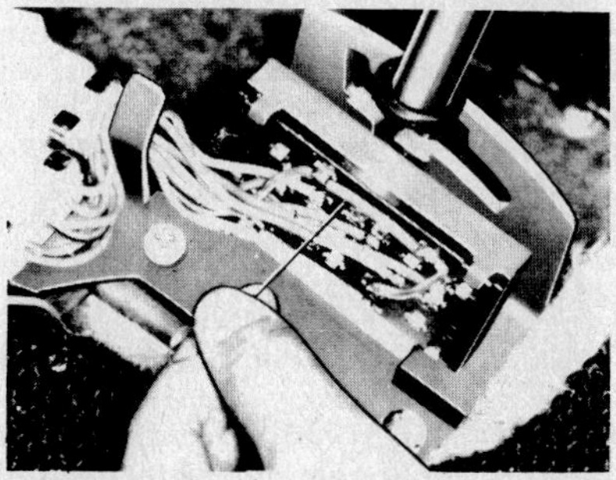

Rotary pick-up neutral safety switch
(© Toyo Kogyo Co. Ltd.)

PAN REMOVAL AND INSTALLATION

1. Raise and support the vehicle.
2. Place a drain pan under the transmission pan.
3. Remove the pan attaching bolts (except the two at the front). Loosen the two at the front slightly. Allow the fluid to drain.
4. Remove the pan.
5. Remove and discard the gasket.
6. Install a new pan gasket and install the pan on the transmission.
7. Lower the vehicle and fill the transmission with fluid. Check the transmission operation.

KICKDOWN SWITCH AND DOWNSHIFT SOLENOID ADJUSTMENT

1. Check the accelerator linkage for smooth operation.
2. Turn the ignition on but do not start the engine.
3. Depress the accelerator pedal fully to the floor. As the pedal nears the end of its travel, a light "click" should be heard from the downshift solenoid.
4. If the kickdown switch operates too soon, loosen the locknut on the switch shaft. Adjust the shaft so that the accelerator linkage makes contact with it when the pedal is depressed $^7/_8$–$^{15}/_{16}$ of the way to the floor. Tighten the locknut.

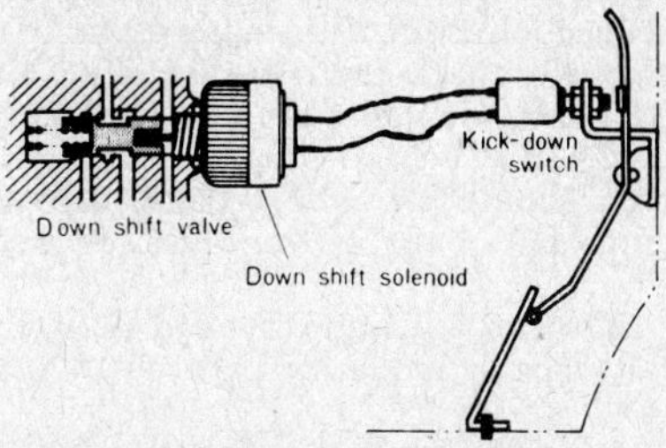

Kickdown switch and downshift solenoid circuit
(© Toyo Kogyo Co. Ltd.)

5. If no noise comes from the solenoid at all, then check the wiring for the solenoid and the switch.
6. If the wiring is in good condition, then remove the wire from the solenoid and connect it to a 12V power source. If the solenoid does not click when connected, it is defective and should be replaced.

NOTE: When the solenoid is removed, about two pints of transmission fluid will leak out; have a container ready to catch it. Remember to add more fluid to the transmission after installing the new solenoid.

BAND ADJUSTMENT

JATCO Model 3N71B

1. Raise and support the vehicle.
2. Drain the transmission fluid and remove the pan.
3. Loosen the locknut and tighten the servo adjusting bolt to 9–11 ft. lbs.
4. Back off the servo bolt exactly two full turns. Hold the bolt in this position and tighten the locknut securely.
5. Install the pan and refill the transmission.

JATCO Model R3A

1. Raise and support the vehicle.
2. The servo is located on the right side of the transmission case. Remove the servo cover.
3. Loosen the locknut and tighten the servo adjusting bolt to 9–11 ft. lbs.
4. Loosen the servo bolt exactly two full turns. Hold the bolt in this position and tighten the locknut securely.
5. Install the servo cover.

DRIVE AXLES

Driveshaft and U-Joints

REMOVAL AND INSTALLATION

1. Raise the rear end of the car and support it using jackstands.

CAUTION: Be sure that the car is securely supported. Remember, you will be working underneath it.

2. Matchmark the flanges on the driveshaft and pinion so that they may be installed in their original position.
3. Remove the four bolts which secure the driveshaft to the pinion flange. Unbolt the center bearing.
4. Lower the back end of the driveshaft and slide the front end out of the transmission.
5. Plug up the hole in the transmission to prevent it from leaking.

NOTE: Use an old U-joint yoke; or, if none is available, place a plastic bag, secured with rubber bands, over the hole.

NOTE: Do not remove the oil seals and the center bearing from the support unless they are defective.

Installation is performed in the reverse order of removal. Tighten the center bearing support bolts to 14–21 ft lbs and the drifeshaft-to-pinion flange bolts to 40–47 ft lbs.

U-JOINT OVERHAUL

Perform this procedure with the driveshaft removed from the car.

1. Matchmark both the yoke and the driveshaft so that they can be returned to their original balancing position during assembly.
2. Remove the bearing snap-rings from the yoke.
3. Use a hammer and a brass drift to drive *in* one of the bearing cups. Remove the cup which is protruding from the other side of the yoke.
4. Remove the other bearing cups by pressing them from the spider.
5. Withdraw the spider from the yoke. Examine the spider journals for rusting or wear. Check the bearings for smoothness or pitting.

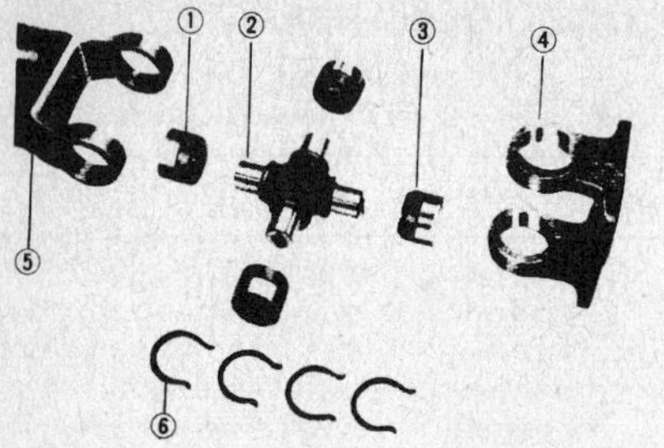

1. Roller bearing (cup)
2. Spider
3. Oil seal
4. Yoke
5. Driveshaft
6. Snap-ring

U-joint components

NOTE: ***The spider and bearing are replaced as a complete assembly only.***

Check the seals and rollers for wear or damage.

Assembly of the U-joint is performed in the following order:

1. Pack the bearing cups with grease.
2. Fit the rollers into the cups and install the dust seals.
3. Place the spider in the yoke and then fit one of the bearing cups into its bore in the yoke.
4. Press the bearing cup home, while guiding the spider into it so that a snap-ring can be installed.
5. Press-fit the other bearings into the yoke.
6. Select a snap-ring to obtain minimum end-play of the spider. Use snap-rings of the same thickness on both sides to center the spider.

NOTE: ***Selective fit snap-rings are available in sizes ranging from 0.048 to 0.054 in.***

7. Install the spider/yoke assembly and bearings to the driveshaft in the same manner as the spider was assembled to the yoke.
8. Test the operation of the U-joint assembly. The spider should move freely with no binding.

Axle Shafts

REMOVAL AND INSTALLATION

Pick-Up Trucks

1. Raise and support the truck.
2. Remove the rear wheel and brake drum.
3. Remove the brake shoes.
4. Remove the parking brake cable retainer.
5. Disconnect and plug the hydraulic brake lines at the wheel cylinders.
6. Unbolt the backing plate and bearing housing.
7. Slide the complete axle shaft from the housing. If necessary, remove the oil seal from the housing.

To install the axle shaft:

8. Install a new axle oil seal in the housing if the old one was removed.
9. Install the axle shaft assembly.
10. Using two bolts and nuts, temporarily install the bearing housing and backing plate to the housing flange.
11. Check the axle shaft end-play with a dial indicator mounted on the backing plate.
12. If only one axle shaft has been removed, the end-play should be 0.002–0.006 in. If both axle shafts have been removed, check the end-play after the first shaft is installed. It should be 0.026–0.033 in. The end-play of the second shaft should then be 0.002–0.006 in. Shims are available to adjust the end-play.
13. After adjusting the end-play, install all bolts and torque them to 12–16 ft lbs.
14. Install the brake shoes.
15. Install the brake drum and wheel.
16. Connect the brake lines.
17. Bleed the brakes.
18. Lower the truck and road-test it.

AXLE SHAFT BEARING AND SEAL REPLACEMENT

1. Remove the rear axle shaft.
2. Using a suitable press, press the axle shaft out of the collar and bearing.

NOTE: ***If the pressure needed to press out the shaft exceeds 10 tons, grind off part of the bearing retaining collar and cut it with a cold chisel, taking care not to damage the shaft surface.***

3. Remove the bearing retainer from the shaft.
4. Clean all parts and inspect the condition of the collar, spacer and shaft.
5. Install the retainer and spacer on the shaft.
6. Position the bearing on the shaft with the sealed side toward the shaft flange. Press it on until the spacer comes in contact with the shoulder of the shaft.
7. Press the bearing retaining collar onto the shaft until it contacts the bearing inner race.

NOTE: ***If the bearing retaining collar can be press fitted with a force less than 2.5 tons, replace the collar.***

8. Install the shaft.

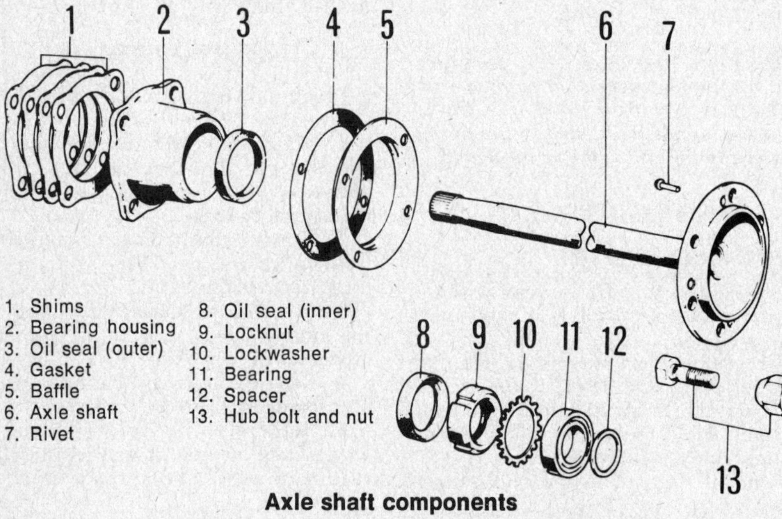

1. Shims
2. Bearing housing
3. Oil seal (outer)
4. Gasket
5. Baffle
6. Axle shaft
7. Rivet
8. Oil seal (inner)
9. Locknut
10. Lockwasher
11. Bearing
12. Spacer
13. Hub bolt and nut

Axle shaft components

Differential

REMOVAL AND INSTALLATION

1. Raise the vehicle and support it with jackstands.
2. Remove the drain (lower) plug from the axle housing and drain the lubricant into a suitable container. Clean and reinstall the plug.
3. Remove the driveshaft as detailed in the appropriate section above.
4. Remove both of the axle shafts as detailed in the section immediately above.
5. Unfasten the nuts which secure the differential carrier to the axle housing and withdraw the carrier assembly from the housing.

Installation is performed in the reverse order of removal. Tighten the carrier-to-housing bolts to 14.5 ft lbs. Fill the axle housing to the level just below the filler plug with one of the following:

Above 0°F-HP SAE 90
Below 0°F-HP SAE 80

OVERHAUL

NOTE: ***Differential overhaul requires the use of special tools and equipment. Proper overhaul cannot be performed without them. The following procedures apply to all Mazda differentials as they are all similar in design.***

Disassembly

1. Mount the carrier on a workstand.
2. Apply identification marks to the carrier, bearing caps, and adjuster, to aid in installation.
3. Unfasten the bolts which secure adjusting nut lockplates and then remove the lockplates.

4. Loosen, but do not remove, the bearing cap securing nuts and then back off on the adjuster, just enough to remove bearing preload.
5. Remove the differential assembly, complete with the outer bearing races.

CAUTION: Be sure that each bearing outer race remains with its bearing.

6. Remove the differential bearings from the gear case with a puller.

NOTE: Use care not to mix up the bearings when setting them aside.

7. Unfasten the bolts which secure the ring gear to the gear case and remove their washers. Separate the ring gear from the case.
8. Straighten out the punched portion of the gear case, then drive the pinion gear shaft locking pin out of the case with a brass drift.
9. Withdraw the pinion gear shaft.
10. Rotate each of the pinion (spider) gears 90° and remove them, complete with thrust washers.
11. Remove the side gears and thrust washers.
12. Hold the pinion flange by screwing two bolts into it and grabbing them with a pipewrench. Remove the pinion nut.
13. Remove the pinion from the carrier.

NOTE: If the pinion is difficult to remove, tap it with a plastic hammer while guiding it out by hand.

14. Remove the collar, if so equipped, and the collapsible spacer from the pinion.
15. Press out the rear bearing and remove the adjustable shim. Save the shim for later reference.
16. Withdraw the oil seal and the front bearing from the carrier.
17. If necessary, the pinion bearing outer races can be driven out with a brass drift placed in the slots which are provided for this purpose.

NOTE: Do not remove the outer races unless they are worn or damaged. If they are replaced, the bearing cones must be replaced as well.

Inspection

1. Check all of the gears for chipping, broken teeth, wear, or other signs of damage. Replace any gears, as required.
2. Examine the carrier and pinion flange for cracks, wear, and other signs of damage. Replace these parts as necessary.
3. Check the clearance between the splines on the side gears and the rear axle shafts. If it is greater than 0.012 in., replace either the side gears or the axle shafts.
4. Inspect the oil seal for wear and/or damage; replace it if either are present.

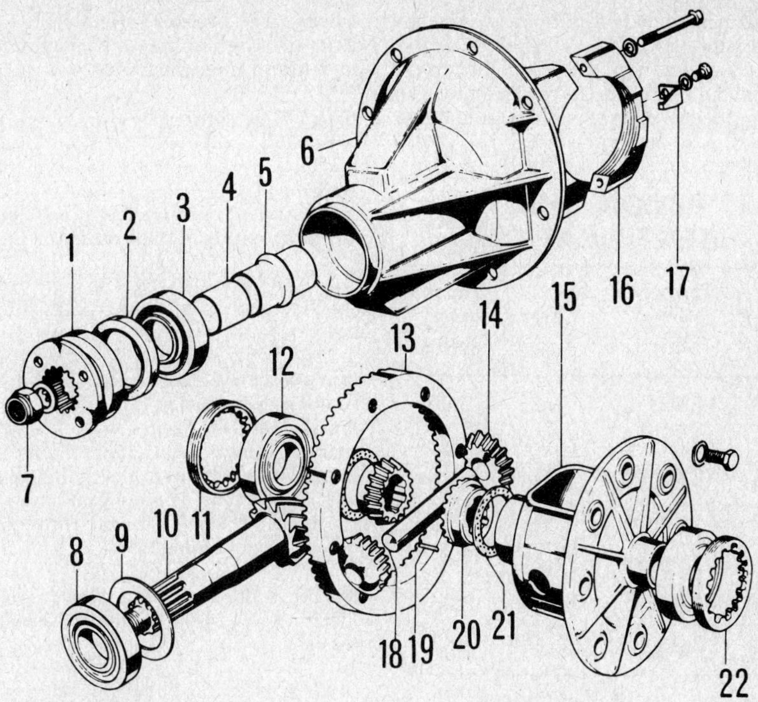

1. Pinion flange
2. Pinion oil seal
3. Pinion front bearing
4. Pinion bearing collar
5. Collapsible pinion bearing spacer
6. Carrier
7. Pinion nut
8. Pinion rear bearing
9. Adjusting washer (adjusting spacer)
10. Drive pinion
11. Pinion side adjusting nut
12. Side bearing
13. Ring gear
14. Pinion gear
15. Differential gear case
16. Bearing cap
17. Adjusting nut lock
18. Pinion shaft
19. Pinion shaft lock pin
20. Side gear
21. Thrust washer
22. Ring gear side adjusting nut

Differential components

ASSEMBLY AND ADJUSTMENT

NOTE: Start out with a handful of collapsible spacers and different sizes of pinion adjusting shims.

1. If the old pinion/ring gear assembly and rear bearing are being used, replace the shim with a new one of the same size (identification marking) as was removed. Use a new collapsible spacer through 1977. On 1978 and later models, use a shim, not a collapsible spacer.
2. If a new pinion/ring gear assembly or rear bearing is being used, determine the correct adjustment shim size in the following manner:
   a. Look at the identification markings on the old pinion and shim which were removed. Record their markings.

NOTE: Pinion markings are given in plus (+) or minus (−) millimeter measurements while the shim has a numbered identification code. Consult the chart below for proper shim identification.

   b. Look at the identification measurement stamped on a new pinion and note its value.
   c. Calculate the difference between the measurements of the new and old pinions by adding or subtracting, as necessary.
   d. If the value on the new pinion is *less* than the value on the old, *add* the difference to the thickness of the old shim (in millimeters). Use a new shim of the total thickness.
   e. If the value on the new pinion is *greater* than the value on the old, *subtract* the difference from the thickness of the old shim (in millimeters). Use a new shim having a thickness of the difference.
   f. If the rear pinion bearing was replaced, measure the difference (in

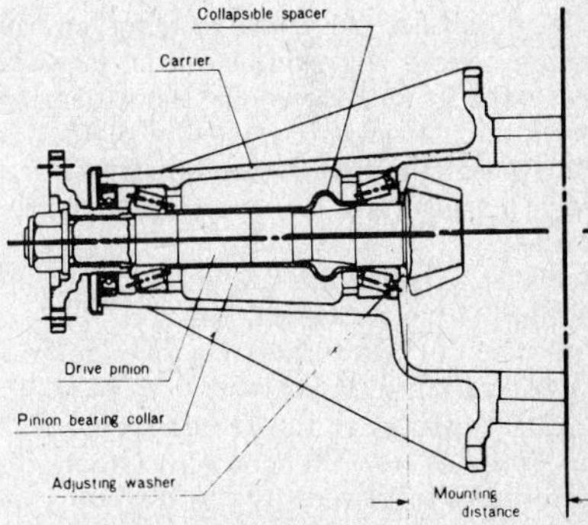

Proper pinion positioning
(© Toyo Kogyo Co. Ltd.)

millimeters) between the new and the old bearing. Add or subtract the difference between the two bearings from the size of the adjusting shim.

g. Select the proper size adjusting shim, as determined in the steps above, from one of the following:

PINION SHIM IDENTIFICATION

Marking	Thickness (mm)	Marking	Thickness (mm)
08	3.08	29	3.29
11	3.11	32	3.32
14	3.14	35	3.35
17	3.17	38	3.38
20	3.20	41	3.41
23	3.23	44	3.44
26	3.26	47	3.47

3. Position the adjusting shim, of the size as determined in steps 1 or 2, and install the rear pinion bearing on the pinion.

4. If they were removed, install the pinion bearing outer races in the carrier. Be sure that they are properly seated.

5. Place the pinion assembly through the collapsible spacer and into the carrier.

NOTE: Use a new collapsible spacer.

6. Position the front bearing on the pinion. Hold the pinion as far forward as it will go and drive the front bearing on to the pinion until it is fully seated.

7. Coat the lips of the pinion oil seal with grease and fit the seal into the carrier.

8. Tap the pinion flange home on the pinion with a rubber mallet.

9. Install the pinion washer and nut but do not tighten the nut.

10. With the nut still loose, i.e., with no preload on the pinion, check the amount of force required to turn the pinion with a torque wrench that is calibrated in inch pounds; this will measure the amount of drag produced by the oil seal.

11. Install two bolts on the pinion flange and hold it with a spanner or pipe wrench to keep it from rotating. Tighten the pinion nut to the specification shown in the chart.

CAUTION: Use care not to overtighten the pinion, as the spacer will collapse and have to be replaced.

12. Release the pinion flange and measure the amount of preload obtained using the inch/pound torque wrench.

13. Continue tightening the pinion nut, if necessary, a little at a time. Check the preload after each small amount of tightening, until the final preload figure is reached.

CAUTION: If the preload is exceeded, the collapsible spacer will be compressed too much. A new spacer will have to be installed and the bearing preload adjusted all over again. Proper preload cannot be obtained by simply backing off on the nut.

14. Install thrust washers on both of the side gears and fit the gears into the case.

15. Fit the two pinion (spider) gears into the case, through the opening, so that they are exactly 180° apart.

16. Turn the gears through 90° so that the pinion shaft holes in the case align with the holes in the pinion gears.

17. Insert the pinion gear shaft into the holes in the case and through the holes in the pinion gears.

NOTE: Align the pinion shaft so that the lockpin holes in it align with the holes in the case.

18. Check the backlash between the side gears and the pinion gears with a dial indicator. The backlash between the gear teeth should be 0-0.004 in. If backlash exceeds 0.008 in., adjust it to specifications by selecting one of the following side gear thrust washers:

NOTE: Use the same thickness thrust washers for both side gears.

19. Install and stake the lockpin onto the pinion shaft.

20. Bolt the ring gear up to the gear case. Torque the bolts evenly, and in sequence, 40-47 ft lbs for the B-1600, B-1800 and the rotary pickup, and to 54-61 ft lbs for the B-2000. Lock the bolts in place with their lockplates.

21. Install the gear bearings in the gear case hub and fit each of the outer races into its respective bearing.

22. Place the differential gearset in the carrier.

NOTE: Be sure that the marks used for backlash adjustment, which are stamped on the faces of the ring gear and pinion teeth, are aligned.

23. Install the adjusters on their respective sides by consulting the identification marks made during their removal.

24. Install the bearing cups properly by consulting the identification marks made on them during removal.

25. Rotate the adjusters until the bearings are properly positioned in their outer races and their end-play is eliminated.

26. Finger tighten one of the bearing cap bolts on each bearing.

27. Attach a dial indicator to the flange on the carrier so that its plunger comes into contact with the ring gear at right angles to its teeth.

28. Check the backlash between the pinion and the ring gear teeth:

a. If backlash is *more* than specified, loosen the adjusting nut on the pinion side one notch and tighten the ring gear adjusting nut on notch.

b. If the backlash is *less* than specified, loosen the adjusting nut on the ring gear side one notch and tighten the pinion adjusting nut one notch.

c. Repeat the procedure until the specified backlash of 0.0075-0.0083 in. is obtained.

29. Tighten the adjusting nut on the differential bearings to obtain proper preload. Proper preload is determined when the distance between the pilot sections of the bearing caps is 8.0485-8.0513 in. Measure the distance with a vernier caliper.

NOTE: Be careful not to disturb the backlash between the pinion and the ring gear teeth while adjusting the bearing preload.

30. Tighten the bearing cap securing bolts to 47-56 ft lbs. Install the lockplate on the bearing adjuster so that they cannot loosen.

31. Coat both sides of about six to eight ring gear teeth with red lead. Move the ring gear back and forth several times and then examine the contact pattern made. Compare it to the illustrations. Adjust the preload or backlash, as required to obtain proper tooth contact.

32. Install the carrier in the axle housing, as outlined above.

Ring Gear Contact Patterns

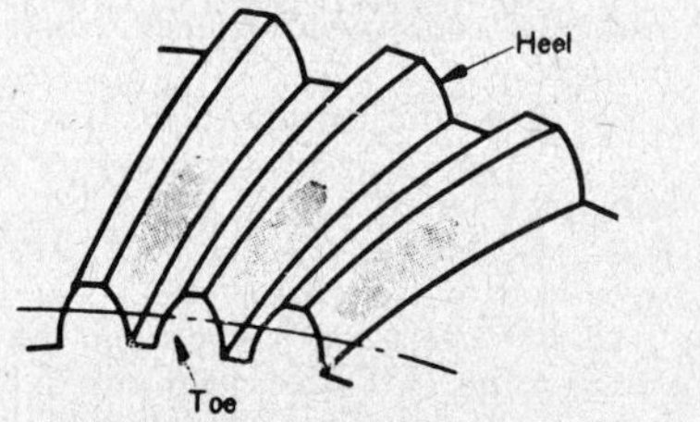

Correct tooth pattern
(© Toyo Kogyo Co. Ltd.)

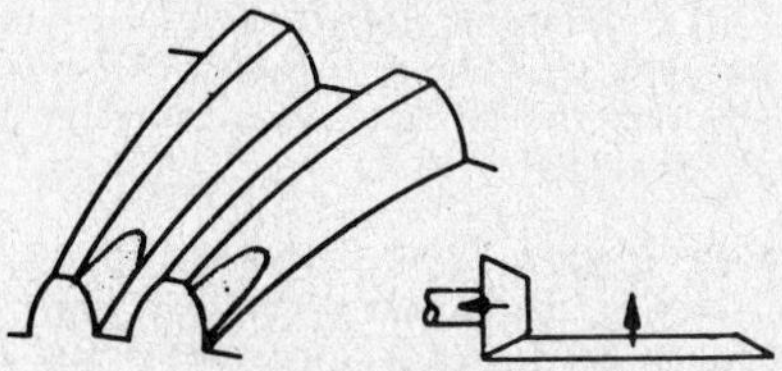

Too much toe contact
(© Toyo Kogyo Co. Ltd.)

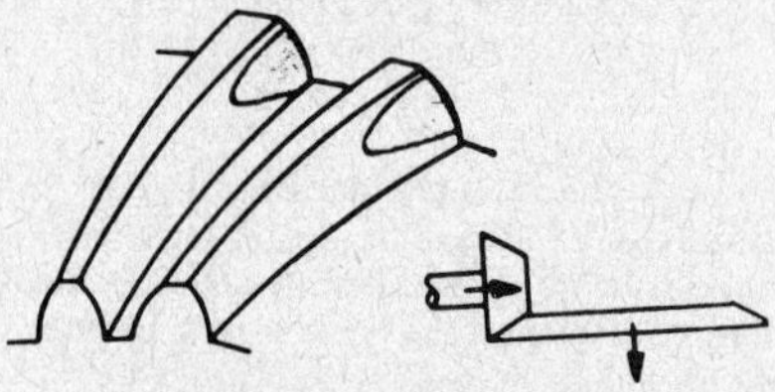

Too much heel contact
(© Toyo Kogyo Co. Ltd.)

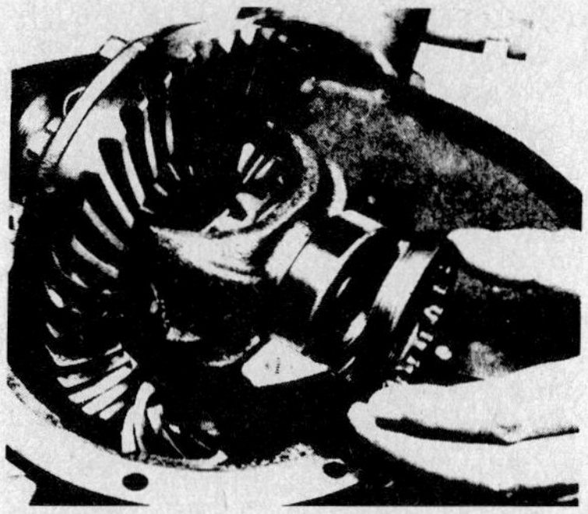

Installing the differential bearing adjuster
(© Toyo Kogyo Co. Ltd.)

REAR SUSPENSION

Springs

REMOVAL AND INSTALLATION

1. Raise and support the truck, allowing the spring to hang freely.
2. Support the rear axle with jackstands.
3. Disconnect the rear shock absorber at the lower mount.
4. Remove the spring clip nuts and the spring plate.
5. Remove the spring pin nut and remove the two bolts and nuts attaching the spring pin to the frame bracket.
6. Remove the spring pin and remove the front end of the spring from the truck.
7. Remove the shackle plate nuts and the shackle plate.
8. Remove the spring from the truck.
9. Installation is the reverse of removal.

Shock Absorbers

REMOVAL AND INSTALLATION

1. Remove the nuts, washers and bushings from the upper and lower shock mounts.

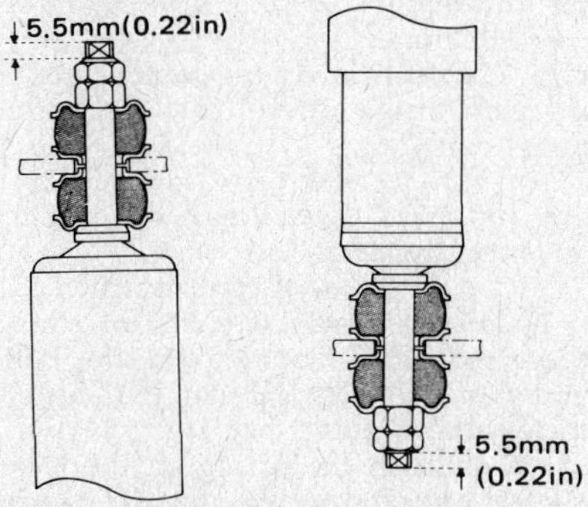

Tightening the rear shock absorber nuts—1976 and later
(© Toyo Kogyo Co. Ltd.)

2. Remove the shock absorber.
3. To install, reverse the installation procedure. On trucks through 1974, tighten all mounts to 18-26 ft. lbs. On 1975-80 trucks, both the lower and upper mounts must be tightened to provide 0.138 in. between the end of the rod and the outside nut in 1975, and 0.217 in. 1976 and later.

FRONT SUSPENSION

The Mazda truck front suspension uses a wishbone-type suspension arm with a coil spring. Shock absorbers are hydraulic double-action.

Front Shock Absorber

TESTING

The simplest test for any shock absorber is to bounce the suspect corner of the vehicle until it is bouncing quickly. Let go of the vehicle and count the number of bounces before it comes to rest. A good shock absorber should come to rest in 2-3 bounces at the most.

As an alternative:

1. Remove the shock absorber.
2. Hold the shock in an upright position and work it up and down 4-5 times through its full travel.
3. If strong resistance is felt, the shock is functioning properly. If no resistance is felt, or, if there is a sudden free movement in the stroke, replace the shock absorber with a new one. It is also a good idea to replace a shock absorber if an *excessive* amount of oil is visible on its exterior.

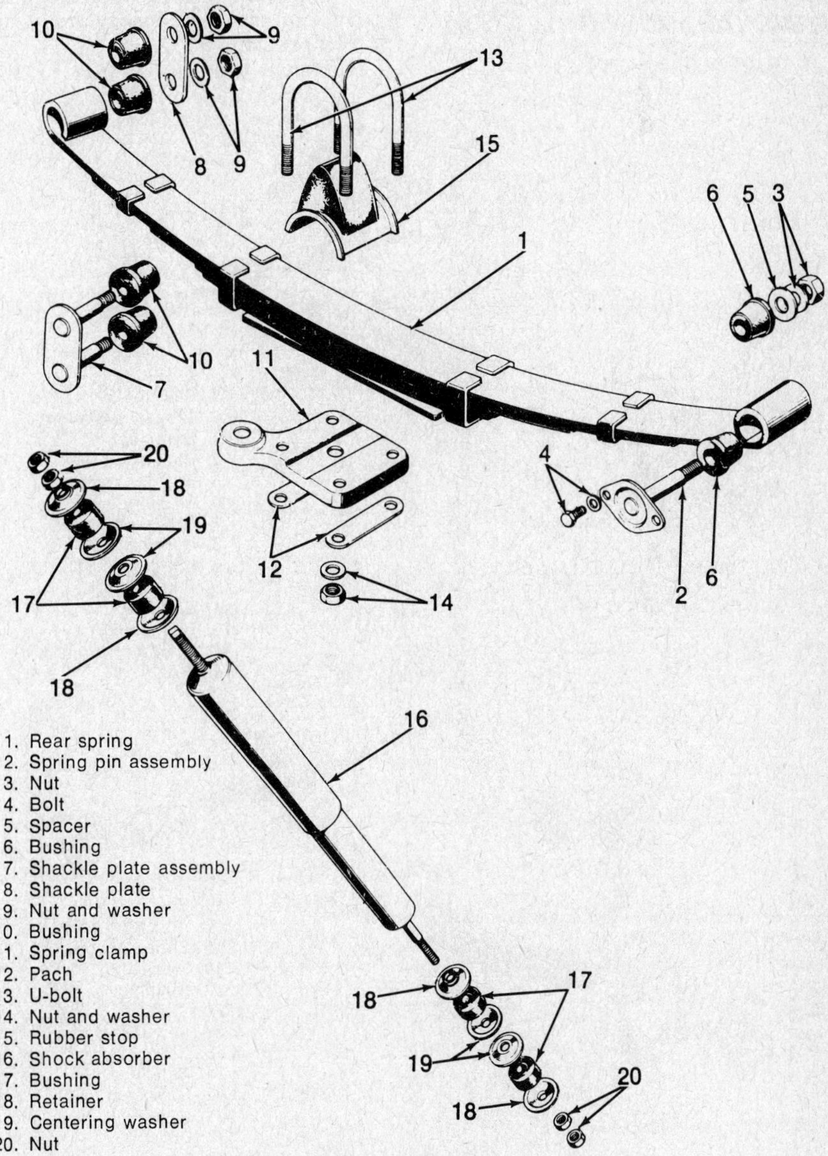

1. Rear spring
2. Spring pin assembly
3. Nut
4. Bolt
5. Spacer
6. Bushing
7. Shackle plate assembly
8. Shackle plate
9. Nut and washer
10. Bushing
11. Spring clamp
12. Pach
13. U-bolt
14. Nut and washer
15. Rubber stop
16. Shock absorber
17. Bushing
18. Retainer
19. Centering washer
20. Nut

Rear suspension

REMOVAL AND INSTALLATION

1. Raise and support the truck.
2. Remove the nuts attaching the upper end of the shock absorber to the cross-member.
3. Remove the rubber bushings and washers.
4. Remove the bolts attaching the lower end of the shock absorber to the lower control arm.
5. Remove the shock from under the lower control arm.
6. Installation is the reverse of removal. Tighten the lower mount to 12-17 ft. lbs. Attach the upper end of the shock to the crossmember and tighten the upper mount to 18-26 ft. lbs. through 1974. For 1975 and later, tighten the nuts so that there is 0.256 in. between the top of the shock absorber rod and the top of the upper nut.
7. Lower the truck.

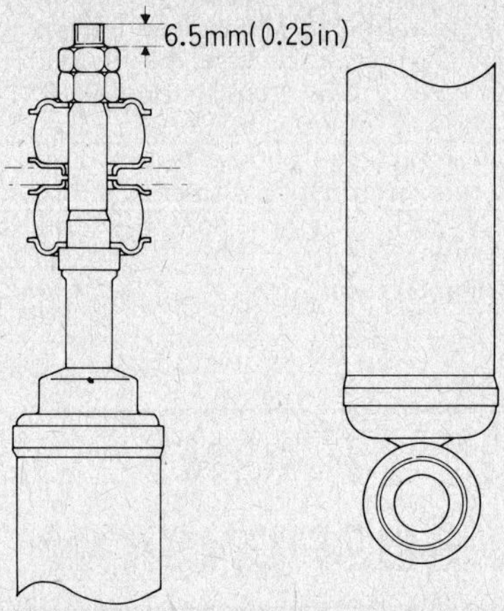

Tightening the front shock absorber nuts
(© Toyo Kogyo Co. Ltd.)

Upper Control Arm

REMOVAL AND INSTALLATION

1. Raise and support the truck.
2. Position jackstands under the lower control arm.
3. Lower the vehicle on the jackstands until the upper control arm is off the bumper stop.
4. Remove the wheel. Install a chain around the coil spring as a safety measure.
5. Remove the cotter pin and nut retaining the upper ball joint.
6. Break the tapered fit loose by striking it with a hammer and separate the ball joint from the spindle.
7. From under the hood, remove the two upper arm retaining bolts and remove the arm from the vehicle. Note the number and position of shims.
8. Remove the three ball joint retaining bolts and remove the ball joint from the upper arm.

To install the upper control arm:

9. Install the ball joint in the upper control arm.
10. Position the upper control arm in the truck and install the alignment shims from where they were removed. Install the retaining nuts and bolts on the shaft and torque them to 62-76 ft lbs.
11. Position the spindle on the ball joint and install the retaining nut (40-55 ft. lbs.) and a new cotter pin.
12. Remove the safety chain.
13. Install the wheel.
14. Remove the jackstands and lower the truck. Have the front end alignment checked.

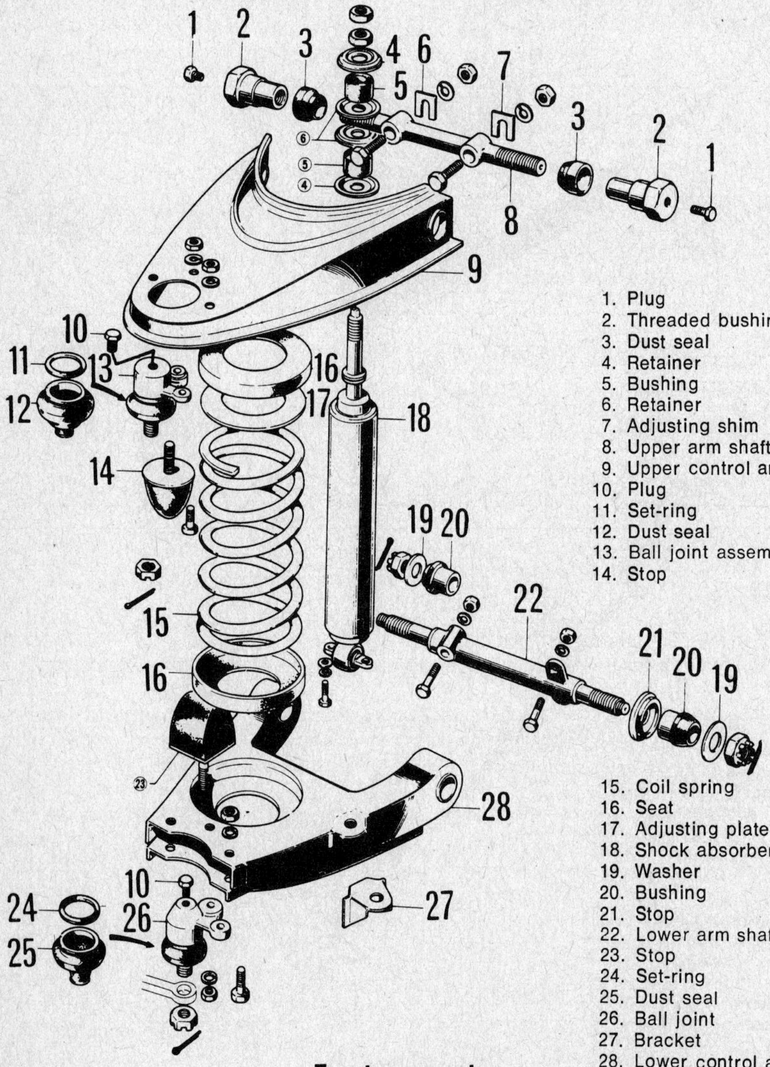

1. Plug
2. Threaded bushing
3. Dust seal
4. Retainer
5. Bushing
6. Retainer
7. Adjusting shim
8. Upper arm shaft
9. Upper control arm
10. Plug
11. Set-ring
12. Dust seal
13. Ball joint assembly
14. Stop
15. Coil spring
16. Seat
17. Adjusting plate
18. Shock absorber
19. Washer
20. Bushing
21. Stop
22. Lower arm shaft
23. Stop
24. Set-ring
25. Dust seal
26. Ball joint
27. Bracket
28. Lower control arm

Front suspension

Lower Control Arm

REMOVAL AND INSTALLATION

1. Raise the front of the truck and position jackstands under both sides of the frame just behind the lower control arms.
2. Remove the wheel.
3. Remove the lower shock absorber retaining bolts and push the shock up into the spring.
4. Remove the front stabilizer bar retaining bolt, nut and bushings and disconnect the stabilizer bar from the lower control arm.
5. Position a floor jack under the lower control arm and raise the arm to take the spring pressure off. Install a safety chain on the spring.
6. Unbolt the ball joint from the lower control arm.
7. Pull the spindle and ball joint away from the lower arm.
8. If necessary, the lower ball joint can be removed by removing the cotter pin and nut and loosening the ball joint with a hammer.
9. Carefully lower the control arm on the jack, being careful that the spring does not fly out.
10. Remove the three lower control arm retaining bolts and remove the lower control arm.

To install the lower control arm:

11. Position the lower control arm in place and install the three retaining bolts and nuts. Do not tighten. If removed, install the ball joint.
12. Position the spring on the lower control arm and in the upper frame retaining pocket.
13. Use a C-clamp to clamp the spring to the lower control arm.

14. Raise the lower control arm with a floor jack and position the ball joint and spindle in the lower arm.
15. Loosely install the three lower arm-to-ball bolts. Remove the safety chain from the spring, and remove the floor jack and C-clamp.
16. Torque the three ball joint retaining nuts to 60-70 ft lbs.
17. Pull the shock absorber down and install the bolts and nuts.
18. Install the stabilizer bar on the lower control arm.
19. Install the front wheel. Lower the truck and have the front wheel alignment checked.

Ball Joints

CHECKING

1. Check the ball joint dust seals and replace them if they are defective.
2. Check the end-play of the upper and lower ball joints. If the end-play exceeds 0.039 in., replace the ball joint.

REPLACEMENT

Use the applicable procedures under "Upper Control Arm Removal and Installation", or "Lower Control Arm Removal and Installation".

Front End Alignment

CASTER

Caster is the forward or rearward tilt of the upper ball joint. Rearward tilt is referred to as positive caster, while forward tilt is referred to as negative caster.

Caster is adjusted by changing the shim(s) between the upper arm shaft and the frame, or, by turning the shaft until the correct angle is obtained.

CAMBER

Camber is the outward tilting of the front wheels, at the top, from the vertical.

Camber is adjusted by adding or subtracting the shim(s) between the upper arm shaft and the frame. Shims are available in thicknesses of 0.039 in., 0.063 in., 0.079 in., and 0.126 in.

TOE-IN

Toe-in is the amount, measured in a fraction of an inch, that the wheels are

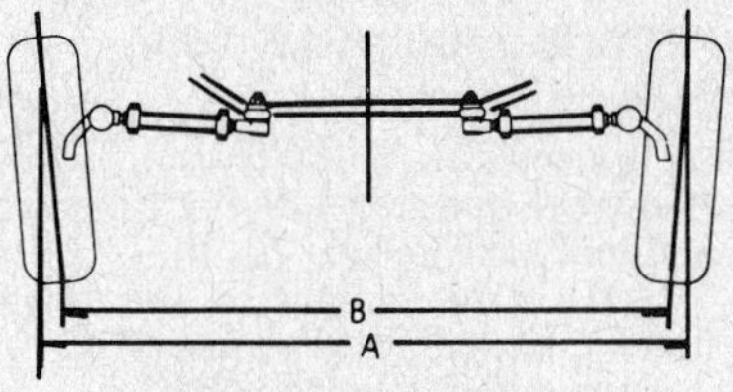

A−B= 0～6 mm (0～0.24 in)

Measuring toe-in
(© Toyo Kogyo Co. Ltd.)

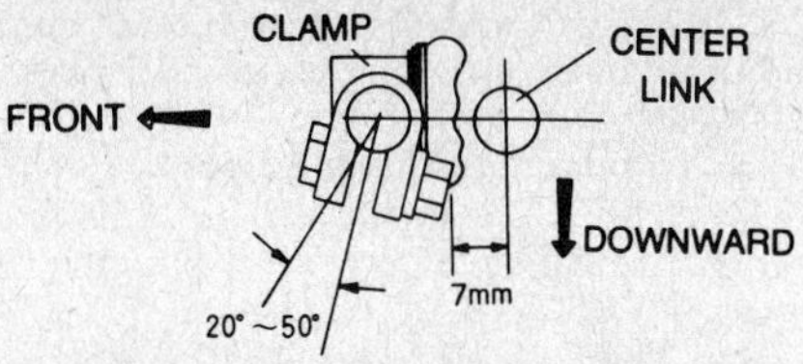

Correct positioning of the tie-rod clamps
(© Toyo Kogyo Co. Ltd.)

closer together in the front than at the rear.

Toe-in can be increased or decreased by changing the length of the tie-rods. Threaded sleeves on the tie-rods are provided for this purpose. The clamps on the tie rods must be positioned to prevent interference with the center link on the Rotary Pick-Up.

FRONT WHEEL TURNING ANGLE

The turning stop screws are located at the steering knuckle. If necessary, the screws can be adjusted to alter the turning angle.

STEERING

Steering Wheel

REMOVAL AND INSTALLATION

1. Remove the screws which secure the crash pad/horn button assembly to the steering wheel. Remove the assembly. On four-spoke steering wheels, pull the center cap toward the wheel top.
2. Punch matchmarks on the steering wheel and steering shaft.
3. Unfasten the steering wheel hub nut and remove the steering wheel with a puller.

CAUTION: The steering column is collapsible; pounding on it or applying excessive pressure to it may cause it to deform, in which case, the entire column will have to be replaced.

Installation of the steering wheel is performed in the reverse order of removal. Tighten the steering wheel nut to 25 ft lbs.

COMBINATION (TURN SIGNAL) SWITCH REPLACEMENT

1. Disconnect the ground cable from the battery.
2. Remove the steering wheel, as detailed above.
3. Unfasten the left-hand column shroud securing screws and remove the shroud.
4. Remove the retaining ring from the combination (turn signal) switch.

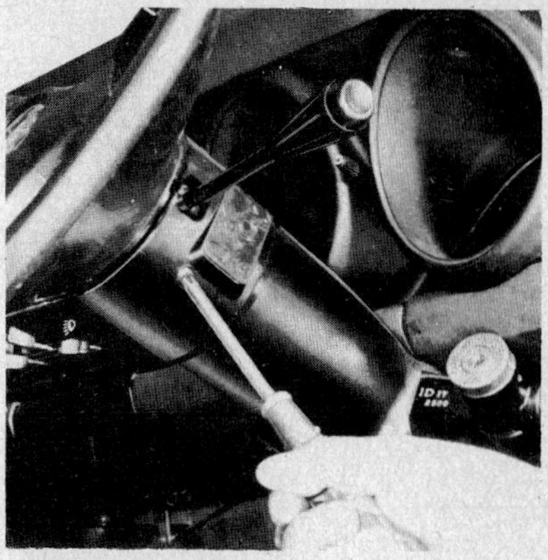

Removing the steering column shroud
(© Toyo Kogyo Co. Ltd.)

5. Withdraw the switch over the steering column, after unfastening its multiconnector from underneath the dash panel.

Installation is performed in the reverse order of removal.

Steering Linkage

REMOVAL AND INSTALLATION

Manual or Power Steering

1. Turn the steering wheel so that the front wheels are pointing straight ahead. Then raise the front end of the vehicle and support it with jackstands.
2. Remove the cotter pins and the castellated nuts which secure the ends of the tie-rods to the center link and the steering knuckle.
3. Use a ball joint puller to disconnect the tie-rods from the center link and steering knuckle. Remove the tie-rods.
4. Remove the cotter pin and the castellated nut which secure the idler arm to the center link.
5. Use the ball joint puller to detach the idler arm from the center link.
6. Unfasten the nuts at the other end of the idler arm and remove the arm from its bracket.
7. Perform steps 4-5 for the pitman arm. Remove the center link.
8. Unfasten the nut which secures the pitman arm to the sector shaft and use a puller to separate them.

Installation is performed in the reverse order of removal. Align the marks on the pitman arm and the sector shaft to ensure proper steering linkage alignment. Torque the removed nuts and bolts to the specifications given at the end of this section. Check and adjust the toe-in, as outlined above.

IDLER ARM REPLACEMENT

1. Remove the cotter pin and nut from the idler arm. Disconnect the center link from the idler arm with a puller.
2. Unbolt and remove the idler arm from the frame.
3. Remove the cotter pin, nut and

washer, and remove the idler arm from the bracket.

4. To install, assemble the arm to the bracket, first lubricating the arm and bushings with lithium grease. Install all parts in the reverse order of removal, using new cotter pins.

REPLACING THE PITMAN ARM

1. Raise and support the front end.
2. Remove the wheels.
3. Disconnect the center link at the pitman arm.
4. Remove the nut attaching the pitman arm to the sector shaft and remove the arm with a puller.
5. Install the pitman arm onto the sector shaft, aligning the identification marks. Tighten the nut to 108–130 ft lbs.
6. Connect the center link to the pitman arm and torque the nut to 22–29 ft lbs. Install a new cotter pin.

REPLACING THE TIE-ROD

1. Raise and support the front end.
2. Disconnect the tie-rod from the center link and knuckle arm. A puller will be necessary.
3. Install the tie-rod to the center link and knuckle arm. Tighten the nuts to 22–28 ft lbs and install new cotter pins.

REPLACING THE CENTER LINK

1. Raise and support the front end.
2. Remove the center link from both tie-rods, pitman arm and idler arm by removing the cotter pins and nuts. A puller will also be necessary.
3. Install the center link and tighten the nuts as follows: center link to pitman arm—22–29 ft lbs; center link to idler arm—31–47 ft lbs through 1976, 36–58 ft lbs for 1977 and later. Install new cotter pins.

Steering Gear

STEERING GEAR ADJUSTMENT

Worm Bearing Preload

1. Remove the gear from the vehicle.
2. Rotate the worm shaft with a torque wrench and check the torque. Rotating torque should be 8–10 in. lb. for rotary pickup; 5–7 in. lb. for B-1600, 5–8 in. lbs. for the B-1800 and B-2000. If not adjust as follows on all models:
3. Remove the end cover and shims.
4. If the preload was too light, remove shims; if too heavy, add shims.
5. Install the end cover.

Sector Gear and Ball Nut Backlash

The sector shaft adjusting screw, located in the cover, raises or lowers the sector shaft to provide proper mesh with the sector gear and rack. Adjust as follows:

1. Turn the wormshaft gently and stop it at the center position.
2. Loosen the locknut and turn the adjuster in or out. The standard backlash is zero.
3. Tighten the adjusting screw.

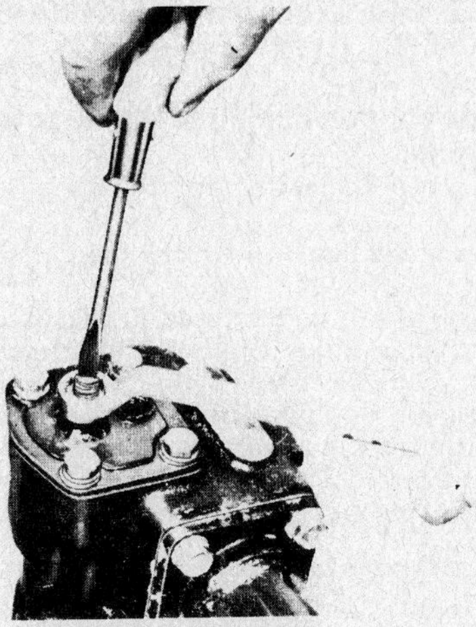

Adjusting backlash
(© Toyo Kogyo Co. Ltd.)

Power Steering Pump

REMOVAL AND INSTALLATION

1. Disconnect the fluid hoses from the pump.
2. Loosen the pump belt adjusting bolt, slide the pump to one side and remove the belt.
3. Support the pump, remove the mounting bolts and lift out the pump.

Installation is the reverse of removal. Adjust belt to give a $1/2''$ deflection at the mid-point of its longest straight stretch. Fill the reservoir and bleed the system.

BRAKE SYSTEMS

Adjustments

FRONT OR REAR DISCS

The front disc brakes are self-adjusting by design. As the brake pads and discs wear, fluid pressure compensates for the amount of wear. Because this action causes the fluid level to go down, the level should be checked and replenished as often as is necessary.

FRONT DRUM BRAKES

B-1600

The brake shoes should be at normal room temperature. Adjust each front brake shoe as follows:

1. Raise and support the truck. The wheels must be free to turn freely.
2. Remove the adjusting slot covers from the brake backing plate.
3. Insert a brake adjusting spoon (a screwdriver will do in a pinch) to grab the starwheel of the wheel cylinder.
4. Rotate the starwheel of one wheel cylinder toward the inside of the brake drum until the wheel is locked. Then back off the starwheel five notches.
5. Repeat step 4 for each wheel cylinder of each wheel.
6. Install the adjusting slot covers.
7. Check the brake adjustment by spinning the wheel by hand. There should be no drag.
8. Lower the truck.

REAR DRUM BRAKES

Through 1975

1. Block the front wheels, raise the car, and support it with jackstands.
2. Release the parking brake completely. Disconnect the equalizer clevis pin.
3. Remove the adjusting hole plugs from the backing plate.
4. Engage the adjuster with a screwdriver. Turn the adjuster in the direction of the arrow stamped on the backing plate until the brake shoes are fully expanded, i.e., the wheel will not turn.
5. Pump the brake pedal several times to be sure that the brake shoe contracts the drum evenly.

NOTE: If the wheel turns after you remove your foot from the brake pedal, continue turning the adjuster until the wheel will no longer rotate.

6. Back off on the adjuster about five notches. The wheel should rotate freely, without dragging. If it does not, turn the adjuster an additional notch.
7. Pump the brake pedal several times and check wheel rotation again.
8. Fit the plug into the adjusting procedure for the three other rear brake shoes.

BRAKE PEDAL

Rotary Pick-up

1. Detach the wiring from the brake light switch terminals.
2. Loosen the locknut on the switch.
3. Turn the switch until the distance between the pedal and the floor is 7.3 in.
4. Tighten the locknut on switch.
5. Loosen the locknut located on the pushrod.
6. Rotate the pushrod, until a pedal free travel of 0.2–0.6 in. is obtained.
7. Tighten the pushrod locknut.

B-1600, B-1800 and B-2000

There should be 0.02–0.09 in. (0.28–0.35 in. on the B-1800 and B-2000) brake pedal free-travel before the pushrod contacts the piston.

1. Loosen the locknut on the master cylinder pushrod at the clevis, which attaches the pushrod to the pedal.
2. Turn the master cylinder pushrod either in or out to obtain the specified clearance.

3. When the adjustment is complete, tighten the locknut to 8–13 ft lbs.

Master Cylinder

REMOVAL AND INSTALLATION

1. Detach all of the hydraulic lines from the master cylinder. Detach the fluid level sensor lead if equipped.

***NOTE:** On models which have a fluid reservoir located separately from the master cylinder, remove the lines which run between the two and plug the lines to prevent leakage.*

2. Unfasten the nuts which secure the master cylinder to the power brake unit or firewall.
3. Withdraw the master cylinder assembly straight out and away from the power brake unit or the firewall and pushrod.

***CAUTION:** Be careful not to spill brake fluid on the painted surfaces of the car, as it makes an excellent paint remover.*

Installation of the master cylinder is performed in the reverse order of its removal. Fill up its reservoir and bleed the brake system, as detailed below.

OVERHAUL

1. Clean the outside of the master cylinder and drain any brake fluid remaining in it.
2. Remove the fluid reservoir from the top of the cylinder, if so equipped.
3. Remove the boot from the rear of the cylinder if present; earlier models do not have the boot.
4. Depress the primary piston and withdraw the snap-ring from the rear of the cylinder bore.
5. Withdraw the washers, piston, cups, spacer, seat and return spring from the cylinder bore.
6. Before removing the secondary piston stop bolt and O-ring, and the secondary piston, you must fabricate a guide pin to be inserted into the stop bolt hole. The guide pin will enable the secondary piston to pass over the hole without catching and tearing. The guide pin should be approximately 8.5 mm in length, with a smooth chamfered tip. Depress the secondary piston with a screwdriver. Remove the secondary stop bolt and O-ring and insert the guide pin. Allow the secondary piston to pass over the guide pin and out.
7. Remove the secondary piston assembly from the bore.

***NOTE:** Blow out the assembly with compressed air, if necessary.*

8. Unfasten the hydraulic line fittings from the master cylinder outlet.
9. Withdraw the check valves and springs from the outlets.

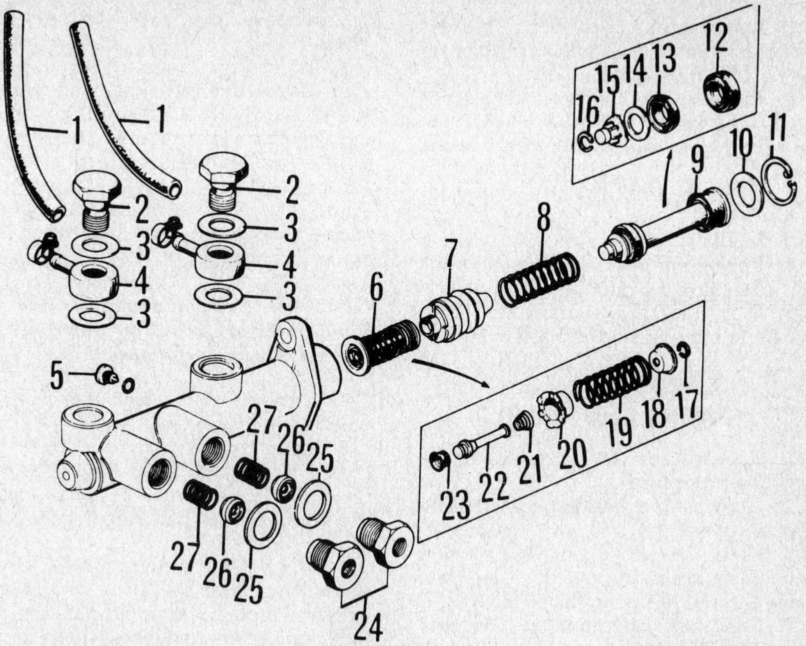

1. Hydraulic line
2. Connector bolt
3. Washer
4. Union
5. Stop bolt
6. Valve and spring
7. Secondary piston
8. Return spring
9. Primary piston
10. Washer
11. Retaining ring
12. Secondary cup
13. Primary cup
14. Spacer
15. Spring seat
16. Stop ring
17. Stop ring
18. Spring seat
19. Return spring
20. Valve case
21. Spring
22. Valve rod
23. Valve
24. Outlet fitting
25. Washer
26. Check valve
27. Spring

Master cylinder components

10. Wash all of the components in clean brake fluid.

***CAUTION:** Never use kerosene or gasoline to clean the master cylinder components.*

Examine all of the piston cups and replace any that are worn, damaged, or swollen.

Check the cylinder bore for roughness or scoring. Check the clearance between the piston and cylinder bore with a feeler gauge. Replace either the piston or the cylinder if the clearance exceeds 0.006 in.

Blow the dirt and the remaining brake fluid out of the cylinder with compressed air.

Master cylinder assembly is performed in the following order:

1. Dip all of the components, except for the cylinder, in clean brake fluid.
2. Install the check valve assemblies in the master cylinder outlets.
3. Insert the return spring and the valve components into the cylinder bore.
4. Fit the secondary cup and the primary cup over the secondary piston. The flat side of the cups should face the piston.
5. Fit the guide pin into the stop-bolt hole. Place the secondary piston components into the cylinder bore.
6. Depress the secondary piston as far as it will go and withdraw the guide pin. Screw the stop bolt into the hole.
7. Place the primary cups on the primary piston with the flat side of the cups facing the piston.
8. Insert the return spring and the primary piston into the bore.
9. Depress the primary piston, then install the stop-washer and snap-ring.

***NOTE:** Be sure that the piston cups do not cover up the compensating ports.*

10. Install the dust boot on the end of the cylinder.

Brake Failure Warning Valve

CENTRALIZING

1. Turn the ignition switch to the ON position.
2. Make sure that the fluid level in the master cylinder is at the $^3/_4$ mark.
3. Depress the brake pedal and the piston will center itself causing the light to go off.
4. Turn the switch to OFF and check the fluid level. Check for a firm pedal.

Bleeding

DISC BRAKES

***NOTE:** Keep the master cylinder reservoir at least $^3/_4$ full during the bleeding operation.*

1. Remove the cap from the bleeder screw on that wheel cylinder which is farthest from the master cylinder.
2. Install a vinyl tube over the bleeder screw. Submerge the other end of the tube in a jar half-full of clean brake fluid.
3. Open the bleeder valve. Fully depress the brake pedal and allow it to return slowly.
4. Repeat this operation until air bubbles cease flowing into the jar.
5. Close the valve, remove the tube, and install the cap on the bleeder valve.

DRUM BRAKES (FRONT AND REAR)

1. Repeat steps 1–2 of the disc brake bleeding procedure.
2. Depress the brake pedal rapidly several times.
3. Keep the brake pedal depressed and open the bleeder valve. Close the valve without releasing the pedal.
4. Repeat this operation until bubbles cease to appear in the jar.
5. Remove the tube and install the cap on the bleeder valve.

FRONT DISC BRAKES

Disc Brake Pads

REMOVAL AND INSTALLATION

1. Raise the front of the vehicle and securely support it with jackstands.
2. Remove the hub cap and the wheel.
3. Depending on the type of brake used, either remove the hair pin retainer and withdraw the pad locating pins, or remove the hairpin retainer, the stopper plates (wedges), the caliper assembly and the anti-rattle spring. Support the caliper by a length of wire suspended from the body. Do not allow it to hang by the hydraulic hose.

CAUTION: Do not disconnect the hydraulic line from the caliper when only pad removal is being performed.

4. Remove the return spring and withdraw the pad.
5. Take the rubber cap off of the bleeder screw and fit a vinyl tube over the screw. Submerge the other end of the tube in a jar half-filled with brake fluid.
6. Open the bleeder screw. Use a screwdriver with its blade wrapped in electrical tape, a c-clamp, or a large pair of locking pliers to depress the piston in the cylinder.
7. Tighten the bleeder screw. Remove the vinyl tube. Fit the rubber cap back on the bleeder screw.
8. Install new pads with shims in the caliper.
9. Install all of the parts which were removed during disassembly.
10. Bleed the brake system, as outlined below.

CAUTION: Replace all of the front brake pads at the same time. Do not use pads of different materials for replacement.

Disc Brake Calipers

REMOVAL AND INSTALLATION

Locating Pin Type Calipers

1. Perform the disc brake pad removal.

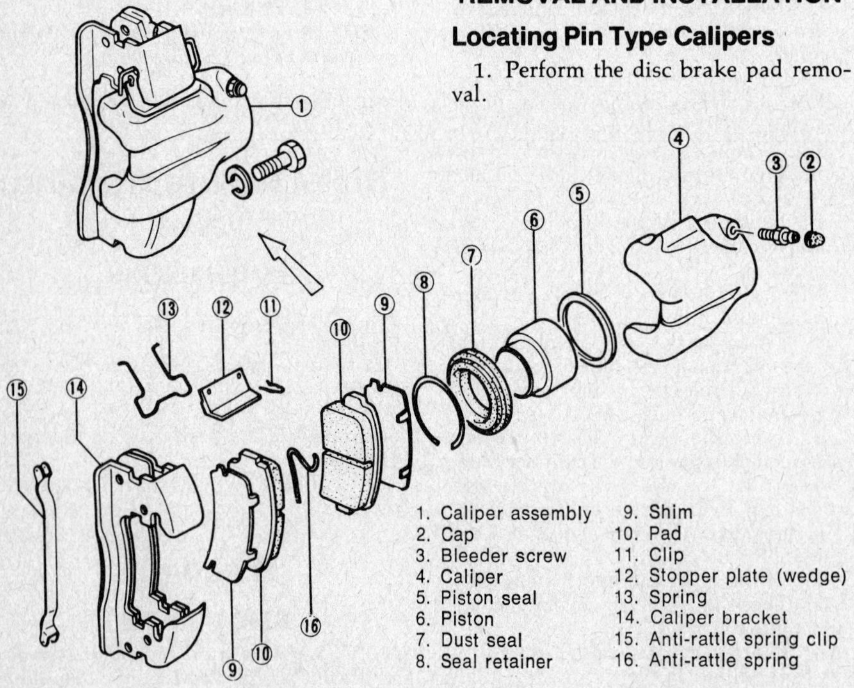

1. Caliper assembly
2. Cap
3. Bleeder screw
4. Caliper
5. Piston seal
6. Piston
7. Dust seal
8. Seal retainer
9. Shim
10. Pad
11. Clip
12. Stopper plate (wedge)
13. Spring
14. Caliper bracket
15. Anti-rattle spring clip
16. Anti-rattle spring

Stopper plate (wedge) disc brake caliper

2. Detach the hydraulic line from the caliper. Plug the end of the line to prevent the entrance of dirt or the loss of fluid.
3. Unfasten the bolts which secure the caliper to the support and remove the caliper.

Follow the caliper removal procedure in reverse order for installation. Bleed the hydraulic system after completing installation.

Stopper Plate (Wedge) Type Calipers

Perform steps 1–3 of the disc brake pad removal procedure, as outlined. In addition, disconnect and plug the hydraulic line at the caliper.

Caliper installation is performed in the reverse order of removal. Bleed the hydraulic system after completing installation.

OVERHAUL

1. Thoroughly clean the outside of the caliper.
2. Remove the dust boot retainer and the boot.
3. Place a piece of hardwood in front of the piston.
4. Gradually apply compressed air through the hydraulic line fitting and withdraw the piston.

NOTE: If the piston is frozen and cannot be removed from the caliper, tap lightly around it while the air pressure is being applied.

5. Withdraw the piston and seal from the caliper bore.
6. If necessary, remove the bleeder screw.
7. Wash all of the parts in clean brake fluid. Dry them off with compressed air.

CAUTION: Do not wash the parts in kerosene or gasoline.

Examine the caliper bore and piston for scores, scratches, or rust. Replace either part as required. Minor scratches, rust, or scoring can be corrected by dressing with crocus cloth.

NOTE: Discard the old piston seal and dust boot. Replace them with new ones.

Apply clean brake fluid to the piston and bore. Assemble the caliper in the reverse order of disassembly. Install it on the car and bleed the brake system.

Brake Disc

REMOVAL AND INSTALLATION

1. Remove the caliper assembly, as detailed in the appropriate section above.

NOTE: It is unnecessary to completely remove the caliper from the vehicle. Leave the hydraulic line attached and wire the

caliper to the underbody of the car so that it is out of the way.

2. Check disc runout, as detailed below, before removing it from the vehicle.
3. Withdraw the grease cap, cotter pin, nut-lock, adjusting nut, and washer from the spindle.
4. Take the thrust washer and outer bearing off the hub.
5. Pull the brake disc/wheel hub assembly off of the spindle.
6. Unbolt and separate the brake disc from the hub after matchmarking them for proper installation.

CAUTION: Do not drive the disc off the hub.

Installation of the disc and hub is performed in the reverse order of removal. Adjust the bearing preload, as detailed below.

INSPECTION

1. With a dial indicator, measure the lateral runout of the disc while the disc is still installed on the spindle.

NOTE: Be sure that the wheel bearings are adjusted properly before checking runout.

2. If runout exceeds more than 0.004 in., replace or resurface the disc.
3. Inspect the surface of the disc for scores or pits and resurface it, if necessary.
4. If the disc is resurfaced, its thickness should be no less than 0.4331 in.

Checking the front brake disc runout
(© Toyo Kogyo Co. Ltd.)

Front Drum Brakes
Brake Drum

REMOVAL AND INSTALLATION

1. Raise and support the truck.
2. Remove the wheel.
3. Remove the brake drum attaching screws and install them in the tapped holes in the brake drum.
4. Turn these screws in evenly to force the brake drum away from the wheel hub.
5. Remove and inspect the brake drum. See "Inspection".

To install the brake drum:

6. Install the brake drum with the attaching screw holes aligned with the holes in the hub.
7. Transfer the attaching screw from the tapped holes in the brake drum to the attaching holes in the hub.
8. Tighten the screws evenly to secure the hub.
9. Install the wheel.
10. Lower the truck and check the brake adjustment.

INSPECTION

1. Brush all dust from the inside of the brake drum.
2. Check the brake drum diameter with a brake drum gauge. Replace any drums which have a diameter greater than 10.28 in.
3. Inspect the brake drums for cracks. Replace any cracked drums.
4. Look carefully for any scoring of the drums. If the drums are scored, have them reground.

Brake Shoes

INSPECTION

1. Wipe out the accumulated dust and grit.
2. Inspect for excessive lining wear or shoe damage. Replace any cracked shoes.
3. If the lining is worn to within 0.039 in. of the shoe or if the shoes are damaged, they must be replaced.
4. Replace any linings that are contaminated with grease or brake fluid from leaking wheel cylinders. Replace linings in axle sets only.
5. Check the condition of the shoes, retracting springs and hold-down springs for signs of overheating. If the shoes have a slight blue color, this indicates overheating and replacement of the springs as well as the linings is recommended.
6. If signs of overheating are present, the wheel cylinders should be rebuilt as a precaution against future problems.

REMOVAL AND INSTALLATION

1. Raise and support the truck.
2. Remove the wheel.
3. Remove the brake drum.
4. Remove the brake shoe retracting springs.
5. Remove the shoe retaining spring guide pin and the retaining spring, by holding the guide pin to the backing plate and compressing and turning the spring 90°. Use a brake spring tool to do this.
6. Remove the brake shoes, noting their positions.

To install new brake shoes:

7. Lubricate the threads of the adjusting screw with brake paste and one or two spots on the adjuster wheel inside threads. Lubricate the backing plate shoe pads.
8. Position each brake shoe on the brake backing plate so that the slot in the shoe web is toward the starwheel in the wheel cylinder.
9. Install the shoe retaining spring guide pin. Install the retaining spring over the guide pin, holding the guide pin in place and depress the retaining spring. Turn it 90° to lock the spring in place.
10. Install the brake shoe retracting spring. Be careful not to bend the springs or stretch the hooks.
11. Install the brake drum.
12. Install the wheel.
13. Adjust the brakes.
14. Bleed the brakes.
15. Lower the truck and check for proper operation.

Wheel Cylinder

REMOVAL AND INSTALLATION

1. Raise and support the truck.
2. Remove the wheel.
3. Remove the brake drum and brake shoes.
4. Disconnect and plug the brake line at the wheel cylinder.

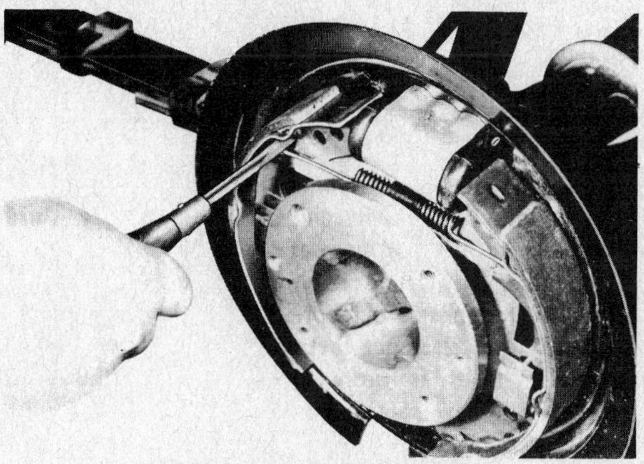

Shoe return spring removal
(© Toyo Kogyo Co. Ltd.)

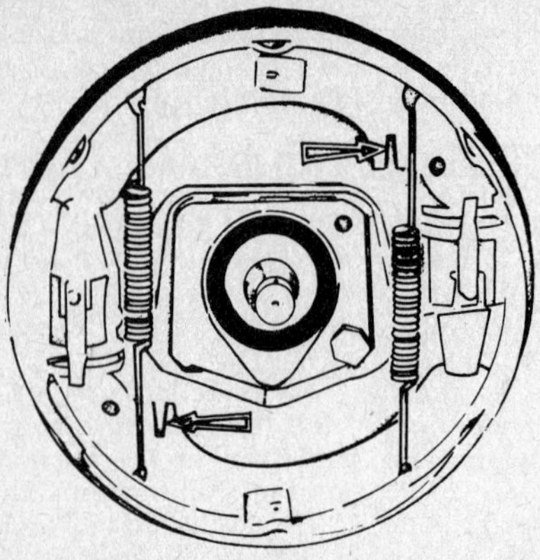

Front brake shot installation—B-1600
(© Toyo Kogyo Co. Ltd.)

5. Remove the stud nuts and bolt attaching the wheel cylinder to the backing plate and remove the wheel cylinder.

To install the wheel cylinder:

6. Install the wheel cylinder on the backing plate.
7. Clean the end of the brake line and attach it to the wheel cylinder. Tighten the tube fitting nut.
8. Install the links in the end of the wheel cylinder.
9. Install the shoes and adjuster assemblies.
10. Install the brake drum and wheel.
11. Adjust the brakes.
12. Bleed the brakes.
13. Lower the truck.

OVERHAUL

1. Remove the wheel cylinder.
2. Remove the piston and adjusting screw with the boot attached to the cylinder. Separate the adjuster and boot from the adjuster.
3. Using compressed air (if possible), remove the piston cup, cup expander and spring. Lay the cylinder face down and apply air pressure to the brake line port.
4. Wash all parts in isopropyl alcohol, except the rubber boot.
5. Examine the cylinder bore, piston and adjuster for wear, roughness or damage. Check the clearance between the piston and cylinder bore. If the clearance is greater than 0.006 in., replace with new parts. Discard the piston cups.

To assemble the wheel cylinder:

6. Lubricate the cylinder bore, adjuster and new piston cup with clean brake fluid.
7. Position the piston return spring in the piston cup expander. Install the return spring, piston cup expander and piston cup in the cylinder. The flat side of the piston cup goes toward the piston.
8. Install the piston boot to the piston adjuster (smaller lip of the boot in the groove of the piston adjuster.)
9. Insert the piston adjuster into the cylinder and install the larger lip of the boot in the groove on the cylinder body.
10. Install the adjusting screw in the piston adjuster.
11. Install the wheel cylinder.

Front Wheel Bearings

ADJUSTMENT

The front wheel bearings should be adjusted if the wheel is loose on the spindle or if the wheel does not rotate freely.

1. Raise and support the vehicle.
2. Remove the wheel and tire.
3. Attach a spring scale onto a hub bolt.
4. Pull the spring scale squarely and read the pull as the hub begins to turn. It should be 1.3–2.4 lbs. for all pick-ups.
5. If the reading is not correct, remove the grease cap and cotter pin. Adjust the bearings with the large nut on the end of the spindle until the proper reading is obtained.
6. Align the holes of the adjusting nut and spindle and install a new cotter pin.
7. Install the grease cap, wheel and tire.
8. Lower the vehicle.

Alternate Procedure

If a spring scale is not available, the following procedure can be used.

1. Raise and support the vehicle.
2. Remove the wheel and tire and the grease cap.
3. Remove the cotter pin.
4. Rotate the hub and tighten the adjusting nut until the hub binds.
5. Back the adjusting nut off $^1/_6$ turn. Be sure that the hub rotates freely with no side-play.
6. Align the holes of the nut and spindle and install a new cotter pin.
7. Install the grease cap, wheel and tire.
8. Lower the vehicle.

REMOVAL, INSTALLATION AND PACKING

1. Raise and support the vehicle.
2. Remove the wheel cover.
3. Remove the wheel and tire.
4. Remove the grease cap from the hub. Remove the cotter pin, nut lock, adjusting nut and flat washer from the spindle.
5. Remove the hub and drum from the wheel spindle.
6. Remove and discard the old grease retainer. Remove the inner bearing cone and roller from the hub.
7. Clean the grease from the inner and outer bearing cups with solvent and inspect the cups for scratches, pits, or wear.
8. If the cups are worn or damaged, remove them with a drift.
9. Thoroughly clean the inner and outer bearing cones and rollers. *Do not spin the bearings to dry them.* Allow them to air dry.
10. Inspect the cones and rollers for wear and replace as necessary. The cone and roller assembles should be replaced as a set. Do not use new bearings or cups with old bearings or cups.
11. Clean the spindle and the inside of the hub with solvent to remove all of the old grease.
12. Cover the spindle with a cloth and clean the dirt from the dust shield. Remove the cloth carefully. Do not get dirt on the spindle.
13. If the inner or outer bearing cups were removed, install the new replacement cups in the hub. Be sure that they are seated squarely and properly.
14. Pack the inside of the hub with wheel bearing grease. Add grease to the hub until grease is flush with the inside diameter of both bearing cups.

NOTE: It is important that all the old grease is removed, because the more popular lithium base grease is not compatible with the sodium base grease that was originally installed (on earlier models).

15. Pack the bearing cone and roller with wheel bearing grease. Work as much grease as possible between the cone and rollers. Lubricate the outside cone surfaced with grease.
16. Install the inner bearing cone and roller in the inner cup. Apply a light film of grease to the grease seal and install the seal. Be sure that the seal is properly seated.
17. Install the hub and drum on the spindle. Keep the hub centered on the spindle to prevent damaging the grease seal.

Checking front wheel bearing preload
(© Toyo Kogyo Co. Ltd.)

18. Install the outer bearing cone and roller and the flat washer on the spindle. Install the adjusting nut.
19. Install the wheel and tire.
20. Adjust the wheel bearings.
21. Install the hub cap.

Rear Drum Brakes
Brake Drums

REMOVAL AND INSTALLATION

1. Remove the wheel cover and loosen the lug nuts.
2. Raise the rear of the vehicle and securely support it with jackstands.
3. Remove the lug nuts and the rear wheel.
4. Be sure that the parking brake is fully released.
5. Remove the bolts which secure the drum to the rear axle shaft flange.
6. Pull the brake drum off the flange.

NOTE: If the drum will not come off easily, screw the drum securing bolts into the two tapped holes in the drum. Tighten the bolts evenly in order to force the drum away from the flange.

Rear brake drum installation is performed in the reverse order of removal. Adjust the shoes after installation is completed.

INSPECTION

1. Examine the drum for cracks or overheating spots. Replace the drum if either of these are present.
2. Check the drum for scoring. Light scoring can be corrected with sandpaper.
3. Check the drum with a dial indicator for out-of-roundness; turn the drum if it exceeds 0.0059 in.
4. If the drum must be turned because of excessive scoring or out-of-roundness, the drum's inside diameter should not exceed 10.2758 inches.

NOTE: If one drum is turned, the opposite drum should also be turned to the same size.

Brake Shoes

REMOVAL AND INSTALLATION

1. Perform the brake drum removal procedure, as detailed above.
2. Remove the return springs from the upper side of the shoe with a brake spring removal tool.
3. Remove the return springs from the lower side of the shoes in the same manner, as in step 2.
4. Remove the shoe retaining spring by compressing the retaining spring while turning the pin 90°.
5. Withdraw the primary shoes and the parking brake link.
6. Disengage the parking brake lever from the secondary shoes by unfastening its retaining clip.
7. Remove the secondary shoe.

CAUTION: Be careful not to get oil or grease on the lining material.

Inspect the linings; replace them if they are badly burned or if worn 0.039 in. beyond the specification for a new lining. (See "Brake Specification" chart).

Replace the linings if they are saturated with oil or grease.

Brake shoe installation is performed in the following manner:

1. Lubricate the threads of the adjusting screw, the sliding surfaces of the shoes, and the backing plate flanges with a small quantity of grease.

CAUTION: Be careful not to get grease on the lining surfaces.

2. Install the eye of the parking brake cable through the parking brake lever which has previously been installed on the secondary shoe and secured with its retaining clip.
3. Fit the link between the shoes.
4. Engage the shoes with the slots in the anchor (adjusting screw) and the wheel cylinder.
5. Fasten the shoes to the backing plate with the retaining springs and pins.
6. Install the shoe return springs with the tool used during removal.
7. Install the drums and adjust the shoes, as detailed elsewhere.

NOTE: If a slight amount of grease has gotten on the shoes during installation, it may be removed by light sanding.

Wheel Cylinders

REMOVAL AND INSTALLATION

1. Remove the brake drums and shoes.
2. Disconnect the hydraulic line from the wheel cylinder by unfastening the nut on the rear of the backing plate.
3. Plug the line to prevent dirt from entering the system or brake fluid from leaking out.
4. Unfasten the nuts which secure the wheel cylinder to the backing plate and remove the cylinder.

Installation of the wheel cylinder is performed in the reverse order of removal. Bleed the hydraulic system and adjust the brake shoes after installation is completed.

OVERHAUL

1. Remove the wheel cylinder from the backing plate.
2. Remove the piston and adjusting screw with the boot attached to the adjuster.
3. Separate the adjuster screw and boot from the adjuster.

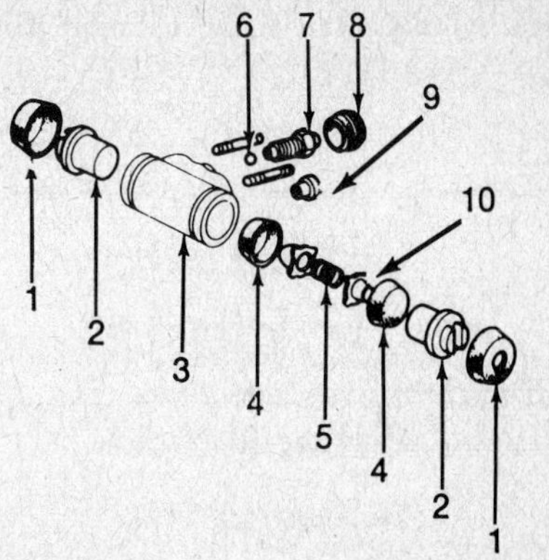

1. Boot	6. Steel ball
2. Piston	7. Bleeder screw
3. Cylinder body	8. Bleeder screw cap
4. Piston cup	9. Hydraulic line seat
5. Return spring	10. Push rod

Rear wheel cylinder components

4. Remove the other piston and boot and separate the boot from the piston.
5. Press in on either piston cup and force the piston cups, cup expanders, and return spring from the cylinder.
6. Wash all parts (except the boots) in clean isopropyl alcohol. Examine the cylinder bore for roughness or scoring.
7. Check the piston-to-cylinder bore clearance. If it exceeds 0.006 in., replace with new parts.

To assemble the wheel cylinder:

8. Lubricate the cylinder bore, adjuster and new piston cups with clean brake fluid, before assembly. Always use new piston cups.
9. Install the piston return spring in a piston cup expander. Place the other piston cup expander and new piston cup on the return spring. Install the return spring, piston cup expanders and piston cups into the cylinder.
10. Install the piston boot to the piston adjuster with the smaller lip of the boot on the groove of the piston adjuster.
11. Insert the piston adjuster into the cylinder assembly and install the larger lip of the boot in the groove of the cylinder.
12. Install the adjusting screw in the piston adjuster.
13. Install the wheel cylinder as detailed above.

PARKING BRAKE

ADJUSTMENT

1. Adjust the service brakes before attempting to adjust the parking brake.
2. Use the adjusting nut to adjust the length of the front cable so that the rear brakes are locked when the parking brake lever is pulled out 5–10 notches.
3. After adjustment, apply the parking brake several times. Release the parking brake and make sure that the

rear wheels rotate without dragging. If they drag, repeat the adjustment.

CHASSIS ELECTRICAL

Wiper Motor

REPLACEMENT

1. Remove the wiper arm attaching screws and remove the wiper arms.
2. Remove the cowl plate screws, move the cowl plate up at the front and disconnect the washer hose. Remove the cowl plate.
3. Disconnect the wires from the wiper motor.
4. Unbolt and remove the motor.
5. Installation is the reverse of removal.

Instrument Cluster

REMOVAL AND INSTALLATION

Rotary Pick-Up

1. Remove the two bolts which secure the steering column bracket to the instrument panel.
2. Unfasten the four instrument cluster securing screws.
3. To disconnect the speedometer cable, reach up under the dash and depress the flat plastic connector tab while pulling the cable away from the head.

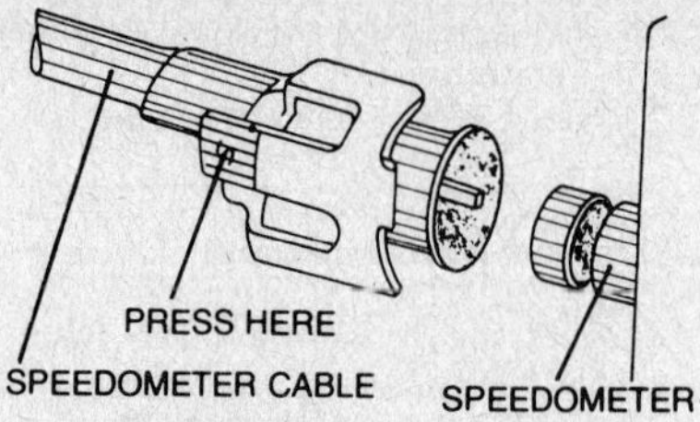

Speedometer cable removal
(© Toyo Kogyo Co. Ltd.)

4. Unfasten the wiring harness from the instrument cluster.
5. Lift the cluster out.

Installation is performed in the reverse order of removal.

B-1600, B-1800 and B-2000

1. Disconnect the cable from the negative (–) battery terminal.
2. Remove the four instrument cluster securing screws.
3. Move the cluster rearward, so that you can gain access to the back of it.
4. To disconnect the speedometer cable, reach up under the dash and depress the flat plastic connector tab while pulling the cable away from the head.
5. Disconnect the cluster wiring harness from the printed circuit. Note the position of the ammeter leads and disconnect them as well.
6. Remove the screw which secures the ground lead to the cluster. On models with air injection, unfasten the two speedometer sensor lead connectors.
7. Remove the cluster.

Installation is the reverse of removal.

Fuses

FUSE BOX LOCATION

Rotary Pick-Up

The main fuse block is mounted behind the seat at the right side of the cab. Another fuse box is attached to the firewall at the left, rear corner of the engine compartment. Fuse amperage and location are printed on the inside of the fuse box cover.

B-1600 and B-1800

The main fuse is located behind the battery. The fuse box is located at the left, rear corner of the engine compartment. Fuse amperage and location are printed on the inside of the cover.

B-2000

The fuse box is located in the engine compartment at the rear left corner.

FUSIBLE LINKS

On all models except the B-2000, these are located in either one or two boxes next to the battery in the engine compartment. On the B-2000, the fusible link is located on the right fender apron. If these links blow, they must be replaced with the specified parts by disconnecting the battery, disconnecting wiring to each link requiring replacement, removing the attaching screws and the link, and installing the new links or links in the reverse of the removal procedure.

INDEX

VEHICLE IDENTIFICATION

Model/Type	Year	Series Identification Number*
Hi-Lux 2000 (Pick-up)		
Standard Wheelbase	1973-74	RN22
Long Wheelbase	1973-74	RN27
Hi-Lux 2200 (Pick-up)		
Standard Wheelbase	1975-78	RN23
Long Wheelbase	1975-78	RN28
Hi-Lux 2200 (Pick-up)		
Standard Wheelbase	1979-80	RN32
Long Wheelbase	1979-80	RN42
Hi-Lux 2200 4X4 (Four Wheel Drive Pick-up)		
Standard Wheelbase	1980	RN37
Long Wheelbase	1980	RN47
Land Cruiser		
2-door	1973-74	FJ40
Station Wagon	1973-74	FJ55
Land Cruiser		
2-door	1975-80	FJ40
Station Wagon	1975-80	FJ55

* The suffixes L, V, KA, etc., may not appear in the serial number; a typical Toyota serial number would appear: RN23L-KRA3.

ENGINE IDENTIFICATION

Model	Year	Displacement cu in. (cc)	Number of Cylinders	Type	Engine Series Identification
Hi-Lux (Pick-up)					
2000	1973-74	120.0 (1980)	4	OHC	18R-C
2200	1975-80	133.6 (2189)	4	OHC	20R
Hi-Lux 4X4 (Four Wheel Drive Pick-up)					
2200	1980	133.6 (2189)	4	OHC	20R
Land Cruiser	1973-74	236.7 (3878)	6	OHV	F
	1975-80	256.0 (4200)	6	OHV	2F

OHV = Overhead valve   OHC = Overhead cam

GENERAL ENGINE SPECIFICATIONS

Year	Engine Type	Engine Displacement cu in. (cc)	Carburetor Type	Horsepower @ rpm	Torque @ rpm (ft-lb)	Bore x Stroke (in.)	Compression Ratio
1973-74	18R-C	123.0 (1980)	2-bbl	97 @ 5500	106 @ 3600	3.48 x 3.15	8.5:1
	F	236.7 (3878)	2-bbl	135 @ 4000	213 @ 2000	3.54 x 4.00	7.8:1

GENERAL ENGINE SPECIFICATIONS

Year	Engine Type	Engine Displacement cu in. (cc)	Carburetor Type	Horsepower @ rpm	Torque @ rpm (ft-lb)	Bore x Stroke (in.)	Compression Ratio
1975-77	20R	133.6 (2189)	2-bbl	96 @ 4800	120 @ 2800	3.48 x 3.50	8.4:1
	2F	257.9 (4200)	2-bbl	125 @ 3600	200 @ 1800	3.70 x 4.00	7.8:1
1978-80	20R	133.6 (2189)	2-bbl	95 @ 4800	122 @ 2400	3.48 x 3.50	8.4:1
	2F	257.9 (4200)	2-bbl	125 @ 3600	200 @ 1800	3.70 x 4.00	7.8:1

TUNE-UP SPECIFICATIONS

(When analyzing compressing test results, look for uniformity among cylinders rather than specific pressures)

Year	Engine Type	Spark Plugs Type (ND)	Spark Plugs Gap (in.)	Distributor Point Dwell (deg.)	Distributor Point Gap (in.)	Ignition Timing (deg.)② Man. Trans	Ignition Timing (deg.)② Auto Trans	Fuel Pump Pressure (psi)	Idle Speed (rpm) Man. Trans	Idle Speed (rpm) Auto Trans	Valve Clearance** (in.) Intake	Valve Clearance** (in.) Exhaust
1973	18R-C	W20EP	0.031	52	0.018	7B	7B	2.8-4.3	650	650	0.008	0.014
	F	W17ES	0.030	41	0.018	7B	—	3.4-4.8	650	—	0.008	0.014
1974	18R-C	W20EP	0.031	52	0.018	7B	7B	2.8-4.3	650	800	0.008	0.014
	F	W14ES①	0.030	41	0.018	7B	—	3.4-4.8	650	—	0.008	0.014
1975-77	20R	W16EP	0.030	52	0.018	8B	8B	2.2-4.2	850	850	0.008	0.012
	2F	W14EX	0.037	41	0.018	7B	—	3.4-4.7	650	—	0.008	0.014
1978-80	20R	W16EP	0.030	Electronic		8B	8B	2.1-4.3	800	850	0.008	0.012
	2F	W14EX	0.39	Electronic		7B	—	3.4-4.7	800	—	0.008	0.014

NOTE: If the information given in this chart disagrees with the information on the engine tune-up decal, use the specifications on the decal—they are current for the engine in your car.

** Valve clearance checked with the engine HOT.

① California F engines: W14EX.

② With manual transmission in Neutral and automatic transmission in Drive (D) (1973) or Neutral (1974-80).

FIRING ORDERS

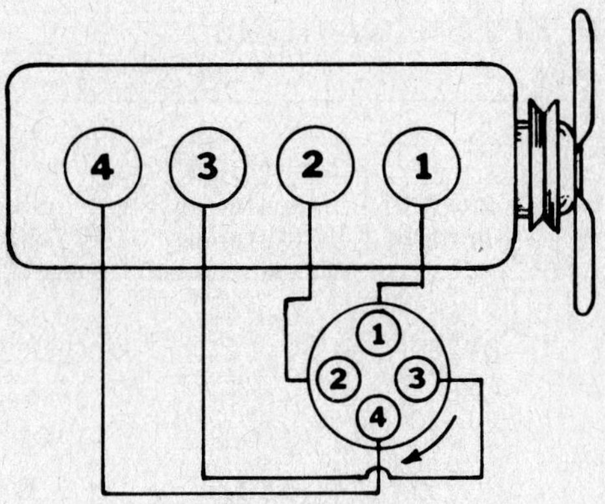

18R-C engine

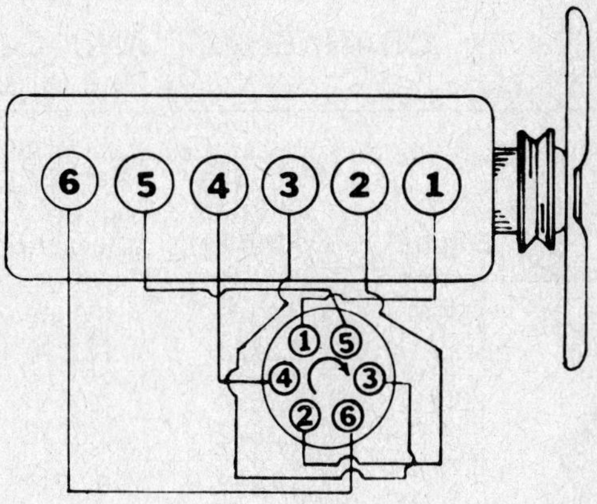

F engines

FIRING ORDERS

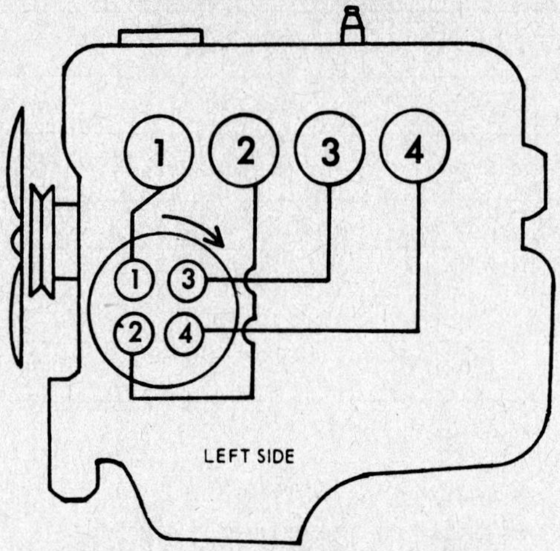

20R engine

CAPACITIES

Year	Engine Type	Engine Crankcase Add 1 Qt. for New Filter	Transmission (pts.) Automatic	Transmission (pts.) Manual 3-speed	Transmission (pts.) Manual 4-speed	Transfer Case	Axle (pts.) Front	Axle (pts.) Rear	Gasoline Tank (gal.)	Cooling System w/Heater (Qts.)
Pick-up										
1973	18R-C	4.3	14.8	—	3.6	—	—	2.2	12.1	7.8
1974	18R-C	4.3	13.6	—	4.0	—	—	3.6	13.7	9.0
1975-78	20R	3.9	14.0⑥	—	4.0①	—	—	3.6	12.1②	8.5③
1979-80	20R	4.2	13.4	—	4.0①	—	—	3.6	13.7②	8.9
4X4 Pick-up										
1980	20R	4.2	—	—	4.0	3.4	4.0	4.2	13.7②	8.9
Land Cruiser										
1973-74	F	7.4	—	3.6	6.6	3.6	5.2	5.2	16.4④	17.7
1975-80	2F	7.4	—	3.6	6.6	3.6	5.2	5.2	22.2④	17.5⑤

① 5 Speed: 5.6 pts.
② Long Bed 1975-80: 16.1
③ 7.4 1978 only
④ 21.7 gals. on Station Wagon
⑤ 1978-80 2 door: 19.9 qts.
1978-80 Station Wagon: 18.3 qts.
⑥ 13.4 1978 only

CRANKSHAFT AND CONNECTING ROD SPECIFICATIONS

(All measurements given in inches)

Year	Engine	Crankshaft Main Brg. Journal Dia.	Crankshaft Main Brg. Oil Clearance	Crankshaft Shaft End-Play	Crankshaft Thrust on No.	Connecting Rod Journal Diameter	Connecting Rod Oil Clearance	Connecting Rod Side Clearance
1973-77	18R-C	2.3613-2.3622	0.0008-0.0020	0.0008-0.0080	3	2.0857-2.0866	0.0010-0.0021	0.0060-0.0100
	20R	2.3614-2.3622	0.0010-0.0022	0.0008-0.0079	3	2.0862-2.0866	0.0010-0.0022	0.0063-0.0102
	F	2.6366-2.6378	0.0012-0.0018	0.0024-0.0065	3	2.1252-2.1260	0.0008-0.0024	0.0040-0.0090

CRANKSHAFT AND CONNECTING ROD SPECIFICATIONS

(All measurements given in inches)

		Crankshaft				Connecting Rod		
Year	Engine	Main Brg. Journal Dia.	Main Brg. Oil Clearance	Shaft End-Play	Thrust on No.	Journal Diameter	Oil Clearance	Side Clearance
1973-77	2F	①	0.0008-0.0017	0.0024-0.0063	3	2.1252-2.1260	0.0008-0.0024	0.0043-0.0091
1978-80	20R	2.3614-2.622	0.0010-0.0022	0.0010-0.0080	3	2.0862-2.0866	0.0010-0.0022	0.0063-0.0102
	2F	①	0.0008-0.0017	0.0024-0.0063	3	2.1252-2.1260	0.0008-0.0024	0.0043-0.0091

Dia. = Diameter Brg. = Bearing

① No. 1—2.6367 2.6376
No. 2—2.6957-2.6967
No. 3—2.7548-2.7557
No. 4—2.8139-2.8148

VALVE SPECIFICATIONS

Engine Type	Seat Angle (deg)	Face Angle (deg)	Spring Test Pressure (lbs) Inner	Spring Test Pressure (lbs) Outer	Spring Installed Height (in.) Inner	Spring Installed Height (in.) Outer	Stem to Guide Clearance (in.) Intake	Stem to Guide Clearance (in.) Exhaust	Stem Diameter (in.) Intake	Stem Diameter (in.) Exhaust
18R-C	45	45	15.2	50.6	1.480	1.640	0.0010-0.0022	0.0014-0.0030	0.3140	0.3136
20R	45	44.5	—	60.0①	—	1.594	0.0006-0.0024	0.0012-0.0026	0.3141	0.3140
F	45	45	—	71.5	—	1.324	0.0010-0.0026	0.0014-0.0028	0.3141	0.3137
2F	45	44.5	—	71.6	—	1.693	0.0012-0.0024	0.0016-0.0028	0.3140	0.3137

① 1978-80; 55.1 lbs.

PISTON AND RING SPECIFICATIONS

(All measurements given in inches)

			Ring Side Clearance			Ring Gap		
Year	Engine	Piston to Bore Clearance	Top Compression	Bottom Compression	Oil Control	Top Compression	Bottom Compression	Oil Control
1973-74	18R-C	0.0020-0.0030	0.0012-0.0028	0.0012-0.0028	0.0008-0.0028	0.004-0.012	0.004-0.012	0.004-0.012
	F	0.0012-0.0020	0.0012-0.0028	0.0008-0.0024	①	0.008-0.016	0.006-0.014	②
1975-80	20R	0.0012-0.0020	0.008	0.008	Snug	0.004-0.012	0.004-0.012	Snug
	2F	0.0012-0.0020	0.0012-0.0024	0.0008-0.0024	—	0.008-0.016	0.008-0.016	—

① Oil control gap:
Top—0.006-0.018 in.
Bottom—0.006-0.016 in.

② Control clearance:
Top—0.0016-0.0031 in.
Bottom—0.0016-0.0033 in.

TORQUE SPECIFICATIONS

(All readings in ft-lbs)

Engine Type	Cylinder Head Bolts	Rod Bearing Bolts	Main Bearing Bolts	Crankshaft Pulley Bolt	Flywheel to Crankshaft Bolts	Intake	Manifold	Exhaust
18R-C	72-82	39-48	69-83	43-51	51-58		30-35①	
20R	52-64	39-48	69-83	80-94②	62-69③	11-15		29-36
F	83-98	35-55	90-108④	—	43-51		14-22①	
2F	83-98	35-55	90-108④	116-145	59-62	28-37		28-37

① Intake and exhaust manifolds combined

② 1978-80: 102-130

③ 1978-80: 73-79

④ Rear bearing—76-94 ft-lb

TORQUE SEQUENCES

Cylinder Head

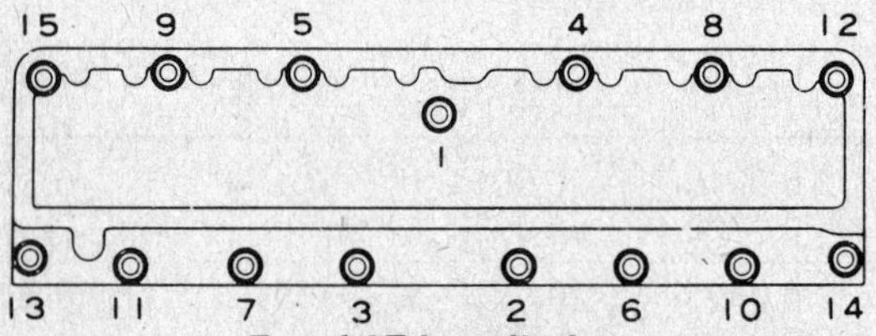

F and 2F installation

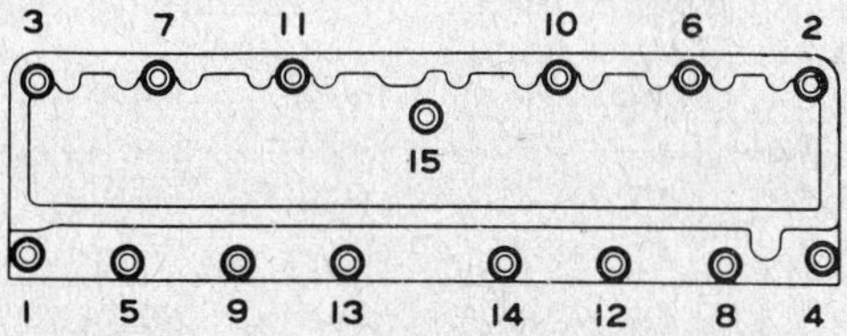

F and 2F removal

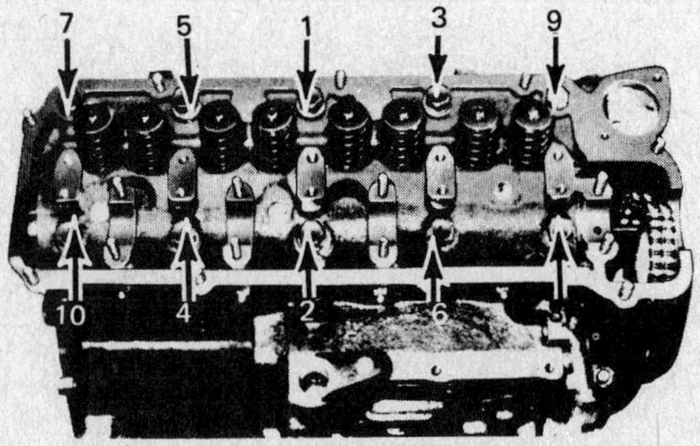

18R-C installation

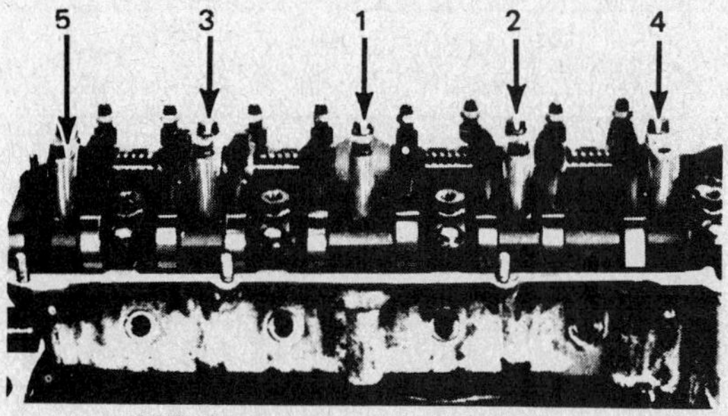

18R-C rocker arm installation sequence

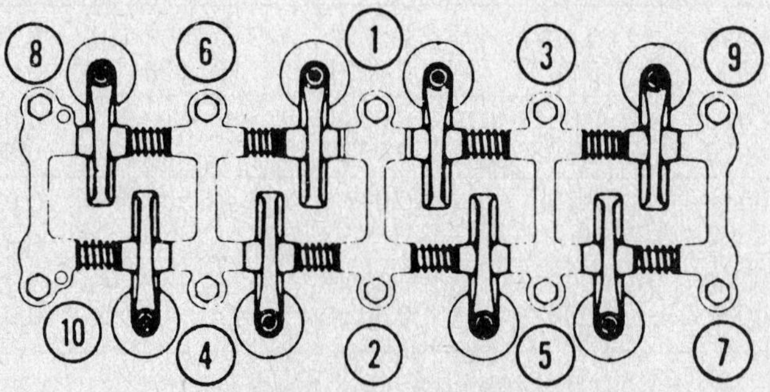

20R cylinder head installation sequence

ALTERNATOR AND REGULATOR SPECIFICATIONS

Engine Type	Alternator Manufacturer	Output (amps)	Regulator Manufacturer	Field Relay Contact Spring Deflection (in.)	Field Relay Point Gap (in.)	Field Relay Volts to Close	Regulator Air Gap (in.)	Regulator Point Gap (in.)	Regulator Volts
18R-C	Nippondenso	40	Nippondenso	0.008-0.018	0.016-0.047	4.5-5.8	0.008	0.010-0.018	13.8-14.8
20R	Nippondenso	40①	Nippondenso	0.008-0.24	0.016-0.047	4.5-5.8	0.012	0.010-0.018	13.8-14.8②
F	Nippondenso	38	Nippondenso	—	—	4.5-5.8	—	0.001-0.018	13.6-14.8
2F	Nippondenso	45③	Nippondenso	Not Adustable					13.8-14.8④

① Optional 55 amp alternator available
② W/55 amp alternator: 14.0-14.7
③ 1979-80: 40 amp and optional 55 amp alternators
④ 1979-80, 40 amp: 13.8-14.8; 55 amp: 14.0-14.7

BRAKE SPECIFICATIONS

(All measurements given are (in.) unless noted)

Year, Model	Lug Nut Torque (ft-lb)	Master Cylinder Bore	Brake Disc Minimum Thickness	Brake Disc Maximum Run-Out	Brake Drum Diameter	Brake Drum Max. Machine O/S	Brake Drum Max. Wear Limit	Minimum Lining Thickness Front	Minimum Lining Thickness Rear
Hi-Lux (Pick-up)									
1973-78	65-68	1.001	0.45	0.006	10.0	10.07	10.08	0.04	0.04
1979-80	65-86	N/A	0.45	0.006	N/A	N/A	10.08	0.04	0.04
Hi-Lux 4X4 (Four Wheel Drive Pick-up)									
1980	65-86	N/A	0.45	0.006	N/A	N/A	10.08	0.04	0.04
Land Cruiser									
1973-75	65-86	0.997	—	—	11.4	11.54	11.54	0.16	0.16
1976-78	65-86	0.997	0.74	0.005	11.4	11.54	11.54	0.04	0.06

WHEEL ALIGNMENT SPECIFICATIONS

Year, Model	Model	CASTER Range (deg)	CASTER Pref Setting (deg)	CAMBER Range (deg)	CAMBER Pref Setting (deg)	Toe-in (in.)	Steering Axis Inclin. (deg)	WHEEL PIVOT RATIO (deg) Inner Wheel	WHEEL PIVOT RATIO (deg) Outer Wheel
Pick-up									
1973-74	RN22, RN27	¼P-1¼N	½N	¼P-1¾P	1P	0.08-0.28	7¼	36-39	27½-31½
1975-78	RN23, RN28	0-1P	½P	½P-1½P	1P	0.20-0.27	7¼	33	26
1979-80	RN32, RN42	0-1P	½P	½P-1½P	1P	0.16-0.24	7⅙	36	29
4X4 Pick-up									
1980	RN37, RN47	NA	3½P①	NA	1P	0.11-0.20②	9½	30½	29
Land Cruiser									
1973-78	FJ40, FJ55	½P-1½P	1P	½P-1½P	1P	0.12-0.20	9½	32③	27③
1979-80	FJ40, FJ55	½P-1½P	1P	½P-1½P	1P	0.10-0.20④	9½	32	30

① Unloaded; 4½° loaded
② For H78-15 Tire; 0-0.008 for HR78-15B Tire
③ Station Wagon, 1973-75: inner 30°; outer 23°; 1976 and later: inner 32°; outer 30°
④ For H78-15B Tire; 0.04N-0.04P for HR78-15B Tire
NA: Not Applicable

TUNE-UP PROCEDURES

***NOTE:** The procedures outlined below are the specific procedures for Toyota vehicles; general tune-up procedures may be found in the section at the end of this book.*

Spark Plugs

Check, clean, and adjust the spark plugs every 6,000 miles. Replace them every 12,000 miles.

Clean any foreign material from around the spark plugs before removing them. Use the spark plug wrench supplied in the tool kit.

Clean any plugs which appear to be dirty and file their electrodes flat. Adjust the gap to the figure given in the "Tune-up Specifications" chart, above, using a wire feeler gauge.

***NOTE:** Do not use a flat gauge; an inaccurate reading will result.*

Inspect the spark plug hole threads for rust and, if necessary, use a 14 mm plug tap to clean them.

Lightly oil the threads and torque the plugs to 11-14 ft lbs. Use caution when tightening the plugs, as most Toyota models use aluminum heads.

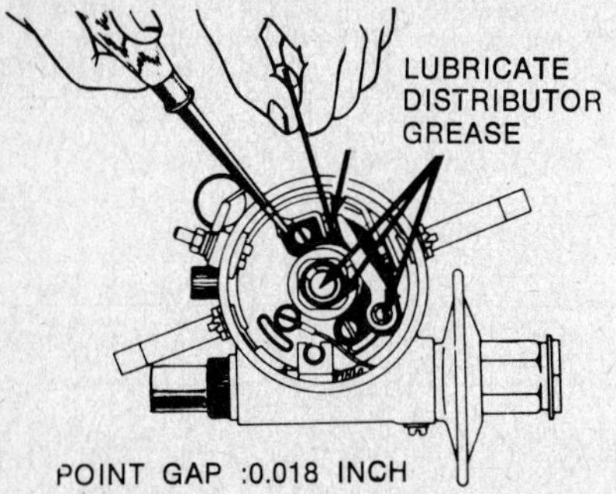

Adjusting breaker point gap at points

Breaker Points and Condenser

Loosen the clips which attach the distributor cap to the distributor body and lift the cap straight up. Leave the leads connected to the cap. Remove the rotor and dust cover.

Clean the distributor cap and rotor with alcohol. Inspect them for cracks and other signs of wear or damage. Polish the points with a point file.

***NOTE:** Do not use emery cloth or sandpaper; these may leave particles on the points, causing them to arc.*

If the points are badly pitted or worn, replace them as follows:

1. Unfasten the point lead connector.
2. Remove the point retaining clip and remove the point hold-down screw.
3. Remove the point set.
4. Installation is the reverse of removal.

After replacing the points, or as routine maintenance, adjust the points to the specifications given in the tune-up chart at the beginning of this section as follows:

1. Rotate the engine by hand or by using a remote starter switch, so that the rubbing block is on the high point of the cam lobe.
2. Insert a 0.018 in. feeler gauge between the points; a slight drag should be felt.

***NOTE:** Some 20R engines with breaker points have a plastic cap over the contact points, making it necessary to adjust the point gap at the rubbing block. Set the rubbing block between two cam lobes and adjust the clearance to 0.018 in. (See illustration). Always check the dwell angle after setting the points.*

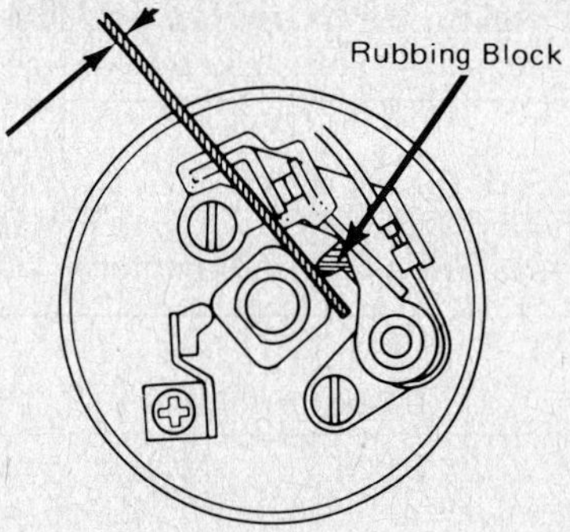

Some 20R engines with breaker points are adjusted at the rubbing block rather than the contact points. See text.

3. If no drag is felt or if the feeler gauge cannot be inserted at all, loosen, but do not remove, the point hold-down screw.
4. Insert a screwdriver into the adjustment slot. Rotate the screwdriver until the proper point gap is attained. The point gap is increased by rotating the screwdriver counterclockwise and decreased by rotating it clockwise.
5. Tighten the point hold-down screw. Lubricate the cam lobes, breaker arm, rubbing block, arm pivot, and distributor shaft with special high-temperature distributor grease.

Check the operation of the centrifugal advance mechanism by moving the rotor clockwise. Release the rotor; it should return to its original position. If it does not, check it for binding.

Check the vacuum advance unit by removing the cap and pressing in on the octane selector. Release the octane selector. It should snap back to its original position. Check for binding if it fails to do so.

Replace the condenser if it is suspect or as routine maintenance during the point replacement operation, in the following manner:

1. Remove the nut and washer from the condenser lead terminal.
2. Remove the condenser mounting screw and withdraw the condenser.
3. Installation is the reverse of removal.

***NOTE:** The condenser is mounted on the outside of the distributor body on all models, except the Land Cruiser, which has it mounted inside the body.*

Install the dust cover, rotor and the distributor cap on the distributor. Adjust the dwell and timing, as outlined below.

Dwell Angle

Connect a dwell/tachometer, in accordance with its manufacturer's instructions, between the distributor primary lead and a ground.

***CAUTION:** On models with electronic ignition, hook the dwell meter or tachometer to the negative (−) side of the coil, not to the distributor primary lead; damage to the ignition control unit will result.*

With the engine warmed up and running at the specified idle speed (see the tune-up chart), take a dwell reading.

If the point dwell is not within specifications, shut the engine off and adjust the point gap, as outlined above.

***NOTE:** Increasing the point gap decreases the dwell angle and vice versa.*

Install the dust cover, rotor, and cap. Check the dwell reading again.

ELECTRONIC DISTRIBUTOR

Setting the points (in this case an air gap) is accomplished almost the same as in a conventional system, but for a few things.

The air gap should be set using a brass or plastic feeler gauge and *extreme* care must be taken to eliminate the possibility of mixing wiring.

Set the air gap to 0.008–0.012 in.

Ignition Timing

1. Warm up the engine. Connect a tachometer and check the engine idle speed to see that it is within specifications. Adjust it as outlined below if it is not.

***CAUTION:** On models with electronic ignition, hook the dwell meter or tachometer to the negative (−) side of the coil, not to the distributor primary lead; damage to the ignition control unit will result.*

If the timing mark is difficult to see, use chalk or a dab of paint to make it more visible.

2. Connect a timing light to the engine, as outlined in the instructions supplied by the manufacturer of the light.

3. Disconnect the vacuum line from the distributor vacuum unit and plug the line.

4. Allow the engine to run at the specified idle speed with the gear shift in neutral for vehicles with manual transmissions, and in Drive (D) for vehicles with automatic transmissions.

CAUTION: Be sure that the parking brake is firmly set and that the wheels are chocked.

5. Point the timing light at the timing marks indicated in the chart below. With the engine at idle, timing should be at the specification given in the tune-up chart at the beginning of this section. If it is not, loosen the pinch bolt at the base and rotate the distributor to advance or retard the timing, as required.

6. Stop the engine and tighten the pinch bolt. Start the engine and recheck the timing.

7. Stop the engine and disconnect the timing light and the tachometer. Connect the vacuum line to the vacuum advance unit.

TIMING MARK LOCATIONS

Engine Type	Location	Type of Mark
18R-C, 20R	Crankshaft pulley	Pointer and painted slot
F, 2F	Flywheel	Ball and pointer

Timing Marks

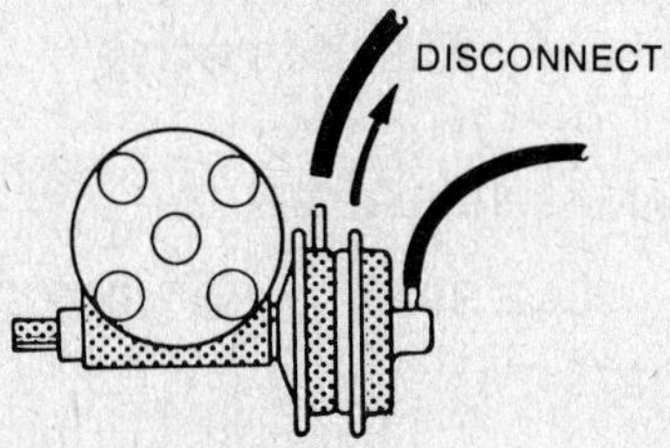

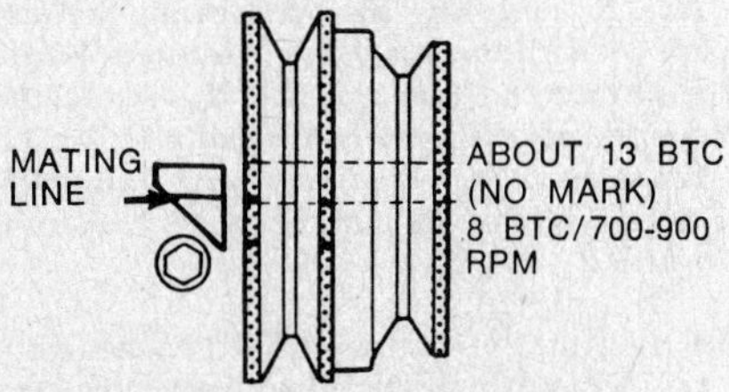

20R timing marks (with High Altitude Compensation system)

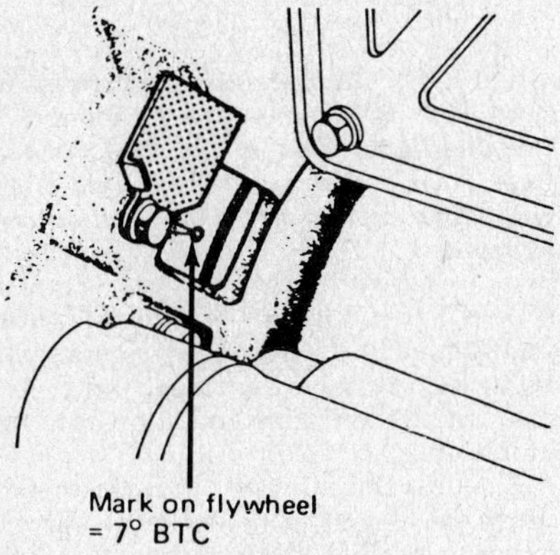

2F engines

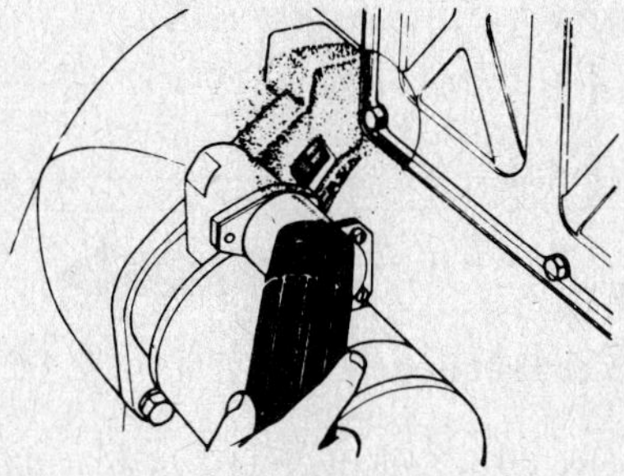

F engine

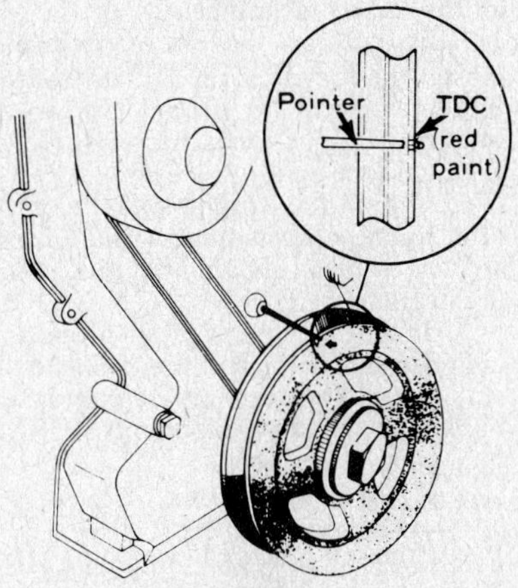

18R-C

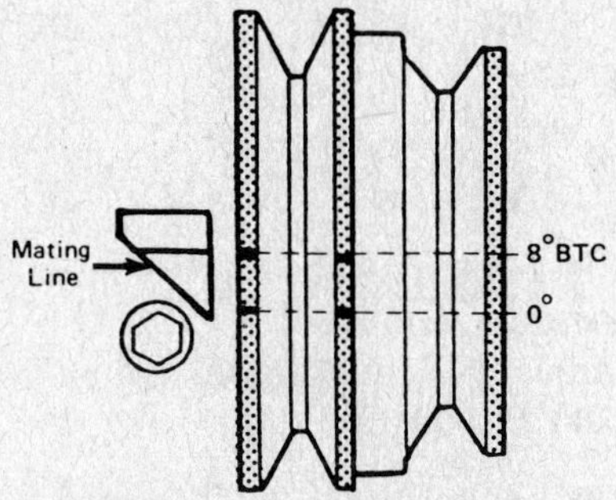

20R timing marks (without High Altitude Compensation system)

Octane Selector

The octane selector is used as a fine adjustment to match the vehicle's ignition timing to the grade of gasoline being used. It is located near the distributor vacuum unit, beneath a plastic dust cover. Normally the octane selector should not require adjustment, however, if necessary, adjustment is as follows:

1. Align the setting line with the threaded end of the housing and then align the center line with the setting mark on the housing.

OCTANE SELECTOR TEST SPEEDS

Engine Type	Test Speed (mph)
18R-C, 20R	16-22
F, 2F	20

2. Drive the vehicle to the speed specified on the chart below, in high gear, on a level road.

3. Depress the accelerator pedal all the way to the floor. A slight "pinging" sound should be heard. As the vehicle accelerates, the sound should gradually go away.

4. If the pinging sound is loud or if it fails to disappear as the vehicle speed increases, retard the timing by turning the knurled knob toward "R" (Retard).

5. If there is no pinging sound at all, advance the timing by turning the knob toward "A" (Advance).

6. When the adjustment is completed, replace the plastic dust cover.

NOTE: One graduation of the octane selector is equal to about ten degrees of crankshaft angle.

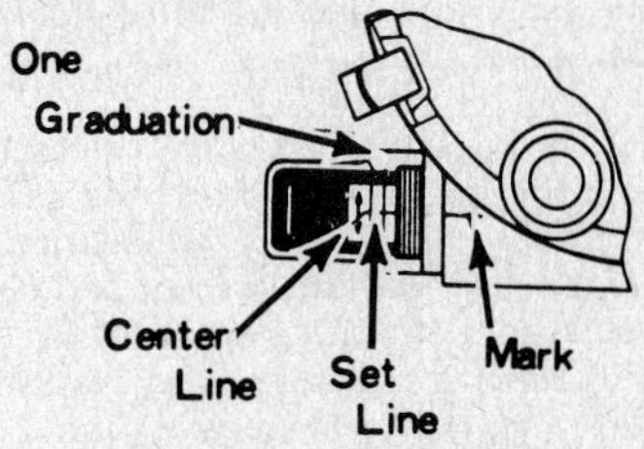

Pick-up octane selector

Valve Lash

18R-C Engine

1. Start the engine and allow it to reach normal operating temperature (above 175°F).

2. Stop the engine. Remove the air cleaner assembly, its hoses, and bracket. Remove any other cables, hoses, wires, etc. which are attached to the valve cover. Remove the valve cover.

3. Check the torque of the valve rocker shaft bolts and the camshaft bearing bolts; they should be 12–17 ft lbs.

4. Check the torque specification of

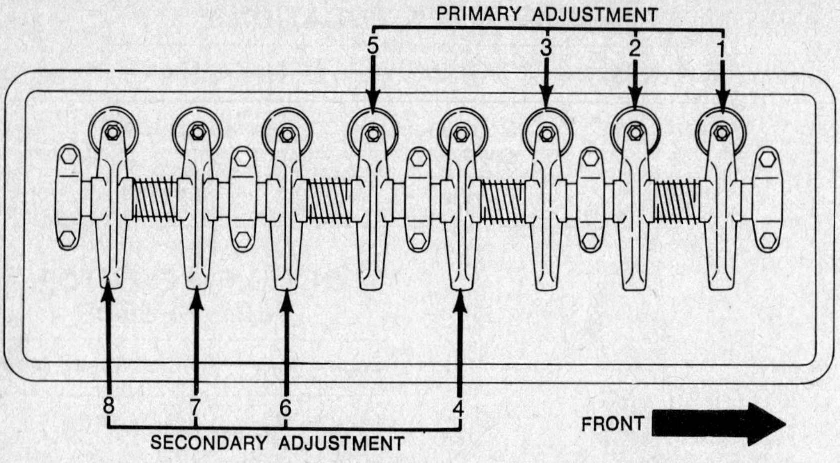

18R-C valve adjustment sequence

the bearing cap union bolts. They should be torqued to 11–16 ft lbs.

5. Set the number one cylinder to TDC on its compression stroke. Remove the spark plug from the number one cylinder and place a finger over the hole. Crank the engine until a pressure is felt, then line the V-notch on the crankshaft pulley with the pointer on the timing chain cover. The number one cylinder is now at TDC.

NOTE: Do not start the engine. Valve clearances are checked with the engine stopped to prevent hot oil from being splashed out by the timing chain.

6. Check the clearances (see the tune-up chart) and adjust valves 1, 2, 3, and 5 to the proper specifications, if necessary.

NOTE: The clearance is measured with a feeler gauge between the valve stem and the adjusting screw.

7. To adjust the valve clearance, loosen the locknut and turn the adjusting screw until the specified clearance is obtained. Tighten the locknut and check the clearance again.

8. Crank the engine one revolution (360°) and perform steps 6 and 7 for valves 4, 6, 7, and 8 in the illustration.

9. Install the spark plug in the number one cylinder. Install the valve cover, air cleaner assembly, and any other components which are removed.

20R Engine

1. Start the engine and allow it to reach normal operating temperature (above 180°F).

2. Stop the engine. Remove the air cleaner assembly, its hoses, and bracket. Remove any other cables, hoses, wires, etc., which are attached to the valve cover. Remove the valve cover.

3. Set the no. 1 cylinder at top dead center (TDC) of its compression stroke, with the TDC notch aligned with the pointer.

4. Measure the clearance between the valve stem and the rocker arm with a feeler gauge for the valves shown in the first illustration. See the tune-up chart for the correct clearance.

5. To adjust the valve clearance, loosen the locknut and turn the adjusting screw until the proper clearance is obtained. Tighten the locknut and check the clearance again.

6. Crank the engine *one* revolution (360°) and perform steps 4 and 5 for the set of valves shown in the second illustration.

7. Install the spark plug in the no. 1 cylinder and reconnect the coil lead. Install the valve cover, air cleaner assembly and any other components that were removed.

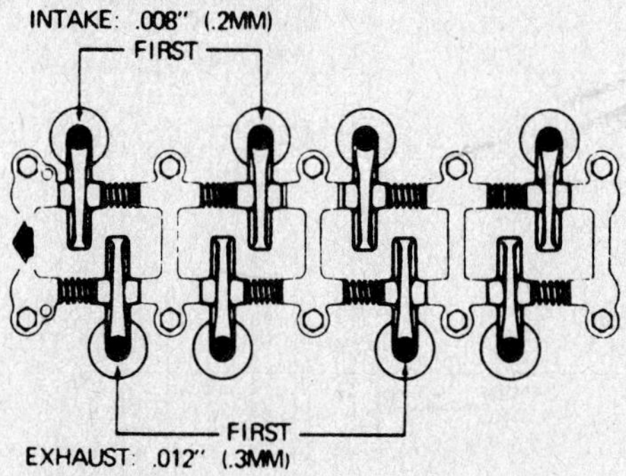

Adjust this set of valves first on the 20R engine

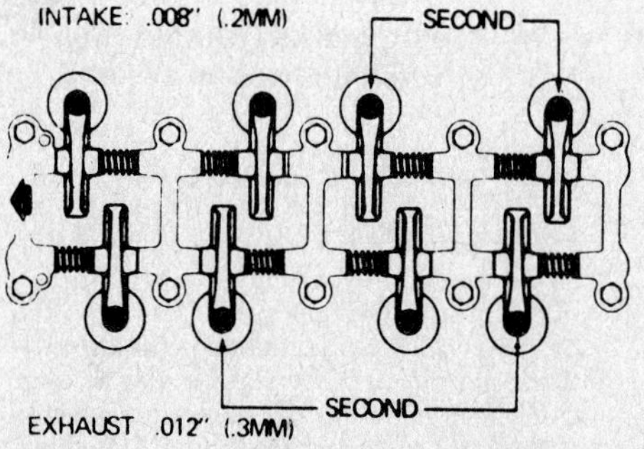

Turn the crankshaft one full turn and then adjust this set of valves on the 20R engine

F and 2F Engine

1. Warm the engine up to normal operating temperature (167–185°F).

2. Stop the engine. Remove the valve cover after removing the air cleaner assembly and any other components which might be in the way.

3. Tighten the cylinder head bolts to 83–93 ft lbs; the manifold retaining nuts to 14–22 ft lbs; and the rocker support nuts or bolts to 25–30 ft lbs (10 mm) and 14–22 ft lbs (8 mm).

NOTE: See above for the proper tightening sequences. Tighten the three stages.

4. Adjust the engine idle speed to 500 rpm.

5. Check the clearances between the rocker arm and the valves stem with a feeler gauge of the specified size. (See the tune-up chart.)

6. If the clearance is not according to specifications, loosen the locknut and turn the adjusting screw as required. Tighten the locknut and recheck the clearance.

7. When finished checking all of the valves, install the valve cover and any other components which were removed.

8. Adjust the idle speed to specification as outlined in the appropriate section below.

Carburetor

NOTE: See "Fuel System," above, for other carburetor adjustments.

IDLE SPEED AND MIXTURE

1973–74

NOTE: Perform the following adjustments with the air cleaner in place. While adjusting the idle speed and mixture the gear selector should be placed in Drive (D) range on models equipped with automatic transmissions. Be sure to block the front wheels.

1. Run the engine until it reaches normal operating temperature. Stop the engine.

2. Connect a tachometer to the engine, as detailed in its manufacturer's instructions.

CAUTION: On models with electronic ignition, do not connect the tachometer to the distributor side of the coil, instead hook it up to the negative (–) side of the coil to prevent damage to the ignition control unit.

3. Remove the plug and install a vacuum gauge in the manifold vacuum port by using a suitable metric adaptor.

4. Start the engine and allow it to run at idle speed.

5. Turn the mixture screw in or out, until the engine runs smoothly at the lowest possible engine speed without stalling.

6. Turn the idle speed screw until the vacuum gauge indicates the highest specified reading (see the chart below) at the specified idle speed. (See the tune-up chart at the beginning of the section.)

7. Tighten the idle speed screw to the point just before the engine rpm and vacuum readings drop off.

8. Remove the tachometer and the vacuum gauge. Install the plug back in the manifold vacuum port. Road-test the vehicle.

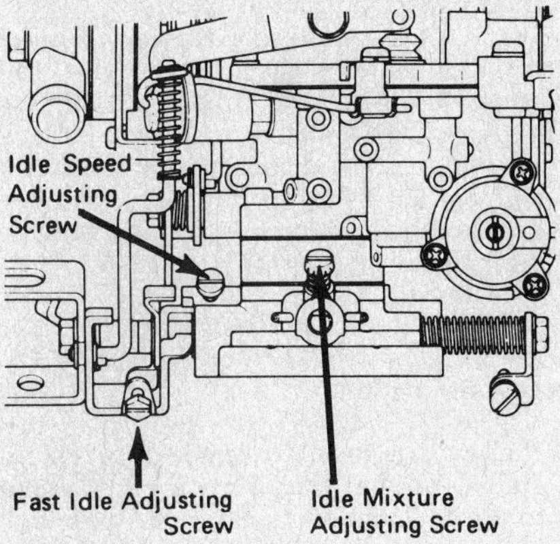

20R

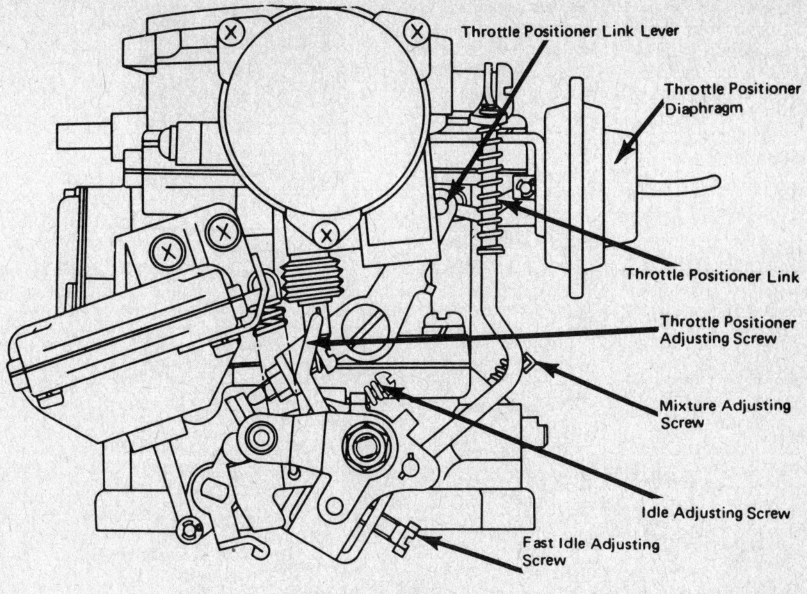

18R-C

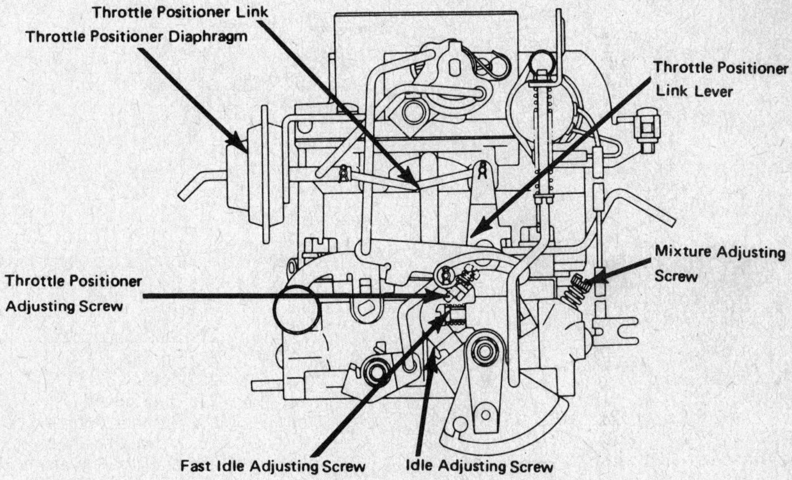

F and 2F engines

1975–80

The idle speed and mixture should be adjusted under the following conditions: the air cleaner must be installed, the choke fully opened, the transmission should be in Neutral (N), all accessories should be turned off, all vacuum lines should be connected, and the ignition timing should be set to specification.

1. Start the engine and allow it to reach normal operating temperature (180°F).

2. Check the float setting; the fuel level should be just about even with the spot on the sight glass. If the fuel level is too high or low, adjust the float level. (See the float adjustment procedure, below).

3. Connect a tachometer in accordance with its manufacturer's instructions. However, connect the tachometer positive (+) lead to the coil Negative (−) terminal. Do NOT hook it up to the distributor side; damage to the transistorized ignition could result.

4. Turn the idle speed adjusting screw to obtain one of the following initial idle speeds:
20R—900 rpm
2F—690 rpm

5. Turn the idle mixture adjusting screw to increase the idle speed as much as is possible.

6. Next, turn the idle speed screw to again obtain the same idle speed figure given in step 4.

7. If possible, turn the idle mixture screw to increase the idle speed again.

8. Keep repeating steps 6 and 7 until the idle mixture adjusting screw will no longer increase the idle speed above the figure specified in stap 4.

9. Slowly turn the idle mixture screw *clockwise,* until the idle speed specified in the "Tune-Up Specifications" chart is reached. (This makes the mixture leaner.)

10. Disconnect the tachometer.

VACUUM AT IDLE

Engine	Year	Minimum Vacuum Gauge (in. Hg)
18R-C	1973-74	17.7
F and 2F	1973-80	16.5

ENGINE ELECTRICAL

Distributor

REMOVAL

1. Unfasten the cables from the spark plugs, after marking the wiring order. Remove the high tension cable from the coil.

2. Remove the primary wire and the vacuum line from the distributor. Remove the distributor cap.

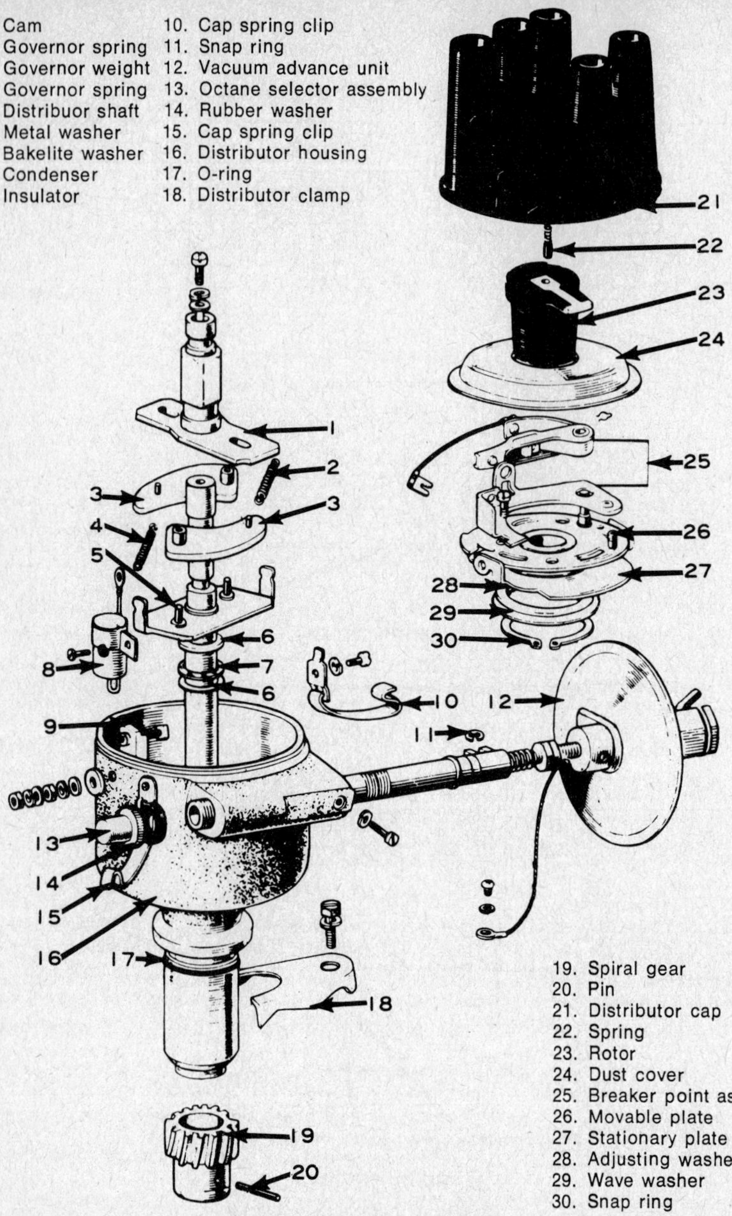

1. Cam
2. Governor spring
3. Governor weight
4. Governor spring
5. Distribuor shaft
6. Metal washer
7. Bakelite washer
8. Condenser
9. Insulator
10. Cap spring clip
11. Snap ring
12. Vacuum advance unit
13. Octane selector assembly
14. Rubber washer
15. Cap spring clip
16. Distributor housing
17. O-ring
18. Distributor clamp
19. Spiral gear
20. Pin
21. Distributor cap
22. Spring
23. Rotor
24. Dust cover
25. Breaker point assembly
26. Movable plate
27. Stationary plate
28. Adjusting washer
29. Wave washer
30. Snap ring

Distributor components

3. Match-mark the distributor housing and the engine block; mark the rotor position in the distributor as well. This will aid in correct positioning of the distributor during installation.
4. Remove the clamp from the distributor. Withdraw the distributor from the block.

***NOTE:** It is easier to install the distributor if the engine timing is not disturbed while it is removed. If the timing has been lost, see "Installation—Timing Disturbed" below.*

INSTALLATION—TIMING NOT DISTURBED

1. Insert the distributor in the block and align the matchmarks made during removal.
2. Engage the distributor drive with the oil pump drive shaft.
3. Install the distributor clamp, cap, high tension wire, primary wire, and vacuum line.
4. Install the wires on the spark plugs.
5. Start the engine. Check the timing and adjust the octane selector.

INSTALLATION—TIMING DISTURBED

If the engine has been cranked, dismantled, or the timing otherwise lost, proceed as follows:

1. Determine top dead center (TDC) of the number one (no. 1) cylinder's compression stroke by removing the spark plug from the no. 1 cylinder and placing a finger or a compression gauge over the spark plug hole.

Crank the engine until compression pressure starts to build up. Continue cranking the engine until the timing marks indicate TDC (or 0°).

2. Next, align the timing marks to the specifications given in the "Ignition Timing" column of the tune-up chart at the beginning of the Toyota section.
3. Temporarily install the rotor in the distributor shaft so that the rotor is pointing toward the number one terminal in the distributor cap. The points should just be about to open.
4. Use a small screwdriver to align the slot on the distributor drive (oil pump driveshaft) with the key on the bottom of the distributor shaft.
5. Install the distributor in the block by rotating it slightly (no more than one gear tooth in either direction) until the driven gear meshes with the drive.

***NOTE:** Oil the distributor spiral gear and the oil pump driveshaft end before distributor installation.*

6. Rotate the distributor, once it is installed, so that the points are just about to open. Temporarily tighten the pinch bolt.
7. Remove the rotor and install the dust cover. Replace the rotor and the distributor cap.
8. Install the primary wire and the vacuum line.
9. Install the no. 1 cylinder spark plug. Connect the cables to the spark plugs in the proper order by using the marks made during removal. Install the high tension wire on the coil.
10. Start the engine. Adjust the ignition timing and the octane selector, as outlined above.

Alternator

ALTERNATOR PRECAUTIONS

1. Always observe proper polarity of the battery connections; be especially careful when jump-starting the car.
2. Never ground or short out any alternator or alternator regulator terminals.
3. Never operate the alternator with any of its or the battery's leads disconnected.
4. Always remove the battery or disconnect its output lead while charging it.
5. Always disconnect the ground cable when replacing any electrical components.
6. Never subject the alternator to excessive heat or dampness if the engine is being steam-cleaned.
7. Never use arc-welding equipment with the alternator connected.

REMOVAL AND INSTALLATION

***NOTE:** On some models the alternator is mounted very low on the engine. On these models it may be necessary to remove the gravel shield and work from underneath*

the car in order to gain access to the alternator.

1. Unfasten the starter-to-battery cable at the battery end.
2. Remove the air cleaner, if necessary, to gain access to the alternator.
3. Unfasten the bolts which attach the adjusting link to the alternator. Remove the alternator drive belt.
4. Unfasten the tag and alternator wiring connection.
5. Remove the alternator attaching bolt and then withdraw the alternator from its bracket.
6. Installation is the reverse order of removal. After installing the alternator, adjust the belt tension.

BELT TENSION ADJUSTMENT

Inspection and adjustment to the alternator drive belt should be performed every 3,000 miles or if the alternator has been removed.

1. Inspect the drive belt to see that it is not cracked or worn. Be sure that its surfaces are free of grease or oil.
2. Push down on the belt halfway between the fan and the alternator pulleys, (or crankshaft pulley) with thumb pressure. Belt deflection should be $^3/_8$–$^1/_2$ in.
3. If the belt tension requires adjustment, loosen the adjusting link bolt and move the alternator until the proper belt tension is obtained.

*CAUTION: **Do not overtighten the belt; damage to the alternator bearings could result.***

4. Tighten the adjusting link bolt.

ON-CAR CHARGING TEST

1. Disconnect wire from terminal "B" at back of alternator and connect negative lead of ammeter to the wire, and positive lead to terminal "B". Connect positive lead of voltmeter to terminal "B" also, while connecting negative voltmeter lead to ground.
2. Run engine at approximately 2,000 rpm with all lights and accessories turned on. The ammeter should read at least 30 amperes with a voltmeter reading of between 13.8 and 14.8.

*NOTE: **If amperage reading is less than 30 amperes, it may be because the battery is fully charged. To discharge battery, disconnect coil lead from distributor and use the starter to turn engine for about five or ten seconds before running test again.***

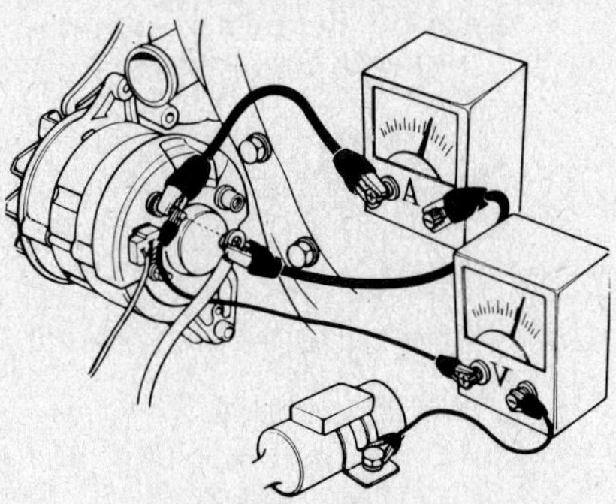

Alternator test

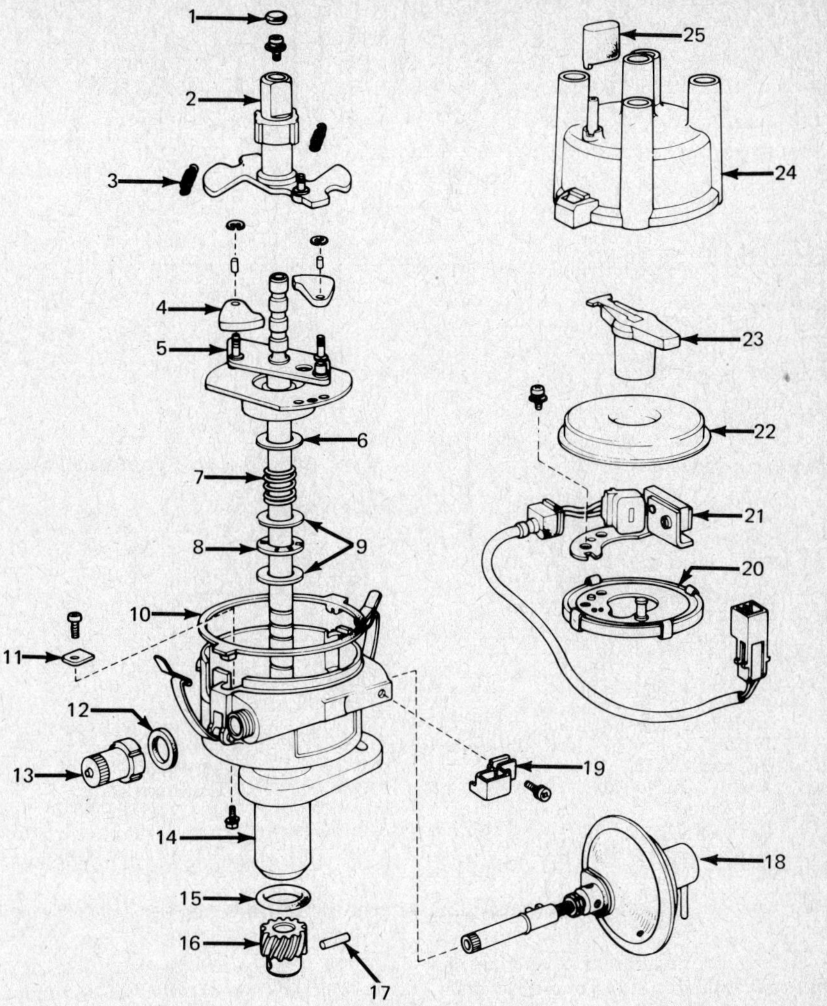

1. Cam grease stopper
2. Signal rotor
3. Governor spring
4. Governor weight
5. Governor shaft
6. Plate washer
7. Compression coil spring
8. Thrust bearing
9. Washer
10. Dustproof packing
11. Steel plate washer
12. Rubber washer
13. Octane selector cap
14. Housing
15. O-ring
16. Spiral gear
17. Pin
18. Vacuum advancer
19. Cord clamp
20. Breaker plate
21. Signal generator
22. Dustproof cover
23. Distributor rotor
24. Distributor cap
25. Rubber cap

20R electronic distributor

OVERHAUL

1. Remove alternator from car.
2. Remove three body screws from pully drive end frame. Pry drive end frame from alternator housing, being careful not to damage rotor coil wires. Firmly anchor rotor in soft-jawed vise. Remove pulley nut, pully, fan and spacer collar.
3. Press rotor from drive end frame. Remove spacer frame. Check rear shaft bearing for wear. Replace if worn or rough.
4. Remove rectifier support nuts and terminal insulators from rear of alternator. Remove rear cover from stator assembly.
5. Remove brush assembly by unscrewing it from leads. On later models, it is necessary to unsolder leads.

*CAUTION: **When unsoldering leads, hold rectifier leads with long nose pliers to protect rectifier from heat.***

6. Remove brush holder assembly.

*NOTE: **On some models it is necessary to press brush terminals from rectifier plate.***

7. Measure length of brush protruding from brush holder. It must protrude at least 0.217 in. If not, replace by:

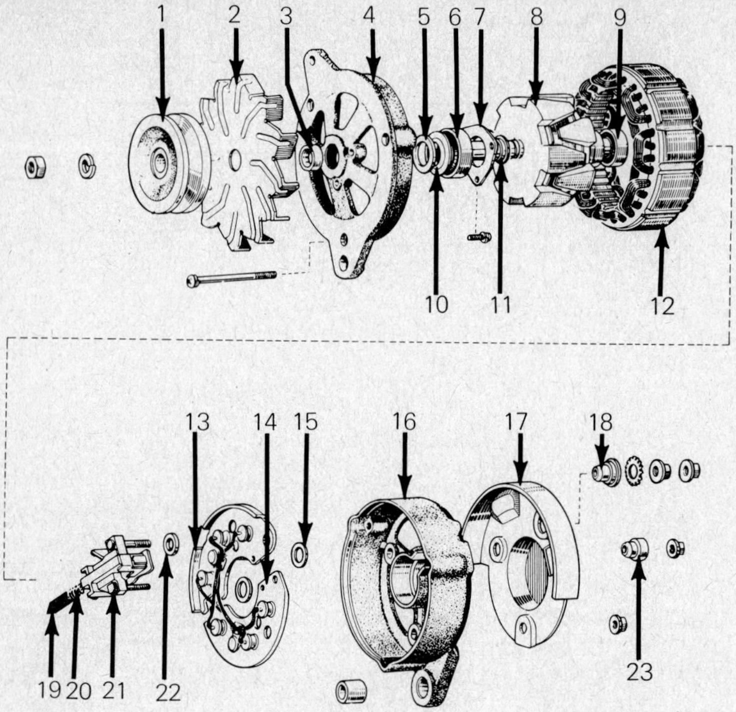

1. Pulley
2. Fan
3. Spacer collar
4. Drive end frame
5. Felt ring
6. Bearing
7. Bearing retainer
8. Rotor
9. Bearing
10. Felt cover
11. Spacer ring
12. Stator assembly
13. (+) Rectifier holder
14. (−) Rectifier holder
15. Insulator
16. Rear end frame
17. Rear end cover
18. Insulator
19. Brush
20. Brush spring
21. Brush holder
22. Insulator
23. Insulator

Exploded view of 20R Alternator (others similar)

8. Unsoldering brush wire from end of brush holder and removing old brush and spring. Place new brush and spring in holder and solder into place. Trim excess wire. The new brush should protrude from the holder 0.492 in.: 2F engines with IC regulator, 16.5 mm (0.65 in.); without IC regulator, 12.5 mm (0.492 in.); F engines, 10 mm (0.04 in.).

NOTE: ***Do not allow more than specified amount of brush to protrude from holder.***

9. Check brush for ease of movement in holder.

To test rotor:

10. Connect a circuit tester with one lead on each of the two slip rings located behind the drive end frame bearing. If there is no conductance, the coil is opened and should be replaced.

11. Connect circuit tester from either of the slip rings to the rotor or rotor shaft and check the insulation between them. If the tester needle moves, the rotor coil or the slip rings are defective and the rotor should be replaced.

12. Check slip rings for roughness and scores. If defective, replace rotor.

To test stator:

13. Check the stator coil for insulation. Connect circuit tester between the stator coil and the stator core. If the tester needle moves, the coil is grounded and must be repaired or replaced.

NOTE: ***For the next test it is necessary to unsolder the stator from the rectifiers. If test is attempted, unsolder leads as quickly as possible to avoid overheating rectifiers. Be sure to note the order in which the leads are attached.***

14. Remove stator from recitifiers. With circuit tester, check the four leads of the stator coil for conductance between them. If the tester indicates no reading, the stator coil is opened and must be replaced. The resistance should be zero.

Assembly is the reverse of disassembly with the following notes:

a. Do not forget to install insulating washers between the rectifier positive holder (Side of rectifier connected directly to leads from stator) and the rectifier end frame. Also reinstall the "B" terminal insulator and insulators on the positive side retaining bolts.

b. When assembling the rectifier end frame, use a piece of wire to hold the brush away from the rotor end to facilitate refitting rotor.

Regulator

REMOVAL AND INSTALLATION

1. Disconnect the battery-to-starter cable at the battery end.

2. Disconnect the wiring harness connector from the regulator.

NOTE: ***On Land Cruisers disconnect the leads from their screw terminals after noting their position for installation.***

3. Remove the regulator securing bolts. Remove the regulator, complete with its condenser.

4. Installation is the reverse order of removal.

VOLTAGE ADJUSTMENT

1. Connect a voltmeter to the battery terminals.

2. Start the engine and gradually increase its speed to about 1,500 rpm (2,000 rpm on Land Cruisers).

3. At this speed, the voltage reading should fall within the range specified in the chart above.

4. If the voltage does not fall within the specifications, remove the cover from the regulator and adjust it by bending the adjusting arm.

5. Repeat steps 2 and 3; if the voltage cannot be brought to specifications, proceed with the mechanical adjustments, outlined below.

MECHANICAL ADJUSTMENTS

NOTE: ***Perform the preceding voltage adjustment before beginning the mechanical adjustments.***

Field Relay

NOTE: ***This adjustment does not apply to Land Cruisers***

1. Remove the cover from the regulator assembly.

2. Use a feeler gauge to check the amount that the contact spring is deflected while the armature is being depressed.

3. If the measurement is not within specifications (see the chart above), adjust the regulator by bending point holder P (See illustration.)

4. Check the point gap with a feeler gauge against the specifications in the chart.

5. Adjust the point gap, as required, by bending the point holder P (See illustration.)

6. Clean off the points with emery cloth if they are dirty and wash them with solvent.

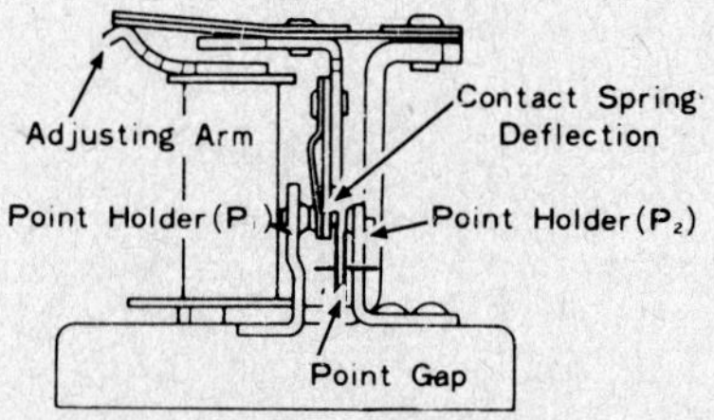

Field relay components

Voltage Regulator

***NOTE:** Step 1 does not apply to Land Cruisers.*

1. Use a feeler gauge to measure the air (armature) gap. If it is not within the specifications (see chart), adjust it by bending the *low*-speed point holder. (See illustration.)
2. Check the point gap with a feeler gauge. If it is not within specifications, adjust it by bending the *high*-speed point holder. (See illustration.) Clean the points with emery cloth and wash them off with solvent.
3. Check the amount of contact spring deflection while depressing the armature. The specification should be the same as that for the contact spring on the field relay. If the amount of deflection is not within specification, replace, do not adjust, the voltage regulator.

Go back and perform the steps outlined under "Voltage Adjustment," above. If the voltage cannot be brought within specifications, replace the voltage regulator. If the voltage still fails to come within specifications after regulator replacement, the alternator is probably defective and should be replaced.

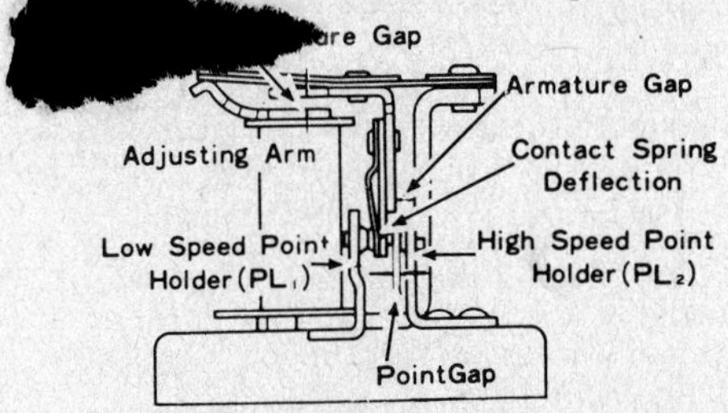

Voltage regulator components

Starter

REMOVAL AND INSTALLATION

1. Disconnect the cable which runs from the starter to the battery, at the battery end.
2. Remove the air cleaner assembly, if necessary, to gain access to the starter.

***NOTE:** On some models with automatic transmissions, it may be necessary to disconnect the throttle linkage connecting rod.*

3. Disconnect all the wiring at the starter.
4. Remove the starter toward the front of the vehicle.
5. Installation is the reverse order of removal.

STARTER DRIVE REPLACEMENT

1. Disconnect wiring and remove starter from engine.
2. Remove solenoid from starter.

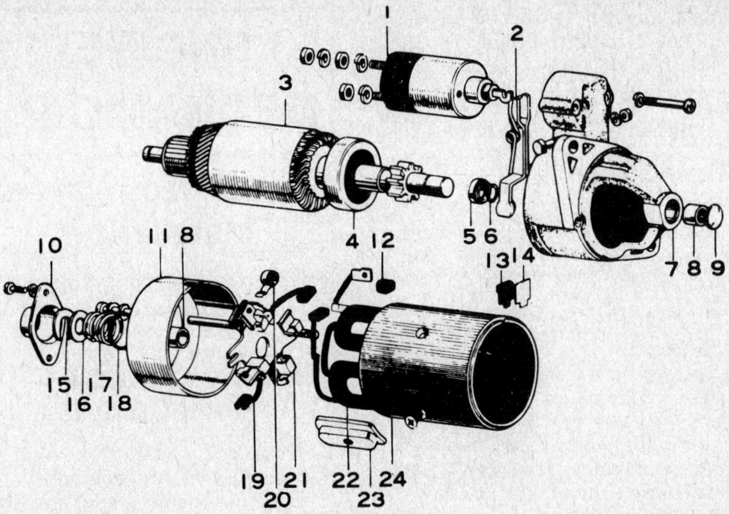

1. Solenoid
2. Engagement lever
3. Armature
4. Overrunning clutch
5. Clutch stop
6. Snap ring
7. Drive housing
8. Bushing
9. Bearing cover
10. Bearing cover
11. Commutator end frame
12. Rubber bushing
13. Rubber grommet
14. Plate
15. Lock plate
16. Washer
17. Brake spring
18. Gasket
19. Brush
20. Brush spring
21. Brush holder
22. Field coil
23. Pole shoes
24. Field yoke

Direct-drive starter components

3. Remove through bolts and take off end plate.
4. Slide armature shaft far enough out to disengage clutch forks.
5. Remove retaining clip and washer from shaft.
6. Slide starter drive assembly from shaft.

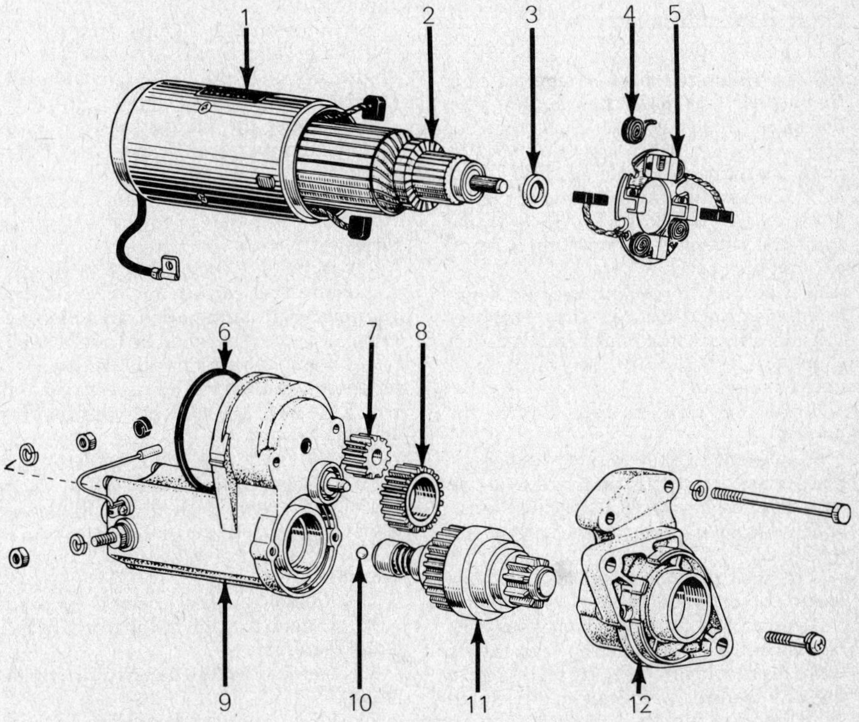

1. Field frame assembly
2. Armature
3. Felt seal
4. Brush spring
5. Brush holder
6. O-ring
7. Pinion gear
8. Idler gear
9. Magnetic switch assembly
10. Steel ball
11. Clutch assembly
12. Starter housing

Reduction type starter components

7. Install in reverse of removal. Always use a new retaining clip.

STARTER SOLENOID AND BRUSH REPLACEMENT

Direct Drive Starter

NOTE: The starter must be removed from the vehicle in order to perform this operation.

1. Remove the field coil lead from the solenoid terminal.
2. Unfasten the solenoid retaining screws. Remove the solenoid by tilting it upward and withdrawing it.
3. Remove the end frame bearing cover screws and remove the cover.
4. Remove the thru-bolts. Remove the commutator end-frame.
5. Withdraw the brushes from their holder if they are to be replaced.
6. Check the brush length against the specification in the "Battery and Starter Specifications" chart, above. Replace the brushes with new ones if required.
7. Dress the new brushes with emery cloth so that they will make proper contact.
8. Use a spring scale to check the brush spring tension against the specification in the chart. Replace the springs if they do not meet specification.

Assembly is the reverse of disassembly. Pack the end bearing cover with multipurpose grease before installing it.

Gear Reduction Type

NOTE: The starter must be removed from the vehicle, in order to perform this operation.

1. Disconnect the solenoid lead.
2. Loosen the two bolts on the starter housing and separate the field frame from the solenoid. Remove the O-ring and felt dust seal.
3. Remove the two screws and separate the starter drive from the solenoid.
4. Withdraw the clutch and gears. Remove the ball from the clutch shaft bore or solenoid.
5. Remove the brushes from the holder.
6. Measure brush length and compare it to the specification given in the "Battery and Starter Specifications" chart. Replace the brushes if they are too short.
7. Check the gears for wear or damage. Replace as required.

Assembly is the reverse of disassembly. Lubricate all bearings and gears with high temperature grease. Grease the ball before inserting in the clutch shaft bore. Align the tab on the brush holder with the notch on the field frame. Check the positive (+) brush leads to see that they aren't grounded. Align the mark on the solenoid with the bolt anchors on the field frame.

ENGINE MECHANICAL

Engine Removal and Installation

CAUTION: Be sure that the vehicle is supported securely, during engine removal.

20R AND 18R-C ENGINES—TWO WHEEL DRIVE

1. Drain the radiator, cooling system, transmission, and engine oil.
2. Disconnect the battery-to-starter cable at the positive battery terminal.
3. Scribe marks on the hood and its hinges to aid in alignment during installation.
4. Remove the hood supports from the body. Remove the hood.

NOTE: Do not remove the supports from the hood.

5. Remove the headlight bezel and the radiator grille.
6. Remove the fan shroud, the hood lock base and the base support.
7. Detach both the upper and lower hoses from the radiator. On cars with automatic transmissions, disconnect the lines from the oil cooler. Remove the radiator.
8. Unfasten the clamps and remove the heater and bypass hoses from the engine. Remove the heater control cable from the water valve.
9. Remove the wiring from the coolant temperature and oil pressure sending units.
10. Remove the air cleaner from its bracket, complete with its attendant hoses.
11. Unfasten the accelerator torque rod from the carburetor. On models equipped with automatic transmissions, remove the transmission linkage as well.
12. Remove the emission control system hoses and wiring, as necessary.
13. Remove the clutch hydraulic line support bracket.
14. Unfasten the high-tension and primary wires from the coil.
15. Mark the spark plug cables and remove them from the distributor.
16. Detach the right-hand front engine mount.
17. Remove the fuel line at the pump.
18. Detach the downpipe from the exhaust manifold.
19. Detach the left-hand front engine mount.
20. Disconnect all the wiring harness multiconnectors.

Perform the following steps on models with manual transmissions:

21. Remove the center console if so equipped.
22. Remove the shift lever boot(s).
23. Unfasten the four shift lever cap retaining screws. Remove the cap and withdraw the shift lever assembly.

Perform the following steps on models equipped with automatic transmissions:

24. Remove the transmission selector linkage:
    a. On models equipped with a floormounted selector, disconnect the control rod from the transmission.
    b. On column-mounted gear selector models, remove the shifter rod.
25. Disconnect the neutral safety switch wiring connector.

Perform the following steps on all models:

26. Raise the rear of the vehicle with jacks and support it on jackstands.
27. Remove the retaining screws and remove the parking brake equalizer support bracket. Disconnect the cable which runs between the lever and the equalizer.
28. Remove the speedometer cable from the transmission. Disconnect the back-up light wiring.
29. Detach the driveshaft from the rear of the transmission.

NOTE: If oil runs out of the transmission, an old U-joint yoke sleeve makes an excellent plug.

30. Detach the clutch release cylinder assembly, complete with hydraulic lines. Do not disconnect the lines.
31. Unbolt the rear support member mounting insulators.
32. Support the transmission and detach the rear support member retaining bolts. Withdraw the support member from under the car.
33. Install lifting hooks on the engine lifting brackets. Attach a suitable hoist to the engine.
34. Remove the jack from under the transmission.
35. Raise the engine and move it toward the front of the car. Use care to avoid damaging the components which remain on the car.
36. Support the engine on a workstand. Install the engine in the reverse order of removal. Adjust all of the linkages as detailed in the appropriate section. Install the hood and adjust it. Replenish the fluid levels in the engine, radiator, and transmission.

20R ENGINES—4 WHEEL DRIVE

NOTE: On the 4x4 Pick-up, it is less cumbersome to remove the transmission/transfer case as a separate unit. Refer to transmission removal and installation section, below.

CAUTION: Be sure to support the rear of the engine with a jack to avoid damage to the front motor mounts while performing engine removal procedures!

1. Complete steps 1-12, 14-17, 19-20 under 20R Engine—2 Wheel Drive removal, above.

2. Complete steps 33–36 under 20R Engine—2 Wheel Drive removal, above.

Installation is the reverse of removal.

F and 2F Engine

1. Scribe marks on the hood and hinges to aid in alignment during installation. Remove the hing bolts from the hood and then remove the hood.
2. Drain the cooling system and engine oil.
3. Unfasten the radiator grille mounting bolts and remove the grille.

NOTE: On station wagon models, remove the parking light assembly and wiring first.

4. Remove the hood latch support rod. Detach the hood latch assembly from the radiator upper bracket. Remove the bracket.
5. Disconnect the heater hose from the radiator.
6. Detach the upper radiator hose at the water outlet housing and the lower hose at water pump.
7. Remove the six bolts which secure the radiator and lift the radiator out of the vehicle.
8. Remove the heater hoses from the water valve and heater box. Disconnect the temperature control cable from the water valve.
9. Detach both of the battery cables and remove the battery.
10. Remove the wires from the starter solenoid terminal.
11. Detach the fuel lines from the pump and remove the fuel filter assembly.
12. Disconnect the primary wire from the ignition coil.
13. Detach both of the intermediate rods from the shifter shafts (column-shift models only).
14. Remove the air cleaner assembly complete with hoses, from its bracket.
15. Remove the emission control system cables and hoses as necessary.
16. Disconnect the alternator multi-connector.
17. Disconnect the hand throttle, accelerator, and choke linkages from the carburetor.
18. On Land Cruisers with vacuum assisted 4WD engagement, remove the control unit vacuum hose from its manifold fitting.
19. Disconnect the oil pressure and water temperature gauge sender's wiring.
20. Unfasten the downpipe from the exhaust manifold.
21. Detach the parking brake cable from the intermediate lever.
22. Unbolt the front driveshaft from the flange on the transfer case output shaft.
23. Remove both the left and right engine stone shields. Remove the transmission skid-plate.
24. Remove the cotter pin and disconnect both the high- and low-range shifter rods from their respective inner levers.
25. Remove the high/low range shifter link lever and the high/low shift rod.
26. Disconnect the clutch release fork spring. Remove the clutch release cylinder from its mounting bracket at the rear of the engine.
27. Unfasten the clamp screws and withdraw the vacuum lines from the transfer case control unit vacuum chamber (only on models with vacuum-assisted 4WD engagement).
28. Remove the 4WD indicator switch assembly.
29. Unfasten the speedometer cable from the transmission.
30. Disconnect the rear driveshaft from the transmission.
31. Detach the gearshift rod and gear selector rod from the shift outer lever and the gear selector outer lever, respectively.
32. Unbolt the rear engine mounts from the frame.
33. Perform Step 32 to the front engine mounts.
34. Install lifting hooks on the engine lift-points and connect a hoist.
35. Lift the engine slightly and toward the front, so the engine/transmission assembly clears the front of the vehicle.

Engine removal is performed in the reverse order of its installation. Refill the engine with coolant and lubricant, as specified above. Check and adjust all linkages, as outlined in the appropriate section. Install the hood and align the matchmarks.

Cylinder Head

CAUTION: Do not perform this operation on a warm engine. Remove the head bolts in the sequence and in several steps. Loosen the head bolts evenly, not one at a time. Keep the pushrods in their original order. Do not attempt to slide the cylinder head off of the block, as it is located with dowel pins. Lift the head straight up and off the block.

REMOVAL AND INSTALLATION

18R-C Engine

1. Disconnect the battery and drain the cooling system.
2. Remove the air cleaner assembly from its bracket, complete with its attendant hoses.
3. Detach the accelerator cable from its support on the cylinder head cover and also from the carburetor throttle arm.
4. Remove the choke cable and fuel lines from the carburetor.
5. Remove the water hose bracket from the cylinder head cover.
6. Unfasten the water hose clamps and remove the hoses from the water pump and the water valve. Detach the heater temperature control cable from the water valve.
7. Disconnect the PCV line from the cylinder head cover.
8. Remove the vacuum lines from the distributor vacuum unit. Remove the lines which run from the vacuum switching valve to the various emission control system components on the cylinder head.
9. Remove the fuel and vacuum lines from the carburetor.
10. Remove the pipes from the automatic choke stove.
11. Unfasten the wires from the spark plugs. Remove the spark plugs.
12. Remove the cylinder head cover retaining bolts and withdraw the cover.

NOTE: Use a clean cloth, placed over the timing cover opening, to prevent anything from falling down into it.

13. Remove the upper radiator hose from the cylinder head water outlet.
14. Remove the outlet elbow and thermostat.
15. Unfasten the downpipe clamp from the exhaust manifold. Remove the manifold from the head.
16. Remove the valve rocker assembly mounting bolts and the oil delivery pipes. Withdraw the valve rocker shaft assembly.

CAUTION: When removing the rocker shaft securing bolts, loosen them in two or three stages and in the proper sequence.

17. Remove the timing gear from the camshaft. Support it so that the chain does not fall down into the cover.
18. Remove the camshaft bearing caps and withdraw the camshaft. Remove the camshaft bearings.

NOTE: Temporarily assemble the bearings and caps to keep them with their mates. Be sure to keep the bearings in proper order.

19. Remove the gear from the timing chain. Support the timing chain so that it does not fall into the cover.
20. Loosen the head bolts in two or three stages; in the sequence illustrated. Lift the head assembly off the block.

Installation is in the following order:

1. Remove any water from the cylinder head bolt holes.
2. Clean the mating surfaces of the cylinder head and block. Use liquid sealer around the oil holes on the head and cylinder block. Do not get sealer in the holes.
3. Lower the cylinder head on to the block.
4. Tighten the cylinder head bolts in the proper sequence (see diagrams, above) and in three or four stages. Tighten them to specifications.
5. Install each lower bearing half into the seat from which it was removed.
6. Place the camshaft in the cylinder head.
7. Install each bearing into the cap from which it was removed.

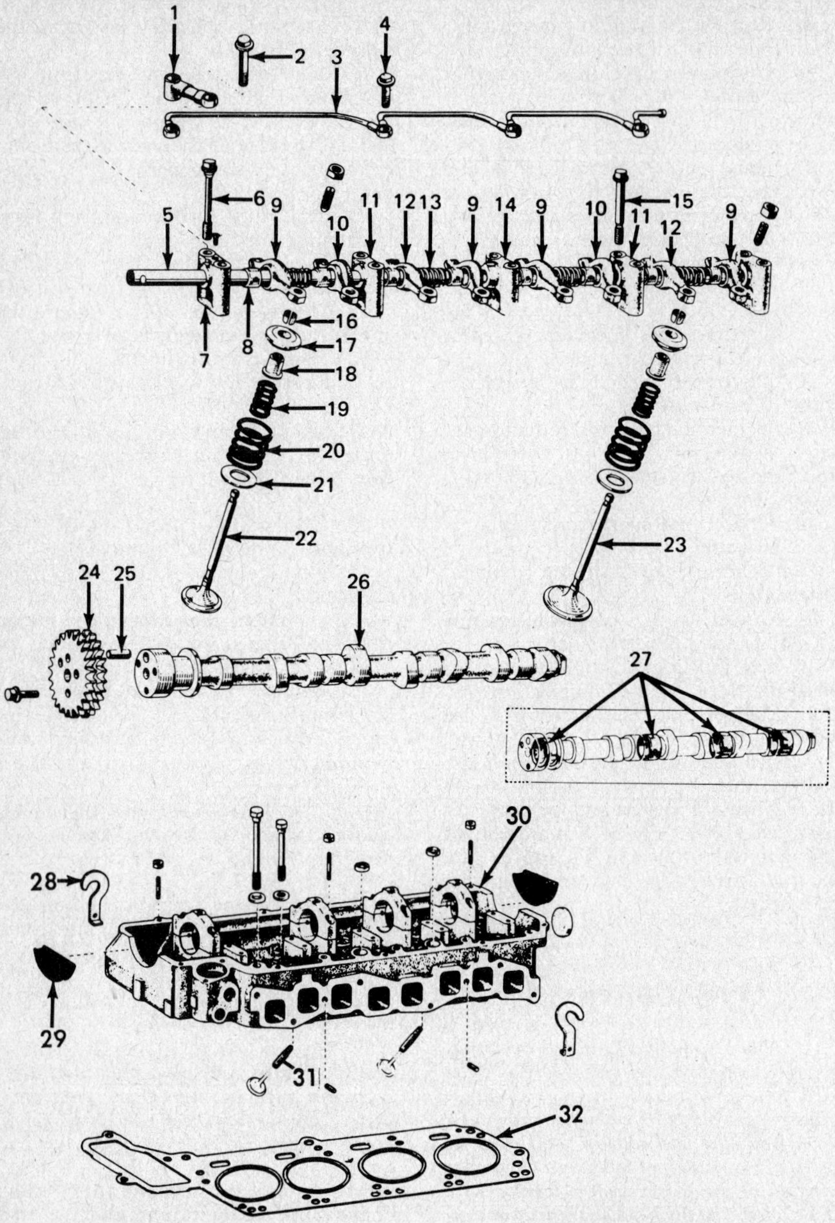

1. Oil banjo fitting
2. Bolt
3. Oil pipe assembly
4. Bolt
5. Valve rocker shaft
6. Bolt
7. Valve rocker support type #1
8. Bushing
9. Rocker arm type #1
10. Rocker arm type #2
11. Valve rocker support type #2
12. Rocker arm type #3
13. Spring
14. Valve rocker support type #3
15. Bolt
16. Valve keeper
17. Spring retainer
18. Valve stem oil seal
19. Inner valve spring
20. Outer valve spring
21. Spring seat
22. Exhaust valve
23. Intake valve
24. Camshaft sprocket
25. Dowel pin
26. Camshaft
27. Camshaft bearing set
28. Engine lifting hook
29. Half circle cam seal
30. Cylinder head
31. Valve guide
32. Head gasket

18R-Cylinder head components

8. Install the camshaft bearing caps on the head, in their numbered sequence, with the numbers facing forward. Tighten to 12–17 ft lbs.

9. First, check the camshaft bearing clearance using Plastigage®, and end-play.

NOTE: For the procedure see "Engine Rebuilding".

The oil clearance should be 0.001–0.002 in.; the end-play should be 0.0017–0.0066 in.

10. Crank the engine so that no. 1 piston is at TDC of its compression stroke.

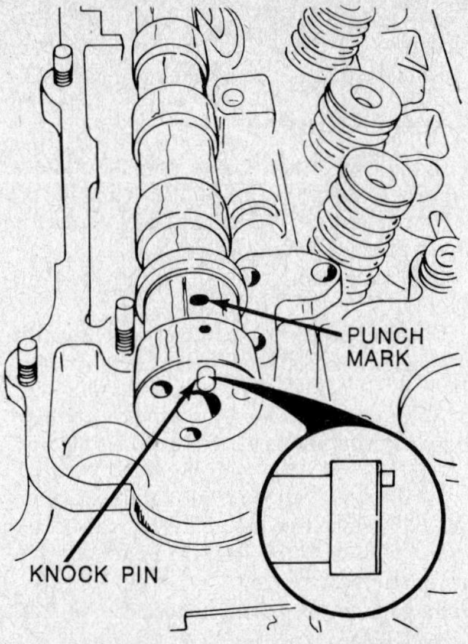

Position 18R-C cam shaft with punch mark and knock pin at top and refit cam shaft sprocket with colored links flanking mark at cam teeth

11. Align the mark on the timing chain with the dowel hole on the camshaft timing gear and the stamped mark on the camshaft.

NOTE: All three marks should be aligned so that they are facing upward.

12. Install the valve rocker assembly. Tighten its securing bolts to 12–17 ft lbs, in the sequence illustrated, and in two or three stages.

13. Attach the oil delivery pipe to the valve rocker assembly and camshaft bearing caps. Tighten their securing bolts to 11–16 ft lbs.

14. Adjust the valve clearance as outlined above to the following *cold* specifications:

Intake—0.007 in.

Exhaust—0.013 in.

15. The rest of installation is performed in the reverse order of removal.

20R Engine

1. Disconnect the battery.

2. Remove the three exhaust pipe flange nuts and separate the pipe from the manifold.

3. Drain the cooling system (both radiator and block). Save the coolant to be reused.

4. Remove the air cleaner, complete with hoses, from the carburetor.

NOTE: Cover the carburetor with a clean rag so that nothing can fall into it.

5. Mark all vacuum hoses to aid installation, and disconnect them. Remove all linkages, fuel lines, etc. from the carburetor, cylinder head, and manifolds. Remove the wire supports.

6. Mark the spark plug leads and disconnect them from the plugs.

7. Matchmark the distributor housing and block. Disconnect the primary lead and remove the distributor. Installation will be easier if you leave the cap leads in place.
8. Remove the valve cover.
9. Remove the rubber camshaft seals. Use a 19mm wrench to remove cam sprocket bolt. Slide the distributor drive gear off of the cam and wire the cam sprocket in place.
10. Remove the timing chain cover 14mm bolt at the front of the head. This must be done before the head bolts are removed.
11. Remove the cylinder head bolts in the order shown under "Torque Sequences". Improper removal could cause head damage.
12. Using pry bars applied evenly at the front and the rear of the valve rocker assembly, pry the assembly off of its mounting dowels.
13. Lift the head off of its dowels. Do NOT pry it off. Support the head on a workbench.
14. Drain the engine oil from the crankcase *after* the head has been removed, because the oil will become contaminated with coolant while the head is being removed.

Installation is in the following order:
1. Apply liquid sealer to the front corners of the block and install the head gasket.
2. Lower the head over the locating dowels. Do not attempt to slide it into place.

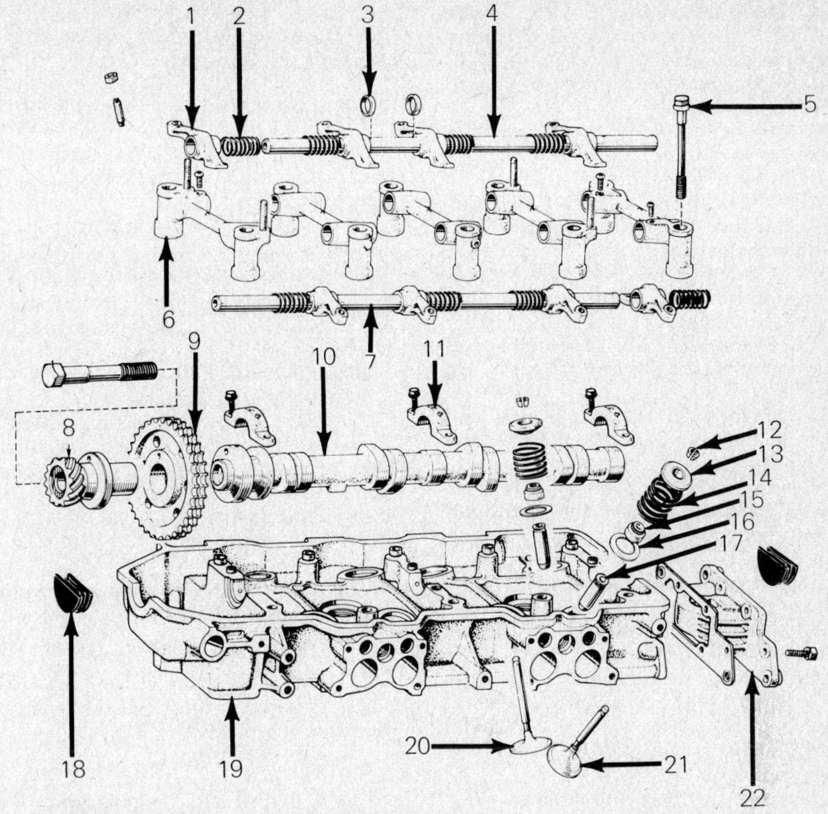

1. Rocker arm
2. Spring
3. Spacer
4. Rocker shaft (Intake)
5. Head bolt
6. Rocker stand
7. Rocker shaft (Exhaust)
8. Distributor drive gear
9. Cam sprocket
10. Camshaft
11. Camshaft bearing cap
12. Valve keeper
13. Spring retainer
14. Valve spring
15. Valve seal
16. Spring seat
17. Valve guide
18. Half circle seal
19. Cylinder head
20. Intake valve
21. Exhaust valve
22. Rear cover (EGR cooler)

20R cylinder head components

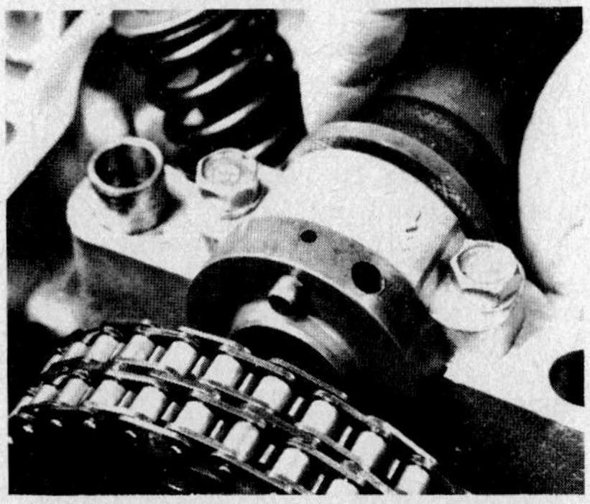

Position 20R cam shaft with dowel at top—note arrow is pointing forward on front cam bearing cap

3. Rotate the camshaft so that the sprocket aligning pin is at the top. Remove the wire and hold the cam sprocket. Manually rotate the engine so that the sprocket hole is also at the top. Wire the sprocket in place again.
4. Install the rocker arm assembly over its positioning dowels.
5. Tighten the cylinder head bolts evenly, in three stages, and in order to 52–63 ft lbs.
6. Install the timing chain cover bolt and tighten it to 7–11 ft lbs.
7. Remove the wire and install the sprocket over the camshaft dowel. If the chain won't allow the sprocket to reach, rotate the crankshaft back and forth, while lifting up on the chain and sprocket.
8. Install the distributor drive gear and tighten the crankshaft bolt to 51–65 ft lbs.
9. Set the no. 1 piston at TDC of its compression stroke and adjust the valves.
10. After completing valve adjustment, rotate the crankshaft one turn, so that 8°-BTDC mark on the pulley aligns with the pointer.
11. Install the distributor, as outlined above.
12. Install the spark plugs and leads.
13. Make sure that the oil drain plug is installed. Fill the engine with oil after installing the rubber cam seals. Pour the oil over the distributor drive gear and the valve rockers.
14. Install the rocker cover and tighten the bolts to 8–11 ft lbs.
15. Connect all the vacuum hoses and electrical leads that were removed during disassembly. Install the spark plug lead supports. Fill the cooling system. Install the air cleaner.
16. Tighten the exhaust pipe to manifold flange bolts to 25–33 ft lbs.
17. Reconnect the battery. Start the engine and allow it to reach normal operating temperature. Check and adjust the timing and valve clearance. Adjust the idle speed and mixture. Road test the vehicle.

F and 2F Engine

1. Disconnect the battery and drain the cooling system.
2. Remove the air cleaner assembly from its bracket, complete with its attendant hoses.
3. Detach the accelerator cable from its support on the cylinder head cover and also from the carburetor throttle arm.
4. Remove the choke cable and fuel lines from the carburetor.
5. Remove the water hose bracket from the cylinder head cover.
6. Unfasten the water hose clamps and remove the hoses from the water pump and the water valve. Detach the heater temperature control cable from the water valve.
7. Disconnect the PCV line from the cylinder head cover.
8. Disconnect the vacuum lines, which run from the vacuum switching valve, at the various components of the emission control system.

9. Drain the engine oil. Unfasten the oil lines from the oil filter and remove the filter assembly from the manifold.

10. Detach the vacuum valve solenoid wire from the coil.

11. Disconnect any remaining lines from the carburetor and remove the carburetor from the manifold.

12. Unfasten the alternator adjusting link and then remove the drivebelt and the alternator.

13. Disconnect the distributor vacuum line from the distributor. Remove the wire from its supports on the head.

14. Disconnect the carburetor fuel line from the fuel pump. Remove the line.

15. Disconnect the spark plug and coil cables, after marking their respective locations.

16. Unfasten the primary wire from the distributor. Remove the distributor clamp bolts and withdraw the distributor.

17. Remove the oil gauge sending unit.

18. Remove the coil from its bracket on the cylinder head.

19. Remove the fuel pump.

20. Remove the oil filler tube clamping bolt from the valve lifter (side) cover. Drive the oil filler tube out of the cylinder block.

21. Remove the combination intake/exhaust manifold from the cylinder block.

22. Take off the cylinder head cover and its gasket.

23. Unfasten the oil delivery union, spring, and sleeve from the valve rocker shafts.

24. Unfasten the securing nuts and bolts from the valve rocker shaft supports. Withdraw the rocker assembly.

25. Withdraw the pushrods from their bores. Be sure to keep them in the same order in which they were removed.

26. Remove the valve lifter (side) cover and gasket.

27. Withdraw the valve lifters from the block.

NOTE: The valve lifters should be kept, with their respective pushrods, in the sequence in which they were removed.

28. Unfasten the oil delivery union from the oil feed pipe.

29. Loosen the cylinder head bolts in two or three stages and in the order illustrated above.

30. Lift off the cylinder head and the gasket.

Installation of the cylinder head is performed in the following order:

1. Clean the gasket mounting surfaces of both the cylinder head and block.

2. Place a *new* head gasket over the dowels on the block.

3. Lower the cylinder head on to the block with the air cleaner mounting bracket attached.

4. Tighten the bolts, in stages, and in the sequence illustrated, to the specified torque.

5. Install the oil feed pipe.

6. Place each valve lifter in the original position from which it came.

NOTE: Do not interchange valve lifters.

7. Perform step 6 for the pushrods, being careful to mate each pushrod with its original lifter.

8. Install the valve rocker assembly, oil delivery union, spring, and connecting sleeve in the head. Tighten the rocker assembly support nuts and bolts to the following torque specifications, in several stages:

10mm nuts and bolts—25–30 ft lbs
8mm bolts—14–22 ft lbs

9. Adjust the valves, as outlined above, to the following *cold* specifications (each piston TDC of its compression stroke):

Intake—0.008 in.
Exhaust—0.014 in.

NOTE: Adjust the valve clearance again after the engine is assembled and warmed up.

10. The rest of cylinder head installation is performed in the reverse order of the removal procedure.

Rocker Arm Shafts

REMOVAL AND INSTALLATION

18R-C, Engines

1. Remove air cleaner.
2. Remove PCV valve.
3. Remove spark plug wires.
4. Remove valve cover.
5. Loosen rocker shaft bolts, alternating front to rear.
6. Remove shaft assembly and oil tube.
7. Install in reverse of removal. Torque bolts in alternating, front to rear sequence, to 14–16 ft lb. Torque oil pipe bolts to 14 ft lb. Check valve clearance.

F Engine

1. Remove the PCV valve.
2. Remove the air cleaner.
3. Remove the spark plug wires.
4. Remove the valve cover.
5. Disconnect the rocker shaft oil delivery joint, spring and the oil connection sleeve from the rocker shaft.
6. Remove the rocker shaft bolts and lift off the shaft assembly.
7. Install in reverse of removal. Torque rocker shaft bolts, in front to rear sequence to: 10mm–30 ft lb., 8mm–22 ft lb. Check valve clearance.

20R Engine

1. Remove the air cleaner.
2. Disconnect all hoses and linkage clipped to the valve cover.
3. Remove the spark plug wires.
4. Remove the carburetor.
5. Remove the valve cover.
6. Remove the distributor.
7. Set the # 1 piston at TDC of the compression stroke.
8. Paint mating marks on the timing chain and sprocket, and drive gear.
9. Remove the distributor drive gear, leaving the chain and sprocket in position.
10. Remove the one 14mm chain cover bolt in the front of the head. This must be done before the head bolts, which also serve as rocker shaft bolts, are removed.
11. Remove the head bolts in a diagonal pattern. Start at the front carburetor side. This must be done to prevent head warpage.
12. Remove the shaft assemblies from the head. It may be necessary to use a pry bar to evenly lift the assemblies from the dowels.
13. Install in reverse of removal. Torque the head bolts, in a diagonal pattern, starting at the center. Tighten in three equal stages to 64 ft lb. Torque the chain cover bolt to 12 ft lb. Torque drive gear bolt to 65 ft lb.

Intake Manifold

REMOVAL AND INSTALLATION

20R Engine

1. Disconnect the battery.
2. Drain the cooling system.
3. Remove the air cleaner, complete with hoses, from the carburetor.
4. Disconnect the vacuum lines from the EGR valve and carburetor. Mark them first, to aid in installation.
5. Remove the fuel lines, electrical leads, accelerator linkage, and water hose from the carburetor.
6. Remove the water by-pass hose from the manifold.
7. Unbolt and remove the intake manifold, complete with carburetor and EGR valve.
8. Cover the cylinder head ports with clean rags to keep anything from falling into the cylinder head or block.

Installation is the reverse of removal. Replace the gasket with a new one. Torque the mounting bolts to specifications. Tighten the bolts in several stages working, from the inside bolts outward. Refill the cooling system.

Exhaust Manifold

REMOVAL AND INSTALLATION

CAUTION: Do not perform this operation on a warm or hot engine.

20R Engine

1. Remove the three exhaust pipe flange bolts and disconnect the exhaust pipe from the manifold.
2. Disconnect the spark plug leads.
3. Matchmark the distributor rotor, housing and the engine block. Remove the distributor.

4. Remove the air cleaner tube from the heat stove. Remove the outer part of the heat stove.

5. Remove the manifold (14mm nuts), complete with air injection tubes and the inner portion of the heat stove.

6. Separate the inner portion of the heat stove from the manifold.

Installation is the reverse of removal. Tighten the retaining nuts to 29–36 ft lbs, working from the inside out. Install the distributor and set the timing. Tighten the exhaust pipe flange nuts to 25–32 ft lbs.

Combination Manifold

REMOVAL AND INSTALLATION

CAUTION: Do not perform this procedure on a warm engine.

F Engines

1. Remove the air cleaner assembly, complete with hoses.
2. Disconnect the accelerator and choke linkages from the carburetor, as well as the fuel and vacuum lines. Remove the hand throttle linkage.
3. Remove, or move aside, any of the emission control system components which are in the way.
4. Disconnect the oil filter lines and remove the oil filter assembly from the intake manifold. Unfasten the solenoid valve wire from the ignition coil terminal. Remove the EGR pipes from the exhaust gas cooler, if so equipped.
5. Unfasten the retaining bolts and remove the carburetor from the manifold.
6. Loosen the manifold retaining nuts, working from the inside out, in two or three stages.
7. Remove the intake/exhaust manifold assembly from the cylinder head as a complete unit.

Installation is performed in the reverse order of removal. Always use *new* gaskets. Tighten the bolts, working from the inside out.

NOTE: Tighten the bolts in two or three stages

18R-C Engines

1. Remove the air cleaner assembly, complete with hoses, from its mounting bracket.
2. Remove the fuel line, vacuum line, automatic choke stove hoses, PCV hose, and accelerator linkage from the carburetor.
3. Unfasten the carburetor securing nuts. Remove the torque rod support, carburetor, and heat insulator.
4. Use a jack to raise the front of the car. Support the vehicle with jackstands.
5. Unfasten the bolts which attach the downpipe flange to the exhaust manifold.

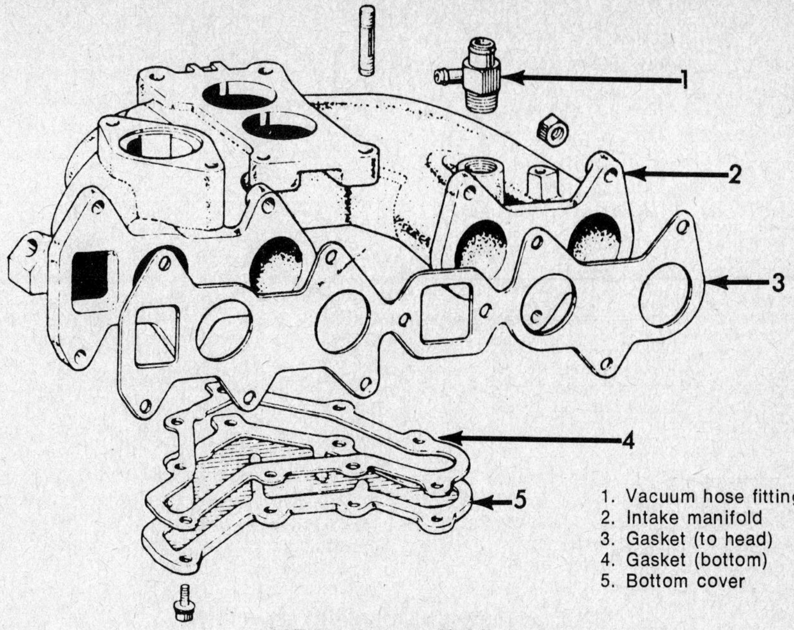

1. Vacuum hose fitting
2. Intake manifold
3. Gasket (to head)
4. Gasket (bottom)
5. Bottom cover

20R intake manifold

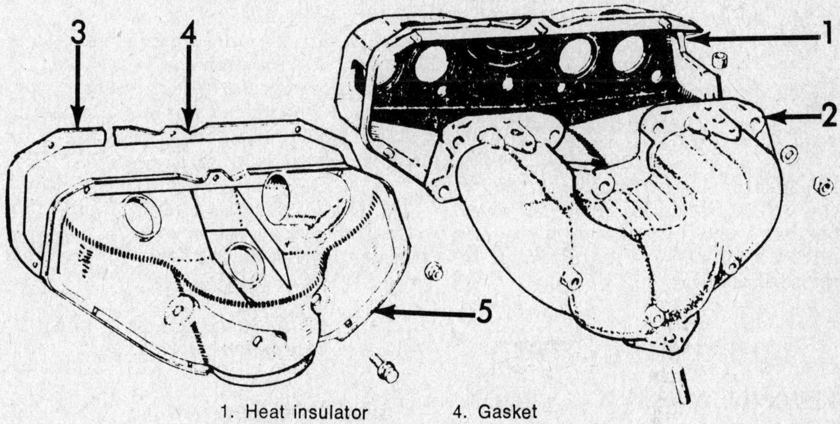

1. Heat insulator
2. Exhaust manifold
3. Gasket
4. Gasket
5. Manifold heat stove

20R exhaust manifold

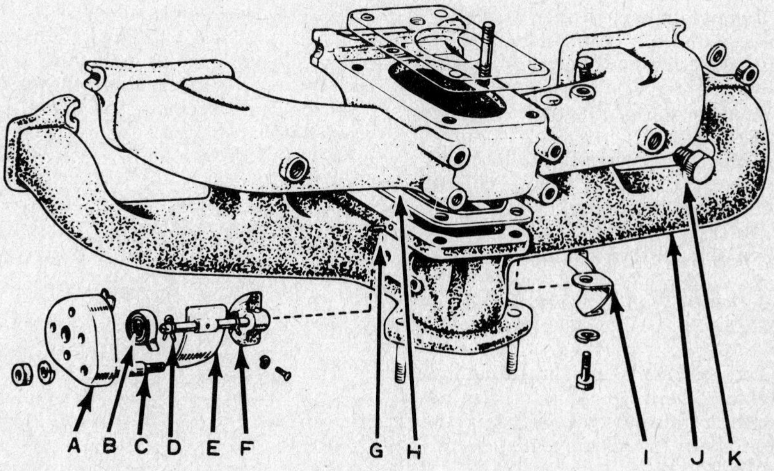

a. Heat control valve bimetal case
b. Valve coil
c. Bolt
d. Retaining spring
e. Heat control valve
f. Heat control valve shaft
g. Dowel
i. Counter weight stop
h. Manifold gasket
j. Exhaust manifold
k. Screw plug

F engine combination manifold assembly

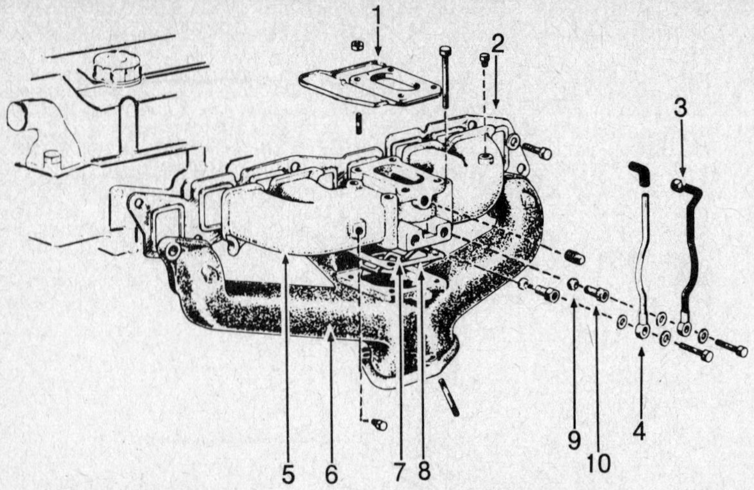

1. Heat insulator
2. Manifold gasket (manifold-to-car)
3. Choke stove outlet pipe
4. Choke stove intake pipe
5. Intake manifold
6. Exhaust manifold
7. Choke stove pipe
8. Manifold gasket (intake-to-exhaust)
9. Sleeve
10. Union

18R-C combination manifold assembly

6. In order to remove the manifold assembly, unfasten the manifold retaining bolts.

CAUTION: Remove and tighten the bolts in two or three stages, working from the inside out.

Installation is performed in the reverse order of removal. Always use *new* gaskets. Tighten the manifold securing bolts to specifications, in the reverse sequence of removal.

Timing Gear Cover

REMOVAL AND INSTALLATION

F and 2F Engines

1. Drain the cooling system and the crankcase.
2. Disconnect the battery.
3. Remove the air cleaner assembly, complete with hoses, from its bracket.
4. Remove the hood latch as well as its brace and support.
5. Remove the headlight bezels and grille assembly.
6. Unfasten the upper and lower radiator hose clamps and remove both of the hoses from the engine.
7. Unfasten the radiator securing bolts and remove the radiator.

NOTE: Take off the shroud first, if so equipped.

8. Loosen the drive belt adjusting link and remove the drive belt. Unfasten the alternator multiconnector, withdraw the retaining bolts, and remove the alternator.
9. Perform step 8 to the air injection pump, if so equipped. Disconnect the hoses from the pump before removing it.
10. Remove the fan and water pump as an assembly.
11. Remove the crankshaft pulley with a gear puller.
12. Remove the gravel shield from underneath the engine.
13. Remove the front driveshaft.
14. Remove the front oil pan bolts, to gain access to the bottom of the timing chain cover.

NOTE: It may be necessary to insert a thin knife between the pan and the gasket in order to break the pan loose. Use care not to damage the gasket.

Installation is the reverse of removal. Be sure to adjust the drive belts.

18R-C, 20R Engines

1. Perform the cylinder head removal procedure as detailed in the appropriate section.
2. Remove the radiator.
3. Remove the alternator.
4. On engines equipped with air pumps, unfasten the adjusting link bolts and the drivebelt. Remove the hoses from the pump; remove the pump and bracket from the engine.

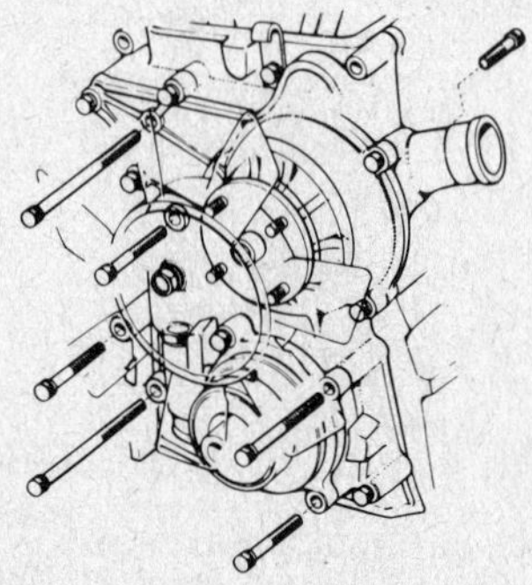

Remove these seven bolts to remove timing chain cover—20R engine

NOTE: If the car is equipped with power steering, see below for its pump removal procedure.

5. Remove the fan and water pump as a complete assembly.

CAUTION: To prevent the fluid from running out from the fan coupling, do not tip the assembly over on its side.

6. Unfasten the crankshaft pulley securing bolt and remove the pulley with a gear puller.

CAUTION: Do not remove the 10mm bolt from its hole, if installed, as it is used for balancing.

7. Loosen the bolts which secure the front of the oil pan, after draining the engine oil. Lower the front of the oil pan.
8. Remove the bolts which secure the timing chain cover. Withdraw the cover.

Installation is performed in the reverse order of removal. Apply sealer to the gaskets for both the timing chain cover and the oil pan.

Tighten the timing chain cover bolts to the specifications below:

18R-C engines:
All bolts—11–15 ft lbs
20R engines:
All bolts—8–11 ft lbs.

TIMING CHAIN COVER OIL SEAL REPLACEMENT

All Engines

1. Remove the timing chain cover, as detailed in the appropriate section above.
2. Inspect the oil seal for signs of wear, leakage, or damage.
3. If worn, pry the old oil seal out, using a large flat-bladed screwdriver. Remove it toward the *front* of the cover.

NOTE: Once the oil seal has been removed, it must be replaced.

4. Use a socket, pipe, or block of wood and a hammer to drive the oil seal into place. Work from the *front* of the cover.

CAUTION: Be extremely careful not to damage the seal.

5. Install the timing chain cover as outlined above.

Timing Chain and Tensioner

REMOVAL AND INSTALLATION

18R-C Engines

1. Remove the cylinder head and timing chain cover as detailed above.
2. Remove the timing chain (front) together with the camshaft drive sprocket.

3. Remove the crankshaft sprocket and oil pump jack shaft, complete with the pump drive chain (rear). Remove the chain vibration damper.

*CAUTION: **Both timing chains are identical; tag them for proper identification during installation.***

4. Inspect the chains and sprockets for wear or damage. Clean the chains with solvent.
5. Use a vernier caliper to measure the amount of stretch of both chains. Measure any 17 links while pulling the chain that is being measured taut.
6. Repeat step 5 at two other places on each chain. Replace either of the chains if any of the 17 link measurements exceed 5.792 in. or if the difference between the minimum and maximum readings is more than 0.0078 in., on any one chain.
7. Remove the plunger and spring from one of the chain tensioners. Inspect all of the parts of the tensioner for wear or damage. Fill it with oil and assemble it if it is not defective.
8. Repeat step 7 for other tensioner.

*CAUTION: **Do not mix the parts of the two chain tensioners together.***

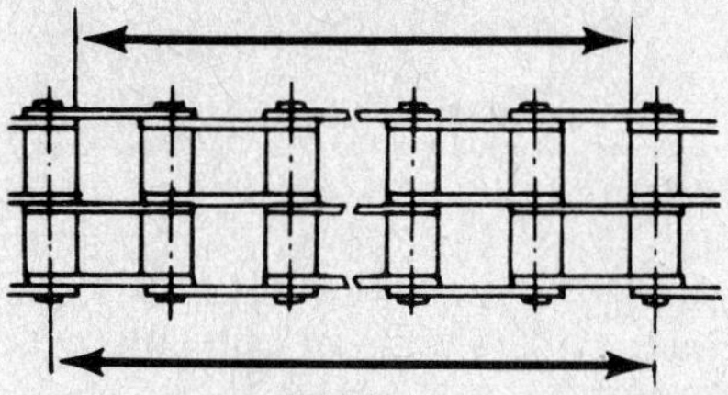

Timing chain stretch measurement —18R-C engine

Installation is performed in the following manner:
1. When the keyway in the crankshaft is pointing straight up and is perpendicular to the cylinder head, the No. 1 piston is at top dead center (TDC). Turn the engine by hand to achieve this configuration.
2. Align the oil pump shaft so that its keyway is facing in the same direction as that on the crankshaft.
3. Align the marks on the timing sprocket and the oil pump drive sprocket with each of the marks on the chain.
4. Install the chain and sprocket assembly over the keyways, while retaining alignment of the chain/sprocket timing marks.

*CAUTION: **Use care not to disengage the plug at the rear of the oil pump driveshaft, by forcing the sprocket over its keyway.***

5. Install the oil pump drive chain vibration damper.
6. Install the gasket for the timing chain cover.

*NOTE: **Use liquid sealer on the gasket before installation.***

7. Install both the chain tensioners in their respective places, being careful not to mix them up. Tighten No. 1 to 15–22 ft-lb, and No. 2 to 22–29 ft-lb. Use liquid sealer on the threads of the bolts without drilled holes.

*CAUTION: **Use care when installing the chain tensioner bolts; they have oil holes tapped in them.***

*NOTE: **If oil remains in the body of tensioner No. 2, it will be difficult to install the camshaft timing gear. If the plunger does not sink when pressed, loosen the bolts holding the vibration damper and drain out the oil.***

8. Fit the camshaft drive sprocket over the keyway on the oil pump driveshaft. Tighten its securing nut to 58–72 ft lb.
9. Install the camshaft drive chain over the camshaft drive sprocket. Align the mating marks on the chain and sprocket.
10. Apply tension to the chain by tying it to the chain tensioner. This will prevent it from falling back into the timing chain cover once it is installed.
11. Install the timing chain cover and cylinder head as outlined above.

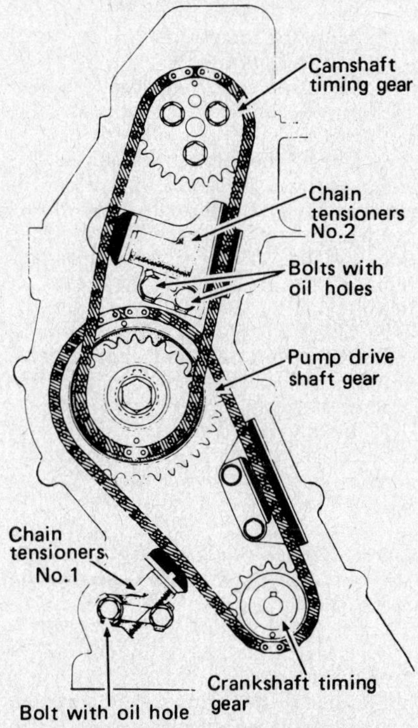

18R-C engine timing chain layout

20R Engine

1. Remove the cylinder head and timing chain cover as outlined above.
2. Separate the chain from the damper, and remove the chain, complete with the camshaft sprocket.
3. Remove the crankshaft sprocket and the oil pump drive with a puller.
4. Inspect the chain for wear or damage. Replace it, if necessary.
5. Inspect the chain tensioner for wear. If it measures less than 0.43 in., replace it.
6. Check the dampers for wear. If they are below specification replace them:

Upper damper—0.20 in.
Lower damper—0.18 in.

Installation is performed in the following order:
1. Rotate the crankshaft until its key is at TDC. Slide the sprocket in place over the key.
2. Place the chain over the sprocket so that its *single* bright link aligns with the mark on the crank sprocket.
3. Install the cam sprocket so that the timing mark falls between the *two* bright links on the chain.
4. Fit the oil pump drive spline over the crankshaft key.
5. Install the timing cover gasket on the front of the block.
6. Rotate the camshaft sprocket counterclockwise to remove the slack from the chain.
7. Position the No. 1 piston at TDC by having the crankshaft keyway point straight up (perpendicular to), toward the cylinder head.
8. Align the pump jackshaft, with its keyway pointing straight up as well.
9. Align the marks on the timing sprocket and the oil pump drive sprocket with each of the marks on the chain.
10. Install the chain and sprocket assembly over the keyways, while retaining alignment of the chain/sprocket timing marks.

*CAUTION: **Use care not to dislodge the welch plug at the rear of the oil pump drive shaft, by forcing the sprocket over its keyway.***

11. Install the oil pump drive chain vibration damper.
12. Install the gasket for the timing chain cover.

*NOTE: **Use liquid sealer on the gasket before installation.***

13. Install both of the chain tensioners in their respective places, being careful not to mix them up. Tighten their securing bolts to 12–17 ft lbs.

*CAUTION: **Use care when installing the chain tensioner bolts; they have oil holes tapped in them.***

14. Fit the camshaft drive sprocket over the keyway on the oil pump drive shaft.
Tighten its securing nut to 58–72 ft lbs.

15. Install the camshaft drive chain over the camshaft drive sprocket. Align the mating marks on the chain and sprocket.

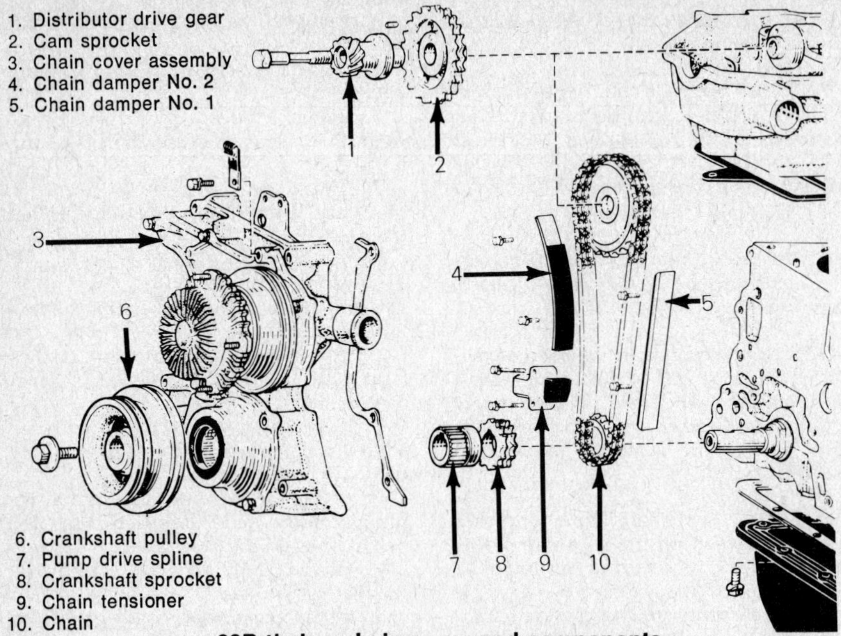

20R timing chain cover and components

16. Apply tension to the chain by tying it to the chain tensioner. This will prevent it from falling back into the timing chain cover once it is installed.

17. Install the timing chain cover and cylinder head as outlined above.

Timing Gears

REMOVAL AND INSTALLATION

F and 2F Engines

NOTE: This procedure contains camshaft removal and installation.

1. Perform the cylinder head and timing cover removal procedures, outlined above.
2. Slip the oil slinger off the crankshaft.
3. Remove the camshaft thrust plate retaining bolts by working through the holes provided in the camshaft timing gear.
4. Remove the camshaft through the front of the cylinder block. Support the camshaft while removing it, so as not to damage its bearings or lobes.

NOTE: The timing gear is a press-fit and cannot be removed without removing the camshaft.

5. Inspect the crankshaft timing gear. Replace it if it has worn or damaged teeth.
6. To remove it, remove the sliding key from the crankshaft. Withdraw the timing gear with a gear puller.

Installation is performed in the following order:

1. Use a large piece of pipe to press the timing gear onto the crankshaft. Lightly and evenly tap the end of the pipe until the gear is in its original position.
2. Apply a coat of engine oil to the camshaft journals and bearings.
3. Insert the camshaft into the block.

CAUTION: Use care not to damage the camshaft lobes, bearings, or journals.

4. Align the mating marks on each of the gears as illustrated.
5. Slip the camshaft into position. Tighten the camshaft thrust plate bolts to 14.5 ft lbs.
6. Check the gear backlash with a feeler gauge, inserted between the crankshaft and the camshaft timing gears. The backlash should be no more than 0.002–0.005 in.; if it exceeds this, replace one or both of the gears, as required.
7. Check the gear run-out with a dial indicator. Run-out, for both gears, should not exceed 0.008 in.; if it does, replace the gear.
8. Install the oil nozzle, if it was removed, by screwing it in place with a screwdriver and punching it in two places, to secure it.

NOTE: Be sure that the oil hole in the nozzle is pointed toward the timing gear before securing it.

9. Install the oil slinger on the crankshaft.
10. Install the timing gear cover and cylinder head, as outlined above.

Camshaft

REMOVAL AND INSTALLATION

18R-C, 20R Engines

All of these engines utilize a chain-driven overhead camshaft (OHC). Therefore, the procedure for removing the camshaft is given as part of the cylinder head removal procedure. Consult the appropriate section, above, for details.

20R engine—install cam sprocket in chain so that timing mark is located between two bright chain links

20R engine—turn crankshaft until the shaft key is at TDC, slide sprocket over key and position chain with single bright link over sprocket

NOTE: It will not be necessary to completely remove the cylinder head in order to remove the camshaft. Therefore, proceed only as far as is necessary, to remove the camshaft, with the cylinder head removal procedure.

F and 2F Engine

The procedure for removing the camshaft is given as part of the timing gear

Alignment of the F engine timing marks

removal procedure, above; the timing gear is press-fit onto the camshaft and cannot be removed separately from it.

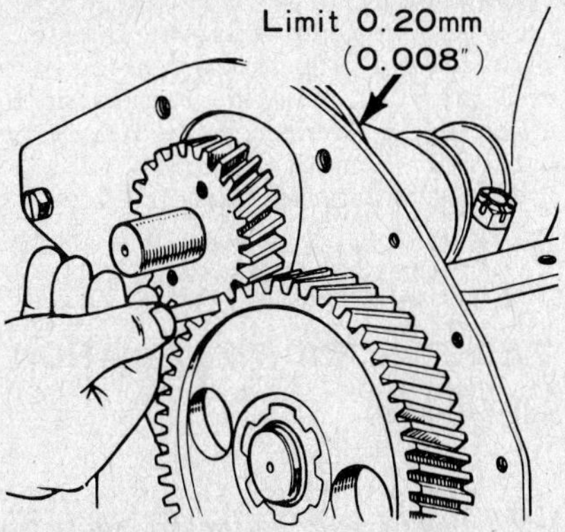

Checking timing gear backlash with a feeler gauge

Pistons and Connecting Rods

REMOVAL AND INSTALLATION

All Engines

See the procedure in the "Engine Rebuilding Section".

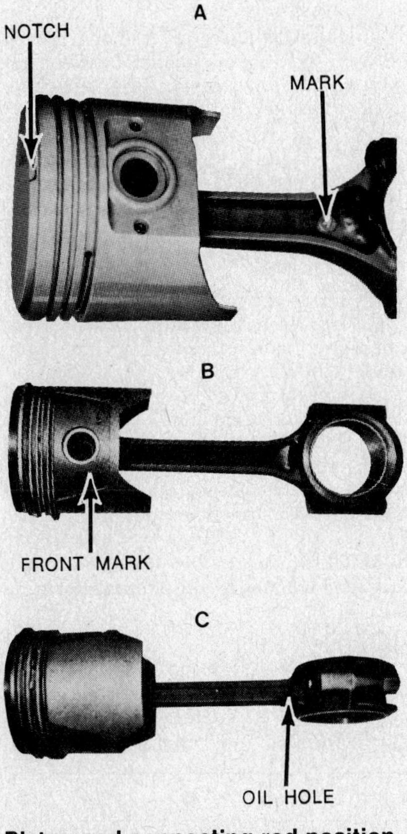

Piston and connecting rod position ing: a) 20R, 18R-C, b) F engine, c) F engine-connecting rod oil hole

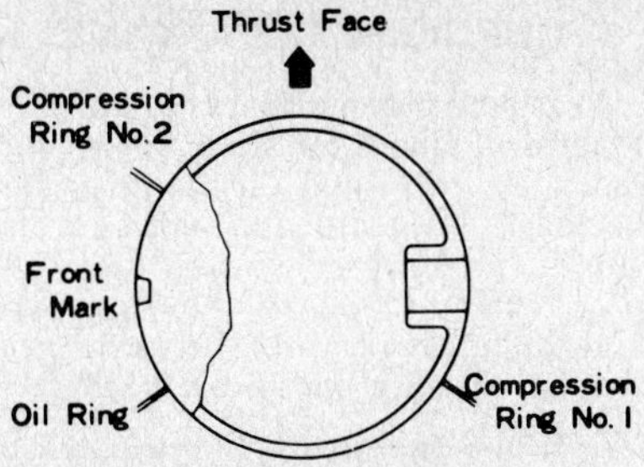

Piston and ring installation of the 20R and 18R-C engines

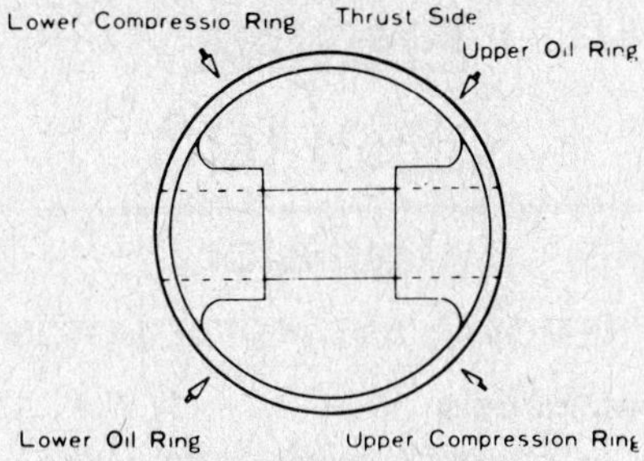

Piston and ring installation of F engines

ENGINE LUBRICATION

Oil Pan

REMOVAL AND INSTALLATION

Pick-up, 4x4 Pick-up

1. Drain the oil.
2. Raise the front end of the vehicle with jacks and support it with jackstands.

CAUTION: Be sure that the vehicle is supported securely. Remember, you will be working underneath it.

3. Detach the steering relay rod and the tie rods from the idler arm, pitman arm, and steering knuckles, as detailed below.
4. Remove the engine stiffening plates.
5. Remove the splash shields from underneath the engine.
6. Support the front of the engine with a jack and remove the front engine mount attaching bolts.
7. Raise the front of the engine *slightly* with the jack.
8. Unbolt and withdraw the oil pan.

Installation is performed in the reverse order of removal. Torque the oil pan securing bolts to the following specifications:

18R-C engines:
3–5 ft lbs.
20R engines:
3–5 ft lbs.

Land Cruiser

1. Remove the engine skid plates.
2. Remove the flywheel side cover and skid plate.
3. Disconnect the front driveshaft from the engine.
4. Drain the engine oil.
5. Remove the bolts which secure the oil pan; remove the pan and its gasket.
6. Installation is performed in the reverse order from removal. Always use a new pan gasket.

Real Main Oil Seal

REPLACEMENT

All Engines

1. Remove the transmission.
2. Remove the clutch cover assembly and flywheel.
3. Remove the oil seal retaining plate, complete with the oil seal.
4. Use a screwdriver to pry the old seal from the retaining plate. Be careful not to damage the plate.
5. Install the new seal, carefully, by using a block of wood to drift it into place.

CAUTION: Do not damage the seal; a leak will result.

6. Lubricate the lips of the seal with multipurpose grease.

Installation is the reverse of removal.

Oil Pump

REMOVAL AND INSTALLATION

All Engines (except 20R)

1. Remove the oil pan, as outlined in the appropriate section above.
2. On pick-up trucks, unbolt the oil pump securing bolts and remove it as an assembly.
3. On Land Cruisers:
   a. Remove the oil strainer and unfasten the union nuts on the oil pump pipe.
   b. Remove the lock wire and the oil pump retaining bolt and pipe from the engine.

Installation is the reverse of removal.

20R Engine

1. Remove the oil pan.
2. Remove the three bolts which secure the oil strainer.
3. Remove the drive belts, the pulley bolt, and the crankshaft pulley.
4. Unfasten the bolts which secure the oil pump housing and remove the pump assembly.
5. Remove the oil pump drive spline and the rubber O-ring.

Installation is the reverse of removal. Apply sealer to the top oil pump housing bolt. Use a new oil strainer gasket.

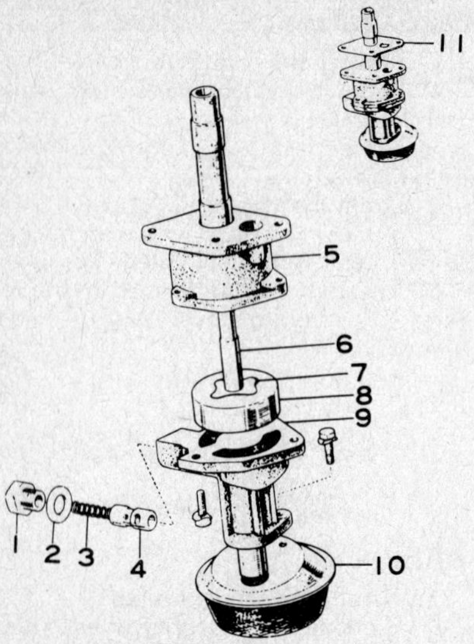

1. Oil pump relief valve plug
2. Relief valve gasket
3. Relief valve spring
4. Relief valve
5. Oil pump body
6. Oil pump shaft
7. Drive rotor
8. Driven rotor
9. Cover
10. Oil strainer
11. Gasket

18R-C oil pump

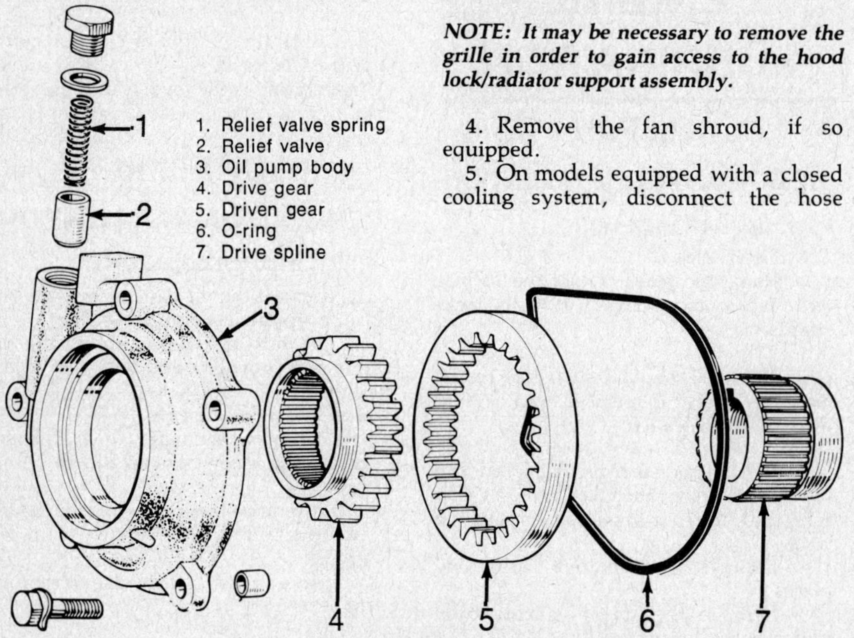

1. Relief valve spring
2. Relief valve
3. Oil pump body
4. Drive gear
5. Driven gear
6. O-ring
7. Drive spline

Exploded view of 20R engine oil pump

CHECKING CLEARANCE

Wash the pump thoroughly and allow to air dry. Check for shiny spots which indicate wear and scuffling. Check backlash of gears and measure free length of relief valve spring, then check play between gears and housing, gears and pump cover and between gears themselves. See specification chart for tolerances.

ENGINE COOLING

Radiator

REMOVAL AND INSTALLATION

All Models

1. Drain the cooling system.
2. Unfasten the clamps and remove the radiator upper and lower hoses. If equipped with an automatic transmission, remove the oil cooler lines.
3. Detach the hood lock cable and remove the hood lock from the radiator upper support.

NOTE: It may be necessary to remove the grille in order to gain access to the hood lock/radiator support assembly.

4. Remove the fan shroud, if so equipped.
5. On models equipped with a closed cooling system, disconnect the hose from the thermal expansion tank and remove the tank from its bracket.
6. Unbolt and remove the radiator upper support.
7. Unfasten and remove the radiator.

Installation is performed in the reverse order of removal. Remember to check the transmission fluid level on cars with automatic transmissions.

Fill the radiator to the specified level.

Water Pump

REMOVAL AND INSTALLATION

All Engines

1. Drain the cooling system.
2. Unfasten the fan shroud securing bolts and remove the fan shroud, if so equipped.
3. Loosen the alternator adjusting link bolt and remove the drive belt.
4. Repeat step 3 for the air pump, air conditioning compressor, or power steering pump drive belts, if so equipped.
5. Detach the bypass and radiator hoses from the water pump.
6. Unfasten the water pump retaining bolts and remove the water pump and fan assembly, using care not to damage the radiator with the fan.

CAUTION: If the fan is equipped with a fluid coupling, do not tip the fan/pump assembly on its side, as the fluid will run out.

Installation is the reverse of removal. Always use a new gasket between the pump body and its mounting. Check for leaks after installation is completed.

Thermostat

REMOVAL AND INSTALLATION

All Engines

1. Drain the cooling system.
2. Unfasten the clamp and remove the upper radiator hose from the water outlet elbow.
3. Unbolt and remove the water outlet (thermostat housing).
4. Withdraw the thermostat.

Installation is performed in the reverse order of removal procedure. Use a new gasket on the water outlet.

CAUTION: Be sure that the thermostat is installed with the spring pointing down.

OIL PUMP CLEARANCE SPECIFICATIONS

(in.)

Engine	Tip Clearance	Side Clearance	Body Clearance	Relief Valve Spring Installed Length
18R-C	0.008	0.006	0.008	1.45
20R	0.012	0.006	0.008	—
F/2F	0.012	0.002	0.002	—

FLUID COOLING FAN

To reduce fan noise and improve power and fuel consumption, the 1977 and later 2F engines are equipped with a fluid coupling cooling fan.

Filled with silicon oil, the fan will vary its RPM by means of a bimetal spring opening and closing a valve with the temperature. Opening allows more oil passage and more RPM.

ELECTRIC COOLING FAN—2F

Starting in 1978, Land Cruisers are equipped with an electric cooling fan to remove hot air from the carburetor, brake booster and some rubber parts, to protect them during high rpm, low ground speed operation.

Disassembly

1. Remove the three screws and lift off the cover and foam gasket.
2. Remove the fan shaft nut and pull off the fan.
3. Remove the three screws, fan motor and rubber gasket.
4. Assembly is the reverse of disassembly. Replace any damaged gaskets.

EMISSION CONTROLS

Positive Crankcase Ventilation (PCV) System

A positive crankcase ventilation (PCV) system is used on all Toyotas sold in the United States. Blow-by gases are routed from the crankcase to the carburetor, where they are combined with the fuel/air mixture and burned during combustion.

A (PCV) valve is used in the line to prevent the gases in the crankcase from being ignited in case of a backfire. The amount of blow-by gases entering the mixture is also regulated by the PCV valve, which is spring-loaded and has a variable orifice.

The valve is either mounted on the valve cover or in the line which runs from the intake manifold to the crankcase.

REMOVAL AND INSTALLATION

Remove the PCV valve from the cylinder head cover on 18R-C engines. Remove the hose from the valve.

On the remainder of the engines, remove the valve from the manifold-to-crankcase hose.

Installation is the reverse of removal.

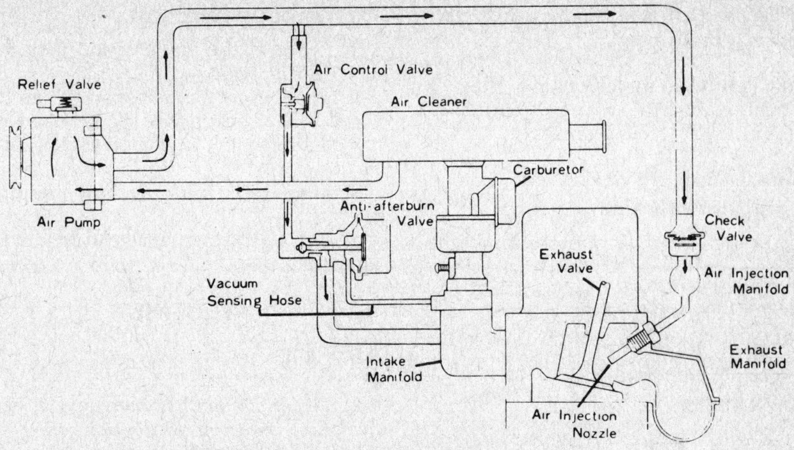

Schematic for the air injection system

TESTING

Check the PCV system hoses and connections, to see that there are no leaks; then replace or tighten, as necessary.

To check the valve, remove it and blow through both of its ends. When blowing from the side which goes toward the intake manifold, very little air should pass through it. When blowing from the crankcase (valve cover) side, air should pass through freely.

Replace the valve with a new one, if the valve fails to function as outlined.

NOTE: Do not attempt to clean or adjust the valve; replace it with a new one.

Air Injection System

A belt-driven air pump supplies air to an injection manifold which has nozzles in each exhaust port. Injection of air at this point causes combustion of unburned hydrocarbons in the exhaust manifold rather than allowing them to escape into the atmosphere. An anti-backfire valve controls the flow of air from the pump to prevent backfiring which results from an overly rich mixture under closed throttle conditions.

A check valve prevents hot exhaust gas backflow into the pump and hoses, in case of a pump failure, or when the antibackfore valve is working.

In addition newer engines have an air switching valve. On engines without catalytic converters, the ASV is used to stop air injection under a constant heavy engine load.

On engines with catalytic converters the ASV is used to protect the catalyst from overheating, by blocking the air necessary for the reaction.

On all engines, except the 2F, the relief valve is built into the ASV.

REMOVAL AND INSTALLATION

Air Pump

1. Disconnect the air hoses from the pump.
2. Loosen the bolt on the adjusting link and remove the drive belt.
3. Remove the pump.

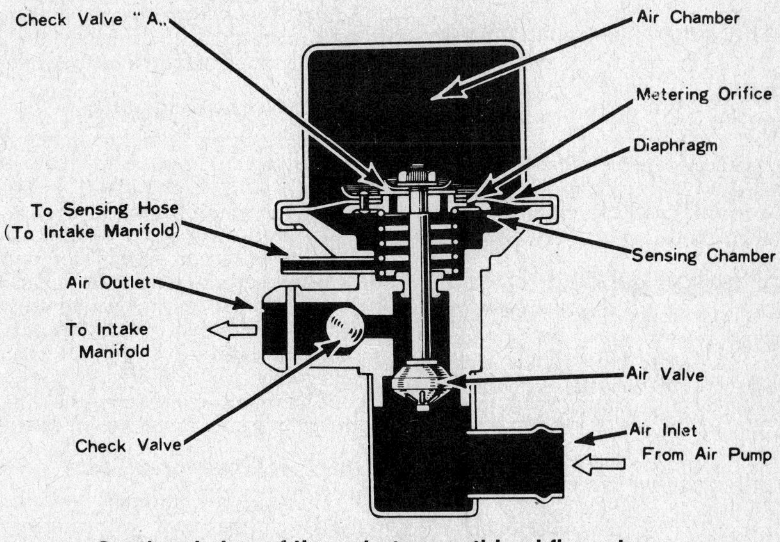

Sectional view of the gulp-type anti-backfire valve

CAUTION: Do not pry on the pump housing; it may be distorted.

Installation is in the reverse order of removal. Adjust the drive belt tension to 1/2–3/4 in. under thumb pressure.

Antibackfire Valve and Air Switching Valve

1. Detach the air hoses from the valve.
2. Remove the valve securing bolt.
3. Withdraw the valve.

Installation is performed in the reverse order of removal.

Check Valve

1. Detach the intake hose from the valve.
2. Use an open-end wrench to remove the valve from its mounting.

Installation is the reverse of removal.

Relief Valve

1. Remove the air pump from the vehicle.
2. Support the pump so that it cannot rotate.

CAUTION: Never clamp the pump in a vise; the aluminum case will be distorted.

3. Use a jaw-type puller to remove the relief valve from the top of the pump.
4. Position the new relief valve over the opening in the pump.

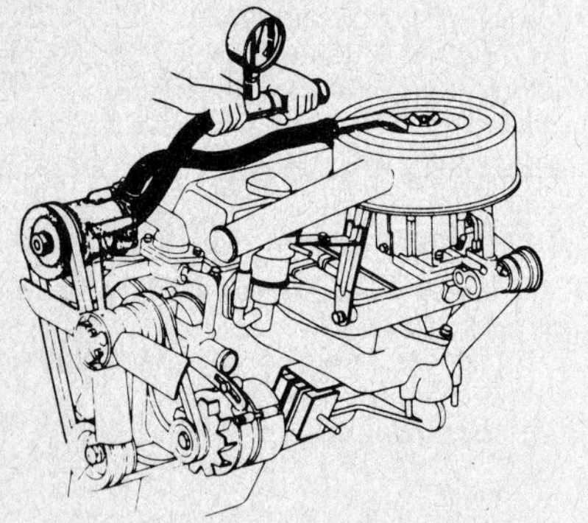

Checking the air pump output

NOTE: The air outlet should be pointing toward the left.

5. Gently tap the relief valve home, using a block of wood and a hammer.
6. Install the pump on the engine, as outlined above.

Air Injection Manifold

1. Remove the check valve, as outlined above.
2. Loosen the air injection manifold attachment nuts and withdraw the manifold.

NOTE: On 20R engines, it will first be necessary to remove the exhaust manifold.

Installation is the reverse order of removal.

Air Injection Nozzles

1. Remove the air injection manifold as outlined above.
2. Remove the cylinder head, as detailed in the appropriate section, above.
3. Place a new nozzle on the cylinder head.
4. Install the air injection manifold over it.
5. Install the cylinder head on the engine block.

TESTING

Air Pump

CAUTION: Do not hammer, pry, or bend the pump housing while tightening the drive belt or testing the pump.

Belt Tension and Air Leaks

1. Before proceeding with the tests, check the pump drive belt tension to see if it is within specifications.
2. Turn the pump by hand. If it has seized, the belt will slip, making a noise. Disregard any chirping, squealing, or rolling sounds from inside the pump; these are normal when it is turned by hand.
3. Check the hoses and connections for leaks. Hissing or a blast of air is indicative of a leak. Soapy water, applied lightly around the area in question, is a good method for detecting leaks.

Air Output

1. Disconnect the air supply hose at the antibackfire valve.
2. Connect a pressure gauge, using a suitable adaptor, to the air supply hose.

NOTE: If there are two hoses, plug the second one.

3. With the engine at normal operating temperature, increase the idle speed to 1,000–1,500 rpm and watch the vacuum gauge.
4. The air flow from the pump should be steady and fall between 2 and 6 psi. If it is unsteady of falls below this, the pump is defective and must be replaced.

Pump Noise Diagnosis

The air pump is normally noisy; as engine speed increases, the noise of the pump will rise in pitch. The rolling sound the pump bearings make is normal. But if this sound becomes objectionable at certain speeds, the pump is defective and will have to be replaced.

A continual hissing sound from the air pump pressure relief valve at idle, indicates a defective valve. Replace the relief valve.

If the pump rear bearing fails, a continual knocking sound will be heard.

Antibackfire Valve Tests

There are two different types of antibackfire valve used with air injection systems. A bypass valve is used on all

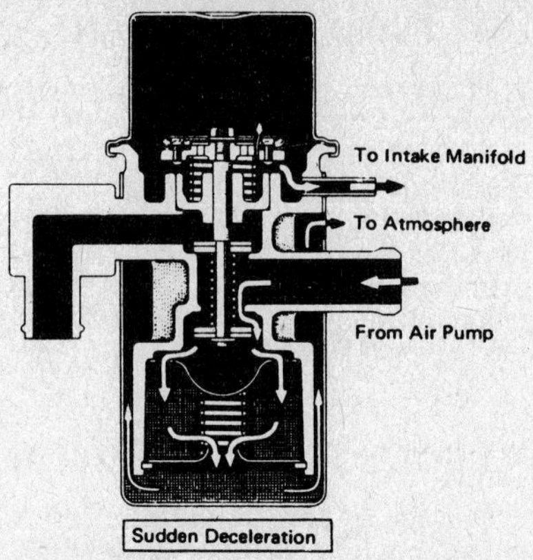

Sectional view of the bypass anti-backfire valve

engines, while 1974 F engines for California use a gulp type of antibackfire valve. Test procedures for both types are given below.

Gulp Valve

1. Detach the air supply hose which runs between the pump and the gulp valve.
2. Connect a tachometer and run the engine to 1,500–2,000 rpm.
3. Allow the throttle to snap closed. This should produce a loud sucking sound from the gulp valve.
4. Repeat this operation several times. If no sound is present, the valve is not working or else the vacuum connections are loose.
5. Check the vacuum connections. If they are secure, replace the gulp valve.

Bypass Valve

1. Detach the hose which runs from the bypass valve to the check valve, at the bypass valve hose connection.
2. Connect a tachometer to the engine. With the engine running at normal idle speed, check to see that air is flowing from the bypass valve hose connection.
3. Speed up the engine so it is running at 1,500–2,000 rpm. Allow the throttle to snap shut. The flow of air from the bypass valve at the check valve hose connection should stop momentarily and air should then flow from the exhaust port on the valve body or the silencer assembly.
4. Repeat step 3 several times. If the flow of air is not diverted into the atmosphere from the valve exhaust port or if it fails to stop flowing from the hose connection, check the vacuum lines and connections. If these are tight, the valve is defective and requires replacement.
5. A leaking diaphragm will cause the air to flow out both the hose connection and the exhaust port at the same time. If this happens, replace the valve.

Air Switching Valve (ASV) Tests

1975–80 20R ENGINES

1. Start the engine and allow it to reach normal operating temperature.

2. At curb idle, the air from the bypass valve should be discharged through the hose which runs to the ASV.

3. When the vacuum line to the ASV is disconnected, the air from the bypass valve should be diverted out through the ASV-to-air cleaner hose. Reconnect the vacuum line.

4. Disconnect the ASV-to-check valve hose and connect a pressure gauge to it.

5. Increase the engine speed. The relief valve should open when the pressure gauge registers 2.7–6.5 psi.

6. If the ASV fails any of the above tests, replace it. Reconnect all hoses.

Vacuum Delay Valve Test

1975–80 20R ENGINES

The vacuum delay valve is located in the line which runs from the intake manifold to the vacuum surge tank. To check it, proceed as follows:

1. Remove the vacuum delay valve from the vacuum line. Be sure to note which end points toward the intake manifold.

2. When air is blown in from the ASV (surge tank) side, it should pass through the valve freely.

3. When air is blown in from the intake manifold side, a resistance should be felt.

4. Replace the valve if it fails either of the above tests.

5. Install the valve in the vacuum line, being careful not to install it backwards.

Check Valve Test

1. Before starting the test, check all of the hoses and connections for leaks.

2. Detach the air supply hose from the check valve.

3. Insert a suitable probe into the check valve and depress the plate. Release it; the plate should return to its original position against the valve seat. If binding is evident, replace the valve.

4. With the engine running at normal operating temperature, gradually increase its speed to 1,500 rpm. Check for exhaust gas leakage. If any is present, replace the valve assembly.

NOTE: Vibration and flutter of the check valve at idle speed is at normal condition and does not mean that the valve should be replaced.

Evaporative Emission Control System

To prevent hydrocarbon emissions from entering the atmosphere, Toyota vehicles use evaporative emission control (EEC) systems. All models use a "charcoal canister" storage system.

The charcoal canister storage system stores fuel vapors in a canister filled with activated charcoal. All models use a vacuum switching valve to purge the system. The air filter is an integral part of the charcoal canister.

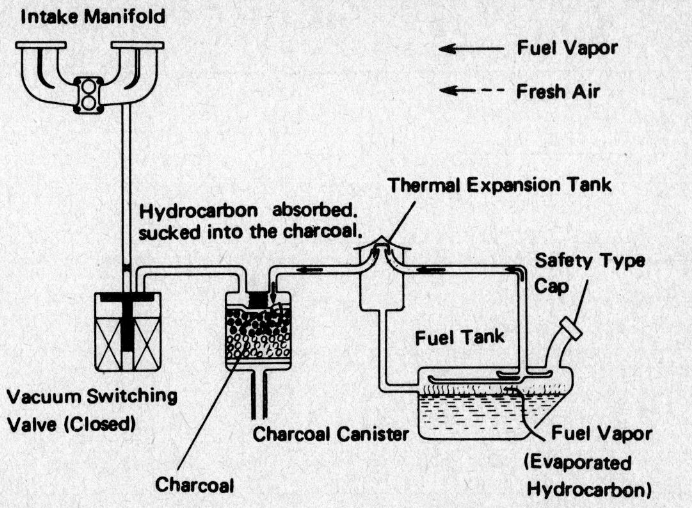

Schematic for charcoal storage system w/thermal expansion tank

REMOVAL AND INSTALLATION

Removal and installation of the various evaporative emission control system components consists of disconnecting hoses, loosening securing screws, and removing the part which is to be replaced from its mounting bracket. Installation is the reverse of removal.

NOTE: When replacing any EEC system hoses, always use hoses that are fuel-resistant or are marked "EVAP."

TESTING

EEC System Troubleshooting

There are several things which may be checked if a malfunction of the evaporative emission control system is suspected.

1. Leaks may be traced by using a hydrocarbon tester. Run the test probe along the lines and connections. The meter will indicate the presence of a leak by a high hydrocarbon (HC) reading. This method is much more accurate than visual inspection which would only indicate the presence of leaks large enough to pass liquid.

2. Leaks may be caused by any of the following:

a. Defective or worn hoses;
b. Disconnected or pinched hoses;
c. Improperly routed hoses;
d. A defective filler cap or safety valve (sealed cap system).

NOTE: If it becomes necessary to replace any of the hoses used in the evaporative emission control system, use only hoses which are fuel-resistant or are marked "EVAP."

3. If the fuel tank, storage case, or thermal expansion tank collapse, it may be the fault of clogged or pinched vent lines, a defective vapor separator, or a plugged or incorrect filler cap.

4. To test the filler cap (if it is the safety valve type), clean it and place it against your mouth. Blow into the relief valve housing. If the cap passes pressure with light blowing or if it fails to release with hard blowing, it is defective and must be replaced.

NOTE: Use the proper cap for the type of system used; either a sealed cap or safety valve cap, as required.

Check Valve

Rough idling when the gas tank is full is probably caused by a defective check valve. To test it, proceed as follows:

1. Run the engine at idle.

2. Clamp the hose between the vacuum switching valve and the charcoal canister.

3. If the engine idle becomes smooth, replace the check valve.

Throttle Positioner

On Toyotas with an engine modification system, a throttle positioner is included to reduce exhaust emissions during deceleration. The positioner prevents the throttle from closing completely. Vacuum is reduced under the throttle valve which, in turn, acts on the retard chamber of the distributor vacuum unit (if so equipped). This compensates for the loss of engine braking caused by the partially open throttle.

Once the vehicle drops below a predetermined speed, the vacuum switching valve provides vacuum to the throttle positioner diaphragm; the throttle positioner retracts allowing the throttle valve to close completely. The distributor also is returned to normal operation.

ADJUSTMENT

1. Start the engine and allow it to reach normal operating temperature.

2. Adjust the idle speed.

THROTTLE POSITIONER SETTINGS

(rpm)

Year	Engine	Engine rpm (Positioner Set)
1973-74	18R-C	1,400
	F	1,200
1975-76	20R	1,400 MT 1,050 AT
	2F	1,200
1977-80	20R	1,400 MT 1,050 AT
	2F	1,200 1,400 (Calif.)

MT—Manual Transmission OT—Automatic Transmission

***NOTE:** Leave the tachometer connected after completing the idle adjustments, as it will be needed in step 5, below.*

3. Detach the vacuum line from the positioner diaphragm unit and plug the line.
4. Accelerate the engine slightly to set the throttle positioner.
5. Check the engine speed with a tachometer when the throttle positioner is set.
6. If necessary, adjust the engine speed, with the throttle positioner adjusting screw, to the specifications.
7. Connect the vacuum hose to the positioner diaphragm.
8. The throttle lever should be freed from the positioner as soon as the vacuum hose is connected. Engine idle should return to normal.
9. If the throttle positioner fails to function properly, check its linkage, and vacuum diaphragm. If there are no defects in either of these, the fault probably lies in the vacuum switching valve or the speed marker unit.

***NOTE:** Due to the complexity of these two components they require special test equipment.*

CHOKE OPENER SYSTEM

If a cold engine is driven soon after starting, the automatic choke system will close the choke plate, resulting in high levels of emissions. To combat the situation all 1978–79 engines are equipped with a system that forcibly holds the choke plate open.

When the coolant is below 140°F. the thermo wax in the TVSV closes the valve and prohibits any vacuum from acting on the choke diaphragm. This keeps the choke open. Above 140° F. the wax expands, opening the valve, and allows the choke plate to operate normally. Should the system malfunction, replace the TVSV.

POWER VALVE CONTROL SYSTEM-2F

In order to minimize CO while ensuring good driveability, the Land Cruiser 2F engines for California are equipped with a power valve control system on the carburetor.

Dependent on coolant temperature, the power system opens or closes turning the VSV "On." It is also influenced by the amount of pressure on the accelerator pedal. Various combinations of pedal pressure and temperature will result in more or less fuel available for use. Any breakdown in the system requires replacement of the part involved.

Auxiliary System

An auxiliary enrichment system, which Toyota calls an "Auxiliary System", is used on all models, starting in 1975.

When the engine is cold, an auxiliary enrichment circuit in the carburetor is operated to squirt extra fuel into the acceleration circuit in order to prevent the mixture from becoming too lean.

TESTS

1. Check for clogged, pinched, disconnected, or misrouted vacuum lines.
2. With the engine cold (below 75°F), remove the top of the air cleaner, and allow the engine to idle.
3. Disconnect the vacuum line from the carburetor AAP unit. Gasoline should squirt out the accelerator pump jet.

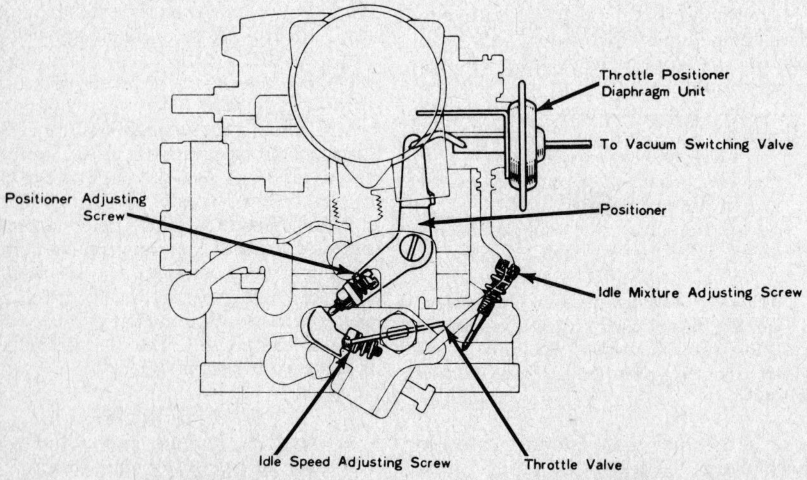

Components of the throttle positioner system

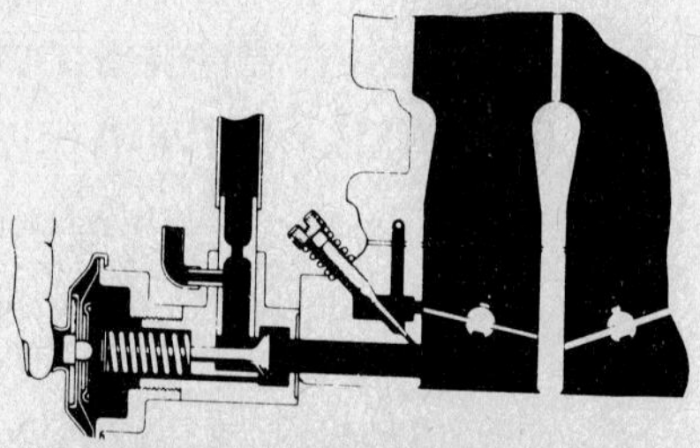

Testing the diaphragm on the auxiliary slow system

4. If gas doesn't squirt out of the jet, check for vacuum at the AAP vacuum line with the engine idling. If there is no vacuum and the hoses are in good shape, the thermostatic vacuum valve is defective and must be replaced.

5. If the gas doesn't squirt out and vacuum is present at the vacuum line in step 4, the AAP unit is defective and must be replaced.

6. Repeat step 3 with the engine at normal operating temperature. If gasoline squirts out of the pump jet, the thermostatic vacuum valve is defective and must be replaced.

7. Reconnect all of the vacuum lines and install the top on the air cleaner.

HIGH ALTITUDE COMPENSATION SYSTEM

For all engines to be sold in areas over 4,000 ft. in altitude, a system has been installed to automatically lean out the fuel mixture by supplying additional air. This also results in lower emissions.

Low atmospheric pressure allows the bellows in the system to expand and close a port, allowing more air to enter from different sources.

In 20R engines, this also results in a timing advance to improve driveability.

All parts in this system must be replaced. The only adjustment available is in the timing.

HOT AIR INTAKE—ALL ENGINES

In order to keep the temperature of the air drawn into the carburetor as constant as possible, all engines are equipped with a Hot Air Intake System (HAI).

In all engines but the 2F, the system depends on a thermo valve to control the temperature. In the 2F (Land Cruiser), the temperature and valve are controlled by thermo wax.

At normal temperatures the air is drawn through the inlet in the air filter. When the temperature drops, the valve switches position, opening the way for air to be drawn from around the exhaust manifold.

When inspecting, check all hoses for poor connections or damage and visually check the air control valve in their air duct.

NOTE: When checking valve movement, do not push too strongly on the control face.

Should there be a malfunction, replace the part involved.

Dual-Diaphragm Distributor

NOTE: 1973–75 Land Cruisers have a vacuum retard unit only; no vacuum advance is used.

Some Toyota models are equipped with a dual-diaphragm distributor unit. This distributor has a retard diaphragm, as well as a diaphragm for advance. Retarding the timing helps to reduce exhaust emissions, as well as making up for the lack of engine braking on models equipped with a throttle positioner.

TESTING

1. Connect a timing light to the engine. Check the ignition timing.

NOTE: Before proceeding with the tests, disconnect any spark control devices, distributor vacuum valves, etc. If these are left connected, inaccurate results may be obtained.

2. Remove the retard hose from the distributor and plug it. Increase the engine speed. The timing should advance. If it fails to do so, then the vacuum unit is faulty and must be replaced.

3. Check the timing with the engine at normal idle speed. Unplug the retard hose and connect it to the vacuum unit. The timing should instantly be retarded from 4 to 10 degrees. If this does not occur, the retard diaphragm has a leak and the vacuum unit must be replaced.

Spark Control System

In 1978–80 all non-California 20R engines are equipped with the spark control system. The valve has a small orifice in it, which slows down the vacuum flow to the vacuum advance unit on the distributor. By delaying the vacuum to the distributor, a reduction in HC and CO emissions is possible.

When the coolant temperature is below 95°F–140°F (1975–77) or 104°F (20R) a coolant temperature operated vacuum control valve is opened, allowing the distributor to receive undelayed, ported vacuum through a separate vacuum line. Above 95°F–140°F this line is blocked, and all ported vacuum must go through the spark delay valve.

SPARK CONTROL VALVE OPERATING TEMPERATURES

Closed	Degrees F
1978–79 20R	104
Open	
1978–79 20R	129

TESTING

1. Allow the engine to cool, so that the coolant temperature is below that required. See the chart.

2. Disconnect the vacuum line which runs from the coolant temperature operated vacuum valve to the vacuum advance unit at the advance unit end. Connect the vacuum gauge to this line.

3. Start the engine. Increase the engine speed; the gauge should indicate a vacuum.

4. Allow the engine to warm-up to normal operating temperature. Increase the engine speed; this time the vacuum gauge should read zero.

5. Replace the coolant temperature operated vacuum valve, if it fails either of these tests. Disconnect the vacuum gauge and reconnect the vacuum lines.

6. Remove the spark delay valve from the vacuum line, noting which side faces the distributor.

7. Connect a hand-operated vacuum pump which has a built-in vacuum gauge to the carburetor side of the spark delay valve.

8. Connect a vacuum gauge to the distributor side of the valve.

9. Operate the hand pump to create a vacuum. The vacuum gauge on the distributor side should show a hesitation before registering.

10. The gauge reading on the pump side should drop slightly, taking several seconds for it to balance with the reading on the other gauge.

11. If steps 9 and 10 are negative, replace the spark delay valve.

12. Remove the vacuum gauge from the distributor side of the valve. Cover the distributor side of the valve with your finger and operate the pump to create a vacuum of 15 in. Hg.

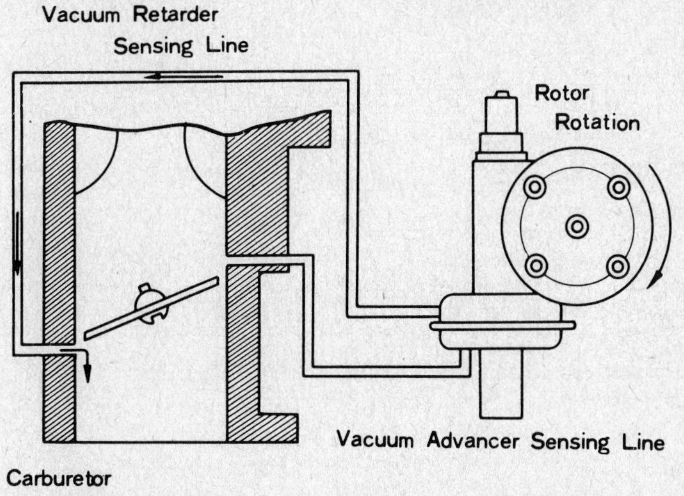

Dual-diaphragm distributor—without the vacuum switching valve

13. The reading on the pump gauge should remain steady, if the gauge reading drops, replace the valve.

14. Remove your finger; the reading on the gauge should drop slowly. If the reading goes to zero rapidly, replace the valve.

Engine Modifications System

Toyota also uses an assortment of engine modifications to regulate exhaust emissions. Most of these devices fall into the category of engine vacuum controls. There are three principal components used on the engine modifications system, as well as a number of smaller parts. The three major components are: a speed sensor; a computer (speed marker); and a vacuum switching valve.

The vacuum switching valve and computer circuit operates most of the emission control components. Depending upon year and engine usage, the vacuum switching valve and computer may operate the purge control for the evaporative emission control system; the transmission controlled spark (TCS) or speed controlled spark (SCS); the dual-diaphragm distributor; and the throttle positioner systems.

The functions of the evaporative emission control system, the throttle positioner, and the dual-diaphragm distributor are described in detail in the sections above. However, a word is necessary about the functions of the TCS and SCS systems before discussing the operation of the vacuum switching valve/computer circuit.

The major difference between the transmission controlled spark and speed controlled spark systems is in the manner in which systems operation is determined.

Below a predetermined speed, or any gear other than fourth, the vacuum advance unit on the distributor is rendered inoperative or, on F engines, timing is retarded. By changing the distributor advance curve in this manner, it is possible to reduce emissions of oxides of nitrogen (NOx).

NOTE: Some engines are equipped with a thermo-sensor so that the TCS or SCS system only operates when the coolant temperature is 140°–212°F.

Aside from determining the conditions outlined above, the vacuum switching valve computer circuit operates other devices in the emission control system.

The computer acts as a speed marker, at certain speeds it sends a signal to the vacuum switching valve which acts as a gate, opening and closing the emission control system vacuum circuits.

The valve used in 1973 contains several solenoid and valve assemblies so that different combinations of opened and closed vacuum ports are possible. This allows greater flexibility of operation for the emission control system.

SYSTEM CHECKS

Due to the complexity of the components involved, about the only engine modification system checks which can be made without the use of special test equipment, are the following:

1. Examine the vacuum lines to see that they are not clogged, pinched, or loose.
2. Check the electrical connections for tightness and corrosion.
3. Be sure that the vacuum sources for the vacuum switching valve are not plugged.
4. On models equipped with speed controlled spark, a broken speedometer cable could also render the system inoperative.
5. Test the thermo-sensor in the following manner:

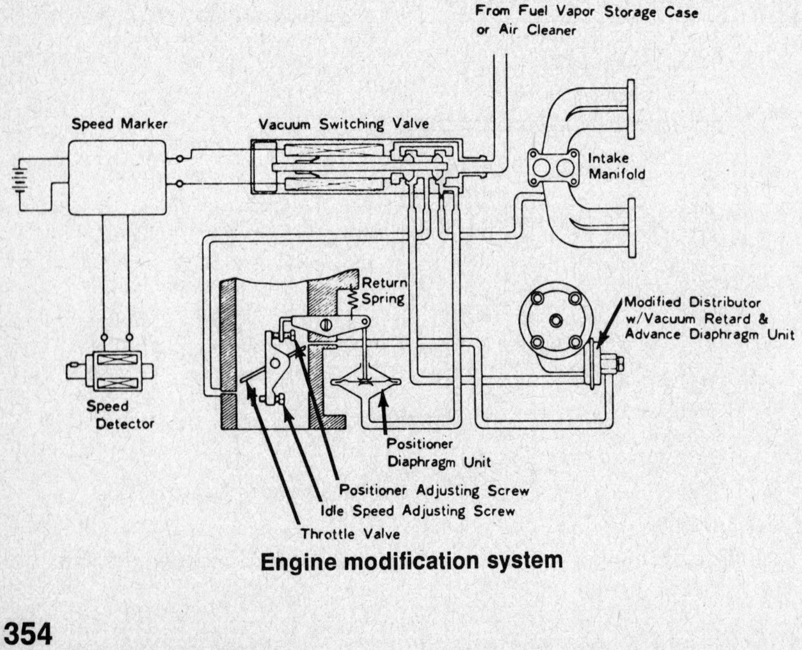

Engine modification system

a. Remove the lead from its center terminal.

b. Touch one test prod of an ohmmeter to the sensor housing.

c. Connect the other test prod in series with a 10 ohm resistor to the center terminal of the sensor.

d. If the engine temperature is between about 140°–212°F (or 113°–217°F on 1974 California F engines), the meter should show no conductivity.

e. If the engine is above or below these temperatures, the meter should show conductivity.

f. Replace the thermo-sensor if it isn't working properly.

6. If everything else is in good working order, the fault probably lies in the vacuum switching valve or the computer (speed marker). About the only way to test these, without using special equipment, is by substitution of new units.

NOTE: A faulty vacuum switching valve or computer could cause more than one of the emission control systems to fail. Therefore, if several systems are out, these two units (and the speedometer cable) would be the first things to check.

Exhaust Gas Recirculation (EGR)

Starting with 1974 models, exhaust gas recirculation (EGR) is used on 18R-C and F engines on vehicles sold in California; in 1975 EGR usage is extended to all US engines.

In all cases, the EGR valve is controlled by the same computer and vacuum switching valve which is used to operate other emission control system components.

On 18R-C and F engines, the EGR valve is operated by vacuum supplied from a port above the throttle blades and fed through the vacuum switching valve.

The vacuum from the port opens the vacuum control valve which then allows venturi vacuum to act on the chamber *above* the EGR valve diaphragm, causing the EGR valve to open. When exhaust gas recirculation is not required, the vacuum switching valve stops sending the advance port vacuum signal to the EGR vacuum control valve which closes, sending intake manifold vacuum to the chamber *below* the EGR valve diaphragm. This closes the EGR valve, blocking the flow of exhaust gases to the intake manifold.

On all engines there are several conditions, determined by the computer and vacuum switching valve, which permit exhaust gas recirculation to take place:

1. Vehicle speed
2. Engine coolant temperature
3. EGR valve temperature (18R-C an F)
4. Carburetor flange temperature (18R-C)

On 18R-C and F engines equipped with EGR, the exhaust gases are carried from the exhaust manifold to the EGR valve and from the EGR valve to the carburetor, via external tubing. The F engine has an exhaust gas cooler mounted on the exhaust manifold.

EGR VALVE CHECKS

ALL EXCEPT F AND 2F

1. Allow the engine to warm up and remove the top from the air cleaner.

NOTE: Do not remove the entire air cleaner assembly.

2. Disconnect the hose (white tape coded), which runs from the vacuum switching valve to the EGR valve, at its EGR valve end.
3. Remove the intake manifold hose (red coded) from the vacuum switching valve and connect it to the EGR valve. When the engine is at idle, a "hollow" sound should be heard coming from the air cleaner.
4. Disconnect the hose from the EGR valve; the hollow sound should disappear.
5. If the sound doesn't vary, the EGR valve is defective and must be replaced.
6. Reconnect the vacuum hoses as they were originally found. Install the top on the air cleaner.

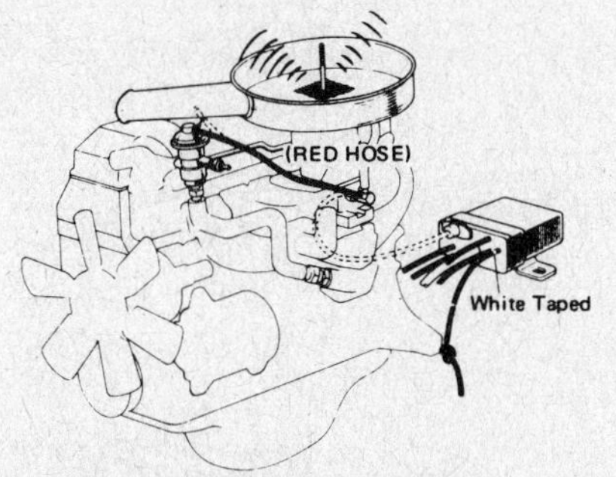

Checking the EGR valve on the 18R-C engine—20R similar

F AND 2F ENGINES

1. Start the engine and allow it to warm up.
2. Connect a tachometer to the engine. Be sure that the engine idle is set to specifications (650 rpm).
3. Disconnect the EGR valve vacuum line (yellow coded) from the vacuum switching valve.
4. Connect a vacuum line directly to either manifold vacuum or to an alternate vacuum source (vacuum pump).
5. When the vacuum is applied to the EGR valve, the engine speed should drop about 50 rpm (to 600 rpm). If the engine speed remains the same, replace the EGR valve.
6. Disconnect the tachometer and reconnect the EGR valve vacuum line to the vacuum switching valve.

EGR VALVE THERMO-SENSOR

18R-C, 2F AND F ENGINES

1. Disconnect the electrical lead which runs to the EGR valve thermo-sensor.
2. Remove the thermo-sensor from the side of the EGR valve.
3. Heat the thermo-sensor in a pan of water to one of the following temperatures:
   260°F—18R-C engine
   320°—F engine
4. Connect an ohmmeter, in series with a 10 ohm resistor, between the thermo-sensor terminal and case.
5. With the ohmmeter set on the k-ohm scale, the following readings should be obtained:
   2.55k-ohms—18R-C engine
   2.00k-ohms—F engines
6. Replace the thermo-sensor if the ohmmeter readings vary considerably from those specified.
7. To install the thermo-sensor on the EGR valve, tighten it 15–21 ft lbs.

CAUTION: Do not tighten the thermo-sensor with an impact wrench.

EGR VACUUM CONTROL VALVE

1. Connect the EGR vacuum control valve hoses up, so that carburetor advance port vacuum operates directly on its diaphragm (top hose connection).
2. Disconnect the two hoses from the EGR vacuum control valve which run to the upper and lower diaphragm chambers of the EGR valve.
3. Take two vacuum gauges and connect one to each of the ports from which you removed a hose in Step 2.
4. Race the engine; the vacuum gauges should indicate the following:
   Upper chamber port—Venturi vacuum
   Lower chamber port—Atmospheric pressure
5. Disconnect the sensing hose from the carburetor advance port.
6. The vacuum gauges should now show the following:
   Upper chamber port-Atmospheric pressure
   Lower chamber port-Intake manifold vacuum

NOTE: The atmospheric pressure reading should be nearly equal to that obtained in Step 4.

7. Replace the EGR vacuum control valve if the readings on the vacuum gauges are incorrect.
8. Hook up the vacuum lines as they were originally found.

SYSTEM CHECKS

If, after having completed the above tests, the EGR system still doesn't work right and everything else checks out OK, the fault probably lies in the computer or the vacuum switching valve systems. Proceed with the tests outlined under "System Checks" in the Engine Modification Section above.

NOTE: A good indication that the fault doesn't lie in the EGR system, but rather in the vacuum supply system, would be if several emission control systems were not working properly.

2F Thermal Reactor System and Heat Control Valve

Installed in place of the exhaust manifold on the Land Cruiser 2F engine for California, is the Thermal Reactor System. It collects the exhaust gases in a common area in order to keep their temperatures higher for a longer period of time to increase the efficiency of the exhaust gas and secondary air, restricting the release of unburned emissions.

Check the manifold for undue noises, leakage or damage and for movement of the head control valve. Replace the manifold, if there's a problem.

CATALYTIC CONVERTERS

In 1977, all Toyota vehicles sold in this country were equipped with catalytic converters. The converters are used to oxidize hydrocarbons (HC) and carbon monoxide (CO). The converters are necessary because of the stricter emission level standards for the 1975 models.

The catalysts are made of noble metals (platinum and palladium) which are bonded to individual pellets. These catalysts cause the HC and CO to break down into water and carbon dioxide (CO_2) without taking part in the reaction; hence, a catalyst life of 50,000 miles may be expected under normal conditions.

An air pump is used to supply air to the exhaust system to aid in the reaction. A thermosensor, inserted into the convertor, shuts off the air supply if the catalyst temperature becomes excessive.

The same sensor circuit also causes a dash warning light labled 'EXH TEMP" to come on when the catalyst temperature gets too high.

NOTE: It is normal for the light to come on temporarily if the vehicle is being driven downhill for long periods of time (such as descending a mountain).

The light will come on and stay on if

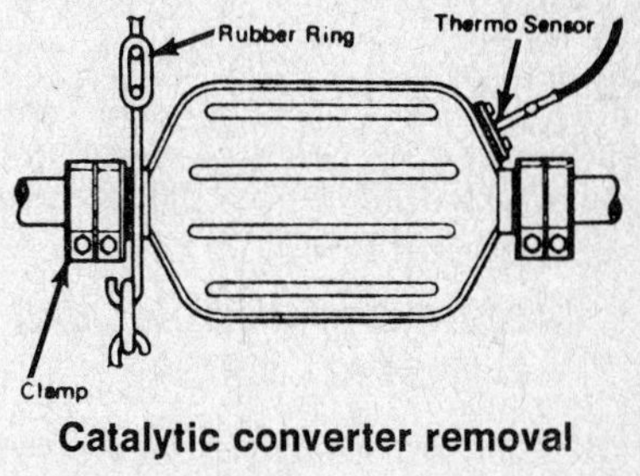

Catalytic converter removal

the air injection system is malfunctioning or if the engine is misfiring.

Precautions

1. Use only unleaded fuel.
2. Avoid prolonged idling; the engine should run no longer than 20 minutes at curb idle, nor longer than 10 minutes at fast idle.
3. Reduce the fast idle speed, by quickly depressing and releasing the accelerator pedal, as soon as the coolant temperature reaches 120°F.
4. Do not disconnect any spark plug leads while the engine is running.
5. Make engine compression checks as quickly as possible.
6. Do not dispose of the catalyst in a place where anything coated with grease, gas, or oil is present; spontaneous combustion could result.

CATALYST TESTING

At the present time there is no known way to reliably test catalytic converter operation in the field. The only reliable test is a 12 hour and 40 minute "soak test" (CVS) which must be done in a laboratory.

An infrared HC/CO tester is not sensitive enough to measure the higher tailpipe emissions from a partially-failed converter. Thus, a bad converter may allow enough HC and CO emissions to escape, so that the car is not in compliance with Federal (or state) standards, but still will not cause the needle on the HC/CO tester to move off zero.

A *completely* failed converter should cause the tester to show a slight reading. As a result, it should be possible to spot one of these in the shop.

As long as the driver of the vehicle avoids severe overheating or use of leaded fuels and the car has less than 50,000 miles on it, it is safe to assume that the converter is working.

WARNING LIGHT CHECKS

NOTE: The warning light comes on while the engine is being cranked, to test its operation, just like any of the other warning lights.

1. If the warning light comes on and stays on, check the components of the air injection system, as outlined above. If these are not defective, check the ignition system for faulty leads, plugs, points, or control box.
2. If no problems can be found in step 1, check the wiring for the light for shorts or opened circuits.
3. If nothing else can be found wrong in steps 1 and 2 above, check the operation of the emission control system computer, either by substitution of a new unit, or by taking it to a service facility which has Toyota's special emission control system checker.

CONVERTER REMOVAL AND INSTALLATION

CAUTION: Do not perform the operation on a hot (or even warm) engine. Catalyst temperatures may go as high as 1700°F, so that any contact with the catalyst could cause severe burns.

1. Disconnect the lead from the converter thermosensor.
2. Remove the wiring shield.
3. Unfasten the pipe clamp securing bolts at either end of the converter. Remove the clamps.
4. Push the tailpipe rearward and remove the converter, complete with thermosensor.
5. Carry the converter with the thermosensor upward to prevent the catalyst from falling out.
6. Unfasten the screws and withdraw the thermosensor and gasket.

Installation is performed in the following order:

1. Place a new gasket on the thermosensor. Push the thermosensor into the converter and secure it with its two bolts. Be careful not to drop the thermosensor.

NOTE: Service replacement converters are provided with a plastic thermosensor guide. Slide the sensor into the guide to install it. Do not remove the guide.

2. Install new gaskets on the converter mounting flanges.
3. Secure the converter with its mounting clamps.
4. If the converter is attached to the body with rubber O-rings, install the O-rings over the body and converter mounting hooks.
5. Install the wire protector and connect the lead to the thermosensor.

FUEL SYSTEM

Fuel Filter

REPLACEMENT

All engines employ a disposable, inline filter, when dirty, or at recommended intervals, remove from line and replace.

Mechanical Fuel Pump

All 1973–74 Toyota vehicles use a mechanically operated fuel pump of diaphragm construction. A separate fuel filter is incorporated into the fuel line.

REMOVAL AND INSTALLATION

1. Disconnect both of the fuel lines from the pump.
2. Unfasten the bolts which attach the fuel pump to the cylinder block.
3. Withdraw the pump assembly.

Installation is performed in the reverse order of removal. Always use a new gasket when installing the fuel pump. After the pump is installed check its discharge rate. See "Testing" below.

NOTE: Failure to use a gasket of the correct thickness could result in an improper pump discharge rate.

TESTING

1. Remove the line which runs from the carburetor to the fuel pump, at the fuel pump end.

NOTE: Be sure that there is enough gasoline left to operate the engine briefly.

2. Attach a pressure gauge to the pump outlet.
3. Run the engine and note the discharge pressure.
4. Check the pump discharge pressure against the specification given at the beginning of the section.
5. If the pump output is not up to specifications, replace the diaphragm spring or the entire pump assembly.
6. Reconnect the carburetor fuel line.

Electric Fuel Pump

Starting in 1975 all models use an electric pump.

The fuel pump is located inside the gas tank. It is serviced as unit; if it breaks, replace it.

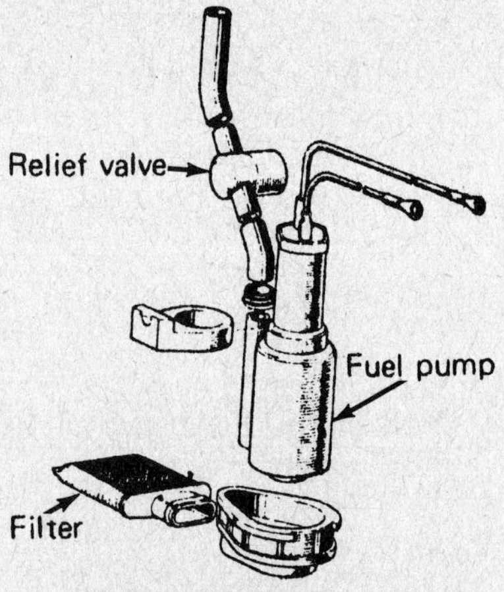

Electric fuel pump

REMOVAL AND INSTALLATION

1. Disconnect the negative (−) cable from the battery.

2.a. On sedans and hardtops, remove the trim panel from inside the trunk.

b. On station wagons, raise the rear of the vehicle, in order to gain access to the pump.

c. On pick-ups remove the fuel tank.

3. Remove the screws which secure the pump access plate to the tank. Withdraw the plate, gasket, and pump assembly.
4. Disconnect the leads and hoses from the pump.

Installation is performed in the reverse order of removal. Use a new gasket on the pump access plate.

TESTING

CAUTION: ***Do not operate the fuel pump unless it is immersed in gasoline and connected to its resistor.***

1. Disconnect the lead from the oil pressure warning light sender.
2. Unfasten the line from the outlet side of the fuel filter.
3. Connect a pressure gauge to the filter outlet with a length of rubber hose.
4. Turn the ignition switch to the "ON" position, but do not start the engine.
5. Check the pressure gauge reading against the figure given in the "Tune-Up Specifications" chart above.
6. Check for a clogged filter or pinched lines if the pressure is not up to specification.
7. If there is nothing wrong with the filter or lines, replace the fuel pump.
8. Turn the ignition off and reconnect the fuel line to the filter. Connect the lead to the oil pressure sender.

Fuel Return Cut Valve

The fuel return cut valve controls the amount of fuel returned to the gas tank according to engine load. This prevents percolation then the engine is hot and the load light.

INSPECTION

Attach a long tube to the return pipe of the valve. Put a container under it to catch the fuel. With the engine at idle, fuel should go into the container.

Pinch-off the vacuum line. If valve is operating correctly, the fuel flow should stop.

Fuel Cut-Off Valve

In case of an accident, a fuel cut-off valve was added to all systems in 1976. The valve, installed between the fuel filter and the carburetor, consists of two check balls that clog the fuel line if the automobile is in other than the normal wheels down position.

Combined with a check on the carburetor and specially designed fuel lines, the fuel cut-off system almost eliminates the chance of spilled fuel during an accident.

Carburetors

The carburetors used on Toyota models are conventional two-barrel, downdraft types similar to domestic carburetors. The main circuits are: *primary,* for normal operational requirements; *secondary,* to supply high-speed fuel needs; *float,* to supply fuel to the primary and secondary circuits; *accelerator,* to supply fuel for quick and safe acceleration; *choke,* for reliable starting in cold weather; and *power valve,* for fuel economy. Although slight differences in appearance may be noted, these carburetors are basically alike. Of course, different jets and settings are demanded by the different engines to which they are fitted.

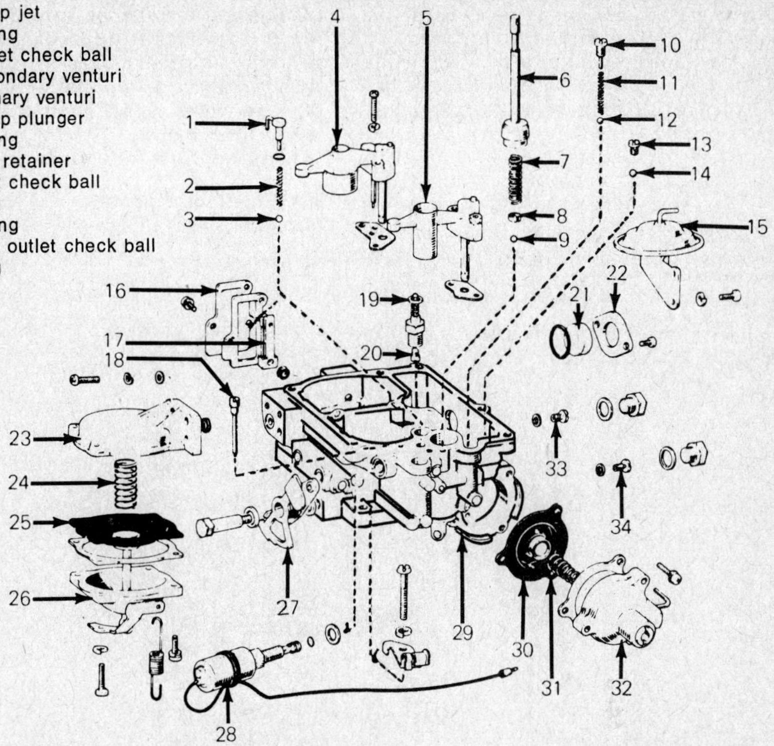

1. Pump jet
2. Spring
3. Outlet check ball
4. Secondary venturi
5. Primary venturi
6. Pump plunger
7. Spring
8. Ball retainer
9. Inlet check ball
10. Plug
11. Spring
12. AAP outlet check ball
13. Plug
14. AAP inlet check ball
15. Throttle positioner
16. Thermostatic valve cover
17. Thermostatic valve
18. Primary slow jet
19. Power valve
20. Power jet
21. Sight glass
22. Glass retainer
23. Diaphragm housing cap
24. Spring
25. Diaphragm
26. Housing
27. Fast idle cam
28. Solenoid valve
29. Carburetor body
30. Diaphragm
31. Spring
32. AAP housing
33. Secondary main jet
34. Primary main jet

Main body assembly—20R

REMOVAL AND INSTALLATION

1. Remove the air cleaner housing, disconnect all air hoses from the air cleaner base, and disconnect the battery ground cable.

NOTE: ***On 20R engines, drain the coolant to prevent it from running into the intake manifold when the carburetor is removed.***

2. Disconnect the fuel line, choke pipe, and distributor vacuum line. On 20R engines disconnect the choke coolant hose.
3. Remove the accelerator linkage. (With an automatic transmission, also remove the throttle rod to the transmission.)

NOTE: ***On Land Cruisers disconnect the magnetic valve wire from the coil terminal, if equipped.***

4. Remove the four nuts that secure the carburetor to the manifold and lift off the carburetor and gasket.
5. Cover the open manifold with a clean rag to prevent small objects from dropping into the engine.

Installation is performed in the reverse order of removal. After the engine is warmed up, check for fuel leaks and float level settings.

OVERHAUL

Efficient carburetion depends greatly on careful cleaning and inspection during overhaul since dirt, gum, water, or varnish in or on the carburetor parts are often responsible for poor performance.

Overhaul your carburetor in a clean, dust-free area. Carefully disassemble the carburetor, referring often to the exploded views. Keep all similar and look-alike parts segregated during disassembly and cleaning to avoid accidental interchange during assembly. Make a note of all jet sizes.

When the carburetor is disassembled, wash all parts (except diaphragms, electric choke units, pump plunger, and any other plastic, leather, fiber, or rubber parts) in clean carburetor solvent. Do not leave parts in the solvent any longer than is necessary to sufficiently loosen the deposits. Excessive cleaning may remove the special finish from the float bowl and choke valve bodies, leaving these parts unfit for service. Rinse all parts in clean solvent and blow them dry with compressed air or allow them to air dry. Wipe clean all cork, plastic, leather, and fiber parts with a clean lint-free cloth.

Blow out all passages and jets with compressed air and be sure that there are no restrictions or blockages. Never use wire or similar tools to clean jets, fuel passages, or air bleeds. Clean all jets and valves separately to avoid accidental interchange.

Check all parts for wear or damage. If wear or damage is found, replace the defective parts. Especially check the following:

1. Check the float needle and seat for wear. If wear is found, replace the complete assembly.
2. Check the float hinge pin for wear

a. Choke valve relief spring
b. Choke lever
c. Choke valve spring
d. Choke level adapter
e. Adapter gasket
f. Choke wire support
g. Choke valve
h. Plug
i. Economizer jet
j. Air bleeder
k. Air horn
l. Main passage plug
m. Plug gasket
n. Strainer
o. Power piston stopper
p. Power piston spring
q. Fitting
r. Needle valve seat gasket
s. Air horn gasket
t. Float pin
u. Needle valve seat
v. Power piston
w. Needle valve
x. Needle valve spring
y. Needle valve push pin
z. Float
aa. Lifter rod
ab. Slow jet
ac. Primary main jet
ad. Gasket
ae. Pump jet screw
af. Pump jet gasket
ag. Pump jet
ah. Spare jet
ai. Power valve
aj. Power jet
ak. Pump discharge weight
al. Level gauge retainer
am. Level gauge glass
an. Level gauge gasket
ao. Primary small venturi
ap. Main body
aq. Discharge check valve
ar. Plug gasket
as. Pump connecting link
at. Choke shaft
au. Plunger washer
av. Fast idle connector
aw. Secondary main jet
ax. Gasket
ay. Gasket
az. Gasket
ba. Pump damping spring
bb. Gasket
bc. Secondary small venturi
bd. Secondary main venturi
be. High speed valve stop lever
bf. Fast idle cam
bg. High speed valve stop
bh. High speed shaft
bi. High speed valve shaft lever
bj. Stop lever attaching screw
bk. High speed valve stop lever spring
bl. Fast idle attaching screw
bm. Throttle adjusting screw
bo. Secondary throttle back spring
bp. Secondary throttle lever
bq. Throttle shaft link
br. Fast idle adjusting screw
bs. Fast idle adjusting screw spring
bt. Primary throttle shaft arm
bu. Throttle lever
bw. Secondary throttle valve
bx. High speed valve
by. Primary throttle valve
bz. Flange
ca. Body to flange gasket
cb. Secondary throttle valve shaft
cd. Idle port plug
ce. Idle adjusting screw spring
cf. Primary throttle valve shaft
cg. Idle adjusting screw

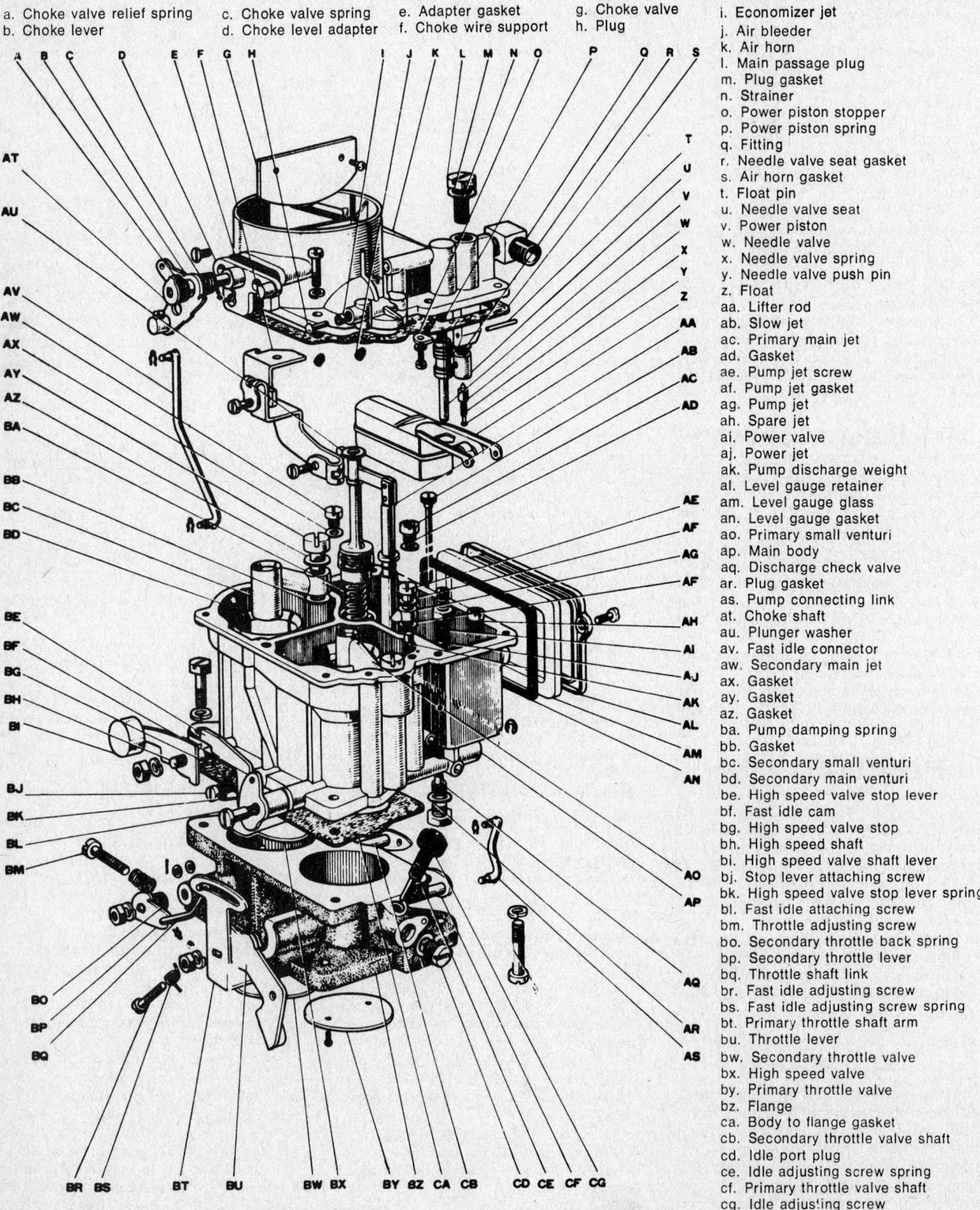

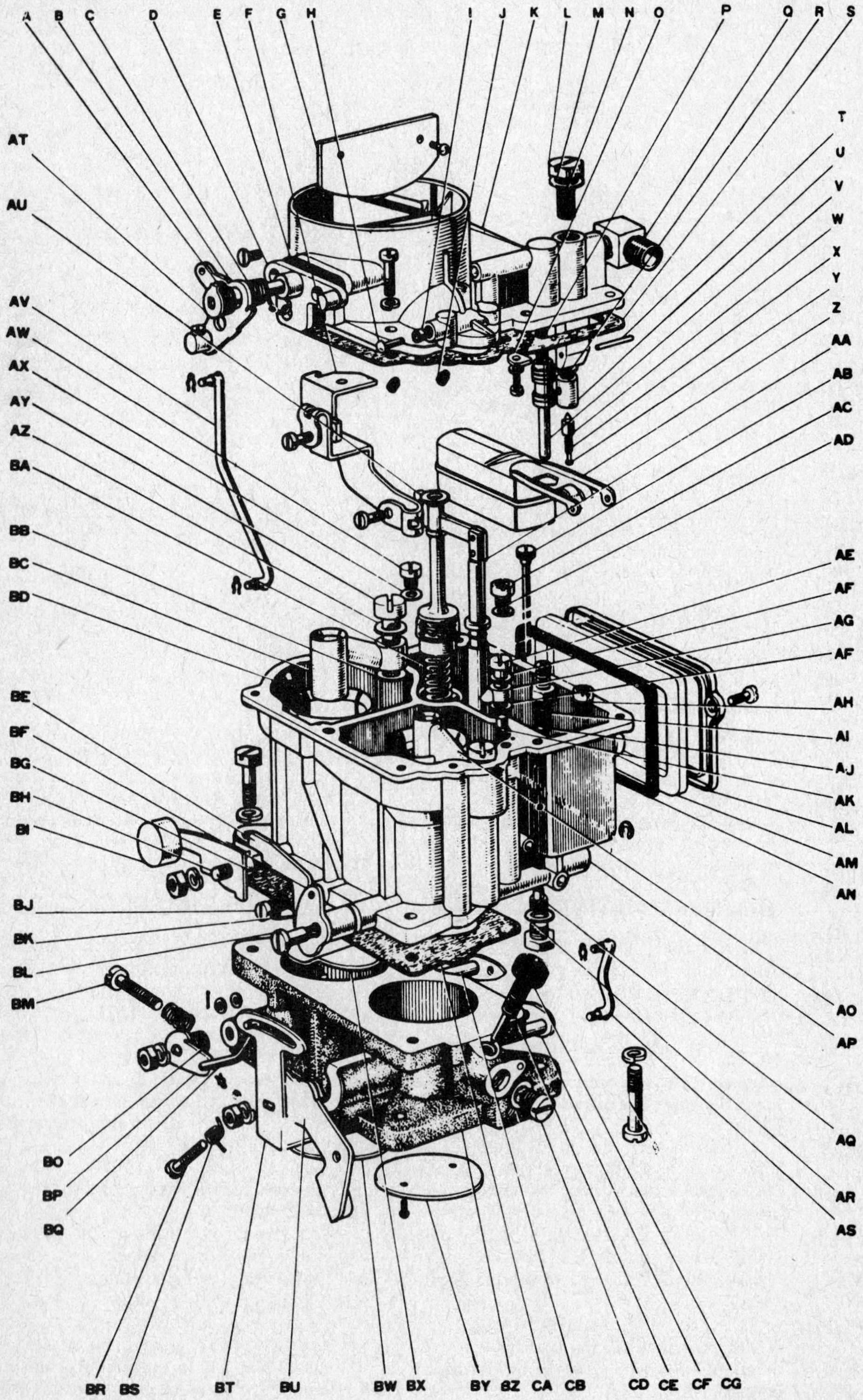

F engine—2 bbl

and the float(s) for dents or distortion. Replace the float if fuel has leaked into it.

3. Check the throttle and choke shaft bores for wear or an out-of-round condition. Damage or wear to the throttle arm, shaft, or shaft bore will often require replacement of the throttle body. These parts require a close tolerance of fit; wear may allow air leakage, which could affect starting and idling.

NOTE: Throttle shafts and bushings are not included in overhaul kits. They can be purchased separately.

4. Inspect the idle mixture adjusting needles for burrs or grooves. Any such condition requires replacement of the needle, since you will not be able to obtain a satisfactory idle.

5. Test the accelerator pump check valves. They should pass air one way but not the other. Test for proper seating by blowing and sucking on the valve. Replace the valve if necessary. If the valve is satisfactory, wash the valve again to remove breath moisture.

6. Check the bowl cover for warped surfaces with a straightedge.

7. Closely inspect the valves and seats for wear and damage, replacing as necessary.

8. After the carburetor is assembled,

a. Thermostat bimetal
b. Coil housing gasket
c. Fast idle cam follower
d. Coil housing plate
e. Piston connector
f. Choke shaft
g. Fast idle cam
h. Fast idle cam spring
i. Thermostat case
k. Pump arm spring
j. Thermostat case gasket
l. Choke valve
m. Pump lever
n. Pump arm securing screw
o. Pump connecting link
p. Air horn
q. Power piston stopper
r. Power piston spring
s. Air horn gasket
t. Union nipple
u. Plug with strainer
v. Needle valve seat
w. Needle valve
x. Needle valve spring
y. Needle valve push pin
z. Float
aa. Power piston
ab. Slow circuit plug
ac. Float lever pin
ad. Slow jet
ae. Power valve
af. Pump plunger
ag. Plunger guide
ah. Power jet
ai. O-ring
aj. Level gauge clamp
ak. Level gauge glass
al. Gasket
am. Main passage plug
an. Pump damping spring
ao. Primary main jet
ap. Secondary main jet
aq. Primary air bleeder
ar. Body
as. Discharge check valve
at. Main passage plug
au. Idle adjusting screw
av. Primary throttle shaft
aw. Secondary throttle shaft
ax. Spring
ay. Main passage plug
az. Thermostatic valve
ba. Primary throttle valve
bb. Flange
bc. Secondary throttle valve
bd. Fast idle adjusting lever
be. Retaining ring
bf. Fast idle adjusting bolt
bg. Fast idle lever
bh. Spring
bi. Throttle lever collar
bj. High speed valve
bk. Primary throttle arm
bl. Spring
bm. Thottle adjusting screw
bn. Secondary throttle back spring
bo. Throttle shaft link
bp. Secondary throttle lever
bq. Gasket
br. High speed valve stop lever
bs. Retaining ring
bt. High speed valve stop lever spring
bu. Stop lever securing screw
bv. High speed valve shaft
bw. High speed valve stopper
bx. High speed valve weight
bz. Weight
ca. Pump jet
cb. Secondary small venturi
cc. Pump jet screw
cd. Pump connecting rod
ce. Connecting rod
cf. Vacuum piston
cg. Piston pin
ch. Sliding rod
ci. Primary main air bleeder
cj. Coil housing

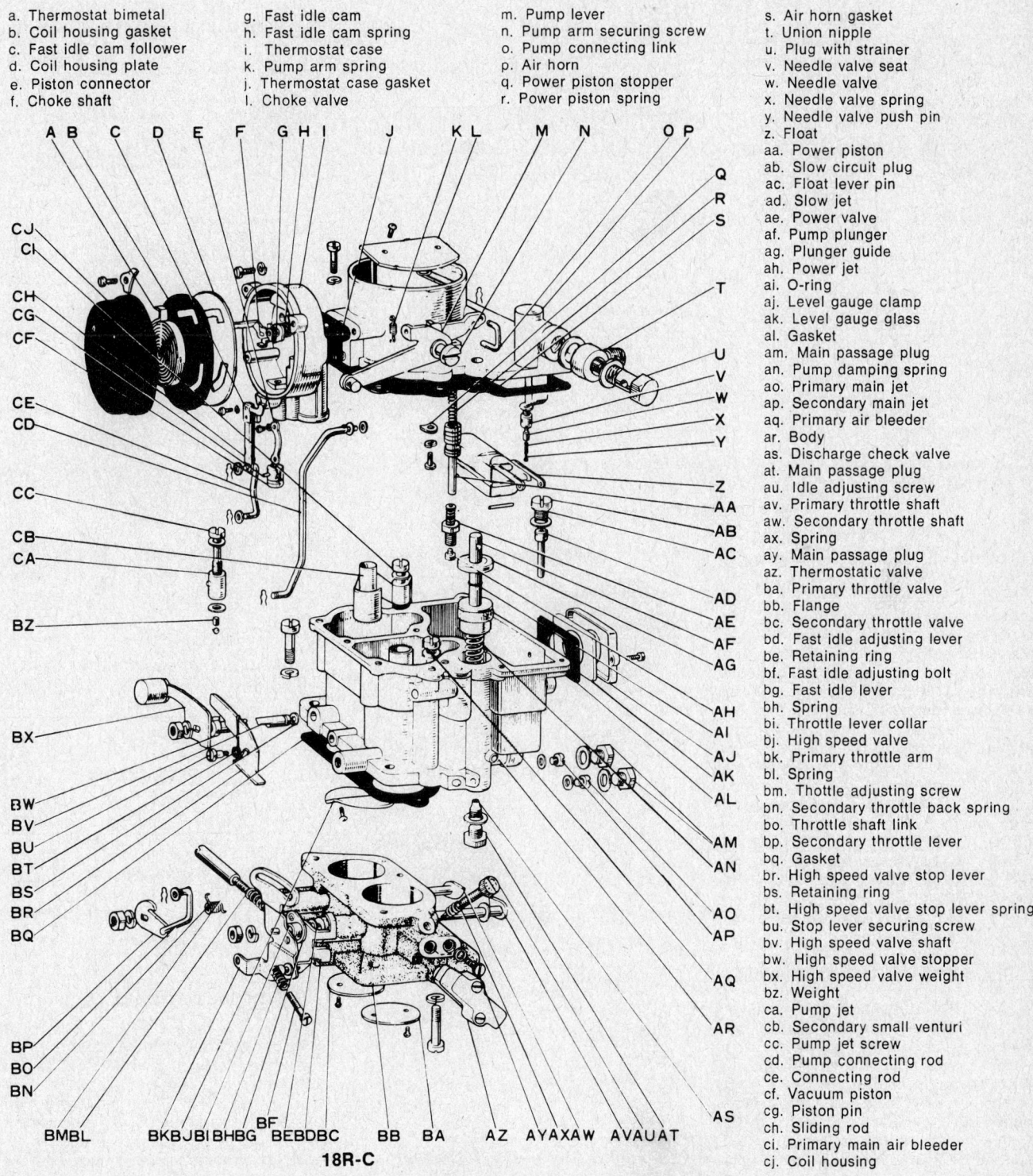

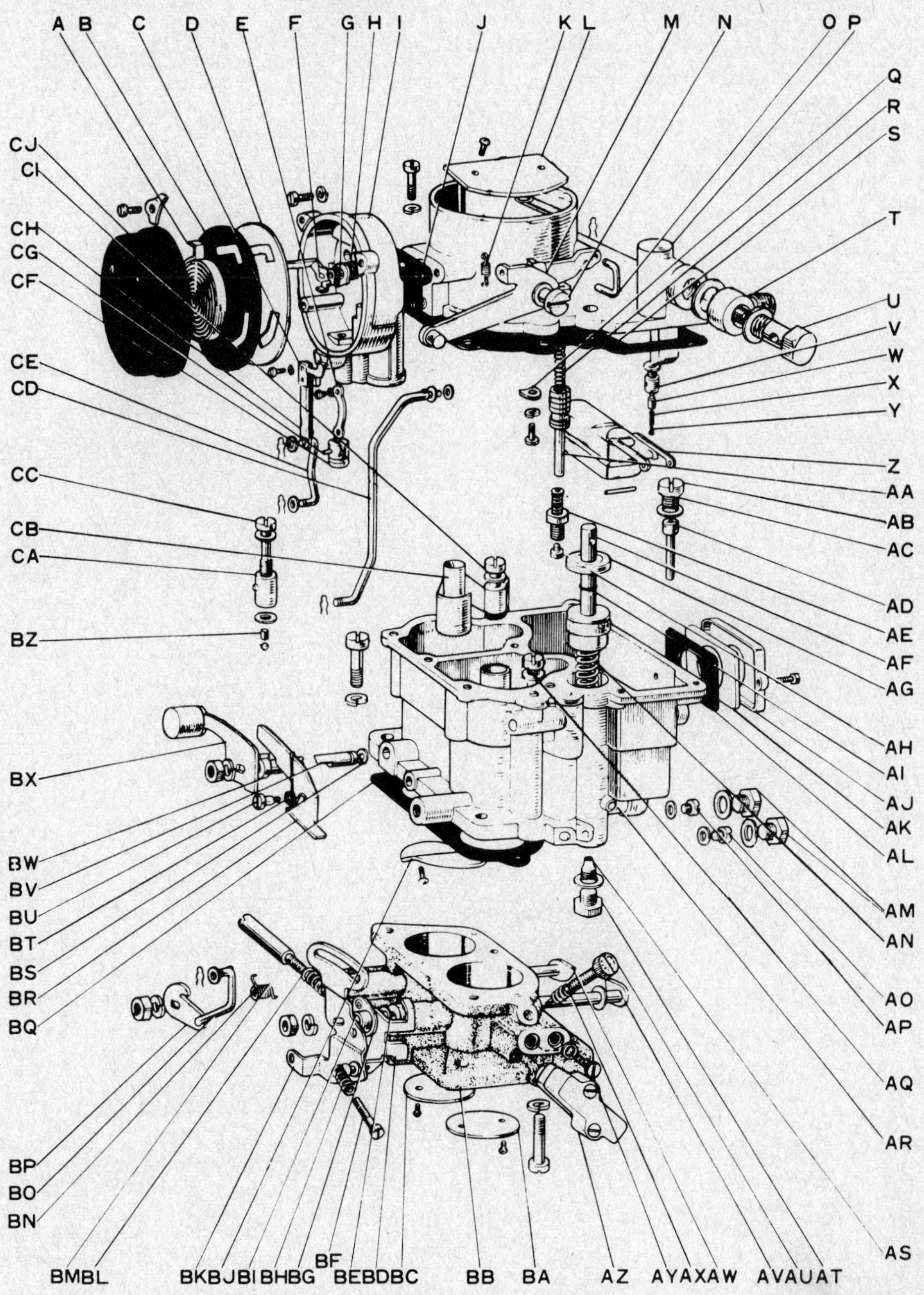

18R-C

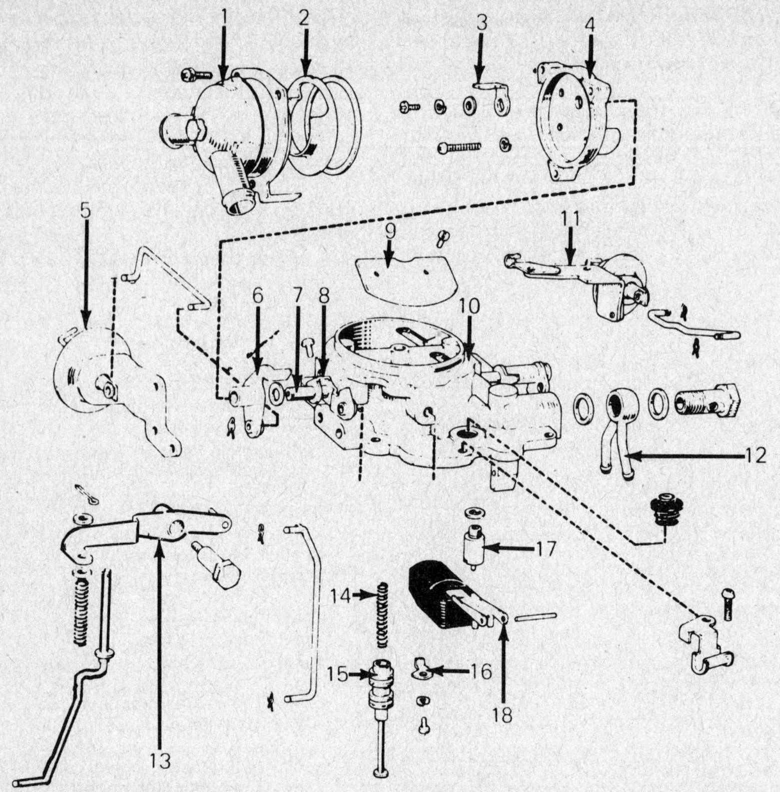

1. Choke coil water housing
2. Choke housing plate
3. Choke lever
4. Choke housing body
5. Choke breaker
6. Relief lever
7. Choke shaft
8. Connecting lever
9. Choke valve
10. Air horn
11. Choke opener
12. Union
13. Pump arm
14. Spring
15. Power piston
16. Piston retainer
17. Needle valve set
18. Float

Air horn assembly—20R

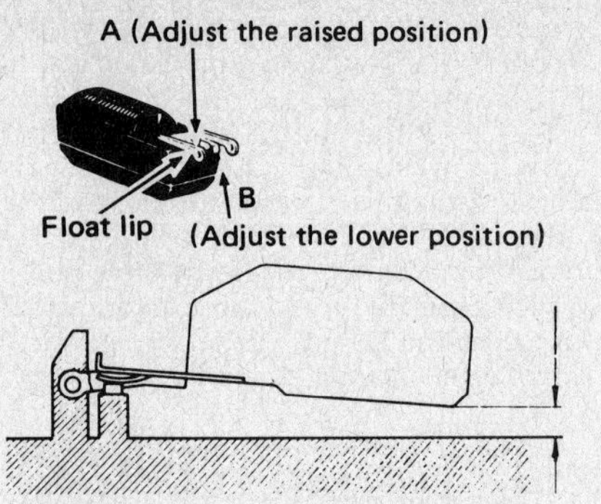

Measuring float level raised position

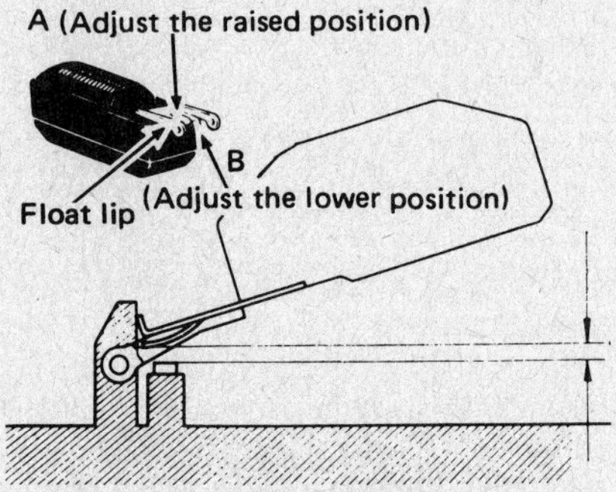

Measuring float level lowered position

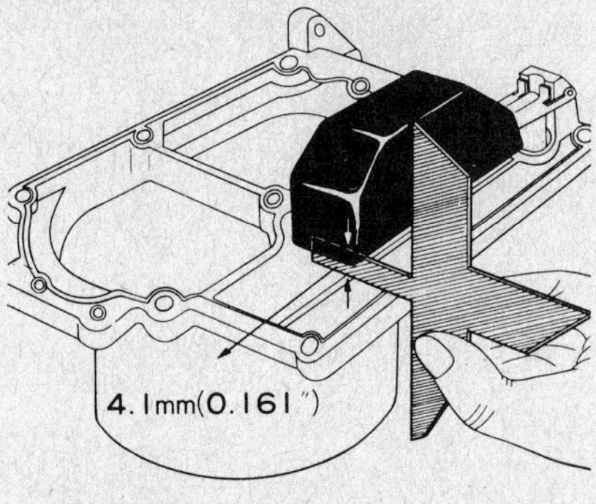

Adjusting F engine float—raised position

check the choke valve for freedom of operation.

Carburetor overhaul kits are recommended for each overhaul. These kits contain all gaskets and new parts to replace those that deteriorate most rapidly. Failure to replace all parts supplied with the kit (especially gaskets) can result in poor performance later.

After cleaning and checking all components, reassemble the carburetor, using new parts and referring to the exploded view. When reassembling, make sure that all screws and jets are tight in their seats, but do not overtighten, as the tips will be distorted. Tighten all screws gradually, in rotation. Do not tighten needle valves into their seats; uneven jetting will result. Always use new gaskets. Be sure to adjust the float level when reassembling.

FLOAT LEVEL ADJUSTMENT

Float level adjustments are unnecessary on models equipped with a carburetor sight glass, if the fuel level falls within the lines or aligns with the dot when the engine is running.

There are two float level adjustments which may be made on Toyota carburetors. One is with the air horn inverted, so that the float is in a fully *raised* position; the other is with the air horn in an upright position, so that the float falls to the bottom of its travel.

The float level is either measured with a special carburetor float level gauge, which comes with a rebuilding kit, or with a standard wire gauge. For the

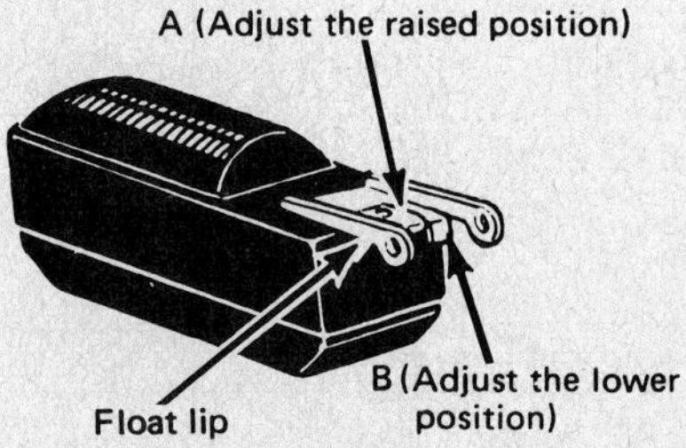

Float level adjusting tabs

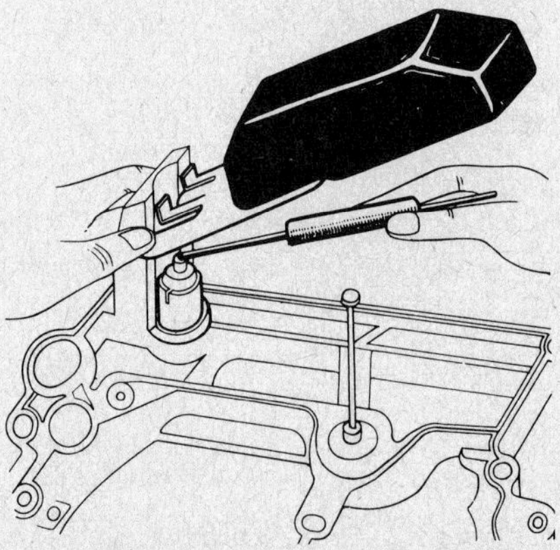

F engine float—lowered position

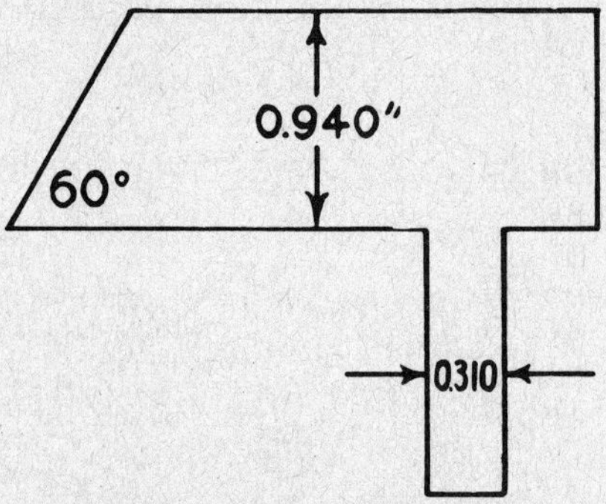

F engine carburetor gauge

FLOAT LEVEL ADJUSTMENT

Engine	FLOAT RAISED Gauge Type	FLOAT RAISED Measure Distance Between	Gap (in.)	FLOAT LOWERED Gauge Type	FLOAT LOWERED Measure Distance Between	Gap (in.)
18R-C	Special	Float and air horn	0.200	Wire	Needle valve bushing pin and float tab	0.039
20R	Special	Float end and air horn	0.197	Special	Needle valve bushing pin and float tab	0.039
F	Special	Float end and air horn gasket surface	0.161	Special	Float end and air horn gasket surface	0.039
2F	Special	Float end and air horn	0.200	Special	Float end and air horn	0.040

FAST IDLE ADJUSTMENT

Engine	Throttle Valve to Bore Clearance (in.)	Primary Throttle Angle (deg.)	To Adjust Fast Idle
18R-C	0.041	13—from closed	Turn the fast idle adjusting screw
20R	0.047	—	Turn the fast idle adjusting screw
F	0.039	12—from closed	Bend the fast idle lever
2F	0.051	30—from closed	Bend the fast idle lever

— Not Available

proper type of gauge, as well as the points to be measured, see the chart at the end of this section.

NOTE: Gap specifications are also given so that a float level gauge may be fabricated.

Adjust the float level by bending the tabs on the float levers, either upper or lower, as required.

FAST IDLE ADJUSTMENT

Off Vehicle-All Years

The fast idle adjustment is performed with the choke valve fully *closed,* except on 18R-C engines which should have the choke valve fully *opened.*

Adjust the gap between the throttle wire gauge to determine the gap.

The chart below also gives the proper valve edge and bore to the specifications, where given, in the chart below. Use a primary throttle valve opening angle, where necessary, and the proper means of fast idle adjustment.

NOTE: The throttle valve opening angle is measured with a gauge supplied in the carburetor rebuilding kit. It is also possible to make one out of cardboard by using a protractor to obtain the correct angle.

On Vehicle—1975–80

NOTE: Disconnect the EGR valve vacuum line on 20R engines.

1. Adjust the idle speed/mixture. Leave the tachometer connected.
2. Remove the top of the air cleaner.
3. Open the throttle valve slightly and close the choke valve. Hold the choke valve with your finger and close the throttle valve. The choke valve is now fully closed.
4. Without depressing the accelerator pedal, start the engine.
5. Check the engine fast idle speed against the chart below.
6. If the reading on the tachometer is not within specifications, adjust the fast idle speed by turning the fast idle screw.
7. Disconnect the tachometer, install the air cleaner cover, and connect the EGR valve vacuum line if it was disconnected.

FAST IDLE SPEED—1975–80

20R—2,400 rpm
2F—1,800 rpm

AUTOMATIC CHOKE ADJUSTMENT

NOTE: The automatic choke should be adjusted with the carburetor installed and the engine running. On 20R engines do no loosen the center bolt; the coolant will leak out.

1. Check to see that the choke valve will close from fully opened when the coil housing is turned counterclockwise.
2. Align the mark on the coil housing with the center line on the thermostat

When adjusting automatic choke, align body scale center line (1), V notch of plate (2) and coil housing line (3) and tighten the three screws

case. In this position, the choke valve should be fully closed when the ambient temperature is 77°F.

3. If necessary, adjust the mixture by turning the coil housing. If the mixture is too *rich,* rotate the housing *clockwise;* if the *lean,* rotate the housing *counterclockwise.*

NOTE: Each graduation on the thermostat case is equivalent to 9°F.

CHOKE BREAK ADJUSTMENT

20R Engine

1. Push the rod which comes out of

CHOKE UNLOADER ADJUSTMENT

Engine	Throttle Valve Fully Closed (deg)	Choke Valve Angle (deg) From Closed to Fully Open (deg)	Throttle Valve Open (Total) (deg)	To Adjust Bend
1973-75				
18R-C	—	27	47	Fast idle cam follower or choke shaft tip
20R	30	—	50	Fast idle lever
1976-80				
20R	—	50	90	Fast idle lever, follower or choke shaft tab
2F	—	38	90	Fast idle lever, follower or choke shaft tab

— Not Available

the upper (choke break) diaphragm so that the choke valve opens.

2. Measure the choke valve opening angle. It should be 40° (38° 1976–80).

3. Adjust the angle, if necessary, by bending the relief lever link.

INITIAL IDLE MIXTURE SCREW ADJUSTMENT

When assembling the carburetor, turn the idle mixture screw the number of turns specified below. After the carburetor is installed, perform the appropriate idle speed/mixture adjustment as outlined above.

18R-C engine–2½ turns from fully closed

20R engine—1¾ turns from fully closed

F/2F engines–1¼–1½ turns out

CAUTION: Seat the idle mixture screw lightly; overtightening will damage its tip.

UNLOADER ADJUSTMENT

Make the unloader adjustment with the primary valve fully opened. The total angle of choke valve opening, in the chart, is measured with either a special gauge, supplied in the carburetor rebuilding kit, or a gauge of the proper angle fabricated from cardboard.

CLUTCH

The clutch is a single-plate, dry disc type. Some early models, and all Land Cruisers, use a coil-spring pressure plate. Later models use a diaphragm-spring pressure plate. Clutch release bearings are sealed ball bearings units which need no lubrication and should never be washed in any kind of solvent. All clutches are hydraulically operated.

FREE-PLAY ADJUSTMENT

1. Adjust the clearance between the master cylinder piston and the pushrod to the specifications given in the chart below. Loosen the pushrod locknut and rotate the pushrod while depressing the clutch pedal lightly with your finger.

2. Tighten the locknut when finished the adjustment.

3. Adjust the release cylinder free-

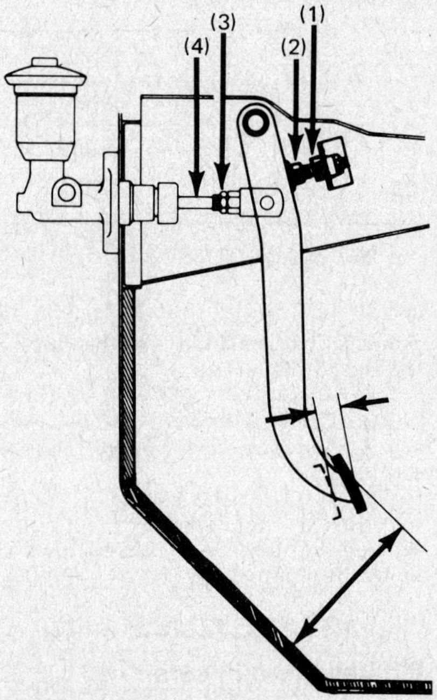

Adjusting Pick-up clutch pedal: (1) lock nut, (2) stop bolt, (3) lock nut, (4) push rod

CLUTCH PEDAL FREE-PLAY ADJUSTMENTS

Model	Master Cylinder Piston to Pushrod Clearance	Release Cylinder to Release Fork Free-Play (in.)	Pedal Free-Play (in.)
Pick-up (all)	Adjust by feel	0.08-0.145①④	1.30②⑤
Land Cruiser—2 dr.	③	0.12-0.16	1.00
Land Cruiser—Station Wagon	③	0.12-0.16	1.38

① 1978-80: not adjustable
② 1978-80: 0.2-0.6 in.
③ Adjust so that pushrod pin will fit through clevis
④ 4X4 Pick-up: 0.08-0.12 in.
⑤ 4X4 Pick-up: 1.0-1.8 in.

play by loosening the release cylinder pushrod locknut and rotating the pushrod until the specification in the chart is obtained.

4. Measure the clutch pedal free-play after performing the above adjustments. If it fails to fall within specifications, repeat steps 1–3 until it does.

Clutch Master Cylinder

REMOVAL AND INSTALLATION

CAUTION: Do not spill fluid on the painted surfaces of the vehicle.

1. Remove the clevis pin.
2. Detach the hydraulic line from the tube.
3. Unfasten the bolts which secure the master cylinder to the firewall. Withdraw the assembly.

Installation is performed in the reverse order of removal. Bleed the system as detailed below. Adjust the clutch pedal height and free-play.

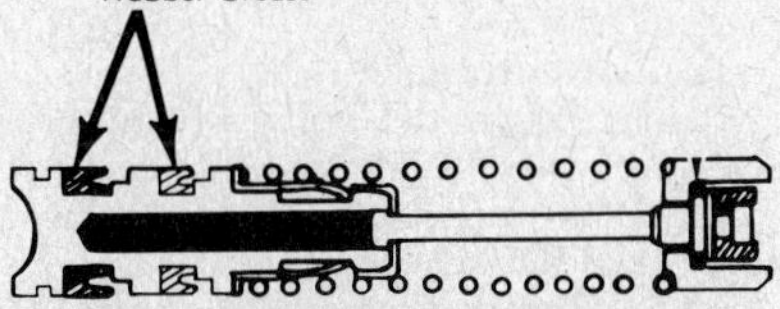

Pick-up master cylinder piston assembly—note direction of rubber cylinder cups marked with arrows

OVERHAUL

1. Remove master cylinder.
2. Remove the reservoir.
3. Disengage the snap ring and take out the pushrod and piston.
4. Inspect all parts for pitting and wear and replace as necessary.
5. Apply a grease compatible with rubber to the piston seals.
6. Install the push rod and piston and secure with a snap ring and washer.
7. Install the reservoir. Torque to 22 ft lb.
8. Install master cylinder.
9. Bleed the system.

Clutch Release Cylinder

REMOVAL AND INSTALLATION

1. Plug the master cylinder cap to prevent fluid leakage.
2. Raise the front of the vehicle and support it with jackstands.
3. Remove the gravel shield, if necessary, to gain access to the release cylinder.
4. Unfasten the clutch fork return spring at the fork.
5. Detach the hydraulic line from the release cylinder.
6. Screw the release cylinder push rod in.
7. Loosen and remove the securing nuts from the release cylinder. Remove the cylinder.

Installation is performed in the reverse order of removal. Adjust the release fork-to-release cylinder free-play and bleed the hydraulic system, after installation is completed.

OVERHAUL

1. Remove the release cylinder.
2. Remove the pushrod, boot, piston and cup.
3. Inspect all parts for pitting and wear. Replace as necessary.
4. Coat piston seal and cup with a grease compatible with rubber.
5. Install all parts.
6. Install cylinder.
7. Bleed the system.

CLUTCH REMOVAL AND INSTALLATION

CAUTION: Do not allow grease or oil to get on any of the disc, pressure plate, or flywheel surfaces.

1. Remove the transmission from the vehicle as detailed below.
2. Remove the clutch cover and disc from the bellhousing.
3. Unfasten the release fork bearing clips. Withdraw the release bearing hub, complete with the release bearing.
4. Remove the tension spring from the clutch linkage.
5. Remove the release fork and support.
6. Punch matchmarks on the clutch cover and the pressure plate so the pressure plate can be returned to its original position during installation.
7. Slowly unfasten the screws which attach the retracting springs.

NOTE: If the screws are released too fast, the clutch assembly will fly apart, causing possible injury or loss of parts.

8. Separate the pressure plate from the clutch cover/spring assembly.

Inspect the parts for wear or deterioration. Replace parts as required.

Installation is performed in the reverse order of removal. Several points should be noted, however:

1. Be sure to align the matchmarks on the clutch cover and pressure plate which were made during disassembly.
2. Apply a thin coating of multipurpose grease to the release bearing hub and release fork contact points. Also, pack the groove inside the clutch hub with multipurpose grease.
3. Center the clutch disc by using a clutch pilot tool or an old input shaft. Insert the pilot into the end of the input shaft front bearing and bolt the clutch to the flywheel.

NOTE: Bolt the clutch assembly to the flywheel in two or three stages.

4. Adjust the clutch as outlined following

MANUAL TRANSMISSION

SHIFT LINKAGE ADJUSTMENT

Land Cruiser—Column Shift

Shift lever adjustment:

The only adjustments which may be performed on the column shift linkages are for the length of the column-to-transmission rods. Adjust these so that the transmission operates smoothly.

FLOOR SHIFTER ADJUSTMENT

All Toyota models equipped with a floor shifter have internally-mounted shift linkages. On older models, the linkage is contained in the side cover which is bolted on the transmission case.

No external adjustment is needed or possible.

REMOVAL AND INSTALLATION

Pick-up

1. Unfasten the cable from the positive battery terminal.
2. Remove the accelerator torque rod from its valve cover mounting.
3. Separate the downpipe from the flange and remove the flange. Remove the exhaust pipe bracket. Raise the vehi-

PEDAL HEIGHT SPECIFICATIONS

Model	Height (in.)	Measure Between
Pick-up (all)	6.3	Pedal and toe-board
Land Cruiser 2-dr.	7.8①	Pedal pad and firewall
Station Wagon	6.7②	Pedal pad and firewall

① 1979-80: 8.5 in. ② 1979-80: 7.3 in.

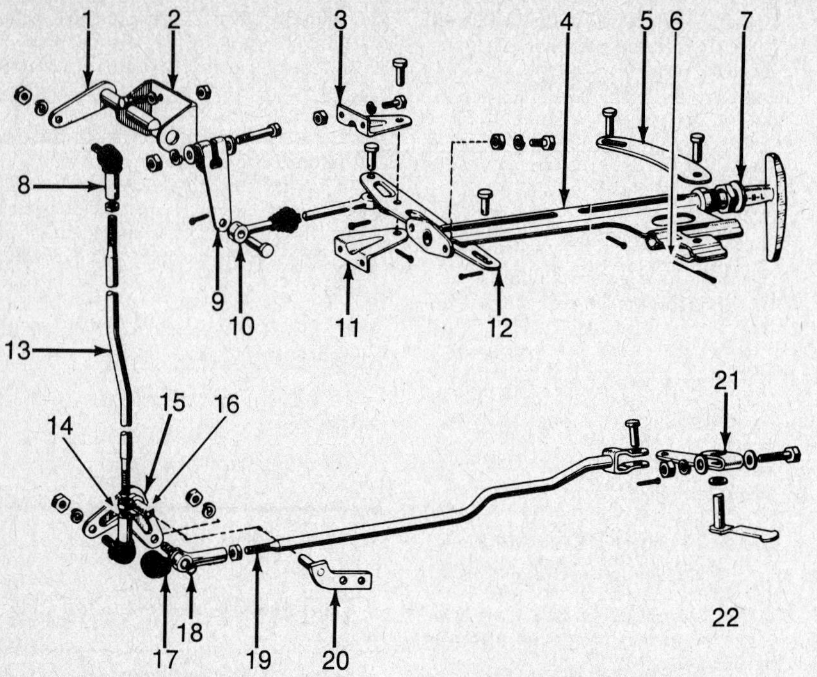

1. High/low shift link
2. Shift link bracket
3. Bracket
4. Shift lever housing
5. Lever
6. Cotter pin
7. Transfer range selector lever
8. Connecting rod end—upper
9. Shift link lever
10. High/low shift intermediate rod
11. Bracket
12. Front drive engagement lever
13. High/low connecting rod
14. Connecting rod end—lower
15. Bell crank
16. Bushing
17. Dust cap
18. Snap ring
19. High/low shift rod
20. Support
21. Transfer case high/low shift lever
22. Lever

Land Cruiser transfer case shift linkage—station wagon

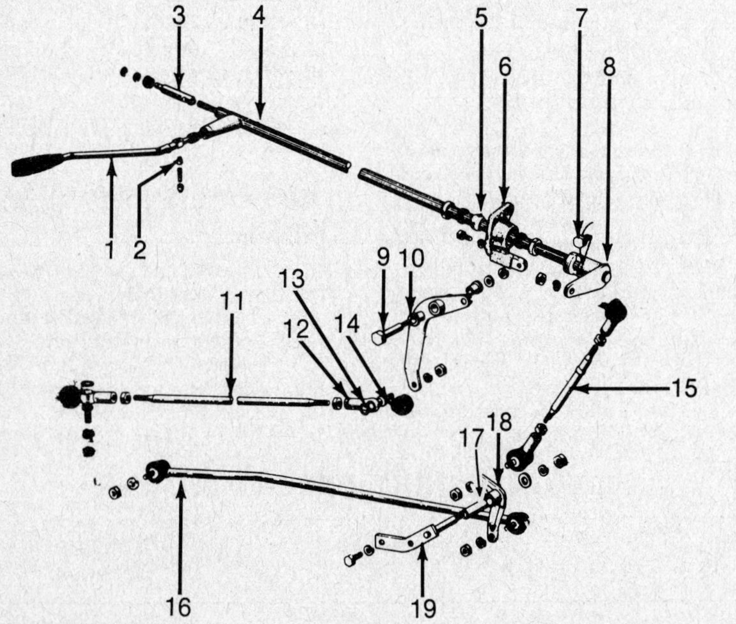

1. Gear selector lever
2. Pin
3. Control shaft—upper end
4. Control shaft
5. Control shaft bushing
6. Control shaft bracket
7. Lock bolt
8. Control shaft lever
9. Selector shaft
10. Bushing
11. Gear selecting rod
12. Connecting rod end
13. Snap ring
14. Dust cap
15. Intermediate
16. Gear shifting rod
17. Bushing
18. Bell crank
19. Support

Land Cruiser station wagon column-shift linkage

cle with a jack and support it with jackstands.

4. Remove the parking brake equalizer support bracket.
5. Disconnect the speedometer cable and back-up lamp wiring harness from the transmission.
6. Remove the control shaft lever retainer.
7. Remove the clutch release cylinder from the transmission and set it up, out of the way.

NOTE: Do not disconnect the hydraulic line from the release cylinder.

8. Drain the transmission oil.
9. Remove the driveshaft.

NOTE: To prevent oil from draining out of the transmission, install a spare U-joint or, if none is available, cover the opening with a plastic bag secured by a rubber band.

10. Support the transmission with a jack.
11. Unfasten the rear engine mounts and remove the engine rear supporting crossmember.
12. Lower the jack.
13. Unfasten the bolts which secure the clutch housing to the cylinder block.
14. Remove the transmission toward the rear of the vehicle.

Installation is the reverse of removal, but observe the following:

Apply a light coating of multipurpose grease to the input shaft end, input shaft spline, clutch release bearing, and driveshaft end.

After installation:

1. Fill the transmission and cooling system.
2. Adjust the clutch as detailed below.
3. Check to see that the back-up lamps function when Reverse is selected.

4x4 Pick-up

1. Disconnect positive battery terminal.
2. Drain radiator and remove top hose.
3. Remove console boot or floor mat. Remove shift lever boot retainer and, using a pair of channel locks, remove the shift lever assembly by pressing down on the cap and turning it at the same time. Remove the four wheel drive shaft lever boot retainer. Unfasten the small dust boot and pull up out of the way. Using a pair of needle nose pliers remove the snap ring and remove shift lever.
4. Disconnect the accelerator link at the carburetor.
5. Jack up the vehicle placing jack stands under front and rear axle shafts.
6. If the transmission and transfer cases are to be overhauled, drain the oil from both using the drain plugs at the bottom of each case. Remove gravel shields.

7. Unbolt exhaust down-pipe from manifold.
8. Disconnect the starter wiring and remove starter along with clutch line bracket.

NOTE: Do not unfasten clutch fluid tube from the master or slave cylinders. It is not necessary.

9. Remove front and rear drive shafts after matchmarking all yokes for reassembly.
10. Disconnect the speedometer cable, back up light switch and four wheel drive indicator switch.
11. Remove exhaust pipe clamp on bell housing.
12. Remove clutch slave cylinder and hang it out of the way.

NOTE: Do not remove the clutch fluid pipe.

13. Support the transmission case on a jack and remove the rear support crossmember.
14. Place a block of wood on a support stand under the engine oil pan so that the engine comes to rest on the wood when transmission is lowered.

NOTE: It is important to gauge the distance between the oil pan and the jack accurately to prevent engine components from damage when the transmission is lowered.

15. Loosen but do not remove the bellhousing-to-engine bolts. Lower the transmission slightly and remove the bellhousing bolts. The transmission must be drawn toward the rear of the truck for removal.

CAUTION: The transmission/transfer case will be very heavy. It would be wise to enlist the aid of an assistant when removing it.

Installation is the reverse of removal with the following notes:

Apply a light coat of multipurpose grease to the transmission spline, clutch release bearing and the socket balls of the shift lever and four wheel drive shift lever. Be sure to align all drive shaft yokes with the correct matchmarks. Tighten the transmission-to-engine mounting bolts to 37-57 ft-lb. Refill transmission, transfer case and radiator with fluid and adjust the clutch if necessary.

Land Cruiser

1. Raise the vehicle and support it with jackstands.
2. Remove the transmission skid plate.
3. Drain the transmission and transfer case.
4. On two-door models only:
   a. Remove the passenger seat.
   b. Remove the fuel tank (only if it is under the passenger seat).
5. Remove the transmission cover.
6. Detach the parking brake cable from the end of the parking brake lever.
7. Disconnect the speedometer cable from the transmission.
8. Loosen the clamps and disconnect the hoses from the transfer case (vacuum operated transfer case only).
9. On models equipped with a column shift, remove the rod pins and cotter pins, then detach the intermediate rods.
10. Disconnect the high and low shift rods.
11. Disconnect the wires from the front drive indicator light switch.
12. Raise the transmission with a jack.
13. Disconnect both front and rear U-joint yokes from the transfer case.
14. Remove the clutch housing skid plate.
15. Unfasten the bolts which attach the transmission to the transfer case.
16. Slide the transmission toward the rear of the vehicle so that the input shaft clears the clutch housing.
17. Remove the transmission transfer case assembly from under the vehicle, complete with the parking brake assembly.

Installation is the reverse of removal. Tighten the transmission mounting bolts to 52-57 ft lbs. Refill the transmission, and check the clutch linkage and shift linkage operation, after installation.

OVERHAUL

Pick-up, 4x4 Pick-up—Four Speed

NOTE: See section below for removing the transfer case from the transmission on 4x4 Pick-up.

1. Remove speedometer drive unit in the extension housing (Except 4x4 Pick-up).
2. Some models have a drive shaft flange and crimped nut at the end of the extension housing. Remove them. Unbolt and remove the extension housing.
3. Unbolt and remove the case cover assembly.
4. Remove the release fork and bearing. Remove the front bearing retainer inside the bell housing.
5. Unbolt and remove the clutch bell housing.
6. Using a brass rod, gently tap the reverse idler gear shaft toward the rear and remove it. Remove the reverse idler gear.
7. Check the counter gear thrust clearance with a feeler gauge, record the reading, then pick the proper adjusting gear side thrust washer to obtain the specified clearance of 0.004-0.010 in. (1973-78); 0.004-0.008 in. (1979-80).
8. Using a dummy shaft, drive out the countershaft and the woodruff key to the rear. Allow the counter gear to drop into the case.
9. Shift the hub sleeve toward the top speed and draw out the output shaft. Be careful not to lose the synchronizer ring.
10. Turn the input shaft assembly so that one of the flat sides of the synchronizer engagement teeth on the input shaft clears the counter gear and remove the input shaft.
11. Remove the counter gear along with its thrust washers.
12. Secure the output shaft in a softjawed vise. Remove the spacer and snap ring at the rear end of the output shaft if so equipped. Remove the snap ring behind the speedometer drive gear and remove the gear along with its woodruff key and second snap ring.
13. Check and record the following

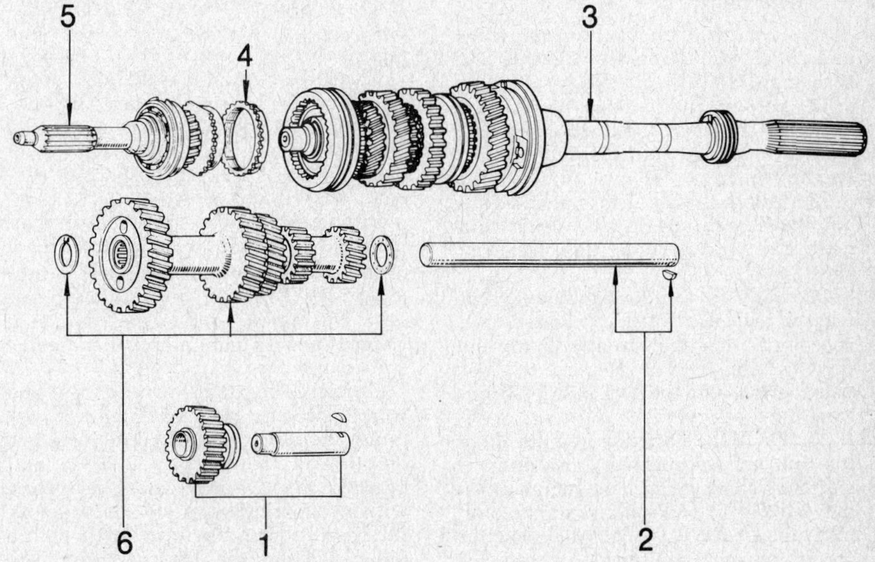

1. Reverse idler gear shaft and gear
2. Counter gear shaft and key
3. Output shaft assembly
4. Synchronizer ring
5. Input shaft assembly
6. Counter gear and thrust washers

Pick-up 4 speed transmission components

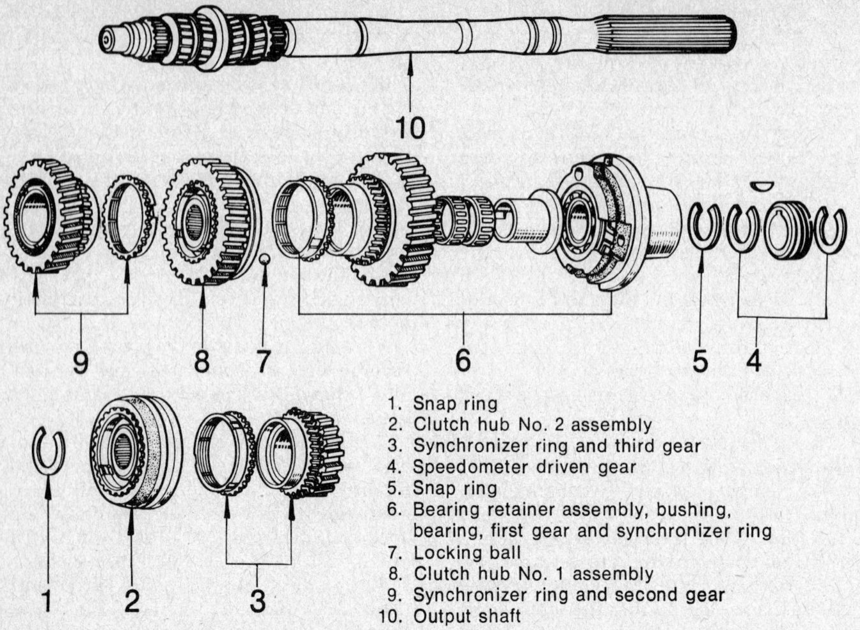

1. Snap ring
2. Clutch hub No. 2 assembly
3. Synchronizer ring and third gear
4. Speedometer driven gear
5. Snap ring
6. Bearing retainer assembly, bushing, bearing, first gear and synchronizer ring
7. Locking ball
8. Clutch hub No. 1 assembly
9. Synchronizer ring and second gear
10. Output shaft

Pick-up 4 speed output shaft components

clearances: first gear thrust clearance, second gear thrust clearance, third gear thrust clearance and clearance between snap ring and clutch hub.

14. Remove the snap ring holding the clutch hub in place and remove clutch hub and third speed gear.

15. Remove the snap ring behind the rear bearing and press the bearing off the shaft with the first speed gear.

NOTE: Be careful not to lose the small locking ball.

CAUTION: Do not attempt to force the bearing and first speed gear off by striking on the end of the output shaft, or you may damage the shaft.

16. Remove the synchronizer rings and clutch hub along with reverse and second gears.

17. Loosen and remove the backup light switch. Move the third and fourth shift fork into the fourth speed position (to the front).

18. Using a long drift punch, drive out the slotted spring pin which connects the shift fork to the shift fork shaft.

19. Slide the shift fork shaft out of the rear of the case cover gradually, preventing the lock ball from popping out under spring tension. Remove the lock ball, spring and the two interlock pins from the case cover.

20. Drive the slotted spring pin out of the first and second shift fork and the shift fork shaft in the same manner. Remove the shift fork shaft and the shift fork, then remove the lock ball and the spring from the case cover.

21. Remove the shift arm pivot locknut. Remove the shift arm from the case cover. Drive out the slotted spring pin, and remove the reverse shift head and the shift fork shaft. Remove the lock ball and the spring. Remove the selector outer lever and the selector lever shaft.

22. Remove the shift lever shaft lockbolt, slide out the shift lever shaft from the case cover. Be careful to prevent the lock ball from popping out under spring tension.

23. Remove the sliding shift lever, lock ball and spring. Remove the wire and shift lever lockbolt.

24. Remove the shift and selector lever shaft toward the rear side of the case.

Wash all disassembled parts thoroughly. Check the transmission case, case cover and the extension housing for cracks; check the bearing fitting portions and gasket surfaces for burrs and nicks.

Check the output shaft splines, snapring grooves, bearing contact surfaces, bearing fitting portions and oil seal lip contact surface for wear, scores, or damage. Check the output shaft for runout. If the runout exceeds 0.0024 in. replace the shaft. To measure runout, place a dial indicator on the center point of the shaft and rotate the shaft slowly to read the maximum and minimum values. The runout equals the maximum value minus the minimum value divided by two.

Check the bearings for roughness and wear. Check for noise or damage by rotating the bearing after applying a few drops of oil. To remove the input shaft bearing, remove the shaft snap-ring with a snap-ring expander, then remove the bearing from the input shaft with a puller. Check the bushings and the bearing rollers for abnormal wear. If the wear is excessive, replace the bushings or the bearing rollers.

Inspect the extension housing bushing for wear or scoring. To replace the bushing, press the bushing out of the extension housing to the front side. To install, align the oil grooves of the bushing and the extension housing, and press the bushing into the housing. After installing the bushing, ream the bushing to fit the outer diameter of the universal joint sleeve yoke.

SPECIFIED GEAR BACKLASH

Input shaft gear to countergear: 0.004 in.

Third gear to countergear: 0.004–0.008 in.

Second gear to countergear: 0.004–0.008 in.

First gear to countergear: 0.004–0.008 in.

Reverse idler gear to countergear: 0.004–0.008 in.

Reverse idler gear to reverse gear: 0.004–0.008 in.

ASSEMBLY

Assembly is performed in the following order:

NOTE: Always install new gaskets, apply liquid sealer or gasket cement when assembling. Apply a thin coating of transmission lubricant on all parts before installation. Thrust clearances of gears and bearings are important factors for smooth shifting. Therefore, select and assemble thrust washers, snap rings and spacers of proper thickenss.

1. If you have disassembled the shifting hubs, reassemble them by:
   a. Install the two shifting springs in the inner hub with the spring ends 120° apart, so that the spring tension on each shifting key will be uniform.
   b. Place the three shifting keys into the clutch hub key slots and onto the shifting springs.

NOTE: The shifting keys for each hub are of different sizes. The keys with the shorter straddle length should be installed on the third and fourth gear synchronizer unit.

   c. Next, slide the hub sleeve onto the clutch hub. The clutch hubs and the hub sleeves of the gear are matched, and should be kept together as an assembly for smooth operation.

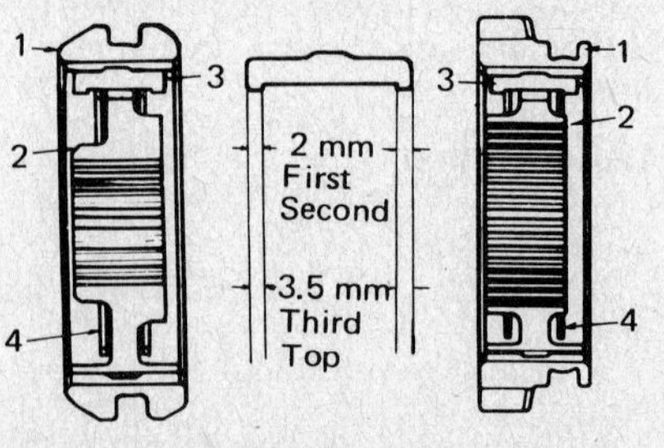

Cut-away view of clutch hubs in Pick-up 4 speed. Note direction of hubs inside sleeves

NOTE: The hubs fit into the clutch sleeves directionally, that is, they must fit into the clutch sleeves facing a certain way. Check the illustration to make sure you fit them correctly.

2. Install the second gear and its synchronizer ring on the output shaft. Install the first and second gear clutch hub behind second gear. Be sure to align the grooves in the synchronizer ring with the shift keys in the clutch hub. Place the small steel lock ball in its slot on the output shaft.
3. Oil and place the roller bearings on the bushing. Slide the bushing into the first speed gear with the collared end of the bushing butting the flat side of the gear. Fit the synchronizer ring on the other side of the gear and insert the gear on the output shaft. Take care to fit the notch in the bushing over the steel lock ball and align the notches in the synchronizer ring with those in the clutch hub.
4. Press the bearing retainer assembly on the output shaft. Check the gears for smooth rotation. Select a snap ring that will give 0–0.006 in. clearance on the output shaft and install. Five different snap ring thicknesses are available.
5. Check the second and first gear thrust clearances. The allowable limits are 0.004–0.010 in.
6. Install first speedometer snap ring and woodruff key on the output shaft and install speedometer gear and second snap ring.
7. Oil and install the third speed gear on the front of the output shaft. Fit its synchronizer ring and install the clutch hub, making sure to align the grooves in the synchronizer with the keys in the clutch hub.
8. Select a snap ring that will give an allowable thrust clearance of 0–0.006 in. between the hub end and the snap ring. Fit the snap ring.
9. Measure the thrust clearance of the third speed gear. Allowable limit for clearance is 0.004–0.010 in.
10. Assemble the counter gear by placing the spacers and greased roller bearings in both ends and fitting a tube or rod that is the exact length of the counter gear with the thrust washers on its ends and fit it into the counter gear.
11. Referring to the thrust measurement you made on the counter gear when disassembling, select thrust washers that give an allowable clearance of 0.004–0.010 in. (1973–78); 0.004–0.008 in. (1979–80). Adjust clearance by replacing the rear thrust washer.
12. Install the thrust washers on the ends of the counter gear. Rear thrust washers are identified by number 1,2,3, or 4 stamped on their outside face. Be sure to install the washers with their protruding groove facing out.
13. Place the counter gear assembly into the case with the notches in the thrust washers facing up and align the notches with the case grooves.
14. Allow the counter gear to drop down into the case. Do not replace the counter gear shaft at this point!
15. Install the input shaft in the same manner of removal, aligning one of the flat sides of the clutch hub with the large counter shaft gear and, using a brass drift, drive the input shaft bearing into the case, tapping it around the outer ball race.
16. Fit the synchronizer ring on the input shaft. Shift the clutch hub on the end of the output shaft forward.
17. Fit the output shaft into the case, making sure the slotted spring pin in the bearing retainer aligns with its groove in the case, and align the grooves in the synchronizer ring with the clutch hub keys.
18. Oil the counter shaft. Raise the counter gear assembly so that it aligns with the case holes and, making sure the thrust washers are in place, insert the counter gear shaft from the rear of the case with the woodruff key slot at the rear. The counter gear shaft will push the tube out of the case. Install the woodruff key and fit it into its slot in the case.
19. Install the reverse idler gear with its toothed end facing forward. Slide the reverse idler gear shaft in with its woodruff key slot end facing the rear. Install the woodruff key and tap the shaft in so that the key is in its seat in the case.
20. Install the front bearing retainer. Be sure to align the oil seal slot in the retainer with the oil hole in the case. Coat the bolt threads with sealer and tighten to 2.9–5.1 ft-lb. (1973–78); 5-6 ft-lb. (1979–80).
21. Install the clutch bell housing. Coat the bolt threads with sealer and tighten to 37–50 ft-lb.
22. Install clutch release fork assembly.
23. Apply grease to the extension housing rear oil seal and install the extension housing.

NOTE: Be careful not to damage the oil seal on the output shaft when assembling.

24. Coat the extension housing bolts with sealer and tighten to 22–32 ft-lb.
25. Oil the speedometer gear assembly and fasten to the extension housing.
26. To assemble the transmission case cover, install the shift arm pivot onto the reverse shift arm, and insert into the case.
27. Assemble the shift and selector lever shaft together with the shift and selector lever, and secure the bolt with a wire.
28. Insert the reverse shift fork shaft compression spring and lock ball into the case, and insert the fork shaft from the rear side, then secure the shift head with a new slotted spring pin.
29. Align the fork shaft positioning groove with the shift interlock pin groove.
30. Align the reverse shift arm knob with the reverse shift fork shaft, and install the O-ring, washer and nut onto the shift arm pivot. Insert the shift interlock pin into the rear side of the case cover and the compression spring and lock ball into the front side, and assemble the shift fork together with the first and second shift fork shaft. Secure the shift fork with a new slotted spring pin.
31. Align the shift fork shaft positioning groove with the shift interlock pin groove. Insert the two shift interlock pins into the front side of the case cover.
32. Insert the compression spring and the lock ball, and assemble the shift fork together with the third and fourth shift fork shaft, then secure the shift fork with a new slotted spring pin.
33. Install the lock ball, compression spring and reverse restricting ball holder.
34. Check all shift forks for smooth movement. Tighten to 27–32 ft lbs.
35. Install the back-up light switch on the case cover.
36. Align each shift fork and the reverse shift arm with the respective gears, and install the transmission case cover, with the gasket, onto the transmission. Torque the case cover retaining bolts to 11–16 ft lbs.
37. To adjust the shift arm pivot, loosen the locknut on the shift arm pivot, turn the shift arm pivot clockwise until friction is felt, when the reverse idler gear contacts with the first gear and/or the countergear.
38. Next from this position, turn the shift arm pivot counterclockwise approximately 90 degrees. Tighten the pivot locknut securely.
39. With the input shaft rotating, make sure that there is no noise and that the reverse idler gear does not contact other gears in the transmission.
40. If no friction is felt when the shift arm pivot is turned clockwise, set the pivot line mark at 60 degrees rearward from its horizontal position to the case cover surface.
41. If necessary, replace the oil seal in the extension housing after assembling the transmission using the oil seal puller, and pull out the oil seal together with the dust seal.

5-Speed W-50

1. Drain the oil from the transmission, if you have not already done so.
2. Unbolt and remove the clutch housing from the transmission case, with the release fork, bearing and hub still attached.
3. Unbolt the back-up light switch. Remove the two reverse restrictor pins by removing their plugs in the extension housing.
4. Remove the gearshift lever retainer.
5. Rotate the shift rod housing counterclockwise (viewed from behind) and then disconnect the rod from the shift fork shafts.
6. Unbolt and remove the extension housing.
7. Drive out the slotted pin and separate the shift rod, housing and spring.

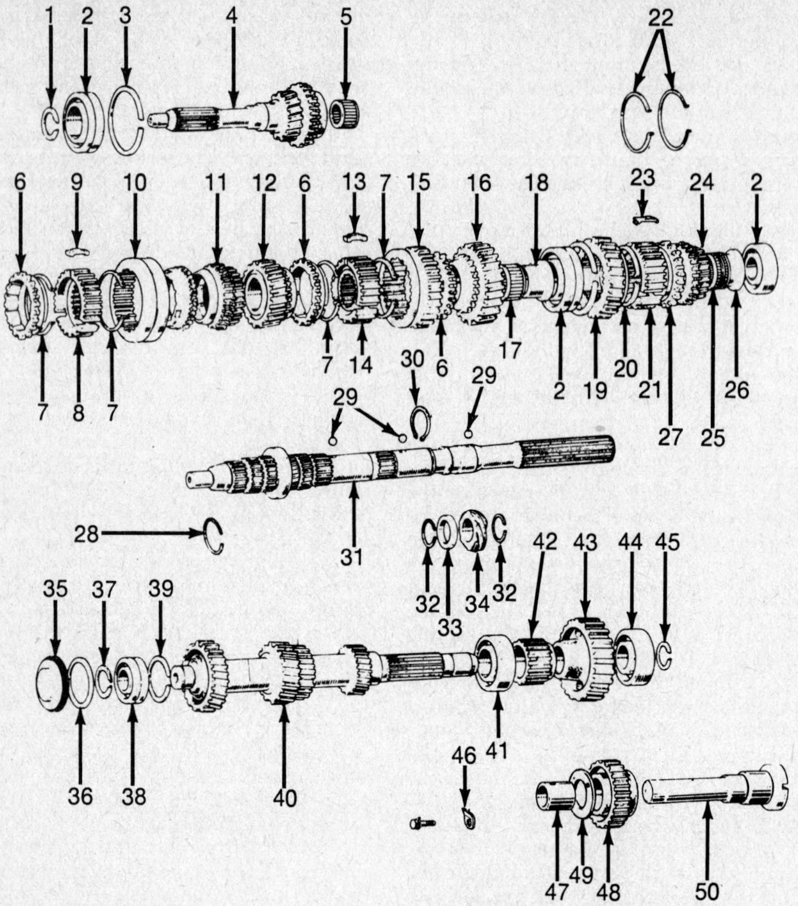

1. Snap-ring
2. Bearing
3. Snap-ring
4. Input shaft
5. Bearing
6. Synchronizer ring
7. Synchromesh shifting key spring
8. Transmission clutch hub
9. Synchromesh shifting key
10. Transmission hub sleeve
11. Third gear
12. Second gear
13. Synchromesh shifting key
14. Transmission clutch hub
15. Reverse gear
16. First gear
17. Bearing
18. First bearing inner race
19. Reverse gear
20. Snap-ring
21. Transmission clutch hub
22. Synchromesh shifting key spring
23. Synchromesh shifting key
24. Fifth gear
25. Bearing
26. Fifth gear inner race
27. Synchronizer ring
28. Snap-ring
29. Ball
30. Snap-ring
31. Output shaft
32. Snap-ring
33. Spacer
34. Speedometer drive gear
35. Countershaft cover
36. Spacer
37. Snap-ring
38. Bearing
39. Snap-ring
40. Countergear
41. Bearing
42. Countershaft reverse gear
43. Countershaft fifth gear
44. Bearing
45. Snap-ring
46. Stop
47. Bushing
48. Reverse idler gear
49. Reverse idler gear shaft spacer
50. Reverse idler gear shaft

Five speed transmission components

8. Unbolt and remove the front bearing retainer. Remove the back-up light switch.

9. Take off both of the front countershaft covers, as well as the spacer.

10. Using an expander, remove the snap-rings from the input and countershaft bearings.

11. Remove the rear cover from the transmission case, by unfastening the bolts which secure it.

***NOTE:** Use a hammer and a wooden drift to break the rear cover free of the case, if necessary.*

12. When removing the rear cover leave all of the gears and the other parts attached. Mount the cover in a vise.

***CAUTION:** Use a copper sheet and clamp the rear cover in the vise at the cross-hatched area, to prevent damage to its joining surfaces.*

13. Withdraw the speedometer driven gear from the output shaft, using care not to lose its lockball.

14. Remove the straight screw plugs from the shift forks and withdraw the springs.

15. Drive the slotted spring pins out of each shift fork.

16. Slide the gear shift fork shafts back and remove the forks. Be careful not to lose the two interlock pins and three balls.

17. Use an expander to remove the speedometer drive gear snap-ring and remove the drive gear. Be careful not to loose the drive gear ball.

18. Remove the snap-ring with an expander and remove the output shaft bearing with a puller.

19. Perform step 5 for the countershaft bearing.

20. Remove the fifth and reverse gears from the countershaft.

21. Remove the snap-ring, fifth gear, its synchronizer ring, needle roller bearing, and fifth gear bearing inner race from the output shaft. Be careful not to lose the fifth gear to inner race lockball.

22. Remove the reverse gear and clutch hub from the output shaft.

23. Loosen the bolt and remove the reverse idler gear stop from the rear cover. Withdraw the reverse idler shaft from the rear; remove the reverse idler gear and spacer.

24. Remove the output shaft rear bearing retainer. Remove the rear bearing snap-ring.

25. Push the countergear bearing outer race rearward, and remove the bearing. Separate the countergear from the rear cover.

26. Separate the input shaft and synchronizer ring from the output shaft.

27. Remove the output shaft from the rear cover.

28. Use an expander to remove the snap-ring and remove the hub and synchronizer ring, followed by third gear.

***NOTE:** Remove the clutch hub by tapping it lightly with a plastic hammer.*

29. Remove the rear bearing snap-ring and press off the rear bearing.

30. Remove the following items from the output shaft, in the order listed:

a. First gear
b. Roller bearing with inner race

***NOTE:** Do not lose the lockballs from the inner race.*

c. Synchronizer ring
d. Reverse gear
e. Clutch hug
f. Second gear
g. Synchronizer ring

Clean all of the parts and inspect them for wear or damage. Replace any parts which are defective.

Use a dial indicator to check output shaft runout, which is measured at the rear bearing installation point. Runout should not exceed 0.001 in. Replace the output shaft, if it does.

Replace the input shaft bearing only if it is rough or noisy. Remove the snap-ring and press the bearing off the shaft. When installing a new bearing, use a snap-ring to obtain *minimum* thrust clearance. Snap-rings are available in six sizes, ranging from 0.081–0.93 in.

ASSEMBLY

Assembly is performed in the following order:

CAUTION: The transmission case and extension housing are aluminum alloy. Take extreme care with mating surfaces.

1. Apply a thin coating of gear oil to all rotating surfaces, prior to assembly.
2. Fit the sleeve over the third gear synchronizer hub. Insert the three shift keys into the hub and sleeve keyways. Install the two hub springs.
3. Assemble the synchronizer ring to third gear, and fit both of them on the output shaft.
4. Insert the third/fourth synchronizer hub on the output shaft, until it contacts the shoulder of the shaft.

NOTE: If the hub is tight on the shaft, lightly tap it home with a wooden mallet.

5. Select a snap-ring to provide 0.002 in. end play for the synchronizer hub and fit it onto the shaft. Snap-rings are available in a range of sizes.
6. Measure third gear thrust clearance with a feeler gauge. The clearance should be 0.004–0.010 in. (1979-80); 0.006–0.010 (1975–78). Replace third gear if the clearance exceeds the limit of 0.010 in.
7. Install the synchronizer ring for second gear to the gear and install the assembly on the output shaft.
8. Install the reverse gear over its clutch hub. Examine them to see that they are properly positioned and slide smoothly.
9. Install the reverse gear and hub on the output shaft so that they contact the shoulder.
10. Measure second gear thrust clearance; it should be between 0.004–0.010 in. (1979–80); 0.006–0.010 (1975–78). Replace the gear if the clearance is more than 0.010 in.
11. Coat the locking ball with grease. Insert it, and the roller bearing inner race, on the output shaft.

NOTE: Be sure that the locking ball does not protrude from the shaft.

12. Assemble first gear with its synchronizer ring, bearing and bearing inner race. Install them on the output shaft, so that the end of the inner race contacts the clutch hub and the groove on the inner race aligns with the locking ball.
13. Press the rear bearing onto the output shaft.
14. Measure first gear thrust clearance; it should be 0.004–0.010 in. (1979–80); 0.006–0.010 (1975–78). Replace the gear if the clearance exceeds 0.010 in.
15. Use a press to insert the straight pin into the rear cover, until it protrudes 1/4–5/16 in. from the cover front side.
16. Clamp the rear cover in a vise, as detailed in step 12 of the disassembly procedure.
17. Install the output shaft on the rear cover.
18. Coat the roller bearing with grease and fit it over the input shaft.
19. Apply gear oil to the front synchronizer ring on the output shaft.
20. Assemble the output shaft and the input shaft.
21. Install the countergear on the rear cover.
22. Install the cylindrical roller bearing into the rear cover, and then install the spacer.
23. Assemble the output shaft and countergear, then fit them through the holes in the rear cover. Push them in until the snap-ring sticks out beyond the rear cover. Install the snap-ring and then push the shafts back until the snap-ring is flush with the rear cover surface.
24. Install the shaft through the reverse idler gear. Insert the end of the shaft into the end of the rear cover.
25. Install the spacer on the idler shaft and secure it with a snap-ring.
26. Lock the reverse idler shaft on the rear cover with its stop. Check the reverse idler gear thrust clearance, it should be 0.006–0.10 in. The thrust clearance limit is 0.012 in.
27. Install the reverse clutch hub on the reverse gear and check it for smooth engagement.
28. Fit the three shift keys into the hub keyways and secure them with the two springs and a snap-ring.
29. Slide the reverse gear hub over the output shaft until it registers against the inner race of the rear cover bearing.

NOTE: Tap the hubs lightly into place with a wooden or plastic mallet, if necessary.

30. Insert the inner race lockball into the output shaft bore, after greasing it so that it can't fall out.
31. Assemble fifth gear, its synchronizer ring, needle roller bearing, and race. Slide the assembly onto the output shaft until the inner bearing face rests against the reverse clutch hub. Be sure that the inner face groove is aligned with the lockball.
32. Secure fifth gear with a snap-ring. Select the snap-ring from one of 13 sizes available, to obtain minimum axial play.
33. Measure fifth gear thrust clearance; it should be 0.004 to 0.010 in. (1975–78); 0.006–0.010 in. (1979–80). The thrust clearance limit is 0.012 in.
34. Install the countershaft reverse gear so that it just rests against the bearing inner race. Install the countershaft fifth gear and then install the countershaft bearing with a brass drift.
35. Fit a snap-ring on the countershaft; select a snap-ring from one of the four available sizes.
36. Fit snap-ring on the output shaft, and drive its bearing into place with a brass drift. Coat the bearing with grease first.
37. Install the spacer ball, and speedometer drive gear on the output shaft. Grease the ball so that it can't fall out. Secure them with a snap-ring.
38. Install the three shift forks in their hub sleeve grooves. Install the first and third shift fork shafts and secure them with their interlocked pins. Coat the pins with grease first. Install the second shift fork shaft next.

NOTE: Place each shift fork shaft in Neutral during assembly.

39. Secure the shift fork shafts to the end cover by inserting the lockballs into their bores, followed by the lockball springs. Tighten the lockball plugs to 14–22 ft lbs, after coating the threads with sealer.
40. Use a new gasket between the transmission case and the rear cover. Slide the case into place.
41. Fit snap-rings on the input shaft and countershaft front bearings.
42. Install the shift lever housing on the end of the shifter shaft. Slide the shifter shaft into the extension housing and secure it with a slotted spring pin.
43. Install a new gasket and slide the extension housing into place, until there is about an inch of clearance between it and the rear cover.
44. Rotate the shift lever housing clockwise (as viewed from the rear) to engage the shifter shaft with the selector lever and the shift fork shaft.
45. Slide the extension housing the rest of the way home and tighten its securing bolts to 22–32 ft lbs.
46. Install the spacer and then the countershaft end covers.
47. Align the front bearing retainer gasket with the oil holes. Fit the bearing retainer over the gasket and tighten its securing bolts to 4.3–6.5 ft lbs evenly, in two or three stages.
48. Bolt the clutch housing onto the front of the transmission case, evenly, in two or three stages, 36–50 ft lbs.
49. Fit the restrictor pins and springs into their extension housing bores. Install the gaskets and tighten the plugs to 27–32 ft lbs.
50. Fit the shift lever retainer over the oil baffle on the extension housing and tighten it to 9–13 ft lbs.
51. Install the shift lever conical spring, large side down, and install the ball seat in the shift lever retainer.
52. Install the speedometer driven gear and secure it with its lockplate. Tighten it to 7.2–11.6 ft lbs.
53. Install the components of the back-up light switch in the reverse order of their removal. Tighten the switch to 27–33 ft lbs.

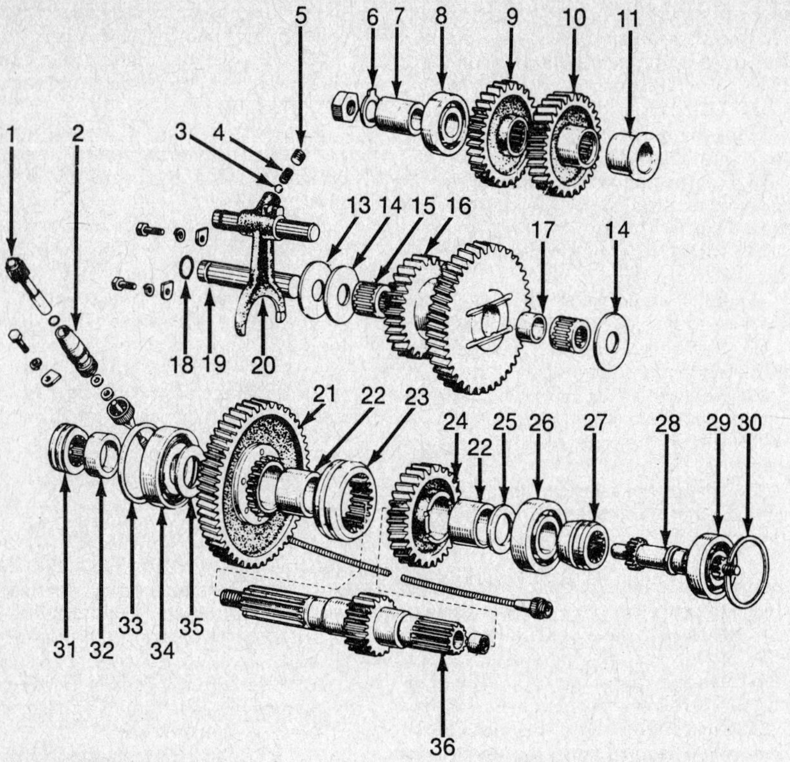

1. Speedometer driven gear
2. Speedometer shaft sleeve
3. Shift fork lockball
4. Compression spring
5. Screw plug
6. Lockwasher
7. Transfer input shaft spacer
8. Bearing
9. Power take-off drive gear
10. Transfer input gear
11. Transfer input gear stop
12. Transfer high & low shift fork shaft
13. Transfer idler gear spacer
14. Washer
15. Needle roller bearing
16. Transfer idler gear
17. Spacer
18. O-ring
19. Transfer idler gear shaft
20. Transfer high and low shift fork
21. Transfer low speed output gear
22. Bushing
23. Transfer high and low clutch sleeve
24. Transfer high speed output gear
25. Washer
26. Bearing
27. Front drive clutch sleeve
28. Transfer output shaft (front)
29. Bearing
30. Snap-ring
31. Speedometer drive gear
32. Spacer
33. Adjusting shim
34. Bearing
35. Washer
36. Transfer output shaft

Land Cruiser 3 speed

54. Install the drain plug and its gasket. Tighten the plug to 27–33 ft lbs.

55. Check to see that the input shaft has no more than 0.020 in. end-play. Put the transmission in Neutral and see if the output shaft can be rotated freely by hand.

Land Cruiser 3-Speed

1. Remove the transfer case shift lever guide, cotter pin, and lockbolt. Remove the shift lever and linkage; do not lose the link lever shoe.
2. Remove the back-up light switch and gasket from the transmission cover.
3. Remove the transfer case cover, complete with gasket. Remove the power take-off cover and gasket.
4. Straighten out the tabs on the input shaft nut lockwasher and remove the nut. Slide the spacer off.

NOTE: Lock the power take-off drive gear with a wooden block or brass drift to keep the shaft from turning while the nut is being removed.

5. Loosen the five bolts which secure the transfer case to the transmission case and separate the cases with a puller. Hold the power take-off drive gear, spacer, and input gear, so that they don't drop out.
6. Unfasten the bolt and remove the gear selector outer lever.
7. Unfasten the bolts and remove the transmission case cover, complete with gasket.
8. Loosen the bolts and remove the front bearing retainer, with gasket, from the transmission case.
9. Drive the shift fork shaft out toward the front of the case with a hammer and a brass drift. Use care not to lose the fork balls, springs and pin.
10. Withdraw the first/reverse shift fork and the second/third shift fork from the transmission case. Remove the lock balls and springs.
11. Drive the countershaft rearward with a brass drift. Remove the countershaft Woodruff key.

NOTE: The countergear should remain in the case.

12. Remove the input shaft and bearing with a puller. Install the puller on the front of the input shaft.
13. Use a hammer and a brass drift to drive the output shaft rearward until the output shaft bearing clears the case. Do not pound on the output shaft; tap it gently.
14. Separate the bearing from the output shaft with a puller.
15. Remove the output shaft and the related components from the transmission case.
16. Use a snap-ring expander to remove the snap-ring from the front of the output shaft. Slide the synchronizer clutch hub, sleeve, synchronizer ring, second gear, and the first/reverse gearset off of the shaft.
17. Remove the countershaft drive gear, spacer, roller bearing, and washers. Note the placement of the gear thrust washers. Use care not to lose the rollers.
18. Drive the reverse idler gear shaft rearward and remove its Woodruff key.
19. Remove the reverse idler gear, rollers, and thrust washers from the case.

Wash all parts thoroughly. Check the case for cracks and burrs. Inspect the gears, replace any that are worn, cracked, or chipped. Check all internal parts for wear or damage; replace as required.

GEAR/BACKLASH

Input shaft gear-to-countershaft drive gear—0.004 in.

Second-to-countergear—0.004 in.

First/reverse gear-to-countergear—0.008 in.

Countergear-to-reverse idler gear—0.008 in.

Reverse gear-to-reverse idler gear—0.008 in.

Synchronizer ring-to-gear—0.039 in.

ASSEMBLY

Transmission assembly is performed in the following order:

NOTE: Use new gaskets, oil seals, and dust deals. Coat the gaskets with sealer.

1. Apply a light coating of gear oil to all components, prior to assembly.
2. Grease the bore of the reverse idler gear. Insert the bearing rollers and washer in the bore.
3. Install the reverse idler gear and the two thrust washers into the case. Drive the reverse idler gear shaft through the case, by gently tapping it into place from behind. Lock the shaft into place with the Woodruff key.

4. Grease the bore of the countershaft drive gear and fit its spacer. Install the rollers in the bore and hold them in place with a heavy coating of grease. Install the washers in the bore.

5. Place the countershaft drive gear, thrust washer, and side thrust washers in the case.

6. If the bearing was removed from the input shaft, press it into place on the shaft.

7. Select a snap-ring that will give the input shaft minimum end-play, and install it on the shaft.

8. Grease bore of the input shaft, install the rollers, and then fit the snap-ring.

9. Carefully drive the input shaft assembly and bearing into the transmission case.

10. Lift the countershaft drive gear up and install the countershaft from the rear of the case. Secure the countershaft with its Woodruff key.

11. Use a feeler gauge to measure the countershaft thrust clearance; it should be 0.002–0.008 in. Select a countergear side thrust washer of the proper size to obtain the specified thrust clearance.

12. Install the two synchronizer shifting key springs into the clutch hub, so that the open ends are 120° apart. Place the three shifting keys into the clutch hub key slots.

13. Slide the clutch hub sleeve into the clutch hub.

14. Fit second gear, its synchronizer ring, and the synchronizer assembly on the output shaft. Check second gear thrust clearance with a feeler gauge. It should be 0.003–0.009 in. Select and install the proper front output shaft snap-ring to obtain this clearance.

15. Working from the rear, slide the first/reverse gear set on the output shaft.

16. Install the output shaft assembly in the transmission case. Using a suitable brass drift, install the rear bearing over the output shaft and into the case.

17. Install both shift forks and retain them with their balls and lockpins.

18. Depress the shift fork lockballs with a screwdriver, then drive the shift fork shaft through the case, and into shift forks.

19. Install a new O-ring on the shift fork shaft and lock it in place with its pin.

20. Coat the front bearing retainer with liquid sealer and install the bearing retainer over it. Tighten the bearing retainer bolts to 11–14 ft lbs.

21. Check all parts for smooth operation and freedom of movement.

22. Install a suitable size pipe over the transmission output shaft. Place the transfer case input gear, power takeoff drive gear, and the spacers over the pipe, which should be projecting through the transfer case.

23. Coat a new gasket with liquid sealer and place the gasket between the transmission case and the transfer case.

24. Install the transfer case on the transmission case and tighten the retaining bolts to 25–30 ft lbs. Be sure to install the two short bolts from the inside of the transfer case.

25. Remove the pipe from the output shaft and transfer case.

26. Install the bearing over the end of the transmission output shaft and into the transfer case with a drift.

27. Fit the transfer case input shaft spacer and tighten the bearing nut to 101–108 ft lbs. Use the lockwasher to secure the nut.

28. Install the transfer case cover over its gasket.

29. Coat the gasket with liquid sealer and install the power take-off cover.

30. Install the back-up light switch and gasket.

31. Install the transfer front drive fork and its gasket on the transfer case extension housing.

32. Check all parts for smooth operation.

Land Cruiser 4-Speed

1. Perform steps 1 through 5 of the Land Cruiser three-speed transmission disassembly procedure.

2. Remove the transfer case input shaft gear stop from the transmission rear bearing retainer.

3. Remove the rear bearing retainer and gasket.

4. Remove the front bearing retainer and gasket from the transmission case.

5. Remove the input shaft and front bearing from the case with a puller.

NOTE: Prior to removing the input shaft, align the slot in the input shaft with the countershaft drivegear. While removing the input shaft, use care not to drop the needle bearings and spacer into the transmission case.

6. Remove the synchronizer ring.

1. Oil seal
2. Snap-ring
3. Bearing
4. Input shaft
5. Bearing roller
6. Bearing spacer
7. Synchronizer ring No. 2
8. Snap-ring
9. Shift-key spring
10. Clutch hub No. 2
11. Shift key No. 2
12. Hub sleeve
13. Third gear
14. Snap-ring
15. Second gear thrust washer
16. Second gear
17. Output shaft
18. Second synchronizer outer ring
19. Snap-ring
20. Synchronizer ring No. 1
21. Compression spring
22. Lockball
23. First synchronizer outer ring
24. First gear
25. First gear thrust washer
26. Straight pin
27. Reverse idler gear
28. Bushing
29. Reverse idler gear shaft
30. Woodruff key
31. Woodruff key
32. Bolt
33. Lockbolt washer
34. Lockbolt plate
35. Bearing
36. Front bearing spacer
37. Countershaft drive gear
38. Spacer
39. Counter shaft third speed gear
40. Countershaft
41. Bearing
42. Snap-rng

Land Cruiser 4 speed

7. Use an expander to remove the snap-ring on the output shaft rear bearing. Remove the bearing with a puller.
8. Withdraw the output shaft and gear-set from the transmission case.
9. Straighten out the tabs on the countershaft front bearing retainer and remove the bolts, then remove the retainer and lockwasher.
10. Use a puller to remove the front countershaft bearing. Remove the bearing spacer. Remove the rear countershaft bearing, as well.
11. Remove the countershaft assembly from the case.
12. Remove the reverse shift arm pivot and shift arm.
13. Install a puller on the reverse idler shaft, and pull the gear shaft and key from the transmission case. Remove the reverse idler gear from the case.
14. Slide the first gear and its thrust washer off the back end of the output shaft.
15. Remove the snap-ring from the front of the output shaft; then remove the clutch hub, sleeve, synchronizer ring, and third gear from the shaft.
16. Remove the snap-ring and slide second gear and thrust washer off the shaft.
17. Slide the reverse gear synchronizer ring off the output shaft.
18. Press the countershaft drive gear off of the countershaft. Remove the Woodruff key and spacer from the shaft.
19. Repeat step 18 for the third gear and Woodruff key.
20. Move the shift forks into neutral. Drive the slotted spring pin out of the third/fourth shift fork with a long dirft.
21. Without using excessive force, drive the third/fourth shift fork shaft and plug forward with a brass drift. Remove the shift fork, lockball, and spring.
22. Drive the spring pins out of the reverse shift fork and boss with a long drift.
23. Remove the plug from the rear of the transmission case. Drive the first/second shift fork shaft forward with a brass drift. Remove the shift fork, boss, lockball, and spring.
24. Drive the spring pins out of the reverse shift fork and boss. Loosen and remove the tapered screw plugs from the transmission cover; then push the interlock rollers out with a long drift.
25. Remove the cotter pin, spring, and lockball from the shift fork boss.
26. Remove the C-washer, then withdraw the reverse return spring the plunger from the boss.

Wash all parts thoroughly. Check the case for cracks and burrs. Inspect the gears, replace any that are worn, cracked, or chipped. Check all internal parts for wear or damage; replace as required.

GEAR BACKLASH

Input gear-to-countershaft drivergear —0.004 in.

Third gear-to-countershaft gear—0.004 in.

Second gear-to-countershaft gear—0.004 in.

First gear-to-countershaft gear—0.004 in.

Reverse gear-to-reverse idler gear—0.005 in.

ASSEMBLY

To assemble the transmission:

NOTE: Use new gaskets, oil seals, and dust seals. Coat the gaskets with sealer.

1. Apply a light coating of gear oil to all components, prior to assembly.
2. Place the reverse idler gear in the case with its fork groove facing forward.
3. Align the Woodruff key, groove, and slot. Carefully drive the reverse idler shaft through the holes in the case, and into the gear.

NOTE: If you install new bushings in the idler gear, be sure that their openings are at least 90° apart.

4. Adjust the reverse idler gear position by turning the shaft arm pivot to obtain a distance of 4.49 in. between the outer rear of the transmission case and the reverse idler gear. Tighten the shift arm pivot nut. Move the gear to neutral; the distance between the front end of the gear and outer rear of the transmission case should now be 2.71 in. Adjust by rotating the shift arm pivot.
5. Install the Woodruff key into the groove of the countershaft and align its keyway with the countershaft third gear. Place the gear on the shaft with the long hub facing forward.
6. Slide the spacer on the countershaft and press its drivegear on, in a similar manner to third gear (step 5), with its long hub facing rearward.
7. Place the countershaft assembly into the transmission case and install the countershaft rear bearing with a press. Install the snap-ring over the end of the countershaft.
8. Install the front bearing spacer, protruded end forward, on the countershaft. Press the front bearing on, until its snap-ring registers firmly against the transmission case.

CAUTION: Apply pressure to the outer bearing race only, to prevent damage to the bearing.

9. Place the bearing retainer and lockwasher on the front of the countershaft. Tighten the bearing retainer bolts to 11–16 ft lbs. Bend the lockwasher tabs upward.
10. Slide second gear on the output shaft so that its synchronizer outer ring faces rearward. Select a snap-ring so that second gear has a thrust clearance of 0.004–0.012 in.
11. Slide third gear on the output shaft, so that its synchronizer cone faces forward.
12. Perform steps 12 and 13 of the Land Cruiser three-speed transmission assembly procedure.
13. Install the synchronizer ring and slide the synchronizer assembly over the output shaft. The grooves should face the rear.
14. Select a snap-ring to provide 0.008 in. thrust clearance for the clutch hub.
15. Slide the reverse gear synchronizer ring over the output shaft. Check the ring for smooth movement.
16. Slide first gear on the output shaft.
17. Place the output shaft assembly in the transmission case.
18. Fit the first gear thrust washer on the output shaft. Align the slot in the thrust washer with output shaft pin.
19. Install the output shaft rear bearing with a press. Be sure to apply pressure on the bearing *outer* race only. Install the rear bearing and its gasket.
20. Press-fit the bearing on the input shaft. Grease the bearing on the input shaft. Grease the bearing rollers and install all 18 in the input shaft.
21. Place the input shaft in the transmission case, so that the synchronizer ring keyways align with the shift keys. Install the input shaft bearing spacer in the input shaft.

CAUTION: Be sure the bearing rollers or the spacer do not fall into the transmission case during installation.

22. Install the input shaft bearing retainer and gasket. Tighten the retainer bolts to 7–11 ft lbs.

NOTE: Make sure that all shift fork shafts are in neutral during the shift fork shaft assembly steps, below.

23. Install the spring and return plunger in the reverse shift boss. Secure them witht he C-washer. Install the ball and spring then secure them with a cotter pin.
24. Place the reverse shift fork and boss in the transmission cover. Install the fork lock-spring and ball in the cover.
25. Slide the reverse shift fork shaft through the front of the cover its bore, shift fork and into its boss, while depressing the lockball with a screwdriver.
26. Align the holes and drive the slotted spring pin through the reverse shift fork and boss to secure them to the shaft.
27. Coat the roller with grease and install it into the interlock hole in the cover.
28. Place the first/second shift boss and fork into the cover. Install the first/second shift fork shaft and spacer from the front of the cover, after fitting its pin, and while depressing the lockball with a screwdriver.
29. Secure the first/second shift fork and boss with their slotted spring pins. Install another roller into the hole in the cover.

30. Install the third/fourth shift fork lock-spring and ball in the shift fork. Install the shift fork and shaft in the cover and secure them with a slotted spring pin.

31. Check the shift fork assembly for smooth operation. Apply liquid sealer to the plugs and screw plug threads. Install the plugs.

32. Perform steps 22 through 31 of the Land Cruiser three-speed transmission assembly procedure.

33. Place the transmission and shift forks in neutral and install the transmission cover with gasket on the transmission case.

34. Check the transmission and transfer case for smooth operation.

AUTOMATIC TRANSMISSION

FRONT BAND ADJUSTMENT

3 Speed (1973–77)

1. Remove the pan as outlined above.
2. Pry the engagment lever toward the band with a screwdriver.
3. The gap between the end of the piston rod and the engagement bolt should be 0.138 in.
4. If the gap does not meet the specification, adjust it by turning the engagement bolt.
5. Install the pan and refill the transmission as outlined above.

REAR BAND ADJUSTMENT

3 Speed (1973–77)

The rear band adjusting bolt is located on the outside of the case, so it is not necessary to remove the pan in order to adjust the band.

1. Loosen the adjusting bolt locknut and fully screw in the adjusting bolt.
2. Loosen the adjusting bolt one turn.
3. Tighten the locknut while holding the bolt so that it cannot turn.

BAND ADJUSTMENT

3 Speed (1978–80)

This type transmission, the A-40, has no bands, and therefore, no band adjustments are possible. The only external adjustments are throttle and shift linkages.

NEUTRAL SAFETY SWITCH ADJUSTMENT

3 Speed—Console Shift

Models with a console-mounted selector have the neutral safety switch on the linkage located beneath the console. To adjust it, proceed in the following manner:

1. Remove the screws which secure the center console.
2. Unfasten the console multiconnector, if so equipped, and completely remove the console.
3. Adjust the switch in the manner outlined in the column selector section, above.
4. Install the console in the reverse order of removal after completion of the switch adjustment.

SHIFT LINKAGE ADJUSTMENT

3 Speed Toyoglide (1973–77)

1. Check all of the shift linkage bushings for wear. Replace any worn bushings.
2. Loosen the connecting rod swivel locknut.
3. Move the selector lever and check movement of the pointer in the shift quadrant.
4. When the control shaft is set in the neutral position the quadrant pointer should indicate "N" (Neutral), as well.

Steps 5–7 apply only to cars equipped with column-mounted shift levers.

5. If the pointer does not indicate Neutral, then check the drive cord adjustment.
6. Remove the steering column shroud.
7. Turn the drive cord adjuster with a phillips screwdriver until the pointer indicates Neutral.

Steps 8–10 apply to both column-mounted and floor-mounted selectors:

8. Position the manual valve lever on the transmission so that it is in the Neutral position.
9. Lock the connecting rod swivel, with the locknut so that the pointer, selector, and manual valve lever are all positioned in Neutral.
10. Check the operation of the gear selector by moving it through all ranges.

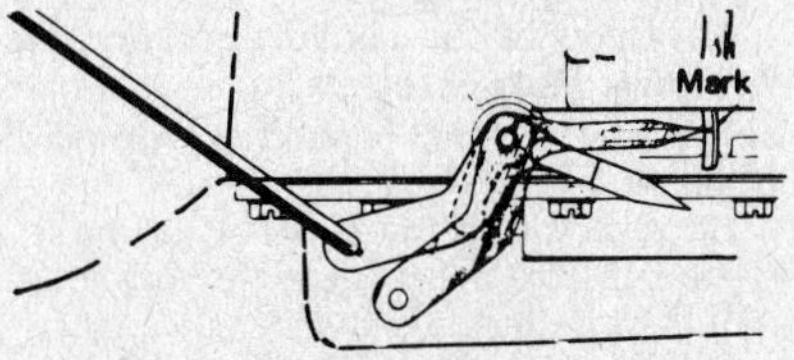

Throttle linkage aligning marks

3-Speed A-40 (1978–80).

1. Check the linkage for freedom of movement.
2. Push the manual valve lever toward the front of the car, as far as it will go.
3. Bring the lever back to its third notch (Neutral).
4. Have someone hold the shift lever in Neutral, while you tighten the linkage so that it can't slip.

THROTTLE LINKAGE ADJUSTMENT

3 Speed Toyoglide (1973–1977)

1. Loosen the locknut at each end of the linkage adjusting turnbuckle.

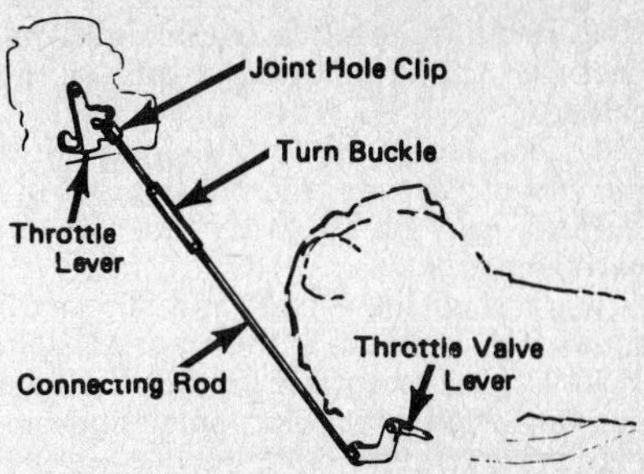

Throttle linkage components

2. Detach the throttle linkage connecting rod from the carburetor.
3. Align the pointer on the throttle valve lever with the mark stamped on the transmission case.
4. Rotate the turnbuckle so that the end of the throttle linkage rod and the carburetor throttle lever are aligned.

NOTE: ***The carburetor throttle valve must be fully opened during this adjustment.***

5. Tighten the turnbuckle locknuts and reconnect the throttle rod to the carburetor.
6. Open the throttle valve and check the pointer alignment with the mark on the transmission case.
7. Road-test the vehicle. If the transmission "hunts," i.e., keeps shifting rapidly back and forth between gears at certain speeds or if it fails to downshift properly when going up hills, repeat the throttle linkage adjustment.

3-Speed A-40 (1978–80)

1. Remove the air cleaner.
2. Confirm that the accelerator linkage opens the throttle fully. Adjust the link as necessary.
3. Peel the rubber dust book back from the throttle cable.
4. Loosen the adjustment nuts on the throttle cable bracket (rocker cover) just enough to allow cable housing movement.
5. Have some depress the accelerator pedal fully.
6. Adjust the cable housing so that the distance between its end the cable stop collar is 2.05 in.
7. Tighten the adjustment nuts. Make sure that the adjustment hasn't changed. Install the dust boot and the air cleaner.

PAN REMOVAL

1. Remove the plug and drain the fluid from the transmission.
2. Unfasten the pan securing bolts.
3. Remove the pan.

Installation is the reverse of removal. Torque the pan securing bolts to 4–6 ft lbs. Refill the transmission with fluid.

REMOVAL AND INSTALLATION

3-Speed Toyoglide (1973–77)

1. Disconnect the battery.

2. Remove the air cleaner and disconnect the accelerator torque link or the cable.

3. Disconnect the throttle link rod at the carburetor side, then disconnect the backup light wiring at the firewall (on early models).

4. Jack up the vehicle and support it on stands, then drain the transmission. (Use a clean receptacle so that the fluid can be checked for color, smell and foreign matter.)

5. Disconnect all shift linkage.

6. On early models, remove the cross shaft from the frame.

7. Disconnect the throttle link rod at the transmission side and remove the speedometer cable, cooler lines and parking brake equalizer bracket.

8. Loosen the exhaust flange nuts and remove the exhaust pipe clamp and bracket.

9. Remove the drive shaft and the rear mounting bracket, then lower the rear end of the transmission carefully.

10. Unbolt the torque converter from the drive plate. Support the engine with a suitable jack stand and remove the seven bolts that hold the transmission to the engine.

Reverse the order of the removal procedures with the following precautions.

1. Install the drive plate and ring gear, tighten the attaching bolts to 37–43 ft lbs.

2. After assembling the torque converter to the transmission, check the clearance, it should be about 0.59 in.

3. Before installing the transmission, install the oil pump locator pin on the torque converter to facilitate installation.

4. While rotating the crankshaft, tighten the converter attaching bolts, a little at a time.

5. After installing the throttle connecting second rod, make sure the throttle valve lever indicator aligns with the mark on the transmission with the carburetor throttle valve fully opened. If required, adjust the rod.

6. To install the transmission control rod correctly, move the transmission lever to N (Neutral), and the selector lever to Neutral. Fill the transmission with automatic transmission fluid (Type F only), then start the engine. Run the engine at idle speed and apply the brakes while moving the selector lever through all positions, then return it to Neutral.

7. After warming the engine, move the selector lever through all positions, then back to Neutral, and check the fluid level. Fill as necessary.

8. Adjust the engine idle to 550–650 rpm with the selector at Drive. Road test the vehicle.

9. With the selector lever at 2 or Drive check the point at which the transmission shifts. Check for shock, noise and slipping with the selector lever in all positions. Check for leaks from the transmission.

3-Speed A-40 (1978–80)

To remove and install the transmission, proceed in the following manner:

1. Perform steps 1 through 3 of the three-speed Toyoglide removal procedure.

2. Remove the upper starter mounting nuts using a socket wrench with a long extension.

3. Raise the vehicle and support it securely with jackstands. Drain the transmission.

4. Remove the lower starter mounting bolt and lay the starter along side of the engine. Don't let it hang by the wires.

5. Unbolt the parking brake equalizer support.

6. Matchmark the driveshaft and the companion flange, to ensure correct installation. Remove the bolts securing the driveshaft to the companion flange.

7. Slide the driveshaft straight back and out of the transmission. Use a spare U-joint yoke or tie a plastic bag over the end of the transmission to keep any fluid from dripping out.

8. Remove the bolts from the cross-shaft body bracket, the cotter pin fron the manual lever, and the cross-shaft socket from the transmission.

9. Remove the exhaust pipe bracket from the torque converter bell housing.

10. Disconnect the oil cooler lines from the transmission and remove the line bracket from the bell housing.

11. Disconnect the speedometer cable from the transmission.

12. Unbolt both support braces from the bell housing.

13. Use a transmission jack to raise the transmission slightly.

14. Unbolt the rear crossmember and lower the transmission about 3 in.

15. Pry the two rubber torque converter access plugs out of their holes at the back of the engine.

16. Remove the six torque converter mounting bolts through the access hole. Rotate the engine with the crankshaft pulley.

17. Cut the head off a bolt to make a guide pin for the torque converter. Install the pin on the converter.

18. Remove the converter bell housing-to-engine bolts.

19. Push on the end of the guide pin in order to remove the converter with the transmission. Remove the transmission rearward and then bring it out from under the car.

CAUTION: Don't catch the throttle cable during removal.

Installation is the reverse of removal. Be sure to note the following, however:

1. Install the two long bolts on the upper converter housing and tighten them to 36–58 ft lbs.

2. Tighten the converter-to-flex-plate bolts finger-tight, and then tighten them with a torque wrench to 11–16 ft lbs.

3. When installing the speedometer cable, make sure that the felt dust protector and washer are on the cable end.

4. Tighten the cooling line and exhaust pipe bracket mounting bolts to 37–58 ft lbs. Tighten the cooling lines to 14–22 ft lbs.

5. Align the matchmarks made on the driveshaft and the companion flange during removal. Tighten the driveshaft mounting bolts to 11–16 ft lbs.

6. Be sure to install the oil pan drain plug. Tighten it to 11–14 ft lbs.

7. Adjust the throttle cable.

8. Fill the transmission to the proper capacity. Use only type "F" (ATF) fluid. Start the engine, run the selector through all gear ranges and place it in Park (P). Check the level on the dipstick and add type F fluid, as necessary.

9. Road test the vehicle and check for leaks.

TRANSFER CASE

REMOVAL AND INSTALLATION

4x4 Pick-up

See transmission removal and installation section above. Be sure to drain both transmission and transfer cases if overhaul is to be done.

To separate transfer case from transmission proceed as follows.

1. Remove four bolts holding the crossmember mounting brace to the transfer case.

2. Remove transmission shift lever retainer from right side of transfer case.

3. Remove five bolts holding transfer case adapter mounting to transmission and separate transfer case from transmission.

Installation is the reverse of removal. Coat gasket and mounting bolts with sealer.

CAUTION: Do not pry on transmission/transfer case interface when separating.

Three Speed and Four Speed Land Cruiser

See appropriate sections under transmission above for removal and installation procedures.

OVERHAUL

4x4 Pick-up

1. Separate transfer case from transmission as outlined above.

2. Remove speedometer drive gear and sleeve.

3. Remove shift lever retainer and oil deflector. Remove transfer indicator switch.

4. Remove nut from front wheel drive output companion flange by freeing the nut lock on the face of the nut with a

small punch and clamping the flange so it will not turn. Remove flange washer and flange.

5. Remove the six bolts holding the transfer adapter to the reduction gear case. Tap the adapter loose with a plastic hammer.

6. Unbolt the reduction gear case and remove it together with the input gear and the counter gear by tapping on it with a plastic hammer.

7. Remove snap rings holding input shaft and bearing and counter gear and bearing in the reduction gear case.

Remove by alternately tapping the input gear and counter gear down through the case with a plastic hammer.

NOTE: To perform the above operation place reduction gear case on two blocks of wood to prevent bottom face of case from damage.

8. Remove needle roller bearing from the end of the input gear.

NOTE: Needle bearing may stay in the end of the output shaft. Remove it so that it does not get lost.

9. Remove the nut from rear output shaft by clamping companion flange and remove companion flange and washer.

10. Unbolt extension housing and remove. Drive speedometer drive gear and steel ball off output shaft with flat punch. Be careful not to damage gear. Remove oil pump screw and O ring.

11. Unbolt rear case and remove together with the idler gear by tapping on it with a plastic hammer.

12. Remove idler gear snap ring from outside of bearing and remove in the same manner as output gear and counter gear.

CAUTION: Always lay front case with the output shaft side up or the clutch hub and steel ball may fall out.

13. Remove two oil pipes.

14. Remove front drive gear bearing retainer.

15. Position front case in a soft vise so that it remains upright and remove snap ring around front drive gear shaft bearing. Remove front drive gear shaft and bearing by tapping on the threaded end of the shaft with a plastic hammer.

16. Move the shift fork shafts to the high-two position.

17. Drive the slotted spring pin from shift fork number one on the output shaft side of the case.

18. Remove the shift fork together with the clutch sleeve.

19. Remove clutch hub, transfer drive seat, needle roller bearing and output spacer and steel ball.

20. Drive slotted spring pin from shift head on the front drive shift fork shaft and remove shift head.

21. Drive slotted spring pin from shift fork number two on high and low

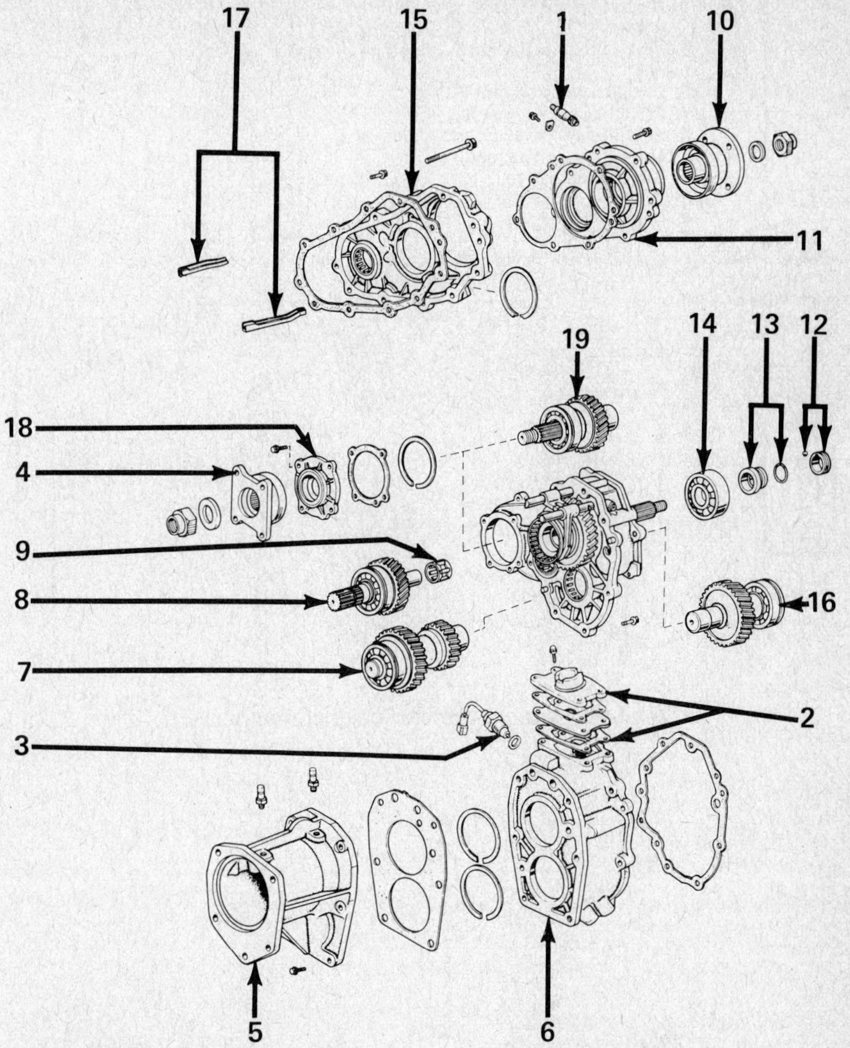

1. Speedometer driven gear & sleeve
2. Shift lever & retainer & oil deflector
3. Transfer indicator switch
4. Companion flange
5. Adapter
6. Reduction gear case
7. Counter gear
8. Input gear
9. Needle roller bearing
10. Companion flange
11. Extension housing
12. Speedometer drive gear & steel ball
13. Oil pump screw & O-ring
14. Radial ball bearing
15. Rear case
16. Idler gear
17. Oil pipe
18. Front drive gear bearing retainer
19. Front drive gear

4x4 Pick-up transfer case

shift fork shaft and remove fork along with clutch sleeve.

22. Remove the detent ball plugs from both sides of the case with an alan wrench and remove springs and steel balls from holes with a magnet.

NOTE: When assembling, coat plug threads with sealer.

23. Remove front drive shift fork shaft. Remove interlock pin through detent hole with a magnet.

24. Remove high and low shift fork shaft.

25. Remove output shaft front bearing retainer and snap ring from around output shaft bearing.

26. Position front case on two blocks of wood and remove output shaft by tapping on the threaded side of the shaft with a plastic hammer.

Wash all disassembled parts thoroughly. Check the transfer case and its covers for cracks. Check the bearing fitting portions and gasket surfaces for burrs and nicks. Inspect all parts for wear or damage and check all bearings for roughness and drag under pressure. Replace any parts which are defective.

27. To replace the input gear bearing, remove the snap ring and press the bearing off shaft. Press new bearing on, install snap ring and check the bearing free play. The play limit between the bearing and snap ring is 0.006 in. Replace with new snap ring if necessary.

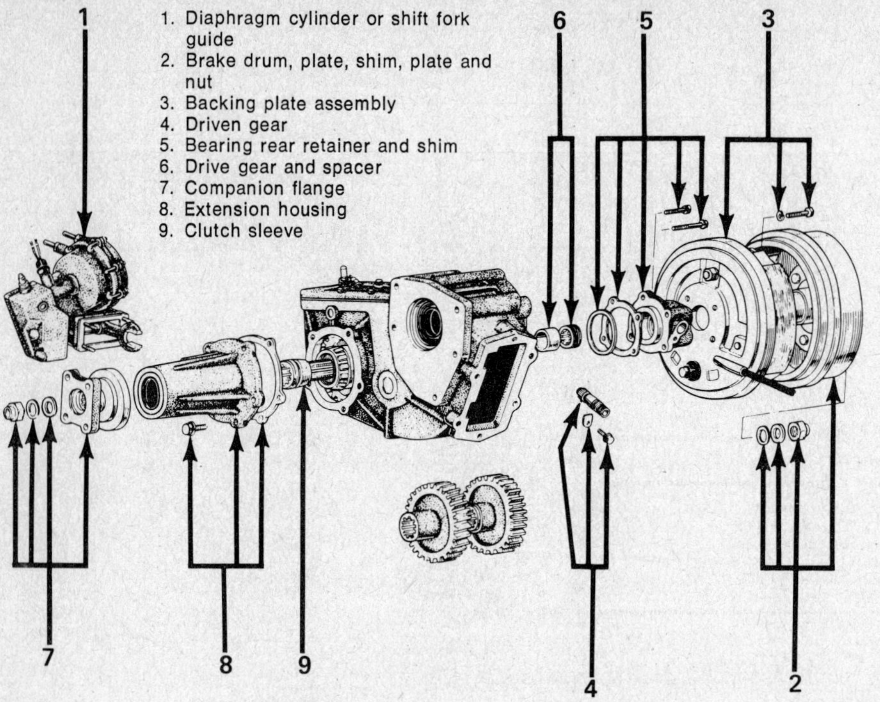

1. Diaphragm cylinder or shift fork guide
2. Brake drum, plate, shim, plate and nut
3. Backing plate assembly
4. Driven gear
5. Bearing rear retainer and shim
6. Drive gear and spacer
7. Companion flange
8. Extension housing
9. Clutch sleeve

Land Cruiser transfer case components

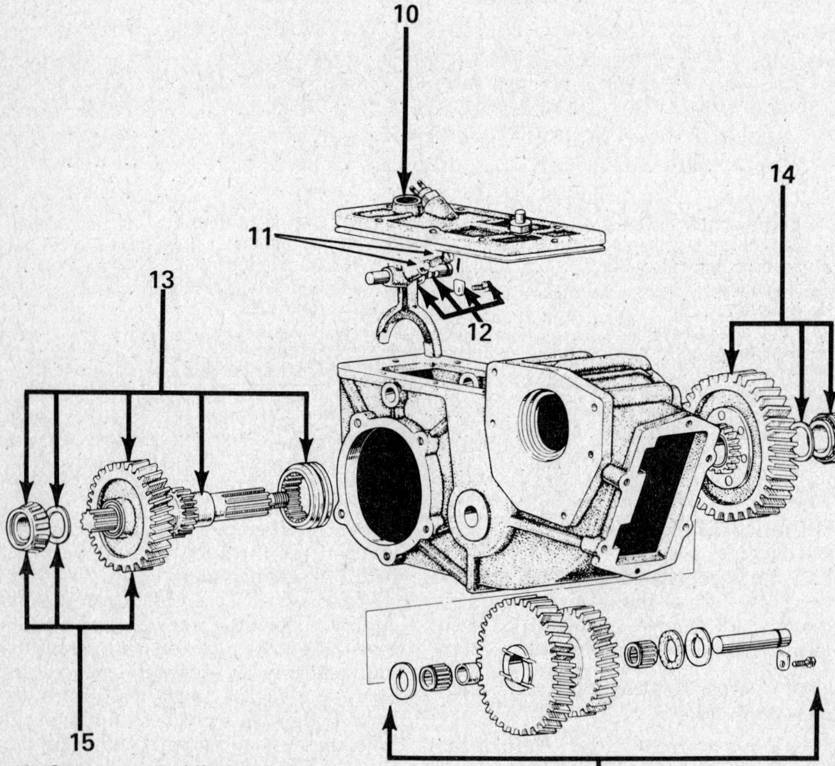

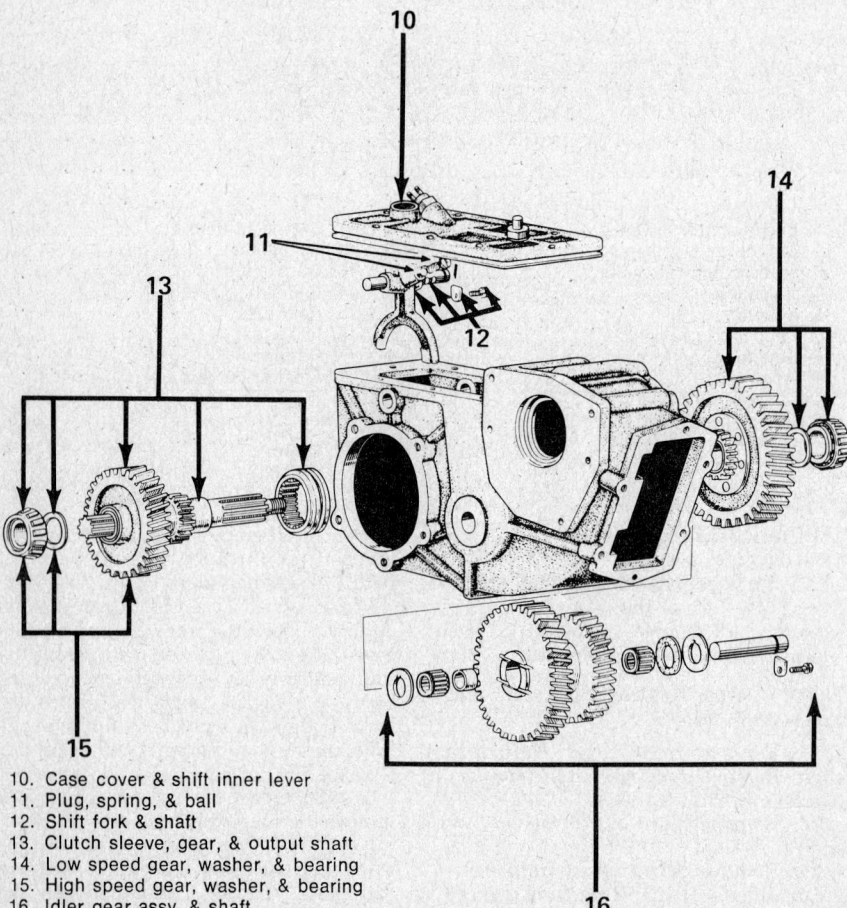

10. Case cover & shift inner lever
11. Plug, spring, & ball
12. Shift fork & shaft
13. Clutch sleeve, gear, & output shaft
14. Low speed gear, washer, & bearing
15. High speed gear, washer, & bearing
16. Idler gear assy. & shaft

Land Cruiser transfer case—exploded view of gears

28. On the output shaft, check the low-gear oil clearance with a dial gauge. Standard clearance ranges from 0.004–0.0022 in. Maximum limit is 0.0030 in.

29. Check the low gear thrust clearance. Standard clearance is between 0.004–0.010 in. with a maximum limit of 0.012 in.

30. To remove bearing and lower gear, remove the snap ring and press lower gear and bearing off. Be careful not to lose the positioning ball. Inspect the lower gear roller beating for wear. Check the output shaft runout. Runout limit is 0.001 in. When replacing, coat lower gear roller bearing with gear oil. Replace lower gear roller bearing and lower gear. Install positioning ball and spacer with notch sliding over ball. Press bearing on, install snap ring and check free play. Free play limit is 0.004 in.

31. Inspect counter gear for wear or damage. Make sure there is no drag on the bearing when it is turned under pressure. To replace bearing, remove snap ring and press bearing off shaft.

NOTE: Removing counter gear bearing requires a Toyota special tool because of the minimum clearance between bearing and gear.
Replace bearing by pressing it in shaft. Install snap ring and check play. Play limit: 0.006 in.

32. Inspect front gear for damage or wear and front gear bearing for drag under pressure. Remove and install bearing with a press.

33. Inspect transfer gear and component parts for wear. Inspect clutch hub and clutch sleeve for wear.

NOTE: Both clutch sleeves are identical.

34. Make sure clutch sleeve slides smoothly on hub. Make sure output shaft sleeve rides smoothly on shaft.

35. Check clearance between sleeve and shift fork number one and sleeve and shift fork number two. Clearance limit: 0.04 in.

36. Inspect shift fork shafts and shift forks for damage. Make sure shafts slide smoothly in their respective bores.

37. Check oil pump screw and oil pipes for wear. Make sure O ring in oil pump screw is not damaged.

38. Make sure oil seals, dust covers and bearings in component transfer cases are in good condition. Replace as necessary.

NOTE: Always install new gaskets, and apply liquid sealer or gasket cement when assembling. Apply a thin coating of transmission lubricant on all parts before installation. Apply multipurpose grease to all oil seals.

Assembly is the reverse of disassembly with the following notes.

1. When the shift fork shafts are installed, make sure the front drive shift

fork shaft does not move when the high and low shift fork shaft is shifted to the neutral or low speed position. After testing, shift fork shafts to the high two position.

2. When installing spacer on output shaft, make sure you position it with steel ball in groove.

3. After transfer drive gear and clutch hub are installed on output shaft, check the transfer drive gear oil clearance. Standard clearance: 0.0004–0.0020 in. Allowable limit: 0.0028 in.

4. Check the transfer gear thrust clearance. Standard clearance: 0.004–0.0011 in. Allowable limit: 0.013 in.

5. When installing the bearing retainer to the front drive gear, make sure you match the oil passages in the case and retainer.

6. Install the oil pipes with their cutout sides facing up.

7. Make sure you install the needle roller bearing in the end of the output shaft.

Transfer case torque specifications:

NOTE: All major case bolts are tightened to 22-32 ft-lb.

Tighten the following to 8-11 ft-lb.: Output shaft front bearing retainer bolts; detent plugs; transfer case shift lever retainer bolts; speedometer drive gear bolt; rear engine mounting bolts.

Tighten the following to the indicated torques:

Transmission shift lever retainer bolts: 11–18 ft–lb.

Front drive gear bearing retainer bolts: 11–15 ft–lb.

Front and rear flange nuts: 80–101 ft–lb.

Land Cruiser

1. Remove diaphragm cylinder or shift fork guide from side of extension housing. Check for smooth operation.

2. Unstake nut at end of emergency brake drum with a punch and loosen. Put system in front drive and clamp or lock front companion flange. Remove nut and shims. Remove brake drum.

3. Remove nuts holding brake drum backing plate and remove plate.

4. Remove speedometer drive gear.

5. Remove rear bearing retainer and shim behind brake drum backing plate, remove drive gear and spacer.

6. Loosen staked nut on front drive companion flange and remove nut, washer and companion flange.

7. Remove bolts from front drive extension housing and tap housing loose with a plastic hammer. Remove clutch sleeve from front drive output shaft.

8. Remove upper case cover and shift inner lever.

9. Remove plug, spring and ball from shifting fork. Remove nut and lock securing shift fork shaft.

10. Using a brass drift, tap shifting shaft out toward the rear. Remove shifting fork.

11. Using special tool Toyota SST (09318–60011) or its equivalent, press output shaft toward the front of the case and off the low speed gear and bearing.

12. Inspect gears and bearings for wear or damage. Replace as necessary. Replace high speed gear with a press.

CAUTION: When removing high speed gear, make sure it is reassembled with gear facing the right way.

13. Measure idler gear thrust clearance. Limit: 0.0016 in.

14. Remove bolt and lock from idler gear shaft. Select a bolt that fits in the end of the idler gear shaft. Place a washer on bolt and insert it in an appropriate size metal tube or deep socket. Screw bolt into the end of the idler gear shaft and withdraw idler gear shaft by tightening bolt. Remove gear assembly and inspect for wear.

15. If equipped with a magnet-type clutch shifter (Identifiable by diaphragm assembly), remove diaphragm cover and inspect diaphragm for tears or cracks.

Wash all parts and inspect for damage. Check transfer case and cover for cracks or chips. Inspect all oil seals for hardness or damage.

16. Check high and low speed output gears for oil clearance on the output shaft. Standard clearance: 0.0038–0.00319 in.

17. Inspect bearing races in transfer case. To replace, drive them out with an appropriate size metal pipe.

18. Check clearance of shifting forks on their sleeves. Limit: 0.04 in.

19. Check extension housing assembly and bearing for roughness and wear. To replace, remove oil seal and bearing snap ring. Press bearing out along with the shaft. To install shaft and bearing in extension housing, use a metal pipe to press bearing and shaft in together. Replace oil seal.

When assembling, use new gaskets and gasket sealer. Coat all moving parts with a thin layer of multipurpose grease.

1. Replace idler gear assembly. Be sure to insert spacer between the two needle bearings and refit gear spacer on small gear side of assembly. Check the thrust clearance between the gear spacer and the thrust washer with a feeler gauge. Standard clearance is 0.004–0.012 in.) Replace gear spacer if clearance is too great. Replacement gear spacers range in thickness from 0.047-0.059 in. Install nut and lock.

2. Replace low speed gear, washer and bearing inside case.

NOTE: Make sure gear is facing the right way

3. Install correct cltuch sleeve on the output shaft, install output shaft in case through the low speed gear, washer and bearing.

4. Press output shaft on low speed bearing using a metal pipe.

5. Install shifting fork on clutch fork shaft. Refit plug, spring and steel ball. Replace nut and lock.

6. Refit upper case cover, making sure to align the lever tip in the cover with the shift fork groove.

7. Install clutch sleeve on output shaft with its thick tapered side toward the bearing.

8. Install extension housing assembly and output flange assembly. Tighten flange nut to 80–101 ft–lb.

9. Refit spacer and drive gear on output shaft.

10. Install bearing retainer and shim.

11. Install brake drum backing plate. Tighten bolts to 14–22 ft–lb.

NOTE: Be sure to put short bolt in proper hole.

12. Refit brake drum and tighten nut to 80–101 ft–lb.

NOTE: It will be necessary to place unit in front drive and clamp or lock front drive flange to tighten brake drum nut.

13. Disengage front drive and wrap a spring scale cord around brake drum, anchoring it on a drive shaft stud. Test preload. With new bearing, preload should be between 2.6–9.0 lbs. With old bearing, preload should be more than 1.04 lbs. If preload is within limits, stake nut. If not, replace shim. Replacement shims range from 0.0039–0.0098 in.

14. Replace speedometer drive gear and nut and lock.

15. Refit diaphragm cylinder or shift fork guide.

NOTE: Be sure to insert shift fork into sleeve groove.

DRIVELINE

Driveshaft

REMOVAL AND INSTALLATION

Standard Bed Pick-up

1. Jack up the rear of the truck and support the rear axle housing with jack stands.

2. Paint a mating mark on the two halves of the rear universal joint flange.

3. Remove the bolts which hold the rear flange together.

4. Remove the splined end of the driveshaft from the transmission.

NOTE: Plug the end of the transmission with a rag or dummy flange to avoid losing transmission oil.

5. Remove the driveshaft from under the truck.

Installation is the reverse of removal. Grease the splined end of the shaft before installing. Tighten bolts to 11-16 ft-lb.

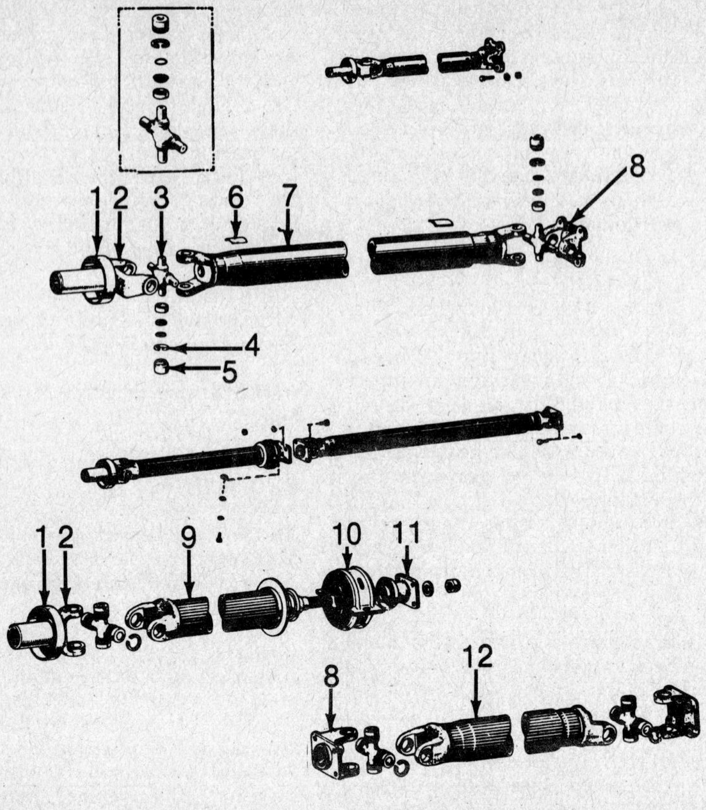

1. Transmission end of the driveshaft
2. U-joint yoke and sleeve
3. U-joint spider
4. Snap ring
5. U-joint spider bearing
6. Balancing weight
7. Driveshaft
8. U-joint yoke flange
Two-piece driveshaft only:
9. Intermediate driveshaft assembly
10. Center bearing support
11. U-joint flange assembly
12. Driveshaft

Driveshaft components—the upper illustration shows a single piece driveshaft

Long Bed Pick-up

1. Jack up truck and rest on support stands.
2. Paint or otherwise make mating lines on all six flange halves.
3. Remove the bolts attaching the rear universal joint flange to the drive pinion flange.
4. Drop the rear section of the shaft slightly and pull the unit out of the center bearing sleeve yoke.
5. Remove the center bearing support from the crossmember.
6. Unbolt the driveshaft flange from the rear of the transmission and remove driveshaft along with center bearing support.

To install:

1. Connect the output flange of the transmission to the flange on the front half of the shaft.
2. Install the center bearing support to the crossmember, but do not fully tighten the bolts.
3. Install the rear section of the shaft making sure that all mating marks are aligned. Make sure line on bearing in the center support mount is in the middle of the hole at the bottom of center mount.
4. Tighten all flange bolts to 11-16 ft-lb.

4x4 Pick-up

1. Jack the truck off the ground and place support stands under both the front and rear axles.
2. Match-mark all driveshaft flanges BEFORE removing bolts.
3. Unbolt the rear driveshaft flange from the rear pinion flange.
4. Unbolt the rear driveshaft flange from the rear transfer case flange and remove driveshaft.
5. Repeat steps 3 and 4 on front driveshaft.
6. Reverse order for reassembly. Tighten flange bolts to 29–43 ft-lb.

NOTE: For 4x4 Long Bed Pickups, see above for rear driveshaft removal and installation.

Land Cruiser

Land Cruiser models are equipped with two driveshafts; one runs from the transfer case to the rear differential and the other from the transfer case to the front differential. Removal and installation of both driveshafts is performed in the same manner.

1. Raise the vehicle and support it with jackstands.
2. Unfasten the bolts which secure the universal joint flange to the differential pinion flange.
3. Perform step 2 for the U-joint-to-transfer case flange bolts.
4. Withdraw the driveshaft from beneath the vehicle.

Installation is performed in the reverse order of removal.

NOTE: Lubricate the U-joints and sliding joints with multipurpose grease before installation.

U-Joint Overhaul

1. Mark the flange yoke and shaft for reassembly.
2. Remove the snap rings and, using a hammer and drift, drive one bearing cap most of the way out. Remove it with pliers.
3. Drive the opposite cap out.
4. Repeat this procedure for the other two caps.
5. Remove the spider.
6. Install a new spider in the yoke.
7. Press bearing caps over spider using a vise.
8. Install snap rings.
9. Assemble drive shaft and check for smoothness of operation.

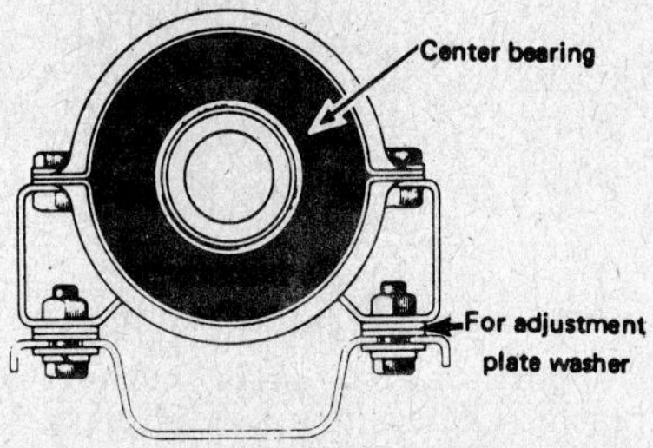

Center bearing adjustment

Center Bearing

REMOVAL AND INSTALLATION

1. Remove driveshaft as described above.
2. Matchmark center flange halves and separate.
3. Matchmark center flange and intermediate shaft for reassembly.
4. Loosen the nut stake and, placing driveshaft in vise, remove nut.
5. Hold flange yoke in vise and drive shaft off using a brass drift.
6. Inspect center support bearing for wear.

To install, slide new bearing on shaft, coat shaft splines with multi-purpose grease and replace flange yoke.

NOTE: Be sure to align match marks on flange and shaft.

7. Tighten flange nut to 123–144 ft-lb.

NOTE: If at all possible, use a new nut.

8. Loosen the nut and retighten to 19–25 ft-lb.
9. Stake the nut and reassemble driveshaft, being sure to align all matchmarks.

DRIVE AXLE

Axle Shaft, Bearing and Seal

REMOVAL AND INSTALLATION

Pick-up

1. Loosen the lug nuts on the wheel, and raise the truck and support it on jack stands.
2. Drain the axle housing.
3. Remove the lug nuts and remove the wheel.
4. Remove the brake drum securing nut and remove the drum.
5. Refer to the appropriate section on removing the rear brake.
6. Remove the brake springs and the retracting spring clamp bolt. Remove the lower springs and shoe strut. Remove the brake shoes, screws and the parking brake lever. Disengage the parking brake cable from the lever and the backing plate.
7. Plug the master cylinder reservoir inlet to prevent the fluid from running out. Disconnect the brake line from the wheel cylinder, being careful not to damage the fitting. Plug the brake line.
8. Remove the four nuts retaining the brake backing plate to the axle housing.
9. Pull the backing plate and the axle from the axle housing.

To remove bearing and seal:

1. Remove the shaft snap ring.
2. The axle shaft must be pressed from the bearing case. To do this, you must support the bearing case and press on the splined end of the axle. Toyota makes a special tool which bolts onto the bearingcase. This tool can then be held while the axle shaft is pressed through.
3. Remove the bearing from the bearing case.
4. Pry the old seals from the axle housing and bearing case with a plastic or wooden pry bar.
5. If the brake drum oil deflector or gaskets are to be replaced, the hub bolts will have to be pressed from the hub. Install the new deflector and gaskets and press the hub bolts back into the hub.
6. Drive a new axle shaft oil seal into the axle housing with a large socket or pipe. Apply a coating of grease to the lip of the seal after installation.
7. Install a new oil seal into the bearing case with a large socket or pipe.
8. Position a new bearing into the

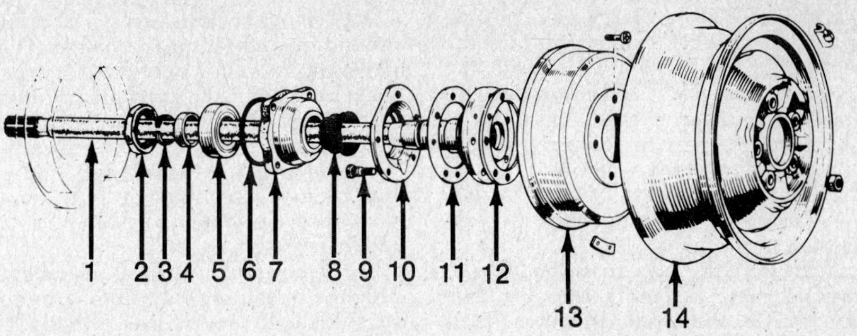

1. Rear axle shaft
2. Type "S" oil seal
3. Shaft snap-ring
4. Rear axle bearing retainer
5. Bearing
6. O-ring
7. Rear axle bearing case
8. Type "K" oil seal
9. Hub bolt
10. Brake drum oil deflector
11. Brake drum oil deflector gasket
12. Brake drum gasket
13. Brake drum
14. Disc wheel subassembly

Pick-up rear axle shaft and related components

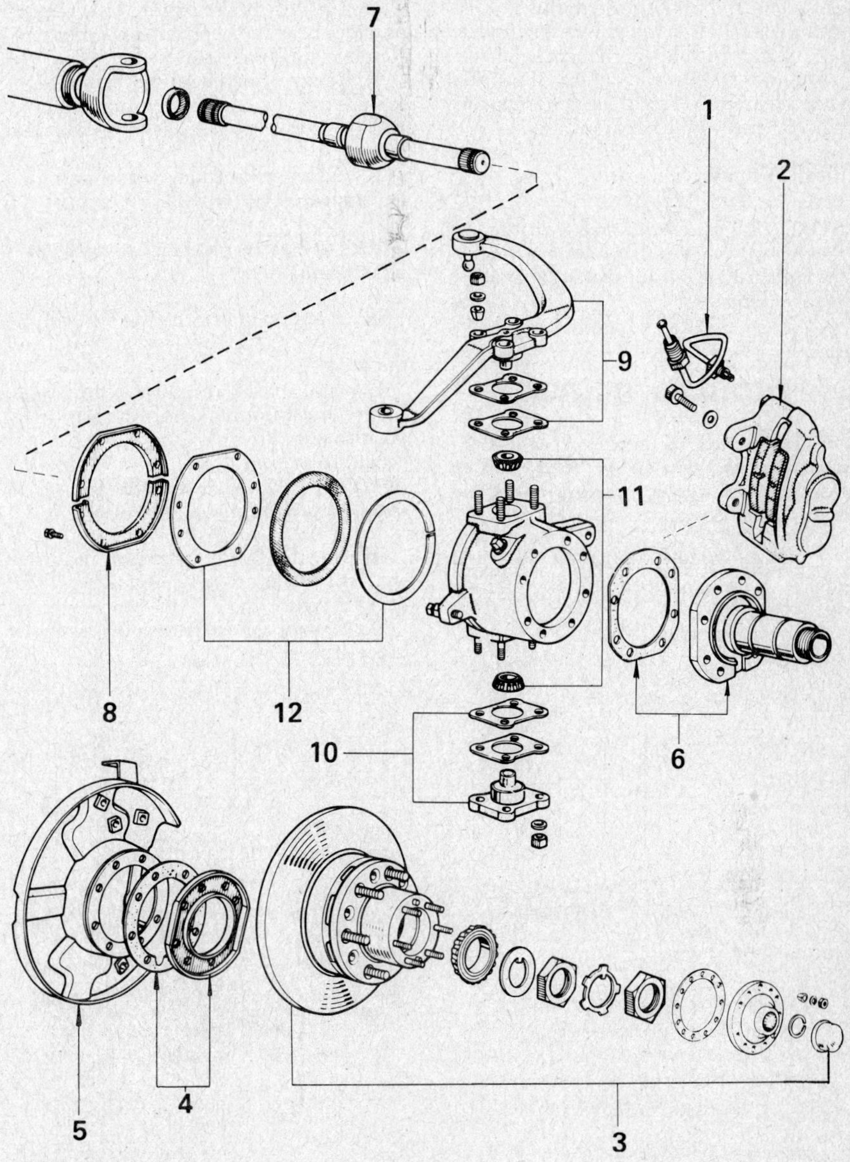

1. Brake tube
2. Disc brake cylinder
3. Front axle hub with brake disc
4. Dust seal & gasket
5. Dust cover
6. Knuckle spindle gasket
7. Drive shaft
8. Oil seal retainer
9. Knuckle arm & shim
10. Bearing cap & shim
11. Steering knuckle & bearing
12. Oil seal set

4x4 Pick-up front axle and steering knuckle assembly—Land Cruiser similar

bearing case. Place a large piece of pipe of a diameter which will support the inner race of the bearing underneath the brake backing plate, and press the axle shaft into the bearing case.

9. Slide the bearing retainer onto the axle shaft. Install the snap ring.

To install axle shaft:

1. Install new O-ring onto the axle housing.

2. Install the axle shaft and brake backing plate assembly into the axle housing. Be careful not to damage the oil seal with the axle splines. Rotate the axle back and forth until the shaft splines mesh with the differential gear splines.

3. Install the brake backing plate nuts and tighten to 44–58 ft-lb.

4. Install the brake shoes and lever assembly. Connect the parking brake cable and the brake shoe springs. Connect the brake line to the wheel cylinder.

5. After installing the brake drum, bleed the brakes and adjust the brake shoe clearance. Refill the axle housing with SAE 90W GL5 gear oil.

4x4 Pick-up

NOTE: The rear axle shafts on the 4x4 Pick-up are removed in the same manner as the regular Pick-up axle shafts. Refer above for operation.

Front Axle Shaft

NOTE: If truck is equipped with free-wheeling hubs, turn dial to "Free". Jack up front of truck, support, remove wheel and drain axle housing.

1. Remove free-wheel hub cover and gasket, if so equipped. Remove flange dust cover.

2. Remove snap ring from around axle shaft.

3. Remove six nuts and washers from around free-wheel hub or flange. To remove washers, it is necessary to expand them by driving a tapered punch into the washer slit. Be careful not to damage stud threads during the above operation.

4. Remove free-wheel hub body or hub flange. To remove hub flange, screw bolts into the two given holes and alternately tighten.

5. Remove disc brake fluid tube and plug the remaining tub running to master cylinder to prevent loss of fluid.

6. Remove the two bolts holding the disc brake caliper to the steering knuckle and remove caliper.

7. With a screwdriver or a punch, pry the metal lock tab away from the lock nut on the axle shaft and remove lock nut and tab. Remove adjusting nut under lock nut.

8. Tilt the brake rotor and remove outside bearing washer and bearing. Remove hub/brake rotor assembly.

9. Remove bolts holding the brake rotor dust cover to the steering knuckle. Remove dust seal, gasket and dust cover.

10. Remove knuckle spindle and gasket from steering knuckle assembly.

NOTE: It may be necessary to tap spindle off with a drift.

11. Position one of the flat sides of the outer drive shaft upwards and pull out the drive shaft.

Clean all parts and inspect for wear. Inspect bushing inside of knuckle spindle for wear.

NOTE: A bushing puller must be used to remove knuckle spindle bushing.

Inspect the Birfield joint on the drive shaft for looseness, cage cracks and ball bearing wear.

To remove the Birfield joint from the inner drive shaft:

Clamp the inner drive shaft in a vise. Place a drift against the inner bearing race on the Birfield joint and drive the joint off the shaft.

CAUTION: Make sure the drift is clear of the outer ball race and the ball cage before driving off joint.

To disassemble the Birfield joint, tilt the inner bearing race and cage as far as they will go inside the outer race and remove the exposed bearing. Repeat this process until all bearings are out. Turn the inner race and cage so that half of it is protruding from the outer race. Line up the two large openings in the cage with the protruding areas between the ball bearing slots and pull the cage along with the inner race out. Turn the inner race sideways inside the cage and, lining it up with the large openings in the cage, pull out. Check all parts for wear and check the ball bearing cage for cracks. Reassembly is the reverse of disassembly. Be sure to pack inside of joint with Molybdenum disulphide lithium grease.

CAUTION: When assembling the inner race and the cage, make sure the wide outer edge of the cage is on the same side as the protruding side of the inner race.

CAUTION: When installing inner race and cage assembly in the outer race, make sure the protruding end of the race and the wide side of the cage are facing out.

To remount the Birfield joint on the inner drive shaft:

1. Secure outer drive shaft in vise.

2. Install new snap rings on the inner drive shaft.

3. Line up the splines on the inner drive shaft with the splines on the inner race of the Birfield joint. Using a screw driver, compress the snap ring that is butting the inner race splines and tap drive shaft onto Birfield joint.

NOTE: Make sure the inner drive shaft cannot be pulled out of Birfield joint. Check the oil seal inside the axle shaft housing for wear. To replace, use a bushing puller mounted on a slide hammer. Refit using an appropriately sized tube as a seating tool.

To install axle shaft, reverse removal procedures at the beginning of this section witht he following notes:

1. When installing axle shaft into axle shaft housing, rotate the shaft from side to side so that the spindles on the shaft can mesh with the spindles in the differential.

2. After axle shaft is meshed with differential, pack the knuckle housing that holds the Birfield joint about three quarters full with Molybdenum disulphide lithium grease.

Observe the following torques when assembling:

Rotor dust cover to steering knuckle; 29–39 ft-lb.

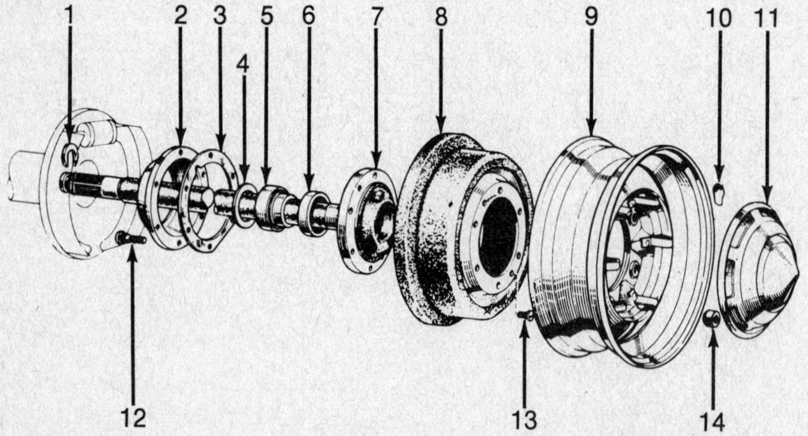

1. Rear axle shaft lock
2. Brake drum oil deector
3. Gasket
4. Spacer
5. Wheel bearing
6. Oil seal
7. Axle shaft
8. Brake drum
9. Wheel
10. Wheel balancing weight
11. Hub cap
12. Hub bolt
13. Brake drum set bolt
14. Lug nut

Land Cruiser rear axle shaft components

Disc brake caliper to steering knuckle; 55–75 ft-lb.

NOTE: BE sure to consult section on front hub installation when replacing hub adjusting nut and lock nut.

CAUTION: Be sure to refill axle with 90W gear oil before driving.

Land Cruiser—Rear

1. Remove the hub cap and loosen the wheel nuts.
2. Raise the rear axle housing with a jack and support the rear of the vehicle with jackstands.
3. Drain the oil from the differential.
4. Remove the wheel nuts and take off the wheels.
5. Remove the brake drum and related parts, as detailed below.
6. Remove the cover from the back of the differential housing.
7. Remove the pin from the differential pinion shaft.
8. Withdraw the pinion shaft and its spacer from the case.
9. Use a mallet to *tap* the rear axle shaft toward the differential, to aid in removal of the axle shaft C-lock.
10. Remove the C-lock.
11. Withdraw the axle shaft from the housing.

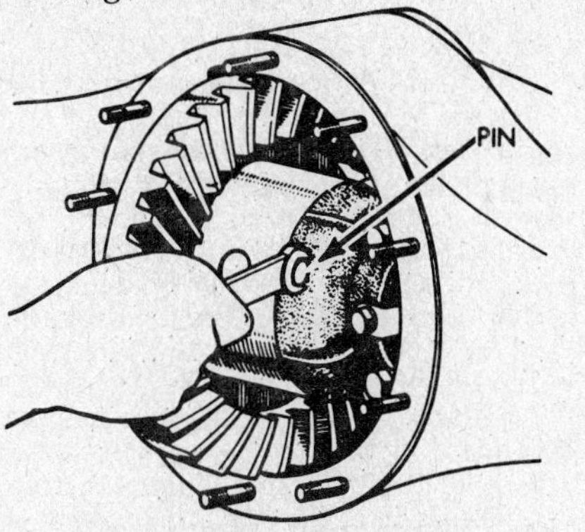

Pinion shaft pin removal—Land Cruiser

12. Repeat the removal procedure for the opposite side.
13. To remove oil seal and bearing, use a bearing puller and remove axle bearing and oil seal together. To replace, use a metal tube to drive bearing and seal into seat.

CAUTION: Do not mix the parts of the left and right axle shaft assemblies.

Installation is performed in the reverse order of removal. After installing the axle shaft, C-lock, spacer, and pinion shaft, measure the clearance between the axle shaft and the pinion shaft spacer with a feeler gauge. The clearance should fall between 0.0024–0.0181 in. If the clearance is not within specifications, use one of the following spacers to adjust it:

1.172–1.173 in.
1.188–1.189 in.
1.204–1.205 in.

The rest of the axle shaft installation is the reverse of removal. Remember to fill the axle with lubricant.

Land Cruiser Front

1. Raise and support the vehicle securely and remove the wheel/tire assembly.
2. Plug the brake master cylinder reservoir to prevent brake fluid leakage from the disconnected brake flexible hose.
3. Remove the outer axle shaft flange cap, and then remove the shaft snapring on the outer shaft. If equipped with free wheel locking hubs, complete steps 1–4 under 4x4 Pick-up axle shaft removal.
4. Remove the bolts retaining the outer axle shaft flange onto the front axle hub, and then, screw in two service bolts into the shaft flange alternately, and remove the shaft flange with its gasket.
5. Remove the brake drum set screws and remove the brake drum. If equipped with disc brakes, remove the caliper and disc.
6. Straighten the lockwasher, and remove the front wheel bearing adjusting nuts with a front wheel adjusting nut wrench or similar tool.
7. Remove the front axle hub together with its claw washer, bearings, and oil seal.
8. Remove the clip and disconnect the brake flexible hose from the brake tube.
9. Cut and remove the lock wire and remove the bolts retaining the brake backing plate onto the steering knuckle. Remove the brake backing plate together with the brake shoes, tension springs, and the wheel cylinder still assembled to the backing plate.
10. Tap the steering knuckle spindle lightly with a soft mallet, and remove the spindle with its gasket.

NOTE: When removing the steering knuckle spindle on a vehicle equipped with the ball joint type axle shaft joint, be prepared for the disconnection of the outer axle shaft from the joint. The joint ball will fall from the joint. Try to cushion its fall or catch it if you can.

11. On those models equipped with the ball type axle shaft joint, slide the inner front axle shaft out of the axle housing. On those models equipped with the Birfield constant velocity joint type of axle joint, remove the entire axle shaft assembly from the axle housing.
12. Remove bushing from inside of knuckle spindle with a bearing puller. Install new bushing using a metal tube as a seating tool.
13. Remove axle housing oil seal with a bearing puller. To install, use a metal tube as a seating tool.

Install the axle shaft in the reverse order of removal.

14. On those models equipped with the ball joint type axle joint, install the inner axle with its proper spacer in position until the splines are fully meshed with the differential side gear splines. Next, fill the steering knuckle three quarters full with grease and place the joint ball on the inner shaft end. Install the outer shaft and the front axle shaft spacer into the steering knuckle spindle and install the spindle with its gasket onto the steering knuckle.
15. On those models equipped with the Birfield constant velocity joint axle joint, install the axle into the housing and rotate the axle shaft until its splines mesh with the splines in the differential. Fill the steering knuckle housing three quarters full with grease and install the steering knuckle spindle.
16. Install and assemble the remaining components in the reverse order of removal. Adjust the wheel bearing preload.

NOTE: See brake drum or disk removal section for wheel bearing preload instructions.

NOTE: For Birfield joint overhaul, see 4x4 Pick-up axle shaft removal and installation section above.

DIFFERENTIAL ASSEMBLY

REMOVAL AND INSTALLATION

NOTE: Drive axle assembly servicing is a complex operation. Repair should not be attempted unless the special tools and knowledge required are readily available. Be sure to use all new gaskets and gasket sealer.

Rear Assembly—All Models

1. Remove drive shaft assembly. See above for procedures.
2. Disconnect the drive shaft from the pinion shaft flange.
3. Unfasten the carrier securing nuts and remove the carrier assembly. Installation is performed in the reverse order of removal. Be sure to apply liquid sealer to both the carrier gasket and the lower carrier securing nuts.

Front Assembly—Land Cruiser, 4x4 Pick-up

1. Remove front axle shafts as described above.
2. Remove drive shaft. See above for procedures.
3. Remove differential assembly retaining nuts. Remove differential assembly. Installation is performed in the reverse order of removal. Be sure to apply liquid sealer to both the carrier gasket and the lower carrier assembly nuts.

OVERHAUL

1. Throughly wash and rinse the carrier and blow dry with compressed air.

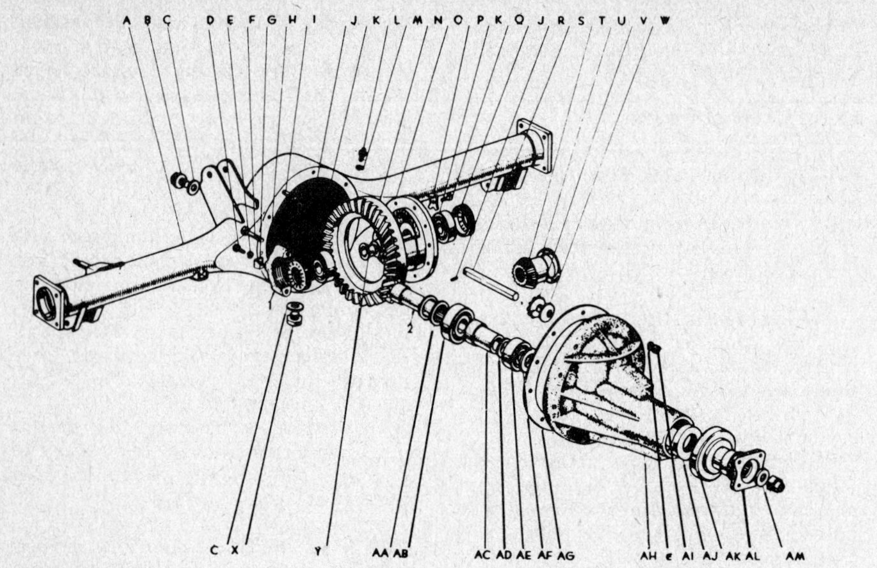

a. Housing assembly
b. Filler plug
c. Gasket
d. Bolt
e. Lock washer
f. Hexagon bolt
g. Bearing adjusting nut lock
h. Lockwasher
i. Stud
j. Bearing adjusting nut
k. Bearing
l. Breather plug
m. Lockwasher
n. Ring gear and drive pinion 1 and 2
o. Case
p. Lockplate
q. Bolt
r. Lockpin
s. Pinion shaft
t. Side gear
u. Thrust washer
v. Pinion
w. Thrust washer
x. Drain plug
y. Oil reservoir
aa. Shim
ab. Bearing
ac. Spacer
ad. Shim
ae. Bearing
af. Oil slinger
ag. Gasket
ah. Carrier
ai. Nut
aj. Oil seal
ak. Dust deflector
al. Universal joint flange
am. Flat washer

Differential components

2. Securely clamp the carrier in a vise or suitable stand.
3. Apply a light coating of mechanic's blue to the teeth of the ring gear.
4. Applying a slight drag on the ring gear to avoid backlash, rotate the pinion in a smooth and continuous manner to obtain a good tooth pattern on the ring gear.
5. Next, attach a dial indicator gauge to the carrier base and check the ring gear backlash.
6. Also check ring gear runout at this time. If the tooth pattern obtained is correct, and the backlash and runout are within limits, any gear noise must come from the side gear.
7. With the dial indicator gauge set up on the carrier, check the backlash between the pinion gears and side gears. Excessive backlash usually is due to either worn thrust washers or a worn pinion shaft.
8. Check side gear thrust clearance with a feeler gauge.
9. If everything is within specifications, test the preload on the differential drive pinion nut. Punch mark both pinion and nut in their original positions, then loosen the pinion nut about 1/2 turn and torque to specifications. If the punch marks line up again (within 60°) the pinion preload was correct.
10. Punch mark both the carrier and the side bearing caps for identification, remove the lock-nuts and take off the caps.
11. Remove the differential case assembly from the carrier. Do not mix the bearing cups; paint mark them for identification.
12. Remove the differential pinion nut (do not let the pinion drop out), then remove the pinion spacer, yoke and oil seal.
13. With a brass punch, drive out the pinion bearing cups.

NOTE: This should be done only when the bearings are to be replaced.

14. Press or pull off the drive pinion rear bearing. Avoid damaging the flat spacer behind the bearing.
15. Measure the spacer thickness and note the measurement for future use. Remove both side bearings from the differential case and mark them "L" and "R" for identification.

NOTE: Remove side bearings only if they must be replaced.

16. Punch mark the differential case and cover, then remove the cover bolts and the cover (where fitted).
17. Remove the shaft and pinions, the side gears and all thrust washers.

NOTE: Some differential types have four spider pinion gears; punch mark the gears before removal so they can be correctly reinstalled.

Check all bearing cones and cups for wear. Inspect the tooth surfaces of all gears carefully and inspect all thrust washers for wear and signs of slipping in their seats. Check all gear shafts for scoring, wear or distortion. Finally, inspect the case and carrier housing for cracks or other damage. Also check the case for signs of wear at the side gear bores, bearing cap and mounting hubs.

Assembly is performed in the following order:

1. Wash and clean all parts before installation.
2. Lightly oil all bearings and gear shafts, except the ring gear and drive pinion teeth.
3. Place the side gears and the pinion gears, with their thrust washers, into the differential case.
4. Insert the shaft and align the lock pin holes in the case and shaft.

DIFFERENTIAL SPECIFICATIONS

Model	Backlash (in.) Ring Gear and Pinion	Backlash (in.) Side Gears	Runout (in.) Ring Gear	Torque (ft-lb) Side Bearing Cap	Torque (ft-lb) Differential Pinion Nut	Pinion Bearing Preload (in.-lb) New	Pinion Bearing Preload (in.-lb) Old
Pick-up (all)	0.005-0.007	0.002-0.008	0.002 (1)(2)	51-65	120-153 (3)	17-23 (5)	4-13 (5)(6)
Land Cruiser (all)	0.006-0.008	0.0008-0.0079 (4)	0.004	65-80	145-175	16-23 (5)	5-8 (5)(6)

(1) 1976-77: 0.004 in.; 1978-80: 0.0028 in.
(2) 4X4 Pick-up: 0.004 in.
(3) 1979-80 2 wheel drive Pick-up: 80-173 ft-lb
(4) 1979-80: 0.001-0.008 in.
(5) Without oil seal and differential gears installed
(6) 1977-80: 8-11 in. lb

5. Install the case cover in place and install the lock pin (bolt) and tighten the cover bolts to specification; check the play.

6. If the side bearings were removed, install them now. If the ring gear was removed, install it now. Tighten the bolts in symmetrical sequence to avoid distortion and runout.

7. Install the drive pinion bearing cups into the carrier housing, using a suitable installing tool. Make sure the cups are seated solidly.

8. Assemble the drive pinion rear bearing to the drive pinion and insert it into the carrier housing. Install the spacer and front bearing to the drive pinion; install the yoke and tighten the nut to specifications.

CAUTION: The drive pinion oil seal is NOT installed at this point.

9. The drive pinion preload is measured in in. lbs (not ft lbs). Adjust the preload by changing the length of the bearing spacer (between the front and rear bearings) until the required preload is obtained.

10. Place the previously assembled differential case into position in the bearing hubs and put the caps into position as marked (L and R).

11. Set the case so that there will be the least amount of backlash between the ring gear and pinion (in order to save time adjusting).

12. Install the adjusting nuts (also marked L and R) and take care not to cross-thread them.

13. Finger-tighten the bearing caps until the threads are lined up correctly, then tighten slowly.

14. Back off the right-hand adjusting nut (ring gear teeth side) and screw in the other nut until almost no backlash is felt.

15. Attach a dial indicator gauge so that it reads at right angles to the back of the ring gear, then screw in the right-hand adjusting nut until the gauge indicates that all side play has been eliminated.

16. Tighten the adjusting nut another 1 or 1½ notches (depending on the fit of the lock tabs).

17. Recheck the preload on the drive pinion as before; this time the specifications are different.

18. If too loose, readjust the side bearing preload; if too tight, adjust the ring gear backlash.

19. Install the dial indicator gauge so that it contacts the ring gear teeth at right angles. Adjust the backlash to specifications.

20. If too great, adjust by loosening the bearing cap bolts slightly and screwing the right-hand adjusting nut (ring gear teeth side) out about two notches.

21. Tighten the left-hand adjusting nut the same amount.

NOTE: One notch of the adjusting nut equals about 0.002 in. of backlash.

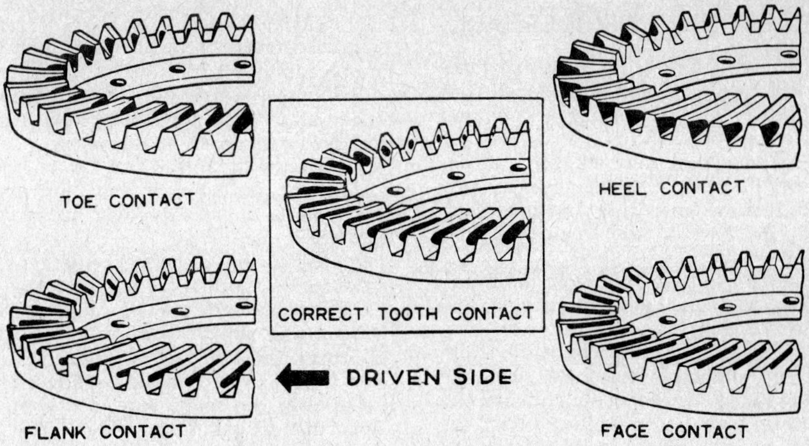

Ring gear tooth contact pattern

22. Recheck the backlash, then tighten the bearing cap nuts.

23. Using a dial indicator recheck all runout dimensions (ring gear back, ring gear outer circumference and differential case).

24. Apply a thin coat of mechanic's blue, red lead or even lipstick to the ring gear teeth. Rotate the gear several times, applying a light drag to the ring gear. Rotate the gear in both directions.

25. Inspect the tooth pattern. There are four basic tooth patterns: heel, toe, flank and face. Most often the tooth pattern obtained will be a combination of two of these patterns and the adjustments must be made accordingly.

Heel contact Move the drive pinion in by increasing the thickness of the spacer (between the pinion head and rear bearing). Readjust backlash by moving the ring gear away from the pinion.

Face contact Adjust same as above.

Toe contact Adjust by moving the drive pinion out by reducing the thickness of the spacer. Readjust backlash.

Flank contact Adjust same as toe contact.

Continue assembling as follows:

26. Remove the drive pinion nut and install the seal into the differential carrier housing, then install the oil slinger, dust shield and yoke and retorque the pinion nut as specified.

27. Install the differential carrier assembly into the axle housing.

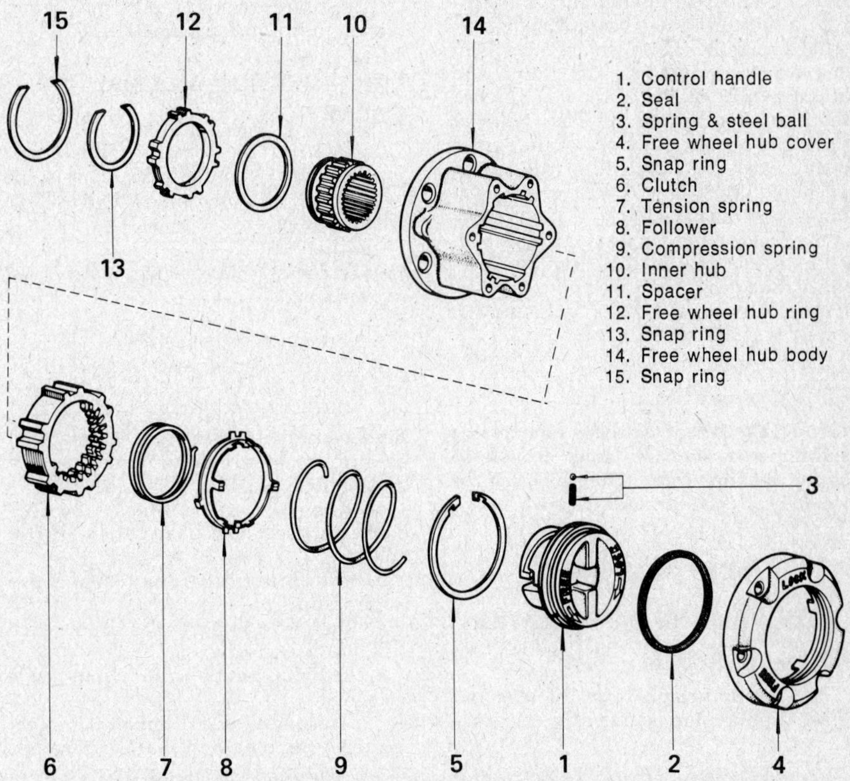

Free-wheel hub assembly—same on 4x4 Pick-up and Land Cruiser

FREE WHEEL HUB OVERHAUL

Certain models of both the 4x4 Pick-up and Land Cruiser are equipped with free wheel locking hubs. The same unit is used on both vehicles.

1. Remove the free wheel hub as described in the front axle removal section.
2. Remove snap ring and inner hub from the base of the free wheel hub body.
3. Remove snap ring from inner hub and remove free wheel hub ring and spacer from inner hub.
4. Remove the clutch assembly from the control knob by turning it clockwise to the knob. When the clutch assembly will turn no more, press it in toward the knob, turn it over the locking notch and remove along with compression spring.
5. Remove the snap ring holding the knob in the free-wheel hub cover and remove the knob.

CAUTION: Do not lose steel ball and spring in control knob when removing from hub cover.

Clean all parts and check for wear. Make sure all meshing teeth are not burred or chipped. Check hub cover oil seal for damage.

If it is necessary to replace part of the clutch assembly, proceed as follows:

6. Pry anchoring end of tension spring from the follower pawl on clutch assembly and push the spring down into the clutch. Remove follower pawl.

CAUTION: Do not distort spring.

7. When reassembling clutch assembly, if the spring has been moved or removed from the clutch, screw the unbent end of the spring into the clutch and align it with the end of the last notched tooth in the clutch. Replace follower pawl and pry the other end of the spring over it with the bent end of the spring anchored under one of the two protruding lips on the pawl.
8. Apply a light coating of multipurpose grease to the teeth on the free-wheel hub ring, the inner hub, and the clutch. Also grease the oil ring and the outsides of the control knob.

Reassembly is the reverse of disassembly.

CAUTION: When replacing compression spring, make sure the larger end of the spring is on the control knob side and the smaller end is on the follower pawl.

Axle Housing

REMOVAL AND INSTALLATION

Rear—All Models

1. Jack up vehicle from the rear and place support stands under the chassis.

NOTE: Do not place jacks under axle housing.

2. Remove wheels.
3. Disconnect driveshaft. See above for procedures.
4. Remove torque rod, stabilizer bar or load sensing proportioning valve arm from the top of differential housing.
5. Remove brake lines at brake line holders on axle housing and plug end that runs to master cylinder to avoid fluid loss.
6. On Pick-up, disconnect emergency brake cables at brake drums.
7. Place a jack under differential housing and unbolt bottoms of shock absorbers. Pull shocks from mounts.
8. Adjust jack so that all tension is off leaf springs but make sure jack is still supporting differential housing.
9. Remove the two bolts at the front of the leaf spring that hold the front leaf spring through-bolt. Remove through-bolt. Carefully pry leaf spring from mount.
10. Have an assistant steady the axle housing and remove shackle bolts and shackles from the rear of leaf springs. Carefully pry leaf spring from mount. Lower axle housing.

Installation is the reverse of removal.

NOTE: When installing the front and rear leaf spring bolts, finger tighten them at first, then, after you have replaced and fully tightened all other components, place a jack under the axle housing and raise the vehicle off the support stands. Now fully tighten the spring bolts.

CAUTION: Do not tighten the spring bolts from under the vehicle!

See spring removal and installation section for torque specifications.

Front—4x4 Pick-up, Land Cruiser

1. Jack up the front of vehicle and place support stands under chassis. Be careful not to damage steering linkage when jacking.

NOTE: Do not place stands under front axle housing.

2. Remove front wheels.
3. Remove brake lines at the brake line holder behind brake assembly and plug to prevent fluid from leaking out. Remove shim holding brake line that goes to master cylinder and remove brake line. Repeat for other side.
4. Remove bottom shock absorber bolts and raise shock absorbers out of holders.
5. Disconnect drive shaft. See above for procedure.
6. Unbolt stabilizer bar from each side of axle housing.
7. Unbolt torque rod from axle housing.
8. On Land Cruiser, unbolt the steering relay rod ball joint that is connected to the steering tie rod and drive off with a ball joint remover. Tie up out of the way. On Pick-up, remove the cotter pin in the end of the drag link that attaches to the steering knuckle arm. Unscrew screw in the end of the drag link and remove screw, spring holder, spring and the outer socket holder. Remove drag link from the steering knuckle arm. Be careful not to lose or displace inner socket holder.
9. On Land Cruiser, remove steering damper from axle housing.
10. Place a jack under differential housing and adjust it to take the weight of the axle housing without putting pressure on the leaf springs.
11. On the Pick-up, have an assistant steady axle housing and unbolt the U-bolts holding the axle housing to the leaf springs. Carefully lower axle housing.

CAUTION: Do not lay under axle housing when unbolting U-bolts.

12. On Land Cruiser, see steps 9 and 10 for rear axle housing removal above.

Installation is the reverse of removal with the following notes:

13. Finger tighten the front and rear leaf spring mounting bolts. Fully assemble and tighten all other components, jack the axle housing up so that the vehicle clears its support stands and fully tighten the leaf spring bolts.

CAUTION: Do not get under the vehicle to tighten the leaf spring bolts!

14. On 4x4 pick-up when installing the drag link, tighten the cap as far as it will go then loosen it 1-1/3 turns and install the new cotter key. Be sure to grease the socket assembly through the grease nipple.

See spring and steering removal and installation sections below for torque specifications.

FRONT SUSPENSION

Springs

REMOVAL AND INSTALLATION

1973–78 Pick-up

1. Remove the hubcap and loosen the lug nuts.
2. Raise the front end of the truck and support the front suspension crossmember with jackstands.
3. Remove the lug nuts and the wheel.
4. Remove the stabilizer bar connecting bolts and remove the bracket parts, being careful to note their removal sequence in order to aid in installation.
5. Remove the tie rod cotter pin and nut. Use a puller to remove the end of the tie rod from the knuckle arm.

6. Remove the shock absorber, as detailed in the appropriate section. Detach the brake hose.

7. Raise the lower control arm, using a jack, so that the arm is free of the steering knuckle.

8. Loosen the ball joint attachment nut and remove the ball joint puller.

9. Slowly lower the jack underneath the control arm.

CAUTION: If the jack is lowered too fast, the spring could suddenly release, causing damage or injury.

10. Remove the coil spring and its insulator from underneath the truck.

Inspect the coil spring, its insulator; and bumper for cracks, wear, or damage. Replace parts as necessary.

Installation is basically performed in the reverse order of removal. However, a coil spring compressor should be used to install the spring, rather than the method used for removing it.

Torque the suspension components to the following specifications:

Lower control arm—51–65 ft lbs (1976–78 33–43 ft lbs)

Ball joint—87–123 ft lbs

1979–80 Pick-up

1979–80 Pick-up models are equipped with torsion bar front springs.

CAUTION: Great care must be take to make sure springs are not mixed after removal. It is strongly suggested that before removal, each spring be marked with paint, showing front and rear of spring and from which side of the truck it was taken. If springs are installed backwards or on the wrong sides of the truck, they could fracture. If replacing springs, it is not necessary to mark them.

1. Jack up truck and support the frame on stands. Remove the wheel.

2. Slide the boot from the rear of torsion bar spring and paint an exact mark from spring housing onto spring.

3. Follow the same procedure on the front of the spring.

CAUTION: Be sure to make a mark showing front of spring from back of spring!

4. On the rear torsion bar spring holder, there is a long bolt that passes through the arm of the holder and up through the frame crossmember. REMOVE THE LOCKING NUT ONLY FROM THIS BOLT.

5. Using a small ruler, measure the length from the bottom of the remaining nut to the threaded tip of the bolt and record this measurement.

CAUTION: Be sure to complete step five accurately.

6. Place a jack under the rear torsion bar spring holder arm and jack up the arm to remove the spring pressure from the long bolt. Remove the adjusting nut from the long bolt.

7. SLOWLY lower jack.

8. Remove long bolt and its spacers and remove rear holder. You should be able to pull the torsion bar out of the front and rear holders.

Inspect all parts for wear damage or cracks. Check the boots for rips and wear. Inspect the splined ends of the torsion bar spring and the splined holes in the rear holder and the front torque arm for damage. Replace as necessary.

On the rear ends of the torsion bar springs, there are markings to show which is right and which is the left bar. Do not confuse them.

To install:

9. Coat the splined ends of the torsion bar with multipurpose grease.

10. If refitting old torsion bars:

a. Slide the front of the bar into the opening on the torque arm, making sure you line up the marks you made earlier on the torsion bar spring and the torque arm.

b. Repeat the above step with the rear spring holder and replace the long bolt and its spacers.

c. Place a pipe that will fit in the notch on the rear holder arm on a jack and jack up the arm.

d. Tighten the adjusting nut so that it is the same length as it was before removal.

NOTE: Do not replace the lock nut yet.

11. When installing a new torsion bar spring:

a. Slide the front of the torsion bar into the opening on the torque arm.

b. Fit the rear holder in place and install the rear of the torsion in it so that when the long bolt and spacers are installed, the distance from the top

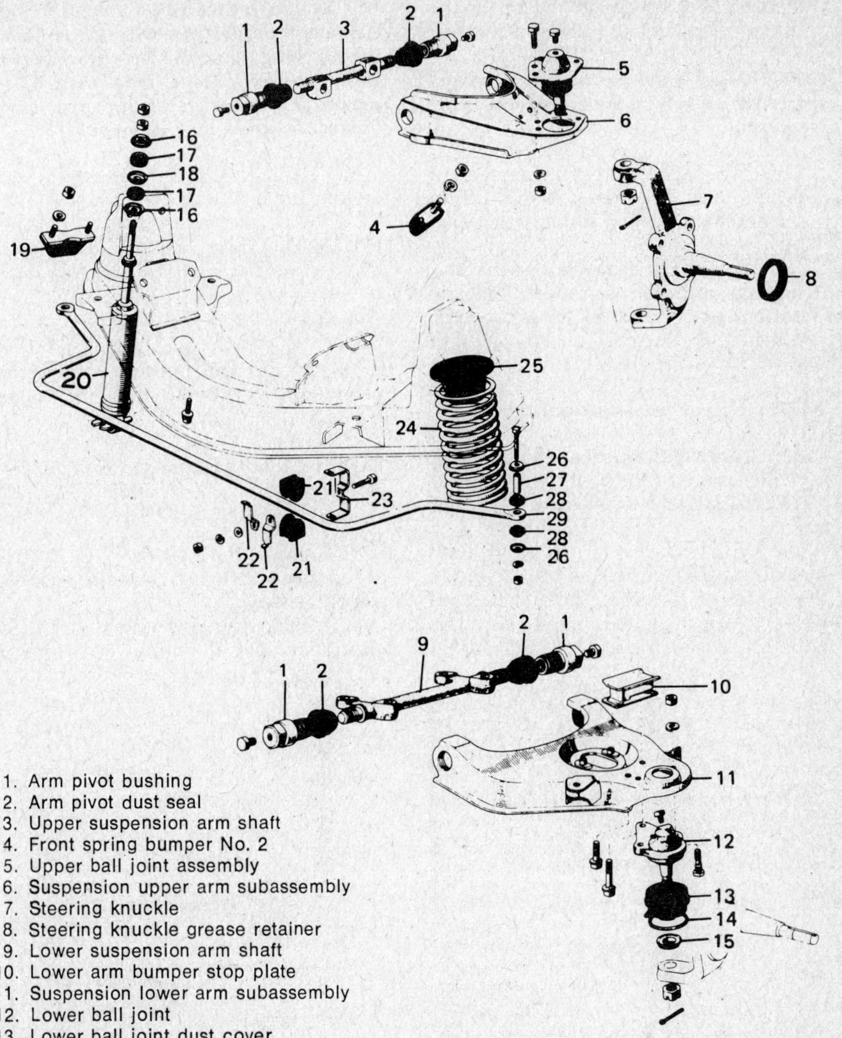

1. Arm pivot bushing
2. Arm pivot dust seal
3. Upper suspension arm shaft
4. Front spring bumper No. 2
5. Upper ball joint assembly
6. Suspension upper arm subassembly
7. Steering knuckle
8. Steering knuckle grease retainer
9. Lower suspension arm shaft
10. Lower arm bumper stop plate
11. Suspension lower arm subassembly
12. Lower ball joint
13. Lower ball joint dust cover
14. Set ring
15. Lower ball joint dust cover plate
16. Cushion retainers
17. Shock absorber cushion
18. Cushion retainer
19. Front spring bumper No. 1
20. Front shock absorber
21. Stabilizer bushing
22. Stabilizer link cover
23. Stabilizer link
24. Front coil spring
25. Front coil spring insulator
26. Cushion retainer
27. Collar
28. Stabilizer cushion
29. Stabilizer bar

1973-78 Pick-up front suspension

of the upper spacer to the tip of the threaded end of bolt is 0.7–1.0 in.

NOTE: Make sure the bolt and bottom spacer are snuggly in the holder arm while measuring.

c. When the correct measurement is achieved, fit a pipe or round bar in the notch on the rear holder arm. Jack up arm on pipe.

d. Replace the adjusting nut and tighten until the distance from the bottom of the nut to the tip of the threaded end of the bolt is 71–89mm (2.8–3.5 in.).

NOTE: Do not install the lock nut yet.

12. Apply multipurpose grease to the boot lips and refit the boots over splines.
13. Replace the wheel and lower the truck.
14. With the wheels on the ground, measure the distance from the ground to the center of the lower arm shaft (See chart). Adjust vehicle height with the adjusting nut on the rear spring holder.

NOTE: If, after achieving the correct vehicle height, the distance from the bottom of the adjusting nut to the top of the threaded end of the long bolt is more than 3.8 in., change the position of the rear spring holder arm spline and reassemble.

15. Replace and tighten the lock nut on the long bolt.

CAUTION: Make sure the adjusting nut does not move when tightening lock nut.

4x4 Pick-up

1. Jack up the front of vehicle and place support stands under the chassis frame.

NOTE: Do not place supports under front axle housing.

2. Remove wheel.
3. Remove the bolt from the bottom of the shock absorber and raise shock up out of the way.
4. If removing driver's side front leaf spring, remove the cotter pin from the end of the steering drag link at the axle housing. Unscrew the slitted bolt in the end of the drag link and remove the bolt, spring holder, spring, and outer socket holder. Remove drag link from steering knuckle arm.

NOTE: Be careful not to lose inner socket holder.

5. Remove stabilizer bar bolt and spacer and washer assembly.
6. Disconnect brake line at the holder behind the brake assembly. Drive out shim holding brake line to holder and withdraw brake line. Plug end of brake line running to master cylinder to prevent fluid loss.
7. Place a jack under the front axle housing and raise to put pressure on the leaf spring. Remove the four nuts holding the two U-bolts to the axle housing and remove the U-bolts.
8. Lower the jack enough to take the pressure off the leaf spring but so it still supports the axle housing.
9. Remove the bolts holding the leaf spring to its hangers and carefully pry the spring from its holders.

NOTE: It may be necessary to lower the jack under the axle housing to remove spring.

Installation is the reverse of removal.

CAUTION: Be sure to refill brake master cylinder reservoir and bleed brakes!

NOTE: Finger tighten the front and rear leaf spring hanger pin nuts. After the spring is attached to the axle housing and chassis, jack up the axle housing until the vehicle clears its support stands and then torque pin nuts.

Observe the following torques:
U-bolt nuts: 73–108 ft-lb.
Front hanger pin placer bolts: 8–11 ft-lb.
Front hanger pin nut: 55–79 ft-lb.
Rear shackle pin nuts: 55–79 ft-lbs.

Land Cruiser

Land Cruiser models are equipped with leaf springs in the front and rear. Thus, front spring removal is performed in almost the same manner as rear spring removal. Follow the procedure outlined in the rear suspension section, below.

CAUTION: Be careful when raising or lowering the front suspension with a jack so as not to damage any of the steering system components.

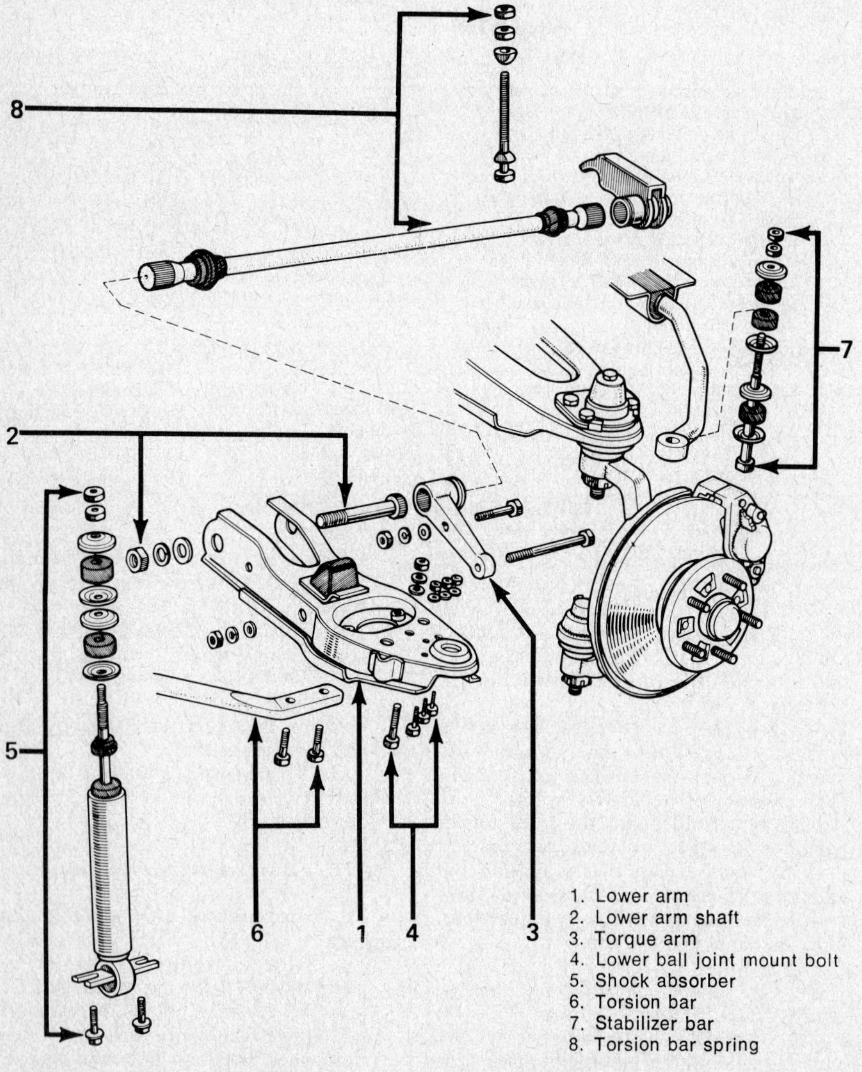

1979-80 Pick-up front suspension

Front Shock Absorber

REMOVAL AND INSTALLATION

Pick-up

1. Remove the hubcap and loosen the lug nuts.

2. Raise the front of the car and support it with jack stands.
3. Remove the lug nuts and the wheel.
4. Unfasten the double nuts at the top end of the shock absorber. Remove the cushions and cushion retainers.
5. Remove the two bolts which secure the lower end of the shock absorber to the lower control arm.
6. Remove the shock absorber.
Installation is the reverse of removal.

4x4 Pick-up

Removal and installation is the same as standard Pick-up, except there is only one through-bolt holding the bottom of the shock in place.

Land Cruiser

Complete steps 1–3 for Pick-up shock absorber removal.

CAUTION: Be careful not to damage steering assembly when jacking up front of vehicle.

Remove bolts holding the top and bottom of the shock in place and remove shock. Installation is the reverse of removal.

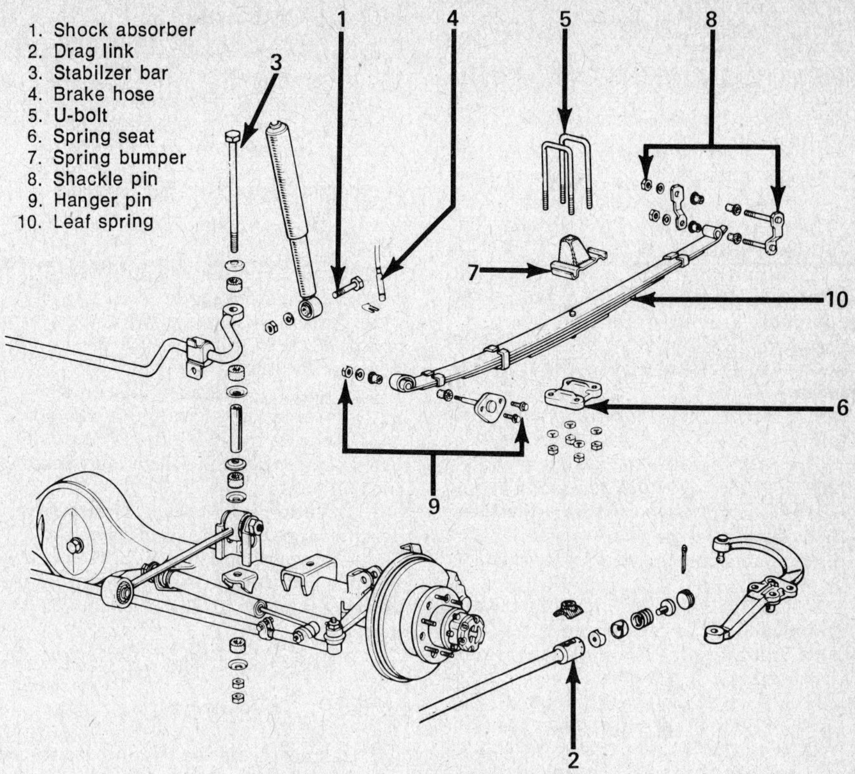

4x4 Pick-up front suspension

Steering Knuckle

REMOVAL AND INSTALLATION

Pick-up

NOTE: On Pick-ups with coil springs, it will be necessary to obtain a spring compresser for installation.

1. Jack up front of vehicle and support on stands.
2. Remove wheel.
3. If vehicle has front disk brakes, remove brake caliper.
4. Remove axle hub dust cap. Remove cotter key, lock, front nut and front nut washer from axle hub. Remove front bearing and remove brake disk or drum.
5. On drum brakes, remove brake line and plug.
6. Remove cotter keys and four bolts holding the brake backing plate and brake shoes on drum and the rotor dust cover on disk brakes. Remove the plate or cover.
7. Remove steering link from back of knuckle.
8. Support the lower arm with a jack and raise to put pressure on spring.

CAUTION: Be careful not to unbalance vehicle support stands when jacking up lower arm!

9. Remove cotter key and large lower ball joint nut and separate the ball joint from the steering knuckle with a gear puller.
10. Repeat step 9 on upper ball joint.

NOTE: Do not let the steering knuckle fall after removing upper ball joint.

Installation is the reverse of removal.
11. On Pick-ups with coil springs, use a spring compressor when reassembling. Observe the following torques:
Large nut on upper ball joint: 66–94 ft–lb
Large nut on lower ball joint: 87–123 ft–lb
Rotor dust cover or drum backing plate to steering knuckle: 66–94 ft–lb

NOTE: See brake section for hub nut installation procedures.

CAUTION: Be sure to bleed brakes.

4x4 Pick-up, Land Cruiser

1. Complete front axle shaft removal procedures in drive axle section, above.
2. Unbolt and remove the tie rod from the knuckle arm with a gear puller. On the Pick-up, if removing the driver's side knuckle see section on steering adjustment below for removal of the steering drag link.
3. Remove the oil seal retainer at the back of the steering knuckle.
4. Remove the four nuts on the top steering knuckle cap along with the cone washers. See section on axle shaft removal for procedures in removing cone washers.
5. Remove the four nuts on the bottom steering knuckle cap along with cone washers.
6. Using a small drift and hammer, tap the knuckle beating caps out from inside the steering knuckle.

CAUTION: Do not tap on the bearings!

NOTE: Do not mix or lose the upper and lower bearing cap shims.

Installation is the reverse of removal.
To test the knuckle bearing preload, attach a spring scale to the end hole in the steering knuckle at a right angle to the arm. The force required to move the knuckle from side to side should be 4–8 lbs. (4x4 Pick-up); 4–5 lbs. (Land Cruiser). If the preload is not correct, adjust by replacing shims.

Upper Control Arm

REMOVAL AND INSTALLATION

Pick-up

1. Raise and support the truck under the frame.
2. Remove the wheel.
3. Raise the lower control arm with a jack.
4. Remove the nut from the upper ball joint stud.
5. Separate the ball joint from the steering knuckle.
6. Unbolt and remove the upper arm at the two bolts holding the inner shaft to the frame, taking note of the number and size of the aligning shims.
7. Installation is the reverse of removal. Replace the shims as found. Tighten fasteners, but do not torque them until the truck in on the ground.
8. Lower the truck and torque the upper arm mounting bolts to 95–153 ft-lb.

Lower Control Arm

REMOVAL AND INSTALLATION

Pick-up

1. Raise and support the front end.
2. On 1973–78 Pick-ups, remove the coil spring as outlined above. On 1979–80 Pick-ups, remove the torsion bar spring as outlined above.
3. Remove the stabilizer bar and the strut bar from the lower arm if so equipped.
4. On 1979–80 Pick-ups, remove the bottom of the shock absorber from the lower arm.
5. Unbolt and remove lower ball joint.

NOTE: If the lower ball joint is not to be replaced, simply unbolt it from the lower control arm. It is not necessary to separate the ball joint from the steering knuckle.

6. On 1973–78 Pick-ups, unbolt and remove the lower control arm at the four bolts mounting the lower control arm on the frame. On 1979–80 Pick-ups, unbolt and remove the nut from the lower arm shaft. Remove the spring torque arm from the other side of the lower control arm and remove the lower arm shaft bolt and the lower arm.

Installation is the reverse of removal. Tighten the bolt(s) holding the lower control arm to the frame but do not torque them until the vehicle is on the ground.

Observe the following torques:
Ball joint retainer bolts:
1979–80
Big bolt: 29–39 ft–lb.
Small bolts: 15–21 ft–lb.
1973–78
Big bolt: 21–32 ft–lb.
Small bolts: 21–28 ft–lb.
1979–80:
Strut bar: 55–75 ft–lb.
Torque arm: 29–39 ft–lb.

7. Lower the truck and torque the lower arm mounting bolt(s) to 33–43 ft–lb. (1973–78 Pick-up) or 145–217 ft–lb. (1979–80 Pick-up)

Lower Ball Joints

INSPECTION

Jack up the lower suspension arm. Check the front wheel play. Replace the lower ball joint if the play at the wheel rim exceeds 0.1 in. vertical motion or 0.25 in. horizontal motion. Be sure that the dust covers are not torn and that they are securely glued to the ball joints.

REMOVAL AND INSTALLATION

NOTE: On models equipped with both upper and lower ball joints—if both ball joints are to be removed, always remove the lower and then the upper ball joint.

Pick-up Coilspring

Perform steps 1–8 of the Pick-up coil spring removal procedure. Skip step 6.

Installation is performed in the reverse order of removal. Lubricate the ball joint. Check front end alignment.

Pick-up—Torsion Bar Spring

1. Jack up vehicle, support on stands and remove wheel.
2. Remove cotter key and large nut from bottom of ball joint.
3. Place a jack under the control arm and jack up to put pressure on the torsion bar spring.
4. Using a gear puller, disconnect the ball joint from the steering knuckle.
5. Remove the ball joint mount bolts.
6. Lower the jack a little and remove the ball joint.

Installation is the reverse of removal. Torque large ball joint mount bolt to 29–39 ft–lb., small bolts to 15–21 ft–lb., and the nut connecting the ball joint to the steering knuckle to 87–123 ft–lb.

Upper Ball Joint

INSPECTION

Disconnect the ball joint from the steering knuckle and check free-play by hand. Replace the ball joint, if it is noticeably loose.

REMOVAL AND INSTALLATION

NOTE: On models equipped with both upper and lower ball joints—if both are to be removed, always remove the lower one first.

Pick-up

Remove and install the upper ball joint in the same manner as outlined for the lower ball joint.

REAR SUSPENSION

Springs

REMOVAL AND INSTALLATION

Pick-up and Land Cruiser, 4x4 Pick-up

1. Loosen the rear wheel lug nuts.
2. Raise the rear of the vehicle. Support the frame and rear axle housing with stands.
3. Remove the lug nuts and the wheel.
4. Remove the cotter pin, nut, and washer from the lower end of the shock absorber.
5. On Land Cruiser models, perform the following:
   a. Remove the cotter pins and nuts from the lower end of the stabilizer link.
   b. Detach the link from the axle housing.
6. Detach the shock absorber from the spring seat pivot pin.
7. Remove the parking brake cable clamp (except Land Cruiser).

NOTE: Remove the parking brake equalizer, if necessary.

8. Unfasten the U-bolt nuts and remove the spring seat assemblies.
9. Adjust the height of the rear axle housing so that the weight of the rear axle is removed from the rear springs.
10. Unfasten the spring shackle retaining nuts. Withdraw the spring shackle inner plate. Carefully pry out the spring shackle with a bar.
11. Remove the spring bracket pin from the front end of the spring hanger and remove the rubber bushings.
12. Remove the spring.

CAUTION: Use care not to damage the hydraulic brake line or the parking brake cable.

Installation is performed in the following order:

1. Install the rubber bushings in the eye of the spring.
2. Align the eye of the spring with the spring hanger bracket and drive the pin through the bracket holes and rubber bushings.

NOTE: Use soapy water as lubricant, if necessary, to aid in pin installation. Never use oil or grease.

3. Finger-tighten the spring hanger nuts and/or bolts.
4. Install the rubber bushings in the spring eye at the opposite end of the spring.
5. Raise the free end of the spring. Install the spring shackle through the bushings and the bracket.
6. Install the shackle inner plate and finger-tighten the retaining nuts.
7. Center the bolt head in the hole which is provided in the spring seat on the axle housing.
8. Fit the U-bolts over the axle housing. Install the lower spring seat.
9. Tighten the U-bolt nuts.

NOTE: Some models have two sets of nuts, while others have a nut and lockwasher.

10. Install the parking brake cable clamp. Install the equalizer, if it was removed.
11. Pick-up and Land Cruiser:
    a. Raise the rear axle with the jack so that the stands no longer support the frame.
    b. Tighten the hanger pin and shackle nuts.
    c. Install the shock absorber bushings and washers. Tighten and install the cotter pins.

d. Install the stabilizer link and hand-tighten its retaining nuts (Land Cruiser).

e. Install the wheels, remove the stands, and lower the vehicle to the ground.

f. Tighten the stabilizer link bolts, bounce the vehicle, and tighten them again (Land Cruiser).

Rear Shock Absorbers

REMOVAL AND INSTALLATION

1. Jack up the rear end of the vehicle.
2. Support the rear axle housing with jackstands.
3. Unfasten the upper shock absorber retaining nuts and/or bolts from the upper frame member.
4. Depending upon the type of rear springs used, either disconnect the lower end of the shock absorber from the spring seat, or the rear axle housing, by removing its cotter pins, nuts, and/or bolts.
5. Remove the shock absorber.

Inspect the shock for wear, leaks, or other signs of damage. Test it as outlined in the front suspension shock absorber section.

Installation is performed in the reverse order from removal.

STEERING

Steering Wheel

REMOVAL AND INSTALLATION

Three-Spoke

CAUTION: Do not attempt to remove or install the steering wheel by hammering on it. Damage to the energy-absorbing steering column could result.

1. Unfasten the horn and turn signal multiconnector(s) at the base of the steering column shroud.
2. Loosen the trim pad retaining screws from the back side of the steering wheel.
3. Lift the trim pad and horn button assembly(ies) from the wheel.
4. Remove the steering wheel hub retaining nut.
5. Scratch matchmarks on the hub and shaft to aid in correct installation.
6. Use a steering wheel puller to remove the steering wheel.

Installation is the reverse of removal. Tighten the wheel retaining nut to 15–22 ft–lbs. except for 1970–80 Pick-up and 4x4 Pick-up, which should be tightened to 22–29 ft lbs.

Two-Spoke

The two-spoke steering wheel is removed in the same manner as the three-spoke, except that the trim pad should be pried off with a screwdriver. Remove the pad by lifting it toward the top of the wheel.

Four-Spoke

CAUTION: Do not attempt to remove or install the steering wheel by hammering on it. Damage to the energy absorbing steering column could result.

1. Unfasten the horn and turn signal connectors at the base of the steering column shroud, underneath the instrument panel.
2. Gently pry the center emblem off the front of the steering wheel.
3. Insert a wrench through the hole and remove the steering wheel retaining nut.
4. Scratch matchmarks on the hub and shaft to aid installation.
5. Use a steering wheel puller to remove the steering wheel.

Installation is the reverse of removal. Tighten the steering wheel retaining nut to 15–22 ft lbs.

Steering Column

REMOVAL AND INSTALLATION

Standard Steering Column

1. Disconnect the negative battery terminal.
2. Working inside the engine compartment, paint or scribe a match mark across the steering column worm-shaft and the steering column coupling to insure that when re-installing steering column shaft into coupling, it is in the exact position of removal.
3. Remove clamp lock bolt.
4. Working inside the driver's compartment, unplug turn signal/multi-connection plug. Unplug ignition wiring harness.
5. Down at the fire-wall of the driver's compartment, unbolt the outer bolts holding the base plate of the steering column to the fire-wall.
6. Remove the bolts holding the steering column tube under the dash and remove steering column.

Installation is the reverse of removal.

NOTE: Be sure to align marks on steering shaft with marks on coupling, or steering wheel will not center with wheels.

Tilt-Type Steering Column

1. Complete steps 1–3 under standard steering column removal.
2. Remove lower column cover behind steering wheel.
3. Unplug turn signal multi-connection plug and remove the two screws holding it to the column. Unplug ignition switch wiring harness.
4. Complete steps 5–6 under standard steering column removal.

Installation is reverse of removal.

NOTE: Be sure to align marks on steering shaft with marks on coupling, or steering wheel will not be true in relation to the front wheels.

Ignition Lock/Switch

REMOVAL AND INSTALLATION

1. Disconnect the negative (–) battery cable.
2. Unfasten the ignition switch connector underneath the instrument panel.
3. Remove the screws which secure the upper and lower halves of the steering column cover.
4. Turn the lock cylinder to the "ACC" position with the ignition key.
5. Push the lock cylinder stop in with a small, round object (cotter pin, punch, etc.)

NOTE: On some models it may be necessary to remove the steering wheel and turn signal switch first.

6. Withdraw the lock cylinder from the lock housing while depressing the stop tab.
7. To remove the ignition switch, unfasten its securing screws and withdraw the switch from the lock housing.

Installation is performed in the following order:

1. Align the locking cam with the hole in the ignition switch and insert the switch in the lock housing.
2. Secure the switch with its screw(s).
3. Make sure that both the lock cylinder and the column lock are in the "ACC" position. Slide the cylinder into the lock housing until the stop tab engages the hole in the lock.
4. The rest of installation is performed in the reverse order of removal.

Turn Signal Switch

REPLACEMENT

1. Disconnect negative (–) battery cable.
2. Remove the steering wheel, as outlined in the appropriate section above.
3. Unfasten the screws which secure the upper and lower steering column shroud halves.
4. Unfasten the screws which retain the turn signal switch and remove the switch from the column. On 1979–80 Pick-ups and 4x4 Pick-ups, the windshield wiper switch is part of the assembly, and will be removed as well.

Installation is performed in the reverse order of removal.

Steering Linkage

REMOVAL AND INSTALLATION

Pick-Up

1. Raise the front of the vehicle and support it with jack stands.

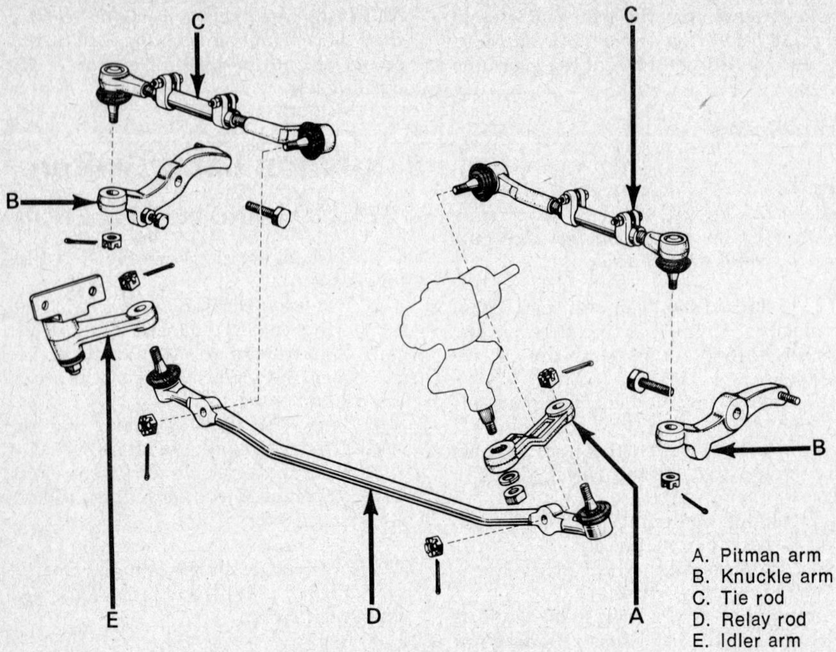

A. Pitman arm
B. Knuckle arm
C. Tie rod
D. Relay rod
E. Idler arm

Pick-up steering linkage

2. Remove the front wheels.
3. Remove the nut on the pitman arm and using a puller remove it from the steering sector shaft.
4. Unfasten the idler arm support securing bolts and remove the support from the frame.
5. Remove the castle nuts and cotter pins from the tie-rod ends and separate them from the steering knuckle arms with a puller.
6. Remove the relay rod complete with the tie-rods, pitman arm and idler arm.

Installation is the reverse of removal with the following notes.

7. Align the marks on the pitman arm and sector shaft before installing the pitman arm.
8. Torque all of the following to 55–79 ft lbs.: tie-rod ends to steering knuckles and relay rod; relay rod to pitman arm. Torque the relay rod to the idler arm at 37–50 ft lb. Torque the pitman arm to the sector shaft at 80–90 ft lb.

4x4 Pick-up

1. Jack up the vehicle and support it on stands.
2. Remove the front wheels.
3. Remove cotter pin and nut from the shimmy damper at the tie-rod and remove shimmy damper from the tie-rod with a puller. Remove the lock nut from other end of the damper. Be sure to note the order of the rubber spacers and washers, and remove damper.
4. Repeat the above procedure where the tie-rod ends connect to the steering knuckles. Remove the tie-rod.
5. To remove the drag link, remove the cotter pin from the steering knuckle end of the drag link, and, using a screw driver, unscrew the cap at the end of the drag link.

NOTE: The cap may be tight, so you may have to use a wrench or pliers to turn the screw driver.

6. When the cap is removed, you should be able to dislodge the spring seat, spring and outer socket holder inside the drag link by working the steering knuckle back and forth. The steering knuckle socket in the drag link can now be removed.

NOTE: Be sure to note the order in which the spring seat, spring and outer socket come out of the drag link. Their order will be reversed on the side of the drag link that attaches to the pitman arm.

7. Repeat steps 5 and 6 on the pitman arm side of the drag link.

Installation is the reverse of removal. Be sure to insert assemblies in drag link in their correct orders. On drag link, screw in caps completely then loosen 1-1/3 turns.

Observe the following torques:

Shimmy damper to axle housing mount: 8–11 ft-lb.

Tie-rod end to steering knuckle arm: 55–79 ft-lb.

Shimmy damper to tie-rod end: 37–50 ft-lb.

NOTE: Be sure to grease drag link ends at their grease nipples, and, when installing drag link end caps, you tighten them completely and then loosen them 1-1/3 turns.

Land Cruiser

1. Remove the hubcaps and loosen the lug nuts.
2. Jack up the front of the vehicle and support it on stands. Remove the wheels.
3. Unfasten the pitman arm retaining nut.

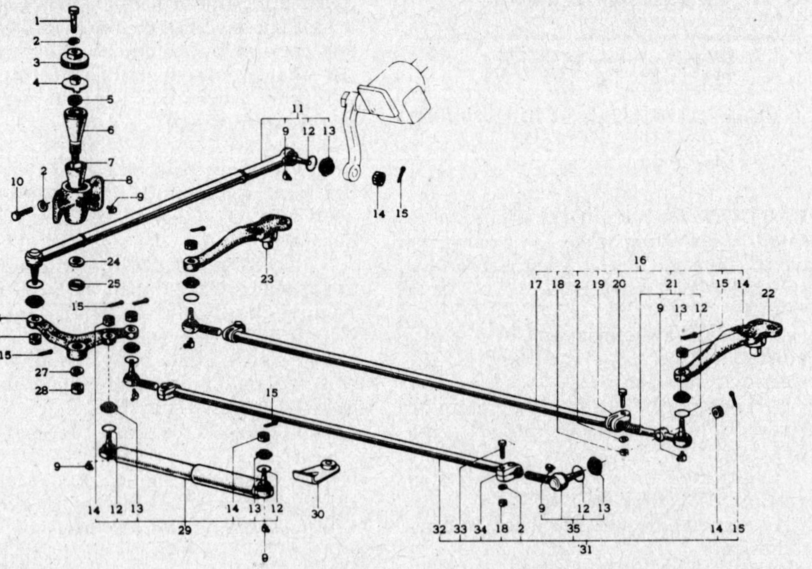

1. Bolt
2. Lock washer
3. Center arm shaft nut
4. Center arm nut lock plate
5. Compression spring
6. Center arm shaft
7. Shaft bushing
8. Center arm bracket
9. Grease fitting
10. Bolt
11. Steering drag link assembly
12. Set ring
13. Joint dust seal
14. Lock nut
15. Cotter pin
16. Tie-rod assembly
17. Steering tie-rod
18. Lock nut
19. Tie-rod end clamp
20. Bolt
21. Tie-rod end assembly
22. Steering knuckle arm
23. Steering knuckle arm
24. Dust seal
25. Center arm dust lower seal
26. Steering center arm
27. Lock washer
28. Nut
29. Steering damper
30. Damper bracket
31. Steering relay rod assembly
32. Steering relay rod
33. Bolt
34. Tie-rod end clamp
35. Relay rod end assembly

Components of the Land Cruiser steering linkage

4. Punch matchmarks on the pitman arm and the sector shaft to aid reinstallation.
5. Remove the pitman arm from the sector shaft with a puller.
6. Detach the drag link from the center arm with a tie-rod puller. Remove the link together with the pitman arm.
7. Detach the tie rod ends from the steering knuckle arm with a puller.
8. Detach the relay rod ends from the center arm. Remove the tie rod/relay rod assembly.
9. Disconnect the end of the steering damper from its bracket on the front crossmember.
10. Remove the center arm attaching nut and use a puller to remove the arm, complete with damper.
11. Remove the skid plate and then remove the center arm bracket from the frame.

Installation is the reverse of removal.

12. Be sure to align the matchmarks, which were made during removal, on the pitman arm and the sector shaft. Tighten the mounting bolt to 120–140 ft-lb.
13. Lubricate all of the rod ends and damper ends with multipurpose grease.
14. After the linkage is installed, adjust the toe-in to the proper specifications.

Manual Steering Gear

REMOVAL AND INSTALLATION

Pick-up

1. Remove the pitman arm from the sector shaft with a puller.
2. Match mark the flexible coupling and worm-shaft and remove the lock bolt.
3. Unbolt and remove the steering gear housing.
4. Install in reverse of removal. Torque the housing bolts to 26–36 ft-lb., and the pitman arm to 80–90 ft-lb. Tighten the coupling yoke bolt to 15–20 ft-lb.

4x4 Pick-up

1. Remove the pitman arm from the sector shaft with a puller.
2. Match mark and then loosen the intermediate shaft coupling at the steering gear worm shaft.
3. Loosen the bolt holding the intermediate shaft at the coupling near the fire wall and slide the shaft up off the steering gear worm shaft.
4. Remove the four bolts on the steering gear base and remove the steering gear.
5. Installation is the reverse of removal.

Observe the following torques:

Steering gear housing to frame: 37–47 ft-lb. Pitman arm to sector shaft: 116–137 ft-lb. Worm shaft coupling lock bolt: 22–32 ft-lb.

Land Cruiser 55 Series

1. Remove the worm yokes from the worm and main shaft.
2. Remove the intermediate shaft assembly.
3. Remove the pitman arm from the sector shaft.
4. Unbolt and remove the gear housing.
5. Install in reverse of removal. Torque the pitman arm to 119–141 ft lb.

*NOTE: **The intermediate shaft must be installed with the wheels in a straight ahead position and the steering wheel straight ahead.***

40 Series

1. Remove the horn button assembly and, using a puller, remove the steering wheel.
2. Remove the steering column jacket lower clamp.
3. Remove the turn signal switch assembly.
4. Remove the steering column access plate.
5. Remove the carburetor and oil filter. (Not necessary on 1975–76)
6. Disconnect the #1 shift rod and select rod at the ends of the shift control and select levers.
7. Remove the lower shift control bracket clamp.
8. Remove the shift control lever, select lever, control shaft lower bracket, control shaft low speed lever, and control shaft lower bracket.
9. Pull the control shaft out toward the driver's side.
10. Remove the pitman arm with a puller.
11. Remove the steering gear box bracket cap and lift out the gear box.
12. Installation is the reverse of removal. Torque the gear box bracket cap to 75–90 ft lb. (30–40 for 1975–76); the pitman arm to 120–140 ft lb. the steering wheel nut to 30–50 ft lb.

ADJUSTMENTS

Adjustments to the manual steering gear are not necessary during normal service. Adjustments are performed only as part of overhaul.

OVERHAUL

Pick-up

1. Remove oil filler plug and drain oil.
2. If you have not done so, remove the pitman arm from the sector shaft.
3. Remove the locknut and bolts from the end cover. Screw in the threaded adjusting screw in the cover and remove the cover. Remove adjusting screw and thrust washer from the end of the sector shaft.
4. Pour out the remaining oil and remove the sector shaft.
5. Remove the large locknut over the worm shaft.

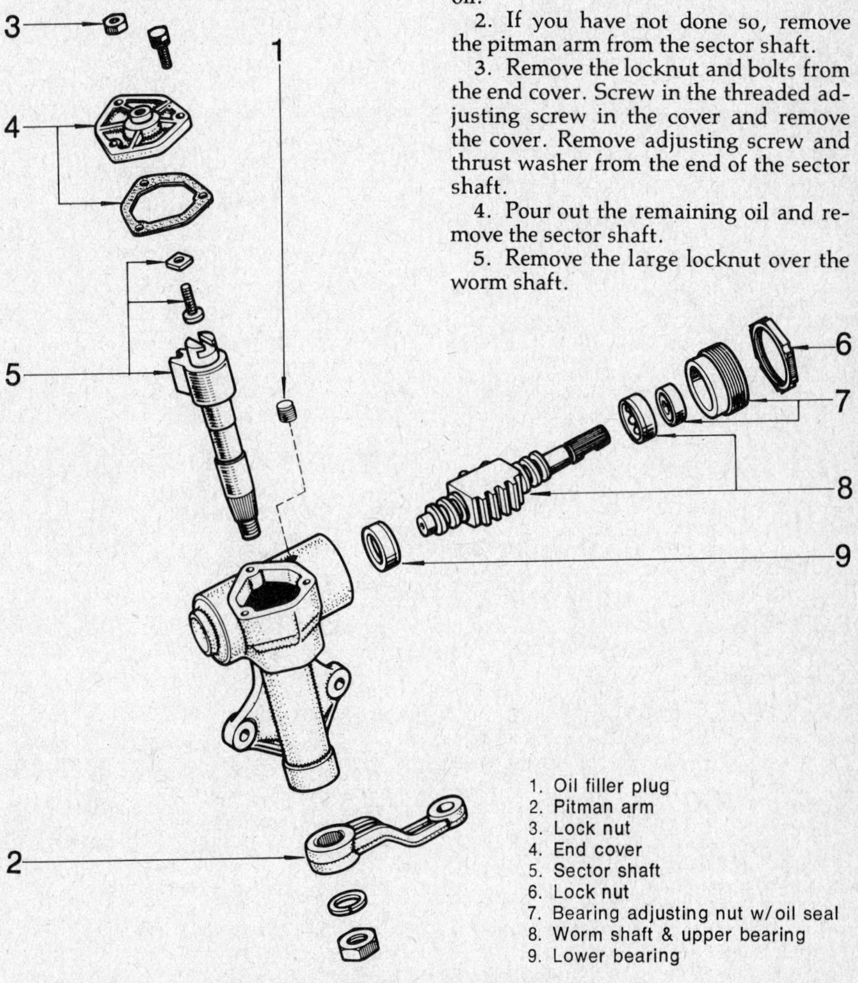

Pick-up manual steering gearbox

6. Using a pair of long needle nosed pliers, unscrew the bearing adjusting screw by lodging the tips of the pliers against the notches inside the screw and turning it out. Remove the worm shaft together with the bearing.

CAUTION: Do not remove the two screws holding the bent pipes in the steering worm ball nut!

7. Clean all parts and inspect for wear.

8. Check the worm shaft ball nut for smooth operation on the shaft. When set on its end, the nut should slide down the shaft by its own weight. If ball nut or worm shaft is defective, replace as a unit.

NOTE: Do not force the ball nut to the ends of its travel or you may damage the internal ball bearings.

9. Inspect all bushings, bearings, races, needle bearings and oil seals for wear. Replace as necessary.

NOTE: Later models may have needle bearings instead of bushings. Make sure none are lost.

10. With thrust washer in place, check the clearance under the head of the adjusting screw in the end of the sector shaft. Thrust limit is 0.002 in. If clearance is greater, replace thrust washer. Replacement washers come in thicknesses from 0.077–0.087 in.

11. Assembly in the reverse of teardown. Replace all gaskets and use gasket sealer when assembling. Observe the following notes.

12. Apply multipurpose grease to all bushings, bearings, races and oil seals.

13. When replacing worm shaft and its bearing adjustment screw, use a spring scale to test the preload BEFORE replacing sector shaft. Preload for steering gear assemblies with four frame mounting bolt holes should be 6.6–13.2 lb., assemblies with two frame bolt holes should be 6.6–11.0 lb. Move the adjusting screw until correct preload is achieved.

NOTE: Before testing preload, tighten down the adjusting screw to seat the bearing.

14. Replace the locknut and tighten, being careful not to move adjusting screw. Torque settings for the two bolt hole assembly is 167–188 ft-lb., and for four bolt hole assembly 58–72 ft-lb.

15. Replace sector shaft so that the middle tooth on the shaft meshes with the two center teeth on the worm gear.

NOTE: Make sure the sector shaft adjustment screw and thrust washer are in position on the sector shaft.

16. Install cover by screwing it on the sector shaft adjustment screw. Before tightening cover bolts, completely loosen adjusting screw with a screw driver.

17. Set sector shaft at center and take up the looseness in the adjusting screw. Again test the worm shaft preload. For two bolt assemblies 13–19 lb., for four bolt assemblies 15–24 lb. Adjust preload with adjusting screw. Replace lock nut, being careful not to move screw.

See removal and installation section for mounting bolt and pitman arm torques.

NOTE: Be sure to refill assembly with gear oil after replacing on vehicle. Leave about 3/4 in. space between oil and filler hole.

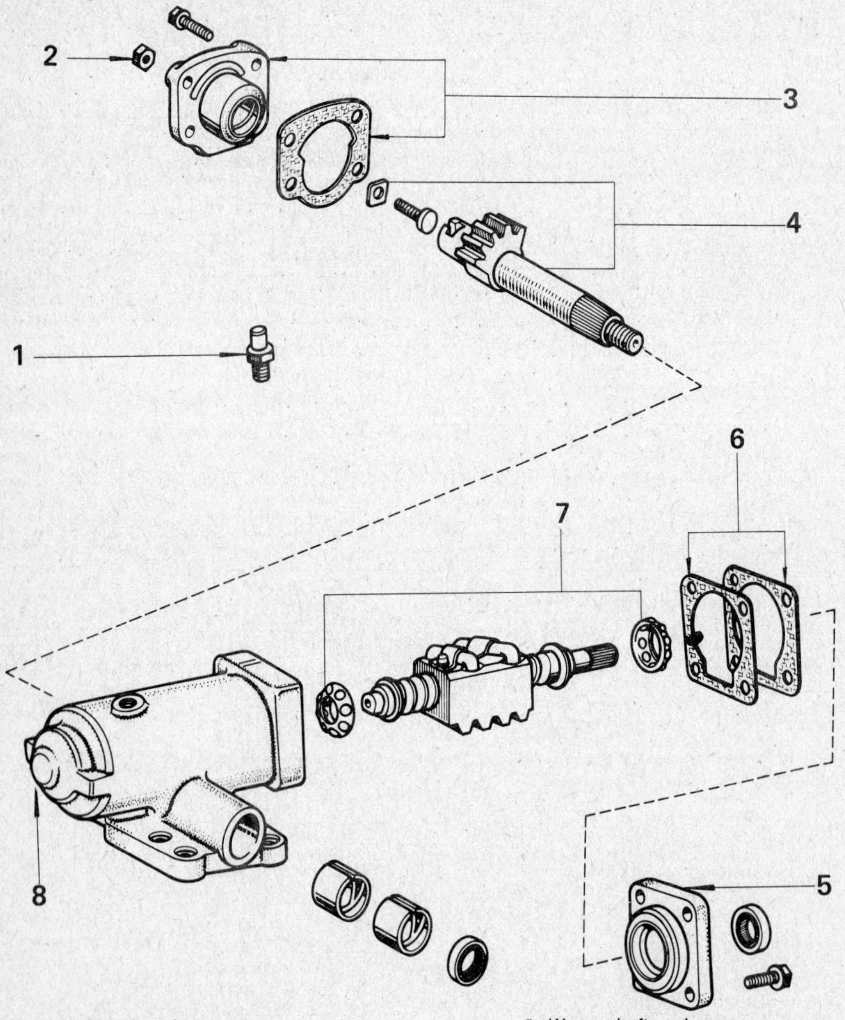

1. Oil filler plug
2. Lock nut
3. Sector shaft end cover & gasket
4. Sector shaft
5. Worm shaft end cover
6. Shim
7. Worm shaft & bearing
8. Gear housing

4x4 Pick-up manual steering gearbox—Land Cruiser similar

4x4 Pick-up, Land Cruiser

1. Complete steps 1–4 under Pick-up overhaul above.

2. Remove bolts holding worm shaft cover and remove cover, noting how many shims are between cover and assembly.

3. Remove the worm assembly, be sure to tag both bearings to avoid confusion when reassembling.

CAUTION: Do not remove the two screws holding the bent pipes in the steering worm ball nut!

4. Complete steps 7–9 under Pick-up, omit note below step 9.

5. For 4x4 Pick-up, complete steps 10–12 under Pick-up.

6. For Land Cruiser, with thrust washer in place, check the clearance under the head of the adjusting screw in the end of the sector shaft. Thrust clearance limit is 0.004 in. If clearance is greater, replace thrust washer. Replacement washers range from .079–.089 in.

7. For Land Cruiser, complete steps 11–12 under Pick-up.

8. When replacing worm shaft, be sure to put the bearings on the correct ends of the shaft. Replace worm shaft cover, making sure you install all of the attendant shims.

NOTE: When tightening cover bolts, keep checking to insure the worm turns freely in the housing.

9. Before installing sector shaft, test the preload on the worm shaft with a spring scale. 4x4 Pick-up preload: 7.7–14.3 lb. Land Cruiser: 8.8–13.2 lb. Adjust the preload by replacing shims.
10. Complete steps 15–16 under Pick-up.
11. Set the sector shaft at center. Take up the looseness in the adjustment screw. Again test the worm shaft preload. Preload: 17.6–24.2 lb. Adjust the preload with the adjusting screw. Replace the lock nut, being careful not to remove the screw.
12. Fill assembly with gear oil after replacing on vehicle. Leave about 1/2–3/4 in. space between oil and filler hole.

Power Steering

PUMP REMOVAL AND INSTALLATION

1. Remove the fan shroud.
2. Unfasten the nut from the center of the pump pulley.

NOTE: Use the drive belt as a brake to keep the pulley from rotating.

3. Withdraw the drive belt.
4. Remove the pulley and the Woodruff key from the pump shaft.
5. Detach the intake and outlet hoses from the pump reservoir.

NOTE: Tie the hose ends up high so the fluid cannot flow out of them. Drain or plug the pump to prevent fluid leakage.

6. Remove the bolt from the rear mounting brace.
7. Remove the front bracket bolts and withdraw the pump.

Installation is performed in the reverse order of removal. Note the following, however:

1. Tighten the pump pulley mounting bolt to 25–39 ft lbs.
2. Adjust the pump drive belt tension. The belt should deflect 0.31–0.39 in. under thumb pressure applied midway between the air pump and the power steering pump.
3. Fill the reservoir with "Dexron" automatic transmission fluid. Bleed the air from the system.

BLEEDING

1. Raise the front of the car and support it securely with jackstands.
2. Fill the pump reservoir with "Dexron" automatic transmission fluid.
3. Rotate the steering wheel from lock to lock several times. Add fluid as necessary.
4. With the steering wheel turned fully to one lock, crank the starter while watching the fluid level in the reservoir.

NOTE: Do not start the engine. Operate the starter with a remove starter switch or have an assistant do it from inside of the car. Do not run the starter for prolonged periods.

5. Repeat step 4 with the steering wheel turned to the opposite lock.
6. Start the engine. With the engine idling, turn the steering wheel from lock to lock two or three times.
7. Lower the front of the car and repeat step 6.
8. Center the wheel at the midpoint of its travel. Stop the engine.
9. The fluid level should not have risen more than 0.2 in. If it does, repeat step 7.
10. Check for fluid leakage.

FRONT-END ALIGNMENT

Front-end alignment measurements require the use of special equipment. Before measuring alignment or attempting to adjust it, always check the following points:

1. Be sure that the tires are properly inflated.
2. See that the wheels are properly balanced.
3. Check the ball joints to determine if they are worn or loose.
4. Check front wheel bearing adjustment.
5. Be sure that the car is on a level surface.
6. Check all suspension parts for tightness.

CASTER AND CAMBER ADJUSTMENTS

Measure the caster and camber angles. If they are not within specifications, adjust them by adding or subtracting the shims on the mounting bolts between the upper control arm and the suspension member:

1. To *increase* camber, *remove* shims equally from both of the control shaft mounting bolts. Do the reverse to decrease camber.
2. To *increase* caster, add camber adjusting shims to the *rear* mounting bolt, or remove them from the front mounting bolt. Do the reverses to decrease caster.

NOTE: Caster and camber adjustments should always be performed in a single operation.

TOE-IN ADJUSTMENT

Measure the toe-in. Adjust it, if necessary, by loosening the tie rod end clamping bolts and rotating the tie rod adjusting tubes. Tighten the clamping bolts when finished.

NOTE: Both tie rod ends should be the same length. If they are not, perform the adjustment until the toe-in is within specifications and the tie rod ends are equal in length.

BRAKE SYSTEMS

Rear Drum Brakes

ADJUSTMENTS

1973–74 Pick-up, Land Cruiser

These models are equipped with rear drum brakes which require manual adjustment. Perform the adjustment in the following order:

1. Chock the front wheels and fully release the parking brake.
2. Raise the rear of the vehicle and support it with jackstands.
3. Remove the adjusting hole plug from the backing plate.
4. Expand the brake shoes by turning the adjusting wheel with a star-wheel adjuster or a thin-bladed screw driver.
5. Pump the brake pedal several times, while expanding the shoes, so that the shoe contacts the drum evenly.

NOTE: If the wheel still turns when your foot is removed from the brake pedal, continue expanding the shoes until the wheel locks.

6. Back off on the adjuster, just enough so that the wheel rotates without dragging.
7. After this point is reached, continue backing off for *five* additional notches

NOTE: On models which have two wheel cylinders at each wheel, adjust each set of brakes separately; never adjust both at once.

8. If the wheel still does not turn freely, back off one or two more notches. If after this, it still drags, check for worn or defective parts.
9. Pump the brake pedal again, and check wheel rotation.
10. Reverse steps 1–3.

1975–80 Pick-up, 4x4 Pick-up

These models are equipped with self-adjusting rear drum brakes. No adjustment is necessary.

Front Drum Brakes

Perform the adjustments in the same manner as detailed for the rear drum brakes.

Front Disc Brakes

Front disc brakes require no adjustment. Hydraulic pressure maintains the proper brake pad-to-disc contact all times.

NOTE: Because of this, the brake fluid level should be checked regularly.

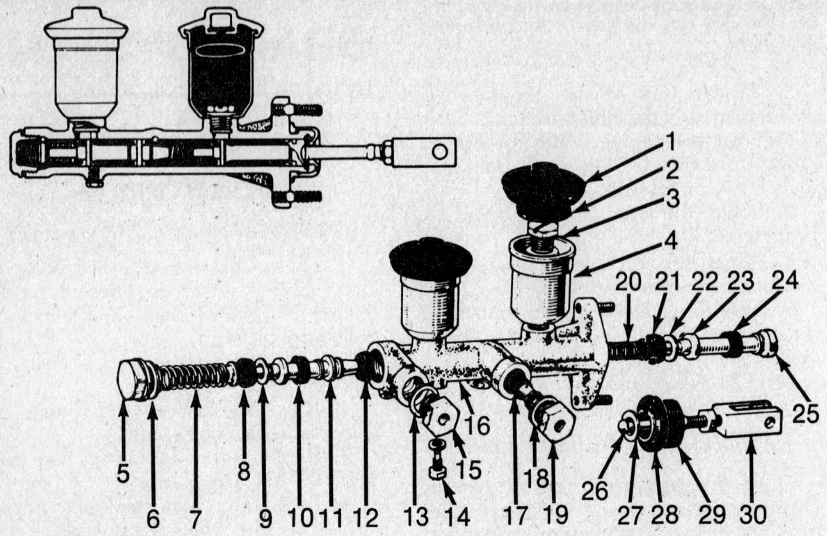

1. Reservoir filler cap
2. Reservoir float
3. Reservoir set bolt
4. Master cylinder reservoir
5. Master cylinder plug
6. Gasket
7. Compression spring
8. Cylinder cup
9. Piston cup spacer
10. Cylinder cup
11. Master cylinder piston No. 2
12. Cylinder cup
13. Gasket
14. Piston stop bolt
15. Valve plug
16. Tandem master cylinder body
17. Compression spring
18. Master cylinder outlet check valve
19. Valve plug
20. Compression
21. Piston return spring retainer
22. Cylinder cup
23. Master cylinder piston cup spacer
24. Cylinder cup
25. Master cylinder piston No. 1
26. Master cylinder pushrod
27. Master cylinder piston stop plate
28. Hole snap-ring
29. Master cylinder boot
30. Master cylinder pushrod clevis

Components of the dual-tandem master cylinder

Master Cylinder

REMOVAL AND INSTALLATION

CAUTION: Be careful not to spill brake fluid on the painted surfaces of the vehicle; it will damage the paint.

1. Unfasten the hydraulic line from the master cylinder.
2. Detach the hydraulic fluid pressure differential switch wiring connectors.
3. Loosen the master cylinder reservoir mounting bolt.
4. Then do one of the following:
   a. On models with manual brakes, remove the master cylinder securing bolts and the clevis pin from the brake pedal. Remove the master cylinder.
   b. On other models with power brakes, unfasten the nuts and remove the master cylinder assembly from the power brake unit.

Installation is performed in the reverse order of removal. Note the following however:

1. Before tightening the master cylinder mounting nuts or bolts, screw the hydraulic line into the cylinder body, a few turns.
2. After installation is completed, bleed the master cylinder and the brake system.

OVERHAUL

1. Remove the reservoir caps and floats and unscrew the bolts that hold the reservoir to the main body.
2. Remove warning switches (where fitted), then remove from the rear of the cylinder, in order: boot and snap-ring, stop plate (washer), piston No. 1 with spacer, cylinder cup, spring retainer and spring.
3. Remove the end plug and gasket from the front of the cylinder, then remove the front piston stop bolt from underneath. Pull out the spring and its retainer, piston No. 2, the spacer and the cylinder cup.
4. Remove the two outlet fittings, washers, check valves and springs.
5. Remove the piston cups from their seats on the pistons only if they are to be replaced.

After washing all parts in clean brake fluid, dry with compressed air. Inspect the cylinder bore for wear, scuff marks or nicks. Cylinders may be honed slightly, but the limit is 0.006 in. It is recommended that it be replaced rather than overhauled.

Reverse the sequence of disassembly. Absolute cleanliness is important, and all parts must be coated with clean brake fluid. Bleed the master cylinder and make sure all lines are tightened correctly and do not leak. Use fluid that meets specifications (for standard brakes) and use the special disc brake fluid (DOT-3) for disc brake equipped cars.

Proportioning Valve

A proportioning valve is used on all models to reduce the hydraulic pressure to the rear brakes because of weight transfer during high speed stops. This helps to keep the rear brakes from locking up by improving front to rear brake balance.

REMOVAL AND INSTALLATION

1. Disconnect the brake lines from the valve unions.
2. Remove the valve mounting bolt, if used, and remove the valve.

NOTE: If the proportioning valve is defective, it must be replaced as an assembly; it cannot be rebuilt.

Installation is the reverse of removal. Bleed the brake system after it is completed.

Bleeding

CAUTION: Do not reuse brake fluid which has been bled from the brake system.

1. Insert a clear vinyl tube into the bleeder plug on the master cylinder or the wheel cylinders.

NOTE: If the master cylinder has been overhauled or if air is present in it, start the bleeding procedure with the master cylinder. Otherwise, (and after bleeding the master cylinder) start with the wheel cylinder which is farthest from the master cylinder.

2. Insert the other end of the tube into a jar which is half filled with brake fluid.
3. Slowly depress the brake pedal (have an assistant do it) and turn the bleeder plug $1/3$–$1/2$ of a turn at the same time.

NOTE: If the brake pedal is depressed too fast, small air bubbles will form in the brake fluid which will be very difficult to remove.

4. Close the bleeder plug before hydraulic pressure decreases in the cylinder.
5. Repeat this procedure until the air bubbles are removed and then go on to the next wheel cylinder.

CAUTION: Replenish the brake fluid in the master cylinder reservoir, so that it does not run out during bleeding.

Disc Brakes

PAD REMOVAL AND INSTALLATION

1. Remove the hub cap and loosen the lug nuts.
2. Raise the front of the vehicle with a jack and support it with stands on the chassis pads provided.
3. Remove the lug nuts and the wheel.
4. Remove the clips, springs, and the pins (which have the holes).
5. Withdraw the anti-squeal shims and the pads.
6. Check pad thickness against the specifications.

Install the pads in the following order:

1. Clean the back of the pistons, cylinder boots and the caliper surfaces which contact the brake pads.
2. Fit the pads and anti-squeal shims into the caliper.

NOTE: Install the shims with their arrows pointing toward the rotational direction of the disc.

3. Install the spring so that it presses correctly against the pads.
4. After completing installation, depress the brake pedal several times before lowering the car. This will provide proper operating clearance for the wheel cylinder components.
5. Install the wheel and lower the vehicle.

CALIPER REMOVAL AND INSTALLATION

CAUTION: Do not unfasten the bridge bolt and separate the caliper halves.

1. Remove the wheel covers and loosen the lug nuts.
2. Raise the front of the vehicle and support it with jackstands.
3. Remove the lug nuts and the wheel.
4. Plug the master cylinder inlet, so that the brake fluid will not run out when the hydraulic line is disconnected.
5. Remove the hydraulic line from the caliper by unfastening the union bolt.
6. Remove the lockwire and unfasten the caliper securint bolts. Withdraw the caliper assembly.

NOTE: Shims are installed between the caliper mounting points and its body to center the caliper over the disc. Count the number of shims at each mounting point. Use care not to mix the shims from the upper and lower mounting points.

OVERHAUL

Pick-up, 4x4 Pick-up

1. Remove the caliper assembly from the vehicle, and separate the pads from the caliper.

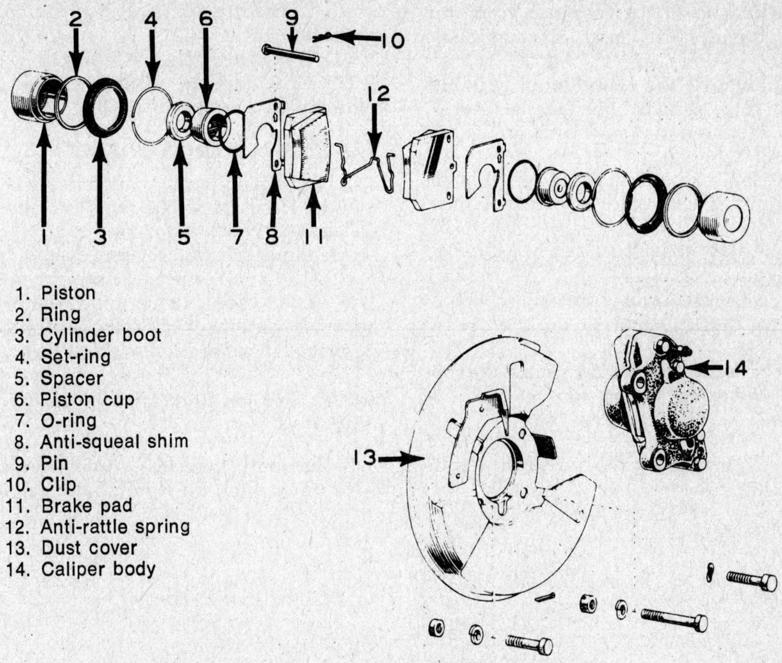

1. Piston
2. Ring
3. Cylinder boot
4. Set-ring
5. Spacer
6. Piston cup
7. O-ring
8. Anti-squeal shim
9. Pin
10. Clip
11. Brake pad
12. Anti-rattle spring
13. Dust cover
14. Caliper body

Pick-up front disc brake components

2. Remove the snap-ring and the dust boot from caliper bores.
3. Place a block of wood between the pistons and below them out of their bores by applying compressed air to the brake line union. Use of the wood block is to keep the pistons from striking each other.
4. Withdraw the sealing rings from the caliper bores. Do not mix the pistons; they must be returned to their original bores.

CAUTION: Do not loosen or remove the bridge bolts which secure the halves of the caliper body.

Check the caliper body for cracks and/or distortion. Examine the caliper bores for wear, damage, or corrosion. Replace the guide pins (with holes) if they are bent.

Assembly is performed in the following order:

1. Replace all rubber parts with new ones.
2. Coat the sealing rings and the caliper bore with the rubber grease supplied in the rebuilding kit; do not use any other type of lubricant.
3. Fit the sealing rings into the grooves in the caliper bores.
4. Install the O-rings and spacers (if used) on the pistons and carefully insert each piston into its original bore. Use only finger-pressure to seat the pistons.
5. Install the boots over the bores and secure them with the snap-rings.
6. Install the calipers and the brake pads, then bleed the brake system.

Land Cruiser

NOTE: Do not separate the caliper halves.

1. Remove the caliper.
2. Remove the retaining pin and antirattle spring.
3. Remove the brake pads.
4. Remove the piston retaining ring.
5. Remove the piston boot and piston.
6. Remove the piston seal.
7. Assembly is the reverse of disassembly.

ROTOR REMOVAL AND INSTALLATION

Pick-up

1. Remove the brake pads and the caliper.
2. Check the disc run-out, as detailed under Inspection, below, at this point.

Make a note of the results for use during installation.

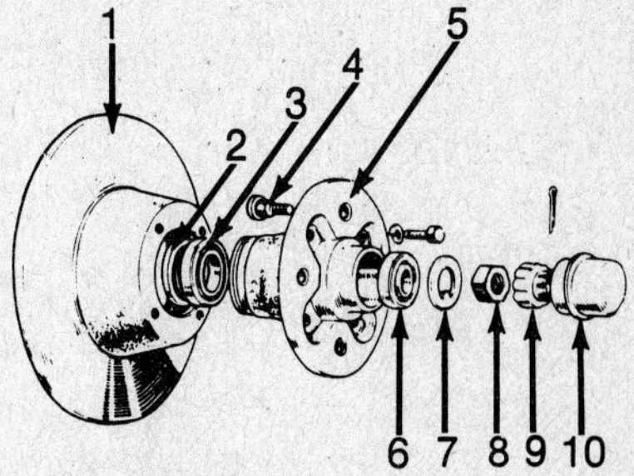

1. Disc
2. Oil seal
3. Tapered roller bearing
4. Hub bolt
5. Hub
6. Tapered roller bearing
7. Washer
8. Nut
9. Adjusting lock cap
10. Grease cap

Pick-up brake disc and hub assembly

3. Remove the grease cap from the hub. Remove the cotter pin and castle nut.
4. Remove the wheel hub with the brake rotor attached, inspect the rotor.
5. Installation is performed in the following order:
6. Coat the hub oil seal lip with multipurpose grease and install the rotor/hub assembly.
7. Adjust the wheel bearing preload as detailed below.
8. Measure rotor run-out. Check it against specifications.

NOTE: ***If the wheel bearing nut is improperly tightened, rotor run-out will be affected.***

9. Tighten the caliper securing bolts to 65–87 ft-lb.
10. Install the remainder of the components.
11. Bleed the brake system.
12. Road test the vehicle. Check the rolling resistance of the wheel.

4x4 Pick-up, Land Cruiser

1. For 4x4 Pick-up, complete steps 1–8 under front drive axle removal, above. Be sure to check rotor run-out, as described in Inspection section, below.
2. For Land Cruiser, complete steps 1–7 under front drive axle removal, above. Be sure to check rotor run-out, as described in Inspection section, below.

NOTE: ***Run-out limit for Land Cruiser is 0.005 in.***

3. For both vehicles, complete steps 5–12 under Pick-up Rotor Removal and Installation, above, with the following notes:
4. When replacing the adjusting nut on the 4x4 Pick-up, tighten the nut to 43 ft-lb. and then loosen it again. Tighten the nut to 3–5 ft-lb. and test preload. Lock the adjusting nut and tighten the lock nut over it to 58–72 ft-lb.

NOTE: ***Reverse steps taken from other sections to complete assembly procedures.***

NOTE: ***Tighten Land Cruiser caliper securing bolts to 54–76 ft-lb.***

INSPECTION

Examine the disc. If it is worn, warped or scored, it must be replaced.

Check the thickness of the disc against specifications. If it is below specifications, replace it. Use a micrometer to measure the thickness. Disc run-out should be measured *before* the disc is removed and again *after* the disc is installed. Use a dial indicator mounted on a stand to determine run-out. If run-out exceeds 0.006 in. (all models), replace the disc.

NOTE: ***Be sure that the wheel bearing nut is properly tightened. If it is not, an inaccurate run-out reading may be obtained. If different run-out readings are obtained with the same disc, between removal and installation, this is probably the cause.***

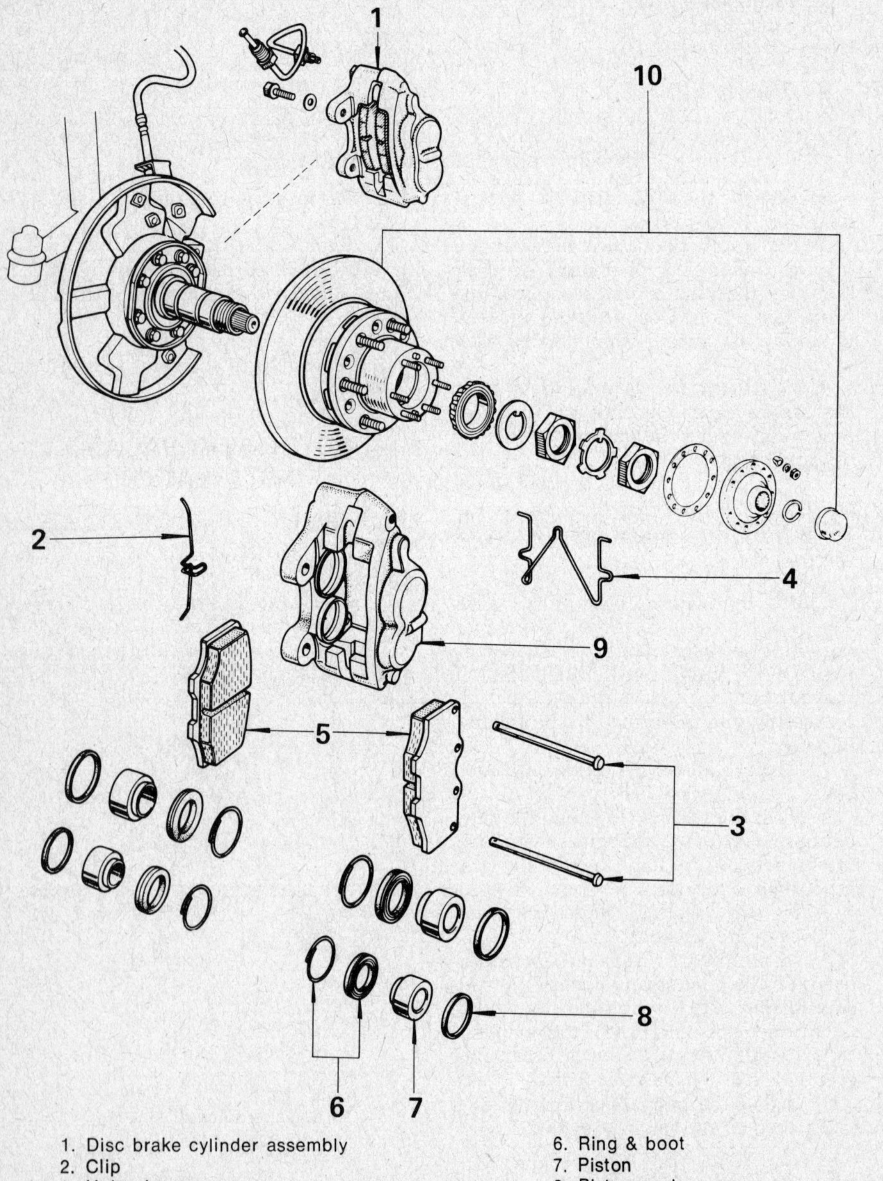

1. Disc brake cylinder assembly
2. Clip
3. Hole pin
4. Anti-rattle spring
5. Pad
6. Ring & boot
7. Piston
8. Piston seal
9. Disc brake cylinder
10. Axle hub with disc

4x4 Pick-up front disc brake, hub and caliper assembly

Wheel Bearings

REMOVAL AND INSTALLATION

1. Remove the disc/hub assembly, as detailed above.
2. If either the disc or the entire hub assembly is to be replaced, unbolt the hub from the disc.

NOTE: ***If only the bearings are to be replaced, do not separate the disc and hub.***

3. Using a brass rod as a drift, tap the inner bearings cone out. Remove the oil seal and the inner bearing.

NOTE: ***Throw the old oil seal away.***

4. Drive out the inner bearing cup.
5. Drive out the outer bearing cup.

Inspect the bearings and the hub for signs of wear or damage. Replace components, as necessary.

Installation is performed in the following order:

1. Install the inner bearing cup and then the outer bearing cup, by driving them into place.

CAUTION: ***Use care not to cock the bearing cups in the hub.***

2. Pack the bearings, hub inner well and grease cap with multipurpose grease.
3. Install the inner bearing into the hub.

4. Carefully install a new oil seal with a soft drift.
5. Install the hub on the spindle. Be sure to install all of the washers and nuts which were removed.
6. Adjust the bearing preload.
7. Install the caliper assembly.

PRELOAD ADJUSTMENT

1. With the front hub/disc assembly installed, tighten the castellated nut to the torque figure specified.
2. Rotate the disc back and forth, two or three times, to allow the bearing to seat properly.
3. Loosen the castellated nut until it is only finger-tight.
4. Tighten the nut firmly, using a box wrench.
5. Measure the bearing preload with a spring scale attached to a wheel mounting stud. Check it against the specifications.
6. Install the cotter pin.

NOTE: If the hole does not align with the nut (or cap) holes, tighten the nut slightly until it does.

7. Finish installing the brake components and the wheel.

Front Drum Brakes

NOTE: The 1976–79 Land Cruisers are equipped with front wheel disc brakes. Refer to front disc brake section

Brake Drums

REMOVAL AND INSTALLATION

1973–75 Pick-up and Land Cruiser

1. Remove the hub cap and loosen the lug nuts.
2. Raise the front of the vehicle and support it with jackstands.
3. Remove the lug nuts and the wheel.
4. On Pick-up models:
   a. Remove the axle hub grease cap.
   b. Remove the cotter pin and claw washer.
   c. Unfasten the nut and withdraw the drum, complete with the hug.
5. On Land Cruiser models:
   a. Unfasten the brake drum retaining screws.
   b. Tap the drum lightly with a mallet to free it.

CAUTION: Do not depress the brake pedal once the drum has been removed.

Inspect the brake drum as detailed in the section below.

Installation is performed in the reverse order of removal. On Pick-up models adjust the wheel bearing preload.

INSPECTION

1. Clean the drum.
2. Inspect the drum for scoring, cracks, grooves, and out of roundness. Replace or turn the drum, as required.
3. Light scoring may be removed by dressing the drum with *fine* emery cloth.
4. Heavy scoring will require the use of a brake drum lathe to turn the drum. The service limits of the drum inside diameter are as follows:
   Pick-up—9.134 in.
   Land Cruiser—11.540 in.

Brake Shoes

REMOVAL AND INSTALLATION

Pick-up

1. Remove the drum.
2. Remove the following parts in the order listed:
   a. Shoe retaining spring pins
   b. Shoe retaining springs
   c. Shoe tension (return) springs
   d. Shoes

NOTE: Use a brake shoe removal tool to aid in removal of the tension springs.

3. After removal, keep the brake shoes in their proper order.

CAUTION: Be careful to keep oil or grease from contacting the lining surface.

Inspect the brake shoes for wear, rust or damage. Inspect the brake linings for wear. The shoes should be relined if the lining thickness is less than 0.06 in.

Inspect the tension spring for deformation or weakness.

Installation is performed in the following order:

1. Coat all of the points where the brake shoes make contact with other brake assembly parts, with grease.

CAUTION: Be careful not to get grease on the surface of the lining.

2. Fit the upper and lower shoes into the grooves on the wheel cylinders and adjusting bolts. Install the spring pins in the shoes and then attach the retaining springs.
3. Hook the brake shoe tension springs on the upper and lower shoes with the aid of the tool used during removal.
4. Install the drum.

Land Cruiser

1. Remove the brake drum.
2. Remove the upper shoe by pulling out the end, while applying an upward force on it.
3. Depress the lower shoe and repeat the removal procedure for it.

CAUTION: Do not interchange the upper and lower shoes. Do not allow grease to contact the lining surface.

Inspect the shoes for wear, rust or damage. Check the linings for wear. The service limit of lining thickness is 0.16 in.; have the shoes relined if it is less.

PRELOAD SPECIFICATIONS

Model	Initial Torque Setting (ft-lb)	Procedure
Pick-up		
1973-78	36①	Tighten to correct ft-lb, loosen 1/6 to 1/3 turn after bearing is seated
1979-80	36①	Tighten to correct ft-lb, loosen and retighten as much as possible with a socket turned by hand
Land Cruiser	43	Tighten to 43 ft-lb, loosen 1/8 to 1/5 turn
4X4 Pick-up	43	Tighten to 43 ft-lb, loosen and tighten to 2.9-5.0 ft-lb

Inspect the springs for weakness and deformation.

Installation is performed in the following order:

1. Grease all points at which the brake shoe makes contact with other brake components.

CAUTION: Do not allow grease to contact the lining surface.

2. Fit the ends of the lower brake shoe into the grooves on the wheel cylinder piston and the adjusting bolt.
3. Push up on the upper brake shoe and fit it into the grooves on the piston and the adjusting bolt.
4. Hook the return springs on the brake shoes.
5. Install the brake drum.

Wheel Cylinders

REMOVAL AND INSTALLATION

Pick-up and Land Cruiser

1. Perform the brake drum and brake shoe removal procedures.
2. Plug the master cylinder reservoir inlet, to prevent fluid from leaking out.
3. Remove the hydraulic lines from the wheel cylinders by unfastening the union bolt.
4. Remove the wheel cylinder attachment screws and withdraw the wheel cylinders.

CAUTION: Do not mix the right and left wheel cylinders.

To install the wheel cylinders, proceed in the following manner:

1. Use the attaching screws to install the wheel cylinder to the backing plate.

NOTE: The wheel cylinder adjusting nut and bolt on the right side of the brake have left-hand threads; while those on the left side have right-hand threads. Be careful not to mix them.

2. Connect the hydraulic line to the wheel cylinders.

CAUTION: Use care to see that the hydraulic line is not twisted.

3. Install the brake drum and shoes. Bleed the brake system.

GENERAL OVERHAUL

Remove the boots, pistons and the cups and closely inspect the bores for signs of wear, scoring and/or scuffing. When in doubt, replace or hone the wheel cylinders with a special brake hone, using clean brake fluid as lubricant. Wash residue from the bores using clean fluid; never use oil or any other solvent on any brake components. Blow dry with air and install with fresh brake fluid. The general limit for a honed cylinder is 0.005 in. oversize (Do not try to save money by reusing brake components such as cylinders and cups.) The self-adjuster screws should be taken apart and all dirt and rust removed with a wire brush. Lightly coat with Lubriplate before assembly; components should turn freely.

Wheel Bearings

REMOVAL AND INSTALLATION

Pick-up

1. Remove the brake drum. Do not separate the drum from the hub, unless either one is to be replaced.

NOITE: The outer bearing comes off with the brake drum.

2. Use a puller to remove the inner bearing and the steering knuckle grease retainer.
3. Use a brass drift to remove the bearing cups from the axle hub.

Check the bearings for worn or pitted rollers. Examine the cup for signs of wear or damage. Inspect the hub itself, for defects.

Installation and packing are performed in the following order:

1. Use the brass drift to install the bearing cups in the hub.

CAUTION: Be careful not to cock the bearing cups in the hub.

2. Coat both the inner and outer bearings with multipurpose grease. Work the grease into the roller cages.
3. Drift the inner bearing and the steering knuckle grease retainer on the spindle.
4. Clean all of the old grease out of hub. Pack the inside of the hub with multipurpose grease.
5. Install the hub and brake drum assembly over the steering knuckle.
6. Install the outer bearing in the axle hub and adjust the preload, as detailed below.
7. Pack the grease cap with multipurpose grease and fit it over the hub.
8. Check and adjust the brake shoe clearance. Lower the vehicle.

Land Cruiser

1. Perform steps 1–3 of the front brake drum removal procedure.
2. Remove the cap from the axle shaft outer flange. Remove the snap-ring from the shaft.
3. Remove the bolts which secure the axle shaft outer flange to the hub.
4. Install the two service bolts into the holes evenly in order to loosen the flange. Withdraw the flange, complete with gasket.

CAUTION: Never remove the flange by prying off; oil leaks will result.

5. Remove the set screws and withdraw the brake drum.
6. Straighten out the lockwasher and remove the adjusting nut, using a spindle nut wrench.

CAUTION: Do not use a hammer and chisel to remove the nut.

7. Remove the hub assembly, complete with the claw washer, bearings and oil seal.

NOTE: If the bearings or cups are difficult to remove, use a puller.

Installation and packing are performed in the following order:

1. Install the oil seal and the inner bearing cone.
2. Pack the hub with multipurpose grease, after assembling both inner and outer bearing cups to it.
3. Assemble the axle hub and brake drum.
4. Install the hub/drum assembly over the spindle then install the outer bearing.
5. Install the claw washer and adjusting nut with the spindle nut wrench.
6. Adjust the bearing preload, then install the locknut and washer.
7. Install the axle shaft flange and gasket. Tighten the retaining bolts to 11–16 ft lbs.
8. Install the bolt on the end of the outer shaft. Pull out on the shaft while installing the snap-ring.
9. Install the flange cap.
10. Install the wheel and the hub cap. Lower the vehicle.

PRELOAD ADJUSTMENT

Pick-up

1. Fit the claw washer and tighten the retaining nut to 36 ft lbs (1973–74).
2. Rotate the axle hub back and forth to set the bearings.
3. Retorque the bearing nut to the proper specification. Loosen the nut $^1/_6$–$^1/_3$ of a turn, so that the cotter pin can be inserted through the castellated nut and into the spindle.
4. Install the front wheel and the lug nuts.
5. Check the wheel for free rotation. Check the axial play of the wheel by shaking it back and forth; the bearing free play should feel like it is about zero.
6. Install a new cotter pin and lock the retaining nut.

Land Cruiser

1. After tightening the adjusting nut with the spindle nut wrench, rotate the wheel back and forth in order to seat the bearing.
2. Loosen the adjusting nut $^1/_8$–$^1/_5$ of a turn.
3. Check the brake drum for free rotation.
4. Install the lockwasher and the locknut. Use the spindle nut wrench to tighten the locknut.
5. Bend the tabs on the lockwasher up.

Rear Drum Brakes
Brake Drums

REMOVAL AND INSTALLATION

The rear brake drum removal and installation procedure for all models is performed in the same manner as that for the front brake drum.

NOTE: Release the parking brake before attempting rear drum removal. Do not depress the brake pedal, once the drum has been removed.

Inspection

Inspection for the rear brake drum is performed in the same way as that for the front brake drum (see above).

Brake Shoes

REMOVAL AND INSTALLATION

Pick-up, 4x4 Pick-up, Land Cruiser

Land Cruiser rear brake shoe removal and installation procedures are identical to those for the Land Cruiser front brake shoes.

The procedures for the Pick-up and the 4x4 Pick-up are also similar to the Land Cruiser front shoe removal procedure, except for the following points:

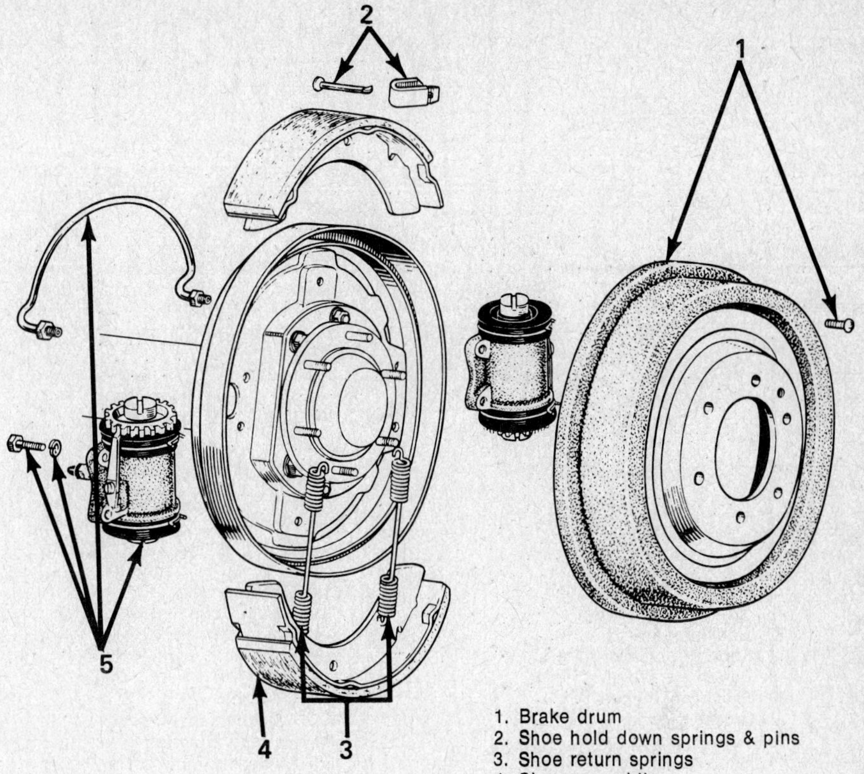

1. Brake drum
2. Shoe hold down springs & pins
3. Shoe return springs
4. Shoe assemblies
5. Wheel cylinders

Land Cruiser rear drum brakes

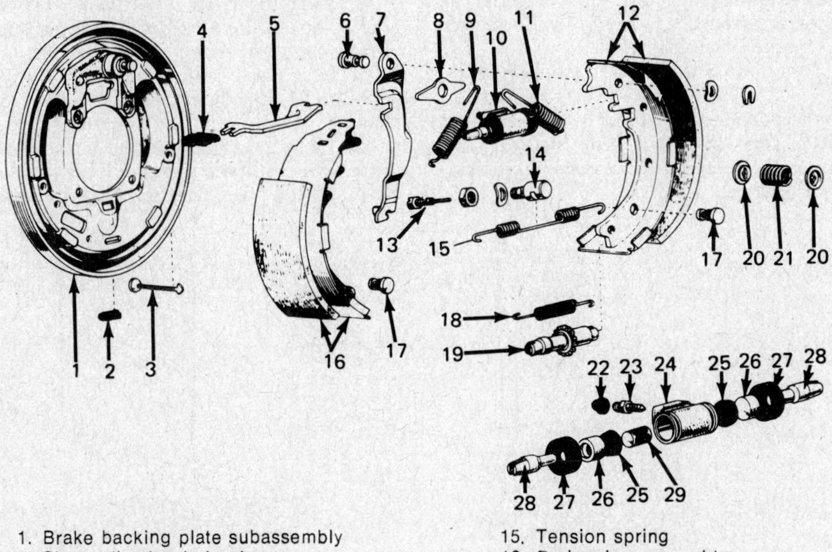

1. Brake backing plate subassembly
2. Shoe adjusting hole plug
3. Shoe hold-down spring pin
4. Compression spring
5. Parking brake shoe strut
6. Parking lever pin
7. Parking brake shoe lever
8. Rear brake shoe guide plate
9. Tension spring
10. Wheel brake rear cylinder assembly
11. Tension spring
12. Brake shoe assembly
13. Retracting spring clamp bolt subassembly
14. Shoe retracting clamp holder
15. Tension spring
16. Brake shoe assembly
17. Tension spring pin
18. Tension spring
19. Adjuster assembly
20. Shoe hold-down spring cup
21. Spring
22. Bleeder plug cap
23. Bleeder plug
24. Wheel brake cylinder rear body
25. Cylinder cup
26. Wheel brake cylinder piston
27. Wheel cylinder boot
28. Wheel cylinder connecting link
29. Compression spring

Pick-up rear brake components 1973-74

Check to see if your vehicle has front drum or disc brakes.

On vehicles with front drum brakes, remove and install the parking brake strut and springs along with the front shoe.

On vehicles with front disc brakes, release the spring on the self adjusting cable where it fastens to the self adjusting rachet arm at the bottom of the brake assembly. Remove the rachet arm and its spring. Remove the top of the cable and remove the parking brake strut in the same manner as described on the vehicle with front drum brakes.

On 2 wd and 4 wd Pick-ups:

1. Disconnect the parking brake cable from the shoe lever. Remember to connect it during installation.
2. Remove and install the rear shoe complete with the parking shoe lever.

The service limits of the brake lining thickness are as follows:

Pick-up: 0.04 in.
4x4 Pick-up: 0.04 in.
Land Cruiser: 0.06 in.

Wheel Cylinders

REMOVAL AND INSTALLATION

Pick-up and 4x4 Pick-up

1. Plug the master cylinder inlet to prevent hydraulic fluid from leaking.
2. Remove the brake drums and shoes as detailed in the appropriate section above.

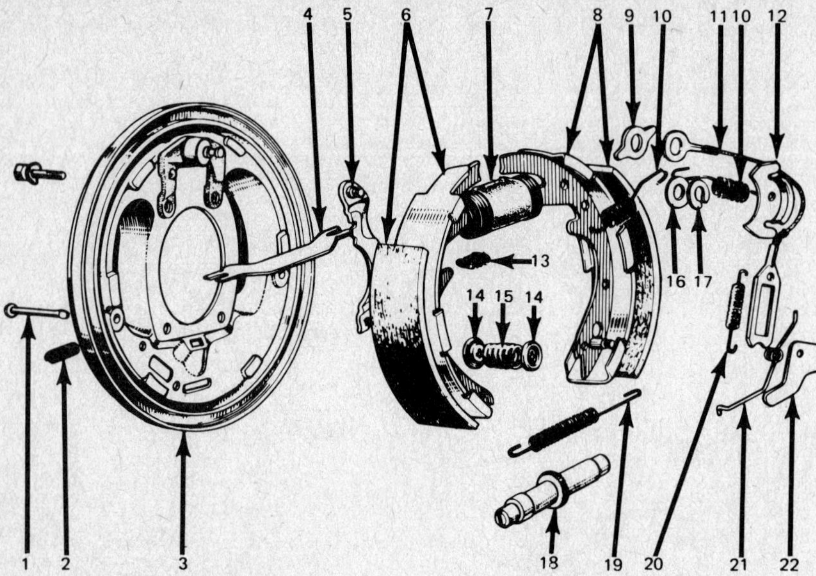

1. Shoe hold down spring pin
2. Adjusting hole plug
3. Backing plate
4. Parking brake shoe strut
5. Parking brake shoe lever
6. Front brake shoe
7. Wheel cylinder
8. Rear brake shoe
9. Shoe guide plate
10. Return spring
11. Automatic adjuster cable
12. Cable guide
13. Parking brake strut spring
14. Hold down spring seat
15. Shoe hold down spring
16. Washer
17. C washer
18. Adjusting screw set
19. Retracting spring
20. Adjusting cable spring
21. Adjusting lever spring
22. Adjusting lever

Pick-up self adjusting rear brakes—1975 and later

3. Working from behind the backing plate, disconnect the hydraulic line from the wheel cylinder.

4. Unfasten the screws retaining the wheel cylinder and withdraw the cylinder.

Installation is performed in the reverse order of removal.

Remember to bleed the brake system after completing wheel cylinder, brake shoe and drum installation.

Land Cruiser

The front brake wheel cylinder removal procedure is performed in the same manner as the procedure for the Pick-up and Land Cruiser rear brakes. For details see the section dealing with these vehicles.

Overhaul

See "General Overhaul" for a description of wheel cylinder overhaul procedures.

Power Brake Booster

REMOVAL AND INSTALLATION

1. Remove brake master cylinder. See above for instructions.

2. Remove the air line running from the brake booster to the manifold.

3. Working inside the driver's compartment, remove the clevis pin that connects the brake pedal to the booster rod. Remove the four nuts holding the booster assembly to the fire wall and remove the assembly.

Installation is the reverse of removal.

NOTE: When installing a new booster, make sure there is a little clearance between the push rod end and the master cylinder piston.

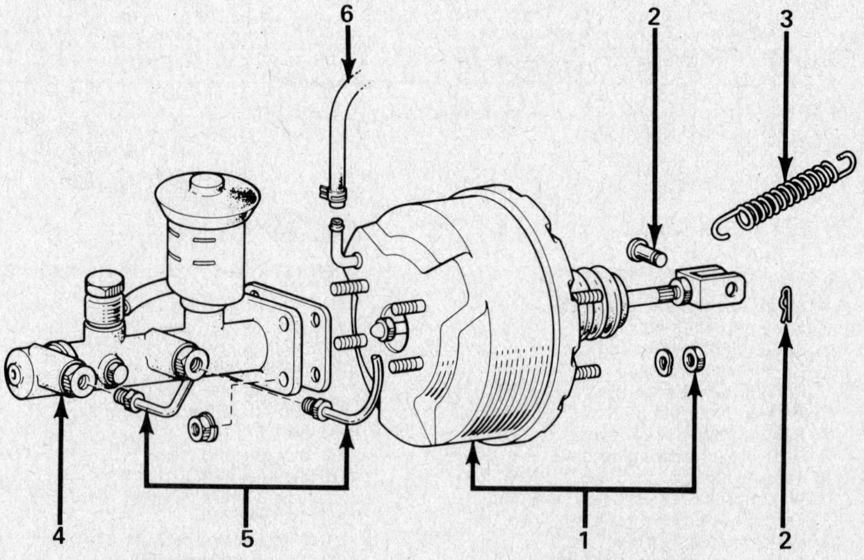

1. Brake booster
2. Push rod pin & snap ring
3. Spring
4. Master cylinder
5. Brake tube
6. Vacuum hose

Power brake booster

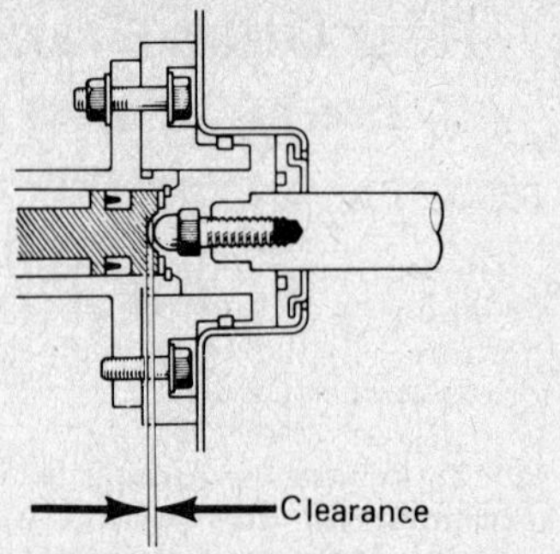

Make sure there is a little clearance between the brake booster push rod and the master cylinder piston

Parking Brake Adjustments

Pick-up, 4x4 Pick-up

NOTE: Adjust the rear brake shoes, as detailed at the beginning of this chapter, before attempting to adjust the parking brake.

1. Loosen the parking brake warning light switch bracket.

2. Push the parking brake lever in until it is stopped by the pawl.

3. Move the switch so that it will be "off" at this position but "on" when the handle is pulled out.

4. Tighten the switch bracket and push the brake lever in again.

5. Working from underneath the vehicle, loosen the locknut on the parking brake cable equalizer.

6. Screw the adjusting nut *in,* just enough so that the brake cables have no slack.

7. Hold the adjusting nut in this position while tightening the locknut.

8. Check the rotation of the rear

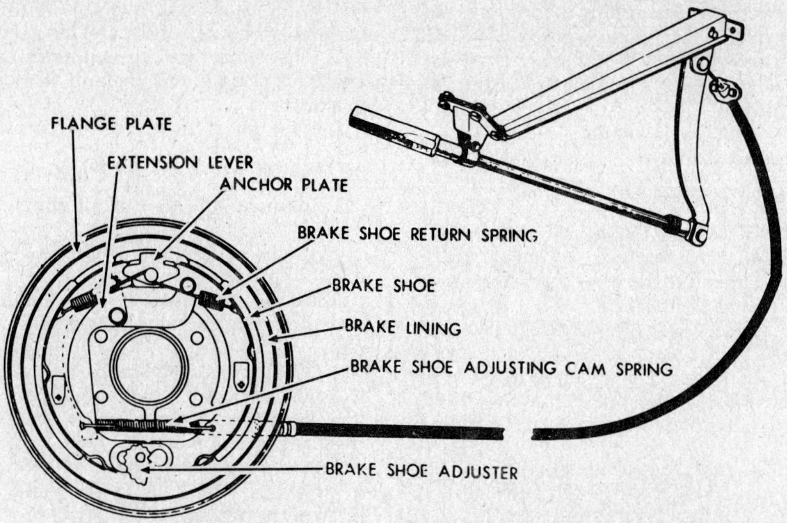

The components of the Land Cruiser parking brake system

wheels to make sure that the brakes are not dragging.

9. Pull out on the parking brake lever, and count the number of notches needed to apply the parking brake. Check the number against the figures given in the chart.

Land Cruiser

Land Cruiser models use a separate drum brake assembly, operating on the driveshaft, to serve as a parking brake. Adjust it as follows:

1. Push the parking brake lever all the way in, so that the brake is released.
2. Raise the rear of the vehicle and support it with jackstands.
3. Turn the parking brake adjustment shaft, which is located at the bottom of the parking brake backing plate, counterclockwise until the shoes seat against the drum.
4. Back the adjuster off one notch.
5. Apply the parking brake; the drum should be locked. Release the brake; the drum should rotate freely.

NOTE: If the drum does not rotate freely with the brake off, loosen the adjuster one more notch.

6. Adjust the turnbuckles on the parking brake intermediate levers and the adjusting nuts on the end of the parking brake cables, so that 6–9 notches are required to apply the parking brake (1973–75). Set for 7–12 notches for 1976–80.

PARKING BRAKE ADJUSTMENT

Model	Range of Adjustment (Notches)
Pick-up (all)	7-15
Land Cruiser (all)	7-15

CHASSIS ELECTRICAL

Heater Blower

REMOVAL AND INSTALLATION

1973-78 Pick-up

NOTE: On models equipped with air conditioning, the heater and air conditioner are completely separate units. The heater removal procedure is the same as outlined here. However, be certain when working under the dashboard that only the heater hoses are disconnected. The air conditioning hoses are under pressure; if disconnected, the escaping refrigerant will freeze any surface with which it comes in contact, including your skin and eyes. Refer all air conditioning work to a qualified mechanic.

1. Drain the cooling system.
2. Remove the package tray from beneath the dashboard.
3. Unfasten the two water hoses from the heater.

NOTE: Have a container ready to catch any water which remains in the system.

4. Unfasten the clamp and remove the defroster hose.
5. Unfasten the three heater control cables from the heater box.
6. Remove the fresh air duct.
7. Unfasten the electrical connections.
8. Unfasten the four heater box attachment bolts and withdraw the heater box.
9. Loosen the fan attachment nut by tapping it lightly and then withdraw the fan from the shaft.

CAUTION: Do not remove the balancing weight from the fan.

10. Unfasten the blower motor securing screws and remove the motor.

Installation is the reverse of removal. Be sure that the fan does not contact the blower housing when it is assembled. Hold the fan adapter in place, on the armature shaft while tightening the fan locknut.

1979-80 Pick-up, 4x4 Pick-up

Proceed as described under 1973–78 Pick-up removal and installation, above, and including the following:

1. Remove the three heater box retainer bolts, one at the top and one on each side of the unit.
2. Remove the radiator unit pipes along with the heater box/radiator assembly.
3. Disconnect the blower motor assembly from the heater box and remove.

Land Cruiser

1. Loosen the air duct clamping screws and remove the ducts.
2. Remove the air duct screen.
3. Unfasten the mounting bolts and remove the blower motor complete with fan.

Installation is the reverse of removal.

Heater Core

REMOVAL AND INSTALLATION

1973–78 Pick-up

1. Complete steps 1-8 under heater blower removal, above.
2. Remove the heater control panel and heater lower case cover as a unit. The core may then be taken out of the heater case.

Installation is the reverse of removal.

1979–80 Pick-up, 4x4 Pick-up

1. Remove heater unit as described above.
2. Remove the two metal unit pipes from the radiator assembly.
3. Remove the set screw and six clips holding the two halves of the radiator case together and separate the cases. Remove the core.

Installation is the reverse of removal.

Land Cruiser

FRONT HEATER

1. Turn off the water valve.
2. Detach both hoses from the heater core.
3. Unfasten the air duct clamp.
4. Detach the defroster hoses from the heater box.
5. Unfasten its attachment bolts and withdraw the core.

Installation is the reverse of removal.

REAR HEATER

1. Shut the water valve.
2. Detach both of the hoses from the rear heater core.
3. Detach the wiring from the rear heater.

4. Unfasten the bolts and lift out the core.

Installation is the reverse of removal.

Radio

CAUTION: Never operate the radio without a speaker; severe damage to the output transistors will result. If the speaker must be replaced, use a speaker of the correct impedance (ohms) or else the output transistors will be damaged and require replacement.

REMOVAL AND INSTALLATION

1973–78 Pick-up

1. Remove the knobs from the radio.
2. Remove the nuts from the radio control shafts.
3. Detach the antenna lead from the jack on the radio case.
4. Detach the power and speaker leads.
5. Remove the radio support nuts and bolts.
6. Remove the radio from beneath the dashboard.

Installation is the reverse of removal.

1979–80 Pick-up, 4X4 Pick-up

1. Disconnect positive lead from battery.
2. Remove steering column upper and lower covers.
3. Remove the five screws holding the instrument cluster trim panel and remove trim panel.
4. Remove the knobs from the radio and remove the securing nuts from the control shafts.
5. Remove the heater/air conditioner knobs from their control arms. Do not remove the blower fan control knob.
6. Remove the two screws holding the heater control dash light. Remove the ash-tray and remove all of the screw holding the center dash facade onto the dash.
7. Pull the facade out, and carefully disconnect the cigaret lighter and the blower fan control at their plugs.
8. Unscrew any remaining screws holding the radio and pull it out part way. Disconnect the power source, speaker coupling and antenna from the radio and remove through the dash.

Installation is the reverse of removal.

Windshield Wiper Motor

REMOVAL AND INSTALLATION

All Pick-up Models

1. Disconnect the wiring from the wiper motor and unbolt it from the fire wall.
2. Remove the arm nut and the crank arm from the wiper motor (1973–78 Pick-up). On 1979–80 Pick-up and 4x4 Pick-up, pry the wiper link from the crank arm.
3. Remove the motor.

Installation is the reverse of removal.

Land Cruiser

1. Detach the wiper link from the motor with a screwdriver.
2. Unfasten the two bracket bolts at the rear of the motor.
3. Disconnect the wiper motor wiring.
4. Unfasten the wiper motor screws and withdraw the motor.

Installation is the reverse of removal.

Wiper Linkage

REMOVAL AND INSTALLATION

Pick-up, 4x4 Pick-up

1. Remove the wiper motor as described above.
2. Remove the wiper arms by removing their retaining nuts and working them off their shafts.
3. Remove the nuts and spacers holding the wiper shafts and push the shafts down into the body cavity. Pull the linkage out of the cavity through the wiper motor hole.

Installation is the reverse of removal.

Land Cruiser—2 Door

1. Remove the wiper arm assemblies.
2. Remove the end plate from the pivot housing.
3. Remove the wiper motor complete with the linkage cable.
4. Separate the wiper motor and transmission.
5. Remove the linkage cable.

Installation is performed in the reverse order of removal.

Land Cruiser—Station Wagon

1. Perform the wiper motor removal procedures above.
2. Remove the wiper arm assemblies.
3. Remove the instrument cluster, as detailed below.
4. Loosen the throttle cable to improve access to the wiper linkage.
5. Remove the linkage attachment bolts and withdraw the linkage.

Installation is the reverse of removal.

Instrument Panel

REMOVAL AND INSTALLATION

1973–78 Pick-up

1. Loosen the steering column clamp bolts at the base of the instrument panel. This will allow the steering column to drop slightly.
2. Remove the three retaining screws on the instrument group and pull out gently on the hood of the cluster.
3. Disconnect the speedometer cable and the wiring connector and withdraw the cluster.

Installation is the reverse of removal.

1979–80 Pick-up, 4x4 Pick-up

1. Remove the positive battery terminal.
2. Remove the upper and lower steering column covers.
3. Remove the five screws holding the instrument trim panel and remove the panel.
4. Disconnect the speedometer cable from the back of the speedometer.
5. Remove the four screws holding the instrument panel in place and pull the panel forward. Unplug the two connectors from the back of the panel and remove the panel.

Installation is the reverse of removal.

Land Cruiser

1. Disconnect the speedometer cable.
2. Remove the instrument panel attaching screws.
3. Loosen the steering column clamp by removing the attaching bolts.
4. Pull out the instrument panel and the speedometer, disconnect the wiring connectors, and remove the panel.

Install the panel in the reverse order from removal.

Speedometer Cable Removal and Installation

Pick-up, 4x4 Pick-up

1. Remove the instrument cluster and disconnect the cable at the speedometer.
2. Disconnect the other end of the speedometer cable at the transmission extension housing and pull the cable from its jacket at the transmission end. If you are replacing the cable because it is broken, don't forget to remove both pieces of the broken cable.
3. Lubricate the new cable with graphite speedometer cable lubricant, and feed it into the cable jacket from the lower end.
4. Connect the cable to the transmission, then to the speedometer. Plug the electrical connector into the instrument cluster, and replace the cluster.

Fuses and Fusible Links

The fuse box is located on the left-hand side, underneath the dashboard, on all models. All models are equipped with fusible links on the battery cables running from the positive (+) battery terminal.

INDEX

INTRODUCTION

The Volkswagen pick-up is new for 1980. It is the first VW ever to be both designed and built by Volkswagen of America and is also the only small pick-up available with a diesel engine.

The new pick-up is based on the Rabbit, and like the Rabbit is available with either a fuel injected gasoline engine or a diesel. The available transmissions are a four or five-speed manual, or a three-speed automatic.

The engines are all water cooled, transversely mounted units. The truck has an independent front suspension, rack and pinion steering and power assisted brakes (disc in the front, self-adjusting drums in the rear).

MODEL IDENTIFICATION

1980 Volkswagen Pickup

SERIAL NUMBER IDENTIFICATION

Vehicle Identification Plate

On the Rabbit pick-up, the plate is on top of the body crossmember above the grille. On the plate are the date of manufacture and the chassis number.

Chassis Number

The chassis number is located on the left front corner of the instrument panel on the Rabbit pick-up, and is visible through the windshield. The chassis number is also on top of the right suspension strut mounting. It also appears on the vehicle identification plate.

Engine Number

The Engine number is stamped on the front of the engine block between the fuel pump and the distributor.

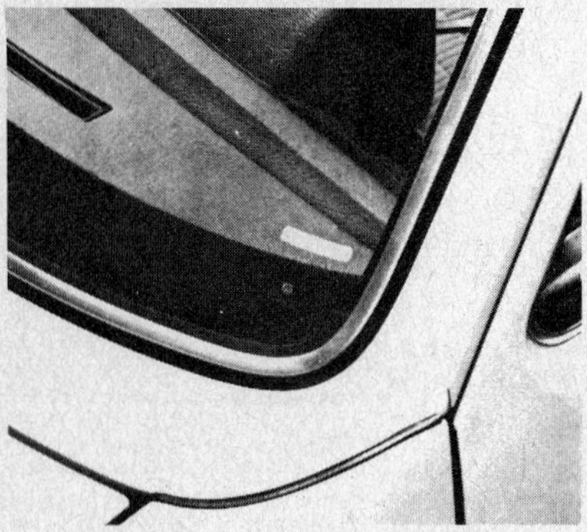

Vehicle identification plate

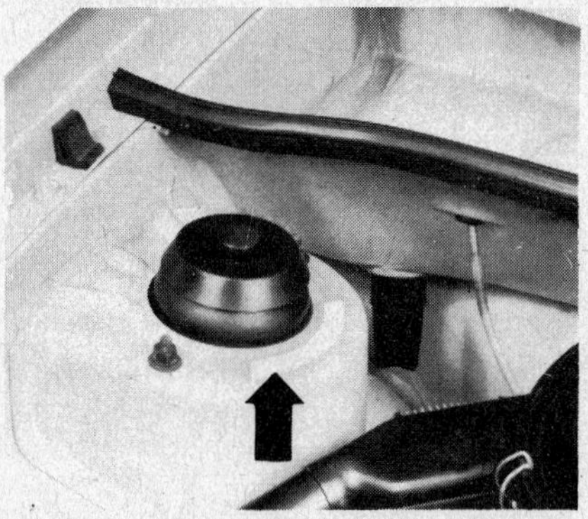

Chassis number

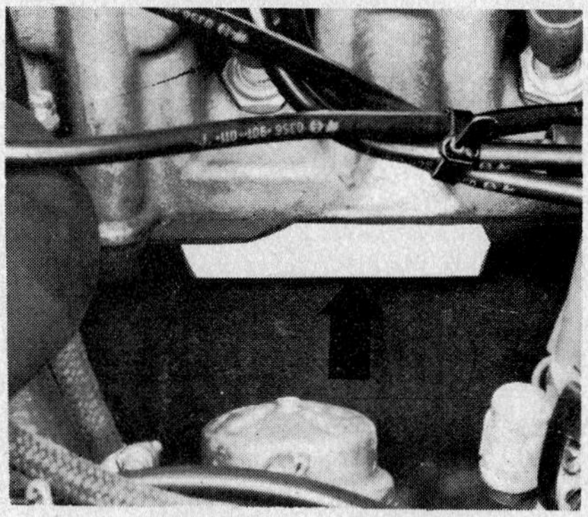

Engine number

GENERAL ENGINE SPECIFICATIONS

Year	Engine Displacement cu in. (cc)	Carburetor Type	Horsepower @ rpm (SAE)	Torque @ rpm (ft lbs) (SAE)	Bore x Stroke (in.)	Compression Ratio	Oil Pressure @ rpm (psi)
1980	88.9 (1457)	Fuel inj.	71 @ 5800	73 @ 3500	3.13 x 2.89	8:1	28 @ 2000
	89.7 (1471)	Diesel	48 @ 5000	56.5 @ 3000	3.01 x 3.15	23.5:1	27 @ 2000

GASOLINE TUNE-UP SPECIFICATIONS

Year	Engine Displacement cm³	Spark Plugs Type	Spark Plugs Gap (in.)	Distributor Point Dwell (deg)	Distributor Point Gap (in.)	Ignition Timing (deg)	Intake Valve Opens (deg)	Compression Pressure (psi)	Idle Speed (rpm)	Valve Clearance (in.) In	Valve Clearance (in.) Ex
1980	1457	W175 T30 N8Y	.024-.028	44-50	.016	3A @ idle	4B	142-184	850-1000	.008-.012	.016-.020

A—After Top Dead Center B—Before Top Dead Center

NOTE: The underhood specifications sticker often reflects tune-up specification changes made in production. Sticker figures must be used if they disagree with those in this chart.

DIESEL TUNE-UP SPECIFICATIONS

Year	Valve Clearance (cold) Intake (in.)	Valve Clearance (cold) Exhaust (in.)	Intake Valve Opens (deg)	Injection Pump Setting (deg)	Injection Nozzle Pressure (psi) New	Injection Nozzle Pressure (psi) Used	Idle Speed (rpm)	Cranking Compression Pressure (psi)
1980	.008-.012	.016-.020	NA	Align marks	1849	1706	770-870	398 minimum

NOTE: Valve clearance need not be adjusted unless it varies more than 0.002 in. from specification.

NA: Information not available

FIRING ORDER

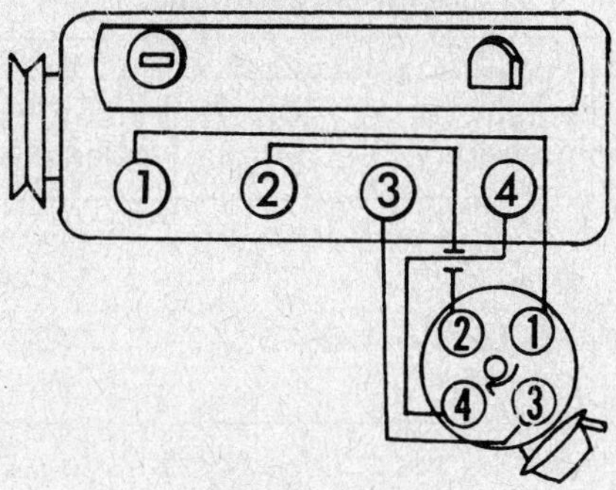

Firing order: 1-3-4-2

CAPACITIES

Year	Engine Displacement cu in. (cc)	Engine Crankcase (qts) With Filter	Engine Crankcase (qts) Without Filter	Transmission (pts) Manual	Transmission (pts) Automatic	Drive Axle (pts)	Gasoline Tank (gals)	Cooling System (pts)
1980	Gasoline	3.7	3.2	3.2①	6.4	1.6	15	9.8
	Diesel	3.7	3.2	2.6	—	1.6	15	12.6

① 5-speed—4.2

CRANKSHAFT AND CONNECTING ROD SPECIFICATIONS

(All measurements are given in inches)

	Crankshaft				Connecting Rod		
Year	Main Brg. Journal Dia.	Main Brg. Oil Clearance	Shaft End-Play	Thrust on No.	Journal Diameter	Oil Clearance	Side Clearance (max.)
1980	2.126	0.001-0.003	0.003-0.007	3	1.811	0.001-0.003	0.015

NOTE: Main and connecting rod bearings are available in three undersizes.

VALVE SPECIFICATIONS

			Stem to Guide Clearance (in.)		Stem Diameter (in.)	
Year	Seat Angle (deg)	Spring Test Pressure (lbs. @ in.)	Intake	Exhaust	Intake	Exhaust
1980	45	96-106① @ 0.92 in.	0.001-0.002	0.001-0.002	0.314	0.314

NOTE: Exhaust valves must be ground by hand.

① Outer spring, inner spring test pressure is 46-51 lbs. @ 0.72 in.

PISTON AND RING SPECIFICATIONS

(All measurements in inches)

		Ring Gap			Ring Side Clearance		
Year, Model	Piston Clear-ance	Top Compression	Bottom Compression	Oil Control	Top Compression	Bottom Compression	Oil Control
Gasoline Engine	0.001-0.003	0.012-0.018	0.012-0.018	0.010-0.016	0.001-0.002	0.001-0.002	0.001-0.002
Diesel Engine	0.001-0.003	0.012-0.020	0.012-0.020	0.010-0.016	0.002-0.400	0.002-0.003	0.001-0.002

NOTE: Three piston sizes are available to accommodate overbores up to 0.040 in.

TORQUE SPECIFICATIONS

(All readings in ft lbs)

						Manifold	
Year	Cylinder Head Bolts	Rod Bearing Bolts	Main Bearing Bolts	Crankshaft Pulley Bolt	Flywheel To Crankshaft Bolts	Intake	Exhaust
1980	61①	33	47	56	54②	18	18

① 69 ft. lbs. warm

② Pressure plate to crankshaft bolts

TORQUE SEQUENCES

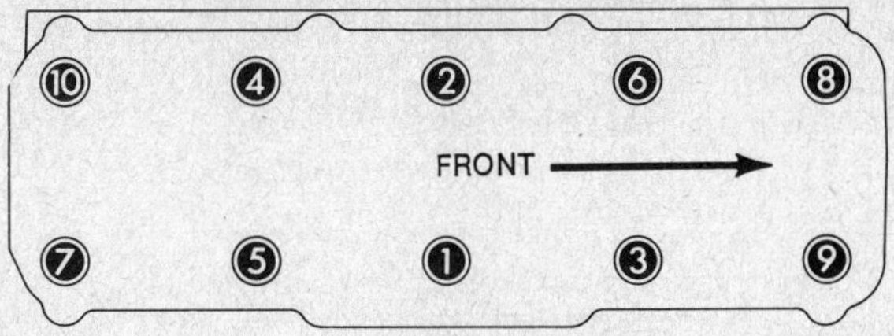

Cylinder head

BATTERY AND STARTER SPECIFICATIONS

(All models use 12 volt, negative ground system)

Year	Battery Amp Hour Capacity	Lock Test Amps	Lock Test Volts	Lock Test Torque (ft/lbs)	No Load Test Amps	No Load Test Volts	No Load Test RPM	Brush Spring Tension (oz.)	Minimum Brush Length (in.)
1980	45/54*	280-370	7.5	2.42	33-55	11.5	6000-8000	35.5	0.5

* w/AC

WHEEL ALIGNMENT

Year	Caster Range (deg)	Caster Pref Setting (deg)	Camber Range (deg)	Camber Pref Setting (deg)	Toe-in (in.)	Steering Axis Inclination (deg)
1980	+1°20′-2°20′	+1°50′	−10′-+50′	+20′	0.08	10°30′

TUNE-UP PROCEDURES

VW recommends a tune-up, including new points and plugs, at 15,000 mile intervals. The only procedure required for diesel engines in this section is the valve lash adjustment.

Spark Plugs

The firing order is 1–3–4–2, with No. 1 cylinder at the right of the engine.

1. Grasp the spark plug boot and pull it straight out. Don't pull on the wire. Either number the wires or remove them one at a time to avoid mixups.
2. Place the spark plug socket firmly on the plug and screw the spark plug out.

NOTE: The cylinder head is aluminum alloy, which is easily stripped of threads. Remove the plugs only when the engine is cold.

If removal is difficult, loosen the plug only slightly and drip penetrating oil onto the threads.

3. Inspect the plugs and clean or discard them. The recommended spark plug gap is listed in the "Tune-Up Specifications" chart. Use a round wire feeler gauge to check the gap between the plug electrodes. If the gap is incorrect, gently bend the side electrode to correct. Do not bend the center electrode.
4. Torque the new spark plugs to 22 ft lbs. Install the ignition wire boots firmly.

Breaker Points and Condenser

Snap off the two retaining clips on the distributor cap. Remove the cap and examine it for cracks, deterioration, or carbon tracking. Replace the cap, if necessary, by transferring one wire at a time from the old cap to the new one. Examine the rotor for corrosion or wear and replace it if questionable. Remove the dust shield. Check the points for pitting and burning. Slight imperfections on the contact surface may be filed off with a point file. It is best to replace the breaker point set. Always replace the condenser when you replace the point set.

To replace the breaker points:

1. Remove the rotor.
2. Unsnap the point connector from the terminal at the side of the distributor. Remove the retaining screw, and lift out the point set.
3. Install the new point set, making

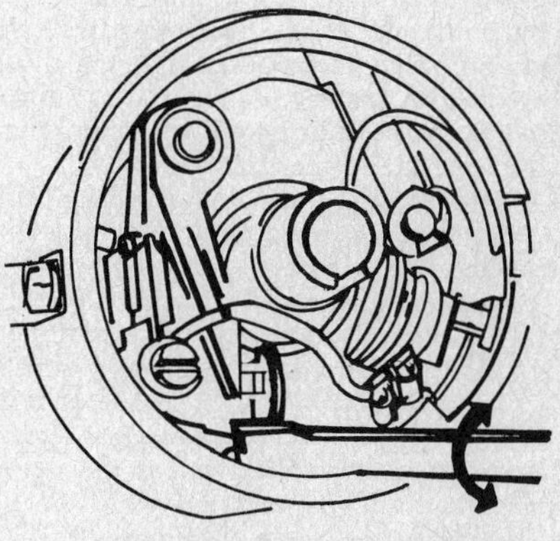

Adjusting the point gap

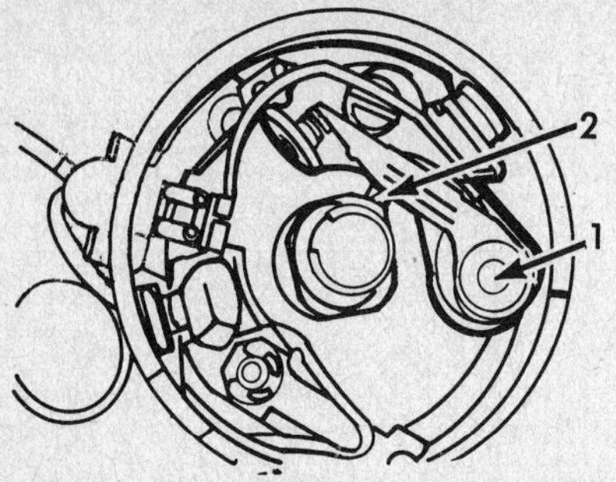

Breaker points and condenser. Lub ricate at (1) with a drop of engine oil and at (2) with high melting point grease

sure that the pin on the bottom engages the hole in the breaker plate.

4. Install the wire connector and the retaining screws (hand-tight).

5. Turn the engine with a wrench on the crankshaft pulley until the breaker arm rubbing block is on the high point of one of the cam lobes. Turn the engine only in the direction of normal rotation to avoid damage to the timing belt.

6. A 0.016 in. feeler gauge should just slip through the points. If the gap is incorrect, pivot a screwdriver in the point set notch and the two projections on the breaker plate to bring it within specifications.

7. When the gap is correct, tighten the retaining screw. Recheck the adjustment.

8. Lubricate the distributor cam with silicone grease.

9. Install the dust cover, rotor and distributor cap.

10. Check the dwell angle and the ignition timing.

11. The condenser is mounted on the outside of the distributor. Undo the mounting screw and the terminal block to replace.

Dwell Angle

Note: The diesel engine has no distributor nor provision for dwell adjustment.

The dwell angle or cam angle is the number of degrees that the distributor cam rotates while the points are closed. There is an inverse relationship between dwell angle and point gap. Increasing the point gap will decrease the dwell angle and vice versa. Checking the dwell angle with a meter is a far more accurate method of measuring point opening than the feeler gauge method.

After setting the point gap to specification with a feeler gauge, check the dwell angle. Attach the dwell meter. The negative lead is grounded and the positive lead is connected to the primary wire, Terminal No. 1 that runs from the coil to the distributor. Start the engine, let it idle and reach operating temperature, and observe the dwell on the meter. The reading should fall within the allowable range. If it does not, the gap will have to be reset. Dwell can also be checked with the engine cranking. In this case, dwell will vary between 0° and the dwell figure for that setting.

Ignition Timing

NOTE: There is no ignition system on the diesel engine.

Ignition timing is always adjusted after the points are gapped (dwell angle changed) since altering the dwell affects the timing.

1. Attach a timing light. Hook up a dwell/tachometer.

2. Locate the timing mark opening in the clutch or torque converter housing at the rear of the engine directly behind the distributor. The 0°T Mark stands for TDC or 0°. The 3 mark to the right means 3° ATDC. Mark them with chalk so that they will be more visible. Don't disconnect the vacuum line.

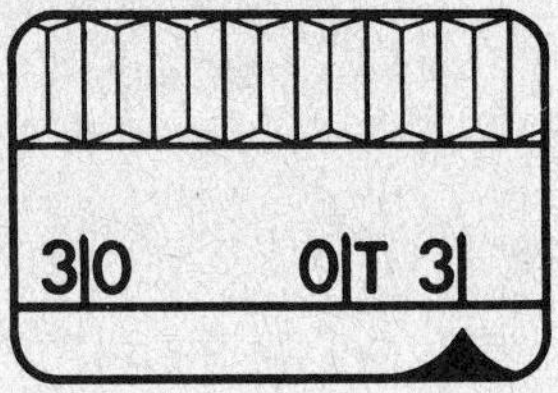

Timing mark aligned at 3°ATDC

3. Start the engine and allow it to reach normal operating temperature. The engine should be at normal idle speed.

4. Shine the timing light at the marks.

5. The 3° line and the V-shaped pointer should be aligned.

6. If not, loosen the distributor hold down bolt and rotate the distributor very slowly to align the marks.

7. Tighten the mounting nut when the ignition timing is correct.

8. Recheck the timing when the distributor is secured.

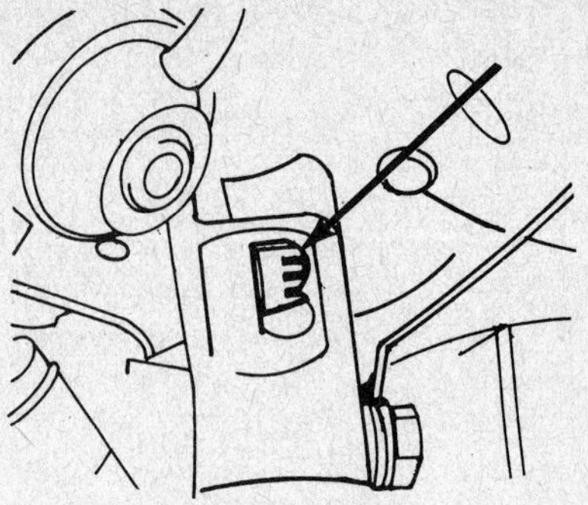

Timing window

Valve Lash

Check the valve clearance every 20,-000 miles in firing order, with the engine at normal operating temperature.

1. Remove the camshaft cover and the distributor cap.

2. Set the engine at TDC on No. 1 cylinder by aligning the 0°T mark on the fly wheel with the pointer and aligning the distributor rotor with the No. 1 cylinder mark on the rim of the distributor body.

NOTE: Always turn the crankshaft in the normal direction of rotation. Do not turn the engine by means of the timing belt (or camshaft bolt), because the belt will stretch or lose teeth.

3. The valve clearances of cylinder No. 1 should be checked when the valves of No. 4 cylinder overlap, i.e. when both No. 4 cylinder valves move in opposite directions simultaneously. It may be necessary to move the crankshaft slightly to find this position. When this happens, the exhaust valve is closing and the intake opening. Check and note the clearance of both the intake and exhaust valves for No. 1 cylinder.

4. Turn the crankshaft 180° (90° at the distributor rotor) in the normal di-

Checking the valve clearance with a feeler gauge

rection of rotation. Check and note the valve clearances of cylinder No. 3 at the overlap position of cylinder No. 2.

5. Turn the crankshaft 180°. Check and note the valve clearances of cylinder No. 4 at the overlap position of cylinder No. 1.

6. Turn the crankshaft 180°. Check and note the valve clearances of cylinder No. 2 at the overlap position of cylinder No. 3.

7. Compare the noted clearances with those listed in the Tune-Up Specifications Chart. Adjustment is made by replacing the tappet clearance disc in the top of each tappet. These are available in 26 sizes ranging from 3.0 mm (0.119 in) to 4.25 mm (0.166 in) in increments of 0.05 mm (0.002 in). The thickness of each disc is marked on the bottom.

NOTE: If a valve clearance deviates 0.002 in or less from the specified clearance, it need not be adjusted.

8. To remove a tappet clearance disc, turn the cylinder to TDC and press down the tappet so that the disc can be lifted out.

NOTE: When adjusting clearances on a diesel, the pistons must not be at TDC.

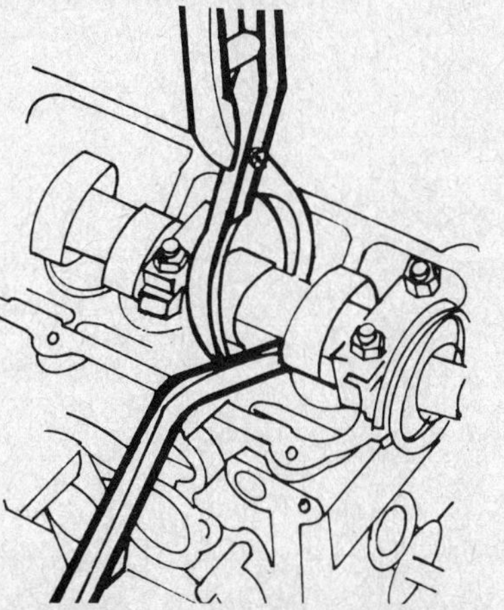

Using special tools to depress the tappet and remove the tappet clearance disc

Adjust the diesel engine idle speed at the screw (arrow) on the injection pump

Turn the crankshaft 1/4 turn past TDC, so that the valves do not contact the pistons when the tappets are depressed.

A special tool is available from VW for this operation. Once the disc is removed, check its size and determine what size will be needed to produce the required adjustment.

9. Install the required disc. When all the clearances have been corrected, recheck valve clearances.

CIS Fuel Injection

IDLE AND CO ADJUSTMENT

The following adjustments can be made *only* with a CO meter and the CO adjusting tool (VW-P377).

1. Run the engine until it reaches normal operating temperature.
2. Adjust the ignition timing to specification with the vacuum hoses connected and the engine at idle.
3. Adjust the idle speed to specification.
4. Remove the charcoal filter hose from the air cleaner except on Canadian models.
5. Turn on the headlight high beams.
6. Remove the plug from the CO adjusting hole and insert adjusting tool VW-P377. Turn the adjustment screw clockwise to raise the percentage of CO and counterclockwise to lower the percentage of CO.

CAUTION: Do Not push the adjustment tool down or accelerate the engine with the tool in place.

7. Remove the tool after each adjustment and accelerate the engine briefly before reading the percentage of CO. The correct CO values are as follows:

49 States, Canada: 1.5%, M/T
1.0%, A/T
California, 1974–76: 0.5%
1977–79: 0.3%

Diesel Fuel Injection

IDLE AND CO ADJUSTMENT

The idle speed must be adjusted with the engine warm (normal operating temperature). Because the diesel engine has no conventional ignition, you will need a special adaptor (VW 1324) to connect your tachometer, or use the tachometer in the instrument panel, if equipped. You should check with the manufacturer

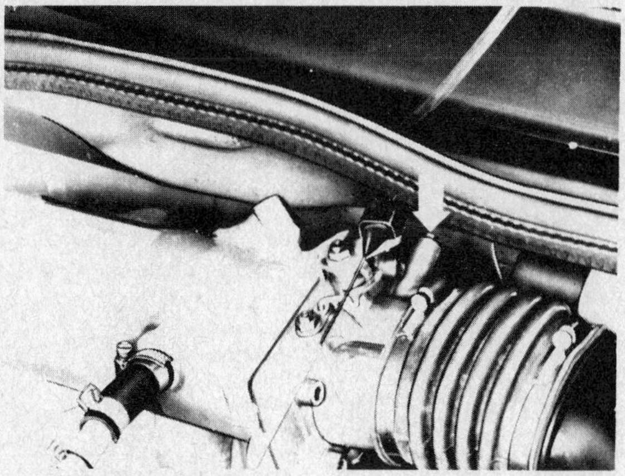

Idle speed adjustment screw—CIS fuel injection

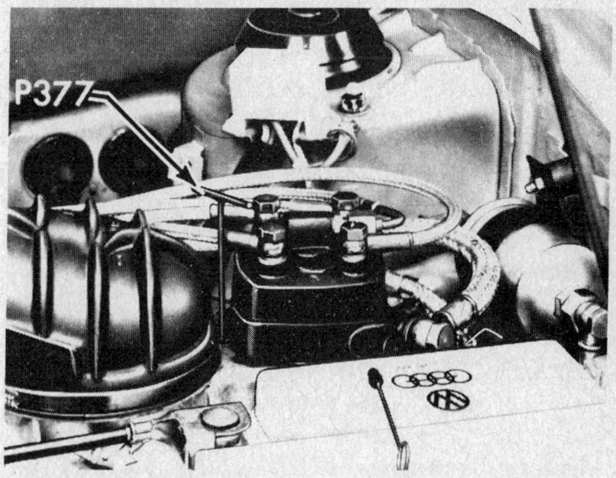

CO adjusting tool installed—CIS fuel injection

A special adapter (VW 1324) is nec essary to use an external tachometer on diesel engines

of your tachometer to see if it will work with diesel engines.

Adjust the idle speed to 850–950 rpm by means of the idle adjusting screw. When finished, lock the screw with a dab of paint or non-hardening thread sealer.

ENGINE ELECTRICAL

Distributor

The distributor is a single breaker point unit. It has both centrifugal and vacuum advance mechanisms. A vacuum retard system works only at idle.

The distributor is gear driven by an intermediate shaft which also drives the fuel pump. The distributor shaft also turns the oil pump.

REMOVAL AND INSTALLATION

1. Disconnect the coil high tension wire.
2. Detach the primary wire.

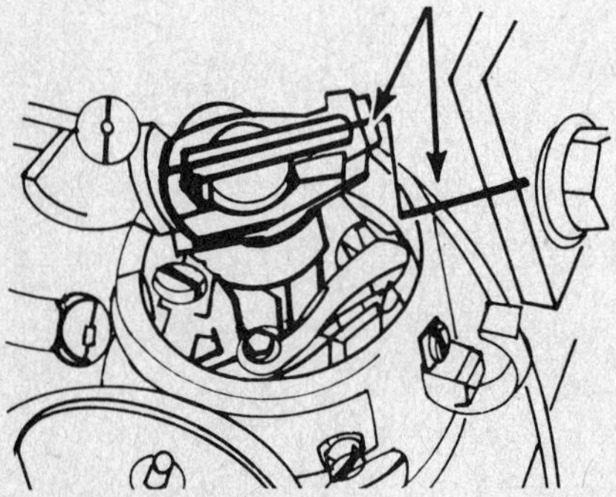

Rotor adjustment with the notch for cylinder No. 1

3. Remove the distributor cap.
4. Turn the engine until the rotor aligns with the index mark on the outer edge of the distributor. This is the No. 1 position. Mark the bottom of the distributor housing and its mounting flange on the engine.
5. Remove the bolt and lift off the retaining flange. Lift the distributor straight out of the engine.

If the engine has not been distributed while the distributor was out i.e., the crankshaft was not turned, then reinstall the distributor in the reverse order of removal. Carefully align the marks.

If the engine has been rotated while the distributor was out, then proceed as follows:

1. Turn the crankshaft so that No. 1 piston is on its compression stroke and

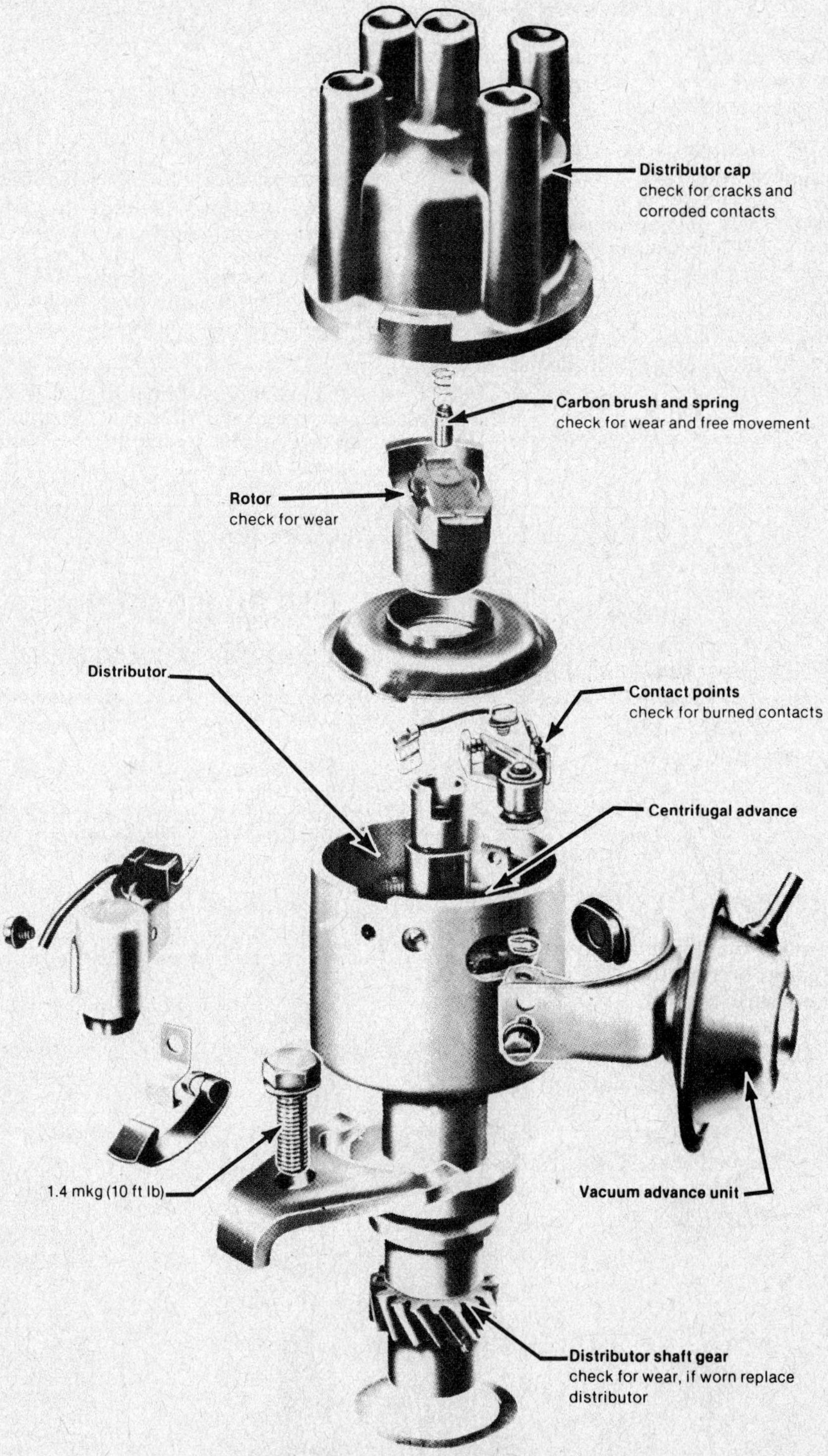

Exploded view of the distributor

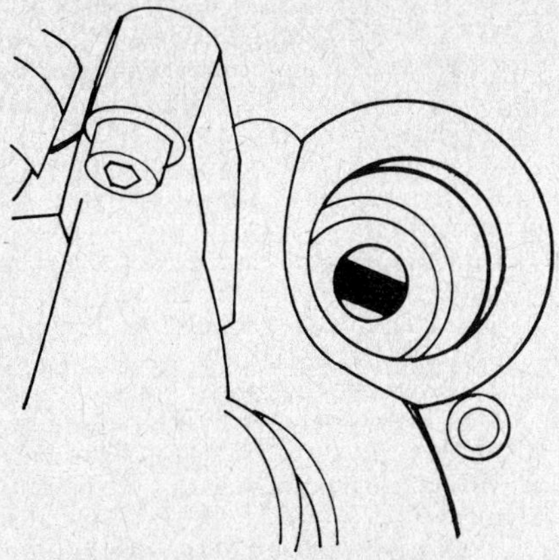

The oil pump drive should be parallel to the crankshaft

the 0°T timing mark is aligned with the V-shaped pointer.

2. Turn the distributor so that the rotor points approximately 15° before the No. 1 cylinder position on the distributor.

3. Insert the distributor into the engine block. If the oil pump drive doesn't engage, remove the distributor and, using a long screwdriver turn the pump shaft so that it is parallel to the centerline of the crankshaft.

4. Install the distributor, aligning the marks. Tighten the retaining nut.

5. Install the cap. Adjust the ignition timing.

Alternator

ALTERNATOR PRECAUTIONS

An alternating current (AC) generator (alternator) is used. Unlike the direct current (DC) generators used in many older cars, there are several precautions which must be strictly observed in order to avoid damaging the unit.

1. Reversing the battery connections will result in damage to the diodes.

2. Booster batteries should be connected from negative to negative, and positive to positive.

3. Never use a fast charger as a booster to start cars with AC circuits.

4. When servicing the battery with a fast charger, always disconnect the car battery cables.

5. Never attempt to polarize an AC generator.

6. Avoid long soldering times when replacing diodes or transistors. Prolonged heat is damaging to AC generators.

7. Do not use test lamps of more than 12 volts (V) for checking diode continuity.

8. Do not short across or ground any of the terminals on the AC generator.

9. The polarity of the battery, generator, and regulator must be matched and considered before making any electrical connections within the system.

10. Never operate the AC generator on an open circuit. Make sure that all connections within the circuit are clean and tight.

11. Disconnect the battery terminals when performing any service on the electrical system. This will eliminate the possibility of accidental reversal of polarity.

12. Disconnect the battery ground cable if arc welding is to be done on any part of the car.

REMOVAL AND INSTALLATION

The alternator and voltage regulator are combined in one housing. No voltage adjustment can be made with this unit. The regulator can be replaced without removing the alternator. Unbolt the regulator and remove from the rear.

1. Disconnect the battery cables.

2. Remove the multi-connector retaining bracket and unplug the connector from the rear of the alternator.

3. Loosen and remove the top mounting nut and bolt.

4. Using a socket inserted through the timing belt cover (it is not necessary to remove the cover), loosen the lower mounting bolt.

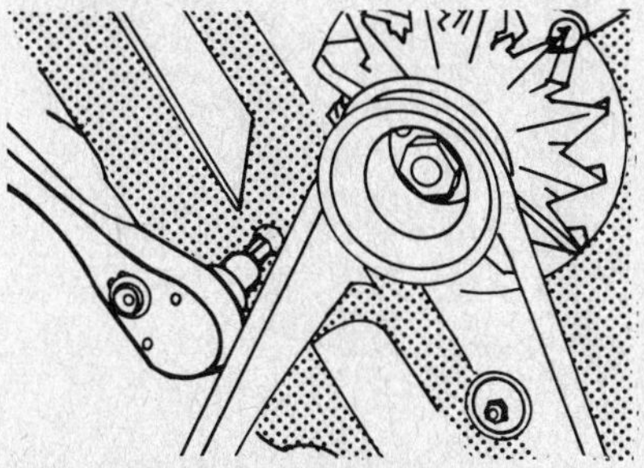

Removing the lower alternator bolt through the timing cover

5. Swing the alternator over and remove the alternator belt.

6. Remove the lower nut and bolt.

7. Remove the alternator.

8. Install the alternator with the lower bolt. *Do not* tighten it at this point.

9. Install the alternator belt over the pulleys.

10. Loosely install the top mounting bolt and pivot the alternator until the belt is correctly tensioned.

11. Tighten the top and bottom bolts to 14 ft lbs.

12. Connect the alternator and battery wires.

BELT REPLACEMENT AND TENSIONING

1. Loosen the top alternator mounting bolt.

2. Using a socket inserted through the timing belt cover loosen the lower mounting bolt.

3. Use a wooden hammer handle or a broomstick to lever the alternator over and remove the belt.

4. Slip the new belt over the pulleys.

5. Pry the alternator over until the belt deflection midway between the crankshaft pulley and the alternator pulley is 3/8–9/16 in. (10–15 mm).

6. Securely tighten the mounting bolts.

Starter

REMOVAL AND INSTALLATION

1. Disconnect the battery ground cable.

2. Raise the front of the car.

3. Mark with tape and then disconnect the wires from the starter solenoid.

4. Disconnect the large cable.

5. Remove the starter retaining nuts.

6. Unscrew the bolt. Remove the starter.

7. Installation of the starter is carried out in reverse order of removal.

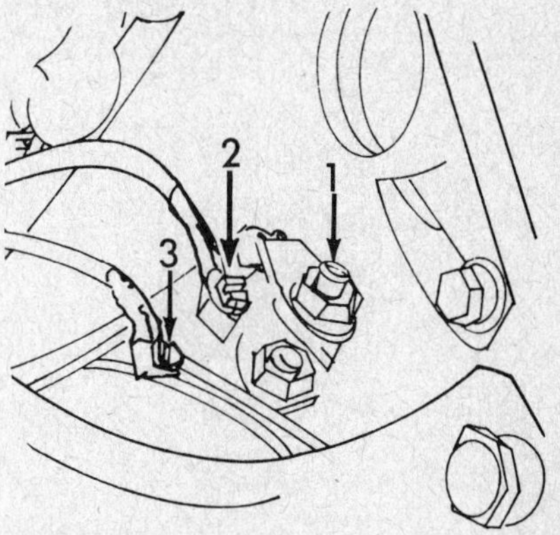

Starter electrical connections: (1) solenoid, (2) coil, (3) positive battery cable

OVERHAUL

Use the following procedure to replace brushes or starter drive.

1. Remove the solenoid.

2. Remove the end bearing cap.

3. Loosen both of the long housing screws.

4. Remove the lockwasher and spacer washers.

5. Remove the long housing screws and remove the end cover.

6. Pull the two field coil brushes out of the brush housing.

7. Remove the brush housing assembly.

8. Loosen the nut on the solenoid housing, remove the sealing disc, and remove the solenoid operating lever.

9. Loosen the large screws on the side of the starter body and remove the field coil along with the brushes.

NOTE: If the brushes require replacement, the field coil and brushes and/or the brush housing and its brushes must be replaced as a unit.

10. If the starter drive is being replaced, push the stop ring down and remove the circlip on the end of the shaft. Remove the stop-ring and remove the drive.

11. Assembly of the starter is carried

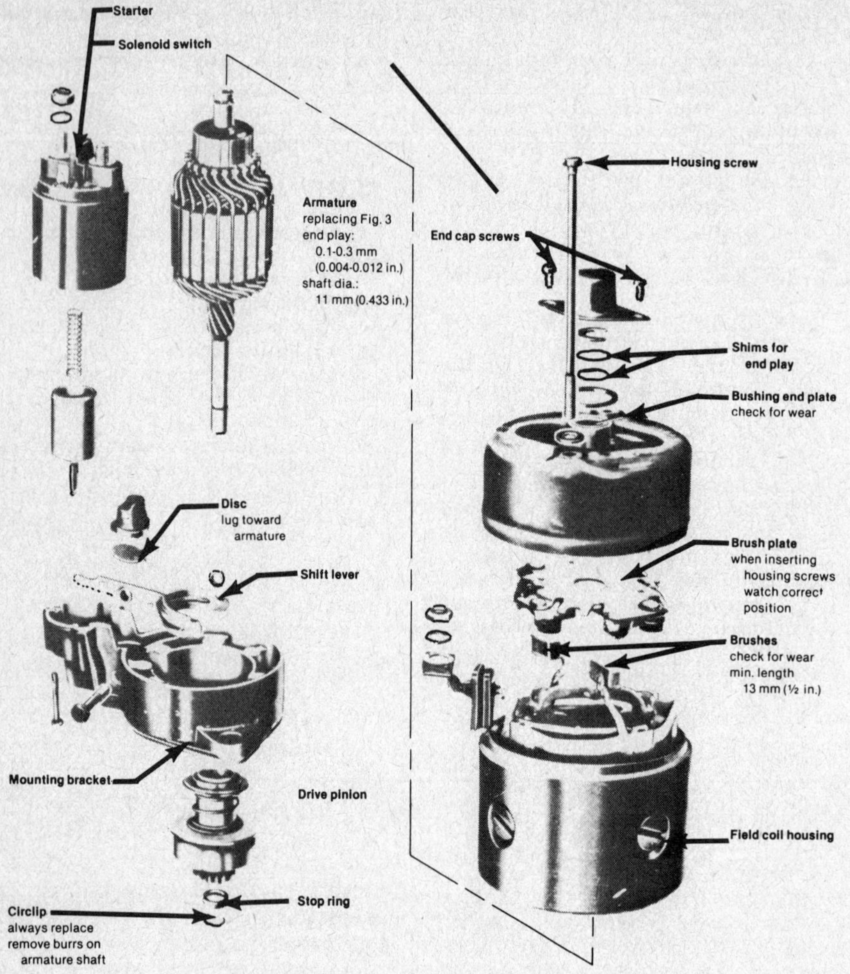

Exploded view of the starter

out in the reverse order of disassembly. Use a gear puller to install the stop-ring in its groove. Use a new circlip on the shaft.

SOLENOID REPLACEMENT

1. Remove the starter.
2. Remove the nut which secures the connector strip on the end of the solenoid.
3. Take out the two retaining screws on the mounting bracket and pull out the solenoid after it has been unhooked from the operating lever.
4. Installation is the reverse of removal. In order to facilitate engagement of the lever, the pinion should be pulled out as far as possible when inserting the solenoid.

ENGINE MECHANICAL

The engine is an inline four cylinder unit with single overhead camshaft. It is inclined 30° to the rear. The crankshaft runs in five bearings with thrust taken on the center bearing. The cylinder block is cast iron. A steel reinforced rubber belt drives the intermediate shaft and camshaft. The intermediate shaft drives the oil pump, distributor and fuel pump.

The cylinder head is lightweight aluminum alloy. The intake and exhaust manifolds are mounted on the same side of the cylinder head. The valves are opened and closed by camshaft lobes operating on cupped cam followers which fit over the valves and springs. This design results in lighter valve train weight and fewer moving parts.

Engine

REMOVAL AND INSTALLATION

Gasoline Engines with Manual Transmission

The engine and transmission are removed as an assembly.

1. Disconnect the battery ground cable.
2. Drain the coolant by unbolting the lower water pump flange or by removing the hoses.

CAUTION: Do Not disconnect or loosen any refrigerant hose connections during engine removal on cars equipped with air conditioning.

3. On trucks equipped with air conditioning:
   a. Loosen the compressor support bolts and remove the compressor.
   b. Remove the radiator cooling fan, air ducts and radiator.
   c. Remove the condenser.
   d. Place the air conditioning compressor and condenser out of the way without disconnecting any refrigerant lines.
4. Remove the radiator with the air ducts and fan.
5. Detach and label all the electrical wires connecting the engine to the body.
6. Disconect and plug the fuel line at the fuel pump. Detach the coolant hoses at the left end of the engine. Disconnect the accelerator cable and remove the air cleaner.
7. Disconnect the speedometer cable from the transmission. Detach the clutch cable.
8. Remove the engine support to the right of the starter.
9. Remove the headlight caps inside the engine compartment.
10. Unbolt the driveshafts from the transmission and wire them up.
11. Unbolt the exhaust pipe from the manifold and unbolt the exhaust pipe brace.
12. Unbolt the transmission rear mount from the body (alongside the tunnel).
13. Detach the ground strap from the transmission and body.
14. Remove the shift linkage.
15. Attach a chain sling to the alternator bracket and the lifting eye at the left end of the engine. Lift the engine and transmission slightly.
16. Detach the engine carrier from the body and remove the left transmission carrier.
17. Lift the engine/transmission assembly carefully out of the truck.
18. To separate the engine and transmission, turn the flywheel to align the lug on the flywheel (to the left of TDC) with the pointer in the opening. The engine and transmission can only be separated in this position. Remove the cover plate over the driveshaft flange and remove the engine to transmission bolts and the transmission housing cover plate.

To install the engine:

19. To attach the transmission to the engine, the recess in the flywheel edge must be at 3:00 o'clock (facing the left end of the engine). Torque the engine to transmission bolts to 40 ft lbs. Lift the engine/transmission assembly into place. Loosen the bolts for the engine and transmission mounts. Move the engine assembly from side to side until the rear transmission mount is straight. Center the left and right transmission mounts and tighten all transmission

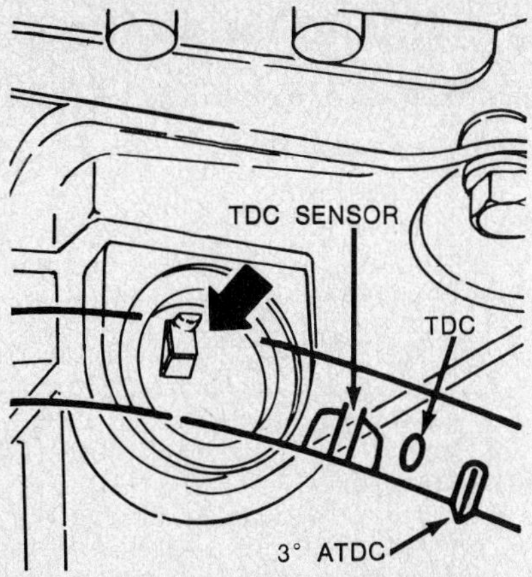

Aligning the flywheel for manual transmission and engine separation

bolts. Push the front mount upward to center the rubber cone, then tighten the mount. Loosen the exhaust pipe clamps, release any strain, then tighten the clamps. Torque the 10 mm bolts to 29 ft lbs. Torque the driveshaft flange bolts to 32 ft lbs. Refill the cooling system.

Gasoline Engines with Automatic Transmission

The engine and transmission are removed as an assembly.

1. Shift the transmission into "Park." Disconnect both battery cables.
2. Drain the coolant by unbolting the lower water pump flange or by removing the hoses.

CAUTION: Do Not disconnect or loosen any refrigerant hose connections during engine removal on cars equipped with air conditioning.

3. On trucks equipped with air conditioning, proceed as follows:
   a. Loosen the compressor support bolts and remove the compressor.
   b. Remove the radiator cooling fan, air ducts, and radiator.
   c. Remove the condenser.
   d. Place the air conditioning components out of the way without disconnecting any refrigerant lines.
4. Remove the radiator with the air ducts and fan.
5. Remove the air cleaner.
6. Detach the speedometer cable from the transmission.
7. Detach and label all electrical wires connecting the engine to the body. Detach the coolant hoses.
8. Remove the screws holding the accelerator cable bracket to the carburetor float bowl (do not disassemble linkage), detach the end of the gearshift selector cable from the transmission, detach the accelerator cable and pedal cable at the transmission, and remove the two bracket bolts behind this linkage on the transmission.
9. Unbolt the exhaust pipe from the manifold.
10. Remove the rear transmission mount. Unbolt the driveshafts and wire them up out of the way.
11. Remove the converter cover plate and remove the three torque converter to drive plate bolts.
12. Attach a chain sling to the alternator bracket and the lifting eye at the left end of the engine. It may be necessary to remove the alternator. Lift the engine and transmission slightly.
13. Detach the engine front mounting support; remove the left transmission carrier and the right engine carrier.
14. Lift the engine/transmission assembly carefully out of the truck.
15. The transmission can now be detached from the engine.

To install the engine:

16. The engine to transmission bolts should be torqued to 40 ft lbs. Lift the engine/transmission assembly into place and install the left transmission carrier, tightening first the body, then the transmission bolts. Lower the assembly to attach the engine carrier to the body, tightening the bolts to 40 ft lbs. Install the engine mounting support. Check that all mounts and clamps are free of strain. Torque converter bolts should be torqued to 21 ft lbs and drive shaft bolts to 32 ft lbs. Refill the cooling system. Check the adjustment of transmission and carburetor linkages.

Diesel Engines

The diesel engine is removed with the transmission attached.

1. Disconnect the battery.
2. Disconnect the radiator hoses and drain the coolant. It can be saved for reuse, if it's not too old.
3. Remove the radiator complete with fan.
4. Remove the alternator.
5. Disconnect the fuel filter and set it aside near the windshield washer reservoir.
6. Detach the supply and return lines from the injection pump.
7. Disconnect the accelerator cable from the lever on the injection pump and remove the injection pump complete with bracket.
8. Disconnect the cold start cable from the pump.
9. Disconnect and label all electrical wires and leads.
10. Remove the front transmission mount.
11. Disconnect the clutch cable.
12. Remove the relay rod and connecting rod from the transmission and turn the relay lever shaft to the rear.
13. Disconnect the selector rod.
14. Unbolt the driveshafts and wire them up out of the way. Remove the rear support.
15. Disconnect the exhaust pipe at the manifold and remove the rear transmission mount.
16. Attach a lifting sling to the engine and take the weight from the engine mounts. Remove the left and right transmission mounts.
17. Carefully guide the engine out of the truck while turning it slightly.
18. To separate the engine from the transmission, unscrew the plug from the TDC sensor opening and turn the flywheel to align the mark on the flywheel with the pointer. The engine/transmission can only be separated in this position.
19. Remove the cover plate over the driveshaft flange and remove the engine-to-transmission bolts.
20. Press the engine off the transmission.
21. Installation is the reverse of removal. Turn the flywheel so that the recess in the flywheel is level with the driveshaft flange. Lower the engine into the car and attach the left transmission mount to the transmission first. Align the rear transmission mount, center the engine/transmission and center the front transmission mount. Adjust the accelerator and cold start cables and bleed the injection system.

Cylinder Head

REMOVAL AND INSTALLATION

The engine should be cold before the cylinder head can be removed. The head is retained by 10 socket head bolts. It can be removed without removing the intake and exhaust manifolds.

NOTE: 12 point socket head bolts are used. These should be used in complete sets only and need not be retorqued after the mileage interval.

Gasoline Engines

1. Disconnect the battery ground cable.
2. Drain the cooling system.
3. Disconnect the air duct from the throttle valve assembly.
4. Disconnect the throttle cable from the throttle valve assembly.
5. Remove the injectors and disconnect the line from the cold start valve.
6. Disconnect the radiator and heater hoses.
7. Disconnect the vacuum and PCV lines (label lines for installation).
8. Remove the auxiliary air regulator from the intake manifold.
9. Disconnect all electrical lines and remove the spark plugs (label all lines and wires for installation).
10. Separate the exhaust manifold from the exhaust pipe.
11. Remove the EGR line from the exhaust manifold.
12. Remove the intake manifold.
13. Remove the timing belt cover and belt.
14. Loosen the cylinder head bolts in the reverse of the tightening sequence.
15. Remove the bolts and lift the head straight off.
16. Check the flatness of the cylinder block.

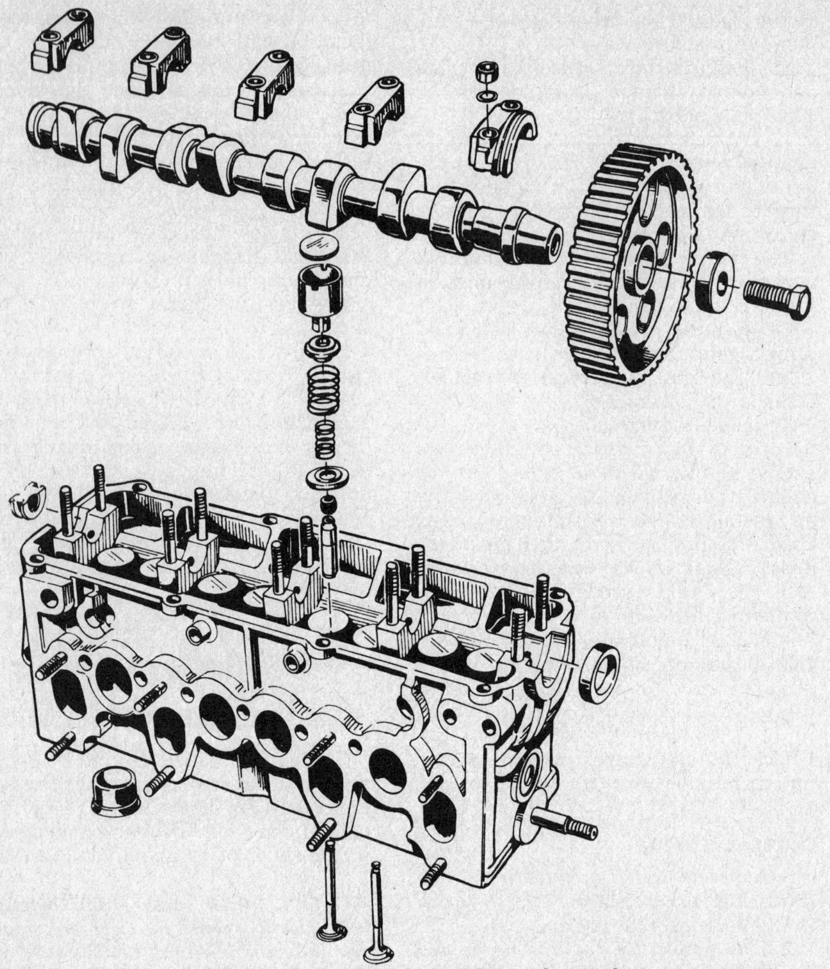

Exploded view of the cylinder head showing valve train components

17. Install the new cylinder head gasket with the word TOP or OBEN facing upward.
18. Install bolts No. 10 and 8 first; these holes are smaller and will properly locate the gasket and cylinder head.
19. Install the remaining bolts. Tighten them in three stages using the sequence shown in the illustration. Cylinder head bolts must be torqued cold to 55 ft. lbs. 12 point bolts should be tightened to 55 ft. lbs., then tightened 1/4 turn more.
20. Install the remaining components in the reverse order of removal.

Diesel Engines

The head is retained by Allen bolts. The engine should be cold when the head is removed. The word TOP or OBEN on the new gasket should face up.

1. Disconnect the battery ground cable.
2. Drain the cooling system.
3. Remove the air cleaner.
4. Disconnect the fuel lines. Disconnect and tag all electrical wires and leads.
5. Separate the exhaust manifold from the pipe. Disconnect the radiator and heater hoses.
6. Remove the timing cover and belt (See timing belt replacement).
7. Loosen the cylinder head bolts in the reverse order of the tightening sequence.
8. Remove the head. Do not lay the head on the gasket surface with the injectors installed. Support it at the ends on strips of wood.
9. Install the cylinder head with a new gasket. Be sure the new gasket has the same number of notches and the same identifying number as the old one, unless the pistons were also replaced.

Install bolts 8 and 10 first and torque the bolts to the specification in the proper sequence. After 1000 miles, loosen all bolts 1/3 turn and retorque the bolts.

OVERHAUL

Valve guides are a shrink fit. Always install new valve seals when doing a valve job. Valve seats are not replaceable; the cylinder head should be replaced if the seat width and face angle cannot be maintained.

Refer to general information section under Engine Overhaul.

Intake Manifold

REMOVAL AND INSTALLATION

Gasoline Models

1. Disconnect the air duct from the throttle valve body. Drain the cooling system.
2. Disconnect the accelerator cable.
3. Remove the injectors and disconnect the line from the cold start valve.
4. Disconnect all coolant hoses.
5. Disconnect all vacuum and emission control hoses (label all hoses for installation).
6. Remove the auxiliary air regulator.
7. Disconnect all electrical lines (label all wires for installation).
8. Disconnect the EGR line from the exhaust manifold.
9. Loosen and remove the retaining bolts and lift off the manifold.
10. Install a new gasket. Install the manifold and tighten the bolts to 18 ft. lbs.
11. Install the remaining components in the reverse order of removal.

Exhaust Manifold

REMOVAL AND INSTALLATION

1. Disconnect the EGR tube from the exhaust manifold.
2. Remove the interfering air pump components if so equipped.
3. Remove the air cleaner hose from the exhaust manifold.
4. Disconnect the intake manifold support.
5. Separate the exhaust pipe from the manifold.
6. Remove the retaining nuts and remove the manifold.
7. Clean the cylinder head and manifold mating surfaces.
8. Install the exhaust manifold using a new gasket.
9. Tighten the nuts to 18 ft lbs. Work from the inside out.
10. Install the remaining components in the reverse order of removal. Use a new manifold flange gasket.

Timing Belt Cover

REMOVAL AND INSTALLATION

1. Loosen the alternator mounting bolts.
2. Pivot the alternator and slip the drive belt off the sprockets.
3. Unscrew the cover retaining nuts and remove the cover.
4. Reposition the spacers on the studs and then install the washers and nuts.
5. Install the alternator belt and adjust its tension.

Timing Belt

NOTE: The timing belt is designed to last for more than 60,000 miles and does not normally require tension adjustments. If

the belt is removed or replaced, the basic valve timing must be checked and the belt retensioned.

REMOVAL, INSTALLATION, AND TENSIONING

Gasoline Engines

Timing belt installation will be easier if the engine is set to TDC prior to belt removal. The 0°T mark will be aligned with the pointer on the bell housing, and the mark on the rear face of the camshaft pulley will align with the camshaft covers gasket on the left. Also, the V-notch in the crankshaft pulley should align with the dot mark on the intermediate shaft, and the distributor rotor should be pointing toward the mark on the rim of the housing.

If the belt has broken and timing is off, remove the belt cover and belt, then set the engine to TDC before installing the belt, as outlined in Steps 5, 6, and 7.

1. Remove the timing belt cover.
2. While holding the large hex on the tension sprocket, loosen the pulley locknut.
3. Release the tensioner from the timing belt.
4. Slide the belt off the three toothed sprockets and remove it.
5. Turn the crankshaft until No. 1 cylinder is at TDC. At this point, the 0°T mark will be aligned with the pointer on the bell housing.
6. Align the timing mark on the rear face of the camshaft pulley with the camshaft cover gasket on the left.

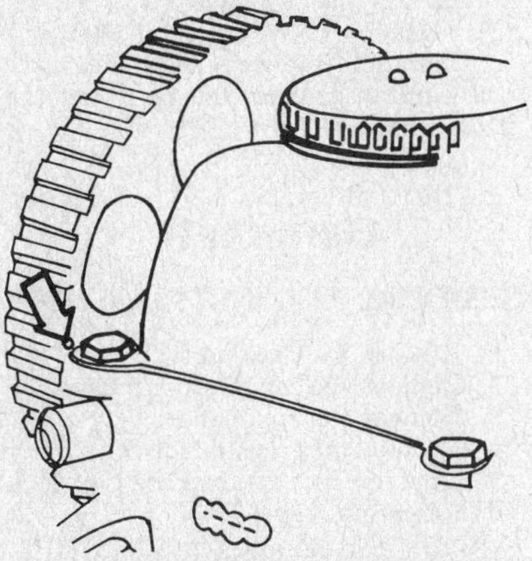

Camshaft sprocket alignment

7. Align the V-notch in the crankshaft pulley with the dot mark on the intermediate shaft. The distributor rotor should be pointing to the No. 1 cylinder mark on the rim of the distributor.

CAUTION: If the timing marks are not correctly aligned, valve timing will be incorrect. Poor performance and serious engine damage can result from improper valve timing. Steps 5, 6, and 7 should not be necessary if the engine was in time and set to TDC prior to belt removal.

8. Install the belt on the sprockets.

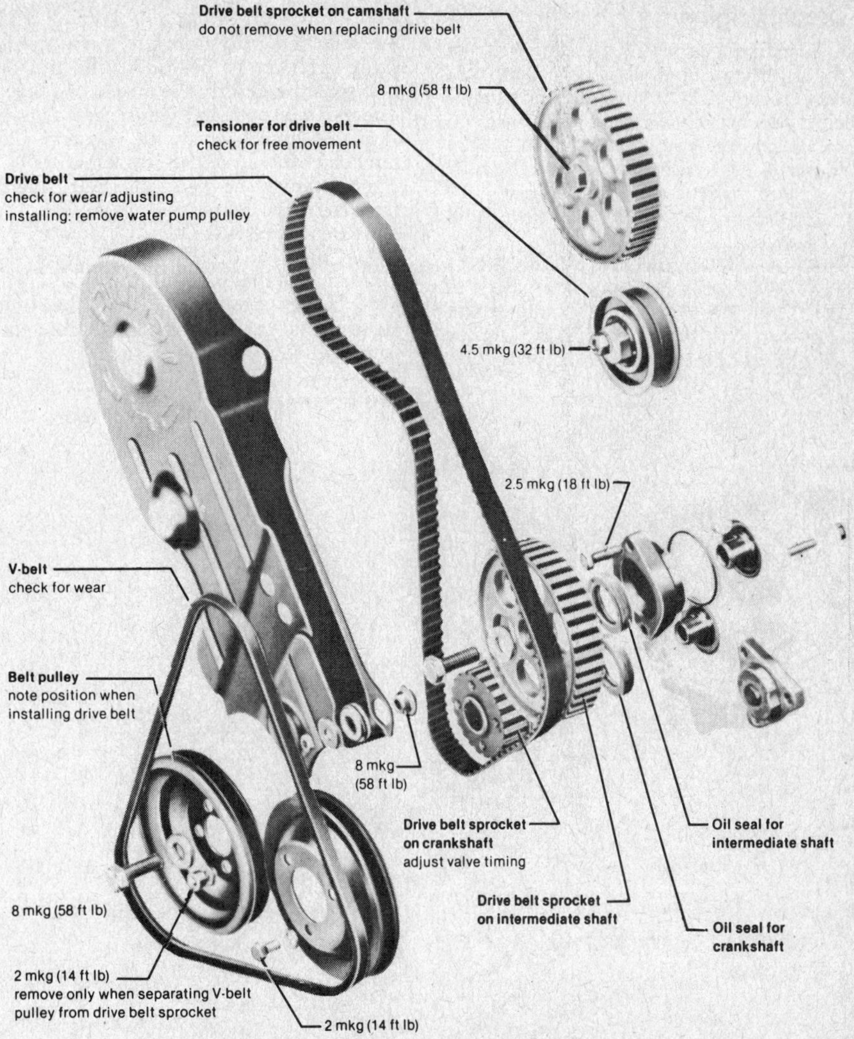

Exploded view of the timing belt assembly

9. Adjust the tensioner by turning the large tensioner hex to the right. Tension is correct when you can twist the belt 90° with two fingers at the midpoint. Tighten the locknut to 32 ft. lbs.
10. Install the timing belt cover and check the ignition timing.

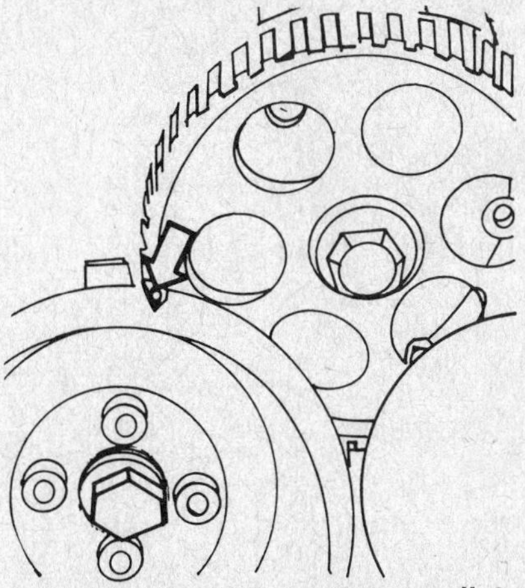

Crankshaft pulley and intermediate shaft sprocket alignment

Turn the tensioner (R) toward (a) to tighten the belt and toward (b) to loosen. Check the tension at (c)

Diesel Engine

The drive belt on the diesel also drives the injection pump. It is necessary that this procedure be followed exactly to ensure proper valve timing and injection pump timing. You will also need special tool VW 210 to properly tension the belt.

1. Remove the alternator belt.
2. Remove the timing belt cover and rocker cover.
3. Set the engine at TDC on No. 1 cylinder. In this position both valves of No. 1 cylinder will be closed and the OT mark on the flywheel will be aligned with the pointer on the bell housing.
4. Use a pin or suitable bolt to hold the injection pump sprocket and camshaft sprocket in position. The pin or bolt must be exactly the size of the hole. There can be no "slop" in the gears.
5. Loosen the tensioner. Remove the fan belt pulley from the crankshaft.
6. Remove the belt and belt shield from the drive gears.

To install the belt:

7. Check that the TDC mark is aligned with the flywheel mark.
8. Loosen the camshaft sprocket bolt 1/2 turn and tap the gear loose from the camshaft with a rubber mallet.
9. Install the drive belt and remove the pin from the camshaft and injection pump gears.
10. Tension the belt by turning the tensioner to the right.
11. Check the belt tension between the camshaft and injection pump sprockets. On VW 210 special tool, the scale should read 12–13.
12. Tighten the camshaft sprocket bolt to 32 ft. lbs.
13. Turn the crankshaft 2 complete turns in the direction of normal rotation and check belt tension again.

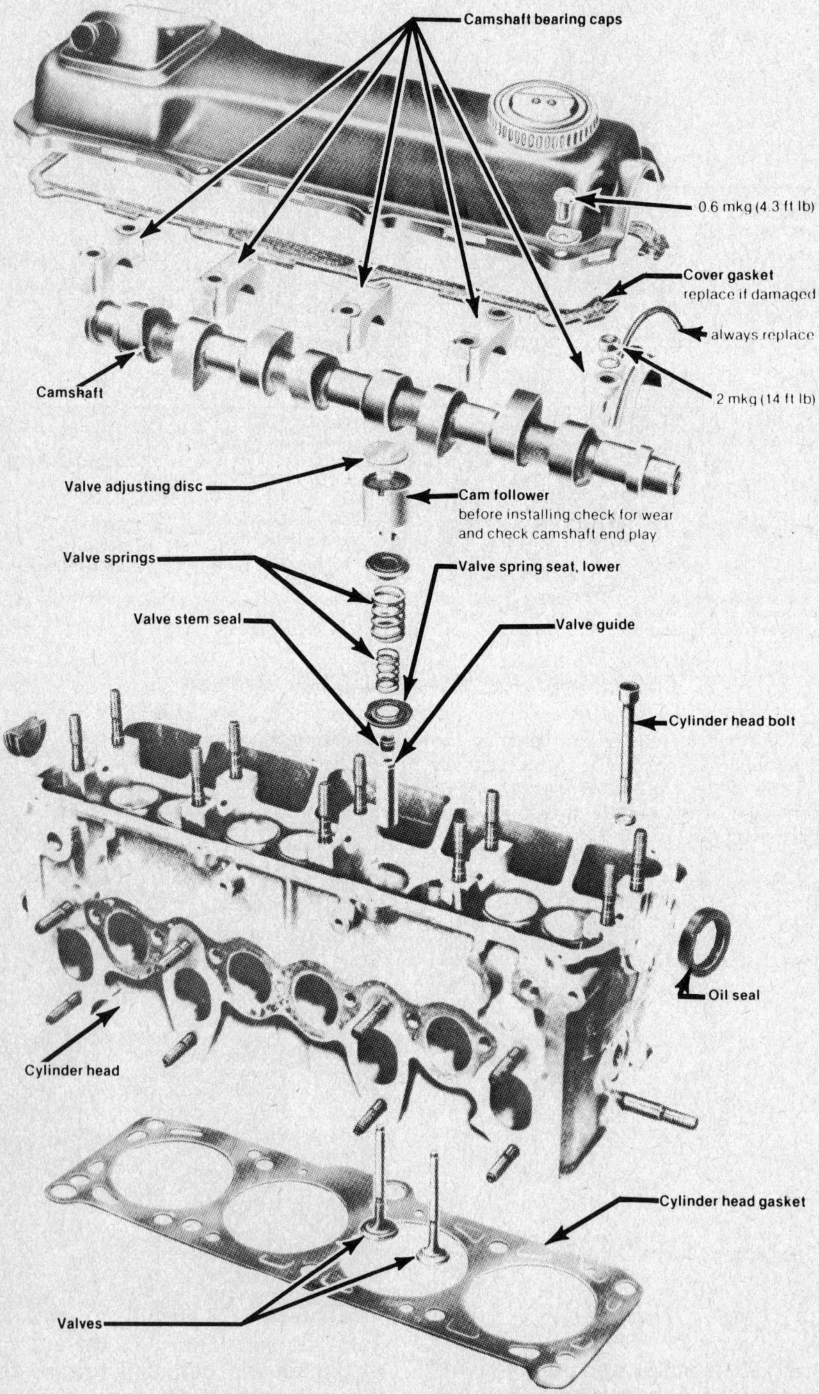

Exploded view of the camshaft assembly

Timing Sprockets

REMOVAL AND INSTALLATION

The camshaft, intermediate shaft, and crankshaft sprockets are located by keys on their respective shafts and each is retained by a bolt. To remove any or all of the pulleys, first remove the timing belt cover and belt.

NOTE: When removing the crankshaft pulley, don't remove the four allen head bolts which hold the outer belt pulley to the timing belt sprocket.

1. Remove the center bolt.
2. Gently pry the sprocket off the shaft. If the gear does not come off easily, use a gear puller. Don't hammer on the sprocket.
3. Remove the sprocket and key.
4. Install in the reverse order of removal.
5. Tighten the center bolt to 58 ft. lbs.
6. Install the timing belt, check the valve timing, tension the belt, and install the cover.

Camshaft

REMOVAL AND INSTALLATION

1. Remove the timing belt.
2. Remove the camshaft sprocket.
3. Remove the air cleaner.
4. Remove the camshaft cover.
5. Unscrew and remove the No. 1, 3, and 5 bearing caps (No. 1 is at the front).
6. Unscrew the No. 2 and 4 bearing caps, diagonally and in increments.
7. Lift the camshaft out of the cylinder head.
8. Lubricate the camshaft journals and lobes with assembly lube or gear oil before installing it in the cylinder head.
9. Replace the camshaft oil seal with a new one whenever the cam is removed.
10. Install the No. 1, 3, and 5 bearing caps and tighten the nuts to 14 ft. lbs. Note that the bores are offset, and the numbers are not always on the same side.
11. Install the No. 2 and 4 bearing caps and diagonally tighten the nuts to 14 ft. lbs.

NOTE: If checking end play, install a dial indicator so that the feeler touches the camshaft snout. Endplay should be no more than 0.006 in. (0.15 mm).

12. Replace the seal in the No. 1 bearing cap. If necessary replace the end plug in the cylinder head.
13. Install the camshaft cover.
14. Install the camshaft pulley and the timing belt.
15. Check the valve clearance.

Pistons and Connecting Rods

Gasoline Engines

The pistons must be installed in the block with the arrow at the edge of the crown facing to the front of the car. The connecting rod and cap alignment casting grooves must face the intermediate shaft. New connecting rod bolts must always be used. The pistons must be heated to 140°F in an oven before the piston pins can be pressed in. Three piston oversizes are available to accommodate overbores up to 0.040 in.

There is a piston size code stamped on the cylinder block above the water pump.

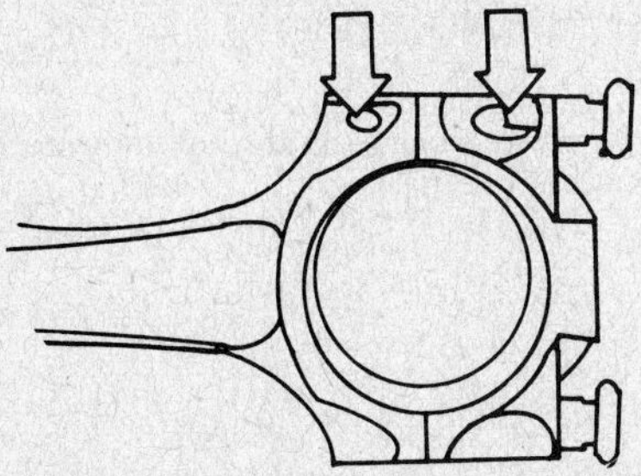

The connecting rod and cap alignment casting grooves must face the intermediate shaft

Diesel Engines

The same installation procedures apply to the diesel as to the gas engine. However, whenever new pistons or a short block are installed, the piston projection must be checked.

A spacer (VW 385/17) and bar with a micrometer are necessary, and must be set up to measure the maximum amount of piston projection above the deck height. The following chart should be used to select a head gasket of the correct thickness to match piston projection.

Piston Projection (mm)	*Gasket Identification No. of Notches*	*Part Number*
0.43-0.63	2	068 103 383
0.63-0.82	3	068 103 383C
0.82-0.92	4	068 103 383G
0.92-1.02	5	068 103 383H

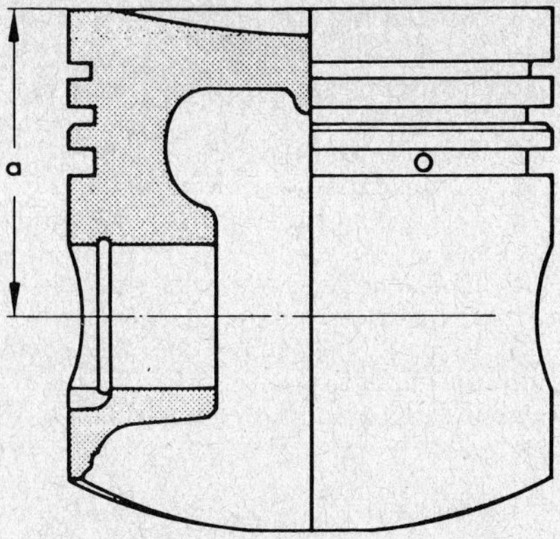

The piston height (A) on diesel engines is 1.768 in.

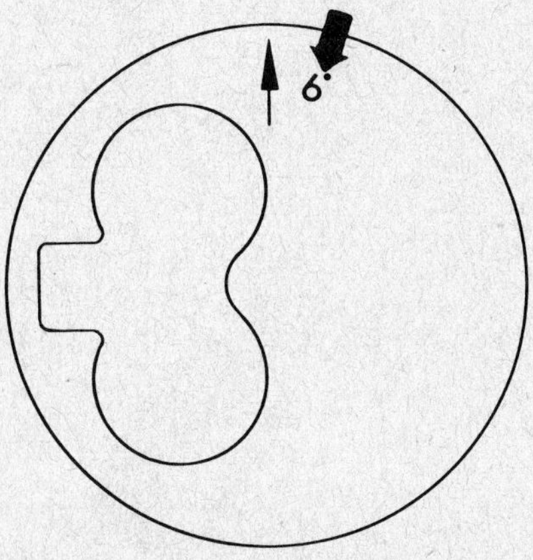

Diesel pistons are identified by the number "9" next to the arrow denoting installation direction

ENGINE LUBRICATION

The lubrication system is a conventional wet-sump design. The gear type oil pump is driven by the intermediate shaft. A pressure relief valve limits pressure and prevents extreme pressure from developing in the system. All oil pressure switch is located at the end of the cylinder head gallery (the end of the system) to assure accurate pressure readings.

Oil Pan

REMOVAL AND INSTALLATION

1. Drain the engine oil.
2. Loosen and remove the bolts retaining the oil pan.
3. Lower the pan from the car.
4. Install the pan using a new oil pan gasket.
5. Tighten the retaining bolts in a criss-cross pattern. Tighten hex bolts to 14 ft. lbs., or Allen head bolts to 7 ft. lbs.
6. Refill the engine with oil. Start the engine and examine the pan for leaks.

Rear Main Oil Seal

REPLACEMENT

The rear main oil seal is located in a housing on the rear of the cylinder block. The engine should be removed from the car.

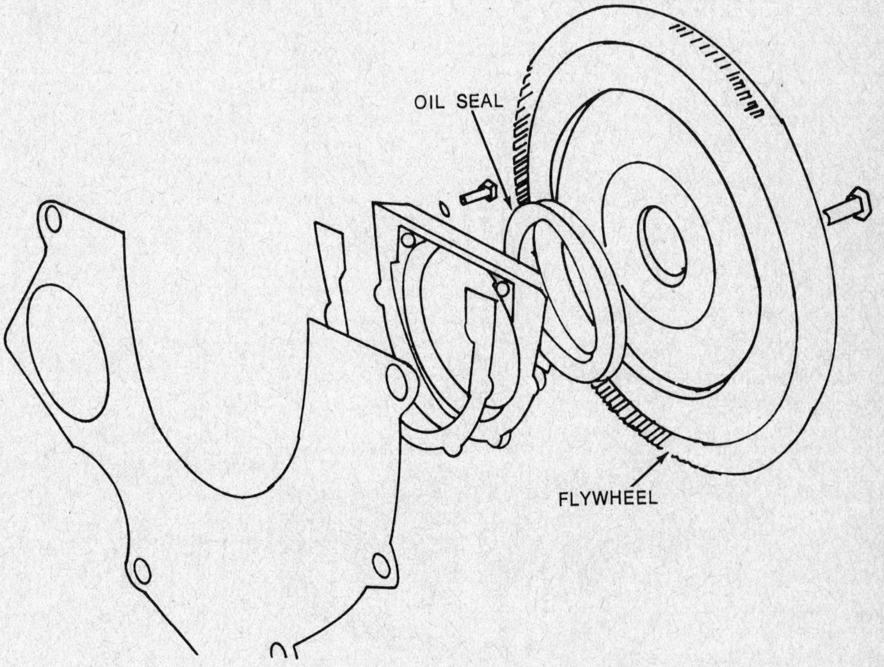

Rear main oil seal assembly

1. Remove the transmission and flywheel.
2. Using a small pry bar, very carefully pry the old seal out of the support ring.
3. Remove the seal.
4. Lightly oil the replacement seal and then press it into place using a circular piece of flat metal. Be careful not to damage the seal or score the crankshaft.
5. Install the flywheel and transmission. Flywheel-to-engine bolts are tightened to 36 ft. lbs.

Oil Pump

REMOVAL AND INSTALLATION

1. Remove the oil pan.
2. Remove the two mounting bolts.
3. Pull the oil pump down and out of the engine.
4. Unscrew the two bolts and separate the pump halves.
5. Remove the driveshaft and gear from the upper body.
6. Clean the bottom half in solvent. Pry up the metal edges to remove the filter screen for cleaning.
7. Examine the gears and driveshaft for wear or damage. Replace them if necessary.
8. Reassemble the pump halves.
9. Prime the pump with oil and install in the reverse order or removal.

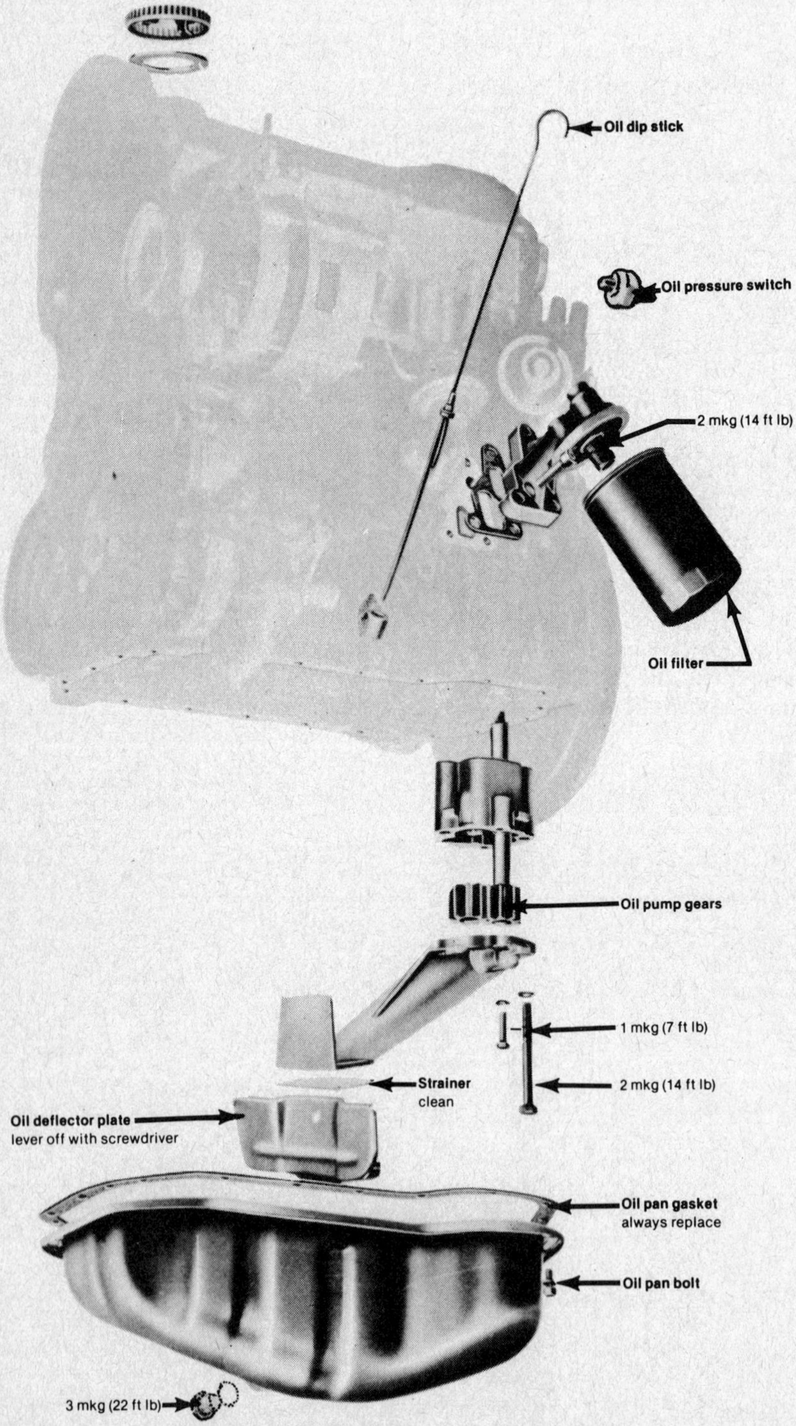

Lubrication system components

ENGINE COOLING

The cooling system consists of a belt driven, external water pump, thermostat, radiator, and thermostatically controlled electric cooling fan. When the engine is cold the thermostat is closed and blocks the water from the radiator so the coolant is circulated only through the engine. When the engine warms up, the thermostat opens and the radiator is included in the coolant circuit. The thermostatic switch is in the bottom of the radiator and turns the electrical fan on at 199°F, off at 186°F. This reduces power loss and engine noise.

Radiator and Fan

REMOVAL AND INSTALLATION

1. Drain the cooling system.
2. Remove the inner shroud mounting bolts.
3. Disconnect the lower radiator hose.
4. Disconnect the thermostatic switch lead.
5. Remove the lower radiator shroud.
6. Remove the lower radiator mounting units.
7. Disconnect the upper radiator hose.
8. Detach the upper radiator shroud.
9. Disconnect the heater and intake manifold hoses.
10. Remove the side mounting bolts and lift the radiator and fan out as an assembly.
11. Installation is the reverse of removal.

Thermostat

REMOVAL AND INSTALLATION

The thermostat is located in the bottom radiator hose neck on the water pump.

1. Drain the cooling system.
2. Remove the two retaining bolts from the lower water pump neck.

***NOTE:** It isn't necessary to disconnect the hose.*

3. Move the neck, with the hoses attached, out of the way.
4. Remove the thermostat.

5. Install a new seal on the water pump neck.
6. Install the thermostat with the spring end up.
7. Replace the water pump neck and tighten the two retaining bolts.

Water Pump

REMOVAL AND INSTALLATION

1. Drain the cooling system.
2. Remove the alternator and drive belt.
3. Remove the timing belt cover.
4. Disconnect the lower radiator hose, engine hose, and heater hose from the water pump.
5. Remove the four pump retaining bolts. Notice where the different length bolts are located.
6. Turn the pump slightly and lift it out of the engine block.
7. Installation is the reverse of removal. Use a new seal on the mating surface with the engine.

EMISSION CONTROLS

Crankcase Ventilation

The crankcase ventilation system keeps harmful vapor byproducts of combustion from escaping into the atmosphere and prevents the building of crankcase pressure which can lead to oil leaking. Crankcase vapors are recirculated from the camshaft cover through a hose to the air cleaner. Here they are mixed with the air/fuel mixture and burned in the combustion chamber.

SERVICE

The only maintenance required on the crankcase ventilation system is a periodic check. At every tune up, examine the hoses for clogging or deterioration. Clean or replace the hoses as necessary.

Evaporative Emission Control System

This system prevents the escape of raw fuel vaport (unburned hydrocarbons or HC) into the atmosphere. The system consists of a sealed carburetor, unvented fuel tank filler cap, fuel tank expansion chamber, an activated charcoal filter canister and connector hoses. Fuel vapors which reach the filter deposit hydrocarbons on the surface of the charcoal filter element. Fresh air enters the filter when the engine is running and forces the hydrocarbons to the air cleaner where they join the air/fuel mixture and are burned.

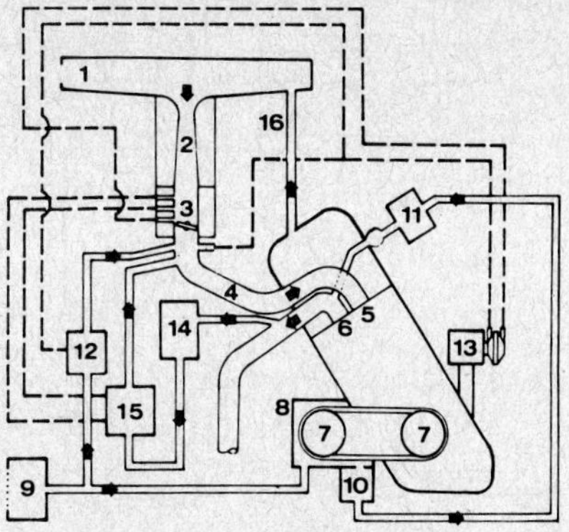

1. Air cleaner
2. Carburetor venturi
3. Throttle valve
4. Intake manifold
5. Cylinder head intake port
6. Cylinder head exhaust port
7. Belt drive for air pump
8. Air pump
9. Air pump filter
10. Pressure relief valve
11. Check valve
12. Diverter valve
13. Distributor
14. EGR filter
15. EGR valve
16. Crankcase ventilation

Emission control system schematic. The arrows indicate flow

SERVICE

Maintenance of the system requires checking the condition of the various connector hoses and the charcoal filter at 10,000 mile intervals. The charcoal filter should be replaced at 50,000 mile intervals.

Dual Diaphragm Distributors

The purpose of the dual diaphragm distributor is to improve exhaust emissions during one of the engine's dirtier operating modes—idling. The distributor has a vacuum retard diaphragm, in addition to a vacuum advance diaphragm. A temperature valve shuts off vacuum from the carburetor when coolant temperatures are below 130°F.

TESTING

Advance Diaphragm

1. Connect a timing light to the engine. Check the ignition timing.
2. Remove the retard hose from the distributor and plug it. Increase the engine speed. The ignition timing should advance. If it doesn't, then the vacuum unit is faulty and must be replaced.

Temperature Valve

1. Remove the temperature valve and place the threaded portion in hot water.
2. Create a vacuum by sucking on the angled connection.
3. The valve must be open above approximately 130°F.

Exhaust Gas Recirculation (EGR)

To reduce NOx (oxides of nitrogen) emissions, metered amounts of exhaust gases are added to the air/fuel mixture. The recirculated exhaust gas lowers the peak flame temperature during combustion. Exhaust gas from the manifold passes through a filter where it is cleaned. The vacuum operated EGR valve controls the volume of this exhaust gas which is allowed into the intake manifold. There is no EGR at idle, partial at slight throttle and full EGR at mid-throttle.

TESTING

EGR Valve

Be sure the vacuum lines are not leaking. Replace any that are leaking or cracked.

1. Warm the engine to normal operating temperature.
2. Run the engine at idle.
3. Remove the vacuum hose from the EGR valve.
4. Connect the line from the brake booster to the EGR valve (this can be done by installing a Tee in the vacuum line to the retard side of the distributor diaphragm and running a separate hose from there to the EGR valve).
5. If the engine speed does not change, the EGR valve is clogged or damaged.

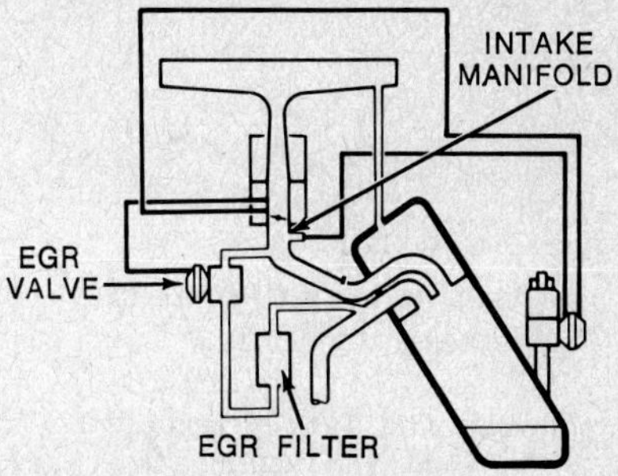

EGR system schematic

EGR Temperature Valve

Warm the engine to normal operating temperature. With the engine at idle, attach a vacuum gauge between the EGR temperature control valve and the EGR valve. The valve should be replaced if the gauge shows less than 2 in./Hg.

EGR Deceleration Valve

1. Remove the hose from the deceleration valve. Plug the hose.
2. Run the engine for a few seconds at 3000 rpm.
3. Snap the throttle valve closed.
4. With your finger, check for suction at the hose connection.
5. Remove the hose from the connector.
6. Run the engine at about 3000 rpm. No suction should be felt.

EGR Vacuum Amplifier

1. Run the engine at idle.
2. Connect a vacuum gauge between the vacuum amplifier and the throttle valve port.
3. The gauge should read 0.2–0.3 in./Hg. If not, check the throttle plate for correct position or check the port for obstruction.
4. Connect a vacuum gauge between the vacuum amplifier and the temperature valve.
5. Replace the vacuum amplifier if the gauge reads less than 2 in./hg.

MAINTENANCE

The only maintenance is to reset the EGR elapsed mileage switch.

Resetting the Elapsed Mileage Switch

The EGR reminder light in the speedometer should light up every 15,000 miles as a reminder for maintenance.

Resetting the EGR mileage odometer

To reset the light switch, press the white button. The speedometer light should go out.

REMOVAL AND INSTALLATION

EGR Valve

1. Disconnect the vacuum hose from the EGR valve.
2. Unbolt the EGR line fitting on the opposite side of the valve.
3. Remove the two retaining bolts and lift the EGR valve from the intake manifold.
4. Install the EGR valve in the reverse order of removal. Use a new gasket at the intake manifold.

Air Injection

This system includes a belt-driven air pump, filter, check valve, anti-backfire valve or gulp valve, and connecting hoses and air lines. The system reduces exhaust emissions by pumping fresh air to the exhaust manifold where it combines with the hot exhaust gas to burn away excess hydrocarbons and reduce carbon monoxide.

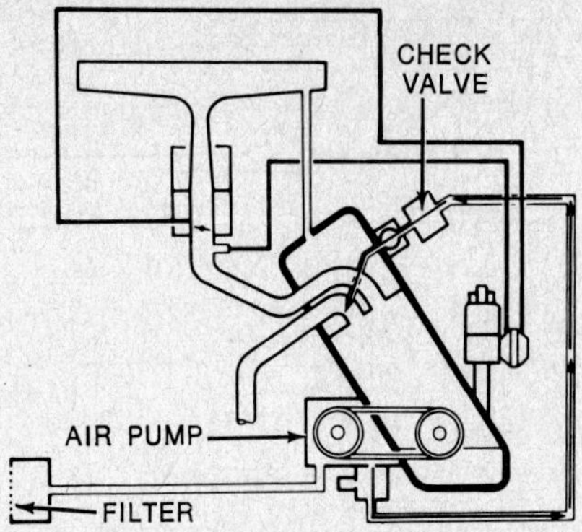

Air injection system schematic. The arrows indicate the air flow

MAINTENANCE

Required maintenance on the air pump involves visually checking the pump, control valves, hoses and lines every 10,000 miles. Clean the air pump filter element at this interval. The filter element should be replaced every 20,000 miles or two years.

TESTING AND SERVICE

Air Pump System

1. Remove and clean the air manifold.
2. Blow compressed air into the anti-backfire valve in the direction of the air flow.
3. Clean or replace the air pump filter.
4. Start the engine.
5. Exhaust gas should flow equally from each air inlet.
6. With the engine idling, block the relief valve air outlet—only a slight pressure should be felt if the system is operating properly.

Anti-Backfire Valve

1. Disconnect the air pump filter line from the anti-backfire valve.
2. Briefly disconnect the anti-backfire valve vacuum line with the engine running. There should be a noticeable vacuum.
3. Replace the anti-backfire valve if the engine backfires.

Catalytic Converter

MAINTENANCE

Required maintenance on the catalytic converter involves checking the condition of the ceramic insert every 30,000 miles. As this interval is reached, a indicator light on the dash will glow. Once service to the converter is performed, the odometer must be reset.

TESTING AND SERVICE

CAUTION: Do not drop or strike the converter assembly or damage to the ceramic insert will result.

Damage and overheating of the catalytic converter, indicated by the flickering of the "CAT" warning light, can be caused by the following:

1. Engine misfire caused by faulty spark plug, ignition wires and so on.
2. Improper ignition timing.
3. CO valve set too high.
4. Faulty air pump diverter valve.
5. Faulty temperature sensor.
6. Engine under strain caused by trailer hauling, high speed driving in hot weather, etc.

A faulty converter is indicated by one of the following symptoms:

1. Poor engine performance.
2. The engine stalls.
3. Rattling in the exhaust system.
4. A CO reading greater than 0.4% at the tail pipe.

Check or replace the converter as follows:

1. Disconnect the temperature sensor.

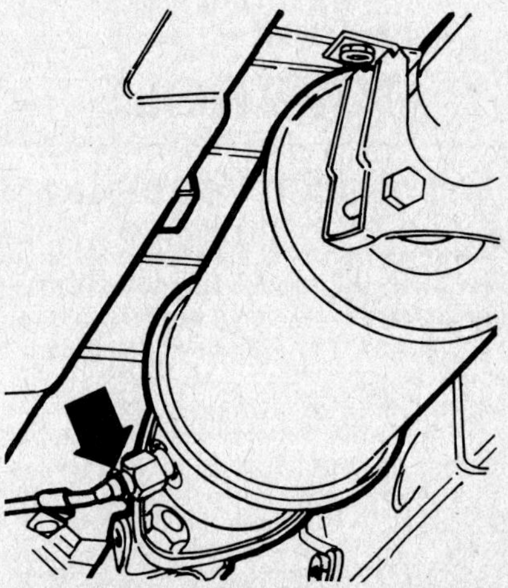

Checking the catalytic converter—the arrow indicates the temperature sensor

Resetting the catalytic converter elapsed mileage odometer

2. Loosen and remove the bolts holding the converter to the exhaust system and the chassis.
3. Remove the converter.
4. Hold the converter up to a strong light and look through both ends, checking for blockages. If the converter is blocked, replace it.
5. Install the converter in the reverse order of removal.
6. Reset the elapsed mileage odometer by pushing the white button marked "CAT".

FUEL SYSTEM

Fuel Pump—CIS Engines (Fuel Injection)

TESTING—ELECTRICAL

1. Have an assistant operate the starter. Listen at the rear wheel to determine if the pump is running.
2. If the pump is not running, check the fuse on the front of the fuel pump relay.
3. If the fuse is good, replace the fuel pump relay.
4. If the fuel pump still does not operate, the fuel pump is faulty and must be replaced.

TESTING—FUEL PUMP DELIVERY

1. Check the condition of the fuel filter, make sure it is clean.
2. Connect a jumper wire between the #1 terminal on the ignition coil and ground.
3. Disconnect the return fuel line and hold it in a measuring container with a capacity of 1 quart of 1000cc.
4. Have an assistant run the starter for 30 seconds while watching the quantity of fuel delivered.
5. If less than 3/4 quart or 750cc of fuel is delivered in 30 seconds, replace the fuel pump.

REMOVAL AND INSTALLATION

1. Support the car on a lift and remove the right rear wheel.
2. Remove the gas tank filler cap to release the pressure.
3. Clean all fuel line connections *thoroughly.*
4. Disconnect the fuel line from the gas tank and the line to the fuel accumulator.
5. Disconnect the electrical connector.
6. Loosen and remove the retaining nuts and remove the fuel pump.
7. Install the new fuel pump in the reverse order of removal. Make sure that new seal washers are installed on the fuel discharge line.

CIS Fuel Injection

AIR FLOW SENSOR-TESTING AND ADJUSTMENT

Sensor Plate Lever and Control Plunger

1. Run the engine for a short time at idle.
2. Remove the air duct from the air flow sensor assembly.
3. Using a magnet, lift the sensor plate. A light even resistance must be felt over the sensor plates entire travel.

NOTE: Make certain that the air sensor plate is centered in the air cone. If adjustment is necessary, proceed as follows:
a. Loosen the centering bolt slightly.
b. Run a 0.004 in. (0.10 mm) feeler gauge around the perimeter of the air gap.
c. Tighten the centering bolt.

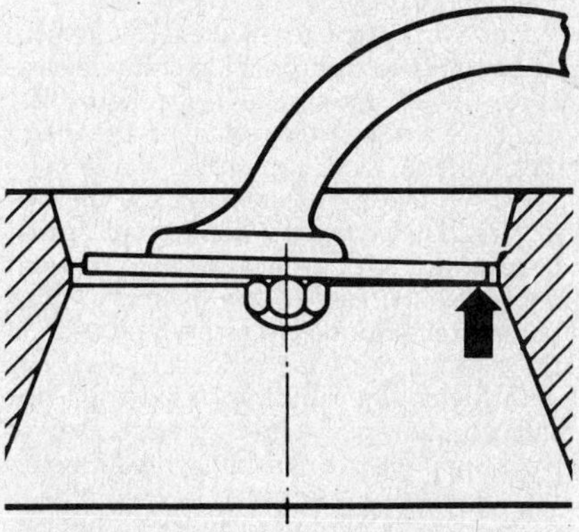

Aligning the air flow sensor plate with the edge of the air cone

4. No resistance must be felt when the sensor plate is moved rapidly up and down. If resistance is felt, the air sensor must be replaced.
5. If the sensor plate is hard to move upward but moves freely down, the control plunger is sticking. Remove the fuel distributor and clean the control plunger in solvent. If after installation the plunger is still sticking, the fuel distributor must be replaced.

Sensor Plate Height Adjustment

The height adjustment of the sensor plate must be checked under fuel pressure. You will also need a bridging adaptor (US 4480/3).
1. Install a pressure gauge in the line between the fuel distributor and control pressure regulator.
2. Remove the rubber elbow from the air flow sensor housing.
3. Remove the fuel pump relay from the fuse panel and install a bridging adaptor (US 4480/3).
4. Switch the adaptor ON and wait until pressure reads 49–54 psi.

Adjusting the air flow sensor spring stop

5. Switch the bridging adaptor OFF; the pressure should fall to 28–37 psi.
6. The upper edge of the sensor plate must be even with the bottom of the air cone taper or no more than 0.020 in. below the bottom of the taper.
7. Bend the clip to adjust the height.
8. Recheck the pressure readings after adjusting.
9. Remove the pressure gauge, reconnect the fuel lines and install the fuel pump relay.

THERMO-TIME SWITCH-TESTING

NOTE: To properly perform the following tests, the engine must be cold with the water temperature below 95 F (35 C).

1. Disconnect the electrical connector from the cold start valve on the end of the intake manifold.
2. Connect a test light across the cold start valve terminals.
3. Connect a jumper wire from the #1 terminal on the ignition coil to a good ground.
4. Have an assistant operate the starter. If the test light fails to light after 8 seconds, the thermo-time switch is defective and should be replaced.

COLD START VALVE—TESTING

1. Remove the electrical connector from the cold start valve.

NOTE: Do not remove the fuel line from the cold start valve.

2. Remove the cold start valve from the manifold and point the nozzle into a measuring container.
3. Connect a jumper wire from one terminal of the cold start valve to terminal #15 on the ignition coil.
4. Connect a second jumper wire from the other cold start valve terminal to ground.
5. Remove the fuel pump relay and bridge the relay plate terminals #L13 and #L14 with a fused (8 amp) jumper wire.
6. Have an assistant turn the ignition switch on while observing the fuel spray

pattern from the cold start valve. The spray pattern from the nozzle must be cone-shaped and steady, if not replace the valve.

7. Turn the ignition switch off.

8. Wipe the nozzle dry with clean rag and check for leakage. If drops form within one minute, the valve is defective and must be replaced.

AUXILIARY AIR REGULATOR—TESTING

NOTE: The engine must be cold to perform this test.

1. Remove the hose from the auxiliary air regulator and plug.
2. Observe gate valve with the aid of a mirror. The valve must be open. If the valve is not open, replace the regulator.
3. Run the engine at idle for 5 minutes. Again check the gate valve, it should be closed. If the valve did not close, replace the auxiliary air regulator.

CONTROL PRESSURE REGULATOR—TESTING

NOTE: The engine must be warm.

1. Remove the electrical connector from the control pressure regulator.
2. Connect an ohmmeter across the terminals in the regulator socket and measure the resistance. The reading should be approximately 20 ohms. If reading is not within specifications, replace the control pressure regulator.

FUEL INJECTORS—TESTING

1. Remove the injector but leave it connected to the fuel line.
2. Point the injector into a measuring container.
3. Remove the fuel pump relay and bridge the relay plate terminals #L13 and L14 with a fused (8 amp) jumper wire.
4. Remove the air duct from the air flow sensor.
5. Have an assistant turn the ignition switch on.
6. Lift the air flow sensor plate with a magnet and observe the injector nozzle spray pattern. The spray pattern must be cone shaped and even, if not replace the injector.
7. Turn the ignition off and hold the injector horizontally. It should not drip.

NOTE: One or more injectors may be checked at the same time.

8. Moisten the rubber seals on the injectors with fuel before installing.
9. Press the injectors firmly into place.

FUEL DISTRIBUTOR—REMOVAL AND INSTALLATION

1. Clean the fuel line connections at the fuel distributor. Disconnect the lines, making sure that they are labled for installation.
2. Remove the fuel distributor retaining bolts.

NOTE: When removing the fuel distributor watch underneath to make sure that the control plunger does not fall out.

3. Carefully remove the fuel distributor.
4. If the control plunger has been removed, moisten it with gasoline before installing. The small shoulder on the plunger is inserted first.
5. Reinstall the fuel distributor using new O-rings.

Diesel Fuel Injection

The diesel fuel system is an extremely complex and sensitive system. Very few repairs or adjustments are possible by the owner. Any service other than that listed here should be referred to an authorized VW dealer or diesel specialist. The injection pump itself is not repairable; it can only be replaced.

Any work done to the diesel fuel injection should be done with absolute cleanliness. Even the smallest specks of dirt will have a disastrous effect on the injection system.

Do not attempt to remove the fuel injectors. They are very delicate and must be removed with a special tool to prevent damage. The fuel in the system is also under tremendous pressure (1700–1850 psi), so it's not wise to loosen any lines with the engine running. Exposing your skin to the spray from the injector at working pressure can cause fuel to penetrate the skin.

CHECKING INJECTION PUMP TIMING

Checking the injection pump timing also involves checking the valve timing. To alter the injection pump timing, the camshaft gear must be removed and repositioned. This also changes the valve timing. Special tool (VW 210) is necessary to properly tension the injection pump drive belt on the diesel engine.

1. Set the engine at TDC on No. 1 cylinder. In this position, the TDC mark on the flywheel should be aligned with boss on the bell housing and both valves of No. 1 cylinder should be closed.
2. The marks on the pump and mounting plate should also be aligned.
3. If the valve timing is incorrect, set the valve timing as detailed in the engine section.

ACCELERATOR CABLE ADJUSTMENT

The ball pin on the pump lever should be pointing up and be aligned with the mark in the slot. The accelerator cable should be attached at the upper hole in the bracket. With the pedal in the full throttle position, adjust the cable so that the pump lever contacts the stop with no binding or strain.

COLD START CABLE ADJUSTMENT

When the cold start knob on the dash is pulled out, the fuel injection pump timing is advanced 2.5°. This improves cold starting and running until the engine warms up.

1. Insert the washer on the cable.
2. Insert the cable in the bracket with the rubber bushing. Install the cable in the pin.
3. Install the lockwasher.
4. Move the lever to zero position (direction of arrow). Pull the inner cable tight and tighten the clamp screw.

CHECKING GLOW PLUGS CURRENT SUPPLY

1. Connect a test light between No. 4 cylinder glow plug and ground.
2. Turn the key to the heat position. The test light should light up.
3. If not, check the glow plug relay, ignition switch, or fuse box relay plate.

CHECKING GLOW PLUGS

Make this check after establishing that there is current to the glow plugs.

1. Remove the wire and glow plug bus bar.
2. Connect the test light between the battery positive terminal and each glow plug in turn.
3. If the light lights, the glow plug is OK. If not, the glow plug is defective and must be replaced.

MANUAL TRANSMISSION

Transaxle

REMOVAL AND INSTALLATION

The engine and transaxle may be removed together as explained under Engine Removal and Installation or the transaxle may be removed alone, as explained here.

1. Disconnect the battery ground cable.
2. Support the left end of the engine at the lifting eye.
3. Remove the left transmission mount (between the transmission and the firewall).
4. Turn the engine until the lug on the flywheel (to the left of the TDC mark) aligns with the flywheel timing pointer.
5. Detach the speedometer drive cable, backup light wire, and clutch cable.
6. Remove the engine to transmission bolts.

7. Disconnect the shift linkage.
8. Detach the transmission ground strap.
9. Remove the starter.
10. Remove the engine mounting support near the starter.
11. Remove the rear transmission mount.
12. Unbolt and wire up the driveshafts.
13. From underneath, remove the bolts for the large cover plate, but don't remove it. Unbolt the small cover plate on the firewall side of the engine. Remove the engine to transmission nut immediately below the small plate.
14. Press the transmission off the dowels and remove it from below the truck.

To install the transaxle:

15. The recess in the flywheel edge must be at 3:00 o'clock. Tighten the engine to transmission bolts to 47 ft lbs. Tighten the engine mounting support bolts to 47 ft lbs. Tighten the driveshaft bolts to 32 ft lbs.
16. Check the adjustment of the shift linkage.

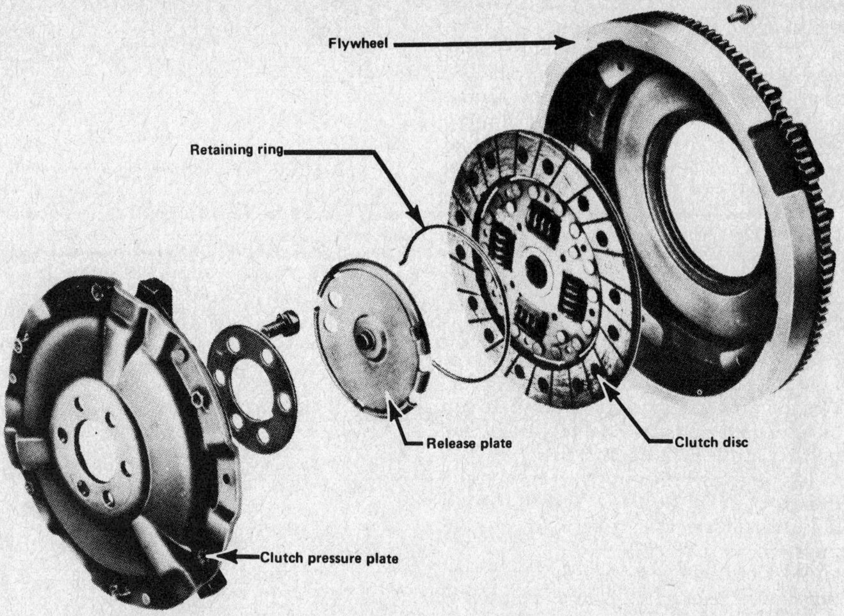

Clutch assembly; the pressure plate is bolted to the crankshaft and the clutch is actuated by a pushrod working on the release plate

SHIFT LINKAGE ADJUSTMENT

1. Align the holes of the lever housing plate with the holes of the lever bearing plate.
2. Loosen the shift rod clamp. Pull the boot off the lever housing and push it out of the way. It may be necessary to loosen the screws in the cover plate to free the boot.
3. Check that the shift finger is in the center of the stopping plate.
4. Adjust the shift rod end so that it is $^3/_4$ in. from the right side of the lever housing. Tighten the shift rod clamp and check the shifter operation.

Selector Shaft Lockbolt Adjustment

Make this adjustment after linkage adjustment, if the linkage still feels spongy or jams.

1. Disconnect the shift linkage and put the transmission in Neutral.
2. Loosen the locknut and turn the adjusting sleeve in until the lockring lifts off the sleeve.
3. Turn the adjusting sleeve back until the lockring just contacts the sleeve. Tighten the locknut.
4. Turn the shaft slightly. The lockring should lift as soon as the shaft is turned.
5. Reconnect the linkage.

CLUTCH

PEDAL FREE PLAY ADJUSTMENT

Clutch pedal free play should be $^5/_8$ in. Pedal free play is the distance the pedal can be depressed before the linkage starts to act on the throwout bearing.

1. Adjust the clutch pedal free play by loosening the two nuts on the cable on the front of the transmission.
2. After obtaining the correct free play, tighten the adjusting nuts.

REMOVAL AND INSTALLATION

1. Remove the transmission.
2. Attach a toothed flywheel holder and gradually loosen the flywheel to pressure plate bolts one or two turns at a time in a crisscross pattern to prevent distortion.
3. Remove the flywheel and the clutch disc.
4. Use a screwdriver to remove the release plate retaining ring. Remove the release plate.
5. Lock the pressure plate in place and unbolt it from the crankshaft. Loosen the bolts one or two turns at a time in a crisscross pattern to prevent distortion.

Check the pressure plate and clutch disc for wear and scoring. Also check the throwout bearing and clutch fork for wear or looseness. If any of the above are noticed, replace the necessary part.

6. On installation, use new bolts to attach the pressure plate to the crankshaft. Use a thread locking compound and torque the bolts in a diagonal pattern to 54 ft lbs.
7. Lubricate the clutch disc splines with multi-purpose grease. Lubricate the release plate contact surface and pushrod socket with multi-purpose grease. Install the release plate, retaining ring, and clutch disc.
8. Install a dummy shaft to align the clutch disc.
9. Install the flywheel, tightening the bolts one or two turns at a time in a criss-cross pattern to prevent distortion. Torque the bolts to 14 ft lbs.
10. Replace the transmission.

AUTOMATIC TRANSMISSION

Transaxle

REMOVAL AND INSTALLATION

The engine and transaxle may be removed together as explained under Engine Removal and Installation or the transaxle may be removed alone, as explained here.

1. Disconnect both battery cables.
2. Disconnect the speedometer cable at the transmission.
3. Support the left end of the engine at the lifting eye. Attach a hoist to the transaxle.
4. Unbolt the rear transmission carrier from the body then from the transaxle. Unbolt the left side carrier from the body.
5. Unbolt the driveshafts and wire them up.
6. Remove the starter.
7. Remove the three converter to drive plate bolts.
8. Shift into P and disconnect the floorshift linkage at the transmission.
9. Remove the accelerator and carburetor cable bracket at the transmission.
10. Unbolt the left side transmission carrier from the transmission.

11. Unbolt the front transmission mount from the transmission.

12. Unbolt the bottom of the engine from the transmission. Lift the transaxle slightly, remove the rest of the bolts, pull the transmission off the mounting dowels, and lower the transaxle out of the truck. Secure the converter so it doesn't fall out.

CAUTION: Don't tilt the torque converter.

13. Be sure the torque converter is fully seated on the one-way clutch support. Push the transmission onto the mounting dowels and install two bolts. Lift the unit until the left driveshaft can be installed and install the rest of the bolts. Torque them to 39 ft lbs.

14. Tighten the front transmission mount bolts to 39 ft lbs. Install the left side transmission carrier to the transmission.

15. Connect the accelerator and carburetor cable bracket. Connect the floorshift linkage.

16. Tighten the torque converter to drive plate bolts to 22 ft lbs. Torque the driveshaft bolts to 32 ft lbs.

17. Install the rear transmission carrier and make sure that the left side carrier is aligned in the center of the body mount. Bolt the left side carrier to the body.

18. Connect the speedometer cable and the battery cables.

PAN REMOVAL AND INSTALLATION, STRAINER SERVICE

1. Remove the drain plug and let the fluid drain into a pan.
2. Remove the pan bolts and take off the pan.
3. Discard the old gasket and clean the pan out. Be very careful not to get any threads or lint from rags into the pan.
4. The filter needn't be replaced unless the fluid is dirty or smells burnt. The specified torque for the strainer screws is 2 ft lbs.
5. Replace the pan with a new gasket and tighten the bolts, in a criss-cross pattern, to 14 ft lbs.
6. Using a long-necked funnel, pour in $2^1/_2$ qts of Dexron® automatic transmission fluid through the dipstick tube. Start the engine and shift through all the transmission ranges with the car stationary. Check the level on the dipstick with the lever in Neutral. It should be up to the lower end of the dipstick. Drive the car until it is warmed up and recheck the level.

LINKAGE ADJUSTMENT

Check the cable adjustment as follows:

1. Run the engine at 1000–1200 rpm with the parking brake on.

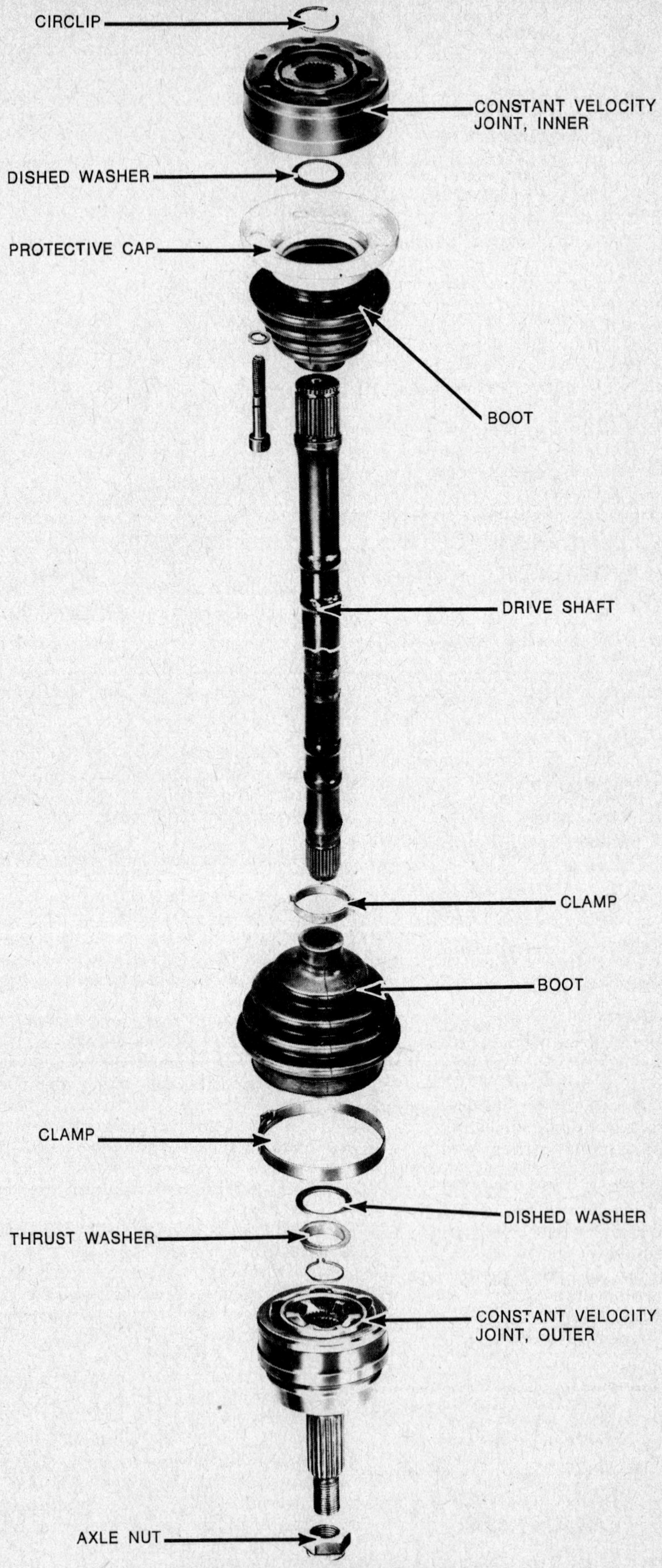

Axle shaft—exploded view

2. Select Reverse—a drop in engine speed should be noticed.
3. Select Park—engine speed should increase. Pull the shift lever against Reverse, the engine speed shouldn't drop.
4. Move the shift lever to Neutral—an increase in engine speed should be noticed.
5. Shift the lever into Drive—a noticeable drop in engine speed should result.
6. Shift into 1—the lever must engage without having to overcome any resistance.
7. To adjust the cable—Shift into Park. Loosen the cable clamp at the transmission end of the cable.
8. Press the transmission lever all the way to the left.
9. Hold the lever in place and tighten the cable clamp.

TRANSMISSION CABLE ADJUSTMENT

1. At the carburetor, make sure that the throttle is closed, the choke is off, and the fast idle cam is out of action. Detach the cable end at the transmission.
2. Press the lever at the transmission end of the cable toward the cable.
3. You should be able to insert the cable end into the transmission lever without moving the lever.
4. Adjust the cable length to correct.

SECOND GEAR (REAR) BAND ADJUSTMENT

NOTE: The transmission must be horizontal when band adjustments are performed. The first gear band has a narrow point adjusting screw, the second gear band a wide screw.

1. Tighten the second gear band adjusting screw to 7.2 ft. lb. (86 in. lb).
2. Loosen the screw and tighten it again to 3.6 ft. lb (43 in. lb).
3. Turn the screw out exactly $2^1/_2$ turns and then tighten the locknut.

NEUTRAL START SWITCH

The combination neutral start and backup light switch is mounted inside the shifter housing.

DRIVE AXLES

Halfshaft

REMOVAL AND INSTALLATION

1. Remove the front axle nut.

NOTE: Use a long breaker bar with an extension (length of pipe).

2. Raise and support the car.

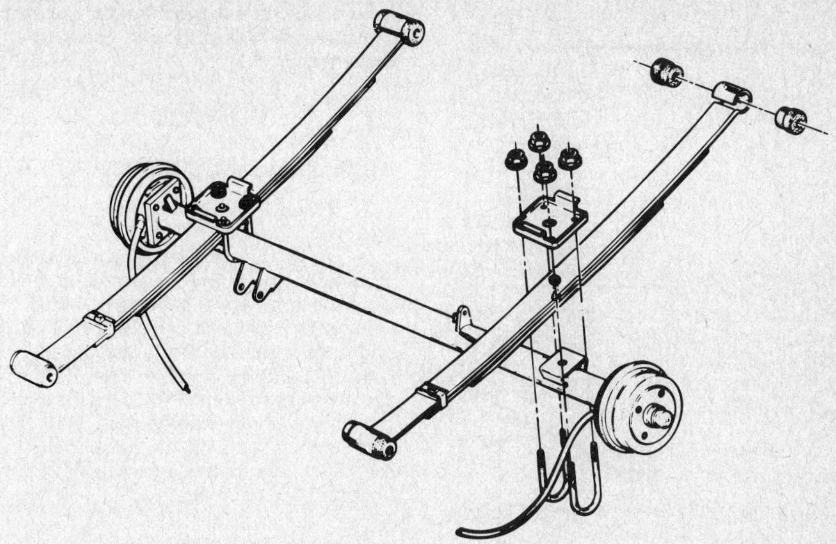

Rear suspension

3. Remove the allen head bolts retaining the axle shaft to the transaxle.

NOTE: If you are removing the right axle shaft, detach the exhaust pipe from the manifold and the transaxle bracket.

4. Pull the axle shaft out and up and place it on top of the transaxle.
5. Turn the steering wheel all the way to the side of the shaft being removed. Pull the axle shaft from the steering knuckle.
6. Installation is the reverse of removal. Tighten the transaxle bolts to 25 ft. lbs. The axle nut is tightened to 175 ft. lbs.

REAR SUSPENSION

Leaf Springs

REMOVAL AND INSTALLATION

CAUTION: The springs are under a considerable amount of tension. Be very careful when removing or installing them; they can exert enough force to cause serious injuries.

1. Jack up the rear of the truck and support it with jackstands placed under the frame.
2. Disconnect the shock absorbers at their lower end.
3. Remove the nuts securing the U-bolts around the axle housing.
4. Place a jack under the rear axle housing and raise the housing to remove the weight off the springs.
5. Remove the nuts from the spring shackles, drive out the shackle pins and remove the spring from the vehicle.
6. Install the spring in the reverse order of removal. The weight of the truck must be on the rear wheels before tightening the front pin, shackle, and shock absorber attaching nuts. Tighten the front pin and shackle nuts, the U-bolt nuts and the shock absorber lower end nut.

Shock Absorbers

REMOVAL AND INSTALLATION

The rear shock absorbers are removed simply by removing the upper and lower attaching nuts, and removing the component from the vehicle. They are installed in the reverse order. The weight of the vehicle must be on the rear wheels before tightening the shock absorber attaching nuts.

FRONT SUSPENSION

The front suspension is a simple strut design. It consists of a lower control arm, ball joint, and suspension strut. In a MacPherson strut design, such as this, the shock absorber strut serves as a locating member of the suspension as well as a damper. A shock absorber insert is located inside the strut. A coil spring is used.

Ball Joint

REMOVAL AND INSTALLATION

1. Jack up the front of the truck and support it on stands.
2. Remove the retaining bolt and nut.
3. Pry the lower control arm and ball joint down and out of the strut.

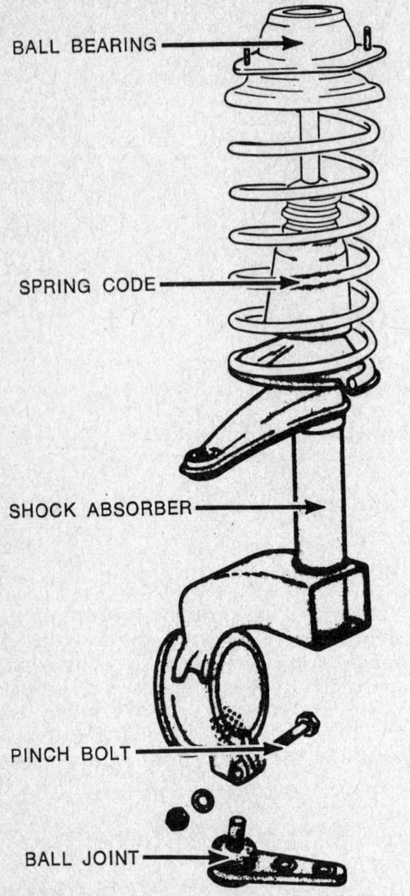

A pinch bolt holds the ball joint to the combination strut and steering knuckle

4. Drill out the rivets; enlarge the holes to 21/64 in.
5. Remove the ball joint assembly.
6. Bolt the new ball joint in place. Torque the bolts to 18 ft lbs. Tighten the retaining bolt for the ball joint stud to 21 ft lbs.

Shock Absorber

REMOVAL AND INSTALLATION

Since the shock absorber cartridge is contained within the strut assembly, it is necessary to remove the strut and then compress the coil spring in order to remove the shock.

Strut

REMOVAL AND INSTALLATION

1. Remove the brake hose from the strut clip.
2. Mark the position of the camber adjustment bolts before removing them from the hub (wheel bearing housing).
3. Remove the upper mounting nuts and remove the strut from the car.
4. Installation is the reverse. The upper nuts are tightened to 14 ft. lbs., and the lower strut-to-hub bolts to 58 ft. lbs. Use new washers on the lower bolts. If the shock absorber was replaced, camber will have to be adjusted.

Coil Spring

REMOVAL AND INSTALLATION

To remove the spring, the strut must be mounted in a large vise, the spring compressed, the retaining nut and cover removed, and the spring slowly released. A special tool is needed to remove the shock absorber retainer, after which the shock absorber is easily removed. Assembly is the reverse of removal.

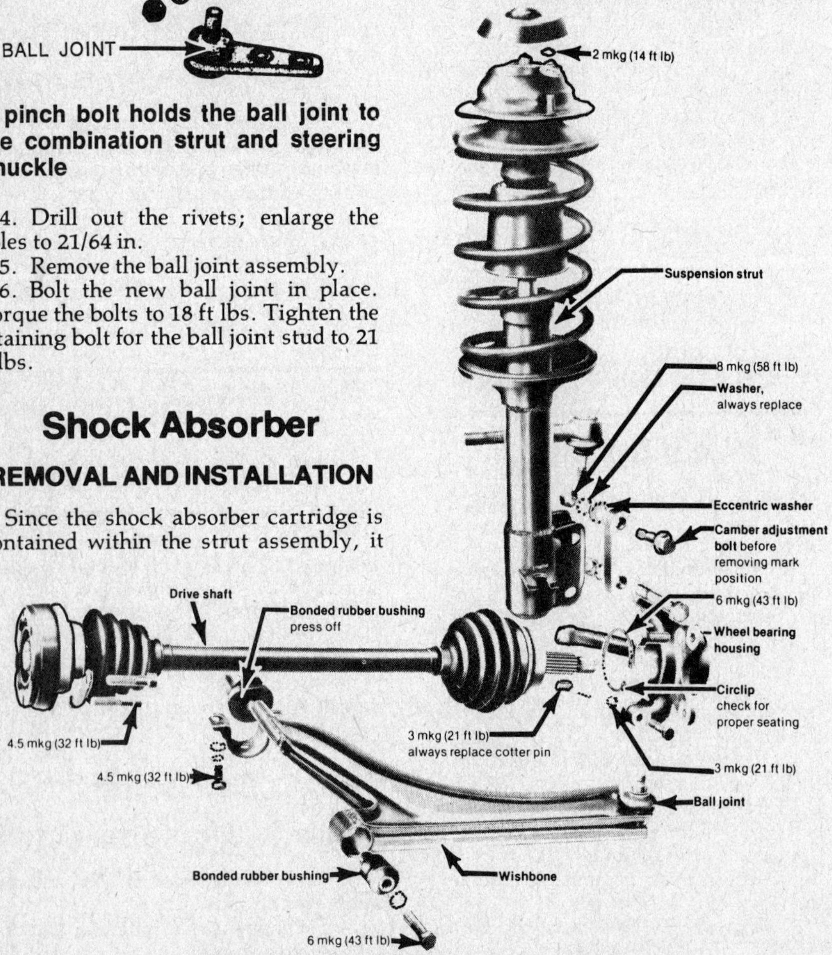

Exploded view of the front suspension

Front End Alignment

CAMBER ADJUSTMENT

Camber is adjusted by loosening the nuts of the two bolts holding the top of the wheel bearing housing to the bottom of the strut, and turning the top eccentric bolt. The range of adjustment is 2°.

CASTER

Other than the replacement of damaged suspension components, caster is not adjustable.

TOE-IN ADJUSTMENT

Toe-in is checked with the wheels straight ahead. Only the right tie-rod is adjustable, but replacement left tie-rods are adjustable. Replacement left tie-rods should be set to the same length as the original. Toe-in should be adjusted only with the right tie-rod. If the steering wheel is crooked, remove and align it.

STEERING

The Rabbit pick-up has rack and pinion steering with end-mounted tie-rods. No periodic maintenance is required on either rack and pinion steering system.

Steering Wheel

REMOVAL AND INSTALLATION

1. Grasp the center cover pad and pull it from the wheel.
2. Loosen and remove the steering shaft nut.
3. Pull the wheel off the shaft. A puller isn't normally needed.
4. Disconnect the horn wire.
5. Replace the wheel in the reverse order of removal. Tighten the nut to 36 ft lb.

Turn Signal and Headlight Dimmer Switch

REPLACEMENT

1. Disconnect the battery ground cable.
2. Remove the steering wheel.
3. Remove the switch retaining screws.
4. Pry the switch housing off the column.
5. Disconnect the electrical plugs at the back of the switch.
6. Remove the switch housing.

7. Replace in the reverse order of removal.

Ignition Switch and Steering Lock

REMOVAL AND INSTALLATION

NOTE: The access hole for removing the lock cylinder may be missing. Before the lock cylinder can be removed, drill a hole according to following dimensions:
a=12 mm (0.472 in.)
b=10 mm (0.393 in.)
Drill the hole 1/8 in. deep.

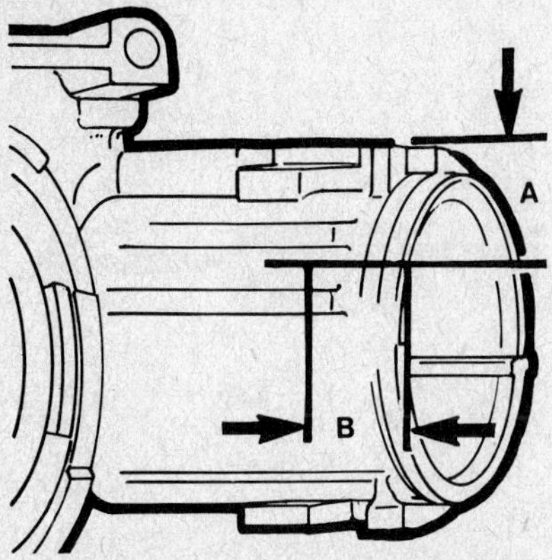

Dimensions for drilling the ignition lock cylinder hole (if not equipped)

1. Remove the steering wheel and turn signal switch. Remove the steering column shaft covers.
2. The lock is clamped to the steering column with special bolts whose heads shear off on installation. These must be drilled out in order to remove the switch.
3. On replacement, make sure that the lock tang is aligned with the slot in the steering column.

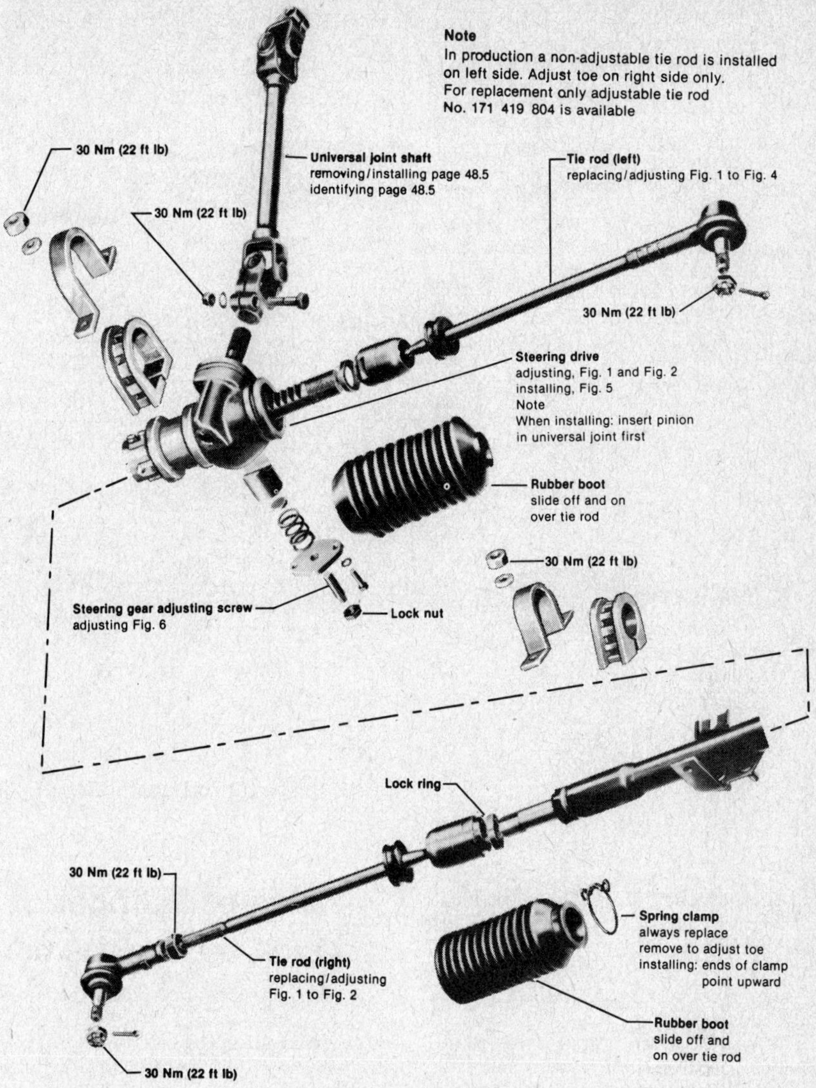

Rabbit steering gear

Steering Gear

REMOVAL AND INSTALLATION

1. Disconnect the steering shaft universal joint and wire up out of the way.
2. Disconnect the tie rods at the steering rack and wire up and out of the way.
3. Remove the steering rack and drive.
4. Install the steering rack and drive and torque the attaching hardware to 14 ft. lbs.
5. Set the steering rack with equal distances between the housing on the right side and left side.
6. Install the tie rods and screw both sides in until an equal distance is reached on both rods.
7. Tighten the steering gear adjusting screw until it touches the thrust washer. Tighten the lock nut.
8. Install the steering shaft.
9. Check the front end alignment.

Steering Linkage

TIE-ROD REMOVAL AND INSTALLATION

1. Center the steering rack.
2. Remove the cotter pin and nut from the tie rod end.
3. Disconnect the tie rod from the steering rack.
4. If the left side tie rod is being replaced, adjust it to 14.92 in. (379 mm).
5. Adjust the steering rack and tie rods as outlined in steps 5 and 6 of the "Steering Gear Removal and Installation".
6. Tighten the tie rod end retaining nut to 21 ft. lbs. and install a new cotter pin.

BRAKE SYSTEMS

The hydraulic system is a dual circuit type that has the advantage of retaining 50% braking effectiveness in the event of failure in one system. The circuits are arranged so that you always have one front and one rear brake for a more con-

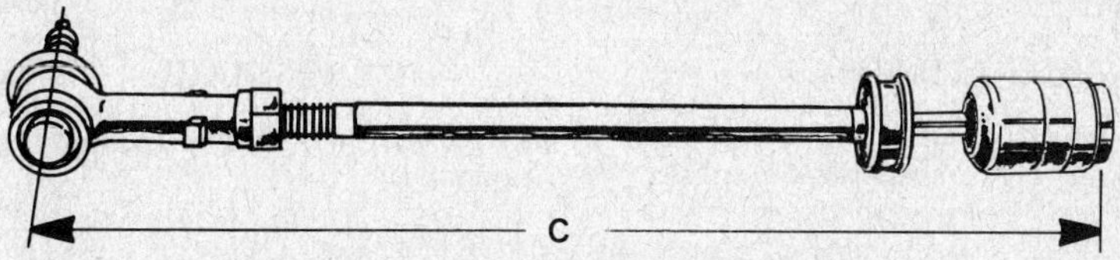

Right side tie rod adjustment

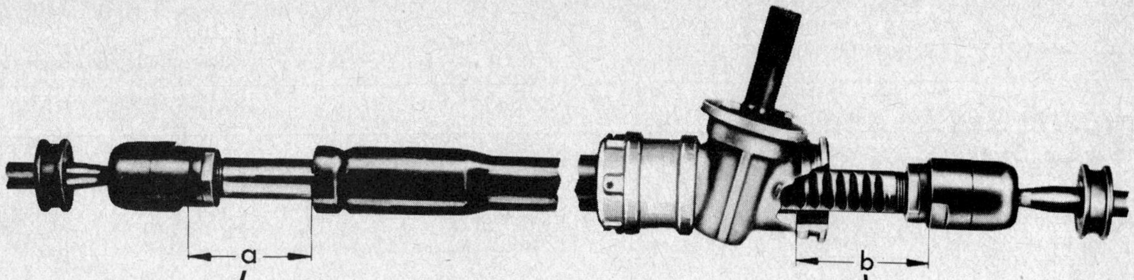

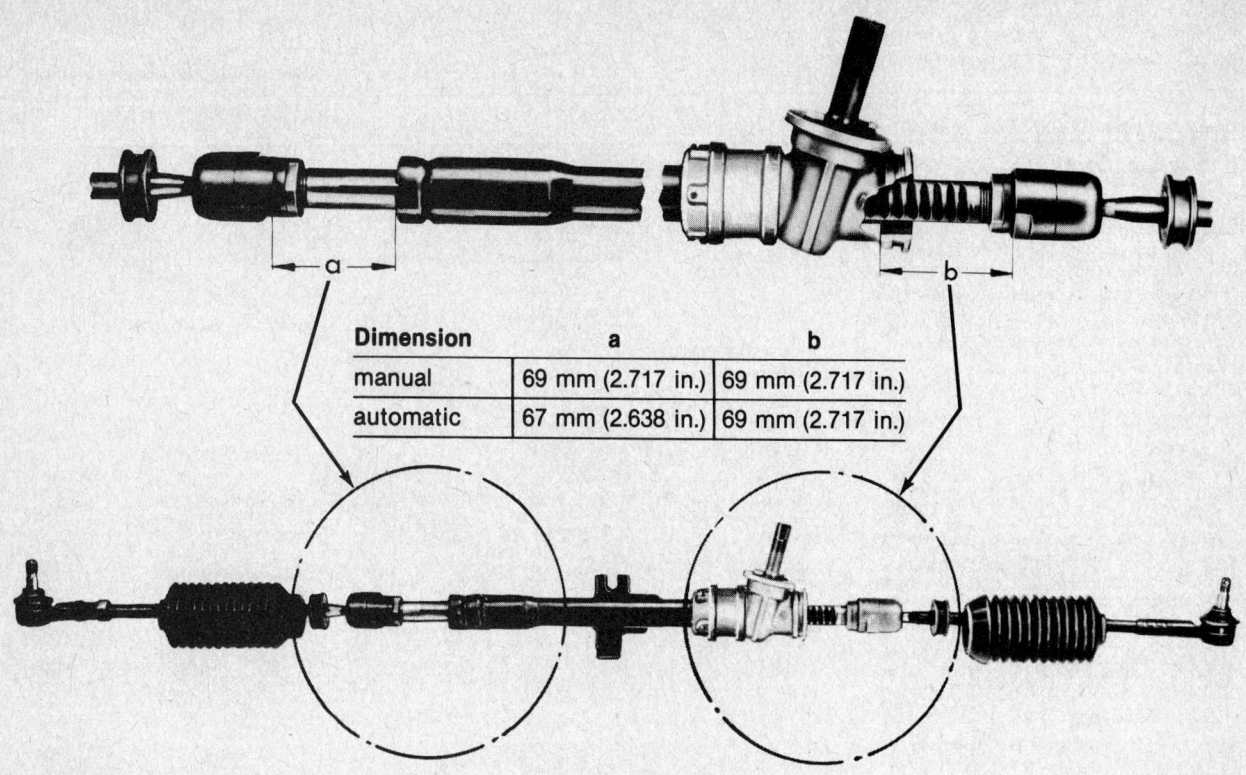

Dimension	a	b
manual	69 mm (2.717 in.)	69 mm (2.717 in.)
automatic	67 mm (2.638 in.)	69 mm (2.717 in.)

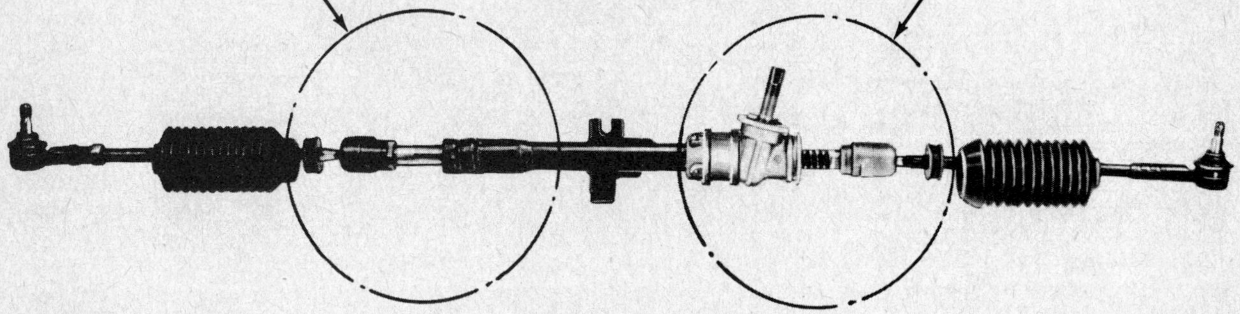

Adjusting the tie rod position. b = 2.64 in.

trolled emergency stop. The right front and left rear are in one circuit; the left front and right rear are in the second circuit.

There is also a brake failure switch and a proportioning valve.

The brake failure unit is a hydraulic valve/electrical switch which warns of brake problems by the warning light on the instrument panel. A piston inside the switch is kept centered by one brake system pressure on one side and the other system pressure on the opposite side. Should a failure occur in one system, the piston would go to the "failed" side and complete an electrical circuit to the warning lamp. This switch also functions as a parking brake reminder light and will go out when the parking brake is released. The proportioning valve provides balanced front-to-rear braking during hard stops.

Extreme brake line pressure will overcome the spring pressure on the piston within the valve causing it to proportionately restrict pressure to the rear brakes. In this manner, the rear brakes are kept from locking. The proportioner doesn't operate under normal braking conditions.

ADJUSTMENT

The front disc brakes require no adjustment, as disc brakes automatically adjust themselves to compensate for pad wear. The VW pick-up has self-adjusting rear drum brakes.

Master Cylinder

REMOVAL AND INSTALLATION

1. Disconnect and plug the brake lines.
2. Disconnect the electrical plug from the sending unit for the brake failure switch.
3. Remove the two master cylinder mounting nuts.
4. Lift the master cylinder and reservoir out of the engine compartment being careful not to spill any fluid on the fender. Empty out and discard the brake fluid.

***CAUTION:** Do not depress the brake pedal while the master cylinder is removed.*

5. Position the master cylinder and reservoir assembly onto the studs for the booster and install the washers and nuts. Tighten the nuts to no more than 9 ft. lbs.
6. Remove the plugs and connect the brake lines.
7. Bleed the entire brake system.

OVERHAUL

1. Remove the master cylinder from the booster.
2. Firmly mount the master cylinder in a vise. Use clean rags to protect the cylinder from the vise jaws.
3. Grasp the plastic reservoir and pull it out of the rubber plugs. Remove the plugs.
4. In the center of the cylinder there is a stop screw; remove it. Discard the stop screw seal; there should be a new one in the rebuilding kit.
5. At the end of the master cylinder is a snap-ring (circlip). Remove it, using snap-ring pliers.
6. Shake out the secondary piston assembly. If the primary piston remains lodged in the bore, it can be forced by applying compressed air to the open line fitting.
7. Disassemble the secondary piston. The two secondary springs will be replaced with those in the rebuilding kit. Save the washers and spacers.
8. Carefully clamp the secondary piston. Slightly compress the spring and screw out the stroke limiting bolt.
9. Remove the secondary piston stop sleeve bolt, spring, spring seat, and support washer.
10. Replace all the parts with those supplied in the overhaul kit. Be careful not to interchange the piston cups and the piston seals.
11. Clean all metal parts in alcohol and dry them with compressed air.
12. Check every part you are reusing. Pay close attention to the cylinder bores. If there is any scoring or rust, have the master cylinder honed or replace it.
13. Lightly coat the bores and cups with brake fluid. Assemble the cylinder

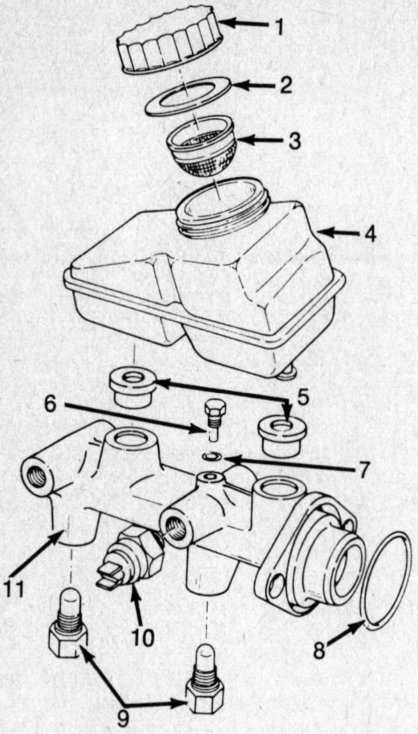

1. Reservoir cap
2. Washer
3. Filter screen
4. Reservoir
5. Master cylinder plugs
6. Stop screw
7. Stop screw seal
8. Master cylinder seal
9. Residual pressure valves
10. Warning light sender unit
11. Brake master cylinder housing

Master cylinder body and reservoir

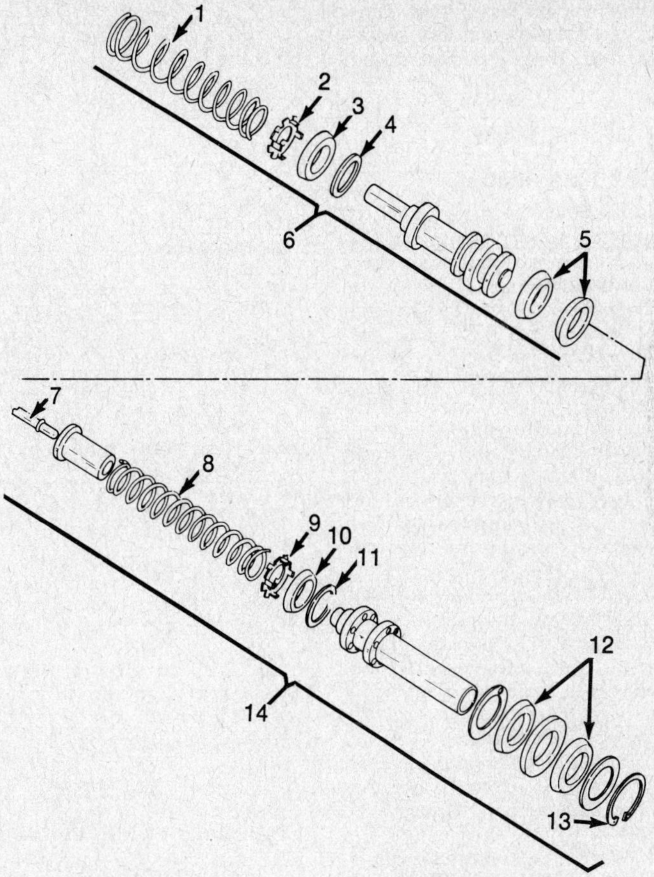

1. Conical spring
2. Spring seat
3. Primary cup
4. Washer
5. Secondary cups
6. Primary piston assembly
7. Stroke limiting screw
8. Cylindrical spring
9. Spring seat
10. Primary cup
11. Washer
12. Secondary cups
13. Circlip
14. Secondary piston assembly

Exploded view of the master cylinder components

components in the exact sequence shown in the illustration.

14. Install the primary piston assembly; notice that the primary spring is conically shaped. Be sure that you aren't using the secondary spring.

15. Using a plastic rod or other non-metallic tool, push the primary piston assembly into the housing until the stop bolt (with a new seal) can be screwed in and tightened.

16. Assemble the secondary piston. Fasten the spring, spring seat, primary cup, and stop sleeve to the piston with the stroke limiting bolt.

17. Assemble the remaining master cylinder components in the reverse order of disassembly. Ensure that the snap-ring is properly positioned. Install the secondary piston with master cylinder opening facing down.

18. Install and tighten the brake failure warning sending unit.

BLEEDING

Anytime a brake line has been disconnected the hydraulic system should be bled. The brakes should also be bled when the pedal travel becomes unusually long ("soft pedal") or the car pulls to one side during braking. The proper bleeding sequence is: right rear wheel, left rear wheel, right front caliper, and left front caliper. You'll need a helper to pump the brake pedal while you open the bleeder valves.

NOTE: If the system has been drained, first refill it with fresh brake fluid. Following the above sequence, open each bleeder valve by 1/2 to 3/4 of a turn and pump the brake pedal until fluid runs out of the valve. Proceed with the bleeding as outlined below.

1. Remove the bleeder valve dust cover and install a clear rubber bleeder hose.

2. Insert the other end of the hose into a container about 1/3 full of brake fluid.

3. Have an assistant pump the brake pedal several times until the pedal pressure increases.

4. Hold the pedal under pressure and then start to open the bleeder valve about 1/2 to 3/4 of a turn. At this point, have your assistant depress the pedal all the way and then quickly close the valve. The helper should allow the pedal to return slowly.

NOTE: Keep a close check on the brake fluid in the reservoir and top it up as necessary throughout the bleeding process.

5. Keep repeating this procedure until no more air bubbles can be seen coming from the hose in the brake fluid.

6. Remove the bleeder hose and install the dust cover.

7. Continue the bleeding at each wheel in sequence.

NOTE: Don't splash any brake fluid on the paintwork. Brake fluid is very corrosive and will eat paint away. Any fluid accidentally spilled on the body should be immediately flushed off with water.

Front Disc Brakes

Single piston floating caliper disc brakes are used. In this design, the single piston forces one pad against the rotating disc brake. Counter pressure forces against the floating frame and the frame then pushes the second pad into the disc. The advantages of the floating caliper are better heat dissipation, simpler repair, fewer leaks, and less sensitivity to variance in disc thickness and parallelism.

BRAKE PADS

Removal and Installation

Brake pads should be replaced when there is no visible clearance between the pads and the cross-spring or when they are worn to a thickness of 1/4 in.

1. Jack up the front of the car and support it on stands. Remove the wheels.
2. Pry the clip out of both retaining pins.
3. While pressing down on the cross-spring, push the pad retaining pins out with a drift or small screwdriver.
4. Reference mark positions of the brake pads if they are being reused.
5. Remove the cross-spring from the caliper.
6. Remove the inner brake pad. VW has a special tool for this purpose, but by using a small drift or punch you can pry the pad out of the caliper until it can be gripped by a pair of pliers and removed.
7. The outer brake pad is positioned in a notch. Use a flat, smooth piece of hardwood or metal to press the floating caliper frame and piston cylinder outward.
8. Grip the outer pad and remove it.
9. Siphon out about half of the brake fluid in the reservoir to prevent it from overflowing when the piston is pushed in and new thicker pads are inserted. Press the piston back into the cylinder with the flat piece of wood or metal. *Do not apply the brakes with the pads removed.*
10. Check that piston is at the proper 20° angle. You can make a gauge out of stiff cardboard.

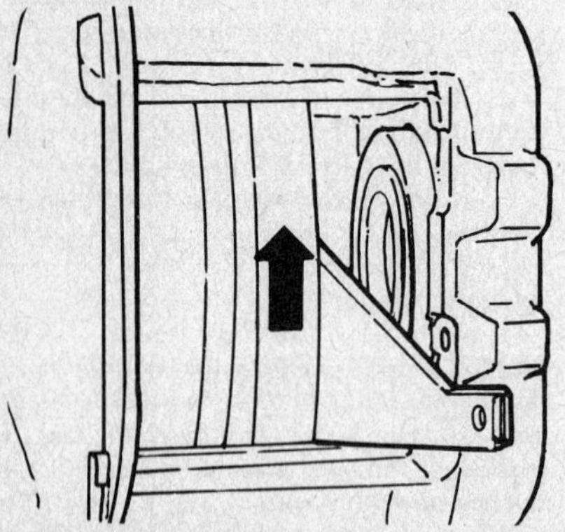

Checking that the piston is at the correct 20° angle

11. Install the brake pads into the caliper.

NOTE: Replace used pads in the side of the caliper from which they were removed. When installing new pads always replace the pads on the opposite wheel at the same time.

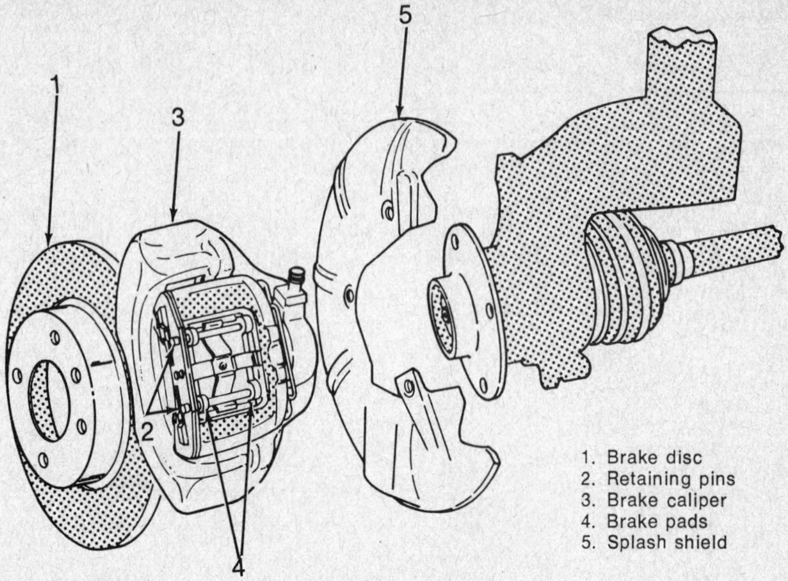

Caliper and disc mounting

12. Position the cross-spring in the caliper and then carefully tap the pad retaining pins into place with a small hammer. Install the pin clip.

CALIPERS

Removal and Installation

1. Jack up and support the front of the car.
2. Remove the brake pads.
3. If you are removing the caliper for overhaul, disconnect and plug the brake line at the caliper. If not, do not remove the hose—hang the caliper by a wire.
4. Remove the two caliper-to-strut retaining bolts and remove the caliper.
5. Install the caliper using the reverse of the removal procedure. Tighten the two retaining bolts to 43 ft. lbs.
6. Bleed the brakes.

Overhaul

1. Remove the caliper.
2. Mount the caliper in a soft-jawed vise or place cloths over the jaws to protect the caliper.
3. Pry the fixed mounting frame off the floating frame.
4. Separate the caliper cylinder from the floating frame by prying it and the guide spring off the frame. Use a brass drift to lightly tap on the cylinder and place a piece of wood under the piston to protect it.

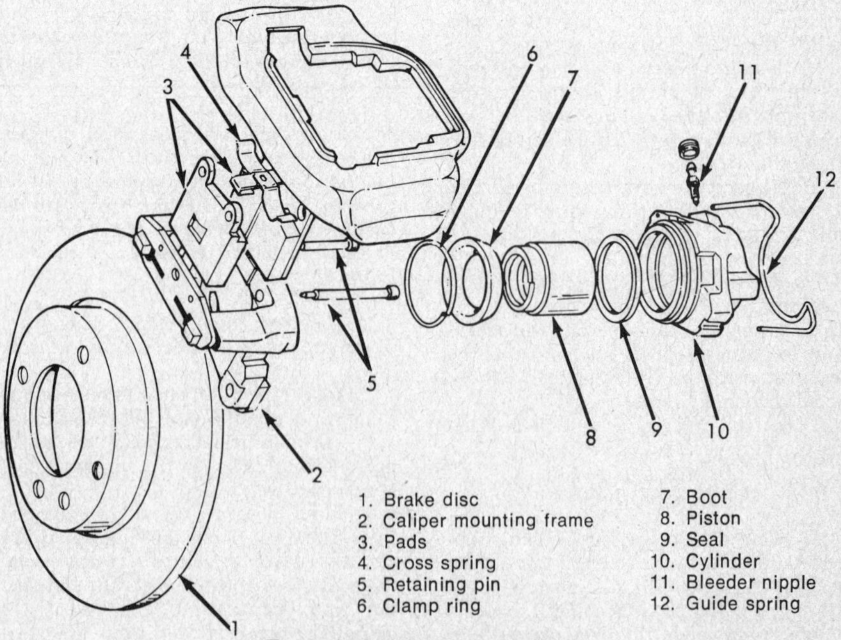

Exploded view of the caliper

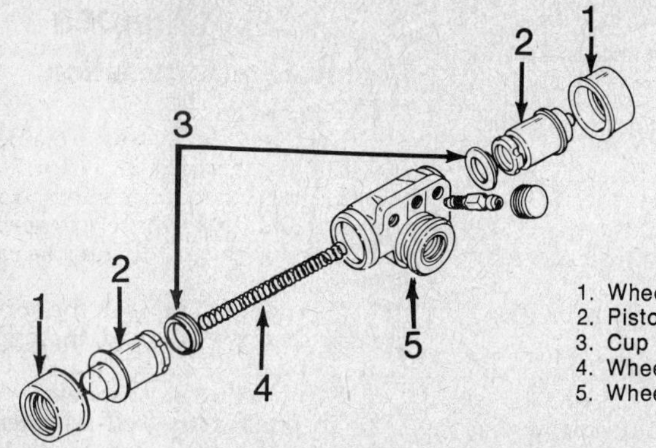

Exploded view of the brake cylinder

of the cylinder, on the back of the ng plate.

Inspect the inside of the wheel cyl-. If it is scored in any way, the der must be honed with a wheel der hone or fine emery paper, and ed with crocus cloth if emery paper ed. If the inside of the cylinder is sively worn the cylinder will have replaced, as only 0.003 in. of mate-an be removed from the cylinder . Whenever honing or cleaning cylinders, keep a small amount of fluid in the cylinder to serve as a ant.

Clean any foreign matter from the s. The sides of the pistons must be smooth for the wheel cylinders to operate properly.

8. Clean the cylinder bore with alcohol and a lint-free rag. Pull the rag through the bore several times to remove all foreign mater and dry the cylinder.

9. Install the bleeder screw and the return spring in the cylinder.

10. Coat new cylinder cups with new brake fluid and install them in the cylinder. Make sure they are square in the bore or they will leak.

11. Install the pistons in the cylinder after coating them with new brake fluid.

12. Coat the insides of the boots with new brake fluid and install them on the cylinder. Install and bleed the brakes.

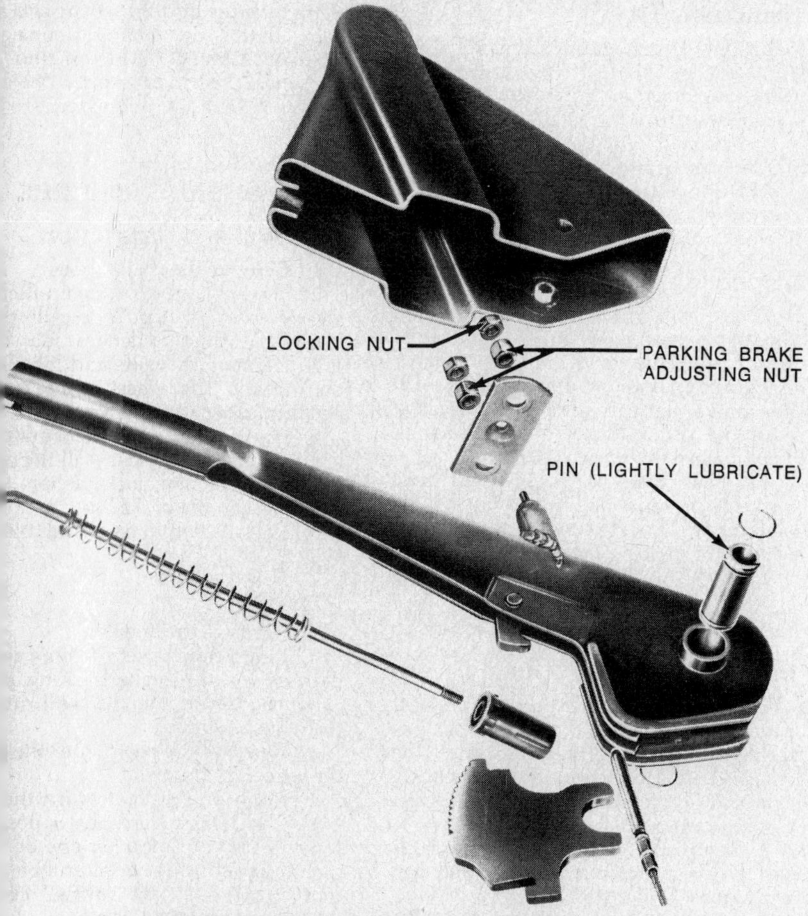

Parking brake; only one of the two cables is shown

REAR WHEEL BEARINGS

Rear wheel bearing adjustment is covered under Brake Drum Removal and Installation.

Parking Brake

CABLE

Adjustment

On the Rabbit pick-up, adjustment is made at the cable end nuts on top of the handbrake lever.

1. Block the front wheels. Raise the rear of the car.
2. Apply the parking brake so that the lever is on the second notch.
3. Tighten the compensator nut or adjusting nuts until both rear wheels can not be turned by hand.
4. Release the parking brake lever and check that both wheels can be easily turned.

CHASSIS ELECTRICAL

Heater

The heater core and blower are contained in the heater assembly which is removed and disassembled to service either component. The heater assembly is located in the passenger compartment under the center of the dash.

REMOVAL AND INSTALLATION

1. Disconnect the battery ground cable.
2. Drain the cooling system.
3. Remove the windshield washer container from its mounts. Remove the ignition coil.
4. Disconnect the two hoses from the heater core connections at the firewall.
5. Unplug the electrical connector.
6. Remove the heater control knobs on the dash.
7. Remove the two retaining screws and remove the controls from the dash complete with brackets.
8. Pull the cable connection off the electric motor.
9. Disconnect the cable from the lever on the round knob.
10. Using a screwdriver, pry the retaining clip off the fresh air housing (the front portion of the heater).
11. Remove the fresh air housing complete with the controls.
12. Detach the left and right air hoses.
13. Remove the heater-to-dash panel mounting screws and lower the heater assembly.
14. Pull out the two pins and remove the heater cover. Unscrew and remove the fan motor.

5. Using pliers remove the piston clamp ring. Remove and discard the rubber dust cover, a new one should be supplied with the rebuilding kit.

6. Remove the piston from the cylinder. If it is stubborn, remove the bleeder screw and blow it out with compressed air.

CAUTION: Hold the piston over a block of wood when doing this as the piston will fly out with considerable force.

7. When the piston pops out of the caliper, remove the rubber seal with a wood or plastic pin to avoid damaging the seal groove.

8. Clean all metal parts in alcohol. Inspect the pistons and their bores, they must be free of scoring and pitting. Replace the cylinder if there is any damage.

9. Discard all rubber parts. The caliper rebuilding kit includes new boots and seals which should be used as the caliper is reassembled.

10. Lightly coat the cylinder bore, piston, and seal with brake assembly paste or fresh brake fluid.

11. Using a vise, install the piston into the cylinder.

12. Piston the guide spring in the groove of the brake cylinder and using a brass drift install the cylinder on the floating frame.

13. Place the mounting frame in the guide spring and slip it onto the floating frame. The fixed frame has two grooves which position it over the raised ribs of the floating frame.

14. Install the caliper and bleed the brakes.

BRAKE DISC

Inspection

Brake discs may be checked for lateral run-out while on the car. This check will require a dial indicator and stand to mount it on the caliper. VW has a special tool for this purpose which mounts the dial indicator to the caliper, but it can also be mounted on the shaft of a C-clamp attached to the outside of the caliper.

1. Remove the wheel and reinstall the wheel bolts to retain the disc to the hub.

2. Mount the dial indicator securely to the caliper. The feeler should touch the disc about $^1/_2$-in. below the outer edge.

3. Rotate the disc and observe the gauge. Radial run-out (wobble) must not exceed 0.004 in. A disc which exceeds this specification must be replaced or refinished.

4. Brake discs which have excessive radial runout, sharp ridges, or scoring can be refinished. Finish grinding must be done on both sides of disc to prevent squeaking and vibrating. Discs which have only light grooves and are otherwise acceptable can be used without refinishing.

The standard disc is 0.47 in thick. It should not be ground to less than 0.41 in.

Removal and Installation

1. Loosen the wheel bolts. Remove the hub cap.

2. Jack up the front of the truck and place it on stands. Remove the wheel(s).

3. Remove the caliper.

4. Remove the disc-to-hub retaining screw.

5. Remove the disc with a sharp pull by hand or use a puller.

6. The disc is installed in the reverse order of removal. Install the caliper and bleed the brakes.

7. Install the wheel and lower the truck. Tighten the wheel bolts diagonally to 65 ft lbs.

FRONT WHEEL BEARINGS

There is no front wheel bearing adjustment. The bearing is pressed into the steering knuckle. Axle nut torque is 175 ft. lbs. The axle nut should be tightened only with the wheels resting on the ground.

Drum Brakes

BRAKE DRUMS

Removal

1. Remove one wheel bolt.

2. Insert a screwdriver through the wheel bolt hole and push the adjusting wedge upward.

3. Reinstall the wheel bolt and tighten to 65 ft. lbs.

4. Remove the grease cap, axle nut, and cotter pin, and remove the drum. See the inspection procedure.

Inspection

Check the brake drum for any cracks, scores, grooves, or an out-of-round condition. Replace a drum that shows cracking. Smooth out light scoring with fine emery cloth. If scoring is extensive have the drum turned. Never have a drum turned more than 0.020 in.

The stub axle bearings in the rear brake drum must be pressed out for replacement. Always use new seals on reassembly.

After greasing the bearings and installing them in the drum with new seals, place the drum onto the stub axle.

Installation

1. Install the washer and the hex nut. Tighten the nut and then loosen it. Retighten the nut slightly so that the washer between the nut and the bearing can just be moved with a screwdriver. Correct bearing play is 0.001–.003 in.

2. Install the castellated nut and insert a new cotter pin. Fill the hub cap with grease and install it.

3. Install the wheel and adjust the brakes.

BRAKE SH

Removal and Install

1. Remove the drum.
2. Remove the spri
pressing in and turning
3. Remove the brake
supports and the lower
4. Unhook the parki
the lever.
5. Use pliers to unho
the adjusting wedge a
turn spring.
6. Remove the brake
7. To remove the s
rod, place the push r
unhook the tensioning
8. See Steps 8, 9
preceding brake drur
dure for inspection.
9. To install, place
vise, attach the brake
rod to install the ten
rod and shoe.
10. Install the adju
the lug toward the bac
11. Attach the bral
ver to the push rod.
return spring.
12. Hook the park
the lever. Place the sh
pistons and hook the
into the shoes.
13. Mount the b
support and hook th
justing wedge into th
14. Install the re
retainers. Install th
the wheel bearings
firmly to set the self-

WHEEL C

Removal and Ins

1. Remove the b
2. Loosen the br
the cylinder, but
away from the cyli
3. Remove the b
that attach the w
backing plate and
4. Position the
the backing plate
attaching bolts an
5. Attach the b
6. Install the
system.

Overhaul

1. Remove the
2. Place the b
pers under the b
catch the brake f
the wheel cylinde
3. Remove the
the wheel cylinde
4. Push one p
of the cylinder t
ton and cup out
inder. Reach in
inder and push
piston out of the
5. Remove th

15. Separate the heater halves to remove the heater core.
16. Installation is the reverse of removal. Refill the cooling system.

Windshield Wiper Motor

REMOVAL AND INSTALLATION

When removing the wiper motor, leave the mounting frame in place. Do not remove the wiper drive crank from the motor shaft—if it must be removed for any reason, matchmark the shaft, motor, and crank for reinstallation.

1. Access is with the hood open. Disconnect the battery ground cable.
2. Detach the connecting rods from the motor crank arm.
3. Pull off the wiring plug.
4. Remove the 4 mounting bolts. You may have to energize the motor for access to the top bolt.
5. Remove the motor. Reverse the procedure for installation.

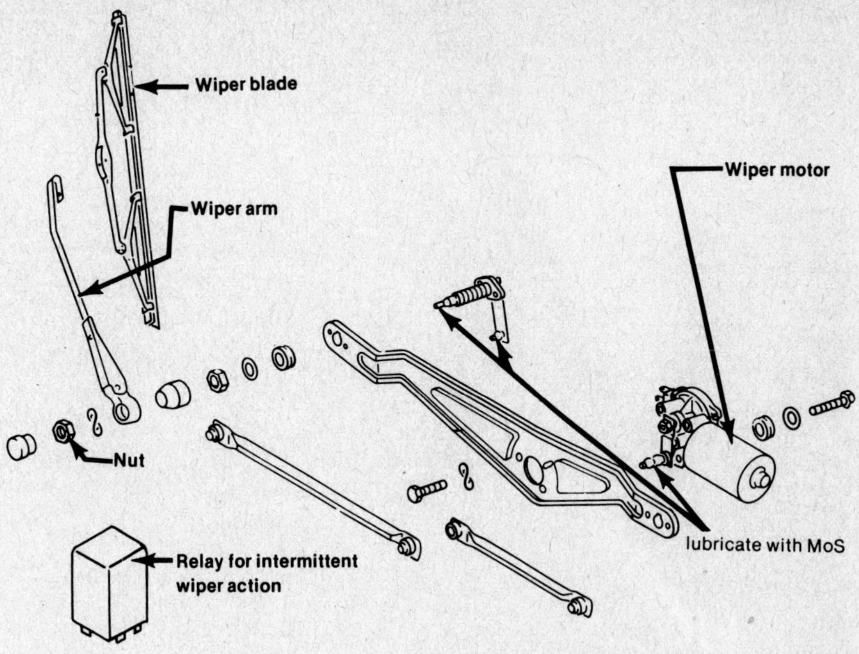

Wiper linkage—exploded view

Instrument Cluster

REMOVAL AND INSTALLATION

1. Disconnect the battery ground cable.
2. Remove the fresh air controls trim plate.
3. Remove the radio or glove box.
4. Unscrew the speedometer drive cable from the back of the speedometer. Detach the electrical plug.
5. Remove the attaching screw inside the radio/glove box opening.
6. Remove the instrument cluster. Reverse the procedure for installation.